BOOKS IN PRINT®

2000–2001

This edition of
BOOKS IN PRINT 2000-2001
was prepared by R.R. Bowker's Database Publishing Group in
collaboration with the Information Technology Department.

Drew Meyer, President & Chief Executive Officer
Michael Cairns, Vice President, Business Development
Dean Hollister, Vice President, Database Production
Randy Mysel, Vice President, Sales & Marketing
Andrew Grabois, Senior Managing Director, Bibliographies
Roy Crego, Managing Director, Books in Print Editorial
Angela D'Agostino, Senior Director, Product Development
Marin Mixon, Director, Marketing

International Standard Book Number/Standard Address Number Agency Publishers Authority Database
Doreen Gravesande, Director
Don Riseborough, Senior Managing Editor
Margot Cronin and Paula Kurdi, Senior Editors
Beverly Palacio and Joy Zichichi, Associate Editors
Kareem Douglas and Janet Weiss, Assistant Editors
Diana Fumando, SAN Senior Editor

Data Acquisition, Bibliographies Group
Joseph Kalina, Managing Editor
Nina Liana, Senior Editor
Gladys Osofisan, Assistant Editor

Quality Assurance & Web Content
Constance Harbison, Director, Quality Assurance
George Krubski, Managing Editor, Web Content, booksinprint.com
Christian Nielsen, Content Specialist Fiction, booksinprint.com
Myriam Nunez, Manager/Data Analysis, QA & Test
Brian Pickton, Senior Editor, Authority Control
Lisa Heft, Senior Editor, Quality Assurance
Jocelyn Kwiatkowski, Thomas Lucas, Michaela Weiland, Lynda Williams and
Steve Zaffuto, Assistant Editors

Subject Guide
Paula Entin, Senior Editor
Angela Barrett, Senior Associate Editor
Joseph V. Tondi, Associate Editor
Adrene Broomes, Assistant Editor

Electronic Data Interchange Group
Frank Accurso, Director
Mary Craig Daley, Managing Editor
Kathleen Keiderling, Managing Editor, Data Integration
Christopher Voser, Senior Editor
Brock Brunson, Associate Editor
Ila Joseph-Corley, Assistant Editor

Data Collection & Processing Group
Valerie Harris, Director of Operations, Tampa
Mervaine Ricks, Production Manager
Cheryl Patrick, Lead Project Coordinator
Rhonda McKendrick, Project Coordinator
Lori Burnett, Senior Data Entry Leader

Production
Carlton Dyce, Senior Director
Mitch Letterman, Senior Managing Editor
Melanie Koserowski, Xyvision Administrator/Senior Associate Desktop Publisher
Megan Roxberry, Senior Associate Desktop Publisher
Jeanne Audino, Monalisa Massiah and Maria Pirovano, Associate Desktop Publishers
Clarice D. Isaacs, Assistant Desktop Publisher

Editorial Systems Group
Gary Aiello, Vice President, Information Technology
Mark Heinzelman, Director
Frank Morris, Project Manager
Nana Rizinashvili and Youliang Zhou, Programmers

Computer Operations Group
Keith Moore, Manager, UNIX/Internet Systems
Nick Wikowski, Director, Network/Computer Operations
Jack Murphy, Supervisor

BOOKS IN PRINT®

2000–2001

VOLUME 3

AUTHORS ◆ L–R

New Providence, New Jersey

Published by
R.R. Bowker
A division of Reed Elsevier
121 Chanlon Rd., New Providence
New Jersey 07974

Drew Meyer, President and Chief Executive Officer

Telephone: 908-464-6800; Toll-free: 1-888-BOWKER2 (1-888-269-5372); Fax: 908-665-6688
E-mail address: info@bowker.com
URL: http://www.bowker.com

Readers may send any corrections and/or updates to the information in this work to R. R. Bowker through the corrections option on the Bowker Web site at http://www.bowker.com or may send e-mail directly to the address: Corrections@bowker.com. Publishers may update or add to their listings by accessing the Bowker Link Publisher Access System at http://www.bowkerlink.com. Books In Print is also available via subscription on the web at www.booksinprint.com.

International Standard Book Numbers
Set: 0-8352-4291-9
Volume 1: 0-8352-4292-7
Volume 2: 0-8352-4293-5
Volume 3: 0-8352-4294-3
Volume 4: 0-8352-4295-1
Volume 5: 0-8352-4296-X
Volume 6: 0-8352-4297-8
Volume 7: 0-8352-4298-6
Volume 8: 0-8352-4299-4
Volume 9: 0-8352-4300-1

International Standard Serial Number
0068-0214

Library of Congress Control Number
74-643574

Printed in the United States of America

ISBN 0-8352-4291-9
9 780835 242912

Contents of Volume 1

Contents of Volume 2

Contents of Volume 3

Contents of Volume 4

Contents of Volume 5

Contents of Volume 6

Contents of Volume 7

Contents of Volume 8

Contents of Volume 9

BOOKS IN PRINT®
2000 - 2001

Volume 3

AUTHORS
L - R

L

Lders, Hans Otto & Comair, Youssef G. Epilepsy Surgery. 2nd ed. 1,000p. text 199.00 (*0-7817-1442-7*) Lppncott W & W.

***L. A. Information Services Group.** Guidelines for Reference & Information Services in Public Libraries. 72p. 1999. pap. 35.00 (*1-85604-350-9*, LAP3509, Pub. by Library Association) Bernan Associates.

L. A. Soard Staff. Bridges: A Guide for All Members of the Adoption Triangle. 230p. 1998. mass mkt. 9.95 (*1-58365-006-7*, Timeless Romance) BT Pub.

L-Baha, Abdu, jt. auth. see Fitzgerald, Michael.

l-Bahba, Oabdu. Wisdom of the Master: The Spiritual Teachings of 0abdu.l-bahba. Scholl, Steven, ed. LC 97-29993. xiv, 111p. 1997. write for info. (*1-883991-23-4*) Whte Cloud Pr.

L., Barry. Yesterday's Tomorrow: Recovery Meditations for Hard Cases. LC 97-15767. 384p. pap. 12.00 (*1-56838-160-3*) Hazelden.

L, Brian. Perfectionism. 20p. (Orig.). 1985. pap. 1.55 (*0-89486-259-6*, 1404B) Hazelden.

***L., Chris.** How to Get Sober & Stay Sober: A Workbook for Steps One Through Five. Hazelden Publishing Staff, ed. 90p. 2000. pap. 11.00 (*1-56838-357-6*) Hazelden.

L. E. A., 1981 Staff. 3rd Annual Conference C. S. S. 1988. 100.00 (*0-8058-0182-0*) L Erlbaum Assocs.

L., Edward. How to Stay Away from Lust One Day at a Time: New Thought & Sex Addicts, Vol. 1. large type ed. LC 97-220894. 76p. (Orig.). 1997. pap. 9.95 (*1-890316-00-8*) E L Billroy.

— How to Stay Away from Lust One Day at a Time: New Thought & Sex Addicts, Vol. 2. large type ed. 64p. (Orig.). 1998. pap. 14.95 (*1-890316-01-6*) E L Billroy.

— How to Stay Away from Lust One Day at a Time: New Thought & Sex Addicts, Vol. 3. large type ed. 56p. (Orig.). 1998. pap. 14.95 (*1-890316-02-4*) E L Billroy.

— How to Stay Away from Lust One Day at a Time: New Thought & Sex Addicts, Vol. 4. large type ed. 96p. (Orig.). 1998. pap. 14.95 (*1-890316-03-2*) E L Billroy.

L., Elisabeth. Comedores Compulsivos.Tr. of Food for Thought. (SPA.). 400p. pap. 15.95 (*968-39-0929-9*, Pub. by Edit Patria) Hazelden.

— Food for Thought: Daily Meditations for Overeaters. 400p. pap. 10.00 (*0-89486-090-9*, 1074A) Hazelden.

L., Elizabeth. Twelve Steps for Overeaters: An Interpretation of Twelve Steps of Overeaters Anonymous. 130p. pap. 10.00 (*0-89486-905-1*) Hazelden.

L. F. Garlinghouse Company Staff. Vacation, Retirement & Leisure Home Plans. 5th ed. LC 97-77619. (Illus.). 256p. 1998. pap. 6.95 (*0-938708-77-5*) L F Garlinghouse Co.

L. J., Lawrence, tr. see Furtwangler, Wilhelm.

L. L. Bean, Inc. Staff, jt. auth. see Talleur, Richard W.

***L. L. Cool J & Hunter, Karen.** I Make My Own Rules, Vol. 1. (Illus.). 234p. 1998. mass mkt. 5.99 (*0-312-96731-4*, Pub. by Tor Bks) St Martin.

L-L Research Staff, jt. auth. see Hatonn, Gyeorgos C.

L. Livermore National Lab Staff. Inertial Confinement Fusion. (Physics Ser.). 398p. 1998. 52.50 (*0-7637-0363-X*) Jones & Bartlett.

L., Mary, jt. auth. see R., Mark.

L Milosz, O. V. De, see De L. Milosz, O. V.

L. Vander Lugt, Joyce, see Vander Lugt, Joyce L.

L-W Book Publishing Staff. Collectible Lanterns. LC 97-120842. 144p. 1996. pap. text 19.95 (*0-89538-081-1*) L-W Inc.

L-W Book Publishing Staff, ed. see Wood, Jack P.

L-W Book Sales (Firm). Price Guide to Majolica. LC 97-120017. (Illus.). 1997. write for info. (*0-89538-080-3*) L-W Inc.

L-W Book Sales (Firm), jt. auth. see Bridges, Moe.

L-W Book Sales (Firm) Staff. Indiana Cabinets: With Prices. LC 98-102368. 104 p. 1997. 24.95 (*0-89538-094-3*) L-W Inc.

L-W Book Sales Staff, ed. Griswold Vol. 2: A Price Guide, Vol. II. 2nd ed. (Illus.). 136p. 1994. pap. 19.95 (*0-89538-058-7*) L-W Inc.

L-W Books Staff, ed. Griswold Cast Iron Vol. 1: A Price Guide, Vol. 1. 2nd rev. ed. LC 93-221453. (Illus.). 182p. 1998. reprint ed. pap. 19.95 (*0-89538-023-4*) L-W Inc.

L-W Books Staff & Wood, Neil L., eds. Old Magazines Price Guide, One. rev. ed. (Illus.). 112p. 1994. pap. 9.95 (*0-89538-064-1*) L-W Inc.

L-W Publishers Staff, ed. Collector's Digest to Beer Cans. 158p. 1996. pap. 12.00 (*0-89145-230-3*) L-W Inc.

L-Z Fang & Li, S. X. Creation of the Universe. 192p. (C). 1993. text 52.00 (*9971-5-0600-9*); pap. text 23.00 (*9971-5-0601-7*) World Scientific Pub.

L&L Sponberg Staff. From Here to There. 504p. (Orig.). 1994. pap. text. write for info. (*0-9643904-0-X*) LoLen Pubs.

La. La Litterature Personnelle. LC PQ3908.L57. (Revue d'Histoire Litteraire du Quebec & du Canada Francais Ser.: Vol. 9). (FRE.). 178p. 1985. reprint ed. pap. 55.20 (*0-608-02208-X*, 206287900004) Bks Demand.

La-Anyane, Seth. Economics of Agricultural Development in Tropical Africa. fac. ed. LC 82-13510. 169p. pap. 52.40 (*0-7837-7501-6*, 204700500005) Bks Demand.

La Barca, Frances Calderon De, see Calderon de la Barca, Frances.

la Barquera Arroyo, Elvia C. Sanchez de, see Sanchez de la Barquera Arroyo, Elvia C.

La Barra, Tomas De, see De la Barra, Tomas.

***La Barre, Frances.** Non-Verbal Behavior in Psychodynamic Psychotherapy & Psychoanalysis. LC 00-38089. 2000. write for info. (*0-88163-316-X*) Analytic Pr.

La Barre, Harriet. Blackwood's Daughter. large type ed. (Ulverscroft). 496p. 1994. 27.99 (*0-7089-3060-3*) Ulverscroft.

— Stranger in Vienna. large type ed. 640p. 1995. 27.99 (*0-7089-3332-7*) Ulverscroft.

La Barre, Weston. Culture in Context. (C). 1994. text 40.00 (*1-885809-00-X*); pap. text 19.95 (*1-885809-01-8*) An LaBarre.

— Human Animal. LC 54-12371. 1993. pap. 2.25 (*0-226-46706-6*, P45) U Ch Pr.

— Muelos: A Stone Age Superstition about Sexuality. LC 84-14232. 168p. 1984. text 52.50 (*0-231-05960-4*) Col U Pr.

— The Peyote Cult. 5th ed. LC 89-40225. (Illus.). 352p. 1989. pap. 18.95 (*0-8061-2214-5*) U of Okla Pr.

— They Shall Take up Serpents: Psychology of the Southern Snake-Handling Cult. (Illus.). 208p. (C). 1992. reprint ed. pap. text 11.95 (*0-88133-663-7*) Waveland Pr.

La Barrera y Leirado, Cayetano A. De, see De la Barrera Y Leirado, Cayetano A.

La Bastille, Anne. Woodswoman. 1991. pap. 12.95 (*0-14-015334-9*, Penguin Bks) Viking Penguin.

La Bath, Octave A., jt. auth. see Imwalle, D. E.

La Bathie, H. Perrier De, see De La Bathie, H. Perrier.

La Baume, Cecile De, see De La Baume, Cecile.

La Bedoyere, Charlotte De, see De la Bedoyere, Charlotte, tr.

la Bedoyere, Guy de, see de la Bedoyere, Guy.

La Bedoyere, Michael De, see De La Bedoyere, Michael.

La Bedoyere, Quentin De, see De la Bedoyere, Quentin.

La Bella, A., jt. ed. see Bianco, Lucio.

La Belle, Jenijoy. The Echoing Wood of Theodore Roethke. LC 76-3265. (Princeton Essays in Literature Ser.). 189p. reprint ed. pap. 58.60 (*0-8357-8865-2*, 203338700085) Bks Demand.

— Herself Beheld: The Literature of the Looking Glass. LC 88-47734. 240p. 1990. reprint ed. pap. text 15.95 (*0-8014-9704-3*) Cornell U Pr.

La Belle, Thomas J. & Ward, Christopher R. Ethnic Studies & Multiculturalism. LC 95-73748. (SUNY Series, Frontiers in Education). 155p. (C). 1996. text 49.50 (*0-7914-2983-0*); pap. text 16.95 (*0-7914-2984-9*) State U NY Pr.

— Multiculturalism & Education: Diversity & Its Impact on Schools & Society. LC 93-5712. (SUNY Series, Frontiers in Education). 211p. (C). 1994. pap. text 19.95 (*0-7914-1940-1*) State U NY Pr.

La Belle, Thomas J., jt. ed. see Hawkins, John N.

La Belle, Tim, jt. auth. see Reynolds, Larry A.

La Berge, Ann F. Mission & Method: The Early Nineteenth-Century French Public Health Movement. (Cambridge History of Medicine Ser.). (Illus.). 396p. (C). 1992. text 80.00 (*0-521-40406-1*) Cambridge U Pr.

La Bern, Arthur. Goodbye Piccadilly, Farewell Leicester. 1976. 21.95 (*0-8488-0176-8*) Amereon Ltd.

La Billardiere, Jean J. de, see De La Billardiere, Jean J.

La Blanc. Contemporary Black Biography, Vol. 2. 275p. 1992. text 60.00 (*0-8103-8554-6*, 101344) Gale.

— Contemporary Black Biography, Vol. 3. 275p. 1992. text 60.00 (*0-8103-8555-4*, 101345) Gale.

— Contemporary Black Biography, Vol. 4. 275p. 1993. text 60.00 (*0-8103-8556-2*, 101346) Gale.

— Contemporary Black Biography, Vol. 5. 275p. 1993. text 60.00 (*0-8103-8557-0*, 101347) Gale.

— Contemporary Black Biography, Vol. 6. 275p. 1994. text 60.00 (*0-8103-8558-9*, 101348) Gale.

— Contemporary Black Biography, Vol. 7. 275p. 1994. text 60.00 (*0-8103-8559-7*, 101349) Gale.

— Contemporary Black Biography, Vol. 8. 275p. 1994. text 60.00 (*0-8103-5739-9*, 101733) Gale.

— Contemporary Musicians, Vol. 11. 320p. 1994. text 81.00 (*0-8103-8552-X*, 004903) Gale.

— Contemporary Musicians, Vol. 12. 320p. 1994. text 81.00 (*0-8103-8553-8*, 004904) Gale.

La Blanc, Michael. Contemporary Black Biography, Vol. 1. 275p. 1991. text 60.00 (*0-8103-5546-9*) Gale.

La Blanca, N. P. De, see De La Blanca, N. P.

La Bo. Looking Black. 31p. (Orig.). 1993. pap. 5.95 (*1-56411-123-7*) Untd Bros & Sis.

La Borderie, Rene. Lexique de L'Education. (FRE.). 1998. 24.95 (*0-320-00150-4*) Fr & Eur.

La Bossiere, Camille R. The Victorian Fol Sage: Comparative Readings on Carlyle, Emerson, Melville & Conrad. LC 87-480005. 136p. 1989. 29.50 (*0-8387-5145-8*) Bucknell U Pr.

La Botz, Dan. The Crisis of Mexican Labor. LC 88-2707. 228p. 1988. 49.95 (*0-275-92600-1*, C2600, Greenwood Pr) Greenwood.

— Democracy in Mexico: Peasant Rebellion & Political Reform. 276p. 1995. 35.00 (*0-89608-508-2*) South End Pr.

— Edward L. Doheny: Petroleum, Power, & Politics in the United States & Mexico. LC 90-20670. 224p. 1991. 57.95 (*0-275-93599-X*, C3599, Praeger Pubs) Greenwood.

— Mask of Democracy: Labor Suppression in Mexico Today. 224p. (Orig.). 1992. 35.00 (*0-89608-438-8*); pap. 14.00 (*0-89608-437-X*) South End Pr.

— Rank & File Rebellion: Teamsters for a Democratic Union. (Haymarket Ser.). 360p. (C). 1991. pap. 20.00 (*0-86091-505-0*, A4502, Pub. by Verso) Norton.

— A Troublemaker's Handbook: How to Fight Back Where You Work - & Win! (Illus.). 262p. (Orig.). 1991. pap. text 17.00 (*0-914093-04-5*) Labor Notes.

La Bounty, Blanca A., jt. auth. see Rice, Dona.

La Brack, Bruce, ed. The Sikhs of Northern California, 1904-1975. LC 87-45787. (Immigrant Communities & Ethnic Minorities in the U. S. & Canada Ser.: No. 22). 1988. 67.50 (*0-404-19432-X*) AMS Pr.

***La Brack, Joy.** Babe: Christmas in the Barn. LC 98-32397. (Illus.). 24p. (J). (ps-1). 1999. pap. 3.25 (*0-375-80216-9*, Pub. by Random Bks Yng Read) Random.

— Elmo's Animal Adventure. (J). 2000. 4.99 (*0-375-80331-9*, Pub. by Random Bks Yng Read) Random.

La Bras, Yvon, tr. see Allen, Diane & Frederick, Larry.

La Brecque, Jennifer, jt. auth. see Shalvis, Jill.

La Bree, Ben, ed. Camp Fires of the Confederacy. (Illus.). 560p. 1994. reprint ed. lib. bdg. 55.00 (*0-8328-4350-4*) Higginson Bk Co.

La Bretonne, Nicholas E. Restif De, see Restif De La Bretonne, Nicholas E.

La Brie, Henry G. The Black Press in America: A Bibliography. 1974. pap. 3.50 (*0-89080-003-0*) Mercer Hse.

La Brie, Henry G., III, intro. A Survey of Black Newspapers in America. LC 80-80551. (Mass Communication & Journalism Ser.). 72p. (Orig.). 1980. 6.00 (*0-89080-034-0*) Mercer Hse.

La Brie, Vicki G. A Learning Disabilities Activity Guide for the Elementary Classroom. 50p. (Orig.). 1975. pap. 3.50 (*0-89080-029-4*) Mercer Hse.

La Brier, DeJoly. Diary of a Survivor: In Art & Poetry. (Illus.). 84p. 1997. pap. 25.00 (*0-937025-08-9*) Shadowood Pubns.

La Brosse, Olivier de, see De la Brosse, Olivier.

La Bruyere. Les Caracteres. (FRE.). (C). pap. 11.95 (*0-8442-1982-7*, VF1982-7) NTC Contemp Pub Co.

La Cabada, Juan De, see De La Cabada, Juan.

La Calprenede. La Mort des Enfans D'Herodes. Smith, ed. (Exeter French Texts Ser.: Vol. 69). (FRE.). 116p. Date not set. pap. text 19.95 (*0-85989-259-X*, Pub. by Univ Exeter Pr) Northwestern U Pr.

La Cambre, Genevieve, et al. Gustave Moreau: Between Epic & Dream. LC 98-73863. (Illus.). 308p. 1999. pap. 19.95 (*0-86559-168-7*) Art Inst Chi.

La Campa, Romban de, see De la Campa, Romban.

La Capra, Dominick. Representing the Holocaust: History, Theory, Trauma. LC 93-33885. 248p. 1994. text 37.50 (*0-8014-2997-8*) Cornell U Pr.

La Carrera, Rosalina De, see De la Carrera, Rosalina.

***La Cava, Gloria.** Italians in Brazil: The Post World War II Experience. LC 98-4986. (Studies in Modern European History: Vol. 30). xxi, 174p. (C). 1999. text 47.95 (*0-8204-3971-1*) P Lang Pubng.

***La Cava, Gloria & Nanetti, Rafaella Y.** Albania: Filling the Vulnerability Gap. (Technical Paper Ser.: No. 460). 88p. 2000. 22.00 (*0-8213-4667-9*, 14667) World Bank.

La Cavera, Anthony, jt. auth. see Thomas, George.

La Cerda, Diego De, see De La Cerda, Diego.

La Cerra, Charles. Franklin Delano Roosevelt & Tammany Hall of New York. LC 97-20588. 124p. (C). 1997. 29.50 (*0-7618-0808-6*) U Pr of Amer.

La Cerva, Victor. Pathways to Peace: Forty Steps to a Less Violent America. 2nd rev. ed. (Illus.). 256p. 1997. pap. 15.00 (*0-9661575-0-8*) HEAL Found.

La Chance, Albert. Jonah: A Prophecy at the Millenium. 56p. 1996. 12.50 (*0-8059-4007-3*) Dorrance.

La Chance, Paul R., ed. Asian Arts in America: Seeds of the Inner Life. LC 88-72074. (West & the Wider World Ser.: Vol. 5). (Illus.). 314p. (C). 1988. 29.85 (*0-940121-11-5*) Cross Cultural Pubns.

The breadth of topics discussed is exceptional. After several years of presenting to college students the wonders & beauties of various of the Asian art forms, the editor gathered all into one volume, featuring extensive & clear explanations of the activities & rituals, as well as remarkable photographs demonstrating & exemplifying the best of each. This is an invaluable tool in international education, while presenting much of interest to the general reader. *Publisher Paid Annotation.*

L

La Chanson de Roland. Chanson de Roland (Medieval & Modern French) (Folio Ser.: No. 1155). (FRE.). pap. 10.95 (2-07-037150-6) Schoenhof.

***La Chapelle, David.** Navigating the Tides of Change: With Stories from Science, the Sacred & a Wise Planet. 256p. 2001. pap. 16.95 (0-86571-424-X, Pub. by New Soc Pubs) Consort Bk Sales.

La Charite, Raymond C. Recreation, Reflection & Re-Creation: Perspectives on Rabelais's Pantagruel. LC 79-53402. (French Forum Monographs: No. 19). 137p. (Orig.). 1980. pap. 10.95 (0-917058-18-6) French Forum.

La Charite, Raymond C., ed. O un Amy! Essays on Montaigne in Honor of Donald M. Frame. LC 76-47501. (French Forum Monographs: No. 5). (ENG & FRE.). 341p. (Orig.). 1977. pap. 16.95 (0-917058-04-6) French Forum.

— Rabelais's Incomparable Book: Essays on His Art. LC 85-80421. (French Forum Monographs: No. 62). 247p. (Orig.). 1986. pap. 17.95 (0-917058-63-1) French Forum.

— Writing the Renaissance: Essays on Sixteenth-Century French Literature in Honor of Floyd Gray. LC 91-73985. (French Forum Monographs: No. 77). 266p. (Orig.). 1992. pap. 17.95 (0-917058-81-X) French Forum.

La Charite, Virginia A. The Dynamics of Space: Mallarme's Un Coup De Des Jamais N' abolira le Hasard. LC 86-82794. (French Forum Monographs: No. 67). 192p. (Orig.). 1987. pap. 13.95 (0-917058-68-2) French Forum.

— Twentieth-Century French Avant-Garde Poetry, 1907-1990. LC 92-71330. (French Forum Monographs: No. 80). 185p. (Orig.). 1992. pap. 17.95 (0-917058-85-2) French Forum.

La Cicciolina, intro. Erotic Tales. 256p. 1993. 7.98 (1-55521-868-7) Bk Sales Inc.

***La Civita, Michael J. L., et al.** Pontifical Mission for Palestine: 50 Years of Papal Concern. Packard, Helen C. & Maron, Margaret, eds. (Illus.). 250p. 1999. write for info. (0-9676262-0-X) Cath Nr E Welfare.

La Clair, Ruth, ed. see Cunningham, John T.

La Claire, John, jt. auth. see Bold, Harold C.

La Colina, Jose De, see De la Colina, Jose.

La Colombiere, Claude De, see Saint-Jure, Jean B. & De La Colombiere, Claude.

La Concepcion Valdes, Gabriel De, see Manzano, Juan F. & De La Concepcion Valdes, Gabriel.

la Concha, Victor Garcia De, see Garcia de la Concha, Victor, ed.

La Conte, Ellen. Free Radical: A Reconsideration of the Good Death of Scott Nearing. 26p. (Orig.). 1997. pap. 6.00 (0-9656077-2-0, Pub. by Loose Leaf) Chelsea Green Pub.

la Costa, Fernando De, see De la Costa, Fernando.

la Costa, Horacio de, see De la Costa, Horacio, ed.

La Coste, Warren. Holy Rider: The Priest & the Gang. LC 92-60565. 304p. 1992. 22.95 (0-88282-114-8) New Horizon NJ.

La Cotardiere, Philippe de. Dictionnaire Astronomie. (FRE.). 412p. 1996. 39.95 (0-320-00658-1) Fr & Eur.

— Larousse Dictionnaire de l'Espace. 280p. 1993. 55.00 (0-7859-5605-0, 2037490054) Fr & Eur.

La Cour, Marshall & Lathrop, Irvin T. Photo Technology. (Illus.). 320p. (YA). (gr. 9-12). 1992. 34.64 (0-87006-899-7) Goodheart.

La Court, Pieter De, see De La Court, Pieter.

La Cova, Antonio De, see De La Cova, Antonio.

La Croix. Womens Kama Sutra. 1999. text 24.95 (0-312-18823-4) St Martin.

— The Women's Kama Sutra. 1999. 24.95 (0-312-20627-5, Thomas Dunne) St Martin.

La Croix, Eric, jt. auth. see La Croix, Isobyl.

La Croix, I. F., et al. Orchids of Malawi. (Illus.). 277p. 1991. 99.00 (90-6191-808-1, Pub. by A A Balkema) Ashgate Pub Co.

La Croix, Isobyl & La Croix, Eric. African Orchids in the Wild & in Cultivation. LC 96-54603. (Illus.). 423p. 1997. 39.95 (0-88192-405-9) Timber.

La Croix, Otto De, see De La Croix, Otto.

La Croix, Richard R. Proslogion A Third Interpretation of Anselm's Argument, Vols. II & III. LC 73-157410. xii, 137 p. 1972. write for info. (90-04-03436-6) Brill Academic Pubs.

La Croix, Richard R., ed. Augustine on Music: An Interdisciplinary Collection of Essays. LC 87-22012. (Studies in the History & Interpretation of Music: Vol. 6). 120p. 1988. lib. bdg. 59.95 (0-88946-431-6) E Mellen.

La Croix, Sumner J., et al, eds. Emerging Patterns of East Asian Investment in China: From Korea, Taiwan, & Hong Kong. LC 94-44252. 316p. (C). (gr. 13). 1994. text 81.95 (1-56324-542-6, East Gate Bk); pap. text 32.95 (1-56324-543-4, East Gate Bk) M E Sharpe.

La Croix, Sumner J. & Wolff, David J. Asia-Pacific Airline Industry: Economic Boom & Political Conflict. (Illus.). 37p. (Orig.). (C). 1996. pap. text 15.00 (0-7881-2621-0) DIANE Pub.

***La Crosse County Historical Society Staff.** La Crosse. (Images of America Ser.). 1999. pap. 18.99 (0-7524-1361-9) Arcadia Publng.

La Cruz, Bartolomei De, see De la Cruz, Bartolomei.

la Cruz, Enrique B. De, see De la Cruz, Enrique B.

La Cruz, Felix De, see Lubs, Herbert A. & De La Cruz, Felix, eds.

la Cruz, Irving De, see De la Cruz, Irving.

la Cruz, Juana I. de, see De la Cruz, Juana I.

la Cruz, Juana Inez De, see De la Cruz, Juana Inez.

la Cruz, Martin De, see De la Cruz, Martin.

La Cruz, San Juan De. Obras Escogidas. (SPA.). 148p. 1979. 5.95 (0-8288-7170-1, S7768) Fr & Eur.

— Poesias Completas y Otras Paginas. (SPA.). 125p. 1976. 12.95 (0-8288-7167-1, S39827) Fr & Eur.

la Cruz, San Juan de, see San Juan de la Cruz.

La Cruz, Sor J. De, see De La Cruz, Sor J.

la Cruz, Sor Juana Ines De, see De la Cruz, Sor Juana Ines.

La Cuesta, Felipe Arroyo De, see Arroyo De La Cuesta, Felipe.

La Cueva, Juan De, see De la Cueva, Juan.

La Curne De Sainte Palaye, Jean B. Dictionnaire Historique de l'Ancien Langage Francois Ou Glossaire de la Langue Francoise, 10 vols., Set. (FRE.). lxxxvi, 4775p. 1972. reprint ed. write for info. (3-487-04251-7) G Olms Pubs.

La Dage, John H. Modern Ships: Elements of Their Design, Construction & Operation. 2nd ed. LC 65-21747. (Illus.). 391p. reprint ed. pap. 121.30 (0-8357-8228-X, 203396800087) Bks Demand.

La Dage, John H. & Van Gemert, Lee. Stability & Trim for the Ship's Officer. 3rd rev. ed. George, William E., ed. LC 82-74137. (Illus.). 359p. 1983. text 27.50 (0-87033-297-X) Cornell Maritime.

La Dell, T. Trees & Shrubs for Landscaping. (Illus.). 400p. 1997. text. write for info. (0-419-20800-3, E & FN Spon) Routledge.

***La Due, William J.** The Chair of Saint Peter: A History of the Papacy. 374p. 2000. pap. 24.00 (1-57075-335-0) Orbis Bks.

La Due, William J. The Chair of Saint Peter: A History of the Papacy. rev. ed. LC 98-50146. (Illus.). 384p. 1999. 35.00 (1-57075-249-4) Orbis Bks.

La Duke, Betty. Companeras: Women, Art & Social Change in Latin America. (Illus.). 176p. (Orig.). 1985. pap. 14.95 (0-87286-172-4) City Lights.

La Encina, J. De, see De La Encina, J.

La Esclava del Senor. The History of the Universe & the Origin of Man: The Bible & the Message to the Men of the "New Earth" Gonzales, Bertha, tr. from SPA. LC 87-71559. (Illus.). 152p. 1987. pap. 15.99 (0-9607590-5-0) Action Life Pubns.

***La Esclava del Senor.** Woman: Help, Temptation & Complementarity of Man. Gonzales, Bertha, tr. from SPA. LC 98-73901.Tr. of La Mujar: Ayuda, Tentacion, y Complementaridad del Hombre. 114p. 1999. pap. 6.99 (0-936707-04-6) Action Life Pubns.

La Falaise, Maxime De, see De la Falaise, Maxime.

La Fane, Pamela. It's a Lovely Day Outside. large type ed. 352p. 1995. 27.99 (0-7089-3333-5) Ulverscroft.

La Farge, John. An American Artist in the South Seas. (Pacific Basin Ser.). 1998. pap. 31.00 (0-7103-0256-8, Pub. by Kegan Paul Intl) Col U Pr.

— An Artist's Letter from Japan. LC 74-130311. (Library of American Art). (Illus.). 1970. reprint ed. lib. bdg. 45.00 (0-306-70064-6) Da Capo.

***La Farge, John.** An Artist's Letters from Japan. 310p. 2000. text 110.00 (0-7103-0690-3) Col U Pr.

La Farge, John. An Artist's Letters from Japan. (Notable American Authors Ser.). 1999. reprint ed. lib. bdg. 125.00 (0-7812-3683-5) Rprt Serv.

— Considerations on Painting. LC 70-9611. (Library of American Art). 1969. reprint ed. lib. bdg. 42.50 (0-306-71824-3) Da Capo.

— Considerations on Painting. (Notable American Authors Ser.). 1999. reprint ed. lib. bdg. 125.00 (0-7812-3681-9) Rprt Serv.

— The Gospel Story in Art. (Notable American Authors Ser.). 1999. reprint ed. lib. bdg. 125.00 (0-7812-3688-6) Rprt Serv.

— Great Masters. LC 68-16945. (Essay Index Reprint Ser.). 1977. reprint ed. 30.95 (0-8369-0604-7) Ayer.

— Great Masters. (Notable American Authors Ser.). 1999. reprint ed. lib. bdg. 125.00 (0-7812-3684-3) Rprt Serv.

— The Higher Life in Art. (Notable American Authors Ser.). 1999. reprint ed. lib. bdg. 125.00 (0-7812-3685-1) Rprt Serv.

— Hokusai. (Notable American Authors Ser.). 1999. reprint ed. lib. bdg. 125.00 (0-7812-3682-7) Rprt Serv.

— Interracial Justice. 1978. 21.95 (0-405-10839-7, 11846) Ayer.

— One Hundred Masterpieces of Painting. (Notable American Authors Ser.). 1999. reprint ed. lib. bdg. 125.00 (0-7812-3686-X) Rprt Serv.

— Reminiscences of the South Seas. (Notable American Authors Ser.). 1999. reprint ed. lib. bdg. 125.00 (0-7812-3687-8) Rprt Serv.

La Farge, Mabel, ed. see Adams, Henry (Brooks).

La Farge, Oliver. All the Young Men. LC 75-41169. reprint ed. 36.00 (0-404-14566-3) AMS Pr.

— La Costumbre en Santa Eulalia. Penalosa, Fernando, tr. (SPA., Illus.). 242p. (Orig.). 1994. pap. 11.95 (1-886502-06-4, Ediciones Yax Te) Yax Te Found.

— Eagle in the Egg. LC 78-169425. (Literature & History of Aviation Ser.). 1972. reprint ed. 33.95 (0-405-03767-8) Ayer.

— Laughing Boy. 192p. Date not set. 20.95 (0-8488-2350-8) Amereon Ltd.

— Laughing Boy. (YA). 1971. mass mkt. 5.95 (0-451-52467-5) NAL.

— Laughing Boy. 259p. (J). 1981. reprint ed. lib. bdg. 21.95 (0-89967-041-5, Harmony Rain) Buccaneer Bks.

La Farge, Oliver & Byers, Douglas. El Pueblo del Cargador del Ano. Montejo, Victor & Velazquez, Oscar, trs. (SPA., Illus.). 377p. (Orig.). 1997. pap. 24.95 (1-886502-16-1) Yax Te Found.

La Farge, Oliver & Morgan, Arthur N. Santa Fe: The Autobiography of a Southwestern Town. LC 59-7958. 436p. 1985. pap. 19.95 (0-8061-1696-X) U of Okla Pr.

La Farge, Oliver, jt. auth. see Reichard, Gladys A.

La Farge, Phyllis & Berman, Sheldon, eds. Promising Practices in Teaching Social Responsibility. LC 92-11632. (SUNY Series, Democracy & Education). 267p. (C). 1993. pap. text 21.95 (0-7914-1398-5) State U NY Pr.

La Farge, Phyllis, tr. see Giraudoux, Jean.

La Farge, Tom. The Crimson Bears, Pt. 1. (New American Fiction Ser.: No. 26). 208p. (Orig.). 1993. pap. 12.95 (1-55713-074-4) Sun & Moon CA.

— A Hundred Doors: The Crimson Bears, Pt. II. (New American Fiction Ser.: No. 31). 232p. (Orig.). 1995. pap. 12.95 (1-55713-192-9) Sun & Moon CA.

— Terror of Earth. LC 96-24616. (Sun & Moon Classics Ser.: No. 136). 136p. 1996. pap. 11.95 (1-55713-261-5) Sun & Moon CA.

***La Fata, Vito.** Existence Reality. unabridged ed. (Illus.). 167p. 1999. 24.99 (1-57529-026-X) Kabel Pubs.

La Fave, Wayne R. Criminal Procedure, 1995 Pocket Part for Use in 1995-96. 2nd ed. Israel, Jerold H., ed. (Hornbook Ser.). 77p. 1995. pap. text, student ed. 7.50 (0-314-06873-2) West Pub.

La Fave, Wayne R. & Israel, Jerold H. Criminal Procedure, Vol. 3. 2nd ed. (Criminal Practice Ser.). 912p. text. write for info. (0-314-87381-3) West Pub.

La Fay, Vivienne. The Mistress. (Black Lace Ser.). 272p. (Orig.). 1996. mass mkt. 5.95 (0-352-33057-0, Pub. by Virgin Bks) London Brdge.

La Fayette, Bernard, Jr. & Jehnsen, David C. The Briefing Booklet: An Orientation to Kingian Nonviolence Conflict Reconciliation & the Leader's Manual - A Structured Guide & Introduction to Kingian Nonviolence. LC 96-135053. 39p. (Orig.). 1995. pap. text 20.00 (1-888615-01-X) Inst Human Rghts.

— The Leaders Manual: A Structural Guide & Introduction to Kingian Nonviolence (The Philosophy & Methodology) LC 96-169176. 155p. 1995. pap. text 40.00 (1-888615-00-1) Inst Human Rghts.

La Fayette, Marie-Madeleine De, see De La Fayette, Marie-Madeleine.

La Ferle, Cynthia G. Old Houses, Good Neighbors: Reflections & Celebrations of Everyday Life in a Small Town. 112p. (Orig.). 1994. pap. 10.00 (0-9642404-0-8) Self Rel Pubng.

La Flesche, Francis. Dictionary of the Osage Language. (Bureau of American Ethnology Bulletins Ser.). (ENG & OSA.). 406p. 1995. lib. bdg. 109.00 (0-7812-4109-X) Rprt Serv.

— Dictionary of the Osage Language. LC 90-43115. (ENG & OSA.). 412p. 1990. reprint ed. pap. 39.00 (1-878592-19-X); reprint ed. lib. bdg. 59.00 (1-878592-20-3) Native Amer Bk Pubs.

— Ke-ma-ha: The Omaha Stories of Francis La Flesche. Littlefield, Daniel & Parins, James W., eds. LC 94-9362. xli, 134p. 1995. pap. 10.00 (0-8032-7977-9) U of Nebr Pr.

— The Middle Five: Indian Schoolboys of the Omaha Tribe. LC 78-17409. (Illus.). xxiv, 156p. 1978. reprint ed. text 25.00 (0-8032-2852-X) U of Nebr Pr.

— The Middle Five: Indian Schoolboys of the Omaha Tribe. LC 78-17409. (Illus.). xxiv, 156p. 1978. reprint ed. pap. text 12.00 (0-8032-7901-9, Bison Books) U of Nebr Pr.

— The Osage & the Invisible World: From the Works of Francis La Flesche. Bailey, Garrick A., ed. & intro. by. LC 95-17999. (Civilization of the American Indian Ser.: Vol. 217). (Illus.). 344p. 1995. 29.95 (0-8061-2743-0) U of Okla Pr.

— War Ceremony & Peace Ceremony of the Osage Indians. (Bureau of American Ethnology Bulletins Ser.). 280p. 1995. lib. bdg. 89.00 (0-7812-4101-4) Rprt Serv.

La Flesche, Francis, jt. auth. see Fletcher, Alice C.

La Fleur, William R. Buddhism. 160p. 1988. pap. text 21.40 (0-13-084724-0) P-H.

La Follette, L., et al. Rome Papers: The Baths of Trajan Decius, Iside e Serapide Nel Palazzo, a Late Domus on the Palatine, & Nero's Golden House. (JRA Supplementary Ser.: No. 11). (Illus.). 254p. 1994. 89.50 (1-887829-11-3) Jour Roman Arch.

La Follette, Maryly & Purdie, Robert A. La Follette & Purdie: A Guide to the Family Law Act 1996. (Butterworths Annotated Legislation Service Ser.). 1996. pap. write for info. (0-406-08160-3, PGFH, MICHIE) LEXIS Pub.

La Follette, Robert M. LaFollette's Autobiography: A Personal Narrative of Political Experiences. Nevins, Allan, ed. 362p. 1960. reprint ed. pap. 15.95 (0-299-02194-7) U of Wis Pr.

La Follette, Robert M., ed. The Making of America: Industry & Finance. LC 73-2516. (Big Business; Economic Power in a Free Society Ser.). 1973. reprint ed. 34.95 (0-405-05096-8) Ayer.

La Follette, Suzanne. Art in America. 361p. 1993. reprint ed. lib. bdg. 89.00 (0-7812-5277-6) Rprt Serv.

— Concerning Women. LC 72-2610. (American Women Ser.: Images & Realities). 320p. 1978. reprint ed. 24.95 (0-405-04464-X) Ayer.

La Fond, Elizabeth B., ed. see Cullen, Noreen P.

***La Fond, James.** The Fighting Edge: Using Your Martial Arts to Fight Better. 296p. 2000. 24.00 (1-58160-063-1) Paladin Pr.

La Fond, John Q., jt. auth. see Durham, Mary L.

La Fond, John Q., jt. auth. see Singer, Richard G.

La Fontaine, J. S. Speak of the Devil: Tales of Satanic Abuse in Contemporary England. LC 97-9822. 236p. (C). 1998. text 59.95 (0-521-62082-1) Cambridge U Pr.

La Fontaine, Jean de. City Mouse, Country Mouse: Story Pak. (Graphic Learning Literature Program Series: Folk Tales). (ENG & SPA., Illus.). (J). 1992. 45.00 (0-87746-239-9) Graphic Learning.

— A Concordance to the Fables & Tales of Jean de la Fontaine. Tyler, J. Allen & Parrish, Stephen M., eds. LC 73-8388. (Cornell Concordances Ser.). 1104p. 1974. text 99.95 (0-8014-0811-3) Cornell U Pr.

— Contes, 3 tomes, Set. (FRE.). 49.95 (0-8288-9926-6, F37932) Fr & Eur.

— Contes et Nouvelles. (Illus.). 1972. pap. 495.00 (0-7859-5276-4) Fr & Eur.

— Contes et Nouvelles en Vers. (Folio Ser.: No. 1404). (FRE.). 576p. 1982. pap. 13.95 (2-07-037404-1) Schoenhof.

— Discours a Madame de la Sabliere sur l'Ame des Animaux. (FRE.). 107p. 1950. 9.95 (0-8288-9929-0, F37970) Fr & Eur.

— Fables, 2 vols. in 1. (FRE., Illus.). (C). 10.95 (0-8288-9928-2, F37956) Fr & Eur.

— Fables. (FRE.). 320p. 1974. pap. 11.95 (0-7859-4646-2) Fr & Eur.

***La Fontaine, Jean de.** Fables. 1999. pap. 9.95 (2-266-08304-X) Midwest European Pubns.

La Fontaine, Jean de. Fables. (FRE.). (C). 1972. pap. 10.95 (0-8442-1962-2, VF1962-2) NTC Contemp Pub Co.

— Fables. (Folio Ser.: No. 2246). (FRE.). 1991. pap. 12.95 (2-07-038346-6) Schoenhof.

— Fables. unabridged ed. (FRE.). pap. 7.95 (2-87714-121-7, Pub. by Bookking Intl) Distribks Inc.

— Fables, Vol. 2. (FRE.). 320p. 1974. pap. 11.95 (0-7859-4480-X, 207032138X) Fr & Eur.

— Fables of La Fontaine. (Illus.). 1997. 30.00 (1-56584-404-1, Pub. by New Press NY) Norton.

***La Fontaine, Jean de.** Fables, Tome II.Tr. of Fables, Vol. II. 2000. pap., boxed set 12.95 incl. audio (2-89517-061-4, Pub. by Coffragants) Penton Overseas.

— Fables, Tome One.Tr. of Fables, Vol. 1. (FRE.). 1998. pap., boxed set 16.95 incl. audio compact disk (2-921997-43-6, Pub. by Coffragants) Penton Overseas.

La Fontaine, Jean de. Fables, Tome 1, (Coffragants Ser.).Tr. of Fables, Vol. 1. (FRE., Illus.). 1998. boxed set 12.95 incl. audio (2-921997-44-4) Penton Overseas.

— Fifty Fables of La Fontaine. Shapiro, Norman R., tr. from FRE. LC 87-28750. (Illus.). 192p. 1988. 29.95 (0-252-01513-4) U of Ill Pr.

***La Fontaine, Jean de.** Forbidden Fruit: Selected Tales in Verse. Waldman, Guido, tr. from FRE. (Illus.). 96p. 1998. 15.00 (1-86046-491-2, Pub. by Harvill Press) FS&G.

La Fontaine, Jean de. The Fox & the Stork. LC 98-55238. 20p. 1999. pap. 3.95 (0-15-202267-8) Harcourt.

— The Fox & the Stork. LC 98-55238. 20p. (J). 1999. 10.95 (0-15-202343-7, Harcourt Child Bks) Harcourt.

— La Fontaine's Bawdy: Of Libertines, Louts, & Lechers. Shapiro, Norman R., tr. (Lockert Library of Poetry in Translation). (Illus.). 224p. 1992. text 45.00 (0-691-06956-5, Pub. by Princeton U Pr) Cal Prin Full Svc.

— The Little Goat: Story Pak. (Graphic Learning Literature Program Series: Folk Tales). (ENG & SPA., Illus.). (J). 1992. 45.00 (0-87746-243-7) Graphic Learning.

— The Mouse, the Rooster & the Cat: Story Pak. (Graphic Learning Literature Program Series: Folk Tales). (ENG & SPA., Illus.). (J). 1992. 45.00 (0-87746-245-3) Graphic Learning.

— Oeuvres Completes, 2 tomes. Incl. Tome I. Fables, Contes et Nouvelles. 99.95 (2-07-011202-0); Tome II. Oeuvres Diverses. deluxe ed. 62.95 (2-07-010297-1); (Pleiade Ser.). write for info. (0-318-52142-3) Schoenhof.

— Oeuvres Completes: Fables, Contes et Nouvelles, Vol. 1. Collinet, Jean-Pierre, ed. (FRE.). 1728p. 1991. lib. bdg. 195.00 (0-7859-3761-7, 2070102963) Fr & Eur.

***La Fontaine, Jean de.** The Rich Man & the Shoe-maker. (Illus.). 32p. 2000. pap. 8.95 (0-19-272402-9) OUP.

La Fontaine, Jean de. Selected Fables. 1976. 19.95 (0-8488-0556-9) Amereon Ltd.

— Selected Fables. Slater, Maya, ed. Wood, Christopher, tr. (World's Classics Ser.). 418p. 1995. pap. 8.95 (0-19-282440-6) OUP.

— Selected Fables. Slater, Maya, ed. Wood, Christopher, tr. (Oxford World Classics Ser.). 424p. 2000. pap. 9.95 (0-19-283785-0) OUP.

— Selected Fables (Fables Choisies) A Dual-Language Book. Appelbaum, Stanley, ed. & tr. by. LC 96-35538. (ENG & FRE.). 224p. (Orig.). 1997. pap. text 8.95 (0-486-29574-5) Dover.

La Fontaine, Jean de & Calder, Alexander. Selected Fables. Clark, Eunice, tr. (Illus.). 89p. 1968. pap. 5.95 (0-486-21878-3) Dover.

***La Fontaine, Jean de & Thornbury, Walter.** Selected Fables. LC 99-47450. 2000. pap. 1.00 (0-486-41106-0) Dover.

La Fontaine, Jean de, et al. Fifty More Fables of La Fontaine. Shapiro, Norman R., tr. LC 96-49336. 200p. 1997. 24.95 (0-252-06650-2); text 39.95 (0-252-02346-3) U of Ill Pr.

— Poetry of the Literary Revolution in Haiti. (B. E. Ser.: No. 77). 1958. 60.00 (0-8115-3028-0) Periodicals Srv.

La Fontaine, Ray, tr. see Martorell, Joanot.

La Force, Beatrice. Alpine: History of a Mountain Settlement. 6th ed. (Illus.). 529p. 1994. reprint ed. pap. 25.00 (0-9643749-0-0) Sky Mesa Pr.

— Psalm for a Winter Twilight. LC 97-221482. 91p. 1997. pap. 9.99 (0-88092-320-2, 3202) Royal Fireworks.

La Forest, Gary B., jt. auth. see Goerlitz, David B.

la Forge, Bill, jt. auth. see Morganthal, J. P.

La Forge, Raymond W., jt. ed. see Hills, Gerald E.

La Forte, Robert S. & Marcello, Ronald E., eds. Remembering Pearl Harbor: Eyewitness Accounts by U. S. Military Men & Women. LC 90-40179. (Illus.). 320p. 1991. 24.95 (0-8420-2371-2) Scholarly Res Inc.

La Franboise, Clifford, jt. ed. see Gordon, John.

***La Frenierre, Jeff.** San Juan Adventure Guide: A Guide to Hiking, Biking & Skiing in Southwestern Colorado. LC 99-87507. (Illus.). 2000. pap. 25.00 (0-87108-909-2) Pruett.

La Fresnaye, Lavon H. Northwest Weekend Gardener Organizer: A Three Year Planner. (Illus.). 160p. 1998. pap. 17.95 (*0-9662674-0-0*) La Fresnaye.
la Fuente, Angel de, see de la Fuente, Angel.
la Fuente, Ariel de, see de la Fuente, Ariel.
La Fuente, Jose De, see De La Fuente, Jose.
la Fuente, Jose Iturriaga de, see Iturriaga de la Fuente, Jose, ed.
La Fuente, Julio De, see Malinowski, Bronislaw & De La Fuente, Julio.
La Fuente, Patricia De, see De La Fuente, Patricia, ed.
La Fuente, Vincent M. De, see De La Fuente, Vincent M.
La Fuye, Allotte De, see De La Fuye, Allotte.
***La Gamma, Alisa.** Art & Oracle. (Illus.). 2000. pap. 39.95 (*0-300-08678-4*) Yale U Pr.
— Art & Oracle: African Art & Rituals of Divination. LC 99-86494. (Illus.). 80p. 2000. 22.50 (*0-8109-6545-3*, Pub. by Abrams) Time Warner.
La Garza, Beatriz De, see De la Garza, Beatriz.
La Garza, Phyllis De, see De La Garza, Phyllis.
La Garza, Phyllis De, see De la Garza, Phyllis.
La Garza, Phyllis De, see De La Garza, Phyllis.
La Garza, Phyllis De, see De la Garza, Phyllis.
La Garza, Phyllis De, see De La Garza, Phyllis.
La Garza, Rodolfo De, see Desipio, Louis & De La Garza, Rodolfo.
la Garza, Rodolfo O. De, see DeSipio, Louis & De la Garza, Rodolfo O.
la Garza, Rodolfo O. De, see De la Garza, Rodolfo O.
La Garza, Velda De, see De La Garza, Velda.
la Garza, Velda De, see De la Garza, Velda.
La Gattuta, Margo, ed. see Stefaniuk, Myroslava, et al.
La Gorce, Pierre F. Histoire de la Seconde Republique Francaise, 2 vols. LC 76-171635. reprint ed. 155.00 (*0-404-07135-X*) AMS Pr.
— Histoire du Second Empire, 7 vols. LC 77-90101. (FRE.). reprint ed. 595.00 (*0-404-01960-9*) AMS Pr.
— Histoire Religieuse de la Revolution Francaise, 5 vols. LC 71-88239. (FRE.). reprint ed. 382.50 (*0-404-03810-7*) AMS Pr.
La Gory, Mark, jt. auth. see Fitzpatrick, Kevin M.
La Gourasana, Kalindi. Ultimate Freedom: Union with God. LC 98-76369. (Illus.). 116p. 1998. pap. text 29.95 (*0-9651626-1-3*) Miracle of Love.
La Grange, Clementine de, see de La Grange, Clementine.
La Grange, Henry L. De, see De La Grange, Henry L.
La Grange, Henry-Louis de, see De La Grange, Henry-Louis.
La Greca, Annette M., et al, eds. Stress & Coping in Child Health. LC 91-38224. (Advances in Pediatric Psychology Ser.). 413p. 1991. lib. bdg. 46.95 (*0-89862-112-7*) Guilford Pubns.
La Greca, G., et al, eds. Continuous Ambulatory Peritoneal Dialysis: A Decade of Experience. (Contributions to Nephrology Ser.: Vol. 89). (Illus.). x, 288p. 1991. 49.75 (*3-8055-5307-2*) S Karger.
La Greca, G., jt. ed. see Ronco, C.
La Gregor. Hazardous Waste Management. 2nd ed. 2000. 69.25 (*0-07-039365-6*) McGraw.
La Gueriniere, Francois R. De, see De La Gueriniere, Francois R.
La Guma, Alex. In the Fog of the Season's End. LC 72-93381. 1973. 8.95 (*0-89388-058-2*) Okpaku Communications.
— In the Fog of the Seasons' End. LC 72-93381. 180p. 1973. 6.95 (*0-685-28732-7*, 89388-2) Okpaku Communications.
— Time of the Butcherbird. LC 79-670199. (African Writers Ser.). 119p. (C). 1979. pap. 9.95 (*0-435-90758-1*, 90758) Heinemann.
La Guma, Alex, ed. Apartheid: A Collection of Writings on South African Racism. LC 74-188757. 239p. (Orig.). reprint ed. pap. 74.10 (*0-7837-0584-0*, 204092800019) Bks Demand.
La Halle, Adam De, see De La Halle, Adam.
La Harpe, Jean-Baptiste De, see De la Harpe, Jean-Baptiste.
la Harpe, P. De, see Ghys, E.
La Harpe, Pierre De, see De La Harpe, Pierre.
La Hausse, Paul. Brewers, Beerhalls & Boycotts: A History of Liquor in South Africa. (History Workshop Topic Ser.: No. 2). (Illus.). 67p. (C). 1988. pap. text 9.95 (*0-86975-332-0*, Pub. by Ravan Pr) Ohio U Pr.
La Haye, Ross. A Hill Without a Name. 48p. 1998. pap. 5.95 (*1-884778-56-9*) Old Mountain.
La Hey, Carolyn De, see De la Hey, Carolyn.
la Higuera, Colin de, see Miclet, Laurent & De La Higuera, Colin.
La Hodde, Lucien De, see De La Hodde, Lucien.
La Huerta, Garcia De, see De La Huerta, Garcia.
La Hunt, Thomas J. De, see De la Hunt, Thomas J.
La Iglesia, Felix A. De, see Welling, Peter G. & De La Iglesia, Felix A., eds.
La Iglesia, Felix A. De, see De La Iglesia, Felix A.
La Iglesia, Felix De, see Feuer, George & De La Iglesia, Felix.
***La Jars, David.** Is Anyone at Home. rev. ed. (Talk Together Ser.). (Illus.). (J). 2000. 9.95 (*1-58728-014-0*); pap. 4.95 (*1-58728-018-3*) Two Can Pub.
— My Animal Friends. rev. ed. (Talk Together Ser.). (Illus.). (J). 2000. 9.95 (*1-58728-013-2*); pap. 4.95 (*1-58728-017-5*) Two Can Pub.
— One, Two, Red & Blue. rev. ed. (Talk Together Ser.). (Illus.). (J). 2000. 9.95 (*1-58728-015-9*); pap. 4.95 (*1-58728-019-1*) Two Can Pub.
***La Joie, Denise.** Whispers from Within. unabridged ed. 1999. mass mkt. 7.95 (*1-891371-13-4*) Angel Ministries.
La Lama, Luis de, see De La Lama, Luis.
La Lama, Luisa De, see De La Lama, Luisa.
La Lande, Michael. The Hot Tub Cooks. Gilbert, Helen et al, eds. 74p. 1980. 1.95 (*0-9605582-0-9*) HTC Pub.
La Lansun, A., pseud. Patterns: Personality Expressions of an Evolving Consciousness. (Solar Ser.: Bk. II). Date not set. pap. write for info. (*0-935861-01-7*) Solarium Analy.
— What Are Your Dreams Telling You? 2nd rev. ed. (Solar Ser.: Bk. I). 136p. 1986. pap. 8.95 (*0-935861-00-9*) Solarium Analy.
La Laurencie, Lionel D. Les Createurs De l'Opera Francais. LC 80-2287. reprint ed. 26.00 (*0-404-18854-0*) AMS Pr.
— Lully. LC 77-3976. (Music Reprint Ser.). (FRE., Illus.). 1977. reprint ed. lib. bdg. 32.50 (*0-306-70894-9*) Da Capo.
— Lully. 2nd ed. LC 76-43923. (Music & Theatre in France in the 17th & 18th Centuries Ser.). (FRE.). reprint ed. 39.50 (*0-404-60167-7*) AMS Pr.
La Leche League International Staff. The Womanly Art of Breastfeeding. 480p. 1997. pap. 15.95 (*0-452-27908-9*, Plume) Dutton Plume.
— Womanly Art of Breastfeeding. 1991. pap. 9.95 (*0-452-26726-9*, Plume) Dutton Plume.
La Leche League International Staff. The Womanly Art of Breastfeeding. 4th rev. ed. LC 87-15355. (Illus.). 384p. 1983. pap. 8.95 (*0-452-26000-0*, Plume) Dutton Plume.
La Loca. The Mayan. Karol, Pamala, ed. (Illus.). 39p. 1988. pap. 10.00 (*0-9619965-0-1*) Bone Scan Pr.
La Lone, jt. auth. see Hall.
La Lone, Mary B., ed. Appalachian Coal Mining Memories: Life in the Coal Fields of Virginia's New River Valley. LC 97-13985. (Appalachian Connection Ser.). (Illus.). 386p. (Orig.). 1997. pap. 25.00 (*0-936015-66-7*) Pocahontas Pr.
La Luz, Antonio De, see De La Luz, Antonio.
La Maiza, Maria Sainz De, see Foster, C. Stephen & Sainz De La Maiza, Maria.
La Malraux. Condition Humaine. (FRE.). (C). pap. 11.95 (*0-8442-1750-6*, VF1750-6) NTC Contemp Pub Co.
La Mance, Lora S., jt. auth. see Stowe, A. A.
La Mann, Angela. Mom Is Going to Stop It. (Foundations Ser.). 27p. (J). (gr. k). 1992. pap. text 4.50 (*1-56843-064-7*) EMG Networks.
— Mom Is Going to Stop It: Big Book. (Foundations Ser.). 27p. (J). (gr. k). 1992. pap. text 23.00 (*1-56843-014-0*) EMG Networks.
La Mantia, F. P., ed. Thermotropic Liquid Crystal Polymer Blends. LC 92-61560. 190p. 1992. pap. text 84.95 (*0-87762-960-9*) Technomic.
La Mar, Gerd N., ed. Nuclear Magnetic Resonance of Paramagnetic Macromolecules. LC 94-48061. (NATO ASI Ser.: Series C, Mathematical & Physical Sciences: Vol. 457). 1995. text 213.50 (*0-7923-3348-9*) Kluwer Academic.
La Mar, Virginia A., ed. see Shakespeare, William.
La Mara, jt. auth. see Liszt, Franz.
La Marque, Martin, tr. see Jackins, Harvey.
***La—aveleine Chefs & Loomis, Susan Herrmann.** Les Recettes de la Saison. Dube, Kathy A., ed.Tr. of Recipes of the Season. (Illus.). 128p. 1999. 19.95 (*0-9643955-1-7*) La Madeleine.
la Maza, E. R. De, see De la Maza, E. R.
La Maza, L. M. De, see De la Maza, L. M., ed.
La Mer, Lia. Advent: Meditations on Belief in Haiku. (Illus.). viii, 49p. 1998. 14.00 (*1-58486-011-1*) LyricLine Pr.
— A Bard in Britain. (Illus.). 168p. 1997. pap. 14.00 (*1-58486-012-X*) LyricLine Pr.
— In Oregon's Ocean: Haiku. (Illus.). viii, 64p. 1998. 14.00 (*1-58486-004-9*) LyricLine Pr.
— Kanaloa's Kin: Haiku of Hawaii. (Illus.). 96p. 1998. 14.00 (*1-58486-003-0*) LyricLine Pr.
— Moonlight Mustangs: Haiku. (Illus.). v, 87p. 1998. 14.00 (*1-58486-000-6*) LyricLine Pr.
— Mother Earth Muse. (Illus.). 140p. 1997. 14.00 (*1-58486-009-X*) LyricLine Pr.
— NW Naiad: Scuba Diving Poetry. (Illus.). 118p. 1998. 14.00 (*1-58486-008-1*) LyricLine Pr.
— Sea Spatters: Haiku. (Illus.). 114p. 1998. 14.00 (*1-58486-001-4*) LyricLine Pr.
La Meres, Clare. The Winner's Circle - Yes, I Can! Self-Esteem Lessons for the Secondary Classroom. (Illus.). 272p. 1990. pap., teacher ed. 29.95 (*0-9644261-3-7*) LaMeres Lifestyles.
La Meri. The Gesture Language of the Hindu Dance. LC 63-23185. (Illus.). 118p. 1979. reprint ed. 26.95 (*0-405-08723-3*, Pub. by Blom Pubns) Ayer.
La Mers, Joyce. Grandma Rationalizes an Enthusiasm for Skydiving. 40p. (Orig.). 1996. pap. 6.00 (*0-9638843-7-9*) Mille Grazie.
La Mesangere, Pierre De, see De La Mesangere, Pierre.
La Meza, L. M. De, see De la Meza, L. M., ed.
La Mina, Don F. Del, see Del La Mina, Don F.
La Moille, T. G. & Parsons, Eugene, compiled by. Favorite Speaker. enl. rev. ed. LC 72-5591. (Granger Index Reprint Ser.). 1977. reprint ed. 17.95 (*0-8369-6373-3*) Ayer.
La Mondia, Susan A., jt. auth. see Gonsalves, Kelly A.
La Monica, Elaine L. Management in Nursing: An Experiential Approach That Makes Theory Work for You. LC 90-9455. 464p. 1990. 51.95 (*0-8261-6580-X*) Springer Pub.
— Nursing Leadership & Management: An Experiential Approach. LC 82-20193. 300p. (C). 1983. reprint ed. pap. 40.00 (*0-86720-377-3*) Jones & Bartlett.
La Mont Johnson, D., et al, eds. Computers in the Special Education Classroom. LC 86-22834. (Computers in the Schools Ser.: Vol. 3, No. 3-4). 194p. 1987. text 49.95 (*0-86656-257-5*) Haworth Pr.
La Monte, Robert R. & Mencken, H. L. Men Versus the Man: A Correspondence Between Robert Rives La Monte, Socialist & H. L. Mencken, Individualist. LC 79-172220. (Right Wing Individualist Tradition in America Ser.). 1975. reprint ed. 23.95 (*0-405-00429-X*) Ayer.
La Morte, Michael W. School Law: Cases & Concepts. 6th ed. LC 98-13180. 453p. 1998. 84.00 (*0-205-29064-7*) Allyn.
La Mothe, Gordon De, see De La Mothe, Gordon.
La Motta, Jake, et al. Raging Bull: My Story. LC 97-15581. (Illus.). 246p. 1997. reprint ed. pap. 15.00 (*0-306-80808-0*) Da Capo.
La Motte, Ellen N. Civilization: Tales of the Orient. LC 76-122727. (Short Story Index Reprint Ser.). 1977. 19.95 (*0-8369-3560-8*) Ayer.
— Snuffs & Butters. LC 74-125226. (Short Story Index Reprint Ser.). 1977. 19.95 (*0-8369-3593-4*) Ayer.
La Motte, Fouque De, see De La Motte, Fouque.
La Motte Fouque, Friedrich De, see De La Motte Fouque, Friedrich.
La Motte-Haber, Helga De, see Flesch, Martin & De La Motte-Haber, Helga.
la Motte, Helga De, see De la Motte, Helga.
La Noceda, Joaquin Garcia De, see Garcia de La Noceda, Joaquin.
LA Notary Association Staff. Louisiana New Notary Kit. 1996. ring bd. 30.00 (*0-87511-805-4*, LLANOT) Claitors.
La Nuez Caballero, Sebastian De, see De la Nuez Caballero, Sebastian, ed.
La Nuez, Manuel De, see De La Nuez, Manuel.
La Obrera 57. Inter Nos: Poemas. LC 97-60764. (Coleccion Hispanica/Literaria Ser.: No. 8). (SPA.). 96p. (Orig.). 1997. pap. 12.00 (*0-89729-844-6*, 844-6) Ediciones.
la Paix, Yvonne De, see De la Paix, Yvonne.
La Para, Marco A. De, see De La Para, Marco A.
La Pasture, Edmee E. De, see De La Pasture, Edmee E.
La Paz, Myrna J. De, see De La Paz, Myrna J.
La Paz, Orlando De, see De La Paz, Orlando.
La Paz, Orlando De, see Bollinger, Marilyn.
la Pedraja, Rene de, see De La Pedraja, Rene.
la Pena, Alvaro Ruiz de, see Palacio Valdes, Armando.
La Pena, Augustin De, see De la Pena, Augustin.
La Pena Ernesto De. Las Contro Versias de La Fe. (SPA.). 1998. 17.95 (*968-19-0403-6*) Santillana.
La Pena, Guillermo De, see De la Pena, Guillermo.
La Pena, Luis De, see De La Pena, Luis.
La Pena McCook, Kathleen De, see De La Pena McCook, Kathleen.
La Pena, Terri De, see Chin-Lee, Cynthia & De la Pena, Terri.
La Pena, Terri De, see De la Pena, Terri.
la Pena, Victor de, see De La Pena, Victor.
la Penn, M. De, see De la Penn, M.
La Penna, jt. ed. see Luzzatto.
La Pensee, Clive. The Historical Companion to House Brewing. 156p. 1990. pap. 35.00 (*0-9515685-0-7*, Pub. by Montag Pubns) St Mut.
— You Should Brew Too! 1992. pap. 35.00 (*0-9515685-2-3*, Pub. by Montag Pubns) St Mut.
La Penta. Travel Fun. (High Q Wipe-Off Bks.). (Illus.). 24p. (J). (ps-1). 1999. mass mkt. 4.99 (*0-7681-0129-8*, McClanahan Book) Learn Horizon.
La Perchia, Alexander. All God's Children. LC 86-91204. 1987. 9.95 (*0-87212-197-6*) Libra.
La Perouse, Jean F. De, see De La Perouse, Jean F.
La Perriere, Guillaume D. Le Theatre des Bons Engins. LC 63-7783. 224p. 1963. reprint ed. 50.00 (*0-8201-1036-1*) Schol Facsimiles.
La Peruse. Medee. Coleman, ed. (Exeter French Texts Ser.: Vol. 56). (FRE.). 136p. Date not set. pap. text 19.95 (*0-85989-216-6*, Pub. by Univ Exeter Pr) Northwestern U Pr.
— Poesies Completes. Coleman, ed. (Exeter French Texts Ser.: Vol. 81). (FRE.). 125p. Date not set. pap. text 19.95 (*0-85989-363-4*, Pub. by Univ Exeter Pr) Northwestern U Pr.
La Pierre, Dominique, jt. auth. see Collins, Larry.
La Pierre, Sharon D. & Zimmerman, Enid, eds. Methods & Methodologies for Art Education. 264p. 1997. pap. text 22.00 (*0-937652-97-0*, 234) Natl Art Ed.
La Pierre, Yvette. Mapping a Changing World. (Illus.). 64p. 1996. 17.95 (*0-9650308-4-9*) Lickle Pubng.
— Native American Rock Art: Messages from the Past. LC 94-13659. (Illus.). 48p. 1994. 16.95 (*1-56566-064-1*) Lickle Pubng.
La Pietra, Ugo, ed. Gio Ponti. LC 95-72948. (Illus.). 448p. 1996. 75.00 (*0-8478-1950-7*, Pub. by Rizzoli Intl) St Martin.
la Pina, Terri de, see Chin-Lee, Cynthia & de la Pina, Terri.
La Place, Viana. Panini, Bruschetta, Crostini: The Sandwich, Italian Style. LC 93-39917. 144p. 1994. 23.00 (*0-688-11325-7*, Hearst) Hearst Commns.
— An Unplugged Kitchen: A Return to the Simple, Authentic Joys of Cooking. 1996. 25.00 (*0-614-95779-6*, Wm Morrow) Morrow Avon.
— Verdura: Vegetables Italian Style. LC 98-27777. 1999. write for info. (*0-88001-663-9*, Ecco Press) HarperTrade.
La Place, Viana & Kleiman, Evan. Cucina Fresca. LC 84-48466. (Illus.). 304p. 1987. pap. 17.00 (*0-06-096211-9*, PL 6211, Perennial) HarperTrade.
— Cucina Rustica. Schwartz, Justin, ed. (Illus.). 384p. 1998. reprint ed. pap. 12.00 (*0-688-16063-8*, Wm Morrow) Morrow Avon.
— Pasta Fresca: An Exuberant Collection Of Fresh, Vivid, And Simple Pasta Recipes, 1. LC 88-9294. (Illus.). 272p. 1999. pap. 12.00 (*0-688-17011-0*, Grenwillow Bks) HarpC Child Bks.
— Pasta Fresca: An Exuberant Collection of Fresh, Vivid & Uncomplicated Pasta Recipes from the Authors of Cucina Fresca. Bramson, Ann, ed. LC 88-9294. (Illus.). 224p. 1988. 19.95 (*0-688-07763-3*, Wm Morrow) Morrow Avon.
La Place Viana Staff. Verdura: Vegetables Italian Style. 1998. pap. 16.00 (*0-688-15802-1*, Hearst) Hearst Commns.
***La Plante, Clare & LaPlante, Alice.** Heaven Help Us: The Worrier's Guide to the Patron Saints. LC 99-24176. 224p. 1999. pap. 9.95 (*0-440-50865-7*, Dell Trade Pbks) Dell.
La Plante, Lynda. Bella Mafia. 768p. 1991. pap. 16.95 (*0-330-31538-2*, Pub. by Macmillan) Trans-Atl Phila.
***La Plante, Lynda.** Cold Blood: A Lorraine Page Mystery. 462p. 1999. mass mkt. 6.99 (*0-515-12479-6*, Jove) Berkley Pub.
La Plante, Lynda. Cold Shoulder. 464p. 1997. mass mkt. 6.99 (*0-515-12128-2*, Jove) Berkley Pub.
— Hog Fever. 288p. 1997. pap. 14.95 (*0-312-85830-2*) St Martin.
— Trial & Retribution. large type ed. LC 98-17700. 398p. 1998. 24.95 (*0-7838-0179-3*, G K Hall & Co) Mac Lib Ref.
La Plante, Richard. Hog Fever. 288p. 1995. 22.95 (*0-312-85884-1*, Pub. by Tor Bks) St Martin.
— Leopard. 336p. 1995. 5.99 (*0-8125-3020-9*, Pub. by Tor Bks) St Martin.
— Mantis. 352p. 1995. 5.99 (*0-8125-3019-5*) Tor Bks.
— Mind Kill. 320p. 1999. mass mkt. 6.99 (*0-8125-8405-8*, Pub. by Tor Bks) St Martin.
— Mind Kill. large type ed. 464p. 1998. 29.99 (*0-7089-3954-6*) Ulverscroft.
— Mindkill. LC 98-3147. 320p. 1998. text 23.95 (*0-312-86055-2*) St Martin.
— Steroid Blues. 1996. pap. 6.99 (*0-614-98099-2*) Tor Bks.
— Steroid Blues, Vol. 1. 1996. mass mkt. 6.99 (*0-8125-5073-0*, Pub. by Tor Bks) St Martin.
— Tegne. 1995. write for info. (*0-614-32236-7*) Tor Bks.
— Tegne: Warlord of Zendow. LC 95-34765. 352p. 1995. 23.95 (*0-312-85977-5*) Tor Bks.
— Tegne Vol. 1: Soul Warrior. 1996. mass mkt. 5.99 (*0-8125-5270-9*, Pub. by Tor Bks) St Martin.
***La Plante, Royal.** Cottage Cove: A Chechako in Alaska, 1. (Lords of the Secret Inner Circle Ser.). 1998. 12.95 (*1-881116-92-1*) Black Forest Pr.
— Uncle Jack's Creek. 277p. 1999. pap. 12.95 (*1-58275-006-8*) Black Forest Pr.
La Plante Royal Staff. The Myrtlewood Grove. 1994. pap. text 12.95 (*1-881116-94-8*) Black Forest Pr.
La Platiere, Marie J. Roland De, see Roland De La Platiere, Marie J.
La Point, June L. And How Are We Today? LC 84-70048. (Illus.). 96p. 1984. pap. 4.95 (*0-930422-32-5*) Dennis-Landman.
La Pointe, P. R. & Hudson, J. A. Characterization & Interpretation of Rock Mass Joint Patterns. LC 84-24750. (Geological Society of America Ser.: Vol. 199). (Illus.). 46p. 1985. reprint ed. pap. 30.00 (*0-608-07728-3*, 206781600010) Bks Demand.
La Pointe, P. R., jt. auth. see Barton, C. C.
La Pointe, Robert. Bibliography of Welding Research Supplements Published in the American Welding Society "Welding Journal" from 1950-1996. 1997. pap. 100.00 (*0-9656164-8-7*, 424) Welding Res Coun.
La Porte, Todd R., ed. Organized Social Complexity: Challenge to Politics & Policy. LC 74-25606. 388p. 1975. reprint ed. pap. 120.30 (*0-7837-9366-9*, 206010900004) Bks Demand.
— Social Responses to Large Technical Systems: Control or Anticipation. (C). 1991. text 137.50 (*0-7923-1192-2*) Kluwer Academic.
La Portilla, Nicolas De, see De La Portilla, Nicolas.
La Potin, Armand S. The Minisink Patent. Bruchey, Stuart, ed. LC 78-56697. (Management of Public Lands in the U. S. Ser.). 1979. lib. bdg. 25.95 (*0-405-11340-4*) Ayer.
La Potin, Armand S., ed. Native American Voluntary Organizations. LC 86-25764. (Ethnic American Voluntary Organizations Ser.). 204p. 1987. lib. bdg. 49.95 (*0-313-23633-X*, LAN/, Greenwood Pr) Greenwood.
La Potterie, Ignace De, see De la Potterie, Ignace.
La Primaudaye, Peter P. De, see De La Primaudaye, Peter P.
La Prise, Larry, et al. The Hokey Pokey. LC 95-43533. (Illus.). 32p. (J). (ps-2). 1997. 16.00 (*0-689-80519-5*) S&S Bks Yung.
La Puebla, Manuel De, see De La Puebla, Manuel, ed.
La Puente, Rene de, see De la Puente, Rene.
La Puma, John. Ethics Consultation: A Practical Guide. LC 93-28098. 1994. pap. 40.00 (*0-86720-797-3*) Jones & Bartlett.
La Puma, John & Schiedermayer, David L. The McGraw-Hill Pocket Guide to Managed Care. 200p. 1996. reprint ed. pap. text 14.95 (*1-57066-105-7*, ME108) Practice Mgmt Info.
***La Raja, Taryn & Pruger, Elizabeth.** Smart Start! A Preparatory Guide. (Illus.). 64p. (YA). (gr. 8). 1999. pap. 5.95 (*1-893110-05-2*) Silver Moon.
La Ramee, Louise De, see De La Ramee, Louise.
La Ramee, Pierre D. The Latine Grammar of P. Ramus. LC 78-26236. (English Experience Ser.: No. 289). 1971. reprint ed. 25.00 (*90-221-0289-0*) Walter J Johnson.
la Regina, Adriano, ed. Scripta Latina. (Illus.). 682p. 1993. 125.00 (*88-7097-023-X*, Pub. by J P Getty Trust) OUP.
La Rey, E. De, see De La Rey, E.

L

La Riche, William. Alexandria: The Sunken City. LC 97-149843. (Illus.). 136p. 1997. 35.00 (*0-297-82180-6*, Pub. by Weidenfeld & Nicolson) Trafalgar.

La Riva, Gloria, tr. see Castro, Fidel.

La Rivers, Ira. Fishes & Fisheries of Nevada. (Illus.). 800p. 1994. text 49.95 (*0-87417-256-X*) U of Nev Pr.

la Rocha, Mercedes Gonzalez De, see Gonzalez de la Rocha, Mercedes, ed.

La Roche, Catherine De, see Dickinson, Thorold & De La Roche, Catherine.

La Roche, Jacob. Die Homerische Textkritik im Alterthum. (GER.). viii, 496p. 1992. write for info. (*3-487-09636-6*) G Olms Pubs.

La Rochefoucauld, Francois de. Maximes. unabridged ed. (FRE.). pap. 5.95 (*2-87714-203-5*, Pub. by Bookking Intl) Distribks Inc.

— Maximes et Pensees. pap. 16.95 (*0-685-34232-8*) Fr & Eur.

— Maximes et Reflexions Diverses. 1976. write for info. (*0-318-63490-2*) Fr & Eur.

***La Rochefoucauld, Francois de.** The Maxims. 200p. 2000. 19.00 (*1-890318-42-6*, Pub. by St Augustines Pr) U Ch Pr.

La Rochefoucauld, Francois de. The Maxims. Tancock, Leonard W., tr. & intro. by. (Classics Ser.). 128p. 1982. pap. 10.95 (*0-14-044095-X*, Penguin Classics) Viking Penguin.

— Maxims of la Rochefoucauld. Heard, John, tr. 1982. pap. 5.95 (*0-8283-1448-9*) Branden Bks.

— Oeuvres Completes. Incl. Dernieres Oeuvres. 95.00 Tome Recapitulatif (1910-1965) 95.00: 1910-1929. 95.00: 1929-1934. 95.00: 1934-1938. 95.00: 1938-1946. 95.00: 1947-1951. 95.00: 1952-1957. 95.00: 1957-1965. 95.00 write for info. (*0-318-52163-6*) Fr & Eur.

— Oeuvres Completes. Martin-Chauffier, Robert, ed. (FRE.). 1056p. 1935. lib. bdg. 110.00 (*0-7859-3762-5*, 2070103013) Fr & Eur.

— Reflexions ou Sentences et Maxims Morales: Reflexions Diverses. 286p. 1967. write for info. (*0-318-63585-2*) Fr & Eur.

La Rochefoucauld, Francois de & Lafond, Jean. Maximes et Reflexions Diverses. (Folio Ser.: No. 728). (FRE.). 286p. 1976. 8.95 (*2-07-036728-2*) Schoenhof.

La Rochelle, Pierre Drieu. The Comedy of Charleroi & Other Stories. (Illus.). 236p. 1980. 9.95 (*0-903747-03-0*) Writers & Readers.

— Secret Journal & Other Writings. Hamilton, Alastair, tr. from FRE. 112p. 1980. 9.95 (*0-903747-02-2*) Writers & Readers.

la Rochere, Martine Hennard Dutheil de, see de la Rochere, Martine Hennard Dutheil.

La Rocque, G. Dictionary Pratique Anglais Affaires: French/English/French. (ENG & FRE.). 1998. 35.00 (*0-320-00304-3*) Fr & Eur.

— Dictionary Pratique Espanol Affaires: French/Spanish/French. (FRE & SPA.). 1998. 35.00 (*0-320-00305-1*) Fr & Eur.

la Ronciere, Delort de, see De La Ronciere, Delort.

La Roque, Guillaume De, see De La Roque, Guillaume.

La Roque, Sieur. 1752 Census of Ile Royale (Cap Breton) 172p. 1997. pap. 16.00 (*1-886560-48-X*) Quintin Pub RI.

La Rosa, Mathilde, tr. see Boni, Ada.

La Rosa, Pablo. Forbidden Fruit & Other Stories. LC 95-37665. 141p. (Orig.). 1996. pap. 11.95 (*1-55885-097-X*) Arte Publico.

La Rosa, Sheila De, see De La Rosa, Sheila.

La Rouche, Lyndon, Jr., tr. see Glazyev, Sergei.

La Roux, Madame. The Practice of Classical Palmistry. LC 92-5951. (Illus.). 288p. 1993. pap. 14.95 (*0-87728-720-1*) Weiser.

la Rubia, Tomas Diaz de, see Diaz de la Rubia, Tomas.

La Rue, Andre & Casciani, Clement. Dictionnaire d'Argot et des Principales Locutions Populaires: Histoire de l'Ar. (FRE.). 190p. 1986. pap. 14.95 (*0-8288-1939-4*, F136760) Fr & Eur.

La Rue, Asenath. Aging & Neuropsychological Assessment. (Critical Issues in Neuropsychology Ser.). (Illus.). 361p. (C). 1991. text 54.00 (*0-306-44062-8*, Kluwer Plenum) Kluwer Academic.

La Rue, Asenath, jt. auth. see Spar, James E.

la Rue, Colin De, see De la Rue, Colin, ed.

***La Rue, Don G.** Washo Land. (Illus.). 368p. 2000. mass mkt. 7.99 (*0-9679614-0-8*) D La Rue.

La Rue, Linda, ed. see Batchlor, Larry G.

La Rue, Richard M. De, see Marsh, John H. & De La Rue, Richard M., eds.

La Russo, Louis, II. Momma's Little Angels. 1979. pap. 5.25 (*0-8222-0769-9*) Dramatists Play.

La Salle, C. W., 2nd, ed. see Taylor, Bayard.

La Salle, Joseph P., ed. see Applied Mathematics Symposium Staff.

la Selva, Ma E. De, see Traversari, Gabriel & De la Selva, Ma E.

la Selva, Teresa de, see De la Selva, Teresa.

La Serna, Ramon G. Dali. 1990. 29.98 (*1-55521-342-1*) Bk Sales Inc.

La Serna, Ramon G. De, see De La Serna, Ramon G.

la Serna, Ramon Gomez De, see Gomez de la Serna, Ramon.

La Serre, Francoise De, see De La Serre, Francoise.

La Sizeranne, Robert De, see De La Sizeranne, Robert.

la Solana, Alberto Gutierrez de, see Gutierrez de la Solana, Alberto.

La Soledad, Rosalia De, see De La Soledad, Rosalia.

La Sor, William S., et al. Old Testament Survey: The Message, Form & Background of the Old Testament. 2nd ed. (Illus.). 877p. (C). 1996. text 45.00 (*0-8028-3788-3*) Eerdmans.

La Sorte, Michael A. La Merica: Images of Italian Greenhorn Experience. LC 84-16169. 224p. 1985. 29.95 (*0-87722-382-3*) Temple U Pr.

La Sota, Ann De, see De la Sota, Ann.

La Taille, Jean De, see De la Taille, Jean.

la Teja, Jesus F. De, see De la Teja, Jesus F.

La Torre, Adela De, see De La Torre, Adela, ed.

La Torre, Augusto De, see De la Torre, Augusto.

La Torre, Jack C. De, see De La Torre, Jack C.

La Torre, Massimo. European Citizenship: An Institutional Challenge. LC 98-21657. (European Forum Ser.: Vol. 3). 492p. 1998. 143.00 (*90-411-9659-5*) Kluwer Law Intl.

La Torre, Rafael De, see Segura, Jordi & De La Torre, Rafael.

la Torre, Rogelio De, see De la Torre, Rogelio.

La Torre, Teodoro De, see De La Torre, Teodoro, contrib. by.

la Torre Villar, Ernesto De, see De la Torre Villar, Ernesto.

La Touche, Louise M. De, see De La Touche, Louise M.

La Tour, Kathy. For Those Who Live: Helping Children Cope with the Death of a Brother or Sister. 145p. 1983. 9.95 (*0-9612870-0-4*) K LaTour.

La Tour-Landry, Geoffroy D. The Book of the Knight of la Tour-Landry. Taylor, G. S., ed. LC 79-8366. reprint ed. 28.00 (*0-404-18350-6*) AMS Pr.

— Book of the Knight of la Tour-Landry. Wright, T., ed. (EETS, OS Ser.: No. 33). 1972. reprint ed. 45.00 (*0-527-00033-7*) Periodicals Srv.

la Tour, Richard De, see De la Tour, Shatoiya & De la Tour, Richard.

la Tour, Shatoiya De, see De la Tour, Shatoiya.

La Tourelle, Maggie & Courtenay, Anthea. Thorson's Introductory Guide to Kinesiology: Touch for Health. 1993. pap. 11.00 (*0-7225-2699-7*) Thorsons PA.

La Tourrette, Joe. Washington Wildlife Viewing Guide. LC 92-53272. (Illus.). 96p. 1995. pap. 8.95 (*1-56044-150-X*) Falcon Pub Inc.

— Watching Wildlife: The National Wildlife Federation Guide to Observing Animals in the Wild. LC 96-44345. (Illus.). 192p. 1995. pap. 12.95 (*0-8050-4685-2*, Owl) H Holt & Co.

La Vail, Matthew M., et al, eds. Degenerative Retinal Diseases: Proceedings of the VIIth International Symposium Held in Sendai, Japan, October 5-9, 1996. LC 97-27725. 440p. 1997. 120.00 (*0-306-45701-6*, Kluwer Plenum) Kluwer Academic.

La Valdene, Guy De, see De la Valdene, Guy.

La Valette, Desiree & Fehrle, Gerdt. Keith Haring: I Wish I Didn't Have to Sleep. LC 97-2950. (Adventures in Art Ser.). (Illus.). 32p. (J). (gr. 1 up). 1997. 14.95 (*3-7913-1815-2*, Pub. by Prestel) te Neues.

La Valle, Deanna, ed. Profiles in Management. Date not set. text 695.00 incl. cd-rom (*0-07-912243-4*) McGraw.

— Profiles in Management. 1994. text 595.00 incl. cd-rom (*0-07-103610-5*); text 495.00 (*0-07-103609-1*) McGraw.

— Profiles in Management. 2nd ed. 1995. 595.00 incl. cd-rom (*0-07-103639-3*) McGraw.

La Valle, John. Everything You Need to Know When You Are the Male Survivor of Rape or Sexual Assault. LC 94-44981. (Need to Know Library). (Illus.). 64p. (YA). (gr. 7-12). 1997. lib. bdg. 17.95 (*0-8239-2084-4*) Rosen Group.

La Valle, John J. Coping When a Parent Is in Jail. LC 94-8245. (YA). (gr. 7-12). 1995. lib. bdg. 17.95 (*0-8239-1967-6*) Rosen Group.

La Valle, Maria T., tr. see Grant, Wilson W.

La Valle, Victor D. Slapboxing with Jesus. LC 99-26222. 1999. pap. 11.00 (*0-375-70590-2*) Knopf.

La Vallee, Elisabeth R. De, see Larre, Claude.

La Vallee Poussin, Louis D. The Way to Nirvana: Six Lectures on Ancient Buddhism As a Discipline of Salvation. LC 77-27154. (Hibbert Lectures: 1916). reprint ed. 39.50 (*0-404-60417-X*) AMS Pr.

La Vars, Lauren P. De, see Benzel, Kathryn N. & De La Vars, Lauren P., eds.

La Vega, Aurelio De, see De La Vega, Aurelio.

la Vega, Inca Carcilaso de, see Carcilaso de la Vega, Inca.

La Verdiere, Eugene. The Breaking of the Bread: The Development of the Eucharist According to Acts. LC 98-9770. 249p. 1998. pap. 12.00 (*1-56854-148-1*, ACTS) Liturgy Tr Pubns.

La Verdiere, L. Luke. 1989. pap. 21.00 (*0-86217-008-7*, Pub. by Veritas Pubns) St Mut.

La Vere, David. The Caddo Chiefdoms: Caddo Economics & Politics, 700-1835. LC 98-13860. (Illus.). xv, 199p. 1998. text 45.00 (*0-8032-2927-5*) U of Nebr Pr.

***La Vere, David.** Contrary Neighbors: Southern Plains & Removed Indians in Indian Territory. LC 00-23051. (Civilization of the American Indian Ser.: Vol. 237). (Illus.). 304p. 2000. 29.95 (*0-8061-3251-5*) U of Okla Pr.

La Vere, David. Life among the Texas Indians: The WPA Narratives. LC 97-32891. (Elma Dill Russell Spencer Series in the West & Southwest: Vol. 18). (Illus.). 288p. 1998. 29.95 (*0-89096-809-8*) Tex A&M Univ Pr.

La Verendrye, Pierre G. Journals & Letters of Pierre Gaultier de Varennes de la Verendrye & His Sons, with Correspondence Between the Governors of Canada & the French Court, Touching the Search for the Western Sea, Vol. 16. Burpee, Lawrence J., ed. LC 68-28605. 548p. 1969. reprint ed. lib. bdg. 85.00 (*0-8371-5055-8*, LAJL) Greenwood.

La Verne, Walker & Planadeball, Marta J. Stories Made Easy for Spanish Speakers. LC 86-6913. 75p. 1986. pap. 6.00 (*0-8477-3344-0*) U of PR Pr.

La Vey, Anton S. Satanic Bible. 272p. 1976. mass mkt. 6.99 (*0-380-01539-0*, Avon Bks) Morrow Avon.

la Vieja, M. Teresa Lopez de, see Lopez de la Vieja, M. Teresa.

La Vigne, Nancy, jt. auth. see Eck, John E.

La Villeguerin, Y. Dictionnaire Fiduciaire Social 1998. (FRE.). 1998. 105.00 (*0-320-00382-5*) Fr & Eur.

La Villeguerin, Yves-Robert De, see De La Villeguerin, Yves-Robert.

La Villguerin, Erik De, see De La Villguerin, Erik.

La Vopa, Anthony J. Grace, Talent & Merit: Poor Students, Clerical Careers & Professional Ideology in Eighteenth Century Germany. (Illus.). 432p. 1988. text 89.95 (*0-521-35041-7*) Cambridge U Pr.

LA 411 Pub Co Staff. NY 411, 1. 1999. pap. text 49.00 (*1-879930-11-0*) LA Four-Eleven.

***LA 411 Publishing Staff.** 411 Digital North America: North America's Professional Reference Guide for Visual Effects & Post Production. 408p. 2000. spiral bd. 49.00 (*1-879930-12-9*, Pub. by Media Pub Intl) SCB Distributors.

Laabi, Abdellatif. Rue du Retour. Kaye, Jacqueline, tr. from FRE. LC 88-63241. 200p. (Orig.). 1989. 17.95 (*0-930523-64-4*); pap. 9.95 (*0-930523-65-2*) Readers Intl.

Laache, N. J., ed. see Rosenius, Carl O.

***Laade, Wolfgang.** Music & Culture in South-East New Britain: Unesco Territorial Survey of Oceanic Music Report on Field Research Conducted in August-October 1988. 262p. 2000. pap. text 35.95 (*3-906760-41-3*) P Lang Pubng.

Laage-Hellman, Jens. Business Networks in Japan: Supplier-Customer Interaction in Product Development. LC 96-16039. 176p. (C). 1997. 80.00 (*0-415-14869-3*) Routledge.

Laak, Jan J., et al, eds. Developmental Tasks: Towards a Cultural Analysis of Human Development. LC 94-12546. 285p. (C). 1994. lib. bdg. 165.50 (*0-7923-2905-8*) Kluwer Academic.

Laakaniemi, Ray. Newswriting in Transition. (Mass Communication Ser.). 1995. pap. text 34.95 (*0-8304-1347-2*) Thomson Learn.

Laakmann, G. Psychopharmaco-Endocrinology & Depression Research. (Illus.). xii, 219p. 1990. 79.95 (*0-387-52075-9*) Spr-Verlag.

Laakso, Liisa, jt. ed. see Olukoshi, Adebayo O.

Laakso, Lila. E. J. Pratt: An Annotated Bibliography. 220p. (C). 1980. pap. text 9.00 (*0-920763-60-X*, Pub. by ECW) Genl Dist Srvs.

Laakso, Toini P., ed. see Hannula, Reino.

Laaksonen, Oiva. Management in China: During & after Mao in Enterprises, Government & Party. (Studies in Organization: No. 12). 379p. (C). 1988. text 57.95 (*3-11-009958-6*) De Gruyter.

Laaly, Heshmat O. The Science & Technology of Traditional & Modern Roofing Systems: "The New Bible of Roofing", 2 Vols. LC 91-90263. (Illus.). 3152p. (C). 1992. 350.00 (*0-9629669-0-8*) Roofing Mtls Sci.

Laan, Carrie Van Der, see Van Der Laan, Carrie.

Laan, H. L. Van Der, see Van Der Laan, H. L.

Laan, H. Laurens Van Der, see Van Der Laan, H. Laurens.

Laan, H. Van der, see Van der Laan, H.

Laan, Hans Van der, see Van der Laan, Hans.

Laan, Lambert Van Der, see Van Der Laan, Lambert, ed.

Laan, P. A. Van der, see Duffels, J. P. & Van der Laan, P. A.

Laan, Ray Van der, see Van der Laan, Ray.

Laan, T. Van, see Smith, R. P. & Van Laan, T.

Laanatza, Marianne, et al. Egypt under Pressure. 152p. 1986. write for info. (*91-7106-255-6*, Pub. by Nordic Africa) Transaction Pubs.

Laane, J. Structure & Dynamics of Electronic Excited States. 1998. 59.95 (*3-540-63908-X*) Spr-Verlag.

Laane, Jaan, ed. Structures & Conformations of Non-Rigid Molecules: Proceedings of the NATO Advanced Research Workshop, Reisenburg, Germany, September 6-10, 1992. (NATO Advanced Science Institutes Series C: Mathematical & Physical Sciences). 656p. (C). 1993. text 353.00 (*0-7923-2415-3*) Kluwer Academic.

Laanpere, H. Finnish-Esthonian-Finnish Dictionary: Suomi-Eesti-s. (EST & FIN.). 499p. 1977. pap. 49.95 (*0-8288-5436-X*, M9641) Fr & Eur.

Laansma, Jon. I Will Give You Rest: The Rest Motif in the New Testament with Special Reference to Mt. 11 & Heb. 3-4. LC 97-226717. (WissUNT Zum Neuen Testament Ser.: Vol. 2, No. 98). 459p. 1997. pap. 87.50 (*3-16-146639-X*, Pub. by JCB Mohr) Coronet Bks.

Laaper, Ben. Procurement Reengineering. LC 97-40468. (Orig.). 1998. pap. 14.95 (*0-945456-31-X*) PT Pubns.

Laar, E. T. Van De, see Van De Laar, E. T.

Laar, H. H. Van, see Goudriaan, J. & Van Laar, H. H.

Laar, H. H. Van, see Kropff, M. J. & Van Laar, H. H., eds.

Laar, Mart. War in the Woods: Estonia's Struggle for Survival, 1944-56. Ets, Tiina, tr. from EST. (Illus.). 272p. 1992. 38.00 (*0-929590-08-2*); pap. 18.95 (*0-929590-09-0*) Compass Pr.

Laar, Timothy Van, see Van Laar, Timothy.

Laar, Timothy Van, see Diepeveen, Leonard & Van Laar, Timothy.

Laarhoven, P. J. Van, see Van Laarhoven, P. J.

Laarhoven, Q. L., jt. auth. see Gosling, P. E.

Laarhoven, Ruurdje. Triumph of Moro Diplomacy: The Maguindanao Sultanate in the 17th Century. 287p. (Orig.). (C). 1989. pap. 17.50 (*971-10-0390-2*, Pub. by New Day Pub) Cellar.

Laarman, Jan, et al. Choice of Technology in Forestry: A Philippine Case Study. (Illus.). (C). 1981. pap. 12.50 (*0-686-30446-2*, Pub. by New Day Pub) Cellar.

Laarman, Jan G. & Sedjo, Roger A. Global Forestry: Issues for Six Billion People. 337p. (C). 1991. 76.56 (*0-07-035702-1*) McGraw.

Laas, Andrew F., jt. auth. see Kesaris, Paul.

Laas, Virginia J. Love & Power in the Nineteenth Century: The Marriage of Violet Blair. (Illus.). 192p. 1998. 32.00 (*1-55728-505-5*); pap. 16.00 (*1-55728-506-3*) U of Ark Pr.

***Laas, Virginia J.** Wartime Washington: The Civil War Letters of Elizabeth Blair Lee. 2000. pap. 24.95 (*0-252-06859-9*) U of Ill Pr.

Laas, Virginia J., ed. Wartime Washington: The Civil War Letters of Elizabeth Blair Lee. (Illus.). 588p. 1991. text 39.95 (*0-252-01802-8*) U of Ill Pr.

Laas, Virginia J., ed. & intro. see Blair, Emily N.

Laasar, Mark & Hopkins, Nancy, eds. Restoring the Soul of a Church: Congregations Wounded by Clergy Sexual Misconduct. pap. 19.95 (*1-56699-164-1*) Alban Inst.

Laasch, Jack & Benton, Scott. Fishing Lake Michigan Illinois - Indiana. (Lake Michigan Ser.). (Illus.). 84p. 1988. pap. 6.95 (*0-939314-19-3*) Fishing Hot.

Laasch, Jack & Brich, Steve. Fishing Lake Michigan Southern Wisconsin. (Lake Michigan Ser.). (Illus.). 80p. 1988. pap. 6.95 (*0-939314-18-5*) Fishing Hot.

Laasch, Jack & Knops, Bob. Fishing Lake Michigan: Central Wisconsin. (Lake Michigan Ser.). (Illus.). 88p. 1988. pap. 6.95 (*0-939314-17-7*) Fishing Hot.

Laase, Lois. Helping Students Write the Best Research Reports Ever. (Illus.). 128p. (J). 1998. pap. 14.95 (*0-590-96386-4*) Scholastic Inc.

Laase, Lois, jt. auth. see Clemmons, Joan.

Laaser, Georg. Vergleichende Systematische Studien an Basidiomycetenhefen Unter Besonderer Beruecksichtigung der Hefestadien. (Bibliotheca Mycologica: Vol. 130). (GER., Illus.). viii, 335p. 1989. 77.00 (*3-443-59031-4*, Pub. by Gebruder Borntraeger) Balogh.

Laaser, Mark. Talking to Your Kids about Sex. LC 99-26336. 256p. 1999. pap. 11.95 (*1-57856-199-X*) Waterbrook Pr.

Laaser, Mark R. Faithful & True: Sexual Integrity in a Fallen World. 208p. 1996. pap. 10.99 (*0-310-20836-X*) Zondervan.

Laaser, Mark R. & Hopkins, Nancy, eds. Restoring the Soul of a Church: Healing Congregations Wounded by Clergy Sexual Misconduct. 280p. 1995. pap. 19.95 (*0-8146-2333-6*, Liturg Pr Bks) Liturgical Pr.

Laaser, Mark R., jt. auth. see Friberg, Nils.

Laaser, U., et al, eds. Costs & Benefits in Health Care & Prevention: An International Approach to Priorities in Medicine. (Illus.). 180p. 1990. 34.95 (*0-387-52708-7*) Spr-Verlag.

Laaser, Ulrich, jt. ed. see Hurrelman, Klaus.

Laat, A. De, see Van Steenberghe, D. & De Laat, A., eds.

***Laato, Antti.** About Zion I Will Not Be Silent: The Book of Isaiah as an Ideological Unity. (Coniectanea Biblica Old Testament Ser.: No. 44). 241p. 1998. pap. 47.50 (*91-22-01811-5*, Pub. by Almqvist Wiksell) Coronet Bks.

Laato, Antti. History & Ideology in the Old Testament Prophetic Literature: A Semiotic Approach to the Reconstruction of the Proclamation of the Historical Prophets. (Coniectanea Biblica Old Testament Ser.: Vol. 41). 445p. (Orig.). 1996. pap. 62.50 (*91-22-01701-1*) Coronet Bks.

— Josiah & David Redivivus: The Historical Josiah & the Messianic Expectations of Exilic & Postexilic Times. (Coniectanea Biblica. Old Testament Ser.: No. 33). 416p. (Orig.). 1992. pap. 66.00 (*91-22-01475-6*) Coronet Bks.

***Laato, Antti.** Monotheism, the Trinity & Mysticism: A Semiotic Approach to Jewish-Christian Encounter. 159p. 1999. pap. 31.95 (*3-631-34531-3*) P Lang Pubng.

— Monotheism, the Trinity & Mysticism: A Semiotic Approach to Jewish-Christian Encounter. 159p. (C). 1999. pap. 31.95 (*0-8204-4312-3*) P Lang Pubng.

Laato, Antti. The Servant YHWH & Cyrus: A Reinterpretation of the Exilic Messianic Programme in Isaiah 40-55. (Coniectanea Biblica. Old Testament Ser.: No. 35). 307p. (Orig.). 1992. pap. 52.50 (*91-22-01529-9*) Coronet Bks.

***Laats, Alar.** Doctrines of the Trinity in Eastern & Western Theologies: A Study with Special Reference to K. Barth & V. Lossky. (Studies in the Intercultural History of Christianity). 171p. 1999. pap. 35.95 (*3-631-34278-0*) P Lang Pubng.

— Doctrines of the Trinity in Eastern & Western Theologies: A Study with Special Reference to K. Barth & V. Lossky. LC 99-39944. (Studies in the Intercultural History of Christianity: Vol. 114). 171p. (C). 1999. pap. 35.95 (*0-8204-3645-3*) P Lang Pubng.

Lab, Doug & Lab, Olivia K. My Life in My Hands: Living on with Cystic Fibrosis. Witkin, Robyn, ed. 163p. 1990. pap. 7.50 (*0-9629216-0-2*) LabPro Pr.

Lab, Olivia K., jt. auth. see Lab, Doug.

Lab, Steven, ed. Crime Prevention at a Crossroads. LC 97-70841. (ACJS/Anderson Monograph Ser.). 210p. 1997. pap. 23.95 (*0-87084-511-X*) Anderson Pub Co.

Lab, Steven P. Crime Prevention: Approaches, Practices & Evaluations. 3rd ed. LC 97-72025. 328p. (C). 1997. pap. text 32.95 (*0-87084-513-6*) Anderson Pub Co.

Lab, Steven P., jt. auth. see Doerner, William G.

Lab, Steven P., jt. auth. see Whitehead, John T.

Lab, Susan V., jt. ed. see Cunningham, Patricia A.

Lab, Susan V., jt. ed. see Cunningham, Patricia.

Lab-Volt, Ltd. Staff. AC/DC Motors & Generators. LC 98-13083. Date not set. write for info. (*2-89289-403-4*) Lab-Volt.

Lab-Volt Ltd. Staff. Analog Communications System Simulation Software: LVSIM-COM. LC 98-14468. (Illus.). 47p. 1998. write for info. (*2-89289-404-2*) Lab-Volt.

— Exploring Electronics: Student's Manual. LC 98-14467. (Exploring Technology Ser.). (Illus.). 1998. student ed. write for info. (*2-89289-401-8*) Lab-Volt.

An Asterisk (*) at the beginning of an entry indicates that the title is appearing for the first time.

— Exploring Industrial Controls: Student's Manual. LC 98-14466. (Exploring Technology Ser.). (Illus.). 1998. student ed. write for info. (*2-89289-402-6*) Lab-Volt.

— Fundamentos de las Antenas: Guia del Professor. LC 98-14345. (Antenas Ser.). (ENG & SPA., Illus.). 1998. teacher ed. write for info. (*2-89289-395-X*) Lab-Volt.

— Multiprocess Station. LC 98-13084. Date not set. write for info. (*2-89289-398-4*) Lab-Volt.

Lab-Volt Staff. Experiments in Electricity for Use with Lab-Volt EMS Equipment. 23p. 1993. teacher ed. 15.00 (*0-8273-5996-9*) Delmar.

Lab-Volt Systems, Inc. Staff. ACI Fundamentals, Vol. 3. 2nd ed. (F.A.C.E.T. Ser.). (Illus.). 294p. (Orig.). (C). 1988. pap. text, student ed. write for info. (*0-86657-065-9*, TM90862-00) Lab-Volt.

— Analog Communications, Vol. 18. (F.A.C.E.T. Ser.). (Illus.). 345p. (Orig.). (C). 1995. pap. text, student ed. write for info. (*0-86657-080-2*, TM90877-00) Lab-Volt.

— Analog Communications, Vol. 18. (F.A.C.E.T. Ser.). (Illus.). 90p. (Orig.). (C). 1995. pap. text, teacher ed. write for info. (*0-86657-090-X*, TM90877-10) Lab-Volt.

— Commander Student PC Troubleshooting & Repair Manual. rev. ed. (Illus.). 332p. 1995. ring bd. write for info. (*0-86657-076-4*, PIN55177-1) Lab-Volt.

— Digital Circuit Fundamentals No. 2, Vol. 16. (F.A.C.E.T. Ser.). (Illus.). 80p. (Orig.). (C). 1991. pap. text, teacher ed. write for info. (*0-86657-039-X*, TM90875-10) Lab-Volt.

— The F.A.C.E.T. Authoring System User's Manual. (F.A.C.E.T. Ser.). (Illus.). 418p. (Orig.). (C). 1992. pap. text. write for info. (*0-86657-045-4*, TI91421-00) Lab-Volt.

— F.A.C.E.T. Computer Based Laboratory Course II Vol. 11: Thyristor & Power Control Circuits. (F.A.C.E.T. Ser.). (Illus.). 94p. (Orig.). (C). 1995. pap. text, teacher ed. write for info. (*0-86657-067-5*, TM91570-10) Lab-Volt.

— F.A.C.E.T. Computer Based Laboratory Course 1 Vol. 1: DC Fundamentals. (F.A.C.E.T. Ser.). (Illus.). 103p. (Orig.). (C). 1992. pap. text, teacher ed. write for info. (*0-86657-051-9*, TM91560-10) Lab-Volt.

— F.A.C.E.T. Computer Based Laboratory Course 10 Vol. 10: FET Fundamentals. (F.A.C.E.T. Ser.). (Illus.). 118p. (Orig.). (C). 1995. pap. text, teacher ed. write for info. (*0-86657-066-7*, TM91569-10) Lab-Volt.

— F.A.C.E.T. Computer Based Laboratory Course 12 Vol. 12: OP AMP Fundamentals. (F.A.C.E.T. Ser.). (Illus.). 93p. (Orig.). (C). 1993. pap. text, teacher ed. write for info. (*0-86657-056-X*, TM91571-10) Lab-Volt.

— F.A.C.E.T. Computer Based Laboratory Course 13 Vol. 13: OP AMP Applications. (F.A.C.E.T. Ser.). (Illus.). 100p. (Orig.). (C). 1995. pap. text, teacher ed. write for info. (*0-86657-061-6*, TM91572-10) Lab-Volt.

— F.A.C.E.T. Computer Based Laboratory Course 15 Vol. 15: Digital Circuit Fundamentals 1. (F.A.C.E.T. Ser.). (Illus.). 92p. (Orig.). (C). 1995. pap. text, teacher ed. write for info. (*0-86657-062-4*, TM91574-10) Lab-Volt.

— F.A.C.E.T. Computer Based Laboratory Course 17 Vol. 17: 32 Bit Microprocessor. (F.A.C.E.T. Ser.). (Illus.). 169p. (Orig.). (C). 1995. pap. text, teacher ed. write for info. (*0-86657-069-1*, TM91577-10) Lab-Volt.

— F.A.C.E.T. Computer-Based Laboratory Course 18 Vol. 18: Analog Communications. (F.A.C.E.T. Ser.). (Illus.). 94p. (Orig.). (C). 1995. pap. text, teacher ed. write for info. (*0-86657-070-5*, TM91578-10) Lab-Volt.

— F.A.C.E.T. Computer Based Laboratory Course 19 Vol. 19: Transducer Fundamentals. (F.A.C.E.T. Ser.). (Illus.). 146p. (Orig.). (C). 1995. pap. text, teacher ed. write for info. (*0-86657-071-3*, TM91579-10) Lab-Volt.

— F.A.C.E.T. Computer Based Laboratory Course 2 Vol. 2: DC Network Theorems. (F.A.C.E.T. Ser.). (Illus.). 138p. (Orig.). (C). 1995. pap. text, teacher ed. write for info. (*0-86657-048-9*, TM91561-10) Lab-Volt.

— F.A.C.E.T. Computer Based Laboratory Course 3A Vol. 3: ACI Fundamentals. (F.A.C.E.T. Ser.). (Illus.). 85p. (Orig.). (C). 1992. pap. text, teacher ed. write for info. (*0-86657-047-0*, TM91562-10) Lab-Volt.

— F.A.C.E.T. Computer Based Laboratory Course 4 Vol. 4: ACZ Fundamentals. (F.A.C.E.T. Ser.). (Illus.). 73p. (Orig.). (C). 1993. pap. text, teacher ed. write for info. (*0-86657-055-1*, TM91563-10) Lab-Volt.

— F.A.C.E.T. Computer Based Laboratory Course 5 Vol. 5: Semiconductor. (F.A.C.E.T. Ser.). (Illus.). 77p. (Orig.). (C). 1992. pap. text, teacher ed. write for info. (*0-86657-050-0*, TM91564-10) Lab-Volt.

— F.A.C.E.T. Computer Based Laboratory Course 7 Vol. 7: Transistor Power Amplifiers. (F.A.C.E.T. Ser.). (Illus.). 82p. (Orig.). (C). 1995. pap. text, teacher ed. write for info. (*0-86657-059-4*, TM91566-10) Lab-Volt.

— F.A.C.E.T. Computer Based Laboratory Course 8 Vol. 8: Transistor Feedback Circuits. (F.A.C.E.T. Ser.). (Illus.). 90p. (Orig.). (C). 1995. pap. text, teacher ed. write for info. (*0-86657-060-8*, TM91567-10) Lab-Volt.

— F.A.C.E.T. Computer Based Laboratory Course 9 Vol. 9: Power Supply Regulation Circuits. (F.A.C.E.T. Ser.). (Illus.). 73p. (Orig.). (C). 1993. pap. text, teacher ed. write for info. (*0-86657-052-7*, TM91568-10) Lab-Volt.

— F.A.C.E.T. Computer Based Laboratory Digital Logic Fundamentals Course 14, Vol. 14. (Illus.). 100p. (Orig.). (C). 1993. pap. text, teacher ed. write for info. (*0-86657-049-7*, TM91573-10) Lab-Volt.

— F.A.C.E.T. Computer Based Laboratory Network Supervisors Manual. (F.A.C.E.T. Ser.). (Illus.). 42p. (Orig.). (C). 1992. pap. text. write for info. (*0-86657-046-2*, TI91498-00) Lab-Volt.

— F.A.C.E.T. Computer Based Laboratory User's Guide. (F.A.C.E.T. Ser.). (Illus.). 108p. (Orig.). (C). 1992. pap. text. write for info. (*0-86657-063-2*, TM91598-00) Lab-Volt.

— F.A.C.E.T. Computer Based Laboratory 1.6 Course 6 Vol. 6: Transistor Amplifier Circuits. (F.A.C.E.T. Ser.). (Illus.). 120p. (Orig.). (C). 1996. pap. text, teacher ed. write for info. (*0-86657-058-6*, TM91565-10) Lab-Volt.

— The F.A.C.E.T. Manager (Network) User's Manual, Vol. 6. (F.A.C.E.T. Ser.). (Illus.). 46p. (Orig.). (C). 1992. pap. text. write for info. (*0-86657-053-5*, TI91575-00) Lab-Volt.

— The F.A.C.E.T. Manager (Non Network) User's Manual. (F.A.C.E.T. Ser.). (Illus.). 46p. (Orig.). (C). 1992. pap. text. write for info. (*0-86657-057-8*, TI91596-00) Lab-Volt.

— Investigations in Electric Power Technology. 2nd ed. (Illus.). 372p. (Orig.). 1992. pap. text, teacher ed. 23.00 (*0-86657-042-X*, TM11627-01) Lab-Volt.

— Investigations in Electric Power Technology. 2nd ed. (Illus.). 372p. (Orig.). (C). 1995. pap. text 18.00 (*0-86657-041-1*, TM11627-00) Lab-Volt.

— Magnetism & Electromagnetism, Vol. 20. (F.A.C.E.T. Ser.). (Illus.). 86p. (Orig.). (C). 1993. pap. text. write for info. (*0-86657-064-0*, TM90879-00) Lab-Volt.

— Magnetism & Electromagnetism, Vol. 20. (F.A.C.E.T. Ser.). (Illus.). 20p. (Orig.). (C). 1993. pap. text, teacher ed. write for info. (*0-86657-093-4*, TM90879-10) Lab-Volt.

— Practical Electricity & Electronics Vol. 11: Fundamentals for Digital Communication: Pulse Modulation. (Illus.). 92p. (Orig.). (C). 1985. pap. text. write for info. (*0-86657-054-3*, TM19616-00) Lab-Volt.

— 32 Bit Microprocessor, Vol. 17. (F.A.C.E.T. Ser.). (Illus.). 496p. (Orig.). (C). 1995. pap. text, student ed. write for info. (*0-86657-079-9*, TM90876-00) Lab-Volt.

— 32 Bit Microprocessor, Vol. 17. (F.A.C.E.T. Ser.). (Illus.). 165p. (Orig.). (C). 1995. pap. text, teacher ed. write for info. (*0-86657-089-6*, TM90876-10) Lab-Volt.

— Transducer Fundamentals, Vol. 19. (F.A.C.E.T. Ser.). (Illus.). 146p. (Orig.). (C). 1995. pap. text, teacher ed. write for info. (*0-86657-091-8*, TM90878-10); pap. text, student ed. write for info. (*0-86657-081-0*, TM90878-00) Lab-Volt.

Laba, Dennis, ed. Rheological Properties of Cosmetics & Toiletries. (Cosmetic Science & Technology Ser.: Vol. 13). (Illus.). 440p. 1993. text 210.00 (*0-8247-9090-1*) Dekker.

Laba, Martin, jt. ed. see Narvaez, Peter.

Labacus, Thelma. A Genuine Antique Person Is. (Illus.). 1993. pap. write for info. (*0-9639812-1-8*) Laid Back Ent.

— Lifestyles of the Rich & Flatulent. (Illus.). 1996. pap. write for info. (*0-9639812-2-6*) Laid Back Ent.

Labadie, J. W., et al, eds. Computerized Decision Support Systems for Water Managers. 992p. 1989. pap. text 11.00 (*0-87262-717-9*, 717) Am Soc Civil Eng.

Labadie, Jeff W., jt. ed. see Hedrick, James L.

Labadie, Joseph A. Anarchism. 1976. 250.00 (*0-87700-231-2*) Revisionist Pr.

— What Is Love? (Men & Movements in the History & Philosophy of Anarchism Ser.). 1979. lib. bdg. 250.00 (*0-87700-311-4*) Revisionist Pr.

Labadie, Laurance. Selected Essays. LC 78-78149. (Libertarian Broadsides Ser.: No. 7). (Illus.). 1978. pap. 1.50 (*0-87926-022-X*) R Myles.

— A Way Out: Anarchist, Mutualist & Individualist Essays. (Men & Movements in the History & Philosophy of Anarchism Ser.). 1980. lib. bdg. 250.00 (*0-686-60065-7*) Revisionist Pr.

Labadie, Pamela, jt. auth. see Altug, Sumru.

***Labahn, Michael.** Jesus Als Lebensspender: Untersuchungen Zu Einer Geschichte der Johanneischen Tradition Anhand Ihrer Wundergeschichten. x, 559p. 1999. 172.00 (*3-11-016301-2*) De Gruyter.

Labairon, Cassandra. Growing Season. 20p. 1999. 5.00 (*0-944024-37-8*) Spoon Riv Poetry.

Labaky, Lordys. Visual Dictionary Botany: English-Arabic. (Large Bks.). (ARA., Illus.). 18.95 (*0-86685-605-6*, LDL6056, Pub. by Librairie du Liban) Intl Bk Ctr.

Labaky, Mansour. The Roads of Nowhere: A Child of Lebanon. Annelyse, Allen, tr. LC 87-32305. Orig. Title: Enfant du Liban: les Chemins de Nulle Part. 96p. 1988. pap. 8.95 (*0-932506-61-5*) St Bedes Pubns.

LaBan, A. Cheap Chow Chicago. rev. ed. LC 98-20442. 240p. (Orig.). 1999. pap. 10.95 (*1-55652-293-2*) Chicago Review.

Laban, Brian. Classic Mercedes-Benz. (Illus.). 160p. 1994. 19.98 (*0-89660-045-9*, Artabras) Abbeville Pr.

— Classic Porsches: Generations of Genius. (Illus.). 160p. 1993. 19.98 (*0-89660-044-0*, Artabras) Abbeville Pr.

— Mercedes SL Series: The Complete Story. (Illus.). 192p. 1992. 35.95 (*1-85223-595-0*) MBI Pubg.

— MGB: The Complete Story. (Illus.). 192p. 1990. pap. 35.95 (*1-85223-358-3*) MBI Pubg.

LaBan, Ric, jt. auth. see Wood, Kent.

Laban, Richard J. Chemical Dependency Treatment Planning Handbook. LC 97-8006. 174p. 1997. spiral bd. 29.95 (*0-398-06776-7*) C C Thomas.

LaBan, Terry. International Bob. 96p. 1993. pap. 9.95 (*1-56097-135-5*) Fantagraph Bks.

— Love's No Three Dollar Fare. 128p. 1995. pap. 14.95 (*1-56097-165-7*) Fantagraph Bks.

Labana, K. S., et al, eds. Breeding Oilseed Brassicas. (Monographs on Theoretical & Applied Genetics: Vol. 19). 296p. 1993. 152.95 (*0-387-55854-3*) Spr-Verlag.

Labana, S. S. & Dickie, R. A., eds. Characterization of Highly Cross-Linked Polymers. LC 83-25733. (ACS Symposium Ser.: No. 243). 321p. 1984. lib. bdg. 54.95 (*0-8412-0824-7*) Am Chemical.

— Characterization of Highly Cross-Linked Polymers: Based on a Symposium. LC 83-25733. (ACS Symposium Ser.: No. 243). (Illus.). 332p. 1984. reprint ed. pap. 103.00 (*0-608-04337-0*, 206511700001) Bks Demand.

Labana, Sandy, pref. Advanced Coatings Technology. (Illus.). 256p. 1991. 85.00 (*1-56378-001-1*) ESD.

Labana, Santokh S. Ultraviolet Light Induced Reactions in Polymers: An International Symposium. LC 76-3421. (ACS Symposium Ser.: Vol. 25). (Illus.). 503p. 1976. pap. 156.00 (*0-608-04804-6*, 205258100004) Bks Demand.

Labanaris, Faye. Blossom by the Sea: Making Wire-Edged Ribbon Flowers for Quilts. 196p. 1996. pap. 24.95 (*0-89145-862-X*, 4593, Am Quilters Soc) Collector Bks.

— Quilts with a View: A Fabric Adventure. LC 98-43388. 96p. 1998. 16.95 (*1-57432-713-5*, Am Quilters Soc) Collector Bks.

Laband, David N. & Lentz, Bernard F. The Roots of Success: Why Children Follow in Their Parents' Career Footsteps. LC 84-26309. 181p. 1985. 45.00 (*0-275-90132-7*, C0132, Praeger Pubs) Greenwood.

Laband, David N., jt. auth. see Lentz, Bernard F.

Laband, John. Anglo-Zulu War. (War Correspondents Ser.). 1997. 33.95 (*0-7509-0882-3*, Pub. by Sutton Pub Ltd) Intl Pubs Mktg.

— Lord Chelmsford's Zululand Campaign, 1878-1879. LC 94-26112. 1997. 53.95 (*0-7509-0665-0*, Pub. by Sutton Pub Ltd) Intl Pubs Mktg.

— Rise & Fall of the Zulu Nation. LC 97-190382. (Illus.). 576p. 1997. 45.00 (*1-85409-421-1*, Pub. by Arms & Armour) Sterling.

— The Rise & Fall of the Zulu Nation. (Illus.). 576p. 1998. pap. 27.95 (*1-85409-494-7*) Sterling.

***Laband, John & Thompson, Paul.** The Field Guide to the Anglo-Zulu War. (Illus.). 210p. 1999. pap. 16.15 (*0-86980-946-6*, Pub. by Univ Natal Pr) Intl Spec Bk.

Laband, John P. Kingdom in Crisis: The Zulu Response to the British Invasion of 1879. Beckett, Ian F., ed. (War, Armed Forces & Society Ser.). 240p. 1992. 59.95 (*0-7190-3582-1*, Pub. by Manchester Univ Pr) St Martin.

Laband, John P. & Haswell, Robert, eds. Pietermaritzburg, 1838-1988: A New Portrait of an African City. 320p. 1988. 25.00 (*0-86980-639-4*, Pub. by Univ Natal Pr) Intl Spec Bk.

Laband, John P. & Thompson, Paul. Kingdom & Colony at War: 16 Studies on the Anglo-Zulu War of 1879. (Illus.). 376p. 1990. 51.50 (*0-86980-766-8*, Pub. by Univ Natal Pr); pap. 32.50 (*0-86980-765-X*, Pub. by Univ Natal Pr) Intl Spec Bk.

Laband, John P. & Thompson, Paul S. Field Guide to the War in Zululand & the Defence of Natal, 1879. (Illus.). 132p. 1983. pap. 14.95 (*0-86980-313-1*, Pub. by Univ Natal Pr) Intl Spec Bk.

Labandeira, J. J. Torres, ed. see International Symposium on Cyclodextrins Staff.

Labanowich, Stan. Wheelchair Basketball. (Wheelchair Sports Ser.). (Illus.). 48p. (J). (gr. 3-7). 1997. lib. bdg. 19.00 (*0-531-11473-2*, Rivr Front Bks) Capstone Pr.

— Wheelchair Basketball. LC 97-19254. (Wheelchair Sports Ser.). (J). 1998. lib. bdg. write for info. (*1-56065-614-X*) Capstone Pr.

— Wheelchair Track Events. (Wheelchair Sports Ser.). (Illus.). 48p. (J). (gr. 3-7). 1997. lib. bdg. 19.00 (*0-531-11476-7*, Rivr Front Bks) Capstone Pr.

— Wheelchair Track Events. LC 97-19255. (Wheelchair Sports Ser.). 1998. lib. bdg. write for info. (*1-56065-616-6*) Capstone Pr.

Labanowich, Stan & Little, Jim. Wheelchair Sports. (Illus.). 48p. 63.80 (*0-7368-0460-9*, Capstone Bks) Capstone Pr.

Labanowski. Neurology Pearls of Wisdom. (Pearls of Wisdom Ser.). (Illus.). 1998. pap. 88.00 (*1-890369-12-8*) Boston Medical.

Labanowski, J. K. & Andzelm, J. W., eds. Density Functional Methods in Chemistry. (Illus.). xv, 443p. 1994. 79.95 (*0-387-97512-8*) Spr-Verlag.

***Labanyi, Jo.** Gender & Modernization in the Spanish Realist Novel. (Oxford Hispanic Studies). 240p. 2000. 72.00 (*0-19 815178-0*); pap. 24.95 (*0-19-816009-7*) OUP.

Labanyi, Jo, intro. Galdos. LC 92-12957. (Modern Literatures in Perspective Ser.). 280p. (C). 1993. text 57.50 (*0-582-08529-2*, 79633); pap. text 30.50 (*0-582-08530-6*, 79632) Longman.

Labanyi, Jo, jt. ed. see Charnon-Deutsch, Lou.

Labanyi, Jo, jt. ed. see Graham, Helen.

Labanyi, Jo, tr. see Traba, Marta.

Labanyi, Jo, tr. see Vazquez, Rial H.

Labanyi, Jo, tr. & intro. see Galdos, Benito Perez.

Labanyi, Peter, tr. see Negt, Oskar & Kluge, Alexander.

Labarca. Our Global Village. 2nd ed. LC 98-87493. (C). 1999. pap. text 24.00 (*0-03-022256-7*, Pub. by Harcourt Coll Pubs) Harcourt.

Labarca, Angela. Nuevas Dimensions. (College Spanish Ser.). (C). 1988. pap., teacher ed. 19.00 (*0-8384-1588-1*) Wadsworth Pub.

— Vision y Vos. (College Spanish Ser.). (C). 1993. mass mkt., student ed., wbk. ed. 7.95 (*0-8384-3456-8*) Heinle & Heinle.

— Vision y Voz. (College Spanish Ser.). (SPA.). (C). 1994. pap., lab manual ed. 13.00 (*0-8384-5585-9*) Heinle & Heinle.

Labarca, Angela, et al, eds. Issues in L2: Theory As Practice - Practice As Theory. LC 89-37180. (Delaware Symposia on Language Studies: Vol. 7). 296p. (C). 1990. text 73.25 (*0-89391-521-1*) Ablx Pub.

Labarca, Angela & Hendrickson. Nuevas Dimensiones. 2nd ed. (C). 1992. pap., student ed. 30.75 (*0-8384-2336-1*) Heinle & Heinle.

— Nuevas Dimensiones. 2nd ed. (C). 1992. pap., student ed. 32.95 (*0-8384-2334-5*) Heinle & Heinle.

Labarca, Angela & Hendrickson, James M. Nuevas Dimensiones. 2nd ed. (C). 1992. pap. 40.95 (*0-8384-2335-3*) Heinle & Heinle.

Labarca, Angela, et al. Workbook to Accompany De Perlas Intermediate Spanish & Audio to Accompany Workbook to Accompany De Perlas Intermediate Spanish. 1997. pap. text, wbk. ed. 59.95 (*0-471-25331-6*) Wiley.

Labarca, Angela, jt. auth. see Galloway, Vicki.

Labarca, Angela, jt. auth. see Halty-Pfaff.

Labarca, Angella. De Perlas: Intermediate Spanish. 320p. 1997. pap. 48.95 (*0-471-17712-1*) Wiley.

LaBare, Martha. Shooting Star & Other Poems. 64p. (Orig.). 1982. pap. 4.50 (*0-9609090-2-8*) Swollen Magpie.

Labaree, Benjamin W. America's Nation-Time: 1607-1789. 272p. 1976. reprint ed. pap. 10.95 (*0-393-00821-5*) Norton.

— The Boston Tea Party. LC 79-5423. (Illus.). 360p. 1979. reprint ed. text 47.50 (*0-930350-16-2*); reprint ed. pap. text 18.00 (*0-930350-05-7*) NE U Pr.

— Supplement (1971-1986) to Robert G Albion's Naval & Maritime History: An Annotated Bibliography. 232p. 1988. pap. 13.95 (*0-913372-46-3*) Mystic Seaport.

Labaree, Benjamin W., et al. America & the Sea Vol. 15: A Maritime History - American Maritime Library. 704p. 1998. 50.00 (*0-913372-81-1*) Mystic Seaport.

Labaree, David F. How to Succeed in School Without Really Learning: The Credentials Race in American Education. LC 97-7793. 320p. 1997. 40.00 (*0-300-06993-6*) Yale U Pr.

— How to Succeed in School Without Really Learning: The Credentials Race in American Education. 320p. 1999. pap. text 18.00 (*0-300-07867-6*) Yale U Pr.

— The Making of an American High School: The Credentials Market & Central High School of Philadelphia. LC 87-10595. 272p. (C). 1988. 42.50 (*0-300-04091-1*) Yale U Pr.

— The Making of an American High School: The Credentials Market & the Central High School of Philadelphia, 1838-1939. 222p. (C). 1992. reprint ed. pap. 19.00 (*0-300-05469-6*) Yale U Pr.

Labaree, Leonard W., ed. see Franklin, Benjamin.

Labaree, Robert V. The Federal Trade Commission: A Guide to Sources. Nasrallah, Wahib, ed. (Research & Information Guides in Business, Industry, & Economic Institutions Ser.). 500p. Date not set. text 75.00 (*0-8153-1296-2*) Garland.

Labarge, Margaret W. Simon de Montfort. LC 75-22643. (Illus.). 312p. 1975. reprint ed. lib. bdg. 35.00 (*0-8371-8359-6*, LASM, Greenwood Pr) Greenwood.

— A Small Sound of the Trumpet: Women in Medieval Life. LC 86-47509. (Illus.). 288p. 1988. reprint ed. pap. text 18.00 (*0-8070-5627-8*) Beacon Pr.

LaBarge, R. L. Fitting the Pieces Together. (Illus.). 1997. write for info. (*0-614-13996-1*) Allfit.

LaBarge, Randy R. The Joy of Pizza: How to Make Great Gourmet & Traditional Pizzas at Home. 96p. (Orig.). 1995. pap. 8.95 (*1-887856-00-5*) Badger Mtn.

LaBarge, S., jt. auth. see Gackenbach, J.

LaBarge, William H. Sweetwater Gunslinger 201. 1986. text 14.95 (*0-07-156064-5*, OP9604) TAB Bks.

Labarge, William H. Sweetwater Gunslinger 201. 1991. 14.95 (*0-8306-8515-4*) McGraw-Hill Prof.

LaBarge, William H. & Holt, Robert L. Sweetwater Gunslinger 201. (Illus.). 192p. 1990. pap. 14.95 (*0-685-47251-5*, 28515, TAB-Aero) TAB Bks.

LaBarge, William H., jt. auth. see Holt, Robert L.

Labarre, jt. auth. see Patton.

LaBarre, Alice, et al. Sexual Abuse! What Is It? An Informational Book for People Who Are Deaf or Hard of Hearing. (Illus.). 71p. (Orig.). (J). (ps-12). 1995. reprint ed. pap. text 9.00 (*0-9629302-1-0*) Ramsey Found.

LaBarre, George H. Collecting Stocks & Bonds, 3 vols., Set. (Illus.). 368p. 1981. pap. 30.00 (*0-941538-00-1*) G H LaBarre.

— Collecting Stocks & Bonds, Vol. I. rev. ed. (Illus.). 108p. 1981. pap. 4.95 (*0-941538-01-X*) G H LaBarre.

— Collecting Stocks & Bonds, Vol. II. (Illus.). 128p. 1981. pap. 4.95 (*0-941538-02-8*) G H LaBarre.

— Collecting Stocks & Bonds, Vol. III. (Illus.). 132p. 1981. pap. 4.95 (*0-941538-03-6*) G H LaBarre.

Labarre, James & Mitchell, William M. Producing Business Documents: Integrated Projects & In-Basket Exercises, Practice set. 1992. pap. text 20.95 (*1-56118-361-X*) Paradigm MN.

LaBarre, James, et al. Paradigm Keyboarding & Applications: A Mastery Approach for Microcomputers & Typewriters, Short Course. (C). 1990. pap. text 23.95 (*1-56118-154-4*) Paradigm MN.

— Producing Business Documents: Integrated Projects & In-Basket Exercises, Instructor's guide. 1992. teacher ed. 9.95 (*1-56118-362-8*) Paradigm MN.

***Labarta, Luis.** Spanish Decorative Ironwork. (Pictorial Archive Ser.). (Illus.). 2000. pap. 13.95 (*0-486-40962-7*) Dover.

Labarthe, Darwin R. Epidemiology & Prevention of Cardiovascular Diseases: A Global Public Health Challenge. LC 97-45221. 704p. 1998. 65.00 (*0-8342-0659-5*, 06595) Aspen Pub.

Labarthe, Phillippe L. Musica Ficta: Figures of Wagner. McCarren, Felicia, tr. LC 94-15594. xxvi, 161p. 1995. pap. 13.95 (*0-8047-2385-0*) Stanford U Pr.

Labastida, Aurora, jt. auth. see Ets, Marie H.

Labastida, Jaime. Animal de Silencios (Animal of Silence) (SPA.). 343p. 1996. 16.99 (*968-16-4858-7*, Pub. by Fondo) Continental Bk.

LaBastille, Anne. Beyond Black Bear Lake: Life at the Edge of the Wilderness. (Illus.). 1988. pap. 12.95 (*0-393-30539-2*) Norton.

–Jaguar Totem: The Woodswoman Explores New Wildlands & Wildlife. unabridged ed. LC 99-70821. (Illus.). 272p. 1999. pap. 16.00 (*0-9632846-2-2*) W Wind Pubns.

L

L

Jaguar Totem is the riveting account of Anne LaBastille's "other life" & the exciting counterpoint to the WOODSWOMAN Trilogy. From her log cabin at the edge of wilderness, Anne LaBastille fares out on fast-paced ecological consultancies which include teeming wildlife, dazzling land - & seascapes, world renowned scientists, glamorous conferences, & daring field trips. Climb with Anne into magnificent cloud forests on Volcano Atitlan in Guatemala to establish a Quetzal Reserve. Camp on the beautiful beaches of remote Anegada Island in the Caribbean as she mist-nets birds & bats new to the area. Run rapids by dugout canoe in the Darien jungle of Panama where Anne meets a wondrous young female jaguar, "Mancha," while on a National Geographic assignment. Zodiak over the stormy North Atlantic to photograph huge gannet colonies off St. Kilda, Scotland. Jaguar Totem rivals anything in the WOODSWOMAN Trilogy. It tells of life intensely lived -- of life as vibrant as this book's cover. It reinforces Dr. LaBastille's strong belief that wildlands & wildlife everywhere need constant, compassionate care. *Publisher Paid Annotation.*

— Mama Poc: An Ecologist's Account of the Extinction of a Species. (Illus.). 320p. 1991. pap. 10.95 (*0-393-30800-6*) Norton.

— Women & Wilderness. LC 80-14369. (Paperback Library). (Illus.). 320p. 1984. reprint ed. pap. 14.00 (*0-87156-828-4*, Pub. by Sierra) Random.

— Woodswoman III: Book Three of the Woodswoman's Adventures. LC 97-60130. 256p. (Orig.). 1997. pap. 15.00 (*0-9632846-1-4*) W Wind Pubns.

***LaBastille, Anne.** Woodswoman II: Beyond Black Bear Lake. 2000. pap. 13.95 (*0-393-32059-6*) Norton.

Labat, Carla. Satisfy Your Soul: A Guide to African American, African & Caribbean Restaurants. LC 97-93896. 224p. (Orig.). 1997. pap. 13.95 (*0-9659204-0-2*) Impressions Bks.

***Labat, Carla.** Steppin' Out: An African American Guide to Our 20 Favorite Cities. (Illus.). 300p. 2000. pap. 17.95 (*1-56261-544-0*, Pub. by Avalon Travel) Publishers Group.

Labat, Jackie. Weight Management for Type II Diabetes: An Action Plan. 224p. (Orig.). 1997. pap. 14.95 (*0-471-34750-7*) Wiley.

Labat, Jackie & Maggi, Annette. Weight Management for Type II Diabetes: An Action Plan. LC 98-231263. 224p. (Orig.). 1997. pap. 12.95 (*1-56561-114-4*) Wiley.

Labat, Jean B. Nuevo Viaje a Islas de la America, Vol. 1. Cardenas-Ruiz, Manuel, ed. LC 83-3591. Orig. Title: Nouveau Vouage aux Isles de l'Amerique. (SPA., Illus.). 279p. 1984. pap. 6.50 (*0-8477-0876-4*) U of PR Pr.

Labat, Joseph. Des Identites Culturelles et des Paradigmes de l'Occident dans Leur Relativite. (FRE.). 1995. write for info. (*0-7734-2914-X*) E Mellen.

— Des Traces sur le Sable: Reflexions sur l'Identite Culturelle. (FRE.). 314p. 1998. 74.95 (*1-57309-248-7*); pap. 54.95 (*1-57309-247-9*) Intl Scholars.

Labat, Karen L. & Nelson, Nancy J. Contemporary Irish Textile Art: The Women of Annaghmakerrig. LC 96-75785. (Illus.). 64p. 1996. pap. 20.00 (*0-939719-07-X*) UMN Goldstein Gall.

***Labat, N. & Touboul, A., eds.** Proceedings of the 10th European Symposium on the Reliability of Electron Devices, Failure Physics & Analysis (ESREF'99) 450p. 1999. pap. 91.00 (*0-08-043419-3*); pap. text 152.00 (*0-08-043421-5*) Elsevier.

Labat, Rene. L' Akkadien de Boghaz-Koi. LC 78-72748. (Ancient Mesopotamian Texts & Studies). reprint ed. 37.50 (*0-404-18189-9*) AMS Pr.

LaBate, Jim. Let's Go, Gaels: A Novella by Jim LaBate. LC 98-165634. (Illus.). 60p. (YA). (gr. 7-12). 1998. pap. 5.95 (*0-9662100-4-2*) Mohawk River Pr.

— Mickey Mantle Day in Amsterdam: Another Novella by Jim LaBate. LC 99-70005. (Illus.). 64p. (YA). (gr. 7-12). 1999. pap. 7.95 (*0-9662100-7-7*) Mohawk River Pr.

L'Abate, Luciano. Building Family Competence: Primary & Secondary Prevention Strategies. (Illus.). 240p. (C). 1990. text 38.00 (*0-8039-3488-2*) Sage.

***L'Abate, Luciano.** Distance Writing & Computer-Assisted Interventions in Psychiatry & Mental Health. LC 00-27546. (Developments in Clinical Psychology Ser.). (Illus.). 2000. write for info. (*1-56750-525-2*) Ablx Pub.

L'Abate, Luciano. Family Evaluation: A Psychological Approach. (C). 1994. text 45.00 (*0-8039-4238-9*); pap. text 21.00 (*0-8039-4239-7*) Sage.

— Family Psychology II: Theory, Therapy, Enrichment & Training. 300p. (Orig.). (C). 1988. pap. text 26.50 (*0-8191-6680-4*) U Pr of Amer.

— Family Psychopathology: The Relational Roots of Dysfunctional Behavior. LC 98-13462. 528p. 1998. 57.00 (*1-57230-369-7*) Guilford Pubns.

— The Handbook of Family Psychology & Therapy, 2 vols., I. LC 84-71293. (Professional Bks.). (C). 1985. text 79.95 (*0-534-10443-6*) Brooks-Cole.

— A Theory of Personality Development. Bryson, Charles H., ed. LC 93-12795. (Personality Processes Ser.). 313p. 1993. 95.00 (*0-471-30303-8*) Wiley.

***L'Abate, Luciano, ed.** Distance Writing & Computer-Assisted Interventions in Psychiatry & Mental Health. (Developments in Clinical Psychology). 2000. write for info. (*1-56750-524-4*) Greenwood.

L'Abate, Luciano, ed. Handbook of Developmental Family Psychology & Psychopathology. LC 93-17725. (Series on Personality Processes). 480p. 1993. 87.50 (*0-471-53527-3*) Wiley.

L'Abate, Luciano & Bagarozzi, Dennis A. Sourcebook of Marriage & Family Evaluation. LC 92-22541. 336p. 1993. text 41.95 (*0-87630-676-8*) Brunner-Mazel.

L'Abate, Luciano & Baggett, Margaret. The Self in the Family: A Classification of Personality, Criminality, & Psychopathology. LC 96-19639. (Wiley Series in Couples & Family Dynamics & Treatment). 404p. 1996. 75.00 (*0-471-12247-5*) Wiley.

L'Abate, Luciano & Baggett, Margaret S. Manual: Distance Writing & Computer Assisted Training in Mental Health. 101p. 1997. pap. 19.95 (*0-9662839-0-2*) Inst Life Empower.

L'Abate, Luciano & Cox, Janet. Programmed Writing: A Self-Administered Approach for Intervention with Individuals, Couples & Families. LC 90-27793. 300p. (C). 1992. text 80.95 (*0-534-14484-5*) Brooks-Cole.

L'Abate, Luciano & McHenry, Sherry. Handbook of Marital Interventions. 414p. pap. 32.00 (*1-56821-203-8*) Aronson.

L'Abate, Luciano, jt. auth. see Weeks, Gerald R.

LaBath, Octave A. Rating Trend Differences Between AGMA & ISO Vehicle Gears. (Technical Papers: Vol. 209.12). 24p. 1981. pap. text 30.00 (*1-55589-138-1*) AGMA.

***Labatt, Mary.** Aliens in Woodford. (Sam: Dog Detective Ser.). (Illus.). 116p. (J). (gr. 2-5). 2000. 12.95 (*1-55074-611-1*, Pub. by Kids Can Press); pap. 4.95 (*1-55074-607-3*, Pub. by Kids Can Press) Genl Dist Srvs.

— The Ghost of Captain Briggs. LC 99-931528. (Sam: Dog Detective Ser.). (Illus.). 120p. (J). (gr. 2-5). 1999. 16.95 (*1-55074-638-3*); pap. text 4.95 (*1-55074-636-7*) Kids Can Pr.

Labatt, Mary. Spying on Dracula. LC 99-931529. (Sam: Dog Detective Ser.). 120p. (J). (gr. 2-5). 1999. pap. text 4.95 (*1-55074-632-4*) Kids Can Pr.

— Spying on Dracula. (Sam: Dog Detective Ser.). (Illus.). 120p. (J). (gr. 2-5). 1999. 16.95 (*1-55074-634-0*) Kids Can Pr.

***Labatt, Mary.** Strange Neighbors. unabridged ed. (Sam: Dog Detective Ser.). 116p. (J). (gr. 2-5). 2000. 12.95 (*1-55074-605-7*, Pub. by Kids Can Pr) Genl Dist Srvs.

— Strange Neighbors. unabridged ed. (Sam: Dog Detective Ser.). (Illus.). 116p. (J). (gr. 2-5). 2000. pap. 4.95 (*1-55074-603-0*, Pub. by Kids Can Pr) Genl Dist Srvs.

Labatut, Jean & Lane, Wheaton J., eds. Highways in Our National Life: A Symposium. LC 72-5058. (Technology & Society Ser.). (Illus.). 554p. 1972. reprint ed. 35.95 (*0-405-04710-X*) Ayer.

Labaune, J. P. Handbook of Pharmacokinetics: Toxicity Assessment of Chemicals. 1990. text 128.00 (*0-470-21572-0*) P-H.

— Pharmacokinetic Profiles of Drugs. (Pharmaceutical Sciences Ser.). 500p. 1996. 125.00 (*0-7484-0559-3*) Taylor & Francis.

LaBauve, Sandy & Kehoe, George. Shave Ten Strokes in Twelve Days: A Woman Golfer's Guide to a More Successful Game. (Illus.). 128p. (Orig.). 1994. pap. 9.95 (*0-399-51860-6*, Perigee Bks) Berkley Pub.

Labaw, George W. Preakness & the Preakness Reformed Church, Passaic County: A History, 1695-1902, with Genealogical Notes, the Records of the Church & Tombstone Inscriptions. (Illus.). 344p. 1997. reprint ed. lib. bdg. 39.50 (*0-8328-6075-1*) Higginson Bk Co.

LaBaw, Jeanine L. & Lepley, Mary M. The Mother's Guide to a Healthier Pregnancy & Easier Birth. (Illus.). 1991. 24.95 incl. audio (*0-9627583-0-2*) Lifesounds.

Labaw, Patricia. Advanced Questionnaire Design. LC 80-69665. 183p. 1983. text 22.50 (*0-89011-553-2*) Abt Bks.

LaBay, Mary Lee, jt. auth. see Hogan, Kevin.

LaBay, Mary Lee, jt. auth. see Hogan, Kevin L.

Labbance, Bob. The Centennial History of the Keene Country Club. (Illus.). 72p. (Orig.). 1997. write for info. (*0-9622354-5-8*); pap. write for info. (*0-9622354-4-X*) NEGS.

— The Centennial History of the Woodstock Country Club. 26p. 1995. 40.00 (*0-9622354-2-3*); pap. text 12.00 (*0-9622354-3-1*) NEGS.

— Golf Courses of New Hampshire: From the Mountains to the Sea. (Illus.). 184p. (Orig.). 1989. pap. 13.95 (*0-9622354-0-7*) NEGS.

***Labbance, Bob.** The Old Man: The Biography of Walter J. Travis. (Illus.). 300p. 2000. 29.95 (*1-886947-91-0*) Sleeping Bear.

L'Abbate, Antonia, ed. The Role of Oxygen Radicals in Cardiovascular Disease. (C). 1988. text 173.50 (*0-89838-407-9*) Kluwer Academic.

Labbate, Carlos, ed. see Haven, Girard.

***Labbe, Dolores E. & University of Southwestern Louisiana Staff.** The Louisiana Purchase & its Aftermath, 1800-1830. LC 98-209973. (Bicentennial Series in Louisiana History). x, 637p. 1998. 40.00 (*1-887366-21-0*) Univ LA Lafayette.

Labbe. Foodborne Pathogens. 288p. write for info. (*0-471-35034-6*) Wiley.

Labbe, Armand J. Guardians of the Life Stream: Shamans, Art & Power in Prehispanic Central Panama. Rodriguez, Aleida, ed. (Illus.). 168p. (C). 1995. 19.95 (*0-9633959-3-9*) Bowers Mus.

Labbe, Armand J., ed. Tribute to the Gods: Treasures of the Museo del Oro. Inga, Maria & De Rhodes, Hanka, trs. from SPA. (Illus.). 82p. 1992. pap. 19.95 (*0-9633959-1-2*) Bowers Mus.

Labbe, Armand J. & Apodaca, Paul. Images of Power: Masterworks of the Bowers Museum of Cultural Art. Bryant, J. et al, eds. (Illus.). 176p. 1992. 35.00 (*0-9633959-0-4*) Bowers Mus.

Labbe, Armand J., et al. Shamans, Gods, & Mythic Beasts: Colombian Gold & Ceramics in Antiquity. LC 98-24090. 1998. 35.00 (*1-885444-10-9*) Am Fed Arts.

— Shamans, Gods, & Mythic Beasts: Colombian Gold & Ceramics in Antiquity. LC 98-24090. (Illus.). 215p. 1998. 40.00 (*0-295-97755-8*) U of Wash Pr.

L'Abbe-D'Aubignac. Disseratations Contre Corneille. Hammond, Nicholas & Mawcroft, Michael, eds. (Exeter French Texts Ser.: No. 95). (FRE.). 154p. 1996. pap. text 19.95 (*0-85989-493-2*, Pub. by Univ Exeter Pr) Northwestern U Pr.

Labbe, Dolores E. Jim Crow Comes to Church: The Establishment of Segregated Catholic Parishes in South Louisiana. 1978. 17.95 (*0-405-10838-9*, 11845) Ayer.

***Labbe, Jacqueline M.** The Romantic Paradox: Love, Violence & the Uses of Romance 1700. 2000. text 59.95 (*0-312-23412-0*) St Martin.

Labbe, John T. & Goe, Vernon. Railroads in the Woods. LC 95-52314. 258p. 1995. 39.95 (*0-9647521-0-7*) Oso Pubng.

Labbe, John T. & Replinger, Peter J. Logging to the Salt Chuck: Over 100 Years of Railroad Logging in Mason County Washington. Martin, F. Raoul, ed. (Logging Railroads of Washington State Ser.). (Illus.). 186p. (Orig.). 1989. pap. 36.95 (*0-915370-09-3*) NW Short Line.

Labbe, John T., jt. auth. see Carranco, Lynwood.

Labbe, M., et al, eds. Operations Research & Decision Aid Methodologies in Traffic & Transportation Management: Proceedings of the NATO ASI in Balatonfured, March 10-21, 1997. (NATO ASI Ser.: Vol. 166). 400p. 1998. 99.00 (*3-540-64562-3*) Spr-Verlag.

Labbe, Marilyn, jt. auth. see Crouch, Eleanor.

Labby, David. The Demystification of Yap: Dialectics of Culture on a Micronesian Island. LC 75-21270. (Illus.). 176p. 1995. lib. bdg. 18.00 (*0-226-46711-2*) U Ch Pr.

***Labe, Louise.** Debate of Folly & Love: A New English Translation with the Original French Text. Bourbon, Anne-Marie, tr. from FRE. LC 96-53919. (History & Language Ser.: Vol. 8). 165p. (C). 2000. text 48.95 (*0-8204-3752-2*) P Lang Pubng.

Labe, Louise. Oeuvres Poetiques, Rymes de Pernette du Guille, Blasons du Corps Feminin. (Poesie Ser.). (FRE.). 188p. 1983. pap. 11.95 (*2-07-032238-6*) Schoenhof.

Labedz, Leopold. The Use & Abuse of Sovietology. 372p. 1988. 49.95 (*0-88738-252-5*) Transaction Pubs.

Labedz, Leopold, ed. Revisionism: Essays on the History of Marxist Ideas. (Essay Index Reprint Ser.). 1977. reprint ed. 26.95 (*0-518-10166-5*) Ayer.

Labedz, Leopold & Urban, George, eds. Sino-Soviet Conflict. LC 65-18351. 1965. 18.95 (*0-8023-1070-2*) Dufour.

Labedz, Leopold, jt. ed. see Hayward, Max.

Label, Lorne S. Injuries & Disorders of the Head & Brain. LC 98-222999. 1997. 59.95 (*0-8205-2763-7*) Bender.

Label, Wayne. 10 Minute Guide to Accounting. 180p. 1997. pap. text 10.95 (*0-02-861407-0*, Pub. by Macmillan) S&S Trade.

Labella, Vincenzo. A Season of Giants, 1492-1508: Michelangelo, Leonardo, Raphael. (Illus.). 1990. 45.00 (*0-316-85646-0*) Little.

Labelle, Brandon & Roden, Steve. Site of Sound: Of Architecture & the Ear. (Illus.). 96p. 1998. pap. 13.00 (*0-9655570-2-2*) Errant Bodies.

LaBelle, Charlene G. A Guide to Backpacking with Your Dog. LC 92-33143. (Illus.). 96p. (Orig.). 1992. pap. 9.95 (*0-931866-59-6*) Alpine Pubns.

LaBelle, Dave. Lessons in Death & Life. Judd, Alan & Perry, Rex, eds. (Illus.). 112p. (C). 1994. text 24.95 (*0-9630770-0-7*) D LaBelle.

Labelle, G. & Leroux, Pierre, eds. Combinatoire Enumerative: Proceedings of the "Colloque de Combinatoire Enumerative" Held at Universite du Quebec a Montreal, May 28-June 1, 1985. (Lecture Notes in Mathematics Ser.: Vol. 1234). xiv, 387p. 1987. 59.95 (*0-387-17207-6*) Spr-Verlag.

Labelle, Jacques & LeClere, Christian, eds. Lexiques-Grammaires Compares en Francais: Actes Du Colloque International De Montreal (3-5 Juin 1992) LC 95-15436. (Lingvisticae Investigationes Supplementa Ser.: No. 17). 217p. 1995. lib. bdg. 45.00 (*1-55619-257-6*) J Benjamins Pubng Co.

LaBelle, Jenijoy, ed. see Blake, William.

Labelle, Micheline. Ideologie De Couleur et Classes Sociales En Haiti. LC 80-477747. (Collection Recherches Caraibes). (FRE., Illus.). 393p. reprint ed. pap. 121.90 (*0-7837-6941-5*, 204677000003) Bks Demand.

Labelle, Nicole. Les Differents Styles de la Musique En France Vol. 1: Le Psaume; Commentaire. (Wissen-schaftliche Abhnadlungen-Musicological Studies: Vol. 31). (FRE.). 268p. 1981. lib. bdg. 6.00 (*0-912024-97-6*) Inst Mediaeval Mus.

— Les Differents Styles De la Musique En France Vol. 2: Le Psaume; Transcriptions A. (Wissenschaftliche Abhandlungen-Musicological Studies: Vol. 31). (FRE.). 168p. 1981. lib. bdg. 6.00 (*0-912024-98-4*) Inst Mediaeval Mus.

— Les Differents Styles De la Musique En France Vol. 3: Le Psaume; Music. (Wissenschaftliche Abhandlungen - Musicological Studies: Vol. 31). (FRE.). 168p. 1981. lib. bdg. 6.00 (*0-912024-99-2*) Inst Mediaeval Mus.

LaBelle, Patti. Don't Block the Blessings: Revelations of a Lifetime. 1998. mass mkt. 7.50 (*0-425-16998-7*) Berkley Pub.

— LaBelle Cuisine: Recipes to Sing About. LC 98-49145. (Illus.). 240p. 1999. 25.00 (*0-7679-0314-5*) Broadway BDD.

Labelle, Patti & Randolph, Laura B. Don't Block the Blessings. 1997. mass mkt. 6.99 (*1-57297-324-2*) Blvd Books.

LaBelle, Patti & Randolph, Laura B. Don't Block the Blessings: Revelations of a Lifetime. large type ed. LC 96-52283. 401p. 1997. 26.95 (*0-7838-8069-3*, G K Hall Lrg Type) Mac Lib Ref.

Labelle, Susan W. Bunny Rabbit Birthday Stickers. (Illus.). (J). (gr. k-3). 1992. pap. 1.00 (*0-486-27326-1*) Dover.

LaBelle, Susan W. Country Rabbit Stickers. (Illus.). (J). 1991. pap. text 1.00 (*0-486-26596-X*) Dover.

LaBelle, Susan W. Peter Rabbit Postcards in Full Color. 12p. 1984. pap. 4.50 (*0-486-24617-5*) Dover.

Labelle, Susan Whited. Bunny Rabbit Christmas Sticker Book. (Little Activity Bks.). (Illus.). (J). 1993. pap. 1.00 (*0-486-27519-1*) Dover.

LaBelle, Thomas J. Nonformal Education & the Poor in Latin America & the Caribbean: Stability, Reform, or Revolution. LC 85-25783. 384p. 1986. 36.95 (*0-275-92078-X*, C2078, Praeger Pubs) Greenwood.

LaBello, Susan, tr. see Derossi, Flavia.

Labensky & Hause. Cooking. 2nd ed. 1998. pap. text, student ed. write for info. (*0-13-973256-X*) P-H.

Labensky, Sarah R. Applied Math for Food Service. LC 97-22923. 143p. (C). 1997. pap. text 22.60 (*0-13-849217-4*) P-H.

— Applied Math for Food Service Professionals. LC 97-22923. (C). 1997. teacher ed. write for info. (*0-13-860768-0*) P-H.

Labensky, Sarah R. & Hause, Alan M. On Cooking: A Textbook of Culinary Fundamentals. LC 94-12053. 896p. 1994. text 77.00 (*0-13-194515-7*) P-H.

— On Cooking: A Textbook of Culinary Fundamentals. 2nd ed. LC 98-17965. 1157p. (C). 1998. 80.00 (*0-13-862640-5*) P-H.

— On Cooking: Techniques from Expert Chefs. 2nd ed. LC 98-17966. (Illus.). 1125p. 1998. 49.95 (*0-13-924101-9*) P-H.

***Labensky, Sarah R. & Hause, Alan M.** On Cooking (trade Version) Techniques from Expert Chefs, 2. 2nd ed. 327p. 1999. 10.00 (*0-13-018785-2*) P-H.

— On Cooking (trade Version) Techniques from Expert Chefs, 3. 2nd ed. 1999. 22.00 (*0-13-018786-0*) P-H.

Labensky, Sarah R. & Van Damme, Eddy. On Baking. (C). 2002. 48.00 (*0-13-533647-3*, Macmillan Coll) P-H.

***Labensky, Steven, et al.** Webster's New World Dictionary of Culinary Arts. 2nd ed. LC 99-47361. 2000. write for info. (*0-13-096622-3*) P-H.

— Webster's New World Dictionary of Culinary Arts. 2nd ed. LC 99-47361. 528p. 2000. pap. text 25.95 (*0-13-026430-X*) P-H.

Labeo, Notker. De Interpretatione. Firchow, Evelyn S., ed. (GER.). xx, 664p. (C). 1995. lib. bdg. 306.15 (*3-11-014394-1*) De Gruyter.

Laber-Laird, Kathy, et al, eds. Handbook of Rabbit & Rodent Medicine. LC 94-45569. (Pergamon Veterinary Handbook Ser.). 1995. text 110.00 (*0-08-042505-4*, Pergamon Pr); pap. text 55.00 (*0-08-042504-6*, Pergamon Pr) Elsevier.

Laber, Robert. Group Process: Working Effectively by Committee. LC 96-61886. 108p. 1996. pap. text 24.95 (*1-56676-501-3*) Scarecrow.

Labercane, jt. auth. see Hunsberger.

LaBerge, David. Attentional Processing: The Brain's Art of Mindfulness. LC 94-38071. (Illus.). 256p. 1995. text 41.00 (*0-674-05268-4*, LABATT) HUP.

LaBerge, Gene. Geology of the Lake Superior Region. LC 93-80796. (Illus.). 320p. (Orig.). 1994. pap. 20.00 (*0-945005-15-6*) Geoscience Pr.

LaBerge, Jeanne M. Interventional Radiology Review. 304p. 130.00 (*0-7817-2010-9*) Lppncott W & W.

LaBerge, Jeanne M. & Darcy, Michael D., eds. Peripheral Vascular Interventions. LC 94-69675. (Illus.). 407p. 1997. write for info. (*1-928625-00-2*) Socy Cardio & Inter.

LaBerge, Jeanne M. & Venbrux, Anthony C., eds. Biliary Interventions. LC 95-68148. (Illus.). 487p. 1997. write for info. (*1-928625-02-9*) Socy Cardio & Inter.

LaBerge, Monique. Cracking the GRE Chemistry. (Illus.). 304p. 2000. pap. 16.00 (*0-375-75346-X*, Pub. by PRP NY) Random.

Laberge, Pierre, ed. see Congres d'Ottawa sur Kant Dans les Traditions Angl.

Laberge, Stephen. Exploring the World of Lucid Dreaming. (Illus.). 1997. pap. 12.00 (*0-345-42012-8*) Ballantine Pub Grp.

LaBerge, Stephen. Lucid Dreaming. 304p. 1986. mass mkt. 5.95 (*0-345-33355-1*) Ballantine Pub Grp.

Laberge, Stephen & Rheingold, Howard. Exploring the World of Lucid Dreaming. 1991. mass mkt. 5.99 (*0-345-37410-X*) Ballantine Pub Grp.

Labersky, David, jt. auth. see Gallagher, Christopher J.

Laberthonniere, Lucien. Etudes Sur Descartes. (FRE.). 836p. 1935. pap. 59.95 (*0-7859-1539-7*, 2711640809) Fr & Eur.

Labesse, J. P., et al, eds. Cohomology of Arithmetic Groups & Automorphic Forms: Proceedings of a Conference Held in Luminy-Marseille, May 22-27, 1989. (Lecture Notes in Mathematics Ser.: Vol. 1447). v, 358p. 1990. 57.95 (*0-387-53422-9*) Spr-Verlag.

Labetoulle, J., ed. see Fourteenth International Teletraffic Congress-ITC.

Labeyrie, L. D., jt. ed. see Berger, W. H.

Labeyrie, V., ed. The Ecology of Bruchids Attacking Legumes: Proceedings of the International Symposium Held at Tours, 1980. (Series Entomologica: No. 19). 1981. text 184.00 (*90-6193-883-X*) Kluwer Academic.

Labeyrie, V., et al, eds. Insects - Plants. (Series Entomologica). (C). 1987. text 278.50 (*90-6193-642-X*) Kluwer Academic.

Labh, Baidyanath. Panna in Early Buddhism: Philosophy Analysis with Special Reference to the Visuddhimagga. (C). 1991. text 17.50 (*0-8364-2654-1*, Pub. by Manohar) S Asia.

An Asterisk (*) at the beginning of an entry indicates that the title is appearing for the first time.

— Panna in Early Buddhism: With Special Reference to Visuddhimagga. xii, 163p. 1991. 14.00 (*0-685-62638-5*, Pub. by Eastern Bk Linkers) Nataraj Bks.

Labhart, A. Clinical Endocrinology: Theory & Practice. LC 75-11535. 1976. 60.00 (*0-387-90175-2*) Spr-Verlag.

Labhart, Toni P. Aarmassiv und Gotthardmassiv. (Sammlung Geologischer Fuehrer Ser.: Band 63). (GER., Illus.). xi, 173p. 1977. spiral bd. 22.00 (*3-443-15019-5*, Pub. by Gebruder Borntraeger) Balogh.

LaBianca, Alice. No More Tomorrows. LC 90-61382. (Illus.). 426p. 1991. 24.95 (*0-9626453-0-3*) MCM Entertainment.

LaBianca, Oystein S. Sedentarization & Nomadization: Food System Cycles at Hesban & Vicinity in Transjordan. Geraty, Lawrence T., ed. LC 89-82543. (Heshbon Excavations Final Reports: Vol. 1). (Illus.). 380p. (C). 1990. text 45.99 (*0-943872-00-6*) Andrews Univ Pr.

LaBianca, Oystein S. & Lacelle, Larry, eds. Environmental Foundations: Studies of Climatical, Geological, Hydrological & Phytological Conditions in Hesban & Vicinity. LC 86-72952. (Heshbon Excavations Final Reports: Vol. 2). 184p. (C). 1986. text 45.99 (*0-943872-15-4*) Andrews Univ Pr.

LaBianca, Oystein S. & Von den Driesch, Angela. Faunal Remains: Taphonomical & Zooarchaeological Studies of the Animal Remains from Tell Hesban & Vicinity. LC 95-77028. (Heshbon Excavations Final Reports: Vol. 13). 236p. (C). 1995. text 45.99 (*0-943872-29-4*) Andrews Univ Pr.

LaBianca, Oystein S., ed. see Ibach, Robert D., Jr.

Labib, Muhammad. The Seven Martyrs of Hurmuzak. Momen, Moojan, tr. & frwd. by. (Illus.). 80p. 1981. 11.50 (*0-85398-105-1*); pap. 5.50 (*0-85398-104-3*) G Ronald Pub.

Labib, Nadya, jt. ed. see Eisenberg, Diane U.

Labica, G. & Bensussan, G. Critical Dictionary of Marxism: Dictionnaire Critique de Marxisme. (FRE.). 1256p. 1985. 150.00 (*0-8288-2252-2*, F70761) Fr & Eur.

Labiche, Eugene. L' Affaire de la Rue de Lourcine. (FRE.). 64p. 1989. pap. 13.95 (*0-7859-1551-6*, 2851812416) Fr & Eur.

— Le Baron de Fourchevif. (FRE.). pap. 10.95 (*0-7859-5349-3*) Fr & Eur.

— La Cagnotte. (FRE.). 182p. 1990. pap. 9.95 (*0-7859-1257-6*, 2038712123) Fr & Eur.

— Celimare le Bien Aime. (FRE.). 1978. pap. 14.95 (*0-7859-5350-7*) Fr & Eur.

— Un Chapeau de Paille d'Italie. (FRE.). 160p. 1987. pap. 9.95 (*0-7859-5351-5*) Fr & Eur.

— La Cigale Chez les Fourmis. (FRE.). pap. 10.95 (*0-7859-5352-3*) Fr & Eur.

— La Commode de Victorine. (FRE.). pap. 12.95 (*0-7859-5353-1*) Fr & Eur.

— La Fille Bien Gardee. (FRE.). 92p. 1986. pap. 8.95 (*0-7859-4651-9*) Fr & Eur.

— Grammaire. (FRE.). 74p. 1986. pap. 12.95 (*0-7859-4581-4*) Fr & Eur.

— Un Jeune Homme Presse. 9.95 (*0-686-54228-2*) Fr & Eur.

— J'Invite le Colonel. 9.95 (*0-686-54229-0*) Fr & Eur.

— La Main Teste. 9.95 (*0-686-54230-4*) Fr & Eur.

— Maman Sabouleux. 9.95 (*0-686-54231-2*) Fr & Eur.

— Mon Ismenie. 9.95 (*0-686-54232-0*) Fr & Eur.

— Un Monsieur Qui a Brule une Dame. 9.95 (*0-686-54233-9*) Fr & Eur.

— Un Monsieur Qui Prend la Mouche. 9.95 (*0-686-54234-7*) Fr & Eur.

— Nouveau Theatre Choisi. 9.95 (*0-686-54235-5*) Fr & Eur.

— L' Omelette a la Follembuche. Marc, Michel, ed. (FRE.). 50p. 1947. pap. 9.95 (*0-7859-5360-4*) Fr & Eur.

— La Perle de la Canebiere. 9.95 (*0-686-54245-2*) Fr & Eur.

— Permettez, Madame. 9.95 (*0-686-54246-0*) Fr & Eur.

— Les Petits Oiseaux. 9.95 (*0-686-54247-9*) Fr & Eur.

— La Piece de Chambertin. 9.95 (*0-686-54248-7*) Fr & Eur.

— Un Pied dans le Crime. 9.95 (*0-686-54249-5*) Fr & Eur.

— La Poudre aux Yeux. 9.95 (*0-686-54250-9*) Fr & Eur.

— A Slap in the Farce & a Matter of Wife & Death. Shapiro, Norman, tr. (Farce Ser.: Vol. 2). 1988. pap. 7.95 (*0-936839-82-1*) Applause Theatre Bk Pubs.

— La Station Champbaudet. 9.95 (*0-686-54251-7*); pap. 4.95 (*0-686-54252-5*) Fr & Eur.

— Les Suites d'Un Premier Lit. 9.95 (*0-686-54253-3*) Fr & Eur.

— Theatre, Vol. 1. (FRE.). 1990. pap. 16.95 (*0-7859-3002-7*) Fr & Eur.

— Theatre, Vol. 2. (FRE.). 1991. pap. 14.95 (*0-7859-3003-5*) Fr & Eur.

— Theatre, Vol. 3. (FRE.). 509p. 1964. 10.95 (*0-8288-9835-9*, F108552) Fr & Eur.

***Labiche, Eugene.** Threesome. (Absolute Classics Ser.). 144p. 2000. pap. 15.95 (*1-84002-155-1*) Theatre Comm.

Labiche, Eugene. Les Trente - Sept Sous de Monsieur Montaudouin. 9.95 (*0-686-54256-8*) Fr & Eur.

— Two Plays by Eugene Labiche: Ninety Degrees in the Shade, & Dust in Your Eyes. 1962. pap. 5.25 (*0-8222-0343-X*) Dramatists Play.

— Vingt-Neuf Degres a l'Ombre. 9.95 (*0-686-54257-6*) Fr & Eur.

— Les Vivacites du Capitaine Tic. 9.95 (*0-686-54258-4*) Fr & Eur.

— Voyage Autour de Ma Marmite. 9.95 (*0-686-54259-2*) Fr & Eur.

— Le Voyage de M. Perrichon. Barsacq, Andre, ed. (FRE.). 1954. 7.95 (*0-7859-0011-X*, F65490); pap. 5.95 (*0-686-54261-4*) Fr & Eur.

— Le Voyage de Monsieur Perrichon. (Coll. Mises en Scene). pap. 9.50 (*0-685-34925-X*) Fr & Eur.

Labiche, Eugene & Sigaux, Gilbert. Oeuvres Completes: Deux Profonds Sclerats, un Mari qui Prende du Ventre, Espagnolas et Boyardinos, Vol. 4. (FRE., Illus.). 1967. 85.00 (*0-7859-5356-6*) Fr & Eur.

— Oeuvres Completes: Il Est de la Police, la Memoir d'Hortense, Doit-on le Dire?, Vol. 8. (FRE., Illus.). 1968. 85.00 (*0-7859-5359-0*) Fr & Eur.

— Oeuvres Completes: J'ai Compromis ma Femme, le Vivacite du Capitaine Tic, L'Amour En Sabot, Vol. 6. (FRE., Illus.). 1968. 85.00 (*0-7859-5557-7*) Fr & Eur.

— Oeuvres Completes: Je Croque ma Tante, le Clou aux Maris, L'Avare aux gants Jaunes, Vol. 5. (Illus.). 1968. 55.00 (*0-7859-5357-4*) Fr & Eur.

— Oeuvres Completes: Monsieur de Coylin, l'Avocat Loubet, L'Article, Vol. 1. (FRE., Illus.). 960p. 1966. 85.00 (*0-7859-5354-X*) Fr & Eur.

— Oeuvres Completes: Premier Prix de Piano, l'homme qui manque le Coche, le Bergere de la Rue Monthabar, Vol. 7. (FRE., Illus.). 1968. 85.00 (*0-7859-5358-2*) Fr & Eur.

— Oeuvres Completes: Un Jeune Homme Presse, le Club Champen, Vol. 2. (FRE., Illus.). 1967. 85.00 (*0-7859-5355-8*) Fr & Eur.

— Oeuvres Completes: Une Clarinette qui Passe, la Femme qui perd ses Jarretiers, on Demande Deux Culottieres, Vol. 3. (FRE., Illus.). 1967. 85.00 (*0-7859-5556-9*) Fr & Eur.

LaBier, Douglas. Can We Make It Last? Practicing Love in a Culture of Disconnection. 320p. 2000. 24.95 (*0-7868-6479-6*, Pub. by Hyprn Child) Time Warner.

— Modern Madness. 1986. 16.30 (*0-201-11775-4*) Addison-Wesley.

Labig, Charles E. Preventing Violence in the Workplace. LC 95-117. 224p. 1995. 24.95 (*0-8144-0287-9*) AMACOM.

Labignan, Italo, jt. auth. see Waszczuk, Henry.

Labije, J. Ten & Balner, H., eds. Coping with Cancer & Beyond: Cancer Treatment & Mental Health. (Publications of the Helen Dowling Institute for Biopsychosocial Medicine: Vol. 5). 194p. 1991. pap. 47.00 (*90-265-1223-6*) Swets.

Labillardiere, Jacques-Julien H. De, see De Labillardiere, Jacques-Julien H.

Labine, Clem & Flaherty, Carolyn, eds. The Old-House Journal Compendium. LC 78-4360. (Illus.). 400p. 1983. pap. 22.95 (*0-87951-186-9*, Pub. by Overlook Pr) Penguin Putnam.

Labine, P., jt. ed. see Raman, A.

Labine, Paul, jt. ed. see Moran, George C.

Labiner, Norah. Our Sometime Sister. LC 97-43268. 452p. 1998. 21.95 (*1-56689-072-1*) Coffee Hse.

***Labiner, Norah.** Our Sometime Sister. 442p. 2000. pap. 15.95 (*1-56689-095-0*) Coffee Hse.

Labinger, Andrea, tr. see Giardinelli, Mempo.

Labinger, Andrea G., tr. see Berman, Sabina.

Labinger, Andrea G., tr. see Cerda, Carlos.

Labinger, Andrea G., tr. see Steimberg, Alicia.

Labinger, Andrea G., tr. see Valenzuela, Luisa.

Labini, Paolo S. Economic Growth & Business Cycles: Prices & the Process of Cyclical Development. (Economists of the Twentieth Century Ser.). 256p. 1993. 110.00 (*1-85278-833-X*) E Elgar.

Labinowicz, Ed. Learning from Children: New Beginnings for Teaching Numerical Thinking. LC 84-234917. 1985. text 26.95 (*0-201-20321-9*) Addison-Wesley.

Labinski, Paul. Macroeconomics Rational Expectations Approach. 2nd ed. (C). 1990. 49.00 (*0-536-57766-8*) Pearson Custom.

Labinsky, Daria & Hieronymus, Stan. The Brewpub Cookbook: Favorite Recipes from Great Brewpub Kitchens. LC 96-50877. 160p. (gr. 11). 1999. pap. 12.95 (*0-7835-4906-7*) Time-Life.

Labinsky, Daria, jt. auth. see Hieronymus, Stan.

Labiosa-Cassone, Libyan. Team Language Learning for French, Spanish & German. Rose, Diana, ed. (Illus.). (Orig.). 1991. pap., student ed. 199.00 incl. VHS (*0-685-54740-X*, Pub. by Accel Lrn Sys) McClelland & Stewart.

Labistour, Leon. Making Ships in Bottles: Beginners to Advanced. 1995. pap. 17.95 (*0-8128-8558-9*, Scrbrough Hse) Madison Bks UPA.

Labit, C., jt. auth. see Tziritas, G.

***Labitzke, K. G. & Van Loon, H.** The Stratosphere: Phenomena, History & Relevance. LC 99-34569. (Illus.). 195p. 1999. 62.00 (*3-540-65784-3*) Spr-Verlag.

***Labitzke, R.** Manual of Cable Osteosyntheses. 200p. 2000. (*3-540-66508-0*) Spr-Verlag.

Labivitz, George, et al. Making Quality Work: A Leadership Guide for the Results-Driven Manager. 208p. 1995. pap. 18.95 (*0-471-13211-X*) Wiley.

Lablanc, Louise. Sophie Fait des Folies. (Novels in the Premier Roman Ser.). (FRE., Illus.). 64p. (J). (gr. 2-5). 1995. pap. 8.95 (*2-89021-244-0*, Pub. by La Courte Ech) Firefly Bks Ltd.

LaBlanc, Michael L. Contemporary Musicians, Vol. 1. 320p. 1989. text 81.00 (*0-8103-2211-0*) Gale.

— Contemporary Musicians Vol. 2: Profiles of the People in Music, Vol. 2. 350p. 1989. text 81.00 (*0-8103-2212-9*) Gale.

LaBlanc, Michael L. Hotdogs, Heroes & Hooligans: The Story of Baseball's Major League Teams, 2 vols. (Illus.). 593p. 1994. pap. 16.95 (*0-8103-9748-X*) Visible Ink Pr.

LaBlanc, Michael L., ed. Contemporary Musicians, Vol. 3. 340p. 1990. text 81.00 (*0-8103-2213-7*) Gale.

Lablanc, Michael L., jt. auth. see Henshaw, Richard.

LaBlaude, Pierre A. The Gardens of Versailles. (Illus.). 160p. 1994. 39.95 (*1-85759-043-0*, Pub. by P Wilson) Scala Books.

— The Gardens of Versailles. LC 96-109742. (Illus.). 192p. 1995. 40.00 (*0-302-00659-1*, Pub. by Scala Books) Antique Collect.

Labno-Falecka, Ewa. Phraseologie und Uebersetzen: Eine Untersuchung der Uebersetzbarkeit Kreativ-Innovativ Gebrauchter "Wiederholter Rede" Anhand von Beispielen aus der Polnischen und Deutschen Gegenwartsliteratur. (Europaische Hochschulschriften Ser.: Reihe 21, Band 148). (GER.). X, 542p. 1994. pap. 79.95 (*3-631-48182-9*) P Lang Pubng.

LaBo. Looking Black. 31p. (Orig.). 1993. pap. text 3.95 (*1-56411-055-9*) Untd Bros & Sis.

Laboda, Amy, ed. see Thom, Trevor.

Laboda, Gene. A Peek at Life from Another Planet. LC 83-62346. 96p. (Orig.). 1983. pap. 4.95 (*0-914279-00-9*) Pyramid Pub Co.

Laboda, Lawrence R. From Selma to Appomattox: The History of the Jeff Davis Artillery. LC 94-41925. (Illus.). 385p. 1995. 30.00 (*0-942597-80-X*) White Mane Pub.

— From Selma to Appomattox: The History of the Jeff Davis Artillery. LC 96-19970. (Illus.). 400p. 1996. reprint ed. pap. 16.95 (*0-19-510997-X*) OUP.

Laboissonniere, Wade. Blueprints of Fashion: Home-Sewing Patterns of the Twentieth Century, 1940. LC 97-17115. 176p. 1997. pap. 29.95 (*0-7643-0304-X*) Schiffer.

***Laboissonniere, Wade.** Blueprints of Fashion Home Sewing Patterns Of The 1950s. (Illus.). 176p. 1999. pap. 29.95 (*0-7643-0919-6*) Schiffer.

LaBombard, Joan. The Counting of Grains. Iddings, Kathleen, ed. LC 90-60172. (American Bk.). 99p. (Orig.). 1983. pap. text, per. 10.00 (*0-931289-03-3*) San Diego Poet Pr.

— The Winter Watch of the Leaves. Iddings, Kathleen, ed. LC 92-60839. (American Bk.). 98p. (Orig.). 1993. per. 10.00 (*0-931289-10-6*) San Diego Poet Pr.

Labon, Don & Evans, Peter. Post-Compulsory Education for Disabled People in OECD Countries. LC 97-224789. 92p. 1997. pap. 19.00 (*92-64-15601-1*, 96-97-06-1, Pub. by Org for Econ) OECD.

Labon, Don & Evans, Peter, eds. Implementing Inclusive Education. LC 98-121131. 192p. 1997. pap. 19.00 (*92-64-15589-9*, 96-97-03-1, Pub. by Org for Econ) OECD.

Labon, Joanna, ed. Balkan Blues: Writing Out of Yugoslavia. LC 95-25082. (Writings from an Unbound Europe). 276p. (C). 1995. pap. 15.95 (*0-8101-1325-2*) Northwestern U Pr.

LaBonte, Gail. The Llama. LC 88-16407. (Remarkable Animals Ser.). (Illus.). 60p. (J). (gr. 3 up). 1988. text 13.95 (*0-87518-393-X*, Dillon Silver Burdett) Silver Burdett Pr.

— The Miniature Horse. LC 89-26046. (Remarkable Animals Ser.). (Illus.). 60p. (J). (gr. 3 up). 1990. lib. bdg. 13.95 (*0-87518-424-3*, Dillon Silver Burdett) Silver Burdett Pr.

— The Tarantula. (Remarkable Animals Ser.). (Illus.). 60p. (J). (gr. 3 up). 1991. lib. bdg. 13.95 (*0-87518-452-9*, Dillon Silver Burdett) Silver Burdett Pr.

— The Tarantula. (Remarkable Animals Ser.). (Illus.). 60p. (J). (gr. 4). 1995. pap. 5.95 (*0-382-39235-3*, Dillon Silver Burdett) Silver Burdett Pr.

LaBonte, George. Fishing for Sailfish. Barrett, Linda, ed. (Illus.). 232p. (Orig.). 1994. pap. 18.95 (*0-923155-21-X*) Fisherman Lib.

LaBonte, Larry. The First Ballet. (Illus.). 24p. 1995. 7.50 (*1-887390-01-4*) Kiki Coll.

— In the Beginning. (Illus.). 160p. 1995. 50.00 (*1-887390-00-6*) Kiki Coll.

LaBonte, Marie L. Conversations with Angels: You'll Remember the Love. 2nd ed. Orig. Title: Voice of the Healing Angels. 216p. 1997. pap. 16.95 (*1-891099-00-0*, 1949) Blu Prl Pr.

Labonte, Marie Lise & Prevost, Ninon. Wings of Light: The Art of Spiritual Angelic Healing. unabridged ed. (Illus.). 97p. 2000. pap. 14.95 (*1-891099-04-3*, Pub. by Blu Prl Pr) Hushion Hse.

***LaBonte, Richard.** Best of Best Gay Erotica. (Illus.). 250p. 2000. pap. 14.95 (*1-57344-104-X*) Cleis Pr.

Labonte, Richard, ed. Best Gay Erotica, 1998. 200p. 1998. pap. 14.95 (*1-57344-031-0*) Cleis Pr.

LaBonte, Richard, ed. Best Gay Erotica, 2000. 200p. pap. 14.95 (*1-57344-092-2*, Pub. by Cleis Pr) Publishers Group.

LaBonte, Richard, ed. see Maney, Mabel.

LaBonty, Dennis, ed. Integrating the Internet into the Business Curriculum. (Nineteen Ninety Eight NBEA Yearbk.). 183p. 1998. pap. 15.00 (*0-933964-51-X*) Natl Busn Ed Assoc.

LaBonty, Jan, jt. auth. see Danielson, Kathy E.

LaBoo, Deborah, ed. A Treasured Token. 1997. 69.95 (*1-57553-421-5*) Nat Lib Poetry.

***LaBoone, Thomas.** Wine Notes: Pocket Guide & Personal Tasting Journal. (Illus.). 96p. 1999. 9.95 (*0-9672651-1-8*) Notable Concpts.

Labor Center Reporter Editorial Board Staff. Labor & the Economy: A Guide for Trade Unionists. (Orig.). 1989. pap. 7.50 (*0-937817-06-6*) CLRE UCAL Berk.

Labor Department, Labor Statistics Bureau Staff, contrib. by. BLS Handbook of Methods. 250p. 1997. per. 20.00 (*0-16-049038-3*) USGPO.

— Occupational Outlook Handbook, 1994-95. (Illus.). 282p. 1998. per. 23.00 (*0-16-049346-3*) USGPO.

Labor Dept., Labor Statistics Bureau Staff, contrib. by. Occupational Outlook Handbook, 1998-99. 23rd ed. (Illus.). 540p. 1998. per. 42.00 (*0-16-049348-X*); boxed set 46.00 (*0-16-049347-1*) USGPO.

Labor, Earl G. & Reesman, Jeanne C. Jack London. rev. ed. LC 93-49825. (Twayne's United States Authors Ser.: No. 230). 208p. 1994. 32.00 (*0-8057-4033-3*, Twyne) Mac Lib Ref.

Labor, Earle, ed. see London, Jack.

Labor, Earle G., ed. see London, Jack.

Labor Institute Staff. Hazardous Materials Workbook. 8th rev. ed. (Illus.). 327p. (Orig.). 1996. pap. 22.50 (*0-945257-70-8*) Apex Pr.

Labor Secretariat of the Commission. Incomes & Productivity in North America: Papers of the 1997 Seminar. (SPA.). 1998. pap. 32.00 (*0-89059-089-3*) Bernan Pr.

— Incomes & Productivity in North America: Papers of the 1997 Seminar. (FRE.). 1998. pap. 32.00 (*0-89059-088-5*) Bernan Pr.

— Plant Closings & Labor Rights: The Effects of Sudden Plant Closings on Freedom of Association & the Right to Organize in Canada, Mexico, & the United States. (SPA.). 240p. 1998. pap. 27.50 (*0-89059-079-6*) Bernan Pr.

Labor Secretariat of the Commission Staff. North American Labor Markets: A Comparative Profile. (North American Labor Ser.). (FRE.). 200p. 1997. pap. 35.00 (*0-89059-074-5*, BPF0745) Bernan Pr.

Labor Staff. Diccionario Enciclopedica Labor, 10 vols., Set. (SPA.). 3758p. 1990. 1795.00 (*0-7859-5911-4*, 8433503901) Fr & Eur.

— Diccionario Enciclopedica Labor, Vol. 1. (SPA.). 374p. 1990. 195.00 (*0-7859-6462-2*) Fr & Eur.

— Diccionario Enciclopedica Labor, Vol. 2. (SPA.). 374p. 1990. 195.00 (*0-7859-5912-2*, 8433503928) Fr & Eur.

— Diccionario Enciclopedica Labor, Vol. 3. (SPA.). 374p. 1990. 195.00 (*0-7859-5913-0*, 8433503936) Fr & Eur.

— Diccionario Enciclopedica Labor, Vol. 4. (SPA.). 374p. 1990. 195.00 (*0-7859-5914-9*, 8433503944) Fr & Eur.

— Diccionario Enciclopedica Labor, Vol. 5. (SPA.). 374p. 1990. 195.00 (*0-7859-5915-7*, 8433503952) Fr & Eur.

— Diccionario Enciclopedica Labor, Vol. 6. (SPA.). 374p. 1990. 195.00 (*0-7859-5916-5*, 8433503960) Fr & Eur.

— Diccionario Enciclopedica Labor, Vol. 7. (SPA.). 374p. 1990. 195.00 (*0-7859-5917-3*, 8433503979) Fr & Eur.

— Diccionario Enciclopedica Labor, Vol. 8. (SPA.). 374p. 1990. 195.00 (*0-7859-5918-1*, 8433503987) Fr & Eur.

— Diccionario Enciclopedica Labor, Vol. 9. (SPA.). 374p. 1990. 195.00 (*0-7859-5919-X*, 8433503995) Fr & Eur.

— Diccionario Enciclopedica Labor, Vol. 10. (SPA.). 1990. 195.00 (*0-7859-5920-3*, 8433504002) Fr & Eur.

— Enciclopedia Labor: La Enciclopedia Organica de Nuestro Tiempo, 12 vols., Set. 3rd ed. (SPA.). 10000p. 1976. 1795.00 (*0-8288-5668-0*, S12295) Fr & Eur.

— Enciclopedia Labor de la Mujer y del Hogar: La Mujer, los Hijos, la Casa y la Alimentacion, 4 vols., Set. 2nd ed. (SPA.). 1280p. 1976. 250.00 (*0-8288-5669-9*, S50457) Fr & Eur.

— Enciclopedia Labor 3, 3 vols., Set. 2nd ed. (SPA.). 1193p. 1972. 195.00 (*0-8288-6384-9*, S-12294) Fr & Eur.

— Lexicolabor: Diccionario Enciclopedico Ilustrado, 4 vols., Set. (SPA.). 2216p. 1977. 395.00 (*0-8288-5484-X*, S50443) Fr & Eur.

Laboratory Evaluation Committee. Handbook for the Interpretation & Application of ANSI-NCL Z540-1-1964. unabridged ed. 70p. 1995. 20.00 (*1-58464-004-9*) Natl Conf Stds Labs.

***Laboratory Facilities Committee.** Guide to Selecting Standards-Laboratory Environments: RP-14. unabridged ed. 16p. 1999. 15.00 (*1-58464-023-5*) Natl Conf Stds Labs.

Laboratory Manual for Medical Microbiology Staff. Laboratory Manual for Medical Microbiology. Schools of Medicine & Dentistry, State University, ed. LC QR0046.L30. (Microbiology Ser.: No. 11). (Illus.). 195p. reprint ed. pap. 60.50 (*0-7837-0617-0*, 204096200019) Bks Demand.

Laboratory Network Program Staff. Facilitating Systemic Change in Science & Mathematics Education: A Toolkit for Professional Developers. 800p. (C). 1995. text. write for info. (*1-878234-08-0*) Reg Lab Educ IOT NE Isls.

Laborde, A. M. Le Marquis et la Marquise de Sade. (American University Studies: Romance Languages & Literature: Ser. II, Vol. 108). 216p. (C). 1990. text 41.95 (*0-8204-0899-9*) P Lang Pubng.

Laborde, Alice M. Diderot et l'Amour. (Stanford French & Italian Studies: No. 17). (FRE.). vi, 114p. 1979. pap. 56.50 (*0-915838-22-2*) Anma Libri.

— Diderot et Mme. de Puisieux. (Stanford French & Italian Studies: Vol. 36). 1985. pap. 56.50 (*0-915838-54-0*) Anma Libri.

LaBorde, Allyson, ed. Corporate Image: Communicating Visions & Values. (Report: No. 1038). 57p. (Orig.). 1993. pap. text 100.00 (*0-8237-0510-2*) Conference Bd.

***Laborde, Cecile.** Pluralist Thinking & the State in Britain & France, 1900-25 LC 99-42554. (St. Antony's Ser.). 2000. text 65.00 (*0-312-22934-8*) St Martin.

Laborde, Claude. Dictionnaire des Histoires Droles Super Erotiques. (FRE.). 1993. pap. 45.00 (*0-7859-8051-2*, 2840690543) Fr & Eur.

Laborde, E. D., tr. see Robequain, Charles.

Laborde, Errol. The Buzzard Wore a Tutu: Chronicles of Life & Adventures in New Orleans. (Illus.). 112p. (Orig.). 1994. pap. 8.95 (*0-9643874-0-9*) Urban Press.

— Mardi Gras! A Celebration. Rogers, Mary A., ed. (Illus.). 200p. 1981. 29.95 (*0-937430-03-X*); pap. 15.95 (*0-937430-02-1*) Picayune Pr.

Laborde, Genie Z. Fine Tune Your Brain: When Everything's Going Right & What to Do When It Isn't. 1988. 24.95 (*0-933347-30-8*); pap. 13.95 (*0-933347-20-0*) Syntony Inc Pub.

— Influencing with Integrity: Management Skills for Communication & Negotiation. LC 83-51129. (Illus.). 235p. 1988. 24.95 (*0-9613172-0-5*); pap. 12.95 (*0-933347-10-3*) Syntony Inc Pub.

— Ninety Days to Communication Excellence. (Communication Ser.). 100p. 1985. 9.95 (*0-317-53169-7*) Syntony Inc Pub.

Laborde, Jean B. Essai sur la Musique Ancienne et Moderne, 4 vols., Set. LC 76-43922. (Music & Theatre in France in the 17th & 18th Centuries Ser.). (FRE.). reprint ed. 355.00 (*0-404-60180-4*) AMS Pr.

L

Laborde, Jean-Marie, ed. Intelligent Learning Environments: The Case of Geometry. (NATO ASI Ser.: Series F, Vol. 117). 1995. write for info. (3-540-56807-7) Spr-Verlag.

Laborde, Jeane-Marie. Intelligent Learning Environments: The Case of Geometry. (NATO ASI Series F: Computer & Systems Sciences, Special Programme AET: Vol. 117). 255p. 1995. 69.00 (0-387-56807-7) Spr-Verlag.

Laborde, Karen, ed. see Baker, Robert P.

Laborde, Leon De, see De Laborde, Leon.

LaBorde, Mason H. Trick or Treatment: How to Avoid Abuse in Psychotherapy. 190p. 2000. pap. 15.95 (1-879899-15-9) Newjoy Pr.

Laborde, Michael, jt. auth. see Ritter, Beverly L.

Laborde Printers Staff, ed. see Alfonso, Betty A.

Laborecky, J. Hudobny Terminologicky Slovnik (Dictionary of Musical Expressions) (SLO.). 420p. 1997. write for info. (80-08-01037-1, Pub. by Slov Pegagog Naklad) IBD Ltd.

Laborit, Emmannuelle. The Cry of the Gull. Mitchell, Constantina T. & Cote, Paul R., trs. LC 98-8775. (Illus.). 160p. 1998. 29.95 (1-56368-072-6) Gallaudet Univ Pr.

***Laborit, Emmanuelle.** Cry of the Gull. 1999. pap. 9.95 (1-56368-086-6) Gallaudet Univ Pr.

LaBoskey, Vicki K. Development of Reflective Practice: A Study of Preservice Teachers. LC 93-46110. 192p. (C). 1994. pap. 18.95 (0-8077-3334-2); text 38.00 (0-8077-3335-0) Tchrs Coll.

LaBossiere, Mike, jt. auth. see Pass, Geoff.

LaBotz, Dan. Mask of Democracy: Labour Suppression in Mexico Today. 223p. write for info. (1-895431-59-X); pap. write for info. (1-895431-58-1) Black Rose.

Labouchere, Rachel. Abiah Darby. 1999. 30.00 (1-85072-018-5, Pub. by W Sessions); pap. 21.00 (1-85072-017-7, Pub. by W Sessions) St Mut.

— Deborah Darby of Coalbrookdale (1754-1810) (Illus.). 468p. 1999. pap. 21.00 (1-85072-100-9, Pub. by W Sessions) St Mut.

LaBouliere, Raymond H. Book of Electrical Formulas Solving Unknown Values: Solving Unknown Values. 140p. (Orig.). 1995. pap. text. write for info. (0-9644626-0-5) R H LaBouliere.

***Labounsky, Ann.** Jean Langlais: The Man & His Music. LC 99-42129. (Illus.). 392p. 2000. 34.95 (1-57467-054-9, Amadeus Pr) Timber.

LaBounty, Char. How to Establish & Maintain Service Level Agreements. Etchison, Jim et al, eds. (Illus.). (Orig.). pap. text. write for info. (1-57125-009-3) Help Desk Inst.

— Outsourcing Trends in the Customer Support Industry. Bultema, Patrick et al, eds. (Illus.). 70p. (Orig.). pap. write for info. (1-57125-017-4) Help Desk Inst.

LaBounty, William P., compiled by. Index to the Map of McLean County, Illinois: By J. L. Spaulding. LC 94-44406. 1994. 30.00 (0-943788-06-4) McLean County.

Labour Housing Group Staff. Right to a Home. Griffiths, David, ed. 194p. 1984. 42.50 (0-85124-399-1, Pub. by Spkesman) Coronet Bks.

— The Roof over Your Head: A Housing Programme for Labour. Darke, Jane, ed. 128p. (Orig.). 1992. pap. 33.50 (0-85124-531-5, Pub. by Spkesman) Coronet Bks.

Labourdette, J. P., jt. auth. see Auzias, D.

Labourdette, Rodolfo. Yagruma Nights. LC 96-60475. 295p. (Orig.). 1996. pap. 15.00 (0-9653347-0-8) Transpersonal.

Laboureur, Sylvain. Laboureur's Graphic Work: Catalogue Raisonne. (FRE., Illus.). 828p. 1989. 185.00 (1-55660-056-9) A Wofsy Fine Arts.

— Laboureur's Illustrated Books. (FRE.). 664p. 1990. 185.00 (1-55660-139-5) A Wofsy Fine Arts.

— Laboureur's Paintings, Watercolors & Couaches. (FRE., Illus.). 516p. 1991. 195.00 (1-55660-260-X) A Wofsy Fine Arts.

Labouvie-Vief, Gisela. Adulthood & Aging. 1996. pap. text. write for info. (0-7167-2931-8) W H Freeman.

— Psyche & Eros: Mind & Gender in the Life Course. LC 93-21292. 345p. (C). 1994. text 59.95 (0-521-43340-1); pap. text 19.95 (0-521-46824-8) Cambridge U Pr.

Labov. Principles of Linguistic Philosophy. 1994. 36.95 (0-631-17914-3) Blackwell Pubs.

LaBov, Larry. How to Sell & Be Yourself. LC 95-95258. 104p. (Orig.). 1995. per. 15.95 (0-9649727-0-0) LaBov & Beyond.

***Labov, William.** Principles of Linguistic Change Vol. 2: Social Factors. (Language in Society Ser.: Vol. 29). (Illus.). 400p. 2000. text 74.95 (0-631-17915-1); pap. text 34.95 (0-631-17916-X) Blackwell Pubs.

Labov, William. The Social Stratification of English in New York City. LC 66-24073. 513p. reprint ed. pap. 159.10 (0-8357-3348-3, 203958100013) Bks Demand.

— Sociolinguistic Patterns. (Conduct & Communication Ser.). 362p. 1973. pap. 20.95 (0-8122-1052-2) U of Pa Pr.

***Labov, William, et al, eds.** Atlas of North American English: Phonetics, Phonology & Sound Change. 2000. 278.00 (3-11-016746-8) De Gruyter.

Labovitz, Annette & Labovitz, Eugene. Time for My Soul: A Treasury of Jewish Stories for Our Holy Days. LC 86-32243. 448p. 1987. 30.00 (0-87668-954-3) Aronson.

— Time for My Soul: A Treasury of Jewish Stories for Our Holy Days. LC 86-32243. 448p. 1997. reprint ed. pap. 30.00 (1-56821-924-5) Aronson.

Labovitz, Annette, jt. auth. see Labovitz, Eugene.

Labovitz, Arthur J. & Pearson, Anthony. Transesophageal Echocardiography: Basic Principles & Clinical Applications. (Illus.). 157p. 1993. pap. text 45.00 (0-8121-1578-3) Lppncott W & W.

Labovitz, Arthur J. & Williams, George A. Doppler Echocardiography: The Quantitative Approach. 3rd ed. (Illus.). 131p. 1992. text 35.00 (0-8121-1429-9) Lppncott W & W.

Labovitz, Esther K. The Myth of the Heroine: The Female Bildungsroman in the Twentieth-Century. 2nd ed. (American University Studies: General Literature: Ser. XIX, Vol. 4). 272p. 1987. text 49.95 (0-8204-0360-1) P Lang Pubng.

Labovitz, Eugene & Labovitz, Annette. A Sacred Trust: Stories of Jewish Heritage & History, Vols. 2 & 3. 2nd rev. ed. 368p. 1997. reprint ed. pap. text 24.00 (0-914615-02-5) I Nathan Pub Co.

— A Sacred Trust Vol. 1: Talmudic Age, Medieval Age, & Sephardic Age, Vol. 1. LC 94-68316. 303p. 1995. pap. 18.00 (0-914615-12-2) I Nathan Pub Co.

— A Touch of Heaven: Spiritual & Kabbalistic Stories for Jewish Living. 2nd rev. ed. 240p. 1998. pap. text 20.00 (0-914615-04-1) I Nathan Pub Co.

Labovitz, Eugene, jt. auth. see Labovitz, Annette.

Labovitz, George & Rosansky, Victor. The Power of Alignment: How Great Companies Stay Centered & Accomplish Extraordinary Things. LC 97-12815. 256p. 1997. 27.95 (0-471-17790-3) Wiley.

Labovitz, George, et al. Making Quality Work: A Leadership Guide for the Results-Driven Manager. LC 93-61340. 200p. (C). 1993. pap. 16.00 (0-939246-54-6) Wiley.

Labovitz, John R. Presidential Impeachment. LC 77-76300. 268p. 1978. 45.00 (0-300-02213-1) Yale U Pr.

Labovitz, Sherman. Being Red in Philadelphia: A Memoir of the McCarthy Era. LC 97-14527. (Illus.). 192p. 1998. 22.00 (0-940159-42-2) Camino Bks.

***Labovitz, Trudy.** Deadly Embrace. (Zoe Kergulin Mystery Ser.: Vol. 1). 224p. 2000. pap. 12.00 (1-883523-38-9, Pub. by Spinsters Ink) Words Distrib.

Labovitz, Trudy. Ordinary Justice: A Zoe Kergulin Mystery. LC 99-19045. 248p. 1999. pap. 12.00 (1-883523-31-1, Pub. by Spinsters Ink) SPD-Small Pr Dist.

Labowitz, Shoni. God, Sex & Women of the Bible: Discovering Our Sensual, Spiritual Selves. LC 98-23304. 320p. 1998. 23.00 (0-684-83717-X) Simon & Schuster.

— Miraculous Living. 336p. 1998. per. 12.00 (0-684-83556-8) S&S Trade.

— Miraculous Living: A Guided Journey Through the 10 Gates of the Tree of Life. LC 96-19269. 336p. 1996. 22.50 (0-684-81444-7) S&S Trade.

Labozzetta, Marisa. Stay with Me, Lella. LC 98-75280. (Prose Ser.: Vol. 54). 172p. 1999. pap. 13.00 (1-55071-076-1) Guernica Editions.

Labra, Carilda O. Dust Disappears. Barkan, Stanley H., ed. Gioseffi, Daniella & Garcia, Enildo, trs. (Review Latin-American Writers (Cuban) Chapbook Ser.: No. 1). (ENG & SPA., Illus.). 48p. 1991. 15.00 (0-89304-150-5) Cross-Cultrl NY.

— Dust Disappears. Barkan, Stanley H., ed. Gioseffi, Daniela & Garcia, Enildo, trs. (Review Latin-American Writers (Cuban) Chapbook Ser.: No. 1). (ENG & SPA., Illus.). 48p. 1991. 15.00 (0-89304-152-1) Cross-Cultrl NY.

— Dust Disappears. Barkan, Stanley H., ed. Gioseffi, Daniella & Garcia, Enildo, trs. (Review Latin-American Writers (Cuban) Chapbook Ser.: No. 1). (ENG & SPA., Illus.). 48p. 1991. 5.00 (0-89304-153-X); pap. 5.00 (0-89304-151-3) Cross-Cultrl NY.

— Dust Disappears. Barkan, Stanley H., ed. Gioseffi, Daniela & Garcia, Enildo, trs. (Review Latin-American Writers (Cuban) Chapbook Ser.: No. 1). (ENG & SPA., Illus.). 48p. 1991. audio 10.00 (0-89304-154-8) Cross-Cultrl NY.

Labraca. Convocacion. (College Spanish Ser.). (SPA.). (C). 1991. mass mkt., teacher ed. 21.95 (0-8384-2203-9) Heinle & Heinle.

***Labrack, Joy.** Baby's Shower. (Illus.). (J). 2000. mass mkt. 4.99 (0-375-81040-4) Random.

— Little Fire Truck. (Illus.). (J). 2000. mass mkt. 4.99 (0-375-81041-2) Random.

— Whale Baby. (Illus.). 5p. (J). (ps). 2000. 4.99 (0-375-80481-1) Random Bks Yng Read.

Labrada, Emilio B., ed. see Betancourt De Hita, Armando.

Labrada, R., et al. Weed Management for Developing Countries. LC 95-221679. (Plant Production & Protection Papers: Vol. 12). 402p. 1994. 50.00 (92-5-103427-3, F34273, Pub. by FAO) Bernan Associates.

LaBrake, Mary L. Ssri Test Differences. LC 92-16719. 1992. pap. text 16.95 (0-201-63411-2) Addison-Wesley.

LaBrake, Tammy, ed. How to Get Families More Involved in the Nursing Home: Four Programs That Work & Why. LC 96-20595. (Illus.). 103p. (C). 1996. 29.95 (0-7890-0056-3) Haworth Pr.

— How to Get Families More Involved in the Nursing Home: Four Programs That Work & Why. LC 96-20595. 103p. (C). 1997. pap. 14.95 (0-7890-0205-1) Haworth Pr.

***LaBranche, George M.** The Dry Fly & Fast Water. 218p. 2000. pap. 19.95 (1-56833-156-8) Madison Bks UPA.

LaBranche, George M. & Schullery, Paul. The Dry Fly & Fast Water. expanded ed. LC 98-16080. (Illus.). 264p. 1998. reprint ed. per. 24.95 (0-9626663-6-X) Greycliff Pub.

— The Dry Fly & Fast Water. limited ed. (Illus.). 264p. 1998. reprint ed. boxed set 50.00 (1-890373-01-X) Greycliff Pub.

Labre, R. M., ed. Accidents in the Year 2000. (C). 1989. pap. text 90.50 (0-7923-0475-6) Kluwer Academic.

Labrecque, Jeff, jt. auth. see Herzog, Brad.

LaBrecque, John L., ed. Ocean Margin Drilling Program Atlases Vol. 13. (Regional Atlas Ser.). 1986. pap. 295.00 (0-86720-263-7) Jones & Bartlett.

Labrecque, Lisa, ed. Unity: A Celebration of Gay Games IV & Stonewall. 168p. (Orig.). 1994. pap. 29.95 (0-9643182-0-2) Labrecque Pub.

Labrecque, Marie-France, ed. L' Egaliti Devant Soi: Sexes, Rapports Sociaux et Developpement International. 353p. 1994. pap. 24.00 (0-88936-686-1, Pub. by IDRC Bks) Stylus Pub VA.

LaBrecque, Rodney. Effective Department & Team Leaders: A Practical Guide. LC 97-78325. 350p. 1998. text 49.95 (0-926842-76-5) CG Pubs Inc.

LaBrecque, Ron, jt. auth. see Markman, Ronald.

Labrie. Androgens & Prostate Cancer. 1992. 14.95 (0-8493-5824-8) CRC Pr.

Labrie, Fernand, et al. DHEA & Sex Steroids: Intracrinology in Target Tissues. 319p. 1996. text 75.00 (1-898099-10-3) Blackwell Sci.

— Localised Prostate Cancer: Recent Advances in Diagnosis & Treatment. 319p. (Orig.). 1997. pap. text 65.00 (1-898099-11-1) Blackwell Sci.

Labrie, Fernand, jt. auth. see Mauvais-Jarvis, P.

Labrie, Roger P., et al. United States Arms Sales Policy: Background & Issues. LC 87-72491. (AEI Studies: No. 359). 96p. reprint ed. pap. 30.00 (0-8357-4539-2, 203743000008) Bks Demand.

Labrie, Roger P., jt. ed. see Pranger, Robert J.

Labrie, Ross. The Catholic Imagination in American Literature. LC 96-37254. 320p. 1997. spiral bd. 39.95 (0-8262-1110-0) U of Mo Pr.

— The Writings of Daniel Berrigan. (Illus.). 284p. (C). 1989. lib. bdg. 50.00 (0-8191-7495-5) U Pr of Amer.

Labriola, Albert C. Essais sur la Conception Materialiste de L'Histoire. (Reimpressions G & B Ser.). (FRE.). iv, 316p. 1972. pap. text 49.00 (0-677-50415-2) Gordon & Breach.

***Labriola, Albert C.** John Milton: The Writer in His Works. (Milton Studies: Vol. 38). 2000. 50.00 (0-8229-4120-1) U of Pittsburgh Pr.

Labriola, Albert C. Milton Studies, Vol. 36. (Illus.). 286p. 1998. text 50.00 (0-8229-4073-6) U of Pittsburgh Pr.

Labriola, Albert C., ed. Milton Studies, Vol. 29. LC 69-12335. 208p. (C). 1993. text 49.95 (0-8229-3732-8) U of Pittsburgh Pr.

— Milton Studies, Vol. 30. (Illus.). 224p. 1994. text 49.95 (0-8229-3772-7) U of Pittsburgh Pr.

— Milton Studies, Vol. 31. 242p. (C). 1995. text 49.95 (0-8229-3861-8) U of Pittsburgh Pr.

— Milton Studies, Vol. 32. 272p. (C). 1996. text 49.95 (0-8229-3914-2) U of Pittsburgh Pr.

— Milton Studies, Vol. 35. (Illus.). 380p. 1998. text 50.00 (0-8229-4038-8) U of Pittsburgh Pr.

— Milton Studies 34. 256p. 1996. text 49.95 (0-8229-3958-4) U of Pittsburgh Pr.

***Labriola, Albert C., ed.** Milton Studies 39, 39 vols., Vol. 39. (Milton Studies: Vol. 39). 312p. 2001. 50.00 (0-8229-4130-9) U of Pittsburgh Pr.

Labriola, Albert C., ed. Milton Studies 37. 320p. (C). 2000. text 50.00 (0-8229-4106-6) U of Pittsburgh Pr.

Labriola, Albert C. & Lieb, Michael, eds. Milton Studies 33: The Miltonic Samson. (Illus.). 240p. 1995. text 49.95 (0-8229-3949-5) U of Pittsburgh Pr.

Labriola, Albert C. & Sichi, Edward, Jr., eds. Milton's Legacy in the Arts. LC 86-43037. (Illus.). 239p. 1988. 30.00 (0-271-00497-5) Pa St U Pr.

Labriola, Albert C. & Smeltz, John W. The Bible of the Poor (Biblia Pauperum) A Facsimile & Edition of the British Library Blockbook C.9 d.2. LC 90-38474. (Illus.). 200p. 1990. text 38.00 (0-8207-0229-3); pap. text 22.50 (0-8207-0230-7) Duquesne.

Labriola, Antonio. Socialism & Philosophy. LC 79-90007. 223p. (C). 1980. 26.00 (0-914386-21-2); pap. 14.00 (0-914386-22-0) Telos Pr.

Labriola, Dan. Complementary Cancer Therapies: Combining Traditional & Alternative Approaches for the Best... LC 99-15123. (Illus.). 336p. 2000. pap. 18.95 (0-7615-1922-X, Prima Health) Prima Pub.

***Labriola, Jerry.** Murders at Hollings General. Jud, Brian, ed. LC 99-70735. 357p. 1999. 19.95 (1-928782-00-0, Pub. by Pubg Directions) ACCESS Pubs Network.

Labriolle, Piere C. De, see De Labriolle, Piere C.

Labriolle, Pierre C. History & Literature of Christianity from Tertullian to Boethius. LC 70-399932. (History of Civilization Ser.). xiii, 555 p. 1968. write for info. (0-7100-6104-8) Routledge.

Labriolle, Pierre C. Les Sources de l'Histoire du Montanisme. LC 80-13175. (Heresies of the Early Christian & Medieval Era Ser.: Second Ser.). reprint ed. 57.50 (0-404-16184-7) AMS Pr.

Labrique, F., jt. auth. see Seguier, G.

Labro, M. T. Host Defense & Infection. (Illus.). 72p. 1994. text 35.00 (0-8247-9218-1) Dekker.

Labro, Philippe. Dark Tunnel, White Light: My Journey to Death & Beyond. Coverdale, Linda, tr. LC 97-25405. 240p. 1997. 20.00 (1-56836-200-5) Kodansha.

— Des Bateaux Dans la Nuit. (Folio Ser.: No. 1645). (FRE.). pap. 10.95 (2-07-037645-1) Schoenhof.

— Ete dans l'Ouest. (Folio Ser.: No. 2169). (FRE.). 297p. 1988. pap. 9.95 (2-07-038258-3) Schoenhof.

— Etudiant Etranger. (Folio Ser.: No. 1961). (FRE.). 302p. (Orig.). 1988. pap. 10.95 (2-07-038043-2) Schoenhof.

— Des Feux Mal Eteints. (Folio Ser.: No. 1162). (FRE.). pap. 9.95 (2-07-037162-X) Schoenhof.

— Le Petit Garcon. Coverdale, Linda, tr. 320p. 1992. text 23.00 (0-374-18448-8) FS&G.

— Le Petit Garcon. (Folio Ser.: No. 2389). (FRE.). pap. 9.95 (2-07-038526-4) Schoenhof.

***Labrosse, Jean J.** Embedded Systems Building Blocks. 2nd ed. 640p. 2000. 69.95 incl. cd-rom (0-87930-604-1, Pub. by C M P Books) Publishers Group.

Labrosse, Jean J. Micro/OS-II: The Real-Time Kernel. 2nd ed. (Illus.). 524p. 1992. 69.95 incl. disk (0-87930-543-6) C M P Books.

Labrot, Gerard, ed. Collections of Paintings in Naples, 1600-1780, Vol.1. (Documents for the History of Collecting Ser.). 806p. 1994. 155.00 (3-598-21692-0) K G Saur Verlag.

Labrot, Syl. Pleasure Beach. 1976. 100.00 (0-614-18204-2) Visual Studies.

Labrousse, Elisabeth. L' Entree de Saturne au Lion: L'Eclipse de Soleil du 12 aout 1654. (Archives Internationales D'Histoire des Idees Ser.: No. 14). (FRE.). 115p. 1974. pap. text 57.00 (90-247-1625-X, Pub. by M Nijhoff) Kluwer Academic.

— Esquisse du Mouvement de Prix et Des Revenus Sur France Au XVIIIe Siecle, 2 vols. (FRE.). 695p. 1984. write for info. (2-903928-11-8) Gordon & Breach.

— Pierre Bayle Tome I: Du Pays de Foix a la Cite d'Erasme. (International Archives of the History of Ideas Ser.: No. 1). 296p. 1985. lib. bdg. 184.00 (90-247-3136-4, Pub. by M Nijhoff) Kluwer Academic.

— Pierre Bayle Tome II: Heterodoxie & Rigorisme. (International Archives of the History of Ideas Ser.: No. 6). 655p. 1964. lib. bdg. 250.00 (90-247-0182-1) Kluwer Academic.

Labrousse, Henri L., jt. auth. see Koburger, Charles W., Jr.

Labrousse, P. Dictionary de Poche Indonesien-Francais. (FRE.). 179p. 1985. 29.95 (0-320-00944-0) Fr & Eur.

— Dictionary General Indonesian-Francais. (FRE.). 934p. 1984. 150.00 (0-320-00945-9) Fr & Eur.

Labrozzi, Douglas, ed. see Robinson, Blake.

LaBruce, Bruce. Bruce LaBruce: Ride, Queer, Ride! (Illus.). 255p. 1997. pap. 22.50 (0-921381-12-3, Pub. by Plug In Editions) RAM Publications.

LaBrucherie, Roger. Puerto Rico - Magnifico! A Celebration of an Enchanted Island. Trelles, Maria D., tr. (ENG & SPA., Illus.). 176p. Date not set. 45.00 (0-939302-34-9) Imagenes.

— Puerto Rico - Magnifico! A Celebration of an Enchanted Island. deluxe ed. Trelles, Maria D., tr. (ENG & SPA., Illus.). 192p. Date not set. 55.00 (0-939302-35-7) Imagenes.

LaBrucherie, Roger A. Barbados, a World Apart. (Illus.). 132p. 1993. 30.00 (0-939302-28-4) Imagenes.

— A Barbados Journey. (Illus.). 112p. 1982. 20.00 (0-939302-07-1) Imagenes.

Labrucherie, Roger A. Barbados, Sun Sea, Superb! (Illus.). 80p. 1996. 25.00 (0-939302-30-6); pap. 15.00 (0-939302-31-4) Imagenes.

— Bermuda, a World Apart. (Illus.). 156p. 1996. 35.00 (0-939302-32-2); 50.00 (0-939302-33-0) Imagenes.

LaBrucherie, Roger A. Hawaiian World, Hawaiian Heart. (Illus.). 228p. 1989. 35.00 (0-939302-16-0); 55.00 (0-939302-17-9) Imagenes.

— Imagenes de Puerto Rico. Zayas, Carmen D. et al, trs. (SPA., Illus.). 144p. 1985. 30.00 (0-939302-38-1) Imagenes.

— Imagenes de Puerto Rico. limited ed. Zayas, Carmen D. et al, trs. (SPA., Illus.). 144p. 1985. 45.00 (0-939302-13-6) Imagenes.

— Imagenes De Santo Domingo: A Reminiscence of the Dominican Republic. Espinosa, Mayra C., tr. (Illus.). 112p. (Orig.). 1978. pap. 12.00 (0-939302-00-4) Imagenes.

— Images of Barbados. 2nd ed. (Illus.). 112p. 1979. pap. 12.00 (0-939302-01-2) Imagenes.

— Images of Bermuda. deluxe rev. ed. (Illus.). 144p. 1989. 30.00 (0-939302-22-5) Imagenes.

— Images of Puerto Rico. (Illus.). 144p. 1985. pap. 15.00 (0-939302-24-1) Imagenes.

— Images of Puerto Rico. deluxe ed. (Illus.). 144p. 1985. 25.00 (0-939302-23-3) Imagenes.

— Puerto Rico, Borinquen Querida: A Loving Portrait of an Island. (Illus.). 156p. 1995. 35.00 (0-939302-26-8) Imagenes.

Labrum, Beverley E. One Small Gift. (Illus.). 47p. 1997. pap. 6.95 (0-9659639-0-X) B E Labrum.

Labrum, Bronwyn, jt. ed. see Dalley, Bronwyn.

Labrum, E. A., ed. Civil Engineering Heritage: Eastern & Central England. LC 96-106312. 288p. 1994. 24.00 (0-7277-1970-X, 1970-X) Am Soc Civil Eng.

Labrum, Marian B., ed. The Changing Scene in World Languages: Issues & Challenges. (American Translators Association Scholarly Monograph Ser.: Vol. IX). 160p. 1997. pap. 49.00 (1-55619-628-8) J Benjamins Pubng Co.

LaBruzza, Anthony L. Using DSM-IV: A Clinician's Guide to Psychiatric Diagnosis. 472p. 1996. pap. 45.00 (0-7657-0053-0) Aronson.

Labruzza, Anthony L. & Mendez-Villarrubia, Jose M. Using DSM-IV: A Clinician's Guide to Psychiatric Diagnosis. LC 94-28534. (Illus.). 459p. 1995. 60.00 (1-56821-333-6) Aronson.

Labs, Eric J. The Role of Foreign Aid in Development. (Illus.). 78p. 1997. pap. text 25.00 (0-7881-4709-9) DIANE Pub.

Labs, James. The Wisconsin Dells: A Completely Unauthorized Guide. LC 99-24582. 1999. 9.95 (1-879483-56-4) Prairie Oak Pr.

Labuda, Michael. Creative Reading for Gifted Learners: A Design for Excellence. 2nd ed. LC 85-10789. 178p. reprint ed. pap. 55.20 (0-8357-2640-1, 204012800014) Bks Demand.

LaBuda, Michele C. & Grigorenko, Elena L., eds. On the Way to Individuality: Current Methodological Issues in Behavioral Genetics. 14p. (C). 1998. lib. bdg. 85.00 (1-56072-427-7) Nova Sci Pubs.

LaBue, Andrea, jt. auth. see Marcus, Marsea.

Labuhn, F., ed. see International Astronomical Union Staff.

Labunka, Miroslav & Rudnytzky, Leonid, eds. The Ukrainian Catholic Church, 1945-1975. LC 76-26753. 1976. 7.50 (0-686-28475-5) St Sophia Religious.

Labunski, Richard E. The First Amendment Under Siege: The Politics of Broadcast Regulation, 62. LC 80-39675. (Contributions in Political Science Ser.: No. 62). 184p. 1981. 52.95 (*0-313-22756-X*, LFA/, Greenwood Pr) Greenwood.

— Libel & the First Amendment: Legal History & Practice in Print & Broadcasting. LC 85-24656. 327p. (Orig.). 1989. pap. 24.95 (*0-88738-790-X*) Transaction Pubs.

*__Labunski, Richard E.__ The Second Constitutional Convention: How the American People Can Take Back Their Government. LC 99-69250. xii, 579p. 2000. 29.50 (*0-9677498-7-5*) Marley & Beck Pr.

Labunsky, A. V., et al. Multiple Gravity Assist Interplanetary Trajectories. (Earth Space Institute Book Series on Public & Private Sector Interest in Space: Vol. 2). (Illus.). 292p. 1998. text 84.00 (*90-5699-090-X*, ECU120, Harwood Acad Pubs) Gordon & Breach.

Laburna, Stanley S. Optical Spanish Manual. LC 96-36007. 176p. 1996. pap. text 16.50 (*0-7506-9674-5*) Buttrwrth-Heinemann.

Laburna, Stanley S., jt. auth. see Ishchenko.

Labus, James B. The Physician Assistant Medical Handbook. LC 94-17891. (Illus.). 752p. 1995. pap. text 41.00 (*0-7216-5169-0*, W B Saunders Co) Harcrt Hlth Sci Grp.

— The Physician Assistant Surgical Handbook. Allen, Andrew, ed. LC 96-49868. (Illus.). 480p. 1997. pap. text 39.95 (*0-7216-6815-1*, W B Saunders Co) Harcrt Hlth Sci Grp.

*__Labuschagne, C. J.__ Numerical Secrets of the Bible: Rediscovering the Bible Codes. LC 00-9699. 2000. write for info. (*0-941037-67-3*, BIBAL Press) D & F Scott.

Labuschagne, E., jt. auth. see Malan, F. R.

Labuszewski, John W. Trading Options on Futures: Markets, Methods, Strategies & Tactics. 2nd ed. 288p. 1996. 39.95 (*0-471-30393-3*) Wiley.

Labuszewski, John W. & Nyhoff, John E. Trading Financial Futures: Markets, Methods, Strategies, & Tactics. 2nd ed. (Wiley Finance Editions Ser.). 288p. 1997. 49.95 (*0-471-30394-1*) Wiley.

*__Labuta, Joseph A.__ Basic Conducting Techniques. 4th ed. LC 99-46733. 339p. 2000. 48.00 (*0-13-085296-1*) P-H.

Labuta, Joseph A. & Smith, Deborah. Music Education. 158p. (C). 1996. 51.00 (*0-13-489444-8*) P-H.

Labute, J., jt. auth. see Kisilevsky, H.

*__Labute, Neil.__ Bash: Latterday Plays. (Illus.). 112p. 2000. pap. 11.95 (*1-58567-024-3*, Pub. by Overlook Pr) Penguin Putnam.

Labute, Neil. In the Company of Men. LC 98-100438. 1997. pap. 12.95 (*0-571-19931-3*) Faber & Faber.

— Your Friends & Neighbors. (Illus.). 112p. (Orig.). 1998. pap. 13.00 (*0-571-19791-4*) Faber & Faber.

*__Labuz, J. F., et al.__ Trends in Rock Mechanics: Proceedings of Sessions of Geo-Denver 2000: August 5-8, 2000, Denver, Colorado. LC 00-44166. (Geotechnical Special Publications). 2000. write for info. (*0-7844-0514-X*) Am Soc Civil Eng.

Labuz, J. F., ed. see American Society of Civil Engineers Staff.

Labuz, Ronald A. Pocket Guide to Digital Design. (Graphic Communications Ser.). 352p. 1996. pap. 12.95 (*0-8273-7591-3*) Delmar.

Labuza, T., jt. auth. see Schmidl, M.

Labuza, Theodore P. Shelf-Life Dating of Foods. 500p. 1982. 77.00 (*0-917678-14-1*) Food & Nut Pr.

Labuza, Theodore P., et al, eds. Maillard Reactions in Chemistry, Food, & Health: Proceedings of the Fifth International Symposium on the Maillard Reaction, Held at the University of Minnesota, 1993. 458p. 1994. 157.00 (*0-85186-802-9*, R6802) CRC Pr.

Labuza, Theodore P. & Erdman, John. Food Science & Nutritional Health: An Introduction. (Illus.). 558p. 1984. pap. text, teacher ed. write for info. (*0-314-78015-7*) West Pub.

Labuza, Theodore P., jt. auth. see Bell, Leonard N.

Laby. WordPerfect 6.0 for DOS. (Step-by-Step Ser.). 1995. teacher ed. write for info. (*0-02-800962-2*) Glencoe.

Laby, Lorraine J., et al. Step by Step: WiordPerfect 6.0, Lotus 1-2-3, dBASE IV, DOS 6.0. LC 94-17416. (Increasing Your Productivity Ser.). 1994. 27.00 (*0-02-800958-4*) Glencoe.

*__Labys, Walter C.__ Modeling Mineral & Energy Markets. LC 98-46233. 6p. 1999. write for info. (*0-7923-8372-9*) Kluwer Academic.

Labys, Walter C. Primary Commodity Markets & Models: An International Bibliography. 298p. 1987. text 96.95 (*0-566-05324-1*, Pub. by Avebry) Ashgate Pub Co.

Labys, Walter C., ed. Quantitative Methods for Market Oriented Economic Analysis over Space & Time. (Illus.). 337p. 1989. text 91.95 (*0-566-07024-3*, Pub. by Avebry) Ashgate Pub Co.

Labys, Walter C. & Nadiri, M. Ishaq, eds. Commodity Markets & Latin American Development: A Modeling Approach; Conference on Commodity Models in Latin America. LC 79-16533. 296p. reprint ed. pap. 91.80 (*0-608-11108-2*, 205197400020) Bks Demand.

Labys, Walter C., jt. auth. see Cromwell, Jeff B.

Labys, Walter C., jt. auth. see Park, Se-Hark.

Labzowsky, L., et al. Relativistic Effects in the Spectra of Atomic Systems. (Illus.). 352p. 1993. 159.00 (*0-7503-0223-2*) IOP Pub.

Lacaine, F., jt. auth. see Fingerhut, A.

Lacaj, Henrik & Fishta, Filip. Latin-Albanian Dictionary (Fjalor Latinisht-Shqip) (ALB & LAT.). 556p. 1980. 24.95 (*0-8288-1089-3*, F89900) Fr & Eur.

Lacal, Juan Carlos. Microinjection. LC 98-43502. (Methods & Tools in Biosciences & Medicine Ser.). 1999. write for info. (*0-8176-5973-0*); pap. write for info. (*0-8176-6019-4*) Birkhauser.

— Ras Superfamily of GTPases. 544p. 1993. lib. bdg. 229.00 (*0-8493-5214-2*, RC268) CRC Pr.

Lacal, Juan Carlos, et al, eds. Microinjection. LC 98-43502. (Methods & Tools in Biosciences & Medicine Ser.). 350p. 1999. spiral bd. 98.00 (*3-7643-6019-4*) Birkhauser.

Lacalamita, M. & Di Gammateo, F., eds. Filmlexicon Degli Autori e Delle Opere, 7 vols., Set. (ITA., Illus.). 1968. 234.95 (*0-405-08505-2*) Ayer.

— Filmlexicon Degli Autori e Delle Opere, 7 vols., Vol. 1. (ITA., Illus.). 1972. 36.95 (*0-405-08506-0*) Ayer.

— Filmlexicon Degli Autori e Delle Opere, 7 vols., Vol. 2. (ITA., Illus.). 1972. 33.95 (*0-405-08507-9*) Ayer.

— Filmlexicon Degli Autori e Delle Opere, 7 vols., Vol. 3. (ITA., Illus.). 1972. 33.95 (*0-405-08508-7*) Ayer.

— Filmlexicon Degli Autori e Delle Opere, 7 vols., Vol. 4. (ITA., Illus.). 1972. 33.95 (*0-405-08509-5*) Ayer.

— Filmlexicon Degli Autori e Delle Opere, 7 vols., Vol. 5. (ITA., Illus.). 1972. 33.95 (*0-405-08510-9*) Ayer.

— Filmlexicon Degli Autori e Delle Opere, 7 vols., Vol. 6. (ITA., Illus.). 1972. 33.95 (*0-405-08511-7*) Ayer.

— Filmlexicon Degli Autori e Delle Opere, 7 vols., Vol. 7. (ITA., Illus.). 1972. 33.95 (*0-405-08512-5*) Ayer.

*__Lacalamita, Tom.__ The All-New Ultimate Bread Machine Cookbook: More Than 95 All New Irresistible Foolproof Recipes. LC 99-31352. 208p. 1999. pap. 15.00 (*0-684-85528-3*) S&S Trade.

Lacalamita, Tom. The Ultimate Bread Machine Cookbook: An Insider's Guide to Automatic Bread Making. LC 93-1513. 208p. 1993. 24.50 (*0-671-88023-3*) S&S Trade.

— The Ultimate Espresso Machine Cookbook. 192p. 1995. 27.00 (*0-684-81336-X*) Simon & Schuster.

LaCalamita, Tom. Ultimate Pasta Machine Cookbook. (Illus.). 192p. 1994. 24.50 (*0-671-50102-X*) S&S Trade.

Lacalamita, Tom. The Ultimate Pressure Cooker Cookbook. LC 96-40229. 192p. 1997. 24.50 (*0-684-82496-5*) S&S Trade.

LaCalle, Guadalupe M., ed. see Rojas, Fernando De.

Lacambra-Ayala, Tita. Camels & Shapes of Darkness in a Time of Olives. LC 98-947569. 1998. write for info. (*971-542-155-5*) U of Philippines Pr.

— Pieces of String & Other Stories. 138p. (Orig.). 1984. pap. 12.50 (*971-10-0186-1*, Pub. by New Day Pub) Cellar.

Lacambre, Genevieve. Gustave Moreau: Magic & Symbols. LC 98-42707. (Discoveries Ser.). 1999. pap. 12.95 (*0-8109-2877-9*, Pub. by Abrams) Time Warner.

— Painting the Orient. (Art & Architecture Ser.). (Illus.). 360p. 1999. 39.95 (*3-89508-892-7*, 520587) Konemann.

Lacambre, Genevieve, et al. Painting in the Musee d'Orsay. (Illus.). 160p. 1987. text 30.00 (*0-85667-228-9*) Scala Books.

Lacan, Ernest. Esquisses Photographiques a Propos de L'Exposition Universelle et de la Guerre D'Orient. Bunnell, Peter C. & Sobieszek, Robert A., eds. LC 76-24665. (Sources of Modern Photography Ser.). (FRE.). 1979. reprint ed. lib. bdg. 15.95 (*0-405-09642-9*) Ayer.

Lacan, Jacques. Ecrits, Vol. 1. (FRE.). 1970. pap. 16.95 (*0-7859-2669-0*) Fr & Eur.

— Ecrits, Vol. 2. (FRE.). 1971. pap. 14.95 (*0-7859-2671-2*) Fr & Eur.

— Ecrits: A Selection. Sheridan, Alan, tr. 352p. 1982. pap. 15.95 (*0-393-30047-1*) Norton.

— The Four Fundamental Concepts of Psycho-Analysis. 1995. 24.50 (*0-8446-6852-4*) Peter Smith.

— The Four Fundamental Concepts of Psychoanalysis. (Seminar of Jacques Lacan Ser.: Bk. XI). 304p. 1998. pap. 17.95 (*0-393-31775-7*) Norton.

— On Feminine Sexuality, the Limits of Love & Knowledge. 160p. 1999. pap. 15.95 (*0-393-31916-4*) Norton.

— Les Psychoses. Date not set. 24.95 (*0-393-01925-X*) Norton.

— Le Seminaire Vol. 11: Les Quatre Concepts Fodaementaux de la Psychanalyse. (FRE.). 1990. pap. 19.95 (*0-7859-2719-0*) Fr & Eur.

— The Seminar of Jacques Lacan: The Psychoses 1955-1956, Bk. 3. Miller, Jacques-Alain, ed. Grigg, Russell, tr. LC 92-28360. 352p. 1993. 35.00 (*0-393-03467-4*) Norton.

— The Seminar of Jacques Lacan Bk. III: The Psychoses, 1955-1956, Bk. 3. Miller, Jacques-Alain, ed. 352p. (C). 1997. pap. 18.95 (*0-393-31612-2*) Norton.

— The Seminar of Jacques Lacan Bk. VII: The Ethics of Psychoanalysis, 1959-1960. Miller, Jacques-Alain, ed. 352p. (C). 1997. pap. 18.95 (*0-393-31613-0*) Norton.

— The Seminars of Jacques Lacan: Freud's Writings on Technique 1953-1954. Miller, Jacques-Alain, ed. Forrester, John & Tomaselli, Sylvana, trs. from FRE. (Lacan's Series of Seminars: Bk. 1). 1988. 24.95 (*0-393-01895-4*) Norton.

— Television: A Challenge to the Psychoanalytic Establishment. 1990. 24.95 (*0-393-02496-2*) Norton.

La'Cancela, Victor De, see De La'Cancela, Victor.

LaCancela, Kathleen. Less Than Half, More Than Whole. (gr. 1-3). 1998. pap. text. write for info. (*0-87358-734-0*) Northland AZ.

Lacapa, Kathleen & Lacapa, Michael. Less Than Half, More Than Whole. LC 94-13132. (Illus.). 40p. (J). (gr. 1-3). 1994. lib. bdg. 14.95 (*0-87358-592-5*, Rising Moon Bks) Northland AZ.

LaCapa, Kathleen & LaCapa, Michael. Less Than Half, More Than Whole. (Illus.). 40p. (J). (gr. 1-3). 1998. pap. 7.95 (*0-87358-731-6*, Rising Moon Bks) Northland AZ.

Lacapa, Michael. Antelope Woman: An Apache Folktale. LC 92-14098. (Illus.). 48p. (J). (gr. 2-3). 1995. reprint ed. pap. 7.95 (*0-87358-647-6*, Rising Moon Bks) Northland AZ.

— The Flute Player: An Apache Folktale. LC 89-63749. (Illus.). 48p. (J). (gr. 1-3). 1995. reprint ed. pap. 7.95 (*0-87358-627-1*, Rising Moon Bks) Northland AZ.

Lacapa, Michael. Native American Coyote Stories. 1996. 12.00 incl. audio (*0-9666415-0-7*, SBP001) Sage Prod AZ.

LaCapa, Michael, jt. auth. see LaCapa, Kathleen.

Lacapa, Michael, jt. auth. see Lacapa, Kathleen.

LaCapra, Dominick. Emile Durkheim: Sociologist & Philosopher. LC 85-1190. xii, 318p. 1985. reprint ed. pap. text 12.95 (*0-226-46726-0*) U Ch Pr.

— History & Criticism. LC 84-16990. 152p. (C). 1987. pap. text 12.95 (*0-8014-9324-2*) Cornell U Pr.

*__Lacapra, Dominick.__ History & Reading: Tocqueville & Foucault. (Green College Lectures). 192p. 2000. pap. text 14.95 (*0-8020-8200-9*) U of Toronto Pr.

LaCapra, Dominick. History, Politics, & the Novel. LC 87-6686. 240p. (C). 1987. text 39.95 (*0-8014-2033-4*); pap. text 15.95 (*0-8014-9577-6*) Cornell U Pr.

— A Preface to Sartre. LC 78-58022. 256p. 1978. pap. text 14.95 (*0-8014-9448-6*) Cornell U Pr.

— Representing the Holocaust: History, Theory, Trauma. 248p. 1996. pap. text 14.95 (*0-8014-8187-2*) Cornell U Pr.

— Rethinking Intellectual History: Texts, Contexts, Language. LC 83-7218. 352p. 1983. pap. text 18.95 (*0-8014-9886-4*) Cornell U Pr.

*__LaCapra, Dominick.__ Writing History, Writing Trauma. LC 00-24994. (Parallax Ser.). 208p. 2001. 39.95 (*0-8018-6495-X*) Johns Hopkins.

*__Lacapra, Dominick.__ Writing History, Writing Trauma. (Parallax Ser.). 208p. 2000. pap. 17.95 (*0-8018-6496-8*) Johns Hopkins.

LaCapra, Dominick, ed. The Bounds of Race: Perspectives on Hegemony & Resistance. LC 91-11896. 360p. 1991. text 52.50 (*0-8014-2553-0*) Cornell U Pr.

LaCapra, Dominick & Kaplan, Steven L., eds. Modern European Intellectual History: Reappraisals & New Perspectives. LC 82-7418. 318p. 1982. pap. text 18.95 (*0-8014-9881-3*) Cornell U Pr.

Lacar, Luis Q. Muslim-Christian Marriages in the Philippines: Studies Made in North Cotabato. (Humanities Publications Ser., Silliman University: No. 2). (Illus.). 100p. (C). 1981. pap. 7.50 (*0-686-31074-8*, Pub. by New Day Pub) Cellar.

Lacarra, J. M., ed. see Menendez Pidal, Ramon.

Lacarra, Marcel. Le Temps des Verbes. 2nd ed. (FRE.). 96p. 1984. pap. 19.95 (*0-8288-3355-9*, 2801105260) Fr & Eur.

Lacarra, Maria E., ed. see Rojas, Fernando De.

Lacarra, Maria J., ed. see Juan Manuel, Don.

Lacarriere, Jacques. Alain-Fournier. 2nd ed. (Maison D'Ecrivain Collection). (FRE., Illus.). 1995. pap. 49.95 (*0-614-14004-8*) Intl Scholars.

— Flaner en France. (FRE., Illus.). 234p. 1995. pap. 54.95 (*0-614-14007-2*) Intl Scholars.

— The Gnostics. Rootes, Nina, tr. (FRE.). 138p. (Orig.). 1989. pap. 7.95 (*0-87286-243-7*) City Lights.

Lacarriere, Jacques, photos by. The Wisdom of Ancient Greece. LC 96-17066. (Illus.). 56p. 1996. 8.95 (*0-7892-0243-3*) Abbeville Pr.

LaCarrubba, Joseph & Zimmer, Louis. How to Buy, Install, & Maintain Your Own Telephone Equipment. 4th rev. ed. LC 81-8047. (Illus.). 52p. (Orig.). (C). 1981. pap. 5.00 (*0-930256-09-3*, Vestal Pr) Madison Bks UPA.

Lacasa, Jaime, jt. auth. see Noble, Judith.

Lacasa, R. & Bustamante, I. D. Spanish-English, English-Spanish Political, Legal & Economics Dictionary: Diccionario de Derecho, Economia y Politica Espanol-Ingles-Espanol. 4th ed. (ENG & SPA.). 763p. 1991. 125.00 (*0-8288-0404-4*, S39842) Fr & Eur.

Lacassagne, Jean Pierre, ed. see Sand, George, et al.

Lacassagne, Joseph. Traite General des Elemens du Chant. fac. ed. (Monuments of Music & Music Literature in Facsimile Ser., Series II: Vol. 27). 1967. lib. bdg. 40.00 (*0-8450-2227-X*) Broude.

Lacasse, Francois, ed. Managing the Cost of Transfer Programmes. LC 98-133448. (Public Management Occasional Papers: No. 16). 180p. 1997. pap. 33.00 (*92-64-15500-7*, 42-97-66-1, Pub. by Org for Econ) OECD.

LaCasse, Maurice A. Nostradamus: The Voice That Echoes Through Time. (Illus.). 208p. (Orig.). 1992. 19.95 (*1-56167-088-X*) Noble Hse MD.

Lacasse, Michael A., ed. Science & Technology of Building Seals, Sealants, Glazing & Waterproofing, Vol. 5. (Special Technical Publication Ser.: No. 1271). (Illus.). 320p. Date not set. text 63.00 (*0-8031-2049-4*, STP1271) ASTM.

Lacasse, Norman, ed. see Thorpe, R. R.

Lacasse, Suzanne, jt. ed. see Singh, Sushil Kumar.

Lacava, Ann, ed. Guide to the Preparation of Theses & Dissertations. 8th ed. 144p. (C). 1994. pap. text 7.95 (*0-9625933-2-X*) Univ TN Grad Schl.

LaCaze, Alfred, Jr. Picture of Happiness. LC 96-67039. 76p. 1996. pap. 9.95 (*1-57197-015-0*) Pentland Pr.

Lacaze, J., jt. ed. see Lesoult, G.

Lacaze, Pierre-Camille, ed. Organic Coatings: Proceedings of the International Meeting of Physical Chemistry, Paris, France 1995. (AIP Conference Proceedings Ser.: No. 354). (Illus.). 560p. 1996. 145.00 (*1-56396-535-6*, AIP Pr) Spr-Verlag.

Lacaze, Yvon. France & Munich: A Study in Decision-Making in International Affairs. 366p. 1995. 42.00 (*0-88033-329-4*, 432, Pub. by East Eur Monographs) Col U Pr.

Lacc, Eugenia. Tales of Thieves. LC 90-64277. 80p. 1991. pap. text 14.00 (*0-914265-13-X*) New Eng Pub MA.

Laccetti, Silvio R., ed. New Jersey Profiles in Public Policy. 1990. 22.00 (*0-940390-05-1*) Comwealth Bks NJ.

Lace, William W. The Alamo. LC 97-9863. (World History Ser.). (Illus.). 96p. (YA). (gr. 4-12). 1997. lib. bdg. 22.45 (*1-56006-450-1*) Lucent Bks.

— The British Empire: The End of Colonialism. LC 99-57228. (History's Great Defeats Ser.). 133p. (YA). (gr. 4-12). 2000. 18.96 (*1-56006-683-0*) Lucent Bks.

Lace, William W. The Dallas Cowboys Football Team. LC 96-26411. (Great Sports Teams Ser.). 48p. (J). (gr. 4-10). 1997. lib. bdg. 18.95 (*0-89490-791-3*) Enslow Pubs.

Lace, William W. The Death Camps. LC 97-36192. (Holocaust Library). (Illus.). 112p. (YA). (gr. 4-12). 1997. lib. bdg. 22.45 (*1-56006-094-8*) Lucent Bks.

Lace, William W. Defeat of the Spanish Armada. LC 96-21508. (J). (gr. 5-12). 1996. lib. bdg. 26.20 (*1-56006-458-7*) Lucent Bks.

— Elizabethan England. (World History Ser.). (Illus.). 128p. (J). (gr. 5-9). 1995. lib. bdg. 22.45 (*1-56006-278-9*, 2789) Lucent Bks.

— England. LC 96-40121. (Overview Ser.). (Illus.). (YA). (gr. 4-12). 1997. lib. bdg. 22.45 (*1-56006-194-4*) Lucent Bks.

*__Lace, William W.__ Hitler & the Nazis (WWII) LC 99-24600. (American War Library). (Illus.). 144p. (YA). (gr. 6-9). 2000. lib. bdg. 23.70 (*1-56006-372-6*) Lucent Bks.

Lace, William W. The Houston Rockets Basketball Team. LC 96-26413. (Great Sports Teams Ser.). (Illus.). 48p. (YA). (gr. 4-10). 1997. lib. bdg. 18.95 (*0-89490-792-1*) Enslow Pubs.

Lace, William W. The Houston Rockets Basketball Team. LC 96-26413. (Great Sports Teams Ser.). (Illus.). 48p. (YA). (gr. 4-10). 1997. pap. 9.95 (*0-7660-1749-4*) Enslow Pubs.

Lace, William W. Ireland. LC 98-55676. (Overview Ser.). (Illus.). 144p. (YA). (gr. 4-12). 1999. lib. bdg. 23.70 (*1-56006-448-X*) Lucent Bks.

*__Lace, William W.__ Leaders & Generals (WWII) LC 99-33487. (American War Library). (Illus.). 144p. (YA). (gr. 6-9). 2000. lib. bdg. 23.70 (*1-56006-664-4*) Lucent Bks.

Lace, William W. The Little Princes in the Tower. LC 96-21509. (Mysterious Deaths Ser.). (Illus.). (YA). 1996. lib. bdg. 22.45 (*1-56006-262-2*) Lucent Bks.

— The Los Angeles Lakers Basketball Team. LC 97-20074. (Great Sports Teams Ser.). (Illus.). 48p. (YA). (gr. 4-10). 1998. lib. bdg. 18.95 (*0-7660-1020-1*) Enslow Pubs.

*__Lace, William W.__ The Los Angeles Lakers Basketball Team. LC 97-20074. (Great Sports Teams Ser.). (Illus.). 48p. (YA). (gr. 4-10). 1998. pap. 9.95 (*0-7660-1750-8*) Enslow Pubs.

Lace, William W. The Nazis. LC 97-21376. (Holocaust Library). (Illus.). (YA). (gr. 6 up). 1997. lib. bdg. 22.45 (*1-56006-091-3*) Lucent Bks.

— The Pittsburgh Steelers Football Team. LC 98-9664. (Great Sports Teams Ser.). 48p. (J). (gr. 4-10). 1999. lib. bdg. 18.95 (*0-7660-1099-6*) Enslow Pubs.

*__Lace, William W.__ Scotland. LC 00-8757. (Modern Nations of the World Ser.). (Illus.). (J). 2000. write for info. (*1-56006-703-9*) Lucent Bks.

Lace, William W. Sports Great Nolan Ryan. LC 92-41693. (Sports Great Bks.). (Illus.). 64p. (J). (gr. 4-10). 1993. lib. bdg. 17.95 (*0-89490-394-2*) Enslow Pubs.

— Tiger Woods: Star Golfer. LC 98-36958. (Sports Reports Ser.). 104p. (YA). (gr. 4-10). 1999. lib. bdg. 20.95 (*0-7660-1081-3*) Enslow Pubs.

— Top 10 Football Quarterbacks. LC 93-40469. (Sports Top 10 Ser.). (Illus.). 48p. (J). (gr. 4-10). 1994. lib. bdg. 18.95 (*0-89490-518-X*) Enslow Pubs.

— Top 10 Football Rushers. LC 93-40470. (Sports Top 10 Ser.). (Illus.). 48p. (J). (gr. 4-10). 1994. lib. bdg. 18.95 (*0-89490-519-8*) Enslow Pubs.

— Winston Churchill. (Importance of...Ser.). (Illus.). 112p. (J). (gr. 5-9). 1995. lib. bdg. 22.45 (*1-56006-067-0*, 0670) Lucent Bks.

Lacelle, Larry, jt. ed. see LaBianca, Oystein S.

LaCelle-Peterson, Mark W., jt. ed. see Finkelstein, Martin J.

*__Lacendre, Darncy.__ The Bushman & the Spirits. 148p. 1999. pap. 0.00 (*0-88965-156-6*) Horizon Books.

LaCentra, Walter. The Authentic Self: Toward a Philosophy of Personality. (American University Studies: Philosophy: Ser. V, Vol. 36). 211p. (C). 1987. text 35.95 (*0-8204-0460-8*) P Lang Pubng.

Lacerda de Azevedo, Jose. Spirit & Matter: New Horizons for Medicine. LC 95-74972. (Illus.). 320p. (Orig.). 1997. pap. 16.95 (*1-56184-083-1*) New Falcon Pubns.

*__Lacerda, Francisco J., et al, eds.__ Emerging Cognitive Abilities in Early Infancy. 350p. 2000. write for info. (*0-8058-2669-6*); pap. write for info. (*0-8058-2670-X*) L Erlbaum Assocs.

Lacerda, Luiz D. De, see De Lacerda, Luiz D.

LaCerra, Charles, jt. auth. see Krase, Jerome.

*__Lacerra, Peggy.__ Only You. 2001. 23.00 (*0-609-60558-5*) Harmony Bks.

Lacerte, Michael, jt. ed. see Shrey, Donald E.

Lacerte, Michel. The Disability Evaluation: Practical Guide for Physicians. 180p. 1995. lib. bdg. 49.95 (*1-57444-037-3*, SL0373) St Lucie Pr.

LaCerva, Victor. Pathways to Peace: 40 Steps to a Less Violent America. (Illus.). 256p. (Orig.). 1996. pap. 15.00 (*0-9649104-0-3*) Heartsongs Publn.

— World Words: Global Wisdom to Awaken the Spirit. (Illus.). 200p. 1999. pap. 15.00 (*0-9661575-9-1*) HEAL Found.

Lacey. God's Plan for the Local Church. 1994. pap. 4.99 (*0-946462-07-0*, Pub. by Evangelical Pr) P & R Pubng.

— Image & Representation: Key Concepts in Media Studies. LC 97-41487. 288p. 1998. text 55.00 (*0-312-21202-X*) St Martin.

*__Lacey.__ MCSD Visual C++ 6 Desktop Exam Cram. (Programming Ser.). (C). 1999. pap. 15.60 (*0-619-01610-8*) Course Tech.

— MCSD Visual C++ 6 Distributed Exam Cram. (Programming Ser.). (C). 2000. pap. 15.60 (*0-619-01611-6*) Course Tech.

L

Lacey. Precalculus with Applications. (C). 1990. pap. text, teacher ed., suppl. ed. 40.50 (0-03-032727-X, Pub. by Harcourt Coll Pubs) Harcourt.

Lacey & Shephard. Discovering Nazi Germany. 1997. text 45.00 (0-7195-7220-7, Pub. by John Murray) Trafalgar.

Lacey, A. A., jt. ed. see Brown, K. J.

Lacey, A. R. Bergson. 240p. 1989. 39.95 (0-415-03007-2, A3519) Routledge.

— Bergson. LC 93-15348. (Arguments of the Philosophers Ser.). 256p. (C). 1993. pap. 18.95 (0-415-08763-5, B2453) Routledge.

— Modern Philosophy: An Introduction. 296p. 1982. pap. 10.95 (0-7100-0974-7, Routledge Thoemms) Routledge.

Lacey, A. R., tr. see Philoponus, John.

Lacey, Alan. Dictionary of Philosophy. 3rd ed. 400p. 1996. pap. 14.99 (0-415-13332-7) Routledge.

Lacey, Alan J. Light Microscopy in Biology: A Practical Approach. 2nd ed. (The Practical Approach Ser.: No. 195). (Illus.). 474p. 1999. pap. text 60.00 (0-19-963669-9) OUP.

***Lacey, Alan J.** Light Microscopy in Biology: A Practical Approach. 2nd ed. LC 99-461881. (The Practical Approach Ser.: No. 195). (Illus.). 474p. 1999. text 120.00 (0-19-963670-2) OUP.

Lacey, Alice R. The Story of Brinkerhoff Home: On the Campus of Springfield College in Illinois - Springfield, Illinois. LC 95-72579. (Illus.). 128p. 1996. 21.95 (0-9622491-2-2); pap. 12.95 (0-9622491-3-0) Pheasant Pr.

Lacey, Ann H. & Pratt, Barbara W. Dr. Rickey: Wednesday's Promise. LC 98-114664. (Illus.). 17p. (J). (ps-6). 1997. pap. 8.95 (0-9658395-0-8) Love on a Leash.

***Lacey, Brenda.** Hidden Identity. large type ed. 216p. 1999. pap. 18.99 (0-7089-5614-9, Linford) Ulverscroft.

Lacey, Brian. Colum Cille & His Legacy. LC 98-105638. 140p. 1997. pap. 9.95 (1-85182-321-2, Pub. by Four Cts Pr) Intl Spec Bk.

— Manus O'Donnell's Life of Colum Cille. LC 98-233154. 256p. 1998. pap. 19.95 (1-85182-395-6, Pub. by Four Cts Pr) Intl Spec Bk.

— Manus O'Donnell's Life of Colum Cille. limited ed. LC 98-233154. 256p. 1998. 120.00 (1-85182-394-8, Pub. by Four Cts Pr) Intl Spec Bk.

Lacey, Charles V. Rosary Novenas to Our Lady. (Illus.). 48p. 1997. reprint ed. pap. 4.95 (0-87946-173-X) ACTA Pubns.

***Lacey, Charles V.** Rosary Novenas to Our Lady: Large Print Version. large type ed. (Illus.). 48p. 1999. pap. 5.95 (0-87946-197-7, 278) ACTA Pubns.

Lacey, Cheryl. Moving on in Spelling. 112p. (J). (gr. k-4). 1994. pap. 14.95 (0-590-49636-0) Scholastic Inc.

***Lacey, Chris.** Chocolate Temptations. 2000. pap. text 4.99 (1-56245-410-2) Great Quotations.

Lacey, Christina K., et al. South Dakota's American Mother: The Life Story of Christina K. Lacey - South Dakota State Mother - 1946. LC 89-8452. (Illus.). 160p. (Orig.). 1989. 12.95 (0-9622491-0-6); pap. 9.95 (0-9622491-1-4) Pheasant Pr.

Lacey, Debbi, jt. auth. see Lewis, Michael.

Lacey, Debbi, jt. auth. see Lewis, Mike.

Lacey, Douglas. The Latin Plus. 1986. student ed. 12.50 (0-89894-020-6); student ed. 12.50 (0-685-11183-0); student ed. 12.95 (0-89894-021-4); pap. text 12.50 (0-89894-018-4) Advocate Pub Group.

Lacey, E. A., tr. from FRE. The Delight of Hearts: Or, What You Will Not Find in Any Book. (Illus.). 240p. (Orig.). 1988. lib. bdg. 25.00 (0-940567-08-3) Gay Sunshine.

Lacey, E. A., tr. see Caminha, Adolfo.

Lacey, E. A., tr. see Leyland, Winston, ed.

Lacey, E. A., tr. see Zapata, Luis.

Lacey, Earnest E. FreeJoe: A Story of Faith Love & Perseverance. Stewart, Dagny, ed. (Illus.). 545p. 1996. 27.95 (0-9669076-1-2) Freejoe Pubns.

***Lacey, Eileen A.** Life Underground: The Biology of Subterranean Rodents. LC 99-51019. (Illus.). 1999. pap. text 24.00 (0-226-46728-7); lib. bdg. 65.00 (0-226-46727-9) U Ch Pr.

Lacey, Frank, ed. & illus. see Janis, C. J.

Lacey, George. If I Be Lifted Up: Reflections for the Season of Lent. LC 97-22788. 64p. 1998. pap. 4.95 (0-8091-3761-5, 3761-5) Paulist Pr.

Lacey, Geraldine. Creating Topiary. (Illus.). 148p. 1987. 39.50 (1-870673-00-X, Pub. by Garden Art Pr) Antique Collect.

Lacey, Graham, jt. auth. see Dowden, Angela.

Lacey, H. E. The Isometric Theory of Classical Banach Spaces. LC 74-394. (Grundlehren der Mathematischen Wissenschaften Ser.: Vol. 208). 270p. 1974. 89.00 (0-387-06562-8) Spr-Verlag.

***Lacey, Harry.** God & the Nations. 296p. 1999. reprint ed. pap. 12.99 (1-882701-56-9, Gospel Folio Pr) Uplook Min.

Lacey, Henry C. To Raise, Destroy, & Create: The Poetry, Drama & Fiction of Imamu Amiri Baraka (Le Roi Jones) LC 80-50078. xii, 206p. 1981. 35.00 (0-87875-185-8) Whitston Pub.

***Lacey, Hoda.** How to Resolve Conflict in the Workplace. LC 00-21273. 224p. 2000. 59.95 (0-566-08073-7, Pub. by Ashgate Pub) Ashgate Pub Co.

Lacey, Hugh. Is Science Value Free? Values & Scientific Understanding LC 99-10016. 1999. text. write for info. (0-415-20820-3) Routledge.

Lacey, Hugh, jt. auth. see Schwartz, Barry.

Lacey, Hugh, ed. see Ellacuria, Ignacio, et al.

Lacey, J. H., jt. ed. see Jones, R. K.

***Lacey, James.** MCSD Visual C++ 6 Desktop. LC 99-38873. (Exam Cram Ser.). 601p. 1999. pap. 29.99 (1-57610-373-0) Coriolis Grp.

— MCSD Visual C++6 Distributed Exam Cram. LC 99-55320. (C). 1999. 29.99 (1-57610-372-2) Coriolis Grp.

Lacey, Jim & Keough, Allen H. Radiation Curing: A Discussion of Advantages, Features & Applications. LC 80-52815. 97p. pap. 30.10 (0-608-11577-0, 201912000010) Bks Demand.

— Radiation Curing: A Discussion of Advantages, Features & Applications. (Illus.). 98p. 1983. 48.00 (0-938648-15-2, 2004) T-C Pr CA.

Lacey, Joel. Compact & Digital Camera Handbook: The Comprehensive Guide to Choosing & Using the New Digital Imaging Technology. (Illus.). 1999. pap. 19.95 (0-609-80423-5) Crown.

— Essential Camera Skills: The Complete Introductory Guide to SLR Photography. (Illus.). 128p. 1995. pap. text 14.95 (0-600-58627-8, Focal) Buttrwrth-Heinemann.

Lacey, John M., jt. auth. see Flamholtz, Eric G.

Lacey, John R. The Law & Policy of International Business: Selected Issues: A Featschrift for William Sprague Barnes. 300p. (C). 1991. lib. bdg. 49.00 (0-8191-8232-X) U Pr of Amer.

Lacey, Julia S., et al. How to Survive Your Computer Workstation: Fifteen Easy Steps to Workstation Comfort. 2nd ed. (Illus.). 240p. 1997. pap. 17.95 (0-9623656-0-2) CRT Servs.

Lacey, Kate. Feminine Frequencies: Gender, German Radio & the Public Sphere 1923-1945. 320p. (Orig.). 1996. pap. text 24.95 (0-472-06616-1, 06616) U of Mich Pr.

— Feminine Frequencies: Gender, German Radio & the Public Sphere 1923-1945. 320p. (Orig.). 1996. text 57.50 (0-472-09616-8, 09616) U of Mich Pr.

***Lacey, Kathy.** Making Mentoring Happen: A Simple & Effective Guide to Implementing a Successful Mentoring Program. 2000. pap. text 14.95 (1-875680-68-3) Woodslane.

Lacey, Kenneth. Profit Measurement & Price Changes. LC 82-48370. (Accountancy in Transition Ser.). 148p. 1982. text 10.00 (0-8240-5323-0) Garland.

Lacey, Laurie. Micmac Medicines: Remedies & Recollections. (Illus.). 128p. 1993. pap. 10.95 (1-55109-041-4) Nimbus Publ.

Lacey, Lawrence A., ed. Manual of Techniques in Insect Pathology. (Biological Techniques Ser.). (Illus.). 432p. 1997. boxed set 110.00 (0-12-432555-6) Morgan Kaufmann.

***Lacey, Lawrence A. & Kaya, Harry K.** Field Manual of Techniques in Invertebrate Pathology: Application & Evaluation of Pathogens for Control Insects & Other Invertebrate Pests. LC 00-29628. 2000. write for info. (0-7923-6269-1, Kluwer Acad) Kluwer Academic.

***Lacey, Lois.** Rockie & the Baby Bunnies. (Illus.). 24p. (J). (gr. k-3). 1999. pap. 11.00 (0-9667395-3-1) In the BAG.

Lacey, Malcolm, jt. auth. see Ward, David.

Lacey, Margaret. Silent Friends: A Quaker Quilt. LC 91-66321. 108p. 1992. 14.95 (0-935153-15-2) Stormline Pr.

Lacey, Mark S., jt. auth. see Hedges, Stoy A.

Lacey, Meg, jt. auth. see Daly, Barbara.

Lacey, Meg. Sexy As Sin. (Temptation Ser.: No. 734). 1999. per. 3.75 (0-373-25834-8, 1-25834-2, Harlequin) Harlequin Bks.

Lacey, Michael J., ed. Government & Environmental Politics: Essays on Historical Developments since World War II. LC 89-22761. 336p. 1991. reprint ed. pap. text 16.95 (0-943875-15-3) Johns Hopkins.

— Religion & Twentieth-Century American Intellectual Life. (Woodrow Wilson Center Ser.). 224p. (C). 1989. text 59.95 (0-521-37560-6) Cambridge U Pr.

— Religion & Twentieth-Century American Intellectual Life. (Woodrow Wilson Center Ser.). 224p. (C). 1991. pap. text 16.95 (0-521-40775-3) Cambridge U Pr.

— The Truman Presidency. (Woodrow Wilson Center Ser.). 480p. (C). 1989. text 74.95 (0-521-37559-2) Cambridge U Pr.

— The Truman Presidency. (Woodrow Wilson Center Ser.). 478p. (C). 1991. pap. text 21.95 (0-521-40773-7) Cambridge U Pr.

Lacey, Michael J. & Furner, Mary O., eds. The State & Social Investigation in Britain & the United States. (Woodrow Wilson Center Ser.). 452p. (C). 1993. text 64.95 (0-521-41638-8) Cambridge U Pr.

Lacey, Michael J. & Haakonssen, Knud, eds. A Culture of Rights: The Bill of Rights in Philosophy, Politics & Law, 1791 & 1991. (Woodrow Wilson Center Ser.). (Illus.). 482p. (C). 1991. text 80.00 (0-521-41637-X) Cambridge U Pr.

— A Culture of Rights: The Bill of Rights in Philosophy, Politics & Law, 1791 & 1991. (Woodrow Wilson Center Ser.). 482p. (C). 1992. pap. text 22.95 (0-521-44653-8) Cambridge U Pr.

Lacey, Nelson J., jt. auth. see Chambers, Donald R.

***Lacey, Nick.** Narrative & Genre: Key Concepts in Media Studies. LC 99-49754. 2000. pap. 21.95 (0-312-23013-3); text 55.00 (0-312-23012-5) St Martin.

Lacey, Nicola. State Punishment: Political Principles & Community Values. (International Library of Philosophy). 256p. 1988. text 49.95 (0-415-00171-4) Routledge.

— State Punishment: Political Principles & Community Values. LC 94-17878. (International Library of Philosophy). 256p. (C). 1994. pap. 27.99 (0-415-10938-8, B4695) Routledge.

— Unspeakable Subjects: Essays in Feminist Legal & Social Theory. LC 98-198167. 256p. 1998. 60.00 (1-901362-33-7, Pub. by Hart Pub) Northwestern U Pr.

Lacey, Nicola, ed. A Reader on Criminal Justice. (Oxford Readings in Socio-Legal Studies). 416p. 1995. pap. 19.95 (0-19-876361-1) OUP.

— A Reader on Criminal Justice. (Oxford Readings in Socio-Legal Studies). 416p. 1995. 65.00 (0-19-876362-X) OUP.

Lacey, Nicola, jt. auth. see Frazer, Elizabeth.

Lacey, Pat. Master of the Titanic. large type ed. (Magna Large Print Ser.). 574p. 1997. 27.99 (0-7505-1067-6) Ulverscroft.

— Master of the Titanic: The Career of Captain Ted Smith. 359p. 1996. 22.50 (1-85776-221-5, Pub. by Book Guild Ltd) Trans-Atl Phila.

— Rosemary Cottage. large type ed. 1990. pap. 16.99 (0-7089-6930-5) Ulverscroft.

— Summer at Saint Pierre. large type ed. 1991. pap. 16.99 (0-7089-6979-8) Ulverscroft.

— The Vintage Year. large type ed. (Linford Romance Library). 288p. 1992. pap. 16.99 (0-7089-7282-9) Ulverscroft.

***Lacey, Pat.** The Washerwoman's Daughters. large type ed. 592p. 1999. 31.99 (0-7089-4110-9, Linford) Ulverscroft.

Lacey, Paul A. Education & the Inward Teacher. LC 88-60795. (Orig.). 1988. pap. 4.00 (0-87574-278-5) Pendle Hill.

Lacey, Paul A. The Inner War: Forms & Themes in Recent American Poetry. LC 78-171500. x, 132 p. 1972. write for info. (0-8006-0413-X) Augsburg Fortress.

Lacey, Paul A. The Inner War Forms & Themes in Recent American Poetry. LC 78-171500. 142p. reprint ed. pap. 44.10 (0-608-16912-9, 202695400053) Bks Demand.

— Leading & Being Led. LC 85-63379. (Orig.). 1985. pap. 4.00 (0-87574-264-5) Pendle Hill.

— Quakers & the Use of Power. LC 81-85558. 32p. (Orig.). 1982. pap. 4.00 (0-87574-241-6) Pendle Hill.

***Lacey, Paul A. & Friends Council on Education Staff.** Growing into Goodness: Essays on Quaker Education LC 98-44919. 1998. pap. 20.00 (0-87574-930-5) Pendle Hill.

Lacey, Paul A. & Friends Council on Education Staff. Growing into Goodness: Essays on Quaker Education. LC 98-44919. 291p. 1999. pap. 18.00 (0-87574-933-X, 6266) Pendle Hill.

Lacey, Penny. People with Profound & Multiple Learning Disabilities; A Collaborative Approach to Meeting 1998. pap. text 32.95 (1-85346-488-0) Taylor & Francis.

Lacey, Penny & Lomas, Jeanette. Support Services & the Curriculum: A Practical Guide to Collaboration. 224p. 1993. pap. 29.00 (1-85346-222-5, Pub. by David Fulton) Taylor & Francis.

Lacey, Penny, jt. auth. see Collis, Mark.

Lacey, R. Kevin & Poole, Francis, eds. Mirrors on the Maghrib: Critical Reflections on Paul & Jane Bowles & Other American Writers in Morocco. LC 96-5758. 226p. 1996. 50.00 (0-88206-087-2) Caravan Bks.

***Lacey, Richard.** Poison on a Platc: The Dangers in the Food We Eat & How to Avoid Them. (Illus.). 288p. 1999. pap. 19.95 (1-900512-45-9, Pub. by Metro Bks) Trafalgar.

Lacey, Richard, jt. auth. see Clark, Terry.

Lacey, Richard W. Hard to Swallow: A Brief History of Food. LC 93-20808. (Illus.). 352p. (C). 1994. 26.95 (0-521-44001-7) Cambridge U Pr.

Lacey, Rick. Cat Fever. LC 94-36091. 1994. 24.95 (0-9642466-0-0) Karson Pubng.

Lacey, Robert. Ford: The Men & the Machine. 832p. 1987. mass mkt. 6.99 (0-345-34312-3) Ballantine Pub Grp.

— Grace. 496p. 1996. mass mkt. 7.50 (0-425-15125-5) Berkley Pub.

— Grace. large type ed. LC 94-42978. 613p. 1995. 26.95 (0-7838-1199-3, G K Hall Lrg Type) Mac Lib Ref.

— Grace. (Illus.). 463p. 1999. reprint ed. text 25.00 (0-7881-6157-1) DIANE Pub.

— Henry VIII. (Life & Times Ser.). (Illus.). 224p. 1998. pap. 18.95 (1-56649-199-1) Welcome Rain.

— The Kingdom. 656p. 1983. mass mkt. 5.95 (0-380-61762-5, Avon Bks) Morrow Avon.

— The Life & Times of Henry VIII. Fraser, Antonia, ed. (Kings & Queens of England Ser.). (Illus.). 224p. 1992. 24.95 (1-55859-451-5) Abbeville Pr.

— Little Man: Meyer Lansky & the Gangster Life. (Illus.). 704p. 1992. mass mkt. 5.99 (0-316-51163-3) Little.

***Lacey, Robert.** The Queen Mother's Century. 132p. (gr. 8). 1999. 25.95 (0-316-51154-4) Little.

Lacey, Robert. Retreat from Moscow, 1812. 1971. pap. 6.95 (0-670-59566-7, Viking) Viking Penguin.

Lacey, Robert. The Rise of Napoleon. 39.00 (1-56696-119-X) Jackdaw.

Lacey, Robert. Sotheby's: Bidding for Class, Vol. 1. LC 97-47639. (Illus.). 352p. (gr. 8). 1998. 27.95 (0-316-51139-0) Little.

Lacey, Robert, compiled by. Drake & the Golden Hinde. 39.00 (1-56696-166-1) Jackdaw.

— The French Revolution. 39.00 (1-56696-056-8) Jackdaw.

***Lacey, Robert & Danziger, Danny.** The Year 1000. large type ed. 248p. 2000. write for info. (0-7089-9145-9) Ulverscroft.

Lacey, Robert & Danziger, Danny. The Year 1000: What Life Was Like at the Turn of the First Millennium. (Illus.). 256p. (gr. 8). 1999. 23.00 (0-316-55840-0) Little.

***Lacey, Robert & Danziger, Danny.** The Year 1000: What Life Was Like at the Turn of the First Millennium: An Englishman's World. LC 98-31254. (Illus.). 240p. 2000. pap. 12.95 (0-316-51157-9, Back Bay) Little.

Lacey, Robert E., ed. see Membrane Processes for Industry Symposium Staff.

Lacey, S. Scent in Your Garden. 192p. 1998. pap. 60.00 (0-7112-1044-6, Pub. by F Lincoln) St Mut.

Lacey, Sarah. File Under - Jeopardy. LC 96-43320. 1997. 21.95 (0-312-15127-6, Thomas Dunne) St Martin.

— File Under - Missing. large type ed. 393p. 1995. pap. 18.99 (1-85389-499-0, Dales) Ulverscroft.

Lacey, Stephen. British Realist Theatre: The New Wave in Its Context, 1956-1965. LC 94-44677. 224p. (C). 1995. pap. 25.99 (0-415-12311-9) Routledge.

— Gardens of the National Trust. (Illus.). 320p. 1996. 45.00 (0-8109-6321-3, Pub. by Abrams) Time Warner.

— The Startling Jungle: Colour & Scent in the Romantic Garden. LC 88-46166. (Illus.). 253p. 1989. reprint ed. 19.95 (0-87923-712-0) Godine.

Lacey, Stephen H., jt. auth. see Smith, Anthony A.

***Lacey, Sue.** Animals. LC 99-39013. (Start with Art Ser.). (Illus.). 32p. (J). (gr. 2-5). 1999. lib. bdg. 21.90 (0-7613-3263-4, Copper Beech Bks) Millbrook Pr.

— Landscapes. (Start with Art Ser.). (Illus.). (J). 2000. 22.90 (0-7613-1167-X, Copper Beech Bks); pap. 6.95 (0-7613-0843-1, Copper Beech Bks) Millbrook Pr.

— People. LC 99-35496. (Start with Art Ser.). (Illus.). 32p. (J). (gr. 2-5). 1999. lib. bdg. 21.90 (0-7613-3262-6, Copper Beech Bks) Millbrook Pr.

— Sports & Leisure. (Start with Art Ser.). (Illus.). (J). 2000. pap. 6.95 (0-7613-0844-X, Copper Beech Bks) Millbrook Pr.

— Still Life. (Start with Art Ser.). (Illus.). (J). 2000. 22.90 (0-7613-1166-1, Copper Beech Bks); pap. 6.95 (0-7613-0842-3) Millbrook Pr.

Lacey, Sylvia, jt. auth. see Esser, Aristide H.

Lacey, Thersa Jensen. Tennessee Curiosities. 1999. pap. write for info. (1-55853-790-2) Rutledge Hill Pr.

Lacey, Thomas A. The Reformation & the People. LC 83-45583. reprint ed. 22.00 (0-404-19901-1) AMS Pr.

Lacey, Vincent A., jt. ed. see Allen, Howard W.

Lacey, W. & Wilson, B. Res Publica: Roman Politics & Society According to Cicero (Sources in Translation) 343p. 1978. reprint ed. 25.95 (0-906515-09-2, Pub. by Brist Class Pr) Focus Pub-R Pullins.

Lacey, W. G., ed. Census of India, 1931: Bihar & Orissa. 1987. reprint ed. 145.00 (0-8364-2070-5, Pub. by Usha) S Asia.

Lacey, W. K., ed. see Cicero, Marcus Tullius.

Lacey, Walt. Time Management. 1992. ring bd. 54.95 incl. audio (1-57052-071-2) Chrch Grwth VA.

Lacey, Walter A. Empowering Church Volunteers: To Develop a Passion for Service. Spear, Cindy G., ed. 21p. 1997. pap., wbk. ed. 54.95 incl. audio (1-57052-077-1) Chrch Grwth VA.

Lach. Asia Making Europe, Vol. 3, Bk. 1. 1998. pap. text 35.00 (0-226-46765-1) U Ch Pr.

— Asia Making Europe, Vol. 3, Bk. 2. 1998. pap. text 30.00 (0-226-46767-8) U Ch Pr.

— Asia Making Europe, Vol. 3, Bk. 3. 1998. pap. text 28.00 (0-226-46768-6) U Ch Pr.

— Asia Making Europe, Vol. 3, Bk. 4. 1998. pap. text 35.00 (0-226-46769-4) U Ch Pr.

Lach, Alma. The Hows & Whys of French Cooking. 1998. 15.99 (0-7858-0926-0) Bk Sales Inc.

Lach, Donald F. Asia in the Eyes of Europe: Sixteenth Through Eighteenth Centuries. LC 90-26873. (Illus.). 1991. pap. 6.00 (0-943056-14-4) Univ Chi Lib.

— Asia in the Making of Europe, 2 vols. Incl. Vol. 2. Century of Wonder Bk. 1: The Visual Arts. LC 64-19848. 1970. lib. bdg. 30.00 (0-226-46750-3); LC 64-19848. (Illus.). 1993. Set lib. bdg. 60.00 (0-226-46751-1) U Ch Pr.

— Asia in the Making of Europe Vol. I: The Century of Discovery. 568p. 1994. pap. text 29.95 (0-226-46731-7) U Ch Pr.

— Asia in the Making of Europe, Vol. I: The Century of Discovery, Book 2. 504p. 1994. pap. text 27.50 (0-226-46732-5) U Ch Pr.

— Asia in the Making of Europe, Vol. II: A Century of Wonder, Book 1: The Visual Arts. 424p. 1994. pap. text 24.95 (0-226-46730-9) U Ch Pr.

— Asia in the Making of Europe, Vol. II: A Century of Wonder, Book 2: The Literary Arts. xxiv, 432p. 1994. pap. text 24.95 (0-226-46733-3) U Ch Pr.

— Asia in the Making of Europe, Vol II: A Century of Wonder, Book 3: The Scholarly Disciplines. 440p. 1994. pap. text 24.95 (0-226-46734-1) U Ch Pr.

— India in the Eyes of Europe: The Sixteenth Century. LC 64-19848. 1993. pap. text 1.95 (0-226-46745-7, P293) U Ch Pr.

— Japan in the Eyes of Europe: The Sixteenth Century. LC 64-19848. 1993. pap. text 1.45 (0-226-46747-3, P295) U Ch Pr.

— Southeast Asia in the Eyes of Europe: The Sixteenth Century. LC 64-19848. 1993. pap. text 1.95 (0-226-46746-5, P294) U Ch Pr.

Lach, Donald F. & Van Kley, Edwin J. Asia in the Making of Europe Vol. III: A Century of Advance, 4 bks., Bk. 1. (Illus.). 674p. 1993. 85.00 (0-226-46753-8) U Ch Pr.

— Asia in the Making of Europe Vol. III: A Century of Advance, 4 bks., Bk. 2. (Illus.). 568p. 1993. 75.00 (0-226-46754-6) U Ch Pr.

— Asia in the Making of Europe Vol. III: A Century of Advance, 4 bks., Bk. 3. (Illus.). 504p. 1997. 65.00 (0-226-46755-4) U Ch Pr.

— Asia in the Making of Europe Vol. III: A Century of Advance, 4 bks., Bk. 4. (Illus.). 627p. 1993. 85.00 (0-226-46756-2) U Ch Pr.

— Asia in the Making of Europe Vol. III: A Century of Advance, 4 bks., Set. (Illus.). 2379p. 1993. 300.00 (0-226-46757-0) U Ch Pr.

Lach, Donald F., jt. auth. see Gottschalk, Louis.

Lach, Donald F., tr. see Leibniz, Gottfried Wilhelm.

Lach, E. M. New York Practice Guide: Business & Commercial, 4 vols. (New York Practice Guides Ser.). 1987. ring bd. 510.00 (0-8205-1517-5) Bender.

Lach, Pamela A. The Bride's Etiquette Guide: Etiquette Made Easy. LC 98-18501. 96p. 1998. pap. 6.95 (1-55652-299-1) Chicago Review.

Lach, Stanley. GOD/god: The Dissident, the Reality Principle. vii, 658p. 1996. 29.00 (0-8059-3808-7) Dorrance.

An Asterisk (*) at the beginning of an entry indicates that the title is appearing for the first time.

Lach, William. A Green Sound: Nature Writing from the Living Tradition of Unitarian Universalism. LC 92-20332. 1992. pap. 6.00 (*1-55896-301-4*, Skinner Hse Bks) Unitarian Univ.

***Lach, William & Metropolitan Museum of Art Staff.** I Imagine Angels: Poems & Prayers for Parents & Children. LC 00-24836. (Illus.). 2000. write for info. (*0-689-84080-2*) Atheneum Yung Read.

Lach, William, ed. see Metropolitan Museum Staff.

Lachance, Albert J. Greenspirit: Twelve Steps in Ecological Spirituality. 208p. 1991. pap. 13.95 (*1-85230-263-1*, Pub. by Element MA) Penguin Putnam.

LaChance, Carol W. The Way of the Mother: The Lost Journey of the Feminine. 160p. 1991. pap. 12.95 (*1-85230-267-4*, Pub. by Element MA) Penguin Putnam.

Lachance, D. The Real World of Engineering: Case History, No. 58. 3.50 (*0-614-05227-0*, CHN05805923.5M) ASFE.

Lachance, Denis, jt. ed. see Manion, Paul D.

Lachance, Gerald R., et al. Quantitative X-Ray Fluorescence Analysis: Theory & Application. LC 94-10486. 424p. 1995. 285.00 (*0-471-95167-6*) Wiley.

LaChance, Karen. Valdez: A Brief Oral History. 110p. 1995. pap. 10.00 (*0-9647662-0-5*) Prince William.

LaChance, Paul, tr. Angela of Foligno: Complete Works. LC 92-38830. (Classics of Western Spirituality Ser.). (Illus.). 448p. 1993. 26.95 (*0-8091-0460-1*); pap. 18.95 (*0-8091-3366-0*) Paulist Pr.

Lachance, Paul, tr. see Brunette, Pierre.

LaChance, Paul, tr. see Flood, David & Matura, Thaddee.

Lachance, Paul, tr. see Matura, Thaddbee.

Lachance, Paul, tr. see Matura, Thaddee.

Lachance, Paul, tr. see Vorreux, Damien.

Lachance, Paul A., ed. Nutraceuticals - Designer Foods III: Garlic, Soy & Licorice. LC 97-60572. (Illus.). 375p. 1997. 110.00 (*0-917678-40-0*, 3308) Food & Nut Pr.

Lachance, Paul A., jt. ed. see Bauernfeind, J. Christopher.

LaChance, Stephen, ed. see Mohan, Claire J.

Lachant, Neil A., jt. ed. see Skeel, Roland T.

Lachapell, Mark, jt. auth. see Duquet, Denis.

***LaChapelle, David.** Hotel LaChapelle. (Illus.). 168p. 1999. 60.00 (*0-8212-2636-3*, Pub. by Bulfinch Pr) Little.

LaChapelle, Dolores. D. H. Lawrence: Future Primitive. LC 95-51087. (Philosophy & the Environment Ser.: Vol. 5). 223p. 1996. 26.50 (*1-57441-007-5*) UNTX Pr.

— Deep Powder Snow: Forty-Years of Ecstatic Skiing, Avalanches, & Earth Wisdom. (Illus.). 112p. (Orig.). 1993. pap. text 6.95 (*1-882308-21-2*) Kivaki Pr.

— Sacred Land, Sacred Sex - Rapture of the Deep: Concerning Deep Ecology & Celebrating Life. 384p. (C). 1992. reprint ed. pap. 24.95 (*1-882308-11-5*) Kivaki Pr.

LaChapelle, E. R. The ABC of Avalanche Safety. 2nd ed. LC 85-21393. (Illus.). 112p. 1985. pap. 6.95 (*0-89886-103-9*) Mountaineers.

LaChapelle, Edward R., jt. auth. see Post, Austin.

Lachapelle, G., jt. ed. see Schwarz, K. P.

LaChappelle, Nancy B., jt. auth. see Abbate, Marcia S.

***LaCharite, Norman.** The Federal Manager's Guide to Measuring Organizational Performance. 54p. 1998. pap. 14.95 (*0-936295-97-X*) FPMI Comns.

***LaCharite, Raymond C.** The Fans of Captain Marvel. LC 00-190185. 311p. 2000. pap. 18.00 (*0-7388-1505-5*) Xlibris Corp.

— A Spirit in the Wind. 2000. write for info. (*1-58235-444-8*) Watermrk Pr.

LaCharite, Raymond C. & Brooks, Richard A., eds. A Critical Bibliography of French Literature: The 16th Century, Vol. 2. rev. ed. (Critical Bibliography of French Literature Ser.). 872p. 1985. text 125.00 (*0-8156-2308-9*) Syracuse U Pr.

***LaCharite, Raymond C., et al.** The Fans of Captain Marvel. LC 00-190185. 311p. 2000. 25.00 (*0-7388-1504-7*) Xlibris Corp.

LaChat, Michael R., jt. ed. see Myers, Max A.

Lachavanne, Jean-Bernard & Juge, Raphaelle, eds. Biodiversity in Land/Inland Water Ecotones. LC 96-3310. (Man in the Biosphere Ser.). (Illus.). 326p. 1997. 85.00 (*1-85070-735-9*) Prthnon Pub.

Lachecki, Marina & Kasperson, James. More Teaching Kids to Love the Earth. (Illus.). 192p. (Orig.). (YA). 1994. pap. 14.95 (*1-57025-040-5*) Pfeifer-Hamilton.

Lachecki, Marina, et al. Teaching Kids to Love the Earth. LC 90-62852. (Illus.). 192p. 1991. pap. 16.95 (*0-938586-42-4*) Pfeifer-Hamilton.

Lachecki, Marina D., jt. auth. see Kasperson, James.

Lachelin, Gillian C. Miscarriage: The Facts. 2nd ed. LC 95-39063. (Facts Ser.). (Illus.). 96p. (C). 1996. pap. text 19.95 (*0-19-262613-2*) OUP.

Lacheman, Ernest R., et al, eds. The Eastern Archives of Nuzi & Excavations at Nuzi, No. 4. LC 93-20366. (Studies on the Civilization & Culture of Nuzi & the Hurrians Ser.: Bk. 4). (Illus.). xii, 450p. 1993. text 79.50 (*0-931464-64-1*) Eisenbrauns.

Lacheman, Ernest R. & Maidman, Maynard P. Joint Expedition with the Iraq Museum at Nuzi VII: Miscellaneous Texts. LC 89-1382. (Studies on the Civilization & Culture of Nuzi & the Hurrians Ser.: Bk. 3). (Illus.). xii, 307p. 1989. text 59.50 (*0-931464-45-5*) Eisenbrauns.

Lacheman, Ernest R., jt. ed. see Owen, David I.

Lachenmayr, Bernhard J. & Vivell, Patrick M. Perimetry & Its Clinical Correlations.Tr. of Perimetrie. 320p. 1993. 99.00 (*0-86577-480-3*) Thieme Med Pubs.

Lachenmeyer, Charles W. Democracy As a Planning System. (Analysis Ser.). 33p. (Orig.). 1981. pap. text 18.00 (*0-938526-03-0*) Inst Analysis.

— Productive Performance. (Analysis Ser.). 51p. (Orig.). 1980. pap. text 18.00 (*0-938526-01-4*) Inst Analysis.

— Thought Control in America: A New Technology Analysis. 140p. 1982. pap. 10.00 (*0-938526-04-9*) Inst Analysis.

Lachenmeyer, Nathaniel. The Outsider: A Journey into My Father's Struggle with Madness. 288p. 2000. 24.00 (*0-7679-0190-8*) Broadway BDD.

Lacher, John. Visual Basic for Applications Database Solutions. 1000p. 1996. pap. text 59.99 incl. cd-rom (*0-7897-0802-7*) Que.

Lacher, Thomas & Savitsky, Basil. GIS Methodologies for Developing Conservation Strategies: Tropical Forest Recovery & Wildlife Management in Costa Rica. LC 97-38069. (Biology & Resource Management in the Tropics Ser.). (Illus.). 278p. 1998. 50.00 (*0-231-10026-4*) Col U Pr.

Lachica, Alan, jt. auth. see Werner, Doug.

Lachica, Eduardo, et al. Asian Issues (Nineteen Eighty-Five) (Asian Agenda Reports: No. 3). (Illus.). 86p. (Orig.). (C). 1986. lib. bdg. 28.00 (*0-8191-5342-7*) U Pr of Amer.

***Lachica, Joe.** Into the Night. (Illus.). 52p. 1998. pap. 7.99 (*0-9669333-0-3*) J Lachica.

Lachieze-Rey, Marc. Cosmology: A First Course. (Illus.). 144p. (C). 1995. text 59.95 (*0-521-47441-8*); pap. text 20.95 (*0-521-47966-5*) Cambridge U Pr.

***Lachieze-Rey, Marc & Gunzig, Edgard.** The Cosmological Background Radiation, 2 vols., Set. (International Hydrology Ser.). (Illus.). 247p. (C). 1999. pap. 34.95 (*0-521-57437-4*) Cambridge U Pr.

Lachieze-Rey, Marc & Gunzig, Edgard. The Cosmological Background Radiation: Echo of the Early Universe, 2 vols., Set. (Illus.). 264p. (C). 1999. 80.00 (*0-521-57398-X*) Cambridge U Pr.

Lachieze-Rey, Marc, jt. auth. see Klein, Etienne.

***Lachin, John M., III.** Biostatistics Methods: The Assessment of Relative Risks. LC 99-59413. 544p. 2000. 89.95 (*0-471-36996-9*) Wiley.

Lachkar, Joan. The Many Faces of Abuse: Treating the Emotional Abuse of High-Functioning Women. 240p. 1998. 50.00 (*0-7657-0065-4*) Aronson.

— The Narcissistic - Borderline Couple: A Psychoanalytic Perspective on Marital Treatment. LC 91-28228. 224p. 1992. text 33.95 (*0-87630-634-2*) Brunner-Mazel.

Lachman. Midlife Development. 832p. (C). 2000. 89.95 (*0-471-33331-X*) Wiley.

Lachman, Barbara. Hildegard, the Last Year. LC 97-7506. 160p. 1997. 20.00 (*1-57062-315-5*, Pub. by Shambhala Pubns) Random.

— Hildegard, the Last Year. 1998. pap. 13.00 (*1-57062-393-7*, Pub. by Shambhala Pubns) Random.

— The Journal of Hildegard of Bingen. 1995. pap. 12.00 (*0-517-88390-2*) Bell T.

Lachman, Beth E. Linking Sustainable Community Activities to Pollution Prevention: A Sourcebook. LC 97-8330. 86p. 1997. pap. 15.00 (*0-8330-2500-7*, MR-855-OSTP) Rand Corp.

Lachman, Beth E., jt. auth. see Camm, Frank A.

Lachman-Chapin, Mildred. Reverberations: Mothers & Daughters. 2nd ed. (Illus.). 48p. (Orig.). 1996. reprint ed. pap. 19.95 (*0-9643728-4-3*) Perry Pubng.

Lachman-Chapin, Mildred, ed. Reverberations: Mothers & Daughters. 44p. (Orig.). 1995. pap. 19.95 (*1-879260-32-8*) Evanston Pub.

Lachman, Charles, ed. from CHI. Evaluations of Sung Dynasty Painters of Renown: Liu Tao-Chiun's Sung-Ch'ao Ming-Hua P'ing. (T'oung Pao Monographies: No. XVI). (Illus.). xii, 115, [60]p. 1990. pap. 76.00 (*90-04-08966-7*) Brill Academic Pubs.

Lachman, David C. The Marrow Controversy, 1718-1723: An Historical & Theological Analysis. LC 92-5154. (Rutherford Studies in Historical Theology). 516p. 1992. reprint ed. lib. bdg. 119.95 (*0-7734-1649-8*) E Mellen.

Lachman, Desmond, et al. Challenges to the Swedish Welfare State. LC 95-40487. (Occasional Papers: No. 130). 1995. 15.00 (*1-55775-486-1*) Intl Monetary.

Lachman, Elizabeth, tr. see Hoffmann, Nicolas, ed.

Lachman, Frank M., jt. auth. see Stolorow, Robert D.

***Lachman, Larry.** Cats on the Couch. 2000. text 21.95 (*0-312-26566-2*) St Martin.

Lachman, Larry & Mickadeit, Frank. Dogs on the Couch: Behavior Therapy for Training & Caring for Your Dog. LC 98-48067. (Illus.). 320p. 1999. text 24.95 (*0-87951-922-3*, Pub. by Overlook Pr) Penguin Putnam.

Lachman, Leon, et al, eds. The Theory & Practice of Industrial Pharmacy. 3rd ed. LC 84-27806. (Illus.). 902p. 1986. text 105.00 (*0-8121-0977-5*) Lppncott W & W.

Lachman, Ludwig M. MarktprozeB und Erwartungen: Studien zur Theorie der Marktwirtschaft. Walentik, Leonhard & Grinder, W., trs. from ENG. 336p. 1984. 105.00 (*3-88405-035-4*) Philosophia Pr.

Lachman, Margie E. & James, Jacquelyn B. Multiple Paths of Midlife Development. LC 96-29289. (Studies on Successful Midlife Development). 1997. 52.00 (*0-226-46758-9*) U Ch Pr.

Lachman, Marvin. A Reader's Guide to the American Novel of Detection. (G. K. Hall Reference Ser.). 200p. 1993. 50.00 (*0-8161-1803-5*, Hall Reference) Macmillan.

Lachman, Ralph S., jt. auth. see Tabyi, Hooshang.

Lachman, Roy, et al. Cognitive Psychology & Information Processing: An Introduction. 592p. (C). 1979. text 99.95 (*0-89859-131-7*) L Erlbaum Assocs.

Lachman, Roy, ed. see Kasschau, Richard A.

Lachman, Sheldon J. The Foundations of Science. 1992. pap. 10.50 (*0-911586-95-4*) Wahr.

Lachman, Vicki D. Stress Management: A Manual for Nurses. 227p. 1983. pap. 19.50 (*0-685-06533-2*, 792424, Grune & Strat) Harcrt Hlth Sci Grp.

***Lachmann, Frank.** Transforming Aggression: Psychotherapy with the Difficult Patient. 2001. 45.00 (*0-7657-0293-2*) Aronson.

Lachmann, G. Boundary Layer & Flow Control: Its Principles & Application, 2 vols., Set. LC 60-9645. 1961. 594.00 (*0-08-009346-9*, Pub. by Pergamon Repr) Franklin.

Lachmann, Karl, ed. Nibelunge Noth und die Klage: Nach den Aeltesten Ueberlieferungen mit Bezeichnung des Unechten und mit den Abweichungen der gemeinen Lesart. 6th ed. (C). 1960. 18.55 (*3-11-000177-2*); pap. 20.75 (*3-11-000178-0*) De Gruyter.

Lachmann, Karl, et al, eds. Schriften der Romischen Feldmesser. xx, 952p. 1967. reprint ed. 225.00 (*0-318-71222-9*) G Olms Pubs.

Lachmann, Karl, ed. see Lessing, Gotthold Ephraim.

Lachmann, Karl, ed. see Von der Vogelweide, Walther.

Lachmann, Karl, ed. see Von Eschenbach, Wolfram.

Lachmann, Ludwig M., et al. Subjectivism & Economic Analysis: Essays in Memory of Ludwig M. Lachmann. LC 98-7044. 208p. (C). 1998. 85.00 (*0-415-11058-0*) Routledge.

Lachmann, P. J., et al, eds. Clinical Aspects of Immunology. 5th ed. LC 92-48808. (Illus.). 2328p. 1993. 299.95 (*0-86542-297-4*) Blackwell Sci.

— Fourteenth International Complement Workshop, Cambridge, U. K., September 1991 Abstracts: Complement & Inflammation Journal, Vol. 8, Nos. 3-4. (Journal: Complement & Inflammation). 136p. 1991. pap. 81.75 (*3-8055-5472-9*) S Karger.

Lachmann, Renate. Memory & Literature: Intertextuality in Russian Modernism. Sellars, Roy & Wall, Anthony, trs. LC 96-50354. (Theory & History of Literature Ser.: Vol. 87). (Illus.). 512p. (C). 1997. pap. 34.95 (*0-8166-2907-2*); text 49.95 (*0-8166-2906-4*) U of Minn Pr.

Lachmann, Richard. Captitalists in Spite of Themselves: Elite Conflict & European Transitions. LC 98-37405. (Illus.). 328p. 2000. text 49.95 (*0-19-507568-4*) OUP.

— Encyclopedic Dictionary of Sociology. 4th ed. 1991. pap. 16.56 (*0-87967-886-0*, Dshkn McG-Hill) McGrw-H Hghr Educ.

— Encyclopedic Dictionary of Sociology. 4th ed. (C). 1991. text. write for info. (*1-56134-044-8*, Dshkn McG-Hill) McGrw-H Hghr Educ.

Lachmund, Carl. Living with Liszt: From the Diary of Carl Lachmund, an American Pupil of Liszt, 1882-1884. rev. ed. Walker, Alan, ed. & anno. by. LC 98-30048. (Franz Liszt Studies: Vol. 4). 1998. 54.00 (*0-945193-56-4*) Pendragon NY.

Lachmund, Margarethe. With Thine Adversary in the Way: A Quaker Witness for Reconciliation. Kite, Florence, tr. LC 79-91957. (Orig.). 1979. pap. 4.00 (*0-87574-228-9*) Pendle Hill.

Lachner, Bert. Milwaukee - Wisconsin: Heimat in the Heartland. Paradis, Trudi, ed. Becker, Claudia et al, trs. LC 95-76780. (ENG & GER., Illus.). 224p. 1995. 45.00 (*0-9640659-2-4*) Lachner & Assocs.

Lachner, Bert & Ott, Ernst. Heimat North America: English-German. Johnson, Bruni, tr. LC 97-73455. Orig. Title: Heimat America, German Americans Today. (ENG & GER., Illus.). 336p. 1997. 60.00 (*0-9640659-3-2*) Lachner & Assocs.

Lachner, Dorothea. Andrew's Angry Words. LC 94-40031. (Illus.). 32p. (J). (gr. k-3). 1995. 15.95 (*1-55858-435-8*); lib. bdg. 15.88 (*1-55858-436-6*, Pub. by North-South Bks NYC) Chronicle Bks.

— Andrew's Angry Words. LC 94-40031. (Illus.). 32p. (J). (gr. k-3). 1997. pap. 6.95 (*1-55858-769-1*, Pub. by North-South Bks NYC) Chronicle Bks.

***Lachner, Dorothea.** Danny, the Angry Lion. (Illus.). 32p. (gr. k-3). 2000. 15.95 (*0-7358-1386-8*); lib. bdg. 15.88 (*0-7358-1387-6*) North-South Bks NYC.

— The Gift from Saint Nicholas. LC 95-953.Tr. of Geschenk vom Nikolaus. (Illus.). 32p. (J). (gr. k-3). 1999. pap. 6.95 (*0-7358-1195-4*, Pub. by North-South Bks NYC) Chronicle Bks.

Lachner, Dorothea. Meredith, the Witch Who Wasn't. James, J. Alison, tr. LC 97-7545. (Illus.). 32p. (J). (gr. k-3). 1997. 15.95 (*1-55858-781-0*, Pub. by North-South Bks NYC); lib. bdg. 15.88 (*1-55858-782-9*, Pub. by North-South Bks NYC) Chronicle Bks.

***Lachner, Dorothea.** Meredith, the Witch Who Wasn't. LC 97-7545. (Illus.). 32p. (J). (gr. k-3). 1999. pap. 6.95 (*0-7358-1196-2*, Pub. by North-South Bks NYC) Chronicle Bks.

— Meredith's Mixed-Up Magic. (Illus.). 32p. (gr. k-3). 2000. 15.95 (*0-7358-1190-3*); pap. 15.88 (*0-7358-1191-1*) North-South Bks NYC.

Lachner, Ernest A., jt. auth. see Fraser, Thomas H.

Lachney, Ann. The HACCP Cookbook & Manual. 213p. 1996. pap. text 59.95 (*0-9659957-0-4*) Nutrit Dev Systs.

***Lachney, Ann.** The HACCP Cookbook & Manual. 3rd rev. ed. 213p. (C). 1999. reprint ed. pap. text 59.95 (*0-9659957-2-0*) Nutrit Dev Systs.

Lachnit, Carroll. Akin to Death. 384p. 1998. mass mkt. 5.99 (*0-425-16409-8*) Berkley Pub.

— A Blessed Death. 336p. 1996. mass mkt. 5.99 (*0-425-15347-9*, Prime Crime) Berkley Pub.

***Lachnit, Carroll.** Janie's Law. (Hannah Barlow Ser.: No. 4). 336p. 1999. mass mkt. 6.50 (*0-425-17150-7*, Prime Crime) Berkley Pub.

Lachnit, Carroll. Murder in Brief. 272p. (Orig.). 1995. mass mkt. 4.99 (*0-425-14790-8*) Berkley Pub.

Lacho, Lubomir & Biros, Florence K. Reason for Treason: A True Story of Intrigue & Romance. LC 95-101957. (Illus.). 250p. 1994. pap. 8.95 (*0-936369-07-8*) Son-Rise Pubns.

Lachocki, Eugene. No Return. LC 96-37246. (Illus.). 150p. (Orig.). 1997. pap. 12.50 (*1-877633-35-6*) Luthers.

***Lachocki, Gryzelda N.** Goodbye Tomorrow. LC 99-31949.Tr. of Niezapomniane Jutro. (ENG & POL., Illus.). 144p. 1999. 19.95 (*1-55618-181-7*); pap. 14.95 (*1-55618-183-3*) Brunswick Pub.

— Niezapomiane Jutro. LC 99-28765.Tr. of Goodbye Tomorrow. (ENG & POL., Illus.). 144p. 1999. pap. 14.95 (*1-55618-180-9*) Brunswick Pub.

Lachouque, Henry & Brown, Anne S. The Anatomy of Glory: Napoleon & His Guard: A Study in Leadership. 4th ed. LC 97-5034. (C). 1997. 69.95 (*1-85367-264-5*, Pub. by Greenhill Bks) Stackpole.

Lachowicz, Mike, jt. auth. see Hale, Monica.

Lachowski, Henry. Guidelines for the Use of Digital Imagery for Vegetation Mapping. (Illus.). 125p. 1996. reprint ed. pap. text 35.00 (*0-7881-3331-4*) DIANE Pub.

Lachs, Gerald. Fiber Optic Communications: Systems Analysis & Enhancements. LC 97-44032. (Telecommunications Ser.). (Illus.). 450p. 1998. 70.00 (*0-07-038279-4*) McGraw.

Lachs, John. In Love with Life: Reflections on the Joy of Living & Why We Hate to Die. LC 98-25379. (Vanderbilt Library of American Philosophy). 128p. 1998. 17.95 (*0-8265-1328-X*) Vanderbilt U Pr.

— Intermediate Man. LC 81-4806. 152p. (C). 1981. 27.50 (*0-915145-12-X*); pap. text 9.95 (*0-915145-13-8*) Hackett Pub.

— Mind & Philosophers. LC 87-2076. 256p. (Orig.). 1987. pap. 17.50 (*0-8265-1222-4*) Vanderbilt U Pr.

— The Relevance of Philosophy to Life. LC 94-44987. (Vanderbilt Library of American Philosophy). 296p. 1995. 29.95 (*0-8265-1262-3*) Vanderbilt U Pr.

Lachs, John, ed. Animal Faith & Spiritual Life: Previously Unpublished & Uncollected Writings by George Santayana with Critical Essays on His Thought. LC 67-20665. (Century Philosophy Ser.). 1967. 42.50 (*0-89197-607-8*) Irvington.

Lachs, John, jt. auth. see Hodges, Michael P.

Lachs, John, ed. & tr. see Fichte, Johann G.

Lachs, Manfred. The Teacher in International Law. 1982. lib. bdg. 120.00 (*90-247-2566-6*) Kluwer Academic.

— The Teacher in International Law: Teachings & Teaching. 2nd rev. ed. LC 86-2540. 1986. pap. text 75.00 (*90-247-3313-8*) Kluwer Academic.

Lachs, Samuel T. Humanism in Talmud & Midrash. LC 91-58956. 152p. 1993. 32.50 (*0-8386-3468-0*) Fairleigh Dickinson.

— Rabbinic Commentary on the New Testament: The Gospels of Matthew, Mark & Luke. 600p. 1987. 39.50 (*0-88125-089-9*); pap. 24.95 (*0-88125-115-1*) Ktav.

Lachterman, David, tr. see Scheler, Max Ferdinand.

Lachterman, David R. The Ethics of Geometry: A Genealogy of Modernity. 288p. 1989. 49.50 (*0-415-90053-0*) Routledge.

Lachtman, Ofelia D. Big Enough (Bastante Grande) Canetti, Yanitzia, tr. (ENG & SPA.). (J). (ps-2). 1998. 14.95 (*1-55885-221-2*, Pinata Bks) Arte Publico.

— The Girl from Playa Blanca. LC 95-9864. 259p. (YA). (gr. 6 up). 1995. pap. 9.95 (*1-55885-149-6*, Pinata Bks) Arte Publico.

— Leticia's Secret. LC 97-24772. 128p. (YA). 1997. 14.95 (*1-55885-208-5*, Pinata Bks) Arte Publico.

— Leticia's Secret. LC 97-24772. 128p. (YA). (gr. 3-7). 1997. pap. text 7.95 (*1-55885-209-3*, Pinata Bks) Arte Publico.

— Pepita Talks Twice (Pepita Habla Dos Veces) LC 95-9869. (Illus.). 32p. (J). (gr. k-3). 1995. 14.95 (*1-55885-077-5*, Pinata Bks) Arte Publico.

— Pepita Thinks Pink (Pepita y el Color Rosado) LC 97-29676. (ENG & SPA., Illus.). 32p. (J). (ps-2). 1998. 14.95 (*1-55885-222-0*, Pinata Bks) Arte Publico.

— A Shell for Angela. LC 94-36140. 214p. (Orig.). 1995. pap. 9.95 (*1-55885-123-2*) Arte Publico.

***Lachtman, Ofelia D., et al.** Pepita Takes Time/Pepita, Siempre Tarde. 32p. (J). (ps-2). 2000. 14.95 (*1-55885-304-9*) Arte Publico.

LaChuisa, John, jt. auth. see Essman, Jeffrey.

LaChuisa, Michael J. First Lady Suite: Musical. LC 97-201215. 1995. pap. 6.00 (*0-8222-1408-3*) Dramatists Play.

— Hello Again: Musical. 1995. pap. 6.00 (*0-8222-1407-5*) Dramatists Play.

— Lucky Nurse & Other Musical Plays. 1993. spiral bd. 16.00 (*0-8222-1354-0*) Dramatists Play.

Lachuk, J. Frank Pachmayr: The Story of America's Master Gunsmith & His Guns. limited ed. (Illus.). 254p. 1996. boxed set 85.00 (*1-57157-031-4*) Safari Pr.

LaChuk, J. Frank Pachmayr, the Story of America's Master Gunsmith & His Guns. (Illus.). 254p. 1996. 50.00 (*1-57157-017-9*) Safari Pr.

***Lacinski, Paul & Bergeron, Michel.** Serious Straw Bale: A Home Construction Guide for All Climates. (Illus.). 380p. 2000. pap. 30.00 (*1-890132-64-0*) Chelsea Green Pub.

Lacirignola, Cosimo, jt. auth. see Khakee, Abdul.

Lacity, Mary C. & Hirschheim, Rudy. Beyond the Inform Syst Outsour. LC 95-12057. (Information Systems Ser.). 262p. 1995. 118.95 (*0-471-95822-0*) Wiley.

— Information Systems Outsourcing: Myths, Metaphors & Realities. LC 92-41996. (Information Systems Ser.). 290p. 1995. pap. 54.95 (*0-471-95604-X*) Wiley.

Lacity, Mary C. & Hirschheim, Rudy A. Information Systems Outsourcing: Myths, Metaphors & Realities. LC 92-41996. (Series in Information Systems). 290p. 1993. 139.95 (*0-471-93882-3*) Wiley.

Lacity, Mary C., jt. auth. see Willcocks, Leslie P.

LaCivita, Peter. Heroes under the Big Dipper: A True Story. LC 97-94028. 1997. pap. 12.95 (*1-57502-539-6*, PO1583) Morris Pubng.

Lack. AFIP Atlas of Tumor Pathology: Tumors of the Adrenal Gland & Extra Adrenal Paraganglia. (Illus.). 468p. 1997. pap. text 70.00 (*1-881041-28-X*) Am Registry Path.

Lack, jt. auth. see Campbell.

Lack, David. Ecological Isolation in Birds. LC 70-151286. (Illus.). 416p. 1971. 43.50 (*0-674-22442-6*) HUP.

L

Lack, Davie L. Island Biology: Illustrated by the Land Birds of Jamaica. LC 75-7194. (Studies in Ecology: No. 3). (Illus.). 463p. reprint ed. pap. 143.60 (*0-7837-4831-0*, 204447800003) Bks Demand.

Lack, Eddie. Crazy Ancient Egypt Game. (Crazy Games Ser.). (J). (gr. 1 up). 1997. pap. 3.99 (*0-8431-7977-5*, Price Stern) Peng Put Young Read.

— Crazy Dolphin Game. (Crazy Games Ser.). (J). (gr. 1 up). 1996. boxed set, bds. 3.50 (*0-8431-8208-3*, Price Stern) Peng Put Young Read.

Lack, Elizabeth, jt. ed. see Campbell, Bruce.

Lack, Ernest E. Pathology of Adrenal & Extra-Adrenal Paragaglia. LC 93-32870. (Major Problems in Pathology Ser.: Vol. 29). 1994. text 79.00 (*0-7216-5263-8*, W B Saunders Co) Harcrt Hlth Sci Grp.

Lack, Ernest E., ed. Pathology of the Adrenal Glands. LC 89-22177. (Contemporary Issues in Surgical Pathology Ser.: No. 14). (Illus.). 399p. 1990. reprint ed. pap. 123.70 (*0-7837-6812-5*, 204664400003) Bks Demand.

Lack, H. W. & Mabberley, David. The Flora Graeca Story: Sibthorp, Bauer & Hawkins in the Levant. LC 98-7563. (Illus.). 360p. 1999. text 450.00 (*0-19-854897-4*) OUP.

Lack, John & Templeton, Jacqueline, eds. Bold Experiment: A Documentary History of Australian Immigration since 945. (Illus.). 328p. 1995. pap. text 45.00 (*0-19-553548-0*) OUP.

Lack, Leon C. Selective Attention & the Control of Binocular Rivalry. (Psychological Studies: No. II). 1978. pap. text 66.15 (*90-279-7644-9*) Mouton.

Lack, Paul D. The Texas Revolutionary Experience: A Political & Social History, 1835-1836. LC 91-23368. (Texas A&M Southwestern Studies: No. 10). 360p. 1996. pap. 19.95 (*0-89096-721-0*) Tex A&M Univ Pr.

Lack, Peter, compiled by. The Atlas of Wintering Birds in Britain & Ireland. (Illus.). 352p. 1990. text (*0-85661-043-7*, 784643) Poyser.

Lack, Richard W. Accident Prevention Manual for Business & Industry: Security Management. LC 97-11923. 487p. 1997. 69.95 (*0-87912-198-X*, 12182-0000) Natl Safety Coun.

Lack, Richard W., ed. Essentials of Safety & Health Management. LC 95-52101. 736p. 1996. lib. bdg. 75.00 (*1-56670-054-X*, L1054) Lewis Pubs.

Lack, Roland-Fran, jt. auth. see Ffrench, Patrick.

Lack, Roland-Fran C., jt. ed. see Ffrench, Patrick.

Lack, Roland-Francois. Poetics of the Pretext: Reading Lautreamont. 250p. 1998. 60.00 (*0-85989-498-3*, Pub. by Univ Exeter Pr) Northwestern U Pr.

***Lack, Russell.** Twenty Four Frames Under: A Buried History of Film Music. 288p. 1999. pap. 16.95 (*0-7043-8045-5*, Pub. by Quartet) Interlink Pub.

Lack, S., jt. auth. see Piggin, C.

Lack, Sylvia A., jt. auth. see Twycross, Robert G.

Lack, T. J., ed. Environmental Protection: Standards & Compliance. LC 84-15644. (Water & Waste Water Technology Ser.). 329p. 1984. text 79.00 (*0-470-20095-2*) P-H.

Lack, Tony & Gifford, Nigel. Equipment & Catering. (C). 1992. 35.00 (*0-907649-55-6*, Pub. by Expedit Advisory Ctr) St Mut.

Lacke, John, et al, eds. Cell Behaviour: Control & Mechanism of Motility. (Biochemical Society Symposia Ser.: No. 5). (Illus.). 1998. pap. text 110.50 (*1-85578-124-7*, Pub. by Portland Pr Ltd) Ashgate Pub Co.

Lackes, R. & Mack, D. Computer Based Training on Neural Nets: Basics, Development, & Practice. 50p. 1997. 39.95 incl. cd-rom (*3-540-14660-1*) Spr-Verlag.

Lackey, Bradley C., jt. auth. see Antonelli, Peter L.

Lackey, Dale, jt. auth. see Sunderland, Bill.

Lackey, Douglas P. The Ethics of War & Peace. 208p. (C). 1988. pap. text 20.80 (*0-13-290925-1*) P-H.

— Moral Principles & Nuclear Weapons. LC 84-11540. (Philosophy & Society Ser.). (Illus.). 284p. (C). 1984. 56.50 (*0-8476-7116-X*) Rowman.

— Moral Principles & Nuclear Weapons. 288p. 1986. pap. 22.50 (*0-8476-7515-7*) Rowman.

Lackey, Ellen A., jt. auth. see Armstrong, Thomas J.

Lackey, George H., Jr., jt. auth. see Friedman, Myles I.

Lackey, Joe. From the Other Side of Death. 69p. (Orig.). 1995. pap. 10.00 (*0-942292-13-8*) Warthog Pr.

Lackey, Kris. RoadFrames: The American Highway Narrative. LC 96-49443. 164p. 1997. text 40.00 (*0-8032-2924-0*, Bison Books) U of Nebr Pr.

— RoadFrames: The American Highway Narrative. LC 96-49443. 180p. 1999. pap. text 15.00 (*0-8032-7981-7*, Bison Books) U of Nebr Pr.

Lackey, Larry A., Sr. How to Survive in Today's Economy. 112p. 1994. pap. 29.95 (*1-885102-00-3*); student ed. 207.00 incl. audio (*1-885102-01-1*) Busn Mgmt Inst.

Lackey, Louana M. The Pottery of Acatlan: A Changing Mexican Tradition. LC 81-40280. (Illus.). 176p. 1991. pap. 19.95 (*0-8061-2301-X*) U of Okla Pr.

Lackey, Mary. Fifty Years of Recipes from the Ravelled Sleeve. LC 88-82333. 582p. (Orig.). 1988. pap. 12.95 (*0-9621301-0-9*) Ravelled Sleeve.

Lackey, Mercedes. Arrow's Fall. (Heralds of Valdemar Ser.: Bk. 3). 320p. 1988. reprint ed. mass mkt. 5.99 (*0-88677-400-4*, Pub. by DAW Bks) Penguin Putnam.

— Arrow's Flight. (Heralds of Valdemar Ser.: Bk. 2). 320p. 1987. reprint ed. mass mkt. 5.99 (*0-88677-377-6*, Pub. by DAW Bks) Penguin Putnam.

— Arrows of the Queen. (Heralds of Valdemar Ser.: Bk. 1). 320p. 1987. reprint ed. mass mkt. 5.99 (*0-88677-378-4*, Pub. by DAW Bks) Penguin Putnam.

— Bedlam's Bard. 1998. per. 6.99 (*0-671-87863-8*) Baen Bks.

***Lackey, Mercedes.** Black Swan. 416p. 2000. mass mkt. 6.99 (*0-88677-890-5*, Pub. by DAW Bks) Penguin Putnam.

Lackey, Mercedes. The Black Swan. 376p. (YA). 1999. 24.95 (*0-88677-833-6*, Pub. by DAW Bks) Penguin Putnam.

***Lackey, Mercedes.** Brightly Burning. 416p. 2000. 24.95 (*0-88677-889-1*, Pub. by DAW Bks) Penguin Putnam.

Lackey, Mercedes. Burning Water. 320p. 1992. mass mkt. 4.99 (*0-8125-2485-3*, Pub. by Tor Bks) St Martin.

— By the Sword. (kerowyn's tale). 1991. mass mkt. 6.99 (*0-88677-463-2*, Pub. by DAW Bks) Penguin Putnam.

— Children of the Night: A Diana Tregarde Investigation. 320p. 1992. mass mkt. 4.99 (*0-8125-2272-9*, Pub. by Tor Bks) St Martin.

— The Eagle & the Nightingales. LC 94-27320. (Bardic Voices Ser.: Bk. 3). 416p. 1995. 22.00 (*0-671-87636-8*) Baen Bks.

— The Eagle & the Nightingales. (Bardic Voices Ser.: Bk. 3). 416p. 1996. mass mkt. 5.99 (*0-671-87706-2*) Baen Bks.

— Elvenborn. 1999. text. write for info. (*0-312-86456-6*) St Martin.

— Fiddler Fair. 1998. per. 5.99 (*0-671-87866-2*) Baen Bks.

— The Fire Rose. LC 95-24110. 1995. 22.00 (*0-671-87687-2*) Baen Bks.

— The Fire Rose. 448p. 1996. per. 6.99 (*0-671-87750-X*) Baen Bks.

— Firebird. 1997. mass mkt. 6.99 (*0-8125-5074-9*, Pub. by Tor Bks) St Martin.

— Four & Twenty Blackbirds. LC 97-29672. (Bardic Voices Ser.: Bk. 4). 1997. 22.00 (*0-671-87853-0*) Baen Bks.

— Four & Twenty Blackbirds. (Bardic Voices Ser.: Bk. 4). 1998. reprint ed. mass mkt. 6.99 (*0-671-57778-6*) Baen Bks.

— The Free Bards. LC 97-637. 720p. 1997. per. 15.00 (*0-671-87778-X*) Baen Bks.

— Friends of Valdemar. 352p. 1997. mass mkt. 5.99 (*0-88677-720-8*, Pub. by DAW Bks) Penguin Putnam.

— Heralds, Harpers & Havoc Songbook. Lee, Teri, ed. (Arrows Trilogy - Heralds of Valdemar Ser.). (Illus.). 40p. (Orig.). pap. 10.00 (*1-879795-01-9*) Firebird Arts.

— Jinx High. 320p. (Orig.). 1991. mass mkt. 4.99 (*0-8125-2114-5*, Pub. by Tor Bks) St Martin.

— The Lark & the Wren. (Bardic Voices Ser.: Bk. 1). 496p. 1992. mass mkt. 5.99 (*0-671-72099-6*) Baen Bks.

— Magic's Pawn. (Last Herald-Mage Ser.: Bk. 1). 352p. 1989. mass mkt. 5.99 (*0-88677-352-0*, Pub. by DAW Bks) Penguin Putnam.

— Magic's Price. (Last Herald-Mage Ser.: Bk. 3). 352p. 1990. mass mkt. 6.99 (*0-88677-426-8*, Pub. by DAW Bks) Penguin Putnam.

— Magic's Promise. (Last Herald-Mage Ser.: Bk. 2). 320p. 1990. mass mkt. 5.99 (*0-88677-401-2*, Pub. by DAW Bks) Penguin Putnam.

— The Oathbound. (Vows & Honor Ser.: Bk. 1). 302p. 1988. mass mkt. 5.99 (*0-88677-414-4*, Pub. by DAW Bks) Penguin Putnam.

— Oathbreakers. (Vows & Honor Ser.: Bk. 2). 1989. mass mkt. 5.99 (*0-88677-454-3*, Pub. by DAW Bks) Penguin Putnam.

***Lackey, Mercedes.** Owlknight. 2000. mass mkt. 6.99 (*0-88677-916-2*, Pub. by DAW Bks) Penguin Putnam.

— The River's Gift. LC 99-14509. 122p. 1999. mass mkt. 14.95 (*0-451-45759-5*, ROC) NAL.

Lackey, Mercedes. The Robin & the Kestrel. LC 93-11286. (Bardic Voices Ser.: Bk. 2). 432p. 1993. 20.00 (*0-671-72183-6*) Baen Bks.

— The Robin & the Kestrel. (Bardic Voices Ser.: Bk. 2). 432p. 1994. mass mkt. 5.99 (*0-671-87628-7*) Baen Bks.

— Sacred Ground. 384p. 1995. 5.99 (*0-8125-1965-5*, Pub. by Tor Bks) St Martin.

— Storm Breaking. LC 96-228065. (Mage Storms Ser.). 448p. 1996. 21.95 (*0-88677-713-5*, Pub. by DAW Bks) Penguin Putnam.

— Storm Breaking. (Mage Storms Ser.). 416p. 1997. mass mkt. 6.99 (*0-88677-755-0*, Pub. by DAW Bks) Penguin Putnam.

— Storm Rising. (Mage Storms Ser.). 416p. 1996. mass mkt. 6.99 (*0-88677-712-7*, Pub. by DAW Bks) Penguin Putnam.

— Storm Warning. (Mage Storms Ser.: Bk. 1). 432p. 1994. 21.95 (*0-88677-611-2*, Pub. by DAW Bks) Penguin Putnam.

— Storm Warning. (Mage Storms Ser.: Bk. 1). 432p. 1995. mass mkt. 6.99 (*0-88677-661-9*, Pub. by DAW Bks) Penguin Putnam.

— Vows & Honor. (Vows & Honor Ser.). 400p. 1998. pap. 6.99 (*0-88677-773-9*, Pub. by DAW Bks) Penguin Putnam.

— Werehunter. 274p. 1999. mass mkt. 6.99 (*0-671-57805-7*) Baen Bks.

— Winds of Fate. (Mage Winds Ser.: Bk. 1). (Illus.). 416p. 1991. 18.95 (*0-88677-489-6*, Pub. by DAW Bks) Penguin Putnam.

— Winds of Fate. (Mage Winds Ser.: Bk. 1). 464p. 1992. mass mkt. 6.99 (*0-88677-516-7*, Pub. by DAW Bks) Penguin Putnam.

— Winds of Fury. (Mage Winds Ser.: Bk. 3). 448p. 1994. reprint ed. mass mkt. 5.99 (*0-88677-612-0*, Pub. by DAW Bks) Penguin Putnam.

Lackey, Mercedes & Carter, David A. Bed Bugs Pop-Up Book: A Pop-Up Bedtime Book. (Illus.). 6p. (J). (ps-2). 1998. per. 14.95 (*0-689-81863-7*) S&S Childrens.

Lackey, Mercedes & Dixon, Larry. The Black Gryphon. (mage wars). 464p. 1995. mass mkt. 6.99 (*0-88677-643-0*, Pub. by DAW Bks) Penguin Putnam.

— Born to Run. 336p. 1992. per. 5.99 (*0-671-72110-0*) Baen Bks.

— Chrome Circle. (Orig.). 1994. mass mkt. 5.99 (*0-671-87615-5*) Baen Bks.

— Owlflight. LC 98-103995. (Darian's Tale Ser.: Vol. 1). 304p. 1997. 21.95 (*0-88677-754-2*, Pub. by DAW Bks) Penguin Putnam.

— Owlflight. (Darian's Tale Ser.: Vol. 1). (Illus.). 342p. 1998. pap. 6.99 (*0-88677-804-2*, Pub. by DAW Bks) Penguin Putnam.

— Owlknight. (Darian's Tale Ser.: Vol. 3). 326p. 1999. 24.95 (*0-88677-851-4*, Pub. by DAW Bks) Penguin Putnam.

— Owlsight. LC 99-188017. (Darian's Tale Ser.: Vol. 2). (Illus.). 389p. 1998. 24.95 (*0-88677-802-6*, Pub. by DAW Bks) Penguin Putnam.

— Owlsight. (Darian's Tale Ser.: Vol. 2). 450p. 1999. mass mkt. 6.99 (*0-88677-803-4*, Pub. by DAW Bks) Penguin Putnam.

— The Silver Gryphon. (mage wars). 352p. 1996. 21.95 (*0-88677-684-8*, Pub. by DAW Bks) Penguin Putnam.

— The Silver Gryphon. (mage wars). 1997. mass mkt. 6.99 (*0-88677-685-6*, Pub. by DAW Bks) Penguin Putnam.

— The White Gryphon. (mage wars). 384p. 1996. mass mkt. 6.99 (*0-88677-682-1*, Pub. by DAW Bks) Penguin Putnam.

Lackey, Mercedes & Emerson, Ru. Fortress of Frost & Fire. (Bard's Tale Ser.). 304p. 1993. per. 5.99 (*0-671-72162-3*) Baen Bks.

Lackey, Mercedes & Greenberg, Martin H., eds. Flights of Fantasy. 320p. 1999. mass mkt. 6.99 (*0-88677-863-8*, Pub. by DAW Bks) Penguin Putnam.

Lackey, Mercedes & Guon, Ellen. Freedom Flight: Wing Commander, No. 1. 1992. mass mkt. 4.99 (*0-671-72145-3*) Baen Bks.

— A Knight of Ghosts & Shadows. (Orig.). 1990. mass mkt. 5.99 (*0-671-69885-0*) Baen Bks.

Lackey, Mercedes & Lisle, Holly. When the Bough Breaks. (Serrated Edge Ser.). 288p. 1993. per. 5.99 (*0-671-72154-2*) Baen Bks.

Lackey, Mercedes & Shepherd, Mark. Prison of Souls. (Bard's Tale Ser.). 368p. (Orig.). 1993. mass mkt. 5.99 (*0-671-72193-3*) Baen Bks.

— Wheels of Fire. (Serrated Edge Ser.). 400p. 1992. mass mkt. 5.99 (*0-671-72138-0*) Baen Bks.

Lackey, Mercedes & Sherman, Josepha. A Cast of Corbies. 320p. 1994. mass mkt. 6.99 (*0-671-72207-7*) Baen Bks.

— Castle of Deception. (Bard's Tale Ser.). 320p. (Orig.). 1992. per. 5.99 (*0-671-72125-9*) Baen Bks.

***Lackey, Mercedes, et al.** The Otherworld. 640p. 2000. per. 6.99 (*0-671-57852-9*) Baen Bks.

Lackey, Mercedes, jt. auth. see Anthony, Piers.

Lackey, Mercedes, jt. auth. see Bradley, Marion Zimmer.

Lackey, Mercedes, jt. auth. see Cherryh, C. J.

Lackey, Mercedes, jt. auth. see McCaffrey, Anne.

Lackey, Mercedes, jt. auth. see Norton, Andre.

Lackey, Richard S., ed. Cite Your Sources: A Manual for Documenting Family Histories & Genealogical Records. LC 85-20371. 94p. 1985. pap. 11.95 (*0-87805-286-0*) U Pr of Miss.

Lackey, Richard S., jt. ed. see Barnes, Donald R.

Lackey, Scott A. The Rebirth of the Habsburg Army: Friedrich Beck & the Rise of the General Staff, 161. LC 95-7897. (Contributions in Military Studies Ser.: 161). 272p. 1995. 65.00 (*0-313-29361-9*, Greenwood Pr) Greenwood.

Lackey, Walter F. History of Newton County, Arkansas. (Illus.). 432p. 1994. reprint ed. lib. bdg. 45.00 (*0-8328-4000-9*) Higginson Bk Co.

***Lacki, Al Francis.** Staying Connected in Your Marriage: Daily Reflections & Dialogue. 2nd rev. ed. LC 99-72918. 376p. 1999. reprint ed. pap. 14.00 (*0-9641428-7-2*) Uplift Ent.

Lackie, Ann M., ed. Immune Mechanisms in Invertebrate Vectors. (Symposian of the Zoological of London: No. 56). (Illus.). 300p. 1987. text 75.00 (*0-19-854004-3*) OUP.

Lackie, Gordon L., ed. see De Grott, Anton C.

***Lackie, J. M.** Cell Behaviour: Control & Mechanism of Motility, Vol. 65. LC 98-89202. 1999. 75.00 (*0-691-00950-3*, Pub. by Princeton U Pr) Cal Prin Full Svc.

Lackie, J. M. Cell Movement & Cell Behaviour. (Illus.). 224p. (C). 1986. pap. text 34.95 (*0-04-574035-6*) Routledge.

Lackie, J. M., jt. ed. see Armitage, J. P.

***Lackie, John M. & Dow, Julian.** The Dictionary of Cell & Molecular Biology. 3rd ed. 504p. 1999. 29.95 (*0-12-432565-3*) Acad Pr.

Lackie-Tarry, Helen. Language & Context: A Functional Linguistic Theory of Register. Birch, David, ed. LC 95-3907. 1995. 64.95 (*1-85567-271-5*) St Martin.

Lackman, Ron. Women of the Western Frontier in Fact, Fiction & Film. LC 97-34075. (Illus.). 215p. 1997. boxed set 45.00 (*0-7864-0400-0*) McFarland & Co.

Lackmann, Dorothy H., jt. ed. see Fischer, Justine.

***Lackmann, Ronald W.** The Encyclopedia of American Radio: An A-Z Guide to Radio from Jack Benny to Howard Stern. LC 99-35263. 1999. 18.95 (*0-8160-4077-X*, Checkmark) Facts on File.

— Encyclopedia of American Radio: An A-Z Guide to Radio from Jack Benny to Howard Stern. rev. ed. LC 99-35263. (Illus.). 347p. 2000. 60.00 (*0-8160-4137-7*, Checkmark) Facts on File.

Lackmann, Ronald W. Same Time . . . Same Station: An A-Z Guide to Radio from Jack Benny to Howard Stern. LC 95-5662. (Illus.). 384p. 1995. 45.00 (*0-8160-2862-1*) Facts on File.

Lackner, Bede K., ed. Stephen of Sawley: Treatises. O'Sullivan, Jeremiah F., tr. 1984. 17.95 (*0-87907-636-4*) Cistercian Pubns.

Lackner, Bede K., jt. ed. see Stark, Gary D.

Lackner, Bernhard. Segnung und Gebot. (Regensburger Studien Zur Theologie Ser.: Bd. 41). (GER.). 355p. 1994. 55.95 (*3-631-46840-7*) P Lang Pubng.

Lackner, Helen. P. D. R. Yemen: Outpost of Socialist Development in Arabia. 219p. 1985. 30.00 (*0-685-13333-8*) Evergreen Dist.

Lackner, Karl, et al, eds. Festschrift fuer Wilhelm Gallas zum 70. Geburtstag. 457p. (C). 1973. 126.95 (*3-11-004062-X*) De Gruyter.

Lackner, Lucas. Internal Exile. 64p. (Orig.). 1984. pap. 6.95 (*0-915643-02-2*) Santa Barb Pr.

Lackner, Marie & Paterno, Cynthia. Practice RCT Reading Exam. 1982. pap. 11.95 (*0-937820-34-2*); pap. 11.95 (*0-937820-35-0*) WestSea Pub.

— RCT Reading. rev. ed. 198p. 1989. pap. 7.95 (*0-937820-58-X*) WestSea Pub.

— RCT Reading Answer Key. rev. ed. 20p. 1989. pap., teacher ed. 3.25 (*0-937820-59-8*) WestSea Pub.

***Lackner, Martin.** Our Family Saga: The True Story of My Life, 1930-1965. LC 99-91798. 2000. 25.00 (*0-7388-1274-9*); pap. 18.00 (*0-7388-1275-7*) Xlibris Corp.

***Lackner, Michelle Myers & Powers, Daniel.** Toil in the Soil. LC 00-36150. (Illus.). 2001. lib. bdg. write for info. (*0-7613-1807-0*) Millbrook Pr.

Lackner, Stephan. Old World Tales: Stories. LC 98-34548. 192p. 1999. pap. 12.00 (*1-56474-291-1*) Fithian Pr.

Lackner, Wayne. Health Insurance: Understanding It, & Medicare. LC 91-72257. 1992. pap. 9.95 (*0-9629538-0-6*) Fee Pub.

Lackney, Jeffery A. Educational Facilities: The Impact & Role of the Physical Environment of the School on Teaching, Learning & Educational Outcomes. (Illus.). vi, 118p. (C). 1995. per. 15.00 (*0-938744-85-2*, R94-4) U of Wis Ctr Arch-Urban.

Lackney, Jeffery A. Environmental quality Assessment Final Report to Baltimore City Schools 1996. 285p. 1996. pap. 17.00 (*1-886437-09-2*) U of Wis Ctr Arch-Urban.

Lackney, Jeffery A., et al. The Costs of Facility Development: A Comparative Analysis of Public & Private Sector Facility Development Processes & Costs. (Illus.). vi, 175p. (C). 1995. per. 20.00 (*0-938744-90-9*, R94-9) U of Wis Ctr Arch-Urban.

Lackney, Jeffrey A., jt. auth. see Moore, Gary T.

***Lackney, Robert.** Christ: Praise & Thanksgiving & Prayer. 2000. 24.95 (*0-7880-1493-5*, Fairway Pr) CSS OH.

***Lackova, Ilona.** A False Dawn: My Life As a Gypsy Woman in Slovakia. Hubschmannova, Milena, ed. & intro. by. (Interface Collection: Vol. 16). (Illus.). 230p. (C). 2000. pap. 23.95 (*1-902806-00-X*, Pub. by Univ of Herfordshire) Bold Strummer Ltd.

Lackovic, V., jt. ed. see Borecky, L.

Lackritz, James R., jt. auth. see Oltman, Debra O.

Lackritz, Wendy, ed. see Whiddon, Debra.

Lacks, Cissy. Downtown Lady. LC 76-41077. 1976. pap. 2.95 (*0-933530-00-5*) Beanie Bks.

***Lacks, Patricia.** Bender Gestalt Screening for Brain Dysfunction, 1. 2nd ed. LC 98-7635. 264p. 1998. 69.50 (*0-471-24257-8*) Wiley.

LaClaire, Jude. Beginning the Journey. (Life Weaving Ser.: Vol. 1). (Illus.). 64p. 1995. spiral bd. 9.95 (*0-9629385-1-3*) Heartlnd Personal.

— Life Weaving: A Practical Integrative Problem Solving Model, Set, Vols. 1-5. (Illus.). 1995. spiral bd. 49.95 (*0-9629385-6-4*) Heartlnd Personal.

— Reaching for Wisdom. (Life Weaving Ser.: Vol. 4). (Illus.). 64p. 1995. spiral bd. write for info. (*0-9629385-4-8*) Heartlnd Personal.

— Receiving a Gift & Giving It Back. (Life Weaving Ser.: Vol. 5). (Illus.). 64p. 1995. spiral bd. 9.95 (*0-9629385-5-6*) Heartlnd Personal.

— Using the Compass. (Life Weaving Ser.: Vol. 2). (Illus.). 64p. 1995. spiral bd. 9.95 (*0-9629385-2-1*) Heartlnd Personal.

— Walking the Path. (Life Weaving Ser.: Vol. 3). (Illus.). 64p. 1995. spiral bd. write for info. (*0-9629385-3-X*) Heartlnd Personal.

Laclau, Ernesto. Emancipation(s) LC 96-10251. (Phronesis Ser.). 144p. 1996. pap. 19.00 (*1-85984-165-1*, Pub. by Verso) Norton.

— The Making of Political Identities. LC 93-50722. (Phronesis Ser.). 320p. (C). 1994. pap. 20.00 (*0-86091-663-4*, Pub. by Verso) Norton.

Laclau, Ernesto & Mouffe, Chantal. Hegemony & Socialist Strategy: Towards a Radical Democratic Politics. 197p. (C). 1985. pap. 20.00 (*0-86091-769-X*, Pub. by Verso) Norton.

Laclavetine, Jean-Marie. Rabelais. (Maison D'Ecrivain Collection). (FRE., Illus.). 1995. pap. 49.95 (*2-86808-065-0*) Intl Scholars.

LaClaviere, R., jt. auth. see De Maulde, L.

Laclos. Les Liaisons Dangereuses. (FRE.). (C). 1987. pap. 11.95 (*0-8442-1971-1*, VF1971-1) NTC Contemp Pub Co.

Laclos, Choderlos De. Les Liaisons Dangereuses. 1992. 17.00 (*0-679-41325-1*) Everymns Lib.

— Les Liaisons Dangereuses. (Coll. GF). pap. 8.95 (*0-685-34038-4*) Fr & Eur.

— Les Liaisons Dangereuses. (Coll. Prestige Ser.). 382p. 1958. pap. 10.95 (*0-7859-1417-X*) Fr & Eur.

— Les Liaisons Dangereuses. (Folio Ser.: No. 894). pap. 11.95 (*2-07-036894-7*) Schoenhof.

***Laclos, Choderlos de.** Les Liaisons Dangereuses. Parmee, Douglas, ed. (Oxford World's Classics Ser.). 442p. 1999. pap. 8.95 (*0-19-283867-9*) OUP.

Laclos, Choderlos De. Les Liaisons Dangereuses. unabridged ed. (FRE.). pap. 7.95 (*2-87714-153-5*, Pub. by Bookking Intl) Distribks Inc.

— Oeuvres Completes. deluxe ed. Allen, ed. (Pleiade Ser.). 1943. 72.95 (*2-07-010937-2*) Schoenhof.

Laclotte, Michel. Le Larousse des Grands Peintres, Vol. 2. (FRE.). 1984. pap. 32.95 (*0-7859-3945-8*) Fr & Eur.

— The Louvre. (Illus.). 1996. pap. 4.95 (*0-89659-097-6*) Abbeville Pr.

— Treasures of the Louvre. (Tiny Folios Ser.). (Illus.). 384p. 1997. 11.95 (*0-7892-0406-1*) Abbeville Pr.

Laclotte, Michel, ed. Les Avions Vol. 1: Des Origines a la Premiere Guerre Mondiale. (FRE.). 480p. 1984. pap. 32.95 (*0-7859-4828-7*) Fr & Eur.

Laclotte, Michel & Cuzin, Jean-Pierre. The Louvre: European Painting. LC 82-61016. (Illus.). 256p. 1983. 40.00 (*0-935748-49-0*) Scala Books.

— The Louvre: European Paintings. (Illus.). 288p. 1997. 40.00 (*1-85759-026-0*) Scala Books.

Laclotte, Michel, jt. auth. see Ziegler.

Laco, V. I. English - Czech, Czech - English Dictionary. 576p. 1993. 39.95 (*0-8288-8454-4*) Fr & Eur.

Lacob, Miriam, jt. auth. see Stix, Gary.

Lacobucci, Ed. OS/2 Programmer's Guide, Vol. 1. 2nd ed. 1990. pap. text 29.95 (*0-07-881533-9*) McGraw.

Lacocque, Andre, jt. auth. see Ricoeur, Paul.

***LaCocque, Andre C.** Romance She Wrote: A Hermeneutical Essay on Song of Songs. LC 98-9421. 256p. 1998. pap. 19.00 (*1-56338-233-4*) TPI PA.

Lacoe, Addie. One, Two, & Three: What Does Each One See? (Illus.). 32p. (J). (gr. k-3). 1995. lib. bdg. 21.40 (*1-56294-523-8*) Millbrook Pr.

Lacoff, Cheryl K., ed. Parapsychology, New Age & the Occult - A Source Encyclopedia. 526p. 1994. 80.00 (*1-879583-01-1*); pap. 24.95 (*1-879583-00-3*) Ref Pr Intl.

— Who's Who in the Peace Corps. 725p. 1994. 95.00 (*1-879583-03-8*); pap. 75.00 (*1-879583-02-X*) Ref Pr Intl.

Lacoff, Cheryl Klein, see Klein Lacoff, Cheryl, ed.

Lacoius-Petruccelli, A. Perinatal Asphyxia. (Illus.). 188p. (C). 1987. text 65.00 (*0-306-42358-8*, Kluwer Plenum) Kluwer Academic.

Lacomara, Aelred, ed. The Language of the Cross. 149p. 1977. 5.95 (*0-8199-0617-4*, Frncscn Herld) Franciscan Pr.

Lacomba, E. A. & Llibre, J. Hamilton System & Celestial Mechanics. (Advanced Series in Nonlinear Dynamics). 216p. 1993. text 78.00 (*981-02-1370-0*) World Scientific Pub.

Lacombe, Aimee. Delos: Island of Light. 399p. 1999. 21.95 (*0-9662061-5-0*) Mnstne Pub.

Lacombe, D. J. Reliability Control for Electrical Systems. LC 99-14996. (Electrical Engineering & Electronics Ser.). (Illus.). 344p. 1999. text 150.00 (*0-8247-9958-5*) Dekker.

Lacombe, Dany. Blue Politics: Pornography & the Law in the Age of Feminism. 288p. (C). 1994. text 50.00 (*0-8020-2854-3*); pap. text 18.95 (*0-8020-7352-2*) U of Toronto Pr.

Lacombe, Dany, jt. ed. see Chunn, Dorothy E.

Lacombe de Prezel, Honore. Dictionnaire Iconologique. (FRE.). 1972. write for info. (*0-7859-8042-3*, 2-8266-0209-8) Fr & Eur.

Lacombe, G., jt. auth. see Hirsch, Francis.

***LaCombe, Herve.** The Keys to French Opera in the Nineteenth Century: Bizet & the Search for Stylistic Mobility. LC 00-29869. (Illus.). 442p. 2001. 40.00 (*0-520-21719-5*, Pub. by U CA Pr) Cal Prin Full Svc.

Lacombe, J. M., et al. English Style Skill-Builders: A Self-Improvement Program for Information Processors. 4th ed. 308p. 1985. text 17.12 (*0-07-011317-3*) McGraw.

Lacombe, J. M., jt. auth. see Cleary, J. B.

LaCombe, Joan, jt. auth. see Fruehling, Rosemary T.

***Lacombe, Michael & Paquette, Yanick.** Harem Nights Collection. (Eros Graphic Novels Ser.: Vol. 39). (Illus.). 112p. 1999. pap. 14.95 (*1-56097-354-4*, Eros Comics) Fantagraph Bks.

LaCombe, Michael A. Medicine Made Clear: House Calls from a Maine Country Doctor. Francis, Edward L., ed. (Illus.). 400p. 1989. 21.95 (*0-9623199-0-2*) Dirigo Bks.

***LaCombe, Michael A.** On Being a Doctor II: Voices of Physicians & Patients. LC 99-40565. 363p. 1999. 26.00 (*0-943126-82-7*) Amer Coll Phys.

LaCombe, Michael A. The Pocket Doctor: 500 Medical Tips You Need to Stay Healthy & Calm Your Fears. LC 96-7960. 374p. (Orig.). 1996. pap. 5.95 (*0-8362-2166-4*) Andrews & McMeel.

LaCombe, Michael A., ed. On Being a Doctor. 192p. 1995. reprint ed. pap. 18.00 (*0-943126-65-7*) Amer Coll Phys.

Lacombe, Michele, jt. ed. see Lennox, John.

Lacome, Julie. I'm a Jolly Farmer. LC 92-47374. (Illus.). 32p. (J). (ps up). 1994. 13.95 (*1-56402-318-4*) Candlewick Pr.

— I'm a Jolly Farmer. LC 92-47374. 1996. 11.19 (*0-606-09453-9*, Pub. by Turtleback) Demco.

— I'm a Jolly Farmer. LC 92-47374. (Illus.). 32p. (J). (ps-3). 1996. reprint ed. pap. 5.99 (*1-56402-839-9*) Candlewick Pr.

***Lacome, Julie.** Ruthie's Big Old Coat. LC 99-28785. 32p. (J). 2000. 13.99 (*0-7636-0969-2*) Candlewick Pr.

Lacome, Julie. Walking Through the Jungle. LC 98-53018. (Reading Together Ser.). (Illus.). 32p. (J). 1999. pap. write for info. (*0-7636-0876-9*) Candlewick Pr.

— Walking Through the Jungle. 1995. 10.19 (*0-606-08349-9*, Pub. by Turtleback) Demco.

Lacome, Julie. Noah's Ark. (Sticker Stories Ser.). 16p. (J). (ps-1). 1996. pap. text 4.99 (*0-448-41256-X*, G & D) Peng Put Young Read.

Lacome, Susie. Easy Country Crafts. LC 98-85571. 128p. 1998. pap. 24.95 (*0-8230-4804-7*) Watsn-Guptill.

Lacon Watson, E. H. Lectures to Living Authors. LC 68-54354. (Essay Index Reprint Ser.). 1977. 19.95 (*0-8369-0603-9*) Ayer.

Laconi. Fundamentals of Professional. 1995. pap. text, teacher ed. write for info. (*0-471-30621-5*) Wiley.

Laconi, Donald V. Fundamentals of Professional Food Preparation: A Laboratory Text-Workbook. 192p. 1995. pap., teacher ed. 54.95 (*0-471-59523-3*) Wiley.

Laconia Historical Society Staff, jt. auth. see Huse, Warren D.

LaConte, Ellen. On Light Alone: A Guru Meditation on the Good Death of Helen Nearing. (Illus.). 125p. 2000. pap. 13.00 (*0-9656077-0-4*, Pub. by Loose Leaf) Chelsea Green Pub.

LaConte, Ellen, ed. see Hall, Bolton.

LaConte, Greg. Well Versed in Business: Straight Talk Can You Relate? (Illus.). 128p. 1994. pap. 10.00 (*0-9642872-0-X*) LaConte & Assocs.

LaConte, P. & Haines, Y. Y. Water Resources & Land-Use Planning: A Systems Approach. 1982. lib. bdg. 191.50 (*90-247-2726-X*) Kluwer Academic.

LaConte, P., et al. Human & Energy Factors: Factors in Urban Planning; A Systems Approach. 1982. 50.00 (*90-247-2688-3*) Kluwer Academic.

Laconte, Pierre, ed. see World Environment & Resources Council (WERC) Staff.

***LaCook, Lewis.** Cling. (Poetry Chapbks.: No. 5). 60p. 2000. pap. 8.00 (*1-930259-04-2*) Anabasis.

Lacoque, A. & Vasquez, F. R. The Newcomer & the Bible. 24p. 1971. 3.00 (*0-913256-46-3*) CMS.

Lacordaire, Henry D. Henri Dominique Lacordaire: Essay on the Re-establishment in France of the Order of Preachers. Tugwell, Simon, ed. (Dominican Sources in English Ser.). 70p. 1983. pap. 4.00 (*0-9511202-1-2*, Pub. by Dominican Sources) Parable.

Lacoren, Nestor R. The New Woman: A Tribute to Mercedes Sosa. Latin Culture Productions Staff, ed. LC 90-61383. (ENG & SPA., Illus.). 150p. (Orig.). 1990. pap. 14.95 (*0-9627004-0-1*) Latin Cul Prod.

LaCosse-Kennedy, Jean. Tau. 1998. pap. write for info. (*1-57553-874-1*) Watermrk Pr.

Lacosta, Francisco C., ed. see Poncela, Enrique J.

Lacoste, Auguste. Henri Arnaud und die Waldenser. (Basler und Berner Studien zur Historischen und Systematischen Theologie: Vol. 47). 216p. 1982. 31.00 (*3-261-04890-5*) P Lang Pubng.

Lacoste, Elaine. Street Names & Picayune Histories of New Orleans. LC 96-80319. 34 p. 1997. write for info. (*0-9656409-0-6*) Hoolauna Hl.

Lacoste, J. Dictionnaire Critique Theologie. (FRE.). 1998. 395.00 (*0-320-00405-8*) Fr & Eur.

Lacoste, Yves. Dictionnaire de Geopolitique. (FRE.). 1679p. 1993. 185.00 (*0-7859-8616-2*, 208035101x) Fr & Eur.

— Dictionnaire de Geopolitique. (FRE.). 1728p. 1995. 225.00 (*0-7859-9241-3*) Fr & Eur.

Lacoue-Labarthe, Philippe. Musica Ficta: Figures of Wagner. LC 94-15594. xxvi, 161p. 1995. 35.00 (*0-8047-2376-1*) Stanford U Pr.

— Poetry As Experience. Tarnowski, Andrea, tr. LC 98-33880. (Meridian Ser.). 180p. 1998. 39.50 (*0-8047-3426-7*) Stanford U Pr.

— Poetry As Experience. Tarnowski, Andrea, tr. LC 98-33880. (Meridian Ser.). 180p. 1999. pap. 14.95 (*0-8047-3427-5*) Stanford U Pr.

— The Subject of Philosophy. Trezise, Thomas et al, trs. LC 92-29837. (Theory & History of Literature Ser.: Vol. 83). (ENG & FRE.). 232p. (C). 1993. pap. 19.95 (*0-8166-1698-1*); text 49.95 (*0-8166-1697-3*) U of Minn Pr.

Lacoue-Labarthe, Philippe & Fynsk, Christopher. Typography: Mimesis, Philosophy, Politics. LC 97-41649. (Meridian Crossing Aesthetics Ser.). 1998. pap. write for info. (*0-8047-3282-5*) Stanford U Pr.

Lacoue-Labarthe, Philippe & Nancy, Jean-Luc. The Literary Absolute. Barnard, Philip & Lester, Cheryl, trs. from FRE. LC 87-10047. (SUNY Series, Intersections: Philosophy & Critical Theory). 169p. (C). 1988. pap. text 19.95 (*0-88706-661-5*) State U NY Pr.

— The Literary Absolute: The Theory of Literature in German Romanticism. Barnard, Philip & Lester, Cheryl, trs. from FRE. LC 87-10047. (SUNY Series, Intersections: Philosophy & Critical Theory). 169p. (C). 1988. text 59.50 (*0-88706-660-7*) State U NY Pr.

Lacoue-Labarthe, Philippe, jt. auth. see Nancy, Jean-Luc.

Lacoue-Labarthe, Phillipe. Typography: Mimesis, Philosophy, Politics. Fynsk, Christopher, ed. LC 88-36989. 312p. 1989. 47.95 (*0-674-91700-6*) HUP.

Lacoue-Labarthe, Phillippe, jt. auth. see Nancy, Jean-Luc.

Lacour, Barbara B. Called to Action: The Knights of Columbus in Louisiana, 1962-1992. Gomez, Irvon J. et al, eds. LC 94-76030. (Illus.). 480p. 1994. 28.00 (*0-9640808-1-8*) LA St Council.

Lacour, Christian. Dictionnaire des Noms Propres de l'Academie de Nimes. (FRE.). 155p. 1990. pap. 105.00 (*0-7859-8168-3*, 2869712324) Fr & Eur.

Lacour, Claudia B. Lines of Thought: Discourse, Architectonics, & the Origin of Modern Philosophy. LC 95-40105. 176p. 1996. text 49.95 (*0-8223-1777-X*); pap. text 16.95 (*0-8223-1774-5*) Duke.

Lacour, Claudia Brodsky, jt. ed. see Morrison, Toni.

Lacour, Jean-Pierre. Lexique du Marketing. 128p. 1993. pap. 19.95 (*0-7859-5641-7*, 2735208230) Fr & Eur.

Lacour, Nicole, et al. Dictionnaire Francais-Pyreneen, Pyreneen-Francais. (FRE.). 1991. write for info. (*0-7859-8170-5*, 2-86971-317-7) Fr & Eur.

LaCourse, Donald E., ed. The Handbook of Solid Modeling. LC 95-4022. 512p. 1995. 89.50 (*0-07-035788-9*) McGraw.

LaCourse, Jon, jt. auth. see Haynes, J. H.

Lacourse, William R. Pulsed Electrochemical Detection in High Performance Liquid Chromatography. LC 97-548. (Techniques in Analytical Chemistry Ser.). 352p. 1997. 79.95 (*0-471-11914-8*) Wiley.

Lacoursiere, Roy B. The Life Cycle of Groups: Group Developmental Stage Theory. LC 79-27112. 317p. 1980. 42.95 (*0-87705-469-X*, Kluwer Acad Hman Sci) Kluwer Academic.

Lacoutre, Jean, tr. see Friedlander, Saul & Hussein, Mahmoud.

Lacouture, Jean. De Gaulle: The Rebel 1890-1944. O'Brian, Patrick, tr. (Illus.). 640p. 1993. pap. 15.95 (*0-393-30999-1*) Norton.

— De Gaulle: The Rebel 1890-1944, Vol. 1. O'Brian, Patrick & Sheridan, Alan, trs. 1990. 29.95 (*0-393-02699-X*) Norton.

— Jesuits: A Multibiography. (Illus.). 560p. 1997. pap. 18.50 (*1-887178-60-0*, Pub. by Counterpt DC) HarpC.

— Leon Blum. Holoch, George, tr. from FRE. LC 81-20083. 571p. 1982. 49.95 (*0-8419-0775-7*); pap. 29.50 (*0-8419-0776-5*) Holmes & Meier.

— Pierre Mendes France. Holoch, George, tr. LC 84-10912. (FRE.). 494p. 1984. 45.00 (*0-8419-0856-7*) Holmes & Meier.

— Sports Heroes. (Illus.). 200p. 1998. pap. 12.95 (*2-85025-569-6*) Dist Art Pubs.

Lacovara, Peter. Deir El-Ballas: Preliminary Report on the Deir el-Ballas Expedition, 1980-1986. (American Research Center in Egypt, Reports: Vol. 12). (Illus.). x, 67p. 1990. text 31.50 (*0-936770-24-4*, Pub. by Amer Res Ctr Egypt) Eisenbrauns.

— The New Kingdom Royal City. LC 96-11773. (Studies in Egyptology). 282p. 1996. 161.50 (*0-7103-0544-3*, Pub. by Kegan Paul Intl) Col U Pr.

Lacovetta, Franca. Such Hardworking People: Italian Immigrants in Postwar Toronto. (Illus.). 336p. 1992. 65.00 (*0-7735-0874-0*, Pub. by McG-Queens Univ Pr) CUP Services.

Lacquinniti, Francesco & Viviani, Paolo, eds. Neural Bases of Motor Behaviour: Proceedings of the NATO Advanced Study Institute on Multi-Sensory Control of Movement, Trieste, Italy, 3-12 July 1994. (NATO Advanced Science Institutes: Series D, Vol. 85). 356p. (C). 1996. text 180.50 (*0-7923-4009-4*) Kluwer Academic.

Lacret-Subirat, Fabian. American Middle & Jr. High Schools Math Basic Skills: Solved Problems. (Illus.). 68p. (J). (gr. 7-8). 1997. pap. 13.33 (*0-943144-37-X*) Lacret Pub.

— American Middle & Jr. High Schools Math Basic Skills Workbook. (Illus.). 186p. (J). (gr. 7-8). 1997. pap., wbk. ed. 12.00 (*0-943144-35-3*) Lacret Pub.

— High School Math Basic Skills. (Illus.). 236p. (YA). (gr. 9-11). 1997. pap., wbk. ed. 12.00 (*0-943144-36-1*) Lacret Pub.

— High School Math Basic Skills: Solved Problems. (Illus.). 100p. (YA). (gr. 9-11). 1997. pap. 13.33 (*0-943144-38-8*) Lacret Pub.

— Lacret 8th Grade Early Warning Test (EWT) - Math Basic Skills Workbook. (Illus.). 186p. (J). (gr. 7-8). 1996. pap., wbk. ed. 12.00 (*0-943144-34-5*) Lacret Pub.

— Lacret 11th Grade High School Proficiency Test (HSPT) - Math Skills Workbook. (Illus.). 252p. (YA). (gr. 9-11). 1995. pap., wbk. ed. 12.00 (*0-943144-32-9*) Lacret Pub.

***Lacret-Subirat, Fabian.** Lacret HS-Math Self-Tutoring (Solving Word-Problems) (Illus.). 220p. (YA). (gr. 9-12). 2000. pap. 32.00 (*0-943144-45-0*) Lacret Pub.

Lacret-Subirat, Fabian. Lacret 11th Grade High School Proficiency Test (HSPT) - Math Skills Solved Problems: Solved Problems. (Illus.). 70p. (YA). (gr. 9-11). 1997. pap. 13.33 (*0-943144-39-6*) Lacret Pub.

— Mastering Math Basic Skills Workbook. (Illus.). 251p. (J). (gr. 7). 1987. pap. 8.48 (*0-943144-21-3*) Lacret Pub.

Lacroix, A., ed. see Shenoi, B. A.

Lacroix, A., ed. see Smirnov, Alexandre J.

Lacroix, A., ed. see Venetsanopoulos, A. & Plataniotis, K.

Lacroix, Arild & Witte, Karl-Heinz. Design Tables for Discrete Time Normalized Low-Pass Filters. LC 86-70818. (Artech House Microwave Library). 303p. 1986. reprint ed. pap. 94.00 (*0-608-01415-X*, 206217800002) Bks Demand.

Lacroix, Christian. Pieces of a Pattern: Lacroix by Lacroix. Mauries, Patrick, ed. LC 92-60343. (Illus.). 192p. 1997. pap. 34.95 (*0-500-27933-0*, Pub. by Thames Hudson) Norton.

LaCroix, Darren, jt. auth. see Segel, Rick.

Lacroix, Eric & Wells, Linton. Japanese Cruisers of the Pacific War. LC 90-30887. (Illus.). 904p. 1997. 89.95 (*0-87021-311-3*) Naval Inst Pr.

Lacroix, Hendrik. The Optimal Surgical Approach for Elective Reconstruction of the Infra- & Juxta-Renal Abdominal Aorta: A Randomised Prospective Study. (Acta Biomedica Lovaniensia Ser.: No. 157). 127p. 1997. pap. 37.50 (*90-6186-841-6*, Pub. by Almqvist Wiksell) Coronet Bks.

Lacroix-Hopson, Eliane, compiled by. Abdul-Baha in New York, the City of the Covenant. rev. enl. ed. LC 99-20286. 1999. pap. 7.95 (*0-87961-255-X*) Naturegraph.

LaCroix, Jean, jt. auth. see Carmona, Rene.

Lacroix, Jean-Michel, jt. ed. see Remie, Cornelius H.

Lacroix, M., jt. auth. see Magnien, Victor.

LaCroix, Mary. The Remnant. 6th ed. LC 80-69604. 535p. 1987. reprint ed. pap. 14.95 (*0-87604-201-9*, 544) ARE Pr.

LaCroix, Michael J. Minitex & Illinet: Two Library Networks. (Occasional Papers: No. 178). 1987. pap. 2.50 (*0-685-34541-6*) U of Ill Grad Sch.

Lacroix, Nitya. The Art of Tantric Sex. LC 96-33597. 144p. 1997. 24.95 (*0-7894-1477-5*) DK Pub Inc.

LaCroix, Nitya. Book of Massage & Aromatherapy. (Illus.). 160p. 1996. 16.99 (*0-517-10256-0*) Random Hse Value.

— Learn Massage in a Weekend. LC 92-53046. 1992. 16.00 (*0-679-41675-7*) Knopf.

LaCroix, Nitya. Massage. (101 Essential Tips Ser.). (Illus.). 72p. 1995. pap. 4.95 (*1-56458-990-0*) DK Pub Inc.

***Lacroix, Nitya.** Massage, Aromatherapy & Yoga. (Practical Handbook Ser.). 1999. pap. 12.95 (*0-7548-0023-7*, Lorenz Bks) Anness Pub.

LaCroix, Nitya. Sensual Massage. LC 90-4101. 128p. (Orig.). 1995. pap. 15.95 (*0-8050-1231-1*, Owl) H Holt & Co.

***Lacroix, Nitya & Gallagher-Mundy, Chrissie.** Relaxation: An Illustrated Programme of Exercises, Techniques & Meditations. (Illus.). 128p. 2000. reprint ed. pap. text 17.00 (*0-7881-9135-7*) DIANE Pub.

Lacroix, Nitya, ed. see Gallagher-Mundy, Chrissie.

Lacroix, Richard, jt. auth. see Christensen, Garry.

LaCroix, W. L. Four Questions on Persons: A Philosophical Dialectic. LC 81-43510. 214p. (Orig.). 1982. pap. text 26.50 (*0-8191-2094-4*) U Pr of Amer.

— War & International Ethics: Tradition & Today. 316p. (Orig.). (C). 1988. pap. text 26.00 (*0-8191-6708-8*); lib. bdg. 51.00 (*0-8191-6707-X*) U Pr of Amer.

Lacron-Foster, jt. auth. see Rubenstein.

LaCrosse, John. Randy. 224p. 1980. 10.95 (*0-932282-47-4*) Caledonia Pr.

— The Story of Ch'ing. 1979. pap. 3.00 (*0-932282-46-6*) Caledonia Pr.

LaCrosse, Richard B., Jr. The Frontier Rifleman. 1989. pap. 17.50 (*0-913150-57-6*) Pioneer Pr.

Lacroux, Jean-Pierre, jt. auth. see Haury, Pierre.

Lacson, Christopher, ed. & illus. see Lacson, John M. & Carrothers, Scott.

Lacson, Daniel L., Jr. The Philippines Yesterday, Today & Tomorrow: Political & Socio-Economic Developments. (Institute for Policy Studies Regional Speakers Lecture Ser.). 40p. 1991. 5.50 (*981-210-004-0*, Pub. by Times Academic) Intl Spec Bk.

Lacson, John M. & Carrothers, Scott. So You're Going to Be a House Daddy: A Survival Manual for Happiness & Sanity in the Home. Lacson, Christopher, ed. & illus. by. (House Daddy Bks.). 64p. (Orig.). 1996. pap. 16.95 (*0-9656632-0-5*) HouseDaddies.

Lacson-Locsin, Ma. S., tr. see Rizal, Jose.

Lactantius. Divine Institutes, Bks. 1-7. McDonald, Mary F., tr. LC 64-18669. (Fathers of the Church Ser.: Vol. 49). 561p. 1964. 31.95 (*0-8132-0049-0*) Cath U Pr.

— Lactantius: De Mortibus Persecutorm. Creed, J. L., ed. (Oxford Early Christian Texts Ser.). 1985. 59.00 (*0-19-826813-0*) OUP.

— Minor Works. McDonald, Mary F., tr. LC 64-18669. (Fathers of the Church Ser.: Vol. 54). 245p. 1965. 17.95 (*0-8132-0054-7*) Cath U Pr.

Lacue, Juan J., tr. see Francisco, C. T.

LaCugna, Catherine M. God for Us: The Trinity & Christian Life. LC 91-55444. 448p. 1993. reprint ed. pap. 21.00 (*0-06-064913-5*, Pub. by Harper SF) HarpC.

LaCugna, Catherine M., ed. Freeing Theology: The Essentials of Theology in Feminist Perspective. LC 92-56129. 272p. 1993. pap. 18.00 (*0-06-064935-6*, Pub. by Harper SF) HarpC.

LaCugna, Charles S. An Introduction to Labor Arbitration. LC 88-5810. 292p. 1988. 62.95 (*0-275-93047-5*, C3047, Praeger Pubs) Greenwood.

LaCure, Jeffrey R. Adopted Like Me. 24p. (J). (ps-2). 1993. pap. 9.95 (*0-9635717-0-2*) Adoption Advocate.

— Remembering: Reflections of Growing up Adopted. 96p. (Orig.). 1995. pap. text 12.95 (*0-9635717-1-0*) Adoption Advocate.

Lacure, Jeffrey R., jt. auth. see Doucette-Dudman, Deborah.

LaCure, Jon. Rhetorical Devices of the Kokinshu: A Structural Analysis of Japanese Waka Poetry. LC 97-24083. (Japanese Studies: No. 4). 224p. 1997. text 89.95 (*0-7734-8510-4*) E Mellen.

Lacuria, Paul F. Les Harmonies De L'etre Exprimees Par les Nombres. LC 75-36848. (Occult Ser.). (FRE.). 1976. reprint ed. 60.95 (*0-405-07964-8*) Ayer.

Lacy. Silent Abduction. LC 98-48571. 1999. 30.00 (*0-7862-1747-2*) Thorndike Pr.

***Lacy, Al.** Battles of Destiny, 4 vols. 1999. spiral bd 19.99 (*1-57673-670-9*) Multnomah Pubs.

Lacy, Al. Beloved Enemy. (Battles of Destiny Ser.: Vol. 3). 356p. 1994. pap. 9.99 (*0-88070-809-3*, Multnomah Bks) Multnomah Pubs.

— Blizzard. LC 99-24867. 1999. pap. 23.95 (*0-7862-1947-5*) Mac Lib Ref.

— Blizzard, (Journeys of the Stranger Ser.: Vol. 3). 276p. 1995. pap. 9.99 (*0-88070-702-X*, Multnomah Bks) Multnomah Pubs.

— Captive Set Free. (Angel of Mercy Ser.: Vol. 3). 278p. 1996. pap. 10.99 (*0-88070-872-7*, Multnomah Bks) Multnomah Pubs.

***Lacy, Al.** Circle of Fire. LC 00-28801. (Journeys of the Stranger Ser.). 2000. write for info. (*0-7862-2571-8*) Five Star.

Lacy, Al. Circle of Fire. (Journeys of the Stranger Ser.: No. 5). 272p. 1996. pap. 9.99 (*0-88070-893-X*, Multnomah Bks) Multnomah Pubs.

— A Dream Fulfilled. (Angel of Mercy Ser.: Vol. 4). 273p. 1996. pap. 10.99 (*0-88070-940-5*, Multnomah Bks) Multnomah Pubs.

— Faithful Heart. LC 95-37377. (Angel of Mercy Ser.: Vol. 2). 307p. 1995. pap. 10.99 (*0-88070-835-2*, Multnomah Bks) Multnomah Pubs.

***Lacy, Al.** Far above Rubies. (Angel of Mercy Ser.: Vol. 10). 300p. 2000. pap. 10.99 (*1-57673-499-4*, Pub. by Multnomah Pubs) GL Services.

Lacy, Al. Final Justice. LC 98-5547. (Angel of Mercy Ser.: Vol. 7). 1998. pap. 10.99 (*1-57673-260-6*, Multnomah Fiction) Multnomah Pubs.

— A Heart Divided: Mobile Bay. (Battles of Destiny Ser.: Vol. 2). 320p. 1993. pap. 9.99 (*0-88070-591-4*, Multnomah Bks) Multnomah Pubs.

***Lacy, Al.** Journeys of the Stranger, 4 vols. 1999. boxed set 19.99 (*1-57673-671-7*) Multnomah Pubs.

Lacy, Al. Joy from Ashes: Fredericksburg. (Battles of Destiny Ser.: Vol. 5). 306p. 1995. pap. 9.99 (*0-88070-720-8*) Multnomah Pubs.

L

— Legacy. LC 98-39759. 1998. 22.95 (0-7862-1651-4) Thorndike Pr.

— Legacy, Vol. 1. (Journeys of the Stranger Ser.: Bk. 1). 320p. 1994. pap. 10.99 (0-88070-619-8, Multnomah Bks) Multnomah Pubs.

— Not by Might. (Angel of Mercy Ser.: Vol. 8). 350p. 1998. pap. 10.99 (1-57673-242-8, Multnomah Fiction) Multnomah Pubs.

— Pillow of Stone. LC 98-29213. (Hannah of Fort Bridger Ser.: Vol. 4). 306p. 1998. pap. 10.99 (1-57673-234-7, Multnomah Fiction) Multnomah Pubs.

— A Promise for Breanna. (Angel of Mercy Ser.: Vol. 1). 321p. 1985. pap. 10.99 (0-88070-797-6, Multnomah Bks) Multnomah Pubs.

— A Promise Unbroken: A Battle of Destiny. (Battles of Destiny Ser.: Vol. 1). 320p. 1993. pap. 9.99 (0-88070-581-7, Multnomah Bks) Multnomah Pubs.

— Quiet Thunder. LC 96-42351. (Journeys of the Stranger Ser.: Vol. 6). 248p. 1996. pap. 9.99 (0-88070-975-8, Multnomah Bks) Multnomah Pubs.

— Season of Valor: Gettysburg, Vol. 6. (Battles of Destiny Ser.: No. 6). 294p. 1996. pap. 9.99 (0-88070-865-4, Multnomah Bks) Multnomah Pubs.

— Secrets of the Heart. LC 98-19418. (Mail Order Bride Ser.: Vol. 1). 320p. pap. 10.99 (1-57673-278-9, Multnomah Fiction) Multnomah Pubs.

— Secrets of the Heart. large type ed. LC 98-53622. 1999. 24.95 (0-7862-1803-7) Thorndike Pr.

— Shadowed Memories: Shiloh. (Battles of Destiny Ser.: Vol. 4). 307p. 1995. pap. 9.99 (0-88070-657-0, Multnomah Bks) Multnomah Pubs.

— Silent Abduction: Journeys of the Stranger. (Journeys of the Stranger Ser.: Vol. 2). 320p. 1994. pap. 9.99 (0-88070-877-8, Multnomah Bks) Multnomah Pubs.

— Snow Ghost. LC 97-11834. (Journeys of the Stranger Ser.: Vol. 7). 300p. 1997. pap. 9.99 (1-57673-047-6, Multnomah Bks) Multnomah Pubs.

— Suffer the Little Children. LC 97-277. (Angel of Mercy Ser.: Vol. 5). 300p. 1997. pap. 10.99 (1-57673-039-5, Multnomah Bks) Multnomah Pubs.

— Tears of the Sun. (Journeys of the Stranger Ser.: Vol.4). 270p. 1995. pap. 9.99 (0-88070-838-7, Multnomah Bks) Multnomah Pubs.

***Lacy, Al.** Tears of the Sun. (Christian Fiction Ser.). 2000. 24.95 (0-7862-2446-0) Thorndike Pr.

Lacy, Al. Things Not Seen. LC 99-24570. (Angel of Mercy Ser.: Vol. 9). 320p. 1999. pap. 10.99 (1-57673-413-7) Multnomah Pubs.

— Turn of Glory. LC 97-48890. (Battles of Destiny Ser.: Vol. 8). 300p. 1998. pap. 9.99 (1-57673-217-7) Multnomah Pubs.

— Whither Thou Goest. LC 97-29863. (Angel of Mercy Ser.: Vol. 6). 300p. 1997. pap. 10.99 (1-57673-078-6, Multnomah Bks) Multnomah Pubs.

***Lacy, Al & Lacy, JoAnna.** Beyond the Valley. (Hannah of Fort Bridger Ser.: Vol. 7). 2000. pap. 10.99 (1-57673-618-0, Pub. by Multnomah Pubs) GL Services.

— Blessed Are the Merciful. LC 99-34878. (Mail Order Bride Ser.: Vol. 4). 300p. 1999. pap. 10.99 (1-57673-417-X) Multnomah Pubs.

***Lacy, Al & Lacy, Joanna.** Blessed Are the Merciful. large type ed. (Christian Fiction Ser.). 2000. 26.95 (0-7862-2520-3) Thorndike Pr.

Lacy, Al & Lacy, Joanna. Consider the Lilies, Vol. 2. LC 97-17922. (Hannah of Fort Bridger Ser.: Vol. 2). 300p. 1997. pap. 10.99 (1-57673-049-2, Multnomah Bks) Multnomah Pubs.

Lacy, Al & Lacy, JoAnna. No Place for Fear, LC 97-32512. (Hannah of Fort Bridger Ser.: Vol. 3). 300p. 1998. pap. 10.99 (1-57673-083-2, Multnomah Fiction) Multnomah Pubs.

— The Perfect Gift. LC 99-11742. (Hannah of Fort Bridger Ser.: Vol. 5). 300p. 1999. pap. text 10.99 (1-57673-407-2) Multnomah Pubs.

***Lacy, Al & Lacy, JoAnna.** Ransom of Love. (Mail Order Bride Ser.: Vol. 5). 300p. 2000. pap. 10.99 (1-57673-609-1, Pub. by Multnomah Pubs) GL Services.

Lacy, Al & Lacy, JoAnna. The Tender Flame. LC 98-53481. (Mail Order Bride Ser.: Vol. 3). 1999. pap. 10.99 (1-57673-399-8) Multnomah Pubs.

***Lacy, Al & Lacy, JoAnna.** The Tender Flame. large type ed. LC 99-38786. 1999. 23.95 (0-7862-2156-9) Mac Lib Ref.

Lacy, Al & Lacy, JoAnna. A Time to Love. LC 98-19240. (Mail Order Bride Ser.: Vol. 2). 312p. 1998. pap. 10.99 (1-57673-284-3) Multnomah Pubs.

— A Time to Love. large type ed. LC 99-33152. 1999. pap. 24.95 (0-7862-2052-X) Mac Lib Ref.

— Touch of Compassion. LC 99-40168. (Hannah of Fort Bridger Ser.: Vol. 6). 320p. 1999. pap. 10.99 (1-57673-422-6) Multnomah Pubs.

***Lacy, Al & Lacy, JoAnna.** Until the Daybreak. (Mail Order Bride Ser.: No. 6). 2000. pap. 10.99 (1-57673-624-5) Multnomah Pubs.

Lacy, Al & Lacy, Lew A. Wings of the Wind. LC 96-46777. (Battles of Destiny Ser.: No. 7). 300p. 1997. pap. 9.99 (1-57673-032-8, Multnomah Bks) Multnomah Pubs.

Lacy, Al, et al. Under the Distant Sky. LC 96-40158. (Hannah of Fort Bridger Ser.: Vol. 1). 274p. 1997. pap. 10.99 (1-57673-033-6, Multnomah Bks) Multnomah Pubs.

Lacy, Alan C., jt. auth. see Hastad, Douglas N.

Lacy, Alex B., Jr., ed. Power in American State Legislatures, Vol. 11. LC 74-216. 1966. 11.00 (0-930598-10-5) Tulane Stud Pol.

— Power in American State Legislatures: The Case Studies of the Arkansas, Louisiana, Mississippi, & Oklahoma Legislatures. LC 74-216. (Tulane Studies in Political Science: No. 11). 187p. Date not set. reprint ed. pap. 58.00 (0-608-20655-5, 207209200003) Bks Demand.

Lacy, Allen. American Gardener. 1990. pap. 10.95 (0-374-52217-0) FS&G.

Lacy, Allen. Farther Afield: A Gardener's Excursions. 273p. 1986. text 17.95 (0-374-15355-8) FS&G.

Lacy, Allen. Farther Afield: A Gardener's Excursions. 288p. 1988. pap. 8.95 (0-374-52063-1) FS&G.

— The Garden in Autumn. 88p. 1995. pap. 25.00 (0-8050-4067-6) H Holt & Co.

— The Gardener's Eyes & Other Essays. LC 95-1574. 304p. 1995. pap. 14.95 (0-8050-3952-X) H Holt & Co.

— The Glory of Roses. LC 90-34496. (Illus.). 240p. 1990. 50.00 (1-55670-155-1) Stewart Tabori & Chang.

— The Glory of Roses. (Illus.). 240p. 1999. pap. 27.50 (1-55670-448-8) Stewart Tabori & Chang.

— Home Ground: A Gardener's Miscellany. 1995. 22.00 (0-8446-6864-8) Peter Smith.

***Lacy, Allen.** In a Green Shade: Writings from Homeground. LC 99-86379. (Illus.). 304p. 2000. 24.00 (0-618-00378-9) HM.

Lacy, Allen. The Inviting Garden: Gardening for the Senses, Mind, & Spirit. LC 97-27539. 1995. write for info. (0-8050-3742-X) H Holt & Co.

Lacy, Allen, ed. The American Gardener: A Sampler. LC 87-37965. 324p. 1988. text 18.95 (0-374-10404-2) FS&G.

Lacy, Allen, ed. see Lawrence, Elizabeth.

***Lacy, Ann.** Concorde. 450p. 2000. pap. 10.00 (0-939965-16-X) Macedon Prod.

Lacy, Barbara L. Cooking with Beer: In the Spirit of Things. (Illus.). 56p. 1987. pap. 5.95 (0-9617721-0-7) Golightly Pubns.

— From Grandma Lacy's Kitchen. (Illus.). 105p. 1989. spiral bd. 6.95 (0-9617721-1-5) Golightly Pubns.

— The Life & (Cooking) Times of an American Missionary in India: Recipes & Adventures of Rosetta Gempler Bell. (Illus.). 60p. 1993. pap. text 5.95 (0-9617721-2-3) Golightly Pubns.

— Texas Trash: And Other Great Recipes from Good Friends in the Lone Star State. (Illus.). 123p. (Orig.). 1991. spiral bd. 6.95 (0-9617721-3-1) Golightly Pubns.

Lacy, Bill & DeMenil, Susan, eds. Angels & Franciscans: Innovative Architecture from Los Angeles & San Francisco. LC 92-19583. (Illus.). 126p. 1992. pap. 29.95 (0-8478-1630-3) Gagosian Gallery.

Lacy, Brian. Siege City: The Story of Derry & Londonderry. (Town History Ser.). 288p. (Orig.). 1990. pap. 26.00 (0-85640-443-8, Pub. by Blackstaff Pr) Dufour.

Lacy, C. Rosary Novenas. 1974. pap. 2.74 (0-02-645810-1) Macmillan.

Lacy, Charles. Drug Information Handbook, 1998-99. 6th ed. 1600p. 1998. pap. text 38.75 (0-916589-66-8) Lexi-Comp.

Lacy, Charles, et al. Drug Information Handbook: Pocket Edition. 3rd ed. (Clinical Reference Library). 1300p. 1998. pap. 33.75 (0-916589-67-6) Lexi-Comp.

***Lacy, Charles F.** Drug Information Handbook: 1999-2000, Vol. 1. 7th ed. 1999. pap. text 41.95 (0-916589-76-5) Lexi-Comp.

— Drug Information Handbook 1999-2000. (Illus.). 1999. pap. 35.95 (0-916589-77-3) Lexi-Comp.

Lacy, Claud H. Astronomy Laboratory Exercises. (Illus.). 96p. 1981. 17.95 (0-8403-8322-3) Kendall-Hunt.

Lacy, Creighton B. The Word-Carrying Giant: The Growth of the American Bible Society. LC 77-22655. 311p. 1977. pap. 6.95 (0-87808-425-8) William Carey Lib.

Lacy, Dan. From Grunts to Gigabytes: Communications & Society. 192p. 1996. 14.95 (0-252-06531-X); text 29.95 (0-252-02228-9) U of Ill Pr.

Lacy, Dan M. Freedom & Communications. 2nd ed. LC 65-19107. 122p. reprint ed. pap. 37.90 (0-8357-6120-7, 203445000090) Bks Demand.

Lacy, Donald C. Healing Echoes: Values for Christian Unity. Sherer, Michael L., ed. (Orig.). 1986. pap. 6.75 (0-89536-826-9, 6835) CSS OH.

— Jewels from John. (Orig.). 1993. pap. 4.95 (1-55673-531-6) CSS OH.

***Lacy, Donald Charles.** A Taste of Glory: Explorations into John 6:53-58. 55p. 2000. pap. 4.95 (0-7880-1495-1, Fairway Pr) CSS OH.

Lacy, Donna, jt. auth. see Guy, Suzanne.

Lacy, E. Readings on Historical Method. 1969. pap. text 10.95 (0-8290-1180-3) Irvington.

Lacy, Ed, ed. see Gongola, Len.

Lacy, Edward A. & Hoss, Robert J. Fiber Optics. 2nd ed. LC 92-42130. (C). 1993. text 42.80 (0-13-321241-6) P-H.

Lacy, Eric R. Antebellum Tennessee. 314p. 1980. pap. 10.95 (0-932807-06-2) Overmountain Pr.

Lacy, Ernest. Chatterton. Mollo, Michele, ed. (Illus.). 34p. 1998. reprint ed. pap. 12.99 (1-892355-00-0) Fifth Season.

Lacy, Ernest Edward. Search for FreeJoe, 1. 1999. pap. text 24.95 (0-9669076-0-4) Freejoe Pubns.

Lacy, Gary. Head Start Social Services: How African American Mothers Use & Perceive Them. rev. ed. LC 99-41203. (Children of Poverty Ser.). 136p. 1999. 40.00 (0-8153-3384-6) Garland.

— The Mark. 48p. 2000. pap. 8.00 (0-8059-4832-5) Dorrance.

Lacy, George W., jt. auth. see Barzelay, Martin E.

Lacy, Gerald M., ed. see Lawrence, D. H.

Lacy, Harold R. The Complete Guide to Financing a Small Business: How to Finance Your Business Dreams with Other People's Money. Date not set. pap. 19.95 (1-890439-02-9) Money Inst.

— Financing Your Business Dreams with Other People's Money: How & Where to Find Money for Start-Up & Growing Businesses. LC 97-76470. 224p. 1998. pap. 15.95 (1-890394-11-4, Sage Creek) Rhodes & Easton.

Lacy, Hermagene P. The Descendants of Frederick & Caroline Palenske of Wabaunsee County, Kansas. (Illus.). vii, 225p. text 20.00 (0-938717-50-2) Shumway Family Hist.

Lacy, Jack. S. H. O. R. T. S. Some Humorous Opinions Regarding Today's Society. Gilliland, Mary E., ed. (Illus.). 120p. (Orig.). 1995. pap. 9.95 (0-9643918-0-5) Triple J Pr.

Lacy, James A. Systems Engineering Management: Achieving Total Quality. 336p. 1991. 36.95 (0-8306-2304-3) McGraw-Hill Prof.

— Systems Engineering Management: Achieving Total Quality. LC 91-21576. (Illus.). 336p. 1995. reprint ed. text 70.00 (0-9644627-0-2) J Lacy Consult.

Lacy, JoAnna, jt. auth. see Lacy, Al.

Lacy, Joe. Prescription for Life. LC 98-107142. 160p. 1997. 5.99 (0-310-97375-9) Zondervan.

Lacy, John. Discover Love: Finding the Marriage that Works. 200p. 1999. pap. 13.95 (1-893075-03-6) Spirit Pr OR.

— Dramatic Works of John Lacy, Comedian. Maidment, James & Logan, W. H., eds. LC 67-18423. 1972. reprint ed. 24.95 (0-405-08722-5) Ayer.

Lacy, John C., jt. auth. see Miranda, Fausto C.

Lacy, John F. The Remington 700: A History & User's Manual. LC 89-91161. (Illus.). 208p. 1989. 44.95 (0-9622303-0-8) J F Lacy.

Lacy, Laurie. Black Spirit: The Way of the Crow. (Illus.). 104p. (Orig.). 1996. pap. 12.95 (1-55109-152-6) Nimbus Publ.

Lacy, Lew A., jt. auth. see Lacy, Al.

Lacy, M., ed. Understanding Computer Systems Architecture. 400p. (C). 1991. 75.00 (1-870941-81-0) St Mut.

Lacy, Madison S. & Morgan, Don. Hollywood Cheesecake. (Illus.). 288p. 1983. reprint ed. pap. 19.95 (0-8065-0830-2, Citadel Pr) Carol Pub Group.

Lacy, Margaret S., tr. & afterword by see Martinson, Moa.

Lacy, Margriet B., ed. The Low Countries: Multidisciplinary Studies. LC 89-24778. (Publications of the American Association for Netherlandic Studies: Vol. 3). (Illus.). 266p. (C). 1990. lib. bdg. 45.00 (0-8191-7587-0) U Pr of Amer.

Lacy, Marie L. Know Yourself Through Color. rev. ed. 1987. pap. 24.00 (0-85030-825-9, Pub. by Aqrn Pr) Harper SF.

Lacy, Maryanne, jt. auth. see McCall, Peter.

***Lacy, Norris J.** The Lancelot-Grail Reader: Selections from the Medieval French Arthurian Cycle. LC 99-39114. (Reference Library of the Humanities). 350p. 2000. 24.95 (0-8153-3419-2) Garland.

Lacy, Norris J. Reading Fabliaux. LC 93-8245. 192p. 1993. text 10.00 (0-8153-1510-4, H1805) Garland.

— Reading Fabliaux. 2nd ed. LC 98-61743. 198p. 1999. reprint ed. pap. 29.95 (1-883479-24-X) Summa Pubns.

Lacy, Norris J., ed. Arthurian Archives: The Early French Tristan Poems. (Arthurian Archives Ser.). 200p. 1998. text 30.00 (0-8153-2368-9) Garland.

— Early French Tristan Poems, Vol. I. LC 98-33615. (Arthurian Archives Ser.). (FRE.). 324p. 1998. 75.00 (0-85991-535-2) Boydell & Brewer.

— Early French Tristan Poems, Vol. II. LC 98-33615. (Arthurian Archives Ser.). (FRE.). 72p. 1998. 75.00 (0-85991-542-5) Boydell & Brewer.

— Lancelot-Grail: The Old French Arthurian Vulgate & Post-Vulgate in Translation. LC 92-1674. 296p. 1995. text 35.00 (0-8153-0748-9, H1896) Garland.

— Lancelot-Grail: The Old French Arthurian Vulgate & Post-Vulgate in Translation, Vol. I. LC 92-1674. 456p. 1992. text 35.00 (0-8240-7733-4, H941) Garland.

— Lancelot-Grail: The Old French Arthurian Vulgate & Post-Vulgate in Translation, Vol. II. LC 92-1674. 342p. 1993. text 35.00 (0-8153-0746-2, H1826) Garland.

— Lancelot-Grail: The Old French Arthurian Vulgate & Post-Vulgate in Translation, Vol. 3. LC 92-1674. (Garland Reference Library of the Humanities: Vol. 941). 338p. 1995. text 35.00 (0-8153-0747-0, H1878) Garland.

— Lancelot-Grail: The Old French Volgate & Post-Vulgate Cycles in Translation, 5 vols., Set. 3500p. 375.00 (0-8240-0700-X) Garland.

Lacy, Norris J., et al, eds. The New Arthurian Encyclopedia. LC 90-237000. (Illus.). 615p. 1991. text 95.00 (0-8240-4377-4, H931) Garland.

— The New Arthurian Encyclopedia. rev. ed. LC 95-36107. (Reference Library of the Humanities: Vol. 931). (Illus.). 656p. 1995. pap. text 32.95 (0-8153-2303-4, H931) Garland.

Lacy, Norris J. & Ashe, Geoffrey. The Arthurian Handbook. LC 87-32873. (Illus.). 455p. 1988. pap. text 20.95 (0-8240-7597-8) Garland.

Lacy, Norris J. & Asher, Martha. Lancelot-Grail: The Old French Arthurian Vulgate & Post-Vulgate in Translation, Vol. 5. LC 92-1674. 456p. 1996. text 35.00 (0-8153-0757-8, H1964) Garland.

Lacy, Norris J. & Nash, Jerry C., eds. Essays in Early French Literature, Presented to Barbara M. Craig. 186p. 1982. 16.00 (0-917786-28-9) Summa Pubns.

Lacy, Norris J., et al. The Arthurian Handbook. 2nd ed. LC 97-17495. (Literature Reference Ser.). 456p. 1997. text 66.00 (0-8153-2082-5) Garland.

— The Arthurian Handbook. 2nd rev. ed. LC 97-17495. 456p. 1997. pap. text 22.95 (0-8153-2081-7) Garland.

Lacy, Norris J., jt. auth. see Fenster, Thelma S.

Lacy, Norris J., jt. auth. see Goodrich, Peter.

Lacy, Norris J., ed. see Busby, Keith.

Lacy, Norris J., ed. see Claassens, Geert & Johnson, David.

Lacy, Norris J., ed. see Kalinke, Marianne E.

Lacy, Norris J., ed. see Kleinhenz, Christopher.

Lacy, Norris J., ed. see Walters, Lori J.

Lacy, Norris J., tr. see Grigsby, John, ed.

Lacy, Robert. The Natural Father. Truesdale, C. W., ed. LC 97-65063. (Minnesota Voices Project Ser.: Vol. 81). 200p. (Orig.). 1997. pap. 14.95 (0-89823-176-0) New Rivers Pr.

Lacy, Robert T. Diagnosis: Cataract. LC 82-73668. (Illus.). (Orig.). 1982. pap. 7.95 (0-9611782-0-5) Britton Inc.

Lacy, Robin T. A Biographical Dictionary of Scenographers: 500 B. C. to 1900 A. D. LC 90-14004. 784p. 1990. lib. bdg. 105.00 (0-313-27429-0, LBD/, Greenwood Pr) Greenwood.

Lacy, Ruby. Searcy County Arkansas Marriages, Vol. III. 53p. (Orig.). 1987. pap. write for info. (0-942977-25-4) Lacy Pubs.

Lacy, Sam & Newson, Moses. Fighting for Fairness: The Life Story of Hall of Fame Sportswriter Sam Lacy. LC 98-45957. (Illus.). 272p. 1998. 29.95 (0-87033-512-X) Cornell Maritime.

Lacy, Sarah C., ed. see Cordova, Maria.

Lacy, Sondra, jt. auth. see Kenna, Peggy.

Lacy, Stanhope, Jr. Mukate & Will Underwood. 300p. 1984. 14.95 (0-9612362-1-3) L Stanhope.

Lacy, Stephen & Simon, Todd F. The Economy & Regulation of United States Newspapers. LC 91-36511. (Communication & Information Science Ser.). 312p. 1993. pap. 39.50 (0-89391-820-2); text 73.25 (0-89391-753-2) Ablx Pub.

Lacy, Stephen, et al. Media Management: A Casebook Approach. (Communication Textbook Journalism Subseries). 408p. 1993. pap. 32.50 (0-8058-1308-X); text 79.95 (0-8058-0659-8) L Erlbaum Assocs.

Lacy, Stephen, jt. auth. see Folkerts, Jean.

Lacy, Susana B., ed. see Salazar, William B.

Lacy, Suzanne, ed. Mapping the Terrain: New Genre Public Art. LC 94-35417. (Illus.). 296p. (Orig.). 1995. pap. 18.95 (0-941920-30-5) Bay Pr.

Lacy, Terry G. Ring of Seasons. (Illus.). 328p. pap. 19.95 (0-472-08661-8, 08661) U of Mich Pr.

Lacy, Terry G. Ring of Seasons: Iceland--Its Culture & History. LC 97-48294. (Illus.). 328p. (C). 1998. 29.95 (0-472-10926-X, 10926) U of Mich Pr.

Lacy, Thomas C. The Tie That Binds: Marriage: How to Make It Last for Ever. (Illus.). 166p. 1997. pap. text. write for info. (0-9659822-0-3) New Hope Couns.

Lacy, Thomas F. Kaniksu: Stories of the Northwest. LC 94-210692. (Illus.). 128p. (Orig.). 1994. pap. 11.95 (1-879628-06-6) Keokee ID.

Lacy, Willard. An Introduction to Geology & Hard Rock Mining, 1. (Science & Technology Ser.: Vol. 1). (Illus.). 151p. 1998. pap. text 25.00 (0-929047-76-1) Rocky Mtn Mineral Law Found.

Lacy, William J., et al, eds. Hazardous & Industrial Solid Waste Testing & Disposal, Vol. 6. LC 86-25944. (Special Technical Publication Ser.: No. 933). (Illus.). 470p. 1986. text 63.00 (0-8031-0931-8, STP933) ASTM.

Lacy, William J., jt. ed. see Petros, James K., Jr.

Laczko, Frank & Phillipson, Chris. Changing Work & Retirement: Social Policy & the Older Worker. 192p. 1991. 113.00 (0-335-09931-9); pap. 35.95 (0-335-09930-0) OpUniv Pr.

Laczko, Gina. Iroquois Silverwork: From the Museum of the American Indian - Heye Foundation. (Illus.). 17p. 1980. 10.00 (0-685-70932-9) Gal Assn NY.

Laczko, Leslie S. Pluralism & Inequality in Quebec. 288p. 1995. text 55.00 (0-312-10064-7) St Martin.

— Pluralism & Inequality in Quebec. 252p. 1996. text 55.00 (0-8020-0892-5) St Martin.

Laczk'o, Tibor. The Syntax of Hungarian Noun Phrases: A Lexical-Functional Approach. LC 95-48818. (MetaLinguistica Ser.: Bd. 2). (Illus.). 207p. 1995. pap. 42.95 (0-8204-2960-0, 68728) P Lang Pubng.

***Laczkovich, Miklos.** Conjecture & Proof. 100p. 1999. pap. 18.00 (963-7546-88-X, Pub. by Akade Kiado) Intl Spec Bk.

Laczniak, Gene R., jt. auth. see Murphy.

Lad, Frank. Operational Subjective Statistical Methods. LC 96-6197. (Series in Probability & Statistics, Applied Probability & Statistics). 484p. 1996. 89.95 (0-471-14329-4) Wiley.

Lad, P. A., jt. auth. see Dalvi, Jayavant D.

Lad, Pramod M., et al, eds. Signal Transduction in Leukocytes: G Protein-Related & Other Pathways. LC 95-16903. 400p. 1995. boxed set 189.95 (0-8493-6694-1, 6694) CRC Pr.

Lad, Usha & Lad, Vasant. Ayurvedic Cooking for Self-Healing. LC 94-71732. (Illus.). 240p. (Orig.). 1993. pap., per. 15.95 (1-883725-00-3) Ayurvedic Pr.

— Ayurvedic Cooking for Self-Healing. 2nd ed. LC 97-70608. (Illus.). 240p. (Orig.). 1997. pap. 15.95 (1-883725-05-4) Ayurvedic Pr.

Lad, Vasant. Ayurveda, the Science of Self-Healing: A Practical Guide. LC 83-80620. (Illus.). 175p. (Orig.). 1990. pap. text 10.95 (0-914955-00-4) Lotus Pr.

— The Complete Book of Ayurvedic Home Remedies: Based on the Timeless Wisdom of India's 5,000 Year Old Medical System. (Illus.). 336p. 1999. pap. 15.00 (0-609-80286-0) Crown Pub Group.

***Lad, Vasant.** Textbook of Ayurveda: A History & Philosophy of Ayurveda. (Illus.). xix, 275p. 2000. pap. write for info. (1-883725-07-0) Ayurvedic Pr.

Lad, Vasant, jt. auth. see Frawley, David.

Lad, Vasant, jt. auth. see Lad, Usha.

Lad, Vasant D. & Peet, Margaret S. Secrets of the Pulse: The Ancient Art of Ayurvedic Pulse Diagnosis. LC 96-86347. (Illus.). 232p. (Orig.). 1996. pap. 21.95 (1-883725-03-8) Ayurvedic Pr.

***Lada, Charles J. & Kylafis, N.** The Origin of Stars & Planetary Systems. LC 99-40948. (NATO Science Ser.). (Illus.). 1999. write for info. (0-7923-5908-9) Kluwer Academic.

Lada, Charles J., jt. ed. see Kylafis, Nikolaos D.

***Lada-Mocarski, Valerian.** Bibliography of Books on Alaska Published Before 1868. vii, 567p. 1998. reprint ed. 95.00 (*1-57898-088-7*) Martino Pubng.

Lada-Richards, Ismene. Initiating Dionysus: Ritual & Theatre in Aristophanes' Frogs. LC 98-25549. (Illus.). 412p. 1999. text 145.00 (*0-19-814981-6*) OUP.

Ladak, Mohamed S. Nutty from Nut. 82p. 1986. pap. 15.00 (*0-7855-1716-2*, Pub. by A H S Ltd) St Mut.

Ladame, F., jt. auth. see Perret-Catipovic, Maja.

Ladame, Paul Alexis. Defending Switzerland: Then & Now. LC 99-34517. 162p. 1999. 25.00 (*0-88206-094-5*) Caravan Bks.

Ladan, A., jt. auth. see Groen-Prakken, Han.

Ladany, L. The Catholic Church in China. LC 87-23. (Perspectives on Freedom Ser.: No. 7). (Orig.). 1987. pap. 16.25 (*0-932088-12-0*) Freedom Hse.

Ladany, Laszlo. The Communist Party of China & Marxism, 1921-1985: A Self Portrait. (Publication Ser.: No. 362). 588p. 1992. pap. text 24.95 (*0-8179-8622-7*) Hoover Inst Pr.

— Law & Legality in China: The Testament of a China-Watcher. Nath, Marie-Luise, ed. 224p. 1992. text 38.00 (*0-8248-1473-8*) UH Pr.

Ladanyi, Hans. SQL Unleashed. LC 97-66950. 936p. 1997. 49.99 (*0-672-31133-X*, Pub. by Macmillan) S&S Trade.

Ladas, Alice K., et al. The G Spot. 256p. 1983. mass mkt. 6.99 (*0-440-13040-9*) Dell.

Ladas, G., jt. auth. see Kocic, V. L.

Ladas, G., ed. see Gyori, I.

Ladas-Gaskin, Carol. Instant Stress Relief: A Book & Reflexology Tool, Incl. reflexology tool. 96p. 1998. pap. text 10.95 (*0-8362-3669-6*) Andrews & McMeel.

Ladas, Gerasimons, jt. auth. see Finizio, Norman.

Ladas, Stephen. Patents, Trademarks, & Related Rights: National & International Protection, 3 vols. LC 73-89709. 1888p. 1975. 197.00 (*0-674-65775-6*) HUP.

Ladas, Stephen P. The Exchange of Minorities: Bulgaria, Greece & Turkey. LC 77-87521. (Illus.). reprint ed. 56.00 (*0-404-16596-6*) AMS Pr.

Ladbrooke, Alan, jt. auth. see Crix, Bernard.

Ladbrooke, Peter H. MMIC Design: GaAs FETs & HEMTs. LC 88-34959. (Artech House Microwave Library). (Illus.). 394p. 1989. reprint ed. pap. 122.20 (*0-7837-9696-X*, 206042600005) Bks Demand.

Ladbury, John E. Evaluation of the Nasa Langley Research Center Mode-Stirred Chamber Facility. 286p. 1999. per. 24.00 (*0-16-056899-4*) USGPO.

***Ladbury, John E. & Chowdhry, Babur Z.** Biocalorimetry: Applications of Calorimetry in the Biological Sciences. LC 98-2780. 354p. 1998. 149.95 (*0-471-97781-0*) Wiley.

Ladbury, John E. & Connelly, Pat R. Structure-Based Drug Design: Thermodynamics, Modeling & Strategy. LC 97-21929. (Biotechnology Intelligence Unit (SV) Ser.). 183p. 1997. 109.00 (*1-57059-469-4*) Landes Bioscience.

Ladbury, John E. & Connelly, Pat R., eds. Structure-Based Drug Design: Thermodynamics, Modeling & Strategy. LC 97-21929. (Biotechnology Intelligence Unit (SV) Ser.). (Illus.). 183p. 1997. 102.00 (*3-540-63250-6*) Spr-Verlag.

***Ladd.** Double Diamond Duderanch. 7th ed. 1998. mass mkt. 3.99 (*1-55902-656-1*) Tor Bks.

— Double Diamond Duderanch. 8th ed. 1998. mass mkt. 3.99 (*1-55902-657-X*) Tor Bks.

— Double Diamond Duderanch #3. 1998. mass mkt. 3.99 (*0-8125-5354-3*) Tor Bks.

— Double Diamond Duderanch #4. 1998. mass mkt. 3.99 (*0-8125-5355-1*) St Martin.

— Double Diamond Duderanch #5. 1998. mass mkt. 3.99 (*0-8125-5357-8*) Tor Bks.

— Double Diamond Duderanch #6. 1998. mass mkt. 3.99 (*0-8125-5358-6*) Tor Bks.

— Ladd 1988 Election Update. (Illus.). pap. 0.00 (*0-393-99991-2*) Norton.

Ladd. Reading Group Guide. 1997. pap. write for info. (*0-684-00545-X*, Scribner Pap Fic) S&S Trade Pap.

Ladd, jt. auth. see McLaren, Paul.

Ladd, Sweetie. Sweetie Ladd's Historic Fort Worth. LC 98-48790. 76p. 1999. 39.95 (*0-87565-196-8*) Tex Christian.

Ladd, Alex, tr. see Capoeira, Nestor.

Ladd, Andrew, jt. auth. see Curran, Thomas.

Ladd, Andrew, jt. auth. see Focazio, Robert L.

Ladd, Barbara. Nationalism & the Color Line in George W. Cable, Mark Twain, & William Faulkner. LC 96-21711. (Southern Literary Studies). 232p. 1996. text 32.50 (*0-8071-2065-0*) La State U Pr.

Ladd, Barry. Reflections of a Country Doctor. LC 95-77536. 200p. 1995. 20.95 (*0-944435-37-8*) Glenbridge Pub.

Ladd, Brian. The Ghosts of Berlin: Confronting German History in the Urban Landscape. LC 96-28562. 272p. 1997. 29.95 (*0-226-46761-9*) U Ch Pr.

— Ghosts of Berlin: Confronting German History in the Urban Landscape. 1998. pap. 15.00 (*0-226-46762-7*) U Ch Pr.

— Urban Planning & Civic Order in Germany, 1860-1914. (Historical Studies: Vol. 105). (Illus.). 334p. 1990. 37.50 (*0-674-93115-7*) HUP.

Ladd, D., et al, eds. Protection for Semiconductor Chip Masks in the United States: Analysis of the Semiconductor Chip Protection Art of 1984. (IIC Studies Ser.: Vol. 8). 99p. 1986. pap. 69.50 (*3-527-26003-X*, Wiley-VCH) Wiley.

Ladd, D. Robert. Intonational Phonology. (Cambridge Studies in Linguistics: No. 79). 349p. (C). 1997. pap. text 23.95 (*0-521-47575-9*) Cambridge U Pr.

— The Structure of Intonational Meaning: Evidence from English. LC 79-3093. 250p. reprint ed. pap. 77.50 (*0-608-17068-2*, 205623500056) Bks Demand.

Ladd, D. Robert, jt. ed. see Docherty, Gerard J.

Ladd, D. Robert, tr. see Pascu, Stefan.

Ladd, Dean. Faithful Warriors. Shepherd, Sylvia, ed. (Illus.). 264p. 1994. reprint ed. pap. 15.95 (*0-9638217-0-9*) Ladd Communs.

***Ladd, Dean.** Thomas H. Elsom: Telephone Pioneer. Bamonte, Tony et al, eds. (Illus.). 128p. 2000. 13.95 (*0-9652219-5-4*) Tornado Creek.

Ladd, Doris M. The Making of a Strike: Mexican Silver Workers' Struggles in Real del Monte, 1766-1775. LC 87-5897. 215p. 1988. reprint ed. pap. 66.70 (*0-608-03485-1*, 206419900008) Bks Demand.

— Mexican Women in Anahuac & New Spain: Three Study Units: Aztec Roles, Spanish Notary Revelations, Creole Genius. (Latin American Curriculum Units for Junior & Community Colleges Ser.). vii, 87p. (Orig.). (C). 1979. pap. text 4.95 (*0-86728-003-4*) U TX Inst Lat Am Stud.

Ladd, Doug. Tallgrass Prairie Wildflowers: A Field Guide. LC 95-6990. (Nature Conservancy Bks.). (Illus.). 264p. 1995. pap. 24.95 (*1-56044-299-9*) Falcon Pub Inc.

Ladd, Douglas M., jt. auth. see Mohlenbrock, Robert H.

***Ladd, Edmund J.** The Zuni. LC 99-23362. (Indian Nation Ser.). (Illus.). 48p. (ps-3). 1999. 25.69 (*0-8172-5454-4*) Raintree Steck-V.

Ladd, Eldon. Steelheader's Reference Guide: Washington & Oregon. LC 99-176046. 110p. 1998. spiral bd. 19.95 (*1-57188-173-5*) F Amato Pubns.

***Ladd, Eric.** Using HTML 4, XML & Java 1.2: Platinum Edition. LC 98-86971. (Using... Ser.). 1998. 59.99 (*0-7897-1759-X*) Que.

Ladd, Eric & O'Donnell, Jim. Internet Explorer Starter Kit. 500p. 1997. 34.99 (*0-7897-1110-9*) Que.

— Platinum Edition Using HTML 3.2, Java 1.1, & CGI: 8 Contemporary Photographers. LC 96-71191. 1520p. 1996. 70.00 (*0-7897-0932-5*) Que.

— Using HTML 4.0, Java 1.1 AND JavaScript 1.2: Platinum Edition. 2nd ed. LC 97-75539. 1395p. 1998. 59.99 (*0-7897-1477-9*) Que.

Ladd, Eric, et al. Using HTML, Java & CGI, Platinum Edition. 1996. 69.99 incl. cd-rom (*0-614-20289-2*, Que New Media) MCP SW Interactive.

Ladd, Everett C. The American Ideology: An Exploration of the Origins, Meaning, & Role of American Political Ideas. (Occasional Papers & Monographs Ser.: No. 1). (Illus.). 90p. (Orig.). (C). 1994. pap. text 9.95 (*1-887415-00-9*) RCPOR.

— American Polity: 1992 Election. 5th ed. (C). Date not set. pap. write for info. (*0-393-99834-7*) Norton.

Ladd, Everett C., Jr. Ideology in America: Change & Response in a City, a Suburb, & a Small Town. (Illus.). 404p. (C). 1986. reprint ed. pap. text 32.00 (*0-8191-5219-6*) U Pr of Amer.

Ladd, Everett C. The Ladd Report: Startling New Research Shows How an Explosion of Voluntary Groups, Activities & Charitable Donations are Transforming Our Towns & Cities. LC 98-31380. 256p. 1999. 26.00 (*0-684-83735-8*) Free Pr.

Ladd, Everett C. & Bowman, Karlyn H. Attitudes Toward Economic Inequality. LC 98-159805. (AEI Studies in Understanding Economic Inequality). 75p. 1998. pap. 9.95 (*0-8447-7090-6*, AEI Pr) Am Enterprise.

— Attitudes Toward the Environment: Twenty-Five Years after Earth Day. (AEI Studies in Public Policy Ser.). 60p. (Orig.). 1995. pap. 5.00 (*0-8447-7032-9*) Am Enterprise.

— What's Wrong: A Survey of American Satisfaction & Complaint. LC 98-4046. 167p. 1998. pap. 14.95 (*0-8447-3955-3*, AEI Pr) Am Enterprise.

— What's Wrong? American Satisfaction & Complaint. 100p. 1996. text 19.95 (*0-8447-3954-5*, AEI Pr) Am Enterprise.

Ladd, Everett C., Jr. & Hadley, Charles D. Transformations of the American Party System: Political Coalitions from the New Deal to the 1970's. (Illus.). 371p. (C). 1975. pap. text 10.00 (*0-393-09203-8*) Norton.

Ladd, Everett C., jt. auth. see Roper Center for Public Opinion Research Staff.

Ladd, Everett C., ed. see Roper Center for Public Opinion Research Staff.

Ladd, Everett C., jt. ed. see Serow, Ann G.

***Ladd, Everett Carll & Bowman, Karlyn H.** Public Opinion about Abortion. 56p. 1999. pap. 9.95 (*0-8447-7126-0*, Pub. by Am Enterprise) Pub Resources Inc.

Ladd, Florence. Sarah's Psalm. 320p. 1996. 22.50 (*0-684-80410-7*) S&S Trade.

Ladd, Forrest E. You Can Break That Habit. (Christian Living Ser.). 32p. 1988. pap. 3.50 (*0-8341-0056-8*) Beacon Hill.

Ladd-Franklin, Christine. Colour & Colour Theories. LC 73-2971. (Classics in Psychology Ser.). 1977. reprint ed. 23.95 (*0-405-05143-3*) Ayer.

Ladd, Gary. Lake Powell: A Photographic Essay of Glen Canyon National Recreation Area. Schlenz, Mark A., ed. (Illus.). 96p. 1994. 34.95 (*0-944197-30-2*); pap. 19.95 (*0-944197-29-9*) Companion CA.

— Landforms--Heart of the Colorado Plateau: The Story Behind the Scenery. LC 95-75094. (Illus.). 48p. 1995. pap. 7.95 (*0-88714-090-4*) KC Pubns.

— Landforms--Heart of the Colorado Plateau: The Story Behind the Scenery. Morales, Brigitte, tr. (GER., Illus.). 48p. 1995. pap. 8.95 (*0-88714-804-2*) KC Pubns.

— Rainbow Bridge: The Story Behind the Scenery. LC 98-65025. (Illus.). 48p. 1998. pap. 7.95 (*0-88714-136-6*) KC Pubns.

— Rainbow Bridge: The Story Behind the Scenery. Morales, Brigitte, tr. (GER., Illus.). 48p. 1998. pap. 8.95 (*0-88714-821-2*) KC Pubns.

— Rainbow Bridge: The Story Behind the Scenery. Le Bras, Yvon, tr. (FRE., Illus.). 48p. 1998. pap. 8.95 (*0-88714-822-0*) KC Pubns.

Ladd, Gary W., jt. ed. see Berndt, Thomas J.

Ladd, Gary W., jt. ed. see Parke, Ross D.

Ladd, George E. The Blessed Hope. 167p. (C). 1990. pap. text 12.00 (*0-8028-1111-6*) Eerdmans.

— Commentary on the Book of Revelation of John. 1972. pap. 18.00 (*0-8028-1684-3*) Eerdmans.

— Critica Del Nuevo Testamento. Chavez, Moises, tr. (Estudios Biblicos Basicos Ser.).Tr. of New Testament & Criticism. (SPA.). 176p. (Orig.). 1990. pap. 7.99 (*0-311-04365-8*) Casa Bautista.

— The Gospel of the Kingdom. 143p. (C). 1990. pap. text 12.00 (*0-8028-1280-5*) Eerdmans.

— The Presence of the Future. 384p. pap. 16.00 (*0-8028-1531-6*) Eerdmans.

— A Theology of the New Testament. rev. ed. Hagner, Donald A., ed. 740p. (C). 1993. pap. text 35.00 (*0-8028-0680-5*) Eerdmans.

***Ladd, George Eldon.** Crucial Questions about the Kingdom of God. 199p. 1998. pap. 22.00 (*1-57910-189-5*) Wipf & Stock.

Ladd, George T. Elements of Physiological Psychology. 712p. 145.00 (*1-85506-676-9*) Thoemmes Pr.

Ladd, George T. Introduction to Philosophy: An Inquiry after a Rational System of Scientific Principles in the Relation to the Ultimate Reality. LC 75-3220. reprint ed. 37.50 (*0-404-59216-3*) AMS Pr.

— Knowledge, Life & Reality: An Essay in Systemic Philosophy. LC 75-3221. reprint ed. 37.50 (*0-404-59217-1*) AMS Pr.

— Philosophy of Conduct: A Treatise of the Facts, Principles, & Ideals of Ethics. LC 75-3222. reprint ed. 46.50 (*0-404-59218-X*) AMS Pr.

— Philosophy of Knowledge: An Inquiry into the Nature, Limits & Validity of Human Cognitive Faculty. LC 75-3223. reprint ed. 57.50 (*0-404-59219-8*) AMS Pr.

— Philosophy of Mind: An Essay in the Metaphysics of Psychology. LC 82-45804. 432p. reprint ed. 55.00 (*0-404-59220-1*) AMS Pr.

— The Philosophy of Religion, 2 vols. LC 75-3225. 1976. reprint ed. 82.50 (*0-404-59221-X*) AMS Pr.

— Psychology, Descriptive & Explanatory: A Treatise of the Phenomena, Laws & Development of Human Mental Life. LC 75-3226. reprint ed. 46.50 (*0-404-59224-4*) AMS Pr.

— The Teacher's Practical Philosophy: A Treatise of Education As a Species of Conduct. LC 75-3228. reprint ed. 32.50 (*0-404-59226-0*) AMS Pr.

Ladd, George T., tr. see Lotze, Rudolf Hermann.

Ladd, George W. Imagination in Research: An Economist's View. LC 86-27591. 154p. reprint ed. pap. 47.80 (*0-608-09059-X*, 206969300005) Bks Demand.

Ladd, Gloria D., ed. see Sundance, G. L.

Ladd, H. S. & Hoffmeister, J. E. Geology of Lau, Fiji. (BMB Ser.: No. 181). 1969. reprint ed. 80.00 (*0-527-02289-6*) Periodicals Srv.

— Geology of Vitilevu Fiji. (BMB Ser.: No. 119). 1969. reprint ed. 40.00 (*0-527-02225-X*) Periodicals Srv.

Ladd, Helen F. The Challenge of Fiscal Disparities for State & Local Governments: The Selected Essays of Helen F. Ladd. LC 98-45784. (Studies in Fiscal Federalism & State-Local Finance). 512p. 1999. 100.00 (*1-85898-687-7*) E Elgar.

— Local Government Tax & Land Use Policies in the United States: Understanding the Links. LC 97-27158. (Studies in Fiscal Federalism & State-Local Finance). 288p. (C). 1998. 90.00 (*1-85898-657-5*) E Elgar.

Ladd, Helen F., ed. Holding Schools Accountable: Performance-Based Reform in Education. LC 95-46845. 382p. 1996. 42.95 (*0-8157-5104-4*) Brookings.

Ladd, Helen F., jt. auth. see Fiske, Edward B.

Ladd, Helen F., ed. see National Research Council Staff.

Ladd, Jerrold. Out of the Madness: From the Projects to a Life of Hope. 208p. 1996. reprint ed. mass mkt. 10.99 (*0-446-67105-3*, Pub. by Warner Bks) Little.

Ladd, Jim. Radio Waves: Life & Revolution on the FM Dial. (Illus.). 320p. 1992. pap. 12.95 (*0-312-07786-6*) St Martin.

Ladd, John. Archeological Investigations in the Parita & Santa Maria Zones of Panama. (Bureau of American Ethnology Bulletins Ser.). 291p. 1995. lib. bdg. 89.00 (*0-7812-4193-6*) Rprt Serv.

— The Metaphysical Element of Justice: Kant. 192p. (C). 1965. pap. text 7.00 (*0-02-367100-9*, Macmillan Coll) P-H.

Ladd, John, ed. Ethical Relativism. 152p. 1985. reprint ed. pap. text 16.00 (*0-8191-4567-X*) U Pr of Amer.

Ladd, John, tr. see Kant, Immanuel.

Ladd, John W. & Buffler, Richard T. Ocean Margin Drilling Program Atlases, Vol. 7. (Regional Atlas Ser.). 1p. 1986. pap. 295.00 (*0-86720-257-2*) Jones & Bartlett.

Ladd, Joseph B. Literary Remains. 1972. reprint ed. lib. bdg. 21.50 (*0-8422-8141-X*) Irvington.

— Literary Remains of Joseph Brown Ladd, M. D. (Notable American Authors Ser.). 1999. reprint ed. lib. bdg. 125.00 (*0-7812-3680-0*) Rprt Serv.

— The Poems of Arouet. (Notable American Authors Ser.). 1999. reprint ed. lib. bdg. 125.00 (*0-7812-3679-7*) Rprt Serv.

Ladd, Justin. Abilene: The Peacemaker. large type ed. (Nightingale Ser.: Bk. 1). 313p. 1995. pap. 17.95 (*0-7838-1137-3*, G K Hall Lrg Type) Mac Lib Ref.

Ladd, Karol. Party Mix: 21 Creative Plans for Fun Fellowship. LC 96-26872. 256p. 1996. pap. 10.99 (*0-8054-6095-0*, 4260-95) Broadman.

Ladd, Kaye. A New Owner's Guide to Dachshunds: AKC Rank #7. (New Owner's Guide to Ser.). (Illus.). 160p. 1996. 12.95 (*0-7938-2759-0*, JG-110) TFH Pubns.

Ladd, Keith, jt. auth. see Hakim, Simon.

Ladd, Kevin. Gone to Texas: Genealogical Abstracts from "The Telegraph & Texas Register" 1835-1841. 322p. (Orig.). 1994. pap. text 25.00 (*0-7884-0005-3*) Heritage Bk.

Ladd, Linda. Dragon Fire. 368p. 1992. mass mkt. 4.99 (*0-380-75698-6*, Avon Bks) Morrow Avon.

— Dreamsong. 320p. (Orig.). 1988. pap. 3.95 (*0-380-75205-0*, Avon Bks) Morrow Avon.

— Fireglow. 336p. 1986. mass mkt. 4.50 (*0-380-89640-0*, Avon Bks) Morrow Avon.

— Forever, My Love. 1997. mass mkt. 5.99 (*0-614-27796-5*, Topaz) NAL.

— Frostfire. 1990. mass mkt. 4.50 (*0-380-75695-1*, Avon Bks) Morrow Avon.

— Lilacs on Lace. 1996. pap. 5.99 (*0-614-98096-8*, Topaz) NAL.

— Love So Fine. 352p. 1999. mass mkt. 6.99 (*0-451-19509-4*, Topaz) NAL.

— Midnight Fire. 384p. 1991. mass mkt. 4.50 (*0-380-75696-X*, Avon Bks) Morrow Avon.

— Moonspell. 368p. 1985. pap. 3.95 (*0-380-89639-7*, Avon Bks) Morrow Avon.

— My Lady Belinda. 1997. mass mkt. 5.99 (*0-451-40557-9*, Onyx) NAL.

— Silverswept. (Avon Romance Ser.). 368p. 1987. pap. 3.95 (*0-380-75204-2*, Avon Bks) Morrow Avon.

— Wildstar. 272p. 1984. mass mkt. 3.95 (*0-380-87171-8*, Avon Bks) Morrow Avon.

Ladd, Louise. The Anywhere Ring: Miracle Island, No. 1. 176p. (Orig.). (J). 1995. mass mkt. 3.99 (*0-425-14879-3*) Berkley Pub.

— The Anywhere Ring Bk. 2: Castle in Time. 160p. (Orig.). (J). 1995. mass mkt. 4.50 (*0-425-15048-8*) Berkley Pub.

— The Anywhere Ring No. 4: Cherry Blossom Moon. (J). (gr. 3-7). 1996. mass mkt. 4.50 (*0-425-15294-4*) Berkley Pub.

— The Anywhere Ring Book No. 3: Lost Valley. 224p. (Orig.). (J). (gr. 3-7). 1996. mass mkt. 4.50 (*0-425-15192-1*) Berkley Pub.

— Call Me Just Plain Chris. (Double Diamond Dude Ranch Ser.). 1998. mass mkt. 3.99 (*0-8125-5352-7*, Pub. by Tor Bks) St Martin.

— Wrangler's Secret. (Double Diamond Dude Ranch Ser.). 1998. mass mkt. 3.99 (*0-8125-5353-5*, Pub. by Tor Bks) St Martin.

Ladd, M. F. Symmetry in Molecules & Crystals. 1989. text 51.95 (*0-470-21376-0*) P-H.

Ladd, M. F. & Palmer, R. A. Structure Determination by X-Ray Crystallography. 3rd ed. LC 94-6538. (Illus.). 612p. (C). 1994. text 37.50 (*0-306-44751-7*, Kluwer Plenum) Kluwer Academic.

— Structure Determination by X-Ray Crystallography. 3rd ed. (Illus.). 600p. (C). 1993. 59.50 (*0-306-44290-6*, Plenum Trade) Perseus Pubng.

Ladd, M. F. & Palmer, R. A., eds. Theory & Practice of Direct Methods in Crystallography. LC 79-10566. (Illus.). 436p. 1980. 95.00 (*0-306-40223-8*, Plenum Trade) Perseus Pubng.

Ladd, Mark. Chemical Bonding in Solids & Fluids. 350p. (C). 1995. 69.00 (*0-13-474933-2*) P-H.

— Dobermans: An Owner's Companion. LC 90-5370. 1991. pap. 25.00 (*0-87605-114-X*) Howell Bks.

— Introduction to Physical Chemistry. 3rd ed. LC 96-37799. (Illus.). 534p. (C). 1998. text 100.00 (*0-521-48000-0*); pap. text 47.95 (*0-521-57881-7*) Cambridge U Pr.

— Symmetry & Group Theory in Chemistry. LC 99-495098. 300p. 1998. pap. 29.95 (*1-898563-39-X*, Pub. by Horwood Pub) Paul & Co Pubs.

Ladd, Mason, et al. Model Code of Evidence. xxiii, 435p. 1942. 63.50 (*0-686-91052-4*, 5070) Am Law Inst.

Ladd, Paula. Microsoft Word 97: Economy Pack. (Illus.). (C). 1998. pap. text 25.99 (*1-57676-010-3*) Scott Jones Pubng.

***Ladd, Paula & Ruby, Ralph.** Lab Activities for the World Wide Web. 1999. pap. text 14.44 (*1-57676-039-1*) Scott Jones Pubng.

Ladd, R. S., ed. see American Society for Testing & Materials Staff.

Ladd, Richard & Girard, Colette. AP French: A Guide for the Language Course. 154p. 1992. 18.45 (*0-8013-0640-X*, 78580); teacher ed. 11.95 (*0-8013-0641-8*, 78581) Longman.

— AP French: A Guide for the Language Course, Set. 154p. 1992. audio 39.95 (*0-8013-0642-6*, 78582) Longman.

Ladd, Richard S., ed. Treasure Maps & Charts in the Library of Congress: A Descriptive List by a Reference Librarian. LC 64-60033. 1988. pap. 5.00 (*0-87380-161-X*) Popular E Commerce.

Ladd, Rosalind E. Children's Rights Re-Visioned: Philosophical Readings. LC 95-3845. 224p. 1995. pap. 30.95 (*0-534-23532-8*) Wadsworth Pub.

Ladd, Rosalind E., jt. auth. see Forman, Edwin N.

Ladd, Sally K., jt. ed. see Hall, Patricia.

Ladd, Scott R. Active Visual J++ LC 97-20719. 425p. 1997. pap. text 39.99 incl. cd-rom (*1-57231-609-8*) Microsoft.

— Applying Zortech C. 1992. pap. write for info. (*0-201-56302-9*) Addison-Wesley.

— Applying Zortech C Plus Plus with Disks. 1992. pap. write for info. (*0-201-56303-7*) Addison-Wesley.

— C++ I/O Streams, Containers & Standard Classes. 89p. 1996. pap. 39.95 incl. disk (*1-55851-463-5*, M&T Bks) IDG Bks.

— C++ Components & Algorithms. 2nd ed. LC 94-26770. 476p. 1994. pap. 39.95 incl. disk (*1-55851-408-2*, M&T Bks) IDG Bks.

— C++ Components & Algorithms. 3rd ed. LC 96-21247. 600p. 1996. pap. 39.95 incl. disk (*1-55851-466-X*, M&T Bks) IDG Bks.

— C++ Simulations & Cellular Automata. LC 95-23320. 89p. 1995. pap. 39.95 incl. disk (*1-55851-447-3*, M&T Bks) IDG Bks.

— C++ Templates & Tools. LC 95-9703. 428p. 1995. pap. 39.95 incl. disk (*1-55851-437-6*, M&T Bks) IDG Bks.

L

— C++ Templates & Tools. 2nd ed. LC 96-35499. 89p. 1996. pap. 39.95 incl. disk (*1-55851-465-1*, M&T Bks) IDG Bks.

— C++ After Stroustrup. 1995. pap. 29.95 (*1-55851-467-8*, M&T Bks) IDG Bks.

— Dynamic HTML Complete. 600p. 1998. pap. 44.95 (*0-07-913701-6*) McGraw.

— Java Algorithms. LC 97-46544. 1997. pap. 44.95 incl. cd-rom (*0-07-913696-6*) Osborne-McGraw.

— Win 32 API: A Programmers Reference. 1994. pap. 39.95 (*1-55851-427-9*, M&T Bks) IDG Bks.

Ladd, Shawn. Titanic & Her Sisters: Remembering the Dream. Van, Jack, ed. 70p. 1999. pap. 10.00 (*0-7392-0145-X*, PO3082) Morris Pubng.

Ladd, Stephen G. Three Years in a Twelve-Foot Boat. LC 99-93603. (Illus.). 390p. 1999. 21.95 (*0-9669337-4-5*) Seekers Pr.

***Ladd, Stephen G.** Three Years in a Twelve-Foot Boat. LC 99-93603. (Illus.). 390p. 2000. pap. 15.95 (*0-9669337-3-7*, Pub. by Seekers Pr) IPG Chicago.

Ladd-Taylor, Molly. Mother-Work: Women, Child Welfare, & the State, 1890-1930. LC 93-9926. (Women in American History Ser.). 232p. 1994. 39.95 (*0-252-02044-8*) U of Ill Pr.

— Mother-Work: Women, Child Welfare, & the State, 1890-1930. 224p. (C). 1995. pap. text 14.95 (*0-252-06482-8*) U of Ill Pr.

Ladd-Taylor, Molly & Umansky, Lauri. "Bad" Mothers: The Politics of Blame in Twentieth-Century America. LC 97-21142. 1997. 60.00 (*0-8147-5119-9*); pap. 22.95 (*0-8147-5120-2*) NYU Pr.

Ladd, Tony & Mathisen, James A. Muscular Christianity: Evangelical Protestants & the Development of American Sport. LC 99-10255. (Illus.). 288p. 1999. pap. 20.99 (*0-8010-5847-3*, Bridgept Bks) Baker Bks.

Ladd, Veronica, jt. auth. see Rule, Ann.

Ladd, W. Ladd Family: The Descendants of Daniel of Haverhill, Mass., Joseph of Portsmouth, New Hampshire, John of Burlington, New Jersey, John of Charles City County, Virginia. (Illus.). 425p. reprint ed. pap. 64.00 (*0-8328-0744-3*); reprint ed. lib. bdg. 72.00 (*0-8328-6568-0*) Higginson Bk Co.

Ladd, W. H. Auditing Advertising Agencies. Campbell, Lee A., ed. (Briefing Ser.). 44p. 1993. pap. text 20.00 (*0-89413-279-2*, A855) Inst Inter Aud.

Ladd, William. Dissertation on the Subject of a Congress of Nations: For the Adjustment of International Disputes Without Recourse to Arms. 156p. 1994. reprint ed. 47.50 (*0-8377-2415-5*, Rothman) W S Hein.

— An Essay on a Congress of Nations for the Adjustment of International Disputes Without Resort to Arms. LC 72-137550. (Peace Movement in America Ser.). 162p. 1972. reprint ed. lib. bdg. 25.95 (*0-89198-078-4*) Ozer.

— On the Duty of Females to Promote the Cause of Peace. 1972. lib. bdg. 59.95 (*0-8490-0765-8*) Gordon Pr.

Ladde, G. S. & Sambandham, M., eds. Proceedings of Dynamic Systems & Applications, Vol. 1. (Illus.). 438p. (C). 1994. 100.00 (*0-9640398-4-2*); pap. 75.00 (*0-9640398-5-0*) Dynamic Pubs.

— Proceedings of Dynamic Systems & Applications, Vol. 2. (Illus.). 600p. (C). 1996. lib. bdg. 150.00 (*0-9640398-1-8*) Dynamic Pubs.

Laddie, Hugh, et al. The Modern Law of Copyright & Designs, 2 vols. 2nd ed. 916p. 1995. text 649.00 (*0-406-61697-3*, 87607, MICHIE) LEXIS Pub.

***Laddon, Judy.** Awakening: The Upside of Y2K, 1. 1998. pap. text. write for info. (*0-9667030-0-6*) Printed Word WA.

Laddon, Judy. Awakening: The Upside of Y2k. 2nd ed. 1999. pap. text 10.00 (*0-9667030-1-4*) Printed Word WA.

Lade, Arnie. Acupuncture Points: Images & Functions. LC 88-82703. 363p. (C). 1989. text 29.50 (*0-939616-08-4*) Eastland.

***Lade, Arnie.** Energetic Healing: Embracing the Life Force. (Illus.). 280p. 1999. pap. 17.95 (*0-914955-46-2*) Lotus Pr.

Lade, Arnie, jt. auth. see Svoboda, Robert.

Lade, John, ed. see Headington, Christopher.

Lade, Poul V. & Yamamuro, Jerry A., eds. Physics & Mechanics of Soil Liquidification: Proceedings of the International Workshop, Baltimore, MD, USA, 10-11 September 11. (Illus.). 385p. (C). 1999. 98.00 (*90-5809-038-8*, TA710, Pub. by A A Balkema) Ashgate Pub Co.

Lade, Roger. The Most Excellent Book of How to Be a Puppeteer. LC 96-12641. (Illus.). 32p. (J). (gr. 4-6). 1996. 5.95 (*0-7613-0505-X*, Copper Beech Bks); lib. bdg. 19.90 (*0-7613-0526-2*, Copper Beech Bks) Millbrook Pr.

Lade, Val & Singleton, Nerida. Decoupage with Painted Backgrounds. (Illus.). 64p. 1997. pap. 14.95 (*1-86351-198-9*, Pub. by Sally Milner) Sterling.

Ladefoged. A Course in Phonetics. 4th ed. (C). 2000. pap. write for info. (*0-15-507319-2*) Harcourt Coll Pubs.

Ladefoged, Peter. A Course in Phonetics. 3rd ed. LC 91-78390. (Illus.). 300p. (Orig.). (C). 1993. pap. text 48.00 (*0-15-500173-6*, Pub. by Harcourt Coll Pubs) Harcourt.

— Elements of Acoustic Phonetics. LC 62-8349. 128p. 1999. pap. text 11.95 (*0-226-46785-6*) U Ch Pr.

— Elements of Acoustic Phonetics. 2nd ed. LC 95-9057. 224p. 1995. pap. text 15.00 (*0-226-46764-3*) U Ch Pr.

— Elements of Acoustic Phonetics. 2nd ed. LC 95-9057. 224p. 1995. lib. bdg. 39.95 (*0-226-46763-5*) U Ch Pr.

— Preliminaries to Linguistic Phonetics. 128p. 1980. pap. text 15.95 (*0-226-46787-2*) U Ch Pr.

***Ladefoged, Peter.** Vowels & Consonants: An Introduction to the Sounds of Languages. 256p. 2000. 74.95 (*0-631-21411-9*); pap. 34.95 (*0-631-21412-7*) Blackwell Pubs.

Ladefoged, Peter & Maddieson, Ian. The Sounds of the World's Languages. (Phonological Theory Ser.). (Illus.). 400p. (C). 1996. pap. 35.95 (*0-631-19815-6*) Blackwell Pubs.

Ladeira, E. A., ed. Brazil Gold Ninety-One - the Economics, Geology, Geochemistry & Genesis of Gold Deposits: Proceedings of the Symposium Brazil Gold '91, Belo Horizonte, Minas Gerais, Brazil, 13-17 May, 1991. (Illus.). 844p. (C). 1991. text 168.00 (*90-6191-195-8*, Pub. by A A Balkema) Ashgate Pub Co.

Ladeira, M. J., ed. Health in the New Communications Age. LC 95-79593. (Studies in Health Technology & Informatics). 733p. (YA). (gr. 12). 1995. 120.00 (*90-5199-224-6*) IOS Press.

Ladell, J. L. Needle Density, Pith Size & Tracheid Length in Pine. 1963. 50.00 (*0-7855-7181-7*) St Mut.

Lademan, Miriam A. & Brindle, Susan A. The Butterfly That Found Her Way Home (La Mariposa que Encontro el Carmino a Cosa) A Story of Forgiveness (Un Cuento de Perdon) Emmanuelli Klosterman, Carmen A., tr. (Seven Sacraments Ser.). (ENG & SPA., Illus.). 52p. (gr. k-10). 1994. pap. 9.95 (*1-889733-00-8*) Precious Life Bks.

— Father Phillip Tells a Ghost Story (Padre Phillip Hoce un Cuento de Fantasmas) A Story of Divine Mercy (Un Cuento de la Divina Misericordia) Emmanuelli Klosterman, Carmen A., tr. (Stories of the Faith Ser.). (ENG & SPA., Illus.). 64p. (gr. k-10). 1996. pap. 9.95 (*1-889733-02-4*, 01004) Precious Life Bks.

— The Little Turtledove Finds His Mate (El Tortolito Encuentra su Companera) Emmanuelli Klosterman, Carmen A., tr. (Seven Sacraments Ser.). (ENG & SPA., Illus.). 56p. (gr. k-10). 1997. pap. 9.95 (*1-889733-06-7*, 01008) Precious Life Bks.

— My Guardian Dear (Mi Angel de la Guarda) A Story of the Angels (Un Cuento Acerca de los Angeles) Emmanuelli Klosterman, Carmen A., tr. (Stories of the Faith Ser.). (ENG & SPA., Illus.). 64p. (gr. k-10). 1996. pap. 9.95 (*1-889733-03-2*, 01005) Precious Life Bks.

Lademan, Miriam A., jt. auth. see Brindle, Susan A.

Lademan, Miriam A., ed. see Hooker, Irene H. & Brindle, Susan A.

Lademann-Priemer, Gabriele. Heilung Als Zeichen Fur die Einheit der Welten: Religiose Vorstellungen von Krankheit und Heilung in Europa Im Vorigen Jahrhundert und Unter Den Zulu Mit Einem Ausblick in Unsere Zeit. (Europaische Hochschulschriften Ser.: Reihe 23, Bd. 382). (GER., Illus.). 337p. 1990. 63.80 (*3-631-42485-X*) P Lang Pubng.

Laden, Elizabeth. Mystic Warriors of the Yellowstone. large type ed. Cooper, Jan, ed. (Orig.). 1996. pap. 12.95 (*0-9654107-1-4*) My Office Pubng.

Laden, Hyman N. & Gildersleeve, Thomas R. System Design for Computer Applications. LC 63-17363. 336p. reprint ed. pap. 104.20 (*0-608-10769-7*, 200707500060) Bks Demand.

Laden, Janis. Fires in the Snow. 320p. 1992. mass mkt. 3.99 (*0-8217-3809-7*, Zebra Kensgtn) Kensgtn Pub Corp.

— Noble Mistress. 1987. mass mkt. 3.95 (*0-8217-2169-0*, Zebra Kensgtn) Kensgtn Pub Corp.

— A Whisper of Scandal. 448p. 1993. mass mkt. 3.99 (*0-8217-4106-3*, Zebra Kensgtn) Kensgtn Pub Corp.

Laden, Jenny & Elaine Tin Nyo, eds. Update, 1995: White Columns Annual Catalogue. 56p. (Orig.). 1995. pap. 15.00 (*0-9648468-0-2*) White Columns.

Laden, Karl. Antiperspirants & Deodorants. 2nd rev. ed. LC 98-50967. (Cosmetic Science & Technology Ser.). (Illus.). 408p. 1999. text 185.00 (*0-8247-1746-5*) Dekker.

Laden, Marie-Paule. Self-Imitation in the Eighteenth-Century Novel. LC 86-25541. 205p. reprint ed. pap. 63.60 (*0-608-06393-2*, 206675400008) Bks Demand.

***Laden, Nina.** Bad Dog. 32p. (J). 2000. 15.95 (*0-8027-8747-9*) Walker & Co.

— Bad Dog. LC 00-24233. (Illus.). 32p. (J). 2000. lib. bdg. 16.85 (*0-8027-8748-7*) Walker & Co.

Laden, Nina. My Family Tree: A Bird's Eye View. LC 96-9633. (Illus.). 32p. (J). 1997. pap. 9.95 (*0-8118-1528-5*) Chronicle Bks.

— The Night I Followed the Dog. LC 93-31008. (Illus.). 40p. (J). (ps-5). 1994. 14.95 (*0-8118-0647-2*) Chronicle Bks.

***Laden, Nina.** Peek-a-Who? LC 99-44248. (Illus.). 11p. (J). (ps). 2000. bds. 6.95 (*0-8118-2602-3*) Chronicle Bks.

Laden, Nina. Private I. Guana: The Case of the Missing Chameleon. LC 95-2828. (Illus.). 32p. (J). (gr. k-5). 1999. 14.95 (*0-8118-0940-4*); pap. 6.95 (*0-8118-2463-2*) Chronicle Bks.

***Laden, Nina.** Roberto: The Insect Architect. LC 99-50851. (Illus.). (J). 2000. 15.95 (*0-8118-2465-9*) Chronicle Bks.

Laden, Nina. When Pigasso Met Mootisse. LC 98-2611. 40p. (J). (ps-5). 1998. 15.95 (*0-8118-1121-2*) Chronicle Bks.

Laden, Patrick. Flexographic Inks. (Illus.). 500p. 2000. 185.00 (*1-885067-07-0*) Jelmar Pub.

Laden, Patrick, ed. Chemistry & Technology of Water Based Inks. LC 96-83829. 345p. 1997. pap. write for info. (*0-7514-0165-X*) Kluwer Academic.

Ladenburg, R. W., et al, eds. Physical Measurements in Gas Dynamics & Combustion. LC 54-13127. 606p. reprint ed. pap. 187.90 (*0-608-10245-8*, 200009700025) Bks Demand.

Ladenburg, Thomas. The Federalist Era. (American History Ser.). (Illus.). 86p. (Orig.). 1989. pap. 19.50 (*0-89994-327-6*) Soc Sci Ed.

Ladenburg, Thomas, jt. auth. see Tegnell, Geoffrey.

Ladendecker, Dianne. Holidays & Holy Days, Vol. 2. 44p. 1989. pap. text 6.95 (*0-8497-4856-9*, C8811) Kjos.

Ladendecker, Dianne, jt. auth. see Frazee, Jane.

Ladendorf, Sandra F. Successful Southern Gardening: A Practical Guide for Year-round Beauty. LC 88-20634. (Illus.). x, 294p. (C). 1989. 32.50 (*0-8078-1831-3*) U of NC Pr.

Ladendorf, Sandra F. Successful Southern Gardening: A Practical Guide for Year-round Beauty. LC 88-20634. (Illus.). x, 294p. (C). 1989. pap. 14.95 (*0-8078-4241-9*) U of NC Pr.

Ladenheim, Kala. Patching the Safety Net: Shifting Health Care Costs & State Policies. LC 98-116504. 32p. 1997. 35.00 (*1-55516-751-9*, 6735) Natl Conf State Legis.

Ladenheim, Melissa. Birds in Wood: The Carvings of Andrew Zergenyi. LC 95-42172. (Folk Art & Artists Ser.). (Illus.). 72p. (C). 1996. 32.50 (*0-87805-862-1*); pap. 16.95 (*0-87805-863-X*) U Pr of Miss.

— The Sauna in Central New York. (Illus.). xiv, 25p. (Orig.). 1986. pap. 2.95 (*0-942690-35-4*) DeWitt Hist.

Ladenis, Nico. Nico: Recipes & Recollections from One of Our Most Brilliant & Controversial Chefs. (Illus.). 240p. 1997. pap. 37.50 (*0-333-71102-5*, Pub. by Macmillan) Trans-Atl Phila.

Ladenson, Alex. Library Law & Legislation in the United States. LC 81-23176. (Library Administration Ser.: No. 1). 203p. 1982. 24.00 (*0-8108-1513-3*) Scarecrow.

Ladenson, Alex, ed. American Library Laws. LC 83-21543. 2019p. reprint ed. pap. 200.00 (*0-7837-5915-0*, 204571400007) Bks Demand.

Ladenson, Elisabeth. Proust's Lesbianism. LC 98-38248. 1999. 32.50 (*0-8014-3595-1*) Cornell U Pr.

Ladenson, Paul W. The Consultation Guide. LC 98-23835. 1998. 49.00 (*0-683-30525-5*) Lppncott W & W.

Ladenson, Robert F. Ethics in the American Workplace: Policies & Decisions. 500p. (Orig.). 1995. pap. 34.90 (*0-934753-41-5*) LRP Pubns.

Ladenthin, Volker. Modern Literatur und Bildung. ix, 405p. 1991. write for info. (*3-487-09504-1*) G Olms Pubs.

Lader, Curt. How to Prepare for the Advanced Placement Test: AP U.S. Government & Politics. 2nd ed. LC 97-37287. (Illus.). 508p. 1998. pap. 14.95 (*0-7641-0368-7*) Barron.

— Painless American History LC 98-50020. (Painless... Ser.). 1999. 8.95 (*0-7641-0620-1*) Barron.

Lader, Curt, jt. auth. see Klose, Nelson.

Lader, Errol. Diagnosis & Treatment of Temporomandibular Joint & Myofascial Pain Dysfunctions. Hogue, Calvin, tr. LC 83-50819. (Illus.). 150p. 1983. pap. text 75.00 (*0-9610782-4-3*) Vadare.

— Handbook of Exercises for Eliminating Headaches. (Illus.). 65p. 1983. pap. 2.95 (*0-9610782-6-X*) Vadare.

— Managing Chronic Orofacial Pain with Transcutaneous Electroneural Stimulation. LC 85-50702. (Illus.). 300p. 1986. pap. text 85.00 (*0-9610782-5-1*) Vadare.

— TMJ: Clinical & Practice Managememt. 116p. ring bd. 85.00 (*0-9610782-0-0*) Vadare.

— TMJ: Systems Manual of Insurance & Practice Management. 97p. spiral bd. 65.00 (*0-9610782-1-9*) Vadare.

Lader, I. Will. PM & the Art of Not Taking Out the Garbage. 1991. pap. write for info. (*1-878515-41-1*) W S Dawson.

Lader, Lawrence. Abortion. LC 66-18592. 1966. 5.95 (*0-672-50601-7*, Bobbs) Macmillan.

— The Margaret Sanger Story & the Fight for Birth Control. LC 73-11855. (Illus.). 348p. 1975. reprint ed. lib. bdg. 69.50 (*0-8371-7076-1*, LAMS, Greenwood Pr) Greenwood.

— A Private Matter: RU-486 & the Abortion Crisis. LC 95-20257. (Illus.). 254p. 1995. 25.95 (*1-57392-012-6*) Prometheus Bks.

— RU 486: The Pill That Could End the Abortion Wars & Why American Women Don't Have It. 1991. 16.30 (*0-201-57069-6*) Addison-Wesley.

— RU 486: The Pill That Could End the Abortion Wars & Why American Women Don't Have It. 1992. pap. 9.57 (*0-201-60819-7*) Addison-Wesley.

— RU 486: The Pill That Could End the Abortion Wars & Why American Women Don't Have It. rev. ed. 1992. 18.95 (*0-201-63203-9*) Addison-Wesley.

Lader, Malcolm H. The Age of Anxiety: A Reassessment. 24p. 1984. pap. 6.00 (*0-904674-09-6*, Pub. by Octagon Pr) ISHK.

Lader, Malcolm H., ed. Priorities in Psychiatric Research. LC 80-40583. 245p. reprint ed. pap. 76.00 (*0-608-12314-5*, 202428000035) Bks Demand.

— Psychopharmacology of Addiction. (British Association for Psychopharmacology Monographs: No. 10). (Illus.). 192p. 1988. 55.00 (*0-19-261626-9*) OUP.

— Studies of Schizophrenia: Papers Read at the World Psychiatric Association Symposium, "Current Concepts of Schizophrenia", London, November, 1972. LC 76-382728. (British Journal of Psychiatry. Special Publication Ser.: No. 10). 170p. reprint ed. pap. 52.70 (*0-608-15852-6*, 203146500074) Bks Demand.

Lader, Malcolm H., et al, eds. The Nature of Alcohol & Drug-Related Problems. (Society for the Study of Addiction Monograph Ser.: No. 2). (Illus.). 228p. 1992. text 69.95 (*0-19-262138-6*) OUP.

Lader, Malcolm H. & Herrington, Reginald. Biological Treatments in Psychiatry. (Illus.). 416p. 1990. text 80.00 (*0-19-261644-7*); pap. text 37.50 (*0-19-261939-X*) OUP.

Lader, Malcolm H., et al. Patterns of Improvement in Depressed In-Patients. (Maudsley Monographs: No. 30). 128p. 1987. 45.00 (*0-19-712154-3*) OUP.

Lader, Malcolm H., jt. auth. see Bond, Alyson J.

Lader, Malcolm H., jt. auth. see Edwards, J. G.

Lader, Malcolm H., jt. auth. see Herrington, Reginald.

Lader, Malcolm H., jt. ed. see Clare, A. W.

Lader, Malcolm H., jt. ed. see Edwards, Griffith.

Lader, Melvin P. Arshile Gorky. LC 84-24268. (Modern Masters Ser.). (Illus.). 128p. 1985. pap. 14.95 (*1-55859-249-0*) Abbeville Pr.

Lader, Melvin P., contrib. by. Arshile Gorky: Three Decades of Drawings. LC 90-62329. (Illus.). 72p. 1990. pap. 20.00 (*0-935037-38-1*) G Peters Gallery.

Laderer, Mandy. Fit-Kids: Getting Kids Hooked on Fitness Fun. LC 93-74028. 200p. 1994. pap. 19.95 (*0-9639178-1-1*) Allure Pubng.

Laderman, Aimlee D., ed. Coastally Restricted Forests. LC 96-13758. (Biological Resource Management Ser.). (Illus.). 352p. 1997. text 85.00 (*0-19-507567-6*) OUP.

Laderman, Carol. Taming the Wind of Desire: Psychology, Medicine, & Aesthetics in Malay Shamanistic Performance. LC 90-38031. (Comparative Studies of Health Systems & Medical Care: Vol. 29). (Illus.). 386p. 1991. pap. 18.95 (*0-520-08258-3*, Pub. by U CA Pr) Cal Prin Full Svc.

— Wives & Midwives: Childbirth & Nutrition in Rural Malaysia. LC 83-47664. (Comparative Studies of Health Systems & Medical Care: Vol. 7). (Illus.). 267p. (C). 1984. pap. 15.95 (*0-520-06036-9*, Pub. by U CA Pr) Cal Prin Full Svc.

Laderman, Carol & Roseman, Marina, eds. The Performance of Healing. LC 95-24568. 330p. (C). 1995. pap. 21.99 (*0-415-91200-8*) Routledge.

— The Performance of Healing. LC 95-24568. 330p. (C). (gr. 13). 1996. 80.00 (*0-415-91199-0*) Routledge.

Laderman, E. Concerto: For Flute & Orchestra Piano Reduction. 56p. 1993. pap. 32.00 (*0-7935-0996-3*) H Leonard.

— MBL Suite: 2 Flutes, String Quartet, Score & Parts. 80p. 1993. pap. 35.00 (*0-7935-2363-X*) H Leonard.

— Partita for Solo Violin. 24p. 1993. per. 12.95 (*0-7935-2294-3*) H Leonard.

— Quintet for Clarinet & String Quartet. 60p. 1993. per. 45.00 (*0-7935-2870-4*) H Leonard.

Laderman, Gary. The Sacred Remains: American Attitudes Toward Death, 1799-1883. LC 96-10373. (Illus.). 240p. 1996. 32.00 (*0-300-06432-2*) Yale U Pr.

— The Sacred Remains: American Attitudes Toward Death, 1799-1883. (Illus.). 240p. 1999. pap. text 16.00 (*0-300-07868-4*) Yale U Pr.

Laderman, Gary, jt. auth. see Leon, Luis.

Laderman, Gary, jt. auth. see Pulcini, Theodore.

Laderman, Jeffrey. The Insider's Guide to Mutual Funds. 128p. 1995. pap. 12.00 (*0-07-036016-2*) McGraw.

***Laderman, Jeffrey M.** Business Week Guide to Mutual Funds. 10th ed. 224p. 2000. pap. 14.95 (*0-07-135891-9*) McGraw.

Laderman, Jeffrey M. Business Week's Guide to Mutual Funds. 7th ed. (Illus.). 224p. 1997. pap. 14.95 (*0-07-036774-4*) McGraw.

Laderman, Jeffrey M., ed. BusinessWeek Guide to Mutual Funds. annuals 8th ed. (Illus.). 240p. 1998. pap. 14.95 (*0-07-038200-X*, BusinessWeek Bks) McGraw.

Laderman, Jeffrey M., jt. auth. see Business Week Staff.

Ladeveze, P. & Simmonds, J. G. Nonlinear Computational Structural Mechanics: New Approaches & Non-Incremental Methods of Calculation. Ling, F. F., ed. LC 98-29990. (Mechanical Engineering Ser.). (Illus.). 240p. 1998. 59.95 (*0-387-98594-8*) Spr-Verlag.

Ladeveze, P. & Zienkiewicz, O. C., eds. New Advances in Computational Structural Mechanics: Proceedings of the European Conference on New Advances in Computational Structural Mechanics, Giens, France, 2-5 April 1991. LC 92-9902. (Studies in Applied Mechanics: Vol. 32). 484p. 1992. 240.75 (*0-444-89057-2*) Elsevier.

Ladeveze, Pierre & Oden, J. Tinsley. Advances in Adaptive Computational Methods in Mechanics. LC 98-15962. (Studies in Applied Mechanics). 1998. 227.00 (*0-08-043327-8*) Elsevier.

Ladew, Donald P. How to Supervise People: Techniques for Getting Results Through Others. LC 98-10418. 128p. 1998. pap. 10.99 (*1-56414-363-5*) Career Pr Inc.

Ladewig, D., ed. Basic & Clinical Science of Substance Related Disorders: Congress, Basel, May, 1998. 2nd ed. LC 99-32981. (Bibliotheca Psychiatrica Ser.: Vol. 168 (1999)). (Illus.). viii, 68p. 1999. 75.00 (*3-8055-6870-3*) S Karger.

— Drogen & Alkohol Series Vol. 3: Folgestudien und Therapieabbruch. (GER., Illus.). vi, 174p. 1984. pap. 50.50 (*3-8055-3874-X*) S Karger.

Ladewig, D., jt. ed. see Pletscher, A.

***Ladewig, David.** Come Travel with Me to the Other Side of Sunset. (Illus.). 296p. (Orig.). 1999. pap. 29.95 (*1-55212-243-3*, 99-0011) Trafford.

Ladewig, James. Antonio Mortaro, Primo De Canzoni Da Sonare a Quattra Voci. LC 88-754002. (Italian Instrumental Music of the Sixteenth & Early Seventeenth Centuries Ser.: Vol. 13). 168p. 1989. text 30.00 (*0-8240-4512-2*) Garland.

— Giovanni Domenico Rognoni Taeggio: Canzoni a 4. & 8. Voci...Libro Primo (Milan, 1605) LC 92-34416. (Italian Instrumental Music of the Sixteenth & Early Seventeenth Centuries Ser.: Vol. 16). 264p. 1993. text 94.00 (*0-8240-4515-7*) Garland.

Ladewig, James, ed. Agostino Soderini: Canzoni a 4. & 8. Voci...Libro Primo (Milan, 1608) LC 91-760648. (Italian Instrumental Music of the Sixteenth & Early Seventeenth Centuries Ser.: Vol. 19). 264p. 1992. text 88.00 (*0-8240-4518-1*) Garland.

— Annibale Padovano: Il Primo Libro de Ricercari a Quattro Voci, Venice, 1556. LC 93-48854. (Italian Instrumental Music of the Sixteenth & Early Seventeenth Centuries Ser.: Vol. 4). 208p. 1994. text 83.00 (*0-8240-4503-3*) Garland.

— Canzonas & Capricio from the Seconda Aggiunta Alli Concerti Raccolti Dal Molto Reverendo Don Francesco Lucino a Due, Tre e Quattro Voci, di Diversi Eccellenti Autori...Novamente Raccolta, & Data in Luce Da Filippo Lomazzo, (Milan, 1617) & Nicolo Corradini il Primo Libro De Canzoni Francese a 4. & Alcune Suonate (Venice, 1624) LC 94-43627. (Italian Instrumental Music of the Sixteenth & Seventeenth Centuries Ser.: Vol. 29). 224p. 1995. text 94.00 (*0-8240-4528-9*) Garland.

— Claudio Merulo: Il Primo Libro de Recercari da Cantare, a

An Asterisk (*) at the beginning of an entry indicates that the title is appearing for the first time.

Quattro Voci. Venice, 1574. LC 87-750977. (Italian Instrumental Music of the Sixteenth & Early Seventeenth Centuries Ser.). 235p. 1987. text 25.00 (*0-8240-4504-1*) Garland.

— Claudio Merulo: Ricercari da Cantare a Quattro Voci--Libro Terzo - Venice 1608, Vol. 7. LC 87-754765. (Italian Instrumental Music of the Sixteenth & Early Seventeenth Centuries Ser.). 240p. 1988. text 30.00 (*0-8240-4506-8*) Garland.

— Claudio Merulo: Ricercari da Cantare a Quattro Voci...Libro Secondo, Venice, 1607. LC 87-752604. (Italian Instrumental Music of the Sixteenth & Early Seventeenth Centuries Ser.: Vol. 6). 274p. 1987. text 30.00 (*0-8240-4505-X*) Garland.

— Giovanni Antonio Cangiasi: Scherzi Forastieri Per Suonare a Quattro Voci (Milan, 1614) LC 91-751636. (Italian Instrumental Music of the Sixteenth & Early Seventeenth Centuries Ser.: Vol. 24). 181p. 1991. text 30.00 (*0-8240-4523-8*) Garland.

— Jacques Buus: Il Secondo Libro di Recercari, da Cantare, & Sonare d'Organo & Altri Stromenti, a Quatro Voci, Venice, 1549. LC 92-43817. (Italian Instrumental Music of the Sixteenth & Early Seventeenth Centuries Ser.: Vol. 3). 192p. 1993. text 79.00 (*0-8240-4502-5*) Garland.

— Lodovico Viadana: Sinfonie Musicali a Otto Voci . . . Commod Per Concertare Con O i Sorte Di Stromen . . . Opera XVIII (Venice, 1610), Pt. 1 & 2. LC 93-29317. (Italian Instrumental Music of the Sixteenth & Early Seventeenth Centuries Ser.: Vol. 21). (Illus.). 504p. 1994. text 182.00 (*0-8240-4520-3*) Garland.

— Ottavio Bariolla: Caprici, Overo Canzoni a Quatro...Libro Terzo (Milan, 1594) LC 94-47251. (Italian Instrumental Music of the Sixteenth & Seventeenth Centuries Ser.: Vol. 12). 216p. 1995. text 94.00 (*0-8240-4511-4*) Garland.

— Rovigo & Ruggier Trofeo Canzoni da Suonare a Quattro et a otto (Milan) (1613) LC 88-750072. (Italian Instrumental Music of the Sixteenth & Early Seventeenth Centuries Ser.). 174p. 1988. text 30.00 (*0-8240-4521-1*) Garland.

— Stefano Bernardi: Sonatas & Sinfonias from the "Motetti in Cantilena a Quattro Voci, con Alcune Canzoni per Sonare con Ogni Sorte di Strumenti" (Venice, 1613) & the "Concerti Academici con Varia di Sinfonie a Sei Voci...Libro Primo" (Venice, 1615-1616) LC 91-761355. (Italian Instrumental Music of the Sixteenth & Early Seventeenth Centuries Ser.: Vol. 23). 192p. 1992. text 83.00 (*0-8240-4522-X*) Garland.

Ladewig, James, ed. see Grillo, Giovanni B.

Ladewig, Patricia. Essentials of Maternal Newborn Nursing. 4th ed. LC 97-37686. 896p. (C). 1997. pap. text 71.24 (*0-8053-5622-3*) Addison-Wesley.

Ladewig, Patricia A., et al. Essentials of Maternal-Newborn Nursing. 700p. (C). 1986. text. write for info. (*0-201-12680-X*, Health Sci) Addison-Wesley.

— Essentials of Maternal-Newborn Nursing. 2nd ed. Hunter, Debra, ed. 889p. (C). 1990. text 56.95 (*0-201-13238-9*) Addison-Wesley.

— Maternal Newborn. 2nd ed. Hunter, Debra, ed. 889p. (C). 1990. pap. text 9.95 (*0-201-53238-7*) Addison-Wesley.

Ladewig, Patricia W. Clinical Handbook to Accompany Essentials of Maternal Newborn Nursing. 4th ed. LC 97-41302. 368p. (C). 1997. pap. text 27.19 (*0-8053-5629-0*) Addison-Wesley.

— Maternal-Newborn Nursing Care: The Nurse, the Family & the Community. 4th ed. 288p. (C). 1997. pap. text, wbk. ed. 27.19 (*0-8053-5628-2*) Addison-Wesley.

Ladewig, Theodor, et al, eds. Vergils Gedichte Band 1: Bukolika und Georgika. (GER.). xiii, 292p. 1973. write for info. (*3-296-15871-5*) G Olms Pubs.

— Vergils Gedichte Band 2: Buch I-VI der Aneis. (GER.). vi, 341p. write for info. (*3-296-15872-3*) G Olms Pubs.

— Vergils Gedichte Band 3: Buch VII-XII der Aneis. (GER.). vi, 308p. 1973. write for info. (*3-296-15873-1*) G Olms Pubs.

Ladewig, Wilfried. Widerstand als Sprachliche Gemeinschaft: Die Romane von Kingsley Amis als Selbstreflexive Texte. (Europaische Hochschulschriften, Reihe 14: Bd. 324). (GER.). 387p. 1996. 63.95 (*3-631-30696-2*) P Lang Pubng.

Ladha, J. K., et al, eds. Biological Nitrogen Fixation for Sustainable Agriculture: Extended Version of Papers Presented in the Symposium, Role of Biological Nitrogen Fixation in Sustainable Agriculture, at the 13th Congress of Soil Science, Kyoto, Japan, 1990. LC 92-10783. (Developments in Plant & Soil Sciences Ser.: Vol. 49). (C). 1992. text 160.50 (*0-7923-1774-2*) Kluwer Academic.

— Management of Biological Nitrogen Fixation for the Development of More Productive & Sustainable Agricultural Systems: Extended Versions of Papers Presented at the Symposium on Biological Nitrogen Fixation for Sustainable Agriculture at the 15th Congress of Soil Science, Acapulco, Mexico, 1994. (Developments in Plant & Soil Sciences Ser.: Vol. 65). 308p. (C). 1995. text 161.50 (*0-7923-3413-2*) Kluwer Academic.

Ladha, J. K., et al. Opportunities for Biological Nitrogen Fixation in Rice & Other Non-Legumes: Papers Presented at the Second Working Group Meeting of the Frontier Project on Nitrogen Fixation in Rice Held at the National Institute for Biotechnology & Genetic Engineering (Nibge), Faislabad, Pakistan, 13-15 October 1996. LC 97-30255. 1997. text. write for info. (*0-7923-4747-1*) Kluwer Academic.

Ladha, Jagdish K., et al, eds. Opportunities for Biological Nitrogen Fixation in Rice & Other Non-Legumes. (Developments in Plant & Soil Sciences Ser.: No. 75). 232p. 1997. text 167.00 (*0-7923-4514-2*) Kluwer Academic.

Ladies Aid Society Staff. The Kelly Cook Book. 2nd ed. 28p. 1981. pap. 3.00 (*0-9617036-1-X*) Bandar Log.

Ladies Auxiliary Hadar Zion Staff. The Plain & Simple Family Cookbook. 189p. 1992. spiral bd. 11.95 (*0-944070-37-X*, Pub. by Targum Pr) Feldheim.

Ladies' Home Journal Editors. Can This Marriage Be Saved? Rosen, Margery D., ed. LC 94-4541. (Illus.). 352p. 1994. pap. 9.95 (*1-56305-628-3*, 3628) Workman Pub.

Ladies Home Journal Editors & Christian Science Monitor Editors. America's Twelve Great Women Leaders During the Past Hundred Years As Chosen by the Women of America. LC 74-90600. (Essay Index Reprint Ser.). 1977. 17.95 (*0-8369-1202-0*) Ayer.

***Ladies' Home Journal Staff.** 100 Most Important Women of the 20th Century. LC 98-66257. (Illus.). 192p. 1998. 34.95 (*0-696-20823-7*) Meredith Bks.

Ladies of the Mission Staff. Old Brewery & the New Mission House at the Five Points. LC 72-112563. (Rise of Urban America Ser.). (Illus.). 1976. reprint ed. 29.95 (*0-405-02461-4*) Ayer.

***Ladies Professional Golf Association Staff.** LPGA's Guide to Every Shot. LC 99-89363. (Illus.). 200p. 2000. pap. 19.95 (*0-88011-980-2*) Human Kinetics.

Ladies Sewing Soc. of St. Luke's Church. The Catskill Cookbook. (Illus.). 150p. pap. 12.95 (*0-941567-46-X*) J C & A L Fawcett.

Ladiges, P. Y. & Martinelli, L. W. Plant Systematics in the Age of Molecular Biology. (Illus.). 172p. 1990. pap. 50.00 (*0-643-05098-1*, Pub. by CSIRO) Accents Pubns.

Ladiges, Pauline Y., jt. ed. see Littlejohn, M. J.

Ladiges, Werner & Vogt, Dieter. Die Suesswasserfische Europas Bis Zum Oral und Kaspischen Meer (Freshwater Fish of Europe to the Urals & Caspian Sea) 2nd ed. (Illus.). 299p. 1979. 20.00 (*3-8263-8163-7*, Pub. by Blckwell Wissenschafts) Balogh.

Ladik, Janos. Quantum Theory of Polymers As Solids. LC 87-29159. (Illus.). 431p. reprint ed. pap. 133.70 (*0-608-08572-3*, 206909500002) Bks Demand.

Ladik, Janos & Forner, Wolfgang. The Beginnings of Cancer in the Cell: An Interdisciplinary Approach. LC 94-21255. 1994. 59.95 (*0-387-57962-1*) Spr-Verlag.

Ladik, Janos J. & Andre, Jean-Marie, eds. Quantum Chemistry of Polymers: Solid State Aspects. LC 84-3367. 1984. text 200.00 (*90-277-1741-9*) Kluwer Academic.

Ladik, Katalin. Stories of the Seven-Headed Sewing Machine. limited ed. B'Racz, Emoke, tr. from HUN. 28p. 1992. pap. 4.50 (*0-685-64797-8*) New Native Pr.

***Ladimer, Bethany.** Colette, Beauvoir & Duras: Age & Women Writers. LC 99-33017. 224p. 1999. 39.95 (*0-8130-1700-9*) U Press Fla.

Ladimer, Irving & McCarthy, Jane. Resolving Faculty Disputes. LC 81-67937. 80p. 1981. pap. 8.00 (*0-943001-12-9*) Am Arbitration.

Lading, L., et al. Optical Diagnostics for Flow Processes. (Illus.). 406p. (C). 1994. text 132.00 (*0-306-44817-3*, Kluwer Plenum) Kluwer Academic.

Ladinsky, Daniel. I Heard God Laughing: Renderings of Hafiz. LC 96-67524. xvii, 161p. (Orig.). 1996. pap. 14.00 (*0-915828-18-9*) Sufism Reoriented.

— The Subject Tonight Is Love: 60 Wild & Sweet Poems of Hafiz. LC 96-92272. 86p. (Orig.). 1996. pap. 10.00 (*0-9657637-0-6*) Pmpkn House.

— The Sun's Breath: Poems of Hafiz. (Illus.). (Orig.). 1997. pap. 15.00 (*0-9657637-5-7*) Pmpkn House.

Ladinsky, Daniel, tr. see Hafiz.

Ladis, Andrew. The Brancacci Chapel, Florence. LC 93-6995. (Great Fresco Cycles of the Renaissance Ser.). (Illus.). 120p. 1993. 25.00 (*0-8076-1311-8*) Braziller.

— Italian Renaissance Maiolica from Southern Collections. Eiland, William U., ed. (Illus.). 118p. 1989. pap. 25.00 (*0-915977-03-6*) Georgia Museum of Art.

Ladis, Andrew, ed. Giotto & the World of Early Italian Art: An Anthology of Literature, 4 vols. Incl. Vol. 1. Giotto As an Historical & Literary Figure: Miscellaneous Specialized Studies. LC 98-29360. (Illus.). 392p. 1998. reprint ed. 90.00 (*0-8153-2773-0*); Vol. 2. Arena Chapel & the Genius of Giotto: Padua. LC 98-29357. 432p. 1998. reprint ed. 95.00 (*0-8153-2774-9*); Vol. 3. Giotto, Master Painter & Architect: Florence. LC 98-29359. 336p. 1998. reprint ed. 85.00 (*0-8153-2725-0*); Vol. 4. Franciscanism, the Papacy, & Art in the Age of Giotto: Assisi & Rome. LC 98-29361. 456p. 1998. reprint ed. 95.00 (*0-8153-2726-9*); 365.00 (*0-8153-2772-2*) Garland.

Ladis, Andrew, et al, eds. The Craft of Art: Originality & Industry in the Italian Renaissance & Baroque Workshop. LC 93-40992. (Illus.). 288p. (C). 1995. 40.00 (*0-8203-1648-2*) U of Ga Pr.

Ladis, Andrew, et al. Brooks Museum Bulletin Vol. II: Essays on the Collection. Lawrence, Patricia B., ed. (Illus.). 44p. (Orig.). (C). 1996. mass mkt. write for info. (*0-915525-04-6*) Memphis Brooks Museum.

Ladis, Andrew, jt. auth. see Brumbaugh, Thomas B.

Ladisch, Michael R., et al, eds. Protein Purification: From Molecular Mechanisms to Large-Scale Processes. LC 90-35551. (ACS Symposium Ser.: No. 427). (Illus.). 302p. 1990. text 75.00 (*0-8412-1790-4*, Pub. by Am Chemical) OUP.

Ladisch, Michael R. & Bose, Arindam, eds. Harnessing Biotechnology for the 21st Century: Proceedings of the Ninth International Biotechnology Symposium & Exposition, Crystal City, Virginia, August 19-21, 1992. LC 92-21791. (ACS Conference Proceedings Ser.). (Illus.). 612p. 1992. text 165.00 (*0-8412-2477-3*, Pub. by Am Chemical) OUP.

Ladislas, Robert & Hornebeck, William, eds. Elastin & Elastases, Vol. I. 328p. 1989. lib. bdg. 229.00 (*0-8493-6428-0*, QP552) CRC Pr.

Ladizinsky, Eric. Magical Science. rev. ed. (Illus.). 80p. (J). (gr. 3-6). 1998. pap. 6.95 (*1-56565-980-5*, 09805W, Pub. by Lowell Hse Juvenile) NTC Contemp Pub Co.

***Ladizinsky, Eric.** More Magical Science: Magic Tricks for Young Scientists. (Illus.). (J). 2000. pap. 6.95 (*0-7373-0513-4*) Lowell Hse Juvenile.

— 150 Nifty Super Rainy-Day Activities. (Illus.). (J). 2000. pap. 9.95 (*0-7373-0515-0*) Lowell Hse Juvenile.

Ladizinsky, Eric, jt. auth. see Amato, Carol.

Ladizinsky, Eric, jt. auth. see Melton, Lisa.

***Ladizinsky, Gideon.** Plant Evolution under Domestication. 262p. 1999. 140.00 (*0-412-82210-5*) Kluwer Academic.

Ladj, M. Lexique de la Scene. (FRE.). 1998. 95.00 (*0-320-00151-2*) Fr & Eur.

Ladjevardi, Habib. Reference Guide to the Iranian Oral History Project. 2nd ed. LC 93-61276. (Orig.). 1993. pap. 9.95 (*0-932885-10-1*) Harvard CMES.

Ladjevardi, Habib, ed. Memoirs of Abdolmadjin Madjidi. LC 98-70949. (Harvard Iranian Oral History Ser.: Vol. 5). (PER.). 270p. (Orig.). 1998. pap. 15.00 (*0-932885-18-7*) Harvard CMES.

— Memoirs of Ali Amini: Prime Minister of Iran. LC 95-81862. 244p. (C). 1995. pap. 15.00 (*0-932885-11-X*) Harvard CMES.

— Memoirs of Fatemeh Pakravan. LC 98-72971. (Harvard Iranian Oral History Ser.: Vol. 6). (Illus.). 155p. (Orig.). 1998. pap. 15.00 (*0-932885-19-5*) Harvard CMES.

— Memoirs of Hamid Kadjar. LC 96-77487. (Iranian Oral History Ser.: Vol. 3). 120p. (Orig.). 1996. pap. 15.00 (*0-932885-15-2*) Harvard CMES.

***Ladjevardi, Habib, ed.** Memoirs of Jafar Sharif-Emami. (Iranian Oral History Ser.: Vol. 7). (PER.). 328p. 1999. pap. 15.00 (*0-932885-22-5*) Harvard CMES.

Ladjevardi, Habib, ed. Memoirs of M. E. Amirteymour Kalali: Tribal Leader, Majles Deputy, Cabinet Minister. LC 97-73990. (Iranian Oral History Ser.: Vol. 4). 330p. (Orig.). 1997. pap. 19.95 (*0-932885-17-9*) Harvard CMES.

— Memoirs of Shapour Bakhtiar, Vol. 2. (Iranian Oral History Ser.). (PER.). 140p. (Orig.). 1996. pap. 15.00 (*0-932885-14-4*) Harvard CMES.

Ladley, A. & Rishworth, P. Public Law in New Zealand: 25 Years of Change. 350p. 1995. pap. write for info. (*0-409-78898-8*, MICHIE) LEXIS Pub.

Ladley, Anne. Moriah's Magic. large type ed. LC 93-15497. 1993. pap. 13.95 (*1-56054-749-9*) Thorndike Pr.

— Prescription for Love. large type ed. 235p. 1992. reprint ed. lib. bdg. 13.95 (*1-56054-478-3*) Thorndike Pr.

Ladmore, Richard. Civil Litigation. (C). 1992. text 48.00 (*1-85431-231-6*, Pub. by Blackstone Pr) Gaunt.

Ladner, Benjamin, ed. The Humanities in Precollegiate Education, 83rd Yearbook of the National Society for the Study of Education, Pt. II. LC 83-62345. x, 212p. 1985. pap. text 8.00 (*0-226-60143-9*) U Ch Pr.

Ladner-Bischoff, Nathalie. An Angel's Touch: True Stories about Angels, Miracles & Answers to Prayers. LC 97-41473. 1998. pap. 8.99 (*0-8163-1577-9*) Pacific Pr Pub Assn.

Ladner, Gerhart B. God, Cosmos, & Humankind: The World Of Early Christian Symbolism. Dunlap, Thomas, tr. from GER. (Illus.). 260p. 1995. 50.00 (*0-520-08549-3*, Pub. by U CA Pr) Cal Prin Full Svc.

Ladner, Joyce, jt. ed. see Edelman, Peter.

***Ladner, Joyce A.** The New Urban Leadership. 2000. 22.95 (*0-8157-5108-7*) Brookings.

Ladner, Joyce A. The Ties That Bind: Timeless Values for African American Families. LC 98-38571. 224p. 1999. text 22.95 (*0-471-19953-2*) Wiley.

— Tomorrow's Tomorrow: The Black Woman. LC 95-22989. xxxiv, 306p. (C). 1995. pap. text 20.00 (*0-8032-7956-6*, Bison Books) U of Nebr Pr.

Ladner, Joyce A., ed. The Death of White Sociology. LC 97-73660. 500p. (C). 1998. reprint ed. pap. 18.95 (*1-57478-007-7*) Black Classic.

Ladner, Joyce A., jt. ed. see Gbadegesin, Segun.

***Ladner, Lorne, compiled by.** The Wheel of Great Compassion: The Practice of the Prayer Wheel in Tibetan Buddhism. (Illus.). 168p. 2000. pap. 19.95 (*0-86171-174-2*) Wisdom MA.

***Ladnier, Gene S.** Fame's Eternal Camping Ground: The Civil War Battle of Brice's Crossroads. LC 99-91483. 1999. 25.00 (*0-7388-0820-2*); pap. 18.00 (*0-7388-0821-0*) Xlibris Corp.

— Rebel Chronicles: Book Two - Rebel's Revenge. 310p. 2000. pap. 18.00 (*0-7388-2097-0*) Xlibris Corp.

Lado. Beginning Picture. (Lado English Ser.). 1993. pap. text, wbk. ed. 11.93 (*0-13-521501-3*) P-H.

Lado. Intermediate Workbook for the Lado Picture Dictionary. rev. ed. (C). 1996. pap. text, wbk. ed. 11.93 (*0-13-521519-6*) P-H.

Lado. Lado Book 3. 3rd ed. 192p. 1989. pap. 15.73 (*0-13-522285-0*) P-H.

Lado. Teacher's Edition. 3rd ed. (Lado English Ser.: Vol. 5). 1990. pap. text, teacher ed. 24.40 (*0-13-522491-8*) P-H.

Lado, Carlos & Pando, Francisco. Myxomycetes, I. Ceratiomyxales, Echinosteliales, Liceales, Trichiales. (Flora Mycologica Iberica Ser.: Vol. 2). (ENG & SPA., Illus.). 323p. 1997. pap. 71.00 (*3-443-65007-4*, Pub. by Gebruder Borntraeger) Balogh.

Lado International College Staff & Lado, Robert. Branching Out, No. One. rev. ed. (Illus.). 229p. (C). 1993. pap. text 14.95 (*1-879580-55-1*) Lado Intl Pr.

— Branching Out, No. Two. rev. ed. (Illus.). 203p. (C). 1993. pap. text 14.95 (*1-879580-56-X*) Lado Intl Pr.

Lado, Lucia. Lado, Bk. 5. 3rd ed. (Lado English Ser.: Vol. 5). 1990. pap. text, wbk. ed. 10.40 (*0-13-522483-7*) P-H.

— Teacher's Edition. 3rd ed. (Lado English Ser.: 6). 1990. pap. text 24.40 (*0-13-522517-5*) P-H.

— Teacher's Edition, Bk. 1. 3rd ed. (Lado English Ser.: Vol. 1). 1989. pap. text, teacher ed. 24.40 (*0-13-522376-8*) P-H.

— Teacher's Edition, Bk. 2. 3rd ed. (Lado English Ser.: Vol. 2). 1990. pap. text, teacher ed. 24.40 (*0-13-522400-4*) P-H.

— Teacher's Edition, Bk. 5. 3rd ed. (Lado English Ser.: Vol. 4). 1990. pap. text, teacher ed. 24.40 (*0-13-522467-5*) P-H.

— Workbook. 3rd ed. (Lado English Ser.: Vol. 6). 1990. pap. text, wbk. ed. 10.40 (*0-13-522509-4*) P-H.

— Workbook, Bk. 1. 3rd ed. (Lado English Ser.: Vol. 1). 1989. pap. text, wbk. ed. 10.40 (*0-13-522368-7*) P-H.

— Workbook, Bk. 2. 3rd ed. (Lado English Ser.: Vol. 2). 1989. pap. text, wbk. ed. 10.40 (*0-13-522392-X*) P-H.

— Workbook, Bk. 4. 3rd ed. (Lado English Ser.: Vol. 4). 1990. pap. text, wbk. ed. 10.40 (*0-13-522442-X*) P-H.

Lado, Robert. Basic Conversations in English. 2nd rev. ed. Kellert, A. Lynne, ed. (Illus.). 100p. 1998. pap. text 12.95 (*1-879580-70-5*) Lado Intl Pr.

— Basic Conversations in English, Bk. 2. (Illus.). 131p. (C). 1993. pap. text 8.95 (*1-879580-54-3*) Lado Intl Pr.

— Basic Conversations in English: Book I. (Illus.). (Orig.). (C). 1992. pap. text 8.95 (*1-879580-50-0*) Lado Intl Pr.

— The Big Bad Wolf: Level 2. (Reading Playhouse Ser.). (Illus.). 24p. (J). (ps). 1985. pap. 3.95 (*1-879580-53-5*); 1.95 (*1-879580-52-7*) Lado Intl Pr.

— Lado. 3rd ed. (Lado English Ser.: Vol. 2). 192p. (C). 1989. pap. 15.73 (*0-13-522269-9*) P-H.

— Lado, Bk. 1. 3rd ed. 183p. (C). 1989. pap. 15.73 (*0-13-522244-3*) P-H.

Lado, Robert. Lado, Bk. 4. 3rd ed. 192p. (C). 1989. pap. 15.73 (*0-13-522301-6*) P-H.

Lado, Robert. Lado, Bk. 5. 3rd ed. (English Ser.). 192p. (C). 1990. pap. text 15.73 (*0-13-522327-X*) P-H.

— Lado, Bk. 6. 3rd ed. 192p. (C). 1990. pap. 15.73 (*0-13-522343-1*) P-H.

— Lado English Series. 3rd ed. (C). 1989. pap. text, wbk. ed. 10.40 (*0-13-522418-7*) P-H.

— Lado English Series. 3rd ed. (C). 1990. pap. text, teacher ed. 24.40 (*0-13-522426-8*) P-H.

— Lado English Series, Bk. 2. 2nd ed. 1987. teacher ed. 11.00 (*0-13-522137-4*, 18758); student ed. 4.50 (*0-13-522079-3*, 18752) Prentice ESL.

— Lado English Series, Bk. 4. 2nd ed. 1987. teacher ed. 11.00 (*0-13-522152-8*, 18754) Prentice ESL.

— Lado English Series, Bk. 5. 2nd ed. (Illus.). 198p. (gr. 7-12). 1987. teacher ed. 11.00 (*0-13-522160-9*, 18761) Prentice ESL.

— Lado English Series, Bk. 6. 2nd ed. (Illus.). 1987. teacher ed. 11.00 (*0-13-522178-1*, 18762) Prentice ESL.

— The Lado Picture Dictionary. rev. ed. LC 92-36959. (Illus.). 128p. (C). 1993. pap. text 13.87 (*0-13-061680-X*) P-H.

— Linguistics Across Cultures: Applied Linguistics for Language Teachers. 160p. 1957. pap. text 19.95 (*0-472-08542-5*, 08542) U of Mich Pr.

— My First Thirty-Two Words: Level 1. (Reading Playhouse Ser.). (Illus.). 34p. (J). (ps). 1985. 9.95 (*1-879580-51-9*) Lado Intl Pr.

— Teaching English Across Cultures. 1988. text 14.95 (*0-07-035769-2*) McGraw.

Lado, Robert, jt. auth. see Lado International College Staff.

Ladoo, Harold S. No Pain Like This Body. (Caribbean Writers Ser.). 141p. (C). 1987. pap. 8.95 (*0-435-98874-3*, 98874) Heinemann.

— Yesterdays. 110p. (Orig.). 1974. pap. 4.95 (*0-88784-329-8*, Pub. by Hse of Anansi Pr) Genl Dist Srvs.

***Ladopoulos, E. G.** Singular Integral Equations: Linear & Non-Linear Theory & Its Applications in Science & Engineering. LC 00-38814. 2000. write for info. (*3-540-67230-3*) Spr-Verlag.

Ladou. Occupational & Environmental Medicine. 3rd ed. (C). 2001. 42.95 (*0-8385-7219-7*) Appleton & Lange.

Ladou, Joseph. Occupational & Environmental Medicine. 2nd ed. 864p. (C). 1997. pap. text 49.95 (*0-8385-7216-2*, A-7216-3, Apple Lange Med) McGraw.

Ladouceur, David J. Plutarch Themistocles. (Bryn Mawr Greek Commentaries Ser.). 80p. (Orig.). (C). 1989. pap. text 6.00 (*0-929524-60-8*) Bryn Mawr Commentaries.

Ladouceur, Norman. Inside Pro-Surface: Moving from Solid Modeling to Surface Design. LC 97-18906. 400p. (C). 1997. pap. 100.95 (*1-56690-134-0*) Thomson Learn.

Ladouceur, Norman & McKeen, John. Pro/Engineer & Plastic Design. LC 98-54937. (Illus.). 400p. (C). 1999. pap. 68.95 (*1-56690-188-X*) Thomson Learn.

Ladouceur, Paul, ed. Sacred Words: A Selection of Spiritual Writings of All Ages. 272p. (Orig.). 1996. pap. 14.95 (*1-899171-65-7*, Pub. by Findhorn Pr) Words Distrib.

Ladouceur, Paul A. Chiefs & Politicians: The Politics of Regionalism in Northern Ghana. LC 79-670408. (Legon History Ser.). 318p. reprint ed. pap. 98.60 (*0-608-13140-7*, 202523000043) Bks Demand.

Ladousse, Gillian P. Speaking Personally: Quizzes & Questionnaires for Fluency Practice. 128p. 1983. pap. text 14.95 (*0-521-28869-X*) Cambridge U Pr.

Ladousse, Gillian P., jt. auth. see Collie, Joanne.

Ladoux, Rita. Iowa. (Hello U. S. A. Ser.). (Illus.). 72p. (J). 1997. pap. text 5.95 (*0-8225-9763-2*) Lerner Pub.

— Montana. (Hello U. S. A. Ser.). (Illus.). 72p. (J). (gr. 3-6). 1997. pap. text 5.95 (*0-8225-9782-9*) Lerner Pub.

LaDoux, Rita C. Georgia. (Hello U. S. A. Ser.). (Illus.). 72p. (J). (gr. 3-6). 1991. lib. bdg. 19.93 (*0-8225-2703-0*, Lerner Publctns) Lerner Pub.

Ladoux, Rita C. Georgia: Hello U. S. A. (Illus.). 72p. (J). 1996. pap. text 5.95 (*0-8225-9734-9*) Lerner Pub.

LaDoux, Rita C. Iowa. Lerner Geography Department Staff, ed. (Hello U. S. A. Ser.). (Illus.). 72p. (J). (gr. 3-6). 1992. lib. bdg. 19.93 (*0-8225-2724-3*, Lerner Publctns) Lerner Pub.

— Louisiana. LC 92-13365. (Hello U. S. A. Ser.). (Illus.). 72p. (J). (gr. 3-6). 1993. lib. bdg. 19.93 (*0-8225-2740-5*, Lerner Publctns) Lerner Pub.

— Missouri. (Hello U. S. A. Ser.). (Illus.). 72p. (J). (gr. 3-6). 1991. lib. bdg. 19.93 (*0-8225-2710-3*, Lerner Publctns) Lerner Pub.

L

— Montana. (Hello U. S. A. Ser.). (Illus.). 72p. (J). (gr. 3-6). 1992. lib. bdg. 19.93 (0-8225-2714-6, Lerner Publctns) Lerner Pub.
— Oklahoma. Lerner Geography Department Staff, ed. (Hello U. S. A. Ser.). (Illus.). 72p. (J). (gr. 3-6). 1992. lib. bdg. 19.95 (0-8225-2717-0, Lerner Publctns) Lerner Pub.
— Oklahoma. (Hello U. S. A. Ser.). (Illus.). 72p. (J). (gr. 3-6). 1997. pap. text 5.95 (0-8225-9783-7) Lerner Pub.
Ladovic, Zdravko J., jt. auth. see Harris, Mark A.
***Ladow, Beth.** The Medicine Line: Life & Death in an American Borderland. 2001. pap. 25.00 (0-415-92764-1) Routledge.
Ladowsky, Ellen, jt. auth. see Fillion, Kate.
Ladra, Kathleen M., ed. see Steinbrecher, Thomas P.
Ladrech. Social Democratic Parties, in the European Union. LC 98-30660. 256p. 1999. text 72.00 (0-312-22007-3) St Martin.
***Ladrech, Robert.** Social Democracy & the Challenge of European Union. LC 00-24782. 175p. 2000. lib. bdg. 49.95 (1-55587-902-0) L Rienner.
Ladson-Billings, Gloria. The Dreamkeepers: Successful Teachers of African-American Children. LC 94-10316. 206p. 1997. pap. 18.00 (0-7879-0338-8) Jossey-Bass.
Ladson-Billings, Gloria, jt. auth. see Grant, Carl A.
Ladson, Etta M. Live Long & Prosper. (Illus.). 33p. 1992. teacher ed. 11.95 (0-9630574-2-1) Jewelgate.
Ladson, Etta M. Reading Tests for Strange Land Songs. 74p. 1991. spiral bd. 8.95 (0-9630574-1-3) Jewelgate.
— Strange Land Songs. (Illus.). 146p. 1992. text 14.95 (0-9630574-0-5) Jewelgate.
Ladu, Edgar E. Early & Late Mosinee. (Illus.). 228p. 1997. reprint ed. lib. bdg. 32.50 (0-8328-6978-3) Higginson Bk Co.
Ladue Chapel, Missouri Staff. Celebrating Our Past, Building for the Future: Ladue Chapel, 1943-1993. (Illus.). 128p. (Orig.). 1993. pap. text 9.95 (1-881576-18-3) Providence Hse.
Ladue, Myron. The Newcomers. 389p. (Orig.). 1989. pap. 15.00 (0-9623443-0-3) M Ladue.
LaDuke, Betty. Africa: Through the Eyes of Women Artists. LC 91-72496. (Illus.). 1991. 45.95 (0-685-56372-3) Africa World.
— Africa: Through the Eyes of Women Artists. LC 91-72496. (Illus.). 1991. pap. 15.95 (0-86543-199-X) Africa World.
— Africa: Women's Art, Women's Lives. LC 96-41841. 1995. pap. 18.95 (0-86543-435-2) Africa World.
Laduke, Betty. Africa: Women's Art, Women's Lives. LC 96-41841. (Illus.). 208p. 1996. 24.95 (0-86543-434-4) Africa World.
LaDuke, Betty. Africa Through the Eyes of Women Artists. (Illus.). 1996. 45.95 (0-86543-198-1) Africa World.
Laduke, Betty. Women Against Hunger: A Sketchbook Journey. LC 97-13313. 125p. 1997. write for info. (0-86543-605-3); pap. write for info. (0-86543-606-1) Africa World.
LaDuke, Betty. Women Artists: Multi-Cultural Visions. LC 91-68511. (Illus.). 205p. 1992. 49.95 (0-932415-77-6); pap. 16.95 (0-932415-78-4) Red Sea Pr.
LaDuke, Kelly, photos by. All Stars: One Team, One Season. LC 95-80232. (Illus.). 1996. 14.95 (1-56352-272-1) Longstreet.
LaDuke, Winona. All Our Relations: Native Struggles for Land & Life. LC 99-16813. (Illus.). 256p. 1999. 40.00 (0-89608-600-3, Pub. by South End Pr); pap. 16.00 (0-89608-599-6, Pub. by South End Pr) Consort Bk Sales.
— Last Standing Woman: A Novel. LC 97-1886. 304p. 1997. 14.95 (0-89658-278-7) Voyageur Pr.
***LaDuke, Winona.** Last Standing Woman: A Novel. LC 97-1886. 304p. 1999. pap. 14.95 (0-89658-452-6) Voyageur Pr.
Ladurie. Montaillou. 376p. 1978. 69.95 (0-85967-403-7) Ashgate Pub Co.
Ladurie, Emmanuel L. The Ancient Regime: A History of France, 1610-1770. (History of France Ser.). (Illus.). 544p. (C). 1996. 58.95 (0-631-17028-6) Blackwell Pubs.
— The Ancient Regime: A History of France, 1610-1774. (History of France Ser.). (Illus.). 544p. 1998. reprint ed. pap. 29.95 (0-631-21196-9) Blackwell Pubs.
— The Beggar & the Professor. Goldhammer, Arthur, tr. 408p. 1998. pap. 15.00 (0-226-47324-4) U Ch Pr.
— Jasmin's Witch. Pearce, Brian, tr. from FRE. LC 87-9393. (Illus.). 222p. 1987. 17.95 (0-8076-1181-6) Braziller.
— Montaillou: The Promised Land of Error. Bray, Barbara, tr. from FRE. (Illus.). 1979. pap. 11.96 (0-394-72964-1) Vin Bks.
— The Peasants of Languedoc. Day, John, tr. from FRE. LC 74-4286. (Illus.). 382p. 1977. reprint ed. pap. text 16.95 (0-252-00635-6) U of Ill Pr.
***Ladurie, Emmanuel Le Roy.** Saint Simon. 1998. 37.00 (0-226-47320-1) U Ch Pr.
— Saint Simon. 1998. pap. 24.00 (0-226-47322-8) U Ch Pr.
Ladurie, LeRoy. Beggar & the Professor. LC 96-23340. 408p. 1997. 29.95 (0-226-47323-6) U Ch Pr.
Ladusaw, William A., jt. auth. see Pullum, Geoffrey K.
Ladwai, Z., jt. auth. see Ch Lai.
Ladwig, Arnold W. From the Farm to the Fire. 53p. 1997. pap. 7.00 (0-8059-4050-2) Dorrance.
Ladwig, Dieter. Slot Machines. 1994. 12.98 (0-7858-0072-7) Bk Sales Inc.
Ladwig, Gail B. Nursing Diagnosis Handbook: A Guide to Planning Care. 3rd ed. Ackley, Betty J., ed. LC 96-47933. (Illus.). 528p. (C). (gr. 13). 1997. pap. text 27.00 (0-8151-0912-1, 28737) Mosby Inc.
Ladwig, James G. Academic Distinctions: Theory & Methodology in the Sociology of School Knowledge. LC 95-540. 208p. (C). 1995. pap. 19.99 (0-415-91188-5, B7171) Routledge.
— Academic Distinctions: Theory & Methodology in the Sociology of School Knowledge. LC 95-540. 208p. (C). (gr. 13). 1995. 65.00 (0-415-91187-7, B7167) Routledge.
Ladwig, Lewis R., jt. auth. see Kirkham, Robert M.
***Ladwig, Tim.** The Lord's Prayer. LC 98-52477. (Illus.). 32p. (J). (ps). 2000. 16.00 (0-8028-5180-0, Eerdmans Bks) Eerdmans.
Ladwig, Tim. Psalm 23. LC 97-14082. 40p. (J). 1997. 16.00 (0-8028-5160-6, Eerdmans Bks); pap. 8.00 (0-8028-5163-0, Eerdmans Bks) Eerdmans.
Ladwig, Tom. Granny Had a Word for It. LC 88-60751. (Illus.). 58p. 1988. pap. 3.95 (0-914546-75-9) Rose Pub.
Ladwig, Tom. How to Talk Dirty Like Grandad. LC 85-60070. 42p. 1985. pap. 3.95 (0-914546-59-7) Rose Pub.
Lady Chablis & Bouloukos, Theodore. Hiding My Candy. 208p. 1997. per. 14.00 (0-671-52095-4) PB.
Lady Dorchester, ed. see Broughton, John C.
Lady Dowding Muriel. Beauty-Not the Beast. (Illus.). 292p. pap. 19.95 (0-8464-4206-X) Beekman Pubs.
Lady Durning-Lawrence. Notes & Illustrations Concerning the Family History of James Smith. (Illus.). 156p. 1991. reprint ed. pap. 24.00 (0-8328-2170-5) Higginson Bk Co.
Lady Easthope, tr. see Ubicini, M. A.
Lady Evans. Hair-Dressing of Roman Ladies as Illustrated on Coins. (Illus.). 44p. 1994. reprint ed. pap. 12.50 (0-9644376-0-0) Paaka Enter.
Lady Fortescue. Return to Sunset House: A Continuation of Beauty for Ashes. large type ed. 1998. 24.95 (0-7531-5051-4, Pub. by ISIS Lrg Prnt) T T Beeler.
Lady Green. The Compleat Spanker. (Illus.). 96p. (Orig.). 1997. pap. 11.95 (1-890159-00-X) Greenery Pr.
Lady Gregory. Irish Myths & Legends: Miniature Edition. (Illus.). 128p. 1999. 4.95 (0-7624-0451-5) Running Press Min.
— Poets & Dreamers: Studies & Translations from the Irish. LC 73-17133. (Studies in Irish Literature: No. 16). 1974. lib. bdg. 75.00 (0-8383-1725-1) M S G Haskell Hse.
Lady Gregory, Isabella A. Irish Folk-History Plays, 2 vols., Set. 1988. reprint ed. lib. bdg. 99.00 (0-7812-0470-4) Rprt Serv.
Lady Hong of Hyegyong Palace. Memoirs of a Korean Queen. Choe-Wall, Yang-hi, ed. (Illus.). 200p. 1985. text 32.50 (0-7103-0052-2) Routledge.
Lady J. 1996 Who's Who in Christian Hip-Hop Artist Directory. Lynch, Fred D. et al, eds. (Illus.). 74p. (Orig.). 1996. pap., spiral bd. 17.95 (1-889133-01-9) Rising Son Media.
— The Voice of a Christian Heart: A Poetic Anthology by Jacqueline M. Gines. 68p. (Orig.). 1993. pap. 6.25 (1-889133-00-0) Rising Son Media.
— Who's Who in Christian Hip-Hop Resource Directory. (Illus.). 64p. (Orig.). 1997. 6.95 (1-889133-02-7) Rising Son Media.
Lady Llanover, ed. see Delany, Mary.
Lady Morgan. The Wild Irish Girl, 1807. LC 94-44534. (Revolution & Romanticism, 1789-1834 Ser.). 1995. 85.00 (1-85477-189-2) Continuum.
Lady Queenborough. Judaism. 1982. lib. bdg. 250.00 (0-87700-410-2) Revisionist Pr.
Lady Queenborough. Occult Theocracy. unabridged ed. 741p. 1933. reprint ed. 30.00 (0-945001-23-1) GSG & Assocs.
***Lady, Sabrina.** Wicca for Beginners A Guide to the Beliefs, Rites & Customs for the Wiccan Religion. 1999. pap. text 12.00 (0-8065-2153-8) Carol Pub Group.
Lady Sandys. The Awakening Letters, Vol. 2. Sandys, Cynthia & Lehmann, Rosamond, eds. 104p. (Orig.). pap. 17.95 (0-8464-4211-6) Beekman Pubs.
Ladybird Book Staff. Games We Like. (Key Words Readers Ser.: A Series, No. 641-9a). (Illus.). (J). (ps-5). pap. 3.50 (0-7214-0555-X, Ladybrd) Penguin Putnam.
Ladybird Books Staff. ABC. (First Steps Ser.). 32p. (J). 1998. 2.50 (0-7214-1874-0, Ladybrd) Penguin Putnam.
— ABC, Vol. 1. (First Steps Ser.). 24p. (J). 1998. pap. 1.99 (0-7214-2606-9, Ladybrd) Penguin Putnam.
— The Airplane Ride. (Kitten Tales Ser.). (Illus.). 28p. (J). (ps-2). 1992. 3.95 (0-7214-5311-2, S915-4 SER., Ladybrd) Penguin Putnam.
— The Alphabet Book. (Sunbird Ser.: No. 792-1). (Illus.). (J). (ps). 3.50 (0-7214-8100-0, Ladybrd) Penguin Putnam.
— Animals. (Talkabouts Ser.: No. 735-1). (Illus.). (J). (ps). pap. 3.50 (0-7214-1096-0, Ladybrd) Penguin Putnam.
— Baby. (Talkabouts Ser.: No. 735-5). (Illus.). (J). (ps). pap. 3.50 (0-7214-1121-5, Ladybrd) Penguin Putnam.
— Baby's Green Picture Book. (Baby Picture Bks.: No. 886-5). (Illus.). (J). (ps). pap. 3.50 (0-7214-1101-0, Ladybrd) Penguin Putnam.
— Baby's Red Picture Book. (Baby Picture Bks.: No. 886-2). (Illus.). (J). (ps). pap. 3.50 (0-7214-1088-X, Ladybrd) Penguin Putnam.
— Baby's Yellow Picture Book. (Baby Picture Bks.: No. 886-4). (Illus.). (J). (ps). pap. 3.50 (0-7214-1100-2, Ladybrd) Penguin Putnam.
— A Balloon for Katie Kitten. (Kitten Tales Ser.). (Illus.). 28p. (J). (ps-2). 1992. 3.95 (0-7214-5308-2, S915-1, Ladybrd) Penguin Putnam.
— The Big Secret. (Read with Me Key Words to Reading Ser.: No. 9010-11). (Illus.). (J). (ps-2). 1990. 3.50 (0-7214-1324-2, Ladybrd) Penguin Putnam.
— The Birthday Party Prize. (Kitten Tales Ser.). (Illus.). 28p. (J). (ps-2). 1992. 3.95 (0-7214-5310-4, S915-3 SER., Ladybrd) Penguin Putnam.
— Christmas Is Coming. (Christmas Board Bks.: No. S8823-3). (Illus.). (J). (ps). 1990. pap. 3.95 (0-7214-9133-2, Ladybrd) Penguin Putnam.
— Cinderella. (First Fairy Tales Ser.: No. S852-1). (Illus.). (J). (ps-2). pap. 3.95 (0-7214-5058-X, Ladybrd) Penguin Putnam.
— Dinosaurs. LC 72-91418. (Ladybird Learners Ser.: No. 8911-1). (J). (gr. 1-4). 1991. pap. 3.95 (0-7214-5319-8, Ladybrd) Penguin Putnam.
— The Dolphin Chase. (Read with Me Key Words to Reading Ser.: No. 9010-14). (Illus.). (J). (ps-2). 1990. 3.50 (0-7214-1327-7, Ladybrd) Penguin Putnam.
— The Dream. (Read with Me Key Words to Reading Ser.: No. 9010-6). (Illus.). (J). (ps-2). 1990. 3.50 (0-7214-1319-6, Ladybrd) Penguin Putnam.
— Eye to Eye Underwater. (J). 1999. pap. 11.99 (0-7214-5751-7, Ladybrd) Penguin Putnam.
— The Fierce Giant. (Read with Me Key Words to Reading Ser.: No. 9010-12). (Illus.). (J). (ps-2). 1990. 3.50 (0-7214-1325-0, Ladybrd) Penguin Putnam.
— First Facts About Space. (First Facts Ser.: No. S898-1). (J). 1989. pap. 3.95 (0-7214-5200-0, Ladybrd) Penguin Putnam.
— First Picture Book: Animals. (First Picture Bks.: No. 832-3). (Illus.). (J). (ps). pap. 3.50 (0-7214-0751-X, Ladybrd) Penguin Putnam.
— First Picture Book: Toys. (First Picture Bks.: No. 832-2). (Illus.). (J). (ps). pap. 3.50 (0-7214-0750-1, Ladybrd) Penguin Putnam.
— First Words. (Read with Me Key Words to Reading Ser.: No. 9010-0). (Illus.). (J). (ps-2). 1990. 3.50 (0-7214-1338-2, Ladybrd) Penguin Putnam.
— First Xmas. (J). 1997. pap. 19.99 (0-7214-5783-5, Ladybrd) Penguin Putnam.
— The Georgians. (History of Britain Ser.: No. F895-6). (Illus.). (YA). (gr. 5 up). 1990. pap. 3.95 (1-85543-011-8, Ladybrd) Penguin Putnam.
— Humpty Dumpty. 1999. text 2.50 (0-7214-2018-4) Ladybird Bks.
— Incy Wincy. 32p. 1999. text 2.50 (0-7214-2019-2) Ladybird Bks.
— Kings & Queens of England: Book One (Great Rulers), Bk. 1. (History Ser.: No. 561-24 & 25). (Illus.). (YA). (gr. 5 up). pap. write for info. (0-7214-0560-6, Ladybrd) Penguin Putnam.
— Kings & Queens of England: Book Two (Great Rulers), Bk. 2. (History Ser.: No. 561-24 & 25). (Illus.). (YA). (gr. 5 up). pap. write for info. (0-7214-0561-4, Ladybrd) Penguin Putnam.
***Ladybird Books Staff.** Lazy Lions. 48p. 1999. pap. 4.99 (0-7214-8035-7) Ladybird Bks.
Ladybird Books Staff. Let's Play. (Read with Me Key Words to Reading Ser.: No. 9010-1). (Illus.). (J). (ps-2). 1990. 3.50 (0-7214-1314-5, Ladybrd) Penguin Putnam.
— Little Bunnies All Through the Year: A Word Picture Book. (Little Bunnies Word Books Ser.: No. S9012-2). (J). 1990. pap. 3.95 (0-7214-5289-2, Ladybrd) Penguin Putnam.
— Little Bunnies at Home: A Picture Word Book. (Little Bunnies Word Books Ser.: No. S9012-1). (J). 1990. pap. 3.95 (0-7214-5288-4, Ladybrd) Penguin Putnam.
— Little Bunnies on the Move: A Word Picture Book. (Little Bunnies Word Books Ser.: No. S9012-4). (J). 1990. pap. 3.95 (0-7214-5291-4, Ladybrd) Penguin Putnam.
— Little Bunnies on Vacation: A Word Picture Book. (Little Bunnies Word Books Ser.: No. S9012-5). (J). 1990. pap. 3.95 (0-7214-5292-2, Ladybrd) Penguin Putnam.
— Little Kittens Dress-Up. (Kitten Tales Ser.). (Illus.). 28p. (J). (ps-2). 1992. 3.95 (0-7214-5312-0, S915-5, Ladybrd) Penguin Putnam.
— The Little Red Hen. (Square Format Fairy Tales Ser.: No. S874-1). (Illus.). 28p. (J). (ps up). 1987. 3.95 (0-7214-5028-8, Ladybrd) Penguin Putnam.
***Ladybird Books Staff.** Mad Millennium Joke Book. 1999. text 6.99 (0-7214-9743-8) Ladybird Bks.
Ladybird Books Staff. Magic Music. (Read with Me Key Words to Reading Ser.: No. 9010-10). (Illus.). (J). (ps-2). 1990. 3.50 (0-7214-1323-4, Ladybrd) Penguin Putnam.
— The Middle Ages. (History of Britain Ser.: No. F895-3). (Illus.). (YA). (gr. 5 up). 1990. pap. 3.95 (1-85543-008-8, Ladybrd) Penguin Putnam.
— Moses. (Bible Stories Ser.: No. S846-3). (Illus.). (J). (ps-2). 1990. pap. 3.00 (0-7214-5066-0, Ladybrd) Penguin Putnam.
— My Book of Baby Forest Animals. (Early Readers Ser.: No. S8711-12). (Illus.). (J). (ps-2). 1989. 3.95 (0-7214-5150-0, Ladybrd) Penguin Putnam.
— My Book of Baby Pet Animals. (Early Readers Ser.: No. S8711-9). (Illus.). (J). (ps-2). 1989. 3.95 (0-7214-5151-9, Ladybrd) Penguin Putnam.
— My Book of Baby Zoo Animals. (Early Readers Ser.: No. S8711-11). (Illus.). (J). (ps-2). 1989. 3.95 (0-7214-5149-7, Ladybrd) Penguin Putnam.
— My Book of Shapes & Colors. (Early Readers Ser.: No. S8711-7). (Illus.). (J). (ps-2). 1992. 3.95 (0-7214-5148-9, Ladybrd) Penguin Putnam.
— My Counting Book. (Early Readers Ser.: No. S8711-6). (Illus.). (J). (ps-2). 3.95 (0-7214-5146-2, Ladybrd) Penguin Putnam.
— My First Christmas Book. (Christmas Board Bks.: No. S8823-1). (Illus.). (J). (ps). 1990. pap. 3.95 (0-7214-9093-X, Ladybrd) Penguin Putnam.
— Noah's Ark. (Bible Stories Ser.: No. S846-2). (Illus.). (J). (ps-2). pap. 3.95 (0-7214-5065-2, Ladybrd) Penguin Putnam.
— Les Nombres. (French Language Editions Ser.: No. 563F-2). (FRE., Illus.). (J). 1990. 3.50 (0-7214-1427-3, Ladybrd) Penguin Putnam.
— 1,2,3. (First Steps Ser.). 32p. (J). 1998. 2.50 (0-7214-1875-9, Ladybrd) Penguin Putnam.
— Picture Book for Baby. (First Picture Bks.: No. 832-1). (Illus.). (J). (ps). pap. 3.50 (0-7214-0749-8, Ladybrd) Penguin Putnam.
— Pinocho: Grade 2 Well Loved Tales Series 700. (Spanish Well Loved Tales Ser.: No. 700-2). (SPA.). (J). (gr. 2). 1990. boxed set 3.50 (0-7214-1412-5, Ladybrd) Penguin Putnam.
— Piper's Park. (Read with Me Key Words to Reading Ser.: No. 9010-13). (Illus.). 1990. 3.50 (0-7214-1326-9, Ladybrd) Penguin Putnam.
— Plants. (Ladybird Learners Ser.: No. 8911-9). (J). 1991. pap. 3.95 (0-7214-5327-9, Ladybrd) Penguin Putnam.
— Red Riding Hood. (First Fairy Tales Ser.: No. S852-10). (Illus.). (J). (ps-2). pap. 3.95 (0-7214-5103-9, Ladybrd) Penguin Putnam.
— The Robbery. (Read with Me Key Words to Reading Ser.: No. 9010-15). (Illus.). (J). (ps-2). 1990. 3.50 (0-7214-1328-5, Ladybrd) Penguin Putnam.
— The Saxons & the Normans. (History of Britain Ser.: No. F895-2). (Illus.). (YA). (gr. 5 up). 1990. pap. 3.95 (1-85543-007-X, Ladybrd) Penguin Putnam.
— Scaredy Kitten. (Kitten Tales Ser.). (Illus.). 28p. (J). (ps-2). 1992. 3.95 (0-7214-5309-0, S915-2, Ladybrd) Penguin Putnam.
— Scary Storytime. (Storytime Ser.: No. 887-6). (Illus.). (J). (ps-2). 1990. 3.50 (0-7214-1340-4, Ladybrd) Penguin Putnam.
***Ladybird Books Staff.** Smokey the Bear Nature Diary. 1999. pap. text 17.00 (0-7214-5642-1) Ladybird Bks.
Ladybird Books Staff. Snow White & the Seven Dwarfs. (First Fairy Tales Ser.: No. S852-5). (Illus.). (J). (ps-2). 1996. pap. 3.95 (0-7214-5062-8, Ladybrd) Penguin Putnam.
— The Space Boat. (Read with Me Key Words to Reading Ser.: No. 9010-3). (Illus.). (J). (ps-2). 1990. 3.50 (0-7214-1316-1, Ladybrd) Penguin Putnam.
— The Sports Day. (Read with Me Key Words to Reading Ser.: No. 9010-9). (Illus.). (J). (ps-2). 1990. 3.50 (0-7214-1322-6, Ladybrd) Penguin Putnam.
— Storytime for Seven Year Olds. (Storytime Ser.: No. 887-5). (Illus.). (J). (gr. 2). 1990. pap. 3.50 (0-7214-1347-1, Ladybrd) Penguin Putnam.
— Tattoo You: Aquarius. 1999. pap. 4.99 (0-7214-5734-7, Ladybrd) Penguin Putnam.
— Tattoo You: Aries. 1999. pap. 4.99 (0-7214-5724-X, Ladybrd) Penguin Putnam.
— Tattoo You: Cancer. 1999. pap. 4.99 (0-7214-5727-4, Ladybrd) Penguin Putnam.
— Tattoo You: Capricorn. 1999. pap. 4.99 (0-7214-5733-9, Ladybrd) Penguin Putnam.
— Tattoo You: Gemini. 1999. pap. 4.99 (0-7214-5726-6, Ladybrd) Penguin Putnam.
— Tattoo You: Leo. 1999. pap. 4.99 (0-7214-5728-2, Ladybrd) Penguin Putnam.
— Tattoo You: Sagittarius. 1999. pap. 4.99 (0-7214-5732-0, Ladybrd) Penguin Putnam.
— Tattoo You: Scorpio. 1999. pap. 4.99 (0-7214-5731-2, Ladybrd) Penguin Putnam.
— Tattoo You: Taurus. 1999. pap. 4.99 (0-7214-5725-8, Ladybrd) Penguin Putnam.
— Tattoo You: Virgo. 1999. pap. 4.99 (0-7214-5729-0, Ladybrd) Penguin Putnam.
— Three Little Pigs. (First Fairy Tales Ser.: No. S852-2). (Illus.). (J). (ps-2). pap. 3.95 (0-7214-5059-8, Ladybrd) Penguin Putnam.
— Tom's Storybook. (Read with Me Key Words to Reading Ser.: No. 9010-8). (Illus.). (J). (ps-2). 1990. 3.50 (0-7214-1321-8, Ladybrd) Penguin Putnam.
***Ladybird Books Staff.** Travel Teasers. 1999. pap. 4.99 (0-7214-2794-4, Ladybrd) Penguin Putnam.
Ladybird Books Staff, ed. Little Red Car. (Little Vehicle Stories Ser.). 32p. (J). 1998. text 2.50 (0-7214-1931-3, Ladybrd) Penguin Putnam.
Ladybird Books Staff1. Daisy Little Dancer. (Little Dancing Stories Ser.). 32p. (J). 1998. text 2.50 (0-7214-1924-0, Ladybrd) Penguin Putnam.
Ladybird Series. Downy Duckling. (Rhyming Stories Ser.: No. 401-5). (Illus.). (J). (ps). pap. 3.50 (0-7214-0210-0, Ladybrd) Penguin Putnam.
— Ladybird Tables & Other Facts & Figures. (Basic Math Ser.: No. 678-5). (Illus.). (gr. 1-3). pap. 3.50 (0-7214-0663-7, Ladybrd) Penguin Putnam.
— Nursery Rhymes. (First Bks.: No. S808-5). (Illus.). (J). (ps). pap. 3.95 (0-7214-5056-3, Ladybrd) Penguin Putnam.
Ladybird Staff. Aim, Focus, Shoot! A Beginning Photographer's Start-Up Kit. (J). (gr. 2). 1999. pap. 19.99 (0-7214-5780-0, Ladybrd) Penguin Putnam.
— The All-Time Classics Collection. (J). 1997. pap. 12.50 (0-7214-4579-9, Dutton Child) Peng Put Young Read.
— Amazing Birthday Card. 1999. pap. 6.99 (0-7214-5721-5, Ladybrd) Penguin Putnam.
— Aztecs, Incas & Mayas. (J). 1999. pap. 9.99 (0-7214-5779-7, Dutton Child) Peng Put Young Read.
— Favorite Fairy Sand. (J). 1999. pap. 6.99 (0-7214-5720-7, Ladybrd) Penguin Putnam.
— The Ladybird Castles Book & Stamp Kit. (J). (gr. 2-6). 1997. 7.99 (0-614-29249-2, Ladybrd) Penguin Putnam.
— The Ladybird Sharks Book & Stamp Kit. (J). (gr. 2-6). 1997. 7.99 (0-614-29250-6, Ladybrd) Penguin Putnam.
— Migrations. (J). 1999. pap. 9.99 (0-7214-5758-4, Ladybrd) Penguin Putnam.
— 100 Favourite Nursery Rhymes. 1999. text 4.99 (0-7214-2020-6, Ladybrd) Penguin Putnam.
— First Steps Activity 2: 1, 2, 3. (First Steps Ser.). 24p. (J). 1998. pap. 1.99 (0-7214-2607-7, Ladybrd) Penguin Putnam.
— Protect the Panda. (J). 1999. pap. 4.99 (0-7214-5722-3, Ladybrd) Penguin Putnam.
— Protect the Tiger. (J). 1999. pap. 4.99 (0-7214-5723-1) Penguin Putnam.
— Seek n' Peek Mummy. (Seek n' Peek Ser.). (J). 1999. pap. 9.99 (0-7214-5737-1, Ladybrd) Penguin Putnam.
— Seek n' Peek Tyrannosaurus Rex. (Seek n' Peek Ser.). (J). 1999. pap. 9.99 (0-7214-5738-X, Ladybrd) Penguin Putnam.
— Smokey the Bear's Little Story Book. 1996. pap. 1.49 (0-7214-5662-6, Ladybrd) Penguin Putnam.

An Asterisk (*) at the beginning of an entry indicates that the title is appearing for the first time.

— Victoria Rose's Tea Party. (Illus.). (J). (ps). 1997. pap. 19.99 (0-7214-5781-9, Dutton Child) Peng Put Young Read.

Ladybug Magazine Staff. Babybug Triplets. (J). 1998. bds. 12.95 (0-8126-0065-7) Open Court.

— I've Got Rainbows! Songbook. 1998. 15.95 (0-8126-0028-2); 19.95 incl. audio (0-8126-0138-6) Open Court.

Ladyman, David. Dawn of War: Prima's Official Strategy Guide. 244p. 1998. per. 19.99 (0-7615-1740-5) Prima Pub.

— Populous III: Beginning. 240p. 1999. per. 19.99 (0-7615-1205-5) Prima Pub.

— Privateer 3: Prima's Official Strategy Guide. 244p. 2000. pap. 19.99 (0-7615-1586-0) Prima Pub.

— Sid Meier's Alpha Centauri: Prima's Offical Strategy Guide. LC 98-65458. 288p. 2000. pap. 19.99 (0-7615-1584-4) Prima Pub.

— Ultima IX: Ascension: Prima's Official Strategy Guide. 244p. 1999. pap. 19.99 (0-7615-1585-2) Prima Pub.

— Ultima Online: The Second Age. LC 98-66898. 352p. 1998. per. 19.99 (0-7615-1771-5) Prima Pub.

— Wing Commander Prophecy Gold: Prima's Official Strategy Guide. 336p. 1998. per. 19.99 (0-7615-1772-3) Prima Pub.

— World War II Fighters: Official Strategy Guide. 244p. 1998. pap. 19.99 (0-7615-1859-2) Prima Pub.

Ladyman, David & Tyler, Melissa. Sid Meier's Gettysburg: The Official Strategy Guide. LC 97-69766. (Secrets of the Game Ser.). 304p. 1997. per. 19.99 (0-7615-1283-7) Prima Pub.

Ladyman, David, ed. see Addams, Shay.

Ladyman, David, jt. ed. see Addams, Shay.

Ladyman, Heather M., jt. ed. see Ritter, Mary A.

Ladywood, Viscount. Gynecocracy. 1999. pap. text 9.95 (1-56201-133-2) Blue Moon.

— Gynecocracy. 416p. 1999. mass mkt. 9.95 (1-56201-112-X) Blue Moon Bks.

— Gynecocracy. 1997. pap. 9.95 (1-56333-511-5) Masquerade.

Ladyzgenskaja, Olga A., ed. see Steklov Institute of Mathematics, Academy of Scien.

Ladyzhenskaja, Olga A., ed. Boundary Value Problems of Mathematical Physics. LC 67-6187. (Proceedings of the Steklov Institute of Mathematics Ser.: Vol. 127). 179p. 1977. pap. 59.00 (0-8218-3027-9, STEKLO/127) Am Math.

— Boundary Value Problems of Mathematical Physics. LC 67-6187. (Proceedings of the Steklov Institute of Mathematics Ser.: Vol. 147). 213p. 1981. pap. 101.00 (0-8218-3068-6) Am Math.

— Boundary Value Problems of Mathematical Physics No. V: Proceedings. (Proceedings of the Steklov Institute Math Ser.: No. 102). 185p. 1979. pap. 57.00 (0-8218-3002-3, STEKLO/102) Am Math.

— Boundary Value Problems of Mathematical Physics No. XII. LC 67-6187. (Proceedings of the Steklov Institute Math Ser.: No. 159). 226p. 1992. reprint ed. pap. 77.00 (0-8218-3084-8, STEKLO/159) Am Math.

Ladyzhenskaja, Olga A., et al. Linear & Quasilinear Equations of Parabolic Type. LC 68-19440. (Translations of Mathematical Monographs: Vol. 23). 648p. 1969. reprint ed. pap. 49.00 (0-8218-1573-3, MMONO/23) Am Math.

Ladyzhenskaja, Olga A., ed. see Steklov Institute of Mathematics, Academy of Scien.

Ladyzhenskaja, Olga A., ed. see Steklov Institute of Mathematics Staff.

Ladyzhenskaya, O. Boundary Value Problems of Mathematical Physics XIII. LC 67-6187. (STEKLO Ser.: Vol. 179). 266p. 1989. pap. 139.00 (0-8218-3127-5, STEKLO/179) Am Math.

Ladyzhenskaya, O. A. The Mathematical Theory of Viscous Incompressible Flow, Vol. 2. 2nd ed. (Mathematics & Its Applications Ser.). (Illus.). xviii, 224p. 1969. text 332.00 (0-677-20760-3) Gordon & Breach.

— Proceedings of the St. Petersburg Mathematical Society Volume IV, Vol. IV. (American Mathematical Society Translations Ser. 2: Vol. 188). 250p. 1998. 115.00 (0-8218-0613-0) Am Math.

Ladyzhenskaya, O. A., ed. Boundary Value Problems of Mathematical Physics & Related Aspects of Function Theory. LC 69-12506. (Seminars in Mathematics Ser.: Vol. 14, Pt. 4). (RUS., Illus.). 163p. reprint ed. pap. 50.60 (0-8357-7369-8, 202069800018) Bks Demand.

— Boundary Value Problems of Mathematical Physics, XIV. LC 67-6187. (Proceedings of the Steklov Institute of Mathematics Ser.: Vol. 188). 239p. 1991. reprint ed. pap. 132.00 (0-8218-3141-0, STEKLO/188) Am Math.

— Proceeding of the St. Petersburg Mathematical Society, Vol. III. (Translations Ser.: Series 2, Vol. 166). 267p. 1995. text 92.00 (0-8218-0387-5, TRANS2/166) Am Math.

— St. Petersburg Mathematical Society: Proceedings. (Translations Ser.: Vol. 159). 225p. 1994. text 115.00 (0-8218-7510-8, TRANS2/159) Am Math.

Ladyzhenskaya, O. A. & Vershik, A. M., eds. Proceedings of the St. Petersburg Mathematical Society, Vol. I. (Translations Ser.: Series 2, Vol. 155). 223p. 1993. text 99.00 (0-8218-7505-1, TRANS2/155C) Am Math.

Ladyzhenskaya, Olga A. Boundary Value Problems of Mathematical Physics. Lohwater, A. J., tr. from RUS. (Applied Mathematical Sciences Ser.: Vol. 49). 350p. 1985. 99.95 (0-387-90989-3) Spr-Verlag.

Ladyzhenskaya, Olga A., ed. see Steklov Institute of Mathematics, Academy of Scien.

Laederach, Jurg. Sixty-Nine Ways to Play the Blues. Wortsmann, Peter, tr. from GER. (Foreign Agents Ser.). 192p. (Orig.). (C). 1990. pap. 6.00 (0-936756-62-4) Autonomedia.

Laee & Ioffe, A. D. Soviet Law & Economy. 1986. lib. bdg. 130.50 (90-247-3265-4, Pub. by M Nijhoff) Kluwer Academic.

Laegaard, S. & Borchsenius, F., eds. Nordic Botanical Research in the Andes & Western Amazonia. (AAU Reports: No. 25). (Illus.). 88p. (C). 1990. pap. 12.95 (87-87600-33-1, Pub. by Aarhus Univ Pr) David Brown.

Laegreid, M., et al. Agriculture, Fertilizers & the Environment. LC 99-23430. (CABI Publishing Ser.). 240p. 2000. pap. text 40.00 (0-85199-358-3) OUP.

Laegreid, Per, jt. ed. see Egeberg, Morten.

Lael, Richard L. Arrogant Diplomacy: U. S. Policy Toward Colombia, 1903-1922. LC 87-12987. 216p. 1987. 45.00 (0-8420-2287-2) Scholarly Res Inc.

— The Yamashita Precedent: War Crimes & Command Responsibility. LC 82-17024. 177p. 1982. lib. bdg. 45.00 (0-8420-2202-3) Scholarly Res Inc.

Laemmel-Serrano, Sibylla. Juan Larrea ou le Suicide en Poesie. (Publications Universitaires Europeennes Ser.: Series 24, Vol. 47). (FRE.). 288p. 1995. 45.95 (3-906754-23-5, Pub. by P Lang) P Lang Pubng.

Laemmlen, Ann & Owen, Jackie. The Articles of Faith Learning Book. 171p. (J). (gr. 3-6). 1990. pap., student ed. 9.95 (0-87579-400-9) Deseret Bk.

Laenen, Antonius & Dunnette, David A. River Quality: Dynamics & Restoration. LC 96-22308. 480p. 1997. lib. bdg. 110.00 (1-56670-138-4) Lewis Pubs.

Laennec, Christine M., jt. ed. see Wilson, Deborah S.

Laennec, Christine M., tr. see Paulhan, Jean.

Laenzlinger, Christopher. Comparative Studies in Word Variation: Adverbs, Pronouns, & Clause Structure in Romance & Germanic. LC 98-17510. (Linguistik Aktuell/Linguistics Today Ser.: Vol. 20). x, 371p. (C). 1998. 79.00 (1-55619-904-X) J Benjamins Pubng Co.

Laer, A. J. Van, see Van Laer, A. J., ed.

Laer, Arnold J. Van, see Van Laer, Arnold J., ed.

Laermer, Richard. The Gay & Lesbian Handbook to New York City. 1994. write for info. (0-318-72470-7, Plume) Dutton Plume.

— Native's Guide to New York. 4th rev. ed. LC 97-47585. 320p. 1998. pap. 15.00 (0-393-31810-9) Norton.

— Native's Guide to New York: 750 Ways to Have the Time of Your Life in the City. 2nd rev. ed. (Illus.). 336p. 1991. pap. 12.95 (1-55958-114-X) Prima Pub.

— Native's Guide to New York: 750 Ways to Have the Time of Your Life in the City. 3rd rev. ed. LC 95-1533. (Illus.). 416p. 1995. pap. 16.95 (0-7615-0020-0) Prima Pub.

Laertius, Diogenes. De Vitis, Dogmatis et Apophthegmatis Clarorum Philosophorum, 4 vols., Set. (GER.). xxxii, 2587p. 1981. reprint ed. write for info. (3-487-07067-7) G Olms Pubs.

— La Vie de Pythagore de Diogene Laerce. (Memoires de l'Academie Royale de Belgique. Classe des Lettres et des Sciences Morales et Politiques Ser. 2). (GER.). 272p. 1988. reprint ed. write for info. (3-487-09032-5) G Olms Pubs.

Laerum, Ole D. & Bjerknes, R., eds. Flow Cytometry in Hematology. (Analytical Cytology Ser.). (Illus.). 272p. 1992. text 115.00 (0-12-432940-3) Acad Pr.

Laes, Ronald G. The Art of Hula, Vol. 1. (ENG & HAW., Illus.). 64p. (Orig.). 1996. pap. 8.95 (0-9644546-3-7) Goldsmiths.

Laess, Thomas E. & Lincoff, Gary. Mushrooms. LC 97-44418. (Eyewitness Handbooks Ser.). 304p. 1998. 29.95 (0-7894-3286-2) DK Pub Inc.

Laessig, Robert E., jt. auth. see Mandel, B. J.

Laessoe, Thomas. The Mushroom Book: How to Identify, Gather & Cook Wild Mushrooms & Other Fungi. LC 96-10835. 256p. 1996. 29.95 (0-7894-1073-7) DK Pub Inc.

Laet, Joannes de. The Empire of the Great Mogol. Hoyland, J. S., tr. 266p. reprint ed. text 22.00 (0-685-13403-2) Coronet Bks.

Laet, S. J. De, see UNESCO Staff & De Laet, S. J., eds.

Laeufer, Christiane & Morgan, Terrell A., eds. Theoretical Analyses in Romance Linguistics: Selected Papers from the Linguistic Symposium on Romance Languages XIX, Ohio State University, April 21-23, 1989. LC 92-15113. (Current Issues in Linguistic Theory Ser.: No. 74). viii, 515p. 1992. 156.00 (1-55619-130-8) J Benjamins Pubng Co.

Laevastu, Taivo. Marine Climate, Weather & Climate Changes in Fisheries & Ocean Resources. 204p. 1993. text 69.95 (0-470-22049-X) Halsted Pr.

Laevers, F., ed. Defining & Assessing Quality in Early Childhood Education. (Studia Paedagogica: No. 16). 292p. (Orig.). 1994. pap. 42.50 (90-6186-586-7, Pub. by Leuven Univ) Coronet Bks.

Laevestu, T. Exploitable Marine Ecosystems: Nature & Dynamics of Marine Ecosystems: Their Productivity, Bases for Fisheries, & Ecosystem Management. 352p. 1995. 95.00 (0-85238-225-1) Blackwell Sci.

Laface, P. & De Mori, Renato, eds. Speech Recognition & Understanding: Recent Advances, Trends & Applications. (NATO ASI Series F: Computer & Systems Sciences, Special Programme AET: Vol. 75). 576p. 1992. 144.00 (0-387-54032-6) Spr-Verlag.

Lafaille, Robert & Fulder, Stephen, eds. Towards a New Science of Health. LC 93-3282. 208p. (C). 1993. 85.00 (0-415-08171-8) Routledge.

LaFaive, Douglas L. The Claims Game - How to Play to Win: How to Present, Evaluate & Settle Your Automobile Injury Claim. Urband, Vesta, ed. 80p. (Orig.). 1991. pap. 19.95 (0-9629403-0-5) Puck Pr.

Lafakis, Irene V. Gladsome Rose: A Bereaved Mother's Journey into Faith. LC 95-80538. 185p. (Orig.). 1995. pap. 10.95 (1-880971-12-7) Light&Life Pub Co MN.

LaFantasie, Glenn W., ed. see Williams, Roger.

Lafar, Uz, jt. ed. see Chaghtai, Mirza S.

*__LaFarge, Albert.__ George Washington. 2000. 11.95 (962-217-660-7) China Guides.

LaFarge, Albert. The U. S. Flea Market Directory. 2nd ed. 496p. (Orig.). 1996. pap. 6.99 (0-380-78494-7, Avon Bks) Morrow Avon.

*__LaFarge, Albert.__ U. S. Flea Market Directory: The Complete Guide to America's Best Flea Markets. 3rd ed. (Illus.). 2000. pap. 15.95 (0-312-26405-4) St Martin.

LaFarge, Albert. United States Flea Market Directory. 432p. (Orig.). 1993. pap. 7.00 (0-380-77079-2, Avon Bks) Morrow Avon.

LaFarge, Albert, ed. see Whyte, William Hollingsworth.

LaFarge, Albert, tr. see Breton, Jean-Francois.

LaFarge, Albert, tr. see Breton, Jean Francois.

LaFarge, Ann. Christmas Gift. 1995. mass mkt. 4.99 (0-8217-5140-9, Zebra Kensgtn) Kensgtn Pub Corp.

LaFarge, Ann, ed. Home for Christmas. 352p. 1992. mass mkt. 3.99 (0-8217-3979-4, Zebra Kensgtn) Kensgtn Pub Corp.

— The Joy of Christmas. 512p. 1994. mass mkt. 4.99 (0-8217-4749-5, Zebra Kensgtn) Kensgtn Pub Corp.

— Merry Christmas, My Love. 480p. 1996. mass mkt. 4.50 (0-8217-4379-1, Zebra Kensgtn) Kensgtn Pub Corp.

— To Mother with Love. 480p. 1993. mass mkt. 4.50 (0-8217-4138-1, Zebra Kensgtn) Kensgtn Pub Corp.

LaFarge, Ann, ed. see Dailey, Janet, et al.

Lafarge, Catherine, ed. Dilemmes du Roman. LC 89-84497. (Stanford French & Italian Studies: Vol. 65). (FRE.). 364p. 1990. pap. 56.50 (0-915838-80-X) Anma Libri.

LaFarge, Oliver. Behind the Mountains. LC 94-72322. 200p. 1994. reprint ed. pap. 12.95 (0-912880-07-4) Charles Pub.

— Laughing Boy. 245p. (J). 1981. reprint ed. lib. bdg. 24.95 (0-89966-367-2) Buccaneer Bks.

— The Mother Ditch: How Water Came to a New Mexico Town. Ortego, Pedro R., tr. LC 82-10712. (ENG & SPA., Illus.). 64p. 1983. pap. 8.95 (0-86534-009-9) Sunstone Pr.

LaFarge, Paul. The Artist of the Missing. LC 98-32152. (Illus.). 256p. 1999. pap. text 13.00 (0-374-52580-3) FS&G.

LaFarge, Phyllis, jt. ed. see Berman, Sheldon.

Lafarge, Rene. Jean-Paul Sartre: His Philosophy. LC 75-105727. 208p. reprint ed. pap. 64.50 (0-608-12684-5, 202436800037) Bks Demand.

LaFargue, Michael. The Tao of the Tao Te Ching: A Translation & Commentary. LC 91-18284. (SUNY Series in Chinese Philosophy & Culture). 270p. (C). 1992. pap. text 18.95 (0-7914-0986-4) State U NY Pr.

Lafargue, Michael, jt. ed. see Kohn, Livia.

Lafargue, Paul. Karl Marx, the Man. 4th ed. 1972. pap. 0.50 (0-935534-36-9) NY Labor News.

— Religion of Capital. 9th ed. 1961. pap. 0.50 (0-935534-38-5) NY Labor News.

— The Right to Be Lazy. Bracken, Len, tr. from FRE. (Illus.). 80p. 1999. pap. 12.95 (1-892355-03-5) Fifth Season.

— The Right to Be Lazy. 1972. 250.00 (0-87968-039-3) Gordon Pr.

— The Right to Be Lazy. (Revolutionary Classics Ser.). (Illus.). 128p. (C). 1975. reprint ed. pap. 12.00 (0-88286-181-6) C H Kerr.

— Selected Marxist Writings of Paul Lafargue. Broadhead, Richard, ed. 530p. (C). 1984. pap. 10.50 (0-916695-05-0) Ctr Social Hist.

LaFargue, Thomas E. China's First Hundred: Educational Mission Students in the United States, 1872-1881. LC 87-10404. (Washington State University Press Art Ser.). (Illus.). 184p. 1987. reprint ed. pap. 11.25 (0-87422-035-1) Wash St U Pr.

LaFaro, Lydia. AAA Rated: Unscrambling the Bond Market. (RUSA Occasional Papers: Vol. 22). 40p. 1997. pap. 20.00 (0-8389-7921-1, 79211) ALA.

LaFaso, Vanessa. Kiss It Where It Hurts. 28p. 1996. pap. 4.00 (0-9637704-4-6) Red Dragon VA.

LaFasto, Frank M., jt. auth. see Larson, Carl E.

LaFaue, Wayne & Israel, Jerold H. Criminal Procedure, 1996 Pocket Part for Use in 1996-1997. (Hornbook Ser.). 105p. 1996. write for info. (0-314-20827-5) West Pub.

Lafaurie, Andre-Jean & Lefevre, Jean-Francois. Golf: Great Courses of the World. (Illus.). 192p. 1991. 19.98 (0-89660-016-5, Artabras) Abbeville Pr.

LaFave, Francis E., ed. see Headley, Barbara J.

LaFave, Helen. Stratham. LC 98-87320. (Images of America Ser.). (Illus.). 128p. 1998. pap. 18.99 (0-7524-0999-9) Arcadia Publng.

Lafave, Kim. I Am Small. 32p. 1997. pap. 4.95 (0-385-25589-6) Doubleday.

LaFave, Kim, jt. auth. see Bourgeois, Paulette.

LaFave, Kim, jt. auth. see Bourgeois, Peter.

LaFave, Kim, jt. auth. see Oppel, Kenneth.

LaFave, Kim, jt. auth. see Wilson, Budge.

LaFave, Martha. Love's Medallion. Severn, Liz, ed. (Illus.). 180p. 1997. pap. 8.95 (1-888701-04-8) Jarrett Pr.

LaFave, Wayne R. Criminal Law. (Hornbook Ser.). 73p. 1997. pap. text, suppl. ed. write for info. (0-314-22788-1) West Pub.

*__LaFave, Wayne R.__ Criminal Law. 3rd ed. 2000. 49.00 (0-314-24817-X) West Pub.

LaFave, Wayne R. Criminal Law, 1995 Pocket Part. 2nd ed. (Hornbook Ser.). 46p. 1995. pap. text 7.00 (0-314-07063-X) West Pub.

— Criminal Law, 1996 Pocket Part. (Handbook Ser.). 54p. 1996. text. write for info. (0-314-20245-5) West Pub.

— Modern Criminal Law: Cases, Comments, & Questions. 2nd ed. (American Casebook Ser.). 903p. (C). 1988. reprint ed. 60.00 (0-314-82177-5) West Pub.

— Search & Seizure: A Treatise on the Fourth Amendment, 4 vols. 2nd ed. 2400p. 1986. text. write for info. (0-314-30073-2) West Pub.

— Search & Seizure, a Treatise on the Fourth Amendment, Vol. 1. 3rd ed. LC 95-61662. 800p. 1995. text. write for info. (0-314-07613-1) West Pub.

— Search & Seizure, a Treatise on the Fourth Amendment, Vol. 2. 3rd ed. 800p. 1995. text. write for info. (0-314-07614-X) West Pub.

— Search & Seizure, a Treatise on the Fourth Amendment, Vol. 3. 3rd ed. 800p. 1995. text. write for info. (0-314-07615-8) West Pub.

— Search & Seizure, a Treatise on the Fourth Amendment, Vol. 4. 3rd ed. 800p. 1995. text. write for info. (0-314-07612-3) West Pub.

LaFave, Wayne R. & Israel, Jerold H. Criminal Procedure, Vols. 1-5. LC 84-10391. (Criminal Practice Ser.). 2283p. 1993. reprint ed. text. write for info. (0-314-79279-1) West Pub.

— Hornbook on Criminal Procedures. 2nd ed. (Paralegal). 1309p. (C). 1998. reprint ed. text 41.00 (0-314-79327-5) West Pub.

LaFave, Wayne R. & Isreal, Jerold H. Criminal Procedure. 2nd ed. (Hornbook Ser.). 75p. 1997. suppl. ed. write for info. (0-314-22733-4) West Pub.

*__LaFave, Wayne R. & Scott, Austin W., Jr.__ Hornbook on Criminal Law. 2nd ed. (Paralegal). 918p. 1998. reprint ed. text 37.00 (0-314-26045-5) West Pub.

LaFave, Wayne R. & Scott, Austin W., Jr. Substantive Criminal Law. 2nd ed. LC 86-7795. (Criminal Practice Ser.). 1300p. 1986. text. write for info. (0-314-98403-8) West Pub.

Lafave, Wayne R., jt. auth. see Dalton, Sheila.

LaFave, Wayne R., jt. auth. see Israel, Jerold H.

LaFave, Wayne R., jt. auth. see Kamisar, Yale.

Lafave, Wayne R., ed. see Kamisar, Yale & Israel, Jerold H.

LaFavor, Carole. Along the Journey River. LC 96-1458. 192p. 1996. pap. 10.95 (1-56341-070-2); lib. bdg. 22.95 (1-56341-071-0) Firebrand Bks.

— Evil Dead Center: A Mystery. LC 97-44328. 224p. 1997. pap. 11.95 (1-56341-088-5); lib. bdg. 24.95 (1-56341-089-3) Firebrand Bks.

Lafavore, Michael. Men's Health Today. LC 96-48142. (Illus.). 288p. 1997. pap. 12.95 (0-87596-417-6) Rodale Pr Inc.

LaFavore, Michael, ed. The Male Almanac: Essential New Information about Sex, Fitness, Health & Life. LC 95-37601. 320p. 1996. pap. 9.95 (0-87596-345-5) Rodale Pr Inc.

LaFay, Bob, jt. auth. see Koenig, Harry.

LaFay, Bob, ed. see Koenig, Harry.

Lafay, J. F. System Structure & Control. LC 99-173327. 1998. pap. write for info. (0-08-043035-X, Pergamon Pr) Elsevier.

LaFay, Vivienne. The Actress. 256p. (Orig.). 1997. mass mkt. 5.95 (0-352-33119-4, Pub. by BLA4) London Brdge.

— Artistic Licence. (Orig.). 1997. mass mkt. 5.95 (0-352-33210-7, Pub. by BLA4) London Brdge.

Lafay, Vivienne. The Seductress. (Black Lace Ser.). 1995. mass mkt. 5.95 (0-352-32997-1, Pub. by Virgin Bks) London Brdge.

Lafaye. Dad. (J). 2000. mass mkt. 16.00 (0-689-81514-X) S&S Trade.

Lafaye, A. Nissa's Place. LC 99-12257. (Illus.). 224p. (J). 1999. per. 16.00 (0-689-82610-9) S&S Bks Yung.

— Strawberry Hill. LC 98-26887. 272p. (J). (gr. 3-7). 1999. per. 16.00 (0-689-82441-6) S&S Bks Yung.

— The Year of the Sawdust Man. (Illus.). 224p. (J). 1999. per. 4.99 (0-689-83106-4) Aladdin.

— The Year of the Sawdust Man. LC 97-14501. 224p. (J). (gr. 5 up). 1998. per. 16.00 (0-689-81513-1) S&S Childrens.

Lafaye, Alexandria. Edith Shay. LC 98-16832. (YA). (gr. 6 up). 1998. 15.99 (0-670-87598-8) Viking Penguin.

Lafaye, Jacques. Los Conquistadores. (Fondo 2000 Ser.). (SPA.). pap. 2.99 (968-16-5275-4, Pub. by Fondo) Continental Bk.

— Quetzalcoatl & Guadalupe: The Formation of Mexican National Consciousness, 1531-1813. Keen, Benjamin, tr. from FRE. LC 75-20889. 1976. lib. bdg. 26.00 (0-226-46794-5) U Ch Pr.

— Quetzalcoatl & Guadalupe: The Formation of Mexican National Consciousness, 1531-1813. Keen, Benjamin, tr. LC 75-20889. xxx, 366p. (C). 1987. pap. text 18.00 (0-226-46788-0) U Ch Pr.

— Quetzalcoatl y Guadalupe (Quetzalcoatl & Guadalupe) 2nd ed. (SPA.). 485p. 1992. pap. 14.99 (968-16-1444-5, Pub. by Fondo) Continental Bk.

Lafayette, Madame De, see Lafayette, Madame De.

LaFayette, Bernard & Jehnsen, David C. The Briefing Booklet: An Orientation to Kingian Nonviolence Conflict Reconciliation & the Leader's Manual- A Structured Guide & Introduction to Kingian Nonviolence. (SPA., Illus.). 39p. 1995. pap. text 20.00 (1-888615-03-6) Inst Human Rghts.

LaFayette, Bernard, jt. auth. see Jehnsen, David C.

*__Lafayette, Carla.__ Friends. (Pulse Ser.: No. 3). 1999. pap. text 14.99 (0-8307-2419-2) Gospel Lght.

Lafayette, J. Maximillien De, see De Lafayette, J. Maximillien.

Lafayette Journal & Courier Staff, ed. Memorable Moments in Purdue Basketball History. (Illus.). 250p. 1998. 29.95 (1-57167-256-7) Sports Pub.

Lafayette Junior League Members. Talk about Good. 450p. 1967. 11.95 (0-935032-00-2) Jr League Lafayette.

— Talk about Good II. (YA). 1980. 11.95 (0-935032-50-9) Jr League Lafayette.

Lafayette, Le Marquis de. Lafayette in the Age of the American Revolution, Selected Letters & Papers, 1776-1790, Vol. I: December 7th, 1776-March 30th,

1778. Idzerda, Stanley J. & Smith, Roger E., eds. LC 76-50268. (Lafayette Papers). (Illus.). 535p. 1977. text 62.50 (*0-8014-1031-2*) Cornell U Pr.

— Lafayette in the Age of the American Revolution, Selected Letters & Papers, 1776-1790, Vol. II: April 10th, 1778-March 20th, 1780. Idzerda, Stanley J. et al, eds. LC 76-50268. (Lafayette Papers). (Illus.). 520p. 1979. text 62.50 (*0-8014-1246-3*) Cornell U Pr.

— Lafayette in the Age of the American Revolution, Selected Letters & Papers, 1776-1790, Vol. III: April 27th, 1780-March 29th, 1781. Idzerda, Stanley J. et al, eds. LC 76-50268. (Lafayette Papers). (Illus.). 577p. 1980. text 62.50 (*0-8014-1335-4*) Cornell U Pr.

— Lafayette in the Age of the American Revolution, Selected Letters & Papers, 1776-1790, Vol. IV: April 1st, 1781-December 23rd, 1781. Idzerda, Stanley J. et al, eds. LC 76-50268. (Lafayette Papers). (Illus.). 600p. 1981. text 62.50 (*0-8014-1336-2*) Cornell U Pr.

— Lafayette in the Age of the American Revolution, Selected Letters & Papers, 1776-1790, Vol. V: January 4th, 1782-December 29th, 1785. Idzerda, Stanley J. & Crout, Robert R., eds. LC 76-50268. (Lafayette Papers). (Illus.). 528p. 1983. text 62.50 (*0-8014-1576-4*) Cornell U Pr.

Lafayette, Lenore. Shelter Cove: The Early Years. LC 97-94940. (Illus.). 115p. (Orig.). 1997. pap. 16.95 (*0-9661779-9-1*) Cherry Orch Bks.
This is a true story about life in a small coastal community in Northern California's San Mateo County. The secluded beach at Shelter Cove & the quaint cottages lining the Cove, as well as the surrounding environs, are rich in history. The outermost part of Shelter Cove is Pedro Point which is adjacent to formidable Devil's Slide. The Cove is now part of the city of Pacifica. This book relates many historical facts about the California coastline from the Eighteenth to the Twentieth Centuries. A chapter is devoted to the now defunct Ocean Shore Railroad which carried passengers & freight to & from San Francisco during the period of 1907 to 1920. Other chapters include tales of the Prohibition years, sea stories of doomed vessels that went aground at Pedro Point & yarns about life at the Cove for a San Francisco family during the Thirties. Send orders to: Cherry Orchard Books, P.O. Box 1995.Los Altos, CA 94023-1995, Price: $16.95 + Shipping/Handling & California Sales Tax where applicable. *Publisher Paid Annotation.*

Lafayette, Madame De. Princesse de Cleves: The Princesse de Montpensier; The Comtesse de Tende. (Oxford World Classics Ser.). 274p. 1999. pap. 8.95 (*0-19-283726-5*) OUP.

Lafayette, Madame De, see De Lafayette, Madame.

Lafayette, Marie J. The Princess of Cleves. LC 77-22941. 210p. 1977. reprint ed. lib. bdg. 38.50 (*0-8371-9729-5*, LAFPC, Greenwood Pr) Greenwood.

Lafayette, Marie J., et al. The Letters of Lafayette & Jefferson. LC 78-19274. 1979. 35.95 (*0-405-10593-2*) Ayer.

Lafayette, Robert C. National Standards: A Catalyst for Reform. LC 96-220759. (ACTFL Foreign Language Education Ser.). 230p. 1996. pap. 16.90 (*0-8442-9395-4*) NTC Contemp Pub Co.

***Lafe, Olurinde.** Cellular Automata Transforms: Theory & Applications in Multimedia Compression, Encryption & Modeling. LC 00-38635. (Multimedia Systems & Applications Ser.). 2000. pap. write for info. (*0-7923-7857-1*, Kluwer Plenum) Kluwer Academic.

LaFeber, Walter. America, Russia, & the Cold War: 1945-1984. 5th ed. 320p. (C). 1985. pap. text. write for info. (*0-318-62574-1*, KnopfC) Knopf.

Lafeber, Walter. America, Russia & the Cold War, 1945-1996. 8th ed. LC 96-34844. (America in Crisis Ser.). 416p. (C). 1996. pap. 28.13 (*0-07-036064-2*) McGraw.

LaFeber, Walter. The American Age: U. S. Foreign Policy at Home & Abroad, from 1750 to the Present, 2nd ed. (Illus.). (C). 1994. pap. text 35.50 (*0-393-96474-4*) Norton.

— The American Age 1750-1920: U. S. Foreign Policy at Home & Abroad, from 1750 to the Present, Vol 1. 2nd ed. (Illus.). (C). 1994. pap. text. write for info. (*0-393-96475-2*) Norton.

— The American Age 1896-Present: U. S. Foreign Policy at Home & Abroad, from 1750 to the Present, Vol. 2. 2nd ed. Vol. 2. (Illus.). (C). 1994. pap. text 21.50 (*0-393-96476-0*) Norton.

— The Cambridge History of American Foreign Relations: The American Search for Opportunity, 1865-1913. LC 92-36165. 281p. 1993. 44.95 (*0-521-38185-1*) Cambridge U Pr.

— The Cambridge History of American Foreign Relations Vol. 2: The American Search for Opportunity, 1865-1913. (Illus.). 281p. (C). 1995. pap. text 17.95 (*0-521-48383-2*) Cambridge U Pr.

— The Clash: U. S.-Japanese Relations Throughout History. LC 96-48565. (Illus.). 544p. 1997. 29.95 (*0-393-03950-1*) Norton.

— The Clash: U. S.-Japanese Relations Throughout History. LC 98-34387. (Illus.). 544p. 1998. pap. 15.95 (*0-393-31837-0*) Norton.

— Inevitable Revolutions: The United States in Central America. 2nd rev. ed. 448p. 1993. pap. 15.95 (*0-393-30964-9*) Norton.

— Liberty & Power: U. S. Diplomatic History, 1750-1945. 2nd expanded rev. ed. (New American History Ser.). 20p. (C). 1997. reprint ed. pap. 5.00 (*0-87229-089-1*) Am Hist Assn.

LaFeber, Walter. Michael Jordan & the New Global Capitalism. LC 98-55910. (Illus.). 160p. 1999. 22.95 (*0-393-04747-4*) Norton.

***LaFeber, Walter.** Michael Jordan & the New Global Capitalism. 192p. 2000. pap. text 12.95 (*0-393-32037-5*) Norton.

Lafeber, Walter. New Empire: An Interpretation of American Expansion, 1860-1898. LC 99-160552. 1998. pap. text 16.95 (*0-8014-8595-9*) Cornell U Pr.

LaFeber, Walter. The Panama Canal: The Crisis in Historical Perspective. rev. ed. (Illus.). 288p. 1990. pap. 13.95 (*0-19-506192-6*) OUP.

Lafeber, Walter, et al. The American Century: A History of the United States since the 1890s. 5th ed. LC 97-12374. 656p. 1997. pap. 40.94 (*0-07-036012-X*) McGraw.

***LaFeber, Walter, et al.** The American Century: A History of the United States since 1941. 5th ed. LC 97-207447. (Illus.). 1998. pap. write for info. (*0-07-036014-6*) McGrw-H Hghr Educ.

LaFeber, Walter, jt. ed. see McCormick, Thomas.

LaFemina, Gerry. A Print of Wild Flowers. 32p. (Orig.). 1997. pap. text 8.00 (*1-56439-065-9*) Ridgeway.

Lafemina, Gerry. Shattered Hours. 112p. (Orig.). 1997. pap. 12.95 (*1-881168-09-3*) Red Danceflr.

LaFemina, Gerry. 23 Below. 56p. (Orig.). 1994. pap. 6.95 (*0-9642273-2-0*) Back Porch Pr.

Lafer, Stephen & Tchudi, Stephen N. The Interdisciplinary Teacher's Handbook: Integrated Teaching Across the Curriculum. LC 95-47264. 270p. (Orig.). 1996. pap. text 29.50 (*0-86709-398-6*, 0398, Pub. by Boynton Cook Pubs) Heinemann.

Laferia, Jane, ed. see Kobayashi, Kazuo, et al.

***Laferiere, Eric.** International Relations Theory & Ecological Thought: Towards a Synthesis. LC 98-44174. 1999. pap. write for info. (*0-415-16479-6*) Routledge.

LaFerla, Jane. Fresh Paint! New Looks for Unfinished Furniture: 45 Fun & Festive Projects. LC 98-39947. (Illus.). 144p. 1999. 24.95 (*1-57990-087-9*, Pub. by Lark Books) Random.

Laferla, Jane. Gilding: Easy Techniques & Elegant Projects with Metal Leaf. LC 96-48695. (Illus.). 112p. 1997. 17.95 (*0-8069-9554-8*) Sterling.

LaFerla, Jane. Make Your Own Great Earrings: Beads, Wire, Polymer Clay, Fabric, Found Objects. LC 97-26423. (Illus.). 128p. 1998. 24.95 (*1-57990-031-3*); pap. 14.95 (*1-57990-014-3*, Pub. by Lark Books) Random.

***LaFerla, Jane.** Making the New Baskets: Alternative Materials, Simple Techniques. (Illus.). 128p. 2000. 27.95 (*1-57990-151-4*, Pub. by Lark Books) Sterling.

Laferla, Jane. 100 Ways to Say I Love You: Handmade Gifts & Heartfelt Expressions. LC 98-18892. 128p. 1998. pap. 18.95 (*1-57990-064-X*, Pub. by Lark Books) Random.

LaFerla, Jane, ed. see Ciletti, Barbara.

LaFerla, Jane, ed. see Diamond, Anna.

LaFerla, Jane, ed. see Henderson, Stevie.

LaFerla, Jane, ed. see Kobler, Chris.

LaFerla, Jane, ed. see Yow, Cathy.

Laferriere, Daniel. Sign & Subject: Semiotic & Psychoanalytic Investigations into Poetry. (Studies in Semiotics: No. 14). 103p. 1978. pap. 17.00 (*90-316-0138-1*, Pub. by B R Gruner) Humanities.

Laferty, et al. Microtech U. S. A. MCSE Training Guide: SQL Server 6.5 Administration. 1998. 53.49 (*1-56205-907-6*, New Riders Sftwre) MCP SW Interactive.

Lafeuer, Carolyn. The Murals of Charles Newcomb: A Story of Hagerstown, Indiana. 105p. 1994. 30.00 (*0-932970-96-6*) Prinit Pr.

Lafever, Carolyn. A Pictorial History of Wayne County, Indiana. LC 98-10951. 1998. write for info. (*1-57864-029-6*) Donning Co.

LaFever, Greg, jt. illus. see Maggard, John.

***LaFever, Malcolm & Root, Lawrence.** Guns That Talk: Firearms with Unique Histories. (Illus.). 257p. 1999. 40.00 (*1-884849-31-8*) R&R Bks.

LaFevor, C. S., jt. auth. see Hendrix, T. G.

Lafevre, John L. How You Really Get Hired: The Inside Story from a College Professor. 3rd ed. LC 92-17054. 256p. 1993. pap. 11.00 (*0-13-444159-1*, Arco) Macmillan Gen Ref.

Laffaille, Gilbert. La Ballade Des Pendules. (FRE., Illus.). 1995. pap. 49.95 (*2-86808-086-3*) Intl Scholars.

Laffaille, Maurice. Dufy's Complete Paintings, 4 vols. & suppl., Set. (FRE.). 1513p. 1977. suppl. ed. 2100.00 (*1-55660-265-0*) A Wofsy Fine Arts.

Laffal, Ken. Vivolo & His Wooden Children. LC 76-11492. (Illus.). 144p. 1976. 19.95 (*0-913622-04-4*) Gallery Pr.

Laffan, Barry. Communal Organization & Social Transition: A Case Study from the Counterculture of the Sixties & Seventies. LC 90-19209. (American University Studies: No. XI, Vol. 46). (Illus.). XXIV, 288p. (C). 1997. pap. text 27.95 (*0-8204-1193-0*) P Lang Pubng.

Laffan, Brigid, et al. Europe's Experimental Union: Rethinking Integration. LC 99-22357. 1999. pap. 29.99 (*0-415-10261-8*) Routledge.

***Laffan, Brigid, et al.** Europe's Experimental Union: Rethinking Integration. LC 99-22357. 240p. (C). 1999. text. write for info. (*0-415-10260-X*) Routledge.

***Laffan, Michael.** The Resurrection of Ireland: The Sinn Fein Party, 1916-1923. LC 99-11331. (Illus.). 450p. (C). 1999. 69.95 (*0-521-65073-9*) Cambridge U Pr.

Laffeaty, Christina. Where the Hills Reply. 359p. 1992. 24.95 (*0-340-54674-3*, Pub. by Hodder & Stought Ltd) Trafalgar.

Laffell, David. Total Skin. 352p. 2000. pap. 15.95 (*0-7868-8400-2*, Pub. by Hyprn Ppbks) Little.

Laffer, Arthur B. Private Short-Term Capital Flows. LC 75-159. (Business Economics & Finance Ser.: No. 5). 160p. reprint ed. pap. 49.60 (*0-7837-0651-0*, 204099000019) Bks Demand.

Laffer, Arthur B., jt. ed. see Canto, Victor A.

Laffer, U., ed. Regional Chemotherapy. (Antibiotics & Chemotherapy Ser.: Vol. 40). (Illus.). viii, 100p. 1988. 77.50 (*3-8055-4670-X*) S Karger.

Laffer, U., et al, eds. Implantable Drug Delivery Systems. (Illus.). viii, 68p. 1991. pap. 35.00 (*3-8055-5434-6*) S Karger.

— Modelle Interdisziplinaeren Handelns: 25 Jahre Department Chirurgie Basel. (Basler Beitraege zur Chirurgie Ser.: Vol. 5). (Illus.). viii, 162p. 1992. pap. 85.25 (*3-8055-5708-6*) S Karger.

— Traumatologie und Rehabilitation No. 2: Organverletzungen. (Basler Beitraege zur Chirurgie Ser.: Vol. 4). (Illus.). vi, 118p. 1992. 77.50 (*3-8055-5459-1*) S Karger.

Laffer, U. & Duerig, M., eds. Chirurgische Traumatologie & Rehabiltation. (Basler Beitraege zur Chirurgie Ser.: Vol. 3). (Illus.). vi, 118p. 1990. 71.50 (*3-8055-5164-9*) S Karger.

— Ethik, Technik, Konzepte. (Basler Beitraege zur Chirurgie Ser.: Vol. 1). (Illus.). x, 138p. 1988. pap. 50.50 (*3-8055-4926-1*) S Karger.

Laffer, U., jt. ed. see Duerig, M.

***Laffere, Eric.** International Relations Theory & Ecological Thought: Towards a Synthesis. LC 98-44174. 1999. write for info. (*0-415-16478-8*) Routledge.

Lafferranderie. Outlook on Space Law over the Next 30 Years. 1997. 195.00 (*90-411-0405-4*) Kluwer Law Intl.

Lafferranderie, Gabriel & Crowther, Daphne, eds. Outlook on Space Law over the Next 30 Years: Essays Published for the 30th Anniversary of the Space Treaty. LC 97-12996. 1997. lib. bdg. 195.00 (*90-411-0402-X*) Kluwer Academic.

Laffernty, William M. & Meadowcroft, James, eds. Democracy & the Environment: Problems & Prospects. LC 95-49827. 304p. 1996. 95.00 (*1-85898-325-8*) E Elgar.

Lafferty, jt. auth. see Baird.

Lafferty, jt. auth. see Pickles.

Lafferty & Assoc. Staff, ed. see Fife, Lynn H.

Lafferty, Carolyn K., jt. auth. see Huang, Jianshi.

Lafferty, Deborah, ed. see Summit, Steve.

Lafferty, Edward L., et al. Parallel Computing: An Introduction. LC 93-866. (Illus.). 134p. 1993. 45.00 (*0-8155-1329-1*) Noyes.

Lafferty, Eileen. Out of the Frying Pan, onto the Freeway: A Cookbook for Soccer Moms (And Dads) & Other Working Cooks. LC 84-72116. (Illus.). 346p. (Orig.). Date not set. pap. 12.00 (*0-9613994-0-6*) Bird Hand Pub.

Lafferty, Elaine. When You Hear Hoof. 1992. pap. 18.95 (*0-13-957440-9*) P-H.

Lafferty, J. M. Foundations of Vacuum Science & Technology. LC 96-29895. 728p. 1998. 165.50 (*0-471-17593-5*) Wiley.

Lafferty, James R., Sr. Ben Messick. LC 89-92682. (Illus.). 96p. 1993. 70.00 (*1-883246-01-6*); pap. 45.00 (*1-883246-02-4*) Eclectic Gal.

— Ben Messick. deluxe limited ed. LC 89-92682. (Illus.). 96p. 1993. boxed set 350.00 (*1-883246-00-8*) Eclectic Gal.

Lafferty, Janet, ed. see Fife, Lynn H.

Lafferty, Jerry. Learning Power: A Student's Guide to Success. Moore, Melissa, ed. LC 92-72769. (Illus.). 138p. (Orig.). (YA). (gr. 7-12). 1993. 34.95 incl. audio (*1-881843-29-7*) Alpha Educ Inst.

Lafferty, Joan M., jt. auth. see Pynes, Joan E.

Lafferty, Kevin & Rennie, John A., eds. Concise Surgery: An Illustrated Introduction. (An Arnold Publication). (Illus.). 512p. 1998. pap. text 32.95 (*0-340-70611-2*) OUP.

Lafferty, Kevin J., jt. ed. see Eisenbarth, George S.

Lafferty, Larry. The Angels Came. Self, Sandra, ed. (Illus.). 78p. 1995. 19.95 (*0-9647492-2-X*) One Winged Angel.

— Flutters, the One Winged Angel. Self, Sandra, ed. (Illus.). 72p. (YA). 1996. 19.95 (*0-9647492-0-3*) One Winged Angel.

Lafferty, Libby. Earthquake Preparedness for Office, Home, Family & Community. (Illus.). 32p. 1994. pap. 5.00 (*0-9641072-1-X*) Lafferty & Assocs.

Lafferty, Libby & Lafferty, Tina. Be Ready, Be Safe for Earthquakes: A Child's Guide to Preparedness. (Illus.). 32p. (Orig.). (J). (gr. k-4). 1994. pap. text 3.50 (*0-9641072-0-1*) Lafferty & Assocs.

Lafferty, Lida & Flood, Bo. Born Early: A Premature Baby's Story. LC 97-33156. (Illus.). 38p. (J). 1998. pap. 9.95 (*1-57749-064-9*) Fairview Press.

— Born Early: A Premature Baby's Story for Children. LC 94-92186. (Illus.). 40p. (J). (ps-4). 1995. pap. 8.95 (*0-9641413-0-2*) Songbird Pubng.

Lafferty, Mark. Adam 3.0. 200p. 1998. pap. text, student ed., lab manual ed. 25.00 (*0-8053-4350-4*) Benjamin-Cummings.

Lafferty, Perry. The Downing of Flight Six Heavy. 384p. 1992. mass mkt. 4.99 (*1-55817-622-5*, Pinncle Kensgtn) Kensgtn Pub Corp.

Lafferty, Peter. Force & Motion. LC 92-6927. (Eyewitness Books). (Illus.). 64p. (J). (gr. 4-7). 1992. 15.95 (*1-879431-85-8*) DK Pub Inc.

***Lafferty, Peter.** Forces & Motion. LC 99-44324. (Science Fact Files Ser.). 2001. 27.12 (*0-7398-1007-3*) Raintree Steck-V.

Lafferty, Peter. Radio & Television. LC 96-9199. (Worldwise Ser.). (Illus.). (J). 1997. lib. bdg. 23.00 (*0-531-14440-2*) Watts.

— Radio & Television. LC 96-9199. (Worldwise Ser.). (Illus.). (J). 1998. pap. write for info. (*0-531-15317-7*) Watts.

— What's Inside Everyday Things? LC 95-2060. (What's Inside? Ser.). (Illus.). 44p. (YA). (gr. 3 up). 1995. lib. bdg. 17.95 (*0-87226-396-7*, P Bedrick Books) NTC Contemp Pub Co.

— The World & Its Wonders. LC 96-68267. (Child Horizons Ser.). (J). (gr. 4-6). 1996. 22.95 (*0-87392-309-X*) Ferguson.

— The World of Science. LC 94-20019. (One Hundred One Questions & Answers Ser.). (Illus.). 48p. (J). (gr. 4-9). 1994. 11.95 (*0-8160-3219-X*) Facts on File.

Lafferty, Peter & Fryer, George. New Science Library, 6 vols. LC 95-21537. (Illus.). (J). 1995. write for info. (*0-89434-160-X*) Ferguson.

Lafferty, R. A. Heart of Stone, Dear & Other Stories. (Booklet Ser.: No. 12). 43p. (Orig.). 1983. pap. 2.00 (*0-936055-09-X*) C Drumm Bks.

— It's down the Slippery Cellar Stairs. (Booklet Ser.: No. 14). 42p. 1984. pap. 2.00 (*0-936055-11-1*) C Drumm Bks.

— It's Down the Slippery Cellar Stairs: Thoughts on Fiction, Writing, & Science Fiction. 2nd expanded rev. ed. LC 95-5201. (I. O. Evans Studies in the Philosophy & Criticism of Literature: No. 17). 104p. 1995. pap. 17.00 (*0-8095-1901-1*) Millefleurs.

— Laughing Kelly & Other Verses. (Booklet Ser.: No. 11). 16p. (Orig.). 1983. pap. 1.00 (*0-936055-08-1*) C Drumm Bks.

— The Man Who Made Models & Other Stories. (Booklet Ser.: No. 18). 51p. (Orig.). 1984. pap. 2.50 (*0-936055-16-2*) C Drumm Bks.

— My Heart Leaps Up, Chapters 7 & 8. (Booklet Ser.: No. 29). 49p. (Orig.). 1988. pap. text 2.75 (*0-936055-37-5*) C Drumm Bks.

— My Heart Leaps Up, Chapters 9 & 10. (Booklet Ser.: No. 35). 63p. (Orig.). 1990. pap. text 3.50 (*0-936055-41-3*) C Drumm Bks.

— My Heart Leaps Up, Chapters 9 & 10. deluxe ed. (Booklet Ser.: No. 35). 63p. (Orig.). 1990. pap. 6.00 (*0-936055-42-1*) C Drumm Bks.

— My Heart Leaps Up, Chs. 5 & 6. (Booklet Ser.: No. 28). 53p. (Orig.). 1987. pap. 2.95 (*0-936055-33-2*) C Drumm Bks.

— My Heart Leaps Up: Chapters 3 & 4, Chpts. 3 & 4. (Drumm Booklet Ser.: No. 26). 44p. (Orig.). 1987. pap. 2.75 (*0-936055-30-8*) C Drumm Bks.

— Okla Hannali. LC 91-50692. 240p. 1991. pap. 12.95 (*0-8061-2349-4*) U of Okla Pr.

— Sinbad, the Thirteenth Voyage. 176p. (Orig.). 1989. pap. 9.95 (*0-9623824-1-8*) Broken Mirrors Pr.

— Slippery & Other Stories. (Booklet Ser.: No. 19). 39p. (Orig.). 1985. pap. 2.00 (*0-936055-18-9*) C Drumm Bks.

— Snake in His Bosom & Other Stories. (Booklet Ser.: No. 13). 44p. (Orig.). 1983. pap. 2.00 (*0-936055-10-3*) C Drumm Bks.

Lafferty, Robert H., 3rd, et al. Settlement Predictions in Sparta. (Illus.). 299p. 1981. pap. 6.50 (*1-56349-038-2*, RS14) AR Archaeol.

Lafferty, Robert H., ed. see Watkins, Beverly, et al.

Lafferty, Sarah R. Gary Rieveschi: Projects & Proposals, 1973-1987. (Illus.). 1987. 9.95 (*0-917562-49-6*) Contemp Arts.

— Photovisions. (Illus.). 1987. 9.95 (*0-917562-48-8*) Contemp Arts.

Lafferty, Tina, jt. auth. see Lafferty, Libby.

Lafferty, William M. & Meadowcraft, James, eds. Democracy & the Environment: Problems & Prospects. LC 95-49827. 304p. 1998. pap. text 30.00 (*1-85898-773-3*) E Elgar.

***Lafferty, William M. & Meadowcroft, James.** Implementing Sustainable Development: Strategies & Initiatives in High Consumption Societies. 380p. 2000. pap. 29.95 (*0-19-924201-1*); text 85.00 (*0-19-829436-0*) OUP.

Lafferty, William M. & Rosenstein, Eliezer, eds. The Challenge of New Technology & Macro Political Change. LC 93-9607. (International Handbook of Participation in Organizations Ser.: No. III). (Illus.). 532p. 1993. text 95.00 (*0-19-828382-2*) OUP.

Laffey, Alice L. Appreciating God's Creation Through Scripture. LC 97-1681. (Illumination Bks.). (Illus.). (Orig.). 1997. pap. 5.95 (*0-8091-3714-3*) Paulist Pr.

— First & Second Chronicles. (Collegeville Bible Commentary - Old Testament Ser.). 96p. 1985. pap. 4.95 (*0-8146-1417-5*) Liturgical Pr.

— Introduction to the Old Testament: A Feminist Perspective. LC 86-46436. 256p. 1988. pap. 20.00 (*0-8006-2078-X*, 1-2078, Fortress Pr) Augsburg Fortress.

— Pentateuch: A Liberation-Critical Reading. LC 98-18082. 1998. pap. text 21.00 (*0-8006-2872-1*, Fortress Pr) Augsburg Fortress.

Laffey, Alice L., ed. see Bergant, Dianne.

Laffey, James L. Methods of Reading Instruction. LC 77-31440. (Reading Research Profiles Ser.). 72p. reprint ed. pap. 30.00 (*0-608-18002-5*, 202625300049) Bks Demand.

Laffey, John. Imperialism & Ideology: An Historical Perspective. 205p. 1999. pap. 19.99 (*1-55164-146-1*, Pub. by Black Rose) Consort Bk Sales.

Laffey, John F. Civilization & Its Discontented. LC 93-70388. 180p. (Orig.). 1993. text 45.99 (*1-895431-71-9*, Pub. by Black Rose); pap. text 16.99 (*1-895431-70-0*, Pub. by Black Rose) Consort Bk Sales.

— Imperialism & Ideology: An Historical Perspective. 1999. 48.99 (*1-55164-147-X*, Pub. by Black Rose) Consort Bk Sales.

Laffey, Mark, jt. ed. see Barkawi, Tarak.

Laffey, Mark, ed. see Weldes, Jutta.

An Asterisk (*) at the beginning of an entry indicates that the title is appearing for the first time.

***Laffi, Domenico.** A Journey to the West: The Diary of a Seventeenth-Century Pilgrim from Bologna to Santiago de Compostela. Hall, James, tr. from ITA. LC 98-110196. (Illus.). 192p. 1998. pap. text 25.00 (90-74310-28-1, Verlag Kunst) Gordon & Breach.

Laffie, Lynn, ed. see Bryant, Gary.

Laffin, Arthur J. & Montgomery, Anne, eds. Swords into Plowshares. 350p. 1996. pap. 18.00 (1-879175-18-5) Fortkamp.

Laffin, John. The Australian Army at War 1899-1975. (Men-at-Arms Ser.: No. 123). (Illus.). 48p. pap. 11.95 (0-85045-418-2, 9056, Pub. by Ospry) Stackpole.

— Brassey's Battles: 3,500 Years of Conflict, Campaigns & Wars from A-Z. rev. ed. (Illus.). 484p. 1995. pap. 34.95 (1-85753-176-0, Pub. by Brasseys) Brasseys.

— Brassey's Book of Espionage. (Illus.). 160p. 1996. pap. 24.95 (1-85753-144-2, Pub. by Brasseys) Brasseys.

— British Butchers & Bunglers of World War One. LC 92-18632. (Illus.). 224p. 1996. pap. 17.95 (0-7509-0179-9, Pub. by Sutton Pub Ltd) Intl Pubs Mktg.

— British VC's of World War 2: A Study in Heroism. LC 97-164984. (Illus.). 288p. 1997. 33.95 (0-7509-1026-7, Pub. by Sutton Pub Ltd) Intl Pubs Mktg.

— Combat Surgeons. 1999. 42.95 (0-7509-2173-0) Sutton Pub Ltd.

— Guide to Australian Battlefields of the Western Front 1916-1918. (Illus.). 192p. (Orig.). 1993. pap. 19.95 (0-86417-468-3, Pub. by Kangaroo Pr) Seven Hills Bk.

— Hitler Warned Us. (Illus.). 176p. 1995. pap. 21.95 (1-85753-103-5, Pub. by Brasseys) Brasseys.

— The Israeli Army in the Middle East Wars, 1948-73. (Men-at-Arms Ser.: No. 127). (Illus.). 48p. 1984. pap. 11.95 (0-85045-450-6, 9059, Pub. by Ospry) Stackpole.

— The Man the Nazis Couldn't Catch. (Illus.). 224p. (Orig.). 1997. pap. 17.95 (0-7509-1442-4, Pub. by Sutton Pub Ltd) Intl Pubs Mktg.

— Raiders: Great Military Actions of the Second World War. LC 99-215370. 1999. 35.00 (0-7509-1525-0) A Sutton.

— Western Front Companion, 1914-1918: A-Z Source to the Battles, Weapons, People, Places & Air Companies. 1997. pap. text 19.95 (0-7509-1520-X, Pub. by Sutton Pub Ltd) Intl Pubs Mktg.

— The Western Front Illustrated, 1914-1918. (Illus.). 192p. 1997. pap. 22.95 (0-7509-1438-6, Pub. by Sutton Pub Ltd) Intl Pubs Mktg.

— The World in Conflict: War Annual 7: Contemporary Warfare Described & Analysed. (Illus.). 150p. 1996. 39.95 (1-85753-196-5, Pub. by Brasseys) Brasseys.

— The World in Conflict: War Annual 8 - Contemporary Warfare Described & Analyzed. (War Annual Ser.). (Illus.). 200p. 1997. 39.95 (1-85753-216-3, Pub. by Brasseys) Brasseys.

— The World in Conflict No. 6: War Annual Six: Contemporary Warfare Described & Analysed. (War Annual Ser.: No. 6). (Illus.). 500p. 1994. 39.95 (0-08-041330-7, Pub. by Brasseys) Brasseys.

— The World in Conflict, 1991: War Annual Five: Contemporary Warfare Described & Analysed. (War Annual Ser.: No. 5). (Illus.). 240p. 1991. 39.95 (0-08-040712-9, Pub. by Brasseys) Brasseys.

Laffin, Martin, ed. Beyond Bureaucracy? The Profession in the Contemporary Public Sector. LC 98-73021. 238p. 1998. text 59.95 (1-84014-161-1, Pub. by Ashgate Pub) Ashgate Pub Co.

Laffin, Richard F. The Jewelers' Guide to Creative Pricing. Holmes, George, ed. 64p. (Orig.). 1990. pap. 19.95 (0-931744-15-6, CR-027) Jewlrs Circular-Keystone.

— Jeweler's Inventory Manual. rev. ed. 170p. 1988. spiral bd. 49.95 (0-931744-13-X, CR-020) Jewlrs Circular-Keystone.

Laffineur, Robert & Vandenabeele, Frieda, eds. Coprus of Cypriote Antiquities: Cypriote Antiquities in Belgium. (Studies in Mediterranean Archaeology: Vol. XX: 13). (Illus.). 124p. (Orig.). 1990. pap. 87.50 (91-86098-96-9, Pub. by P Astroms) Coronet Bks.

Laffite, Jean. The Journal of Jean Laffite: The Privateer-Patriot's Own Story. 153p. 1994. reprint ed. pap. 12.95 (0-9646846-0-8) Dogwood TX.

Laffling, John. Toward High Precision Machine Translation: Based on Contrastive Textology. LC 91-33903. (Distributed Language Translation Ser.: No. 7). xiv, 178p. (C). 1991. lib. bdg. 75.40 (3-11-013388-1) Mouton.

Laffoley, Paul. Architectonic Thought Forms: A Survey of the Art of Paul Laffoley, 1968-1999. (Illus.). 96p. 1999. pap. 24.95 (0-9670952-1-2) Austin Mus.

— Paul Laffoley: The Phenomenology of Revelation. Wasilik, Jeanne M., ed. (Illus.). 112p. 1989. 30.00 (1-878607-06-5) Kent Gallery.

Laffoni, Robert, ed. The Illustrated History of Paris & the Parisians. (Illus.). 292p. 1958. lib. bdg. 35.00 (0-8288-3996-4) Fr & Eur.

Laffont, Bompiani. Dictionnaire des Oeuvres de Tous les Temps et de Tous les Pays. (FRE.). 1981. lib. bdg. 275.00 (0-8288-2600-5) Fr & Eur.

— Dictionnaire des Personnages Litteraires et Dramatiques de Tous les Tempes et de Tous les Pays. (FRE.). 83.95 (0-8288-9900-2, F12885) Fr & Eur.

— Dictionnaires Oeuvres Contemporaines.Tr. of Dictionary of Contemporary Works. (FRE.). 1977. 225.00 (0-8288-5462-9, M6129) Fr & Eur.

Laffont, Jean-Jacques. The Economics of Uncertainty & Information. Bonin, John P. & Bonin, Helene, trs. from FRE. 312p. 1989. 42.00 (0-262-12136-0) MIT Pr.

— Essays in the Economics of Uncertainty. LC 79-19771. (Economic Studies: No. 149). (Illus.). 150p. 1980. 15.00 (0-674-26555-6) HUP.

— The Fundamentals of Public Economics. Bonin, John P. & Bonin, Helene, trs. from FRE. (Illus.). 288p. (Orig.). 1988. 39.50 (0-262-12127-1) MIT Pr.

— Incentives & Political Economy. (Clarendon Lectures in Economics). 240p. 2000. text 35.00 (0-19-829424-7) OUP.

Laffont, Jean-Jacques, ed. Advances in Economic Theory Vol. 1: Sixth World Congress. (Econometric Society Monographs: No. 20). 337p. (C). 1995. pap. text 21.95 (0-521-48459-6) Cambridge U Pr.

— Advances in Economic Theory Vol. 2: Sixth World Congress. (Econometric Society Monographs: No. 21). 462p. (C). 1995. pap. text 24.95 (0-521-48460-X) Cambridge U Pr.

Laffont, Jean-Jacques & Moreaux, Michel, eds. Dynamics, Incomplete Information & Industrial Economics. Laisney, Francois, tr. 288p. (C). 1991. text 60.95 (0-631-16967-9) Blackwell Pubs.

Laffont, Jean-Jacques & Senik-Leygonie, Claudia. Price Controls & the Economics of Institutions in China. LC 99-172753. (Development Centre Studies). 100p. 1997. pap. 19.00 (92-64-15473-6, Pub. by Org for Econ) OECD.

***Laffont, Jean-Jacques & Tirole, Jean.** Competition in Telecommunications. LC 99-41518. (Center for Economic Studies - Munich Lectures). (Illus.). 415p. 1999. 30.00 (0-262-12223-5) MIT Pr.

Laffont, Jean-Jacques & Tirole, Jean. A Theory of Incentives in Regulation & Procurement. (Illus.). 731p. 1993. 57.50 (0-262-12174-3) MIT Pr.

Laffont, Robert. Dictionnaire des Auteurs Vol. 1: Aa-Des, 4 vols., Set. (FRE.). 1980. lib. bdg. 150.00 (0-8288-2614-5, F12570) Fr & Eur.

— Dictionnaire des Auteurs Vol. 4: Qa-Zw. (FRE.). 759p. 1980. pap. 45.00 (0-7859-4429-X, 2221501756) Fr & Eur.

— Dictionnaire des Oeuvres de Tous les Temps et de Tous les Pays: Litterature.Tr. of Dictionary of the Works of All Times & Places. (FRE.). 882p. pap. 45.00 (0-7859-4622-5) Fr & Eur.

— Dictionnaire Encyclopedique de la Litterature Francaise. (FRE.). 1140p. 1997. pap. 75.00 (0-7859-9504-8) Fr & Eur.

Laffont, Robert, ed. Dictionnaire des Oeuvres de Tous les Temps et de Tous les Pays Vol. 6: Sa-Zu. (FRE.). 1980. pap. 45.00 (0-7859-4426-5) Fr & Eur.

Laffont, Robert & Bompiani, Valentino. Dictionnaire des Oeuvres de Tous les Temps et de Tous les Pays Litterature, Philosophie, Musique, Sciences, 7 vols. (FRE.). 1980. 265.00 (0-7859-8630-8, 222101183x) Fr & Eur.

— Dictionnaire des Personnages. 3rd ed. (FRE.). 776p. 1984. pap. 49.95 (0-7859-5120-2) Fr & Eur.

Laffont Staff. Dictionnaire de la Sagesse Orientale Bouddhisme, Hindouisme, Taoisme, Zen. (FRE.). 780p. 1989. pap. 45.00 (0-7859-7805-4, 2221056116) Fr & Eur.

— Dictionnaire du Cinema Vol. 2: Les Acteurs. (FRE.). 1128p. 1984. pap. 55.00 (0-7859-7811-9, 2221071638) Fr & Eur.

***Lafford, Stuart & Greenaway, Theresa.** Caterpillars. LC 98-34068. (Minipets Ser.). (Illus.). 32p. (gr. 1-5). 1999. lib. bdg. 22.83 (0-8172-5585-0) Raintree Steck-V.

Laffort, Paul, jt. ed. see Martin, Guy.

Laffort, Paul, jt. ed. see Martin, G.

Laffra, C., et al, eds. Object-Oriented Programming for Graphics. (Focus on Computer Graphics Ser.). 278p. 1996. 74.95 (0-387-58314-9) Spr-Verlag.

Laffrey, David C., jt. ed. see Medlock, Ronald D.

Lafhail-Molino, Raphael. Paysages Unbains dans "Les Beaux Quartiers" d'Aragon: Pour une Theorie de la Description dans le Roman. (Publications Universitaires Europeennes Ser.: Series 13, Vol. 224). (FRE.). 538p. 1997. 58.95 (3-906757-84-6, Pub. by P Lang) P Lang Pubng.

Lafili, Louis, et al, eds. Survey of the International Sale of Goods. 375p. 1986. lib. bdg. 96.50 (90-6544-241-3) Kluwer Academic.

Lafili, Louis, jt. ed. see Campbell, Dennis.

Lafitte, Francois. The Internment of Aliens. 260p. 1988. 37.50 (1-870352-55-6) Denali Press.

Lafkeur, William R. Liquid Life: Abortion & Buddhism in Japan. 275p. 1992. pap. text 16.95 (0-691-02965-2, Pub. by Princeton U Pr) Cal Prin Full Svc.

Laflamme, Gilles, et al, eds. Flexibility & Labour Markets in Canada & the United States. (Research Ser.: No. 94). 315p. 1989. pap. 27.00 (92-9014-462-9) Intl Labour Office.

Laflamme, Joan M., ed. see Drewermann, Eugen.

LaFlamme, Nicole, ed. see Brenneman, Tim.

Laflamme, Simon. La Cociete Integree: De la Circulation Des Biens, Des Idees et Des Personnes. LC 91-45433. (Worcester Polytechnic Institute Studies in Science, Technology, & Culture: Vol. 12). (FRE.). XIV, 310p. 1993. 54.95 (0-8204-1869-2) P Lang Pubng.

***Lafleche, Veronique.** Venice. (Illus.). 98p. 2000. 20.00 (1-85995-765-X) Parkstone Pr.

***Laflen, John M.** Soil Erosion & Dryland Farming. LC 00-23701. (Illus.). 744p. 2000. boxed set. write for info. (0-8493-2349-5) CRC Pr.

Lafler, Joanne. The Celebrated Mrs. Oldfield: The Life & Art of an Augustan Actress. LC 88-34654. (Illus.). 240p. (C). 1989. 31.95 (0-8093-1485-1) S Ill U Pr.

***Lafler, Steve.** Bug House. (Illus.). 192p. 2000. pap. 14.95 (1-891830-13-9, Pub. by Top Shelf Prodns) LPC InBook.

Lafler, Steve. Bughouse. (Illus.). 136p. (Orig.). 1996. pap. 12.95 (1-889059-00-5) Regent Pr.

— Jonk! A Bughouse Fable. (Illus.). 56p. 1998. pap. 8.95 (1-889059-15-3) Regent Pr.

LaFlesche, Francis, jt. auth. see Fletcher, Alice C.

***Lafleur.** Exploring Medical Language. 5th ed. 2001. text. write for info. (0-323-01218-3) Mosby Inc.

LaFleur, Amanda J. Tonnerre Mes Chiens! A Glossary of Louisiana French Figures of Speech. LC 99-61503. (Illus.). xxii, 202p. 1999. 34.95 (0-9670838-8-5, Pub. by Renouveau Pubg); pap. 16.95 (0-9670838-9-3, Pub. by Renouveau Pubg) Forest Sales & Dist.

***LaFleur Brooks, Myrna.** Exploring Medical Language. 4th ed. (Illus.). 704p. 1998. write for info. (0-323-00040-1); teacher ed. write for info. (0-323-00075-4); text. write for info. (0-323-00071-1) Mosby Inc.

LaFleur-Brooks, Myrna, ed. Health Unit Coordinating. 3rd ed. (Illus.). 541p. 1993. pap., teacher ed. write for info. (0-7216-4304-3, W B Saunders Co) Harcrt Hlth Sci Grp.

— Health Unit Coordinating. 4th ed. (Illus.). 555p. 1998. pap. write for info. (0-7216-7187-X, W B Saunders Co) Harcrt Hlth Sci Grp.

LaFleur-Brooks, Myrna & Gillingham, Elaine. Certification Review to Accompany Health Unit Coordinating. 3rd ed. Kaszczuk, Selma, ed. LC 97-36631. 192p. (C). 1998. pap. text 22.50 (0-7216-7283-3, W B Saunders Co) Harcrt Hlth Sci Grp.

Lafleur-Brooks, Myrna & Gillingham, Elaine T. Skills Practice Manual to Accompany Health Unit Coordinating. 4th ed. LC 97-44166. (C). 1998. pap. text 27.00 (0-7216-7613-8, W B Saunders Co) Harcrt Hlth Sci Grp.

LaFleur Brooks, Myrna & LaFleur, Danielle. Programmed Medical Language. (Illus.). 352p. (C). (gr. 13). 1995. spiral bd. 27.00 (0-8016-7835-8, 07835) Mosby Inc.

***LaFleur Brooks, Myrna & LaFleur, Danielle.** Programmed Medical Language. 1998. write for info. (0-8151-5417-8); teacher ed. write for info. (0-8151-7852-2); text. write for info. (0-323-00112-2); text. write for info. incl. audio (0-323-00113-0) Mosby Inc.

LaFleur-Brooks, Myrna & LaFleur, Danielle. Programmed Medical Language Packaged with Accompanying Audiotape. 1996. pap. text 31.00 incl. audio (0-8151-1278-5) Mosby Inc.

LaFleur Brooks, Myrna & Starr, Winnifred K. Exploring Medical Language. 3rd ed. 1994. teacher ed. write for info. (0-8151-4600-0); text. write for info. (0-323-00110-6) Mosby Inc.

LaFleur-Brooks, Myrna W. Health Unit Coordinating. 4th ed. Kaszczuk, Selma, ed. LC 97-36857. (Illus.). 560p. (C). 1998. text 39.95 (0-7216-7186-1, W B Saunders Co) Harcrt Hlth Sci Grp.

LaFleur, Bruce & Lafleur, Terri, eds. LaFleur's 1995 European Lottery Abstract. 208p. 1995. pap. write for info. (1-883567-71-8) TLF Pubns.

LaFleur, Bruce, jt. auth. see LaFleur, Terri.

LaFleur, Bruce, jt. ed. see LaFleur, Teresa.

Lafleur, Bruno. Dictionary of Idiomatic French Expressions. (ENG & FRE.). 670p. 1991. 65.00 (0-685-62923-6, 2801109479) Fr & Eur.

— Dictionary of Idiomatic French Expressions. 2nd ed. (ENG & FRE.). 670p. 1991. lib. bdg. 65.00 (0-8288-3314-1, 2801109479) Fr & Eur.

— Dictionnaire des Expressions. (FRE.). 672p. 1984. 59.95 (0-7859-7698-1, 2040152679) Fr & Eur.

— Dictionnaire des Locutions Idiomatiques Francaises. (FRE.). 669p. 1980. pap. 105.00 (0-7859-8292-2, 3261048042) Fr & Eur.

LaFleur, Danielle, jt. auth. see LaFleur Brooks, Myrna.

LaFleur, Danielle, jt. auth. see LaFleur-Brooks, Myrna.

LaFleur, Danielle, jt. auth. see LaFleur Brooks, Myrna.

LaFleur, Doug & Brethower, Dale. The Transformation: Business Strategies for the 21st Century. (Illus.). 177p. 1998. pap. 19.95 (0-9663185-0-1) Impact Grpwrks.

Lafleur, J., ed. see Bentham, Jeremy.

LaFleur, Kathryn. Louise de Marillac: A Light in the Darkness. LC 96-6432. 254p. 1996. pap. 12.95 (1-56548-075-9) New City.

Lafleur, Laurence J. Descartes: Discourse on Method. 72p. (C). 1956. pap. text 6.20 (0-02-367160-2, Macmillan Coll) P-H.

— Descartes: Meditation on First Philosophy. 104p. (C). 1960. pap. text 5.80 (0-02-367170-X, Macmillan Coll) P-H.

— Discourse Method & Meditations. (C). 1960. pap. text 6.00 (0-02-367260-9, Macmillan Coll) P-H.

— Philosophical Essays - Descartes. (Library of Liberal Arts: No. 99). 264p. (C). 1964. pap. text 10.00 (0-02-367240-4, Macmillan Coll) P-H.

Lafleur, Laurence J., tr. see Descartes, Rene.

LaFleur, Matt, jt. auth. see Conrad, Hy.

LaFleur, Richard, jt. auth. see Comeau, Paul T.

LaFleur, Richard A. Latin Poetry. 1987. teacher ed. 28.00 (0-8013-0140-8, 75804); pap. text 12.57 (0-8013-0133-5, 75797) Longman.

***Lafleur, Richard A. & Ovid.** Love & Transformation: An Ovid Reader. 2nd ed. LC 98-218230. x, 192 p. 1999. write for info. (0-673-58920-X) Addison-Wesley.

LaFleur, Robert G., ed. Groundwater As a Geomorphic Agent. (Binghamton Symposia in Geomorphology: International Ser.: No. 13). (Illus.). 384p. (C). 1984. text 80.00 (0-04-551069-5) Routledge.

LaFleur, Teresa & LaFleur, Bruce, eds. LaFleur's 1997 World Lottery Almanac. 5th ed. 425p. pap. text. write for info. (1-883567-75-0) TLF Pubns.

LaFleur, Terri. Compendium of Lottery Statistics 1992. 207p. 1992. pap. 100.00 (1-883567-50-5) TLF Pubns.

— LaFleur's Lottery Interim Report: Fiscal 1992 Sales & Analysis. 54p. 1992. pap. 40.00 (1-883567-57-2) TLF Pubns.

— LaFleur's Ninety One North American Gambling Abstract. 258p. 1991. pap. 139.00 (1-883567-55-6) TLF Pubns.

— The Lottery Book. 167p. 1991. pap. 100.00 (1-883567-52-1) TLF Pubns.

— 1994 World Lottery Almanac. 388p. 1994. pap. text 149.00 (1-883567-64-5) TLF Pubns.

LaFleur, Terri & Lafleur, Bruce. LaFleur World Gambling Abstract, 1993. 297p. 1992. pap. 175.00 (1-883567-56-4) TLF Pubns.

LaFleur, Terri & LaFleur, Bruce. LaFleur's European Lottery Abstract. 202p. 1992. pap. 100.00 (1-883567-53-X) TLF Pubns.

— LaFleur's Lottery Interim Report Vol. 2: Fiscal 1993 Sales & Analysis. 55p. 1993. pap. 45.00 (1-883567-59-9) TLF Pubns.

— LaFleur's Principles of Contemporary Lottery Marketing. 192p. 1992. pap. 100.00 (1-883567-51-3) TLF Pubns.

LaFleur, Terri & Lafleur, Bruce. LaFleur's Video Lottery Terminal & Keno Report. 70p. 1993. pap. 45.00 (1-883567-58-0) TLF Pubns.

LaFleur, Terri & LaFleur, Bruce. LaFleur's Video Lottery Terminal Report. 68p. 1992. pap. 40.00 (1-883567-54-8) TLF Pubns.

— LaFleur's World Gambling Almanac, 1994. 325p. 1993. pap. 185.00 (1-883567-60-2) TLF Pubns.

— World Lottery Almanac, 1993. 394p. 1993. pap. 139.00 (1-883567-61-0) TLF Pubns.

Lafleur, Terri, jt. ed. see LaFleur, Bruce.

LaFleur, Tom & Brennan, Gale. Bingo the Bear. (Illus.). 16p. (Orig.). (J). (gr. k-6). 1981. pap. 1.25 (0-685-02454-7) Brennan Bks.

— Henry the Hound. (Illus.). 16p. (Orig.). (J). (gr. k-6). 1982. pap. 1.25 (0-685-05556-6) Brennan Bks.

— Isadore the Dinosaur. (Illus.). 16p. (Orig.). (J). (gr. k-6). 1981. pap. 1.25 (0-685-02456-3) Brennan Bks.

— Spunky the Monkey. (Illus.). 16p. (Orig.). (J). (gr. k-6). 1981. pap. 1.25 (0-685-02457-1) Brennan Bks.

— Tuffy the Tiger. (Illus.). 16p. (J). (gr. k-6). 1982. pap. 1.25 (0-685-05557-4) Brennan Bks.

— Woolly the Wolf. (Illus.). 16p. (Orig.). (J). (gr. k-6). 1981. pap. 1.25 (0-685-02459-8) Brennan Bks.

LaFleur, William R. The Karma of Words: Buddhism & the Literary Arts in Medieval Japan. LC 82-45909. 232p. (C). 1983. pap. 16.95 (0-520-05622-1, Pub. by U CA Pr) Cal Prin Full Svc.

LaFleur, William R., ed. Dogen Studies. LC 85-16427. (Studies in East Asian Buddhism: No. 2). 172p. 1985. pap. text 19.00 (0-8248-1011-2) UH Pr.

LaFleur, William R., ed. & intro. see Abe, Masao.

Laflin, Patricia B. Coachella Valley, California: A Pictorial History. LC 98-33803. 1998. write for info. (1-57864-049-0) Donning Co.

LaFluer, Belinda D. Optimum Use of Space: Time Spent in Alaska. LC 98-65167. 64p. 1998. pap. 9.95 (1-888125-25-X) Publ Consult.

Lafo, Rachel, jt. auth. see Danly, Susan.

Lafo, Rachel R. Anne Griffith Johnson Paintings: Orleonok Pitkin. (Illus.). 1981. pap. 1.00 (0-914435-05-1) Marylhurst Art.

— Belief in the Underground: The Art of Marcy Hermansader. LC 90-80631. (Orig.). 1990. pap. 12.00 (0-945506-05-8) DeCordova Mus.

— Carlos Dorrien: The Nine Muses & Other Projects. LC 97-67434. (Illus.). 8p. 1997. pap. 1.00 (0-945506-21-X) DeCordova Mus.

— Eight Artists - Eight Visions: 1990. LC 90-82380. (Orig.). 1990. bds. 7.00 (0-945506-06-6) DeCordova Mus.

— Ten Artists - Ten Visions, 1989. LC 89-51080. (Orig.). 1989. bds. 6.00 (0-945506-03-1) DeCordova Mus.

Lafo, Rachel R. & Capasso, Nicholas. Eleven Artists - Eleven Visions: 1992. 1992. bds. 6.00 (0-945506-08-2) DeCordova Mus.

— Eleven Artists - Eleven Visions: 1993. 1993. bds. 6.00 (0-945506-13-9) DeCordova Mus.

— Nine Artists - Nine Visions, 1991. 1991. bds. 6.00 (0-945506-07-4) DeCordova Mus.

Lafo, Rachel R. & Capasso, Nick. 9 Artists/9 Visions: 1996. LC 96-84236. (Illus.). 13p. (Orig.). Date not set. pap. write for info. (0-945506-19-8) DeCordova Mus.

— 10 Artists 10 Visions, 1997. LC 97-67435. (Illus.). 13p. 1997. pap. 7.95 (0-945506-22-8) DeCordova Mus.

Lafo, Rachel R. & Roberts, Sara R. 10 Artists/10 Visions: 1994. LC 94-72173. (Orig.). Date not set. pap. write for info. (0-945506-16-3) DeCordova Mus.

Lafo, Rachel R. & Westfall, Stephen. Gregory Amenoff: Works on Paper, 1975-1992. (Illus.). 40p. (Orig.). 1993. pap. write for info. (0-945506-12-0) DeCordova Mus.

Lafo, Rachel R., et al. Body & Soul: Contemporary Art & Healing. LC 93-74679. 80p. (Orig.). Date not set. pap. write for info. (0-945506-15-5) DeCordova Mus.

— The Sudbury River: A Celebration: Photographs by Frank Gohlke. LC 93-72473. (Illus.). 40p. (Orig.). Date not set. pap. write for info. (0-945506-14-7) DeCordova Mus.

Lafo, Rachel Rosenfield & DeCordova Museum & Sculpture Park Staff. 1998 DeCordova Annual Exhibition, 13 June-September 7: Bethany Bristow, Tom Chapin, Stephanie Chubbuck, Vico Fabbris, Ben Freeman, Thomas Halloran, John Hughes, Abelardo Morell, Irene Valincius, Lucy White. LC 98-71568. 24p. 1998. write for info. (0-945506-26-0) DeCordova Mus.

***Lafo, Rachel Rosenfield & Nagler, Gillian, eds.** Photography in Boston, 1955-1985. (Illus.). 204p. 2000. 39.95 (0-262-12229-4) MIT Pr.

Lafollete Summerskill, Mimi. In the Land of Solomon & Sheba. 200p. 1998. 59.95 (1-56902-092-2); pap. 18.95 (1-56902-093-0) Red Sea Pr.

LaFollette, Hugh. Persons & Personal Relationships: Love, Identity & Ethics. 256p. (C). 1995. 58.95 (0-631-19684-6); pap. 25.95 (0-631-19685-4) Blackwell Pubs.

***LaFollette, Hugh, ed.** Blackwell Guide to Ethical Theory. LC 99-33934. (Philosophy Guides Ser.). 500p. 1999. 64.95 (0-631-20118-1) Blackwell Pubs.

LaFollette, Hugh, ed. Ethics in Practice: An Anthology. LC 96-16025. (Philosophy Anthologies Ser.). 672p. (C). 1996. 88.95 (1-55786-639-2); pap. 34.95 (1-55786-640-6) Blackwell Pubs.

L

***LaFollette, Hugh, ed.** Guide to Ethical Theory. LC 99-33934. (Philosophy Guides Ser.). 500p. 1999. pap. 34.95 (*0-631-20119-X*) Blackwell Pubs.

Lafollette, Hugh & Shanks, Niall. Brute Science: Dilemmas of Animal Experimentation. LC 96-18248. (Philosophical Issues in Science Ser.). 304p. (C). 1997. 85.00 (*0-415-13113-8*); pap. 24.99 (*0-415-13114-6*) Routledge.

LaFollette, Hugh, jt. ed. see Aiken, William.

LaFollette, Karen, jt. auth. see Roberts, Paul C.

LaFollette, Marcel C. Making Science Our Own: Public Images of Science, 1910-1955. LC 89-20555. (Illus.). 312p. 1995. pap. text 19.95 (*0-226-46779-1*) U Ch Pr.

— Making Science Our Own: Public Images of Science, 1910-1955. LC 89-20555. (Illus.). 312p. 1995. lib. bdg. 54.00 (*0-226-46778-3*) U Ch Pr.

— Stealing into Print: Fraud, Plagiarism, & Misconduct in Scientific Publishing. 1992. 45.00 (*0-520-07831-4*, Pub. by U CA Pr) Cal Prin Full Svc.

— Stealing into Print: Fraud, Plagiarism, & Misconduct in Scientific Publishing. LC 91-41669. 293p. (C). 1996. pap. 15.95 (*0-520-20513-8*, Pub. by U CA Pr) Cal Prin Full Svc.

LaFollette, Marcel C. & Stine, Jeffrey K., eds. Technology & Choice: Readings from Technology & Culture. (Illus.). 352p. 1991. pap. 19.50 (*0-226-46777-5*) U Ch Pr.

— Technology & Choice: Readings from Technology & Culture. (Illus.). 352p. 1991. lib. bdg. 40.50 (*0-226-46776-7*) U Ch Pr.

LaFollette, Robert M., ed. The Making of America: Labor. LC 72-89744. (American Labor, from Conspiracy to Collective Bargaining Ser., No. 1). 433p. 1970. reprint ed. 34.95 (*0-405-02132-1*) Ayer.

Lafon, Jacqueline L., jt. auth. see Volcansek, Mary L.

Lafon, Michel. 15 Days of Prayer with Charles de Foucauld. Hebert, Victoria & Sabourin, Denise, trs. from FRE. LC 99-34425. 128p. (Orig.). 1999. reprint ed. pap. 7.95 (*0-7648-0489-8*) Liguori Pubns.

— French-Comorian (Shingazidja) Lexicon. (FRE.). 239p. 1991. 69.95 (*0-8288-6922-7*, 2738411010) Fr & Eur.

Lafon, Robert. Diccionario de Psicopedagogia y Psiqiatria del Nino: French - Spanish. 5th ed. (FRE & SPA.). 1056p. 1993. lib. bdg. write for info. (*0-7859-3677-7*, 8428107556) Fr & Eur.

— Vocabulaire de Psychopedagogie et de Psychiatrie de L'Enfant: Vocabulary of Child Psychiatry & Educational Psychology. 3rd ed. (FRE.). 868p. 1973. 95.00 (*0-8288-6335-0*, F-19440) Fr & Eur.

LaFon, Ron, ed. Euphoria Journal, Vol. 1. 270p. (C). 1982. 55.00 (*0-912647-00-0*) Strawberry.

— Euphoria Journal, Vol. 2. 270p. (C). 1983. 45.00 (*0-912647-01-9*) Strawberry.

— Euphoria Journal, Vol. 3. 270p. (C). 1984. 45.00 (*0-912647-02-7*) Strawberry.

— Euphoria Journal, Vol. 4. 270p. (C). 1985. 45.00 (*0-912647-08-6*) Strawberry.

— Euphoria Journal, Vol. 5. 270p. (C). 1987. 45.00 (*0-912647-05-1*) Strawberry.

— Euphoria Journal, Vol. 6. 270p. (C). 1989. 45.00 (*0-912647-06-X*) Strawberry.

— Euphoria Journal, Vol. 7. 270p. (C). 1991. 45.00 (*0-912647-04-3*) Strawberry.

LaFon, Ron, jt. auth. see Foust, Jeff.

LaFon, Ron, ed. see Rowley, Gorden.

LaFond, Anne. Sustaining Primary Health Care. LC 95-16318. 1995. text 55.00 (*0-312-12732-4*) St Martin.

LaFond, Carolyn Street. The Painter's Daughter: The Story of Sandro Botticelli & Alessandra Lippi. LC 99-22016. (Illus.). 432p. 2000. 35.00 (*0-913720-78-X*) Beil.

Lafond, D., et al. Living with Aphasia: Psychosocial Issues. LC 92-49888.Tr. of L'Aphasie. (Illus.). 308p. (Orig.). (C). 1992. pap. text 49.95 (*1-56593-067-3*, 0372) Thomson Learn.

Lafond, Jean, jt. auth. see La Rochefoucauld, Francois de.

Lafond, Patrick. L' Anglais de l'Expert Compatable: French & English Accounting Dictionary. (ENG & FRE.). 160p. 1993. 69.95 (*0-7859-9459-9*) Fr & Eur.

Lafond, Patrick & Vaughan, Richard. L' Anglais de l'Expert-Comptable. (FRE.). 159p. 1993. pap. 69.95 (*0-7859-1661-X*, 2906471054) Fr & Eur.

Lafond, Paul. Hieronymus Bosch - The Complete Prints: Catalogue Raisonne. rev. ed. (Illus.). 256p. 1999. 150.00 (*0-614-26236-4*) A Wofsy Fine Arts.

LaFond, Richard E., ed. Cancer: The Outlaw Cell. 2nd ed. LC 88-14517. (Illus.). 289p. 1988. text 33.00 (*0-8412-1419-0*, Pub. by Am Chemical); pap. text 22.00 (*0-8412-1420-4*, Pub. by Am Chemical) OUP.

Lafond, Virginia. Grieving Mental Illness: A Guide for Patients & Their Caregivers. 96p. 1994. text 30.00 (*0-8020-0614-0*); pap. text 12.95 (*0-8020-7578-9*) U of Toronto Pr.

Lafont, Antoine & Topol, Eric J. Arterial Remodeling: Critical Factor in Restenosis. LC 97-33314. (Developments in Cardiovascular Medicine Ser.). 600p. 1997. text 247.50 (*0-7923-8008-8*) Kluwer Academic.

Lafont, B. & Yildiz, F. Tablettes Cuneiformes de Tello au Musee d'Istambul: Datant De l'Epoque De la IIIe Dynastie d'Ur. 296p. 1989. pap. text 56.00 (*90-6258-065-3*, Pub. by Netherlands Inst) Eisenbrauns.

LaFont, Betrand & Yildiz, Fatma. Tablettes Cuneiformes de Tello au Musee D'Istanbul: Datant de l'Epoque de la III Dynastie d'Ur/ITT II/1, 2544-2819, 3158-4342, 4708-4713. (FRE.). 395p. 1996. pap. text 46.75 (*90-6258-077-7*, Pub. by Netherlands Inst) Eisenbrauns.

***Lafont, Cristina.** Heidegger, Language & World-Disclosure. (Modern European Philosophy Ser.). 320p. (C). 2000. text 59.95 (*0-521-66247-8*) Cambridge U Pr.

Lafont, Cristina. The Linguistic Turn in Hermeneutic Philosophy. Medina, Jose, tr. from SPA. LC 99-23900. (Studies in Contemporary German Social Thought Ser.). 377p. 1999. 45.00 (*0-262-12217-0*) MIT Pr.

Lafont, Ghislain. God, Time & Being. Maluf, Leonard, tr. from FRE. LC 91-27423. 348p. (Orig.). 1992. pap. 29.95 (*0-932506-89-5*) St Bedes Pubns.

***Lafont, Ghislain.** Imagining the Catholic Church: Structural Communion in the Spirit. Burkhard, John, tr. 224p. 2000. pap. 29.95 (*0-8146-5946-2*) Liturgical Pr.

LaFont, Jan. The Mirror on the Town Hall. 150p. (Orig.). 1982. pap. 3.50 (*0-9603596-3-X*) Fontastic.

LaFont, Suzanne. The Emergence of an Afro-Caribbean Legal Tradition: Gender Relations & Family Courts in Kingston, Jamaica. LC 94-29005. 250p. (C). 1996. pap. 49.95 (*1-880921-91-X*) Austin & Winfield.

— The Emergence of an Afro-Caribbean Legal Tradition: Gender Relations & Family Courts Use in Kingston, Jamaica. LC 94-29005. 250p. (C). 1996. 69.95 (*1-880921-92-8*) Austin & Winfield.

LaFont, Suzanne, ed. Women in Transition: Voices from Lithuania. LC 97-28022. 160p. (C). 1998. text 44.50 (*0-7914-3811-2*); pap. text 14.95 (*0-7914-3812-0*) State U NY Pr.

LaFontaine. Famous Buildings of F. L. Wright. 1998. pap. 2.95 (*0-486-29362-9*) Dover.

— History of Trucks. 1998. pap. 2.95 (*0-486-29278-9*) Dover.

— Oeuvres Completes: Poemes, Theatre. (FRE.). 1196p. 1978. 125.00 (*0-7859-9748-2*) Fr & Eur.

Lafontaine, B. History of the Sword. 1998. pap. text 2.95 (*0-486-40139-1*) Dover.

***Lafontaine, B.** Learning about the Solar System. (Learning about Bks.). (Illus.). (J). 2000. pap. 1.00 (*0-486-41009-9*) Dover.

— Modern Experimental Aircraft. (Pictorial Archive Ser.). 2000. pap. 2.95 (*0-486-41037-4*) Dover.

LaFontaine, Bruce. Bridges of the World Coloring Book. (Illus.). (J). 1995. pap. 2.95 (*0-486-28358-5*) Dover.

— Classic Airplanes. (Illus.). 2000. pap. 1.00 (*0-486-41073-0*) Dover.

— Classic Motorcycles Sticker Book. (Illus.). (J). 1999. pap. 1.00 (*0-486-40603-2*) Dover.

— Classic Racing Cars. (Illus.). 2000. pap. 1.00 (*0-486-41072-2*) Dover.

— Classic Sports Cars Stickers. (Illus.). (J). 1999. pap. 1.00 (*0-486-40604-0*) Dover.

LaFontaine, Bruce. Exploring the Solar System. (Illus.). 48p. (J). 1998. pap. 2.95 (*0-486-40361-0*) Dover.

— Great Inventors & Inventions. (Illus.). (J). pap. 2.95 (*0-486-29784-5*) Dover.

— History of Space Exploration Coloring Book. (Illus.). (J). pap. 2.95 (*0-486-26152-2*) Dover.

***LaFontaine, Bruce.** Homes of the American Presidents Coloring Book. (Illus.). (J). 2000. pap. 2.95 (*0-486-40801-9*) Dover.

LaFontaine, Bruce. Lindbergh & the Spirit of St. Louis. 1999. pap. text 2.95 (*0-486-40567-2*) Dover.

— Solar System. 1998. pap. 1.00 (*0-486-40308-4*) Dover.

— Spacecraft. 1998. pap. text 1.00 (*0-486-40309-2*) Dover.

***LaFontaine, Bruce.** Sports Cars. (Illus.). 1999. pap. text 2.95 (*0-486-40802-7*) Dover.

LaFontaine, Bruce. Submarines & Underwater Exploration. 2000. pap. text 2.95 (*0-486-40803-5*) Dover.

— Train. 1998. pap. 1.00 (*0-486-40310-6*) Dover.

***LaFontaine, Bruce.** Trains Stained Glass Coloring Book. (Little Activity Bks.). (Illus.). (J). 2000. pap. 1.00 (*0-486-40972-4*) Dover.

LaFontaine, Gary. Caddisflies. LC 97-223773. (Illus.). 336p. 1989. 40.00 (*0-941130-98-3*) Lyons Pr.

— The Dry Fly: New Angles. LC 91-202676. (Illus.). 320p. 1990. 39.95 (*0-9626663-0-0*) Greycliff Pub.

— Fly Fishing the Mountain Lakes. LC 98-28039. 186p. (Orig.). 1998. pap. 14.95 (*0-9626663-7-8*) Greycliff Pub.

— Trout Flies: Proven Patterns. LC 93-1075. (Illus.). 280p. 1993. 39.95 (*0-9626663-1-9*) Greycliff Pub.

LaFontaine, Gary, jt. auth. see Cordes, Ron.

LaFontaine, Gary, jt. auth. see Grove, Eric.

LaFontaine, Gary, jt. auth. see Peper, Eric.

LaFontaine, H. C. Apollonius of Tyana. (Orig.). 1993. pap. 6.95 (*1-55818-234-9*) Holmes Pub.

LaFontaine, Henri. Pasicrisie Internationale, 1794-1900: Histoire Documentaire des Arbitrage Internationaux. LC 97-17793. 1997. 209.00 (*90-411-0454-2*) Kluwer Law Intl.

Lafontaine, Henry C. De, see De Lafontaine, Henry C.

Lafontaine, J., et al. Riemannian Geometry. (Universitext Ser.). x, 248p. 1987. pap. 29.00 (*0-387-17923-2*) Spr-Verlag.

Lafontaine, J. Donald. The Moths of America North of Mexico: Fascicle 27.2-Noctuoidea, Noctuidae: Noctuinae (Part-Euxoa) Hodges, R. W. et al, eds. LC 87-50657. (Illus.). 235p. (C). 1987. pap. text 75.00 (*0-933003-03-X*) Wedge Entomological.

— The Moths of America North of Mexico: Noctuoidea - Noctuidae. (Illus.). 349p. 1998. pap. 115.00 (*0-933003-09-9*) Wedge Entomological.

Lafontaine, J. Donald & Poole, Robert W. The Moths of America North of Mexico, Fascicle 25.1: Noctuoidea, Noctuidae (Part), Plusiinae. Hodges, R. W. et al, eds. LC 91-65196. (Illus.). 182p. (C). 1991. pap. text 70.00 (*0-933003-06-4*) Wedge Entomological.

Lafontaine, Jacques, jt. ed. see Audin, Michele.

Lafontaine, Marie-Jo. Marie-Jo LaFontaine. 1999. 42.95 (*3-89322-947-7*) Dist Art Pubs.

LaFontaine, Mary, jt. auth. see LaFontaine, Ray.

Lafontaine, Monique, ed. see Lafontaine, Steve.

***Lafontaine, Oskar.** The Heart Beats on the Left. 2000. 59.95 (*0-7456-2581-9*, Pub. by Polity Pr); pap. 24.95 (*0-7456-2582-7*, Pub. by Polity Pr) Blackwell Pubs.

Lafontaine, Oskar & Muller, Christa. No Fear of Globalization: Welfare & Work for All. 2000. 27.00 (*1-85984-751-X*, Pub. by Verso) Norton.

Lafontaine, Pierre. Chevrolet Small-Block V-8 Id Guide: Covers All Chevy Small Block Engines since 1955. LC 96-13064. 128p. 1996. pap. text 19.95 (*0-7603-0175-1*) MBI Pubg.

LaFontaine, Ray & LaFontaine, Mary. Oswald Talked: The New Evidence in the JFK Assassination. LC 94-45945. (Illus.). 456p. 1996. reprint ed. 25.00 (*1-56554-029-8*) Pelican.

Lafontaine, Steve. Mazda Wankel Rotary Aviation Conversion Resource Book. Lafontaine, Monique, ed. (Illus.). 32p. (Orig.). 1990. pap. text 10.00 (*0-9625685-0-3*) Lafontaine Pr.

— Oildrum Cookbook: Fifty-Five Back to Basic, Appropriate Technology Devices You Can Build from a Steel Oildrum. Lafontaine, Monique, ed. (Illus.). 200p. (Orig.). 1990. pap. text 10.00 (*0-9625685-1-1*) Lafontaine Pr.

Lafontant, Raymond. Fuerte Allen: La Diaspora Haitiana. (SPA., Illus.). 192p. 1996. pap. 7.95 (*1-56328-107-4*) Edit Plaza Mayor.

Lafora, Nicholas De, see De Lafora, Nicholas.

Lafora, Nicolbas de & Kinnaird, Lawrence. New York Film Festival Programs, 1963-1975. 1977. 65.95 (*0-405-07619-3*, 11479) Ayer.

Laforcade, Geoffroy De, see Horowitz, Donald L. & Noiriel, Gerard, eds.

Laforcade, Geoffroy De, see Noiriel, Gerard.

LaForce, Beatrice. Devil's Cuspidor. 1981. pap. 1.75 (*0-686-37157-7*) Eldridge Pub.

Lafore, Laurence. The Long Fuse: An Interpretation of the Origins of World War I. 2nd ed. (Illus.). 284p. (C). 1997. reprint ed. pap. text 13.95 (*0-88133-954-7*) Waveland Pr.

Lafore, Laurence D. The Long Fuse. LC 81-1514. (Critical Periods of History Ser.). 282p. 1981. reprint ed. lib. bdg. 67.50 (*0-313-22969-4*, LALF, Greenwood Pr) Greenwood.

Lafore, Robert. Object-Oriented Programming in C++ 2nd rev. ed. 912p. 1995. 34.99 (*1-878739-73-5*) Sams.

— Teach Yourself Data Structures & Algorithms in 24 Hours. 1999. pap. text 24.99 (*0-672-31633-1*) Sams.

— The Waite Group's C Programming Using Turbo C++ 2nd ed. 778p. 1993. 34.95 (*0-672-30399-X*) Sams.

— Waite Group's Object-Oriented Programming in C++ 3rd ed. LC 98-85905. (Illus.). 925p. 1998. pap. 34.99 (*1-57169-160-X*) Sams.

Lafore, Robert & Waite, Mitchell. Data Structures & Algorithms in Java with CD-ROM. LC 97-32172. (Mitchell Waite Signature Ser.). 656p. 1998. write for info. (*1-57169-095-6*) Sams.

***Laforest, Anne.** Therese of Lisieux: The Way of Love. 160p. 2000. pap. 15.95 (*1-58051-082-5*) Sheed & Ward WI.

Laforest, T. J., ed. & tr. see Saintonge, Jacques.

Laforest, Thomas J., ed. & tr. see Lebel, Gerard.

LaForest, Thomas J., ed. & tr. see Lebel, R. P.

Laforest, Thomas J., ed. & tr. see Saintonge, Jacques.

LaForest, Thomas J., tr. see Lebel, Gerard & Saintonge, Jacques.

Laforet, Andrea. The Book of the Grand Hall. (Illus.). 80p. 1992. pap. 16.95 (*0-660-14001-2*, Pub. by CN Mus Civilization) U of Wash Pr.

Laforet, Andrea & York, Annie. Spuzzum: Fraser Canyon Histories, 1808-1939. 1999. pap. text 22.95 (*0-7748-0667-2*) U BC Pr.

Laforet, Carmen. Isla y los Demonios. 2nd ed. 312p. 1991. pap. 19.95 (*0-7859-5142-3*) Fr & Eur.

— Nada. 286p. (Orig.). 1958. pap. text 21.95 (*0-19-500942-8*) OUP.

— Nada. Ennis, Glafyra, tr. from SPA. LC 92-31936. (Catalan Studies: Vol. 8). 250p. (Orig.). (C). 1993. pap. text 29.95 (*0-8204-2064-6*) P Lang Pubng.

LaForet, Carmen. Nada. (SPA.). pap. 19.95 (*84-233-0989-4*, Pub. by Destino) Continental Bk.

LaForge, Ann. Tantrums: Secrets to Calming the Storm. 96p. 1996. mass mkt. 5.99 (*0-671-88039-X*) PB.

— What Really Happens in School: A Guide to Your Child's Emotional, Social & Intellectual Development, Grades K-5. LC 98-43988. 320p. 1999. pap. 14.95 (*0-7868-8211-5*, Pub. by Hyperion) Time Warner.

Laforge, Larry, ed. Boston Rocks. 1987. pap. 10.00 (*0-685-19188-5*) MIT Outing.

Laforge, Raymond W., jt. ed. see Hills, Gerald E.

LaForgia, Gerard M. Local Organizations for Rural Health in Panama: Community Participation, Bureaucratic Reorientation, & Political Will. (Special Series on Rural Local Organization: No. 8). 153p. 1985. 7.50 (*0-86731-035-9*) Cornell CIS RDC.

LaForgue, Jules. Berlin: The City & the Court. Smith, William J., tr. & intro. by. (Illus.). 219p. (Orig.). 1996. pap. 13.95 (*1-885983-02-6*) Turtle Point Pr.

Laforgue, Jules. Berlin, la Cour et la Ville. LC 77-10273. reprint ed. 26.00 (*0-404-16325-4*) AMS Pr.

— Lettres a un Ami: 1880-1886, avec le Fac-Simile d'Une Lettre Inedite a Stephane Mallarme. LC 77-10274. 240p. reprint ed. 47.50 (*0-404-16326-2*) AMS Pr.

— Moral Tales. Smith, William J., tr. from FRE. LC 84-25498. (Illus.). 224p. 1985. 9.95 (*0-8112-0942-3*, Pub. by New Directions) Norton.

— Moralites Legendaires. (Folio Ser.: No. 855). (FRE.). 243p. 1977. pap. 8.95 (*2-07-036855-6*) Schoenhof.

LaForgue, Jules. Poems of Jules Laforgue. Terry, Patricia, tr. LC 86-4617. 217p. 1986. reprint ed. lib. bdg. 59.50 (*0-313-25210-6*, LFPO, Greenwood Pr) Greenwood.

Laforgue, Jules. Poesies Completes Tome 1: Les Complaintes. Premiers Poemes. (Poesie Ser.). (FRE.). 1979. pap. 15.95 (*2-07-032181-9*) Schoenhof.

LaForgue, Jules. Poesies Completes Tome 2: L'Imitation de Notre Dame la Lune. Le Concile Feerique. Etc... (Poesie Ser.). (FRE.). 1979. pap. 11.95 (*2-07-032182-7*) Schoenhof.

Laforgue, Jules. Selected Poems. 336p. 1999. pap. 12.95 (*0-14-043626-X*, PuffinBks) Peng Put Young Read.

— Six Moral Tales from Jules Laforgue. Newman, Frances, ed. LC 77-10275. 296p. reprint ed. 49.50 (*0-404-16327-0*) AMS Pr.

Laforgue, Jules & Dale, Peter. Poems of Jules Laforgue. 456p. 1986. pap. 19.95 (*0-85646-146-6*, Pub. by Anvil Press) Dufour.

Laforgue, Jules, tr. see Whitman, Walt.

Laforgue, Rene. Clinical Aspects of Psychoanalysis. Hall, Joan, tr. from FRE. (Psychoanalysis: Examined & Re-Examined Ser.). 300p. 1984. reprint ed. lib. bdg. 35.00 (*0-306-76235-8*) Da Capo.

Laforre, Timmy R. Acidosis--Index of New Information & Medical Research Bible. 150p. 1994. 47.50 (*0-7883-0086-5*); pap. 44.50 (*0-7883-0087-3*) ABBE Pubs Assn.

— Alkalosis--Index of New Information & Medical Bible of Research. 150p. 1994. 47.50 (*0-7883-0088-1*); pap. 44.50 (*0-7883-0089-X*) ABBE Pubs Assn.

***Laforsch, Matthias.** Kosten der Luftreinhaltung: Ein Ansatz Zur Erstellung von Kostenfunktionen Fur die Emissionsminderung Zur Unterstutzung Internationaler Umweltpolitischer Verhandlungen. (Europaische Hochschulschriften Ser.: Bd. 2507). xvi, 314p. 1999. 52.95 (*3-631-35077-5*) P Lang Pubng.

Laforse, Martin W. & Drake, James A. Popular Culture & American Life: Selected Topics in the Study of Twentieth Century American Popular Culture. LC 80-27809. 264p. (C). 1981. pap. text 24.95 (*0-88229-778-3*) Burnham Inc.

LaForte, Robert S., et al, eds. With Only the Will to Live: Accounts of Americans in Japanese Prison Camps, 1941-1945. LC 93-42419. 320p. 1994. 24.95 incl. audio (*0-8420-2464-6*, SR Bks) Scholarly Res Inc.

Lafortezza, Angela, ed. see Matrullo, Fondano.

Lafortune, M., tr. see Fruhwald, Franz X. & Blackwell, D. Eric, eds.

***LaFosse, Michael.** Origami-Do: The Art of Paper Folding. 2000. 35.00 (*1-56496-639-9*) Rockport Pubs.

LaFosse, Michael. Paper Animals. (Make It with Paper Ser.). (Illus.). 72p. 1997. pap. 9.95 (*1-56010-385-X*, RPO1) W Foster Pub.

— Paper Animals: 8 Step-by-Step Projects. (Make It with Paper Ser.). (Illus.). 72p. 1997. pap. 19.99 (*1-56496-276-8*, Quarry Bks) Rockport Pubs.

— Paper Boxes: 8 Step-by-Step Projects. (Make It with Paper Ser.). (Illus.). 114p. 1997. pap. 19.99 (*1-56496-277-6*, Quarry Bks) Rockport Pubs.

— Paper Flowers: 8 Step-by-Step Projects. (Make It with Paper Ser.). (Illus.). 72p. 1997. pap. 19.99 (*1-56496-275-X*, Quarry Bks) Rockport Pubs.

— Paper Pop-Ups. (Make It with Paper Ser.). (Illus.). 72p. 1997. pap. 9.95 (*1-56010-386-8*, RPO2) W Foster Pub.

— Paperart: Sculpting with Paper. (Illus.). 144p. 1998. 29.99 (*1-56496-378-0*, Quarry Bks) Rockport Pubs.

***LaFosse, Michael G.** Paper Art: The Art of Sculpting with Paper. (Illus.). 144p. 1998. text. write for info. (*90-5703-132-9*, Harwood Acad Pubs) Gordon & Breach.

LaFosse, Michael G. Paper Flowers. (Make It with Paper Ser.). (Illus.). 72p. 1997. pap. 9.95 (*1-56010-387-6*, RPO3) W Foster Pub.

Lafouge, Jean-Pierre. Etude Sur l'Orientalisme d'Eugene Fromentin dans ses "Recits Algeriens" (American University Studies: Romance Languages & Literature: Ser. II, Vol. 100). 258p. (C). 1988. text 36.50 (*0-8204-0820-4*) P Lang Pubng.

LaFountain, Marc J. Dali & Postmodernism: This Is Not an Essence. LC 96-48415. (SUNY Series in Postmodern Culture). 173p. (C). 1997. text 50.50 (*0-7914-3325-0*); pap. text 16.95 (*0-7914-3326-9*) State U NY Pr.

LaFountain, Rebecca M. & Garner, Nadire E. A School with Solutions: Implementing a Solution-Focused/Adlerian-Based Comprehensive School Counseling Program. 161p. 1998. pap. text 16.95 (*1-929289-00-6*, SWS01) Am Sch Coun.

LaFountain, William. Setting Limits: Parents, Kids & Drugs. 36p. 1982. 3.00 (*0-89486-145-X*, 1418B) Hazelden.

Lafourcade, Bernard, jt. auth. see Morrow, Bradford.

Lafourcade, Bernard, ed. see Lewis, Wyndham.

Lafourcade, Georges. Arnold Bennett: A Study. LC 70-148345. reprint ed. 37.50 (*0-404-08859-7*) AMS Pr.

— Arnold Bennett: A Study. LC 74-176494. (English Literature Ser.: No. 33). 1971. reprint ed. lib. bdg. 75.00 (*0-8383-1360-4*) M S G Haskell Hse.

Lafourche Heritage Society. Historical Scenes of Thibodaux: A Sesquicentennial Volume. (Illus.). 200p. 1988. 30.00 (*0-9617559-2-X*) Oubres Bks.

LaFoy, Leslie. Daring the Devil. 368p. 1999. mass mkt. 5.50 (*0-553-58042-6*) Bantam.

— It Happened One Night. 384p. 1997. mass mkt. 5.50 (*0-553-57745-X*, Fanfare) Bantam.

— Lady Reckless. 320p. 1998. mass mkt. 5.50 (*0-553-57747-6*) Bantam.

***LaFoy, Leslie.** Maddie's Justice. 304p. 2000. mass mkt. 5.50 (*0-553-58045-0*) Bantam.

Laframboise, Larry, jt. auth. see Cocks, David.

Laframboise, Leon W. History of the Administrative & Technical Services Branch of Service Insignia. (Branch of Service Insignia Ser.). (Illus.). 542p. (C). 1986. text 40.00 (*0-9613855-0-2*) L W Laframboise.

LaFranc, Elsie, jt. ed. see Blustain, Harvey.

LaFrance, Arthur B. Bioethics: Health Care, Human Rights, & the Law LC 99-13521. 1999. 58.00 (*0-8205-4072-2*) Bender.

An Asterisk (*) at the beginning of an entry indicates that the title is appearing for the first time.

LaFrance, Arthur B. & Loewy, Arnold H. Criminal Procedure: Trial & Sentencing. LC 93-46987. 718p. 1994. 55.95 (*0-87084-179-3*) Anderson Pub Co.

LaFrance, Arthur B., jt. auth. see Loewy, Arnold H.

LaFrance, Danielle, ed. Berkeley! A Literary Tribute. 256p. (Orig.). 1997. pap. 14.95 (*0-930588-94-0*) Heyday Bks.

LaFrance, David G. The Mexican Revolution in Puebla, 1908-1913: The Maderista Movement & the Failure of Liberal Reform. LC 88-34923. 272p. 1989. 45.00 (*0-8420-2293-7*) Scholarly Res Inc.

LaFrance, David G. & Jones, Errol D., eds. Latin American Military History: An Annotated Bibliography. LC 92-12606. (Military History Bibliographies Ser.: Vol. 12). 752p. 1992. text 40.00 (*0-8240-4634-X*, H01024) Garland.

LaFrance, David G., jt. auth. see Thomson, Guy P.

LaFrance, Edward. Pak: Men, Media, & Masculinity. 48p. (C). 1995. student ed. write for info. (*0-7872-1769-7*); pap., per. write for info. (*0-7872-1577-5*); 41.93 (*0-7872-1770-0*) Kendall-Hunt.

Lafrance, Jean. My Vocation Is Love. 175p. (C). 1990. 45.00 (*0-85439-393-5*, Pub. by St Paul Pubns) St Mut.

Lafrance, John C., ed. see Paugh, Jon.

LaFrance, Peter. Beer Basics: A Quick & Easy Guide. LC 94-49717. 208p. 1995. pap. 14.95 (*0-471-11936-9*) Wiley.

— Cooking & Eating with Beer: 50 Chefs, Brewmasters & Restauranteurs Talk about Beer & Food. LC 96-49039. 211p. 1997. 24.95 (*0-471-13564-X*) Wiley.

— Cooking With Beer: 50 Chefs, Brewmasters & Resauranteurs Talk about Beer & Food. 224p. 1998. pap. 16.95 (*0-471-31879-5*) Wiley.

LaFrance, Scott, jt. auth. see Duis, Perry.

LaFrance, Vincent A. Sources of Japanese Industrial Success: The Case of the Television Receiver Industry. LC 96-535. (Contributions in Economics & Economic History Ser.: No. 179). 1997. text. write for info. (*0-313-26070-2*, Greenwood Pr) Greenwood.

***LaFranchi, Guy.** Archonpoison. 120p. 1999. pap. 19.95 (*3-211-83294-7*) Spr-Verlag.

LaFray, Joyce. Country Cookin' 200p. 1996. 16.95 (*0-942084-41-1*) SeaSide Pub.

— Cuba Cocina! The Tantalizing World of Cuban Cooking--Yesterday, Today, & Tomorrow. LC 94-1594. 288p. 1994. 25.00 (*0-688-11067-3*, Hearst) Hearst Commns.

— Famous Florida! Florida Orange Recipes. 48p. 1989. pap. 5.95 (*0-942084-69-1*) SeaSide Pub.

— Famous Florida! Seafood Recipes. 32p. 1989. pap. 5.95 (*0-942084-36-5*) SeaSide Pub.

— Famous Florida Classic Crab. 48p. 1996. 5.95 (*0-942084-63-2*) SeaSide Pub.

— Famous Florida! Favorite Recipes Index. 1990. pap. 12.95 (*0-942084-88-8*) SeaSide Pub.

Lafray, Joyce. Famous Florida! Key Lime Cookin' Famous Recipes from Famous Places. (Famous Florida! Ser.). 1994. pap. text 5.95 (*0-942084-30-6*) SeaSide Pub.

LaFray, Joyce. Famous Florida! Key Lime Desserts. 48p. 1996. 5.95 (*0-942084-65-9*) SeaSide Pub.

— Famous Florida! Seafood! 1990. pap. 16.95 (*0-942084-20-9*) SeaSide Pub.

— Guide to Famous Florida! Restaurants. 1990. pap. 9.95 (*0-942084-93-4*) SeaSide Pub.

Lafray, Joyce. Restaurants & Recipes. (Famous Florida! Ser.). 1998. pap. text 16.95 (*0-942084-49-7*) SeaSide Pub.

LaFray, Joyce. Secrets of Great Miami Chefs. 1986. pap. 5.95 (*0-942084-32-2*) SeaSide Pub.

Lafray, Joyce. Underwater Gourmet: The Great Seafood Book. (Famous Florida! Ser.). 1998. pap. text 14.95 (*0-942084-57-8*) SeaSide Pub.

LaFray, Joyce & Altschul, B. J. Drifting & Dreaming: The Biography of Songwriter Haven Gillespie. LC 97-62107. (Illus.). 140p. 1983. 1.50 (*0-942084-05-5*) SeaSide Pub.

LaFray, Joyce & Kushnir, Millie. Millie's Jewish Kitchen. Altschul, B. J., ed. LC 97-62108. 105 p. 1982. 0.95 (*0-942084-03-9*) SeaSide Pub.

LaFray, Joyce, jt. auth. see Cayla, Edward.

LaFray, Joyce, jt. auth. see Polvay, Marina.

LaFray, Joyce, jt. auth. see Sandvik, Mary.

LaFray, Joyce, ed. see Schoolsky, Robert.

LaFray Young, Joyce S., ed. see Simos, Michele & O'Keefe, Timothy.

Lafree, Gary. Losing Legitimacy: Street Crime & the Decline of Social Institutions in America. LC 98-13957. (Crime & Society Ser.). 1998. 27.00 (*0-8133-3450-0*, Pub. by Westview) HarpC.

— Losing Legitimacy: Street Crime & the Decline of Social Institutions in America. (Crime & Society Ser.). (C). 1999. pap. text 20.00 (*0-8133-3451-9*) Westview.

***Lafreniere, Bree.** Music Through the Dark: A Tale of Survival in Cambodia. LC 99-53430. (Intersections Ser.). 176p. 2000. pap. 17.95 (*0-8248-2266-8*); text 36.00 (*0-8248-2227-7*) UH Pr.

Lafreniere, Joan G. Low-Back Patient: Treatment by Physical Therapy. (C). (gr. 13). 1979. 31.50 (*0-89352-033-0*) Mosby Inc.

Lafreniere, Kenneth. El Duque: The Story of Orlando Hernandez. LC 99-13618. (YA). (gr. 3-7). 1999. pap. 4.99 (*0-375-80197-9*) Knopf.

— El Duque: The Story of Orlando Hernandez. LC 99-13618. (J). (gr. 3-7). 1999. lib. bdg. 11.99 (*0-375-90197-3*) Random.

Lafreniere, Kenny. Babe: If Pigs Could Fly. 24p. (J). 1999. 1.99 (*0-679-89450-0*) Random.

LaFreniere, Peter J. Emotion, Development & Adaptation. LC 99-32542. (Psychology Ser.). 331p. 1999. pap. text 72.95 (*0-534-34808-4*) Brooks-Cole.

Lafrentiere, Joan G. Body Techniques. (C). (gr. 13). 1984. 26.50 (*0-89352-205-8*) Mosby Inc.

LaFromboise, Teresa D. American Indian Life Skills Development Curriculum. LC 95-6546. (Illus.). 522p. 1995. pap., wbk. ed. 22.95 (*0-299-14924-2*) U of Wis Pr.

Lafser, Christine O. An Empty Cradle, a Full Heart: Reflections for Mothers & Fathers after Miscarriage, Stillbirth, or Infant Death. LC 98-15190. 260p. 1998. pap. 10.95 (*0-8294-1173-9*) Loyola Pr.

Lafuma, Louis, jt. auth. see Pascal, Blaise.

Lag, Jul, ed. Geomedicine. 256p. 1990. lib. bdg. 184.95 (*0-8493-6755-7*, RA792) CRC Pr.

Lagace, Paul A., ed. Composite Materials Vol. 2: Fatigue & Fracture. (Special Technical Publication Ser.: No. STP 1012). (Illus.). 420p. 1989. text 64.00 (*0-8031-1190-8*, STP1012) ASTM.

Lagache, Daniel. The Works of Daniel Lagache: Selected Papers, 1938-1964. 446p. 1993. pap. text 25.00 (*0-946439-89-3*, Pub. by H Karnac Bks Ltd) Other Pr LLC.

Lagadec, Patrick. Major Technological Risk: An Assessment of Industrial Disasters. (Illus.). 536p. 1982. 235.00 (*0-08-028913-4*, Pub. by Pergamon Repr) Franklin.

— Preventing Chaos in a Crisis: Strategies for Prevention, Control, & Damage Limitation. LC 92-33415. 356p. 1993. 29.95 (*0-07-707774-1*) McGraw.

***Lagadic, Laurent.** Use of Biomarkers for Environmental Quality Assessment. LC 00-32229. 2000. write for info. (*1-57808-095-9*) Science Pubs.

Lagae, L. A Neurophysiological Study of Optic Flow Analysis in the Monkey Brain. No. 47. 189p. (Orig.). 1991. pap. 44.50 (*90-6186-479-8*, Pub. by Leuven Univ) Coronet Bks.

Lagal, Roy. Find an Ounce of Gold a Day. Dawson, Hal, ed. LC 88-60013. (Guidebook Ser.). (Illus.). 52p. (Orig.). 1988. pap. 3.00 (*0-915920-52-2*) Ram Pub.

— Gold Panning Is Easy. rev. ed. LC 92-61347. (Illus.). 120p. (Orig.). 1992. pap. 9.95 (*0-915920-79-4*) Ram Pub.

Lagally, M. C. Kinetics of Ordering & Growth at Surfaces. (NATO ASI Ser.: Vol. 239). (Illus.). 530p. (C). 1990. text 145.00 (*0-306-43702-3*, Kluwer Plenum) Kluwer Academic.

Lagaly, G. & Kremer, F., eds. Horizons 2000 - Aspects of Colloid & Interface Science at the Turn of the Millennium. (Progress in Colloid & Polymer Science Ser.: Vol. 109). 285p. 1998. 119.00 (*3-7985-1113-6*) Spr-Verlag.

Lagaly, G., jt. auth. see Porte, G.

Lagana, Antonio, ed. Supercomputer Algorithms for Reactivity, Dynamics & Kinetics of Small Molecules. (C). 1989. text 223.00 (*0-7923-0226-5*) Kluwer Academic.

Lagana, Kathleen, jt. auth. see Duderstadt, Karen.

Lagane, Rene, jt. auth. see Dubois, Jean.

LaGarce. Beyond ADA. (Interior Design Ser.). 1998. text 69.95 (*0-442-02127-5*, VNR) Wiley.

Lagarce, Jean-Luc. Madame Knipper's Journey to Eastern Prussia. Antal, Paul, tr. from FRE. 92p. (Orig.). 1984. pap. text 8.95 (*0-913745-10-3*) Ubu Repertory.

Lagarde, A. & Michard, L. Collection Litteraire, 6 vols. Incl. Vol. 1. Moyen Age. 23.95 (*2-04-016207-0*); Vol. 2. Seizieme Siecle. 24.95 (*2-04-016209-7*); Vol. 3. Dix-Septieme Siecle. 28.95 (*2-04-016211-9*); Vol. 4. Dix-Huitieme Siecle. 28.95 (*2-04-016213-5*); Vol. 5. Dix-Neuvieme Siecle. 31.95 (*2-04-016216-X*); Vol. 6. Vingtieme Siecle. 39.95 (*2-04-018000-1*); (FRE., Illus.). write for info. (*0-318-55654-5*) Schoenhof.

Lagarde, A. & Raous, M., eds. Engineering Systems Design & Analysis Conference: Photomechanics Contact Mechanics & Tribology. 217p. 1996. pap. text 130.00 (*0-7918-1499-8*, TA355) ASME Pr.

Lagarde, Deborah. Battle of the Band: The Saga of the Prodigal Band Begins. LC 96-226458. (Prodigal Band Trilogy Ser.: Vol. 1). 212p. 1996. pap. 13.95 (*0-9649566-0-8*) OmegaBooks.

— The Prophesied Band: The Saga of the Prodigal Band Continues. (Prodigal Band Trilogy Ser.: Vol. 2). 112p. (Orig.). 1998. pap. 13.95 (*0-9649566-1-6*) OmegaBooks.

Lagarde, Francois. Rene Girard Ou la Christinaisation des Sciences Humanies. LC 93-23078. (Sociocriticism: Literature, Society & History Ser.: Vol. 7). 212p. (C). 1994. text 45.95 (*0-8204-2289-4*) P Lang Pubng.

Lagarde, M. & Knapp, H. R. Fatty Acids & Lipids from Cell Biology to Human Disease: Proceedings of the 2nd International Congress of the ISSFAL. Galli, Claudio et al, eds. (Illus.). 336p. (Orig.). 1996. pap. 60.00 (*0-614-14862-6*) Am Oil Chemists.

Lagarde, Michel. Index du Grand Commentaire de Fahr al-Din al-Razi. (Handbuch der Orientalistik, I: Abteilung - Der Nahe und der Mittlere Osten Ser.: No. 22). (ARA & FRE.). lxxxii, 360p. 1996. 174.50 (*90-04-10362-7*) Brill Academic Pubs.

***Lagarde, Michel.** Le Livre des Haltes--Kitcab Al-Mawcaqif. LC 00-21146. (FRE.). 2000. write for info. (*90-04-11568-4*) Brill Academic Pubs.

— Le Livre des Haltes, Kitab Al-Mawaqif, Tome I. (FRE.). 650p. 2000. text 193.00 (*90-04-11567-6*) Brill Academic Pubs.

Lagarde, Paul De, see De Lagarde, Paul.

Lagarde, Philippe. Practical Dictionary to Understand the Study of Cancer: Dictionnaire Pratique du Cancer: Pour Comprendre le Langage du Cancerologue. (FRE.). 1984. 59.95 (*0-8288-1812-6*, M404) Fr & Eur.

Lagardere, Jean Paul, et al. Advances in Invertebrates & Fish Telemetry: Proceedings of the Second Conference on Fish Telemetry in Europe, Held in La Rochelle, France, 5-9 April 1997. LC 98-31665. (Developments in Hydrobiology Ser.). xi, 360 p. 1999. write for info. (*0-7923-5211-4*) Kluwer Academic.

Lagarias, J. & Todd, M. Mathematical Developments Arising from Linear Programming: Proceedings of the Conference. LC 90-22942. (Contemporary Mathematics Ser.: Vol. 114). 341p. 1991. pap. 61.00 (*0-8218-5121-7*, CONM/114) Am Math.

Lagarias, Peter C. Effective Closing Argument. 817p. 1991. suppl. ed. 80.00 (*0-87473-434-7*, 64195-10, MICHIE) LEXIS Pub.

— Effective Closing Arguments: 1990 Supplement. 1990. write for info. (*0-87473-633-1*, 64196-10, MICHIE) LEXIS Pub.

***Lagarius, Peter C.** Effective Closing Argument. 2nd ed. 800p. 1999. write for info. (*0-327-10019-2*, 6419512) LEXIS Pub.

Lagarkov, A. N. & Rutkevich, Igor M. Ionization Waves in Electrical Breakdown of Gases. 240p. 1993. write for info. (*3-540-94075-8*) Spr-Verlag.

Lagarrigne, Jerome, jt. auth. see Wiles, Debie.

Lagarrigne, Jerome, jt. auth. see Hartfield, Claire.

Lagasse, E. Lee, jt. auth. see Reney, Caren.

***Lagasse, Emeril.** Emeril Kids' Cookbook. 2000. write for info. (*0-688-17706-9*) Lothrop.

Lagasse, Emeril. Emeril's Creole Christmas. LC 97-15138. (Illus.). 192p. 1997. 23.00 (*0-688-14691-0*, Wm Morrow) Morrow Avon.

— UNTI. Portuguese Cookbook. 1924. write for info. (*0-688-16431-5*, Hearst) Hearst Commns.

Lagasse, Emeril & Bienvenu, Marcelle. Emeril's Creole Christmas. Koenig, Pam, ed. 1997. 25.00 (*0-614-30563-2*, Wm Morrow) Morrow Avon.

— Louisiana Real & Rustic. LC 95-46653. (Illus.). 288p. 1996. 25.00 (*0-688-12721-5*, Wm Morrow) Morrow Avon.

Lagasse, Emeril & Tirsch, Jessie. Emeril's New New Orleans. LC 92-33497. (Illus.). 354p. 1993. 25.00 (*0-688-11284-6*, Wm Morrow) Morrow Avon.

***Lagasse, Emeril, et al.** Emeril's Tv Dinners: Kickin' It Up A Notch With Recipes From Emeril Live And Essence Of Emeril. Hoenig, Pam, ed. LC 98-25857. (Illus.). 288p. 1998. 25.00 (*0-688-16378-5*, Wm Morrow) Morrow Avon.

— Every Day's a Party: Louisiana Recipes for Celebrating with Family & Friends. LC 99-29341. (Illus.). 352p. 1999. 26.00 (*0-688-16430-7*, Wm Morrow) Morrow Avon.

Lagasse, Paul, jt. ed. see Columbia University Press Staff.

Lagatree, Kirsten. Feng Shui at Work: Arranging Your Office Work Space to Achieve Peak Performance. LC 97-44828. 112p. 1998. pap. 13.95 (*0-375-75010-X*) Villard Books.

Lagatree, Kirsten, jt. auth. see Bredin, Alice.

Lagatree, Kirsten M. Feng Shui: Arranging Your Home to Change Your Life. (Illus.). 84p. 1996. pap. 13.95 (*0-679-76543-3*) Random.

***Lagatree, Kirstin M.** Checklists for Life: 104 Lists to Help You Get Organized, Save Time & Unclutter Your Life. 320p. 1999. pap. 12.95 (*0-375-70733-6*) Random Ref & Info.

LaGattuta, Margo. Embracing the Fall. 86p. (Orig.). 1994. pap. text 12.95 (*0-911051-71-6*) Plain View.

— Variations on the Ordinary: A Woman's Reader. (Illus.). 220p. (Orig.). 1995. pap. text 17.95 (*0-911051-81-3*) Plain View.

LaGattuta, Margo, ed. Almost Touching: A Reader for Men & Women. 260p. 1996. 17.95 (*0-911051-84-8*) Plain View.

LaGattuta, Margo & Speltus, Carol. The Dream Givers. 88p. 1990. pap. 9.95 (*0-941363-12-0*) Lake Shore Pub.

LaGattuta, Margo, jt. ed. see Bright, Susan.

LaGattuta, Margo, ed. see Matthews, Stephanie, et al.

Lagauskas, Valerie, ed. see International Festivals & Events Assoc. Staff.

Lagayette, Pierre, ed. Strategies of Difference in Modern Poetry: Case Studies in Poetic Composition. LC 97-39277. 184p. 1998. 35.50 (*0-8386-3698-5*) Fairleigh Dickinson.

Lagden, Keith. Chicken Soup for Starters: The Recipe - "Secrets" Car Dealers Don't Want You to Know When Buying Your New Car. 158p. (Orig.). 1995. pap. 15.95 (*0-9647333-0-7*) L K Lagden Pub.

Lage, Dietmar. Martin Luther's Christology & Ethics. LC 89-77128. (Texts & Studies in Religion: Vol. 45). 192p. 1990. lib. bdg. 79.95 (*0-88946-834-6*) E Mellen.

Lage, Gustavo A. & Nathan, Harvey K. Psychotherapy, Adolescents, & Self-Psychology. LC 90-4924. 500p. 1991. 67.50 (*0-8236-5403-6*) Intl Univs Pr.

Lageira, Jacinto, et al. Jean-Marc Bustamante. 128p. 1995. pap. 23.50 (*2-906571-44-X*) Dist Art Pubs.

Lageman, August G. The Moral Dimensions of Marriage & Family Therapy. LC 92-33573. 138p. (Orig.). (C). 1993. pap. text 21.50 (*0-8191-8966-9*); lib. bdg. 42.50 (*0-8191-8965-0*) U Pr of Amer.

Lagemann, Ellen Condiffe. Education Research: Problems & Possibilities. LC 99-11010. (Jossey-Bass Education Ser.). 464p. 1999. text 39.95 (*0-7879-4810-1*) Jossey-Bass.

Lagemann, Ellen C. A Generation of Women: Education in the Lives of Progressive Reformers. LC 79-13528. (Illus.). 215p. 1979. 29.00 (*0-674-34471-5*) HUP.

— The Politics of Knowledge: The Carnegie Corporation, Philanthropy, & Public Policy. LC 89-16634. xvi, 364p. 1992. pap. text 18.95 (*0-226-46780-5*) U Ch Pr.

— The Politics of Knowledge: The Carnegie Corporation, Philanthropy & Public Policy. LC 89-16634. 363p. 1989. reprint ed. pap. 112.60 (*0-608-03014-7*, 206346400006) Bks Demand.

Lagemann, Ellen C., ed. Nursing History: New Perspectives, New Possibilities. LC 82-10320. 229p. 1983. pap. 71.00 (*0-7837-8950-5*, 204966200002) Bks Demand.

— Philanthropic Foundations: New Scholarship, New Possibilities. LC 98-55922. (Philanthropic Studies). (Illus.). 464p. 1999. text 35.00 (*0-253-33500-0*) Ind U Pr.

Lagemann, Ellen C. & Miller, LaMar P., eds. Brown vs. Board of Education: The Challenge for Today's Schools. 224p. (C). 1996. pap. text 17.95 (*0-8077-3524-8*) Tchrs Coll.

***Lagemann, Ellen Condliffe.** Elusive Science: The Troubling History of Education Research. LC 99-86832. 2000. 25.00 (*0-226-46772-4*) U Ch Pr.

***Lagemann, Robert T. & Holladay, Wendell G.** To Quarks & Quasars: A History of Physics & Astronomy at Vanderbilt University. LC 00-8611. (Illus.). 2000. 0.00 (*0-9679271-0-2*) U of Alaska Pr.

Lagendijk, Reginald L. & Biemond, Jan. Iterative Identification & Restoration of Images. (International Series in Engineering & Computer Science, VLSI, Computer Architecture, & Digital Screen Processing). 224p. (C). 1990. text 116.50 (*0-7923-9097-0*) Kluwer Academic.

Lagendijk, Reginald L., jt. ed. see Sezan, Ibrahim.

Lagendonck, Willy Van, see Van Belle, William & Van Lagendonck, Willy, eds.

Lagenscheidt Staff. Technical Dictionary, German-English. (ENG & GER.). 784p. 1996. 250.00 (*0-7859-9679-6*) Fr & Eur.

Lager, Carl H., jt. auth. see Snell, Daniel C.

Lager, Carole. L' Europe en Quete de Ses Symboles. (Euroclio Ser.). (FRE.). 129p. 1995. 29.95 (*3-906751-71-6*, Pub. by P Lang) P Lang Pubng.

Lager, Cathy C. Fingernail Moon: Mama's Journal. Stiefel, Dorthy, ed. 68p. 1995. pap. 8.95 (*0-9646714-0-9*) Taylor Made Pubns.

Lager, Claude. Jeanette & Josie. 1999. pap. write for info. (*0-14-050989-5*) NAL.

Lager, Eric & Zwerling, Isreal. Psychotherapy in the Community: A Psychoanalytically Based Guide to the Treatment of the Adult. Gardner, Alvin F., ed. (Allied Health Professions Monograph). 208p. (C). 1983. 22.50 (*0-87527-315-7*) Green.

Lager, Ioan E. Finite Element Modeling of Static & Stationary Electric & Magnetic Fields. (Illus.). 240p. (Orig.). 1996. pap. 57.50 (*90-407-1386-3*, Pub. by Delft U Pr) Coronet Bks.

Lager, James L. Leica Vol. 3-Accessories: An Illustrated History. (Illus.). 352p. 1997. write for info. (*0-9636973-3-1*) Lager Ltd Edits.

— Leica - An Illustrated History, Vol. 1: Cameras. (Illus.). 320p. 1993. 149.95 (*0-9636973-1-5*) Lager Ltd Edits.

— Leica - An Illustrated History, Vol. 2: Lenses. (Illus.). 320p. 1995. 149.95 (*0-9636973-2-3*) Lager Ltd Edits.

Lagerberg, R., jt. ed. see Gregory, F.

Lagerborg, Mary B., jt. auth. see Wilson, Mimi.

Lagerborg, Mary Beth. Incessant Drumbeat. (Illus.). 224p. (Orig.). 1992. pap. 9.25 (*0-87508-968-2*) Chr Lit.

— Though Lions Roar: The Story of Helen Roseveare. LC 96-132746. 124p. (Orig.). (YA). (gr. 9-11). 1995. mass mkt. 5.99 (*0-87508-663-2*, 663) Chr Lit.

Lagerborg, Mary Beth, compiled by. A Cure for the Growly Bugs & Other Tried-&-True Tips for Moms. LC 97-10361. 128p. 1997. pap. 6.99 (*0-310-21135-2*) Zondervan.

Lagerborg, Mary Beth & Parks, Karen J., eds. Beyond Macaroni & Cheese: Mom-Tested, Kid-Approved Recipes. LC 98-20277. 256p. 1998. pap. 14.99 (*0-310-21978-7*) Zondervan.

Lagerborg, Mary Beth, jt. auth. see Wilson, Mimi.

Lagerborg, Mary E., jt. auth. see Wilson, Marilyn S.

Lagercrantz, David, jt. auth. see Kropp, Goran.

Lagercrantz, Hugo, jt. ed. see Von Euler, Curt.

***Lagercrantz, Olof.** Epic of the Afterlife. Hallengren, Anders, tr. from SWE. (Swedenborg Studies: Vol. 12). 160p. 2000. pap. 16.95 (*0-87785-248-0*, Pub. by Swedenborg) Words Distrib.

Lagercrantz, Rose & Lagercrantz, Samuel. Is It Magic? Norlen, Paul, tr. from SWE. LC 89-63054. (Illus.). (J). (gr. k-3). 1990. 13.95 (*91-29-59182-1*, Pub. by R & S Bks) FS&G.

Lagercrantz, Samuel, jt. auth. see Lagercrantz, Rose.

Lagerfeld, Karl. La Brochure. (Illus.). 1998. 24.95 (*3-88243-547-X*) Steidl.

— Casa Malaparte. Pfrunder, Eric & Steidl, Gerhard, eds. LC 98-216131. (Illus.). 56p. 1999. 34.95 (*3-88243-564-X*, 910732, Pub. by Steidl) Dist Art Pubs.

— Claudia Schiffer. Date not set. 35.00 (*0-7493-2470-8*) Heinemann.

— German House. 1998. 34.95 (*3-88243-535-6*) Steidl.

***Lagerfeld, Karl.** Karl Lagerfeld: Escape from Circumstances. 2000. pap. 19.95 (*3-88243-703-0*) Steidl.

Lagerfeld, Karl. Karl Lagerfeld: Off the Record. 1995. 49.95 (*1-881616-37-1*, Pub. by Scalo Pubs) Dist Art Pubs.

— Madonna Superstar: Photographs. 1991. pap. 10.95 (*0-393-30766-2*) Norton.

— Modern Italian Architecture: Casa Malaparte/The House in The Trees. (Illus.). 112p. 1999. 54.95 (*3-88243-661-1*, Pub. by Steidl) Dist Art Pubs.

— Nadja Auermann. (Illus.). 144p. 1999. 45.00 (*3-8238-1000-6*) te Neues.

***Lagerfeld, Karl.** Tadao Ando-Vitra House. Pfrunder, Eric & Steidl, Gerhard, eds. (Illus.). 72p. 1999. pap. 19.95 (*3-88243-622-0*, 910731, Pub. by Steidl) Dist Art Pubs.

Lagerkvist, C. I., et al, eds. Asteroids, Comets & Meteors, Vol. 3: Proceedings of a Meeting Held at the Astronomical Observatory of Uppsala University, June 12-16, 1989. (Illus.). 620p. (Orig.). 1990. pap. 375.00 (*91-506-0777-4*) Coronet Bks.

Lagerkvist, Par. Barabbas. Blair, Alan, tr. (Vintage International Ser.). 1989. pap. 10.00 (*0-679-72544-X*) Vin Bks.

L

— The Dwarf. Dick, Alexandra, tr. from SWE. 288p. (Orig.). 1958. pap. 11.00 (0-374-52135-2) FS&G.
— Evening Land - Aftonland. Auden, W. H. & Sjoberg, Leif, trs. LC 75-16172. (ENG & SWE.). 195p. reprint ed. pap. 60.50 (0-7837-3621-5, 204348700009) Bks Demand.
— Five Early Works. Swanson, Roy A., tr. from SWE. LC 87-35394. 200p. 1989. lib. bdg. 89.95 (0-88946-019-1) E Mellen.
— Sibyl. Walford, Naomi, tr. 1963. pap. 10.00 (0-394-70240-9) Vin Bks.
Lagerkvist, Par, jt. auth. see Bekessy, Emery.
Lagerkvist, Ulf. DNA Pioneers & Their Legacy. LC 97-37281. 184p. 1998. 20.00 (0-300-07184-1) Yale U Pr.
***Lagerlof, Margaretha.** The Sculptures of the Parthenon: Aesthetics & the Interpretation of Antiquity. LC 99-47026. (Illus.). 224p. 2000. 30.00 (0-300-07391-7) Yale U Pr.
Lagerlof, Selma. Algunas Leyendas de Cristo. (Fondo 2000 Ser.). (SPA.). pap. 2.99 (968-16-5052-2, Pub. by Fondo) Continental Bk.
— The Changeling. 1992. pap. 15.99 (0-685-52495-7) McKay.
— Christ Legends. pap. 10.95 (0-86315-524-3, 929, Pub. by Floris Bks) Anthroposophic.
— From a Swedish Homestead. Brochner, Jessie, tr. LC 73-116959. (Short Story Index Reprint Ser.). 1977. 24.95 (0-8369-3463-6) Ayer.
— The Further Adventures of Nils. rev. ed. Johnson, Nancy, ed. Howard, Velma S., tr. from SWE. (Travels of Nils Holgersson Ser.: Bk. 2). (Illus.). 250p. (J). (gr. 4-12). 1992. pap. 12.95 (0-9615394-4-5) Skandisk.
— The Girl from the Marsh Croft. Zug, John, ed. 1996. pap. 12.95 (1-57216-014-4) Penfield.
— Gosta Berling's Saga. LC 97-65667. 358p. 1997. pap. 18.95 (1-57216-033-0) Penfield.
— Invisible Links. Anderson, Greta, ed. 1995. pap. 12.95 (1-57216-001-2) Penfield.
— Jerusalem. Brochner, Jessie, tr. LC 76-98777. 396p. 1970. reprint ed. lib. bdg. 65.00 (0-8371-3120-0, LAJE, Greenwood Pr) Greenwood.
— The Lowenskold Ring. Schenck, Linda, tr. from SWE. (Norvik Press Series B: No. 8). 117p. 1991. pap. 19.95 (1-870041-14-3, Pub. by Norvik Pr) Dufour.
— Memories of Marbacka. 200p. 1996. pap. 18.95 (1-57216-048-9) Penfield.
— Selma Lagerlof's Words of Love & Wisdom. Crum, Dorothy & Bradnan, Melinda, eds. (Illus.). 60p. 2000. pap. 12.95 (1-57216-032-2) Penfield.
— Three Stories Scandinavian Kings & Queens: Astrid, Sigrid Storrade & the Silver Mine. 80p. 1996. pap. 10.95 (1-57216-023-3) Penfield.
— The Wonderful Adventures of Nils. Howard, Velma S., tr. from SWE. LC 94-41647. (Illus.). xii, 219p. (J). (gr. 4-12). 1995. pap. text 6.95 (0-486-28611-8) Dover.
— The Wonderful Adventures of Nils. 540p. (J). (gr. 4-12). 1992. reprint ed. lib. bdg. 36.95 (0-89966-936-0) Buccaneer Bks.
— The Wonderful Adventures of Nils, Bk. 1. rev. ed. Howard, Velma S., tr. from SWE. (Travels of Nils Holgersson Ser.). (Illus.). 250p. (J). (gr. 4-12). 1991. pap. 12.95 (0-9615394-3-7) Skandisk.
— The Wonderful Adventures of Nils; The Further Adventures of Nils, 2 bks. in 1. 420p. (YA). (gr. 5 up). 2000. reprint ed. pap. 12.95 (1-57216-036-5) Penfield.
Lagerquest, Syble. Philip Johnston & the Navajo Code Talkers. 2nd ed. (Indian Culture Ser.). (Illus.). 32p. 1996. reprint ed. pap. 4.95 (0-89992-139-6) Coun India Ed.
Lagerquist, Donna. Hunting for Easter. 1998. pap. 15.00 (0-310-67764-5) Zondervan.
— Milestone. 1998. pap. 15.00 (0-310-67798-X) Zondervan.
Lagerquist, Kay & Lenard, Lisa. The Complete Idiot's Guide to Numerology. (Complete Idiot's Guide Ser.). 400p. 1999. pap. 16.95 (0-02-863201-X) Macmillan.
Lagerquist, L. DeAne. In America the Men Milk the Cows: Factors of Gender, Ethnicity & Religion in the Americanization of Norwegian-American Women. LC 91-26844. (Chicago Studies in the History of American Religion Ser.: Vol. 12). 190p. 1991. 50.00 (0-926019-49-X) Carlson Pub.
— The Lutherans. (Denominations in America Ser.: No. 9). 192p. 1999. pap. 19.95 (0-275-96393-4, Greenwood Pr) Greenwood.
— The Lutherans, 9. LC 99-22099. 272p. 1999. lib. bdg. 69.50 (0-313-27549-1, Greenwood Pr) Greenwood.
Lagerquist, Sally L. Addison-Wesley's Nursing Examination. 2nd ed. 1982. pap. 26.50 (0-201-14190-6, Health Sci) Addison-Wesley.
— Addison-Wesley's Nursing Examination Review. 3rd ed. 1987. pap. 23.75 (0-201-14497-2) Addison-Wesley.
— Little, Brown's Nursing Q&A: Critical-Thinking Exercises. LC 96-10793. (RN NCLEX Review Ser.). 350p. 1996. pap. text 26.95 (0-316-51298-2) Lppncott W & W.
— Little, Brown's Psychiatric-Mental Health Nursing Review. LC 96-9116. 1997. pap. text 22.95 (0-316-51299-0) Lppncott W & W.
Lagerquist, Sally L., jt. auth. see Colombraro, Geraldine C.
Lagerquist, Sally L., ed. see Bobak, Irene M., et al.
Lagerqvisi, Bosse. The Conservation Information System: Photogrammetry As a Base for Designing Documentation in Conservation & Cultural Resources Management. (Goteborg Studies in Conservation: No. 4). (Illus.). 156p. 1997. pap. 52.50 (91-7346-302-7, Pub. by Almqvist Wiksell) Coronet Bks.
Lagers, G. H. Design Adjustments of a Jack up for Production or Extended Well Testing. 1989. 125.00 (90-6314-512-8, Pub. by Lorne & MacLean Marine) St Mut.
— Design Adjustments of a Jack-up for Production or Extended Well Testings. (C). 1989. 95.00 (0-89771-728-7, Pub. by Lorne & MacLean Marine) St Mut.
Lagerspetz, Eerik. The Opposite Mirrors: An Essay on the Conventionalist Theory of Institutions. LC 94-42237. (Law & Philosophy Library: Vol. 22). 240p. 1995. lib. bdg. 110.50 (0-7923-3325-X, Pub. by Kluwer Academic) Kluwer Academic.
Lagerspetz, Olli. Trust: The Tacit Demand. LC 97-32492. 177p. 1998. text 110.50 (0-7923-4874-5) Kluwer Academic.
Lagerstam, Catharina. Hedging of Contracts, Anticipated Positions, & Tender Offers: A Study of Corporate Foreign Exchange Rate Risk & - or Price Risk. 202p. (Orig.). 1990. pap. 72.50 (91-7258-306-1) Coronet Bks.
Lagerstrom, Birgitta. Och Vi Tog Till Vapen: Kvinna i Angola. (Kvinna i U-Land Ser.). 144p. 1980. write for info. (91-7106-171-1, Pub. by Nordic Africa) Transaction Pubs.
Lagerstrom, James, jt. auth. see Cooper, Jeff.
Lagerstrom, P. A. Laminar Flow Theory. 288p. 1996. pap. text 19.95 (0-691-02598-3, Pub. by Princeton U Pr) Cal Prin Full Svc.
— Matched Aymptotic Expansions. (Applied Mathematical Sciences Ser.: Vol. 76). (Illus.). xiii, 251p. 1988. 65.95 (0-387-96811-3) Spr-Verlag.
***Lagerwall, Sven T.** Ferroelectric & Antiferroelectric Liquid Crystals. 446p. 1999. 220.00 (3-527-29831-2) Wiley.
Lagerwerff, Ellen. Astrology Can Make Sense. 84p. 1985. 9.00 (0-86690-260-0, L2457-014) Am Fed Astrologers.
Lagerwey, Mary D. Reading Auschwitz. LC 98-19715. (Ethnographic Alternatives Ser.: Vol. 5). 184p. (C). 1998. pap. 62.00 (0-7619-9186-7) AltaMira Pr.
— Reading Auschwitz. LC 98-19715. (Ethnographic Alternatives Ser.: Vol. 5). 184p. (C). 1998. 22.95 (0-7619-9187-5) AltaMira Pr.
Lageson, David R. & Spearing, Darwin R. Roadside Geology of Wyoming. LC 88-1650. (Roadside Geology Ser.). (Illus.). 288p. (Orig.). 1988. pap. 18.00 (0-87842-216-1) Mountain Pr.
***Lageson, David R., et al.** Colorado & Adjacent Areas. LC 99-48043. (Field Guide Ser.). 1999. write for info. (0-8137-0001-9) Geol Soc.
Lageson, Ernest B. Battle at Alcatraz: A Desparate Attempt to Escape the Rock. LC 98-41824. (Illus.). 283p. 1999. pap. 16.95 (1-886039-37-2) Addicus Bks.
Laget, Mokha, tr. see Sinoue, Gilbert.
Laggner, A. N., jt. ed. see Lenz, K.
Laggner, P. & Glatter, O., eds. Trends in Colloid & Interface Science VII. (Progress in Colloid & Polymer Science Ser.: Vol. 93). 412p. 1994. 159.95 (0-387-91454-4) Spr-Verlag.
***Laggoon Bks. Staff.** Trivia Quiz: The Complete Guide to Bar-Room Banality. 1999. 6.95 (1-899712-21-6) Lagoon Bks.
Lagier, Jennifer. Second Class Citizen. (VIA Folios Ser.: Vol. 19). 55p. 1999. pap. 9.00 (1-884419-29-1) Bordighera.
***Lagier, Jennifer.** Where We Grew Up. 98p. 1999. pap. 12.00 (0-9676487-0-X) Paisano Pr CA.
Lagler, Karl F., et al. Ichthyology. 2nd ed. 528p. 1977. text 96.95 (0-471-51166-8) Wiley.
Lagnado, Lucette M. & Dekel, Sheila C. Children of the Flames: Dr. Josef Mengele & the Untold Story of the Twins of Auschwitz. (Illus.). 320p. 1992. pap. 13.95 (0-14-016913-8) Viking Penguin.
Lagnan, Pierre. La Commissaire Dans la Truffiere. (FRE.). 250p. 1991. pap. 11.95 (0-7859-4348-X, 2070383245) Fr & Eur.
Lagneborg, Rune, jt. ed. see Pipes, R. Byron.
Lagnese, John E. Boundary Stabilization of Thin Plates. LC 89-11316. (Studies in Applied Mathematics: No. 10). viii, 176p. 1989. 48.00 (0-89871-237-8) Soc Indus-Appl Math.
Lagnese, John E., et al, eds. Control & Optimal Design of Distributed Parameter Systems. LC 95-2606. (IMA Volumes in Mathematics & Its Applications: Vol. 70). (Illus.). 264p. 1995. 71.95 (0-387-94490-7) Spr-Verlag.
Lagnese, John E., et al. Modeling, Analysis & Control of Dynamic Elastic Multi-Link Structures. LC 94-3096. (Systems & Control Ser.). 388p. 1994. 78.50 (0-8176-3705-2) Birkhauser.
Lagnese, John E., jt. auth. see Lions, J. L.
Lagnio, Irene. The Best-Ever Guide to the Monterey Peninsula & Carmel Area. 3rd rev. ed. 192p. 1997. pap. 14.95 (0-9623209-3-5) Kaskaskia Pr.
Lago, Amy, ed. see Lago, Ray.
Lago, Armando M., jt. auth. see Brown, Charles J.
Lago, Colin & Thompson, Joyce. Race, Culture, & Counselling. LC 95-24920. 192p. 1996. pap. 29.95 (0-335-19294-7) OpUniv Pr.
***Lago, M. T. & Blanchard, A.** The Non-Sleeping Universe LC 99-37370. 1999. write for info. (0-7923-5877-5, Kluwer Plenum) Kluwer Academic.
Lago, M. T., jt. ed. see Dupree, A. K.
Lago, Mary. Christiana Herringham & the Edwardian Art Scene. (Illus.). 344p. (C). 1995. text 39.95 (0-8262-1024-4) U of Mo Pr.
***Lago, Mary.** India's Prisoner: A Biography of Edward John Thompson, 1886-1946. (Illus.). 392p. 2000. 39.95 (0-8262-1299-9) U of Mo Pr.
Lago, Mary, ed. see Burne-Jones, Edward C.
Lago, Mary M. & Beckson, Karl, eds. Max & Will: Max Beerbohm & William Rothenstein, Their Friendship & Letters, 1893-1945. LC 74-30853. (Illus.). 200p. 1976. 31.00 (0-674-55661-5) HUP.
Lago, Mary M., ed. see Forster, E. M.
Lago, Mary M., ed. see Rothenstein, William & Tagore, Rabindranath.
Lago, Ray. Ray Lago: Heroes & Angels. Lago, Amy, ed. (Illus.). 80p. 1998. pap. 20.00 (1-892519-00-3, AAE-4015) Archangel Ent.
Lagoe, J. Arthur. First Steps: A New Believer's Survival Guide. LC 94-76861. 111p. 1996. reprint ed. pap. 5.50 (0-9641761-0-6) Aletheia WA.
Lagoe, J. Arthur, jt. auth. see Owen, Mac.
Lagomarcino, Virgil. The Owl, the Elephant, & the Other Side of the Mountain: An Academic Odyssey. LC 96-222834. (Illus.). 186p. 1997. pap. text 14.95 (0-8138-2877-5) Iowa St U Pr.
— A Window on Main Street: Life above the Corner Drug. (Illus.). 136p. 1994. pap. 10.95 (0-8138-2949-6) Iowa St U Pr.
Lagomarsino, David & Wood, Charles T., eds. The Trial of Charles I: A Documentary History. LC 89-40356. (Illus.). 167p. 1989. pap. text 15.95 (0-87451-499-1) U Pr of New Eng.
Lagomarsino, Nancy. The Secretary Parables. LC 91-16373. 72p. (Orig.). 1991. pap. 9.95 (0-914086-92-8) Alice James Bks.
— Sleep Handbook. LC 86-72477. 72p. (Orig.). (C). 1987. 6.95 (0-914086-68-5); pap. 9.95 (0-914086-69-3) Alice James Bks.
Lagon, Mark P. The Reagan Doctrine: Sources of American Conduct in the Cold War's Last Chapter. LC 93-23676. 208p. 1994. 55.00 (0-275-94798-X, Praeger Pubs) Greenwood.
Lagoni, Laurel S., et al, eds. The Human-Animal Bond & Grief. (Illus.). 496p. 1994. pap. text 50.00 (0-7216-4577-1, W B Saunders Co) Harcrt Hlth Sci Grp.
***Lagoni, Rainer.** Legal Aspects of High Voltage Direct Current (HVDC) Cables. 120p. 1999. pap. 32.95 (3-8258-3888-9, Pub. by CE24) Transaction Pubs.
Lagoon Bks Staff. After Dinner Games. (Illus.). 96p. 1996. 6.95 (1-899712-42-9, Pub. by Lagoon Bks) Midpt Trade.
— Death after Dinner. (Illus.). 96p. 1997. 6.95 (1-899712-46-1, Pub. by Lagoon Bks) Midpt Trade.
— Fantastic Optical Illusions & Puzzles, No. 1. (Illus.). 96p. 1996. 6.95 (1-899712-40-2, Pub. by Lagoon Bks) Midpt Trade.
— Fifty of the Finest Drinking Games. (Illus.). 104p. 1995. 6.95 (1-899712-17-8, Pub. by Lagoon Bks) Midpt Trade.
— Five-Minute Adventure Lateral Thinking Puzzles. (Illus.). 96p. 1998. 6.95 (1-899712-60-7, Pub. by Lagoon Bks) Midpt Trade.
— Five-Minute Classic Lateral Thinking Puzzles. (Illus.). 96p. 1998. 6.95 (1-899712-29-1, Pub. by Lagoon Bks) Midpt Trade.
— Five-Minute Crime Lateral Thinking Puzzles. (Illus.). 96p. 1998. 6.95 (1-899712-28-3, Pub. by Lagoon Bks) Midpt Trade.
— Five-Minute Murder Lateral Thinking Puzzles. (Illus.). 96p. 1998. 6.95 (1-899712-33-X, Pub. by Lagoon Bks) Midpt Trade.
— Mind-Bending Challenging Logic, No. 1. (Mind-Bending Puzzle Bks.). (Illus.). 96p. 1998. 6.95 (1-899712-24-0, Pub. by Lagoon Bks) Midpt Trade.
— Mind-Bending Classic Logic Puzzles, No. 1. (Mind-Bending Puzzle Bks.). (Illus.). 96p. 1994. 6.95 (1-899712-18-6, Pub. by Lagoon Bks) Midpt Trade.
— Mind-Bending Conundrums & Puzzles, No. 1. (Mind-Bending Puzzle Bks.). (Illus.). 96p. 1994. 6.95 (1-899712-03-8, Pub. by Lagoon Bks) Midpt Trade.
— Mind-Bending Lateral Thinking Puzzles, 1, No. 1. (Mind-Bending Puzzle Bks.). (Illus.). 96p. 1994. 6.95 (1-899712-06-2, Pub. by Lagoon Bks) Midpt Trade.
— Mind-Bogglers. (Illus.). 96p. 1996. 6.95 (1-899712-44-5, Pub. by Lagoon Bks) Midpt Trade.
— More Mind-Bending Lateral Thinking Puzzles, Vol. 2. (Mind-Bending Puzzle Bks.). (Illus.). 96p. 1996. 6.95 (1-899712-19-4, Pub. by Lagoon Bks) Midpt Trade.
— Murder at Thrippleton Hall. (Illus.). 96p. 1997. 6.95 (1-899712-49-6, Pub. by Lagoon Bks) Midpt Trade.
— Murder in Manhattan. (Illus.). 96p. 1997. 6.95 (1-899712-48-8, Pub. by Lagoon Bks) Midpt Trade.
— Murder on the Riviera Express. (Illus.). 96p. 1997. 6.95 (1-899712-47-X, Pub. by Lagoon Bks) Midpt Trade.
— Pub Trivia Quiz. rev. ed. (Illus.). 96p. 1996. 6.95 (1-899712-50-X, Pub. by Lagoon Bks) Midpt Trade.
— Sports Trivia Quiz. (Illus.). 96p. 1998. 6.95 (1-899712-26-7, Pub. by Lagoon Bks) Midpt Trade.
— Where in the World Am I? (Illus.). 96p. 1996. 6.95 (1-899712-41-0, Pub. by Lagoon Bks) Midpt Trade.
— Who in the World Am I? (Illus.). 96p. 1998. 6.95 (1-899712-27-5, Pub. by Lagoon Bks) Midpt Trade.
Lagoon Books Staff. The Bumper Compendium of Mind-Bending Puzzles. (Illus.). 96p. 1998. 14.95 (1-899712-61-5, Pub. by Lagoon Bks) Midpt Trade.
— Mind-Bending Challenging Optical Puzzles. 1999. 6.95 (1-899712-69-0) Lagoon Bks.
— Mind-Bending Maze Puzzles. 1999. 6.95 (1-899712-72-0) Lagoon Bks.
— Pocket Personality Quiz. 1999. 6.95 (1-899712-90-9) Lagoon Bks.
— 16 Puzzles. (Illus.). 96p. 1998. 7.95 (1-899712-68-2, Pub. by Lagoon Bks) Midpt Trade.
— Sporting Record Breakers. 1999. 6.95 (1-899712-75-5) Lagoon Bks.
— Ultimate Golf Quiz. 1999. 6.95 (1-899712-73-9) Lagoon Bks.
— X Is for Unexplained. (Illus.). 96p. 1997. 6.95 (1-899712-25-9, Pub. by Lagoon Bks) Midpt Trade.
***Lagoon Books Staff, ed.** A Cookbook for a Man Who Probably Only Owns One Saucepan: Idiot-Proof Recipes. 64p. 2000. 5.95 (1-902813-14-6, Pub. by Lagoon Bks) Midpt Trade.
— Dr. C. K. Fortune & the Lost City Labyrinth. (Soft Bath Book Ser.). (Illus.). 20p. (J). (gr. 2-9). 2000. 9.95 (1-902813-12-X, Pub. by Lagoon Bks) Midpt Trade.
— How to Become a Dinner Party Legend & Avoid Crippling Psychological Damage: Easy Dinner Party Recipes. 64p. 2000. 5.95 (1-902813-16-2, Pub. by Lagoon Bks) Midpt Trade.
— How to Drink Wine Out of Fish Heads While Cooking Lobster in a Volkswagen Hub Cap: Easy Seafood Recipes. 64p. 2000. 5.95 (1-902813-13-8, Pub. by Lagoon Bks) Midpt Trade.
— The Mafia Just Moved in Next Door & They're Dropping by for Dinner Cookbook: Easy Italian Recipes. 64p. 2000. 5.95 (1-902813-15-4, Pub. by Lagoon Bks) Midpt Trade.
— Wanda the Witch & the Magical Maze. (Illus.). 20p. (J). (gr. 2-7). 2000. 9.95 (1-902813-11-1, Pub. by Lagoon Bks) Midpt Trade.
Lagoon Books Staff, ed. see Claybourne, Anna & King, David.
Lagoon Books Staff, ed. see Garner, Richard & Shute, Helen.
Lagoon Books Staff, ed. see Hooper, Joanna & Ireland, Roya.
Lagoon, Steve, jt. auth. see Devore, Steve.
Lagopoulos, Alexandros P. & Boklund-Lagopoulou, Karin. Meaning & Geography: The Social Conception of the Region in Northern Greece. LC 91-43000. (Approaches to Semiotics Ser.: No. 104). xiv, 453p. (C). 1992. lib. bdg. 183.10 (3-11-012956-6) Mouton.
Lagorio-Anthony, Jeanne. Everyday Heroes: Secrets Shared by Those with L. D. LC 98-92878. (Illus.). 80p. (YA). (gr. 5 up). 1998. pap. 8.95 (0-9633195-5-8) Empower in Act.
Lagorio, Henry J. Earthquakes: An Architect's Guide to Nonstructural Seismic Hazards. LC 90-35605. 336p. 1990. 120.00 (0-471-63302-X) Wiley.
Lagorio, Henry J. & Mader, George G. Earthquake in Campania-Basilicata, Italy, November 23, 1980: Architectural & Planning Aspects. 103p. 1981. pap. 12.00 (0-318-17285-2, EP-43) Earthquake Eng.
Lagorio, Irene R. Art History's Innovators. (Illus.). 93p. (Orig.). 1992. pap. 8.95 (0-9633541-0-8) Arina Pr.
Lagorio, Jeanne. The Life Cycle Education Manual: A Guide for Teachers & Helping Professionals: To Help Children Cope with Daily Change & Loss. rev. ed. 216p. (Orig.). 1992. pap. text 20.00 (0-9633195-9-0) Empower in Act.
— Life Cycles: Activites for Helping Children Cope with Daily Change & Loss. rev. ed. Orig. Title: Life Cycle Education Manual. 128p. (J). (ps-6). 1997. pap. 13.95 (0-9633195-0-7) Empower in Act.
Lagos, Maria L. Autonomy & Power: The Dynamics of Class & Culture in Rural Bolivia. LC 93-48809. (Ethnohistory Ser.). 224p. (Orig.). (C). 1994. text 39.95 (0-8122-3213-5); pap. text 16.50 (0-8122-1500-1) U of Pa Pr.
Lagos-Pope, Maria-Ines, ed. Exile in Literature. LC 87-47726. 144p. 1988. 29.50 (0-8387-5126-1) Bucknell U Pr.
Lagos, Ramona. Varia Coleccion: Ensayos sobre Literatura Hispano-Americana. (American University Studies: Ser. XXII, Vol. 5). 320p. (C). 1989. text 44.95 (0-8204-1059-4) P Lang Pubng.
Lagoudas, D. C., jt. ed. see Allen, D. H.
Lagowski, Barbara. 888 Reasons to Hate Democrats: A to Z Guide to Everything Loathsome About the Party of Big Gover. 160p. 1996. 6.95 (1-55972-365-3, Birch Ln Pr) Carol Pub Group.
— 888 Reasons to Hate Republicans: A To Z Guide to Everything Loathsome about Tte Party of the... 160p. 1996. 19.95 (1-55972-370-X) Carol Pub Group.
Lagowski, Barbara, jt. auth. see Rabin, Susan.
Lagowski, Barbara, jt. auth. see Sullivan, George A.
Lagowski, Barbara J., jt. auth. see Rabin, Susan.
Lagowski, Joseph J. Chemistry, 4 vols. LC 97-1824. (Macmillan Information Now Encyclopedias Ser.). 2400p. 1997. 400.00 (0-02-897225-2) Macmillan.
— Modern Inorganic Chemistry. LC 72-90374. (Undergraduate Chemistry Ser.: No. 6). 824p. reprint ed. pap. 200.00 (0-7837-3363-1, 204332100008) Bks Demand.
Lagowski, Joseph J., jt. auth. see Sorum, C. Harvey.
LaGoy, Peter K. Risk Assessment: Principles & Applications for Hazardous Waste & Related Sites. LC 94-2510. (Illus.). 244p. 1994. 79.00 (0-8155-1349-6) Noyes.
Lagrakov, Andrei N. & Rutkevich, Igor M. Ionization Waves in Electrical Breakdown of Gases. LC 93-27847. (Illus.). 240p. 1993. 79.95 (0-387-94075-8) Spr-Verlag.
LaGrand, James. The Earliest Christian Mission to "All Nations" in Light of Matthew's Gospel. LC 99-27308. 304p. 1999. pap. 32.00 (0-8028-4653-X) Eerdmans.
Lagrand, Louis E. After Death Communication: Final Farewells. LC 97-9262. 256p. (Orig.). 1997. pap. 12.95 (1-56718-405-7) Llewellyn Pubns.
***LaGrand, Louis E.** Messages & Miracles: Extraordinary Experiences of the Bereaved. LC 99-33212. (Illus.). 336p. 1999. pap. 12.95 (1-56718-406-5) Llewellyn Pubns.
Lagrange, Anne-Marie, et al, eds. High Angular Resolution in Astrophysics. LC 97-29303. (NATO ASI Series C, Mathematical & Physical Sciences). 398p. 1997. text 197.50 (0-7923-4767-6) Kluwer Academic.
Lagrange, J. L. Analytical Mechanics. Boissonnade, Auguste & Vagliente, Victor N., trs. LC 96-49523. (Boston Studies in the Philosophy of Science: Vol. 191). 640p. (C). 1997. text 217.50 (0-7923-4349-2) Kluwer Academic.
LaGrange, Mike. Ballistics in Perspective: A Guide for Weapon Choice in the Hunting of Game in Zimbabwe. rev. ed. 1990. reprint ed. 12.95 (0-9624807-2-X) PHS Pub Div.
LaGrange, Randy L. Policing American Society. 2nd ed. LC 97-3889. (Illus.). 572p. (C). 1997. text 63.95 (0-8304-1471-1) Thomson Learn.

LaGravanese, Richard. The Fisher King: The Illustrated Screenplay. LC 91-35217. (Screenplay Ser.). (Illus.). 320p. 1991. pap. 12.95 (*1-55783-098-3*) Applause Theatre Bk Pubs.

LaGreca, Annette. Helping Children Prepare for & Cope with Natural Disasters: A Manual for Professionals Working with Elementary School Children. (Illus.). 100p. (Orig.). (C). 1995. pap. text 30.00 (*0-7881-1624-X*) DIANE Pub.

Lagree, Michel, ed. see Mayeur, Jean-Marie & Hilaire, Yves-Marie.

Lagrega, Michael D. Hazardous Waste Management. 1025p. (C). 1994. 87.81 (*0-07-019552-8*) McGraw.

Lagro. Site Analysis. 2000. text 49.95 (*0-471-34412-5*) Wiley.

LaGrone, Oliver. Dawnfire & Other Poems. LC 88-83008. (Illus.). 133p. (YA). (gr. 9-12). 1989. pap., per. 9.00 (*0-916418-72-3*) Lotus.

***Lagrou, Pieter.** The Legacy of Nazi Occupation: Patriotic Memory & National Recovery in Western Europe, 1945-1965. (Studies in the Social & Cultural History of Modern Warfare: No. 8). (Illus.). 342p. (C). 2000. 59.95 (*0-521-65180-8*) Cambridge U Pr.

***Laguard, Alice.** Piriphiriques M.i.n.n.e.s.o.t.a. Architectural Projects & Cultural Productions. (Illus.). 288p. 2000. pap. 28.00 (*3-7643-6299-5*) Birkhauser.

LaGuardia & Guth. Access. 1999. pap. text, wbk. ed. 20.00 (*0-205-28621-6*) Allyn.

Laguardia & Guth. Access Handbook. LC 99-51328. 553p. 2000. spiral bd. 33.00 (*0-205-28620-8*) Allyn.

***Laguardia & Guth.** The Access Handbook: Interactive Edition. 2000. cd-rom 30.00 (*0-205-32213-1*) Allyn.

LaGuardia, Cheryl. The CD-ROM Primer: The ABCs of CD-ROM. LC 94-7086. 250p. 1994. pap. 49.95 (*1-55570-167-1*) Neal-Schuman.

LaGuardia, Cheryl, ed. The Upside of Downsizing: Using Library Instruction to Cope. LC 95-13157. 250p. 1995. pap. 49.95 (*1-55570-217-1*) Neal-Schuman.

***LaGuardia, Cheryl & Oka, Christine K.** Becoming a Library Teacher. (New Library Ser.: Vol. 3). 115p. 2000. pap. 49.95 (*1-55570-378-X*) Neal-Schuman.

***LaGuardia, Cheryl & Vasi, John.** Designing, Building, & Teaching in the Electronic Library Classroom. (New Library Ser.: Vol. 5). 175p. 2000. pap. 55.00 (*1-55570-380-1*) Neal-Schuman.

LaGuardia, Cheryl M., ed. Recreating the Academic Library: Breaking Virtual Ground. LC 98-16605. (New Library Ser.: Vol. 1). 250p. 1998. pap. 65.00 (*1-55570-293-7*) Neal-Schuman.

LaGuardia, Cheryl M. & Mitchell, Barbara A., eds. Finding Common Ground: Creating the Library of the Future Without Diminishing the Library of the Past. LC 97-51663. (New Library Ser.: No. 3). 478p. 1998. pap. 82.50 (*1-55570-290-2*) Neal-Schuman.

LaGuardia Community College Staff. Basic Speech Communication. 128p. (C). 1994. spiral bd. 15.95 (*0-8403-8168-9*) Kendall-Hunt.

Laguardia, David. The Iconography of Power: The French Nouvelle at the End of the Middle Ages. LC 98-24414. 176p. 1999. 33.50 (*0-87413-669-5*) U Delaware Pr.

LaGuardia, Dolores & Guth, Hans P. American Visions: Multi-Cultural Literature for Writers. LC 94-6444. xix, 742p. (C). 1995. pap. text 37.95 (*1-55934-322-2*, 1322) Mayfield Pub.

***LaGuardia, Dolores & Guth, Hans P.** American Voices: Culture & Community. 4th ed. LC 99-24016. xxvii, 692p. 1999. pap. text 31.95 (*0-7674-1129-3*, 1129-3) Mayfield Pub.

LaGuardia, Dolores & Guth, Hans P. Issues Across the Curriculum: Reading, Writing, Research. LC 96-21081. xvii, 701p. (C). 1996. pap. text 34.95 (*1-55934-570-5*, 1570) Mayfield Pub.

— Issues Across the Curriculum, Instructor's Manual: Reading, Writing, Research. 302p. 1997. pap. text. write for info. (*1-55934-571-3*, 1571) Mayfield Pub.

LaGuardia, Dolores & Guth, Hans P., eds. American Voices: Multicultural Literacy & Critical Thinking. 692p. 1999. reprint ed. pap. text 20.00 (*0-7881-6024-9*) DIANE Pub.

LaGuardia, Dolores, et al. American Visions: Multicultural Literature for Writers, Instructor's Manual. LC 94-6444. 185p. (Orig.). (C). 1994. pap. text, teacher ed. write for info. (*1-55934-323-0*, 1323) Mayfield Pub.

— American Voices Instructor's Manual. 3rd ed. (Illus.). vii, 167p. 1997. pap. text 28.95 (*0-7674-0062-3*, 20062) Mayfield Pub.

LaGuardia, Fiorello H. The Making of an Insurgent: An Autobiography, 1882-1919. LC 85-24782. (Illus.). 222p. 1986. reprint ed. lib. bdg. 59.50 (*0-313-22769-1*, LAMI, Greenwood Pr) Greenwood.

Lagud, Jose A. The Cross Before the Crown. 170p. Date not set. pap. write for info. (*0-9649770-0-1*) Lagud Chrstian.

Lague, Louise. The Working Mom's Book of Hints, Tips, & Everyday Wisdom. LC 95-5094. 192p. (Orig.). 1995. pap. 9.95 (*1-56079-461-5*, Petersons Pacesetter) Petersons.

LaGue, Peter, jt. auth. see Pochocki, Ethel.

Laguerie, Claude, jt. ed. see Large, Jean-Francoise.

Laguerre. Global Ethnopolis. LC 99-31478. 199p. 2000. text 59.95 (*0-312-22612-8*) St Martin.

Laguerre, Danielle V. Black Ties. 424p. 1995. pap. 15.00 (*0-9646413-0-5*) Tenaj Pub Hse.

Laguerre, E. Oeuvres, 2 Vols. LC 70-125075. 1971. reprint ed. text 69.50 (*0-8284-0263-9*) Chelsea Pub.

Laguerre, Enrique A. Los Amos Benevolos. 2nd ed. LC 76-21797. 258p. 1990. pap. 7.95 (*0-8477-3523-0*) U of PR Pr.

Laguerre, Enrique A., jt. auth. see Melon.

Laguerre, Enrique A., jt. auth. see Melon, Ester.

Laguerre, Michel S. American Odyssey: Haitians in New York City. LC 83-21078. (Anthropology of Contemporary Issues Ser.). (Illus.). 200p. 1984. pap. text 15.95 (*0-8014-9270-X*) Cornell U Pr.

— Minoritized Space: An Inquiry into the Spatial Order of Things. LC 99-19278. 152p. 1999. pap. 15.00 (*0-87772-387-7*) UCB IGS.

LaGuma, Alex. In the Fog of the Season's End. 2nd ed. (African Writers Ser.). 181p. (C). 1992. pap. 9.95 (*0-435-90980-0*, 90980) Heinemann.

— Walk in the Night & Other Stories. 129p. 1967. pap. 10.95 (*0-8101-0139-4*) Northwestern U Pr.

LaGumina, Salvatore J. From Steerage to Suburb: Long Island Italians. LC 87-20842. (CMS Migration & Ethnicity Ser.). 285p. 1989. 19.50 (*0-934733-33-3*) CMS.

Lagumina, Salvatore J. New York at Mid-Century: The Impellitteri Years, 147. LC 92-8844. 272p. 1992. 55.00 (*0-313-27205-0*, LBC, Greenwood Pr) Greenwood.

— WOP: A Documentary History of Anti-Italian Discrimination, Vol. 1. 2nd rev. ed. LC 97-78146. (Illus.). 319p. 1999. pap. 18.00 (*1-55071-047-8*) Guernica Editions.

LaGumina, Salvatore J., et al, eds. The Italian American Experience: An Encyclopedia. LC 99-38629. (Special Reference Ser.). (Illus.). 735p. 1999. 110.00 (*0-8153-0713-6*, H1535) Garland.

Lagumina, Salvatore J., jt. auth. see Cavaioli, Frank J.

Laguna, Asela R. De, see De Laguna, Asela R., ed.

Laguna, Asela Rodriguez-Seda De, see Rodriguez-Seda de Laguna, Asela.

Laguna, Fred, jt. auth. see Glover, Fred.

***Laguna, Lance.** Dance! Dance! Dance! 2000. 4.95 (*0-7624-0826-X*) Running Pr.

Laguna, Theodore De, see De Laguna, Theodore.

Lagunoff, Susan, jt. auth. see Dempsey, K. Ann.

Lagus, P. L. & Trechsel, Heinz R., eds. Measured Air Leakage of Building, STP 904. LC 86-10953. (Special Technical Publication Ser.). (Illus.). 428p. 1986. text 54.00 (*0-8031-0469-3*, STP904) ASTM.

Laha, R. G., jt. auth. see Lukacs, E.

Laham, Martha. Essentials of Selling. 160p. (C). 1995. pap. text, per. 41.95 (*0-7872-1811-1*, 41181101) Kendall-Hunt.

Laham, Nicholas. A Lost Cause: Bill Clinton's Campaign for National Health Insurance. LC 96-2197. 272p. 1996. 65.00 (*0-275-95611-3*, Praeger Pubs) Greenwood.

— The Reagan Presidency & the Politics of Race: In Pursuit of Colorblind Justice & Limited Government. LC 98-14907. 256p. 1998. 59.95 (*0-275-96182-6*, Praeger Pubs) Greenwood.

***Laham, Nicholas.** Ronald Reagan & the Politics of Immigration Reform. LC 99-45987. 264p. 2000. 65.00 (*0-275-96723-9*, Praeger Pubs) Greenwood.

Laham, Nicholas. Why the United States Lacks a National Health Insurance Program. 216p. 1993. pap. 22.95 (*0-275-94779-3*, Praeger Pubs) Greenwood.

— Why the United States Lacks a National Health Insurance Program, 331. LC 93-3167. (Contributions in Political Science Ser.: No. 331). 216p. 1993. 59.95 (*0-313-28745-7*, GM8745) Greenwood.

Lahane, Dennis. Darkness, Take My Hand. LC 95-23609. 384p. 1997. mass mkt. 6.99 (*0-380-72628-9*, Avon Bks) Morrow Avon.

Lahav, Noam. Biogenesis: Theories of Life's Origins. (Illus.). 368p. 1999. text 65.00 (*0-19-511754-9*); pap. text 29.95 (*0-19-511755-7*) OUP.

Lahav, O., et al, eds. Gravitational Dynamics. (Cambridge Contemporary Astrophysics Ser.). (Illus.). 271p. (C). 1996. text 69.95 (*0-521-56327-5*) Cambridge U Pr.

Lahav, Pnina. Judgement in Jerusalem: Simon Agranat & the Zionist Century. LC 96-40381. 352p. 1997. 29.95 (*0-520-20595-2*, Pub. by U CA Pr) Cal Prin Full Svc.

Lahav, Ran & Venza Tillmanns, Maria da, eds. Essays on Philosophical Counseling. 234p. (C). 1995. lib. bdg. 38.50 (*0-8191-9973-7*) U Pr of Amer.

Lahay, O. Thrombospondin. 320p. 1993. lib. bdg. 199.00 (*0-8493-4929-X*, QP552) CRC Pr.

LaHaye, Beverly. Como Desarrollar el Temperamento de Su Hijo.Tr. of How to Develop Your Child's Temperament. 182p. 1979. 8.99 (*0-88113-036-2*) Caribe Betania.

— La Mujer Sujeta al Espiritu.Tr. of Spirit-Controlled Woman. 208p. 1978. 9.99 (*0-88113-210-1*) Caribe Betania.

— The Restless Woman. 176p. 1984. pap. 6.95 (*0-310-27091-X*, 18337P) Zondervan.

— The Spirit-Controlled Woman. rev. ed. LC 94-29312. 1995. pap. 9.99 (*1-56507-223-5*) Harvest Hse.

— Understanding Your Child's Temperament. 224p. 1999. pap. 9.99 (*1-56507-939-6*) Harvest Hse.

LaHaye, Beverly & Blackstock, Terri. Seasons Under Heaven. LC 98-56104. 2000. 14.97 (*0-310-22137-4*) HarpC.

***LaHaye, Beverly & Blackstock, Terri.** Showers in Season. 2000. 16.99 (*0-310-22138-2*) Zondervan.

LaHaye, Beverly & LaHaye, T. Contra la Corriente.Tr. of Against the Tide. (SPA.). 9.99 (*1-56063-947-4*, 497669) Editorial Unilit.

LaHaye, Beverly, jt. auth. see LaHaye, Tim F.

Lahaye, Jacques & Ehrburger, Pierre, eds. Fundamental Issues in Control of Carbon Gasification Reactivity. (C). 1991. text 287.50 (*0-7923-1080-2*) Kluwer Academic.

Lahaye, Jacques & Prado, G., eds. Fundamentals of the Physical-Chemistry of Pulverized Coal Combustion. (C). 1987. text 251.50 (*90-247-3573-4*) Kluwer Academic.

***LaHaye, T. & Jenkins, T.** Dejados Atras. (Serie Dejados Atras - Left Behind Ser.: No. 1).Tr. of Left Behind. (SPA.). 2000. 8.99 (*0-7899-0373-3*, 497475) Editorial Unilit.

LaHaye, T., jt. auth. see LaHaye, Beverly.

LaHaye, Tim. Cuatro Pasos Hacia la Intimidad/Matrimonio. (Serie Guia de Bolsillo - Pocket Guides Ser.).Tr. of Four Steps to an Intimate Marriage. (SPA.). pap. 2.79 (*1-56063-231-3*, 498064) Editorial Unilit.

Lahaye, Tim. Jesus, Who Is He. 1996. 17.99 (*0-345-40515-3*) Ballantine Pub Grp.

Lahaye, Tim. Revelation Unveiled. LC 99-18860. 384p. 1999. pap. 15.99 (*0-310-23005-5*) Zondervan.

— Understanding the Male Temperament: What Women Want to Know about Men but Don't Know How to Ask. 2nd rev. ed. LC 95-40963. (Illus.). 288p. 1996. 15.99 (*0-8007-1719-8*) Revell.

LaHaye, Tim & Jenkins. El Comando Tribulacion. (Serie Dejados Atras - Left Behind Ser.: Vol. 2).Tr. of Tribulation Force. (SPA.). 2000. 9.99 (*0-7899-0374-1*, 497476) Editorial Unilit.

***LaHaye, Tim & Jenkins, Jerry B.** Are We Living in the End Times? LC 99-41424. 1999. 16.97 (*0-8423-0098-8*) Tyndale Hse.

LaHaye, Tim & Jenkins, Jerry B. Have You Been Left Behind? (Illus.). 1999. 12.99 (*0-8423-5196-5*) Tyndale Hse.

LaHaye, Tim, jt. auth. see Ice, Thomas.

LaHaye, Tim, jt. auth. see Jenkins, J. B.

Lahaye, Tim, jt. auth. see Jenkins, Jerry B.

LaHaye, Tim F. Aumente el Poder de su Peresonalidad. (Serie Guia de Bolsillo - Pocket Guides Ser.).Tr. of Increase Your Personality Power. (SPA.). 92p. 1987. pap. 2.79 (*0-8423-6516-8*, 498040) Editorial Unilit.

— Bible Prophecy: What You Need to Know. (Quick Reference Guides Ser.). 16p. 1999. pap. 1.99 (*0-7369-0035-7*) Harvest Hse.

— Casados Pero Felices.Tr. of How to Be Happy Though Married. (SPA.). 176p. 1986. pap. 4.50 (*0-8423-6252-5*, 490210) Editorial Unilit.

— El Comienzo del Fin.Tr. of Beginning of the End. (SPA.). 232p. 1986. pap. write for info. (*0-614-27007-3*) Editorial Unilit.

— Comienzo Del Fin (The Beginning of the End) (SPA.). 1992. 3.99 (*0-8423-6253-3*, 490211) Editorial Unilit.

— Como Estudiar la Biblia por Si Mismo.Tr. of How to Study the Bible for Yourself. 192p. 1977. 8.99 (*0-88113-042-7*) Caribe Betania.

— Faith of Our Founding Fathers. LC 94-77270. 276p. 1996. pap. 10.95 (*0-89051-201-9*, FAFOFA) Master Bks.

— Homosexualidad - Lo que Es, Lo que Hace y Como Superarla: What Everyone Should Know about Homosexuality. Duffer, Hiram, tr. from ENG. (Una Respuesta Cristiana Ser.). (SPA.). 144p. (Orig.). 1991. pap. 6.99 (*0-311-46126-3*) Casa Bautista.

— How to Be Happy Though Married. (Living Bks.). 160p. 1979. mass mkt. 4.99 (*0-8423-1499-7*) Tyndale Hse.

— How to Manage Pressure: Before Pressure Manages You. 240p. 1983. pap. 7.95 (*0-310-27081-2*, 18336P) Zondervan.

— How to Win over Depression. 224p. 1974. pap. 8.95 (*0-310-26981-4*, 18072P) Zondervan.

— How to Win over Depression. 244p. 1983. pap. 7.95 (*0-310-25837-5*) Zondervan.

— How to Win over Depression. rev. ed. 240p. 1996. pap. 10.99 (*0-310-20326-0*) Zondervan.

— If Ministers Fall, Can They Be Restored? 176p. 1990. mass mkt. 8.99 (*0-310-52131-9*) Zondervan.

— Jesus, Who Is He? LC 96-50940. 316p. 1997. 19.99 (*1-57673-042-5*, Multnomah Bks) Multnomah Pubs.

— Manual del Temperamento: Descubra Su Potencial.Tr. of Your Temperament: Discover Its Potential. (SPA.). 1987. 16.99 (*0-8423-6322-X*, 490214); write for info. (*0-614-27078-2*) Editorial Unilit.

***LaHaye, Tim F.** Nicolas. (Left Behind Ser.: Vol. 3). (SPA.). 2000. pap. 9.99 (*0-7899-0457-8*) Editorial Unilit.

LaHaye, Tim F. No Fear of the Storm: Why Christians Will Escape All the Tribulation. 256p. 1994. pap. 12.99 (*0-88070-788-7*) Multnomah Pubs.

— No Temas a la Tormenta.Tr. of No Fear of the Storm. (SPA.). 260p. 1992. pap. 7.99 (*1-56063-708-0*, 498554) Editorial Unilit.

— Opposites Attract. LC 98-5767. 276p. 1998. 10.99 (*1-56507-952-3*) Harvest Hse.

***LaHaye, Tim F.** El Poseido. (Left Behind Ser.: Vol. 7). (SPA.). 2000. pap. 9.99 (*0-7899-0755-0*) Editorial Unilit.

LaHaye, Tim F. Power of the Cross. Date not set. pap. 8.99 (*0-8297-1686-6*) Vida Pubs.

— Power of the Cross: Real Stories - Real People - a Real God. LC 97-45539. 256p. 1998. 19.99 (*1-57673-212-6*) Multnomah Pubs.

— Raising Sexually Pure Kids: How to Prepare Your Children for the Act of Marriage. LC 98-226789. 260p. 1998. pap. 12.99 (*1-57673-392-0*) Multnomah Pubs.

— Rapture under Attack: Will You Escape the Tribulation. 256p. 1998. pap. 12.99 (*1-57673-391-2*) Multnomah Pubs.

— Revelation-Illustrated & Made Plain. 1999. pap. 10.99 (*0-8297-2073-1*) HarpC.

— Revelation-Illustrated & Made Plain. rev. ed. 325p. 1974. pap. 10.99 (*0-310-26991-1*, 18073P) Zondervan.

— Sex Education Is for the Family. 192p. (J). (gr. 9-12). 1985. 12.95 (*0-310-27010-3*, 18343) Zondervan.

— Spirit-Controlled Temperament. 251p. 1993. pap. 9.99 (*0-8423-6220-7*) Tyndale Hse.

— Spirit-Controlled Temperament. large type ed. 1986. 13.95 (*0-8027-2563-5*) Walker & Co.

— Te Amo Por Que Somos Differentes!Tr. of I Love You, Why Are We So Different?. (SPA.). 240p. 1995. pap. 10.99 (*0-8297-1989-X*) Vida Pubs.

— Temperamentos Controlados.Tr. of Spirit Controlled Temperaments. (SPA.). 125p. 1986. pap. 4.50 (*0-8423-6254-1*, 490212) Editorial Unilit.

— Temperamentos Transformados.Tr. of Transformed Temperaments. (SPA.). 1986. 4.99 (*0-8423-6255-X*, 490213); pap. write for info. (*0-614-27142-8*) Editorial Unilit.

— Ten Steps to Victory over Depression. 1974. pap. 3.99 (*0-310-27002-2*, 18074P) Zondervan.

— Transformed Temperaments. 293p. 1993. mass mkt. 5.99 (*0-8423-7304-7*) Tyndale Hse.

— Transforming Your Temperament. 512p. 1991. 11.99 (*0-88486-040-X*, Inspirational Pr) Arrowood Pr.

— Trifunto Sabre la Depresion.Tr. of How to Win over Depression. (SPA.). 256p. 1975. pap. 6.99 (*0-8297-0515-5*) Vida Pubs.

— Understanding the Last Days: Making Sense of Bible Prophecy. LC 97-44851. (Illus.). 160p. 1998. pap. 8.99 (*1-56507-862-4*) Harvest Hse.

— Usted Se Enoja Porque Quiere.Tr. of Anger Is a Choice. (SPA.). 240p. (Orig.). 1984. pap. 5.99 (*0-8297-1402-2*) Vida Pubs.

— El Varon y Su Temperamento. 217p. 1978. 4.95 (*0-88113-340-X*) Caribe Betania.

— Why You Act the Way You Do. 342p. 1988. mass mkt. 5.99 (*0-8423-8212-7*) Tyndale Hse.

***LaHaye, Tim F. & Jenkins, Jerry.** Asesinos. (Left Behind (Spanish) Ser.: Vol. 6). (SPA.). 1999. pap. 9.99 (*0-7899-0725-9*) Spanish Hse Distributors.

— El Clandestino. (SPA.). (J). (gr. 4-7). 2000. mass mkt. 3.99 (*0-7899-0724-0*) Spanish Hse Distributors.

— Secundaria Nicolas. (SPA.). (J). (gr. 4-7). 2000. mass mkt. 3.99 (*0-7899-0723-2*) Spanish Hse Distributors.

***LaHaye, Tim F. & Jenkins, Jerry B.** Apolion. (Left Behind (Spanish) Ser.: Vol. 5). (SPA.). 2000. pap. 9.99 (*0-7899-0655-4*) Spanish Hse Distributors.

LaHaye, Tim F. & Jenkins, Jerry B. Apollyon: The Destroyer is Unleashed, 5. LC 98-32064. (Left Behind Ser.: Bk. 5). 400p. 1999. 19.97 (*0-8423-2916-1*) Tyndale Hse.

— Apollyon: The Destroyer Is Unleashed, 5. (Left Behind Ser.: Bk. 5). 400p. 1999. pap. 13.99 (*0-8423-2926-9*) Tyndale Hse.

— Assassins: The Destroyer is Unleashed. LC 99-23466. (Left Behind Ser.: Bk. 6). 2000. pap. 13.99 (*0-8423-2927-7*) Tyndale Hse.

— Assassins: The Destroyer is Unleashed, Vol. 6. LC 99-23466. (Left Behind Ser.: Bk. 6). 1999. 19.97 (*0-8423-2920-X*) Tyndale Hse.

***LaHaye, Tim F. & Jenkins, Jerry B.** Cosecha de Almas. Vol. 4. (SPA.). 2000. pap. 9.99 (*0-7899-0577-9*) Spanish Hse Distributors.

— Despojado. (SPA.). (J). (gr. 4-7). 2000. pap. 3.99 (*0-7899-0837-9*) Spanish Hse Distributors.

— The Indwelling: The Beast Takes Possession. (Left Behind Ser.: Bk. 7). 300p. 2000. 22.99 (*0-8423-2928-5*); pap. write for info. (*0-8423-2929-3*) Tyndale Hse.

LaHaye, Tim F. & Jenkins, Jerry B. Left Behind: A Novel of the Earth's Last Days. LC 95-19132. (Left Behind Ser.: Bk. 1). 468p. 1995. 19.99 (*0-8423-2911-0*) Tyndale Hse.

— Left Behind: A Novel of the Earth's Last Days. (Left Behind Ser.: Bk. 1). 320p. 1996. pap. 13.99 (*0-8423-2912-9*) Tyndale Hse.

***LaHaye, Tim F. & Jenkins, Jerry B.** Left Behind: A Novel of the Earth's Last Days. large type ed. LC 99-87745. (Left Behind Ser.). 575p. 2000. 29.95 (*0-7862-2468-1*) Thorndike Pr.

LaHaye, Tim F. & Jenkins, Jerry B. Nicolae: The Rise of Antichrist. LC 97-20356. (Left Behind Ser.: Bk. 3). 432p. 1997. 16.95 (*0-8423-2914-5*) Tyndale Hse.

— Nicolae: The Rise of Antichrist. (Left Behind Ser.: Bk. 3). 415p. 1998. pap. 13.99 (*0-8423-2924-2*, 910666Q) Tyndale Hse.

***LaHaye, Tim F. & Jenkins, Jerry B.** Nicolae: The Rise of Antichrist. large type ed. LC 99-87744. (Left Behind Ser.: Bk. 3). 2000. write for info. (*0-7862-2469-X*) Thorndike Pr.

— Soul Harvest: The World Takes Sides. LC 98-20929. (Left Behind Ser.: Bk. 4). 438p. 1998. 19.97 (*0-8423-2915-3*) Tyndale Hse.

LaHaye, Tim F. & Jenkins, Jerry B. Soul Harvest: The World Takes Sides. (Left Behind Ser.: Bk. 4). 425p. 1999. pap. 13.99 (*0-8423-2925-0*) Tyndale Hse.

— Tribulation Force: The Continuing Drama of Those Left Behind. (Left Behind Ser.: Bk. 2). 450p. 1996. 19.99 (*0-8423-2913-7*) Tyndale Hse.

— Tribulation Force: The Continuing Drama of Those Left Behind. 450p. 1996. pap. 13.99 (*0-8423-2921-8*) Tyndale Hse.

***LaHaye, Tim F. & Jenkins, Jerry B.** Tribulation Force: The Continuing Drama of Those Left Behind. (Left Behind Ser.: Bk. 2). 1999. text 19.99 incl. audio (*0-8423-3583-8*) Tyndale Hse.

— Tribulation Force: The Continuing Drama of Those Left Behind. large type ed. LC 99-87743. (Left Behind Ser.: Bk. 2). 517p. 2000. 29.95 (*0-7862-2471-1*) Thorndike Pr.

LaHaye, Tim F. & LaHaye, Beverly. The Act of Marriage: The Beauty of Sexual Love. expanded ed. 324p. 1998. mass mkt. 6.99 (*0-310-21200-6*) Zondervan.

— The Act of Marriage: The Beauty of Sexual Love. rev. ed. LC 97-39953. 304p. 1998. pap. 12.99 (*0-310-21177-8*) Zondervan.

— Alike in Love: When Opposites Attract. LC 97-75864. (Hearth & Home Ser.). (Illus.). 80p. 1998. 9.99 (*0-89221-369-8*) New Leaf.

— La Familia Sujeta al Espiritu.Tr. of Spirit-Controlled Family. 208p. 1992. 8.99 (*0-88113-085-0*) Caribe Betania.

— Family: The Real Measure of Success. LC 97-75865. (Hearth & Home Ser.). 80p. 1998. 9.99 (*0-89221-370-1*) New Leaf.

L

An Asterisk (*) at the beginning of an entry indicates that the title is appearing for the first time.

— Gathering Lilies from among the Thorns: Finding the Mate God Has for You. LC 97-75863. (Hearth & Home Ser.). (Illus.). 80p. 1998. 9.99 (*0-89221-368-X*) New Leaf.

— Hearth & Home: Gathering Lilies among the Thorns; Alike in Love; When Opposites Attract Family: the Real Measure of Success, 3 bks., Set. gif. ed. 1998. 34.95 (*0-89221-417-1*) New Leaf.

— Practical Answers to Common Questions about Sex in Marriage. 72p. (Orig.). 1984. pap. 1.70 (*0-310-27042-1*, 18340P) Zondervan.

LaHaye, Tim F. & Phillips, Bob. Anger Is a Choice. 160p. (Orig.). 1982. pap. 9.99 (*0-310-27071-5*, 18335P) Zondervan.

LaHaye, Tim F., jt. auth. see Jenkins, Jerry B.

LaHaye, Tina. Como Estudiar la Profecia Biblica por Si Mismo.Tr. of How to Study Bible Prophecy for Yourself. (SPA.). 192p. 1992. 8.99 (*0-88113-102-4*, B023-1024) Caribe Betania.

Lahee, A., tr. see Ibach, Harald & Luth, Hans.

Lahee, A., tr. see Schwabl, F.

Lahee, Henry C. Annals of Music in America. LC 72-107810. (Select Bibliographies Reprint Ser.). 1977. 23.95 (*0-8369-5185-9*) Ayer.

— Annals of Music in America. LC 78-97889. reprint ed. 32.50 (*0-404-03801-8*) AMS Pr.

— Annals of Music in America: A Chronological Record of Significant Musical Events. 298p. 1990. reprint ed. lib. bdg. 69.00 (*0-7812-9031-7*) Rprt Serv.

— Famous Singers of Today & Yesterday. reprint ed. lib. bdg. 59.00 (*0-7812-0765-7*) Rprt Serv.

— Grand Opera in America. LC 72-2050. reprint ed. 36.00 (*0-404-09909-2*) AMS Pr.

— Grand Opera in America. LC 76-154157. (Select Bibliographies Reprint Ser.). 1977. reprint ed. 25.95 (*0-8369-5773-3*) Ayer.

***Lahens, Yanick.** La Petite Corruption. (FRE.). 123p. 1999. pap. write for info. (*1-58437-006-8*) Edit Memo.

Laheta, Bob. The Key Guidelines for Quickly Finding a Professional Position. Tedeschi, Frank, ed. 77p. (Orig.). (C). 1988. pap. text 12.00 (*0-929403-00-2*) T&H Pr.

Lahey. Psycholog An Introduction. 7th ed. 1999. 42.00 (*0-07-235829-7*) McGraw.

— Psychology: An Introduction. 5th ed. 1994. student ed. 6.25 (*0-697-23284-0*) McGraw.

— Psychology: An Introduction. 5th ed. 1994. 86.87 (*0-697-22875-4*, WCB McGr Hill) McGrw-H Hghr Educ.

— Psychology: An Introduction. 6th ed. 272p. 1997. pap., student ed. 22.50 (*0-697-25314-7*) McGraw.

— Psychology: An Introduction - Text Index File, No. 2. 5th ed. 1995. 20.62 (*0-697-26612-5*, WCB McGr Hill) McGrw-H Hghr Educ.

— Psychology: An Introduction with Student Study Guide. 5th ed. 1994. 59.74 (*0-697-23285-9*) McGraw.

— Psychology Pract. Test. 6th ed. 1997. 44.25 (*0-07-561122-8*) McGraw.

Lahey, Benjamin B. Psychology: An Introduction. 5th ed. 784p. (C). 1994. text. write for info. (*0-697-27484-5*) Brown & Benchmark.

— Psychology: An Introduction. 6th ed. LC 96-78737. 752p. (C). 1997. text. write for info. (*0-697-25310-4*, WCB McGr Hill) McGrw-H Hghr Educ.

— Psychology: An Introduction, Language Enhancement Guide. 5th ed. 112p. (C). 1994. text. write for info. (*0-697-26250-2*) Brown & Benchmark.

— Psychology: An Introduction, Study Guide. 5th ed. 400p. (C). 1994. text, student ed. 18.75 (*0-697-14521-2*) Brown & Benchmark.

— Psychology: An Introduction, Study Guide. 5th ed. (C). 1995. text, student ed. 15.62 (*0-697-26753-9*) Brown & Benchmark.

— Psychology: An Introduction with Student Practice Test. 272p. 1995. student ed. write for info. (*0-614-03036-6*); student ed. write for info. incl. audio (*0-614-03037-4*) Brown & Benchmark.

Lahey, Benjamin B. & Kazdin, Alan E., eds. Advances in Clinical Child Psychology, Vol. 3. LC 77-643411. (Illus.). 494p. 1980. 55.00 (*0-306-40374-9*, Plenum Trade) Perseus Pubng.

— Advances in Clinical Child Psychology, Vol. 4. LC 77-643411. 380p. 1981. 65.00 (*0-306-40705-1*, Plenum Trade) Perseus Pubng.

— Advances in Clinical Child Psychology, Vol. 5. LC 77-643411. 392p. 1982. 65.00 (*0-306-41043-5*, Plenum Trade) Perseus Pubng.

— Advances in Clinical Child Psychology, Vol. 6. LC 77-643411. 344p. 1983. 65.00 (*0-306-41330-2*, Plenum Trade) Perseus Pubng.

— Advances in Clinical Child Psychology, Vol. 7. LC 77-643411. 368p. 1984. 65.00 (*0-306-41659-X*, Plenum Trade) Perseus Pubng.

— Advances in Clinical Child Psychology, Vol. 8. LC 77-643411. 344p. 1985. 65.00 (*0-306-41963-7*, Plenum Trade) Perseus Pubng.

— Advances in Clinical Child Psychology, Vol. 9. LC 77-643411. 420p. 1986. 65.00 (*0-306-42241-7*, Plenum Trade) Perseus Pubng.

— Advances in Clinical Child Psychology, Vol. 10. LC 77-643411. 378p. 1987. 65.00 (*0-306-42536-X*, Plenum Trade) Perseus Pubng.

— Advances in Clinical Child Psychology, Vol. 11. LC 77-643411. (Illus.). 414p. (C). 1988. 102.00 (*0-306-42892-X*, Plenum Trade) Perseus Pubng.

— Advances in Clinical Child Psychology, Vol. 12. (Illus.). 270p. (C). 1989. 102.00 (*0-306-43271-4*, Plenum Trade) Perseus Pubng.

— Advances in Clinical Child Psychology, Vol. 13. LC 77-643411. (Illus.). 426p. (C). 1990. 85.00 (*0-306-43479-2*, Plenum Trade) Perseus Pubng.

— Advances in Clinical Child Psychology, Vol. 14. (Illus.). 325p. (C). 1991. 85.00 (*0-306-43957-3*, Plenum Trade) Perseus Pubng.

Lahey, Carol H., ed. see Lahey, Lyle.

Lahey Clinic Staff. Global Outreach Cookbook. LC 93-71223. 1993. pap. write for info. (*0-87197-371-5*) Favorite Recipes.

Lahey, David. Athletic Scholarships: Making Your Sports Pay. 200p. 1992. pap. 12.95 (*1-895629-06-3*) Warwick Publ.

Lahey, G. F. Gerard Manley Hopkins. LC 72-95435. (Studies in Poetry: No. 38). 1969. reprint ed. lib. bdg. 75.00 (*0-8383-0986-0*) M S G Haskell Hse.

Lahey, Gerald. Gerard Manley Hopkins. (BCL1-PR English Literature Ser.). 172p. 1992. reprint ed. lib. bdg. 69.00 (*0-7812-7565-2*) Rprt Serv.

Lahey, Gerald F. Gerard Manley Hopkins. 1973. 250.00 (*0-87968-030-X*) Gordon Pr.

Lahey, Jayme P. Experimental Design for Injection Molding LC 98-94190. 201p. 1998. write for info. (*0-9636093-5-1*) Launsby Cnslting.

***Lahey, Joy.** Abandoned Premises. (Illus.). 32p. 1999. pap. 3.00 (*0-9663846-4-4*) Lavender Ink.

Lahey, Kathleen A. Are We 'Persons' Yet: Law & Sexuality in Canada. 512p. 1999. text 80.00 (*0-8020-4205-8*); pap. text 24.95 (*0-8020-8062-6*) U of Toronto Pr.

Lahey, Lyle. The Packer Chronicles Vol. 1: Waiting for the Pack to Come Back... Lahey, Carol H., ed. LC 97-94198. (Illus.). 224p. 1997. pap. 14.95 (*0-9659774-0-4*) Green Bay News.

Lahey, Margaret. Language Disorders & Language Development. LC 87-22059. 550p. (C). 1988. 101.00 (*0-02-367130-0*, Macmillan Coll) P-H.

Lahey, Miriam P., et al. Recreation, Leisure, & Chronic Illness: Therapeutic Rehabilitation As Intervention in Health Care. LC 93-16983. (Loss, Grief & Care Ser.: Vol. 6, No. 4). (Illus.). 162p. 1993. lib. bdg. 39.95 (*1-56024-418-6*) Haworth Pr.

Lahey, R. T., Jr., et al, eds. Multiphase Science & Technology, Vol. 8. 808p. 1995. 99.50 (*1-56700-023-1*) Begell Hse.

Lahey, R. T. & Moody, Frederick J. The Thermal Hydraulics of a Boiling Water Nuclear Reactor. 2nd ed. LC 93-12785. 1993. 65.00 (*0-89448-037-5*) Am Nuclear Soc.

Lahey, R. T., ed. see Basic Mechanisms in Two-phase Flow & Heat Transfer.

Lahey, Richard T. & Wallis, Graham B., eds. Non-Equilibrium Two-Phase Flows: Papers Presented at the Winter Annual Meeting of ASME, Houston, TX, November 30-December 5, 1975. LC 75-25192. 67p. reprint ed. pap. 30.00 (*0-608-30626-6*, 201683000005) Bks Demand.

Lahickey, Beth, ed. All Ages: Reflections on Straight Edge. (Illus.). 250p. (Orig.). 1998. pap. 12.00 (*1-889703-00-1*) Revelation CA.

Lahidji, Behrooz, jt. auth. see Lin, S. C. Jonathon.

Lahiff, James M., jt. auth. see Penrose, John M.

Lahiji, Nadir, jt. ed. see Friedman, Daniel S.

Lahiri, Aloka. Chaitanya Movement in Eastern India. (C). 1993. 30.00 (*81-85094-67-5*, Pub. by Punthi Pus) S Asia.

Lahiri, Ashok K., jt. ed. see Citrin, Daniel A.

***Lahiri, Jhumpa.** Interpreter of Maladies. 2000. 23.00 (*0-618-10136-5*) HM.

Lahiri, Jhumpa. Interpreter of Maladies: Stories. LC 98-50895. 198p. 1999. pap. 12.00 (*0-395-92720-X*, Mariner Bks) HM.

Lahiri, Kajal & Moore, Geoffrey H., eds. Leading Economic Indicators: New Approaches & Forecasting Records. (Illus.). 480p. (C). 1992. pap. text 30.95 (*0-521-43858-6*) Cambridge U Pr.

Lahiri, Latika, tr. see Ching, I.

Lahiri, Latika, tr. see I-Ching.

Lahiri-Munir, Devjani & Garcia, C. Retinal Pigment Epithelial Transplantation. LC 95-7452. (Medical Intelligence Unit Ser.). 133p. 1995. 79.00 (*1-57059-255-1*) Landes Bioscience.

Lahiri, Nayanjot. The Archaeology of Indian Trade Routes up to the Century 200 B. C. Resource Use, Resource Access & Lines of Communication. (Illus.). 480p. 1992. 42.00 (*0-19-562814-4*) OUP.

— Pre-Ahom Assam. (C). 1991. 16.00 (*0-685-50019-5*, Pub. by M Manoharial) S Asia.

Lahiri, Pradip K. Bengali Muslim Thought 1818-1947. (C). 1991. 14.00 (*81-7074-067-3*, Pub. by KP Bagchi) S Asia.

Lahiri, R. M. The Annexation of Assam. (C). 1994. text 16.00 (*81-7102-008-9*, Pub. by Firma KLM) S Asia.

***Lahiri, Shompa.** Indians in Britain: Anglo-Indian Encounters, Race & Identity, 1880-1930. LC 99-24206. 272p. 1999. 59.50 (*0-7146-4986-4*, Pub. by F Cass Pubs); pap. 24.50 (*0-7146-8049-4*, Pub. by F Cass Pubs) Intl Spec Bk.

Lahiri, Sukhamay, et al, eds. Response & Adaptation to Hypoxia: Organ to Organelle. (Clinical Physiology Series - An American Physiological Society Book). (Illus.). 272p. 1991. text 68.00 (*0-19-506244-2*) OUP.

Lahiri, Sukhamay, jt. ed. see West, John B.

Lahiri, Tarapada. Crime & Punishment in Ancient India. xiii, 207p. 1986. text 22.50 (*81-7027-093-6*, Pub. by Radiant Pubs) S Asia.

***Lahita, Robert G.** Arthritis Solution: The Newest Treatments to Help You Live Pain-Free. 256p. 1999. mass mkt. 5.99 (*0-380-80778-5*, Avon Bks) Morrow Avon.

Lahita, Robert G. Systemic Lupus Erythematosus. 2nd ed. (Illus.). 1002p. 1992. text 210.00 (*0-443-08785-7*) Church.

Lahita, Robert G., ed. Systemic Lupus Erythematosus. LC 86-11007. (Illus.). 1024p. reprint ed. pap. 200.00 (*0-7837-2586-8*, 204274800006) Bks Demand.

— Systemic Lupus Erythematosus. 3rd ed. LC 98-35859. (Illus.). 1051p. (C). 1998. boxed set 189.95 (*0-12-433900-X*) Acad Pr.

Lahita, Robert G. & Phillips, Robert H. Lupus: Everything You Need to Know. LC 97-34718. 224p. 1999. pap. 12.95 (*0-89529-833-3*, Avery) Penguin Putnam.

Lahita, Robert G., et al. Textbook of the Autoimmune Diseases. 912p. text 149.00 (*0-7817-1505-9*) Lppncott W & W.

Lahita, Robert G., jt. auth. see Moore, P. M.

Lahita, Robert G., jt. ed. see Moore, Patricia M.

Lahlou, B. & Vitiello, P., eds. Aquaculture: Fundamental & Applied Research. LC 93-38053. (Coastal & Estuarine Studies: Vol. 43). 1993. 42.00 (*0-87590-257-X*) Am Geophysical.

Lahlou, B., jt. ed. see Kirsch, R.

Lahlou, B., jt. ed. see Truchot, J.

Lahlou, Moncef, jt. auth. see Hanger, Catherine.

Lahm, Frank P., jt. auth. see Chandler, Charles D.

Lahman, James R. Prayers of the Hours: Morning, Midday, & Evening. LC 95-61503. 136p. (Orig.). 1996. pap. 9.95 (*0-89622-677-8*) Twenty-Third.

Lahman, Lois E., compiled by. Teacher's Guide for Reuben & the Fire. (Illus.). 24p. 1995. pap., teacher ed. 3.95 (*1-56148-140-8*) Good Bks PA.

Lahn, Dean, jt. auth. see Dunbar, Andrew.

***Lahoda, Gary.** Life's Little Prayer Book. 192p. 2000. pap. 7.99 (*0-517-16198-2*) Random Hse Value.

Lahoda, Gary, compiled by. Life's Little Prayer Book. (Illus.). 192p. 1996. pap. 11.00 (*0-8092-3178-6*, 317860, Contemporary Bks) NTC Contemp Pub Co.

Lahodny, Jan. Competitive Drills for Winning Basketball. 240p. (C). 1986. text 27.95 (*0-13-154949-9*, Parker Publishing Co) P-H.

LaHood, Charles G. & Sullivan, Robert C. Reprographic Services in Libraries: Organization & Administration. LC 75-25585. (LTP Publication Ser.: No. 19). 80p. reprint ed. pap. 30.00 (*0-608-12592-X*, 202395400034) Bks Demand.

LaHood, Marvin J., ed. Stories of Tragedy & Triumph. 308p. (C). 1997. pap. text 38.00 (*0-536-00227-4*) Pearson Custom.

— Tender Is the Night: Essays in Criticism. LC 77-85091. 222p. reprint ed. pap. 68.90 (*0-8357-9246-3*, 201762500007) Bks Demand.

Lahore, J. & Rothnie, W. Butterworths Annotated Acts: Copyright Act. write for info. (*0-409-31001-8*, Austral, MICHIE) LEXIS Pub.

Lahori, Maulane A. Commentators of the Holy Quran. 130p. (Orig.). 1995. text 22.50 (*1-56744-506-3*) Kazi Pubns.

Lahoz, S. Colet. Conquering Yeast Infections: The Non-Drug Solution for Men & Women. LC 96-67040. (Illus.). 147p. 1996. reprint ed. pap. 13.95 (*0-9678999-0-7*) East West.

Lahoz, S. Colet. Conquering Yeast Infections - The Non-Drug Solution for Men & Women. LC 96-67040. 139p. 1996. pap. 17.95 (*1-57197-016-9*) Pentland Pr.

Lahr, Christopher J. Shining Light on Constipation: Rectal Descent & Other Colon, Rectal & Anal Problems. Lindgren, Brian J., ed. (Illus.). 112p. (Orig.). 1997. pap. 12.95 (*0-9648176-4-0*) Pink Hse.

Lahr, Grace, ed. see Waconia Heritage Association Staff.

Lahr, Jana, jt. ed. see Ferrer, Linda.

Lahr, Jane. The Celtic Quest in Art & Literature: An Anthology from Merlin to Van Morrison. LC 98-41255. (Illus.). 240p. 1998. 50.00 (*0-941807-23-1*) Stewart Tabori & Chang.

Lahr, Jane & Tabori, Lena, eds. Love: A Celebration in Art & Literature. LC 82-5680. (Illus.). 240p. 1982. 45.00 (*0-941434-20-6*) Stewart Tabori & Chang.

Lahr, Jeff. Christmas Carol: A Cradle, Cross & Crown. 48p. (Orig.). 1992. pap. text 3.49 (*0-87227-175-7*, RBP5209) Reg Baptist.

— Coconut Christmas. 47p. (Orig.). 1996. pap. 3.49 (*0-87227-190-0*, RBP5229) Reg Baptist.

Lahr, Jeff. Countdown to Christmas. 48p. Date not set. pap. 3.49 (*0-87227-204-4*) Reg Baptist.

Lahr, Jeff. Light of Life. LC 97-191592. 48p. 1997. pap. 3.49 (*0-87227-194-3*, RBP5234) Reg Baptist.

— Music of the Manger. 40p. (Orig.). 1994. pap. 3.49 (*0-87227-183-8*, RBP5220) Reg Baptist.

— Time of Miracles. 40p. 1991. pap. 3.49 (*0-87227-170-6*, RBP5202) Reg Baptist.

Lahr, John. Coward the Playwright. LC 82-47991. (Illus.). 176p. (C). 1983. pap. 16.95 (*0-413-48050-X*, A0065, Methuen Drama) Methn.

— Coward the Playwright. 200p. 1983. pap. 3.95 (*0-380-64683-8*, Avon Bks) Morrow Avon.

***Lahr, John.** Dame Edna Everage & the Rise of Western Civilization: Backstage with Barry Humphries. LC 99-47196. (Illus.). 254p. 2000. pap. 14.95 (*0-520-22305-5*, Pub. by U CA Pr) Cal Prin Full Svc.

Lahr, John. Diary of a Somebody: Based on the Orton Diaries. LC 88-37726. 79p. (Orig.). 1989. pap. 7.95 (*0-87910-124-5*) Limelight Edns.

***Lahr, John.** Notes on a Cowardly Lion: The Biography of Bert Lahr. LC 99-43657. (Illus.). 417p. 2000. pap. 16.95 (*0-520-22304-7*, Pub. by U CA Pr) Cal Prin Full Svc.

Lahr, John. The Orton Diaries. Date not set. pap. 11.99 (*0-7493-2183-0*) Heinemann.

***Lahr, John.** Prick Up Your Ears: The Biography of Joe Orton. (Illus.). 320p. 2000. pap. 16.95 (*0-520-22666-6*) U CA Pr.

— Show & Tell: New Yorker Profiles. 240p. 2000. 27.95 (*1-58567-062-6*, Pub. by Overlook Pr) Penguin Putnam.

Lahr, John, jt. ed. see Orton, Joe.

Lahr, Luralyn & Hinkle, Harry, eds. Arts Express Teacher's Guide. (Arts Express TV Ser.). 56p. 1983. pap. 3.50 (*0-910475-93-8*) KET.

Lahr, Marta M. The Evolution of Modern Human Diversity: A Study on Cranial Variation. (Studies in Biological Anthropology: No. 18). (Illus.). 432p. (C). 1996. text 74.95 (*0-521-47393-4*) Cambridge U Pr.

Lahr, Michael L., jt. auth. see Stevens, Benjamin H.

Lahr Schier, Mary. Take Your Victories As They Come: The Carlson Years in Minnesota Politics. Benson, Brooke, ed. (Illus.). 240p. 1998. 21.95 (*0-9641908-3-4*) MSP Communs.

Lahrson-Fisher, Ann. Foundations of Homeschooling: Building Excellence in Family-Based Education. 200p. (Orig.). 2002. pap. 18.95 (*0-9640813-6-9*) Nettlepatch Pr.

— Homeschooling in Oregon: The 1998 Handbook. 2nd rev. expanded ed. LC 98-84767. Orig. Title: Homeschooling in Oregon: The Handbook. (Illus.). 398p. 1998. pap. 18.95 (*0-9640813-8-5*) Nettlepatch Pr.

— Mudpies & Building Blocks: Homeschooling Young Children. 250p. 1999. pap. write for info. (*0-9640813-4-2*) Nettlepatch Pr.

***Lahs-Gonzales, Olivia.** My Nature: Works with Paper by Kiki Smith. Steiner, Mary Ann, ed. 1999. pap. 19.95 (*0-89178-081-5*) St Louis Art Mus.

Lahs-Gonzales, Olivia & Lippard, Lucy. Defining Eye: Women Photographers of the 20th Century: Organized by the Saint Louis Art Museum. Steiner, Mary A., ed. LC 97-68149. (Illus.). 158p. 1997. pap. 29.95 (*0-89178-047-5*) St Louis Art Mus.

Lahti, Arto, ed. Contact Urticaria Syndrome. LC 97-12227. (Illus.). 384p. 1997. lib. bdg. 99.95 (*0-8493-7352-2*) CRC Pr.

Lahti, Kai, jt. auth. see Hedlund, Laura.

Lahti, N. E. The Language of Art from A to Z. rev. ed. LC 97-60020. Orig. Title: Plain Talk about Art. 185p. 1997. pap. text 11.00 (*0-9620147-3-7*) York Bks.

— Plain Talk about Art: The Language of Art from A to Z. 4th rev. ed. LC 94-90022. 203p. 1994. pap. 11.00 (*0-9620147-1-0*) York Bks.

***Lahti, Paul M.** Magnetic Properties of Organic Materials LC 99-26161. (Illus.). 752p. 1999. text 195.00 (*0-8247-1976-X*) Dekker.

Lahti, Pekka J. The Foundations of Modern Physics, 1990: Symposium. Mittelstaedt, P., ed. 540p. 1990. text 147.00 (*981-02-0387-X*) World Scientific Pub.

Lahti, Pekka J., jt. ed. see Mittelstaedt, P.

Lahti, Pekka J., jt. ed. see Mittlestaedt, P.

Lahti, Robert E. Innovative College Management. LC 73-10938. (Jossey-Bass Higher Education Ser.). 198p. reprint ed. pap. 61.40 (*0-608-14799-0*, 202566000045) Bks Demand.

Lahti-Wagner, Jean, jt. auth. see Schwanke, Dik.

Lahti, Will & Salmela, David W. Karhun Otsa: Bear's Forehead. 52p. (Orig.). 1992. pap. text 6.95 (*0-9632975-1-1*) Sampo Pub.

***Lahtti, Marku.** Alvar Aalto: A Gentler Structure for Life. (Illus.). 176p. 2000. 115.00 (*951-682-475-7*, Pub. by Rakennustieto) Gingko Press.

Lahue. Volvo Stern Drive Shop Manual. 1989. 14.50 (*0-07-155087-9*) McGraw.

Lahue, Fabian. Electronic Troubleshooting. 1994. teacher ed. 10.08 (*0-02-819905-7*) Glencoe.

Lahue, Fabian J. Electronic Troubleshooting. LC 93-24452. 1993. 23.16 (*0-02-819904-9*) Glencoe.

Lahue, Kalton. Mercruiser Stern Drive Shop Manual, 1964-1987 (Also Includes 1986-1987 TR & TRS Models) 7th rev. ed. LC 93-79848. (Illus.). 616p. 1993. pap. 36.95 (*0-89287-613-1*, B740) Intertec Pub.

Lahue, Kalton C. All about Roofs & Sidings. Smith, Cheryl, ed. LC 90-86165. 112p. 1991. pap. 9.95 (*0-89721-237-1*, Ortho Bks) Meredith Bks.

— Auto Chassis. Date not set. pap. text, teacher ed. write for info. (*0-314-07192-X*) West Pub.

— Auto Undercar. Date not set. pap. text, teacher ed. write for info. (*0-314-08742-7*) West Pub.

— Automotive Brakes. Date not set. pap. text, teacher ed. write for info. (*0-314-03361-0*) West Pub.

— Automotive Brakes & Antilock Braking Systems. LC 93-46889. (Automotive Ser.). 618p. (C). 1995. pap. 77.95 (*0-314-02838-2*) West Pub.

— Automotive Chassis: Suspension, Steering, & Brakes. LC 94-43215. (West's Automotive Ser.). 1995. pap. text 38.25 (*0-314-04551-1*) West Pub.

— Automotive Chassis: Suspension, Steering, & Brakes. LC 94-42860. (West's Automotive Ser.). (C). 1995. mass mkt. 31.25 (*0-314-04549-X*) West Pub.

— Electronic Automatic Transmissions. LC 93-31296. 1994. 70.96 (*0-02-801365-4*) Glencoe.

— Interior Lighting. Smith, Cheryl, ed. LC 90-84632. (Illus.). 112p. (Orig.). 1991. pap. 9.95 (*0-89721-227-4*, Ortho Bks) Meredith Bks.

— Mercury Outboard Shop Manual 45-225 HP, 1972-1989. 4th rev. ed. (Illus.). 424p. 1989. pap. 34.95 (*0-89287-396-5*, B726) Clymer Pub.

— OMC Stern Drive Shop Manual, 1964-1986. 4th rev. ed. (Illus.). 456p. (Orig.). 1988. pap. 34.95 (*0-89287-398-1*, B730) Clymer Pub.

Lahue, Kalton C., ed. see Leigh, Bob, et al.

Lahue, Robert, ed. Methods in Neurobiology, Vol. 1. LC 80-15623. 614p. 1981. 110.00 (*0-306-40517-2*, Plenum Trade) Perseus Pubng.

— Methods in Neurobiology, Vol. 2. LC 80-15623. 682p. 1981. 110.00 (*0-306-40518-0*, Plenum Trade) Perseus Pubng.

LaHue, Sanford P., Sr., ed. Solutions for Pavement Rehabilitation Problems. 304p. 1986. 31.00 (*0-87262-578-8*) Am Soc Civil Eng.

Lahunta, Alexander De, see De Lahunta, Alexander.

An Asterisk (*) at the beginning of an entry indicates that the title is appearing for the first time.

Lahunta, Alexander De, see Evans, Howard E. & De Lahunta, Alexander.

LaHurd, Jeff. Come on Down! Pitching Paradise During the Roaring 20s. 96p. 1995. 29.95 (*1-888438-50-9*); pap. 19.95 (*1-888438-00-2*) Sarasota Alliance.

— Quintessential Sarasota: Stories & Pictures from the 1920's-1950's. (Illus.). 128p. (Orig.). 1990. pap. 8.95 (*1-879026-00-7*) Clubhouse Pub.

*__LaHurd, Jeff.__ Sarasota. LC 99-98268. (Illus.). 83p. 2000. pap. 16.95 (*0-9676539-0-8*) Lobo Media Grp Inc.

LaHurd, Jeff. Sarasota, a Sentimental Journey. 120p. 1991. pap. 8.95 (*1-888438-75-4*) Sarasota Alliance.

— Sarasota, Then & Now. 96p. 1994. pap. 12.00 (*1-888438-25-8*) Sarasota Alliance.

Lahusen, Christian. The Rhetoric of Moral Protest: Public Campaigns, Celebrity Endorsement, & Political Mobilization. LC 96-24877. (Studies in Organization: Vol. 76). (Illus.). xvi, 425p. (C). 1996. text 82.95 (*3-11-015093-X*, 134/96) De Gruyter.

*__Lahusen, Thomas.__ Harbin & Manchuria: Place, Space & Identity. 280p. 2000. pap. 12.00 (*0-8223-6475-1*) Duke.

Lahusen, Thomas. How Life Writes the Book: Real Socialism & Socialist Realism in Stalin's Russia. LC 97-19261. 256p. 1997. 29.95 (*0-8014-3394-0*); pap. write for info. (*0-8014-8423-5*) Cornell U Pr.

— Socialist Realism Without Shores. 1995. pap. 12.00 (*0-8223-6430-1*) Duke.

Lahusen, Thomas & Dobrenko, Evgeny, eds. Socialist Realism Without Shores. LC 96-43217. (Post-Contemporary Interventions Ser.). (Illus.). 392p. 1997. pap. text 19.95 (*0-8223-1941-1*); lib. bdg. 59.95 (*0-8223-1935-7*) Duke.

Lahusen, Thomas & Kuperman, Gene, eds. Late Soviet Culture: From Perestroika to Novostroika. LC 92-28051. (Post-Contemporary Interventions Ser.). 344p. 1993. text 54.95 (*0-8223-1290-5*); pap. text 19.95 (*0-8223-1291-3*) Duke.

Lai, C., jt. auth. see Hromadka, Theodore V., II.

Lai, C. H., ed. Gauge Theory of Weak & Electromagnetic Interactions. 458p. 1981. text 52.00 (*9971-83-023-X*); pap. text 30.00 (*9971-83-022-1*) World Scientific Pub.

— Ideals & Realities: Selected Essays of Abdus Salem. 2nd ed. 400p. 1987. text 59.00 (*9971-5-0315-8*); pap. text 37.00 (*9971-5-0316-6*) World Scientific Pub.

Lai, C. H., jt. ed. see Hassan, Z.

Lai, C. H., jt. ed. see Mohapatra, R. N.

Lai, C. L., et al, eds. Viral Hepatitis B Infection: Vaccine & Control. 304p. 1984. 85.00 (*9971-950-80-4*) World Scientific Pub.

Lai, Cheng-chung. Adam Smith Across the Nations: Translation & Receptions of the Wealth of Nations. LC 99-17607. 450p. 2000. text 105.00 (*0-19-823339-6*) OUP.

Lai, Christopher C. Operation: Prosperity: Fixing America's Economy, a Practical & Ecological Guide for Individuals & Governments. (Illus.). 336p. 1997. pap. 14.95 (*0-9652728-1-8*) Candor Pr.

Lai, David. Photoshop Type Magic, Vol. 2. 2nd ed. LC 96-77856. 272p. 1996. pap. text 39.99 incl. cd-rom (*1-56830-329-7*) Hayden.

— Photoshop 4 Type Magic 1. LC 97-71008. 264p. 1997. 39.99 (*1-56830-380-7*) Hayden.

Lai, David, ed. Global Perspectives: International Relations, U. S. Foreign Policy, & the View from Abroad. LC 97-3828. 356p. 1997. 55.00 (*1-55587-719-2*); pap. 22.50 (*1-55587-729-X*) L Rienner.

Lai, David & Simsic, Greg. Photoshop Type Magic. LC 95-77739. (Illus.). 240p. 1995. 35.00 (*1-56830-220-7*, Alpha Ref) Macmillan Gen Ref.

Lai, David C. Land of Genghis Khan: The Rise & Fall of Nation-States in China's Northern Frontiers. LC 97-107190. (Illus.). 88p. 1995. pap. 9.95 (*0-919838-20-0*) U of Wash Pr.

Lai, David C. & Madoff, Pamela. Building & Rebuilding Harmony: The Gateway to Victoria's Chinatown. LC 97-200465. (Illus.). 90p. 1997. pap. 11.95 (*0-919838-22-7*) U of Wash Pr.

Lai, Eric & Birren, Bruce W., eds. Electrophoresis of Large DNA Molecules: Theory & Applications. (Current Communications in Cell & Molecular Biology Ser.: No. 1). (Illus.). 180p. (C). 1991. text 20.00 (*0-87969-360-6*) Cold Spring Harbor.

Lai, Eric, jt. auth. see Birren, Bruce W.

Lai, Eric, jt. ed. see Birren, Bruce W.

Lai, G. Y. High Temperature Corrosion of Engineering Alloys. 230p. 1990. 117.00 (*0-87170-411-0*, 6130) ASM.

Lai, G. Y. & Sorrell, G., eds. Materials Performance in Waste Incineration Systems. (Illus.). 538p. 1992. 32.00 (*1-877914-31-2*) NACE Intl.

Lai, Him M., et al. Island: Poetry & History of Chinese Immigrants on Angel Island, 1910-40. LC 91-8372. (CHI & ENG., Illus.). 174p. 1991. pap. 17.95 (*0-295-97109-6*) U of Wash Pr.

Lai, Hong-Jian, jt. auth. see Liu, Bolian.

Lai, Hongyi, tr. see Teiwes, Frederick C. & Sun, Warren, eds.

Lai, Ivan, jt. auth. see Bartlett, Frances.

Lai, James. Materials of Construction. 368p. (C). 1997. 53.90 (*0-7872-4404-X*) Kendall-Hunt.

*__Lai, James.__ Materials of Construction. 2nd ed. 308p. (C). 1999. per. 61.95 (*0-7872-6108-4*, 41610801) Kendall-Hunt.

Lai, James S., jt. ed. see Nakanishi, Donald T.

Lai, Jane, jt. ed. see Cheung, Martha P.

Lai, Jerry. Tolley's Company Secretary's Handbook Eighth Edition. 8th ed. 1998. pap. 195.00 (*1-86012-795-9*) Tolley Pubng.

Lai, Juey H. Polymers for Electronic Applications. LC 89-9860. 272p. 1989. 140.00 (*0-8493-4704-1*, TK7871) Franklin.

Lai, Junbiao. Non-Linear Time-Dependent Deformation Behaviour of High Density Polyethylene. vi, 159p. (Orig.). 1995. pap. 59.50 (*90-407-1136-4*, Pub. by Delft U Pr) Coronet Bks.

*__Lai, Karen M.__ An Unconditional Love Story: Meeting the People of the Sea. 208p. 1999. pap. 7.95 (*0-9673673-0-1*) Mall Pubng.

Lai, Kuo-Yann. Liquid Detergents. LC 96-44787. (Surfactant Science Ser.: Vol. 67). (Illus.). 576p. 1996. text 225.00 (*0-8247-9391-9*) Dekker.

Lai, Kwok-Wing. Words Have Wings: Teaching & Learning with Computer Networks. 1996. 29.95 (*0-614-18889-X*, Pub. by Univ Otago Pr) Intl Spec Bk.

*__Lai, Kwok-Wing, ed.__ Net--Working: Teaching, Learning & Professional Development. 224p. 1999. pap. 39.95 (*1-877133-68-X*, Pub. by Univ Otago Pr) Intl Spec Bk.

Lai, Kwok-Wing, ed. Words Have Wings: Teaching & Learning with Computer Networks. LC 96-218768. 176p. 1996. pap. 34.95 (*1-877133-05-1*, Pub. by Univ Otago Pr) Intl Spec Bk.

Lai, Larissa. When Fox Is a Thousand. (Illus.). 216p. 1995. pap. 14.95 (*0-88974-041-0*, Pub. by Press Gang Pubs) LPC InBook.

Lai, Lawrence Wai-Chung, see Wai-Chung Lai, Lawrence.

Lai, M. M. & Stohlman, S. A., eds. Coronaviruses. LC 87-22034. (Advances in Experimental Medicine & Biology Ser.: Vol. 218). (Illus.). 604p. 1987. 125.00 (*0-306-42672-2*, Plenum Trade) Perseus Pubng.

Lai, Man O., jt. auth. see Lu, Li.

Lai, Mary, et al. Am I Covered for...? A Comprehensive Guide to Insuring Your Non-Profit Organization. 2nd ed. (Illus.). 286p. (C). 1992. pap. text 14.95 (*0-9631553-0-X*) Consort Human.

Lai, Melisa W., jt. auth. see Lai, Ralph W.

Lai, Michael W., et al. Introduction to Continuum Mechanics. 3rd ed. 570p. 1996. pap. text 56.95 (*0-7506-2894-4*) Buttrwrth-Heinemann.

Lai, Ming-Chiu, jt. ed. see Cheung, Frederick H.

Lai, Ralph W. The Overlooked Law of Nature: A New Concept in Kinetics Analysis. (Illus.). 210p. (C). 1991. 45.00 (*0-9628526-1-9*) Toshi Co.

Lai, Ralph W. & Lai, Melisa W. Theory on the Relationship of Two Associated Variables: A New Mathematical Concept for Description of Two Related Variables. (C). 1997. 49.95 (*0-9628526-4-3*) Toshi Co.

Lai, Ralph W., et al. Modern Proportionality Law for Science, Medicine, & Engineering Applications: A Graphical Description of the Law of Nature. (Illus.). 368p. (C). 1995. text 85.00 (*0-9628526-2-7*) Toshi Co.

Lai, Richard & Jirachiefpattana, Ajin. Communication Protocol Specification & Verification. LC 98-39003. (International Series in Engineering & Computer Science). 304p. 1998. 139.95 (*0-7923-8284-6*) Kluwer Academic.

Lai, Robert S. & Waite Group Staff. Writing MS-DOS Device Drivers. (Illus.). 400p. 1987. pap. 24.95 (*0-201-13185-4*) Addison-Wesley.

— Writing MS-DOS Device Drivers. 2nd ed. 576p. (C). 1992. pap. text 29.95 (*0-201-60837-5*) Addison-Wesley.

Lai, S. T. Gas Chromatography - Mass Spectrometry Operation. LC 88-90572. (Illus.). 153p. (Orig.). (C). 1988. pap. text 55.00 (*0-945846-00-2*, R541) Realistic Syst.

*__Lai, Stanley.__ The Copyright Protection of Computer Software in the United Kingdom. 320p. 1999. 72.00 (*1-84113-087-7*, Pub. by Hart Pub) Intl Spec Bk.

Lai, T. C. Ch'i Pai-shih. LC 73-76338. (Illus.). 208p. 1973. 20.00 (*0-295-95315-2*) U of Wash Pr.

Lai, T. L. & Siegmund, D., eds. Herbert Robbins: Selected Papers. (Illus.). 560p. 1985. 99.95 (*0 387 96137 2*) Spr-Verlag.

Lai Tse-Han, et al. A Tragic Beginning: The Taiwan Uprising of February 28, 1947. LC 90-39218. (Illus.). 288p. 1991. 39.50 (*0-8047-1829-6*) Stanford U Pr.

Lai, W. Michael, et al. An Introduction to Continuum Mechanics. LC 72-10904. (C). 1978. text 105.00 (*0-08-022698-1*, Pergamon Pr) Elsevier.

Lai, W. Michael, jt. auth. see Lin, S. P.

Lai, Wai S., et al, eds. Broadband Access Systems, Vol. 2917. 512p. 1996. 85.00 (*0-8194-2319-X*) SPIE.

Lai, Wai S. & Cooper, Robert B., eds. Performance & Control of Network Systems II, Vol. 3530. LC 99-159854. 1998. 80.00 (*0-8194-2991-0*) SPIE.

Lai, Wai Sum, et al. Performance & Control of Network Systems: 3-5 November 1997, Dallas, Texas. LC 98-122055. (Proceedings Ser.). xi, 596p. 1997. 99.00 (*0-8194-2664-4*) SPIE.

Lai, Walton L. Indentured Labor, Caribbean Sugar: Chinese & Indian Migrants to the British West Indies, 1838-1918. LC 92-33812. (Studies in Atlantic History & Culture). (Illus.). 384p. (C). 1993. text 45.00 (*0-8018-4465-7*) Johns Hopkins.

Lai, Y. Yang, tr. see Shen, Terry C.

Lai Yen-Jen, ed. see Huang Su Huei.

Lai, Young-Jou & Hwang, Ching-Lai. Fuzzy Mathematical Programming: Methods & Applications. LC 92-27311. (Lecture Notes in Economics & Mathematical Systems Ser.: Vol. 394). 1995. 71.00 (*0-387-56098-X*) Spr-Verlag.

Laib, Nevin K. Rhetoric & Style: Strategies for Advanced Writers. LC 92-22827. 408p. (C). 1993. pap. text 20.40 (*0-13-478967-9*) P-H.

Laib, Wolfgang. Wolfgang Laib: A Journey. 1997. pap. text 14.95 (*3-89322-315-0*, Pub. by Edition Cantz) Dist Art Pubs.

Laibman, David. Value, Technical Change & Crisis: Explorations in Marxist Economic Theory. LC 91-11246. 400p. (C). (gr. 13). 1992. text 88.95 (*0-87332-735-7*) M E Sharpe.

Laibman, David. Value, Technical Change & Crisis: Explorations in Marxist Economic Theory. LC 91-11246. 400p. (C). (gr. 13). 1992. pap. text 40.95 (*0-87332-736-5*) M E Sharpe.

Laibman, David, et al. Soviet Union Socialist or Social-Imperialist: Essays Toward the Debate on the Nature of Soviet Society. LC 83-559. 210p. (Orig.). 1983. pap. 6.95 (*0-89851-062-7*) RCP Pubns.

Laichen, Sun. Chinese Historical Sources on Burma: A Bibliography of Primary & Secondary Works. (Journal of Burma Studies: Vol. 2). 116p. 1997. pap. 16.00 (*1-877979-36-8*) SE Asia.

Laichena, S. F., tr. see Luck, Erich & Jager, Martin.

Laider, Keith J., jt. auth. see Meiser.

Laidi, Zaki. The Superpowers & Africa: The Constraints of a Rivalry, 1960-1990. Baudoin, Patricia, tr. LC 90-10832. (Illus.). 256p. 1990. lib. bdg. 54.00 (*0-226-46781-3*) U Ch Pr.

— The Superpowers & Africa: The Constraints of a Rivalry, 1960-1990. Baudoin, Patricia, tr. LC 90-10832. (Illus.). 268p. 1996. pap. text 17.95 (*0-226-46782-1*) U Ch Pr.

— A World Without Meaning: The Crisis of Meaning in International Politics. Burnham, June & Coulon, Jenny, trs. LC 98-2515. 240p. (C). 1998. 90.00 (*0-415-16717-5*) Routledge.

— A World Without Meaning: The Crisis of Meaning in International Politics. Burnham, June & Coulon, Jenny, trs. LC 98-2515. 224p. (C). 1998. pap. 25.99 (*0-415-16718-3*) Routledge.

Laidi, Zaki, ed. Power & Purpose after the Cold War. McPhail, Helen, tr. (World Time Ser.). 256p. 1995. 47.50 (*0-85496-807-5*); pap. 19.50 (*1-85973-077-9*) Berg Pubs.

Laidi, Zaki, ed. see De Senarclens, Pierre.

Laidig, Jean, ed. see Werkley, Vicki.

Laidig, Wyn D., jt. ed. see Burquest, Donald A.

Laidlar, John, compiled by. Lisbon. LC 98-109802. (World Bibliographical Ser.: Vol. 199). 304p. 1997. lib. bdg. 54.00 (*1-85109-268-4*) ABC-CLIO.

Laidlaw, Andrew & Roberts, G. Law Relating to Banking Services. 389p. 1990. pap. 125.00 (*0-85297-320-9*, Pub. by Chartered Bank) St Mut.

Laidlaw, Christine W., ed. see Longfellow, Charles A.

Laidlaw, Frances J. Acceleration of Technology Development by the Advanced Technology Program: The Experience of 28 Projects Funded in 1991. (Illus.). 60p. (C). 1998. pap. text 20.00 (*0-7881-7233-6*) DIANE Pub.

Laidlaw, Harry H. Contemporary Queen Rearing. LC 79-50568. (Illus.). 199p. (C). 1997. reprint ed. pap. 8.95 (*0-915698-05-6*) Dadant & Sons.

— Instrumental Insemination of Honey Bee Queens: Pictorial Instructional Manual. (Illus.). (C). 1977. 12.95 (*0-915698-03-X*) Dadant & Sons.

Laidlaw, Harry H., Jr. & Page, Robert E., Jr. Queen Rearing & Bee Breeding. LC 96-27881. (Illus.). 216p. 1996. text 25.00 (*1-878075-08-X*) Wicwas Pr.

Laidlaw, James, ed. see Leach, Edmund.

Laidlaw, James A. Riches & Renunciation: Religion, Economy, & Society among the Jains. (Oxford Studies in Social & Cultural Anthropology). (Illus.). 448p. 1996. text 89.00 (*0-19-828031-9*); pap. text 29.95 (*0-19-828042-4*) OUP.

Laidlaw, James A., jt. auth. see Humphrey, Caroline.

Laidlaw-Johnson, Elizabeth A. Plato's Epistemology: How Hard It Is to Know. (American University Studies V: Vol. 173). X, 137p. (C). 1997. text 33.95 (*0-8204-2721-7*) P Lang Pubng.

Laidlaw, L. & Roberts, Graham. Law Relating to Banking Services. (C). 1989. 190.00 (*0-85297-277-6*, Pub. by Chartered Bank) St Mut.

Laidlaw, Marc. Gadget: The Third Force. 256p. 1996. per. 11.00 (*0-684-82245-8*) S&S Trade.

*__Laidlaw, Mark.__ The 37th Mandala. 368p. 1999. mass mkt. 4.99 (*0-8439-4658-X*, Leisure Bks) Dorchester Pub Co.

Laidlaw, P. Richard. The Godly Women: Based on Titus 2:3-5. 84p. 2000. per. 15.95 (*1-884816-05-3*) M M Moe.

Laidlaw, Renton, ed. The Royal & Ancient Golfer's Handbook, 1999. (Illus.). 992p. 1999. 87.50 (*0-333-72571-9*); pap. 37.50 (*0-333-72572-7*) Trans-Atl Phila.

Laidlaw, Robert A. La Razon por Que. (Serie Realidades - Realities Ser.).Tr. of Reason Why. (SPA.). 36p. 1989. pap. 1.99 (*1-56063-004-3*, 498100) Editorial Unilit.

— The Reason Why. (Christian Classics Ser.). 1995. pap. 2.99 (*1-56570-011-2*) Meridian MI.

— Reason Why. 1996. pap. text 14.95 (*1-56570-060-0*) Meridian MI.

— The Reason Why. LC 93-70313. 60p. 1994. reprint ed. pap. text 1.50 (*0-88270-649-7*) Bridge-Logos.

Laidlaw, Toni A. Vitamins & Cancer Prevention Contemporary Issues in Clinical Nutrition, Vol. 14. LC 90-44657. (Contemporary Issues in Clinical Nutrition Ser.: Vol. 14). 145p. 1991. 155.00 (*0-471-56066-9*) Wiley.

Laidler. Understanding Annual Reports & Accounts. LC 98-204162. 1998. pap. 18.99 (*1-86152-109-X*) Thomson Learn.

Laidler, David. Fabricating the Keynesian Revolution: Studies of the Inter-War Literature on Money, the Cycle, & Unemployment. LC 98-38614. (Historical Perspectives on Modern Economics Ser.). (Illus.). 392p. (C). 1999. text 74.95 (*0-521-64173-X*); pap. text 27.95 (*0-521-64596-4*) Cambridge U Pr.

Laidler, David, ed. The Foundations of Monetary Economics, 3 vols. LC 99-45643. (Mini Ser.). 1768p. 2000. 615.00 (*1-85898-997-3*) E Elgar.

Laidler, David E. The Demand for Money: Theories, Evidence & Problems. 4th ed. LC 92-11945. 210p. (C). 1997. pap. 55.00 (*0-06-501098-1*) Addson-Wesley Educ.

Laidler, David E. Essays on Money & Inflation. LC 75-22170. xiv, 246p. 1994. pap. text 6.95 (*0-226-46792-9*, P817) U Ch Pr.

— Essays on Money & Inflation. (Studies in Inorganic Chemistry: No. 3). 272p. 1993. reprint ed. text 56.95 (*0-7512-0198-7*, Pub. by Gregg Revivals) Ashgate Pub Co.

— Monetarist Perspectives. 232p. 1983. 37.95 (*0-674-58240-3*) HUP.

— Money & Macroeconomics: The Selected Essays of David Laidler. LC 97-14360. (Economists of the Twentieth Century Ser.). 424p. (C). 1997. 100.00 (*1-85898-596-X*) E Elgar.

— Taking Money Seriously. 200p. 1990. 32.95 (*0-262-12148-4*) MIT Pr.

Laidler, David E., jt. ed. see Purdy, D. L.

Laidler, Harry W. Social-Economic Movements: An Historical & Comparative Survey of Socialism. (Essay Index Reprint Ser.). 1977. reprint ed. 48.95 (*0-518-10149-5*) Ayer.

Laidler, John & Donaghy, Peter. The Coopers & Lybrand Multilingual Dictionary of Financial Reporting Terms: 3000 Financial Reporting Terms in English, French, German, Italian & Spanish. 400p. 2000. mass mkt. 105.95 (*0-412-59850-7*) Chapman & Hall.

Laidler, John, jt. auth. see Donaghy, Peter.

Laidler, Keith, jt. auth. see Laidler, Liz.

Laidler, Keith J. Physical Chemistry. (C). 1995. text 81.16 (*0-395-64153-5*) HM.

— Physical Chemistry. (C). 1995. pap., student ed. 25.96 (*0-395-72410-4*) HM.

— Reaction Kinetics, 2 vols., 1. LC 62-22037. 1963. pap. 100.00 (*0-08-009833-9*, Pub. by Pergamon Repr) Franklin.

— To Light a Candle: Chapters in the History of Science & Technology. (Illus.). 396p. 1998. 55.00 (*0-19-850056-4*) OUP.

— The World of Physical Chemistry. (Illus.). 488p. 1995. pap. text 65.00 (*0-19-855919-4*) OUP.

Laidler, Keith J. & Keith, J. Chemical Kinetics. 3rd ed. 490p. (C). 1997. 129.00 (*0-06-043862-2*) Addson-Wesley Educ.

Laidler, Keith J. & Meiser, John H. Physical Chemistry. 3rd ed. LC 98-72056. xvii, 1019p. 1999. text 69.87 (*0-395-91848-0*) HM.

Laidler, Keith J., jt. auth. see Meiser.

Laidler, Liz. China's Threatened Wildlife. 1999. pap. text 17.95 (*0-7137-2705-5*) Blandford Pr.

Laidler, Liz & Laidler, Keith. China's Threatened Wildlife. (Illus.). 192p. 1996. 29.95 (*0-7137-2372-6*, Pub. by Blandford Pr) Sterling.

Laidler, P. Stroke Rehabilitation: Structure & Strategy. 336p. 1994. 49.95 (*1-56593-208-0*, 0522) Thomson Learn.

Laidler, Terry, jt. auth. see Naughtin, Gerry.

Laidley, W. S. History of Charleston & Kanawha County, & Representative Citizens. (Illus.). 1021p. 1997. reprint ed. lib. bdg. 99.00 (*0-8328-6943-0*) Higginson Bk Co.

Laidlow, Philip. Tolley's Tax Planning for Post Death Variations. 150p. 1993. 90.00 (*0-85459-684-4*, Pub. by Tolley Pubng) St Mut.

Laidman, Hugh. Animals: How to Draw Them. LC 75-11930. (Illus.). 160p. (YA). (gr. 7 up). 1979. pap. 12.95 (*0-685-46950-6*, Dutt) Dutton Plume.

Laie. Practical ESD Control for Small & Medium Companies. (Electrical Engineering Ser.). 1991. write for info. (*0-442-23815-0*, VNR) Wiley.

Laifer, Miryam. Edmond Jabes: Un Judaisme Apres Dieu. (American University Studies: Romance Languages & Literature: Ser. II, Vol. 39). XI, 151p. 1986. pap. 33.70 (*0-8204-0283-4*) P Lang Pubng.

Laignel-Lavastine, Maxime. French Medicine. LC 75-23666. (Clio Medica Ser.: 15). (Illus.). reprint ed. 37.50 (*0-404-58915-4*) AMS Pr.

Laik, Judy. Under Whose Influence? LC 93-86233. (Decision Is Yours Ser.). (Illus.). 64p. (J). (gr. 3-7). 1994. pap. 5.95 (*0-943990-97-1*); lib. bdg. 16.95 (*0-943990-98-X*) Parenting Pr.

Laik, Judy, jt. auth. see Moen, Lynn.

Laik, Madeleine. Deck Chairs. Schein, Gideon Y., tr. from FRE. 106p. (Orig.). 1984. pap. text 8.95 (*0-913745-05-7*) Ubu Repertory.

Laikari, H., ed. River Basin Management V: Proceedings of the Conference Held in Rovaniemi, Finland, 31 July-4 August 1989. (Advances in Water Pollution Control Ser.: Vol. 9). (Illus.). 438p. 1989. 126.00 (*0-08-037379-8*, Pergamon Pr) Elsevier.

Laiken, Deidre S. Death among Strangers. 256p. 1988. pap. 3.95 (*0-380-70521-4*, Avon Bks) Morrow Avon.

— Killing Time in Buffalo. 1990. 18.95 (*0-316-51223-0*) Little.

Laiken, Nora, ed. Interpretation of Electrocardiograms: A Self-Instructional Approach. 2nd ed. (Illus.). 264p. 1988. spiral bd. 37.00 (*0-88167-388-9*) Lppncott W & W.

Laikin, Milton. Frank: A Novel. 112p. 1998. pap. 13.95 (*1-887750-97-5*) Rutledge Bks.

— Lens Design. 2nd expanded rev. ed. LC 94-44816. (Optical Engineering Ser.: Vol. 48). (Illus.). 464p. 1995. text 135.00 (*0-8247-9602-0*) Dekker.

Laikko, Paul, jt. auth. see Flegle, Janice.

Lail Hopkins, Margaret & Hopkins Phillips, Nancy. The Anglican Parishes of Loudoun County Virginia: Truro, Cameron & Shelburne, 1736-1805. (Illus.). 136p. 1997. pap. 14.00 (*1-888265-24-8*) Willow Bend.

Lailhacar, Christine De, see De Lailhacar, Christine.

Laili, Anthony F. Tailored Urologic Imaging. LC 80-16566. (Illus.). 335p. reprint ed. pap. 103.90 (*0-608-17811-X*, 203229800079) Bks Demand.

Laim, Sheryl. A Poem for Every Student: Creating Community in a Public School Classroom. (Illus.). 116p. 1998. pap. 11.00 (*1-883920-13-2*) Nat Writing Proj.

L

L

Laiman, Leah. Bride & Groom: Another Summer of Love. 1995. mass mkt. 5.99 (0-671-53406-8, PB Trade Paper) PB.
— The Bridesmaid: Another Summer of Love. 1995. mass mkt. 5.99 (0-671-53405-X, Pocket Books) PB.
— For Better, for Worse. Marrow, Linda, ed. 304p. (Orig.). 1994. mass mkt. 5.50 (0-671-86483-1) PB.
— For Richer, for Poorer. Marrow, Linda, ed. 320p. (Orig.). 1994. mass mkt. 5.50 (0-671-86482-3) PB.
— To Love & to Cherish. 1994. mass mkt. 5.50 (0-671-86484-X) PB.
***Laimo, Michael.** Demons, Freaks & Other Abnormalities. limited ed. (Illus.). 1999. lib. bdg. 25.00 (1-929653-01-8, DB-002) Delirium Bks.
Lain. Advertising Survival Kit. 64p. 1992. 2.00 (0-318-60010-2) Quill & Scroll.
Lain, Barb, jt. auth. see Lain, Larry.
Lain Entralgo, Pedro. Tan Solo Hombres. (Nueva Austral Ser.: Vol. 250). (SPA.). 1991. pap. text 24.95 (84-239-7250-X) Elliots Bks.
Lain, J. Brooklyn City Directory, 1859. 1972. 59.95 (0-87968-796-7) Gordon Pr.
***Lain, Larry.** London for Families. 2nd ed. (Illus.). 2000. pap. 14.95 (1-56656-337-2) Interlink Pub.
— Paris for Families. 2000. pap. 15.00 (1-56656-360-7) Interlink Pub.
Lain, Larry & Griffin, Jeff. The Students Guide to London. LC 98-28147. (Illus.). 296p. 1998. pap. 17.95 (0-939923-80-7) M & W Pub Co.
Lain, Larry & Lain, Barb. London for Lovers. LC 99-41374. 272p. 2000. pap. 15.00 (1-56656-345-3) Interlink Pub.
Laine. Frommer's Comprehensive Travel Guide Colorado. 3rd ed. 1996. per. 15.95 (0-671-51940-9) S&S Trade.
Laine, Andrew F., et al, eds. Wavelet Applications in Signal & Imaging Processing VI, Vol. 3458. LC 99-192667. 1998. 69.00 (0-8194-2913-9) SPIE.
Laine, Andrew, ed. Wavelet Theory & Application. LC 93-10594. 140p. (C). 1993. text 141.50 (0-7923-9357-0) Kluwer Academic.
Laine, Andrew, et al. Wavelet Applications in Signal & Image Processing Iii: 12-14 July, 1995, San Diego, California. LC 99-170368. (Proceedings / the International Society for Optical Engineering). 1995. write for info. (0-8194-1928-1) SPIE.
Laine, Barbara. Frommer's America on Wheels: Southwest 1997. (Illus.). 1996. 14.95 (0-02-861112-8, P-H Travel) Prntice Hall Bks.
Laine, Barbara, jt. auth. see Laine, Don.
***Laine Carol Publishing Staff.** Best of Cleveland & Northeast Ohio. (Illus.). 2000. pap. 14.95 (0-9678255-0-4) L Carol Pubng.
Laine, Claude, ed. Combinatory Vocabulary of CAD-CAM in Mechanical Engineering. (FRE & ENG.). 145p. (Orig.). 1993. pap. 15.95 (0-660-58029-2, Pub. by Canadian Govt Pub) Accents Pubns.
Laine, Cleo. Cleo. LC 97-16367. 1997. 24.50 (0-684-83762-5) S&S Trade.
***Laine, Cleo.** Cleo. (Illus.). 352p. 2000. reprint ed. text 25.00 (0-7881-6977-7) DIANE Pub.
***Laine, Daniel.** African Kings: Portraits of a Disappearing Era. (Illus.). 160p. 2000. 40.00 (1-58008-224-6) Ten Speed Pr.
Laine, Don. Frommer's Denver, Boulder & Colorado Springs. 4th ed. 1996. 13.95 (0-02-860921-2, P-H Travel) Prntice Hall Bks.
Laine, Don & Laine, Barbara. Frommer's Colorado: With Denver & the Best of Rocky Mountain National Park. 5th ed. 420p. 1999. pap. 15.95 (0-02-862611-7, Pub. by Macmillan) S&S Trade.
***Laine, Don & Laine, Barbara.** Frommer's Rocky Mountain National Park. (Illus.). 170p. 1999. pap. 9.95 (0-02-863085-8, Frommer) Macmillan Gen Ref.
Laine, Don & Laine, Barbara. New Mexico & Arizona State Parks: A Complete Recreation Guide. LC 97-43393. (State Parks Ser.). (Illus.). 250p. 1998. pap. 16.95 (0-89886-559-X) Mountaineers.
Laine, Ecro J. Learning a Second National Language: A Research Report. LC 95-30855. (Scandinavian University Studies in the Humanities & Social Sciences: Vol. 8). 169p. 1995. 42.95 (3-631-48813-0) P Lang Pubng.
Laine, Gary J., jt. auth. see Penny, Morris M.
Laine, I., et al, eds. Complex Analysis. (Lecture Notes in Mathematics Ser.: Vol. 1351). 415p. 1988. 52.95 (0-387-50370-6) Spr-Verlag.
Laine, Ilpo. Nevalinna Theory & Complex Differential Equations. LC 92-35852. (Studies in Mathematics: Vol. 15). viii, 341p. (C). 1992. lib. bdg. 92.95 (3-11-013422-5) De Gruyter.
Laine, Ilpo, et al, eds. XVIth Rolf Nevanlinna Colloquium: Proceedings of the International Conference Held in Joensuu, Finland, August 1-5, 1995. LC 96-28630. ix, 353p. (C). 1996. lib. bdg. 158.95 (3-11-014746-7) De Gruyter.
Laine, J. Gary, jt. auth. see Penny, Morris M.
Laine, Loren. Endoscopic Interpretation. 2nd ed. LC 97-16692. 600p. 1998. text 185.00 (0-7817-0290-9) Lppncott W & W.
Laine, Michael, ed. A Cultivated Mind: Essays on J. S. Mill Presented to John M. Robson. 192p. 1991. text 60.00 (0-8020-5915-5) U of Toronto Pr.
Laine, Michael, ed. see Robson, John M.
Laine, Michael D., jt. auth. see Chidsey, Thomas C., Jr.
Laine, Pascal. Dentelliere. (Folio Ser.: No. 726). (FRE.). (Orig.). pap. 8.95 (2-07-036726-6) Schoenhof.
— Jeanne du Bon Plaisir Ou les Hasards de la Fidelite. (Folio Ser.: No. 1730). (FRE.). 1986. pap. 8.95 (2-07-037730-X) Schoenhof.
— Monsieur Vous Oubliez Votre Cadavre. (Folio Ser.: No. 2186). (FRE.). 1970. pap. 9.95 (2-07-038276-1) Schoenhof.
— Petites Egarees. (Folio Ser.: No. 2170). (FRE.). pap. 14.95 (2-07-038259-1) Schoenhof.
— Plutot Deux Fois Qu'une. (Folio Ser.: No. 2063). (FRE.). pap. 9.95 (2-07-038150-1) Schoenhof.
— Trois Petits Meurtres . . . et Puis S'en Va. (Folio Ser.: No. 2026). (FRE.). 281p. 1985. pap. 9.95 (2-07-038114-5) Schoenhof.
Laine, R. M., et al, eds. Organic - Inorganic Hybrid Materials Vol. 519: Proceedings Materials Research Society Symposium. 415p. 1998. text 81.00 (1-55899-425-4) Materials Res.
***Laine, R. M., et al, eds.** Organic/Inorganic Hybrid Materials -- 2000: Materials Research Society Symposium Proceedings, Vol. 628. 2000. text 82.00 (1-55899-536-6) Materials Res.
Laine, Richard M., ed. Inorganic & Organometallic Polymers with Special Properties: Proceedings of the NATO Advanced Research Workshop, Cap d'Agde, France, September 9-14, 1990. (C). 1991. text 234.00 (0-7923-1514-6) Kluwer Academic.
— Transformation of Organometallics into Common & Exotic Materials: Design & Activation. (C). 1988. text 191.00 (90-247-3661-7) Kluwer Academic.
Laine, Richard M., jt. ed. see Harrod, John F.
Laine, Tom, ed. see Brass, Perry.
Lainer, Rhudiger, jt. auth. see Zschokke, Walter.
Laing. Medieval Britain: The Age of Chivalry. (Illus.). 224p. 1998. pap. 16.95 (0-312-21793-5) St Martin.
Laing, Adrian C. R. D. Laing: A Biography. LC 95-118981. 248p. 1995. 50.00 (0-7206-0934-8, Pub. by P Owen Ltd) Dufour.
Laing, Alastair. In Trust for the Nation: Paintings from National Trust Houses. (Illus.). 256p. 1996. 55.00 (0-7078-0260-1, Pub. by Merrell Holberton) U of Wash Pr.
Laing, Alastair, ed. see Braham, Allan & Hager, Hellmut.
Laing, Alastair, ed. see Branner, Robert.
Laing, Alastair, ed. see Downes, Kerry.
Laing, Alastair, ed. see Garstang, Donald.
Laing, Alastair, ed. see Herrmann, Wolfgang.
Laing, Alastair, ed. see Leach, Peter.
Laing, Alastair, ed. see Stillman, Damie.
Laing, Alastair, ed. see Tadgell, Christopher.
Laing, Alastair, ed. see Watkin, David.
Laing, Alexander, ed. Haunted Omnibus. LC 96-76466. (Illus.). 848p. 1996. reprint ed. 14.98 (1-56731-119-9, MJF Bks) Fine Comms.
Laing, Alison. Speaking As a Woman. 40p. 1989. pap. 10.00 (1-880715-03-1) Creat Des Srvs.
Laing Communications Staff. Pioneers. 1999. 16.99 (0-525-67504-3) NAL.
Laing, D. G., et al, eds. The Human Sense of Smell. (Illus.). 395p. 1991. 174.95 (0-387-53355-9) Spr-Verlag.
Laing, David, ed. Collection of Ancient Scottish Prophecies in Alliterative Verse. LC 70-144433. (Bannatyne Club, Edinburgh. Publications: No. 44). reprint ed. 37.50 (0-404-52754-X) AMS Pr.
— Original Letters Relating to the Ecclesiastical Affairs of Scotland, 2 vols. LC 73-171637. (Bannatyne Club, Edinburgh. Publications: No. 92). reprint ed. 95.00 (0-404-52833-3) AMS Pr.
— Registrum Cartarum Ecclesie Sancti Egidii de Edinburgh. LC 76-174803. (Bannatyne Club, Edinburgh. Publications: No. 105). reprint ed. 47.50 (0-404-52860-0) AMS Pr.
— Registrum Domus de Soltre. LC 77-171638. (Bannatyne Club, Edinburgh. Publications: No. 109). reprint ed. 42.50 (0-404-52863-5) AMS Pr.
— Royal Letters, Charters, & Tracts. LC 70-171639. (Bannatyne Club, Edinburgh. Publications: No. 114). reprint ed. 42.50 (0-404-52869-4) AMS Pr.
Laing, David, ed. see Baillie, Robert.
Laing, David, ed. see Bannatyne Club Staff.
Laing, David, ed. see Barbour, John.
Laing, David, ed. see Clerk, John.
Laing, David, ed. see Colville, John.
Laing, David, ed. see Ferguson, David.
Laing, David, ed. see Knox, John.
Laing, David, ed. see Rolland, John.
Laing, David L. Dance of the Dance. (Illus.). 150p. (Orig.). 1998. pap. 14.95 (0-9646264-1-1) Elohim Art & Bks.
— Willing Evolution. (Illus.). 50p. (Orig.). 1995. pap. write for info. (0-9646264-0-3) Elohim Art & Bks.
Laing, Elizabeth. Glory Days: Real-Life Answers for Teens. 135p. 1999. pap. 9.99 (1-57782-060-6) Discipleshp.
Laing, Ellen J. Chinese Paintings in Chinese Publications, 1956-1968: An Annotated Bibliography & an Index to the Paintings. LC 77-151498. (Michigan Monographs in Chinese Studies: No. 6). (Illus.). 320p. 1969. text 50.00 (0-89264-124-X) Ctr Chinese Studies.
— An Index to Reproductions of Paintings by Twentieth-Century Chinese Artists. LC 98-2855. (Michigan Monographs in Chinese Studies: Vol. 76). 1998. 75.00 (0-89264-126-6) Ctr Chinese Studies.
Laing, Evelyn, jt. auth. see McCulloch, William.
Laing, G. S. Accident & Emergency Medicine. 225p. 1988. 32.95 (0-387-19508-4) Spr-Verlag.
Laing, Geri, jt. auth. see Laing, Sam.
Laing, Gordon J., tr. see Gentili, Alberico.
Laing, Henry. Descriptive Catalogue of Impressions from Ancient Scottish Seals. LC 75-171640. (Maitland Club, Glasgow. Publications: No. 68). reprint ed. 47.50 (0-404-53081-8) AMS Pr.
Laing, Ian A. & McIntosh, Neil. Paediatric History & Examination. (Illus.). 95p. 1994. text 15.95 (0-7020-1809-0, Pub. by W B Saunders) Saunders.
Laing, Jennifer. Art & Society in Roman Britain. 224p. 1999. pap. text 19.95 (0-7509-2149-8) A Sutton.
— Art & Society in Roman Britain. (Illus.). 224p. 1998. 35.95 (0-7509-0895-5, Pub. by Sutton Pub Ltd) Intl Pubs Mktg.
— The Art of Making Teddy Bears. (Illus.). 76p. 1993. pap. 12.95 (1-86351-099-0, Pub. by Sally Milner) Sterling.
— Teddy Bear Art: How to Design & Make Great Teddy Bears. LC 98-190356. (Illus.). 96p. 1998. pap. 17.95 (0-87588-517-9, H5460) Hobby Hse.
Laing, Jennifer & Laing, Lloyd Robert. Celtic Britain & Ireland, A. D. 200-800. 240p. 1990. 14.95 (0-7165-2415-5, I2415, Pub. by Irish Acad Pr) Intl Spec Bk.
Laing, Jennifer, jt. auth. see Laing, Lloyd.
Laing, Jennifer, jt. auth. see Laing, Lloyd Robert.
Laing, John. One Cool Cat. (Methuen Young Drama Ser.). 43p. (J). (gr. 1). 1988. pap. 5.95 (0-413-54220-3, A0197) Heinemann.
Laing, John, jt. auth. see Halkett, Samuel.
Laing, Judith M. Care or Custody? Mentally Disordered Offenders in the Criminal Justice System. LC 99-16147. 384p. 2000. text 74.00 (0-19-826818-1) OUP.
Laing, Kojo. Godhorse. (African Writers Ser.). (Illus.). 57p. (Orig.). (C). 1989. pap. 8.95 (0-435-90552-X, 90552) Heinemann.
— Major Gentl & the Achimoto Wars. (African Writers Ser.). 185p. (C). 1992. pap. 8.95 (0-435-90978-9, 90978) Heinemann.
Laing, Lesley, jt. auth. see Breckenridge, Jan.
Laing, Linda & Freeman, Jack. Guide to Adirondack Trails: Southern Region. 2nd rev. ed. Burdick, Neal S., ed. LC 93-28567. (Forest Preserve Ser.: Vol. VII). (Illus.). 256p. 1998. reprint ed. pap. 16.95 (0-935272-65-8) ADK Mtn Club.
***Laing, Lloyd & Laing, Jennifer.** Warriors of the Dark Ages. (Illus.). 224p. 2000. 29.95 (0-7509-1920-5) Sutton Publng.
Laing, Lloyd Robert. Britain's European Heritage. LC 95-194380. (Themes in History Ser.). 1997. 30.95 (0-7509-0463-1, Pub. by Sutton Pub Ltd) Intl Pubs Mktg.
***Laing, Lloyd Robert.** Later Celtic Art in Britain & Ireland. LC 88-115996. (Archaeology Ser.: No. 48). (Illus.). 56p. 1999. pap. 10.50 (0-85263-874-4, Pub. by Shire Pubns) Parkwest Pubns.
Laing, Lloyd Robert. Picts & the Scots. 1997. pap. text 19.95 (0-7509-0677-4, Pub. by Sutton Pub Ltd) Intl Pubs Mktg.
Laing, Lloyd Robert & Laing, Jennifer. Ancient Art: The Challenge to Modern Thought. (Illus.). 256p. (C). 1993. 14.95 (0-7165-2473-2, Pub. by Irish Acad Pr) Intl Spec Bk.
— Art of the Celts: From 700 B. C. to the Celtic Revival. LC 91-66018. (World of Art Ser.). (Illus.). 216p. 1992. pap. 14.95 (0-500-20256-7, Pub. by Thames Hudson) Norton.
— Celtic Britain & Ireland: Art & Society. LC 95-16925. (Illus.). 224p. 1995. text 45.00 (0-312-12613-1) St Martin.
— Early English Art & Architecture. LC 96-35991. (Illus.). 240p. 1996. 44.95 (0-7509-0462-3, Pub. by Sutton Pub Ltd) Intl Pubs Mktg.
— A Guide to the Dark Age Remains in Britain LC 79-311108. 318 p. 1979. write for info. (0-09-462230-2) Constable & Co.
— The Picts & the Scots. (Illus.). 172p. 1999. reprint ed. text 30.00 (0-7881-6124-5) DIANE Pub.
Laing, Lloyd Robert, jt. auth. see Laing, Jennifer.
Laing, M. E. Metropolitan Museum Journal, Vol. 19-20, 1984-1985. LC 68-28799. 268p. 1986. 75.00 (0-226-52117-6) U Ch Pr.
Laing, M. E., ed. see Balken, Deborah, et al.
Laing, Malcolm, jt. auth. see Ryle, E. Brown.
Laing, Margaret. Catalogue of Sources for a Linguistic Atlas of Early Medieval English. LC 93-18969. 196p. 1993. 75.00 (0-85991-384-8, DS Brewer) Boydell & Brewer.
— Edward Heath: Prime Minister. LC 72-95089. 258p. 1973. 30.00 (0-89388-086-8) Okpaku Communications.
— Middle English Dialectology: Essays on Some Principles & Problems. 272p. 1989. text 50.00 (0-08-036404-7, Pub. by Aberdeen U Pr) Macmillan.
Laing, Margaret & Williamson, Keith, eds. Speaking in Our Tongues: Proceedings of a Colloquium on Medieval Dialectology & Related Disciplines. LC 93-38900. (Illus.). 243p. (C). 1994. 75.00 (0-85991-403-8, DS Brewer) Boydell & Brewer.
Laing, R. D. Divided Self. 1965. pap. 12.95 (0-14-013537-5, Viking) Viking Penguin.
***Laing, R. D.** The Divided Self: An Existential Study in Sanity & Madness. LC 99-220349. 1999. write for info. (0-415-19818-6) Routledge.
— Eros, Love & Lies. unabridged ed. (C). 1995. 10.95 incl. audio (1-56176-912-6, MYS-76912) Mystic Fire.
Laing, R. D. Interpersonal Perception: A Theory & a Method of Research. LC 99-165283. (R. D. Laing, Selected Works). 179p. 1998. 75.00 (0-415-19823-2) Routledge.
— Knots. 96p. 1972. pap. 10.00 (0-394-71776-7) Vin Bks.
***Laing, R. D.** Knots. LC 99-220342. (Illus.). 1999. write for info. (0-415-19824-0) Routledge.
Laing, R. D. The Politics of Experience. 1983. pap. 10.00 (0-394-71475-X) Pantheon.
***Laing, R. D.** The Politics of the Family & Other Essays LC 99-194016. 133p. 1999. write for info. (0-415-19822-4) Routledge.
Laing, R. D. Selected Works of R. D. Laing, 7 vols., Vols. 1-7. 1324p. (C). 1998. reprint ed. 655.00 (0-415-19825-9, D6393) Routledge.
— Wisdom, Madness & Folly. 1999. pap. 11.95 (0-86241-831-3) Interlink Pub.
Laing, R. D., jt. auth. see Russell, Roberta.
Laing Research Services Staff. Correlating Museum & Exhibition Attendance with Book & Catalog Sales. 121p. 1996. 95.00 (0-938106-19-8) Laing Res Servs.
— Sales & Distribution Practices of Independent Presses, 1989-1990. 56p. 1990. 45.00 (0-938106-12-0) Laing Res Servs.
— Survey of Independent Presses, 1989-1990: Sorted & Analyzed by Number of Titles in Print. 70p. 1990. 95.00 (0-938106-08-2) Laing Res Servs.
— Survey of Independent Presses, 1989-1990: Sorted & Analyzed by Publisher's Annual Gross Revenue. 70p. 1990. 95.00 (0-938106-11-2) Laing Res Servs.
— Survey of University Presses, 1989-1990. 70p. 1990. 95.00 (0-938106-09-0) Laing Res Servs.
Laing, Robert A., jt. ed. see Hirsch, Christian R.
***Laing, Ronald D.** El Yo y los Ostros. rev. ed. 185p. 1999. pap. 6.99 (968-16-0146-7) Fondo CA.
Laing, Sam. Be Still, My Soul. 136p. 1998. pap. 9.99 (1-57782-056-8) Discipleshp.
***Laing, Sam.** A Mighty Man of God: A Return to the Glory of Manhood. 160p. 1999. pap. 9.99 (1-57782-118-1) Discipleshp.
Laing, Sam & Laing, Geri. Friends & Lovers. 175p. 1996. pap. 11.99 (1-884553-95-8) Discipleshp.
— Raising Awesome Kids in Troubled Times. 218p. 1994. pap. 12.99 (1-884553-23-0) Discipleshp.
— Raising Awesome Kids in Troubled Times: Criando Ninos Ejemplares. (SPA.). 218p. 1997. pap. 12.99 (1-884553-97-4) Discipleshp.
Laing, Samuel, tr. see Snorri Sturluson.
Laing, Stuart, jt. auth. see Mercer, David.
Laing, Susan, jt. auth. see Bruess, Clint E.
Laing, Susan J. Nutrition & Body Image. (Comprehensive Health for Middle Grades Ser.). (J). (gr. 6-9). 1996. 24.00 (1-56071-470-0, H572) ETR Assocs.
Lainhart, Ann S. State Census Records. 116p. 2000. reprint ed. 17.95 (0-8063-1362-5, Pub. by Clearfield Co) ACCESS Pubs Network.
Lainhart, Ann S., ed. First Boston City Directory,(1789) Including Extensive Annotations by John Haven Dexter (1791-1876) 152p. 1989. 20.00 (0-88082-020-9, S2-76750) New Eng Hist.
Lainhart, Ann S., jt. auth. see Dunkle, Robert J.
Lainhart, Ann S., jt. auth. see New England Historical & Genealogical Society Staf.
Lainiotis, Demetrios G., jt. ed. see Tzannes, Nicolaos S.
Lainiotis, Dmitri G., jt. ed. see Ray.
Laino, E. J. Girl Hurt. LC 95-34545. 72p. 1996. pap. 9.95 (1-882295-07-2) Alice James Bks.
***Laino, Jane.** The Telephony Book. 350p. 1999. pap. 34.95 (1-57820-035-0) Telecom Bks.
Laino, Jane. Telephony for Computer Professionals. 1997. write for info. (0-936648-49-X) Telecom Bks.
Lainoff. Hannah Arendt. 1998. 22.95 (0-8057-4027-9) Macmillan.
Lainsbury, Andrew. Once upon an American Dream: The Story of Euro Disneyland. LC 99-37813. (CultureAmerica Ser.). 280p. 2000. 35.00 (0-7006-0989-X) U Pr of KS.
Laiou, Angeliki E. Constantinople & the Latins: The Foreign Policy of Andronicus the 2nd, 1282-1328. LC 78-176042. (Historical Studies: No. 88). (Illus.). 400p. 1972. 27.50 (0-674-16535-7) HUP.
— Gender, Society & Economic Life in Byzantium. (Collected Studies: Vol. CS370). 336p. 1992. 113.95 (0-86078-322-7, Pub. by Variorum) Ashgate Pub Co.
— Wills from Late Medieval Venetian Crete, 1312-1420. McKee, Sally, ed. LC 97-42311. 1248p. (C). 1998. pap. 65.00 (0-88402-245-5) Dumbarton Oaks.
Laiou, Angeliki E., ed. Consent & Coercion to Sex & Marriage in Ancient & Medieval Societies. LC 93-3070. 308p. 1993. 28.00 (0-88402-213-7) Dumbarton Oaks.
— Consent & Coercion to Sex & Marriage in Ancient & Medieval Societies. (Illus.). 308p. (C). 1997. pap. 16.95 (0-88402-262-5) Dumbarton Oaks.
— Dumbarton Oaks Papers, No. 44. LC 42-6499. (Illus.). 396p. 1991. 85.00 (0-88402-189-0, DP44) Dumbarton Oaks.
— Dumbarton Oaks Papers, No. 45. LC 42-6499. (Illus.). 272p. 1992. 60.00 (0-88402-196-3, DP45) Dumbarton Oaks.
***Laiou, Angeliki E. & Mottahedeh, Roy P.** Byzantium & the Muslim World: The Crusades from the Eastern Perspective. LC 00-22785. 2000. write for info. (0-88402-277-3) Dumbarton Oaks.
Laiou, Angeliki E. & Simon, Dieter, eds. Law & Society in Byzantium: Ninth-Twelfth Centuries. LC 93-29343. (Illus.). 308p. 1994. 35.00 (0-88402-222-6) Dumbarton Oaks.
Laiou, Angeliki E., jt. auth. see May, Ernest R.
Laiou, Angeliki E., jt. ed. see Ahrweiler, Helene G.
Laiou, Angeliki E., jt. ed. see Maguire, Henry P.
Lair. Until Then . . . 1993. pap. 8.95 (1-883748-00-3) Chrstian Stewardshp.
Lair, Cynthia. Feeding the Whole Family: Whole Foods Recipes for Babies, Young Children & Their Parents. 2nd rev. ed. (Illus.). 270p. 2000. pap. 18.00 (0-9660346-1-9, Pub. by Moon Smile Pr) Chelsea Green Pub.
Lair, George S. Counseling the Terminally Ill: Sharing the Journey. LC 96-12921. (Series in Death Education, Aging, & Health Care). 207p. 1996. 49.95 (1-56032-516-X, Pub. by Tay Francis Ltd); pap. 22.95 (1-56032-517-8, Pub. by Tay Francis Ltd) Taylor & Francis.
Lair, Gerald, jt. auth. see Nawrocki, Susan.
Lair, James J., Jr. Dear Pen Pal. 144p. 1998. pap. 13.00 (0-8059-4510-5) Dorrance.
Lair, Jess. I Ain't Much Baby, but I'm All I've Got. 1985. mass mkt. 5.99 (0-449-20802-8, Crest) Fawcett.

An Asterisk (*) at the beginning of an entry indicates that the title is appearing for the first time.

Laird. The Alphabet Zoo. LC 74-190264. (Illus.). 32p. (J). (ps-2). 1972. lib. bdg. 9.95 (*0-87783-053-3*) Oddo.
— Business Telecomuncations. (C). 1991. write for info. (*0-673-46139-4*) Addison-Wesley.
— Don't Talk to Me about Giving. 1993. pap. 3.95 (*1-883748-02-X*) Chrstian Stewardshp.
— Psychology. (C). 1992. pap. 59.56 (*0-395-63342-7*) HM.
— Simon & Spy. 1990. pap. text. write for info. (*0-582-04611-4*, Pub. by Addison-Wesley) Longman.
***Laird.** The Storm: Penguin Readers Level 2. 144p. (J). 1999. pap. text 7.00 (*0-582-37456-1*) Addison-Wesley.
Laird. Welcome to Great Britain & the U. S. A. 1993. pap. text. write for info. (*0-582-08955-7*, Pub. by Addison-Wesley) Longman.
— Why Worry? 1993. pap. 9.95 (*1-883748-01-1*) Chrstian Stewardshp.
Laird, Alma. Complete George Washington Anniversary Programs for Every School Grade: New Ways to Honor the Father of Our Country. 1977. 15.95 (*0-8369-6389-X*, 7453) Ayer.
Laird, Andrew. Powers of Expression, Expressions of Power: Speech Presentation in Latin Literature. LC 98-52497. (Oxford Classical Monographs Ser.). 382p. 2000. text 85.00 (*0-19-815276-0*) OUP.
***Laird, Andrew & Kahane, Ahuvia, eds.** A Companion to the Prologue to Apuleius' Metamorphoses. 300p. 2000. text 75.00 (*0-19-815238-8*) OUP.
Laird, Archibald. The Near Great, Chronicle of the Vice-Presidents. (Illus.). 1980. 17.50 (*0-8158-0381-8*) Chris Mass.
— Profitable Company: Milestones & Monuments of the Signers of the Declaration of Independence. LC 84-71719. 1987. 19.50 (*0-8158-0425-3*) Chris Mass.
Laird, Betty A. & Laird, Roy D., eds. To Live Long Enough: The Memoirs of Naum Jasny, Scientific Analyst. LC 75-33900. x, 190p. 1976. 19.95 (*0-7006-0140-6*) U Pr of KS.
Laird, Brian A. To Bury the Dead. LC 96-34916. 176p. 1997. 20.95 (*0-312-15224-8*, Thomas Dunne) St Martin.
Laird, Brian B., et al, eds. Chemical Applications of Density-Functional Theory. LC 96-14753. (ACS Symposium Ser.: No. 629). (Illus.). 488p. 1996. text 130.00 (*0-8412-3403-5*, Pub. by Am Chemical) OUP.
Laird-Brown, May, tr. see Steiner, Rudolf.
Laird-Brown, May, tr. see Steiner, Rudolf & Sardello, Robert J.
Laird, Cameron, jt. auth. see Stone, Mark.
Laird, Carobeth. Limbo: A Memoir about Life in a Nursing Home by a Survivor. LC 79-10937. 190p. 1979. pap. 12.95 (*0-88316-536-8*) Chandler & Sharp.
— Mirror & Pattern. LC 83-62710. 1984. 25.00 (*0-939046-30-X*) Malki Mus Pr.
***Laird, Charlton.** Pocket Thesaurus. 2nd ed. 320p. 2000. pap. 4.95 (*0-7645-6148-0*) IDG Bks.
Laird, Charlton. Webster's New World Thesaurus. Shannon, Scott, ed. 512p. 1995. reprint ed. pap. 11.00 (*0-671-89450-1*, PB Trade Paper) PB.
Laird, Charlton & Webster's New World Dictionaries Editors. Roget's A-Z Thesaurus. LC 99-13475. (Webster's New World Ser.). 894p. 1999. pap. 12.95 (*0-02-863123-4*) Macmillan.
— Webster's New World Roget's A-Z Thesaurus. Agnes, Michael, ed. LC 99-13475. (Webster's New World Ser). 894p. 1999. 24.95 (*0-02-863281-8*) Free Pr.
— Webster's New World Roget's A-Z Thesaurus. Agnes, Michael, ed. LC 99-13475. (Webster's New World Ser.). 894p. 1999. 19.95 (*0-02-863122-6*) Macmillan.
Laird, Charlton A. Webster's New World Thesaurus. 1995. pap. text 20.00 (*0-205-19987-9*) P-H.
— Webster's New World Thesaurus. 1995. pap. 10.95 (*0-671-84871-2*) S&S Trade.
Laird, Charlton G. Iowa Legends of Buried Treasure. Hutchinson, Stephen K., ed. LC 90-19777. 187p. 1990. pap. 8.95 (*0-934988-23-4*) Foun Bks.
— Webster's New World Thesaurus. 512p. 1995. per. 4.99 (*0-671-51983-2*) PB.
— Webster's New World Thesaurus. 1986. mass mkt. 3.50 (*0-446-31418-8*, Pub. by Warner Bks) Little.
— Webster's New World Thesaurus. rev. ed. 854p. 1985. 16.00 (*0-671-60437-6*, Webstrs New) Macmillan Gen Ref.
— Webster's New World Thesaurus. rev. ed. 512p. 1990. mass mkt. 10.95 (*0-446-39165-4*, Pub. by Warner Bks) Little.
Laird, Charlton G., ed. Walter Van Tilburg Clark: Critiques. LC 83-6789. (Illus.). 312p. 1983. 24.95 (*0-87417-077-X*) U of Nev Pr.
— World Through Literature. LC 77-99639. (Essay Index Reprint Ser.). 1977. 36.95 (*0-8369-1359-0*) Ayer.
Laird, Charlton G. & Webster's New World Dictionaries Editors. Webster's New World Thesaurus. 3rd ed. Agnes, Michael, ed. LC 96-2072. (Illus.). 1996. 18.95 (*0-02-861320-1*) Macmillan.
— Webster's New World Thesaurus. 3rd deluxe ed. Agnes, Michael, ed. LC 96-2072. (Illus.). 1996. 22.95 (*0-02-860337-0*) Macmillan.
Laird, Charlton G. & Webster's New World Dictionaties Editors. Webster's New World Thesaurus. 3rd ed. Agnes, Michael, ed. LC 96-2072. (Illus.). 1996. pap. write for info. (*0-614-12738-6*) Macmillan.
Laird, Christa. But Can the Phoenix Sing? LC 94-28422. 224p. (YA). (gr. 7 up). 1995. 16.00 (*0-688-13612-5*, Grenwillow Bks) HarpC Child Bks.
— But Can the Phoenix Sing? 1998. 10.05 (*0-606-13232-5*, Pub. by Turtleback) Demco.
***Laird, Christa.** But Can the Phoenix Sing. 240p. (YA). (gr. 7 up). 1998. mass mkt. 4.95 (*0-688-15860-9*, Wm Morrow) Morrow Avon.
Laird, Christa. Shadow of the Wall. LC 89-34469. 144p. (gr. 6-12). 1997. mass mkt. 4.95 (*0-688-15291-0*, Wm Morrow) Morrow Avon.
— Shadow of the Wall. 1997. 10.05 (*0-606-11832-2*, Pub. by Turtleback) Demco.
Laird, Donald A. Psychology. (C). 1991. pap. text, student ed. 21.16 (*0-395-59231-3*) HM.
— Psychology. (C). 1992. pap. text, teacher ed., suppl. ed. 5.96 (*0-395-59233-X*) HM.
— What Makes People Buy? LC 75-39254. (Getting & Spending: The Consumer's Dilemma Ser.). 1976. reprint ed. 23.95 (*0-405-08027-1*) Ayer.
Laird, Donivee M. Hau Kea & the Seven Menehune. LC 95-77136. (Illus.). 50p. (J). (gr. k-4). 1995. 7.95 (*0-940350-26-2*) Barnaby Bks.
— Keaka & the Lilikoi Vine. LC 82-72452. (J). (gr. k-3). 1982. 8.95 (*0-940350-22-X*) Barnaby Bks.
— The Three Little Hawaiian Pigs & the Magic Shark. LC 81-67047. (Illus.). 40p. (J). (ps-3). 1981. 8.95 (*0-940350-26-3*) Barnaby Bks.
— Ula Li'i & the Magic Shark. LC 86-3390. (Illus.). 42p. (J). (gr. k-3). 1985. 8.95 (*0-940350-25-4*) Barnaby Bks.
— Wili Wai Kula & the Three Mongooses. LC 83-8805. (J). (gr. k-3). 1983. 8.95 (*0-940350-24-6*) Barnaby Bks.
Laird, Donivee M., ed. see Kajiyama, Kats.
Laird, Dugan. Approaches to Training & Development. LC 77-81193. (Illus.). 1978. text 18.95 (*0-201-04112-X*) Addison-Wesley.
Laird, Dugan & Schleger, Peter R. Approaches to Training & Development. 2nd ed. LC 84-24480. (Illus.). 315p. 1985. 35.00 (*0-201-04498-6*) Addison-Wesley.
Laird, Edgar & Fischer, Robert, eds. Pelerin de Prusse on the Astrolabe: Text & Translation of His Practique de Astrolabe. LC 94-8986. (Medieval & Renaissance Texts & Studies: Vol. 127). 128p. 1995. 24.00 (*0-86698-132-2*, MR127) MRTS.
***Laird, Elisabeth.** Anitas Big Day Easystart. 1998. pap. text 7.00 (*0-582-35289-4*) Addison-Wesley.
Laird, Elizabeth. Americans On the Move. (American Background Readers Ser.). (Illus.). 31p. (YA). 1989. pap. text 5.25 (*0-582-01715-7*, 78663) Longman.
— Anitas Big Day Easy Starts. (Longman Easy Starts Ser.). 1996. pap. text 7.35 (*0-582-09693-6*) Addison-Wesley.
***Laird, Elizabeth.** A Book of Promises. LC 99-31531. (Illus.). 32p. (J). (ps-3). 2000. 15.95 (*0-7894-2547-5*, D K Ink) DK Pub Inc.
Laird, Elizabeth. Earthquake: Longman Originals Stage Two, Level 2. (Longman Originals Ser.). 1996. pap. text 7.35 (*0-582-06452-X*, Pub. by Addison-Wesley) Longman.
— Faces of the USA. (YA). 1987. audio 24.95 (*0-582-01896-X*, 78271) Longman.
— Karen & the Artist. 144p. (J). 1999. pap. text 7.00 (*0-582-37174-0*) Addison-Wesley.
— Kiss the Dust. 288p. (J). (gr. 5 up). 1994. pap. 5.99 (*0-14-036855-8*, PuffinBks) Peng Put Young Read.
— Kiss the Dust. LC 91-43517. 1994. 10.09 (*0-606-06513-X*, Pub. by Turtleback) Demco.
***Laird, Elizabeth.** Secret Friends. LC 97-47728. 80p. (YA). (gr. 5 up). 1999. 14.99 (*0-399-23334-2*) Putnam Pub Group.
— When the World Began. (Oxford Myths & Legends Ser.). (Illus.). 96p. 2000. 25.00 (*0-19-274535-2*) OUP.
Laird, Ellen & Brunhouse, Barbara. The Network to Home Repair & Decorating Services: Northern New Jersey Edition. (Illus.). 250p. 1999. pap. 18.95 (*0-9660791-2-4*, Lairhse Guide); pap. 18.95 (*0-9660791-3-2*) Lairhse Pubns.
Laird, Ellen, et al. The Network to Home Repair & Decorating Services: Central New Jersey. 1998. pap. 16.95 (*0-9660791-0-8*) Lairhse Pubns.
Laird-Fryer, Barbara, ed. Blood Group Systems: Kell. LC 90-949. 91p. (C). 1990. text 35.00 (*0-915355-80-9*) Am Assn Blood.
Laird-Fryer, Barbara, jt. auth. see Unger, Phyllis.
Laird-Fryer, Barbara, jt. ed. see Kasprisin, Christina A.
Laird-Fryer, Barbara, jt. ed. see Moulds, JoAnn M.
Laird, Gerald F. & Dunn, Louise M. Frames & Framing: The Ultimate Illustrated How-to-Do-It Guide. (Illus.). 208p. 1987. pap. 14.95 (*0-8306-2909-2*) McGraw-Hill Prof.
— Frames & Framing: The Ultimate Illustrated How to Guide. 200p. 1988. pap. 18.95 (*0-07-155848-9*) McGraw.
Laird, Holly A. Self & Sequence: The Poetry of D. H. Lawrence. LC 87-23047. 304p. reprint ed. pap. 94.30 (*0-608-08552-9*, 206907500002) Bks Demand.
***Laird, Holly A.** Women Coauthors. LC 99-6863. 288p. 2000. 29.95 (*0-252-02547-4*) U of Ill Pr.
Laird, Hugh E., II, jt. ed. see Jobe, Phillip C.
Laird, J. T., ed. On All Fronts: Australian Stories of World War II. 250p. (Orig.). 1989. pap. 16.95 (*0-7022-2160-0*, Pub. by Univ Queensland Pr) Intl Spec Bk.
Laird, James D. & Thompson, Nicholas S. Psychology. (C). 1991. text 65.96 (*0-395-47090-0*) HM.
— Psychology. 561p. (C). 1992. text, teacher ed. 3.96 (*0-395-59232-1*) HM.
Laird, James D., jt. ed. see Flack, William F., Jr.
Laird, Jean, jt. auth. see Hartman.
Laird, Jean E. The Homemaker's Book of Energy Savers. LC 82-1295. 1982. pap. write for info. (*0-672-52712-X*) Macmillan.
— Your Condo-Co-Op: Tips for Living Comfortably in a Small Space. 1983. pap. 7.95 (*0-8289-0515-0*) Viking Penguin.
Laird, Joan. Ageless Exercise: A Gentle Approach for the Inactive or Physically Limited. LC 93-60903. (Illus.). 64p. 1994. spiral bd. 15.95 (*0-9638390-0-4*) Angelwood Pr.
— Lesbians & Lesbian Families: Reflections on Theory & Practice. LC 98-36503. 363p. 1999. 49.50 (*0-231-10252-6*); 21.50 (*0-231-10253-4*) Col U Pr.
Laird, Joan, intro. Revisioning Social Work Education: A Social Constructionist Approach. LC 94-2853. (Journal of Teaching in Social Work). (Illus.). 326p. 1994. lib. bdg. 49.95 (*1-56024-615-4*) Haworth Pr.
Laird, Joan & Green, Robert-Jay, eds. Lesbians & Gays in Couples & Families: A Handbook for Therapists. (Psychology Ser.). 352p. 1996. 40.95 (*0-7879-0222-5*) Jossey-Bass.
Laird, Joan & Hartman, Ann, eds. A Handbook of Child Welfare: Context, Knowledge & Practice. 752p. (C). 1985. 70.00 (*0-02-918090-2*) Free Pr.
Laird, Joan, jt. auth. see Hartman, Ann.
Laird, Joe. How to Overcome Worry. 11p. (Orig.). 1995. pap. 0.50 (*1-56794-097-8*, C-2385) Star Bible.
Laird, Joe, ed. Often Asked Questions. 180p. (Orig.). 1995. pap. 5.00 (*1-56794-098-6*, C-2386) Star Bible.
Laird, John. As I See It. (Illus.). 49p. 1996. pap. 10.00 (*0-9658253-0-2*) J Laird.
— Enquiry into Moral Notions. LC 76-114045. reprint ed. 37.50 (*0-404-03802-6*) AMS Pr.
— Idea of the Soul. LC 76-107811. (Select Bibliographies Reprint Ser.). 1977. 20.95 (*0-8369-5207-3*) Ayer.
— The Idea of Value. LC 68-58973. (Reprints of Economic Classics Ser.). xx, 384p. 1969. reprint ed. 45.00 (*0-678-00460-9*) Kelley.
— Recent Philosophy. LC 73-5955. 1977. 19.95 (*0-518-19054-4*) Ayer.
— Salmon & Trout Farming. (Aquaculture & Fisheries Support Ser.). 272p. 1988. text 62.95 (*0-470-21087-7*) P-H.
— A Study in Realism. LC 77-152991. (Select Bibliographies Reprint Ser.). 1977. reprint ed. 20.95 (*0-8369-5743-1*) Ayer.
— Theism & Cosmology. LC 74-84317. (Essay Index Reprint Ser.). 1977. 23.95 (*0-8369-1147-4*) Ayer.
Laird, John, ed. Machine Learning International Workshop on Machine Learning: Proceedings of the 5th International Conference. 467p. (C). 1998. pap. text 19.95 (*0-934613-64-8*) Morgan Kaufmann.
Laird, John, et al. Universal Subgoaling & Chunking: The Automatic Generation & Learning of Goal Hierarchies. 1986. text 102.00 (*0-89838-213-0*) Kluwer Academic.
Laird, Lisa, tr. see Tracqui, Valerie.
Laird, M. Avian Malaria in the Asian Tropical Subregion. (Illus.). 180p. 1998. 69.00 (*981-3083-19-0*, Pub. by Spr-Verlag) Spr-Verlag.
Laird, M. R., intro. Conservative Papers. LC 74-117774. (Essay Index Reprint Ser.). 1977. 21.95 (*0-8369-1748-0*) Ayer.
Laird, MacGregor & Oldfield, R. A. Narrative of an Expedition into the Interior of Africa, 2 vols., Set. (Illus.). 1971. reprint ed. 45.00 (*0-7146-1826-8*, Pub. by F Cass Pubs) Intl Spec Bk.
Laird, Margaret. We Are the World We Walk Through. 297p. 1993. pap. 12.95 (*0-9638172-0-5*) M Laird Fnd.
***Laird, Mark.** Flowering of the Landscape Garden: English Pleasure Grounds, 1720-1800. LC 98-22949. (Penn Studies in Landscape Architecture). (Illus.). 446p. 1998. 49.95 (*0-8122-3457-X*) U of Pa Pr.
***Laird, Marnie.** Water Rat. (Illus.). 196p. (J). (gr. 4-7). 1998. 15.95 (*1-890817-08-2*, Pub. by Winslow Pr) Publishers Group.
Laird, Marshall. Biocontrol of Medical & Veterinary Pests. LC 81-12083. 235p. 1981. 69.50 (*0-275-91346-5*, C1346, Praeger Pubs) Greenwood.
Laird, Marshall, ed. Commerce & the Spread of Pests & Disease Vectors. LC 83-16627. (Illus.). 354p. 1984. 59.95 (*0-275-91208-6*, C1208, Praeger Pubs) Greenwood.
Laird, Marshall, et al, eds. Safety of Microbial Insecticides. 272p. 1990. boxed set 229.95 (*0-8493-4793-9*, SB933) CRC Pr.
Laird, Marshall & Miles, James W., eds. Integrated Mosquito Control Methodologies, Vol. 2. 1985. text 157.00 (*0-12-434002-4*) Acad Pr.
Laird, Nick L. & Roosevelt, Rita K. Quantifying Impacts (QI) Handbook: A Comprehensive Guide to Quantifying Bottom-Line Impacts of Public & Government Affairs Activities. (Illus.). 82p. (Orig.). (C). 1994. pap. text 29.95 (*0-9644865-0-4*) Laird & Assoc.
Laird, Pamela W. Advertising Progress: American Business & the Rise of Consumer Marketing. LC 97-52039. (Studies in Industry & Society). (Illus.). 480p. 1998. 35.95 (*0-8018-5841-0*) Johns Hopkins.
Laird, Paul R. Towards a History of the Spanish Villancico. LC 97-2393. (Detroit Monographs in Musicology). 1997. 35.00 (*0-89990-075-5*) Harmonie Park Pr.
Laird, Peter, jt. auth. see Lawson, Jim.
Laird, Philip D. Learning from Good & Bad Data. (C). 1988. text 91.00 (*0-89838-263-7*) Kluwer Academic.
Laird, R. F. The Boomer Bible. LC 91-50385. (Illus.). 880p. (Orig.). 1991. pap. 14.95 (*1-56305-075-7*, 3075) Workman Pub.
Laird, Rebecca. Leslie Weatherhead's the Will of God a Workbook. 96p. (Orig.). 1995. pap. 7.95 (*0-687-00840-9*) Abingdon.
— Ordained Women in the Church of the Nazarene: The First Generation. 167p. (Orig.). 1993. pap. 10.99 (*0-8341-1452-6*, 85257) Beacon Hill.
Laird, Rick. Improvising Jazz Bass. 1980. pap. 16.95 (*0-8256-4091-1*, AM27939) Music Sales.
— Jazz Riffs for Bass, EFS205. (Illus.). 48p. 1978. pap. 12.95 (*0-8256-2205-0*, AM24605) Music Sales.
Laird, Robbin. French Security Policy in Transition: Dynamics of Continuity & Change. 55p. (C). 1996. reprint ed. pap. text 25.00 (*0-7881-3675-5*) DIANE Pub.
Laird, Robbin F. Bonn & Moscow: A Partnership in Progress? (C). 1990. 65.00 (*0-907967-97-3*, Pub. by Inst Euro Def & Strat) St Mut.
Laird, Robbin F., ed. West European Arms Control Policy. LC 89-16819. (Duke Press Policy Studies). 210p. 1989. text 49.95 (*0-8223-0955-6*) Duke.
Laird, Robbin F. & Clark, Susan L. The U. S. S. R. & the Western Alliance. 288p. 1989. 55.00 (*0-04-445392-2*) Routledge.
Laird, Robbin F. & Hoffmann, Erik P., eds. Soviet Foreign Policy in a Changing World. LC 85-18712. 993p. (Orig.). 1986. pap. text 36.95 (*0-202-24167-X*); lib. bdg. 69.95 (*0-202-24166-1*) Aldine de Gruyter.
***Laird, Robbin F. & Mey, Holger H.** The Revolution in Military Affairs: Allied Perspectives. 105p. (C). 1999. pap. text 25.00 (*0-7881-8392-3*) DIANE Pub.
Laird, Robbin F., jt. ed. see Hoffmann, Erik P.
Laird, Robin F., jt. auth. see Clark, Susan.
Laird, Roland O. Still I Rise: A Cartoon History of African Americans. LC 97-8417. (Illus.). xvi, 206p. 1997. pap. 15.95 (*0-393-31751-X*) Norton.
Laird, Roland Owen, Jr. & Laird, Taneshia N. Still I Rise: A Cartoon History of African Americans. LC 97-8417. (Illus.). 204p. 1997. 21.95 (*0-393-04538-2*) Norton.
***Laird, Ronald A.** Fast Walking. LC 00-29702. 2000. pap. 13.95 (*0-8117-2758-0*) Stackpole.
Laird, Ronald A. Some Low Level Walks in Strathspey. (C). 1986. pap. 29.00 (*0-906664-11-X*, Pub. by Mercat Pr Bks) St Mut.
Laird, Ross. Moanin' Low: A Discography of Female Popular Vocal Recordings, 1920-1933, 67. LC 96-21947. (Discographies Ser.: Vol. 67). 768p. 1996. lib. bdg. 105.00 (*0-313-29241-8*, Greenwood Pr) Greenwood.
Laird, Roy D. The Soviet Legacy. LC 92-41617. 240p. 1993. 59.95 (*0-275-94558-8*, C4558, Praeger Pubs) Greenwood.
Laird, Roy D., jt. ed. see Laird, Betty A.
***Laird, Sally, ed.** Voices of Russian Literature: Interviews with Ten Contemporary Writers. (Illus.). 259p. 1999. text 45.00 (*0-19-815181-0*) OUP.
Laird, Sally, jt. auth. see Petrushevskakila, Lkiludmila.
Laird, Sandra. Handcoloring Photographs Step by Step. LC 96-79314. (Illus.). 112p. 1997. pap. text 29.95 (*0-936262-54-0*) Amherst Media.
Laird, Suzanne. Choices in Child Care: What's Best for Your Child. (Illus.). 138p. (Orig.). 1992. pap. 12.95 (*1-55059-043-X*) Temeron Bks.
Laird, Taneshia N., jt. auth. see Laird, Roland Owen, Jr.
Laird, Thomas. Blue Collar & Other Stories. Danbury, Richard S., III, ed. LC 94-66610. 120p. (Orig.). 1994. pap. 10.95 (*0-89754-086-7*) Dan River Pr.
Laird, Thomas, jt. auth. see Baker, Ian.
***Laird, Tom.** Into Tibet: America's Last Secret Expedition to Tibet. (Illus.). 320p. 2000. 25.00 (*0-06-019396-4*) HarperTrade.
Laird, Tom. Tibet. 2000. pap. 14.00 (*0-06-093206-6*) HarpC.
Laird, W. David. Hopi Bibliography: Comprehensive & Annotated. LC 77-95563. 735p. 1977. pap. 38.50 (*0-8165-0566-7*) U of Ariz Pr.
Laird, Walter. Technique of Latin Dancing. (Ballroom Dance Ser.). 1984. lib. bdg. 79.95 (*0-87700-510-9*) Revisionist Pr.
Laird, Winona I., jt. auth. see Chambers, Anna R.
***Lairdon, Roberts.** Breaking Controlling Powers: A Compilation of Breaking Controlling Powers, Learning to Say No Without Feeling Guilty & How to Survive an Attack. 272p. 2000. pap. 10.99 (*1-57778-155-4*) Albury Pub.
Lairdon, Roberts, ed. I Saw Heaven. 31p. 1983. pap. 2.00 (*0-915693-00-3*) Christian Pub.
Lairson, Thomas D. & Skidmore, David. International Political Economy: The Struggle for Power & Wealth. 2nd ed. LC 96-76310. 480p. (C). 1996. pap. text 40.00 (*0-15-503026-4*, Pub. by Harcourt Coll Pubs) Harcourt.
***Laisk, A. & Oja, V.** Dynamics of Leaf Photosynthesis: Rapid Response Measurements & Their Interpretations. (Techniques in Plant Sciences Ser.). (Illus.). 176p. 1998. pap. 59.95 (*0-643-06378-1*, Pub. by CSIRO) Accents Pubns.
Laisney, Francois, jt. auth. see Lefebvre, Marcel.
Laisney, Francois, tr. see Laffont, Jean-Jacques & Moreaux, Michel, eds.
Laistner, Max L. Greek Economics. LC 79-171641. (Library of Greek Thought: No. 3). reprint ed. 41.00 (*0-404-07802-8*) AMS Pr.
— Thought & Letters in Western Europe, A. D. 500-900. 1972. 59.95 (*0-8490-1207-4*) Gordon Pr.
Laistner, Max L., et al, eds. Glossaria Latina, Bd. IV: Placidi Glossae. xxi, 1990p. 1965. reprint ed. write for info. (*0-318-71134-6*) G Olms Pubs.
Lait, Jack. Beef, Iron & Wine. LC 78-116960. (Short Story Index Reprint Ser.). 1977. 21.95 (*0-8369-3464-4*) Ayer.
Laita, Luis M. Traveler's Spanish Dictionary. 1993. pap. 6.95 (*0-8050-2908-7*) H Holt & Co.
Laita, Luis M. & Gil de Montes, Carmen. Cortina - Holt Traveler's Spanish Dictionary: English-Spanish - Spanish-English. Berberi, Dilaver & Winje, Edel A., eds. LC 93-3673. (ENG & SPA.). 1993. pap. 6.95 (*0-8327-0721-X*) Cortina.
Laite, Ben. Maritime Air Operations. (Air Power: Aircraft, Weapons Systems & Technology Ser.: Vol. 11). (Illus.). 200p. 1992. 40.00 (*0-08-040705-6*, Pub. by Brasseys); 25.00 (*0-08-040706-4*, Pub. by Brasseys) Brasseys.
Laithwaite, Eric. An Inventor in the Garden of Eden. (Illus.). 303p. (C). 1994. 26.95 (*0-521-44106-4*) Cambridge U Pr.
Laitier, Gabriel. Dictionnaire de Physique. (FRE.). 276p. 1968. pap. 55.00 (*0-8288-6632-5*, M-6328) Fr & Eur.
Laitin, Anna, jt. auth. see Curtis, Patrick.
Laitin, David, ed. see Anderson, Benedict R.
Laitin, David, ed. see Desan, Suzanne.
Laitin, David, ed. see Given, James B.

An Asterisk (*) at the beginning of an entry indicates that the title is appearing for the first time.

L

Laitin, David D. Hegemony & Culture: Politics & Religious Change among the Yoruba. (Illus.). xiv, 266p. 1986. pap. text 19.00 (*0-226-46790-2*) U Ch Pr.
— Hegemony & Culture: Politics & Religious Change among the Yoruba. (Illus.). xiv, 252p. 1995. lib. bdg. 30.00 (*0-226-46789-9*) U Ch Pr.
— Identity in Formation: The Russian-Speaking Populations in the Near Abroad. LC 97-48670. (Wilder House Series in Politics, History, & Culture). 448p. 1998. pap. 22.50 (*0-8014-8495-2*) Cornell U Pr.
— Identity in Formation: The Russian-Speaking Populations in the Near Abroad. LC 97-48670. (Wilder House Series in Politics, History, & Culture). (Illus.). 448p. 1998. text 57.50 (*0-8014-3495-5*) Cornell U Pr.
— Language Repertoires & State Construction in Africa. (Cambridge Studies in Comparative Politics). (Illus.). 219p. (C). 1992. text 59.95 (*0-521-41343-5*) Cambridge U Pr.
Laitin, David D. Politics, Language, & Thought: The Somali Experience. LC 76-22958. (Illus.). 280p. 1977. lib. bdg. 28.00 (*0-226-46791-0*) U Ch Pr.
Laitin, Ken & Laitin, Steve. Playing Soccer. LC 79-63980. (Illus.). (J). (gr. 2-7). 1979. pap. 9.95 (*0-916802-22-1*) Soccer for Am.
Laitin, Steve, jt. auth. see Laitin, Ken.
Laitinen, Mauri, jt. auth. see Fayad, Mohamed.
Laitl, J., jt. auth. see Janos, K.
Laitner, Bill. The Dee-Troit Diet. 144p. 1989. spiral bd. 9.95 (*0-937247-15-4*) Detroit Pr.
Laitner, Skip & Goldberg, Marshall. Regional Energy & Economic Self-Sufficiency Indicators in the Southeastern United States. (Illus.). 76p. (Orig.). (C). 1997. pap. text 30.00 (*0-7881-3744-1*) DIANE Pub.
Laitner, Skip, jt. auth. see Hoerner, J. Andrew.
Laitos, Jan. Law of Property Rights Protection: Limitations on Governmental Powers. LC 98-34101. 1998. boxed set 195.00 (*0-7355-0152-1*) Aspen Law.
Laitos, Jan G. Cases & Materials on Natural Resources Law. LC 85-13787. (American Casebook Ser.). 938p. (C). 1985. 62.50 (*0-314-90413-1*) West Pub.
— Natural Resources Law: Cases & Materials. LC 85-13787. (American Casebook Ser.). 283p. (C). 1985. teacher ed. write for info. (*0-314-95851-7*) West Pub.
Laitos, Jan G. & Tomain, Joseph P. Energy & Natural Resources Law in a Nutshell. (Nutshell Ser.). 554p. (C). 1992. pap. 23.50 (*0-314-00118-2*) West Pub.
Laity, Annabel, tr. see Hanh, Thich Nhat.
Laity, Annabell, tr. see Hanh, Thich Nhat.
Laity, Cassandra. H.D. & the Victorian Fin de Siecle: Gender, Modernism, Decadence. (Cambridge Studies in American Literature & Culture Ser.: No. 104). 236p. (C). 1996. text 57.95 (*0-521-55414-4*) Cambridge U Pr.
Laity, Cassandra, ed. & intro. see H. D., pseud.
Laity, Edward. Priesthood, Old & New. 1980. 4.50 (*0-86544-012-3*) Salv Army Suppl South.
— Tabernacle Types & Teaching. 1980. pap. 3.95 (*0-86544-011-5*) Salv Army Suppl South.
Laity, Sally. Better Than Friends. (Heartsong Ser.). 1994. pap. text 1.66 (*1-55748-511-9*) Barbour Pub.
Laity, Sally & Crawford, Dianna. The Embers of Hope. LC 96-14241. (Freedom's Holy Light Ser.: Vol. 5). 350p. 1996. pap. 10.99 (*0-8423-1362-1*) Tyndale Hse.
— Fires of Freedom. (Freedom's Holy Light Ser.: Vol. 4). 388p. 1996. pap. 10.99 (*0-8423-1353-2*) Tyndale Hse.
— The Tempering Blaze. LC 94-23236. (Freedom's Holy Light Ser.: Vol. 3). 393p. 1995. pap. 10.99 (*0-8423-6902-3*) Tyndale Hse.
— Torch of Triumph. LC 96-47576. (Freedom's Holy Light Ser.: Vol. 6). 421p. 1997. pap. 10.99 (*0-8423-1417-2*) Tyndale Hse.
***Laity, Sally, et al.** The Painting. 352p. 1999. pap. 4.97 (*1-57748-640-4*) Barbour Pub.
Laizer, Sheri. Into Kurdistan: Frontiers under Fire. LC 91-8856. (Illus.). 128p. (C). 1991. text 55.00 (*0-86232-898-5*, Pub. by St Martin); text 19.95 (*0-86232-899-3*, Pub. by St Martin) St Martin.
— Martyrs, Traitors, & Patriots: Kurdistan after the Gulf War. LC 95-25552. 240p. (C). 1996. text 62.50 (*1-85649-395-4*, Pub. by Zed Books); text 22.50 (*1-85649-396-2*, Pub. by Zed Books) St Martin.
Laj, Carlo, jt. ed. see Kissel, Catherine.
Lajarrige, Jacques, jt. ed. see Camion, Arlette.
LaJaune, Tom. Masonry Supervision: Playing the Game to Win, Not Just to Stay in the Game. 116p. 1996. per. 21.95 (*0-7872-2387-5*) Kendall-Hunt.
LaJaune, Tom & Seymour, Arthur. Basic Construction Supervision. 66p. per. write for info. (*0-7872-6702-3*) Kendall-Hunt.
Laje, Zilia L. La Cortina De Bagazo. LC 95-94272. (SPA.). 576p. (Orig.). 1995. pap. 19.00 (*0-9646224-0-8*) Guarina Pub.
***Laje, Zilia L.** The Sugar Cane Curtain. LC 00-91110. Orig. Title: Bagasse Curtain. 552p. 2000. pap. 19.95 (*0-9646224-1-6*) Guarina Pub.
Laje, Zilia L., ed. see Warns, E. Fredy & Boulette, Jack.
Lajer-Burcharth, Ewa. Necklines: The Art of Jacques-Louis David after the Terror. LC 98-47971. (Illus.). 374p. 1999. 50.00 (*0-300-07421-2*) Yale U Pr.
Lajeunesse, Nicholas. Sex Inc. (Illus.). 128p. 1998. pap. 14.95 (*1-56097-320-X*) Fantagraph Bks.
Lajimi, Ahmed & Tanlak, Acar. International Directory of Islamic Cultural Institutions. 344p. 1987. pap. 59.50 (*0-7103-0201-0*, 02010) Routledge.
Lajoie, Bob, jt. auth. see Lajoie, Gesele.
Lajoie, Gesele & Lajoie, Bob. Tennis Handbook. (Illus.). 46p. pap. 5.95 (*0-318-32568-3*) Hancock House.
LaJoie, Jim & Plumb, Ron. Year of the 'Cats: A Look Back at Northern Michigan University's 1990-91 Championship Hockey Season. 150p. 1991. pap. 9.95 (*0-9630901-0-0*) J LaJoie.
Lajoie, Jose, jt. auth. see Lippman, Stanley B.
Lajoie, Susanne & Derry, Sharon. Computers As Cognitive Tools. (Technology & Education Ser.). 416p. 1993. pap. 45.00 (*0-8058-1082-X*); text 89.95 (*0-8058-1081-1*) L Erlbaum Assocs.
Lajoie, Susanne P., ed. Reflections on Statistics: Agendas for Learning, Teaching, & Assessment in K-12. LC 97-7357. (Studies in Mathematical Thinking & Learning). 350p. 1997. write for info. (*0-8058-1971-1*); pap. write for info. (*0-8058-1972-X*) L Erlbaum Assocs.
Lajolo, Davide. An Absurd Vice: A Biography of Cesare Pavese. Pietralunga, Mario & Pietralunga, Mark, trs. LC 82-14482. (ITA.). 288p. 1983. 18.50 (*0-8112-0850-8*, Pub. by New Directions); pap. 9.25 (*0-8112-0851-6*, NDP545, Pub. by New Directions) Norton.
Lajonquiere, Etienne E. Lunet De, see Lunet De Lajonquiere, Etienne E.
Lajos, B. Pszichologiai Ertelmezo Szotar: Explanatory Psychological Dictionary. (HUN.). 1981. 24.95 (*0-8288-2220-4*, M172) Fr & Eur.
Lajos, Fury. Vasarnap Farkaspusztan. 1978. boxed set 12.00 (*0-912404-11-6*) Alpha Pubns.
Lajos, Hegedus. Learn English for Hungarian Speakers, 2 vols., Set. Incl. Advanced Vol. 2. pap. 20.95 (*0-87557-122-0*); Beginners Vol. 1. pap. 20.95 (*0-87557-094-1*); Set pap. 36.00 (*0-87557-095-X*) Saphrograph.
— Resz Haladoknak, Vol. 2. 180p. pap. write for info. (*0-318-55622-7*, 094-1X) Saphrograph.
Lajos, Ivicsics. Hydraulic Models. 1980. 42.00 (*0-918334-38-1*) WRP.
Lajos, Mari & Henzo, Karoly. 99 Casserole Dishes with 33 Colour Photographs. (Illus.). 64p. 1999. 25.00 (*963-13-2774-4*, Pub. by Corvina Bks) St Mut.
***Lajos, Mari & Henzo, Karoly.** 99 Hungarian Dishes with 33 Colour Photographs. 64p. 1999. 25.00 (*963-13-4790-7*, Pub. by Corvina Bks) St Mut.
Lajos, Mari & Henzo, Karoly. 99 Salads with 33 Colour Photographs. 2nd ed. (Illus.). 64p. 1999. 25.00 (*963-13-2664-0*, Pub. by Corvina Bks) St Mut.
Lajoux, Alexandra R. Art of M & A: Due Diligence: Navigating Critical Steps & Uncovering Crucial Data. 250p. 2000. 49.95 (*0-7863-1150-9*, Irwn Prfssnl) McGraw-Hill Prof.
— The Art of M&A Financing & Refinancing: Sources & Instruments for Growth. LC 99-18008. (Art of M & A Ser.). (Illus.). 457p. 1999. 49.95 (*0-07-038303-0*) McGraw-Hill Prof.
— The Art of M&A Integration: A Guide to Merging Resources, Processes, & Responsibilities. LC 97-8663. 1997. 49.95 (*0-7863-1127-4*, Irwn Prfssnl) McGraw-Hill Prof.
Lajoux, Alexandra R., jt. auth. see Reed, Stanley F.
LaJoyce, Martin. Coriander Seed & Honey: Pint-Sized Manna for Every Day of the Year. 190p. 1998. pap. write for info. (*1-57502-926-X*, PO2554) Morris Pubng.
— A Single Worry. LC 93-18944. 200p. (Orig.). 1993. pap. 8.99 (*1-56722-011-8*) Word Aflame.
Lajpat, Lala, jt. auth. see Lajpat, Rai.
***Lajpat, Rai.** Problem of Indian Education. 1999. 30.00 (*81-7020-450-X*, Pub. by Cosmo Pubn) S Asia.
Lajpat, Rai & Lajpat, Lala. The Arma Samaj: An Account of Its Origin, Doctrines & Activities. (C). 1989. 47.00 (*81-85199-30-2*, Pub. by Renaiss Publng Hse) S Asia.
Lajpat Rai, Lala. Unhappy India. 2nd enl. rev. ed. LC 72-171642. reprint ed. 49.50 (*0-404-03803-4*) AMS Pr.
Lajpuri, Abdur R. Fatawa Rahimiyah, 3 vols., Set. 1992. 56.85 (*1-56744-453-9*) Kazi Pubns.
— Fatawa Rahimiyah, Vol. 1. 360p. 1992. 18.95 (*1-56744-450-4*) Kazi Pubns.
— Fatawa Rahimiyah, Vol. 2. 354p. 1992. 18.95 (*1-56744-451-2*) Kazi Pubns.
— Fatawa Rahimiyah, Vol. 3. 250p. 1992. 18.95 (*1-56744-452-0*) Kazi Pubns.
Lajtha, Abel, ed. Handbook of Neurochemistry, Vol. 1: Chemical Architecture of the Nervous Syste. LC 68-28097. 508p. reprint ed. pap. 157.50 (*0-608-12932-1*, 202470100001) Bks Demand.
— Handbook of Neurochemistry, Vol. 1: Chemical & Cellular Architecture. 2nd ed. LC 82-493. 516p. 1982. 120.00 (*0-306-40861-9*, Plenum Trade) Perseus Pubng.
— Handbook of Neurochemistry, Vol. 10: Pathological Neurochemistry. 2nd ed. LC 82-493. 822p. 1985. 145.00 (*0-306-41744-8*, Plenum Trade) Perseus Pubng.
— Handbook of Neurochemistry, Vol. 2: Experimental Neurochemistry. 2nd ed. LC 82-493. 498p. 1983. 120.00 (*0-306-40972-0*, Plenum Trade) Perseus Pubng.
Lajtha, Abel, ed. Handbook of Neurochemistry, Vol. 3: Metabolism in the Nervous System. 2nd ed. LC 82-493. 724p. 1983. 130.00 (*0-306-41153-9*, Plenum Trade) Perseus Pubng.
— Handbook of Neurochemistry, Vol. 4: Enzymes in the Nervous System. LC 82-493. 572p. 1983. 120.00 (*0-306-41210-1*, Plenum Trade) Perseus Pubng.
— Handbook of Neurochemistry, Vol. 5: Metabolic Turnover in the Nervous System. 2nd ed. LC 82-493. 518p. 1983. 120.00 (*0-306-41323-X*, Plenum Trade) Perseus Pubng.
— Handbook of Neurochemistry, Vol. 7: Structural Elements of the Nervous System. 2nd ed. LC 82-493. 734p. 1984. 130.00 (*0-306-41440-6*, Plenum Trade) Perseus Pubng.
— Handbook of Neurochemistry, Vol. 8: Neurochemical Systems. 2nd ed. LC 82-493. 700p. 1985. 140.00 (*0-306-41579-8*, Plenum Trade) Perseus Pubng.
Lajtha, Abel, ed. The Handbook of Neurochemistry, Vol. 9: Alterations of Metabolites in the Nervous System. 2nd ed. LC 82-493. 622p. 1985. 135.00 (*0-306-41743-X*, Plenum Trade) Perseus Pubng.
— Protein Metabolism of the Nervous System. LC 74-85373. 754p. reprint ed. pap. 200.00 (*0-608-14551-3*, 202471800038) Bks Demand.
Lajtha, K. & Michener, R. Stable Isotopes in Ecology & Environmental Science. (Illus.). 250p. 1994. 39.95 (*0-632-03154-9*) Blackwell Sci.
Laka, Itzial. On Syntax of Negation. LC 94-598. (Outstanding Dissertations in Linguistics Ser.). 1994. write for info. (*0-8153-0696-2*) Garland.
Laka, Itziar. On the Syntax of Negation. LC 94-598. (Outstanding Dissertations in Linguistics Ser.). 200p. 1994. text 20.00 (*0-8153-1728-X*) Garland.
Lakatos, E. Proofs & Refutations. Worrall, J., ed. LC 75-32478. 174p. 1976. pap. text 23.95 (*0-521-29038-4*) Cambridge U Pr.
Lakatos, Geza. As I Saw It: The Tragedy of Hungary. Fenyo, Mario D., tr. from HUN. LC 93-95028. Orig. Title: Ahogyan en Lattam. (Illus.). 301p. 1996. 25.00 (*0-935484-16-7*) Universe Pub Co.
Lakatos, Imre. Philosophical Papers: Mathematics, Science & Epistemology, Vol. 2. Worrall, J. & Currie, Gregory, eds. LC 77-14374. 295p. 1980. pap. text 35.95 (*0-521-28030-3*) Cambridge U Pr.
— Philosophical Papers: The Methodology of Scientific Research Programmes, Vol. 1. Worrall, J. & Currie, Gregory, eds. LC 77-71415. 258p. 1980. pap. text 35.95 (*0-521-28031-1*) Cambridge U Pr.
Lakatos, Imre & Feyerabend, Paul K. For & Against Method: Including Lakatos's Lecturese on Scientific Method & the Lakatos-Feyerabend Correspondence. Motterlini, Matteo, ed. LC 99-13581. (Illus.). 416p. 1999. 34.00 (*0-226-46774-0*) U Ch Pr.
Lakatos, Imre & Musgrave, Alan E., eds. Criticism & the Growth of Knowledge. LC 78-105496. 282p. 1970. pap. text 26.95 (*0-521-09623-5*) Cambridge U Pr.
Lakatos, Imre, et al. For & Against Method: Including Lakatos's Lectures on Scientific Method & the Lakatos-feyerabend Correspondence. LC 99-13581. 1997. pap. text 19.95 (*0-226-46775-9*) U Ch Pr.
***Lakatos, Istvan, ed.** Challenges of an Interdisciplinary Science Vol. 1: Progress in Mining & Oilfield Chemistry. 358p. 1999. 68.00 (*963-05-7655-4*, Pub. by Akade Kiado) Intl Spec Bk.
Lakatta, E. G., ed. Vascular Disease in the Older Person. LC 97-41937. (Novartis Foundation for Gerontological Research Ser.: Vol. 1). 166p. 1998. 48.00 (*1-85070-010-9*) Prthnon Pub.
Lake. Advances in Anesthesia, 16. (Illus.). 352p. 1998. text 81.00 (*0-8151-9802-7*, 25039) Mosby Inc.
***Lake.** Desktop Publishing in 10 Hours. LC 99-12942. (Keyboarding Ser.). (Illus.). 76p. 1999. pap. 16.95 (*0-538-68754-1*) S-W Pub.
Lake. Images of the Past. (Jersey Heritage Editions Ser.). 1991. 40.00 (*0-86120-018-7*, Pub. by Aris & Phillips) David Brown.
— Pediatric Cardiac Anesthesia. 3rd ed. LC 97-11876. 698p. (C). 1998. 150.00 (*0-8385-7680-X*, A-7680-0, Apple Lange Med) McGraw.
— These Haunted Islands: A Story of Witchcraft in the Channel Islands. 1991. 35.00 (*0-318-68515-9*, Pub. by Aris & Phillips) David Brown.
Lake, A. L. The Pony Express. (Wild West in American History Ser.). (Illus.). 32p. (J). (gr. 3-8). 1989. lib. bdg. 23.93 (*0-86625-368-8*) Rourke Pubns.
— Women of the West. (Wild West in American History Ser.). (Illus.). 32p. (J). (gr. 3-8). 1990. lib. bdg. 18.00 (*0-86625-373-4*) Rourke Pubns.
Lake, Alexander. Hunter's Choice. LC 95-49383. 1995. pap. 16.95 (*1-57090-026-4*) Alexander Dist.
— Killers in Africa: The Truth about Animals Lying in Wait & Hunters Lying in Print. 2nd ed. Resnick, Mike et al, eds. LC 95-78530. (Illus.). 272p. 1995. reprint ed. pap. 12.95 (*1-57090-013-2*) Alexander Dist.
Lake, Alice. Our Own Years. 244p. (C). 1982. reprint ed. 8.95 (*0-86683-667-5*) Harper SF.
Lake, Alizarin. Clara. 3rd ed. 1997. reprint ed. mass mkt. 6.95 (*1-56333-548-4*) Masquerade.
— The Instruments of the Passion. 2nd ed. 1998. reprint ed. mass mkt. 6.95 (*1-56333-659-6*) Masquerade.
— Miss High Heels. 2nd ed. 1998. reprint ed. mass mkt. 6.95 (*1-56333-632-4*) Masquerade.
— Sex on Dr.'s Orders. 2nd ed. 1996. mass mkt. 5.95 (*1-56333-402-X*) Masquerade.
Lake, Anthony. Six Nightmares. 352p. 2000. 27.95 (*0-316-55976-8*) Little.
— Somoza Falling: A Case Study of Washington at Work. LC 90-34788. 336p. 1990. reprint ed. pap. 19.95 (*0-87023-733-0*) U of Mass Pr.
— The "Tar Baby" Option: American Policy Toward Southern Rhodesia. LC 76-2455. 316p. 1976. text 57.50 (*0-231-04066-0*) Col U Pr.
— Third World Radical Regimes: U. S. Policy under Carter & Reagan. LC 85-81057. (Headline Ser.: No. 272). (Illus.). 56p. (Orig.). 1985. pap. 5.95 (*0-87124-099-8*) Foreign Policy.
Lake, Anthony, et al. After the Wars: Reconstruction in Afghanistan, Indochina, Central America, Southern Africa, & the Horn of Africa. (U. S. Third World Policy Perspectives Ser.: No. 16). 240p. (C). 1990. text 39.95 (*0-88738-392-0*); pap. text 21.95 (*0-88738-880-9*) Transaction Pubs.
Lake, Austen, jt. auth. see Atkinson, Leroy.
Lake, Bambi & Orloff, Alvin. The Unsinkable Bambi Lake: A Fairy Tale Containing the Dish on Cockettes, Punks & Angels. LC 96-10093. (Illus.). 160p. (Orig.). 1996. pap. 11.95 (*0-916397-42-4*) Manic D Pr.
Lake, Brian, jt. auth. see Ash, Russell.
Lake, Brian, jt. auth. see Heard, Dorothy.
Lake, Brian D., jt. ed. see Filipe, M. Isabel.
Lake, Brian G., jt. ed. see Gibson, G. Gordan.
Lake, Bruce. Fifteen Hundred Feet over Vietnam: A Marine Helicopter Pilot's Diary. LC 90-14421. 372p. (Orig.). 1990. pap. 14.00 (*0-9623500-2-8*) Ministry Two.
Lake, Carlton. Confessions of a Literary Archaeologist. LC 89-13707. (Illus.). 256p. 1990. 21.95 (*0-8112-1130-4*, Pub. by New Directions) Norton.
— No Symbols Where None Intended: Samuel Beckett at the Harry Ransom Humanities Research Center. (Illus.). 185p. 1984. 20.00 (*0-87959-101-3*) U of Tex H Ransom Ctr.
Lake, Carlton & Ashton, Linda. Henri-Pierre Roche: An Introduction. (Illus.). 240p. 1991. 20.00 (*0-87959-113-7*) U of Tex H Ransom Ctr.
Lake, Carlton, jt. auth. see Gilot, Francoise.
Lake, Carney. Reflected Glory: An Account of a British Soldier in Northern Ireland. 240p. 1994. 39.50 (*0-85052-366-4*, Pub. by Leo Cooper) Trans-Atl Phila.
Lake, Carol L. Advances in Anesthesia, 15. (Illus.). 464p. (C). (gr. 13). 1997. text 81.00 (*0-8151-5278-7*, 23021) Mosby Inc.
— Advances in Anesthesia, 18. 18th ed. (Illus.). 350p. 2000. text 81.00 (*0-8151-1216-5*, 31772) Mosby Inc.
— Advances in Anesthesia, 19. 19th ed. 2000. 81.00 (*0-8151-1217-3*, 31773) Mosby Inc.
— Advances in Anesthesia, 20. 2002. 81.00 (*0-8151-1218-1*, 31774) Mosby Inc.
— Cardiovascular Anesthesia. (Illus.). 480p. 1984. 98.00 (*0-387-96028-7*) Spr-Verlag.
— Cherry Blossom Tea: A Collection of Short Stories. 124p. 1994. pap. 8.95 (*0-9642362-4-9*) White Hart Pr.
— The Horse Is Out of Order: And Other Essays about the Writing Life. 70p. 1994. pap. 5.95 (*0-9642362-2-2*) White Hart Pr.
Lake, Carol L. & Moore, Roger A., eds. Blood: Hemostasis, Transfusion, & Alternatives in the Perioperative Period. LC 94-42192. (Illus.). 528p. 1995. text 141.00 (*0-7817-0267-4*) Lppncott W & W.
Lake, Carol L., et al. Clinical Monitoring: Practical Applications for Anesthesia & Critical Care. (Illus.). 525p. 2000. text. write for info. (*0-7216-8698-2*, W B Saunders Co) Harcrt Hlth Sci Grp.
Lake, Carole, ed. see Taggart, Jean.
Lake, Carole L., ed. Clinical Monitoring for Anesthesia & Critical Care. 2nd ed. LC 93-41600. (Illus.). 590p. 1994. text 145.00 (*0-7216-5269-7*, W B Saunders Co) Harcrt Hlth Sci Grp.
Lake, Carolyn. Under Cover for Wells Fargo: The Unvarnished Recollections of Fred Dodge. 336p. 1999. pap. text 13.95 (*0-8061-3106-3*) U of Okla Pr.
Lake, Carolyn, ed. see Dodge, Fred.
Lake County Historical Society Staff, contrib. by. History of Lake County 1881. 328p. 1997. pap. 12.95 (*1-884995-10-1*) Word Dancer.
Lake, D. J. & Hammond, Gene P. Hammond's Edition of the Atlas of Shenandoah & Page Counties, Virginia by D. J. Lake - 1885: With Added Maps. expanded rev. ed. LC 90-3379. 60p. 1991. pap. text 26.00 (*1-878014-03-X*) G P Hammond Pub.
Lake, Dale, jt. auth. see Ulrich, Dave.
Lake, Dale G. Perceiving & Behaving. LC 72-77891. 116p. reprint ed. pap. 36.00 (*0-608-14858-X*, 202603800048) Bks Demand.
***Lake, David.** Entangling Relations: American Foreign Policy In Its Century. LC 98-37330. 1999. 60.00 (*0-691-05990-X*, Pub. by Princeton U Pr) Cal Prin Full Svc.
Lake, David, ed. The International Political Economy of Trade, 2 vols., Set. (Library of International Political Economy: Vol. 1). 1168p. 1993. 385.00 (*1-85278-583-7*) E Elgar.
Lake, David & Rothchild, Donald. Ethnic Fears & Global Engagement: The International Spread & Management of Ethnic Conflict. (IGCC Policy Paper: No. 20). 62p. (Orig.). 1996. pap. 3.50 (*0-934637-35-0*) U of CA Inst Global.
***Lake, David A.** Entangling relations: American Foreign Policy in Its Century. LC 98-37330. 1999. 17.95 (*0-691-05991-8*, Pub. by Princeton U Pr) Cal Prin Full Svc.
Lake, David A. Power, Protection, & Free Trade: International Sources of U. S. Commercial Strategy, 1887-1939. LC 87-47869. (Cornell Studies in Political Economy). 264p. 1988. text 42.50 (*0-8014-2134-9*) Cornell U Pr.
— Power, Protection, & Free Trade: International Sources of U. S. Commercial Strategy, 1887-1939. LC 87-47869. (Cornell Studies in Political Economy). 264p. 1990. reprint ed. pap. text 17.95 (*0-8014-9753-1*) Cornell U Pr.
Lake, David A. & Morgan, Patrick M. Regional Orders: Building Security in a New World. LC 96-50186. 1997. 55.00 (*0-271-01703-1*); pap. 19.95 (*0-271-01704-X*) Pa St U Pr.
Lake, David A. & Powell, Robert. Strategic Choice & International Relations LC 99-12215. 1999. 16.95 (*0-691-02697-1*, Pub. by Princeton U Pr) Cal Prin Full Svc.
Lake, David A. & Powell, Robert, eds. Strategic Choice & International Relations. (Illus.). 248p. 49.50 (*0-691-02698-X*, Pub. by Princeton U Pr) Cal Prin Full Svc.
Lake, David A. & Rothchild, Donald S. The International Spread of Ethnic Conflict: Fear, Diffusion, & Escalation. LC 97-15031. 424p. 1998. text 60.00 (*0-691-01691-7*, Pub. by Princeton U Pr); pap. text 18.95 (*0-691-01690-9*, Pub. by Princeton U Pr) Cal Prin Full Svc.
Lake, David A., jt. auth. see Frieden, Jeffry A.
Lake, David A., jt. auth. see Long, Wallace.
Lake, David C. Feelings Are for Sharing. LC 86-80550. 128p. 1987. 11.75 (*0-9616471-0-8*) Intl Enlightenment.
Lake, David J. The Canon of Thomas Middleton's Plays: Internal Evidence for the Major Problems of Authorship. LC 74-25661. 314p. reprint ed. pap. 89.50 (*0-608-12063-4*, 2024487) Bks Demand.

An Asterisk (*) at the beginning of an entry indicates that the title is appearing for the first time.

Lake, E. & Porter, F., eds. Livy: Hannibal the Scourge of Rome: Selections from Book X. (Bristol Latin Texts Ser.). (LAT.). 103p. 1976. reprint ed. 16.95 (0-86292-131-7, Pub. by Brist Class Pr) Focus Pub-R Pullins.

Lake, E. D. Lowriders & Other Customized Cars. (Wheels Ser.). (Illus.). 48p. (J). (gr. 3-6). 1995. 19.00 (0-516-35217-2) Childrens.

Lake Editors. The Classroom Resource Book: One-A-Day Language Lessons - People at Work. 192p. (YA). (gr. 6-12). 1995. pap. 49.50 (0-7854-0832-0, 40272) Am Guidance.

— The Teacher's Daybook: One-A-Day Language Lessons - People at Work. LC 95-80019. 192p. 1995. teacher ed., spiral bd. 49.50 (0-7854-0831-2, 40271) Am Guidance.

Lake, Elizabeth, ed. see Harris, Roger.

Lake, Elizabeth, ed. see Hunt, Glen & Smith, Eugene.

Lake, GeorgeTombe. Southern Sudan: The Foundation of a War Economy. LC 93-43060. (Illus.). 98p. 1994. 29.00 (3-631-46579-3) P Lang Pubng.

***Lake, Gina.** Symbols of the Soul: Discovering Your Karma Through Astrology. LC 99-58551. (Illus.). 240p. 2000. pap. 12.95 (1-56718-407-3) Llewellyn Pubns.

Lake, H. S., tr. see Lievegoed, Bernard.

Lake, Inez H. Road from Pompey's Head: The Life & Work of Hamilton Basso. LC 98-34406. (Southern Literary Studies). 256p. 1999. 29.95 (0-8071-2294-7) La State U Pr.

Lake, J. W. Mythos of the Ark. 1993. reprint ed. pap. 8.95 (1-55818-199-7, Sure Fire) Holmes Pub.

— Tree & Serpent Worship. 1994. reprint ed. pap. 8.95 (1-55818-274-8, Sure Fire) Holmes Pub.

Lake, James A., jt. auth. see Flaws, Robert.

Lake, Jane. Riding Western. 88p. (C). 1990. pap. 30.00 (0-85131-432-5, Pub. by J A Allen) St Mut.

Lake, Janet & Zilker, Sandra. Nourish & Flourish: How to Feast Nutritiously. 174p. 1990. text 12.50 (0-9640010-1-2) Peace Pubng.

Lake, John. Jane's Pocket Guide: A.T. F. 144p. 1999. pap. 15.00 (0-00-472135-7, Harper Ref) HarpC.

— John G. Lake. (Living Classics Ser.). 160p. 1996. mass mkt. 5.99 (0-89274-985-7, HH985) Harrison Hse.

Lake, John G. Adventures in God. 131p. 1981. pap. 6.99 (0-89274-206-2) Harrison Hse.

— Adventures in God. rev. ed. 96p. 1991. pap. 6.99 (0-89274-819-2, HH-819) Harrison Hse.

— John G. Lake: The Complete Collection of His Life Teachings. 1200p. 1998. 29.99 (1-57778-075-2) Albury Pub.

Lake, Jon. Blenheim Units of World War 2. (Illus.). 96p. 1998. pap. 17.95 (1-85532-723-6, 126377AE, Pub. by Osprey) Motorbooks Intl.

— Halifax Units of World War II, Vol.14. (Combat Aircraft Ser.). 1999. pap. text 17.95 (1-85532-892-5) Osprey.

***Lake, Jon.** Jane's MiG-29: At the Controls. (Jane's at the Controls Ser.). 96p. 1998. pap. 18.00 (0-00-472144-6) HarpC.

Lake, Jon. SBD Dauntless Units of World War 2. (Combat Aircraft Ser.: No. 10). (Illus.). 96p. 1998. pap. 16.95 (1-85532-732-5, Pub. by Osprey) Motorbooks Intl.

***Lake, Jon.** Sunderland Squadrons of World War 2. (Combat Aircraft Ser.: Vol. 20). (Illus.). 112p. 2000. pap. 17.95 (1-84176-025-0, Pub. by Osprey) Motorbooks Intl.

Lake, Jon. Top Spy. LC 95-76744. (Ten-Minute Thrillers Ser.). 32p. (YA). (gr. 6-12). 1995. pap. 2.95 (0-7854-1071-6, 40823) Am Guidance.

— Top Spy Readalong. (Ten-Minute Thrillers Ser.). 32p. (YA). (gr. 6-12). 1995. pap. 12.95 incl. audio (0-7854-1082-1, 40825) Am Guidance.

Lake, Jon, ed. Grumman F-14 Tomcat: Shipborne Superfighter. (Illus.). 224p. 1998. 34.95 (1-880588-13-7, Aerospace) AIRtime Pub.

— Phantom: Spirit in the Skies. 232p. 1993. 34.95 (1-880588-04-8) AIRtime Pub.

***Lake, Jon & Jane's Staff.** Jane's F-117 Stealth Fighter: At The Controls. (Jane's at the Controls Ser.). (Illus.). 96p. 1998. pap. 18.00 (0-00-472109-8, Pub. by Harper SF) HarpC.

Lake, Jon, jt. auth. see Dorr, Robert.

Lake, Jon, ed. see Aerospace Publishing Ltd. Staff.

Lake, Jon, jt. ed. see Donald, David.

Lake, Julian. Guess Who's Coming Out at Dinner? Vol. 1: Coming Out Cartoons. LC 98-68356. (Illus.). 96p. 1999. pap. 8.95 (0-9663454-1-X) Rubicon Media.

***Lake, Julian.** Please Don't Come Out While We're Eating: Coming Out Cartoons. LC 99-98253. (Illus.). 100p. 2000. pap. 8.95 (0-9663454-3-6, Pub. by Rubicon Media) Bookazine Co Inc.

Lake, Kirsopp, tr. Ecclesiastical History, 2 vols., 1. (Loeb Classical Library: No. 153, 265). 582p. 1926. 18.95 (0-674-99169-9) HUP.

Lake, Larry W. Enhanced Oil Recovery. 600p. (C). 1988. text 74.25 (0-13-281601-6) P-H.

Lake, Laura M. Environmental Regulation: The Political Effects of Implementation. LC 82-12305. 152p. 1982. 47.95 (0-275-90844-5, C0844, Praeger Pubs) Greenwood.

Lake, Laura M., ed. Environmental Mediation: The Search for Consensus. (Social Impact Assessment Ser.). 1980. text 48.50 (0-89158-587-7) Westview.

Lake, Linda K., jt. auth. see Connor, Patrick E.

Lake, Liz, ed. see Gutteridge, Marianne.

Lake, M. D. Amends for Murder. 224p. (Orig.). 1989. mass mkt. 4.99 (0-380-75865-2, Avon Bks) Morrow Avon.

— Cold Comfort. 224p. 1990. mass mkt. 5.99 (0-380-76032-0, Avon Bks) Morrow Avon.

— Death Calls the Tune: A Peggy O'Neill Mystery. (Peggy O'Neill Mystery Ser.). 256p. 1999. mass mkt. 5.99 (0-380-78760-1, Avon Bks) Morrow Avon.

— Flirting with Death. 288p. (Orig.). 1996. mass mkt. 5.99 (0-380-77522-0, Avon Bks) Morrow Avon.

— Gift for Murder. 256p. 1992. mass mkt. 5.50 (0-380-76855-0, Avon Bks) Morrow Avon.

— Grave Choices: A Peggy O'Neill Mystery. 256p. (Orig.). 1995. mass mkt. 5.99 (0-380-77521-2, Avon Bks) Morrow Avon.

— Midsummer Malice. (Peggy O'Neill Mystery Ser.). 256p. 1997. mass mkt. 5.99 (0-380-78759-8, Avon Bks) Morrow Avon.

— Murder by Mail. 256p. (Orig.). 1993. mass mkt. 5.99 (0-380-76856-9, Avon Bks) Morrow Avon.

— Once upon a Crime. 275p. (Orig.). 1995. mass mkt. 5.50 (0-380-77520-4, Avon Bks) Morrow Avon.

— Poisoned Ivy. 256p. 1992. mass mkt. 5.50 (0-380-76573-X, Avon Bks) Morrow Avon.

***Lake, Marilyn.** Getting Equal: The History of Australian Feminism. 272p. 2000. pap. 24.95 (1-86508-137-X, Pub. by Allen & Unwin Pty) Paul & Co Pubs.

Lake, Marilyn. Limits of Hope: Soldier Settlement in Victoria, 1915-1938. (Illus.). 272p. 1987. 39.00 (0-19-554666-0) OUP.

Lake, Marilyn, jt. ed. see Damousi, Joy.

Lake, Marilyn, jt. ed. see Holmes, Katie.

Lake, Mary D. My Circus Family. LC 95-17745. (Illus.). 8p. (J). (ps-1). 1995. pap. 2.95 (1-57255-034-1) Mondo Pubng.

— The Royal Drum: An Ashanti Tale. LC 95-33612. (Illus.). 24p. (J). (gr. 1-5). 1996. 14.95 (1-57255-140-2) Mondo Pubng.

Lake, Matthew. Breaking into Windows. 241p. 1993. pap. 24.95 incl. disk (1-56276-144-7, Ziff-Davis Pr) Que.

Lake Medicine Grizzly Bear. Native Healer: Initiation into an Ancient Art. 1991. pap. 13.00 (0-8356-0667-8, Quest) Theos Pub Hse.

Lake, Monte B. Immigration Act of 1990: An Employer's Handbook. 354p. (Orig.). 1992. pap. 50.00 (0-916559-37-8) EPF.

Lake, Nara. A Court for Owls. large type ed. 336p. 1996. 27.99 (0-7089-3450-1) Ulverscroft.

— Goldrush Girl. large type ed. 352p. 1996. 27.99 (0-7089-3488-9) Ulverscroft.

— Hostage of Love. large type ed. (Linford Romance Large Print Ser.). 368p. 1997. pap. 16.99 (0-7089-7983-1, Linford) Ulverscroft.

***Lake, Nara.** Lost Woman. large type ed. 272p. 2000. 31.99 (0-7089-4170-2) Ulverscroft.

Lake, Nara. Man from Kanpur. large type ed. (Linford Romance Library). 368p. 1996. pap. 16.99 (0-7089-7966-1, Linford) Ulverscroft.

— The Painted Girl. large type ed. 1995. 27.99 (0-7089-3275-4) Ulverscroft.

***Lake, Nara.** The Secret Man. large type ed. 304p. 1999. 31.99 (0-7089-4150-8) Ulverscroft.

— The Smiling Stranger. 264p. 2000. 31.99 (0-7089-4217-2) Ulverscroft.

Lake, Nara. The Traitor Heart. large type ed. 352p. 1995. 27.99 (0-7089-3334-3) Ulverscroft.

Lake, Neal E. The Preacher's Notebook. 1994. pap. 5.95 (1-55673-594-4, 7993) CSS OH.

***Lake, Neville.** Third Principle: How to Get 20More out of Your Business. 2000. pap. text 19.95 (1-875680-70-5) Woodslane.

Lake, Obiagele. RastafarI Women: Subordination in the Midst of Liberation Theology. LC 98-11542. 214p. 1998. pap. 22.95 (0-89089-836-7) Carolina Acad Pr.

Lake of the Ozarks General Hospital Auxiliary Staf. A Taste of the Lake. LC 93-70696. 1993. write for info. (0-87197-369-3) Favorite Recipes.

Lake, Patricia, jt. auth. see Miller, Somi A.

Lake, Paul. Among the Immortals: A Novel. 302p. 1994. pap. 14.95 (0-934257-73-6) Story Line.

— Another Kind of Travel. LC 87-14705. (Phoenix Poets Ser.). 80p. 1987. pap. 9.95 (0-226-46808-9) U Ch Pr.

— Another Kind of Travel. (Phoenix Poets Ser.). 80p. 1994. lib. bdg. 20.00 (0-226-46807-0) U Ch Pr.

— Bull Dancing, Vol. 5. 1977. pap. 3.95 (0-685-50008-X) Brick Hse Bks.

— Walking Backward. LC 99-22540. 88p. 1999. pap. 12.95 (1-885266-72-3, Pub. by Story Line) Consort Bk Sales.

Lake, Peter & Dowling, Maria. Protestantism & the National Church in 16th Century England. 224p. 1987. lib. bdg. 55.00 (0-7099-1681-7, Pub. by C Helm) Routldge.

***Lake, Peter & Questier, Michael C., eds.** Conformity & Orthodoxy in the English Church, c. 1560-1660. (Studies in Modern British Religious History: Vol. 1464-6625). (Illus.). 302p. 2000. 90.00 (0-85115-797-1) Boydell & Brewer.

Lake, Peter, jt. ed. see Sharpe, Kevin.

Lake, Peter F., jt. auth. see Bickel, Robert D.

Lake, R. D., et al. The Wakefield District - A Concise Account of the Geology: Memoir for 1:50 000 Sheet 78 (England & Wales) (British Geological Survey Memoirs Ser.). (Illus.). viii, 97p. 70.00 (0-11-884554-3, Pub. by Statnry Office) Balogh.

Lake, Ralph B. & Draetta, Ugo. Lake & Draetta: Letters of Intent & Other Precontractual Documents. 2nd ed. 1995. write for info. (0-406-05047-3, LLI2, MICHIE) LEXIS Pub.

— Letters of Intent & Other Precontractual Documents: Comparative Analysis & Forms. 2nd ed. 350p. 1994. 95.00 (0-250-40740-X, MICHIE) LEXIS Pub.

Lake, Ralph B., et al. Lake, Nanda & Draetta: Breach & Adaption of International Contracts. 1992. write for info. (0-406-02055-8, DLNB, MICHIE) LEXIS Pub.

***Lake, Rick & Lake, Ronald.** Private Equity & Venture Capital: A Practical Guide for Investors & Practioners. 323p. 2000. pap. text 170.00 (1-85564-691-9, Pub. by Euromoney) Am Educ Systs.

Lake, Robert. Blood Trail to Kansas. 1991. mass mkt. 3.50 (0-8217-3541-1, Zebra Kensgtn) Kensgtn Pub Corp.

— Mountain Man's Vengeance. 1991. mass mkt. 3.50 (0-8217-3619-1, Zebra Kensgtn) Kensgtn Pub Corp.

Lake, Robert W. Locational Conflict: Community Capital & the State. 208p. (C). 1999. 70.00 (0-415-11571-X) Routledge.

Lake, Robert W. & Fitzgerald, Thomas E., Jr. Real Estate Tax Delinquency in the Central City: Private Disinvestment & Public Response. LC 79-12207. 268p. 1979. 1.00 (0-88285-046-6) Ctr Urban Pol Res.

Lake, Ron, et al. How-to Make Folding Knives: A Step-by-Step How to. 193p. 1994. pap. 13.95 (0-87341-390-3) Krause Pubns.

Lake, Ronald, ed. Evaluating & Implementing Hedge Fund Strategies. 2nd ed. 296p. 1999. pap. 195.00 (1-85564-660-9, Pub. by Euromoney) Am Educ Systs.

Lake, Ronald, jt. auth. see Lake, Rick.

Lake, Rosemary. Once upon a Time When the Princess Beat the Dragon. (Once upon a Time When the Princess...Ser.). (Illus.). 100p. (Orig.). (J). (gr. 4-10). 2001. pap. 10.00 (0-940918-51-X) Dragon Tree.

— Once upon a Time When the Princess Cast the Spell. (Once upon a Time When the Princess...Ser.). (Illus.). 100p. (Orig.). (J). (gr. 4-10). 2000. pap. 10.00 (0-940918-52-8) Dragon Tree.

— Once upon a Time When the Princess Got the Treasure. (Once upon a Time When the Princess...Ser.). (Illus.). 100p. (Orig.). (J). (gr. 4-10). 2002. pap. 10.00 (0-940918-53-6) Dragon Tree.

— Once upon a Time When the Princess Rescued the Prince. (Once upon a Time When the Princess...Ser.). (Illus.). 100p. (Orig.). (J). (gr. 4-10). 2000. pap. 10.00 (0-940918-50-1) Dragon Tree.

Lake, Russ K., ed. see Gallagher, Mark.

Lake, Russell W. Thank God for Prayer. LC 83-50397. 292p. 1983. 3.48 (0-87159-159-6) Unity Bks.

Lake, Stuart N. Wyatt Earp: Frontier Marshall. Grad, Doug, ed. 416p. 1994. reprint ed. mass mkt. 6.99 (0-671-88537-5) PB.

Lake, Susan E. Unit Based Planning: A Guide for the Secondary English Teacher. 135p. (Orig.). (C). 1994. pap. 15.00 (1-881459-10-1) Eagle Pr SC.

Lake, Tela S. Hawk Woman Dancing with the Moon. LC 97-44970. 256p. 1998. pap. 14.95 (0-87131-846-6) M Evans.

— Hawk Woman Dancing with the Moon: The Last Female Shaman. LC 95-51463. (Illus.). 256p. 1996. 19.95 (0-87131-802-4) M Evans.

Lake-Thom, Bobby. Spirits of the Earth: A Guide to Native American Symbols, Stories & Ceremonies. LC 97-11026. (Illus.). 224p. 1997. pap. 13.95 (0-452-27650-0, Plume) Dutton Plume.

Lake, Thomas T. Endo Nasal, Aural & Allied Techniques: Ear, Eye, Nose & Throat. 109p. 1996. reprint ed. spiral bd. 11.00 (0-7873-0521-9) Hlth Research.

— The Fundamentals of Applied Psychiatry for Non-Medical Physicians. 102p. 1996. reprint ed. spiral bd. 16.50 (0-7873-0520-0) Hlth Research.

— Treatment by Neuropathy & the Encyclopedia of Physical & Manipulative Therapeutics. 684p. 1996. reprint ed. spiral bd. 38.50 (0-7873-0519-7) Hlth Research.

***Lake, Tom, ed.** Hudson River Almanac, Vol. 5. (Illus.). 128p. 1999. pap. 10.00 (1-930098-03-0) Purple Mnt Pr.

Lake, Tom, ed. The Hudson River Almanac, 1997-1998, Vol. 4. (Illus.). 128p. 1998. pap. 10.00 (0-916346-66-8) Purple Mnt Pr.

— The Hudson River Almanac 1995-1996, Vol. II. (Illus.). 128p. 1996. pap. 10.00 (0-935796-84-3) Purple Mnt Pr.

Lake, Tony. Overcoming Nervous Breakdown. 107p. 1989. reprint ed. pap. 7.95 (1-878290-01-0) Intl Hlth MD.

Lake, Van M. Book of the I AM. LC 98-90838. 1999. 7.95 (0-533-12934-6) Vantage.

Lake, Vicki. Firm up Your Flabby Faith. (Women's Inductive Bible Study Ser.). 96p. 1990. pap. 6.50 (0-89693-783-6, 6-1783, Victor Bks) Chariot Victor.

Lakein, Alan. Give Me a Moment & I'll Change Your Life: Tools for Moment Management. 112p. 1998. pap. 7.95 (0-8362-6943-8) Andrews & McMeel.

— How to Get Control of Your Time & Your Life. 10.95 (0-317-63116-0) McKay.

— How to Get Control of Your Time & Your Life. 1989. mass mkt. 6.99 (0-451-16772-4) NAL.

Lakeland, Jo, tr. see Mernissi, Fatima.

Lakeland, Mary J., tr. see Mernissi, Fatima.

Lakeland, Paul. Freedom in Christ: An Introduction to Political Theology. 2nd ed. LC 86-80021. 151p. reprint ed. pap. 46.90 (0-7837-5609-7, 204551500005) Bks Demand.

— The Politics of Salvation: The Hegelian Idea of the State. LC 83-17875. (SUNY Series in Hegelian Studies). 197p. (C). 1985. pap. text 21.95 (0-87395-847-0) State U NY Pr.

— Postmodernity: Christian Identity in a Fragmented Age. LC 97-23817. (Guide to Theological Inquiry Ser.). 128p. 1997. pap. 14.00 (0-8006-3098-X, 1-3098, Fortress Pr) Augsburg Fortress.

Lakeman, Sandra D. Natural Light & the Italian Piazza: Siena, As a Case Study. LC 93-206345. (Illus.). 110p. 1995. pap. 24.95 (0-295-97418-4) U of Wash Pr.

Lakemeyer, Gerhard & Nebel, Bernhard, eds. Foundations of Knowledge Representation & Reasoning. LC 94-20768. (Lecture Notes in Computer Science, Vol. 810; Lecture Notes in Artificial Intelligence). 1994. 55.95 (0-387-58107-3) Spr-Verlag.

Lakemeyer, Gerhard, jt. auth. see Levesque, Hector J.

Laken, Donna D. Prevent Complications Due to Impaired Mobility. 1995. pap. 3.95 (0-915708-43-4, 3164) Cheever Pub.

Laken, M. P. & Hutchins, E. Recruitment & Retention of Substance-Using Pregnant Women & Parenting Women: Lessons Learned. LC 96-69415. (Illus.). 72p. 1996. pap. write for info. (1-57285-033-7) Nat Ctr Educ.

Laken, M. Poland & Hutchins, E. Building & Sustaining Systems of Care for Substance-Using Pregnant Women & Their Infants. LC 95-71705. 68p. 1995. pap. text. write for info. (1-57285-021-3) Nat Ctr Educ.

Laker. Clinical Biochemistry for Medicine. 1995. pap. text 33.00 (0-7020-1690-X, W B Saunders Co) Harcrt Hlth Sci Grp.

***Laker, Anthony.** Beyond the Boundaries of Physical Education: Educating Young People for Citizenship & Social Responsibility. LC 99-53989. 2000. write for info. (0-7507-0930-8, Falmer Pr) Taylor & Francis.

L

Laker, Kenneth R. Design of Analog Integrated Circuits & Systems. LC 93-49574. 896p. (C). 1994. 103.44 (0-07-036060-X) McGraw.

Laker, Mark. Nursing Home Activities for the Handicapped. 98p. 1980. pap., spiral bd. 23.95 (0-398-04074-5) C C Thomas.

***Laker, Rosalind.** Banners of Silk. large type ed. 768p. 1999. 31.99 (0-7505-1440-X, Pub. by Mgna Lrg Print) Ulverscroft.

— Jewelled Path. 512p. 2000. 31.99 (0-7505-1521-X) Ulverscroft.

Laker, Rosalind. The Sugar Pavilion. large type ed. LC 94-1780. 697p. 1994. lib. bdg. 24.95 (0-7862-0225-4) Thorndike Pr.

***Laker, Rosalind.** This Shining Land. LC 99-14897. 1999. pap. 27.95 (0-7838-8620-9, G K Hall Lrg Type) Mac Lib Ref.

Laker, Rosalind. The Venetian Mask. large type ed. 691p. 1993. reprint ed. lib. bdg. 23.95 (1-56054-585-2) Thorndike Pr.

— What the Heart Keeps. 1986. pap. 3.95 (0-8217-1810-X) NAL.

***Laker, Rosalind.** What the Heart Keeps. large type ed. LC 99-45559. (Thorndike Romance Ser.). 1999. 28.95 (0-7862-2262-X) Thorndike Pr.

Lakers, John J. Christian Ethics: An Ethics of Intimacy. LC 96-16811. 1996. 16.95 (0-8199-0972-6) Franciscan Pr.

Lakervi, E. & Holmes, E. J. Electricity Distribution Network Design. 2nd ed. (Power Ser.: No. 21). 336p. 1995. boxed set 99.00 (0-86341-308-0, PO021) INSPEC Inc.

— Electricity Distribution Network Design. 2nd ed. (I. E. E. Poewr Ser.: No. 212). 336p. 1995. pap. 40.00 (0-86341-309-9) INSPEC Inc.

Lakes, R. S., jt. auth. see Park, J. B.

Lakes Region General Hospital Auxiliary Staff. Lakes Region Cuisine: A Centennial Celebration, 1893-1993. LC 93-70329. 1993. spiral bd. 12.50 (0-87197-365-0) Favorite Recipes.

Lakes, Richard D. Critical Education for Work: Multidisciplinary Approaches. 224p. (Orig.). 1994. pap. 24.95 (1-56750-110-9) Ablx Pub.

— Youth Development & Critical Education: The Promise of Democratic Action. LC 96-21038. (SUNY Series, Democracy & Education). (Illus.). 181p. (C). 1997. text 49.50 (0-7914-3349-8); pap. text 16.95 (0-7914-3350-1) State U NY Pr.

Lakes, Richard D., ed. Critical Education for Work: Multidisciplinary Approaches. 224p. (Orig.). 1994. text 73.25 (1-56750-109-5) Ablx Pub.

Lakes, Roderic S. Viscoelastic Solids. LC 98-26280. (Mechanical Engineering Ser.). 496p. 1998. boxed set 84.95 (0-8493-9658-1) CRC Pr.

***Lakeshore Learning Materials Staff.** Best-Loved Writers & Their Work Reading Program, Set. 1999. pap. write for info. (1-929255-05-5, RA468) Lkeshore Learn Mats.

— First Chapter Book Collection, Set. 1998. pap. write for info. (1-929255-03-9) Lkeshore Learn Mats.

— High Interest Transitional Readers, Set. 1998. pap. write for info. (1-929255-02-0, LK953) Lkeshore Learn Mats.

— Learning Phonics Through Literature Program, Set. 1997. pap. write for info. (1-929255-00-4, LK600X) Lkeshore Learn Mats.

— Phonemic Awareness Literature Packets Set. 1999. pap. write for info. (1-929255-01-2, RR910X) Lkeshore Learn Mats.

— Really Readable Books: Green Level, Set. 1997. pap. write for info. (1-929255-04-7, LA496) Lkeshore Learn Mats.

Lakey, Berit, et al. Grassroots & Non-Profit Leadership: A Guide for Organizations in Changing Times. 224p. 1995. pap. 16.95 (0-86571-328-6) New Soc Pubs.

Lakey, George. Non-Violent Action: How it Works. LC 63-17661. (C). 1963. pap. 4.00 (0-87574-129-0) Pendle Hill.

Lakey, Steven D. Bamboo Horses: Wooden Dragons - Twenty-Two Hornet. LC 80-69812. 60p. (Orig.). 1980. text 4.95 (0-685-01609-9, 0003); pap. text 3.25 (0-936748-04-4) Fade In.

— The Nickel Chimera. LC 80-65824. (Illus.). 60p. (C). 1980. 4.95 (0-936748-00-1); pap. 2.95 (0-936748-01-X) Fade In.

Lakha, Salim, jt. ed. see Pinches, Michael.

Lakhakia, A., ed. Selected Papers on Natural Optical Activity. 624p. 1990. pap. 35.00 (0-8194-0436-5, VOL. MS15) SPIE.

Lakhan, V. C. & Trenhaile, Alan S., eds. Applications in Coastal Modeling. (Elsevier Oceanography Ser.: No. 49). 388p. 1989. 184.75 (0-444-87452-6) Elsevier.

Lakhani, Mayur, et al. Evidence-Based Audit. LC 98-26928. (Illus.). 128p. 1998. pap. text 35.00 (0-7506-3104-X) Buttrwrth-Heinemann.

Lakhani, Sunil, et al. Basic Pathology: An Introduction to the Mechanisms of Disease. 2nd ed. (An Arnold Publication). (Illus.). 336p. 1998. pap. text 24.50 (0-340-67787-2) OUP.

Lakhani, Sunil R., jt. ed. see Al-Sam, S.

Lakhanpal, P. L. A Rebel at Law. (C). 1987. 135.00 (0-7855-4778-9) St Mut.

An Asterisk (*) at the beginning of an entry indicates that the title is appearing for the first time.

L

Lakhanpal, T. N. & Mukerji, K. G. Taxonomy of the Indian Myxomycetes. (Bibliotheca Mycologica Ser.: No. 78). (Illus.). 532p. 1981. lib. bdg. 112.00 (*3-7682-1287-4*) Lubrecht & Cramer.

Lakhanpal, T. N., jt. auth. see Monga, Pradeep.

Lakhnech, Y., jt. ed. see Berghammer, R.

Lakhno, V. D. & Chuev, G. N., eds. Physics of Clusters. 360p. 1998. 68.00 (*981-02-3307-8*) World Scientific Pub.

Lakhno, Victor D., ed. Polarons & Applications. (Proceedings in Nonlinear Science Ser.). 528p. 1995. text 250.00 (*0-471-95514-0*) Wiley.

— Spin Wave Amplification: Electron Mechanisms. 148p. (C). 1992. text 175.00 (*1-56072-067-0*) Nova Sci Pubs.

Lakhotia, R. N. Tax Planning Through Trusts & Wills. 2nd ed. (C). 1988. 60.00 (*0-7855-3660-4*) St Mut.

— Zero to Hero in Income Tax. (C). 1990. 65.00 (*0-89771-267-6*) St Mut.

Lakhovsky, G. The Secret of Life: Cosmic Rays & Radiations & Radiations of Living Beings & Electro-Magnetic Waves. (Alternative Energy Ser.). 1991. lib. bdg. 79.95 (*0-8490-4275-5*) Gordon Pr.

Lakhovsky, Georges. The Secret of Life. 213p. 1996. reprint ed. pap. 17.50 (*0-7873-0522-7*) Hlth Research.

Lakhtakia, Akhlesh. Beltrami Fields in Chiral Media. LC 95-105786. (Contemporary Chemical Physics Ser.: No. 2). 556p. 1994. text 86.00 (*981-02-1403-0*) World Scientific Pub.

— Models & Modelers of Hydrogen. 400p. 1996. text 58.00 (*981-02-2302-1*) World Scientific Pub.

Lakhtakia, Akhlesh, ed. Essays on the Formal Aspects of Electromagnetic Theory. 550p. 1993. text 140.00 (*981-02-0854-5*) World Scientific Pub.

— Selected Papers on Linear Optical Composite Materials. LC 95-53169. (SPIE Milestone Ser.: Vol. MS120). 1996. 118.00 (*0-8194-2152-9*) SPIE.

Lakhtakia, Akhlesh, et al. Time-Harmonic Electromagnetic Fields in Chiral Media. (Lecture Notes in Physics Ser.: Vol. 335). vii, 121p. 1989. 34.95 (*0-387-51317-5*) Spr-Verlag.

Lakhtakia, Akhlesh, jt. ed. see Singh, Onkar N.

Lakhtin, Y. Engineering Physical Metallurgy. (Russian Monographs & Texts on the Physical Sciences). 472p. 1965. text 412.00 (*0-677-20240-7*) Gordon & Breach.

Laki, Koloman. Fibrinogen. LC 67-22482. 412p. reprint ed. pap. 127.80 (*0-608-16925-0*, 202709600054) Bks Demand.

Laki, Koloman, ed. Contractile Proteins & Muscle. LC 72-134784. (Illus.). 622p. reprint ed. pap. 192.90 (*0-7837-0949-8*, 204125400019) Bks Demand.

Laki, Peter. Bartok & His World. LC 95-13368. 250p. 1995. text 59.50 (*0-691-00634-2*, Pub. by Princeton U Pr); pap. text 20.95 (*0-691-00633-4*, Pub. by Princeton U Pr) Cal Prin Full Svc.

Laki, Peter & Kantor, Barna, trs. from HUN. Brassai: Letters to My Parents. LC 97-10099. 274p. 1997. 29.95 (*0-226-07146-4*) U Ch Pr.

Lakic, Nikola, jt. auth. see Gardiner, Frederick P.

Lakier, Aleksandr B. A Russian Looks at America: The Journey of Aleksandr Borisovich Lakier in 1857. Schrier, Arnold & Story, Joyce, eds. LC 79-11205. 1993. 15.95 (*0-226-46795-3*) U Ch Pr.

— A Russian Looks at America: The Journey of Aleksandr Borisovich Lakier in 1857. Schrier, Arnold & Story, Joyce, eds. & trs. by. LC 79-11205. (Illus.). 330p. reprint ed. pap. 102.30 (*0-608-09460-9*, 205426000005) Bks Demand.

Lakin, Chuck, jt. auth. see Lancy, Michael.

Lakin, Dennis. Lyme Disease - The Untold Story. 174p. 1998. pap. 20.00 (*1-890622-15-X*) Leathers Pub.

Lakin, Joan, jt. auth. see Meyers, Susan.

Lakin, K. M., jt. auth. see Chazov, Eugene I.

Lakin, Leonard & Beane, Leona. Materials in the Law of Business Contracts. 3rd ed. 368p. (C). 1995. pap. text, per. 30.95 (*0-8403-9236-2*) Kendall-Hunt.

Lakin, Leonard, jt. auth. see Schiff.

Lakin, Martin. Coping with Ethical Dilemmas. 264p. (C). 1991. pap. text 40.00 (*0-205-14401-2*, H4401) Allyn.

— Ethical Issues in the Psychotherapies. 192p. 1988. text 45.00 (*0-19-504446-0*) OUP.

— The Helping Group: Therapeutic Principles & Issues. 288p. 1987. 19.95 (*0-317-66348-8*, Pergamon Pr) Elsevier.

— Personality Factors in Mothers of Excessively Crying Infants. (SRCD M Ser.: Vol. 22, No. 1). 1957. pap. 25.00 (*0-527-01569-5*) Periodicals Srv.

***Lakin, Pat.** Subway Sonata. LC 00-29209. (Illus.). (J). 2001. lib. bdg. write for info. (*0-7613-1464-4*) Millbrook Pr.

Lakin, Patricia. Aware & Alert. LC 94-19718. (My Community Ser.). (Illus.). 32p. (J). (ps-4). 1995. lib. bdg. 21.40 (*0-8114-8261-8*) Raintree Steck-V.

— Dad & Me in the Morning. LC 93-36169. (Illus.). 32p. (J). (gr. 1-3). 1994. lib. bdg. 14.95 (*0-8075-1419-5*) A Whitman.

— Don't Forget. LC 93-20341. (Illus.). 32p. (J). 1994. lib. bdg. 13.93 (*0-688-12076-8*, Wm Morrow) Morrow Avon.

***Lakin, Patricia.** Don't Forget. LC 93-20341. (Illus.). 32p. (YA). (gr. k-3). 2000. pap. 5.95 (*0-688-17522-8*, Wm Morrow) Morrow Avon.

Lakin, Patricia. Family: Around the World. Glassman, Bruce, ed. LC 94-41713. (We All Share Ser.). (Illus.). 32p. (J). (gr. 3-5). 1995. lib. bdg. 16.95 (*1-56711-143-2*) Blackbirch.

— Food: Around the World. LC 98-50549. (We All Share Ser.). (Illus.). 32p. (J). (gr. 3-6). 1999. lib. bdg. 16.95 (*1-56711-147-5*) Blackbirch.

— Grandparents: Around the World. LC 98-46854. (We All Share Ser.). (Illus.). 32p. (J). (gr. 3-6). 1999. lib. bdg. 16.95 (*1-56711-146-7*) Blackbirch.

— Information, Please. LC 94-22495. (My Community Ser.). (Illus.). 32p. (J). (ps-4). 1995. lib. bdg. 21.40 (*0-8114-8260-X*) Raintree Steck-V.

— Jennifer Capritati. LC 93-18131. (Winning Spirirt Ser.). 48p. (J). (gr. 4-8). 1993. lib. bdg. 21.27 (*0-86592-090-7*) Rourke Enter.

— The Palace of Stars. LC 92-36796. (Illus.). 32p. (J). (ps up). 1993. 14.00 (*0-688-11176-9*, Wm Morrow) Morrow Avon.

— Play: Around the World. Glassman, Bruce, ed. LC 94-38497. (We All Share Ser.). (Illus.). 32p. (J). (gr. 3-5). 1995. lib. bdg. 16.95 (*1-56711-141-6*) Blackbirch.

— Red Letter Day: The Mail Carrier. LC 94-28680. (My Community Ser.). (Illus.). 32p. (J). (ps-4). 1995. lib. bdg. 21.40 (*0-8114-8264-2*) Raintree Steck-V.

— Signs of Protest. LC 94-19717. (My Community Ser.). (Illus.). 32p. (J). (ps-4). 1995. lib. bdg. 21.40 (*0-8114-8263-4*) Raintree Steck-V.

— A Summer Job. LC 94-19720. (My Community Ser.). (Illus.). 32p. (J). (ps-4). 1995. lib. bdg. 21.40 (*0-8114-8259-6*) Raintree Steck-V.

— Where There's Smoke. LC 94-19706. (My Community Ser.). (Illus.). 32p. (J). (ps-4). 1995. lib. bdg. 21.40 (*0-8114-8262-6*) Raintree Steck-V.

Lakin, R. D. American Passport. 60p. 1992. 35.00 (*0-930126-38-6*) Typographeum.

— The MacDowell Poems. limited ed. 1977. bds. 20.00 (*0-930126-00-9*) Typographeum.

Lakin, Ruth. Kettle River Country. rev. ed. (Illus.). 300p. (Orig.). (C). 1987. pap. write for info. (*0-318-62465-6*) Statesman-Exam.

Lakin, Susan, photos by. Hollywood TV's in Bondage!!!, Vol. 2. (Illus.). 28p. 1998. 19.95 (*0-9666596-1-9*, 2) Calendar Girl.

Laking, Guy F. A Record of European Armour & Arms Through Seven Centuries, 5 vols., Set. LC 79-8365. (Illus.). reprint ed. 295.00 (*0-404-18344-1*) AMS Pr.

Lakis, Chris, ed. The New York Political Almanac: The Constitutional Officers, the Senate, the Assembly, & the U. S. Congressional Delegation, 1995 Edition. rev. ed. 355p. 1995. 19.95 (*0-926766-14-7*) Ctr Leader Stu.

Lakis, Cynthia. Modern Marine Engineer's Manual, Vol. I. 3rd ed. Hunt, Everett C. et al, eds. LC 99-14987. (Illus.). 1280p. 1999. text 85.00 (*0-87033-496-4*) Cornell Maritime.

Lakke, E. A. The Projections to the Spinal Cord of the Rat During Development: A Time-Table of Descent. LC 96-39080. (Advances in Anatomy, Embryology & Cell Biology Ser.). 1997. pap. write for info. (*3-540-61878-3*) Spr-Verlag.

Lakmann, M. L. Der Platoniker Tauros in der Darstellung des Aulus Gellius. (GER.). xi, 294p. 1994. 105.50 (*90-04-10096-2*, PHA, 63) Brill Academic Pubs.

Lakner, Armand A. & Anderson, Ronald T. Reliability Engineering for Nuclear & Other High Technology Systems: A Practical Guide. (Illus.). 424p. 1985. ring bd. 300.00 (*0-85334-286-5*, Chap & Hall CRC) CRC Pr.

Lako, Gyorgy. The Proto-Finno-Ugric Antecedents of the Hungarian Phonetic Stock. LC 67-66163. (Uralic & Altaic Ser.: Vol. 80). 1966. reprint ed. spiral bd. write for info. (*0-87750-030-4*) Curzon Pr Ltd.

— Swedish-Hungarian Dictionary: Sved-Magyar Szotar. 4th ed. (HUN & SWE.). 1024p. 1985. 49.95 (*0-8288-1674-3*, M8583) Fr & Eur.

Lako, Gyorgy, jt. auth. see Feher, Janos.

Lakoff, George. Moral Politics: What Conservatives Know That Liberals Don't. LC 95-47690. 432p. 1996. 24.95 (*0-226-46796-1*) U Ch Pr.

— Moral Politics: What Conservatives Know That Liberals Don't. xii, 414p. 1997. pap. 14.95 (*0-226-46805-4*) U Ch Pr.

— Women, Fire, & Dangerous Things. LC 86-19136. xxvi, 642p. 1990. pap. 20.00 (*0-226-46804-6*) U Ch Pr.

— Women, Fire, & Dangerous Things: What Categories Reveal about the Mind. LC 86-19136. (Illus.). xviii, 614p. (C). 1987. 29.95 (*0-226-46803-8*) U Ch Pr.

Lakoff, George & Johnson, Mark. Metaphors We Live By. LC 80-10783. xiv, 242p. 1980. lib. bdg. 20.00 (*0-226-46800-3*) U Ch Pr.

— Metaphors We Live By. LC 80-10783. xiv, 256p. 1981. pap. 13.00 (*0-226-46801-1*) U Ch Pr.

— Philosophy in the Flesh: The Embodied Mind & Its Challenge to Western Thought. LC 98-37113. 826p. 1999. 32.00 (*0-465-05673-3*, Pub. by Basic) HarpC.

***Lakoff, George & Johnson, Mark.** Philosophy in the Flesh: The Embodied Mind & Its Challenge to Western Thought. 550p. 1999. pap. 20.00 (*0-465-05674-1*) HarpC.

***Lakoff, George & Nunez, Rafael.** Where Mathematics Come From: How the Embodied Mind Brings Mathematics into Being. 448p. 2000. 30.00 (*0-465-03770-4*) HarpC.

Lakoff, George & Turner, Mark. More Than Cool Reason: A Field Guide to Poetic Metaphor. LC 88-29306. 242p. 1989. pap. text 13.00 (*0-226-46812-7*) U Ch Pr.

— More Than Cool Reason: A Field Guide to Poetic Metaphor. LC 88-29306. 240p. 1998. lib. bdg. 29.95 (*0-226-46811-9*) U Ch Pr.

Lakoff, George, ed. see Borkin, Ann.

***Lakoff, Robin.** The Language War. LC 99-55386. 2000. 24.95 (*0-520-22296-2*) U CA Pr.

***Lakoff, Robin T.** The Language War. LC 99-55386. 352p. 2000. 24.95 (*0-520-21666-0*, Pub. by U CA Pr) Cal Prin Full Svc.

Lakoff, Robin T. & Coyne, James C. Father Knows Best: The Use & Abuse of Power in Freud's Case of Dora. (Athene Ser.). 160p. (C). 1992. text 36.00 (*0-8077-6267-9*); pap. text 16.95 (*0-8077-6266-0*) Tchrs Coll.

Lakoff, Sanford. Democracy: History, Theory, Practice. LC 96-24373. 400p. (C). 1996. pap. text 30.00 (*0-8133-3228-1*, Pub. by Westview) HarpC.

— Max Lerner: Pilgrim in the Promised Land. LC 97-52640. (Illus.). 308p. 1998. 25.00 (*0-226-46831-3*) U Ch Pr.

Lakoff, Sanford & York, Herbert F. A Shield in Space? Technology, Politics, & the Strategic Defense Initiative. (California Studies in Global Conflict & Cooperation: Vol. 1). 1989. 45.00 (*0-520-06650-2*, Pub. by U CA Pr) Cal Prin Full Svc.

Lakoff, Sanford, ed. see Kolkowicz, Roman, et al.

Lakofka, Lenard. Assassin's Knot. 1983. 6.00 (*0-394-51835-7*) Random.

Lakomia. Microbiology for Health Careers. 6th ed. LC 98-53502. (Allied Health Ser.). 464p. (C). 1998. text 37.95 (*0-7668-0917-X*) Delmar.

***Lakomia.** Microbiology for Health Careers: Instructor's Manual. 6th ed. 96p. 1999. teacher ed. 14.95 (*0-7668-0918-8*) Delmar.

Lakomski, G., jt. ed. see Keeves, J. P.

Lakomski, Gabriele, jt. auth. see Evers, C. W.

Lakomski, Gabriele, jt. auth. see Evers, Colin W.

***Lakomsky, V. I.** Alloying Liquid Metal by Nitrogen from Electric Arc Plasma. 230p. 1999. boxed set 99.00 (*1-898326-53-3*, Pub. by CISP) Balogh.

Lakond, Wladimir, tr. see Tchaikovsky, Peter Illich.

Lakos, John. Large Scale C++ Software Design. (Professional Computing Ser.). 896p. (C). 1996. pap. text 43.95 (*0-201-63362-0*) Addison-Wesley.

Lakoski, Joan M., et al. Cocaine: Pharmacology, Physiology & Clinical Strategies. 464p. 1991. lib. bdg. 149.00 (*0-8493-8813-9*, QP801) CRC Pr.

— Cocaine: Pharmacology, Physiology & Clinical Strategies. 500p. 1990. 65.00 (*0-936923-42-3*); pap. 32.50 (*0-936923-43-1*) Telford Pr.

Lakowicz, J. R. Principles of Fluorescence Spectroscopy. LC 85-28251. (Illus.). 510p. (C). 1983. text 59.50 (*0-306-41285-3*, Kluwer Plenum) Kluwer Academic.

— Principles of Fluorescence Spectroscopy. 2nd ed. LC 99-30047. (Illus.). 725p. (C). 1999. text. write for info. (*0-306-46093-9*, Kluwer Plenum) Kluwer Academic.

— Topics in Fluorescence Spectroscopy Vol. 3: Biochemical Applications. (Illus.). 408p. (C). 1991. text 110.00 (*0-306-43954-9*, Kluwer Plenum) Kluwer Academic.

Lakowicz, J. R., ed. Topics in Fluorescence Spectroscopy, Vol. 4. (Illus.). 520p. (C). 1994. text 115.00 (*0-306-44784-3*, Kluwer Plenum) Kluwer Academic.

Lakowicz, Joseph R., ed. Time-Resolved Laser Spectroscopy in Biochemistry III. 1992. 20.00 (*0-8194-0786-0*, 1640) SPIE.

— Topics in Fluorescence Spectroscopy Vol. 1: Techniques, Vol. 1. (Illus.). 472p. (C). 1991. text 110.00 (*0-306-43874-7*, Kluwer Plenum) Kluwer Academic.

— Topics in Fluorescence Spectroscopy Vol. 2: Principles, Vol. 2. (Illus.). 448p. (C). 1991. text 110.00 (*0-306-43875-5*, Kluwer Plenum) Kluwer Academic.

— Topics in Fluorescence Spectroscopy Vol. 5: Nonlinear & Two-Photon Induced Fluoresence. (Illus.). 560p. (C). 1997. text 135.00 (*0-306-45553-6*, Kluwer Plenum) Kluwer Academic.

***Lakowicz, Joseph R., et al, eds.** Advances in Fluorescence Sensing Technology IV. 452p. 1999. pap. text 92.00 (*0-8194-3072-2*) SPIE.

Lakowicz, Joseph R. & Ross, J. B., eds. Advances in Optical Biophysics, Vol. 3256. LC 98-227310. 290p. 1998. 69.00 (*0-8194-2695-4*) SPIE.

Lakra, Arun & Gimbel, Howard V. In Search of 20-20: Everything You Need to Know about Laser Eye Surgery. LC 97-910013. (Illus.). 262p. 1997. 14.95 (*0-9681756-0-0*, 738800Q, Pub. by Gibbel Eye) IPG Chicago.

Lakritz, Andrew M. Modernism & the Other in Stevens, Frost, & Moore. 232p. 1996. 39.95 (*0-8130-1460-3*) U Press Fla.

Lakritz, Esther. Battlelines. LC 98-87014. 192p. 1999. pap. 11.95 (*1-56315-155-3*) SterlingHse.

— Developing Library Skills. 112p. (J). (gr. 4-8). 1989. 12.99 (*0-86653-481-4*, GA1081) Good Apple.

Lakritz, Ken & Knoblauch, Thomas. Elders on Love: Dialogues on the Consciousness, Cultivation & Expression of Love. 240p. 1999. 24.95 (*0-930407-41-5*) Parabola Bks.

***Lakritz, Kenneth R.** Elders on Love: Dialogues on the Consciousness, Cultivation & Expression of Love, Vol. 1. large type ed. LC 99-22494. 259p. 1999. 26.95 (*0-7862-1955-6*, G K Hall Lrg Type) Mac Lib Ref.

Lakritz, Kenneth R. & Knoblauch, Thomas M. Elders on Love: Dialogues on the Consciousness, Cultivation, & Expression of Love. LC 98-44297. 1999. pap. 15.95 (*0-930407-45-8*) Parabola Bks.

Laks, Andre & Most, Glenn W., eds. Studies on the Derveni Papyrus. 212p. 1997. text 55.00 (*0-19-815032-6*) OUP.

Laks, Andre & Schofield, Malcolm, eds. Justice & Generosity: Studies in Hellenistic Social & Political Philosophy. (Proceedings of the Sixth Symposium Hellenisticum Ser.). (Illus.). 314p. (C). 1995. text 69.95 (*0-521-45293-7*) Cambridge U Pr.

Laks, Michael M., ed. Computerized Interpretation of the Electrocardiogram, No. VII. 414p. (Orig.). 1983. pap. 30.00 (*0-939204-19-3*, 82-09) Eng Found.

Laks, P. E., jt. auth. see Hemingway, R. W.

***Laks, Szymon.** Music of Another World. LC 99-88812. (Jewish Lives Ser.). 2000. pap. 15.95 (*0-8101-1802-5*) Northwestern U Pr.

Lakshamma, C. Impact of Ramanuja's Teaching on Life & Conditions in Society. 1990. 39.00 (*81-85067-46-5*, Pub. by Sundeep Prak) S Asia.

Lakshiminarayana, B., ed. see Joint Fluids Engineering Gas Turbine Conference &.

***Lakshman, Bulusu.** Oracle Developer Forms Techniques. LC 99-68916. 248p. 2000. 34.99 (*0-672-31846-6*) Sams.

Lakshman Sarup, jt. auth. see Woolner, Alred C.

***Lakshman, Weliqamage & Tisdell, Clement.** SRL Lankas Development Since Independence: Socio-Economic Perspectives & Analysis. LC 00-20745. 287p. 2000. lib. bdg. 59.00 (*1-56072-784-5*) Nova Sci Pubs.

Lakshmana, Mamta. Population Control & Family Planning in India. (C). 1988. 24.00 (*81-7141-026-X*) S Asia.

Lakshmana Rao, V. Industrial Entrepreneurship in India. (C). 1987. 26.00 (*81-85076-05-7*, Pub. by Chugh Pubns) S Asia.

Lakshmana Ras, V. Economic Development of India. (C). 1987. 35.00 (*81-85076-27-8*, Pub. by Chugh Pubns) S Asia.

Lakshmanan, M. Solitons. (Nonlinear Dynamics Ser.). (Illus.). 420p. 1988. 72.95 (*0-387-18588-7*) Spr-Verlag.

Lakshmanan, M. & Daniel, M., eds. Symmetries & Singularity Structures: Integrability & Chaos in Nonlinear Dynamical Systems. (Research Reports in Physics). (Illus.). 256p. 1991. 71.95 (*0-387-53092-4*) Spr-Verlag.

Lakshmanan, M. & Murali, K. Chaos in Nonlinear Oscillators: Controlling & Synchronization. LC 96-217265. (World Scientific Series on Nonlinear Science: Vol. 13). 300p. 1996. text 66.00 (*981-02-2143-6*) World Scientific Pub.

Lakshmanan, T. R. & Nijkamp, Peter, eds. Economic-Environmental-Energy Interactions. (Studies in Applied Regional Science: Vol. 16). 224p. 1980. lib. bdg. 111.00 (*0-89838-023-5*) Kluwer Academic.

— Structure & Change in the Space Economy: Festschrift in Honor of Martin H. Beckmann. LC 93-16821. 1993. 119.95 (*0-387-56490-X*) Spr-Verlag.

Lakshmanan, Usha. Universal Grammar in Child Second Language Acquisition: Null Subjects & Morphological Uniformity. LC 94-26067. (Language Acquisition & Language Disorders (LALD) Ser.: Vol. 10). x, 162p. 1994. pap. 19.95 (*1-55619-783-7*) J Benjamins Pubng Co.

Lakshmi. Ripples in the River. Ananthakrishnan, Indira, tr. (C). 1992. text 4.00 (*81-7201-045-1*, Pub. by National Sahitya Akademi) S Asia.

Lakshmi, J. Vijaya & Kumari, M. Krishna. Kamesvara Temple at Gallavalli. (C). 1991. 55.00 (*0-8364-2771-8*, Pub. by Agam Kala Prakashan) S Asia.

Lakshmi, K. P. Communications Across the Borders: The U. S., the Non-Aligned & the New Information Order. (C). 1993. text 16.00 (*81-7027-204-1*, Pub. by Radiant Pubs) S Asia.

Lakshmi, M. S., jt. auth. see Sherbet, G. V.

Lakshmi, M. Vijay. A Critical Study of Sangita Makaranda of Narada. LC 96-904744. (Illus.). 282p. (C). 1996. 32.00 (*81-212-0526-3*, Pub. by Gyan Publishing Hse) Nataraj Bks.

***Lakshmi, Padma.** Easy Exotic: A Model's Low-Fat Recipes from Around the World. (Illus.). 120p. 2000. pap. 16.95 (*0-7868-8612-9*, Pub. by Talk Miramax Bks) Time Warner.

Lakshmi, Padma. Easy Exotic: One-Dish Wonders from Around the World. LC 98-26336. (Illus.). 128p. (J). 1999. 24.45 (*0-7868-6459-1*, Pub. by Hyperion) Time Warner.

Lakshmibai, V., jt. auth. see Billey, S.

Lakshmikantham, et al. Stability Analysis of Nonlinear Systems. (Pure & Applied Mathematics Ser.: Vol. 125). (Illus.). 336p. 1988. text 175.00 (*0-8247-8067-1*) Dekker.

Lakshmikantham, V. Nonlinear Analysis & Applications. (Lecture Notes in Pure & Applied Mathematics Ser.: Vol. 109). (Illus.). 680p. 1987. pap. text 190.00 (*0-8247-7810-3*) Dekker.

— Theory of Differential Equations with Unbounded Delay. LC 94-27710. (Mathematics & Its Applications Ser.). 350p. (C). 1994. text 220.50 (*0-7923-3003-X*) Kluwer Academic.

— Theory of Integro-Differential Equations. 384p. 1995. text 108.00 (*2-88449-000-0*) Gordon & Breach.

— Trends in Theory & Practice of Nonlinear Differential Equations. (Lecture Notes in Pure & Applied Mathematics Ser.: Vol. 90). (Illus.). 592p. 1984. pap. text 170.00 (*0-8247-7130-3*) Dekker.

Lakshmikantham, V., ed. World Congress of Nonlinear Analysts, '92: Proceedings of the First, Tampa, Florida, August 19-26, 1992, 4 vols., Set. LC 95-42044. xlvi, 3954p. 1995. lib. bdg. 798.95 (*3-11-013215-X*) De Gruyter.

Lakshmikantham, V. & Deo, S. G. Method of Variation of Parameters for Dynamics Systems. (Mathematical Analysis & Applications Ser.: Vol. 1). 328p. 1998. text 54.00 (*90-5699-160-4*, ECU71) Gordon & Breach.

***Lakshmikantham, V. & Leela, S.** The Origins Of Mathematics. 104p. 2000. 44.00 (*0-7618-1736-0*); pap. 24.50 (*0-7618-1737-9*) U Pr of Amer.

Lakshmikantham, V. & Vatsala, A. S. Generalized Quasilinearization for Nonlinear Problems. LC 98-13117. (Mathematics & Its Applications Ser.). 1998. 140.00 (*0-7923-5038-3*) Kluwer Academic.

Lakshmikantham, V. & Xinzhi Liu. Stability Analysis in Terms of Two Measures. LC 93-14063. 250p. 1993. text 61.00 (*981-02-1389-1*) World Scientific Pub.

Lakshmikantham, V., et al. Dynamic Systems on Measure Chains. LC 96-9016. (Mathematics & Its Applications Ser.). 1996. text 161.50 (*0-7923-4116-3*) Kluwer Academic.

— Practical Stability of Nonlinear Systems. 220p. (C). 1990. text 53.00 (*981-02-0351-9*); pap. text 36.00 (*981-02-0356-X*) World Scientific Pub.

— Vector Lyapunov Functions & Stability Analysis of Nonlinear Systems. (C). 1991. text 144.00 (*0-7923-1152-3*) Kluwer Academic.

Lakshmikantham, V., jt. auth. see Agarwal, Ravi P.

Lakshmikantham, V., jt. auth. see Heikkila, Seppo.

Lakshmikanthamma, S. Sustainability of Dryland Agriculture in India: A Case Study of Watershed Development Approach. LC 97-901612. 339p. 1997. pap. 288.00 (*81-7533-033-3*, Pub. by Print Hse) St Mut.

Lakshmilcantham, V., et al, eds. Theory of Impulsive Differential Equations. 288p. (C). 1989. text 74.00 (*9971-5-0970-9*) World Scientific Pub.

Lakshminarayan, P. G. Tradeoffs in Balancing Multiple Objectives of an Integrated Agricultural Economic & Environmental System. LC 96-85287. (Card Monographs: Vol. 96-M8). (Illus.). 142p. (Orig.). 1996. pap. 15.00 (*0-936911-08-5*) Ctr Agri & Rural Dev.

Lakshminarayana, Budugur. Fluid Dynamics & Heat Transfer of Turbomachinery. LC 94-41844. 848p. 1995. 140.00 (*0-471-85546-4*) Wiley.

Lakshminarayana, H. D. Democracy in Rural India: Problems & Process. 180p. 1980. 15.95 (*0-940500-42-6*) Asia Bk Corp.

Lakshminarayana, H. D. & Tyagi, S. S. Changes in Agrarian Structure in India. 163p. 1982. 21.95 (*0-318-36789-0*) Asia Bk Corp.

Lakshminarayana, J. S., jt. ed. see Nriagu, Jerome O.

Lakshminarayana, K., et al. Flora of Krishna District, Andhra Pradesh, India. LC 97-901608. 356p. 1997. pap. 300.00 (*81-7533-036-8*, Pub. by Print Hse) St Mut.

Lakshminarayanan. Basic & Clinical Applications of Vision Science the Professor Jay M. Enoch Festschrift. LC 96-49524. 1996. text 176.50 (*0-7923-4348-4*) Kluwer Academic.

Lakshminath, A. Precedent in the Indian Legal System. (C). 1989. 125.00 (*0-89771-768-6*, Pub. by Eastern Book); 125.00 (*0-89771-759-7*, Pub. by Eastern Book) St Mut.

— Precedent in the Indian Legal System. (C). 1990. text 125.00 (*0-89771-485-7*) St Mut.

Lakshmiswaramma, M., jt. auth. see Chandra, Shanta K.

Lakshmivarahan, S. Learning Algorithms Theory & Applications. 279p. 1981. 76.95 (*0-387-90640-1*) Spr-Verlag.

Lakshmivarahan, S. & Dhall, S. K. Parallel Computing Using the Prefix Problem. (Illus.). 320p. 1994. text 80.00 (*0-19-508849-2*) OUP.

Lakusta, Boris H. West's California Code Forms with Practice Commentaries-Public Utilities: Contains Pocket Parts. 3rd ed. LC 82-50923. (Illus.). xi, 366p. 1984. 32.00 (*0-685-07262-2*) West Pub.

***Lal.** The Changing Bhangis of India: A Study of Caste Association. LC 99-935835. 1999. 32.00 (*81-85809-29-1*, Pub. by Abhinav Pubns) S Asia.

Lal, A. K. Dalits in Action: An Evaluation of Bihar Dalit Vikas Samiti LC 98-900040. 95p. 1997. write for info. (*81-7022-604-X*) Concept.

— Seculiarism: Concept & Practice. LC 98-909208. 191p. 1998. write for info. (*81-7022-729-1*) Concept.

Lal, B. B. Earliest Civilization of South Asia. LC 98-903824. (C). 1997. 175.00 (*81-7305-107-0*, Pub. by Aryan Bks Intl) S Asia.

— India 1947-1997: New Light on the Indus Civilization. LC 98-907055. xix, 135 p. 1998. 78.00 (*81-7305-129-1*, Pub. by Aryan Bks Intl) S Asia.

Lal, B. K. Contemporary Indian Philosophy. 364p. 1978. 15.95 (*0-318-37017-4*) Asia Bk Corp.

Lal, Basant K. Contemporary Indian Philosophy. xxi, 345p. (C). 1992. 18.00 (*81-208-0260-8*, Pub. by Motilal Bnarsidass) S Asia.

***Lal, Basant K.** Contemporary Indian Philosophy. 1998. pap. 10.00 (*81-208-0261-6*) Motilal Bnarsidass.

Lal, Basant K. Contemporary Indian Philosophy. rev. ed. 1978. pap. text 17.00 (*0-89684-013-1*, Pub. by Motilal Bnarsidass) S Asia.

— Contemporary Indian Philosophy. 2nd rev. ed. 1978. 22.50 (*0-89684-012-3*, Pub. by Motilal Bnarsidass) S Asia.

Lal, Bhawani. Extraordinary Trials from Law Courts. 135p. 1961. pap. 80.00 (*0-7855-1301-9*) St Mut.

— Extraordinary Trials from Law Courts. (C). 1961. 6.00 (*0-7855-5397-5*) St Mut.

— Interpretation of Statutes. 326p. 1964. pap. 75.00 (*0-7855-1300-0*) St Mut.

Lal, Brij V. Broken Waves: A History of the Fiji Islands in the Twentieth Century. LC 92-17786. (Pacific Islands Monographs: No. 11). (Illus.). 424p. 1992. text 39.00 (*0-8248-1418-5*) UH Pr.

***Lal, Brij V. & Fortune, Kate.** The Pacific Islands: An Encyclopedia. LC 99-34571. 2000. 100.00 incl. cd-rom (*0-8248-2265-X*) UH Pr.

Lal, Chaman. Punjabi & Dalit Images in Indian Literature. 1998. 35.00 (*81-7488-917-5*) Anmol.

Lal-Das, Bhagirath. Trade & Development Issues & the World Trade Organization: The WTO Agreements: Deficiences, Imbalances & Required Changes, Vol. II. 128p. 1998. pap. 17.50 (*1-85649-584-1*) St Martin.

Lal De, Satyendra, see De, Satyendra Lal.

Lal, Deepak. Against Dirigisme: The Case for Unshackling Economic Markets. LC 94-1702. 1994. pap. 19.95 (*1-55815-324-1*) ICS Pr.

— The Hindu Equilibrium, Vol. I: Cultural Stability & Economic Stagnation in India, 1500 B.C. - 1980 A.D. (Illus.). 374p. 1989. text 85.00 (*0-19-828498-5*) OUP.

— The Hindu Equilibrium, Vol. II: Aspects of Indian Labour. (Illus.). 210p. 1989. text 49.95 (*0-19-828499-3*) OUP.

— India. 51p. 1988. pap. 9.95 (*1-55815-016-1*) ICS Pr.

— A Liberal International Economic Order: The International Monetary System & Economic Development. LC 80-22523. (Essays in International Finance Ser.: No. 139). 50p. reprint ed. pap. 30.00 (*0-608-18075-0*, 203211800078) Bks Demand.

— Political Economy & Public Policy. 36p. 1990. pap. 9.95 (*1-55815-101-X*) ICS Pr.

— The Poverty of "Development Economics" (Illus.). 144p. 1986. pap. 12.95 (*0-674-69471-6*) HUP.

***Lal, Deepak.** The Poverty of Development Economics. LC 00-21974. (Illus.). 175p. 2000. 24.95 (*0-262-12234-0*) MIT Pr.

— The Poverty of Development Economics. 2nd ed. 193p. 1997. 27.50 (*0-255-36410-5*, Pub. by Inst Economic Affairs) Coronet Bks.

Lal, Deepak. The Repressed Economy: Causes, Consequences, Reform. (Economists of the Twentieth Century Ser.). 624p. 1993. 120.00 (*1-85278-888-7*) E Elgar.

— Unfinished Business: India in the World Economy. LC 99-938559. (Illus.). 306p. 1999. text 35.00 (*0-19-564548-0*) OUP.

Lal, Deepak, ed. Development Economics, 4 vols., Set. (International Library of Critical Writings in Economics: No. 18). 1976p. 1992. 650.00 (*1-85278-196-3*) E Elgar.

Lal, Deepak & Myint, H. The Political Economy of Poverty, Equity, & Growth: A Comparative Study. (Illus.). 476p. 1999. reprint ed. pap. text 24.95 (*0-19-829432-8*) OUP.

Lal, Deepak, jt. auth. see Collier, Paul.

Lal, Deepak, jt. ed. see Scott, Maurice F.

Lal, Deepak K. Unintended Consequences: The Impact of Factor Endowments, Culture, & Politics on Long-Run Economic Performance. LC 98-38290. (Ohlin Lectures). (Illus.). 297p. 1998. 39.95 (*0-262-12210-3*) MIT Pr.

Lal Dhody, Chandan, tr. The Adhyatma Ramayana: Concise English Version. LC 96-900946. 291p. 1995. pap. 350.00 (*81-85880-77-8*, Pub. by Print Hse) St Mut.

Lal Dhody, Chandan, tr. The Bhagavata: Glimpses Glorious: Gajendra Moksha & Some Other Gems. 125p. (C). 1994. pap. 75.00 (*81-85880-46-8*, Pub. by Print Hse) St Mut.

Lal, H. City & Urban Fringe. 1987. 18.50 (*81-7022-190-0*, Pub. by Concept) S Asia.

Lal, H. & Marangos, Paul J., eds. Emerging Strategies in Neuroprotection. (Advances in Neuroprotection Ser.). (Illus.). xviii, 359p. 1992. 109.00 (*0-8176-3544-0*) Birkhauser.

Lal, Harbans, jt. ed. see Van Bever, William.

Lal Hazra, Kanai. Rise & Decline of Buddhism in India. LC 95-905207. 462p. (C). 1995. 48.00 (*81-215-0651-4*, Pub. by M Manoharial) Coronet Bks.

Lal, J. B. Environmental Conservation. 126p. 1987. 85.00 (*0-7855-3114-9*, Pub. by Intl Bk Distr); 65.00 (*0-7855-6545-0*, Pub. by Intl Bk Distr) St Mut.

— India's Forest. (C). 1987. 145.00 (*0-7855-3103-3*, Pub. by Intl Bk Distr) St Mut.

Lal, Joginder & Mark, James E., eds. Advances in Elastomers & Rubber Elasticity. LC 86-25416. 454p. 1986. 105.00 (*0-306-42472-X*, Plenum Trade) Perseus Pubng.

Lal, Joginder, jt. ed. see Mark, James E.

Lal, K., jt. auth. see Aagrawal, A. N.

Lal, K. M. Population Settlements: Development & Planning. 1988. 32.00 (*81-85076-48-0*, Pub. by Chugh Pubns) S Asia.

Lal, K. S. Legacy of Muslim Rule in India. (C). 1992. 34.00 (*81-85689-03-2*, Pub. by Aditya Prakashan) S Asia.

— The Mughal Harem. (C). 1988. 72.00 (*81-85179-03-4*, Pub. by Aditya Prakashan) S Asia.

— Muslim Slave System in Medieval India. LC 94-905167. (C). 1995. 17.50 (*81-85689-67-9*, Pub. by Aditya Prakashan) S Asia.

***Lal, K. S.** Theory & Practice of Muslim State in India. 1999. 32.00 (*81-86471-72-3*, Pub. by Aditya Prakashan) S Asia.

***Lal, Kishan.** Revolutionary Activities in Delhi. LC 99-938053. 1999. 32.00 (*81-7320-042-4*, Pub. by Agam Kala Prakashan) S Asia.

Lal, L., jt. auth. see Goyal, G.

***Lal, Lakshmi.** Ramayana. (Illus.). 1998. 36.00 (*0-86131-805-6*, Pub. by Sangam Bks Ltd) S Asia.

***Lal, M., et al, eds.** Supramolecular & Colloidal Structures in Biomaterials & Biosubstrates. 500p. 2000. 96.00 (*1-86094-236-9*, Pub. by Imperial College) World Scientific Pub.

Lal, Malashri. Feminist Spaces: Cultural Readings from India & Canada. LC 98-900457. (Occasional Monograph Series / University of Delhi, Centre for Canadian Studies). xxiii, 236p. 1997. 38.00 (*81-7023-703-3*, Pub. by Allied Pubs) S Asia.

Lal, Mohan. Rural Industrialisation & Regional Development. 168p. 1987. 21.00 (*0-8364-2031-4*, Pub. by Deep & Deep Pubns) S Asia.

Lal, Mukandi. Garhwal Painting. (Illus.). 120p. 1982. 55.00 (*0-318-36335-6*) Asia Bk Corp.

Lal, Muni. Mini Mughals. (Illus.). 340p. 1990. text 37.50 (*81-220-0174-2*, Pub. by Konark Pubs Pvt Ltd) Advent Bks Div.

— Mughal Glory: Stories of Love, Loyalty, Honour, Courage... 127p. 1989. text 15.95 (*81-220-0076-2*, Pub. by Konark Pubs Pvt Ltd) Advent Bks Div.

***Lal, Muni.** The Structure & Dynamics of Materials in the Mesoscopic Domain. LC 99-40858. 300p. 1999. 96.00 (*1-86094-190-7*) World Scientific Pub.

Lal Nagar, Shanti. Surya & Sun Cult in Indian Art, Culture, Literature, Thought. LC 95-901256. (C). 1995. 120.00 (*81-7305-056-2*, Pub. by Aryan Bks Intl) S Asia.

Lal, Nathuni. Benami Transactions. (C). 1990. 125.00 (*0-89771-268-4*) St Mut.

— Law of Arbitration. 4th rev. ed. (C). 1983. 85.00 (*0-7855-5647-8*) St Mut.

Lal, P. The Mahabharata of Vyasa. 400p. 1980. 15.95 (*0-7069-1033-8*); 29.95 (*0-318-37171-5*) Asia Bk Corp.

Lal, P., ed. Great Sanskrit Plays in Modern Translation. LC 63-21383. 1964. pap. 15.00 (*0-8112-0079-5*, NDP142, Pub. by New Directions) Norton.

Lal Pandit, Moti. Sunyata: The Essence of Mahayana Spirituality. LC 98-906997. xv, 399 p. 1998. write for info. (*81-215-0845-2*, Pub. by M Manoharial) Coronet Bks.

Lal, Parag K., ed. Satellite Perturbations & Orbital Determination. (Advances in Space Research Ser.: Vol. 1, No. 6). (Illus.). 95p. 1981. pap. 14.50 (*0-08-028380-2*, Pergamon Pr) Elsevier.

Lal, Premila. Complete Book of Indian Cooking. 288p. 1996. pap. text 19.95 (*0-572-02264-6*, Pub. by W Foulsham) Trans-Atl Phila.

Lal, R. Genetic Engineering of Plants for Crop Improvement. 256p. 1993. lib. bdg. 125.00 (*0-8493-6424-8*, SB123) CRC Pr.

— Management of Carbon Sequestration in Soil. LC 97-18398. (Advances in Soil Science Ser.). 480p. 1997. boxed set 119.95 (*0-8493-7442-1*) CRC Pr.

— Methods for Assessment of Soil Degradation. LC 97-24696. (Advances in Soil Science Ser.). 576p. 1997. boxed set 84.95 (*0-8493-7443-X*) CRC Pr.

— Pesticides & the Nitrogen Cycle, Vol. I. 152p. 1987. 90.00 (*0-8493-4351-8*, CRC Reprint) Franklin.

— Pesticides & the Nitrogen Cycle, Vol. II. 168p. 1987. 46.00 (*0-8493-4352-6*) CRC Pr.

— Soil Processes & the Carbon Cycle. LC 97-29442. 624p. 1997. boxed set 119.95 (*0-8493-7441-3*) CRC Pr.

— Tropical Ecology & Physical Edaphology. LC 85-16906. (Illus.). 744p. reprint ed. pap. 200.00 (*0-608-20222-3*, 207148100012) Bks Demand.

Lal, R. & Greenland, D. J., eds. Soil Physical Properties & Crop Production in the Tropics. LC 79-40583. 573p. 1979. reprint ed. pap. 177.70 (*0-608-04600-0*, 206537000003) Bks Demand.

Lal, R. & Sanchez, P. A. Myths & Science of Soils of the Tropics. (SSSA Special Publications: No. 29). 185p. 1992. 15.00 (*0-89118-800-2*) Soil Sci Soc Am.

Lal, R., ed. see International Conference on Soil Conservation & Ma.

***Lal, R. B.** Novel Materials & Crystal Growth Techniques for Nonlinear Optical Devices: Proceedings of a Conference Held 23 January 2000, San Jose, California. SPIE Staff, ed. LC 00-20243. (Critical Reviews of Optical Science & Technology Ser.). 2000. pap. write for info. (*0-8194-3543-0*) SPIE.

Lal, R. B. Principles & Practices of Range Management. (C). 1989. text 125.00 (*0-89771-578-0*, Pub. by Intl Bk Distr) St Mut.

— Principles & Practices of Range Management. 120p. 1990. pap. 175.00 (*81-7089-129-9*, Pub. by Intl Bk Distr) St Mut.

Lal, R. M. & Lal, Sukayna, eds. Crop Improvement Utilizing Biotechnology. 368p. 1989. lib. bdg. 295.00 (*0-8493-5082-4*, SB123) CRC Pr.

Lal, Ramji. Political India, 1935-42: Anatomy of Indian Politics. 308p. 1986. 28.00 (*81-202-0160-4*, Pub. by Ajanta) S Asia.

Lal, Rattan. Assessment Methods for Soil, 001. 2000. lib. bdg. 64.95 (*0-8493-4134-5*) CRC Pr.

— Assessment Methods for Soil Carbon. 2000. ring bd. 69.95 (*1-56670-461-8*) CRC Pr.

— Global Climate Change. LC 99-35811. 320p. 1999. boxed set 69.95 (*1-56670-458-8*) CRC Pr.

***Lal, Rattan.** Global Climate Change: Pedogenic Carbonates. 300p. 1999. 54.95 (*0-8493-4133-7*) CRC Pr.

Lal, Rattan. Integrated Watershed Management in the Global Ecosystem. LC 99-21035. 480p. 1999. boxed set 69.95 (*0-8493-0702-3*) CRC Pr.

— Introduction to Soil Physics, 001. 2000. lib. bdg. 49.95 (*0-8493-4135-3*) CRC Pr.

— Introduction to Soil Physics. (C). 2000. ring bd. 59.95 (*1-56670-477-4*) CRC Pr.

— Soil Physical Properties & Crop Production in the Tropics. 551p. 1989. pap. 625.00 (*0-7855-2719-2*, Pub. by Intl Bk Distr) St Mut.

— Soil Physical Properties & Crop Production in the Tropics. 551p. (C). 1989. 65.00 (*0-7855-6883-2*, Pub. by Intl Bk Distr); pap. 45.00 (*0-7855-6884-0*, Pub. by Intl Bk Distr) St Mut.

— Soil Physical Properties & Crop Production in the Tropics. 551p. 1989. pap. 1250.00 (*81-7089-104-3*, Pub. by Intl Bk Distr) St Mut.

— Soil Quality & Agricultural Sustainability. LC 98-9659. (Illus.). 400p. 1998. ring bd. 74.95 (*1-57504-082-4*) CRC Pr.

***Lal, Rattan.** Soil Quality & Agricultural Sustainability. 400p. 1999. 69.95 (*0-8493-4116-7*) CRC Pr.

Lal, Rattan. Soil Quality & Soil Erosion. LC 99-166567. 330p. 1998. lib. bdg. 79.95 (*1-57444-100-0*, SL1000) St Lucie Pr.

— Tropical Agricultural Hydrology Watershed Management & Land-Use. 494p. 1990. pap. 750.00 (*81-7089-120-5*, Pub. by Intl Bk Distr) St Mut.

Lal, Rattan, ed. Soil Erosion Research Methods. 2nd ed. LC 93-45352. (Illus.). 352p. (Orig.). 1994. per. 57.95 (*1-884015-09-3*) St Lucie Pr.

— Soil Management & Greenhouse Effect. 400p. 1995. lib. bdg. 95.00 (*1-56670-117-1*, L1117) Lewis Pubs.

Lal, Rattan, et al, eds. Soils & Global Change. LC 95-2343. 464p. 1995. lib. bdg. 110.00 (*1-56670-118-X*, L1118) Lewis Pubs.

— Sustainable Agricultural Systems. (Illus.). 696p. 1990. lib. bdg. 79.95 (*0-935734-21-X*) Soil & Water Conserv.

Lal, Rattan & Stewart, B. A., eds. Sustainable Management of Soils. (Advances in Soil Science Ser.). 576p. 1995. lib. bdg. 95.00 (*1-56670-076-0*, L1076) Lewis Pubs.

Lal, Rattan, et al. Global Climate Change: Cold Regions Ecosystems. (Advances in Soil Science Ser.). 280p. 1999. boxed set 69.95 (*1-56670-459-6*) Lewis Pubs.

— Global Climate Change & Tropical Ecosystems: Cold. LC 99-47136. 456p. 1999. boxed set 69.95 (*1-56670-485-5*) Lewis Pubs.

***Lal, Rattan, et al.** The Potential of Us Cropland to Sequester Carbon & Mitigate the Greenhouse Effect. LC 99-184688. 1998. boxed set 54.95 (*1-57504-112-X*) CRC Pr.

Lal, Rattan, jt. ed. see Russell, E. W.

Lal, Rattan, jt. ed. see Stewart, B. A.

***Lal, Ravindra B. & Frazier, Donald O., eds.** Operational Characteristics & Crystal Growth of Nonlinear Optical Materials. 246p. 1999. pap. text 72.00 (*0-8194-3279-2*) SPIE.

Lal, Rup, ed. Pesticides & Nitrogen Cycle: Pesticides, Chemists & Soil Scientists, 3 vol., Set. 1988. 90.00 (*0-8493-4350-X*, QH545, CRC Reprint) Franklin.

Lal, S. & Singh, V., eds. Schrodinger Centenary: Surveys in Physics. 312p. 1988. text 84.00 (*9971-5-0694-7*) World Scientific Pub.

Lal, Sheo K. Rural Social Transformation. (C). 1992. text 32.00 (*81-7033-159-5*, Pub. by Rawat Pubns) S Asia.

Lal, Sheo K. & Nahar, Umed R. Extent of Untouchability & Pattern of Discrimination. 1990. 19.50 (*81-7099-221-4*, Pub. by Mittal Pubs Dist) S Asia.

Lal, Shirley R., et al. Handbook on Gangs in Schools: Strategies to Reduce Gang-Related Activities. Herman, Janice L., ed. LC 93-27431. 88p. 1993. pap. 14.95 (*0-8039-6071-9*) Corwin Pr.

Lal, Shiv. Bangla-Pak Politics. 430p. 1986. 120.00 (*0-7855-1800-2*, Pub. by Archives Pubs) St Mut.

— British History of Elections (Olden Days) 260p. 1986. 125.00 (*0-7855-1801-0*, Pub. by Archives Pubs) St Mut.

— British History of Elections (Recent) 224p. 1986. 145.00 (*0-7855-1802-9*, Pub. by Archives Pubs) St Mut.

— The Death of Party System in India, 1982. 268p. 1986. 130.00 (*0-7855-1803-7*, Pub. by Archives Pubs) St Mut.

— Documents on Muslim States: Iran: Selected Political Documents. 224p. 1986. 150.00 (*0-7855-1804-5*, Pub. by Archives Pubs) St Mut.

— Documents on Muslim States: Morocco & Other African Nations. 300p. 1986. 125.00 (*0-7855-1806-1*, Pub. by Archives Pubs) St Mut.

— Documents on Muslim States: Politics in Iraq. 160p. 1986. 120.00 (*0-317-61947-0*, Pub. by Archives Pubs) St Mut.

— Documents on Muslim States: Select Constitutions. 248p. 1986. 120.00 (*0-7855-1807-X*, Pub. by Archives Pubs) St Mut.

— Elections & the Constitution: The Question of Amendment. 412p. 1977. 120.00 (*0-7855-1808-8*, Pub. by Archives Pubs) St Mut.

— Global Election Records, 7 vols., Set. 1986. 1850.00 (*0-7855-1812-6*, Pub. by Archives Pubs) St Mut.

— Indian Political Thought. (C). 1989. 540.00 (*0-7855-4750-9*) St Mut.

— International Encyclopedia of Politics & Laws. 14000p. 1987. 3900.00 (*0-7855-3014-2*, Pub. by Archives Pubs) St Mut.

— Malaysian Democracy: An Indian Perspective (1982) 432p. 1986. 120.00 (*0-7855-1820-7*, Pub. by Archives Pubs) St Mut.

— A Non-Muslim among Muslim States: Israel. 152p. 1986. 135.00 (*0-7855-1838-X*, Pub. by Archives Pubs) St Mut.

— Politico-Legal India, 5 vols. 1986. 1950.00 (*81-7051-000-7*, Pub. by Archives Pubs) St Mut.

— The Two Leftist Parties of India, 1982. 200p. 1986. 165.00 (*0-7855-1832-0*, Pub. by Archives Pubs) St Mut.

Lal, Shyam. Tribals & Christian Missionaries. 176p. (C). 1994. text. write for info. (*81-85445-58-3*, Pub. by Manak Pubns Pvt Ltd) Nataraj Bks.

Lal, Sukayna, jt. ed. see Lal, R. M.

Lal, Victor. Fiji: Coups in Paradise. LC 88-14217. 256p. (C). 1990. pap. 25.00 (*0-86232-777-6*, Pub. by St Martin); text 65.00 (*0-86232-776-8*, Pub. by St Martin) St Martin.

Lal, Vinay. South Asian Cultural Studies: A Bibliography. (C). 1996. 34.00 (*81-7304-134-2*, Pub. by Manohar) S Asia.

***Lal, Vinay, ed.** Dissenting Knowledges, Open Futures: The Multiple Selves & Strange Destinations of Ashis Nandy. 352p. 2000. text 24.95 (*0-19-565115-4*) OUP.

Lala, Chhaganlal. Philosophy of Bhakti. (C). 1989. 28.50 (*81-7018-557-2*, Pub. by BR Pub) S Asia.

Lala, Frank J., Jr. Counseling the Deaf Substance Abuser. LC 98-66640. 416p. 1998. pap. text 28.95 (*0-9663753-0-0*) Midas Mngmt.

Lala, Marco. The Ultimate Weapon. (Illus.). 70p. (Orig.). 1987. pap. 16.95 (*0-939427-82-6*, 05052) Alpha Pubns OH.

Lala, Parag K. Digital Circuit Testing & Testability. LC 96-42114. (Illus.). 199p. 1997. text 69.95 (*0-12-434330-9*) Morgan Kaufmann.

— Digital System Design Using Programmable Logic Devices. 288p. 1990. boxed set 44.00 (*0-685-44717-0*) P-H.

— Practical Digital Logic Design & Testing. LC 95-20486. 420p. (C). 1995. 96.00 (*0-02-367171-8*, Macmillan Coll) P-H.

***Lala, Parag K.** Self-Checking & Fault-Tolerant Digital Design. LC 98-52157. 250p. 2000. 59.95 (*0-12-434370-8*) Acad Pr.

Lalagia. Spanish Dancing. Ivanova, Ana, ed. (Illus.). 168p. 1995. pap. 19.95 (*0-903102-88-9*, Pub. by Dance Bks) Princeton Bk Co.

Lalaguna, Juan. A Traveller's History of Spain. 4th ed. 1999. pap. text 14.95 (*1-56656-324-0*) Interlink Pub.

Lalaire, Louis. La Variation Modale dans les Subordonnees a Temps Fini du Francais Moderne: Approche Syntaxique. (Linguistique Ser.: Vol. 195). (FRE.). x, 377p. 1998. 48.95 (*3-906759-77-6*) P Lang Pubng.

LaLance & Short. The Tennis Trek. 3rd ed. LC 97-21443. 162p. (C). 1997. per. 30.95 (*0-7872-3764-7*, 41376401) Kendall-Hunt.

Laland, Avar & Laland, Stephanie. How to Meet Men: And Make Them Fall in Love with You. 215p. (Orig.). 1989. pap. 8.95 (*0-685-30138-9*) C C T P Reddick.

Laland, John F., 2nd, tr. see Gut, Martin.

An Asterisk (*) at the beginning of an entry indicates that the title is appearing for the first time.

L

Laland, Stephanie. Animal Angels: Amazing Acts of Love & Compassion. LC 98-36868. (Illus.). 256p. 1998. pap. 12.95 (*1-57324-142-3*) Conari Press.
— Fifty-One Ways to Entertain Your Housecat While You're Out. 112p. (Orig.). 1994. pap. 7.50 (*0-380-77431-3*, Avon Bks) Morrow Avon.
— Peaceful Kingdom Vol. 1: Random Acts of Kindness by Animals. (Illus.). 224p. (Orig.). 1997. pap. 11.95 (*1-57324-094-X*) Conari Press.
— Random Acts of Kindness by Animals. 1998. pap. 6.98 (*1-56731-270-5*) Fine Comms.
Laland, Stephanie, jt. auth. see Laland, Avar.
LaLande, John, et al. Activities Manual: First Year German. (GER.). 176p. (C). 1985. pap. text 19.00 (*0-07-554344-3*) McGraw.
Lalande, John F., II & Condray, Kathleen, eds. Teaching Ideas, Vol. 5. 140p. ring bd. 17.00 (*0-942017-66-8*, 4-643536) Amer Assn Teach German.
Lalande, John F., II, et al. Deutsch Heute: Grundstufe, 6 vols. 6th ed. (GER.). 539p. (C). 1996. text 61.16 (*0-395-74418-0*) HM.
— Deutsch Heute: Grundstufe, 6 vols. 6th ed. (GER.). (C). 1996. text, teacher ed. 11.96 (*0-395-76688-5*) HM.
— Deutsch Heute: Grundstufe, 6 vols. 6th annot. ed. (GER.). (C). 1996. text, teacher ed. 62.36 (*0-395-76686-9*) HM.
Lalande, John F., II, tr. see Gutl, Martin.
Lalande, Michel R. De Profundis: Grand Motet for Soloists, Chorus, Woodwinds, Strings, & Continuo. Anthony, James R., ed. LC 79-29740. (Early Musical Masterworks Ser.). 182p. reprint ed. pap. 56.50 (*0-8357-3897-3*, 203662900004) Bks Demand.
Lalande, Roxanne D. Intruders in the Play World: The Dynamics of Gender in Moliere's Comedies. LC 95-32324. 232p. 1996. 37.50 (*0-8386-3592-X*) Fairleigh Dickinson.
— A Labor of Love: Critical Reflections on the Writings of Marie-Catherine Desjardins (Mme de Villedieu) LC 99-33242. 224p. 2000. 37.50 (*0-8386-3824-4*) Fairleigh Dickinson.
Lalani, Nazir & Joint Committee of Traffic Engineering, Council & Transportation Planning Council. Access Management - A Key to Safety & Mobility. (Illus.). 20p. 1998. pap. text 5.00 (*0-935403-26-4*, IR-095) Inst Trans Eng.
Lalani, Suleiman & Jamsa, Kris. Java Programmers Library. LC 96-204060. 560p. 1996. pap. 49.95 incl. cd-rom (*1-884133-26-6*, Jamsa Press) Gulf Pub.
Lalani, Suleiman S. & Chandak, Ramesh. ActiveX Programmer's Library. LC 98-112182. (Illus.). 512p. (Orig.). 1997. pap. 49.95 incl. cd-rom (*1-884133-52-5*, Jamsa Press) Gulf Pub.
Lalani, Zane. Ugandan Asian Expulsion: 90 Days & Beyond Through the Eyes of the International Press. (Illus.). 192p. 1997. 30.00 (*0-9658740-0-1*) Expulsion Pubns.
LaLanne, Elaine & Benyo, Richard. The Joy of Juicing: The Complete Guide to Healthy & Delicious Fresh Fruit & Vegetable Juices. LC 92-34876. 320p. 1992. pap. 13.95 (*0-452-26928-8*, Plume) Dutton Plume.
Lalanne, J. R. Optical Spectroscopies of Electronic Absorption. (World Scientific Series in Contemporary Chemical Physics - Vol. 17: Vol. 17). 300p. 1999. 58.00 (*981-02-3861-4*) World Scientific Pub.
Lalanne, J. R., et al. Laser Molecule Interaction: Laser Physics & Molecular Nonlinear Optics. Orrit, L., tr. from FRE. LC 95-24308. 323p. 1996. 84.95 (*0-471-12066-9*) Wiley.
Lalanne, Jack. Revitalize Your Life after 50: Improve Your Health, Your Sex Life, & Your Looks after Age Fifty. 208p. 1995. pap. 13.95 (*0-8038-9356-6*, Pub. by Hastings) Midpt Trade.
Lalanne, M. & Ferraris, Guy. Rotordynamics Prediction in Engineering. 2nd ed. LC 97-22472. 266p. 1998. 75.00 (*0-471-97288-6*) Wiley.
Lalanne, Michel, et al. Mechanical Vibrations for Engineers. Nelson, Frederick C., tr. & adapted by by. LC 83-6908. (Illus.). 274p. reprint ed. pap. 85.00 (*0-8357-3097-2*, 203935400012) Bks Demand.
Lalanne, P. & Chavel, P., eds. Perspectives for Parallel Optical Interconnects: Project 3199 WOIT. (ESPRIT Basic Research Ser.). xiii, 417p. 1993. 89.00 (*0-387-56786-0*) Spr-Verlag.
Lalas, Alexi & Wright, Thomas L. Kickin Balls: The Alexi Lalas Story. (Illus.). 256p. 1996. 22.00 (*0-684-80387-9*) Simon & Schuster.
Lalas, Demetri P. & Ratto, Corrado F., eds. Modelling of Atmospheric Flow Fields. LC 95-45327. 768p. 1996. write for info. (*981-02-2509-1*) World Scientific Pub.
Lalbachan, Pamela. The Complete Caribbean Cookbook. (Illus.). 304p. 1994. 34.95 (*0-8048-3038-X*) Tuttle Pubng.
Lale, Cissy S., jt. auth. see Knight, Oliver.
Lale, Tim & Habada, Patricia A. Ten Who Came Back: Their Own Stories & What They Can Teach Us about Reclaiming Our Friends & Family. LC 97-25908. 1998. pap. 9.99 (*0-8163-1406-3*) Pacific Pr Pub Assn.
Lale, Tim, jt. auth. see Cornforth, Fred.
Lale, Tim, ed. see Beach, Bert Beverly, et al.
Lale, Tim, ed. see Finley, Mark & Mosley, Steven.
Lale, Tim, ed. see Finley, Mark & Mosley, Steven R.
Lale, Tim, ed. see Johnson, Kim Allan.
Lale, Tim, ed. see Melashenko, E. Lonnie & Jones, Brian D.
Lale, Tim, ed. see Robinson, Glen.
Lale, Tim, ed. see Williams, Hyveth.
Laleger, Grace E. Vocational Interests of High School Girls As Inventoried by the Strong & Manson Blanks. LC 76-176970. (Columbia University. Teachers College. Contributions to Education Ser.: No. 857). reprint ed. 37.50 (*0-404-55857-7*) AMS Pr.
Laleng, Per, jt. auth. see Ireland, Paddy.
Laliberte, Jacqueline. Driving a Heavy Vehicle. 2nd ed. (Illus.). 165p. 1999. reprint ed. pap. text 30.00 (*0-7881-7165-8*) DIANE Pub.
Laliberte, Katherine & Watson, Ben. Passport to Gardening: A Sourcebook for the Twenty-First Century Gardener. LC 97-31662. (Illus.). 320p. 1999. pap. 24.95 (*1-890132-00-4*) Chelsea Green Pub.
Laliberte, Lucie, jt. auth. see Harrison, Deborah.
Laliberte, Norman, jt. auth. see Mogelon, Alex.
Laliberte, Richard, et al. The Men's Health Guide to Peak Conditioning. LC 96-34087. 1997. pap. 29.95 (*0-87596-323-4*) Rodale Pr Inc.
Lalic, Bogdan. Budapest Game. (Batsford Chess Openings Ser.). (Illus.). 144p. 1998. pap. text 23.95 (*0-7134-8456-X*, Pub. by B T B) Branford.
— The Grunfeld for the Attacking Player. LC 97-71881. (Illus.). 224p. (Orig.). 1997. pap. 22.50 (*1-879479-62-1*) ICE WA.
— The Queen's Indian Defense. 192p. 1996. pap. 22.95 (*1-85744-157-5*, Pub. by Cadgn Bks) Macmillan.
Lalic, Ivan V. Fading Contact. LC 97-214894. 80p. 1997. pap. 15.95 (*0-85646-281-0*, Pub. by Anvil Press) Dufour.
— The Passionate Measure. 94p. 1989. pap. 17.95 (*0-85646-222-5*, Pub. by Anvil Press) Dufour.
— The Passionate Measure. (C). 1989. 23.00 (*0-948268-60-3*, Pub. by Dedalus) St Mut.
— Roll Call of Mirrors: Selected Poems of Ivan V. Lalic. Simic, Charles, tr. from SER. LC 87-21185. (Wesleyan Poetry in Translation Ser.). 80p. 1988. pap. 12.95 (*0-8195-1152-8*, Wesleyan Univ Pr) U Pr of New Eng.
Lalic, Ivan V. & Jones, Francis R. Last Quarter. 30p. 1987. pap. 9.95 (*0-85646-191-1*, Pub. by Anvil Press) Dufour.
— A Rusty Needle. LC 96-135484. 196p. 1997. pap. 18.95 (*0-85646-241-1*) Anvil Press.
Lalich, Janja & Tobias, Madeleine L. Captive Hearts, Captive Minds: Freedom & Recovery from Cults & Abusive Relationships. LC 93-33938. 320p. 1994. 24.95 (*0-89793-145-9*) Hunter Hse.
Lalich, Janja, jt. auth. see Singer, Margaret T.
Lalich, Janja, jt. auth. see Tobias, Madeleine L.
Lalich, Richard, jt. auth. see Stovall, Pamela.
*__Lalicki, Tom.__ Spellbinder: The Life of Harry Houdini. LC 99-45629. (Illus.). 96p. (J). (gr. 3-7). 2000. 18.95 (*0-8234-1499-X*) Holiday.
Lalini, V. Rural Leadership in India. 1991. 28.50 (*81-212-0333-3*, Pub. by Gian Publng Hse) S Asia.
Lalique, Marie-Claude. Lalique. (FRE.). 640p. 1993. lib. bdg. 295.00 (*0-7859-3655-6*, 2883000018) Fr & Eur.
Lalique, Rene. Lalique Glass: The Complete Illustrated Catalogue for 1932.Tr. of Catalogue Des Verreries de Rene Lalique. (Illus.). 149p. 1981. reprint ed. pap. 14.95 (*0-486-24122-X*) Dover.
Lalique, Rene, et al. The Jewels of Lalique. LC 97-48532. 224p. 1998. pap. write for info. (*2-08-013631-3*) Flammarion.
Lalita, K., jt. ed. see Tharu, Susie J.
Lalitananda, Swami. Yoga in Life. (Illus.). 1972. pap. 4.99 (*0-934664-17-X*) Yoga Res Foun.
— Yoga Mystic Songs for Meditation, 7 Vols. 1975. pap. 4.99 (*0-934664-19-6*) Yoga Res Foun.
Lalitananda, Swami, ed. Yoga Quotations from the Wisdom of Swami Jyotirmayananda. (Illus.). 1974. pap. 6.95 (*0-934664-27-7*) Yoga Res Foun.
*__Lalithakumari, D.__ Fungal Protoplast: A Biotechnological Tool. LC 00-37192. 2000. write for info. (*1-57808-093-2*) Science Pubs.
Lalithambal, K. S. Dharmakirti's Rupavatara-A Critical Study: A Critical Study. (C). 1995. 30.00 (*81-7030-437-7*, Pub. by Sri Satguru Pubns) S Asia.
Lalive D'Epinay, Th., jt. ed. see Rodd, Mike G.
Lalkaka, R. & Mingyu, Wu. Managing Science Policy & Technology Acquisitions: Strategies for China. 544p. 1984. 40.00 (*0-86346-050-X*, Tycooly Pub) Weidner & Sons.
Lall. Chip-Scale Packaging. 2000. ring bd. 59.95 (*0-8493-9626-3*) CRC Pr.
Lall, Arthur. Modern International Negotiation. LC 66-17587. 404p. 1966. text 69.00 (*0-231-02935-7*) Col U Pr.
Lall, B. Kent & Jones, Daniel L., Jr., eds. Major Development & Transportation Projects: Public-Private Partnerships. LC 90-980. 381p. 1990. pap. text 6.00 (*0-87262-764-0*) Am Soc Civil Eng.
— Transportation Congress: Civil Engineers - Key to the World Infrastructure: Proceedings of the 1995 Conference, San Diego, California, October 22-26, 1995, 2 vols. 2229p. 1995. 225.00 (*0-7844-0129-2*) Am Soc Civil Eng.
Lall, B. Kent, jt. auth. see Khisty, C. Jotin.
Lall, Betty G. Security Without Starwars: Verifying a Ban on Ballistic Missile Defense. 106p. 1987. pap. 6.00 (*0-87871-052-3*) CEP.
Lall, Bhagirath, jt. ed. see Marks, George V.
Lall, Chaman. Soft Magnetism: Fundamentals for Powder Metallurgy & Metal Injection Molding. LC 92-19313. (Monographs in P-M Ser.: No. 2). (Illus.). (C). 1992. pap. 60.00 (*1-878954-17-2*) Metal Powder.
Lall, Chaman & Neupaver, Albert J., compiled by. Advances in Powder Metallurgy & Particulate Materials - 1994: Proceedings of the 1994 International Conference & Exhibition on Powder Metallurgy & Particulate Materials, May 8-11, Toronto, Canada, 7 vols., Set. (Advances Ser.). 2400p. 1994. 300.00 (*1-878954-44-X*) Metal Powder.
Lall, J. S., ed. Selections from the Himalaya: Aspects of Change. (Oxford India Paperbacks Ser.). (Illus.). 244p. 1995. pap. 14.95 (*0-19-563263-X*) OUP.
Lall, J. S. & Moddie, A. D., eds. The Himalaya: Aspects of Change. (Illus.). 1981. 49.95 (*0-19-561254-X*) OUP.
Lall, K. B. Struggle for Change: (International Economic Relations) 327p. 1983. 34.95 (*0-318-37215-0*) Asia Bk Corp.
Lall, K. B., ed. The EEC in the Global Systems. 1984. 20.00 (*0-8364-1177-3*, Pub. by Allied Pubs) S Asia.
Lall, K. B., et al, eds. EC '92: United Germany & the Changing World Order. 260p. 1992. 30.00 (*81-7027-188-6*, Pub. by Radiant Pubs) S Asia.
— The European Community & SAARC. 114p. 1992. 25.00 (*81-7027-190-8*, Pub. by Radiant Pubs) S Asia.
— European Union & Transformation of Europe's Economy. 262p. 1992. 35.00 (*81-7027-189-4*, Pub. by Radiant Pubs) S Asia.
— India, Germany & the European Community. 164p. 1992. 27.50 (*81-7027-191-6*, Pub. by Radiant Pubs) S Asia.
Lall, Kesar. An Encounter with the Yeti & Other Stories. 1991. 30.00 (*0-7855-0268-8*, Pub. by Ratna Pustak Bhandar) St Mut.
— Folk Tales from the Himalayan Kingdom of Nepal-Black Rice & Other Stories. 1993. 20.00 (*0-7855-0274-2*, Pub. by Ratna Pustak Bhandar) St Mut.
— Folk Tales from the Kingdom of Nepal. 1991. 20.00 (*0-7855-0275-0*, Pub. by Ratna Pustak Bhandar) St Mut.
— Nepal: Off the Beaten Path. 1992. 40.00 (*0-7855-0280-7*, Pub. by Ratna Pustak Bhandar) St Mut.
— Nepal: Off the Beaten Path. (C). 1992. 30.00 (*0-7855-0200-9*, Pub. by Ratna Pustak Bhandar) St Mut.
— Nepal Miscellany. 1993. 30.00 (*0-7855-0279-3*, Pub. by Ratna Pustak Bhandar) St Mut.
— The Nepalese Customs & Manners. 1992. 30.00 (*0-7855-0282-3*, Pub. by Ratna Pustak Bhandar) St Mut.
— The Seven Sisters & Other Nepalese Tales. 1988. 25.00 (*0-7855-0286-6*, Pub. by Ratna Pustak Bhandar) St Mut.
— The Seven Sisters & Other Nepalese Tales. (Illus.). (C). 1988. 45.00 (*0-89771-082-7*, Pub. by Ratna Pustak Bhandar) St Mut.
Lall, Kesar, ed. The Nepalese Customs & Manners. 76p. (C). 1990. 35.00 (*0-89771-073-8*, Pub. by Ratna Pustak Bhandar) St Mut.
Lall, Rajiv, jt. auth. see Harrold, Peter.
Lall, Rajiv B. Multinationals from the Third World: Indian Firms Investing Abroad. 112p. 1987. 14.95 (*0-19-561895-5*) OUP.
Lall, Sanjaya. Attracting Foreign Investment, No. 31. 62p. 1997. pap. 11.95 (*0-85092-506-1*, Pub. by Comm Sec) Stylus Pub VA.
— Promoting Industrial Competitiveness in Developing Countries No. 39: Lessons from Asia. (Economic Paper Ser.). 84p. 2000. pap. 17.95 (*0-85092-623-8*, Pub. by Comm Sec) Stylus Pub VA.
Lall, Sanjaya. Technological Response to Import Liberalization in Sub-Saharan Africa. LC 98-25288. 256p. 1999. text 75.00 (*0-312-21800-1*) St Martin.
Lall, Sanjaya, ed. Conflict & Bargaining. 1976. pap. 19.75 (*0-08-021060-0*, Pergamon Pr) Elsevier.
— Transnational Corporations & Economic Development. (Readings in Transnational Corporations Ser.). 428p. 1996. pap. 29.95 (*0-415-14110-9*) Routledge.
Lall, Sanjaya, jt. auth. see Najmabadi, Farrokh.
Lalla, Barbara. Arch of Fire: A Child in Nazi Germany. LC 98-170447. 523 p. 1998. write for info. (*976-625-089-8*) Kingston Pub.
— Defining Jamaican Fiction: Marronage & the Discourse of Survival. LC 95-31869. (CRP & FRE.). 240p. (C). 1996. pap. text 29.95 (*0-8173-0782-6*) U of Ala Pr.
Lalla, Barbara & D'Costa, Jean. Language in Exile: Three Hundred Years of Jamaican Creole. LC 88-34012. 276p. 1990. text 44.95 (*0-8173-0447-9*) U of Ala Pr.
Lalla, Barbara, jt. ed. see D'Costa, Jean.
Lalleman, Josine A. Dutch Language Proficiency of Turkish Children Born in the Netherlands. (Functional Grammar Ser.). xvi, 237p. 1986. pap. 53.85 (*90-6765-160-5*) Mouton.
Lalleman, Josine A., jt. auth. see Jordens, Peter.
Lalleman, Josine A., jt. ed. see Jordens, Peter.
*__Lallemand, Henri.__ Manet: A Visionary Impressionist. 1998. 16.98 (*1-880908-14-X*) Todtri Prods.
*__Lallemand, Serge.__ La Subduction Oceanique. (FRE.). 212p. 1998. pap. text 40.00 (*90-5699-205-8*) Gordon & Breach.
Lallemand, Sylvie. The Tastes & Colors of Provence: A Unique Experience in the South of France. Kalb, C. W., Jr., ed. (Illus.). 1998. pap. 19.95 (*0-9661828-0-4*) Dove Byrd.
Lalley, Edward P. Corporate Uncertainty & Risk Management. LC 82-60961. (Illus.). 187p. 1982. 19.95 (*0-937802-03-4*) RMSP.
Lalley, Jacqueline, ed. see Larner, Mary.
Lalli. Fun & Games. 128p. 1998. pap. 35.00 (*0-7893-0138-5*) St Martin.
*__Lalli.__ Sex Machine. 1999. pap. 17.95 (*3-86187-148-3*) B Gmunder.
*__Lalli, Biancamaria Tedeschini, et al, eds.__ Brave New Words: Strategies of Language & Communication in the United States of the 1930s. 267p. 2000. 59.90 (*90-5383-592-X*, Pub. by VU Univ Pr) Paul & Co Pubs.
Lalli, Carol M. & Gilmer, Ronald W. Pelagic Snails: The Biology of Holoplanktonic Gastropod Mollusks. LC 88-20116. (Illus.). 288p. 1989. 55.00 (*0-8047-1490-8*) Stanford U Pr.
Lalli, Carole. Stuffings: 45 International Recipes to Enhance Fish, Poultry, Meat, Vegetables, & Fruit. LC 97-223530. (Illus.). 96p. 1997. 16.95 (*0-06-757502-1*) HarpC.
— Yesterday's Bread: 100 Creative Recipes for Not-Quite-Fresh Bread. LC 99-26365. 160p. 1999. pap. 12.95 (*0-06-095314-4*) HarpC.
Lalli, Cele G. Modern Bride Guide to Etiquette: Answers to the Questions Today's Couples Really Ask. LC 92-42166. 240p. (Orig.). 1993. pap. 16.95 (*0-471-58299-9*) Wiley.
Lalli, Cele G. & Dahl, Stephanie H. Modern Bride Wedding Celebrations: The Complete Wedding Planner for Today's Bride. 2nd rev. ed. LC 96-6327. (Illus.). 237p. 1996. pap. 15.95 (*0-471-14111-9*) Wiley.
Lalli, Judy. I Like Being Me: Poems for Children about Feeling Special, Appreciating Others, & Getting Along. LC 97-11653. (Illus.). 64p. (J). 1997. pap. text 8.95 (*1-57542-025-2*) Free Spirit Pub.
— Make Someone Smile & 40 More Ways to Be a Peaceful Person. LC 95-39198. (Illus.). 80p. (J). (gr. k up). 1996. pap. 9.95 (*0-915793-99-7*) Free Spirit Pub.
Lalli, Judy & Whitworth, Mary M. Leaders Guide to I Like Being Me: Poems for Children about Feeling Special, Appreciating Others & Getting Along. (Illus.). 80p. 1997. pap. text, teacher ed. 14.95 (*1-57542-026-0*) Free Spirit Pub.
Lalli, Nicholas. Seeds of Knowledge. (Minister's Manna Ser.: Vol. 1). v, 101p. 1997. pap. 8.00 (*0-9662519-1-1*) TKM Pubns WV.
— Seeds of Knowledge, Vol. 1. iii, 21p. 1994. pap. 5.00 (*0-9662519-0-3*) TKM Pubns WV.
Lalli, Sergio, jt. auth. see Bonanno, Joseph.
Lalli, Vincent A., et al. Using Plants to Bridge the Generations: Horticulture & Intergenerational Learning As Therapy (HILT) (Illus.). 68p. 1998. pap. 14.75 (*1-57753-224-4*, 141L10) Corn Coop Ext.
Lallier, Adalbert G. Sovereignty Association: Economic Realism or Utopia? 86p. 1991. pap. 10.95 (*0-88962-477-1*) Mosaic.
Lallier, Katherine G. & Marino, Nancy R. The Persona Book: Curriculum-Based Enrichment for School Librarians & Teachers. LC 96-37655. 180p. 1997. pap. text, teacher ed. 24.50 (*1-56308-443-0*) Teacher Ideas Pr.
Lallier-Verges, Elisabeth, et al, eds. Organic Matter Accumulation: The Organic Cyclicities of the Kimmeridge Clay Formation (Yorkshire, GB) & the Recent Maar Sediments (Lac du Bouchet, France) LC 95-12984. (Lecture Notes in Earth Sciences Ser.: Vol. 57). 1995. write for info. (*0-387-59170-2*) Spr-Verlag.
Lalljee, Barbara, jt. ed. see Holderness, Jackie.
Lalljee, Yousuf N. Know Your Islam. LC 81-51707. 255p. 1981. pap. 7.00 (*0-940368-02-1*, 60) Tahrike Tarsile Quran.
Lally, Dale V., Jr., tr. see Klauprecht, Emil.
Lally, Dick. Hit Men. (Baseball's Best Ser.). (Illus.). 24p. (J). (gr. 1 up). 1991. pap. 3.95 (*0-671-73637-X*) Litle Simon.
— Home Run Kings. (Baseball's Best Ser.). (Illus.). 24p. (J). (gr. 1 up). 1991. pap. 3.95 (*0-671-73636-1*) Litle Simon.
— Record Breakers. (Baseball's Best Ser.). (Illus.). 24p. (J). (gr. 1 up). 1991. pap. 3.95 (*0-671-73634-5*) Litle Simon.
Lally, Frank E. As Lord Acton Says. 1942. 30.00 (*0-686-17394-5*) R S Barnes.
Lally, J. Ronald, ed. Infant - Toddler Caregiving: A Guide to Social-Emotional Growth & Socialization. (Program for Infant - Toddler Caregivers Ser.). (Illus.). 104p. 1990. pap. 12.50 (*0-8011-0876-4*) Calif Education.
— Module I, Social-Emotional Growth & Socialization: Trainer's Manual. (Program for Infant - Toddler Caregivers Ser.). (Illus.). 164p. 1993. pap. 20.00 (*0-8011-1084-X*) Calif Education.
Lally, J. Ronald, et al, eds. Infant - Toddler Caregiving: A Guide to Language Development & Communication. (Program for Infant - Toddler Caregivers Ser.). (Illus.). 78p. 1991. pap. 12.50 (*0-8011-0880-2*) Calif Education.
Lally, J. Ronald & Stewart, Jay. Infant - Toddler Caregiving: A Guide to Setting up Environments. (Program for Infant - Toddler Caregivers Ser.). (Illus.). 78p. 1990. pap. 12.50 (*0-8011-0879-9*) Calif Education.
Lally, J. Ronald, et al. Caring for Infants & Toddlers in Groups: Developmentally Appropriate Practice. LC 95-62132. 94p. (Orig.). 1995. pap. text 17.00 (*0-943657-34-2*) ZERO TO THREE.
Lally, J. Ronald, jt. auth. see Honig, Alice S.
Lally, James, jt. auth. see Baldock, Cora V.
Lally, Kelly A. The Historic Architecture of Wake County, North Carolina. LC 93-85281. (Illus.). 448p. 1994. 35.00 (*0-9639198-0-6*) Wake County.
Lally, Kevin. Wilder Times: The Life & Times of Billy Wilder. 1995. pap. 14.95 (*0-8050-3120-0*) H Holt & Co.
— Wilder Times: The Life & Times of Billy Wilder. LC 95-33668. (Illus.). 89p. 1995. 30.00 (*0-8050-3119-7*) H Holt & Co.
Lally, Linda. The Volkswagen Beetle. LC 98-48552. (On the Road Ser.). 1999. 19.00 (*0-7368-0185-5*, Rivr Front Bks) Capstone Pr.
Lally, Linda Jean. Volkswagen Beetle. 1999. 19.00 (*0-531-11812-6*) Capstone Pr.
Lally, Linda Jean, jt. auth. see Burgan, Michael.
Lally, Margaret. The Nursery Teacher in Action. 194p. 1991. pap. 27.00 (*1-85396-131-0*, Pub. by P Chapman) Taylor & Francis.
Lally, Maureen & Stimpson, Cynthia, eds. Where Shall We Meet? 2nd ed. 54p. pap. 11.95 (*0-685-44384-1*) WOW Pub.
Lally, Michael. Attitude: Uncollected Poems of the Seventies. 1982. pap. 7.50 (*0-914610-31-7*) Hanging Loose.
— Cant Be Wrong: Poems 1985-1992. LC 96-11110. 144p. (Orig.). (C). 1996. pap. 11.95 (*1-56689-046-2*) Coffee Hse.
— It's Not Nostalgia, 1. LC 99-51344. 250p. 1999. 27.50 (*1-57423-112-X*); pap. 16.00 (*1-57423-111-1*); boxed set 35.00 (*1-57423-113-8*) Black Sparrow.
— Mentally, He's a Sick Man. LC PS3562.A414Z. (Salt Lick Samplers Ser.). 19p. 1975. reprint ed. pap. 30.00 (*0-7837-9160-7*, 204986000003) Bks Demand.
*__Lally, Michael.__ Of. 106p. 1999. pap. 9.95 (*1-882550-35-8*, Pub. by Quiet Lion Pr) SPD-Small Pr Dist.
Lally, Richard, jt. auth. see Morgan, Joe.
Lally, Rosemarie, jt. auth. see Bradbery, Angela.
Lally, Rosemarie, ed. see Wise, Patricia A.

An Asterisk (*) at the beginning of an entry indicates that the title is appearing for the first time.

Lally, Rosemary, ed. see DeSimone, Peter.

Lally, Soinbhe. A Hive for the Honeybee. LC 98-17145. (Illus.). (J). 1999. pap. write for info. (*0-590-51045-2*, A A Levine) Scholastic Inc.

— A Hive for the Honeybee. LC 98-17145. (Illus.). 224p. (YA). (gr. 5-9). 1999. 16.95 (*0-590-51038-X*, A A Levine) Scholastic Inc.

Lally, Steven. Using NMAKE. (C). 1996. pap. text. write for info. (*0-201-63350-7*) Addison-Wesley.

Lally, Steven, jt. auth. see Gehani, Narain.

Lalman, David, jt. auth. see Bueno de Mesquita, Bruce.

Lalmas, Mounia. Information Retrieval: Uncertainty & Logics: Advanced Models for the Representation & Retrieval of Information. LC 98-41652. (Kluwer International Series on Information Retrieval). 1998. 136.00 (*0-7923-8302-8*) Kluwer Academic.

Lalo. Symphonie Espagnole in Full Score. 1998. pap. 12.95 (*0-486-29532-X*) Dover.

Lalo, Eduardo. En el Burger King de la Calle San Francisco. (Illus.). 98p. 1986. pap. 7.00 (*0-317-01397-1*) Ed Astrolabio.

LaLoca. Adventures on the Isle of Adolescence. 128p. (Orig.). 1989. pap. 5.95 (*0-87286-236-4*) City Lights.

L'Aloge, Bob. Ghosts & Mysteries of the Old West: True Accounts of New Mexico & the Old West. rev. ed. LC 91-66180. (Illus.). 112p. 1991. pap. 9.95 (*0-9622940-5-5*) Yucca Tree Pr.

— Knights of the Sixgun: A Diary of Gunfighters, Outlaws & Villains in New Mexico. LC 91-65342. (Illus.). 192p. (Orig.). 1991. pap. 9.95 (*0-9622940-3-9*) Yucca Tree Pr.

L'Aloge, Bob. Pistols & Petticoats: 13 Female Trailblazers of the Old West. LC 95-90642. (Illus.). 272p. 1995. pap. 14.95 (*0-938147-99-4*, Pub. by Flying Eagle) Yucca Tree Pr.

L'Aloge, Bob. Riders along the Rio Grande: A Collection of Outlaws, Prostitutes & Vigilantes. LC 92-60658. (Illus.). 212p. 1992. pap. 9.95 (*1-881481-00-X*) Yucca Tree Pr.

— Yesterdays . . . Today! Authentic Accounts of the Old West. Nelson-L'Aloge, Virginia, ed. (Illus.). 208p. (Orig.). (YA). (gr. 5 up). 1995. pap. text 12.95 (*0-938147-97-8*) Flying Eagle.

— Yesterdays . . . Today! Authentic Accounts of the Past, Vol. 2. Nelson-L'Aloge, Virginia, ed. (Illus.). 256p. (Orig.). (YA). (gr. 5 up). 1995. pap. text 12.95 (*0-938147-98-6*) Flying Eagle.

***Laloggia, Charles.** Superstock Investor: Proviting from Wall Street's Best Undervalued Companies. 2000. 27.95 (*0-07-136083-2*) McGraw.

Laloggia, Nicole Shay & Wurmfeld, Eden H. Independent Filmmaker's Manual. LC 99-19198. 288p. 1999. pap. 36.95 (*0-240-80389-2*, Focal) Buttrwrth-Heinemann.

LaLond, David E. & Ross, John A. Experiments in Principles of Electronic Devices & Circuits. 88p. 1994. pap., teacher ed. 21.00 (*0-8273-4665-4*) Delmar.

— Principles of Electronic Controls & Devices: Printed Test Bank. 182p. 1994. pap. 32.50 (*0-8273-6385-0*) Delmar.

— Principles of Electronic Devices & Circuits: Computerized Testmaker & Testbank for DOS Compatible Computers. 1994. 49.95 (*0-8273-6510-1*) Delmar.

Lalond, David E., jt. auth. see Ross, John A.

Lalonde. 301 Startling Proofs & Prophecies. 1996. pap. 13.95 (*0-9680758-0-0*) Prophecy Partners.

Lalonde Alenier, Karren. Looking for Divine Transportation: Poetry by Karren Lalonde Alenier. Cavalieri, Grace, ed. 75p. (Orig.). 1999. pap. 10.00 (*0-938572-24-5*, Pub. by Bunny Crocodile) WrdWrks Pub.

Lalonde, Beverly, ed. see Birmingham, Kelly J.

LaLonde, Beverly, ed. see Blackwell, Thomas T.

Lalonde, Catherine, jt. auth. see Burchell, Louise.

LaLonde, Christopher A. William Faulkner & the Rites of Passage. 208p. (C). 1995. text 25.00 (*0-86554-482-4*, MUP/H378) Mercer Univ Pr.

Lalonde, Francois, ed. Geometry, Topology, & Dynamics. LC 98-13428. (CRM Proceedings & Lecture Notes Ser.: Vol. 15). (Illus.). 148p. 1998. pap. 35.00 (*0-8218-0877-X*, CRMP/15) Am Math.

Lalonde, Gerald V., et al. Inscriptions, Horoi, Poletai Records, Leases of Public Lands. LC 90-49463. (Athenian Agora Ser.: Vol. 19). (Illus.). xiv, 245p. 1991. 90.00 (*0-87661-219-2*) Am Sch Athens.

LaLonde, Jane, jt. auth. see O'Shea, Tracy.

Lalonde, Lawrence J. Legends of BAKA. 52p. 1984. pap. write for info. (*0-9608136-0-8*) L J Lalonde.

Lalonde, M., et al, eds. Frankia & Actinorhizal Plants. (Developments in Plant & Social Sciences Ser.). 1985. text 147.00 (*90-247-3214-X*) Kluwer Academic.

***Lalonde, Marc P.** Critical Theology & the Challenge of Jurgen Habermas: Toward a Critical Theory of Religious Insight. LC 98-30627. (Studies in Religion, Politics, & Public Life: Vol. 1). 118p. (C). 1999. text 41.95 (*0-8204-3762-X*) P Lang Pubng.

Lalonde, Marc P., ed. The Promise of Critical Theology: Essays in Honour of Charles Davis. LC 96-110739. xii, 146p. (C). 1995. pap. 21.95 (*0-88920-254-0*) W Laurier U Pr.

Lalonde, Patti, jt. auth. see Lalonde, Peter.

Lalonde, Paul, jt. auth. see Lalonde, Peter.

LaLonde, Paul, jt. auth. see LaLonde, Peter.

Lalonde, Paul, jt. auth. see Lalonde, Peter.

LaLonde, Peter. Revelation. 1999. pap. text 8.95 (*0-9680758-6-X*) Prophecy Partners.

Lalonde, Peter & Lalonde, Patti. Left Behind. (Orig.). 1995. pap. 9.99 incl. VHS (*1-56507-364-9*) Harvest Hse.

***LaLonde, Peter & LaLonde, Paul.** 2000 D. C. Esta Preparado? 1998. pap. text 9.99 (*0-88113-503-8*) Caribe Betania.

— La Marca de La Bestia.Tr. of Mark of the Beast. (SPA.). 184p. 1998. pap. 8.99 (*0-88113-500-3*) Caribe Betania.

Lalonde, Peter & Lalonde, Paul. The Mark of the Beast: Your Money, Computers, & the End of the World. LC 93-43734. 1994. pap. 9.99 incl. VHS (*1-56507-218-9*) Harvest Hse.

LaLonde, Peter & LaLonde, Paul. Los Que Se Quedaron.Tr. of Left Behind. 1997. 8.99 (*0-88113-449-X*) Caribe Betania.

— 301 Sorprendentes Pruebas y Profecias. (SPA.). 1997. 12.99 (*0-88113-458-9*, B109-4589) Caribe Betania.

Lalonde, Peter & Lalonde, Paul. 301 Startling Proofs & Prophecies: Proving That God Exists. 1997. pap. 6.99 (*0-9680758-1-9*) Prophecy Partners.

— 2000 A. D. Are You Ready? LC 97-9831. 192p. 1997. pap. 12.99 (*0-7852-7188-0*) Nelson.

Lalonde, Robert J. Regulation & Labor. (Case; Hb - Economics Ser.). 1997. mass mkt. 3.75 (*0-538-85804-4*) S-W Pub.

Lalonde, Robert J., jt. ed. see Ashenfelter, Orley C.

LaLonde, Wilf. Discovering Smalltalk. (Object Oriented Software Engineering Ser.). 576p. (C). 1993. pap. 47.95 (*0-8053-2720-7*) Addison-Wesley.

Lalone. Statistics. 1996. 30.74 (*0-07-036679-9*) McGraw.

LaLone, Jodi. Broken Butterflies. Zagury, Carolyn & Vaughn, Helen, eds. LC 97-61602. 240p. 1998. pap. 14.95 (*1-880254-49-2*) Vista.

LaLong, David. The Eight Thousand Eighty, Eight Thousand Eighty-Five, & Seven Hundred Eighty: Hardware, Software, Programming, Interfacing & Troubleshooting. (Illus.). 416p. 1988. text 54.20 (*0-13-247008-X*) P-H.

Lalor, Brian. Blue Guide Ireland. 8th ed. LC 99-223829. (Illus.). 448p. 1998. pap. 24.95 (*0-393-31801-X*) Norton.

***Lalor, Brian.** The Irish Round Tower: Origins & Architecture Explored. LC 99-198078. (Illus.). 1999. 35.95 (*1-898256-64-0*, Pub. by Collins Press) Dufour.

Lalor, Brian. The Laugh of Lost Men: An Irish Journey. (Illus.). 192p. 1998. 29.95 (*1-85158-858-2*, Pub. by Mainstream Pubng) Trafalgar.

Lalor, Francis R. Leisuregrams. LC 80-83525. 1981. 7.95 (*0-87212-144-5*) Libra.

Lalor, James F. Collected Writings, 1918. LC 96-35549. (Hibernia Ser.). 1997. 65.00 (*1-85477-219-8*) Continuum.

Lalor, John J., tr. see Nohl, Louis.

Lalor, John J., tr. see Von Jhering, Rudolph.

Lalor, Paule, jt. auth. see Morgan, Sally.

Lalos, Peter. SlowBurn. LC 99-90661. 432p. 1999. pap. 14.95 (*1-56167-488-5*, Five Star Spec Ed) Am Literary Pr.

Lalou, Elizabeth, ed. see Bautier, Robert-Henri.

Lalou, Rene. Roman Francais Depuis, 1900. 127p. 1966. 9.95 (*0-8288-7413-1*) Fr & Eur.

— Theatre en France Depuis, 1900. 127p. 1951. 9.95 (*0-8288-7412-3*) Fr & Eur.

Lalouette, Jaques. Agawa Poems. 1986. 5.00 (*0-920806-85-6*, Pub. by Penumbra Pr) U of Toronto Pr.

Laloy, J. R., jt. auth. see Dany, M.

Laloy, Louis. La Musique Chinoise: A Study of Chinese Music. (Illus.). 96p. 1993. pap. 18.50 (*0-910704-75-9*) Hawley.

Lalrymple, Douglas J., et al. Cases in Marketing Management. LC 91-28624. 608p. (C). 1991. text 78.95 (*0-471-54746-8*) Wiley.

Lalumandier, Lillian H. When Only the Best Will Do. large type ed. (Illus.). 190p. 1996. spiral bd. 14.95 (*0-9656047-0-5*) Lillians LA Kitchen.

Lalumia, Joseph. Ettore Majorana & the Atomic Bomb. 80p. 1993. pap. 12.95 (*1-880365-96-0*); pap. 12.95 (*1-880365-67-7*) Prof Pr NC.

Lalumia, Matthew P. Realism & Politics in Victorian Art of the Crimean War. LC 83-24284. (Studies in the Fine Arts: Iconography: No. 9). (Illus.). 304p. reprint ed. pap. 94.30 (*0-8357-1499-3*, 207050200097) Bks Demand.

Lalumiere, Martin L., jt. auth. see Quinsey, Vernon L.

Laluzerne & Tsuk. Tell Me about It! (J). 1993. audio 18.00 (*0-8384-3609-9*) Heinle & Heinle.

— Tell Me about It! (J). 1993. mass mkt., teacher ed. 9.95 (*0-8384-4202-1*) Heinle & Heinle.

Laluzerne, Sally & Tsukamoto, Cynthia McKeag. Tell Me about It! (J). 1993. pap. text 21.95 (*0-8384-3608-0*) Heinle & Heinle.

Lalvani, Suren. Photography, Vision, & the Production of Modern Bodies. LC 95-36567. (SUNY Series, Interruptions). (Illus.). 265p. (C). 1995. pap. text 17.95 (*0-7914-2718-8*) State U NY Pr.

Lalvani, Vimla. Classic Yoga for Stress Relief. 128p. 1999. pap. text 14.95 (*0-8069-1961-2*) Sterling.

Lalwani, Anil K. & Grundfast, Kenneth M., eds. Pediatric Otology & Neurotology. LC 97-30730. (Illus.). 400p. 1997. text 149.00 (*0-397-51466-2*) Lppncott W & W.

Lalwani, K. C. Kalpa Sutra. 207p. 1979. 18.00 (*0-89684-039-5*, Pub. by Motilal Bnarsidass) S Asia.

Lalwani, Rajesh. Power Programming with SQL Windows. 1994. pap. 29.95 incl. disk (*0-13-179306-3*) P-H.

***Lam.** Cognitive Therapy for Bipolar Disorder: A Therapist's Guide to Concepts, Methods & Practice. 320p. 1999. 59.95 (*0-471-97939-2*) Wiley.

Lam, et al. Basic Clinical Microbiology & Pathology. 182p. (C). 1997. spiral bd. 30.95 (*0-7872-4425-2*, 41442501) Kendall-Hunt.

Lam, Adrienne, tr. see Loo, Andre.

Lam, Agnes, jt. auth. see Ngok, Lee.

Lam, Alex W. & Tantaratana, Sawasd. Theory & Applications of Spread Spectrum Systems. Zaputowycz, Roman & Maric, Svetislav, eds. 300p. 1994. student ed. 259.00 (*0-7803-0374-1*, HL4671) Inst Electrical.

Lam, Alven H. S. & Robinson, Dennis W., eds. Land Systems Technology: Background Papers Prepared for the Lincoln Institute of Land Policy Seminar on Land Systems Technology. LC G 0070.2.L36. (Lincoln Institute of Land Policy Monograph: No. 86-11). (Illus.). 52p. reprint ed. pap. 30.00 (*0-7837-5755-7*, 204541700006) Bks Demand.

Lam, Arthur M., ed. Anesthetic Management of Acute Head Injury. LC 93-49496. (Illus.). 304p. 1994. text 59.00 (*0-07-036127-4*) McGraw-Hill HPD.

Lam, Arthur M., jt. auth. see Chung, David C.

Lam, C. Eat in Hong Kong. 150p. 1996. pap. 7.00 (*962-8141-01-5*) World Scientific Pub.

Lam, Chan F. Techniques for the Analysis & Modelling of Enzyme Kinetic Mechanisms. LC 81-188222. (Medical Computing Ser.: No. 4). (Illus.). 412p. reprint ed. pap. 127.80 (*0-8357-7049-4*, 203334300085) Bks Demand.

Lam, Chun H. & Hempel, George H. Microcomputer Applications in Banking. LC 85-32322. 221p. 1986. 57.95 (*0-89930-117-7*, HMI/, Quorum Bks) Greenwood.

Lam, D. C., et al. Effluent Transport & Diffusion Models for the Coastal Zone. (Lecture Notes on Coastal & Estuarine Studies: Vol. 5). (Illus.). 170p. 1984. pap. 39.00 (*0-387-90928-1*) Spr-Verlag.

Lam, David C. L. & Schertzer, William M. Potential Climate Change Effects on Great Lakes Hydrodynamics & Water Quality. LC 98-55322. 232p. 1999. 32.00 (*0-7844-0413-5*) Am Soc Civil Eng.

Lam, Dominic. Cognitive Therapy for Biopolar Disorder: A Therapist's Guide to Concepts, Methods, & Practice. LC 99-20568. (Clinical Psychology Ser.). 320p. 1999. pap. 37.00 (*0-471-97945-7*) Wiley.

Lam, Dominic M. & Bray, Garth M., eds. Regeneration & Plasticity in the Mammalian Visual System, Vol. 4. (Illus.). 262p. 1992. 78.00 (*0-262-12169-7*, Bradford Bks) MIT Pr.

Lam, Dominic M. & Gilbert, Charles D., eds. Proceedings of the Retina Research Foundation Symosia Vol. 1: Cellular & Molecular Biology of the Retina. (Illus.). 200p. 1991. pap. text 45.00 (*0-262-62083-9*) MIT Pr.

Lam, Dominic M. & Shatz, Carla J., eds. Development of the Visual System. (Bradford - Proceedings of the Retina Foundation Symposium Ser.: Vol. 3). (Illus.). 312p. 1991. 70.00 (*0-262-12154-9*, Bradford Bks) MIT Pr.

Lam, Eric W. Bankruptcy in Iowa. LC 91-45696. 1992. 58.00 (*0-87414-085-4*) Iowa Law Schl.

Lam, Gladys S., jt. auth. see Ross, Ronald G.

Lam, James C. Life of Goodrich. LC 87-82702. 160p. 1987. pap. text 5.50 (*0-940043-26-2*) Evangel Lit.

Lam, James C., ed. Beloved Saints. (CHI.). 129p. 1998. pap. 35.00 (*0-940043-39-4*) Evangel Lit.

***Lam, Jermain T. M.** The Political Dynamics of Hong Kong under the Chinese Sovereignty. LC 00-28422. 251p. 2000. lib. bdg. 59.00 (*1-56072-806-X*) Nova Sci Pubs.

Lam, Joseph & Bray, William. China: The Last Superpower. LC 97-65165. 240p. 1997. pap. 12.95 (*0-89221-343-4*) New Leaf.

Lam, Joseph S. State Sacrifices & Music in Ming China: Orthodoxy, Creativity, & Expressiveness. LC 97-36909. (SUNY Series in Chinese Studies). (Illus.). 256p. (C). 1998. text 74.50 (*0-7914-3705-1*); pap. text 24.95 (*0-7914-3706-X*) State U NY Pr.

Lam, Joseph S., jt. ed. see Yung, Bell.

Lam, K. D., et al. Total Quality: A Textbook of Strategic Quality Leadership & Planning. 360p. (C). 1991. pap. 35.00 (*0-9622176-9-7*) Air Acad Pr.

Lam, K. Y., jt. auth. see Tay, A. A.

Lam, Kam C. The Way of Energy: A Gaia Original. (Illus.). 192p. (Orig.). 1991. pap. 15.95 (*0-671-73645-0*, Fireside) S&S Trade Pap.

Lam Kam Chuen. Step-by-Step Tai Chi: The Natural Way to Strength & Health. LC 94-7581. 144p. 1994. per. 15.00 (*0-671-89247-9*) S&S Trade.

***Lam, Kwok Yan, et al, eds.** Advances in Cryptology - ASIACRYPT'99: Proceedings of the International Conference on the Theory & Application of Cryptology & Information Security, Singapore, November 14-18, 1999. LC 99-51451. (Lecture Notes in Computer Science Ser.: Vol. 1716). xi, 414p. 1999. pap. 69.00 (*3-540-66666-4*) Spr-Verlag.

Lam, Kwong W. & Mancuso, Ted. Northern Sil Lum Form #7: Plum Flower Fist (or Moi Fah) LC 83-50020. (Illus.). 150p. 1984. pap. 8.95 (*0-86568-044-2*, 213) Unique Pubns.

Lam, L. The Analysis of Doubly Censored Survival Data: An Application to Data Collected from the Amsterdam Cohort Studies on HIV Infection & AIDS. (WBBM Report Ser.: No. 36). (Illus.). 75p. 1997. pap. 25.00 (*90-407-1561-0*, Pub. by Delft U Pr) Coronet Bks.

Lam, Lai Sing. Mao Tse-Tung's Purposive Contention with the Superpowers: The Theory of Ch'i. LC 94-13504. 216p. 1994. text 89.95 (*0-7734-2289-7*) E Mellen.

— The Role of Ch'i in Mao Tse-Tung's Leadership Style. LC 93-29019. 336p. 1993. text 99.95 (*0-7734-2224-2*) E Mellen.

Lam, Loh N. & Batchelor, Andrew W. Materials Degradation & Its Control by Surface Engineering. 500p. 1998. 68.00 (*1-86094-072-2*, Pub. by Imperial College) World Scientific Pub.

— Materials Degradation & Its Control by Surface Engineering. LC 99-17069. 500p. 1998. 78.00 (*1-86094-083-8*, Pub. by Imperial College) World Scientific Pub.

Lam, Lui, ed. Introduction to Nonlinear Physics. LC 96-14764. 417p. 1996. 59.95 (*0-387-94758-2*) Spr-Verlag.

— Nonlinear Physics for Beginners. 250p. (C). 1997. text 55.00 (*981-02-0140-0*); pap. text 21.00 (*981-02-0141-9*) World Scientific Pub.

Lam, Lui, et al, eds. Solitons in Liquid Crystals. (Partially Ordered Systems Ser.). (Illus.). 368p. 1991. 89.95 (*0-387-96878-4*) Spr-Verlag.

Lam, Lui & Morris, H. C., eds. Nonlinear Structures in Physical Systems: Pattern Formation, Chaos, & Waves: Proceedings of the Second Woodward Conference, San Jose State University, November 17-18, 1989. (Woodward Conference Ser.). (Illus.). x, 331p. 1990. 83.95 (*0-387-97344-3*) Spr-Verlag.

— Wave Phenomena. (Illus.). xii, 275p. 1988. 96.95 (*0-387-96921-7*) Spr-Verlag.

Lam, Lui & Naroditsky, V., eds. Modeling Complex Phenomena. (Woodward Conference Ser.). (Illus.). 320p. 1992. 96.95 (*0-387-97821-6*) Spr-Verlag.

Lam, Lui, jt. ed. see Shibaev, Valery.

***Lam, Maivan Clech.** At the Edge of the State: Indigenous Peoples & Self-Determination. (Innovation in International Law Ser.). 300p. 2000. 95.00 (*1-57105-076-0*) Transnatl Pubs.

***Lam, Maria Lai-Ling.** Working with Chinese Expatriates in Business Negotiations: Portraits, Issues & Applications. LC 99-56361. 208p. 2000. 65.00 (*1-56720-327-2*, Q327, Quorum Bks) Greenwood.

Lam, Martin & Shimizu, Kaoru. Kanji from the Start: A Comprehensive Japanese Reader. Hirowatari, Taro & Hulbert, Paul, eds. 360p. 1995. pap. 25.00 (*4-7700-1936-X*) Kodansha.

Lam, Michael, jt. auth. see Markovitz, Morris J.

Lam, Monica S. A Systolic Array Optimizing Compiler. (C). 1988. text 91.50 (*0-89838-300-5*) Kluwer Academic.

Lam, My-Yen. A Review of Food Research in Vietnam with Emphasis on Postharvest Losses. 111p. 1993. pap. 75.00 (*1-86320-097-5*, Pub. by ACIAR) St Mut.

Lam, Paul K., jt. auth. see Dudgeon, David.

Lam, Peng E., jt. auth. see Tan, Kevin.

***Lam, Peng Er.** Green Politics in Japan. LC 99-212070. (Illus.). 1999. write for info. (*0-415-19938-7*) Routledge.

Lam, Peter K. Y., jt. ed. see Hui, Humphrey K. F.

Lam, Peter Y. K. 2000 Years of Chinese Lacquer. 246p. 1994. 165.00 (*962-7101-26-5*, Pub. by Chinese Univ of Hong Kong) St Mut.

Lam, Peter Y. K., ed. Elegant Vessels for the Lofty Pavillion: The Zande Lou Gift of Porcelain with Studio Marks. 74p. 1993. 84.00 (*962-7101-23-0*, Pub. by Chinese Univ of Hong Kong) St Mut.

— Qing Imperial Porcelain of the Kangxi, Yongzheng & Qianlong Reigns. 270p. 1995. 165.00 (*962-7101-31-1*, Pub. by Chinese Univ of Hong Kong) St Mut.

Lam, Peter Y. K. & Hok-wa, Yau, trs. A Legacy of the Ming. 143p. 1996. pap. 120.00 (*962-7101-32-X*, Pub. by Chinese Univ of Hong Kong) St Mut.

Lam, Pun-Lee & Chan, Sylvia. Competition in Hong Kong's Gas Industry. (Illus.). 144p. (C). pap. text 18.00 (*962-201-906-4*, Pub. by Chinese Univ) U of Mich Pr.

Lam, Raymond W., ed. Seasonal Affective Disorder & Beyond: Light Treatment for SAD & Non-SAD Conditions. LC RC545.S42 1998. 327p. 1998. text 47.00 (*0-88048-867-0*, 8867) Am Psychiatric.

Lam, Richard, jt. auth. see Giblin, Daniel.

Lam, Richard B. The Netscape Programmer's Guide: Using OLE to Build Componentware Apps. 416p. 1998. pap. 39.95 (*0-521-64820-3*) Cambridge U Pr.

Lam, Richard B., jt. auth. see Cooper, James W.

Lam, Roger. The Cuckoo Clock Adventure. Gibb, George, ed. LC 82-99848. (Illus.). (Orig.). (J). (gr. 5-12). 1983. pap. 2.25 (*0-943310-01-6*) Six Pr.

Lam, S. F., et al. X-Ray Diagnosis: A Physician's Approach. LC 97-13226. (Illus.). 200p. (C). 1998. pap. 35.00 (*981-3083-24-7*, Pub. by Spr-Verlag) Spr-Verlag.

Lam, S. K., ed. Update on Hepatobiliary Diseases, 1996. (Falk Symposium Ser.). 336p. (C). 1997. text 157.50 (*0-7923-8715-5*) Kluwer Academic.

Lam, S. P. & Shum, K. P., eds. Algebraic Structures & Number Theory: Proceedings of the First International Symposium, Hong Kong, 8-13 Aug. 1988. 344p. (C). 1990. text 101.00 (*981-02-0291-1*) World Scientific Pub.

Lam, Sau-Hai, jt. auth. see Li, Wen-Hsiung.

Lam, Shiu-Kum, ed. The Health of the Elderly in Hong Kong. LC 98-170579. 232p. (Orig.). 1997. pap. 29.50 (*962-209-431-7*, Pub. by HK Univ Pr) Coronet Bks.

Lam, Shui F. How the Family Influences Children's Academic Achievement. rev. ed. LC 96-39982. (Children of Poverty Ser.). (Illus.). 144p. 1997. text 39.00 (*0-8153-2620-3*) Garland.

Lam, Stanley K., jt. auth. see Fong, Goodwin W.

Lam, Stephen T. & Pang, Calvin C., eds. Neonatal & Perinatal Screening: The Asian Pacific Perspective. LC 98-139431. 1997. 34.50 (*962-201-765-7*, Pub. by Chinese Univ) U of Mich Pr.

***Lam, Syrine K.** Portraits of Successful Entrepreneurs & High-Flyers: A Psychological Perspective. 270p. 1999. text 69.95 (*1-84014-791-1*, Pub. by Inst Materials) Ashgate Pub Co.

Lam, T. Y. The Algebraic Theory of Quadratic Forms. 343p. (C). 1980. pap. text 36.75 (*0-8053-5666-5*) Addison-Wesley.

— Exercises in Classical Ring Theory. LC 94-19976. (Problem Books in Mathematics). 1994. 59.95 (*0-387-94317-X*) Spr-Verlag.

— A First Course in Noncommutative Ring. (Graduate Texts in Mathematics Ser.: Vol. 131). xv, 397p. 1991. 54.95 (*0-387-97523-3*) Spr-Verlag.

— Lectures on Rings & Modules. LC 98-18389. (Graduate Tests in Mathematics Ser.: Vol. 189). 420p. 1998. 54.95 (*0-387-98428-3*) Spr-Verlag.

— Orderings, Valuations & Quadratic Forms. LC 83-11729. (CBMS Regional Conference Series in Mathematics: No. 52). 143p. 1983. pap. 25.00 (*0-8218-0702-1*, CBMS/52) Am Math.

Lam, Tony. How to Beat Stress. 88p. 6.75 (*0-317-31556-0*) Chans Corp.

— Vietnamese Cooking. 128p. 1993. 12.98 (*1-55521-907-1*) Bk Sales Inc.

***Lam, Tri.** Encyclopedia of Chinese Astrology. (Illus.). 318p. 2000. pap. 25.00 (*0-9685735-0-9*) Lam Inter Media.

***Lam, Truong B.** Colonialism Experienced: Vietnamese Writings on Colonialism (1900-1931) LC 99-58296. (Illus.). 416p. (C). 2000. text 69.50 (*0-472-09712-1*, 09712); pap. text 19.95 (*0-472-06712-5*, 06712) U of Mich Pr.

Lam, Wai F. Governing Irrigation Systems in Nepal: Institutions, Infrastructure & Collective Action. LC 97-42569. 1998. pap. 24.95 (*1-55815-505-8*) ICS Pr.

Lam, William K. & Brayton, Robert K. Timed Boolean Functions: A Unified Formalism for Exact Timing Analysis. LC 94-8519. (International Series in Engineering Computer Science, Computer Architecture & Digital Signal Processing Ser.). 296p. (C). 1994. text 133.50 (*0-7923-9454-2*) Kluwer Academic.

Lam, Willy W. China after Deng Xiaoping: The Power Struggle in Beijing since Tiananmen. 497p. 1995. 34.95 (*0-471-13114-8*) Wiley.

***Lam, Willy Wo-Lap.** The Era of Jiang Zemin. LC 98-474002. 452p. 1999. pap. text 19.99 (*0-13-083701-6*) P-H.

Lam, Y. L., ed. Canadian Public Education System: Issues & Prospects. 337p. (Orig.). (C). 1990. pap. text 21.95 (*1-55059-019-7*) Temeron Bks.

***Lam, Yee L., et al, eds.** Photonic Systems & Applications in Defense & Manufacturing. 1999. pap. text 103.00 (*0-8194-3500-7*) SPIE.

***Lama, Dalai.** The Meaning of Life: Buddhist Perspectives on Cause & Effect. Hopkins, Jeffrey, ed. & tr. by. 164p. 2000. pap. 15.95 (*0-86171-173-4*) Wisdom MA.

Lama, Dalai, jt. auth. see Lozoff, Bo.

LAMA Development Committee Staff. Staff Development: A Practical Guide. 2nd ed. Lipow, Anne G. & Carver, Deborah A., eds. LC 91-18962. 104p. (C). 1991. pap. text 25.00 (*0-8389-3402-1*) ALA.

Lama, Luisa De La, see De La Lama, Luisa.

Lama, M. & Thapar, A. Nepal: The Himalayan Kingdom. 1997. pap. 110.00 (*0-7855-7465-4*, Pub. by Ratna Pustak Bhandar) St Mut.

Lama, Mahendra P., ed. Sikkim: Society, Polity, Economy, Environment. (C). 1994. text 30.00 (*81-7387-013-6*, Pub. by Indus Pub) S Asia.

Lama Mi-pham. Golden Zephyr. Kawamura, Leslie S., tr. from TIB. LC 75-5259. (Tibetan Translation Ser.: Vol. 4). (Illus.). 185p. (Orig.). 1975. pap. 12.95 (*0-913546-21-6*) Dharma Pub.

Lama, Nino. A CPA's Guide to Understanding Business Insurance. 1998. pap. 36.00 (*0-87051-229-3*) Am Inst CPA.

Lama, R. D. & Vutukuri, V. S. Handbook on Mechanical Properties of Rocks, Vol. III. (Rock & Soil Mechanics Ser.). (Illus.). (C). 1978. 75.00 (*0-87849-022-1*, Pub. by Trans T Pub) Enfield Pubs NH.

— Handbook on Mechanical Properties of Rocks, Vol. IV. (Rock & Soil Mechanics Ser.). (Illus.). (C). 1978. 75.00 (*0-87849-023-X*, Pub. by Trans T Pub) Enfield Pubs NH.

Lamac, Miroslav. Osma a Skupina Vytvarnych Umelcu, 1907-1917, Cesky Kubismus. (CZE., Illus.). 544p. 1988. 70.00 (*0-317-03838-9*) Szwede Slavic.

***Lamacraft, Jane & Wilson, Vicky.** Kids' London: A Guide for Parents. 320p. 2000. pap. 15.00 (*1-84166-029-9*, Pub. by Ellipsis) Norton.

Lamacz, Margaret, jt. auth. see Money, John.

Lamada. Discussion. 150p. 1998. pap. 13.95 (*1-870259-71-8*, Pub. by Oberon Bks Ltd) Theatre Comm.

Lamadrid, Enrique E., ed. En Breve: Minimalism in Mexican Poetry, 1900-1985. Mares, E. A., tr. from SPA. 80p. 1988. pap. 6.00 (*0-940510-17-0*) Tooth of Time.

LaMadrid, Enrique E., et al, eds. An Eye Through the Wall: Mexican Poetry, 1970-1985. Brandi, John et al, trs. (Poetry Ser.). (ENG & SPA., Illus.). 220p. (Orig.). 1985. pap. 10.00 (*0-940510-14-6*) Tooth of Time.

Lamadrid, Enrique E., et al. Communicating in Spanish: A First Course. 2nd ed. LC 83-81321. 768p. 1984. VHS. write for info. (*0-395-32715-6*); disk. write for info. (*0-318-57690-2*) HM.

Lamadrid, Enrique R., jt. auth. see Howarth, Sam.

Lamagna, Joseph. Coins: The Collector's Guide. 2nd rev. ed. (Illus.). 88p. pap. 10.00 (*0-9610464-4-9*) J Lamagna.

— God's Last Will & Testament for Earth. (Illus.). 56p. 1999. pap. 10.00 (*0-9610464-7-3*) J Lamagna.

— Lamagna Genealogy. (Illus.). 44p. (Orig.). 1992. pap. write for info. (*0-9610464-2-2*) J Lamagna.

— Trout Fishing U. S. A. (Illus.). 80p. pap. 10.00 (*0-9610464-6-5*) J Lamagna.

— Wild Game Cookbook & Other Recipes. 3rd enl. expanded ed. 134p. pap. 10.00 (*0-9610464-5-7*) J Lamagna.

— Write Right: Not Almost Right. (Illus.). 48p. (Orig.). pap. 10.00 (*0-9610464-3-0*) J Lamagna.

Lamaison, Jean-Louis & Polese, Jean-Mari. Great Encyclopedia of Mushrooms. (Illus.). 240p. 1999. 19.95 (*3-8290-1728-6*, 521076) Konemann.

Lamal, P. A., ed. Behavioral Analysis of Societies & Cultural Practices. (Series in Health Psychology & Behavioral Medicine). 325p. 1991. 68.95 (*1-56032-123-7*) Hemisp Pub.

— Cultural Contingencies: Behavior Analytic Perspectives on Cultural Practices. LC 97-1919. 312p. 1997. 69.50 (*0-275-95776-4*, Praeger Pubs) Greenwood.

Lamalle, Cecile. Appetite for Murder. (Culinary Mystery Ser.). (Illus.). 290p. 1999. mass mkt. 6.50 (*0-446-60762-2*, Pub. by Warner Bks) Little.

Lamalle, Cecile. Glutton for Punishment: A Culinary Mystery. mass mkt. 6.50 (*0-446-60937-4*) Warner Bks.

Laman, Jennifer. When Health Care Is Not Enough: Support Services for Pregnant Women & Infants. (State Legislative Report Ser.: Vol. 19, No. 8). 9p. 1994. 15.00 (*1-55516-226-6*, 7302-1908) Natl Conf State Legis.

Lamancusa, Jim. Dynamite Crafts for Special Occasions. (J). (gr. 4-7). 1993. pap. 12.95 (*0-8306-4272-2*) McGraw-Hill Prof.

Lamancusa, Joe. Kid Cash: Creative Money-Making Ideas. 1993. pap. 9.95 (*0-07-036158-4*) McGraw.

— Kid Cash: Creative Money-Making Ideas. (J). (gr. 4-7). 1993. pap. 9.95 (*0-8306-4265-X*) McGraw-Hill Prof.

Lamancusa, Kathy. Bridal Creations. (Illus.). 28p. (Orig.). 1987. pap. 5.95 (*0-933491-18-2*) Hot off Pr.

— The Bride's Bouquet. (Illus.). 28p. (Orig.). 1986. pap. 5.95 (*0-933491-10-7*) Hot off Pr.

— Decorative Painting. 1991. 19.95 (*0-8306-1933-X*); pap. 10.95 (*0-8306-1931-3*) McGraw-Hill Prof.

— Floral Fundamentals, Vol. 1. (Illus.). 28p. (Orig.). 1985. pap. 5.95 (*0-933491-08-5*) Hot off Pr.

— Floral Fundamentals, Vol. 2. (Illus.). 28p. (Orig.). 1986. pap. 5.95 (*0-933491-09-3*) Hot off Pr.

— Floral Fundamentals, Vol. 3. (Illus.). 28p. (Orig.). 1987. pap. 5.95 (*0-933491-17-4*) Hot off Pr.

***Lamancusa, Kathy.** Flowers Are for Love. 2001. write for info. (*0-7432-0608-8*, Fireside) S&S Trade Pap.

Lamancusa, Kathy. Flowers Feed the Soul: A Glorious Bouquet of a Hundred Inspirational Stories. 256p. 2000. per. 12.00 (*0-684-85737-5*) S&S Trade.

— For Your Wedding Day. (Illus.). 28p. (Orig.). 1988. pap. text 5.95 (*0-685-22198-9*) Hot off Pr.

— Great Ideas for Gift Baskets, Bags, & Boxes. (Illus.). 144p. 1992. pap. 12.95 (*0-8306-4035-5*, 3899) McGraw-Hill Prof.

— Kathy Lamancusa's Guide to Floral Design. (Creative Home Design Ser.). (Illus.). 128p. 1990. pap. 12.95 (*0-8306-3491-6*) McGraw-Hill Prof.

— Kathy Lamancusa's Guide to Wearable Art. 1992. pap. text 10.95 (*0-07-157850-1*) McGraw.

— Kathy Lamancusa's Guide to Wreath Making. (Creative Home Design Ser.). (Illus.). 128p. 1991. pap. 10.95 (*0-8306-3492-4*) McGraw-Hill Prof.

— Treasures from the Earth: Creating with Flowers & Nature. LC 97-80619. (Illus.). 160p. 1998. pap. 22.95 (*0-87341-561-2*, TREA) Krause Pubns.

— Wearable Art. (Creative Home Design Ser.). 128p. 1992. 19.95 (*0-8306-4027-4*, 3900); pap. 10.95 (*0-8306-4026-6*, 3900) McGraw-Hill Prof.

Lamanna. Group Exercises Marriages & Families. 6th ed. (Sociology Ser.). 1996. 14.50 (*0-534-50552-X*) Wadsworth Pub.

— Marriages & Families. 4th ed. (Sociology - Intro Level Ser.). 1991. pap. 39.00 (*0-534-12723-1*) Wadsworth Pub.

— Marriages & Families. 7th ed. LC 99-33896. (Sociology - Intro Level). 1999. pap. 73.95 (*0-534-52507-5*) Wadsworth Pub.

— Transparencies: Marriages & Families. 4th ed. 1991. write for info. (*0-534-12724-X*) Wadsworth Pub.

Lamanna & Riedmann. Marriages & Families. 2nd ed. (Sociology - Introductory Level Ser.). 1985. pap. 7.25 (*0-534-04048-9*) Wadsworth Pub.

— Marriages & Families. 3rd ed. (Sociology - Introductory Level Ser.). 1988. pap., student ed. 10.00 (*0-534-08665-9*) Wadsworth Pub.

— Marriages & Families. 4th ed. (Sociology - Intro Level Ser.). 1991. pap., student ed. 12.00 (*0-534-12721-5*); mass mkt., teacher ed. write for info. (*0-534-12722-3*) Wadsworth Pub.

Lamanna & Riedmann, Agnes. Marriages & Families. 5th ed. (Sociology Ser.). 1993. mass mkt., student ed. 15.00 (*0-534-18740-4*) Wadsworth Pub.

***Lamanna, Dean.** The Doom Factory. 2001. write for info. (*0-380-80601-0*, HarpEntertain) Morrow Avon.

LaManna, Joseph C., jt. ed. see Nemoto, Edwin M.

Lamanna, Mary A. Marriages & Families. 6th ed. (Sociology Ser.). 1996. pap., student ed. 18.00 (*0-534-50555-4*) Wadsworth Pub.

— Marriages & Families. 7th ed. (Sociology - Intro Level). 1999. pap., student ed. 20.25 (*0-534-52508-3*) Wadsworth Pub.

— Portrait of a Family: Telecourse Guide. 4th ed. (Sociology Ser.). 1996. pap. 23.50 (*0-534-50562-7*) Wadsworth Pub.

Lamanna, Mary A. & Riedmann, Agnes. Marriages & Families. 6th ed. LC 96-18509. (Sociology - Intro Level). (C). 1996. pap. 49.00 (*0-534-50553-8*) Wadsworth Pub.

— Marriages & Families: Making Choices & Facing Change. 3rd ed. 656p. (C). 1988. pap. write for info. (*0-534-08664-0*) Wadsworth Pub.

— Marriages & Families: Making Choices & Facing Change. 4th ed. 711p. (C). 1991. pap. 48.95 (*0-534-12720-7*) Wadsworth Pub.

— Marriages & Families: Making Choices & Facing Change. 5th ed. 709p. (C). 1993. mass mkt. 42.00 (*0-534-18738-2*) Wadsworth Pub.

— Marriages & Families: Making Choices Throughout the Life Cycle. 2nd ed. 704p. (C). 1985. pap. write for info. (*0-534-04047-0*) Wadsworth Pub.

Lamanno, Angela. Imagine. LC 98-47303. (Illus.). (J). 2000. 6.95 (*0-87868-744-0*) Child Welfare.

Lamant, Hubert. Dictionnaire des Francs-Macons. (FRE.). 750p. 1995. 125.00 (*0-7859-9921-3*) Fr & Eur.

Lamantia, Philip. Bed of Sphinxes: Selected Poems. 200p. (Orig.). 1997. pap. 12.95 (*0-87286-320-4*) City Lights.

— Meadowlark West. 104p. (Orig.). 1986. pap. 6.95 (*0-87286-176-7*) City Lights.

— Touch of the Marvelous. 1966. pap. 1.95 (*0-685-04678-8*) Oyez.

LaMaout, E. I. General System of Botany: Descriptive & Analytical, 2 pts. 1066p. 1985. reprint ed. pap. 2250.00 (*81-7089-029-2*, Pub. by Intl Bk Distr) St Mut.

Lamar. Papers of Mirabeau Buonaparte, 6 vols., Set. 1993. reprint ed. lib. bdg. 450.00 (*0-7812-5941-X*) Rprt Serv.

Lamar, Angela M., jt. auth. see Goggins, Alfonza R.

Lamar, Celita. Our Voices, Ourselves: Women Writing for the French Theatre. LC 90-21539. (Currents in Romance Languages & Literature Ser.: Vol. 5). XIV, 213p. (C). 1991. text 37.00 (*0-8204-1499-9*) P Lang Pubng.

Lamar, Curt, ed. History of Rosedale, Mississippi, 1876-1976. LC 76-25443. 1976. 20.00 (*0-87152-246-2*) Reprint.

Lamar, Derek. Man Is Dead. 250p. 1999. pap. 14.95 (*1-893075-00-1*) Spirit Pr OR.

LaMar, Donna F. Transcending Turmoil: Survivors of Dysfunctional Families. Tilson, Bonnie, ed. 328p. (Orig.). Date not set. pap. 13.95 (*1-884570-39-9*) Research Triangle.

LaMar, Frank J. Buying into Condomania: Delight or Delusion. 90p. (Orig.). 1997. pap. 8.95 (*1-886383-29-4*, Keystone) Pride & Imprints.

***Lamar, Glenn J.** Jerome Bonaparte: The War Years, 1800-1815, 189. LC 99-46039. (Contributions in Military Studies Ser.). 136p. 2000. 55.00 (*0-313-30997-3*) Greenwood.

Lamar, H. Arthur. I Saw Stars: Memories of Adam Nimitz's Flag Lt. 1985. pap. 2.00 (*0-934841-03-9*) Adm Nimitz Foun.

Lamar, Howard. Dakota Territory, 1861-1889: A Study of Frontier Politics. LC 97-72631. (Illus.). 225p. 1997. reprint ed. 25.00 (*0-911042-47-4*) NDSU Inst Reg.

***Lamar, Howard R.** The Far Southwest, 1846-1912: A Territorial History. rev. ed. 2000. reprint ed. pap. 24.95 (*0-8263-2248-4*) U of NM Pr.

Lamar, Howard R. The Trader on the American Frontier: Myth's Victim. LC 76-51650. (Elma Dill Russell Spencer Series in the West & Southwest: No.2). (Illus.). 56p. 1977. 12.95 (*0-89096-033-X*) Tex A&M Univ Pr.

Lamar, Howard R., ed. The New Encyclopedia of the American West. LC 98-6231. (Illus.). 1324p. 1998. 60.00 (*0-300-07088-8*) Yale U Pr.

Lamar, Howard R., ed. see Perlot, Jean-Nicolas.

***Lamar, Howard Roberts.** The Far Southwest, 1846-1912: A Territorial History. rev. ed. LC 00-29883. 2000. write for info. (*0-8263-2288-3*) U of NM Pr.

Lamar, Jake. Close to the Bone: A Novel. LC 98-21773. 352p. 1999. 23.00 (*0-517-70407-2*) Crown Pubns.

***Lamar, Jake.** If 6 Was 9. 2001. write for info. (*0-609-60537-2*) Crown Pub Group.

Lamar, John. Cowboy Songs & Ballads. 1997. 19.99 (*0-517-18505-9*) Random Hse Value.

Lamar, Laura. Desktop Design. Gerould, Phil, ed. LC 89-81517. (Illus.). 96p. 1990. pap. 11.95 (*1-56052-001-9*) Crisp Pubns.

Lamar, Linda, ed. see Johns, Betty S. N.

***LaMar, Linda L.** Poems of Love & Faith. 54p. 1999. pap. 6.00 (*1-929302-00-2*, 001) FnQualPoets Pubg Servs.

— Poems of Love & Faith. deluxe rev. ed. 78p. 2000. pap. 12.95 (*1-929302-07-X*) FnQualPoets Pubg Servs.

LaMar, Linda L., ed. see Johns, Betty S. N.

Lamar, Mario. Escape from Castro. LC 98-54097. 237p. 1999. pap. 14.00 (*1-883911-20-6*) Brandylane.

***LaMar, Melinda.** Gentle Giant. ed. 2000. 4.50 (*1-928670-73-3*) Awe Struck E Bks.

Lamar, Mirabeau B. Papers, 6 vols. Gulick, Charles A. et al, eds. LC 76-171643. reprint ed. 560.00 (*0-404-03820-4*) AMS Pr.

Lamar, N. How to Speak the Written Word. 1987. 15.95 (*0-933062-25-7*) R H Sommer.

LaMar, Nat R., ed. see Read, Joan R.

Lamar, Rene, ed. see Butler, Samuel.

LaMar, Virginia A. Travel & Roads in England. LC 61-1916. (Folger Guides to the Age of Shakespeare Ser.). 1961. 4.95 (*0-918016-23-1*) Folger Bks.

Lamar, Virginia A., ed. see Shakespeare, William.

Lamar, William. The World's Most Spectacular Reptiles & Amphibians. Ohr, Tim & Williams, Winston, eds. (World's Most Ser.). (Illus.). 208p. 1996. 29.95 (*1-884942-07-5*); pap. 22.95 (*1-884942-06-7*) Wrld Tampa.

Lamar, William W., jt. auth. see Campbell, Jonathan A.

Lamarca, Geoerge. Iowa Pleading & Causes Action, Vol. ISS.4. 224p. 1997. ring bd. 50.00 (*0-86678-785-2*, 81054-14, MICHIE) LEXIS Pub.

LaMarca, George A. Iowa Pleading & Causes of Action, 1989-1993, 2 vols. 700p. 1993. suppl. ed. 60.00 (*0-250-40797-3*, MICHIE) LEXIS Pub.

— Iowa Pleading & Causes of Action, 1989-1993, 2 vols., Set. 700p. 1994. spiral bd. 160.00 (*0-86678-784-4*, 81050-10, MICHIE) LEXIS Pub.

Lamarca, Maureen, jt. auth. see Bowman, Daria P.

***Lamarche, Caroline.** Night in the Afternoon & Other Erotica. Curtis, Howard, tr. from FRE. 96p. 2000. pap. 12.00 (*0-8021-3709-1*, Pub. by Grove-Atltc) Publishers Group.

Lamarche, Caroline & De, Jephan. Leg Ours - The Bears: Gardiens du People D'Arbonie - Guardiens of the People of Arbonia. (FRE.). 64p. 1976. 40.00 (*0-9672487-0-1*) R Koener Art Gall.

Lamarche, Gara, ed. Speech & Equality: Do We Really Have to Choose? 150p. (C). 1996. text 45.00 (*0-8147-5091-5*); pap. text 18.50 (*0-8147-5105-9*) NYU Pr.

***LaMarche, Jacq.** From Petoskey to Prague. 182p. 2000. 11.95 (*0-9701342-0-7*) Point Net.

Lamarche, Jim. The Raft. LC 99-35546. (Illus.). 40p. (YA). (gr. 1-4). 2000. 15.95 (*0-688-13977-9*) Morrow Avon.

— The Raft. LC 99-35546. (Illus.). 40p. (YA). (ps-3). 2000. 15.89 (*0-688-13978-7*) Morrow Avon.

LaMarche, Robert J., jt. auth. see Connors, Jimmy.

Lamarck, Jean Baptiste. Memoirs sur les Fossiles des Environs de Paris No. 15: Special Publication. 380p. 1978. 15.00 (*0-87710-374-7*) Paleo Res.

— Philosophie Zoologique, 2 vols. in 1. 1960. reprint ed. 75.00 (*3-7682-0028-0*) Lubrecht & Cramer.

— Zoological Philosophy: An Exposition with Regard to the Natural History of Animals. Elliot, Hugh, tr. 500p. 1993. pap. 16.95 (*0-226-46810-0*) U Ch Pr.

— Zoological Philosophy: An Exposition with Regard to the Natural History of Animals. Elliot, Hugh, tr. LC 82-45842. reprint ed. 57.50 (*0-404-19353-6*) AMS Pr.

Lamare. Texas Politics. 7th ed. (Political Science Ser.). 2000. 31.75 (*0-534-56997-8*) Wadsworth Pub.

Lamare, James W. California Politics: Economics,power & Policy. Perlee, Clyde, ed. LC 93-25933. (Political Science). 250p. (C). 1993. 33.75 (*0-314-02677-0*) West Pub.

— Tax Politics: Testbank. 5th ed. Date not set. pap. text, teacher ed., suppl. ed. write for info. (*0-314-03265-7*) West Pub.

— Texas Politics: Economics, Power, & Policy. 5th ed. Perlee, Clyde, ed. LC 94-4546. 250p. (C). 1994. pap. 37.00 (*0-314-02849-8*) West Pub.

— Texas Politics:economics,power& Policy. 6th ed. LC 97-23747. (Political Science). (C). 1997. pap. 51.95 (*0-314-20481-4*) Wadsworth Pub.

— What Rules America? 203p. (C). 1988. pap. text 30.00 (*0-314-64228-5*) West Pub.

Lamare, James W., ed. International Crisis & Domestic Politics: Major Political Conflicts in the 1980s. LC 90-7803. 200p. 1991. 52.95 (*0-275-93304-0*, C3304, Praeger Pubs) Greenwood.

Lamarque, Ariel, tr. see Kuntz, Darcy, ed.

Lamarque, C. H., jt. ed. see Jezequel, L.

Lamarque, L. Niger: Profile of Agricultural Potential. 1993. pap. 25.00 (*0-85954-361-7*, Pub. by Nat Res Inst) St Mut.

Lamarque, Martin, ed. see Werner, David B.

Lamarque, Martin, tr. see Wipfler, Patricia.

Lamarque, Martin, tr. see Wipfler, Patty.

Lamarque, P., ed. Concise Encyclopedia of Philosophy Language. LC 97-28781. 480p. 1997. text 157.00 (*0-08-042991-2*, Pergamon Pr) Elsevier.

Lamarque, Peter. Fictional Points of View. 240p. 1996. text 37.50 (*0-8014-3216-2*) Cornell U Pr.

Lamarque, Peter & Olsen, Stein H. Truth, Fiction, & Literature: A Philosophical Perspective. (Clarendon Library of Logic & Philosophy). 494p. 1997. reprint ed. pap. text 29.95 (*0-19-823681-6*) OUP.

Lamarr, Tom. October Revolution. LC 98-26116. 168p. 1998. 19.95 (*0-87081-501-6*) Univ Pr Colo.

LaMarre, ed. see Barrow, Georgia M. & Shuttlesworth, Guy.

LaMarre, ed. see Fogel, Alan.

LaMarre, ed. see Hatch, Kathryn L.

LaMarre, ed. see Heffernan, Joseph, et al.

Lamarre, Helene M. Career Focus: A Personal Job Search Guide. 2nd ed. LC 97-36708. 156p. 1997. pap. text 28.20 (*0-13-748989-7*) P-H.

Lamarre, Paul. E.I.D.I.A. Catalogue Everything I Do Is Art: My Life Is Not My Own. (Illus.). 40p. (C). 1989. pap. 12.00 (*0-9619021-2-4*) Eidia Bks.

Lamarre, Paul & Wolf, Melissa. The Starving Artists' Cookbook: Food, Sex, Art. (Illus.). 162p. (Orig.). (C). 1991. pap. 60.00 (*0-9619021-1-6*, TXU 290827) Eidia Bks.

***LaMarre, Thomas.** Project Insider. LC 00-190792. 311p. 2000. 25.00 (*0-7388-1862-3*); pap. 18.00 (*0-7388-1863-1*) Xlibris Corp.

— Uncovering Heian Japan: An Archaeology of Sensation & Inscription. LC 99-49889. (Asia-Pacific Ser.). 232p. 2000. pap. 17.95 (*0-8223-2518-7*) Duke.

LaMarsh, Jeannenne. Changing the Way We Change: Gaining Control of Major Operational Change. (Engineering Process Improvement Ser.). 240p. (C). 1995. 36.00 (*0-201-63364-7*) Addison-Wesley.

Lamarsh, John R. Introduction to Nuclear Engineering. 3rd ed. 736p. (C). 1999. text 96.00 (*0-201-82498-1*, Prentice Hall) P-H.

— Introduction to Nuclear Reactor Theory. 1966. 34.00 (*0-201-04120-0*) Addison-Wesley.

Lamartine, Alphonse. Oeuvres Poetiques Completes, deluxe ed. Guyard, Jean, ed. (Pleiade Ser.). (FRE.). 1963. 93.95 (*2-07-010298-X*) Schoenhof.

Lamartine, Alphonse D. Le Livre du Centenaire. (FRE.). 380p. 1971. pap. 49.95 (*0-686-54277-0*, 2082103161) Fr & Eur.

— Le Manuscrit de Ma Mere. 200p. 65.00 (*0-686-54278-9*) Fr & Eur.

— Sur la Politique Rationnelle. 164p. 1978. reprint ed. 49.95 (*0-7859-5361-2*) Fr & Eur.

Lamartine, Alphonse M. Histoire des Girondins, 8 vols. 3rd ed. LC 70-171644. reprint ed. 280.00 (*0-404-07330-1*) AMS Pr.

— History of the French Revolution of 1848, 2 vols. in 1. LC 73-171645. reprint ed. 62.50 (*0-404-07138-4*) AMS Pr.

Lamartine, Alphorse De, see De Lamartine, Alphorse.

Lamartine, M. Alphonse De, see De Lamartine, M. Alphonse, tr.

Lamartine Yates, Paul, et al. Mexico's Agricultural Dilemma. LC 81-10279. 307p. 1981. reprint ed. pap. 95.20 (*0-7837-9237-9*, 204998800004) Bks Demand.

Lamas, Blanca Rosa, tr. see Romanelli, Serena.

Lamas, Blanca Rosas, tr. see Romanelli, Serena.

Lamas, G., et al. Bibliography of Butterflies, Vol. 124. (Atlas of Neotropical Lepidoptera Ser.). 1995. pap. 62.95 (*0-945417-31-4*) Sci Pubs.

LaMay, Craig, jt. auth. see Minow, Newton.

***LaMay, Craig L., et al.** Television Autonomy & the State. LC 99-201932. (Communications & Society Ser.). xii, 146p. 1999. pap. 12.00 (*0-89843-255-3*) The Aspen Inst.

LaMay, Craig L., jt. ed. see Dennis, Everette E.

LaMay, Graig, et al, eds. Publishing Books. LC 96-30691. 190p. (Orig.). 1997. pap. text 19.95 (*1-56000-905-5*) Transaction Pubs.

LaMay, Michael Robert & Barkan, Elliott Robert, eds. Issues of Immigration & Naturalization in America: A Documentary History. LC 98-55343. (Primary Documents in American History & Contemporary Issues Ser.). 384p. 1999. 49.95 (*0-313-30156-5*, Greenwood Pr) Greenwood.

Lamay, Paul G., ed. Language Maintenance & Language Shift in Canada: New Dimensions in the Use of Census Language Data. LC 78-319608. (Research Monographs in the Social Sciences: Vol. 3). 113p. 1977. reprint ed. pap. 35.10 (*0-608-02184-9*, 20628530003) Bks Demand.

Lamazares, Ivonne. The Sugar Island: A Novel. 224p. 2000. 23.00 (*0-395-86040-7*) HM.

Lamaze, Fernand. Journal Perinatal Education, 1993, No. 2. 72p. (C). 1993. pap. text. write for info. (*0-318-72517-7*) Jones & Bartlett.

— Journal Perinatal Education 1993, No. 3. (C). 1993. pap. text. write for info. (*0-318-72518-5*) Jones & Bartlett.

— Journal Perinatal Education 1993, No. 4. (C). 1993. pap. text. write for info. (*0-318-72519-3*) Jones & Bartlett.

Lamb. Biogeography. pap. text. write for info. (*0-471-49094-6*) Wiley.

— Early Modern Englishwoman, Pt. 2. 2000. 42.95 (*1-84014-215-4*) Ashgate Pub Co.

Lamb. Exploration & Exchange. 1998. pap. text 18.00 (*0-226-46846-1*); lib. bdg. 49.00 (*0-226-46845-3*) U Ch Pr.

Lamb. Multiple Discovery. 1985. pap. 39.95 (*0-86127-025-8*) Ashgate Pub Co.

Lamb. Physical Science, 1989: Records of the District of West Augusta & Ohio & Yohogania Counties, Virginia 1775-1780. 542p. 1989. reprint ed. pap. 53.75 (*0-614-09954-4*, 1260) H Holt & Co.

— Physical Science, 1994. 1994. text, teacher ed. 105.75 (*0-03-097539-5*) H Holt & Co.

***Lamb & Briney, D.** Between Husband & Wife. 2000. 17.95 (*1-57734-609-2*) Covenant Comms.

Lamb & Hair. Essentials of Marketing. LC 98-23040. (SS - Marketing Management Ser.). (C). 1998. pap. 52.95 (*0-538-87926-2*) S-W Pub.

— Grademaker. 4th ed. (Miscellaneous/Catalogs Ser.). (C). 1997. mass mkt., student ed. 19.95 (*0-538-87012-5*) S-W Pub.

***Lamb & Hair.** Grademaker. 5th ed. (Swc-Marketing Ser.). 1999. pap., student ed. 21.00 (*0-324-01440-6*) Thomson Learn.

Lamb & Kenaga, E. E., eds. Avian & Mammalian Wildlife Toxicology: Second Conference - STP 757. 170p. 1981. pap. 18.50 (*0-8031-0759-5*, STP757) ASTM.

***Lamb, et al.** Web Tutor on Webct to Accompany Marketing. 5th ed. 1999. pap. 19.00 (*0-534-76554-8*) Wadsworth Pub.

Lamb, jt. auth. see Hair.

Lamb, A. F. Pinus Caribaea, Vol. 1. 1978. 50.00 (*0-85074-015-0*) St Mut.

Lamb, Albert, ed. see Neill, Alexander S.

Lamb, Albert R., Jr. The Second General Hospital Vol. 1: An Account of the Army Affiliated Unit of the Presbyterian Hospital of New York City in the European Theater of Operations, World War II, 1942-1945. (Illus.). xiii, 193p. 1996. lib. bdg. write for info. (*0-9654040-0-5*) Col U Ofc Univ Publns.

Lamb, Allan R. Framing Photography, Vol. 6. (Library of Professional Picture Framing: Vol. 6). (Illus.). 96p. 1997. pap. 19.00 (*0-938655-05-1*, B051) Columba Pub.

Lamb, Andrew. Jerome Kern in Edwardian London. LC 85-80274. (I.S.A.M. Monographs: No. 22). (Illus.). 96p. 1985. pap. 10.00 (*0-914678-24-8*) Inst Am Music.

***Lamb, Andrew.** 150 Years of Popular Musical Theatre. LC 00-25281. 2000. write for info. (*0-300-07538-3*) Yale U Pr.

Lamb, Andrew. U-Musik und Osterreich: Max Schonherr in Seinen Schriften und Erinnerungen - Light Music from Austria: Writings & Reminiscences of Max Schonherr. LC 91-29172. (Austrian Culture Ser.: Vol. 6). (ENG & GER.). XVII, 262p. (C). 1993. text 62.95 (*0-8204-1671-1*) P Lang Pubng.

Lamb, Annette. Building Treehouses for Learning: Technology in Today's Classrooms. 2nd ed. (Illus.). 615p. (J). (gr. k-12). 1999. pap. 34.95 (*1-891917-00-5*) Vision to Action.

— Emerging Technologies & Instruction: Hypertext, Hypermedia, & Interactive Multimedia. Milheim, William D., ed. LC 91-4704. (Educational Technology Selected Bibliography Ser.: Vol. 4). 64p. 1991. pap. 24.95 (*0-87778-234-2*) Educ Tech Pubns.

— HyperCard (Mac) Creativity Tool: Student Version for Writing, Organizing & Multimedia. Saari, Joani, ed. 700p. 1992. pap., teacher ed. 60.00 (*0-89262-328-4*) Career Pub.

— IBM LinkWay Authoring Tool for Presentations, Tutorials, & Information Exploration. Saari, Joani, ed. 800p. 1993. pap. text 39.95 (*0-89262-353-5*) Career Pub.

— MacPac for Teachers: Hands-On Macintosh Applications. (Illus.). 148p. (C). 1997. pap. text 19.95 (*0-9641581-4-0*) Vision to Action.

— The Magic Carpet Ride: Integrating Technology into the K-12 Classroom. (Illus.). 211p. (C). 1997. pap. text 23.95 (*0-9641581-5-9*) Vision to Action.

— The Magic Carpet Ride: Integrating Technology into the K-12 Classroom. 2nd ed. 211p. (C). 1998. pap. 28.95 (*0-9641581-8-3*) Vision to Action.

— Spinnin' the Web: Designing & Developing Web Projects. 308p. (C). 1998. pap. 26.95 (*0-9641581-9-1*) Vision to Action.

Lamb, Annette & Johnson, Larry. Cruisin' the Information Highway: Internet in the K-12 Classroom. 2nd ed. (Illus.). 234p. (Orig.). (C). 1997. pap. text 23.95 (*0-9641581-6-7*) Vision to Action.

— Strap on Your Spurs: Technology & Change Cowboy Style. (Illus.). 173p. (C). 1994. pap. text 23.95 (*0-9641581-0-8*) Vision to Action.

Lamb, Annette & Smith, William L. Virtual Sandcastles: Teaching & Learning at a Distance. (Illus.). 224p. 1999. pap. 23.95 (*1-891917-01-3*) Vision to Action.

Lamb, Annette, et al. Surfin' the Internet: Practical Ideas from A to Z. 2nd ed. (Illus.). 331p. (Orig.). (C). 1998. pap. text 26.95 (*0-9641581-7-5*) Vision to Action.

Lamb, Annette, jt. auth. see Myers, Dennis.

Lamb, Anthony, jt. auth. see Phillipps, Anthea.

Lamb, Arnette. Beguiled. 320p. 1996. per. 6.50 (*0-671-88219-8*, PB Trade Paper) PB.

— Betrayed. 1995. mass mkt. 6.50 (*0-671-88218-X*, PB Trade Paper) PB.

— Betrayed. large type ed. LC 96-24029. 1996. 22.95 (*0-7862-0819-8*, G K Hall Lrg Type) Mac Lib Ref.

— Betrothal. Tolley, Carolyn, ed. 384p. 1992. mass mkt. 6.50 (*0-671-73002-9*, Pocket Star Bks) PB.

— The Betrothal. large type ed. LC 92-27928. 521p. (Orig.). 1992. reprint ed. lib. bdg. 17.95 (*1-56054-546-1*) Thorndike Pr.

— Border Bride. Tolley, Carolyn, ed. 320p. 1993. mass mkt. 6.50 (*0-671-77933-8*) PB.

— Border Lord. Tolley, Carolyn, ed. 336p. 1993. per. 6.50 (*0-671-77932-X*) PB.

— Chieftain. 1994. mass mkt. 6.50 (*0-671-77937-0*) PB.

— Chieftain. large type ed. LC 95-2474. 402p. 1995. pap. 19.95 (*0-7838-1279-5*, G K Hall Lrg Type) Mac Lib Ref.

— Maiden of Inverness. Tolley, Carolyn, ed. 339p. (Orig.). 1995. mass mkt. write for info. (*0-671-88220-1*) PB.

— Secreto Conyugal. 1998. pap. 6.95 (*84-01-50800-2*) Lectorum Pubns.

— Threads of Destiny. 1998. per. 6.50 (*0-671-01422-6*, Pocket Books) PB.

— True Heart. 1997. per. 5.99 (*0-671-88217-1*) PB.

Lamb, Art. Sanderson's Lunch. 288p. 1998. pap. 14.95 (*1-890622-30-3*) Leathers Pub.

Lamb, Artemus. The Odyssey of the Soul. 96p. (Orig.). 1995. pap. 11.95 (*0-85398-401-8*) G Ronald Pub.

Lamb, Arthur W. Take Back Your Life: How to Regain Your Personal Freedom. 168p. 1992. pap. 12.95 (*0-9631757-6-9*) Pin Oak Pr.

Lamb, B., jt. auth. see Court, S.

Lamb, B. C. Applied Genetics. 300p. 1999. 44.00 (*1-86094-179-6*) World Scientific Pub.

Lamb, Beth & Logsdon, Phyllis. Positively Kindergarten: A Classroom-Proven, Theme-Based, Developmental Guide for the Kindergarten Teacher. 141p. (Orig.). 1991. pap. 14.95 (*0-935493-48-4*) Modern Learn Pr.

Lamb, Bonnie, ed. see Lamb, George.

Lamb, Brian. Booknotes. (Illus.). 440p. 1998. pap. 15.00 (*0-8129-3029-0*, Times Bks) Crown Pub Group.

— Booknotes: America's Finest Authors on Reading, Writing, & the Power of Ideas. LC 98-142445. (Illus.). 423p. 1997. 25.00 (*0-8129-2847-4*, Times Bks) Crown Pub Group.

— Booknotes: America's Finest Authors on Reading, Writing & the Power of Ideas. 1997. 25.00 (*0-614-27818-X*, Times Bks) Crown Pub Group.

***Lamb, Brian.** Life Stories. (Illus.). 496p. 2000. pap. 16.95 (*0-8129-3339-7*, Times Bks) Crown Pub Group.

— Who's Buried in Grant's Tomb? A Tour of Presidential Gravesites. (Illus.). 2000. 24.95 (*1-881846-08-3*) C-Span.

Lamb, Brian, ed. Booknotes: Life Stories: Notable Biographers on the People Who Shaped America. LC 98-41374. (Illus.). 400p. 1999. 27.50 (*0-8129-3081-9*, Times Bks) Crown Pub Group.

Lamb, Brian, jt. auth. see C-Span Staff.

***Lamb, C.** Deep & Silent Waters. 1998. text 35.00 (*0-340-71282-1*, Pub. by Hodder & Stought Ltd) Trafalgar.

— Walking In Darkness. mass mkt. 13.95 (*0-340-72866-3*, Pub. by Hodder & Stought Ltd) Trafalgar.

Lamb, Caroline P. Glenarvon. LC 93-17429. 264p. 1993. reprint ed. 80.00 (*1-85477-132-9*) Continuum.

— Glenarvon, 3 vols. in 1. LC 71-161933. 272p. 1972. reprint ed. 50.00 (*0-8201-1093-0*) Schol Facsimiles.

— Glenarvon, 3 vols., Set. 3rd ed. LC 70-37709. reprint ed. 97.50 (*0-404-56767-3*) AMS Pr.

Lamb, Catherine. Milady's Life Management Skills for Cosmetology, Barber-Styling & Nail Technology. LC 95-21218. (Career Development Ser.). (Illus.). 136p. 1996. 10.95 (*1-56253-252-9*) Thomson Learn.

Lamb, Charles. Charles Lamb: Prose & Poetry. LC 77-28850. 216p. 1978. reprint ed. lib. bdg. 35.00 (*0-313-20274-5*, LAPP0, Greenwood Pr) Greenwood.

— Elia, 1823. LC 91-31468. (Revolution & Romanticism Ser.). 358p. 1991. reprint ed. 55.00 (*1-85477-074-8*) Continuum.

— Howard Barker's Theatre of Seduction. (Contemporary Theatre Studies). 160p. 1997. text 59.00 (*3-7186-5874-7*, Harwood Acad Pubs); pap. text 20.00 (*3-7186-5884-4*, Harwood Acad Pubs) Gordon & Breach.

— Lamb & Hazlitt. LC 76-168954. reprint ed. 30.00 (*0-404-07359-X*) AMS Pr.

— Lamb's Criticism: A Selection from the Literary Criticism of Charles Lamb. (BCL1-PR English Literature Ser.). 1992. reprint ed. lib. bdg. 69.00 (*0-7812-7015-4*) Rprt Serv.

— Life, Letters & Writings of Charles Lamb, 6 vols, Set. Fitzgerald, Percy H., ed. LC 77-148887. (Select Bibliographies Reprint Ser.). 1977. reprint ed. 192.95 (*0-8369-5654-0*) Ayer.

***Lamb, Charles.** More Meanderings from Doc's Diary. Wightman, Christina Case, ed. 125p. 2000. pap. write for info. (*1-888911-18-2*) Benson Smythe.

Lamb, Charles. Roast Pig & Other Essays. large type ed. (YA). (gr. 10 up). reprint ed. 10.00 (*0-318-65692-2*) NAVH.

— Rosamund Gray, 1789. LC 91-16915. (Revolution & Romanticism Ser.). 146p. 1991. reprint ed. 48.00 (*1-85477-075-6*) Continuum.

Lamb, Charles. Tales from Shakespeare. 1986. 11.05 (*0-606-03275-4*, Pub. by Turtleback) Demco.

Lamb, Charles. The Works of Charles & Mary Lamb, 7 vols., Set. (BCL1-PR English Literature Ser.). 1992. reprint ed. lib. bdg. 630.00 (*0-7812-7584-9*) Rprt Serv.

Lamb, Charles & Lamb, Mary. Illustrated Tales from Shakespeare. (Illus.). 207p. 10.99 (*1-57215-217-6*, JG2176) World Pubns.

— Lamb's Poetry for Children. LC 78-108585. (Granger Index Reprint Ser.). 1977. 19.95 (*0-8369-6113-7*) Ayer.

— The Letters of Charles & Mary Anne Lamb, 3 vols. Lucas, E. V., ed. LC 68-59268. reprint ed. write for info. (*0-404-03840-9*) AMS Pr.

— Tales from Shakespeare. LC 79-89991. (Illus.). 1988. 40.00 (*0-918016-04-5*) Folger Bks.

— Tales from Shakespeare. 336p. 1986. mass mkt. 5.95 (*0-451-52391-1*, Sig Classics) NAL.

— Tales from Shakespeare. (Puffin Classics Ser.). (Illus.). 346p. (YA). (gr. 5 up). 1995. pap. 4.99 (*0-14-036677-6*, PuffinBks) Peng Put Young Read.

— Tales from Shakespeare. (J). (gr. k-6). 1986. 8.98 (*0-685-16860-3*, 621568) Random Hse Value.

— Tales from Shakespeare. (Illus.). 318p. 1995. 6.95 (*0-460-87638-4*, Everyman's Classic Lib) Tuttle Pubng.

— Tales from Shakespeare. 1993. reprint ed. lib. bdg. 24.95 (*1-56849-117-4*) Buccaneer Bks.

Lamb, Charles & Lamb, Mary. Tales from Shakespeare, Set. unabridged ed. (YA). 1990. 41.95 incl. audio (*1-55685-581-8*) Audio Bk Con.

Lamb, Charles & Lamb, Mary. The Works of Charles & Mary Lamb, Set. Lucas, E. V., ed. LC 68-59332. (Illus.). reprint ed. write for info. (*0-404-03830-1*) AMS Pr.

— The Works of Charles & Mary Lamb, 7 vols., Set. Lucas, E. V., ed. LC 70-115252. 1970. reprint ed. 450.00 (*0-403-00366-0*) Scholarly.

Lamb, Charles & Lamb, Mary A. The Letters of Charles & Mary Anne Lamb, Vol. I: 1796-1801. Marrs, Edwin W., Jr., ed. (Illus.). 352p. 1975. text 59.95 (*0-8014-0930-6*) Cornell U Pr.

— The Letters of Charles & Mary Anne Lamb, Vol. III: 1809-1817. Marrs, Edwin W., Jr., ed. (Illus.). 320p. 1978. text 59.95 (*0-8014-1129-7*) Cornell U Pr.

Lamb, Charles, et al. The Letters of Charles & Mary Anne Lamb, Vol. II: 1801-1809. (Illus.). 336p. 1976. text 59.95 (*0-8014-0977-2*) Cornell U Pr.

Lamb, Charles E., jt. auth. see Owen, Lisa B.

Lamb, Charles F. Doc's Diary: Encounters Humorous & Inspirational. Wightman, Heather & Wightman, Christina, eds. LC 96-69732. 122p. 1996. 12.00 (*1-888911-00-X*) Benson Smythe.

Lamb, Charles M. & Halpern, Stephen C., eds. The Burger Court: Political & Judicial Profiles. (Illus.). 528p. 1991. text 49.95 (*0-252-01733-1*); pap. text 19.95 (*0-252-06135-7*) U of Ill Pr.

Lamb, Charles M., jt. ed. see Goldman, Sheldon.

Lamb, Charles R., jt. auth. see Coleman, Patrick K.

Lamb, Charles W. Marketing Plan Project - Marketing. 3rd ed. (SB - Marketing Education Ser.). 1995. mass mkt. 15.95 (*0-538-84951-7*) S-W Pub.

Lamb, Charles W., Jr., et al. Marketing. 3rd ed. LC 95-2874. 1995. pap. 75.95 (*0-538-84948-7*) S-W Pub.

Lamb, Charles W., jt. auth. see Hair.

Lamb, Charles W., jt. auth. see Matulich.

Lamb, Charlotte. Angry Desire. 1996. per. 3.50 (*0-373-11846-5*, 1-11846-2) Harlequin Bks.

— Angry Desire. large type ed. (Harlequin Romance Ser.). 1996. 19.95 (*0-263-14576-X*) Thorndike Pr.

— Besieged. (Presents Ser.). 1992. pap. 2.89 (*0-373-11498-2*, 1-11498-2) Harlequin Bks.

— Body & Soul. large type ed. 1994. 19.95 (*0-263-13907-7*) Thorndike Pr.

— Le Coeur Aventurier. (Azur Ser.: No. 776). (FRE.). 1999. mass mkt. 3.99 (*0-373-34776-6*, 1-34776-4) Harlequin Bks.

— Dark Fate. large type ed. (Harlequin Romance Ser.). 1995. lib. bdg. 18.95 (*0-263-14075-X*) Mac Lib Ref.

— Dark Fate: Wedlocked. 1995. per. 3.25 (*0-373-11763-9*) Harlequin Bks.

— Dark Fever. (Presents Ser.). 1996. per. 3.50 (*0-373-11840-6*, 1-11840-5) Harlequin Bks.

— Dark Fever. large type ed. (Harlequin Romance Ser.). 1996. 19.95 (*0-263-14510-7*) Thorndike Pr.

— Dark Music. (Presents Ser.: No. 1410). 1991. per. 2.79 (*0-373-11410-9*) Harlequin Bks.

— Dark Pursuit. (Presents Ser.: No. 1370). 1991. per. 2.75 (*0-373-11370-6*) Harlequin Bks.

— Deadly Rivals. (Harlequin Presents Ser.: No. 1822). 1996. per. 3.50 (*0-373-11822-8*, 1-11822-3) Harlequin Bks.

— Dreaming. (Presents Ser.). 1994. per. 2.99 (*0-373-11618-7*, 1-11618-5) Harlequin Bks.

— Dying for You. LC 95-6892. (Presents Ser.). 188p. 1995. per. 3.25 (*0-373-11743-4*, 1-11743-1) Harlequin Bks.

— En El Lado Oscuro Del Deseo - Dark Fever. (Bianca Ser.). (SPA.). 1997. per. 3.50 (*0-373-33391-9*, 1-33391-3) Harlequin Bks.

— Enemigos Mortales - Deadly Rivals. (SPA.). 1996. per. 3.50 (*0-373-33379-X*, 1-33379-8) Harlequin Bks.

— An Excellent Wife? (Presents Ser.). 1998. per. 3.75 (*0-373-11949-6*, 1-11949-4) Harlequin Bks.

— Falling in Love: (Presents Plus) (Presents Ser.). 1994. per. 2.99 (*0-373-11672-1*, 1-11672-2) Harlequin Bks.

***Lamb, Charlotte.** Fiance Malgre Lui. (Azur Ser.: No. 806). (FRE.). 2000. mass mkt. 3.99 (*0-373-34806-1*, 1-34806-9, Harlequin French) Harlequin Bks.

Lamb, Charlotte. Fire in the Blood. 1994. per. 2.99 (*0-373-11658-6*, 1-11658-1) Harlequin Bks.

— Fire in the Blood. large type ed. (Harlequin Ser.). 1994. lib. bdg. 19.95 (*0-263-13659-0*) Thorndike Pr.

— Forbidden Fruit. large type ed. 1992. reprint ed. 18.95 (*0-263-13037-1*) Mac Lib Ref.

— Forbidden Fruit: Presents Plus. (Presents Ser.). 1993. per. 2.99 (*0-373-11584-9*, 1-11584-9) Harlequin Bks.

— Guerra Matrimonial. (Bianca Ser.: Vol. 123).Tr. of Marriage War. 1998. per. 3.50 (*0-373-33473-7*, 1-33473-9) Harlequin Bks.

— Guilty Love. (Presents Ser.). 1994. per. 2.99 (*0-373-11706-X*, 1-11706-8) Harlequin Bks.

— Guilty Love. large type ed. (Harlequin Romance Ser.). 1994. lib. bdg. 19.95 (*0-263-13874-7*) Thorndike Pr.

— Hambre Salvaje: Wild Hunger. (Bianca Ser.). (SPA.). 1996. per. 3.50 (*0-373-33387-0*, 1-33387-1) Harlequin Bks.

— Haunted Dreams. (Presents Ser.). 1996. per. 3.50 (*0-373-11828-7*, 1-11828-0) Harlequin Bks.

— Heart on Fire. (Presents Ser.: No. 467). 1992. per. 2.89 (*0-373-11467-2*, 1-11467-7) Harlequin Bks.

— Hot Blood. 1996. per. 3.50 (*0-373-11852-X*, 1-11852-0) Harlequin Bks.

— Hot Surrender. 1999. per. 3.75 (*0-373-12046-X*, 1-12046-8) Harlequin Bks.

— Hot Surrender. large type ed. (Harlequin Ser.). 1999. 21.95 (*0-263-16103-X*, Pub. by Mills & Boon) Ulverscroft.

— In Still of the Night, Vol. 1. 1997. mass mkt. 5.99 (*0-312-96280-0*) St Martin.

— Lovestruck. (Presents Ser.: No. 1935). 1998. per. 3.75 (*0-373-11935-6*, 1-11935-3) Harlequin Bks.

— Lovestruck. large type ed. (Harlequin Romance Ser.). 288p. 1998. 20.95 (*0-263-15491-2*) Thorndike Pr.

— Un Macho au Coeur Tendre. (Azur Ser.: No. 782). (FRE.). 1999. mass mkt. 3.99 (*0-373-34782-0*, 1-34782-2) Harlequin Bks.

— The Marriage War. 1997. per. 3.50 (*0-373-11913-5*, 1-11913-0) Harlequin Bks.

— Marriage War. large type ed. (Harlequin Romance Ser.). 288p. 1997. 20.95 (*0-263-15289-8*) Thorndike Pr.

— Miedo a Quererte: Angry Desire. (SPA.). 1997. per. 3.50 (*0-373-33395-1*, 1-33395-4) Harlequin Bks.

— Obsesion Secreta: Secret Obsession. (Bianca Ser.). (SPA.). 1996. per. 3.50 (*0-373-33375-7*, 1-33375-6) Harlequin Bks.

— Passion Conjugale. (Azur Ser.: No. 722). (FRE.). 1998. mass mkt. 3.50 (*0-373-34722-7*, 1.-34722-8) Harlequin Bks.

— Perseguido por un Sueno. (Bianca Ser.: No. 383). (SPA.). 1996. per. 3.50 (*0-373-33383-8*, 1-33383-0) Harlequin Bks.

***Lamb, Charlotte.** Rendicion Ardiente. (Bianca Ser.: No. 182).Tr. of Hot Surrender. (SPA.). 1999. per. 3.50 (*0-373-33532-6*, 1-33532-2) Harlequin Bks.

Lamb, Charlotte. Rites of Possession. (Presents Ser.: No. 1345). 1991. per. 2.75 (*0-373-11345-5*) Harlequin Bks.

— Rites of Possession. large type ed. 1990. reprint ed. lib. bdg. 18.95 (*0-263-12270-0*) Mac Lib Ref.

— Runaway Wife. large type ed. 1990. reprint ed. lib. bdg. 18.95 (*0-263-12078-3*) Mac Lib Ref.

— Sangre Caliente. (Bianca Ser.: No. 33399).Tr. of Hot Blood. (SPA.). 1997. per. 3.50 (*0-373-33399-4*, 1-33399-6) Harlequin Bks.

— Secret Obsession. (Top Author/Sins Ser.). 1996. per. 3.50 (*0-373-11816-3*, 1-11816-5) Harlequin Bks.

— Secret Obsession. large type ed. (Harlequin Romance Ser.). 1995. 20.95 (*0-263-14262-0*) Mac Lib Ref.

***Lamb, Charlotte.** Seduction Business. (Presents Ser.: Vol. 208). 2000. mass mkt. 3.99 (*0-373-12085-0*) Harlequin Bks.

— Seduction Business. large type ed. (Harlequin Romance Ser.). 2000. 22.95 (*0-263-16309-1*) Mills & Boon.

Lamb, Charlotte. Shotgun Wedding. (Presents Ser.: No. 480). 1992. per. 2.89 (*0-373-11480-X*) Harlequin Bks.

— Shotgun Wedding. large type ed. 285p. 1991. reprint ed. 18.95 (*0-263-12805-9*) Thorndike Pr.

— Sleeping Partners. (Presents Ser.). 1993. per. 2.99 (*0-373-11560-1*, 1-11560-9) Harlequin Bks.

— Sleeping Partners. large type ed. 285p. 1992. reprint ed. 18.95 (*0-263-12838-5*) Thorndike Pr.

— Spellbinding. (Presents Ser.: No. 1393). 1991. per. 2.79 (*0-373-11393-5*) Harlequin Bks.

— Spellbinding. large type ed. 1990. lib. bdg. 18.95 (*0-263-12418-5*) Mac Lib Ref.

— Surrender. (Presents Ser.). 1993. pap. 2.89 (*0-373-11540-7*, 1-11540-1) Harlequin Bks.

— A Sweet Addiction. (Presents Ser.). 1993. per. 2.89 (*0-373-11530-X*, 1-11530-2) Harlequin Bks.

— Un Tendre Secret. (FRE.). 1994. pap. 3.50 (*0-373-34438-4*, 1-34438-1) Harlequin Bks.

— The Threat of Love. (Presents Ser.: No. 435). 1992. per. 2.79 (*0-373-11435-4*, 1-11435-4) Harlequin Bks.

— The Threat of Love. large type ed. 1991. reprint ed. lib. bdg. 18.95 (*0-263-12623-4*) Thorndike Pr.

— Vampire Lover: (Presents Plus) LC 94-4575. (Presents Ser.). 189p. 1995. pap. 3.25 (*0-373-11720-5*, 1-11720-9) Harlequin Bks.

— Wild Hunger. (Presents Ser.). 1996. per. 3.50 (*0-373-11834-1*, 1-11834-8) Harlequin Bks.

— Wounds of Passion. 1994. per. 2.99 (*0-373-11687-X*, 1-11687-0) Harlequin Bks.

— Wounds of Passion. large type ed. (Harlequin Ser.). 1994. lib. bdg. 19.95 (*0-263-13777-5*) Thorndike Pr.

— Yuletide Child. 1999. 21.95 (*0-263-15985-X*, G K Hall & Co) Mac Lib Ref.

***Lamb, Charlotte.** The Yuletide Child: Expecting! (Harlequin Presents Ser.). 1999. mass mkt. 3.75 (*0-373-12070-2*, Harlequin) Harlequin Bks.

L

L

Lamb, Charlotte & Clair, Daphne. Body & Soul. LC 95-7126. (Presents Ser.). 186p. 1995. per. 3.25 (*0-373-11733-7*, 1-11733-2) Harlequin Bks.
Lamb, Charlotte, et al. Snowbound: Shotgun Wedding, Murder by the Book, On a Wing & a Prayer. 1998. per. 5.99 (*0-373-20143-5*, 1-20143-3) Harlequin Bks.
Lamb, Christopher & Bryant, M. Darrol, eds. Religious Conversion: Contemporary Practices & Controversy. LC 99-10551. 342p. 1999. pap. 24.95 (*0-304-33843-5*) Continuum.
***Lamb, Christopher & Bryant, M. Darrol, eds.** Religious Conversion: Contemporary Practices & Controversy. 1999. 75.00 (*0-304-33842-7*) Continuum.
Lamb, Christopher J. Belief Systems & Decision Making in the Mayaguez Crisis. LC 88-12039. 328p. 1989. 49.95 (*0-8130-0900-6*) U Press Fla.
Lamb, Christopher R. Diagnostic Imaging of the Dog & Cat: Self Assessment Picture Tests in Veterinary Medicne. (Illus.). 144p. (C). (gr. 13). 1994. pap. text 32.95 (*0-8151-5323-6*, 22956) Mosby Inc.
Lamb, Clarence. Multimedia Animation. LC 97-65589. (Illus.). 100p. 1997. 49.99 (*1-57576-706-6*) Sams.
Lamb, Clarice, jt. auth. see Nunan, David.
Lamb County History Book Committee, jt. auth. see Ogletree, Madema.
Lamb, Cynthia. Brigid's Charge. LC 96-78573. vi, 296p. 1997. 22.00 (*0-9654694-0-9*); pap. 14.00 (*0-9654694-1-7*) Bay Island.
Lamb, D. Psychotherapy with Adolescent Girls. 2nd ed. LC 86-12211. (Illus.). 278p. (C). 1986. 54.50 (*0-306-42242-5*, Plenum Trade) Perseus Pubng.
Lamb, D. J. Problems & Solutions in Complete Denture Fabrication. (Illus.). 168p. 1993. text 52.00 (*1-85097-021-1*) Quint Pub Co.
Lamb, Dana & Lamb, Ginger. Quest for the Lost City. LC 84-50124. (Illus.). 352p. 1984. reprint ed. pap. 10.95 (*0-915643-00-6*) Santa Barb Pr.
Lamb, Dana S. Bright Salmon & Brown Trout. (Illus.). 112p. 1996. reprint ed. 50.00 (*1-886967-04-0*) Meadow Run Pr.
— On Trout Streams & Salmon Rivers. (Illus.). 97p. 1996. reprint ed. 50.00 (*1-886967-03-2*) Meadow Run Pr.
Lamb, Daniel S., ed. Howard University Medical Department, Washington, D. C. LC 78-37309. (Black Heritage Library Collection). 1977. reprint ed. 44.95 (*0-8369-8946-5*) Ayer.
Lamb, Davd A. Studies of Software Design: ICSE '93 Workshop, Baltimore Maryland, U. S. A., May 17-18, 1993, Selected Papers, Vol. 107. LC 96-8638. (Lecture Notes in Computer Science Ser.). 188p. 1996. pap. 36.00 (*3-540-61285-8*) Spr-Verlag.
Lamb, David. The Africans. rev. ed. 1987. pap. 14.00 (*0-394-75308-9*) Vin Bks.
— Death, Brain Death & Ethics. (Avebury Series in Philosophy). 144p. 1996. text 65.95 (*1-85972-506-6*, Pub. by Avebry) Ashgate Pub Co.
— Discovery, Creativity & Problem-Solving, 183p. 1991. text 72.95 (*1-85628-043-8*, Pub. by Avebry) Ashgate Pub Co.
— Do Platanos Go Wit' Collard Greens? LC 94-96061. 140p. (Orig.). 1994. pap. 8.95 (*0-9640692-1-0*) I Write.
— Hegel: From Foundations to System. (Philosophy Library: No. 1). 254p. 1980. text 106.00 (*90-247-2359-0*) Kluwer Academic.
— Organ Transplants & Ethics. (Avebury Series in Philosophy). 172p. 1996. text 68.95 (*1-85972-507-4*, Pub. by Avebry) Ashgate Pub Co.
— A Sense of Place: Listening to Americans. large type ed. LC 93-24125. 370p. 1993. lib. bdg. 22.95 (*0-7862-0005-7*) Thorndike Pr.
— Therapy Abatement, Autonomy & Futility: Ethical Decisions at the Edge of Life. LC 95-78193. 146p. (C). 1995. 61.95 (*1-85972-202-4*, Pub. by Avebry) Ashgate Pub Co.
— The Trumpet Is Blown. 240p. 1997. pap. 14.95 (*0-9640692-2-9*) I Write.
Lamb, David, ed. Hegel: Vol. I: Law & Morality; Vol. II: The Philosophy of Hegel, 2 vols. LC 98-17299. (International Library of Critical Essays in the History of Philosophy: No. 3). 500p. 1998. text 333.95 (*1-84014-010-0*, Pub. by Ashgate Pub) Ashgate Pub Co.
— Hegel & Modern Philosophy. 272p. 1987. lib. bdg. 62.00 (*0-7099-4168-4*, Pub. by C Helm) Routldge.
— New Horizons in the Philosophy of Science. (Philosophy of Science Ser.). 200p. 1992. 72.95 (*1-85628-296-1*, Pub. by Avebry) Ashgate Pub Co.
— Perspectives in Exercise Science & Sports Medicine Vol. 7: Physiology & Nutrition of Competitive Sport. LC 88-70343. (Illus.). 400p. (C). 1994. text 49.00 (*1-884125-09-3*) Cooper Pubng.
Lamb, David, et al, eds. Exercise & the Female - A Life Span Approach. (Perspectives in Exercise Science & Sports Medicine Ser.: Vol. 9). (Illus.). 450p. (C). 1996. text 49.00 (*1-884125-28-X*) Cooper Pubng.
— Perspectives in Exercise Science & Sports Medicine: Exercise, Heat, & Thermoregulation, Vol. 6. LC 92-73445. (Illus.). 405p. 1993. text 49.00 (*1-884125-37-9*) Cooper Pubng.
— Perspectives in Exercise Science & Sports Medicine Vol. 8: Exercise in Older Adults. LC 88-70343. (Illus.). 400p. 1995. text 49.00 (*1-884125-20-4*) Cooper Pubng.
Lamb, David & Gisolfi, Carl V., eds. Perspectives in Exercise Science & Sports Medicine: Energy Metabolism in Exercise & Sport, Vol. 5. LC 91-73932. (Illus.). 495p. 1992. reprint ed. text 49.00 (*1-884125-36-0*) Cooper Pubng.
Lamb, David & Williams, Melvin, eds. Perspectives in Exercise Science & Sports Medicine Vol. 4: Ergogenics: Enhancement of Athletic Performance. LC 88-70343. (Illus.). 444p. 1991. reprint ed. text 49.00 (*1-884125-08-5*) Cooper Pubng.
Lamb, David, jt. ed. see Gisolfi, Carl V.
Lamb, David J., jt. auth. see Figures, Keith H.
Lamb, David R. & Murray, Robert, eds. Perspectives in Exercise Science & Sports Medicine: Prolonged Exercise, Vol. 1. LC 88-70343. (Illus.). 494p. 1988. reprint ed. text 49.00 (*1-884125-34-4*) Cooper Pubng.
— Perspectives in Exercise Science & Sports Medicine Vol. 10: Optimizing Sport Performance. 450p. 1997. text 49.00 (*1-884125-63-8*) Cooper Pubng.
— Perspectives in Exercise Science & Sports Medicine Vol. 11: Exercise, Nutrition, & Weight Control. LC 95-67366. 450p. 1998. text 49.00 (*1-884125-70-0*) Cooper Pubng.
— Perspectives in Exercise Science & Sports Medicine Vol. 12: The Metabolic Basis of Performance in Sport & Exercise. 450p. (C). 1999. text 49.00 (*1-884125-73-5*) Cooper Pubng.
Lamb, David R., et al. Perspectives in Exercise Science & Sports Medicine. LC 88-70343. 1988. write for info. (*0-936157-34-8*) Brown & Benchmark.
Lamb, David R., ed. see McKeag, Douglas B. & Hough, David.
Lamb, Donald Q. & Patterson, Joseph, eds. Cataclysmic Variables & Low-Mass X-Ray Binaries. 1985. text 203.00 (*90-277-1947-0*) Kluwer Academic.
Lamb, Doris. Psychotherapy with Adolescent Girls. LC 78-62560. (Jossey-Bass Social & Behavioral Science Ser.). 224p. reprint ed. pap. 69.50 (*0-8357-4900-2*, 203783000009) Bks Demand.
***Lamb, Dorothy M.** The Call of the Mountain. (Illus.). (J). (gr. k-3). 1999. 10.95 (*0-533-12938-9*) Vantage.
Lamb, Doug. Pepper Sprays: Practical Self-Defense for Anyone, Anywhere. (Illus.). 120p. 1994. pap. 16.00 (*0-87364-794-7*) Paladin Pr.
Lamb, Douglas W. & Law, Hamish. Upper Limb Deficiencies in Children. 152p. 1987. 100.00 (*0-316-51269-9*, Little Brwn Med Div) Lppncott W & W.
Lamb, Edgar. Colorful Cacti of American Desert. 11.95 (*0-02-567670-9*) Macmillan.
Lamb, Elizabeth S. Casting into a Cloud: Southwest Haiku. (Xtras Ser.: No. 11). (Illus.). 72p. (Orig.). 1985. pap. 3.95 (*0-89120-024-X*) From Here.
— Thirty-Nine Blossoms. 28p. 1982. pap. 2.00 (*0-913719-59-5*, High Coo Pr) Brooks Books.
— Today & Every Day. 190p. 1970. 3.48 (*0-87159-154-5*) Unity Bks.
***Lamb, Elizabeth Searle.** Across the Windharp: Collected & New Haiku. 115p. 2000. pap. 12.00 (*1-888809-18-3*, Pub. by La Alameda Pr) U of NM Pr.
Lamb, Ella Condie, jt. auth. see Seeley, Barea Lamb.
Lamb, Ellen C. A Profile of State Chartered Banking. 300p. 1996. spiral bd. 60.00 (*0-614-13712-8*) Conf St Bank.
Lamb, F. Bruce. Rio Tigre & Beyond: The Amazon Jungle Medicine of Manuel Cordova. (Illus.). 256p. (Orig.). 1985. pap. 14.95 (*0-938190-59-8*) North Atlantic.
— The Wild Bunch: An Annotated Bibliography. LC 93-77747. (Illus.). 160p. 1993. 23.50 (*1-881019-05-5*) High Plns WY.
Lamb, F. Bruce & Cordova-Rios, Manuel. Wizard of the Upper Amazon: The Story of Manuel Cordova-Rios. 204p. 1987. reprint ed. pap. 15.95 (*0-938190-80-6*) North Atlantic.
Lamb, F. Bruce & Rios, Manual C. Kidnapped in the Amazon Jungle. LC 93-44837. (Illus.). 160p. (Orig.). (YA). 1994. pap. 14.95 (*1-55643-173-2*) North Atlantic.
Lamb-Faffelberger, Margarete. Valie Export und Eldfriede Jelinek Im Spiegel der Presse: Zur Rezeption der Feministischen Avantgarde Osterreichs. LC 92-20676. X, 224p. (C). 1993. text 39.95 (*0-8204-1980-X*) P Lang Pubng.
Lamb-Faffelberger, Margarete, ed. Out from the Shadows: Essays on Contemporary Austrian Women Writers & Filmmakers. LC 96-9842. (Studies in Austrian Literature, Culture, & Thought). 306p. 1997. 36.95 (*1-57241-037-X*) Ariadne CA.
Lamb, Frank B. Cowan. Henry Cowan Family of Virginia. Kuhns, Maude P., ed. 43p. 1996. reprint ed. pap. 9.00 (*0-8328-5290-2*); reprint ed. lib. bdg. 19.00 (*0-8328-5289-9*) Higginson Bk Co.
Lamb, Franklin, ed. Reason Not the Need: Eyewitness Chronicles of Israel's War in Lebanon. 936p. 1986. 60.00 (*0-85124-432-7*); pap. 40.00 (*0-85124-433-5*) St Mut.
***Lamb, G. F.** Apt & Amusing Quotations. 192p. 2000. pap. 8.95 (*0-7160-2037-8*, Pub. by Elliot RW Bks) Midpt Trade.
Lamb, G. L. Introductory Applications of Partial Differential Equations: With Emphasis on Wave Propagation & Diffusion. LC 94-33111. 496p. 1995. 89.95 (*0-471-31123-5*) Wiley.
Lamb, George. GSM Made Simple. Lamb, Bonnie, ed. (Illus.). 185p. 1997. pap. 29.00 (*0-9665752-0-2*, 63139) Cordero Consult.
— The TDMA Book. Lamb, Bonnie, ed. (Illus.). 215p. 1998. pap. 29.00 (*0-9665752-1-0*, TDMA) Cordero Consult.
Lamb, George, tr. see Marrou, Henri I.
***Lamb, George H.** The Unwritten History of Braddock's Field (PA) (Illus.). 342p. 1999. reprint ed. pap. 26.50 (*0-7884-1237-X*, L050) Heritage Bk.
***Lamb, Gerri, et al.** Case Management: A Guide to Strategic Evaluation. 256p. (C). 1998. write for info. (*0-323-00086-X*) Mosby Inc.
Lamb, Ginger, jt. auth. see Lamb, Dana.
Lamb, Gordon H. Choral Techniques. 3rd ed. 316p. (C). 1988. text. write for info. (*0-697-00612-3*) Brown & Benchmark.
— Guide for the Beginning Choral Director. (Monographs: No. 1). 41p. (C). 1972. pap. 5.00 (*1-882648-00-5*) Am Choral Dirs.
Lamb, H. H. Climate: Present, Past & Future, Vol. 2. 835p. 1977. 150.00 (*0-416-11540-3*, NO.2283) Routledge.
— Climate, History & the Modern World. (Illus.). 480p. 1982. pap. 29.95 (*0-416-33440-7*, NO. 3696) Routledge.
— Climate, History & the Modern World. 2nd ed. LC 94-44666. 432p. (C). 1995. pap. 29.99 (*0-415-12735-1*) Routledge.
Lamb, H. Richard. Rehabilitation in Community Mental Health. LC 76-168989. (Jossey-Bass Behavioral Science Ser.). 222p. reprint ed. pap. 68.90 (*0-608-16958-7*, 202776000056) Bks Demand.
— Treating the Long-Term Mentally Ill. LC 82-48391. (Jossey-Bass Social & Behavioral Science Ser.). 270p. reprint ed. pap. 83.70 (*0-7837-6514-2*, 204562600007) Bks Demand.
Lamb, H. Richard, et al, eds. Handbook of Community Mental Health Practices: The San Mateo Experience. LC 72-92886. (Jossey-Bass Behavioral Science Ser.). 512p. reprint ed. pap. 158.80 (*0-8357-9323-0*, 201393000087) Bks Demand.
— Treating the Homeless Mentally Ill: A Task Force Report of the American Psychiatric Association. LC 92-10470. 315p. 1992. text 11.95 (*0-89042-236-2*, 2236) Am Psychiatric.
Lamb, H. Richard, et al. Community Survival for Long-Term Patients. LC 75-44883. (Jossey-Bass Behavioral Science Ser.). 208p. reprint ed. pap. 64.50 (*0-8357-4992-4*, 203792500009) Bks Demand.
Lamb, H. Richard, ed. see American Psychiatric Association Staff.
***Lamb, Hair-McDaniel.** Essentials of Marketing. 2nd ed. LC 99-87757. (SWC-General Business Ser.). (C). 2000. text 47.00 (*0-324-04376-7*); text, student ed., wbk. ed. 15.50 (*0-324-04378-3*) Thomson Learn.
Lamb, Harold. Alexander of Macedon. 412p. 27.95 (*0-8488-2645-0*) Amereon Ltd.
— Durandal. (Illus.). 1981. 15.00 (*0-937986-45-3*); 35.00 (*0-937986-64-X*) D M Grant.
— Emperor of All Men. 22.95 (*0-88411-798-7*) Amereon Ltd.
— John Gideon Shaw. large type ed. (Dales Large Print Ser.). 199p. 1997. pap. 18.99 (*1-85389-747-7*, Dales) Ulverscroft.
***Lamb, Harold.** The Mexican. large type ed. 264p. 1999. pap. 18.99 (*0-7089-5619-X*, Linford) Ulverscroft.
Lamb, Harold. Return to Silver City. large type ed. (Dales Large Print Ser.). 224p. 1996. pap. 18.99 (*1-85389-659-4*, Dales) Ulverscroft.
— The Sea of the Ravens. (Illus.). 1983. 15.00 (*0-937986-58-5*); 35.00 (*0-937986-59-3*) D M Grant.
— Tamerlane the Earth Shaker. 1976. 26.95 (*0-8488-1072-4*) Amereon Ltd.
— The Three Palladins. 1977. 12.00 (*0-686-27901-8*) D M Grant.
Lamb, Helen B. Studies on India & Vietnam. Lamont, Corliss, ed. LC 76-1668. 267p. reprint ed. pap. 82.80 (*0-7837-3922-2*, 204377000010) Bks Demand.
— Vietnam's Will to Live: Resistance to Foreign Aggression from Early Times Through the Nineteenth Century. LC 72-81760. 352p. 1972. reprint ed. pap. 109.20 (*0-7837-9612-9*, 206036900005) Bks Demand.
Lamb, Holly, et al. Journey Through Drama. Tyre, Travis, ed. (Illus.). 178p. (Orig.). (J). (gr. 4-6). 1996. pap., wbk. ed. 26.00 (*1-887710-02-7*, ArtCan Drama) Promise Prodns.
Lamb, Horace. Hydrodynamics. 3rd ed. 1991. 85.00 (*0-521-05515-6*) Cambridge U Pr.
— Hydrodynamics. 6th ed. (Cambridge Mathematical Library). (Illus.). 764p. (C). 1993. pap. text 19.95 (*0-521-45868-4*) Cambridge U Pr.
— Hydrodynamics. 6th ed. (Illus.). 738p. 1945. pap. text 16.95 (*0-486-60256-7*) Dover.
Lamb, Howard. The Fatbook. 133p. 1982. ring bd. 39.95 (*0-9609150-0-1*) H Lamb.
Lamb, Hubert H. Historic Storms of the North Sea. 216p. 1991. text 110.00 (*0-521-37522-3*) Cambridge U Pr.
— Weather, Climate & Human Affairs. 416p. 1988. text 99.00 (*0-415-00674-0*) Routledge.
Lamb, Hugh, ed. see Capes, Bernard.
Lamb, Hugh, ed. see Chambers, Robert W.
Lamb, Hugh, ed. see Cowles, Frederick.
Lamb, I. M. Antarctic Lichens Vol. I: The Genera Usnea, Ramalina, Himantormia, Alectoria, Cornicularia. (British Antarctic Survey Report Ser.: No. 38). 86p. 1964. 25.00 (*0-85665-772-7*, Pub. by Brit Antarctic Surv) Balogh.
— Antarctic Lichens Vol. II: The Genera Buellia & Rinodina (with an Ontogenetic Section) (British Antarctic Survey Report Ser.: No. 61). 162p. 1964. 28.00 (*0-85665-038-2*, Pub. by Brit Antarctic Surv) Balogh.
Lamb, I. Mackenzie & Zimmerman, Martin H. Benthic Marine Algae of the Antarctic Peninsula: Paper 4 in Biology of the Antarctic Seas V. Pawson, David L., ed. (Antarctic Research Ser.: Vol. 23). 104p. 1977. pap. 53.00 (*0-87590-128-X*) Am Geophysical.
***Lamb, Iner.** Relics of Ancient America. (LC History-America-E). 52p. 1999. reprint ed. lib. bdg. 69.00 (*0-7812-4345-9*) Rprt Serv.
Lamb, J. D. & Preece, D. A., eds. Surveys in Combinatorics 1999. LC 99-23537. (London Mathematical Society Lecture Note Ser.: No. 267). 300p. 1999. pap. 39.95 (*0-521-65376-2*) Cambridge U Pr.
Lamb, J. Dayne. A Question of Preference: A Teal Stewart Mystery. 1995. mass mkt. 4.99 (*0-8217-5099-2*, Zebra Kensgtn) Kensgtn Pub Corp.
— Questionable Behavior. 288p. 1993. mass mkt. 3.99 (*0-8217-4333-3*, Zebra Kensgtn) Kensgtn Pub Corp.
— Unquestioned Loyalty: A Teal Stewart Mystery. 352p. 1996. mass mkt. 4.99 (*1-57566-054-7*, Knsington) Kensgtn Pub Corp.
Lamb, J. Parker. Classic Diesels of the South. 1997. 26.95 (*1-883089-20-4*) TLC VA.
— Classic Diesels of the South. (Illus.). 126p. 1997. 26.95 (*1-883089-28-X*) TLC VA.
— KATY Diesels to the Gulf. (Illus.). 108p. (Orig.). 1991. pap. 39.95 (*0-944119-05-0*) Andover Junction.
Lamb, J. R., jt. auth. see Owen, M. J.
***Lamb, J. S.** The Practice of Oxygen Measurement for Divers. LC 98-86313. (Illus.). 120p. 1999. pap. 19.95 (*0-941332-68-3*, B0990) Best Pub Co.
Lamb, Jack, ed. Classic Festival Solos: Horn in F (Solo Book) 16p. (C). 1992. pap. text 4.95 (*0-7692-1759-1*, EL03740) Wrner Bros.
Lamb, Jackie & Lamb, Wesley. Parent Education & Elementary Counseling. LC 77-12942. (New Vistas in Counseling Ser.: Vol. V). 151p. 1978. 29.95 (*0-87705-318-9*, Kluwer Acad Hman Sci) Kluwer Academic.
***Lamb, James B.** The Corvette Navy: True Stories from Canada's Atlantic War. 2nd rev. ed. (Illus.). 224p. 2000. 20.95 (*0-7737-3225-X*) Stoddart Publ.
Lamb, Jane H. The Aerie. 56p. 1981. pap. 3.95 (*0-614-24765-9*) Tesseract SD.
— Remembrance Framed. 30p. 1992. pap. 3.00 (*0-614-24767-5*) Tesseract SD.
Lamb, Jane M. & Dodge, Nancy C. Sharing with Thumpy: My Story of Love & Grief. (Illus.). 48p. (J). (gr. k-12). 1985. pap. text, student ed. 9.95 (*0-918533-10-4*) SHARE.
Lamb, Jeremy. So Idle a Rogue: The Life & Death of Lord Rochester. (Illus.). 336p. 1995. write for info. (*0-7490-0291-3*); 21.95 (*0-85031-958-7*) Allison & Busby.
Lamb, Jessia. Highland Rogue. Tolley, Carolyn, ed. 304p. 1991. mass mkt. 6.50 (*0-671-73001-0*) PB.
Lamb, Joann L. Woman's Health Journal. 112p. 2000. spiral bd. 17.95 (*1-58238-046-5*, Whitman Coin) St Martin.
Lamb, John D. Chemistry Tutor Workbook - Preliminary. (Chemistry Ser.). 300p. Date not set. pap. 16.25 (*0-7637-0349-4*) Jones & Bartlett.
Lamb, John D., et al. Chemistry Tutor Student Workbook & CD-ROM. (Chemistry Ser.). 192p. 1997. pap., wbk. ed. 37.50 incl. cd-rom (*0-7637-0350-8*) Jones & Bartlett.
***Lamb, John J.** San Diego Specters: Ghosts, Poltergeists & Phantasmic Tales. LC 99-33384. (Illus.). 192p. 1999. pap. 12.95 (*0-932653-32-4*) Sunbelt Pubns.
Lamb, John L. The End of Summer. 1996. pap. 10.00 (*0-614-97795-9*, WSP) PB.
— The End of Summer. 176p. 1996. pap. 10.00 (*0-671-53616-8*) S&S Trade.
Lamb, John L. The End of the Summer. LC 94-46865. 1995. 18.45 (*0-684-80358-5*) S&S Trade.
***Lamb, John M.** Lockport. (Images of America Ser.). 1999. pap. 18.99 (*0-7524-1281-7*) Arcadia Publng.
Lamb, John P. Lotus Notes & Domino 5 Scalable Network Design. LC 99-34198. 752p. 1999. pap. 49.95 incl. cd-rom (*0-07-913792-X*) McGraw.
— Lotus Notes Network Design. 1996. pap. 44.95 (*0-07-036160-6*) McGraw.
Lamb, John P., jt. auth. see Lew, Peter.
***Lamb, Jonathan.** Preserving Self in South Seas. 1999. pap. text 18.00 (*0-226-46849-6*); lib. bdg. 45.00 (*0-226-46848-8*) U Ch Pr.
Lamb, Jonathan. The Rhetoric of Suffering: Reading the Book of Job in the Eighteenth Century. (Illus.). 342p. 1995. text 65.00 (*0-19-818264-3*) OUP.
Lamb, Jonathan R., jt. ed. see Dallman, Margaret J.
Lamb, Joyce, jt. auth. see Nation, Edna.
Lamb, Judy, jt. auth. see Fairchild, Joice.
***Lamb, Julia, compiled by.** Teaching Resources on Asia for the Classroom. (Illus.). 37p. 1999. teacher ed., ring bd. 9.95 (*1-891134-01-9*) SE Asia.
— Teaching Resources on Asia for the Classroom, Set. (Illus.). 37p. 1999. teacher ed., ring bd. 49.95 (*1-891134-02-7*) SE Asia.
Lamb, Karl A. As Orange Goes: Twelve California Families & the Future of American Politics. (C). 1974. pap. text. write for info. (*0-393-09235-6*) Norton.
— As Orange Goes: Twelve California Families & the Future of American Politics. (C). 1974. 10.50 (*0-393-05520-5*) Norton.
— Reasonable Disagreement: Two U. S. Senators & the Choices They Make. Shull, Steven A., ed. LC 98-19160. (Politics & Policy in American Institutions Ser.: Vol. 2). (Illus.). 192p. 1998. 55.00 (*0-8153-2801-X*, SS1157); pap. 26.95 (*0-8153-2802-8*, SS1157) Garland.
Lamb, Kathleen, jt. auth. see Westerbeck, Colin.
Lamb, Kathryn. One Ewe over the Cuckoo's Nest. (Illus.). 96p. 1991. pap. 8.95 (*0-85236-227-7*, Pub. by Farming Pr) Diamond Farm Bk.
Lamb, Keith W. The Lord's Freedman. 266p. (Orig.). 1995. pap. 10.99 (*1-56043-829-0*, Treasure Hse) Destiny Image.
Lamb, Kenya, ed. & illus. see Lamb, Pat.
Lamb, Lady Caroline. Glenarvon. Watson, Frances, ed. 336p. (Orig.). 1995. pap. 7.50 (*0-460-87468-3*, Everyman's Classic Lib) Tuttle Pubng.
Lamb, Larry, jt. auth. see Parshall, Jim.
Lamb, Lawrence E. The Weighting Game: The Truth about Weight Control. 196p. 1988. 15.95 (*0-8184-0487-6*) Carol Pub Group.
— The Weighting Game: The Truth about Weight Control. 1991. pap. 10.95 (*0-8184-0551-1*) Carol Pub Group.
Lamb, Linda. Learning the VI Editor. 5th rev. ed. (Computer Science). 192p. 1990. reprint ed. pap. 24.95 (*0-937175-67-6*) Thomson Learn.
Lamb, Linda & Peek, Jerry. Using Email Effectively. LC 96-140813. 160p. 1995. pap. 14.95 (*1-56592-103-8*) Thomson Learn.
Lamb, Linda & Robbins, Arnold. Learning the vi Editor. 6th ed. (Illus.). 348p. 1998. pap. 24.95 (*1-56592-426-6*) OReilly & Assocs.
Lamb, Linda, ed. see Babbit, Nikki.
Lamb, Linda, ed. see Finn, Bob.
Lamb, Linda, ed. see Finn, Robert.

An Asterisk (*) at the beginning of an entry indicates that the title is appearing for the first time.

Lamb, Linda, ed. see Green, Reg.
Lamb, Linda, ed. see Janes-Hodder, Honna & Keene, Nancy.
Lamb, Linda, ed. see Johnston, Lorraine.
Lamb, Linda, ed. see Karp, Gary.
Lamb, Linda, ed. see Keene, Nancy & Prentice, Rachel.
Lamb, Linda, ed. see Keene, Nancy, et al.
Lamb, Linda, ed. see Mayer, Musa.
Lamb, Linda, ed. see Toporek, Chuck & Robinson, Kellie.
Lamb, Linda, ed. see Waltz, Mitzi.
Lamb, M., jt. auth. see Checkland, O.
Lamb, Malcolm. Directory of Officials & Organizations in China: A Quarter-Century Guide. LC 94-12103. (Contemporary China Papers - Australian National University: Vol. 22). 1392p. (gr. 13). 1994. text 245.95 (*1-56324-427-6*, East Gate Bk) M E Sharpe.
— Directory of Officials & Organizations in China, 1968-1983. LC 84-1297. (Contemporary China Papers). 751p. 1984. reprint ed. pap. 200.00 (*0-7837-9978-0*, 206070500006) Bks Demand.
Lamb, Marcia, jt. auth. see Lamb, Roger.
Lamb, Margaret. Antony & Cleopatra on the English Stage. LC 78-66803. 248p. 1970. 32.50 (*0-8386-2198-8*) Fairleigh Dickinson.
Lamb, Marion J., jt. auth. see Jablonka, Eva.
Lamb, Martha J. Wall Street in History. LC 92-71285. (Illus.). 95p. (Orig.). 1992. reprint ed. pap. 15.00 (*0-87034-104-9*) Fraser Pub Co.
Lamb, Mary. Mrs. Leicester's School, 1809. LC 94-44530. (Revolution & Romanticism, 1789-1834 Ser.). 1995. 48.00 (*1-85477-182-5*) Continuum.
Lamb, Mary, jt. auth. see Lamb, Charles.
Lamb, Mary A., jt. auth. see Lamb, Charles.
Lamb, Mary E. Gender & Authorship in the Sidney Circle. LC 90-50092. 288p. (Orig.). (C). 1991. text 22.95 (*0-299-12690-0*); pap. text 8.95 (*0-299-12694-3*) U of Wis Pr.
Lamb, Matthew L. Creativity & Method: Studies in Honor of Rev. Bernard Lonergan, S. J. LC 81-80327. 600p. 1981. pap. 20.00 (*0-87462-533-5*) Marquette.
— History, Method & Theology: A Dialectical Comparison of Wilhelm Dilthey's Critique of Historical Reason & Bernard Lonergan's Meta-Methodology. LC 78-18707. (American Academy of Religion. Dissertation Ser.: No. 25). 562p. reprint ed. pap. 174.30 (*0-7837-5463-9*, 204522800005) Bks Demand.
Lamb, Matthew L., ed. Creativity & Method: Studies in Honor of Rev. Bernard Lonergan, S.J. LC 81-80327. 600p. 1981. pap. 20.00 (*0-87462-524-6*) Marquette.
Lamb, May W. Life in Alaska: The Reminiscences of a Kansas Woman, 1916-1919. Zimmerman, Dorothy W., ed. LC 87-30023. (Illus.). 181p. reprint ed. pap. 56.20 (*0-608-05994-3*, 206632200008) Bks Demand.
***Lamb, Michael, ed.** The Effects of Quality Care on Child Development: A Special Issue of Applied Developmental Science. 65p. 2000. pap. write for info. (*0-8058-9752-6*) L Erlbaum Assocs.
Lamb, Michael, ed. New Research & Child Witnesses Pt. I: A Special Issue of Applied Developmental Science. 72p. 1999. pap. 20.00 (*0-8058-9800-X*) L Erlbaum Assocs.
Lamb, Michael E. The Role of the Father in Child Development. 3rd ed. LC 96-4899. 432p. 1996. 79.95 (*0-471-11771-4*) Wiley.
Lamb, Michael E., ed. New Research on Child Witnesses Pt. II: A Special Issue in Applied Developmental Science. 80p. 1999. pap. 20.00 (*0-8058-9795-X*) L Erlbaum Assocs.
— Non-Traditional & Traditionally Understudied Families: Parenting & Child Development. LC 98-18422. 400p. 1998. write for info. (*0-8058-2747-1*); pap. write for info. (*0-8058-2748-X*) L Erlbaum Assocs.
— Nontraditional Families: Parenting & Child Development. (Illus.). 372p. 1982. text 79.95 (*0-89859-178-3*) L Erlbaum Assocs.
Lamb, Michael E., et al, eds. Advances in Developmental Psychology, Vol. 3. 312p. (C). 1984. text 59.95 (*0-89859-366-2*) L Erlbaum Assocs.
— Advances in Developmental Psychology, Vol. 4. 376p. 1986. 79.95 (*0-89859-675-0*) L Erlbaum Assocs.
— Child Care in Context: Cross-Cultural Perspectives. 560p. 1991. text 89.95 (*0-8058-0797-7*) L Erlbaum Assocs.
— Social Interaction Analysis: Methodological Issues. LC 78-53287. (Illus.). 333p. reprint ed. pap. 103.30 (*0-608-07012-2*, 206721900009) Bks Demand.
Lamb, Michael E. & Brown, Ann L., eds. Advances in Developmental Psychology, Vol. 1. (Advances in Developmental Psychology Ser.). 256p. 1981. text 49.95 (*0-89859-103-1*) L Erlbaum Assocs.
— Advances in Developmental Psychology, Vol. 2. 224p. (C). 1982. text 49.95 (*0-89859-244-5*) L Erlbaum Assocs.
Lamb, Michael E. & Sagi, Abraham, eds. Fatherhood & Family Policy. 288p. (C). 1983. text 59.95 (*0-89859-190-2*) L Erlbaum Assocs.
Lamb, Michael E. & Sherrod, Lonnie R., eds. Infant Social Cognition: Theoretical & Empirical Considerations. LC 80-21137. 448p. 1981. text 79.95 (*0-89859-058-2*) L Erlbaum Assocs.
Lamb, Michael E. & Sutton-Smith, Brian, eds. Sibling Relationships: Their Nature & Significance Across the Lifespan. 416p. 1982. 79.95 (*0-89859-189-9*) L Erlbaum Assocs.
Lamb, Michael E., jt. auth. see Bornstein, Marc H.
Lamb, Michael E., jt. auth. see Poole, Debra A.
Lamb, Michael E., jt. ed. see Bornstein, Marc H.
Lamb, Michael E., jt. ed. see Elster, Arthur B.
Lamb, Michael E., jt. ed. see Keller, Heidi.
Lamb, Michael E., jt. ed. see Ketterlinus, Robert D.
***Lamb, Mondy, ed.** K-LINE Collector's Guide: Trains 1985-1998. (Illus.). 304p. 1999. 59.95 (*0-934580-22-7*) MDK Inc.
Lamb, Nancy. The Great Mosquito, Bull, & Coffin Caper. LC 91-31125. (Illus.). 128p. (YA). (gr. 5 up). 1994. reprint ed. mass mkt. 4.95 (*0-688-12944-7*, Wm Morrow) Morrow Avon.
— The World's Greatest Toe Show. (Canal Street Kids Book Ser.). (J). 1994. 7.70 (*0-606-08400-2*, Pub. by Turtleback) Demco.
Lamb, Nancy & Singer, Muff. The Vampires Went Thataway! LC 95-14844. (Canal Street Kids Bks.). (Illus.). 80p. (J). (gr. 2-5). 1995. pap. 2.95 (*0-8167-3718-5*, Little Rainbow) Troll Communs.
— The Vampires Went Thataway! LC 95-14844. (Illus.). 80p. (J). (gr. 2-5). 1997. lib. bdg. 14.00 (*0-8167-3950-1*, Little Rainbow) Troll Communs.
— The World's Greatest Toe Show. LC 93-28440. (Illus.). 64p. (J). (gr. 2-5). 1996. 13.95 (*0-8167-3322-8*) BrdgeWater.
— The World's Greatest Toe Show. LC 93-28440. (Illus.). 64p. (J). (gr. 2-5). 1997. pap. 3.95 (*0-8167-3323-6*, Little Rainbow) Troll Communs.
Lamb, Nancy, et al. One April Morning: Children Remember The Oklahoma City Bombing. LC 95-39210. (Illus.). 48p. (YA). (gr. 5 up). 1996. 16.00 (*0-688-14666-X*) Lothrop.
Lamb, Nancy, jt. auth. see Gelman, Rita G.
Lamb, Norman, pref. EPHOS - At a Glance: The European Procurement Handbook for Open Systems. (Illus.). 39p. (C). 1995. pap. text 20.00 (*0-7881-2345-9*) DIANE Pub.
Lamb, Norman & Cook, Susan J. Guide to Teaching Strings. 6th ed. 224p. (C). 1993. text. write for info. (*0-697-12499-1*) Brown & Benchmark.
Lamb, Pat. Diamonds by the Side of the Road. Lamb, Kenya, ed. & illus. by. 119p. (Orig.). 1995. pap. 9.95 (*0-9652363-0-7*) Publng Plus.
Lamb, Patrica F., ed. see Clotfelter, Charles R.
Lamb, Patricia C. All Men by Nature. 48p. (Orig.). 1993. pap. 4.00 (*0-9615145-2-3*) Harbottle Pr.
— The Long Love: New & Collected Poems, 1957-1998. LC 98-93640. 220p. 1998. 14.95 (*0-9615145-3-1*) Harbottle Pr.
Lamb, Paul. Diary of the Trail. iii, 239p. (Orig.). 1995. pap. text 10.00 (*0-9639719-1-3*) Lambs Fold Ranch.
— Memories from the Trail. iii, 122p. (Orig.). 1994. pap. text 10.00 (*0-9639719-0-5*) Lambs Fold Ranch.
— Roses on the Trail. 135p. (Orig.). 1995. pap. text 10.00 (*0-9639719-3-X*) Lambs Fold Ranch.
Lamb, Peter & Coyle, Matthew. Registry of Death. Garnier, Catherine, ed. LC 96-22478. (Illus.). 56p. 1997. pap. 15.95 (*0-87816-448-0*) Kitchen Sink.
Lamb, Peter, ed. see International Conference on Applications of Statis.
Lamb, Philip. NYAT! (National Yiddish Art Theater) 120p. 1987. pap. 6.95 (*0-918537-02-9*) Justin Bks.
***Lamb, Rebecca Ann & Erickson, David.** God's Precious Gift in a Manger. LC 00-37602. (Illus.). 2000. write for info. (*0-7814-3265-0*, Bible Discovery) Chariot Victor.
Lamb, Richard. Churchill As War Leader. 416p. 1993. 22.95 (*0-88184-937-5*) Carroll & Graf.
— Following Jesus in the Real World: Discipleship for the Post-College Years. LC 94-45410. 192p. (Orig.). 1995. pap. 10.99 (*0-8308-1608-9*, 1608) InterVarsity.
— Lamb Instructor's Guide. (Illus.). 500p. (C). 1986. teacher ed. 10.75 (*0-8053-5831-5*) Benjamin-Cummings.
— Mussolini & the British. LC 98-180709. (Illus.). 336p. 1998. 45.00 (*0-7195-5592-2*, Pub. by John Murray) Trafalgar.
— Mussolini As Diplomat: Il Duce's Italy on the World Stage. LC 99-38378. (Illus.). 368p. 1999. 30.00 (*0-88064-244-0*, Pub. by Fromm Intl Pub) FS&G.
— The Prophet King: A New Look at the Historical Jesus. 195p. (Orig.). 1997. pap. 13.95 (*0-9657750-0-3*) Earth Heart Pr.
— War in Italy, 1943-1945: A Brutal Story. LC 95-41048. (Illus.). 363p. 1996. reprint ed. pap. 14.95 (*0-306-80688-6*) Da Capo.
Lamb, Richard & Mittelberger, Ernest. In Celebration of Wine & Life. 2nd ed. (Illus.). 245p. 1980. 19.95 (*0-932664-12-1*); pap. 9.95 (*0-932664-13-X*) Wine Appreciation.
Lamb, Richard G. Availability Engineering & Management for Manufacturilng Plant Performance. 416p. (C). 1995. 53.20 (*0-13-324112-2*) P-H.
Lamb, Ridgeway H. Hard Times in Natal & the Way Out. (Colin Webb Natal & Zululand Ser.: No. 3). (Illus.). 56p. 1992. pap. 16.50 (*0-86980-879-6*, Pub. by Univ Natal Pr) Intl Spec Bk.
Lamb, Robert. Promising the Earth. (Illus.). 248p. (C). 1996. 65.00 (*0-415-14443-4*); pap. 17.99 (*0-415-14444-2*) Routledge.
— Striking Out. LC 90-53327. 264p. 1991. 22.00 (*1-877946-06-0*) Permanent Pr.
Lamb, Robert, et al, eds. Advances in Strategic Management, Vol. 4. 301p. 1987. 78.50 (*0-89232-668-9*) Jai Pr.
Lamb, Robert & Horn, Chris. The Class Menagerie: A Collection of Short Stories Out of USC. LC 97-80992. 190p. 1998. pap. write for info. (*0-9661199-0-8*) Red Letter.
Lamb, Robert & Rappaport, Stephen P. Municipal Bonds: The Comprehensive Review of Municipal Securities & Public Finance. 2nd ed. LC 86-27539. 288p. 1987. 34.95 (*0-07-036084-7*) McGraw.
Lamb, Robert B. The Mule in Southern Agriculture. LC 63-63464. (University of California Publications in Social Welfare: vol. 15). 106p. reprint ed. pap. 32.90 (*0-608-18652-X*, 202127200022) Bks Demand.
Lamb, Robert B., jt. auth. see Grubb, Thomas M.
Lamb, Robert B., jt. auth. see Leigland, James.
Lamb, Robert B., ed. see Foster, Lawrence W.
Lamb, Robert O., jt. ed. see Hoddinott, Keith B.
Lamb, Robert P., jt. auth. see Swaggart, Jimmy.
Lamb, Roger. Original & Authentic Journal of Occurrences During the Late American War. LC 67-29033. (Eyewitness Accounts of the American Revolution Ser.). 1968. reprint ed. 19.95 (*0-405-01118-0*) Ayer.
Lamb, Roger, ed. Love Analyzed. LC 96-38902. 288p. (C). 1996. pap. 27.00 (*0-8133-3223-0*, Pub. by Westview); text 75.00 (*0-8133-8891-0*, Pub. by Westview) HarpC.
Lamb, Roger & Lamb, Marcia. This Doesn't Feel Like Love: Trusting God When Bad Things Happen. 210p. 1996. pap. 12.99 (*1-884553-82-6*) Discipleshp.
Lamb, Ron K. Micro Focus Workbench & Toolset Developer's Guide. 1995. pap. 40.00 (*0-07-036122-3*) McGraw.
***Lamb, Roy R.** Sorbonne. LC 00-20776. 2000. pap. write for info. (*0-87770-713-8*) Ye Galleon.
Lamb, Ruth D. American Chamber of Horrors: The Truth about Food & Drugs. LC 75-39255. (Getting & Spending: The Consumer's Dilemma Ser.). (Illus.). 1976. reprint ed. 35.95 (*0-405-08028-X*) Ayer.
***Lamb, Ruth M. & Cooper Back, Mary W.** Mary's Way: A Memoir of the Life of Mary Cooper Back. (Illus.). vii, 280p. 1999. pap. 13.00i (*0-9671734-0-X*) FuturePrep Corp.
Lamb, Samuel H. Native Trees & Shrubs of the Hawaiian Islands: A Guide. LC 80-19715. 160p. 1981. pap. 14.95 (*0-913270-91-1*) Sunstone Pr.
— Woody Plants of the Southwest: A Guidebook. LC 76-357696. (Illus.). 1977. pap. 14.95 (*0-913270-50-4*) Sunstone Pr.
Lamb, Samuel H., jt. auth. see Miller, Howard A.
Lamb, Sandra. How to Write It. 352p. 1998. pap. 19.95 (*1-58008-001-4*) Ten Speed Pr.
Lamb, Sandra C., jt. auth. see Bellows, Dena K.
Lamb, Sandra E. Rape in America: A Reference Handbook. LC 95-12012. (Contemporary World Issues Ser.). 210p. 1995. lib. bdg. 45.00 (*0-87436-730-1*) ABC-CLIO.
Lamb, Sara, ed. see Institute of Medicine Staff.
***Lamb, Sarah.** White Saris & Sweet Mangoes: Aging, Gender, & Body in North India. LC 99-88195. (Illus.). 323p. 2000. 55.00 (*0-520-22000-5*, Pub. by U CA Pr); pap. 22.50 (*0-520-22001-3*, Pub. by U CA Pr) Cal Prin Full Svc.
Lamb, Sharon. New Versions of Victims: Feminists Struggle with the Concept. LC 99-17521. 1999. pap. text 18.50 (*0-8147-5153-9*) NYU Pr.
— The Trouble with Blame: Victims, Perpetrators, & Responsibility. LC 95-47457. 256p. (C). 1996. 22.95 (*0-674-91010-9*) HUP.
***Lamb, Sharon.** The Trouble with Blame: Victims, Perpetrators, & Responsibility. 1999. pap. text 14.00 (*0-674-91011-7*) HUP.
Lamb, Sharon, ed. New Versions of Victims: Feminists Struggle with the Concept. LC 99-17521. 192p. 1999. text 55.00 (*0-8147-5152-0*) NYU Pr.
Lamb, Sharon, jt. ed. see Kagan, Jerome.
Lamb, Sherry. A Royal Storybook. (Illus.). 50p. (J). (gr. 5-8). 1999. 10.95 (*0-533-12883-8*) Vantage.
Lamb, Sidney, ed. King Henry IV, part 1: Complete Study Edition. 101p. 1965. pap. 6.95 (*0-8220-1425-4*, Cliff) IDG Bks.
— King Lear Complete Study Edition. 101p. 1964. pap. text, student ed. 6.95 (*0-8220-1422-X*, Cliff) IDG Bks.
— Merchant of Venice Complete Study Guide. 101p. 1965. pap. text, student ed. 6.95 (*0-8220-1431-9*, Cliff) IDG Bks.
— Othello Complete Study Edition. (Cliffs Notes Ser.). 101p. 1966. pap. 6.95 (*0-8220-1434-3*, Cliff) IDG Bks.
— Romeo & Juliet Complete Study Edition. 101p. 1965. pap. text 6.95 (*0-8220-1438-6*, Cliff) IDG Bks.
— Tempest Complete Study Edition. 101p. 1965. pap. text, student ed. 6.95 (*0-8220-1441-6*, Cliff) IDG Bks.
Lamb, Sidney, ed. see Shakespeare, William.
Lamb, Sidney M. Pathways of the Brain: The Neurocogntivie Basis of Language. LC 98-31816. (Current Issues in Linguistic Theory Ser.: Vol. 170). xii, 418p. 1999. pap. 34.95 (*1-55619-888-4*) J Benjamins Pubng Co.
Lamb, Simon & Sington, David. Earth Story: The Shaping of Our World. LC 98-17380. 240p. 1998. 29.95 (*0-691-00229-0*, Pub. by Princeton U Pr) Cal Prin Full Svc.
***Lamb, Stephen, ed.** Practical Handbook of Stainless Steels & Nickel Alloys. 360p. 1999. 90.00 (*1-894038-23-1*, 06819G, Pub. by Csti Pubng); 166.00 incl. cd-rom (*1-894038-24-X*, 06817AZ, Pub. by Csti Pubng) ASM.
Lamb, Steven. Sexual Purity: Gospel & Medical Perspectives on Sexual Intimacy & Sin. 224p. (Orig.). 1996. pap. 16.98 (*0-88290-586-4*) Horizon Utah.
Lamb, Susan. Channel Islands National Park. LC 98-27863. (Illus.). 64p. 2000. pap. 9.95 (*1-877856-74-6*) SW Pks Mnmts.
— Grand Canyon: The Vault of Heaven. Frazier, Pam, ed. LC 95-79191. (Illus.). 68p. 1998. 34.95 (*0-938216-59-7*) GCA.
— Grand Canyon Vol. 1: The Vault of Heaven. Frazier, Pam, ed. LC 95-79191. (Illus.). 68p. 1995. reprint ed. pap. 18.95 (*0-938216-53-8*) GCA.
— Guide to Navajo Rugs. Foreman, Ronald J. & Priehs, T. J., eds. LC 92-62470. (Illus.). 32p. (Orig.). 1992. pap. 3.95 (*1-877856-26-6*) SW Pks Mnmts.
— A Guide to Pueblo Pottery. LC 96-34657. (Illus.). 48p. 1996. pap. 3.95 (*1-877856-62-2*) SW Pks Mnmts.
***Lamb, Susan.** Mesa Verde National Park. Nicholas, Jeff, ed. (Pocket Portfolio Ser.: Vol. 14). (Illus.). 32p. 1999. pap. 5.95 (*1-58071-001-8*, Pub. by Panorama Intl) Falcon Pub Inc.
Lamb, Susan. Montezuma Castle National Monument. Foreman, Ronald J. & Priehs, T. J., eds. LC 92-62157. (Illus.). 16p. (Orig.). 1992. pap. 3.95 (*1-877856-19-3*) SW Pks Mnmts.
— Petroglyph National Monument. Foreman, Ronald J., ed. LC 92-62155. (Illus.). 16p. (Orig.). 1993. pap. 3.95 (*1-877856-22-3*) SW Pks Mnmts.
— Pueblo & Mission: Cultural Roots of the Southwest. LC 96-39593. (Illus.). 160p. 1997. pap. 19.95 (*0-87358-653-0*) Northland AZ.
— The Smithsonian Guides to Natural America: The Southern Rockies - Colorado & Utah. LC 95-9041. 304p. 1996. pap. 19.95 (*0-679-76472-0*, Pub. by Smithsonian Bks) Random.
— Tumacacori National Historical Park. Priehs, T. J. & Scott, Sandra, eds. LC 93-86297. (Illus.). 16p. (Orig.). 1993. pap. 3.95 (*1-877856-37-1*) SW Pks Mnmts.
— Wildflowers of the Pacific Northwest. (Illus.). 136p. 1999. 34.95 (*0-944197-58-2*, Pub. by Companion CA); pap. 19.95 (*0-944197-57-4*, Pub. by Companion CA) U of Nev Pr.
— Wildflowers of the Pacific Northwest: Twenty Postcards. (Illus.). 24p. 1999. pap. 8.95 (*0-944197-59-0*, Pub. by Companion CA) U of Nev Pr.
— Wildflowers of the Plateau & Canyon Country. (Illus.). 136p. 1996. 34.95 (*0-944197-42-6*); pap. 18.95 (*0-944197-41-8*) Companion CA.
— Wildflowers of the Plateau & Canyon Country: Twenty Postcards. (Illus.). 24p. 1996. pap. 8.95 (*0-944197-43-4*) Companion CA.
— Wupatki National Monument. Scott, Sandra, ed. LC 94-66873. (Illus.). 16p. 1995. pap. 3.95 (*1-877856-47-9*) SW Pks Mnmts.
Lamb, Susan, ed. Best of Grand Canyon Nature Notes. LC 94-75654. 168p. 1995. pap. 11.95 (*0-938216-49-X*) GCA.
Lamb, Sydney M. Pathways of the Brain: The Neurocogntivie Basis of Language. LC 98-31816. (Current Issues in Linguistic Theory Ser.: Vol. 170). xii, 418p. 1999. 95.00 (*1-55619-886-8*) J Benjamins Pubng Co.
Lamb, Sydney M. & Mitchell, E. Douglas, eds. Sprung from Some Common Source: Investigations into the Prehistory of Languages. LC 90-46495. (Illus.). 432p. 1991. 52.50 (*0-8047-1897-0*) Stanford U Pr.
Lamb, Sydney M. & Newell, Leonard E. An Outline of Stratificational Grammar. LC 66-28562. (Illus.). 115p. reprint ed. pap. 35.70 (*0-7837-6331-X*, 204604400010) Bks Demand.
***Lamb, Terri S.** Sams Teach Yourself E-Genealogy Today: Finding Your Family Roots Online. (Teach Yourself Today Ser.). (Illus.). 300p. 1999. pap. 17.99 (*0-672-31816-4*) Sams.
Lamb, Terry. Born to Be Together: Love Relationships, Astrology & the Soul. LC 98-9763. 336p. 1998. pap. 12.95 (*1-56170-471-7*, 868) Hay House.
Lamb, Toni, ed. see Molina, Tarea.
Lamb, Trevor. Colour: Art & Science. Bourriau, Janine, ed. (Darwin College Lectures). (Illus.). 243p. (C). 1995. pap. 26.95 (*0-521-49963-1*) Cambridge U Pr.
Lamb, Ursula. Cosmographers & Pilots of the Spanish Maritime Empire. (Variorum Collected Studies Ser.: Vol. 499). 288p. 1995. 97.95 (*0-86078-473-8*, Pub. by Variorum) Ashgate Pub Co.
— The Globe Encircled - The World Revealed. LC 95-22339. (Expanding World Ser.: Vol. 3). 350p. 1995. 124.95 (*0-86078-502-5*, Pub. by Variorum) Ashgate Pub Co.
Lamb, V. B. The Betrayal of Richard the Third: An Introduction to the Controversy. LC 97-149102. (Illus.). 128p. (C). 1996. pap. 13.95 (*0-86299-778-X*, Pub. by Sutton Pub Ltd) Intl Pubs Mktg.
Lamb, V. R., jt. auth. see Rieber, J. E.
Lamb, W. E. Croquet. 1994. pap. 19.95 (*1-85223-816-X*, Pub. by Crolwood) Trafalgar.
— Croquet. (Know the Sport Ser.). (Illus.). 48p. 1997. pap. 5.95 (*0-8117-2833-1*) Stackpole.
Lamb, W. R., tr. Charmides, Alcibiades First & Second, Hipparchus, the Lovers, Theages, Minos, Epinomis, Vol. XII. (Loeb Classical Library: No. 201). 512p. 1927. text 18.95 (*0-674-99221-0*) HUP.
— Laches, Protagoras, Meno & Euthydemus, Vol. II. (Loeb Classical Library: No. 165). 530p. 1924. reprint ed. 18.95 (*0-674-99183-4*) HUP.
— Lysias. LC 76-29460. reprint ed. 45.00 (*0-404-15315-1*) AMS Pr.
— Lysis, Symposium, Gorgias, Vol. III. (Loeb Classical Library: No. 166). 558p. 1925. text 18.95 (*0-674-99184-2*) HUP.
Lamb, Wallace E. Historic Lake George Illustrated. 3rd ed. LC 47-204. (Lake George Facts & Anecdotes Ser.). (Illus.). 52p. (Orig.). 1984. reprint ed. pap. text 4.25 (*0-317-06216-6*) Lake George Hist.
Lamb, Wally. I Know This Much Is True. 912p. 1999. pap. 16.00 (*0-06-098756-1*) HarpC.
— I Know This Much Is True. 2000. mass mkt. 7.50 (*0-06-109764-0*) HarpC.
— I Know This Much Is True. 2000. write for info. (*0-06-039280-0*) HarpC.
— I Know This Much Is True. LC 98-167337. 912p. 1998. 27.50 (*0-06-039162-6*, ReganBks) HarperTrade.
— I Know This Much Is True. large type ed. LC 98-36935. 949 p. 1998. 29.95 (*1-57490-164-8*) T T Beeler.
***Lamb, Wally.** I Know This Much Is True: Howard,&Ken, Set. abr. ed. 1998. audio 25.00 (*0-694-51940-5*, 695741, Pub. by HarperAudio) Lndmrk Audiobks.
Lamb, Wally. She's Come Undone. 465p. 1993. mass mkt. 9.99 (*0-671-75921-3*, WSP) PB.
— She's Come Undone. 480p. 1996. per. 14.00 (*0-671-00375-5*, WSP) PB.
— She's Come Undone. 1997. 23.00 (*0-671-01473-0*, Pocket Books) PB.
— She's Come Undone. 1998. per. 7.99 (*0-671-02100-1*, Pocket Books) PB.

An Asterisk (*) at the beginning of an entry indicates that the title is appearing for the first time.

— She's Come Undone. large type ed. LC 97-15909. (Compass Press Large Print Book Ser.). 1997. lib. bdg. 27.95 (*1-56895-460-3*, Compass) Wheeler Pub.

Lamb, Walter. Always Begin Where You Are: Themes in Poetry & Song. LC 78-32108. (Illus.). 1979. text 17.22 (*0-07-035921-0*) McGraw.

Lamb, Wesley, jt. auth. see Lamb, Jackie.

Lamb, William, jt. auth. see Schimmels, Cliff.

***Lamb, Yanick R.** Black Star Power: BET Celebrating 20 Years. (Illus.). 2000. 32.00 (*1-58314-191-X*) BET Bks.

Lamba, B. P. Graham Greene: His Mind & Art. LC 87-70632. 150p. 1987. text 13.95 (*0-86590-793-5*) Apt Bks.

Lamba, Juginder, et al, eds. Beyond Frontiers: South Asian Visual Arts. (Illus.). 240p. (Orig.). 1996. pap. 32.99 (*1-85242-539-3*) Serpents Tail.

***Lamba, Krishan G.** Dynamics of Punjabi Suba Movement. LC 98-915215. 1999. write for info. (*81-7629-129-3*) Deep & Deep Pubns.

Lamba, P. S., ed. Impact of Urbanization & Industrialization on Rural Society. (C). 1992. 19.00 (*81-224-0412-X*) S Asia.

Lamba, S. S. & Walker, C. A. Antibiotics & Microbial Transformations. LC 86-29908. 224p. 1987. 128.00 (*0-8493-6408-6*, QR88, CRC Reprint) Franklin.

Lambakis, Steven J. Winston Churchill - Architect of Peace: A Study of Statesmanship & the Origins of the Cold War, 322. LC 92-42674. (Contributions in Political Science Ser.: No. 322). 208p. 1993. 55.00 (*0-313-28823-2*, GM8823, Greenwood Pr) Greenwood.

Lambard, Creede, ed. see Blankenship, Loyd.

Lambard, Neil. Pocket Dictionary of Banjo Chords. 1966. pap. 2.95 (*0-934286-19-1*) Kenyon.

Lambarde, William. William Lambarde & Local Government: His "Ephemeris" & Twenty-Nine Charges to Juries & Commissions. Read, Conyers, ed. (Documents Ser.). 1978. 29.50 (*0-918016-36-3*) Folger Bks.

Lambardi, Francesco, et al. A Neapolitan Festa a Ballo "Delizie Di Posilipo Boscarecce, a Maritime & Selected Instrumental Ensemble Pieces. Jackson, Roland, ed. (Recent Researches in Music of the Baroque Era Ser.: Vol. RRB25). (Illus.). xx, 69p. 1978. pap. 30.00 (*0-89579-093-9*, RRB25) A-R Eds.

Lambdin, Dewey. The French Admiral. 1999. mass mkt. write for info. (*0-449-00359-0*, Crest) Fawcett.

— The French Admiral. 1991. mass mkt. 4.95 (*1-55817-491-5*, Pinncle Kensgtn) Kensgtn Pub Corp.

***Lambdin, Dewey.** The French Admiral. large type ed. LC 99-46549. (G. K. Hall Core Ser.). 1999. 27.95 (*0-7838-8788-4*, G K Hall Lrg Type) Mac Lib Ref.

Lambdin, Dewey. The Gun Ketch: An Alan Lewrie Naval Adventure. 1996. mass mkt. 5.99 (*0-449-22450-3*) Fawcett.

— H.M.S. Cockerel: An Alan Lewrie Naval Adventure. 1997. mass mkt. 5.99 (*0-449-22448-1*) Fawcett.

— H.M.S. Cockerel: An Alan Lewrie Naval Adventure. 1996. text 23.95 (*0-07-036237-8*) McGraw.

— Jester's Fortune: An Alan Lewrie Naval Adventure. LC 98-41800. (Illus.). 384p. 1999. 26.95 (*0-525-94482-6*) NAL.

— Jester's Fortune: An Alan Lewrie Naval Adventure. large type ed. LC 99-32484. (Core Ser.). 1999. pap. 26.95 (*0-7838-8681-0*, G K Hall Lrg Type) Mac Lib Ref.

***Lambdin, Dewey.** King's Captain. (Alan Lewrie Naval Adventure Ser.). 352p. 2000. 23.95 (*0-312-26885-8*, Thomas Dunne) St Martin.

Lambdin, Dewey. The King's Coat. 1998. mass mkt. 5.99 (*0-449-00360-4*, Crest) Fawcett.

— The King's Coat. large type ed. LC 98-46671. 1999. 27.95 (*0-7838-0440-7*, G K Hall Lrg Type) Mac Lib Ref.

— A King's Commander. LC 96-31029. 384p. 1997. pap. 24.95 (*1-55611-504-0*, Pub. by D I Fine) Penguin Putnam.

— A King's Commander. 1998. mass mkt. 5.99 (*0-449-00022-2*, Crest) Fawcett.

— The King's Commission. 1996. mass mkt. 5.99 (*0-449-22452-X*) Fawcett.

— The King's Privateer: An Alan Lewrie Naval Adventure. 1996. mass mkt. write for info. (*0-449-22451-1*, Crest) Fawcett.

Lambdin, Diana V., et al, eds. Emphasis on Assessment: Readings from NCTM's School-Based Journals. LC 96-14938. (Illus.). 152p. 1996. pap. 13.95 (*0-87353-428-X*) NCTM.

Lambdin, Edward D. Beyond Feather or Flesh. (Orig.). (YA). (gr. 8 up). 1997. pap. 8.95 (*0-9643419-1-3*) Wrd Weaver Pub.

— The Cloud Master. 208p. 1994. pap., per. 8.95 (*0-9643419-0-5*) Wrd Weaver Pub.

Lambdin, Laura C. & Lambdin, Robert T. Camelot in the Nineteenth Century: Arthurian Characters in the Poems of Tennyson, Arnold, Morris & Swinburne, 97. LC 99-21707. (Contributions to the Study of World Literature Ser.: Vol. 97). 2000. write for info. (*0-313-31124-2*) Greenwood.

***Lambdin, Laura C. & Lambdin, Robert T.** A Companion to Jane Austen Studies. LC 99-49693. 344p. 2000. lib. bdg. 79.50 (*0-313-30662-1*) Greenwood.

Lambdin, Laura C. & Lambdin, Robert T., eds. Chaucer's Pilgrims: An Historical Guide to the Pilgrims in The Canterbury Tales. LC 95-34160. 416p. 1996. lib. bdg. 85.00 (*0-313-29334-1*, Greenwood Pr) Greenwood.

Lambdin, Laura C., jt. ed. see Lambdin, Robert T.

Lambdin, Laura T. & Lambdin, Robert, eds. Chaucer's Pilgrims: An Historical Guide to the Pilgrims in The Canterbury Tales. 416p. 1999. pap. 29.95 (*0-275-96629-1*, Praeger Pubs) Greenwood.

Lambdin, Robert, jt. ed. see Lambdin, Laura T.

Lambdin, Robert T. & Lambdin, Laura C., eds. Encyclopedia of Medieval Literature. LC 97-13713. 560p. 2000. lib. bdg. 89.50 (*0-313-30054-2*) Greenwood.

Lambdin, Robert T., jt. auth. see Lambdin, Laura C.

Lambdin, Robert T., jt. ed. see Lambdin, Laura C.

Lambdin, Thomas O. An Introduction to Biblical Hebrew. (C). 1985. pap. text 25.00 (*0-684-41322-1*, Scribners Ref) Mac Lib Ref.

— Introduction to Classical Ethiopic (Ge'ez) LC 78-12895. (Harvard Semitic Studies: No. 24). 462p. reprint ed. pap. 143.30 (*0-7837-5409-4*, 204517300005) Bks Demand.

Lambdin, William S., jt. auth. see Bronaugh, Edwin L.

Lambe, Dwight W., Jr., ed. see International Symposium on Anaerobic Bacteria Staf.

Lambe, John. A Briefe Description of the Notorious Life of J. Lambe. LC 76-57394. (English Experience Ser.: No. 811). 1977. reprint ed. lib. bdg. 15.00 (*90-221-0811-2*) Walter J Johnson.

Lambe, Larry A. & Radford, David E. Introduction to the Quantum Yang-Baxter Equation & Quantum Groups: An Algebraic Approach. LC 97-26710. (Mathematics & Its Applications Ser.: No. 423). 320p. 1997. 142.00 (*0-7923-4721-8*) Kluwer Academic.

Lambe, Miriam. A Tipperary Landed Estate: Castle Otway, 1750-1853. (Maynooth Studies in Local History). 64p. 1998. pap. 9.95 (*0-7165-2705-7*) Intl Spec Bk.

Lambe, Philip C. & Hansen, Lawrence A., eds. Design & Performance of Earth Retaining Structures. LC 90-771. 904p. 1990. pap. text 76.00 (*0-87262-761-6*) Am Soc Civil Eng.

Lambe, T. William & Whitman, Robert V. Soil Mechanics. (Geotechnical Engineering Ser.). 576p. (C). 1969. 120.00 (*0-471-51192-7*) Wiley.

Lambeck, Raymond P. Hydraulic Pumps & Motors: Selection & Application for Hydraulic Power Control Systems. (Fluid Power & Control Ser.: Vol. 1). (Illus.). 176p. 1983. text 125.00 (*0-8247-7014-5*) Dekker.

Lambee, Joshua B. What I Saw at the Dance: A Poem to A Friend. Darden, Daniel Y., ed. LC 93-91549. 355p. (Orig.). (C). 1994. pap. 15.95 (*0-9637078-3-3*) HourGlass TX.

Lambeis, Barbara & Ratliff, Susan. Making More Money Retailing: Low Cost Ideas for Successful Merchandising & Boosting Profits from Your Retail Store. 140p. 1994. pap. 10.95 (*0-9624798-8-8*) Mktg Methods Pr.

Lambek, J., jt. auth. see Anglin, W. S.

Lambek, Joachim. Lectures in Rings & Modules. 3rd ed. LC 75-41494. viii, 184p. 1986. 16.95 (*0-8284-2283-4*) Chelsea Pub.

Lambek, Michael. Knowledge & Practice in Mayotte: Local Discourses of Islam, Sorcery, & Spirit Possession. (Anthropological Horizons Ser.: No. 3). 656p. 1993. text 70.00 (*0-8020-2960-4*); pap. text 24.95 (*0-8020-7783-8*) U of Toronto Pr.

Lambek, Michael & Messer, Ellen, eds. Ecology & the Sacred: Engaging the Anthropology of Roy A. Rappaport. (Illus.). 304p. (C). text 49.50 (*0-472-11170-1*, 11170) U of Mich Pr.

Lambek, Michael & Strathern, Andrew, eds. Bodies & Persons: Comparative Perspectives from Africa & Melanesia. 312p. (C). 1998. text 59.95 (*0-521-62194-1*); pap. text 19.95 (*0-521-62737-0*) Cambridge U Pr.

Lambek, Michael, jt. ed. see Antze, Paul.

Lambek, Ruth. A Passion for the Divine. 1979. pap. 5.95 (*0-87516-289-4*) DeVorss.

Lambelet, Philippe, jt. ed. see Keller, Walter.

Lamberg-Karlovsky, C. C. Old World Archaeology: Foundations of Civilization: Readings from Scientific American. LC 72-1961. 260p. 1972. write for info. (*0-7167-0860-4*) W H Freeman.

Lamberg-Karlovsky, C. C., ed. Archaeological Thought in America. (Illus.). 365p. (C). 1991. pap. text 29.95 (*0-521-40643-9*) Cambridge U Pr.

Lamberg-Karlovsky, C. C. & Sabloff, Jeremy A. Ancient Civilizations: The Near East & Mesoamerica. 2nd ed. (Illus.). 406p. (C). 1995. pap. text 28.95 (*0-88133-834-6*) Waveland Pr.

Lamberg-Karlovsky, C. C., ed. see Beale, Thomas W.

Lamberg, Lynne, jt. auth. see Smolensky, Michael.

***Lamberg, Stanford I.** Little Black Book of Dermatology. (Little Black Book Ser.). (Illus.). 300p. 2000. pap. 39.95 (*0-632-04519-1*) Blackwell Sci.

Lambers, Bill. The Battle of Britain. (Illus.). 72p. (YA). (gr. 7-12). 1994. pap. 7.50 (*0-9656520-0-9*) B Lambers.

***Lambers, Bill.** The Battle of Britain. 72p. (YA). (gr. 6-12). 1998. 14.95 (*0-9656520-1-7*) B Lambers.

Lambers, Elke, jt. ed. see Thorne, Brian.

Lambers, H., et al, eds. Fundamental, Ecological & Agricultural Aspects of Nitrogen Fixation. (Developments in Plant & Soil Sciences Ser.). 1986. text 304.50 (*90-247-3258-1*) Kluwer Academic.

Lambers, H. & Van der Plas, L. H., eds. Molecular, Biochemical & Physiological Aspects of Plant Respiration. 635p. 1992. 174.00 (*90-5103-079-7*, Pub. by SPB Acad Pub) Balogh.

Lambers, H., et al. Plant Physiology Ecology. LC 97-33273. (Illus.). 456p. 1998. text 44.95 (*0-387-98326-0*) Spr-Verlag.

Lambers, Hans, et al, eds. Causes & Consequences of Variation in Growth Rate & Productivity of Higher Plants. (Illus.). x, 364p. 1989. 115.00 (*90-5103-033-9*, Pub. by SPB Acad Pub) Balogh.

***Lambers, Vincent.** CPA Exam: An Introduction with Test Taking Tips & Past Exam Questions with Solutions. (Illus.). 2000. pap. 14.95 (*1-892115-42-5*) Lambers CPA Rev.

— CPA Exam Preparation. (Illus.). 1999. pap. 120.00 (*1-892115-22-0*) Lambers CPA Rev.

— CPA Exam Preparation 2000. (Illus.). 2000. pap. 200.00 (*1-892115-41-7*) Lambers CPA Rev.

Lambers, Vincent & DelGaudio, Richard. Auditing Vol. 3: CPA Exam Preparation. rev. ed. 480p. 1999. pap. text 35.00 (*1-892115-20-4*) Lambers CPA Rev.

Lambers, Vincent, et al. Accounting & Reporting Vol. 2: CPA Exam Preparation. 684p. 1999. pap. text 35.00 (*1-892115-19-0*) Lambers CPA Rev.

— Financial Accounting & Reporting Vol. 1: CPA Exam Preparation. rev. ed. 752p. 1999. pap. text 35.00 (*1-892115-21-2*) Lambers CPA Rev.

***Lambers, William.** From War to Peace: The Story of Great Britain & the U. S. (Illus.). 70p. (YA). (gr. 7-12). 1999. pap. 7.50 (*0-9656520-2-5*) B Lambers.

— From War to Peace: The Story of Great Britain & the United States (from the American Revolution, the War of 1812 to the Oregon Treaty) (Illus.). 2000. pap. 15.00 (*0-9656520-4-1*) B Lambers.

Lamberson, L. R., jt. auth. see Kapur, K. C.

Lambersy, Werner. Despite My Growling Heart. 58p. 1990. pap. 8.00 (*0-920717-38-1*) Guernica Editions.

Lambert. Antibiotics & Chemotherapy. 7th ed. 1997. text 140.00 (*0-443-05255-7*, 00202) Church.

Lambert. Banking: Legal Environment. 1993. pap. write for info. (*0-415-05625-X*) Thomson Learn.

Lambert. Book of Dinosaurs. (Reference Library). 204p. 1998. pap. 6.95 (*1-85326-754-6*, 7546WW, Pub. by Wrdsworth Edits) NTC Contemp Pub Co.

***Lambert.** Cheese Lover's Cookbook & Guide. 240p. 2000. 29.50 (*0-684-86318-9*) S&S Trade.

— Curriculum Guide for Programming. 2nd ed. 2001. pap. 12.95 (*0-538-69563-3*) Thomson Learn.

Lambert. Fundamentals of Program Design & Data. (DF - Computer Applications Ser.). 1997. 63.95 (*0-314-20492-X*) S-W Pub.

— Fundamentals of Programming & Problem Solving. LC 97-156734. (DF - Computer Applications Ser.). 1997. 63.95 (*0-314-20493-8*) S-W Pub.

Lambert & Nance, Douglas W. Fundamentals of C++, Understanding Programming & Problem Solving. LC 96-204612. 1996. mass mkt. 16.25 (*0-314-07739-1*) West Pub.

Lambert & Rothschild. Adolescence Transition. (Psychology Ser.). 1972. pap. 11.75 (*0-8185-0040-9*) Brooks-Cole.

Lambert & Schniedman, Rose. Being a Nursing Assistant Pocket Guide. 6th ed. (C). 1991. pap. 12.40 (*0-89303-121-6*, Medical Exam) Appleton & Lange.

Lambert, jt. auth. see Schneider.

Lambert, jt. ed. see Dost.

Lambert, Carol J. Field Trips & Events Made Easy. LC 98-67572. ix, 85p. (Orig.). 1998. pap. 14.95 (*0-9668002-0-6*) Lighthse Inst.

Lambert, S. W. J. Diagnosis & Treatment of Pituitary Insufficiency. 1998. 79.95 (*1-901978-00-1*) Blackwell Sci.

Lambert, Adam. The Gallery Guide: Art & Fine Crafts on Cape Cod, Martha's Vineyard, & Nantucket. Reckford, Laura, ed. & intro. by. (Illus.). 161p. (Orig.). 1996. pap. 14.95 (*0-9622782-5-4*) Cape Cod Life Mag.

Lambert, Agnew & Lambert, Grace. Online System Migration Guide. (LITA Monographs: No. 7). 47p. 1996. pap. 15.00 (*0-8389-7832-0*) ALA.

Lambert, Alan & Scott-Hughes, Brian. Junior Drama Workshop. (Drama Anthologies Ser.). (Illus.). 96p. (Orig.). (YA). 1990. pap. 15.00 (*0-333-43459-5*, Pub. by Macmillan Ed) Players Pr.

Lambert, Alan, jt. auth. see O'Neill, Cecily.

***Lambert, Andrew.** Foundations of Naval History: John Knox Laughton, the Royal Navy & the Historical Profession. (Illus.). 1999. write for info. (*1-86176-057-4*, Chatham Pubg); 55.00 (*1-86176-086-8*, Chatham Pubg) G Duckworth.

— History of Warfare: War at Sea in the Age of Sail. 2000. 29.95 (*0-304-35246-2*, Pub. by Cassell) Sterling.

Lambert, Andrew D., ed. Warship, Vol. IX. LC 78-55455. (Illus.). 288p. 1986. 41.95 (*0-87021-984-7*) Naval Inst Pr.

— Warship, Vol. X. LC 78-55455. (Illus.). 288p. 1987. 41.95 (*0-87021-985-5*) Naval Inst Pr.

Lambert, Andrew D., jt. auth. see Badsey, Stephen.

Lambert, Angela. 1939: The Last Season of Peace. large type ed. 387p. 1990. 10.97 (*0-685-56331-6*, Pub. by ISIS Lrg Prnt); 21.95 (*1-85089-370-5*, Pub. by ISIS Lrg Prnt) Transaction Pubs.

***Lambert, Ann.** Very Heaven. 64p. 2000. pap. 10.95 (*0-921368-92-5*) Blizzard Publ.

Lambert, Anne T. New Reflections on Women: By the Marchioness de Lambert. Hine, Ellen M., tr. from FRE. (Writing about Women Ser.: Vol. 17). 90p. (C). 1995. text 33.95 (*0-8204-2705-5*) P Lang Pubng.

Lambert, Anne W., jt. auth. see Lambert, Walter N.

Lambert, Anthony J. On the Rails Around Eastern Europe: A Comprehensive Guide to Travel by Train. (On the Rails Around . . . Ser.). (Illus.). 352p. (Orig.). 1996. pap. 16.95 (*0-8442-9992-8*, 99982, Passprt Bks) NTC Contemp Pub Co.

***Lambert, Anthony J.** Switzerland: Rail, Road, Lake - The Bradt Travel Guide. 2nd ed. (Illus.). 448p. 2000. pap. 18.95 (*1-84162-014-9*, Pub. by Bradt Pubns) Globe Pequot.

Lambert, Anthony J. Switzerland by Rail. LC 95-11392. (Bradt Rail Guides Ser.). (Illus.). 404p. (Orig.). 1996. pap. 17.95 (*1-56440-701-2*, Pub. by Bradt Pubns) Globe Pequot.

Lambert, Barrie. How Safe Is Safe? Radiation Controversies Explained. (Illus.). 208p. 1990. pap. text 14.95 (*0-04-440347-X*) Routledge.

Lambert, Becky J. Beyond Five in a Row, Vol. 1. (Illus.). 107p. 1997. pap. text 24.95 (*1-888659-05-X*) Five in a Row.

— Beyond Five in a Row, Vol. 2. (Illus.). 183p. 1998. pap. text 24.95 (*1-888659-07-6*) Five in a Row.

— Beyond Five in a Row: Christian Character, Bible Study Supplement, Vol. 1. 22p. 1997. pap. text 9.95 (*1-888659-06-8*) Five in a Row.

— Beyond Five in a Row: Christian Character, Bible Study Supplement, Vol. 2. 19p. 1998. pap. text 9.95 (*1-888659-08-4*) Five in a Row.

***Lambert, Becky Jane.** Beyond Five in a Row, Vol. 3. (Illus.). 264p. 1999. pap. text, teacher ed. 24.95 (*1-888659-09-2*) Five in a Row.

— Beyond Five in a Row Vol. 3: Christian Character, Bible Study Supplement. 18p. 1999. pap. text 9.95 (*1-888659-10-6*) Five in a Row.

— The Five in a Row Cookbook. 150p. 1999. spiral bd. 22.95 (*1-888659-11-4*) Five in a Row.

***Lambert, Bette.** A Farm Wife's Journal. 100p. 1999. pap. 14.95 (*0-9670962-0-0*) Stephen Pubg.

Lambert, Betty. Jennie's Story, 2 bks. in 1. 194p. 1997. pap. 12.95 (*0-88754-462-2*) Theatre Comm.

Lambert, Brian K., ed. Milling, Methods & Machines. LC 82-61032. (Manufacturing Update Ser.). (Illus.). 268p. reprint ed. pap. 83.10 (*0-8357-6483-4*, 203585400097) Bks Demand.

Lambert, Byron C. The Rise of the Anti-Mission Baptists: Sources & Leaders, 1800-1840. Gaustad, Edwin S., ed. LC 79-52573. (Baptist Tradition Ser.). 1980. lib. bdg. 42.95 (*0-405-12441-4*) Ayer.

Lambert, C., jt. ed. see Healey, P.

Lambert, C. J., jt. ed. see Giovannella, C.

Lambert, Camille, Jr. & Freeman, Howard E. The Clinic Habit. 1967. pap. 17.95 (*0-8084-0083-5*) NCUP.

***Lambert, Carol I.** Visiting Ventura County. LC 99-73132. ix, 124p. 1999. pap. 14.95 (*0-9668002-1-4*) Lighthse Inst.

***Lambert, Carol J.** Field Trips & Events Made Easy. 2nd rev. ed. LC 98-67572. ix, 115p. 1999. pap. 14.95 (*0-9668002-2-2*) Lighthse Inst.

Lambert, Carrole, ed. The Empty Cross: Medieval Hopes, Modern Futility in the Theater of Mauriace Masterlink, Paul Claudel, August Strindberg, & George Kaiser. LC 90-34401. (Studies in Comparative Literature). 352p. 1990. reprint ed. 25.00 (*0-8240-0002-1*) Garland.

Lambert, Charles. The Boss. 288p. 1997. pap. 17.95 (*0-575-60221-X*, Pub. by V Gollancz) Trafalgar.

— Pink Pencil. LC 96-95244. 132p. (Orig.). 1997. pap. 7.95 (*1-57502-372-5*, PO1192) Morris Pubng.

Lambert, Charles, tr. see Vernant, Jean-Pierre, ed.

Lambert, Charles E. & Stone, Donald. Orthopaedic Physician's Assistant Techniques. LC 74-77819. (Allied Health Ser.). 1975. pap. 7.05 (*0-672-61388-3*, Bobbs) Macmillan.

Lambert, Charles J. Sweet Waters, a Chilean Farm. LC 75-14091. (Illus.). 212p. 1975. reprint ed. lib. bdg. 59.50 (*0-8371-8201-8*, LASWA, Greenwood Pr) Greenwood.

Lambert, Cindy, ed. see James, Mark.

Lambert, Colin R. You Too Can Heal: Energy Key of the Future. 220p. (Orig.). 1993. pap. text 16.50 (*0-908807-03-1*) Ka Io Prods.

Lambert-Colombda, Lorelei. Keepers of the Central Fire: Issues in Ecology for Indigenous Peoples. LC 97-51179. (Illus.). 320p. 1998. pap. 23.95 (*0-88737-742-4*, 14-7424) Natl League Nurse.

Lambert Colomeda, Lorelei A. Keepers of the Central Fire: Issues in Ecology for Indigenous Peoples. LC 97-51179. 1998. write for info. (*0-7637-0923-9*) Jones & Bartlett.

Lambert, Constant. Music Ho. 1967. 8.95 (*0-8079-0086-9*) October.

— Music Ho! A Study of Music in Decline. (Music Book Index Ser.). 342p. 1992. reprint ed. lib. bdg. 89.00 (*0-7812-9507-6*) Rprt Serv.

Lambert, Craig. Mind over Water: Lessons on Life from the Art of Rowing. LC 98-34450. 160p. 1998. 22.00 (*0-395-85716-3*) HM.

***Lambert, Craig.** Mind over Water: Lessons on Life from the Art of Rowing. 160p. 1999. pap. 12.00 (*0-618-00184-0*, Mariner Bks) HM.

Lambert, D. L., ed. Frontiers of Stellar Evolution. (ASP Conference Series Proceedings: Vol. 20). 626p. 1991. 34.00 (*0-937707-39-2*) Astron Soc Pacific.

Lambert, Dale. The Pacific Northwest: Past, Present & Future. (Illus.). 480p. (YA). (gr. 8-12). 1986. teacher ed. 7.95 (*0-685-10071-5*); teacher ed. 2.95 (*0-939688-18-2*); student ed. 3.95 (*0-939688-17-4*); text 19.95 (*0-939688-14-X*); 9.95 (*0-939688-16-6*) Directed Media.

— Washington: Past & Present LC 98-93610. 188p. 1998. write for info. (*0-939688-70-0*) Directed Media.

Lambert-Dannen, Evelyn. In My Mother's House. (Illus.). 94p. (Orig.). 1996. pap. 5.95 (*0-9654960-0-7*) E Lambert-Dannen.

Lambert, Darwin. Great Basin Drama: The Story of a National Park. (Illus.). 268p. 1991. pap. 12.95 (*0-911797-95-5*) Roberts Rinehart.

— The Undying Past of Shenandoah National Park. 352p. 1989. 29.95 (*0-911797-58-0*); pap. 18.95 (*0-911797-57-2*) Roberts Rinehart.

***Lambert, Dave.** Trouble Times Ten. (KidWitness Tales Ser.). (Illus.). 128p. (J). (gr. 2-5). 2000. pap. 5.99 (*1-56179-883-5*) Bethany Hse.

Lambert, Dave, jt. auth. see Campbell, Ross.

Lambert, Dave, jt. auth. see Davis, Ken.

Lambert, David. Asia. LC 96-40278. (Continents Ser.). 48p. (J). 1997. lib. bdg. 25.69 (*0-8172-4781-5*) Raintree Steck-V.

— Body Language. (Collins Gem Ser.). (GER.). 1996. pap. 8.00 (*0-00-470918-7*) Collins.

— Calcium Signaling Protocols. LC 98-44482. (Methods in Molecular Biology Ser.: Vol. 114). (Illus.). 376p. 1999. 84.50 (*0-89603-597-2*) Humana.

— The Children's Animal Atlas. LC 91-30147. (Children's Atlases Ser.). (Illus.). 96p. (J). (gr. 2-6). 1992. 16.95 (*1-56294-101-1*); pap. 14.95 (*1-56294-720-6*); lib. bdg. 27.40 (*1-56294-167-4*) Millbrook Pr.

An Asterisk (*) at the beginning of an entry indicates that the title is appearing for the first time.

— The Children's Animal Atlas. LC 92-30147. (Illus.). 96p. (J). (gr. 2-6). 1993. pap. 10.95 (*1-56294-716-8*) Millbrook Pr.
— Dictionnaire Francais-Anglais de l'Economie. (ENG & FRE.). 264p. 1975. pap. 49.95 (*0-8288-5857-8*, M63299) Fr & Eur.
— Dinosaur! Build Your Own Model Triceratops from the Inside Out, & Discover a Lost World! (Science Action Bks.). (Illus.). 20p. (J). (gr. 4-7). 1998. 19.95 (*0-7624-0259-8*) Running Pr.
— Dinosaur Data Book. LC 97-47096. 320p. 1998. 8.99 (*0-517-18843-0*) Random Hse Value.
— Fires & Floods. LC 92-8687. (Repairing the Damage Ser.). (Illus.). 48p. (YA). (gr. 6 up). 1992. lib. bdg. 21.00 (*0-02-751350-5*, Mac Bks Young Read) S&S Childrens.
— Forests. LC 89-20311. (Our Planet Ser.). (Illus.). 32p. (J). (gr. 4-6). 1990. pap. 4.95 (*0-8167-1972-1*); lib. bdg. 17.25 (*0-8167-1971-3*) Troll Communs.
— Green Pieces. 160p. 1992. pap. text 18.95 (*0-521-40991-8*) Cambridge U Pr.
— Joy in Suffering: Receiving Your Reward. (Beatitudes Ser.). 64p. 1993. mass mkt. 5.99 (*0-310-59673-4*) Zondervan.
Lambert, David. The Mediterranean Sea. LC 96-31163. (Seas & Oceans Ser.). (Illus.). 48p. (J). (gr. 5-9). 1997. lib. bdg. 24.26 (*0-8172-4512-X*) Raintree Steck-V.
Lambert, David. The Pacific Ocean. LC 96-28228. (Seas & Oceans Ser.). (Illus.). 48p. (J). 1997. lib. bdg. 24.26 (*0-8172-4507-3*) Raintree Steck-V.
— People of the Deserts. LC 98-10915. (Wide World Ser.). 48p. (J). 1999. 25.69 (*0-8172-5063-8*) Raintree Steck-V.
— People of the Grasslands. LC 97-28058. (Wide World Ser.). 48p. (J). 1998. 25.69 (*0-8172-5060-3*) Raintree Steck-V.
— Polar Regions. (Our World Ser.). (Illus.). 48p. (J). (gr. 5-8). 1987. lib. bdg. 12.95 (*0-382-09502-2*) Silver Burdett Pr.
— Seas & Oceans. (Our World Ser.). (Illus.). 48p. (J). (gr. 5-8). 1987. lib. bdg. 12.95 (*0-382-09503-0*) Silver Burdett Pr.
— Showing Mercy: Getting What You Give. (Beatitudes Ser.). 64p. 1993. mass mkt. 5.99 (*0-310-59663-7*) Zondervan.
— Society Pieces. 160p. 1993. pap. text 18.95 (*0-521-40990-X*) Cambridge U Pr.
— Stars & Planets. (New View Ser.). (J). (gr. 4-7). 1995. pap. text 6.95 (*0-8114-6449-0*) Raintree Steck-V.
— The Ultimate Dinosaur Book. LC 93-21885. (Illus.). 192p. 1993. 29.95 (*1-56458-304-X*) DK Pub Inc.
— Weather. LC 89-20304. (Our Planet Ser.). (Illus.). 32p. (J). (gr. 4-6). 1990. pap. 4.95 (*0-8167-1980-2*) Troll Communs.
— Weather. LC 89-20304. (Our Planet Ser.). (Illus.). 32p. (J). (gr. 4-6). 1997. lib. bdg. 17.25 (*0-8167-1979-9*) Troll Communs.
Lambert, David & Balderstone, David. Learning to Teach Geography in the Secondary School. LC 98-56529. 208p. (C). 1999. pap. write for info. (*0-415-15676-9*) Routledge.
***Lambert, David & Diagram Group Staff.** The Field Guide to Early Man. (Illus.). 256p. (YA). (gr. 8-12). 1999. pap. 32.95 (*0-7351-0215-5*) Replica Bks.
Lambert, David & Diagram Group Staff. The Field Guide to Geology. (Illus.). 256p. 1998. 27.95 (*0-8160-3840-6*) Facts on File.
— The Field Guide to Geology. rev. ed. (Illus.). 256p. 1998. pap. 14.95 (*0-8160-3823-6*) Facts on File.
Lambert, David & Kingfisher Books Staff. The Kingfisher Young People's Book of Oceans. LC 96-50971. (Illus.). 96p. (J). (gr. 4-8). 1997. 21.95 (*0-7534-5098-4*, Kingfisher) LKC.
Lambert, David, et al. The Field Guide to Prehistoric Life. LC 84-21237. (Illus.). 256p. reprint ed. pap. 79.40 (*0-8357-4250-4*, 203704000007) Bks Demand.
Lambert, David, tr. see Lavigne, Marie.
Lambert, David M. Successful Mentor-Protege Relationships. 237p. Date not set. ring bd. 124.00 (*1-56726-026-8*, B566) Mgmt Concepts.
Lambert, David M. & Spencer, Hamish G., eds. Speciation & the Recognition Concept: Theory & Application. (Illus.). 528p. 1994. text 65.00 (*0-8018-4740-0*); pap. text 35.00 (*0-8018-4741-9*) Johns Hopkins.
Lambert, David R., ed. see Blacker, Keith.
Lambert, David W. Oswald Chambers. LC 97-4646. (Men of Faith Ser.). 128p. 1997. mass mkt. 4.99 (*1-55661-942-1*) Bethany Hse.
Lambert, Dean M. The Advent Jesse Tree: Devotions for Children Adults to Prepare for the Coming of the Christ Child at Christmas. 96p. 1990. 13.95 (*0-687-00908-1*) Abingdon.
Lambert, Dean W. When the Ripe Pears Fell: The Battle of Richmond, Kentucky. LC 95-14688. (Illus.). 325p. 1996. lib. bdg. 32.50 (*0-9615162-3-2*) Madison Cty KY Hist.
Lambert, Derek. Beau Blackstone. LC 73-175085. 224p. (J). 1973. write for info. (*0-413-44960-2*) Heinemann.
— Beau Blackstone. LC 73-91847. 224p. (J). 1974. write for info. (*0-8128-1670-6*) Madison Bks UPA.
— Blackstone's Fancy. LC 73-177441. 189p. (J). 1973. write for info. (*0-413-44950-5*) Heinemann.
— English Garden Ponds. (Illus.). 64p. 1998. 12.95 (*0-7938-0224-5*, WW058) TFH Pubns.
— Fishkeepers Guide to Water Gardening. (Illus.). 64p. 12.95 (*0-7938-0238-5*, WW072) TFH Pubns.
***Lambert, Derek.** The Killing House. large type ed. 400p. 1999. 31.99 (*0-7089-4111-7*) Ulverscroft.
Lambert, Derek. Rainbowfishes of Australia & Papua New Guinea. 64p. 1998. 6.95 (*0-7938-0376-4*) TFH Pubns.
***Lambert, Derek.** Spanish Lessons: Beginning a New Life in Spain. 240p. 2000. 24.00 (*0-7679-0415-X*) Broadway BDD.
Lambert, Derek. Vendetta. 176p. 1990. 16.95 (*0-8027-1120-0*) Walker & Co.
Lambert, Derek J. Gardener's Guide to Water Gardens. (Illus.). 64p. 1998. 12.95 (*0-7938-0246-6*, WW080) TFH Pubns.
— Identifying Fresh Water Aquarium Fish. (Illus.). 80p. 1997. 7.98 (*0-7858-0867-1*) Bk Sales Inc.
Lambert, Dobbie E. 25th Virginia Cavalry. (Virginia Regimental Histories Ser.). (Illus.). 148p. 1994. 19.95 (*1-56190-072-9*) H E Howard.
Lambert, Douglas M. & Stock, James R. Strategic Logistics Management. 3rd ed. 820p. (C). 1992. text 68.95 (*0-256-08838-1*, Irwn McGrw-H) McGrw-H Hghr Educ.
Lambert, Douglas M., et al. Fundamentals of Logistics Management. LC 97-42279. 1997. text 47.96 (*0-256-14117-7*, Irwn McGrw-H) McGrw-H Hghr Educ.
Lambert, Eddie & Norsworthy, Elaine. Duke Ellington: A Listener's Guide. LC 98-36431. (Studies in Jazz: Vol. 26). 560p. 1998. 95.00 (*0-8108-3161-9*) Scarecrow.
Lambert, Edie. Millie's China. 240p. 1998. pap. 9.95 (*0-939497-48-4*) Promise Pub.
Lambert, Elizabeth. Wings of Desire. 384p. (Orig.). 1989. mass mkt. 3.95 (*0-380-75599-8*, Avon Bks) Morrow Avon.
Lambert, Ellen Z. Placing Sorrow: A Study of the Pastoral Elegy Convention from Theocritus to Milton. LC 76-23154. (Studies in Comparative Literature: No. 60). xxxiv, 231p. 1977. lib. bdg. 37.50 (*0-8078-7060-9*) U of NC Pr.
Lambert, Ellen Zetzel. The Face of Love: Feminism & the Beauty Question. LC 94-37969. 256p. 1999. pap. 16.00 (*0-8070-6501-3*) Beacon Pr.
Lambert, Emolyn. From the Back of My Bible: Timeless Truths for the Soul. LC 99-207824. 1998. pap. text 4.97 (*1-57748-164-X*) Barbour Pub.
Lambert, Erin, jt. auth. see Lambert, Lee R.
Lambert, Ernest. Cowboys & Indians. LC 97-66368. 200p. 1997. pap. 10.00 (*1-884522-00-9*) SW Aspen.
Lambert, F. J., jt. ed. see Antoniou, Ioannis.
Lambert, Frank. Inventing the "Great Awakening" LC 98-26646. (Illus.). 320p. 1999. 35.00 (*0-691-04379-5*, Pub. by Princeton U Pr) Cal Prin Full Svc.
— Pedlar in Divinity: George Whitefield & the Transatlantic Revivals, 1737-1770. LC 93-1345. (Illus.). 264p. 1994. text 32.50 (*0-691-03296-3*, Pub. by Princeton U Pr) Cal Prin Full Svc.
Lambert, Frederick. Letter Forms: 110 Complete Alphabets. 110p. 1972. pap. 6.95 (*0-486-22872-X*) Dover.
Lambert, Gary. Access All Areas: Backstage with the Grateful Dead. (Illus.). 80p. 22.95 (*1-888358-16-5*) Acid Test Prodns.
***Lambert, Gavin.** The Goodby People. 1999. pap. 12.00 (*1-85242-442-7*, Pub. by Serpents Tail) Consort Bk Sales.
— The Goodbye People. 1999. pap. 9.98 (*0-671-77508-1*, Pocket Books) PB.
Lambert, Gavin. Inside Daisy Clover. (Midnight Classics Ser.). 265p. 1996. pap. 11.99 (*1-85242-424-9*) Serpents Tail.
***Lambert, Gavin.** Lindsay Anderson. LC 99-59305. (Illus.). 320p. 2000. 29.95 (*0-679-44598-6*) Knopf.
— On Cukor. Trachtenberg, Robert, ed. (Illus.). 208p. 2000. 50.00 (*0-8478-2297-4*) Rizzoli Intl.
— Running Time. (Midnight Classics Ser.). 524p. 2001. pap. 15.00 (*1-85242-443-5*) Serpents Tail.
Lambert, Gavin. The Slide Area. LC 97-69091. (Midnight Classics Ser.). 229p. (Orig.). 1998. pap. 11.99 (*1-85242-441-9*) Serpents Tail.
Lambert, George H., jt. auth. see Kacew, Sam.
Lambert, Grace, jt. auth. see Lambert, Agnew.
Lambert, H., et al. Dictionnaire Francais de Medicine et de Biologie, Vol. 4. (FRE.). 580p. 1975. 1195.00 (*0-8288-5856-X*, M15420) Fr & Eur.
— Dictionnaire Francais de Medicine et de Biologie Vol. 4: Annexes. (FRE.). 580p. 1975. 325.00 (*0-7859-4432-X*, 2225287767) Fr & Eur.
Lambert, H., ed. see Blake, P.
Lambert, H. E. Kikuyu Social & Political Institutions. LC DT0429.L3. 157p. reprint ed. pap. 48.70 (*0-608-14381-2*, 201941900011) Bks Demand.
Lambert, Hannah E. & Blake, Peter R., eds. Gynaecological Oncology. (Illus.). 248p. 1992. pap. 39.50 (*0-19-262203-X*) OUP.
Lambert, Harold P. & O'Grady, Francis, eds. Antibiotic & Chemotherapy. 6th ed. (Illus.). 561p. 1991. text 149.95 (*0-443-03203-3*) Church.
***Lambert, Howard, photos by.** Classic Fishing Lures & Tackle: An Entertaining History of Collectible Fishing Gear. LC 00-27759. (Illus.). 144p. 2000. 29.95 (*0-89658-379-1*) Voyageur Pr.
Lambert, Hugh K., jt. auth. see Parker, Watson.
Lambert, Isaac E. The Public Accepts: Stories Behind Famous Trade-Marks, Names, & Slogans. LC 75-39256. (Getting & Spending: The Consumer's Dilemma Ser.). (Illus.). 1976. reprint ed. 20.95 (*0-405-08029-8*) Ayer.
Lambert, J. D. Numerical Methods for Ordinary Differential Systems: The Initial Value Problem. LC 90-28513. 304p. 1991. 99.95 (*0-471-92990-5*) Wiley.
Lambert, J. H. Qvod Temptabam. (C). 1982. pap. text 39.00 (*0-900269-08-1*, Pub. by Old Vicarage) St Mut.
***Lambert, Jack.** Atlantic Air War: Sub Hunters vs. U-Boats. (Air Combat Photo History Ser.: Vol. 4). (Illus.). 112p. 1999. pap. 18.95 (*1-58007-015-9*, Pub. by Specialty Pr) Voyageur Pr.
Lambert, Jack. Bombs, Torpedoes & Kamikazes. (Air Combat Photo History Ser.). 1997. pap. 18.95 (*0-933424-82-5*) Specialty Pr.
— Low Level Attack: The Pacific. (Air Combat Photo History Ser.). 1997. pap. 18.95 (*0-933424-83-3*) Specialty Pr.
Lambert, Jame. Porn in America: The Drift Toward Decadence in Our Society. LC 97-74264. 1997. pap. text 11.99 (*1-56384-145-2*) Huntington Hse.
Lambert, James F. Luther's Hymns. LC 83-45646. reprint ed. 34.50 (*0-404-19855-4*) AMS Pr.
Lambert, James F. & Reinhard, Henry J. History of Catasauqua in Lehigh County. (Illus.). 408p. 1997. reprint ed. lib. bdg. 43.00 (*0-8328-6400-5*) Higginson Bk Co.
Lambert, James G. & Perry, C. Michael. Curses, Foiled Again! An Old Fashioned Musical Melodrama. 39p. (Orig.). 1993. pap. 3.50 (*1-57514-217-1*, 0043) Encore Perform Pub.
Lambert, Jane, ed. see Brooks, Brian S. & Pinson, James L.
Lambert, Jane C. Before Five in a Row. (Illus.). 156p. 1997. pap. text 24.95 (*1-888659-04-1*) Five in a Row.
— Five in a Row, Vol. 1. 2nd rev. ed. (Illus.). 159p. 1997. pap. text 19.95 (*1-888659-00-9*) Five in a Row.
— Five in a Row, Vol. 2. 2nd rev. ed. (Illus.). 107p. 1997. pap. text 24.95 (*1-888659-01-7*) Five in a Row.
— Five in a Row, Vol. 3. 2nd rev. ed. (Illus.). 144p. 1997. pap. text 19.95 (*1-888659-02-5*) Five in a Row.
— Five in a Row: Christian Character & Bible Study Supplement, Vol. 1. 2nd rev. ed. 95p. 1997. pap. text 17.95 (*1-888659-03-3*) Five in a Row.
Lambert, Janet. Candy Kane. 20.95 (*0-8488-0125-3*) Amereon Ltd.
— Confusion: By Cupid. 20.95 (*0-8488-0127-X*) Amereon Ltd.
— Don't Cry, Little Girl. 20.95 (*0-8488-0131-8*) Amereon Ltd.
— Just Jennifer. 1976. 20.95 (*0-8488-0126-1*) Amereon Ltd.
— Little Miss Atlas. 20.95 (*0-8488-0129-6*) Amereon Ltd.
— Myself & I. 20.95 (*0-8488-0128-8*) Amereon Ltd.
— Practically Perfect. 20.95 (*0-8488-0130-X*) Amereon Ltd.
— Whoa, Matilda. 183p. Date not set. 19.95 (*0-8488-2351-6*) Amereon Ltd.
Lambert, Janet, et al, eds. Transect Through Time: The Archaeological Landscape of the Shell North Western Ethylene Pipeline. LC 96-164802. (Lancaster Imprint Ser.: No. 1). (Illus.). 1995. pap. 36.00 (*0-901800-74-0*, Pub. by Lancaster U Archaeol) David Brown.
Lambert, Jean. No Change? No Chance! The Politics of Choosing Green. LC 96-166142. 128p. 1998. pap. 16.95 (*1-897766-23-8*, Pub. by Jon Carpenter) Paul & Co Pubs.
Lambert, Jean-Clarence. Los Artistas Cobra. (SPA., Illus.). 1993. write for info. (*0-614-00039-4*); write for info. (*0-614-00145-5*) Elliots Bks.
— Los Artistas Cobra. Vol. 1. (SPA., Illus.). 1993. write for info. (*0-614-00250-8*) Elliots Bks.
— Botero: Sculptures. 1999. 75.00 (*958-9393-64-0*, Pub. by Rizzoli Intl) St Martin.
— Cobra. LC 83-21419. (Illus.). 264p. 1994. 75.00 (*0-89659-416-5*) Abbeville Pr.
— La Imaginacion Material. (SPA., Illus.). 1993. write for info. (*0-614-00040-8*) Elliots Bks.
— La Imaginacion Material. Vol. 2. (SPA., Illus.). 1993. write for info. (*0-614-00146-3*); write for info. (*0-614-00251-6*) Elliots Bks.
— Reino Imaginal, 2 vols. (Grandes Monografias). (SPA., Illus.). 358p. 1993. 225.00 (*84-343-0736-7*) Elliots Bks.
— Sugai. (Grandes Monografias). (SPA., Illus.). 224p. 1993. 175.00 (*84-343-0639-5*) Elliots Bks.
Lambert, Jean-Clarence, jt. ed. see Strahan, Bradley R.
Lambert, Jeanette. African-American Legacies for the 21st Century: A Bibliography of Biographies for Children about Notable African-Americans. 25p. (Orig.). (J). (gr. k-8). 1994. pap. 4.95 (*0-9632736-3-9*) Edit Cetera.
— Black Images in Contemporary Children's Books: An Annotated Bibliography. 20p. (Orig.). 1991. pap. 5.50 (*0-9632736-0-4*) Edit Cetera.
— In First Place: A Bibliography of Books & Materials about Girls Involved in Sports. 25p. (Orig.). (J). (gr. k-9). 1994. pap. 5.95 (*0-9632736-2-0*) Edit Cetera.
— Twenty-First Century African-American Legacies: A Bibliography of Biographies for Children about Notable African-Americans. 25p. (Orig.). (J). (gr. k-8). 1994. pap. 5.95 (*0-9632736-1-2*) Edit Cetera.
Lambert, Jill. Scientific & Technical Journals. LC 85-116142. (Illus.). 191p. reprint ed. pap. 59.30 (*0-7837-5324-1*, 204506300005) Bks Demand.
Lambert, Joan D. Circles of Stone: A Novel. LC 96-30904. 416p. 1997. 23.00 (*0-671-55285-6*) PB.
Lambert, Joan Dahr. Circles of Stone: A Novel. 480p. 1999. mass mkt. 6.99 (*0-671-55286-4*) PB.
Lambert, Joanna, jt. auth. see Myers, Selma.
***Lambert, Jock.** Low Level Attack Vol. 3: The Mediterranean & Europe. (Illus.). 112p. 1998. pap. 18.95 (*1-58007-005-1*) Specialty Pr.
Lambert, Johann H. La Perspective Affranchie. (FRE., Illus.). 208p. 1998. reprint ed. pap. 240.00 (*1-85297-028-6*, Pub. by Archival Facs) St Mut.
Lambert, John. Betrayed Trust: Africans & the State in Colonial Natal. 216p. 1996. pap. 28.00 (*0-86980-909-1*, Pub. by Univ Natal Pr) Intl Spec Bk.
— Solidarity & Survival: A Vision for Europe. 148p. 1994. 72.95 (*1-85628-871-4*, Pub. by Avebry) Ashgate Pub Co.
— 30 Day Turn Around. 144p. 1995. pap. text, per. 16.95 (*0-7872-1490-6*) Kendall-Hunt.
Lambert, John & Hill, David. The Submarine Alliance. LC 86-60258. (Anatomy of the Ship Ser.). (Illus.). 96p. 1986. 39.95 (*0-87021-688-0*) Naval Inst Pr.
Lambert, John & Ross, Al. Allied Coastal Forces of World War II: Vosper MTBs & US ELCOs, Vol. 2. LC 93-87261. (Illus.). 256p. 1994. 47.95 (*1-55750-035-5*) Naval Inst Pr.
Lambert, John, et al. Medicinal Plants: An Expanding Role in Development. LC 96-13421. (World Bank Technical Papers: No. 320). 32p. 1996. pap. 22.00 (*0-8213-3613-4*, 13613) World Bank.
— Medicinal Plants: Rescuing a Global Heritage. LC 96-52234. (Technical Paper Ser.: No. 355). 80p. 1997. pap. 22.00 (*0-8213-3856-0*, 13856) World Bank.
Lambert, John, jt. auth. see Rees, Gareth.
Lambert, John C. The Romance of Missionary Heroism, 1. 1979. pap. 5.99 (*0-88019-103-1*) Schmul Pub Co.
— The Romance of Missionary Heroism, 2. 1979. pap. 5.99 (*0-88019-104-X*) Schmul Pub Co.
Lambert, John R. Crime, Police & Race Relations: A Study in Birmingham. (Illus.). (C). 1970. 12.00 (*0-19-218188-2*) OUP.
***Lambert, John W.** Assault on the Empire Vol. 1: Stemming the Tide of Conquest, 1942-1943. (Illus.). 112p. 2000. pap. 18.95 (*1-58007-024-8*) Specialty Pr.
— Assault on the Empire Vol. 2: Return to the Philippines, 1944. (Illus.). 112p. 2000. pap. 18.95 (*1-58007-033-7*) Specialty Pr.
Lambert, John W. The Pineapple Air Force: Pearl Harbor to Tokyo. LC 90-60558. (Illus.). 220p. (C). 1990. 34.95 (*0-9625860-0-5*) Specialty Pr.
— Sortie: A Bibliography of Combat Aviation Unit Histories of World War II. 48p. (C). 1993. pap. 10.95 (*0-9625860-6-4*) Specialty Pr.
Lambert, John W. & Mullins, John D., eds. An Escort of P-38s: The 1st Fighter Group in World War II. LC 94-65588. (Illus.). 192p. (C). 1995. 32.95 (*1-883809-03-7*) Specialty Pr.
Lambert, John W., ed. see Hagedorn, Dan.
Lambert, John W., ed. see MacGlashing, John W.
Lambert, John William. The Long Campaign: History of the Fifteenth Fighter Group World War II. 1982. 45.00 (*0-89745-032-9*) Beachcomber Bks.
Lambert, Jonamay & Myers, Selma. Activities for Diversity Training. 1994. ring bd. 139.95 (*0-87425-980-0*) HRD Press.
Lambert, Jonamay, jt. auth. see Myers, Selma.
***Lambert, Jonathan.** Colors. (Picture Magic Ser.). (Illus.). 12p. (J). (ps-1). 2000. 6.95 (*0-439-11206-0*, Cartwheel) Scholastic Inc.
Lambert, Jonathan. Twelve Days of Christmas. (J). (ps-3). 1992. pap. 12.00 (*0-671-78396-3*) S&S Bks Yung.
***Lambert, Jonathan.** Weather. (Picture Magic Ser.). (Illus.). 12p. (J). (ps-1). 2000. 6.95 (*0-439-11207-9*, Cartwheel) Scholastic Inc.
Lambert, Jonathan, jt. auth. see Faulkner, Keith.
Lambert, Joseph B. Physical Organic Chemistry Through Solved Problems. 1978. pap. text 26.95 (*0-8162-4921-0*) Holden-Day.
— Traces of the Past: Unraveling the Secrets of Archaeology Through Chemistry. 336p. 1998. pap. text 18.00 (*0-7382-0027-1*) Perseus Pubng.
Lambert, Joseph B., ed. Archaeological Chemistry, Vol. III. LC 83-15736. (Advances in Chemistry Ser.: No. 205). 487p. 1983. lib. bdg. 89.95 (*0-8412-0767-4*) Am Chemical.
— Archaeological Chemistry III. LC 83-15736. (Advances in Chemistry Ser.: Vol. 205). 500p. 1984. reprint ed. pap. 155.00 (*0-608-03501-7*, 206422000008) Bks Demand.
Lambert, Joseph B. & Grupe, Gisela, eds. Prehistoric Human Bone: Archaeology at the Molecular Level. LC 93-21141. 1993. 174.95 (*0-387-55393-2*) Spr-Verlag.
Lambert, Joseph B. & Riddell, Frank G., eds. The Multinuclear Approach to NMR Spectroscopy. 1983. text 247.50 (*90-277-1582-3*) Kluwer Academic.
Lambert, Joseph B. & Takeuchi, Yoshito. Cyclic Organonitrogen Stereodynamics. (Methods in Stereochemical Analysis Ser.). 304p. 1991. text 125.00 (*0-89573-773-6*, Wiley-VCH) Wiley.
Lambert, Joseph B. & Takeuchi, Yoshito, eds. Acyclic Organonitrogen Stereodynamics. (Methods in Stereochemical Analysis Ser.). 304p. 1991. text 125.00 (*1-56081-555-8*, Wiley-VCH) Wiley.
— Organonitrogen Stereodynamics, 2 vols., Set, Pts. I & II. (Methods in Stereochemical Analysis Ser.). 692p. 1992. text 195.00 (*1-56081-556-6*, Wiley-VCH) Wiley.
Lambert, Joseph B., et al. Organic Structural Spectroscopy. LC 97-40522. 568p. (C). 1997. 94.67 (*0-13-258690-8*) P-H.
Lambert, Joseph C., tr. see Giraud, Marcel.
Lambert, Joseph J., ed. Terrorism & Hostages in International Law: A Commentary on the Hostages Convention 1979. 454p. (C). 1990. 220.00 (*0-949009-46-6*, Pub. by Grotius Pubns Ltd) St Mut.
Lambert, Judith & Peterson, Jane. From Course to Course: A Beginner's Guide to College Writing. LC 87-17290. (Illus.). 523p. reprint ed. pap. 162.20 (*0-7837-4744-6*, 204455300004) Bks Demand.
Lambert, Julien, jt. auth. see Dougherty, Lisa.
Lambert, Karel. The Logical Way of Doing Things. LC 69-15450. 338p. reprint ed. pap. 104.80 (*0-608-30820-X*, 201318400086) Bks Demand.
Lambert, Karel, ed. Philosophical Problems in Logic: Some Recent Developments. (Synthese Library: No. 29). 183p. 1970. text 94.00 (*90-277-0079-6*, D Reidel) Kluwer Academic.
Lambert, Karel & Brittan, Gordon G., Jr. An Introduction to the Philosophy of Science. rev. ed. xviii, 173p. 1987. pap. text 15.00 (*0-924922-10-9*) Ridgeview.
— An Introduction to the Philosophy of Science. 4th rev. ed. xviii, 173p. 1987. lib. bdg. 33.00 (*0-924922-60-5*) Ridgeview.
Lambert, Karel & Ulrih, William. The Nature of Argument. 282p. (C). 1988. reprint ed. pap. text 24.00 (*0-8191-6747-9*) U Pr of Amer.

L

L

Lambert, Kathy K. Martin Luther King, Jr. Civil Rights Leader. (Junior Black Americans of Achievement Ser.). (Illus.). 76p. (J). (gr. 3-6). 1992. pap. 4.95 (0-7910-1954-3) Chelsea Hse.

— Martin Luther King, Jr. Civil Rights Leader. LC 91-34986. (Junior Black Americans of Achievement Ser.). (Illus.). 76p. (J). (gr. 5-7). 1993. lib. bdg. 15.95 (0-7910-1759-1) Chelsea Hse.

Lambert, Kelly. Zonefully Easy: The Sane Way to Better Health. 1999. pap. 14.95 (0-9653846-7-5) McGregor Pub.

Lambert, Kenneth. Java. LC 98-33484. (C). 1998. pap. 58.95 (0-534-95116-3) PWS Pubs.

— Java: Complete Course of Programming & Problem Solving. LC 98-35332. (Computer Applications Ser.). 1998. pap. 51.95 (0-538-68707-X); pap., wbk. ed. 12.95 (0-538-68710-X) S-W Pub.

Lambert, Kenneth & Nance, Douglas W. Understanding Programming & Problem Solving with C++ rev. ed. 558p. pap. 64.95 (0-534-95203-8, Pub. by Brooks-Cole) Thomson Learn.

***Lambert, Kenneth & Osborne Martin** Java: A Framework for Program Design & Data Structures. LC 99-58171. 2000. pap. 58.95 (0-534-36691-0) Brooks-Cole.

Lambert, Kenneth & Osborne, Martin. Java: Complete Course in Programming & Problem Solving. LC 98-35332. 1999. pap. 51.95 (0-538-68711-8) Sth-Wstrn College.

Lambert, Kenneth A. & Nance, Douglas W. Understanding Programming & Problem Solving with C++ LC 95-34794. 650p. (C). 1996. pap. text 48.00 (0-314-06743-4) West Pub.

Lambert, Kenneth A. & Naps, Thomas L. Program Design & Data Structures with C++ LC 95-45571. 550p. (C). 1996. mass mkt. 67.95 (0-314-07340-X) West Pub.

Lambert, Kenneth A., et al. Introduction to Computer Science with C++ LC 95-43868. 950p. (C). 1996. text 57.50 (0-314-07339-6) West Pub.

***Lambert, Kenneth Alfred, et al.** Introduction to Computer Science with C++ 2nd ed. LC 99-26729. 2000. 81.95 (0-534-36893-X) Brooks-Cole.

Lambert, Kirby, ed. see Russell, Charles M.

Lambert, L. La Proteccion Espiritual.Tr. of Spiritual Protection. (SPA.). 93p. 1995. 3.50 (1-56063-432-4, 550016) Editorial Unilit.

Lambert, L., jt. auth. see Rowe, J.

***Lambert, L. Gary.** Pratique, Pratique: Manuel de Conversation Guidee. 256p. 1999. pap. 34.50 (0-7618-1468-X) U Pr of Amer.

Lambert, L. Gary, jt. ed. see Hancock, Ralph C.

***Lambert-Lagace, Louise.** Feeding Your Baby the Healthiest Foods: From Breast Milk to Table Foods. 304p. 2000. pap. 24.95 (0-7737-6112-8) Stoddart Publ.

Lambert-Lagace, Louise. The Nutrition Challenge for Women. 192p. 1990. pap. 12.95 (0-923521-06-2) Bull Pub.

Lambert, Larry & Carpenter, Dave. Sportoons. Silliman, Stan, ed. (Illus.). 88p. (Orig.). 1997. pap. text 6.50 (1-886682-03-8) Comedy Emp Pr.

Lambert, Laurie J., jt. auth. see Harper, Andrew C.

Lambert, Lee. Basic Library of the World's Greatest Music. (Illus.). (YA). (gr. 7 up). 1988. pap. text 39.00 (0-9621630-1-5) L Lambert.

— Basic Library of the World's Greatest Music. 2nd rev. ed. 384p. (J). (gr. k-12) 1995. reprint ed. 39.00 (0-9621630-3-1) L Lambert.

— Basic Library of the World's Greatest Music: Musical Learning System. (Illus.). 356p. (Orig.). 1990. pap., teacher ed. 19.00 (0-9621630-0-7) L Lambert.

— Basic Library of the World's Greatest Music: Text. 296p. 1996. text 29.00 (0-9621630-4-X) L Lambert.

— Basic Video Library of the World's Greatest Music (Lectures) Vol. I: Video-Lecture Series. 56p. (Orig.). 1996. pap. 9.50 (0-9621630-8-2) L Lambert.

Lambert, Lee R. & Lambert, Erin. The Other Kuwait: An American Father & Daughter's Personal Impressions. Berry, Connie & Wampler, Nan, eds. (Illus.). 250p. (Orig.). (C). 1992. pap. text 16.95 (0-9626397-1-0) L R Lambert & Assocs.

***Lambert, Lee R. & Lambert, Erin.** Project Management: The CommonSense Approach: Using Earned Value to Balance the Triple Constraint. 2000. pap. 24.99 (0-9626397-8-8) L R Lambert & Assocs.

Lambert, Leo, et al, eds. University Teaching: A Guide for Graduate Students. 200p. 1995. pap. 17.95 (0-8156-2637-1) Syracuse U Pr.

Lambert, Leo & Tice, Stacey L., eds. Preparing Graduate Students to Teach: A Guide to Programs That Improve Undergraduate Education & Develop Tomorrow's Faculty. 150p. 1993. pap. 22.00 (1-56377-029-6, TI9201) Am Assn Higher Ed.

Lambert, Leo M., jt. auth. see Wilbur, Franklin P.

Lambert, Leo P. Soldering for Electronic Assemblies. (Manufacturing Engineering & Materials Processing Ser.: Vol. 25). (Illus.). 368p. 1987. text 145.00 (0-8247-7681-X) Dekker.

Lambert, Linda. Building Leadership Capacity in Schools. LC 98-40095. 135p. 1998. pap. 13.95 (0-87120-307-3, 198058) ASCD.

— The Constructivist Leader. 240p. (C). 1995. text 48.00 (0-8077-3463-2); pap. text 22.95 (0-8077-3462-4) Tchrs Coll.

Lambert, Linda, et al. Who Will Save Our Schools? Teachers As Constructivist Leaders. (Illus.). 224p. 1996. 61.95 (0-8039-6462-5) Corwin Pr.

Lambert, Lisa A. The Leakeys. LC 92-46046. (Pioneers Ser.). 112p. (J). 1993. lib. bdg. 25.27 (0-86625-492-7) Rourke Pubns.

Lambert, Lynda, jt. auth. see Graham, Bob.

Lambert, Lyndsay, jt. auth. see Lambert, Timothy.

Lambert, M. W. & Laval, J., eds. DNA Repair Mechanisms & Their Biological Implications in Mammalian Cell. LC 89-72122. (NATO ASI Series A, Life Sciences: Vol. 182). (Illus.). 694p. 1990. 149.50 (0-306-43411-3, Plenum Trade) Perseus Pubng.

Lambert, Malcolm. The Cathars. (Illus.). 368p. 1998. 68.95 (0-631-14343-2); pap. 31.95 (0-631-20959-X) Blackwell Pubs.

— Franciscan Poverty. LC 98-87936. (History Ser.). 365p. 1996. pap. 25.00 (1-57659-001-1) Franciscan Inst.

— Medieval Heresy: Popular Movements from the Gregorian Reform to the Reformation. rev. ed. 400p. 1992. reprint ed. pap. 30.95 (0-631-17432-X) Blackwell Pubs.

Lambert, marc, ed. see Oksenberg, Michel.

Lambert, Margaret. English Popular Art. (C). 1989. text 35.00 (0-85036-372-1, Pub. by MRLN) Paul & Co Pubs.

***Lambert, Marilyn.** Franny & Roxxy. (J). (gr. k-3). 1999. pap. 6.95 (0-533-12820-X) Vantage.

Lambert, Marjie. Bread Machine Book. 128p. 1996. 12.98 (0-7858-0577-X) Bk Sales Inc.

— Cooking of the Pacific Rim. 1995. 17.98 (0-7858-0244-4) Bk Sales Inc.

— Microwave Craft Magic. 112p. 1996. write for info. (1-57215-178-1) World Pubns.

— The New Bread Machine Book. (Illus.). 128p. 1999. 12.99 (0-7858-1134-6) Bk Sales Inc.

***Lambert, Marjie.** Ocean Pacific: Fresh Modern Flavors from North America's Pacific Coast. (Illus.). 160p. 2000. 29.95 (962-593-815-X) Tuttle Pubng.

Lambert, Marjie. Salsa Cooking. 1994. 17.98 (0-7858-0023-9) Bk Sales Inc.

— Southern Cooking. 144p. 1994. 17.98 (0-7858-0025-5) Bk Sales Inc.

Lambert, Mark. Brain & Nervous System. (How Our Bodies Work Ser.). (Illus.). 48p. (J). (gr. 5-8). 1988. lib. bdg. 12.95 (0-382-09703-3) Silver Burdett Pr.

— The Compleat Cardiologist: Heart Attack Handbook. 200p. 1997. pap. 21.95 (0-9641170-0-2) Gosport Pubng.

— Dickens & the Suspended Quotation. LC 80-22072. 200p. reprint ed. pap. 62.00 (0-8357-3751-9, 203647700003) Bks Demand.

— Lungs & Breathing. (How Our Bodies Work Ser.). (Illus.). 48p. (J). (gr. 5-8). 1988. lib. bdg. 12.95 (0-382-09701-7) Silver Burdett Pr.

— Malory: Style & Vision in La Morte d'Arthur. LC 74-29727. (Yale Studies in English: No. 186). 241p. reprint ed. pap. 74.80 (0-8357-8213-1, 203379300087) Bks Demand.

— Plastics. (Spotlight on Resources Ser.). (Illus.). 48p. (J). (gr. 5 up). 1985. 12.95 (0-685-58326-0) Rourke Corp.

— Reptiles. LC 97-18505. (Pockets Ser.). 128p. (J). (gr. 3 up). 1997. 6.95 (0-7894-2046-5) DK Pub Inc.

Lambert, Martha. But I Won't Get Lost. (Illus.). 32p. (J). (ps-2). 15.95 (0-06-028960-0); 15.89 (0-06-028961-9); 5.95 (0-06-443679-9) HarpC.

Lambert, Martha L., jt. auth. see Schlessinger, Laura C.

***Lambert, Mary.** Introduction to Reiki: Healing Energy for Mind, Body & Spirit. 2000. pap. 12.95 (1-85585-747-2) Collins & Br.

Lambert, Mary, jt. auth. see Skinner, Stephen.

Lambert, Mary H., ed. & illus. see Lambert, W. L.

Lambert, Matthew. Joey's Birthday Wish. LC 94-40451. (Publish-a-Book Ser.). (Illus.). (J). (gr. 1-6). 1995. lib. bdg. 22.83 (0-8114-7273-6) Raintree Steck-V.

Lambert, Maureen K. The Theory & Practice of Marriage at the Premier Institute of Marriage. (Illus.). 72p. 1999. pap. 12.00 (0-8059-3558-4) Dorrance.

Lambert, Merryl. Dolphin Sponsorship Kit. (Friends of the Ocean Ser.). 1994. 19.95 (0-9641742-5-1) Pequot Pubng.

— Grizzly Sponsorship Kit. 1995. 19.95 (0-9641742-9-4) Pequot Pubng.

— Rain Forest Preservation Kit. (Friends of the Forest Ser.). 1991. 19.95 (0-9641742-6-X) Pequot Pubng.

— Siberian Tiger Sponsorship Kit. 1995. 19.95 (0-9641742-7-8) Pequot Pubng.

— Wetlands Preservation Kit. 2nd ed. 1992. 19.95 (0-614-06229-2) Pequot Pubng.

— Whale Adoption Kit. (Friends of the Ocean Ser.). 1992. 19.95 (0-9641742-3-5) Pequot Pubng.

— Wild Mustang Sponsorship Kit. pap. 19.95 (1-886738-01-7) Pequot Pubng.

— Wolf Sponsorship Kit. 1993. 19.95 (0-9641742-4-3) Pequot Pubng.

Lambert, Michael E., et al, eds. Eukaryotic Transposable Elements As Mutagenic Agents. (Banbury Reports: No. 30). (Illus.). 362p. 1988. text 77.00 (0-87969-230-8) Cold Spring Harbor.

Lambert, Michael J. The Effects of Psychotherapy, Vol. II. (Psychotherapy Research Review Ser.). 288p. 1982. 42.95 (0-89885-099-1, Kluwer Acad Hman Sci) Kluwer Academic.

Lambert, Mike & Pearson, Alan. Instant Guide to Birds. LC 98-29074. (Instant Guide Ser.). (Illus.). 128p. 1988. 4.99 (0-517-46891-3) Random Hse Value.

Lambert, Miles. Fashion in Photographs, 1860-1880. (Illus.). 144p. (C). 1992. text 82.50 (0-7134-6392-9) B&N Imports.

Lambert, N., et al. De Ferri Metallographia Vol. 4: Recent Examination Methods in Metallography - the Metallography of Welds. 448p. 1983. 395.00 (3-514-00214-2, Pub. by Woodhead Pubng) Am Educ Systs.

Lambert, Nadine M. & McCombs, Barbara L., eds. How Students Learn: Reforming Schools Through Learner-Centered Education. (Illus.). 540p. 1997. pap. text 29.95 (1-55798-464-6) Am Psychol.

Lambert, Neal. George Frederick Ruxton. LC 74-1974. (Western Writers Ser.: No. 15). 44p. 1974. pap. 4.95 (0-88430-014-5) Boise St U W Writ Ser.

Lambert, Neal E., ed. Literature of Belief. (Monograph Ser.: Vol. 5). 1981. 4.95 (0-88494-409-3) Bookcraft Inc.

Lambert, Nevin & Patel, Manish. PC Week Microsoft Windows NT Security: System Administrator's Guide. 416p. 1997. 39.99 (1-56276-457-8, Ziff-Davis Pr) Que.

Lambert, Nicholas. Sir John Fisher's Naval Revolution. LC 99-6012. (Illus.). 7p. 1999. text 39.95 (1-57003-277-7) U of SC Pr.

Lambert, Norma K. Cumulative Indices to Military Affairs 1937-1969. (Libraries Bibliography: No. 6). 1979. pap. 4.50 (0-686-20808-0) KSU.

Lambert, O. C. Catholicism Against Itself. 127p. (Orig.). 1991. pap. 2.50 (0-933672-94-2, C-2102) Star Bible.

— Catholicism Against Itself, Vol. 1. (Orig.). 1956. pap. 9.95 (0-89315-005-3) Lambert Bk.

— Catholicism Against Itself, Vol. 2. (Orig.). 1965. 12.95 (0-89315-006-1) Lambert Bk.

— Russellism Unveiled. 1940. pap. 3.50 (0-88027-090-X) Firm Foun Pub.

Lambert Ortiz, Elisabeth. The Encyclopedia of Herbs, Spices & Flavorings. LC 92-6537. (Illus.). 288p. 1992. 34.95 (1-56458-065-2) DK Pub Inc.

Lambert, P. Blud. Bathroom Humor: Passing Wind, Vol. 1. LC 88-81771. 200p. (Orig.). 1988. pap. 9.99 (0-317-91202-X) Fulcort Pr.

Lambert, P. H., et al, eds. From Antigen Presentation to Immunity & Allergy: Abstracts. (Journal: International Archives of Allergy & Applied Immunology: Vol. 83, Suppl. 1). iv, 44p. 1987. pap. 19.25 (3-8055-4602-5) S Karger.

Lambert, Page. In Search of Kinship: Modern Pioneering on the Western Landscape. 272p. 1996. 23.95 (1-55591-266-4) Fulcrum Pub.

— Shifting Stars. 1999. mass mkt. 5.99 (0-8125-7149-5, Pub. by Tor Bks) St Martin.

Lambert, Patricia. Bioarchaeological Studies of Life in the Age of Agriculture: A View from the Southeast. 294p. 2000. pap. text 29.95 (0-8173-1007-X) U of Ala Pr.

— False Witness: The Real Story of Jim Garrison's Investigation & Oliver Stone's Film, "JFK" (Illus.). 400p. 1999. 24.95 (0-87131-879-2, Pub. by M Evans) Natl Bk Netwk.

***Lambert, Patricia.** False Witness: The Real Story of Jim Garrison's Investigation & Oliver Stone's Film JFK. 400p. 2000. pap. 16.95 (0-87131-920-9) M Evans.

Lambert, Patricia, et al. Color & Fiber. LC 86-61295. (Illus.). 255p. 1990. 49.50 (0-88740-065-5) Schiffer.

***Lambert, Paul, et al.** Washington County: A Centennial History. Campbell, Gini Moore, ed. LC 98-68081. (Oklahoma County History Ser.). 424p. 1999. 39.95 (1-885596-10-3) OK Heritage.

Lambert, Paul F. & Franks, Kenny A., eds. Voices from the Oil Fields. LC 84-7327. (Illus.). 288p. 1984. 26.95 (0-8061-1799-0) U of Okla Pr.

***Lambert, Paul F., et al.** Historic Oklahoma: An Illustrated History. Campbell, Gini Moore, ed. LC 99-80130. (Oklahoma Horizons Ser.). (Illus.). 384p. (YA). 2000. 49.95 (1-893619-04-4) OK Heritage.

Lambert, Paul F., jt. auth. see Franks, Kenny A.

Lambert, Paul H., et al, eds. Recent Advances in Systemic Lupus Erythematosus. 1984. text 104.00 (0-12-434620-0) Acad Pr.

Lambert, Paul R., jt. auth. see Canalis, Rinaldo F.

Lambert, Paulette, jt. auth. see Pietruszka, Marvin.

Lambert, Paulette L. Evening: An Appalachian Lullaby. LC 95-69276. (Illus.). 32p. (J). (ps-3). 1995. 15.95 (1-57098-012-8) Roberts Rinehart.

Lambert, Peter J. The Distribution & Redistribution of Income: A Mathematical Analysis. 2nd ed. LC 93-17870. 1993. text 27.95 (0-7190-4059-0, Pub. by Manchester Univ Pr) St Martin.

Lambert, Philip. The Music of Charles Ives. LC 96-38979. (Composers of the Twentieth Century Ser.). 256p. 1997. 35.00 (0-300-06522-1) Yale U Pr.

— Sea Cucumbers of British Columbia: Including Puget Sound & Southern Alaska. LC 98-124713. (Illus.). 192p. 1997. pap. 24.95 (0-7748-0607-9) U of Wash Pr.

Lambert, Philip, ed. Ives Studies. LC 97-7588. (Illus.). 312p. (C). 1998. text 64.95 (0-521-58277-6) Cambridge U Pr.

Lambert, Phyllis, ed. Viewing Olmsted: Photographs by Robert Burley, Lee Friedlander, & Geoffrey James. (Illus.). 119p. 1997. pap. text 26.50 (0-262-62116-9) MIT Pr.

Lambert, Phyllis & Stewart, Alan, eds. Opening the Gates of Eighteenth-Century Montreal. (Centre Canadien d'Architecture Ser.). (Illus.). 96p. (Orig.). 1992. pap. text 15.95 (0-262-62086-3) MIT Pr.

Lambert, Phyllis H. Turning Every Stone: Autism with Love - Reality Therapy. (Illus.). 96p. 1990. pap., per. 18.00 (0-9624737-4-X) Old Barn Entrprs.

Lambert, Pierre. Dictionnaire Pratique des Mathematiques Vol. 1: Analyse. (FRE.). 284p. 1989. pap. 22.95 (0-7859-7793-7, 2218079429) Fr & Eur.

— Dictionnaire Pratique des Mathematiques Vol. 2: Algebre. (FRE.). 285p. 1990. pap. 22.95 (0-7859-7786-4, 2218025760) Fr & Eur.

— Mickey Mouse. deluxe ed. LC 98-26026. (Illus.). 240p. (J). 1998. 150.00 (0-7868-6453-2, Pub. by Hyperion) Time Warner.

— Pinocchio. LC 98-146716. (Illus.). 236p. 1997. 150.00 (0-7868-6247-5, Pub. by Hyperion) Time Warner.

Lambert, R. Aeronautic Dictionary English-French/French-English. Orig. Title: Dictionnaire Technique de l'Aeronautique. 336p. 1996. pap. 59.00 (2-85428-422-4, Pub. by Cepadues) IBD Ltd.

— Dictionnaire Technique Aeronautique. 3rd ed. (FRE.). 336p. 1996. 69.95 (0-320-00649-2) Fr & Eur.

Lambert, R. M., jt. ed. see Thomas, J. M.

Lambert, Rae. Mungo Goes East: A Window Board Book. 12p. (J). (ps). 1996. bds. 4.99 (1-900207-15-X, Pub. by Little Wizard) Assoc Pubs Grp.

— Mungo Goes North: A Window Board Book. 12p. (J). (ps). 1996. bds. 4.99 (1-900207-05-2, Pub. by Little Wizard) Assoc Pubs Grp.

— Mungo Goes South: A Window Board Book. 12p. (J). (ps). 1996. bds. 4.99 (1-900207-10-9, Pub. by Little Wizard) Assoc Pubs Grp.

— Mungo Goes West: A Window Board Book. 12p. (J). (ps). 1996. bds. 4.99 (1-900207-20-6, Pub. by Little Wizard) Assoc Pubs Grp.

— Mungo's Hedgerow Tale: A Stopframe Book. 12p. (J). (ps). 1996. 7.99 (1-900207-35-4, Pub. by Little Wizard) Assoc Pubs Grp.

— Mungo's Rainforest Tale: A Stopframe Book. 12p. (J). (ps). 1996. 7.99 (1-900207-40-0, Pub. by Little Wizard) Assoc Pubs Grp.

— Mungo's Riverbank Tale: A Stopframe Book. 12p. (J). (ps). 1996. 7.99 (1-900207-25-7, Pub. by Little Wizard) Assoc Pubs Grp.

— Mungo's Woodland Tale: A Stopframe Book. 12p. (J). (ps). 1996. 7.99 (1-900207-30-3, Pub. by Little Wizard) Assoc Pubs Grp.

— Mungo's World Tour. (Comes to Life Bks.). 16p. (J). (ps-2). 1995. write for info. (1-57234-058-4) YES Ent.

— Mungo's World Tour: The Exciting Adventures of Munog, Lemmy & Albert Ross. 32p. (J). (ps-3). 1996. 5.99 (1-900207-00-1, Pub. by Little Wizard) Assoc Pubs Grp.

Lambert, Rebecca T., jt. auth. see McComish, Charles D.

Lambert, Rene. Aeronautical Dictionary, French-English/English-French. (ENG & FRE.). 1996. 95.00 (0-7859-9717-2) Fr & Eur.

— French-English, English-French Technical Aeronautics Dictionary. (ENG & FRE.). 304p. 1991. 95.00 (0-8288-6957-X, 2854281640) Fr & Eur.

Lambert, Richard, et al. Once upon a Time: The Storytelling Card Game. 1995. 18.95 (1-887801-00-6, Atlas Games) Trident MN.

Lambert, Richard, ed. see Calligaro, Keith D., et al.

Lambert, Richard, ed. see Rosenbaum, Arthur L. & Santiago, Alvina P.

Lambert, Richard D., ed. America's Most Challenging Objectives. LC 76-160739. (Annals Ser.: 396). 1971. 28.00 (0-87761-140-8); pap. 18.00 (0-87761-139-4) Am Acad Pol Soc Sci.

— China in the World Today. LC 72-78295. (Annals Ser.: 402). 300p. 1972. 28.00 (0-685-00180-6); pap. 18.00 (0-87761-150-5) Am Acad Pol Soc Sci.

— Foreign Language Instruction: A National Agenda. (Annals Ser.: Vol. 490). 1987. 26.00 (0-8039-2931-5); pap. 17.00 (0-8039-2932-3) Sage.

— Foreign Language Policy: An Agenda for Change. LC 93-85875. (Annals of the American Academy of Political & Social Science Ser.: Vol. 532). 1994. 28.00 (0-8039-5586-3); pap. 18.00 (0-8039-5587-1) Am Acad Pol Soc Sci.

— New Directions in International Education. LC 80-65243. (Annals of the American Academy of Political & Social Science Ser.: No. 449). 1980. pap. text 18.00 (0-87761-251-X) Am Acad Pol Soc Sci.

Lambert, Richard d., et al, eds. Language Planning Around the World: Contexts & Systemic Change. LC 94-5826. (National Foreign Language Center Monographs). 1994. 10.00 (1-880671-03-4) NFLC Pubns.

Lambert, Richard D. & Heston, Alan W., eds. The Annals Ninetieth Anniversary Index: 1976-1980. 192p. 1981. 26.00 (0-8039-1762-7); pap. 17.00 (0-8039-1763-5) Sage.

***Lambert, Richard D. & Shohamy, Elana, eds.** Language Policy & Pedagogy: Essays in Honor of A. Ronald Walton. LC 99-58745. xii, 270p. 2000. 65.00 (1-55619-763-2, JB8007) J Benjamins Pubng Co.

Lambert, Richard D., et al. The Transformation of an Indian Labor Market: The Case of Pune. LC 86-26900. (University of Pennsylvania Studies on South Asia: No. 3). ix, 249p. 1986. 65.00 (0-915027-63-1) J Benjamins Pubng Co.

Lambert, Richard D., jt. auth. see Jorden, Eleanor H.

Lambert, Richard D., jt. auth. see Lyons, Gene M.

Lambert, Richard D., jt. ed. see Alexander, Herbert E.

Lambert, Richard D., jt. ed. see Altbach, Philip G.

Lambert, Richard D., ed. see American Academy of Political & Social Science.

Lambert, Richard D., jt. ed. see Blake, David H.

Lambert, Richard D., ed. see Bradway, John S.

Lambert, Richard D., jt. ed. see Bressler, Marvin.

Lambert, Richard D., ed. see Charlesworth, James C.

Lambert, Richard D., jt. ed. see Charlesworth, James C.

Lambert, Richard D., jt. ed. see Clemente, Frank.

Lambert, Richard D., jt. ed. see Cook, Philip J.

Lambert, Richard D., ed. see Ferman, Louis A.

Lambert, Richard D., jt. ed. see Fox, Renee C.

Lambert, Richard D., jt. ed. see Fox, William T.

Lambert, Richard D., jt. ed. see Galnoor, Itzhal.

Lambert, Richard D., jt. ed. see Gordon, Milton M.

Lambert, Richard D., jt. ed. see Gross, Bertram M.

Lambert, Richard D., ed. see Hart, Parker T.

Lambert, Richard D., jt. ed. see Holland, Kenneth.

Lambert, Richard D., jt. ed. see Hollingsworth, J. Rogers.

Lambert, Richard D., jt. ed. see Mott, George F.

Lambert, Richard D., jt. ed. see Ornstein, Norman J.

Lambert, Richard D., jt. ed. see Park, Richard L.

Lambert, Richard D., ed. see Shur, Irene G. & Littell, Franklin H.

Lambert, Richard D., jt. ed. see Taeuber, Conrad.

Lambert, Richard D., jt. ed. see Weintraub, Sidney.

Lambert, Richard D., ed. see Wilcox, Wayne.

Lambert, Richard D., jt. ed. see Windmuller, John P.

Lambert, Richard D., jt. ed. see Wolfgang, Marvin E.

Lambert, Richard M. & Pacchioni, Gianfranco, eds. Chemisorption & Reactivity on Supported Clusters & Thin Films: Towards an Understanding of Microscopic Processes in Catalysis. LC 97-3730. 1997. text 264.50 (*0-7923-4448-0*) Kluwer Academic.

Lambert, Rob. Labour & State in Indonesia: State & Labour in New Order Indonesia. (Asia Papers: No. 6). pap. write for info. (*1-875560-71-8*, Pub. by Univ of West Aust Pr) Intl Spec Bk.

Lambert, Robert. How to Make a Rope & Washer Pump. 32p. 1989. pap. 12.00 (*1-85339-022-4*, Pub. by Intermed Tech) Stylus Pub VA.

Lambert, Robert, jt. auth. see Davis, Jan.

Lambert, Robert A. Species History in Scotland: Introductions & Extinctions since the Ice Age. 176p. 1997. pap. 39.00 (*1-84017-011-5*) St Mut.

Lambert, Robert G., Jr. A Critical Study of Emily Dickinson's Letters: The Prose of a Poet. LC 96-8301. 256p. 1996. text. write for info. (*0-7734-2270-6*) E Mellen.

— Emily Dickinson's Use of Anglo-American Legal Concepts & Vocabulary in Her Poetry: Muse at the Bar. LC 97-25076. (Studies in American Literature: Vol. 24). 144p. 1997. text 69.95 (*0-7734-8639-9*) E Mellen.

Lambert, Rosemary. The Twentieth Century. (Cambridge Introduction to Art Ser.). 96p. (C). 1981. pap. text 16.95 (*0-521-29622-6*) Cambridge U Pr.

Lambert, Royston. Beloved & God: The Story of Hadrian & Antinous. 352p. reprint ed. pap. 9.95 (*0-8216-2003-7*) Carol Pub Group.

Lambert, Ruth D. One Hundred One Survival Tactics for New & Used Parents. (Illus.). (Orig.). 1991. pap. 11.95 (*0-927054-15-9*) H Sq Co.

Lambert, Ruth D. & Harrison, Henry S. Houses Cookbook. (Illus.). 1991. reprint ed. pap. 11.95 (*0-927054-16-7*) H Sq Co.

Lambert, Ruth D., ed. see Harrison, Henry S. & Highnote, David F.

Lambert, S. D. The Phratries of Attica. LC 92-41140. (Monographs in Classical Antiquity). (Illus.). 440p. (C). 1994. text 77.50 (*0-472-10388-1*, 10388) U of Mich Pr.

— The Phratries of Attica. 440p. (C). 1998. pap. text 34.50 (*0-472-08399-6*, 08399) U of Mich Pr.

— Rationes Centesimarum: Land Sales by Corpoorate Groups in Lykouran Athens. LC 97-217916. (Archaia Hellas Ser.: Vol. 3). (Illus.). 344p. 1997. lib. bdg. 94.00 (*90-5063-157-6*, Pub. by Gieben) J Benjamins Pubng Co.

Lambert, Samuel W. When Mr. Pickwick Went Fishing. LC 74-3271. (Studies in Dickens: No. 52). 1974. lib. bdg. 57.00 (*0-8383-2063-5*) M S G Haskell Hse.

Lambert, Sheila. Bills & Acts: Legislative Procedures in Eighteenth-Century England. LC 78-163054. 256p. reprint ed. pap. 73.00 (*0-8357-7211-X*, 2031680) Bks Demand.

Lambert, Sheila, ed. The House of Commons Sessional Papers of the Eighteenth Century Pt. 1: George I & II, 20 vols., Set, incl. List Vol. I. 1975. 2200.00 (*0-8420-2014-4*) Scholarly Res Inc.

— The House of Commons Sessional Papers of the Eighteenth Century Pt. 2: George III, 127 vols., Set, incl. List Vol. II. 1975. 13800.00 (*0-8420-2016-0*) Scholarly Res Inc.

Lambert, Simon, ed. Managing Tertiary & Sixth Form Colleges. LC 88-2687. 134p. reprint ed. pap. 41.60 (*0-7837-5179-6*, 204490900004) Bks Demand.

Lambert, Stephen & DeCotis, Ruth. Math Majors. LC 98-7868. (Great Jobs for... Ser.). 304p. 1998. pap. 11.95 (*0-8442-6422-9*, 64229, VGM Career) NTC Contemp Pub Co.

Lambert, Stephen, jt. auth. see Degalan, Julie A.

Lambert, Stephen, jt. auth. see Goodhart, Pippa.

Lambert, Stephen E. Great Jobs for Business Majors. (Great Jobs Ser.). (Illus.). 192p. (C). 1996. pap. 11.95 (*0-8442-4357-4*, 43574, VGM Career) NTC Contemp Pub Co.

— Great Jobs for Sociology Majors. (Illus.). 246p. 1996. pap. 11.95 (*0-8442-4358-2*, 43582, VGM Career) NTC Contemp Pub Co.

Lambert, Stephen E. & DeGalan, Julie. Great Jobs for English Majors. LC 93-45866. (Illus.). 192p. 1995. pap. 11.95 (*0-8442-4350-7*, VGM Career) NTC Contemp Pub Co.

Lambert, Stephen E., jt. auth. see DeGalan, Julie.

Lambert, Steve, jt. auth. see Cox, Joyce.

Lambert-Stock. Strategic Logistics Management. 4th ed. 2000. 66.00 (*0-256-13687-4*) McGraw.

Lambert, Susan. Form Follows Function? Design in the Twentieth Century. (Illus.). 72p. 1993. pap. 14.95 (*1-85177-122-0*, Pub. by V&A Ent) Antique Collect.

***Lambert, Susan.** Prints: Art & Techniques. (Illus.). 96p. 2000. pap. 19.95 (*1-85177-288-X*, Pub. by V&A Ent) Antique Collect.

***Lambert, Sylvie.** The Ring. (Illus.). 272p. 2000. write for info. (*2-88046-317-3*, Rotovision) Watsn-Guptill.

Lambert, Sylvie & Moser-Mercer, Barbara, eds. Bridging the Gap: Empirical Research in Simultaneous Interpretation. LC 94-9728. (Benjamins Translation Library: Vol. 3). 362p. 1994. 69.00 (*1-55619-481-1*) J Benjamins Pubng Co.

Lambert, T. Making Change Pay. 1996. pap. 129.00 (*1-85953-041-9*, Pub. by Tech Comm) St Mut.

Lambert, Thomas F., Jr. The Case for Punitive Damages: A New Audit. (ATLA Monograph Ser.). 34p. (Orig.). 1988. pap. 6.00 (*0-941916-47-2*) West Group.

***Lambert, Timothy & Lambert, Lyndsay.** THSC - Texas Home School Coalition 1999 Handbook for Texas Home Schoolers. Orig. Title: Handbook for TX Homeschoolers HOPE for Texas. (Illus.). 94p. 1999. pap. 15.00 (*0-9676073-0-2*) Texas Home Schl.

Lambert, Tom. High Income Consulting: How to Build & Market Your Professional Practice. 2nd rev. ed. (Illus.). 348p. 1997. 40.00 (*1-85788-164-8*); pap. 19.95 (*1-85788-169-9*) Nicholas Brealey.

— High Value Consulting: Managing & Maximizing External & Internal Consultants for Massive Added Value. (Illus.). 224p. 1998. 30.00 (*1-85788-173-7*) Nicholas Brealey.

— The Power of Influence: Intensive Influencing Skills at Work. (People Skills for Professionals Ser.). (Illus.). 214p. (Orig.). 1996. pap. 17.95 (*1-85788-115-X*) Nicholas Brealey.

Lambert, Tony. Resurrection of the Chinese Church. 319p. (C). 1991. pap. 15.95 (*0-340-54997-1*, Pub. by Hodder & Stought Ltd) Trafalgar.

Lambert, Vicki. Garnishment: A Practial Guide. 250p. 1998. pap. 69.00 (*0-8080-0212-0*) CCH INC.

— Garnishment: A Practical Guide. (Payroll Management Professional Ser.). 300p. 1998. pap. text 69.00 (*0-8080-0248-1*) CCH INC.

***Lambert, Vicki.** Garnishment: A Practical Guide. 2nd ed. LC 99-228031. (Employment & Human Resources Management Professional Ser.). 200p. 1999. pap. 69.00 (*0-8080-0372-0*) CCH INC.

Lambert, Vicki. Payroll Year-End Survival Guide. 350p. 1998. pap. 69.00 (*0-8080-0275-9*) CCH INC.

***Lambert, Vickie A.** Payroll Year-End Survival Guide, 2000. 500p. 1999. pap. 69.00 (*0-8080-0415-8*) CCH INC.

Lambert, W. A., tr. see Luther, Martin.

Lambert, W. C., et al. Basic Mechanisms of Physiologic & Aberrant Lymphoproliferation in the Skin. (NATO ASI Ser.: 265). (Illus.). 664p. (C). 1994. text 145.00 (*0-306-44736-3*, Kluwer Plenum) Kluwer Academic.

Lambert, W. G. Babylonian Wisdom Literature. LC 96-34017. xix, 359p. 1996. reprint ed. text 75.00 (*0-931464-94-3*) Eisenbrauns.

Lambert, W. G., et al. Atra-Hasis: The Babylonian Story of the Flood. LC 99-24265. (ENG & SUX., Illus.). xii, 198p. 1999. text 29.50 (*1-57506-039-6*) Eisenbrauns.

Lambert, W. G., jt. ed. see George, Andrew R.

Lambert, W. L. Sandscripts Vol. I: Word Pictures of Life. 2nd ed. Lambert, Mary H., ed. & illus. by. LC 88-91181. 102p. (C). 1991. reprint ed. pap. 7.95 (*0-929357-00-0*) Sandscript Creations.

— Sandscripts Vol. II: Word Pictures of Life. LC 88-91181. (Illus.). 102p. 1991. pap. 7.95 (*0-929357-01-9*) Sandscript Creations.

Lambert, Wallace E. & Klineberg, Otto. Children's Views of Foreign People: A Cross-National Study. LC 66-24057. (Century Psychology Ser.). (Illus.). 1967. 31.00 (*0-89197-076-2*) Irvington.

Lambert, Wallace E. & Taylor, Donald M. Coping with Cultural & Racial Diversity in Urban America. LC 89-16097. 202p. 1990. 52.95 (*0-275-93174-9*, C3174, Praeger Pubs) Greenwood.

Lambert, Walter N. Cooking with the Noonday Chef, Vol. 3. 200p. 1997. pap. 8.95 (*0-9660904-1-1*) Taste Matters.

— Kinfolks & Custard Pie: Recollections & Recipes from an East Tennessean. LC 88-14342. (Illus.). 224p. 1988. 16.95 (*0-87049-585-2*) U of Tenn Pr.

Lambert, Walter N. & Lambert, Anne W. Cooking with the Noonday Chef, Vol. 1. 136p. 1993. pap. 8.95 (*0-9660904-0-3*) Taste Matters.

***Lambert, Willi.** Directions for Communication: Discoveries with Ignatius Loyola. 216p. 2000. pap. write for info. (*0-8245-1853-5*, Pub. by Crossroad NY) Natl Bk Netwk.

***Lambert, Yon.** New Choices for South Carolina: Preserve, Promote & Protect. Smith, Kit, ed. (Illus.). 48p. 2000. pap. 6.50 (*0-9679016-1-8*, Pub. by Palmetto Conservat) Parnassus Bk Dist.

Lamberth, David C. William James & the Metaphysics of Experience. LC 98-30668. (Cambridge Studies in Religion & Critical Thought: No. 5). 296p. (C). 1999. text 59.95 (*0-521-58163-X*) Cambridge U Pr.

Lamberti, C. Diccionario Enciclopedico De Astronomia. (SPA.). 284p. 1989. 39.95 (*0-7859-6406-1*, 8486761131) Fr & Eur.

Lamberti, F., et al, eds. Durable Resistance in Crops. LC 82-18980. (NATO ASI Series A, Life Sciences: Vol. 55). 464p. 1983. 115.00 (*0-306-41183-0*, Plenum Trade) Perseus Pubng.

Lamberti, F. & Taylor, C. E., eds. Cyst Nematodes. LC 86-25381. (NATO ASI Series A, Life Sciences: Vol. 121). 478p. 1986. 110.00 (*0-306-42475-4*, Plenum Trade) Perseus Pubng.

Lamberti, F., et al. Advances in Molecular Plant Nematology. (NATO ASI Ser.: 268). (Illus.). 320p. (C). 1994. text 132.00 (*0-306-44822-X*, Kluwer Plenum) Kluwer Academic.

Lamberti, Gary A., jt. ed. see Hauer, F. Richard.

***Lamberti, Irene.** Spirit in Action: Moving Mediations for Peace, Insight & Personal Power. 288p. 2000. pap. 18.00 (*0-345-43482-X*) Ballantine Pub Grp.

Lamberti, Jean-Claude. Tocqueville & the Two Democracies. Goldhammer, Arthur, tr. from FRE. LC 88-18758. 323p. 1989. 56.00 (*0-674-89435-9*) HUP.

Lamberti, Jean-Claude, ed. see De Tocqueville, Alexis.

***Lamberti, Stafania.** Maldives. 2nd ed. (Globetrotter Travel Guides Ser.). (Illus.). 128p. 2000. pap. 10.95 (*1-85974-364-1*) New5 Holland.

***Lambertini, Marco.** A Naturalist's Guide to the Tropics. Veneralla, John, tr. LC 99-32802. (Illus.). 344p. 2000. pap. 25.00 (*0-226-46828-3*) U Ch Pr.

— Naturalists Guide to Tropics. 1997. 55.00 (*0-226-46827-5*) U Ch Pr.

Lamberto, Charlanne, ed. see Overlook Hospital Auxilary Staff.

Lamberton, D. Introduction to Stochastic Calculus Applied to Finance. LC 96-84905. 200p. 1996. boxed set 56.95 (*0-412-71800-6*, Chap & Hall CRC) CRC Pr.

Lamberton, Donald M. The Theory of Profit. LC 70-1657. vii, 211p. 1965. 35.00 (*0-678-06259-5*) Kelley.

Lamberton, Donald M., ed. Beyond Competition: The Future of Telecommunications. LC 95-36211. 434p. 1995. text 145.75 (*0-444-82252-6*) Elsevier.

— Communication & Trade: Essays in Honor of Meheroo Jussawalla. (Communication Ser.). 320p. (C). 1998. pap. text 26.50 (*1-57273-111-7*) Hampton Pr NJ.

— Communication & Trade: Essays in Honor of Meheroo Jussawalla. (Communication Ser.). 320p. (C). 1998. text 65.00 (*1-57273-110-9*) Hampton Pr NJ.

— The Economics of Communication & Information. (International Library of Critical Writings in Economics: Vol. 70). 592p. (C). 1996. 215.00 (*1-85898-294-4*) E Elgar.

Lamberton, Ken. Wilderness & Razor Wire. LC 99-33539. (Illus.). 224p. 1999. pap. 14.95 (*1-56279-116-8*) Mercury Hse Inc.

Lamberton, Lowell, jt. auth. see Minor, Leslie.

Lamberton, Robert. Homer the Theologian: Neoplatonist Allegorical Reading & the Growth of the Epic Tradition. LC 85-1184. (Transformation of the Classical Heritage Ser.: No. IX). 375p. (C). 1986. pap. 17.95 (*0-520-06607-3*, Pub. by U CA Pr) Cal Prin Full Svc.

Lamberton, Robert, tr. Porphyry: Cave of Nymphs. LC 82-16969. 64p. 1983. 35.00 (*0-930794-71-0*) Station Hill Pr.

Lamberton, Robert, jt. auth. see Rotroff, Susan I.

Lamberton, Robert, jt. ed. see Keaney, John J.

Lamberton, Sharon, ed. see Rogers, Leon & Weidman, Brent.

Lamberton, Sharon, ed. see Russell, Philip & Hemmer, Joe.

Lamberton, Sharon, ed. see Story, Quenda B.

Lamberton, W. M. Standard Review Plan on Antitrust Reviews: Final Report. 31p. 1997. pap. 3.50 (*0-16-062716-8*) USGPO.

Lamberts, Emiel. Christian Democracy in the European Union, 1945-1995: Proceedings of the Leuven Colloquium, 15-18 November 1995. LC 98-209512. (KADOC-Studies). 511p. 1997. 87.50 (*90-6186-808-4*, Pub. by Leuven Univ) Coronet Bks.

Lamberts, David W. & Potter, David E. Clinical Ocular Pharmacology. 560p. 1987. 89.95 (*0-316-51286-9*, Little Brwn Med Div) Lppncott W & W.

— Clinical Ophthalmic Pharmacology. 608p. 1987. text 55.00 (*0-318-37135-9*, Little Brwn Med Div) Lppncott W & W.

Lamberts, E., jt. ed. see Blom, J. C.

Lamberts, Henk, et al, eds. The International Classification of Primary Care in the European Community: With a Multi-Language Layer. (Illus.). 254p. 1993. text 95.00 (*0-19-262298-6*) OUP.

Lamberts, Koen & Shanks, David R., eds. Knowledge, Concepts & Categories. LC 96-52838. (Studies in Cognition Ser.). (Illus.). 384p. 1997. pap. text 31.50 (*0-262-62118-5*) MIT Pr.

Lamberts, W. J., jt. ed. see Van Wimersma Greidanus, T.

Lambertsen, Isaac. Holy New Hieromartyr Maximus Sandovich: Protomartyr of the Lemko People, Vol. III. 48p. 1999. pap. 5.00 (*0-912927-94-1*, X055) St John Kronstadt.

Lambertsen, Isaac, tr. The Complete Octoechos. 160p. 1998. 35.00 (*0-912927-93-3*) St John Kronstadt.

— Menaion of the Orthodox Church, No. XI, July. 448p. 1998. 125.00 (*0-912927-92-5*, D049) St John Kronstadt.

— Menaion of the Orthodox Church, Vol. VII. 224p. 1999. 75.00 (*0-912927-97-6*) St John Kronstadt.

— Menaion of the Orthodox Church: Provisional Edition, First Recension, Vol. VI (February) 1998. write for info. (*0-912927-91-7*, D047) St John Kronstadt.

— Menaion of the Orthodox Church: Provisional Edition, First Recension, Vol. XII (August) 351p. 1997. 100.00 (*0-912927-87-9*, D045) St John Kronstadt.

— Menaion of the Orthodox Church, Vol. III, November: Protomartyr of the Lemko People. 367p. 1998. 100.00 (*0-912927-95-X*, X055) St John Kronstadt.

— St. Job of Pochaev: Life, Service & Akathist Hymn. 96p. Date not set. pap. 5.00 (*0-912927-79-8*, X050) St John Kronstadt.

Lambertsen, Isaac, et al, trs. from GRE. St. Spyridon of Tremithus: Life, Miracles, Liturgical Service & Akathist Hymn. 64p. 1997. pap. 5.00 (*0-912927-89-5*, X053) St John Kronstadt.

Lambertsen, Isaac & Lardas, George, trs. from GRE. Menaion of the Orthodox Church Vol. VIII: Provisional Edition, First Recension, April. 192p. 1997. 75.00 (*0-912927-82-8*, D044) St John Kronstadt.

Lambertsen, Isaac, tr. see Clader, Timothy, ed.

Lambertsen, Isaac E., tr. from GRE. The Eleven Resurrectional Gospels of Matins: With the Resurrectional Exapostilaria & Their Theotokia & the Evangelical Stichera. (Illus.). 32p. (Orig.). 1992. pap. 4.00 (*0-912927-50-X*, X045) St John Kronstadt.

— The Holy Hieromartyr Philip, Metropolitan of Moscow. 28p. 1995. pap. 4.00 (*0-912927-60-7*, D028) St John Kronstadt.

— The Holy Martyrs Adrian & Natalia: Account of Their Suffering, Liturgical Service, Akathist Hymn. 48p. (Orig.). 1989. pap. 3.50 (*0-912927-35-6*, X035) St John Kronstadt.

— The Holy Myrrh-Bearer Mary Magdalen: Life & Akathist Hymn. 48p. (Orig.). 1989. pap. 3.00 (*0-912927-34-8*, X034) St John Kronstadt.

— The Kazan' Icon of the Mother of God: History, Service, & Akathist Hymn. (Illus.). 48p. (Orig.). 1985. pap. 3.50 (*0-912927-13-5*, X013) St John Kronstadt.

— Life of St. Anna of Novgorod. 16p. (Orig.). 1983. pap. 1.00 (*0-912927-06-2*, X006) St John Kronstadt.

— The Life of the Holy Apostle & Evangelist Luke: And the Liturgical Service in His Honor. (Illus.). 32p. (Orig.). 1989. pap. 2.50 (*0-912927-32-1*, X032) St John Kronstadt.

— Life of the Holy Prince Vladimir the Great of Kiev: With Liturgical Service, & Akathist Hymn. (Illus.). 48p. (Orig.). 1993. pap. 3.00 (*0-912927-55-0*, X046) St John Kronstadt.

— Menaion of the Orthodox Church: Provisional Edition, First Recension. 1996. write for info. (*0-912927-65-8*) St John Kronstadt.

— Menaion of the Orthodox Church: Provisional Edition, First Recension, Vol. I: September. 432p. 1996. 135.00 (*0-912927-72-0*) St John Kronstadt.

— Menaion of the Orthodox Church: Provisional Edition, First Recension, Vol. IV: December. 432p. 1996. 135.00 (*0-912927-77-1*) St John Kronstadt.

— Menaion of the Orthodox Church: Provisional Edition, First Recension, Vol. IX: May. 256p. 1996. 85.00 (*0-912927-71-2*, D037) St John Kronstadt.

— Prayers for the Blessing & Sanctification of Icons of Various Kinds, & of an Iconostasis. 24p. (Orig.). 1993. pap. 3.00 (*0-912927-51-8*, D014) St John Kronstadt.

— The Reigning, Kolomna Icon of the Mother of God: Account of Appearance, Liturgical Service, Akathist Hymn. (Illus.). 48p. (Orig.). 1989. pap. 4.00 (*0-912927-37-2*, X037) St John Kronstadt.

— The Rite of Holy Matrimony. 16p. (Orig.). 1991. pap. 2.00 (*0-912927-46-1*, D008) St John Kronstadt.

— St. Benedict of Nursia: Life from the Menology of St. Dimitri of Rostov, Orthodox Liturgical Service, Akathist Hymn, Rule for Monasteries. (Illus.). 80p. (Orig.). 1989. reprint ed. pap. 5.00 (*0-912927-38-0*, X038) St John Kronstadt.

— St. John of Kronstadt: Life, Service, & Akathist Hymn. 64p. (Orig.). 1996. pap. 3.50 (*0-912927-03-8*, X003) St John Kronstadt.

— Saints Euthymius, Ignatius & Acacius: Holy New Venerable-Martyrs of Athos. 32p. (Orig.). 1984. pap. 2.50 (*0-912927-10-0*, X010) St John Kronstadt.

— Service of Supplication Chanted in Time of Drought. 20p. (Orig.). 1991. pap. 2.00 (*0-912927-45-3*, D002) St John Kronstadt.

— The Service of the Lesser Sanctification of Water: Customarily Used on the 1st Day of August. 12p. (Orig.). 1992. pap. 3.00 (*0-912927-48-8*, D011) St John Kronstadt.

— Suffering of St. Eleutherius. 16p. (Orig.). 1983. pap. 1.00 (*0-912927-05-4*, X005) St John Kronstadt.

— The Suffering of the Holy Venerable-Martyr Stephen the New. 32p. (Orig.). 1985. pap. 2.50 (*0-912927-14-3*, X014) St John Kronstadt.

— The Translation of the Precious Relics of Our Father among the Saints Nicholas, Archbishop of Myra in Lycia from Myra, to Bari in Italy: Account of the Translation, & the Liturgical Service for Its Commemoration. (Illus.). 32p. (Orig.). 1987. pap. 2.50 (*0-912927-26-7*, X026) St John Kronstadt.

— The Wonderworking Kursk-Root Icon of the Mother of God: Discovery & History, Recent Miracles, Liturgical Service, Akathist Hymn. (Illus.). 64p. (Orig.). 1989. pap. 3.50 (*0-912927-33-X*, X033) St John Kronstadt.

Lambertsen, Isaac E., tr. see Clader, Timothy.

Lambertsen, Isaac E., tr. see Clader, Timothy, ed.

Lambertsen, Isaac E., tr. see Von Gardner, Ivan.

Lambertsen, Issac E., jt. auth. see Holy Apostles Convent Staff.

Lamberty, B. George, jt. auth. see Cormack, George C.

Lamberty, G., et al, eds. Research Priorities: Proceedings of the Fourth National Title V Maternal & Child Health Research Priorities Conference. LC 96-70894. 144p. 1996. pap. write for info. (*1-57285-037-X*) Nat Ctr Educ.

Lamberty, G. & Coll, C. G., eds. Puerto Rican Women & Children: Issues in Health, Growth & Development. (Topics in Social Psychiatry Ser.). (Illus.). 306p. (C). 1994. text 47.50 (*0-306-44615-4*, Kluwer Plenum) Kluwer Academic.

Lamberty, Gontran, ed. Maternal & Child Health Research Program: Active Projects Fiscal Year 1994 & Fiscal Year 1995. (Illus.). 192p. (C). 1998. pap. text 40.00 (*0-7881-7376-6*) DIANE Pub.

Lamberty, Kim, tr. see Committee for National Security & Harriman, W. Averell, Institute for Advanced Study.

Lamberty, Steve, ed. Insurance Department Resources Report, Vol. 15, No. 2. 8th rev. ed. 58p. (C). 1997. pap. 45.00 (*0-89382-375-9*, STA-BB) Nat Assn Insurance.

— State Average Expenditures & Premiums for Personal Automobile Insurance in 1995. 7th rev. ed. 32p. (C). 1997. pap. 35.00 (*0-89382-447-X*, AUS-PB) Nat Assn Insurance.

— State Insurance Department Resources Report. rev. ed. 74p. (C). 1995. pap. 35.00 (*0-89382-376-7*, STA-BB94) Nat Assn Insurance.

Lambesis, Barbara. One Hundred One Big Ideas for Promoting a Business on a Small Budget. LC 89-91071. 112p. (Orig.). 1989. pap. 12.95 (*0-9624798-0-2*) Mktg Methods Pr.

Lambesis, Barbara, ed. The Healthy Senior Workbook: Your Personal Health Management Planner. 160p. 1991. pap. 11.95 (*0-9624798-1-0*) Mktg Methods Pr.

Lambeth, Benjamin S. Russia's Air Power in Crisis. Hardesty, Von, ed. LC 98-53121. (Smithsonian History of Aviation Ser.). 1999. 29.95 (*1-56098-991-2*) Smithsonian.

***Lambeth, Benjamin S.** The Transformation of American Air Power. (Studies in Security Affairs). 2000. 29.95 (*0-8014-3816-0*) Cornell U Pr.

Lambeth, Benjamin S. The Warrior Who Would Rule Russia: A Profile of Aleksandr Lebed. LC 96-41162. (Illus.). 153p. 1996. pap. 15.00 (*0-8330-2447-7*, MR-805-AF) Rand Corp.

Lambeth, Courtney, jt. ed. see Im, Hun B.

L

Lambeth, Edmund B., et al, eds. Assessing Public Journalism. LC 98-6621. 304p. 1998. pap. 22.50 (0-8262-1158-5) U of Mo Pr.

Lambeth, James & James, Miles. Cuisine of the Creative: A Cookbook. LC 97-49870. (Illus.). 230p. 1998. 49.00 (0-9601678-3-8) Miami Dog Pr.

— Cuisine of the Creative: A Cookbook. LC 97-49870. 1999. pap. 39.00 (0-9601678-4-6) Miami Dog Pr.

Lambeth, Joseph A. Lambeth Method of Cake Decoration & Practical Pastries. LC 80-65654. (Illus.). 362p. 1980. reprint ed. 75.00 (0-916096-23-8) Books Bakers.

Lambeth, M. Discovering Corn Dollies. (Handbook Ser.: No. 199). (Illus.). 48p. 1985. reprint ed. pap. 5.75 (0-85263-283-5, Pub. by Shire Pubns) Parkwest Pubns.

Lambeth, R. J. Marine Insurance: Templeman on Principles & Practice. 6th ed. (C). 1986. 600.00 (0-7855-4086-5, Pub. by Witherby & Co) St Mut.

— Templeman on Marine Insurance: Its Principles & Practice. 6th ed. 628p. 1986. text 99.50 (0-273-02537-6) Sheridan.

Lambi, Ivo N. The Navy & German Power Politics, 1862-1914. 356p. (C). 1984. text 65.00 (0-04-943035-1) Routledge.

Lambiase, J. J., ed. Hydrocarbon Habitat in Rift Basins. (Geological Society Special Publication: No. 80). 370p. (C). 1994. 108.00 (1-897799-15-2, 299, Pub. by Geol Soc Pub Hse) AAPG.

Lambie, Dolores Z., et al. Home Teaching with Mothers & Infants: Ypsilanti-Carnegie Infant Education Project - an Experiment. LC 74-16863. (Monographs of the High/Scope Educational Research Foundation: No. 2). 129p. 1980. pap. 12.95 (0-931114-01-2) High-Scope.

Lambie, Jack. Composite Construction. (Illus.). 240p. 19.95 (0-614-13167-7, 21-17409) EAA Aviation.

— Composite Construction for Homebuilt Aircraft: The Basic Handbook of Composite Aircraft Aerodynamics, Construction, Maintenance & Repair Plus, How-to & Design Information. 2nd rev. ed. Markowski, Mike, ed. (Illus.). 240p. 1995. pap. 19.95 (0-938716-26-3) Markowski Intl.

— Ultralight Airmanship: How to Master the Air in an Ultralight. Markowski, Michael A., ed. LC 81-71888. (Ultralight Aviation Ser.: No. 2). (Illus.). 144p. (Orig.). 1984. pap. 11.95 (0-938716-02-6, Aviation Pubs) Markowski Intl.

Lambie-Nairn, Martin. Brand Identity for Television: With Knobs On. (Illus.). 240p. 1997. 69.95 (0-7148-3447-5, Pub. by Phaidon Press) Phaidon Pr.

***Lambie, Rosemary.** Family Systems Within Educational Contexts: Understanding At-Risk & Special Needs Students. 2nd ed. 544p. (C). 1999. pap. text 52.00 (0-89108-265-4, 9903) Love Pub Co.

Lambillion, Paul. Being Loving Is Being Healthy: Self Heal Through the Power of Love. 147p. 1999. pap. 19.95 (0-8464-4942-0) Beekman Pubs.

— Communications from Heartstar. 90p. 1999. pap. 14.95 (0-8464-4944-7) Beekman Pubs.

Lambin, Helen R. Death of a Husband: Reflections for a Grieving Wife. 1998. pap. text 8.95 (0-87946-179-9) ACTA Pubns.

— From Grief to Grace: Images for Overcoming Sadness & Loss. 96p. (Orig.). 1997. pap. 8.95 (0-87946-154-3, 257) ACTA Pubns.

***Lambin, Jean-Jacques.** Market-Driven Management: An Introduction to Marketing. LC 00-21421. 608p. 2000. text 85.00 (0-312-23185-7) St Martin.

Lambin, Jean-Jacques. Marketing Strategy: A New European Approach. LC 93-21714. (Marketing for Professionals Ser.).Tr. of Marketing Strategique. 1993. 22.50 (0-07-707795-4) McGraw.

— Strategic Marketing Management. LC 96-27234. 1996. pap. write for info. (0-07-709227-9) McGraw.

***Lambin, Rosine A.** Le Voile des Femmes. (Studia Religiosa Helvetica Altera Ser.: Vol. 3). 272p. 1999. 33.95 (3-906762-87-4, Pub. by P Lang Pubng) P Lang Pubng.

Lambin, Thomas O. An Introduction to Biblical Hebrew. 345p. (C). 1971. 87.00 (0-02-367250-1, Macmillan Coll) P-H.

Lambing, Frank, ed. Alabama Manufacturers Register. 10th rev. ed. 1999. 79.00 (1-58202-038-8) Manufacturers.

— Alaska Manufacturers Directory. 4th rev. ed. 1999. 46.00 (1-58202-039-6) Manufacturers.

— Arkansas Manufacturers Register. 4th rev. ed. 1998. 68.00 (1-58202-040-X) Manufacturers.

— Connecticut Manufacturers Register. 3rd rev. ed. 1999. 72.00 (1-58202-041-8) Manufacturers.

— Delaware Manufacturers Register. 4th rev. ed. 1999. 48.00 (1-58202-042-6) Manufacturers.

— Florida Manufacturers Register. 14th rev. ed. 1999. 149.00 (1-58202-043-4) Manufacturers.

— Georgia Manufacturers Register. 12th rev. ed. 1999. 104.00 (1-58202-044-2) Manufacturers.

— Hawaii Manufacturers Directory. 4th rev. ed. 1999. 54.00 (1-58202-045-0) Manufacturers.

— Illinois Manufacturers Directory. 16th rev. ed. 1999. 54.00 (1-58202-046-9) Manufacturers.

— Illinois Services Directory. 16th rev. ed. 1998. 179.00 (1-58202-047-7) Manufacturers.

— Indiana Manufacturers Directory. 18th rev. ed. 1999. 110.00 (1-58202-048-5) Manufacturers.

— Iowa Manufacturers Register. 17th rev. ed. 1999. 76.00 (1-58202-049-3) Manufacturers.

— Kansas Manufacturers Directory. 4th rev. ed. 1999. 69.00 (1-58202-050-7) Manufacturers.

— Kentucky Manufacturers Register. 15th rev. ed. 1998. 76.00 (1-58202-051-5) Manufacturers.

— Louisiana Manufacturers Register. 9th rev. ed. 1999. 71.00 (1-58202-052-3) Manufacturers.

— Maine Manufacturers Register. rev. ed. 1998. 55.00 (1-58202-074-4) Manufacturers.

— Maryland-D. C. Manufacturers Directory. 7th rev. ed. 1999. 73.00 (1-58202-053-1) Manufacturers.

— Massachusetts Manufacturers Register. 1998. 79.00 (1-58202-077-9) Manufacturers.

— Minnesota Manufacturers Register. 16th rev. ed. 1998. 106.00 (1-58202-054-X) Manufacturers.

— Mississippi Manufacturers Register. 5th rev. ed. 1999. 66.00 (1-58202-055-8) Manufacturers.

— Missouri Manufacturers Register. 12th rev. ed. 1998. 101.00 (1-58202-056-6) Manufacturers.

— Nebraska Manufacturers Register. 7th rev. ed. 1999. 67.00 (1-58202-057-4) Manufacturers.

— New Hampshire Manufacturers Register. 1998. 55.00 (1-58202-075-2) Manufacturers.

— New Jersey Manufacturers Register. 2nd rev. ed. 1999. 105.00 (1-58202-058-2) Manufacturers.

— New Mexico Manufacturers Register. 3rd rev. ed. 1999. 62.00 (1-58202-059-0) Manufacturers.

— New York Manufacturers Register. 2nd rev. ed. 1999. 145.00 (1-58202-060-4) Manufacturers.

— North Carolina Manufacturers Register. 6th rev. ed. 1999. 106.00 (1-58202-061-2) Manufacturers.

— North Dakota Manufacturers Register. 4th rev. ed. 1999. 54.00 (1-58202-062-0) Manufacturers.

— Ohio Manufacturers Directory. 17th rev. ed. 1998. 157.00 (1-58202-063-9) Manufacturers.

— Oklahoma Manufacturers Register. 8th rev. ed. 1998. 75.00 (1-58202-064-7) Manufacturers.

— Pennsylvania Manufacturers Register. 14th rev. ed. 1999. 157.00 (1-58202-065-5) Manufacturers.

— Rhode Island Manufacturers Register. 3rd rev. ed. 1999. 57.00 (1-58202-066-3) Manufacturers.

— South Carolina Manufacturers Register. 5th rev. ed. 1998. 69.00 (1-58202-067-1) Manufacturers.

— South Dakota Manufacturers Register. 3rd rev. ed. 1998. 55.00 (1-58202-068-X) Manufacturers.

— Tennessee Manufacturers Register. 3rd rev. ed. 1998. 74.00 (1-58202-069-8) Manufacturers.

— Texas Manufacturers Register. 15th rev. ed. 1999. 157.00 (1-58202-070-1) Manufacturers.

— Vermont Manufacturers Register. 1998. 55.00 (1-58202-076-0) Manufacturers.

— Virginia Manufacturers Directory. 7th rev. ed. 1999. 79.00 (1-58202-071-X) Manufacturers.

— West Virginia Manufacturers Register. 12th rev. ed. 1998. pap. 59.00 (1-58202-072-8) Manufacturers.

— Wisconsin Manufacturers Register. 16th rev. ed. 1999. 111.00 (1-58202-073-6) Manufacturers.

Lambing, Frank, jt. ed. see West, Louise M.

Lambing, Peggy A. Entrepreneurship. 2nd ed. LC 98-47768. (Illus.). 301p. (C). 1999. pap. text 52.00 incl. disk (0-13-020043-3) P-H.

Lambiotte, Judith, jt. auth. see Fenker, Richard M., Jr.

Lambiris, A. J. Frogs & Toads of the Natal Drakensberg. (Ukhahlamba Ser.: No. 3). 72p. 1989. pap. 11.95 (0-86980-612-2, Pub. by Univ Natal Pr) Intl Spec Bk.

Lambiris, Michael. The Historical Context of Roman Law. LC 98-152318. 250p. 1997. pap. 49.00 (0-455-21498-0, 14588, Pub. by LawBk Co) Gaunt.

Lambirth, Frank. Now I Lay Me down to Sleep. 240p. 1989. mass mkt. 3.95 (0-445-20672-1, Pub. by Warner Bks) Little.

Lambkin, Brian K. Opposite Religions Still? Interpreting Northern Ireland after the Conflict. 224p. (C). 1996. 63.95 (1-85972-163-X, Pub. by Avebry) Ashgate Pub Co.

Lambkin, David. The Hanging Tree. 400p. 1998. pap. 15.00 (1-887178-71-6, Pub. by Counterpt DC) HarpC.

Lambkin, Laura C., jt. ed. see Lambkin, Robert T.

Lambkin, Mary. European Perspectives on Consumer Behavior. 352p. 1997. pap. 39.40 (0-13-552382-6, Prentice Hall) P-H.

Lambkin, Robert T. & Lambkin, Laura C., eds. Encyclopedia of Medieval Literature. 1999. lib. bdg. 95.00 (1-57958-054-8) Fitzroy Dearborn.

Lambkin, Romie. Echo of Seals. (YA). 1997. pap. 6.95 (0-86327-398-X, Pub. by Wolfhound Press) Irish Amer Bk.

Lamble, Phillip, tr. see Marx, Siegfried & Pfau, Werner.

Lambley, Peter. Middle Aged Rebel: Embracing the Challenge of Midlife, a Dynamic Approach. 1995. pap. 10.95 (1-85230-644-0, Pub. by Element MA) Penguin Putnam.

Lamblin, Bianca. A Disgraceful Affair: Simone de Beauvoir, Jean-Paul Sartre & Bianca Lamblin. Plovnick, Julie, tr. (Women's Life Writings from Around the World Ser.). (Illus.). 224p. 1996. text 28.95 (1-55553-251-9) NE U Pr.

Lambo, T. A. & Day, S. B. Issues in Contemporary International Health. LC 89-72169. (Illus.). 360p. (C). 1990. text 90.00 (0-306-43344-3, Kluwer Plenum) Kluwer Academic.

Lamboon, Raymond E. Geology of Coshocton Co., Ohio. 245p. 1993. reprint ed. lib. bdg. 34.50 (0-8328-2992-7) Higginson Bk Co.

Lambooy, J. G., jt. ed. see Kuklinski, Antoni.

Lamborn, Edmund A. Shakespeare, the Man. LC 76-30695. (Studies in Shakespeare: No. 24). 1977. lib. bdg. 75.00 (0-8383-2173-9) M S G Haskell Hse.

Lamborn, Edmund A. & Harrison, George B. Shakespeare: The Man & His Stage. LC 73-153336. reprint ed. 29.50 (0-404-03805-0) AMS Pr.

Lamborn, Florence, jt. auth. see Lindgren, Astrid.

Lamborn, Florence, tr. see Lindgren, Astrid.

Lamborn, Frances, tr. see Lindgren, Astrid.

Lamborn, S. The Genealogy of the Lamborn Family with Extracts from History, Biographies & Anecdotes, Etc. (Illus.). 487p. reprint ed. pap. 73.00 (0-8328-0746-X); reprint ed. lib. bdg. 81.00 (0-8328-0745-1) Higginson Bk Co.

Lambot, Ian. Norman Foster, Buildings & Projects, 1982-1989, Vol. 4. (Norman Foster Ser.). (Illus.). 256p. 1996. 85.00 (3-7643-5428-3, Pub. by Birkhauser) Princeton Arch.

Lambot, Ian, ed. Norman Foster - Buildings & Projects, 1964-1973, Vol. 1. (Norman Foster Ser.). (Illus.). 260p. 1996. 85.00 (3-7643-5446-1, Pub. by Birkhauser) Princeton Arch.

— Norman Foster - Buildings & Projects, 1971-1978, Vol. 2. (Norman Foster Ser.). (Illus.). 240p. 1996. 85.00 (3-7643-5447-X, Pub. by Birkhauser) Princeton Arch.

— Norman Foster - Buildings & Projects, 1978-1982, Vol. 3. (Norman Foster Ser.). (Illus.). 264p. 1996. 85.00 (3-7643-5448-8, Pub. by Birkhauser) Princeton Arch.

Lambot, Ian & Davies, Colin, eds. Commerzbank Frankfurt: Prototype for an Ecological High-Rise. LC 97-31968. (GER., Illus.). 316p. 1997. text 70.00 (3-7643-5740-1, Pub. by Birkhauser) Princeton Arch.

Lambot, Isobel. Blood Ties. large type ed. 1989. 27.99 (0-7089-2092-6) Ulverscroft.

— Come Back & Die. large type ed. 296p. 1989. 27.99 (0-7089-1977-4) Ulverscroft.

— Deadly Return. large type ed. (Lythway Ser.). 232p. 1990. 20.95 (0-7451-1211-0, G K Hall Lrg Type) Mac Lib Ref.

— Grip of Fear. (Lythway Adult Ser.). 208p. 1991. 18.95 (0-7451-1359-1, G K Hall Lrg Type) Mac Lib Ref.

— The Identity Trap. large type ed. 288p. 1989. 27.99 (0-7089-2013-6) Ulverscroft.

— Let the Witness Die. large type ed. 240p. 1990. 19.95 (0-7451-1144-0, G K Hall Lrg Type) Mac Lib Ref.

— Rooney's Gold. large type ed. (Lythway Ser.). 256p. 1991. 21.95 (0-7451-1274-9, G K Hall Lrg Type) Mac Lib Ref.

— Shroud of Canvas. (Black Dagger Crime Ser.). 200p. 1997. 19.50 (0-7451-8706-4, Black Dagger) Chivers N Amer.

— Still Waters Run Deadly. large type ed. 384p. 1989. 27.99 (0-7089-2040-3) Ulverscroft.

— Watcher on the Shore. large type ed. 336p. 1988. 27.99 (0-7089-1914-6) Ulverscroft.

Lambotte, H., jt. auth. see Taerwe, L.

Lambotte, H., jt. ed. see Taerwe, L.

Lambou, Andreas. Fountain Pens in the World. (Illus.). 328p. 1995. 190.00 (0-302-00668-0) Sothebys Pubns.

Lambourne, Lionel. The Aesthetic Movement. LC 96-173011. (Illus.). 240p. 1996. 59.95 (0-7148-3000-3, Pub. by Phaidon Press) Phaidon Pr.

— Madame Tussauds. 1999. pap. 19.95 (0-525-48425-6) NAL.

— Victorian Painting. 512p. 1999. 59.95 (0-7148-3776-8) Phaidon Press.

Lambourne, Lionel, jt. auth. see Sato, Tomoko.

Lambourne, Maureen. The Art of Bird Illustration: Visual Tribute to the Lives & Achievements of the Classic Bird Illustrations. 1997. pap. text 25.95 (1-57715-024-4) Knckerbocker.

— Gould's Exotic Birds. (Victoria & Albert Natural History Illustrators Ser.). (Illus.). 64p. 1988. student ed. 13.00 (0-929655-58-3) Abrams.

Lambourne, Mike. Down the Hatch! Find Out about Your Food. LC 91-22686. (Lighter Look Bk.). (Illus.). 40p. (J). (gr. 2-6). 1992. lib. bdg. 20.90 (1-56294-150-X) Millbrook Pr.

Lambourne, R. & Strivens, T. A., eds. Paint & Surface Coatings: Theory & Practice. 2nd ed. 950p. 1999. boxed set 225.00 (1-85573-348-X, Pub. by Woodhead Pubng) Am Educ Systs.

***Lambourne, R. & Strivens, T.A.** Paint & Surface Coatings: Theory & Practice. 2nd ed. 950p. 1999. 285.00 (1-884207-73-1) William Andrew.

***Lambourne, R. & Tinker, M.** Basic Mathematics for the Physical Sciences. 688p. 2000. pap. 35.00 (0-471-85207-4) Wiley.

Lambourne, R., et al. Close Encounters? Science & Science Fiction. LC 90-33934. (Illus.). 200p. 1990. pap. 37.00 (0-85274-141-3) IOP Pub.

Lambourne, R. A., ed. Community, Church & Healing. (C). 1990. pap. 30.00 (0-85305-279-4, Pub. by Arthur James) St Mut.

***Lambourne, Robert & Tinker, Michael.** Basic Mathematics for the Physical Sciences. LC 99-35925. 688p. 2000. 105.00 (0-471-85206-6) Wiley.

Lambourne, Robert, jt. auth. see Tinker, Michael.

Lambrecht, Andrea L., jt. auth. see Henderson, Carrol.

***Lambrecht, Barbara.** One Bike, One Dream. LC 00-100106. (Illus.). 256p. 2000. pap. 14.00 (0-9678578-4-8) E Bks.

Lambrecht, Frank L. In the Shade of an Acacia Tree: Memoirs of a Health Officer in Africa: 1945-59. LC 90-56110. (Memoirs Ser.: Vol. 194). (Illus.). 420p. (C). 1991. 30.00 (0-87169-194-9, M194-LAF) Am Philos.

— Pawa: A Memoir from the Belgian Congo, 1945-1949. Lane, Richard, ed. LC 98-104087. (Illus.). 112p. 1994. 17.95 (0-9643780-0-0) F L Lambrecht.

— Where the Mopane Bloom: A Biologist in Ngamiland, Botswana. LC 89-8101. 1990. 25.00 (0-89341-577-4, Longwood Academic) Hollowbrook.

Lambrecht, J. Thomas. 3-D Modeling Technology in Oral & Maxillofacial Surgery. LC 94-48366. (Illus.). 160p. 1995. text 140.00 (0-86715-287-7, B2877) Quint Pub Co.

Lambrecht, Jan. Out of the Treasure: The Parables in the Gospel of Matthew. (Louvain Theological & Pastoral Monographs). 296p. (Orig.). (C). 1992. pap. 25.00 (0-8028-0662-7) Eerdmans.

— Second Corinthians. Harrington, Daniel J., ed. LC 98-19294. (Sacra Pagina Ser.: No. 8). 256p. 1999. 29.95 (0-8146-5810-5, M Glazier) Liturgical Pr.

— The Wretched "I" & Its Liberation: Paul in Romans 7 & 8. (Louvain Theological & Pastoral Monographs). 165p. 1993. pap. 25.00 (0-8028-0570-1) Eerdmans.

Lambrecht, Judith J. & Edgmand, Nina M. Microsoft Excel 5.0: A Professional Approach. LC 93-42004. 1994. write for info. (0-02-801955-5) Glencoe.

Lambrecht, K. & Quenstedt, W. A. Paleontologi: A Biographical & Bibliographical Register of Paleontologists, Vol. 72. Albritton, Claude C., Jr., ed. LC 77-6526. (History of Geology Ser.). 1978. reprint ed. lib. bdg. 44.95 (0-405-10445-6) Ayer.

Lambrecht, Knud. Information Structure & Sentence Form: Topic, Focus & the Mental Representations of Discourse Referents. (Cambridge Studies in Linguistics: No. 71). 404p. 1996. pap. text 24.95 (0-521-58704-2) Cambridge U Pr.

— Topic, Antitopic & Verb Agreement in Non-Standard French. (Pragmatics & Beyond Ser.: II: 6). vii, 113p. (Orig.). 1981. pap. 29.00 (90-272-2526-5) J Benjamins Pubng Co.

Lambrecht, Richard M. Biological Models in Radiopharmaceutical Development. LC 95-43931. (Developments in Nuclear Medicine Ser.: No. 27). 288p. (C). 1996. text 144.00 (0-7923-3836-7) Kluwer Academic.

Lambrecht, Richard M. & Morcos, Nabil, eds. Nuclear & Radiochemistry Applications. LC 82-9111. (Illus.). 592p. 1982. 68.00 (0-08-029389-1, Pub. by Pergamon Repr) Franklin.

Lambrechts, Eric & Salu, Luc. Photography & Literature: An International Bibliography of Monographs. LC 91-34752. 320p. 1992. text 120.00 (0-7201-2113-2, Z1023) Continuum.

***Lambrechts, James R. & American Society of Civil Engineers Staff.** Special Geotechnical Testing for Central Artery/Tunnel Project in Boston, Massachusetts. LC 99-40797. (Geotechnical Special Publication Ser.). 184p. 1999. 30.00 (0-7844-0453-4) Am Soc Civil Eng.

Lambrechts, James R., et al. Big Digs Around the World: Proceedings of Sessions of Geo-Congress 98, Sponsored by the Geo-Institute of the American Society of Civil Engineers, October 18-21, 1998, Boston, Massachusetts. LC 98-40669. (Geotechnical Special Publication Ser.). 432p. 1998. 55.00 (0-7844-0398-8) Am Soc Civil Eng.

***Lambrechtse, Rudi.** Hiking the Escalante. 1999. pap. 11.95 (0-87480-631-3) U of Utah Pr.

Lambrechtse, Rudi. Hiking the Escalante. LC 84-63000. (Illus.). 192p. 1985. pap. 11.95 (0-915272-27-X) Wasatch Pubs.

Lambregts, B. W. & Spaans, M. The Development & Financing of Public Real Property in Urban Areas in Belgium, Germany, France & Great Britain. LC 98-230172. (Housing & Urban Policy Studies: No. 14). 126p. 1998. pap. 32.50 (90-407-1692-7, Pub. by Delft U Pr) Coronet Bks.

Lambregtse, Cornelius. He Gathers the Lambs. LC 96-39176. (J). 1996. 12.90 (0-921100-77-9) Inhtce Pubns.

***Lambreth, James & James, Miles.** A Tuscan Seduction: A Romantic Cookbook for Two. 144p. 2000. 34.50 (0-9601678-6-2) Miami Dog Pr.

***Lambrew, Costas, et al, eds.** Rapid Identification & Treatment of Patients with Acute Myocardial Infarction. (Illus.). 73p. 1999. reprint ed. pap. text 20.00 (0-7881-8193-9) DIANE Pub.

Lambrichs, Louise. Hannah's Diary. Reynolds, Sian, tr. 1999. pap. 12.95 (0-7043-8081-1) Interlink Pub.

Lambright, W. Henry. Powering Apollo: James E. Webb of NASA. LC 94-29063. (New Series in NASA History). (Illus.). 296p. 1995. text 39.95 (0-8018-4902-0) Johns Hopkins.

— Presidential Management of Science & Technology: The Johnson Presidency. (Administrative History of the Johnson Presidency Ser.). 238p. 1985. text 25.00 (0-292-76494-4) U of Tex Pr.

Lambright, W. Henry & Rahm, Dianne, eds. Technology & U. S. Competitiveness: An Institutional Focus, 139. LC 92-8845. (Contributions in Economics & Economic History Ser.: No. 139). 200p. 1992. 55.00 (0-313-28560-8, LRH, Greenwood Pr) Greenwood.

Lambright, W. Henry, jt. ed. see Rahm, Dianne.

Lambrinos, James & Kelly, William A., Jr. The Effects of Member Income Levels on Credit Union Financial Performance. 93p. 1996. pap. 100.00 (1-880572-24-9) Filene Res.

Lambris, J. D., ed. The Third Component of Complement. (Current Topics in Microbiology & Immunology Ser.: Vol. 153). (Illus.). 248p. 1989. 123.00 (0-387-51513-5) Spr-Verlag.

Lambris, John D. & Holers, V. Michael, eds. Therapeutic Interventions in the Complement System. (Contemporary Immunology Ser.). 269p. 2000. 119.50 (0-89603-587-5) Humana.

***Lambrix, P.** Part-Whole Reasoning in an Object-Centered Framework. (Lecture Notes in Computer Science Ser.: Vol. 1771). xii, 195p. 2000. pap. 45.00 (3-540-67225-7) Spr-Verlag.

Lambrix, Robert J. & Singhvi, Suren S., eds. Global Finance 2000: A Handbook of Strategy & Organization. (Illus.). 256p. (Orig.). 1996. pap. text 17.95 (0-8237-0590-0) Conference Bd.

Lambropoulos, Peter & Walther, H. Multiphoton Processes, 1996: Proceedings of the 7th International Conference on Multiphoton Processes Held in Garmisch-Partenkirchen, Germany, 30 September-4 October 1996. LC 97-3611. (Conference Ser.). 1997. 168.00 (0-7503-0443-X) IOP Pub.

Lambropoulos, Peter, ed. see Eberlein, Harold D. & VanDyke Hubbard, Cortland.

Lambropoulos, V., jt. ed. see Alexiou, M.

An Asterisk (*) at the beginning of an entry indicates that the title is appearing for the first time.

Lambropoulos, Vassilis. Literature As National Institution: Studies in the Politics of Modern Greek Criticism. LC 87-32712. 271p. reprint ed. pap. 84.10 (*0-608-06399-1*, 206676000008) Bks Demand.

— The Rise of Eurocentrism: Anatomy of Interpretation. 480p. 1992. text 47.50 (*0-691-06949-2*, Pub. by Princeton U Pr) Cal Prin Full Svc.

Lambropoulos, Vassilis, ed. Ethical Politics. 360p. 1996. pap. 12.00 (*0-8223-6440-9*) Duke.

Lambropoulos, Vassilis & Miller, David N., eds. Twentieth-Century Literary Theory: An Introductory Anthology. LC 86-5837. (SUNY Series, Intersections). 521p. (Orig.). (C). 1987. pap. text 24.95 (*0-88706-266-0*) State U NY Pr.

Lambros, Anna V. Culture & the Literary Text: The Case of Flaubert's Madame Bovary. LC 94-1889. (American University Studies Series II: Romance Languages & Literatures: Vol. 162). 96p. (C). 1996. text 29.95 (*0-8204-2588-5*) P Lang Pubng.

Lambros, Nick. Americanization of Odysseus. 189p. 1988. pap. 8.95 (*0-89697-286-0*) Intl Univ Pr.

Lambros, Paul. The Coins of the Genoese Rulers of Chios (1314-1429) Barozzi, A., tr. (Illus.). 27p. 1968. pap. 5.00 (*0-916710-00-9*) Obol Intl.

— Gold Coins of Philippi. (Illus.). 1975. pap. 5.00 (*0-916710-20-3*) Obol Intl.

— Unpublished Coins of the Medieval Kingdom of Cyprus. Toumazou, Michael, tr. from GRE. (ENG, FRE & GRE., Illus.). 170p. 1980. 30.00 (*0-916710-76-9*) Obol Intl.

— Unpublished Coins Struck at Glarentza in Imitation of Venetian by Robert of Taranto, Sovereign of the Peloponnese: 1346-1364. Gardiakos, B., tr. (Illus.). 30p. 1969. pap. 5.00 (*0-916710-01-7*) Obol Intl.

Lambros, Spyridon P., ed. Ecthesis Chronica & Chronicon Athenarum. LC 76-24931. (Byzantine Texts: No. 3). reprint ed. 30.00 (*0-404-60003-4*) AMS Pr.

Lambrou, Andreas. Fountain Pens: For Collectors. (Illus.). 208p. 1989. 50.00 (*0-85667-362-5*) Sothebys Pubns.

Lambrou, G. N. & Greve, E. L., eds. Ocular Blood Flow in Glaucoma: Means, Methods & Measurements. LC 89-19833. (Illus.). 295p. 1989. lib. bdg. 86.00 (*90-6299-053-3*, Pub. by Kugler) Kugler Pubns.

Lambrou, Nicholas C., et al. The Johns Hopkins Manual of Gynecology & Obstetrics. LC 98-47453. 1999. write for info. (*0-7817-1890-2*) Lppncott W & W.

Lambrou, Peter T. & Pratt, George J. Instant Emotional Healing: Acupressure for the Emotions. LC 99-36506. (Illus.). 288p. 2000. 25.00 (*0-7679-0392-7*) Bantam.

Lambrou, Peter T., jt. auth. see Alman, Brian M.

Lambrou-Phillipson, C. Hellenorientalia: The Near Eastern Presence in the Bronze Age Aegean, ca. 3000-1100 B. C. - A Catalogue of Egyptian, Mesopotamian, Mitannian, Syro-Palestinian, Cypriot & Asia Minor Objects from the Bronze Age Aegean. (Studies in Mediterranean Archaeology & Literature: No. 95). (Illus.). 575p. (Orig.). 1990. pap. 97.50 (*91-86098-87-X*, Pub. by P Astroms) Coronet Bks.

Lambrova, Golda, tr. see Boudjedra, Rachid.

Lambroza, Shlomo. Boris Yeltsin. (World Leaders Ser.). 112p. (J). Date not set. lib. bdg. 25.27 (*1-57103-476-5*) Rourke Pr.

— Boris Yeltsin. (World Leaders Ser.). 112p. (J). 1993. lib. bdg. 26.60 (*0-86625-476-5*) Rourke Pubns.

— World Leaders - Boris Yeltsin. LC 92-46479. (Biographies Ser.). (YA). 1993. 19.93 (*0-86625-482-X*) Rourke Pubns.

Lambroza, Shlomo, jt. ed. see Klier, John D.

Lambton, Ann K. Landlord & Peasant in Persia: A Study of Land Tenure & Land Revenue Administration. 550p. 1991. text 65.00 (*1-85043-293-7*, Pub. by I B T) St Martin.

— Persian Grammar. 290p. (C). 1953. pap. text 44.95 (*0-521-09124-1*) Cambridge U Pr.

— Persian Vocabulary. (PER.). 406p. (C). 1953. pap. text 44.95 (*0-521-09154-3*) Cambridge U Pr.

— State & Government in Medieval Islam: An Introduction to the Study of Islamic Political Theory; the Jurists. (London Oriental Ser.: No. 36). 382p. 1981. 65.00 (*0-19-713600-1*) OUP.

Lambton, Edward, jt. auth. see Lapenkova, Valentina.

Lambton, George. Men & Horses I Have Known. 320p. 1990. pap. 34.00 (*0-85131-031-1*, Pub. by J A Allen) St Mut.

Lambton, Gunda. Stealing the Show: Seven Women Artists in Canadian Public Art. (Illus.). 240p. 1994. 65.00 (*0-7735-1188-1*, Pub. by McG-Queens Univ Pr); pap. 27.95 (*0-7735-1189-X*, Pub. by McG-Queens Univ Pr) CUP Services.

Lambton, Lucinda. An Album of Curious Houses. 1989. 24.95 (*0-7011-3119-5*) Random.

Lamda. Lamda Guide to English Literature. 109p. 1998. pap. 13.95 (*1-84002-011-3*, Pub. by Oberon Bks Ltd) Theatre Comm.

***Lamdan, Ruth.** A Separate People: Jewish Women in Palestine, Syria & Egypt in the 16th Century. LC 00-39776. (Jewish Studies). 2000. write for info. (*90-04-11747-4*) Brill Academic Pubs.

Lamden, Charles W. The Securities & Exchange Commission: A Case Study in the Use of Accounting As an Instrument of Public Policy. Brief, Richard P., ed. LC 77-87302. (Development of Contemporary Accounting Thought Ser.). 1978. lib. bdg. 37.95 (*0-405-10941-5*) Ayer.

Lamdin, Griffith D. Odyssey to Guadalajara. LC 86-64031. (Hindsight Saga Ser.). (Illus.). 120p. 1987. pap. 10.95 (*0-915433-14-1*) Packrat WA.

Lamdin, Lois. Earn College Credit for What You Know. 2nd rev. ed. (Illus.). 256p. 1992. pap. 19.95 (*0-9628073-2-X*) CAEL.

Lamdin, Lois, ed. Roads to the Learning Society. 180p. (C). 1991. text 25.00 (*0-9628073-1-1*) CAEL.

Lamdin, Lois & CAEL Staff. Earn College Credit for What You Know. 3rd rev. ed. LC 97-197351. (Illus.). 256p. 1997. per. 24.95 (*0-7872-3573-3*, 41357301) Kendall-Hunt.

Lamdin, Lois S. & Fugate, Mary C. Elderlearning: New Frontier in an Aging Society. LC 96-29843. (American Council on Education/Oryx Press Series on Higher Education). 216p. 1997. boxed set 34.95 (*0-89774-959-6*) Oryx Pr.

Lame Deer, Archie Fire, see Erdoes, Richard & Fire Lame Deer, Archie.

Lame Deer, John, jt. auth. see Erdoes, Richard.

Lamech, Ranjit, jt. auth. see Jenkins, Glenn.

Lameer, Joep. Al-Farabi & Aristotelian Syllogistics: Greek Theory & Islamic Practice. LC 94-25189. 1994. 88.00 (*90-04-09884-4*) Brill Academic Pubs.

***Lameire, N. & Ronco, C., eds.** Haemodialysis & Oxidant Stress. (Reprint of Blood Purification Ser.: Vol. 17, Nos. 2-3 (1999)). (Illus.). iv, 120p. 1999. 98.00 (*3-8055-6918-1*) S Karger.

***Lameiro, Carlos.** Historias Que Tenho para Contar... A Importancia do Turismo Na Minha Vida. unabridged ed. Peregrinacao Publications Staff, ed. (Documentos Ser.: No. 3). (POR.). 96p. 2000. boxed set 12.95 (*1-889358-07-X*, 23) Peregrinacao.

Lamela, Susan & Meals, Hank. Yuba Trails - A Selection of Historic Hiking Trails in the Yuba River Watershed. 2nd ed. 200p. 1996. pap. text 13.95 (*0-9640817-1-7*) S E Lamela.

Lamelas, Diego. The Sale of Gibraltar in 1474. (C). 1988. pap. text 35.00 (*0-948466-20-0*, Pub. by Gibraltar Bks) St Mut.

Lamendella, John, ed. see Bissonnette, Denise.

Lamendola, John. The Storyteller: Tales of Stories & Dreams. 72p. (J). (gr. 6-9). 1998. pap. 9.00 (*0-8059-4482-6*) Dorrance.

LaMendola, Walter, et al, eds. A Casebook of Computer Applications in the Social & Human Services. 316p. 1989. 79.95 (*0-86656-867-0*); pap. 24.95 (*0-86656-870-0*) Haworth Pr.

Lamendola, Walter, jt. auth. see Glastonbury, Bryan.

Lamensdorf, Len. The Crouching Dragon. LC 99-90176. (Will to Conquer Ser.: Bk. 1). (Illus.). 278p. (YA). (gr. 7-12). 1999. 19.95 (*0-9669741-5-8*) SeaScape Pr Ltd.

— Gino, the Countess & Chagall. LC 99-90211. 432p. 2000. 24.95 (*0-9669741-6-6*) SeaScape Pr Ltd.

***Lamensdorf, Len.** The Raging Dragon. (Will to Conquer Ser.: Vol. 2). 350p. (YA). (gr. 5-12). 2000. 19.95 (*0-9669741-7-4*) SeaScape Pr Ltd.

Lamer, Hans. Woerterbuch der Antike. 8th ed. (GER.). 1976. 59.95 (*0-8288-5768-7*, M7042) Fr & Eur.

LaMer, Lia. Fetters: Handicapped Poet Sings in Defiance. rev. ed. (Illus.). 124p. 1996. 14.00 (*1-58486-007-3*) LyricLine Pr.

Lamer, Timothy W., jt. auth. see Pines, Burton Y.

Lamers, C. B., ed. Clinical Impact of H Plus, K Plus-ATP-ase Inhibitors: Journal: Digestion, Vol. 44, Suppl. 1, 1989. 98p. 1989. pap. 32.25 (*3-8055-5111-8*) S Karger.

Lamers, Henny G. & De Loore, Camiel W., eds. Instabilities in Luminous Early Type Stars. (C). 1987. text 161.50 (*90-277-2522-5*) Kluwer Academic.

Lamers, Henny J., jt. ed. see Habing, Harm J.

Lamers, Henny J., jt. ed. see Nota, Antonella.

Lamers, Henry & Cassinelli, Joseph P. Introduction to Stellar Winds. LC 98-15182. (Illus.). 415p. (C). 1999. 74.95 (*0-521-59398-0*); pap. 29.95 (*0-521-59565-7*) Cambridge U Pr.

Lamers, Joseph M., ed. Biochemistry of Signal Transduction in Myocardium. LC 96-19183. (Developments in Molecular & Cellular Biochemistry Ser.). 282p. (C). 1996. text 272.50 (*0-7923-4067-1*) Kluwer Academic.

Lamers, William M. Edge of Glory: A Biography of General William S. Rosecrans, U. S. A. LC 98-49269. (Illus.). 520p. 1999. pap. 19.95 (*0-8071-2396-X*) La State U Pr.

Lamersdorf, Winfried, et al, eds. Trends in Electronic Commerce: International Conference, TREC '98, Hamburg, Germany, June 3-5, 1998, Proceedings, Vol. 140. LC 98-22218. (Lecture Notes in Computer Science Ser.: Vol. 1402). xii, 255p. 1998. pap. 49.00 (*3-540-64564-0*) Spr-Verlag.

Lamet, Eric. You Can Be the Life of the Party. 112p. 1999. pap. 9.95 (*0-9666808-0-4*) Viva Commun.

Lamet, Jerome S. & Orton, Michelle D. How to Fix Your Credit Report Yourself. LC 97-95083. (Illus.). 272p. 1998. pap. 24.95 (*0-9662219-0-7*) J S Lamet.

Lamet, Rosalie. City of Diamonds. 314p. 1996. 18.95 (*1-56871-097-6*, Pub. by Targum Pr) Feldheim.

Lametschwandtner, A., jt. auth. see Aharinejad, S. H.

Lamey. Sapt Dentistry: Oral Dis. 1996. text 34.00 (*0-7234-2397-0*) Harcourt.

Lamey, Robert W. The Illustrated Guide to PSpice for DOS. LC 94-2662. (Illus.). 219p. (C). 1994. mass mkt. 37.75 (*0-8273-6524-1*) Delmar.

— The Illustrated Guide to PSpice for Windows. LC 94-44412. (C). 1995. pap. 60.95 (*0-8273-7068-7*) Delmar.

Lamfalussy, Alexandre. La Banca Central en Transicion. LC HG1811.L35. (Conferencia Per Jacobsson Ser.: Vol. 1994). (SPA.). 35p. reprint ed. pap. 30.00 (*0-608-08764-5*, 206940300004) Bks Demand.

— Les Banques Centrales en Transition. LC HG1811.L35. (Conference Per Jacobsson Ser.: Vol. 1994). (FRE.). 33p. reprint ed. pap. 30.00 (*0-608-08765-3*, 206940400004) Bks Demand.

— Central Banking in Transition. LC HG1811.L35. (Per Jacobsson Lecture Ser.: Vol. 1994). 33p. reprint ed. pap. 30.00 (*0-608-08763-7*, 206940200004) Bks Demand.

***Lamfalussy, Alexandre.** Financial Crises in Emerging Markets: An Essay on Financial Globalisation & Fragility. LC 99-59157. (Henry L. Stimson Lectures). (Illus.). 224p. 2000. 25.00 (*0-300-08230-4*) Yale U Pr.

Lamford, Paul. The Amazing Book of Casino Games. 1998. 14.99 (*0-7858-0820-5*) Bk Sales Inc.

***Lamford, Paul.** Gem Lottery. 2000. pap. 7.95 (*0-00-472463-1*, Pub. by HarpC) Trafalgar.

Lamia, Tony L. Blame It on the System. Hackbarth, Greg M., ed. LC 99-60175. (Illus.). 261p. 1999. 25.00 (*0-910941-24-6*) JGC.

Lamichhane, Padmini, ed. Communicating in Nepali: A Practical Handbook of Useful Nepali Dialogues, Expressions, Prase & Terminology. 1997. pap. 22.00 (*0-7855-7371-2*, Pub. by Ratna Pustak Bhandar) St Mut.

Lamie, Edward L. Pascal Programming. LC 86-26779. 427p. reprint ed. pap. 132.40 (*0-7837-2819-0*, 205765300006) Bks Demand.

Lamie, Judith, jt. auth. see Moore, George.

Lamiell, James T. The Psychology of Personality: An Epistemological Inquiry. (Critical Assessments of Contemporary Psychology Ser.). (Illus.). 256p. 1987. text 57.50 (*0-231-06020-3*) Col U Pr.

Lamiell, James T., tr. see Stern, Clara & Stern, William.

Lamigueiro, Fernando, ed., see Henrichsen, Walter A.

Lamigueiro, Fernando, tr. see Baxter, Mary K.

Laminack, Lester. Learning with Zachar. (J). 1995. pap. 10.95 (*0-590-73823-2*) Scholastic Inc.

Laminack, Lester L. The Sunsets of Miss Olivia Wiggins. LC 97-40949. (Illus.). 32p. (J). (gr. 1-5). 1998. 15.95 (*1-56145-139-8*) Peachtree Pubs.

— Trevor's Wiggly-Wobbly Tooth. LC 98-7210. (Illus.). 32p. (J). (ps-2). 1998. 15.95 (*1-56145-175-4*, Peachtree) Peachtree Pubs.

— Volunteers Working with Young Readers. LC 98-15541. 133p. 1998. pap. 14.95 (*0-8141-3410-6*) NCTE.

Laming, D. J., jt. ed. see Furrance, E. M.

Laming, D. J., jt. ed. see Stow, D. A.

***Laming, Denis.** Invisible Tensions. 2000. pap. 25.00 (*88-7838-054-7*) L'Arca IT.

Laming, Donald. The Measurement of Sensation. LC 97-3966. (Oxford Psychology Ser.: No. 30). (Illus.). 276p. 1997. text 120.00 (*0-19-852342-4*) OUP.

Laming, Donald, jt. ed. see Fischer, Gerhard H.

Laming, Peter B., jt. auth. see Rijsdijk, Jan F.

Laming, Peter R., et al, eds. Glial Cells: Their Role in Behaviour. LC 98-10902. (Illus.). 440p. (C). 1998. text 150.00 (*0-521-57368-8*) Cambridge U Pr.

***Laming, Tim.** Airbus A320. (Illus.). 128p. 2000. pap. 24.95 (*0-7603-0902-7*, 130214AP, Pub. by MBI Pubg) Motorbooks Intl.

Laming, Tim. Avro Shackleton. (Illus.). 192p. 1998. 44.95 (*1-86126-125-X*, Pub. by Crolwood) Motorbooks Intl.

— Buccaneer. LC 98-70523. (Illus.). 224p. 1998. 39.95 (*1-85260-478-6*) Haynes Manuals.

— V-Bombers: Vulcan, Victor & Valiant, Britain's Airborne Nuclear Deterrent LC 96-78558. 200 p. 1997. 37.95 (*1-85260-529-4*) P Stephens.

Lamirande, Carole A. Able & the Tree of Life. (Illus.). 128p. (J). (gr. 3-9). 1997. pap. 9.95 (*0-9661385-0-3*) Dream Catcher.

Lamiroy, Beatrice. Les Verbes de Mouvement en Francais et en Espagnol: Etude Comparee de Leurs Infinitives. (Lingvisticae Investigationes Supplementa Ser.: No. 11). (FRE.). xiv, 323p. 1984. 62.00 (*90-272-3121-4*) J Benjamins Pubng Co.

Lamis, Alexander P., ed. Ohio Politics. LC 94-7637. (Illus.). 417p. 1994. 24.00 (*0-87338-507-1*); pap. 17.00 (*0-87338-509-8*) Kent St U Pr.

— Southern Politics in the 1990s. LC 98-50424. 552p. 1999. 39.95 (*0-8071-2374-9*) La State U Pr.

Lamls, Alexander P. & Sharkey, Mary A. Ohio Politics. LC 98-13737. 1998. pap. 24.00 (*0-87338-613-2*) Kent St U Pr.

Lamison-White, Leatha. Income, Poverty, & Wealth in the United States: A Chart Book. (Illus.). 50p. 1996. reprint ed. pap. text 25.00 (*0-7881-3285-7*) DIANE Pub.

— Poverty in the United States, 1996. (Illus.). 59p. (C). 1998. pap. text 25.00 (*0-7881-3187-7*) DIANE Pub.

Lamit, L. Gary. Technical Drawing & Design. Conty, ed. LC 92-43902. 1184p. (C). 1993. text 76.75 (*0-314-01264-8*) West Pub.

Lamit, L. Gary & Kitto, Kathleen L. Principles of Engineering Drawing. Conty, ed. LC 93-33033. 700p. (C). 1994. pap. text 43.25 (*0-314-02805-6*) West Pub.

Lamit, Louis G. Basic Pro Engineer. LC 97-35748. (General Engineering Ser.). (C). 1997. mass mkt. 69.95 (*0-534-95068-X*) PWS Pubs.

— Principles of Engineering Drawing. Date not set. pap. text, student ed. write for info. (*0-314-03409-9*) West Pub.

***Lamit, Louis G.** Pro/Engineer 2000 I. rev. ed. LC 99-33302. 1999. pap. 80.95 (*0-534-37038-1*) Brooks-Cole.

— Pro/Engineer 2000 I. rev. ed. LC 99-33302. 1999. pap. text 83.95 (*0-534-37786-6*) Brooks-Cole.

Lamit, Louis G. Technical Drawing & Design. Date not set. pap. text, student ed. write for info. (*0-314-02913-3*) West Pub.

Lamit, Louis G. & Kitto, Kathleen L. Engineering Graphics & Design. LC 96-2078. 1200p. 1997. write for info. (*0-314-06733-7*) West Pub.

— Fundamentals of Engineering Graphics & Design. LC 96-31572. 1000p. (C). 1996. pap. 75.95 (*0-314-20540-3*) West Pub.

Lamit, Louis G. & Lloyd, Sandra J. Drafting for Electronics. 3rd ed. LC 98-17353. 594p. (C). 1998. 74.00 (*0-13-602137-9*) P-H.

Lamit, Louis G., et al. Drafting for Electronics. 2nd ed. (Illus.). 256p. (C). 1993. pap. text, wbk. ed. 60.00 (*0-02-367345-1*, Macmillan Coll) P-H.

Lamizet & Silem, Ahmed. Encyclopedie Dictionary Info Sciences, Communication, French to English. (ENG & FRE.). 590p. 1997. 95.00 (*0-320-00476-7*) Fr & Eur.

Lamke, Sue, jt. auth. see Lamke, Tony.

***Lamke, Tony & Lamke, Sue.** My Pal Grubby. (Illus.). 112p. (Orig.). (J). 2000. pap. 9.95 (*1-882203-68-2*) Orange Frazer.

Lamkin, Geraldine E. Lovey - A Book of Poems. 72p. 1983. pap. 5.00 (*0-9612632-0-2*) Lamkin.

Lamkin, Jeffrey C. The Massachusetts Eye & Ear Infirmary Review Manual for Ophthalmology. LC 92-49469. (Illus.). 672p. 1993. pap. text 76.00 (*0-316-51293-1*) Lppncott W & W.

Lamkin, Jeffrey C. & Massachusetts Eye & Ear Infirmary Staff. The Massachusetts Eye & Ear Infirmary Review Manual for Ophthalmology. 2nd ed. LC 98-27315. 1998. write for info. (*0-7817-1763-9*) Lppncott W & W.

Lamkin, Selma H. Accounting, Self-Instruction Manual. (Orig.). (C). 20.00 (*0-686-32949-X*) Nikmal Pub.

— Do It Right the First Time: Guide to Computer Installation. 1983. 15.00 (*0-686-37906-3*) Nikmal Pub.

— How to Start & Succeed in Business: Small Business Development. abr. ed. 120p. 1991. pap. text 35.00 (*0-686-37907-1*) Nikmal Pub.

— The Shoebox Syndrome (Record-Keeping) (Orig.). (C). 15.00 (*0-686-32948-1*) Nikmal Pub.

— Small Business Survival Manual: Applied Management for Small Non-Profit. (Orig.). (C). 20.00 (*0-686-32947-3*) Nikmal Pub.

Lamkin, Speed. Comes a Day. 1959. pap. 5.25 (*0-8222-0231-X*) Dramatists Play.

Lamley, Harry J., ed. see University of Hawaii (Honolulu), Asian Studies Pro.

Lamm. Pirates. LC 98-52662. 32p. (J). 2000. 10.45 (*0-7868-0392-4*, Pub. by Hyperion); lib. bdg. 15.49 (*0-7868-2343-7*, Pub. by Hyperion) Little.

Lamm & Cross. Human Western Culture. 10th ed. 1995. teacher ed. 20.00 (*0-697-26405-X*, WCB McGr Hill) McGrw-H Hghr Educ.

Lamm, Barbara. The American Constitution in Context. (Illus.). 227p. (C). 1997. lib. bdg. 55.00 (*1-56072-363-7*) Nova Sci Pubs.

— This Is You, America: The Constitution Explained. LC 96-26531. (Illus.). 227p. (Orig.). 1996. pap. 18.95 (*1-56072-326-2*, Nova Kroshka Bks) Nova Sci Pubs.

Lamm, C. Drew. Cottontail at Clover Crescent. LC 94-28697. (Smithsonian's Backyard Ser.). (Illus.). 32p. (J). (ps-2). 1995. 15.95 (*1-56899-108-8*); 19.95 incl. audio (*1-56899-112-6*, BC5005); audio 5.00 (*1-56899-113-4*, C5005) Soundprints.

— Cottontail at Clover Crescent, Incl. 12" plush toy. LC 94-28697. (Smithsonian's Backyard Ser.). (Illus.). 32p. (J). (ps-2). 1995. 32.95 (*1-56899-110-X*) Soundprints.

— Cottontail at Clover Crescent, Micro bk. LC 94-28697. (Smithsonian's Backyard Ser.). (Illus.). 32p. (J). (ps-2). 1995. 4.95 (*1-56899-109-6*) Soundprints.

— Cottontail at Clover Crescent, Micro bk., incl. 6" plush toy. LC 94-28697. (Smithsonian's Backyard Ser.). (Illus.). 32p. (J). (ps-2). 1995. 12.95 (*1-56899-111-8*) Soundprints.

— The Prog Frince: A Mixed-Up Tale. LC 98-12379. (Illus.). 32p. (J). (ps-2). 1999. 16.95 (*0-531-30135-4*); lib. bdg. 17.99 (*0-531-33135-0*) Orchard Bks Watts.

— Screech Owl at Midnight Hollow. (Smithsonian's Backyard Ser.). (Illus.). 32p. (J). (ps-2). 1996. 15.95 (*1-56899-264-5*) Soundprints.

Lamm, C. Drew. Screech Owl at Midnight Hollow. (Smithsonian's Backyard Ser.). (Illus.). 32p. (J). (ps-2). 1996. 19.95 incl. audio (*1-56899-268-8*, BC5010) Soundprints.

Lamm, C. Drew. Screech Owl at Midnight Hollow, Incl. 10" stuffed animal toy. (Smithsonian's Backyard Ser.). (Illus.). 32p. (J). (ps-2). 1996. 32.95 (*1-56899-266-1*) Soundprints.

— Screech Owl at Midnight Hollow, Micro bk. (Illus.). 32p. (J). (ps-2). 1996. 4.95 (*1-56899-265-3*) Soundprints.

— Screech Owl at Midnight Hollow, Micro bk., incl. 6" stuffed animal toy. (Smithsonian's Backyard Ser.). (Illus.). 32p. (J). (ps-2). 1996. 12.95 (*1-56899-267-X*) Soundprints.

— Sea Lion Roars. (Smithsonian Oceanic Collection). (Illus.). 32p. (J). (ps-2). 1997. 15.95 (*1-56899-400-1*); 19.95 incl. audio (*1-56899-406-0*, BC4013) Soundprints.

— Sea Lion Roars, Incl. Large Toy. (Smithsonian Oceanic Collection). (Illus.). 32p. (J). (ps-2). 1997. 34.95 incl. audio (*1-56899-405-2*) Soundprints.

— Sea Lion Roars, Incl. Sm. & Lg. Plush Toy. (Smithsonian Oceanic Collection). (Illus.). 32p. (J). (ps-2). 1996. 38.95 incl. audio (*1-56899-656-X*) Soundprints.

— Sea Lion Roars, Incls. Large Book & Large Toy. (Smithsonian Oceanic Collection). (Illus.). (J). (ps-2). 1997. 29.95 (*1-56899-403-6*) Soundprints.

— Sea Lion Roars, Micro bk. (Smithsonian Oceanic Collection). (Illus.). 32p. (J). (ps-2). 1997. 4.95 (*1-56899-401-X*) Soundprints.

— Sea Lion Roars, Micro bk. & small toy. (Smithsonian Oceanic Collection). (Illus.). 32p. (J). (ps-2). 1997. 9.95 (*1-56899-404-4*) Soundprints.

— Woodchuck at Blackberry Road. (Smithsonian's Backyard Ser.). (Illus.). 32p. (J). (ps-2). 1994. 15.95 (*1-56899-087-1*) Soundprints.

Lamm, C. Drew. Woodchuck at Blackberry Road. (Smithsonian's Backyard Ser.). (Illus.). 32p. (J). (ps-2). 1994. 19.95 incl. audio (*1-56899-091-X*, BC5004) Soundprints.

Lamm, C. Drew. Woodchuck at Blackberry Road, Incl. 10" toy. (Smithsonian's Backyard Ser.). (Illus.). 32p. (J). (ps-2). 1994. 32.95 (*1-56899-089-8*) Soundprints.

— Woodchuck at Blackberry Road, Micro bk. (Smithsonian's Backyard Ser.). (Illus.). 32p. (J). (ps-2). 1994. 4.95 (*1-56899-088-X*) Soundprints.

L

— Woodchuck at Blackberry Road, Micro bk., incl. 6" toy. (Smithsonian's Backyard Ser.). (Illus.). 32p. (J). (ps-2). 1994. 12.95 (*1-56899-090-1*) Soundprints.

Lamm-Cross. The Humanities in Western Culture: A Search for Human Values. 5th ed. 1998. pap. text 35.00 (*0-697-34425-8*) McGraw.

— Humanities Western Culture, Vol. 2. 10th ed. 1996. pap. 13.44 (*0-697-35475-X*) McGraw.

Lamm, D. L., ed. Advances in the Treatment of Superficial Bladder Cancer: Optimizing BCG Immunotherapy. (Journal Ser.: Vol. 27, Suppl. 1, 1995). (Illus.). iv, 34p. 1995. pap. 21.75 (*3-8055-6137-7*) S Karger.

— BCG - A New Standard for Superficial Bladder Cancer: Journal: European Urology, Vol. 21, Suppl. 2, 1992. (Illus.). iv, 48p. 1992. pap. 15.75 (*3-8055-5620-9*) S Karger.

Lamm, David V. Contract Negotiation Cases: Government & Industry. 271p. (C). 1993. text 37.50 (*0-941448-06-1*) Wordcraft MD.

— Instructor's Manual to Accompany Contract Negotiation Cases: Government & Industry. 233p. (C). 1993. pap. 25.00 (*0-941448-07-X*) Wordcraft MD.

Lamm, E., jt. auth. see Vasilenko, E.

Lamm, E., jt. ed. see Vasilenko, E.

Lamm, G. The Cardiovascular Disease Programme of WHO in Europe. (Public Health in Europe Ser.: No. 15). 139p. 1981. pap. text 11.00 (*92-890-1151-3*) World Health.

Lamm, Jay. How to Restore British Sports Cars. LC 91-33927. (Illus.). 224p. 1991. pap. 29.95 (*0-87938-567-7*) MBI Pubg.

Lamm, John. America's Supercar: Corvette. 1995. 14.95 (*0-7858-0341-6*) Bk Sales Inc.

— Mercedes-Benz M-Class: The Complete Story Behind the All-New Sport Utility Vehicle. LC 97-25607. 160p. 1997. pap. text 21.95 (*0-7603-0431-9*) MBI Pubg.

— Porsche Boxster: Color Tech. LC 98-23723. (ColorTech Ser.). (Illus.). 128p. 1998. pap. 17.95 (*0-7603-0519-6*) Motorbooks Intl.

Lamm, Julia A. The Living God: Schleiermacher's Theological Appropriation of Spinoza. 1996. 42.50 (*0-271-01540-3*) Pa St U Pr.

Lamm, Kathryn. 10,000 Ideas for Term Papers: Projects, Reports & Speeches. 5th ed. LC 97-81090. 448p. 1998. 12.95 (*0-02-862512-9*, Arc) IDG Bks.

Lamm, Lawrence, jt. ed. see Copeland, Lewis.

Lamm, Leonard J. The Idea of the Past: History, Science, & Practice in American Psychoanalysis. LC 92-44651. (Psychoanalytic Crosscurrents Ser.). 288p. (C). 1993. text 50.00 (*0-8147-5073-7*) NYU Pr.

Lamm, Leonard Johnathan. Idea of the Past. 1997. pap. text 20.00 (*0-8147-5139-3*) NYU Pr.

Lamm, Martin. August Strindberg. Carlson, Harry G., ed. LC 69-16323. 1972. 27.95 (*0-405-08724-1*) Ayer.

***Lamm, Martin.** Emanuel Swedenborg: A Biography. Spiers, Tomas & Hallengren, Anders, trs. from SWE. (Swedenborg Studies: Vol. 9). 400p. 2000. 24.95 (*0-87785-193-X*, Pub. by Swedenborg) Words Distrib.

Lamm, Maurice. Becoming a Jew. 500p. 1991. 25.00 (*0-8246-0350-8*) Jonathan David.

***Lamm, Maurice.** Jewish Way in Death & Mourning. LC 99-88942. 2000. 25.00 (*0-8246-0423-7*); pap. 16.95 (*0-8246-0422-9*) Jonathan David.

Lamm, Maurice. Jewish Way in Death & Mourning. rev. ed. LC 69-11684. 1972. pap. 15.00 (*0-8246-0126-2*) Jonathan David.

— Jewish Way in Love & Marriage. 1991. pap. 18.95 (*0-8246-0353-2*) Jonathan David.

— Living Torah in America. Cutter, William, ed. (Illus.). 182p. (YA). (gr. 8-10). 1993. 30.00 (*0-87441-513-6*) Behrman.

— The Power of Hope. 1997. per. 10.00 (*0-684-82547-3*, Fireside) S&S Trade Pap.

— The Power of Hope: The One Essential of Life & Love. 288p. 1995. text 22.95 (*0-89256-361-3*, Rawson Assocs) Macmillan.

Lamm, Michael. The Fabulous Firebird. 3rd ed. LC 79-89981. (Illus.). 160p. 1998. reprint ed. 39.95 (*0-932128-01-7*) Lamm-Morada Pub.

Lamm, Michael & Holls, Dave. A Century of Automotive Style: 100 Years of American Car Design. 2nd ed. (Illus.). 306p. 1996. 59.95 (*0-932128-07-6*) Lamm-Morada Pub.

Lamm, Norman. Faith & Doubt: Studies in Traditional Jewish Thought. Date not set. pap. 11.95 (*0-88125-100-3*) Yeshiva Univ Pr.

— A Hedge of Roses: Jewish Insights into Marriage. LC 66-19539. 1977. pap. 6.95 (*0-87306-095-4*) Feldheim.

— The Shema: Spirituality & Law in Judaism. 214p. 1998. 29.95 (*0-8276-0655-9*) JPS Phila.

— Torah Lishmah: The Study of Torah for Torah's Sake in the Work of Rabbi Hayyim of Volozhin & His Contemporaries. (Studies & Sources in Kabbalah, Hasidism & Jewish Thought Ser.: Vol. I). 1988. 25.00 (*0-88125-117-8*); pap. 16.95 (*0-88125-133-X*) Ktav.

— Torah Umadda: The Encounter of Religious Learning & Worldly Knowledge in the Jewish Tradition. LC 89-18519. 264p. 1990. 40.00 (*0-87668-810-5*) Aronson.

— Torah Umadda: The Encounter of Religious Learning & Worldly Knowledge in the Jewish Tradition. LC 89-18519. 264p. 1994. pap. 30.00 (*1-56821-231-3*) Aronson.

Lamm, Norman, ed. Hasidic Religious Thought: Sources & Commentary. LC 98-52553. 624p. 1999. 49.50 (*0-88125-501-7*) Ktav.

— The Religious Thought of Hasidism: Text & Commentary. LC 98-52553. 711p. 1997. pap. 29.50 (*0-88125-440-1*) Ktav.

***Lamm, Richard D.** Mountains of Colorado. LC 99-25301. 1999. 35.00 (*1-55868-470-0*) Gr Arts Ctr Pub.

Lamm, Richard D. & Grossman, Arnold. 1988: A Novel of Politics. 1986. pap. 3.95 (*0-685-43593-8*) St Martin.

Lamm, Robert C. & Cross, Neal. The Humanities in Western Culture: A Search for Human Values. 3rd ed. 624p. (C). 1992. text. write for info. (*0-697-12562-9*) Brown & Benchmark.

— The Humanities in Western Culture: A Search for Human Values. 4th ed. 608p. (C). 1997. per. write for info. (*0-07-114992-9*) McGraw.

— Humanities in Western Culture: A Search for Human Values. 10th ed. 84p. (C). 1996. text 11.87 (*0-697-35474-1*) Brown & Benchmark.

— The Humanities in Western Culture: A Search for Human Values - Brief Version. 4th ed. LC 95-76176. 583p. (C). 1995. text 52.20 (*0-697-25425-9*) Brown & Benchmark.

— Humanities in Western Culture Vol. I: A Search for Human Values. 9th ed. 496p. (C). 1992. text, ring bd. write for info. incl. audio (*0-697-10949-6*) Brown & Benchmark.

— Humanities in Western Culture, Vol. 2: A Search for Human Values. 9th ed. 512p. (C). 1992. text. write for info. (*0-697-10667-5*) Brown & Benchmark.

— Humanities Western Culture Vol. I: A Search for Human Values. (C). 1995. audio. write for info. (*0-697-25428-3*) Brown & Benchmark.

— Humanities Western Culture Vol. I: A Search for Human Values. 10th ed. 496p. (C). 1995. text. write for info. (*0-697-25427-5*) Brown & Benchmark.

— Humanities Western Culture Vol. II: A Search for Human Values. (C). 1995. audio. write for info. (*0-697-25430-5*) Brown & Benchmark.

— Humanities Western Culture Vol. II: A Search for Human Values. 10th ed. 496p. (C). 1995. text. write for info. (*0-697-25429-1*) Brown & Benchmark.

Lamm, Robert C., et al. The Humanities in Western Culture: A Search for Human Values. 2nd ed. 560p. (C). 1988. text. write for info. (*0-697-10299-8*) Brown & Benchmark.

Lamm, Robert P., jt. auth. see Schaefer, Richard T.

Lamm, Ruediger. Highway Design & Traffic Engineering Handbook. LC 98-41928. (Illus.). 1088p. 1998. 164.95 (*0-07-038295-6*) McGraw-Hill Prof.

Lamm, Spencer. The Matrix. pap. 24.95 (*1-55704-432-5*, Pub. by Newmarket) Norton.

***Lamm, Spencer, ed.** The Art of the Matrix. aut. ed. (Illus.). 500p. 2000. 60.00 (*1-55704-405-8*, Pub. by Newmarket) Norton.

— The Art of the Matrix. limited aut. ed. (Illus.). 500p. 2000. 250.00 (*1-55704-433-3*, Pub. by Newmarket) Norton.

Lamm, Steven. The Virility Solution: Everything You Need to Know About Viagra, the Potency Pill That Can Restore & Enhance Male Sexuality. LC 98-5837. 224p. (YA). 1998. 22.50 (*0-684-84780-9*) S&S Trade.

— Younger at Last: Discover the Age-Defying Powers of Vitality Medicine. 1998. per. 6.99 (*0-671-02291-1*, Pocket Star Bks) PB.

Lamm, Steven & Couzens, Gerald S. Younger at Last. LC 97-13557. 1997. 22.50 (*0-684-83438-3*) S&S Trade.

Lamm, Steven & Couzens, Gerald Secor. The Virility Solution: Everything You Need to Know about Viagra, the Potency Pill That Can Restore & Enhance Male Sexuality. 224p. 1999. per. 12.00 (*0-684-85431-7*, Fireside) S&S Trade Pap.

Lamm-Tennant, Joan. Mutual Funds: Analysis, Allocation, & Performance Evaluation. LC 94-73423. 200p. (C). 1995. text 43.00 (*0-943590-66-3*) Amer College.

Lamm, V., jt. auth. see Kilenyi, G.

Lamm, V., jt. auth. see Kilenyi, Geza.

Lamm, V., jt. auth. see Peteri, Z.

Lamm, Vanda, jt. ed. see Peteri, Zoltan.

Lamma, E. & Mello, P., eds. Extensions of Logic Programming: Third International Workshop, ELP '92, Bologna, Italy, February 26-28, 1992, Proceedings. LC 92-45283. (Lecture Notes in Computer Science, Lecture Notes in Artificial Intelligence Ser.). 1993. 61.95 (*0-387-56454-3*) Spr-Verlag.

Lamma, E., ed. see Associazione Italiana per l'intelligenza Artificiale Staff.

Lammas, David. Adhesives & Sealants. (Orig.). pap. 19.95 (*1-85486-048-8*, Pub. by Nexus Special Interests) Trans-Atl Phila.

— Adhesives & Sealants. (Workshop Practice Ser.: No. 21). (Illus.). 144p. (Orig.). 1991. pap. 19.95 (*0-85486-048-7*, Pub. by Nexus Special Interests) Trans-Atl Phila.

***Lammasniemi, Jorma, et al, eds.** Diagnostic Imaging Technologies & Industrial Applications. 170p. 1999. pap. text 72.00 (*0-8194-3313-6*) SPIE.

Lamme, Ary J., III. America's Historic Landscapes: Community Power & the Preservation of Four National Historic Sites. LC 89-4925. (Illus.). 230p. 1990. text 27.00 (*0-87049-614-X*) U of Tenn Pr.

Lamme, Ary J. Florida: A Geography. 1996. text 39.50 (*0-8133-0008-8*) Westview.

Lamme, Linda, jt. ed. see Hoffman, Stevie.

Lamme, Linda L., et al. Literature-Based Moral Education: Children's Books & Activities to Enrich the K-5 Curriculum. LC 92-31390. 160p. 1992. pap. 29.95 (*0-89774-723-2*) Oryx Pr.

Lammel, George. Open Spaces in Vienna: A Guide to Contemporary Landscaping. 1998. write for info. (*3-211-83178-9*) Spr-Verlag.

Lammens, Henri. Islam: Beliefs & Institutions. 1976. lib. bdg. 59.95 (*0-8490-2080-8*) Gordon Pr.

— Islam: Beliefs & Institutions. Ross, E. Denison, tr. from FRE. 265p. reprint ed. text 23.50 (*0-685-13406-7*) Coronet Bks.

Lammens, Letty & Scholte, Els. Beaded Animals in Jewelry. 56p. 1994. pap. 14.00 (*0-916896-61-7*) Lacis Pubns.

Lammens, Martin. Developmental Neuropathology in Etiology & Pathogenesis of Human Malformations: A Personal Contribution. (Acta Biomedica Lovaniensia Ser.: No. 154). (Illus.). 177p. 1997. pap. 62.50 (*90-6186-825-4*, Pub. by Almqvist Wiksell) Coronet Bks.

Lammer, Helmut & Lammer, Marion. Milabs! Military Mind-Control & Alien Abductions. LC 99-14041. (Illus.). 168p. 1999. 14.95 (*1-881532-18-6*) IllumiNet Pr.

Lammer, Jutta. Cross-Stitch a Beautiful Christmas. LC 91-12851. (Illus.). 64p. 1992. pap. 9.95 (*0-8069-8311-6*) Sterling.

Lammer, L., jt. auth. see Topping, B. H. V.

Lammer, Marion, jt. auth. see Lammer, Helmut.

Lammer, Victoria, ed. Survivor's Guide to Computer Viruses: Virus Bulletin '93. (Illus.). 346p. 1999. reprint ed. pap. text 20.00 (*0-7881-6513-5*) DIANE Pub.

Lammermeyr, Horst U. Human Relations: The Key to Quality. (Illus.). 296p. 1990. text 32.95 (*0-527-91628-5*, 916285) Productivity Inc.

Lammers, Ann C. In God's Shadow: The Collaboration of Victor White & C. G. Jung. LC 94-15329. (Jung & Spirituality Ser.). 352p. 1994. pap. 19.95 (*0-8091-3489-6*) Paulist Pr.

Lammers, Bernard. Fragmented Government. LC 96-49720. 94p. 1997. pap. 19.50 (*0-7618-0651-2*) U Pr of Amer.

— Legislative Process & Drafting U. S. Law Schools. LC 77-79655. ix, 86p. 1977. 20.00 (*0-910058-87-3*, 304940) W S Hein.

Lammers, Cornelius J. & Szell, Gyorgy, eds. International Handbook of Participation in Organizations Vol. 1: For the Study of Organizational Democracy, Co-Operation & Self-Management: Organizational Democracy: Taking Stock. (Illus.). 372p. 1990. text 125.00 (*0-19-877259-9*) OUP.

Lammers, Hendrik. Synthesis & Coordination Behaviour of N-alkylamino Sugars & Derivatives. (Illus.). 199p. (Orig.). 1995. pap. 59.50 (*90-407-1187-9*, Pub. by Delft U Pr) Coronet Bks.

Lammers, J. G., jt. ed. see Kiss, A.-Ch.

Lammers, Jane, photos by. America's National Historic Trails. (Illus.). 363p. 1999. pap. 19.95 (*0-8061-3089-X*) U of Okla Pr.

Lammers, Jeff & Blackburn, Ken. World Record Paper Airplane Kit. 32p. 1992. pap. 9.95 (*0-9634845-0-8*) Wrld Rec Paper.

Lammers, Jeff, jt. auth. see Blackburn, Ken.

Lammers, Johan G. Pollution of International Watercourses. 1984. lib. bdg. 283.00 (*90-247-2955-6*) Kluwer Academic.

Lammers, Johan G., jt. ed. see Kiss, A. C.

Lammers, Johan G., jt. ed. see von Hebel, Herman A. M.

Lammers, Laura, ed. A Hero Born: A Tribute to John Glenn. LC 99-60640. (Illus.). 100p. (Orig.). (YA). (gr. 5 up). 1999. pap. 19.99 (*1-893231-01-1*, B2JG1) Poet Born.

— Poetry of the Web Vol. I: 1999. LC 99-90294. 150p. (YA). (gr. 9 up). 1999. pap. 19.99 (*1-893231-02-X*) Poet Born.

Lammers, Laura, ed. see Chilson, Steve.

Lammers, Laura, ed. see Skye, Laura.

Lammers, Lawrence P., jt. auth. see Hardy, Owen B.

Lammers, Mark. Nordic Instrumental Music for Colleges & Universities. 236p. (Orig.). (C). 1991. pap. 15.00 (*0-9630771-0-4*) M Lammers.

Lammers, Nadine B. Birthday Stars. 32p. (J). (gr. k-5). 1994. pap. 5.95 (*0-9642971-1-6*) N B Lammers.

— Night Time Twinkles. 20p. (J). (gr. k-5). 1994. pap. 4.95 (*0-9642971-0-8*) N B Lammers.

Lammers-Prior, Teri, ed. 301 Great Ideas for Selling Smarter. 352p. 1998. pap. 14.95 (*1-880394-76-6*) Thomson Learn.

Lammers, Stephen E. & Verhey, Allen, eds. On Moral Medicine: Theological Perspectives in Medical Ethics. 667p. 1987. pap. 20.00 (*0-8028-0293-1*) Eerdmans.

— On Moral Medicine: Theological Perspectives in Medical Ethics. 2nd expanded rev. ed. LC 97-35605. 1000p. 1998. pap. 49.00 (*0-8028-4249-6*) Eerdmans.

Lammers, Susan. All about Houseplants. rev. ed. Orthos Books Staff, ed. LC 81-86183. (Illus.). 96p. (Orig.). 1982. pap. 9.95 (*0-89721-002-6*, Ortho Bks) Meredith Bks.

Lammers, Susan M., jt. auth. see Hodgson, Larry.

Lammers, Thomas F. & Woodruff, Everett B. Steam-Plant Operation. 7th ed. LC 97-46056. 818p. 1998. 84.95 (*0-07-036150-9*) McGraw.

Lammers, Thomas G. Systematics of Clermontia (Campanulaceae-Lobelioideae) Anderson, Christiane, ed. (Systematic Botany Monographs: Vol. 32). (Illus.). 97p. 1991. pap. 13.00 (*0-912861-32-0*) Am Soc Plant.

Lammers, Wayne & Morrison, Clinton D., trs. Treasures 3: Stories & Art by Students in Japan & Oregon. LC 96-132186. (Illus.). 258p. (Orig.). (J). (gr. k-12). 1994. pap. 11.95 (*0-9616058-6-3*) OR Students Writing.

Lammers, Wayne P. Mangajin's Japanese Grammar Through Comics. (JPN., Illus.). 256p. (Orig.). (C). 1997. pap. write for info. (*0-9634335-5-5*) Mangajin.

Lammers, Wayne P., tr. from JPN. The Tale of Matsura: Fujiwara Teika's Experiment in Fiction. LC 90-42197. (Michigan Monographs in Japanese Studies: No. 9). xii, 207p. 1992. 35.00 (*0-939512-48-3*) U MI Japan.

Lammers, Wayne P., jt. auth. see Freye, Kurt.

Lammers, Wayne P., jt. auth. see Simmons, Vaughan P.

Lammers, Wayne P., ed. & tr. see Shohei, Ooka.

Lammers, Wayne P., tr. see Shono, Junzo.

***Lammers, William W.** Presidency & Domestic Policy: Comparing Leadership Styles, FDR to Clinton. 330p. 2000. 38.95 (*1-56802-125-9*) CQ Pr.

***Lammers, William W. & Genovese, Michael A.** The Presidency & Domestic Policy: Comparing Leadership Styles, F. D. R. to Clinton. LC 99-88686. 2000. 28.95 (*1-56802-124-0*) CQ Pr.

***Lammert.** Microbiology. 2002. pap. text. write for info. (*0-7167-2867-2*); pap. text, student ed. write for info. (*0-7167-3942-9*) W H Freeman.

Lammert & Boer, eds. Ptolemaei, Claudii Vol. III, Fascicule 2: Peri Kriteriu Kai Hegemoniku. (GRE.). 1961. 22.95 (*3-322-00908-4*, T1966, Pub. by B G Teubner) U of Mich Pr.

***Lammert-Reeves, Ruth.** Kaplan Newsweek Law School Admissions Adviser. 240p. 2000. pap. text 22.00 (*0-684-87337-0*) S&S Trade.

Lammerts Van Bueren, E. M. & Duivenvoorden, J. F. Towards Priorities of Biodiversity Research in Support of Policy & Management of Tropical Rain Forests: A Contribution to the Conservation & Wise Use of Tropical Rain Forests. (Tropenbos Technical Ser.). (Illus.). 32p. 1996. 17.00 (*90-5113-029-5*, Pub. by Backhuys Pubs) Balogh.

Lammerts, Walter E., intro. Scientific Studies in Special Creation. 2nd ed. LC 70-150955. (Illus.). 343p. 1990. reprint ed. pap. 10.00 (*0-940384-08-6*) Creation Research.

Lammey, William C. Karmic Tarot: A Profound System for Finding Your Life's Path. enl. rev. ed. Gross, Gina R. & Buryn, Ed, eds. (Illus.). 256p. 1993. pap. 16.95 (*0-87877-136-0*) Newcastle Pub.

Lammey, William L., ed. see Lawrence, Shirley B.

Lammi, O. Paradigm Visual Series: Microsoft Powerpoint 7: Text with data disk, 3.5 IBM. 128p. text 14.95 (*0-7638-0017-1*) EMC-Paradigm.

Lammi, Outi & Kolari, Jukka. Microsoft Word 97: Text with Data Disk, 3.5. LC 97-35439. (Paradigm Visual Ser.). 128p. 1997. pap. write for info. incl. 3.5 hd (*0-7638-0087-2*) Paradigm MN.

— Microsoft Word 97. LC 97-35439. (Paradigm Visual Ser.). 1997. write for info. (*0-7638-0086-4*) Paradigm MN.

Lammie, Todd. CCNP Exam Notes: Advanced Cisco Certified Router. 3rd ed. LC 99-65193. (Certification Ser.). 432p. 1999. pap. 19.99 (*0-7821-2540-9*) Sybex.

— Cisco Certified Design Associate Study Guide. 4th ed. 640p. 1999. 49.99 (*0-7821-2534-4*) Sybex.

***Lammie, Todd.** Cisco Certified Network Associate. 2nd ed. (CCNA Exam Notes Ser.). (Illus.). 400p. 2000. pap. 19.99 (*0-7821-2648-0*) Sybex.

— Cisco Certified Network Associate Study Guide. 2nd ed. (CCNA Study Guides). 800p. 2000. 49.99 (*0-7821-2647-2*) Sybex.

***Lammie, Todd & Tedder, Bill.** CCNA Virtual Lab E-Trainer. 2000. pap. 99.99 incl. cd-rom (*0-7821-2728-2*) Sybex.

Lammiman, jt. auth. see Syrett.

Lammiman, Jean, jt. auth. see Syrett, Michel.

Lamming. In the Castle of My Skin. Date not set. pap. text. write for info. (*0-582-64267-1*, Pub. by Addison-Wesley) Longman.

Lamming, Douglas. A Scottish Internationalists' Who's Who, 1872-1986. 250p. 1987. 80.00 (*0-907033-47-4*) St Mut.

Lamming, G. E., ed. Marshall's Physiology of Reproduction Vol. 2: Reproduction Function in the Male. 4th ed. (Illus.). 704p. 1990. text 125.00 (*0-443-01967-3*) Church.

Lamming, G. E., ed. see Easter School in Agricultural Science (14th 1967,.

Lamming, George. Conversations: Essays, Addresses, & Interviews 1953-1990. Drayton, Richard & Andaiye, eds. 300p. Date not set. pap. 14.95 (*0-472-06575-0*); text 42.50 (*0-472-09575-7*) U of Mich Pr.

— The Emigrants. LC 80-40599. 274p. 1987. pap. 6.95 (*0-8052-8036-7*) Schocken.

— The Emigrants. LC 94-2141. 280p. 1994. reprint ed. pap. 15.95 (*0-472-06470-3*, 06470, Ann Arbor Bks) U of Mich Pr.

— In the Castle of My Skin. LC 91-42068. (Ann Arbor Paperbacks Ser.). 314p. (C). 1991. reprint ed. pap. 17.95 (*0-472-06468-1*, 06468); reprint ed. text 49.50 (*0-472-09468-8*, 09468) U of Mich Pr.

— Natives of My Person. (Ann Arbor Paperbacks Ser.). 300p. (C). 1991. reprint ed. pap. 17.95 (*0-472-06467-3*, 06467); reprint ed. text 49.50 (*0-472-09467-X*, 09467) U of Mich Pr.

— The Pleasures of Exile. (Ann Arbor Paperbacks Ser.). 300p. (C). 1991. reprint ed. pap. 17.95 (*0-472-06466-5*, 06466); reprint ed. text 49.50 (*0-472-09466-1*, 09466) U of Mich Pr.

— Season of Adventure. LC 86-673901. 366p. 1979. write for info. (*0-85031-291-4*) Black Moss.

— Season of Adventure. LC 99-19113. 368p. (C). 1999. pap. 17.95 (*0-472-06655-2*, 06655); text 49.50 (*0-472-09655-9*, 09655) U of Mich Pr.

Lamming, Michael G., jt. auth. see Newman, William H.

Lammle, Todd. Advanced Cisco Router Configuration. LC 98-88911. (CCNP Ser.). 800p. 1999. 49.99 (*0-7821-2403-8*) Sybex.

***Lammle, Todd.** CCDA Exam Notes: Cisco Certified Design Associate. (Illus.). 400p. 2000. pap. text 24.99 (*0-7821-2776-2*, Network Pr) Sybex.

— CCNA Certification Kit. 2000. pap. text 139.98 (*0-7821-2729-0*, Network Pr) Sybex.

— CCNP: Remote Access Exam Notes. (CCNP Exam Notes Ser.). 2000. pap. 24.99 (*0-7821-2714-2*, Network Pr) Sybex.

— CCNP: Remote Access Study Guide. 704p. 2000. pap. 49.99 incl. cd-rom (*0-7821-2710-X*) Sybex.

— CCNP: Routing Study Guide. (CCNP Study Guides Ser.). 2000. pap. 49.99 (*0-7821-2712-6*, Network Pr) Sybex.

— CCNP: Support Exam Notes. 2000. pap. 24.99 (*0-7821-2717-7*) Sybex.

— CCNP: Switching Study Guide. 704p. 2000. pap. 49.99 incl. cd-rom (*0-7821-2711-8*) Sybex.

— CCNP CISCO Certified Network Professionals Study Kit. 1999. pap. 199.95 incl. cd-rom (*0-7821-2575-1*) Sybex.

— CCNP Support Study Guide. 2000. pap. 49.99 (0-7821-2713-4) Sybex.

— Cisco Certified Network Associate. LC 99-61311. (Certification Ser.). (Illus.). 352p. 1999. 49.99 (0-7821-2535-2) Sybex.

Lammle, Todd. Cisco Certified Network Associate Study Guide. LC 98-87589. 768p. 1998. 49.99 (0-7821-2381-3) Sybex.

***Lammle, Todd.** Cisco Internetwork Troubleshooting. 3rd ed. (Certification Ser.). 384p. 1999. pap. text 19.99 (0-7821-2541-7) Sybex.

— Cisco LAN Switching Configuration. 3rd ed. (CCNP Ser.). (Illus.). 416p. 1999. pap. text 19.99 (0-7821-2542-5) Sybex.

Lammle, Todd. Configuring, Monitoring & Troubleshooting Dial-Up Services. 720p. 1999. student ed. 49.99 (0-7821-2544-1); pap. 19.99 (0-7821-2543-3) Sybex.

***Lammle, Todd.** MCSE, TCP/IP for NT Server 4 Study Guide. 4th ed. 2000. pap. write for info. (0-7821-2725-8) Sybex.

Lammle, Todd & Chellis, James. MCSE TCP/IP for NT Server 4 Study Guide. 2nd ed. LC 97-61719. 640p. 1997. pap. text, student ed. 49.99 (0-7821-2173-X) Sybex.

Lammle, Todd & Spangenberg, Ward. CCNP: Cisco LAN Switching Configuration Study Guide. 3rd ed. 656p. 1999. text, student ed. 49.99 (0-7821-2571-9) Sybex.

***Lammle, Todd & Swartz, John.** CCIE: Cisco Certified Internetwork Expert Study Guide. 1008p. 2000. 69.99 (0-7821-2657-X) Sybex.

Lammle, Todd, et al. CCNP: Cisco Internetwork Troubleshooting Study Guide. LC 99-62998. 784p. 1999. 49.99 (0-7821-2536-0) Sybex.

— MCSE Test Success - Networking Essentials. LC 98-84010. 384p. 1998. pap. text 24.99 incl. cd-rom (0-7821-2146-2, Network Pr) Sybex.

— MCSE Test Success - NT Workstation 4. LC 98-84012. 384p. 1998. pap. text 24.99 incl. cd-rom (0-7821-2149-7, Network Pr) Sybex.

Lammle, Todd, jt. auth. see Syngress Media, Inc. Staff.

Lammon, Carol B., et al. Clinical Nursing Skills. LC 93-44872. (Illus.). 784p. 1995. pap. text 47.00 (0-7216-6680-9, W B Saunders Co) Harcrt Hlth Sci Grp.

— Clinical Nursing Skills: Textbook/Checklist Package, Textbook/Checklist Package. (Illus.). 811p. 1995. text 58.00 (0-7216-6217-X, W B Saunders Co) Harcrt Hlth Sci Grp.

Lammon, Martin. News from Where I Live: Poems by Martin Lammon. LC 97-39769. 1998. 20.00 (1-55728-507-1); pap. 12.00 (1-55728-508-X) U of Ark Pr.

Lammon, Martin, ed. Written in Water, Written in Stone: Twenty Years of Poets on Poetry. LC 96-43380. 304p. (Orig.). 1996. pap. 16.95 (0-472-06634-X, 06634); text 42.50 (0-472-09634-6, 09634) U of Mich Pr.

Lammond, D. Thomas Carlyle. LC 73-18127. (Studies in Thos. Carlyle: No. 53). 1974. lib. bdg. 75.00 (0-8383-1740-5) M S G Haskell Hse.

Lamnabhi-Lagarrigue, F., jt. ed. see Jacob, G.

Lamo-Jimenez, Mario. Discovering Dinosaurs: Dinosaur Giants of South America. LC 96-6063. (Illus.). (J). 1996. pap. 5.95 (0-382-39683-9, Silver Pr NJ); lib. bdg. 15.95 (0-382-39682-0, Silver Pr NJ) Silver Burdett Pr.

Lamoine, Georges. Changes to the Grand Jury, 1689-1803. (Camden Fourth Ser.: No. 43). 256p. (C). 45.00 (0-86193-130-0) David Brown.

Lamola, Angelo A., ed. Creation & Detection of the Excited State, Vol. 1, Pt. A. LC 76-134785. (Illus.). 391p. 1971. reprint ed. pap. 121.30 (0-7837-0943-9, 204124800001) Bks Demand.

— Creation & Detection of the Excited State, Vol. 1, Pt. B. LC 76 134785. (Illus.). 301p. 1971. reprint ed. pap. 93.40 (0-7837-0944-7, 204124800002) Bks Demand.

LaMon, Dana. The Soul's Mirror: Reflections on the Fullness of Life. LC 97-93087. 336p. 1997. 24.95 (0-9656633-2-9) ImageWorth.

Lamon, Lester C. Black Tennesseans, Nineteen Hundred to Nineteen Thirty. LC 76-49583. (Twentieth-Century America Ser.). 338p. reprint ed. pap. 104.80 (0-8357-7299-3, 202556100044) Bks Demand.

— Blacks in Tennessee, 1791-1970. LC 81-3396. (Tennessee Three Star Ser.). (Illus.). 136p. 1981. pap. 7.00 (0-87049-324-8) U of Tenn Pr.

Lamon, Robert S. Megiddo Water System F. 1994. lib. bdg. 2.00 (0-226-46798-8) U Ch Pr.

Lamon, Susan J. More: In-Depth Discussion of the Reasoning Activities in "Teaching Fractions & Ratios for Understanding" LC 99-193054. 192p. 1999. pap. 24.50 (0-8058-3299-8) L Erlbaum Assocs.

— Teaching Fractions & Ratios for Conceptual Understanding: Essential Content Knowledge & Instructional Strategies for Teachers. LC 98-51379. xiv, 272p. 1999. pap. 24.50 (0-8058-2940-7) L Erlbaum Assocs.

***Lamon, Susan J.** Teaching Fractions & Ratios for Understanding: Essential Content Knowledge & Instructional Strategies for Teachers, 2 vols., Set. 1999. pap. 32.50 (0-8058-3321-8) L Erlbaum Assocs.

Lamon, Susan J., jt. ed. see Lesh, Richard.

Lamon, Ward H. The Life of Abraham Lincoln: From His Birth to His Inauguration As President. LC 99-10195. (Illus.). 592p. 1999. pap. 22.00 (0-8032-7985-X, Bison Books) U of Nebr Pr.

— Recollections of Abraham Lincoln, 1847-1865. Teillard, Dorothy L., ed. LC 94-18220. (Illus.). 1326p. 1994. reprint ed. pap. 15.95 (0-8032-7950-7, Bison Books) U of Nebr Pr.

Lamond, Frederick. Religion Without Beliefs: Essays in Pantheist Theology, Comparative Religion & Ethics. LC 98-116923. 184p. 1998. pap. 16.95 (1-85756-341-7) Paul & Co Pubs.

Lamond, John & Tucek, Robin. The Malt Whisky File. 2nd ed. LC 98-123552. (Illus.). 256p. 1998. 24.95 (1-55821-669-3) Lyons Pr.

— The Malt Whisky File: The Connoisseur's Guide to Malt Whiskies & Distilleries. (Illus.). 225p. 1997. 19.95 (0-932664-93-8, 6830) Wine Appreciation.

Lamond, Joseph F. & Klieger, Paul, eds. Significance of Testing & Properties of Concrete & Concrete-Making Materials. 4th ed. LC 94-16746. (Special Technical Publications: Vol. 169C). (Illus.). 630p. 1994. 110.00 (0-8031-2053-2, STP169C) ASTM.

Lamond, Margrete. Plague & Pestilence: Deadly Diseases That Changed the World. (True Stories Ser.). (Illus.). 100p. (Orig.). (J). (gr. 3-8). 1997. pap. 6.95 (1-86448-456-X, Pub. by Allen & Unwin Pty) IPG Chicago.

Lamond, Ross, jt. auth. see Jochle, Wolfgang.

Lamond, Thomas C. Manufactured & Patented Spokeshaves & Similar Tools: Identification of the Artifacts & Profiles of the Makers & Patentees. LC 97-93162. (Illus.). 450p. 1997. 95.00 (0-9655401-0-3) T C Lamond.

Lamonica, Tom, ed. see Bloodworth, Bryan & Cushman, Roger.

Lamont. Puritanism & the English Revolution, Vol. 2. 1992. 56.95 (0-7512-0002-6) Ashgate Pub Co.

— Puritanism & the English Revolution, Vol.1. 1992. 56.95 (0-7512-0001-8) Ashgate Pub Co.

— Puritanism & the English Revolution, Vol.3. 1992. 63.95 (0-7512-0003-4) Ashgate Pub Co.

Lamont. Vascular Surgery. LC 98-37284. (Illus.). 224p. 1999. text 145.00 (0-19-262523-3) OUP.

Lamont, Alonzo D., Jr. That Serious He-Man Ball. 1992. pap. 5.25 (0-8222-1127-0) Dramatists Play.

Lamont, Billy. The Gallery of Light. 100p. 1993. pap. 9.95 (0-9632881-0-5); audio 11.95 (0-9632881-2-1) Natl Post Modern.

Lamont-Brown, Raymond. Discovering Fife. (Discovering Ser.). 216p. (C). 1996. pap. 26.85 (0-85976-204-1, Pub. by J Donald) St Mut.

— The Grey Widow-Maker: Twenty-Four Disasters at Sea. large type ed. (Lythway Ser.). 280p. 1991. 24.95 (0-7451-1337-0, G K Hall Lrg Type) Mac Lib Ref.

***Lamont-Brown, Raymond.** John Brown: Queen Victoria's Highland Servant. 2000. 29.95 (0-7509-2252-4, Pub. by Sutton Publng) Intl Pubs Mktg.

Lamont-Brown, Raymond. Kamikaze: Japan's Suicide Samurai. LC 98-111024. (Illus.). 192p. 1998. 24.95 (1-85409-367-3, Pub. by Arms & Armour) Sterling.

***Lamont-Brown, Raymond.** Kamikaze: Japan's Suicide Samurai. (Military Classics). 2000. pap. 9.95 (0-304-35200-4) Continuum.

Lamont-Brown, Raymond. Kempeitai: Japan's Dreaded Military Policy. LC 99-171188. 1998. 35.95 (0-7509-1566-8, Pub. by Sutton Pub Ltd) Intl Pubs Mktg.

— The Life & Times of Berwick-upon-Tweed. 200p. (C). 1989. pap. text 30.00 (0-85976-233-5, Pub. by J Donald) St Mut.

— The Life & Times of St. Andrews. 220p. (C). 1996. pap. 35.00 (0-85976-236-X, Pub. by J Donald) St Mut.

— Scotland of One Hundred Years Ago. (Illus.). 128p. 1997. 33.95 (0-7509-1421-1, Pub. by Sutton Pub Ltd) Intl Pubs Mktg.

— Scottish Folklore. LC 97-129243. (Traditional Scotland Ser.). 154p. pap. 11.95 (1-874744-58-0, Pub. by Birlinn Ltd) Dufour.

— Tutor to the Dragon Emperor: The Life of Sir Reginald Fleming Johnston. 1999. 34.95 (0-7509-2106-4, Pub. by Sutton Publng) Intl Pubs Mktg.

Lamont, Claire, ed. & intro. see Scott, Sir Walter.

Lamont-Clarke, Ginette & Stevens, Florence. Et Si Papa Se Perd au Zoo? LC 91-65364. (FRE., Illus.). 24p. (J). (ps-2). 1991. 12.95 (0-88776-266-2); pap. 6.95 (0-88776-273-5) Tundra Bks.

Lamont-Clarke, Ginette, jt. auth. see Stevens, Florence.

Lamont, Corliss. Humanist Funeral Service. 3rd ed. LC 77-76001. 48p. 1977. pap. 9.95 (0-87975-090-1) Prometheus Bks.

— A Humanist Wedding Service. 3rd ed. 28p. 1972. pap. 7.95 (0-87975-000-6) Prometheus Bks.

— Lover's Credo: Poetry. LC 82-13909. 1994. pap. 8.95 (0-87233-114-8) Bauhan.

Lamont, Corliss, ed. Man Answers Death. LC 79-99031. (Granger Index Reprint Ser.). 1977. 23.95 (0-8369-6106-4) Ayer.

Lamont, Corliss, ed. see Lamb, Helen B.

Lamont, Daveda, ed. see Buttwinick, Marty.

Lamont, Douglas. Global Marketing. LC 95-11202. 1995. 72.95 (1-55786-493-4) Blackwell Pubs.

— Salmon Day: The End of the Beginning for Global Business, 1. 312p. 1998. 24.95 (1-900961-19-9) Capstone Pub NH.

Lamont, Douglas, ed. Protectionism: Can American Business Overcome It? (ITT Key Issues Lecture). 127p. (Orig.). (C). 1986. pap. write for info. (0-937137-01-4) Bookscraft.

Lamont, E. Taxonomy of Eupatorium Section Verticillata (Asteraceae) (Memoirs of the New York Botanical Garden Ser.: Vol. 72). (Illus.). 67p. 1995. pap. 14.00 (0-89327-391-0) NY Botanical.

Lamont, Edward M. Ambassador from Wall Street: The Story of Thomas W. Lamont, J. P. Morgan's Chief Executive. LC 93-27773. 1993. 26.95 (1-56833-018-9) Madison Bks UPA.

LaMont, J. T., jt. ed. see Rambaud, J. P.

Lamont, J. Thomas. Gastrointestinal Infections: Diagnosis & Management. LC 97-18585. (Gastroenterology Ser.). (Illus.). 504p. 1997. text 140.00 (0-8247-0055-4) Dekker.

Lamont, John. Diary. LC 78-171649. (Maitland Club, Glasgow. Publications: No. 7). reprint ed. 37.50 (0-404-52933-X) AMS Pr.

LaMont Johnson, D. & Maddux, Cleborne. Computers & Technology in Education: A Self-paced Study Guide for Learning to Use Computers & Technology in Te. 2nd ed. 180p. (C). spiral bd. 27.95 (0-7872-6436-9) Kendall-Hunt.

***Lamont, Kate.** Kate Lamont: Family, Food & Friends. (Illus.). 120p. 2000. pap. 24.95 (1-86368-293-7, Pub. by Fremantle Arts) Intl Spec Bk.

***LaMont, Mark.** A Graceful Age: Reflections for the Wisdom Years. 168p. 2000. pap. 12.95 (0-88489-617-X) St Marys.

***Lamont, Michaele.** The Dignity of Working Men: Morality & the Boundaries of Race, Class & Immigration. LC 00-31087. 432p. 2000. write for info. (0-674-00306-3) HUP.

Lamont, Michele. Cultural Territories of Race: Black & White Boundaries: Black & White Boundaries. LC 98-48863. 448p. 1999. pap. text 25.00 (0-226-46836-4); lib. bdg. 55.00 (0-226-46835-6) U Ch Pr.

— Money, Morals & Manners: The Culture of the French & the American Upper- Middle Class. LC 92-7270. (Morality & Society Ser.). (Illus.). 350p. 1992. 39.95 (0-226-46815-1) U Ch Pr.

— Money, Morals & Manners: The Culture of the French & the American Upper-Middle Class. (Morality & Society Ser.). xxx, 350p. 1994. pap. text 15.00 (0-226-46817-8) U Ch Pr.

Lamont, Michele & Fournier, Marcel, eds. Cultivating Differences: Symbolic Boundaries & the Making of Inequality. LC 92-15204. 364p. (C). 1992. pap. text 19.95 (0-226-46814-3); lib. bdg. 57.50 (0-226-46813-5) U Ch Pr.

***Lamont, Michele & Thevenot, Laurent, eds.** Rethinking Comparative Cultural Sociology: Repertoires of Evaluation in France & the United States. LC 99-462248. (Cambridge Cultural Social Studies Ser.). 400p. 2000. pap. write for info. (0-521-78794-7) Cambridge U Pr.

— Rethinking Comparative Cultural Sociology: Repertoires of Evaluation in France & the United States. LC 99-462248. (Cambridge Cultural Social Studies Ser.). (Illus.). 400p. 2000. write for info. (0-521-78263-5) Cambridge U Pr.

Lamont, Priscilla. Our Mammoth Goes to School. LC 86-26939. (Illus.). 32p. (J). (ps-3). 1988. 11.95 (0-15-258837-X, Harcourt Child Bks) Harcourt.

— Playtime Rhymes: And Songs for the Very Young. LC 97-36187. (Illus.). 29p. (J). (ps-4). 1998. 12.95 (0-7894-2861-X) DK Pub Inc.

***Lamont, Priscilla.** Ring O'Roses: Nursery Rhymes, Action Rhymes & Lullabies. (Illus.). (J). 1999. pap. text 10.99 (0-7112-1245-7) F Lincoln.

Lamont, Rosette, tr. see Deforges, Regine.

Lamont, Rosette C. Ionesco's Imperatives: The Politics of Culture. LC 92-43167. (Theater: Theory - Text - Performance Ser.). 344p. (C). 1993. text 52.50 (0-472-10310-5, 10310) U of Mich Pr.

— Shakespeare & the World: Quarterly Report, October, 1982. (CNL/World Reports: No. 4). (Illus.). 40p. 1982. pap. 2.50 (0-918680-19-0) Griffon House.

Lamont, Rosette C., ed. Women on the Verge: Seven Avant-Garde American Plays. 1992. pap. 14.95 (1-55783-148-3) Applause Theatre Bk Pubs.

Lamont, Rosette C., et al. New Literary Continents: Selected Papers of the Fifth Annual NDEA Seminar on Foreign Area Studies Held February, 1981. (CNL/World Report Ser.: Vol. 1). 68p. 1984. pap. 4.95 (0-918680-25-5) Griffon House.

Lamont, Rosette C., tr. see Delbo, Charlotte.

Lamont, Rosette C., tr. see Dunant, Ghislaine.

Lamont, Stewart. In Good Faith. 118p. (C). 1989. pap. 30.00 (0-7855-6819-0, Pub. by St Andrew) St Mut.

— In Good Faith. 118p. (C). 1988. pap. text 30.00 (0-7152-0636-2) St Mut.

Lamont, Susan J., jt. ed. see Schook, Lawrence B.

Lamont, Thomas W. Henry P. Davison: The Record of a Useful Life. LC 75-2644. (Wall Street & the Security Market Ser.). (Illus.). 1975. reprint ed. 39.95 (0-405-06969-3) Ayer.

Lamont, W. D. Law & the Moral Order: A Study in Ethics & Jurisprudence. 128p. 1981. text 23.90 (0-08-025742-9, Pergamon Pr); pap. text 12.95 (0-08-025746-1, Pergamon Pr) Elsevier.

Lamont, William. Historical Controversies & Historians. LC 98-182748. 1998. 75.00 (1-85728-739-8, Pub. by UCL Pr Ltd); pap. 22.95 (1-85728-740-1, Pub. by UCL Pr Ltd) Taylor & Francis.

— Puritanism & Historical Controversy. (McGill-Queen's Studies in the History of Religion Ser.). 256p. 1996. 60.00 (0-7735-1445-7, Pub. by McG-Queens Univ Pr); pap. text 22.95 (0-7735-1446-5, DA375, Pub. by McG-Queens Univ Pr) CUP Services.

— Puritanism & the English Revolution, 3 vols. (Modern Revivals in History Ser.). 810p. 1992. 177.95 (0-7512-0004-2, Pub. by Gregg Revivals) Ashgate Pub Co.

Lamont, William, ed. see Baxter, Richard.

Lamontagne, Gisele. Journey Out of Hades. 226p. 1998. pap. 14.95 (0-7414-0011-1) Buy Books.

Lamontagne, Greg. Syllabification & Consonant Cooccurrence Conditions. LC 96-53690. (Outstanding Dissertations in Linguistics Ser.). 270p. 1997. 59.00 (0-8153-2559-2) Garland.

Lamontagne, Tara, tr. see Becker, Catherine.

***Lamontaine, Grace.** Discovering the Spirit. 196p. 1999. pap. write for info. (0-7392-0194-8, PO3183) Morris Pubng.

LaMonte, Edward S. Politics & Welfare in Birmingham, 1900-1975. LC 94-7186. 320p. 1995. text 34.95 (0-8173-0754-0) U of Ala Pr.

LaMonte, J. L. Feudal Monarchy in the Latin Kingdom of Jerusalem, 1100-1291. (Mediaeval Academy of America Publications: Vol. 11). 1932. 40.00 (0-527-01685-3) Periodicals Srv.

Lamoreau, John & Beebe, Ralph. Waging Peace: A Study in Biblical Pacifism. 1980. pap. 3.95 (0-913342-31-9) Barclay Pr.

Lamoreaux, Denise, jt. ed. see Sherfy, Elizabeth J.

***Lamoreaux, J. C.** The Life of Stephen of Mar Sabas. (Corpus Scriptorum Christianorum Orientalium Ser.). xii,137p. 1999. 57.00 (90-429-0691-X, Pub. by Peeters Pub) Bks Intl VA.

LaMoreaux, James W. Medical Waste Solutions. Date not set. 64.95 (0-87371-712-0, L712) Lewis Pubs.

***Lamoreaux, John C.** The Life of Stephen of Mar Sabas. LC 99-510754. (Corpus Scriptorum Christianorum Orientalium Ser.). xiv,153p. 1999. write for info. (90-429-0690-1, Pub. by Peeters Pub) Bks Intl VA.

Lamoreaux, John C., jt. auth. see Rorem, Paul.

Lamoreaux, Matthew, ed. Minute Math Drills: Grade 1-3. (Illus.). 64p. (J). (gr. 1-3). 1998. pap. text 8.95 (0-88724-453-X, CD-0901) Carson-Dellos.

— Minute Math Drills: Grade 3-6. (Illus.). 64p. (J). (gr. 3-6). 1998. pap. text 8.95 (0-88724-454-8, CD-0902) Carson-Dellos.

Lamoreaux, Naomi R. The Great Merger Movement in American Business, 1895-1904. (Illus.). 224p. 1988. pap. text 17.95 (0-521-35765-9) Cambridge U Pr.

— Insider Lending: Banks, Personal Connections & Economic Development in Industrial New England. (Illus.). 182p. 1996. pap. text 17.95 (0-521-56624-X) Cambridge U Pr.

— Insider Lending: Banks, Personal Connections, & Economic Development in Industrial New England. (Illus.). 182p. (C). 1994. text 54.95 (0-521-46096-4) Cambridge U Pr.

Lamoreaux, Naomi R., et al, eds. Learning by Doing in Markets, Firms, & Countries. LC 98-8558. 328p. 1999. pap. text 22.50 (0-226-46834-8); lib. bdg. 65.00 (0-226-46832-1) U Ch Pr.

Lamoreaux, Naomi R. & Raff, Daniel M., eds. Coordination & Information: Historical Perspectives on the Organization of Enterprise. LC 94-41674. 350p. 1995. pap. text 22.50 (0-226-46821-6) U Ch Pr.

— Coordination & Information: Historical Perspectives on the Organization of Enterprise. LC 94-41674. (National Bureau of Economic Research Conference Report Ser.). 345p. 1995. lib. bdg. 68.00 (0-226-46820-8) U Ch Pr.

Lamoreaux, P. E. & Wanfang, Z., eds. Springs & Bottled Waters of the World: Ancient History, Source, Occurrence, Quality & Use. (Illus.). 250p. 1998. 69.95 (3-540-61841-4) Spr-Verlag.

Lamoreaux, Steve K., jt. auth. see Khriplovich, I. B.

Lamoreux, Diana J. Red Bows on White Lambs. (Illus.). 128p. 1994. pap. 9.95 (1-881576-40-X) Providence Hse.

Lamorey, Suzanne & Robinson, Bryan E. Latchkey Kids: Unlocking Doors for Children & Their Families. 2nd ed. LC 98-40064. 224p. 1998. 36.00 (0-7619-1259-2); pap. 15.99 (0-7619-1260-6) Sage.

Lamorisse, Albert. The Red Balloon. LC 57-9229. (Illus.). 48p. (J). (ps-3). 1967. 16.95 (0-385-00343-9) Doubleday.

— The Red Balloon. LC 57-9229. (Illus.). 48p. (J). (ps-3). 1978. pap. 10.95 (0-385-14297-8) Doubleday.

— The Red Balloon. 1978. 16.15 (0-606-12496-9, Pub. by Turtleback) Demco.

***Lamorisse, Albert.** Red Balloon. (Oberon Bks.). 2000. pap. 13.95 (1-84002-079-2) Theatre Comm.

Lamorisse, Albert, jt. auth. see Prevert, Jacques.

LaMorte, Kathy & Lewis, Sharen. Ecology Green Pages for Students & Teachers. Keeling, Jan, ed. (Illus.). 64p. (Orig.). (J). (gr. 2-8). 1993. pap. text 8.95 (0-86530-269-3, 269-3) Incentive Pubns.

— U. S. Social Studies Yellow Pages for Students & Teachers. Keeling, Jan, ed. LC 92-74235. (Illus.). 64p. (Orig.). (J). (gr. 2-8). 1993. pap. text 8.95 (0-86530-267-7, 267-7) Incentive Pubns.

— World Social Studies Yellow Pages for Students & Teachers. Newton, Rebecca, ed. (Illus.). 64p. (Orig.). (J). (gr. 2-8). 1993. pap. text 8.95 (0-86530-268-5, 268-5) Incentive Pubns.

Lamos, Colleen. Deviant Modernism: Sexual & Textual Errancy in T. S. Eliot, James Joyce & Marcel Proust. LC 98-16594. (Studies in Nineteenth-Century Literature & Culture). 288p. (C). 1999. text 59.95 (0-521-62418-5) Cambridge U Pr.

Lamos, F. Matematika V Poistovnictve (Mathematics in the System of Insurance) (SLO.). 136p. 1997. pap. write for info. (80-08-02552-2, Pub. by Slov Pegagog Naklad) IBD Ltd.

Lamothe, Andre. Black Art of 3D Game Programming: Writing Your Own High-Speed 3D Polygon Video Games in C. (Illus.). 1224p. 1995. pap. 49.95 (1-57169-004-2) Sams.

***Lamothe, Andre & IDG Books Staff.** Windows 98 Game Programming for Dummies. (For Dummies Ser.). 496p. 1998. pap. 29.99 incl. cd-rom (0-7645-0337-5) IDG Bks.

Lamothe, Denise C. The Taming of the Chew: A Holistic Guide to Stopping Compulsive Eating. Blakeney, Laurie, ed. (Illus.). 185p. (Orig.). 1998. pap. 11.95 (0-9663653-0-5) Questover Bks.

Lamothe, Irene, ed. see Chauvin, Lilyan.

Lamothe, Lee, jt. auth. see Nicaso, Antonio.

Lamothe, Solange, jt. auth. see Judge, Anne.

***Lamott, Anne.** All New People. 176p. 1999. pap. text 13.00 (1-58243-054-3, Pub. by Counterpt DC) HarpC.

Lamott, Anne. Bird by Bird: Instructions on Writing & Life. LC 94-5448. 288p. 1994. 23.00 (0-679-43520-4) Pantheon.

— Bird by Bird: Some Instructions on Writing & Life. LC 95-10225. 239p. 1995. reprint ed. pap. 12.95 (0-385-48001-6, Anchor NY) Doubleday.

— Crooked Little Heart. LC 97-39450. 326p. 1998. pap. 12.95 (0-385-49180-8, Anchor NY) Doubleday.

— Crooked Little Heart. LC 96-47718. 352p. 1997. 24.00 (0-679-43521-2) Pantheon.

— Crooked Little Heart. large type ed. (Niagara Large Print Ser.). 512p. 1997. 29.50 (0-7089-5883-4) Ulverscroft.

— Hard Laughter: A Novel. LC 86-62832. 304p. 1979. pap. 13.00 (0-86547-280-7) N Point Pr.

— Operating Instructions: A Journal of My Son's First Year. 251p. 1994. reprint ed. pap. 9.50 (0-449-90928-X, Columbine) Fawcett.

— Rosie. 288p. 1997. pap. 12.95 (0-14-026479-5) Viking Penguin.

***Lamott, Anne.** Traveling Mercies: Signed Edition. 1999. 23.00 (0-375-40880-0, Pub. by Knopf) Random House.

— Traveling Mercies: Some Thoughts on Faith. 2000. pap. 13.00 (0-385-49609-5, Anchor NY) Doubleday.

Lamott, Anne. Traveling Mercies: Some Thoughts on Faith. LC 98-30487. 288p. 1999. 23.00 (0-679-44240-5) Pantheon.

***Lamott, Anne.** Traveling Mercies: Some Thoughts on Faith. ed. 1999. 18.40 (0-375-40917-3) Random.

Lamott, Anne. Traveling Mercies: Some Thoughts on Faith. large type ed. 1999. 28.95 (0-7862-1961-0) Mac Lib Ref.

LaMotta, Toni. Recognition: The Quality Way. LC 95-1339. 240p. 1995. 31.00 (0-527-76223-7) Productivity Inc.

Lamotte, Andree, jt. auth. see Calais-Germain, Blandine.

Lamotte, E. & Boin, S., trs. from SAN. The Teaching of Vimalakirti. (C). 1976. 79.00 (0-86013-077-0, Pub. by Pali Text) Elsevier.

LaMotte, Ellen N. The Ethics of Opium. Grob, Gerald N., ed. LC 80-1260. (Addiction in America Ser.). 1981. reprint ed. lib. bdg. 20.95 (0-405-13601-3) Ayer.

Lamotte, Etienne. Karmasiddhiprakarana: The Treatise on Action by Vasubandhu. Pruden, Leo M., tr. LC 87-71232. 133p. 1988. reprint ed. pap. 38.00 (0-608-01777-9, 2062435) Bks Demand.

Lamotte, Etienne, tr. The Suramgamasamadhi Sutra. 320p. 1998. text 50.00 (0-7007-1024-8, Pub. by Curzon Pr Ltd) UH Pr.

LaMotte, Frank, ed. see Ward, Ben.

Lamotte, Michel, jt. ed. see Garrigues, Philippe.

L'Amour, Angelique, compiled by. A Trail of Memories: The Quotations of Louis L'Amour. large type ed. (General Ser.). 216p. 1989. lib. bdg. 21.95 (0-8161-4728-0, G K Hall Lrg Type) Mac Lib Ref.

L'Amour, Louis. Bendigo Shafter. 336p. 1983. mass mkt. 5.50 (0-553-26446-X) Bantam.

— Beyond the Great Snow Mountains. LC 99-11757. 282p. 1999. 16.95 (0-553-10963-4) Bantam.

— Beyond the Great Snow Mountains. LC 99-15814. 1950. 30.00 (0-7862-2041-4) Thorndike Pr.

***L'Amour, Louis.** Beyond the Great Snow Mountains. large type ed. LC 99-15814. 1999. 28.95 (0-7862-2040-6) Thorndike Pr.

— Beyond the Great Snow Mountains. 224p. 2000. reprint ed. mass mkt. 4.99 (0-553-58041-8) Bantam.

L'Amour, Louis. The Black Rock Coffin Makers. unabridged ed. 1990. pap. 7.95 incl. audio (1-882071-25-5, 027) B&B Audio.

— Borden Chantry. 176p. 1995. mass mkt. 4.50 (0-553-27863-0) Bantam.

— Bowdrie. 192p. 1990. mass mkt. 4.50 (0-553-28106-2) Bantam.

— Bowdrie's Law. LC 85-824. 224p. (Orig.). 1984. mass mkt. 4.50 (0-553-24550-3) Bantam.

— Brionne. 160p. (Orig.). 1995. mass mkt. 4.50 (0-553-28107-0) Bantam.

— Brionne. large type ed. (Special Ser.). 192p. (Orig.). 1993. reprint ed. 18.95 (1-56054-653-0) Thorndike Pr.

— The Broken Gun. LC 85-2817. 160p. 1984. mass mkt. 4.50 (0-553-24847-2) Bantam.

— The Broken Gun. large type ed. (Special Ser.). 213p. 1993. reprint ed. 18.95 (1-56054-649-2) Thorndike Pr.

— Buckskin Run. 192p. 1981. mass mkt. 4.50 (0-553-24764-6) Bantam.

— The Burning Hills. 160p. 1985. mass mkt. 4.50 (0-553-28210-7) Bantam.

— The Burning Hills. large type ed. LC 96-42396. 1999. 20.00 (0-7838-1958-7, G K Hall Lrg Type) Mac Lib Ref.

— The Californios. 192p. (Orig.). 1985. reprint ed. mass mkt. 4.50 (0-553-25322-0) Bantam.

— Callaghen. 192p. 1998. mass mkt. 4.50 (0-553-24759-X) Bantam.

— Catlow. 160p. (Orig.). 1984. reprint ed. mass mkt. 4.50 (0-553-24767-0) Bantam.

— Catlow. 160p. (Orig.). 1998. reprint ed. mass mkt. 3.99 (0-553-22901-X) Bantam.

— Chancy. 176p. 1973. mass mkt. 4.50 (0-553-28085-6) Bantam.

— The Cherokee Trail. 208p. 1996. mass mkt. 4.50 (0-553-27047-8) Bantam.

— The Cherokee Trail. (J). 1982. 9.09 (0-606-01540-X, Pub. by Turtleback) Demco.

— Comstock Lode. 432p. 1982. mass mkt. 5.50 (0-553-27561-5) Bantam.

— Comstock Lode. large type ed. (Special Ser.). 718p. 1993. reprint ed. 18.95 (1-56054-648-4) Thorndike Pr.

— Conagher. 160p. 1979. mass mkt. 4.50 (0-553-28101-1) Bantam.

— Conagher. 1994. mass mkt. 4.99 (0-553-85025-3) Bantam.

— Crossfire Trail. 176p. 1983. mass mkt. 4.50 (0-553-28099-6) Bantam.

— Dark Canyon. (Illus.). 160p. 1996. mass mkt. 4.50 (0-553-25324-7) Bantam.

— Dark Canyon. large type ed. LC 96-41419. 1999. 20.00 (0-7862-0876-7) Thorndike Pr.

— The Daybreakers. 1996. mass mkt. 4.99 (0-553-85144-6) Bantam.

L'Amour, Louis. The Daybreakers. 1960. 9.09 (0-606-02082-9, Pub. by Turtleback) Demco.

L'Amour, Louis. The Daybreakers. large type ed. (Ulverscroft Large Print Ser.). 1975. 27.99 (0-85456-381-4) Ulverscroft.

— The Daybreakers, No. 3. 224p. 1979. mass mkt. 4.50 (0-553-27674-3) Bantam.

— Desert, Death Song. unabridged ed. 1990. pap. 7.95 incl. audio (1-882071-26-3, 028) B&B Audio.

— Down the Long Hills. 160p. 1984. mass mkt. 4.50 (0-553-28081-3) Bantam.

L'Amour, Louis. Down the Long Hills. 1992. 9.09 (0-606-00341-X, Pub. by Turtleback) Demco.

L'Amour, Louis. Down the Long Hills. large type ed. (Special Ser.). 222p. 1993. reprint ed. 18.95 (1-56054-651-4) Thorndike Pr.

— Dutchman's Flat. 256p. 1986. mass mkt. 4.50 (0-553-28111-9) Bantam.

— Education of a Wandering Man. 272p. 1990. mass mkt. 5.99 (0-553-28652-8) Bantam.

L'Amour, Louis. Education of a Wandering Man. 1990. 11.09 (0-606-04660-7, Pub. by Turtleback) Demco.

L'Amour, Louis. The Empty Land. 192p. (Orig.). 1995. mass mkt. 4.50 (0-553-25306-9) Bantam.

— The Empty Land. large type ed. LC 96-36270. (Orig.). 1999. 20.00 (0-7838-1956-0, G K Hall Lrg Type) Mac Lib Ref.

— End of the Drive. large type ed. LC 97-34310. 1997. 26.96 (1-56895-490-5, Compass) Wheeler Pub.

— End of the Drive. 272p. 1998. reprint ed. mass mkt. 4.99 (0-553-57898-7) Bantam.

— Fair Blows the Wind. 288p. 1981. mass mkt. 4.50 (0-553-27629-8) Bantam.

— Fallon. 160p. (Orig.). 1994. mass mkt. 4.50 (0-553-28083-X) Bantam.

— Far Blue Mountains. 1996. mass mkt. 4.99 (0-553-85150-0) Bantam.

— The Ferguson Rifle. 192p. 1985. mass mkt. 4.50 (0-553-25303-4) Bantam.

— The First Fast Draw. 160p. 1998. mass mkt. 4.50 (0-553-25224-0) Bantam.

— Flint. 192p. 1997. mass mkt. 4.50 (0-553-25231-3); mass mkt. 3.99 (0-553-20337-1) Bantam.

— Frontier. LC 84-45178. (Illus.). 224p. 1984. 34.95 (0-553-05078-8) Bantam.

— Galloway. 176p. 1970. mass mkt. 4.50 (0-553-27675-1) Bantam.

— Galloway. large type ed. LC 96-41328. 232p. 1998. 20.00 (0-7862-0872-4) Thorndike Pr.

— Grub Line Rider. abr. ed. 1990. audio 9.99 (0-553-45245-2) Bantam.

— A Gun for Kilkenny. abr. ed. 1997. audio 9.99 (0-553-47754-4) BDD Aud Pub.

— Guns of the Timberlands. 160p. (Orig.). 1984. mass mkt. 4.50 (0-553-24765-4) Bantam.

— Hanging Woman Creek. 160p. (Orig.). 1994. mass mkt. 4.50 (0-553-24762-X) Bantam.

— The Haunted Mesa. 384p. (Orig.). 1988. mass mkt. 5.50 (0-553-27022-2) Bantam.

— Heller with a Gun. 160p. 1998. mass mkt. 4.50 (0-553-25206-2) Bantam.

— The High Graders. 176p. 1989. mass mkt. 4.50 (0-553-27864-9) Bantam.

— High Lonesome. 160p. 1962. mass mkt. 4.50 (0-553-25972-5) Bantam.

— High Lonesome. large type ed. LC 96-36037. 1996. 23.95 (0-7838-1947-1, G K Hall Lrg Type) Mac Lib Ref.

— The Hills of Homicide. 256p. 1984. mass mkt. 4.50 (0-553-24134-6) Bantam.

L'Amour, Louis. His Brother's Debt. 1994. 8.31 (1-55935-144-6) Soundelux.

— His Brother's Debt. unabridged ed. 1990. pap. 7.95 incl. audio (1-882071-27-1, 029) B&B Audio.

L'Amour, Louis. Hondo. 1994. mass mkt. 4.99 (0-553-85028-8) Bantam.

— Hondo. 192p. 1997. mass mkt. 4.50 (0-553-28090-2) Bantam.

— Hondo. 1997. pap. 12.95 (0-553-05033-8) Bantam.

— How the West Was Won. 256p. (YA). (gr. 7-12). 1984. mass mkt. 4.50 (0-553-26913-5) Bantam.

L'Amour, Louis. How the West Was Won: A Novel. 1963. 9.60 (0-606-02135-3, Pub. by Turtleback) Demco.

L'Amour, Louis. The Iron Marshall. 192p. 1993. mass mkt. 4.50 (0-553-24844-8) Bantam.

— Jubal Sackett. 368p. 1986. mass mkt. 5.50 (0-553-27739-1) Bantam.

L'Amour, Louis. Jubal Sackett. 1986. 10.60 (0-606-02260-0, Pub. by Turtleback) Demco.

L'Amour, Louis. The Key-Lock Man. 160p. 1984. mass mkt. 4.50 (0-553-28098-8) Bantam.

— Kid Rodelo. 160p. 1995. mass mkt. 4.50 (0-553-24748-4) Bantam.

— Kid Rodelo. large type ed. LC 96-42397. 176p. 1999. 20.00 (0-7838-1957-9, G K Hall Lrg Type) Mac Lib Ref.

— Kilkenny. Date not set. mass mkt. 2.50 (0-553-23142-1) Bantam.

— Kilkenny. 160p. 1984. mass mkt. 4.50 (0-553-24758-1) Bantam.

— Killoe. 160p. 1997. mass mkt. 4.50 (0-553-25742-0) Bantam.

— Killoe. large type ed. LC 96-41326. 1998. 24.95 (0-7862-0870-8) Thorndike Pr.

— Kilrone. (Western Ser.). 160p. 1981. mass mkt. 4.50 (0-553-24867-7) Bantam.

— Kilrone. large type ed. LC 96-41418. 1999. 20.00 (0-7862-0875-9) Thorndike Pr.

— Kiowa Trail. 160p. 1994. mass mkt. 4.50 (0-553-24905-3) Bantam.

— Lando. 176p. 1979. mass mkt. 4.50 (0-553-27676-X) Bantam.

— Lando. large type ed. (Special Ser.). 222p. 1993. 18.95 (1-56054-652-2) Thorndike Pr.

— Last of the Breed. 384p. 1987. mass mkt. 5.50 (0-553-28042-2) Bantam.

L'Amour, Louis. Last of the Breed. (J). 1987. 10.60 (0-606-03599-0, Pub. by Turtleback) Demco.

L'Amour, Louis. Last Stand at Papago Wells. 144p. 1998. mass mkt. 4.50 (0-553-25807-9) Bantam.

— The Law of the Desert Born. 256p. 1984. mass mkt. 4.50 (0-553-24133-8) Bantam.

— The Law of the Desert Born. 192p. 1983. 16.95 (0-671-06697-8) Boulevard.

— The Law of the Desert Born. large type ed. (Special Ser.). 359p. 1993. reprint ed. 18.95 (1-56054-646-8) Thorndike Pr.

— The Lonely Men. 192p. 1984. mass mkt. 4.50 (0-553-27677-8) Bantam.

— Lonely on the Mountain. 208p. 1984. mass mkt. 4.50 (0-553-27678-6) Bantam.

— Lonely on the Mountain. 1996. mass mkt. 4.99 (0-553-85153-5) Bantam.

— The Lonesome Gods. 464p. 1984. mass mkt. 5.50 (0-553-27518-6) Bantam.

— Long Ride Home. 192p. 1998. mass mkt. 4.50 (0-553-28181-X) Bantam.

L'Amour, Louis. Long Ride Home. 1989. 9.09 (0-606-01765-8, Pub. by Turtleback) Demco.

L'Amour, Louis. Long Ride Home. large type ed. LC 96-36267. 228p. 1998. 25.95 (0-7838-1954-4, G K Hall Lrg Type) Mac Lib Ref.

— Lonigan. 192p. 1988. mass mkt. 4.50 (0-553-27536-4) Bantam.

***L'Amour, Louis.** Louis L'Amour: Sackett Boxed Set. 1999. mass mkt., boxed set 18.00 (0-553-66738-6) Bantam.

L'Amour, Louis. Louis L'Amour: The Sacketts, 4 vols., Set. 1990. boxed set 17.50 (0-553-60928-9) Bantam.

***L'Amour, Louis.** Louis L'Amour Boxed Gift Set. 1999. mass mkt. 14.97 (0-553-66737-8) Bantam.

L'Amour, Louis. The Man Called Noon. 192p. 1984. mass mkt. 4.50 (0-553-24753-0) Bantam.

— The Man Called Noon. large type ed. (Special Ser.). 271p. 1993. reprint ed. 18.95 (1-56054-645-X) Thorndike Pr.

— The Man from Skibbereen. 192p. (Orig.). 1983. mass mkt. 4.50 (0-553-24906-1) Bantam.

— The Man from the Broken Hills. 224p. 1996. reprint ed. mass mkt. 4.50 (0-553-27679-4) Bantam.

— Matagorda. 176p. 1985. mass mkt. 4.50 (0-553-28108-9) Bantam.

— Matagorda. large type ed. LC 96-36194. 1999. 20.00 (0-7862-0874-0) Thorndike Pr.

— Milo Talon. 224p. 1981. mass mkt. 4.50 (0-553-24763-8) Bantam.

— Mojave Crossing. 160p. 1979. mass mkt. 4.50 (0-553-27680-8) Bantam.

— Monument Rock. large type ed. LC 98-30790. 1998. 27.95 (0-7862-1645-X) Thorndike Pr.

— Monument Rock. large type ed. LC 98-30790. 1999. pap. 25.95 (0-7862-1646-8) Thorndike Pr.

— Monument Rock. 244p. 1999. reprint ed. mass mkt. 4.99 (0-553-58082-5) Bantam.

— The Mountain Valley War. 208p. 1997. mass mkt. 4.50 (0-553-25090-6) Bantam.

— The Mountain Valley War. large type ed. LC 96-36268. (Westerm Ser.). 281p. 1998. 25.95 (0-7838-1953-6, G K Hall Lrg Type) Mac Lib Ref.

— Mustang Man. 176p. 1966. mass mkt. 4.50 (0-553-27681-6) Bantam.

— Mustang Man. LC 96-41329. (Thorndike Large Print Western Ser.). 248 p. 1999. write for info. (0-7540-3670-7) Chivers N Amer.

— Mustang Man. large type ed. LC 96-41329. 1999. 20.00 (0-7862-0873-2, G K Hall Lrg Type) Mac Lib Ref.

— Night over the Solomons. 192p. 1986. mass mkt. 4.50 (0-553-26602-0) Bantam.

— North to the Rails. 192p. 1987. mass mkt. 4.50 (0-553-28086-4) Bantam.

***L'Amour, Louis.** Off the Mangrove Coast. LC 99-86061. 288p. 2000. 16.95 (0-553-80160-0, Spectra) Bantam.

— Off the Mangrove Coast: A Collection of Short Stories. large type ed. LC 00-21656. 448p. 2000. 16.95 (0-375-43062-8) Random Hse Lrg Prnt.

L'Amour, Louis. The Outlaws of Mesquite: Frontier Stories. 240p. 1990. mass mkt. 4.50 (0-553-28714-1) Bantam.

— The Outlaws of Mesquite: Frontier Stories. 1990. 9.09 (0-606-04997-5, Pub. by Turtleback) Demco.

— Over on the Dry Side. 192p. 1985. mass mkt. 4.50 (0-553-25321-2) Bantam.

— Passin' Through. 208p. (Orig.). 1985. mass mkt. 4.50 (0-553-25320-4) Bantam.

— The Proving Trail. 224p. 1985. mass mkt. 4.50 (0-553-25304-2) Bantam.

— The Quick & the Dead. 160p. 1978. mass mkt. 4.50 (0-553-28084-8) Bantam.

— Radigan. 160p. 1986. mass mkt. 4.50 (0-553-28082-1) Bantam.

— Reilly's Luck. 224p. 1985. mass mkt. 4.50 (0-553-25305-0) Bantam.

— Ride the Dark Trail. 176p. 1981. mass mkt. 4.50 (0-553-27682-4) Bantam.

— Ride the River, No. 17. 192p. 1983. mass mkt. 4.50 (0-553-27683-2) Bantam.

— Ride the River, Vol. 17. 1996. mass mkt. 4.99 (0-553-85147-0) Bantam.

— Ride, You Tonto Raiders! unabridged ed. 1990. pap. 7.95 incl. audio (1-882071-28-X, 030) B&B Audio.

— The Rider of Lost Creek. 160p. (Orig.). 1982. mass mkt. 4.50 (0-553-25771-4) Bantam.

— The Rider of Ruby Hills. 400p. 1986. mass mkt. 4.50 (0-553-28112-7) Bantam.

— The Riders of High Rock. 272p. 1994. mass mkt. 4.99 (0-553-56782-9) Bantam.

— The Riders of High Rock: A Hopalong Cassidy Novel. large type ed. LC 96-36266. 303p. 1998. 25.95 (0-7838-1955-2, G K Hall Lrg Type) Mac Lib Ref.

— Riding for the Brand. 256p. 1993. mass mkt. 4.50 (0-553-28105-4) Bantam.

— Riding for the Brand. large type ed. LC 96-42514. 398p. 1999. 20.00 (0-7838-1982-X, G K Hall Lrg Type) Mac Lib Ref.

— Rivers West. 160p. (Orig.). 1993. mass mkt. 4.50 (0-553-25436-7) Bantam.

— The Rustlers of West Fork: A Hopalong Cassidy Novel. 288p. 1992. mass mkt. 4.99 (0-553-29539-X) Bantam.

— The Rustlers of West Fork: A Hopalong Cassidy Novel. large type ed. LC 94-9291. 353p. 1994. pap. 19.95 (0-8161-5798-7, G K Hall Lrg Type) Mac Lib Ref.

— Sackett. 160p. 1981. mass mkt. 4.50 (0-553-27684-0) Bantam.

— Sackett. 1994. mass mkt. 4.99 (0-553-85022-9) Bantam.

— Sackett. 1996. mass mkt. 4.99 (0-553-85138-1) Bantam.

L'Amour, Louis. Sackett. 1961. 9.09 (0-606-00580-3, Pub. by Turtleback) Demco.

L'Amour, Louis. The Sackett Brand. 160p. 1979. mass mkt. 4.50 (0-553-27685-9) Bantam.

— The Sackett Companion: A Personal Guide to the Sackett Novels. 352p. 1992. pap. 13.95 (0-553-37102-9) Bantam.

— Sackett's Land. 208p. 1980. mass mkt. 4.50 (0-553-27686-7) Bantam.

— Sackett's Land. 1996. mass mkt. 4.99 (0-553-85141-1) Bantam.

L'Amour, Louis. Sackett's Land. 1975. 9.09 (0-606-00582-X, Pub. by Turtleback) Demco.

L'Amour, Louis. Sackett's Land. large type ed. LC 96-41327. 1998. 23.95 (0-7862-0871-6) Thorndike Pr.

— Shadow Riders. 208p. 1982. mass mkt. 4.50 (0-553-23132-4) Bantam.

L'Amour, Louis. Shalako. 176p. 1995. reprint ed. pap., mass mkt. 4.50 (0-553-24858-8) Bantam.

L'Amour, Louis. Showdown at Yellow Butte. 192p. 1997. mass mkt. 4.50 (0-553-27993-9) Bantam.

— Showdown at Yellow Butte. 1997. 9.95 (0-553-06278-6) Bantam.

— Silver Canyon. 176p. 1957. mass mkt. 4.50 (0-553-24743-3) Bantam.

— Sitka. 245p. 1984. mass mkt. 4.99 (0-553-27881-9) Bantam.

***L'Amour, Louis.** Sitka. large type ed. (Famous Authors Ser.). 2000. 27.95 (0-7862-2435-5) Thorndike Pr.

L'Amour, Louis. The Sky-Liners. Vol. 12. 208p. 1980. mass mkt. 4.50 (0-553-27687-5) Bantam.

— The Sky-Liners. large type ed. (Special Ser.). 264p. 1993. reprint ed. 18.95 (1-56054-650-6) Thorndike Pr.

— Smoke from This Altar. 96p. 1990. 16.00 (0-553-07349-4) Bantam.

— Son of a Wanted Man. 176p. 1997. mass mkt. 4.50 (0-553-24457-4) Bantam.

— Son of a Wanted Man. large type ed. (Special Ser.). 269p. 1993. reprint ed. 18.95 (1-56054-654-9) Thorndike Pr.

— The Strong Shall Live. 176p. 1981. mass mkt. 4.50 (0-553-25200-3) Bantam.

— The Strong Shall Live. large type ed. (Special Ser.). 242p. 1993. reprint ed. 18.95 (1-56054-647-6) Thorndike Pr.

— Taggart. 160p. 1982. mass mkt. 4.50 (0-553-25477-4) Bantam.

— Taggart. 1996. reprint ed. mass mkt. 3.99 (0-553-24577-5) Bantam.

— The Tall Stranger. 128p. 1986. mass mkt. 4.50 (0-553-28102-X) Bantam.

— To Tame a Land. 22.95 (0-89190-159-0) Amereon Ltd.

— To Tame a Land. 160p. 1997. mass mkt. 4.50 (0-553-28031-7) Bantam.

— To the Far Blue Mountains. (Sackett Titles Ser.). 1976. 9.09 (0-606-02297-X, Pub. by Turtleback) Demco.

— To the Far Blue Mountains. unabridged ed. 288p. 1984. mass mkt. 4.50 incl. audio (0-553-27688-3) Bantam.

— A Trail of Memories: The Quotations of Louis L'Amour. LC 88-965. 224p. 1988. 12.95 (0-553-05271-3) Bantam.

— The Trail to Crazy Man. 368p. 1986. mass mkt. 4.50 (0-553-28035-X) Bantam.

— The Trail to Seven Pines: A Hopalong Cassidy Novel. 256p. 1993. mass mkt. 4.99 (0-553-56178-2) Bantam.

— The Trail to Seven Pines: A Hopalong Cassidy Novel. large type ed. LC 93-45637. 269p. 1994. pap. 19.95 (0-8161-5799-5, G K Hall Lrg Type) Mac Lib Ref.

— Treasure Mountain. 208p. (Orig.). 1979. mass mkt. 4.50 (0-553-27689-1) Bantam.

— Trouble Shooter: A Hopalong Cassidy Novel. 240p. 1995. mass mkt. 4.99 (0-553-57187-7) Bantam.

— Trouble Shooter: A Hopalong Cassidy Novel. large type ed. LC 96-36478. 2000. 20.00 (0-7862-0896-1) Thorndike Pr.

— Tucker. 192p. 1981. mass mkt. 4.50 (0-553-25022-1) Bantam.

— Under the Sweetwater Rim. 192p. 1996. mass mkt. 4.50 (0-553-24760-3) Bantam.

— Utah Blaine. 176p. 1984. mass mkt. 4.50 (0-553-24761-1) Bantam.

An Asterisk (*) at the beginning of an entry indicates that the title is appearing for the first time.

— Valley of the Sun: Frontier Stories. 192p. 1996. mass mkt. 4.99 (*0-553-57444-2*) Bantam.
— Valley of the Sun: Frontier Stories. 1996. 10.09 (*0-606-10010-5*, Pub. by Turtleback) Demco.
— Valley of the Sun: Frontier Stories. large type ed. 1996. 21.95 (*0-7862-0587-3*) Thorndike Pr.
— Walking Drum. 480p. 1985. mass mkt. 5.50 (*0-553-28040-6*) Bantam.
L'Amour, Louis. Walking Drum. (J). 1985. 10.60 (*0-606-01789-5*, Pub. by Turtleback) Demco.
L'Amour, Louis. War Party. 160p. 1982. mass mkt. 4.50 (*0-553-25393-X*) Bantam.
— War Party. large type ed. LC 96-36269. 190p. 1998. 25.95 (*0-7838-1952-8*, G K Hall Lrg Type) Mac Lib Ref.
— The Warrior's Path. 240p. 1980. mass mkt. 4.50 (*0-553-27690-5*) Bantam.
— West from Singapore. 176p. 1987. mass mkt. 4.50 (*0-553-26353-6*) Bantam.
— West of Dodge: Fontier Stories. 240p. 1997. mass mkt. 4.99 (*0-553-57697-6*) Bantam.
— West of Dodge: Frontier Stories. large type ed. LC 96-20872. (Western Ser.). 380p. 1996. 21.95 (*0-7862-0803-1*) Thorndike Pr.
— Westward the Tide. 224p. (Orig.). 1995. mass mkt. 4.50 (*0-553-24766-2*) Bantam.
— Where the Long Grass Blows. 192p. 1988. mass mkt. 4.50 (*0-553-28172-0*) Bantam.
— Yondering. rev. ed. 1989. pap. 4.50 (*0-553-28203-4*) Random Hse Value.
Lamoureux. Community Action & Politics: Organising for Social Change. Aronoff, Phyllis & Scott, Howard, trs. 248p. 1989. pap. 16.99 (*0-921689-20-9*, Pub. by Black Rose) Consort Bk Sales.
Lamoureux, Charles H. Trailside Plants of Hawaii's National Parks. rev. ed. (Illus.). 80p. 1996. reprint ed. pap. 12.95 (*0-940295-09-1*) HI Natural Hist.
Lamoureux, Dorothy. The Arts & Crafts Studio of Dirk Van Erp. LC 89-61391. (Illus.). 60p. (Orig.). 1989. pap. 15.00 (*1-877742-01-5*) SF Craft & Folk.
Lamoureux, Marie E. Index to Clerical Biographies in William Buell Sprague's 'Annals of the American Pulpit' 25p. 1994. pap. 9.50 (*0-944026-59-1*) Am Antiquarian.
Lamoureux, Nancy. By Prescription Only. Zagury, Carolyn S., ed. LC 97-60582. 184p. 1997. pap. 12.95 (*1-880254-44-1*) Vista.
Lamoureux, Normand J., jt. auth. see Comeau, Raymond.
Lamoureux, Normand J., jt. auth. see Comeau, Raymond F.
Lamoureux, Paul E., ed. Massachusetts Appellate Division Reports, 1980-1994. 366p. 1984. 56.90 (*0-318-03673-8*) Lawyers Weekly.
Lamoureux, Vincent B. Guide to Ship Sanitation. (ENG, FRE & RUS.). 119p. 1967. pap. text 17.10 (*92-4-154010-9*, 1150055) World Health.
Lamoy, Victor. Echoes from the High Peaks: Adventures of Adirondack Youth. LC 96-16795. 1997. pap. 15.00 (*0-925168-52-1*) North Country.
Lamp, C. O. Distant Love. large type ed. 544p. 1984. 27.99 (*0-7089-1129-3*) Ulverscroft.
— The Return of Glenn Miller. LC 99-27017. 256p. 1999. pap. 14.95 (*1-880090-84-8*) Galde Pr.
Lamp, David. Astronomy for the Masses: Astronomy 1100 Lab Manual. 2nd ed. 80p. (C). 1998. spiral bd., lab manual ed. 20.95 (*0-7872-5290-5*, 41529001) Kendall-Hunt.
Lamp, Frederick. Art of the Baga: A Drama of Cultural Re-Invention. (Illus.). 272p. 1996. 75.00 (*3-7913-1725-3*, Pub. by Prestel) te Neues.
Lamp, Frederick, et al. Art of the Baga: A Drama of Cultural Reinvention. LC 96-77336. 267 p. 1996. write for info. (*0-945802-18-8*) Museum African.
***Lamp, Jeffrey S.** 1st Corinthians 1-4 in Light of Jewish Wisdom Traditions: Christ, Wisdom & Spirituality. LC 99-54863. (Studies in Bible & Early Christianity: Vol. 42). 260p. 2000. 89.95 (*0-7734-7833-7*) E Mellen.
***Lamp, Jennifer J.** His Chosen Bride: Applying Proverbs 31 as a Single Young Woman. rev. ed. 226p. 2000. pap. 9.99 (*1-929125-24-0*) Loyal Pubng.
Lamp Light Press Staff. Advertising Black Markets: A Directory of Slang, Jargon & Chocolate Grammar. 70p. 1993. ring bd. 49.95 (*0-917593-21-9*, Lamp Light Pr) Prosperity & Profits.
— Advertising Cheaper with Telemarketing: Script Presentations Directory. 200p. (C). 1993. ring bd. 94.95 (*0-917593-18-9*, Lamp Light Pr) Prosperity & Profits.
— Advertising Food Businesses with Recipe Greetings: Samples Directory for Licensing. 60p. 1993. ring bd. 39.95 (*0-917593-19-7*, Lamp Light Pr) Prosperity & Profits.
— Advertising with Flowers: Clip Art Directory. (Illus.). 60p. 1993. ring bd. 39.95 (*0-917593-20-0*, Lamp Light Pr) Prosperity & Profits.
— Alfreda's Fragrantis Dictionary. rev. ed. (Illus.). 55p. 1993. ring bd. 29.95 (*0-917593-33-2*, Lamp Light Pr) Prosperity & Profits.
— Alfreda's Reading Theatre: Business Theatre - Skits & Plays for Meetings, Conferences, Schools, Etc. 70p. 1993. ring bd. 29.95 (*0-917593-32-4*, Lamp Light Pr) Prosperity & Profits.
— Clip Art: Food Illustrations & Recipe Greeting Rhymes to Duplicate & Use. (Illus.). 50p. 1993. ring bd. 49.95 (*0-917593-12-X*, Lamp Light Pr) Prosperity & Profits.
— Coffee Substitutes: Poetry, Greetings, Etc. (Illus.). 18p. (Orig.). (C). 1995. ring bd. 19.95 (*0-917593-37-5*, Lamp Light Pr) Prosperity & Profits.
— Copy Service Business Possibilities. 112p. (C). 1993. ring bd. 32.95 (*0-917593-14-6*, Lamp Light Pr) Prosperity & Profits.
— Entrepreneur's Home School. (Illus.). 360p. 1993. ring bd. 179.00 (*0-917593-16-2*, Lamp Light Pr) Prosperity & Profits.
— Greeting Card Service Agency, Gift Shops: Greetings to Duplicate & Use. (Illus.). 60p. 1993. ring bd. 75.00 (*0-917593-24-3*, Lamp Light Pr) Prosperity & Profits.
— Greetings That Educate, Entertain & Rhyme to Duplicate & Use. (Illus.). 60p. 1993. ring bd. 29.95 (*0-917593-23-5*, Lamp Light Pr) Prosperity & Profits.
— Immune System Herbal Greetings to Duplicate & Use. (Illus.). 60p. 1993. student ed., ring bd. 29.95 (*0-917593-26-X*, Lamp Light Pr) Prosperity & Profits.
— Immune System Herbals, Approaches, Folklore: A How to Find or Locate Workbook. (Illus.). 70p. 1993. ring bd. 25.95 (*0-917593-28-6*, Lamp Light Pr) Prosperity & Profits.
— Index to Prayer Books, Pamphlets, Etc. 50p. 1984. pap. 5.95 (*0-917593-01-4*, Lamp Light Pr) Prosperity & Profits.
— Kids Businesses: Telemarketing Script Presentations. 75p. 1993. ring bd. 39.95 (*0-917593-27-8*, Lamp Light Pr) Prosperity & Profits.
— Love Theme Greetings to Duplicate & Use. (Illus.). 70p. 1993. ring bd. 29.95 (*0-917593-22-7*, Lamp Light Pr) Prosperity & Profits.
— Make It Tasty Spice Recipe Greetings to Duplicate & Use. 60p. 1993. ring bd. 29.95 (*0-917593-29-4*, Lamp Light Pr) Prosperity & Profits.
— Money Saving Frugal Consumer Workshop Notebook. (Illus.). 93p. 1993. ring bd. 37.95 (*0-917593-15-4*, Lamp Light Pr) Prosperity & Profits.
— Noah's Ark: A Story Rhyme. (Illus.). 23p. (J). (ps-6). 1992. pap. text 8.95 (*0-917593-11-1*, Lamp Light Pr) Prosperity & Profits.
— Song Send Greetings to Duplicate & Use. (Illus.). 52p. 1993. ring bd. 29.95 (*0-917593-31-6*, Lamp Light Pr) Prosperity & Profits.
Lamp Light Press Staff, jt. auth. see Doyle, A. C.
Lamp, Scott P., jt. auth. see Benjamin, Patricia.
Lampa, jt. auth. see King.
Lampa, Steven, jt. auth. see King, Douglas.
Lamparczyk, Henryk. Analysis & Characterization of Steroids. 176p. 1992. lib. bdg. 179.00 (*0-8493-3008-4*, QP752) CRC Pr.
Lampard, Eric E. The History of Cities in the Economically Advanced Areas. (Reprint Series in Social Sciences). (C). 1993. reprint ed. pap. text 4.50 (*0-8290-2650-9*, S-440) Irvington.
Lampard, Liz. Business Information from Government, 1998. LC 98-3093. 1998. write for info. (*1-85739-270-1*) Bowker-Saur.
***Lampard, Marie Turbow, et al, eds.** The Uncommon Vision of Sergei Konenkov, 1874-1971: A Russian Sculptor & His Times. LC 00-39038. (Illus.). 240p. (C). 2001. text 55.00 (*0-8135-2854-2*) Rutgers U Pr.
Lamparello, Christopher. Cold Cash Vol. 1: How to Become Rich from One Five-Minute Phone Call. 94p. (Orig.). 1996. per. 39.95 (*1-889628-00-X*) City Books Pub.
— The Complete Get Rich Encyclopedia. 148p. 1998. pap. 19.95 (*1-889628-01-8*) City Books Pub.
Lamparski, Beata J., jt. auth. see Beaubien, Richard F.
Lamparski, Richard. Lamparski's Hidden Hollywood: Where the Stars Lived, Loved & Died. 1981. pap. 8.95 (*0-671-41885-8*, Fireside) S&S Trade Pap.
Lampe, B. P., jt. auth. see Rosenwasser, E. N.
Lampe, Betsy, ed. see Whelan, Robert F.
Lampe, David, ed. The Legend of Being Irish: A Collection of Irish-American Poetry. 120p. 1988. pap. 9.00 (*0-934834-23-7*) White Pine.
— Myths & Voices: New Canadian Short Fiction. 420p. 1993. pap. 17.00 (*1-877727-28-8*) White Pine.
Lampe, Diana. Diana Lampe's Embroidery from the Garden. (Illus.). 104p. 1997. 24.95 (*1-86351-206-3*, Pub. by Sally Milner) Sterling.
— Embroider a Garden. (Illus.). 124p. 1994. 19.95 (*1-86351-122-9*, Pub. by Sally Milner) Sterling.
— Little Book of Embroidered Garden Flowers. 1999. 9.95 (*1-86351-226-8*) Sally Milner.
Lampe, Frederick, jt. auth. see Allcock, Harry.
Lampe, G. W., ed. The Cambridge History of the Bible, 3 vols. Incl. Vol. 2. West from the Fathers to the Reformation. LC 63-24435. 1969. 95.00 (*0-521-04255-0*); Vol. 2. West from the Fathers to the Reformation. LC 63-24435. 576p. 1975. pap. text 69.95 (*0-521-29017-1*); LC 63-24435. 1975. 155.00 (*0-521-08778-3*); Set pap. 120.00 (*0-521-29018-X*) Cambridge U Pr.
— Patristic Greek Lexicon. (GRE.). 1,616p. 1969. text 295.00 (*0-19-864213-X*) OUP.
Lampe, Gayle. Riding for Success; Both in & Out of the Ring. (Illus.). 320p. 1996. text 29.95 (*0-9655501-0-9*) Saddle & Bridle.
Lampe, Gerald E., ed. Justice & Human Rights in Islamic Law. 114p. 1997. 35.00 (*0-935328-84-X*) Intl Law Inst.
Lampe, Gerald E. & Shaybani Society of International Law Staff. Justice & Human Rights in Islamic Law. LC 98-160065. xvi, 98 p. 1997. write for info. (*0-03-532984-X*) Holt R&W.
Lampe, Gregory P. Frederick Douglass: Freedom's Voice, 1818-1845. LC 98-10830. (Rhetoric & Public Affairs Ser.). 350p. (C). 1998. pap. 22.95 (*0-87013-480-9*) Mich St U Pr.
Lampe, John A. Will You Help Me Save America? 116p. 1989. 12.95 (*0-9627376-0-7*) J A Lampe.
Lampe, John F. A Plain & Compendious Method of Teaching Thorough Bass. fac. ed. (Monuments of Music & Music Literature in Facsimile Ser., Series II: Vol. 29). 1969. lib. bdg. 45.00 (*0-8450-2229-6*) Broude.
Lampe, John R. Yugoslavia As History: Twice There Was a Country. LC 96-10390. (Illus.). 441p. (C). 1996. pap. text 21.95 (*0-521-46705-5*) Cambridge U Pr.
***Lampe, John R.** Yugoslavia As History: Twice There Was a Country. 2nd ed. (Illus.). 480p. 2000. 64.95 (*0-521-77357-1*); pap. 24.95 (*0-521-77401-2*) Cambridge U Pr.
Lampe, John R., ed. Creating Capital Markets in Eastern Europe. (Woodrow Wilson Center Press Ser.). 110p. (Orig.). 1992. pap. text 10.95 (*0-943875-42-0*) Johns Hopkins.
Lampe, John R. & Nelson, Daniel N., eds. East European Security Reconsidered. (Woodrow Wilson Center Press Ser.). 175p. (Orig.). 1993. pap. text 14.95 (*0-943875-47-1*) Johns Hopkins.
Lampe, John R., et al. Yugoslav-American Economic Relations since World War II. LC 90-38619. 262p. (C). 1990. text 42.95 (*0-8223-1061-9*) Duke.
Lampe, Kenneth F., ed. see Inter-American Conference in Toxicology & Occupati.
Lampe, Laszlo G., ed. see Wolf, Merrill.
Lampe, Maud Von, see Von Lampe, Maud.
***Lampe, Owen.** Millburn - Short Hills: New Jersey. LC 00-100181. (Images of America Ser.). (Illus.). 128p. 2000. pap. 18.99 (*0-7385-0413-0*) Arcadia Publng.
Lampe, Peter. From Paul to Valentinus: Christians at Rome in the First Two Centuries. Steinhauser, Michael, tr. 528p. 1999. 42.00 (*0-8006-2702-4*, Fortress Pr) Augsburg Fortress.
Lampe, Philip E., ed. Hispanics in the Church: Up from the Cellar. LC 93-33338. 1994. 54.95 (*1-883255-19-8*); pap. 34.95 (*1-883255-18-X*) Intl Scholars.
Lampe, Susan. Butterfly Chazu. (Illus.). 24p. (Orig.). (YA). 1995. pap. 6.95 (*1-883893-21-6*) WinePress Pub.
— Chart Forms. 260p. (Orig.). 1991. pap. 50.00 (*0-9621520-8-0*) Creative Nursing.
— Focus Charting: Documentation for Patient Centered Care. 7th rev. ed. 431p. 1997. pap. 35.00 (*1-886624-06-2*, B250) Creative Nursing.
— Focus Charting, What We Have Learned: A Collection of Articles from Primarily Nursing Newsletter. 69p. 1992. pap. 10.00 (*0-9621520-4-8*) Creative Nursing.
— Tiny Shooting Stars. LC 98-61100. 48p. 1998. pap. 6.95 (*1-57921-145-3*) WinePress Pub.
Lampe, Thomas R. Idea to Marketplace: How to Turn Your Good Ideas into Moneymakers. (Illus.). 240p. (Orig.). 1991. reprint ed. pap. 9.95 (*0-929923-44-8*) Lowell Hse.
Lampel, Tzvi, anno. Maimonides' Introduction to the Talmud: A Translation of Maimonides Introduction to His Commentary on the Mishna with Complete Original Hebrew Text. 3rd rev. ed. 288p. 1998. pap. 15.95 (*1-880582-28-7*) Judaica Pr.
Lampel, Zvi. The Dynamics of Dispute: Machlokess in Talmudic Times. 288p. 1991. pap. 16.95 (*0-910818-99-1*) Judaica Pr.
Lampen, Betty. Knitted Bears & Dolls. 1997. pap. 7.00 (*0-9634890-4-6*) B Lampen Knit.
— Miniature Sweaters, Bk. I. 2nd ed. 1990. 7.00 (*0-9634890-0-3*) B Lampen Knit.
— More Miniature Sweater Designs, Bk. 2. (Knitting Books Ser.: Vol. 5, Bk. III). (Illus.). 16p. 1994. pap. 7.00 (*0-9634890-3-8*, MS3) B Lampen Knit.
Lampen, Dorothy. Economic & Social Aspects of Federal Reclamation. Bruchey, Stuart, ed. LC 78-56686. (Management of Public Lands in the U. S. Ser.). (Illus.). 1979. reprint ed. lib. bdg. 15.95 (*0-405-11338-2*) Ayer.
Lampen, John. Findings: Poets & the Crisis of Faith. LC 93-85638. (Orig.). 1993. pap. 4.00 (*0-87574-310-2*) Pendle Hill.
Lampen, L. Finnish-Swedish Dictionary. (FIN & SWE.). 571p. 1980. 49.95 (*0-8288-4699-5*, M9655) Fr & Eur.
— Finnish-Swedish Dictionary: Ruotsalais-Suomalainen Suursanakirja. 6th ed. (FIN & SWE.). 857p. 1985. 150.00 (*0-8288-1079-6*, F64080) Fr & Eur.
— Finnish-Swedish-Finnish Dictionary: Suomi-Ruotsi-Suomi Taskusanakirja. 9th ed. (FIN & SWE.). 633p. 1987. 19.95 (*0-8288-1693-X*, M9647) Fr & Eur.
— Finnish-Swedish Students Dictionary: Suomalais-Ruotsalainen Opiskelusanakirja. (FIN & SWE.). 571p. 1985. 59.95 (*0-8288-1679-4*, M9656) Fr & Eur.
Lampen, Stephen H. Wire, Cable, & Fiber Optics for Video & Audio Engineers. LC 97-16148. (Video/Audio Engineering Ser.). (Illus.). 288p. 1997. 55.00 (*0-07-037148-2*); pap. 34.95 (*0-07-038134-8*) McGraw.
Lampert, Ada. The Evolution of Love. LC 97-11073. (Human Evolution, Behavior & Intelligence Ser.). 144p. 1997. 49.95 (*0-275-95907-4*, Praeger Pubs) Greenwood.
Lampert, Carl M., et al, eds. Optical materials Technology for Energy Efficiency & Solar Energy. LC 98-122052. 24p. 1997. pap. 59.00 (*0-8194-2560-5*) SPIE.
***Lampert, Carl M. & Granqvist, Claes G., eds.** Solar Optical Materials XVI. 1999. pap. text 62.00 (*0-8194-3275-X*) SPIE.
Lampert, Catherine. Rodin: Sculpture & Drawings. LC 86-50765. 256p. 1987. pap. 30.00 (*0-300-03832-1*) Yale U Pr.
Lampert, Dan & Woodley, Douglas R. Site Selection & Investigation. 170p. 1991. text 74.95 (*0-566-09090-2*, Pub. by Gower) Ashgate Pub Co.
Lampert, Diane, jt. auth. see Farrow, Peter.
Lampert, E. The Apocalypse of History: Problems of Providence & Human Destiny. 1948. 49.50 (*0-317-07646-9*) Elliots Bks.
Lampert, Emily. A Little Touch of Monster. LC 85-26847. (Illus.). 32p. (J). (ps-3). 1986. lib. bdg. 12.95 (*0-316-51287-7*, 512877, Joy St Bks) Little.
Lampert, Erv, ed. see Anderson, Dorothy & Anderson, Robert.
Lampert, Erv, ed. see Anderson, Robert.
Lampert, Erv, ed. see Berkowitz, Henry.
Lampert, Erv, ed. see Bruce, Hank.
Lampert, Erv, ed. see Bruce, Hank & Bruce, Marlene.
Lampert, Erv, ed. see Bruce, Hank, et al.
Lampert, Eva, ed. see Anderson, Dorothy & Anderson, Robert.
Lampert, Eva, ed. see Anderson, Robert.
Lampert, F., et al, eds. Cancer in the First Year of Life: Leukemia, Neuroblastomas, Soft Tissue Sarcomas. (Beitraege Zur Onkologie, Contributions to Oncology Ser.: Vol. 41). (Illus.). viii, 174p. 1991. 61.75 (*3-8055-5233-5*) S Karger.
Lampert, Gary B. God's Website: Light, Color & Perception. large type ed. Spinney, Jonathon, ed. LC 97-4406. (Illus.). 87p. 1998. pap. 24.95 (*1-891850-05-9*, Pub. by Med Bear) Partners Pubs Grp.
***Lampert, Gunther & Lampert, Martina.** The Conceptual Structure of Modality: Essences & Ideologies: A Study in Linguistic (Meta-)Categorization. 328p. 2000. pap. 47.95 (*0-8204-4738-2*) P Lang Pubng.
Lampert, Harry. The Fun Way to Advanced Bridge. 11.95 (*0-910791-77-5*, 0575) Devyn Pr.
— The Fun Way to Serious Bridge. 160p. 1986. pap. 10.00 (*0-671-63027-X*) S&S Trade.
Lampert, Hebara M. Tunesische Spezialitaten: 3000 Jahre Esskultur. 2nd ed. (GER., Illus.). 191p. (C). 1993. 40.00 (*3-8170-0014-6*, Pub. by Knstvrlag Weingrtn) Intl Bk Import.
Lampert, Jay. Synthesis & Backward Reference in Husserl's Logical Investigations. LC 94-23102. (Phaenomenologica Ser.: Vol. 131). 232p. 1995. lib. bdg. 110.50 (*0-7923-3105-2*, Pub. by Kluwer Academic) Kluwer Academic.
Lampert, Jeri, tr. see Defazio, Alex S.
Lampert, Junko. The Tofu Cookbook: Recipes for Traditional & Modern Cooking. LC 85-25546. (Illus.). 102p. (Orig.). 1986. pap. 12.95 (*0-87701-383-7*) Chronicle Bks.
Lampert, Junko, jt. auth. see Barber.
Lampert, Laurence. Leo Strauss & Nietzsche. LC 95-10467. 238p. 1995. 22.50 (*0-226-46825-9*) U Ch Pr.
— Leo Strauss & Nietzsche. x, 230p. 1997. pap. text 16.95 (*0-226-46826-7*) U Ch Pr.
— Nietzsche & Modern Times: A Study of Bacon, Descartes, Nietzsche. 1995. pap. 19.00 (*0-300-06510-8*) Yale U Pr.
— Nietzsche's Teaching: An Interpretation of "Thus Spake Zarathustra" LC 86-9209. 400p. (C). 1989. reprint ed. pap. 19.00 (*0-300-04430-5*) Yale U Pr.
Lampert, Laurence, ed. see Bacon, Francis.
Lampert, Lawrence D. The Pro's Edge: Vision Training for Golf. Orloff, Erica, ed. (Illus.). 176p. 1998. pap. 14.95 (*1-885843-06-2*) Saturn Press.
Lampert, Lincoln M. Modern Dairy Products: Composition, Food Value, Processing, Chemistry, Bacteriology, Testing, Imitation Dairy Products. LC HD9275.L34. 425p. reprint ed. pap. 131.80 (*0-7837-1961-2*, 204224700001) Bks Demand.
Lampert, Lyndon J. Lake City Hiking. 136p. 1999. pap. 7.50 (*1-928590-00-4*) Golden Stone CO.
— Lake City Places. 136p. 1999. pap. 7.50 (*1-928590-01-2*) Golden Stone CO.
Lampert, Lyndon J., jt. auth. see Borneman, Walter R.
Lampert, Magdalene & Ball, Deborah. Teaching Multimedia: Investigations of Real Practice. LC 98-17105. (Practitioner Inquiry Ser.). 1998. 53.00 (*0-8077-3758-5*) Tchrs Coll.
Lampert, Magdalene & Ball, Deborah l. Teaching Multimedia: Investigations of Real Practice. LC 98-17105. (Practitioner Inquiry Ser.). 244p. 1998. pap. 24.95 (*0-8077-3757-7*) Tchrs Coll.
Lampert, Magdalene & Blunk, Merrie, eds. Talking Mathematics in School: Studies of Teaching & Learning. LC 97-35236. (Learning in Doing Ser.). (Illus.). 304p. (C). 1998. 59.95 (*0-521-62136-4*) Cambridge U Pr.
Lampert, Martin D., jt. ed. see Edwards, Jane A.
Lampert, Martina, jt. auth. see Lampert, Gunther.
Lampert, Nick & Rittersporn, Gabor T., eds. Stalinism: Its Nature & Aftermath: Essays in Honor of Moshe Lewin. LC 91-15051. 200p. (C). (gr. 13). 1991. text 85.95 (*0-87332-876-0*) M E Sharpe.
Lampert, Nigel. Through Much Tribulation: Stewart Spiers & the Planemakers of Ayr. (Illus.). 128p. 1998. pap. 30.00 (*0-646-36426-X*) Astragal Pr.
Lampert, Rachel & Rotman, Leslie. What's Remembered: Labanotation Score. (Educational Performance Collection). 231p. 1986. pap. write for info. (*0-932582-46-X*) Dance Notation.
Lampert, Richard, ed. see Andrassy, Richard J.
Lampert, Richard, ed. see Andrews, James R. & Harrelson, Gary L.
Lampert, Richard, ed. see Andrews, James R. & Timmerman, Laura A.
Lampert, Richard, ed. see Ashcraft, Keith W.
Lampert, Richard, ed. see Benjamin, William J.
Lampert, Richard, ed. see Borenstein, David G., et al.
Lampert, Richard, ed. see Browner, Bruce D., et al.
Lampert, Richard, ed. see Canellos, George P., et al.
Lampert, Richard, ed. see Eagle, Ralph C.
Lampert, Richard, ed. see Eiff, M. Patricia, et al.
Lampert, Richard, ed. see Elander, Richard E., et al.
Lampert, Richard, ed. see Green, David P., et al.
Lampert, Richard, ed. see Green, Neil E. & Swiontkowski, Marc F.
Lampert, Richard, ed. see Greenbaum, Scott.
Lampert, Richard, ed. see Guten, Gary N.
Lampert, Richard, ed. see Guyer, David R., et al.
Lampert, Richard, ed. see Herkowitz, Harry N., et al.
Lampert, Richard, ed. see Hohl, H. Mason.
Lampert, Richard, ed. see Leibowitz, Howard M. & Waring, George O.
Lampert, Richard, ed. see Levine, Alan M.
Lampert, Richard, ed. see Miller, Mark D.

L

Lampert, Richard, ed. see Miller, Mark D., et al.
Lampert, Richard, ed. see Moody, Frank G.
Lampert, Richard, ed. see Nathan, David G. & Orkin, Stuart H.
Lampert, Richard, ed. see Nelson, Leonard B.
Lampert, Richard, ed. see Putterman, Allen M.
Lampert, Richard, ed. see Ranney, Don.
Lampert, Richard, ed. see Reider, Bruce.
Lampert, Richard, ed. see Reuder, Bruce.
Lampert, Richard, ed. see Rondinelli, Robert D. & Katz, Richard T.
Lampert, Richard, ed. see Spaide, Richard F.
Lampert, Richard, ed. see Tubiana, Raoul.
Lampert, Richard, ed. see Weber, Jorg & Caprioli, Joseph.
Lampert, Richard, ed. see Wiesel, Sam W. & Delahay, John N.
Lampert, Richard, ed. see Wu, Gloria.
Lampert, Richard, ed. see Yim, Anthony P., et al.
Lampert, Richard, ed. see Zadnik, Karla.
Lampert, Vera. Modern Masters. rev. ed. (New Grove Ser.). 1997. pap. 16.95 (0-393-31592-4) Norton.
Lampert, Winfried, ed. Food Limitation & the Structure of Zooplankton Communities: Proceedings of an International Symposium Held at Pion, W. Germany, July 9-13, 1984. (Advances in Limnology Ser.: Vol. 21). (GER., Illus.). viii, 497p. 1985. pap. text 111.00 (3-510-47019-2, Pub. by E Schweizerbartsche) Balogh.
Lampert, Winfried & Sommer, Ulrich. Limnoecology: The Ecology of Lakes & Streams. Haney, James G., tr. (Illus.). 400p. (C). 1997. text 59.95 (0-19-509592-8) OUP.
Lamperti, Claudia M., ed. Woman Space: Future & Fantasy Stories by Women. LC 80-83471. 96p. (Orig.). 1981. pap. 4.95 (0-934678-04-9) New Victoria Pubs.
Lamperti, Gainfranco, jt. auth. see Cacace, Philippe.
Lamperti, Giovanni B., jt. auth. see Brown, William E.
Lamperti, J. Stochastic Processes: A Survey of the Mathematical Theory. LC 77-24321. (Applied Mathematical Sciences Ser.: Vol. 23). 1997. pap. 36.00 (0-387-90275-9) Spr-Verlag.
Lamperti, John. What Are We Afraid Of? An Assessment of the "Communist Threat" in Central America. NARMIC-AFSC Staff, ed. LC 88-6690. 110p. 1988. 25.00 (0-89608-339-X); pap. 8.00 (0-89608-338-1) South End Pr.
Lamperti, John W. Probability: A Survey of the Mathematical Theory. 2nd ed. LC 96-9559. (Wiley Probability & Mathematics Ser.). 189p. 1996. 79.95 (0-471-15407-5, Wiley-Interscience) Wiley.
Lamperti, Noelle. Brown Like Me. 2nd large type ed. LC 98-51132. 32p. (gr. 4-7). 1999. 12.95 (1-892281-03-1) New Victoria Pubs.
Lamphear, F. Charles & Roesler, Theodore W. Input-Output Model of the Nebraska Economy, 1970. 1975. 2.50 (0-318-42808-3) Bur Busn Res U Nebr.
Lamphear, John. The Scattering Time: Turkana Responses to Colonial Rule. (Illus.). 332p. 1992. text 75.00 (0-19-820226-1) OUP.
Lamphear, John. The Traditional History of the Jie of Uganda. (Oxford Studies in African Affairs). (Illus.). 282p. 1976. text 55.00 (0-19-821692-0) OUP.
Lamphere, Louise. Anthropology: Discipline Analysis. LC 98-227025. (Women in the Curriculum Ser.: Vol. 7a). 40p. (Orig.). 1997. pap. 7.00 (1-885303-16-5) Towson St Univ.
— From Working Daughters to Working Mothers: Immigrant Women in a New England Industrial Community. LC 86-32952. (Anthropology of Contemporary Issues Ser.). (Illus.). 411p. 1987. reprint ed. pap. 127.50 (0-608-01687-X, 206234300002) Bks Demand.
Lamphere, Louise, ed. Structuring Diversity: Ethnographic Perspectives on the New Immigration. LC 91-41183. (Illus.). 268p. 1992. pap. text 16.95 (0-226-46819-4) U Ch Pr.
— Structuring Diversity: Ethnographic Perspectives on the New Immigration. LC 91-41183. (Illus.). 268p. 1996. lib. bdg. 44.00 (0-226-46818-6) U Ch Pr.
Lamphere, Louise, et al, eds. Newcomers in the Workplace: Immigrants & the Restructuring of the U. S. Economy. LC 93-15205. (Labor & Social Change Ser.). 320p. (C). 1994. pap. 22.95 (1-56639-131-8); text 69.95 (1-56639-124-5) Temple U Pr.
— Situated Lives: Gender & Culture in Everyday Life. LC 96-51900. 500p. (C). 1997. pap. 28.99 (0-415-91807-3) Routledge.
— Situated Lives: Gender & Culture in Everyday Life. LC 96-51900. 500p. (C). 1997. 75.00 (0-415-91806-5) Routledge.
Lamphere, Louise, et al. Sunbelt Working Mothers: Reconciling Family & Factory. LC 92-56789. (Anthropology of Contemporary Issues Ser.). (Illus.). 352p. 1993. text 45.00 (0-8014-2788-6); pap. text 16.95 (0-8014-8066-3) Cornell U Pr.
Lamphere, Louise, jt. ed. see Rosaldo, Michelle Z.
Lamphere, Robert J. FBI - KGB War: A Special Agent's Story. (C). 1995. pap. text 24.95 (0-86554-477-8, MUP-P123) Mercer Univ Pr.
Lamphier, Mary J. Zany Characters of the Ad World, Collector's Identification & Value Guide: 1995 Values. 176p. 1995. pap. 16.95 (0-89145-652-X, 3979) Collector Bks.
Lamphier, Sheldon, jt. auth. see Heiney, Sue P.
Lampietti, Heidi. Afterday. (Best Ideas Series). 100p. 1998. pap. 4.75 (1-892619-04-0) RedJack.
— Best Science Fiction of the Dark Ages. (The Best Ideas Series). 100p. 1998. pap. 4.75 (1-892619-05-9) RedJack.
— Black & White Abstract. (Color Me Notebooks Ser.). 100p. 1998. pap. 4.75 (1-892619-02-4) RedJack.
— Book. 100p. 1998. pap. 4.75 (1-892619-00-8) RedJack.
— Plain White. (Color Me Notebooks Ser.). 100p. 1998. pap. 4.00 (1-892619-03-2) RedJack.
— What You Can Do with Your Degree. 100p. 1998. pap. 4.75 (1-892619-01-6) RedJack.
Lampignano, John P., jt. auth. see Bontrager, Kenneth L.
Lampikoski, Karl & Emden, Jack B. Igniting Innovation: Inspiring Organisations by Managing Creativity. LC 95-50659. 232p. 1996. 84.95 (0-471-96367-4) Wiley.
Lamping, Alwena. NTC's Italian Grammar. LC 97-34565. (Grammar Ser.). (ENG & ITA., Illus.). 192p. 1997. pap. 10.95 (0-8442-8080-1, 80801) NTC Contemp Pub Co.
Lamping, Alwena. Talk Italian. LC 98-33754. (Talk Short Language Courses Ser.). (ENG & FRE.). 1999. write for info. (0-8442-1364-0, Passprt Bks); pap. 18.95 incl. audio (0-8442-1387-X, 1387X, Passprt Bks) NTC Contemp Pub Co.
Lampinig, David A. Electrical Power System Reliability Handbook: For Industrial & Commercial Facilities. (Illus.). 512p. 1998. 69.95 (0-07-036081-2) McGraw.
Lampitt, Bob. A Manager's Introduction to Tendering. (C). 1991. pap. 60.00 (0-85171-097-2, Pub. by IPM Hse) St Mut.
Lampkin, N. H. & Padel, S., eds. The Economics of Organic Farming: An International Perspective. 480p. 1994. text 105.00 (0-85198-911-X) OUP.
Lampkin, Nicolas. Organic Farming. (Illus.). 720p. 1990. 49.95 (0-85236-191-2, Pub. by Farming Pr) Diamond Farm Bk.
Lampkin, Richard H. Clericalism Impeached, Vol. 1. LC 96-86277. 384p. 1998. 26.95 (0-8158-0524-1) Chris Mass.
— Lampkin Genealogy: A Genealogcal History of the Ancestors of David P. Lampkin, Vol. 1. LC CS0071.. 870p. 1989. reprint ed. pap. 200.00 (0-8357-6288-2, AU0038800001) Bks Demand.
— Lampkin Genealogy: A Genealogcal History of the Ancestors of David P. Lampkin, Vol. 2. LC CS0071.. 868p. 1989. reprint ed. pap. 200.00 (0-8357-6289-0, AU0038800002) Bks Demand.
— Selected Readings in Scripture & Morals: Twelve Canonical Scriptures Considered As Sources of True Propositions about the Morality of Eating Meat & of Drinking Alcohol, of Making War & of Making Love. LC BJ0047.. 327p. reprint ed. pap. 101.40 (0-7837-2031-9, AU0041800003) Bks Demand.
— Variability in Recognizing Scientific Inquiry: An Analysis of High School Science Textbooks. LC 70-176971. (Columbia University. Teachers College. Contributions to Education Ser.: No. 955). reprint ed. 37.50 (0-404-55955-7) AMS Pr.
Lampkin, Rita. Easy Kana Workbook: Basic Practice in Hiragana & Katakana for Japanese Language Students. (Illus.). 104p. 1991. pap. 9.95 (0-8442-8532-3, Natl Textbk Co) NTC Contemp Pub Co.
— Learning & Using Japanese Numbers: Beginning Through Intermediate. LC 96-151824. (JPN.). 96p. (C). pap., student ed. 10.95 (0-8442-8439-4, E8439-4) NTC Contemp Pub Co.
Lampkin, Rita L. Easy Japanese Crossword Puzzles: Using Kana. (ENG & JPN.). 64p. 1997. pap. 5.95 (0-8442-8345-2, 83452) NTC Contemp Pub Co.
— Easy Japanese Crossword Puzzles: Using Roomaji. (ENG & JPN.). 64p. 1997. pap. 5.95 (0-8442-8346-0, 83460) NTC Contemp Pub Co.
Lampkin, Rita L. Japanese Verbs & Essentials of Grammar. LC 99-88197. (BBC Phrase Bks.). (JPN & ENG.). 160p. 1995. pap. 8.95 (0-8442-8406-8, 84068, Passprt Bks) NTC Contemp Pub Co.
Lampkin, Rita L. Learning & Using Japanese Numbers, 2 cass., Set. (JPN.). 96p. 1996. 19.95 incl. audio (0-8442-8520-X, Natl Textbk Co) NTC Contemp Pub Co.
Lampkin, Rita L. & Christensen, John. The ABCs of ESL Business Letter Writing. (Illus.). 98p. 1989. 12.95 (1-877591-09-2) Excellence Education.
Lampkin, Rita L., jt. auth. see Takada, Norika.
Lampkin, Viola. Viola's Favorite Recipes. (Illus.). 74p. (Orig.). 1988. pap. write for info. (0-9621378-0-4) B Clagett.
Lampl-de Groot, Jeanne. Development of the Mind: Psychoanalytic Papers on Clinical & Theoretical Problems. LC 65-21749. 391p. 1965. 57.50 (0-8236-1240-6) Intl Univs Pr.
— Man & Mind. ix, 441p. 1985. 65.00 (0-8236-3087-0) Intl Univs Pr.
Lampl, Elizabeth J. & Protho Williams, Kimberly. Chevy Chase: A Home Suburb for the Nation's Capital. LC 98-46749. (Illus.). 168p. 1998. pap. 25.00 (1-878399-75-6) Div Hist Cult Progs.
Lampl, Hans. Turning Notes into Music: An Introduction to Musical Interpretation. LC 96-7833. 152p. 1996. pap. 26.00 (0-8108-3165-1) Scarecrow.
— Turning Notes into Music: An Introduction to Musical Interpretation. LC 96-7833. 152p. 1996. 44.00 (0-8108-3164-3) Scarecrow.
Lampland, Martha. The Object of Labor: Commodification of Agrarian Life in Socialist Hungary. LC 95-11554. 410p. 1995. pap. text 17.95 (0-226-46830-5); lib. bdg. 39.95 (0-226-46829-1) U Ch Pr.
Lample, Paul, compiled by. A Wider Horizon: Selected Messages of the Universal House of Justice 1983-1992. x, 257p. (Orig.). 1992. pap. 10.00 (1-890101-11-7) Palabra Pubns.
Lamplight Press Staff. Dude Ranches, Vacation Guest Ranches: A How to Find or Locate Reference & Planning Guide. rev. ed. (Illus.). 70p. 1995. ring bd. 24.95 (0-917593-13-8, Lamp Light Pr) Prosperity & Profits.
— Home Economics: Home School. 120p. 1993. ring bd. 25.95 (0-917593-17-0, Lamp Light Pr) Prosperity & Profits.
Lamplugh, Diana & Pagan, Barbara. Personal Safety for People Working in Education. LC 95-86202. 326p. 1996. pap. 33.95 (1-85742-194-9, Pub. by Arena) Ashgate Pub Co.
Lamplugh, Diana, et al. Working Alone: Surviving & Thriving. (Institute of Management Ser.). 208p. (Orig.). 1993. pap. 37.50 (0-273-60196-2, Pub. by Pitman Pub) Trans-Atl Phila.
Lamplugh, F. The Gnosis of the Light: A Translation of the Untitled Apocalypse Contained in the Codex Brucianus. 89p. 1994. reprint ed. pap. 14.95 (1-56459-431-9) Kessinger Pub.
Lamplugh, George R. Politics on the Periphery: Factions & Parties in Georgia, 1783-1806. LC 85-40662. (Illus.). 224p. 1986. 38.50 (0-87413-288-6) U Delaware Pr.
Lamplugh, Rick. Job Search That Works: A Proven 10-Step Plan. Gerould, Philip, ed. LC 91-70077. (Fifty-Minute Ser.). (Illus.). 110p. (Orig.). 1991. pap. 10.95 (1-56052-105-8) Crisp Pubns.
Lampman & Peters, A. T., eds. Ferroalloys & Other Additives to Liquid Iron & Steel- STP 739. 216p. 1981. 24.75 (0-8031-0744-7, STP739) ASTM.
Lampman, Ben H. How Could I Be Forgetting. (Illus.). 158p. 1956. pap. 4.95 (0-8323-0379-8) Binford Mort.
Lampman, Evelyn S. Treasure Mountain. (Eager Beaver Bks.). (Illus.). 207p. (J). (gr. 4). 1990. reprint ed. pap. 6.95 (0-87595-231-3) Oregon Hist.
Lampman, Greg R. Magic & Loss. LC 95-131071. 184p. (Orig.). 1994. 18.95 (1-57174-017-1); pap. 9.95 (1-57174-015-5) Hampton Roads Pub Co.
Lampman, Linda, tr. & illus. see Tritt, Marilyn.
Lampman, Lisa B., ed. God & the Victim: Theological Reflections on Evil, Victimization, Justice & Forgiveness. LC 99-37659. 341p. 1999. pap. 16.00 (0-8028-4546-0) Eerdmans.
***Lampman, Lisa Barnes.** Helping a Neighbor in Crisis. rev. ed. LC 99-33445. 1999. pap. 11.99 (0-8423-3608-7) Tyndale Hse.
Lampman, M. Jerista. Parousia: . . . And Man Made God. 1997. pap. 11.95 (0-9673430-0-3) Da Hood Pubg Inc.
Lampman, Richard M., jt. auth. see Campaigne, Barbara.
Lampman, Robert J. Changes in the Share of Wealth Held by Top Wealth-Holders, 1922-1956. (Occasional Papers: No. 71). 38p. 1960. reprint ed. 20.00 (0-87014-385-9) Natl Bur Econ Res.
— The Share of Top Wealth-Holders in National Wealth, 1922-56. (General Ser.: No. 74). 316p. 1975. reprint ed. 82.20 (0-87014-073-6) Ayer.
— The Share of Top Wealth-Holders in National Wealth, 1922-56. LC 84-19118. 286p. 1984. reprint ed. lib. bdg. 79.50 (0-313-24425-1, LAST, Greenwood Pr) Greenwood.
— Social Welfare Spending: Accounting for Changes from Nineteen Fifty to Nineteen Seventy-Eight. (Institute for Research on Poverty Policy Analysis Ser.). 1984. text 60.00 (0-12-435260-X) Acad Pr.
Lampman, Steve, ed. Weld Integrity & Performance. LC 97-10740. 417p. 1997. 153.00 (0-87170-600-8, 6593) ASM.
Lampman Symposium, 1975, University of Ottawa Staf. The Lampman Symposium. McMullen, Lorraine, ed. & intro. by. LC 77-367781. (Re-Appraisals, Canadian Writers Ser.). 148p. 1976. reprint ed. pap. 45.90 (0-608-02201-2, 206287100004) Bks Demand.
Lampmann, L. E., et al. CT Densitometry in Osteoporosis: The Impact on Management of the Patient. (Series in Radiology). 124p. 1984. text 122.00 (0-89838-633-0) Kluwer Academic.
Lampner, Carl. Recipes for Parent Survival: Revealing the Amazing Secrets of SUPERCHEF, the Great. LC 95-23140. (Illus.). 324p. 1995. pap. 19.95 (0-942963-63-6) Distinctive Pub.
Lampo, Richard G., jt. ed. see Williams, Mark F.
Lampola, R. Gastronomic Terms. 5th ed. (ENG & FIN.). 80p. 1985. 35.00 (0-8288-0844-9, F42684) Fr & Eur.
Lamport, F. J. German Classical Drama: Theatre, Humanity & Nation, 1750-1870. 255p. (C). 1992. pap. text 19.95 (0-521-42828-9) Cambridge U Pr.
— Lessing & the Drama. 254p. (C). 1982. text 39.00 (0-19-815767-3) OUP.
Lamport, F. J., ed. Schiller: Die Rauber. (German Texts Ser.). (GER.). 192p. 1996. pap. 18.95 (1-85399-318-2, Pub. by Brist Class Pr) Focus Pub-R Pullins.
Lamport, F. J., tr. & intro. see Schiller, Friedrich.
Lamport, F. J., tr. & notes see Schiller, Friedrich.
Lamport, Leslie. Concurrent Program Verification. (Computer Science Ser.). (Illus.). 400p. (C). 1996. text. write for info. (0-201-50421-9) Addison-Wesley.
— Latex: A Document Preparation System User's Guide & Reference Manual. 2nd ed. (Illus.). 288p. (C). 1994. pap. text 36.95 (0-201-52983-1) Addison-Wesley.
Lamport, Nancy K., et al. Activity Analysis & Application: Building Blocks of Treatment. 3rd ed. (Illus.). 264p. 1996. pap. text 29.00 (1-55642-321-7, 33217) SLACK Inc.
***Lamport, Nancy K., et al.** Activity Analysis & Application: Building Blocks of Treatment. 4th ed. (C). 2000. pap. text 32.00 (1-55642-487-6) SLACK Inc.
Lampou. English-Greek & Greek-English Dictionary of Financial & Commercial Terms. (ENG & GRE.). 404p. pap. 150.00 (0-7859-9055-0) Fr & Eur.
Lamprati, L. M. Industrial Relations in Australia. 4th ed. 304p. 1985. pap. text 26.95 (0-471-33390-5) Wiley.
Lamprecht. Lamprecht, der Pfaffe, Alexander: Gedicht Des Zwolften Jahrhunderts, 2 vols. cxxx, 1164p. 1971. reprint ed. write for info. (0-318-71265-2); reprint ed. write for info. (0-318-71266-0) G Olms Pubs.
— Lamprecht, der Pfaffe, Alexander: Gedicht Des Zwolften Jahrhunderts, 2 vols., Set. cxxx, 1164p. 1971. reprint ed. write for info. (0-318-71264-4) G Olms Pubs.
Lamprecht, E. Heating & Cooling on Board. (Illus.). 112p. 1994. pap. 18.50 (0-7136-3528-2) Sheridan.
***Lamprecht, Gerlinde.** Die F. M. Alexander-Technik: Eine Ganzheitliche Methode Zur Wieder-Erlangung Der Naturlichen Korperkoordination Und Ihre Bedeutung in Der Sprachtherapeutischen Praxis. (Illus.). 182p. 1999. 37.95 (3-631-34064-8) P Lang Pubng.
Lamprecht, I. & Zotin, A. I., eds. Thermodynamics & Pattern Formation in Biology. xiii, 518p. (C). 1988. lib. bdg. 306.15 (3-11-011368-6) De Gruyter.
— Thermodynamics & Regulation of Biological Processes. LC 84-23302. (Illus.). xiv, 573p. 1985. 207.70 (3-11-009789-3) De Gruyter.
***Lamprecht, James L.** For the Sake of Quality: Compliance of Complaints in Supply Chain Management. (Illus.). 342p. 2000. 29.95 (0-7506-7343-5) Buttrwrth-Heinemann.
Lamprecht, James L. ISO 14000: Issues & Implementation Guidelines for Responsible Environmental Management. LC 96-42575. 240p. 1996. 27.95 (0-8144-0353-0) AMACOM.
— ISO 9000: Preparing for Registration. LC 92-4932. 254p. 1992. 49.75 (0-8247-8741-2, H0776) ASQ Qual Pr.
— ISO 9000 & the Service Sector: A Critical Interpretation of the 1994 Revisions. LC 94-27380. 265p. 1994. 38.00 (0-87389-313-1, H0871) ASQ Qual Pr.
— ISO 9000 Implementation for Small Business. LC 95-37171. (Illus.). 209p. 1996. text 41.75 (0-87389-350-6, H0907) ASQ Qual Pr.
Lamprecht, Sterling P. Metaphysics of Naturalism. LC 67-18049. (Century Philosophy Ser.). 1967. 42.50 (0-89197-302-8) Irvington.
Lamprecht, Sterling P., ed. see Hobbes, Thomas.
Lampreia, J. P., et al. Iteration Theory, ECIT 91. 372p. 1992. text 95.00 (981-02-1109-0) World Scientific Pub.
Lamprell, K. & Whitehead, T. Bivalves of Australia, Vol. 1. (Illus.). 196p. 1992. 52.00 (1-86333-039-9, Pub. by Backhuys Pubs) Balogh.
Lamprell, Klay, ed. Sex in Long-Term Relationships: Men & Women Talk about Sex. 185p. (Orig.). 1997. pap. 14.95 (1-86448-234-6, Pub. by Allen & Unwin Pty) IPG Chicago.
Lamprell, Klay & Young Discoveries Staff. Scaly Things. LC 96-12346. (Nature Company Young Discoveries Ser.). (Illus.). 32p. (J). (ps-2). 1999. 10.00 (0-7835-4842-7) Time-Life.
Lamprey, Louise. Children of Ancient Gaul. LC 60-16708. (Illus.). (J). (gr. 7-11). 1968. 22.00 (0-8196-0109-8) Biblo.
— Children of Ancient Rome. LC 61-12876. (Illus.). (J). (gr. 7-11). 1967. pap. 20.00 (0-8196-0114-4) Biblo.
Lamprichs, Ronald. Die Westexpansion des Neuassyrischen Reiches: Eine Strukturanalyse. (Alter Orient und Altes Testament Ser.: Vol. 239). (GER.). x, 452p. 1995. text 95.00 (3-7887-1533-2, Pub. by NeukirchenerV) Eisenbrauns.
Lampright, Richard L. Gold Placer Deposits in East Central Alaska. (Illus.). 102p. (Orig.). 1996. pap. 19.95 (0-9645366-3-3) Iron Fire Pubns.
— Gold Placer Deposits in NorthCentral Alaska. LC 99-474400. (Illus.). 112p. 1999. pap. 19.95 (1-892279-01-0) Iron Fire Pubns.
— Gold Placer Deposits in Northeast Alaska (Dalton Highway) LC 97-171184. (Illus.). 104p. (Orig.). 1997. pap. 19.95 (0-9645366-4-1) Iron Fire Pubns.
— Gold Placer Deposits in NorthWest Alaska. LC 99-474398. (Illus.). 134p. 1999. pap. 19.95 (1-892279-02-9) Iron Fire Pubns.
— Gold Placer Deposits in Southeast Alaska. LC 99-163660. (Illus.). 96p. 1998. pap. 19.95 (0-9645366-8-4) Iron Fire Pubns.
— Gold Placer Deposits in SouthWest Alaska. LC 99-474397. (Illus.). 112p. 1999. pap. 19.95 (0-9645366-9-2) Iron Fire Pubns.
— Gold Placer Deposits in WestCentral Alaska. LC 99-474399. (Illus.). 112p. 1999. pap. 19.95 (1-892279-00-2) Iron Fire Pubns.
— Gold Placer Deposits near Anchorage, Alaska. 2nd ed. LC 98-116447. (Illus.). 118p. 1997. pap. 19.95 (0-9645366-5-X) Iron Fire Pubns.
— Gold Placer Deposits Near Fairbanks Alaska. LC 96-207745. (Illus.). 140p. (Orig.). 1996. pap. 19.95 (0-9645366-1-7) Iron Fire Pubns.
— Gold Placer Deposits Near Nome Alaska: Centennial Edition. (Illus.). 134p. 1998. pap. 19.95 (0-9645366-7-6) Iron Fire Pubns.
— Gold Placer Deposits Near Talkeetna, Alaska. 2nd ed. LC 98-161008. (Illus.). 104p. 1997. pap. 19.95 (0-9645366-6-8) Iron Fire Pubns.
Lampropoulos, G. A. & Lessard, R. A. Applications of Photonic Technology: Communications, Sensing, Materials, & Signal Processing, Vol. 2. LC 98-134578. (Illus.). 910p. (C). 1998. 234.00 (0-306-45808-X, Plenum Trade) Perseus Pubng.
Lampropoulos, George A., et al, eds. Applications of Photonic Technology: Proceedings of an International Conference on Applications of Photonic Technology, Sensing, Signal Processing, & Communications, Held in Toronto, Ontario, Canada, June 21-23, 1994. LC 96-33160. (Illus.). 580p. (C). 1995. 155.00 (0-306-45011-9, Kluwer Plenum) Kluwer Academic.
Lampros, Angelique, jt. auth. see Ballare, Antonia.
Lampson, B. W., et al, eds. Distributed Systems: Architecture & Implementation, An Advanced Course. (Springer Study Edition Ser.). 510p. 1988. 54.95 (0-387-12116-1) Spr-Verlag.
Lampson, Butler W. Research in Man-Machine Communications Using Time Shared Computer Systems. LC 77-131392. 73p. 1969. 19.00 (0-403-04513-4) Scholarly.
Lampson, Marc. From Profanity Hill, King County Bar Association's Story. LC 93-71147. 29.95 (0-935503-10-2) Document Bk.

Lampton, Christopher. Bathtubs, Slides, Roller Coaster Rails: Simple Machines That Are Really Inclined Planes. (Gateway Simple Machines Ser.). (Illus.). 32p. (J). (gr. 2-4). 1991. pap. 4.80 (*1-878841-44-0*) Millbrook Pr.
— Blizzard. (Disaster! Ser.). (Illus.). 64p. (J). (gr. 4-6). 1991. pap. 5.95 (*1-56294-775-3*) Millbrook Pr.
— Blizzard: A Disaster Book. (J). (gr. 4-7). 1992. pap. 5.70 (*0-395-63641-8*) HM.
— Chemical Accident. (Disaster! Ser.). (Illus.). 48p. (J). (gr. 4-6). 1994. lib. bdg. 19.90 (*1-56294-316-2*) Millbrook Pr.
— Cutting Edge 3D Game Programming with CD-ROM. 10th ed. 500p. (C). 1996. pap., mass mkt. 39.99 incl. cd-rom (*1-883577-70-5*) Coriolis Grp.
— Drought. LC 91-18053. (Disaster! Ser.). (Illus.). 64p. (J). (gr. 4-6). 1992. pap. 5.95 (*1-878841-91-2*) Millbrook Pr.
— Drought. (Disaster Zone Ser.). (J). 1992. 11.15 (*0-606-02601-0*, Pub. by Turtleback) Demco.
— Drought: A Disaster Book. (J). (gr. 4-7). 1992. pap. 5.70 (*0-395-62465-7*) HM.
— Earthquake. (Disaster! Ser.). (Illus.). 64p. (J). (gr. 4-6). 1991. pap. 5.95 (*1-56294-777-X*) Millbrook Pr.
— Earthquake. (Disaster Zone Ser.). (J). 1991. 11.15 (*0-606-02611-8*, Pub. by Turtleback) Demco.
— Earthquake: A Disaster Book. (J). (gr. 4-7). 1992. pap. 5.70 (*0-395-63642-6*) HM.
— Epidemic. LC 91-21413. (Illus.). 64p. (J). (gr. 4-6). 1992. pap. 5.95 (*1-878841-92-0*); lib. bdg. 19.90 (*1-56294-126-7*) Millbrook Pr.
— Epidemic. (Disaster Zone Ser.). (J). 1992. 11.15 (*0-606-02633-9*, Pub. by Turtleback) Demco.
— Epidemic: A Disaster Book. (J). (gr. 4-7). 1992. pap. 5.70 (*0-395-62466-5*) HM.
— Famine. LC 93-9428. (Disaster! Ser.). (Illus.). 48p. (J). (gr. 4-6). 1994. lib. bdg. 19.90 (*1-56294-317-0*) Millbrook Pr.
— Forest Fire. (Disaster! Ser.). (Illus.). 64p. (J). (gr. 4-6). 1991. pap. 5.95 (*1-56294-779-6*) Millbrook Pr.
— Forest Fire. (Disaster Zone Ser.). (J). 1991. 11.15 (*0-606-02643-6*, Pub. by Turtleback) Demco.
— Forest Fire: A Disaster Book. (J). (gr. 4-7). 1992. pap. 5.70 (*0-395-63646-9*) HM.
Lampton, Christopher. Home Page: An Introduction to Web Page Design. (First Book Ser.). (Illus.). (J). 1997. 12.30 (*0-606-18151-2*) Turtleback.
Lampton, Christopher. Home Page: An Introduction to Web Page Design. (First Bk.). (J). (gr. 4-6). 1997. lib. bdg. 22.00 (*0-531-20255-0*) Watts.
— Home Page: An Introduction to Web Page Design. LC 96-41130. (First Bks.). (J). (gr. 4-6). 1997. pap. text 6.95 (*0-531-15854-3*) Watts.
— Hurricane. (Disaster! Ser.). (Illus.). 64p. (J). (gr. 4-6). 1991. pap. 5.95 (*1-56294-780-X*) Millbrook Pr.
Lampton, Christopher. Hurricane. (Disaster Zone Ser.). (J). 1991. 11.15 (*0-606-02679-7*, Pub. by Turtleback) Demco.
Lampton, Christopher. Hurricane: A Disaster Book. (J). (gr. 4-7). 1992. pap. 5.70 (*0-395-63643-4*) HM.
— Insect Attack. LC 91-26155. (Disaster! Ser.). 64p. (J). (gr. 4-6). 1992. pap. 5.95 (*1-878841-93-9*) Millbrook Pr.
— Insect Attack. (Disaster Zone Ser.). (J). 1992. 11.15 (*0-606-02691-6*, Pub. by Turtleback) Demco.
— Insect Attack: A Disaster Book. (J). (gr. 4-7). 1992. pap. 5.70 (*0-395-62467-3*) HM.
— Marbles, Roller Skates, Doorknobs: Simple Machines That Are Really Wheels. LC 92-34332. (Gateway Simple Machines Ser.). (Illus.). 32p. (J). (gr. 2-4). 1991. pap. 4.80 (*1-878841-45-9*) Millbrook Pr.
— Nuclear Accident. LC 91-43564. (Disaster! Ser.). (Illus.). 64p. (J). (gr. 4-6). 1992. pap. 5.95 (*1-56294-782-6*) Millbrook Pr.
— Oil Spill. LC 91-43565. (Disaster! Ser.). (Illus.). 64p. (J). (gr. 4-6). 1992. pap. 5.95 (*1-56294-783-4*) Millbrook Pr.
— Science of Chaos: Complexity in the Natural World. LC 91-40896. (Venture Bks.). (Illus.). 112p. (YA). (gr. 7-12). 1992. lib. bdg. 24.00 (*0-531-12513-0*) Watts.
— Seesaws, Nutcrackers, Brooms: Simple Machines That Are Really Levers. (Gateway Simple Machines Ser.). (Illus.). 32p. (J). (gr. 2-4). 1991. pap. 4.80 (*1-878841-43-2*) Millbrook Pr.
— Tidal Wave: A Disaster Book. (J). (gr. 4-7). 1992. pap. 5.70 (*0-395-62464-9*) HM.
— Tornado. (Disaster! Book). (Illus.). 64p. (J). (gr. 4-6). 1991. pap. 5.95 (*1-56294-785-0*) Millbrook Pr.
— Tornado. (Disaster Zone Ser.). (J). 1991. 11.15 (*0-606-02950-8*, Pub. by Turtleback) Demco.
— Tornado: A Disaster Book. (J). (gr. 4-7). 1992. pap. 5.70 (*0-395-63644-2*) HM.
— Volcano. (Disaster! Ser.). (Illus.). 64p. (J). (gr. 4-6). 1991. pap. 5.95 (*1-56294-786-9*) Millbrook Pr.
— Volcano. (Disaster Zone Ser.). (J). 1991. 11.15 (*0-606-02964-8*, Pub. by Turtleback) Demco.
— Volcano: A Disaster Book. (J). (gr. 4-7). 1992. pap. 5.70 (*0-395-63645-0*) HM.
— The World Wide Web. LC 96-36145. 1997. lib. bdg. 22.00 (*0-531-20262-3*) Watts.
— The World Wide Web. (First Bks.). (J). 1997. pap. text 6.95 (*0-531-15842-X*) Watts.
Lampton, Christopher & Radtke, Mick. Build Your Own Flight Sim in C++ 2nd ed. 660p. 1996. pap. 39.95 (*1-57169-022-0*) Sams.
Lampton, Christopher, jt. auth. see Vergoth, Karin.
Lampton, David M. Paths to Power: Elite Mobility in Contemporary China. (Michigan Monographs in Chinese Studies: No. 55). (Illus.). 379p. (Orig.). 1986. pap. text 25.00 (*0-89264-064-2*) Ctr Chinese Studies.
— Paths to Power: Elite Mobility in Contemporary China. LC 85-16601. (Michigan Monographs in Chinese Studies: No. 55). (Illus.). 379p. (Orig.). 1988. text 50.00 (*0-89264-063-4*) Ctr Chinese Studies.
***Lampton, David M.** Same Bed, Different Dreams: Managing U.S.-China Relations, 1989-2000. LC 00-28712. (Illus.). 485p. 2001. 35.00 (*0-520-21590-7*) U CA Pr.
Lampton, David M. & Madancy, Joyce A. A Relationship Restored: Trends in U. S. - China Educational Exchanges, 1978-1984. LC 86-61028. 286p. reprint ed. pap. 88.70 (*0-7837-1797-0*, 204199800001) Bks Demand.
Lampton, David M. & Wilhelm, Alfred D., Jr., eds. U. S. & China Relations at a Crossroads. 306p. (Orig.). (C). 1995. lib. bdg. 62.50 (*0-8191-9888-9*) U Pr of Amer.
— United States & China Relations at a Crossroads. 306p. (Orig.). (C). 1995. pap. 34.00 (*0-8191-9889-7*) U Pr of Amer.
Lampton, David M., jt. ed. see Lieberthal, Kenneth G.
Lampton, Patrice. A Touch of Tiffany. (Illus.). 40p. 1989. pap. 14.95 (*0-935133-25-9*) CKE Pubns.
Lampton, William. The Complete Communicator. LC 98-75588. 160p. 1999. 24.95 (*1-57736-133-4*, Hillsboro Pr) Providence Hse.
Lampugnani. Berlin Tomorrow, Vol. 1. 1991. pap. 21.95 (*0-312-07142-6*) St Martin.
Lampugnani, Vittorio M. Berlin Tomorrow: International Architectural Visions. (Orig.). 1992. pap. 19.95 (*0-312-06783-6*) St Martin.
***Lampugnani, Vittorio M.** Museums for a New Millennium: Concepts, Projects & Buildings. (Illus.). 224p. 1999. 65.00 (*3-7913-2219-2*, Pub. by Prestel) te Neues.
Lampugnani, Vittorio M. Renzo Piano, 1987-1994. (Illus.). 272p. 1995. pap. 49.50 (*3-7643-5159-4*, Pub. by Birkhauser) Princeton Arch.
Lampugnani, Vittorio M., ed. Museum Architecture in Frankfurt, 1980-1990. (Illus.). 200p. 1990. 75.00 (*3-7913-1096-8*, Pub. by Prestel) te Neues.
Lampugnani, Vittorio M., et al, eds. Hong Kong Architecture: The Aesthetics of Density. (Illus.). 160p. 1993. 50.00 (*3-7913-1324-X*, Pub. by Prestel) te Neues.
Lamrim Chenmo Translation Committee, tr. see Tsong-kha-pa.
Lamrimpa, Gen. Calming the Mind: Tibetan Buddhist Teachings on Cultivating Meditative Quiescence. Sprager, Hart, ed. Wallace, B. Alan, tr. LC 92-28543. (TIB.). 152p. 1992. pap. 12.95 (*1-55939-051-4*) Snow Lion Pubns.
— Realizing Emptiness: Madhyamaka Cultivation of Insight. Posman, Ellen, ed. Wallace, B. Alan, tr. LC 99-31832. 184p. 1999. pap. 14.95 (*1-55939-118-9*) Snow Lion Pubns.
— Transcending Time: An Explanation of the Kalachakra Six-Session Guru Yoga. Wallace, B. Alan, tr. LC 99-19501. 320p. 1999. pap. 21.95 (*0-86171-152-1*) Wisdom MA.
***Lams, Victor J.** Anger, Guilt & the Psychology of the Self in "Clarissa" LC 98-27378. (American University Studies IV: Vol. 191). (Illus.). XVII, 210p. (C). 1999. text 46.95 (*0-8204-4160-0*) P Lang Pubng.
Lamsa, G. M., jt. auth. see Emhardt, William C.
Lamsa, George M. Idioms in the Bible Explained & a Key to the Original Gospels. LC 85-42782. 128p. 1985. pap. 14.00 (*0-06-064927-5*, Pub. by Harper SF) HarpC.
Lamsa, George M., tr. The Modern New Testament: Translated from the Original Aramaic Sources. 560p. 1998. reprint ed. pap. 23.00 (*0-87516-716-0*) DeVorss.
Lamsky, Bruce, ed. Golf: It's Just a Game. (Illus.). 110p. (Orig.). 1996. pap. write for info. (*0-671-90438-8*) Meadowbrook.
***Lamsley, Terry.** Dark Matters. (Illus.). xii, 252p. 2000. 41.50 (*1-55310-002-6*) Ash-Tree.
Lamson, jt. auth. see Tibbetts.
Lamson, Amy. Guide for the Beginning Therapist: Relationship Between Diagnosis & Treatment. 2nd ed. LC 78-4061. 130p. 1986. 32.95 (*0-89885-293-5*, Kluwer Acad Hman Sci); pap. 19.95 (*0-89885-295-1*, Kluwer Acad Hman Sci) Kluwer Academic.
— Psychology of Juvenile Crime. 123p. 1982. 32.95 (*0-89885-060-6*, Kluwer Acad Hman Sci); pap. 18.95 (*0-89885-290-0*, Kluwer Acad Hman Sci) Kluwer Academic.
Lamson, Byron S., ed. see Watson, C. Hoyt.
Lamson, Christy. The Movie Critic's Journal. (Orig.). 1993. pap. 8.95 (*0-9638778-0-1*) Lamson Ent.
Lamson, Cynthia, ed. The Sea Has Many Voices: Oceans Policy for a Complex World. 336p. 1994. 65.00 (*0-7735-1112-1*, Pub. by McG-Queens Univ Pr) CUP Services.
Lamson, Cynthia, jt. ed. see VanderZwaag, David L.
Lamson, Darryl B., jt. auth. see Tibbetts, Leonard F.
Lamson, David R. Two Years Experience among the Shakers. LC 71-134418. reprint ed. 40.00 (*0-404-08477-X*) AMS Pr.
Lamson, Martha. Duval's Svengali on Singing. pap. 5.00 (*0-8315-0111-1*) Speller.
Lamson, Mary S. Life & Education of Laura Dewey Bridgman: The Deaf, Dumb & Blind Girl. LC 74-21419. (Classics in Child Development Ser.). (Illus.). 420p. 1975. lib. bdg. 36.95 (*0-405-06469-1*) Ayer.
Lamson, Richard, jt. auth. see Bromley, Hank.
Lamson, Roy & Smith, Hallett D., eds. Golden Hind. rev. ed. (Illus.). (C). 1956. text 57.75 (*0-393-09483-9*) Norton.
Lamson-Scribner, F., tr. see Hackel, Eduard.
Lamson, Sharon & Tuitel, Johnnie. The Barn at Gun Lake. LC 97-66781. (Gun Lake Gang Adventure Ser.: No. 1). (Illus.). (J). (gr. 4-6). 1997. pap. 5.99 (*0-9658075-0-9*) Cedar Tree Pub.
Lamson, Sharon E., jt. auth. see Tuitel, Johnnie.
Lamson, Suzy. A Rose Between Her Teeth. 76p. 1998. pap. text 10.00 (*1-887012-15-X*) Hanovr Pr.
Lamson, Theresa. ADD: The Facts, the Fables, Hope for Your Family. LC 96-60585. 208p. 1996. pap. 11.99 (*1-56384-121-5*, Vital Issue Pr) Huntington Hse.
Lamson, W. Descendants of William Lamson of Ipswich, Massachusetts, 1634-1917. (Illus.). 414p. 1993. reprint ed. pap. 65.00 (*0-8328-3044-5*); reprint ed. lib. bdg. 75.00 (*0-8328-3043-7*) Higginson Bk Co.
Lamstein, Sarah, jt. auth. see Shrestha, Kavita R.
Lamstein, Sarah M. Annie's Shabbat. LC 96-53607. (Illus.). 40p. (J). (gr. 1-5). 1997. lib. bdg. 15.95 (*0-8075-0376-2*) A Whitman.
— I Like Your Buttons! LC 98-29561. (Illus.). 32p. (J). (ps-3). 1999. lib. bdg. 15.95 (*0-8075-3510-9*) A Whitman.
Lamster, Frederick. Souls Made Great Through Love & Adversity: The Film Work of Frank Borzage. LC 80-28441. 242p. 1981. 24.00 (*0-8108-1404-8*) Scarecrow.
***Lamster, Mark, ed.** Architecture & Film. LC 99-57029. (Illus.). 256p. 2000. pap. 24.95 (*1-56898-207-0*) Princeton Arch.
Lamthean, Judith. Lecturer Practitioners. LC 97-24976. 192p. 1995. pap. text 28.95 (*0-7506-2449-3*) Buttrwrth-Heinemann.
Lamut, Sonja. ABC with Sticker, Vol. 1. (Made by Me Ser.). (Illus.). 26p. (ps-k). 1999. pap. 9.99 (*0-8431-7452-8*, Price Stern) Peng Put Young Read.
— Dress Up, 1 vol. (J). (ps-2). 1999. pap. text 4.99 (*0-448-41989-0*) Putnam Pub Group.
***Lamut, Sonja.** Halloween Costumes. (My Turn Bks.). (Illus.). 12p. (J). (ps). 2000. bds. 4.99 (*0-448-41991-2*, G & D) Peng Put Young Read.
— Halloween Shapes. (My Turn Bks.). (Illus.). 12p. (J). (ps). 2000. pap. 4.99 (*0-448-41992-0*, G & D) Peng Put Young Read.
Lamut, Sonja. 123, Vol. 1. (Made by Me Ser.). (Illus.). 26p. (ps-k). 1999. pap. 9.99 (*0-8431-7453-6*, Price Stern) Peng Put Young Read.
— Pirates, 1 vol. (J). (ps-2). 1999. pap. text 4.99 (*0-448-41988-2*) Putnam Pub Group.
— Too Noisy! LC 95-81406. (All Aboard Reading Picture Readers Ser.). (Illus.). 32p. (J). (ps-3). 1996. pap. text 3.95 (*0-448-41306-X*, G & D) Peng Put Young Read.
Lamut, Sonja. Bugs: A Nature Sticker Stories Book. (Nature Sticker Stories Ser.). 16p. (Orig.). (J). (ps-1). 1997. pap. 4.95 (*0-448-41599-2*, G & D) Peng Put Young Read.
— Christmas at Our House. (Sticker Stories Ser.). 16p. (Orig.). (J). (ps-1). 1996. pap. 4.95 (*0-448-41343-4*, G & D) Peng Put Young Read.
***Lamut, Sonja.** Christmas Numbers. (My Turn Bks.). 12p. (J). (ps). 2000. bds. 4.99 (*0-448-42027-9*, Planet Dexter) Peng Put Young Read.
— Christmas Rhyme Time. (My Turn Bks.). 12p. (J). (ps). 2000. bds. 4.99 (*0-448-42026-0*, Planet Dexter) Peng Put Young Read.
Lamut, Sonja. Colors. (My Turn Bks.). 12p. (J). (ps). 1997. mass mkt. 4.99 (*0-448-41631-X*, G & D) Peng Put Young Read.
— 1-2 Peek-a-Boo! LC 96-78085. (Lift & Look Board Bks.). 12p. (J). (ps). 1997. bds. 4.95 (*0-448-41610-7*, G & D) Peng Put Young Read.
Lamut, Sonja, jt. auth. see Hest, Amy.
***LaMuth, John E.** A Revolution in Family Values: Spirituality for a New Millennium. LC 00-190777. (Illus.). 320p. 2000. 24.95 (*1-929649-64-9*, 1012) Fairhaven Bk Pubs.
— A Revolution in Family Values: Spirituality for a New Millennium. expanded ed. (Illus.). 330p. 2000. pap. 16.95 (*1-929649-65-7*) Fairhaven Bk Pubs.
— The Ultimate Guide to Family Values: A Grand Unified Theory of Ethics & Morality. LC 99-90853. (Illus.). 185p. 1999. 19.95 (*1-929649-27-4*) Fairhaven Bk Pubs.
Lamy. Jersey Folk Lore. (Jersey Heritage Editions Ser.). 1991. 40.00 (*0-86120-000-4*, Pub. by Aris & Phillips) David Brown.
Lamy, Bernard. Perspective Made Easie. (Illus.). 256p. 1998. reprint ed. pap. 240.00 (*1-85297-029-4*, Pub. by Archival Facs) St Mut.
Lamy, J. P. The Insider's Guide to Buying a Powerboat. LC 99-42564. 192p. 1999. pap. 14.95 (*0-07-135150-7*) McGraw.
Lamy, Jean & Lamy, Josette, eds. Invertebrate Oxygen-Binding Proteins: Structure, Active Site, & Function. LC 81-5570. (Illus.). 864p. reprint ed. pap. 200.00 (*0-7837-0790-8*, 204110400019) Bks Demand.
Lamy, Josette, jt. ed. see Lamy, Jean.
Lamy, Lucie. Egyptian Mysteries: New Light on Ancient Knowledge. LC 88-51329. (Art & Imagination Ser.). (Illus.). 160p. 1989. pap. 15.95 (*0-500-81024-9*, Pub. by Thames Hudson) Norton.
Lamy, M., jt. ed. see Thijs, L. G.
Lamy, Marge. Cross Country Ski Inns of the Northeastern U. S. & Quebec. 168p. 1991. pap. 16.95 (*0-9630607-0-8*) R Reid Assocs.
Lamy, Marie-Noelle. The Cambridge French-English Thesaurus. LC 96-29914. (ENG & FRE., Illus.). 344p. (C). 1998. pap. text 24.95 (*0-521-42581-6*) Cambridge U Pr.
Lamy, P., jt. ed. see Giese, R. H.
Lamy, Paul, ed. Language Planning & Identity Planning. (International Journal of the Sociology of Language Ser.: No. 20). 1979. pap. text 60.00 (*90-279-7768-2*) Mouton.
Lamy, Peter P. Prescribing for the Elderly. LC 78-55289. 714p. reprint ed. pap. 200.00 (*0-8357-7865-7*, 203628200002) Bks Demand.
Lamy, Philip. Millennium Rage: Survivalists, White Supremacists & the Doomsday Prophecy. LC 96-32896. (Illus.). 306p. (C). 1996. 25.95 (*0-306-45409-2*, Plenum Trade) Perseus Pubng.
Lan. Building Another Superpower. 63.95 (*1-84014-569-2*) Ashgate Pub Co.
Lan, C. T., jt. auth. see Roskam, Jan.
Lan, Darna, ed. see Covan, Penney.
***Lan, David.** David Lan Plays: Painting a Wall; Red Earth; Flight; Desire; The Ends of the Earth, Vol. 1. 304p. 2000. pap. 16.95 (*0-413-73680-6*) Methn.
Lan, David. Flight. (Methuen New Theatrescripts Ser.). 40p. (C). 1988. pap. write for info. (*0-413-14590-5*, A0107, Methuen Drama) Methn.
— Guns & Rain: Guerillas & Spirit Mediums in Zimbabwe. LC 85-40287. (Perspectives on Southern Africa Ser.: No. 38). 1985. pap. 18.95 (*0-520-05589-6*, Pub. by U CA Pr) Cal Prin Full Svc.
— Sergeant Ola & His Followers. 45p. (C). 1988. pap. write for info. (*0-413-47590-5*, A0260, Methuen Drama) Methn.
Lan, Ho S. Guide to Condominium Housing in Singapore, Central, Vol. 1. 214p. (Orig.). 1992. pap. 32.50 (*9971-69-174-4*, Pub. by Sngapore Univ Pr) Coronet Bks.
— Guide to Condominium Housing in Singapore, Central, Vol. 2. 184p. (Orig.). 1992. pap. 32.50 (*9971-69-175-2*, Pub. by Sngapore Univ Pr) Coronet Bks.
Lan, Hua R. & Fong, Vanessa L. Women in Republican China: A Sourcebook. LC 99-10680. (Asia & the Pacific Ser.). 280p. 1999. pap. text 24.95 (*0-7656-0343-8*, East Gate Bk) M E Sharpe.
***Lan, Hua R. & Fong, Vanessa L., eds.** Women in Republican China: A Sourcebook. LC 99-10680. (Asia & the Pacific Ser.). 280p. 1999. text 73.95 (*0-7656-0342-X*, East Gate Bk) M E Sharpe.
Lan, Kam Y. Lonely Planet Cantonese. 3rd ed. 256p. 1999. pap. 6.95 (*0-86442-645-3*) Lonely Planet.
Lan, Michael, jt. auth. see Crotty, James.
Lan, Ping. Technology Transfer to China Through Foreign Direct Investment. 260p. 1996. text 68.95 (*1-85972-205-9*, Pub. by Avebry) Ashgate Pub Co.
Lan Tak Lam-Chang, Gladys. Parenting in Stepfamilies: Social Attitudes, Parental Perceptions & Parenting Behaviours in Hong Kong. LC 98-74644. (Social & Political Studies from Hong Kong). 9p. 1999. text 69.95 (*1-84014-969-8*, Pub. by Ashgate Pub) Ashgate Pub Co.
lan Winterton. Last Rites: Four Present-Day Adventures for Call of Cthulhu. (Call of Cthulhu Roleplaying Ser.). 1999. pap. 14.95 (*1-56882-137-9*) Chaosium.
Lan-Ying, jt. auth. see Light.
Lana, Robert E. Assumptions of Social Psychology: A Reexamination. 160p. (C). 1991. pap. 19.95 (*0-8058-1023-4*); text 39.95 (*0-8058-1022-6*) L Erlbaum Assocs.
— The Mass Flights of Italo Balbo: The Flights of 1928, 1929, 1930 & 1933 - A History & Catalog of Their Postal Artifacts. LC 95-83532. (Illus.). 144p. (Orig.). 1996. pap. 10.00 (*0-939429-15-2*) Am Air Mail.
Lanagan, B. J. Bushwhackers, Vol. 1. (Bushwhackers Ser.). 256p. 1997. mass mkt. 5.99 (*0-515-12102-9*, Jove) Berkley Pub.
— Bushwhackers: Rebel County. 192p. 1997. mass mkt. 4.99 (*0-515-12142-8*, Jove) Berkley Pub.
— Bushwhackers No. 3: The Killing Edge. 192p. 1997. mass mkt. 4.99 (*0-515-12177-0*, Jove) Berkley Pub.
— Bushwhackers No. 4. 192p. 1998. mass mkt. 4.99 (*0-515-12232-7*, Jove) Berkley Pub.
— Death Pass, Vol. 8. (Bushwhackers Ser.). 1999. mass mkt. 4.99 (*0-515-12658-6*, Jove) Berkley Pub.
— Epitaph. (Bushwhackers Ser.: Vol. 6). 1998. mass mkt. 4.99 (*0-515-12290-4*, Jove) Berkley Pub.
***Lanagan, B. J.** Hangman's Drop. (Bushwhackers Ser.: Vol. 9). 192p. 2000. mass mkt. 4.99 (*0-515-12731-0*, Jove) Berkley Pub.
Lanagan, B. J. Mexican Standoff. (Bushwhackers Ser.: Vol. 5). 1998. mass mkt. 4.99 (*0-515-12263-7*, Jove) Berkley Pub.
— Time for Killing, 1 vol., Vol. 7. (Bushwhackers Ser.). 1999. mass mkt. 4.99 (*0-515-12574-1*, Jove) Berkley Pub.
Lanahan, M. A. Within a Delirium. 23p. 1986. pap. 40.00 (*0-7223-2046-9*, Pub. by A H S Ltd) St Mut.
Lanari, Riccardo, jt. auth. see Franceschetti, Giorgio.
Lanasa, Philip J., III, jt. auth. see Criscoe, Betty L.
Lanave, Kevin. Christian Justice: Sharing God's Goodness. Allaire, Barbara, ed. (Illus.). 313p. 1995. teacher ed., spiral bd. 24.95 (*0-88489-331-6*) St Marys.
Lanb, Richard F. Metropolitan Impacts on Rural America. LC 74-84782. (University of Chicago, Department of Geography, Research Paper Ser.: No. 162). 210p. 1975. reprint ed. pap. 65.10 (*0-608-02288-8*, 206292900004) Bks Demand.
***Lancas, John.** The Contracting Universe. LC 00-91395. (Illus.). viii, 56p. 2000. 25.00 (*0-9700230-0-6*) J Lancas.
Lancaser, J. L. & Meisch, M. V. Arthropods in Livestock & Poultry Production. 1986. text 131.00 (*0-470-20243-2*) P-H.
Lancashire, Anne, ed. Editing Renaissance Dramatic Texts: English, Italian, & Spanish: Papers Given at the Eleventh Annual Conference on Editorial Problems, University of Toronto, 31 October-1 November, 1975. LC 76-7324. (Conference on Editorial Problems Ser.: No. 11). 1987. 42.50 (*0-404-63661-6*) AMS Pr.
Lancashire, Anne, ed. see Leech, Clifford.
Lancashire, Anne B. The Second Maiden's Tragedy. LC 77-4604. (Revels Plays Ser.). 337p. reprint ed. pap. 104.50 (*0-608-06032-1*, 206636300008) Bks Demand.
Lancashire, Anne B., ed. see Lyly, John.
Lancashire, Ian. Dramatic Texts & Records of Britain: A Chronological Topography to 1558. (Studies in Early English Drama). 633p. 1984. text 85.00 (*0-8020-5592-3*) U of Toronto Pr.
Lancashire, Ian, ed. Two Tudor Interludes: The Interlude of Youth, Hick Scorner. LC 79-3123. (Revels Plays Ser.). 303p. reprint ed. pap. 94.00 (*0-7837-0337-6*, 204065600018) Bks Demand.

L

L

Lancashire, Ian, et al. Using TACT with Electronic Texts: A Guide to "Text-Analysis Computing Tools" LC 95-48850. xiii, 361p. (Orig.). 1996. pap. 50.00 incl. cd-rom (0-87352-569-8, NTACT) Modern Lang.

***Lancaster.** The Complete Sql Training Course. 2000. 109.99 (0-13-089727-2); student ed. 78.00 (0-13-089726-4) P-H.

Lancaster & Martin. Advertising Media: Site License Adlab. 1992. 600.50 (0-697-17022-5) McGraw.

Lancaster & Withey. Marketing Fundamentals. pap. text. write for info. (0-7506-4366-8) Buttrwrth-Heinemann.

Lancaster, jt. auth. see Massingham.

Lancaster, jt. ed. see Urry, John.

Lancaster, Ann, ed. see Rosenbaum, Claire M.

Lancaster, Barbara M. Choosing Your New Home: A Consumer Guide to Living Styles for Retirees, New Jersey Edition, 1993. Gonzalez, Liane, ed. (Illus.). 259p. (Orig.). 1993. pap. text 19.95 (1-57108-000-7) Lancashire Intl.

— Choosing Your New Home: A Consumer Guide to Living Styles for Retirees, New Jersey Edition, 1993. Gonzalez, Liane, ed. Pease, Suzanne, tr. & illus. by. 268p. (Orig.). 1994. pap. 24.95 (1-57108-001-5) Lancashire Intl.

— Choosing Your New Home: A Consumer Guide to Living Styles for Retirees, New Jersey Edition, 1993. LC 94-75143. (Illus.). 660p. (Orig.). 1994. pap. 29.95 (1-57108-002-3) Lancashire Intl.

— Directory of Senior Facilities: Delaware, District of Columbia, Maryland, New Jersey, New York. Gonzalez, Liane L., ed. 416p. 1997. pap. text 159.95 (1-57108-014-7) Lancashire Intl.

— Guide to Living Styles for Retirees: Professional Edition 1994. Gonzalez, Liane, ed. 190p. (Orig.). 1994. ring bd. 89.95 (1-57108-005-8) Lancashire Intl.

— Retirement: A Consumer Guide for Planning & Housing New Jersey 1996. Gonzalez, Liane, ed. 260p. 1995. pap. text 24.95 (1-57108-011-2) Lancashire Intl.

Lancaster, Beverly, jt. auth. see Woods, Elsa.

Lancaster, Bill, jt. ed. see Coles, Robert.

Lancaster, Bob. The Jungles of Arkansas: A Personal History of the Wonder State. LC 89-30818. 245p. 1989. pap. 16.00 (1-55728-109-2) U of Ark Pr.

Lancaster, Brian. Elements of Judaism. LC 93-36028. (Illus.). 144p. 1993. pap. 9.95 (1-85230-402-2, Pub. by Element MA) Penguin Putnam.

— Mind, Brain & Human Potential: The Quest for an Understanding of Self. 204p. 1993. pap. 17.95 (1-85230-209-7, Pub. by Element MA) Penguin Putnam.

***Lancaster-Brown, Peter.** Megaliths, Myths & Men: An Introduction to Astro-Archaeology. LC 99-52590. 2000. pap. 12.95 (0-486-41145-1) Dover.

Lancaster, Bruce. The American Revolution. LC 85-3982. (American Heritage Library). (Illus.). 334p. 1985. pap. 15.00 (0-8281-0281-3) HM.

— Blind Journey. 1976. reprint ed. lib. bdg. 24.95 (0-88411-685-9) Amereon Ltd.

— Bride of a Thousand Cedars. (Illus.). 344p. 1975. reprint ed. lib. bdg. 25.95 (0-89190-883-8, Rivercity Pr) Amereon Ltd.

— Bright to the Wanderer. (Illus.). 451p. 1975. reprint ed. lib. bdg. 29.95 (0-89190-885-4, Rivercity Pr) Amereon Ltd.

— For Us the Living. (Illus.). 556p. 1975. reprint ed. lib. bdg. 32.95 (0-89190-882-X, Rivercity Pr) Amereon Ltd.

— Guns of Burgoyne. (Illus.). 425p. 1975. reprint ed. lib. bdg. 27.95 (0-89190-881-1, Rivercity Pr) Amereon Ltd.

— No Bugles Tonight. 1999. lib. bdg. 26.95 (1-56723-142-X, 151) Yestermorrow.

— Phantom Fortress. 1976. reprint ed. lib. bdg. 24.95 (0-88411-683-2) Amereon Ltd.

— The Scarlet Patch. 1976. reprint ed. lib. bdg. 30.95 (0-88411-682-4) Amereon Ltd.

— The Secret Road. 22.95 (0-89190-217-1) Amereon Ltd.

— Trumpet to Arms. 1976. reprint ed. lib. bdg. 26.95 (0-88411-681-6) Amereon Ltd.

— Venture in the East. 1976. reprint ed. lib. bdg. 24.95 (0-88411-684-0) Amereon Ltd.

— Wide Sleeve of Kwannon. (Illus.). 307p. 1975. reprint ed. lib. bdg. 24.95 (0-89190-884-6, Rivercity Pr) Amereon Ltd.

Lancaster, Carol. Aid to Africa: So Much to Do, So Little Done. 272p. 1999. pap. text 22.00 (0-226-46839-9); lib. bdg. 55.00 (0-226-46838-0) U Ch Pr.

— An Irresistable Force Meets an Immovable Object: The United States at UNCTAD I. (Pew Case Studies in International Affairs). 50p. (C). 1992. pap. text 3.50 (1-56927-108-9) Geo U Inst Dplmcy.

***Lancaster, Carol.** Transforming Foreign Aid! Purpose, Programs & Organization for a New Century. 350p. 2000. pap. 25.00 (0-88132-291-1) Inst Intl Eco.

Lancaster, Carol & Williamson, John, eds. African Debt & Financing. LC 86-7421. (Institute for International Economics. Special Report Ser.: No. 5). 236p. (Orig.). reprint ed. pap. 73.20 (0-7837-4219-3, 204390800012) Bks Demand.

Lancaster, Carol J. United States & Africa: Into the Twenty-First Century. LC 93-19138. (Policy Essay Ser.: No. 7). (Illus.). 72p. (C). 1993. pap. text 9.95 (1-56517-010-5) Overseas Dev Council.

Lancaster, Clay. The American Bungalow, 1880-1930. unabridged ed. (Illus.). 256p. 1995. reprint ed. pap. text 17.95 (0-486-28678-9) Dover.

— Antebellum Architecture of Kentucky. LC 91-2419. (Illus.). 352p. 1991. 55.00 (0-8131-1759-3) U Pr of Ky.

— Architectural Domestication: An Album of 24 Original Residence Designs in the Federal & Greek Revival Styles. LC 98-90410. (Illus.). 113p. 1999. 50.00 (1-892106-13-2) Warwick Pubns.

— Architectural Edification: An Album of 24 Original Designs in Traditional American Styles. rev. ed. LC 95-61949. (Illus.). 101p. 1997. 50.00 (1-892106-11-6) Warwick Pubns.

— Architectural Exotica: An Album of 24 Original Designs in Mannerist, Romantic, & Fantasy Styles. LC 97-61120. (Illus.). 117p. 1998. 50.00 (1-892106-12-4) Warwick Pubns.

***Lancaster, Clay.** Architectural Residuum: An Album of 24 Original Designs in 17th to 20th Century Styles. LC 99-95061. (Illus.). 116p. 2000. 50.00 (1-892106-16-7) Warwick Pubns.

Lancaster, Clay. The Arts & Crafts of the Animals. LC 93-94294. (Illus.). xi, 62p. 1993. pap. 6.00 (1-892106-07-8) Warwick Pubns.

— The Blue Plaid Riders: or The Candy Shop Kidnapping. LC 94-90495. 81p. 1995. 16.00 (1-892106-08-6) Warwick Pubns.

— The Breadth & Depth of East & West: A Survey & an Assessment of Civilization Based on Universal Considerations. LC 95-61948. (Illus.). vi, 576p. 1996. 42.50 (1-892106-09-4) Warwick Pubns.

— The Crucified Joshua & the Resurrected Jesus. viii, 15p. 1993. pap. 3.00 (1-892106-05-1) Warwick Pubns.

— Dharmapala's Key to Religion. vi, 23p. 1993. pap. 3.00 (1-892106-06-X) Warwick Pubns.

— Figi. LC 89-62793. (Illus.). 63p. 1989. 16.00 (1-892106-02-7) Warwick Pubns.

— The Flight of the Periwinkle. LC 87-92074. (Illus.). 57p. 1987. 16.00 (1-892106-00-0) Warwick Pubns.

— From Ur to Uncle Remus: Five Thousand Years of Animal Fable Illustration. LC 94-60588. (Illus.). 120p. 1997. write for info. (0-917519-06-X) U of KY Libs.

— Holiday Island. Michael, Gayl, ed. (Illus.). 1992. pap. write for info. (0-9607340-9-0) Nantucket Hist Assn.

— The Inception of Universal Ethics in Ancient Asia & Modern America. (Illus.). 43p. 1991. pap. 4.50 (1-892106-03-5) Warwick Pubns.

***Lancaster, Clay.** The Japanese Influence in America: The First Century Following Ratification of Perry's Treaty. 3rd rev. ed. LC 99-70774. (Illus.). 320p. 1999. 45.00 (1-892106-15-9) Warwick Pubns.

Lancaster, Clay. Nantucket in the 19th Century. LC 77-75512. (Illus.). 160p. 1979. pap. 12.95 (0-486-23747-8) Dover.

— Old Brooklyn Heights. (Illus.). 1980. pap. 8.95 (0-486-23872-5) Dover.

***Lancaster, Clay.** Pleasant Hill - Shaker Canaan in Kentucky: An Architectural & Social Study. LC 98-90411. (Illus.). 134p. 2000. 35.00 (1-892106-14-0) Warwick Pubns.

Lancaster, Clay. The Runaway Prince. LC 90-92001. (Illus.). 71p. 1991. 16.00 (1-892106-04-3) Warwick Pubns.

— The Toy Room. LC 88-71507. (Illus.). 85p. 1988. 16.00 (1-892106-01-9) Warwick Pubns.

Lancaster, Clay & Grow, Lawrence, eds. Waiting for Five O Five: Terminal, Station, & Depot in America. LC 76-56632. (Illus.). 1977. text 8.95 (0-87663-957-0, Pub. by Universe) St Martin.

Lancaster, Clay, jt. auth. see Gillon, Edmund V., Jr.

Lancaster, Dallas M., jt. intro. see Lancaster, Mary H.

Lancaster, Daniel B. The Bagbys of Brazil: The Life & Work of William Buck & Anne Luther Bagby. LC 98-28967. (Texas Baptist Leaders Ser.: Vol. 3). (Illus.). 156p. 1999. 21.95 (1-57168-251-1, Eakin Pr) Sunbelt Media.

Lancaster, David. Christie's Collectibles: Art Nouveau Jewelry. 80p. 1996. 12.95 (0-8212-2270-8, Pub. by Bulfinch Pr) Little.

Lancaster, Derek. Picture America: States & Capitals. Anderson, Stevens, ed. (Illus.). 136p. (YA). (gr. 5). 1991. pap. 4.95 (1-880184-02-8) Compact Classics.

Lancaster, Dianne. Reclaiming the Authentic Self. LC 96-90739. 208p. (Orig.). 1996. pap. 14.95 (0-9655069-4-0) Four-Sight Pr.

Lancaster, Don. Active Filter Cookbook. (Illus.). 240p. (C). 1995. reprint ed. pap. 28.50 (1-882193-31-8) Synergetics Pr.

— Blatant Opportunist Vol. I: Selected Reprints from Midnight Engineering. (Illus.). 144p. (Orig.). 1994. pap. 24.50 (1-882193-21-0) Synergetics Pr.

— Book-on-Demand Resource Kit. (Illus.). 200p. (C). 1994. pap. 39.50 (1-882193-50-4) Synergetics Pr.

— The Case Against Patents: Selected Reprints from "Midnight Engineering" & "Nuts & Volts" Magazines. 2nd ed. 170p. (Orig.). 1996. pap. 28.50 (1-882193-71-7) Synergetics Pr.

— CMOS Cookbook. 2nd ed. (Illus.). 512p. 1997. pap. text 26.95 (0-7506-9943-4) Buttrwrth-Heinemann.

— Hardware Hacker Vol. II. (Illus.). 152p. (Orig.). 1990. pap. 24.50 (1-882193-02-4) Synergetics Pr.

— Hardware Hacker Vol. III. (Illus.). 182p. (Orig.). 1994. pap. 24.50 (1-882193-03-2) Synergetics Pr.

— Hardware Hacker Vol. IV. (Illus.). 186p. (Orig.). 1994. pap. 24.50 (1-882193-04-0) Synergetics Pr.

— Incredible Secret Money Machine II. 2nd ed. (Illus.). 192p. 1992. pap. 18.50 (1-882193-65-2) Synergetics Pr.

— Resource Bin Vol. I: Selected Reprints from Nuts & Volts. 154p. (Orig.). 1994. pap. 24.50 (1-882193-11-3) Synergetics Pr.

— TTL Cookbook. LC 73-90295. (Illus.). 336p. (Orig.). 1974. 24.95 (0-672-21035-5) Sams.

Lancaster, E. L. Caribbean Holiday. 4p. 1993. pap. 2.50 (0-7390-0762-9, 5470) Alfred Pub.

— Dream Echoes. 4p. 1995. pap. 2.50 (0-7390-0763-7, 14721) Alfred Pub.

— Favorite Classics, Solo Book 1. 48p. 1991. pap. 7.95 (0-7390-0381-X, 6023) Alfred Pub.

***Lancaster, E. L. & Kowalchyk, Gayle.** Christmas Carol Activity Book. 32p. 1999. pap. 6.95 (0-7390-0393-3, 18198) Alfred Pub.

— Easy Classical Piano Duets for Teacher & Student, No. 3. 64p. 1999. pap. 7.95 (0-7390-0029-2) Alfred Pub.

Lancaster, E. L. & Renfrow, Kenon D. Alfred's Basic Group Piano Course, Bk. 2. 1996. pap. 34.95 (0-88284-700-7) Alfred Pub.

— Alfred's Basic Group Piano for Adults, Bk. 1. 1995. pap. 34.95 (0-88284-653-1, 2723) Alfred Pub.

— Group Piano for Adults, 12 CD Set, Bk. 1. 1995. pap. 125.00 incl. audio compact disk (0-88284-836-4, 14028) Alfred Pub.

***Lancaster, E. L. & Renfrow, Kenon D.** Piano 101: An Exciting Group Course for Adults, Bk. 1. 160p. 1999. spiral bd. 24.95 (0-7390-0255-4, 14588) Alfred Pub.

— Piano 101: An Exciting Group Course for Adults, Bk. 2. 152p. 1999. spiral bd. 24.95 (0-7390-0257-0, 4591) Alfred Pub.

— Piano 101, the Short Course. 56p. 1999. 8.95 (0-7390-0343-7, 17176) Alfred Pub.

— Piano 101, the Short Course. 1999. 19.95 incl. audio compact disk (0-7390-0607-X, 17179) Alfred Pub.

— Piano 101: Teacher's Handbook, Bks. 1 & 2. 64p. 1999. pap., teacher ed. 8.95 (0-7390-0254-6, 14594) Alfred Pub.

Lancaster, E. L. & Renfrow, Kenon D., eds. Joplin/Maple Leaf Rag. 4p. 1996. pap. 2.50 (0-7390-0880-3, 14330) Alfred Pub.

Lancaster, E. L., et al. Music for Little Mozarts. (Music Flashcards Ser.: Bk. 3). (J). (ps-1). Date not set. write for info. (0-7390-0646-0, 17183); pap. write for info. (0-7390-0645-2, 17182); pap. write for info. (0-7390-0644-4, 17180) Alfred Pub.

— Music for Little Mozarts. (Music Flashcards Ser.: Bk. 4). (J). (ps-1). Date not set. write for info. (0-7390-0653-3, 17189); pap. write for info. (0-7390-0650-9, 17186); pap. write for info. (0-7390-0652-5, 17188) Alfred Pub.

— Music for Little Mozarts. (Music Workbks.: No. 4). (J). (ps-1). Date not set. pap., wbk. ed. write for info. (0-7390-0651-7, 17187) Alfred Pub.

— Music for Little Mozarts, Workbk. 3. wbk. ed. write for info. (0-7390-0643-6, 17181) Alfred Pub.

— Music for Little Mozarts: Deluxe Package. deluxe ed. 1999. 69.95 (0-7390-0796-3, 17194) Alfred Pub.

— Music for Little Mozarts, Teacher's Handbook, Nos. 3 & 4. Date not set. pap. write for info. (0-7390-0656-8, 17192) Alfred Pub.

Lancaster, E. L., jt. auth. see Kowalchyk, Gayle.

Lancaster, E. M. Guide to Negro Marketing Information. 1991. lib. bdg. 77.95 (0-8490-4511-8) Gordon Pr.

Lancaster, F. T. Administration of Public Solid Waste. 178p. 1992. spiral bd. 37.00 (0-918334-79-9) WRP.

Lancaster, F. W. If You Want to Evaluate Your Library. 2nd ed. (Illus.). (C). 1993. text 39.50 (0-87845-091-2) U of Ill Grad Sch.

— Indexing & Abstracting in Theory & Practice. 1991. 39.50 (0-87845-083-1) U of Ill Grad Sch.

— Indexing & Abstracting in Theory & Practice. 2nd rev. ed. LC 98-218053. (Illus.). 412p. (C). 1998. 47.50 (0-87845-102-1) U of Ill Grad Sch.

Lancaster, F. W., ed. Ethics & the Librarian: Proceedings of the 31st Allerton Institute. 1991. 20.00 (0-87845-085-8) U of Ill Grad Sch.

— Libraries & the Future: Essays on the Library in the Twenty-First Century. LC 92-42380. (Original Book Ser.). (Illus.). 195p. (C). 1994. lib. bdg. 49.95 (1-56024-382-1) Haworth Pr.

— Library Automation As a Source of Management Information: Proceedings of the Clinic on Library Applications of Data Processing, 1982. LC 83-9110. 200p. 1983. 10.00 (0-87845-068-8) U of Ill Grad Sch.

— What Is User Friendly? (C). 1988. text 10.00 (0-87845-076-9) U of Ill Grad Sch.

Lancaster, F. W. & Fayen, Emily G. Information Retrieval On-Line. LC 73-9697. (Information Sciences Ser.). 613p. reprint ed. pap. 190.10 (0-8357-9911-5, 201584000097) Bks Demand.

Lancaster, F. W. & Sandore, Beth. Technology & Management in Library & Information Services. LC 97-146794. 322p. 1997. 39.50 (0-87845-099-8) U of Ill Grad Sch.

***Lancaster, F. W. & Smith, Linda.** Intelligent Technologies & the Special Library of the Future. 2000. 39.50 (1-57387-063-3) Info Today Inc.

Lancaster, F. W. & Warner, Amy. Information Retrieval Today. LC 93-77931. 350p. 1993. pap. 38.00 (0-87815-064-1) Info Resources.

Lancaster, F. W., jt. auth. see Haricombe, Lorraine J.

Lancaster, F. W., ed. see Clinic on Library Applications of Data Processing.

Lancaster, F. Wilfrid. Vocabulary Control for Information Retrieval. 2nd ed. LC 84-82260. (Illus.). xvii, 270p. 1992. reprint ed. text 27.50 (0-87815-053-6) Info Resources.

Lancaster, F. Wilfrid & Baker, Sharon L. The Measurement & Evaluation of Library Services. 2nd ed. LC 91-72908. xviii, 411p. 1991. text 49.95 (0-87815-061-7) Info Resources.

Lancaster, Fidelity, jt. auth. see Lancaster, William.

Lancaster, Francine. Favorite Animal Songs, Set. (Francine Sings Keepsake Collection). 40p. (J). (gr. k up). 16.95 incl. audio (0-930647-01-7) Lancaster Prodns.

— Favorite Holiday Songs, Set. (Francine Sings the Keepsake Collection). 48p. (J). 1997. 16.95 incl. audio (0-930647-02-5) Lancaster Prodns.

— Nursery Songs & Lullabies. (Francine Sings Keepsake Collection). (J). (gr. k up). 1984. 16.95 incl. audio (0-930647-00-9); audio. write for info. (0-318-58469-7) Lancaster Prodns.

Lancaster, Geoff. Introduction to Marketing. (C). 1992. pap. text. write for info. (0-201-54440-7) Addison-Wesley.

— Marketing. 258p. 1995. pap. text 37.95 (0-7506-2055-2) Buttrwrth-Heinemann.

Lancaster, Geoff & Reynolds, Paul. Introduction to Marketing. (Marketing in Action Ser.). 160p. 1998. pap. 19.95 (0-7494-2095-2) Kogan Page Ltd.

Lancaster, Geoff, jt. auth. see Jobber, David.

Lancaster, Geoffrey & Massingham, Lester. Essentials of Marketing: Text & Cases. 2nd ed. LC 93-19905. 1993. write for info. (0-07-707728-8) McGraw.

— Marketing Management. LC 92-25428. 1993. 16.95 (0-07-707420-3) McGraw.

Lancaster, Gordon. Introduction to Fields & Circuits. (Textbks. in Electrical & Electronic Engineering: No. 1). (Illus.). 406p. (C). 1992. pap. text 45.95 (0-19-853931-2) OUP.

Lancaster, Guy, ed. see Kyle, Linda Davis, et al.

Lancaster, H. Carrington, ed. Creole Voices. (FRE.). 1990. 15.00 (0-87498-009-7) Assoc Pubs DC.

Lancaster, H. L. Lancaster Family: Thomas & Phebe Lancaster of Bucks County, Penn., & Their Descendants, 1711-1902. (Illus.). 302p. reprint ed. pap. 45.00 (0-8328-0748-6); reprint ed. lib. bdg. 53.00 (0-8328-0747-8) Higginson Bk Co.

Lancaster, H. O. Bibliography of Statistical Bibliographies. 1968. 18.00 (0-934454-12-4) Lubrecht & Cramer.

— Expectations of Life. (Illus.). 592p. 1990. 105.00 (0-387-97105-X) Spr-Verlag.

— Quantitative Methods in Biological & Medical Sciences: A Historical Essay. LC 94-8063. 297p. 1994. 89.95 (0-387-94279-3) Spr-Verlag.

Lancaster, Henry C. Adventures of a Literary Historian: A Collection of His Writings Presented to H. C. Lancaster by His Former Students & Other Friends in Anticipation of His Sixtieth Birthday November 10, 1942. LC 68-14907. (Essay Index Reprint Ser.). 1977. 23.95 (0-8369-0605-5) Ayer.

— French Tragi-Comedy. LC 66-29465. 216p. 1966. reprint ed. 50.00 (0-87752-059-3) Gordian.

— History of French Dramatic Literature in the Seventeenth Century, 9 vols., Set. Incl. Period of Racine, 1673-1700. LC 66-20028. 1966. 75.00 (0-87752-260-X); Recapitulation, 1610-1700. LC 66-20028. 1966. 75.00 (0-87752-261-8); Vol. 1, Pt. 1. Pre-Classical Period, 1610-1634. LC 66-20028. 1966. 75.00 (0-87752-253-7); Vol. 1, Pt. 2. Period of Corneille, 1635-1651. LC 66-20028. 1966. 75.00 (0-87752-255-3); Vol. 1, Pt. 3. Period of Moliere, 1652-1672. LC 66-20028. 1966. 75.00 (0-87752-257-X); Vol. 1, Pt. 4. Period of Racine, 1673-1700. LC 66-20028. 1966. 75.00 (0-87752-259-6); Vol. 2, Pt. 1. Pre-Classical Period, 1610-1634. LC 66-20028. 1966. 75.00 (0-87752-254-5); Vol. 2, Pt. 2. Period of Corneille, 1635-1651. LC 66-20028. 1966. 75.00 (0-87752-256-1); Vol. 2, Pt. 3. Period of Moliere, 1652-1672. LC 66-20028. 1966. 75.00 (0-87752-258-8); LC 66-20028. 3698p. 1966. reprint ed. 600.00 (0-87752-060-7) Gordian.

— Sunset: A History of Parisian Drama in the Last Years of Louis XIV, 1701-1715. LC 76-29737. 1977. reprint ed. lib. bdg. 69.50 (0-8371-9278-1, LASH, Greenwood Pr) Greenwood.

Lancaster, J. Handbook of Structural Welding: Processes, Materials & Methods Used in the Welding of Major Structures, Pipelines & Process Plant. 444p. 1997. pap. 63.00 (1-85573-343-9, Pub. by Woodhead Pubng) Am Educ Systs.

Lancaster, J. F. Metallurgy of Welding. 4th ed. 352p. 1987. text 105.00 (0-04-669010-7); pap. text 44.95 (0-04-669011-5) Routledge.

— Metallurgy of Welding. 6th ed. 446p. 1999. pap. 89.00 (1-884207-80-4) William Andrew.

Lancaster, J. F. & Mills, K. C. Recommendations for the Avoidance of Variable Penetration in Gas Tungsten Arc Welding. (Illus.). 44p. 1994. pap. 98.00 (1-85573-160-6) Am Educ Systs.

Lancaster, J. R., ed. The Bioinorganic Chemistry of Nickel. 337p. 1988. 165.00 (0-471-18692-9) Wiley.

Lancaster, Jack, Jr., ed. Nitric Oxide: Principles & Actions. (Illus.). 355p. 1996. text 79.95 (0-12-435555-2) Acad Pr.

Lancaster, Jack R., Jr., ed. The Bioinorganic Chemistry of Nickel. LC 88-140028. 337p. 1988. lib. bdg. 115.00 (0-89573-338-2, Wiley-VCH) Wiley.

Lancaster, Jack R. & Parkinson, J. F., eds. Nitric Oxide, Cytochromes P450, & Sexual Steroid Hormones. LC 97-25453. (Ernst Schering Research Foundation Workshop Ser.: Vol. 21). (Illus.). 307p. write for info. (3-540-63050-3) Spr-Verlag.

Lancaster, James. Risk Capital. LC 99-461777. 185p. 1998. pap. 7.50 (1-892614-10-3, BWP-RC-11) Briarwood VA.

Lancaster, Jane B., et al, eds. Parenting Across the Life Span: Biosocial Dimensions. (Evolutionary Foundations of Human Behavior Ser.). (Illus.). 486p. (C). 1987. lib. bdg. 59.95 (0-202-30332-2) Aldine de Gruyter.

Lancaster, Jane B., jt. ed. see Gelles, Richard J.

Lancaster, Jane F. Removal Aftershock: The Seminoles' Struggles to Survive in the West, 1836-1866. LC 94-129. (Illus.). 248p. (C). 1994. pap. text 16.00 (0-87049-846-0); lib. bdg. 32.00 (0-87049-845-2) U of Tenn Pr.

Lancaster, Jeanette. Nursing Issues in Leading & Managing Change. LC 98-26134. 544p. 1998. pap. text 34.95 (0-323-00250-1) Mosby Inc.

Lancaster, Jeanette, jt. auth. see Stanhope, Marcia.

Lancaster, Jeanette, jt. ed. see Stanhope, Marcia.

Lancaster, John. Engineering Catastrophes: Causes & Effects of Major Accidents. 304p. 1997. pap. 69.95 (1-85573-342-0, Pub. by Woodhead Pubng) Am Educ Systs.

— Handbook of Structural Welding. LC 92-29915. 240p. 1993. 65.50 (0-07-031684-8) McGraw.

Lancaster, John, jt. ed. see Maslen, Keith.

Lancaster, John, ed. see Wilde, Oscar.

Lancaster, John F. Metallurgy of Welding. 6th ed. 350p. 1999. pap. 81.00 (1-85573-428-1) Am Educ Systs.

An Asterisk (*) at the beginning of an entry indicates that the title is appearing for the first time.

Lancaster, Joseph. Improvements in Education: As It Respects the Industrious Classes of the Community. 3rd ed. LC 68-56241. xvi, 211p. 1974. reprint ed. 39.50 (*0-678-00697-0*) Kelley.
— Manual of the System of Teaching: 1816 Edition. Stern, Jeffrey, ed. & intro. by. (Classics in Education Ser.). 96p. 1996. reprint ed. 65.00 (*1-85506-274-7*) Bks Intl VA.
Lancaster, Kathy. Keys to Adopting a Child. LC 94-5222. (Parenting Keys Ser.). 208p. (Orig.). 1994. pap. 6.95 (*0-8120-1925-3*) Barron.
— Keys to Parenting an Adopted Child. LC 95-20864. (Parenting Keys Ser.). 208p. 1996. pap. 6.95 (*0-8120-9104-3*) Barron.
Lancaster, Kelvin. Mathematical Economics. xiii, 411p. 1987. reprint ed. pap. text 12.95 (*0-486-65391-9*) Dover.
Lancaster, Kelvin J. Modern Consumer Theory. 256p. 1990. 95.00 (*1-85278-384-2*) E Elgar.
— Trade, Markets & Welfare. LC 95-38731. (Illus.). 288p. 1996. 95.00 (*1-85278-975-1*) E Elgar.
Lancaster, Kelvin J., ed. Consumer Theory, Vol. 100. LC 98-31081. (The International Library of Critical Writings in Economics Ser.: No. 100). 656p. 1999. 220.00 (*1-85278-956-5*) E Elgar.
Lancaster, Kent & Katz, Helen T. Strategic Media Planning. 320p. 1993. pap. 39.95 incl. disk (*0-8442-3475-3*, NTC Business Bks) NTC Contemp Pub Co.
— Strategic Media Planning. 2nd ed. Knudsen, Anne, ed. 1995. 79.95 (*0-8442-3537-7*, NTC Business Bks) NTC Contemp Pub Co.
Lancaster, Kent & Martin, Thomas C. Adlab: Advertising Media Planning on the IBM, Macintosh & Compatibles. 64p. (C). 1989. text, spiral bd. write for info. incl. disk (*0-697-11164-4*) Brown & Benchmark.
Lancaster, Kirk, jt. ed. see Concus, Paul.
Lancaster, Kurt. Warlocks & Warpdrive: Contemporary Fantasy Entertainments with Interactive & Virtual Environments. LC 99-44740. 198p. 1999. lib. bdg. 32.50 (*0-7864-0634-8*) McFarland & Co.
Lancaster, L. & Yu, C. S. Assimilation of Buddhism in Korea: Religious Maturity & Innovation in the Silla Dynasty. LC 87-71274. 264p. (C). 1991. text 30.00 (*0-89581-878-7*) Asian Humanities.
Lancaster, Lane. Hegel to Dewey, 3 vols. (Essay Index Reprint Ser.: Vol. 3). 1977. reprint ed. 22.95 (*0-518-10156-8*) Ayer.
Lancaster, Lane W. Government in Rural America. 2nd ed. LC 74-2686. (Illus.). 375p. 1974. reprint ed. lib. bdg. 75.00 (*0-8371-7425-2*, LAGR, Greenwood Pr) Greenwood.
Lancaster, Lewis R. & Yu, C. S., eds. Introduction of Buddhism to Korea: New Cultural Patterns. LC 87-71273. (Studies in Korean Religions & Culture: No. 3). 239p. 1989. pap. 68.20 (*0-608-04958-1*, 2065537) Bks Demand.
Lancaster, Lewis R., et al. Religion & Society in Contemporary Korea. LC 97-2424. (Korea Research Monographs). 1998. pap. 20.00 (*1-55729-055-5*) IEAS.
Lancaster, Lewis R., jt. ed. see Gomez, Luis O.
Lancaster, M. J. Passive Microwave Device Applications of High Temperature Superconductors. LC 96-14062. (Illus.). 356p. (C). 1997. text 85.00 (*0-521-48032-9*) Cambridge U Pr.
Lancaster, Mary H. & Lancaster, Dallas M., intros. The Civil War Diary of Anne S. Frobel. LC 92-21439. (Illus.). 320p. 1992. pap. 14.95 (*0-939009-69-2*, EPM) Howell Pr VA.
Lancaster, Michael. Colourscape. LC 97-130080. (Illus.). 129p. (Orig.). 1996. pap. 38.00 (*1-85490-451-5*) Academy Ed UK.
Lancaster, Michael. The New European Landscape. LC 94-15507. (Illus.). 144p. 1995. text 76.95 (*0-7506-1546-X*, Butterwrth Archit) Buttrwrth-Heinemann.
Lancaster, Nicholas. The Geomorphology of Desert Dunes. (Physical Environment Ser.). (Illus.). 312p. (C). 1995. pap. 29.99 (*0-415-06094-X*) Routledge.
— The Namib Sand Sea: Dune Forms, Processes & Sediments. 192p. (C). 1989. text 110.00 (*90-6191-697-6*, Pub. by A A Balkema) Ashgate Pub Co.
Lancaster, Nicholas, jt. ed. see Pye, K.
Lancaster, Osbert, jt. auth. see Scott-James, Anne.
Lancaster, Otis E. Jet Propulsion Engines. LC 58-5030. (High Speed Aerodynamics & Jet Propulsion Ser.: No. 12). (Illus.). 841p. reprint ed. pap. 200.00 (*0-8357-4398-5*, 205706800007) Bks Demand.
Lancaster, P. & Rodman, L. Algebraic Riccati Equations. (Oxford Mathematical Monographs). 498p. 1995. text 115.00 (*0-19-853795-6*) OUP.
Lancaster, Patricia J. Overcoming Barriers to Construction: Social, Economic, Environmental & Political. (Civil Engineering - Advisors Ser.). 1999. 69.95 (*0-8493-7486-3*, 7486) CRC Pr.
Lancaster, Paul. Gentleman of the Press: The Life & Times of an Early Reporter, Julian Ralph of the Sun. LC 91-17818. (Illus.). 322p. 1992. 39.95 (*0-8156-2552-9*) Syracuse U Pr.
Lancaster, Peggy. Abby & the Assassin. LC 97-215979. (Adventures of Abby Smith Ser.: Vol. 2). 64p. (J). (gr. 3-5). 1997. pap. 6.95 (*0-87588-487-3*) Hobby Hse.
— Abby & the Enchanted Crystal. LC 97-216110. (Adventures of Abby Smith Ser.: Vol. 1). 64p. (J). (gr. 3-5). 1997. pap. 6.95 (*0-87588-486-5*) Hobby Hse.
— Abby & the Golden Goddess. LC 97-215973. (Adventures of Abby Smith Ser.: Vol. 3). 64p. (J). (gr. 3-5). 1997. pap. 6.95 (*0-87588-488-1*) Hobby Hse.
— Abby & the Silken Secret. LC 97-215965. (Adventures of Abby Smith Ser.: Vol. 5). 64p. (J). (gr. 3-5). 1997. pap. text 6.95 (*0-87588-490-3*) Hobby Hse.
— Abby Rescues Rascal. LC 98-102946. (Adventures of Abby Smith Ser.: Vol. 4). 64p. (J). (gr. 3-5). 1997. pap. text 6.95 (*0-87588-489-X*) Hobby Hse.
Lancaster, Peter & Salkauskas, Kestutis. Curve & Surface Fitting. (Computational Mathematics & Applications Ser.). 1986. text 146.00 (*0-12-436060-2*); pap. text 54.00 (*0-12-436061-0*) Acad Pr.
— Transform Methods in Applied Mathematics: An Introduction. LC 95-48302. (Canadian Mathematical Society Series & Advanced Texts). 332p. 1996. 84.95 (*0-471-00810-9*) Wiley.
Lancaster, Peter & Tismenetsky, Miron. The Theory of Matrices. 2nd ed. (Computer Science & Applied Mathematics Ser.). (C). 1985. text 81.00 (*0-12-435560-9*) Acad Pr.
Lancaster, Peter, ed. see Bottcher, Albrecht, et al.
Lancaster, Phil A. Merchandising New & Used Cars. 15.95 (*0-87359-030-9*, AM 202) Northwood Univ.
Lancaster, Phil A. & Wangberg, David I. Dealership Business Management. LC 81-83717. 315p. 1981. write for info. (*0-87359-027-9*) Northwood Univ.
Lancaster, Ray. Plant Hunting in Nepal. (C). 1988. 74.00 (*0-685-25851-3*) St Mut.
Lancaster, Robert S. The Better Parts of a Life. (Illus.). 249p. (Orig.). 1990. pap. 14.95 (*0-9627687-1-5*) Proctors Hall Pr.
— The Better Parts of a Life. (Orig.). 1990. pap. 14.95 (*0-918769-33-7*) Univ South Pr.
Lancaster, Roger & Di Leonardo, Micaela, eds. The Gender/Sexuality Reader: Culture, History, Political Economy. LC 96-39187. (Illus.). 550p. 1997. pap. 27.99 (*0-415-91005-6*) Routledge.
— The Gender/Sexuality Reader: Culture, History, Political Economy. LC 96-39187. (Illus.). 550p. (C). 1997. 80.00 (*0-415-91004-8*) Routledge.
Lancaster, Roger N. Life Is Hard: Machismo, Danger & the Intimacy of Power in Nicaragua. LC 91-45764. 1994. pap. 16.95 (*0-520-08929-4*, Pub. by U CA Pr) Cal Prin Full Svc.
Lancaster, Ronald, et al. Fireworks: Principles & Practice. 3rd ed. (Illus.). 450p. (C). 1998. 105.00 (*0-8206-0354-6*) Chem Pub.
Lancaster, Roy. Mediterranean Plants & Gardens. (Illus.). 144p. 1990. pap. 17.95 (*0-903001-64-0*, Pub. by Burall Floraprint) J Markham Assocs.
— A Plantsman in Nepal. (Illus.). 240p. 1995. 69.50 (*1-85149-179-1*) Antique Collect.
— Roy Lancaster Travel in China: A Plantsman Paradise. 1989. 79.50 (*1-85149-019-1*) Antique Collect.
— Travels in China: A Plantsman's Paradise. (Illus.). 520p. 1989. 79.50 (*1-85149-175-9*) Antique Collect.
— Trees for Your Garden. (Illus.). 1993. 35.00 (*0-85628-232-4*, Pub. by Aidan Ellis Pub) Antique Collect.
— What Perennials Where. LC 97-16627. 160p. 1997. 19.95 (*0-7894-2087-2*) DK Pub Inc.
— What Plant Where. LC 95-8172. (Illus.). 256p. 1995. 24.95 (*0-7894-0151-7*, 6-70482) DK Pub Inc.
Lancaster, Roy & Biggs, Matthew. What Houseplant Where. LC 98-19945. 128p. 1998. 19.95 (*0-7894-3522-5*) DK Pub Inc.
Lancaster, Ryan. Top Forty Things Considerate Golfers Do. Westheimer, Mary, ed. (Illus.). 44p. (Orig.). 1994. pap. 10.00 (*1-885001-04-5*) Via Press.
Lancaster, Samuel. Lancaster Family of Maryland & Kentucky: History of English Ancestry, Emigration to Colony of Maryland, Pioneers of Kentucky. (Illus.). 200p. 1993. reprint ed. pap. 32.50 (*0-8328-3360-6*); reprint ed. lib. bdg. 42.50 (*0-8328-3359-2*) Higginson Bk Co.
Lancaster, Sheila. Mistress of Fortune. large type ed. 576p. 1984. 27.99 (*0-7089-1113-7*) Ulverscroft.
Lancaster-Smith, M. Gastroenterology. (Management of Common Diseases in Family Practice Ser.). 1985. 22.00 (*0-88416-529-9*) Mosby Inc.
Lancaster, Sue, ed. see Radel, Cliff.
Lancaster, Theo, ed. The Corner. 128p. (C). 1988. pap. 35.00 (*0-7212-0769-3*, Pub. by Regency Pr GBR) St Mut.
Lancaster, Thomas D. Policy Stability & Democratic Change: Energy in Spain's Transition. LC 87-43185. (Illus.). 256p. 1990. lib. bdg. 30.00 (*0-271-00634-X*) Pa St U Pr.
Lancaster, Thomas D. & Prevost, Gary, eds. Politics & Change in Spain. LC 84-18107. 240p. 1985. 55.00 (*0-275-90133-5*, C0133, Praeger Pubs) Greenwood.
Lancaster, Tony. The Econometric Analysis of Transition Data. (Econometric Society Monographs: No. 17). (Illus.). 364p. (C). 1992. pap. text 23.95 (*0-521-43789-X*) Cambridge U Pr.
Lancaster, Wade, jt. ed. see Venkatesan, M.
Lancaster, William. The Department Store: A Social History. 240p. 1995. 79.00 (*0-7185-1374-6*); pap. 22.95 (*0-7185-1985-X*) Bks Intl VA.
— The Rwala Bedouin Today. 2nd rev. ed. (Illus.). 203p. (C). 1997. pap. text 12.50 (*0-88133-943-1*) Waveland Pr.
***Lancaster, William & Lancaster, Fidelity.** People, Land & Water in the Bilad-Ash Sham, the Arabian Peninsula: Indigenous Systems in the Countryside. 454p. 1999. text 83.00 (*90-5702-322-9*, Harwood Acad Pubs) Gordon & Breach.
Lancaster, Yvonne E. From the Heart--Sketches from Life. (Illus.). 96p. 1986. pap. 7.95 (*0-940573-00-8*) Genesis Pub MA.
Lance. Hoarded Vengeance. unabridged ed. (Orig.). 1995. pap. 19.95 (*0-930400-49-6*, 216HV) Pleasure Trove.
***Lance, David L.** The Brotherhood of the Scroll. LC 00-190867. 366p. 2000. 25.00 (*0-7388-2053-9*); pap. 18.00 (*0-7388-2054-7*) Xlibris Corp.
Lance, Derek. Developmental Mathematics Graphing. 4th ed. 272p. (C). 1996. pap. text, lab manual ed. 26.00 (*0-201-82438-8*) Addison-Wesley.
— Graphing Calculator: Custom Version to Accompany Developmental Mathematics. 3rd ed. (C). 1994. pap. text, lab manual ed. 25.00 (*0-201-82394-2*) Addison-Wesley.
Lance, Donald M., jt. ed. see Glowka, Wayne.
Lance, Donald M., ed. see Kenyon, John S.
Lance, E. Christopher. Hilbert C*-Modules: A Toolkit for Operator Algebraists. (London Mathematical Society Lecture Note Ser.: No. 210). 140p. (C). 1995. pap. text 32.95 (*0-521-47910-X*) Cambridge U Pr.
Lance, Fran, jt. ed. see King, Pat.
Lance, G. N. & Deland, E. C. The Steady, Axially Symmetric Flow of a Viscous Fluid in a Deep Rotating Cylinder Heated from Below. LC 58-9085. (California University Publications in Engineering: Vol. 5, No. 6). 20p. reprint ed. pap. 30.00 (*0-608-11105-8*, 202118800022) Bks Demand.
Lance, H. Darrell. The Old Testament & the Archaeologist. Tucker, Gene M., ed. LC 80-2387. (Guides to Biblical Scholarship: Old Testament Ser.). 112p. (Orig.). 1981. pap. 12.00 (*0-8006-0467-9*, 1-467, Fortress Pr) Augsburg Fortress.
Lance, H. Darrell, jt. ed. see Dever, William G.
Lance, J. & Pfaffenrath, V., eds. Sumatripian - From Molecule to Man: An Official Session at the 8th Migraine Trust Symposium - Journal: European Neurology, Vol. 31, No. 5, 1991. (Illus.). 72p. 1991. pap. 31.50 (*3-8055-5437-0*) S Karger.
Lance, James W. Mechanisms & Management of Headache. 5th ed. 288p. 1993. text 85.00 (*0-7506-0575-8*) Buttrwrth-Heinemann.
— Migraine & Other Headaches. 256p. 1999. per. 13.00 (*0-684-86846-6*) S&S Trade.
— Migraine & Other Headaches: A Practical Guide to Understanding, Preventing & Treating Headaches. 1998. pap. text. write for info. (*0-7318-0740-5*) Simon & Schuster.
Lance, James W. & Goadsby, Peter J. Mechanism & Management of Headache. 6th ed. LC 98-15127. 336p. 1998. text 95.00 (*0-7506-3728-5*) Buttrwrth-Heinemann.
Lance, Janice. First Literature Experiences. (Illus.). 48p. 1991. pap. 7.95 (*1-879287-01-3*, BL011) Pieces of Lrning.
Lance, John, jt. auth. see Rost, Michael A.
Lance, Kathryn, jt. auth. see Cooper, Jay.
Lance, Keith C., et al. The Impact of School Library Media Centers on Academic Achievement. (Illus.). 125p. 1993. pap. text 25.00 (*0-931510-48-1*) Hi Willow.
***Lance, Keith Curry, et al.** How School Librarians Help Kids Achieve Standards: The Second Colorado Study. 102p. 2000. pap. 25.00 (*0-931510-76-7*) Hi Willow.
Lance, Larry R. & Hinton, John R. Computer Mathematics. 4th ed. 513p. (C). 2000. pap. 35.00 (*0-923231-38-2*) Mohican Pub.
— Elementary Mathematics for Computing. LC 85-1258. 543p. 1986. text. write for info. (*0-201-05123-0*) Addison-Wesley.
Lance, Leonard L. Drug Information Handbook for the Allied Health Professional. 6th ed. 1999. pap. text 32.95 (*0-916589-72-2*) Lexi-Comp.
— Quick Look Drug Book, 1998. 1998. write for info. (*0-683-40174-2*) Lppncott W & W.
Lance, Leonard L., et al. Drug Information Handbook for the Allied Health Professional: With Indication/ Therapeutic Catego. 5th ed. (Clinical Reference Library). 825p. 1998. pap. 32.75 (*0-916589-63-3*) Lexi-Comp.
— 1995 Quick Look Drug Book. 729p. 1995. pap. 34.00 (*0-683-07046-0*) Lppncott W & W.
— Quick Look Drug Book, 1997. 719p. 1997. pap. 34.95 (*0-683-40057-6*) Lppncott W & W.
— Quick Look Drug Book, 1996. 787p. (Orig.). 1996. pap. 34.95 (*0-683-07045-2*) Lppncott W & W.
Lance, Leslie. Nurse Verena at Weirwater. large type ed. 1991. 27.99 (*0-7089-2463-8*) Ulverscroft.
— The Return of the Cuckoo. large type ed. 1990. 27.99 (*0-7089-2124-8*) Ulverscroft.
— Someone Who Cares. large type ed. 288p. 1995. 27.99 (*0-7089-3432-3*) Ulverscroft.
— Spun by the Moon. large type ed. 336p. 1988. 27.99 (*0-7089-1900-6*) Ulverscroft.
— The Young Curmudgeon. large type ed. 352p. 1987. 27.99 (*0-7089-1686-4*) Ulverscroft.
Lance, Lynn H. Jesus: His Time, His Place, His Friends. (J). (gr. 5-6). 1984. 18.00 (*1-881678-31-8*) CSEE.
Lance, Mark N. & O'Leary-Hawthorne, John. The Grammar of Meaning: Normativity & Semantic Discourse. LC 96-46022. (Cambridge Studies in Philosophy). 464p. (C). 1998. text 69.95 (*0-521-58300-4*) Cambridge U Pr.
Lance, Peter. First Degree Burn. 1997. mass mkt. 5.99 (*0-614-27729-9*, Prime Crime); mass mkt. 5.99 (*0-425-15698-2*, Prime Crime) Berkley Pub.
Lance, Steven. Written Out of Television: A TV Lover's Guide to Cast Changes 1945-1994. LC 95-47417. (Illus.). 505p. 1996. pap. 24.95 (*1-56833-071-5*) Madison Bks UPA.
— Written Out of Television: The Complete Couch Potato's Guide to Cast Changes & Character Replacements, 1945-1994. LC 95-47417. 1996. text. write for info. (*1-56833-070-7*) Madison Bks UPA.
— Written Out of Television: The Encyclopedia of Cast Changes & Character Replacements, 1945-Present. LC 94-15370. 528p. 1996. text 89.50 (*0-8108-2902-9*) Scarecrow.
Lance, Steven C. Immortal Invisible God. 1.25 (*0-687-50372-8*) Abingdon.
— In a Garden Long Ago. 1.25 (*0-687-05853-8*) Abingdon.
Lance, Victory, jt. auth. see Robbins, Thomas.
Lance, William L. Life Insurance, Spend It & Keep It: How to Make a Tax-Free Exchange of Your Life Insurance & Earn Tax-Deferred Interest. (Illus.). 52p. 1980. pap. 8.00 (*0-686-27280-3*) Truth Pub AZ.
Lancee, Charles T., ed. Echocardiology. (Developments in Cardiovascular Medicine Ser.: No. 1). 1979. text 220.00 (*90-247-2209-8*) Kluwer Academic.
Lancel, Serge. Carthage: A History. Nevill, Antonia, tr. from FRE. (Illus.). xvii, 474p. 1995. 73.95 (*1-55786-468-3*) Blackwell Pubs.
— Carthage: A History. Nevill, Antonia, tr. from FRE. (Illus.). xvii, 474p. 1997. pap. 31.95 (*1-57718-103-4*) Blackwell Pubs.
— Hannibal. Nevill, Antonia, tr. from FRE. LC 97-37371. (Illus.). 368p. (C). 1998. text 31.95 (*0-631-20631-0*) Blackwell Pubs.
— Hannibal. Nevill, Antonia, tr. (Illus.). 256p. 1999. pap. 24.95 (*0-631-21848-3*) Blackwell Pubs.
Lanceley, Frederick J. On-Scene Guide for Crisis Negotiators. LC 99-28068. 232p. (C). 1999. per. 39.95 (*0-8493-0784-8*) CRC Pr.
Lancellotti, Sadie. Letters to Jacob. LC 98-85371. 192p. 1999. pap. 11.95 (*1-56315-199-5*, Pub. by SterlingHse) Natl Bk Netwk.
Lancelot, Claude, jt. auth. see Arnauld, Antoine.
Lancelot-Harrington, Katherine. America - Past & Present: The Continuing Quest, Vol. III. (J). 1985. mass mkt. 19.25 (*0-8384-2786-3*, Newbury) Heinle & Heinle.
— America: Past & Present, Vols. 1-3. 2nd rev. ed. LC 92-31762. (J). 1992. mass mkt. 25.95 (*0-8384-3439-8*) Heinle & Heinle.
— America: Past & Present, Vols. 1-3. 2nd rev. ed. LC 92-31762. (J). 1993. pap. 25.95 (*0-8384-3441-X*); text 25.95 (*0-8384-3440-1*) Heinle & Heinle.
Lancelot, Harry B., 3rd, jt. ed. see Senkiw, George A.
Lancelotta, A. Geotechnical Engineering. (Illus.). 400p. (C). 1994. pap. 59.00 (*90-5410-179-2*, Pub. by A A Balkema) Ashgate Pub Co.
— Geotechnical Engineering. (Illus.). 400p. (C). 1995. text 118.00 (*90-5410-178-4*, Pub. by A A Balkema) Ashgate Pub Co.
***Lancelotta, Victoria.** Here in the World: 13 Stories. 2000. 23.00 (*1-58243-099-3*, Pub. by Counterpt DC) HarpC.
Lancer, Bob. The Soulmate Process. 128p. (Orig.). 1992. pap. 9.98 (*0-87554-501-7*, B928) Valley Sun.
Lancester, Edwin R. DeRieux: Our French Ancestors & How They Came to Virginia. 31p. 1997. reprint ed. pap. 6.00 (*0-8328-8276-3*); reprint ed. lib. bdg. 16.00 (*0-8328-8275-5*) Higginson Bk Co.
Lancet, ed. see Kodansha Ltd. Staff.
Lancet, Barry, ed. see Kobayashi, Tadashi.
Lancet, Barry, ed. see Kodansha Ltd. Staff.
Lancet, Barry, ed. see Levy, Ran.
Lancet, Barry, ed. see Richie, Donald.
Lancet, Barry, ed. see Slivka, Rose & Tsujimoto, Karen.
Lancet, Barry, ed. see Udesky, James.
Lanchais, A., jt. auth. see Crozon, Alain.
Lanchais, Aurelie, jt. auth. see Crozon, Alain.
Lanchbery, Edward, jt. auth. see Duke, Neville.
Lanchester, F. W. Aircraft in Warfare: The Dawn of the Fourth Arm. LC 95-77628. (Illus.). 224p. (C). 1995. 24.95 (*1-57321-002-1*) Lanchester Pr.
***Lanchester, Fw.** Aircraft in Warfare: The Dawn of the Fourth Arm, 1. 1999. pap. text 28.00 (*1-57321-017-X*) Lanchester Pr.
Lanchester, John. The Debt to Pleasure. LC 95-34658. (Illus.). 88p. 1995. 20.00 (*0-8050-4388-8*) H Holt & Co.
— The Debt to Pleasure. 272p. 1997. pap. 10.00 (*0-8050-5130-9*) H Holt & Co.
— The Debt to Pleasure. 256p. 1996. pap. 26.99 (*0-7710-4585-9*) McCland & Stewart.
— The Debt to Pleasure. 256p. 1998. pap. 14.99 (*0-7710-4587-5*) St Martin.
***Lanchester, John.** Mr. Phillips. 304p. 2000. 23.95 (*0-399-14604-0*, Marion Wood) Putnam Pub Group.
Lanchner, Carolyn. Fernand Leger. LC 97-75510. (Museum of Modern Art Book Ser.). (Illus.). 304p. 1998. 60.00 (*0-8109-6185-7*, Pub. by Abrams) Time Warner.
— Fernand Leger. (Illus.). 320p. 1998. 60.00 (*0-87070-052-9*, 0-8109-6185-7, Pub. by Mus of Modern Art); pap. 29.95 (*0-87070-053-7*) Mus of Modern Art.
— Joan Miro. (Illus.). 480p. 1993. 75.00 (*0-8109-6123-7*, Pub. by Abrams) Time Warner.
— Joan Miro. (Illus.). 480p. 1993. 75.00 (*0-87070-434-6*, 0-8109-6123-7, Pub. by Mus of Modern Art); pap. 29.95 (*0-87070-430-3*, 0-8109-6162-8) Mus of Modern Art.
***Lanci-Altomare, Michele.** The Resting Place: Pet Cemeteries & Memorials. LC 00-9258. (Illus.). 96p. 2000. 26.95 (*1-889540-57-9*) Bowtie Press.
Lanci, John R. A New Temple for Corinth: Rhetorical & Archaeological Approaches to Pauline Imagery. LC 96-33594. (Studies in Biblical Literature: Vol. 1). 155p. (C). 1997. text 39.95 (*0-8204-3676-3*) P Lang Pubng.
Lancia, Enrico. Italian Movie Goddesses: Over Eighty of the Greatest Women in Italian Cinema. 1996. 29.95 (*88-7301-071-7*, Pub. by Gremese Intl) Natl Bk Netwk.
Lanciani, R. Notes from Rome. (Illus.). 464p. 1988. pap. 30.00 (*0-904152-12-X*, Pub. by British Schl Rome) David Brown.
Lanciani, Rodolfo. Ancient Rome in the Light of Recent Discoveries. LC 67-13335. (Illus.). 1972. reprint ed. 31.95 (*0-405-08725-X*, Pub. by Blom Pubns) Ayer.
— The Destruction of Ancient Rome. LC 67-23855. (Illus.). 1972. reprint ed. 20.95 (*0-405-08726-8*, Pub. by Blom Pubns) Ayer.
— Forma Urbis Romae. (Illus.). 1994. 75.00 (*88-7097-013-2*) OUP.
— New Tales of Old Rome. LC 67-29707. (Illus.). 1972. reprint ed. 22.95 (*0-405-08727-6*, Pub. by Blom Pubns) Ayer.

L

An Asterisk (*) at the beginning of an entry indicates that the title is appearing for the first time.

L

— Pagan & Christian Rome. LC 67-23856. (Illus.). 1972. reprint ed. 39.95 (*0-405-08728-4*, Pub. by Blom Pubns) Ayer.
— The Ruins & Excavations of Ancient Rome. LC 67-29706. (Illus.). 1972. reprint ed. 52.95 (*0-405-08729-2*, Pub. by Blom Pubns) Ayer.
Lancini, G. & Lorenzetti, R. Biotechnology of Antibiotics & Other Bioactive Microbial Metabolites. (Illus.). 244p. (C). 1993. text 69.50 (*0-306-44603-0*, Kluwer Plenum) Kluwer Academic.
Lancini, Giancarlo L. & Parenti, Francesco. Antibiotics: An Integrated View. (Microbiology Ser.). (Illus.). 250p. 1982. 124.00 (*0-387-90630-4*) Spr-Verlag.
Lancioni, Judith A., jt. auth. see Kloskey, Thomas A.
***Lanciotti, Joseph.** River Island: The Summer People at Barley Point. LC 99-96151. (Illus.). x, 128p. 2000. pap. 9.95 (*0-9675740-0-5*) Overview Ltd.
Lanciotti, Judi. Prayers with Pizzazz for Junior High Teens. Stamschror, Robert P., ed. 76p. (YA). 1996. spiral bd. 12.95 (*0-88489-376-6*) St Marys.
Lancis, Antonio. Grau: Estadista y Politico (Cincuenta Anos en la Historia de Cuba) LC 85-80250. (Coleccion Cuba y sus Jueces). (SPA., Illus.). 160p. (Orig.). 1985. pap. 9.95 (*0-89729-374-6*) Ediciones.
Lancour, Harold. American Art Auction Catalogues, 1785-1942: A Union List. 377p. 1999. reprint ed. 65.00 (*1-57898-133-6*) Martino Pubng.
Lanctot. Medical Mafia. 1995. pap. 14.95 (*0-9644126-0-8*) Heres The Key.
Lanctot, Barbara. A Walk Through Graceland Cemetery: A Chicago Architecture Foundation Walking Tour. 3rd ed. (Illus.). 68p. 1988. pap. 6.95 (*0-9620562-0-0*) Chi Arch Fndtn.
— A Walk Through Graceland Cemetery: A Chicago Architecture Foundation Walking Tour. 4th ed. (Illus.). 68p. 1992. reprint ed. pap. text. write for info. (*0-318-69176-0*) Chi Arch Fndtn.
Lanctot, Gustave. A History of Canada: From the Treaty of Utrecht to the Treaty of Paris, 1713-1763, Vol. 3. Cameron, Margaret M., tr. LC 63-2859. (Illus.). 318p. 1965. 36.95 (*0-674-39602-2*) HUP.
Lanctot, Neil. Fair Dealing & Clean Playing: The Hilldale Club & the Development of Black Professional Baseball, 1910-1932. LC 94-16432. (Illus.). 304p. 1994. lib. bdg. 25.95 (*0-89950-988-6*) McFarland & Co.
Lancy, David F. Children's Emergent Literacy: From Research to Practice. LC 93-23475. 416p. 1994. 69.50 (*0-275-94589-8*, Praeger Pubs) Greenwood.
— Playing on the Mother-Ground: Cultural Routines for Children's Development. (Culture & Human Development Ser.). 240p. 1996. pap. text 21.00 (*1-57230-215-1*, 0215); lib. bdg. 39.95 (*1-57230-142-2*) Guilford Pubns.
— Qualitative Research in Education: An Introduction to the Major Traditions. LC 92-20128. 352p. (C). 1993. text 46.95 (*0-8013-0309-5*, 78014) Longman.
Lancy, Michael. Alice. 64p. 1983. pap. 5.00 (*1-890298-33-6*) Centerstage Pr.
— Bill & Me. 76p. 1983. pap. 5.00 (*1-890298-03-4*) Centerstage Pr.
— The Five Rings. 124p. 1983. pap. 6.00 (*1-890298-30-1*) Centerstage Pr.
— Going Up. 56p. 1988. pap. 5.00 (*1-890298-00-X*) Centerstage Pr.
— Hansel & Gretel. 42p. 1983. pap. 5.00 (*1-890298-39-5*) Centerstage Pr.
— Heidi. 82p. 1984. pap. 6.00 (*1-890298-15-8*) Centerstage Pr.
— It Happened at the Snack Bar. 76p. 1987. pap. 5.00 (*1-890298-18-2*) Centerstage Pr.
— Michael & the Pied Piper. 54p. 1983. pap. 5.00 (*1-890298-21-2*) Centerstage Pr.
— Mollie & the Last Bookworm. 52p. 1985. pap. 5.00 (*1-890298-24-7*) Centerstage Pr.
— Pinocchio II: One Little Puppet. 68p. 1983. pap. 5.00 (*1-890298-36-0*) Centerstage Pr.
— Wizard of Oz. 76p. 1983. pap. 5.00 (*1-890298-42-5*) Centerstage Pr.
— Year of the Child. 80p. 1983. pap. 5.00 (*1-890298-12-3*) Centerstage Pr.
Lancy, Michael & Lakin, Chuck. Cindi - Cinderella. 60p. 1983. pap. 5.00 (*1-890298-09-3*) Centerstage Pr.
— Oliver Twist. 80p. 1981. pap. 5.00 (*1-890298-27-1*) Centerstage Pr.
— Tom & Huck. 64p. 1983. pap. 5.00 (*1-890298-06-9*) Centerstage Pr.
Lanczik, M., jt. ed. see Beckmann, H.
Lanczos, Cornelius. Applied Analysis. (Illus.). 559p. 1988. reprint ed. pap. text 13.95 (*0-486-65656-X*) Dover.
— Linear Differential Operators. LC 96-14933. (Classics in Applied Mathematics Ser.: No. 18). xviii, 564p. 1996. pap. 53.00 (*0-89871-370-6*, CL18) Soc Indus-Appl Math.
— Linear Differential Operators. unabridged ed. LC 97-26069. (Illus.). 576p. 1997. reprint ed. pap. 14.95 (*0-486-68035-5*) Dover.
— The Variational Principles of Mechanics. (Illus.). 418p. 1986. reprint ed. pap. text 12.95 (*0-486-65067-7*) Dover.
— The Variational Principles of Mechanics. 2nd ed. LC QA0845.L229.. (Mathematical Expositions Ser.: No. 4). 393p. reprint ed. pap. 121.90 (*0-7837-0497-6*, 204082100019) Bks Demand.
Land. Behind the Headlines. Date not set. pap. text. write for info. (*0-582-79344-0*, Pub. by Addison-Wesley) Longman.
***Land & Coe.** Tools for Schools: Microsoft Office. 2001. pap. 36.00 (*0-534-52229-7*) Thomson Learn.
Land- en Volkenkunde (Netherlands)Koninklijk Instituut voor Taal-, jt. auth. see Collins, William A.
Land, A. H. Materials for Display & Printing Technologies. write for info. (*0-444-00909-4*) Elsevier.
Land, Ailsa H. & Powell, S. FORTRAN Codes for Mathematical Programming: Linear, Quadratic & Discrete. LC 73-2789. (Illus.). 265p. reprint ed. pap. 82.20 (*0-608-17856-X*, 203265700080) Bks Demand.
Land, Barbara. Las Vegas with Kids: Where to Go, What to Do in America's Hottest Family Destination. LC 95-2703. (Illus.). 272p. 1995. pap. 12.95 (*0-7615-0014-6*) Prima Pub.
Land, Barbara, et al. A Sierra Mosaic: Reno-Sparks-Lake Tahoe. LC 94-3035. (Urban Tapestry Ser.). (Illus.). 256p. 1994. 39.50 (*1-881096-07-6*) Towery Pub.
Land, Barbara, jt. auth. see Land, Myrick.
Land, Barbara N., jt. auth. see Land, Myrick E.
Land, Betty L. Reading 571 (Literacy Strategies) (C). 1998. pap. text 10.88 (*1-56870-277-9*) RonJon Pub.
Land, Bobby L. How to Make It in the Music Business: For the Recording Artist. LC 97-179441. 166p. (Orig.). 1997. pap. text 9.95 (*0-9657754-0-2*, 674) Hit One.
Land, Bonnie G. Down Home Dining in Mississippi. LC 99-93015. 320p. 1999. 15.00 (*0-9670070-0-3*) MS Home Volunteers.
Land, C. M. Van't, see Van't Land, C. M.
Land, Dixie, ed. see Wassell, Irene.
Land, E. Waverly. Moves from Arm to Arm. Bayes, Ronald H., ed. 76p. (Orig.). 1993. pap. 8.95 (*1-879934-07-8*) St Andrews NC.
Land, Frederick S. Current Issues in Public Administration. 5th ed. 496p. 1993. pap. text 36.95 (*0-312-08413-7*) St Martin.
Land, Gary. Essentials of U. S. History since 1941. rev. ed. LC 95-69370. (Illus.). 112p. 2000. pap. text 6.95 (*0-87891-717-9*) Res & Educ.
Land, Gary, ed. Adventism in America: A History. rev. ed. LC 98-14095. 262p. (Orig.). 1998. pap. text 12.99 (*1-883925-19-3*) Andrews Univ Pr.
Land, Gary, ed. see Dick, Everett N.
Land, George & Jarman, Beth. Break-Point & Beyond: Mastering the Future - Today. 1992. 20.00 (*0-88730-547-4*, HarpBusn) HarpInfo.
— Breakpoint & Beyond: Mastering the Future - Today. 261p. 1998. reprint ed. pap. 15.00 (*0-9626605-2-3*) Leadership Two Thousand.
Land, Greg, ed. see O'Neil, Dennis & Grant, Alan.
Land, Helen, ed. AIDS: A Complete Guide to Psychosocial Intervention. LC 92-18565. 318p. 1992. pap. 25.95 (*0-87304-258-1*) Manticore Pubs.
Land, Hilary & Ward, Sue. Social Security Review & Women. 1986. 20.00 (*0-946088-26-8*, Pub. by NCCL) St Mut.
Land, Jeff. Active Radio: Pacifica's Brash Experiment. LC 98-56538. (Commerce & Mass Culture Ser.). 184p. 1999. 42.95 (*0-8166-3156-5*); pap. 16.95 (*0-8166-3157-3*); pap. 16.95 (*0-8166-2711-8*) U of Minn Pr.
Land, John. Lucifer Directive. 1984. mass mkt. 4.95 (*0-8217-3354-0*, Zebra Kensgtn) Kensgtn Pub Corp.
Land, Jon. Day of the Delphi. 432p. (Orig.). 1993. mass mkt. 5.99 (*0-8125-3434-4*, Pub. by Tor Bks) St Martin.
— Dead Simple. 1999. mass mkt. 6.99 (*0-8125-4001-8*, Pub. by Forge NYC) St Martin.
— Dead Simple. LC 97-39737. 1998. text 23.95 (*0-312-86489-2*) St Martin.
***Land, Jon.** Dolphin Key. 192p. 1999. 17.95 (*0-312-87249-6*, Pub. by Forge NYC) St Martin.
Land, Jon. The Doomsday Spiral. 1983. mass mkt. 2.95 (*0-8217-1175-X*, Zebra Kensgtn) Kensgtn Pub Corp.
— Fires of Midnight. 1996. mass mkt. 6.99 (*0-8125-5252-0*, Pub. by Forge NYC) St Martin.
— Hope Mountain. LC 98-21313. 192p. 1998. 17.95 (*0-312-86772-7*, Pub. by Forge NYC) St Martin.
***Land, Jon.** Hope Mountain. 2001. pap. 11.95 (*0-312-87267-4*) St Martin.
Land, Jon. Kingdom of the Seven. 432p. (Orig.). 1994. pap. 5.99 (*0-8125-3435-2*, Pub. by Forge NYC) St Martin.
— The Pillars of Solomon. LC 98-46710. 352p. 1999. 24.95 (*0-312-86819-7*, Pub. by Forge NYC) St Martin.
***Land, Jon.** The Pillars of Solomon, 1. LC 98-46710. 438p. 2000. mass mkt. 6.99 (*0-8125-6672-6*, Pub. by Forge NYC) St Martin.
— Return to Hope Mountain. text 23.95 (*0-312-87266-6*) St Martin.
Land, Jon. The Vengeance of the Tau. (Orig.). 1993. mass mkt. 5.99 (*0-449-14776-2*, GM) Fawcett.
***Land, Jon.** A Walk in the Darkness. LC 99-98190. 352p. 2000. 25.95 (*0-312-87265-8*, Pub. by Forge NYC) St Martin.
Land, Jon. The Walls of Jericho. LC 96-27427. 1997. 23.95 (*0-312-86267-9*, Pub. by Forge NYC) St Martin.
— The Walls of Jericho. 1998. mass mkt. 6.99 (*0-8125-6456-1*, Pub. by Tor Bks) St Martin.
Land, Kenneth C. & Schneider, Stephen H., eds. Forecasting in the Social & Natural Sciences. (C). 1987. text 176.50 (*90-277-2616-7*) Kluwer Academic.
Land, Kenneth C. & Spilerman, Seymour, eds. Social Indicator Models. LC 74-79447. 412p. 1975. 45.00 (*0-87154-505-5*) Russell Sage.
Land, Leslie. Modern Country Cooking. 1999. pap. 13.00 (*0-14-017825-2*, Penguin Bks) Viking Penguin.
Land, Lisa, ed. Knowledge Based System Usage: Benefits Experienced & Lessons Learned. LC 94-31236. 1994. write for info. (*0-07-709048-9*) McGraw.
Land, Lynton S. Dolomitization. LC QE0471.15.D6. (Education Course Note Ser.: Vol. 24). 22p. 1983. reprint ed. pap. 30.00 (*0-608-03023-6*, 206347300006) Bks Demand.
Land, Mary. Louisiana Cookery. 1972. pap. 8.95 (*0-87511-070-3*) Claitors.
***Land, Marybelle.** Poetic Tales of the Longhorn Trail. unabridged ed. (Illus.). 20p. 1998. spiral bd. 7.00 (*1-929326-37-8*) Hal Bar Pubg.
Land, Marybelle S. A Collage of Poetry. LC 97-61799. (Illus.). 60p. 1997. pap. 5.00 (*1-886467-23-4*) WJM Press.
— Heartsongs. LC 97-61798. (Illus.). 60p. 1997. pap. 5.00 (*1-886467-21-8*) WJM Press.
Land, Marybelle S. & Middleton, William J. Sette Bellos: Acrostic Poetry. LC 97-81022. (Illus.). 76p. 1997. pap. 4.00 (*1-886467-29-3*) WJM Press.
Land, Michael. Tools for Schools: Clarisworks 5.0. LC 98-49643. 1999. text 56.95 (*0-534-52462-1*) Wadsworth Pub.
Land, Michael & Turner, Sandra. Tools for Schools: Claris Works Edition. LC 96-36362. (Education Ser.). 320p. (C). 1997. pap. 35.25 (*0-534-21492-4*) Wadsworth Pub.
Land, Michael, jt. auth. see Turner, Sandra.
Land, Myrick & Land, Barbara. A Short History of Las Vegas. LC 98-41746. (Illus.). 200p. 1999. pap. 15.95 (*0-87417-326-4*) U of Nev Pr.
Land, Myrick E. The Fine Art of Literary Mayhem: A Lively Account of Famous Writers & Their Feuds. 2nd rev. ed. LC 82-49332. 272p. 1983. pap. 9.95 (*0-938530-11-9*, 11-9) Lexikos.
Land, Myrick E. & Land, Barbara N. A Short History of Reno. LC 94-32428. (Illus.). 136p. 1995. pap. 14.95 (*0-87417-262-4*) U of Nev Pr.
Land-Nellist, Cassandra. Colors in Hawaiian. (Hawaiian Treasures Ser.). (ENG & HAU., Illus.). 10p. (J). (ps). 1993. 3.95 (*0-916630-72-2*) Pr Pacifica.
— Counting Hawaiian Petroglyphs. (Hawaiian Treasures Ser.). (Illus.). 10p. (J). (ps). 1993. 3.95 (*0-916630-74-9*) Pr Pacifica.
— Hawai'i Pono'i. (Hawaiian Treasures Ser.). (Illus.). 10p. (J). (ps). 1993. 3.95 (*0-916630-73-0*) Pr Pacifica.
— Hawaiian Words & Pictures. LC 95-37584. 139p. 1996. 15.95 (*0-916630-76-5*) Pr Pacifica.
Land, Norman E. The Potted Tree: Essays in Venetian Art. LC 93-40775. (ARTHIS Ser.). xiv, 188p. 1994. 65.00 (*1-879751-85-2*) Camden Hse.
— The Viewer As Poet: The Renaissance Response to Art. LC 93-4469. 1994. 45.00 (*0-271-01004-5*) Pa St U Pr.
Land, Norman E., jt. auth. see Collins, Marcia.
Land, Norman E., ed. see Museum of Art & Archaeology, University of Missouri, Columbia Staff.
Land O Lakes Staff. American Heritage Cookbook: Time-Honored Recipes from the Family Farm. LC 99-44754. (Land O'Lakes Ser.). (Illus.). 96p. 1999. 15.95 (*0-86573-172-1*) Creat Pub Intl.
— Chicken. LC 94-16805. (Land O Lakes Collector Ser.). (Illus.). 128p. 1994. pap. 9.95 (*0-86573-953-6*) Creat Pub Intl.
— Treasury of Country Recipes. 1994. 24.95 (*2-89429-058-6*, Pub. by Tormont) Creat Pub Intl.
Land O Lakes Staff & Creative Publishing International Staff. Simply Delicious: Cookies, Bars, Desserts. LC 99-27799. (Land O'Lakes Ser.). (Illus.). 224p. 1999. 24.95 (*0-86573-897-1*) Creat Pub Intl.
Land O'Lakes Staff. Land O'Lakes Baking. (Land O'Lakes Cooking Traditions Ser.). (Illus.). 132p. 2000. pap. 14.95 (*0-9663558-3-0*, Pub. by Tiger Oak) Natl Bk Netwk.
— Land O'Lakes Comfort Foods. (Land O'Lakes Cooking Traditions Ser.: No. I). (Illus.). 1999. pap. 14.95 (*0-9663558-5-7*, Pub. by Tiger Oak) Natl Bk Netwk.
— Land O'Lakes Cookies. (Land O'Lakes Cooking Traditions Ser.). (Illus.). 132p. (Orig.). 1999. pap. 14.95 (*0-9663558-2-2*, Pub. by Tiger Oak) Natl Bk Netwk.
— Land O'Lakes Desserts. (Land O'Lakes Cooking Traditions Ser.). (Illus.). 132p. 2000. pap. 14.95 (*0-9663558-4-9*, Pub. by Tiger Oak) Natl Bk Netwk.
— Land O'Lakes Holiday Cooking. (Land O'Lakes Cooking Traditions Ser.). (Illus.). 132p. (Orig.). 1999. pap. 14.95 (*0-9663558-6-5*, Pub. by Tiger Oak) Natl Bk Netwk.
Land O'Lakes Staff & Time-Life Books Editors. Land O' Lakes Best-Loved Recipes: Celebrating 75 Years of Quality Cooking. LC 96-25442. (Illus.). 96p. (gr. 11). 1999. 14.95 (*0-7835-4860-5*) Time-Life.
Land, Peter A. Managing to Get the Job Done: How to Make Sure Your Employees Are Ready, Willing, & Able to Succeed. (Illus.). 110p. 1998. 24.95 (*0-939975-14-9*) Exec Pr NC.
— Managing to Get the Job Done: How to Make Sure Your Employees Are Ready, Willing, & Able to Succeed. 128p. 1994. 24.95 (*0-471-11279-8*) Wiley.
Land, Philip. Shaping Welfare Consensus: U. S. Catholic Bishops Contribution. 217p. (Orig.). (C). 1988. pap. text 7.95 (*0-934255-07-5*) Center Concern.
Land Planning Committee, U.S. National Resources B. Report of the Land Planning Committee, Vol. 2. LC 75-26322. (World Food Supply Ser.). (Illus.). 1976. reprint ed. 20.95 (*0-405-07798-X*) Ayer.
Land Planning, Public Works & Rural Land Use Commi, jt. auth. see United States National Resources Committee.
Land, Richard, jt. ed. see George, Timothy F.
Land, Richard D. Send a Message to Mickey: The ABC's of Making Your Voice Heard at Disney. LC 98-24223. 1998. pap. 5.95 (*0-8054-9308-5*) Broadman.
Land, Richard D. & Hollaway, Lee, eds. Christians in the Public Square: Faith in Practice? LC 96-84947. 160p. (Orig.). 1996. pap. 9.99 (*1-888880-01-5*, ERLC Pubns) ERCSBC.
Land, Robert D., jt. auth. see Huggins, Kenneth.
Land, Stephen K. Challenge & Conventionality in the Fiction of E. M. Forster. LC 87-45795. (Studies in Modern Literature: No. 19). 1989. 34.50 (*0-404-61589-9*) AMS Pr.
— Conrad & the Paradox of Plot LC 86-673517. vii, 311 p. 1984. write for info. (*0-333-36932-7*) Macmillan.
— The Philosophy of Language in Britain: Major Theories from Hobbes to Thomas Reid. LC 83-45287. (Studies in the Seventeenth Century: No. 2). 1986. 39.50 (*0-404-61722-0*) AMS Pr.
Land, Steven J. Pentecostal Spirituality: A Passion for the Kingdom. (JPT Supplement Ser.: No. 1). 239p. 1993. pap. 21.95 (*1-85075-442-X*, Pub. by Sheffield Acad) CUP Services.
Land Tenure Center Staff, et al, contrib. by. Empresas Forestales Comunitarias en las Americas: Estudios de Caso Presentados en el Simposio "Aprovechamientos Forestales en las Americas: Manejo Comunitario y Sostenibilidad." Universidad de Wisconsin-Madison, 3-4 Febrero, 1995. (SPA., Illus.). xi, 192p. 1995. pap. 12.00 (*0-934519-03-X*) U of Wis Land.
Land, Tesse, jt. auth. see Lang, Moshe.
Land Trust Alliance & National Trust for Historic. Appraising Easements: Guidelines for Valuation of Historic Preservation & Land Conservation Easements. rev. ed. 70p. 1990. pap. text 17.00 (*0-943915-05-8*) Land Trust DC.
Land Trust Alliance Staff. Starting a Land Trust: A Guide to Forming a Land Conservation Organization. 200p. (Orig.). 1990. pap. 16.00 (*0-943915-06-6*) Land Trust DC.
Land Trust Exchange Staff, jt. auth. see Montana Land Reliance Staff.
Land, W., ed. Optimal Use of Sandimmun in Organ Transplantation. (Illus.). 40p. 1987. 40.95 (*0-387-17865-1*) Spr-Verlag.
Land, W. & Dossetor, J. B., eds. Organ Replacement Therapy: Ethics, Justice & Commerce: First Joint Meeting of ESOT & EDTA - ERA Munich, December 1990. (Illus.). xxiii, 578p. 1991. 185.00 (*0-387-53687-6*) Spr-Verlag.
***Land-Weber, Ellen.** To Save a Life: Stories of Holocaust Rescue. LC 99-50499. (Illus.). 368p. 1999. 34.95 (*0-252-02515-6*) U of Ill Pr.
Landa. Graphic Design Solutions. 2nd ed. (C). 2000. pap. 55.95 (*0-7668-1360-6*) Delmar.
Landa, Douglas C., jt. auth. see Landa, Henry C.
Landa, E. R. Buried Treasure to Buried Waste: The Rise & Fall of the Radium Industry. LC 87-22233. (Colorado School of Mines Quarterly Ser.: Vol. 82, No. 2). (Illus.). 336p. 1987. pap. text 20.00 (*0-918062-75-6*) Colo Sch Mines.
Landa, Gertrude, see Aunt Naomi, pseud.
Landa, Gertrude, jt. auth. see Aunt Naomi, pseud.
Landa, Henry C. Automotive Aerodynamics Handbook. 7th ed. (Illus.). 1991. 28.50 (*0-931974-15-1*) FICOA.
— Silencer Theory. (Illus.). 1979. pap. 11.00 (*0-931974-09-7*) FICOA.
— Solar Energy Handbook. 5th ed. (Illus.). (C). 1977. pap. 15.00 (*0-931974-00-3*) FICOA.
Landa, Henry C. & Landa, Douglas C. The Political Handbook for Student Government Operations: A Guide to Candidacy, Campaigning, Leadership & Management & Advisory Functions. 158p. (Orig.). 1998. pap. 18.00 (*0-931974-17-8*) FICOA.
Landa, Janet T. Trust, Ethnicity, & Identity: Beyond the New Institutional Economics of Ethnic Trading Networks, Contract Law, & Gift-Changing. LC 94-1727. 248p. 1995. text 57.50 (*0-472-10361-X*, 10361) U of Mich Pr.
Landa, Jose A., jt. auth. see Onega, Susana.
Landa, Judah. How to Study Physics. (Illus.). 384p. 1994. 19.50 (*0-9639716-0-3*) Jay-El Pubns.
— Torah & Science. 1990. 39.50 (*0-88125-320-0*) Ktav.
Landa, Jutta, ed. I Am Too Many People: Peter Turrini: Poet, Playwright, Essayist. LC 97-19133. (Studies in Austrian Literature, Culture & Thought). ii, 276 p. 1998. 32.50 (*1-57241-040-X*) Ariadne CA.
Landa, L. A., ed. see Swift, Jonathan.
Landa, L. N. Algorithmization in Learning & Instruction. Kopstein, Felix F., ed. Bennett, Virginia, tr. from RUS. LC 73-11044. 752p. 1974. reprint ed. 69.95 (*0-87778-063-3*) Educ Tech Pubns.
— Instructional Regulation & Control: Cybernetics, Algorithmization & Heuristics in Education. Kopstein, Felix F., ed. Desch, Samuel, tr. from RUS. LC 75-44383. 552p. 1976. 69.95 (*0-87778-087-0*) Educ Tech Pubns.
Landa, Louis, ed. see Defoe, Daniel.
Landa, Louis A. Essays in Eighteenth-Century English Literature. LC 80-7541. (Princeton Series of Collected Essays: No. 3). 253p. 1980. reprint ed. pap. 78.50 (*0-7837-1933-7*, 204214800001) Bks Demand.
Landa, M. English-Serbocroatian Dictionary of Economics & Business. (ENG & SER.). 358p. 1986. 59.95 (*0-7859-7511-X*) Fr & Eur.
— English-Serbocroatian Economics & Business Studies Dict. 504p. (C). 1990. 150.00 (*0-89771-929-8*, Pub. by Collets) St Mut.
Landa, Mariasun. The Dancing Flea. White, Linda, tr. (Basque Ser.).Tr. of Errusika. (BAQ & ENG., Illus.). 128p. (J). (gr. 3-5). 1996. pap. 12.00 (*0-87417-281-0*) U of Nev Pr.
— Karmentxu & the Little Ghost. White, Linda, tr. LC 96-30600. (Basque Ser.).Tr. of Txan Fantasma. (BAQ & ENG., Illus.). 88p. (J). (gr. 3-5). 1996. pap. 12.00 (*0-87417-282-9*) U of Nev Pr.
Landa, Norbert. The Little Bear's Christmas. LC 99-25069. (Illus.). 32p. (J). (gr. k-3). 1999. 14.95 (*1-888444-60-6*, Pub. by Little Tiger) Futech Educ Prods.
Landa, Norbert, jt. auth. see Baeuerle, Patrick.
Landa, Norbert, jt. auth. see Baeuerle, Patrick A.
Landa, Norbert, jt. auth. see Bauerle, Patrick.
Landa, P. S. Nonlinear Oscillations & Waves in Dynamical Systems. LC 95-48427. (Mathematics & Its Applications Ser.: Vol. 360). 556p. (C). 1996. text 254.00 (*0-7923-3931-2*) Kluwer Academic.
Landa, P. S., jt. auth. see Neimark, Yu. I.
***Landa, R. K.** Dad Is a "Drinking Man" LC 99-91106. 152p. 1999. 25.00 (*0-7388-0610-2*); pap. 18.00 (*0-7388-0611-0*) Xlibris Corp.

An Asterisk (*) at the beginning of an entry indicates that the title is appearing for the first time.

Landa, Robin. Graphic Design Solutions. (Graphic Communications Ser.). 320p. (C). 1996. mass mkt. 58.95 (*0-8273-6352-4*) Delmar.

— Religious Art: A Workbook for Artists & Designers. 272p. 1985. 29.95 (*0-13-773037-3*); pap. 16.95 (*0-13-773029-2*) P-H.

— Thinking Creatively: New Ways to Unlock Your Visual Imagination. LC 98-18728. (Illus.). 160p. 1998. 32.99 (*0-89134-843-3*, North Lght Bks) F & W Pubns Inc.

Landa, Robin, jt. auth. see Gonnella, Rose.

Landahl, M. T. & Mollo-Christensen, E. Turbulence & Random Processes in Fluid Mechanics. 2nd ed. (Illus.). 180p. (C). 1992. text 69.95 (*0-521-41992-1*); pap. text 24.95 (*0-521-42213-2*) Cambridge U Pr.

Landahl, Marten, jt. auth. see Ashley, Holt.

Landais-Stamp, Paul & Rogers, Paul. Rocking the Boat: New Zealand, the United States & the Nuclear-Free Zone Controversy in the 1980s. 201p. 1989. 19.50 (*0-85496-279-4*) Berg Pubs.

Landale, Anthony. Gower Handbook of Training & Development. 3rd ed. LC 99-18669. 200p. 1999. 131.95 (*0-566-08122-9*, Pub. by Ashgate Pub) Ashgate Pub Co.

Landale, Zoe. Burning Stone. LC 95-173293. 106p. 1999. pap. 10.95 (*0-921870-31-0*, Pub. by Ronsdale Pr) Partners-West.

Landalf, Helen. Moving Is Relating: Developing Interpersonal Skills Through Movement. LC 98-9253. 96p. (J). (gr. 3-6). 1998. pap. 19.95 (*1-57525-123-X*) Smith & Kraus.

— Moving the Earth: Teaching Earth Science Through Movement. LC 97-11379. (Illus.). 144p. (Orig.). (J). (gr. 3-6). 1997. pap. 19.95 (*1-57525-108-6*) Smith & Kraus.

— The Secret Night World of Cats. LC 97-29775. (Illus.). 32p. (J). (gr. k-3). 1998. 16.95 (*1-57525-117-5*) Smith & Kraus.

Landalf, Helen & Gerke, Pamela. Hooves & Horns, Fins & Feathers: Drama Curriculum for Kindergarten & First Grade. LC 99-25281. 240p. 1999. pap. 19.95 (*1-57525-121-3*) Smith & Kraus.

— Mail & Mystery, Family & Friends: Drama Curriculum for Second & Third Grades. LC 99-25288. 268p. 1999. pap. 19.95 (*1-57525-188-4*) Smith & Kraus.

Landau. Adaptive Control: The Model Reference Approach. (Control & Systems Theory Ser.: Vol. 8). (Illus.). 432p. 1979. text 185.00 (*0-8247-6548-6*) Dekker.

— Rethinking the European Union. LC 96-18901. 256p. 1997. text 59.95 (*0-312-16156-5*) St Martin.

— Tropical Rain Forests. (J). 1991. pap. text 5.50 (*0-516-91560-6*) Childrens.

Landau, Alan M. U. S. Special Forces. 384p. 1999. 19.98 (*0-7603-0778-4*) Motorbooks Intl.

Landau, Alan M. & Landau, Frieda W. Airborne Rangers. LC 92-7488. (Power Ser.). (Illus.). 128p. 1992. pap. 16.95 (*0-87938-606-1*) MBI Pubg.

Landau, Asher F. Selected Judgments of the Supreme Court of Israel: Special Volume. 191p. 1971. 39.95 (*0-87855-175-1*) Transaction Pubs.

Landau, Asher F., ed. The Jerusalem Post Law Reports. 270p. (Orig.). 1993. pap. 17.50 (*965-223-827-9*) Gefen Bks.

***Landau, Barbara.** Perception, Cognition & Language: Essays in Honor of Henry & Lila Gleitman. LC 99-88328. 2000. 39.95 (*0-262-12228-6*) MIT Pr.

Landau, Barbara & Gleitman, Lila R. Language & Experience: Evidence from the Blind Child. (Cognitive Science Ser.: Vol. No. 8). (Illus.). 256p. 1985. reprint ed. pap. 18.95 (*0-674-51026-7*) HUP.

Landau, Barbara, jt. ed. see Gleitman, Lila R.

Landau, Betzalel. The Vilna Gaon. 20.99 (*0-89906-441-8*, VILH); pap. 17.99 (*0-89906-442-6*, VILP) Mesorah Pubns.

***Landau, Camille & White, Tiare.** What They Don't Teach You at Film School: 161 Strategies for Making Your Own Movies No Matter What. 256p. 2000. pap. 14.00 (*0-7868-8477-0*, Pub. by Hyperion) Time Warner.

Landau, Carl & Landau, Katie. California Festivals. (Illus.). (Orig.). 1988. pap. 9.95 (*0-929881-25-7*) Landau Comns.

Landau, Carol, et al. The Complete Book of Menopause. 368p. (Orig.). 1995. pap. 15.00 (*0-399-51906-8*, Perigee Bks) Berkley Pub.

Landau, D. P., et al, eds. Computer Simulation Studies in Condensed Matter Physics. (Proceedings in Physics Ser.: Vol. 33). (Illus.). 240p. 1988. 77.95 (*0-387-50449-4*) Spr-Verlag.

— Computer Simulation Studies in Condensed Matter Physics III: Proceedings of the Third Workshop, Athens, GA, USA February 12-16, 1990. (Proceedings in Physics Ser.: Vol. 53). 224p. 1991. 70.95 (*0-387-53607-8*) Spr-Verlag.

— Computer Simulation Studies in Condensed-Matter Physics IV: Proceedings of the Fourth Workshop, Athens, GA, February 18-22, 1991. LC 92-39677. 1993. 119.95 (*0-387-56309-1*) Spr-Verlag.

— Computer Simulation Studies in Condensed-Matter Physics V: Proceedings of the Fifth Workshop, Athens, GA, USA, February 17-21, 1992. LC 93-18578. (Proceedings in Physics Ser.: Vol. 75). 1993. 75.95 (*0-387-56474-8*) Spr-Verlag.

— Computer Simulation Studies in Condensed-matter Physics VI. (Proceedings in Physics Ser.: Vol. 76). 225p. 1993. 108.95 (*0-387-57143-4*) Spr-Verlag.

— Computer Simulation Studies in Condensed-Matter Physics VIII: Recent Developments, Proceedings of the 8th Workshop, Athens, GA, USA, February 20-24, 1995. (Proceedings in Physics Ser.: Vol. 80). 181p. 1995. 130.95 (*3-540-60346-8*) Spr-Verlag.

***Landau, D. P., et al, eds.** Computer Simulation Studies in Condensed-Matter Physics XII: Proceedings of the Twelfth Workshop, Athens, GA, U. S. A. (Proceedings in Physics Ser.: Vol. 85). (Illus.). x, 231p. 2000. 99.00 (*3-540-66565-X*) Spr-Verlag.

Landau, D. P. & Mon, K. K., eds. Computer Simulation Studies in Condensed-Matter Physics VII Vol. 78: Proceedings of the Seventh Workshop Athens, GA. 244p. 1994. 117.95 (*3-540-58481-1*) Spr-Verlag.

Landau, D. P. & Schuttler, H. B., eds. Computer Simulation Studies in Condensed-Matter Physics XI: Proceedings of the 11th Workshop Athens, GA, U. S. A., February 22-27, 1998. (Proceedings in Physics Ser.: Vol. 84). (Illus.). ix, 230p. 1999. 109.00 (*3-540-65519-0*) Spr-Verlag.

Landau, D. P., jt. ed. see Family, F.

Landau, David. Piety & Power: The World of Jewish Fundamentalism. LC 92-37540. 1992. 27.50 (*0-8090-7605-5*) Hill & Wang.

— The Renaissance Print, 1470-1550. (Illus.). 448p. 1996. pap. 35.00 (*0-300-06883-2*) Yale U Pr.

***Landau, David & Binder, Kurt.** A Guide to Monte Carlo Simulations in Statistical Physics. (Illus.). 400p. (C). 2000. write for info. (*0-521-65314-2*); pap. 37.95 (*0-521-65366-5*) Cambridge U Pr.

Landau, David, tr. see Crozier, Michel.

Landau, David P., et al, eds. Computer Simulation Studies in Condensed-Matter Physics X: Proceedings of the 10th Workshop Athens, GA, February 24-28, 1997. LC 97-39888. (Proceedings in Physics Ser.: Vol. 83). (Illus.). xi, 267p. (C). 1997. 94.95 (*3-540-63510-6*) Spr-Verlag.

Landau, Diana, ed. Iowa: The Spirit of America State by State. LC 97-12018. (Art of the State Ser.). 96p. 1998. 12.95 (*0-8109-5550-4*, Pub. by Abrams) Time Warner.

Landau, Diana, ed. see Bix, Cynthia O.

Landau, Diana, ed. see Friedman, Nancy.

Landau, Diana, ed. see Friedman, Nancy J.

Landau, Diana, ed. see Friedman, Nancy & Vincent, Steve.

Landau, Diana, ed. see Harris, Patricia.

Landau, Diana, ed. see Kostyal, K. M.

Landau, Diana, ed. see Mantell, Suzanne.

Landau, Diana, ed. see Palmer, Barbara.

Landau, Diana, ed. see Sonenberg, Nina.

Landau, Diana, ed. see Wanning, Esther.

Landau, Edmund. Algebraische Zahlen. 2nd ed. 9.95 (*0-8284-0062-8*) Chelsea Pub.

— Differential & Integral Calculus. LC 65-4331. 372p. (C). 1981. text 27.50 (*0-8284-0078-4*) Chelsea Pub.

— Elementare Zahlentheorie. LC 49-235. 14.95 (*0-8284-0026-1*) Chelsea Pub.

— Elementary Number Theory. LC 99-15533. 1999. write for info. (*0-8218-2004-4*) Am Math.

— Elementary Number Theory. 2nd ed. LC 57-8494. 1988. 19.95 (*0-8284-0125-X*) Chelsea Pub.

— Foundations of Analysis. 2nd ed. LC 60-15580. (gr. 9 up). 1960. text 13.95 (*0-8284-0079-2*) Chelsea Pub.

— Grundlagen der Analysis: With Complete German-English Vocabulary. 4th ed. LC 60-7485. (ENG & GER.). pap. 4.95 (*0-8284-0141-1*) Chelsea Pub.

— Handbuch der Lehre von der Verteilung der Primzahlen, 2 vols. in 1. 3rd ed. LC 73-21539. 1974. text 55.00 (*0-8284-0096-2*) Chelsea Pub.

Landau, Elaine. The Abenaki. (First Bks.). (Illus.). 64p. (J). (gr. 5-8). 1996. pap. 6.95 (*0-531-15782-2*) Watts.

— Air Crashes. LC 98-49174. (Watts Library: Disasters). 63p. (J). (gr. 4-7). 1999. 24.00 (*0-531-20346-8*) Watts.

***Landau, Elaine.** Air Crashes. (Watts Library). (Illus.). (J). 2000. pap. 8.95 (*0-531-16416-0*) Watts.

Landau, Elaine. Allergies. (Understanding Illness Ser.). (Illus.). 64p. (J). (gr. 5-8). 1995. lib. bdg. 18.90 (*0-8050-2989-3*) TFC Bks NY.

— Alzheimer's Disease. (Venture Bks.). (Illus.). 112p. (YA). (gr. 7-12). 1996. lib. bdg. 24.00 (*0-531-11268-3*) Watts.

— Angelfish. (True Bks.). (Illus.). 48p. (gr. 2-4). 1999. lib. bdg. 6.95 (*0-516-26488-5*) Childrens.

— Angelfish. LC 98-16121. (Animals Ser.). (Illus.). 47p. (J). (gr. 2-4). 1999. 21.50 (*0-516-20660-5*) Childrens.

— Apatosaurus. LC 98-24780. (Dinosaurs Ser.). (J). 1999. 21.00 (*0-516-20434-3*) Childrens.

— Apatosaurus. LC 98-24780. (True Bks.). (Illus.). 48p. (gr. 2-4). 1999. lib. bdg. 6.95 (*0-516-26489-3*) Childrens.

— Apples. LC 98-47327. (Food & Nutrition Ser.). (J). 1999. 21.50 (*0-516-21024-6*) Childrens.

***Landau, Elaine.** Apples. (True Bks.). (J). 2000. pap. text 6.95 (*0-516-26571-7*) Childrens.

Landau, Elaine. The Assyrians. LC 96-46899. (Cradle of Civilization Ser.). 64p. (J). (gr. 4-6). 1997. lib. bdg. 21.40 (*0-7613-0217-4*) Millbrook Pr.

— Australia & New Zealand. LC 98-50881. (Geography Ser.). (J). 1999. 21.50 (*0-516-20981-7*) Childrens.

***Landau, Elaine.** Australia & New Zealand. (True Bks.). 2000. pap. text 6.95 (*0-516-26573-3*) Childrens.

— Autism. LC 00-42643. 2001. write for info. (*0-531-11780-4*) Watts.

Landau, Elaine. The Babylonians. LC 96-46871. (Cradle of Civilization Ser.). 64p. (J). (gr. 4-6). 1997. lib. bdg. 21.40 (*0-7613-0216-6*) Millbrook Pr.

— Bananas. LC 98-47328. (Food & Nutrition Ser.). (J). 1999. write for info. (*0-516-21025-4*) Childrens.

***Landau, Elaine.** Bananas. (True Bks.). (J). 2000. pap. text 6.95 (*0-516-26574-1*) Childrens.

Landau, Elaine. Big Brother Is Watching. (J). 1992. 14.95 (*0-8027-8160-8*); lib. bdg. 15.85 (*0-8027-8161-6*) Walker & Co.

— Bill Clinton. 1993. 11.15 (*0-606-05161-9*, Pub. by Turtleback) Demco.

— Bill Clinton & His Presidency. LC 96-37870. (First Bk.). (J). 1997. lib. bdg. 22.00 (*0-531-20295-X*) Watts.

— Bill Clinton & His Presidency. (First Books). (J). 1997. pap. text 6.95 (*0-531-15841-1*) Watts.

— Blindness. (Understanding Illness Ser.). (Illus.). 64p. (J). (gr. 5-8). 1995. lib. bdg. 15.95 (*0-8050-2992-3*) TFC Bks NY.

— Breast Cancer. LC 95-3831. (Venture Bks.). 112p. (YA). (gr. 7-12). 1995. lib. bdg. 24.00 (*0-531-11242-X*) Watts.

— Canada. LC 99-13662. (True Bks.). (Illus.). 48p. (gr. 3-5). 1999. 21.50 (*0-516-21170-6*) Childrens.

***Landau, Elaine.** Canada. (Illus.). 48p. (J). (gr. 3-5). 2000. pap. 6.95 (*0-516-27021-4*) Childrens.

Landau, Elaine. Cancer. (Understanding Illness Ser.). (Illus.). 64p. (J). (gr. 5-8). 1995. lib. bdg. 18.90 (*0-8050-2990-7*) TFC Bks NY.

***Landau, Elaine.** Chewing Gum: A Sticky Treat. LC 00-22393. (Tasty Treats Ser.). 2000. write for info. (*1-57103-335-1*) Rourke Pr.

Landau, Elaine. Child Abuse: An American Epidemic. 1990. 11.05 (*0-606-04633-X*, Pub. by Turtleback) Demco.

***Landau, Elaine.** Chocolate: Savor the Flavor. LC 00-22392. (Tasty Treats Ser.). 2000. write for info. (*1-57103-336-X*) Rourke Pr.

Landau, Elaine. Corn. LC 98-47332. (Food & Nutrition Ser.). (J). 1999. 21.50 (*0-516-21026-2*) Childrens.

***Landau, Elaine.** Corn. (True Bks.). 2000. pap. text 6.95 (*0-516-26759-0*) Childrens.

Landau, Elaine. The Curse of Tutankhamen. (Mysteries of Science Ser.). (Illus.). 48p. (J). (gr. 3-6). 1996. lib. bdg. 20.90 (*0-7613-0014-7*) Millbrook Pr.

— Deafness. (Understanding Illness Ser.). (Illus.). 64p. (J). (gr. 5-8). 1995. lib. bdg. 18.90 (*0-8050-2993-1*) TFC Bks NY.

— Desert Mammals. LC 96-3891. (True Bk.). 48p. (J). 1996. lib. bdg. 21.00 (*0-516-20038-0*) Childrens.

— Desert Mammals. (True Bks.). 48p. (J). (gr. 3-4). 1997. pap. 6.95 (*0-516-26097-9*) Childrens.

— Diabetes. (Understanding Illness Ser.). (Illus.). 64p. (J). (gr. 5-8). 1995. lib. bdg. 18.90 (*0-8050-2988-5*) TFC Bks NY.

— The Dominican Republic. LC 99-13663. (True Bks.). (Illus.). 48p. (gr. 3-5). 2000. 21.50 (*0-516-21171-4*) Childrens.

***Landau, Elaine.** Dominican Republic. (Illus.). 48p. (J). (gr. 3-5). 2000. pap. 6.95 (*0-516-27022-2*) Childrens.

Landau, Elaine. Egypt. LC 99-25975. (A True Book). (Illus.). 48p. (gr. 3-5). 2000. 21.50 (*0-516-21172-2*) Childrens.

***Landau, Elaine.** Egypt. (Illus.). 48p. (J). (gr. 3-5). 2000. pap. 6.95 (*0-516-27018-4*) Childrens.

Landau, Elaine. Electric Fish. LC 98-16122. (Animals Ser.). 47p. (J). 1999. 21.50 (*0-516-20666-4*) Childrens.

— Electric Fish. (True Bks.). (Illus.). 48p. (gr. 2-4). 1999. lib. bdg. 6.95 (*0-516-26491-5*) Childrens.

— Endangered Plants. (First Bks.). (Illus.). 64p. (J). (gr. 4-6). 1992. pap. 6.95 (*0-531-15645-1*) Watts.

— Epilepsy. (Understanding Illness Ser.). (Illus.). 64p. (J). (gr. 5-8). 1995. lib. bdg. 18.90 (*0-8050-2991-5*) TFC Bks NY.

— ESP. (Mysteries of Science Ser.). (Illus.). 48p. (J). (gr. 3-6). 1996. lib. bdg. 20.90 (*0-7613-0012-0*) Millbrook Pr.

— Fires. LC 98-49175. (Watts Library: Disasters). 1999. 24.00 (*0-531-20343-3*) Watts.

***Landau, Elaine.** Fires. (Watts Library). (Illus.). (J). 2000. pap. 8.95 (*0-531-16423-3*) Watts.

Landau, Elaine. Fortune Telling. LC 95-47687. (Mysteries of Science Ser.). (Illus.). 48p. (J). (gr. 3-6). 1996. lib. bdg. 20.90 (*0-7613-0013-9*) Millbrook Pr.

***Landau, Elaine.** France. (Illus.). 48p. (J). (gr. 3-5). 2000. pap. 6.95 (*0-516-27023-0*) Childrens.

Landau, Elaine. Ghosts. (Mysteries of Science Ser.). (Illus.). 48p. (J). (gr. 3-6). 1995. lib. bdg. 20.90 (*1-56294-544-0*) Millbrook Pr.

— Grassland Mammals. LC 96-3892. (True Bk.). (Illus.). 48p. (J). (gr. 3-5). 1996. lib. bdg. 21.00 (*0-516-20039-9*) Childrens.

— Grassland Mammals. (True Bks.). 48p. (J). (gr. 3-5). 1997. pap. 6.95 (*0-516-26099-5*) Childrens.

***Landau, Elaine.** Hamburgers: Bad News for Cows. LC 00-22394. (Tasty Treats Ser.). 2000. write for info. (*1-57103-337-8*) Rourke Pr.

Landau, Elaine. Hooked: Talking about Addictions. LC 94-41680. (Illus.). 64p. (J). (gr. 4-6). 1995. lib. bdg. 21.90 (*1-56294-469-X*) Millbrook Pr.

***Landau, Elaine.** Independence Day. LC 00-9425. (Finding Out about Holidays Ser.). (Illus.). (J). 2001. write for info. (*0-7660-1571-8*) Enslow Pubs.

Landau, Elaine. India. LC 98-41179. (Geography Ser.). (J). 1999. 21.50 (*0-516-20982-5*) Childrens.

***Landau, Elaine.** India. (True Bks.). (J). 2000. pap. text 6.95 (*0-516-26764-7*) Childrens.

Landau, Elaine. Interracial Dating. LC 92-44814. (YA). (gr. 7 up). 1993. lib. bdg. 13.95 (*0-671-75258-8*, Julian Messner); lib. bdg. 7.95 (*0-671-75261-8*, Julian Messner) Silver Burdett Pr.

— Israel. LC 98-41192. (Geography Ser.). (J). 1999. 21.50 (*0-516-20983-3*) Childrens.

***Landau, Elaine.** Israel. (True Bks.). (J). 2000. pap. text 6.95 (*0-516-26765-5*) Childrens.

Landau, Elaine. Jellyfish. (True Bks.). 1999. lib. bdg. 6.95 (*0-516-26494-X*) Childrens.

— Jellyfish. LC 98-16116. (Animals Ser.). 47p. (J). (gr. 3-5). 1999. 21.50 (*0-516-20676-1*) Childrens.

***Landau, Elaine.** John F. Kennedy, Jr. LC 00-27659. 2000. lib. bdg. write for info. (*0-7613-1857-7*) TFC Bks NY.

Landau, Elaine. Joined at Birth: The Lives of Conjoined Twins. LC 96-38707. (First Bks.). (J). 1997. lib. bdg. 22.00 (*0-531-20331-X*) Watts.

— Jupiter. LC 90-13099. (First Bks.). (Illus.). 64p. (J). (gr. 4-6). 1991. lib. bdg. 22.00 (*0-531-20015-9*) Watts.

— Jupiter. LC 98-9917. (Watts Library: Space). 63p. (J). (gr. 5-7). 1999. 24.00 (*0-531-20387-5*) Watts.

***Landau, Elaine.** Jupiter. LC 98-9917. (Watts Library). (Illus.). (J). 2000. pap. 8.95 (*0-531-16426-8*) Watts.

Landau, Elaine. Jupiter. (First Bks.). (Illus.). 64p. (J). (gr. 4-6). 1996. reprint ed. pap. 6.95 (*0-531-15768-7*) Watts.

— Korea. LC 98-37359. (Geography Ser.). (J). 1999. 21.50 (*0-516-20984-1*) Childrens.

***Landau, Elaine.** Korea. (True Bks.). (J). 2000. pap. text 6.95 (*0-516-26766-3*) Childrens.

— Land Mines: 100 Million Hidden Killers. LC 99-50597. (Issues in Focus Ser.). (Illus.). 128p. (YA). (gr. 6 up). 2000. lib. bdg. 20.95 (*0-7660-1240-9*) Enslow Pubs.

Landau, Elaine. Living with Albinism. LC 97-1771. (First Book Ser.). (Illus.). 64p. (J). (gr. 5-8). 1997. 21.00 (*0-531-20296-8*) Watts.

— The Loch Ness Monster. LC 92-35145. (Mysteries of Science Ser.). (Illus.). 48p. (J). (gr. 3-6). 1993. lib. bdg. 20.90 (*1-56294-347-2*) Millbrook Pr.

***Landau, Elaine.** Lyme Disease. (Illus.). 63p. (J). (gr. 5-7). 2000. reprint ed. text 17.00 (*0-7881-9055-5*) DIANE Pub.

Landau, Elaine. Maritime Disasters. LC 98-46910. (Watts Library). 63p. (J). (gr. 4-7). 1999. 24.00 (*0-531-20344-1*) Watts.

***Landau, Elaine.** Maritime Disasters. (Illus.). (J). 2000. pap. 8.95 (*0-531-16427-6*) Watts.

Landau, Elaine. Mars. LC 90-13097. (First Bks.). (Illus.). 64p. (J). (gr. 4-6). 1991. lib. bdg. 22.00 (*0-531-20012-4*) Watts.

— Mars. LC 98-46327. (First Bks.). 63p. (J). (gr. 5-7). 1999. lib. bdg. 24.00 (*0-531-20388-3*) Watts.

***Landau, Elaine.** Mars. (Illus.). (J). 2000. pap. 8.95 (*0-531-16428-4*) Watts.

Landau, Elaine. Mars. (First Bks.). (Illus.). 64p. (J). (gr. 4-6). 1996. reprint ed. pap. 6.95 (*0-531-15773-3*) Watts.

— Minibeasts As Pets. LC 97-17372. (True Books--Animals Ser.). 1997. lib. bdg. 21.00 (*0-516-20388-6*) Childrens.

— Minibeasts As Pets. LC 97-17372. (True Bks.). (J). 1998. pap. text 6.95 (*0-516-26268-8*) Childrens.

— Mountain Mammals. LC 96-3893. (True Bk.). (Illus.). 48p. (J). 1996. lib. bdg. 21.00 (*0-516-20040-2*) Childrens.

— Mountain Mammals. (True Bks.). 48p. (J). 1997. pap. 6.95 (*0-516-26109-6*) Childrens.

— Multiple Births. LC 96-40224. (First Bk.). 64p. (J). 1997. 22.00 (*0-531-20309-3*) Watts.

— Near-Death Experiences. (Mysteries of Science Ser.). (Illus.). 48p. (J). (gr. 3-6). 1995. lib. bdg. 20.90 (*1-56294-543-2*) Millbrook Pr.

— Neptune. LC 90-13098. (First Bks.). (Illus.). 64p. (J). (gr. 3-5). 1991. lib. bdg. 22.00 (*0-531-20014-0*) Watts.

— Neptune. (Illus.). 64p. (J). (gr. 4-6). 1996. reprint ed. pap. 6.95 (*0-531-15774-1*) Watts.

— Norway. LC 98-37714. (Geography Ser.). (J). 1999. lib. bdg. 21.50 (*0-516-20985-X*) Childrens.

***Landau, Elaine.** Norway. (True Bks.). (J). 2000. pap. text 6.95 (*0-516-26767-1*) Childrens.

— The Nuclear Reality. LC 99-40023. 128p. (J). (gr. 7). 2000. lib. bdg. 22.90 (*0-7613-1555-1*) TFC Bks NY.

Landau, Elaine. Ocean Mammals. LC 96-17885. (True Bk.). 48p. (J). 1996. lib. bdg. 21.00 (*0-516-20041-0*) Childrens.

— Ocean Mammals. (True Bks.). 48p. (J). 1997. pap. 6.95 (*0-516-26110-X*) Childrens.

— The Ottawa. (First Bks.). (Illus.). 64p. (J). (gr. 5-8). 1996. lib. bdg. 22.00 (*0-531-20226-7*) Watts.

— The Ottawa. (First Bks.). (Illus.). 64p. (J). (gr. 5-8). 1996. pap. 6.95 (*0-531-15783-0*) Watts.

— Parkinson's Disease. LC 98-22450. (Venture Ser.). 112 p. (J). 1999. 24.00 (*0-531-11423-6*) Watts.

— Parrots & Parakeets As Pets. LC 97-21768. (True Books--Animals Ser.). 1997. 21.00 (*0-516-20385-1*) Childrens.

— Parrots & Parakeets as Pets. (True Bks.). (J). 1998. pap. text 6.95 (*0-516-26272-6*) Childrens.

***Landau, Elaine.** Peru. LC 99-14955. (True Bks.). (Illus.). 48p. (J). (gr. 3-5). 2000. 21.50 (*0-516-21174-9*) Childrens.

— Peru. (Illus.). 48p. (J). (gr. 3-5). 2000. pap. 6.95 (*0-516-27019-2*) Childrens.

Landau, Elaine. Piranhas. LC 98-16117. (Animals Ser.). (Illus.). 47p. (J). 1999. 21.50 (*0-516-20673-7*) Childrens.

— Piranhas. (True Bks.). (Illus.). 48p. (gr. 2-4). 1999. lib. bdg. 6.95 (*0-516-26498-2*) Childrens.

— The Pomo. LC 93-23264. (First Bks.). (Illus.). 64p. (J). (gr. 4-6). 1994. pap. 6.95 (*0-531-15687-7*) Watts.

— Pterodactyls. 1999. lib. bdg. 6.95 (*0-516-26500-8*) Childrens.

— Pterodactyls. LC 98-8280. (Dinosaurs Ser.). (J). 1999. 21.50 (*0-516-20447-5*) Childrens.

— Puerto Rico. LC 98-45092. (Geography Ser.). (J). 1999. 21.50 (*0-516-20986-8*) Childrens.

***Landau, Elaine.** Puerto Rico. (True Bks.). (J). 2000. pap. text 6.95 (*0-516-26770-1*) Childrens.

Landau, Elaine. The Right to Die. (Impact Bks.). (Illus.). 128p. (YA). (gr. 7-12). 1993. lib. bdg. 24.00 (*0-531-13015-0*) Watts.

— Sasquatch, Wild Man of the Woods. LC 92-35144. (Mysteries of Science Ser.). (Illus.). 48p. (J). (gr. 3-6). 1993. lib. bdg. 20.90 (*1-56294-348-0*) Millbrook Pr.

— Saturn. LC 90-13081. (First Bks.). (Illus.). 64p. (J). (gr. 3-5). 1991. lib. bdg. 22.00 (*0-531-20013-2*) Watts.

— Saturn. LC 98-46526. (Watts Library: Space). (J). (gr. 4-6). 1999. 24.00 (*0-531-20389-1*) Watts.

***Landau, Elaine.** Saturn. (Watts Library). (Illus.). (J). 2000. pap. 8.95 (*0-531-16430-6*) Watts.

Landau, Elaine. Saturn. (First Books). (Illus.). 64p. (J). (gr. 4-6). 1996. reprint ed. pap. 6.95 (*0-531-15771-7*) Watts.

— Sea Horses. (True Bks.). 1999. lib. bdg. 6.95 (*0-516-26503-2*) Childrens.

— Sea Horses. LC 98-16120. (Animals Ser.). 47p. (J). 1999. 21.50 (*0-516-20675-3*) Childrens.

— Sexual Harassment. LC 92-43748. 128p. (J). (gr. 5 up). 1993. 14.95 (*0-8027-8265-5*); lib. bdg. 15.85 (*0-8027-8266-3*) Walker & Co.

L

— The Shawnee. (First Bks.). 64p. (J). 1997. pap. 6.95 (*0-531-15818-7*) Watts.

— The Shawnee. LC 96-5375. (First Books-Indians of the Americas). 64p. (J). (gr. 4-6). 1997. lib. bdg. 22.00 (*0-531-20247-X*) Watts.

— Short Stature: From Folklore to Fact. LC 96-42347. (First Bks.). 1997. lib. bdg. 22.00 (*0-531-20265-8*) Watts.

— Siamese Fighting Fish. (True Bks.). 1999. lib. bdg. 6.95 (*0-516-26504-0*) Childrens.

— Siamese Fighting Fish. LC 98-16119. (Animals Ser.). (J). 1999. 21.50 (*0-516-20678-8*) Childrens.

— Sibling Rivalry: Brothers & Sisters at Odds. (Illus.). 48p. (J). (gr. 4-6). 1994. lib. bdg. 19.90 (*1-56294-328-6*) Millbrook Pr.

— Space Disasters. LC 98-49176. (Watts Library: Disasters). 63p. (J). (gr. 4-7). 1999. 24.00 (*0-531-20345-X*) Watts.

*__Landau, Elaine.__ Space Disasters. (Watts Library). (Illus.). (J). 2000. pap. 8.95 (*0-531-16431-4*) Watts.

Landau, Elaine. Stalking. LC 96-5088. (Individual Titles Ser.). 120p. (J). (gr. 2-7). 1996. lib. bdg. 24.00 (*0-531-11295-0*) Watts.

— Standing Tall: Unusually Tall People. LC 96-41681. (First Bk.). (J). 1997. lib. bdg. 22.00 (*0-531-20257-7*) Watts.

— State Birds: Including the Commonwealth of Puerto Rico. LC 92-8949. (State Symbols Ser.). (Illus.). 64p. (J). 1992. lib. bdg. 24.00 (*0-531-20058-2*) Watts.

— State Flowers: Including the Commonwealth of Puerto Rico. LC 92-8950. (Our State Symbols Ser.). 64p. (YA). 1992. lib. bdg. 24.00 (*0-531-20059-0*) Watts.

— Stegosaurus. LC 98-8278. (True Bks.). 47p. 1999. lib. bdg. 6.95 (*0-516-26505-9*) Childrens.

— Stegosaurus. LC 98-8278. (Dinosaurs Ser.). (Illus.). 48p. (J). (gr. 3-5). 1999. 21.00 (*0-516-20452-1*) Childrens.

— Sugar. LC 98-47334. (Food & Nutrition Ser.). (J). 1999. 21.50 (*0-516-21027-0*) Childrens.

*__Landau, Elaine.__ Sugar. (True Bks.). (J). 2000. pap. text 6.95 (*0-516-26772-8*) Childrens.

Landau, Elaine. The Sumerians. LC 96-46898. (Cradle of Civilization Ser.). (Illus.). 64p. (J). (gr. 4-6). 1997. lib. bdg. 21.40 (*0-7613-0215-8*) Millbrook Pr.

— Teenage Drinking. LC 94-40. (Issues in Focus Ser.). (Illus.). 104p. (YA). (gr. 6 up). 1994. lib. bdg. 20.95 (*0-89490-575-9*) Enslow Pubs.

— Teenagers Talk about School. Steltenpohl, Jane, ed. LC 88-23065. 120p. (YA). (gr. 7 up). 1989. pap. 5.95 (*0-671-68148-6*, Julian Messner) Silver Burdett Pr.

— Temperate Forest Mammals. LC 96-3889. (True Bk.). (Illus.). 48p. (J). (gr. 3-5). 1996. lib. bdg. 21.00 (*0-516-20043-7*) Childrens.

— Temperate Forest Mammals. (True Bks.). 48p. (J). (gr. 3-4). 1997. pap. 6.95 (*0-516-26115-0*) Childrens.

— Tomatoes. LC 98-49387. (Food & Nutrition Ser.). (J). 1999. 21.50 (*0-516-21028-9*) Childrens.

*__Landau, Elaine.__ Tomatoes. (True Bks.). (J). 2000. pap. text 6.95 (*0-516-26773-6*) Childrens.

Landau, Elaine. Tourette's Syndrome. (Venture Ser.). (J). (gr. 5 up). 1998. lib. bdg. 24.00 (*0-531-11399-X*) Watts.

— Triceratops. LC 98-8276. (True Bks.). 47p. 1999. lib. bdg. 6.95 (*0-516-26506-7*) Childrens.

— Triceratops. LC 98-8276. (Dinosaurs Ser.). (J). 1999. 21.50 (*0-516-20453-X*) Childrens.

— Tropical Forest Mammals. LC 96-3890. (True Bk.). (Illus.). 48p. (J). 1996. lib. bdg. 21.00 (*0-516-20044-5*) Childrens.

— Tropical Forest Mammals. (True Bks.). 48p. (J). 1997. pap. 6.95 (*0-516-26116-9*) Childrens.

— Tropical Rain Forests Around the World. (First Bks.). (Illus.). 64p. (J). (gr. 5-8). 1991. pap. 6.95 (*0-531-15600-1*) Watts.

— Tuberculosis. LC 94-39305. (Venture-Health & the Human Body Ser.). (Illus.). 112p. (YA). (gr. 7-12). 1995. lib. bdg. 22.00 (*0-531-12555-6*) Watts.

— Tyrannosaurus Rex. LC 98-8277. (True Books: Continents Ser.). 1999. lib. bdg. 6.95 (*0-516-26507-5*) Childrens.

— Tyrannosaurus Rex. LC 98-8277. (Dinosaurs Ser.). (Illus.). 48p. (J). 1999. 21.50 (*0-516-20454-8*) Childrens.

— UFOs. (Mysteries of Science Ser.). (Illus.). 48p. (J). (gr. 3-6). 1995. lib. bdg. 20.90 (*1-56294-542-4*) Millbrook Pr.

— Velociraptor. (True Bks.). 1999. lib. bdg. 6.95 (*0-516-26509-1*) Childrens.

— The Warsaw Ghetto Uprising. LC 92-15851. (Illus.). 144p. (YA). (gr. 6 up). 1992. lib. bdg. 19.00 (*0-02-751392-0*, Mac Bks Young Read) S&S Childrens.

— We Survived the Holocaust. LC 91-16982. (International Affairs Ser.). (Illus.). 144p. (YA). (gr. 9-12). 1991. lib. bdg. 24.00 (*0-531-11115-6*) Watts.

— Wheat. LC 98-47333. (Food & Nutrition Ser.). (J). 1999. 21.50 (*0-516-21029-7*) Childrens.

*__Landau, Elaine.__ Wheat. (True Bks.). (J). 2000. pap. text 6.95 (*0-516-26792-2*) Childrens.

Landau, Elaine. Why Are They Starving Themselves? Understanding Anorexia Nervosa & Bulimia. LC 82-24913. (Teen Survival Library). 160p. (J). (gr. 7 up). 1983. mass mkt. 13.98 (*0-671-45582-6*, Julian Messner); mass mkt. 5.95 (*0-671-49492-9*, Julian Messner) Silver Burdett Pr.

— Wildflowers Around the World. (First Bks.). 64p. (J). (gr. 5-8). 1992. pap. 6.95 (*0-531-15649-4*) Watts.

— Yeti, Abominable Snowman of the Himalayas. LC 92-35147. (Mysteries of Science Ser.). (Illus.). 48p. (J). (gr. 3-6). 1993. lib. bdg. 20.90 (*1-56294-349-9*) Millbrook Pr.

— Your Legal Rights. LC 94-42718. 128p. (YA). 1995. 13.95 (*0-8027-8359-7*); lib. bdg. 14.85 (*0-8027-8360-0*) Walker & Co.

— Your Pet Cat. LC 97-15626. (True Books--Animals Ser.). (J). (gr. 2-4). 1997. 21.00 (*0-516-20381-9*) Childrens.

— Your Pet Cat. (True Bks.). (J). 1998. pap. text 6.95 (*0-516-26260-2*) Childrens.

— Your Pet Dog. LC 97-15627. (True Books--Animals Ser.). (J). (gr. 2-4). 1997. 20.00 (*0-516-20382-7*) Childrens.

— Your Pet Dog. (True Bks.). (J). 1998. pap. text 6.95 (*0-516-26263-7*) Childrens.

— Your Pet Gerbil. LC 97-17179. (True Books--Animals Ser.). (J). (gr. 2-4). 1997. lib. bdg. 21.00 (*0-516-20384-3*) Childrens.

— Your Pet Gerbil. (True Bks.). (J). 1998. pap. text 6.95 (*0-516-26264-5*) Childrens.

— Your Pet Hamster. LC 97-15625. (True Books--Animals Ser.). (J). (gr. 2-4). 1997. lib. bdg. 21.00 (*0-516-20383-5*) Childrens.

— Your Pet Hamster. (True Bks.). (J). 1998. pap. text 6.95 (*0-516-26265-3*) Childrens.

— Your Pet Iguana. LC 97-17311. (True Books--Animals Ser.). (J). (gr. 2-4). 1997. lib. bdg. 21.00 (*0-516-20387-8*) Childrens.

— Your Pet Iguana. (True Bks.). (J). 1998. pap. text 6.95 (*0-516-26267-X*) Childrens.

— Your Pet Tropical Fish. LC 97-17378. (True Books--Animals Ser.). (J). (gr. 2-4). 1997. 21.00 (*0-516-20386-X*) Childrens.

— Your Pet Tropical Fish. (True Bks.). (J). 1998. pap. text 6.95 (*0-516-26278-5*) Childrens.

*__Landau, Eliot A.__ U. S. Stamp Facts, 19th Century. LC 99-27081. 1999. write for info. (*0-940403-81-1*) Linns Stamp News.

Landau, Ellen, et al. Twenty-Five Years: A Retrospective. (Illus.). 78p. 1993. pap. text 20.00 (*1-880353-04-0*) Cleveland Ctr.

Landau, Ellen G. Jackson Pollock. (Illus.). 283p. 1989. 75.00 (*0-8109-3702-6*, Pub. by Abrams) Time Warner.

— Lee Krasner: A Catalogue Raisonne. LC 94-41535. (Illus.). 336p. 1995. 150.00 (*0-8109-3513-9*, Pub. by Abrams) Time Warner.

Landau, Erica. Courage to Be Gifted. 1992. pap. 14.99 (*0-89824-527-3*) Trillium Pr.

Landau, Frieda W., jt. auth. see Landau, Alan M.

Landau, Fuller J. & Landau, Mann J. The Accounting Profession in Canada. LC HF5616.C2A33. (Professional Accounting in Foreign Countries Ser.). 75p. reprint ed. pap. 30.00 (*0-7837-0278-7*, 204059900017) Bks Demand.

Landau, George W., et al. Latin America at a Crossroads: The Challenge to the Trilateral Countries. (Triangle Papers: Vol. 39). 1990. 6.00 (*0-930503-62-7*) Trilateral Comm.

Landau, Gertrude, jt. auth. see Kubie, Susan H.

Landau, H. Moments in Mathematics. LC 87-19384. (Proceedings of Symposia in Applied Mathematics Ser.: Vol. 37). 154p. 1987. pap. 33.00 (*0-8218-0114-7*, PSAPM/37) Am Math.

*__Landau, Herbert.__ Full Deck. 2000. pap. write for info. (*1-58235-434-0*) Watermrk Pr.

Landau, I. D., et al. Adaptive Control. Dickinson, B. W. et al, eds. LC 97-29211. (Communications & Control Engineering Ser.). (Illus.). xx, 562p. 1997. 109.00 (*3-540-76187-X*) Spr-Verlag.

Landau, Jacob, jt. auth. see Hoffmann, E. T. A.

Landau, Jacob M. The Arab Minority in Israel, 1967-1991: Political Aspects. LC 92-26238. (Illus.). 246p. 1993. text 39.95 (*0-19-827712-1*, Clarendon Pr) OUP.

Landau, Jacob M. Arabs in Israel: A Political Study. (Royal Institute of International Affairs Ser.). 1969. 14.50 (*0-19-214977-6*) OUP.

— The Hejaz Railway & the Muslim Pilgrimage: A Case of Ottoman Political Propaganda. LC 78-12918. 295p. reprint ed. pap. 91.50 (*0-608-16602-2*, 202767600055) Bks Demand.

— Middle Eastern Themes: Papers in History & Politics. 309p. 1973. 49.50 (*0-7146-2969-3*, Pub. by F Cass Pubs) Intl Spec Bk.

— Pan-Turkism: From Irredentism to Cooperation. 2nd rev. ed. LC 94-42974. 256p. 1995. pap. 14.95 (*0-253-20960-9*); text 35.00 (*0-253-32869-1*) Ind U Pr.

— The Politics of Pan-Islam: Ideology & Organization. 448p. 1990. 110.00 (*0-19-827709-1*) OUP.

— The Politics of Pan-Islam: Ideology & Organization. 448p. 1994. reprint ed. pap. 22.00 (*0-19-827948-5*) OUP.

Landau, Jacob M., jt. ed. see Heper, Metin.

Landau, Jennifer H., jt. auth. see Westcott, Jean.

Landau, John. A Thing Divided: Representation in the Late Novels of Henry James. 1995. write for info. (*0-614-96419-9*) Fairleigh Dickinson.

— A Thing Divided: Representation in the Late Novels of Henry James. LC 95-53134. 192p. 1996. 32.50 (*0-8386-3626-8*) Fairleigh Dickinson.

Landau, Julie. Beyond Spring: TZU Poems of the Sung Dynasty. 1997. pap. text 17.00 (*0-231-09679-8*) Col U Pr.

Landau, Julie, tr. Beyond Spring: Tzu Poems of the Sung Dynasty. (Translations from the Asian Classics Ser.). 275p. 1994. 34.50 (*0-231-09678-X*) Col U Pr.

Landau, Katie, jt. auth. see Landau, Carl.

Landau, Ken, ed. see Nenshel, Robert P.

Landau, L., jt. auth. see Taussig, Lynn.

Landau, L. D. Course of Theoretical Physics Vol. 7: Theory of Elasticity. 3rd ed. 195p. 2000. pap. text 56.95 (*0-7506-2633-X*) Buttrwrth-Heinemann.

— Course of Theoretical Physics Vol. 8: Electro Dynamic. 2nd ed. 460p. 2000. pap. text 56.95 (*0-7506-2634-8*) Buttrwrth-Heinemann.

— Course of Theoretical Physics Vol. 9: Statistical Physics, Pt. 2, 1980. 387p. 2000. pap. text 56.95 (*0-7506-2636-4*, Prgamon Press) Buttrwrth-Heinemann.

— Fluid Mechanics. (Course of Theoretical Physics Ser.: No. 6). 536p. 1959. pap. 22.00 (*0-317-66821-8*, Pergamon Pr) Elsevier.

— Fluid Mechanics. 2nd ed. 552p. 2000. pap. text 56.95 (*0-7506-2767-0*) Buttrwrth-Heinemann.

— Quantum Mechanics, Vol. 3. 3rd ed. 689p. 2000. pap. text 49.95 (*0-7506-3539-8*) Buttrwrth-Heinemann.

Landau, L. D. & Lifshitz, E. M. Fluid Mechanics. 2nd ed. LC 86-30498. (Illus.). 551p. 1987. pap. text 48.00 (*0-08-033932-8*, Prgamon Press) Buttrwrth-Heinemann.

— Fluid Mechanics. 2nd ed. LC 86-30498. No. 6. (Illus.). 551p. 1987. text 130.00 (*0-08-033933-6*, Prgamon Press) Buttrwrth-Heinemann.

— Quantum Mechanics. LC 74-167927. (Shorter Course Theoretical Physics Ser.: Vol. 2). 1974. 166.00 (*0-08-017801-4*, Pub. by Pergamon Repr) Franklin.

— A Shorter Course of Theoretical Physics, Set. Incl. Vol. 1. Mechanics & Electrodynamics. LC 74-167927. 1972. text 135.00 (*0-08-016739-X*, CRC Reprint); LC 74-167927. 1992. text. write for info. (*0-08-025049-1*, Pub. by Pergamon Repr) Franklin.

— Statistical Physics, Vol. 1. 3rd rev. enl. ed. Sykes, J. B. & Kearsley, M. J., trs. from RUS. LC 78-40140.Tr. of Statisticheskaia fizika. (Illus.). 1980. text 160.00 (*0-08-023039-3*, Pergamon Pr) Elsevier.

Landau, L. D., jt. auth. see Berestetskii, V. B.

Landau, L. D., jt. auth. see Smorodinskii, Iakov A.

Landau, L. D., jt. ed. see Khalatnikov, Isaac M.

Landau, Laura G., jt. auth. see Myers, Lois M.

Landau, Lawrence J. & Taylor, John G., eds. Concepts for Neural Networks: A Survey. LC 97-23815. (Perspectives in Neural Computing Ser.). xv, 307p. 1997. pap. 69.95 (*3-540-76163-2*) Spr-Verlag.

Landau, Lois & Myers, Laura G. Too Many Tomatoes, Squash, Beans, & Other Good Things: A Cookbook for When Your Garden Explodes. LC 75-34581. (Illus.). 304p. 1991. reprint ed. pap. 16.00 (*0-06-096857-5*, Perennial) HarperTrade.

Landau, Luis. Poland Country Assistance Review: Partnership in a Transition Economy. LC 97-17871. (Operations & Evaluation Study Ser.). 152p. 1997. pap. 22.00 (*0-8213-3980-X*, 13980) World Bank.

Landau, Mann J., jt. auth. see Landau, Fuller J.

Landau, Marsha, jt. ed. see Lesh, Richard.

Landau, Matthew. Introduction to Aquaculture. LC 91-4714. 464p. (C). 1991. text 87.95 (*0-471-61146-8*) Wiley.

— Poisonous & Venomous Animals. 84p. 1996. pap. text, per. 29.95 (*0-7872-0731-4*) Kendall-Hunt.

— Poisonous, Venomous, & Electric Marine Organisms of the Atlantic Coast, Gulf of Mexico, & the Caribbean. (Illus.). 218p. 1997. 29.95 (*0-937548-36-7*); pap. 19.95 (*0-937548-33-2*) Plexus Pub.

Landau, Michael. Accountant - Auditor. 8th ed. 208p. 1983. per. 14.95 (*0-671-87427-6*, Arc) IDG Bks.

Landau, Michael, jt. auth. see Lindey, Alexander.

Landau, Misia. Narratives of Human Evolution. (Illus.). 216p. (C). 1991. 32.50 (*0-300-04940-4*) Yale U Pr.

— Narratives of Human Evolution. LC 90-45177. 216p. (C). 1993. reprint ed. pap. 16.00 (*0-300-05431-9*) Yale U Pr.

Landau, Nathan. Heavenly Deceptor. 337p. (Orig.). 1994. pap. 6.50 (*0-9620285-1-7*) Sound Music Pub.

Landau, Norman J., et al. Premises Liability: Law & Practice, 4 vols. 1987. 590.00 (*0-8205-1568-X*) Bender.

Landau, Paul S. The Realm of the Word: Language, Gender & Christianity in a Southern African Kingdom. LC 94-24942. (Social History of Africa Ser.). 249p. 1995. 60.00 (*0-435-08963-3*, 08963); pap. 24.95 (*0-435-08965-X*, 08965) Heinemann.

*__Landau, Peter, et al.__ Karl von Amira Zum Gedachtnis. (Rechtshistorische Reihe Ser.). 308p. 1999. 52.95 (*3-631-35425-8*) P Lang Pubng.

Landau, Ralph. Uncaging Animal Spirits: Essays on Engineering, Entrepreneurship, & Economics. Gottron, Martha V., ed. LC 94-817. (Illus.). 380p. 1994. 46.50 (*0-262-12183-2*) MIT Pr.

Landau, Ralph, et al, eds. The Mosaic of Economic Growth. LC 95-22572. 512p. 1996. 55.00 (*0-8047-2599-3*); pap. 18.95 (*0-8047-2604-3*) Stanford U Pr.

Landau, Ralph & Jorgenson, Dale, eds. Technology & Economic Policy. 376p. 1986. text 34.95 (*0-88730-068-5*, HarpBusn) HarpInfo.

*__Landau, Ralph, et al.__ Pharmaceutical Innovation: Revolutionizing Health Care. LC 99-52121. 1999. write for info. (*0-941901-21-1*) Chem Heritage Fnd.

Landau, Ralph, jt. ed. see Jorgenson, Dale W.

Landau, Robert & Evenhuis, Frans. Hollywood Poolside: Classic Images of Legendary Stars. LC 97-4574. (Illus.). 128p. 1997. 29.95 (*1-883318-02-5*) Angel City Pr.

Landau, Robert & Kreuger, John. Corporate Trust Administration & Management. 5th ed. LC 97-44745. 512p. 1998. 63.00 (*0-231-11048-0*) Col U Pr.

Landau, Robert I. Corporate Trust Administration & Management. 4th ed. 424p. 1992. text 61.50 (*0-231-07670-3*) Col U Pr.

Landau, Robert I. & Kennedy, Joseph C. Corporate Trust Administration & Management. 3rd ed. LC 85-2607. 1985. text 63.00 (*0-231-05962-0*) Col U Pr.

Landau, Robert M., et al, eds. Emerging Office Systems. LC 82-4086. (Communication & Information Science Ser.). 336p. 1982. text 78.50 (*0-89391-075-9*) Ablx Pub.

Landau, Rom. God Is My Adventure. 417p. 1977. 27.95 (*0-8369-2848-2*) Ayer.

— Ignace Paderewski: Musician & Statesman. LC 74-24137. reprint ed. 37.50 (*0-404-12999-4*) AMS Pr.

Landau, Ronald I. The Hour of the Milk Is No Longer White. LC 92-90089. 156p. (Orig.). 1992. pap. 8.95 (*1-881215-00-8*) Landau & Assocs.

Landau, Ronnie S. The Nazi Holocaust. 372p. 1994. pap. 14.95 (*1-56663-052-5*, Elephant Paperbacks); text 27.50 (*1-56663-054-1*) I R Dee.

— Studying the Holocaust: Issues, Readings, & Documents. LC 97-51127. 208p. (YA). 1998. pap. 22.99 (*0-415-16144-4*) Routledge.

— Studying the Holocaust: Issues, Readings, & Documents. LC 97-51127. (Illus.). 197p. (C). 1998. 75.00 (*0-415-16143-6*) Routledge.

Landau, Rubin & Mejia, Manuel J. Computational Physics: Problem Solving with Computers. LC 96-51776. 552p. 1997. 79.95 incl. disk (*0-471-11590-8*) Wiley.

Landau, Rubin H. Quantum Mechanics II: A Second Couse in Quantum Theory. 2nd ed. LC 95-17502. 520p. 1995. pap. 69.95 (*0-471-11608-4*, Wiley-Interscience) Wiley.

Landau, Rubin H., et al. A Scientist's & Engineer's Guide to Workstations & Supercomputers: Coping with UNIX, RISC, Vectors, & Programming. LC 92-19556. 416p. 1992. 89.95 incl. disk (*0-471-53271-1*) Wiley.

Landau, Sarah B. George B. Post, Architect: Picturesque Designer & Determined Realist. LC 98-20359. 224p. 1998. 45.00 (*1-885254-92-X*, Pub. by Monacelli Pr) Penguin Putnam.

Landau, Sarah B. & Condit, Carl W. Rise of the New York Skyscraper, 1865-1913. LC 95-34061. (Illus.). 465p. 1996. 55.00 (*0-300-06444-6*) Yale U Pr.

Landau, Saul. The Guerrilla Wars of Central America: Nicaragua, El Salvador & Guatemala. 211p. 1993. 35.00 (*0-297-82114-8*) Inst Policy Stud.

— My Dad Was Not Hamlet. Ferry, Carol, ed. 85p. (Orig.). 1993. pap. 9.95 (*0-89758-049-4*) Inst Policy Stud.

— Red Hot Radio: Sex, Violence & Politics at the End of the American Century. LC 98-39680. 247p. 1998. pap. 16.95 (*1-56751-146-5*); lib. bdg. 29.95 (*1-56751-147-3*) Common Courage.

Landau, Sidney, ed. The New International Webster's Compact Dictionary of the English Language: Encyclopedic Edition. rev. ed. (Illus.). 864p. 1999. 24.95 (*1-888777-97-4*) Trident Pr Intl.

— The New International Webster's Family Dictionary. deluxe rev. ed. (Illus.). 864p. 1999. 24.95 (*1-888777-99-0*) Trident Pr Intl.

Landau, Sidney I. Bantam Collegiate Roget's Thesaurus. 1987. 10.60 (*0-606-03048-4*, Pub. by Turtleback) Demco.

— Cambridge Dictionary of American English. LC 99-33397. (Illus.). 1088p. 1999. pap. 15.95 (*0-521-47761-1*); pap. 20.95 incl. cd-rom (*0-521-77974-X*) Cambridge U Pr.

Landau, Sidney I., ed. International Dictionary of Medicine & Biology. (Illus.). 3200p. 1988. text 495.00 (*0-471-01849-X*) Church.

— The New International Webster's Concise Dictionary of the English Language: Deluxe Padded Edition. rev. ed. Orig. Title: The Illustrated Contemporary Dictionary-Encyclopedic. (Illus.). 1070p. 1998. 49.95 (*1-888777-10-9*) Trident Pr Intl.

— The New International Webster's Concise Dictionary of the English Language: Standard Edition. rev. ed. Orig. Title: The Illustrated Contemporary Dictionary-Encyclopedia. (Illus.). 1070p. 1997. 39.95 (*1-888777-09-5*) Trident Pr Intl.

Landau, Sidney I., et al, eds. The New International Webster's Concise Dictionary: International Encyclopedic Edition. Orig. Title: Webster's Illustrated Contemporary Dictionary - Encyclopedic Edition. (Illus.). 1070p. 1998. reprint ed. 49.95 (*1-888777-91-5*) Trident Pr Intl.

Landau, Sidney I. & Bogus, Ronald. Doubleday Roget's Thesaurus in Dictionary Form. rev. ed. LC 86-24184. 816p. 1987. 14.95 (*0-385-23997-1*) Doubleday.

Landau, Sidney I. & Bogus, Ronald J., eds. The New International Webster's Student Dictionary. rev. ed. Orig. Title: Illustrated Contemporary Dictionary-Encyclopedic Edition. (Illus.). 864p. 1998. pap. 14.99 (*1-888777-08-7*) Trident Pr Intl.

— The New International Webster's Student Dictionary of the English Language: International Encyclopedic Edition. rev. ed. Orig. Title: Illustrated Contemporary Dictionary-Encyclopedic Edition. (Illus.). 864p. 1998. 24.95 (*1-888777-01-X*, 2495) Trident Pr Intl.

Landau, Sidney M. & Bogus, Ronald J., eds. The Bantam Roget's Thesaurus. 804p. 1991. mass mkt. 5.99 (*0-553-28769-9*) Bantam.

Landau, Sol. Turning Points. 1986. 13.95 (*0-88282-017-6*) New Horizon NJ.

— Turning Points: Self-Renewal at Mid-Life. 1992. pap. 11.95 (*0-88282-109-1*) New Horizon NJ.

Landau-Stanton, Judith & Clements, Colleen D. AIDS, Health, & Mental Health: A Primary Sourcebook. LC 92-30578. 360p. 1993. text 41.95 (*0-87630-688-1*) Brunner-Mazel.

Landau, Susan, jt. auth. see Diffie, Whitfield.

Landau-Tasseron, Ella, tr. History of al-Tabari No. 39: Biographies of the Prophet's Companions & Their Successors: al-Tabari's Supplement to His History. 320p. 1996. pap., suppl. ed. 21.95 (*0-614-21148-4*, 1488) Kazi Pubns.

— The History of al-Tabari Vol. 39: Biographies of the Prophet's Companions & Their Successors: al-Tabari's Supplement to His "History" LC 97-45138. (SUNY Series in Near Eastern Studies). 320p. (C). 1998. text 74.50 (*0-7914-2819-2*); pap. text 27.95 (*0-7914-2820-6*) State U NY Pr.

Landau, Ted. Sad Macs, Bombs & Other Disasters: And What to Do about Them. LC 92-38361. 640p. (C). 1993. pap. text 24.95 (*0-201-62207-6*) Addison-Wesley.

— Sad Macs, Bombs & Other Disasters: And What to Do about Them. 3rd ed. LC 97-220302. 992p. (C). 1997. pap. text 29.95 (*0-201-68810-7*, Pub. by Peachpit Pr) Addison-Wesley.

*__Landau, Ted.__ Sad Macs, Bombs & Other Disasters: And What to Do about Them. 4th ed. 1008p. (C). 2000. pap. 34.99 (*0-201-69963-X*) Addison-Wesley.

Landau, Ted. The Simple Process of Getting Healthy: The Total Book for Good Health & Well-Being. 66p. (Orig.). 1994. pap. 10.95 (*0-9640599-0-8*) Apollo Pub OR.

Landau, Toby, jt. auth. see Hunter, Martin.

An Asterisk (*) at the beginning of an entry indicates that the title is appearing for the first time.

L

An Asterisk (*) at the beginning of an entry indicates that the title is appearing for the first time.

Landers, Mary F. & Weaver, H. Roberta. Inclusive Education: A Process, Not a Placement. LC 96-61913. (Illus.). 268p. (Orig.). (C). 1997. pap. text 37.95 (*0-9628917-2-X*) Watersun MA.

Landers, Ray. Second Piano Accompaniments for Students & Teachers, Vol. A. 64p. 1982. pap. text 8.95 (*0-87487-922-1*) Summy-Birchard.

— Second Piano Accompaniments for Students & Teachers, Vol. B. 72p. 1982. pap. text 8.95 (*0-87487-923-X*) Summy-Birchard.

Landers, Ray, contrib. by. Is Suzuki Education Working in America? 64p. 1996. pap. text 10.95 (*0-87487-924-8*) Summy-Birchard.

Landers, Rich & Hansen, Dan. Paddle Routes of the Inland Northwest: 50 Flatwater & Whitewater Trips for Canoe & Kayak. LC 97-45681. (Illus.). 272p. 1998. pap. 14.95 (*0-89886-556-5*) Mountaineers.

***Landers, Richard A.** Western County Prison. LC 99-53529. 144p. 2000. pap. 10.95 (*1-56474-324-1*) Fithian Pr.

Landers, Robert, jt. ed. see Chase, Leslie R.

Landers, Robert K. Honest Writer. 1995. 35.00 (*0-8050-2580-4*) H Holt & Co.

Landers, Roger Rice, ed. see Ellis, Thomas B., Sr.

Landers, Sam, jt. auth. see Maday, Tom.

Landers, Susan. Advanced First Aid. (C). 1993. student ed. 14.00 (*1-881592-00-6*) Hayden-McNeil.

Landers, T. A. Professional Grooming & Care of the Racehorse. Equine Research, Inc. Research Staff, ed. & illus. by. 480p. (C). 1995. text 48.00 (*0-935842-10-1*) Equine Res.

Landers, Thomas L., et al. Electronics Manufacturing Processes. LC 93-5980. 564p. 1994. 70.60 (*0-13-176470-5*) P-H.

Landes, Cheryl. Beautiful America's Seattle. 1999. pap. text 12.95 (*0-89802-707-1*) Beautiful Am.

***Landes, Cheryl.** Beautiful America's Seattle. 1999. 19.95 (*0-89802-708-X*) Beautiful Am.

Landes, Alison. Pariswalks. 4th ed. 1995. pap. 12.95 (*0-8050-1186-2*, Owl) H Holt & Co.

Landes, Alison & Landes, Sonia. Pariswalks. rev. ed. LC 98-42822. (Henry Holt Walks Ser.). (Illus.). 320p. 1999. pap. 15.95 (*0-8050-6127-4*, Pub. by H Holt & Co) VHPS.

Landes, Burton R. The Making of a Senator, 1974: A Biography of Richard S. Schweiker. LC 75-7003. 120p. 1974. 2.50 (*0-614-13003-4*) B R Landes.

— A Study of the International Press the Shaping of Public Opinion: Supreme Court Edition - Study/Sarah Churchill Cause. 5th ed. 400p. (Orig.). 1985. pap. write for info. (*0-915568-08-X*) B R Landes.

Landes, Daniel, ed. Confronting Omnicide: Jewish Reflections on Weapons of Mass Destruction. LC 90-48358. 312p. 1991. 40.00 (*0-87668-851-2*) Aronson.

Landes, David S. Bankers & Pashas: International Finance & Economic Imperialism in Egypt. (Illus.). 370p. 1980. pap. 17.50 (*0-674-06165-9*) HUP.

— Revolution in Time: Clocks & the Making of the Modern World. (Illus.). 502p. 1985. pap. text 15.95 (*0-674-76802-7*) Belknap Pr.

— Revolution in Time: Clocks & the Making of the Modern World. LC 83-8489. (Illus.). 502p. 1983. 32.00 (*0-674-76800-0*) HUP.

***Landes, David S.** Revolution in Time: Clocks & the Making of the Modern World. (Illus.). 528p. 2000. pap. 16.95 (*0-674-00282-2*) HUP.

Landes, David S. Unbound Prometheus: Technological Change & Industrial Development in Western Europe from 1750 to the Present. 576p. (C). 1969. pap. text 29.95 (*0-521-09418-6*) Cambridge U Pr.

— The Wealth & Poverty of Nations: Why Some Are So Rich & Some So Poor. LC 97-27508. (Illus.). 650p. 1998. 30.00 (*0-393-04017-8*) Norton.

— The Wealth & Poverty of Nations: Why Some Are So Rich & Some So Poor. LC 99-462547. 658p. 1999. pap. 15.95 (*0-393-31888-5*) Norton.

Landes, Deborah. Competence in Cloze: Level B, Science. 56p. 1990. student ed. 4.25 (*0-910307-81-4*) Comp Pr.

— Competence in Cloze: Level B, Social Studies. 55p. 1989. student ed. 4.25 (*0-910307-84-9*) Comp Pr.

Landes, G. M. Report on Archaeological Work at Suw-Wanet Et-Thaniya, Tananir & Khirbet Minha (Munhata) (Bulletin of the American Schools of Oriental Research Supplements Ser.: No. 21). 117p. 1975. pap. 17.95 (*0-89130-036-8*, Pub. by Sheffield Acad) CUP Services.

***Landes, George M.** On the Way to Nineveh: Studies in Honor of George M. Landes. Cook, Stephen L. & Winter, S. C., eds. LC 99-43279. (ASOR Bks.: Vol. 4). 368p. 1999. pap. 49.95 (*0-7885-0585-8*, 855004, Pub. by Am Sch Orient Res) David Brown.

Landes, George M., ed. Report on Archaeological Work at Suwannet eth-Thaniya, Tananir, & Khirbet Minha. LC 75-30540. (American Schools of Oriental Research, Supplement Ser.: Vol. 21). 117p. 1975. text 17.50 (*0-89757-317-X*); pap. text 13.50 (*0-89757-321-8*) Am Sch Orient Res.

Landes, J. D., et al, eds. Elastic-Plastic Fracture - STP 668. 786p. 1981. 58.75 (*0-8031-0330-1*, STP668) ASTM.

— Nonlinear Fracture Mechanics Vol. II: Elastic-Plastic Fracture. LC 88-38147. (Special Technical Publication Ser.: No. STP 995). (Illus.). 625p. 1989. text 78.00 (*0-8031-1257-2*, 04-995002-30) ASTM.

Landes, Joan, jt. auth. see Levine, Sura.

Landes, Joan B. Women & the Public Sphere in the Age of the French Revolution. LC 88-3723. (Illus.). 296p. 1988. text 42.50 (*0-8014-2141-1*); pap. text 15.95 (*0-8014-9481-8*) Cornell U Pr.

Landes, Joan B., ed. Feminism, the Public & the Private. LC 97-39266. (Oxford Readings in Feminism Ser.). 518p. 1998. text 75.00 (*0-19-875203-2*); pap. text 19.95 (*0-19-875202-4*) OUP.

Landes, John D., et al, eds. Fracture Mechanics, Vol. 24. 830p. 1994. 199.00 (*0-8031-1990-9*, STP1207) ASTM.

Landes, John D., ed. see Metallurgical Society of AIME Staff.

Landes-Levi, Louise. Extinction. 1990. pap. 9.00 (*0-916258-24-6*) Woodbine Pr.

— Extinction. 32p. 1992. reprint ed. pap. 9.00 (*1-880516-10-1*) Left Hand Bks.

***Landes, Michael.** Back Door Guide to Short Term Adventures. rev. ed. LC 99-59529. 496p. 2000. pap. 19.95 (*1-58008-147-9*) Ten Speed Pr.

Landes, Michael. The Back Door Guide to Short-Term Job Adventures. LC 97-9441. 496p. 1997. pap. 21.95 (*0-89815-954-7*) Ten Speed Pr.

Landes, Richard, jt. ed. see Head, Thomas.

Landes, Richard A. Relics, Apocalypse, & the Deceits of History: Ademar of Chabannes, 989-1034. LC 94-39890. (Harvard Historical Studies). (Illus.). 416p. 1995. text 55.00 (*0-674-75530-8*, LANREL) HUP.

Landes, Richard A., ed. see Berkshire Reference Works Staff.

Landes, Rob, jt. auth. see Berger, Sidney.

Landes, Ruth. City of Women. 251p. 1994. 17.95 (*0-8263-1555-0*); pap. 17.95 (*0-8263-1556-9*) U of NM Pr.

— The Mystic Lake Sioux: Sociology of the Mdewakantonwan Santee. LC 68-9019. 232p. reprint ed. pap. 72.00 (*0-7837-5589-9*, 204538200005) Bks Demand.

— Ojibwa Sociology. LC 79-84467. (Columbia Univ. Contributions to Anthropology Ser.: Vol. 29). reprint ed. 22.00 (*0-404-50579-1*) AMS Pr.

— The Ojibwa Woman. LC 97-24489. xxx, 247p. 1997. pap. 13.00 (*0-8032-7969-8*, Bison Books) U of Nebr Pr.

— Ojibwa Woman. LC 70-82362. (Columbia Univ. Contributions to Anthropology Ser.: Vol. 31). reprint ed. 27.50 (*0-404-50581-3*) AMS Pr.

Landes, S. H., tr. see Aristophanes.

Landes, S. H., tr. see Euripides.

Landes, S. H., tr. see Ibsen, Henrik.

Landes, S. H., tr. see Moliere.

Landes, S. H., tr. see Schnitzler, Arthur.

Landes, S. H., tr. see Strindberg, August.

Landes, Sonia, jt. auth. see Landes, Alison.

Landes, William A., ed. see Ferguson, Alistair.

Landes, William A., ed. see Kemp, Robert.

Landes, William A., ed. see Morton, Carlos.

Landes, William-Alan. Aladdin n' His Magic Lamp. rev. ed. LC 89-43679. (Wondrawhopper Ser.). 51p. (J). (gr. 3-12). 1985. pap. 6.00 (*0-88734-102-0*) Players Pr.

— Aladdin n' His Magic Lamp: Director's Guide Book. LC 89-43679. (Wondrawhopper Ser.). 80p. (J). (gr. 3-12). 1985. pap., wbk. ed. 30.00 (*0-88734-003-2*) Players Pr.

— Aladdin n' His Magic Lamp: Music & Lyrics. rev. ed. (Wondrawhopper Ser.). (J). (gr. 3-12). 1985. pap. text 15.00 (*0-88734-002-4*) Players Pr.

— Alice n' Wonderland. LC 89-63870. (Wondrawhopper Ser.). (Orig.). (J). (gr. 3 up). 1984. pap. 6.00 (*0-88734-112-8*) Players Pr.

— The Ambassador. LC 92-50271. 13p. (Orig.). 1992. pap. 5.00 (*0-88734-123-3*) Players Pr.

— Jack 'n the Beanstalk: Director's Guide Book. rev. ed. LC 89-43681. (Wondrawhopper Ser.). (J). (gr. 3-12). 1985. pap., teacher ed. 30.00 (*0-88734-001-6*) Players Pr.

— Jack 'n the Beanstalk: Music & Lyrics. rev. ed. (Wondrawhopper Ser.). (J). (gr. 3-12). 1985. pap. text 15.00 (*0-88734-000-8*) Players Pr.

— Jack 'n the Beanstalk: Playscript. rev. ed. LC 89-43681. (Wondrawhopper Ser.). (J). (gr. 3-12). 1985. pap. 6.00 (*0-88734-101-2*) Players Pr.

— Monologues & Scenes from World Theatre - American. LC 93-16180. (World Theatre Ser.: Vol. 5). 62p. (Orig.). 1993. pap. 8.00 (*0-88734-129-2*) Players Pr.

— Monologues & Scenes from World Theatre - Ancient Greek & Roman, Vol. 1. LC 93-16180. 100p. (Orig.). 1999. pap. 8.00 (*0-88734-125-X*) Players Pr.

— Monologues & Scenes from World Theatre - Belgian, Austrian, Scandinavian, Irish, Vol. 3. LC 93-16180. 100p. (Orig.). 1993. pap. 8.00 (*0-88734-127-6*) Players Pr.

— Monologues & Scenes from World Theatre - German, French, Spanish, Italian, Russian, Vol. 2. 100p. (Orig.). 1993. pap. 8.00 (*0-88734-126-8*) Players Pr.

— A New Competitor: Playscript. LC 91-58033. 24p. (Orig.). 1991. pap. 5.00 (*0-88734-121-7*) Players Pr.

— Performance One: Monologues for Women. 128p. (Orig.). 1991. pap. 10.00 (*0-88734-122-5*) Players Pr.

— Peter 'n the Wolf: Acting Edition. rev. ed. LC 89-69871. (Wondrawhopper Ser.). (J). (gr. 3-12). 1988. pap. 6.00 (*0-88734-106-3*) Players Pr.

— Peter 'n the Wolf: Director's Guide Book. rev. ed. LC 89-69871. (Wondrawhopper Ser.). (J). (gr. 3-12). 1988. pap., teacher ed. 30.00 (*0-88734-013-X*) Players Pr.

— Rapunzel 'n the Witch. rev. ed. LC 89-43682. (Wondrawhopper Ser.). (J). (gr. 3-12). 1985. pap. 6.00 (*0-88734-107-1*) Players Pr.

— Rapunzel 'n the Witch: Director's Guide Book. rev. ed. LC 89-43682. (Wondrawhopper Ser.). (J). (gr. 3-12). 1985. pap., teacher ed. 30.00 (*0-88734-007-5*) Players Pr.

— Rapunzel 'n the Witch: Music & Lyrics. rev. ed. (Wondrawhopper Ser.). (J). (gr. 3-12). 1985. pap. 15.00 (*0-88734-006-7*) Players Pr.

— Rhyme Tyme: Director's Guide. LC 87-62593. (Wondrawhopper Ser.). 1988. pap., teacher ed. 30.00 (*0-88734-009-1*) Players Pr.

— Rhyme Tyme: Playscript. rev. ed. LC 87-62593. (Wondrawhopper Ser.). (J). (gr. 3-12). 1985. pap. 6.00 (*0-88734-108-X*) Players Pr.

— Rumpelstiltskin: Director's Guide. rev. ed. LC 89-43683. (Wondrawhopper Ser.). 52p. (J). (gr. 3-12). 1985. pap., teacher ed. 30.00 (*0-88734-005-9*) Players Pr.

— Rumpelstiltskin: Playscript. rev. ed. LC 89-43683. (Wondrawhopper Ser.). 52p. (J). (gr. 3-12). 1985. pap. 6.00 (*0-88734-104-7*) Players Pr.

Landes, William-Alan, ed. Monologues & Scenes from World Theatre Vol. 4: English. 1993. pap. 8.00 (*0-88734-128-4*) Players Pr.

— Punch & Judy. LC 95-37906. (Illus.). 24p. 1995. pap. 7.00 (*0-88734-290-6*) Players Pr.

— Swan Song. Ponomarov, Sergius, tr. (Chekhov Collection). pap. 6.00 (*0-88734-375-9*) Players Pr.

Landes, William-Alan, ed. Everyman. 36p. 1995. pap. 7.00 (*0-88734-275-2*) Players Pr.

Landes, William-Alan & Lasky, Mark A. Grandpa's Bedtime Story. rev. ed. LC 89-63868. (J). (gr. 3-12). 1985. pap. 6.00 (*0-88734-505-0*) Players Pr.

Landes, William-Alan & Rizzo, Jeff. Rhyme Tyme: Music & Lyrics. rev. ed. (Wondrawhopper Ser.). (J). (gr. 3-12). 1985. pap. text 15.00 (*0-88734-008-3*) Players Pr.

— Rumpelstiltskin: Music & Lyrics. rev. ed. (Wondrawhopper Ser.). (J). (gr. 3-12). 1985. pap. text 15.00 (*0-88734-004-0*) Players Pr.

Landes, William-Alan & Standish, Marilyn. Diary of a Madman: Playscript. rev. ed. LC 90-52545. 1985. pap. 5.00 (*0-88734-109-8*) Players Pr.

— The Wizard of Oz. rev. ed. LC 89-63872. (Wondrawhopper Ser.). (J). (gr. 3-12). 1985. pap. 6.00 (*0-88734-105-5*) Players Pr.

— The Wizard of Oz: Director's Guide. rev. ed. LC 89-63872. (Wondrawhopper Ser.). (J). (gr. 3-12). 1985. pap., teacher ed. 30.00 (*0-88734-011-3*) Players Pr.

— The Wizard of Oz: Music & Lyrics. rev. ed. (Wondrawhopper Ser.). (J). (gr. 3-12). 1985. pap. 15.00 (*0-88734-010-5*) Players Pr.

Landes, William-Alan, jt. auth. see Brooke, Iris.

Landes, William-Alan, jt. auth. see Crawford, David W.

Landes, William-Alan, jt. auth. see Evans, Mary.

Landes, William-Alan, jt. auth. see Galsworthy, John.

Landes, William-Alan, jt. auth. see Jans, Martin.

Landes, William-Alan, jt. auth. see Miller, Ev.

Landes, William-Alan, ed. see Adam, Agnes.

Landes, William-Alan, ed. see Aeschylus.

Landes, William-Alan, ed. see Alvarez Quintero, Serafin & Alvarez Quintero, Joaquin.

Landes, William-Alan, ed. see Aristophanes.

Landes, William-Alan, ed. see Barker, Granville.

Landes, William-Alan, ed. see Barr, Robert.

Landes, William-Alan, ed. see Barrie, J. M.

Landes, William-Alan, ed. see Brandl, Dave.

Landes, William-Alan, ed. see Brooke, Rupert.

Landes, William-Alan, ed. see Chekhov, Anton.

Landes, William-Alan, ed. see Cook, Stephen.

Landes, William-Alan, ed. see Countryman, Ruth & Hopper, Elizabeth W.

Landes, William-Alan, ed. see Crawford, David W.

Landes, William-Alan, ed. see Davis, R. I.

Landes, William-Alan, ed. see Doyle, Arthur Conan & Reyburn, Stanley.

Landes, William-Alan, ed. see Dunsany, Lord.

Landes, William-Alan, ed. see Euripides.

Landes, William-Alan, ed. see Fass, Gertrude.

Landes, William Alan, ed. see Fife, Bruce.

Landes, William Alan, ed. see Freeman, Lynne.

Landes, William-Alan, ed. see Gilbert, W. S.

Landes, William-Alan, ed. see Gilbert, William S.

Landes, William-Alan, ed. see Gorky, Maxim.

Landes, William-Alan, ed. see Gregory, Lady A.

Landes, William-Alan, ed. see Heath, Timothy.

Landes, William-Alan, ed. see Heiss, Rolland L.

Landes, William-Alan, ed. see Hess, Michael W.

Landes, William Alan, ed. see Hezlep, William.

Landes, William-Alan, ed. see Ibsen, Henrik.

Landes, William-Alan, ed. see Kluger, Garry M.

Landes, William-Alan, ed. see Korty, Carol.

Landes, William-Alan, ed. see Langner, Lawrence.

Landes, William-Alan, ed. see Marlowe, Christopher.

Landes, William-Alan, ed. see Maxfield, John.

Landes, William-Alan, ed. see McCaslin, Nellie.

Landes, William-Alan, ed. see Middlemass, Robert & Holworthy Hall Staff.

Landes, William-Alan, ed. see Mill, Kristin L.

Landes, William-Alan, ed. see Miller, Ev.

Landes, William-Alan, ed. see Moliere.

Landes, William-Alan, ed. see Morton, Carlos.

Landes, William-Alan, ed. see Najera, Rick.

Landes, William-Alan, ed. see Orr, Bob & Orr, Helen.

Landes, William-Alan, ed. see Orr, Helen & Orr, Bob.

Landes, William-Alan, ed. see Pinero, Arthur W.

Landes, William-Alan, ed. see Pirandello, Luigi.

Landes, William-Alan, ed. see Porter, Stephen.

Landes, William-Alan, ed. see Potter, Jonathan.

Landes, William-Alan, ed. see Prior, Judith.

Landes, William-Alan, ed. see Racine, Jean.

Landes, William-Alan, ed. see Reyburn, Stanley S.

Landes, William-Alan, ed. see Richardson, Alan.

Landes, William-Alan, ed. see Ryback, Jeffrey W.

Landes, William-Alan, ed. see Sabato, George F.

Landes, William-Alan, ed. see Schnitzler, Arthur.

Landes, William-Alan, ed. see Scotland, James.

Landes, William-Alan, ed. see Shakespeare, William.

Landes, William-Alan, ed. see Shaw, George Bernard.

Landes, William-Alan, ed. see Sinclair, Jean.

Landes, William-Alan, ed. see Sitarj, Oaula G.

Landes, William-Alan, ed. see Sitarz, Paula Gaj.

Landes, William-Alan, ed. see Slesar, Henry.

Landes, William-Alan, ed. see Sophocles.

Landes, William-Alan, ed. see Sophocles, et al.

Landes, William-Alan, ed. see Steelsmith, Mary.

Landes, William-Alan, ed. see Stewart, Hal D.

Landes, William-Alan, ed. see Strindberg, August.

Landes, William-Alan, ed. see Thistle, Louise.

Landes, William-Alan, ed. see Thornton, Charles.

Landes, William-Alan, ed. see Tibbets, Mike.

Landes, William-Alan, ed. see Tracy, Jack.

Landes, William-Alan, ed. see Welch, Kevin.

Landes, William-Alan, ed. see Yeats, William Butler.

Landes, William-Alan, ed. & frwd. see Dickens, Charles.

Landes, William-Alan, ed. & frwd. see Lillo, George.

Landes, William-Alan, ed. & intro. see Addison, Joseph.

Landes, William-Alan, ed. & intro. see Chekhov, Anton.

Landes, William-Alan, ed. & intro. see Dryden, John.

Landes, William-Alan, ed. & intro. see Dunseny, Edward J.

Landes, William-Alan, ed. & intro. see Goldsmith, Oliver.

Landes, William-Alan, ed. & intro. see Marlowe, Christopher.

Landes, William-Alan, ed. & intro. see Rowe, Nicholas.

Landes, William-Alan, ed. & intro. see Shakespeare, William.

Landes, William-Alan, ed. & intro. see Shaw, George Bernard.

Landes, William-Alan, ed. & intro. see Sheridan, Richard Brinsley.

Landes, William-Alan, ed. & intro. see Sophocles.

Landes, William-Alan, ed. & intro. see Wilde, Oscar.

Landes, William-Alan, ed. & photos by see Wheeler, Jacque & Laughlin, Haller.

Landes, William-Alan, ed. & pref. see Aeschylus.

Landes, William-Alan, ed. & pref. see Shaw, George Bernard.

Landes, William-Alan, ed. & pref. see Synge, John Millington.

Landes, William-Allan, ed. see Howard, Vernon.

Landes, William-Allan, ed. & intro. see Synge, John Millington.

Landes, William M. & Posner, Richard A. The Economic Structure of Tort Law. LC 86-18450. (Illus.). 352p. 1987. 43.50 (*0-674-23051-5*) HUP.

Landes, William M., jt. ed. see Becker, Gary Stanley.

Landes, William-Alan, ed. see Gilbert, William S.

Landesco, John. Illinois Crime Survey. unexpurgated ed. Incl. Organized Crime in Chicago. LC 68-55774. 1968. LC 68-55774. (Crimson Crystal Adventures Ser.: No. 9). 1968. 40.00 (*0-87585-009-X*) Patterson Smith.

— Organized Crime in Chicago (Unexpurgated) 1968. reprint ed. write for info. (*0-318-62185-1*) Patterson Smith.

Landesman, Alter F. Brownsville. 430p. 1989. 27.50 (*0-8197-0151-3*); pap. 16.95 (*0-8197-0563-2*) Bloch.

Landesman, Charles. Color & Consciousness: An Essay in Metaphysics. LC 88-29442. 149p. (C). 1989. 24.95 (*0-87722-616-4*) Temple U Pr.

— Discourse & Its Presuppositions. LC 72-75201. 174p. reprint ed. pap. 54.00 (*0-608-14018-X*, 202201000024) Bks Demand.

— The Eye & the Mind: Reflections on Perception & the Problem of Knowledge. (Philosophical Studies in Philosophy). 170p. (C). 1993. lib. bdg. 134.50 (*0-7923-2586-9*, Pub. by Kluwer Academic) Kluwer Academic.

— An Introduction to Epistemology. LC 96-13100. 256p. 1996. 60.95 (*0-631-20212-9*); pap. 25.95 (*0-631-20213-7*) Blackwell Pubs.

Landesman, Charles, jt. ed. see Care, Norman S.

Landesman, Dovid. A Practical Guide to Torah Learning. LC 94-32902. 248p. 1996. 30.00 (*1-56821-320-4*) Aronson.

Landesman, Dovid, tr. As the Rabbis Taught: Studies in the Aggados of the Talmud - A Tishah b'Av Reader. LC 96-24685. (Tishah b'Av Reader Ser.: Vol. 2). 128p. 1996. 30.00 (*1-56821-995-4*) Aronson.

Landesman, Dovid, tr. Megillath Esther. (Illus.). 1993. 9.95 (*1-58330-164-X*) Feldheim.

Landesman, Dovid, tr. As the Rabbis Taught: The Aggados of the Talmud. LC 96-1864. 328p. 1996. 40.00 (*1-56821-949-0*) Aronson.

Landesman, Dovid, jt. auth. see Kranzler, Dovid.

Landesman, Dovid, ed. see Kitov, Eliyahu, et al.

Landesman, Dovid, tr. see Greenwald, Ze'ev.

Landesman, Earl S. The CFO Reach Awards: The Best Practices of World-Class Companies 1998. 98th ed. 1998. pap. 99.00 (*0-15-606289-5*) Harcourt Coll Pubs.

— Corporate Financal Management: Strategies for Maximizing Shareholder Wealth. LC 95-32070. 368p. 1996. 130.00 (*0-471-12353-6*) Wiley.

Landesman, Fran. Ballad of the Sad Young Men. LC 81-85724. 64p. 1982. 16.00 (*0-932966-18-7*) Permanent Pr.

— Invade My Privacy. LC 83-63244. 64p. (Orig.). 1984. pap. 16.00 (*0-932966-44-6*) Permanent Pr.

— More Truth Than Poetry. LC 80-85345. 64p. (Orig.). 1981. pap. 16.00 (*0-932966-13-6*) Permanent Pr.

Landesman, Jay. Rebel Without Applause. LC 86-62451. 286p. 1987. 22.00 (*0-932966-75-6*) Permanent Pr.

***Landesman, Peter.** Blood Acre. 272p. 2000. pap. 12.95 (*0-14-028236-X*) Penguin Putnam.

Landesman, Peter. Blood Acre. LC 98-21330. 262p. 1999. 23.95 (*0-670-78181-9*); 23.95 (*0-670-88207-0*) Viking Penguin.

— The Raven. 356p. 1995. 23.00 (*1-880909-37-5*) Baskerville.

— Raven. 368p. 1997. pap. 11.95 (*0-14-026345-4*) Viking Penguin.

— Ten Ways to Wreck a Date. (Full House Stephanie Ser.). 144p. (J). (gr. 4-7). 1996. per. 3.99 (*0-671-53548-X*, Minstrel Bks) PB.

— Two for One Christmas Fun. (Full House Stephanie Ser.). 144p. (J). (gr. 4-6). 1995. per. 3.99 (*0-671-53546-3*) PB.
Landesman, Peter, jt. auth. see Simon, Lisa.
Landesmann, Michael A. Unemployment in Europe. LC 99-15424. 1999. text 85.00 (*0-312-22630-6*) St Martin.
Landesmann, Michael A. & Scazzieri, Robert, eds. Production & Economic Dynamics. (Illus.). 373p. (C). 1996. text 69.95 (*0-521-46251-7*) Cambridge U Pr.
Landesmann, Michael A. & Szekely, Istvan P., eds. Industrial Restructuring & Trade Reorientation in Eastern Europe. (Department of Applied Economics, Occasional Papers: No. 60). 391p. (C). 1995. text 69.95 (*0-521-48085-X*) Cambridge U Pr.
Landesmusem Joanneum, ed. Shiny Shapes: Arms & Armor from the Zeughaus Graz. (Illus.). 220p. 1999. 50.00 (*3-211-83098-7*, Pub. by Spr-Verlag) Princeton Arch.
Landess, Thomas, jt. auth. see Quinn, Richard.
Landess, Thomas H. The Short Fiction of Caroline Gordon: A Critical Symposium. LC 72-81278. 133p. 1972. 4.95 (*0-911005-34-X*) Dallas Inst Pubns.
Landey, Peter M., jt. auth. see Reicha, Anton.
Landfester, Manfred. Das Griechische Nomen "Philos" und Seine Ableitungen. (GER.). xi, 196p. 1966. write for info. (*0-318-70616-4*) G Olms Pubs.
— Handlungsverlauf und Komik in den Fruehen Komoedien des Aristophanes. (Untersuchungen zur Antiken Literatur und Geschichte Ser.: Vol. 17). (C). 1977. 115.40 (*3-11-006950-4*) De Gruyter.
Landfield, Alvin W. & Epting, Franz R. Personal Construct Psychology: Clinical & Personality Assessment. LC 86-10477. 327p. 1986. 51.95 (*0-89885-315-X*, Kluwer Acad Hman Sci); pap. 24.95 (*0-89885-318-4*, Kluwer Acad Hman Sci) Kluwer Academic.
Landfield, Alvin W., jt. ed. see Epting, Franz R.
Landfield, Alvin W., ed. see Nebraska Symposium on Motivation Staff.
Landfield, Lonie, ed. see Andringa, Patty P.
Landfried, Christine, ed. Constitutional Review & Legislation: An International Comparison. 266p. 1988. 81.00 (*3-7890-1640-3*, Pub. by Nomos Verlags) Intl Bk Import.
Landgarten, Helen. Magazine Photo Collage: A Multicultural Assessment & Treatment Technique. LC 93-16792. (Illus.). 224p. 1993. text 31.95 (*0-87630-706-3*) Brunner-Mazel.
Landgarten, Helen B. Clinical Art Therapy: A Comprehensive Guide. LC 80-22564. 416p. 1987. text 34.95 (*0-87630-237-1*) Brunner-Mazel.
— Family Art Psychotherapy: A Clinical Guide & Casebook. LC 86-28380. (Illus.). 320p. 1987. text 38.95 (*0-87630-456-0*) Brunner-Mazel.
Landgarten, Helen B. & Lubbers, Darcy, eds. Adult Art Psychotherapy: Issues & Applications. LC 90-15103. (Illus.). 224p. 1991. text 32.95 (*0-87630-593-1*) Brunner-Mazel.
Landgraf, Anne K. Na Wahi Pana o Ko'olau Poko: Legendary Places of Ko'olau Poko. Meinecke, Fred K., tr. from HAW. LC 94-12427. (Illus.). 176p. (C). 1994. text 34.00 (*0-8248-1578-5*) UH Pr.
Landgraf, Arthur. Commentarius Cantabrigiensis in Epistolas Pauli e Schola Petri Abaelardi, 3 vols. Incl. Vol. 1. In Epistolam Ad Romanos. 223p. 1937. 17.95 (*0-268-00133-2*); Vol. 2. In Epistolam Ad Corinthios Iam et Iiam, Ad Galatas et Ad Ephesios. 1223p. 1960. 17.95 (*0-268-00134-0*); Vol. 3. In Epistolam ad Philippenses, ad Colossenses, ad Thessalonicenses Primam et Secundam, ed Timotheam Priman et Secundam, ad Titum et Philemonem. 447p. 1944. 17.95 (*0-268-00132-4*); (Mediaeval Studies Ser.: No. 2). write for info. (*0-318-56117-4*) U of Notre Dame Pr.
Landgraf, Ed. Luxury in the Rough. LC 97-75984. 144p. 1998. pap. 12.95 (*1-57197-102-5*) Pentland Pr.
Landgraf, Gustav. Kommentar Zu Ciceros Rede Pro Sexto Roscio Amerino. vii, 290p. 1978. reprint ed. write for info. (*3-487-01183-2*) G Olms Pubs.
Landgraf, John R. Creative Singlehood & Pastoral Care. LC 82-7439. (Creative Pastoral Care & Counseling Ser.). 95p. reprint ed. pap. 30.00 (*0-608-17914-0*, 202909800058) Bks Demand.
— Singling: A New Way to Live the Single Life. 180p. (Orig.). 1990. pap. 15.95 (*0-664-25086-6*) Westminster John Knox.
Landgraf, Michael. Mind States: An Introduction to Light & Sound Technology. unabridged ed. LC 97-97223. (Illus.). 92p. 1997. pap. 12.98 (*0-9662596-0-2*) Little Minnies.
Landgraf, Otto. Oldtimer Sewing Machine. Forsdyke, Graham, tr. from GER. (Illus.). 192p. 1992. reprint ed. 29.00 (*3-926879-06-8*, Pub. by Weppert GmbH) A Stitch Back.
Landgraf, R., jt. ed. see Mitchell, M. R.
Landgraf, R. W., jt. ed. see Mitchell, M. R.
Landgraf, Sherry. Love's Voyage. Bradbury, Dianne & Bare, Wanda, eds. LC 95-67506. 436p. 1995. 23.95 (*0-9644981-0-3*) Donnabelle Pub.
Landgrebe, A. R., et al, eds. Proceedings of the Workshop on Direct Methanol-Air Fuel Cells. LC 92-81870. (Proceedings Ser.: Vol. 92-14). 224p. 1992. 46.00 (*1-56677-015-7*) Electrochem Soc.
— Proton Conducting Membrane Fuel Cells. LC 95-61596. (Proceedings Ser.: Vol. 95-23). (Illus.). 318p. 1995. 61.00 (*1-56677-118-8*) Electrochem Soc.
Landgrebe, A. R. & Holmes, Curtis F., eds. Batteries for Portable Applications & Electric Vehicles. LC 97-211260. (Proceedings Ser.: Vol. 97-18). 996p. 1997. 98.00 (*1-56677-146-3*) Electrochem Soc.
Landgrebe, A. R. & Takehara, Z. R., eds. Proceedings of the Symposium on Batteries & Fuel Cells for Stationary & Electric Vehicle Applications. LC 93-70052. (Proceedings Ser.: Vol. 93-8). 342p. 1993. 43.00 (*1-56677-055-6*) Electrochem Soc.
Landgrebe, A. R., jt. ed. see Doddapaneni, N.
***Landgrebe, Gary.** Tofu Goes West. LC 99-33921. 128p. 1999. pap. 12.95 (*1-58091-047-5*) Crossing Pr.
Landgrebe, John A. Theory & Practice in the Organic Laboratory: With Microscale & Standard Scale Experiments. 4th ed. 1993. mass mkt., teacher ed. write for info. (*0-534-16855-8*) Brooks-Cole.
— Theory & Practice in the Organic Laboratory: With Microscale & Standard Scale Experiments. 4th ed. LC 92-32949. 573p. 1993. mass mkt. 54.25 (*0-534-16854-X*) Brooks-Cole.
Landgren, Le. Old Mother Bear's Book of Hug Rhymes. LC 88-38973. (Illus.). 40p. (Orig.). (J). (ps-9). 1989. pap. 6.95 (*0-943367-02-6*) Princess Pub.
Landgren, Le, see Le Landgren.
Landgren, Signe M. The Baltic States: New Participants in the European Security Debate. (SIPRI Research Reports: No. 14). 150p. 2000. text 49.95 (*0-19-829277-5*); pap. text 24.95 (*0-19-829276-7*) OUP.
Landham, Sonny. The Total Man. LC 79-11128. 1981. 21.95 (*0-87949-157-4*) Ashley Bks.
Landheer. World Society. 1971. pap. text 46.00 (*90-247-5088-1*, Pub. by M Nijhoff) Kluwer Academic.
Landholt, Thomas. Automating the Medical Record. Stanley, Kay, ed. 1998. 44.95 (*0-89970-909-5*) AMA.
Landholt, Thomas & Coker Group Staff. Managing the Outpatient Medical Practice: Strategies for a Changing Environment. LC 98-20745. 127p. 1998. 35.00 (*1-55648-242-6*) AHPI.
Landi, Giovanni. An Introduction to Noncommutative Spaces & Their Geometries. Beiglbsck, W. et al, eds. LC 97-31663. (Lecture Notes in Physics Ser.). (Illus.). xi, 200p. 1997. 49.00 (*3-540-63509-2*) Spr-Verlag.
Landi, Nina. 125 Things You Must Know about Being Pregnant. LC 98-2644. (Illus.). 48p. 1998. pap. 9.95 (*0-8050-5860-5*, Owl) H Holt & Co.
Landi, Sheila. Textile Conservator's Manual. 2nd ed. LC 98-160005. 364p. 1998. pap. text 59.95 (*0-7506-3897-4*) Buttrwrth-Heinemann.
***Landi, Stefano.** Stefano Landi - La Morte D'Orfeo: Tragicommedia Pastorale. Herzog, Sylvia, ed. (Illus.). xxxviii, 133p. 1999. pap. 65.00 (*0-89579-444-6*) A-R Eds.
Landies, Douglas C. Sensitive Spots: Nine Drawings. (Illus.). 1978. pap. 4.00 (*0-935350-89-6*) Luna Bisonte.
Landim, Claudio, jt. auth. see Kipnis, Claude.
Landim, Leilah. Defining the Nonprofit Sector: Brazil. Salamon, Lester M. & Anheier, Helmut K., eds. (Working Papers of the Johns Hopkins Comparative Nonprofit Sector Project: No. 9). (Illus.). 22p. 1993. pap. text 6.00 (*1-886333-11-4*) JH Univ Inst Pol Studies.
Landin, Joseph. Introduction to Algebraic Structure. 247p. 1989. pap. 8.95 (*0-486-65940-2*) Dover.
— An Introduction to Ordinary Differential Equations. 304p. 1989. pap. 8.95 (*0-486-65942-9*) Dover.
Landin, Les & Hagelin, Linda. 100 Blackboard Games Series, 4 bks., Set. 26.99 (*1-56417-772-6*, FE0060) Fearon Teacher Aids.
— 100 Blackboard Math Activities. (100 Blackboard Games Ser.). 48p. 6.99 (*0-86653-921-2*, FE0921) Fearon Teacher Aids.
— 100 Blackboard Problem-Solving Activities. (100 Blackboard Games Ser.). 48p. 6.99 (*0-86653-922-0*, FE0922) Fearon Teacher Aids.
— 100 Blackboard Science Activities. (100 Blackboard Games Ser.). 48p. 6.99 (*0-86653-920-4*, FE0920) Fearon Teacher Aids.
Landin, Leslie & Gardner, Mary. Homework Sweet Homework. (YA). 1990. pap. 5.99 (*0-8224-3603-5*) Fearon Teacher Aids.
Landin, Leslie & Hagelin, Linda. 100 Blackboard Games. rev. ed. 48p. (J). (gr. 1-6). 6.99 (*0-86653-919-0*, FE0919) Fearon Teacher Aids.
Landin, Leslie & Meredith, Paul. One Hundred Activities for Gifted Children. 1957. pap. 5.99 (*0-8224-5050-X*) Fearon Teacher Aids.
Landin, Leslie & Thibault, Frank. Creative Chalkboard Activities. 1986. pap., teacher ed. 5.99 (*0-8224-1636-0*) Fearon Teacher Aids.
Landing, B. H., et al, eds. Genetic Metabolic Diseases. (Perspectives in Pediatric Pathology Ser.: Vol. 17). (Illus.). xiv, 190p. 1993. 208.75 (*3-8055-5581-4*) S Karger.
Landing, Benjamin H. Factors in the Distribution of Butterfly Color & Behavior Patterns: Selected Aspects. (Illus.). ii, 200p. 1984. pap. 17.95 (*0-911836-13-6*) Entomological Repr.
Landing, Ed, ed. Dynamic Stratigraphy & Depositional Environments of the Hamilton Group (Middle Devonian) in New York State, Pt. II. (Bulletin Ser.: No. 469). (Illus.). 177p. (Orig.). (C). 1991. pap. text 20.00 (*1-55557-183-2*) NYS Museum.
— Studies in Stratigraphy & Paleontology in Honor of Donald W. Fisher. (Bulletin Ser.: No. 481). (Illus.). 380p. 1994. 25.00 (*1-55557-196-4*) NYS Museum.
Landing, Ed & Westrop, Stephen R., eds. Avalon 1997: The Cambrian Standard. (New York State Museum Bulletin Ser.: No. 492). (Illus.). 92p. 1998. pap. text 14.95 (*1-55557-209-X*) NYS Museum.
Landing, Ed, et al. Silurian Cycles: Linkages of Dynamic Stratigraphy with Atmospheric, Oceanic & Tectonic Changes LC 98-60308. (Bulletin Ser.). ix, 327p. 1998. write for info. (*1-55557-206-5*) NYS Museum.
Landing, Ed, ed. see Goloring, Winifred.
Landing, James E. Reaching Mount Zion: The Origins & Impact of Black Judaism. LC 97-13610. 1997. write for info. (*0-89089-820-0*) Carolina Acad Pr.
Landingham, Hugh F. Van, see Bingulac, Stanoje & Van Landingham, Hugh F.
Landini, Gregory. Russell's Hidden Substitutional Theory. (Illus.). 352p. 1998. text 85.00 (*0-19-511683-6*) OUP.
Landini, Michael J., Jr. ADA Source Book: What You Need to Know about the Americans with Disabilities Act: A Guide for Small & Medium Size Business. 70p. 1991. 9.95 (*0-88713-624-9*) Nat Alliance.
Landis. Sociology. 7th ed. (C). 1998. student ed. 16.75 (*0-534-52867-8*) Wadsworth Pub.
***Landis.** Sociology: Concepts & Characteristics. 11th ed. (Sociology - Intro Level Ser.). 2000. 29.00 (*0-534-57861-6*) Wadsworth Pub.
Landis. Sociology-Concepts. 5th ed. (Sociology - Introductory Level Ser.). 1983. pap., teacher ed. write for info. (*0-534-01382-1*) Wadsworth Pub.
Landis, et al. Building a Healthier Tomorrow: A Manual for Rural Coalition Building, 01. 138p. (C). 1996. 23.95 (*0-7872-2655-6*, 41265501) Kendall-Hunt.
Landis, Andrew. Social Security: The Inside Story. 2nd rev. ed. LC 97-68503. (Professional Ser.). 160p. 1997. pap. 15.95 (*1-56052-452-9*) Crisp Pubns.
Landis, Andy, jt. auth. see Shelton, Bettye.
Landis, Arthur H. Spain, the Unfinished Revolution. LC 75-21091. 463p. reprint ed. pap. 143.60 (*0-7837-0583-2*, 204092700019) Bks Demand.
Landis, Benson Y. An Outline of the Bible: Book by Book. (Illus.). 192p. (Orig.). 1994. pap. 14.00 (*0-06-463263-6*, EH 263, Harper Ref) HarpC.
— Professional Codes: A Sociological Analysis to Determine Applications to the Educational Profession. LC 70-176974. (Columbia University. Teachers College. Contributions to Education Ser.: No. 267). reprint ed. 37.50 (*0-404-55267-6*) AMS Pr.
Landis, Bernard. Ego Boundaries. LC 70-138248. (Psychological Issues Monographs: No. 24, Vol. 6, No. 4). 177p. 1970. 27.50 (*0-8236-1570-7*) Intl Univs Pr.
Landis, Bob. The Remnant. 208p. 1999. pap. write for info. (*0-7392-0204-9*, PO3208) Morris Pubng.
Landis, Brook I. Value Judgments in Arbitration: A Case Study of Saul Wallen. LC 77-8131. (Cornell Studies in Industrial & Labor Relations: No. 19). 200p. 1977. text 16.95 (*0-87546-063-1*, ILR Press) Cornell U Pr.
Landis, Carney & Bolles, M. Marjorie. Personality & Sexuality in the Physically Handicapped Woman. Phillips, William R. & Rosebberg, Janet, eds. LC 79-6912. (Physically Handicapped in Society Ser.). 1980. reprint ed. lib. bdg. 19.95 (*0-405-13121-6*) Ayer.
Landis, Carney & Page, James D. Modern Society & Mental Disease. Grob, Gerald N., ed. LC 78-22571. (Historical Issues in Mental Health Ser.). (Illus.). 1980. reprint ed. lib. bdg. 18.95 (*0-405-11924-0*) Ayer.
Landis, Carolyn P., jt. auth. see Poage, James.
Landis, Carolyn P., jt. auth. see Rowell, Harry.
Landis, Charles S. Hunting with the Twenty-Two. 429p. 1993. 35.00 (*1-884849-01-6*) R&R Bks.
— Twenty-Two Caliber Varmint Rifles. 1991. 32.00 (*0-935632-60-3*) Wolfe Pub Co.
— Woodchucks & Woodchuck Rifle. (Library Classics). 402p. 1988. reprint ed. 42.00 (*0-935632-62-X*) Wolfe Pub Co.
Landis, Christine, jt. ed. see Harris, Maxine.
***Landis, Christopher.** In Search of Eldorado: The Salton Sea. (Illus.). 48p. 2000. pap. 29.95 (*0-9678595-0-6*) C Landis.
Landis, Dan & Bhagat, Rabi, eds. Handbook of Intercultural Training. 2nd ed. 460p. 1995. 65.00 (*0-8039-5833-1*); pap. 29.95 (*0-8039-5834-X*) Sage.
Landis, Dorothy K., ed. Landis. Report of the 31st Reunion of the Landis-Landes Families Held at Perkasie Park, Perkasie, Bucks Co., Pa., 8/19/50. 65p. 1996. reprint ed. pap. 13.00 (*0-8328-5278-3*); reprint ed. lib. bdg. 23.00 (*0-8328-5277-5*) Higginson Bk Co.
Landis, Dwight. Trout Streams of Pennsylvania: An Angler's Guide. 2nd ed. LC 95-75138. (Illus.). 248p. 1995. pap. 18.95 (*1-879475-01-4*) Hempstead-Lyndell.
***Landis, Dwight.** Trout Streams of Pennsylvania: An Angler's Guide. 3rd ed. (Illus.). 238p. 2000. pap. 20.95 (*1-879475-02-2*) Hempstead-Lyndell.
Landis, Dylan. Checklist for Your New Baby: The Indispensable Guide to What to Buy Before Your Baby Arrives. 112p. 1991. pap. 5.95 (*0-399-51657-3*, Perigee Bks) Berkley Pub.
— Designing for Small Homes. (Illus.). 176p. 1996. reprint ed. 34.95 (*0-86636-378-5*) PBC Intl Inc.
***Landis, Dylan.** Elegant & Easy Bedrooms: 100 Trade Secrets for Designing with Style. LC 99-45352. (Illus.). 128p. 2000. pap. 12.95 (*0-440-50861-4*, Dell Trade Pbks) Dell.
— Elegant & Easy Foyers, Hallways: 100 Trade Secrets for Designing with Style. LC 99-45838. (Illus.). 128p. 2000. pap. 12.95 (*0-440-50860-6*, Dell Trade Pbks) Dell.
— Elegant & Easy Living Rooms: 100 Trade Secrets for Designing with Style. LC 99-45821. 128p. 2000. pap. 12.95 (*0-440-50859-2*, Dell Trade Pbks) Dell.
Landis, Dylan. Elegant & Easy Rooms: 250 Trade Secrets for Decorating Your Home. LC 97-816. (Illus.). 240p. 1997. pap. 12.95 (*0-440-50774-X*) Dell.
— Your Healthy Child's Medical Workbook: The Essential Organizer for Parents. 176p. 1997. pap. 9.95 (*0-425-15982-5*) Berkley Pub.
— Your Healthy Pregnancy Workbook. 240p. (Orig.). 1995. pap. 12.00 (*0-425-14952-8*) Berkley Pub.
Landis, E. M. Second Order Equations of Elliptic & Parabolic Type. LC 97-34670. (Translations of Mathematical Monographs Ser.). 203p. 1997. text 99.00 (*0-8218-0857-5*) Am Math.
***Landis, Geoffrey A.** Mars Crossing. 1999. write for info. (*0-8125-7648-9*) Tor Bks.
— Mars Crossing. 2000. text 24.95 (*0-312-87201-1*) Tor Bks.
Landis, Henry K. Canoeing on the Juniata, 1888. (Illus.). 67p. 1993. 15.95 (*0-89271-047-0*, 0421) Pa Hist & Mus.
Landis, J. D. Lying in Bed: A Novel. LC 94-43078. 294p. 1995. 19.95 (*1-56512-068-X*) Algonquin Bks.
Landis, Jacquelyn & Shaw, Eva. The Insider's Guide to San Diego. (Illus.). 584p. 1999. pap. 16.95 (*1-57380-077-5*, The Insiders Guide) Falcon Pub Inc.
Landis, James D. The Band Never Dances. LC 88-28401. 288p. (YA). (gr. 7 up). 1989. 13.95 (*0-06-023721-X*) HarpC Child Bks.
***Landis, James D.** Longing. LC 00-35049. 592p. 2000. 26.00 (*0-15-100453-6*) Harcourt.
Landis, James M., jt. auth. see Frankfurter, Felix.
***Landis, Jamye K.** Sand Springs: Oklahoma. (Images of America Ser.). (Illus.). 128p. 1999. pap. 18.99 (*0-7385-0320-7*) Arcadia Publng.
Landis, Jill M. After All. 336p. (Orig.). 1995. mass mkt. 6.50 (*0-515-11501-0*, Jove) Berkley Pub.
— Blue Moon. 1999. mass mkt. 6.99 (*0-515-12527-X*, Jove) Berkley Pub.
— Come Spring. 384p. 1992. mass mkt. 6.50 (*0-515-10861-8*, Jove) Berkley Pub.
— Day Dreamer. 416p. 1996. mass mkt. 6.50 (*0-515-11948-2*, Jove) Berkley Pub.
— Jade. 1991. mass mkt. 6.50 (*0-515-10591-0*, Jove) Berkley Pub.
— Just Once. 336p. 1997. mass mkt. 6.50 (*0-515-12062-6*, Jove); mass mkt. 6.50 (*0-614-27758-2*, Jove) Berkley Pub.
— Last Chance. 416p. (Orig.). 1995. mass mkt. 5.99 (*0-515-11760-9*, Jove) Berkley Pub.
— Past Promises. 384p. 1993. mass mkt. 6.50 (*0-515-11207-0*, Jove) Berkley Pub.
— Rose. 1990. mass mkt. 6.50 (*0-515-10346-2*, Jove) Berkley Pub.
— Sunflower. 1990. mass mkt. 6.50 (*0-515-10659-3*, Jove) Berkley Pub.
— Until Tomorrow. 368p. (Orig.). 1994. mass mkt. 6.99 (*0-515-11403-0*, Jove) Berkley Pub.
— Wild Flower. 1989. mass mkt. 6.50 (*0-515-10102-8*, Jove) Berkley Pub.
***Landis, Jill Marie.** Glass Beach. 355p. 1998. mass mkt. 6.99 (*0-515-12285-8*, Jove) Berkley Pub.
— The Orchid Hunter. 400p. 2000. mass mkt. 6.99 (*0-515-12768-X*, Jove) Berkley Pub.
— Sweet Hearts. 2000. mass mkt. 5.99 (*0-515-12710-8*, Jove) Berkley Pub.
Landis, John T. Mayflower Descendants & Their Marriages for Two Generations after the Landing. LC 72-158139. 37p. 1998. reprint ed. pap. 8.00 (*0-8063-0206-2*) Clearfield Co.
Landis, Joseph C., ed. from YID. Three Great Jewish Plays. 272p. 1986. pap. 8.95 (*0-936839-04-X*) Applause Theatre Bk Pubs.
***Landis, Joshua & Doran, Michael, eds.** The Arab-Israeli War of 1948: Inter-Arab Rivalry & the Making of the Middle Eastern State System. (Princeton Series on the Middle East). 160p. 2000. text 39.95 (*1-55876-225-6*); pap. text 16.95 (*1-55876-226-4*) Wiener Pubs Inc.
Landis, Judson & Kando, Thomas. Pal: Readings in Criminology. 240p. (C). 1995. 24.95 (*0-7872-1372-1*); student ed. write for info. (*0-7872-1097-8*); pap., per. write for info. (*0-7872-1096-X*) Kendall-Hunt.
Landis, Judson R. Sociology: Concepts & Characteristics. 5th ed. 464p. (C). 1983. pap. write for info. (*0-534-01381-3*) Wadsworth Pub.
— Sociology: Concepts & Characteristics. 6th ed. 417p. (C). 1986. pap. write for info. (*0-534-06438-8*) Wadsworth Pub.
— Sociology: Concepts & Characteristics. 7th ed. 449p. (C). 1989. pap. write for info. (*0-534-10158-5*) Wadsworth Pub.
— Sociology: Concepts & Characteristics. 8th ed. 483p. (C). 1992. pap. 30.95 (*0-534-17256-3*) Wadsworth Pub.
— Sociology: Concepts & Characteristics. 9th ed. LC 94-35558. 482p. 1995. mass mkt. 30.25 (*0-534-23754-1*) Wadsworth Pub.
— Sociology: Concepts & Characteristics. 10th ed. LC 97-39568. (C). 1997. pap. 51.95 (*0-534-52560-1*) Wadsworth Pub.
Landis, Judson T., et al. Personal Adjustment, Marriage & Family Living. 6th ed. 1975. text 26.48 (*0-13-657338-X*) P-H.
Landis, Lauren, jt. auth. see Dec, Jennifer.
Landis, Mark. Joseph McCarthy: The Politics of Chaos. LC 85-63422. 176p. 1987. 32.50 (*0-941664-19-8*) Susquehanna U Pr.
Landis, Mary. ABC Book of God's Creatures. (Jewel Book Ser.: Set 4). (Illus.). 32p. (J). 1993. pap. 2.55 (*0-7399-0043-9*, 2526) Rod & Staff.
— Across the Rose Hedge with Aunt Mary. (Illus.). 134p. (J). (gr. 3-6). 1995. pap. 6.55 (*0-7399-0075-7*, 2103) Rod & Staff.
— Anthony Gets Ready for Church. (Jewel Book Ser.: Set 3). (Illus.). 24p. (J). 1990. pap. 2.55 (*0-7399-0037-4*, 2119) Rod & Staff.
— Betty's Secret & Other Stories by Grandmother Lois. (Illus.). 184p. (J). (gr. 3-6). 1971. 6.55 (*0-7399-0077-3*, 2125) Rod & Staff.
— The Chest in the Attic. 92p. (J). (gr. 4-7). 1980. pap. 3.05 (*0-7399-0307-1*, 2205.2) Rod & Staff.
— Coon Tree Summer. (Illus.). 328p. (YA). (gr. 7-10). 1978. 10.55 (*0-7399-0107-9*, 2180) Rod & Staff.
— David & Susan at the Little Green House. (Illus.). 170p. (J). (gr. 3-6). 1975. 7.80 (*0-7399-0097-8*, 2185) Rod & Staff.
— David & Susan at Wild Rose Cottage. (Illus.). 231p. 1980. 9.10 (*0-7399-0099-4*, 2190) Rod & Staff.
— Dear Princess. (Illus.). 260p. 1973. 9.25 (*0-7399-0135-4*, 2194); pap. 5.90 (*0-7399-0137-0*, 2195.2) Rod & Staff.
— God's Gifts. (Jewel Book Ser.: Set 2). (Illus.). 24p. (J). (ps-2). 1989. pap. 2.55 (*0-7399-0032-3*, 2260) Rod & Staff.

— God's Wonderful Trees. (Jewel Book Ser.: Set 3). (Illus.). 24p. (J). 1990. pap. 2.55 (*0-7399-0038-2*, 2527) Rod & Staff.

— God's Wonderful Water. (Jewel Book Ser.: Set 3). (Illus.). 24p. (J). (ps-2). 1990. pap. 2.55 (*0-7399-0039-0*, 2263) Rod & Staff.

— Helping Mother. (Jewel Book Ser.: Set 2). (Illus.). 32p. (J). (ps-2). 1989. pap. 2.55 (*0-7399-0033-1*, 2272) Rod & Staff.

— Ice Slide Winter. (Illus.). 289p. (YA). (gr. 7-10). 1981. 9.85 (*0-7399-0108-7*, 2290) Rod & Staff.

— Missing Popcorn. (Illus.). 160p. 1975. 7.65 (*0-7399-0079-X*, 2335) Rod & Staff.

— My Blue Book of God's Different Things. (Illus.). 32p. (J). (ps-2). 1993. pap. 2.55 (*0-7399-0045-5*, 2539) Rod & Staff.

— My Blue Book of God's Different Things. (SPA., Illus.). 32p. (J). (ps-2). 1995. pap. 2.05 (*0-7399-0290-3*, 2539.1) Rod & Staff.

— My Green Book of God's Different Things. (Jewel Book Ser.: Set 4). (Illus.). 32p. (J). 1993. pap. 2.55 (*0-7399-0044-7*, 2529) Rod & Staff.

— My Green Book of God's Different Things. (Jewel Book Ser.). (SPA., Illus.). 32p. (J). 1995. pap. 2.05 (*0-7399-0289-X*, 2529.1) Rod & Staff.

— My Thank You Book. (Jewel Book Ser.: Set 3). (Illus.). 24p. (J). (ps-2). 1990. pap. 2.55 (*0-7399-0040-4*, 2333) Rod & Staff.

— Rainbow Promise. (Illus.). 195p. (YA). (gr. 7-10). 1992. 8.25 (*0-7399-0110-9*, 2304) Rod & Staff.

— Summer Days with Treelo Triplets. (Illus.). 191p. (J). (gr. 3-6). 1971. 8.20 (*0-7399-0080-3*, 2415) Rod & Staff.

— Treasured Memories of Our Baby. (Illus.). 52p. 1986. 17.30 (*0-7399-0249-0*, 2123) Rod & Staff.

— Trouble at Windy Acres. (Illus.). 208p. (YA). (gr. 7-10). 1976. 8.30 (*0-7399-0117-6*, 2450) Rod & Staff.

— The Twins Picnic. (Jewel Book Ser.: Set 5). (Illus.). 24p. (J). 1994. pap. 2.55 (*0-7399-0047-1*, 2528) Rod & Staff.

Landis, Milton W. & Taylor, Carl B. The Early History of Cogan House Township (Lycoming County, Pa.) LC 81-50694. (Illus.). 285p. 1982. pap. 16.50 (*0-9605948-0-9*) C B Taylor.

Landis, Paul. Once Saved, Always Saved: Truth or Delusion? (Cornerstone Ser.). 143p. 1991. pap. 4.75 (*0-7399-0198-2*, 2332) Rod & Staff.

— Purity in the Christian Home. 29p. 1978. pap. 1.65 (*0-7399-0213-X*, 2365); pap. 1.35 (*0-7399-0214-8*, 2365.1) Rod & Staff.

— Purity in the Christian Home. (GER.). tpp. 1980. 1.50 (*0-7399-0234-2*, 2365.2) Rod & Staff.

Landis, Paul, ed. Four Famous Greek Plays: Agamemnon; Oedipus; Medea; The Frogs. 20.00 (*0-8196-2016-5*) Biblo.

Landis, Paul, ed. see Browning, Elizabeth Barrett.

Landis, Paul H. Three Iron Mining Towns: A Study in Cultural Change. LC 72-112555. (Rise of Urban America Ser.). 1974. reprint ed. 16.95 (*0-405-02462-2*) Ayer.

Landis, Paul N. Four Famous Greek Plays. 285p. 1977. 20.95 (*0-8369-8224-X*) Ayer.

***Landis, Raymond B.** Studying Engineering: A Road Map to a Rewarding Career. 2nd ed. (Illus.). 256p. 2000. pap. 22.95 (*0-9646969-5-9*) Discover CA.

Landis, Raymond B. Studying Engineering: A Road Map to a Successful Career. (C). 1995. pap. text 22.95 (*0-9646969-0-8*) Discover CA.

Landis, Robyn. BodyFueling: The Ground-Breaking Approach to Eating for Health, Energy, Fitness, & Fat Loss. 368p. 1995. mass mkt. 5.99 (*0-446-60194-2*, Pub. by Warner Bks) Little.

Landis, Robyn & Khalsa, Karta P., eds. Herbal Defense: Positioning Yourself to Truimph over Illness & Aging. LC 97-1817. 576p. 1997. mass mkt. 14.99 (*0-446-67242-4*, Pub. by Warner Bks) Little.

Landis, Scott. The Workbench Book. LC 86-51321. (Illus.). 256p. 1987. 34.95 (*0-918804-76-0*, 70061) Taunton.

— Workbench Book. (Illus.). 256p. 1998. pap. 22.95 (*1-56158-270-0*, 070403) Taunton.

— The Workshop Book. LC 90-26624. (Illus.). 224p. (C). 1991. 34.95 (*0-942391-37-3*, 70094) Taunton.

— Workshop Book. (Illus.). 224p. 1998. pap. 22.95 (*1-56158-271-9*, 070402) Taunton.

Landis, Scott & Wilson, Edward O., eds. Conservation by Design. (Illus.). 160p. (Orig.). 1993. pap. 30.00 (*0-9638593-0-7*) Woodwrks Alliance.

Landis, Stephan. Das Verhaeltnis des Johannesevangeliums zu den Synoptikern: Am Beispiel von Mt. 8, 5-13; Lk. 7, 1-10; Joh. 4, 46-54. (Beiheft zur Zeitschrift fuer die Neuetestamentliche Wissenschaft Ser.: Bd. 74). (GER.). 85p. (C). 1994. pap. text 36.95 (*3-11-014389-5*) De Gruyter.

Landis, Susan M. But Why Don't We Go to War? Finding Jesus' Path to Peace. LC 93-10849. 224p. (Orig.). 1993. pap. 11.99 (*0-8361-3647-0*) Herald Pr.

Landis, Thomas D., et al, eds. Forest & Conservation Nursery Associations: National Proceedings, 1996. (Illus.). 282p. (C). 1998. pap. text 40.00 (*0-7881-7378-2*) DIANE Pub.

Landis, Thomas D. & Dumroese, R. Kasten. Forest & Conservation Nursery Associations: National Proceedings (1994) (Illus.). 319p. (Orig.). (C). 1996. pap. text 45.00 (*0-7881-3014-5*) DIANE Pub.

Landis, Thomas D. & Fischer, James W. Intermountain Nurseryman's Association Meeting (August 13-15, 1985, Fort Collins, Colorado) Proceedings. 124p. 1986. reprint ed. text 18.40 (*0-89904-915-X*, Ecosytems Resrch) Crumb Elbow Pub.

— Intermountain Nurseryman's Association Meeting (August 13-15, 1985, Fort Collins, Colorado) Proceedings. (Illus.). 124p. 1986. reprint ed. pap. 13.40 (*0-89904-914-1*, Ecosytems Resrch) Crumb Elbow Pub.

Landis, Thomas D., jt. ed. see Duryea, Mary L.

Landis, Tom. Home Building Consumer's Guide & Video: How to Save Money by Taking Charge of the Design/Build Process. Incl. (Illus.). (Orig.). 1997. pap. Not sold separately (*0-9641268-0-X*); (Illus.). (Orig.). 1997. VHS Not sold separately (*0-9641268-2-6*); 60.00 (*0-9641268-1-8*) Owner Blder Srvs.

Landis, Tony, jt. auth. see Jenkins, Dennis R.

Landis, W. G. & Van der Schalie, W. H., eds. Aquatic Toxicology & Risk Assessment, Vol. 13. (Special Technical Publication Ser.: No. 1096). (Illus.). 380p. 1990. text 86.00 (*0-8031-1460-5*, STP1096) ASTM.

Landis, Wayne G. Environmental Toxicology. 352p. 1994. lib. bdg. 75.00 (*0-87371-515-2*, L515) Lewis Pubs.

Landis, Wayne G., et al, eds. Environmental Toxicology & Risk Assessment, STP 1179. LC 92-46581. (Special Technical Publication Ser.: No. STP 1179). (Illus.). 240p. 1993. 92.00 (*0-8031-1860-0*, STP1179) ASTM.

Landis, Wayne G. & Yu, Ming-Ho. Introduction to Environmental Toxicology. 2nd ed. LC 97-50324. 400p. 1998. lib. bdg. 69.95 (*1-56670-265-8*, L1265) Lewis Pubs.

Landkof, N. S. Foundations of Modern Potential Theory. Doohovskoy, A. P., tr. from RUS. LC 77-186131. (Grundlehren der Mathematischen Wissenschaften Ser.: Vol. 180). 440p. 1973. 86.95 (*0-387-05394-8*) Spr-Verlag.

Landlow, George P. Hypertext 2.0: The Convergence of Contemporary Critical Theory & Technology. 2nd ed. LC 97-1642. (Parallax Ser.). (Illus.). 384p. 1997. text 48.50 (*0-8018-5585-3*); pap. text 18.95 (*0-8018-5586-1*) Johns Hopkins.

Landman, Alexander, tr. see Terras, Victor.

Landman, Annlee. Learning to Quilt the Traditional Way. (Illus.). 128p. 1996. pap. 14.95 (*0-8069-0630-8*) Sterling.

Landman, Christina. Europe's Role in a South African Methodology: A Sideline & Female Perspective. (European University Studies: Series 23, Vol. 386). 175p. 1991. pap. 36.80 (*3-631-42728-X*) P Lang Pubng.

Landman, Fred. Structures for Semantics. 384p. (C). 1991. lib. bdg. 154.00 (*0-7923-1239-2*, Pub. by Kluwer Academic) Kluwer Academic.

— Structures for Semantics. (Studies in Linguistics & Philosophy: No. 45). 384p. 1994. pap. text 43.00 (*0-7923-1240-6*) Kluwer Academic.

Landman, Hedy B. Chinese Jade Carvings from the Collection of Dr. & Mrs. Harold L. Tonkin: Exhibition Catalogue. (Illus.). 48p. 1983. pap. 6.75 (*0-911209-28-X*) Palmer Mus Art.

— Selection IV: Glass from the Museum's Collection. LC 73-94132. (Illus.). 144p. 1974. pap. 6.50 (*0-911517-36-7*) Mus of Art RI.

Landman, Hedy B., ed. European & American Art from the Princeton Alumni Collection: Publication of the Art Museum, Princeton University. LC 74-188505. (Illus.). 188p. 1972. text 35.50 (*0-691-03882-1*, Pub. by Princeton U Pr) Cal Prin Full Svc.

Landman, Hedy B., jt. auth. see Preisner, Olga K.

Landman, Hedy B., ed. see Preisner, Olga K.

Landman, Jessica, jt. auth. see Adler, Robert.

Landman, Lawrence B. Doing Business in the U. S. Legal Opportunities & Pitfalls. LC 96-35879. 326p. 1997. pap. 38.95 (*0-471-96160-4*) Wiley.

Landman, Leo, ed. Scholars & Scholarship: The Interaction Between Judaism & Other Cultures. 1991. 25.00 (*0-88125-344-8*) Ktav.

Landman, N. H. & Saunders, W. B. Nautilus: The Biology & Paleobiology of a Living Fossil. LC 87-32725. (Topics in Geobiology Ser.: Vol. 6). (Illus.). 666p. (C). 1988. text 135.00 (*0-306-42709-5*, Kluwer Plenum) Kluwer Academic.

Landman, N. H., et al. Ammonoid Paleobiology. (Topics in Geobiology Ser.: Vol. 13). (Illus.). 845p. (C). 1996. text 179.00 (*0-306-45222-7*, Kluwer Plenum) Kluwer Academic.

Landman, Ruth H. Creating Community in the City: Cooperatives & Community Gardens in Washington, D. C. LC 92-42899. (Contemporary Urban Studies). 168p. 1993. 52.95 (*0-89789-316-6*, H316, Bergin & Garvey) Greenwood.

Landman, Silviu, jt. auth. see Danzi, J. Thomas.

Landman, Sylvia. Crafting for Dollars: Turn Your Hobby into Serious Cash. (Illus.). 304p. 1996. per. 14.95 (*0-7615-0442-7*) Prima Pub.

***Landman, Sylvia.** Crocheting for Fun & Profit. (For Fun & Profit Ser.). (Illus.). 320p. 2000. pap. 19.99 (*0-7615-2161-5*) Prima Pub.

Landman, Sylvia. Make Your Quilting Pay for Itself. LC 97-23573. (Illus.). 144p. 1997. pap. 18.99 (*1-55870-446-9*, Betrwy Bks) F & W Pubns Inc.

***Landman, Sylvia.** Official Guide to Pricing Your Crafts. 1999. pap. 16.99 (*0-7615-2123-2*) Prima Pub.

Landman, T. & Veltman, F., eds. Varieties of Formal Semantics: Proceedings of the 4th Amsterdam Colloquium. (Groningen-Amsterdam Studies in Semantics). xii, 425p. 1985. pap. 75.40 (*90-6765-007-2*) Mouton.

***Landman, Todd.** Issues & Methods in Comparative Politics: Introduction. LC 99-48348. 288p. 2000. pap. 25.99 (*0-415-18728-1*) Routledge.

— Issues & Methods in Comparative Politics: Introduction. LC 99-48348. 272p. (C). 2000. text. write for info. (*0-415-18727-3*) Routledge.

Landman, Todd, jt. auth. see Foweraker, Joe.

Landman, Uzi, ed. Aspects of the Kinetics & Dynamics of Surface Reactions. LC 80-68004. (AIP Conference Proceedings Ser.: No. 61). 343p. 1980. lib. bdg. 22.25 (*0-88318-160-6*) Am Inst Physics.

Landmann, Eric & Hynek, Don. Climber's Guide to Gibraltar Rock. 2nd ed. (Illus.). 64p. 1993. pap. text. write for info. (*0-9619571-5-8*) Granite WI.

Landmann, G. & Bonneau, M., eds. Forest Decline & Atmosphere Deposition Effects in the French Mountains. LC 95-6104. (Illus.). 492p. 1995. 117.95 (*3-540-58874-4*) Spr-Verlag.

Landmann, I. Tunnel Warfare Vol. 1: A Treatise on Mines: A Reprinting of the 1815 Classic on Military Mining. Hanesalo, Bruce A., ed. (Illus.). 102p. 1995. reprint ed. vinyl bd. 15.00 (*1-886848-12-2*) Mil-Info.

Landmann, Michael. Fundamental Anthropology. Parent, David J., ed. & tr. by. (Current Continental Research Ser.: No. 403). 354p. (Orig.). 1985. lib. bdg. 52.50 (*0-8191-4842-3*) U Pr of Amer.

— Philosophische Anthropologie: Menschliche Selbstdeutung in Geschichte und Gegenwart. 5th ed. (Sammlung Goeschen Ser.: Vol. 2201). 228p. (C). 1976. pap. 12.95 (*3-11-008997-1*) De Gruyter.

— Reform of the Hebrew Alphabet. Parent, David J., tr. LC 76-14595. (Illinois Language & Culture Ser.: Vol. 1). 345p. reprint ed. pap. 107.00 (*0-8357-0177-8*, 201371500087) Bks Demand.

Landmark College Students. Off the Ground: A Landmark Anthology of Student Writing. 144p. (Orig.). 1996. pap. 9.95 (*0-9655762-0-5*) Landmark College.

Landmark Outreach Program Staff, ed. Learning Disabilities: Information & Resources. 2nd ed. 110p. 1996. pap. 20.00 (*0-9624119-4-9*) Landmark Found.

Landmarks Staff. The European Public Affairs Directory, 1992: The Comprehensive Guide to Opinion-Formers in the Capital of Europe. 252p. (C). 1992. pap. text 99.00 (*0-8133-1607-3*) Westview.

Lando, Miriam. Funny Friday. 28p. (J). 1992. 14.95 (*1-56062-136-2*) CIS Comm.

Lando, Ole & Beale, Hugh, eds. The Principles of European Contract Law: Prepared by the Commission on European Contract Law, Chairman, Ole Lando. LC 94-21316. 1995. lib. bdg. 136.00 (*0-7923-2957-0*) Kluwer Academic.

***Lando, Ole, et al.** The Principles of European Contract Law. LC 99-51943. 1999. 195.00 (*90-411-1305-3*) Kluwer Law Intl.

Landolfi, Suzi. Hot, Sexy, & Safer. pap. 9.95 (*0-87477-750-X*, Tarcher Putnam) Putnam Pub Group.

Landolfi, Tommaso. An Autumn Story. Neugroschel, Joachim, tr. from ITA. LC 88-83031. 145p. 1989. pap. 11.00 (*0-941419-26-6*, Eridanos Library) Marsilio Pubs.

— Gogol's Wife & Other Stories. LC 63-21382. 1963. pap. 8.95 (*0-8112-0080-9*, NDP155, Pub. by New Directions) Norton.

Landoll. Blue's ABCs! 32p. 1999. pap. text 2.25 (*1-56189-049-9*) Amer Educ Pub.

— Blue's Geography! 1999. pap. text 2.25 (*1-56189-065-0*) Amer Educ Pub.

— Blue's Math! With Stickers. 1999. pap. text 2.25 (*1-56189-064-2*) Amer Educ Pub.

— Blue's Reading! 1999. pap. text 2.25 (*1-56189-048-0*) Amer Educ Pub.

— Blue's Science! 1999. pap. text 2.25 (*1-56189-047-2*) Amer Educ Pub.

— Blue's Signs! 1999. pap. text 2.25 (*1-56189-066-9*) Amer Educ Pub.

***Landoll.** Colors & Shapes Workbook. (Beginners Bible Ser.). 2000. pap. text 14.95 (*1-56189-618-7*) Amer Educ Pub.

— English Workbook. (Beginners Bible Ser.). 2000. pap. text 14.95 (*1-56189-621-7*) Amer Educ Pub.

— Letters Workbook. (Beginners Bible Ser.). 2000. pap. text 14.95 (*1-56189-620-9*) Amer Educ Pub.

— Math Workbook. (Beginners Bible Ser.). 2000. pap. text 14.95 (*1-56189-622-5*) Amer Educ Pub.

— Numbers Workbook. (Beginners Bible Ser.). 2000. pap. text 14.95 (*1-56189-619-5*) Amer Educ Pub.

Landolphi, Donald & Russo, Joe. Fundamentals of Coaching & Playing Baseball. LC 97-29276. 175p. 1997. pap. text 29.00 (*0-205-26114-0*) P-H.

Landolphi, Suzi. Best Love: Creating the Best Love, Sex & Intimacy. (Illus.). 128p. (Orig.). 1996. pap. 6.95 (*0-9649699-0-4*) TVFirst.

— The Best Love, the Best Sex: Creating Sensuous, Soulful, Supersatisfying Relationships. 256p. 1997. pap. 13.50 (*0-399-52341-3*, Perigee Bks) Berkley Pub.

— Hot, Sexy & Safer. 176p. (Orig.). 1994. pap. 12.50 (*0-399-51882-7*, Perigee Bks) Berkley Pub.

***Landolphi, Suzi.** My First Time: True Stories of Love & Sex from the Internet. Paddock, Craig & Foldy, Peter, eds. 201p. 1999. pap. 14.95 (*0-9672635-0-6*) Good 2 Go Entertain.

Landolt. Pituitary Adenomas. 1995. text 215.00 (*0-443-05134-8*, W B Saunders Co) Harcrt Hlth Sci Grp.

Landolt, A. M., ed. Complications in Neurosurgery I. (Progress in Neurological Surgery Ser.: Vol. 11). (Illus.). x, 174p. 1984. 85.25 (*3-8055-3691-7*) S Karger.

— Intensive Care & Monitoring of the Neurosurgical Patient. (Progress in Neurological Surgery Ser.: Vol. 12). (Illus.). xiv, 202p. 1987. 115.75 (*3-8055-4414-6*) S Karger.

Landolt, A. M., et al, eds. Advances in Pituitary Adenoma Research: Proceedings of the 4th European Workshop on Pituitary Adenomas, University of Zurich-Irchel, Zurich, Switzerland, September 13-16, 1987. (Advances in the Biosciences Ser.: Vol. 69). 498p. 1988. 110.00 (*0-08-035596-X*, Pergamon Pr) Elsevier.

Landolt, A. M., et al. Applied Anatomy of the Back. Wilson, R. R. & Winstanley, D. P., trs. from GER. LC 85-9937. (Illus.). 425p. 1985. 645.00 (*0-387-15132-X*) Spr-Verlag.

Landolt-Bornstein. Condensed Matter: Magnetic Properties of Non-Metallic Inorganic Compounds Based on Transition Elements. Martienssen, W. & Wijn, H. P., eds. (Numerical Data & Functional Relationships in Science & Technology Ser.: Group III). (Illus.). vii, 150p. 1998. text 688.00 (*3-540-52960-8*) Spr-Verlag.

— Magnetic Properties of Non-Metallic Inorganic Compounds Based on Transition Elements: Part b: Pnictides & Chalcogenides II, Part 2: Lanthanide Monochalcogenides. viii, 459p. 1999. 1092.00 (*3-540-63268-9*) Spr-Verlag.

— Numerical Data & Functional Relationships in Science & Technology Group 4, Vol. 8, Pt. E: Physical Chemistry. (Thermodynamic Properties of Organic Compounds & Their Mixtures Ser.: Vol. 8). viii, 373p. 1998. 2215.00 incl. cd-rom (*3-540-62510-0*) Spr-Verlag.

— Physical Chemistry Vol. 5: Phase Equilibria, Crystallographic Data & Values of Thermodynamic Properties of Binary Alloys. Martienssen, W. et al, eds. (Numerical Data & Functional Relationships in Science & Technology Ser.: Group IV). (Illus.). xxx, 428p. 1997. text 1822.00 (*3-540-61433-8*) Spr-Verlag.

Landolt, C. A., ed. see Metallurgical Society of AIME Staff.

Landolt, E. A Manual of Examination of the Eyes. LC 78-20773. (Classics in Ophthalmology Ser.). 328p. 1979. reprint ed. lib. bdg. 31.50 (*0-88275-843-8*) Krieger.

Landolt, Oliver. Place Coding in Analog VLSI: A Neuromorphic Approach to Computation. LC 98-9929. 216p. 1998. 110.00 (*0-7923-8194-7*) Kluwer Academic.

Landolt, R., ed. Aktuelle Probleme der Paediatrischen Hepatologie. (Paediatrische Fortbildungskurse fuer die Praxis Ser.: Band 44). (GER., Illus.). 1977. 17.50 (*3-8055-2662-8*) S Karger.

Landolt, Robert G. The Mexican-American Workers of San Antonio, Texas. Cortes, Carlos E., ed. LC 76-1291. (Chicano Heritage Ser.). (Illus.). 1977. 33.95 (*0-405-09509-0*) Ayer.

***Landon, Luann.** Dinner at Miss Lady's: Memories & Recipes from a Southern Childhood. LC 98-53264. 240p. 1999. pap. 19.95 (*1-56512-227-5*, 72227) Algonquin Bks.

Landon, Alicia. The Worm Queen: Memoirs of Santa Ynez Valley. LC 91-29351. (Illus.). 112p. (Orig.). 1992. pap. 9.95 (*1-56474-006-4*) Fithian Pr.

Landon, B. A. & Goodall, J. D. An Atlas of Trauma Management: The First Hour. (Encyclopedia of Visual Medicine Ser.). (Illus.). 151p. 1994. 70.00 (*1-85070-411-2*) Prthnon Pub.

Landon, Brooks. The Aesthetics of Ambivalence: Rethinking Science Fiction Film in the Age of Electronic (Re) Production, 52. LC 92-4048. (Contributions to the Study of Science Fiction & Fantasy Ser.: No. 52). 224p. 1992. 55.00 (*0-313-25687-X*, LAA/, Greenwood Pr) Greenwood.

— Thomas Berger. (United States Authors Ser.: No. 550). 200p. 1989. 22.95 (*0-8057-7540-4*, TUSAS 550) Macmillan.

Landon, Carol, ed. see Wordsworth, William.

Landon, Charles. A Text-Critical Study of the Epistle of Jude. LC 96-220508. (JSNTS Ser.: No. 135). 172p. 1996. 52.50 (*1-85075-636-8*, Pub. by Sheffield Acad) CUP Services.

Landon, Donald L. Country Lawyers: The Impact of Context on Professional Practice. LC 89-16220. 186p. 1990. 52.95 (*0-275-93042-4*, C3042, Praeger Pubs) Greenwood.

Landon, Fred. Lake Huron. (American Lakes Ser.). lib. bdg. 27.95 (*0-8488-1989-6*) Amereon Ltd.

Landon, Grelun, jt. auth. see Stambler, Irwin.

Landon, H. C. Beethoven: His Life, Work & World. LC 92-64271. (Illus.). 248p. 1993. 40.00 (*0-500-01540-6*, Pub. by Thames Hudson) Norton.

— Haydn at Eszterhaza 1766-1790. LC 94-61475. (Haydn: Chronicle & Works). (Illus.). 819p. 1995. 100.00 (*0-500-01168-0*, Pub. by Thames Hudson) Norton.

— Haydn: Chronicle & Works. Incl. Vol. V. Haydn: Chronicle & Works. LC 76-14630. (Illus.). 496p. 1977. 72.00 (*0-253-37005-1*); LC 76-14630. write for info. (*0-318-53523-8*) Ind U Pr.

— Haydn: The Early Years 1732-1765. LC 94-61473. (Haydn: Chronicle & Works). (Illus.). 676p. 1995. 100.00 (*0-500-01169-9*, Pub. by Thames Hudson) Norton.

— Haydn: The Late Years 1801-1809. LC 94-61478. (Haydn: Chronicle & Works). (Illus.). 523p. 1995. 100.00 (*0-500-01167-2*, Pub. by Thames Hudson) Norton.

— Haydn: The Years of "The Creation" 1796-1800. LC 94-61477. (Haydn: Chronicle & Works). (Illus.). 676p. 1995. 100.00 (*0-500-01166-4*, Pub. by Thames Hudson) Norton.

— Haydn in England 1791-1795. LC 94-61476. (Haydn: Chronicle & Works). (Illus.). 667p. 1995. 100.00 (*0-500-01164-8*, Pub. by Thames Hudson) Norton.

— Mozart: The Golden Years. 256p. 1989. write for info. (*0-318-66745-2*) Macmillan.

— Vivaldi. LC 93-60428. (Illus.). 240p. 1993. 24.95 (*0-500-01576-7*, Pub. by Thames Hudson) Norton.

— Vivaldi: Voice of the Baroque. (Illus.). 224p. 1996. pap. 15.95 (*0-226-46842-9*) U Ch Pr.

Landon, H. C. Robbins. 1791: Mozart's Last Year. LC 98-61442. (Illus.). 240p. 1999. pap. 17.95 (*0-500-28107-6*, Pub. by Thames Hudson) Norton.

Landon, Harold R., ed. Reinhold Niebuhr: A Prophetic Voice in Our Time. (Essay Index Reprint Ser.). 1977. reprint ed. 13.95 (*0-518-10150-9*) Ayer.

Landon, Harry F. History of the North Country, 3 vols., Set. 1993. reprint ed. lib. bdg. 270.00 (*0-7812-5188-5*) Rprt Serv.

— The North Country: A History Embracing Jefferson, St. Lawrence, Oswego, Lewis & Franklin Counties, 3 vols. (Illus.). 1647p. 1997. reprint ed. lib. bdg. 165.00 (*0-8328-6887-6*) Higginson Bk Co.

Landon, J. & Chard, T., eds. Therapeutic Antibodies. LC 94-38225. (Illus.). 240p. 1994. 118.00 (*0-387-19722-2*) Spr-Verlag.

Landon, James O. Landon Genealogy, Boardman Genealogy. 383p. 1993. reprint ed. pap. 59.50 (*0-8328-2987-0*); reprint ed. lib. bdg. 69.50 (*0-8328-2986-2*) Higginson Bk Co.

Landon, John C. World History & the Eonic Effect: Civilization, Darwinism & Theories of Evolution. LC 99-90491. 365p. 1999. 25.00 (*0-7388-0428-2*); pap. 15.00 (*0-7388-0429-0*) Xlibris Corp.

Landon, John C., jt. ed. see Erwin, J.

Landon, John W. Behold the Mighty Wurlitzer: The History of the Theatre Pipe Organ, 6. LC 83-5557. (Contributions to the Study of Popular Culture Ser.: No. 6). 231p. 1983. 65.00 (*0-313-23827-8*, LPO/, Greenwood Pr) Greenwood.

— The Development of Social Welfare. LC 85-14254. 210p. 1985. 34.95 (*0-89885-258-7*, Kluwer Acad Hman Sci) Kluwer Academic.

Landon, Joseph W. Clinical Practice in Music Education. (Contemporary Music Education Ser.). (Illus.). 128p. (Orig.). 1988. pap. 8.95 (*0-943988-03-9*, 943E) Music Educ Pubns.

— How to Write Learning Activity Packages for Music Education. (Contemporary Music Education Ser.). (Illus.). 109p. (Orig.). 1980. reprint ed. pap. 8.95 (*0-930424-01-8*) Music Educ Pubns.

— Leadership for Learning in Music Education. LC 75-305303. (Contemporary Music Education Ser.). 306p. (Orig.). 1975. reprint ed. pap. 12.95 (*0-943988-02-0*) Music Educ Pubns.

— Music Lab. (Mini-Modular Series in Music Education). (Illus.). 182p. (Orig.). (J). (gr. 3-8). 1982. pap. 14.95 (*0-943988-00-4*) Music Educ Pubns.

— A Notable Beginning: The Founding & Early Years of the CSUF Department of Music, 1959-69. (Illus.). 255p. 1996. text 50.00 (*0-943988-04-7*) Music Educ Pubns.

***Landon, Juliet.** The Golden Lure. 1999. per. 4.99 (*0-373-30339-4*) Harlequin Bks.

Landon, Juliet. The Golden Lure. large type ed. 1995. 23.99 (*0-263-14421-6*, Pub. by Mills & Boon) Ulverscroft.

***Landon, Juliet.** The Goldsmith's Jewel. large type ed. 320p. 1999. 25.99 (*0-263-16035-1*, Pub. by Mills & Boon) Ulverscroft.

Landon, Juliet. A Knight in Waiting. (Historical Ser.: Vol. 4). 1998. mass mkt. 4.99 (*0-373-30313-0*, 1-30313-0) Harlequin Bks.

— The Knight, the Knave & the Lady. 1999. pap. 4.99 (*0-373-30325-4*, 1-30325-4, Harlequin) Harlequin Bks.

— The Knight, the Knave & the Lady. large type ed. (Mills & Boon Large Print Ser.). 350p. 1997. 23.99 (*0-263-15101-8*, Pub. by Mills & Boon) Ulverscroft.

***Landon, Juliet.** The Passionate Pilgrim. 320p. 2000. 26.99 (*0-263-16473-X*, Pub. by Mills & Boon) Ulverscroft.

Landon, Kenneth P. Siam in Transition: A Brief Survey of Cultural Trends in the Five Years Since the Revolution of 1932. LC 68-57615. (Illus.). 328p. 1969. reprint ed. lib. bdg. 38.50 (*0-8371-0521-8*, LASI, Greenwood Pr) Greenwood.

Landon, Letitia E. Ethel Churchill. LC 92-16474. 1008p. 1992. 90.00 (*0-8201-1464-2*) Schol Facsimiles.

— Fate of Adelaide. LC 90-8961. 204p. 1990. reprint ed. 50.00 (*0-8201-1447-2*) Schol Facsimiles.

— The Improvisatrice, 1825. LC 95-41937. (Revolution & Romanticism, 1789-1834 Ser.). 1996. 65.00 (*1-85477-183-3*) Continuum.

— Poetical Works of Letitia Elizabeth Landon "L. E. L." LC 90-8789. 676p. 1990. 75.00 (*0-8201-1443-X*) Schol Facsimiles.

Landon, Letitia Elizabeth. Francesca Carrara, 3 vols. in 1. Sypher, F. J., ed. LC 99-12387. (Scholars' Facsimiles & Reprints Ser.: Vol. 522). 1040p. 1999. reprint ed. lib. bdg. 100.00 (*0-8201-1522-3*) Schol Facsimiles.

— Tales & Sketches. LC 99-23989. (Scholars' Facsimiles & Reprints Ser.: Vol. 521). 1999. 75.00 (*0-8201-1521-5*) Schol Facsimiles.

— Traits & Trials of Early Life. LC 99-25053. (Scholars' Facsimiles & Reprints Ser.: Vol. 523). 330p. 1999. reprint ed. 60.00 (*0-8201-1523-1*) Schol Facsimiles.

Landon, Linda L. Earth Angel Child: You May Be One. (Illus.). (Orig.). (J). (gr. 3 up). 1992. pap. 8.80 (*0-9633759-0-3*) Harmony Hill.

***Landon, Lucinda.** American History Mysteries: More Than 35 Real-life SceneMore Spellbinding Reproducible Mystery Stories That Students, 1 vol. (Illus.). 112p. 1999. pap. text 14.95 (*0-590-49889-4*) Scholastic Inc.

Landon, Lucinda. Meg Mackintosh & the Case of the Curious Whale Watch: A Solve-It-Yourself Mystery. LC 87-2748. (Meg Mackintosh Mysteries Ser.: Vol. 2). (Illus.). 48p. (J). (gr. 2-5). 1996. reprint ed. pap. 4.95 (*1-888695-01-3*) Secret Passage.

— Meg Mackintosh & the Case of the Missing Babe Ruth Baseball: A Solve-It-Yourself Mystery. LC 85-20055. (Meg Mackintosh Mysteries Ser.: Vol. 1). (Illus.). 48p. (J). (gr. 2-5). 1996. reprint ed. pap. 4.95 (*1-888695-00-5*) Secret Passage.

— Meg Mackintosh & the Mystery at Camp Creepy: A Solve-It-Yourself Mystery. LC 89-38466. (Meg Mackintosh Mysteries Ser.: Vol. 4). (Illus.). 64p. (J). (gr. 2-5). 1996. reprint ed. pap. 4.95 (*1-888695-03-X*) Secret Passage.

— Meg Mackintosh & the Mystery at the Medieval Castle. (J). (ps-3). 1993. mass mkt. 4.95 (*0-316-51376-8*) Little.

— Meg Mackintosh & the Mystery at the Medieval Castle: A Solve-It-Yourself Mystery. LC 88-28586. (Meg Mackintosh Mysteries Ser.: Vol. 3). (Illus.). (J). (gr. 2-5). 1996. reprint ed. pap. 4.95 (*1-888695-02-1*) Secret Passage.

— Meg Mackintosh & the Mystery at the Soccer Match: A Solve-It-Yourself Mystery. (Meg Mackintosh Mysteries Ser.: Vol. 6). (Illus.). 48p. (Orig.). (J). (gr. k up). 1997. pap. 4.95 (*1-888695-05-6*) Secret Passage.

— Meg Mackintosh & the Mystery in the Locked Library: A Solve-It-Yourself Mystery. LC 92-19948. (Meg Mackintosh Mysteries Ser.: Vol. 5). (Illus.). 48p. (J). (gr. 2-5). 1996. reprint ed. pap. 4.95 (*1-888695-04-8*) Secret Passage.

***Landon, Margaret.** Anna & the King. abr. ed. LC 99-67663. 208p. (J). (gr. 4-7). 1999. mass mkt. 4.95 (*0-06-440861-2*) HarpC Child Bks.

Landon, Margaret. Anna & the King of Siam. Date not set. lib. bdg. 25.95 (*0-8488-2176-9*) Amereon Ltd.

***Landon, Margaret.** Anna & the King of Siam. LC 96-46570. 416p. 1999. pap. 14.00 (*0-06-095488-4*) HarpC.

Landon, Margaret. Anna & the King of Siam. (Illus.). (J). 1944. 16.95 (*0-381-98135-5*, A05201) HarpC Child Bks.

Landon, Margaret. Anna & the King of Siam. abr. ed. LC 79-740790. 1980. audio 14.00 (*0-694-50334-7*, SWC 1629, Caedmon) HarperAudio.

Landon, Margaret. Anna & the King of Siam. 360p. 1990. reprint ed. lib. bdg. 45.95 (*0-89966-753-8*) Buccaneer Bks.

— Never Dies the Dream. lib. bdg. 24.95 (*0-8488-1990-X*) Amereon Ltd.

Landon, Melville D. Complete Works of Artemus Ward. (Notable American Authors Ser.). 1999. reprint ed. lib. bdg. 125.00 (*0-7812-3692-4*) Rprt Serv.

— Eli Perkins at Large: His Sayings & Doings. (Notable American Authors Ser.). 1999. reprint ed. lib. bdg. 125.00 (*0-7812-3691-6*) Rprt Serv.

— The Franco-Prussian War in a Nut-Shell. (Notable American Authors Ser.). 1999. reprint ed. lib. bdg. 125.00 (*0-7812-3689-4*) Rprt Serv.

— Money: Gold, Silver, of Bimetalism. (Notable American Authors Ser.). 1999. reprint ed. lib. bdg. 125.00 (*0-7812-3696-7*) Rprt Serv.

— Saratoga in 1901. (Notable American Authors Ser.). 1999. reprint ed. lib. bdg. 125.00 (*0-7812-3690-8*) Rprt Serv.

— Thirty Years of Wit. (Notable American Authors Ser.). 1999. reprint ed. lib. bdg. 125.00 (*0-7812-3695-9*) Rprt Serv.

— Wise, Witty, Eloquent Kings of the Platform & Pulpit. (Notable American Authors Ser.). 1999. reprint ed. lib. bdg. 125.00 (*0-7812-3694-0*) Rprt Serv.

Landon, Michael, jt. auth. see Slaughter, William W.

Landon, Perceval. Nepal, 2 vols., Set. (C). 1988. 500.00 (*0-7855-0061-8*, Pub. by Print Hse) St Mut.

— Nepal, 2 vols., Set. 1993. 223.00 (*0-7855-0263-7*, Pub. by Ratna Pustak Bhandar) St Mut.

— Nepal, 2 vols., Set. (C). 1993. reprint ed. text 70.00 (*81-206-0723-6*, Pub. by Asian Educ Servs) S Asia.

— The Opening of Tibet: An Account of Lhasa & the Country & People of Central Tibet & of the Mission Sent There by the English Government in the 1903-1904. 1990. reprint ed. 68.50 (*81-85326-26-6*, Pub. by Vintage) S Asia.

Landon, Perceval, ed. Nepal, 2 vols., Set. 358p. (C). 1987. 600.00 (*0-89771-068-1*, Pub. by Ratna Pustak Bhandar) St Mut.

Landon, Richard, ed. Editing & Editors: A Retrospective: Papers Given at the Twenty-First Annual Conference on Editorial Problems, University of Toronto, 1-2 November, 1985. LC 87-45816. (Conference on Editorial Problems Ser.: No. 21). 1987. 42.50 (*0-404-63671-3*) AMS Pr.

Landon, Robbins H. & Chapman, Roger. Studies in Eighteenth Century Music: A Tribute to Karl Geiringer on His 70th Birthday. (Music Reprint Ser.). 1979. reprint ed. lib. bdg. 49.50 (*0-306-79519-1*) Da Capo.

Landon, Robert P. Practical Surveying for Technicians. 36p. 1992. teacher ed. 14.95 (*0-8273-3942-9*) Delmar.

Landon, Susan M., ed. Interior Rift Basins. (AAPG Memoir Ser.: No. 59). (Illus.). xi, 276p. 1994. 105.00 (*0-89181-339-X*, 587) AAPG.

Landon, William, jt. auth. see Frazee, Irving A.

Landone, Brown. The A-B-C of Truth. 98p. 1996. reprint ed. spiral bd. 12.00 (*0-7873-1108-1*) Hlth Research.

— The A-B-C of Truth: 35 Lessons for Beginners in New Thought Study. 98p. 1996. reprint ed. pap. 11.95 (*1-56459-798-9*) Kessinger Pub.

— Basic Vivid Thinking. 63p. 1996. reprint ed. spiral bd. 9.00 (*0-7873-1254-1*) Hlth Research.

— Beginning Youth. 62p. 1996. reprint ed. spiral bd. 10.50 (*0-7873-1130-8*) Hlth Research.

— Body Purification. 69p. 1994. reprint ed. spiral bd. 10.00 (*0-7873-1132-4*) Hlth Research.

— The Breath of Youth. 75p. 1996. reprint ed. spiral bd. 10.00 (*0-7873-1147-2*) Hlth Research.

— The Christ Men Can Follow. 24p. 1996. reprint ed. spiral bd. 8.00 (*0-7873-1255-X*) Hlth Research.

— Deep, Deep Down in Your Heart. 249p. 1996. reprint ed. spiral bd. 15.50 (*0-7873-1251-7*) Hlth Research.

— Do Four Things Now. 528p. 1996. reprint ed. spiral bd. 29.50 (*0-7873-1253-3*) Hlth Research.

— Do Four Things Now: Positivism the Great New Discovery of Power. 528p. 1996. reprint ed. pap. 28.95 (*1-56459-892-6*) Kessinger Pub.

— Greater Spiritual Responsiveness of Body & Awakening the Brain of Spirit, Pt. 1. 150p. (Orig.). 1994. reprint ed. spiral bd. 14.00 (*0-7873-1105-7*) Hlth Research.

— Hope & Certainty. 36p. 1994. reprint ed. spiral bd. 8.00 (*0-7873-1181-2*) Hlth Research.

— How to Change Any Habit: A Course of 8 Lessons. 50p. 1996. reprint ed. spiral bd. 9.00 (*0-7873-1071-9*) Hlth Research.

— How to Turn Your Desires & Ideals into Realities. 159p. 1994. reprint ed. spiral bd. 14.50 (*0-7873-1185-5*) Hlth Research.

— How to Turn Your Desires & Ideals into Realities (1922) 160p. 1996. reprint ed. pap. 14.25 (*1-56459-793-8*) Kessinger Pub.

— I Reveal, the Landone Epistles. 138p. 1996. reprint ed. spiral bd. 14.00 (*0-7873-0524-3*) Hlth Research.

— Landone Assorted Titles, No. 1. 40p. 1996. reprint ed. spiral bd. 8.00 (*0-7873-1249-5*) Hlth Research.

— Landone Assorted Titles, No. 2. 35p. 1994. reprint ed. spiral bd. 8.00 (*0-7873-1043-3*) Hlth Research.

— Landone Assorted Titles, No. 3. 64p. 1994. reprint ed. spiral bd. 9.00 (*0-7873-1042-5*) Hlth Research.

— Landone Menus for Thirty One Days. 40p. 1994. reprint ed. spiral bd. 9.00 (*0-7873-1101-4*) Hlth Research.

— The Means Which Guarantee Leadership. 299p. 1996. reprint ed. spiral bd. 20.00 (*0-7873-0530-8*) Hlth Research.

— The Means Which Guarantee Leadership: How to Become a Leader. 1991. lib. bdg. 79.95 (*0-8490-4993-8*) Gordon Pr.

— The Methods of Truth Which I Use. 102p. 1996. reprint ed. spiral bd. 10.00 (*0-7873-0528-6*) Hlth Research.

— Mysterious Catalytic Foods. 63p. 1994. reprint ed. spiral bd. 11.00 (*0-7873-1033-6*) Hlth Research.

— Powers That Turn Failure into Success. 73p. 1985. reprint ed. spiral bd. 11.00 (*0-7873-1250-9*) Hlth Research.

— Proof of Proofs, They Live. 149p. 1996. reprint ed. spiral bd. 14.00 (*0-7873-0526-X*) Hlth Research.

— Prophecies of Melchi-Zedek in the Great Pyramid & the Seven Temples. 179p. 1996. reprint ed. pap. 14.50 (*0-7873-0523-5*) Hlth Research.

— Soul Catalysts & How to Use Them. 62p. 1996. reprint ed. spiral bd. 9.50 (*0-7873-1044-1*) Hlth Research.

— Spiritual Revelations of the Bible. 259p. (Orig.). 1996. reprint ed. spiral bd. 18.50 (*0-7873-1097-2*) Hlth Research.

— The Success Process. 233p. 1981. 12.00 (*0-89540-181-9*, SB-181) Sun Pub.

— Transformation of Your Life in Twenty-Four Hours. 16p. 1996. reprint ed. spiral bd. 8.00 (*0-7873-0531-6*) Hlth Research.

— Truth & Its Magnificent Simplicity. 62p. 1994. reprint ed. spiral bd. 9.50 (*0-7873-1086-7*) Hlth Research.

— Unconsciously Freeing the Body: (A Course of 16 Lessons) 36p. 1996. reprint ed. spiral bd. 9.00 (*0-7873-0525-1*) Hlth Research.

— Unknown Powers. 17p. 1994. reprint ed. spiral bd. 6.00 (*0-7873-1252-5*) Hlth Research.

— Your Ears: Reactivating Them. 28p. 1996. reprint ed. spiral bd. 9.00 (*0-7873-0532-4*) Hlth Research.

— Your Electronic Body & Electronic Potentials of Food. 249p. 1996. reprint ed. spiral bd. 27.50 (*0-7873-1072-7*) Hlth Research.

— Your Eyes - Rejuvenating Them. 47p. 1996. reprint ed. spiral bd. 9.00 (*0-7873-1074-3*) Hlth Research.

— Your Path Direct to the Goal You Desire. 518p. 1996. reprint ed. spiral bd. 33.50 (*0-7873-0529-4*) Hlth Research.

Landone Foundation Staff. He Lives. 127p. 1994. reprint ed. spiral bd. 14.00 (*0-7873-1013-1*) Hlth Research.

Landor, A. H. Tibet & Nepal Painted & Described. (C). 1994. 48.50 (*81-206-0852-6*, Pub. by Asian Educ Servs) S Asia.

***Landor, A. Henry Savage.** An Explorer's Adventures in Tibet: A 1987 Epic. 2nd fac. ed. (Illus.). 202p. 2000. pap. 18.00 (*1-879415-31-3*) Mtn n Air Bks.

Landor, Gina & Cleaver, Paul. How to Play the Penny Whistle. (Illus.). 40p. 1980. pap. 5.95 (*0-86001-780-X*, AM27137) Music Sales.

Landor, Lynn. Children's Own Stories: A Literature-Based Language Arts Program. (Illus.). 118p. 1990. pap. 20.00 (*0-936434-25-2*, Pub. by Zellerbach Fam Fund) Intl Spec Bk.

Landor, Walter Savage. Citation & Examination of William Shakespeare. LC 73-16141. (Studies in Shakespeare: No. 24). 1974. reprint ed. lib. bdg. 75.00 (*0-8383-1721-9*) M S G Haskell Hse.

— The Complete Latin Poetry of Walter Savage Landor, Vol. I. Sutton, Dana F., ed. LC 98-29221. (Salzburg Romantic Reassessment Ser.: Vol. 151A). 632p. 1998. text 129.95 (*0-7734-1249-2*) E Mellen.

— The Complete Latin Poetry of Walter Savage Landor, Vol. II. Sutton, Dana F., ed. LC 98-29221. (Salzburg Romantic Reassessment Ser.: Vol. 151B). 455p. 1998. text 109.95 (*0-7734-1251-4*) E Mellen.

— Complete Works, 16 vols., Set. (BCL1-PR English Literature Ser.). 1992. reprint ed. lib. bdg. 1440.00 (*0-7812-7587-3*) Rprt Serv.

— Gebir. LC 93-17427. 92p. 1993. reprint ed. 40.00 (*1-85477-128-0*) Continuum.

— Imaginary Conversations: Poems, Dialogues in Verse, & Epigrams, Longer Prose Works, 10 vols. Crump, Charles G., ed. LC 70-171652. (Illus.). 4126p. 1983. reprint ed. 910.00 (*0-404-07680-7*) AMS Pr.

— Poetry & Prose. LC 76-29435. reprint ed. 24.50 (*0-404-15314-3*) AMS Pr.

— Selected Imaginary Conversations of Literary Men & Statesmen. Proudfit, Charles L., ed. LC 69-10272. 302p. reprint ed. pap. 93.70 (*0-7837-6030-2*, 204584200008) Bks Demand.

Landorf Heatherley, Joyce. Mourning Song. 2nd expanded rev. ed. LC 74-9938. 240p. (gr. 11). 1994. pap. 8.99 (*0-8007-5547-2*) Revell.

Landorf, Joyce. He Began with Eve. large type ed. (Large Print Inspirational Ser.). 1985. pap. 11.95 (*0-8027-2511-2*) Walker & Co.

— His Stubborn Love. 1974. pap. 3.95 (*0-310-27122-3*, 9991P) Zondervan.

— Irregular People. large type ed. 1986. pap. 10.95 (*0-8027-2525-2*) Walker & Co.

— Let's Have a Banquet: Or Will One Dollar & Thirty-Six Cents Be Enough. 1968. pap. 5.95 (*0-310-27131-2*, 9994P) Zondervan.

Landow, George P. Elegant Jeremiahs: The Sage from Carlyle to Mailer. LC 86-47644. 184p. 1986. text 32.50 (*0-8014-1905-0*) Cornell U Pr.

— Hypertext: The Convergence of Contemporary Critical Theory & Technology. LC 91-20068. (Parallax: Re-Visions of Culture & Society Ser.). (Illus.). 240p. 1991. text 48.50 (*0-8018-4280-8*); pap. text 16.95 (*0-8018-4281-6*) Johns Hopkins.

Landow, George P., ed. Hyper-Text-Theory. 377p. 1994. text 48.50 (*0-8018-4837-7*) Johns Hopkins.

Landow, George P., jt. ed. see Delany, Paul.

Landow, R. Kenneth. Handbook of Dermatologic Treatment. LC 83-80541. 219p. 1986. pap. text 19.95 (*0-930010-09-4*) Jones Med.

Landowska, Wanda. Landowska on Music. 434p. reprint ed. lib. bdg. 59.00 (*0-685-14898-X*) Rprt Serv.

— Music of the Past. 185p. 1990. reprint ed. lib. bdg. 59.00 (*0-7812-9012-0*) Rprt Serv.

— Music of the Past. LC 75-181199. 184p. 1924. reprint ed. 39.00 (*0-403-01609-6*) Scholarly.

Landphai, Ted & Highsmith, Carol M. Boston. LC 96-43085. (Photographic Tour Ser.). (Illus.). 128p. 1997. 14.99 (*0-517-18329-3*) Random Hse Value.

— Chicago. LC 96-43089. (Photographic Tour Ser.). (Illus.). 128p. 1997. 14.99 (*0-517-18331-5*) Random Hse Value.

— Manhattan. LC 96-44146. (Photographic Tour Ser.). (Illus.). 128p. 1997. 14.99 (*0-517-18332-3*) Random Hse Value.

— New England. LC 96-43087. (Photographic Tour Ser.). (Illus.). 128p. 1997. 14.99 (*0-517-18333-1*) Random Hse Value.

Landphai, Ted, jt. auth. see Highsmith, Carol.

Landphai, Ted, jt. auth. see Highsmith, Carol M.

Landphair, jt. auth. see Highsmith, C.

Landphair, H. C. New York City. LC 96-43088. (Illus.). 128p. 1997. 14.99 (*0-517-18330-7*) Random Hse Value.

Landphair, H. C. & Klatt, F. Landscape Architecture Construction. 2nd ed. 448p. 1987. 48.25 (*0-444-01286-9*) P-H.

Landphair, H. C. & Motloch, J. L. Site Reconnaissance & Engineering: An Introduction for Architects, Landscape Architects & Planners. xxi, 300p. 1985. 45.00 (*0-444-00900-0*) P-H.

Landphair, Harlow. Materials & Methods for Landscape Architecture Construction. (C). 2000. text 60.00 (*0-13-254954-9*) P-H.

Landphair, Harlow & Klatt, Fred. Landscape Architecture Construction. 3rd ed. LC 98-24744. (Illus.). 432p. (C). 1998. 78.00 (*0-13-254947-6*) P-H.

Landphair, Harlow & Larsen, Terry. Evaluation & Development of Visualization Technology for Highway Transportation. (Illus.). 77p. (C). 1998. reprint ed. pap. text 20.00 (*0-7881-4937-7*) DIANE Pub.

Landphair, Ted. Virginia. LC 97-18035. 64p. 1998. 7.99 (*0-517-18758-2*) Random Hse Value.

Landphair, Ted, jt. auth. see Highsmith, Carol M.

Landre, Debra. Explorations in Statistics & Probability. 288p. (C). 1992. pap. text 28.95 (*0-8403-8099-2*) Kendall-Hunt.

Landre, John K. Spirituality: Personal Growth in the Second Half of Life. (Illus.). 152p. 1999. pap. 13.00 (*0-8059-4562-8*) Dorrance.

Landre, Nikki. Keys to Successful Music Lessons. LC 96-3665. (Parenting Keys Ser.). 160p. 1996. pap. 6.95 (*0-8120-9609-6*) Barron.

***Landre, Ralph W., Jr.** The Broken Center-Line: How to Be a Highway Patrol Officer & Enjoy It! LC 00-190706. 2000. 25.00 (*0-7388-1940-9*); pap. 18.00 (*0-7388-1941-7*) Xlibris Corp.

Landre, Rick, et al. Gangs: A Handbook for Community Awareness. LC 95-25314. (Illus.). 288p. 1997. 22.95 (*0-8160-3359-5*); pap. 12.95 (*0-8160-3724-8*) Facts on File.

Landreau, Anthony N. & Pickering, W. R. From the Bosporus to Samarkand: Flat-Woven Rugs. LC 71-81238. (Illus.). 1969. pap. 15.00 (*0-87405-001-4*) Textile Mus.

Landreau, Anthony N., et al. Flowers of the Yayla: Yoruk Weaving of the Toros Mountains. LC 83-51062. (Illus.). 112p. 1983. pap. 18.50 (*0-87405-021-9*) Textile Mus.

Landregan, Steve. Speak Lord! Reflections on the Ordination Rite for Deacons. 52p. (Orig.). 1987. pap. 3.95 (*1-55586-150-4*) US Catholic.

Landreneau, Raymond L., Jr. The Cajun French Language, Vol. I. LC 89-71246. 112p. 1990. pap. 19.95 (*0-913845-03-5*) Chicot Pr.

Landres, Galina, jt. auth. see Landres, Vlad.

Landres, Miriam D., ed. see Kabaker, Betty.

Landres, Peter & Meyer, Shannon. National Wilderness Preservation System Database: Key Attributes & Trends, 1964 Through 1998. (Illus.). 97p. (C). 1999. pap. text 25.00 (*0-7881-7885-7*) DIANE Pub.

Landres, Peter B., jt. ed. see Knight, Richard L.

***Landres, Vlad & Landres, Galina.** SQR in PeopleSoft & Other Applications. LC 99-20763. (Illus.). 600p. 1999. pap. 59.95 (*1-884777-77-5*) Manning Pubns.

Landreth, Bill. The Bank Secrecy Act: Exemption Regulations Clarified. Zimmerman, Carolyn, ed. LC 88-70571. (Orig.). 1988. pap. 10.00 (*0-317-91177-5*) Amherst Ent.

Landreth, Frank, ed. see Talania, Frank.

Landreth, Frank, ed. see Talania, Franquintin.

Landreth, Garry, jt. auth. see Kraft, Arthur.

Landreth, Garry L. Play Therapy: Dynamics of the Process of Counseling with Children. 380p. 1982. pap. 46.95 (*0-398-06221-8*) C C Thomas.

— Play Therapy: Dynamics of the Process of Counseling with Children. 380p. (C). 1982. text 58.95 (*0-398-04716-2*) C C Thomas.

Landreth, Harry H. History of Economic Theory, 3 vols. 3rd ed. LC 93-78675. (C). 1993. text 70.76 (*0-395-66858-1*) HM.

Landreth, Harry H., jt. auth. see Colander, David.

Landreth, Harry H., jt. ed. see Colander, David C.

L

Landreth, Jane. Gems of Nature. 161p. 1994. pap. text 6.95 (*1-885022-01-8*) Precious Gems.
— Gems of the Home. 151p. 1994. pap. text 6.95 (*1-885022-02-6*) Precious Gems.
— Magnify the Lord. 20p. 1994. 1.50 (*1-885022-00-X*) Precious Gems.
Landreth, John. The Dead Cat Capers. (Illus.). 324p. 1995. pap. 19.95 (*0-935680-56-X*) Kentucke Imprints.
Landreth, Marilyn L. Memories for Mary Ruth: Mieran, Bergtholdt, Sturtz, & Brasfield Families. (Illus.). (Orig.). 1997. pap. 30.00 (*0-9649896-1-1*) Muddy Water.
Landreth, Marilyn L. & Smith, Roy H. The Tie That Binds: Harvey United with Lake, Bridgewater, Clark, Smith, Carter, Dotterer, Other Families. (Illus.). 224p. (Orig.). 1996. pap. 25.00 (*0-9649896-0-3*, 750) Muddy Water.
***Landreth, Marsha.** The Holiday Murders. large type ed. LC 99-47888. 325p. 1999. 23.95 (*0-7838-8827-9*, G K Hall Lrg Type) Mac Lib Ref.
Landreth, Marsha. Vial Murders. LC 94-16398. (Doctor Samantha Turner Mystery Ser.). 224p. 1994. 19.95 (*0-8027-3199-6*) Walker & Co.
Landreth, Patrick, jt. auth. see Linehan, Patricia.
Landreth, Robert E. & Rebers, Paul A. Municipal Solid Wastes: Problems & Solutions. LC 96-31106. (Illus.). 288p. 1996. lib. bdg. 99.95 (*1-56670-215-1*) Lewis Pubs.
***Landrey, Gregory J.** The Winterthur Guide to Caring for Your Collection. (Illus.). 2000. pap. 17.95 (*0-912724-52-8*) Winterthur.
***Landrey, Dave & Landrey, Martha.** One So Precious among Us. Decker, Cynthia, ed. 96p. 1998. pap. text 6.95 (*1-57636-070-9*) SunRise Pbl.
Landrey, David, ed. see Oppenheimer, Joel.
Landrey, Martha, jt. auth. see Landrey, Dave.
Landrey, Wanda A. Boardin' in the Thicket: Recipes & Reminiscences of Early Big Thicket Boarding Houses. LC 89-24868. 192p. 1998. pap. 15.95 (*1-57441-054-7*) UNTX Pr.
— The Historic Belle - Jim Hotel of Jasper: Remembrances & Recipes of Those Who Knew It Best. LC 98-28766. (Illus.). 64p. 1998. pap. 8.95 (*1-57168-271-6*, Eakin Pr) Sunbelt Media.
— Lost in the Big Thicket: A Mystery & Adventure in the Big Thicket of Texas. LC 96-51663. (Illus.). 104p. (Orig.). (J). (gr. 5-6). 1997. pap. 10.95 (*1-57168-116-7*, Eakin Pr) Sunbelt Media.
— Outlaws in the Big Thicket. 128p. 1979. pap. 12.95 (*0-89015-144-X*) Sunbelt Media.
Landrigan, Philip J. & Kazemi, Homayoun, eds. The Third Wave of Asbestos Disease Vol. 643: Exposure to Asbestos in Place. 628p. 1992. 190.00 (*0-89766-677-1*) NY Acad Sci.
— The Third Wave of Asbestos Disease, Exposure to Asbestos in Place: Public Health Control. LC 92-6138. (Annals Ser.: Vol. 643). 628p. 1992. pap. 190.00 (*0-89766-678-X*, Q11) NY Acad Sci.
Landrigan, Philip J., jt. auth. see Needleman, Herbert L.
Landrine, Hope. The Politics of Madness: A Theory of the Function of Madness in a Stratified Society. LC 91-16889. (American University Studies: Psychology: Ser. VIII, Vol. 22). XVI, 217p. 1992. 44.95 (*0-8204-1571-5*) P Lang Pubng.
Landrine, Hope & Klonoff, Elizabeth A. African-American Acculturation: Deconstructing Race & Reviving Culture. LC 95-41809. 182p. 1996. 46.00 (*0-8039-7282-2*); pap. 21.00 (*0-8039-7283-0*) Sage.
— Discrimination Against Women: Prevalence, Consequences, Remedies. LC 97-4766. 297p. 1997. text 46.00 (*0-7619-0954-0*); pap. text 21.95 (*0-7619-0955-9*) Sage.
Landrine, Hope & Klonoff, Elizabeth A., eds. Black Women's Health: A Special Issue of Women's Health. 210p. 1997. pap. 40.00 (*0-8058-9855-7*) L Erlbaum Assocs.
Landrine, Hope, jt. auth. see Klonoff, Elizabeth A.
Landro, Laura. Survivor: Taking Control of Your Fight Against Cancer. LC 98-27002. 235p. 1998. 18.00 (*0-684-84335-8*) S&S Trade.
***Landro, Laura.** Survivor: Taking Control of Your Fight Against Cancer. 224p. 2000. pap. 12.00 (*0-684-85678-6*, Touchstone) S&S Trade Pap.
Landrock, Arthur H. Adhesives Technology Handbook. LC 85-15329. (Illus.). 444p. 1986. 64.00 (*0-8155-1040-3*) Noyes.
Landrock, Arthur H., ed. Handbook of Plastic Foams. LC 94-15236. (Illus.). 488p. 1995. 135.00 (*0-8155-1357-7*) Noyes.
***Landru, H. C.** Blue Parka Man: Alaskan Gold Rush Bandit. 196p. 2000. pap. 9.95 (*1-57833-112-9*) Todd Commns.
***Landrum.** Quincy. (Images of America Ser.). 1999. pap. 18.99 (*0-7385-0127-1*) Arcadia Publng.
Landrum, John B. O. History of Spartanburg County, South Carolina: Embracing an Account of Many Important Events & Biographical Sketches of Statesmen... And the Names of Many Others Worthy of Record in the History of Their County. 739p. 1997. reprint ed. 59.95 (*0-8063-4732-5*) Genealog Pub.
Landrum, Carl & Landrum, Shirley. Landrum's Quincy, Vol. 1. (Illus.). 208p. 1995. 25.00 (*1-884177-50-6*) Justice IL.
— Landrum's Quincy, Vol. 2. (Illus.). 208p. 1996. 25.00 (*1-884177-51-4*) Justice IL.
— Landrum's Quincy, Vol. 3. (Illus.). 208p. 1996. 25.00 (*1-884177-52-2*) Justice IL.
Landrum, Carl & Landrum, Shirley. Landrum's Quincy, Vol. 4. Hunter, Robert S., ed. (Illus.). 208p. 1997. 25.00 (*1-884177-53-0*) Justice IL.
Landrum, Faye. The Final Mile: a Wife's Response to her Husband's Terminal Illness. LC 99-39696. 175p. (Orig.). 1999. pap. text 9.99 (*0-8423-3483-1*) Tyndale Hse.
Landrum, Francis S. Van, see Van Landrum, Francis S.
Landrum, Gene N. Eight Keys to Greatness: How to Unlock Your Hidden Potential. LC 99-13588. (Illus.). 285p. 1999. 25.95 (*1-57392-686-8*) Prometheus Bks.
— Profiles of Black Success: Thirteen Creative Geniuses Who Changed the World. LC 96-39376. (Illus.). 402p. 1997. 25.95 (*1-57392-119-X*) Prometheus Bks.
— Profiles of Female Genius: Thirteen Creative Women Who Changed the World. LC 94-7579. (Illus.). 437p. (C). 1994. 25.95 (*0-87975-892-9*) Prometheus Bks.
— Profiles of Genius: Thirteen Creative Men Who Changed the World. LC 93-18637. 263p. (C). 1993. 25.95 (*0-87975-832-5*) Prometheus Bks.
— Profiles of Power & Success: Fourteen Geniuses Who Broke the Rules. LC 95-54002. (Illus.). 412p. 1996. 25.95 (*1-57392-052-5*) Prometheus Bks.
— Prometheus 2000 - Truth - Vision - Power Creativity, Innovation, Entrepreneurship: Derivation of Success & Power & the Use & Abuse of Libidinal Energy. 421p. 1997. pap. 14.95 (*0-9659355-0-7*) Genie-Vision.
Landrum, Graham. The Famous DAR Murder Mystery. 1995. mass mkt. 4.50 (*0-312-95568-5*, Pub. by Tor Bks) St Martin.
— The Famous DAR Murder Mystery. large type ed. LC 92-14498. 292p. 1992. reprint ed. lib. bdg. 19.95 (*1-56054-444-9*) Thorndike Pr.
— The Rotary Club Murder Mystery. 1996. mass mkt. 4.99 (*0-312-95796-3*, Pub. by Tor Bks) St Martin.
— The Sensational Music Club Mystery. large type ed. LC 95-2758. 250p. 1995. lib. bdg. 21.95 (*0-7838-1278-7*, G K Hall Lrg Type) Mac Lib Ref.
Landrum, Graham & Landrum, Robert. The Garden Club Mystery. LC 98-4991. 224p. 1998. text 20.95 (*0-312-18570-7*) St Martin.
Landrum, Graham Gordan. The Garden Club Mystery. LC 99-11186. 1999. 22.95 (*1-56895-642-8*) Wheeler Pub.
Landrum, J., Jr. Militerrorism: On the Morality of Combating Terror with Terror. LC 95-23001. (Critical Questions Ser.). 1996. text 9.95 (*0-7734-8909-6*) E Mellen.
Landrum, Jeff. Reflections of a Boomtown: A Photographic Essay of the Burkburnett Oil Boom 1912-1982. (Illus.). 1982. 24.95 (*0-9611894-0-1*) J Landrum Pub.
Landrum, John. Colonial & Revolutionary History of Upper South Carolina. LC 61-1396. (Illus.). 376p. 1999. 35.00 (*0-87152-001-X*) Reprint.
— History of Spartanburg County. LC 77-13343. (Illus.). 800p. 1999. reprint ed. 45.00 (*0-87152-255-1*) Reprint.
Landrum, John F. Out of Court: How to Protect Your Business from Litigation. 160p. 1992. pap. 14.95 (*0-9633730-9-9*) Headwaters LA.
Landrum, L. R. Campomanesia et al (Myrtaceae) (Flora Neotropica Monographs: No. 45). (Illus.). 180p. 1986. pap. text 35.50 (*0-89327-301-5*) NY Botanical.
Landrum, L. Wayne. Biscayne: The Story Behind the Scenery. LC 90-61963. (Illus.). 48p. (Orig.). 1990. pap. 7.95 (*0-88714-048-3*) KC Pubns.
Landrum, Larry. American Mystery & Detective Novels: A Reference Guide. LC 98-22916. (American Popular Culture Ser.). 296p. 1999. lib. bdg. 75.00 (*0-313-21387-9*, Greenwood Pr) Greenwood.
Landrum, Leslie R. The Life & Botanical Accomplishments of Boris Alexander Krukoff. LC 86-838. (Advances in Economic Botany Ser.: Vol. 2). (Illus.). 96p. (Orig.). 1986. 17.50 (*0-89327-298-1*) NY Botanical.
Landrum, Mary, jt. ed. see Dettmer, Peggy.
Landrum, Michael. Alternative Dispute Resolution: How to Prepare the Case & Represent Your Client. 1988. audio 150.00 (*1-55917-009-3*); VHS 750.00 (*1-55917-010-7*) Natl Prac Inst.
Landrum, Pat K., et al. Outcome Oriented Rehabilitation: Principles, Strategies & Tools for Effective Program Management. 340p. 1995. 57.00 (*0-8342-0665-X*) Aspen Pub.
Landrum, Phil, jt. auth. see Huggins, Kevin.
Landrum, R. Eric. Introduction to Psychology: A General Guidebook. 2nd ed. 220p. (C). 1997. spiral bd. 31.95 (*0-7872-3894-5*, 41389401) Kendall-Hunt.
Landrum, R. Eric, jt. ed. see Chastain, Garvin.
Landrum, Robert, jt. auth. see Landrum, Graham.
***Landrum, Robert K.** Monica's Tale of Sexual Harassment. 825p. 1999. pap. 39.50 (*0-9674118-0-7*) P A X Pubng.
Landrum, Shirley, jt. auth. see Landrum, Carl.
Landrum, Warren G., Jr. Forty Nine Per Cent. (Illus.). 75p. (Orig.). 1996. pap. 10.00 (*0-964957I-5-9*) Princess Lee.
Landry, Anne G. Represented Discourse in the Novels of Francois Mauriac: Catholic University of America. LC 70-128933. (Studies in Romance Languages & Literatures: No. 44). reprint ed. 37.50 (*0-404-50344-6*) AMS Pr.
Landry, Ashby D., Jr. & Landry, Brenda, eds. Secrets of the Original Don's Seafood & Steakhouse. (Illus.). 82p. 1996. 11.95 (*0-9654883-0-6*) Dons Seafood.
***Landry, Bart.** Black Working Wives: Pioneers of the American Family Revolution. (George Gund Foundation Imprint in Africa Ser.). 273p. 2000. 24.95 (*0-520-21826-4*, Pub. by U CA Pr) Cal Prin Full Svc.
Landry, Bart. The New Black Middle Class. 1987. pap. 15.95 (*0-520-06465-8*, Pub. by U CA Pr) Cal Prin Full Svc.
Landry, Bernard. A Phylogenetic Analysis of the Major Lineages of the Crambinae & of the Genera of Crambini of North America (Lepidoptera: Pyralidae), Vol. 1. Gupta, Virendra K., ed. (Memoirs on Entomology, International Ser.). (Illus.). 248p. 1995. 45.00 (*1-56665-056-9*) Assoc Pubs FL.
Landry, Bernard, jt. auth. see Quebec Province Ministere des Finances Staff.
Landry, Brenda, jt. ed. see Landry, Ashby D., Jr.
***Landry, Carey.** O Healing Light of Christ. 112p. 1999. pap. 9.95 (*1-57992-019-5*) OR Catholic.
Landry, Cat, jt. illus. see Fontenot, Mary Alice.
Landry, Christopher P. & Wilcox, David C. Study Guide for Basic Fluid Mechanics. 2nd ed. LC 99-72858. (Illus.). 246p. (C). 1999. pap. text 20.00 (*0-9636051-9-4*) DCW Industries.
Landry, Clay J. Saving Our Streams Through Water Markets: A Practical Guide. (Illus.). vi, 62p. 1998. spiral bd. 5.00 (*0-9668243-0-X*) Pol Econo Res.
***Landry, Dale A.** Christ Spirit. 1999. pap. 14.95 (*0-9684678-1-4*) B1 Destiny.
Landry, Donna. The Muses of Resistance: Laboring-Class Women's Poetry in Britain 1739-1796. (Illus.). 335p. (C). 1990. text 74.95 (*0-521-37412-X*) Cambridge U Pr.
Landry, Donna, ed. see Spivak, Gayatri Chakravorty.
Landry, Dorothy B. Family Fallout: A Handbook for Families of Adult Sexual Abuse Survivors. Bear, Euan, ed. 76p. 1991. pap. 12.95 (*1-884444-05-9*) Safer Soc.
Landry, Ed. Caribbean Adventures: Classic Cajun Cooking & Tales from the Reign of the Pirates. LC 94-70556. (Illus.). 128p. 1994. pap. 11.95 (*0-9630244-1-8*) Adlai Hse.
Landry, Elaine, et al. A Concordance to the Poems of Hart Crane. LC 72-10663. (Concordances Ser.: No. 4). 1973. 40.00 (*0-8108-0564-2*) Scarecrow.
Landry, Elaine M., et al. Curriculum for Negotiation & Conflict Management: Instructor's Manual. 524p. (C). 1991. 35.00 (*1-880711-01-X*) Prog Negot HLS.
Landry, Garrie, jt. auth. see Reese, William D.
Landry, Greg & Landry, Nancy, eds. Directory of Newsletters Related to Health, Medicine, Nutrition, & Sports. 48p. (Orig.). 1988. write for info. (*0-929363-00-0*) G Landry.
Landry, Hilton J. Interpretations in Shakespeare's Sonnets, 14. LC 76-1901. (Perspectives in Criticism Ser.: No. 14). (Illus.). 185p. 1976. reprint ed. lib. bdg. 65.00 (*0-8371-8749-4*, LAIS, Greenwood Pr) Greenwood.
Landry, Hilton J., ed. New Essays on Shakespeare's Sonnets. LC 71-16167. (Studies in the Renaissance: No. 1). 1976. 34.50 (*0-404-09028-1*) AMS Pr.
Landry, J., jt. auth. see Fontenot, M. A.
Landry, J. C., ed. see Valter, K. & Arrizabalaga, P.
Landry, Janice & Fesmire, Anna H. The World Is Out There Waiting. LC 93-29717. 256p. (C). 1993. pap. text 45.80 (*0-13-474735-6*) P-H.
Landry, Judith, tr. see Cazotte, Jacques.
Landry, Judith, tr. see Fenelon, Fania & Routier, Marcelle.
Landry, Judith, tr. see Germain, Sylvie.
Landry, Judith, tr. see Nodier, Charles.
Landry, Judith, tr. see Toaff, Ariel.
Landry, Judith, tr. see Verga, Giovanni.
Landry, Julie. A Christmas for Carol: A Short Play about an Unhappy Girl. 16p. 1991. pap. 3.25 (*0-88680-360-8*) I E Clark.
Landry, Julie, tr. see Fontenot, Mary A.
Landry, Julie F., tr. see Fontenot, Mary A.
Landry, Julie Fontenot, tr. see Fontenot, Mary A.
Landry, Julie Fontenot, tr. & illus. see Fontenot, Mary Alice.
Landry, Juliette, ed. see Mooney, Blake.
Landry, Linda L., et al. An Advocate's Guide to Surviving the SSI System. Vol. I. 1995. pap. text. write for info. (*0-944490-86-7*) Mass CLE.
***Landry, Lorraine Y.** Marx & the Postmodernism Debates: An Agenda for Critical Theory. LC 99-86107. 240p. 2000. 62.00 (*0-275-96889-8*, C6889, Praeger Pubs) Greenwood.
Landry, Margie, ed. see Bayou Civic Club, Inc. Staff.
Landry, Mim J. Overview of Addiction Treatment Effectiveness. (Illus.). 116p. (Orig.). (C). 1996. pap. text 35.00 (*0-7881-3656-9*) DIANE Pub.
— Understanding Drugs of Abuse: The Processes of Addiction, Treatment & Recovery. 363p. 1993. 22.95 (*0-88048-533-7*, 8533) Am Psychiatric.
Landry, Nancy, jt. ed. see Landry, Greg.
Landry, Paul. Kept in the Pocket of My Poems. 1993. pap. 3.00 (*0-929730-46-1*) Zeitgeist Pr.
Landry, Paul & McNair, Mattie. The Outward Bound Canoeing Handbook. (Illus.). 144p. 1992. pap. 12.95 (*1-55821-149-7*) Lyons Pr.
Landry, Pierre B. & Champ, Claire, eds. Canadian Art Vol. II (G-K) Catalogue of the National Gallery of Canada, Vol. 2, G-K. (Illus.). 108p. 1995. pap. text 74.95 (*0-88884-638-X*) U Ch Pr.
Landry, Pierre B., jt. auth. see Hill, Charles C.
Landry, Roger. Hot Prospects. 1990. mass mkt. 12.95 (*0-446-39129-8*, Pub. by Warner Bks) Little.
***Landry, Sandra.** Perfect Love. (Time Passages Romance Ser.). 2000. mass mkt. 5.99 (*0-515-12885-6*) Berkley Pub.
Landry, Sarah. Peterson 1st Urban Wildlife. LC 93-31279. 1998. pap. 5.95 (*0-395-93544-X*) HM.
***Landry, Sophamae Dean.** A Through Z Animal Poetry. (Illus.). 64p. (J). 2000. 20.00 (*0-8059-4796-5*) Dorrance.
Landry, Tom & Lewis, Gregg. Tom Landry. large type ed. (Illus.). 336p. 1991. reprint ed. pap. 15.95 (*0-8027-2659-3*) Walker & Co.
Lands, Merrilee, ed. Mayi: Some Bush Fruits of Dampeirland. (C). 1990. 30.00 (*0-7855-6627-9*, Pub. by Pascoe Pub) St Mut.
Lands, William E., ed. Biochemistry of Arachidonic Acid Metabolism. LC 85-4853. (Prostaglandins, Leukotrienes, & Cancer Ser.). 1985. text 176.50 (*0-89838-717-5*) Kluwer Academic.
Lands, William E., jt. ed. see Colowick, Sidney P.
Landsberg, Brian K. Enforcing Civil Rights: Race Discrimination & the Department of Justice. LC 96-29501. (Studies in Government & Public Policy). 296p. 1997. 35.00 (*0-7006-0826-5*) U Pr of KS.
***Landsberg, G. S.** Textbook of Elementary Physics, Vol. 1. 520p. 2000. pap. 33.75 (*0-89875-036-9*) U Pr Pacific.
Landsberg, Gary M., et al. Handbook of Behavioural Problems of the Dog & Cat. LC 96-15793. (Veterinary Handbook Ser.). (Illus.). 220p. 2000. pap. text 60.00 (*0-7506-3060-4*) Buttrwrth-Heinemann.
Landsberg, Hans H. Natural Resources for U. S. Growth: A Look Ahead to the Year 2000. LC 64-24348. 269p. reprint ed. pap. 83.40 (*0-7837-3120-5*, 204286700006) Bks Demand.
Landsberg, Hans H., ed. Making National Energy Policy. 151p. 1993. pap. 22.50 (*0-915707-70-5*) Resources Future.
Landsberg, Hans H. & Dukert, Joseph M. High Energy Costs: Uneven, Unfair, Unavoidable? LC 81-15648. 104p. 1981. pap. 9.95 (*0-8018-2782-5*) Resources Future.
Landsberg, Hans H., et al. Energy & the Social Sciences: An Examination of Research Needs. LC 74-16949. (Resources for the Future, RFF Working Papers: EN-3). 786p. reprint ed. pap. 200.00 (*0-608-12539-3*, 202380400034) Bks Demand.
— Resources in America's Future: Patterns of Requirements & Availabilities 1960-2000. LC 62-7233. 1017p. 1963. 50.00 (*0-8018-0357-8*) Resources Future.
Landsberg, Hans H., jt. auth. see Barger, Harold.
Landsberg, Hans H., jt. auth. see Netschert, Bruce C.
Landsberg, Hans H., jt. ed. see Olson, Mancur, Jr.
Landsberg, Helmut. The Urban Climate. LC 80-2766. (International Geophysics Ser.). 1981. text 79.00 (*0-12-435960-4*) Acad Pr.
Landsberg, J. J. & Gower, Stith T. Applications of Physiological Ecology to Forest Management. LC 96-27735. (Physiological Ecology Ser.). (Illus.). 354p. 1996. text 69.95 (*0-12-435955-8*) Morgan Kaufmann.
Landsberg, J. J., jt. ed. see Pereira, J. S.
Landsberg, Louis L. Biology & Psychology of Alcohol Drinking: Index of New Information & Research Reference Book. 150p. 1996. 47.50 (*0-7883-1170-0*); pap. 44.50 (*0-7883-1171-9*) ABBE Pubs Assn.
Landsberg, Marge E. The Genesis of Language & Speech: A Different Judgement of Evidence. xiv, 278p. (C). 1988. lib. bdg. 90.75 (*0-89925-370-9*) Mouton.
Landsberg, Marge E., ed. Syntactic Iconicity & Linguistic Freezes: The Human Dimension. (Studies in Anthropological Linguistics: No. 9). ix, 444p. (C). 1995. lib. bdg. 183.10 (*3-11-014227-9*) Mouton.
Landsberg, Max. The Tao of Coaching: Boost Your Effectiveness by Inspiring Those Around You. LC 97-19284. 200p. 1997. 22.95 (*1-888232-34-X*) Knowldge Exchange.
Landsberg, Melvin. Dos Passos Path to U. S. A. A Political Biography, 1912-1936. LC 72-75880. (Illus.). 304p. reprint ed. pap. 94.30 (*0-8357-9058-4*, 201220200081) Bks Demand.
Landsberg, Melvin, ed. & narrated by see Dos Passos, John.
Landsberg, Michele, jt. auth. see Newman, Fran.
***Landsberg, P. T.** Seeking Ultimates: An Intuitive Guide to Physics. LC 99-55029. 314p. 1999. pap. 21.00 (*0-7503-0657-2*) IOP Pub.
Landsberg, Paul-Louis. The Experience of Death: The Moral Problem of Suicide. Kastenbaum, Robert J., ed. LC 76-19579. (Death & Dying Ser.). 1979. reprint ed. lib. bdg. 21.95 (*0-405-09576-7*) Ayer.
Landsberg, Peter T. & Moss, T. S., eds. Basic Properties of Semiconductors. enl. rev. ed. LC 92-32392. (Handbook on Semiconductors Ser.: Vol. 1). 1218p. 1993. 405.00 (*0-444-88855-1*, North Holland) Elsevier.
— Basic Properties of Semiconductors, Set. write for info. (*0-318-70113-8*, North Holland) Elsevier.
Landsberg, Peter T. & Willoughby, A. F, eds. Recombination in Semiconductors: Selected Proceedings of the International Conference Held at the University of Southampton, England. 30 August - 1st September 1978. 1979. pap. 63.00 (*0-08-024226-X*, Pergamon Pr) Elsevier.
Landsberg, Sylvia. Cat-Logo de Leyes del Ao. (Illus.). 144p. 1992. 150.00 (*0-614-05788-4*, MICHIE) LEXIS Pub.
— The Medieval Garden. LC 95-61563. (Illus.). 144p. 1996. 24.95 (*0-500-01691-7*, Pub. by Thames Hudson) Norton.
Landsberger, Benno. Die Fauna des alten Mesopotamien nach der 14. LC 78-72747. (Ancient Mesopotamian Texts & Studies). reprint ed. 34.50 (*0-404-18190-2*) AMS Pr.
Landsberger, Kurt. The Root Box. 580p. 1997. text. write for info. (*0-9640120-4-9*) Front Desk LLC.
— William Steinitz, Chess Champion: A Biography of the Bohemian Caesar. LC 92-50376. (Illus.). 539p. 1992. lib. bdg. 55.00 (*0-89950-758-1*) McFarland & Co.
Landsberger, Sheldon & Creatchman, Marsha, eds. Elemental Analysis of Airborne Particles. (Advances in Environmental Process Control Technologies Ser.: Vol. 1). 326p. 1999. text 60.00 (*90-5699-627-4*, ECU75, Harwood Acad Pubs) Gordon & Breach.
Landsberger, Stefan. Chinese Propaganda Posters: From Revolution to Modernization. LC 95-9042. (Illus.). 240p. (C). (gr. 13). 1996. 94.95 (*1-56324-688-0*, East Gate Bk) M E Sharpe.
***Landsbergis, Vytautas.** Lithuania, Free at Last: The Autobiography of Vytautas Landsbergis. Packer, Anthony & Sova, Eimutis, trs. (Illus.). 352p. 2000. 35.00 (*0-295-97959-3*) U of Wash Pr.
Landsburg. Price Theory & Applications. 4th ed. LC 98-4436. (Intermediate Microeconomics Ser.). 1998. pap. 93.95 (*0-538-88206-9*) S-W Pub.
Landsburg, Alan. The Insects Are Coming. (Illus.). (Orig.). 1978. mass mkt. 2.25 (*0-446-82595-6*, Pub. by Warner Bks) Little.
Landsburg, Steven E. The Armchair Economist: Economics & Everyday Life. 260p. 1993. 22.95 (*0-02-917775-8*) Free Pr.
— The Armchair Economist: Economics & Everyday Life. 240p. 1995. per. 12.00 (*0-02-917776-6*) Free Pr.

An Asterisk (*) at the beginning of an entry indicates that the title is appearing for the first time.

— Book on Economic Philosophy. 1997. 22.50 (0-02-874103-X) Free Pr.

— Price Theory. 3rd ed. 1995. pap., student ed. 19.00 (0-314-04899-5) West Pub.

— Price Theory & Applications. 3rd ed. LC 94-32600. 832p. (C). 1995. pap. 65.75 (0-314-04059-5) West Pub.

— What Your Child Can Teach You about Economics: A Cheerful Guide to the Dismal Science. LC 97-35813. 224p. 1997. 23.50 (0-684-82755-7) Free Pr.

Landsburg, Steven E. & Feinstone, Lauren. Macroeconomics. (C). 1996. pap. text, student ed. 23.44 (0-07-020498-5) McGraw.

Landsburg, Steven E., jt. auth. see Feinstone, Lauren.

***Landsburgs & University of Rochester Staff.** Price Theory & Applications. 5th ed. (SWC-General Business Ser.). (C). 2001. pap. 65.00 (0-324-05979-5); text, student ed. 25.95 (0-324-05990-6) Sth-Wstrn College.

Landscape Architecture Magazine Staff. Home Landscape, 1982. (Illus.). 1983. pap. 7.95 (0-07-036194-0) McGraw.

Landscape Institute Staff, jt. ed. see Institute of Environmental Assessment Staff.

Landscheid, Ulf. Satze Uber Den Satz: Eine Theorie Der Satzbedeutung und Ihre Anwendung Auf Die Logik. (Studia Philosophica et Historica Ser.: No. 22). (GER., Illus.). 211p. 1997. 42.95 (3-631-32039-6) P Lang Pubng.

Landschulze, Maren. Alternativer Landbau und Feministische Naturwissenschaftskritik: Eine Bibliographie mit Kommentar. (Illus.). 211p. 1997. pap. 42.95 (3-631-31735-2) P Lang Pubng.

***Landsdowne, Judith A.** Lord Nightingale's Love Song. (Zebra Regency Romance Ser.). 2000. mass mkt. 4.99 (0-8217-6688-0, Zebra Kensgtn) Kensgtn Pub Corp.

Landsheere, Gilbert. La Investigacion Educativa. (SPA.). pap. 17.99 (968-16-4513-8, Pub. by Fondo) Continental Bk.

Landshoff, D. I., jt. auth. see Eden, Richard.

Landshoff, Ludwig. Johann Rudolf Zumsteeg (1760-1802) 215p. reprint ed. write for info. (0-318-71923-1) G Olms Pubs.

Landshoff, Peter, et al. Essential Quantum Physics. 2nd ed. LC 97-25151. (Illus.). 214p. (C). 1998. text 64.95 (0-521-62011-2); pap. text 24.95 (0-521-62993-4) Cambridge U Pr.

Landshoff, Ursula. Cats Are Good Company. LC 82-48844. (I Can Read Bks.). (Illus.). 64p. (J). (ps-3). 1983. 9.95 (0-06-023676-0) HarpC Child Bks.

Landshut, Siegfried. Politisches Woerterbuch. (GER.). 1958. pap. 75.00 (0-8288-6852-2, M-7589) Fr & Eur.

Landside Access to Ports Study Committee. Landside Access to U. S. Ports. LC 92-38897. (Special Reports: No. 238). 198p. 1993. 28.00 (0-309-05407-9) Transport Res Bd.

Landskron, Jerry. Remington Rolling Block Pistols. LC 81-50481. (Illus.). 304p. 1981. 60.00 (0-940028-01-8) Rolling Block.

— Remington Rolling Block Pistols. deluxe ed. LC 81-50481. (Illus.). 304p. 1981. 100.00 (0-940028-00-X) Rolling Block.

Landskroner, Ronald A. The Nonprofit Manager's Resource Directory. LC 95-51509. (Nonprofit Law, Finance, & Management Ser.). 522p. 1996. pap. text 84.95 incl. disk (0-471-14839-3) Wiley.

Landsman, Anne. The Devil's Chimney. LC 97-18951. 320p. 1997. 24.00 (1-56947-101-0) Soho Press.

— The Devil's Chimney: A Novel. 304p. 1999. pap. 12.95 (0-14-027746-3) Viking Penguin.

Landsman, Gregory. Balance of Beauty: Explodes the Body Myth. 1996. pap. text 13.95 (0-85572-267-3, Pub. by Hill Content Pubng) Seven Hills Bk.

***Landsman, Joyce, ed.** An A Fare to Remember: All Good Things Are Worth Waiting For. (Illus.). 325p. 1999. pap. 19.95 (0-9649541 0 9) Tcbidinc.

Landsman, Julie. Basic Needs: A Year with Street Kids in a City School. LC 93-16148. 246p. (Orig.). 1993. pap. 14.95 (0-915943-65-4) Milkweed Ed.

— Tips for Creating a Manageable Classroom: Understanding Your Students' Basic Needs. LC 94-31920. 32p. 1994. pap. 3.50 (1-57131-200-5) Milkweed Ed.

Landsman, Julie, jt. ed. see Haynes, David.

Landsman, Mark, jt. auth. see de Pres, Josquin.

Landsman, Michael. Attitude of a Servant: Servant Heart - A Sign of Strength & Inner Peace Like Jesus. 1987. pap. 6.99 (0-88270-700-0) Bridge-Logos.

— Lord, Increase Our Faith. LC 94-70706. 186p. (Orig.). 1994. mass mkt. 5.99 (0-88270-718-3) Bridge-Logos.

— Supportive Ministries. 32p. (Orig.). 1992. pap. 3.99 (0-88270-702-7) Bridge-Logos.

Landsman, Michael, jt. auth. see Harrison, Buddy.

***Landsman, N. P.** Mathematical Topics Between Classical & Quantum Mechanics. LC 98-18391. (Monographs in Mathematics). xix, 529p. 1998. 64.95 (0-387-98318-X) Spr-Verlag.

Landsman, Ned C. American Thought & Culture 1680-1760. LC 97-36274. (Illus.). 1997. 33.00 (0-8057-1626-2) Mac Lib Ref.

***Landsman, Ned C.** From Colorado to Provincials: American Thought & Culture, 1680-1760. 2000. reprint ed. pap. 16.95 (0-8014-8701-3) Cornell U Pr.

Landsman, Ned C. Scotland & Its First American Colony, 1683-1765. LC 84-42891. 375p. 1985. reprint ed. pap. 116.30 (0-608-02509-7, 206315300004) Bks Demand.

Landsman, Sandra G. Found: A Place for Me: The Development, Diagnosis & Treatment of Manic-Depressive Structure. (Illus.). xvi, 149p. (Orig.). 1985. pap. text 14.95 (0-935571-01-9) Treehouse.

— I'm Special: An Experiential Workbook for the Child in Us All. (Illus.). (J). (gr. k up). 1986. pap. 6.95 (0-935571-02-7) Treehouse.

Landsman, Stephan A., ed. American Bar Association Section of Litigation - Readings on Adversarial Justice: The American Approach to Adjudication. (American Casebook Ser.). 217p. (C). 1988. reprint ed. 20.95 (0-314-36115-4) West Pub.

Landsman, Susan. A History Mystery: What Happened to Amelia Earhart? 96p. (Orig.). (J). 1991. pap. 3.50 (0-380-76221-8, Avon Bks) Morrow Avon.

— A History Mystery: Who Shot JFK? 96p. (Orig.). (YA). 1992. pap. 3.50 (0-380-77063-6, Avon Bks) Morrow Avon.

— Survival! At Sea. 112p. (Orig.). 1993. pap. 3.50 (0-380-76603-5, Avon Bks) Morrow Avon.

— Survival! In the Desert. 112p. (Orig.). (J). 1993. pap. 3.50 (0-380-76601-9, Avon Bks) Morrow Avon.

— Survival! In the Jungle. 112p. (Orig.). (YA). 1993. pap. 3.50 (0-380-76605-1, Avon Bks) Morrow Avon.

— Survival! In the Mountains. 112p. (Orig.). (J). 1993. pap. 3.50 (0-380-76602-7, Avon Bks) Morrow Avon.

Landsman, Wayne R., jt. auth. see Beaver, William H.

Landsmann, Liliana T. & Strauss, Sidney, eds. Culture, Schooling, & Psychological Development. (Human Development Ser.). 224p. (C). 1991. text 73.25 (0-89391-529-7) Ablx Pub.

Landsness, Ruthanne N., tr. see Paulus, Trina.

Landson, Davis, ed. Spon's Mechanical & Electrical Services Price Book 1998. 560p. (C). (gr. 13). 1997. pap. 125.00 (0-419-23080-7) Thomson Learn.

Landsowne, Judith A. Camilla's Fate. 288p. 1997. mass mkt. 4.99 (0-8217-5688-5, Zebra Kensgtn) Kensgtn Pub Corp.

Landsteiner, Karl. Specificity of Serological Reactions. 348p. 1990. pap. 8.95 (0-486-66203-9) Dover.

Landstone, Hetty, tr. see Schnitzler, Arthur.

Landstrom, Elsie H. Closing the Circle: An American Family in China. LC 96-17397. (Illus.). 176p. (Orig.). 1997. pap. 16.95 (0-936609-38-9) QED Ft Bragg.

— Friends, Let Us Pray. LC 79-146679. (Orig.). 1970. pap. 4.00 (0-87574-174-6) Pendle Hill.

Landstrom, Elsie H., ed. Hyla Doc in Africa: 1950-1961. LC 93-6280. (Illus.). 104p. (Orig.). 1994. pap. 10.50 (0-936609-32-X) QED Ft Bragg.

Landstrom, Elsie H. & Watters, Hyla S. Hyla Doc: Surgeon in China Through War & Revolution, 1924-1949. LC 90-40637. (Illus.). 312p. (Orig.). 1990. pap. 12.95 (0-936609-19-2) QED Ft Bragg.

Landstrom, Hans, et al, eds. Entrepreneurship & Small Business Research in Europe: An ECSB Survey. 416p. 1997. 83.95 (1-85972-632-1, Pub. by Avebry) Ashgate Pub Co.

Landstrom, Hans, jt. ed. see Sexton, Donald.

Landstrom, Lena. Will Goes to the Beach. Wiberg, Carla, tr. LC 95-67923. (Illus.). 32p. (J). (ps). 13.00 (91-29-62914-4) FS&G.

Landstrom, Lena, jt. auth. see Landstrom, Olof.

***Landstrom, Olof.** Boo & Baa Get Wet. (Illus.). 28p. (J). (ps). 2000. mass mkt. 7.95 (91-29-64752-5) R&S Bks SW.

— Boo & Baa in the Woods. (Illus.). 28p. (J). (ps). 2000. mass mkt. 7.95 (91-29-64754-1) R&S Bks SW.

— Will Gets a Haircut.Tr. of Nisse Hos Fris Oren. (Illus.). 28p. (J). (ps-k). 2000. pap. 4.95 (91-29-64875-0) R&S Bks SW.

— Will's New Cap. (Illus.). 28p. (J). (ps-k). 2000. pap. 4.95 (91-29-64877-7) R&S Bks SW.

Landstrom, Olof & Landstrom, Lena. Boo & Baa at Sea. Sandin, Joan, tr. LC 96-70541. (Illus.). 28p. (J). (ps). 1997. 7.95 (91-29-63921-2) FS&G.

— Boo & Baa in Windy Weather. Sandin, Joan, tr. LC 96-68148. 28p. (J). (ps). 1996. pap. 7.95 (91-29-63920-4, Pub. by R & S Bks) FS&G.

— Boo & Baa on a Cleaning Spree. Sandin, Joan, tr. LC 96-70542. (Illus.). 28p. (J). (ps). 1997. 7.95 (91-29-63919-0) FS&G.

— Will Gets a Haircut. LC 93-660.Tr. of Nisse Hos Fris Oren. (Illus.). 28p. (J). 1993. reprint ed. 13.00 (91-29-62075-9, Pub. by R & S Bks) FS&G.

— Will Goes to the Post Office. LC 94-66898. (Illus.). 32p. (J). (ps-k). 1994. 13.00 (91-29-62950-0) FS&G.

— Will's New Cap. Fisher, Richard E., tr. LC 91-42407. (Illus.). 32p. (J). (ps-2). 1992. 13.00 (91-29-62062-7, Pub. by R & S Bks) FS&G.

Landsverk, Helen P., jt. auth. see Wardian, Jeanne F.

Landsverk, O. G. Runic Records of the Norsemen in America. (Library of Scandinavian Literature). 1974. lib. bdg. 42.50 (0-8057-5457-1) Irvington.

Landt, Artur. Lenses for 35mm Photography. LC 95-73080. (Kodak Workshop Ser.). (Illus.). 112p. (C). 1998. pap. 22.95 (0-87985-765-X, KW-18, Kodak) Saunders Photo.

***Landt, Artur.** Nikon F100. LC 99-39067. (Magic Lantern Guides Ser.). 176p. 1999. pap. 19.95 (1-883403-61-8, Silver Pixel Pr) Saunders Photo.

Landt, Artur. Nikon N60. LC 99-10123. (Magic Lantern Guides Ser.). 176p. 1999. pap. 19.95 (1-883403-56-1, Pub. by Saunders Photo) Sterling.

Landt, Fran, ed. see Collins, Max A.

Landt, Fran, ed. see Starr, Victoria.

Landtman, Gunnar. The Folk-Tales of the Kiwai Papuans. LC 78-63204. (Folktale Ser.). 1980. reprint ed. 42.50 (0-404-16139-1) AMS Pr.

— The Origin of the Inequality of the Social Classes. LC 75-100511. reprint ed. 37.50 (0-404-00623-X) AMS Pr.

— The Origin of the Inequality of the Social Classes. LC 68-56332. (Illus.). 444p. 1969. reprint ed. lib. bdg. 79.50 (0-8371-0522-6, LASC, Greenwood Pr) Greenwood.

Landtroop, Belinda A., jt. auth. see Art, Clip.

Landtsheer, Christ'l de, see Feldman, Ofer & De Landtsheer, Christ'l, eds.

Landtsheer, Christ'l de, see De Landtsheer, Christ'l, ed.

Landua, R., et al, eds. Medium-Energy Antiprotons & the Quark-Gluon Structure of Hadrons. (Ettore Majorana International Science Ser., Life Sciences: Vol. 58). (Illus.). 256p. (C). 1992. text 114.00 (0-306-44087-3, Kluwer Plenum) Kluwer Academic.

Landucci, Luca. Florentine Diary from Fourteen Fifteen to Fifteen Forty-Two. LC 76-88827. (Art Histories Collection). (Illus.). reprint ed. 23.50 (0-405-02225-5) Ayer.

— A Florentine Diary from Fourteen Fifty to Fifteen Sixteen. De Rosen Jervis, Alice, tr. LC 75-169766. (Select Bibliographies Reprint Ser.). 1977. reprint ed. 25.95 (0-8369-5986-8) Ayer.

***Landus, Thomas D.** Container Tree Nursery Manual: Seedling Propagation, 6. 173p. 1999. 24.00 (0-16-050049-4, Agriculture Dept) USGPO.

Landuyt, Sylvia. The Cemetery Gang. LC 96-90026. (Illus.). (J). (gr. 5-8). 1996. 8.95 (0-533-11779-8) Vantage.

Landva, Arvid & Knowles, G. David. Geotechnics of Waste Fills: Theory & Practices. LC 90-44937. (Special Technical Publication Ser.: No. 1070). (Illus.). 370p. 1990. text 45.00 (0-8031-1285-8, STP1070) ASTM.

Landvater, Darryl V. MRP II Standard System - A Handbook for Manufacturing Software Survival. LC 88-50484. 250p. 1993. pap., student ed. 67.50 (0-939246-13-9) Wiley.

— World Class Production & Inventory Management. LC 92-61829. 280p. 1993. 114.00 (0-939246-19-8, TM7525) Wiley.

— World Class Production & Inventory Management. 2nd ed. LC 97-1493. 304p. 1997. 55.00 (0-471-17855-1) Wiley.

Landvater, Darryl V. & Gray, Christopher D. MRP II Standard System - A Handbook for Manufacturing Software. 352p. 1995. 95.00 (0-471-13275-6) Wiley.

— MRP II Standard System - A Handbook for Manufacturing Software Survival. LC 88-50485. 350p. 1993. 201.00 (0-939246-12-0) Wiley.

Landvik, Lorna. Patty Jane's House of Curl. 1999. mass mkt. 6.99 (0-8041-1460-9) Ivy Books.

— Patty Jane's House of Curl. large type ed. (Niagara Large Print Ser.). 488p. 1997. 29.50 (0-7089-5877-X) Ulverscroft.

— Patty Jane's House of Curl: A Novel. LC 95-15731. 292p. 1995. 19.95 (1-882593-12-X) Bridge Wrks.

— Patty Jane's House of Curl: A Novel. 292p. 1996. pap. 11.00 (0-449-91100-4) Fawcett.

— The Tall Pine Polka. LC 99-21849. 304p. 1999. 22.50 (0-345-43317-3) Ballantine Pub Grp.

***Landvik, Lorna.** The Tall Pine Polka. 1999. pap. 25.00 (0-449-00370-1) Fawcett.

— Welcome to the Great Mysterious. 320p. 2000. 23.00 (0-345-43881-7) Ballantine Pub Grp.

Landvik, Lorna. Your Oasis on Flame Lake. 304p. 1998. pap. 12.00 (0-449-00298-5) Fawcett.

Landvogt, Erasmus. A Compactification of the Bruhat-Tits Building. LC 95-44956. (Lecture Notes in Mathematics Ser.: No. 1619). 152p. 1995. 38.95 (3-540-60427-8) Spr-Verlag.

***Landweber, L. H. & Winfree, E., eds.** Evolution As Computation: DIMACS Workshop, Princeton, January 1999. (Natural Computing Ser.). 300p. 2000. 49.00 (3-540-66709-1) Spr-Verlag.

Landweber, Laura & Baum, Eric, eds. DNA Based Computers II: DIMACS Workshop, June 10-12, 1996. LC 98-35278. (DIMACS: Series in Discrete Mathematics & Theoretical Computer Science: Vol. 44). 275p. 1998. 59.00 (0-8218-0756-0) Am Math.

Landweber, Laura F. & Dobson, Andrew P. Genetics & the Extinction of Species: DNA & the Conservation of Biodiversity. LC 99-24114. 1999. pap. 19.95 (0-691-00971-6, Pub. by Princeton U Pr) Cal Prin Full Svc.

Landweber, Laura F. & Dobson, Andrew P., eds. Genetics & the Extinction of Species: DNA & the Conservation of Biodiversity. LC 99-24114. (Illus.). 192p. 1999. 45.00 (0-691-00970-8, Pub. by Princeton U Pr) Cal Prin Full Svc.

Landweber, Lawrence H., jt. auth. see Brainerd, Walter S.

Landwehr, Bernard J. Basic Business Statistics. LC 84-26195. 246p. (C). 1985. lib. bdg. 24.50 (0-89874-823-2) Krieger.

Landwehr, Carl E., et al, eds. Dependable Computing for Critical Applications 3. LC 93-9046. (Dependable Computing & Fault-Tolerant Systems Ser.: Vol. 8). (Illus.). xii, 382p. 1993. 143.95 (0-387-82481-2) Spr-Verlag.

Landwehr, Carl E., et al. Dependable Computing for Critical Applications. LC 93-9046. (Dependable Computing & Fault-Tolerant Systems Ser.: No. 3). 1993. write for info. (3-211-82481-2) Spr-Verlag.

Landwehr, Carl E., jt. ed. see Keefe, Thomas F.

***Landwehr, Ellen.** Rosemaling with Ellen. (Illus.). 32p. 2000. 10.95 (1-57377-096-5) Easl Pubns.

Landwehr, G., ed. Application of High Magnetic Fields in Semiconductor Physics: Proceedings, Grenoble, France, 1982. (Lecture Notes in Physics Ser.: Vol. 177). 552p. 1983. pap. 49.00 (0-387-11996-5) Spr-Verlag.

— High Magnetic Fields in Semiconductor Physics. (Solid-State Sciences Ser.: Vol. 71). (Illus.). 560p. 1987. 86.95 (0-387-17872-4) Spr-Verlag.

— High Magnetic Fields in Semiconductor Physics II. (Solid-State Sciences Ser.: Vol. 87). (Illus.). 648p. 1989. 106.95 (0-387-51227-6) Spr-Verlag.

Landwehr, G., et al, eds. High Magnetic Fields in Semiconductor Physics Three: Quantum Hall Effect, Transport & Optics - Proceedings at the International Conference, Wurzburg, FRG, July 30 to August 3, 1990. (Solid-State Sciences Ser.: Vol. 101). (Illus.). 744p. 1992. 113.00 (0-387-53618-3) Spr-Verlag.

Landwehr, G. & Rashba, E. I., eds. Landau Level Spectroscopy, 2 pts., Set. 1300p. 1990. 617.00 (0-444-88874-8, North Holland) Elsevier.

Landwehr, James M. Exploring Surveys & Information from Samples. pap. 13.95 (0-86651-340-X) Seymour Pubns.

Landwehr, James M. & Watkins, Ann E. Exploring Data: Student. rev. ed. (Quantitative Literacy Ser.). (Illus.). 181p. 1994. teacher ed. 15.95 (0-86651-613-1) Seymour Pubns.

— Exploring Data: Student. 2nd rev. ed. (Quantitative Literacy Ser.). (Illus.). 181p. 1994. pap. text 10.50 (0-86651-610-7) Seymour Pubns.

Landwehr, John. Splendid Ceremonies: State Entries & Royal Funerals in the Low Countries, 1515-1791--A Bibliography. (Illus.). 350p. 1971. text 99.50 (90-6004-287-5, Pub. by B De Graaf) Coronet Bks.

Landwehr, K., ed. Ecological Perception Research, Visual Communication, & Aesthetics. (Recent Research in Psychology Ser.). viii, 143p. 1990. 38.95 (0-387-52200-X) Spr-Verlag.

Landwehr, Richard. Budapest: The Stalingrad of the Waffen-SS. 2nd rev. ed. (Siegrunen Monograph Ser.: Vol. 2). (Illus.). 74p. 1998. 24.95 (1-57638-129-3, SR2) Merriam Pr.

***Landwehr, Richard.** Budapest: The Stalingrad of the Waffen-SS. 2nd rev. ed. (Siegrunen Monograph Ser.: Vol. 2). (Illus.). 74p. 1998. pap. 14.95 (1-57638-128-5, SR2) Merriam Pr.

Landwehr, Richard. Lions of Flanders: Flemish Volunteers of the Waffen-SS, Eastern Front, 1941-1945. 163p. 1998. pap. 32.00 (1-899765-03-4) Intl Spec Bk.

— Steadfast Hussars: The Last Cavalry Divisions of the Waffen-SS. 2nd rev. ed. (Siegrunen Monograph Ser.: Vol. 1). (Illus.). 67p. 1997. 25.00 (1-57638-105-6, SR1); pap. 15.00 (1-57638-130-7, SR1) Merriam Pr.

***Landwehr, Richard & Nielsen, Holger T.** Nordic Warriors: SS-Panzergrenadier-Regiment 24 Danmark, Eastern Front, 1943-45. (Armed Forces of the Third Reich). 194p. 1999. (1-899765-07-7, Pub. by Shelf Bks) Intl Spec Bk.

Landwehr, Richard, et al. The Wallonien: The History of the 5th SS-Sturmbrigade & 28th SS Volunteer Panzergrenadier Division. 2nd rev. ed. (World War II Monograph: Vol. 162). (Illus.). 43p. 1997. 17.95 (1-57638-089-0, M162H); pap. 7.95 (1-57638-088-2, M162S) Merriam Pr.

Landwehr, U. Industrial Mobility & Public Policy. viii, 169p. 1996. pap. 59.00 (3-7908-0949-7) Spr-Verlag.

Landwehr, William C. Watercolor U. S. A., 1986: The Monumental Image. LC 86-61583. (Illus.). 80p. (Orig.). 1986. pap. text 15.00 (0-934306-06-0) Springfield.

Landwehr, William C., ed. see Albin, Edgar A., et al.

Landwehrmeyer, Richard Geleitwort von, see Walravens, Hartmut V., ed.

Landy. Economics. 2nd ed. (C). 1995. text 35.33 (0-201-62875-9) Addison-Wesley.

— Psychology of Work Behavior. 3rd ed. (Psychology Ser.). Date not set. mass mkt., student ed. 10.50 (0-534-10664-1) Brooks-Cole.

Landy, Alice S. The Heath Introduction to Literature. 3rd ed. LC 87-80091. 1085p. (C). 1988. pap. text 29.96 (0-669-14809-1); teacher ed. 2.66 (0-669-14810-5) HM Trade Div.

— The Heath Introduction to Literature. 4th ed. 1142p. (C). 1992. pap. text 29.96 (0-669-24409-0); teacher ed. 31.16 (0-669-24410-4) HM Trade Div.

— The Heath Introduction to Literature. 5th ed. (C). 1996. text, teacher ed. 31.16 (0-669-35511-9); pap. text 29.96 (0-669-35510-0) HM Trade Div.

Landy, Edward, et al, eds. Guidance in American Education, 3 vols., 1. LC 64-54998. 1990. pap. 3.95 (0-674-36500-3) HUP.

— Guidance in American Education, 3 vols., 2. LC 64-54998. 1990. pap. 7.95 (0-674-36501-1) HUP.

— Guidance in American Education, 3 vols., 3. LC 64-54998. 1990. 14.00 (0-674-36503-8) HUP.

***Landy, Elliott.** Remembering Woodstock... 30 Years Later. (Illus.). 33p. 1999. reprint ed. 15.95 (0-9672475-0-0) Woodstock Fest.

— Woodstock Dream. 2000. pap. text 22.50 (3-8238-5452-6) te Neues.

Landy, Francis. Hosea. (Readings Ser.). 192p. 1995. 57.50 (1-85075-549-3, Pub. by Sheffield Acad); pap. 19.50 (1-85075-733-X, Pub. by Sheffield Acad) CUP Services.

Landy, Francis. Paradoxes of Paradise: Identity & Difference in the Song of Songs. (Bible & Literature Ser.). 1983. pap. 10.95 (0-907459-17-X) Dove Bkslrs.

— Paradoxes of Paradise: Identity & Difference in the Song of Songs. (Bible & Literature Ser.: No. 7). 410p. 1983. 95.00 (0-907459-16-1, Pub. by Sheffield Acad) CUP Services.

Landy, Frank J. Psychology: The Science of People. 2nd ed. (Illus.). 672p. (C). 1987. pap. text, student ed. write for info. (0-318-61592-4) P-H.

— Psychology of Work Behavior. 3rd ed. 1985. mass mkt. 39.25 (0-534-10663-3) Brooks-Cole.

Landy, Frank J., et al, eds. Performance Measurement & Theory. 416p. 1983. text 79.95 (0-89859-246-1) L Erlbaum Assocs.

Landy, Gene K. The Software Developer's & Marketer's Legal Companion: Protect Your Software & Your Software Business/Book & Disk. LC 93-19050. 560p. 1993. pap. 36.95 incl. disk (0-201-62276-9) Addison-Wesley.

Landy, Gerald. Military Paintings of Terence Cuneo. (Illus.). 192p. 60.00 (1-872727-51-4) Pincushion Pr.

Landy, Gloria, jt. ed. see Kaltovich, Edith R.

Landy, Jacob. The Architecture of Minard Lafever. LC 69-19461. 227p. reprint ed. pap. 70.40 (0-7837-0420-8, 204074300018) Bks Demand.

L

L

Landy, Joanne. Ready to Use Physical Education Activities. (J). (gr. 5-9). 1993. pap. 27.95 (*0-685-63549-X*) P-H.

Landy, Joanne M. & Burridge, Keith. 50 Simple Things You Can Do to Raise a Child Who Is Physically Fit: Raise a Child Physically Fit. (Illus.). 144p. 1997. 11.95 (*0-02-861984-6*, Arc) IDG Bks.

***Landy, Joanne M. & Burridge, Keith R.** Ready-to-Use Fine Motor Skills & Handwriting Activities for Young Children LC 99-30193. (Complete Motor Skills Activities Program Ser.). 1999. write for info. (*0-13-013942-4*) Aspen Law.

— Ready-to-Use Motor Skills & Movement Station Lesson Plans for Young Children. LC 00-20250. (Complete Motor Skills Activities Program Ser.). 1999. pap. 29.95 (*0-13-013943-2*) P-H.

Landy, Joanne M. & Landy, Maxwell J. Ready-to-Use P.E. Activities for Grades 3-4, Vol. 2. Vol. 2. 392p. (J). (gr. 3-4). 1992. pap. text, student ed. 27.95 (*0-13-673088-4*) P-H.

— Ready-to-Use Physical Education Activities, Bk. 3. 432p. (J). (gr. 5-6). 1993. pap. text, student ed. 27.95 (*0-13-673070-1*) P-H.

— Ready-to-Use Physical Education Activities, Vol. 1. LC 92-21049. 320p. (C). 1992. pap. text 27.95 (*0-13-673054-X*, Parker Publishing Co) P-H.

— Ready to Use Physical Education Activities for Grades 7-9. 464p. (C). 1993. pap. text, student ed. 27.95 (*0-13-673062-0*) P-H.

Landy, Joanne M., jt. auth. see Burridge, Keith R.

Landy, Leigh. Experimental Music Notebooks. (Performing Arts Studies). 146p. 1994. text 30.00 (*3-7186-5553-5*, Harwood Acad Pubs); pap. text 15.00 (*3-7186-5554-3*, Harwood Acad Pubs) Gordon & Breach.

— What's the Matter with Today's Experimental Music? Organized Sound Too Rarely Heard. (Contemporary Music Studies). xiv, 308p. 1991. pap. text 15.00 (*3-7186-5168-8*, Harwood Acad Pubs) Gordon & Breach.

Landy, Leigh, jt. ed. see Denyer, Frank.

Landy, Lynne, jt. auth. see Pyke, Kaye.

***Landy, Marc & Milkis, Sidney M.** Presidential Greatness. LC JK511.L357 2000. 288p. 2000. text 34.95 (*0-7006-1005-7*) U Pr of KS.

Landy, Marc, ed. see De Jouvenel, Bertrand.

Landy, Marc K. The Politics of Environmental Reform: Controlling Kentucky Strip Mining. LC 76-15907. (RFF Working Paper Ser.: PD-2). (Illus.). 414p. reprint ed. pap. 128.40 (*0-608-17386-X*, 203020800067) Bks Demand.

Landy, Marc K., ed. Environmental Impact Statement Directory: The National Network of EIS-Related Agencies & Organizations. LC 80-27909. 380p. 1981. 110.00 (*0-306-65195-5*, Kluwer Plenum) Kluwer Academic.

Landy, Marc K. & Levin, Martin A., eds. The New Politics of Public Policy. LC 94-24379. 384p. 1995. text 49.95 (*0-8018-4877-6*); pap. text 16.95 (*0-8018-4878-4*) Johns Hopkins.

Landy, Marc K., et al. The Environmental Protection Agency: Asking the Wrong Quesstions: From Nixon to Clinton. exp. ed. 368p. (C). 1994. pap. text 23.95 (*0-19-508673-2*) OUP.

Landy, Marc K., ed. see De Jouvenel, Bertrand.

Landy, Marcia. Cinematic Uses of the Past. LC 96-22176. 264p. (C). 1996. pap. 19.95 (*0-8166-2825-4*); text 49.95 (*0-8166-2824-6*) U of Minn Pr.

— Fascism in Film: The Italian Commercial Cinema, 1931-1943. LC 85-43296. 369p. reprint ed. pap. 114.40 (*0-7837-0095-4*, 204037300016) Bks Demand.

— Film, Politics & Gramsci. LC 93-43616. 1994. pap. 19.95 (*0-8166-2391-0*) U of Minn Pr.

— The Folklore of Consensus: Theatricality in the Italian Cinema, 1930-1943. LC 97-44015. (Suny Series, Cultural Studies in Cinema/Video). (Illus.). 352p. (C). 1998. pap. text 22.95 (*0-7914-3804-X*) State U NY Pr.

— The Folklore of Consensus: Theatricality in the Italian Cinema, 1930-1943. LC 97-44015. (Suny Series, Cultural Studies in Cinema/Video). (Illus.). 352p. (C). 1998. text 68.50 (*0-7914-3803-1*) State U NY Pr.

***Landy, Marcia.** Italian Film. LC 99-35247. (National Film Traditions Ser.). (Illus.). 448p. (C). 2000. 64.95 (*0-521-64009-1*); pap. 22.95 (*0-521-64977-3*) Cambridge U Pr.

***Landy, Marcia, ed.** The Historical Film: History & Memory in Media. LC 00-28080. (Depth of Field Ser.). 370p. (C). 2000. text 50.00 (*0-8135-2855-0*); pap. text 20.00 (*0-8135-2856-9*) Rutgers U Pr.

Landy, Marcia & Villarejo, Amy. Queen Christina. LC 96-139030. 79p. 1996. pap. 10.95 (*0-85170-523-5*, Pub. by British Film Inst) Ind U Pr.

Landy, Maxwell J., jt. auth. see Landy, Joanne M.

Landy, Michael S. & Movshon, J. Anthony, eds. Computational Models of Visual Processing. (Illus.). 406p. 1991. 60.00 (*0-262-12155-7*, Bradford Bks) MIT Pr.

Landy, Michale S., ed. see Gaylord, Richard J. & Pavel, Misha.

Landy, R. A., jt. auth. see Rigaud, M. A.

Landy, Robert E. Responsible Presidency. 1997. 24.95 (*0-02-917777-4*) Free Pr.

Landy, Robert J. Collected Essays in Drama Therapy: The Double Life. 268p. 1995. 24.95 (*1-85302-322-1*, Pub. by Jessica Kingsley) Taylor & Francis.

— Drama Therapy: Concepts, Theories & Practices. 2nd ed. LC 94-28228. 294p. (C). 1994. pap. 41.95 (*0-398-05947-0*); text 61.95 (*0-398-05928-4*) C C Thomas.

— Handbook of Educational Drama & Theatre. LC 82-6111. 282p. 1982. lib. bdg. 75.00 (*0-313-22947-3*, LHE/, Greenwood Pr) Greenwood.

— Persona & Performance: The Meaning of Role in Drama, Therapy, & Everyday Life. LC 93-2361. 278p. 1996. pap. text 21.00 (*0-89862-598-X*, 2598) Guilford Pubns.

— Persona & Performance: The Meaning of Role in Drama, Therapy & Everyday Life. 250p. 1993. write for info. (*1-85302-229-2*, Pub. by Jessica Kingsley) Taylor & Francis.

— Persona & Performance: The Meaning of Role in Drama, Therapy & Everyday Life. 250p. 1994. pap. write for info. (*1-85302-230-6*, Pub. by Jessica Kingsley) Taylor & Francis.

Landy, Uta, jt. ed. see Ratnam, S. Shan.

Landynski, Jacob W. Search & Seizure & the Supreme Court: A Study in Constitutional Interpretation. LC 65-13523. (Johns Hopkins University Studies in Historical & Political Science: Ser. 84: No. 1). 296p. reprint ed. pap. 91.80 (*0-608-10211-3*, 200519300050) Bks Demand.

Landzberg, Abraham H., ed. Electronics Manufacturing Diagnostics Handbook. LC 92-18936. 1993. text 99.95 (*0-442-00471-0*, VNR) Wiley.

Lane. Burdens of Intimacy. LC 98-17100. 1999. lib. bdg. 46.00 (*0-226-46859-3*) U Ch Pr.

Lane. Focus on Pronunciation: Principles & Practice for Effective Communication. 1995. 26.83 (*0-201-59284-3*) Addison-Wesley.

Lane. Hospitality World. (Hospitality, Travel & Tourism Ser.). 1996. pap., teacher ed. write for info. (*0-442-02473-8*, VNR) Wiley.

— I Want to Be Baptised. 1994. pap. 3.99 (*0-946462-08-9*, Pub. by Evangelical Pr) P & R Pubng.

— Nutrition Workbook. 11th ed. 1992. pap. 11.96 (*0-314-01328-8*) Wadsworth Pub.

— Student Solutions Manual to Accompany Calculus. 5th ed. (C). 1992. pap. text, student ed. 27.00 (*0-03-096968-9*) Harcourt Coll Pubs.

— Succeeding as a Home/Health Aide. (Home Care Aide Ser.). 1993. pap., teacher ed. 12.00 (*0-8273-3833-3*) Delmar.

— Succeeding As Homemaker - Home-Health Aide. (Home Care Aide Ser.). 1994. wbk. ed. 13.95 (*0-8273-5365-0*) Delmar.

— Succeeding As Homemaker - Home Health Aide Guide. (Home Care Aide Ser.). 1994. 12.95 (*0-8273-5530-0*) Delmar.

***Lane.** Websters Fundamentals of Grant Writing. (Webster's New World Ser.). 224p. 2000. pap. 10.95 (*0-02-863855-7*, Websters New Wrld) Macmillan Gen Ref.

Lane. Writing Clearly: An Editing Guide. 2nd ed. (J). 1999. pap. 31.95 (*0-8384-0949-0*) Heinle & Heinle.

Lane & Otten, eds. Fracture Mechanics: 13th Conference - STP 743. 650p. 1981. 58.50 (*0-8031-0732-3*, STP743) ASTM.

Lane, jt. auth. see Lerner, Alan J.

Lane, A. & Catrice, R. Formulaire International: Modeles D'actes, Formules et Locutions Pour la Pratique Jurisdiques. (FRE & GER.). 724p. 1969. 89.95 (*0-8288-6598-1*, M-6330) Fr & Eur.

Lane, A. N. The Lion Concise Book of Christian Thought LC 85-174392. 239 p. 1984. pap. write for info. (*0-85648-505-5*) Lion USA.

Lane, A. N. S., ed. see Calvin, John.

Lane, A. T. Solidarity or Survival? American Labor & European Immigrants, 1830-1924, 21. LC 86-25735. (Contributions in Labor Studies: No. 21). 242p. 1987. 55.00 (*0-313-25544-X*, LSV/, Greenwood Pr) Greenwood.

Lane, A. Thomas, ed. Biographical Dictionary of European Labor Leaders. LC 94-24945. 1204p. 1995. lib. bdg. 225.00 (*0-313-26456-2*, Greenwood Pr) Greenwood.

— Biographical Dictionary of European Labor Leaders: A-L, Vol. 1. LC 94-24945. 616p. 1995. lib. bdg. 175.00 (*0-313-29899-8*, Greenwood Pr) Greenwood.

— Biographical Dictionary of European Labor Leaders: M-Z, Vol. 2. LC 94-24945. 552p. 1995. lib. bdg. 175.00 (*0-313-29900-5*, Greenwood Pr) Greenwood.

Lane, Abbe. But Where Is Love? 512p. 1994. mass mkt. 5.99 (*0-446-60035-0*, Pub. by Warner Bks) Little.

Lane, Abigail, et al. Abigail Lane. LC 98-3962. 1998. 10.95 (*0-933856-56-3*) Mus Art Chicago.

Lane, Alfred H. Gifts & Exchange Manual. LC 79-7590. 121p. 1980. lib. bdg. 49.95 (*0-313-21389-5*, LGE/, Greenwood Pr) Greenwood.

Lane, Alice. Atlantii! (Illus.). 296p. (Orig.). 1993. pap. 14.95 (*0-9636665-0-9*) Altre Pub.

Lane, Allen. The Queen. LC 78-303872. 186 p. 1977. write for info. (*0-7139-1060-7*, A Lane) Viking Penguin.

***Lane, Allison.** Beleagured Earl. (Regency Romance Ser.). 220p. 2000. mass mkt. 4.99 (*0-451-19972-3*, Sig) NAL.

Lane, Allison. A Bird in Hand. 218p. 1999. mass mkt. 4.99 (*0-451-19790-9*, Sig) NAL.

— Birds of a Feather. (Signet Regency Romance Ser.). 1999. mass mkt. 4.99 (*0-451-19825-5*) NAL.

***Lane, Allison.** Double Deceit. (Signet Regency Romance Ser.). 224p. 1999. mass mkt. 4.99 (*0-451-19854-9*, Sig) NAL.

Lane, Allison. Second Lady Emily. (Signet Regency Romance Ser.). 224p. 1998. mass mkt. 4.99 (*0-451-19518-3*, Sig) NAL.

Lane, Alvin S. & Dreishpoen, Doug. The Terese & Alvin S. Lane Collection: Twentieth-Century Sculpture & Sculptors' Works on Paper. (Illus.). 1995. pap. 34.95 (*0-932900-40-2*) Elvejhem Mus.

Lane, Ambrose I. Return of the Buffalo: The Story Behind America's Indian Gaming Explosion. LC 95-11677. (Illus.). 240p. 1995. 55.00 (*0-89789-432-4*, Bergin & Garvey) Greenwood.

Lane, Amy. Incognito. 100p. 1999. pap. 10.00 (*1-886383-92-8*) Pride & Imprints.

***Lane, Amy.** Lives of the Saints. 20p. 1999. pap. 2.95 (*1-886383-91-X*) Pride & Imprints.

— Rosemilk. 40p. 1999. 5.95 (*1-886383-84-7*) Pride & Imprints.

— Skeleton. 40p. 1999. pap. 4.95 (*1-886383-85-5*) Pride & Imprints.

Lane, Andrew. Motoring Costume. (Album Ser.: No. 197). (Illus.). 32p. 1989. pap. 6.25 (*0-85263-872-8*, Pub. by Shire Pubns) Parkwest Pubns.

Lane, Andy. The Babylon File. 256p. (Orig.). 1997. mass mkt. 5.95 (*0-7535-0049-3*, Pub. by Virgin Bks) London Brdge.

— The Babylon File: The Unofficial Guide to J. Michael Straczynski's Babylon 5, Vol. 2. rev. ed. 286p. 1999. mass mkt. 7.95 (*0-7535-0233-X*, Pub. by Virgin Bks) London Brdge.

— Bond Files: The Definitive Unofficial Guide to Ian Fleming's James Bond. 1998. mass mkt. 7.95 (*0-7535-0218-6*, Pub. by Virgin Bks) London Brdge.

Lane, Andy & Richards, Justin, eds. Dcalog 4: Re-Generations. 5.95p. (Orig.). 1997. mass mkt. 5.95 (*0-426-20505-7*, Pub. by Virgin Bks) London Brdge.

Lane, Ann. Britain, the Cold War & Yugoslav Unity: 1941-1949. LC 96-226649. 220p. 1996. 67.50 (*1-898723-27-3*, Pub. by Sussex Acad Pr) Intl Spec Bk.

Lane, Ann & Temperley, Howard, eds. The Rise & Fall of the Grand Alliance, 1941-1945. LC 95-13886. 212p. 1996. text 69.95 (*0-312-12674-3*) St Martin.

Lane, Ann J. To Herland & Beyond: The Life & Work of Charlotte Perkins Gilman. LC 96-37487. 432p. 1997. reprint ed. pap. text 17.50 (*0-8139-1742-5*) U Pr of Va.

Lane, Ann J., ed. The Debate over Slavery: Stanley Elkins & His Critics. LC 79-141518. (Illini Bks.: No. IB-73). 384p. reprint ed. pap. 119.10 (*0-608-10746-8*, 202225700026) Bks Demand.

— Mary Ritter Beard: A Sourcebook. LC 99-13674. 272p. 2000. pap. 19.95 (*1-55861-219-X*, Pub. by Feminist Pr) Consort Bk Sales.

Lane, Ann J., ed. & intro. see Gilman, Charlotte Perkins.

Lane, Anne W. & Beale, Harriet B. To Walk with God (1920) 120p. 1998. reprint ed. pap. 17.95 (*0-7661-0327-7*) Kessinger Pub.

Lane, Anthony. On Shakespeare. 1999. pap. write for info. (*0-375-70062-5*) Vin Bks.

Lane, Anthony N. S., ed. The Unseen World: Christian Reflection on Angels, Demons & the Heavenly Realm. LC 97-200100. (Tyndale House Studies Ser.). 240p. 1997. pap. 16.99 (*0-8010-2142-1*, Ephesians: Powe) Baker Bks.

Lane, Art, jt. auth. see Lane, Kit.

Lane, Arthur E. An Adequate Response: The War Poetry of Wilfred Owen & Siegfried Sassoon. LC 74-39905. 191p. reprint ed. pap. 59.30 (*0-7837-3795-5*, 204361500010) Bks Demand.

Lane, B. & Gregg, W. Encyclopedia of Serial Killers. 1995. mass mkt. 7.50 (*0-425-15213-8*) Berkley Pub.

Lane, Barbara. Background of Treaty-Making in Western Washington. (Treaty Manuscripts Ser.: No. 3). 32p. 15.00 (*0-944253-25-3*) Inst Dev Indian Law.

— Echoes from Medieval Halls: Past-Life Memories from the Middle Ages. LC 97-6281. (Illus.). 256p. (Orig.). 1997. pap. 12.95 (*0-87604-390-2*, 471) ARE Pr.

— Echoes from the Battlefield: First-Person Accounts of Civil War Past Lives. Robertson, Jon, ed. LC 95-44539. (Illus.). 278p. 1996. pap. 12.95 (*0-87604-355-4*, 465) ARE Pr.

— Sixteen Clues to Your Past Lives. LC 99-10526. 1999. pap. 9.95 (*0-87604-421-6*) ARE Pr.

Lane, Barbara, jt. auth. see Lane, Robert B.

Lane, Barbara M. Architecture & Politics in Germany, 1918-1945. LC 85-8550. (Illus.). 292p. 1985. pap. 20.50 (*0-674-04370-7*) HUP.

Lane, Barry. After "The End" Teaching & Learning Creative Revision. LC 92-32704. 230p. (C). 1992. pap. text 24.00 (*0-435-08714-2*, 08714) Heinemann.

— The Revisers Tool Box. (Illus.). 200p. 1998. 19.00 (*0-9656574-4-2*) Discover Writing.

— Writing As a Road to Self-Discovery. 2nd ed. 1997. reprint ed. pap. 17.00 (*0-9656574-2-6*) Discover Writing.

Lane, Barry, jt. auth. see Ballenger, Bruce.

Lane, Barry, ed. see Boise, Ruth.

Lane, Barry, ed. see Champine, Rosa B.

Lane, Barry, ed. see Cram, Lillian.

Lane, Barry, ed. see Gulliver, Deborah.

Lane, Belden C. The Solace of Fierce Landscapes: Exploring Desert & Mountain Spirituality. LC 98-10842. (Illus.). 296p. 1998. 27.50 (*0-19-511682-8*) OUP.

Lane, Ben, ed. see Fogle, Jeanne S.

Lane, Bethany, tr. see Ballester, Mariano.

***Lane, Bill.** Complete Idiot's Guide to Flying & Gliding. (Complete Idiot's Guides Ser.). 360p. 2000. pap. text 16.95 (*0-02-863885-9*, Alpha Ref) Macmillan Gen Ref.

Lane, Brian. The Butchers. 1995. mass mkt. 5.95 (*0-86369-600-7*, Pub. by Virgin Bks) London Brdge.

— Chronicle of 20th Century Murder, Vol. 1. 288p. 1995. mass mkt. 5.99 (*0-425-14649-9*) Berkley Pub.

***Lane, Brian.** Crime & Detection. (Eyewitness Books). (Illus.). (J). (gr. 4-7). 2000. 19.99 (*0-7894-6622-8*) DK Pub Inc.

— Crime & Detection. (Eyewitness Books). (J). (gr. 4-7). 2000. 15.95 (*0-7894-5882-9*) DK Pub Inc.

— Crime & Detection. LC 97-32376. (Eyewitness Books). (Illus.). 64p. (J). 1998. 19.00 (*0-679-89117-X*) Knopf.

— Crime & Detection. LC 97-32376. (Eyewitness Books). (J). 1998. lib. bdg. 20.99 (*0-679-99117-4*) Random.

Lane, Brian. Forces from Beyond: Shocking True Stories Behind the World's Most Bizarre Murders. LC 96-94951. 1997. mass mkt. 5.99 (*0-380-78554-4*, Avon Bks) Morrow Avon.

— Investigation of Murder. (Crimebusters Ser.). (Illus.). 32p. (J). (gr. 4-6). 1996. lib. bdg. 20.90 (*0-7613-0527-0*, Copper Beech Bks) Millbrook Pr.

— Killer Cults: Murderous Messiahs & Their Fanatical Followers. 310p. 1997. pap. 13.95 (*0-7472-5514-8*, Pub. by Headline Bk Pub) Trafalgar.

— Murder Update: Modern Murders That Made the Headlines. 224p. 1991. pap. 9.95 (*0-88184-740-2*) Carroll & Graf.

Lane, Brian, ed. The Murder Club Regional Guides, 2 vols., No. 5: Eastern & Home Countries. (C). 1989. pap. 39.00 (*0-245-54679-0*) St Mut.

— The Murder Club Regional Guides, 2 vols., No. 6: South-West England & Wales. (C). 1989. pap. 39.00 (*0-245-54686-3*) St Mut.

Lane, Brigitte M. Franco-American Folk Traditions & Popular Culture in a Former Milltown. LC 90-39059. (Harvard Dissertations in Folklore & Oral Literature Ser.). 632p. 1990. reprint ed. text 35.00 (*0-8240-2674-8*) Garland.

Lane, Bruce & Wyatt, Scott. New York's 50 Best Places to Eat Southern. LC 98-2928. 128p. 1998. pap. 12.00 (*1-885492-57-X*) City & Co.

Lane, Byron. Byron's War: I Never Will Be Young Again. Dickinson, C. C., ed. LC 97-27688. (Illus.). 284p. 1997. pap. 21.95 (*1-55571-402-1*, Hellgate Pr) PSI Resch.

Lane, Byron D. Managing People: A Practical Guide. 3rd ed. LC 96-33212. (Successful Business Library). 217p. 1996. pap. 21.95 (*1-55571-380-7*, Oasis Pr) PSI Resch.

Lane, C. E. & Steinberg, R. Discovery of the Neutrino, Franklin Symposium Proceedings in Celebration. 232p. 1993. text 91.00 (*981-02-1567-3*) World Scientific Pub.

Lane, Calvin W. Evelyn Waugh. (English Authors Ser.: No. 301). 192p. (C). 1981. 28.95 (*0-8057-6793-2*) Macmillan.

Lane, Carla, jt. auth. see Portway, Patrick.

Lane, Carole A., et al. Naked in Cyberspace: How to Find Personal Information Online. LC 97-193244. 544p. (Orig.). 1997. pap. 29.95 (*0-910965-17-X*) Info Today Inc.

Lane, Charles. Cooper Henderson & the Open Road. 128p. 1990. 100.00 (*0-85131-392-2*, Pub. by J A Allen) St Mut.

— A Voluntary Political Government: Letters from Charles Lane. LC 82-19787. 104p. (Orig.). 1982. pap. 5.95 (*0-9602574-3-8*) M E Coughlin.

Lane, Charles, ed. Custodians of the Commons: Pastoral Land Tenure in East & West Africa. (Illus.). 192p. 1998. pap. 30.00 (*1-85383-473-4*, Pub. by Escan Pubns) Island Pr.

Lane, Charles E., jt. ed. see Humm, Harold J.

Lane, Charles S. New Hampshire's First Tourists in the Lakes & Mountains. rev. ed. (Illus.). 207p. 1993. pap. 18.00 (*0-9637214-1-0*) Old Print Barn.

Lane, Chris, jt. auth. see Lee, Melinda.

Lane, Christel. Christian Religion in the Soviet Union: A Sociological Study. LC 77-801. 256p. (C). 1978. text 32.50 (*0-87395-327-4*) State U NY Pr.

— Industry & Society in Europe: Stability & Change in Britain, Germany & France. LC 94-43574. (Illus.). 256p. (Orig.). 1995. 95.00 (*1-85278-394-X*) E Elgar.

— Industry & Society in Europe: Stability & Change in Britain, Germany & France. LC 94-43574. 256p. (Orig.). (C). 1996. pap. 30.00 (*1-85898-274-X*) E Elgar.

***Lane, Christel.** Trust Within & Between Organizations: Conceptual Issues & Empirical Applications. LC 99-89127. 352p. 2000. pap. 29.95 (*0-19-924044-2*) OUP.

Lane, Christel & Bachmann, Reinhard, eds. Trust Within & Between Organizations: Conceptual Issues & Empirical Applications. LC 97-51508. (Illus.). 348p. 1998. text 85.00 (*0-19-829318-6*) OUP.

***Lane, Christina.** Feminist Hollywood: From Born in Flames to Point Break. LC 99-53522. 2000. 39.95 (*0-8143-2799-0*); pap. 19.95 (*0-8143-2922-5*) Wayne St U Pr.

***Lane, Christopher.** Burdens of Intimacy. LC 98-17100. 288p. 1999. pap. text 18.00 (*0-226-46860-7*) U Ch Pr.

Lane, Christopher. Christ in the Carols. LC 99-31844. 1999. 12.99 (*0-8423-3521-8*) Tyndale Hse.

— Elements of a Kill. 416p. 1998. mass mkt. 5.99 (*0-380-79870-0*, Avon Bks) Morrow Avon.

— Kingdom Parables. (Illus.). 192p. (J). (gr. k-3). 1994. 16.99 (*1-56476-275-0*, 6-3275, Victor Bks) Chariot Victor.

— The Psychoanalysis of Race. LC 97-38840. (Illus.). 1p. 1998. 52.00 (*0-231-10946-6*); pap. 19.50 (*0-231-10947-4*) Col U Pr.

— The Ruling Passion: British Colonial Allegory & the Paradox of Homosexual Desire. LC 95-6484. 344p. 1995. text 49.95 (*0-8223-1677-3*); pap. text 17.95 (*0-8223-1689-7*) Duke.

— Season of Death: An Inupiat Eskimo Mystery. 352p. 1999. mass mkt. 5.99 (*0-380-79872-7*, Avon Bks) Morrow Avon.

***Lane, Christopher.** A Shroud of Midnight Sun. LC 99-94992. (Inupiat Eskimo Mysteries Ser.). 352p. 2000. mass mkt. 5.99 (*0-380-79873-5*, Avon Bks) Morrow Avon.

Lane, Christopher. Stardust: I Climbed a Rainbow Once. (Illus.). 1993. 4.50 (*0-8378-5304-4*) Gibson.

— Stardust: I Saw an Angel Yesterday. (Illus.). 1993. 4.50 (*0-8378-5305-2*) Gibson.

— Tonopah. LC 98-49556. 2000. pap. 12.99 (*0-310-21568-4*) Zondervan.

Lane, Christopher W. A Guide to Collecting Antique Maps. Cresswell, Donald H., ed. (Illus.). 42p. 1997. pap. 8.00 (*0-9636924-3-7*) Phila Prnt Shop.

— Impressions of Niagara: The Charles Rand Penney Collection. 198p. 1993. 50.00 (*0-9636924-0-2*); pap. 29.50 (*0-9636924-1-0*) Phila Prnt Shop.

An Asterisk (*) at the beginning of an entry indicates that the title is appearing for the first time.

Lane, Christopher W., et al. A Guide to Collecting Antique Historical Prints. (Illus.). 48p. (Orig.). 1995. pap. 8.00 (*0-9636924-2-9*) Phila Prnt Shop.

***Lane, Christy.** Christy Lane's Complete Book of Line Dancing. 2nd ed. LC 99-48366. (Illus.). 208p. 2000. pap. 16.95 (*0-7360-0067-4*) Human Kinetics.

Lane, Clinton F. & Kabalka, George W. A New Hydroboration Reagent. 1976. pap. 12.75 (*0-08-021330-8*, Pergamon Pr) Elsevier.

Lane, Clive. Cottage Garden Annuals: Grown from Seed for Summer-Long Color. LC 97-192527. (Illus.). 160p. 1997. 27.95 (*0-7153-0429-1*) Sterling.

***Lane, Connie.** Reinventing Romeo. 2000. mass mkt. 5.99 (*0-440-23593-6*) Dell.

Lane County Mathematics Project Staff. Problem Solving in Mathematics. 1997. pap. text 19.95 (*0-86651-184-9*); pap. text 19.95 (*0-86651-182-2*); pap. text 19.95 (*0-86651-183-0*) Seymour Pubns.

Lane, Cristy & Stevens, Laura A. How to Help Your Own Troubled Marriage. 1989. pap. 9.95 (*0-9618889-0-3*) L S Records.

Lane, Cynthia, jt. auth. see Reddy, Kumuda.

Lane, Cynthia, ed. see Records, Maryla W.

Lane, D. Preach the Word. 1994. pap. 3.99 (*0-85234-247-0*, Pub. by Evangelical Pr) P & R Pubng.

Lane, D. A., et al, eds. Fibrinogen: Fibrin Formation & Fibrinolysis: Proceedings of a Workshop on Fibrinogen, London, England, April 2-3, 1985. (Illus.). xviii, 396p. 1986. 192.35 (*3-11-010597-7*) De Gruyter.

Lane, D. A., et al. Heparin & Related Polysaccharides. (Advances in Experimental Medicine & Biology Ser.: Vol. 313). (Illus.). 384p. (C). 1992. text 110.00 (*0-306-44212-4*, Kluwer Plenum) Kluwer Academic.

Lane, D. R. Veterinary Nursing, 2 vols. 836p. 1996. pap. text 70.00 (*0-7506-3417-0*) Buttrwrth-Heinemann.

Lane, D. R. & Cooper, B. Veterinary Nursing. 2nd ed. LC 99-18294. 720p. 1999. pap. text 77.50 (*0-7506-3999-7*) Buttrwrth-Heinemann.

Lane, D. R. & Cooper, B., eds. Veterinary Nursing, 2 vols. 2nd ed. 1994. text. write for info. (*0-08-042288-8*) Elsevier.

Lane, D. R., jt. ed. see Cooper, B.

Lane, D. R., ed. see Jones, Bruce V.

Lane, Dakota. Johnny Voodoo. 208p. (YA). (gr. 7 up). 1997. mass mkt. 4.50 (*0-440-21998-1*) BDD Bks Young Read.

— Johnny Voodoo. 1998. 9.60 (*0-606-12971-5*, Pub. by Turtleback) Demco.

Lane, Dame E. Hear the Other Side. 1985. 40.00 (*0-406-50240-4*, U.K., MICHIE) LEXIS Pub.

Lane, Damon W. Seniors Wealth with Safety. 300p. 1998. 34.99 (*1-892046-00-8*) IntegrityDirect.

Lane, David. Law Relating to Unincorporated Associations. 350p. 1996. pap. write for info. (*1-85941-028-6*, Pub. by Cavendish Pubng) Gaunt.

— The Phenomenon of Teilhard: Prophet for a New Age. 192p. 1996. text 21.95 (*0-86554-498-0*, MUP/P131) Mercer Univ Pr.

***Lane, David.** Political Economy of Russian Oil. LC 99-15556. 240p. 1999. text 69.00 (*0-8476-9508-5*) Rowman.

Lane, David. The Roots of Russian Communism: A Social & Historical Study of Russian Social Democracy 1898-1907. LC 74-15196. 1975. pap. text 14.95 (*0-271-01178-5*) Pa St U Pr.

— Soviet Society under Perestroika. 256p. 1990. text 75.00 (*0-04-445166-0*); pap. text 22.95 (*0-04-445167-9*) Routledge.

— Soviet Society under Perestroika. 300p. 1992. pap. 14.95 (*0-00-302060-6*, A8325) Routledge.

Lane, David, ed. Russia in Flux: The Political & Social Consequences of Reform. 272p. 1992. 95.00 (*1-85278-680-9*) E Elgar.

— Russia in Flux: The Political & Social Consequences of Reform. 272p. 1993. pap. 30.00 (*1-85278-713-9*) E Elgar.

— Russia in Transition: Policies, Classes & Inequalities. 292p. (C). 1995. pap. 32.46 (*0-582-27566-0*) Longman.

Lane, David & Lane, Robert. Transistor Radios: A Collector's Encyclopedia & Price Guide. LC 94-16053. (Illus.). 176p. 1994. pap. 19.95 (*0-87069-712-9*, Wllce-Homestd) Krause Pubns.

Lane, David & Stratford, Brian, eds. Current Approaches to Down's Syndrome. LC 85-8842. 447p. 1985. 75.00 (*0-275-90212-9*, C0212, Praeger Pubs) Greenwood.

Lane, David, jt. auth. see Harlow, Ed.

Lane, David, jt. auth. see Lowe, Scott.

Lane, David, jt. auth. see Talsky, M. Aaron.

Lane, David, jt. ed. see Harlow, Ed.

Lane, David A. Heparin. 1989. 143.00 (*0-8493-7100-7*, R) CRC Pr.

Lane, David A. & Miller, Andrew, eds. Child & Adolescent Therapy: A Handbook. LC 92-18914. (Psychotherapy Handbooks Ser.). 1993. pap. 36.95 (*0-335-09890-8*) OpUniv Pr.

Lane, David C. Clash of the Archetypes: The Mummy Meets the Wolfman. (Occam's Razor Ser.). 1992. pap. 2.00 (*1-56543-006-9*) Mt SA Coll Philos.

— The Enchanted Land: A Journey with the Saints of India. 125p. 1999. pap. 9.95 (*1-56543-053-0*, EL1999) Mt SA Coll Philos.

— Exposing Cults: When the Skeptical Mind Confronts the Mystical. LC 94-9197. (Religious Information Systems Ser.: Vol. 10). 304p. 1994. text 25.00 (*0-8153-1275-X*, SS890) Garland.

— Gurus, Swamis, & Vegetarianism. (Occam's Razor Ser.). 53p. (Orig.). 1992. pap. text 2.00 (*1-56543-011-5*) Mt SA Coll Philos.

— Inner Visions & Running Trains: A Comparative Study of the Unknowing Sage & the Tibetan Book of the Dead. (Jewels of India Ser.). 60p. 1992. pap. 2.00 (*1-56543-007-7*) Mt SA Coll Philos.

— The Making of a Spiritual Movement: The Untold Story of Paul Twitchell & Eckankar. rev. ed. (Understanding Cults & Spiritual Movements Ser.). 211p. 1994. pap. 15.00 (*0-9611124-6-8*) Del Mar Pr.

— The Making of a Spiritual Movement: The Untold Story of Paul Twitchell & Eckankar. 4th rev. ed. (Understanding Cults & Spiritual Movements Ser.: No. 1). (Illus.). 171p. 1989. pap. 19.95 (*0-685-26797-0*) Del Mar Pr.

— The Mystical Dimension: An Essay on Unknowingness. (Jewels of India Ser.). (Orig.). 1992. pap. 2.00 (*1-56543-010-7*) Mt SA Coll Philos.

— Why I Don't Eat Faces: The Hierarchical Principle Behind Vegetarianism. (Occam's Razor Ser.). 54p. (Orig.). 1992. pap. 4.95 (*1-56543-019-0*) Mt SA Coll Philos.

Lane, David C., ed. The Teachings of Jesus: A Dialogue Between an Indian Mystic & a Group of Christian Fundamentalists. (Jewels of India Ser.). 50p. 1992. pap. 2.00 (*1-56543-005-0*) Mt SA Coll Philos.

— Understanding Cults & Spiritual Movements. (Understanding Cults & Spiritual Movements Ser.). (Illus.). 200p. (Orig.). 1989. pap. 21.95 (*0-9611124-2-5*) Del Mar Pr.

— The Unknowing Sage: The Life & Work of Baba Fagir Chand. (Enchanted Land Book Ser.). (Illus.). 63p. (Orig.). 1989. pap. 11.95 (*0-9611124-1-7*) Del Mar Pr.

Lane, David C., ed. see Chano, Fagir.

Lane, David C., ed. see Juergensmeyer, Mark.

Lane, David J. The Peshitta of Leviticus. LC 94-569. (Monographs of the Peshitta Institute Leiden: Vol. 6). xv, 184p. 1994. 92.50 (*90-04-10020-2*) Brill Academic Pubs.

***Lane, David S.** The Political Economy of Russian Oil. LC 99-15556. 240p. 1999. pap. text 29.95 (*0-8476-9509-3*) Rowman.

Lane, David S. The Rise & Fall of State Socialism: Industrial Society & the Socialist State. LC 96-42467. (C). 1996. text 55.95 (*0-7456-0742-X*, Pub. by Polity Pr); pap. text 22.95 (*0-7456-0743-8*, Pub. by Polity Pr) Blackwell Pubs.

Lane, Denis. Cloud & the Silver Lining. 1985. pap. 3.99 (*0-85234-193-8*, Pub. by Evangelical Pr) P & R Pubng.

— Man & His God. 1981. pap. 4.99 (*0-85234-155-5*, Pub. by Evangelical Pr) P & R Pubng.

Lane, Denis, ed. In the Spirit of Powys: New Essays. LC 89-42925. 272p. 1990. 39.50 (*0-8387-5173-3*) Bucknell U Pr.

Lane, Denis R. & Guthrie, Sue. Dictionary of Small Animal Nursing. LC 98-53103. (Illus.). 288p. 1998. pap. text 34.00 (*0-7506-3615-7*) Buttrwrth-Heinemann.

Lane, Dermont A. The Reality of Jesus. LC 77-70635. (Exploration Bk.). 180p. 1977. pap. 12.95 (*0-8091-2020-8*) Paulist Pr.

Lane, Dermot A. Christ at the Centre: Selected Issues in Christology. 154p. 1989. pap. 29.00 (*1-85390-058-3*, Pub. by Veritas Pubns) St Mut.

— The Experience of God: An Invitation to Do Theology. LC 81-80873. 96p. (Orig.). 1981. pap. 7.95 (*0-8091-2394-0*) Paulist Pr.

— The Experience of God: An Invitation to Do Theology. 86p. (Orig.). 1989. pap. 22.00 (*0-86217-179-2*, Pub. by Veritas Pubns) St Mut.

— Keeping Hope Alive: Stirrings in Christian Theology. LC 96-19685. 224p. (Orig.). 1996. pap. 14.95 (*0-8091-3684-8*) Paulist Pr.

Lane, Dick. A-Z of Dog Diseases & Health Problems. 288p. 1997. write for info. (*0-87605-042-9*) Howell Bks.

Lane, Don. Trial & Error. 325p. (C). 1990. 90.00 (*0-86439-154-4*, Pub. by Boolarong Pubns) St Mut.

Lane, Donald J. Asthma: The Facts. 3rd ed. (Facts Ser.). (Illus.). 240p. 1996. pap. text 19.95 (*0-19-262151-3*) OUP.

Lane, Dorothy F. The Island As Site of Resistance: An Examination of Caribbean & New Zealand Texts, Vol. 6. LC 94-3675. (Studies of World Literature in English: 6). VIII, 181p. (C). 1995. text 45.95 (*0-8204-2642-3*) P Lang Pubng.

***Lane, Douglas A., ed.** Gas & Particle Phase Measurements of Atmospheric Organic Compounds. 408p. 1999. text 110.00 (*90-5699-647-9*) Gordon & Breach.

Lane, E. W. Arabian Society in the Middle Ages: Studies from the 1001 Nights. 232p. (C). 1988. pap. 25.00 (*0-7007-0195-8*, Pub. by Curzon Pr Ltd) Paul & Co Pubs.

— Arabic English Lexicon, 8 vols. (ARA & ENG.). 1985. reprint ed. 195.00 (*0-8288-8455-2*) Fr & Eur.

— Arabic-English Lexicon, 2 vols., Set. 136p. 1995. 290.00 (*0-946621-03-9*, Pub. by Islamic Texts) Intl Spec Bk.

— Manners & Customs of the Modern Egyptians. 616p. 1986. 360.00 (*1-85077-115-4*, Pub. by Darf Pubs Ltd) St Mut.

Lane, Eamonn, jt. auth. see Collins, Denis.

Lane, Eddie B. African-American Christian Man: Reclaiming the Village. 1998. pap. text 12.95 (*0-9647767-4-X*, Blck Fam Pr) Inst Black Fam.

— African American Christian Woman: The Village Gate Keepers. 1999. pap. text 12.95 (*0-9647767-6-6*, Blck Fam Pr) Inst Black Fam.

— The Christian African American Family: Building Lasting Relationships. 2nd ed. 192p. 1995. pap. text 15.95 (*0-9647767-3-1*, Blck Fam Pr) Inst Black Fam.

— The Christian-African-American Family Vol. 1: Building Lasting Relationships. 192p. 1995. text 15.95 (*0-9647767-1-5*, Blck Fam Pr) Inst Black Fam.

— The Single African-American-Christian Vol. 2: Keeping a Clean Life in a Dirty World. 112p. 1995. text 12.95 (*0-9647767-0-7*, Blck Fam Pr) Inst Black Fam.

Lane, Edmund C., ed. Do Not Be Afraid, I Am with You. 1991. pap. 2.50 (*0-8189-0617-0*) Alba.

Lane, Edmund C., tr. see Amorth, Gabriel.

Lane, Edmund C., tr. see Benigni, Maria L.

Lane, Edmund C., tr. see Contessa, Fabrizio.

Lane, Edmund C., tr. see Giudici, Maria P.

Lane, Edmund C., tr. see Haring, Bernard & Salvoldi, Valentin.

Lane, Edmund C., tr. see Marcucci, Domenico.

Lane, Edmund C., tr. see Massini, Mario.

Lane, Edmund C., tr. see Pasquero, Fedele.

Lane, Edmund C., tr. see Romano, Giuseppe.

Lane, Edmund C., tr. see Schiatti, Lamberto.

Lane, Edmund C., tr. see Tarzia, Antonio.

Lane, Edward W. Arabic-English Lexicon, 2 vols., Set. (ARA.). 3000p. 1984. reprint ed. 420.00 (*0-946621-04-7*, IT1039) Intl Bk Ctr.

***Lane, Edward W.** Lane's Description of Egypt: Notes & Views in Egypt & Nubia. (Illus.). 800p. 1999. 39.50 (*977-424-525-3*, Pub. by Am Univ Cairo Pr) Col U Pr.

Lane, Edward W. & Qamus, Madd A. Lane's Arabic-English Lexicon: Madd al Qamus, 8 vols., Set. (ARA & ENG.). 3064p. 400.00 (*0-86685-087-2*, LDL0872, Pub. by Librairie du Liban) Intl Bk Ctr.

Lane, Elizabeth. Apache Fire. 1998. per. 4.99 (*0-373-29036-5*, 1-29036-0) Harlequin Bks.

— Hometown Wedding. 1996. per. 3.25 (*0-373-19194-4*, 1-19194-9) Silhouette.

— Lydia. LC 96-3683. (Historical Ser.). 299p. 1996. per. 4.50 (*0-373-28902-2*, 1-28902-4) Harlequin Bks.

— MacKenna's Promise. (Historical Ser.). 1994. per. 3.99 (*0-373-28816-6*, 1-28816-6) Harlequin Bks.

— Shawnee Bride. (Historical Ser.: Bk. 492). 2000. mass mkt. 4.99 (*0-373-29092-6*, 1-29092-3) Harlequin Bks.

— The Tycoon & the Townie. 1997. per. 3.25 (*0-373-19250-9*, 1-19250-9) Silhouette.

— Wild Wings, Wild Heart. (Special Edition Ser.). 1995. per. 3.50 (*0-373-09936-3*, 1-09936-5) Silhouette.

Lane, Ellery. Lenten Worship for Young Adults. 56p. (Orig.). 1997. pap. 7.95 (*0-7880-1015-8*) CSS OH.

***Lane, Eric.** Proverbs: Everyday Wisdom for Everyone. 2000. pap. 14.99 (*1-85792-451-7*) Christian Focus.

Lane, Eric. Special Children: The Theology of a Child. 1996. pap. text 10.99 (*0-946462-39-9*, Pub. by Evangelical Pr) P & R Pubng.

Lane, Eric, ed. Telling Tales: And Other New One-Act Plays. 350p. (Orig.). 1993. pap. 15.95 (*0-14-048237-7*, Penguin Bks) Viking Penguin.

Lane, Eric & Lane, Joyce. Eve's Story: A Christian Woman's Search for Fullness & Equality. 1984. pap. 5.99 (*0-85234-181-4*, Pub. by Evangelical Pr) P & R Pubng.

Lane, Eric & Shengold, Nina, eds. The Actor's Book of Scenes from New Plays. 448p. 1988. pap. 12.95 (*0-14-010487-9*, Penguin Bks) Viking Penguin.

Lane, Eric, jt. auth. see Mikva, Abner J.

Lane, Eric, ed. see Deledda, Grazia.

Lane, Eric, jt. ed. see Shengold, Nina.

Lane, Eric, ed. see Verga, Giovanni.

Lane, Ermot. The Reality of Jesus. 180p. 1989. pap. 22.00 (*0-901810-85-1*, Pub. by Veritas Pubns) St Mut.

Lane, Ernest. God Unmasked: The Full Life Revealed. LC 98-85155. 368p. 1998. pap. 24.95 (*0-9654915-2-8*, High Ground) Northwoods Cnslting.

Lane, Ernest P. Metric Differential Geometry of Curves & Surfaces. LC 40-12579. 224p. reprint ed. pap. 69.50 (*0-608-12124-X*, 202412000035) Bks Demand.

Lane, Eugene L., ed. Cybele, Attis & Related Cults: Essays in Memory of M. J. Vermaseren. x, 442p. 1996. 153.00 (*90-04-10196-9*) Brill Academic Pubs.

Lane, Eugene N., jt. ed. see MacMullen, Ramsay.

Lane, Evedine L. They Weave the Spider's Web. LC 97-60859. (Illus.). 212p. 1997. pap. 10.00 (*0-9657909-0-8*, Zawn Bks) Pictures & Pages.

Lane, Ferdinand. Mysterious Sea. LC 73-128268. (Essay Index Reprint Ser.). 1977. 24.95 (*0-8369-1971-8*) Ayer.

Lane, Fintan. The Origins of Modern Irish Socialism, 1881-1896. 172p. 1997. 64.95 (*1-85918-151-1*, Pub. by Cork Univ); pap. 24.95 (*1-85918-152-X*, Pub. by Cork Univ) Intl Spec Bk.

Lane, Francis E. American Charities & the Child of the Immigrant: Study of Typical Child Caring Institutions New York & Massachusetts-1845-1880, Vol. 6. LC 74-1691. (Children & Youth Ser.). 188p. 1974. reprint ed. 20.95 (*0-405-05967-1*) Ayer.

Lane, Franklin K. The Letters of Franklin K. Lane, Personal & Political. (American Biography Ser.). 473p. 1991. reprint ed. lib. bdg. 89.00 (*0-7812-8237-3*) Rprt Serv.

Lane, Fred, ed. Medical Trial Technique Quarterly, 38 vols. LC 72-136152. 1954. 1100.00 (*0-318-42410-X*) West Group.

Lane, Fred & Birnbaum, David A. Lane Medical Litigation Guide, 4 vols. LC 81-10167. 1981. ring bd. 525.00 (*0-685-09243-7*) West Group.

Lane, Fred, jt. auth. see Goldstein, Irving.

Lane, Frederic C. Andrea Barbarigo, Merchant of Venice, 1418-1449. LC 78-64194. (Johns Hopkins University. Studies in the Social Sciences. Thirtieth Ser. 1912: 1). reprint ed. 37.50 (*0-404-61300-4*) AMS Pr.

— Studies in Venetian Social & Economic History. Kohl, Benjamin G. & Mueller, Reinhold C., eds. (Collected Studies: No. CS254). (ENG, FRE & ITA., Illus.). 346p. (C). 1987. reprint ed. lib. bdg. 117.95 (*0-86078-202-6*, Pub. by Variorum) Ashgate Pub Co.

— Venetian Ships & Shipbuilders of the Renaissance. 1979. 28.95 (*0-405-10609-2*) Ayer.

— Venetian Ships & Shipbuilders of the Renaissance. LC 92-11280. (Softshell Bks.). (Illus.). 296p. 1992. reprint ed. pap. text 16.95 (*0-8018-4514-9*) Johns Hopkins.

— Venice: A Maritime Republic. LC 72-12342. (Illus.). 518p. 1973. pap. 19.95 (*0-8018-1460-X*) Johns Hopkins.

— Venice & History: The Collected Papers of Frederic C. Lane. LC 66-14160. 582p. reprint ed. pap. 180.50 (*0-608-14485-1*, 202530400043) Bks Demand.

Lane, Frederic C. & Mueller, Reinhold C. Money & Banking in Medieval & Renaissance Venice, Vol. 1. LC 84-47947. 707p. 1985. reprint ed. pap. 200.00 (*0-608-03712-5*, 206453700001) Bks Demand.

Lane, Frederick C. Profits from Power: Readings in Protection Rent & Violence-Controlling Enterprises. LC 79-13860. 128p. (C). 1979. pap. text 19.95 (*0-87395-420-3*) State U NY Pr.

Lane, Frederick S. Current Issues in Public Administration. 6th ed. LC 97-65192. 576p. 1999. pap. 33.95 (*0-312-15249-3*) St Martin.

***Lane, Frederick S.** Obscene Profits: The Entrepreneurs of Pornography in the Cyber Age. LC 99-35383. 272p. 2000. 27.50 (*0-415-92096-5*) Routledge.

Lane, Frederick S., 3rd, jt. auth. see Berger, Richie E.

Lane, G. B. The Trombone: An Annotated Bibliography. LC 98-28420. 624p. 1999. 65.00 (*0-8108-3465-0*) Scarecrow.

Lane, G. S. Words for Clothing in the Principal Indo-European Languages. (LD Ser.: No. 9). 1931. pap. 25.00 (*0-527-00755-2*) Periodicals Srv.

Lane, Gary. Beating the French. (Batsford Chess Library). 144p. 1995. pap. 16.95 (*0-8050-3292-4*) H Holt & Co.

***Lane, Gary.** Colle Opening. (Chess Bks.). 144p. 2000. pap. text 15.95 (*0-7134-8478-0*) B T B.

Lane, Gary. A Concordance to Personae: Concordance to the Poems of Ezra Pound. LC 72-6462. (Reference Ser.: No. 44). (C). 1972. lib. bdg. 75.00 (*0-8383-1613-1*) M S G Haskell Hse.

— A Concordance to the Poems of Hart Crane. LC 72-1872. (Reference Ser.: No. 44). 356p. (C). 1972. lib. bdg. 75.00 (*0-8383-1437-6*) M S G Haskell Hse.

— A Concordance to the Poems of Marianne Moore. LC 72-6438. (Reference Ser.: No. 44). 1972. lib. bdg. 75.00 (*0-8383-1588-7*) M S G Haskell Hse.

— H. O. T. Chess: Highly Original Thinking Chess. LC 96-78265. (New American Batsford Chess Library). 192p. (Orig.). 1997. pap. 22.50 (*1-879479-43-5*) ICE WA.

— How to Attack in Chess. LC 96-78261. (New American Batsford Chess Library). 128p. (Orig.). 1996. pap. 14.95 (*1-879479-39-7*) ICE WA.

— Sylvia Plath: New Views on the Poetry. LC 78-20515. 280p. reprint ed. pap. 86.80 (*0-608-16363-5*, 202632300049) Bks Demand.

***Lane, Gary.** Victory in the Opening! The Art of Winning Quickly in Chess. (Illus.). 144p. 1999. pap. 10.99 (*0-7134-8427-6*) B T B.

— Victory in the Opening: The Art of Winning Quickly in Chess. 1999. pap. text 12.95 (*0-7134-8546-9*) Branford.

Lane, Gary. Winning with the Bishop's Opening. (Batsford Chess Library). 120p. 1993. pap. 19.95 (*0-8050-2636-3*, Owl) H Holt & Co.

— Winning with the Closed Sicilian. (Batsford Chess Library). 160p. 1995. pap. 19.95 (*0-8050-2637-1*, Owl) H Holt & Co.

— Winning with the Fischer-Sozin Attack. (Batsford Chess Library). 1995. pap. 19.95 (*0-8050-3576-1*) H Holt & Co.

— Winning with the Scotch. (Batsford Chess Library). 160p. 1995. pap. 19.95 (*0-8050-2940-0*) H Holt & Co.

— World Championship, 1995. LC 95-97231. 1995. pap. 15.00 (*0-8050-4231-8*) H Holt & Co.

Lane, Gary, ed. A Word-Index to James Joyce's Dubliners. LC 71-183760. (Reference Ser.: No. 44). 270p. 1972. lib. bdg. 75.00 (*0-8383-1384-1*) M S G Haskell Hse.

***Lane, Geoffrey.** NuSpeak: Become a Powerful Speaker. 144p. 1999. pap. 19.95 (*1-894499-00-X*) Berkana.

Lane, George. Guide for Catholics: The Beliefs of the Church. 1997. pap. 2.50 (*0-8294-0845-2*) Loyola Pr.

Lane, George A. Christian Spirituality: An Historical Sketch. 88p. 1984. pap. 4.95 (*0-8294-0450-3*) Loyola Pr.

— Guide for Catholics: Beliefs of the Church. (SPA.). 1998. pap. 2.50 (*0-8294-0976-9*) Loyola Pr.

Lane, George A., ed. Solar Heat Storage--Latent Heat Materials: Vol. 1, Background & Scientific Principles. 288p. 1983. 143.00 (*0-8493-6585-6*, TJ810, CRC Reprint) Franklin.

— Solar Heat Storage--Latent Heat Materials: Vol. 1, Background & Scientific Principles, II. 288p. 1986. 141.00 (*0-8493-6586-4*, TJ810, CRC Reprint) Franklin.

Lane, George M. Latin Grammar for Schools & Colleges. (Notable American Authors Ser.). 1999. reprint ed. lib. bdg. 125.00 (*0-7812-3698-3*) Rprt Serv.

— Latin Grammar for Schools & Colleges. rev. ed. LC 78-107458. reprint ed. 29.50 (*0-404-00634-5*) AMS Pr.

— Latin Pronunciation. (Notable American Authors Ser.). 1999. reprint ed. lib. bdg. 125.00 (*0-7812-3697-5*) Rprt Serv.

Lane, Gerald R., et al, eds. Technologies for Advanced Land Combat: Proceedings of a Conference Held 17-18 April, 1995, Orlando, Florida. LC 95-9816. (Critical Reviews of Optical Science & Technology Ser.: Vol. 59). 1995. pap. 66.00 (*0-8194-1851-X*) SPIE.

Lane, Gerd R. & Mels, Reinhard. Chronograph Wristwatches: Stop Watches. LC 93-83050. (Illus.). 256p. 1993. 79.95 (*0-88740-502-9*) Schiffer.

Lane, Gilbert M. Flagships - Exploring 194 Nations of the World. (Illus.). 125p. (Orig.). (J). (gr. 3-12). 1995. pap. text 14.95 (*0-9647208-0-9*) Lane & Lane Enter.

Lane, Gilles. Government, Justice, & Contempt. LC 92-34527. 144p. (Orig.). (C). 1993. pap. text 18.50 (*0-8191-8957-X*); lib. bdg. 39.50 (*0-8191-8956-1*) U Pr of Amer.

Lane, Gretchen G. My Memory Book: A Journal for Grieving Children. 2nd ed. 68p. (J). (ps-13). 1997. pap., wbk. ed. 10.95 (*1-888493-12-7*) Chi Rho Pr.

Lane, H. Richard, jt. ed. see Mann, Keith O.

***Lane, Harlan.** The Mask of Benevolence: Disabling the Deaf Community. LC 99-13183. 1999. pap. 11.95 (*1-58121-009-4*) Dawn Sign.

An Asterisk (*) at the beginning of an entry indicates that the title is appearing for the first time.

L

Lane, Harlan. The Mask of Benevolence: Disabling the Deaf Community. LC 93-13107. 1993. pap. 14.00 (*0-679-73614-X*) Vin Bks.

Lane, Harlan. When the Mind Hears. 537p. 1989. pap. 15.96 (*0-679-72023-5*) McKay.

Lane, Harlan. When the Mind Hears: A History of the Deaf. (Illus.). 537p. 1998. pap. text 10.00 (*0-7881-5233-5*) DIANE Pub.

— When the Mind Hears: A History of the Deaf. 1989. pap. 16.95 (*0-685-27139-0*) Vin Bks.

— The Wild Boy of Aveyron. (Illus.). 384p. 1976. pap. 16.50 (*0-674-95300-2*) HUP.

Lane, Harlan, ed. The Deaf Experience: Classics in Language & Education. Philip, Franklin, tr. from FRE. (Illus.). 240p. 1984. 37.95 (*0-674-19460-8*) HUP.

Lane, Harlan & Emmorey, Karen, eds. The Signs of Language Revisited: An Anthology in Honor or Ursula. LC 99-41589. 424p. 2000. write for info. (*0-8058-3246-7*) L Erlbaum Assocs.

Lane, Harlan & Grosjean, Francois, eds. Recent Perspectives on American Sign Language. 176p. 1989. reprint ed. pap. 34.50 (*0-8058-0560-5*) L Erlbaum Assocs.

***Lane, Harlan & Wayser, Christian.** Make Every Minute Count: 750 Tips & Strategies to Revolutionize How You Manage Your Time. (Illus.). 2000. pap. 14.95 (*1-56924-613-0*) Marlowe & Co.

Lane, Harlan, et al. Journey into the Deaf-World. Machemer, Corona, ed. LC 96-19522. (Illus.). 528p. (Orig.). 1996. 39.95 (*0-915035-62-6*, 3650) Dawn Sign.

— Journey into the Deaf-World. 2nd ed. Machemer, Corona, ed. LC 96-19522. (Illus.). 528p. (Orig.). 1997. pap. 24.95 (*0-915035-63-4*, 9652B) Dawn Sign.

Lane, Harlan, jt. auth. see Phillip, F.

Lane, Harlan, jt. ed. see Fischer, Renate.

Lane, Harlan, jt. tr. see Philip, Franklin.

Lane, Harold A. & Straka, Joseph J. Late Mississippian & Early Pennsylvanian Conodonts, Arkansas & Oklahoma. LC 73-90838. (Geological Society of America, Special Paper: No. 152). 204p. reprint ed. pap. 63.30 (*0-608-15183-1*, 202737000055) Bks Demand.

Lane, Harold E. & Dupre, Denise. Hospitality World! An Introduction. (Hospitality, Travel & Tourism Ser.). 560p. 1996. 59.95 (*0-471-28989-2*, VNR) Wiley.

Lane, Harole. Hospitality World. LC 96-8345. 650p. 1996. text 49.95 (*0-442-00118-5*, VNR) Wiley.

Lane, Helen, et al, trs. Blatant Artifice 2-3: An Anthology of Short Fiction by Visiting Writers, 1985-1987. (Illus.). 168p. 1988. pap. 10.00 (*0-936739-16-9*) Hallwalls Inc.

Lane, Helen, tr. see Bastos, Augusto Roa.

Lane, Helen, tr. see De Mier, Fray S.

Lane, Helen, tr. see Gaite, Carmen Martin.

Lane, Helen, tr. see Garcia-Ponce, Juan.

Lane, Helen, tr. see Garcia Ponce, Juan.

Lane, Helen, tr. see Goytisolo, Juan.

Lane, Helen, tr. see Marmol, Jose.

Lane, Helen, tr. see Martinez, Tomas E.

Lane, Helen, tr. see Merino, Jose Maria.

Lane, Helen, tr. see Onetti, Juan Carlos.

Lane, Helen, tr. see Paz, Octavio.

Lane, Helen, tr. see Pinon, Nelida.

Lane, Helen, tr. see Saramago, Jose.

Lane, Helen, tr. see Valenzuela, Luisa.

Lane, Helen, tr. see Vargas Llosa, Mario.

Lane, Helen, tr. see Vargas Llosa, Mario & Bovary, Flaubert & Madame.

Lane, Helen H. History of Dighton, the South Purchase, 1712. 263p. 1995. reprint ed. lib. bdg. 35.00 (*0-8328-4696-1*) Higginson Bk Co.

Lane, Helen R., tr. see Amado, Jorge.

Lane, Helen R., tr. see Barreno, Maria I., et al.

Lane, Helen R., tr. see Breton, Andre.

Lane, Helen R., tr. see Burch, Noel.

Lane, Helen R., tr. see Fernandez-Santos, Jesus.

Lane, Helen R., tr. see Friedlander, Saul.

Lane, Helen R., tr. see Goytisolo, Juan.

Lane, Helen R., tr. see Poniatowska, Elena.

Lane, Helen R., tr. see Quijano, Anibal.

Lane, Helen R., tr. see Rebolledo, Francisco.

Lane, Helen R., tr. see Revel, Jean-Francois.

Lane, Helen R., tr. see Simon, Claude.

Lane, Helen R., tr. see Vargas Llosa, Mario.

Lane, Helen W. & Schoeller, Dale A. Nutrition in Space Flight & Weightlessness Models. LC 99-51978. (Modern Nutrition Ser.). 328p. 1999. boxed set 89.95 (*0-8493-8567-9*) CRC Pr.

***Lane, Henry W.** International Management Behavior: Text, Readings & Cases. 4th ed. 1999. pap. write for info. (*0-631-21831-9*) Blackwell Pubs.

Lane, Henry W., et al. International Management Behavior. 3rd rev. ed. 480p. 1996. pap. text 44.95 (*1-55786-985-5*) Blackwell Pubs.

Lane, Henry W., et al. International Management Behavior: Text, Readings & Cases. 4th ed. 84.95 (*0-631-21830-0*) Blackwell Pubs.

Lane, I. William & Comac, Linda. Sharks Don't Get Cancer: How Shark Cartilage Could Save Your Life. LC 92-782. 224p. pap. 11.95 (*0-89529-520-2*, Avery) Penguin Putnam.

— Sharks Still Don't Get Cancer: The Continuing Story of Shark Cartilage Therapy. LC 96-4749. 272p. 1996. pap. 12.95 (*0-89529-722-1*, Avery) Penguin Putnam.

— The Skin Cancer Answer: The Natural Treatment for Basal & Squamous Cell Carcinomas & Keratoses. LC 98-31180. 148p. Date not set. pap. 9.95 (*0-89529-865-1*, Avery) Penguin Putnam.

***Lane, I. William, et al.** Immune Power: How to Use Your Immune System to Fight Disease - from Cancer to AIDS. LC 99-16122. 192p. 1999. pap. 11.95 (*0-89529-934-8*, Avery) Penguin Putnam.

Lane, Ira M., Jr. The Gospel - Manual for Teachers. Johnson, Joe, ed. LC 98-92390. 32p. 1998. pap., teacher ed. 14.00 (*0-9662647-0-3*, 101) Christ Educ Forum.

Lane, Irving, jt. auth. see Siegel, Laurence.

Lane, Irving M. & Messe, Lawrence A. Equity & the Distribution of Rewards. LC 71-131014. 129p. 1970. 19.50 (*0-685-38425-X*) Scholarly.

Lane, J. A. Microwave Power Measurement. LC TK6553.L3. (IEE Monograph Ser.: No. 12). (Illus.). 80p. reprint ed. pap. 30.00 (*0-8357-8952-7*, 203345400086) Bks Demand.

Lane, J. D., ed. Robotic Welding. (International Trends in Manufacturing Technology Ser.). (Illus.). 380p. 1987. 97.95 (*0-387-16676-9*) Spr-Verlag.

Lane, J. Eric. Moment of Encounter. LC 83-49361. (American University Studies: History: Ser. IX, Vol. 6). XXI, 163p. (Orig.). (C). 1984. pap. text 18.00 (*0-8204-0090-4*) P Lang Pubng.

Lane, J. S. On Optimal Population Paths. LC 77-704. (Lecture Notes in Economics & Mathematical Systems Ser.: Vol. 142). 1977. pap. 26.00 (*0-387-08070-8*) Spr-Verlag.

Lane, Jack, jt. ed. see O'Sullivan, Maurice.

Lane, James B. City of the Century: A History of Gary, Indiana. LC 77-23622. (Illus.). 383p. pap. 118.80 (*0-608-05030-X*, 205969100004) Bks Demand.

Lane, James B. & Escobar, Edward J., eds. Forging a Community: The Latino Experience in Northwest Indiana, 1919-1975. LC 87-10292. (Illus.). 306p. 1987. 32.00 (*0-253-32382-7*); pap. 3.95 (*0-253-21213-8*) Ind U Pr.

Lane, James M. The Complete Golfer's Almanac, 1995. (Orig.). 1995. pap. 13.95 (*0-399-52151-8*, Perigee Bks) Berkley Pub.

— The Complete Golfer's Almanac, 1996. 400p. 1996. pap. 13.95 (*0-399-51992-0*, Perigee Bks) Berkley Pub.

— Peterson's Golf Schools & Resorts. LC 95-7991. 226p. (Orig.). 1995. pap. 13.95 (*1-56079-476-3*) Petersons.

***Lane, James R.** The Wendover Whale: A Nautical Tale from the Great Salt Desert. LC 99-95119. 320p. 1999. pap. 15.00 (*0-87980-443-2*, Shared Vision Bks) Wilshire.

Lane, James R., jt. ed. see Andres, Rachel.

Lane, James W. Lay Speaking Ministry: Guide for Conference & District Committees 1997-2000. 32p. 1997. pap. 7.95 (*0-88177-203-8*, DR203) Discipleship Res.

— Masters in Modern Art. LC 67-22100. (Essay Index Reprint Ser.). 1977. 19.95 (*0-8369-1332-9*) Ayer.

Lane, Jan E., jt. ed. see Pennings, Paul.

Lane, Jan-Erik. Bureaucracy & Public Choice. (Modern Politics Ser.: Vol. 15). (Illus.). 320p. (C). 1987. text 45.00 (*0-8039-8067-1*); pap. text 17.95 (*0-8039-8068-X*) Sage.

— Constitutions & Political Theory. 220p. 1996. text 24.95 (*0-7190-4648-3*, Pub. by Manchester Univ Pr) St Martin.

— Institutional Reform: A Public Policy Perspective. 256p. 1990. text 69.95 (*1-85521-002-9*, Pub. by Dartmth Pub) Ashgate Pub Co.

— The Public Sector: Concepts, Models & Approaches. (Illus.). 240p. (C). 1993. text 65.00 (*0-8039-8818-4*); pap. text 21.95 (*0-8039-8819-2*) Sage.

— The Public Sector: Concepts, Models & Approaches. 288p. 1995. pap. 21.95 (*0-8039-7652-6*) Sage.

— The Public Sector: Concepts, Models & Approaches. 2nd ed. 288p. 1995. 69.95 (*0-8039-7651-8*) Sage.

Lane, Jan-Erik, ed. Public Sector Reform: Rationale, Trends & Problems. 320p. 1997. 85.00 (*0-7619-5366-3*); pap. 29.95 (*0-7619-5367-1*) Sage.

— Understanding the Swedish Model. 1991. text 39.50 (*0-7146-3445-X*, Pub. by F Cass Pubs) Intl Spec Bk.

Lane, Jan-Erik & Errson, Svante O. Comparative Political Economy: A Developmental Approach. 2nd ed. LC 96-34109. 256p. 1997. 85.00 (*1-85567-434-3*) Bks Intl VA.

— Comparative Politics: An Introduction & New Approach. LC 94-32597. 1994. 65.95 (*0-7456-1256-3*); pap. 28.95 (*0-7456-1257-1*) Blackwell Pubs.

Lane, Jan-Erik & Ersson, Svante O. Comparative Political Economy. 1990. text 49.00 (*0-86187-795-0*, Pub. by P P Pubs); pap. text 14.50 (*0-86187-858-2*, Pub. by P P Pubs) Cassell & Continuum.

— Comparative Political Economy: A Developmental Approach. 2nd ed. LC 96-34109. 256p. 1997. pap. 34.95 (*1-85567-435-1*) Bks Intl VA.

— European Politics: An Introduction. 224p. 1996. 69.95 (*0-7619-5286-1*); pap. 22.95 (*0-7619-5287-X*) Sage.

— New Institutional Politics: Outcomes & Consequences. LC 99-32334. 304p. 1999. pap. 27.99 (*0-415-18321-9*) Routledge.

***Lane, Jan-Erik & Ersson, Svante O.** New Institutional Politics: Outcomes & Consequences. LC 99-32334. 304p. (C). 2000. text. write for info. (*0-415-18320-0*) Routledge.

Lane, Jan-Erik & Ersson, Svante O. Politics & Society in Western Europe. rev. ed. (Illus.). 320p. (C). 1991. pap. text 19.95 (*0-8039-8407-3*) Sage.

— Politics & Society in Western Europe. 2nd rev. ed. (Illus.). 320p. (C). 1991. text 55.00 (*0-8039-8406-5*) Sage.

— Politics & Society in Western Europe. 3rd ed. 432p. 1994. 69.95 (*0-8039-7795-6*); pap. 28.00 (*0-8039-7796-4*) Sage.

***Lane, Jan-Erik & Ersson, Svante O., eds.** Politics & Society in Western Europe. 4th ed. LC 98-61733. 432p. 1998. 84.00 (*0-7619-5861-4*) Sage.

Lane, Jan-Erik, et al. Political Data Handbook: OECD Countries. 2nd ed. LC 97-164375. (Comparative Politics Ser.). (Illus.). 366p. 1997. text 95.00 (*0-19-828053-X*) OUP.

Lane, Jan-Erik, jt. ed. see Faure, Murray.

Lane, Jan-Erik, jt. ed. see Moar, Moshe.

Lane, Janet. Writing Clearly. 2nd ed. (J). 1999. pap. text, teacher ed. 8.25 (*0-8384-0985-7*) Heinle & Heinle.

Lane, Janet, et al. Writing Clearly. 246p. (J). 1993. mass mkt. 26.95 (*0-8384-3849-0*); mass mkt., teacher ed. 22.95 (*0-8384-4207-2*) Heinle & Heinle.

Lane, Jay, ed. see Blomstrom, David.

Lane, Jay, ed. see Northwest Seafood Consultant Staff.

Lane, Jay, ed. see Rezvani, Kate A.

Lane, Jay B., ed. Cousins' Cuisine: An All-American Family Cookbook. (Illus.). 134p. (Orig.). 1988. pap. 5.95 (*0-934363-05-6*) Lance Pubns.

***Lane, Jeremy.** Pierre Bourdieu: A Critical Introduction. 224p. 2000. pap. 17.95 (*0-7453-1501-1*, Pub. by Pluto GBR) Stylus Pub VA.

Lane, Jeremy. Yellow Men Sleep. (Illus.). 1983. 15.00 (*0-937986-99-2*) D M Grant.

***Lane, Jeremy F.** Pierre Bourdieu: A Critical Introduction. 2000. 59.95 (*0-7453-1506-2*) Pluto GBR.

Lane, Jill, ed. see Phelan, Peggy.

Lane, Jim, jt. auth. see Grimm, Beth A.

Lane, Jim R. Duty: A Novel. LC 99-18832. 240p. 1999. 22.95 (*1-882593-29-4*) Bridge Wrks.

Lane, Joan. John Hall & His Patients: The Medical Practice of Shakespeare's Son-in-Law. (Illus.). 416p. 1996. 72.00 (*0-7509-1094-1*, Pub. by Sutton Pub Ltd) Intl Pubs Mktg.

Lane, Jodi & Petersilia, Joan, eds. Criminal Justice Policy. LC 98-6259. (International Library of Comparative Public Policy). 672p. 1998. 240.00 (*1-85898-568-4*) E Elgar.

Lane, Jody, jt. auth. see Spurlock, Gordon.

Lane, John. Against Information. Crowe, Thomas R., ed. (Illus.). 8p. 1994. 1.00 (*1-883197-04-X*) New Native Pr.

— Against Information & Other Poems. LC 94-69299. 68p. (Orig.). 1995. pap. 7.95 (*1-883197-06-6*) New Native Pr.

— Aluminum in Building. 185p. 1992. 96.95 (*1-85742-082-9*, Pub. by Avebury Technical) Ashgate Pub Co.

***Lane, John.** In Praise of Devon: A Guide to Its People, Places & Character. LC 99-488072. (Illus.). 192p. 1999. pap. 23.95 (*1-870098-75-7*, Pub. by Green Bks) Chelsea Green Pub.

— Only Connect - Soil, Soul, & Society: The Best of Resurgence Magazine. 320p. 2000. pap. 16.95 (*1-870098-90-0*) Chelsea Green Pub.

Lane, John. A Snake's Tail Full of Ants: Art, Ecology & Consciousness. (Illus.). 256p. 1996. pap. 19.95 (*1-870098-65-X*, Pub. by Green Bks) Chelsea Green Pub.

— Weed Time: Essays from the Edge of a Country Yard. 70p. (Orig.). 1996. pap. 8.00 (*0-9638731-3-X*) Hub City Writers.

— The Woods Stretched for Miles: An Anthology of Contemporary Nature Writing from the South. LC 98-20339. 1999. 40.00 (*0-8203-2087-0*) U of Ga Pr.

Lane, John & Lane, Nina. The Boy Mystic. 164p. (Orig.). 1985. pap. 8.95 (*0-87418-009-0*, 144) Coleman Pub.

Lane, John & Teter, Betsy, eds. Hub City Christmas: Spartanburg Writers Trim the Literary Christmas Tree. 250p. 1997. 25.00 (*1-891885-07-3*) Hub City Writers.

Lane, John, jt. ed. see Teter, Betsy.

Lane, John, jt. ed. see Thurmond, Gerald.

Lane, John E., jt. auth. see Hammel, Eric.

Lane, John H., Jr. Voluntary Associations among Mexican Americans in San Antonio, Texas: Organizational & Leadership Characteristics. Cortes, Carlos E., ed. LC 76-1292. (Chicano Heritage Ser.). 1977. 20.95 (*0-405-09510-4*) Ayer.

Lane, John J., ed. Ferment in Education: A Look Abroad. 220p. 1995. 26.00 (*0-226-46862-3*) U Ch Pr.

Lane, John J. & Epps, Edgar G., eds. Restructuring the Schools: Problems & Prospects. LC 91-66584. (NSSE Series on Contemporary Educational Issues). 217p. 1992. 33.75 (*0-8211-1116-7*) McCutchan.

Lane, John J. & Walberg, Herbert J., eds. Effective School Leadership: Policy & Process. LC 86-63774. (NSSE Series on Contemporary Educational Issues). 218p. (C). 1987. 33.75 (*0-8211-1115-9*) McCutchan.

Lane, John J., jt. ed. see Walberg, Herbert J.

Lane, John R., et al, eds. Carnegie International, 1985. LC 85-25870. (Illus.). 256p. (Orig.). 1985. pap. 10.00 (*0-88039-011-5*) Mus Art Carnegie.

Lane, Joseph M. & Healey, John H., eds. Diagnosis & Management of Pathologic Fractures. LC 92-48561. 192p. 1993. text 115.50 (*0-7817-0062-0*) Lppncott W & W.

Lane, Joseph P., jt. auth. see Mann, William C.

Lane, Joyce, jt. auth. see Adams, Russ.

Lane, Joyce, jt. auth. see Lane, Eric.

Lane, Judith. Buster, Where Are You? LC 98-41293. (Illus.). 32p. (J). (gr. 1-5). 1998. 12.95 (*1-58021-019-8*); pap. 5.95 (*1-58021-020-1*); pap. 9.95 incl. audio (*1-58021-023-6*); pap. 19.95 incl. audio (*1-58021-021-X*) Benefactory.

— Buster, Where Are You? Includes Plush Toy Animal. (Illus.). 32p. (J). (gr. 1-5). 1998. 29.95 (*1-58021-028-7*); pap. 14.95 (*1-58021-022-8*) Benefactory.

— Buster, Where Are You? Includes Tape & Plush Toy Animal. (Illus.). 32p. (J). (gr. 1-5). 1998. 34.95 incl. audio (*1-58021-027-9*) Benefactory.

***Lane, Julian C.** Key & Allied Families. 495p. 2000. reprint ed. pap. 45.00 (*0-8063-4977-8*, Pub. by Clearfield Co) ACCESS Pubs Network.

Lane, Julie. The Life & Adventures of Santa Claus. rev. ed. (Illus.). 154p. (J). 1985. pap. 10.00 (*0-9615664-1-8*) Parkhurst Brook Pubs.

— The Life & Adventures of Santa Claus: A Keepsake. rev. ed. (Illus.). (J). (ps-8). 1995. 18.95 (*1-56888-149-5*) Tapestry MA.

Lane, Karen. The Medical Assisting Examination Guide: A Comprehensive Review for Certification. 2nd ed. (Illus.). 267p. (C). 1995. pap. text 29.95 (*0-8036-0039-9*) Davis Co.

Lane, Karen, ed. Saunders Manual of Medical Assisting Practice. LC 92-49703. (Illus.). 888p. 1992. text 49.95 (*0-7216-3063-4*, W B Saunders Co) Harcrt Hlth Sci Grp.

Lane, Karen & Reed, Linda. Medications: A Guide for the Health Professions. 2nd rev. ed. LC 98-27995. (Illus.). 350p. 1998. pap. 34.95 (*0-8036-0378-9*) Davis Co.

Lane, Kathryn, et al. Israel: Reading & Social Studies Skills Workbook & Activity Guide. 1999. teacher ed. 7.96 (*0-86505-563-7*); student ed. 6.60 (*0-86505-562-9*) Crabtree Pub Co.

Lane, Keith & Speed, Sandra M. Black Relationships the Truth: A Practical Guide to Loving Relationships in the 90s. LC 94-71753. 200p. 1994. pap. 15.00 (*0-9641951-9-4*) Creative Commun.

Lane, Kel. Shadows: A Book of Verse. LC 91-90777. 61p. (Orig.). 1992. pap. 7.00 (*0-9631621-0-1*) K Lane.

Lane, Kelley, et al. Managing in Mexico: A Cultural Perspective. (SPA.). 14p. (C). 1985. pap. text 10.00 (*0-937795-05-4*) Waste-Mgmt Educ.

Lane, Kenneth A. Developing Your Child for Success. LC 90-62570. (Illus.). 230p. (Orig.). 1991. per. 24.95 (*1-878145-00-2*) Learning Potentials.

— Developing Your Child for Success. rev. ed. LC 90-62570. (Illus.). 230p. (Orig.). 1991. pap., per. 24.95 (*1-878145-06-1*) Learning Potentials.

— Reversal Errors: Theories & Procedures. Corngold, Sally M., ed. LC 88-50982. (Illus.). 153p. 1988. pap. 18.00 (*0-929780-00-0*) VisionExtension.

Lane, Kenneth E., et al. The School Safety Handbook: Taking Action for Student & Staff Protection. LC 96-60023. 357p. 1996. pap. 49.95 (*1-56676-397-5*, 763975) Scarecrow.

Lane, Kenneth Jay & Miller, Harrice S. Kenneth Jay Lane: Faking It. LC 96-13671. (Illus.). 160p. 1996. 35.00 (*0-8109-3579-1*, Pub. by Abrams) Time Warner.

Lane, Kenneth S. Field Test Sections Save Cost in Tunnel Support: Report from Underground Construction Research Council. LC 76-378194. 64p. reprint ed. pap. 30.00 (*0-608-30851-X*, 201447700094) Bks Demand.

Lane, Kenneth S., ed. see North American Rapid Excavation & Tunneling Confer.

Lane, Kerry. Marine Pioneers: The Unsung Heroes of World War II. LC 96-70487. (Illus.). 272p. 1997. 29.95 (*0-7643-0227-2*) Schiffer.

Lane, Kit. Between the Bridges: Seven Short Stories Set in Saugatuck, 1834 to 1985. LC 96-71724. (Illus.). 64p. 1997. pap. 5.50 (*1-877703-48-6*) Pavilion Pr.

— Beyond B., M., & D. A Guide to Collecting & Publishing Family History. LC 90-60630. 52p. (Orig.). 1990. pap. 3.84 (*1-877703-18-4*) Pavilion Pr.

— Built on the Banks of the Kalamazoo. LC 93-83589. (Saugatuck Maritime Ser.). (Illus.). 288p. 1993. pap. 17.50 (*1-877703-00-1*) Pavilion Pr.

— Buried Singapore: Michigan's Imaginary Pompeii. LC 93-83589. (Illus.). 64p. 1994. pap. 5.50 (*1-877703-09-5*) Pavilion Pr.

— Chicora: Lost on Lake Michigan. (Saugatuck Maritime Ser.). (Illus.). 160p. (Orig.). 1996. pap. 15.50 (*1-877703-02-8*) Pavilion Pr.

— The Day the Elephant Died & Other Tales of Saugatuck. LC 90-61362. (Illus.). 72p. (Orig.). 1990. pap. 5.50 (*1-877703-19-2*) Pavilion Pr.

— The Dustless Road to Happyland: Chicago-Saugatuck Passenger Boats 1859-1929. LC 95-68184. (Saugatuck Maritime Ser.: Vol. 2). (Illus.). 160p. (Orig.). 1995. pap. 15.50 (*1-877703-01-X*) Pavilion Pr.

***Lane, Kit.** Heroes Rogues & Just Plain Folks: A History of the Saugatuck Area. LC 98-60047. (Illus.). 78p. 1998. pap. 12.00 (*0-9657042-8-9*) Saugatuck-Douglas.

Lane, Kit. John Allen: Michigan's Pioneer Promoter. (Illus.). 224p. 1989. 19.50 (*1-877703-17-6*); pap. 11.50 (*1-877703-16-8*) Pavilion Pr.

— Lake Michigan Shipwrecks: South Haven to Grand Haven. (Saugatuck Maritime Ser.: Vol. 4). (Illus.). 192p. (Orig.). 1997. pap. 15.50 (*1-877703-03-6*) Pavilion Pr.

— The Letters of William G. Butler & Other Tales of Saugatuck. LC 94-66962. (Illus.). 80p. (Orig.). 1994. pap. 5.50 (*1-877703-23-0*) Pavilion Pr.

— Lucius Lyon: An Eminently Useful Citizen. LC 91-60196. (Illus.). 352p. 1991. 19.50 (*1-877703-21-4*) Pavilion Pr.

— Michigan's Victorian Poets. 52p. 1993. pap. 4.00 (*1-877703-10-9*) Pavilion Pr.

— The Popcorn Millionaire & Other Tales of Saugatuck. LC 91-60187. (Illus.). 94p. (Orig.). 1991. pap. 5.50 (*1-877703-20-6*) Pavilion Pr.

— Western Allegan County, Michigan. (Illus.). 541p. 1988. 62.50 (*0-88107-122-6*) Curtis Media.

— The Wreck of the Hippocampus & Other Tales of Saugatuck. LC 92-80010. (Illus.). 96p. (Orig.). 1992. pap. 5.50 (*1-877703-22-2*) Pavilion Pr.

Lane, Kit, ed. Allegan County Historical Atlas & Gazetteer. LC 98-67290. (Illus.). 192p. 1998. pap. 9.50 (*1-877703-47-8*) Pavilion Pr.

***Lane, Kit, ed.** Ottawa County Historical Atlas & Gazetteer. 1999. pap. 9.50 (*1-877703-46-X*) Pavilion Pr.

Lane, Kit & Lane, Art. Australia: A Traveler's Preview. LC 89-62874. (Illus.). 80p. (Orig.). 1989. pap. 5.95 (*1-877703-15-X*) Pavilion Pr.

— Fiji: A Traveler's Preview. LC 89-62878. (Illus.). 64p. (Orig.). 1989. pap. 5.95 (*1-877703-14-1*) Pavilion Pr.

— Galapagos Islands: A Traveler's Preview. LC 89-62879. (Illus.). 64p. (Orig.). 1989. pap. 5.95 (*1-877703-13-3*) Pavilion Pr.

— Winter on Spain's Costa del Sol: A Traveler's Preview. LC 90-62946. (Illus.). (Orig.). 1990. pap. 5.95 (*1-877703-12-5*) Pavilion Pr.

An Asterisk (*) at the beginning of an entry indicates that the title is appearing for the first time.

Lane, Kris E. Pillaging the Empire: Piracy in the Americas, 1500-1750. LC 97-32619. (Latin American Realities Ser.). 264p. (C). 1998. 61.95 (*0-7656-0256-3*) M E Sharpe.
— Pillaging the Empire: Piracy in the Americas, 1500-1750. LC 97-32619. (Latin American Realities Ser.). (Illus.). 264p. (gr. 13). 1998. pap. 21.95 (*0-7656-0257-1*) M E Sharpe.
Lane, Larry. Claim Your Money from Insurance Companies. LC 93-85361. (Illus.). 310p. 1993. pap. 14.95 (*0-9622317-2-X*) Tailight Studio.
Lane, Larry, jt. auth. see Milano, Phillip J.
Lane, Larry M. & Wolf, James F. The Human Resource Crisis in the Public Sector: Rebuilding the Capacity to Govern. LC 90-32647. 240p. 1990. 59.95 (*0-89930-491-5*, WRJ/, Quorum Bks) Greenwood.
Lane, Lauree, jt. auth. see Davis, Flora P.
Lane, Leonard G. Gallaudet Survival Guide to Signing. LC 89-25686. (Illus.). 220p. (Orig.). 1987. pap. 6.95 (*0-930323-67-X*) Gallaudet Univ Pr.
Lane, LeRoy E. By All Means, Communicate: An Introduction to Basic Speech. 384p. (C). 1987. pap. text 27.60 (*0-13-109612-5*) P-H.
Lane, Leroy L. By All Means Communicate. 2nd ed. 384p. (C). 1990. pap. text 58.00 (*0-13-109687-7*) P-H.
Lane, Linda. Basics in Pronunciation. LC 96-50194. 160p. 1997. pap. text 26.83 (*0-201-87806-2*) Addison-Wesley.
— Focus on Pronunciation: Principles & Practice for Effective Communication, 4 cass., Set. LC 92-33239. 1993. audio 72.77 (*0-8013-0807-0*, 78867) Longman.
***Lane, Lori, ed.** Federal Technical Standards Workshop Proceedings, 1998: Standards Management - A World of Change & Opportunities. 562p. (C). 1999. pap. text 50.00 (*0-7881-8353-2*) DIANE Pub.
Lane, Louise & Albert, James. Classic Americans. LC 98-61888. (Illus.). 300p. 1999. pap. 14.00 (*0-9636426-4-2*) Windham Pr.
Lane, M. S. Method & Politics in Plato's "Statesman" LC 97-6077. (Cambridge Classical Studies). 242p. (C). 1998. text 59.95 (*0-521-58229-6*) Cambridge U Pr.
Lane, M. Travis. Night Physics. LC 94-194883. 86p. 1994. pap. 11.95 (*0-919626-70-X*, Pub. by Brick Bks) Genl Dist Srvs.
— Reckonings. 79p. 1988. pap. 6.95 (*0-86492-071-7*, Pub. by Goose Ln Edits) Genl Dist Srvs.
— Temporary Shelter. 98p. 1993. pap. 10.95 (*0-86492-148-9*, Pub. by Goose Ln Edits) Genl Dist Srvs.
Lane, Maggie. Jane Austen & Food. LC 95-5995. 1995. 40.00 (*1-85285-124-4*) Hambledon Press.
— Jane Austen's World. 144p. 1996. 20.00 (*1-55850-748-5*) Adams Media.
— Lessons in Dying: Learning How to Live. LC 96-61543. 144p. (Orig.). 1997. pap. 9.95 (*1-883893-78-X*) WinePress Pub.
Lane, Marc J. Taxation for Engineering & Technical Consultants. LC 80-12065. 182p. reprint ed. pap. 56.50 (*0-608-30516-2*, 205553000026) Bks Demand.
— Taxation for Small Manufacturers. LC 80-11621. 174p. reprint ed. pap. 54.00 (*0-608-30519-7*, 205553200026) Bks Demand.
— Taxation for the Computer Industry. LC 80-12070. 189p. reprint ed. pap. 58.60 (*0-608-30517-0*, 205553100026) Bks Demand.
Lane, Marcia. Picturing the Rose: A Way of Looking at Fairy Tales. LC 93-5777. 121p. 1994. 30.00 (*0-8242-0848-X*) Wilson.
Lane, Marcus, jt. ed. see McDonald, Geoff.
Lane, Margaret. Bronte Story. LC 75-108394. (Illus.). 368p. 1971. reprint ed. lib. bdg. 35.00 (*0-8371-3817-5*, LABS, Greenwood Pr) Greenwood.
— Spider. (Picture Puffin Ser.). 1982. 10.19 (*0-606-06014-6*, Pub. by Turtleback) Demco.
Lane, Margaret, ed. see Thompson, Flora.
Lane, Margaret T. State Publications & Depository Libraries: A Reference Handbook. LC 80-24688. (Illus.). 573p. 1981. lib. bdg. 105.00 (*0-313-22118-9*, LSP/, Greenwood Pr) Greenwood.
Lane, Marion. Guide to Owning a Staffordshire Bull Terrier, AKC Rank No. 104. (Guide to Owning Ser.). (Illus.). 64p. 1998. pap. 6.95 (*0-7938-1880-X*, RE-330) TFH Pubns.
— Yorkshire Terrier: An Owner's Guide to a Happy Healthy Pet. LC 97-3459. 160p. 1996. 12.95 (*0-87605-477-7*) Howell Bks.
Lane, Marion & Humane Society of the United States Staff. The Humane Society of the United States Complete Guide to Dog Care. LC 97-44392. (Illus.). 400p. (gr. 8). 1998. 24.95 (*0-316-51305-9*) Little.
Lane, Mark. Chicago Eyewitness. LC 68-58740. (Illus.). (Orig.). 1968. 14.95 (*0-8392-5013-4*); pap. 10.95 (*0-686-66377-2*) Astor-Honor.
— Plausible Denial: Was the CIA Involved in the Assassination of JFK? LC 98-182700. (Illus.). 416p. 1992. pap. 13.95 (*1-56025-048-8*, Thunders Mouth) Avalon NY.
— Rush to Judgment. 2nd ed. 512p. 1992. pap. 14.95 (*1-56025-043-7*, Thunders Mouth) Avalon NY.
Lane, Mark & Gregory, Dick. Murder in Memphis: The FBI & the Assassination of Martin Luther King. LC 92-44534. 336p. 1993. pap. 13.95 (*1-56025-056-9*, Thunders Mouth) Avalon NY.
Lane, Martha. Teddy Bears at School: An Activities Handbook for Teachers of Young Children. (Illus.). 224p. 1986. reprint ed. lib. bdg. 28.95 (*0-89334-227-0*, 2270X23) Humanics Ltd.
Lane, Martha A. Let's Get Started. (Passport to the World of English Ser.: Bk. 1). (Illus.). 142p. 1996. teacher ed., ring bd. 18.00 incl. audio (*1-877596-21-3*); student ed., ring bd. 15.00 incl. audio (*1-877596-22-1*) Literacy & Evangelism.
— Luke: ESL Study Edition. (Passport to the World of English Ser.: Bk. 4). (Illus.). 194p. 1997. teacher ed., ring bd. 23.00 incl. audio (*1-877596-33-7*); student ed., ring bd. 20.00 incl. audio (*1-877596-34-5*) Literacy & Evangelism.
— Passport to the World of English, 4 vols., Set. (Illus.). 1486p. 1997. ring bd. 87.00 incl. audio (*1-877596-37-X*) Literacy & Evangelism.
— Reading & Writing. (Passport to the World of English Ser.: Bk. 3). (Illus.). 240p. 1997. teacher ed., ring bd. 23.00 incl. audio (*1-877596-29-9*); student ed., ring bd. 20.00 incl. audio (*1-877596-30-2*) Literacy & Evangelism.
— Spelling & Grammar. (Passport to the World of English Ser.: Bk. 2). (Illus.). 248p. 1996. teacher ed., ring bd. 23.00 incl. audio (*1-877596-25-6*); student ed., ring bd. 20.00 incl. audio (*1-877596-26-4*) Literacy & Evangelism.
Lane, Mary. Pot Pourri: A Practical Guide. 100p. 1985. 60.00 (*0-7855-2950-0*, Pub. by Bishopsgate Pr Ltd) St Mut.
— Pot Pourri: A Practical Guide. 100p. 1985. pap. 21.00 (*0-7855-2951-9*) St Mut.
Lane, Mary B. Our Schools - Frontline for the Twenty-First Century: What Our Schools Must Become. Baker, Quentin, ed. LC 98-84765. (Illus.). 140p. 1998. pap. 11.95 (*0-9663364-0-2*) Q Trips.
Lane, Mary B. & Signer, Sheila. Infant - Toddler Caregiving: A Guide to Creating Partnerships with Parents. (Program for Infant - Toddler Caregivers Ser.). (Illus.). 102p. 1990. pap. 12.50 (*0-8011-0878-0*) Calif Education.
Lane, Mary E. A Guide to the Antiquities of the Fayyum. 1985. pap. 17.50 (*977-424-042-1*, Pub. by Am Univ Cairo Pr) Col U Pr.
***Lane, Mary E. Bradley.** Mizora: A Prophecy. Pfaelzer, Jean, ed. & intro. by. LC 00-24976. 146p. 2000. pap. text 14.95 (*0-8156-2839-0*) Syracuse U Pr.
Lane, Mary E. Bradley. Mizora: A World of Women. LC 99-34330. (Bison Frontiers of Imagination Ser.). 147p. 1999. pap. 9.95 (*0-8032-7992-2*) U of Nebr Pr.
Lane, Mary L. & Weinberger, Scott R. Flying with Baby: A Parent's Guide to Making Air Travel with an Infant or Toddler Easy. 20p. (Orig.). 1994. pap. 4.95 (*0-9643266-0-4*) Third St Pr.
Lane, Mary R., jt. auth. see Samuels, Mike.
Lane, Mary Rockwood, jt. auth. see Samuels, Michael.
Lane, Mary T. & Wileman, Ralph E. A Structure for Population Education: Goals, Generalizations, & Behavioral Objectives. 2nd ed. LC 74-77985. 1978. pap. 4.00 (*0-89055-128-6*) Carolina Pop Ctr.
Lane, Max, tr. see Toer, Pramoedya A.
***Lane, Megan, ed.** 2000 Photographer's Market: 2,000 Places to Sell Your Photographs. LC 78-643526. (Illus.). 640p. 1999. pap. 24.99 (*0-89879-912-0*, 10610, Wrtrs Digest Bks) F & W Pubns Inc.
Lane, Mervin, ed. Black Mountain College: Sprouted Seeds-An Anthology of Personal Accounts. LC 90-35968. (Illus.). 368p. 1990. 36.00 (*0-87049-663-8*) U of Tenn Pr.
Lane, Michael. Introduction to Structuralism. 1970. pap. 11.50 (*0-465-03576-0*) Basic.
— A Man's View of Life & Love. Allums, Betty, ed. 57p. (Orig.). 1988. pap. 8.00 (*0-932211-02-X*) BA Cross Ctrl.
— Pink Highways: Tales of Queer Madness on the Open Road. LC 94-20515. 288p. 1995. 19.95 (*1-55972-263-0*, Birch Ln Pr) Carol Pub Group.
***Lane, Michael.** Secrets of the Wealth Makers: Top Money Managers Reveal Their Investing Wisdom. 256p. 2000. 24.95 (*0-07-135574-X*) McGraw.
Lane, Michael, jt. auth. see Crotty, Jim.
Lane, Michael F. & Chambers, Larry. Guaranteed Income for Life: How Variable Annuities Can Cut Your Taxes, Pay You Every Year of Your Life, & Bring You Financial Peace of Mind. LC 98-3163. (Illus.). 244p. 1998. 22.95 (*0-07-038297-2*) McGraw.
Lane, Michael H. Customs Modernization & the International Trade Superhighway. LC 97-48616. (Illus.). 248p. 1998. 59.95 (*1-56720-210-1*, Q210, Quorum Bks) Greenwood.
Lane, Michael K., et al. Style Manual for Political Science. rev. ed. 24p. (C). 1993. pap. 4.00 (*1-878147-09-9*) Am Political.
Lane, Michael R. Britannia Iron Works. 1993. pap. text 50.00 (*1-870948-85-8*, Pub. by Quiller Pr) St Mut.
— Crossroads: The Prophet (& Other Lives) 192p. 2000. pap. 13.95 (*0-89407-112-2*) Strawberry Hill.
Lane, Mike, ed. see Vitale, Mike.
Lane, Mills. Architecture of the Old South. LC 93-1550. (Architecture of the Old South Ser.). (Illus.). 324p. 1993. 67.50 (*1-55859-044-7*) Abbeville Pr.
— Architecture of the Old South: Colonial & Federal. (Illus.). 378p. 1996. 75.00 (*0-88322-033-4*) Beehive GA.
— Architecture of the Old South: Georgia. rev. ed. (Illus.). 240p. 1996. 55.00 (*0-88322-037-7*) Beehive GA.
— Architecture of the Old South: Greek Revival & Romantic. (Illus.). 368p. 1996. 75.00 (*0-88322-034-2*) Beehive GA.
— Architecture of the Old South: Kentucky & Tennessee. (Illus.). 245p. 1993. 55.00 (*0-88322-022-9*) Beehive GA.
— Architecture of the Old South: Louisiana. rev. ed. (Illus.). 204p. 1997. 55.00 (*0-88322-039-3*) Beehive GA.
— Architecture of the Old South: Maryland. rev. ed. (Illus.). 235p. 1996. 55.00 (*0-88322-032-6*) Beehive GA.
— Architecture of the Old South: Mississippi & Alabama. rev. ed. (Illus.). 204p. 1997. 55.00 (*0-88322-038-5*) Beehive GA.
— Architecture of the Old South: North Carolina. rev. ed. (Illus.). 228p. 1997. 55.00 (*0-88322-036-9*) Beehive GA.
— Architecture of the Old South: South Carolina. rev. ed. (Illus.). 252p. 1997. 55.00 (*0-88322-035-0*) Beehive GA.
— Architecture of the Old South: Virginia. rev. ed. (Illus.). 264p. 1996. 55.00 (*0-88322-029-6*) Beehive GA.
— The People of Georgia: An Illustrated History. 2nd ed. (Illus.). 312p. 1992. 50.00 (*0-88322-000-8*) Beehive GA.
— Savannah Revisited: History & Architecture. 4th ed. (Illus.). 218p. 1994. 35.00 (*0-88322-021-0*) Beehive GA.
Lane, Mills, ed. Dear Mother: Don't Grieve about Me, If I Get Killed, I'll Only Be Dead: Letters from Georgia Soldiers in the Civil War. (Illus.). 356p. 1990. 35.00 (*0-88322-009-1*) Beehive GA.
— General Oglethorpe's Georgia: Colonial Letters, 1733-1743, 2 vols., Set. 674p. 1990. 60.00 (*0-88322-001-6*) Beehive GA.
— Georgia, History Written by Those Who Lived It. (Documentary History Ser.). 368p. 1995. 40.00 (*0-88322-020-2*) Beehive GA.
— Neither More nor Less Than Men: Slavery in Georgia. (A Documentary History Ser.). 248p. 1993. 35.00 (*0-88322-016-4*) Beehive GA.
— The Rambler in Georgia: Travellers' Accounts of Frontier Georgia. (Illus.). 233p. 1990. 30.00 (*0-88322-003-2*) Beehive GA.
— Standing upon the Mouth of a Volcano: New South Georgia. (A Documentary History Ser.). 245p. 1993. 35.00 (*0-88322-018-0*) Beehive GA.
— Times That Prove People's Principles: Civil War in Georgia. (Documentary History Ser.). 276p. 1993. 35.00 (*0-88322-017-2*) Beehive GA.
Lane, N. E. Skill Acquisition Rates & Patterns. (Recent Research in Psychology Ser.). (Illus.). 170p. 1987. 56.95 (*0-387-96579-3*) Spr-Verlag.
Lane, N. Gary, jt. auth. see Ausich, William I.
Lane, Nancy. How to Have a Happy New Rear! (Illus.). (Orig.). 1983. pap. 4.95 (*0-912171-00-6*, 50M) World Pr Ltd.
— Saving Face. write for info. (*0-318-58989-3*) World Pr Ltd.
Lane, Nancy, jt. ed. see Chisholm, Margaret.
***Lane, Nancy D., et al, contrib. by.** Techniques for Student Research: A Comprehensive Guide to Using the Library. LC 99-56395. 200p. 2000. pap. 35.00 (*1-55570-367-4*) Neal-Schuman.
Lane, Nancy E., ed. AIDS Allergy & Rheumatology. (Illus.). 112p. 1997. 59.50 (*0-89603-502-6*) Humana.
— The Osteoporosis Book. LC 98-19650. (Illus.). 224p. 1999. 27.50 (*0-19-511602-X*) OUP.
Lane, Nathan M. An Introduction to Professional Responsibility. LC 97-51282. 550p. 1998. pap. text 33.95 (*1-56706-698-4*) Panel Pubs.
***Lane, Neal, ed.** Our Changing Planet: The FY 2000 U. S. Global Change Research Program - Implementation Plan & Budget Overview. (Illus.). 100p. (C). 1999. pap. text 20.00 (*0-7881-8253-6*) DIANE Pub.
Lane, Neal & Varmus, Harold, eds. Investing in Our Future: A National Research Initiative for America's Children for the 21st Century. (Illus.). 88p. (C). 1999. text 20.00 (*0-7881-7928-4*) DIANE Pub.
Lane, Nina, jt. auth. see Lane, John.
Lane, Norman, jt. auth. see Irwin, Robert.
Lane, Norman H. & Zaritsky, Howard M. Federal Income Taxation of Estates & Trusts. 1988. 140.00 (*0-7913-0012-9*, FIET) Warren Gorham & Lamont.
Lane, P. H. Commentary on the Australian Constitution: With Sixth Cumulative Supplement. 298p. 1994. pap., suppl. ed. 75.00 (*0-455-21278-3*, Pub. by LawBk Co) Gaunt.
— A Digest of Australian Constitutional Cases. 4th ed. 483p. 1992. 110.00 (*0-455-21145-0*, Pub. by LawBk Co); pap. 68.00 (*0-455-21146-9*, Pub. by LawBk Co) Gaunt.
— A Digest of Australian Constitutional Cases: A Digest of Australian Constitutional Cases. 5th ed. LC 97-179966. 451p. 1996. pap. 80.00 (*0-455-21423-9*, Pub. by LawBk Co) Gaunt.
— An Introduction to the Australian Constitution. 5th ed. ix, 276p. 1990. pap. 32.00 (*0-455-21012-8*, Pub. by LawBk Co) Gaunt.
— An Introduction to the Australian Constitution. 6th ed. 320p. 1994. text 36.00 (*0-455-21260-0*, Pub. by LawBk Co) Gaunt.
— Lane's Commentary on the Australian Constitution. 766p. 1986. suppl. ed. 195.00 (*0-455-20701-1*, Pub. by LawBk Co) Gaunt.
— Lane's Commentary on the Australian Constitution. 2nd ed. 900p. 1999. 185.00 (*0-455-21440-9*, Pub. by LBC Info Servs) Gaunt.
— A Manual of Australian Constitutional Law. 4th ed. xxii, 565p. 1987. pap. 74.50 (*0-455-20771-2*, Pub. by LawBk Co) Gaunt.
Lane-Palagyi, Addyse. The East River & the Unicorn Tapestries. 160p. 1992. 24.95 (*1-56538-026-6*); pap. 12.95 (*1-56538-025-8*) Addison-Pacific.
Lane, Patrick. Milford & Me. (Illus.). 32p. (J). 1989. pap. 6.95 (*0-919926-97-5*, Pub. by Coteau) Genl Dist Srvs.
— Milford & Me. (Illus.). 32p. (J). (ps-7). 1989. pap. 11.95 (*0-919926-96-7*, Pub. by Coteau) Genl Dist Srvs.
Lane, Patrick. Mortal Remains. 2nd ed. (Picas Ser.: No. 17). 92p. reprint ed. pap. 7.00 (*1-55096-541-7*, Pub. by Exile Edns) Paul & Co Pubs.
Lane, Patrick. Poems New & Selected. 1980. pap. 5.95 (*0-19-540296-0*) OUP.
— Winter. 56p. 1990. reprint ed. pap. 7.95 (*1-55050-002-3*, Pub. by Coteau) Genl Dist Srvs.
Lane, Patrick & Crozier, Lorna, eds. Alden Nowlan Selected Poems. 194p. (Orig.). 1996. pap. 15.95 (*0-88784-573-8*, Pub. by Hse of Anansi Pr) Genl Dist Srvs.
Lane, Patrick R., jt. auth. see Pollack, Cecelia.
***Lane, Patrick T.** Advanced Internet Business Fundamentals. Lane, Susan M. & Oberman, David, eds. (Illus.). 150p. (C). 1999. pap. write for info. (*0-7423-0297-0*) ComputerPREP.
— Advanced Internet Business Fundamentals: A4, Version 3.07. Lane, Susan M. & Oberman, David, eds. (CIW Foundations Track A4 Ser.). (Illus.). 1999. pap. write for info. (*1-58143-060-4*) Prosoft I-net.
— Advanced Internet Business Fundamentals Version 3.17. Lane, Susan M. & Oberman, David, eds. (CIW Foundations Ser.). (Illus.). 2000. pap. write for info. (*1-58143-107-4*) Prosoft I-net.
— Advanced Internet Business Fundamentals Version 3.17 A4. Lane, Susan M. & Oberman, David, eds. (CIW Foundations Ser.). (Illus.). 2000. pap. write for info. (*1-58143-108-2*) Prosoft I-net.
— Advanced TCP/IP Concepts & Practices: A4, Version 3.07. Lane, Susan M., ed. (CIW Internetworking Professional Track A4 Ser.). (Illus.). 1999. pap. write for info. (*1-58143-087-6*) Prosoft I-net.
— Advanced TCP/IP Concepts & Practices: Version 3.07. Lane, Susan M., ed. (CIW Internetworking Professional Track Ser.). 1999. pap. write for info. (*1-58143-051-5*) Prosoft I-net.
— Basic Internet Business Fundamentals. Obermen, David, ed. (Illus.). 123p. (C). 1999. pap. write for info. (*0-7423-0296-2*) ComputerPREP.
— Basic Internet Business Fundamentals. Oberman, David, ed. (CIW Foundations Ser.). (Illus.). 1999. pap. write for info. (*1-58143-029-9*) Prosoft I-net.
— Basic Internet Business Fundamentals: A4, Version 3.07. Oberman, David, ed. (CIW Foundations Track A4 Ser.). (Illus.). 1999. pap. write for info. (*1-58143-059-0*) Prosoft I-net.
— Basic Internet Business Fundamentals Version 3.17. Oberman, David, ed. (Illus.). 2000. pap. write for info. (*1-58143-105-8*) Prosoft I-net.
— Basic Internet Business Fundamentals Version 3.17 A4. Lane, Susan M. & Oberman, David, eds. (CIW3 Foundations Ser.). (Illus.). 2000. pap. write for info. (*1-58143-106-6*) Prosoft I-net.
— Network & Certification Training. Oberman, David, ed. (Illus.). 1999. pap. write for info. (*1-58143-002-7*, PSG1EUE4) Prosoft I-net.
— Network + Certification Training: Version 2.07. Oberman, David, ed. (CIW Internetworking Professional Track Ser.). (Illus.). 1999. pap. write for info. (*1-58143-052-3*) Prosoft I-net.
— Network + X: A4, Version 2.07. Oberman, David, ed. (CIW Internetworking Professional Track A4 Ser.). (Illus.). 1999. pap. write for info. (*1-58143-088-4*) Prosoft I-net.
— TCP/IP Internetworking: A4, Version 2.07. McKenna, Jill, ed. (CIW Internetworking Professional Track A4 Ser.). (Illus.). 1999. pap. write for info. (*1-58143-086-8*) Prosoft I-net.
— TCP/IP Internetworking: Version 2.07. McKenna, Jill, ed. (CIW Internetworking Professional Track Ser.). (Illus.). 1999. pap. write for info. (*1-58143-050-7*) Prosoft I-net.
***Lane, Patrick T. & Stanger, James.** Networking Fundamentals: A4, Version 4.07. McKenna, Jill & Oberman, David, eds. (CIW Foundations Track A4 Ser.). (Illus.). 1999. pap. write for info. (*1-58143-062-0*) Prosoft I-net.
***Lane, Patrick T. & Stranger, James.** Networking Fundamentals. McKenna, Jill, ed. (Illus.). 250p. (C). 1999. pap. write for info. (*0-7423-0298-9*) ComputerPREP.
***Lane, Paul.** Oracle 8/8i DBA Certification. (Oracle Bks.). (Illus.). 1400p. 2000. pap. 99.99 (*0-672-31785-0*) Sams.
Lane, Peter. Ceramic Form. LC 97-76296. (Illus.). 256p. 1998. 45.00 (*0-8478-2113-7*, Pub. by Rizzoli Intl) St Martin.
***Lane, Peter.** Ceramic Form Revised Edition: Design & Decoration. 2nd ed. 256p. 1998. text. write for info. (*90-5703-242-2*, Harwood Acad Pubs) Gordon & Breach.
Lane, Peter. Contemporary Porcelain. (Illus.). 224p. 1995. 39.95 (*0-8019-8635-4*) Krause Pubns.
— Success in British History, 1760-1914. (Success Sportbooks Ser.). (Illus.). 1978. pap. 12.00 (*0-7195-3483-6*) Transatl Arts.
Lane, Peter, ed. The Use of Chemicals in Oil Spill Response. LC 95-22156. (STP Ser.: No. 1252). 340p. 1995. 89.00 (*0-8031-1999-2*, STP1252) ASTM.
Lane, Peter & Peto, Monica. Blackstone's Guide to the Environment Act, 1995. 564p. 1995. 27.95 (*1-85431-491-2*, Pub. by Blackstone Pr) Gaunt.
Lane, Peter, et al. Genstat Five: A Second Course. (Illus.). 256p. 1989. 69.00 (*0-19-852201-0*); pap. text 35.00 (*0-19-852218-5*) OUP.
— Genstat 5: An Introduction. (Illus.). 176p. 1988. text 49.95 (*0-19-852209-6*) OUP.
Lane, Peter B. The United States & the Balkan Crisis of 1940-1941. LC 88-11062. (Modern American History Ser.). 336p. 1988. 20.00 (*0-8240-4332-4*) Garland.
Lane, Pinkie G. Girl at the Window: Poems by Pinkie Gordon Lane. LC 91-4197. 64p. 1991. pap. 7.95 (*0-8071-1714-5*); text 15.95 (*0-8071-1713-7*) La State U Pr.
***Lane, Pinkie Gordon.** Elegy for Etheridge. 80p. 2000. 22.50 (*0-8071-2544-X*); pap. 14.95 (*0-8071-2545-8*) La State U Pr.
Lane-Poole, E. W. Arabic-English Lexicon, Vol. I. 1500p. (C). 1993. text 165.00 (*1-56744-491-1*) Kazi Pubns.
— Arabic-English Lexicon, Vol. II. 1520p. (C). 1993. text 165.00 (*1-56744-492-X*) Kazi Pubns.
Lane-Poole, Stanley. The Barbary Corsairs. 334p. 1984. 200.00 (*1-85077-018-2*, Pub. by Darf Pubs Ltd) St Mut.
— Cairo: Sketches of Its History, Monuments & Social Life. LC 73-6286. (Middle East Ser.). 1979. reprint ed. 33.95 (*0-405-05345-2*) Ayer.
— History of Egypt in the Middle Ages. (Illus.). 382p. 1968. reprint ed. 45.00 (*0-7146-1686-9*, Pub. by F Cass Pubs) Intl Spec Bk.

L

— History of Egypt in the Middle Ages. LC 68-25246. (World History Ser.: No. 48). (C). 1969. reprint ed. lib. bdg. 75.00 (*0-8383-0210-6*) M S G Haskell Hse.
— History of India from the Reign of Akbar the Great to the Fall of the Moghul Empire. LC 72-14391. (History of India Ser.: No. 4). reprint ed. 90.00 (*0-404-09004-4*) AMS Pr.
— The Life of the Right Honourable Stratford Canning, Viscount Stratford de Redcliffe, 2 vols. LC 73-171653. reprint ed. 115.00 (*0-404-07387-5*) AMS Pr.
— Mediaeval India: Under Mohammed Rule. 1990. reprint ed. 12.50 (*0-8364-2517-0*, Pub. by Low Price) S Asia.
— Mediaeval India from the Mohammedan Conquest to the Reign of Akbar the Great. LC 72-14391. (History of India Ser.: No. 3). reprint ed. 110.00 (*0-404-09003-6*) AMS Pr.
— Medieval India under Mohammedan Rule. LC 70-132442. (World History Ser.: No. 48). 1970. reprint ed. lib. bdg. 75.00 (*0-8383-1196-2*) M S G Haskell Hse.
— The Moors in Spain. 212p. 1924. pap. text 22.00 (*0-916157-31-8*) African Islam Miss Pubns.
— The Moors in Spain. 304p. 1984. 190.00 (*1-85077-042-5*, Pub. by Darf Pubs Ltd) St Mut.
— Saladin. 528p. 1985. 300.00 (*1-85077-068-9*, Pub. by Darf Pubs Ltd) St Mut.
— Saladin Vol. 1: And the Fall of the Kingdom of Jerusalem. 1991. pap. text 17.00 (*0-916157-93-8*) African Islam Miss Pubns.
— Saladin Vol. 2: And the Fall of the Kingdom of Jerusalem. 1991. pap. text 17.00 (*0-916157-94-6*) African Islam Miss Pubns.
— Saladin Vol. 3: And the Fall of the Kingdom of Jerusalem. 1991. pap. text 17.00 (*0-916157-95-4*) African Islam Miss Pubns.
— Saladin & the Fall of the Kingdom of Jerusalem. LC 73-14453. (Heroes of the Nations Ser.). reprint ed. 37.50 (*0-404-58270-2*) AMS Pr.
— Social Life in Egypt: A Description of the Country & Its People. LC 77-87653. (Illus.). reprint ed. 32.50 (*0-404-16414-5*) AMS Pr.
— The Speeches & Table Talk of the Prophet Muhammad. 189p. 1990. 8.95 (*0-318-36781-5*) Asia Bk Corp.
— The Story of Cairo. (Mediaeval Towns Ser.: Vol. 11). 1974. reprint ed. pap. 46.00 (*0-8115-0853-6*) Periodicals Srv.
— The Story of the Barbary Corsairs. LC 73-97416. (Illus.). 316p. 1970. reprint ed. lib. bdg. 38.50 (*0-8371-3231-2*, LBC&) Greenwood.
— The Story of the Moors in Spain. LC 90-81538. (Illus.). 274p. 1990. reprint ed. pap. 18.95 (*0-933121-19-9*) Black Classic.
— Studies in a Mosque, Vol. 1. Obaba, Al I., ed. 184p. 1990. pap. text 20.00 (*0-916157-22-9*) African Islam Miss Pubns.
— Studies in a Mosque, Vol. II. 136p. 1990. pap. text 20.00 (*0-916157-58-X*) African Islam Miss Pubns.
— Turkey. 400p. 1986. 300.00 (*1-85077-130-8*, Pub. by Darf Pubs Ltd) St Mut.

Lane, Purvis N. The Immortal Man: A Reality for Today. 85p. 1999. pap. write for info. (*0-7392-0108-5*, PO3003) Morris Pubng.

Lane, R. W. & Otten, G., eds. Power Plant Instrumentation for Measurement of High-Purity Water Quality - STP 742. 235p. 1981. 26.50 (*0-8031-0798-6*, STP742) ASTM.

Lane, Randall. P. O. V.'s Living Large: The Guy's Guide to Getting Ahead, Getting It Right & Getting It Often. LC 98-21260. 384p. 1998. pap. 20.00 (*0-06-273521-7*) HarpC.

Lane, Richard. Fun Songs for Children. (Illus.). 56p. 1987. pap. 9.95 (*0-8256-1094-X*, AM63876) Music Sales.
— The Golden Age of Australian Radio Drama, 1923-1960. 496p. 1996. pap. 34.95 (*0-522-84704-8*, Pub. by Melbourne Univ Pr) Paul & Co Pubs.
— Lane's English As a Second Language, 6 bks. Incl. Lane's English Pronunciation Guide. 44p. 1995. pap. text, per. 9.25 (*0-935606-04-1*); Bk. 1. 76p. 1995. pap. text 9.25 (*0-935606-01-7*); Bk. 2. 98p. 1995. pap. text 9.25 Bk. 3. 128p. 1997. pap. text 9.25 Bk. 4. 112p. 1997. pap. text 9.25 Bk. 5. 95p. 1987. pap. text 9.95 Bk. 6. 105p. 1987. pap. text 9.25 (Illus.). 120p. 1987. Set pap. text 9.25 (*0-685-07057-3*) Lane Pr.
— Swashbuckling: A Step-by-Step Guide to the Art of Stage Combat & Theatrical Swordplay. LC 98-7290. (Illus.). 329p. 1999. pap. 27.50 (*0-87910-091-5*) Limelight Edns.

Lane, Richard, ed. see Lambrecht, Frank L.

Lane, Richard, ed. see Tuttle, Tom.

Lane, Richard B., jt. auth. see Grossman, Stanley I.

Lane, Richard D. & Nadel, Lynn, eds. Cognitive Neuroscience of Emotion. LC 99-17111. (Series in Affective Science). (Illus.). 448p. 1999. text 60.00 (*0-19-511888-X*) OUP.

Lane, Richard J. & Wurts, Jay. In Search of the Woman Warrior. LC 98-25708. 344p. 1998. 19.95 (*1-86204-313-2*, Pub. by Element MA) Penguin Putnam.

Lane, Richard P. & Crosske, Roger W., eds. Medical Insects & Arachnids. LC 92-49000. 1993. write for info. (*0-04-124000-6*) Chapman & Hall.

Lane, Robert. EC Competition Law. (Law Ser.). 160p. (C). 1996. pap. text 14.95 (*0-582-28976-9*, Pub. by Addison-Wesley) Longman.

Lane, Robert. Gambler's Bullets. large type ed. 224p. pap. 18.99 (*0-7089-5432-4*) Ulverscroft.

Lane, Robert, jt. auth. see Lane, David.

Lane, Robert B. & Lane, Barbara. Chehalis River Treaty Council & the Treaty of Olympia. (Treaty Manuscripts Ser.: No. 1). 77p. 15.00 (*0-944253-23-7*) Inst Dev Indian Law.
— The Treaties of Puget Sound, 1854-1855. (Treaty Manuscripts Ser.: No. 6). 60p. 12.50 (*0-944253-28-8*) Inst Dev Indian Law.
— Western Washington Treaty Proceedings. (Treaty Manuscripts Ser.: No. 2). 67p. 12.50 (*0-944253-24-5*) Inst Dev Indian Law.

Lane, Robert C., ed. Psychoanalytic Approaches to Supervision. LC 90-1971. (Current Issues in Psychoanalytic Practice Ser.: No. 2). 224p. 1990. text 35.95 (*0-87630-603-2*) Brunner-Mazel.

Lane, Robert C. & Hyman, Marvin, eds. Special Section on Termination: A Special Issue of Psychoanalytic Psychology. 176p. 1997. pap. 20.00 (*0-8058-9866-2*) L Erlbaum Assocs.

Lane, Robert C. & Meisels, Murray, eds. A History of the Division of Psychoanalysis of the American Psychological Association. 384p. 1994. pap. text 49.95 (*0-8058-1323-3*) L Erlbaum Assocs.

Lane, Robert C., jt. auth. see Edward, David A.

Lane, Robert D. Reading the Bible: Intention, Text, Interpretation. 222p. (Orig.). (C). 1993. pap. text 24.50 (*0-8191-9114-0*) U Pr of Amer.

*__Lane, Robert E.__ The Decline of Happiness in Market Democracies LC 99-29817. (Illus.). 480p. 2000. 35.00 (*0-300-07801-3*) Yale U Pr.

Lane, Robert E. The Fear of Equality. (Reprint Series in Social Sciences). (C). 1993. reprint ed. pap. text 5.00 (*0-8290-2734-3*, PS-162) Irvington.
— The Market Experience. 640p. (C). 1991. pap. text 29.95 (*0-521-40737-0*) Cambridge U Pr.

Lane, Robert G. The Confetti Kid. LC 96-67684. (Illus.). 360p. (Orig.). 1997. pap. text 25.00 (*0-943104-97-1*) Serrell & Simons.
— A Solitary Dance. LC 82-81020. (Illus.). 240p. (Orig.). (C). 1983. 19.00 (*0-943104-82-3*) Serrell & Simons.

Lane, Robert S., jt. auth. see Middlekauff, Woodrow S.

Lane, Robert W. Beyond the Schoolhouse Gate: Free Speech & the Inculcation of Values. LC 94-16430. 224p. (C). 1995. text 69.95 (*1-56639-274-8*); pap. text 19.95 (*1-56639-275-6*) Temple U Pr.

Lane, Rodney, jt. ed. see Cella, Charles P.

Lane, Roger. Murder in America: A History. LC 96-39626. (History of Crime & Criminal Justice Ser.). (Illus.). 416p. 1998. text 42.50 (*0-8142-0732-4*, LANMUR); pap. text 16.95 (*0-8142-0733-2*, LANMUX) Ohio St U Pr.
— Roots of Violence in Black Philadelphia, 1860-1900. (Illus.). 224p. 1986. 35.00 (*0-674-77990-8*) HUP.
— Roots of Violence in Black Philadelphia, 1860-1900. 224p. 1986. reprint ed. pap. 16.50 (*0-674-77978-9*) HUP.
— Violent Death in the City: Suicide, Accident, & Murder in Nineteenth-Century Philadelphia. LC 79-11836. (Commonwealth Fund Publications). 202p. 1979. 36.50 (*0-674-93946-8*) HUP.
— Violent Death in the City: Suicide, Accident & Murder in Nineteenth-Century Philadelphia. 2nd ed. LC 98-47596. 224p. 1999. pap. text 16.95 (*0-8142-5021-1*) Ohio St U Pr.
— William Dorsey's Philadelphia & Ours: On the Past & Future of the Black City in America. (Illus.). 512p. 1991. text 49.95 (*0-19-506566-2*, 11827) OUP.

Lane, Roger & Turner, John J., Jr., eds. Riot, Rout, & Tumult: Readings in American Social & Political Violence, 69. LC 77-84752. (Contributions in American History Ser.: No. 69). 399p. 1978. 49.95 (*0-8371-9845-3*, LRR/, Greenwood Pr) Greenwood.

Lane, Roger B. The Money Workbook: A 30-Day Program to Greater Abundance, Prosperity & Self-Worth. 2nd ed. 79p. Date not set. spiral bd. 29.95 (*1-888388-24-2*) Right Lane.
— The Money Workbook: A 30-Day Program to Greater Abundance, Prosperity & Self-Worth. 3rd ed. Date not set. spiral bd. 19.95 (*1-888388-12-9*) Right Lane.

Lane, Ron. An Introduction to Utilities. LC 75-19284. 176p. reprint ed. pap. 54.60 (*0-608-30932-X*, 201039700069) Bks Demand.

Lane, Ronald E., tr. see Martini, Carlo M.

Lane, Rose W. Discovery of Freedom: Man's Struggle Against Authority. LC 73-172216. (Right Wing Individualist Tradition in America Ser.). 1979. reprint ed. 21.95 (*0-405-00425-7*) Ayer.
— The Discovery of Freedom: Man's Struggle Against Authority. 50th anniversary ed. 262p. 1996. reprint ed. pap. 14.95 (*0-930073-00-2*) Fox & Wilkes.
— Free Land. LC 84-7493. iv, 332p. 1984. reprint ed. pap. 12.95 (*0-8032-7914-0*, Bison Books) U of Nebr Pr.
— Old Home Town. LC 85-8645. vii, 309p. 1985. reprint ed. pap. 12.00 (*0-8032-7917-5*, Bison Books) U of Nebr Pr.
— Young Pioneers. 1976. 17.95 (*0-8488-0557-7*) Amereon Ltd.
— Young Pioneers. LC 97-50447. (Illus.). 192p. (J). (gr. 3-7). 1998. pap. 4.95 (*0-06-440698-9*) HarpC.

Lane, Rose W. & Ahmad, Imadad D. Islam & the Discovery of Freedom. LC 97-33212. 1997. write for info. (*0-915957-73-6*) amana pubns.

Lane, Rose W., jt. auth. see Wilder, Laura Ingalls.

Lane, Rose W., ed. see Wilder, Laura Ingalls.

Lane-Rowley, Ulla V. Using Design Protection in the Fashion & Textile Industry. LC 97-21574. 222p. 1997. pap. 67.50 (*0-471-96925-7*) Wiley.

*__Lane, Ruby.__ In God's Hands. 16p. 2000. pap. 4.95 (*1-56167-576-8*) Am Literary Pr.

Lane, Russel M., et al. Sport Medicine: Protection, Treatment & Nutrition. LC 73-10420. (Sport Medicine Ser.: Vol. 2). 1974. 32.00 (*0-8422-7140-6*) Irvington.

Lane, Russell J. Handbook of Muscle Disease. LC 96-21848. (Neurological Disease & Therapy Ser.: Vol. 42). (Illus.). 768p. 1996. text 215.00 (*0-8247-9494-X*) Dekker.

Lane, Ruth. The Art of Comparative Politics. LC 96-20593. 147p. (C). 1996. pap. text 32.46 (*0-205-26099-3*) Allyn.
— Political Science in Theory & Practice: The 'Politics' Model. LC 96-21984. 188p. (C). (gr. 13). 1996. text 58.95 (*1-56324-939-1*) M E Sharpe.

Lane, Ruth. Political Science in Theory & Practice: The 'Politics' Model. LC 96-21984. 188p. (C). (gr. 13). 1996. pap. text 27.95 (*1-56324-940-5*) M E Sharpe.

Lane, S. Mac. Mathematics: Form & Function. (Illus.). xi, 476p. 1985. 59.95 (*0-387-96217-4*) Spr-Verlag.

Lane, S. Mac, see Mac Lane, S.

Lane, S. N., et al. Landform Monitoring Modelling & Analysis. LC 97-5546. 466p. 1998. 125.00 (*0-471-96977-X*) Wiley.

Lane, Sandra & Gibson, Julia. I'm Special: Fun & Educational Songs for Children. (Illus.). 55p. (Orig.). (J). (gr. k-6). 1997. pap. text 12.00 (*0-9658295-1-0*) Yellow Flowers Mus.

Lane, Sandy L., jt. auth. see Ryan, Gail D.

Lane, Sarah, et al. The Cora: People of the Sierra Madre. 51p. (J). (gr. 6-12). 1989. pap. 9.95 (*0-941379-06-X*, 5114) World Eagle.

Lane, Scott E. Gambling Card Sharps: How to Beat a Cheater. 230p. 1992. pap. 19.95 (*0-9635261-0-3*) CAD-Cam Pubn.

Lane, Shelly J., jt. ed. see Chandler, Lynette S.

Lane, Shelly J., ed. see Porr, Susan M., et al.

Lane, Simon. Fear: A Novel. LC 97-42367. 171p. 1998. 21.95 (*1-882593-22-7*) Bridge Wrks.
— Still Life with Books: A Novel. LC 93-18948. 144p. 1993. 17.95 (*1-882593-02-2*) Bridge Wrks.

Lane Staff. All That Jazz & More... 2nd ed. LC 93-61401. 160p. 1994. pap. text, per. 21.95 (*0-8403-9020-3*) Kendall-Hunt.

Lane, Susan M., jt. auth. see Lange, Alan.

Lane, Susan M., ed. see Bagdonas, Richard.

Lane, Susan M., ed. see Brown, Jeff, et al.

Lane, Susan M., ed. see Cohen, Ken & Frosti, Gregg.

Lane, Susan M., ed. see Cohen, Ken, et al.

Lane, Susan M., ed. see Crothers, Timothy & Stanger, James.

Lane, Susan M., ed. see Eliasen, Alan.

Lane, Susan M., ed. see Koenen, Frank.

Lane, Susan M., ed. see Lane, Patrick T.

Lane, Susan M., ed. see Occhiogrosso, Neill.

Lane, Susan M., ed. see Pease, Lisa.

Lane, Susan M., ed. see Pease, Lisa & Stanger, James.

Lane, Susan M., ed. see Pease, Lisa, et al.

Lane, Susan M., ed. see Roberts, Molly.

Lane, Susan M., ed. see Roberts, Molly J.

Lane, Susan M., ed. see Strack, Paul.

Lane, Susan M., ed. see Teitelbaum, Jeremy.

Lane, Suzie W., jt. auth. see Lee, Scout.

Lane, T. A. & Myllylae, G., eds. Leukocyte-Depleted Blood Products. (Current Studies in Hematology & Blood Transfusion: No. 60). (Illus.). viii, 150p. 1994. 149.75 (*3-8055-5862-7*) S Karger.

Lane, Tamar. What's Wrong with the Movies? LC 78-160237. (Moving Pictures Ser.). 254p. 1971. reprint ed. lib. bdg. 31.95 (*0-89198-038-5*) Ozer.

Lane, Terrance & Serk, Jessie. Australians at Home: A Documentary History of Australian Domestic Interiors from 1788-1914. (Illus.). 462p. 1991. text 175.00 (*0-19-553128-0*) OUP.

Lane, Terry S., jt. auth. see Feins, Judith D.

Lane, Theodore. Measuring Changes in Alaska's Labor Market: Hours Worked vs. People Employed. (Occasional Papers: No. 16). 13p. 1982. pap. write for info. (*0-88353-035-X*) U Alaska Inst Res.

Lane, Theodore, ed. Developing America's Northern Frontier. LC 86-28233. (Illus.). 270p. (Orig.). 1987. pap. text 25.00 (*0-8191-6082-2*) U Pr of Amer.

*__Lane, Thomas.__ MCSD Visual Basic 6.0 Distributed Exam Cram. (Programming Ser.). (C). 1999. pap. 15.60 (*0-619-01608-6*) Course Tech.

Lane, Thomas J. Luke & the Gentile Mission: Gospel Anticipates Acts. (European University Studies: Series 23, Vol. 571). (GER.). 240p. 1996. pap. 44.95 (*3-631-49999-X*) P Lang Pubng.

*__Lane, Tony.__ Changing Ministry in Changing Times. 2000. pap. 11.99 (*0-87148-214-2*) Pathway Pr.

Lane, Tony. Exploring Christian Thought. LC 95-19148. (Christian Cornerstone Ser.). 260p. 1996. pap. 12.99 (*0-7852-1143-8*) Nelson.
— Liverpool: City of the Sea. LC 96-130581. 151p. 1997. 34.95 (*0-85323-780-8*, Pub. by Liverpool Univ Pr) Intl Spec Bk.

Lane, Tony, ed. see Calvin, John.

Lane, Tracy. The Living Organization: Systems of Behavior. LC 88-39746. 229p. 1989. 59.95 (*0-275-93084-X*, C3084, Praeger Pubs) Greenwood.

*__Lane, Travles, ed.__ International Who's Who of Professionals: The Ultimate Professional Directory, 3 vols. 8th ed. (Illus.). 2000. lib. bdg. write for info. (*1-882952-22-7*) Gibralter Pub.

Lane, Vann. Children of Revival. LC 99-167114. 144p. 1998. pap. 9.99 (*1-56043-699-9*, Revival Pr) Destiny Image.

Lane, Vera W., jt. auth. see Molyneaux, Dorothy.

Lane, W. Ben, ed. see Fogle, Jeanne S.

Lane, W. Ben, ed. see Wright, Paul S.

*__Lane, W. Ronald & Russell, J. Thomas.__ Advertising: A Framework. 350p. 2000. pap. 51.33 (*0-13-085220-1*, Prentice Hall) P-H.

Lane, W. Ronald, jt. auth. see Russell, J. Thomas.

Lane, Wheaton J., jt. ed. see Labatut, Jean.

Lane, William. Moonlight Standing in As Cordelia. 1980. pap. 4.00 (*0-914610-20-1*) Hanging Loose.
— Praying with the Saints: Saints' Lives & Prayers. 67p. (Orig.). 1989. pap. 5.95 (*1-85390-034-6*, Pub. by Veritas Pubns) St Mut.

Lane, William, et al. The Newspaperman's Guide to the Law. 5th ed. 352p. 1990. pap. 86.00 (*0-409-05769-X*, SA, MICHIE); boxed set 126.00 (*0-409-05770-3*, SA, MICHIE) LEXIS Pub.

Lane, William C. Tip, Tap, Toe: The Great Tapdancers. write for info. (*0-318-58990-7*) World Pr Ltd.

Lane, William L. Commentary on the Gospel of Mark. rev. ed. (New International Commentary on the New Testament Ser.). 9p. 1974. 40.00 (*0-8028-2502-8*) Eerdmans.
— Hebrews: A Call to Commitment. 184p. 1988. pap. text 9.95 (*0-943575-03-6*) Hendrickson MA.
— Hebrews 9-13. (Biblical Commentary Ser.: Vol. 47B). 29.99 (*0-8499-0935-X*) Word Pub.
— Hebrews 1-8. (Biblical Commentary Ser.: Vol. 47A). 29.99 (*0-8499-0246-0*) Word Pub.

Lane, William L., ed. A Book of New Testament Prayers. 95p. 1988. reprint ed. pap. 4.95 (*1-85390-046-X*, Pub. by Veritas Pubns) St Mut.

Lane, William L., jt. auth. see Oswalt, John N.

Lane, Winthrop D. Civil War in Virginia. 1971. 20.95 (*0-88143-120-6*) Ayer.
— Civil War in West Virginia: A Story of the Industrial Conflict in the Coal Mines. LC 76-89745. (American Labor Ser.). reprint ed. 17.95 (*0-405-02133-X*) Ayer.

Lanecki, Francois. French-English Vocabulary of the Industrial Sewing Machine. (ENG & FRE.). 87p. 1981. reprint ed. pap. 19.95 (*0-8288-0743-4*, M6331) Fr & Eur.
— Lexique de la Machine a Coudre Familiale. Dupre, Celine, ed. (FRE.). 12p. 1974. pap. 9.95 (*0-7859-0800-5*, M-9229) Fr & Eur.

Lanegran, David, jt. auth. see Young, Billie.

Laneham, Robert. Captain Cox, His Ballads & Books, or Robert Laneham's Letter. Furnivall, Frederick J., ed. LC 68-57998. (Ballad Society, London. Publications: No. 7). reprint ed. 30.00 (*0-404-50823-5*) AMS Pr.

Laner, Doris, jt. auth. see Sharp, Thelma.

Laner, Mary R. Dating: Delights, Discontents & Dilemmas. 2nd ed. 290p. (C). 1995. pap. text 17.95 (*1-879215-26-8*) Sheffield WI.

Lanes, Douglas M., jt. auth. see Horowitz, Karen.

*__Lanese, Janet.__ Babies Are Like Blossoms: Every Baby Is a Beautiful Flower in the Garden of Life. LC 99-50012. 128p. 2000. per. 10.00 (*0-684-86216-6*) S&S Trade.
— Grandfathers Are Like Gold: Every Family's Treasure. 128p. 2000. 10.00 (*0-684-86217-4*, Fireside) S&S Trade Pap.

Lanese, Janet. Grandmothers Are Like Snowflakes No Two Are Alike: Are Alike. LC 95-38616. 128p. 1996. 10.95 (*0-440-50717-0*, Dell Trade Pbks) Dell.
— Mothers Are Like Miracles: They Make Everything Possible. LC 97-46849. 128p. 1998. per. 10.00 (*0-684-84251-3*, Fireside) S&S Trade Pap.
— Sisters Are Like Sunshine. LC 98-34134. (Illus.). 112p. 1998. per. 10.00 (*0-684-84252-1*) S&S Trade.

Laney, Al. Following the Leaders: A Reminiscence. 165p. 1997. 24.95 (*0-940889-34-X*) Classics Golf.

*__Laney, Carl.__ God Supersaver ed. Who He Is, What He Does, How to Find Him, 1. (Swindoll Leadership Library). 1999. 19.97 (*0-8499-1586-4*) Word Pub.

Laney, Culbert B. Computational Gasdynamics. LC 97-52717. (Illus.). 650p. (C). 1998. pap. 54.95 (*0-521-62558-0*); text 110.00 (*0-521-57069-7*) Cambridge U Pr.

Laney-Cummings, Karen, jt. auth. see Estes, Mark.

Laney, Dolores, ed. see Ceasor, Ebraska D.

Laney, J. Carl. Answers to Tough Questions from Every Book of the Bible. LC 96-53071. 352p. 1997. pap. 14.99 (*0-8254-3094-1*) Kregel.
— Concise Bible Atlas: A Geographical Survey of Bible History. 278p. 1998. 16.95 (*1-56563-366-0*) Hendrickson MA.
— The Divorce Myth. LC 81-7690. 16p. 1981. pap. 8.99 (*0-87123-892-6*) Bethany Hse.
— Everything I Know about Success I Learned from the Bible. 160p. 1996. pap. 9.99 (*0-8254-3093-3*) Kregel.
— Ezra & Nehemiah. (Everyman's Bible Commentary Ser.). 1982. pap. 9.99 (*0-8024-2014-1*) Moody.

*__Laney, J. Carl.__ God: Who he is, What he does, How to know him better. Swindoll, Charles R. & Zuck, Roy B., eds. LC 98-39064. 1999. 24.99 (*0-8499-1368-3*) Word Pub.

Laney, J. Carl. John. (Gospel Commentaries Ser.). pap. 21.99 (*0-8024-5621-9*, 518) Moody.
— Primero y Segundo de Samuel. (Comentario Biblico Portavoz Ser.). (SPA.). 144p. 1996. pap. 6.99 (*0-8254-1423-7*, Edit Portavoz) Kregel.
— Site Safety. LC 81-19540. (Site Practice Ser.). (Illus.). 226p. reprint ed. pap. 70.10 (*0-8357-3536-2*, 203448400090) Bks Demand.
— Zechariah. (Everyman's Bible Commentaries Ser.). pap. 9.99 (*0-8024-0445-6*, 481) Moody.

Laney, J. Carl, jt. auth. see Hughes, Robert B.

Laney, J. Carl, jt. auth. see Schmitt, John W.

Laney, Joan & Mosser, David. Devotional Companion to the International Lessons, 1994-1995. 112p. (Orig.). 1994. pap. 8.95 (*0-687-08635-3*) Abingdon.

Laney, Mildred, et al, eds. The Heritage of Calhoun County, Alabama. (Heritage of Alabama Ser.: No. 8). (Illus.). 316p. 1998. 55.00 (*1-891647-09-1*) Herit Pub Consult.

Laney, Nancy R. Desert Waters: From Ancient Aquifers to Modern Demands. LC 97-74314. (Illus.). 50p. (Orig.). 1997. pap. 4.95 (*1-886679-08-8*) Ariz-Sonora Des Mus.

Laney, William R. & Gibilisco, Joseph A., eds. Diagnosis & Treatment in Prosthodontics. LC 82-15171. 575p. reprint ed. pap. 178.30 (*0-608-17764-4*, 205651600069) Bks Demand.

An Asterisk (*) at the beginning of an entry indicates that the title is appearing for the first time.

Laney, William R. & Tolman, Dan E., eds. Tissue Integration in Oral, Orthopedic, & Maxillofacial Reconstruction. (Illus.). 396p. 1992. text 72.00 (*0-86715-251-6*) Quint Pub Co.

Laney, William R., jt. auth. see Taylor, Thomas D.

Lanfant, Marie-Francoise, et al, eds. International Tourism: Identity & Change. (Studies in International Sociology: Vol. 47). 240p. (C). 1995. 75.00 (*0-8039-7512-0*); pap. 26.95 (*0-8039-7513-9*) Sage.

Lanfear, Vincent W. Business Fluctuations & the American Labor Movement, 1915-1922. LC 68-57572. (Columbia University. Studies in the Social Sciences: No. 247). reprint ed. 20.00 (*0-404-51247-X*) AMS Pr.

Lanfmead. Wings Like Eagles. 1991. pap. 7.50 (*0-7459-2119-1*, Pub. by Lion Pubng) Trafalgar.

Lanfranc. The Letters of Lanfranc, Archbishop of Canterbury. Clover, Helen & Gibson, Margaret, eds. (Oxford Medieval Texts Ser.). (Illus.). 220p. 1980. text 65.00 (*0-19-822235-1*) OUP.

Lanfranc De Milan, Guido. Text & Concordance of Biblioteca Nacional, MS2165: Arte Complida de Cirugia. Wasick, Cynthia M. & Ardemagni, Enrica J., eds. (Medieval Spanish Medical Texts Ser.: No. 26). (SPA.). 10p. 1988. 10.00 incl. fiche (*0-940639-25-4*) Hispanic Seminary.

***Lanfranchi, Eduardo.** 1500 Fuentes para la PC: Las Mejores True Type Fonts. (SPA.). 191p. 1999. pap. 15.90 incl. cd-rom (*987-526-014-2*, Pub. by MP Ediciones) Am Wholesale.

***Lanfranchi, Pierre & Taylor, Matthew.** Moving with the Ball: The Migration of Professional Footballers. (Illus.). 256p. 2000. 65.00 (*1-85973-302-6*, Pub. by Berg Pubs); pap. 19.50 (*1-85973-307-7*, Pub. by Berg Pubs) NYU Pr.

Lanfranco of Milan. Lanfrank's Science of Cirurgie. Fleischhacker, R. V., ed. (EETS, OS Ser.: No. 102). 1969. 63.00 (*0-527-00103-1*) Periodicals Srv.

Lanfrey, Pierre. History of Napoleon First, 4 vols. 2nd ed. LC 77-171654. reprint ed. 245.00 (*0-404-07340-9*) AMS Pr.

Lanfur, J. Depths of Hell. LC 85-90917. 147p. (Orig.). 1985. pap. write for info. (*0-9615034-0-8*) J Lanfur.

Lang. Age Proof Muscles & Joints. (C). 1997. text 25.95 (*0-13-593021-9*) P-H.

— The Complete Book of Origami. (Illus.). 160p. pap. 8.95 (*0-486-25837-8*) Dover.

— Internet. 400p. 2000. pap. text 39.95 (*0-471-37157-2*) Wiley.

— Multilateral Tax Treaties. LC 98-177772. 1997. lib. bdg. 103.00 (*90-411-0704-5*) Kluwer Law Intl.

— Principles of Air Conditioning. 5th ed. 28p. 1995. teacher ed. 13.95 (*0-8273-6592-6*) Delmar.

— Strategy for Personal Finance. 5th ed. 1993. teacher ed. 84.68 (*0-07-036401-X*) McGraw.

— Structure Charts for Program Design. (C). 1993. pap. text 23.00 (*0-07-036328-5*) McGraw.

— Teaching: Strategies for Student-Centered Curriculum. LC 94-930999. (Illus.). xxiv, 537p. (C). 1994. pap. text 64.00 (*0-03-922866-5*, Pub. by Harcourt Coll Pubs) Harcourt.

Lang, A., jt. ed. see Butcher, S. H.

Lang, A. G., jt. auth. see Amos, H. D.

Lang, A. L. Memoirs of Robert E. Lee. (Illus.). 707p. 1992. 10.98 (*0-89009-694-5*) Bk Sales Inc.

Lang, A. W. Seekarten der Suedlichen Nord- und Ostee. (GER.). x, 106p. 1968. 33.00 (*3-443-39035-8*, Pub. by Gebruder Borntraeger) Balogh.

Lang, Alan R. Alcohol: Teenage Drinking. (Encyclopedia of Psychoactive Drugs Ser.: No. 1). (Illus.). 124p. (YA). (gr. 7 up). 1992. lib. bdg. 19.95 (*0-87754-761-0*) Chelsea Hse.

Lang, Aldon S. Financial History of the Public Lands in Texas. Bruchey, Stuart, ed. LC 78-56692. (Management of Public Lands in the U. S. Ser.). 1979. reprint ed. lib. bdg. 19.95 (*0-405-11339-0*) Ayer.

Lang, Amei. Die Geriefte Drehscheibenkeramik der Heuneburg 1950-1970 & Verwandte Gruppen Heuneburgstudien 3. LC 74-76528. (Roemisch-Germanische Forschungen Ser.: Vol. 34). (Illus.). x, 114p. (C). 1974. 84.60 (*3-11-004516-8*) De Gruyter.

Lang, Andrew. Adventures among Books. LC 73-105023. (Essay Index Reprint Ser.). 1977. 23.95 (*0-8369-1474-0*) Ayer.

— Alfred Tennyson. 2nd ed. LC 70-111615. reprint ed. 27.50 (*0-404-03856-5*) AMS Pr.

— The Arabian Nights Entertainments. (Illus.). 1990. 22.75 (*0-8446-0752-5*) Peter Smith.

***Lang, Andrew.** Blue Book of Poetry. 2001. 9.99 (*0-517-16272-5*) Crown Pub Group.

Lang, Andrew. Blue Poetry Book. LC 77-80375. (Granger Index Reprint Ser.). 1977. 25.95 (*0-8369-6080-7*) Ayer.

— Book of Dreams & Ghosts. LC 71-108815. reprint ed. 37.50 (*0-404-03848-4*) AMS Pr.

— Books & Bookmen. LC 76-115093. (Illus.). reprint ed. 37.50 (*0-404-03818-2*) AMS Pr.

— Cock Lane & Common-Sense. LC 74-110572. reprint ed. 39.50 (*0-404-03846-8*) AMS Pr.

— Custom & Myth. 2nd rev. ed. LC 68-59267. reprint ed. 37.50 (*0-404-03817-4*) AMS Pr.

— Disentanglers. LC 71-112938. reprint ed. 39.50 (*0-404-03859-X*) AMS Pr.

— Essays in Little. 2nd ed. LC 68-59265. reprint ed. 37.50 (*0-404-03839-5*) AMS Pr.

— History of English Literature. LC 75-95357. reprint ed. 38.00 (*0-404-03872-7*) AMS Pr.

— History of Scotland, 4 vols. LC 78-109917. reprint ed. 375.00 (*0-404-03860-3*) AMS Pr.

— Homer & His Age. LC 68-59285. reprint ed. 37.50 (*0-404-03867-0*) AMS Pr.

— Homer & the Epic. LC 71-109918. reprint ed. 38.00 (*0-404-03845-X*) AMS Pr.

— How to Fail in Literature. LC 78-101919. reprint ed. 37.50 (*0-404-03837-9*) AMS Pr.

— Lang's Ballads of Books. LC 75-75714. (Granger Index Reprint Ser.). 1977. 18.95 (*0-8369-6024-6*) Ayer.

— Letters on Literature. LC 68-54277. reprint ed. 37.50 (*0-404-03836-0*) AMS Pr.

— Letters to Dead Authors. LC 68-59284. reprint ed. 37.50 (*0-404-03819-0*) AMS Pr.

— Library. LC 68-59288. reprint ed. 40.00 (*0-404-03816-6*) AMS Pr.

— Library: With a Chapter on Modern English Illustrated Books by Austin Dobson. 2nd enl. ed. LC 72-1657. reprint ed. 40.00 (*0-404-03844-1*) AMS Pr.

— Life & Letters of John Gibson Lockhart, 2 vols. LC 79-110131. 1970. reprint ed. 74.50 (*0-404-03849-2*) AMS Pr.

— Magic & Religion. LC 76-137255. reprint ed. 29.50 (*0-404-03857-3*) AMS Pr.

— Magic & Religion. LC 69-13964. 316p. 1969. reprint ed. lib. bdg. 65.00 (*0-8371-0933-7*, LAMR) Greenwood.

— Making of Religion. LC 68-59286. reprint ed. 51.50 (*0-404-03854-9*) AMS Pr.

— Mark of Cain. LC 68-54278. reprint ed. 37.50 (*0-404-03828-X*) AMS Pr.

— Modern Mythology. LC 68-54279. reprint ed. 40.00 (*0-404-03852-2*) AMS Pr.

— A Monk of Fife. LC 68-59287. reprint ed. 37.50 (*0-404-03847-6*) AMS Pr.

— Mystery of Mary Stuart. LC 78-111771. reprint ed. 52.50 (*0-404-03858-1*) AMS Pr.

— Myth, Ritual & Religion, 2 vols. 1993. 59.00 (*1-881338-46-0*) Nataraj Bks.

— Myth, Ritual & Religion, 2 vols. in 1. LC 68-54280. reprint ed. 55.00 (*0-404-03868-9*) AMS Pr.

— Old Friends. LC 70-101914. reprint ed. 37.50 (*0-404-03838-7*) AMS Pr.

— Pickle the Spy. LC 72-110132. reprint ed. 37.50 (*0-404-03853-0*) AMS Pr.

— Prince Charles Edward. LC 01-25240. reprint ed. 105.00 (*0-404-03855-7*) AMS Pr.

— Secret of the Totem. LC 70-115094. 1970. reprint ed. 34.50 (*0-404-03866-2*) AMS Pr.

— Shakespeare, Bacon & the Great Unknown. LC 75-75982. reprint ed. 40.00 (*0-404-03871-9*) AMS Pr.

— Sir Walter Scott & the Border Minstrelsy. LC 68-59266. reprint ed. 37.50 (*0-404-03869-7*) AMS Pr.

— Valet's Tragedy & Other Studies. LC 75-112939. (Illus.). reprint ed. 39.00 (*0-404-03865-4*) AMS Pr.

— World of Homer. LC 68-54281. reprint ed. 37.50 (*0-404-03870-0*) AMS Pr.

Lang, Andrew, ed. The Annesley Case. (Notable British Trials Ser.). 371p. 1995. reprint ed. 115.00 (*1-56169-119-4*) Gaunt.

— The Arabian Nights Entertainments. 27.95 (*0-89190-085-3*) Amereon Ltd.

— The Arabian Nights Entertainments. LC 69-17098. (Illus.). xv, 424p. (J). (gr. k-6). 1969. reprint ed. pap. 7.95 (*0-486-22289-6*) Dover.

— The Blue Fairy Book. 27.95 (*0-89190-089-6*) Amereon Ltd.

— The Blue Fairy Book. LC 34-28315. (Illus.). 390p. (J). (gr. 1-6). 1965. pap. 8.95 (*0-486-21437-0*) Dover.

— The Blue Fairy Book. (Illus.). 390p. (J). 1994. 9.98 (*1-56731-059-1*, MJF Bks) Fine Comms.

— The Blue Fairy Book. (J). 1990. 22.75 (*0-8446-5495-7*) Peter Smith.

— Blue Fairy Book. large type ed. 540p. 1998. lib. bdg. 24.00 (*0-939495-54-6*) North Bks.

— Blue Fairy Book. 390p. 1998. reprint ed. lib. bdg. 24.00 (*1-58287-018-7*) North Bks.

— The Bookworm: Illustrated Treasury of Old-Time Literature. (Illus.). 415p. 1998. reprint ed. pap. 50.00 (*0-87556-870-X*) Saifer.

— Brown Fairy Book. (Illus.). 350p. (J). (gr. 1-6). 1965. pap. 7.95 (*0-486-21438-9*) Dover.

— The Brown Fairy Book. (J). 1990. 22.25 (*0-8446-5496-5*) Peter Smith.

— The Chronicles of Pantouflia. 20.95 (*0-89190-088-8*) Amereon Ltd.

— Cinderella & Other Stories from "The Blue Fairy Book" (Children's Thrift Editions Ser.). (Illus.). 96p. (Orig.). (J). 1997. pap. text 1.00 (*0-486-29389-0*) Dover.

— Crimson Fairy Book. LC 67-17988. (Illus.). 371p. (J). (gr. 4-6). 1967. pap. 7.95 (*0-486-21799-X*) Dover.

— The Crimson Fairy Book. LC 67-17988. (Illus.). (J). (gr. 4-8). 1990. 22.25 (*0-8446-0753-3*) Peter Smith.

— Green Fairy Book. (Illus.). (J). (gr. 4 up). 1990. 22.75 (*0-8446-5056-0*) Peter Smith.

— The Green Fairy Book. LC 34-28314. (Illus.). 366p. (J). (gr. 4-6). 1965. pap. 8.95 (*0-486-21439-7*) Dover.

— Grey Fairy Book. LC 67-17983. (Illus.). 387p. (J). (gr. 4-6). 1967. pap. 7.95 (*0-486-21791-4*) Dover.

— Grey Fairy Book. (Illus.). (J). (gr. 4 up). 1990. 22.25 (*0-8446-2424-1*) Peter Smith.

— The Lilac Fairy Book. 26.95 (*0-89190-084-5*) Amereon Ltd.

— The Lilac Fairy Book. (Illus.). 369p. (J). (ps-4). 1968. pap. 7.95 (*0-486-21907-0*) Dover.

— The Lilac Fairy Book. (Illus.). (J). (gr. 4-12). 1990. 22.25 (*0-8446-2425-X*) Peter Smith.

— More Favorite Fairy Tales. 1976. 22.95 (*0-8488-0822-3*) Amereon Ltd.

— The Nursery Rhyme Book. 23.95 (*0-89190-082-9*) Amereon Ltd.

— Olive Fairy Book. 24.95 (*0-89190-086-1*) Amereon Ltd.

— Olive Fairy Book. (Illus.). 335p. (J). (gr. 4-6). 1968. pap. 7.95 (*0-486-21908-9*) Dover.

— The Olive Fairy Book. (Illus.). (J). (gr. 2 up). 1990. 22.75 (*0-8446-0754-1*) Peter Smith.

— The Orange Fairy Book. 26.95 (*0-89190-083-7*) Amereon Ltd.

— The Orange Fairy Book. (Illus.). 358p. (J). (gr. 1-6). 1968. pap. 7.95 (*0-486-21909-7*) Dover.

— The Orange Fairy Book. (Illus.). (J). (gr. 4-12). 1990. 22.00 (*0-8446-4770-5*) Peter Smith.

— Pink Fairy Book. (Illus.). 360p. (J). (gr. 4-6). 1967. pap. 7.95 (*0-486-21792-2*) Dover.

— The Pink Fairy Book. 26.95 (*0-89190-080-2*) Amereon Ltd.

— The Pink Fairy Book. (Illus.). (J). (gr. 2 up). 1990. 22.75 (*0-8446-0755-X*) Peter Smith.

— The Red Fairy Book. (Illus.). 370p. (J). 1994. 8.98 (*1-56731-060-5*, MJF Bks) Fine Comms.

— The Red Fairy Book. (Illus.). (J). (gr. 2 up). 1990. 22.75 (*0-8446-0756-8*) Peter Smith.

— Red Fairy Book. 1976. 17.95 (*0-8488-1403-7*) Amereon Ltd.

— Red Fairy Book. (Illus.). 367p. (J). (gr. 4-6). 1966. pap. 7.95 (*0-486-21673-X*) Dover.

— Red Fairy Book. large type ed. 470p. 1998. lib. bdg. 24.00 (*0-939495-53-8*) North Bks.

— The Red Fairy Book. 1987. reprint ed. lib. bdg. 16.95 (*0-89966-602-7*) Buccaneer Bks.

— Red Fairy Book. 365p. 1998. reprint ed. lib. bdg. 24.00 (*1-58287-063-2*) North Bks.

— The Violet Fairy Book. 29.95 (*0-89190-081-0*) Amereon Ltd.

— The Violet Fairy Book. (Illus.). 388p. (J). (gr. 4-6). 1966. pap. 7.95 (*0-486-21675-6*) Dover.

— The Violet Fairy Book. (Illus.). (J). (gr. 2 up). 1990. 22.25 (*0-8446-0757-6*) Peter Smith.

— Yellow Fairy Book. (Illus.). 321p. (J). (gr. 4-6). 1966. pap. 7.95 (*0-486-21674-8*) Dover.

— The Yellow Fairy Book. (Illus.). (J). (gr. 2 up). 1990. 23.25 (*0-8446-0758-4*) Peter Smith.

Lang, Andrew & Henley, W. E. Pictures at Play or Dialogues of the Galleries. LC 70-112940. (Illus.). reprint ed. 37.50 (*0-404-03829-8*) AMS Pr.

Lang, Andrew, jt. auth. see Doyle, Richard.

Lang, Andrew, tr. see De Saint-Pierre, Bernardin J.

Lang, Andrew, tr. see Homer.

Lang, Andrew G. Estate Agency Law & Practice in New South Wales. 3rd ed. xxx, 513p. 1988. pap. 49.50 (*0-455-20768-2*, Pub. by LawBk Co) Gaunt.

— Residential Tenancies Law & Practice (N. S. W.) 2nd ed. xxiii, 328p. 1990. pap. 39.00 (*0-455-20798-4*, Pub. by LawBk Co) Gaunt.

Lang, Andrew M. A Life of George Dempster, Scottish M. P. of Dunnichen, 1732-1818. LC 98-4383. 352p. 1998. text 99.95 (*0-7734-8386-1*) E Mellen.

***Lang, Andrew S.** The Financial Responsibilities of Nonprofit Boards. rev. ed. 40p. 1998. pap. text 12.00 (*0-925299-87-1*) Natl Ctr Nonprofit.

Lang, Andrew S. Nonprofit Financial Management. LC 95-13206. 150p. ring bd. 119.00 (*0-8342-0430-4*, S179) Aspen Pub.

***Lang, Andrew S. & Rocha, Laurie A.** How to Read Nonprofit Financial Statements. LC 00-40600. 2000. write for info. (*0-88034-168-8*) Am Soc Assn Execs.

Lang, Ann C., ed. see Fleming, Richard.

***Lang, Annie.** Rooftop Hoppin' (Illus.). 48p. 1999. pap. 10.95 (*1-57377-073-6*) Easl Pubns.

Lang, Annie, ed. Measuring Psychological Responses to Media Messages. (LEA's Communication Ser.). 256p. 1994. text 49.95 (*0-8058-0717-9*) L Erlbaum Assocs.

Lang, Annie J. AirMailed Penguins. (Illus.). 40p. 1998. pap. 10.95 (*1-57377-051-5*, 01988402242-8) Easl Pubns.

— Bedbugs Don't Bite. (Illus.). 42p. 1999. pap. 10.95 (*1-57377-067-1*) Easl Pubns.

— Bee It Ever So Hummmble. (Illus.). 48p. 1999. pap. 10.95 (*1-57377-079-5*, 0-19884-02304) Easl Pubns.

— Buglets Hugs & Soggy Froggies. (Illus.). 48p. 1999. pap. 10.95 (*1-57377-061-2*) Easl Pubns.

— Christmas in My Stocking Feet. (Illus.). 44p. 1997. 9.95 (*1-57377-019-1*) Easl Pubns.

— Christmas Lights & Snowy Nights. (Illus.). 40p. 1997. 9.95 (*1-57377-025-6*) Easl Pubns.

— Just Bee Happy Vol. 1: Decorative Painting Projects. (Illus.). 38p. 1998. pap. 10.95 (*1-57377-031-0*) Easl Pubns.

— Meadow Mouse Seasons. 2nd ed. 1997. pap. text. write for info. (*1-57377-012-4*) Easl Pubns.

***Lang, Annie J.** Penguin Pond. 50p. 2000. 10.95 (*1-57377-094-9*, 0-1988-4-02326-5) Easl Pubns.

Lang, Annie J. Puddle Pals & Butterfly Buddies. (Illus.). 50p. 1998. pap. 10.95 (*1-57377-040-X*) Easl Pubns.

***Lang, Annie J.** Sea Horsies & Waterbugs. 42p. 2000. pap. 10.95 (*1-57377-089-2*, 019884-02316) Easl Pubns.

Lang, Annie J. & Baagh, Beck. Beeecause Those Kringles Jingle. (Illus.). 30p. 1998. pap. 10.95 (*1-57377-050-7*, 019884-02246) Easl Pubns.

Lang, Anthony E., jt. ed. see Weiner, William J.

Lang, Aubrey. Eagles. (Sierra Club Bks.). (Illus.). 64p. (J). (gr. 3-6). 1995. pap. 7.95 (*0-316-51383-0*) Little.

— Eagles. (Sierra Club Wildlife Library). 1995. 12.90 (*0-606-07459-7*, Pub. by Turtleback) Demco.

— Loons. (Illus.). 144p. 1996. pap. text 19.95 (*1-55209-017-5*) Firefly Bks Ltd.

***Lang, Aubrey & Lynch, Wayne.** Loons. (Illus.). 144p. 2000. 15.98 (*1-57145-241-9*, Thunder Bay) Advantage Pubs.

Lang, Audry, jt. photos by see Mullen, Candy.

Lang, Barbara F. & Halter, Mary. Making Choices Curriculum: Life Skills for Adolelscents. 1995. teacher ed., student ed., ring bd. 89.95 (*0-911655-49-2*) Advocacy Pr.

— Making Choices Workbook: Life Skills for Adolescents. 1994. pap., student ed. 8.95 (*0-911655-37-9*) Advocacy Pr.

Lang, Berel. Act & Idea in the Nazi Genocide. 272p. 1996. lib. bdg. 60.00 (*0-226-46868-2*) U Ch Pr.

— Act & Idea in the Nazi Genocide. 272p. 2000. pap. 17.95 (*0-226-46869-0*) U Ch Pr.

— Art & Inquiry. LC 74-18240. 227p. 1975. lib. bdg. 24.00 (*0-8143-1531-3*) Ridgeview.

— Art & Inquiry. LC 74-18240. 229p. reprint ed. pap. 71.00 (*0-8357-5756-0*, 203271200080) Bks Demand.

— The Future of the Holocaust: Between History & Memory. LC 99-20088. 1999. pap. 17.95 (*0-8014-8569-X*) Cornell U Pr.

— The Future of the Holocaust: Between History & Memory. LC 99-20088. 1999. 45.00 (*0-8014-3588-9*) Cornell U Pr.

***Lang, Berel.** Holocaust Representation: Art Within the Limits of History & Ethics. LC 99-85757. 200p. 2000. 38.00 (*0-8018-6415-1*) Johns Hopkins.

Lang, Berel. Mind's Bodies: Thought in the Act. LC 94-48037. 162p. (C). 1995. text 39.50 (*0-7914-2553-3*); pap. text 12.95 (*0-7914-2554-1*) State U NY Pr.

— Philosophy & the Art of Writing: Studies in Philosophical & Literary Style. LC 81-65865. 248p. 1983. 35.00 (*0-8387-5030-3*) Bucknell U Pr.

Lang, Berel, ed. The Concept of Style. rev. ed. LC 86-16233. (Illus.). 320p. 1987. pap. text 18.95 (*0-8014-9439-7*) Cornell U Pr.

***Lang, Berel, ed.** Race & Racism in Theory & Practice. LC 99-45818. 272p. 2000. pap. 19.95 (*0-8476-9693-6*); text 65.95 (*0-8476-9692-8*) Rowman.

Lang, Berel, ed. Writing & the Holocaust. LC 88-11249. 301p. 1988. 45.00 (*0-8419-1184-3*); pap. 19.95 (*0-8419-1185-1*) Holmes & Meier.

Lang, Berel, et al, eds. The Philosopher in the Community: Essays in Memory of Bertram Morris. LC 84-13224. (Illus.). 190p. (Orig.). 1984. pap. text 20.50 (*0-8191-4188-7*); lib. bdg. 48.00 (*0-8191-4187-9*) U Pr of Amer.

Lang, Berel, et al. The Death of Art. (World of Art Ser.). 220p. 1984. 55.00 (*0-930586-38-7*) Haven Pubns.

Lang, Bernhard. Monotheism & the Prophetic Minority: An Essay in Biblical History & Sociology. (Social World of Biblical Antiquity Ser.: No. 1). 191p. 1983. pap. 15.95 (*0-907459-31-5*, Pub. by Sheffield Acad) CUP Services.

— Sacred Games: A History of Christian Worship. LC 97-60406. 448p. 1997. 40.00 (*0-300-06932-4*) Yale U Pr.

Lang, Bertha F. A Piano Teacher's Words of Wisdom. LC 97-67138. 124p. (Orig.). 1998. pap. 10.95 (*1-57197-078-9*) Pentland Pr.

Lang, Beryl. Heidegger's Silence. 144p. 1996. text 19.95 (*0-8014-3310-X*) Cornell U Pr.

Lang, Bob. Uncle Bobby's Finally Sober. 77p. (Orig.). 1987. pap. 2.95 (*0-9618264-0-1*) Psalm Thirty Pubs.

Lang, Bonnie, et al. Ordinary Women . . . Extraordinary Circumstances. 134p. 1995. 10.00 (*1-879908-09-3*) Milton Pub.

Lang, Brian, jt. auth. see Wilson, Bill.

Lang, C. B., jt. ed. see Gausterer, H.

Lang, C. B., jt. ed. see Mitter, H.

Lang, Candace D. Irony-Humor: Critical Paradigms. LC 87-45483. 256p. 1988. text 38.50 (*0-8018-3528-3*) Johns Hopkins.

Lang, Caroline. Keep Smiling Through: Women in the Second World War. (Women in History Ser.). (Illus.). 48p. (C). 1990. pap. 13.95 (*0-521-37747-1*) Cambridge U Pr.

Lang, Cay. Taking the Leap: Building a Career As a Visual Artist. LC 97-41038. 1998. 16.95 (*0-8118-1815-2*) Chronicle Bks.

Lang, Cecil Y. The Pre-Raphaelites & Their Circle. 2nd ed. LC 75-12233. xxix, 592p. 1975. pap. text 16.95 (*0-226-46866-6*, P651) U Ch Pr.

Lang, Cecil Y., ed. The Letters of Matthew Arnold, 1829-1859, Vol. I. LC 95-50448. (Victorian Literature & Culture Ser.). 600p. (C). 1996. text 60.00 (*0-8139-1651-8*) U Pr of Va.

***Lang, Cecil Y., ed.** The Letters of Matthew Arnold, 1871-1878, Vol. 4. (Victorian Literature & Cultural Ser.). 496p. 2000. 60.00 (*0-8139-1896-0*) U Pr of Va.

Lang, Cecil Y., ed. see Arnold, Matthew.

Lang, Cecil Y., ed. see Swinburne, Algernon Charles.

Lang, Cecil Y., ed. see Tennyson, Alfred Lord.

Lang, Christian B., jt. ed. see Gausterer, H.

Lang Communications Staff. Iron Horse. 1999. 16.99 (*0-525-67519-1*) NAL.

***Lang, D. D.** Deadly Venom. large type ed. 224p. 1999. pap. 20.99 (*1-85389-914-3*, Dales) Ulverscroft.

Lang, D. D. Last Stop Liberty. large type ed. (Linford Western Library Ser.). 224p. 1997. pap. 16.99 (*0-7089-5134-1*, Linford) Ulverscroft.

— Woebegone. large type ed. (Linford Western Large Pr. Ser.). 224p. 1998. pap. 17.99 (*0-7089-5198-8*, Linford) Ulverscroft.

Lang, Daniel A. Medical Staff Peer Review: A Strategy for Motivation & Performance. LC 90-14532. 146p. (Orig.). 1991. pap. 42.50 (*1-55648-065-2*, 145157) AHPI.

Lang, Daniel A., et al. Managing Medical Staff Change Through Bylaws & Other Strategies. 160p. 1995. pap. 56.50 (*1-55648-138-1*, 145104) AHPI.

Lang, Daniel G., jt. ed. see Clinton, David.

Lang, Darrel & Stinston, Bill. Lazy Dogs & Snoozing Frogs: Relaxation & Quieting Activities for Children. 53p. 1988. 10.95 (*0-9611456-4-1*, Coulee Press) Adastra Pub.

Lang, David & Odell, John. Korean Joggers: (Shoe Exports) (Pew Case Studies in International Affairs). 50p. (C). 1992. pap. text 3.50 (*1-56927-129-1*) Geo U Inst Dplmcy.

Lang, David L., et al. Intellectual Property: Cases & Materials. LC 98-117432. (Paralegal). 1100p. (C). 1998. text, suppl. ed. 46.50 (*0-314-21130-6*) West Pub.

L

Lang, David M., ed. Lives & Legends of the Georgian Saints. 179p. 1976. pap. 8.95 (*0-913836-29-X*) St Vladimirs.

***Lang, Denise.** A Call for Justice: A New England Town's Fight to Keep a Stone Cold Serial Killer in Jail. 352p. 2000. mass mkt. 6.50 (*0-380-78077-1*, Avon Bks) Morrow Avon.

Lang, Denise & Territo, Joseph. Coping with Lyme Disease: A Practical Guide to Dealing with Diagnosis & Treatment. 2nd ed. 283p. 1999. pap. text 15.00 (*0-7881-6073-7*) DIANE Pub.

Lang, Denise V. The Dark Son. (Illus.). 416p. (Orig.). 1995. mass mkt. 6.50 (*0-380-77595-6*, Avon Bks) Morrow Avon.

Lang, Doe. The New Secrets of Charisma. LC 98-38352. (Illus.). 336p. 1999. pap. 14.95 (*0-8092-2826-2*, 282620, Contemporary Bks) NTC Contemp Pub Co.

— The Secret of Charisma. 370p. reprint ed. pap. 12.95 (*0-934297-00-2*) New Choices.

***Lang, Donna.** A Gift for Giving: Making the Most of the Present. LC 99-59906. (Illus.). 128p. 2000. 25.00 (*0-609-60590-9*) C Potter.

Lang, Donna. Make It with Style. 1997. pap. write for info. (*0-517-88238-8*) C Potter.

— Make It with Style: Baby Access. 1996. pap. write for info. (*0-517-88731-2*) C Potter.

— Make It with Style - Slipcovers: With Instructions for More Than 30 Designer Looks. LC 97-42918. 1998. pap. 18.00 (*0-517-88241-8*) C Potter.

Lang, Donna & Petersen, Judy. Make It with Style: Draperies & Swags. LC 97-6641. 1997. pap. 18.00 (*0-517-88716-9*) Crown Pub Group.

— Make It with Style: Window Shades & Blinds: Creating Roman, Balloon & Austrian Shades. LC 96-49687. 1997. pap. 18.00 (*0-517-88237-X*) Crown Pub Group.

Lang, E. K., ed. Beta-Blockers in the Elderly. (Illus.). 107p. 1982. 32.00 (*0-387-11682-6*) Spr-Verlag.

Lang, E. K., et al, eds. Radiology of the Upper Urinary Tract. (Medical Radiology, Diagnostic Imaging & Radiation Oncology Ser.). (Illus.). 384p. 1991. 316.00 (*0-387-52546-7*) Spr-Verlag.

Lang, E. K., jt. ed. see Bierwisch, Manfred.

Lang, E. M., tr. see Lepelletier, Edmond A.

Lang, Edgar A. Ludwig Tieck's Early Concept of Catholic Clergy & Church. LC 74-140044. (Catholic University Studies in German: No. 8). reprint ed. 37.50 (*0-404-50228-8*) AMS Pr.

Lang, Edith M. The Effects of Net Interregional Migration on Agricultural Income Growth: The United States, 1850-1860. LC 75-2585. (Dissertations in American Economic History Ser.). (Illus.). 1975. 23.95 (*0-405-07205-8*) Ayer.

Lang, Edith M. & West, George. Musical Accompaniment of Moving Pictures. LC 72-124014. (Literature of Cinema, Ser. 1). 1975. reprint ed. 11.95 (*0-405-01620-4*) Ayer.

Lang, Eleanor M., ed. Art of the Real World. (Masterworks of Literature Ser.). 1979. pap. 14.95 (*0-8084-0424-5*) NCUP.

Lang, Eleanor R. & Bodden, Donna, eds. The Eloquent War: Personal & Public Writings, 1860-1865. 160p. (C). 1999. pap. text 16.50 (*1-881089-31-2*) Brandywine Press.

Lang, Erich K. Roentgenographic Diagnosis of Renal Mass Lesions. LC 70-125008. (Illus.). 190p. 1971. 12.50 (*0-87527-047-6*) Green.

Lang, Erich K., ed. Radiology of the Lower Urinary Tract. LC 93-49790. (Medical Radiology: Diagnostic Imaging & Radiation). 1994. 306.00 (*0-387-53720-1*) Spr-Verlag.

Lang, Erich K. & Ascher, Susan, eds. Radiology of the Female Pelvic Organs. LC 97-50319. (Medical Radiology Ser.). (Illus.). 250p. 1998. 168.00 (*3-540-61119-3*) Spr-Verlag.

Lang, Ewald. The Semantics of Coordination. Pheby, John, tr. LC 84-14541. (Studies in Language Companion: No. 9). 300p. 1984. 91.00 (*90-272-3008-0*) J Benjamins Pubng Co.

Lang, Ewald & Zifonun, Gisela, eds. Deutsch - Typologisch. (Institut fuer Deutsche Sprache - Jahrbuch, 1993 Ser.). (GER., Illus.). vii, 700p. (C). 1996. lib. bdg. 163.00 (*3-11-014983-4*) De Gruyter.

Lang, F. P., ed. Cell Volume Regulation. (Journal: Renal Physiology & Biochemistry: Vol. 11, No. 3-5, 1988). (Illus.). 180p. 1989. pap. 119.25 (*3-8055-4986-5*) S Karger.

— Ion Channels in Renal Epithelia. (Journal: Renal Physiology & Biochemistry: Vol. 13, No. 1-2, 1990). (Illus.). 128p. 1990. pap. 113.25 (*3-8055-5163-0*) S Karger.

— Ion Transport in the Regulation of Cell Proliferation in Cellular Physiology & Biochemistry: Journal: Cellular Physiology & Biochemistry, Vol. 2, No. 3, 1992. (Illus.). 92p. 1992. pap. 38.50 (*3-8055-5638-1*) S Karger.

— The Molecules of Transport Ion Channels. (Journal: Cellular Physiology & Biochemistry: Vol. 3, No. 5-6, 1993). (Illus.). 164p. 1993. pap. 75.75 (*3-8055-5848-1*) S Karger.

— Physiology of Diuretic Action. (Journal: Renal Physiology & Biochemistry: Vol. 10, No. 3, 1987). 92p. 1988. pap. 49.75 (*3-8055-4769-2*) S Karger.

Lang, F. P. & Ohr, R., eds. Openness & Development: Yearbook of Economic & Social Relations 1996. (Studies in Contemporary Economics). (Illus.). 242p. 1996. pap. 71.00 (*3-7908-0958-6*) Spr-Verlag.

Lang, F. P. & Somero, George N. Advances in Comparative & Environmental Physiology Vol. 14: Interaction of Cell Volume & Cell Function. (Illus.). 324p. 1993. 281.95 (*0-387-54854-8*) Spr-Verlag.

Lang-Ferrell, K., ed. Directory of Vocational Rehabilitation Service Projects for American Indians, 1997-98. 8p. 1997. pap. 1.50 (*1-888557-62-1*) No Ariz Univ.

Lang, Fiona, jt. auth. see Patterson, Judy.

Lang, Florian, ed. Cell Volume Regulation. LC 98-38490. (Contributions to Nephrology Ser.: Vol. 123 (1998)). (Illus.). viii, 260p. 1998. 198.25 (*3-8055-6737-5*) S Karger.

Lang, Franz. Performing Arts Resources, Vol. 9: An Essay on Stage Performance, A Translation of Franz Lang's Dissertatio de Actione Scenica (1727) by Alfred Siemon Golding. Cocuzza, Ginnine & Cohen-Stratyner, Barbarba N., eds. Golding, Alfred S., tr. from LAT. LC 75-646287.Tr. of Dissertatio de Actione Scenica. (Illus.). 128p. 1984. reprint ed. 25.00 (*0-932610-06-4*) Theatre Lib.

Lang, Franz P., jt. ed. see Rebe, Bernd.

Lang, G. Metallurgy of Non-Ferrous Metals: Glossary of Technical Terms English-French-German-Spanish. (ENG, FRE, GER & SPA.). 633p. 1994. pap. 154.00 (*3-87017-223-1*) IBD Ltd.

— Metallurgy of Non-Ferrous Metals: Glossary of Technical Terms, English/French/German/Spanish. (ENG, FRE, GER & SPA.). 1994. 205.00 (*0-7859-9426-2*) Fr & Eur.

Lang, G., ed. Swiss Lake & Mire Environments During the Last 15,000 Years. (Dissertationes Botanicae Ser.: No. 87). (Illus.). 428p. 1985. pap. 104.00 (*3-7682-1447-8*) Lubrecht & Cramer.

Lang, G. & Nitsche, J. Extrusion of Metals: Glossary of Technical Terms English-French-German-Spanish. (ENG, FRE, GER & SPA.). 295p. 1991. pap. 70.00 (*3-87017-192-8*) IBD Ltd.

Lang, G. & Schluchter, C., eds. Lake, Mire & River Environment During the Last 150000 Years: Proceedings of the INQUA-IGCP 158 Meetings on the Palaeohydrological Changes During the Last 150000 Years, Bern, June, 1985. (Illus.). 248p. (C). 1988. text 91.00 (*90-6191-849-9*, Pub. by A A Balkema) Ashgate Pub Co.

Lang, G. A., ed. Plant Dormancy: Physiology, Biochemistry & Molecular Biology. LC 97-142321. (CAB International Publication). 408p. 1997. text 105.00 (*0-85198-978-0*) OUP.

***Lang, G. K.** Ophthalmology: A Short Textbook. (Illus.). 664p. 2000. pap. 39.00 (*0-86577-935-X*) Thieme Med Pubs.

Lang, Gehard & Heiss, George D. A Practical Guide to Research Methods. 4th ed. 204p. (Orig.). (C). 1990. pap. text 22.00 (*0-8191-7974-4*); lib. bdg. 43.50 (*0-8191-7973-6*) U Pr of Amer.

Lang, Gene, jt. auth. see DeMont, Philip.

Lang, George. George Lang's Cuisine of Hungary. (Illus.). 495p. 1994. text 30.00 (*0-7881-5244-0*) DIANE Pub.

— Nobody Knows the Truffles I've Seen: A Memoir. LC 97-42598. 416p. 1998. 28.95 (*0-679-45094-7*) McKay.

Lang, George, et al, compiled by. Medal of Honor Recipients, 1863-1994, 2 vols. (Illus.). 928p. 1995. 99.00 (*0-8160-3259-9*) Facts on File.

Lang, George, ed. see Ngate, Jonathan.

Lang, George, ed. see Priebe, Richard K.

Lang, Gerhard. Arado AR 240. (Luftwaffe Profile Ser.: No. 8). (Illus.). 24p. pap. 9.95 (*0-88740-923-7*) Schiffer.

— Heinkel HE 60. LC 96-160378. (Luftwaffe Profile Ser.: No. 7). (Illus.). 40p. pap. 12.95 (*0-88740-922-9*) Schiffer.

Lang, Gerhard & Heiss, George D. A Practical Guide to Research Methods. 5th ed. LC 93-40438. 202p. (C). 1994. pap. text 25.00 (*0-8191-9384-4*); lib. bdg. 51.00 (*0-8191-9383-6*) U Pr of Amer.

— A Practical Guide to Research Methods. 6th ed. LC 97-44434. 200p. (C). 1997. 54.00 (*0-7618-0979-1*); pap. 27.00 (*0-7618-0980-5*) U Pr of Amer.

Lang, Gernot. Glossary of Technical Terms: Extrusion of Metals. (ENG & GER.). 800p. 1982. 195.00 (*0-8288-0595-4*, M6604) Fr & Eur.

Lang, Gernot, compiled by. Glossary of Technical Terms: Non-Ferrous Metal Casting (German/English-English/German) 442p. 1985. 39.00 (*3-88355-094-9*, Pub. by DGM Metallurgy Info) IR Pubns.

Lang, Gernot, tr. see Laue, Kurt & Stenger, Helmut.

Lang, Gladys E. & Lang, Kurt. The Battle for Public Opinion: The President, the Press & the Polls During Watergate. 360p. 1983. text 78.00 (*0-231-05548-X*) Col U Pr.

— Etched in Memory: The Building & Survival of Artistic Reputation. LC 89-70715. 459p. reprint ed. pap. 142.30 (*0-608-20086-7*, 207135800011) Bks Demand.

— Politics & Television Reviewed. LC 84-11637. 223p. 1984. reprint ed. pap. 69.20 (*0-608-01454-0*, 205949800001) Bks Demand.

Lang, Gladys E., jt. auth. see Lang, Kurt.

***Lang, Glenna.** Looking Out for Sarah. LC 00-37714. (Illus.). (J). 2001. write for info. (*0-88106-647-8*, Talewinds) Charlesbridge Pub.

Lang, Gordon. Miller's Antiques Checklist: Pottery. LC 96-147009. (Illus.). 192p. 1995. 15.95 (*1-85732-408-0*, Pub. by Millers Pubns) Antique Collect.

— Miller's Collecting Pottery & Porcelain: The Facts at Your Fingertips. (Illus.). 192p. 1997. 19.95 (*1-84000-040-6*, Pub. by Millers Pubns) Antique Collect.

— Miller's Pottery & Porcelain Marks. LC 96-139077. (Illus.). 400p. 1995. 15.95 (*1-85732-615-6*, Pub. by Reed Illust Books) Antique Collect.

— Porcelain: Antiques Checklist. Miller, Judith & Miller, Martin, eds. (Illus.). 192p. 1991. 15.95 (*0-85533-894-6*, Pub. by Millers Pubns) Antique Collect.

Lang, Gordon, jt. auth. see Caplan, Sandi.

Lang, Gottfried O. A Study in Culture Contact & Culture Change: The Whiterock Utes in Transition. (Utah Anthropological Papers: No. 15). reprint ed. 10.50 (*0-404-60615-6*) AMS Pr.

Lang, Grace. Love a Hostage. large type ed. (Linford Romance Library). 272p. 1993. pap. 16.99 (*0-7089-7324-8*, Linford) Ulverscroft.

— Springboard to Love. large type ed. (Linford Romance Library). 1991. pap. 16.99 (*0-7089-7062-1*) Ulverscroft.

Lang, Graeme & Ragvald, Lars. The Rise of a Refugee God: Hong Kong's Wong Tai Sin. LC 92-47422. (Illus.). 214p. (C). 1993. text 65.00 (*0-19-585755-0*) OUP.

Lang, Greg & Berberich, Chris. All Children Are Special: Creating an Inclusive Classroom. (Illus.). 152p. (C). 1995. pap. text 21.00 (*1-57110-017-2*) Stenhse Pubs.

Lang, Gunther. On Overlapping Generations Models with Productive Capital. LC 96-38441. (Lecture Notes in Economics & Mathematical Systems Ser.: Vol. 443). (Illus.). 98p. 1996. 46.00 (*3-540-61603-9*) Spr-Verlag.

Lang, H. Jack. Dear Wit. 256p. 1990. 17.95 (*0-685-31178-3*, Webstrs New); pap. 9.95 (*0-685-31179-1*, Webstrs New) Macmillan Gen Ref.

Lang, H. O., ed. History of the Willamette Valley: Being a Description of the Valley & Its Resources, with an Account of Its Discovery & Settlement by White Men, & Its Subsequent History, Together with Personal Reminiscences of Its Early Pioneers. (Illus.). 902p. 1997. reprint ed. lib. bdg. 92.50 (*0-8328-6374-2*) Higginson Bk Co.

Lang, Hans J. Cost Analysis for Capital Investment Decisions. (Cost Engineering Ser.: Vol. 14). (Illus.). 400p. 1989. text 210.00 (*0-8247-7894-4*) Dekker.

Lang, Hans J. & Merino, Donald N. The Selection Process for Capital Projects. LC 92-40500. (Engineering & Technology Management Ser.). 720p. 1993. 150.00 (*0-471-63425-5*) Wiley.

***Lang, Harry G.** A Phone of Our Own: The Deaf Insurrection Against Ma Bell. LC 00-28147. (Illus.). 256p. 2000. 29.95 (*1-56368-090-4*) Gallaudet Univ Pr.

Lang, Harry G. Silence of the Spheres: The Deaf Experience in the History of Science. LC 93-20838. 224p. 1994. 55.00 (*0-89789-368-9*, Bergin & Garvey) Greenwood.

Lang, Harry G. & Meath-Lang, Bonnie. Deaf Persons in the Arts & Sciences: A Biographical Dictionary. LC 94-24206. 448p. 1995. lib. bdg. 75.00 (*0-313-29170-5*, Greenwood Pr) Greenwood.

Lang, Harry O., Jr. Letters of Love & War, 1944-1945: A True Story. LC 98-85079. 144p. 1998. pap. 12.95 (*1-890394-26-2*, Sage Creek) Rhodes & Easton.

Lang, Helen S. Aristotle's Physics & Its Medieval Varieties. LC 91-35652. (SUNY Series in Ancient Greek Philosophy). 322p. (C). 1992. text 19.50 (*0-7914-1083-8*) State U NY Pr.

— The Order of Nature in Aristotle's Physics: Place & the Elements. LC 97-51317. 352p. (C). 1998. 64.95 (*0-521-62453-3*) Cambridge U Pr.

Lang, Henry R., frwd. Cancionero de Baena. 380p. 1971. reprint ed. 25.00 (*0-87535-116-6*) Hispanic Soc.

Lang, Herbert H., ed. see Nixon, Pat I.

Lang, Herbert O. History of Tuolumne County Ca. with Biographies. 557p. 1995. reprint ed. lib. bdg. 55.00 (*0-8328-4456-X*) Higginson Bk Co.

Lang, Hermann. Language & the Unconscious: Jacques Lacan's Hermeneutics of Psychoanalysis. Brockelman, Thomas, tr. LC 96-50099. (Contemporary Philosophy & the Human Sciences Ser.). 224p. (C). 1997. text 49.95 (*0-391-04035-9*) Humanities.

Lang, Hilary & Ward, Sue. Women Won't Benefit. (C). 1988. 25.00 (*0-7855-4419-4*, Pub. by NCCL) St Mut.

Lang-Hinrichs, Christine. Extrachromosamale Invitro-Genetik Bei Pilzen: Chondriom-Vektoren Bei Hefen. (Bibliotheca Mycologica: Vol. 102). (GER., Illus.). 124p. 1986. 36.00 (*3-443-59003-9*, Pub. by Gebruder Borntraeger) Balogh.

Lang, Holly, jt. auth. see Polancy, Toni.

Lang, Hua. Lang Hua: Photographs by Lang Hua. Luo, Haibo, ed. Jin, Gang, tr. from CHI. (Contemporary Chinese Artists Ser.). (Illus.). 110p. 1996. pap. 19.95 (*0-9644818-7-1*) Waymont Intl.

— The Picturesque Landscapes of China: Photographys by Lang Hua. Luo, Haibo, ed. (CHI., Illus.). 68p. (Orig.). 1997. pap. 12.95 (*0-9644818-9-8*) Waymont Intl.

Lang, I. Attempts to Restore Economic & Financial Relations... 1980. pap. 50.00 (*963-05-2587-9*, Pub. by Akade Kiado) St Mut.

Lang, I. L., et al. Hungarian-German & German Hungarian Dictionary for Tourists. 304p. (C). 1991. 21.00 (*963-205-262-5*, Pub. by Akade Kiado) St Mut.

Lang, I. L., jt. auth. see Magay, Tamas.

Lang, Ingrid, ed. Naktergalen, Vol. 3. 3rd ed. Elex, Sweden, tr. (Listen & Learn Language Audio Ser.: Vol. LL0399).Tr. of Nightingale. (ENG & SWE., Illus.). 32p. 1999. pap. 9.95 (*1-892623-05-6*) Intl Book.

— Naktergalen: The Nightingale, Vol. 3. 3rd unabridged ed. Elex, Sweden, tr. (Listen & Learn Language Audio Ser.: Vol. LL0399). (ENG & SWE., Illus.). 32p. 1999. pap. 15.95 incl. audio (*1-892623-04-8*) Intl Book.

— Tusenskonan, Vol. 001B. unabridged ed. Bohlmark, Marta, tr. from DAN. (Listen & Learn Language Audio Ser.: Vol. LL1098).Tr. of Daisy. (ENG & SWE., Illus.). 28p. 1998. pap. 9.95 (*1-892623-01-3*) Intl Book.

Lang, Isa. Index to Federal Tax Articles, 5 vols., Set. Goldstein, Gersham et al, eds. 1976. 425.00 (*0-88262-018-5*, IFTA) Warren Gorham & Lamont.

Lang, J. Clinical Anatomy of the Nose, Naval Cavity & Paranasal Sinuses. (Illus.). 144p. 1989. text 129.00 (*0-86577-330-0*) Thieme Med Pubs.

— Color Atlas of Microneurosurgery Vol. 2: Cerebrovascular Lesions. 2nd ed. Koos, Wolfgang T. & Spetzler, Robert F., eds. (Illus.). 415p. 1996. text 335.00 (*0-86577-478-1*) Thieme Med Pubs.

— Topographische Anatomie des Plexus Brachialis und Thoracic-Outlet-Syndrom. (GER., Illus.). 74p. 1985. pap. 43.85 (*3-11-010160-2*) De Gruyter.

Lang, J., jt. ed. see Brown, R.

Lang, J. M., ed. see Casey, Mary.

Lang, J. Spencer. To Awaken a Sleeping Giant. Goodman, Sharon L., ed. (Orig.). 1986. pap. 4.00 (*0-935369-07-4*) In Tradition Pub.

Lang, J. Stephen. Another Big Book of American Trivia. LC 97-7009. 424p. 1997. pap. 11.99 (*0-8423-0155-0*) Tyndale Hse.

— Best of Bible Trivia I: Kings, Criminals, Saints & Sinners. 170p. 1990. mass mkt. 4.99 (*0-8423-0464-9*) Tyndale Hse.

— Best of Bible Trivia II: Palaces, Poisons, Feasts & Beasts. 202p. 1990. mass mkt. 4.99 (*0-8423-0465-7*) Tyndale Hse.

— The Bible: What's in It for Me? LC 96-37666. 316p. 1997. write for info. (*1-56476-612-8*) Chariot Victor.

***Lang, J. Stephen.** Biblical Quotations for All Occasions: From the World's Greatest Source, over 2,000 Timeless Quotes to Enhance Your Message. LC 99-15078. 462p. 1999. pap. 18.00 (*0-7615-1542-9*) Prima Pub.

Lang, J. Stephen. The Book of God's Promises. (Living Books). 173p. 1999. mass mkt. 3.99 (*0-8423-3486-6*) Tyndale Hse.

— The Complete Book of Bible Promises. LC 97-2382. 468p. 1997. pap. 11.99 (*0-8423-4701-1*) Tyndale Hse.

— The Complete Book of Bible Trivia. 494p. 1988. pap. 11.99 (*0-8423-0421-5*) Tyndale Hse.

— The Complete Book of Confederate Trivia. LC 95-52054. (Illus.). 368p. 1996. pap. 14.99 (*1-57249-007-1*) White Mane Pub.

— Drawn to the Civil War. LC 99-47248. (Illus.). 256p. 1999. pap. 14.95 (*0-89587-186-6*) Blair.

— 1,001 Things You Always Wanted to Know about the Bible but Never Thought to Ask. LC 98-44531. 504p. 1999. pap. 9.99 (*0-7852-7346-8*) Nelson.

— 1,001 Things You Always Wanted to Know about the Holy Spirit. LC 99-15323. 516p. 1999. pap. 12.99 (*0-7852-7046-9*) Nelson.

***Lang, J. Stephen.** 1,001 Things You Always Wanted to Know about Angels, Demons & the Afterlife. 516p. 2000. pap. 12.99 (*0-7852-6861-8*) Nelson.

Lang, J. Stephen. The Ultimate Book of Bible Trivia. LC 97-8874. 1997. pap. 11.99 (*0-8423-7949-5*) Tyndale Hse.

Lang, James T. Corpus of Anglo-Saxon Stone Sculpture Vol. III: York & Eastern Yorkshire, Vol. 3. (British Academy Ser.). (Illus.). 456p. 1991. text 215.00 (*0-19-726079-9*) OUP.

— Feeding a Hungry Planet: Rice, Research & Development in Asia & Latin America. LC 95-50150. 224p. (C). 1996. pap. text 18.95 (*0-8078-4593-0*) U of NC Pr.

— Feeding a Hungry Planet: Rice, Research & Development in Asia & Latin America. LC 95-50150. 224p. (C). (gr. 13). 1996. lib. bdg. 39.95 (*0-8078-2284-1*) U of NC Pr.

— Inside Development in Latin America: A Report from the Dominican Republic, Colombia, & Brazil. LC 87-5950. xx, 307p. (C). 1988. 49.95 (*0-8078-1753-8*); pap. 14.95 (*0-8078-4195-1*) U of NC Pr.

— Inside Development in Latin America: A Report from the Dominican Republic, Colombia, & Brazil. LC 87-5950. 327p. 1988. reprint ed. pap. 101.40 (*0-608-02062-1*, 206271500003) Bks Demand.

Lang, James T., jt. auth. see Franke, Christopher.

Lang, Janet, ed. Radiography of Cultural Material. LC 97-14630. 1997. 75.00 (*0-7506-2621-6*) Buttrwrth-Heinemann.

Lang, Jayne. Around the World in 80 Years. 96p. 1998. pap. 10.00 (*0-9649742-3-1*) Boudelang Pr.

Lang, Jeffery B. Struggling to Surrender: Some Impressions of an American Convert to Islam. 1999. pap. text 11.75 (*0-915957-26-4*) Amana Corp.

— Struggling to Surrender: Some Impressions of an American Convert to Islam. 246p. 1996. pap. 11.75 (*0-614-21683-4*, 1379) Kazi Pubns.

Lang, Jeffrey, jt. auth. see Blass, Piotr.

Lang, Jeffrey B. Struggling to Surrender: Some Impressions of an American Convert to Islam. 2nd ed. LC 94-29827. 1995. pap. 11.75 (*0-915957-29-9*) amana pubns.

Lang, Jennifer H. The Crowning City. 416p. 1995. mass mkt. 11.95 (*0-7472-4494-4*, Pub. by Headline Bk Pub) Trafalgar.

Lang, Jennifer H., ed. Larousse Gastronomique: The New American Edition of the World's Greatest Culinary Encyclopedia. LC 88-1178. (Illus.). 1193p. 1988. 60.00 (*0-517-57032-7*, Crown) Crown Pub Group.

Lang, Jim. Great Careers for People Who Want to Be Entrepreneurs, Vol. 5. 2nd ed. LC 94-60781. (Career Connections Ser.: Series 2). 48p. 1994. text 23.00 (*0-8103-9967-9*, UXL) Gale.

Lang, Jim. Make Your Own Breaks: Become an Entrepreneur & Create Your Own Future. 224p. 1994. pap. 15.95 (*1-880030-25-X*) DBM Pub.

Lang, Joan M., et al. Zagat Survey: New York City Marketplace Survey. 200p. 1995. pap. 10.95 (*1-57006-009-6*) Zagat.

Lang, Jochen Von, see Von Lang, Jochen, ed.

Lang, Johannes. Clinical Anatomy of the Cervical Spine. (Illus.). 188p. 1993. text 139.00 (*0-86577-486-2*) Thieme Med Pubs.

— Clinical Anatomy of the Masticatory Apparatus & the Peripharyngeal Spaces. (Illus.). 220p. 1995. 139.00 (*0-86577-551-6*) Thieme Med Pubs.

— Clinical Anatomy of the Posterior Cranial Fossa & Its Forimina. (Illus.). 166p. 1991. text 119.00 (*0-86577-379-3*) Thieme Med Pubs.

Lang, Johannes G. Current, Voltage, Resistance. LC TK0146. (Siemens Programmed Instruction Ser.: 9). 71p. reprint ed. pap. 30.00 (*0-608-13152-0*, 205208600033) Bks Demand.

— The Electric Field. LC QC0661.L3547. (Siemens Programmed Instruction Ser.: 2). 64p. reprint ed. pap. 30.00 (*0-608-16145-4*, 205207900033) Bks Demand.

An Asterisk (*) at the beginning of an entry indicates that the title is appearing for the first time.

— The Magnetic Field. LC QC0754.2.M3M. (Siemens Programmed Instruction Ser.: No. 3). 67p. reprint ed. pap. 30.00 (*0-608-12362-5*, 205208000033) Bks Demand.

Lang, John H. History of Harrison County. (Illus.). 303p. 1997. reprint ed. lib. bdg. 36.50 (*0-8328-6822-1*) Higginson Bk Co.

Lang, John T. Digest of State Lotteries. (Illus.). 96p. (Orig.). 1983. pap. write for info. (*0-913397-00-8*) Hilltop Publishing.

Lang, Jon. Urban Design: The American Experience. 528p. 1994. 75.00 (*0-471-28542-0*, VNR) Wiley.

Lang, Jon, et al. Architecture & Independence: The Search for Identity - India 1880 to 1980. LC 97-914012. (Illus.). 370p. 1998. text 115.00 (*0-19-563900-6*) OUP.

Lang, Jon T. Urban Design: The American Experience. LC 93-15893. 509p. 1994. text 64.95 (*0-442-01360-4*, VNR) Wiley.

Lang, Joseph R., ed. see SEDOS Research Seminar on the Future of Mission St.

Lang, Josephine. Selected Songs. LC 82-2435. (Women Composers Ser.). 1982. 29.50 (*0-306-76097-5*) Da Capo.

Lang, Jovian P. Dictionary of the Liturgy. 1989. 16.95 (*0-89942-273-X*, 273/22) Catholic Bk Pub.

Lang, Jovian P., ed. Unequal Access to Information: Problems & Needs of the World's Information Poor. LC 87-34577. 258p. 1988. pap. 35.00 (*0-87650-239-7*) Pierian.

***Lang, Jovian P. & O'Gorman, Jack.** Recommended Reference Books in Paperback. 3rd ed. LC 99-45461. 320p. 2000. 55.00 (*1-56308-583-6*) Libs Unl.

Lang, Jovian P., ed. see ALA Reference & Adult Services Division Ad Hoc Co.

Lang, Judith. The Angels of God: Understanding the Bible. LC 97-30286. 240p. (Orig.). 1997. pap. 12.95 (*1-56548-101-1*) New City.

Lang, Julian, ed. Ararapikva: Traditional Karuk Indian Literature from Northwestern California. (Illus.). 112p. 1994. pap. 10.95 (*0-930588-65-7*) Heyday Bks.

Lang, Kenneth R. Astrophysical Data: Planets & Stars. (Illus.). 956p. 1993. 65.95 (*0-387-97109-2*) Spr-Verlag.

— Astrophysical Formulae: A Compendium for the Physicist & Astrophysicist. 3rd ed. LC 98-27747. 800p. 1997. 59.00 (*3-540-61267-X*) Spr-Verlag.

—Astrophysical Formulae Vol. II: Space, Time, Matter in Cosmology. 3rd ed. LC 98-27747. (Astronomy & Astrophysics Library). xii, 350p. 1999. 89.95 (*3-540-64664-7*) Spr-Verlag.

— Sun, Earth, & Sky. LC 95-6109. 300p. 1995. 39.95 (*3-540-58778-0*) Spr-Verlag.

— Sun, Earth & Sky. LC 97-8370. 1997. 39.95 (*3-540-62808-8*) Spr-Verlag.

***Lang, Kenneth R.** The Sun from Space. LC 00-41038. (Astronomy & Astrophysics Library). 2000. write for info. (*3-540-66944-2*) Spr-Verlag.

Lang, Kenneth R. Wanderers in Space: Exploration & Discovery in the Solar System. 334p. 1991. pap. text 30.95 (*0-521-42252-3*) Cambridge U Pr.

Lang, Kenneth R. & Gingerich, Owen, eds. A Source Book in Astronomy & Astrophysics, 1900-1975. LC 78-9463. (Source Books in the History of the Sciences). (Illus.). 942p. 1979. 105.50 (*0-674-82200-5*) HUP.

— Source Book on Astronomy & Astrophysics. 922p. 1980. 41.95 (*0-318-13544-2*, B0163) HUP.

Lang, Klaus, et al. International Construction Terminology. (ENG & FRE.). 131p. 1980. pap. write for info. (*0-7859-4855-4*) Fr & Eur.

Lang, Kurt & Lang, Gladys E. The Unique Perspective of Television & Its Effect: A Pilot Study. (Reprint Series in Social Sciences). (C). 1993. reprint ed. pap. text 5.00 (*0-8290-3797-7*, S-160) Irvington.

Lang, Kurt, jt. auth. see Lang, Gladys E.

Lang, Larry. Absorption Spectra in the Infrared Reg., Vol. 5. 1980. pap. 125.00 (*963-05-1768-X*, Pub. by Akade Kiado) St Mut.

— Absorption Spectra in the Infrared Region. 183p. 1975. ring bd. 75.00 (*963-05-0189-9*, Pub. by Akade Kiado) St Mut.

— Absorption Spectra in the Ultraviolet..., Vol. 16. 1972. pap. 145.00 (*963-05-0714-5*, Pub. by Akade Kiado) St Mut.

— Absorption Spectra in the Ultraviolet..., Vol. 17. 1972. pap. 145.00 (*963-05-7411-X*, Pub. by Akade Kiado) St Mut.

— Absorption Spectra in the Ultraviolet..., Vol. 19. 1974. pap. 170.00 (*963-05-0271-2*, Pub. by Akade Kiado) St Mut.

— Absorption Spectra in the Ultraviolet..., Vol. 20. 1975. pap. 170.00 (*963-05-0577-0*, Pub. by Akade Kiado) St Mut.

— Absorption Spectra in the Ultraviolet..., Vol. 21. 1977. pap. 170.00 (*963-05-0993-8*, Pub. by Akade Kiado) St Mut.

— Absorption Spectra in the Ultraviolet & Visible Region, Vol. 1. 400p. 1966. ring bd. 100.00 (*0-7855-2777-X*, Pub. by Akade Kiado) St Mut.

— Absorption Spectra in the Ultraviolet & Visible Region, Vol. 2. 400p. 1966. ring bd. 195.00 (*0-7855-2778-8*) St Mut.

— Absorption Spectra in the Ultraviolet & Visible Region, Vol. 3. 400p. 1966. ring bd. 100.00 (*0-7855-2779-6*, Pub. by Akade Kiado) St Mut.

— Absorption Spectra in the Ultraviolet & Visible Region, Vol. 4. 400p. 1966. ring bd. 100.00 (*0-7855-2780-X*, Pub. by Akade Kiado) St Mut.

— Absorption Spectra in the Ultraviolet & Visible Region, Vol. 5. 400p. 1966. ring bd. 100.00 (*0-7855-2781-8*, Pub. by Akade Kiado) St Mut.

— Absorption Spectra in the Ultraviolet & Visible Region, Vol. 6. 400p. 1966. ring bd. 100.00 (*0-7855-2782-6*, Pub. by Akade Kiado) St Mut.

— Absorption Spectra in the Ultraviolet & Visible Region, Vol. 7. 400p. 1966. ring bd. 100.00 (*0-7855-2783-4*, Pub. by Akade Kiado) St Mut.

— Absorption Spectra in the Ultraviolet & Visible Region, Vol. 8. 400p. 1966. ring bd. 100.00 (*0-7855-2784-2*, Pub. by Akade Kiado) St Mut.

— Absorption Spectra in the Ultraviolet & Visible Region, Vol. 9. 400p. 1966. ring bd. 100.00 (*0-7855-2785-0*, Pub. by Akade Kiado) St Mut.

— Absorption Spectra in the Ultraviolet & Visible Region, Vol. 10. 400p. 1966. ring bd. 120.00 (*0-7855-2786-9*, Pub. by Akade Kiado) St Mut.

Lang, Larry, et al, eds. Absorption Spectra in the Infrared Region, 2 vols., 1. LC 75-647671. 320p. 1974. reprint ed. pap. 99.20 (*0-8357-5021-3*, 202574700001) Bks Demand.

— Absorption Spectra in the Infrared Region, 2 vols., 2. LC 75-647671. 319p. 1976. reprint ed. pap. 98.90 (*0-8357-5022-1*, 202574700002) Bks Demand.

— Research in International Business & Finance, Vol. 12. 1995. 78.50 (*1-55938-919-2*) Jai Pr.

— Research in International Business & Finance: Technology Transfer & Economic Development. (Research in International Business & Finance Ser.: Vol. 2). 320p. 1982. 78.50 (*0-89232-140-7*) Jai Pr.

— Research in International Business & Finance: Uncle Sam As Host, Vol. 5. 381p. 1986. 78.50 (*0-89232-588-7*) Jai Pr.

— Research in International Business & Finance Vol. 1: The Economic Effects of Multinational Corporations. (Research in International Business & Finance Ser.). 330p. 1979. 78.50 (*0-89232-031-1*) Jai Pr.

— Research in International Business & Finance Vol. 3: The Internationalization of Financial Markets & National Economic Policy. (Research in International Business & Finance Ser.: Vol. 3). 352p. 1983. 78.50 (*0-89232-264-0*) Jai Pr.

— Research in International Business & Finance Vol. 4: International Business Strategies in the Asia-Pacific Region. 1984. 157.00 (*0-89232-308-6*) Jai Pr.

— Research in International Business & Finance Vol. 7: The Modern International Environment. 258p. 1989. 78.50 (*0-89232-906-8*) Jai Pr.

— Research in International Business & Finance Vol. 8: Prospects for Canadian-United States Economic Relations under Free Trade. 240p. 1990. 78.50 (*1-55938-050-0*) Jai Pr.

— Research in International Business & Finance Vol. 9: Emerging Challeges for the International Industry. 268p. 1993. 78.50 (*1-55938-234-1*) Jai Pr.

— Research in International Business & Finance Vol. 11: Studies in the Financial Markets of the Pacific Basin, 2 vols. 1995. 157.00 (*1-55938-617-7*) Jai Pr.

— Research in International Business & Finance - Studies in the Financial Markets, Pt. A. 240p. 1995. 78.50 (*1-55938-780-7*) Jai Pr.

— Research in International Business & Finance - Studies in the Financial Markets, Pt. B. 232p. 1995. 78.50 (*1-55938-860-9*) Jai Pr.

Lang, Larry, ed. see Dutta, Jan.

Lang, Larry H. Project Financing in Asia. LC 98-13337. (Advances in Finance, Investment, & Banking Ser.). 1998. write for info. (*0-444-82804-4*) Elsevier.

Lang, Larry R. Strategy for Personal Finance. 5th ed. LC 92-37247. (Series in Finance). (C). 1993. text 64.74 (*0-07-036400-1*); pap. text, student ed. 30.00 (*0-07-036402-8*) McGraw.

***Lang, Laura.** GIS for Health Organizations. 2000. pap. text 19.95 (*1-879102-65-X*) ESR Inst.

Lang, Laura. Managing Natural Resources with GIS. 117p. 1998. pap. text 19.95 (*1-879102-53-6*) ESR Inst.

— Transportation GIS. 118p. 1999. pap. 19.95 (*1-879102-47-1*) ESR Inst.

Lang, Leonora B., tr. see Rambaud, Alfred N.

Lang, Lillian L. Face to Face: A Practicable Novelette (1922) 316p. 1998. reprint ed. pap. 24.95 (*0-7661-0618-7*) Kessinger Pub.

Lang, Louise B. Letter Writing. 1994. pap. 10.00 (*0-00-470702-8*) Collins.

Lang, Lucy. Tomorrow Is Beautiful. (American Autobiography Ser.). 303p. 1995. reprint ed. lib. bdg. 99.00 (*0-7812-8573-9*) Rprt Serv.

Lang, M. Wittgenstein's Philosophische Grammatik: Entstehung und Perspektiven der Strategie eines Radikalen Aufklarers. 160p. 1972. pap. text 71.50 (*90-247-1204-1*) Kluwer Academic.

Lang, M. & Khoury, Colleen A. Federal Tax Elections. 1992. 155.00 (*0-7913-0864-2*) Warren Gorham & Lamont.

Lang, M., jt. auth. see Thomas, M.

Lang, Mabel L. The Athenian Citizen. (Excavations of the Athenian Agora Picture Bks.: No. 4). (Illus.). 32p. 1987. pap. 3.00 (*0-87661-632-5*) Am Sch Athens.

— Cure & Cult in Ancient Corinth: A Guide to the Asklepieion. (Illus.). 32p. 1977. pap. 3.00 (*0-87661-670-8*) Am Sch Athens.

— Graffiti & Dipinti. LC 75-40229. (Athenian Agora Ser.: Vol. 21). (Illus.). x, 116p. 1976. 35.00 (*0-87661-221-4*) Am Sch Athens.

— Graffiti in the Athenian Agora. (Excavations of the Athenian Agora Picture Bks.: No. 14). (Illus.). 1988. pap. 3.00 (*0-87661-633-3*) Am Sch Athens.

— Herodotean Narrative & Discourse. (Martin Classical Lectures: No. 28). (Illus.). 192p. 1984. 20.00 (*0-674-38985-9*) HUP.

— Life, Death & Litigation in the Athenian Agora. (Excavations of the Athenian Agora Picture Bks.: No. 23). (Illus.). 32p. 1994. pap. 3.00 (*0-87661-637-6*) Am Sch Athens.

— Ostraka. LC 90-46998. (Athenian Agora Ser.: Vol. 25). (Illus.). xvi, 188p. 1990. 55.00 (*0-87661-225-7*) Am Sch Athens.

— Socrates in the Agora. (Excavations of the Athenian Agora Picture Bks.: No. 17). (Illus.). 32p. 1978. pap. 3.00 (*0-87661-617-1*) Am Sch Athens.

— Waterworks in the Athenian Agora. LC 69-22670. (Excavations of the Athenian Agora Picture Bks.: No. 11). (Illus.). 32p. 1968. pap. 3.00 (*0-87661-611-2*) Am Sch Athens.

Lang, Margaret A. Modern French Grammar Workbook. Perez, Isabelle, ed. 96p. (C). 1997. pap., wbk. ed. 12.99 (*0-415-12093-4*) Routledge.

Lang, Margaret A., jt. auth. see Perez, Isabelle.

Lang, Marilyn, ed. National Directory of Health Care Critical Pathways: Fall 1996 Edition. 2nd ed. 135p. 1996. pap. text 98.00 (*0-9645360-2-1*) Cor Hlthcare.

Lang, Marjorie. Women Who Made the News: Female Journalists in Canada, 1883-1945. 371p. 1999. 32.95 (*0-7735-1838-X*, Pub. by McG-Queens Univ Pr) CUP Services.

Lang-Marshall, Mary. God Is Mindful of Man. Koger, Dorothy P. & Battle, Jackie, eds. 52p. pap. write for info. (*1-882821-25-4*) DPK Pubns.

Lang, Marvel, ed. Contemporary Urban America: Problems, Issues, & Alternatives. 480p. (Orig.). (C). 1991. pap. text 37.50 (*0-8191-8262-1*); lib. bdg. 65.00 (*0-8191-8261-3*) U Pr of Amer.

Lang, Marvel & Ford, Clinita A., eds. Strategies for Retaining Minority Students in Higher Education. (Illus.). 180p. 1992. pap. 28.95 (*0-398-06222-6*) C C Thomas.

— Strategies for Retaining Minority Students in Higher Education. (Illus.). 180p. (C). 1992. text 41.95 (*0-398-05820-2*) C C Thomas.

Lang, Mary A., et al, eds. AIDS Blindness & Low Vision: A Guide for Service Providers. 36p. 1996. reprint ed. pap. text 15.00 (*0-7881-3128-1*) DIANE Pub.

Lang, Mary A., et al. Toys & Play: A Guide to Fun & Development for Children with Impaired Vision. (Illus.). 56p. 1995. 9.95 (*0-9603444-6-2*, P580) Lighthouse NYC.

Lang, Mary A., jt. auth. see Blakely, Kim S.

Lang, Mary E., jt. auth. see Zigler, Edward F.

Lang, Meredith. Defender of the Faith: The High Court of Mississippi, 1817-1875. LC 77-7971. 184p. reprint ed. pap. 57.10 (*0-7837-1063-1*, 204158500021) Bks Demand.

***Lang, Michael.** The Application of the OECF Model Tax Con: A Critical Analysis of the Report Prepared by the OECD Committee on Fiscal Affairs / LC 00-42662. Pp. 2000. write for info. (*90-411-9791-5*) Kluwer Law Intl.

Lang, Michael H. Designing Utopia: John Ruskin's Urban Vision for Britain & America. 254p. 1998. pap. 24.99 (*1-55164-130-5*, Pub. by Black Rose) Consort Bk Sales.

— Designing Utopia: John Ruskin's Urban Vision for Britain & America. 254p. 1998. 53.99 (*1-55164-131-3*, Pub. by Black Rose) Consort Bk Sales.

***Lang, Michael D. & Taylor, Alison.** Making of a Mediator: Developing Artistry in Practice. LC 99-50521. 240p. 2000. 34.95 (*0-7879-4992-2*, Pfffr & Co) Jossey-Bass.

— Homelessness Amid Affluence: Structure & Paradox in the American Political Economy. LC 89-32271. 247p. 1989. 55.00 (*0-275-93167-6*, C3167, Praeger Pubs) Greenwood.

Lang, Mike. Grand Prix Race by Race Account of F-1 World Championship Motor Racing, Vol. 4. (Illus.). 256p. 1992. 49.95 (*0-85429-733-2*) Haynes Manuals.

— Grand Prix, 1950-73, Vols. 1 & 2. (Illus.). 548p. 1991. 39.95 (*0-85429-861-4*, Pub. by GT Foulis) Haynes Manuals.

***Lang, Monika.** Geistige Behinderung - Bewaltigung und Religioser Glaube. Eine Interviewstudie Mit Muttern Von Jugendlichen und Erwachsenen Mit Einer Geistigen Behinderung. (Illus.). 421p. 1999. 56.95 (*3-631-33964-X*) P Lang Pubng.

***Lang, Monique.** Journey to Wholeness: Healing from the Trauma of Rape. 192p. 1999. 19.95 (*1-55691-147-5*) Learning Pubns.

Lang, Moshe & Land, Tesse. Resilience: Stories of a Family Therapist. LC 97-160525. 258p. 1996. write for info. (*1-86330-459-2*) Mdrin Au.

***Lang, Moshe & McCallum, Peter.** A Family in Therapy. 2000. pap. 17.95 (*0-86431-333-0*, Pub. by Aust Council Educ Res) Stylus Pub VA.

Lang, Nick, jt. auth. see Staffel, J. Gregory.

***Lang, Niklaus P., et al, eds.** Proceedings of the 3rd European Workshop on Periodontology: Implant Dentistry. (Illus.). 613p. 1999. 68.00 (*3-87652-306-0*, Pub. by Quintessenz Verlags) Quint Pub Co.

Lang, Niklaus P., et al, eds. Proceedings of 2nd European Workshop on Periodontology: Chemicals in Periodontics. (Illus.). 428p. 1997. pap. 68.00 (*3-87652-423-7*) Quint Pub Co.

***Lang, Niklaus P., et al, eds.** Proceedings of the European Workshop on Mechanical Plaque Control. 314p. 2000. pap. 42.80 (*3-87652-428-8*, Pub. by Quintessenz Verlags) Quint Pub Co.

Lang, Niklaus P. & Karring, Thorkild, eds. Proceedings of the 1st European Workshop on Periodontology. (Illus.). 478p. 1997. 58.50 (*1-85097-035-1*) Quint Pub Co.

Lang, Niklaus P., et al. Wax-Up for Functional Occlusion. (Illus.). 28p. 1989. ring bd. 24.00 (*0-86715-217-6*) Quint Pub Co.

Lang, Norma C. & Sulman, Joanne, eds. Collectivity in Social Group Work: Concept & Practice. LC 86-31898. (Social Work with Groups Ser.: Vol. 9, No. 4). 125p. 1987. text 3.95 (*0-86656-661-9*) Haworth Pr.

Lang, Olga. Chinese Family & Society. (Illus.). 395p. 1985. reprint ed. pap. 18.00 (*0-89986-373-6*) Oriental Bk Store.

— Pa Chin & His Writings: Chinese Youth Between the Two Revolutions. LC 67-17314. (Harvard East Asian Ser.: No. 28). 418p. 1967. reprint ed. pap. 129.60 (*0-7837-4115-4*, 205793800011) Bks Demand.

Lang, Ossian H., ed. Educational Creeds of the Nineteenth Century. LC 78-165722. (American Education Ser, No. 2). (Illus.). 1972. reprint ed. 17.95 (*0-405-03711-2*) Ayer.

Lang, Patrick, jt. ed. see Kalivas, John H.

Lang, Paul. The English Language Debate: One Nation, One Language? LC 94-31225. (Multicultural Issues Ser.). (Illus.). 112p. (YA). (gr. 6 up). 1995. lib. bdg. 20.95 (*0-89490-642-9*) Enslow Pubs.

— Maria Tallchief: Native American Ballerina. LC 96-52555. (Native American Biographies Ser.). (Illus.). 128p. (YA). (gr. 6 up). 1997. lib. bdg. 20.95 (*0-89490-866-9*) Enslow Pubs.

— Die Speusippi Academici Scriptis. 89p. 1965. reprint ed. write for info. (*0-318-70952-X*) G Olms Pubs.

Lang, Paul H. George Frideric Handel. unabridged ed. LC 96-22869. (Illus.). 768p. 1996. reprint ed. pap. text 18.95 (*0-486-29227-4*) Dover.

Lang, Paul H. Music in Western Civilization. LC 97-5883. 1100p. (C). 1997. 45.00 (*0-393-04074-7*) Norton.

Lang, Paul H., ed. Haydn Commemorative Issue of "The Musical Quarterly." LC 82-1590. (Music Reprint Ser.). 1983. reprint ed. lib. bdg. 29.50 (*0-306-76156-4*) Da Capo.

— One Hundred Years of Music in America. LC 84-1798. (Music Reprint Ser.). 322p. 1984. reprint ed. lib. bdg. 39.50 (*0-306-76242-0*) Da Capo.

— Symphony, 1800-1900. LC 75-77392. (Music Anthology Ser.). (C). 1969. pap. text 42.50 (*0-393-09865-6*) Norton.

Lang, Paul H., et al. Musicology & Performance. LC 96-39636. 272p. 1997. 35.00 (*0-300-06805-0*) Yale U Pr.

Lang, Paul S. & Lang, Susan S. Teen Fathers. (Changing Family Ser.). 128p. (YA). (gr. 9-12). 1995. lib. bdg. 24.00 (*0-531-11216-0*) Watts.

***Lang-Peralta, Linda, ed.** Women, Revolution & the Novels of the 1790s. LC 99-50547. (Early Women Writers Ser.: Vol. 6). (Illus.). 230p. 2000. pap. text 21.95 (*0-87013-519-8*) Mich St U Pr.

Lang, Peter, ed. Affective Education in Europe. (Personal & Social Education Ser.). (Illus.). 224p. 1998. 90.00 (*0-304-33987-3*); pap. 29.95 (*0-304-33988-1*) Continuum.

Lang, Peter J. Suburban Discipline. LC 97-18862. (Storefront Bks.: Vol. 2). (Illus.). 112p. (Orig.). 1997. pap. 14.95 (*1-56898-106-6*) Princeton Arch.

Lang, Peter J., ed. Mortal City: Storefront Books. LC 95-867. (Illus.). 112p. (Orig.). 1995. pap. 12.95 (*1-56898-046-9*) Princeton Arch.

Lang, Peter J., et al, eds. Attention & Orienting: Sensory & Motivational Processes. LC 96-32753. 400p. 1997. 99.95 (*0-8058-2089-2*) L Erlbaum Assocs.

Lang, Peter J., jt. auth. see Stropes, John.

Lang, Peter J., ed. see McGuiness, John.

Lang, Peter J., ed. see Whitaker, Patrick.

Lang-Pickvance, Katy, et al, eds. Environmental & Housing Movements: Grassroots Experience in Hungary, Russia & Estonia. LC 96-79371. 368p. 1997. text 78.95 (*1-85972-400-0*, Pub. by Avebry) Ashgate Pub Co.

Lang, Poiette. Fence Slat Holidays. (Illus.). 30p. 1998. 8.99 (*1-58050-051-X*, HO-6180) Provo Craft.

Lang, Rebecca. Let Tomorrow Come. 1999. mass mkt. 3.50 (*0-373-17409-8*, 1-17409-3, Mira Bks) Harlequin Bks.

***Lang, Rebecca.** Let Tomorrow Come. large type ed. 288p. 1999. 25.99 (*0-263-15906-X*, Pub. by Mills & Boon) Ulverscroft.

Lang, Rebecca. Wedding Song. large type ed. 288p. 1996. 23.99 (*0-263-14633-2*, Pub. by Mills & Boon) Ulverscroft.

Lang, Richard W. & Harris, Arthur. The Faunal Remains from Arroyo Hondo Pueblo, New Mexico: A Study in Short-Term Subsistence Change. LC 84-10514. (Arroyo Hondo Archaeological Ser.: Vol. 5). (Illus.). 140p. 1983. pap. 14.95 (*0-933452-09-8*) Schol Am Res.

Lang, Rick, jt. auth. see Milewski, Ron.

Lang, Robert. American Film Melodrama: Griffith, Vidor, Minnelli. LC 88-17936. 270p. 1989. reprint ed. pap. 83.70 (*0-608-04580-2*, 206535000003) Bks Demand.

— The Land & People of Pakistan. rev. ed. LC 74-792. (Portraits of the Nations Ser.). (Illus.). 160p. (J). (gr. 5-9). 1974. lib. bdg. 12.89 (*0-397-31551-1*) HarpC Child Bks.

Lang, Robert & Kunselman, Joan. Heinrich Schenker, Oswald Jonas, Moriz Violin: A Checklist of Manuscripts & Other Papers in the Oswald Jonas Memorial Collection. LC 94-9207. (Catalogs & Bibliographies Ser.: Vol. 10). 1994. 40.00 (*0-520-09790-4*, Pub. by U CA Pr) Cal Prin Full Svc.

Lang, Robert, jt. auth. see Montroll, John.

Lang, Robert, ed. see Griffith, D. W.

Lang, Robert J. Investment Software Reference Guide. 3rd rev. ed. 128p. 1988. pap. text 11.95 (*0-929777-00-X*) SCIX Corp.

Lang, Robert J. Origami Insects & Their Kin: Step-by-Step Instructions in over 1500 Diagrams. LC 95-50. (Illus.). 160p. 1995. pap. 9.95 (*0-486-28602-9*) Dover.

Lang, Robert J. Origami Zoo. 1990. pap. 15.95 (*0-312-04015-6*) St Martin.

Lang, S. Diophantine Geometry. LC 97-222652. 296p. 1997. pap. text 54.50 (*3-540-61223-8*) Spr-Verlag.

— Introduction to Diophantine Approximations. 2nd ed. 136p. 1995. 43.95 (*0-387-94456-7*) Spr-Verlag.

— Topics in Cohomology of Groups, Vol. 162. LC 96-26607. (Lecture Notes in Mathematics Ser.). 226p. 1996. 43.00 (*3-540-61181-9*) Spr-Verlag.

Lang, S., et al. Solutions Manual for Geometry: A High School Course. LC 93-38093. 1994. 32.95 (*0-387-94181-9*) Spr-Verlag.

Lang, S., jt. auth. see Jorgensen, J.

L

Lang, S. B., jt. auth. see Das Gupta, D. K.

Lang, S. L. Linear Optimization in Applications. 166p. 1999. pap. 23.50 (*962-209-483-X*, Pub. by HK Univ Pr) Coronet Bks.

***Lang, Sabine.** Men As Women, Women As Men: Changing Gender in Native American Cultures. Vantine, John L., tr. from GER. LC 97-34759. xvii, 398p. (C). 1998. pap. 19.95 (*0-292-74701-2*, LANMEP) U of Tex Pr.

Lang, Sabine, ed. see Jacobs, Sue-Ellen.

Lang, Sandra. The Breastfeeding Handbook. (C). 1996. pap. text 22.00 (*0-7020-2020-6*) Harcourt.

Lang, Sean. Parliamentary Reform, 1785-1928. LC 98-31486. (Questions & Analysis in History Ser.). (Illus.). 112p. (C). 1999. pap. 11.99 (*0-415-18399-5*) Routledge.

— The Second World War: Conflict & Cooperation. (Cambridge History Programme Ser.). 96p. (C). 1993. pap. 14.95 (*0-521-43826-8*) Cambridge U Pr.

— The Second World War: Conflict & Cooperation. (History Programme Ser.). 32p. (C). 1994. pap. text 21.95 (*0-521-43827-6*) Cambridge U Pr.

— The Twentieth Century World: War, Revolution & Technology. LC 99-161357. (History Programme Ser.). (Illus.). 112p. (C). 1998. pap. 15.95 (*0-521-48324-7*) Cambridge U Pr.

Lang, Serge. Challenges. LC 94-7180. (Illus.). 816p. 1997. pap. 29.95 (*0-387-94861-9*) Spr-Verlag.

Lang, Serge. Collected Papers, I-IV, 4 vols., Set. Incl. Vol. 1. Selecta, 1952-1970. LC 99-17359. 504p. 1999. 79.00 (*0-387-98802-5*); Vol. 2. Selecta, 1971-1977. 592p. 1999. 79.00 (*0-387-98803-3*); Vol. 3. Selecta, 1978-1980. 400p. 1999. 79.00 (*0-387-98800-9*); Vol. 6. Selecta, 1990-1996. 432p. 1999. 79.00 (*0-387-98804-1*); 1928p. 280.00 (*0-387-91591-5*) Spr-Verlag.

Lang, Serge. Complex Analysis. 4th ed. LC 98-29992. (Graduate Texts in Mathematics Ser.: Vol. 103). 472p. 1999. 64.95 (*0-387-98592-1*) Spr-Verlag.

— Fundamentals of Differential Geometry. 4th ed. LC 98-29993. (Graduate Texts in Mathematics Ser.: Vol. 160). 384p. 1999. 54.95 (*0-387-98593-X*) Spr-Verlag.

***Lang, Serge.** Math Talks for Undergraduates. LC 98-55410. 112p. 1999. 29.95 (*0-387-98749-5*) Spr-Verlag.

Lang, Serge A. Abelian Varieties. 260p. 1983. reprint ed. 46.95 (*0-387-90875-7*) Spr-Verlag.

— Algebra. 2nd ed. 714p. (C). 1984. text 63.50 (*0-201-05487-6*) Addison-Wesley.

— Algebra. 3rd ed. LC 91-36078. (Illus.). 900p. (C). 1992. 101.00 (*0-201-55540-9*) Addison-Wesley.

— Algebraic Number Theory. (Graduate Texts in Mathematics Ser.: Vol. 110). 370p. 1993. reprint ed. 29.80 (*0-387-96375-8*) Spr-Verlag.

— Algebraic Number Theory. 2nd ed. LC 93-50625. (Graduate Texts in Mathematics Ser.: Vol. 110). 376p. 1996. 39.95 (*0-387-94225-4*) Spr-Verlag.

— Basic Mathematics. (Illus.). xv, 475p. 1995. 39.95 (*0-387-96787-7*) Spr-Verlag.

— The Beauty of Doing Mathematics. (Illus.). xi, 127p. 1994. 29.95 (*0-387-96149-6*) Spr-Verlag.

— Calculus of Several Variables. 2nd ed. LC 78-55822. (Mathematics Ser.). (Illus.). 1979. text 31.25 (*0-201-04299-1*) Addison-Wesley.

— Calculus of Several Variables. 3rd ed. (Undergraduate Texts in Mathematics Ser.). (Illus.). 590p. 1996. 49.95 (*0-387-96405-3*) Spr-Verlag.

— Complex Analysis. (Graduate Texts in Mathematics Ser.: Vol. 103). (Illus.). 385p. 1988. 49.00 (*0-387-96085-6*) Spr-Verlag.

— Complex Analysis. 3rd ed. Ewing, J. H. et al, eds. (Graduate Texts in Mathematics Ser.: Vol. 103). (Illus.). 458p. 1995. reprint ed. 64.95 (*0-387-97886-0*) Spr-Verlag.

— Complex Multiplications. (Grundlehren der Mathematischen Wissenschaften Ser.: Vol. 255). 192p. 1983. 95.95 (*0-387-90786-6*) Spr-Verlag.

— Cyclotomic Fields First & Second. (Graduate Texts in Mathematics Ser.: Vol. 121). (Illus.). 432p. 1989. 59.95 (*0-387-96671-4*, 1209) Spr-Verlag.

— Cyclotonic Fields: Two. (Graduate Texts in Mathematics Ser.: Vol. 69). 288p. 1980. 36.00 (*0-387-90447-6*) Spr-Verlag.

— Differential & Riemannian Manifolds. 3rd ed. LC 94-20828. 364p. 1995. 49.50 (*0-387-94338-2*) Spr-Verlag.

— Differential Manifolds. 2nd ed. (Illus.). ix, 230p. 1988. pap. 29.80 (*0-387-96113-5*) Spr-Verlag.

— Elliptic Curves: Diophantine Analysis. LC 77-21139. (Grundlehren der Mathematischen Wissenschaften Ser.: Vol. 231). 1979. 94.95 (*0-387-08489-4*) Spr-Verlag.

— Elliptic Functions. 2nd ed. (Graduate Texts in Mathematics Ser.: Vol. 112). 340p. 1987. 48.95 (*0-387-96508-4*) Spr-Verlag.

— A First Course in Calculus. 4th ed. LC 77-76193. (Mathematics Ser.). (Illus.). 1978. text 27.25 (*0-201-04149-9*) Addison-Wesley.

— A First Course in Calculus. 5th ed. (Undergraduate Texts in Mathematics Ser.). (Illus.). xv, 727p. 1993. reprint ed. 45.95 (*0-387-96201-8*) Spr-Verlag.

— Fundamentals of Diophantine Geometry. (Illus.). 400p. 1983. 79.95 (*0-387-90837-4*) Spr-Verlag.

— Introduction to Algebraic & Abelian Functions, Vol. IX. 2nd rev. ed. Ewing, J. H. et al, eds. (Graduate Texts in Mathematics Ser.: Vol. 89). (Illus.). 169p. 1995. 54.95 (*0-387-90710-6*) Spr-Verlag.

— Introduction to Arakelov Theory. (Illus.). x, 187p. 1988. 59.95 (*0-387-96793-1*) Spr-Verlag.

— Introduction to Complex Hyperbolic Spaces. (Illus.). 300p. 1987. 69.95 (*0-387-96447-9*) Spr-Verlag.

— Introduction to Linear Algebra. LC 70-100872. (Mathematics Ser.). (C). 1970. pap. 10.25 (*0-201-04206-1*) Addison-Wesley.

— Introduction to Linear Algebra. 2nd ed. (Undergraduate Texts in Mathematics Ser.). (Illus.). viii, 291p. 1997. 39.95 (*0-387-96205-0*) Spr-Verlag.

— Introduction to Modular Forms. (Grundlehren der Mathematischen Wissenschaften Ser.: Vol. 222). (Illus.). 1987. 99.95 (*0-387-07833-9*) Spr-Verlag.

— Linear Algebra. 3rd ed. (Undergraduate Texts in Mathematics Ser.). (Illus.). 200p. 1996. 39.95 (*0-387-96412-6*) Spr-Verlag.

— Math! Encounters with High School. (Illus.). 150p. 1995. 34.95 (*0-387-96129-1*) Spr-Verlag.

— Number Theory III: Diophantine Geometry. (Encyclopedia of Mathematical Sciences Ser.: Vol. 60). (Illus.). 304p. 1991. 118.95 (*0-387-53004-5*) Spr-Verlag.

— Real Analysis. 2nd ed. (C). 1983. 45.95 (*0-201-14179-5*) Addison-Wesley.

— Real Analysis. 3rd ed. LC 92-21208. (Illus.). 600p. 1993. 54.95 (*0-387-94001-4*) Spr-Verlag.

— SL 2 (IR) (Graduate Texts in Mathematics Ser.: Vol. 105). (Illus.). xiv, 428p. 1985. reprint ed. 54.95 (*0-387-96198-4*) Spr-Verlag.

— Undergraduate Algebra. (Undergraduate Texts in Mathematics Ser.). (Illus.). 250p. 1986. 36.00 (*0-387-96404-5*) Spr-Verlag.

— Undergraduate Algebra. 2nd ed. Ewing, J. H. et al, eds. (Undergraduate Texts in Mathematics Ser.). (Illus.). xi, 367p. 1994. 43.95 (*0-387-97279-X*) Spr-Verlag.

— Undergraduate Analysis. 2nd ed. LC 96-26339. (Undergraduate Texts in Mathematics Ser.). 642p. 1997. 54.95 (*0-387-94841-4*) Spr-Verlag.

— Undergraduate Analysis, Vol. XIII. rev. ed. Ewing, J. H. et al, eds. (Undergraduate Texts in Mathematics Ser.). (Illus.). 545p. (C). 1996. 45.00 (*0-387-90800-5*) Spr-Verlag.

Lang, Serge A., ed. The File: A Case Study in Correction, (1977 - 1979) 712p. 1981. 69.95 (*0-387-90607-X*) Spr-Verlag.

Lang, Serge A. & Cherry, W. Topics in Nevanlinna Theory. Dold, A. et al, eds. (Lecture Notes in Mathematics Ser.: Vol. 1433). (Illus.). ii, 174p. 1990. 34.95 (*0-387-52785-0*) Spr-Verlag.

Lang, Serge A. & Murrow, Gene. Geometry: A High School Course. 2nd ed. (Illus.). 464p. 1991. pap. text 29.80 (*0-387-90727-0*) Spr-Verlag.

— Geometry: A High School Course. 2nd ed. (Illus.). xii, 394p. 1997. 39.95 (*0-387-96654-4*) Spr-Verlag.

Lang, Serge A., jt. auth. see Fulton, W.

Lang, Serge A., jt. auth. see Jorgenson, Jay.

Lang, Serge A., jt. auth. see Kubert, D. S.

Lang, Serge A., ed. see Artin, Emil.

Lang, Sidney B. Ferroelectrics Computerized Index. 1995. 3.5 hd 220.00 (*2-88449-154-6*) Gordon & Breach.

— Sourcebook of Pyroelectricity, Vol. 2. (Ferroelectricity & Related Phenomena Ser.). xvi, 562p. 1974. text 488.00 (*0-677-01580-1*) Gordon & Breach.

Lang, Simon. Hopeship. 240p. (Orig.). 1994. mass mkt. 4.99 (*0-441-34306-6*) Ace Bks.

Lang-Sims, Lois. Letters to Lalage: The Letters of Charles Williams to Lois Lang-Sims. LC 89-33241. 97p. 1990. pap. 16.50 (*0-87338-398-2*) Kent St U Pr.

Lang, Stephen. The Bible: What's in It for Me? 1997. 16.99 (*0-614-27561-X*) Chariot Victor.

Lang, Stephen & Teninga, Adelaide. Living Long & Loving It! large type rev. ed. (Friendship Ser.). (Illus.). 48p. (Orig.). 1995. pap. 0.70 (*1-882536-11-8*, A100-0035) Bible League.

— Shall We? (Friendship Ser.). (Illus.). 48p. (Orig.). 1993. reprint ed. pap. 0.70 (*1-882536-10-X*, A100-0034) Bible League.

Lang, Stephen A. An Investigation of Image Processing Techniques at Pincevent Habitation, No. 1: An Upper Magdalenian Site in Northern France. (Anthropological Research Papers: No. 43). vii, 110p. (Orig.). 1992. pap. 25.00 (*0-936249-13-7*) AZ Univ ARP.

***Lang, Stephen J.** Bible Trivia 2001. 2000. pap. text 9.99 (*0-8423-3771-7*) Tyndale Hse.

Lang, Stephen J. The Big Book of American Trivia. LC 96-44960. 390p. 1997. 10.99 (*0-8423-0471-1*) Tyndale Hse.

Lang, Susan. More Nature in Your Backyard. LC 97-32181. (Illus.). 48p. (J). (gr. 2-5). 1998. lib. bdg. 22.90 (*0-7613-0308-1*) Millbrook Pr.

— The Ortho Book of Gardening Basics. Rae, Norman, ed. LC 90-86169. (Illus.). 504p. 1991. 24.95 (*0-89721-233-9*, Ortho Bks) Meredith Bks.

Lang, Susan & Beressem, Hanjo. Someone Else with My Fingerprints. (Illus.). 176p. (C). 1997. pap. 30.00 (*3-932189-01-9*) Dist Art Pubs.

Lang, Susan, ed. see Peirce, Pamela K.

Lang, Susan, ed. see Wolf, Rex & McNair, James.

Lang, Susan M. & O'Connor, Martha S., eds. AOTCB Study Guide for the COTA Certification Examination. rev. ed. 72p. (Orig.). (C). 1996. pap. text 20.00 (*0-9639373-0-8*) Am Occupat Ther.

— AOTCB Study Guide for the OTR Certification Examination. rev. ed. 76p. (Orig.). (C). 1996. pap. text 20.00 (*0-9639373-1-6*) Am Occupat Ther.

Lang, Susan S. & Patt, Richard B. You Don't Have to Suffer: A Complete Guide to Relieving Cancer Pain for Patients & Their Families. (Illus.). 384p. 1995. pap. 12.95 (*0-19-508419-5*) OUP.

Lang, Susan S., jt. auth. see Cayuga Nature Center Staff.

Lang, Susan S., jt. auth. see Lang, Paul S.

Lang, Susan S., jt. auth. see Robbins, Lawrence.

Lang, Terry, jt. auth. see Schoenholz, Deborah L.

Lang, Theodore F. Loyal West Virginia, 1861-1865. (Illus.). 476p. 1998. 35.00 (*1-885033-19-2*) Blue Acorn Pr.

Lang, Thomas A. & Secic, Michelle. How to Report Statistics in Medicine: A Guide for Authors, Editors & Reviewers. LC 96-30333. (Medical Writing & Communication Ser.). 376p. 1997. pap. 39.95 (*0-943126-44-4*) Amer Coll Phys.

Lang, Thomas A., jt. auth. see Musser, Doug.

Lang, Thomas A., jt. auth. see Reed, Rosalind.

Lang, Tim & Hines, Colin. The New Protectionism: Protecting the Future Against Free Trade. LC 93-28024. 208p. 1993. pap. 11.95 (*1-56584-135-2*, Pub. by New Press NY) Norton.

Lang, Tim, jt. auth. see Gabriel, Yiannis.

Lang, Timothy. The Victorians & the Stuart Heritage: Interpretations of a Discordant Past. 247p. (C). 1995. text 59.95 (*0-521-47464-7*) Cambridge U Pr.

Lang, Tom. Cat: A Story by Tom Lang. LC 95-83316. (Illus.). 64p. 1996. pap. 5.00 (*0-9649742-8-2*) Boudelang Pr.

— Coffee: A Story by Tom Lang. LC 95-94650. (Illus.). (Orig.). 1995. pap. 5.00 (*0-9649742-9-0*) Boudelang Pr.

— Eagle: A Story by Tom Lang. LC 96-84755. (Illus.). 64p. 1996. pap. text 5.00 (*0-9649742-7-4*) Boudelang Pr.

— Mrs. Claus: A Story by Tom Lang. LC 96-94888. (Illus.). 64p. (J). (gr. 2-12). 1997. pap. 5.00 (*0-9649742-0-7*) Boudelang Pr.

— Salmon: A Short Story by Tom Lang. 64p. 1998. pap. 5.00 (*0-9649742-1-5*) Boudelang Pr.

Lang, Tom & Zier, Don. Jo, the Japanese Short Staff. LC 84-52443. (Illus.). 112p. (Orig.). 1985. pap. 12.95 (*0-86568-058-2*, 310) Unique Pubns.

Lang, Tomas, jt. auth. see Ercegovac, Milos D.

Lang, Tomas, jt. auth. see Moreno, Jaime H.

Lang, Tony. Learn French with Teddy Berlitz. LC 96-20153. 64p. (J). (ps up). 1996. reprint ed. pap. 12.95 incl. audio (*0-689-81128-4*) Litle Simon.

Lang, Tran T. Electronics of Measuring Systems: Practical Implementation of Analogue & Digital Techniques. LC 86-26786. 336p. 1987. 275.00 (*0-471-91157-7*) Wiley.

Lang, V. Paul. Heating & Cooling Safety. LC 76-24983. 1977. 13.95 (*0-8273-1012-9*) Delmar.

— Principles of Air Conditioning. 4th ed. LC 86-32988. 384p. (C). 1987. pap. 46.95 (*0-8273-2759-5*) Delmar.

— Principles of Air Conditioning. 4th ed. LC 86-32988. 384p. (C). 1987. teacher ed. 14.95 (*0-8273-2760-9*) Delmar.

— Principles of Air Conditioning. 5th ed. LC 94-44734. 1995. mass mkt. 79.95 (*0-8273-6591-8*) Delmar.

Lang, Virgil R. & Krug, Samuel E. Perspectives on the Executive Personality. LC 78-27205. 1983. pap. text 25.00 (*0-918296-12-9*) Inst Personality & Ability.

***Lang, Virginia & Nayer, Louise.** How to Bury a Goldfish: 140 New Traditions for Everyday Life. 2000. 22.50 (*1-57954-275-1*, Daybrk) Rodale Pr Inc.

Lang, W., et al, eds. Porous Silicon: Proceedings of Symposium 1 on Porous Silicon: Material, Technology & Devices of the 1995 E-MRS Spring Conference, Strasbourg, France, 22-26 May 1995. LC 96-229437. (European Materials Research Society Symposia Proceedings Ser.: No. 57). 344p. 1996. text 216.25 (*0-444-82414-6*, North Holland) Elsevier.

Lang, W. H. History of Seneca County, Ohio. (Illus.). 691p. 1993. reprint ed. lib. bdg. 69.50 (*0-8328-3228-6*) Higginson Bk Co.

Lang, W. H., jt. auth. see Herino, R.

Lang, W. Harold. Islands of the Pacific. Kubat, Frank J., Jr., ed. LC 87-83228. (Illus.). 168p. (YA). 1988. 44.95 (*0-945201-00-1*) Gannam-Kubat.

Lang, Walter A. J. Job & Science. 2nd rev. ed. (Illus.). 541p. (C). 1993. reprint ed. pap. 29.95 (*0-9633724-0-8*) Genesis Inst.

Lang-Wescott, Martha. Architects of Time. (Illus.). 290p. (Orig.). 1997. 26.00 (*0-9619852-9-1*) Treehouse Mtn.

— Derivative Angles. (Illus.). 30p. (Orig.). 1992. pap. text 10.00 (*0-9619852-0-8*) Treehouse Mtn.

— The Mechanics of Free Will: The Astrology of Perception, Reality & Will. LC 87-51613. (Illus.). 226p. (Orig.). 1987. pap. 22.95 (*0-9619852-5-9*) Treehouse Mtn.

— Mechanics of the Future: Asteroids. rev. ed. (Illus.). 244p. 22.95 (*0-9619852-1-6*) Treehouse Mtn.

— The Orders of Light. (Illus.). 320p. (Orig.). 25.00 (*0-9619852-3-2*) Treehouse Mtn.

Lang-Wescott, Martha, ed. Asteroid Mechanics, 1925-2006, 2 vols., Vol. II. (Asteroid Ephemerides Ser.). 80p. 15.95 (*0-9619852-4-0*) Treehouse Mtn.

Lang, William. Final Play. 64p. 1977. pap. 3.50 (*0-87129-975-5*, F16) Dramatic Pub.

— History of Seneca County (Ohio) From the Close of the Revolutionary War to July, 1880; Embracing Many Personal Sketches of Pioneers, Anecdotes, & Faithful Descriptions of Events Pertaining to the Organization of the County & Its Progress, 2 vols. 771p. 2000. reprint ed. pap. 40.00 (*0-7884-1387-2*, 1387) Heritage Bk.

Lang, William L. A Confederacy of Ambition: William Winlock Miller & the Making of Washington Territory. (Illus.). 368p. 1996. text 30.00 (*0-295-97502-4*) U of Wash Pr.

***Lang, William L. & Carriker, Robert C., eds.** Great River of the West: Essays on the Columbia River. LC 99-41255. (Illus.). 176p. 1999. pap. text 18.95 (*0-295-97777-9*) U of Wash Pr.

Lang, William W., ed. Standards, Regulations & Federal Programs for Noise Control: NOISE-CON 75. (Noise-Con Ser.). ix, 458p. Date not set. pap. 30.00 (*0-614-25016-1*) Noise Control.

Lang, Winfried, ed. Sustainable Development & International Law. LC 95-7301. 1995. lib. bdg. 128.50 (*1-85966-179-3*, Pub. by Graham & Trotman) Kluwer Academic.

***Lang, Zhi-Peng, et al.** Principles of Magnetic Resonance Imaging: A Signal Processing Perspective LC 99-27706. (Series in Biomedical Engineering). 1999. 89.95 (*0-7803-4723-4*) IEEE Standards.

***Langa, Mandla.** The Memory of Stones: A Novel. LC 00-22413. 375p. 2000. pap. 16.00 (*0-89410-866-2*, Three Contnts) L Rienner.

Langa, Mandla. The Naked Song & Other Stories. (Three Continents Ser.). 147p. 1997. pap. 11.95 (*0-89410-855-7*) L Rienner.

Langa Mora, Enriaue. Diccionario de Hacienda Publica. (SPA.). 448p. 1990. pap. 45.00 (*0-7859-5975-0*, 8436802489) Fr & Eur.

***Langabeer, James R., II & Napiewocki, John.** Competitive Business Strategy for Teaching Hospitals. LC 00-20898. 325p. 2000. 70.00 (*1-56720-349-3*, Q349, Quorum Bks) Greenwood.

***Langacker, Paul.** Neutrinos in Physics & Astrophysics. 1999. 179.00 (*981-02-3887-8*) WSC Inst MA Studies.

Langacker, Paul. Precision Tests of the Standard Electroweak Model. 1032p. 1995. text 162.00 (*981-02-1284-4*) World Scientific Pub.

Langacker, Paul, jt. ed. see Cvetic, Mirjam.

Langacker, Ronald W. Concept, Image & Symbol: The Cognitive Basis of Grammar. (Cognitive Linguistics Research Ser.: No. 1). (Illus.). x, 395p. (Orig.). (C). 1991. pap. text 29.95 (*3-11-012863-2*, 152-91) Mouton.

***Langacker, Ronald W.** Foundations of Cognitive Grammar: Vol. 1, Theoretical Prerequisites. 1999. pap. text 27.95 (*0-8047-3851-3*) Stanford U Pr.

— Foundations of Cognitive Grammar: Vol. 2, Descriptive Application. 1999. 27.95 (*0-8047-3852-1*) Stanford U Pr.

Langacker, Ronald W. Foundations of Cognitive Grammar Vol. 1: Theoretical Prerequisites. LC 84-51300. 528p. 1987. 55.00 (*0-8047-1261-1*) Stanford U Pr.

— Foundations of Cognitive Grammar Vol. II: Descriptive Application. LC 84-51300. 608p. 1991. 57.50 (*0-8047-1909-8*) Stanford U Pr.

***Langacker, Ronald W.** Grammar & Conceptualization. LC 99-33328. (Cognitive Linguistics Research Ser.). 1999. 34.95 (*3-11-016604-6*) De Gruyter.

Langan. College Writing Skills. 5th ed. 592p. 1999. pap. 38.13 (*0-07-228322-X*) McGraw.

— English Brushup. 2nd ed. LC 99-184106. 224p. 1997. pap. 16.88 (*0-07-037108-3*) McGraw.

***Langan.** English Skills. 7th ed. 2000. 27.25 (*0-07-238127-2*) McGraw.

Langan. English Skills: All Write. 1997. 29.74 (*0-07-913197-2*) McGraw.

— Read & Study Skills. 6th ed. 640p. 1997. pap. 37.19 (*0-07-036440-0*) McGraw.

— Sentence Skills. 6th ed. LC 97-219193. 560p. 1997. pap. 37.19 (*0-07-036672-1*) McGraw.

***Langan.** Sentence Skills, Form A. 7th ed. 2000. 26.00 (*0-07-238132-9*) McGraw.

Langan, jt. auth. see Fitzpatrick.

Langan, Brian, et al. MCSE Complete NT 4 Certification Exam Guide. (Illus.). 1200p. 1998. 99.00 incl. cd-rom (*0-07-913714-8*) McGraw.

Langan, Celeste. Romantic Vagrancy: Wordsworth & the Simulation of Freedom. (Cambridge Studies in Romanticism: No. 15). (Illus.). 315p. (C). 1995. text 59.95 (*0-521-47507-4*) Cambridge U Pr.

***Langan-Egan, Maureen.** Galway Women in the Nineteenth Century. (Illus.). 148p. 1999. pap. 29.95 (*1-85182-461-8*, Pub. by Four Cts Pr) Intl Spec Bk.

Langan, Elizabeth D., et al, eds. Recommended Standards for a College Health Program. 80p. 1991. pap. 100.00 (*0-614-30085-1*) Am Coll Hlth.

Langan-Fox, Janice, jt. auth. see Poole, Millicent E.

Langan, John. Catholic Universities in Church & Society: A Dialogue on Excorde Ecclesiae. LC 93-22154. 271p. reprint ed. pap. 84.10 (*0-608-08048-9*, 206901300002) Bks Demand.

— College Writing Skills. 4th ed. 493p. (C). 1995. pap. 37.18 (*0-07-036442-7*) McGraw.

— College Writing Skills. 4th ed. (Guide to the Langan Ser.). 1996. pap. text. write for info. (*0-07-036461-3*) McGraw.

— College Writing Skills with Readings. 4th ed. LC 96-28159. 672p. (C). 1996. pap. 40.63 (*0-07-036458-3*) McGraw.

***Langan, John.** College Writing Skills with Readings. 5th ed. LC 00-24280. 2000. write for info. (*0-07-228328-9*) McGraw.

Langan, John. English Skill. (C). 1994. pap. text 6.00 (*0-07-036443-3*) McGraw.

— English Skills. 6th ed. LC 96-19890. 576p. (C). 1996. pap. 38.13 (*0-07-036446-X*) McGraw.

***Langan, John.** English Skills. 7th ed. LC 00-36140. 2001. write for info. (*0-07-238128-0*) McGraw.

Langan, John. English Skills with Readings. 2nd ed. (C). 1991. text 35.00 (*0-07-036374-9*) McGraw.

— English Skills with Readings. 2nd ed. (C). 1992. text. write for info. (*0-07-036399-4*) McGraw.

— English Skills with Readings. 3rd ed. LC 94-17411. 592p. (C). 1994. pap. 40.63 (*0-07-036418-4*) McGraw.

— English Skills with Readings. 4th ed. LC 98-26416. 672p. 1998. pap. 40.63 (*0-07-092063-X*) McGraw.

— Reading & Study Skills: A Workbook for Writers, Form B. 5th ed. LC 93-36861. 576p. (C). 1994. pap. 37.19 (*0-07-036413-3*) McGraw.

— Sentence Skills: A Workbook for Writers. 5th ed. LC 94-31072. (Langan Ser.). 1994. write for info. (*0-07-036424-9*) McGraw.

— Sentence Skills: A Workbook for Writers, Form C. 5th ed. LC 94-34371. 1994. pap. text 29.00 (*0-07-036423-0*) McGraw.

— Sentence Skills: A Workbook for Writers, Form A. 3rd ed. 496p. (C). 1986. pap. text. write for info. (*0-07-036305-6*) McGraw.

An Asterisk (*) at the beginning of an entry indicates that the title is appearing for the first time.

— Sentence Skills: A Workbook for Writers, Form B. 5th ed. LC 93-28530. 520p. 1993. pap. 37.19 *(0-07-036410-9)* McGraw.

***Langan, John.** Sentence Skills: A Workbook for Writers : Form B. 6th ed. LC 99-204699. 1998. write for info. *(0-07-037127-X)* McGrw-H Hghr Educ.

Langan, John. Sentence Skills with Readings. LC 97-204436. 640p. (C). 1996. pap. 40.63 *(0-07-036506-7)* McGraw.

***Langan, John.** Sentence Skills with Readings. 2nd ed. LC 00-30550. 2001. write for info. *(0-07-242981-X)* McGraw.

Langan, John. Ten Steps to Advancing College Reading Skills. 3rd ed. LC 99-204746. 596p. 1998. pap. text 18.00 *(0-944210-45-7)* Townsend NJ.

***Langan, John.** Ten Steps to Building College Reading Skills. 3rd ed. LC 98-164874. (C). 1998. pap. text 18.00 *(0-944210-42-2)* Townsend NJ.

Langan, John. Ten Steps to Improving College Reading Skills. 3rd ed. LC 98-163044. 560p. (C). 1997. pap. text 18.00 *(0-944210-73-2)* Townsend NJ.

Langan, John & Nadell, Judith. Doing Well in College: A Concise Guide to Reading, Writing & Study Skills. Talkington, William A., ed. (Illus.). 208p. (Orig.). (C). 1980. text 47.75 *(0-07-036262-9)* McGraw.

Langan, John, et al. Improving Reading Comprehension Skills. (C). 1992. pap. text 16.00 *(0-944210-54-6)* Townsend NJ.

Langan, John, jt. ed. see Hennelly, Alfred T.

Langan, John P., ed. see Bernardin, Joseph Louis.

Langan, John P., jt. ed. see Weigel, George.

Langan, Katherine, tr. see Pike, Kenneth L.

Langan, Mary. Welfare: Needs, Rights, & Risks. LC 97-48927. (Social Policy--Welfare, Power & Diversity Ser.). 352p. (C). 1998. 75.00 *(0-415-18127-5)*; pap. 22.99 *(0-415-18128-3)* Routledge.

Langan, Mary & Lee, Phil, eds. Radical Social Work Today. 276p. 1989. text 65.00 *(0-04-445368-X)* Routledge.

Langan, Patrick A. & Cohen, Robyn L. State Court Sentencing of Convicted Felons, 1992. (Illus.). 64p. (Orig.). (C). 1996. pap. text 20.00 *(0-7881-3138-9)* DIANE Pub.

Langan, Patrick A. & Farrington, David P. Crime & Justice in the United States & in England & Wales, 1981-96. (Illus.). 105p. (C). 1999. pap. text 25.00 *(0-7881-7654-4)* DIANE Pub.

Langan, Patrick L. & Solari, Richard. National Judicial Reporting Program (1990) (Illus.). 51p. (Orig.). (C). 1995. pap. text 20.00 *(0-7881-2422-6)* DIANE Pub.

***Langan, Ruth.** Angel. 2000. mass mkt. 4.50 *(0-373-82224-3*, 1-82224-6) Harlequin Bks.

Langan, Ruth. Blackthorne. 1998. per. 4.99 *(0-373-29035-7*, 1-29035-2) Harlequin Bks.

— Briana. (Historical Ser.: No. 480). 1999. per. 4.99 *(0-373-29080-2*, 1-29080-8) Harlequin Bks.

— Conor. (Historical Ser.: Bk. 468). 1999. per. 4.99 *(0-373-29068-3*, 1-29068-3) Harlequin Bks.

— The Courtship of Izzy McCree: 10th Anniversary Promotion. anniversary ed. (Historical Ser.: Vol. 425). 1998. per. 4.99 *(0-373-29025-X*, 1-29025-3) Harlequin Bks.

— Malachite. (Historical Ser.). 1998. per. 4.99 *(0-373-29007-1*, 1-29007-1) Harlequin Bks.

***Langan, Ruth.** Rory. 1999. per. 4.99 *(0-373-29057-8*, 1-29057-6, Harlequin) Harlequin Bks.

Langan, Ruth. Ruby. 1997. per. 4.99 *(0-373-28984-7*, 1-28984-2) Harlequin Bks.

***Langan, Ruth.** The Sea Witch. (Historical Ser.). 2000. mass mkt. 4.99 *(0-373-29123-X*, 1-29123-6) Harlequin Bks.

— Snowbound Cinderella. (Fortunes of Texas Ser.: No. 6). 2000. per. 4.50 *(0-373-65035-3*, 1-65035-7, Harlequin) Harlequin Bks.

— Texas Healer. large type ed. 320p. 1999. 25.99 *(0-263-16219-2*, Pub. by Mills & Boon) Ulverscroft.

— The Wildes of Wyoming--Ace. (Intimate Moments Ser.: Bk. 1009). 2000. per. 4.50 *(0-373-27079-8*, 1-27079-2) Silhouette.

— Wildes of Wyoming... Change. (Intimate Moments Ser.: Vol. 985). 2000. per. 4.50 *(0-373-07985-0)* Silhouette.

***Langan, Ruth, et al.** One Christmas Night: Highland Christmas; A Wife for Christmas; Ian's Gift. (Historical Ser.). 304p. 1999. mass mkt. 4.99 *(0-373-29087-X*, Harlequin) Harlequin Bks.

Langan, Ruth, jt. auth. see Coffman, Elaine.

Langan, Ruth, jt. auth. see Potter, Patricia.

Langan, Ruth R. Addy Starr. 352p. 1992. 19.00 *(0-7278-4370-2)* Severn Hse.

— Angel. 1994. per. 3.99 *(0-373-28845-X*, 1-28845-5) Harlequin Bks.

— Deception. (Historical Ser.). 1993. per. 3.99 *(0-373-28796-8*, 1-28796-0) Harlequin Bks.

— Diamond. LC 96-7294. (Historical Ser.). 296p. 1996. per. 4.50 *(0-373-28905-7*, 1-28905-7) Harlequin Bks.

— Dulcie's Gift. (Harlequin Historical Ser.: No. 324). 276p. 1996. per. 4.99 *(0-373-28924-3*, 1-28924-8) Harlequin Bks.

— Highland Heart. (Historical Ser.: No. 711). 1992. mass mkt. 3.99 *(0-373-28711-9*, 1-28711-9) Harlequin Bks.

— Highland Heaven. LC 95-13551. (Historical Ser.). 299p. 1995. per. 4.50 *(0-373-28869-7*, 1-28869-5) Harlequin Bks.

— The Highlander. (Historical Ser.). 1994. per. 3.99 *(0-373-28828-X*, 1-28828-1) Harlequin Bks.

— Jade. (Historical Ser.). 1997. per. 4.99 *(0-373-28952-9*, 1-28952-9) Harlequin Bks.

— Pearl. (Historical Ser.). 1996. per. 4.99 *(0-373-28929-4*, 1-28929-7) Harlequin Bks.

— Texas Hero. (Historical Ser.). 1993. mass mkt. 3.99 *(0-373-28780-1*, 1-28780-4) Harlequin Bks.

— To Love a Dreamer. (Men Made in America Ser.). 1995. mass mkt. 3.59 *(0-373-45192-X*, 1-45192-1) Harlequin Bks.

***Langan, Simon J.** The Impact of Nitrogen Deposition on Natural & Semi-Natural Ecosystems. LC 99-29975. (Environmental Pollution Ser.). 256p. 1999. 118.00 *(0-412-81040-9*, Kluwer Plenum) Kluwer Academic.

Langan, Thomas. Being & Truth. 424p. (C). 1996. text 39.95 *(0-8262-1053-8)* U of Mo Pr.

— The Catholic Tradition. LC 98-27053. 544p. 1998. 34.95 *(0-8262-1183-6)* U of Mo Pr.

— The Meaning of Heidegger: A Critical Study of an Existentialist Phenomenology. LC 83-12737. 247p. (C). 1983. reprint ed. lib. bdg. 55.00 *(0-313-24124-4*, LAMH, Greenwood Pr) Greenwood.

— Surviving the Age of Virtual Reality. 200p. 2000. 29.95 *(0-8262-1252-2)* U of Mo Pr.

— Tradition & Authenticity in the Search for Ecumenic Wisdom. 256p. (C). 1992. text 34.95 *(0-8262-0800-2)* U of Mo Pr.

Langan, Thomas D. The Meaning of Heidegger. LC 59-9976. 258p. (C). reprint ed. 80.00 *(0-8357-9067-3*, 200611400061) Bks Demand.

Langanke, K., et al, eds. Computational Nuclear Physics 1: Nuclear Structure. (Illus.). xii, 209p. 1991. text 74.95 incl. 5.25 hd *(0-387-53571-3)* Spr-Verlag.

— Computational Nuclear Physics 2. LC 92-37450. 216p. 1993. 98.95 *(0-387-97954-9)* Spr-Verlag.

Langari, Reza, jt. auth. see Yen, John.

Langbaine, Gerard. An Account of the English Dramatick Poets. 556p. 1968. reprint ed. write for info. *(0-318-71924-X)* G Olms Pubs.

— An Account of the English Dramatick Poets. (Anglistica & Americana Ser.: No. 9). 556p. 1968. reprint ed. 89.70 *(0-685-66488-0*, 05102000) G Olms Pubs.

— An Account of the English Dramatick Poets, 1691, 2 vols., Set. LC 92-22686. (Augustan Reprints Ser.: No. 5 (1971)). 1992. 75.00 *(0-404-70105-1)* AMS Pr.

— The Lives & Characters of the English Dramatic Poets. LC 70-144618. reprint ed. 49.50 *(0-404-02769-5)* AMS Pr.

— Momus Triumphans. LC 74-121838. reprint ed. 37.50 *(0-404-03873-5)* AMS Pr.

— Momus Triumphans: or The Plagiaries of the English Stage: Expos'd in a Catalogue of All the Comedies, Tragi- Comedies, Masques, Tragedies, Opera's, Pastorals, Interludes. LC 92-24820. (Augustan Reprints Ser.: No. 150). 1971. reprint ed. 14.50 *(0-404-70150-7*, PR625) AMS Pr.

— Momus Truimphans: The Plagiaries of the English Stage-Expos'd in a Catalogue. (English Stage Ser.: Vol. 19). 1974. lib. bdg. 61.00 *(0-8240-0602-X)* Garland.

Langbart, David A., jt. auth. see Haines, Gerald K.

Langbauer, Laurie. Novels of Everyday Life: The Series in English Fiction, 1850-1930. LC 98-39544. 304p. 1999. 47.50 *(0-8014-3497-1)*; pap. 18.95 *(0-8014-8501-0)* Cornell U Pr.

— Women & Romance: The Consolations of Gender in the English Novel. LC 90-55116. (Reading Women Writing Ser.). 288p. 1990. 42.50 *(0-8014-2421-6)*; pap. text 15.95 *(0-8014-9692-6)* Cornell U Pr.

Langbaum, Francesca L. & Husserl-Kapit, Susan, eds. Random House Essential French Dictionary. (FRE.). 1997. mass mkt. 3.99 *(0-345-41079-3)* Ballantine Pub Grp.

Langbaum, Robert. Isak Dinesen's Art: The Gayety of Vision. LC 74-23528. x, 310p. (C). 1992. pap. text 4.95 *(0-226-46871-2*, P628) U Ch Pr.

— The Mysteries of Identity: A Theme in Modern Literature. LC 81-21894. (Phoenix Ser.). 400p. (C). 1998. pap. text 14.95 *(0-226-46873-9)* U Ch Pr.

— The Poetry of Experience: The Dramatic Monologue in Modern Literary Tradition. LC 85-14861. 256p. 1996. reprint ed. pap. text 12.00 *(0-226-46872-0)* U Ch Pr.

— Thomas Hardy in Our Time. 256p. 1997. pap. 18.95 *(0-312-16409-2)* St Martin.

Langbaum, Robert, ed. Victorian Age: Essays in History & in Social & Literary Criticism. 3rd ed. 320p. (C). 1983. reprint ed. pap. 8.00 *(0-89733-055-2)* Academy Chi Pubs.

Langbaum, Robert W. The Word from Below: Essays on Modern Literature & Culture. LC 87-40140. 256p. reprint ed. pap. 79.40 *(0-608-09914-7*, 206925200003) Bks Demand.

Langbein & Wolk. Pension & Employee Benefit Law: 1998 Case Supplement. 2nd ed. 1998. write for info. *(1-56662-647-1)* Foundation Pr.

Langbein, D. Theory of Van der Waals Attraction. LC 25-9130. (Tracts in Modern Physics Ser.: Vol. 72). (Illus.). 150p. 1974. 58.95 *(0-387-06742-6)* Spr-Verlag.

Langbein, Hermann. Against All Hope: Resistance in the Nazi Concentration Camps, 1938-1945. LC 95-32401.Tr. of Nicht Wie Die Schafe Zur Schlachbank. 504p. 1996. pap. 19.95 *(0-8264-0940-7)* Continuum.

— Against All Hope: Resistance in the Nazi Concentration Camps, 1938-1945. Zohn, Henry, tr. from GER. LC 93-16247.Tr. of Nicht Wie Die Schafe Zur Schlachbank. 480p. 1993. 29.95 *(1-55778-363-2)* Paragon Hse.

— Nicht wie die Schafe zur Schlachtbank: Widerstand in den nationalsozialistischen Konzentrationslagern. (GER.). 1997. pap. 18.00 *(3-596-23486-7*, Pub. by Fischer Tasch) Intl Bk Import.

Langbein, John H. Prosecuting Crime in the Renaissance: England, Germany, France. LC 73-81670. (Studies in Legal History). (Illus.). 330p. reprint ed. pap. 102.30 *(0-7837-4165-0*, 205901300012) Bks Demand.

— Torture & the Law of Proof: Europe & England in the Ancien Regime. LC 76-58314. 1992. lib. bdg. 20.00 *(0-226-46806-2)* U Ch Pr.

Langbein, John H. & Waggoner, Lawrence W. Selected Statutes on Trusts & Estates. 851p. 1993. pap. text. write for info. *(1-56662-144-5)* Foundation Pr.

Langbein, John H. & Wolk, Bruce A. Pension & Employee Benefit Law. (University Casebook Ser.). 673p. 1990. text 37.95 *(0-88277-780-7)* Foundation Pr.

— Pension & Employee Benefit Law. 2nd ed. (Illus.). xlix, 923p. 1995. text 44.95 *(1-56662-243-3)* Foundation Pr.

— Pension & Employee Benefit Law: Teacher's Manual. (University Casebook Ser.). 202p. 1990. pap. text. write for info. *(0-88277-848-X)* Foundation Pr.

— Pension & Employee Benefit Law, 1994 Supplement. (University Textbook Ser.). 175p. 1994. 9.00 *(1-56662-203-4)* Foundation Pr.

— Pension & Employee Benefit Law, 1991 Supplement. 87p. (C). 1991. pap. text. write for info. *(0-318-68679-1)* Foundation Pr.

— Pension & Employee Benefit Law, 1997 Supplement. 2nd ed. (University Casebook Ser.). 83p. 1997. pap. text. write for info. *(1-56662-404-5)* Foundation Pr.

Langbein, John H., jt. auth. see Wolk, Bruce A.

Langbein, Laura I. & Lichtman, Allan J. Ecological Inference. LC 77-93283. (Quantitative Applications in the Social Sciences Ser.: Vol. 10). 70p. 1978. pap. 10.95 *(0-8039-0941-1)* Sage.

Langberg, Diane. Counseling Survivors of Sexual Abuse. LC 97-17267. 1997. 24.99 *(0-8423-0487-8)* Tyndale Hse.

Langberg, Diane Mandt. On the Threshold of Hope: Opening the Door to Hope & Healing for Survivors of Sexual Abuse. LC 98-48043. (AACC Counseling Library). 217p. 1999. pap. 10.99 *(0-8423-4362-8)* Tyndale Hse.

Langbort. Building Success in Math. 1985. pap. 17.25 *(0-534-03394-6)* Seymour Pubns.

Langbridge, R. Charlotte Bronte: A Psychological Study. LC 72-3280. (English Literature Ser.: No. 33). 1972. reprint ed. lib. bdg. 75.00 *(0-8383-1529-1)* M S G Haskell Hse.

***Langbroek, P. M. & Fabri, M., eds.** The Challenge of Change for European Judicial Systems: Developing a Public Administration Perspective. (International Institute of Administrative Sciences Monographs: Vol. 14). 250p. 2000. 67.00 *(1-58603-062-0)* IOS Press.

***Langdale, Jonathan.** Professional SQL Server 2000 XML. 800p. 2000. pap. 49.99 *(1-86100-446-X)* Wrox Pr Inc.

Langdell, C. C. A Selection of Cases on the Law of Contracts: With References & Citations. LC 99-28293. 1999. 120.00 *(1-58477-001-5)* Lawbk Exchange.

— Summary of Equity Pleading. 2nd ed. LC 98-23666. xvi, 282p. 1998. reprint ed. 45.00 *(0-8377-2420-1*, Rothman) W S Hein.

— Summary of the Law of Contracts. 2nd ed. xiv, 278p. 1980. reprint ed. 32.50 *(0-8377-0809-5*, Rothman) W S Hein.

***Langdo, Bryan.** Jake. 2002. text 15.95 *(0-8050-6494-X)* St Martin.

Langdon. Malignent Tumor. 1995. 85.00 *(0-340-44794-X*, Pub. by E A) Routldge.

Langdon, jt. ed. see Davis.

Langdon, jt. ed. see Patel.

Langdon, A. B., jt. auth. see Birdsall, C. K.

Langdon, Agnes, jt. auth. see Hoffmann, Dirk.

Langdon, Agnes D., jt. ed. see Guilloton, Doris S.

Langdon, Anthony, jt. auth. see Dunbar, Ian.

Langdon, Arthur G. Old Cornish Crosses. 1977. lib. bdg. 134.95 *(0-8490-2367-X)* Gordon Pr.

Langdon, Barbara T. The Melungeons: An Annotated Bibliography: References in Both Fiction & Nonfiction. large type ed. 70p. 1998. pap. 8.00 *(1-887745-10-6)* Dogwood TX.

Langdon, Betty. The Lion Who Lost His Roar. 51p. 1969. pap. 3.25 *(0-87129-980-1*, L24) Dramatic Pub.

Langdon-Brown, Walter. Thus We Are Men. LC 79-86768. (Essay Index Reprint Ser.). 1977. 23.95 *(0-8369-1148-2)* Ayer.

Langdon, Charlie. The Dandelion Vote: 50 Poems & a Fable. 80p. 1997. pap. 12.95 *(0-9654553-0-0)* Hilton Pub.

Langdon-Dahm, Martha. Trade Secrets: Twenty-Five Proven Success Tools for Working, Dealing & Winning with People. LC 85-82343. 211p. (Orig.). 1986. pap. 14.95 *(0-936585-00-5)* Learn Deve.

Langdon, Danny G. The Adjunct Study Guide. LC 77-25457. (Instructional Design Library). (Illus.). 100p. 1978. 27.95 *(0-87778-105-2)* Educ Tech Pubns.

— The Audio Workbook. LC 77-25109. (Instructional Design Library). (Illus.). 80p. 1978. 27.95 *(0-87778-109-5)* Educ Tech Pubns.

— The Construct Lesson Plan: Improving Group Instruction. LC 77-25406. (Instructional Design Library). (Illus.). 96p. 1978. 27.95 *(0-87778-111-7)* Educ Tech Pubns.

— Interactive Instructional Designs for Individualized Learning. LC 72-89577. 176p. 1973. pap. 24.95 *(0-87778-041-2)* Educ Tech Pubns.

— Leveraging the Language of Work: Improving the Performance of People, Systems, & Organizations. LC 99-6755. 304p. 1999. 44.95 *(0-7879-4736-9)* Jossey-Bass.

Langdon, Danny G., et al, eds. Intervention Resource Guide: 50 Performance Technology Tools. LC 98-39590. xiii, 402 p. 1999. 59.95 *(0-7879-4401-7)* Jossey-Bass.

Langdon, Danny G., ed. see Alden, Jay.

Langdon, Danny G., ed. see Broadwell, Martin M.

Langdon, Danny G., ed. see Bullock, Donald H.

Langdon, Danny G., ed. see Caskey, Owen L.

Langdon, Danny G., ed. see DeVries, David L., et al.

Langdon, Danny G., ed. see Dormant, Diane.

Langdon, Danny G., ed. see Endsley, William R.

Langdon, Danny G., ed. see Esbensen, Thorwald.

Langdon, Danny G., ed. see Feldhusen, John F.

Langdon, Danny G., ed. see Godfrey, Robert C.

Langdon, Danny G., ed. see Horabin, Ivan & Lewis, Brian.

Langdon, Danny G., ed. see Kapfer, Philip G. & Kapfer, Miriam B.

Langdon, Danny G., ed. see Lauridsen, David.

Langdon, Danny G., ed. see Merrill, M. David, et al.

Langdon, Danny G., ed. see Norton, Margaret, et al.

Langdon, Danny G., ed. see Parker, Lorne A. & Monson, Mavis K.

Langdon, Danny G., ed. see Rahmlow, Harold F.

Langdon, Danny G., ed. see Rahmlow, Harold F., et al.

Langdon, Danny G., ed. see Russell, James D.

Langdon, Danny G., ed. see Sherman, J. Gilmour & Ruskin, Robert S.

Langdon, Danny G., ed. see Sherman, Thomas M.

Langdon, Danny G., ed. see Stolovitch, Harold D.

Langdon, Danny G., ed. see Stolovitch, Harold D. & Thiagarajan, Sivasailam.

Langdon, Danny G., ed. see Thiagarajan, Sivasailam.

Langdon, Danny G., ed. see Thiagarajan, Sivasailam & Stolovitch, Harold D.

Langdon, Danny G., ed. see Von Harrison, Grant & Guymon, Ronald E.

Langdon, Danny G., ed. see Wales, Charles E. & Stager, Robert A.

Langdon, Danny G., ed. see Wohlking, Wallace & Gill, Patricia J.

Langdon, Danny G., ed. see Wydra, Frank T.

Langdon-Davies, J. Air Raid. LC 74-16278. (World History Ser.: No. 48). 1974. lib. bdg. 75.00 *(0-8383-1839-8)* M S G Haskell Hse.

Langdon-Davies, John. Seeds of Life. 1955. 12.95 *(0-8159-6808-6)* Devin.

Langdon-Davies, John, compiled by. The Plague & Fire of London. 39.00 *(1-56696-079-7)* Jackdaw.

Langdon-Davies, John, ed. James Watt & Steam Power. 39.00 *(1-56696-073-8)* Jackdaw.

— Magna Carta. 39.00 *(1-56696-062-2)* Jackdaw.

— The Slave Trade & Its Abolition. 39.00 *(1-56696-090-8)* Jackdaw.

— The Spanish Inquisition. 39.00 *(1-56696-010-X)* Jackdaw.

— Young Shakespeare. 39.00 *(1-56696-139-4)* Jackdaw.

Langdon, Davis & Everest Staff & Means, R.S. Staff. European Construction Costs Handbook. 1995. 150.00 *(0-87629-415-8*, 67300) R S Means.

Langdon, Davis, Seah International Staff, ed. Asia-Pacific Construction Costs Handbook. 2nd ed. 1997. 150.00 *(0-87629-459-X*, 67305A) R S Means.

Langdon, E. Jean & Baer, Gerhard, eds. Portals of Power: Shamanism in South America. LC 91-42609. (Illus.). 360p. 1992. reprint ed. pap. 111.60 *(0-608-04135-1*, 206486800011) Bks Demand.

Langdon, Emma F. Cripple Creek Strike: A History of Industrial Wars in Colorado 1903-4-5. LC 75-90402. (Mass Violence in America Ser.). (Illus.). 1975. reprint ed. 46.95 *(0-405-01322-1)* Ayer.

Langdon, Frank, jt. ed. see Akaha, Tsuneo.

Langdon, George D. Pilgrim Colony: A History of New Plymouth, 1620-1691. LC 66-21526. (Yale Publications in American Studies: No. 12). 268p. reprint ed. pap. 83.10 *(0-8357-8268-9*, 203379600087) Bks Demand.

Langdon, Glen G., Jr. Computer Design. LC 81-71785. (Illus.). 577p. (C). 1982. 39.00 *(0-9607864-0-6)* Computeach.

Langdon, Harry. Children Celebrate: 39 Plays for Feasts. 87p. 1993. pap. 7.95 *(0-86716-165-5)* St Anthony Mess Pr.

***Langdon, Helen.** Art Galleries of the World. 2nd ed. (Illus.). 2000. pap. 19.95 *(1-873429-41-X)* Pallas Athene.

— Caravaggio: A Life. LC 98-51195. (Illus.). 432p. 1999. mass mkt. 30.00 *(0-374-11894-9)* FS&G.

— Caravaggio: A Life. 448p. 2000. pap. 17.00 *(0-8133-3794-1)* Westview.

Langdon, Helen. Holbein. (Color Library). (Illus.). 128p. (C). 1994. pap. 14.95 *(0-7148-2867-X*, Pub. by Phaidon Press) Phaidon Pr.

Langdon, Helen, jt. ed. see Chard, Chloe.

Langdon, Henrette W. Hispanic Children & Adults with Communication Disorders: Assessment & Intervention. LC 91-42491. (Excellence in Practice Ser.). 450p. 1992. 61.00 *(0-8342-0288-3)* Aspen Pub.

Langdon, Ida. Milton's Theory of Poetry & Fine Art: And Essay. (BCL1-PR English Literature Ser.). 342p. 1992. reprint ed. lib. bdg. 89.00 *(0-7812-7385-4)* Rprt Serv.

Langdon, J. D. & Henk, J. M., eds. Malignant Tumours of the Mouth, Jaw & Salivary Glands. 288p. 1995. text 145.00 *(0-340-55794-X*, Pub. by E A) OUP.

Langdon, J. H. Functional Morphology of the Miocene Hominoid Foot. (Contributions to Primatology Ser.: Vol. 22). (Illus.). x, 226p. 1986. 85.25 *(3-8055-4258-5)* S Karger.

Langdon, J. Kenneth. A Spy in My House. 136p. 1987. pap. 5.95 *(0-86492-065-2*, Pub. by Goose Ln Edits) Genl Dist Srvs.

Langdon, John. Wordplay: Ambigrams & Reflections on the Art of Ambigrams. 1992. 18.95 *(0-15-198454-9)* Harcourt.

Langdon, John, jt. ed. see Astill, Grenville.

Langdon, John E. Canadian Silversmiths, 1700-1900. (Illus.). 270p. 1998. reprint ed. 95.00 *(1-55660-288-X)* A Wofsy Fine Arts.

Langdon, John H. Human Dissection for the Health Sciences. LC 93-1842. (Spiral Manual Ser.). 336p. 1993. spiral bd. 34.95 *(0-316-51394-6)* Lppncott W & W.

Langdon, John S. Byzantium's Last Imperial Offensive in Asia Minor: The Documentary Evidence for & Hagiographical Lore about John III Ducas Vatatzes's

L

An Asterisk (*) at the beginning of an entry indicates that the title is appearing for the first time.

Crusade Against the Turks, 1222 or 1225 to 1231. (Hellenism: Ancient, Mediaeval, Modern Ser.: No. 7). (Illus.). 172p. 1992. text 45.00 (*0-89241-497-9*) Caratzas.

Langdon, John S., et al, eds. To Hellenikon, Studies in Honor of Speros Vryonis, Jr., 2 vols., Set. 1018p. 1993. lib. bdg. 140.00 (*0-89241-504-5*) Caratzas.

— To Hellenikon, Studies in Honor of Speros Vryonis, Jr. Vol. I: Hellenic Antiquity & Byzantium. 474p. 1993. lib. bdg. 75.00 (*0-89241-512-6*) Caratzas.

Langdon, John W., jt. auth. see Judge, Edward H.

Langdon, Ken. Key Accounts Are Different: Solution Selling for Key Account Managers. 320p. 1995. pap. text 19.95 (*0-273-61780-X*) F T P-H.

Langdon, Ken & Bonham, Alan. Building a Value Portfolio: Learn to Uncover the Hidden Value of Shares. LC 98-150640. 287p. 1997. pap. 62.50 (*0-273-63029-6*, Pub. by F T P-H) Trans-Atl Phila.

Langdon, Ken & Bruce, Andrew. Creating a Market-Sensitive Culture: Anticipate Change, Act Fast, Do It Today. (Millennium Manager Ser.). (Illus.). 338p. (Orig.). 1997. pap. 54.50 (*0-273-62631-0*, Pub. by Pitman Pub) Trans-Atl Phila.

Langdon, Margaret. Comparative Hokan-Coahuiltecan Studies. LC 72-94480. (Janua Linguarum, Ser. Critica: No. 4). (Illus.). 114p. 1974. pap. text 58.50 (*90-279-2717-0*) Mouton.

Langdon, Margaret, ed. Papers from the 1990 Hokan-Penutian Languages Workshop, Held at University of California, San Diego, June 22-23, 1990. (Occasional Papers on Linguistics: No. 15). 201p. 1990. reprint ed. pap. text 21.25 (*1-55567-482-8*) Coyote Press.

Langdon, Margaret & Silver, Shirley. American Indian & Indoeuropean Studies: Papers in Honor of Madison S. Beeler. Klar, Kathryn et al, eds. (Trends in Linguistics, Studies & Monographs: No. 16). 495p. 1980. 103.85 (*90-279-7876-X*) Mouton.

Langdon, Margaret, ed. see Conference on Hokan Languages, San Diego, Californ.

Langdon, Mary Janine. When Meme Came to Live at My House. (Illus.). 25p. (J). 1997. pap. 5.00 (*0-9671688-0-5*) MJ Langdon.

Langdon, Merle K. A Sanctuary of Zeus on Mount Hymettos. LC 76-16777. (Hesperia Supplement Ser.: No. 16). (Illus.). xi, 118p. 1976. pap. 15.00 (*0-87661-516-7*) Am Sch Athens.

Langdon, Nigel. Diana with Love. 1998. 7.95 (*1-85304-979-4*) Assoc Pubs Grp.

Langdon, Nigel & Snape, Charles. A Way with Maths. 48p. 1985. pap. 14.95 (*0-521-27833-3*) Cambridge U Pr.

Langdon, Philip. A Better Place to Live: Reshaping the American Suburb. LC 93-42348. (Illus.). 288p. 1997. pap. 18.95 (*1-55849-106-6*) U of Mass Pr.

Langdon, Philip, jt. auth. see Thomas, Steve.

Langdon, Richard & Rothwell, Roy G., eds. Design & Innovation: Policy & Management. LC 85-26109. 220p. 1986. text 29.95 (*0-312-19448-X*) St Martin.

Langdon, Robert & Tryon, Darrell T. The Language of Easter Island: Its Development & Eastern Polynesian Relationships. (Polynesian Studies: No. 4). 88p. (C). 1983. pap. text 6.95 (*0-939154-32-3*) Inst Polynesian.

Langdon, S. Babylonian Menologies & the Semitic Calendars. (British Academy, London, Schweich Lectures on Biblical Archaeology Series, 1930). 1972. reprint ed. pap. 25.00 (*0-8115-1275-4*) Periodicals Srv.

Langdon, Samuel, tr. Hymn to Ishtar As Venus & Idin-Dagan As Tammuz. 1993. pap. 5.95 (*1-55818-201-2*) Holmes Pub.

Langdon, Simon P., et al, eds. Biology of Female Cancers. LC 96-34494. 320p. 1997. lib. bdg. 139.95 (*0-8493-9443-0*) CRC Pr.

Langdon, Stephen H. Babylonian Liturgies. LC 78-72746. (Ancient Mesopotamian Texts & Studies). (Illus.). reprint ed. 37.50 (*0-404-18191-0*) AMS Pr.

— Babylonian Menologies & the Semitic Calendars. LC 78-72744. (Ancient Mesopotamian Texts & Studies). reprint ed. 32.50 (*0-404-18192-9*) AMS Pr.

— Babylonian Wisdom. 1976. lib. bdg. 34.95 (*0-8490-1468-9*) Gordon Pr.

— Sumerian Grammatical Texts. LC 17-16093. (University of Pennsylvania, the University Museum, Publications of the Babylonian Section: Vol. 12, No. 1). 103p. reprint ed. pap. 32.00 (*0-608-13636-0*, 205202800026) Bks Demand.

— Sumerian Liturgical Texts. LC 17-16092. (University of Pennsylvania, the University Museum, Publications of the Babylonian Section: Vol. 10, No. 2). 163p. reprint ed. pap. 50.60 (*0-608-13637-9*, 205202600027) Bks Demand.

— Tammuz & Ishtar. LC 78-72750. (Ancient Mesopotamian Texts & Studies). reprint ed. 34.50 (*0-404-18193-7*) AMS Pr.

Langdon, Steve J. The Native People of Alaska. 3rd rev. ed. Bovy, Edward, ed. (Illus.). 96p. (Orig.). 1994. pap. text 8.95 (*0-936425-17-2*) Greatland Graphics.

Langdon, Terence G., ed. Superplasticity in Advanced Materials: ICSAM-94. (Materials Science Forum Ser.: Vols. 170-172). (Illus.). 824p. (C). 1995. 258.00 (*0-87849-685-8*, Pub. by Trans T Pub) Enfield Pubs NH.

***Langdon, Thomas P. & Ruckstuhl, William J.** Financial Planning Applications. 2000. 68.00 (*1-57996-028-6*, Pub. by Amer College) Maple-Vail Bk.

Langdon, Thomas P. & Woltmann, Regina. The Descendants of Edward & Esther (Lalor) Greene of Stradbally Parish, Queens County, Ireland & Middletown, CT. (Illus.). 352p. 1997. 60.00 (*0-9656977-0-3*) T P Langdon.

Langdon, W. B. Genetic Programming & Data Structures: Genetic Programming + Data Structures = Automatic Programming! LC 98-3602. (Series in Engineering & Computer Science). 1998. 125.00 (*0-7923-8135-1*) Kluwer Academic.

Langdon, William C. Everyday Things in American Life, 2 vols. Incl. Vol. 1. Everyday Things, 1607-1676. 416p. 1981. 55.00 (*0-684-17415-4*); Vol. 2. Everyday Things, 1776-1876. (Illus.). 448p. 1981. 45.00 (*0-684-17416-2*); write for info. (*0-318-55713-4*) Macmillan.

— Everyday Things in American Life, 2 vols., Set. (BCL1 - U. S. History Ser.). 1991. reprint ed. lib. bdg. 150.00 (*0-7812-6003-5*) Rprt Serv.

Langdon, William G., Jr. Bits & Bitting Manual: Getting the Horse to Understand Man, the Bit, the Rein, & the Leg. LC 93-206482. (Illus.). 113p. 1989. spiral bd. 29.95 (*1-883714-03-6*) Langdon Ent.

— Bits, Patterns & Reining: Teaching Horses to Rein. LC 93-206517. (Illus.). 157p. 1990. spiral bd. 29.95 (*1-883714-04-4*) Langdon Ent.

— Fouler. LC 93-206461. (Illus.). 80p. 1992. spiral bd. 29.95 (*1-883714-02-8*) Langdon Ent.

— Polo a Way of Life. LC 93-206495. (Illus.). 219p. 1964. spiral bd. 29.95 (*1-883714-00-1*) Langdon Ent.

— Ride Right: An Informative Training Manual for the Serious Rider That Wants to Improve. LC 93-91892. (Illus.). 122p. 1993. spiral bd. 29.95 (*1-883714-06-0*) Langdon Ent.

— Saddle Fitting: How to Select the Right Saddle to Fit You & Your Horse. LC 96-94587. (Illus.). 116p. 1997. spiral bd. 29.95 (*1-883714-07-9*) Langdon Ent.

— Team Play Polo. LC 93-206527. (Illus.). 128p. 1985. spiral bd. 29.95 (*1-883714-01-X*) Langdon Ent.

— Training with Bits: Bitting Techniques to Make Training Understandable for the Horse. LC 93-199250. (Illus.). 100p. (Orig.). 1992. spiral bd. 29.95 (*1-883714-05-2*) Langdon Ent.

Lange. Design Dimensioning with Computer Graphics Applications. (Mechanical Engineering Ser.: Vol. 31). (Illus.). 344p. 1984. text 99.75 (*0-8247-7119-2*) Dekker.

— Evidence Dismissed. 1997. mass mkt. 6.99 (*0-671-01938-4*) PB.

— Sorrows Young Werther* 13* 177p. (C). 1949. pap. text 26.50 (*0-03-008900-X*, Pub. by Harcourt Coll Pubs) Harcourt.

***Lange, et al.** Mathematics with Business Applications. rev. ed. 1998. student ed. 39.00 (*0-02-814730-8*) Glencoe.

— Mathematics with Business Applications: Teacher's Wraparound Edition. 1998. teacher ed. 52.50 (*0-02-814731-6*) Glencoe.

Lange, A. H. Catechetical Review. 32p. (J). (gr. 4-12). 1968. pap. 1.00 (*0-570-03520-1*, 14-1102) Concordia.

Lange, Adriaan M. De, see De Lange, Adriaan M.

Lange, Adrianne. El Manual de la Super Mama. (SPA.). 224p. (Orig.). 1987. pap. 4.95 (*0-939193-11-6*) Edit Concepts.

Lange, Adrianne, ed. El Manual de la Mama Perfecta. deluxe ed. (SPA., Illus.). 192p. 1999. pap. 5.95 (*0-939193-37-X*) Edit Concepts.

— Problemas Sexuales de la Mujer. deluxe ed. (SPA., Illus.). 192p. 1999. pap. 5.95 (*0-939193-47-7*) Edit Concepts.

Lange-Akhund, Madine. Macedonian Question: 1893-1908. LC 97-74978. 320p. 1997. lib. bdg. 45.00 (*0-88033-383-9*, 486, Pub. by East Eur Monographs) Col U Pr.

***Lange, Alan.** Intermediate Internet Sales Skills: A4, Version 2.07. McKenna, Jill, ed. (CIW Foundations Track A4 Ser.). (Illus.). 1999. pap. write for info. (*1-58143-065-5*) Prosoft I-net.

— Intermediate Internet Sales Skills: Version 2.07. McKenna, Jill, ed. (CIW Foundations Track Ser.). (Illus.). 1999. pap. write for info. (*1-58143-068-X*) Prosoft I-net.

***Lange, Alan & Lane, Susan M.** Basic Internet Sales Skills: A4, Version 2.07. McKenna, Jill, ed. (CIW Foundations Track A4 Ser.). (Illus.). 1999. pap. write for info. (*1-58143-063-9*) Prosoft I-net.

— Basic Internet Sales Skills: Version 2.07. McKenna, Jill, ed. (CIW Foundations Track Ser.). (Illus.). 1999. pap. write for info. (*1-58143-066-3*) Prosoft I-net.

***Lange, Alexandra.** Zur Differenzierung marktwirtschaftlicher Systeme. 2000. 63.95 (*3-631-35835-0*) P Lang Pubng.

Lange Andersen, K., et al. Habitual Physical Activity & Health. (WHO Regional Publications, European Ser.: No. 6). 188p. 1978. 25.00 (*92-9020-106-1*, 1310006) World Health.

Lange, Andre & Soudart, S. A. Treatise on Cryptography: With Problems in French. 181p. 1981. pap. 26.80 (*0-89412-055-7*) Aegean Park Pr.

Lange, Armin. Computer Aided Text-Reconstruction & Transcription: CATT-Manual. (Illus.). 160p. (Orig.). 1993. pap. 47.50 (*3-16-146149-5*, Pub. by JCB Mohr) Coronet Bks.

— Weisheit und Pradestination: Weisheitliche Urordnung und Pradestination in den Textfunden von Qumran. (Studies on the Texts of the Desert of Judah: No. 18). (GER., Illus.). xii, 345p. 1995. 128.00 (*90-04-10432-1*) Brill Academic Pubs.

— Weisheit und Torheit Bei Kohelet und in Seiner Umwelt: Eine Untersuchung Ihrer Theologischen Implikationen. (Europaische Hochschulschriften Ser.: Reihe 23, Bd. 433). (GER.). VI, 202p. 1991. 43.80 (*3-631-43889-3*) P Lang Pubng.

Lange, Art. Evidence. LC 81-11377. 1981. pap. 3.50 (*0-916328-15-5*) Yellow Pr.

Lange, Art & Mackey, Nathaniel, eds. Moment's Notice: Jazz in Poetry & Prose. LC 93-10151. 370p. (YA). (gr. 11-12). 1993. pap. 17.50 (*1-56689-001-2*, Pub. by Coffee Hse) SPD-Small Pr Dist.

Lange, Arthur J. & Jakubowski, Patricia. Responsible Assertive Behavior: Cognitive-Behavioral Procedures for Trainers. LC 76-1703. 348p. (Orig.). 1976. pap. text 24.95 (*0-87822-174-3*, 1743) Res Press.

Lange, Arthur J., jt. auth. see Ellis, Albert.

Lange, Arthur J., jt. auth. see Jakubowski, Patricia.

Lange, Axel. Von der Fortschreitenden Freiheit Eines Christenmenschen: Glaube und Moderne Welt Bei Karl Gottlieb Bretschneider. (Kontexte Ser.: Bd. 15). (GER., Illus.). 206p. 1994. 37.95 (*3-631-47898-4*) P Lang Pubng.

Lange-Bertalog, H. & Krammer, Kurt. Achnanthes: Eine Monographie der Gattung mit Definition der Gattung Cocconeis und Nachtraegen zu den Naviculaceae. (Bibliotheca Diatomologica Ser.: Vol. 18). (GER., Illus.). iv, 393p. 1989. lib. bdg. 130.00 (*3-443-57009-7*, Pub. by Gebruder Borntraeger) Balogh.

— Bacillariaceae, Epithemiaceae, Surirellaceae: Neue und Wenig Bekannte Taxa, Neue Kombinationen und Synonyme Sowie Bemerkungen und Ergaenzungen zu den Naviculaceae. (Bibliotheca Diatomologica Ser.: Vol. 15). (GER., Illus.). ii, 289p. 1987. lib. bdg. 83.00 (*3-443-57006-2*, Pub. by Gebruder Borntraeger) Balogh.

Lange-Bertalot & Metzelin, Ditmar. Iconographia Diatomologica Vol. 2: Annotated Diatom Micrographs. (Illus.). 390p. 1996. 185.00 (*3-87429-386-6*, Pub. by Koeltz Sci Bks) Lubrecht & Cramer.

Lange-Bertalot, H. & Kramer, Kurt. Naviculaceae, Neue und Wenig Bekannte Taxa, neue Kombinationan und Synonymer sowie Bemerkungen zu Einigen Gattungen. (Bibliotheca Diamatologica Ser.: No. 9). (Illus.). 250p. 1985. lib. bdg. 78.25 (*3-7682-1437-0*) Lubrecht & Cramer.

Lange-Bertalot, H. & Krammer, Kurt. Suesswasserflora von Mitteleuropa Band 2\1: Bacillariophyceae: Naviculaceae. Pascher, A., ed. (Illus.). 876p. 1997. reprint ed. lib. bdg. 161.00 (*3-437-35396-9*) Balogh.

— Suesswasserflora von Mitteleuropa Vol. 2, Pt. 1: Bacillariophyceae Pt. 1: Naviculaceae. Pascher, A., ed. (GER., Illus.). 876p. 1986. lib. bdg. 143.00 (*3-437-30403-8*, Pub. by Gustav Fischer) Balogh.

Lange-Bertalot, H. & Moser, Gert. Brachysira-Monographie der Gattung, Vol. 29. (Bibliotheca Diatomologica Ser.: Band 29). (GER., Illus.). iv, 212p. 1994. lib. bdg. 89.00 (*3-443-57020-8*, Pub. by Gebruder Borntraeger) Balogh.

Lange-Bertalot, H., ed. see Cumming, B. F., et al.

Lange, Bertalot H., ed. see Krammer, Kurt.

Lange-Bertalot, H., ed. see Pascher, A.

Lange-Bertalot, Horst. 85 New Taxa & Much More Than 100 Taxonomic Clarifications Supplementary to Suesswasserflora von Mitteleuropa, 2 vols. in 1, Vol. 2, Pts. 1-4. (Bibliotheca Diatomologica Ser.: Vol. 27). (GER., Illus.). xxiii, 454p. 1993. lib. bdg. 142.00 (*3-443-57018-6*, Pub. by Gebruder Borntraeger) Balogh.

***Lange-Bertalot, Horst & Genkal, S. I.** Iconographia Diatomologica: Annotated Distom Micrographs: Phytogeography-Diversity-Taxonomy Diatoms from Siberia, 6. (Iconographia Diatomologica: 6). (Illus.). 295p. 1999. 145.00 (*3-904144-12-X*, Pub. by Gantner) Lubrecht & Cramer.

***Lange-Bertalot, Horst & Reichardt, Erwin.** Iconographia Diatomologica: Annotated Distom Micrographs: Taxonomy, 8. (Iconographia Diatomologica: 8). (GER., Illus.). 250p. 2000. 150.00 (*3-904144-15-4*, Pub. by Gantner) Lubrecht & Cramer.

Lange-Bertalot, Horst & Witkoski, Andrej. Iconographia Diatomologica: Annotated Distom Micrographs: Diversity-Taxonomy-Identification, 7. (Iconographia Diatomologica). (Illus.). 1000p. text 275.00 (*3-904144-10-3*, Pub. by Gantner) Lubrecht & Cramer.

Lange-Bertalot, Horst, et al. Iconographia Diatomologica Vol. 3: Annotated Diatom Micrographs: Taxa-Diatom Taxa Introduced by Georg Krasske. (Illus.). 358p. 1996. text 125.00 (*3-87429-389-0*, Pub. by Koeltz Sci Bks) Lubrecht & Cramer.

— Iconographia Diatomologica Vol. 4: Annotated Diatom Micrographs: Taxonomy. (Illus.). 286p. 1998. text 125.00 (*3-87429-392-0*, Pub. by Koeltz Sci Bks) Lubrecht & Cramer.

Lange-Bertalot, Horst, ed. see Metzeltin, Ditmar.

Lange, Brian M., et al. Dental Management of the Handicapped: Approaches for Dental Auxiliaries. LC 82-23939. 182p. reprint ed. pap. 56.50 (*0-7837-2852-2*, 205762000006) Bks Demand.

Lange, Charles E. The Humerus of the Long Arm of the Law. 103p. (C). 1989. 67.00 (*0-7223-2219-4*, Pub. by A H S Ltd) St Mut.

Lange, Charles H. & Riley, Carroll L. Bandelier: The Life & Adventures of Adolph Bandelier, American Archaeologist & Scientist. (Illus.). 304p. (C). 1996. 34.95 (*0-87480-499-X*) U of Utah Pr.

Lange, Charles H., ed. see Bandelier, Adolph F.

Lange, Dagmar. Untersuchungen zur Systematik und Taxonomie der Gattung Helictotrichon Besser ex J. A. Schultes & J. H. Schultes (Poaceae) in Sudosteuropa und Vorderasien. (Bibliotheca Botanica: Vol. 144). (GER., Illus.). iv, 238p. 1995. 99.00 (*3-510-48015-5*, Pub. by E Schweizerbartsche) Balogh.

Lange, Dale L. Foreign Language Education: A Reappraisal. (ACTFL Review Ser.: Vol. 4). 1995. pap. 21.25 (*0-8442-9347-4*, Natl Textbk Co) NTC Contemp Pub Co.

Lange, Danny. Programming & Deploying Mobile Agents with Java Aglets. LC 98-20525. 256p. (C). 1998. pap. text 37.95 (*0-201-32582-9*) Addison-Wesley.

Lange, David W. The Complete Guide to Buffalo Nickels. (Illus.). 130p. (Orig.). pap. 25.00 (*1-880731-14-2*) S J Durst.

— The Complete Guide to Lincoln Cents. (Illus.). 384p. (Orig.). 1996. pap. text 34.95 (*0-943161-67-3*) Bowers & Merena.

— The Complete Guide to Mercury Dimes. (Illus.). 180p. 1993. pap. 29.95 (*1-880731-77-0*) DLRC Pr.

Lange, Deborah, jt. auth. see Cook, Richard.

Lange, DeLane. Painting Decorative Heirlooms with DeLane Lange. LC 98-45644. (Illus.). 128p. 1999. pap. 23.99 (*0-89134-869-7*, North Lght Bks) F & W Pubns Inc.

Lange, Dieter & Born, Gary. The Extraterritorial Application of National Laws. LC 87-3300. 1987. 38.00 (*90-6544-306-1*) Kluwer Law Intl.

Lange, Dietz, ed. Religionen - Fundamentalismus - Politik: Vortrage Im Rahmen des Studium Generale der Georg-August-Universitat Gottingen Im Wintersemester, 1994-95. (GER.). 228p. 1996. 32.95 (*3-631-48842-4*) P Lang Pubng.

Lange, Dietz & Widmann, Peter, eds. Kirche Zwischen Heilsbotschaft und Lebenswirklichkeit: Festschrift Fur Theodor Jorgensen Zum 60. Geburtstag. (GER.). 286p. 1996. 37.95 (*3-631-49864-0*) P Lang Pubng.

Lange, Dorothea. Aperture Masters of Photography Series, Vol. 5. 1987. pap. 9.95 (*0-89381-260-9*) Aperture.

— Photographs of a Lifetime. (Illus.). 182p. 1996. 50.00 (*0-89381-657-4*) Aperture.

***Lange, Dorothea, photos by.** American Exodus: A Record of Human Erosion - Dorothea Lange & Paul Taylor. (Illus.). 196p. 2000. reprint ed. pap. 29.95 (*2-85893-513-0*, A20451, Pub. by J M Place Edits) Dist Art Pubs.

Lange, Dorothea, photos by. Dorothea Lange: Photographs of a Lifetime. (Monographs). (Illus.). 182p. 1998. pap. 44.95 (*0-89381-835-6*) Aperture.

Lange, Dorothea & Taylor, Paul S. An American Exodus: A Record of Human Erosion. LC 74-30641. (American Farmers & the Rise of Agribusiness Ser.). (Illus.). 1979. reprint ed. 23.95 (*0-405-06811-5*) Ayer.

Lange, Ed. Family Naturism in America. LC 87-30329. (Nudist Pictorial Classic Ser.). (Illus.). 100p. (Orig.). 1989. pap. 24.95 (*0-910550-54-9*) Events Unltd.

— Family Naturism in Europe. LC 88-6954. (Illus.). 1983. pap. 24.95 (*0-910550-20-4*) Events Unltd.

— Fun in the Sun. LC 95-37059. (Illus.). 1986. pap. 24.95 (*0-910550-51-4*) Events Unltd.

— N Is for Naked. Bancroft, Iris, ed. (Vintage Nudist Classics Ser.). (Illus.). 64p. (Orig.). 1995. pap. 21.95 (*1-55599-052-5*) Events Unltd.

— Nudist Magazines of the '50s & '60s, Bk. 3. Bancroft, Iris, ed. (Nudist Nostalgia Ser.). (Illus.). 100p. (C). 1994. 29.95 (*1-55599-050-9*) Events Unltd.

— Nudist Magazines of the '50s & '60s, Bk. 3. Bancroft, Iris, ed. (Nudist Nostalgia Ser.). (Illus.). 96p. (C). 1995. pap. 24.95 (*1-55599-051-7*) Events Unltd.

— Nudist Nudes. LC 91-9296. (Illus.). 1991. pap. 14.95 (*1-55599-043-6*) Events Unltd.

Lange, Ed, ed. Fun in the Sun Bk. 2: Nudist-Naturist Recreation. LC 90-49181. (Illus.). 64p. 1990. pap. 21.95 (*1-55599-036-3*) Elysium.

— Fun in the Sun Bk. 2: Nudist-Naturist Recreation. LC 90-49181. (Illus.). 64p. 1990. 26.95 (*1-55599-035-5*) Events Unltd.

— The Shameless Nude: A Historic Look at Nudism in the Sixties. LC 91-11562. (Illus.). 140p. 1991. 29.95 (*1-55599-037-1*) Elysium.

Lange, Ed & Sohler, Stan. Nudist Magazines of the '50s & '60s, Bk. 2. Bancroft, Iris, ed. (Nudist Nostalgia Ser.). (Illus.). 96p. 1993. 29.95 (*1-55599-047-9*); pap. 24.95 (*1-55599-048-7*) Events Unltd.

— Nudist Magazines of the '50s & '60s, Bk. 4. Bancroft, Iris & Moran, Chris, eds. (Illus.). 96p. 1996. 29.95 (*1-55599-053-3*); pap. 24.95 (*1-55599-054-1*) Events Unltd.

Lange, Ed, jt. auth. see Sohler, Stan.

Lange, Emma, et al. A Regency Valentine, Vol. 2. large type ed. (Nightingale Series Large Print Bks.). 296p. 1992. pap. 14.95 (*0-8161-5272-1*, G K Hall Lrg Type) Mac Lib Ref.

Lange, Ernst. And Yet It Moves: Dream & Reality in the Ecumenical Movement. Robertson, Edwin H., tr. LC BX0006.W775L. 181p. reprint ed. pap. 56.20 (*0-7837-5993-2*, 204580300008) Bks Demand.

Lange, Even, jt. ed. see Amdam, Rolv P.

Lange, F. G. Handbook of Safety & Accident Prevention. 1991. lib. bdg. 125.95 (*0-8490-4526-6*) Gordon Pr.

Lange, Frauke. Gehalt und Form von Moralitat bei Henry James. (Europaische Hochschulschriften, Reihe 14: Bd. 319). (GER.). 332p. 1996. 57.95 (*3-631-30704-7*) P Lang Pubng.

Lange, Frederick, et al. Yellow Jacket: A Four Corners Anasazi Ceremonial Center. rev. ed. LC 86-82465. (Illus.). 72p. (Orig.). 1986. pap. 5.95 (*1-55566-005-3*) Johnson Bks.

Lange, Frederick A. The History of Materialism: Criticism of Its Present Importance. LC 73-14163. (Perspectives in Social Inquiry Ser.). 380p. 1980. reprint ed. 30.95 (*0-405-05508-0*) Ayer.

Lange, Frederick W., ed. Precolumbian Jade: New Geological & Cultural Interpretations. LC 92-34099. (Illus.). 416p. (C). 1993. text 45.00 (*0-87480-393-4*) U of Utah Pr.

— Wealth & Hierarchy in the Intermediate Area. LC 90-43419. (Illus.). 476p. 1992. 36.00 (*0-88402-191-2*) Dumbarton Oaks.

Lange, Frederick W., et al. The Archaeology of Pacific Nicaragua. LC 90-23536. (Illus.). 345p. reprint ed. pap. 107.00 (*0-608-04111-4*, 206484300011) Bks Demand.

Lange, Frederick W., jt. auth. see Handler, Jerome S.

Lange, Frederick W., jt. ed. see Bishop, Ronald L.

Lange, Friedrich. J. S. Mill: 1866 Edition. 271p. 1996. reprint ed. 60.00 (*1-85506-360-3*) Bks Intl VA.

Lange, Friedrich & Geertz, Otto. Ubungen Zu Den Wichtigsten Kapiteln der Franzosischen Grammatik. (GER.). 60p. 1974. 5.90 (*3-296-60300-X*, Pub. by Weidmann); 5.90 (*3-296-60301-8*, Pub. by Weidmann) Lubrecht & Cramer.

Lange, Friedrich A. Die Arbeiterfrage in Ihrer Bedeutung fur Gegenwart und Zukenf Beleuchtet. (GER.). 196p. 1979. reprint ed. write for info. (*3-487-06716-1*) G Olms Pubs.

Lange, Gerald. Printing Digital Type on the Hand-Operated Flatbed Cylinder Press. 36p. 1999. pap. 20.00 (*0-931460-33-6*, Bieler Pr Monographs) Bieler.

***Lange, Gerald.** Red Crosse. (Illus.). 45p. 2000. 500.00 (*0-931460-32-8*) Bieler.

Lange, Gerald. Wild Parrots & the King of La Brea. (Illus.). 57p. 1998. 590.00 (*0-931460-31-X*) Bieler.

Lange, Gerda G. De, see Grubb, R. & De Lange, Gerda G., eds.

Lange, Glenn-Marie, jt. auth. see Duchin, Faye.

***Lange-Greve, Susanne.** August Sander, 1876-1964. Heiting, Manfred, ed. (Illus.). 251p. 1999. 39.99 (*3-8228-7179-6*) Taschen Amer.

Lange-Greve, Susanne. Die Kulturelle Bedeutung Von Literaturausstellungen. (Germanistische Texte und Studien: Vol. 49). (GER.). xii, 320p. 1995. write for info. (*3-487-09966-7*) G Olms Pubs.

Lange, H. & Birkenhake, C. Complex Tori. LC 99-32326. (Progress in Mathematics Ser.). 272p. 1999. 59.50 (*0-8176-4103-3*) Birkhauser.

Lange, H., jt. auth. see Birkenhake, Christina.

Lange, H., jt. ed. see Barth, W. P.

Lange, Harry De, see Goudzwaard, Bob & De Lange, Harry.

***Lange, Hartmut.** Missing Persons. 2000. write for info. (*1-902881-26-5*, Pub. by Toby Pr Ltd); pap. 15.95 (*1-902881-27-3*, Pub. by Toby Pr Ltd) Toby Pr.

Lange, Heiko, et al, eds. Working Across Cultures: Ethical Perspectives for Intercultural Management. LC 97-45501. (Issues in Business Ethics Ser.). 360p. 1998. text 147.00 (*0-7923-4700-5*) Kluwer Academic.

Lange, Helene. Higher Education of Women in Europe. 1977. lib. bdg. 59.95 (*0-8490-1949-4*) Gordon Pr.

Lange, Hellmuth, et al. Gas Geben? Umsteuern? Bremsen? Die Zukunft von Auto und Verkehr Aus der Sicht der Automobilarbeiter. Ergebnisse einer Reprasentativerhebung in der Autoindustrie und einer Parallelbefragung in Einem Stahlwerk. (GER., Illus.). 246p. 1995. 28.95 (*3-631-47877-1*) P Lang Pubng.

Lange, Herbert. Vox--Enciclopedia Cultural Tomo 8: Plantas. (SPA.). 210p. 1977. 49.95 (*0-7859-0903-6*, S-50501) Fr & Eur.

Lange, Herbert & Birkenhake, Christina. Complex Abelian Varieties. LC 92-23806. (Grundlehren der Mathematischen Wissenschaften Ser.: Vol. 302). 1992. 126.95 (*0-387-54747-9*) Spr-Verlag.

Lange, Horst H. Jazz in Deutschland - Die Deutsche Jazz-Chronik Bis, 1960. (GER., Illus.). 320p. 1996. write for info. (*3-487-08375-2*) G Olms Pubs.

Lange, J. Crime as Destiny: A Study of Criminal Twins. Haldane, Charlotte, tr. from GER. 200p. 1996. reprint ed. pap. 18.00 (*1-878465-21-X*) Scott-Townsend Pubs.

***Lange, J. & Siewert, J. Rhudiger, eds.** Esophageal Carcinoma: State of the Art. LC 99-56373. (Recent Results in Cancer Research Ser.: Vol. 155). (Illus.). 150p. 2000. 106.00 (*3-540-65323-6*) Spr-Verlag.

***Lange, Jack.** Search for the Dragon. LC 99-35367. 270p. 1999. pap. 14.95 (*1-58151-026-8*, Pub. by BookPartners) Midpt Trade.

Lange, Jaochim. Gesammelte Werke: Abteilung: Ergaenzungsreihe, Vol. 17. (Materialien und Dokumente Ser.). (GER.). 1282p. 1984. write for info. (*3-487-07451-6*) G Olms Pubs.

Lange, Jeffrey, jt. ed. see Coleman, Jules.

Lange, Jerome. Solving Mechanical Design Problems with Computer Graphics. (Mechanical Engineering Ser.: Vol. 48). (Illus.). 408p. 1986. text 160.00 (*0-8247-7479-5*) Dekker.

Lange, Jerome C. Kinematics: A Graphical Approach. LC 94-32547. (C). 1995. 58.60 (*0-13-125303-4*) P-H.

Lange, Joachim. Gesammelte Werke Bd. 23: Abteilung: Ergaenzungsreihe. (Materialien und Dokumente Ser.). (GER.). 310p. 1986. reprint ed. write for info. (*3-487-07805-8*) G Olms Pubs.

Lange, Joachim, jt. auth. see Walch, Johann G.

Lange, Joanni, jt. auth. see Willkomm, Mauritio.

Lange, Johannes. Crime & Destiny. Haldane, Charlotte, tr. from GER. (Historical Foundations of Forensic Psychiatry & Psychology Ser.). 250p. 1983. reprint ed. lib. bdg. 25.00 (*0-306-76209-9*) Da Capo.

Lange, John. Cognitivity Paradox: An Inquiry Concerning the Claims of Philosophy. LC 72-90952. 128p. 1970. pap. text 12.95 (*0-691-01967-3*, Pub. by Princeton U Pr) Cal Prin Full Svc.

— The Cognitivity Paradox: An Inquiry Concerning the Claims of Philosophy. LC 72-90952. 125p. 1970. reprint ed. pap. 38.80 (*0-608-03327-8*, 206403900008) Bks Demand.

Lange, Joseph K. How to Photograph Landscapes. LC 97-44031. (How to Photograph Ser.). (Illus.). 115p. 1998. pap. 19.95 (*0-8117-2456-5*) Stackpole.

***Lange, Joseph K.** Photographer's Guide to the Grand Canyon & Northern Arizona. LC 00-39491. (Illus.). 2001. pap. 14.95 (*0-8117-2901-X*) Stackpole.

— Photographer's Guide to Yellowstone & the Tetons. LC 99-43766. (Illus.). 128p. 2000. pap. 14.95 (*0-8117-2895-1*) Stackpole.

***Lange, K. Robert.** Surfactants: A Practical Handbook. LC 99-24733. 237p. 1999. write for info. (*1-56990-270-4*) Hanser-Gardner.

Lange, Karen, ed. see Detzler, Robert E.

Lange, Kelly. Gossip. LC 98-34221. 320p. 1998. 23.00 (*0-684-83263-1*) Simon & Schuster.

Lange, Kenneth. Mathematical & Statistical Methods for Genetic Analysis. LC 96-49533. (Statistics for Biology & Health Ser.). (Illus.). 288p. 1997. 54.95 (*0-387-94909-7*) Spr-Verlag.

— Numerical Analysis for Statisticians. Chambers, J. et al, eds. LC 98-16688. (Statistics & Computing Ser.). 360p. 1999. 69.95 (*0-387-94979-8*) Spr-Verlag.

Lange, Kinley. Allelu! 1.50 (*0-687-07085-6*) Abingdon.

Lange, Klaus. Dictionary for Construction Work Abroad, Contract, Planning, Design, German-English/English-German. (ENG & GER.). 740p. 1995. 150.00 (*0-7859-9882-9*) Fr & Eur.

— International Construction Contracts Terminology. (ENG, FRE & GER.). 131p. 1980. pap. 39.95 (*0-8288-0223-8*, M15022) Fr & Eur.

Lange, Kofi R., tr. see Christaller, J. G.

Lange-Kowal, Ernst E. Langenscheidt French-German Dictionary: Langenscheidt Handwoerterbuch Franzoesisch-Deutsch. 12th ed. (FRE & GER.). 640p. 1982. 59.95 (*0-8288-0341-2*, M6155) Fr & Eur.

— Langenscheidt French-German, German-French Pocket Dictionary: Langenscheidt Taschenwoerterbuch Franzoesisch-Deutsch-Franzoesisch. (FRE & GER.). 1216p. 1982. 39.95 (*0-8288-0343-9*, M8010) Fr & Eur.

— Langenscheidt French-German Pocket Dictionary: Langenscheidt Taschenwoerterbuch Franzoesisch-Deutsch. (FRE & GER.). 575p. 1982. 24.95 (*0-8288-0344-7*, M8220) Fr & Eur.

— Langenscheidt German-French, French-German Dictionary: Langenscheidt Handwoerterbuch Franzoesisch-Deutsch-Franzoesisch. 14th ed. (FRE & GER.). 1314p. 1983. 85.00 (*0-8288-0342-0*, M15629) Fr & Eur.

Lange-Kowal, Ernst E., jt. auth. see Larousse Staff.

Lange-Kuettner, Christiane & Thomas, Glyn. Drawing & Cooking. 288p. (C). 1995. pap. text 38.00 (*0-13-342882-6*) P-H.

Lange, Kurt. Handbook of Metal Forming. LC 83-19897. 1176p. 1995. 131.00 (*0-87263-457-4*) SME.

***Lange, L. J., et al.** Continued Fractions: From Analytic Number Theory to Constructive Approximation: A Volume in Honor of L. J. Lange: Continued Fractions, from Analytic Number Theory to Constructive Approximation, May 20-23, 1998, University of Missouri. LC 99-30750. (Contemporary Mathematics Ser.). 1999. write for info. (*0-8218-1200-9*) Am Math.

Lange, Louise, tr. see Toeplitz, Otto.

Lange, Ludwig. Romiscshe Alterthumer, 3 vols. xxxvi, 2366p. 1974. reprint ed. write for info. (*3-487-05235-0*) G Olms Pubs.

Lange, Lyle W. Church & State. 43p. (Orig.). 1986. pap. 4.00 (*0-8100-0246-9*, 22N0798) Northwest Pub.

— Outline of the Book of Concord. LC 94-67906. 136p. 1994. 19.99 (*0-8100-0538-7*, 15N2047) Northwest Pub.

***Lange, Lyle W.** Sanctification: Alive in Christ. (People's Bible Teachings Ser.). 206p. 1999. pap. 9.99 (*0-8100-0614-6*) Northwest Pub.

— Sanctification: Bible Study. (People's Bible Teachings Ser.). 1999. 37.99 (*0-8100-0987-0*) Northwest Pub.

Lange, Lyle W., ed. Our Great Heritage, Vol. 1. LC 90-63693. 608p. 1991. 36.99 (*0-8100-0371-6*, 15N0481) Northwest Pub.

— Our Great Heritage, Vol. 2. LC 90-63693. 640p. 1991. 36.99 (*0-8100-0378-3*, 15N0482) Northwest Pub.

— Our Great Heritage, Vol. 3. LC 90-63693. 776p. 1991. 38.99 (*0-8100-0379-1*, 15N0483) Northwest Pub.

Lange, Lynda, jt. ed. see Clark, Lorenne.

***Lange, Marc.** Natural Laws in Scientific Practice. LC 99-38157. 368p. 2000. write for info. (*0-19-513148-7*) OUP.

Lange, Margo. Quest for Health & Happiness: A Woman's Guide: Fitness Tips for the Body-Mind-Heart-Soul Plus Dream Planner & Daily Diary. 296p. (Orig.). 1993. pap., student ed. 15.95 (*0-9635020-9-3*) M Lange Comm.

Lange, Marie A. & Mandt, Jinger, eds. Classified Directory of Wisconsin Manufacturers, 1997. 53rd ed. 1100p. 1993. 140.00 (*0-942198-20-4*) WMC Serv.

— Wisconsin Services Directory, 1997. 6th ed. 1000p. 1994. 140.00 (*0-942198-19-0*) WMC Serv.

Lange, Marjory E. Telling Tears in the English Renaissance. LC 95-53245. (Studies in the History of Christian Thought, 0081-8607: Vol. 70). x, 279p. 1996. 99.00 (*90-04-10517-4*) Brill Academic Pubs.

***Lange, Michael, et al, eds.** Niederlaendisches Buergerliches Gesetzbuch Buch 2: Juristische Personen. 2nd ed. 460p. 1998. 108.00 (*90-411-0600-6*) Kluwer Law Intl.

Lange, Monique. The Bathing Huts. Beaumont, Barbara, tr. from FRE. LC 84-29287.Tr. of Les/Cabines de Bain. 128p. 1986. 13.95 (*0-7145-2821-8*) M Boyars Pubs.

— Cannibals in Sicily & the Bathing Huts. Beaumont, Barbara, tr. from FRE. (Iris Ser.). 112p. 1988. 18.95 (*0-7145-2879-X*) M Boyars Pubs.

Lange, N., jt. auth. see Kiessling, R.

Lange, Nicholas de, see De Lange, Nicholas, ed.

Lange, Nicholas T. Case Studies in Biometry. (Series in Probability & Mathematical Statistics). 496p. 1994. 114.95 (*0-471-58885-7*); pap. 69.95 (*0-471-58925-X*) Wiley.

Lange, O. L., et al, eds. Physiological Plant Biology IV: Ecosystems Processes - Mineral Cycling, Productivity, & Man's Influence. (Encyclopedia of Plant Physiology Ser.: Vol. 12 D). (Illus.). 690p. 1983. 362.95 (*0-387-10908-0*) Spr-Verlag.

— Physiological Plant Ecology I: Responses to the Physical Environment. (Encyclopedia of Plant Physiology Ser.: Vol. 12 A). (Illus.). 625p. 1981. 294.95 (*0-387-10763-0*) Spr-Verlag.

— Physiological Plant Ecology III: Responses to the Chemical & Biological Environment. (Encyclopedia of Plant Physiology Ser.: Vol. 12C). (Illus.). 850p. 1983. 362.95 (*0-387-10907-2*) Spr-Verlag.

Lange, O. L. & Mooney, Harold A. Anticipated Effects of a Changing Global Environment in Mediterranean-Type Ecosystems. LC 95-5548. (Ecological Studies: Vol. 117). (Illus.). 488p. 1995. 118.00 (*0-387-94352-8*) Spr-Verlag.

Lange, O. L., et al. Physiological Plant Ecology II: Water Relations & Carbon Assimilation. (Encyclopedia of Plant Physiology Ser.: Vol. 12 B). (Illus.). 153p. 1982. 362.95 (*0-387-10906-4*) Spr-Verlag.

Lange, O. L. De, see De Lange, O. L.

Lange, Oscar R. Price Flexibility & Employment, No. 8--8. LC 78-6631. (Cowles Commission for Research in Economics, Monograph Ser.: No. 8). (Illus.). 114p. 1978. reprint ed. lib. bdg. 35.00 (*0-313-20480-2*, LAPF, Greenwood Pr) Greenwood.

Lange, Oskar. Optimal Decisions. LC 76-143810. 304p. 1972. 139.00 (*0-08-016053-0*, Pub. by Pergamon Repr) Franklin.

Lange, Oskar, et al, eds. Studies in Mathematical Economics & Econometrics in Memory of Henry Schultz. LC 68-8498. (Essay Index Reprint Ser.). 1977. 23.95 (*0-8369-0916-X*) Ayer.

Lange, Owen S. Wind Came All Ways: A Quest to Understand the Winds, Waves & Weather in the Georgia Basin, 1. (Illus.). 123p. 1999. pap. 22.50 (*0-660-17517-7*) CAN1 Commn.

Lange, P. J. De, see De Lange, P. J.

Lange, Patti, jt. auth. see Mallan, Chicki.

Lange, Peter & Regini, Marino, eds. State, Market & Social Regulation: New Perspectives on Italy. (Illus.). 320p. (C). 1989. text 59.95 (*0-521-35453-6*) Cambridge U Pr.

***Lange, Raeburn.** May the People Live: Maori Health Development, 1900-1920. 300p. 2000. pap. 29.95 (*1-86940-214-6*, Pub. by Auckland Univ) Paul & Co Pubs.

Lange, Ralf. Architekturfuhrer Hamburg: Arachitercutral Guide to Hamburg. (ENG & SPA., Illus.). 336p. 1997. pap. text 39.90 (*3-930698-58-7*, Pub. by E J Wasmuth) Dist Art Pubs.

Lange, Richard C. Prehistoric Land Use & Settlement of the Middle Little Colorado River Valley: The Survey of the Homolovi Ruins State Park. (Archaeological Ser.: No. 189). (Illus.). 197p. 1998. 17.95 (*1-889747-67-X*) Ariz St Mus.

Lange, Richard C. & Deaver, William L. The 1979-1983 Testing at Los Morteros (AZ AA-12-57 ASM) A Large Hohokam Village Site in the Tucson Basin, Vol. 177. (Illus.). 352p. 1989. 16.95 (*1-889747-61-0*) Ariz St Mus.

Lange, Ridgley & Wang, Shengwang, eds. New Approaches in Spectral Decomposition. LC 92-6183. (Contemporary Mathematics Ser.: Vol. 128). 273p. 1992. pap. 44.00 (*0-8218-5139-X*, CONM/128C) Am Math.

Lange, Robert. Gender Identity & Madness in the Nineteenth-Century Novel. LC 98-12875. 160p. 1998. text 69.95 (*0-7734-2243-9*) E Mellen.

— Schleiermacher on Workings of the Knowing Mind: New Translations, Resources, & Understandings. Richardson, Ruth, ed. LC 98-17870. 316p. 1998. text 99.95 (*0-7734-8507-4*) E Mellen.

Lange, Robert C. Nuclear Medicine for Technicians. LC 72-95732. 180p. reprint ed. pap. 55.80 (*0-608-12353-6*, 202426600036) Bks Demand.

Lange, Robert C., jt. auth. see Smith, Robert C.

Lange, Roland. Japanese Verbs. (JPN & ENG.). 350p. 1991. pap. 5.95 (*0-8120-4525-4*) Barron.

Lange, Roland A. 501 Japanese Verbs. 2nd ed. LC 98-70001. (ENG & JPN.). xxxvii, 585 p. 1998. pap. 13.95 (*0-7641-0285-0*, 835971Q) Barron.

Lange, Ronald H. Master Your Migraine: The Migraine Home Cure Manual. Reed, Michael, ed. LC 95-83475. (Illus.). 75p. 1996. pap. 17.95 (*0-9648931-0-X*) Enigma Pub.

Lange, S. De, see De Lange, S.

Lange, Samuel G. & Meier, Georg F., eds. Der Gesellige: Eine Moralische Wochenschrift. (GER.). 2512p. 1987. reprint ed. write for info. (*3-487-07952-6*) G Olms Pubs.

— Der Mensch: Eine Moralische Wochenschrift. (GER.). 1992. reprint ed. write for info. (*3-487-09547-5*) G Olms Pubs.

Lange, Sebastian. Radiology of Chest Diseases. (Illus.). 300p. 1989. text 69.00 (*0-86577-313-0*) Thieme Med Pubs.

— Teaching Atlas of Urologic Radiology. LC 94-35149.Tr. of Lehratlanten der Radiologischen Diagnostik. (ENG., Illus.). 300p. 1994. 99.00 (*0-86577-540-0*) Thieme Med Pubs.

Lange, Sebastian, ed. Radiology of Chest Diseases. 2nd rev. ed. Telger, Terry, tr. LC 97-28204. (Illus.). 370p. 1997. 79.00 (*0-86577-637-7*) Thieme Med Pubs.

Lange, Sebastian & Stark, Paul. Teaching Atlas of Thoracic Radiology. LC 92-49323. 1993. 99.00 (*0-86577-467-6*) Thieme Med Pubs.

Lange, Stella, tr. see Pieper, Josef.

Lange, Suzanne. The Year. LC 78-120787. (J). (gr. 8 up). 1970. 26.95 (*0-87599-173-4*) S G Phillips.

Lange, Thomas. Rethinking Higher Education: On the Future of Higher Education in Britain. (Studies in Education: Vol. 6). 59p. 1998. pap. 15.95 (*0-255-36421-0*) Inst Economic Affairs.

Lange, Thomas, ed. Understanding the School-to-Work Transition: An International Perspective. 161p. 49.00 (*1-56072-604-0*) Nova Sci Pubs.

***Lange, Thomas, ed.** Unemployment in Theory & Practice. LC 97-41519. 320p. 1998. 90.00 (*1-85898-595-1*) E Elgar.

***Lange, Thomas & Pugh, Geoffrey.** The Economics of German Unification: An Introduction. LC 97-38249. 240p. 1998. 85.00 (*1-85898-090-9*) E Elgar.

Lange, Thomas & Shackleton, J. R., eds. The Political Economy of German Unification. LC 97-28863. 192p. 1997. 45.00 (*1-57181-880-4*) Berghahn Bks.

Lange, Tom & Vannatter, Philip. Evidence Dismissed: The Inside Story of the Police Investigation of O. J. Simpson. 1997. 24.00 (*0-671-00959-1*) PB.

***Lange, Ursula.** East Germany: What Happened to the Silesians in 1945? 240p. 2000. 32.50 (*1-85776-402-1*, Pub. by Book Guild Ltd) Trans-Atl Phila.

Lange, V. N. Physical Paradoxes & Sophisms. 232p. (C). 1987. 25.00 (*0-7855-4969-2*, Pub. by Collets) St Mut.

Lange, Vern, jt. auth. see Finley, Bob.

Lange, Victor. Classical Age of German Literature, 1740-1815. LC 82-15734. 256p. (Orig.). (C). 1982. pap. 19.50 (*0-8419-0854-0*) Holmes & Meier.

Lange, Victor, et al. German Expressionism. LC 77-126039. (Review of National Literatures Ser.: Vol. 9). 176p. 1979. pap. 6.95 (*0-918680-69-7*) Griffon House.

Lange, Victor, jt. ed. see Amacher, Richard E.

Lange, Victor, ed. see Goethe, Johann Wolfgang Von.

Lange, Victor, ed. & intro. see Hoffmann, E. T. A.

Lange, Victor, ed. & tr. see Goethe, Johann Wolfgang Von.

Lange, Victor, tr. see Goethe, Johann Wolfgang Von.

Lange, Vladimir. Be a Survivor. 1999. pap. 19.95 (*0-7615-1895-9*) Prima Pub.

— Be a Survivor: Your Guide to Breast Cancer Treatment. LC 98-84908. (Illus.). 154p. 1998. pap. 24.95 (*0-9663610-0-8*) Lange Prodns.

***Lange, Vladimir.** Confia En El Manana: Guia Para El Tratamiento Del Cancer. 1999. pap. text 24.95 (*0-9663610-3-2*) Lange Prodns.

***Lange, Vladimir D.** Be a Survivor: Your Guide to Breast Cancer Treatment. (Illus.). 158p. 1999. 89.00 incl. VHS (*0-9663610-4-0*) Lange Prodns.

Lange, W. Efficiency in Plant Breeding. 383p. 1990. pap. 750.00 (*81-7089-125-6*, Pub. by Intl Bk Distr) St Mut.

Lange, W. & Masihi, K. Noel, eds. Immunotherapeutic Prospects of Infectious Diseases. (Illus.). 352p. 1991. 96.95 (*0-387-53214-5*) Spr-Verlag.

Lange, W. Robert. The Doctor's Guide to Protecting Your Health Before, During & after International Travel. LC 97-17148. (Well-Prepared Traveler Ser.). 128p. 1997. pap. 9.95 (*0-87576-209-3*) Pilot Bks.

Lange, Wiesje De, see De Lange, Wiesje.

***Lange, Willem.** Okay, Let's Try It Again. LC 99-34966. 117p. 1999. pap. 12.95 (*1-58465-004-4*) U Pr of New Eng.

Lange, Willem. Tales from the Edge of the Woods. LC 97-35028. 96p. 1998. pap. 12.95 (*0-87451-859-8*) U Pr of New Eng.

Lange, William de, see de Lange, William.

Lange, Wolfgang. Woerterbuch Georgisch-Deutsch, Deutsch-Georgisch. (GEO & GER.). 161p. 1987. 39.95 (*0-7859-8523-9*, 3871188506) Fr & Eur.

Langeback, Carl H. Regional Archaeology in the Muisca Territory: A Study of the Fuquene & Susa Valleys - Arqueologia Regional en el Territorio Musica: Estudio de los Valles de Fuquene y Susa. Jones, Roxanna M., tr. LC 95-21919. (University of Pittsburgh Memoirs in Latin American Archaeology Ser.: No. 9). (ENG & SPA.). 1995. pap. 21.00 (*1-877812-34-X*, M009) UPLAAP.

Langebaek, Carl H. & Cardenas-Arroyo, Felipe, eds. Chieftains, Power & Trade: Regional Interaction in the Intermediate Area of the Americas. (ENG & SPA., Illus.). 262p. 1996. pap. 14.00 (*958-9057-58-6*, UA08, Pub. by Universidad De Los Andes) UPLAAP.

Langebartel, James L. & Koester, Robert. The Complete Timotheus Verinus. LC 96-71341. 156p. 1998. text 39.99 (*0-8100-0672-3*, 15N0594) Northwest Pub.

Langefors, B., et al, eds. Trends in Information Systems: TC 8 Anthology. 450p. 1986. 113.75 (*0-444-87949-8*, North Holland) Elsevier.

Langeheine, R. & Rost, J. Latent Trait & Latent Class Models. LC 88-4141. (Illus.). 328p. (C). 1988. 75.00 (*0-306-42727-3*, Plenum Trade) Perseus Pubng.

Langeher, Frances. Painting Reasons on the Mirror. (Illus.). (Orig.). 1989. pap. text 6.50 (*0-9623824-0-X*) Broken Mirrors Pr.

Langehove, Van, jt. auth. see Harre, Rom.

Langel, Hans. Di Entwicklung des Schulwesens in Preuben unter Franz Albrecht Schultz (1733-1763) (Abhandlungen zur Philosophie und Iher Geschichte Ser.: No. 32). (GER.). xi, 152p. 1985. reprint ed. write for info. (*3-487-07609-8*) G Olms Pubs.

Langel, R. A. & Hinze, W. J. The Magnetic Field of the Earth's Lithosphere: The Satellite Perspective. LC 97-51319. (Illus.). 400p. (C). 1998. text 100.00 (*0-521-47333-0*) Cambridge U Pr.

Langel, Randy. Client/Server: The 10 Percent You Need to Know. LC 94-79114. (Illus.). 167p. (Orig.). 1995. pap., per. 29.95 (*0-9643104-0-6*) IBM So Calif.

Langelaan, James S. The Philosophy & Theology of Love: According to St. Francis de Sales. LC 94-13278. (Toronto Studies in Theology: Vol. 67). 234p. 1994. text 89.95 (*0-7734-9100-7*) E Mellen.

Langeland, Deirdre. Kangaroo Island: A Story of an Australian Mallee Forest. LC 97-47612. (Habitat Ser.). (Illus.). 36p. (J). (gr. 1-4). 1998. 15.95 (*1-56899-543-1*); 19.95 incl. audio (*1-56899-545-8*, BC7007); pap. 5.95 (*1-56899-544-X*); pap. 10.95 incl. audio (*1-56899-546-6*) Soundprints.

— Kangaroo Island: A Story of an Australian Mallee Forest, Incl. toy. (Habitat Ser.). (Illus.). 36p. (J). (gr. 1-4). 1998. 26.95 (*1-56899-547-4*); 31.95 incl. audio (*1-56899-549-0*); pap. 16.95 (*1-56899-548-2*); pap. 19.95 incl. audio (*1-56899-550-4*) Soundprints.

— Octopus' Den. LC 97-8676. (Smithsonian Oceanic Collection). (Illus.). 32p. (J). (ps-2). 1997. 15.95

L

An Asterisk (*) at the beginning of an entry indicates that the title is appearing for the first time.

(1-56899-473-7); 4.95 (1-56899-474-5); 19.95 incl. audio (1-56899-475-3, BC4014); 9.95 incl. audio (1-56899-481-8) Soundprints.
— Octopus' Den, Incl. large toy. (Smithsonian Oceanic Collection). (Illus.). 32p. (J). (ps-2). 1997. 29.95 (1-56899-477-X); 34.95 incl. audio (1-56899-479-6) Soundprints.
— Octopus' Den, Incl. Sm. & Lg. Plush Toy. LC 97-8676. (Smithsonian Oceanic Collection). (Illus.). 32p. (J). (ps-2). 1997. 38.95 incl. audio (1-56899-649-7) Soundprints.
— Octopus' Den, Micro bk., incl. small toy. (Smithsonian Oceanic Collection). (Illus.). 32p. (J). (ps-2). 1997. 14.95 incl. audio (1-56899-480-X) Soundprints.
— Octopus' Den: Incl. small toy. (Smithsonian Oceanic Collection). (Illus.). 32p. (J). (ps-2). 1997. 9.95 (1-56899-478-8) Soundprints.
***Langeland, Frederica.** Main Dish Soups. LC 99-47394. (Illus.). 2000. 19.95 (0-7621-0266-7, Pub. by RD Assn) Penguin Putnam.
Langeland, Frederica. A Passion for Preserves: Jams, Jellies, Marmalades, Conserves & Butters. LC 97-13132. (Illus.). 128p. 1997. write for info. (1-56799-533-0, Friedman-Fairfax) M Friedman Pub Grp Inc.
Langeler, B., jt. auth. see Bendow, Bernard.
Langeler, Freddie. Children of the Earth. (Illus.). 24p. (J). 1996. 12.95 (1-56937-104-0); 12.95 (1-56937-101-6) Kabouter Prods.
— Children of the Stars. (Illus.). 24p. (J). 1996. 12.95 (1-56937-100-8) Kabouter Prods.
Langelier, Lisa A. & Garton, Edward O. Management Guidelines for Increasing Populations of Birds That Feed on Western Spruce Budworm. (Illus.). 24p. 1997. reprint ed. pap. 3.40 (0-89904-655-X, Wildlife Resrch Grp) Crumb Elbow Pub.
Langellier, Alice & Langellier, Paul. Billet Circulaire. LC 66-12110. (FRE.). (C). 1966. reprint ed. pap. text 9.95 (0-89197-516-0) Irvington.
Langellier, J. Phillip. Bluecoats: The U. S. Army in the West, 1848-1897. LC 99-14391. (G.I. Ser.). (Illus.). 84p. (J). 1999. 19.95 (0-7910-5366-0) Chelsea Hse.
***Langellier, J. Phillip.** Fix Bayonets: The U.S. Infantry from the American Civil War to the Surrender of Japan. LC 99-13173. (G.I. Ser.). (Illus.). 84p. 1999. 19.95 (0-7910-5378-4) Chelsea Hse.
Langellier, J. Phillip. Parade Ground Soldiers: Military Uniforms & Headress, 1837-1910, in the Collections of the State Historical Society of Wisconsin. LC 78-4681. 132p. 1978. pap. 5.00 (0-87020-174-3) State Hist Soc Wis.
— Redlegs: The U. S. Artillery from the Civil War to the Spanish-American War, 1861-1898. LC 99-14390. (G.I. Ser.). (Illus.). 84p. (YA). 1999. 19.95 (0-7910-5375-X) Chelsea Hse.
— Redlegs: The U. S. Artillery from the Civil War to the Spanish-American War, 1861-1898. LC 97-40159. (G. I., The Illustrated History of the American Soldier, His Uniform & His Equipment Ser.). 75p. 1998. pap. 12.95 (1-85367-309-9) Stackpole.
— Sound the Charge: The U. S. Cavalry in the American West, 1866-1916. LC 97-38293. (G. I. Ser.). 72p. 1998. 12.95 (1-85367-319-6, Pub. by Greenhill Bks) Stackpole.
***Langellier, J. Phillip.** Sound the Charge: The U.S. Cavalry in the American West, 1861-1916. LC 99-13174. (G.I. Ser.). (Illus.). 84p. 1999. 19.95 (0-7910-5376-8) Chelsea Hse.
Langellier, J. Phillip. Uncle Sam's Little Wars: The Spanish-American War, Philippine Insurrection & Boxer Rebellion. LC 98-49195. (G. I. Ser.). 1999. pap. 13.95 (1-85367-357-9) Stackpole.
— The War in Europe: From the Kasserine Pass to Berlin, 1941-1945. LC 98-19841. (G. I. Ser.). (Illus.). 80p. 1998. 12.95 (1-85367-338-2, Pub. by Greenhill Bks) Stackpole.
Langellier, J. Phillip, et al. Fix Bayonets: The U. S. Infantry from the American Civil War to the Surrender of Japan. LC 98-19875. (G. I. Ser.). (Illus.). 72p. 1998. 12.95 (1-85367-324-2, Pub. by Greenhill Bks) Stackpole.
***Langellier, John P.** American Indians in the U. S. Armed Forces, 1866-1945. LC 00-24790. Vol. 20. (Illus.). 72p. 2000. pap. write for info. (1-85367-408-7, Pub. by Greenhill Bks) Stackpole.
Langellier, John P. Army Blue: The Uniform of Uncle Sam's Regulars. LC 97-80211. (Illus.). 320p. 1998. 79.95 (0-7643-0443-7) Schiffer.
— The Bluecoats: The U. S. Army in the West, 1848-1897. LC 95-15138. (GI: The Illustrated History of the American Soldier, His Uniform, & His Equipment Ser.: Vol. 2). (Illus.). 80p. 1995. pap. 12.95 (1-85367-221-1, Pub. by Greenhill Bks) Stackpole.
***Langellier, John P.** Custer: The Man, the Myth, the Movies. (Illus.). 160p. 2000. pap. 29.95 (0-8117-3201-0) Stackpole.
Langellier, John P. Hats Off: Head Dress of the U. S. Army, 1872-1912. (Illus.). 320p. 1999. 69.95 (0-7643-0956-0) Schiffer.
***Langellier, John P.** Terrible Swift Sword: Union Artillery, Cavalry 7 Infantry, 1861-1865. LC 00-21765. Vol. 19. (Illus.). 72p. 2000. pap. write for info. (1-85367-405-2, Pub. by Greenhill Bks) Stackpole.
Langellier, John P. U. S. Dragoons, 1833-55. (Men-at-Arms Ser.). (Illus.). 48p. 1995. pap. 11.95 (1-85532-389-3, Pub. by Osprey) Stackpole.
— The War in Europe: From the Kasserine Pass to Berlin, 1941-1945. LC 95-15139. (G. I. Ser.: Vol. 1). (Illus.). 80p. 1995. pap. 12.95 (1-85367-220-3, Pub. by Greenhill Bks) Stackpole.
— The War in Europe: From the Kasserine Pass to Berlin, 1942-1945. LC 99-21645. (G.I. Ser.). (Illus.). 84p. 1999. 19.95 (0-7910-5365-2) Chelsea Hse.
Langellier, John P., compiled by. Myles Keogh: The Life & Legend of an Irish Dragoon with the Seventh Cavalry. LC 91-65910. (Montana & the West Ser.: Vol. 9). (Illus.). 206p. 1991. 100.00 (0-912783-21-4) Upton & Sons.
Langellier, John P., ed. Armed Forces on the West Coast. (Illus.). 76p. (Orig.). 1981. pap. text 15.00 (0-89745-023-X) Sunflower U Pr.
Langellier, John P. & McAfee, Michael J. Billy Yank: The Uniform of the Union Army, 1861-1865. (GI: The Illustrated History of the American Soldier, His Uniform, & His Equipment Ser.). (Illus.). 80p. 1996. pap. 12.95 (1-85367-238-6, Pub. by Greenhill Bks) Stackpole.
Langellier, John P. & Rosen, Daniel B. El Presidio de San Francisco: A History under Spain & Mexico, 1776. (Frontier Military Ser.: Vol. XIX). (Illus.). 200p. 1996. 35.50 (0-87062-239-0) A H Clark.
Langellier, John P., jt. auth. see Cox, Kurt H.
Langellier, Paul, jt. auth. see Langellier, Alice.
Langello, Kip. Clinic. 1997. per. 5.99 (0-671-55282-1) PB.
— The Cure. (Orig.). 1999. per. 6.99 (0-671-54085-8, Pocket Books) PB.
***Langelo, Vincent A.** U.S.S. Boise: With All Our Might. LC 99-49991. 2000. write for info. (1-57168-370-4, Eakin Pr) Sunbelt Media.
Langeloh, Tom. Bravara Eagle Thunderbolt. (Illus.). 48p. (Orig.). (J). (gr. 3-6). 1996. pap. 10.95 (1-880812-26-6) S Ink WA.
Langeluttig, Albert. Department of Justice of the United States. (Brookings Institution Reprint Ser.). reprint ed. lib. bdg. 42.50 (0-697-00161-X) Irvington.
Langemo, Mark, jt. auth. see Brathal, Daniel A.
Langen, Annette. Cartas de Felix - Letters from Felix: Un Conejito Da la Vuelta al Mundo - A Little Rabbit on a World Tour. (SPA., Illus.). 32p. (J). 1996. 16.95 (0-7892-0172-0) Abbeville Pr.
— Felix: What Time Is It? LC 98-89882. (Illus.). 22p. (J). 1999. pap. 10.95 (0-7892-0562-9, Abbeville Kids) Abbeville Pr.
***Langen, Annette.** Felix Joins the Circus. LC 99-88113. 36p. (J). 2000. 18.95 (0-7892-0632-3, Abbeville Kids) Abbeville Pr.
Langen, Annette. Felix Travels Back in Time. (Illus.). 32p. (J). (ps-3). 1995. 16.95 (0-7892-0002-3, Abbeville Kids) Abbeville Pr.
— Felix's Christmas Around the World. LC 99-199870. (Illus.). 32p. (J). (ps-5). 1998. bds. 19.95 (0-7892-0452-5, Abbeville Kids) Abbeville Pr.
— Letters from Felix: A Little Rabbit on a World Tour. LC 94-29355. (Illus.). 32p. (J). 1994. 16.95 (1-55859-886-3, Abbeville Kids) Abbeville Pr.
— Pippo: A Little Dog Finds a Home. (Illus.). 40p. (J). (ps-3). 1995. 12.95 (0-7892-0071-6, Abbeville Kids) Abbeville Pr.
Langen, Annette & Droop, Constanza. Felix Explores Planet Earth. LC 97-137887. (Illus.). 32p. (J). 1997. bds. 16.95 (0-7892-0320-0, Abbeville Kids) Abbeville Pr.
Langen, Peter. Beitrage Zur Kritik und Erklarung des Plautus. (GER.). iv, 348p. 1973. reprint ed. write for info. (3-487-04991-0) G Olms Pubs.
— Plautinische Studien. vi, 400p. 1970. reprint ed. write for info. (0-318-71159-1) G Olms Pubs.
Langen, Peter, ed. see Flaccus, Gaius Valerius.
***Langen, Timothy & Weir, Justin, trs.** Eight Twentieth-Century Russian Plays. 352p. 2000. 59.95 (0-8101-1373-2); pap. 21.95 (0-8101-1374-0) Northwestern U Pr.
Langenbach, A. Monotone Potentialoperatoren in Theorie & Anwendung. (GER.). 1977. 37.80 (3-540-08071-6) Spr-Verlag.
Langenbach, Michael. Curriculum Models in Adult Education. 240p. 1993. 29.50 (0-89464-784-9) Krieger.
Langenbach, Michael, et al. Introduction to Educational Research. LC 93-22189. 425p. 1993. text 55.00 (0-205-13902-7) Allyn.
Langenbach, Michael, jt. auth. see Zepeda, Sally J.
Langenbach, Randolph, jt. auth. see Hareven, Tamara K.
Langenbach, Robert, et al, eds. Tumor Promoters: Biological Approaches for Mechanistic Studies & Assay Systems. LC 86-43223. (Progress in Cancer Research & Therapy Ser.: Vol. 34). 480p. 1988. reprint ed. pap. 148.80 (0-608-00303-4, 206102000007) Bks Demand.
Langenbahn, Stacia, jt. auth. see Epstein, Joel.
Langenbeck, K., jt. auth. see Greiner, J.
Langenberg, Carolyn Van, see Van Langenberg, Carolyn.
Langenberg, Mechtild, et al, eds. Qualitative Music Therapy Research: Beginning Dialogues. 276p. (C). 1996. pap. text 25.00 (0-9624080-4-2) Barcelona Pubs.
Langenbrunner, Jim. I Love the Lady Choir Director by Uncle Jim but He Was Kicked-Out for Misbehaving. (Illus.). 1989. write for info. (0-318-65114-9) J Langenbrunner.
Langenderfer, jt. auth. see Bower.
Langenderfer, jt. auth. see Skousen.
Langenderfer, Harold Q. The Federal Income Tax, 1861 to 1872. Brief, Richard P., ed. LC 80-1500. (Dimensions of Accounting Theory & Practice Ser.). 1980. lib. bdg. 88.95 (0-405-13493-2) Ayer.
Langenderfer, Harold Q. & Skousen, K. Fred. Accounting Principles & Applications, Wkg. Papers 2-16. 4th ed. (AB - Accounting Principles Ser.). (C). 1992. mass mkt., wbk. ed. 19.75 (0-538-81165-X) S-W Pub.
— Accounting Principles & Applications, Wkg. Papers 15-28. 4th ed. (AB - Accounting Principles Ser.). (C). 1993. mass mkt., wbk. ed. 19.75 (0-538-81166-8) S-W Pub.
— Accounting Principles & Applications Chapters 1-15. 4th ed. (AB - Accounting Principles Ser.). (C). 1992. mass mkt., student ed. 27.25 (0-538-82629-0) S-W Pub.
— Accounting Principles & Applications Chapters 15-28. 4th ed. (AB - Accounting Principles Ser.). (C). 1993. mass mkt., student ed. 27.25 (0-538-82630-4) S-W Pub.
— Financial Accounting. 5th ed. (AB - Accounting Principles Ser.). (C). 1994. pap., student ed. 20.25 (0-538-82835-8); pap., wbk. ed. 19.75 (0-538-82836-6) S-W Pub.
Langenderfer, Harold Q., et al. Financial Accounting. 5th ed. (C). 1994. mass mkt. 79.00 (0-538-82832-3) S-W Pub.
Langendoen, D. Terence, jt. ed. see Barss, Andrew.
Langendoen, D. Terence, jt. ed. see Fillmore, Charles J.
Langendoen, David & Costa, Dan, eds. The Home Office Computing Handbook (1994) (Illus.). 195p. 1999. reprint ed. pap. text 10.00 (0-7881-6501-1) DIANE Pub.
Langendoen, D. Terence, jt. ed. see Archangeli, Diana B.
Langendonck, Jef Van, see Van Langendonck, Jef, ed.
Langendorf, Adele. Denial. 64p. 1986. pap. 6.00 (0-912449-19-5) Floating Island.
Langendorf, Hans. Woerterbuch der Deutschen und Nierderlaendischen Rechtssprache, Vol. 1. (DUT & GER.). 365p. 1991. 85.00 (0-8288-5771-7, M7025) Fr & Eur.
— Woerterbuch der Deutschen und Nierderlaendischen Rechtssprache, Vol. 2. (DUT & GER.). 426p. 1989. 125.00 (0-8288-5772-5, M7026) Fr & Eur.
Langendorf, Hans, ed. Legal Dictionary Dutch - German. 1991. text 46.00 (90-6544-563-3) Kluwer Law Intl.
Langendorf, Patricia. It's Not a Bad Start. LC 92-60342. 208p. (Orig.). 1992. pap. 14.95 (0-9625714-5-8) Spruce Gulch Pr.
— Logging the Rockies: The Langendorf Olson Story. large type ed. (Illus.). 249p. (Orig.). 1992. pap. 22.50 (0-9625714-9-0); lib. bdg. 40.00 (0-9625714-8-2) Spruce Gulch Pr.
Langendorf, Richard, jt. auth. see Pick, Alfred.
Langendorfer, Stephen J. & Bruya, Lawrence D. Aquatic Readiness: Developing Water Competence in Young Children. LC 93-42159. (Illus.). 224p. 1994. pap. text 28.00 (0-87322-661-1, BLAN0663) Human Kinetics.
Langendorff, T. & Zurcher, Erik J., eds. Humanities in the Nineties. 378p. 1990. 66.25 (90-265-1133-7) Swets.
***Langenfeld, Carol J. & Langenfeld, Douglas E.** Living Better: Every Patient's Guide to Living with Illness. 2001. 14.95 (0-9701545-1-8) Patient Pr.
Langenfeld, Douglas E., jt. auth. see Langenfeld, Carol J.
Langenfeld, Robert. George Moore: An Annotated Secondary Bibliography of Writings about Him. LC 84-48436. (Studies in Modern Literature: No. 13). 1987. 76.50 (0-404-61583-X) AMS Pr.
Langenheim, Ralph L., Jr., jt. auth. see Frost, Stanley H.
Langenkamp, Robert D. Handbook of Oil Industry Terms & Phrases. 5th ed. LC 94-13887. 400p. 1994. 64.95 (0-87814-421-8) PennWell Bks.
— The Illustrated Petroleum Reference Dictionary. LC 94-34489. (Illus.). 1994. 89.95 (0-87814-423-4) PennWell Bks.
Langenohl, Andreas. Die Semantik des Wortnestes Grad-Gorod Im Altrussischen: Unter Kontextuellem, Wortbildendem und Kulturellem Aspekt. Jelitte, Herbert, ed. (Beitragezur zur Slavistik Ser.: Vol. 36). (GER.). 223p. 1998. pap. 39.95 (3-631-32923-7) P Lang Pubng.
Langenscheidt. German-English - English-German Dictionary. (YA). 1993. pap. 5.99 (0-671-72720-6, Pocket Books) PB.
— German/English/German Dictionary Environmental Technology. (ENG & GER.). 272p. 1997. 295.00 (0-320-00446-5) Fr & Eur.
Langenscheidt Editorial Staff. New College German Dictionary. (GER.). (C). 1995. 32.95 (0-88729-020-5) Langenscheidt.
— New College German Dictionary, Thumb-Indexed. (GER.). (C). 1995. 34.95 (0-88729-021-3) Langenscheidt.
— New College Spanish Dictionary. (SPA.). 1020p. (C). 1995. 32.95 (0-88729-126-0) Langenscheidt.
— New College Spanish Dictionary, Thumb-Indexed. (SPA.). 1020p. (C). 1995. 34.95 (0-88729-127-9) Langenscheidt.
— Pocket German. rev. ed. (Pocket Dictionaries Ser.). 1999. vinyl bd. 12.95 (0-88729-121-X) Langenscheidt.
— Pocket Russian. rev. ed. (Pocket Dictionaries Ser.). 1999. vinyl bd. 12.95 (0-88729-120-1) Langenscheidt.
— Pocket Spanish-English Dictionary. rev. ed. (Pocket Dictionaries Ser.). 1999. vinyl bd. 12.95 (0-88729-123-6) Langenscheidt.
— Technical Dictionary, English-German. (ENG & GER.). 1996. 250.00 (0-7859-9385-1) Fr & Eur.
— Universal German-English Dictionary. rev. ed. (Universal Dictionaries Ser.). 1999. vinyl bd. 5.95 (0-88729-122-8) Langenscheidt.
— Universal Polish/English Dictionary. (Universal Dictionaries Ser.). 1999. vinyl bd. 6.95 (0-88729-015-9) Langenscheidt.
Langenscheidt Editorial Staff, ed. Computergestuetzter Fremdsprachenunterricht: Ein Handbuch. 128p. 1985. pap. 23.95 (3-468-49434-3) Langenscheidt.
— Dictionary of Information Technology, German-English & English-German. (ENG & GER.). 430p. 1996. 295.00 (0-7859-9382-7) Fr & Eur.
— Langenscheidt Lilliput Dictionary Little Webster. rev. ed. 640p. 1995. vinyl bd. 3.25 (0-88729-521-5) Langenscheidt.
Langenscheidt Editorial Staff, jt. auth. see Quinalt, R.
Langenscheidt, Florian & Langenscheidt, Gabriele. Wish I May, Wish I Might: Fantastic Thoughts for a Starry Night. (Illus.). 128p. 1993. 8.95 (1-55859-638-0) Abbeville Pr.
Langenscheidt, Gabriele, jt. auth. see Langenscheidt, Florian.
***Langenscheidt Publishers Staff.** Caves, Cliffs & Canyons. (Travel Adventures Ser.). (Illus.). 224p. 2000. pap. 19.95 (1-56331-929-2) Discovery.
Langenscheidt Publishers Staff. Diccionario Basico Langenscheidt: Espanol-Ingles, Ingles-Espanol. (SPA.). 1997. pap. 11.95 (0-88729-083-3) Langenscheidt.
— Jiffy Phrase Book - Spanish. LC 84-203565. (Illus.). 256p. 1986. pap. 6.95 (0-88729-950-4) Langenscheidt.
Langenscheidt Publishers Staff, ed. Langenscheidt French Pocket Dictionary. (Pocket Dictionaries Ser.). 624p. 1983. pap. 11.95 (0-88729-104-X) Langenscheidt.
Langenscheidt Publishing Staff. Langenscheidt Pocket Dictionary Webster English. 903p. 1997. pap. 10.95 (0-88729-199-6) Langenscheidt.
***Langenscheidt Publishing Staff, ed.** Portugal. (Langenscheidt Pocket Menu Reader Ser.). (POR & ENG., Illus.). 2000. pap. text 7.95 (0-88729-314-X, Insight Guides) Langenscheidt.
Langenscheidt-Redaktion. Langenscheidts Eurowortebucher: Italienisch. (ITA.). 1997. pap. write for info. (3-468-12180-6) Langenscheidt.
— Langenscheidts Euroworterbucher: Portugiesisch. (POR.). 1997. pap. write for info. (3-468-12270-5) Langenscheidt.
— Langenscheidts Euroworterbucher: Spanisch. (SPA.). 1997. pap. write for info. (3-468-12340-X) Langenscheidt.
Langenscheidt-Redaktion, jt. auth. see Messinger, H.
Langenscheidt Staff. Bangkok. 3rd ed. (Insight Guides Ser.). 1998. pap. 21.95 (0-88729-488-X) Langenscheidt.
— CC-ROM Bibliothek. (ENG & GER.). 695p. 1994. write for info. (0-614-00359-8, 3468909012) Fr & Eur.
— Diccionario Basico Espanol. (Insight Guides Ser.). (SPA.). 1998. pap. 11.95 (0-88729-106-6) Langenscheidt.
— French. (Insight Guides). 1998. pap. 10.95 (0-88729-222-4) Langenscheidt.
— French Quick & Easy. 1984. pap. 16.95 incl. audio (0-88729-901-6) Langenscheidt.
— German. (Insight Guides). 1998. pap. 10.95 (0-88729-224-0) Langenscheidt.
— German Quick & Easy. 1984. pap. 16.95 incl. audio (0-88729-902-4) Langenscheidt.
— Glossaire Europeen de Terminologie Juridique & Administrative No. 15: Termes de Droit Anglais des Obligations, Anglais-Francais. (ENG & FRE.). 36p. pap. 29.95 (0-7859-0416-6, M9482) Fr & Eur.
— Glossaire Europeen de Terminologie Juridique et Administrative. (ENG & GER.). 127p. 1973. pap. 14.95 (0-685-57825-9, M-9485) Fr & Eur.
— Glossaire Europeen de Terminologie Juridique et Administrative: Regional Policy. (FRE.). 111p. write for info. (0-7859-0417-4, M9484) Fr & Eur.
— Glossaire Europeen de Terminologie Juridique et Administrative No. 1: Droit du Mariage. (FRE & GER.). 96p. 1973. pap. 14.95 (0-8288-6294-X, M-9486) Fr & Eur.
— Glossaire Europeen de Terminologie Juridique et Administrative No. 1: Terminologie Administrative et Secretariat. (FRE & GER.). write for info. (0-318-56667-2, M-9495) Fr & Eur.
— Glossaire Europeen de Terminologie Juridique et Administrative No. 2: Budgeting & Auditing, German-Italian. (GER & ITA.). 144p. 1980. pap. 19.95 (3-468-49076-3) Fr & Eur.
— Glossaire Europeen de Terminologie Juridique et Administrative No. 2: Civil Service Organizations. (ENG & GER.). 83p. 1976. pap. 24.95 (0-8288-5672-9, M9489) Fr & Eur.
— Glossaire Europeen de Terminologie Juridique et Administrative No. 2: Conference Terminology, German-Italian. (GER & ITA.). 72p. 1979. pap. 24.95 (0-8288-4805-X, M9492) Fr & Eur.
— Glossaire Europeen de Terminologie Juridique et Administrative No. 2: Terminologie de Reunions. (GER & ITA.). write for info. (0-318-56674-5, M-9497) Fr & Eur.
— Glossaire Europeen de Terminologie Juridique et Administrative No. 3: Renumeration. (FRE & GER.). write for info. (0-318-56668-0, M-9498) Fr & Eur.
— Glossaire Europeen de Terminologie Juridique et Administrative No. 4: Oroit Administratif. (FRE & GER.). write for info. (0-318-56662-1, M-9499) Fr & Eur.
— Glossaire Europeen de Terminologie Juridique et Administrative No. 6: Droits des Collectivites Locales. (FRE & GER.). write for info. (0-318-56665-6) Fr & Eur.
— Glossaire Europeen de Terminologie Juridique et Administrative No. 7: Budget. (FRE & GER.). write for info. (0-318-56675-3, M-9603) Fr & Eur.
— Glossaire Europeen de Terminologie Juridique et Administrative No. 8: Oroit de al Fonction Publique. (FRE & GER.). write for info. (0-318-56663-X, M-9604) Fr & Eur.
— Glossaire Europeen de Terminologie Juridique et Administrative No. 9: Amenagement du Territoie. (FRE & GER.). write for info. (0-318-56676-1, M-9605) Fr & Eur.
— Glossaire Europeen de Terminologie Juridique et Administrative No. 10: Marches Publics. (FRE & GER.). 72p. 1972. pap. 12.95 (0-8288-6395-4, M-9479) Fr & Eur.
— Glossaire Europeen de Terminologie Juridique et Administrative No. 11: Jeunesse. (Allemand-Francais Ser.). (FRE & GER.). 109p. 1972. pap. 12.95 (0-8288-6394-6, M-9478) Fr & Eur.
— Glossaire Europeen de Terminologie Juridique et Administrative No. 13: Law of Establishment. (FRE.). 100p. 1973. pap. 12.95 (0-8288-6295-8, M-9480) Fr & Eur.

An Asterisk (*) at the beginning of an entry indicates that the title is appearing for the first time.

— Glossaire Europeen de Terminologie Juridique et Administrative No. 20: Local Government. (GER & ITA.). 96p. 1975. pap. 14.95 (*0-8288-5890-X*, M9487) Fr & Eur.

— Glossaire Europeen de Terminologie Juridique et Administrative No. 21: Droits D'Etablissement. (FRE & GER.). 146p. 1976. pap. 18.95 (*0-8288-5671-0*, M9488) Fr & Eur.

— Glossaire Europeen de Terminologie Juridique et Administrative No. 23: Eductions et Enseignment. (FRE & GER.). 168p. pap. 18.95 (*0-7859-0418-2*, M9490) Fr & Eur.

— Glossaire Europeen de Terminologie Juridique et Administrative No. 24: Office Terminology, German-Italian. (GER & ITA.). 79p. 1979. pap. 14.95 (*0-8288-4806-8*, M9491) Fr & Eur.

— Glossaire Europeen de Terminologie Juridique et Administrative No. 27: Motor, Insurance, German-Italian. (GER & ITA.). 152p. 1980. pap. 19.95 (*0-8288-4703-7*, M9494) Fr & Eur.

— Glossaire Europeen de Terminologie Juridique et Administrative No. 29: Environment Policy Protection & Management of the Environment. (ENG & GER.). 160p. pap. 22.50 (*0-7859-0419-0*, M9496) Fr & Eur.

— Italian. (Pocket Grammar Ser.). 1998. pap. 10.95 (*0-88729-223-2*) Langenscheidt.

— Italian Quick & Easy. 1984. pap. 16.95 incl. audio (*0-88729-903-2*) Langenscheidt.

— Jiffy Travel Pack: French. (FRE.). boxed set 12.95 incl. audio (*0-88729-976-8*) Langenscheidt.

— Jiffy Travel Pack: German. (GER.). boxed set 13.95 incl. audio (*0-88729-977-6*) Langenscheidt.

— Jiffy Travel Pack: Italian. (ITA.). boxed set 13.95 incl. audio (*0-88729-978-4*) Langenscheidt.

— Jiffy Travel Pack: Spanish. (SPA.). boxed set 13.95 incl. audio (*0-88729-975-X*) Langenscheidt.

— Langenscheidt Dictionary Building, Civil Engineering: German/English/German. (ENG & GER.). 348p. 1997. 295.00 (*0-320-00440-6*) Fr & Eur.

— Langenscheidt Latin Universal Dictionary. 454p. 1966. vinyl bd. 5.95 (*0-88729-173-2*) Langenscheidt.

— Langenscheidt Picture Dictionary. (ENG & GRE.). (J). (gr. 4-7). 1989. 19.95 (*0-88729-862-1*) Langenscheidt.

— Langenscheidt Picture Dictionary. (ENG & JPN.). 280p. (J). (gr. 4-7). 1990. 24.95 (*0-88729-855-9*); pap. 14.95 (*0-88729-856-7*); pap. 24.95 (*0-88729-861-3*) Langenscheidt.

— Langenscheidt Picture Dictionary. (ENG & SPA.). 190p. (J). (gr. 4-7). 1990. 19.95 (*0-88729-854-0*); 19.95 (*0-88729-851-6*); 19.95 (*0-88729-850-8*) Langenscheidt.

— Langenscheidt Picture Dictionary. (ENG & ITA.). 190p. (J). (gr. 4-7). 1993. 19.95 (*0-88729-853-2*); 19.95 (*0-88729-863-X*); 19.95 (*0-88729-864-8*); 19.95 (*0-88729-865-6*); 19.95 (*0-88729-866-4*); 19.95 (*0-88729-867-2*); pap. 14.95 (*0-88729-859-1*) Langenscheidt.

— Langenscheidt Portuguese Pocket Dictionary. 812p. 1989. vinyl bd. 12.95 (*0-88729-110-4*) Langenscheidt.

— Langenscheidt Portuguese Universal Dictionary. 383p. 1983. vinyl bd. 5.95 (*0-88729-164-3*) Langenscheidt.

— Langenscheidt Russian-English Lilliput Dictionary. 1993. pap. 3.25 (*0-88729-453-7*) Langenscheidt.

— Langenscheidt Turkish Standard Dictionary, Thumb-Indexed. (TUR.). 1046p. 1986. 22.95 (*0-88729-048-5*) Langenscheidt.

— Langenscheidt Universal Dictionary Spanish. (SPA.). 380p. 1994. vinyl bd. 5.95 (*0-88729-064-7*) Langenscheidt.

— Langenscheidt Universal Spanish-German, German-Spanish Dictionary: Langenscheidt Universal Woerterbuch Spanisch-Deutsch-Spanisch. (GER & SPA.). 480p. 1983. 14.95 (*0-8288-0350-1*, S39870) Fr & Eur.

— New College Dictionary. (Insight Guides). 1998. 32.95 (*0-88729-213-5*); 34.95 (*0-88729-216-X*) Langenscheidt.

— New College Thesaurus. (Insight Guides). 1998. 30.95 (*0-88729-214-3*); 32.95 (*0-88729-217-8*) Langenscheidt.

— PC-Woerterbuch English. (ENG & GER.). 495p. 1994. write for info. (*0-614-00362-8*, 3468909128); write for info. (*0-614-00363-6*, 3468909128) Fr & Eur.

— PC-Woerterbuch Franzoesich. (FRE & GER.). 495p. 1994. 150.00 (*0-614-00361-X*, 3468909187) Fr & Eur.

— Pocket Crossword Puzzle Dictionary. (Insight Guides). 1998. pap. 11.95 (*0-88729-215-1*) Langenscheidt.

— Pocket Guide to Punctuation & Style. (Insight Guides Ser.). 1998. pap. 10.95 (*0-88729-218-6*) Langenscheidt.

— Pocket Guide to Synonyms & Antonyms. (Insight Guides Ser.). 1998. pap. 10.95 (*0-88729-220-8*) Langenscheidt.

— Pocket Japanese. (Insight Guides Ser.). 1998. pap. 12.95 (*0-88729-171-6*) Langenscheidt.

— Pocket Thesaurus. (Insight Guides Ser.). 1998. pap. 10.95 (*0-88729-219-4*) Langenscheidt.

— Presupuesto Publico y Fiscalization Glossary German & Spanish, Europa-Glossar der Rechts und Verwaltungssprache, No. 28. (GER & SPA.). 183p. pap. 22.50 (*0-7859-7565-9*, 346849078X) Fr & Eur.

— Spanish. (Insight Guides). 1998. pap. 10.95 (*0-88729-221-6*) Langenscheidt.

— Spanish Quick & Easy. 1984. pap. 16.95 incl. audio (*0-88729-900-8*) Langenscheidt.

— Super Mario Super Englisch: Woerterbuch fur Kids: English-German, German-English. 2nd ed. (ENG & GER.). 576p. 1993. 29.95 (*0-7859-8390-2*, 3468203705) Fr & Eur.

— Universal Dictionary. (Insight Guides Ser.). 1998. pap. 5.95 (*0-88729-084-1*) Langenscheidt.

— Universal German/Turkish/German Dictionary. 4th ed. (GER & TUR.). 448p. 1996. 24.95 (*0-320-00512-7*) Fr & Eur.

— Woerterbuch Franzoesich Langenscheidt CD-ROM. (FRE & GER.). 125p. 1994. write for info. (*0-614-00360-1*, 3468906153) Fr & Eur.

Langenscheidt Staff, jt. auth. see Renyi, Pierre.

Langensiepen, Bernd & Guleryuz, Ahmet. The Ottoman Steam Navy, 1828-1923. Cooper, J., tr. LC 94-69766. (Illus.). 208p. 1995. 55.00 (*1-55750-659-0*) Naval Inst Pr.

Langenus, Gustave. Complete Method for the Clarinet, 3 pts. (Illus.). 118p. pap. 15.95 (*0-8258-0242-3*, 0-1404) Fischer Inc NY.

— Complete Method for the Clarinet, 3 pts. (Illus.). 85p. 1916. pap. 13.00 (*0-8258-0241-5*, 0-1403) Fischer Inc NY.

— Complete Method for the Clarinet, 3 pts. (Illus.). 88p. 1923. pap. 13.00 (*0-8258-0240-7*, 0-1402) Fischer Inc NY.

Langenus, Gustave, ed. see Baermann, Carl.

***Langenwalter, Gary A.** Enterprise Resources Planning & Beyond. (APICS Series on Resource). 424p. 1999. boxed set 44.95 (*1-57444-260-0*) St Lucie Pr.

Langer, jt. auth. see Chasin, Mark.

Langer, Adam. City-Smart: Chicago. (City Smart Ser.). (Illus.). 272p. 1999. pap. 15.95 (*1-56261-450-9*, City Smart) Avalon Travel.

— The Film Festival Guide: For Filmmakers, Film Buffs, & Industry Professionals. LC 97-49209. 256p. 1998. pap. 16.95 (*1-55652-285-1*) Chicago Review.

— The Madness of Art: A Guide to Living & Working in Chicago. LC 96-15362. 268p. (Orig.). 1996. pap. 12.95 (*1-55652-268-1*) Chicago Review.

***Langer, Adam & Barsanti, Chris.** The Film Festival Guide: For Filmmakers, Film Buffs & Industry Professionals. rev. ed. LC 00-35871. 280p. 2000. pap. 16.95 (*1-55652-415-3*, Pub. by Chicago Review) IPG Chicago.

Langer, Angelika, jt. auth. see Kreft, Klaus.

Langer, Anja & Reynolds, Bill. Body Flex - Body Magic. (Illus.). 336p. 1992. pap. 15.95 (*0-8092-3930-2*, 393020, Contemporary Bks) NTC Contemp Pub Co.

Langer, Arne. Der Regisseur und die Aufzeichnungspraxis der Opernregie im 19. Jahrhundert. Maehder, Jurgen & Stenzl, Jurg, eds. (Perspektiven der Opernforschung Ser.: Bd. 4). (GER., Illus.). 496p. 1996. 76.95 (*3-631-31224-5*) P Lang Pubng.

***Langer, Arthur M.** Analysis & Design of Information Systems. LC 00-40046. 2000. write for info. (*0-387-95038-9*) Spr-Verlag.

Langer, Arthur M. The Art of Analysis. LC 96-30097. 192p. 1997. 39.95 (*0-387-94972-0*) Spr-Verlag.

Langer, Arthur W., ed. Polyamine-Chelated Alkali Metal Compounds: A Symposium Co-Sponsored by the Division of Polymer Chemistry & the Organometallic Subdivision of the Division of Inorganic Chemistry at the 164th Meeting of the American Chemical Society, New York, NY, August 28, 1972. LC 74-75334. (Advances in Chemistry Ser.: No. 130). (Illus.). 302p. 1974. reprint ed. pap. 93.70 (*0-608-06775-X*, 206697200009) Bks Demand.

Langer, Burkhard. Zur Energieabhaengigkeit Von Photoelektronensatelliten. LC 92-37269. (Studies of Vacuum Ultraviolet & X-Ray Processes: No. 2). 1992. 45.00 (*0-404-69952-9*) AMS Pr.

Langer, Cassandra. Feminist Art Criticism: An Annotated Bibliography. LC 93-822. 250p. 1994. 65.00 (*0-8161-8948-X*, Hall Reference) Macmillan.

— Home Is Where the Heart Is - Our Family Values. (Illus.). 32p. (Orig.). 1997. pap. 2.00 (*0-9648468-1-0*) White Columns.

Langer, Elinor. Death of Mulugeta Seraw. 1996. write for info. (*0-8050-5098-1*) H Holt & Co.

— Josephine Herbst. LC 94 1506. 384p. 1994. reprint ed. pap. text 18.95 (*1-55553-183-0*) NE U Pr.

— Josephine Herbst: The Story She Could Never Tell. 1985. mass mkt. 3.95 (*0-446-32853-7*, Pub. by Warner Bks) Little.

***Langer, Elky & Berkovits, Masha.** Shades of Gray. 264p. 1999. 18.95 (*1-56871-182-4*, Pub. by Targum Pr) Feldheim.

Langer, Ellen. The Power of Mindful Learning. 1998. pap. 12.00 (*0-201-33991-9*) Addison-Wesley.

Langer, Ellen J. Mindfulness. 1989. 16.30 (*0-201-09502-5*) Addison-Wesley.

— Mindfulness. 1990. pap. 12.50 (*0-201-52341-8*) Addison-Wesley.

— The Power of Mindful Learning. 167p. 1997. 20.00 (*0-614-28237-3*) Addison-Wesley.

— The Psychology of Control. LC 83-11224. (Illus.). 311p. reprint ed. pap. 96.50 (*0-8357-4816-2*, 203775300009) Bks Demand.

Langer, Ellen J., jt. ed. see Alexander, Charles N.

Langer, Ellen J., jt. ed. see Schank, Roger C.

Langer, Erick D. Economic Change & Rural Resistance in Southern Bolivia, 1880-1930. LC 88-31117. 288p. 1989. 47.50 (*0-8047-1491-6*) Stanford U Pr.

Langer, Erick D. & Jackson, Robert H., eds. The New Latin American Mission History. LC 94-43080. (Latin American Studies). xviii, 215p. 1995. text 45.00 (*0-8032-2911-9*); pap. text 22.00 (*0-8032-7953-1*) U of Nebr Pr.

Langer, Ewald. Die Gattung Hyphodontia John Eriksson. (Bibliotheca Mycologica: Vol. 154). (GER., Illus.). 298p. 1994. 77.00 (*3-443-59055-1*, Pub. by Gebruder Borntraeger) Balogh.

Langer, Felicia. These Are My Brothers: Israel & the Occupied Territories. LC 82-186068. iv,145 p. 1979. 6.50 (*0-903729-50-4*) Evergreen Dist.

— With My Own Eyes: Israel & the Occupied Territories, 1967-1973 LC 76-383738. (ENG.). 170 p. 1975. write for info. (*0-903729-10-5*) Evergreen Dist.

Langer, Freddy, ed. Lewis W. Hine: The Empire State Building. LC 98-34624. (Illus.). 104p. 1998. 39.95 (*3-7913-1996-5*) te Neues.

Langer, Fritz. Intellektualmythologie: Betrachtungen Uber das Wesen das Mythus und Die Mythologische Methode. Bolle, Kees W., ed. LC 77-79136. (Mythology Ser.). (GER.). 1978. reprint ed. lib. bdg. 23.95 (*0-405-10546-0*) Ayer.

Langer, Gary F. The Coming of Age of Political Economy, 1815-1825, 72. LC 86-31802. (Contributions in Economics & Economic History Ser.: No. 72). (Illus.). 236p. 1987. 59.95 (*0-313-25645-4*, LCA/, Greenwood Pr) Greenwood.

Langer, Georgia. Teaching As Decision Making. (C). 1996. pap. text. write for info. (*0-8013-1560-3*); pap. text. write for info. (*0-8013-1561-1*) Addison-Wesley.

Langer, Gitta. Die Gattung Botryobasidium DONK (Corticiaceae, Basidiomycetes) (Bibliotheca Mycologica: Vol. 158). (GER., Illus.). 459p. 1994. 100.00 (*3-443-59060-8*, Pub. by Gebruder Borntraeger) Balogh.

***Langer, Glenn.** Understanding Disease Vol. I: How Your Heart, Lungs, Blood & Blood Vessels Function & Respond to Treatment. LC 99-24762. (Illus.). 192p. 1999. text 24.95 (*0-936609-40-0*) QED Ft Bragg.

***Langer, Glenn A.** Understanding Disease. LC 99-24762. 1999. write for info. (*0-09-660940-0*) QED Ft Bragg.

Langer, Glenn A., ed. Calcium & the Heart. LC 90-8049. 401p. 1990. reprint ed. pap. 124.40 (*0-608-03425-8*, 206412400008) Bks Demand.

— The Myocardium. 2nd ed. LC 97-15596. (Illus.). 405p. 1997. text 69.95 (*0-12-436570-1*) Morgan Kaufmann.

Langer, Gloria. Student Sm: Beginning Algebra. 4th ed. (Math). 352p. (C). 1987. mass mkt., student ed. 16.00 (*0-534-91516-7*, 33L4364) PWS Pubs.

Langer, H., jt. ed. see Gohberg, I.

Langer, Heinz & Dijksma, A. Contributions to Operator Theory in Spaces with an Indefinite Metric: The Heinz Langer Anniversary Volume. LC 98-31196. (Operator Theory, Advances & Applications Ser.). 1998. 129.00 (*0-8176-6003-8*) Birkhauser.

Langer, Hermann. Kerle Statt Kopfe! 209p. 1995. 42.95 (*3-631-48658-8*) P Lang Pubng.

Langer, Howard J. American Indian Quotations. LC 95-33151. 288p. 1996. lib. bdg. 55.00 (*0-313-29121-7*, Greenwood Pr) Greenwood.

— The History of the Holocaust: A Chronology of Quotations. LC 96-36636. 328p. 1997. 40.00 (*0-7657-5956-X*) Aronson.

Langer, Howard J., ed. World War II. LC 98-26436. 472p. 1999. lib. bdg. 75.00 (*0-313-30018-6*) Greenwood.

Langer, J. A., ed. see ASTM Committee D-18 on Soil & Rock.

Langer, Jiri. Nine Gates to the Chasidic Mysteries. Jolly, Stephen, tr. LC 92-28679. 312p. 1993. 40.00 (*0-87668-249-2*) Aronson.

Langer, John. Tabloid Television: Popular Journalism & the "Other News" LC 97-12734. (Communication & Society Ser.). 208p. (C). 1997. write for info. (*0-415-06636-0*) Routledge.

— Tabloid Television: Popular Journalism & the Other News. (Communication & Society Ser.). 200p. (C). 1997. pap. 24.99 (*0-415-06637-9*) Routledge.

Langer, Jonas & Killen, Melanie, eds. Piaget, Evolution, & Development. LC 98-12663. (Jean Piaget Symposia Ser.). 270p. 1998. write for info. (*0-8058-2210-0*) L Erlbaum Assocs.

Langer, Josef. Emerging Sociology: An International Perspective. 157p. 1992. 66.95 (*1-85628-279-1*, Pub. by Avebry) Ashgate Pub Co.

Langer, Judith A. Children Reading & Writing: Structures & Strategies. Farr, Marcia, ed. LC 85 31564. (Writing Research Ser.: Vol. 7). 200p. 1986. pap. 39.50 (*0-89391-303-0*); text 73.25 (*0-89391-302-2*) Ablx Pub.

— Envisioning Literature: Literary Understanding & Literature Instruction. (Language & Literacy Ser.). 192p. (C). 1995. text 37.00 (*0-8077-3465-9*); pap. text 18.95 (*0-8077-3464-0*) Tchrs Coll.

— Literature Instruction: A Focus on Student Response. 211p. 1992. pap. 14.95 (*0-8141-3318-5*) NCTE.

Langer, Judith A., ed. Language, Literacy, & Culture: Issues of Society & Schooling. LC 87-11450. 256p. (C). 1987. text 73.25 (*0-89391-437-1*) Ablx Pub.

Langer, Judith A. & Applebee, Arthur N. How Writing Shapes Thinking: A Study of Teaching & Learning. 154p. 1987. 16.95 (*0-8141-2180-2*) NCTE.

Langer, Judith A. & Smith-Burke, M. Trika, eds. Reader Meets Author - Bridging the Gap: A Psycholinguistic & Sociolinguistic Perspective. LC 81-20769. (Illus.). 250p. reprint ed. pap. 77.50 (*0-8357-4310-1*, 203710800007) Bks Demand.

Langer, Judith A., jt. ed. see Flood, James.

Langer, K., et al, eds. Technology Education, Innovation, & Management: Proceedings of WOCATE Conference. LC 95-30836. 336p. 1995. 79.00 (*3-540-60018-3*) Spr-Verlag.

Langer, Karen G., et al, eds. Psychotherapeutic Interventions for Adults with Brain Injury or Stroke A C: A Clinician's Treatment Resource. LC 99-24556. 250p. 1999. 35.00 (*1-887841-23-7*, 65433, Psychosocial) Intl Univs Pr.

Langer, Lawrence L. Admitting the Holocaust: Collected Essays. 224p. (C). 1996. pap. 11.95 (*0-19-510648-2*) OUP.

— Art from the Ashes: A Holocaust Anthology. (Illus.). 720p. (C). 1995. reprint ed. pap. 30.95 (*0-19-507732-6*) OUP.

— The Holocaust & the Literary Imagination. LC 75-8443. 336p. 1975. pap. 19.00 (*0-300-02121-6*) Yale U Pr.

— Holocaust Testimonies: The Ruins of Memory. LC 90-44768. (C). 1993. pap. 16.00 (*0-300-05247-2*) Yale U Pr.

Langer, Lawrence L. Preempting the Holocaust. LC 98-60967. (Illus.). 232p. 1998. 27.50 (*0-300-07357-7*) Yale U Pr.

***Langer, Lawrence L.** Preempting the Holocaust. (Illus.). 232p. 2000. pap. 12.95 (*0-300-08268-1*) Yale U Pr.

Langer, Lawrence L. & Baker, Samuel. The Game Continues: Chess in the Art of Samuel Bak. LC 99-14175. 1999. 39.95 (*1-879985-03-9*) Ind U Pr.

Langer, M., jt. auth. see Hardy, H. R.

Langer, M., jt. auth. see Hardy, H. R., Jr.

Langer, Maria. America Online 3 for Windows 95: Visual QuickStart Guide. LC 97-129145. 288p. (C). 1996. pap. 17.95 incl. disk (*0-201-69401-8*) Peachpit Pr.

— Database Publishing with FileMaker Pro on the Web. 440p. (C). 1998. pap. text 29.95 (*0-201-69665-7*, Pub. by Peachpit Pr) Addison-Wesley.

— Excel 5 for Macintosh: Visual QuickStart Guide. 272p. (C). 1995. pap. text 16.95 (*0-201-88358-9*) Peachpit Pr.

— Excel 98 for Macintosh: Visual QuickStart Guide. LC 98-235165. 280p. (C). 1999. pap. text 17.95 (*0-201-35360-1*, Pub. by Peachpit Pr) Addison-Wesley.

— Excel 2000 for Windows: Visual QuickStart Guide. LC 99-236297. 304p. 1999. pap. text 17.99 (*0-201-35427-6*) Peachpit Pr.

— Excel 95: Visual Quickstart Guide. 1996. pap. write for info. (*0-201-88363-5*) Addison-Wesley.

***Langer, Maria.** FileMaker Pro 5 Companion. (Illus.). 792p. 2000. pap. text 44.95 (*0-12-436151-X*) Morgan Kaufmann.

Langer, Maria. The Filemaker Pro 4 Companion. LC 98-28408. (Illus.). 736p. 1998. pap. 39.95 (*0-12-436575-2*) Morgan Kaufmann.

— Integrating PCs into the Internal Audit Process. Campbell, Lee A., ed. 99p. 1991. pap. text, student ed. 130.00 (*0-89413-255-5*, A6044) Inst Inter Aud.

— Mac OS 8: Visual QuickStart Guide. LC 97-221091. 320p. (C). 1997. pap. text 17.95 (*0-201-69645-2*) Peachpit Pr.

— Mac OS 8.5: Visual QuickStart Guide. LC 99-167854. (Visual QuickStart Guide Ser.). 336p. (C). 1998. pap. text 17.95 (*0-201-35357-1*, Pub. by Peachpit Pr) Addison-Wesley.

***Langer, Maria.** Mac OS 9: Visual QuickStart Guide. 376p. 1999. pap. text 17.99 (*0-201-70004-2*) Peachpit Pr.

Langer, Maria. The Macintosh Bible Guide to Word 6. (Illus.). 750p. (C). 1995. pap. text 24.95 (*1-56609-073-3*) Peachpit Pr.

***Langer, Maria.** Macintosh OS 8.6: Visual QuickStart Guide. 3rd ed. LC 99-462548. 352p. (C). 1999. pap. 17.99 (*0-201-35472-1*, Pub. by Peachpit Pr) Addison-Wesley.

— PageMill 3 for Macintosh & Windows: Visual QuickStart Guide. (Visual QuickStart Guide Ser.). 304p. (C). 1998. pap. text 17.99 (*0-201-35443-8*, Pub. by Peachpit Pr) Addison-Wesley.

Langer, Maria. PageMill 2 for Macintosh: Visual QuickStart Guide. LC 97-127589. (Illus.). 256p. (C). 1996. pap. text 16.95 (*0-201-69402-6*) Peachpit Pr.

***Langer, Maria.** Putting Your Small Business on the Web. 352p. 2000. pap. text 24.99 (*0-201-71713-1*) Peachpit Pr.

Langer, Maria. Quicken 99: The Official Guide. LC 99-167165. 1998. pap. text 24.99 (*0-07-211889-X*) Osborne-McGraw.

— Quicken 2000: The Official Guide. 1999. pap. text 24.99 (*0-07-212140-8*) Osborne-McGraw.

— Quicken 2000 for The Mac: The Official Guide. 1999. pap. text 24.99 (*0-07-212141-6*) Osborne-McGraw.

— Word 98 for Macintosh: Visual QuickStart Guide. Davis, Nancy, ed. LC 99-174786. (Illus.). 272p. (C). 1998. pap. 17.95 (*0-201-35354-7*, Pub. by Peachpit Pr) Addison-Wesley.

***Langer, Maria.** Word 2000 for Windows: Visual QuickStart Guide. LC 00-502523. (Illus.). 304p. 1999. pap. text 17.99 (*0-201-35428-4*) Peachpit Pr.

***Langer, Marie.** Motherhood & Sexuality. LC 00-27427. 2000. 30.00 (*1-892746-64-6*) Other Pr LLC.

Langer, Marie. Motherhood & Sexuality. Hollander, Nancy C., tr. from SPA. 305p. 1998. reprint ed. 42.00 (*1-892746-06-9*, 46069) Other Pr LLC.

Langer, Marshall J. Practical International Tax Planning. 3rd ed. 1050p. 1988. 195.00 (*0-685-69476-3*, J6-1461) PLI.

Langer, Marshall J., jt. auth. see Rhoades, Rufus V.

Langer, Mary. Moon for a Candle, No. 25. (Serenade Saga Ser.). 1985. pap. 2.50 (*0-310-47052-8*, 15558P) Zondervan.

— Wait for the Sun, No. 19. (Serenade Saga Ser.). 1985. pap. 1.49 (*0-310-46792-6*, 15539P) Zondervan.

Langer, Maryn. Divide the Joy. (Serenade Saga Ser.: No. 28). 1986. pap. 1.49 (*0-310-47332-2*) Zondervan.

— Eyes of the Heart. (Heartsong Ser.). 176p. 1994. pap. text 1.66 (*1-55748-463-5*) Barbour Pub.

— Ride with Wings. 224p. 1987. pap. 5.95 (*0-310-47771-9*, 15650P) Zondervan.

Langer, P. & Greer, M. A. Substances & Naturally Occurring Goitrogens. (Illus.). 1978. 67.00 (*3-8055-2659-8*) S Karger.

Langer, Paul, jt. auth. see Swearingen, A. Rodger.

Langer, Paul F. & Zasloff, Joseph J. North Vietnam & the Pathet Lao: Partners in the Struggle for Laos. LC 73-134326. (Rand Corporation Research Studies). (Illus.). 276p. 1970. 29.00 (*0-674-62675-3*) HUP.

Langer, Paul H., jt. ed. see Gupta, Dinesh C.

Langer, Peter, jt. ed. see Chivers, David J.

Langer, R. E., ed. see Applied Mathematics Symposium Staff.

Langer, R. H., ed. Pastures: Their Ecology & Management. (Illus.). 506p. 1990. text 65.00 (*0-19-558174-1*) OUP.

Langer, R. H., jt. auth. see Hill, G. D.

Langer, R. S., jt. ed. see Peppas, Nicholas A.

L

An Asterisk (*) at the beginning of an entry indicates that the title is appearing for the first time.

Langer, Richard. Where There's Smoke There's Flavor: Real Barbecue - The Tastier Alternative to Grilling. 256p. 1996. pap. 14.00 (*0-316-51301-6*) Little.

Langer, Richard W. Bread Machine Bakery Book; How to Bake Wonderful Homemade Breads with Your Bread Machines. 119p. 1991. pap. 10.95 (*0-316-51388-1*) Little.

— The Complete Bread Machine Bakery Book. LC 96-1783. 320p. (gr. 8). 1996. 20.00 (*0-316-51303-2*) Little.

— Grow It! The Beginner's Complete Organic Small-Farm Guide. rev. ed. LC 94-148030. 360p. 1994. pap. 12.00 (*0-374-52390-8*, Noonday) FS&G.

***Langer, Richard W.** Where There's Smoke, There's Flavor: Real Barbecue - The Tastier Alternative to Grilling. 256p. 2000. pap. 14.95 (*0-316-51337-7*) Little.

Langer, Robert, jt. ed. see Cleland, Jeffrey L.

Langer, Robert S. & Wise, Donald L., eds. Medical Applications of Controlled Release, 2 vols., Vol. I: Classes of Systems. 272p. 1985. 155.00 (*0-8493-5405-6*, RS201, CRC Reprint) Franklin.

— Medical Applications of Controlled Release, 2 vols., Vol. II: Applications & Evaluation. 248p. 1985. 137.00 (*0-8493-5406-4*, RS201, CRC Reprint) Franklin.

Langer, Rudolph E. Electromagnetic Waves: Proceedings of a Symposium Conducted by the Mathematics Research Center, United States Army, at the University of Wisconsin, Madison, April 10-12, 1961. LC 62-60005. (Publication of the Mathematics Research Center, U. S. Army, the University of Wisconsin Ser.: No. 6). 408p. reprint ed. pap. 126.50 (*0-7837-6660-2*, 204627200011) Bks Demand.

Langer, Rudolph E., ed. Boundary Problems in Differential Equations: Proceedings of a Symposium Conducted by the Mathematics Research Center at the University of Wisconsin, Madison, April 20-22, 1959. LC 60-60003. (U. S. Army. Mathematics Research Center Publication Ser.: No. 2). 334p. reprint ed. pap. 103.60 (*0-8357-7368-X*, 202113700021) Bks Demand.

— Frontiers of Numerical Mathematics: A Symposium Conducted by the Mathematics Research Center, United States Army & the National Bureau of Standards at the University of Wisconsin, Madison, Wisconsin, October 30 & 31, 1959. LC 60-60026. (U. S. Army. Mathematics Research Center Publication Ser.: No. 4). 144p. reprint ed. pap. 44.70 (*0-608-30388-7*, 204465600045) Bks Demand.

— Nonlinear Problems: Proceedings of a Symposium Conducted by the Mathematics Research Center, United States Army, at the University of Wisconsin, Madison, April 30-May 2, 1962. LC 63-8971. (U. S. Army. Mathematics Research Center Publication Ser.: No. 8). 336p. reprint ed. pap. 104.20 (*0-608-10292-X*, 202113800021) Bks Demand.

— On Numerical Approximation: Proceedings of a Symposium Conducted by the Mathematics Research Center, United States Army, at the University of Wisconsin, Madison, April 21-23 1958. LC 59-9018. (Army Mathematics Research Center Ser.: No. 1). 474p. reprint ed. pap. 147.00 (*0-608-10287-3*, 202113600021) Bks Demand.

— Partial Differential Equations & Continuum Mechanics. LC 61-600003. (U. S. Army. Mathematics Research Center Publication Ser.: No. 5). 413p. reprint ed. pap. 128.10 (*0-608-10257-1*, 201536400094) Bks Demand.

Langer, Russell D. Accounting As a Variable in Mergers. Brief, Richard P., ed. LC 77-87303. (Development of Contemporary Accounting Thought Ser.). 1978. lib. bdg. 26.95 (*0-405-10942-3*) Ayer.

Langer, Ruth. To Worship God Properly: Tensions Between Liturgical Custom & Halakhah in Judaism. LC 98-15069. (Monographs of the Hebrew Union College: No. 22). 350p. 1998. 49.95 (*0-87820-421-0*) Hebrew Union Coll Pr.

***Langer, Ruth.** To Worship God Properly: Tensions Between Liturgical Custom & Halakhah in Judaism. 1999. 49.95 (*0-8143-2850-4*) Wayne St U Pr.

Langer, S., jt. ed. see Dolan, J. E.

Langer, S. Z., ed. Alpha1: Pre-Congress Satellite Symposium, Paris, July 1998, in Connection with the XIIIth International Congress of Pharmacology, Munich, July 1998. 3rd ed. (European Urology Ser.). (Illus.). iv, 100p. 1999. pap. 34.00 (*3-8055-6904-1*) S Karger.

Langer, S. Z., et al, eds. New Vistas in Depression. (Illus.). 339p. 1982. 81.00 (*0-08-027388-2*, Pergamon Pr) Elsevier.

— Presynaptic Receptors & Neuronal Transporters: Proceedings of the Official Satellite Symposium to the IUPHAR 1990 Congress Held in Rouen, France, 26-29 June 1990. (Advances in the Biosciences Ser.: No. 82). (Illus.). 372p. 1992. 181.50 (*0-08-041165-7*, Pergamon Pr) Elsevier.

Langer, S. Z. & Church, Martin K., eds. New Developments in the Therapy of Allergic Disorders & Asthma. (International Academy for Biomedical & Drug Research Ser.: Vol. 6). (Illus.). vi, 136p. 1994. 139.25 (*3-8055-5748-5*) S Karger.

Langer, S. Z., et al. Presynadtic Receptors: Proceedings of the Satellite Symposium, Paris, July 22-23 1978, 7th International Congress of Pharmacology. (Illus.). 340p. 1979. 81.00 (*0-08-023190-X*, Pergamon Pr) Elsevier.

Langer, Sheldon, et al. A Practical Manual for a Basic Approach to Clinical Electrodynography. 68p. 1988. pap. text 24.00 (*0-317-91266-6*); pap. text 24.00 (*0-936445-02-5*) Langer Found BSMR.

Langer, Shirley, tr. see Morgan, Allen.

Langer, Shirley, tr. see Munsch, Robert.

Langer, Stephen. Raise Your IQ Sky High, 1. 1999. mass mkt. 5.99 (*1-57566-342-2*) Kensgtn Pub Corp.

***Langer, Stephen.** Solved - The Riddle of Illness: Your Amazing Thyroid & How You Can Work with It. 256p. 2000. pap. 14.95 (*0-658-00293-7*, 002937, Keats Publng) NTC Contemp Pub Co.

— Super Smarts. 2000. pap. 12.00 (*1-57566-588-3*) Kensgtn Pub Corp.

Langer, Stephen & Scheer, James F. Solved - The Riddle of Weight Loss: Restore Healthy Body Chemistry & Lose Weight Naturally. Orig. Title: How to Win at Weight Loss. 256p. (Orig.). 1989. pap. 12.95 (*0-89281-296-6*, Heal Arts VT) Inner Tradit.

Langer, Stephen E. & Scheer, James F. Solved: The Riddle of Illness. 2nd expanded rev. ed. LC 95-2608. 240p. (Orig.). 1995. pap. 12.95 (*0-87983-667-9*, Keats Publng) NTC Contemp Pub Co.

— Solved: The Riddle of Osteoporosis. LC 97-7975. 96p. 1997. reprint ed. mass mkt. 4.95 (*0-87983-785-3*, Keats Publng) NTC Contemp Pub Co.

Langer, Steven, ed. Available Pay Survey Reports for Other Countries: An Annotated Bibliography. 4th ed. 1995. pap. 160.00 (*0-916506-39-8*) Abbott Langer Assocs.

— Available Pay Survey Reports for the U. S. An Annotated Bibliography. 4th ed. 1995. pap. 450.00 (*0-317-55987-7*) Abbott Langer Assocs.

— Compensation & Benefits in Consulting Engineering Firms - 1995 National Edition. 467p. 1995. pap. 495.00 (*0-614-05741-8*) Abbott Langer Assocs.

— Compensation & Benefits in Consulting Engineering Firms in Indiana. 2nd ed. 208p. 1994. pap. 395.00 (*0-614-05742-6*) Abbott Langer Assocs.

— Compensation & Benefits in Consulting Engineering Firms in New England. 3rd ed. 225p. 1994. pap. 395.00 (*0-614-05744-2*) Abbott Langer Assocs.

— Compensation & Benefits in Consulting Engineering Firms in Utah. 202p. 1994. pap. 395.00 (*0-614-05743-4*) Abbott Langer Assocs.

— Compensation in Food & Beverage Processing. 1995. pap. 450.00 (*0-614-05751-5*) Abbott Langer Assocs.

— Compensation in Manufacturing. 14th ed. 622p. 1994. pap. 450.00 (*0-916506-28-8*) Abbott Langer Assocs.

— Compensation in Medical Equipment Manufacturing. 198p. 1994. pap. 450.00 (*0-614-05750-7*) Abbott Langer Assocs.

— Compensation in Research & Development. 9th ed. 573p. 1995. pap. 650.00 (*0-916506-34-7*) Abbott Langer Assocs.

— Compensation in the Accounting-Financial Field. 14th ed. 353p. 1995. pap. 495.00 (*0-317-55984-2*) Abbott Langer Assocs.

— Compensation in the Human Resources Field. 16th ed. 1071p. 1994. pap. 500.00 (*0-916506-31-2*) Abbott Langer Assocs.

— Compensation in the MIS-dp Field. 12th ed. 687p. 1995. pap. 750.00 (*0-916506-37-1*) Abbott Langer Assocs.

— Compensation in the Security-Loss Prevention Field. 8th ed. 367p. 1994. pap. 395.00 (*0-916506-23-1*) Abbott Langer Assocs.

— Compensation of Plant & Facilities Managers & Engineers. 438p. 1994. pap. 150.00 (*0-614-05752-3*) Abbott Langer Assocs.

— Fringe Benefits & Working Conditions in Nonprofit Organizations. 7th ed. 1233p. 1994. pap. 125.00 (*0-614-05749-3*) Abbott Langer Assocs.

— Income in Sales-Marketing Management. 15th ed. 1071p. 1994. pap. 395.00 (*0-317-55980-X*) Abbott Langer Assocs.

— Inter-City Wage Salary Differentials - 1995. 1995. pap. 225.00 (*0-317-55986-9*) Abbott Langer Assocs.

— Salaries & Bonuses in the Service Department, 1994. 74p. 1994. pap. 295.00 (*0-317-55974-5*) Abbott Langer Assocs.

Langer, Susanne K. Feeling & Form. 431p. (C). 1977. pap. text 40.00 (*0-02-367500-4*, Macmillan Coll) P-H.

— Introduction to Symbolic Logic. 3rd ed. 367p. 1967. pap. text 10.95 (*0-486-60164-1*) Dover.

— Mind: An Essay on Human Feeling, 3 vols., Vol. 1. (Illus.). 512p. 1970. pap. 16.95 (*0-8018-1150-3*) Johns Hopkins.

— Mind: An Essay on Human Feeling, 3 vols., Vol. 2. LC 66-26686. 412p. 1974. pap. 16.95 (*0-8018-1607-6*) Johns Hopkins.

— Mind: An Essay on Human Feeling, 3 vols., Vol. 3. 264p. 1984. pap. 16.95 (*0-8018-2511-3*) Johns Hopkins.

— Philosophical Sketches. 1979. 21.95 (*0-405-10610-6*) Ayer.

— Philosophy in a New Key: A Study in the Symbolism of Reason, Rite & Art. 3rd ed. LC 57-1386. (Illus.). 330p. 1957. pap. text 15.50 (*0-674-66503-1*) HUP.

— Problems of Art. 1985. 15.00 (*0-684-15346-7*) S&S Trade.

— Reflections on Art. 1979. 25.95 (*0-405-10611-4*) Ayer.

Langer, Susanne K. & Danto, Arthur C. Mind: An Essay on Human Feeling. abr. ed. LC 88-45414. 464p. (C). 1988. pap. 17.95 (*0-8018-3706-5*); text 55.00 (*0-8018-3705-7*) Johns Hopkins.

Langer, Susanne K., tr. see Cassirer, Ernst.

Langer, Ullrich. Invention, Death, & Self-Definitions in the Poetry of Pierre de Ronsard. (Stanford French & Italian Studies: Vol. 45). 128p. (Orig.). 1986. pap. 56.50 (*0-915838-61-3*) Anma Libri.

Langer, William H. & Glanzman, V. M. Natural Aggregate: Building America's Future: Public Issues in Earth Science. (Illus.). 39p. (Orig.). (C). 1995. pap. text 20.00 (*0-7881-1942-7*) DIANE Pub.

Langer, William L. European Alliances & Alignments, 1871-1890. LC 77-1767. 509p. 1977. reprint ed. lib. bdg. 45.50 (*0-8371-9518-7*, LAEA, Greenwood Pr) Greenwood.

Langer, William L. Explorations in Crisis: Papers on International History. Schorske, Carl E. & Schorske, Elizabeth, eds. LC 69-18036. 561p. reprint ed. pap. 174.00 (*0-7837-2291-5*, 205737900004) Bks Demand.

— In & Out of the Ivory Tower: The Autobiography of William L. Langer. LC 77-20035. 1978. 20.00 (*0-88202-177-X*) Watson Pub Intl.

Langer, William L., et al, eds. Western Civilization, 2 vols. 2nd ed. Incl. Vol. 1. Prehistory to the Peace of Utrecht. 526p. 1975. pap. text 21.95 (*0-06-043844-4*); (C). 1975. pap. text. write for info. (*0-06-363843-6*) Addson-Wesley Educ.

Langer, William L. & Gleason, S. Everett. The Challenge to Isolation: The World Crisis of 1937-1940 & American Foreign Policy, Vol. 1. 1990. 16.50 (*0-8446-0759-2*) Peter Smith.

Langeraar, W. Surveying & Charting of the Seas. (Elsevier Oceanography Ser.: No. 37). 612p. 1984. 162.50 (*0-444-42278-1*, I-540-83) Elsevier.

Langerbeck, Hermann. Neue Philologische Untersuchungen Heft 10: Doxis Epirhysmie. 132p. 1967. write for info. (*3-296-14190-1*) G Olms Pubs.

Langerdorfer, Stephen J., jt. ed. see Bruya, Lawrence D.

Langeren, Jacob Van, see Van Langeren, Jacob.

Langerfield, Karl, ed. Iwao Yamawaki. (Illus.). 96p. 1999. 54.95 (*3-88243-642-5*) Steidl.

Langerhorst, Christina T. Automated Perimetry in Glaucoma: Fluctuation Behavior & General & Local Reduction of Sensitivity. (Illus.). 172p. 1988. pap. text 54.50 (*90-6299-025-8*, Pub. by Kugler) Kugler Pubns.

Langerman, Neal. OSHA Bloodborne Pathogens Exposure Control Plan. 382p. 1992. lib. bdg. 120.00 (*0-87371-802-X*, L802) Lewis Pubs.

— Precautionary Labels for Chemical Containers. 176p. 1994. lib. bdg. 75.00 (*0-87371-917-4*, L917) Lewis Pubs.

Langerman, Phillip D., ed. see Adult Education Association Staff.

***Langermann, Y. Tzvi.** The Jews & the Sciences in the Middle Ages. LC 99-31956. (Variorum Collected Studies: Vol. 624). 350p. 1999. text 106.95 (*0-86078-675-7*, Pub. by Ashgate Pub) Ashgate Pub Co.

Langermann, Y. Tzvi, tr. see Langermann, Yitzhak T.

Langermann, Yitzhak T. Yeminite Midrash. Langermann, Y. Tzvi, tr. LC 98-15914. 1996. 49.95 (*0-7619-9003-8*) Sage.

Langermann, Yitzhak T. Yemonite Midrash: Philosophical Commentaries on the Torah: An Anthology of Writing from the Golden Age of Judaism in the Yemen. Langermann, Y. Tzvi, tr. LC 96-22669. (Sacred Literature Ser.). 384p. 1996. pap. 24.95 (*0-7619-9004-6*) AltaMira Pr.

***Langess, Robert S. & Mandelglatt, James L.** U. S. S. Albacore: Forerunner of the Future, Vol. 25. LC 99-47504. (Illus.). 1999. 30.00 (*0-915819-24-4*); pap. 15.00 (*0-915819-25-2*) Portsmouth Marine Soc.

***Langeste, Tom.** Words on the Wing: Slang, Aphorisms & Catchphrases & Jargon of Canadian Military Aviation since 1914. (Illus.). 330p. 1999. reprint ed. pap. text 35.00 (*0-7881-4997-0*) DIANE Pub.

Langeston, Lynne E. Marriage Therapy: Index of New Information for the Married, Divorced, Live-Ins & Professional Counselors. 179p. 1997. 47.50 (*0-7883-1604-4*); pap. 44.50 (*0-7883-1605-2*) ABBE Pubs Assn.

***Langetieg, Jackie.** White Shoulders. (Illus.). 24p. 2000. pap. 6.00 (*1-889460-03-6*) CrossplusRds.

Langevin, ed. Light Scattering by Liquid Surfaces & Complementary Techniques. (Surfactant Science Ser.: Vol. 41). (Illus.). 472p. 1991. text 199.00 (*0-8247-8607-6*) Dekker.

Langevin, D., ed. see Meunier, J.

Langevin, Don. How-to-Grow World Class Giant Pumpkins. LC 93-71941. (Illus.). 128p. (Orig.). 1993. pap. 14.95 (*0-9632793-4-3*) Annedawn Pub.

Langevin, Don, jt. auth. see Wiberg, Hugh.

Langevin, Donald. How-to-Grow World Class Giant Pumpkins, II. LC 98-71190. (Illus.). 160p. 1998. pap. 17.95 (*0-9632793-5-1*) Annedawn Pub.

Langevin, Donald G. The Growing & Marketing of Fall Mums: How You Can Turn Your Backyard into ... a Money-Making, Growing Machine! LC 92-71432. (Illus.). 224p. (Orig.). 1992. pap. text 19.95 (*0-9632793-3-5*) Annedawn Pub.

Langevin, Gilbert. Body of Night: Selected Poems. Plourde, Marc, ed. & tr. by. (ENG & FRE.). 135p. 1987. pap. 9.00 (*0-919349-47-1*) Guernica Editions.

Langevin, Leo J. Advanced VSE Systems Programming Techniques. LC 90-8529. 224p. 1990. 34.95 (*0-89435-365-9*) Wiley.

— Advanced VSSE Systems Programming Techniques. 203p. 1993. 49.95 (*0-471-58029-5*) Wiley.

— DOS-VSE-SP Guide for Systems Programming: Programs, Macros, Subroutines. 456p. 1993. 49.95 (*0-89435-299-7*) Wiley.

— DOS-VSE-SP Handbook for System. 1989. pap. text 39.95 (*0-471-58023-6*) Wiley.

— VSE JCL & Subroutines for Application Programmers. 1992. 34.95 (*0-89435-401-9*) Wiley.

— VSE JCL & Subroutines for Application Programmers. 220p. 1993. pap. 54.99 (*0-471-58028-7*, GC4019) Wiley.

Langevin, M. & Waldschmidt, M., eds. Cinquante Ans de Polynomes - Fifty Years of Polynomials. (Lecture Notes in Mathematics Ser.: Vol. 1415). ix, 235p. 1990. 41.95 (*0-387-52190-9*, 3899) Spr-Verlag.

Langevin, Michael & Snider, Jerry, eds. Magical Universe: The Best of Magical Blend Magazine. LC 96-46576. 284p. 1996. pap. 15.95 (*1-893183-22-X*, Swan Raven) Granite Pub.

Langevin, Michael, jt. auth. see Snider, Jerry.

Langevin, R. Sexual Strands: Understanding & Treating Sexual Anomalies in Men. (Illus.). 560p. (C). 1983. text 99.95 (*0-89859-205-4*) L Erlbaum Assocs.

Langevin, Roger G. Customer Focus. Christopher, Bill, ed. LC 98-73102. (Management Library: No. 18). 104p. 1998. pap. 12.95 (*1-56052-485-5*) Crisp Pubns.

Langevin, Ron, ed. Erotic Preference, Gender Identity, & Aggression in Men: New Research Studies. 376p. 1984. text 79.95 (*0-89859-445-6*) L Erlbaum Assocs.

Langevoort, Donald C. Insider Trading: Regulation, Enforcement & Prevention. LC 91-27756. (Securities Law Ser.). 1991. ring bd. 145.00 (*0-87632-758-7*) West Group.

Langewiesche. Devil in Montana. text. write for info. (*0-86547-581-4*) N Point Pr.

***Langewiesche, Dieter.** Liberalism in Germany. 384p. 1999. pap. 24.95 (*0-691-01032-3*, Pub. by Princeton U Pr) Cal Prin Full Svc.

***Langewiesche, Dieter & Breuilly, John.** Liberalism in Germany. 384p. 1999. 65.00 (*0-691-01031-5*, Pub. by Princeton U Pr) Cal Prin Full Svc.

Langewiesche, Karl R. Carl Larsson: Fifty Paintings. Rice, Allan L., tr. from SWE. (Illus.). 104p. 1985. 19.95 (*0-940607-05-0*) Pictura NJ.

— Carl Larsson: On the Sunny Side. Rice, Allan L., tr. from SWE. (Illus.). 62p. 1984. reprint ed. 19.95 (*0-940607-06-9*) Pictura NJ.

Langewiesche, William. Inside the Sky: A Meditation on Flight. LC 97-49844. 240p. 1998. 24.00 (*0-679-42983-2*) Pantheon.

— Inside the Sky: A Meditation on Flight. (Vintage Departures Ser.). (Illus.). 240p. 1999. pap. 12.00 (*0-679-75007-X*) Vin Bks.

— Sahara Unveiled: A Journey Across the Desert. 1997. pap. 13.00 (*0-679-75006-1*) Vin Bks.

Langewiesche, William. Stick & Rudder: An Explanation of the Art of Flying. 70th ed. (Illus.). 400p. 1990. 22.95 (*0-07-036240-8*) McGraw.

Langfeld, Lynne. Decorative Dough Craft: Beautiful Projects for Different Occasions. LC 96-9922. (Illus.). 128p. 1997. 24.95 (*0-8069-9739-7*) Sterling.

Langfeldt, T. & Porter, M. Sexuality & Family Planning: Report of a Consultation & Research Findings. 62p. 1986. pap. 8.00 (*92-890-1042-8*) World Health.

Langfie. Truth about Mormonism. 1995. pap. text 7.95 (*0-9634097-2-7*) W Langfield Pubns.

Langfield, Paul. A Picture Guide to Chess. LC 75-46637. (J). (gr. 5-9). 1977. 11.50 (*0-397-31681-X*) HarpC Child Bks.

Langfield, Weldon. How to Survive & Prosper: A Guidebook for Christian Men. 1992. pap. write for info. (*0-9634097-0-0*) W Langfield Pubns.

— Joy Without Limits: Overcoming the Unhappy Christian Syndrome. 121p. pap. 7.95 (*0-9634097-1-9*) W Langfield Pubns.

Langfitt, Thomas W., et al, eds. Partners in the Research Enterprise: University-Corporate Relations in Science & Technology. LC 83-3508. (Illus.). 224p. 1983. pap. text 25.95 (*0-8122-1150-2*) U of Pa Pr.

Langford. Logistics. 1998. pap. 65.00 (*0-07-134529-9*) McGraw.

— Mosby Handbook of Diseases. 2nd ed. 2000. pap. text 26.95 (*0-323-00895-X*) Mosby Inc.

— Navigating Research. 2000. 35.00 (*0-323-00947-6*) Mosby Inc.

— Navigating Research. 2001. text. write for info. (*0-323-01012-1*); text, teacher ed. write for info. (*0-323-01015-6*) Mosby Inc.

Langford, jt. auth. see Perreau.

Langford, jt. auth. see Zitrin.

Langford, Margaret. One Came Back: A Civil War Adventure.Tr. of UnRevenant. (Illus.). 256p. 2000. 30.00 (*1-884592-22-8*, Pub. by Images from the Past) Koen Bk Distributors.

Langford, A. T. Why Men Marry: Insights from Men about What Makes Them Ready for Marriage. LC 98-11628. 240p. 1998. pap. text 9.95 (*1-58062-069-8*) Adams Media.

Langford, Alec J. Invitations to Communion. LC 86-6116. 112p. (Orig.). 1986. pap. 7.99 (*0-8272-1607-6*) Chalice Pr.

Langford, Andy. Blueprints for Worship: A User's Guide for United Methodist Congregations. LC 92-41992. 96p. (Orig.). 1993. pap. 12.95 (*0-687-03312-8*) Abingdon.

Langford, Andy. Christian Weddings: Macintosh. 30.00 (*0-687-01703-3*) Abingdon.

— Christian Weddings: Resources to Make Your Ceremony Unique. LC 96-142654. 64p. (Orig.). 1995. pap. 5.95 (*0-687-01143-4*) Abingdon.

Langford, Andy. Cokesbury Chorus Book - Words & Music Edition: Praise & Worship Music for Today's Church. 112p. 1996. spiral bd. 14.95 (*0-687-01888-9*) Abingdon.

— Transitions in Worship: Moving from Traditional to Contemporary. LC 98-35786. 144p. 1999. pap. 14.00 (*0-687-08173-4*) Abingdon.

Langford, Andy, compiled by. Abingdon Chorus Book 1: Praise & Worship Music for Today's Church: Words Only. 64p. 1996. pap. 4.95 (*0-687-03131-1*) Abingdon.

Langford, Andy, ed. Christian Weddings: Windows. 30.00 (*0-687-01455-7*) Abingdon.

Langford, Andy, ed. The United Methodist Book of Worship. LC 92-28537. 1992. 24.95 (*0-687-03572-4*) Abingdon.

— The United Methodist Book of Worship. deluxe ed. LC 92-28537. 1992. lthr. 49.95 (*0-687-03573-2*) Abingdon.

Langford, Andy, jt. auth. see Willimon, William H.

Langford, Anna L., jt. auth. see Kadolph, Sara J.

Langford, Anne. Meditation for Little People. LC 75-46191. (Illus.). 40p. (J). (gr. k-4). 1976. reprint ed. pap. 7.95 (*0-87516-211-8*) DeVorss.

Langford, C. M., jt. auth. see Zitrin, R.

Langford, Carl T. Hizzoner the Mayor. LC 75-40537. 1976. 8.95 (*0-88435-005-3*) Chateau Pub.

Langford, Carol M., jt. auth. see Zitrin, Richard A.

Langford, Cooper H. & Beebe, Ralph A. The Development of Chemical Principles. unabridged ed. (Illus.). 384p. 1995. pap. text 12.95 (*0-486-68359-1*) Dover.

An Asterisk (*) at the beginning of an entry indicates that the title is appearing for the first time.

Langford, D. A., ed. Organization & Management of Construction. (Illus.). 1768p. (C). 1996. 375.00 (*0-419-21030-X*, E & FN Spon) Routledge.

Langford, D. A. & Rowland, V. R. Managing Overseas Construction Contracting. LC 95-209398. 192p. 1995. 67.00 (*0-7277-2029-5*) Am Soc Civil Eng.

Langford, Daniel L. Medical Staff Peer Review: Motivation & Performance in the Era of Managed Care. rev. ed. LC 99-16654. 1999. pap. 35.00 (*1-55648-266-3*) AHPI.

— The Pastor's Family: The Challenges of Family Life & Pastoral Responsibilities. LC 98-18461. 175p. 1998. 29.95 (*0-7890-0584-0*, Haworth Pastrl); pap. 14.95 (*0-7890-0585-9*, Haworth Pastrl) Haworth Pr.

***Langford, David.** Josh Kirby: A Cosmic Journey. (Illus.). 2000. pap. 21.95 (*1-85585-731-6*) Collins & Br.

Langford, David. The Silence of the Langford: Essays (And Some Stories) Yalow, Ben, ed. LC 96-69346. (Illus.). 286p. 1996. pap. 15.00 (*0-915368-62-5*) New Eng SF Assoc.

Langford, David, ed. Organization & Management of Construction: Managing Construction Information. 358p. (C). (gr. 13). 1997. 160.00 (*0-419-22250-2*) Routledge.

— Organization & Management of Construction: Managing the Construction Enterprise. 430p. (C). (gr. 13). 1996. 160.00 (*0-419-22230-8*) Routledge.

— Organization & Management of Construction: Shaping Theory & Practice. 908p. (C). (gr. 13). 1996. 160.00 (*0-419-22240-5*) Routledge.

Langford, David P. & Cleary, Barbara A. Orchestrating Learning with Quality. LC 94-45285. 187p. 1995. pap. 24.00 (*0-87389-321-2*, H0867) ASQ Qual Pr.

Langford, Diane. Left for Dead. LC 98-86412. 208p. 1999. pap. 12.99 (*1-85242-369-2*, Pub. by Serpents Tail) Consort Bk Sales.

— Shame about the Street. 160p. 1995. pap. 11.99 (*1-85242-269-6*) Serpents Tail.

Langford, Don. Are We There Yet? (Illus.). 210p. 1999. pap. 12.95 (*0-9668634-0-2*) Graphics Seven.

***Langford, Duncan.** Internet Ethics. LC 99-59607. 2000. text 49.95 (*0-312-23279-9*) St Martin.

Langford, Duncan. Langford Business Computer Ethics. (C). 1999. pap. text. write for info. (*0-201-34279-0*) Addison-Wesley.

— Practical Computer Ethics. LC 95-2503. 1995. pap. write for info. (*0-07-709012-8*) McGraw.

***Langford, Elizabeth.** Mind & Muscle: An Owner's Handbook. 253p. 1999. 45.00 (*90-5350-883-X*, Pub. by Garant Uitgevers) Gaunt.

Langford, Eulalie T. Heritage. 523p. 1991. 39.95 (*0-9630972-0-2*) E T Langford.

Langford-Garstin, Edward. Aspects of Occultism. Kuntz, Darcy, ed. (Golden Dawn Studies Ser.: No. 19). (Orig.). 1998. pap. 8.95 (*1-55818-370-1*) Holmes Pub.

Langford, Gary & Langford, Lauren. The Psychic Almanac, 1991 A. D. 224p. (Orig.). pap. text 6.95 (*0-9627408-0-2*) Forest Light Pr.

Langford, Gerald. Alias O. Henry: A Biography of William Sidney Porter. LC 83-1743. (Illus.). 294p. 1983. reprint ed. lib. bdg. 48.50 (*0-313-23964-9*, LAAL, Greenwood Pr) Greenwood.

Langford, H. Dale, ed. see Rockefeller University Staff, et al.

Langford, H. G., jt. ed. see Blaufox, M. Donald.

Langford, Howard D. Educational Service: Its Functions & Possibilities. LC 74-176975. (Columbia-University. Teachers College. Contributions to Education Ser.: No. 509). reprint ed. 37.50 (*0-404-55509-8*) AMS Pr.

Langford, J. A. Prison Books & Their Authors. 1972. 59.95 (*0-8490-0892-1*) Gordon Pr.

Langford, J. O. & Gipson, Fred. Big Bend: A Homesteader's Story. (Illus.). 191p. 1974. reprint ed. pap. 11.95 (*0-292-70734-7*) U of Tex Pr.

Langford, James R., jt. ed. see Rouner, Leroy S.

Langford, Janet, jt. auth. see Lee, Carol K.

Langford, Jerome J. Galileo, Science & the Church. 3rd ed. LC 98-22638. (Illus.). 245p. 1998. 32.50 (*1-890318-25-6*) St Augustines Pr.

— Galileo, Science & the Church. 3rd ed. 248p. (C). 1992. pap. text 17.95 (*0-472-06510-6*, 06510) U of Mich Pr.

Langford, Jim. Happy Are They... Living the Beatitudes in America. LC 96-47975. 192p. (Orig.). 1997. pap. 12.00 (*0-7648-0059-0*, Liguori Triumph) Liguori Pubns.

Langford, Jim, jt. auth. see Walton, Jerome.

Langford, Joel. Silver: Practical Guide to Collecting Silverware. 1991. 12.98 (*1-55521-710-9*) Bk Sales Inc.

***Langford, John.** Toward a Financially Sustainable Irrigation System: Lessons from the State of Victoria, Australia, 1984-1994, Vol. 423. LC 99-55520. (World Bank Technical Papers). 1998. write for info. (*0-8213-4404-8*) World Bank.

Langford, John, et al. Toward a Financially Sustainable Irrigation System: Lessons from the State of Victoria, Australia, 1984-1994. LC 98-32236. 107p. 1999. pap. 22.00 (*0-8213-4286-X*) World Bank.

Langford, John W. Transport in Transition: The Reorganization of the Federal Transport Portfolio. LC 76-381003. (Canadian Public Administration Ser.). 283p. reprint ed. pap. 87.80 (*0-7837-1165-4*, 204169400022) Bks Demand.

Langford, John W. & Brownsey, K. Lorne. Economic Policy-Making in the Asia-Pacific Region. 342p. 1990. 26.95 (*0-88645-104-3*, Pub. by Inst Res Pub) Ashgate Pub Co.

Langford, John W., jt. auth. see Kernaghan, Kenneth.

Langford, Joseph D. & Burrows, William E. Programming Business Applications with Visual Basic. (Illus.). 512p. (C). 1996. pap. text 50.00 (*0-07-036435-4*) McGraw.

Langford, Joseph D., jt. auth. see Burrows, William E.

Langford, Larry L. Fiction & the Social Contract: Genocide, Pornography, & the Deconstruction of History, Vol. 9. LC 97-13444. (Studies in Literary Criticism & Theory). 175p. (C). 1998. text 42.95 (*0-8204-3849-9*) P Lang Pubng.

Langford, Laura C. The Ladies of the White House. LC 70-171655. (Illus.). reprint ed. 76.50 (*0-404-04608-8*) AMS Pr.

Langford, Lauren, jt. auth. see Langford, Gary.

Langford, Laurie. The Big Talk: Talking to Your Child about Sex & Dating. LC 98-10052. 256p. 1998. pap. 14.95 (*0-471-19586-3*) Wiley.

— If It's Love You Want, Why Settle for (Just) Sex? 288p. 1997. per. 14.00 (*0-7615-0995-X*) Prima Pub.

— If It's Love You Want, Why Settle for (Just) Sex? Practical Steps to Avoid Having Sex Too Soon. 288p. 1996. 18.95 (*0-7615-0309-9*) Prima Pub.

Langford, Les. Understanding Police Traffic RADAR & LIDAR. (Illus.). 173p. 1998. pap. text 19.95 (*0-9667433-0-X*) Law Enforcement.

— Understanding Police Traffic RADAR & LIDAR: Instructor's Course. (Illus.). 243p. 1998. ring bd. 29.95 (*0-9667433-1-8*) Law Enforcement.

Langford, Martha. George Steeves, 1979-1993. 115p. 1994. pap. 34.95 (*0-88884-566-9*) U Ch Pr.

— Tom Gibson: False Evidence Appearing Real. 115p. 1994. pap. 25.00 (*0-88884-567-7*) U Ch Pr.

Langford, Martha, ed. Beau: A Reflection on the Nature of Beauty in Photography. (Illus.). 112p. 1992. pap. 39.95 (*0-88884-562-6*) U Ch Pr.

Langford, Mary J. The Fairest Isle: History of Jamaica Friends. 210p. 1998. pap. 12.00 (*0-944350-42-9*) Friends United.

Langford, Michael J. Advanced Photography. 5th ed. (Illus.). 308p. 1989. pap. 44.95 (*0-240-51088-7*, Focal) Buttrwrth-Heinemann.

— Advanced Photography. 8th ed. LC 97-42017. (Illus.). 336p. 1998. pap. text 47.95 (*0-240-51486-6*, Focal) Buttrwrth-Heinemann.

— Basic Photography. 6th ed. LC 97-210537. (Illus.). 320p. 2000. pap. text 37.95 (*0-240-51485-8*, Focal) Buttrwrth-Heinemann.

***Langford, Michael J.** Basic Photography. 7th ed. (Illus.). 320p. 2000. pap. 37.95 (*0-240-51592-7*, Focal) Buttrwrth-Heinemann.

Langford, Michael J. The Darkroom Handbook. LC 83-49188. 120p. 1984. pap. 29.95 (*0-394-72468-2*) Knopf.

— Learn Photography in a Weekend. LC 92-53044. 1992. 16.95 (*0-679-41674-9*) Knopf.

— Michael Langford's 35mm Handbook. 3rd ed. LC 92-54920. 1993. pap. 22.00 (*0-679-74634-X*) Knopf.

— Starting Photography. 128p. 1976. pap. 13.95 (*0-240-50903-X*, Focal) Buttrwrth-Heinemann.

— Starting Photography. 2nd ed. (Illus.). 160p. (YA). (gr. 7 up). 1993. pap. text 19.95 (*0-240-51348-7*, Focal) Buttrwrth-Heinemann.

— Starting Photography. 3rd rev. ed. LC 99-32434. (Illus.). 191p. 1999. pap. text 22.95 (*0-240-51484-X*, Focal) Buttrwrth-Heinemann.

— Story of Photography. 2nd ed. (Illus.). 224p. 2000. pap. text 29.95 (*0-240-51483-1*, Focal) Buttrwrth-Heinemann.

Langford, Michael J., jt. auth. see Hedgecoe, John.

***Langford, Michele.** ABC's of Title VII Discrimination: Age, Race, Sex, Disability, Nationality Disparity. (Illus.). 64p. 1999. pap. 7.95 (*0-9675234-0-0*) JEMS Pubns.

— 491: Or Seventy x Seven Plus 1: A Collection of Christian Iniquities & Other Stories. (Illus.). 2000. pap. 7.95 (*0-9675234-2-7*) JEMS Pubns.

— Love Pat's from God: How Much My Father Loves Me. fac. ed. (Illus.). 2000. pap. 9.95 (*0-9675234-1-9*) JEMS Pubns.

Langford, Michele K., ed. Contours of the Fantastic: Selected Essays from the Eighth International Conference on the Fantastic in the Arts, 41. LC 89-23308. (Contributions to the Study of Science Fiction & Fantasy Ser.: No. 41). 248p. 1990. 62.95 (*0-313-26647-6*, LCN/) Greenwood.

Langford, Nanci. Politics, Pitchforks & Pickle Jars: 75 Years of Organized Farm Women in Alberta. LC 97-190911. (Illus.). 176p. (Orig.). 1997. pap. write for info. (*1-55059-147-9*) Detselig Ents.

Langford, Nathaniel P. The Ascent of Mt. Hayden. Jones, William R., ed. (Illus.). 1980. reprint ed. pap. 2.00 (*0-89646-066-5*) Vistabooks.

— Discovery of Yellowstone Park: Journal of the Washburn Expedition to the Yellowstone & Firehole Rivers in the Year 1870. LC 78-93106. (Illus.). lxii, 147p. 1972. pap. 9.95 (*0-8032-5705-8*, Bison Books) U of Nebr Pr.

— The Discovery of Yellowstone Park, Journal of the Washburn Expedition to the Yellowstone & Firehole Rivers in the Year 1870. (American Biography Ser.). 125p. 1991. reprint ed. lib. bdg. 59.00 (*0-7812-8238-1*) Rprt Serv.

— Vigilante Days & Ways, 2 vols. LC 76-156021. reprint ed. 95.00 (*0-404-09121-0*) AMS Pr.

— Vigilante Days & Ways. LC 71-160979. (Select Bibliographies Reprint Ser.). 1977. reprint ed. 42.95 (*0-8369-5847-0*) Ayer.

— Vigilante Days & Ways. rev. ed. (Sweetgrass Bks.). 352p. 1996. pap. 14.95 (*1-56037-038-6*) Am Wrld Geog.

Langford, P. E. Modern Philosophies of Human Nature: Their Emergence from Christian Thought. (Martinus Nijhoff Philosophy Library: No. 15). 272p. 1986. lib. bdg. 129.50 (*90-247-3370-7*, Pub. by M Nijhoff) Kluwer Academic.

— Modern Philosophies of Human Nature: Their Emergence from Christian Thought. (Martinus Nijhoff Philosophy Library: No. 15). 272p. 1986. pap. text 59.00 (*90-247-3371-5*, Pub. by M Nijhoff) Kluwer Academic.

Langford, Pat. Embroidery from Sketch to Stitch. 96p. 1996. 34.95 (*0-9629056-7-4*) Quilters Res.

***Langford, Paul.** Englishness Identified: Manners & Character, 1650-1850. LC 99-41373. 400p. 2000. write for info. (*0-19-820681-X*) OUP.

— A Polite & Commercial People: England, 1727-1783. (Illus.). 820p. 1998. 55.00 (*0-19-820733-6*) OUP.

Langford, Paul. A Polite & Commercial People: England, 1727-1783. (New Oxford History of England Ser.). (Illus.). 820p. 1994. reprint ed. pap. text 22.00 (*0-19-285253-1*) OUP.

Langford, Paul. Public Life & Propertied Englishmen, 1689-1798. (Ford Lectures 1990). (Illus.). 622p. 1994. reprint ed. pap. text 32.00 (*0-19-820534-1*) OUP.

— Public Life & Propertied Englishmen, 1689-1798: The Ford Lectures Delivered in the University of Oxford, 1990. (Ford Lectures 1990). (Illus.). 622p. 1991. text 95.00 (*0-19-820149-4*) OUP.

Langford, Paul. Walpole & the Robinocracy. LC 85-6609. (English Satirical Print Ser.). 252p. 1986. lib. bdg. write for info. (*0-85964-175-9*) Chadwyck-Healey.

Langford, Paul, ed. see Burke, Edmund.

Langford, Paul, ed. see McLoughlin, T. O.

Langford, R. Everett, jt. auth. see Campbell, Reginald L.

Langford, R. P. & Combes, J. M. Depositional Environments of Unstable Shelf-Margin Deltas of the Oligocene Vicksburg Formation, McAllen Ranch Field, South Texas. (Reports of Investigations: Vol. RI 219). (Illus.). 60p. 1994. pap. 5.00 (*0-614-01868-4*) Bur Econ Geology.

Langford, R. P., et al. Reservoir Heterogeneity & Permeability Barriers in the Vicksburg S Reservoir, McAllen Ranch Gas Field. (Reports of Investigations: No. RI 222). (Illus.). 64p. 1994. pap. 7.00 (*0-614-06201-2*) Bur Econ Geology.

— Use of Dipmeters in Stratigraphic & Depositional Interpretation of Natural Gas Reservoirs of the Oligocene Vicksburg Formation: An Example from McAllen Ranch Field, Hidalgo County, Texas. (Geological Circular Ser.: No. GC 94-1). (Illus.). 39p. 1994. pap. 5.50 (*0-614-01871-4*) Bur Econ Geology.

***Langford, Rachael.** Jules Valles & the Narration of History: Contesting the French Third Republic in the Jacques Vingtras Trilogy. LC PQ2458.V7Z754 1999. (French Studies of the Eighteenth & Nineteenth Centuries: Vol. 3). 271p. (C). 1999. pap. 42.95 (*0-8204-4249-6*) P Lang Pubng.

— Jules Valles & the Narration of History: Contesting the French 3rd Republic in the Jacques Vingtras Trilogy, 3. Cook, Malcolm & Kearns, James, eds. (French Studies of the Eighteenth & Nineteenth Centuries). 271p. 1999. pap. 42.95 (*3-906762-99-8*, Pub. by P Lang) P Lang Pubng.

Langford, Rae & Thompson, June M. Mosby's Handbook of Diseases. LC 95-52142. 624p. (C). (gr. 13). 1996. text 26.95 (*0-8151-8771-8*, 25183) Mosby Inc.

Langford, Roland E., jt. auth. see Campbell, Reginald L.

Langford, Ronn, jt. auth. see Bentley, Ross.

Langford, T. E., jt. auth. see Dibble, Jerry A.

Langford, Teddy L. Managing & Being Managed: Preparation for Reintegrated Professional Nursing Practice. rev. ed. (Illus.). 352p. (C). 1990. pap. text 26.95 (*0-9626604-1-8*) Landover Pub.

Langford, Thomas A. God Made Known. Brockwell, Charles W., ed. (We Believe Ser.). 144p. (Orig.). 1992. pap. 8.95 (*0-687-17976-9*) Abingdon.

***Langford, Thomas A.** Methodism Theology. 1998. pap. 18.00 (*0-7162-0521-1*) Epworth Pr.

Langford, Thomas A., ed. Doctrine & Theology. 1991. 17.95 (*0-687-11019-X*) Abingdon.

— Practical Divinity Vol. 1: Theology in the Wesleyan Tradition, Vol. 1. rev. ed. LC 98-27227. 320p. 1998. pap. 25.00 (*0-687-07382-0*) Abingdon.

— Practical Divinity Vol. 2: Readings in Wesleyan Theology, Vol. 2. 1999. pap. 25.00 (*0-687-01247-3*) Abingdon.

Langford, Thomas A. & Poteat, William H., eds. Intellect & Hope: Essays in the Thought of Michael Polyani. LC 68-23393. (Lilly Endowment Research Program in Christianity & Politics Ser). (Illus.). xi, 464p. 1968. text 54.95 (*0-8223-0105-9*) Duke.

Langford, Thomas A., et al. Grace upon Grace: Essays in Honor of Thomas A. Langford, Jr. LC 99-28178. 272p. 1999. pap. 25.00 (*0-687-08609-4*) Abingdon.

Langford, Thomas W., Jr., jt. auth. see Isard, Walter.

Langford, W. F., et al, eds. Oscillation, Bifurcation & Chaos: Proceedings of the Canadian Mathematical Society Annual Seminar, 1986. LC 87-11402. (Conference Proceedings of the Canadian Mathematical Society Ser.: Vol. 8). 711p. 1988. reprint ed. pap. 93.00 (*0-8218-6015-5*, CMSAMS/8) Am Math.

Langford, Walter M. The Mexican Novel Comes of Age. LC 77-160486. 239p. 1971. text 21.95 (*0-8290-2401-8*) Irvington.

***Langford, Wendy.** Revolutions of the Heart: Gender, Power & the Delusions of Love. LC 98-50255. 1999. write for info. (*0-415-16297-1*); pap. 22.99 (*0-415-16298-X*) Routledge.

Langford, William F. & Nagata, Wayne, eds. Normal Forms & Homoclinic Chaos. LC 95-20344. (Fields Institute Communications Ser.: Vol. 4). 294p. 1995. text 98.00 (*0-8218-0326-3*, FIC/4) Am Math.

Langguth, A. J. A Noise of War: Caesar, Pompey, Octavian & the Struggle for Rome. 1994. 25.00 (*0-671-70829-5*) S&S Trade.

***Langguth, A. J.** Our Vietnam: The War 1954-1975. (Illus.). 784p. 2000. 34.50 (*0-684-81202-9*) Simon & Schuster.

Langguth, A. J. Patriots: The Men Who Started the American Revolution. 640p. 1989. pap. 16.00 (*0-671-67562-1*) S&S Trade Pap.

Langguth, A. J., ed. see Corwin, Norman.

Langguth, Gerd. In Search of Security: A Socio-Psychological Portrait of Today's Germany. LC 95-31398. 256p. 1995. 65.00 (*0-275-95231-2*, Praeger Pubs); pap. 20.95 (*0-275-95380-7*, Praeger Pubs) Greenwood.

Langguth, Paula E. Bounce Back from Bankruptcy: A Step-by-Step Guide to Getting Back on Your Financial Feet. v, 58p. (Orig.). 1996. pap. 14.95 (*1-889605-00-X*) Pellingham Casper.

Langhaar, Henry L. Energy Methods in Applied Mechanics. LC 88-38817. 364p. (C). 1989. reprint ed. lib. bdg. 43.50 (*0-89464-364-9*) Krieger.

Langham, Barbara A. The Complete Workers' Compensation Guide for Texas Physicians. 2nd rev. ed. LC 97-217475. (C). 1997. 169.00 (*0-9640262-8-7*) TX Med Assn.

— The Pecan Tree: A True Friend. LC 94-96074. (Illus.). 32p. (J). (gr. k-3). 1994. lib. bdg. 12.95 (*0-9640804-0-0*) B A Langham.

Langham Brown, Jo. Tune in or Buy In? 1997. 26.00 (*1-86020-531-3*, Pub. by U of Luton Pr) Bks Intl VA.

Langham, Derald G. Circle Gardening. (Illus.). 1978. pap. 12.95 (*0-8159-5215-5*) Devin.

— Circle Gardening: Producing Food by Genesa Principles LC 77-92698. xii, 93p. 1978. 5.95 (*0-8159-5217-1*) Devin.

Langham, Ian G. The Building of British Social Anthropology. 420p. 1981. lib. bdg. 171.00 (*90-277-1264-6*) Kluwer Academic.

Langham, Ian G., jt. ed. see Oldroyd, David R.

Langham, Josephine. Lights, Camera, Action! Careers in Film, Television, & Video. 2nd rev. ed. (Distributed for the British Film Institute Ser.). 230p. 1996. pap. 19.95 (*0-85170-573-1*, Pub. by British Film Inst) Ind U Pr.

Langham, Josephine & Chrichley, Janine. Radio Research: An Annotated Bibliography, 1975-1988. 368p. 1990. text 96.95 (*0-566-07130-4*, Pub. by Avebry) Ashgate Pub Co.

Langham, M. J., jt. auth. see Hussey, David E.

Langham, Marion. Belleek-Irish Porcelain: An Illustrated Guide to Over 2000 Pieces. (Illus.). 224p. 1993. 79.95 (*1-870948-77-7*, Pub. by Quiller Pr) St Mut.

Langham, Michael, intro. see Sophocles.

***Langham, Murry.** Chocolate Therapy: Dare to Discover Your Inner Center. LC 99-22926. 56p. 1999. pap. text 4.95 (*1-58008-108-8*) Ten Speed Pr.

Langham, Tony, jt. auth. see Breese, Gillian.

Langham, Tony, tr. see Dunselman, Ron.

Langham, Tony, tr. see Locher, Kees & Van Der Brug, Jos.

Langham, Tony, tr. see Van Haren, Wil & Kischnick, Rudolf.

Langham, Tony, tr. see Zoeteman, Kees.

Langhammer, Rolf J. & Hiemenz, Ulrich. Regional Integration among Developing Countries: Opportunities, Obstacles & Options. 112p. (Orig.). (C). 1992. pap. text 36.50 (*0-472-10376-8*) U of Mich Pr.

Langhans, Edward A. Eighteenth Century British & Irish Promptbooks: A Descriptive Bibliography, 6. LC 87-23638. (Bibliographies & Indexes in the Performing Arts Ser.: No. 6). 302p. 1987. lib. bdg. 79.50 (*0-313-24029-9*, LEB/, Greenwood Pr) Greenwood.

— An International Dictionary of Theatre Language. Trapido, Joel & Brandon, James R., eds. LC 83-22756. 1032p. 1985. lib. bdg. 115.00 (*0-313-22980-5*, TDT/, Greenwood Pr) Greenwood.

— Restoration Promptbooks. LC 80-15626. 563p. 1981. 100.00 (*0-8093-0885-1*) S Ill U Pr.

Langhans, Robert W. Greenhouse Management: Guide to Structures, Environmental Control, Materials Handling, Crop Programming & Business Analysis. 3rd ed. (Illus.). 274p. 1990. 30.00 (*0-9604006-2-1*) Halcyon Ithaca.

Langhart, Janet, jt. auth. see Phillips, Colette.

Langhart, Nicholas. Houses of Southold: First Three Hundred Fifty Years. 1976. 27.95 (*0-8488-0870-3*) Amereon Ltd.

***Langhauser, Susan.** Blessings & Rituals for the Journey of Life. LC 99-46789. 144p. 2000. pap. 13.00 (*0-687-07437-1*) Abingdon.

Langheinrich, Gunter. Verformungsanalyse Im Rhenoherzynikum. (Geotektonische Forschungen Ser.: Vol. 51). (GER.). ii, 127p. 1976. 47.00 (*3-510-50017-2*, Pub. by E Schweizerbartsche) Balogh.

Langhoff, June. The Business Traveler's Survival Guide: How to Get Work Done While on the Road. LC 97-73915. (Illus.). 128p. (Orig.). 1997. pap. 9.95 (*1-890154-03-2*) Aegis Pub Grp.

— Phone Company Services: Working Smarter with the Right Telecom Tools. LC 97-73917. (Illus.). 102p. (Orig.). 1997. pap. 9.95 (*1-890154-01-6*) Aegis Pub Grp.

— Telecom Made Easy: Money-Saving, Profit-Building Solutions for Home Businesses, Telecommuters & Small Organizations. 3rd ed. LC 97-72689. (Illus.). 400p. (Orig.). 1997. pap. 19.95 (*0-9632790-7-6*) Aegis Pub Grp.

***Langhoff, June.** Telecom Made Easy: Money-Saving, Profit-Building Solutions for Home Businesses, Telecommuters. 4th ed. 2000. pap. text 19.95 (*1-890154-14-8*) Aegis Pub Grp.

Langhoff, June. The Telecommuter's Advisor: Real World Solutions for Remote Workers. 2nd ed. LC 99-23768. (Illus.). 251p. 1999. pap. 14.95 (*1-890154-10-5*, Pub. by Aegis Pub Grp) Natl Bk Netwk.

Langhoff, Stephen R., ed. Quantum Mechanical Electronic Structure Calculations with Chemical Accuracy. LC 94-39289. (Understanding Chemical Reactivity Ser.: Vol. 13). 1995. text 239.50 (*0-7923-3264-4*) Kluwer Academic.

Langholf, Volker. Medical Theories in Hippocrates: Early Texts & the "Epidemics" (Untersuchungen zur Antiken Literatur und Geschichte Ser.: No. 34). vi, 285p. (C). 1990. lib. bdg. 127.70 (*3-11-011956-0*) De Gruyter.

L

Langholm, Odd. The Legacy of Scholasticism in Economic Thought: Antecedents of Choice & Power. LC 97-26895. (Historical Perspectives on Modern Economics Ser.). 226p. (C). 1998. text 59.95 (*0-521-62159-3*) Cambridge U Pr.

Langholm, Tore. Partiality, Truth & Persistence. LC 88-15015. (CSLI Lecture Notes Ser.: No. 15). 155p. 1988. 54.95 (*0-937073-35-0*); pap. 16.95 (*0-937073-34-2*) CSLI.

Langholtz, Harvey J., ed. The Psychology of Peacekeeping. LC 98-23552. 280p. 1998. 69.50 (*0-275-96232-6*, Praeger Pubs) Greenwood.

Langholz, Gideon & Kandel, Abraham, eds. Fuzzy Control Systems. LC 93-28382. 656p. 1993. boxed set 110.95 (*0-8493-4496-4*, TJ217) CRC Pr.

Langholz, Gideon, jt. auth. see Kandel, Abraham.

Langhorn, Richard & Hamilton, Keith. The Practice of Diplomacy: Its Evolution, Theory & Administration. LC 94-15093. 288p. (C). 1994. pap. 27.99 (*0-415-10475-0*, B4100) Routledge.

Langhorne, Elizabeth. Monticello: A Family Story. (Illus.). 328p. 1987. 24.95 (*0-912697-58-X*) Algonquin Bks.

***Langhorne, Henry.** Tombigbee. 115p. 1999. pap. 15.00 (*0-944206-05-0*) W FL Lit Fed.

Langhorne, Karyn E., jt. auth. see Martin, Eric R.

Langhorne, Mary J., ed. Developing An Information Literacy Program K-12: A How-to-Do-It Manual & CD ROM Package. LC 98-7714. (Illus.). 300p. 1998. pap. 75.00 incl. cd-rom (*1-55570-332-1*) Neal-Schuman.

Langie, Andre. Cryptography: A Study on Secret Writings. rev. ed. 192p. (C). 1984. pap. text 20.80 (*0-89412-061-1*) Aegean Park Pr.

Langill, Ellen. Carroll College: The First Century, 1846-1946. LC 79-54879. (Illus.). 1980. text 20.95 (*0-916120-06-6*) Carroll Coll.

— Pompey Poems... Celebrating a Cat. LC 86-91603. (Illus.). 64p. (YA). (gr. 7-12). 1986. 10.25 (*0-943864-28-3*) Davenport.

Langill, Ellen D. Foley & Lardner: Attorneys at Law, 1842-1992. LC 92-20157. (Illus.). 266p. 1992. 35.00 (*0-87020-267-7*, FOLLA) State Hist Soc Wis.

Langill, Ellen D. & Loerke, Jean P., eds. From Farmland to Freeways: A History of Waukesha County, Wisconsin. (Illus.). 480p. 1984. 10.00 (*0-685-09626-2*) Waukesha.

Langille, Carol. All That Glitters on Water. Raymond, Clarinda H., ed. 64p. 1990. pap. 5.95 (*0-932616-29-1*) Brick Hse Bks.

Langille, Jacqueline, jt. auth. see Kalman, Bobbie.

Langille, P. G. & Canada Staff. A Survey of Chemical Spill Countermeasures. LC 97-40553. 1997. lib. bdg. 65.00 (*1-56670-313-1*) Lewis Pubs.

Langille, Peter. Changing the Guard: Canada's Defense in Transition. 224p. 1990. text 32.50 (*0-8020-5870-1*) U of Toronto Pr.

Langilotti, Frank T. Adjunctive Therapy: 1985 Edition. (Illus.). 152p. 1985. 30.00 (*0-938470-03-5*) NY Chiro Coll.

Langin, Bernd G. Plain & Amish: An Alternative to Modern Pessimism. Thiessen, Jack, tr. from GER. LC 94-8324. (Illus.). 416p. 1994. pap. 16.99 (*0-8361-3665-9*) Herald Pr.

Langin, Chester. An Easy Course in Using DOS. 368p. 1992. pap. 9.95 (*0-931011-40-X*) Grapevine Pubns.

Langino, Charles F., Jr. & Murphy, John W. Reason & Rationality in Health & Human Services Delivery. Pardeck, John T., ed. LC 98-10498. 120p. 1998. 29.95 (*0-7890-0509-3*) Haworth Pr.

Langiulli, Nino. European Existentialism. LC 96-53074. 495p. 1997. pap. text 24.95 (*1-56000-957-8*) Transaction Pubs.

Langius, Gregor. Eine Ausgewaehlte Sammlung Motetten Zu 4, 5, 6 und 8 Stimmen P. Starke, Reinhold, ed. (Publikation Alterer Praktischer und Theoretischer Musikwerke, XV. & XVI. Jhs. Ser.: Vol. 25). (GER & LAT.). 1966. reprint ed. lib. bdg. 75.00 (*0-8450-1725-X*) Broude.

Langjahr, Jenet & Sebree, Anita. Newborn Care Video Step-by-Step: A Parents' Complete Medical Guide to Safe & Happy Beginnings with Your New Baby. 32p. 1995. 19.95 incl. VHS (*0-8431-2288-9*) U Studios Home Vid.

Langjahr, Stephen W. & Brister, Robert D. Coloring Atlas of Human Anatomy. 2nd ed. 202p. (C). 1992. write for info. (*0-8053-4021-1*) Benjamin-Cummings.

— Human Anatomy Coloring Atlas. 2nd ed. 202p. (C). 1992. pap. text 30.60 (*0-8053-4020-3*) Benjamin-Cummings.

Langkau, David A. Civil War Veterans of Winnebago County, Wisconsin, Vol. 2. 384p. (Orig.). 1994. pap. text 27.50 (*0-7884-0035-5*) Heritage Bk.

Langkein, John H. & Waggoner, Laurence W. Selected Statutes on Trusts & Estates, 1995. 908p. 1994. pap. text 21.95 (*1-56662-237-9*) Foundation Pr.

Langlais, Bruno & Reckhow, David R. Ozone in Water Treatment. 592p. 1991. boxed set 99.95 (*0-87371-474-1*, L474) Lewis Pubs.

Langlais, F. & Tomeno, B., eds. Limb Salvage: Major Reconstruction in Oncologic & Nontumoral Conditions, 5th International Symposium - St. Malo. ISOLS-GETO. (Illus.). 880p. 1991. 214.00 (*0-387-52861-X*) Spr-Verlag.

***Langlais, Heather M.** Mummy's Home Town: The Curse of the Amulet. (Illus.). 144p. (J). (gr. 4-8). 1999. pap. 7.95 (*1-930506-00-7*) March Forth.

Langlais, Jean. Four Postludes for Organ. 32p. 1997. pap. text 6.95 (*0-87487-755-5*) Summy-Birchard.

Langlais, K. J. Managing with Integrity for Long Term Care. LC 97-10673. 250p. 1997. 35.00 (*0-7863-1097-9*, Irwn Prfssnl) McGraw-Hill Prof.

Langlais, R. Road News from Tibet. 227p. 1995. 42.95 (*0-387-56965-0*) Spr-Verlag.

Langlais, Robert P., et al, eds. Dental Diagnostic Imaging: Diagnostic Features & Pathology. LC 97-8630. (Illus.). 176p. 1997. text 52.95 (*0-398-06784-8*) C C Thomas.

Langlais, Robert P. & Kasle, Myron J. Exercises in Oral Radiographic Interpretation. 3rd ed. (Illus.). 281p. 1992. pap. text 47.00 (*0-7216-4468-6*, W B Saunders Co) Harcrt Hlth Sci Grp.

Langlais, Robert P. & Langland, Olaf E. Diagnostic Imaging of the Jaws. (Illus.). 661p. 1994. write for info. (*0-683-04809-0*) Lppncott W & W.

Langlais, Robert P. & Miller, Craig S. Color Atlas of Common Oral Diseases. LC 89-12561. (Illus.). 182p. 1992. text 38.00 (*0-8121-1249-0*) Lppncott W & W.

— Color Atlas of Common Oral Diseases. 2nd ed. LC 97-2654. (Illus.). 200p. 1997. pap. 44.00 (*0-683-30173-X*) Lppncott W & W.

Langlais, Robert P., et al. Diagnostic Imaging of the Jaws. (Illus.). 715p. (C). 1994. pap. text 62.95 (*0-683-04849-X*) Lppncott W & W.

Langlais, Robert P., jt. auth. see Langland, Olaf E.

Langlais, Xavier De, see De Langlais, Xavier.

Langland, Elizabeth. Anne Bronte: The Other One. (C). 1989. text 58.00 (*0-389-20865-5*, N8423); pap. text 22.50 (*0-389-20866-3*, N8424) B&N Imports.

— Nobody's Angels: Middle-Class Women & Domestic Ideology in Victorian Culture. LC 94-24393. (Reading Women Writing Ser.). 288p. 1995. text 42.50 (*0-8014-3045-3*); pap. text 16.95 (*0-8014-8220-8*) Cornell U Pr.

— Society in the Novel. LC 83-23597. 279p. reprint ed. pap. 86.50 (*0-7837-2067-X*, 204234200004) Bks Demand.

Langland, Elizabeth & Gove, Walter, eds. A Feminist Perspective in the Academy: The Difference It Makes. LC 82-17520. 168p. 1983. pap. 7.50 (*0-226-46875-5*) U Ch Pr.

Langland, Elizabeth, jt. ed. see Claridge, Laura.

Langland, Joseph. Selected Poems. LC 90-24604. 128p. 1991. lib. bdg. 20.00 (*0-87023-747-0*) U of Mass Pr.

— Selected Poems. LC 90-24604. 1992. pap. 12.95 (*0-87023-800-0*) U of Mass Pr.

— Twelve Poems: With Preludes & Postludes. 40p. (Orig.). 1988. pap. 6.00 (*0-938566-37-7*) Adastra Pr.

Langland, Olaf E. & Langlais, Robert P. Principles of Dental Imaging. LC 97-2361. (Illus.). 467p. 1997. pap. 42.00 (*0-683-18241-2*) Lppncott W & W.

Langland, Olaf E., et al. Textbook of Dental Radiology. 2nd ed. (Illus.). 684p. (C). 1984. 71.95 (*0-398-04910-6*) C C Thomas.

Langland, Olaf E., jt. auth. see Langlais, Robert P.

Langland, Tuck. From Clay to Bronze: A Studio Guide to Figurative Sculpture. LC 99-22169. (Illus.). 208p. 1999. pap. 29.95 (*0-8230-0638-7*) Watsn-Guptill.

Langland, William. Piers Plowman. Kirk, Elizabeth D. & Anderson, Judith H., eds. Donaldson, E. Talbot, tr. (C). 1990. pap. text 14.75 (*0-393-96011-0*) Norton.

— Piers Plowman: A New Translation of the B-Text. Schmidt, A. V., tr. & intro. by. (World's Classics Ser.). 402p. 1992. pap. 8.95 (*0-19-282587-9*) OUP.

***Langland, William.** Piers Plowman: A New Translation of the B-Text. Schmidt, A.V.C., tr. (Oxford World's Classics Ser.). 408p. 2000. pap. 9.95 (*0-19-283646-3*) OUP.

Langland, William. Piers Plowman: An Edition of the C-Text. Pearsall, Derek, ed. 416p. 1995. pap. text 16.95 (*0-85989-429-0*, Pub. by Univ Exeter Pr) Northwestern U Pr.

— Piers Plowman: The Z Version. Rigg, A. G. & Brewer, Charlotte, eds. x, 137p. pap. text 13.71 (*0-88844-059-6*) Brill Academic Pubs.

— Piers Plowman Glossary, Pt. 4. Skeat, Walter W., ed. (EETS, OS Ser.: No. 81). 1974. reprint ed. 70.00 (*0-527-00060-4*) Periodicals Srv.

— Piers the Ploughman. Goodridge, J. F., tr. (Classics Ser.). 320p. (Orig.). 1959. pap. 10.95 (*0-14-044087-9*, Penguin Classics) Viking Penguin.

— Piers the Plowman: A Critical Edition of the A-Version. Knott, Thomas A. & Fowler, David C., eds. LC PR2010.K65. 316p. reprint ed. pap. 98.00 (*0-608-11904-0*, 202312200032) Bks Demand.

— The Vision of Piers Plowman. 352p. 1994. pap. 10.50 (*0-460-87509-4*, Everyman's Classic Lib) Tuttle Pubng.

— The Vision of Piers Plowman. Wells, Henry W., tr. LC 68-55324. 304p. 1969. reprint ed. lib. bdg. 38.50 (*0-8371-0525-0*, LAPP, Greenwood Pr) Greenwood.

— Vision of Piers the Plowman. Skeat, Walter W., ed. LC 66-26827. (Medieval Library). reprint ed. 45.00 (*0-8154-0134-5*) Cooper Sq.

— The Vision of William Concerning Piers the Plowman. (BCL1-PR English Literature Ser.). 216p. 1992. reprint ed. lib. bdg. 79.00 (*0-7812-7183-5*) Rprt Serv.

— The Vision of William Concerning Piers the Plowman, Pt. 4. Skeat, Walter W., ed. (EETS, OS Ser.: No. 67). 1974. reprint ed. 72.00 (*0-527-00059-0*) Periodicals Srv.

Langland, William, et al. Will's Visions of Piers Plowman, Do-Well, Do-Better, & Do-Best. LC 96-45499. (Piers Plowman--the Three Versions Sr.). x, 700 p. 1997. write for info. (*0-485-11408-9*) Athlone Pr.

Langlands, Bell. Frozen Sky. 1998. pap. text 28.95 (*4-7713-3404-8*) Korinsha.

Langlands, Robert P. Euler Products. LC 72-151580. (Yale Mathematical Monographs: Vol. 1). 59p. reprint ed. pap. 30.00 (*0-608-30117-5*, 201679000005) Bks Demand.

Langley. The Dunsmuirs: A Promise Kept. 1992p. 1992. pap. 10.95 (*0-88922-304-1*) LPC InBook.

— Fundamentals of Refrigeration. (Heating, Ventilation & Air Conditioning Ser.). 1995. teacher ed. 14.95 (*0-8273-6567-5*) Delmar.

— Principles of Anatomy & Physiology. 8th ed. Date not set. pap., teacher ed. write for info. (*0-673-55777-4*) Addson-Wesley Educ.

Langley, A. Senior Executives & Their Long Term Incentive Plans. 1996. pap. 145.00 (*1-85953-017-6*, Pub. by Tech Comm) St Mut.

Langley, Adria. A Lion Is in the Streets. lib. bdg. 25.95 (*0-8488-1991-8*) Amereon Ltd.

Langley, Aidan. Senior Executives & Their Long Term Incentive Plans. (Financial Times Management Briefings Ser.). 1997. pap. 94.50 (*0-273-63207-8*, Pub. by F T P-H) Trans-Atl Phila.

Langley, Albert M., Jr., et al. Seaboard Air Line Railway Album. LC 88-50417. (Illus.). 184p. (Orig.). 1988. pap. 27.95 (*0-9615257-2-X*) Union Sta.

Langley, Albert M., Jr., jt. auth. see Beckum, William Forrest, Jr.

Langley, Andrew. Alexander the Great: The Greatest Ruler of the Ancient World. LC 97-24192. (What's Their Story?). (Illus.). 32p. (J). (gr. 1-4). 1998. lib. bdg. 12.95 (*0-19-521402-1*) OUP.

— Amelia Earhart: The Pioneering Pilot. LC 97-27400. (What's Their Story? Ser.). (Illus.). 32p. (J). (gr. 2-4). 1998. lib. bdg. 12.95 (*0-19-521403-X*) OUP.

— Discovering the New World: The Voyages of Christopher Columbus. LC 94-43535. (Great Explorers Ser.). (Illus.). 32p. (J). (gr. 4-7). 1993. lib. bdg. 15.95 (*0-7910-2821-6*) Chelsea Hse.

— Exploring the Pacific: The Expeditions of Captain Cook. LC 94-43513. (Great Explorers Ser.). (Illus.). 32p. (J). (gr. 4-7). 1993. lib. bdg. 15.95 (*0-7910-2819-4*) Chelsea Hse.

— The Great Polar Adventure: The Journey of Roald Amundsen. LC 94-43511. (Great Explorers Ser.). (Illus.). 32p. (J). (gr. 4-7). 1995. lib. bdg. 15.95 (*0-7910-2820-8*) Chelsea Hse.

— Hans Christian Andersen: The Dreamer of Fairy Tales. LC 97-41960. (What's Their Story? Ser.). (Illus.). 32p. (J). (gr. 3-4). 1998. lib. bdg. 12.95 (*0-19-521435-8*) OUP.

— The Illustrated Book of Questions & Answers. LC 96-7972. (Illus.). 96p. 1996. 19.95 (*0-8160-3561-X*) Facts on File.

Langley, Andrew. The Industrial Revolution. (See Through History Ser.). (Illus.). 48p. (J). (gr. 3-7). 1994. 17.99 (*0-670-85835-8*, Viking Child) Peng Put Young Read.

— Leonardo & His Times. (Eyewitness Books). (J). (gr. 4-7). 2000. 15.95 (*0-7894-6290-7*) DK Pub Inc.

— Medieval Life. (Eyewitness Books). (Illus.). (J). (gr. 4-7). 2000. 19.99 (*0-7894-6614-7*) DK Pub Inc.

— Medieval Life. (Eyewitness Books). (J). (gr. 4-7). 2000. 15.95 (*0-7894-6038-6*) DK Pub Inc.

— Oxford First Book of Space. (Illus.). 48p. (YA). 2000. 18.95 (*0-19-521686-5*) OUP.

— The Search for Riches. LC 96-30797. (Remarkable World Ser.). (Illus.). 48p. (J). (gr. 4-7). 1997. lib. bdg. 24.26 (*0-8172-4544-8*) Raintree Steck-V.

Langley, Andrew. Shakespeare's Theatre. (Illus.). 48p. (YA). (gr. 3 up). 1999. 17.95 (*0-19-910565-0*) OUP.

***Langley, Andrew.** Shakespeare's Theatre. 48p. 2000. pap. 10.95 (*0-19-910566-9*) OUP.

Langley, Andrew. Sports & Politics. (World Issues Ser.). (Illus.). 48p. (J). (gr. 5 up). 1990. lib. bdg. 13.95 (*0-685-46458-X*) Rourke Corp.

— Sports & Politics, Set II. (World Issues Ser.). (Illus.). 48p. (J). (gr. 5 up). 1990. lib. bdg. 25.27 (*0-86592-117-2*) Rourke Enter.

Langley, Andrew & Crawford, Andy. Renaissance. LC 98-49766. 1999. lib. bdg. 20.99 (*0-375-90136-1*) Knopf.

***Langley, Andrew & Crawford, Andy.** Renaissance. LC 98-49766. 1999. 19.00 (*0-375-80136-7*) Knopf.

Langley, Andrew & De Souza, Philip. The Roman News. Powell, Anton & Steele, Philip, eds. LC 96-3584. (Illus.). 32p. (J). (gr. 4-9). 1996. 15.99 (*0-7636-0055-5*) Candlewick Pr.

Langley, Andrew, jt. auth. see Brown, Alan.

Langley, Andrew E. Medieval Life. LC 95-25064. (Eyewitness Books). (Illus.). (J). (gr. 5-8). 1996. 19.00 (*0-679-88077-1*); lib. bdg. 20.99 (*0-679-98077-6*) Knopf.

Langley, Ann M., ed. United States Court Directory (1998) 600p. (C). 1999. pap. text 50.00 (*0-7881-7700-1*) DIANE Pub.

Langley, Batty. The Builder's Director. LC 69-16324. (Illus.). 184p. 1972. reprint ed. 19.95 (*0-405-08730-6*, Pub. by Blom Pubns) Ayer.

— Builder's Jewel. LC 69-16325. (Illus.). 1972. reprint ed. 19.95 (*0-405-08731-4*, Pub. by Blom Pubns) Ayer.

— The City & Country Builder's & Workman's Treasury of Designs. LC 67-18424. (Illus.). 240p. 1972. reprint ed. 31.95 (*0-405-08732-2*, Pub. by Blom Pubns) Ayer.

Langley, Batty & Langley, Thomas. Gothic Architecture. LC 73-172512. 1972. reprint ed. 18.95 (*0-405-08733-0*, Pub. by Blom Pubns) Ayer.

Langley, Bill, jt. auth. see Talkington, Bruce.

Langley, Billy C. Air Conditioning & Refrigeration Trouble-Shooting Handbook. LC 80-13578. (Illus.). 650p. 1993. 98.00 (*0-8359-0204-8*) P-H.

Langley, Billy C. Electrical Applications for Air Conditioning & Refrigeration Systems. LC 98-54804. 1999. write for info. (*0-88173-273-7*) Fairmont Pr.

***Langley, Billy C.** Electrical Applications for Air Conditioning & Refrigeration Systems. 459p. 1999. 82.00 (*0-13-014307-3*) P-H.

Langley, Billy C. Electromechanical & Electronic Controls for HVAC R. LC 98-5682. 438p. (C). 1998. 75.00 (*0-13-907569-0*) P-H.

— Fundamentals of Air Conditioning Systems. LC 94-23108. 389p. 1994. 74.00 (*0-88173-176-5*) Fairmont Pr.

***Langley, Billy C.** Fundamentals of Air Conditioning Systems. 2nd ed. LC 00-35434. (Illus.). 2000. write for info. (*0-88173-346-6*) Fairmont Pr.

— Fundamentals of Air Conditioning Systems. 2nd ed. 2000. 92.00 (*0-13-031396-3*) P-H.

Langley, Billy C. Heating System Troubleshooting Handbook. LC 87-14517. (Illus.). 572p. (C). 1987. text 45.00 (*0-8359-2805-5*) P-H.

— Major Appliances: Operation, Maintenance, Troubleshooting & Repair. 547p. 1993. 51.80 (*0-13-544834-4*) P-H.

— Operating at Peak Efficiency: A Technician's Guide to Servicing HVAC-R Equipment. LC 95-15991. 1995. pap. 24.95 (*1-885863-07-1*) Busn News.

— Refrigerant Management: The Recovery, Recycling & Reclaiming of CFCs. LC 92-40577. 155p. 1993. mass mkt. 38.00 (*0-8273-5590-4*) Delmar.

Langley, Bob. Autumn Tiger. large type ed. 480p. 1983. 27.99 (*0-7089-0959-0*) Ulverscroft.

— Blood River. large type ed. 1991. 27.99 (*0-7089-2431-X*) Ulverscroft.

— Conquistadores. large type ed. 448p. 1987. 27.99 (*0-7089-1627-9*) Ulverscroft.

— Falklands Gambit. LC 85-20179. 272p. 1985. 15.95 (*0-8027-0871-4*) Walker & Co.

— Fireball. 320p. 1998. 25.00 (*0-7278-5285-X*) Severn Hse.

Langley, Bob. Fireball. large type ed. 576p. 31.99 (*0-7089-4050-1*) Ulverscroft.

Langley, Bob. Hour of the Gaucho. large type ed. 488p. 1988. 11.50 (*0-7089-1904-9*) Ulverscroft.

— The Third Pinnacle. 256p. 1999. 25.00 (*0-7278-2244-6*, Pub. by Severn Hse) Chivers N Amer.

— Traverse of the Gods. large type ed. 464p. 1982. 27.99 (*0-7089-0879-9*) Ulverscroft.

Langley, Charles. Catherine & Geko: The Adventure Begins. (Illus.). 32p. (Orig.). (J). (gr. k-2). 1996. pap. 9.95 (*1-884570-54-2*) Research Triangle.

Langley, Charles. Catherine, Anna & Geko Go to the Beach. large type ed. (Illus.). 32p. (Orig.). (J). (gr. k-2). 1997. pap. 9.95 (*1-884570-73-9*) Research Triangle.

Langley, Christopher. Women! from Mars. LC 76-15099. 1976. 15.00 (*0-87832-018-0*) Piper.

Langley, Clara B. South Carolina Deed Abstracts, 1719-1772. Incl. Vol. 4. 1768-1772, Books III-ZZZ. 400p. 1983. 37.50 (*0-89308-317-8*); Vol. 1. Books A-T: 1719-1740. 392p. 1983. 37.50 (*0-89308-271-6*); Vol. 2. 1740-1755: Books V-PP. 370p. 1983. 37.50 (*0-89308-272-4*); Vol. 3. 1755-1768: Books QQ-HHH. 386p. 1983. 37.50 (*0-89308-273-2*); 1983. 37.50 (*0-685-73578-8*) Southern Hist Pr.

***Langley-Danos, Eva.** Prison on Wheels: From Ravensbruck to Burgau. 1999. pap. 14.95 (*3-85630-585-8*, Pub. by Daimon Pubs) Cassell & Continuum.

Langley, Donald J. & Blake, Holly J. Tahiti Bound. LC 98-92300. (Illus.). viii, 213p. 1998. pap. 12.95 (*0-9668904-0-X*) A T I Pubg.

Langley, Dorothy. A View from the Red Tees: The Truth about Women & Golf. LC 97-17002. (Illus.). 192p. 1997. 14.95 (*1-55972-440-4*) Carol Pub Group.

Langley, Erika. Lusty Lady. (Illus.). 208p. 1997. pap. 34.95 (*3-931141-59-4*) Dist Art Pubs.

Langley, Ernest. The Poetry of Giacomo Da Lentino: Sicilian Poet of the Thirteenth Century. 1977. lib. bdg. 59.95 (*0-8490-2448-X*) Gordon Pr.

Langley, F. P. & Caldicott, D. A. Workbook in Accounting. 3rd ed. 284p. (C). 1981. pap. 24.95 (*0-408-10680-8*) Buttrwrth-Heinemann.

Langley, F. P., jt. auth. see Hardern, G. S.

Langley, Florence. Glimpse of the Past: A History of Wilmot, New Hampshire. LC 86-22491. (Illus.). 160p. 1986. 14.95 (*0-914659-21-9*) Phoenix Pub.

— When School Bells Rang: The History of Wilmot, NH Schools. LC 76-50006. (Illus.). 80p. 1976. 6.95 (*0-914016-34-2*) Phoenix Pub.

— With Prayer & Psalm: The History of Wilmot, New Hampshire Churches. LC 81-5116. 80p. 1981. 7.95 (*0-914016-77-6*) Phoenix Pub.

***Langley, Garda.** Understanding Horses. 256p. 2000. pap. 15.00 (*0-87980-446-7*) Wilshire.

Langley, Gerald, et al. The Improvement Guide: A Practical Approach to Enhancing Organizational Performance. LC 96-16014. (Business & Management Ser.). 1996. 34.95 (*0-7879-0257-8*) Jossey-Bass.

Langley, Gilbert W. Tricks Your Cat Can Do. (Orig.). 1991. 4.98 (*1-55521-755-9*) Bk Sales Inc.

Langley, Graham & Ronayne, John. Telecommunications Primer. 4th ed. 240p. 1993. pap. 42.50 (*0-273-60157-1*, Pub. by Pitman Pub) Trans-Atl Phila.

Langley, Harold D. A History of Medicine in the Early U. S. Navy. LC 94-31383. (Illus.). 472p. 1995. text 49.95 (*0-8018-4876-8*) Johns Hopkins.

— Social Reform in the United States Navy, 1798-1862. LC 67-10440. 323p. reprint ed. pap. 92.10 (*0-608-30810-2*, 2045402) Bks Demand.

— Social Reform in the United States Navy, 1798-1862. LC 67-10440. 323p. 1967. reprint ed. pap. 100.20 (*0-7837-5741-7*, 204540200006) Bks Demand.

***Langley, I. Lewis, ed.** The American Revolution & the Craft. deluxe ed. LC 00-101513. (Illus.). 820p. 2000. 49.95 (*0-935633-19-7*) Anchor Comm.

Langley, James, et al, eds. Earl O. Heady: His Impact on Agricultural Economics. LC 94-5800. 212p. 1994. text 46.95 (*0-8138-2249-1*) Iowa St U Pr.

Langley, James M., ed. Living with Art Two. LC 83-62194. (Illus.). 134p. (Orig.). 1983. pap. 15.00 (*0-940784-05-X*) Miami Univ Art.

Langley, Jay, ed. see Vuocolo, Sal, Jr.

Langley, Jim. Bicycling Magazine's Complete Guide to Maintenance & Repair: Over 1,000 Tips, Tricks & Techniques to Maximize Performance, Minimize Repairs & Save Money. 4th ed. LC 99-17760. (Illus.). 23p. (Orig.). 1999. pap. 18.95 (*1-57954-009-0*) Rodale Pr Inc.

Langley, Joan & Langley, Wright. Key West Images of the Past. LC 81-71478. (Illus.). 132p. 1982. 24.95 (*0-9609272-1-2*); pap. 13.95 (*0-9609272-0-4*) Images Key.

— Old Key West in Three-D. LC 85-82420. (Illus.). 64p. 1986. pap. 14.95 (*0-911607-04-8*) Langley Pr Inc.

Langley, Joan, jt. auth. see Langley, Wright.

An Asterisk (*) at the beginning of an entry indicates that the title is appearing for the first time.

Langley, Jonathan. Goldilocks & the Three Bears. LC 96-85379. (Nursery Pop-Up Bks.). (Illus.). 10p. (J). 1997. 4.95 (*0-7641-5004-9*) Barron.
— Hansel & Gretel. LC 96-85380. (Nursery Pop-Up Bks.). (Illus.). 10p. (J). 1997. 4.95 (*0-7641-5005-7*) Barron.
— Little Red Riding Hood. (Nursery Pop-Up Bks.). (Illus.). 10p. (J). 1996. 4.95 (*0-8120-6570-0*) Barron.
— Three Little Pigs. LC 95-78328. (Nursery Pop-Up Bks.). (Illus.). 10p. (J). 1996. 4.95 (*0-8120-6571-9*) Barron.

Langley, Jonathan. Rumpelstiltskin. LC 91-11133. 32p. (J). (ps-3). 1992. 14.95 (*0-06-020198-3*); lib. bdg. 14.89 (*0-06-020199-1*) HarpC Child Bks.

Langley, Jonathan, jt. auth. see Oram, Hiawyn.

Langley, Jonathan, jt. auth. see Root, Betty.

Langley, Judy. Bushland Backyard. Kikugawa, Wendy, ed. LC 96-207856. (Land Far Away Ser.). (Illus.). 32p. (J). (ps-k). 1996. pap. text 7.99 (*1-56309-182-8*, N968109, New Hope) Womans Mission Union.

Langley, Judy. The Elephant Path. Kikugawa, Wendy, ed. LC 96-207854. (Land Far Away Ser.). (Illus.). 32p. (J). (ps-k). 1996. per. 7.99 (*1-56309-180-1*, N968107, New Hope) Womans Mission Union.

Langley, Judy & Kikugawa, Wendy. Bush Station Boys. LC 97-197255. (Land Far Away Ser.). (Illus.). 32p. (J). (ps-k). 1997. per. 7.99 (*1-56309-219-0*, N978107, New Hope) Womans Mission Union.
— Clay Homes. LC 96-207855. (Land Far Away Ser.). (Illus.). 32p. (J). (ps-k). 1996. pap. text 7.99 (*1-56309-181-X*, N968108, New Hope) Womans Mission Union.
— Down African Roads. LC 97-197256. (Land Far Away Ser.). (Illus.). 32p. (J). (ps-k). 1997. per. 7.99 (*1-56309-218-2*, N978106, New Hope) Womans Mission Union.

Langley, Leanne, jt. ed. see Bashford, Christina.

Langley, Lee. Persistent Rumours. LC 94-6454. 304p. 1994. 21.95 (*1-57131-001-0*) Milkweed Ed.
— Persistent Rumours. 304p. 1998. pap. 14.95 (*1-57131-014-2*) Milkweed Ed.

Langley, Lester. Mexamerica, Dos Paises un Futuro. (SPA.). pap. 12.99 (*968-16-4288-0*, Pub. by Fondo) Continental Bk.

Langley, Lester D. America & the Americas: The United States in the Western Hemisphere. LC 89-31968. (United States & the Americas Ser.). 304p. 1989. pap. 20.00 (*0-8203-1104-9*) U of Ga Pr.
— The Americas in the Age of Revolution, 1750-1850. LC 96-11598. (Illus.). 400p. 1996. 42.50 (*0-300-06613-9*); pap. 18.95 (*0-300-07726-2*) Yale U Pr.
— Mexico & the United States. (Twayne's International History Ser.: No. 8). 160p. 1991. 27.95 (*0-8057-7912-4*, Twyne); pap. 15.95 (*0-8057-9209-0*, Twyne) Mac Lib Ref.

Langley, Lester D., jt. auth. see Schoonover, Thomas.

***Langley, Liz.** Pop Tart: A Fresh, Frosted Sugar Rush Through Our Pre-Packaged Culture. 188p. 2000. pap. text 9.95 (*0-9673380-0-X*) Octavo Design.

Langley, M. Beth & Lombardino, Linda J., eds. Neurodevelopmental Strategies for Managing Communication Disorders in Children with Severe Motor Dysfunction. LC 90-9166. 342p. 1991. text 39.00 (*0-89079-422-7*, 1942) PRO-ED.

Langley, Michael H. Self-Management Therapy for Borderline Personality Disorder: A Therapist-Guided Approach. LC 93-34656. 216p. 1993. 29.95 (*0-8261-8300-X*) Springer Pub.

Langley, Mike, ed. Rewarding the Sales Force. 100p. (C). 1987. 45.00 (*0-85292-380-5*) St Mut.

***Langley, Myrtle.** Religion. (Eyewitness Books). (Illus.). (J). (gr. 4-7). 2000. 19.99 (*0-7894-6617-1*) DK Pub Inc.
— Religion. (Eyewitness Books). (J). (gr. 4-7). 2000. 15.95 (*0-7894-5886-1*) DK Pub Inc.
— Religion. LC 96-12236. (Eyewitness Books). (J). 1996. 19.00 (*0-679-88123-9*); lib. bdg. 20.99 (*0-679-98123-3*) Knopf.

Langley, Nina, jt. ed. see Shipley, Betty.

Langley, Noel. Edgar Cayce on Reincarnation. Cayce, Charles T., ed. 286p. 1989. mass mkt. 5.99 (*0-446-35784-7*, Pub. by Warner Bks) Little.

Langley, Noel, et al. The Wizard of Oz. 155p. (Orig.). 1997. reprint ed. pap. text 15.00 (*0-7881-5043-X*) DIANE Pub.

Langley, Pat. Elements of Machine Learning. LC 98-29398. 419p. 1995. text 58.95 (*1-55860-301-8*) Morgan Kaufmann.

Langley, Pat, ed. Machine Learning International Workshop, 4th, Irvine, CA: Proceedings. LC 87-3803. 416p. (Orig.). (C). 1998. pap. text 34.95 (*0-934613-41-9*) Morgan Kaufmann.

Langley, Pat, jt. ed. see Shrager, Jeff.

Langley, Patrick, et al. Scientific Discovery: Computational Explorations of the Creative Processes. (Illus.). 344p. 1987. pap. text 19.50 (*0-262-62052-9*) MIT Pr.

Langley, Paul, jt. auth. see Crawshaw, Janet.

Langley, Phillip D., jt. auth. see Boyle, Gregory J.

Langley-Price, Pat & Ouvry, Philip. Competent Crew: An Introduction to the Practice & Theory of Sailing. 2nd ed. (Illus.). 190p. 1991. pap. 19.95 (*0-7136-3421-9*, Pub. by Adlard Coles) Sheridan.

***Langley, R. F.** Collected Poems. 2000. pap. 14.95 (*1-85754-448-X*, Pub. by Carcanet Pr) Paul & Co Pubs.

Langley, Ray. The Pool Players Bible. (Illus.). 1981. 6.00 (*0-686-29667-2*) Langley.

Langley Research Center Staff. Variable Sweep Wings: From Theory to Practice, a Symposium of the Langley Research Center, Hampton, Virginia, March 1981. 1981. pap. 23.95 (*0-89126-103-6*) MA-AH Pub.

Langley, Richard H. Introduction to Organic & Biochemistry Laboratory. 188p. (C). 1998. spiral bd. 32.95 (*0-7872-5321-9*, 41532101) Kendall-Hunt.

Langley, Ricky L., et al. Safety & Health in Agriculture, Forestry & Fisheries. LC 96-46442. 758p. 1997. text 125.00 (*0-86587-552-9*) Gov Insts.

Langley, Robert, et al, eds. Surface Conditioning of Vacuum Systems. LC 89-82542. (Conference Proceedings Ser.: No. 199). (Illus.). 184p. 1990. lib. bdg. 70.00 (*0-88318-756-6*) Am Inst Physics.

Langley, Rod. Bethune. 128p. 1975. reprint ed. pap. 11.95 (*0-88922-088-3*, Pub. by Talonbks) Genl Dist Srvs.
— The Dunsmuirs: Alone at the Edge. 103p. 1991. pap. 11.95 (*0-88922-297-5*, Pub. by Talonbks) Genl Dist Srvs.

Langley, Roland, ed. see Dunnavant, Robert, Jr.

Langley, Russell A. Practical Statistics Simply Explained. 2nd ed. 399p. 1971. pap. 9.95 (*0-486-22729-4*) Dover.

Langley, Stephen. Theatre Management & Production in America: Commercial, Stock, Resident, College, Community, Theatre, & Presenting Organizations. (Illus.). 702p. (C). 1990. pap. 37.50 (*0-89676-143-6*, Drama Pubs) QSMG Ltd.

Langley, Susan. Vintage Hats & Bonnets, 1770-1970, 4955. LC 98-141855. (Illus.). 288p. 1997. 24.95 (*1-57432-028-9*) Collector Bks.

***Langley, Tammy, et al.** Ocular Anatomy & Physiology. LC 99-19851. (Basic Bookshelf for Eyecare Professionals Ser.). (Illus.). 160p. 1999. pap. 30.00 (*1-55642-348-9*, 63489) SLACK Inc.

Langley, Tammy, jt. auth. see Borover, Bill.

Langley, Tania. The London Linnet. large type ed. 416p. 1986. 27.99 (*0-7089-1543-4*) Ulverscroft.

Langley, Thomas, jt. auth. see Langley, Batty.

Langley, Thomas D. & Hawkins, Jerald D. Administration for Exercise - Related Professions. (Health Sciences Ser.). (Illus.). 350p. (C). 1998. text 52.95 (*0-89582-417-5*) Wadsworth Pub.

***Langley, Winston E.** Encyclopedia of Human Rights Issues Since 1945. LC 98-30498. 424p. 1999. 65.00 (*0-313-30163-8*, Greenwood Pr) Greenwood.

Langley, Winston E., ed. Women's Rights in International Documents: A Sourcebook with Commentary. LC 90-53501. 216p. 1991. lib. bdg. 55.00 (*0-89950-548-1*) McFarland & Co.

Langley, Winston E. & Fox, Vivan C., eds. Women's Rights in America: A Documentary History. LC 94-7429. (Primary Documents in American History & Contemporary Issues Ser.). 400p. 1994. 49.95 (*0-313-28755-4*, Greenwood Pr) Greenwood.

Langley, Winston E. & Fox, Vivian C., eds. Women's Rights in the United States: A Documentary History. LC 94-7429. 400p. 1998. pap. 29.95 (*0-275-96527-9*, Praeger Pubs) Greenwood.

Langley, Winston E., jt. ed. see Glasgow, Roy A.

Langley-Wood, R. H. Bacon's Last Captain: A Two-Ocean Novel of World War Two. 2nd rev. ed. LC 98-215858. 342p. (Orig.). 1997. pap. 18.95 (*0-930845-06-4*) Mycotaxon Ltd.

Langley, Wright & Langley, Joan. Key West & the Spanish-American War. LC 97-92760. (Illus.). 72p. (Orig.). 1998. pap. 10.95 (*0-911607-11-0*) Langley Pr Inc.

Langley, Wright, jt. auth. see Langley, Joan.

Langley, Wright, jt. auth. see Windhorn, Stan.

Langlinais, Scott. Mastering Middle Earth, Strategies for Middle Earth - Wizards. 250p. 1997. pap. 14.95 (*1-55622-559-8*) Wordware Pub.

Langlois, Carole S. The Pathway Home: A Journey into Light. 171p. (Orig.). 1996. pap. 12.95 (*0-9637744-3-3*) Thats The Spirit.

Langlois, Claude Victor, jt. auth. see Rigole, Marc.

Langlois, Donald & McAdams, Richard. Performance Appraisal of School Management: Evaluating the Administrative Team. LC 91-67571. 175p. 1996. text 29.95 (*0-87762-892-0*) Scarecrow.

Langlois, E. Chrestomathie du Moyen Age. 366p. 1970. 18.95 (*0-8288-7440-9*) Fr & Eur.

Langlois, E., ed. see De Lorris, Guillaume & De Meur, Jean.

Langlois, Ernest. Genealogies of the Catholic Families of Aroostook County, Maine & the Catholic Diocese of Edmundston, New Brunswick. 2336p. 1979. pap. 200.00 (*1-886560-42-0*) Quintin Pub RI.

Langlois, Florence & Jeunesse, Albin M. The Extraordinary Gift. LC 97-143086. (Illus.). 28p. (J). 1997. 14.95 (*0-7892-0301-4*, Abbeville Kids) Abbeville Pr.

***Langlois, Glennys.** Good & Natural: Delicious High Fiber Low-Fat Cooking & Baking. (Illus.). 102p. 1999. reprint ed. pap. text 15.00 (*0-7881-6338-8*) DIANE Pub.

Langlois, Janet L. Belle Gunness: The Lady Bluebeard. LC 84-43172. (Illus.). 188p. 1985. 9.95 (*0-253-31157-8*) Ind U Pr.
— Belle Gunness, the Lady Bluebeard. LC 84-43172. (Illus.). 185p. Date not set. reprint ed. pap. 57.40 (*0-608-20555-9*, 205446900002) Bks Demand.

***Langlois, Jason.** Wolves at the Door. (Libellus Sanguinis Ser.: Vol. III). 2000. pap. 15.95 (*1-56504-203-4*) White Wolf.

Langlois, John D., Jr., ed. China under Mongol Rule. LC 80-8559. (Illus.). 515p. reprint ed. pap. 159.70 (*0-7837-6497-9*, 204658700003) Bks Demand.

Langlois, Larry K. Inheritance: A Novel. LC 98-90303. 1998. pap. 14.95 (*0-533-12755-6*) Vantage.

Langlois, Richard N., ed. Economics As a Process: Essays in "The New Institutional Economics" (Illus.). 288p. (C). 1989. pap. text 22.95 (*0-521-37859-1*) Cambridge U Pr.

Langlois, Richard N. & Robertson, Paul. Firms, Markets & Economic Change. LC 94-23752. 224p. (C). 1995. pap. 27.99 (*0-415-12385-2*, C0413) Routledge.

Langlois, Richard N., jt. ed. see Fusfeld, Herbert I.

Langlois, Simon, et al, eds. Convergence or Divergence? Comparing Recent Social Trends in Industrial Societies. (Comparative Charting of Social Change Ser.). 340p. 1994. 75.00 (*0-7735-1264-0*, Pub. by McG-Queens Univ Pr) CUP Services.

Langlois, Simon, et al. Recent Social Trends in Quebec, 1960-1990. 620p. 1992. 75.00 (*0-7735-0879-1*, Pub. by McG-Queens Univ Pr) CUP Services.

Langlois, Suzane, jt. auth. see Trudel, Sylvain.

Langlois, T. H. A Study of the Small-Mouth Bass, Micropterus Dolomieu (Lacepede) in Rearing Ponds in Ohio. (Bulletin Ser.: No. 33). 1936. pap. text 2.00 (*0-86727-032-2*) Ohio Bio Survey.

Langlois, Tish. Fault Lines: Sexuality, Incest & Catholic Family Culture. 224p. 1997. pap. 16.95 (*0-929005-98-8*, Pub. by Sec Story Pr) LPC InBook.

Langlos, Ruth & Niemiec, Dennis. Murder, No Doubt: A Widow's Nightmare. 1993. 22.95 (*0-88282-078-8*) New Horizon NJ.

Langmaack, H., et al, eds. Formal Techniques in Real-Time & Fault-Tolerant Systems: Proceedings of the Third International Symposium Organized Jointly with the Working Group Provably Correct Systems - ProCos, Lubeck, Germany, September 19-23, 1994. (Lecture Notes in Computer Science Ser.: Vol. 863). xiv, 787p. 1994. 108.95 (*3-540-58468-4*) Spr-Verlag.
— Formal Techniques in Real-Time & Fault-Tolerant Systems: Third International Symposium Organized Jointly with the Working Group Provably Correct Systems, ProCoS, Lubeck, Germany, September 19-23, 1994 Proceedings. LC 94-33384. (Lecture Notes in Science Ser.: 863). 1994. 102.00 (*0-387-58468-4*) Spr-Verlag.

Langmade, Calvin, jt. auth. see Pischke, Linda.

Langmaid, Roy, jt. auth. see Gordon, Wendy.

Langman, Juliet. Beyond Borders: Remaking Cultural Identities in the New Eastern & Central Europe. Kurti, Laszlo, ed. LC 96-48576. 176p. (C). 1997. text 69.00 (*0-8133-3232-X*, Pub. by Westview) HarpC.

Langman, Larry. American Film Cycles: The Silent Era, 22. LC 97-53128. (Bibliographies & Indexes in the Performing Arts Ser.: Vol. 22). 424p. 1998. lib. bdg. 79.50 (*0-313-30657-5*, Greenwood Pr) Greenwood.

***Langman, Larry.** Destination Hollywood: The Influence of Europeans on American Filmmaking. LC 99-45091. (Illus.). 286p. 1999. boxed set 46.50 (*0-7864-0681-X*) McFarland & Co.

Langman, Larry. A Guide to American Crime Films of the Thirties, 18. LC 94-41519. (Bibliographies & Indexes in the Performing Arts Ser.: Vol. 18). 392p. 1995. lib. bdg. 85.00 (*0-313-29532-8*, Greenwood Pr) Greenwood.
— A Guide to American Film Directors: The Sound Era, 1929-1979, 2 vols. LC 81-14536. 1981. 58.00 (*0-8108-1467-6*) Scarecrow.
— A Guide to Silent Westerns, 13. LC 92-23783. (Bibliographies & Indexes in the Performing Arts Ser.: No. 13). 616p. 1992. lib. bdg. 85.00 (*0-313-27858-X*, LSD, Greenwood Pr) Greenwood.
— The Media in the Movies: An Illustrated Catalog of American Journalism, 1900-1996. LC 97-46949. 341p. 1998. lib. bdg. 65.00 (*0-7864-0433-7*) McFarland & Co.
— Return to Paradise: A Guide to South Sea Island Films. LC 96-47937. 320p. 1997. 48.00 (*0-8108-3268-2*) Scarecrow.

Langman, Larry & Ebner, David. Encyclopedia of American Spy Films. LC 90-3577. (Illus.). 352p. 1990. text 20.00 (*0-8240-5533-0*, H1189) Garland.

Langman, Larry & Finn, Daniel. A Guide to American Crime Films of the Forties & Fifties. (Bibliographies & Indexes in the Performing Arts Ser.). 1996. text. write for info. (*0-313-32926-5*, Greenwood Pr) Greenwood.
— A Guide to American Crime Films of the Forties & Fifties, 19. LC 95-32991. (Bibliographies & Indexes in the Performing Arts Ser.: No. 18). 408p. 1995. lib. bdg. 85.00 (*0-313-29265-5*, Greenwood Pr) Greenwood.
— A Guide to American Silent Crime Films, 15. LC 93-41436. (Bibliographies & Indexes in the Performing Arts Ser.: No. 15). 384p. 1994. lib. bdg. 79.50 (*0-313-28858-5*, Greenwood Pr) Greenwood.

Langman, Larry & Gold, Paul, compiled by. Comedy Quotes from the Movies: Over 4000 Bits of Humorous Dialogue from All Film Genres, Topically Arranged & Indexed. LC 92-56659. 416p. 1993. lib. bdg. 45.00 (*0-89950-863-4*) McFarland & Co.

Langman, Larry & Molinari, Joseph. The New Video Encyclopedia. LC 90-3605. (Illus.). 328p. 1990. text 15.00 (*0-8240-8244-3*, H1221) Garland.

Langman, Larry & Spinelli, Paul. The Complete Video Book. 1984. pap. 3.95 (*0-685-07892-2*, Zebra Kensgtn) Kensgtn Pub Corp.

***Langman, Peter F.** Jewish Issues in Multiculturalism: A Handbook for Educators & Clinicians. LC 99-31750. 464p. 1999. 50.00 (*0-7657-6029-0*) Aronson.

***Langmead, Donald.** The Artists of De Stijl: A Guide to the Literature, 25. LC 00-35332. (Art Reference Collection Ser.: Vol. 25). 512p. 2000. lib. bdg. 95.00 (*0-313-30552-8*) Greenwood.

Langmead, Donald. Dutch Modernism: Architectural Resources in the English Language, 22. LC 96-18777. (Art Reference Collection Ser.: No. 22). 296p. 1996. lib. bdg. 89.50 (*0-313-29618-9*, Greenwood Pr) Greenwood.
— J. J. P. Oud & the International Style: A Bio-Bibliography, 5. LC 98-41648. (Bio-Bibliographies in Art & Architecture Ser.: Vol. 5). 304p. 1999. lib. bdg. 79.50 (*0-313-30100-X*, Greenwood Pr) Greenwood.
— Willem Marinus Dudok, a Dutch Modernist: A Bio-Bibliography, 4. LC 95-46113. (Bio-Bibliographies in Art & Architecture Ser.: No. 4). 304p. 1996. lib. bdg. 85.00 (*0-313-29425-9*, Greenwood Pr) Greenwood.

***Langmead, Donald & Garnaut, Christine.** Encyclopedia of Architectural & Engineering Feats. 2001. lib. bdg. 65.00 (*1-57607-112-X*) ABC-CLIO.

***Langmead, Donald & Johnson, Donald.** Architectural Excursions: Frank Lloyd Wright, Holland & Europe, 6. LC 99-59467. (Contributions to the Study of Art & Architecture Ser.: Vol. 6). 272p. 2000. 59.95 (*0-313-30567-6*, Greenwood Pr) Greenwood.

Langmead, Donald, jt. auth. see Johnson, Donald L.

Langmead, Donald, jt. ed. see Johnson, Donald L.

Langmead, Walter A. Radiation Protection of the Patient in Nuclear Medicine: A Manual of Good Practice, Vol. 2. 1984. pap. 13.95 (*0-19-261422-3*) OUP.

Langmesser, August. Eine Moderne Orientreise. 178p. reprint ed. write for info. (*0-318-71527-9*) G Olms Pubs.

***Langmoen, Iver A., et al, eds.** Management of Aneurysmal: Subarachnoid Haemorrhage. LC 99-19266. (Acta Neurochirurgica Ser.). (Illus.). 100p. 1999. 89.00 (*3-211-83256-4*) Spr-Verlag.

***Langmore.** Endoscopic Evaluation & Treatment of Swallowing Disorders. (Illus.). 224p. 2000. 65.00 (*0-86577-838-8*) Thieme Med Pubs.

Langmore, Diane. Missionary Lives: Papua, 1874-1914. LC 88-26131. (Pacific Islands Monographs: No. 6). (Illus.). 430p. 1989. text 36.00 (*0-8248-1163-1*) UH Pr.

Langmore, John & Quiggin, John. Work for All: Full Employment in the Nineties. LC 94-225465. 400p. 1994. pap. 24.95 (*0-522-84641-6*, Pub. by Melbourne Univ Pr) Paul & Co Pubs.

Langmore, Paul, jt. auth. see Kaye, H. Stephen.

Langmueller, Amalie H. Against All Odds: A Northwestern Pacific Railroad - El River Valley Mystery. LC 98-91623. 312p. 1998. pap. 9.95 (*0-9665024-0-X*) River Valley.

Langmuir. Aqueous Environmental Geochemistry. 1997. pap. text, student ed. write for info. (*0-02-367413-X*) P-H.

Langmuir, David, tr. see Vernadsky, Vladimir.

Langmuir, Donald. Aqueous Environmental Geochemistry. LC 96-37614. 600p. (C). 1996. 88.00 (*0-02-367412-1*, Macmillan Coll) P-H.

Langmuir, Elizabeth C. & Chojnacki, Stanislaw. Ethiopia, the Christian Art of an African Nation. (Illus.). 1978. 6.95 (*0-87577-057-6*, PEMP129, Peabody Museum) Peabody Essex Mus.

Langmuir, Erika. Allegory. (National Gallery Pocket Guides Ser.). 64p. 1997. pap. text 10.00 (*0-300-07320-8*) Yale U Pr.
— Angels. (Illus.). 80p. 1999. pap. text 10.00 (*0-300-07923-0*) Yale U Pr.
— Landscape. LC 97-67663. (National Gallery Pocket Guides Ser.). 80p. 1997. pap. text 10.00 (*0-300-07321-6*) Yale U Pr.
— The National Gallery Companion Guide. enl. rev. ed. (National Gallery Publications). (Illus.). 344p. 1998. pap. 20.00 (*0-300-07481-6*) Yale U Pr.

***Langmuir, Erika & Lynton, Norbert.** The Yale Dictionary of Art & Artists. (Illus.). 800p. 2000. 30.00 (*0-300-08702-0*); pap. 12.95 (*0-300-06458-6*) Yale U Pr.

Langmuir, Erika, jt. auth. see MacGregor, Neil.

Langmuir, G. E., ed. West Highland Steamers. (C). 1987. 175.00 (*0-85174-505-9*) St Mut.

Langmuir, Gavin I. History, Religion, & Antisemitism. 391p. 1990. 55.00 (*0-520-06141-1*, Pub. by U CA Pr) Cal Prin Full Svc.
— History, Religion, & Antisemitism. 1993. pap. 17.95 (*0-520-07728-8*, Pub. by U CA Pr) Cal Prin Full Svc.
— Toward a Definition of Antisemitism. LC 90-41686. 432p. (C). 1996. pap. 18.95 (*0-520-06143-8*, Pub. by U CA Pr) Cal Prin Full Svc.

Langn. Langan: Writing Series 1998. 1998. 0.10 (*0-07-427403-1*) McGraw.
— Langan Writing Series 1999. 1999. 0.10 (*0-07-427404-X*) McGraw.

***Langner, Jhurgen & Ansorge, Siegfried.** Cellular Peptidases in Immune Functions & Diseases. 2nd ed. LC 00-22919. (Advances in Experimental Medicine & Biology Ser.). 2000. write for info. (*0-306-46383-0*, Kluwer Plenum) Kluwer Academic.

Langner, Kathryn A., ed. see Ware, J. Patrick.

Langner, Lawrence. Another Way Out. Landes, William-Alan, ed. LC 97-26683. 18p. (Orig.). 1997. pap. 5.00 (*0-88734-397-X*) Players Pr.

Langner, Lawrence & Robinson, Julian. The Importance of Wearing Clothes. rev. ed. Moran, Chris, ed. (Illus.). 400p. (C). 1991. 24.95 (*1-55599-039-8*) Events Unltd.

Langner, Linda L. & United Nations Staff. Non-Wood Goods & Services of the Forest: Report of ECE/FAO Team of Specialists LC 98-200292. (Geneva Timber & Forest Study Papers). (ENG & RUS.). vi, 44p. 1998. pap. write for info. (*92-1-116691-8*) UN.

Langness, Anna P., jt. auth. see Thurman, Leon.

Langness, L. L. Men & Woman in New Guinea. LC 98-36764. (Publications in Anthropology & Related Fields). 224p. (C). 1999. pap. text 16.95 (*0-88316-594-5*) Chandler & Sharp.
— The Study of Culture. rev. ed. LC 86-32716. (Publications in Anthropology & Related Fields). (Illus.). 288p. 1987. pap. 16.95 (*0-88316-556-2*) Chandler & Sharp.

Langness, L. L. & Hays, Terence E., eds. Anthropology in the High Valleys: Essays on the New Guinea Highlands. LC 86-26415. (Publications in Anthropology & Related Fields). 384p. 1987. 24.95 (*0-88316-555-4*) Chandler & Sharp.

Langness, L. L., ed. see Eastman, Carol M.

Langness, L. L., ed. see Glazer, Ilsa M.

Langness, L. L., ed. see Jones, Rex L. & Jones, Shirley K.

Langness, L. L., ed. see Kearney, Michael.

Langness, L. L., ed. see Lindenbaum, Shirley.

Langness, L. L., ed. see Marshall, Mac.

Langness, L. L., ed. see Meggitt, Mervyn J.

Langness, L. L., ed. see Orans, Martin.

Langness, Lewis L. & Levine, Harold, eds. Culture & Retardation. 1986. lib. bdg. 124.50 (*90-277-2177-7*) Kluwer Academic.

An Asterisk (*) at the beginning of an entry indicates that the title is appearing for the first time.

— Culture & Retardation. 1987. pap. text 59.50 (*90-277-2178-5*) Kluwer Academic.

Langness, Lewis L., ed. see Spiro, Melford E.

Lango, John W. Whitehead's Ontology. LC 78-171184. 102p. (C). 1972. text 28.50 (*0-87395-093-3*) State U NY Pr.

— Whitehead's Ontology. LC 78-171184. 112p. reprint ed. pap. 34.80 (*0-608-10162-1*, 201095800072) Bks Demand.

Langomo, Amando, tr. see Stigen, Terge.

L

Langone, John. Cambridge Rindge & Latin School: Yesterday & Today. unabridged ed. LC 98-74562. (Illus.). 65p. 1998. pap. 10.00 (*1-878284-47-9*) Cmbrdg Hist.

— Harvard Med: The Story Behind America's Premier Medical School & the Making of America's Doctors. 400p. 1996. pap. 14.00 (*1-55850-610-1*) Adams Media.

***Langone, John.** Mystery of Time: Humanity's Quest for Order & Measure. (Illus.). 256p. 2000. 35.00 (*0-7922-7910-7*) Natl Geog.

— The Mystery of Time: Humanity's Quest for Order & Measure. LC 00-41812. 2000. write for info. (*0-7922-7911-5*) Natl Geog.

— National Geographic's How Things Work: Everyday Technology Explained. LC 99-11776. (Illus.). 272p. 1999. 34.50 (*0-7922-7150-5*, Pub. by Natl Geog) S&S Trade.

Langone, John & National Science Resource Center Staff. National Geographic's How Things Work: Everyday Technology Explained. LC 99-11776. 1999. write for info. (*0-7922-7151-3*) Natl Geog.

Langone, John J. AIDS: The Facts. 192p. 1988. pap. 8.95 (*0-316-51412-8*, Little Brwn Med Div) Lppncott W & W.

— Teaching Students with Mild & Moderate Learning Problems. 472p. 1990. pap. text 44.00 (*0-205-12362-7*, H23625) Allyn.

Langone, John J., et al, eds. Antibodies, Antigens, & Molecular Mimicry. (Methods in Enzymology Ser.: Vol. 178). 835p. 1989. text 153.00 (*0-12-182079-3*) Acad Pr.

Langone, John J. & Van Vunakis, Helen, eds. Immunochemical Techniques, Vol. 74, Pt. C. (Methods in Enzymology Ser.). 1981. text 179.00 (*0-12-181974-4*) Acad Pr.

Langone, John J., jt. ed. see Colowick, Sidney P.

Langone, Michael D., ed. Recovery from Cults: Help for Victims of Psychological & Spiritual Abuse. 432p. 1995. pap. 17.95 (*0-393-31321-2*, Norton Paperbks) Norton.

Langone, Michael D., jt. auth. see Ross, Joan C.

Langoni, Carlos G. The Development Crisis: Blueprint for Change. LC 87-29350. 158p. 1987. 29.95 (*0-917616-95-2*); pap. 19.95 (*0-917616-94-4*) ICS Pr.

Langoni, Carlos G., jt. auth. see Shepherd, Geoffrey.

Langoni, Carlos G., ed. see Ronci, Marcio.

Langord, A. C., ed. see Society of Photographic Scientists & Engineers Sta.

Langosch, Karl, ed. Nibelunge Not in Auswahl: Mit Kurzem Woerterbuch. 11th ed. (Sammlung Goeschen Ser.: No. 1). (C). 1966. 6.00 (*3-11-002722-4*) De Gruyter.

Langosch, Karl, et al. Kleine Schriften. (Spolia Berolinensia Ser.: Bd. 1). (GER.). vii, 362p. 1986. 88.00 (*3-615-00031-5*, Pub. by Weidmann) Lubrecht & Cramer.

***Langosch, Sydney L.** Essential Words for the GED. LC 99-13815. 256p. 1999. pap. 8.95 (*0-7641-0882-4*) Barron.

Langosch, Sydney L. Writing American Style: An ESL/EFL Handbook. 2nd rev. ed. LC 98-43402. 208p. 1999. pap. 11.95 (*0-7641-0792-5*) Barron.

Langouche, F., et al. Functional Integration & Semiclassical Expansions. 1982. text 196.50 (*90-277-1472-X*) Kluwer Academic.

Langoulant, Allan, jt. auth. see Gray, Nigel.

***Langr, Jeff.** Essential Java Style: Patterns for Implementation. LC 99-34858. 277p. 1999. pap. text 39.99 (*0-13-085086-1*) P-H.

***Langran.** Government, Business, & the American Economy. 352p. 2000. pap. 38.67 (*0-13-949132-5*) P-H.

— Us Supreme Court. 4th ed. 224p. 1999. pap. text 40.00 (*0-536-02396-4*) Pearson Custom.

Langran, Gail. Time in Geographic Information Systems. (Technical Issues in GIS Ser.). 180p. 1992. 90.00 (*0-7484-0003-6*, Pub. by Tay Francis Ltd); pap. 39.95 (*0-7484-0059-1*, Pub. by Tay Francis Ltd) Taylor & Francis.

Langran, John & Kozlov, Sergei. BBC Russian Phrase Book. (BBC Phrase Bks.). 192p. 1995. pap. 5.95 (*0-8442-9174-9*, 91749) NTC Contemp Pub Co.

Langran, Robert. The United States Supreme Court: An Historical & Political Analysis. 2nd ed. 204p. (C). 1992. pap. text 56.00 (*0-536-57699-8*) Pearson Custom.

Langran, Robert W. The United States Supreme Court: An Historical & Political Analysis. 3rd ed. LC 96-126800. 200p. (C). 1995. pap. text 59.00 (*0-536-59290-X*) Pearson Custom.

Langrana, N. A., et al, eds. 1993 Bioengineering Conference. LC 93-71951. (BED Ser.: Vol. 24). 677p. 1993. 70.00 (*0-7918-0682-0*) ASME.

Langrand, Olivier. Guide to the Birds of Madagascar. 456p. (C). 1990. 70.00 (*0-300-04310-4*) Yale U Pr.

Langrehr, D., jt. ed. see Miranda, D. R.

Langrehr, John. Sharing Thinking Strategies. Presseisen, Barbara Z., ed. 121p. (Orig.). 1990. teacher ed. 22.95 (*1-879639-09-2*) Natl Educ Serv.

— Teaching Students to Think. 110p. 1988. pap., teacher ed. 21.95 (*1-879639-12-2*) Natl Educ Serv.

Langreuter, Jutta. Little Bear & the Big Fight. LC 97-43157. (Little Bear Ser.). (Illus.). 32p. (J). (ps-k). 1998. pap. 6.95 (*0-7613-0375-8*); lib. bdg. 21.40 (*0-7613-0403-7*) Millbrook Pr.

— Little Bear Brushes His Teeth. LC 96-36469. (Illus.). 32p. (J). (ps-k). 1997. pap. 6.95 (*0-7613-0230-1*); lib. bdg. 21.40 (*0-7613-0190-9*) Millbrook Pr.

— Little Bear Goes to Kindergarten. LC 96-35112. (Illus.). 32p. (J). (ps-k). 1997. pap. 6.95 (*0-7613-0231-X*); lib. bdg. 21.40 (*0-7613-0191-7*) Millbrook Pr.

— Little Bear Is a Big Brother. LC 97-44623. (Little Bear Ser.). (Illus.). 32p. (J). (ps-k). 1998. pap. 6.95 (*0-7613-0376-6*) Millbrook Pr.

***Langreuter, Jutta.** Little Bear Won't Go to Bed. LC 99-56178. (Little Bear Collection). (Illus.). (J). 2000. pap. 7.95 (*0-7613-1395-8*) Millbrook Pr.

Langri Tangpa, jt. auth. see Tharchin, Sermey G.

Langridge, Andrew. Zoot Suite. 1998. pap. text 9.95 (*1-56097-295-5*) Fantagraph Bks.

Langridge, Derek, ed. Classification: Its Kinds, Elements, Systems & Applications. 100p. 1992. 50.00 (*0-86291-622-4*) Bowker-Saur.

Langrish, Bob, jt. auth. see Oliver, Robert.

Langrock, Peter F. Addison County Justice: Tales from a Vermont Courthouse. LC 97-20346. (Illus.). 224p. 1997. 21.95 (*0-8397-0097-0*) Eriksson.

— Addison County Justice: Tales from a Vermont Courthouse. 2nd ed. LC 97-20346. (Illus.). 224p. 1998. reprint ed. pap. 14.95 (*0-8397-0098-9*) Eriksson.

— Beyond the Courthouse: Tales of Lawyers & Lawyering. LC 99-38177. (Illus.). 192p. 1999. pap. text 21.95 (*0-8397-1034-8*, Pub. by Eriksson) IPG Chicago.

Langrognet, Michel. Enciclopedia Juvenil Larousse: Childrens Larousse Encyclopedia, 8 vols., Set. 4th ed. (SPA.). 1552p. (J). 1978. 495.00 (*0-8288-5226-X*, S50479) Fr & Eur.

— Enciclopedia Juvenil Larousse (Spanish Edition), 8 vols., Set. 4th ed. (SPA.). 1978. 495.00 (*0-8288-8233-9*, 8471782413) Fr & Eur.

Langs, R. J. The Evolution of the Emotion-Processing Mind. 240p. 1996. pap. text 32.00 (*1-85575-124-0*, Pub. by H Karnac Bks Ltd) Other Pr LLC.

***Langs, R. J.** Ground Rules in Psychotherapy & Counselling. 232p. 1998. pap. 28.00 (*1-85575-171-2*, Pub. by H Karnac Bks Ltd) Other Pr LLC.

Langs, Robert. Dreams & Emotional Adaptation: A Clinical Notebook for Psychotherapists. LC 98-38986. 206p. 1998. 32.95 (*1-891944-05-3*) Zeig Tucker.

Langs, Robert, ed. Current Theories of Psychoanalysis. LC 98-13585. 356p. 1998. 55.00 (*0-8236-1094-2*, 01094) Intl Univs Pr.

Langs, Robert J. The Bipersonal Field. LC 75-42530. 480p. 1976. 50.00 (*0-87668-246-8*) Aronson.

— Classics in Psychoanalytic Technique. rev. ed. LC 90-38548. 512p. 1990. 95.00 (*0-87668-744-3*) Aronson.

— Clinical Practice & the Architecture of the Mind. 160p. 1995. pap. text 28.00 (*1-85575-088-0*, Pub. by H Karnac Bks Ltd) Other Pr LLC.

— Clinical Workbook for Psychotherapists. 528p. 1992. pap. text 50.00 (*1-85575-004-X*, Pub. by H Karnac Bks Ltd) Other Pr LLC.

Langs, Robert J. Death Anxiety & Clinical Practice. LC 98-149910. 264p. 1997. pap. 33.00 (*1-85575-141-0*, Pub. by H Karnac Bks Ltd) Other Pr LLC.

Langs, Robert J. Doing Supervision & Being Supervised. 280p. 1994. pap. text 33.00 (*1-85575-060-0*, Pub. by H Karnac Bks Ltd) Other Pr LLC.

— The Dream Workbook: Simple Exercises to Unravel the Secrets to Your Dreams. LC 95-101066. 208p. (Orig.). 1994. pap. text 15.00 (*0-9641509-1-3*) Allian Pubng.

— Empowered Psychotherapy: Teaching Self Processing. 252p. 1993. pap. text 17.50 (*1-85575-057-0*, Pub. by H Karnac Bks Ltd) Other Pr LLC.

— The Evolution of the Emotion-Processing Mind: With an Introduction to Mental Darwinism. LC 96-24500. 223p. 1996. 35.00 (*0-8236-1775-0*) Intl Univs Pr.

— The Listening Process. LC 78-68010. 688p. 1978. 40.00 (*0-87668-341-3*) Aronson.

— Madness & Cure. 296p. (C). 1995. text 38.95 (*0-89876-218-9*) Gardner Pr.

— A Primer of Psychotherapy. LC 86-22869. 256p. (C). 1993. reprint ed. pap. text 29.50 (*0-89876-197-2*) Gardner Pr.

— The Psychotherapeutic Conspiracy. 1995. pap. text 50.00 (*1-56821-731-5*) Aronson.

— Psychotherapy: A Basic Text. LC 81-17663. 800p. 1982. 70.00 (*0-87668-466-5*) Aronson.

— Science, Systems & Psychoanalysis. 288p. 1992. pap. text 17.50 (*1-85575-036-8*, Pub. by H Karnac Bks Ltd) Other Pr LLC.

— The Technique of Psychoanalytic Psychotherapy Vol. 1: The Initial Contact, Theoretical Framework, Understanding the Patient's Communications, the Therapist's Interventions. LC 72-96542. 672p. 1973. 70.00 (*0-87668-104-6*) Aronson.

— The Technique of Psychoanalytic Psychotherapy Vol. 2: The Patient's Responses to Intervention, the Patient-Therapist Relationship, the Phases of Psychotherapy. LC 72-96542. 544p. 1974. 60.00 (*0-87668-105-4*) Aronson.

— The Therapeutic Environment. LC 79-64458. 592p. 1979. 60.00 (*0-87668-385-5*) Aronson.

— Unconscious Communication in Everyday Life. LC 82-1669. 224p. 1983. 25.00 (*0-87668-492-4*) Aronson.

— Unconscious Communication in Everyday Life. LC 82-1669. 224p. 1993. pap. 40.00 (*1-56821-106-6*) Aronson.

— Workbooks for Psychotherapists: Intervening & Validating, Vol. 3. LC 84-62354. (Workbooks for Psychotherapists Ser.). 302p. 1985. pap. text 33.50 (*0-931231-03-5*) Newconcept Pr.

— Workbooks for Psychotherapists: Listening & Formulating, Vol. 2. LC 84-62354. (Workbooks for Psychotherapists Ser.). 304p. 1985. pap. text 36.00 (*0-931231-02-7*) Newconcept Pr.

— Workbooks for Psychotherapists: Understanding Unconscious Communication, Vol. 1. LC 84-62354. (Workbooks for Psychotherapists Ser.). 144p. 1985. pap. text 20.00 (*0-931231-01-9*) Newconcept Pr.

— The Yearbook of Psychoanalysis & Psychotherapy, Vol. 1-1985. 432p. 1985. text 49.95 (*0-931231-04-3*) Newconcept Pr.

— The Yearbook of Psychoanalysis & Psychotherapy, Vol. 2. LC 86-641022. 356p. 1987. text 45.00 (*0-89876-141-7*) Gardner Pr.

Langs, Robert J., ed. Contemporary Theories in Psychoanalysis. 416p. (C). 1996. pap. text 35.95 (*0-89876-216-2*) Gardner Pr.

— International Journal of Psychoanalytic Psychotherapy, Vol. 8. LC 75-648853. 705p. 1980. 35.00 (*0-87668-428-2*) Aronson.

— Technique in Transition. LC 78-65121. 744p. 1978. 75.00 (*0-87668-349-9*) Aronson.

Langs, Robert J., jt. auth. see Searles, Harold.

Langs, Robert J., jt. auth. see Stone, Leo.

Langs, Robert L. The Daydream Workbook. 1995. pap. 15.00 (*0-9641509-7-2*) Allian Pubng.

Langsam, Avivia. M'Aleph V'ad Tav: Spirit Duplicating Reading Primer. (Illus.). 1997. pap., teacher ed. 18.00 (*0-915152-02-9*, A040) Langsam Publishing Co.

— M'Tishrei V'ad Elul. (Illus.). 86p. 1997. pap., teacher ed. 28.00 (*0-915152-04-5*, A042) Langsam Publishing Co.

— Nichtov M'Aleph V'ad Tav: Spirit Duplicating Writing Primer. (Illus.). 1997. pap., teacher ed. 18.00 (*0-915152-03-7*, A041) Langsam Publishing Co.

Langsam, Walter C., ed. Historic Documents of World War II. LC 76-56108. 192p. 1977. reprint ed. lib. bdg. 45.00 (*0-8371-9426-1*, LAHD, Greenwood Pr) Greenwood.

Langsam, Walter E. Great Houses of the Queen City: Two Hundred Years of Historic & Contemporary Architecture & Interiors in Cincinnati & Northern Kentucky. 2nd ed. (Illus.). 1997. 45.95 (*0-911497-23-4*); pap. 34.95 (*0-911497-24-2*) Cin Mus Ctr.

Langsam, Yedidyah. C. 312p. (C). 1996. text 31.80 (*0-536-59699-9*) Pearson Custom.

Langsam, Yedidyah, et al. Data Structures Using C & C++ 2nd ed. LC 95-25747. 672p. (gr. 1). 1995. 73.00 (*0-13-036997-7*) P-H.

Langsdon, L. R., Sr. Everyman Says - One-Liners for Writing, Speaking & Daily Living: Common Sense Strategies for Winning at the Game of Life. 327p. 1989. 18.95 (*0-9619098-0-3*) Angel Par Pr.

***Langsdon, Phillip R.** Tennessee: A Political History. LC 99-75681. (Illus.). 448p. 2000. 39.95 (*1-57736-125-3*, Hillsboro Pr) Providence Hse.

Langsdorf, Lenore, et al, eds. Phenomenology, Interpretation, & Community. LC 95-19602. (Selected Studies in Phenomenology & Existential Philosophy: Vol. 19). 295p. (C). 1996. text 59.50 (*0-7914-2865-6*); pap. text 19.95 (*0-7914-2866-4*) State U NY Pr.

— Reinterpreting the Political: Continental Philosophy & Political Theory. LC 97-35330. (Selected Studies in Phenomenology & Existential Philosophy: No. 20). 352p. (C). 1998. text 74.50 (*0-7914-3793-0*); pap. text 24.95 (*0-7914-3794-9*) State U NY Pr.

Langsdorf, Lenore & Smith, Andrew R., eds. Recovering Pragmatism's Voice: The Classical Tradition, Rorty, & the Philosophy of Communication. LC 94-1571. (SUNY Series in the Philosophy of the Social Sciences). 336p. (C). 1994. text 59.50 (*0-7914-2213-5*); pap. text 19.95 (*0-7914-2214-3*) State U NY Pr.

Langsdorf, Lenore, jt. ed. see Angus, Ian.

Langsdorff, Georg. Langsdorff's Narrative of the Rezanov Voyage. 1988. 29.95 (*0-87770-449-X*) Ye Galleon.

Langsdorff, Georg H. Von, see Von Langsdorff, Georg H.

Langseth, Jo-Ann, jt. ed. see Stahl, R. James.

Langseth, Marcus G. & Mammerickx, Jacqueline. Ocean Margin Drilling Program Atlases, Vol. 8. (Regional Atlas Ser.). 1986. pap. 295.00 (*0-86720-258-0*) Jones & Bartlett.

Langseth, Muriel, jt. auth. see Frey, William H.

Langshaw, Deborah. Finding a Job without Losing Your Mind! A Survivor's Manual for Job Hunters & Their Families. 96p. (Orig.). 1993. pap. 9.95 (*0-9633939-0-1*) SimonWood Pr.

Langsley, Donald G., ed. Health Policy Issues Affecting Medical Education. 1990. lib. bdg. 44.95 (*0-934277-13-3*) Am Bd Med Spec.

— How to Select Residents. LC 87-73378. 300p. 1988. lib. bdg. 39.95 (*0-934277-11-7*) Am Bd Med Spec.

Langsley, Donald G. & Darragh, James H., eds. Trends in Specialization: Tomorrow's Medicine. LC 85-73107. (Illus.). 128p. 1985. lib. bdg. 29.95 (*0-934277-06-0*) Am Bd Med Spec.

Langsley, Donald G. & Lloyd, John S., eds. Recertification for Medical Specialists. LC 87-72510. 276p. 1987. lib. bdg. 39.95 (*0-934277-10-9*) Am Bd Med Spec.

Langsley, Donald G. & Signer, Mona, eds. Hospital Privileges & Specialty Medicine. LC 86-70590. (Illus.). 352p. 1986. lib. bdg. 34.95 (*0-934277-08-7*) Am Bd Med Spec.

Langsley, Donald G. & Stubblefield, Beauregard, eds. Hospital Privileges & Specialty Medicine. 2nd ed. LC 92-73099. 537p. 1992. lib. bdg. 44.95 (*0-934277-17-6*) Am Bd Med Spec.

Langsley, Donald G., jt. ed. see Lloyd, John S.

***Langslow, D. R.** Medical Latin in the Roman Empire. LC 99-33260. 500p. 2000. text 110.00 (*0-19-815279-5*) OUP.

Langsner, Drew. The Chairmaker's Workshop: Handcrafting Windsor & Post-&-Rung Chairs. Needham, Bobbe, ed. LC 97-8054. (Illus.). 304p. 1997. 34.95 (*1-887374-34-5*, Pub. by Lark Books) Random.

— Green Woodworking: A Hands-on-Approach. 2nd ed. Taylor, Carol, ed. LC 94-42309. (Country Workshop Handbook Ser.). (Illus.). 176p. (Orig.). 1995. reprint ed. pap. 18.95 (*0-937274-82-8*) Lark Books.

Langstaff, Bard & McConnaughy, James, eds. Fifty Years on Fifty-Seventh Street. (Illus.). 72p. (Orig.). 1986. pap. write for info. (*0-9616646-1-4*) S J Shrubsole.

Langstaff, Eleanor. Panama, Vol. 14. 2nd rev. ed. (World Bibliographical Ser.). 250p. 1997. lib. bdg. 79.00 (*1-85109-251-X*) ABC-CLIO.

Langstaff, Eleanor, jt. auth. see McDonough, Kristin.

Langstaff, Eleanor D. Panama. (World Bibliographical Ser.: No. 14). 184p. 1982. lib. bdg. 28.00 (*0-903450-26-7*) ABC-CLIO.

Langstaff, J. David Copperfield's Library. 1972. 59.95 (*0-87968-998-6*) Gordon Pr.

Langstaff, John. Annotated Bibliography, Bk. IV. (Music Makes a Difference Ser.). 12p. 1994. pap. 1.95 (*1-886380-03-1*) Langstaff Vid.

***Langstaff, John.** On Christmas Day in the Morning. LC 98-51122. (Illus.). 32p. (J). 1999. 15.99 (*0-7636-0375-9*) Candlewick Pr.

— What a Morning! the Christmas Story in a Black Spiritual. (J). 1996. 10.19 (*0-606-12068-8*, Pub. by Turtleback) Demco.

Langstaff, John, compiled by. A Revels Garland of Song: In Celebration of Spring, Summer & Autumn. (Illus.). 176p. (Orig.). 1996. pap. 17.95 (*0-8256-9370-5*, RI 10096) Revels MA.

Langstaff, John, jt. auth. see Langstaff, Nancy.

Langstaff, John, ed. see Irving, Washington.

Langstaff, John M. Frog Went A-Courtin' (J). 1955. 12.20 (*0-606-00696-6*, Pub. by Turtleback) Demco.

— I Have a Song to Sing, O! An Introduction to the Songs of Gilbert & Sullivan. (Illus.). 80p. (J). (ps up). 1994. text 17.95 (*0-689-50591-4*) McElderry Bks.

— Oh, A-Hunting We Will Go. LC 91-1987. (Illus.). 32p. (J). (gr. k-3). 1991. reprint ed. mass mkt. 5.99 (*0-689-71503-X*) Aladdin.

— Over in the Meadow. LC 57-8587. (Illus.). 32p. (J). (ps-3). 1992. pap. 19.95 (*0-15-258853-1*) Harcourt.

— What a Morning. 1996. mass mkt. 4.99 (*0-689-80807-0*) S&S Childrens.

Langstaff, John M., jt. auth. see Bryan, Ashley.

Langstaff, John M., jt. auth. see Langstaff, Nancy.

Langstaff, John M., jt. auth. see Mayer, Elizabeth L.

Langstaff, John M., jt. auth. see Rojankovsky, Feodor.

Langstaff, John M., jt. auth. see Sweet, Melissa.

Langstaff, Launcelott. Salmagundi. 1972. reprint ed. lib. bdg. 42.50 (*0-8422-8162-2*) Irvington.

Langstaff, Nancy & Langstaff, John. Sally Go Round the Moon: Revels Songs & Singing Games for Young Children. LC 86-90535. (Illus.). 127p. (J). (ps-4). 1986. pap. 14.95 (*0-9640836-3-9*, RI 10098) Revels Recs.

Langstaff, Nancy & Langstaff, John M. The Christmas Revels Songbook: Carols, Processionals, Rounds, Ritual & Children's Songs in Celebration of the Winter Solstice. 4th rev. ed. (Illus.). 160p. 1995. pap. 16.95 (*0-9640836-1-2*, VI 10095) Revels MA.

Langsted, Jorn, ed. Strategies: Studies in Modern Cultural Policy. 88p. (Orig.). (C). 1990. pap. 11.95 (*87-7288-321-9*, Pub. by Aarhus Univ Pr) David Brown.

Langsted, Lars B., et al. Criminal Law in Denmark. LC 98-16777. 1998. pap. 51.00 (*90-411-0591-3*) Kluwer Law Intl.

Langsten, P., ed. Advanced Computer Applications 1994: Proceedings of the Pressure Vessels & Piping Conference, Minneapolis, MN, 1994. LC 94-71262. (PVP Ser.: Vol. 274). 147p. 1994. pap. 50.00 (*0-7918-1197-2*) ASME.

Langston. Introduction to Law Office Accounting. (Paralegal Ser.). 1996. teacher ed. 14.00 (*0-8273-7444-5*) Delmar.

***Langston.** Research Methods. 2001. 17.00 incl. cd-rom (*0-534-55683-3*) Wadsworth Pub.

Langston, Ann, jt. auth. see Smith, Adrian.

Langston, Diane J. & Smith, Adeline M. Free Magazines for Libraries. 4th ed. LC 94-2427. 303p. 1994. pap. 32.50 (*0-89950-947-9*) McFarland & Co.

Langston, Donna. Kaida: Poems of a Working Feminist. 1985. pap. 6.00 (*0-317-20172-7*) Quixote.

***Langston, Douglas C.** Conscience & Other Virtues. LC 00-27430. 2001. write for info. (*0-271-02070-9*) Pa St U Pr.

Langston, Elaine M. Client Accounting for the Law Office. LC 95-24137. (Paralegal Ser.). 320p. (C). 1996. mass mkt. 63.95 (*0-8273-7443-7*) Delmar.

Langston, Eugene, tr. see Niwano, Nikkyo.

Langston, J. William & Palfreman, Jon. The Case of the Frozen Addicts. 1996. pap. 13.00 (*0-679-74708-7*) Vin Bks.

Langston, Jack M. Lexigrow: A New & Easy Gardening Concept. LC 82-90041. (Illus.). 160p. (Orig.). 1982. pap. 14.95 (*0-910387-00-1*) Lexigrow Intl.

Langston, John M. Freedom & Citizenship. LC 74-79012. (Black Heritage Library Collection). 1977. 29.95 (*0-8369-8618-0*) Ayer.

— From the Virginia Plantation to the National Capitol. LC 69-18567. (American Negro: His History & Literature. Series 2). 1968. reprint ed. 25.95 (*0-405-01877-0*) Ayer.

Langston, L. H. Practical Bank Operation, 2 vols. Bruchey, Stuart, ed. LC 80-1159. (Rise of Commercial Banking Ser.). (Illus.). 1981. reprint ed. lib. bdg. 71.95 (*0-405-13666-8*) Ayer.

Langston, Laura. The Fox's Kettle. LC 97-81097. (Illus.). 32p. (J). (ps-3). 1998. pap. 6.95 (*1-55143-132-7*) Orca Bk Pubs.

— Pay Dirt! The Search for Gold in British Columbia. LC 96-120391. (Illus.). 80p. (YA). (gr. 8-12). 1995. pap. 8.95 (*1-55143-029-0*) Orca Bk Pubs.

Langston, Loup & Corral, Pablo, eds. Discovering Ecuador & the Galapagos Islands. 49.95 (*0-9644049-0-7*) Descubriendo Ecu.

An Asterisk (*) at the beginning of an entry indicates that the title is appearing for the first time.

Langston, Melissa & Durso, Asunta. Thick to Thin: Your Thirty-Day Diet Companion. (Orig.). 1992. pap. 2.95 (*0-399-51703-0*, Perigee Bks) Berkley Pub.

Langston, Nancy. Forest Dreams, Forest Nightmares: The Paradox of Old Growth in the Inland West. LC 95-14973. (Weyerhaeuser Environmental Classics Ser.). (Illus.). 384p. (C). 1995. 30.00 (*0-295-97456-7*) U of Wash Pr.

— Forest Dreams, Forest Nightmares: The Paradox of Old Growth in the Inland West. (Weyerhaeuser Environmental Classics Ser.). (Illus.). 384p. 1996. pap. 16.95 (*0-295-97550-4*) U of Wash Pr.

Langston, Nanda, et al. From the Heart: Recipes from The Taste of Health Restaurant. (Illus.). 130p. (Orig.). 1989. pap. 9.95 (*0-942333-10-1*) Bio-Comns Pr.

Langston, Ruth C., ed. The North Carolina Historical Review: Supplement to Fifty-Year Index, 1974-1983. 243p. (Orig.). 1999. reprint ed. pap. 30.00 (*0-86526-213-6*) NC Archives.

Langston, Ruth C., jt. ed. see Crabtree, Beth G.

Langston, Scott M. Cultic Sites in the Tribe of Benjamin: Benjaminite Prominence in the Religion of Israel. LC 97-13468. (American Univ. Studies, VII: Vol. 200). IX, 275p. (C). 1998. 46.95 (*0-8204-3818-9*) P Lang Pubng.

Langston, Teresa A. Parenting Without Pressure: A Whole Family Approach To. LC 94-65638. 160p. 1994. pap. 14.00 (*0-89109-750-3*) Pinon Press.

Langston, Thomas S. Ideologues & Presidents: From the New Deal to the Reagan Revolution. 272p. 1992. text 40.00 (*0-8018-4361-8*) Johns Hopkins.

— With Reverence & Contempt: How Americans Think about Their President. LC 94-34134. (Interpreting American Politics Ser.). 192p. 1995. 35.00 (*0-8018-5016-9*) Johns Hopkins.

— With Reverence & Contempt: How Americans Think about Their President. (Interpreting American Politics Ser.). 328p. 1997. reprint ed. pap. text 15.95 (*0-8018-5510-1*) Johns Hopkins.

Langston, Tressie L. Tressie-upon These Rocks . . ., Bk. I. (Illus.). 223p. 1997. text 20.00 (*0-9663859-0-X*) T L Lacy Langston.

Langstraat, Patricia, jt. auth. see Mazor, Stanley.

Langstroth, Libby, jt. auth. see Langstroth, Lovell.

***Langstroth, Lovell & Langstroth, Libby.** A Living Bay: The Underwater World of Monterey Bay. LC 00-22014. (Monterey Bay Aquarium Series in Marine Conservation: Vol. 2). (Illus.). 315p. 2000. 60.00 (*0-520-21686-5*) U CA Pr.

***Langstroth, Lovell, et al.** A Living Bay: The Underwater World of Monterey Bay. LC 00-22014. (Monterey Bay Aquarium Series in Marine Conservation : Vol. 2). (Illus.). 315p. 2000. pap. 29.95 (*0-520-22149-4*, Pub. by U CA Pr) Cal Prin Full Svc.

***Langtangen, H. P., et al, eds.** Advances in Software Tools for Scientific Computing. LC 99-57895. (Lecture Notes in Computational Science & Engineering Ser.: Vol. 10). viii, 360p. 2000. pap. 76.00 (*3-540-66557-9*) Spr-Verlag.

***Langteaux, James Alexander.** God.Com: Extreme Intimacy with an Interactive God. LC 00-8507. 2000. 12.99 (*1-57673-707-1*) Multnomah Pubs.

***Langthaler, Herbert.** Sura Za Afrika.Tr. of Voices from Africa. (GER.). 1999. pap. 56.95 (*3-631-33571-7*) P Lang Pubng.

Langthaler, Herbert, ed. Sura za Afrika - Voices from Africa. LC 99-20780. 374p. 1999. pap. text 56.95 (*0-8204-4302-6*) P Lang Pubng.

Langthaler, Rudolf. Kants Ethik als "System der Zwecke" Perspektiven Einer Modifizierten Idee der "Moralischen Teleologie & Ethikotheologie. (Kantstudien Ergaenzungsheft Ser.: Band 125). xiv, 428p. (C). 1990. lib. bdg. 129.25 (*3-11-012620-6*) De Gruyter.

— Organismus und Umwelt. (Studien und Materialien Zur Geschichte der Philosophie Ser.: Bd. 34). (GER.). 270p. 1992. write for info. (*3-487-09638-2*) G Olms Pubs.

Langthorp, Herb, jt. auth. see American Production & Inventory Control Society St.

Langthrop, Herb, ed. Aerospace & Defense Specific Industry Group Resource Book Supplement. 30p. (Orig.). 1995. pap. 8.00 (*1-55822-154-9*) Am Prod & Inventory.

***Langton.** Machinery of Life & Life of Machine. 2000. 29.95 (*0-7382-0193-6*, Pub. by Perseus Pubng) HarpC.

— Pony Activity Book. 2000. pap. 8.95 (*0-85131-587-9*, Pub. by J A Allen) Trafalgar.

— Time Bike. LC 99-39896. 192p. (J). 2001. pap. 4.95 (*0-06-440792-6*) HarpC Child Bks.

Langton, B., jt. auth. see Langton, N.

Langton, Brenda & Stuart, Margaret. The Cafe Brenda Cookbook: Redefining Seafood & Vegetarian Cuisine. LC 91-42049. (Illus.). 240p. 1992. pap. 17.95 (*0-89658-205-1*) Voyageur Pr.

Langton, Charan. Join a Club: Directory of Clubs & Associations of Greater Los Angeles. (Illus.). 270p. (Orig.). 1983. pap. 10.00 (*0-913063-00-2*) Shartec Syst.

Langton, Charlie. Keep Silence, but Speak Out. (Loess Hills Poet Ser.). 64p. 1998. 22.00 (*0-931209-78-1*, Loess Hills Bks); pap. 12.00 (*0-931209-79-X*, Loess Hills Bks) Mid-Prairie Bks.

Langton, Christopher. An Introduction into Physicke. LC 75-25797. (English Experience Ser.: No. 281). 1970. reprint ed. 30.00 (*90-221-0281-5*) Walter J Johnson.

Langton, Christopher G. Artificial Life. (C). 1998. write for info. (*0-201-60808-1*) Addison-Wesley.

— Artificial Life III. (Proceedings, Santa Fe Institute Studies in the Sciences of Complexity: Vol. 17). (Illus.). 599p. (C). 1993. pap. 42.00 (*0-201-62494-X*) Addison-Wesley.

Langton, Christopher G., ed. Artificial Life: An Overview. (Illus.). 352p. 1995. 50.00 (*0-262-12189-1*, Bradford Bks) MIT Pr.

— Artificial Life: An Overview. (Illus.). 352p. 1997. reprint ed. pap. text 25.00 (*0-262-62112-6*, Bradford Bks) MIT Pr.

Langton, Christopher G. & Shimohara, Taksunori, eds. Artificial Life V: Proceedings of the Fifth International Workshop on the Synthesis & Simulation of Living Systems May 16-18, 1996, Nara, Japan. LC 97-9088. 542p. 1997. pap. text 68.00 (*0-262-62111-8*, Bradford Bks) MIT Pr.

Langton, Daniel J. The Inheritance. 48p. 1988. pap. text 10.00 (*0-9615838-1-9*) Cheltenham Pr.

— Life Forms. 245p. 1995. pap. text 15.00 (*0-9615838-2-7*) Cheltenham Pr.

— Querencia: Poems. LC 76-740443. (Devins Award Breakthrough Ser.). 64p. 1976. 7.00 (*0-8262-0192-X*) Cheltenham Pr.

Langton, Daniel J. & Stock, Robert. The Hogarth-Selkirk Letters. 70p. 1985. pap. 7.00 (*0-9615838-0-0*) Cheltenham Pr.

***Langton, Daniel R.** Claude Montefiore & Liberal Jewish Thought. (Illus.). 196p. 2000. (*0-85303-369-2*); pap. (*0-85303-376-5*) Intl Spec Bk.

Langton, Dawn, jt. auth. see DiLeo, Dale.

Langton, Dawn, jt. ed. see DiLeo, Dale.

Langton, Edward. Essentials of Demonology: A Study of Jewish & Christian Doctrine. LC 79-8108. (Illus.). 272p. reprint ed. 34.50 (*0-404-18419-7*) AMS Pr.

— Satan, a Portrait: A Study of the Character of Satan Through All the Ages. 1976. lib. bdg. 59.95 (*0-8490-2568-0*) Gordon Pr.

Langton, H. H., ed. see Campbell, Patrick.

Langton, H. H., tr. see Sagard-Theodat, Gabriel.

***Langton, Helen.** The Child with Cancer: A Textbook of Complete Family-centred Care. LC 99-29466. 2000. text. write for info. (*0-7020-2300-0*) W B Saunders.

Langton, Jane. The Astonishing Stereoscope. LC 74-157894. (Trophy Bk.). (Illus.). 256p. (J). (gr. 5 up). 1983. pap. 3.25 (*0-06-440133-2*, HarpTrophy) HarpC Child Bks.

— The Dante Game: A Homer Kelly Mystery. (Homer Kelly Mystery Ser.). (Illus.). 336p. 1992. pap. 6.99 (*0-14-013887-0*, Penguin Bks) Viking Penguin.

— Dark Nantucket Noon. LC 80-29128. (Fiction Ser.). 304p. 1981. pap. 5.99 (*0-14-005836-2*, Penguin Bks) Viking Penguin.

— Dead as a Dodo: A Homer Kelly Mystery. LC 96-6724. (Illus.). 340p. 1997. pap. 6.95 (*0-14-024795-5*) Viking Penguin.

— The Diamond in the Window. (J). (gr. 5 up). 1990. 19.00 (*0-8446-6414-6*) Peter Smith.

— The Diamond in the Window. 1973. 9.60 (*0-606-07432-5*, Pub. by Turtleback) Demco.

— The Diamond in the Window. LC 62-7312. (Trophy Bk.). (Illus.). 256p. (J). (gr. 5 up). 1973. reprint ed. pap. 4.95 (*0-06-440042-5*, HarpTrophy) HarpC Child Bks.

— Divine Inspiration: A Homer Kelly Mystery. (Illus.). 416p. 1994. reprint ed. pap. 5.99 (*0-14-017376-5*, Penguin Bks) Viking Penguin.

— Emily Dickinson Is Dead. large type ed. 448p. 1992. pap. 16.99 (*0-7089-7162-8*) Ulverscroft.

***Langton, Jane.** The Face on the Wall: A Homer Kelly Mystery. LC 98-51486. 1999. 45.00 (*1-57490-205-9*) T T Beeler.

Langton, Jane. The Face on the Wall: A Homer Kelly Mystery. 288p. 1999. pap. 5.99 (*0-14-028157-6*) Viking Penguin.

— Fledgling. 1980. 10.05 (*0-606-00457-2*, Pub. by Turtleback) Demco.

— The Fledgling. LC 79-2008. (Ursula Nordstrom Bk.). 196p. (J). (ps-3). 1980. lib. bdg. 15.89 (*0-06-023679-5*) HarpC Child Bks.

— The Fledgling. LC 79-2008. (Trophy Bk.). 192p. (J). (gr. 4-7). 1981. pap. 5.95 (*0-06-440121-9*, HarpTrophy) HarpC Child Bks.

— God in Concord: A Homer Kelly Mystery. (Illus.). 352p. 1993. pap. 5.99 (*0-14-016594-0*, Penguin Bks) Viking Penguin.

— Good & Dead. 256p. 1989. pap. 5.95 (*0-14-012687-2*, Penguin Bks) Viking Penguin.

— The Hedgehog Boy. LC 83-47698. (Illus.). 40p. (J). (gr. k-3). 1985. 12.95 (*0-06-023696-5*) HarpC Child Bks.

— The Memorial Hall Murder. 1996. pap. write for info. (*0-14-771166-5*) Penguin Putnam.

— The Memorial Hall Murder. large type ed. LC 86-2365. 393 p. 1986. write for info. (*0-89621-706-X*) Thorndike Pr.

— Murder at the Gardner. 352p. 1989. pap. 6.99 (*0-14-011382-7*, Penguin Bks) Viking Penguin.

— Murder at the Gardner. large type ed. LC 88-14728. 468p. 1988. reprint ed. lib. bdg. 7.95 (*0-89621-170-3*) Thorndike Pr.

— The Queen's Necklace: A Swedish Folktale. LC 93-34817. (Illus.). 40p. (J). (gr. k-3). 1994. 15.95 (*0-7868-0011-9*, Pub. by Hyprn Child); lib. bdg. 15.89 (*0-7868-2007-1*, Pub. by Hyprn Child) Little.

— The Shortest Day: Murder at the Revels. (Illus.). 272p. 1996. pap. 5.95 (*0-14-017377-3*, Viking) Viking Penguin.

***Langton, Jane.** The Thief of Venice: A Homer Kelly Mystery. LC 98-54894. 256p. 1999. 22.95 (*0-670-88210-0*, Viking) Viking Penguin.

— The Thief of Venice: A Homer Kelly Mystery. (Homer Kelly Mystery Ser.). (Illus.). 256p. 2000. pap. 5.99 (*0-14-029189-X*) Viking Penguin.

Langton, Jane. The Time Bike. LC 99-39896. 192p. (J). (gr. 3-7). 2000. 15.95 (*0-06-028437-4*) HarpC Child Bks.

— The Time Bike. LC 99-39896. (Illus.). 192p. (J). (gr. 4-7). 2000. lib. bdg. 15.89 (*0-06-028438-2*) HarpC Child Bks.

***Langton, Jane.** Tom's Case. (Homer Kelly Mystery Ser.). 2001. 22.95 (*0-670-89462-1*, Viking) Viking Penguin.

Langton, Jane & Blegvad, Erik. The Fragile Flag. LC 83-49471. (Illus.). 224p. (J). (gr. 3-7). 1984. 13.00 (*0-06-023698-1*) HarpC Child Bks.

Langton, Jeffrey H. The Victor Story: History of a Bitter Root Valley Town. LC 85-61259. (Illus.). 126p. 1985. 14.95 (*0-933126-62-X*) Pictorial Hist.

Langton, John. Geographical Change & Industrial Revolution: Coalmining in South West Lancashire, 1590-1799. LC 78-67428. (Cambridge Geographical Studies: Vol. 11). 336p. reprint ed. pap. 95.80 (*0-608-16861-0*, 2027241) Bks Demand.

Langton, John & Morris, R. J. Atlas of Industrializing Britain. 280p. 1987. 35.00 (*0-416-30290-4*, 1123) Routledge.

Langton, John, jt. auth. see Hoppe, Goran.

Langton, Loup & Corral, Pablo, eds. Descubriendo Ecuador. (SPA.). 238p. 60.00 (*0-9644049-1-5*) Descubriendo Ecu.

Langton, Mandy & Pilgrim, Anne. The Pony Puzzle Book. 86p. (J). 1990. 21.00 (*0-85131-535-6*, Pub. by J A Allen) Trafalgar.

Langton, Mark. Mountain Biking. unabridged ed. LC 98-102784. (Outdoor Action Guides Ser.). 1997. pap. 6.95 (*0-307-24600-0*, Whitman Coin) St Martin.

Langton, Mark, jt. auth. see Hasenauer, Jim.

***Langton, N. & Langton, B.** The Cat in Ancient Egypt: Illustrated from a Collection of Cat & Egyptian Figures Formed by N. & B. Langton. 100p. 2000. text 161.50 (*0-7103-0710-1*) Col U Pr.

Langton, Phyllis A. Jurisdiction Competition Between Obstetricians & Nurse Midwives in Washington, Vol. O7. 1991. 4.00 (*1-888028-20-3*) GWU Ctr WAS.

— The Social World of Drugs. LC 96-121910. 450p. (C). 1996. 48.95 (*0-314-07165-2*) West Pub.

Langton, Phyllis A., ed. The Challenge of Participatory Research: Preventing Alcohol-Related Problems in Ethnic Communities. (Illus.). 459p. (C). 1998. pap. text 50.00 (*0-7881-4755-2*) DIANE Pub.

Langton, Rae. Epistemic Humility: Kant & the Intrinsic. 246p. 1998. text 65.00 (*0-19-823653-0*) OUP.

Langton, Robert. Childhood & Youth of Charles Dickens. LC 76-148809. reprint ed. 34.50 (*0-404-08875-9*) AMS Pr.

Langton, Stuart, jt. ed. see DeSario, Jack.

Langton, Tom. Snakes & Lizards. (Illus.). 128p. text 19.95 (*0-905483-77-4*, Pub. by Whittet Bks) Diamond Farm Bk.

Langtree, Graham. At the Heart: A Practical Guide to Teaching Religious Education. (Illus.). 122p. (Orig.). 1997. pap. 52.50 (*0-7487-2855-4*, Pub. by S Thornes Pubs) Trans-Atl Phila.

Langtree, Graham, et al. One World Many Issues: Teacher's Resource Guide. 96p. (Orig.). 1997. pap., teacher ed. 26.50 (*0-7487-3010-9*, Pub. by S Thornes Pubs) Trans-Atl Phila.

Langtry, Bruce, ed. All Connected: Universal Service in Telecommunications. 176p. 1998. pap. 29.95 (*0-522-84784-6*, Pub. by Melbourne Univ Pr) Paul & Co Pubs.

Langtry, J. O. & Ball, D., eds. A Vulnerable Country: Civil Resources in the Defence of Australia. 704p. 1986. 62.00 (*0-08-033045-2*, K122,K120,K115, Pergamon Pr) Elsevier.

Langtry, Lillie. The Days I Knew. LC 79-8067. (Illus.). 336p. reprint ed. 37.50 (*0-404-18378-6*) AMS Pr.

Language & Reading in Mathematics Group Staff. Children Reading Mathematics. Shuard, Hilary & Rothery, Andrew, eds. (Illus.). 170p. (C). (gr. k). 1990. pap. text 20.00 (*0-7195-4093-3*, 00653) Heinemann.

Language Arts Staff, ed. see Shostak, Jerome.

Language Center Staff, tr. from GER. Manual Para Tubos Drager. 9th ed.Tr. of Drager-Tube Handbook. 367p. (Orig.). 1995. pap. 25.00 (*0-9650423-0-8*) National Draeger.

Language Inc. Staff, tr. see UNICEF Staff.

Language Institute, Beijing Staff. New Chinese Three Hundred: A Beginning Language Course. LC 83-73591. (C & T Asian Language Ser.). 355p. (C). 1987. pap. 14.95 (*0-88727-001-8*) Cheng & Tsui.

***Language Living Staff.** Living Language Hable Ingles. 1999. 15.95 (*0-609-60533-X*) Crown Bks Yng Read.

Language Living Staff. Your Way: French. (Living Language Ser.). (FRE.). 1995. 60.00 (*0-517-70275-4*) Liv Lang.

Language Services Division of the Foreign Office o, ed. Disarmament Terminology: English, German, French, Spanish, Russian. LC 82-14931. (Terminological Ser.: Vol. 1). 645p. 1982. pap. 81.55 (*3-11-008858-4*) De Gruyter.

Language Studies Centre Staff & Jenkins, Carol. Mathwords: A Word Book for Mathematics. (Illus.). 62p. (C). 1994. 20.95 (*0-521-45527-8*) Cambridge U Pr.

Languages Service Staff. Nuclear Test Ban. (ARA, ENG & FRE.). 300p. 30.00 (*92-1-000057-9*, JX1974) UN.

Languille, Carole G. In Cannon Cave. LC 97-204989. 80p. 1997. pap. 12.95 (*0-919626-91-2*, Pub. by Brick Bks) Genl Dist Srvs.

Languilli, Nino. Possibility, Necessity & Existence: Abbagnano & His Predecessors. (Themes in the History of Philosophy Ser.). 250p. (C). 1992. 59.95 (*0-87722-921-X*) Temple U Pr.

Languis, M. L. Cognitive Science: Contributions to Educational Practice. (Monographs in Psychobiology: Vol. 6). xv, 404p. 1991. text 252.00 (*2-88124-437-8*) Gordon & Breach.

Langum, David J. Crossing over the Line: Legislating Morality & the Mann Act. LC 94-13292. (Chicago Series in Sexuality, History, & Society). (Illus.). 324p. 1994. 24.95 (*0-226-46880-1*) U Ch Pr.

***Langum, David J.** William M. Kunstler: The Most Hated Lawyer in America. LC 99-6393. (Illus.). 480p. 1999. 34.95 (*0-8147-5150-4*) NYU Pr.

Langum, David J., ed. The Law in the West. (Illus.). 96p. 1985. pap. 15.00 (*0-89745-068-X*) Sunflower U Pr.

Langum, David J. & Walthall, Howard P. From Maverick to Mainstream: Cumberland School of Law, 1847-1997. LC 96-51954. (Studies in the Legal History of the South). 1997. 35.00 (*0-8203-1892-2*) U of Ga Pr.

Langum, David J., jt. auth. see Hague, Harlan.

Languuth, Phillip, jt. auth. see Carrington, Mark.

Langvardt, Arlen W. Creditors' Remedies Forms, 1990. (Nebraska Legal Forms Ser.). 140p. ring bd. 50.00 (*0-86678-026-2*, MICHIE); ring bd. 85.00 incl. disk (*0-685-49522-1*, MICHIE) LEXIS Pub.

— Creditors' Remedies Forms, 1990. (Nebraska Legal Forms Ser.). 140p. 1993. suppl. ed. 34.50 (*0-685-74348-9*, MICHIE) LEXIS Pub.

— Nebraska Legal Forms: Creditors' Remedies. 1982. ring bd. 69.95 (*0-327-01001-0*, 81986, MICHIE) LEXIS Pub.

Langville, Alan R., compiled by. Modern World Rulers: A Chronology. LC 79-19294. 372p. 1979. 34.50 (*0-8108-1251-7*) Scarecrow.

Langway, C. C. Jr., et al, eds. Greenland Ice Core: Geophysics, Geochemistry, & the Environment. (Geophysical Monograph Ser.: Vol.33). 118p. 1985. 19.00 (*0-87590-057-7*) Am Geophysical.

Langwell, William H. The Conservation of Books & Documents. LC 73-2640. 114p. 1974. reprint ed. lib. bdg. 35.00 (*0-8371-6810-4*, LACB, Greenwood Pr) Greenwood.

Langwick, John J. Eastern European Technological Business Opportunities: An Executive Report. LC 92-39409. 350p. 1993. 95.00 (*0-88173-170-6*) Fairmont Pr.

— Eastern European Technological Business Opportunities: An Executive Report. 304p. (C). 1993. pap. text 95.00 (*0-13-605890-6*) P-H.

Langworth, R. & Robson, G. Triumph Cars: The Complete Story. (Illus.). 352p. 1996. 39.95 (*0-947981-28-4*, Pub. by Motor Racing) Motorbooks Intl.

Langworth, R. M. New Complete Book of Collectible Cars, 1930-90. 576p. 1989. 19.98 (*1-56173-303-2*) Pubns Intl Ltd.

Langworth, Richard. Illustrated Dodge Buyer's Guide. LC 95-24760. (Motorbooks International Illustrated Buyer's Guide Ser.). (Illus.). 160p. 1995. pap. 17.95 (*0-7603-0064-X*) MBI Pubg.

— Corvettes, 1953-1988: A Collector's Guide. (Collector's Guide Ser.). (Illus.). 128p. 1996. pap. 19.95 (*1-899870-11-3*, Pub. by Motor Racing) Motorbooks Intl.

— Mustangs, 1965-1973: A Collector's Guide. (Collector's Guide Ser.). (Illus.). 128p. 1996. pap. 19.95 (*1-899870-12-1*, Pub. by Motor Racing) Motorbooks Intl.

Langworth, Richard M. Illustrated Chrysler Buyer's Guide. LC 96-6485. (Illustrated Buyer's Guide Ser.). (Illus.). 128p. 1996. pap. 17.95 (*0-7603-0106-9*) MBI Pubg.

Langworth, Richard M. & Redburn, H. Ashley. Churchill Bibliographic Data: Surveys of Works by & about Sir Winston Churchill. (Educational Ser.: No. 4). (Illus.). 52p. 1992. pap. 10.00 (*0-614-04945-8*) Churchill Ctr.

Langworth, Richard M., jt. auth. see Brown, Arch.

Langworth, Richard M., ed. see Russell, Douglas S.

Langworthy, Harry. Africa for the African: The Life of Joseph Booth. 520p. 1996. pap. 59.95 (*99908-16-03-4*, U Pr W Africa) Intl Scholars.

Langworthy, J. Lamont & McNeil, Katherine. Hillside Homes. LC 82-82433. (Illus.). 128p. (Orig.). 1983. pap. 10.00 (*0-9609334-0-9*) IO.

Langworthy, Mark & Finan, Timothy J. Waiting for Rain: Agriculture & Ecological Imbalance in Cape Verde. LC 96-44538. 212p. 1997. 45.00 (*1-55587-709-5*) L Rienner.

Langworthy, Robert H. Policing in America: A Balance of Forces. 2nd ed. LC 98-25251. 460p. 1998. 80.00 (*0-13-646217-0*) P-H.

— The Structure of Police Organizations. LC 86-21173. 176p. 1986. 55.00 (*0-275-92328-2*, C2328, Praeger Pubs) Greenwood.

Langworthy, Robert J., jt. ed. see McCarthy, Belinda R.

Lanham. Electronic Word. 1993. lib. bdg. 19.95 (*0-226-46884-4*) U Ch Pr.

Lanham, Carol C. Pregnancy after a Loss: A Guide to Pregnancy after a Miscarriage, Stillbirth or Infant Death. 1999. pap. 14.95 (*0-425-17047-0*) Berkley Pub.

Lanham, Carol D. Salutatio Formulas in Latin Letters to 1200: Syntax, Style, & Theory. (Munchener Beitrage zur Mediavistik und Renaissance-Forschung Ser.: Bd. 22). (GER.). xii, 140p. 1975. 30.00 (*3-615-00155-9*) G Olms Pubs.

Lanham, Cheryl. Dear Diary No. 2: Remember Me. 208p. (Orig.). (J). (gr. 7-10). 1996. mass mkt. 4.50 (*0-425-15194-8*) Berkley Pub.

***Lanham, Cheryl.** Dying Young. (Dear Diary Ser.: No. 5). 192p. (YA). (gr. 7-12). 2000. mass mkt. 4.50 (*0-425-17430-1*) Berkley Pub.

— Fighting Back. (Dear Diary Ser.: No. 6). (YA). 2000. mass mkt. 4.50 (*0-425-17606-1*) Berkley Pub.

Lanham, Cheryl. Life at Sixteen: Good Intentions. (Life at Sixteen Ser.). (YA). 1998. pap. 4.50 (*0-425-16521-3*, JAM) Berkley Pub.

— No Guarantees. (Life at Sixteen Ser.). 208p. 1997. mass mkt. 4.50 (*0-425-15974-4*) Berkley Pub.

— Second Best. (Life at Sixteen Ser.). 208p. 1997. mass mkt. 4.50 (*0-425-15545-5*) Berkley Pub.

Lanham, David, et al. Criminal Fraud. xli, 629p. 1987. 96.00 (*0-455-20745-3*, Pub. by LawBk Co) Gaunt.

Lanham, Edwin. Wind Blew West. 1993. reprint ed. lib. bdg. 75.00 (*0-7812-5968-1*) Rprt Serv.

Lanham, John C., Jr., ed. see Hannon, Charles-Louis.

Lanham, L. W. & Prinsloo, K. Language & Communication Studies in South Africa. 1978. 15.50 (*0-19-570144-5*) OUP.

Lanham, Richard A. The Electronic Word: Democracy, Technology, & the Arts. 302p. 1996. 22.50 (*0-226-46883-6*) U Ch Pr.

— The Electronic Word: Democracy, Technology & the Arts. 302p. 1994. pap. 15.00 (*0-226-46885-2*) U Ch Pr.

— A Handlist of Rhetorical Terms. 2nd ed. 168p. 1992. pap. 17.95 (*0-520-07669-9*, Pub. by U CA Pr) Cal Prin Full Svc.

— A Hypertext Handlist of Rhetorical Terms: For Macintosh Computers. 1997. 34.95 (*0-520-08838-7*, Pub. by U CA Pr) Cal Prin Full Svc.

***Lanham, Richard A.** Revising Business Prose. 4th ed. LC 99-27672. 117p. 1999. pap. text 25.00 (*0-205-30944-5*) P-H.

— Revising Prose. 4th ed. LC 99-27670. 131p. 1999. pap. text 25.00 (*0-205-30945-3*) Allyn.

Lanham, Richard A. Self-Teaching Exercise Book: Prose. rev. ed. 96p. (C). 1987. pap. text 32.00 (*0-02-367490-3*, Macmillan Coll) P-H.

— Tristram Shandy: The Games of Pleasure. LC 70-174461. 184p. reprint ed. pap. 57.10 (*0-608-18063-7*, 202904800058) Bks Demand.

Lanham, Url. Earth, the Sapphire Planet. LC 98-43891. 1999. pap. text 6.95 (*0-486-40677-6*) Dover.

Lanham, Url N. The Bone Hunters: The Heroic Age of Paleontology in the American West. Orig. Title: The Bone Hunters. (Illus.). 304p. 1992. reprint ed. pap. 9.95 (*0-486-26917-5*) Dover.

— The Insects. LC 64-14235. (Illus.). 1967. pap. text 20.00 (*0-231-08582-6*) Col U Pr.

Lanhei Kim Park. The Heavenly Pomegranate. 76p. (J). (gr. 5-7). 1973. pap. text 3.00 (*0-686-05501-2*) Simpson Pub.

Lanher, Jean & Litaize, Alain. Dictionnaire du Francais Regional de Lorraine. (FRE.). 160p. 1990. 125.00 (*0-8288-9479-5*) Fr & Eur.

Lani-Wayda, Bernhard. Hyperbolic Sets, Shadowing, & Persistence for Noninvertible Mappings in Banach Spaces. (Pitman Research Notes in Mathematics Ser.: Vol. 30). 1995. write for info. (*0-614-09432-1*) Longman.

Lanier. Information is An Alienated Expense. 2000. 26.00 (*0-465-03282-6*) HarpC.

Lanier, jt. auth. see Jaron.

Lanier, Alison R. Living in the U. S. A. 5th ed. LC 95-53161. 240p. 1996. pap. text 15.95 (*1-877864-40-4*, 304R) Intercult Pr.

***Lanier, Alton.** Southern Railway in Color, Vol. 2. (Illus.). 128p. 1999. 49.95 (*1-58248-014-1*) Morning NJ.

Lanier, Ann T. Scientific & Engineering Research Facilities at Universities & Colleges Vol. 1: Analysis. (Illus.). 200p. (Orig.). (C). 1995. pap. text 30.00 (*0-7881-2288-6*) DIANE Pub.

***Lanier, Ann T., ed.** Scientific & Engineering Research Facilities at Colleges & Universities, 1996. (Illus.). 150p. (C). 1999. reprint ed. pap. text 35.00 (*0-7881-8238-2*) DIANE Pub.

Lanier, Catherine B., jt. auth. see Hauser, Karen.

Lanier, Chris. Combustion. (Illus.). 56p. 1999. pap. 7.95 (*1-56097-314-5*) Fantagraph Bks.

Lanier, Clifford. Thorn-Fruit. 1973. reprint ed. lib. bdg. 35.00 (*0-8490-1206-6*) Gordon Pr.

Lanier, Doris. Absinthe - The Cocaine of the Nineteenth Century: A History of the Hallucinogenic Drug & Its Effect on Artists & Writers in Europe & the United States. (Illus.). 195p. 1995. lib. bdg. 35.00 (*0-89950-989-4*) McFarland & Co.

Lanier, Gabrielle M. & Herman, Bernard L. Everyday Architecture of the Mid-Atlantic: Looking at Buildings & Landscapes. LC 96-17883. (Creating the North American Landscape Ser.). (Illus.). 392p. 1997. pap. 29.95 (*0-8018-5325-7*); text 55.00 (*0-8018-5324-9*) Johns Hopkins.

Lanier, Georgiann. The "R" Word: Retention is OK. LC 94-80244. (Illus.). 30p. (Orig.). (J). (gr. 1-5). 1995. pap. 7.95 (*1-884063-50-0*) Mar Co Prods.

Lanier-Graham, Susan D. The Ecology of War: Environmental Impacts of Weaponry & Warfare. LC 92-43568. (Illus.). 208p. 1993. 22.95 (*0-8027-1262-2*) Walker & Co.

— The Nature Directory: A Guide to Environmental Organizations. 304p. 1991. pap. 12.95 (*0-8027-7348-6*) Walker & Co.

Lanier-Graham, Susan D., jt. auth. see Nelson, Paul.

Lanier, Henry W., ed. see Freeman, Mary E. Wilkins.

Lanier, Henry W., ed. see Lanier, Sidney.

Lanier, Janet, jt. auth. see Kish, Karen.

Lanier, Laura. All Things Bright & Beautiful. 1993. 9.95 (*0-8378-6946-3*) Gibson.

Lanier, Laura L. All Things Bright & Beautiful. 1996. 8.95 (*0-614-20839-4*) Gibson.

— All Things Wise & Beautiful. (Illus.). 64p. 1993. 8.95 (*0-8378-7176-X*) Gibson.

— All Things Wise & Wonderful. 1996. 8.95 (*0-614-20838-6*) Gibson.

Lanier, Leon T., Sr. Caveman Psychology: Men Understanding Women. 220p. 1998. pap. 9.99 (*0-9662711-1-4*) Black Renaiss.

— The Innocence of Evil. 240p. 1997. mass mkt. 7.99 (*0-9662711-0-6*) Black Renaiss.

Lanier, Mark M. & Henry, Stuart D. Essential Criminology. LC 97-36850. (C). 1997. pap. text 35.00 (*0-8133-3137-4*, Pub. by Westview) HarpC.

Lanier, Mary D., ed. Poems of Sidney Lanier. 320p. 1999. reprint ed. pap. 17.95 (*0-8203-2155-9*) U of Ga Pr.

***Lanier, Naomi.** Selective Poems. 1999. pap. write for info. (*1-58235-170-8*) Watermrk Pr.

Lanier, Pamela. Cinnamon Mornings & Raspberry Teas. (Illus.). 160p. 1997. 14.95 (*0-89815-960-1*) Ten Speed Pr.

***Lanier, Pamela.** The Complete Guide Bed & Breakfasts, Inns & Guesthouse in the U. S., Canada & Worldwide. 18th ed. 800p. 2000. pap. 16.95 (*1-58008-248-3*) Ten Speed Pr.

— Complete Guide to Bed & Breakfasts, Inns & Guesthouses. 17th ed. 800p. 1999. pap. 16.95 (*1-58008-116-9*) Ten Speed Pr.

Lanier, Pamela. Condo Vacations. 7th ed. 504p. 1998. pap. text 14.95 (*0-89815-986-5*) Ten Speed Pr.

— Elegant Hotels of the Pacific Rim. LC 94-208424. 208p. 1994. pap. 14.95 (*0-89815-583-5*) Ten Speed Pr.

***Lanier, Pamela.** Elegant Small Hotels. 15th anniversary ed. 304p. 2000. pap. 19.95 (*1-58008-247-5*) Ten Speed Pr.

Lanier, Pamela. Elegant Small Hotels: A Connisseur's Guide. 240p. 1998. pap. 19.95 (*1-58008-023-5*) Ten Speed Pr.

***Lanier, Pamela.** Elegant Small Hotels: A Connoisseur's Guide. 14th ed. 304p. 1999. pap. 19.95 (*1-58008-114-2*) Ten Speed Pr.

Lanier, Pamela. Family Travel & Resort: The Complete Guide. 2nd ed. (Illus.). 352p. 1998. pap. 19.95 (*0-89815-987-3*) Ten Speed Pr.

— Family Travel & Resorts. 3rd ed. 464p. 1999. pap. 19.95 (*1-58008-059-6*) Ten Speed Pr.

Lanier, Pamela. Golf Resorts International. 3rd ed. 268p. (Orig.). 1993. pap. 19.95 (*0-89815-534-7*) Ten Speed Pr.

Lanier, Pamela. Sweets & Treats from America's Inns. 134p. 1999. pap. 14.95 (*1-58008-032-4*) Ten Speed Pr.

Lanier, Pamela, jt. auth. see Wright, J. C.

Lanier, Parks, Jr., ed. The Poetics of Appalachian Space. LC 90-45244. (Illus.). 232p. 1991. text 26.00 (*0-87049-692-1*) U of Tenn Pr.

Lanier, Perry E., jt. ed. see Wilcox, Sandra K.

Lanier Publishing International Editors. The Back Almanac: The Best New Thinking on an Age-Old Problem. LC 92-25976. 216p. 1992. pap. 14.95 (*0-89815-508-8*) Ten Speed Pr.

Lanier, Roy H., Jr. Cross Questions & Scripture Answers. 1960. pap. 3.00 (*0-89137-618-6*) Quality Pubns.

— The Epistles of John. 1992. pap. 9.85 (*0-89137-136-2*) Quality Pubns.

Lanier, Roy H., Sr. The Timeless Trinity. 1974. 13.25 (*0-89137-551-1*) Quality Pubns.

— Twenty Years of the Problem Page, Vol. I. 1984. pap. 8.25 (*0-89137-549-X*) Quality Pubns.

— Twenty Years of the Problem Page, Vol. II. 1984. pap. 8.25 (*0-89137-555-4*) Quality Pubns.

Lanier, S., jt. auth. see Feldman, Jane.

***Lanier, Shannon.** Jefferson's Children: The Story of One American Family. (Illus.). 144p. (gr. 4-7). 2000. 21.99 (*0-375-90597-9*) Random Bks Yng Read.

Lanier, Sidney. Bob: The Story of Our Mocking Bird. (Notable American Authors Ser.). 1999. reprint ed. lib. bdg. 125.00 (*0-7812-3728-9*) Rprt Serv.

— The Boy's Froissart. (Notable American Authors Ser.). 1999. reprint ed. lib. bdg. 125.00 (*0-7812-3716-5*) Rprt Serv.

— The Boy's King Arthur. LC 73-13451. (Illustrated Classics Ser.). (Illus.). 336p. (J). 1989. text, lib. bdg. 27.00 (*0-684-19111-3*) Scribner.

— The Boy's King Arthur. (Notable American Authors Ser.). 1999. reprint ed. lib. bdg. 125.00 (*0-7812-3718-1*) Rprt Serv.

— The Boy's Mabinogion. (Notable American Authors Ser.). 1999. reprint ed. lib. bdg. 125.00 (*0-7812-3720-3*) Rprt Serv.

— The Boy's Percy. (Notable American Authors Ser.). 1999. reprint ed. lib. bdg. 125.00 (*0-7812-3722-X*) Rprt Serv.

— The Centennial Edition of the Works of Sidney Lanier Vol. 10: Letters 1878-1881. Anderson, C. R. & Starke, A. H., eds. LC 46-2793. (Illus.). 558p. reprint ed. pap. 173.00 (*0-7837-3396-8*, 204335400010) Bks Demand.

— The English Novel & the Principle of Its Development. (Notable American Authors Ser.). 1999. reprint ed. lib. bdg. 125.00 (*0-7812-3721-1*) Rprt Serv.

— Florida: Its Scenery, Climate & History. A Facsimile Reproduction of the 1875 Edition, with Introduction & Index by Jerrell H. Shofner. LC 72-14330. (Bicentennial Floridian Facsimile Ser.). 318p. reprint ed. pap. 98.60 (*0-8357-6922-4*, 203798100009) Bks Demand.

— Florida: Its Scenery, Climate, & History. (Notable American Authors Ser.). 1999. reprint ed. lib. bdg. 125.00 (*0-7812-3700-9*) Rprt Serv.

— King Arthur & His Knights of the Round Table. Malory, Thomas, ed. (Illustrated Junior Library). (Illus.). 288p. (J). (gr. 4-6). 1950. 15.99 (*0-448-06016-7*, G & D) Peng Put Young Read.

— Letters. (Notable American Authors Ser.). 1999. reprint ed. lib. bdg. 125.00 (*0-7812-3725-4*) Rprt Serv.

— Letters: Selections from His Correspondence. Lanier, Henry W., ed. LC 71-37890. (Select Bibliographies Reprint Ser.). 1977. reprint ed. 23.95 (*0-8369-6727-5*) Ayer.

— Music & Poetry. 1973. lib. bdg. 250.00 (*0-87968-028-8*) Gordon Pr.

— Music & Poetry. LC 68-25292. (Studies in Poetry: No. 38). (C). 1969. reprint ed. lib. bdg. 75.00 (*0-8383-0306-4*) M S G Haskell Hse.

— Music & Poetry. (Notable American Authors Ser.). 1999. reprint ed. lib. bdg. 125.00 (*0-7812-3724-6*) Rprt Serv.

— Poems. (Notable American Authors Ser.). 1999. reprint ed. lib. bdg. 125.00 (*0-7812-3715-7*); reprint ed. lib. bdg. 125.00 (*0-7812-3723-8*) Rprt Serv.

— Poems & Letters. (American Autobiography Ser.). 227p. 1995. reprint ed. lib. bdg. 79.00 (*0-7812-8574-7*) Rprt Serv.

— Poems of Sidney Lanier. 262p. 1998. reprint ed. lib. bdg. 89.00 (*0-7812-4776-4*) Rprt Serv.

— Retrospects & Prospects. (Notable American Authors Ser.). 1999. reprint ed. lib. bdg. 125.00 (*0-7812-3726-2*) Rprt Serv.

— The Science of English Verse. (Notable American Authors Ser.). 1999. reprint ed. lib. bdg. 125.00 (*0-7812-3719-X*) Rprt Serv.

— Selected Poems. LC 83-48838. reprint ed. 34.50 (*0-404-20151-2*) AMS Pr.

— Shakespeare & His Forerunners, 2 vols. (BCL1-PR English Literature Ser.). 1992. reprint ed. lib. bdg. 99.00 (*0-7812-7289-0*) Rprt Serv.

— Shakespeare & His Forerunners. (Notable American Authors Ser.). 1999. reprint ed. lib. bdg. 125.00 (*0-7812-3727-0*) Rprt Serv.

— Shakspere & His Forerunners, 2 vols. LC 74-171656. reprint ed. 95.00 (*0-404-03875-1*) AMS Pr.

— Sidney Lanier: Poems & Letters. LC 76-83323. 239p. reprint ed. pap. 74.10 (*0-608-14633-1*, 202582400046) Bks Demand.

— Some Highways & Byways of American Travel. (Notable American Authors Ser.). 1999. reprint ed. lib. bdg. 125.00 (*0-7812-3717-3*) Rprt Serv.

— Tiger Lilies. (Notable American Authors Ser.). 1999. reprint ed. lib. bdg. 125.00 (*0-7812-3699-1*) Rprt Serv.

Lanier, Sidney, ed. Music & Poetry: Essays upon Some Aspects & Interrelations of the Two Arts. 248p. 1990. reprint ed. lib. bdg. 69.00 (*0-7812-9013-9*) Rprt Serv.

Lanier, Stephen M. & Limbird, Lee, eds. Alpha-2 Adrenergic Receptors: Structure, Function & Therapeutic Implications. 224p. 1997. text 55.00 (*90-5702-019-X*, ECU71, Harwood Acad Pubs) Gordon & Breach.

Lanier, Sterling E. The Curious Quests of Brigadier Fellowes. (Illus.). 1986. 30.00 (*0-937986-89-5*) D M Grant.

— The Peculiar Exploits of Brigadier Fellowes. LC 74-188477. (Illus.). 159 p. (J). 1971. write for info. (*0-8027-5548-8*) Walker & Co.

Lanier, Tyre C. & Lee, Chong M., eds. Surimi Technology. (Food Science & Technology Ser.: Vol. 50). (Illus.). 536p. 1992. text 225.00 (*0-8247-8470-7*) Dekker.

Lanier, Vincent. The Arts We See: A Simplified Introduction to the Visual Arts. (Orig.). 1982. pap. text 13.95 (*0-8077-2699-0*) Tchrs Coll.

— Essays in Art Education: The Development of One Point of View. 2nd ed. 144p. 1976. pap. text 6.95 (*0-8422-0516-0*) Irvington.

— The World of Art Education. 56p. 1991. pap. 15.00 (*0-937652-57-1*) Natl Art Ed.

Lanier, Virginia. Blind Bloodhound Justice: A Jo Beth Sidden Mystery. LC 98-3661. 288p. 1998. 24.00 (*0-06-017547-8*) HarpC.

— Blind Bloodhound Justice: A Jo Beth Sidden Mystery. 352p. 1999. mass mkt. 6.50 (*0-06-109971-6*) HarpC.

— A Bloodhound to Die For. 2000. 24.00 (*0-06-019388-3*); pap. 6.50 (*0-06-109840-X*) HarpC.

— A Brace of Bloodhounds. 448p. 1998. mass mkt. 6.50 (*0-06-101087-1*) HarpC.

— Death in Bloodhound Red. 544p. 1996. mass mkt. 6.50 (*0-06-101025-1*, Harp PBks) HarpC.

— Death in Bloodhound Red. LC 94-43196. 462p. 1995. 19.95 (*1-56164-076-X*) Pineapple Pr.

— The House on Bloodhound Lane. 384p. 1997. mass mkt. 5.99 (*0-06-101086-3*, Harp PBks) HarpC.

— Ten Little Bloodhounds: A Jo Beth Sidden Mystery. LC 98-49470. 288p. 1999. 24.00 (*0-06-017548-6*) HarpC.

***Lanier, Virginia.** Ten Little Bloodhounds: A Jo Beth Sidden Mystery. 352p. 2000. mass mkt. 6.50 (*0-06-109066-2*) HarpC.

Lanier, W. C. A Taste of North Carolina: A Collection of Recipes from Festivals & Events of North Carolina. LC 96-79061. (Illus.). 1997. pap. text 14.95 (*0-9654781-0-6*) Bluewater Mktg.

***Lanier, W. Chandler.** Yallid, Stable Boy of Bethlehem. 70p. (J). (gr. 3-6). 2000. pap. 7.99 (*1-58158-011-8*, Parable Pubns) McDougal Pubng.

Lanig, Indira S. & Chase, Teresa. Practical Guide to Health Promotion after Spinal Cord Injury. 300p. 1995. 62.00 (*0-8342-0628-5*) Aspen Pub.

Lanigan, Anne. Complete Yogurt Cookbook. Adler, Andrew & Adler, Roger, eds. (Illus.). 1978. 9.95 (*0-916844-02-1*); pap. text 5.95 (*0-916844-03-X*) Turtle Pr.

Lanigan, Anni, jt. auth. see Cohen, Matthew M.

Lanigan, Catherine. All or Nothing. 400p. (Orig.). 1989. mass mkt. 4.50 (*0-380-75459-2*, Avon Bks) Morrow Avon.

— At Long Last Love. 416p. (Orig.). 1994. mass mkt. 4.99 (*0-380-76948-4*, Avon Bks) Morrow Avon.

— Becoming. 400p. (Orig.). 1997. mass mkt. 5.99 (*0-8439-4261-4*, Leisure Bks) Dorchester Pub Co.

— California Moon. 376p. 2000. per. 5.99 (*1-55166-578-6*) Harlequin Bks.

— Dangerous Love. 416p. 1996. per. 5.99 (*1-55166-163-2*, 1-66163-6, Mira Bks) Harlequin Bks.

— Elusive Love. 1997. per. 5.99 (*1-55166-286-8*) Harlequin Bks.

— In Love's Shadow. 384p. 1998. per. 5.99 (*1-55166-435-6*, 1-66435-8, Mira Bks) Harlequin Bks.

— The Legend Makers. 384p. 1999. mass mkt. 5.99 (*1-55166-517-4*, 1-66517-3, Mira Bks) Harlequin Bks.

— Montana Bride. 1998. per. 3.75 (*0-373-76151-1*, 1-76151-9) Silhouette.

— A Promise Made. 496p. (Orig.). 1990. mass mkt. 4.95 (*0-380-75694-3*, Avon Bks) Morrow Avon.

— Seduced. 400p. 1996. pap. text, mass mkt. 5.50 (*0-8439-3942-7*) Dorchester Pub Co.

— Tender Malice. (Mira Bks.). 1998. per. 5.99 (*1-55166-420-8*, 1-66420-0, Mira Bks) Harlequin Bks.

— The Texan. (Desire Ser.: No. 1126). 1998. per. 3.75 (*0-373-76126-0*, 1-76126-1) Silhouette.

— The Way of the Wicked. 448p. (Orig.). 1993. mass mkt. 4.99 (*0-380-76947-6*, Avon Bks) Morrow Avon.

— Web of Deceit. 400p. 1987. mass mkt. 4.50 (*0-380-75311-1*, Avon Bks) Morrow Avon.

***Lanigan, Catherine.** Wings of Destiny. LC 99-37207. 500p. 1999. 24.00 (*1-55874-690-0*) Health Comm.

Lanigan, Esther F. Mary Austin: Song of a Maverick. LC 96-42224. (Illus.). 285p. 1997. pap. 19.95 (*0-8165-1714-2*) U of Ariz Pr.

Lanigan, Esther F., ed. A Mary Austin Reader. LC 95-41730. (Illus.). 271p. 1996. 40.00 (*0-8165-1619-7*); pap. 17.95 (*0-8165-1620-0*) U of Ariz Pr.

Lanigan, Katherine & Tyler, Gerald, eds. Kilkenny: Its Architecture & History. 120p. 1982. 40.00 (*0-905140-41-9*) St Mut.

Lanigan, Richard J. Kangaroo Express: The Epic Story of the Submarine Growler. LC 97-69729. (Illus.). 173p. 1997. 14.95 (*0-9659995-0-5*) RJL Express.

Lanigan, Richard L. The Human Science of Communicology: A Phenomenology of Discourse in Foucault & Merleau-Ponty. LC 91-47094. (Illus.). 290p. (C). 1992. text 34.95 (*0-8207-0242-0*) Duquesne.

— Phenomenology of Communication. LC 87-24587. 288p. 1988. text 19.50 (*0-8207-0185-8*) Duquesne.

— Semiotic Phenomenology of Rhetoric: Eidetic Practice in Henry Grattan's Discourse on Tolerance. (Current Continental Research Ser.: No. 203). (Illus.). 248p. (Orig.). 1984. 52.00 (*0-8191-4294-8*); pap. 23.00 (*0-8191-4295-6*) U Pr of Amer.

— Speaking & Semiology: Maurice Merleau-Ponty's Phenomenological Theory of Existential Communication. 2nd ed. LC 91-30860. (Approaches to Semiotics Ser.: No. 22). vi, 257p. 1991. lib. bdg. 106.15 (*3-11-012864-0*) Mouton.

***Lanigan-Schmidt, Therese.** Ghostly Beacons: Haunted Lighthouses of North America. (Illus.). 160p. 2000. pap. 14.95 (*0-7643-1114-X*) Schiffer.

***Lanigan, Sean.** Lasers of Dermatology. LC 00-24606. 2000. write for info. (*1-85233-277-8*) Spr-Verlag.

Laning, Charlotte. Bearded Collie. (SWE., Illus.). 188p. text 40.00 (*0-9644628-1-8*) C Laning.

***Laning, Harris.** An Admiral's Yarn. Shulman, Mark R. & Naval War College Press Staff, eds. LC 99-30641. (Naval War College Historical Monograph Ser.: No. 14). (Illus.). 426p. (C). 1999. pap. 15.00 (*1-884733-12-3*) Naval War Coll.

***Laningham, Ivan.** Python in 24 Hours. LC 99-65588. (Illus.). 528p. 2000. pap. 24.99 (*0-672-31735-4*) Sams.

Lanir, Zvi. Israeli Defense in the 1980's. LC 83-23124. 271p. 1984. 55.00 (*0-275-91209-4*, C1209, Praeger Pubs) Greenwood.

Lanitis, Trudy. Bio-Etheric Healing: A Breakthrough in Alternative Therapies. LC 98-87550. (Illus.). 192p. 1999. pap. 14.95 (*1-56184-139-0*) New Falcon Pubns.

Lanius, Roger D., jt. auth. see Hallwas, John E.

Lanjalley, Paul & Corriez, Paul. Histoire de la Revolution Du 18 Mars. LC 78-171657. reprint ed. 76.50 (*0-404-07139-2*) AMS Pr.

Lanjouw, Jean O., jt. auth. see Howes, Steven.

Lanjouw, Peter & Stern, Nicholas. Economic Development in Palanpur over Five Decades. 300p. 1999. text 125.00 (*0-19-828832-8*) OUP.

Lanjouw, Peter, jt. auth. see Hentschel, Jesko.

Lanjovw, G. J. International Trade Institutions. LC 95-23081. 112p. (C). 1996. pap. text 17.25 (*0-582-27764-7*, Pub. by Addison-Wesley) Longman.

Lank, jt. auth. see Mayo.

Lank, Alden, jt. auth. see Neubauer, Fred.

Lank, David. Audubon's Wilderness Palette: The Birds of Canada. LC 98-203761. (Illus.). 192p. 1999. 39.95 (*1-55013-978-9*, Pub. by Key Porter) Firefly Bks Ltd.

Lank, Edith. Como Comprar o Vender Tu Casa.Tr. of How to Buy or Sell Your Home. (SPA.). 128p. (Orig.). 1997. pap. 7.95 (*0-7931-2698-3*, 1700-0701, Real Estate Ed) Dearborn.

— Essentials of New Jersey Real Estate. 3rd ed. LC 98-26648. 1998. pap. 39.95 (*0-7931-2972-9*) Dearborn.

— The Homebuyer's Kit. 4th ed. LC 97-18830. 208p. 1997. pap. 15.95 (*0-7931-2665-7*, 1913-0604, Real Estate Ed) Dearborn.

— The Homeseller's Kit. 4th ed. LC 97-18829. 240p. 1997. pap. 15.95 (*0-7931-2664-9*, 1913-0504, Real Estate Ed) Dearborn.

***Lank, Edith.** Jane Austen Speaks to Women. 2000. pap. 4.95 (*0-7407-1047-8*) Andrews & McMeel.

Lank, Edith. Modern Real Estate Practice in New York. 6th ed. LC 97-3695. 1997. pap. text 41.95 (*0-7931-2414-X*, 1510-5206) Dearborn.

***Lank, Edith & Deickler, Judith.** Modern Real Estate Practice in New York: For Salespersons & Brokers. 7th ed. LC 99-39630. 2000. pap. 42.95 (*0-7931-3626-1*, Real Estate Ed) Dearborn.

***Lank, Edith & Sobeck, Joan M.** Essentials of New Jersey Real Estate. 4th ed. LC 99-55595. 2000. pap. 39.95 (*0-7931-3599-0*, Real Estate Ed) Dearborn.

Lank, Elizabeth, jt. auth. see Mayo, Andrew.

Lanka, L. Darlene, jt. auth. see Huston, James E.

Lankard, David R., ed. see American Concrete Institute Staff.

Lankard, Frederick, ed. Letters to Dotty B: World War II in the South Pacific. LC 98-134884. (Illus.). 300p. 1998. pap. 22.95 (*0-89745-218-6*) Sunflower U Pr.

Lankavatara-Sutra. Self-Realization of Noble Wisdom. Goddard, Dwight, ed. Suzuki, D. T., tr. LC 78-72461. reprint ed. 37.50 (*0-404-17333-0*) AMS Pr.

Lanken, Paul N. The Intensive Care Unit Manual. Zorab, Richard, ed. LC 98-40583. (Illus.). 830p. 1999. pap. text 47.50 (*0-7216-2197-X*, W B Saunders Co) Harcrt Hlth Sci Grp.

Lankenau, Walter C., ed. see Ronfor, Philip A.

***Lanker, Brian.** I Dream a World: Portrait of Black Women Who Changed America. anniversary ed. 172p. 1999. pap. 24.95 (*1-55670-974-9*) Stewart Tabori & Chang.

Lanker, Brian. I Dream a World: Portraits of Black Women Who Changed America. 10th anniversary ed. (Illus.). 172p. 1999. 40.00 (*1-55670-888-2*) Stewart Tabori & Chang.

***Lanker, Brian.** I Dream a World: Portraits of Black Women Who Changed America: A Tenth Anniversary Celebration. 10th rev. ed. 1999. pap. 24.95 (*1-55670-923-4*) Stewart Tabori & Chang.

Lanker, Brian, photos by. I Dream a World: Portraits of Black Women Who Changed America. LC 88-32697. (Illus.). 160p. 1989. pap. 24.95 (*1-55670-092-X*) Stewart Tabori & Chang.

***Lanker, Brian & Newnham, Nicole.** They Drew Fire: Combat Artists of World War II. LC 99-86620. (Illus.). 192p. 2000. 39.95 (*1-57500-085-7*, Pub. by TV Bks) HarpC.

Lankes, R. David. Building & Maintaining Internet Information Services: K-12 Digital Reference Services. (Illus.). 213p. (Orig.). 1998. pap. 20.00 (*0-937597-46-5*, IR-106) ERIC Clear.

***Lankes, R. David, et al, eds.** Digital Reference Service in the New Millennium: Planning, Management, & Evaluation. (New Library Ser.). 225p. 2000. pap. 85.00 (*1-55570-384-4*) Neal-Schuman.

Lankes, R. David & Kasowitz, Abby S. Ask a Starter Kit: How to Build & Maintain Digital Reference Services. (Illus.). 235p. (Orig.). 1998. pap. 20.00 (*0-937597-47-3*, IR-107) ERIC Clear.

Lankes, Virtual D. The Bread & Butter of the Internet: A Primer & Presentation Packet for Educators. (Illus.). 133p. 1999. reprint ed. pap. text 25.00 (*0-7881-7563-7*) DIANE Pub.

Lankester, Bob, jt. auth. see Farmer, Neil.

Lankester, Edwin R. Diversions of a Naturalist. LC 77-105024. (Essay Index Reprint Ser.). 1977. 29.95 (*0-8369-1471-6*) Ayer.

— Great & Small Things. LC 72-5630. (Essay Index Reprint Ser.). 1977. reprint ed. 23.95 (*0-8369-2995-0*) Ayer.

— Science from an Easy Chair. LC 79-152185. (Essay Index Reprint Ser.: 1). 1977. 26.95 (*0-8369-2194-1*) Ayer.

— Science from an Easy Chair. LC 79-152185. (Essay Index Reprint Ser.: 2). 1977. 23.95 (*0-8369-2210-7*) Ayer.

— Secrets of Earth & Sea. LC 76-93352. (Essay Index Reprint Ser.). 1977. 21.95 (*0-8369-1301-9*) Ayer.

Lankester, Edwin R., ed. see Ray, John.

***Lankester, Ted.** Traveller's Good Health Guide. (Illus.). 2000. pap. 10.95 (*0-85969-827-0*) Sheldon Pr.

Lankevich, George J. American Metropolis: A History of New York City. LC 98-11251. (Illus.). 282p. 1998. pap. 18.95 (*0-8147-5149-0*); text 55.00 (*0-8147-5148-2*) NYU Pr.

— Chief Justices of the U. S. 1995. 20.00 (*0-941980-30-8*) Bronx County.

Lankevich, George J., ed. United Nations Archives, New York: United Nations War Crimes Commission. LC 89-16915. (Archives of the Holocaust Ser.: Vol. 16). 400p. 1990. reprint ed. text 110.00 (*0-8240-5498-9*) Garland.

***Lankevich, George L.** Postcards from Manhattan: Sights & Sentiments from the Last Century. 2000. pap. 8.95 (*0-7570-0101-7*) Square One.

— Postcards from Times Square: Sights & Sentiments from the Last Century. 2000. pap. 8.95 (*0-7570-0100-9*) Square One.

***Lankford.** Pilot's Guide to Aircraft Icing. LC 99-41781. 352p. 1999. pap. 34.95 (*0-07-134139-0*) McGraw.

— Pilots Guide To Weather Report. 3rd ed. LC 99-57417. 470p. 1999. pap. 34.95 (*0-07-135456-5*) McGraw.

Lankford & Blaze. Arizona Laws of Negligence, 1997. 2nd ed. LC 98-124291. 588p. 1997. text 95.00 (*1-55834-519-1*, 64215-11, MICHIE) LEXIS Pub.

Lankford, jt. auth. see Katz, Elizabeth L.

Lankford, E. Louis. Aesthetics: Issues & Inquiry. 106p. 1992. pap. 18.00 (*0-937652-60-1*, 214) Natl Art Ed.

Lankford, E. Louis, et al. Teachers Resource Box: Themes & Foundations of Art. 2nd ed. (Tech Prep-English). 1999. pap. 202.00 (*0-538-43008-7*) Thomson Learn.

Lankford, George. Native American Legends: The Southeast. 2nd ed. 1998. pap. 14.95 (*0-87483-518-6*) August Hse.

Lankford, J., et al. Fatigue Mechanisms: Advances in Quantitative Measurement of Physical Damage- STP 811. LC 82-73773. 498p. 1983. text 50.00 (*0-8031-0250-X*, STP811) ASTM.

Lankford, J., jt. ed. see Ritchie, R. O.

Lankford, Jefferson L. & Blaze, Douglas A. The Law of Negligence in Arizona, 1998 Supplement. 100p. 1998. pap. write for info. (*0-327-00607-2*, 6421614) LEXIS Pub.

***Lankford, Jefferson L. & Blaze, Douglas A.** The Law of Negligence in Arizona, 1999 Supplement. 100p. 1999. write for info. (*0-327-01583-7*, 6421615) LEXIS Pub.

Lankford, John. American Astronomy: Community, Careers & Power, 1859-1940. LC 96-31461. 1997. 65.00 (*0-226-46886-0*) U Ch Pr.

Lankford, John & Rothenberg, Marc, eds. History of Astronomy: An Encyclopedia. LC 96-28558. (Encyclopedias in the History of Science Ser.: No. 1). (Illus.). 650p. 1996. text 105.00 (*0-8153-0322-X*, SS771) Garland.

Lankford, Larry G., jt. auth. see Hearn, Eldo D.

Lankford, Larry G., jt. auth. see Hearn, Eldon D.

Lankford, Mary. Dominoes Around the World. LC 97-20975. (Illus.). 40p. (J). (gr. 1-4). 1998. 16.00 (*0-688-14051-3*, Wm Morrow) Morrow Avon.

***Lankford, Mary.** Dominoes Around the World. LC 97-20975. (Illus.). 40p. (J). (gr. 1-5). 1998. 15.89 (*0-688-14052-1*, Wm Morrow) Morrow Avon.

Lankford, Mary D. Birthdays Around the World. LC 99-49779. (J). 2001. write for info. (*0-688-15431-X*, Wm Morrow); lib. bdg. write for info. (*0-688-15432-8*, Wm Morrow) Morrow Avon.

Lankford, Mary D. Christmas Around the World. LC 93-38566. (Illus.). 48p. (J). (gr. 2 up). 1995. 15.93 (*0-688-12167-5*, Wm Morrow) Morrow Avon.

Lankford, Mary D. Christmas Around the World. LC 93-38566. (Illus.). 48p. (J). (ps-3). 1995. 16.00 (*0-688-12166-7*, Wm Morrow) Morrow Avon.

— Christmas Around the World. (Illus.). 48p. (J). (gr. k-3). 1998. mass mkt. 5.95 (*0-688-16323-8*, Wm Morrow) Morrow Avon.

— Hopscotch Around the World. LC 91-17152. (Illus.). 48p. (J). (gr. 3 up). 1992. 16.00 (*0-688-08419-2*, Wm Morrow) Morrow Avon.

— Hopscotch Around the World. LC 91-17152. (Illus.). 48p. (J). (gr. 4 up). 1992. lib. bdg. 15.93 (*0-688-08420-6*, Wm Morrow) Morrow Avon.

— Hopscotch Around the World. LC 91-17152. (Illus.). 48p. (J). 1997. pap. 8.95 (*0-688-15250-3*, Wm Morrow) Morrow Avon.

— Hopscotch Around the World. LC 91-17152. 1996. 11.15 (*0-606-09430-X*, Pub. by Turtleback) Demco.

— Hopscotch Around the World. (Illus.). (J). (gr. 2 up). reprint ed. pap. 5.95 (*0-614-15677-7*, Wm Morrow) Morrow Avon.

— Hopscotch Around the World: Nineteen Ways to Play the Game. LC 91-17152. 48p. (J). (gr. 4-7). 1996. mass mkt. 5.95 (*0-688-14745-3*, Wm Morrow) Morrow Avon.

— Jacks Around the World. LC 95-22864. (Illus.). 40p. (J). 1996. 16.00 (*0-688-13707-5*, Wm Morrow) Morrow Avon.

Lankford, Mary D. Jacks Around the World. LC 95-22864. (Illus.). 40p. (J). 1996. lib. bdg. 15.93 (*0-688-13708-3*, Wm Morrow) Morrow Avon.

Lankford, Mary D. Mazes Around the World. (J). 1924. write for info. (*0-688-16519-2*, Wm Morrow); lib. bdg. write for info. (*0-688-16520-6*, Wm Morrow) Morrow Avon.

— Quinceanera: A Latina's Journey to Womanhood. (Illus.). 48p. (J). (gr. 6-9). 1994. lib. bdg. 20.90 (*1-56294-363-4*) Millbrook Pr.

— Successful Field Trips. LC 91-38558. 175p. 1992. pap. text 35.00 (*0-87436-638-0*) ABC-CLIO.

Lankford, Mike. Life in Double Time: Confessions of an American Drummer. 256p. 1997. 22.95 (*0-8118-0683-9*) Chronicle Bks.

— Life in Double Time: Confessions of an American Drummer. 272p. 1999. pap. 12.95 (*0-8118-2321-0*) Chronicle Bks.

Lankford, Nelson D., ed. OSS Against the Reich: The World War II Diaries of Colonel David K. E. Bruce. LC 90-47719. (Illus.). 256p. 1991. 28.50 (*0-87338-427-X*) Kent St U Pr.

Lankford, Nelson D., ed. see Hilldrup, Robert P.

Lankford, Perry W. & Eckenfelder, W. Wesley, eds. Toxicity Reduction in Industrial Effluents. 350p. 1990. text 72.95 (*0-442-00234-3*, VNR) Wiley.

Lankford, Perry W. & Eckenfelder, W. Wesley, eds. Toxicity Reduction in Industrial Effluents. 368p. 1990. 84.95 (*0-471-28397-5*, VNR) Wiley.

Lankford, Philip M. Regional Incomes in the United States, 1929-1967: Level, Distribution, Stability, & Growth. LC 72-91224. (University of Chicago Department of Geography Research Paper Ser.: Vol. 145). 150p. 1972. reprint ed. pap. 46.50 (*0-608-02433-3*, 206307600004) Bks Demand.

Lankford, Randall T. & Jacobs-Steward, Paula M. Foundations of Normal & Therapeutic Nutrition. 1989. pap. text 34.95 (*0-8273-4282-9*) Delmar.

Lankford, Robert D. Dream Weaver: Survive until Dawn, Vol. 1, Issue 1. (Illus.). 24p. (YA). (gr. 11 up). 1987. pap. 1.95 (*0-9621811-0-2*) Lankford Comics.

— Dream Weaver in the Face of Fear, Vol. 1, No. 3. (Illus.). 48p. (YA). (gr. 11 up). 1991. pap. 2.75 (*0-9621811-2-9*) Lankford Comics.

— Dreamweaver, Vol. 1. 2nd ed. (Illus.). 24p. (YA). (gr. 10 up). 1988. pap. 1.95 (*0-685-44540-2*) Lankford Comics.

— Dreamweaver, Vol. 1. 4th ed. (Illus.). 24p. (YA). (gr. 10 up). 1989. pap. 1.95 (*0-317-93324-8*) Lankford Comics.

Lankford, Sam, jt. auth. see Mitra, Ananda.

Lankford, Sara S., jt. auth. see Carter, Lucy R.

Lankford, T. Randall. Foundations of Normal Nutrition. 2nd ed. (Nursing Education Ser.). 1994. teacher ed. 18.95 (*0-8273-6543-8*) Delmar.

Lankford, T. Randall & Gribble, Paula V. Foundations of Normal & Therapeutic Nutrition. 2nd ed. LC 93-35725. 656p. (C). 1994. pap. 50.95 (*0-8273-5268-9*) Delmar.

Lankford, Terrill. Angry Moon. LC 97-14500. 320p. 1997. 22.95 (*0-312-85726-8*, Pub. by Tor Bks) St Martin.

— Angry Moon. 1999. mass mkt. 5.99 (*0-8125-4834-5*, Pub. by Tor Bks) St Martin.

— Shooters. LC 96-29344. 1996. 20.95 (*0-312-86272-5*, Pub. by Forge NYC) St Martin.

— Shooters. 224p. 1998. mass mkt. 5.99 (*0-8125-5538-4*) Forge Pr.

***Lankford, Terry T.** Aviation Weather Handbook. (Illus.). 2000. 49.95 (*0-07-136103-0*) McGraw.

Lankford, Terry T. Cockpit Weather Decisions. LC 97-24639. (Practical Flying Ser.). (Illus.). 240p. 1997. pap. 31.95 (*0-07-036719-1*) McGraw.

— The Pilot's Guide to Weather Reports, Forecasts & Flight Planning. 2nd ed. (TAB Practical Flying Series). (Illus.). 400p. 1995. 29.95 (*0-07-036426-5*) McGraw.

— The Pilot's Guide to Weather Reports, Forecasts & Flight Planning. 2nd ed. LC 95-1617. (Illus.). 416p. 1995. pap. 20.95 (*0-07-036427-3*) McGraw-Hill Prof.

— Understanding Aeronautical Charts. (Practical Flying Ser.). 320p. 1992. 27.95 (*0-8306-3912-8*, 1041) McGraw-Hill Prof.

— Understanding Aeronautical Charts. (Practical Flying Ser.). 208p. 1992. pap. 17.95 (*0-8306-3911-X*, 1041) McGraw-Hill Prof.

— Understanding Aeronautical Charts. 2nd ed. 323p. 1996. pap. 29.95 (*0-07-036467-2*) McGraw.

Lankheit, Klaus, ed. see Marc, Franz.

Lankhorst, G. J., et al. Rehabilitation Activities Profile. 80p. 1996. pap. 20.00 (*90-5383-398-6*, Pub. by VUB Univ Pr) Paul & Co Pubs.

Lankin, Aron. Two Lenses. Koronkevich, Dmitriy, ed. & tr. by. (Illus.). 80p. 1995. pap. 15.99 (*0-9643971-3-7*) Isometry.

Lankisch, P. G., ed. Pancreatic Enzymes in Health & Disease. (Illus.). 224p. 1991. 100.00 (*0-387-53187-4*) Spr-Verlag.

Lankisch, P. G. & Banks, Peter A. Pancreatitis. LC 97-21618. (Illus.). 504p. 1997. 109.00 (*3-540-61726-4*) Spr-Verlag.

Lankisch, P. G., et al. A Primer of Pancreatitis. LC 97-28507. (Illus.). vi, 68p. pap. write for info. (*3-540-63259-X*) Spr-Verlag.

Lankisch, Paul G. Pancreatic Disease: State of the Art & Future Aspects of Research. DiMagno, E. P., ed. LC 99-13105. (Illus.). xiii,270p. 1999. pap. 82.00 (*3-540-65357-0*) Spr-Verlag.

Lankow, Edward. How to Breathe Right. 1996. spiral bd. 9.00 (*0-7873-0990-7*) Hlth Research.

Lankowitz, Stanley, jt. auth. see Ellis, David B.

Lankowski, Carl. Germany & the European Community. 1993. text 55.00 (*0-312-06035-1*) St Martin.

Lankowski, Carl, jt. ed. see Ash, Mitchell G.

Lankowski, Carl, jt. ed. see Cafruny, Alan W.

***Lankowski, Carl F., ed.** Breaking up & Breaking Down: Germany's Modernity in State & Society. LC 99-28045. (Policies & Institutions Ser.). 233p. 1999. 49.95 (*1-57181-211-3*) Berghahn Bks.

Lanks, Karl W. Academic Environment: A Handbook for Evaluating Employment Opportunities in Science. 160p. 1995. pap. 20.95 (*1-56032-423-6*) Hemisp Pub.

— Academic Environment: A Handbook for Evaluating Employment Opportunities in Science. 3rd ed. 160p. 1995. 52.95 (*1-56032-422-8*) Hemisp Pub.

— Academic Environment: A Handbook for Evaluating Faculty Employment Opportunities. LC 90-81847. 138p. (Orig.). (C). 1990. pap. text 12.95 (*0-9626658-0-0*) Faculty Brooklyn.

Lankshear, ed. Counternarratives. 208p. (C). 1996. 65.00 (*0-415-90583-4*) Routledge.

Lankshear & Colin. Changing Literacies. LC 96-38317. (Changing Education Ser.). (Illus.). 220p. 1997. pap. 27.95 (*0-335-19636-5*) OpUniv Pr.

Lankshear, Colin. Changing Literacies. LC 96-38317. (Changing Education Ser.). (Illus.). 220p. 1997. 91.00 (*0-335-19637-3*) OpUniv Pr.

Lankshear, Colin & McLaren, Peter L., eds. Critical Literacy: Politics, Praxis, & the Postmodern. LC 91-39669. (SUNY Series, Teacher Empowerment & School Reform). 443p. (C). 1993. text 64.50 (*0-7914-1229-6*); pap. text 21.95 (*0-7914-1230-X*) State U NY Pr.

***Lankshear, Colin, et al.** Teachers & Technoliteracy: Managing Literacy, Technology & Learning in Schools. 200p. 2000. pap. 29.95 (*1-86448-946-4*, Pub. by Allen & Unwin Pty) Paul & Co Pubs.

Lankshear, Colin, jt. ed. see Gerber, Rodney.

Lankshear, Colin, jt. ed. see McLaren, Peter.

Lankshear, David W., jt. ed. see Frances, Leslie.

Lankton, Carol H., jt. auth. see Lankton, Stephen R.

Lankton, Larry D. Beyond the Boundaries: Life & Landscape at the Lake Superior Copper Mines, 1840-1875. LC 96-38552. (Illus.). 288p. 1997. 45.00 (*0-19-510804-3*) OUP.

— Beyond the Boundaries: Life & Landscape at the Lake Superior Copper Mines, 1840-1875. (Illus.). 247p. 1999. pap. 16.95 (*0-19-513243-2*) OUP.

— Cradle to Grave: Life, Work, & Death at the Lake Superior Copper Mines. (Illus.). 352p. 1993. reprint ed. pap. text 19.95 (*0-19-508357-1*) OUP.

Lankton, Stephen. Practical Magic: A Translation of Basic Neuro-Linguistic Programming into Clinical Psychotherapy. LC 80-50148. 1980. pap. 19.95 (*0-916990-08-7*) META Pubns.

Lankton, Stephen R., ed. The Broader Implications of Ericksonian Therapy. LC 89-71310. (Ericksonian Monographs: No. 7). 128p. 1990. 28.95 (*0-87630-582-6*) Brunner-Mazel.

— Elements & Dimensions of an Ericksonian Approach. LC 85-17454. (Ericksonian Monographs: No. 1). 152p. 1985. text 28.95 (*0-87630-411-0*) Brunner-Mazel.

Lankton, Stephen R., et al, eds. Views on Ericksonian Brief Therapy, Process & Action. LC 91-16001. (Ericksonian Monographs: No. 8). 128p. 1991. text 28.95 (*0-87630-646-6*) Brunner-Mazel.

Lankton, Stephen R. & Erickson, Kristina K., eds. The Essence of a Single-Session Success. LC 93-11832. (Ericksonian Monographs: No. 9). 184p. 1993. text 28.95 (*0-87630-727-6*) Brunner-Mazel.

Lankton, Stephen R. & Lankton, Carol H. Advanced Metaphor Demonstrations: Enchantment & Intervention. 1987. 12.95 incl. audio (*0-87630-467-6*) Brunner-Mazel.

Lankton, Stephen R. & Lankton, Carol H. The Answer Within: A Clinical Framework of Ericksonian Hypnotherapy. LC 82-20637. 392p. 1988. text 35.95 (*0-87630-320-3*) Brunner-Mazel.

— Enchantment & Intervention in Family Therapy: Training in Ericksonian Approaches. LC 86-4240. 336p. 1986. text 39.95 (*0-87630-428-5*) Brunner-Mazel.

— Tales of Enchantment: Goal-Oriented Metaphors for Adults & Children in Therapy. LC 89-720. 432p. 1989. text 43.95 (*0-87630-504-4*) Brunner-Mazel.

Lankton, Stephen R. & Zeig, Jeffrey K., eds. Ericksonian Monographs No. 10: Difficult Contexts for Therapy. LC 94-5346. (Ericksonian Monographs: No. 10). 160p. 1994. text 28.95 (*0-87630-749-7*) Brunner-Mazel.

— Extrapolations: Demonstrations of Ericksonian Therapy. LC 89-37590. (Ericksonian Monographs: No. 6). 136p. 1989. text 28.95 (*0-87630-567-2*) Brunner-Mazel.

Lankton, Stephen R., ed. see Zeig, Jeffrey K.

Lankton, Stephen R., jt. ed. see Zeig, Jeffrey K.

Lanly, Andre, ed. see Villon, Francois.

Lanman, Barry A. & Mehaffy, George L. Oral History in the Secondary School Classroom. (Oral History Association Pamphlet Ser.: No. 2). 39p. (Orig.). 1988. pap. 8.00 (*0-317-03929-6*) Oral Hist.

Lanman, Charles. Adventures in the Wilds of America. (Notable American Authors Ser.). 1999. reprint ed. lib. bdg. 125.00 (*0-7812-3736-X*) Rprt Serv.

— Beginnings of Hindu Pantheism. 1972. 35.00 (*0-87968-719-3*) Gordon Pr.

— Biographical Annals of the Civil Government of the United States. 2000. reprint ed. 75.00 (*1-55888-934-5*) Omnigraphics Inc.

— A Canoe Voyage up the Mississippi & Around Lake Superior in 1846. LC 77-85592. 1978. reprint ed. 17.50 (*0-912382-22-8*); reprint ed. pap. 9.00 (*0-912382-23-6*) Black Letter.

— Dictionary of the United States Congress. (Notable American Authors Ser.). 1999. reprint ed. lib. bdg. 125.00 (*0-7812-3737-8*) Rprt Serv.

— Editor - Journal of Alfred Ely. (Notable American Authors Ser.). 1999. reprint ed. lib. bdg. 125.00 (*0-7812-3740-8*) Rprt Serv.

— Essays for Summer Hours. (Notable American Authors Ser.). 1999. reprint ed. lib. bdg. 125.00 (*0-7812-3729-7*) Rprt Serv.

— How-Ho-Noo: or Records of a Tourist. (Notable American Authors Ser.). 1999. reprint ed. lib. bdg. 125.00 (*0-7812-3734-3*) Rprt Serv.

— The Japanese in America. (Notable American Authors Ser.). 1999. reprint ed. lib. bdg. 125.00 (*0-7812-3741-6*) Rprt Serv.

— Letters from a Landscape Painter. (Notable American Authors Ser.). 1999. reprint ed. lib. bdg. 125.00 (*0-7812-3730-0*) Rprt Serv.

— Letters from the Alleghany Mountains. (Notable American Authors Ser.). 1999. reprint ed. lib. bdg. 125.00 (*0-7812-3733-5*) Rprt Serv.

— Life of William Woodbridge. (Notable American Authors Ser.). 1999. reprint ed. lib. bdg. 125.00 (*0-7812-3738-6*) Rprt Serv.

— Private Life of Daniel Webster. (Notable American Authors Ser.). 1999. reprint ed. lib. bdg. 125.00 (*0-7812-3735-1*) Rprt Serv.

— Red Book of Michigan. (Notable American Authors Ser.). 1999. reprint ed. lib. bdg. 125.00 (*0-7812-3739-4*) Rprt Serv.

— A Summer in the Wilderness. (Notable American Authors Ser.). 1999. reprint ed. lib. bdg. 125.00 (*0-7812-3731-9*) Rprt Serv.

— A Tour to the River Saguenay. (Notable American Authors Ser.). 1999. reprint ed. lib. bdg. 125.00 (*0-7812-3732-7*) Rprt Serv.

Lanman, Charles R. Sanskrit Reader: Text & Vocabulary & Notes. LC 11-24320. 425p. 1884. 49.95 (*0-674-78900-8*) HUP.

Lanman, Charles R., ed. see Whitney, William D.

***Lanman, Lisa.** When Alligators Laugh. LC 99-57. 190p. 1999. per. 14.95 (*1-55212-306-5*) Trafford Pub.

Lanmon, Dwight P. Glass from Six Centuries. LC 78-62279. (Illus.). 134p. 1976. pap. 10.00 (*0-317-13582-1*) Wadsworth Atheneum.

Lanmon, Dwight P., compiled by. Evaluating Your Collection: The 14 Points of Connoisseurship. LC 98-43759. (Winterthur Decorative Arts Ser.). (Illus.). 123p. 1999. pap. 17.95 (*0-912724-50-1*) U Pr of New Eng.

Lanmon, Dwight P. & Whitehouse, David B. Glass. (Robert Lehman Collection: Vol. 11). (Illus.). 358p. 1994. text 125.00 (*0-691-03405-2*, Pub. by Princeton U Pr) Cal Prin Full Svc.

Lanmon, Lorraine W. Quarry Farm: A Study of the "Picturesque" (Quarry Farm Papers: No. 3). 36p. 1991. pap. 5.00 (*1-880817-03-9*) EC Ctr Mark T Stu.

— William Lescaze, Architect. LC 83-45295. 216p. 1987. 55.00 (*0-87982-506-5*) Art Alliance.

Lanmuir, G. E., jt. auth. see Duckworth, C. L.

Lann, Irma S., et al, eds. Strategies for Studying Suicide & Suicidal Behavior. 164p. 1989. lib. bdg. 20.95 (*0-89862-383-9*) Guilford Pubns.

Lannacci, Anthony, ed. see Ward, R.

Lannamann, M. P. The Greatest Biggest Golf Book. LC 98-85183. 624p. 1998. pap. 9.95 (*0-8362-6937-3*) Andrews & McMeel.

Lannan Museum Staff. Edward Ruscha. Clearwater, Bonnie et al, eds. (Illus.). 150p. 1988. pap. 24.95 (*0-8109-2405-6*, Pub. by Abrams) Time Warner.

Lanner, Allan. A Critical Edition Of Richard Brathwait's Whimzies. LC 91-15584. (Renaissance Imagination Ser.). 416p. 1991. text 15.00 (*0-8153-0463-3*) Garland.

Lanner, Joseph. Galoppe. (Samtliche Werke fur Klavier Ser.: Vol. 7). (Illus.). 1973. reprint ed. pap. 65.00 (*0-8450-1017-4*) Broude.

— Landler, Polkas & Mazurkas. (Samtliche Werke fur Klavier Ser.: Vol. 6). 1973. reprint ed. pap. 65.00 (*0-8450-1016-6*) Broude.

— Quadrillen, Marsche & Andere Werkes. (Samtliche Werke fur Klavier Ser.: Vol. 8). (Illus.). 1973. reprint ed. pap. 65.00 (*0-8450-1018-2*) Broude.

— Samtliche Werke Fur Klavier, 8 vols. 1973. reprint ed. pap. 425.00 (*0-8450-1010-7*) Broude.

L

L

— Walzer Nr. 1-30. (Samtliche Werke fur Klavier Ser.: Vol. 1). (Illus.). 1973. reprint ed. pap. 65.00 (*0-8450-1011-5*) Broude.
— Walzer Nr. 31-51. (Samtliche Werke fur Klavier Ser.: Vol. 2). 1973. reprint ed. pap. 65.00 (*0-8450-1012-3*) Broude.
— Walzer Nr. 52-70. (Samtliche Werke fur Klavier Ser.: Vol. 3). (Illus.). 1973. reprint ed. pap. 65.00 (*0-8450-1013-1*) Broude.
— Walzer Nr. 71-93. (Samtliche Werke fur Klavier Ser.: Vol. 4). 1973. reprint ed. pap. 65.00 (*0-8450-1014-X*) Broude.
— Walzer Nr. 94-106: Anhang. (Samtliche Werke fur Klavier Ser.: Vol. 5). (Illus.). 1973. reprint ed. pap. 65.00 (*0-8450-1015-8*) Broude.
Lanner, Ron. Autumn Leaves. LC 94-139071. (Illus.). 1990. pap. 9.95 (*1-55971-078-0*, 0191, NorthWord Pr) Creat Pub Intl.
Lanner, Ronald M. Conifers of California. LC 98-52371. (Illus.). 288p. 1998. 36.95 (*0-9628505-4-3*); pap. 24.95 (*0-9628505-3-5*) Cachuma Pr.
— Made for Each Other: A Symbiosis of Birds & Pines. (Illus.). 180p. 1996. 29.95 (*0-19-508902-2*); pap. 15.95 (*0-19-508903-0*) OUP.
— The Pinon Pine: A Natural & Cultural History. LC 81-119. (Illus.). 224p. 1981. 21.95 (*0-87417-065-6*); pap. 13.95 (*0-87417-066-4*) U of Nev Pr.
— Trees of the Great Basin: A Natural History. LC 83-21714. (Max C. Fleischmann Series in Great Basin Natural History). 273p. 1984. reprint ed. pap. 77.90 (*0-608-01262-9*, 2062011) Bks Demand.
Lannering, J. Studies in the Prose Style of Joseph Addison. (Essays & Studies on English Language & Literature: Vol. 9). 1974. reprint ed. pap. 25.00 (*0-8115-0207-4*) Periodicals Srv.
Lanners, Edi. Secrets of One Hundred Twenty-Three Classic Science Tricks & Experiments. (Illus.). 196p. (Orig.). 1987. pap. 8.95 (*0-8306-2821-5*) McGraw-Hill Prof.
— Secrets of 123 Classic Science Tricks & Experiments. 192p. 1987. pap. 12.95 (*0-07-157345-3*) McGraw.
Lanners, Karen & Schwartzenberger, Ken. Therapeutic Stories for Children in Foster Care. 2nd rev. ed. LC 98-90266. (Illus.). x, 60p. (Orig.). (J). (ps-6). 1998. pap. 15.95 (*0-9652163-1-4*) Therapeutic Stories.
Lannert, Paula. Mexican Americans. (American Voices Ser.). 112p. (J). 1991. lib. bdg. 18.95 (*0-86593-139-9*); lib. bdg. 18.60 (*0-685-59187-5*) Rourke Corp.
Lannestock, Gustaf, tr. see Boye, Karin.
Lanni, Deborah. What's a Duck Like You Doing in a Place Like This? (Illus.). iv, 23p. (Orig.). (J). (gr. 3-6). 1984. pap. 2.00 (*0-942788-12-5*) Iris Visual.
Lannin, Joanne. Billie Jean King: Tennis Trailblazer. LC 98-37488. 112p. (YA). (gr. 6-9). 1999. 25.26 (*0-8225-4959-X*, Lerner Publctns) Lerner Pub.
***Lannin, Joanne.** A History of Basketball for Girls & Women: From Bloomers to Big Leagues. LC 99-50643. (Sports Legacy Ser.). (Illus.). 144p. (YA). (gr. 4-7). 2000. pap. 9.95 (*0-8225-9863-9*, LernerSports) Lerner Pub.
— A History of Basketball for Girls & Women: From Bloomers to Big Leagues. LC 99-50643. (Sports Legacy Ser.). (Illus.). 144p. (YA). (gr. 6-10). 2000. lib. bdg. 23.93 (*0-8225-3331-6*, LernerSports) Lerner Pub.
Lanning, ed. Personality. (C). 1999. text. write for info. (*0-321-01191-0*) Addison-Wesley Educ.
Lanning, Andy, jt. auth. see Abnett, Dan.
Lanning, Cynthia, jt. ed. see Anderson, Sara L.
***Lanning, D. D.** Integral Assessment: Frapcon-3. 228p. 1998. per. 18.00 (*0-16-062884-9*) USGPO.
— Modifications to Fuel Rod Material Properties & Performance Models for High-burnup Application: Frapcon-3. 134p. 1997. per. 13.00 (*0-16-062872-5*) USGPO.
Lanning, David D., jt. ed. see White, James D.
Lanning, Edward P. Archaeology of the Rose Spring Site INY-372. Heizer et al, eds. (University of California Publications in American Archaeology & Ethnology: No. 49:3). 97p. (C). 1963. pap. 10.94 (*1-55567-327-9*) Coyote Press.
Lanning, George, jt. auth. see Macauley, Robie.
Lanning, J. Stephen. Marketing Your Consultancy: How to Establish Yourself As the Expert. 28p. 1998. write for info. (*1-891558-05-6*) New Ventures Pub.
***Lanning, J. Stephen.** Starting & Growing a Business in the Quad-State Region. Heerwagen, Peter, ed. 200p. 2000. pap. 24.95 (*0-9678447-0-3*) Quad-State.
Lanning, J. Stephen. $10,000-a-Day Business Opportunities: Seminars, Newsletters, Cassettes, Software & More. 48p. 1998. write for info. (*1-891558-01-3*) New Ventures Pub.
Lanning, J. Stephen, jt. auth. see Qubein, Nido.
Lanning, Jean. The Great Dane. LC 79-183675. 210 p. 1972. write for info. (*0-668-02588-3*, ARCO) Macmillan.
— The Great Dane rev. ed. LC 78-304036. 196p. 1977. write for info. (*0-09-128040-0*) Arrow Bks.
— Great Danes LC 76-11028. 90p. 1976. write for info. (*0-668-03996-5*, ARCO) Macmillan.
Lanning, Jim & Lanning, Judy, eds. Texas Cowboys: Memories of the Early Days. LC 83-40494. (Illus.). 256p. 1995. pap. 14.95 (*0-89096-658-3*) Tex A&M Univ Pr.
Lanning, Joyce A., jt. auth. see Juster, Robert J.
Lanning, Judy, jt. ed. see Lanning, Jim.
Lanning, K. Consistency, Scalability, & Personality Measurement. (Recent Research in Psychology Ser.). (Illus.). viii, 157p. 1990. 54.95 (*0-387-97438-5*) Spr-Verlag.
Lanning, Lee & Hart, Nett. Ripening: An Almanac of Lesbian Lore & Vision, Vol. 1. 160p. 1992. reprint ed. pap. 8.95 (*0-9615605-2-5*) Word Weavers.
Lanning, Michael J. Delivering Profitable Value. 1998. write for info. (*0-201-36098-5*) Addison-Wesley.
***Lanning, Michael J.** Delivering Profitable Value: A Revolutionary Framework to Accelerate Growth, Generate Wealth & Rediscover the Heart of Business. 336p. 2000. pap. text 25.00 (*0-7382-0162-6*, Pub. by Perseus Pubng) HarpC.
Lanning, Michael J., jt. auth. see Josaitis, Norman F.
Lanning, Michael L. The African-American Soldier: From Crispus Attucks to Colin Powell. LC 96-37626. (Illus.). 288p. 1997. 22.50 (*1-55972-404-8*, Birch Ln Pr) Carol Pub Group.
— Defenders of Liberty: African Americans in the Revolutionary War. LC 98-56271. (Illus.). 256p. 1999. 22.50 (*1-55972-513-3*, Birch Ln Pr) Carol Pub Group.
— Inside the LRRPS: Rangers in Vietnam. 256p. 1988. mass mkt. 5.99 (*0-8041-0166-3*) Ivy Books.
— The Military 100: A Ranking of the Most Influential Military Leaders of All Time. (Illus.). 372p. 1999. text 27.00 (*0-7881-6038-9*) DIANE Pub.
— The Military 100: Ranking of the Most Influential Military Leaders of All Time. (Illus.). 352p. Date not set. 27.50 (*0-8065-1828-6*, Citadel Pr) Carol Pub Group.
— Senseless Secrets: The Failures of U. S. Military Intelligence from George Washington to the Present. LC 95-19249. (Illus.). 336p. 1995. 24.95 (*1-55972-322-X*, Birch Ln Pr) Carol Pub Group.
Lanning, Michael L. & Cragg, Dan. Inside the VC & the NVA: The Real Story of North Vietnam's Armed Forces. 1994. mass mkt. 5.99 (*0-8041-0500-6*) Ivy Books.
Lanning, Michael L. & Stubbe, Ray W. Inside Force Recon: Recon Marines in Vietnam. 304p. 1989. mass mkt. 5.99 (*0-8041-0301-1*) Ivy Books.
Lanning, Michael Lee. African-American Soldier: Form Crispus Attucks to Colin Powell. (Illus.). 320p. 1999. pap. 16.95 (*0-8065-2049-3*) Carol Pub Group.
Lanning, Rosemary, jt. auth. see Krischanitz, Raoul.
Lanning, Rosemary, tr. see Colle, Gisela.
Lanning, Rosemary, tr. see Falda, Dominique.
Lanning, Rosemary, tr. see Hanel, Wolfram.
Lanning, Rosemary, tr. see Janisch, Heinz.
Lanning, Rosemary, tr. see Laukel, Hans Gerold.
Lanning, Rosemary, tr. see Pfister, Marcus.
Lanning, Rosemary, tr. see Reider, Katja.
Lanning, Rosemary, tr. see Scheffler, Ursel.
Lanning, Rosemary, tr. see Siegenthaler, Kathrin & Pfister, Marcus.
Lanning, Rosemary, tr. see Velthuijs, Max.
Lanning, Rosemary, tr. see Waas, Uli.
Lanning, Rosemary, tr. see Wagener, Gerda.
Lanning, Rosemary, tr. see Weninger, Brigitte.
Lannom, Jack. Untapped Potential: 12 Steps for Turning Ordinary People into Extraordinary Performers. LC 98-14654. 300p. 1998. pap. 12.99 (*0-7852-7455-3*) Nelson.
***Lannon.** Technical Communication. 8th ed. LC 99-23623. 680p. (C). 1999. pap. 70.00 (*0-321-02395-1*) Addson-Wesley Educ.
Lannon, Albert V. Second String Red: A Biography of Al Lannon, American Communist. 240p. 1998. 45.00 (*0-7391-0002-5*) Lxngtn Bks.
Lannon, Erwan, jt. auth. see Maresceau, Marc.
Lannon, Frances. Privilege, Persecution & Prophecy: The Catholic Church in Spain, 1875-1975. (Illus.). 276p. 1987. 75.00 (*0-19-821923-7*) OUP.
***Lannon, John M.** The Writing Process: A Concise Rhetoric. 7th ed. 496p. 2000. pap. 46.00 (*0-321-07663-X*) Longman.
Lannon, John M. The Writing Process: With MLA Update. 6th ed. 400p. (C). 1999. pap. 46.00 (*0-321-04964-0*) Addison-Wesley Educ.
Lannon, Kathleen, ed. InfoMap Project Manager's Guide. (Illus.). 100p. (Orig.). 1990. pap. 39.95 incl. disk (*0-9606408-5-1*) Info Mgmt Pr.
Lannon, Michael. Insights into Business. 1995. pap. text, student ed. write for info. (*0-17-556883-9*); pap. text, wbk. ed. write for info. (*0-17-557055-8*) Addison-Wesley.
***Lannon, T. Stanley.** The Other Side of the Gray: A Poet's Journey. 20p. 1999. pap. 3.00 (*0-9673765-0-5*, 001) Lemming Line.
Lannon Taylor, Joseph. Joe Taylor's Complete Guide to Breeding & Raising Racehorses, 1. 1999. pap. text 29.95 (*0-929346-61-0*) R Meerdink Co Ltd.
***Lannoo.** European Capital Market. LC 99-32598. 216p. 2000. 79.95 (*0-471-99762-5*) Wiley.
Lannoo, M., et al, eds. Physics & Applications of Defects in Advanced Semiconductors. LC 94-1533. (Materials Research Society Symposium Proceedings Ser.: Vol. 325). 523p. 1994. text 71.00 (*1-55899-224-3*) Materials Res.
Lannoo, M. & Bourgoin, J. Point Defects in Semiconductors I. (Solid-State Sciences Ser.: Vol. 22). (Illus.). 260p. 1981. 53.00 (*0-387-10518-2*) Spr-Verlag.
Lannoo, M. & Friedel, P. Atomic & Electronic Structure of Surfaces: Theoretical Foundations. Ertl, G. & Gomer, R., eds. (Surface Sciences Ser.: Vol. 16). (Illus.). 272p. 1991. 71.95 (*0-387-52682-X*) Spr-Verlag.
Lannoo, M., jt. auth. see Bourgoin, J.
Lannoo, Michael J. Okoboji Wetlands: A Lesson in Natural History. LC 95-43617. (Bur Oak Original Ser.). (Illus.). 190p. 1996. pap. 14.95 (*0-87745-533-3*); text 29.95 (*0-87745-532-5*) U of Iowa Pr.
Lannoo, Michael J., ed. Status & Conservation of Midwestern Amphibians. LC 97-48748. (Illus.). 528p. 1998. text 49.95 (*0-87745-631-3*); pap. text 29.95 (*0-87745-632-1*) U of Iowa Pr.
Lannoy, De, see De Lannoy, ed.
Lannoy, Jacques-Dominique De, see Feyereisen, Pierre & De Lannoy, Jacques-Dominique.
Lannoy, Richard. Anandamayi. 160p. 1996. pap. 30.00 (*1-85230-914-8*, Pub. by Element MA) Penguin Putnam.
***Lannoy, Richard.** Benares Seen from Within. (Illus.). 640p. 1999. 100.00 (*1-902716-00-0*) U of Wash Pr.
— Benares Seen from Within. LC 00-272532. 1999. write for info. (*0-295-97835-X*) U of Wash Pr.
Lannoy, Violet D. Pears from the Willow Tree. LC 86-50770. 151p. (Orig.). 1989. 35.00 (*0-89410-564-7*, Three Contnts); pap. 14.50 (*0-89410-565-5*, Three Contnts) L Rienner.
L'annunziata, Michael F. Handbook of Radioactivity Analysis. LC 98-84367. (Illus.). 771p. (C). 1998. text 125.00 (*0-12-436255-9*) Acad Pr.
L'Annunziata, Michael F. Radionuclide Tracers. 485p. 1987. text 217.00 (*0-12-436252-4*) Acad Pr.
Lannutti, J. E. & Williams, P. K., eds. Current Trends in the Theory of Fields: Tallahassee, 1979. (AIP Conference Proceedings Ser.: No. 48). (Illus.). 1978. lib. bdg. 16.25 (*0-88318-147-9*) Am Inst Physics.
Lano, K. The B Language & Method: A Guide to Practical Formal Development. (Formal Approaches to Computing & Information Technology Ser.). 232p. 1996. pap. 59.95 (*3-540-76033-4*) Spr-Verlag.
Lano, Kevin. Formal Object-Oriented Development. LC 95-32281. (Formal Approaches to Computing & Information Technology Ser.). 436p. 1995. 59.00 (*3-540-19978-0*) Spr-Verlag.
Lano, Kevin & Haughton, Howard. Reverse Engineering & Software Maintenance: A Practical Approach. LC 93-29541. (International Series in Software Engineering). 1993. write for info. (*0-07-707897-7*) McGraw.
— Specification in B: An Introduction Using the B Toolkit. LC 96-215429. 252p. 1996. 48.00 (*1-86094-008-0*); pap. 24.00 (*1-86094-018-8*) World Scientific Pub.
Lano, Kevin & Parry, Clarie, eds. Breaking the Barriers to Desire: New Approaches to Multiple Relationships. 137p. (Orig.). (YA). (gr. 10). 1995. pap. 12.98 (*0-907123-36-8*) AK Pr Dist.
Lano, Kevin, jt. auth. see Haughton, Howard.
Lanois, Daniel, et al, photos by. Bob Dylan: Time Out of Mind. (Illus.). 48p. 1997. pap. 15.95 (*0-8256-1622-0*, AM945120) Music Sales.
Lanoix, J. N., jt. auth. see Wagner, E. G.
Lanon, Frances & Preston, Paul, eds. Elites & Power in Twentieth-Century Spain: Essays in Honour of Sir Raymond Carr. (Illus.). 328p. 1991. text 95.00 (*0-19-822880-5*) OUP.
Lanot, Marra P. Passion & Compassion: Mga Tula Sa Ingles at Pilipino. 153p. 1981. pap. 12.50 (*0-686-32581-8*, Pub. by New Day Pub) Cellar.
Lanou, Steven M., jt. auth. see Miller, Kenton R.
Lanoue, David G. & Wilson, Vivian A., eds. Bard South: Teaching Writing at Historically Black Colleges & Universities. (Occasional Publications: No. 1). 63p. 1988. pap. 6.95 (*1-883275-03-2*) Xavier Rev.
Lanoue, David G., tr. see Kobayashi, Issa.
Lanoue, David J. From Camelot to the Teflon President: Economics & Presidential Popularity Since 1960, 222. LC 88-10251. (Contributions in Political Science Ser.: No. 222). 137p. 1988. 47.95 (*0-313-26393-0*, LFM/, Greenwood Pr) Greenwood.
Lanoue, David J. & Schrott, Peter R. The Joint Press Conference: The History, Impact, & Prospects of American Presidential Debates, 26. LC 90-45322. (Contributions to the Study of Mass Media & Communications Ser.: No. 26). 184p. 1991. 49.95 (*0-313-27248-4*, LPA, Greenwood Pr) Greenwood.
***LaNoue, Deirdre.** The Spiritual Legacy of Henri Nouwen. 176p. 2000. 22.95 (*0-8264-1283-1*) Continuum.
Lanoue, F. Drownproofing: A New Technique for Water Safety. 1978. pap. 3.95 (*0-685-03844-0*) P-H.
Lanoue, Guy. Brothers: The Politics of Violence among the Sekani of Northern British Columbia. 250p. 1992. 25.00 (*0-85496-746-X*) Berg Pubs.
Lanoue, Guy, tr. see Meletinsky, Eleazar M.
Lanouette, William & Silard, Bela. Genius in the Shadows: A Biography of Leo Szilard, the Man Behind the Bomb. Stewart, Robert, ed. (Illus.). 640p. 1993. text 35.00 (*0-684-19011-7*, Scribners Ref) Mac Lib Ref.
— Genius in the Shadows: A Biography of Leo Szilard, the Man Behind the Bomb. (Illus.). 608p. 1994. pap. 18.95 (*0-226-46888-7*) U Ch Pr.
Lanoux, Armand, ed. see Zola, Emile.
Lanoux, Rene, ed. see Zola, Emile.
Lanphear, Roger G. Unified: A Course on Truth & Practical Guidance from Babaji. LC 86-72570. 160p. (Orig.). 1987. pap. 8.95 (*0-87516-585-0*) DeVorss.
Lanpher, Bob. North Attleborough. (Images of America Ser.). 1998. pap. 16.99 (*0-7524-0885-2*) Arcadia Publng.
Lanphere, M. A., et al, eds. Abstracts of the Eighth International Conference on Geochronology, Cosmochronology & Isotope Geology. (Illus.). 384p. (Orig.). (C). 1994. pap. text 75.00 (*0-7881-1349-6*) DIANE Pub.
***Lanphere, Teresa.** Test of Articulation in Context (TAC) (Illus.). 1999. pap. text 110.00 (*1-883315-42-5*) Imaginart Intl.
Lanquetin, Paule, jt. auth. see Boidin, Jacques.
Lanre. Design Consultants Including Design Colleges '97. 1993. 250.00 (*0-9518494-3-3*, Pub. by Janvier Pubng Ltd) St Mut.
— The Professional & Business Guide to Design Services '97. 1993. 250.00 (*0-9518494-1-7*, Pub. by Janvier Pubng Ltd) St Mut.
— The Visual Index of Creative Services, 1997. 1993. pap. 150.00 (*0-9518494-2-5*, Pub. by Janvier Pubng Ltd) St Mut.
Lanros, Nedell. Emergency Nursing: With Certification Preparation & Review. 4th ed. LC 97-456. 692p. (Orig.). (C). 1997. pap. text 54.95 (*0-8385-0437-X*, A0437-2, Apple Lange Med) McGraw.
Lans, Jenni & Hardy. If It Wasn't for the Money, I Wouldn't Be Doing This . . . Finding the Courage to Survive the Job You Hate. 244p. 1998. pap. 12.95 (*0-7322-5679-8*) HarpC.
Lans, Ken, ed. see Kjeldsen, Jim.
Lans, Rick Van Der, see Van der Lans, Rick.
Lansana, Quraysh A. & Morea, J. M., eds. Dream in Yourself: A Collection of Literary Works from Gallery 37. (Illus.). 265p. (YA). (gr. 9-12). 1997. pap. 15.00 (*0-938903-23-3*) Cty of Chicago.
***Lansana, Quraysh Ali.** Southside Rain. 68p. 1999. pap. 10.00 (*0-88378-219-7*) Third World.
Lansberg, Ivan. Succeeding Generations: Realizing the Dream of Families in Business. LC 98-52228. (Illus.). 379p. 1999. 35.00 (*0-87584-742-0*) Harvard Busn.
Lansberry, J. Robert. Police Lieutenants & Captains Handbook, Vol. II. 88p. (Orig.). 1971. pap. 28.95 (*0-685-46276-5*, DH008) Davis Pub Law.
— Police Sergeants Handbook, Vol. II. 279p. (Orig.). 1972. pap. 28.95 (*1-56325-050-0*, DH012) Davis Pub Law.
Lansberry, J. Robert & Hendel, Ralph E. Police Lieutenants & Captains Handbook, Vol. I. (Illus.). 225p. (Orig.). 1971. pap. 28.95 (*1-56325-023-3*, DH007) Davis Pub Law.
Lansbury, jt. auth. see Bamber, B.
Lansbury, Angela. Angela Lansbury's Positive Moves. large type ed. 160p. 1991. lib. bdg. 14.95 (*1-56054-990-4*) Thorndike Pr.
— Angela Lansbury's Positive Moves. large type ed. 160p. 1991. reprint ed. lib. bdg. 22.95 (*1-56054-124-5*) Thorndike Pr.
— Family Matters: Wedding Speeches & Toasts. rev. ed. 96p. 1994. pap. 6.95 (*0-7063-7218-2*, Pub. by WrLock) Sterling.
Lansbury, Coral. The Old Brown Dog: Women, Workers, & Vivisection in Edwardian England. LC 85-40369. 227p. 1985. reprint ed. pap. 70.40 (*0-608-07453-5*, 206768000009) Bks Demand.
— The Reasonable Man: Trollope's Legal Fiction. LC 80-8560. 240p. pap. 74.40 (*0-8357-4649-6*, 203757900008) Bks Demand.
Lansbury, George. My Pilgrimage for Peace. LC 70-147723. (Library of War & Peace; Peace Leaders: Biographies & Memoirs). 1972. lib. bdg. 46.00 (*0-8240-0251-2*) Garland.
Lansbury, Russell, jt. ed. see Bamber, Greg J.
Lansbury, Russell D., jt. auth. see Bamber, Greg J.
Lansche, Jerry. History of the St. Louis Cardinals, Vol. 1. 1998. 25.00 (*0-939995-26-3*) Angel Pr WI.
— Stan "The Man" Musial: Born to Be a Ball Player. LC 93-45459. 240p. 1994. 19.95 (*0-87833-846-2*) Taylor Pub.
Lansdale, et al. Understanding Interfaces: A Handbook of Human Computer Dialogue. 289p. 1999. pap. write for info. (*0-12-436610-4*) Acad Pr.
Lansdale, Bruce. Metamorphosis: or Why I Love Greece. LC 78-75129. (Illus.). 128p. 1979. 30.00 (*0-89241-083-3*) Caratzas.
***Lansdale, Bruce M.** Cultivating Inspired Leaders: Making Participatory Management Work. LC 99-87595. (Illus.). 176p. 2000. pap. 27.95 (*1-56549-110-6*) Kumarian Pr.
Lansdale, Edward G. In the Midst of Wars: An American's Mission to Southeast Asia. 2nd ed. LC 91-70451. xxxii, 386p. 1991. pap. 19.95 (*0-8232-1314-5*) Fordham.
Lansdale, Joe R. Act of Love. 320p. 1995. mass mkt. 4.95 (*0-7867-0288-5*) Carroll & Graf.
— Act of Love. 1990. mass mkt. 3.95 (*0-8217-3080-0*, Zebra Kensgtn) Kensgtn Pub Corp.
— Bad Chili. LC 97-17846. 320p. 1997. 21.50 (*0-89296-619-X*, Pub. by Mysterious Pr) Little.
— Bad Chili. 1997. mass mkt. write for info. (*0-446-60421-6*) Warner Bks.
— Bad Chili. 272p. 1998. mass mkt. 6.50 (*0-446-60602-2*, Pub. by Warner Bks) Little.
— Best Sellers Guaranteed. 224p. (Orig.). 1993. mass mkt. 4.50 (*0-441-05502-8*) Ace Bks.
***Lansdale, Joe R.** Blood Dance. limited unabridged ed. (Lost Lansdale Ser.: Vol. 3). (Illus.). 175p. 2000. 40.00 (*1-892284-66-9*) Subtrrnean Pr.
— Blood Dance: Lettered Edition. deluxe unabridged ed. (Lost Lansdale Ser.: Vol. 3). (Illus.). 175p. 2000. 400.00 (*1-892284-67-7*) Subtrrnean Pr.
— The Bottoms. 304p. 2000. 24.95 (*0-89296-704-8*) Mysterious Pr.
— The Bottoms. limited unabridged ed. (Illus.). 350p. 2000. 150.00 (*1-892284-60-X*) Subtrrnean Pr.
— The Bottoms: Lettered Edition. deluxe unabridged ed. (Illus.). 350p. 2000. 400.00 (*1-892284-61-8*) Subtrrnean Pr.
Lansdale, Joe R. By Bizarre Hands. 256p. 1991. mass mkt. 3.99 (*0-380-71205-9*, Avon Bks) Morrow Avon.
— By Bizarre Hands: Stories. LC 89-51702. xi, 246 p. 1989. write for info. (*0-929480-13-9*) Mark Ziesing.
— Cold in July. 208p. 1995. mass mkt. 5.50 (*0-446-40430-6*, Pub. by Warner Bks) Little.
— Dead in the West. LC 85-27887. (Illus.). 136p. 1986. pap. 10.00 (*0-917053-04-4*) Space And.
— Dead in the West. rev. ed. (Illus.). 155p. 1994. 55.00 (*1-892300-00-1*); 125.00 (*1-892300-01-X*) Crossrds Press.
— The Drive-In: A Double-Feature Omnibus. 352p. 1997. mass mkt. 5.95 (*0-7867-0442-X*) Carroll & Graf.
— Freezer Burn. (Illus.). 250p. 1999. 60.00 (*1-892300-05-2*) Crossrds Press.
— Freezer Burn. LC 99-12075. 245p. 1999. 23.95 (*0-89296-703-X*, Pub. by Mysterious Pr) Little.

An Asterisk (*) at the beginning of an entry indicates that the title is appearing for the first time.

***Lansdale, Joe R.** Freezer Burn. 2000. mass mkt. 6.99 (*0-446-60882-3*) Warner Bks.
— High Cotton: Selected Stories of Joe R. Lansdale. 267p. 2000. 23.95 (*0-9655901-2-7*, Pub. by Golden Gryphon) IPG Chicago.
Lansdale, Joe R. Jonah Hex: Two Gun Mojo. Kahan, Bob, ed. LC 95-110906. (Illus.). 160p. 1994. pap. 12.95 (*1-56389-162-X*, Vertigo) DC Comics.
— The Long Ones. 1999. write for info. (*1-889186-15-5*) Necro Publns.
— Mucho Mojo. 304p. 1995. mass mkt. 5.99 (*0-446-40187-0*, Pub. by Warner Bks) Little.
— The Nightrunners. 248p. 1995. mass mkt. 4.95 (*0-7867-0289-3*) Carroll & Graf.
— Rumble Tumble. LC 97-51213. 256p. 1998. 21.50 (*0-89296-620-3*, Pub. by Mysterious Pr) Little.
— Rumble Tumble. 272p. 1999. mass mkt. 6.50 (*0-446-60757-6*, Pub. by Warner Bks) Little.
— Savage Season. 192p. 1995. mass mkt. 5.50 (*0-446-40431-4*, Pub. by Warner Bks) Little.
— The Two-Bear Mambo. 288p. 1996. mass mkt. 5.99 (*0-446-40188-9*, Pub. by Warner Bks) Little.
— Waltz of Shadows: A Novel of Suspense, 4 vols. deluxe ed. (Lost Lansdale Ser.). (Illus.). 300p. 1999. 195.00 (*1-892284-30-8*) Subtrrnean Pr.
— Waltz of Shadows Vol. 1: A Novel of Suspense, 4 vols. (Lost Lansdale Ser.). (Illus.). 300p. 1999. 50.00 (*1-892284-29-4*) Subtrrnean Pr.
— Writer of the Purple Rage. 320p. 1997. mass mkt. 5.95 (*0-7867-0389-X*) Carroll & Graf.
Lansdale, Joe R. & Klaw, Richard, eds. Weird Business. (Illus.). 420p. 1995. 29.95 (*1-885418-02-7*) MOJO Pr.
Lansdale, Joe R. & Pratt, George. Freezer Burn. (Illus.). 250p. 1999. 130.00 (*1-892300-06-0*) Crossrds Press.
Lansdale, Joe R. & Shiner, Lewis. Private Eye Action As You Like It. unabridged ed. (Illus.). 200p. 1998. 60.00 (*1-892300-03-6*); 125.00 (*1-892300-04-4*); pap. 20.00 (*1-892300-02-8*) Crossrds Press.
Lansdale, Joe R., jt. auth. see Burroughs, Edgar Rice.
Lansdale, Maria H. Paris: Its Sites, Monuments & History. 1977. lib. bdg. 59.95 (*0-8490-2413-7*) Gordon Pr.
Lansdell, Avril. Canal Arts & Crafts. (Album Ser.: No. 300). (Illus.). 32p. 1999. pap. 5.25 (*0-7478-0233-5*, Pub. by Shire Pubns) Parkwest Pubns.
— Fashion a la Carte, 1860-1900. 1989. pap. 30.00 (*0-85263-747-0*, Pub. by Shire Pubns) St Mut.
— Seaside Fashions, 1860-1939. 1989. pap. 40.00 (*0-7478-0066-9*, Pub. by Shire Pubns) St Mut.
— Wedding Fashions, 1860-1980. (Album Ser.: No. 256). (Illus.). 112p. 1989. pap. 10.50 (*0-85263-839-6*, Pub. by Shire Pubns) Parkwest Pubns.
Lansdell, Henry. Russian Central Asia: Including Kuldja, Bokhara, Khiva & Merv. LC 79-115556. (Russia Observed, Series I). 1970. reprint ed. 70.95 (*0-405-03041-X*) Ayer.
— Through Siberia. LC 75-115555. (Russia Observed, Series I). 1970. reprint ed. 46.95 (*0-405-03042-8*) Ayer.
Lansdell, Lyle, jt. auth. see Cunerty, Bill.
Lansden, John M. History of the City of Cairo, Illinois. (Illus.). 303p. 1997. reprint ed. lib. bdg. 36.50 (*0-8328-5719-X*) Higginson Bk Co.
Lansdown, A. R. Molybdenum Disulphide Lubrication. LC 99-29083. (Tribology Ser.). 406p. 1999. 175.00 (*0-444-50032-4*) Elsevier.
Lansdown, A. V. & Campbell, J. South African Criminal Law & Procedure: Criminal Procedure & Evidence, Vol. V. 1192p. 1982. write for info. (*0-7021-1257-7*, Pub. by Juta & Co) Gaunt.
Lansdown, Andrew. Beyond the Open Door. (J). (gr. 4-7). 1993. pap. 2.95 (*0-590-47160-0*) Scholastic Inc.
Lansdown, J. & Earnshaw, Rae A., eds. Computers in Art, Design & Animation. (Illus.). xvii, 305p. 1989. 131.95 (*0-387-96896-2*, 2321) Spr-Verlag.
***Lansdown, Richard.** The Autonomy of Literature: Institutionalism & Its Discontents. LC 00-41517. 2000. write for info. (*0-312-23819-3*) St Martin.
Lansdown, Richard. Byron's Historical Dramas. (Illus.). 272p. 1992. text 59.00 (*0-19-811252-1*) OUP.
— Children in the Hospital: A Guide for Family & Care Givers. (Illus.). 276p. 1996. pap. 29.95 (*0-19-262357-5*) OUP.
— Visibly Different: Coping with Disfigurement. LC 97-23638. 254p. 1997. pap. text 37.50 (*0-7506-3424-3*) Buttrwrth-Heinemann.
***Lansdown, Richard.** Your Child's Development from Birth to Adolescence. 1999. pap. 24.95 (*0-7112-1114-0*) F Lincoln.
Lansdowne, David. Fund Raising Realities Every Board Member Must Face: A 1-Hour Crash Course on Raising Major Gifts for Nonprofit Organizations. LC 96-84332. 112p. (Orig.). 1996. pap. 24.95 (*1-889102-10-5*) Emerson & Church.
— The Relentlessly Practical Guide to Raising Serious Money: Proven Strategies for Nonprofit Organizations. LC 96-86273. 264p. (Orig.). 1997. pap. 34.95 (*1-889102-13-X*) Emerson & Church.
Lansdowne, J. F. Lansdowne's Birds of the Forest. 1989. 49.98 (*0-88486-027-2*) Arrowood Pr.
Lansdowne, Judith. Balmorrow's Bride. 288p. 1998. pap. 4.99 (*0-8217-5930-2*) Kensgtn Pub Corp.
— A Devilish Dilemma. 256p. 1998. mass mkt. 4.99 (*0-8217-5826-8*, Zebra Kensgtn) Kensgtn Pub Corp.
Lansdowne, Judith A. Annabelle's Diamond. (Zebra Regency Romance Ser.). 224p. 1999. mass mkt. 4.99 (*0-8217-6228-1*) Kensgtn Pub Corp.
— Legion's Ladies. 304p. 1996. mass mkt. 4.50 (*0-8217-5465-3*, Zebra Kensgtn) Kensgtn Pub Corp.
***Lansdowne, Judith A.** Lord Nightingale's Debut. 2000. mass mkt. 4.99 (*0-8217-6671-6*) Kensgtn Pub Corp.
— Lord Nightingale's Triumph. (Regency Romance Ser.). 256p. 2000. mass mkt. 4.99 (*0-8217-6704-6*, Zebra Kensgtn) Kensgtn Pub Corp.
Lansdowne, Judith A. Mutiny at Almack's. 1999. mass mkt. 4.99 (*0-8217-6388-1*, Zebra Kensgtn) Kensgtn Pub Corp.
— Season of Virtues. 256p. 1999. mass mkt. 4.99 (*0-8217-6103-X*) Kensgtn Pub Corp.
***Lansdowne, Judith A., et al.** Stocking Stuffers. 256p. 2000. mass mkt. 4.99 (*0-8217-6758-5*, Zebra Kensgtn) Kensgtn Pub Corp.
Lansdowne, Zachary F. The Chakras & Esoteric Healing. LC 84-51108. 160p. 1986. pap. 8.95 (*0-87728-584-5*) Weiser.
— Ray Methods of Healing. LC 92-45541. (Illus.). 176p. (Orig.). 1993. pap. 7.95 (*0-87728-745-7*) Weiser.
— The Rays & Esoteric Psychology. LC 89-5547. 144p. (Orig.). 1989. pap. 8.95 (*0-87728-682-5*) Weiser.
— Rules for Spiritual Initiation. LC 90-38635. 128p. (Orig.). 1990. pap. 7.95 (*0-87728-707-4*) Weiser.
Lansell, Scott, jt. auth. see Edgeworth, Linda.
Lansell, Scott B., jt. auth. see Edgeworth, Linda V.
Lansell, Scott R., et al. Republic of Georgia: Assessment & Voter Information Campaign, September-November 1995. LC 96-3453. ii, 78p. 1996. pap. text 10.00 (*1-879720-17-5*) Intl Fndt Elect.
Lanser, Susan S. Fictions of Authority: Women Writers & Narrative Voice. LC 91-55537. 304p. 1992. 42.50 (*0-8014-2377-5*); pap. text 16.95 (*0-8014-8020-5*) Cornell U Pr.
***Lansfield, Matthew.** My Secret Pal. 2000. 4.99 (*1-56245-400-5*) Great Quotations.
Lansford, Kim D., ed. see Robertson, Lee.
Lansford, Sam. Sex What That. 1993. pap. 7.99 (*0-8054-9967-9*) Broadman.
***Lansford, Tom.** The Lords of Foggy Bottom. LC 99-27661. 1999. write for info. (*0-914746-55-3*) G Kurian.
Lansing. The Balinese. 1996. 20.50 (*0-15-504539-3*, Pub. by Harcourt Coll Pubs) Harcourt.
Lansing, Alfred. Endurance: Shackleton's Incredible Adventure. (Illus.). 288p. 1999. pap. 12.95 (*0-7867-0621-X*) Carroll & Graf.
— Endurance: Shackleton's Incredible Voyage. 282p. 1986. pap. 10.95 (*0-88184-178-1*) Carroll & Graf.
***Lansing, Alfred.** Endurance: Shackleton's Incredible Voyage. LC 99-236005. 247p. 1999. pap. 12.99 (*0-8423-0824-5*) Tyndale Hse.
Lansing, Alfred. Endurance: Shackleton's Incredible Voyage. LC 94-71390. (Adventure Library: Vol. 1). (Illus.). 312p. 1994. reprint ed. lib. bdg. 32.50 (*1-885283-00-8*) Advent Library.
Lansing, Carol. The Florentine Magnates: Lineage & Faction in a Medieval Commune. LC 91-6867. 281p. 1991. reprint ed. pap. 87.20 (*0-608-04589-6*, 206535900003) Bks Demand.
— Power & Purity: Cathar Heresy in Medieval Italy. (Illus.). 288p. (C). 1998. text 45.00 (*0-19-506391-0*) OUP.
Lansing Community College, Science Department Staf. The Science of the Water Planet. (C). 1993. student ed. 12.00 (*1-881592-16-2*) Hayden-McNeil.
***Lansing, David.** The County of Orange: Center of Southern California. Mealer, Cathy, ed. (Illus.). 100p. 1999. 37.95 (*0-9660793-3-7*) Max Co.
— The County of Orange: Center of Southern California. Mealer, Cathy, ed. 100p. 1999. per. 19.95 (*0-9660793-2-9*) Max Co.
Lansing, Dorothy I. That Magnificent Cestrian-William Darlington: Being a Short Biography, 1782-1863. 87p. (Orig.). 1985. pap. 14.95 (*0-9619411-0-3*) Serpentine Pr.
Lansing, Gerrit. Heavenly Tree - Soluble Forest. expanded rev. ed. 214p. 1995. pap. 16.95 (*1-883689-12-0*); lib. bdg. 37.95 (*1-883689-13-9*) Talisman Hse.
— The Heavenly Tree Grows Downward: Poems. 1977. 15.00 (*0-913028-47-9*); pap. 4.00 (*0-913028-40-1*) North Atlantic.
Lansing, J. Stephen. Priests & Programmers: Colonialism, Ecology & the Technologies of Power in the Balinese State. (Illus.). 200p. 1991. text 39.50 (*0-691-09466-7*, Pub. by Princeton U Pr); pap. text 16.95 (*0-691-02863-X*, Pub. by Princeton U Pr) Cal Prin Full Svc.
— Three Worlds of Bali. LC 83-4117. (Illus.). 170p. 1983. 45.00 (*0-275-91720-7*, C1720, Praeger Pubs) Greenwood.
Lansing, John. The Black Eagles No. 11: Duel on the Song Cai. 240p. 1987. mass mkt. 2.50 (*0-8217-2048-1*, Zebra Kensgtn) Kensgtn Pub Corp.
— Hanoi Hellground. (Black Eagles Ser.: Vol. 1). 1983. mass mkt. 2.95 (*0-8217-1249-7*, Zebra Kensgtn) Kensgtn Pub Corp.
Lansing, John B., et al. Planned Residential Environments: A Report Prepared for the U. S. Department of Transportation, Bureau of Public Road. LC 76-632967. (Illus.). 281p. reprint ed. pap. 87.20 (*0-7837-5243-1*, 204497700005) Bks Demand.
Lansing, Karen E. Time to Be a Friend. LC 92-13010. 96p. (J). (gr. 4-8). 1993. pap. 5.99 (*0-8361-3614-4*) Herald Pr.
— Time to Fly. LC 91-14393. 104p. (Orig.). (J). (gr. 4-8). 1991. pap. 5.99 (*0-8361-3560-1*) Herald Pr.
***Lansing, Kathleen J. & Swain, Eric R., eds.** International Law Enforcement Directory - European Union Edition. 388p. 1999. pap. 130.00 (*0-9669405-0-4*) Intl Law.
Lansing, Marion F. Against All Odds. LC 78-84318. (Essay Index Reprint Ser.). 1977. 21.95 (*0-8369-1149-0*) Ayer.
— Liberators & Heroes of Mexico & Central America. LC 72-152186. (Essay Index Reprint Ser.). 1977. reprint ed. 28.95 (*0-8369-2237-9*) Ayer.
— Liberators & Heroes of South America. LC 76-156675. (Essay Index Reprint Ser.). 1977. reprint ed. 31.95 (*0-8369-2321-9*) Ayer.
Lansing, Martha H., jt. auth. see Goodheart, Carol D.
Lansing, Nan. Christmas Customs Cookbook. 346p. 1993. lib. bdg. write for info. (*0-9637976-3-8*) Nickoli Pub.
***Lansing, Richard, ed.** Dante: An Encyclopedia. (Illus.). 800p. 2000. 165.00 (*0-8153-1659-3*) Garland.
***Lansing, Richard D., Jr.** The Blue Moose. 48p. (J). (ps-4). 1999. mass mkt. 6.00 (*0-9661844-5-9*) Purple Gorilla.
Lansing, Richard D., Jr. The Golden Porpoise. (Illus.). 48p. (J). (ps-4). 1998. mass mkt. 6.00 (*0-9661844-3-2*) Purple Gorilla.
***Lansing, Richard D., Jr.** The Green Curly-Tailed Lizard. (Illus.). 48p. (J). (ps-4). 1999. mass mkt. 6.00 (*0-9661844-4-0*) Purple Gorilla.
Lansing, Richard D., Jr. The Purple Gorilla. (Illus.). 48p. (J). (ps-4). 1997. mass mkt. 6.00 (*0-9661844-0-8*) Purple Gorilla.
Lansing, Robert. Big Four, & Others of the Peace Conference. LC 73-177961. (Essay Index Reprint Ser.). 1977. reprint ed. 21.95 (*0-8369-2556-4*) Ayer.
— Peace Negotiations: A Personal Narrative. LC 74-110852. (Illus.). 328p. 1971. reprint ed. lib. bdg. 65.00 (*0-8371-4519-8*, LAPN, Greenwood Pr) Greenwood.
— War Memoirs of Robert Lansing, Secretary of State. LC 78-110853. 383p. 1971. reprint ed. lib. bdg. 65.00 (*0-8371-4520-1*, LAWM, Greenwood Pr) Greenwood.
***Lansing, Robert & Carnegie Endowment for International Peace Staff.** Notes on Sovereignty: From the Standpoint of the State & of the World. LC 99-47540. 1999. write for info. (*1-57588-591-3*) W S Hein.
Lansing, Ronald. Juggernaut: The Whitman Massacre Trial, 1850. 140p. 1993. pap. 15.95 (*0-9635086-0-1*) Ninth Judicial CHS.
Lansing State Journal Staff. One Shining Season: The Amazing Story of Michigan State University's 1998-99 Men's Basketball Team. (Illus.). 92p. 1999. pap. 12.95 (*1-58261-131-9*) Sprts Pubng.
Lansing, Stephen. The Balinese. Spindler, Louise S. & Spindler, George D., eds. (Case Studies in Anthropology). (Illus.). 168p. (C). 1994. pap. text 23.50 (*0-15-500240-6*) Harcourt Coll Pubs.
Lanskey, Bruce, ed. Newfangled Fairy Tales. (J). 1998. 3.95 (*0-88166-299-2*) Meadowbrook.
Lanski, Joseph W., jt. auth. see Drago, Raymond J.
Lansky. Best Birthday Party Game Book. (J). 1997. pap. 3.95 (*0-671-57606-2*) S&S Childrens.
***Lansky.** Games Babies Play - from Birth to 12 Months. 112p. 1998. 5.98 (*1-56731-273-X*, MJF Bks) Fine Comms.
— Getting Your Child to Sleep... & Back to Sleep. 144p. 1998. 5.98 (*1-56731-274-8*, MJF Bks) Fine Comms.
Lansky. Industrial Pneumatic Control. (Fluid Power & Control Ser.: Vol. 6). (Illus.). 264p. 1986. text 145.00 (*0-8247-7494-9*) Dekker.
— Work & Other Occupational Hazards. LC 98-3186. 112p. 1998. pap. 7.00 (*0-671-02387-X*) S&S Trade.
Lansky, Amy, ed. Foundations of Automatic Planning - The Classical Approach & Beyond: Papers from the 1993 Spring Symposium. (Technical Reports). (Illus.). 168p. (Orig.). (C). 1993. spiral bd. 25.00 (*0-929280-40-7*) AAAI Pr.
Lansky, Amy, jt. ed. see Georgeff, Michael.
Lansky, Bruce. The Baby Name Survey Book. 250p. 1998. 9.00 (*0-671-02385-3*) S&S Trade.
— Baby Names Around the World. 300p. 1999. per. 12.00 (*0-671-31658-3*) S&S Trade.
— A Bad Case of the Giggles: Kid's Favorite Funny Poems. LC 94-3336. (Illus.). 128p. (J). 1994. 14.00 (*0-88166-213-5*, 0671899821) Meadowbrook.
— A Bad Case of the Giggles: Kid's Favorite Funny Poems. LC 94-3336. (Illus.). 128p. (J). (gr. 4-7). 1994. 16.00 (*0-671-89982-1*, Pub. by Meadowbrook) S&S Trade.
— The Best Baby Name Book in the Whole Wide World. LC 84-6632. 140p. 1990. reprint ed. pap. text 5.00 (*0-915658-17-8*) Meadowbrook.
— The Best Baby Name Book in the Whole World. rev. ed. LC 84-6632. (Illus.). 150p. 1984. per. 5.00 (*0-671-54463-2*) S&S Trade.
— The Best Birthday Party Game Book. 32p. (J). (gr. 1-7). 1997. lib. bdg. 3.95 (*0-671-57701-8*) PB.
— Best Christmas Party Games. 32p. (J). (gr. 1-7). 1998. pap. 3.95 (*0-689-82213-8*, Pub. by Meadowbrook) S&S Trade.
— The Best Halloween Party Game Book. 32p. (J). (gr. 1-7). 1998. mass mkt. 3.95 (*0-689-82214-6*) S&S Childrens.
— Bruce Lansky's Poetry Party. LC 95-51245. (Illus.). 96p. (J). (gr. 4-7). 1996. 12.00 (*0-671-57303-9*) PB.
— Familiarity Breeds Children: The Best Quotes about Parenthood. 110p. 1994. 7.00 (*0-671-88444-1*) Meadowbrook.
— 15,000 Baby Names. LC 97-7031. 1997. 20.01 (*0-88166-282-8*); pap. 3.95 (*0-614-28107-5*) Meadowbrook.
— 15,000+ Baby Names. LC 97-7031. 184p. 1997. pap. 3.95 (*0-671-52127-6*, Meadowbrook Pr) S&S Childrens.
— For Better & for Worse. rev. expanded ed. LC 96-29458. 112p. 1997. 7.00 (*0-671-52122-5*) S&S Trade.
— For Better & for Worse: The Best Quotes about Marriage. LC 96-29458. 1997. pap. 6.00 (*0-88166-291-7*) Meadowbrook.
— Girls to the Rescue: Tales of Clever, Courageous Girls from Around the World. LC 98-30241. (J). 1998. 3.95 (*0-88166-314-X*) Meadowbrook.
— Girls to the Rescue: Tales of Clever, Courageous Girls from Around the World, 4. 120p. (J). 1998. lib. bdg. 3.95 (*0-671-57703-4*) S&S Childrens.
— Golf: It's Just a Game: The Best Quotes about Golf. 110p. 1996. pap. 7.00 (*0-671-57049-8*, Pub. by Meadowbrook) S&S Trade.
— Happy Birthday to Me! LC 97-42044. (Illus.). (J). 1998. 8.95 (*0-88166-305-0*) Meadowbrook.
— Happy Birthday to Me. (Illus.). 32p. (J). (gr. 3-7). 1998. lib. bdg. 8.95 (*0-671-58062-0*) S&S Childrens.
— Laugh Twice & Call Me In the Morning: The Best Quotes & Cartoons about Calamities & Cures. LC 98-53471. (Illus.). 112p. (Orig.). 1999. per. 7.00 (*0-671-31656-7*) S&S Trade.
— Lighten Up! LC 98-8788. 1998. 5.95 (*0-88166-324-7*) Meadowbrook.
***Lansky, Bruce.** Lighten Up! LC 99-33561. 1999. write for info. (*0-88166-356-5*) Meadowbrook.
— Lighten Up 2: 101 More Funny Little Poems, Vol. 2. Vol. 2. 101p. 1999. per. 5.95 (*0-671-31772-5*) S&S Childrens.
Lansky, Bruce. Lovesick: The Best Quotes about Love & Sex. LC 96-43476. (Orig.). 1997. write for info. (*0-88166-270-4*) Meadowbrook.
— Miles of Smiles: Kids Pick the Funniest Poems. LC 97-52095. (Illus.). 128p. (J). (gr. 2-8). 1998. lib. bdg. 16.00 (*0-689-82183-2*) Meadow Brook.
— Miles of Smiles: Kids Pick the Funniest Poems. LC 97-52095. (Illus.). (J). (gr. 3-7). 1998. 16.00 (*0-88166-313-1*) Meadow Brook.
— Moms Say the Funniest Things. (Illus.). 112p. 1992. pap. 6.00 (*0-671-74183-7*, Pub. by Meadowbrook) S&S Trade.
— Moms Say the Funniest Things: A Collection of Motherly Wit & Wisdom. LC 90-26455. (Illus.). 110p. 1992. pap. 6.00 (*0-88166-178-3*) Meadowbrook.
— Mother Murphy's Law. LC 86-5240. 96p. 1986. pap. 5.00 (*0-88166-080-9*) Meadowbrook.
— Mother Murphy's Law. 108p. 1986. per. 4.50 (*0-671-62274-9*) S&S Trade.
— The New Adventures of Mother Goose: Gentle Rhymes for Happy Times. (Illus.). 32p. (J). (ps up). 1993. 15.00 (*1-881662-01-2*) Meadowbrook.
— The New Adventures of Mother Goose: Gentle Rhymes for Happy Times. (Illus.). 32p. (J). (ps-k). 1993. 15.00 (*0-671-87288-5*) S&S Trade.
— New Rhymes about Animals. (Illus.). 16p. (J). (gr. k up). 1995. lib. bdg. 4.95 (*0-671-51980-8*) Meadowbrook.
— New Rhymes about Animals: The New Adventures of Mother Goose Board Book Collection. (Illus.). 1995. bds. 4.95 (*0-88116-228-0*) Meadowbrook.
— New Rhymes for Bedtime. (Illus.). 16p. (J). (gr. k up). 1995. lib. bdg. 4.95 (*0-671-51978-6*) S&S Trade.
— New Rhymes for Bedtime: The New Adventures of Mother Goose Board Book Collection. (Illus.). (J). 1995. bds. 4.95 (*0-88116-226-4*) Meadowbrook.
— New Rhymes for Mealtime. (Illus.). 16p. (J). (gr. k up). 1995. lib. bdg. 4.95 (*0-671-51979-4*) S&S Trade.
— New Rhymes for Mealtime: The New Adventures of Mother Goose Board Book Collection. (Illus.). (J). 1995. bds. 4.95 (*0-88116-225-6*) Meadowbrook.
— New Rhymes for Playtime. (Illus.). 16p. (J). (gr. k up). 1995. lib. bdg. 4.95 (*0-671-51977-8*) S&S Trade.
— New Rhymes for Playtime: The New Adventures of Mother Goose Board Book Collection. (Illus.). (J). 1995. bds. 4.95 (*0-88116-227-2*) Meadowbrook.
— Newfangled Fairy Tales Bk. 2. 120p. (J). (gr. 2-8). 1998. 3.95 (*0-689-82211-1*, Pub. by Meadowbrook) S&S Trade.
— No More Homework! No More Tests! Kids' Favorite Funny School Poems. LC 97-12729. (Illus.). 80p. (J). (gr. 3-7). 1997. lib. bdg. 8.00 (*0-671-57702-6*) Litle Simon.
— Sweet Dreams: Bedtime Poems & Lullabyes. (Illus.). 32p. (J). (ps-1). 1996. 15.00 (*0-671-57046-3*) Simon & Schuster.
— Sweet Dreams: Bedtime Poems, Songs, & Lullabies. (Illus.). 1996. 15.00 (*0-671-53479-3*); 15.00 (*0-88166-246-1*) Meadowbrook.
— Ten Thousand Baby Names. LC 85-7177. 144p. 1985. pap. 3.50 (*0-88166-067-1*) Meadowbrook.
— 35,000 Baby Names. LC 95-10295. 272p. 1995. 5.95 (*0-671-51975-1*) Meadowbrook.
— 35,000+ Baby Names. LC 95-10295. 220p. 1995. pap. write for info. (*0-88166-216-X*) Meadowbrook.
— The Very Best Baby Name Book. rev. ed. LC 95-46292. 364p. 1996. pap. 8.00 (*0-671-56113-8*, Pub. by Meadowbrook) S&S Trade.
— The Very Best Baby Name Book in the Whole Wide World. 1996. write for info. (*0-88166-247-X*) Meadowbrook.
— You're Invited to Bruce Lansky's Poetry Party. LC 95-51245. (Illus.). (J). 1996. 11.00 (*0-88166-245-3*) Meadowbrook.
Lansky, Bruce, compiled by. If We'd Wanted Quiet, We Would Have Raised Goldfish: Poems for Parents. (Illus.). 90p. 1994. 12.00 (*0-671-89457-9*) Meadowbrook.
— Kids Pick the Funniest Poems. LC 91-31072. (Illus.). 120p. (J). 1991. 15.00 (*0-88166-149-X*) Meadowbrook.
Lansky, Bruce, ed. Age Happens: The Best Quotes about Growing Older. LC 95-44800. (Illus.). 112p. (Orig.). 1996. per. 7.00 (*0-671-56112-X*, Pub. by Meadowbrook) S&S Trade.
— Familiarity Breeds Children: The Best Quotes about Parenthood. (Illus.). 110p. 1994. pap. 5.95 (*0-671-88844-7*, Pub. by Meadowbrook) S&S Trade.
— Familiarity Breeds Children: The Best Quotes & Cartoons about Parenthood. LC 97-30744. (Illus.). 112p. (J). 1998. pap. 7.00 (*0-671-57999-1*) S&S Trade.
— Girls to Rescue, Bks. 1-3. LC 98-30241. (J). (gr. 2-8). 1998. lib. bdg. 9.95 (*0-689-82279-0*) S&S Childrens.
— Girls to the Rescue: Tales of Clever, Courageous Girls from Around the World. LC 95-17733. 120p. (J). (gr. 3-7). 1995. pap. 3.95 (*0-88166-215-1*) Meadowbrook.
— Girls to the Rescue: Tales of Clever, Courageous Girls from Around the World, Bk. 2. LC 95-17733. Vol. 2. 120p. (J). (gr. 2-8). 1996. 12.00 (*0-671-57439-6*) Meadowbrook.

L

L

— Girls to the Rescue: Tales of Clever, Courageous Girls from Around the World, Bk. II. 2nd ed. Vol. 2. 120p. (J). (gr. 2-8). 1996. lib. bdg. 3.95 (*0-671-57375-6*) Meadowbrook.

— Girls to the Rescue: Tales of Clever, Courageous Girls from Around the World, Bk. III. Vol. 3. 120p. (J). (gr. 2-8). 1997. lib. bdg. 3.95 (*0-671-57550-3*) Meadowbrook.

— Girls to the Rescue: Tales of Clever, Courageous Girls from Around the World, No. 6. (J). (gr. 2-8). 1999. pap. 3.95 (*0-689-82574-9*) S&S Childrens.

— Girls to the Rescue Book 5, Bk. 5. (Girls to the Rescue Ser.: Vol. 5). 120p. (J). (gr. 2-8). 1998. pap. 3.95 (*0-689-82210-3*) S&S Childrens.

— Kids Pick the Funniest Poems. LC 91-31072. (Illus.). 100p. (J). (gr. 4-7). 1991. 16.00 (*0-671-74769-X*) S&S Trade.

— Lighten Up! 101 Funny Little Poems. LC 98-8788. 124p. 1998. pap. 12.00 (*0-671-31632-X*) S&S Childrens.

— Lovesick: The Best Quotes about Love & Sex. LC 96-43476. 110p. (Orig.). 1997. 7.00 (*0-671-57499-X*) S&S Trade.

— Newfangled Fairy Tales. (Illus.). 120p. (J). (gr. 3-7). 1998. lib. bdg. 3.95 (*0-671-57704-2*) S&S Childrens.

— No More Homework! No More Tests! Kids' Favorite Funny School Poems. LC 97-12729. (Illus.). (J). 1997. pap. 8.00 (*0-88166-290-9*) Meadowbrook.

— Tales of Clever, Courageous Girls, Bk. 4. (Girls to the Rescue Ser.: Vol. 4). 112p. (J). (gr. 3-6). 1998. pap. 3.95 (*0-88166-301-8*) Meadowbrook.

Lansky, Bruce, ed. Girls to the Rescue: Tales of Clever, Courageous Girls from Around the World, Bk. 1. LC 95-17733. (Girls to the Rescue Ser.: Vol. 1). (Illus.). 120p. (J). (gr. 2-8). 1995. pap. 3.95 (*0-671-89979-1*) S&S Trade.

Lansky, Bruce, selected by. Age Happens: The Best Quotes about Growing Older. LC 95-44800. (Orig.). 1996. 7.00 (*0-88166-244-5*) Meadowbrook.

— Familiarity Breeds Children: The Best Quotes, Quips & Rhymes about Parenthood. LC 97-30744. 1996. write for info. (*0-88166-264-X*) Meadowbrook.

— For Better & for Worse: The Best Quotes about Marriage. 1995. pap. 6.00 (*0-88116-231-0*); pap. 6.00 (*0-88166-231-3*) Meadowbrook.

— For Better & for Worse: The Best Quotes about Marriage. (Illus.). 1995. pap. 6.00 (*0-671-52702-9*) Meadowbrook.

— The Funny Side of Parenthood. (Illus.). 112p. 1994. pap. 5.95 (*0-88166-206-2*) Meadowbrook.

— Golf, It's Just a Game: The Best Quotes about Golf. LC 96-1098. 1996. write for info. (*0-88166-248-8*) Meadowbrook.

— If We'd Wanted Quiet, We Would Have Raised Goldfish: Poems for Parents. (Illus.). 96p. 1994. 12.00 (*0-88166-210-0*) Meadowbrook.

Lansky, Bruce & Johnson, Martha. Girls to the Rescue: Tales of Clever, Courageous Girls from Around the World, Bk. 5. 108p. pap. text. write for info. (*0-88166-315-8*) Meadowbrook.

Lansky, Bruce & Jones, K. L. Dads Say the Dumbest Things. LC 89-29067. 112p. 1989. pap. 6.00 (*0-88166-131-7*) Meadowbrook.

— Dads Say the Dumbest Things. 112p. 1990. 6.00 (*0-671-69613-0*) Meadowbrook.

Lansky, Bruce & Sinrod, Barry. The Baby Name Personality Survey. LC 88-27142. 230p. 1990. pap. 7.00 (*0-88166-164-3*) Meadowbrook.

Lansky, Bryna. Tomorrow's Retiree: A Planning & Resource Publication. (Northeast Edition - 1990-1992 Ser.). 1990. pap. 12.95 (*0-9618885-0-4*) Tomorrows Retiree.

Lansky, Bryna, ed. Tomorrow's Retiree: A National Publication of Local Resources. (Midwest Edition - 1993-1994 Ser.). 144p. 1993. pap. 14.95 (*0-9618885-2-0*) Tomorrows Retiree.

— Tomorrow's Retiree: A National Publication of Local Resources. (West Edition - 1993-1994 Ser.). 1993. pap. 14.95 (*0-9618885-4-7*) Tomorrows Retiree.

— Tomorrow's Retiree: A National Publication of Local Resources. (South Edition - 1993-1994 Ser.). 1993. pap. 14.95 (*0-9618885-3-9*) Tomorrows Retiree.

— Tomorrow's Retiree: A National Publication of Local Resources. rev. ed. (Northeast Edition - 1993-1994 Ser.). 144p. 1993. pap. 14.95 (*0-9618885-1-2*) Tomorrows Retiree.

Lansky, Doug. Up the Amazon Without a Paddle: A Humorist's Offbeat Adventures Around the World. 296p. 1999. per. 8.00 (*0-671-31657-5*) S&S Trade.

— The World's Best Simple Bar Tricks. LC 98-18132. (Illus.). 128p. 1998. pap. 9.95 (*0-440-50826-6*, Dell Trade Pbks) Dell.

Lansky, Doug, ed. There's No Toilet Paper... on the Road Less Traveled: The Best of Travel Humor & Misadventure. (Travelers' Tales Ser.). 207p. 1998. pap. 12.95 (*1-885211-27-9*) Trvlers Tale.

Lansky, Melvin R. Fathers Who Fail: Shame & Psychopathology in the Family System. 264p. 1992. 39.95 (*0-88163-105-1*) Analytic Pr.

Lansky, Melvin R., ed. Essential Papers on Dreams. (Essential Papers in Psychology). 488p. (C). 1992. text 75.00 (*0-8147-5061-3*); pap. text 27.50 (*0-8147-5062-1*) NYU Pr.

— Family Approaches to Major Psychiatric Disorders. LC 85-18494. (Clinical Insights Ser.). 169p. reprint ed. pap. 52.40 (*0-8357-7838-X*, 203621200002) Bks Demand.

— Family Therapy & Major Psychopathology. LC 95-23343. (Master Works). 1995. 55.00 (*1-56821-711-0*) Aronson.

Lansky, Melvin R. & Bley, Carol R. Posttraumatic Nightmares: Psychodynamic Explorations. LC 94-43415. 208p. 1995. 34.50 (*0-88163-193-0*) Analytic Pr.

Lansky, Melvin R. & Morrison, Andrew, eds. The Widening Scope of Shame. LC 97-11431. 416p. 1997. 55.00 (*0-88163-169-8*) Analytic Pr.

Lansky, Vicki. Another Use for... 101 Common Household Items. 2nd rev. ed. (Illus.). 168p. 1999. pap. 8.95 (*0-916773-29-9*) Book Peddlers.

— Baby Proofing Basics: How to Keep Your Child Safe. 148p. (Orig.). 1991. pap. 6.95 (*0-916773-28-0*) Book Peddlers.

***Lansky, Vicki.** The Bag Book: Over 500 Great Uses - And Reuses - For Paper, Plastic & Other Bags to Organize & Enhance Your Life. (Illus.). 120p. 2000. pap. 6.95 (*0-916773-89-2*, Pub. by Book Peddlers) Publishers Group.

Lansky, Vicki. Baking Soda: Over Five Hundred Fabulous, Fun & Frugal Uses You've Probably Never Thought Of. (Illus.). 108p. (Orig.). 1995. pap. 6.95 (*0-916773-42-6*) Book Peddlers.

***Lansky, Vicki.** Birthday Parties: Best Party Tips & Ideas. 150p. 1999. 5.98 (*1-56731-323-X*, MJF Bks) Fine Comms.

Lansky, Vicki. Birthday Parties: Best Party Tips & Ideas. 3rd ed. (Illus.). 160p. 1995. reprint ed. pap. 8.95 (*0-916773-36-1*) Book Peddlers.

— Dear Babysitter Handbook. 60p. (YA). (gr. 5 up). 1990. reprint ed. pap. 4.95 (*0-916773-16-7*) Book Peddlers.

— Don't Throw That Out! (Illus.). 98p. (Orig.). 1994. pap. 6.95 (*0-916773-40-X*) Book Peddlers.

— Feed Me, I'm Yours. 176p. 1982. mass mkt. 4.99 (*0-553-27251-9*) Bantam.

— Feed Me, I'm Yours. 1997. pap. 4.95 (*0-671-57494-9*) S&S Trade.

— Feed Me, I'm Yours. expanded rev. ed. (Illus.). 144p. 1994. 9.00 (*0-671-88443-3*) Meadowbrook.

— Feed Me! I'm Yours. rev. ed. LC 86-8364. 132p. 1986. spiral bd. 8.00 (*0-88166-072-8*) Meadowbrook.

— Feed Me! I'm Yours. rev. ed. LC 86-8364. (Illus.). 130p. 1994. spiral bd. 8.00 (*0-88166-208-9*, 0671884433) Meadowbrook.

— Games Babies Play: From Birth to Twelve Months. 112p. (Orig.). 1993. pap. 8.95 (*0-916773-33-7*) Book Peddlers.

— Getting Your Child to Sleep...& Back to Sleep: Tips for Parents of Infants, Toddlers & Preschoolers. 2nd rev. ed. (Illus.). 140p. (Orig.). 1991. reprint ed. pap. 6.95 (*0-916773-19-1*) Book Peddlers.

— It's Not Your Fault, KoKo Bear: A Read-Together Book for Parents & Young Children During Divorce. LC 98-213927. (Illus.). 32p. (J). (ps-2). 1998. 10.95 (*0-916773-46-9*); pap. 5.99 (*0-916773-47-7*) Book Peddlers.

— It's Not Your Fault, KoKo Bear: A Read-Together Book for Parents & Young Children During Divorce, 2 vols. 1999. pap. 21.95 (*0-916773-74-4*) Book Peddlers.

— KoKo Bear's Big Earache: Preparing for Ear Tube Surgery. 2nd ed. (Illus.). 32p. (Orig.). (J). (ps). 1990. reprint ed. pap. 4.95 (*0-916773-26-4*) Book Peddlers.

— Koko Bear's New Potty, 3 vols. 1999. 17.95 (*0-916773-69-8*) Book Peddlers.

— Koko Bear's New Potty. (Illus.). 32p. (J). 1997. reprint ed. pap. 5.95 (*0-916773-25-6*) Book Peddlers.

— A New Baby at Koko Bear's House. 2nd ed. (Illus.). 32p. (Orig.). (J). 1991. reprint ed. pap. 5.95 (*0-916773-22-1*) Book Peddlers.

— No Es Tu Culpa, Koko Oso (It's Not Your Fault, Koko Bear) (SPA., Illus.). 32p. (J). (ps-2). 1999. pap. 7.99 (*0-916773-45-0*) Book Peddlers.

— 101 Ways to Be a Special Dad. LC 92-41271. 120p. 1993. 6.95 (*0-8092-3820-9*, 382090, Contemporary Bks) NTC Contemp Pub Co.

— 101 Ways to Be a Special Mom. (Illus.). 120p. 1995. 6.95 (*0-8092-3530-7*, 353070, Contemporary Bks) NTC Contemp Pub Co.

— 101 Ways to Make Your Child Feel Special. (Illus.). 120p. 1991. 6.95 (*0-8092-3997-3*, 399730, Contemporary Bks) NTC Contemp Pub Co.

— One Hundred One Ways to Say "I Love You" (Illus.). 128p. 1991. per. 7.95 (*0-671-72350-2*) S&S Trade.

— 101 Ways to Spoil Your Grandchild. (Illus.). 120p. 1996. 6.95 (*0-8092-3231-6*, 323160, Contemporary Bks) NTC Contemp Pub Co.

— 101 Ways to Tell Your Child "I Love You" (Illus.). 120p. 1988. 6.95 (*0-8092-4527-2*, 452720, Contemporary Bks) NTC Contemp Pub Co.

— Practical Parenting Tips. enl. rev. ed. LC 92-17149. (Illus.). 192p. 1992. pap. 8.00 (*0-88166-192-9*) Meadowbrook.

— Practical Parenting Tips for the First Five Years. rev. ed. LC 92-17149. (Illus.). 192p. 1992. 8.00 (*0-671-79205-9*) S&S Trade.

— Sing along Birthday Songs: Favorite Party & Game Songs & Their Words. unabridged ed. (J). (ps-6). 1996. pap. 8.95 incl. audio (*0-916773-51-5*) Book Peddlers.

Lansky, Vicki. Sing along Birthday Songs: Favorite Party & Game Songs & Their Words. unabridged ed. (J). (ps-6). 1996. 9.95 incl. audio (*0-916773-52-3*, Pub. by Book Peddlers) Publishers Group.

Lansky, Vicki. Sing along Travel Songs: Favorite Children's Songs & Their Words. unabridged ed. (J). (ps-6). 1996. 9.95 incl. audio (*0-916773-57-4*, Pub. by Book Peddlers) Publishers Group.

— Taming of the C. A. N. D. Y.* Monster *Continuously Advertised Nutritionally Deficient Yummies: Recipes & Tips for Feeding Junk Food Fans & Picky Eaters: 20th Anniversary Special Edition. 3rd anniversary ed. 180p. 1999. pap. 9.95 (*0-916773-06-X*) Book Peddlers.

— Toilet Training: A Practical Guide to Daytime & Nighttime Training. rev. ed. LC 92-35022. 112p. 1984. pap. 6.99 (*0-553-37140-1*) Bantam.

— Transparent Tape: Over 350 Super, Simple & Surprising Uses You've Probably Never Thought Of. (Illus.). 108p. 1995. pap. 6.95 (*0-916773-44-2*) Book Peddlers.

***Lansky, Vicki.** Trouble-Free Travel with Children: Helpful Hints for Parents on the Go. 144p. 1999. 5.98 (*1-56731-324-8*, MJF Bks) Fine Comms.

Lansky, Vicki. Trouble-Free Travel with Children: Helpful Hints for Parents on the Go. (Illus.). 148p. 1998. reprint ed. pap. text 7.00 (*0-7881-5223-8*) DIANE Pub.

— Trouble-Free Travel with Children: Helpful Hints for Parents on the Go. 2nd rev. ed. (Illus.). 144p. 1996. reprint ed. pap. 8.95 (*0-916773-15-9*) Book Peddlers.

— Vicki Lansky's Divorce Book for Parents: Helping Your Children Cope with Divorce & Its Aftermath. 3rd rev. ed. 240p. 1996. pap. 5.99 (*0-916773-48-5*) Book Peddlers.

— Welcoming Your Second Baby. 2nd ed. (Illus.). 112p. 1990. pap. 6.95 (*0-916773-12-4*) Book Peddlers.

Lansky, Vicki, jt. auth. see Consumer Guide Editors.

Lansky, Z. J., jt. auth. see Pippenger, John J.

Lansley, Alfred, et al. Chula Vista: The Early Years, Vol. 2. (Illus.). 80p. (Orig.). 1993. pap. 7.95 (*0-938711-17-2*) Tecolote Pubns.

Lansley, John, jt. ed. see Jones, Helen.

Lansley, P. & Harlow, P., eds. Managing Construction Worldwide, 3 vols., Set. 1300p. 1988. lib. bdg. 235.00 (*0-419-14030-1*, E & FN Spon) Routledge.

Lanslots, D. I. The Primitive Church. LC 79-67862. 295p. 1980. reprint ed. pap. 10.00 (*0-89555-134-9*) TAN Bks Pubs.

Lansner, Jonathan. How Money Works. 1995. pap. text 19.95 (*1-56276-291-5*, Ziff-Davis Pr) Que.

Lanson, Gerald. Writing & Reporting the News. 2nd ed. LC 93-77400. (C). 1994. pap. text 57.50 (*0-03-079177-4*, Pub. by Harcourt Coll Pubs) Harcourt.

Lanson, Gustave. Bossuet. Mayer, J. P., ed. LC 78-67363. (European Political Thought Ser.). (FRE.). 1979. reprint ed. lib. bdg. 40.95 (*0-405-11711-6*) Ayer.

— Corneille. LC 75-41170. reprint ed. 36.00 (*0-404-14797-6*) AMS Pr.

Lanson, Jerry & Fought, Barbara Croll. News in A New Century: Reporting in An Age of Converging Media. LC 98-25449. 339 p. 1999. write for info. (*0-7619-8506-9*) Sage.

Lansonius, Susanne. Emily, Moonshine & Sister Goose. (Illus.). 32p. (J). (gr. k-6). 1997. 16.95 (*0-88839-403-9*) Hancock House.

Lanspery, Susan & Hyde, Joan, eds. Staying Put: Adapting the Places Instead of the People. LC 95-51473. (Society & Aging Ser.). 295p. 1996. 41.95 (*0-89503-133-7*) Baywood Pub.

Lanstrum, Michael. Pre-GED Mathematics. LC 97-65278. (GED Test Ser.). 256p. 2000. pap. 11.95 (*0-87891-798-5*) Res & Educ.

Lansverk, Marvin D. The Wisdom of Many, the Vision of One: The Proverbs of William Blake. LC 93-35971. (American University Studies, IV, English Language & Literature: Vol. 142). 216p. (C). 1994. text 38.95 (*0-8204-1781-5*) P Lang Pubng.

Lant, A. F., ed. Advanced Medicine, Eleven: Proceedings of the 11th Annual Symposium on Advanced Medicine 1975. (Illus.). 450p. (Orig.). 1975. 42.00 (*0-8464-0112-6*) Beekman Pubs.

Lant, A. F., ed. see Advanced Medicine Symposia Staff & Royal College of Physicians Staff.

Lant, Antonia C. Blackout: Reinventing Women for Wartime British Cinema. (Illus.). 262p. 1991. text 60.00 (*0-691-05540-8*, Pub. by Princeton U Pr); pap. text 18.95 (*0-691-00828-0*, Pub. by Princeton U Pr) Cal Prin Full Svc.

***Lant, Antonia C.** Red Velvet Seat: Women's Writings on the Cinema: The First Fifty Years. 1999. 37.00 (*1-85984-722-6*, Pub. by Verso) Norton.

Lant, Jeffrey. Cash Copy: How to Offer Your Products & Services so Your Prospects Buy Them ... Now! 3rd ed. 480p. 1997. pap. 35.00 (*0-940374-23-4*) JLA Pubns.

— The Consultant's Kit: Establishing & Operating Your Successful Consulting Business. 203p. 1996. pap. 35.00 (*0-940374-29-3*) JLA Pubns.

— Development Today: A Fund Raising guide for Nonprofit Organizations. 5th ed. 282p. 1993. pap. 24.95 (*0-940374-25-0*) JLA Pubns.

— E-Mail El Dorado: Everything You Need to Know to Sell More of Your Products & Services Every Day by E-Mail Without Ever Spamming Anyone! LC 99-158939. 184p. 1998. 29.95 (*0-940374-38-2*) JLA Pubns.

— How to Make a Whole Lot More Than One Million Dollars Writing, Commissioning, Publishing & Selling "How-to" Information. 2nd rev. ed. 552p. 1993. 39.95 (*0-940374-26-9*) JLA Pubns.

— How to Make at Least One Hundred Thousand Dollars Every Year As a Successful Consultant in Your Own Field. 2nd ed. 316p. 1992. pap. 35.00 (*0-940374-21-8*) JLA Pubns.

— Money Making Marketing: Finding the People Who Need What You're Selling & Making Sure They Buy It. 3rd rev. ed. 283p. 1999. 35.00 (*0-940374-30-7*) JLA Pubns.

— Money Talks: The Complete Guide to Creating a Profitable Workshop or Seminar in Any Field. 3rd rev. ed. 302p. (Orig.). 1995. 35.00 (*0-940374-27-7*) JLA Pubns.

— Multi-Level Money: The Complete Guide to Generating, Closing & Working with All the Prospects You Need to Make Real Money Every Month in Network Marketing. 2nd ed. LC 95-187301. 250p. (Orig.). 1995. pap. 19.95 (*0-940374-28-5*) JLA Pubns.

— No More Cold Calls: The Complete Guide to Generating & Closing All the Prospects You Need to Become a Multi-Millionaire by Selling Your Service. 1993. pap. 39.95 (*0-940374-24-2*) JLA Pubns.

— The Unabashed Self-Promoter's Guide: What Every Man, Woman, Child & Organization in America Needs to Know About Getting Ahead by Exploiting the Media. 2nd ed. (Enterprise Ser.: Vol. 2). 366p. (Orig.). 1992. pap. 35.00 (*0-940374-18-8*) JLA Pubns.

— Web Wealth: How to Turn the World Wide Web into a Cash Hose for You & Your Business...Whatever You're Selling. 248p. 1997. pap. 24.95 (*0-940374-37-4*) JLA Pubns.

Lant, Kathleen M. & Thompson, Theresa, eds. Imagining the Worst: Stephen King & the Representation of Women, 67. LC 97-48575. (Contributions to the Study of Popular Culture: Vol. 67). 216p. 1998. 55.00 (*0-313-30232-4*, Greenwood Pr) Greenwood.

***Lant, Theresa K. & Shapira, Zur.** Cognition in Organizations: Computation & Interpretation. LC 99-47155. (Lea Series in Organization & Management). 2000. write for info. (*0-8058-3333-1*) L Erlbaum Assocs.

Lanteigne, Helen. The Seven Chairs. LC 98-13792. (Illus.). 32p. (J). (ps-2). 1998. 14.95 (*0-531-30110-9*) Orchard Bks Watts.

Lanteigne, Nellie M., jt. auth. see Schell, Bernadette H.

Lanter, Wayne. At Float on the Ohta-Gawa. LC 97-30528. 160p. 1997. pap. 14.95 (*0-7734-2838-0*, Mellen Poetry Pr) E Mellen.

— Canonical Hours: Poems. LC 99-11293. 104p. 1999. pap. text 19.95 (*0-7734-3087-3*) E Mellen.

— Threshing Time: A Tribute to James Hearst. LC 96-67071. 55p. (Orig.). 1996. pap. 10.00 (*0-9650764-0-7*) River King.

— The Waiting Room: Poems. LC 95-34703. 1995. pap. 14.95 (*0-7734-2747-3*, Mellen Poetry Pr) E Mellen.

Lanteri, Edouard. Modelling & Sculpting Animals. (Illus.). 352p. 1985. reprint ed. pap. 8.95 (*0-486-25007-5*) Dover.

Lanteri, Edouard. Modelling & Sculpting the Human Figure. (Illus.). 480p. 1985. reprint ed. pap. 10.95 (*0-486-25006-7*) Dover.

Lanterman, E., ed. see Society for Applied Spectroscopy Staff.

Lanterman, Ray, jt. auth. see Barrow, Terence.

Lanterman, Ray, jt. auth. see Kyselka, Will.

Lantermann, Susanne, jt. auth. see Lantermann, Werner.

***Lantermann, Werner.** Amazon Parrots. (Complete Pet Owner's Manual Ser.). (Illus.). 104p. 2000. pap. 6.95 (*0-7641-1036-5*) Barron.

— Cockatoos. 2nd ed. LC 99-86987. (Complete Pet Owner's Manual Ser.). (Illus.). 104p. 2000. pap. text. write for info. (*0-7641-1037-3*) Barron.

Lantermann, Werner. The Encyclopedia of Macaws. (Illus.). 208p. 1996. 35.95 (*0-7938-2183-5*, TS243) TFH Pubns.

— New Parrot Handbook. (Illus.). 144p. 1986. pap. 9.95 (*0-8120-3729-4*) Barron.

Lantermann, Werner & Lantermann, Susanne. Amazon Parrots. (Barron's Pet Owner's Manuals Ser.). 64p. 1988. pap. 6.95 (*0-8120-4035-X*) Barron.

— Cockatoos. (Illus.). 56p. 1989. pap. 6.95 (*0-8120-4159-3*) Barron.

Lantero, Erminie H. Feminine Aspects of Divinity. LC 73-84214. 36p. (Orig.). 1973. pap. 4.00 (*0-87574-191-6*) Pendle Hill.

***Lanters, Josbe.** Unauthorized Versions: Irish Menippean Satire, 1919-1952. LC 99-89814. 2000. 59.95 (*0-8132-0986-2*) Cath U Pr.

Lanthier, Craig J. The Keetzas of Podinn. (Illus.). 47p. (J). (gr. 3 up). 1995. 34.50 (*1-57529-003-0*) Kabel Pubs.

Lanthony, Philippe. Dictionnaire du Strabisme: Phisiologie et Clinique. (FRE.). 202p. 1983. 79.95 (*0-8288-1813-4*, M15412) Fr & Eur.

Lantier, Raymond, jt. auth. see Breuil, Henri.

Lantier-Sampon, Patricia. Wings, 4 bks. Incl. Airplanes. LC 91-50344. (Illus.). 24p. (J). (ps-2). 1994. lib. bdg. 19.93 (*0-8368-0539-9*); Birds. LC 91-50345. (Illus.). 24p. (J). (ps-2). 1991. lib. bdg. 19.93 (*0-8368-0541-0*); Flying Animals. LC 91-50346. (Illus.). 24p. (J). (ps-2). 1991. lib. bdg. 19.93 (*0-8368-0540-2*); Flying Insects. LC 91-50347. (Illus.). 24p. (J). (ps-2). 1991. lib. bdg. 19.93 (*0-8368-0542-9*); Set lib. bdg. 79.73 (*0-8368-0755-3*) Gareth Stevens Inc.

Lantieri, Linda & Patti, Janet. Waging Peace in Our Schools. 1998. pap. 15.00 (*0-8070-3117-8*) Beacon Pr.

Lantieri, Linda, jt. frwd. see Fox, Daniel M.

Lantigua, John. Heat Lightning. 288p. 1989. mass mkt. 4.95 (*0-446-35833-9*, Pub. by Warner Bks) Little.

— Player's Vendetta, 1 vol. 272p. 1999. mass mkt. 5.99 (*0-451-19846-8*) NAL.

Lanting, Frans. Eye to Eye: Intimate Encounters with the Animal World. Eckstrom, Christine, ed. LC 98-84524. (Illus.). 251p. 1997. 39.99 (*3-8228-7745-X*) Taschen Amer.

— Eye to Eye: Intimate Encounters with the Animal World. 1999. pap. 19.99 (*3-8228-6602-4*) Taschen Amer.

— Frente: Encuentros Intimos Con el Reino Animal. 1998. 49.99 (*3-8228-7560-0*) Benedikt Taschen.

— Jungles. 2000. 39.99 (*3-8228-6309-2*) Taschen Amer.

Lanting, Frans. Okavango: Africa's Last Eden. Arrowsmith, Alexandra, ed. LC 93-10296. (Illus.). 168p. 1993. 45.00 (*0-8118-0527-1*) Chronicle Bks.

— Okavango: Africa's Last Eden. (Illus.). 168p. 1995. pap. 24.95 (*0-8118-1182-4*) Chronicle Bks.

— Penguin. Eckstrom, Christine, ed. (Illus.). 168p. 1999. 24.99 (*3-8228-6519-2*) Taschen Amer.

Lanting, Frans, photos by. Madagascar: A World Out of Time. (Illus.). 144p. 1990. 60.00 (*0-89381-422-9*) Aperture.

Lanting, Frans & Cavagnaro, David, photos by. Feathers. LC 82-82344. (Illus.). 96p. 1982. pap. 12.95 (*0-912856-79-3*) Gr Arts Ctr Pub.

Lanting, Frans, jt. auth. see De Waal, Frans.

Lantis, David W., et al. California: The Pacific Connection. (Illus.). 595p. (C). 1988. pap. text 29.95 (*0-9620015-2-X*) Creekside Pr.

Lantis, Jeffrey S. Domestic Constraints & the Breakdown of International Agreements. LC 97-11074. 256p. 1997. 65.00 (*0-275-95948-1*, Praeger Pubs) Greenwood.

An Asterisk (*) at the beginning of an entry indicates that the title is appearing for the first time.

***Lantis, Jeffrey S., et al, eds.** The New International Studies Classroom: Active Teaching, Active Learning. LC 99-56615. 308p. 2000. pap. 26.95 (*1-55587-889-X*); lib. bdg. 59.95 (*1-55587-865-2*) L Rienner.

Lantis, Margaret. Alaskan Eskimo Ceremonialism. LC 84-45514. (American Ethnological Society Monographs: No. 11). 1988. reprint ed. 22.50 (*0-404-62911-3*) AMS Pr.

— Eskimo Childhood & Interpersonal Relationships. LC 84-45528. (American Ethnological Society Monographs: No. 33). 1988. reprint ed. 32.00 (*0-404-62932-6*) AMS Pr.

Lantner, Henry L. What? Again Those Jews! 150p. 1997. 14.95 (*965-229-158-7*) Gefen Bks.

Lanto, Sandra, jt. auth. see Spera, Stephanie.

Lantolf, James P., et al, eds. Research in Second Language Learning: Focus on the Classroom. LC 86-22300. (Delaware Symposia on Language Studies: Vol. 6). 240p. (C). 1987. text 73.25 (*0-89391-363-4*) Ablx Pub.

Lantolf, James P. & Appel, Gabriela, eds. Vygotskian Approaches to Second Language Research. LC 93-49680. (Second Language Learning Ser.). 232p. 1994. text 73.25 (*1-56750-024-2*) Ablx Pub.

Lantolf, James P. & Appel, Gabriela, eds. Vygotskian Approaches to Second Language Research. LC 93-49680. (Second Language Learning Ser.). 232p. 1994. pap. 39.50 (*1-56750-025-0*) Ablx Pub.

Lantolf, James P., ed. see Colloquium on Hispanic & Luso-Brazilian Linguistic.

Lanton, Peter L., jt. auth. see Graham, David I.

Lantos, I., jt. auth. see Hatala, P.

Lantos, John D. Do We Still Need Doctors? LC 97-11424. 214p. 1997. 25.99 (*0-415-91852-9*) Routledge.

— Do We Still Need Doctors? 1997. 24.95 (*0-415-91853-7*) Routledge.

— Do We Still Need Doctors? Physician's Personal Account of Practicing Medicine Today. LC 99-25174. 214p. 1999. pap. 17.95 (*0-415-92495-2*) Routledge.

Lantos, John D., jt. ed. see Burgio, G. Roberto.

Lantos, John D., jt. ed. see Elliott, Carl.

Lantos, Steve. Moon Handbooks: New Hampshire: Including Portsmouth, the Lakes Region, the Upper Valley & the White Mountains. (Illus.). 480p. 1998. pap. 18.95 (*1-56691-111-7*, Moon Handbks) Avalon Travel.

Lantree, Dave. Collecting Court Judgments for Fun & Profit. (Illus.). 120p. (C). 1990. pap. text 19.95 (*0-937309-09-5*) Business Controls Inc.

Lantry, Eileen E. Nature Trails & Animal Tales. LC 96-122228. 96p. (J). 1996. pap. 7.99 (*0-8280-0866-3*) Review & Herald.

Lantry, Eileen E., jt. auth. see Witcombe, John C.

Lantry, Noreen D. & Hummel, Kathy I. Building Baby's Brain Power Vol. I: 365 One-Minute Brain Stimulating Activities for Baby's First Years. (Illus.). vi, 410p. 1999. spiral bd. 19.95 (*0-9671289-0-0*) BETA Ctr Inc.

Lantz, Alma E., et al. Re-Entry Programs for Female Scientists. LC 79-25364. 195p. 1980. 52.95 (*0-275-90510-1*, C0510, Praeger Pubs) Greenwood.

Lantz, Chris. Instructional Video Production. 236p. (C). 1996. pap. text, per. 58.95 (*0-7872-2184-8*, 41218401) Kendall-Hunt.

Lantz, Christopher P. Field Manual for the Performances of the Forty-Nine Symphonies: A Children's Book Written Especially for Grown-Ups. (Illus.). 155p. (Orig.). 1997. pap. 19.95 (*0-9655875-0-9*, A-1) Way of the Turtle.

Lantz, David L. Bill Clinton You're No John F. Kennedy. (Illus.). 151p. (Orig.). 1994. pap. text 9.95 (*0-9639611-0-1*) Joshua Hse.

Lantz, Francess L. Fade Far Away. LC 98-8052. 176p. (YA). (gr. 7-12). 1998. 14.00 (*0-380-97553-X*, Avon Bks) Morrow Avon.

— Fade Far Away. 176p. (YA). (gr. 7-12). 1999. mass mkt. 6.99 (*0-380-79372-5*, Avon Bks) Morrow Avon.

— Marissa's Dance. LC 93-43225. (Boys' School Girls Ser.). (Illus.). 128p. (J). (gr. 3-7). 1994. pap. text 2.95 (*0-8167-3475-5*) Troll Communs.

— Mom, There's a Pig in My Bed! 144p. (Orig.). (J). (gr. 4). 1992. pap. 3.50 (*0-380-76112-2*, Avon Bks) Morrow Avon.

— Randy's Raiders. LC 93-44345. (Boys' School Girls Ser.). (Illus.). 176p. (J). (gr. 3-6). 1994. pap. 3.95 (*0-8167-3474-7*) Troll Communs.

— Rock, Rap, & Rad: How to Be a Rock or Rap Star. 224p. (Orig.). (YA). 1992. mass mkt. 3.99 (*0-380-76793-7*, Avon Bks) Morrow Avon.

***Lantz, Francess L.** A Royal Kiss. 144p. (J). (gr. 7). 2000. pap. 3.99 (*0-689-83422-5*) Aladdin.

— Sing Me a Love Song. LC 99-48902. (You're the One Ser.). 144p. (J). (gr. 4-7). 2000. per. 3.99 (*0-689-83420-9*) Aladdin.

Lantz, Francess L. Someone to Love. LC 96-31434. 224p. (J). (gr. 5). 1997. mass mkt. 14.00 (*0-380-97477-0*, Avon Bks) Morrow Avon.

— Someone to Love. 256p. 1998. mass mkt. 3.99 (*0-380-77590-5*, Avon Bks) Morrow Avon.

***Lantz, Francess L.** Someone to Love. 1998. 9.09 (*0-606-13787-4*, Pub. by Turtleback) Demco.

Lantz, Francess L. Spinach with Chocolate Sauce. (J). 1997. pap. 3.95 (*0-8167-4286-3*) Troll Communs.

— Stepsister from the Planet Weird. LC 96-43938. 170p. (J). (gr. 3-7). 1997. pap. 3.99 (*0-679-87330-9*, Pub. by Random Bks Yng Read) Random.

— Stepsister from the Planet Weird. LC 96-43938. (J). (gr. 3-7). 1997. lib. bdg. 11.99 (*0-679-97330-3*, Pub. by Random Bks Yng Read) Random.

Lantz, Francess L. Stepsister from the Planet Weird. 1997. 9.09 (*0-606-13040-3*, Pub. by Turtleback) Demco.

— You're the One, Vol. 3. LC 99-89184. 144p. (J). (gr. 4-7). 2000. per. 3.99 (*0-689-83421-7*) Aladdin.

Lantz, Francess Lin. The Case of the Missing Mummy. (New Adventures of Mary-Kate & Ashley Ser.). (Illus.). 82p. (J). (gr. 1-3). 1998. pap. 3.99 (*0-590-29404-0*) Scholastic Inc.

Lantz, Herman R. & Snyder, Eloise C. Marriage: An Examination of the Man-Woman Relationship. 2nd ed. LC 69-16038. (Illus.). 278p. reprint ed. pap. 86.20 (*0-608-10751-4*, 201372200087) Bks Demand.

***Lantz, James E.** Meaning-Centered Marital & Family Therapy: Learning to Bear the Beams of Love. LC 99-42368. (Illus.). 166p. 1999. pap. text 23.95 (*0-398-07017-2*) C C Thomas.

— Meaning-Centered Marital & Family Therapy: Learning to Bear the Beams of Love. LC 99-42368. (Illus.). 166p. 2000. text 36.95 (*0-398-07016-4*) C C Thomas.

Lantz, Jim, jt. auth. see Harper, Karen.

Lantz, John. Major Issues in Gerontological Nursing. 3rd rev. ed. Halliburton, Barbara, ed. 127p. 1996. pap. 29.95 (*1-57801-009-8*) Western Schls.

***Lantz, John, ed.** Major Issues in Gereontological Nursing. 4th rev. ed. (Illus.). 143p. 1999. pap. write for info. (*1-57801-037-3*) Western Schls.

Lantz, John, ed. see Cagley-Knight, Joan.

Lantz, K. A., ed. see Leskov, Nikolai S.

Lantz, Kenneth, tr. see Dostoyevsky, Fyodor.

Lantz, Marti, jt. auth. see Brownsey, Lois.

Lantz, Norma R. After Stephen: From Hurting to Healed. LC 87-70625. (Illus.). 175p. (Orig.). 1987. pap. 9.95 (*0-942419-00-6*) Ana Pub.

Lantz, Peggy S. & Hale, Wendy A. The Florida Water Story: From Raindrops to the Sea. LC 97-45043. (Illus.). 132p. (Orig.). (J). (gr. 3-7). 1998. 19.95 (*1-56164-099-9*) Pineapple Pr.

— The Young Naturalist's Guide to Florida. LC 94-15485. (Illus.). 128p. (J). (gr. 5-9). 1994. pap. 12.95 (*1-56164-051-4*) Pineapple Pr.

Lantz, Peggy S., ed. see Huegel, Craig N.

Lantz, Raymond C. Ottawa & Chippewa Indians of Michigan, 1870-1909. 296p. 1991. pap. 21.00 (*1-55613-531-9*) Heritage Bk.

— Seminole Indians of Florida, 1850-1874. 415p. (Orig.). 1994. pap. text 30.00 (*0-7884-0034-7*) Heritage Bk.

— Seminole Indians of Florida, 1875-1879. 436p. 1995. pap. 31.00 (*0-7884-0333-8*) Heritage Bk.

Lantz, Robert B. . . . Let the Children Come: Fifty-Two Object Lessons for Children in Worship. LC 96-52554. 90p. (Orig.). 1997. pap. 10.95 (*0-7880-1059-X*) CSS OH.

Lantz, Roy. The Care & Keeping of Customers: A Treasury of Facts, Tips & Proven Techniques for Keeping Your Customers Coming Back. Scanlon, Kelly & Guthrie, Jane D., eds. LC 95-74669. (Illus.). 80p. (Orig.). 1996. pap. 12.95 (*1-57294-007-7*, 12-0015) SkillPath Pubns.

Lantz, Walter. Woody Woodpecker: Work & Play, a Coloring Book. (J). 1990. pap. text 1.49 (*0-448-09343-X*, G & D) Peng Put Young Read.

Lantzman-Forbes, Arlene G., ed. see Ney, Ronald E., Jr.

Lantzy, Louise M., compiled by. Individuals with Disabilities Education Act: An Annotated Guide to Its Literature & Resources, 1980-1991. LC 92-9676. xi, 148p. 1992. ring bd. 37.50 (*0-8377-9274-6*, Rothman) W S Hein.

Lanusse, Armand, ed. Les Cenelles: Choix de Poesies Indigenes. (B. E. Ser.: No. 53). (FRE.). 1845. 35.00 (*0-8115-3004-3*) Periodicals Srv.

***Lanwrights.** MCSE Test Prep for MS Windows 2000 Professional. (Networking Ser.). (C). 2000. pap. 45.00 (*0-619-01511-X*) Course Tech.

— MCSE Test Prep Networking Essentials. (Networking Ser.). (C). 2000. pap. 45.00 (*0-619-01507-1*) Course Tech.

Lanwrights. Test Prep Windows 2000 Advanced Server. (C). 2000. pap. 20.00 (*0-619-01503-9*) Thomson Learn.

Lanyado, Joseph. Word Was Hebrew. text 24.95 (*1-58063-129-0*) Renaissance.

***Lanyado, Monica.** Handbook of Child & Adolescent Psychotherapy. LC 98-48880. 1999. 85.00 (*0-415-17258-6*); pap. write for info. (*0-415-17259-4*) Routledge.

Lanyen, Milton & Bulmore, Lawrence. Cinnabar Hills. 1967. 22.20 (*0-912314-20-6*) Academy Santa Clara.

Lanyer, Aemelia. The Poems of Aemelia Lanyer: Salve Deus Rex Judaeorum. Woods, Susanne, ed. (Women Writers in English Ser.). (Illus.). 192p. 1993. pap. text 16.95 (*0-19-508361-X*) OUP.

Lanyi, Andrew A. Confessions of a Stockbroker: You, Too Can Find Tomorrow's Blue Chips Before Wall Street Finds Them. LC 92-25479. 274p. (C). 1992. text 21.95 (*0-13-175746-6*) P-H.

Lanyi, Anthony, jt. auth. see Khahkhonen, Satu.

Lanyi, Gabriel. Managing Documentation Projects in an Imperfect World. LC 94-9111. 186p. 1994. pap. text 29.95 (*0-935470-74-3*) Battelle.

Lanyi, Marton. Diagnosis & Differential Diagnosis of Breast Calcifications. (Illus.). 270p. 1987. 154.00 (*0-387-16949-0*) Spr-Verlag.

— Diagnosis & Differential Diagnosis of Breast Calcifications. 252p. 1988. 140.00 (*3-540-16949-0*) Spr-Verlag.

***Lanyon, Anna.** Malinche's Conquest. 2000. pap. 14.95 (*1-86448-780-1*, Pub. by Allen & Unwin Pty) IPG Chicago.

Lanyon, Barbara P., jt. auth. see Lanyon, Richard I.

Lanyon, Ellen. Transformations I, 1973-74. 1977. pap. 12.50 (*0-89439-005-8*) Printed Matter.

Lanyon, Richard I. & Goodstein, Leonard. Personality Assessment. 3rd ed. LC 96-18061. (Series on Personality Processes). 438p. 1996. 74.50 (*0-471-55562-2*) Wiley.

Lanyon, Richard I. & Goodstein, Leonard D. Personality Assessment. 2nd ed. 328p. (C). 1992. pap. text 29.50 (*0-8191-8487-X*) U Pr of Amer.

Lanyon, Richard I. & Lanyon, Barbara P. Behavior Therapy: A Clinical Introduction. LC 77-83022. (Topics in Clinical Psychology Ser.: 7). 1978. pap. text. write for info. (*0-201-04100-6*) Addison-Wesley.

Lanyon, Richard I., jt. ed. see Goodstein, Leonard D.

Lanyon, W. E. & Tavolga, William N. Animal Sound & Communications. 1960. 35.00 (*0-934454-07-8*) Lubrecht & Cramer.

Lanyon, Walter C. Abo Allah, Teacher, Healer. 77p. 1996. spiral bd. 11.00 (*0-7873-0533-2*) Hlth Research.

— And It Was Told of a Certain Potter. LC 78-163038. (Short Story Index Reprint Ser.). 1977. reprint ed. 13.95 (*0-8369-3952-2*) Ayer.

— Demonstration. 78p. 1996. reprint ed. pap. 14.00 (*0-7873-1000-X*) Hlth Research.

— The Eyes of the Blind. 220p. 1983. reprint ed. pap. 10.00 (*1-889870-06-4*) Union Life.

— The Laughter of God. 224p. 1983. reprint ed. pap. 10.00 (*1-889870-04-8*) Union Life.

— London Notes & Lectures. 214p. 1983. reprint ed. pap. 10.00 (*1-889870-02-1*) Union Life.

— London Notes & Lectures. 2nd ed. 213p. 1996. reprint ed. spiral bd. 16.50 (*0-7873-0534-0*) Hlth Research.

— The Temple Not Made with Hands. 184p. (Orig.). 1983. pap. 10.00 (*1-889870-00-5*) Union Life.

— Thrust in the Sickle. 224p. 1983. reprint ed. pap. 10.00 (*1-889870-01-3*) Union Life.

— Without the Smell of Fire. 228p. 1983. reprint ed. pap. 10.00 (*1-889870-05-6*) Union Life.

Lanyon, Wesley E. The Comparative Biology of the Meadowlarks (Sturnella) in Wisconsin. (Publications of the Nuttall Ornithological Club: No. 1). (Illus.). 66p. 1957. pap. 4.00 (*1-877973-10-6*) Nuttall Ornith.

Lanys, Bita, ed. see McLaine, Patricia.

Lanz, David. Sacred Road. 96p. 1996. otabind 14.95 (*0-7935-6896-X*) H Leonard.

Lanz, Hanspeter. Die Romanischen Wandmalereien von San Silvestro in Tivoli: Ein roemisches Apsisprogramm der Zeit Innozenz III. (European University Studies: Ser. 28, Vol. 22). (GER., Illus.). 139p. 1983. 24.00 (*3-261-05080-2*) P Lang Pubng.

Lanz, Henry. Physical Basis of Rime: An Essay on the Aesthetics of Sound. LC 69-10115. (Illus.). 365p. 1969. reprint ed. lib. bdg. 69.50 (*0-8371-0136-0*, LABR, Greenwood Pr) Greenwood.

Lanz, K., jt. auth. see Achterberg, E.

Lanz, K., jt. auth. see Ahterberg, E.

Lanz, Lucille, ed. see Mann, Kirk.

Lanz, Maria E. Como Leer La Celestina. 45.50 (*0-685-69534-4*) Scripta.

***Lanza, Alessandro.** Resources Accounting in China. LC 98-43902. (Economics, Energy & Environment Ser.). 1999. write for info. (*0-7923-5485-0*) Kluwer Academic.

Lanza, Anna T. The Heart of Sicily: Recipes & Reminiscences of Life at Regaleali, a Country Estate. LC 92-45598. (Illus.). 1993. 40.00 (*0-517-58961-3*) C Potter.

***Lanza, Barbara.** The Great Golden Easter Egg Hunt. LC 99-43954. (Illus.). 12p. (J). (ps-1). 2000. 10.95 (*0-439-14262-8*, Cartwheel) Scholastic Inc.

Lanza, Elizabeth. Language Mixing in Infant Bilingualism: A Sociolinguistic Perspective. (Oxford Studies in Language Contact). (Illus.). 412p. 1997. text 90.00 (*0-19-823575-5*) OUP.

Lanza, Giovanni. Pourrait Etre Continue. . . La Poetica dell' "Opera Aperta" e "les Faux=Monnayeurs" di Andre Gide. (GER.). 353p. 1998. 51.95 (*3-631-33575-X*) P Lang Pubng.

Lanza, Janet, jt. auth. see Nelson, Tina.

Lanza, Janet R. & Wilson, Carolyn C. The Word Adolescent: A Program to Build Expressive Vocabulary & Semantic Skills for Adolescents. 270p. 1991. spiral bd. 44.95 (*1-55999-209-3*) LinguiSystems.

Lanza, Joseph. Cocktail. (Illus.). 176p. 1997. pap. 10.00 (*0-312-15248-5*) St Martin.

— The Cocktail. 1997. pap. 10.00 (*0-614-28102-4*, Picador USA) St Martin.

— Elevator Music: A Surreal History of Muzak, Easy Listening, & Other Moodsong. LC 95-14787. 288p. 1995. pap. 11.00 (*0-312-13063-5*) St Martin.

— Fragile Geometry: The Films, Philosophy & Misadventures of Nicolas Roeg. (Illus.). 176p. 1988. 35.00 (*1-55554-033-3*); pap. 13.95 (*1-55554-034-1*) PAJ Pubns.

***Lanza, Louis & Morton, Laura.** Totally Dairy-Free Cooking. LC 99-30472. (Illus.). 256p. 2000. 25.00 (*0-688-16909-0*, Wm Morrow) Morrow Avon.

Lanza, Marco, photos by. Pastissima! Pasta the Italian Way. LC 97-1823. (Pane & Vino Ser.). (Illus.). 128p. (gr. 11). 1997. 17.95 (*0-7835-4942-3*) Time-Life.

***Lanza, Michael.** The AMC Guide to Backcountry Travel. LC 99-41009. (Illus.). 288p. 1999. pap. 16.95 (*1-878239-82-1*, Pub. by AMC Books) Globe Pequot.

Lanza, Michael. Foghorn Outdoors: New England Hiking: The Complete Guide to Nearly 400 of the Best Hikes in New England. 2nd ed. (Illus.). 450p. 1999. pap. 18.95 (*1-57354-057-9*, Foghorn Outdoors) Avalon Travel.

Lanza, Patricia. Lasagna Gardening: A New Layering System for Bountiful Gardens: No Digging, No Tilling, No Weeding, No Kidding! LC 98-25315. (Illus.). 256p. 1998. pap. 15.95 (*0-87596-962-3*) Rodale Pr Inc.

Lanza, Patricia, photos by. Moscow & the Golden Ring. 2nd ed. LC 93-87281. (Illustrated Travel Guides from Thomas Cook Ser.). (Illus.). 272p. 1995. pap. 16.95 (*0-8442-9959-6*, Passprt Bks) NTC Contemp Pub Co.

Lanza, R. P., jt. ed. see Cooper, D. K.

Lanza, Robert. Principles of Tissue Engineering. LC 96-33638. (Illus.). 808p. 1996. text 139.95 (*0-12-436625-2*) Acad Pr.

Lanza, Robert, ed. One World: The Health & Survival of the Human Species in the 21st Century. 334p. 1996. 25.00 (*0-929173-16-3*) Health Press.

***Lanza, Robert P.** Principles of Tissue Engineering. 2nd ed. LC 99-68198. 800p. 2000. 199.95 (*0-12-436630-9*) Acad Pr.

Lanza, Robert P. & Chick, William L., eds. Immunodulation of Pancreatic Islets, II. 130p. 1994. 94.00 (*1-57059-134-2*, LN9134) CRC Pr.

— Immunoisolation of Pancreatic Islets, III. 130p. 1994. 94.00 (*1-57059-135-0*, LN9135) CRC Pr.

— Procurement of Pancreatic Islets, Vol. I. 130p. 1994. 94.00 (*1-57059-133-4*, LN9133) CRC Pr.

— Yearbook of Cell & Tissue Transplantation, 1996-1997. 294p. 1996. text 184.00 (*0-7923-3844-8*) Kluwer Academic.

Lanza, Robert P., jt. auth. see Cooper, David K. C.

Lanza, Susan E. Essentials for the Activity Professional in LTC. LC 96-19631. (Home Care Aide Ser.). (Illus.). 352p. 1996. pap. 66.95 (*0-8273-7387-2*) Delmar.

Lanzafame, Raymond, ed. see Rochester General Hospital Laser Group Staff.

Lanzano, Ellen A. Hardy: The Temporal Poetics. LC 97-34969. (Studies in Nineteenth-Century British Literature: Vol. 10). XI, 157p. (C). 1999. text 43.95 (*0-8204-3835-9*) P Lang Pubng.

Lanzano, Michael, jt. auth. see Bodman, Jean W.

Lanzara, Joseph. Paradise Lost: The Novel. LC 93-87625. 255p. 1994. 24.95 (*0-9639621-4-0*) New Arts Lib.

Lanzarone, Michael, jt. auth. see Kahn, Steven C.

Lanzarotti, Sally, ed. see Anderson, Alex.

Lanzarotti, Sally, ed. see Avery, Virginia.

Lanzarotti, Sally, ed. see Laurg, Jean R.

Lanzarotti, Sally, ed. see Lose, Patrick.

Lanzarotti, Sally, ed. see McDowell, Ruth B.

Lanzarotti, Sally, ed. see Oroyan, Susanna.

Lanzarotti, Sally, ed. see Scherer, Deidre.

Lanzas, Pedro T. Relacion Descriptiva de los Mapas, Planos de Mexico y Floridas. (SPA.). 424p. 1997. reprint ed. 65.00 (*1-57898-014-3*) Martino Pubng.

Lanze, Laura B. Import-Export Can Make You Rich. (Illus.). 192p. (C). 1988. 32.95 (*0-13-451857-8*) P-H.

Lanze, W. Dabi das Abkuerzungsverzeichnis Fuer Den Ingenieur: Index of Abbreviations for Engineers. 2nd ed. (GER & RUS.). 344p. 1981. 75.00 (*0-8288-1164-4*, M15318) Fr & Eur.

Lanzen Harris, Laurie & Henderson, Helene, eds. Twentieth Century Literary Movements Index. (Literary Movements Reference Ser.). 419p. 1991. lib. bdg. 70.00 (*1-55888-306-1*) Omnigraphics Inc.

Lanzendorf, Scott. New Hampshire Militia Officers, 1820-1850: Division, Brigade & Regimental Field & Staff Officers. 232p. (Orig.). 1995. pap. 21.00 (*0-7884-0299-4*) Heritage Bk.

Lanzer, Harriette. The Key to German Grammar for Key Stages 3 & 4. (Illus.). 140p. 1995. pap. 19.95 (*0-7487-1923-7*, Pub. by S Thornes Pubs) Trans-Atl Phila.

Lanzer, Harriette & Parikh, Rachel. Advanced German Vocabulary. 96p. 1994. pap. 14.95 (*1-85234-527-6*, Pub. by S Thornes Pubs) Trans-Atl Phila.

Lanzer, Peter & Roesch, Josef, eds. Vascular Diagnostics: Noninvasive & Invasive Techniques-Periinterventional Evaluations. LC 94-28254. (Illus.). 528p. 1994. 155.00 (*0-387-57939-7*) Spr-Verlag.

Lanzer, Peter, jt. auth. see Lipton, Martin J.

Lanzer, Peter, jt. ed. see Yoganathan, A. P.

Lanzer, Toby. The U. N. Department of Humanitarian Affairs in Angola: A Model for the Coordination of Humanitarian Assistance? LC 96-174854. (Studies on Emergencies & Disaster Relief: No. 5). 41p. 1996. 8.95 (*91-7106-385-4*, Pub. by Nordic Africa) Transaction Pubs.

Lanzerotti, B., ed. Parting Glass: An American Book of Drink. xi, 76p. 1993. pap. 9.95 (*1-891413-00-7*) Twin Willows.

Lanzerotti, Bruce. The Business Traveler's Handbook: Tips & Time Saving Hints for the Business Traveler. (Illus.). 1998. pap. 19.95 (*1-891413-25-2*) Twin Willows.

— The Compleat Golfer of 1783: A Reference & Historical Guide to the Game. (Illus.). xii, 95p. 1996. pap. 14.95 (*1-891413-01-5*) Twin Willows.

— The Self-Publishing Workbook: A Guide to Writing, Printing & Selling Your Own Books or Magazines. (Illus.). 100p. 1998. pap., wbk. ed. 19.95 (*1-891413-75-9*) Twin Willows.

Lanzerotti, L. J. & Park, C., eds. Upper Atmosphere Research in Antarctica. (Antarctic Research Ser.: Vol. 29). (Illus.). 264p. 1977. 50.00 (*0-87590-141-7*) Am Geophysical.

***Lanzetta, Beverly J.** The Other Side of Nothingness: Toward a Theology of Radical Openness. (C). 2001. pap. text. write for info. (*0-7914-4950-5*) State U NY Pr.

— The Other Side of Nothingness: Toward a Theology of Radical Openness. (C). 2001. text. write for info. (*0-7914-4949-1*) State U NY Pr.

Lanzhou Institute of Glaciology & Geocryology Staf, et al, eds. Glaciers & Environment in the Qinghai-Xizang (Tibet) Plateau Pt. I: The Gongga Mountain. 201p. 1996. 38.00 (*7-03-004154-2*, Pub. by Sci Pr) Lubrecht & Cramer.

***Lanzi, Elisa, et al.** Introduction to Vocabularies: Enhancing Access to Cultural Heritage Information. LC 98-36514. (Introduction to Ser.). (Illus.). 80p. (Orig.). 1999. pap. 14.95 (*0-89236-544-7*, Pub. by J P Getty Trust) OUP.

L

Lanzillotti, Robert F., et al. Phase II in Review: The Price Commission Experience. LC 75-5164. (Brookings INstitution Studies in Wage-Price Policy). 223p. reprint ed. pap. 69.20 (0-608-12712-4, 202538700043) Bks Demand.

Lanzillotti, Robert F., ed. see Government-Mandated Costs Seminar Staff.

Lanzkowsky, Philip. Manual of Pediatric Hematology & Oncology. 2nd ed. LC 94-32744. 1994. text 115.00 (0-443-08969-8) Church.

***Lanzkowsky, Philip.** Manual of Pediatric Hematology & Oncology. 3rd ed. (Illus.). 816p. 2000. 99.95 (0-12-436635-X) Acad Pr.

Lanzkowsky, Philip, et al. Manual of Pediatric Hematology & Oncology. LC 89-470. 468p. reprint ed. pap. 145.10 (0-7837-1613-3, 204190500024) Bks Demand.

Lanzl, Lawrence H., jt. auth. see Jayaraman, Subramania.

Lanzmann, Claude. Shoah: The Complete Text of the Acclaimed Holocaust Film. rev. ed. (Illus.). 208p. 1995. reprint ed. pap. 12.95 (0-306-80665-7) Da Capo.

Lanzone, R. V. Dizionario Di Mitologia Egizia, 3 vols. (ITA.). 1312p. 1974. reprint ed. 590.00 (90-272-0931-6, 0932-4) J Benjamins Pubng Co.

— Dizzionario Di Mitologia Egizia, Vol. 4. xv, 205p. 1975. 125.00 (90-272-0934-0) J Benjamins Pubng Co.

Lao, He H. & Lin, Moses. Wrist-Ankle Acupuncture: Methods & Applications. (Illus.). 268p. (Orig.). 1997. pap. text 45.00 (0-9659060-0-0) NY Oriental Hlthcare.

Lao, Kenneth Q. Engineering Optics. (Electrical Engineering Ser.). 1991. text. write for info. (0-442-00685-3, VNR) Wiley.

Lao, Meri. Sirens: Symbols of Seduction. LC 97-15688. (Illus.). 224p. 1997. 40.00 (0-89281-653-8, Park St Pr) Inner Tradit.

— Sirens: Symbols of Seduction. (Illus.). 192p. 1999. pap. 25.00 (0-89281-846-8, Inner Trad Espanol) Inner Tradit.

***Lao She.** Blades of Grass: The Stories of Lao She. Goldblatt, Howard, ed. Lyell, William A. & Chen, Sarah Wei-ming, trs. from CHI. LC 99-11832. (Fiction from Modern China Ser.). 320p. 1999. pap. 18.95 (0-8248-1803-2) UH Pr.

Lao, She. Blades of Grass: The Stories of Lao She. Lyell, William A. & Wei-ming Chen, Sarah, trs. from CHI. LC 99-11832. (Fiction from Modern China Ser.). 320p. 1999. 48.00 (0-8248-1506-8) UH Pr.

Lao She. Rickshaw: The Novel Lo-t'o hsiang Tzu. James, Jean M., tr. from CHI. LC 79-10658. Orig. Title: Lo-to Hsiang Tzu. xi, 249 p. (C). 1979. pap. text 10.00 (0-8248-0655-7) UH Pr.

Lao-Tse, et al. Springs of Chinese Wisdom. (Illus.). 22p. 1997. 4.95 (3-85788-314-6, Pub. by Quellen Verlag) Assoc Pubs Grp.

Lao Tze. Tao Te Ching. Legge, James, tr. LC 97-46018. (Illus.). 112p. 1998. pap. 1.50 (0-486-29792-6) Dover.

Lao-tzu. The Light of China: Selections. 1972. lib. bdg. 250.00 (0-87968-534-4) Krishna Pr.

— Lyrical Translation of Lao Tzu's Tao-Te Ching in English & Korean. LC 90-91956. (Illus.). 300p. (Orig.). 1986. pap. 20.00 (0-942049-03-9) One Mind Pr.

Lao-Tzu. Tao Te Ching. Addiss, Stephen & Lombardo, Stanley, trs. LC 93-21939. (Hackett Classics Ser.). (Illus.). 128p. (Orig.). (C). 1993. pap. text 7.95 (0-87220-232-1); lib. bdg. 27.95 (0-87220-233-X) Hackett Pub.

— Tao-Te-Ching. Bryce, Derek & Wieger, Leon, trs. from CHI. LC 99-24278. (Illus.). 120p. 1999. pap. 12.95 (1-57863-123-8) Weiser.

Lao Tzu. Tao Te Ching. 190p. 1987. reprint ed. lib. bdg. 23.95 (0-89966-610-8) Buccaneer Bks.

— Tao Te Ching: The Classic Book of Integrity & the Way. 192p. 1990. pap. 12.95 (0-553-34935-X) Bantam.

— The Way of Life: Tao Te Ching. 1955. mass mkt. 5.99 (0-451-62674-5, Ment) NAL.

Lao-zi. Dao de Jing: The Old Sage's Classic of the Way of Virtue. Byrne, Patrick M., tr. 162p. 1991. pap. 15.00 (0-89540-160-6, SB-160) Sun Pub.

***Laohe Mahfooz Guild Staff.** Islam: The Divine Choice. LC 98-6779. 143p. 1998. pap. 12.95 (0-9667251-1-5) Laohe Mahfooz.

Laoide-Kemp, Siobhan, jt. ed. see McCracken, Wendy.

Laonhardt, W. Mathematical Principles of Economics. Creedy, John, ed. (Classics in the History of Economics Ser.). 208p. 1992. 90.00 (1-85278-723-6) E Elgar.

Laor, Nathaniel & Agassi, Joseph. Diagnosis: Philosophical & Medical Perspectives. 280p. (C). 1990. lib. bdg. 99.50 (0-7923-0845-X, Pub. by Kluwer Academic) Kluwer Academic.

Laor, Nathaniel, jt. ed. see Jarvie, I. C.

Laor, Ofer. CGI Programming with Visual Basic 5. LC 97-30389. 578p. 1997. pap. 49.95 (0-07-913688-5) McGraw.

Laorr, Alan & Helms, Clyde A. MRI of Musculoskeletal Masses. LC 96-24302. (Illus.). 384p. 1996. text 139.50 (0-89640-320-3) Igaku-Shoin.

Laos, N. K. Topics in Mathematical Analysis & Differential Geometry. LC 97-51928. 600p. 1997. text 86.00 (981-02-3180-6) World Scientific Pub.

Laosa, Luis M. & Sigel, Irving E., eds. Families As Learning Environments for Children. LC 82-18062. 414p. 1982. 65.00 (0-306-40939-9, Plenum Trade) Perseus Pubng.

Laosa, Luis M., jt. ed. see Sigel, Irving E.

Laothamatas. Democratization in Southeast & East Asia. LC 96-52735. 285p. 1997. text 49.95 (0-312-17364-4) St Martin.

Laourdas & Westerink, eds. Photii Patriarchae Constantinopolitani Vol. IV: Amphilochiorum Pars Prima. (GRE.). 1986. 53.50 (3-322-00277-2, T1510, Pub. by B G Teubner) U of Mich Pr.

— Photii Patriarchae Constantinopolitani Vol. V: Amphilochiorum Pars Altera. (GRE.). 1986. 59.50 (3-322-00333-7, T1511, Pub. by B G Teubner) U of Mich Pr.

— Photii Patriarchae Constantinopolitani Vol. VI, Fascicule 1: Amphilochiorum Pars Tertia. (GRE.). 1987. 34.50 (3-322-00361-2, T1512, Pub. by B G Teubner) U of Mich Pr.

— Photii Patriarchae Constantinopolitani Vol. VI, Fascicule 2: Indices. (GRE.). 1988. 37.50 (3-322-00510-0, T1513, Pub. by B G Teubner) U of Mich Pr.

Laoureux, N. Practical Method Pt. 2: Violin in Four Parts. 64p. 1986. pap. 7.95 (0-7935-5454-3, 50326960) H Leonard.

— Practical Method for Violin, Pt. 1. 60p. 1986. pap., suppl. ed. 8.95 (0-7935-5107-2, 50326940) H Leonard.

— Practical Method Violin, Pt. 1 A Cappella. 68p. 1986. pap. 7.95 (0-7935-5440-3, 50326950) H Leonard.

Lap-Chew, Lin, jt. auth. see Wijers, Marjan.

Lap, M. Tamil - French Dictionary: Vocabulaire Tamoul-Francais. (FRE & TAM.). 1984. 24.95 (0-8288-1727-8, F109490) Fr & Eur.

Lapadula, Dorothy. Doing It Right: Making the Most of Your Life. 159p. 1999. reprint ed. text 17.00 (0-7881-6282-9) DIANE Pub.

LaPadula, Thomas. Tonka Big Rigs. LC 00-501730. (Illus.). 12p. (J). (ps-2). 1999. 9.95 (0-439-04519-3, Cartwheel) Scholastic Inc.

***LaPadula, Thomas.** Tonka Big Rigs Display. 1999. 79.60 (0-439-07836-9, Cartwheel) Scholastic Inc.

LaPadula, Thomas. Tonka Busy Builders. (Tonka Wheel Bks.). 32p. (J). (ps-2). 1997. bds. 5.95 (0-590-97303-7) Scholastic Inc.

— Tonka Trucks Around Town. (Tonka Wheel Bks.). 32p. (J). (ps-2). 1997. bds. 5.95 (0-590-97304-5) Scholastic Inc.

Lapage, S. P., et al, eds. International Code of Nomenclature of Bacteria. rev. ed. 232p. 1992. text 47.00 (1-55581-039-X) ASM Pr.

— International Code of Nomenclature of Bacteria, & Statutes of the International Committee on Systematic Bacteriology, & Statutes of the Bacteriology Section of the International Association of Microbiological Societies: Bacteriological Code. rev. ed. LC 75-20730. 216p. reprint ed. pap. 67.00 (0-608-18102-1, 203223300078) Bks Demand.

LaPaglia, Brenda. Forever Changed. 170p. 1999. pap. write for info. (0-7392-0312-6, PO3450) Morris Pubng.

LaPaglia, Nancy. Storytellers: The Image of the Two-Year College in American Fiction & in Women's Journals. LC 93-37645. 182p. 1994. pap. 15.95 (1-879528-07-X) Ed Studies Pr.

LaPaglia, Peter S., jt. auth. see Crutchfield, James A.

LaPaglia, Peter S., jt. ed. see Gardner, James B.

Lapaire, Pierre J. Montherlant et la Parole: Etude d'un Langage Dramatique. LC 93-83301. (FRE.). 149p. 1993. lib. bdg. 33.95 (0-917786-94-7) Summa Pubns.

Lapaire, Sophie, ed. see Ching Hai, Suma.

LaPalma, Marina. Grammars for Jess. (Illus.). 56p. 1981. 4.50 (0-932716-16-4) Kelsey St Pr.

LaPalma, Marina & Rosenwasser, Rena. Hair-Raising. 1976. 3.75 (0-932716-05-9) Kelsey St Pr.

LaPalombara, Joseph. Democracy, Italian Style. LC 87-6124. 320p. (C). 1989. reprint ed. pap. 17.00 (0-300-04411-9) Yale U Pr.

LaPalombara, Joseph G. The Initiative & Referendum in Oregon, 1938-1948. LC 50-62689. (Oregon State Monographs, Studies in Political Science: No. 1). 149p. reprint ed. pap. 46.20 (0-7837-0157-8, 204045400017) Bks Demand.

— The Italian Labor Movement: Problems & Prospects. LC 82-11885. 192p. 1982. reprint ed. lib. bdg. 65.00 (0-313-23553-8, LAIT, Greenwood Pr) Greenwood.

— Italy: The Politics of Planning. LC 66-17523. (National Planning Ser.: No. 7). 204p. reprint ed. pap. 63.30 (0-608-13891-6, 202039800017) Bks Demand.

LaPalombara, Joseph G., jt. ed. see Weiner, Myron.

Lapan, Glenda, et al. Accentuate the Negative: Integers. Anderson, Catherine & Miceli, Stacey, eds. (Connected Matheamtics Ser.). (Illus.). 139p. (Orig.). 1996. pap., teacher ed. 16.50 (1-57232-169-5, 21464) Seymour Pubns.

— Accentuate the Negative: Integers. Anderson, Catherine & Miceli, Stacey, eds. (Connected Matheamtics Ser.). (Illus.). 82p. (Orig.). (J). (gr. 7). 1996. pap., wbk. ed. 5.95 (1-57232-168-7, 21463) Seymour Pubns.

— Comparing & Scaling: Ratio, Proportion, & Present. (Connected Mathematics Ser.). (Illus.). 81p. (Orig.). (J). (gr. 7). 1996. pap., student ed. 5.95 (1-57232-166-0, 21461) Seymour Pubns.

— Comparing & Scaling: Ratio, Proportion, & Present. (Connected Mathematics Ser.). (Illus.). 148p. (Orig.). 1996. teacher ed. 16.50 (1-57232-167-9, 21462) Seymour Pubns.

— Stretching & Shrinking: Similarity. Anderson, Catherine et al, eds. (Connected Mathematics Ser.). (Illus.). 84p. (Orig.). 1996. pap., wbk. ed. 5.95 (1-57232-164-4, 21459) Seymour Pubns.

— Stretching & Shrinking: Similarity. Anderson, Catherine et al, eds. (Connected Mathematics Ser.). (Illus.). 168p. (Orig.). 1996. pap., teacher ed. 16.50 (1-57232-165-2, 21460) Seymour Pubns.

Lapan, Maureen & Houghton, Raymond. Learning & Intelligence: Conversations with Skinner & Wheeler. 142p. 1995. 37.50 (0-7165-2584-4, Pub. by Irish Acad Pr) Intl Spec Bk.

***Lapanja, Margie.** Food Men Love. 2001. pap. 14.95 (1-57324-512-7) Conari Press.

Lapanja, Margie. Goddess' Guide to Love: Timeless Secrets to Divine Romance. LC 98-45503. (Illus.). 250p. 1999. pap. text 12.95 (1-57324-143-1) Conari Press.

— Goddess in the Kitchen: 201 Heavenly Recipes, Spirited Stories & Saucy Secrets. LC 98-4612. (Illus.). 320p. 1998. pap. text 14.95 (1-57324-115-6) Conari Press.

LaPanta, Stephen C. The Long Way Home . . . A Christmas Story. (Illus.). 56p. 1996. 15.95 (0-9659048-0-6) Homewrd Bound.

Lapas, Raimundas M. It Happened on the Silver Screen: Ethnic Lithuanian Cinematographic Activities in the United States, 1909-1979. 1983. 19.95 (0-685-09857-5) Baltic Cinema.

— Ten, Ekrane Suzibus: Amerikos Lietuviu Kinematografija, 1909-1979. LC 81-69029.Tr. of It Happened on the Silver Screen: Ethnic Lithuanian Cinematographic Activities in the United States, 1909-1979. (ENG & LIT., Illus.). 386p. 19.95 (0-941618-00-5) Baltic Cinema.

Lapasin, Romano, jt. auth. see Pricl, Sabrina.

Lapasta, Douglas, ed. see Neuweiler, Phillip F.

LaPasta, Douglas G., ed. see Neuweiler, Phillip F.

Lapati, Americo D. A High School Curriculum for Leadership. 1961. 17.95 (0-8084-0375-3) NCUP.

Lapati, Americo D., ed. see Brownson, Orestes A.

Lapatina, Eduardo G., ed. Advances in Molecular & Cell Biology Vol. 18: The Platelet. 408p. 1997. 128.50 (0-7623-0140-6) Jai Pr.

Lapatine, Sol. Electronics in Communication. 2nd ed. LC 85-22594. (Electronic Technology Ser.). 369p. 1986. text 44.50 (0-471-05787-8) P-H.

Lapatra, Jack, jt. auth. see Temes, Gabor C.

Lapchick, J. Michael. Brand Name Guide to Low-Fat & Fat-Free Foods: A Comprehensive Listing of More Than 1000 Packaged Low-Fat & Fat-Free Foods Found in Almost Every Grocery Store with Complete Nutrition Information. 190p. 1995. pap. 9.95 (1-56561-045-8) Wiley.

Lapchick, Mike. The Label Reader's Pocket Dictionary of Food Additives: A Comprehensive Quick Reference Guide to Mor E Than 250 of Today's Most Common Food Additives. 128p. 1993. pap. 4.95 (0-471-34744-2) Wiley.

Lapchick, Mike & Appleseth, Cindy. The Label Reader's Pocket Dictionary of Food Additives. 128p. (Orig.). 1993. pap. 4.95 (1-56561-027-X) Wiley.

Lapchick, Richard, jt. auth. see Robinson, Eddie.

Lapchick, Richard E. The Politics of Race & International Sport: The Case of South Africa, 1. LC 74-11705. (Studies in Human Rights: No. 1). 268p. 1975. 38.50 (0-8371-7691-3, LPR/, Greenwood Pr) Greenwood.

Lapchick, Richard E. & Benedict, Jeffrey R., eds. Sport in Society: Equal Opportunity or Business As Usual? LC 95-35477. 332p. 1995. 54.00 (0-8039-7280-6); pap. 25.00 (0-8039-7281-4) Sage.

Lapchick, Richard E. & Urdang, Stephanie. Oppression & Resistance: The Struggle of Women in Southern Africa, 29. LC 81-4267. (Contributions in Women's Studies: No. 29). (Illus.). 197p. 1982. 52.95 (0-313-22960-0, LWA/, Greenwood Pr) Greenwood.

Lapchick, Richard S. & Slaughter, John B., eds. Rules of the Game: Ethics in College Sport. (Ace/Oryx Press Series in Higher Education). (C). 1989. reprint ed. pap. 19.95 (1-57356-262-9) Oryx Pr.

Lapchinskii, V. F., jt. auth. see Paton, B. E.

Lape, Fred. A Farm & Village Boyhood. LC 80-17303. (York State Bk.). (Illus.). 175p. reprint ed. pap. 54.30 (0-8357-3124-3, 203938500012) Bks Demand.

— A Garden of Trees & Shrubs: Practical Hints for Planning & Planting an Arboretum. 2nd ed. LC 98-2794. 1998. pap. 17.00 (0-935796-96-7) Purple Mnt Pr.

***Lape, Gene.** Blood on the Rising Sun. 2000. pap. 10.95 (0-533-13261-4) Vantage.

Lape, Harvey, jt. auth. see Schwarze, Sharon.

Lape, Irene & Gilleland, Michael S. The Scarlet Letter Study Guide. 50p. (YA). (gr. 9-12). 1996. student ed., ring bd. 14.99 (1-58609-164-6) Progeny Pr WI.

Lape, Joseph. Why the Book of Revelation? Putting the Pieces of the Puzzle Together. 255p. 1998. pap. 19.95 (1-887002-73-1) Cross Trng.

***Lape, Noreen Grover.** West of the Border: The Multicultural Literature of the Western American Frontiers. 272p. (C). 2000. text 59.95 (0-8214-1345-7); pap. text 24.95 (0-8214-1346-5) Ohio U Pr.

Lapedes, D. N. Encyclopedic Italian-English, English-Italian Scientific & Technical Dictionary: Dizionario Enciclopedico Scientifico e Tecnico: Inglese-Italiano, Italiano-Inglese. (ENG & ITA.). 2122p. 1980. 295.00 (0-8288-4693-6, M9201) Fr & Eur.

— Spanish & English Dictionary of Technical & Scientific Terminology: Diccionario de Terminos Cientificos y Tecnicos, 5 vols., Set. (ENG & SPA.). 2592p. 1981. 895.00 (0-8288-0668-3, S38580) Fr & Eur.

Lapena-Bonifacio, Amelia, ed. 12 Philipine Women Writers. LC 94-943847. 136p. (Orig.). 1995. pap. text 12.00 (971-542-040-0, Pub. by U of Philippines Pr) UH Pr.

***Lapenkova, Valentina & Lambton, Edward.** Russian Food & Drink. (Illus.). 48p. (J). (gr. 5-7). 1999. text 17.00 (0-7881-6420-1) DIANE Pub.

Lapenna, Ivo. Soviet Penal Policy. LC 80-15755. (Background Bk.). 148p. 1980. reprint ed. lib. bdg. 55.00 (0-313-22570-2, LASP, Greenwood Pr) Greenwood.

Lapensohn, Lee. Captain Anderson's Cookbook. (Illus.). 108p. 1997. 9.95 (0-9655680-0-8) Capt Andersons Rest.

Lapensohn, Lee & Patronis, Jimmy, Jr. Captain Anderson's True Greek. (Illus.). 1997. write for info. (0-9655680-1-6) Capt Andersons Rest.

LaPenta, Anthony V., Jr. The Sniper. LC 75-16563. 1976. 21.95 (0-87949-042-X) Ashley Bks.

LaPenta, Barbara L., tr. see Tafuri, Manfredo.

***LaPenta, Marilyn.** Car Fun. (My Little Wipe-Off Board Bks.). (Illus.). 8p. (J). (ps-1). 2000. bds. 4.99 (0-7681-0225-1, McClanahan Book) Learn Horizon.

LaPenta, Marilyn. Music, Songs, & Poems. Evento, Susan, ed. (Macmillan Early Skills Program - Conversion Ser.). 64p. (J). (ps-2). 1995. pap. 9.95 (1-56784-506-1) Newbridge Educ.

— 1 2 3 in the Sea: Including Abacus. (Illus.). 12p. (J). (ps-1). 1999. boxed set 9.95 (0-7641-7256-5) Barron.

— Our America. Evento, Susan, ed. (Macmillan Early Skills Program - Conversion Ser.). 64p. (J). (ps-2). 1995. pap. 9.95 (1-56784-513-4) Newbridge Educ.

LaPenta, Marilyn & Bielitz, Joan. Activity Centers. Evento, Susan, ed. (Macmillan Early Skills Program - Conversion Ser.). 64p. 1995. pap. 9.95 (1-56784-507-X) Newbridge Educ.

LaPenta, Marilyn, jt. auth. see Bielitz, Joan.

Lapera, J. Alvarez. El Greco Identity & Transformation. 1999. 65.00 (88-8118-474-5) Skira IT.

***LaPerchia, Alex.** Satan & the Saint. LC 98-87018. (Illus.). 149p. 1999. pap. 17.95 (1-56315-166-9, Pub. by SterlingHse) Natl Bk Netwk.

Laperle, Patricia J. Under His Wings. LC 86-63915. (Illus.). 52p. (Orig.). 1987. pap. 7.75 (0-910147-41-8) World Poetry Pr.

Laperouse, Jean F. & Chinard, Gilbert. Le Voyage de Laperouse sur les Cotes de l'Alaska et de la Californie (1786) 1979. 21.95 (0-405-10592-4) Ayer.

Lapeyre, B. The International Secretary Dictionary: English-Spanish-French. (ENG, FRE & SPA.). 165p. 1992. pap. 25.00 (0-7859-8905-6) Fr & Eur.

— Practical Business Negotiations in French-English-Spanish. (ENG, FRE & SPA.). 174p. 1992. 24.95 (0-7859-7513-6, 8428319464); pap. 22.00 (0-7859-8919-6) Fr & Eur.

— Secretary's International Dictionary: English-Spanish-French. (ENG, FRE & SPA.). 165p. 1992. 24.95 (0-7859-7512-8, 8428319456) Fr & Eur.

Lapeyre, B. & Sheppard, P. The International Secretary Dictionary: English-Spanish-French. (ENG, FRE & SPA.). 165p. 1992. pap. 26.25 (84-283-1945-6, Pub. by Paraninfo) IBD Ltd.

— Practical Business Negotiations in French-English-Spanish. (ENG, FRE & SPA.). 174p. 1992. pap. 23.25 (84-283-1946-4, Pub. by Paraninfo) IBD Ltd.

Lapeyre, B. J., et al. Understanding Numerical Analysis for Option Pricing. (Illus.). 250p. (C). 1999. text 49.95 (0-521-62114-3) Cambridge U Pr.

Lapeyre, Benedicte & Sheppard, Pamela. Chairing Meetings in French As Well As in English. (ENG & FRE.). 87p. 1992. 39.95 (0-7859-1001-8, 2708114557) Fr & Eur.

— Taking the Floor in Meetings in French As Well As in English. (ENG & FRE.). 109p. 1992. 39.95 (0-7859-1002-6, 2708114565) Fr & Eur.

Lapeyre, Frederic, jt. auth. see Bhalla, A. S.

Lapeyrouse, Norton J. Formulas & Calculations for Drilling, Production & Workover. 224p. 1992. 55.00 (0-88415-011-9, 5011) Gulf Pub.

Lapham, Alice G. Old Planters of Beverly in Massachusetts, & the Thousand Acre Grant of 1635. (Illus.). 133p. 1995. reprint ed. pap. 19.50 (0-8328-4703-8); reprint ed. lib. bdg. 29.50 (0-8328-4695-3) Higginson Bk Co.

Lapham, Burks, ed. see Craig, Dorothy.

Lapham, Dave. Ghosts of St. Augustine. LC 96-49882. (Illus.). 168p. (Orig.). 1997. pap. 8.95 (1-56164-123-5) Pineapple Pr.

Lapham, David D., tr. see Yoon, Suk-Joong.

Lapham, Increase A. The Antiquities of Wisconsin As Surveyed & Described. LC 72-5000. (Antiquities of the New World Ser.: Vol. 4). (Illus.). reprint ed. 42.50 (0-404-57304-5) AMS Pr.

— Wisconsin: Its Geography & Topography, History, Geology & Mineralogy. LC 74-107. (Mid-American Frontier Ser.). 1975. reprint ed. 21.95 (0-405-06874-3) Ayer.

Lapham, Lewis. The Agony of Mammon: The Imperial Global Economy Explains Itself to the Membership in Davos, Switzerland. LC 98-55978. 2000. 15.00 (1-85984-710-2, Pub. by Verso) Norton.

— Lapham's Rules of Influence. LC 98-33212. 224p. 1999. 19.95 (0-679-42605-1) Random.

— Waiting for the Barbarians. 256p. 1997. pap. 15.00 (1-85984-119-8, Pub. by Verso) Norton.

***Lapham, Lewis H.** End of the World. 2000. pap. 15.95 (0-312-25264-1) St Martin.

Lapham, Lewis H. Fortune's Child. 1994. pap. 12.95 (1-879957-21-3) Harpers Mag Found.

— Hotel America: Scenes in the Lobby of the Fin-de-Siecle. LC 95-21592. 384p. 1996. pap. 18.00 (1-85984-062-0, Pub. by Verso) Norton.

— Waiting for the Barbarians. LC 97-45921. 1997. 22.00 (1-85984-882-6, Pub. by Verso) Norton.

Lapham, Lewis H., ed. The End of the World. LC 98-50225. (Illus.). 320p. 1999. text 24.95 (0-312-19264-9) St Martin.

— High Technology & Human Freedom. LC 85-8341. (International Symposia Ser.). (Illus.). 170p. (Orig.). 1985. text 35.00 (0-87474-598-5, LAHT) Smithsonian.

— High Technology & Human Freedom. LC 85-8341. (International Symposia Ser.). (Illus.). 170p. (Orig.). 1986. pap. text 16.95 (0-87474-599-3, LAHTP) Smithsonian.

***Lapham, Lewis H. & Rosenbush, Ellen, eds.** An American Album: One Hundred of Fifty Years of Harper's Magazine. (Illus.). 760p. 2000. 50.00 (1-879957-53-1, Franklin Sq Pr) Harpers Mag Found.

Lapham, Robert & Norling, Bernard. Lapham's Raiders: Guerrillas in the Philippines, 1942-1945. LC 95-20719. (Illus.). 312p. 1996. 27.50 (0-8131-1949-9) U Pr of Ky.

Lapham, Robert W., jt. auth. see Agar, Heather.

Lapham, Samuel, Jr., jt. auth. see Simons, Albert.

Lapham, W. B. Clason, Clawson, Classon, Clesson, Clarson, Stephen Clason of Stamford, Connecticut, in 1654, & Some of His Descendants, Compiled from Data Chiefly Collected by Oliver B. Clason. (Illus.). 160p. 1993. reprint ed. pap. 24.00 (*0-8328-1359-1*); reprint ed. lib. bdg. 34.00 (*0-8328-1358-3*) Higginson Bk Co.

Lapham, William B. Centennial History of Norway, Oxford County, Maine. (Illus.). 822p. 1986. reprint ed. 55.00 (*0-89725-061-3*, 1215) Picton Pr.

— Genealogical Sketches of Robert & John Hazelton & Some of Their Descendants: With Brief Notices of Other New England Families Bearing This Name. (Illus.). 368p. 1989. reprint ed. pap. 55.00 (*0-8328-0650-1*); reprint ed. lib. bdg. 63.00 (*0-8328-0649-8*) Higginson Bk Co.

— History of Bethel (Formerly Sudbury, Canada), Oxford Co., 1768-1890, with a Brief Sketch of Hanover & Family Statistics. (Illus.). 688p. 1997. reprint ed. lib. bdg. 69.50 (*0-8328-5812-9*) Higginson Bk Co.

— History of Bethel, ME, 1768-1890: Formerly Sudbury, Canada, with a Brief Sketch of Hanover. LC 81-82795. (Illus.). 827p. 1986. reprint ed. 50.00 (*0-89725-023-0*, 1199) Picton Pr.

— History of Rumford, Oxford County, Maine from Its First Settlement in 1779 to the Present Time. (Illus.). 432p. 1992. reprint ed. lib. bdg. 45.00 (*0-8328-2521-2*) Higginson Bk Co.

— History of Woodstock, Maine. LC 83-62055. (Illus.). 359p. 1983. reprint ed. 35.00 (*0-89725-041-9*, 1221) Picton Pr.

— History of Woodstock, with Family Sketches & an Appendix. (Illus.). 315p. 1998. reprint ed. lib. bdg. 37.50 (*0-8328-7024-2*) Higginson Bk Co.

Lapham, William B. & Maxim, Silas P. History of Paris, Maine. (Illus.). 816p. 1992. reprint ed. lib. bdg. 44.50 (*0-8328-2528-X*) Higginson Bk Co.

— The History of Paris, Maine. 2nd ed. LC 83-60493. (Illus.). 992p. 1983. 60.00 (*0-89725-037-0*) Picton Pr.

LaPiana, David. Nonprofit Mergers: The Board Responsibility to Consider the Unthinkable, No. 56. 26p. 1994. pap. text 12.00 (*0-925299-32-4*) Natl Ctr Nonprofit.

***LaPiana, David.** The Nonprofit Mergers Workbook: The Leader's Guide to considering, negotiating & Executing a Merger. Hyman, Vincent, ed. 240p. 2000. per. 28.00 (*0-940069-21-0*) A H Wilder.

LaPiana, William P. Logic & Experience: The Origin of Modern American Legal Education. 264p. 1994. text 55.00 (*0-19-507935-3*) OUP.

LaPiana, William P., et al. New York Wills & Trust: 1999 Cumulative Supplement with Disk, 2 vols. 3rd ed. 300p. 1999. 37.00 incl. disk (*0-327-01277-3*, 6892713); ring bd. 74.00 (*0-327-01154-8*, 6892312) LEXIS Pub.

Lapick, Gaetan J. & Geller, Jack. Scientific Fur Servicing: Storage, Cleaning, Repairing & Restyling. LC TS1061.L3. (Illus.). 145p. reprint ed. pap. 45.00 (*0-608-11490-1*, 201175100079) Bks Demand.

Lapicque, F., et al. Electrochemical Engineering & Energy: Proceedings of the Third European Symposium, Held in Nancy, France, March 23-25, 1994. LC 94-44821. (Illus.). 284p. (C). 1995. text 95.00 (*0-306-44887-4*, Kluwer Plenum) Kluwer Academic.

***Lapid, Haim.** Breznitz. 244p. 2000. write for info. (*1-902881-10-9*, Pub. by Toby Pr Ltd); pap. 15.95 (*1-902881-15-X*, Pub. by Toby Pr Ltd) Toby Pr.

Lapid, Yosef & Kratochwil, Friedrich, eds. The Return of Culture & Identity in IR Theory. LC 95-9033. (Critical Perspectives on World Politics Ser.). 255p. (Orig.). 1996. lib. bdg. 49.95 (*1-55587-522-X*, 87522X) L Rienner.

— The Return of Culture & Identity in IR Theory. LC 95-9033. (Critical Perspectives Ser.). 253p. (Orig.). 1996. pap. 19.95 (*1-55587-727-3*, 877273) L Rienner.

Lapide, Phinn E. Hebrew in the Church: The Foundations of Jewish-Christian Dialogue. Rhodes, Erroll F., tr. LC 84-26044. 274p. reprint ed. pap. 85.00 (*0-608-17880-2*, 203273500080) Bks Demand.

Lapide, Phinn E. & Moltmann, Jurgen. Jewish Monotheism & Christian Trinitarian Doctrine: A Dialogue by Pinchas Lapide & Jurgen Moltmann. Swidler, Leonard, tr. LC 80-8058. 93p. reprint ed. pap. 30.00 (*0-608-17983-3*, 202910700058) Bks Demand.

Lapide, Pinchas. The Sermon on the Mount: Utopia or Program for Action? Swidler, Arlene, tr. from GER. LC 85-29810.Tr. of DieBergpre digt-Utopie oder Program?. 160p. (Orig.). reprint ed. pap. 49.60 (*0-8357-2681-9*, 204021700015) Bks Demand.

Lapides, Kenneth. Marx's Wage Theory in Historical Perspective: Its Origins, Development & Interpretation. LC 98-4941. 288p. 1998. 59.95 (*0-275-96271-7*, Praeger Pubs) Greenwood.

Lapides, Kenneth, ed. see Marx, Karl & Engels, Friedrich.

Lapides, Robert, jt. ed. see Adelson, Alan.

Lapidge, Michael. Anglo-Latin Literature, 600-899. LC 96-37649. 520p. 1996. 70.00 (*1-85285-011-6*) Hambledon Press.

— Anglo-Latin Literature, 900-1066. LC 93-20227. 1993. 70.00 (*1-85285-012-4*) Hambledon Press.

Lapidge, Michael, ed. Archbishop Theodore: Commemorative Studies on His Life & Influence. (Cambridge Studies in Anglo-Saxon England: No. 11). 357p. (C). 1995. text 74.95 (*0-521-48077-9*) Cambridge U Pr.

— Columbanus: Studies on the Latin Writings. LC 96-38197. (Studies in Celtic History: Vol. 17). (Illus.). 328p. 1997. 90.00 (*0-85115-667-3*) Boydell & Brewer.

***Lapidge, Michael, et al, eds.** Anglo-Saxon England, Vol. 28. 432p. (C). 2000. Price not set. (*0-521-65203-0*) Cambridge U Pr.

Lapidge, Michael, intro. Bede & His World: The Jarrow Lectures, 1958-1993, 2 vols., Set. (Illus.). 1024p. 1994. 253.95 (*0-86078-449-5*, Pub. by Variorum) Ashgate Pub Co.

Lapidge, Michael & Baker, Peter, eds. Byrhtferth's Enchiridion. (Early English Text Society-Original Ser.: Vol. 15). (Illus.). 614p. (C). 1996. text, suppl. ed. 80.00 (*0-19-722416-4*) OUP.

Lapidge, Michael & Sharpe, Richard. A Bibliography of Celtic-latin Literature, 400-1200 LC 86-125485. xxii, 361 p. 1985. write for info. (*0-901714-43-7*) Royal Irish Acad.

Lapidge, Michael, et al. The Blackwell Encyclopedia of Anglo-Saxon England. LC 98-20814. (Illus.). 640p. 1999. 99.95 (*0-631-15565-1*) Blackwell Pubs.

Lapidge, Michael, jt. auth. see Bischoff, Bernhard.

Lapidge, Michael, ed. see Esposito, Mario.

Lapidge, Michael, jt. ed. see Godden, Malcolm.

Lapidge, Michael, ed. see Lindsay, Wallace M.

Lapidge, Michael, ed. see Wulfstan.

Lapidge, Michael, jt. tr. see Keynes, Simon.

Lapidot, Ema. Borges & Artificial Intelligence: An Analysis in the Style of Pierre Menard. LC 90-5917. (American University Studies: Latin American Literature: Ser. XXII, Vol. 11). IX, 197p. (C). 1991. text 39.95 (*0-8204-1376-3*) P Lang Pubng.

Lapidoth, Ruth. Autonomy: Flexible Solutions to Intrastate Conflicts. LC 96-42468. 1996. 32.50 (*1-878379-63-1*); pap. text 19.95 (*1-878379-62-3*) US Inst Peace.

— The Red Sea & the Gulf of Aden. 1982. lib. bdg. 150.50 (*90-247-2501-1*) Kluwer Academic.

Lapidoth, Ruth, ed. The Jerusalem Question & Its Resolution: Selected Documents. 576p. (C). 1994. lib. bdg. 173.50 (*0-7923-2893-0*) Kluwer Academic.

Lapidoth, Ruth & Hirsh, Moshe. The Arab-Israel Conflict & Its Resolution: Selected Documents. 388p. (C). 1992. lib. bdg. 151.00 (*0-7923-1300-3*) Kluwer Academic.

Lapidus, B. A. & Shevtsoka, S. V. The Learner's Russian-English Dictionary. (ENG & RUS.). 550p. 1977. 19.95 (*0-8288-5452-1*, M9117) Fr & Eur.

Lapidus, Gail W., ed. The Nationality Question in the Soviet Union. LC 92-3618. (Articles on Russian & Soviet History, 1500-1991 Ser.: Vol. 11). 920320p. 1992. text 68.00 (*0-8153-0568-0*) Garland.

— The New Russia: Troubled Transformation. 320p. (C). 1994. pap. 28.00 (*0-8133-2077-1*, Pub. by Westview) HarpC.

— Women, Work, & Family in the Soviet Union. LC 81-9281. 358p. reprint ed. pap. 111.00 (*0-8357-2620-7*, 204010800014) Bks Demand.

Lapidus, Gail W., et al, eds. From Union to Commonwealth: Nationalism & Separatism in the Soviet Republics. (Soviet Paperbacks Ser.: No. 6). 141p. (C). 1992. text 54.95 (*0-521-41706-6*); pap. text 16.95 (*0-521-42716-9*) Cambridge U Pr.

Lapidus, Gail W. & De Wevers, Renee, eds. Nationalism, Ethnic Identity & Conflict Management in Russia Today. LC 96-164644. 98p. 1995. pap. 15.00 (*0-935371-37-0*) CFISAC.

Lapidus, Gail W. & Swanson, Guy E., eds. State & Welfare, U. S. A. - U. S. S. R. Contemporary Policy & Practice. LC 88-15444. (Research Ser.: No. 71). (Illus.). xxii, 467p. 1988. pap. text 22.50 (*0-87725-171-1*) U of Cal IAS.

Lapidus, I. I. & Drobot, D. V. Design of Engineering Technology: Principles & Approaches. 200p. 2000. 99.00 (*1-898326-75-4*, Pub. by CISP) Balogh.

Lapidus, Ira M. Contemporary Islamic Movements in Historical Perspective. LC 83-82308. (Policy Papers in International Affairs: No. 18). viii, 66p. (C). 1983. pap. text 6.50 (*0-87725-518-0*) U of Cal IAS.

— A History of Islamic Societies. (Illus.). 1040p. 1988. text 90.00 (*0-521-22552-3*) Cambridge U Pr.

— A History of Islamic Societies. 1034p. 1990. pap. text 32.95 (*0-521-29549-1*) Cambridge U Pr.

Lapidus, Ira M., jt. ed. see Burke, Edmund, III.

Lapidus, Jacqueline. Ready to Survive. LC 75-9593. 24p. 1975. pap. 4.00 (*0-914610-04-X*) Hanging Loose.

— Ultimate Conspiracy: Poems. 84p. (Orig.). 1987. pap. 7.95 (*0-9619598-0-0*) Lynx Pubns.

Lapidus, Joellen. Lapidus on Dulcimer. (Illus.). 228p. (Orig.). 1978. pap. 9.95 (*0-89705-007-X*) Almo Pubns.

LaPidus, Jules B., jt. ed. see Kohl, Kay J.

Lapidus, June, jt. auth. see Hartmann, Heidi.

Lapidus, Leon & Pinder, George F. Numerical Solution of Partial Differential Equations in Science & Engineering. LC 81-16491. 696p. 1982. 199.50 (*0-471-09866-3*) Wiley.

— Numerical Solution of Partial Differential Equations in Science & Engineering. 677p. 1999. pap. 79.95 (*0-471-35944-0*) Wiley.

Lapidus, M. Bilingual Glossary of Business Terms. (ENG & SPA.). 213p. 1982. pap. 14.95 (*0-8288-0133-9*, S 19416) Fr & Eur.

Lapidus, M., jt. auth. see Johnson, G.

Lapidus, Michel L. & Van Frankenhuysen, M. Fractal Geometry & Number Theory: Complex Dimensions of Fractal Strings & Zeros of Zeta-Functions. LC 99-51583. (Illus.). 205p. 2000. 54.95 (*0-8176-4098-3*, Pub. by Birkhauser) Spr-Verlag.

Lapidus, Michel L., jt. auth. see Andersson, S. I.

Lapidus, Michel L., jt. auth. see He, Christina Q.

Lapidus, Michel L., jt. auth. see Johnson, Gerald W.

Lapidus, Michel L., ed. see Shapiro, Victor L. & Contemporary Mathematics Staff.

Lapidus, Mikhail C., et al. Business in the Russian Free Market. Jezmir, Leonid, tr. from RUS. LC 95-94101. 244p. (Orig.). (C). 1995. pap. 24.95 (*0-9645464-1-8*) MIR Hse.

Lapidus, Mikhail K. & Van De Waal-Palms, Pyotr J. Understanding Russian Banking: Russian Banking System, Securities Market, & Money Settlements. Corbin, Michael D. & Trittin, Paul S., eds. Jezmir, Leonid, tr. from RUS. LC 97-74538. 314p. (C). 1998. pap., per. 34.95 (*0-9645464-2-6*) MIR Hse.

Lapidus, Morris. Architect of the American Dream. 1996. 48.00 (*3-7643-2559-3*) Birkhauser.

Lapidus, Morris. Too Much Is Never Enough: The Autobiography of Morris Lapidus, Architect. LC 96-13259. (Illus.). 304p. 1996. 45.00 (*0-8478-1978-7*, Pub. by Rizzoli Intl) St Martin.

Lapidus, Richard, jt. auth. see Hickey, Michael M.

Lapidus, Roxanne, tr. see Finkielkraut, Alain.

Lapidus, Roxanne, tr. see Serres, Michael.

Lapidus, Todd. High-Impact Training: Getting Results & Respect. LC 99-47338. 208p. 1999. 34.95 incl. disk (*0-7879-4642-7*) Jossey-Bass.

Lapier, Terrence. Competition, Growth Strategies, & the Globalization of Services: Real Estate Advisory Services in Japan, Europe, & the United States. LC 97-45903. (Illus.). 272p. (C). 1998. 90.00 (*0-415-16924-0*) Routledge.

Lapiere, Charles M. & Krieg, Thomas, eds. Connective Tissue Diseases of the Skin. (Basic & Clinical Dermatology Ser.: Vol. 9). (Illus.). 408p. 1993. text 199.00 (*0-8247-9133-9*) Dekker.

***LaPierre, Alexandra.** Artemisa. 1999. 29.95 (*84-08-02943-6*) Planeta.

— Artemisia. 544p. 2000. 25.00 (*0-8021-1672-8*, Grove) Grove-Atltic.

LaPierre, Alexandra. Fanny Stevenson: A Romance of Destiny. Cosman, Carol, tr. (Illus.). 520p. 1995. 26.00 (*0-7867-0127-7*) Carroll & Graf.

Lapierre, Andre. L' Ontario Francais du Sud-Quest: Temoignages Oraux. LC 82-226547. (Cahiers du Centre de Recherche en Civilisation Canadienne-Francaise: Vol. 20). (FRE.). 659p. 1982. reprint ed. pap. 200.00 (*0-608-01987-9*, 206264300003) Bks Demand.

Lapierre, Bob. Bouki ak Malis: Haitian Folktale in Haitian Creole. Vilsaint, Fequiere, ed. 68p. (YA). (gr. 8-12). 1993. pap. 10.00 (*1-881839-42-7*) Educa Vision.

Lapierre, Dominique. Beyond Love. 1992. mass mkt. 12.99 (*0-446-39346-0*, Pub. by Warner Bks) Little.

— The City of Joy. 544p. 1988. mass mkt. 7.99 (*0-446-35556-9*, Pub. by Warner Bks) Little.

***Lapierre, Dominique.** A Thousand Suns. 496p. 2000. mass mkt. 14.95 (*0-446-67595-4*, Pub. by Warner Bks) Little.

Lapierre, Dominique. A Thousand Suns: Witness to History. LC 98-39026. (Illus.). 482p. 1999. 25.00 (*0-446-52535-9*, Pub. by Warner Bks) Little.

Lapierre, Dominique, jt. auth. see Collins, Larry.

***Lapierre, Janet.** Baby Mine: A Port Silva Mystery. LC 99-12940. 256p. 1999. pap. 12.95 (*1-880284-32-4*) J Daniel.

Lapierre, Janet. Children's Games. 1990. mass mkt. 3.50 (*0-373-26052-0*) Harlequin Bks.

— The Cruel Mother. 1991. reprint ed. per. 3.95 (*0-373-26078-4*) Harlequin Bks.

— Grandmother's House. (Mystery Ser.). 1993. per. 3.99 (*0-373-26120-9*, 1-26120-5) Harlequin Bks.

— Old Enemies. 256p. 1993. text 20.00 (*0-684-19614-X*, Scribners Ref) Mac Lib Ref.

Lapierre, L. Vancouver. Date not set. mass mkt. 6.99 (*0-06-109799-3*) HarpC.

LaPierre, Laurier. Sir Wilfred Laurier & the Romance of Canada. 512p. 1996. 29.95 (*0-7737-2979-8*) Stoddart Publ.

— Sir Wilfred Laurier & the Romance of Canada. 512p. 1997. 19.95 (*0-7737-5916-6*) Stoddart Publ.

***Lapierre, Lise.** Le Participe Passe en Francais. (Leipzinger Fachsprachen-Studien: Bd. 13). (Illus.). 175p. 1998. 38.00 (*3-631-33223-8*) P Lang Pubng.

Lapierre, Louis L. Human Rights & Civil Rights: Index of New Information with Authors, Subjects & References. 159p. 1997. 47.50 (*0-7883-1466-1*); pap. 44.50 (*0-7883-1467-X*) ABBE Pubs Assn.

***Lapierre, Michael J.** The Noetical Theory of Gabriel Vasquez, Jesuit Philosopher & Theologian (1549-1604) His View of the Objective Concept. LC 99-45518. (Studies in the History of Philosophy: Vol. 53). 132p. 1999. text 69.95 (*0-7734-7888-4*) E Mellen.

LaPierre, Wayne. Guns, Crime & Freedom. 264p. 1994. 22.95 (*0-89526-477-3*) Regnery Pub.

LaPietra, Mary. The Disguise of Love, No. 21. (Serenade Serenata Ser.). 1985. pap. 2.50 (*0-310-46812-4*, 15540P) Zondervan.

Lapillone, B., jt. auth. see Chateau, B.

Lapin. Modern Engineering. (Statistics Ser.). 1997. pap., student ed. write for info. (*0-534-50885-5*) PWS Pubs.

— Modern Engineering Statistics. (Statistics Ser.). 1997. pap., student ed. 17.95 (*0-534-50884-7*) Wadsworth Pub.

— Probability & Stats F/modern Engineers. (Statistics). 1983. 38.25 (*0-534-01460-7*) Brooks-Cole.

— Quantative Methods. 6th ed. (C). 1994. pap. text 33.50 (*0-03-097816-5*) Harcourt Coll Pubs.

— Quantitative Methods. 6th ed. 1995. 191.00 (*0-534-51052-3*) Brooks-Cole.

— Quantitative Methods. 6th ed. 1995. teacher ed. 9.25 (*0-534-51055-8*) Brooks-Cole.

— QuickQuant Plus. 1994. wbk. ed. 34.95 incl. disk (*1-880075-05-9*) Alamo Pub.

— QuickQuant Plus: Version 4. 1994. wbk. ed. 24.95 (*1-880075-02-4*) Alamo Pub.

— QuickQuant Plus Package to Accompany QuickQuantPlus, Version 4.1 for MS-DOS PC. (C). 1994. wbk. ed. 34.95 incl. disk (*1-880075-03-2*) Alamo Pub.

— QuickQuant Plus Package, Version 4.1 for MS-DOS PC. (C). 1994. wbk. ed. 34.95 incl. disk (*1-880075-04-0*) Alamo Pub.

— Sm Prob Stat F/ Modern Engineer. (Statistics). 1983. student ed. 7.50 (*0-534-01461-5*) Brooks-Cole.

Lapin, Daniel. America's Real War. LC 98-50359. 320p. 1999. 19.99 (*1-57673-366-1*) Multnomah Pubs.

— America's Real War: An Orthodox Rabbi Insists That Judeo-Christian Values Are Vital for Our Nation's Survival. 375p. 2000. pap. 12.99 (*1-57673-655-5*) Multnomah Pubs.

— The Vampire, Dracula & Incest: The Vampire Myth, Stoker's Dracula, & Psychotherapy of Vampiric Sexual Abuse. LC 95-75221. 252p. (Orig.). 1995. pap. 14.95 (*0-9644983-0-8*) Gargoyle Pub.

***Lapin, Gloria.** Fun Times: Little Books to Make & Read with Other. (ps-3). 1999. pap. 0.00 (*1-55254-019-7*) Brighter Vision.

Lapin, Hayim, ed. Religious & Ethnic Communities in Later Roman Palestine. LC 98-29098. (Studies & Texts in Jewish History & Culture, the Joseph & Rebecca Meyerhoff Center for Jewish Studies: No. 5). 305p. (C). 1998. 35.00 (*1-883053-51-5*) Univ Pr MD.

Lapin, Lawrence L. Business Statistics. LC 84-6690. (College Outline Ser.). 341p. (C). 1984. pap. text 13.25 (*0-15-601553-6*) Harcourt Coll Pubs.

— The Home Owner's Guide to Making a Fortune. (Illus.). 168p. 1981. 12.95 (*0-9605140-0-7*) Alamo Pr.

— Instructor's Manual to Accompany Statistics for Modern Business Decisions. 296p. (C). 1995. teacher ed. write for info. (*0-03-013803-5*) Dryden Pr.

— Modern Engineering Statistics. LC 96-35230. (Statistics Ser.). (C). 1997. pap. 91.95 (*0-534-50883-9*) Wadsworth Pub.

— Probability & Statistics for Modern Engineering. 2nd ed. (Illus.). 810p. (C). 1998. reprint ed. text 69.95 (*0-88133-996-2*) Waveland Pr.

— Quantitative Methods for Business Decisions: With Cases. 6th ed. (Illus.). 1250p. (C). 1995. pap. 75.95 (*0-534-51051-5*) Wadsworth Pub.

— Statistics for Modern Business: A First Course. 678p. (C). 1995. pap. 67.95 (*0-534-51117-1*) Wadsworth Pub.

— Statistics for Modern Business Decisions. 5th ed. 1021p. (C). 1990. disk. write for info. (*0-318-67019-4*) Dryden Pr.

— Statistics for Modern Business Decisions. 6th ed. (Business Statistics Ser.). 1993. pap., suppl. ed. 23.95 (*0-534-51064-7*) Wadsworth Pub.

— Statistics for Modern Business Decisions: International Edition. 5th ed. 1021p. (C). 1990. write for info. (*0-318-67020-8*) Dryden Pr.

Lapin, Lawrence L. & Whisler, William D. Cases in Management Science. (Business Statistics Ser.). 300p. (C). 1996. pap. 29.95 (*0-534-51425-1*) Wadsworth Pub.

***Lapin, Lee.** The Covert Catalog, 2000: Survillance, Covert Entry, & Investigative Equipment Suppliers. (Illus.). 210p. 1999. pap. 34.95 (*1-880231-19-0*) Intelligence.

— Hands-On Countermeasures: State-of-the-Art Electronic Surveillance Countermeasures. (Illus.). 90p. 1993. pap. 22.95 (*1-880231-15-8*) Intelligence.

— Hands-On Electronic Surveillance. 54p. 1992. pap. 22.95 (*1-880231-14-X*) Intelligence.

Lapin, Lee. How to Get Anything on Anybody. (Illus.). 272p. 1987. 40.00 (*0-87364-594-4*) Paladin Pr.

***Lapin, Lee.** How to Get Anything on Anybody, Bk. III. (Illus.). 342p. 2000. pap. 49.95 (*1-880231-13-1*) Intelligence.

Lapin, Lee. How to Get Anything on Anybody, Bk. 11. 1991. pap. 34.95 (*1-880231-00-X*) Intelligence.

— The Whole Spy Catalog: A Research Encyclopedia for Researchers, PIs, Spies & Generally Nosy People. (Illus.). 440p. 1995. pap. 44.95 (*1-880231-10-7*) Intelligence.

Lapin, Mark. The Pledge of Allegiance. large type ed. LC 91-18381. 396p. 1991. reprint ed. 19.95 (*1-56054-195-4*) Thorndike Pr.

Lapin, Terence W. The Mosin-Nagant Rifle. (For Collectors Only Ser.). (Illus.). 200p. 1998. pap. 19.95 (*1-882391-21-7*) N Cape Pubns.

***Lapin, Terence W., ed.** The Soviet Mosin-Nagant Manual: The Official Soviet Military Handbook for the M1891/30 Rifle & the M1938 & M1944 Carbines. (Illus.). vii, 136p. 1999. pap. 15.95 (*0-9676896-0-0*) Hyrax Pubs.

Lapina, Ronald P. Estimating Centrifugal Compressor Performance Vol. 1: Process Compressor Technology. fac. ed. LC 82-3124. (Illus.). 221p. 1982. reprint ed. pap. 68.60 (*0-608-00975-X*, 206182900001) Bks Demand.

— Process Compressor Technology, Vol. 2. LC 82-3124. 351p. 1983. reprint ed. pap. 108.90 (*0-608-01575-X*, 206199500002) Bks Demand.

Lapine, James. Sunday in the Park with George. (Musical Library). (Illus.). 256p. 1991. 19.95 (*1-55783-067-3*); pap. 9.95 (*1-55783-068-1*) Applause Theatre Bk Pubs.

— Twelve Dreams. rev. ed. 1996. pap. 5.25 (*0-8222-1506-3*) Dramatists Play.

Lapine, James & Sondheim, Stephen. Into the Woods. LC 89-4402. 160p. 1998. reprint ed. pap. 10.95 (*0-930452-93-3*) Theatre Comm.

— Passion. LC 94-26688. 112p. 1994. 22.50 (*1-55936-087-9*); pap. 10.95 (*1-55936-088-7*) Theatre Comm.

Lapine, James, et al. Wordplays 5: New American Drama. (Wordplays Ser.). 188p. 1986. pap. 15.95 (*1-55554-007-4*) PAJ Pubns.

Lapine, Jennifer & Lapine, Susan. My First Hebrew Alphabet Book. (Illus.). 48p. (J). (ps-1). 1977. pap. 3.95 (*0-8197-0399-0*) Bloch.

Lapine, Kenneth M. Consumer Credit: Laws Transaction & Forms, 4 vols. 1984. ring bd. 720.00 (*0-8205-1084-X*) Bender.

Lapine, Susan, jt. auth. see Lapine, Jennifer.

Lapine, Warren. Absolute Magnitude Anthology. 1998. pap. 16.95 (*0-312-86449-3*) St Martin.

Laping, Francis & Knight, Hans. Remember Hungary, 1956: A Pictorial History of the Hungarian Revolution. (Illus.). 381p. 1992. 45.00 (*0-912404-01-9*) Alpha Pubns.

Lapinksi, Mike. Radical Elk Hunting Strategies. (Illus.). 162p. 1988. 19.95 (*0-912299-41-X*); pap. 14.95 (*0-912299-42-8*) Stoneydale Pr Pub.

Lapinski, Kathie, jt. auth. see Lipinski, Bob.

Lapinski, Kathie, jt. auth. see Lipsinski, Bob.

***Lapinski, Mike.** Elk Mystique. 1998. pap. 19.95 (*0-912299-73-8*) Stoneydale Pr Pub.

Lapinski, Mike. High Pressure Elk Hunting: Secrets of Hunting Educated Elk. (Illus.). 192p. 1996. 19.95 (*0-912299-63-0*); pap. 14.95 (*0-912299-64-9*) Stoneydale Pr Pub.

— Seasonal Pro Trapping. (Illus.). 150p. 1991. pap. 13.95 (*0-912299-48-7*) Stoneydale Pr Pub.

***Lapinski, Mike.** Self Defense for Nature Lovers Handling Dangerous Situations with Wild Critters. 144p. 1998. pap. 12.95 (*0-912299-77-0*) Stoneydale Pr Pub.

Lapinski, Mike. Western Hunting Guide. (Illus.). 172p. 1989. 19.95 (*0-912299-43-6*); pap. 14.95 (*0-912299-44-4*) Stoneydale Pr Pub.

Lapinski, Mike, et al. All about Elk. Miller, Bill, ed. LC 86-63878. (Hunter's Information Ser.). (Illus.). 253p. 1987. write for info. (*0-914697-07-2*) N Amer Outdoor Grp.

Lapirov, Il'ia. Vek: Kniga Stikhov. LC 85-63414. (RUS.). 208p. (Orig.). 1986. pap. 14.00 (*0-89830-108-4*) Russica Pubs.

Lapis, K., ed. Developments of Cancer Chemotherapy. (Journal: Oncology: Vol. 37, Suppl. 1). (Illus.). iv, 120p. 1980. pap. 28.75 (*3-8055-1588-X*) S Karger.

Lapis, K. & Eckhardt, S. Lectures & Symposia of the 14th International Cancer Congress Vol. 1: Cancer Research & Treatment Today: Results, Trends & Frontiers. 266p. (C). 1987. 150.00 (*963-05-4523-3*, Pub. by Akade Kiado) St Mut.

— Lectures & Symposia of the 14th International Cancer Congress Vol. 2: Molecular Biology & Differentiation of Cancer Cells, Oncogenes, Growth Factors, Receptors. 361p. (C). 1987. 190.00 (*963-05-4524-1*, Pub. by Akade Kiado) St Mut.

— Lectures & Symposia of the 14th International Cancer Congress Vol. 3: Cytology, Pathology & Cancer Prognosis. 219p. (C). 1987. 130.00 (*963-05-4525-X*, Pub. by Akade Kiado) St Mut.

— Lectures & Symposia of the 14th International Cancer Congress Vol. 5: Novel Approaches in Cancer Therapy. 387p. (C). 1987. 174.00 (*963-05-4527-6*, Pub. by Akade Kiado) St Mut.

— Lectures & Symposia of the 14th International Cancer Congress Vol. 6: Epidemiology, Prevention, Diagnosis. 365p. (C). 1987. 174.00 (*963-05-4528-4*, Pub. by Akade Kiado) St Mut.

— Lectures & Symposia of the 14th International Cancer Congress Vol. 7: Oncological Surgery. 223p. (C). 1987. 130.00 (*963-05-4529-2*, Pub. by Akade Kiado) St Mut.

— Lectures & Symposia of the 14th International Cancer Congress Vol. 8: Radiotherapy, Paediatric Oncology, Neurooncology. 352p. (C). 1987. 180.00 (*963-05-4530-6*, Pub. by Akade Kiado) St Mut.

— Lectures & Symposia of the 14th International Cancer Congress Vol. 10: Biological Response Modifiers, Leukaemias & Lymphomas. 133p. (C). 1987. 75.00 (*963-05-4532-2*, Pub. by Akade Kiado) St Mut.

— Lectures & Symposia of the 14th International Cancer Congress Vol. 11: Medical Oncology. 339p. (C). 1987. 168.00 (*963-05-4533-0*, Pub. by Akade Kiado) St Mut.

— Lectures & Symposia of the 14th International Cancer Congress Vol. 13: Education, Nursing, Organization. 336p. (C). 1987. 168.00 (*963-05-4535-7*, Pub. by Akade Kiado) St Mut.

— Lectures & Symposia of the 14th International Cancer Congress, 13 vols., Set. (C). 1987. 1875.00 (*963-05-4522-5*) St Mut.

Lapis, K. & Eckhardt, S., eds. Lectures & Symposia of the 14th International Cancer Congress Vol. 4: Carcinogenesis & Tumour Progression. 334p. (C). 1987. 168.00 (*963-05-4526-8*, Pub. by Akade Kiado) St Mut.

— Lectures & Symposia of the 14th International Cancer Congress Vol. 9: Anticancer Drug Research. 256p. 1987. 132.00 (*963-05-4531-4*, Pub. by Akade Kiado) St Mut.

— Lectures & Symposia of the 14th International Cancer Congress Vol. 12: Endocrine Aspects of Malignancies. 293p. (C). 1987. 168.00 (*963-05-4534-9*) St Mut.

Lapis, K. & Jeney, A. Regulation & Control of Cell Proliferation. 512p. (C). 1984. 162.00 (*963-05-3246-8*, Pub. by Akade Kiado) St Mut.

Lapis, Karoly, et al, eds. Biochemistry & Molecular Genetics of Cancer Metastasis. (Developments in Oncology Ser.). 1986. text 127.00 (*0-89838-785-X*) Kluwer Academic.

Lapisardi, Frederick S., ed. see Gore-Booth, Eva.

Lapitajs, Gaida, tr. see Gunzler, H., ed.

Lapitajs, Gaida, tr. see Unzler, Helmut G., ed.

Lapitskii, A., jt. auth. see Stupin, L.

Lapkin, Sharon, ed. French Second-Language Education in Canada: Empirical Studies. LC 99-183428. (Illus.). 336p. 1998. text 70.00 (*0-8020-4333-X*) U of Toronto Pr.

Lapkus, Dānas, ed. & intro. see Paskevicius, Mykolas.

Laplaca, Annette. Finding Your Real ID. 112p. 1998. pap. text 7.99 (*0-87788-233-9*, H Shaw Pubs) Waterbrook Pr.

— A Truly Terrific Grandparent. LC 97-15007. 1997. pap. text 5.99 (*0-87788-241-X*, H Shaw Pubs) Waterbrook Pr.

LaPlaca, Annette H. Are We Almost There? The Kids' Book of Travel Fun. (Illus.). 48p. (Orig.). (J). (gr. 1-5). 1992. pap. text, wbk. ed. 5.99 (*0-87788-051-4*, H Shaw Pubs) Waterbrook Pr.

— How Long 'til Christmas? The Kid's Book of Holiday Fun. (Illus.). 48p. (Orig.). (J). (gr. 3-6). 1993. pap., wbk. ed. 5.99 (*0-87788-369-6*, H Shaw Pubs) Waterbrook Pr.

— The Sunday Morning Fun Book. LC 95-224073. (Illus.). 48p. (J). 1995. pap. 5.99 (*0-87788-569-9*, H Shaw Pubs) Waterbrook Pr.

LaPlaca, Annette H., compiled by. Graduate's Celebration Book of Wit & Wisdom. LC 95-53696. 96p. 1996. pap. 5.99 (*0-87788-814-0*, H Shaw Pubs) Waterbrook Pr.

— Mom's Appreciation Book of Wit & Wisdom. 96p. 1996. pap. 5.99 (*0-87788-548-6*, H Shaw Pubs) Waterbrook Pr.

LaPlaca, Annette H., jt. compiled by see Laplaca, David.

Laplaca, David & LaPlaca, Annette H., compiled by. Dad's Appreciation Book of Wit & Wisdom. LC 95-54016. 96p. 1996. pap. 5.99 (*0-87788-237-1*, H Shaw Pubs) Waterbrook Pr.

Laplaca, Michael. Easter Decorations: Make & Color Your Own. (J). (ps-3). 1997. pap. 1.95 (*0-89375-647-4*) Troll Communs.

LaPlaca, Michael. How to Draw Boats, Trains, & Planes. LC 81-52123. (Illus.). 32p. (J). (gr. 2-6). 1982. lib. bdg. 17.25 (*0-89375-682-2*) Troll Communs.

— How to Draw Boats, Trains, & Planes. LC 81-52123. (Illus.). 32p. (J). (gr. 2-6). 1996. pap. 2.95 (*0-89375-497-8*) Troll Communs.

— How to Draw Cars & Trucks. LC 81-52122. (Illus.). 32p. (J). (gr. 2-6). 1982. lib. bdg. 17.25 (*0-89375-681-4*) Troll Communs.

— How to Draw Cars & Trucks. LC 81-52122. (Illus.). 32p. (J). (gr. 2-6). 1996. pap. 2.95 (*0-89375-498-6*) Troll Communs.

— How to Draw Dinosaurs. LC 81-52118. (Illus.). 32p. (J). (gr. 2-6). 1982. lib. bdg. 17.25 (*0-89375-683-0*) Troll Communs.

— How to Draw Dinosaurs. LC 81-52118. (How to Draw Ser.). (Illus.). 32p. (J). (gr. 2-7). 1996. pap. 2.95 (*0-89375-496-X*) Troll Communs.

Laplaca, Michael. How to Draw Dinosaurs. 1982. 7.15 (*0-606-01058-0*, Pub. by Turtleback) Demco.

Laplace, Jean. Prayer According to the Scriptures. 85p. 1991. pap. 8.95 (*1-85390-167-9*, Pub. by Veritas Pubns) St Mut.

LaPlace, Jean. Preparing for Spiritual Direction. 192p. 1975. pap. 4.95 (*0-8199-0550-X*, Frncscn Herld) Franciscan Pr.

Laplace, Marquis De, see Simon, Pierre & De Laplace, Marquis.

Laplace, Marquis Pierre Simon De. Celestial Mechanics, Vol. 5. LC 63-11316. 1969. reprint ed. text 39.50 (*0-8284-0214-0*) Chelsea Pub.

— Celestial Mechanics, 4 vols., Vols. 1-4. LC 69-11316. text 250.00 (*0-8284-0194-2*) Chelsea Pub.

— Philosophical Essays on Probabilities, 13. Toomer, G. J., ed. Dale, Andrew I., tr. LC 94-25497. 270p. 1994. 79.95 (*0-387-94349-8*) Spr-Verlag.

Laplace, P. S., jt. auth. see Lavoisier, A. L.

Laplace, Theodore, jt. auth. see Pierre, Cyrille.

***LaPlace, Viana.** Verdura: Vegetables Italian-Style. LC 99-89332. (Illus.). 400p. 2000. 30.00 (*0-06-019598-3*, Ecco Press) HarperTrade.

Laplanche, Jean. Life & Death in Psychoanalysis. LC 75-36928. 160p. reprint ed. pap. 49.60 (*0-608-12099-5*, 202413800035) Bks Demand.

— Life & Death in Psychoanalysis. Mehlman, Jeffrey, tr. from FRE. LC 75-36928. 160p. 1985. reprint ed. pap. text 12.95 (*0-8018-2730-2*) Johns Hopkins.

— Das Vokabular der Psychoanalyse: The Vocabulary of Psychoanalysis, 2 vols. (GER.). 1973. pap. 49.95 (*0-8288-6340-7*, M-7680) Fr & Eur.

Laplanche, Jean & Fletcher, John. Essays on Otherness. LC 98-11837. (Warwick Studies in European Philosophy Ser.). 272p. (C). 1998. 85.00 (*0-415-13107-3*) Routledge.

***Laplanche, Jean & Fletcher, John.** Essays on Otherness. LC 98-11837. (Warwick Studies in European Philosophy Ser.). vii, 279p. (C). 1999. pap. 24.99 (*0-415-13108-1*) Routledge.

Laplanche, Jean & Pontalis, Jean-Baptiste. The Language of Psycho-Analysis. Micholson-Smith, Donald, tr. from FRE. LC 73-18418. 510p. (C). 1974. 50.00 (*0-393-01105-4*) Norton.

Laplanche, Jean & Pontalis, Jean-Bertrand. Diccionario del Psicoanalisis. 3rd deluxe ed. Cervantes Gimeno, Fernando, ed. (SPA.). 558p. 1977. 65.50 (*0-7859-0894-3*, S-31445) Fr & Eur.

Laplanche, Jean, jt. auth. see Pontalis, Jean-Baptiste.

Laplanche, Jean, ed. see Pontalis, Jean-Baptiste.

LaPlanche, Shirley, photos by. Stepping Lightly on Australia: A Traveller's Guide to Ecotourism. LC 95-43033. (Illus.). 208p. 1996. pap. 14.95 (*1-56440-904-X*) Globe Pequot.

***LaPlant, Ralph & Sharpe, Amy.** Outdoor & Survival Skills for Nature Photographers. (Illus.). 80p. 2000. pap. 17.95 (*1-58428-017-4*) Amherst Media.

LaPlant, Sarah, jt. auth. see Franklin, Carleen.

Laplante. Real-Time Programming, 1995. LC 96-227020. (IFAC Postprint Ser.). 220p. Date not set. pap. 69.25 (*0-08-042590-9*, Pergamon Pr) Elsevier.

LaPlante, Alice & Seidner, Rich. Playing for Profit: How Digital Entertainment Is Making Big Business Out of Child's Play. LC 98-33166. (Upside Magazine Ser.). 287p. 1999. 29.95 (*0-471-29614-7*) Wiley.

LaPlante, Alice, jt. auth. see La Plante, Clare.

Laplante, Dan & Laplante, Roberta. New England's Best Family Getaways: A Guide to Child-Friendly Inns & B&B's. (Illus.). 192p. (Orig.). 1996. pap. 14.95 (*0-924771-73-9*, Covered Brdge Pr) Douglas Charles Ltd.

LaPlante, Dan & LaPlante, Roberta. New England's Best Family Getaways: Country Inns & Bed & Breakfasts. 2nd rev. ed. LC 94-69865. (Illus.). 300p. (Orig.). 1995. pap. 14.95 (*0-9632294-1-9*) Columbine Pub.

LaPlante, John D. Asian Art. 3rd ed. 304p. (C). 1992. text. write for info. (*0-697-11591-7*) Brown & Benchmark.

LaPlante, Joseph A., jt. auth. see Tait, Colin C.

LaPlante, Josephine M. & Durham, Taylor R. An Introduction to Benefit-Cost Analysis for Evaluating Public Expenditure Alternatives. (Learning Packages in the Policy Sciences Ser.: No. 22). (Illus.). 74p. (C). 1983. pap. text 10.50 (*0-936826-17-7*) PS Assocs Croton.

LaPlante, Joy. Angel Gabriel a True Story. 175p. 1999. pap. 14.95 (*0-9670356-0-0*) J LaPlante.

Laplante, Lisa I. & Kinsley, Carol W., eds. Things That Work in Community Service Learning, Vol. 1. 160p. (Orig.). 1994. pap. 20.00 (*0-9644330-0-1*) Comm Srv Lrning.

LaPlante, Philip. Electrical Engineering Dictionary, CRCnetBase 1999. 750p. 1998. 129.00 incl. cd-rom (*0-8493-9765-0*) CRC Pr.

Laplante, Phillip. The Comprehensive Dictionary of Electrical Engineering. 720p. 1998. boxed set 94.95 (*0-8493-3128-5*) CRC Pr.

Laplante, Phillip. Design & Application of Real-time Systems. 1997. pap. text 351.00 (*0-7803-2339-4*) IEEE Comp Soc.

Laplante, Phillip. Easy PC Maintenance & Repair. 2nd ed. LC 94-37455. 232p. 1994. pap. 19.95 (*0-07-036433-8*, Windcrest) TAB Bks.

***Laplante, Phillip, ed.** Real-Time Systems: Selected Readings. 400p. 1999. 69.95 (*0-7803-4815-X*) Inst Electrical.

Laplante, Phillip A. Design & Application of Real-Time Systems. 100p. 1997. pap. 259.00 (*0-7803-2343-2*, HL5742) Inst Electrical.

— Keys to Successful Software Development: Selected Readings. 350p. 1999. pap. text 69.95 (*0-7803-4803-6*) IEEE Standards.

Laplante, Phillip A. Real-Time Systems Design & Analysis: An Engineer's Handbook. 2nd ed. LC 96-29044. 384p. 1996. 69.95 (*0-7803-3400-0*, PC5383) Inst Electrical.

Laplante, Phillip A. & Stoyenko, Alexander D., eds. Real-Time Imaging: Theory, Techniques, & Application. 328p. 1996. 79.95 (*0-7803-1068-3*, PC4242) Inst Electrical.

Laplante, Phillip A., et al. Real-Time Imaging: 29-30 January, 1996, San Jose, California. LC 95-72256. (Proceedings Ser.). viii, 178p. 1996. pap. write for info. (*0-8194-2035-2*) SPIE.

Laplante, Phillip A., jt. auth. see Dougherty, Edward R.

***LaPlante, Robert J.** The Ten Million Mile Man. (Illus.). 120p. 1999. 19.95 (*1-58244-026-3*) Rutledge Bks.

Laplante, Roberta, jt. auth. see Laplante, Dan.

LaPlante, Roberta, jt. auth. see LaPlante, Dan.

***LaPlante, Royal.** The Myrtlewood Grove-Revisited. Inbody, Mary, ed. 226p. 2000. pap. 12.95 (*1-58275-015-7*) Black Forest Pr.

LaPlante, Royal. Penalomah: The Eagle Soars. (Illus.). 278p. 1997. pap. 12.95 (*1-881116-88-3*) Black Forest Pr.

LaPlantz, David. Artists Anodizing Aluminum. LC 87-61000. (Illus.). 200p. (Orig.). 1988. pap. 19.95 (*0-942002-03-2*) Press LaPlantz.

LaPlantz, David, ed. Jewelry - Metalwork 1991 Survey: Visions - Concepts - Communication. (Illus.). 160p. (Orig.). (C). 1991. pap. text 19.95 (*0-942002-05-9*) Press LaPlantz.

LaPlantz, David & LaPlantz, Shereen, eds. Jewelry-Metalwork Survey: A Way of Communicating, No. 2. (Illus.). 224p. 1992. pap. text 24.95 (*0-942002-07-5*) Press LaPlantz.

Laplantz, Shereen. Cover to Cover. 1998. pap. 16.95 (*0-676-57287-1*) Random.

LaPlantz, Shereen. Cover to Cover: Creative Techniques for Making Beautiful Books, Journals & Albums. Dierks, Leslie, ed. LC 94-24439. (Illus.). 144p. 1995. 24.95 (*0-937274-81-X*) Lark Books.

— Cover to Cover: Creative Techniques for Making Beautiful Books, Journals & Albums. (Illus.). 144p. 1995. reprint ed. pap. 16.95 (*0-937274-87-9*) Lark Books.

— Twill Basketry: A Handbook of Designs, Techniques, & Styles. LC 92-29051. (Illus.). 144p. 1993. 19.95 (*0-937274-64-X*) Lark Books.

LaPlantz, Shereen, jt. ed. see LaPlantz, David.

Lapmardo, Michael C. An Intimate Look at Wine, Vol. 1. unabridged ed. 125p. 1996. pap. 9.99 (*0-9651849-0-0*) MC Productions.

Lapo, Andrey. Traces of Bygone Biospheres. (Illus.). 356p. 1988. pap. 8.95 (*0-907791-06-9*) Synerg CA.

Lapoint, George M. Chess Points: How You Can Win Chess Games. (Illus.). 226p. (Orig.). (C). 1989. pap. 9.95 (*0-9623240-0-0*) Gemla Pub.

LaPoint, James D., jt. auth. see Hamil, Baha M.

LaPoint, Thomas A., et al, eds. Environmental Toxicology & Risk Assessment, Vol. 4, NO. 1262. (Special Technical Publication Ser.). 287p. 1996. text 64.00 (*0-8031-1998-4*, STP1262) ASTM.

LaPoint, Velma, jt. auth. see Washington, Valora.

***LaPointe, Betty.** Picture Letters: Using Visual Links to Remember Letter Names. Shine, Kristy & LaPointe, Don, eds. (Illus.). 30p. (C). 1999. pap. 25.00 (*0-9674918-1-9*) Litracy Links CT.

— Picture Words: Using Visual Links to Remember Early Sight Words. Shine, Kristy et al, eds. (Illus.). 30p. (C). 1999. pap. 25.00 (*0-9674918-0-0*) Litracy Links CT.

LaPointe, Claude. Out of Sight! Out of Mind! LC 94-38165. (Illus.). 32p. (J). (gr. 1-5). 1995. 20.00 (*0-15-200956-6*, Creat Educ) Creative Co.

LaPointe-Crump, Janice D. & Staley, Kimberly T. Discovering Jazz Dance: America's Energy & Soul. 224p. (C). 1992. text. write for info. (*0-697-11392-2*) Brown & Benchmark.

LaPointe, Don, ed. see LaPointe, Betty.

Lapointe, Francois H., compiled by. Ludwig Wittgenstein: A Comprehensive Bibliography. LC 79-6565. 312p. 1980. lib. bdg. 55.00 (*0-313-22127-8*, LAW/, Greenwood Pr) Greenwood.

— Soren Kierkegaard & His Critics: An International Bibliography of Criticism. LC 80-783. 430p. 1980. lib. bdg. 79.50 (*0-313-22333-5*, LKI/, Greenwood Pr) Greenwood.

Lapointe, Francois H., ed. George Lukacs & His Critics: An International Bibliography with Annotations, 1910-1982. LC 83-5613. 403p. 1983. lib. bdg. 65.00 (*0-313-23891-X*, LAG/, Greenwood Pr) Greenwood.

***LaPointe, Joseph.** The Last Real People. (Illus.). 200p. 2000. pap. 14.95 (*0-9632476-8-9*, Pub. by Pinto Pr) North Country.

LaPointe, Leonard L. Aphasia & Related Neurogenic Language Disorders. 2nd rev. ed. LC 96-19737. (Illus.). 256p. (C). 1996. text 49.00 (*0-86577-622-9*) Thieme Med Pubs.

— Base-Ten Response Form. rev. ed. (Illus.). (C). 1991. pap. 51.50 (*1-879105-28-4*, 0212) Thomson Learn.

— Base-Ten Response-Reorder Forms. rev. ed. (Illus.). (C). 1991. 32.50 (*1-879105-27-6*, 0213) Singular Publishing.

Lapointe, Steven G., et al, eds. Morphology & Its Relation to Phonology & Syntax. LC 97-39330. 512p. (C). 1998. pap. 27.95 (*1-57586-112-7*); text 69.95 (*1-57586-113-5*) CSLI.

Lapolla, Garibaldi M. The Fire in the Flesh. LC 74-17935. (Italian American Experience Ser.). 362p. 1975. reprint ed. 24.95 (*0-405-06407-1*) Ayer.

— The Grand Gennaro. LC 74-17937. (Italian American Experience Ser.). 380p. 1975. reprint ed. 25.95 (*0-405-06408-X*) Ayer.

LaPolla, Randy J. & Lowe, John B. Bibliography of the International Conferences on Sino-Tibetan Languages & Linguistics I-XXV. Matisoff, James A., ed. LC 94-72182. (STEDT Monographs: 1A). 308p. (Orig.). (C). 1994. pap. text 28.00 (*0-944613-22-5*) UC Berkeley Ctrs SE Asia.

LaPolla, Randy J., jt. auth. see Van Valin, Robert D., Jr.

Lapomarda, Vincent A. The Boston Mayor Who Became Truman's Secretary of Labor: Maurice J. Tobin & the Democratic Party. LC 93-40602. (American University Studies: Vol. 159). XIII, 342p. (C). 1995. text 58.95 (*0-8204-2448-X*) P Lang Pubng.

— The Jesuit Heritage in New England. LC 76-42896. (Illus.). (Orig.). (C). 1977. pap. 15.00 (*0-9606294-0-8*) Jesuits Holy Cross.

— The Jesuits & the Third Reich. LC 88-27180. (Texts & Studies in Religion: Vol. 39). 392p. 1989. lib. bdg. 99.95 (*0-88946-828-1*) E Mellen.

— The Knights of Columbus in Massachusetts. 158p. (Orig.). 1982. pap. 10.00 (*0-9608258-1-9*) Mass State.

Laponce, J. A. The Government of the Fifth Republic. LC 76-2005. (Illus.). 415p. 1976. reprint ed. lib. bdg. 79.50 (*0-8371-8763-X*, LAGF, Greenwood Pr) Greenwood.

— Languages & Their Territories. Martin-Sperry, A. D., tr. from FRE. 275p. 1987. pap. 19.95 (*0-8020-6631-3*); text 37.50 (*0-8020-5703-9*) U of Toronto Pr.

— Left & Right: The Topography of Political Perceptions. 284p. 1981. text 40.00 (*0-8020-5533-8*) U of Toronto Pr.

Laponce, J. A. & Smoker, Paul, eds. Experimentation & Simulation in Political Science. LC 72-163827. 475p. reprint ed. pap. 147.30 (*0-608-16627-8*, 202636800049) Bks Demand.

Laponce, J. A., jt. ed. see Berry, J. W.

Laponce, Jean A. & Safran, William, eds. Ethnicity & Citizenship: The Canadian Case. LC 95-33459. 128p. 1996. 35.00 (*0-7146-4693-8*, Pub. by F Cass Pubs) Intl Spec Bk.

— Ethnicity & Citizenship: The Canadian Case. LC 95-33459. 128p. 1996. pap. 20.00 (*0-7146-4231-2*, Pub. by F Cass Pubs) Intl Spec Bk.

***Lapore, Janyce.** Ferris Wheel. 72p. 2000. pap. 5.60 (*0-87129-973-9*, F70) Dramatic Pub.

***LaPorta, John.** A Guide to Jazz Improvisation. 96p. 2000. otabind 16.95 incl. audio compact disk (*0-634-00700-9*) H Leonard.

Laporte, Bruno & Ringold, Dena. Trends in Education Access & Financing During the Transition in Central & Eastern Europe. (Technical Papers: No. 361). 56p. 1997. pap. 22.00 (*0-8213-3912-5*, 13912) World Bank.

***Laporte, Dominique.** History of Shit. Benabid, Nadia & Khoury, Rodolpheel, trs. from FRE. LC 99-46032. (Illus.). 192p. 2000. 20.00 (*0-262-12225-1*) MIT Pr.

Laporte, Gilbert, jt. auth. see Crainic, Teodor G.

***Laporte, Gul.** Quilts from Europe: Projects & Inspiration. Aneloski, Liz & Nelleman, Beate, eds. (Illus.). 112p. 2000. pap. 24.95 (*1-57120-095-9*, 10212) C & T Pub.

Laporte, Jean. Eucharistia in Philo. LC 82-25876. (Studies in the Bible & Early Christianity: Vol. 3). 274p. 1983. lib. bdg. 89.95 (*0-88946-601-7*) E Mellen.

LaPorte, Jean. The Role of Women in Early Christianity. LC 82-8281. (Studies in Women & Religion: Vol. 7). 196p. (C). 1982. lib. bdg. 79.95 (*0-88946-545-2*) E Mellen.

Laporte, Jean & Taylor, Finian. Understanding Our Biblical & Early Christian Tradition: An Introductory Textbook in Theology. LC 91-35645. 368p. 1991. pap. 34.95 (*0-7734-9668-8*) E Mellen.

LaPorte, Jean L. Tuttle - Tuthill: One Branch of the Eli Tuthill Family of Liberty Township of Michigan, Descendants of the Tuthill Family of Southold & Orient, Long Island, 1640, & of Tharston, England. (Illus.). 107p. 1992. pap. 15.00 (*0-8328-2358-9*); lib. bdg. 25.00 (*0-8328-2357-0*) Higginson Bk Co.

Laporte, Juan P. & Valdes, Juan A., eds. Tikal y Uaxactun en el Preclasico. 126p. 1993. pap. 9.20 (*968-36-2673-4*, UN010) UPLAAP.

Laporte, L. F., ed. Establishment of a Geologic Framework for Paleoanthropology. (Special Papers: No. 242). (Illus.). 82p. 1990. pap. 12.00 (*0-8137-2242-X*) Geol Soc.

An Asterisk (*) at the beginning of an entry indicates that the title is appearing for the first time.

***Laporte, Leo F.** George Gaylord Simpson: Paleontologist & Evolutionist. LC 00-29030. 2000. 16.00 (0-231-12065-6) Col U Pr.

Laporte, Leo F., ed. Reefs in Time & Space: Selected Examples from the Recent & Ancient. LC 74-165238. (Society of Economic Paleontologists & Mineralogists, Special Publication Ser.: No. 18). 260p. reprint ed. pap. 80.60 (0-608-12949-6, 202474500038) Bks Demand.

***Laporte, Lio K.** George Gaylord Simpson: Paleontologist & Evolutionist. 256p. 2000. text 50.00 (0-231-12064-8) Col U Pr.

LaPorte, Penny & O'Neill, Robert. American Kernel Lessons: Advanced Teacher's Edition. 101p. 1982. 18.95 (0-582-79763-2, 75017) Longman.

LaPorte, Richard H. The Adventures of a Bush Pilot. (Illus.). 222p. 1997. pap., per. 19.95 (0-9658373-0-0) R H LaPorte.

LaPorte, Richard J. Hydrophilic Polymer Coatings for Medical Devices: Structure/Properties, Development, Manufacture & Applications. LC 96-62021. 185p. 1997. pap. text 174.95 (1-56676-504-8) Technomic.

LaPorte, Robert, Jr. & Burki, Shahid J., eds. Pakistan's Development Priorities: Choices for the Future. (UGC Series in Economics). (Illus.). 1985. pap. 18.95 (0-19-577333-0) OUP.

LaPorte, Stephen. Guide to Search & Seizure for Illinois Police. 1996. spiral bd. 5.80 (0-87563-648-9) Stipes.

LaPorte, Valerie & Rubin, Jeffrey, eds. Reform & Regulation in Long Term Care. LC 79-9761. 216p. 1979. 57.95 (0-275-90379-6, C0379, Praeger Pubs) Greenwood.

LaPorte, Valerie, jt. ed. see Rubin, Jeffrey.

***La'Porte, Victoria.** An Attempt to Understand the Muslim Reaction to the Satanic Verses. LC 99-20729. (Symposium Ser.: Vol. 53). 320p. 1999. text 99.95 (0-7734-8031-5) E Mellen.

Lapos-Massey, Freeda. A Royal Buggy Garden. (Illus.). 29p. (J). (gr. 3-6). 1994. lib. bdg. 13.75 (1-886272-00-X) Bugsy-n-Doc.

Laposata. Robbins Clinical Pathology. 1999. text. write for info. (0-7216-7027-X) Harcourt.

Laposata, Michael. SI Unit Conversion Guide. (Illus.). 110p. (Orig.). 1992. spiral bd. 14.95 (0-910133-38-7) Mass Med Pub Div.

Laposata, Michael, et al. Guide to Laboratory Test Selection. LC 96-45495. 1998. pap. text 29.00 (0-443-07610-3) Church.

Lapouge, Gilles. The Battle of Wagram. Brownjohn, J. Maxwell, tr. from FRE. 344p. (C). 1988. 19.95 (0-941533-32-8, NAB) I R Dee.

— The Battle of Wagram. Brownjohn, J. Maxwell, tr. from FRE. 344p. 1990. reprint ed. pap. 12.95 (1-56131-013-1, NAB) I R Dee.

Lapp, Alvin K., et al. The Amish Cookbook. (Illus.). 433p. 1992. 11.25 (0-9637275-0-8) A K Lapp.

Lapp, Barbara L. & Lapp, Rachel B. No Law Against Mercy: Jailed for Sheltering a Child from the State. LC 96-94579. (Illus.). 428p. 1997. 24.95 (0-9653547-0-9) Hand of Hope.

Lapp, Benjamin. Revolution from the Right: Politics, Class, & the Rise of Nazism in Saxony, 1919-1933. LC 96-52073. (Studies in Central European Histories). (Illus.). 248p. (C). 1997. text 55.00 (0-391-04027-8) Humanities.

Lapp, Charles L., jt. auth. see Frank, William.

Lapp, Claudia. Honey. 1977. pap. 3.00 (0-916696-04-9) Cross Country.

Lapp, Danielle C. Don't Forget! Easy Exercises for a Better Memory. expanded ed. LC 95-798. 288p. (C). 1995. pap. 12.00 (0-201-48336-X) Addison-Wesley.

— Maximizing Your Memory Power. 2nd rev. ed. LC 98-16506. (Barron's Business Success Ser.). 160p. 1998. pap. 6.95 (0-7641-0400-4) Barron.

— Nearly Total Recall: A Guide to a Better Memory at Any Age. (Portable Stanford Bks.). 192p. (Orig.). 1992. pap. 12.95 (0-916318-51-6) Stanford Alumni Assn.

Lapp, Diane K., ed. Making Reading Possible Through Effective Classroom Management. LC 80-10444. 248p. reprint ed. pap. 76.90 (0-608-15488-1, 202972700064) Bks Demand.

Lapp, Diane K., jt. auth. see Anderson, Paul S.

Lapp, Diane K., jt. auth. see Flood, James.

Lapp, Elam. Funfilled Games & Activities: For the Creative Teacher. (Illus.). 36p. 1998. pap. 3.00 (1-890050-25-3) Carlisle Press.

Lapp, Elam & Lapp, Naomi. Old Country Cookin' (Illus.). 148p. (Orig.). 1996. spiral bd. 7.95 (0-9642548-9-1) Carlisle Press.

Lapp, Elam D. Hurricane Mitch in Central America. (Illus.). 160p. 1999. 25.95 (0-9670627-2-1); pap. 19.95 (0-9670627-3-X) Brookside Pubs.

Lapp, Elizabeth. Journal of Tears. 1984. pap. 3.50 (0-87813-522-7) Christian Light.

Lapp, Henry. Craftman's Handbook: An Exquisite Reproduction of a Rare Notebook by Amish Furnituremaker Henry Lapp. (Illus.). 94p. 1998. pap. text 16.00 (0-7881-5845-7) DIANE Pub.

Lapp, Henry. A Craftsman's Handbook: Henry Lapp. LC 91-70663. 100p. 1991. pap. 15.95 (1-56148-014-2) Good Bks PA.

Lapp, Janet E. Dancing with Tigers. LC 94-96110. 123p. 1994. pap. 10.95 (1-885365-01-2) Demeter Pr.

— Dancing with Tigers. 237p. 1996. 22.95 (1-885365-02-0) Demeter Pr.

— Plant Your Feet Firmly in Mid-Air: Guidance Through Turbulent Change. LC 95-71616. 235p. 1996. 22.95 (1-885365-00-4) Demeter Pr.

Lapp, John A. The Mennonite Church in India: Eighteen Ninety-Seven to Nineteen Sixty-Two. LC 75-186445. (Studies in Anabaptist & Mennonite History: Vol. 14). 248p. 1972. 12.99 (0-8361-1122-2) Herald Pr.

Lapp, John A., ed. see Dyck, Cornelius J.

Lapp, John C. The Brazen Tower: Essays on Mythological Imagery in French Renaissance & Baroque, 1550-1670. (Stanford French & Italian Studies: No. 7). 198p. 1978. pap. 56.50 (0-915838-35-4) Anma Libri.

Lapp, John C., ed. & tr. see Corneille, Pierre.

***Lapp, Joy.** Hanging on to Hope: Studies in Revelations. (Good Ground Ser.). 43p. 1999. pap. 5.95 (0-87303-363-9) Faith & Life.

Lapp, M., et al, eds. Modern Developments in Energy, Combustion & Spectroscopy: In Honor of S. S. Penner. LC 93-45316. 198p. 1994. text 129.25 (0-08-042019-2, Pergamon Pr) Elsevier.

Lapp, Marshall, et al, eds. Advances in Laser Science, II. LC 87-71962. (AIP Conference Proceedings Ser.: No. 160). 768p. 1987. lib. bdg. 85.00 (0-88318-360-9) Am Inst Physics.

Lapp, Marshall, jt. ed. see Stwalley, William C.

Lapp, Nancy, ed. see Leonard, Albert, Jr.

Lapp, Nancy L. The Third Campaign at Tell el-Ful: The Excavations of 1964. LC 81-3659. (Annuals of the American Schools of Oriental Research Ser.: Vol. 45). (Illus.). 100p. 1981. text 39.50 (0-89757-045-6, Pub. by Sheffield Acad) CUP Services.

Lapp, Nancy L., jt. auth. see Lapp, Paul W.

Lapp, Nancy L., ed. see Lapp, Paul W.

Lapp, Naomi, jt. auth. see Lapp, Elam.

Lapp, Paul W. The Dhahr Mirzbaneh Tombs: Three Intermediate Bronze Age Cemeteries in Jordan. (American Schools of Oriental Research Publications of the Jerusalem School Archaeology: Vol. 4). x, 117p. 1966. pap. text 12.50 (0-317-04129-0) Am Sch Orient Res.

— The 1957 Excavations at Beth-Zur. (Annuals of the American Schools of Oriental Research Ser.: Vol. 38). 87p. 1968. text 39.50 (0-89757-038-3, Pub. by Sheffield Acad) CUP Services.

— The Tale of the Tell, Archeological Studies: Archaeological Studies by Paul W. Lapp. Lapp, Nancy L., ed. LC 75-5861. (Pittsburgh Theological Monographs: No. 5). 1975. pap. 9.25 (0-915138-05-0) Pickwick.

Lapp, Paul W. & Lapp, Nancy L. Discoveries in the Wadi ed-Daliyeh. (Annuals of the American Schools of Oriental Research Ser.: Vol. 41). (Illus.). 106p. 1974. text 39.50 (0-89757-041-3, Pub. by Sheffield Acad) CUP Services.

Lapp, Rachel B., jt. auth. see Lapp, Barbara L.

Lapp, Ralph E. Must We Hide? LC 81-6440. (Illus.). 182p. 1981. reprint ed. lib. bdg. 55.00 (0-313-23102-8, LAMW, Greenwood Pr) Greenwood.

Lapp, Ralph L. My Life with Radiation: Hiroshima Plus 50 Years. LC 95-36596. (Illus.). 168p. 1995. pap. 17.95 (0-944838-52-9, Cogito Bks) Med Physics Pub.

Lapp, Richard M. Memorial Cup: Canada's National Junior Hockey Championship. LC 98-151615. 300p. 1997. pap. 18.95 (1-55017-170-4) Harbour Pub Co.

Lapp, Robert K. Contest for Cultural Authority: Hazlitt, Coleridge & the Distresses of the Regency. LC 99-34718. 1999. 39.95 (0-8143-2833-4) Wayne St U Pr.

Lapp, Rudolph M. Afro-Americans in California. 2nd ed. Hundley, Norris, Jr. & Schutz, John A., eds. (Physical Education). (Illus.). 128p. 1987. pap. 8.75 (0-87835-152-3) Thomson Learn.

— Blacks in Gold Rush California. 1995. pap. 16.00 (0-300-06545-0) Yale U Pr.

Lapp, Sallie Y. Amish Cooking. 48p. 1982. 1.69 (0-9637275-2-4) A K Lapp.

— Amish Treats from My Kitchen. (Illus.). 47p. (Orig.). 1981. 3.29 (0-9637275-1-6) A K Lapp.

Lapp, Susan. I'm Going to Age Well or Die Trying: A Humorous & Practical Look at the Second Half of Our Lives. 80p. (Orig.). 1997. pap. 8.95 (0-9657103-0-0) S Lapp.

— Think Soup: Some of My Favorite Vegetarian Soups - All Delicious, Low-Fat & Easy to Prepare. 16p. 1997. pap. 3.50 (0-9657103-1-9) S Lapp.

— Think Vegetarian Fast Food. 16p. 1998. pap. 3.50 (0-9657103-2-7) S Lapp.

***Lapp, Susan E.** The Secret in the Claw-Feet Box. (Illus.). 190p. (J). (gr. 3-7). 2000. 12.95 (0-615-11327-3) S E Lapp.

Lapp, T. Digital Communication & Signal Processing. 1988. text. write for info. (0-442-26042-3, VNR) Wiley.

Lapp, Warren A. & Silberman, Herbert A., eds. United States Large Cents, 1793-1857. LC 74-27611. (Gleanings from the Numismatist Ser.). (Illus.). 640p. 1975. 50.00 (0-88000-058-9) Quarterman.

Lappan, G. Middle Grades Mathematics Project. 1986. text 82.50 (0-201-21473-3) Addison-Wesley.

Lappan, Glenda. Mouse & Elephant, Measuring Growth: Middle Grades Mathematics Projects. 1986. text 18.95 (0-201-21474-1) Addison-Wesley.

— Probability, Middle Grades Mathematics Projects. 1986. text 18.95 (0-201-21478-4) Addison-Wesley.

— Similarity & Equivalent Fractions: Middle Grades Mathematics Project. 1986. text 18.95 (0-201-21476-8) Addison-Wesley.

— Spatial Visualization: Middle Grades Mathematics Project. 1986. text 18.95 (0-201-21477-6) Addison-Wesley.

Lappan, Glenda, et al. Accentuate the Negative: Integers. rev. ed. Anderson, Catherine et al, eds. (Connected Mathematics Ser.). (Illus.). 159p. (YA). (gr. 7 up). 1997. pap. text, teacher ed. 16.50 (1-57232-634-4, 45829); pap. text, student ed. 5.95 (1-57232-633-6, 45828) Seymour Pubns.

— Bits & Pieces I: Understanding Rational Numbers. Anderson, Catherine et al, eds. (Connected Mathematics Ser.). (Illus.). (Orig.). 1995. pap. text, teacher ed. 16.50 (1-57232-153-9, DS21448) Seymour Pubns.

— Bits & Pieces I: Understanding Rational Numbers. Anderson, Catherine et al, eds. (Connected Mathematics Ser.). (Illus.). (Orig.). (J). (gr. 6). 1995. pap. text, wbk. ed. 5.95 (1-57232-152-0, DS21447) Seymour Pubns.

— Bits & Pieces I: Understanding Rational Numbers. rev. ed. Anderson, Catherine et al, eds. (Connected Mathematics Ser.). (Illus.). 89p. (Orig.). (YA). (gr. 6 up). 1997. pap. text, student ed. 5.95 (1-57232-614-X, 45809) Seymour Pubns.

— Bits & Pieces I: Understanding Rational Numbers. rev. ed. Anderson, Catherine et al, eds. (Connected Mathematics Ser.). (Illus.). 187p. (Orig.). (YA). (gr. 6 up). 1997. pap. text, teacher ed. 16.50 (1-57232-615-8, 45810) Seymour Pubns.

— Bits & Pieces II: Using Rational Numbers. Anderson, Catherine et al, eds. (Connected Mathematics Ser.). (Illus.). (Orig.). (J). (gr. 6). 1996. pap., teacher ed. 16.50 (1-57232-159-8, 21454); pap., wbk. ed. 5.95 (1-57232-158-X, 21453) Seymour Pubns.

— Bits & Pieces II: Using Rational Numbers. rev. ed. Anderson, Catherine et al, eds. (Connected Mathematics Ser.). (Illus.). 82p. (Orig.). (YA). (gr. 6 up). 1997. pap. text, student ed. 5.95 (1-57232-616-6, 45811) Seymour Pubns.

— Clever Counting: Combinations. Anderson, Catherine et al, eds. (Connected Mathematics Ser.). (Illus.). 60p. (Orig.). (YA). (gr. 8 up). 1997. pap. text, student ed. 5.95 (1-57232-192-X, 21487) Seymour Pubns.

— Clever Counting: Combinatorics. Phillips, Elizabeth D. et al, eds. (Connected Mathematics Ser.). (Illus.). 116p. (Orig.). 1997. pap. text, teacher ed. 16.50 (1-57232-193-8, 21488) Seymour Pubns.

— Comparing & Scaling: Ratio, Proportion, & Percent. rev. ed. Anderson, Catherine et al, eds. (Connected Mathematics Ser.). (Illus.). 87p. (YA). (gr. 7 up). 1997. pap. text, student ed. 5.95 (1-57232-635-2, 45830) Seymour Pubns.

— Comparing & Scaling: Ratio, Proportion, & Percent. rev. ed. Anderson, Catherine et al, eds. (Connected Mathematics Ser.). (Illus.). 166p. (J). (gr. 7). 1997. pap. text, teacher ed. 16.50 (1-57232-636-0, 45831) Seymour Pubns.

— Covering & Surrounding: Two-Dimensional Measurement. Apple, Mali, ed. (Connected Mathematics Ser.). (Illus.). (Orig.). 1996. teacher ed. 16.50 (1-57232-155-5, DS21450); wbk. ed. 5.95 (1-57232-154-7, DS21449) Seymour Pubns.

— Covering & Surrounding: Two-Dimensional Measurement. rev. ed. Anderson, Catherine et al, eds. (Connected Mathematics Ser.). (Illus.). 89p. (Orig.). (YA). (gr. 6 up). 1997. pap. text, student ed. 5.95 (1-57232-618-2, 45813) Seymour Pubns.

— Covering & Surrounding: Two-Dimensional Measurement. rev. ed. Anderson, Catherine et al, eds. (Connected Mathematics Ser.). (Illus.). 163p. (Orig.). (YA). (gr. 6 up). 1997. pap. text, teacher ed. 16.50 (1-57232-619-0, 45814) Seymour Pubns.

— Data about Us: Statistics. Anderson, Catherine et al, eds. (Connected Mathematics Ser.). (Illus.). (Orig.). 1995. pap. text, teacher ed. 16.50 (1-57232-149-0, DS21444) Seymour Pubns.

— Data about Us: Statistics. Anderson, Catherine et al, eds. (Connected Mathematics Ser.). (Illus.). (Orig.). (J). (gr. 6). 1995. pap. text, wbk. ed. 5.95 (1-57232-148-2, DS21443) Seymour Pubns.

— Data about Us: Statistics. rev. ed. Anderson, Catherine et al, eds. (Connected Mathematics Ser.). (Illus.). 75p. (Orig.). (YA). (gr. 6 up). 1997. pap. text, student ed. 5.95 (1-57232-612-3, 45807) Seymour Pubns.

— Data about Us: Statistics. rev. ed. Anderson, Catherine et al, eds. (Connected Mathematics Ser.). (Illus.). 137p. (Orig.). (YA). (gr. 6 up). 1997. pap. text, student ed. 16.50 (1-57232-613-1, 45808) Seymour Pubns.

— Data Around Us: Number Sense. Anderson, Catherine et al, eds. (Connected Mathematics Ser.). (Illus.). 69p. (Orig.). (J). (gr. 7). 1996. pap., wbk. ed. 5.95 (1-57232-176-8, 21471) Seymour Pubns.

— Data Around Us: Number Sense. Anderson, Catherine et al, eds. (Connected Mathematics Ser.). (Illus.). 125p. (Orig.). 1996. pap., teacher ed. 16.50 (1-57232-177-6, 21472) Seymour Pubns.

— Data Around Us: Number Sense. rev. ed. Anderson, Catherine et al, eds. (Connected Mathematics Ser.). (Illus.). 72p. (Orig.). (YA). (gr. 7 up). 1997. pap. text, student ed. 5.95 (1-57232-637-9, 45832) Seymour Pubns.

— Data Around Us: Number Sense. rev. ed. Anderson, Catherine et al, eds. (Connected Mathematics Ser.). (Illus.). 140p. (Orig.). (J). (gr. 7). 1997. pap. text, teacher ed. 16.50 (1-57232-638-7, 45833) Seymour Pubns.

— Filling & Wrapping: Three-Dimensional Measurement. Anderson, Catherine et al, eds. (Connected Mathematics Ser.). (Illus.). 72p. (Orig.). (J). (gr. 7). 1996. student ed., wbk. ed. 5.95 (1-57232-172-5, 21467) Seymour Pubns.

— Filling & Wrapping: Three-Dimensional Measurement. Anderson, Catherine et al, eds. (Connected Mathematics Ser.). (Illus.). 137p. (Orig.). 1996. teacher ed. 16.50 (1-57232-173-3, 21468) Seymour Pubns.

— Filling & Wrapping: Three-Dimensional Measurement. Anderson, Catherine et al, eds. (Connected Mathematics Ser.). (Illus.). 158p. (Orig.). (J). (gr. 7). 1997. pap. text, teacher ed. write for info. (1-57232-640-9, 45835) Seymour Pubns.

— Filling & Wrapping: Three-Dimensional Measurement. rev. ed. Anderson, Catherine et al, eds. (Connected Mathematics Ser.). (Illus.). 79p. (Orig.). (J). (gr. 7). 1997. pap. text, student ed. 5.95 (1-57232-639-5, 45834) Seymour Pubns.

— Frogs, Fleas, & Painted Cubes: Quadratic Relationships. Anderson, Catherine et al, eds. (Connected Mathematics Ser.). (Illus.). 89p. (YA). (gr. 8 up). 1997. pap. text, student ed. 5.95 (1-57232-184-9, 21479) Seymour Pubns.

— How Likely Is It? Probability. Anderson, Catherine et al, eds. (Connected Mathematics Ser.). (Illus.). 1996. teacher ed. 16.50 (1-57232-157-1, 21452) Seymour Pubns.

— How Likely Is It? Probability. Anderson, Catherine et al, eds. (Connected Mathematics Ser.). (Illus.). (J). (gr. 6). 1996. wbk. ed. 5.95 (1-57232-156-3, 21451) Seymour Pubns.

— How Likely Is It? Probability. rev. ed. Anderson, Catherine et al, eds. (Connected Mathematics Ser.). (Illus.). 68p. 1997. pap. text, student ed. 5.95 (1-57232-626-3, 45821) Seymour Pubns.

— Kaleidoscopes, Hubcaps, & Mirrors: Symmetry & Transformations. Anderson, Catherine & Miceli, Stacey, eds. (Connected Mathematics Ser.). (Illus.). 82p. (J). (gr. 8). 1997. pap. 5.95 (1-57232-188-1, 21483) Seymour Pubns.

— Kaleidoscopes, Hubcaps, & Mirrors: Symmetry & Transformations. Anderson, Catherine et al, eds. (Connected Mathematics Ser.). (Illus.). 209p. 1997. pap. text, teacher ed. 16.50 (1-57232-189-X, 21484) Seymour Pubns.

— Looking for Pythagoras: The Pythagorean Theorem. Anderson, Catherine et al, eds. (Connected Mathematics Ser.). (Illus.). 160p. (Orig.). 1997. teacher ed. 16.50 (1-57232-181-4, 21476); pap. text 5.95 (1-57232-180-6, 21475) Seymour Pubns.

— Moving Straight Ahead: Linear Relationships. rev. ed. Anderson, Catherine et al, eds. (Connected Mathematics Ser.). (Illus.). 182p. (YA). (gr. 7 up). 1997. pap. text, teacher ed. 16.50 (1-57232-642-5, 45837); pap. text, student ed. 5.95 (1-57232-641-7, 45836) Seymour Pubns.

— Prime Time: Factors & Multiples. Anderson, Catherine & Miceli, Stacey, eds. (Connected Mathematics Ser.). (Illus.). (Orig.). 1995. student ed. 5.95 (1-57232-146-6, DS21441) Seymour Pubns.

— Prime Time: Factors & Multiples. Anderson, Catherine et al, eds. (Connected Mathematics Ser.). (Illus.). (Orig.). 1995. teacher ed. 16.50 (1-57232-147-4, DS21442) Seymour Pubns.

— Prime Time: Factors & Multiples. rev. ed. Anderson, Catherine et al, eds. (Connected Mathematics Ser.). (Illus.). 70p. (Orig.). (YA). (gr. 6 up). 1997. pap. text, student ed. 5.95 (1-57232-620-4, 45815) Seymour Pubns.

— Ruins of Montarek: Spatial Visualization. (Connected Mathematics Ser.). (Illus.). 1996. teacher ed. 16.50 (1-57232-161-X, 21456); wbk. ed. 5.95 (1-57232-160-1, 21455) Seymour Pubns.

— Ruins of Montarek: Spatial Visualization. rev. ed. Anderson, Catherine et al, eds. (Connected Mathematics Ser.). (Illus.). 85p. (YA). (gr. 6 up). 1997. pap. text, student ed. 5.95 (1-57232-622-0, 45817) Seymour Pubns.

— Ruins of Montarek: Spatial Visualization. rev. ed. Anderson, Catherine et al, eds. (Connected Mathematics Ser.). (Illus.). 166p. (YA). (gr. 6 up). 1997. pap. text, teacher ed. 16.50 (1-57232-623-9, 45818) Seymour Pubns.

— Samples & Populations: Data & Statistics. Anderson, Catherine et al, eds. (Investigations in Number, Data, & Space Ser.). (Illus.). 151p. (YA). (gr. 8 up). 1997. pap. text, teacher ed. 16.50 (1-57232-191-1, 21486); pap. text, student ed. 5.95 (1-57232-190-3, 21485) Seymour Pubns.

— Say It with Symbols: Algebraic Reasoning. Anderson, Catherine et al, eds. (Connected Mathematics Ser.). (Illus.). 151p. (J). (gr. 8). 1997. pap. text 16.50 (1-57232-187-3, 21482) Seymour Pubns.

— Shapes & Designs: Two-Dimensional Geometry. Anderson, Catherine et al, eds. (Connected Mathematics Ser.). (Illus.). (Orig.). 1995. pap., wbk. ed. 5.95 (1-57232-150-4, DS21445) Seymour Pubns.

— Shapes & Designs: Two-Dimensional Geometry. Anderson, Catherine et al, eds. (Connected Mathematics Ser.). (Illus.). (Orig.). 1995. pap., teacher ed. 16.50 (1-57232-151-2, DS21446) Seymour Pubns.

— Shapes & Designs: Two-Dimensional Geometry. rev. ed. Anderson, Catherine et al, eds. (Connected Mathematics Ser.). (Illus.). 84p. (Orig.). (YA). (gr. 6 up). 1997. pap. text, student ed. 5.95 (1-57232-624-7, 45819) Seymour Pubns.

— Shapes & Designs: Two-Dimensional Geometry. rev. ed. Anderson, Catherine et al, eds. (Connected Mathematics Ser.). (Illus.). 149p. (Orig.). (YA). (gr. 6 up). 1997. pap. text, teacher ed. 16.50 (1-57232-625-5, 45820) Seymour Pubns.

— Stretching & Shrinking: Similarity. rev. ed. Anderson, Catherine et al, eds. (Connected Mathematics Ser.). (Illus.). 189p. (YA). (gr. 7 up). 1997. pap. text, teacher ed. 16.50 (1-57232-644-1, 45839); pap. text, student ed. 5.95 (1-57232-643-3, 45838) Seymour Pubns.

— Thinking with Mathematical Models: Representing Relationships. Anderson, Catherine et al, eds. (Connected Mathematics Ser.). (Illus.). 139p. (Orig.). 1997. teacher ed. 16.50 (1-57232-179-2, 21474); pap. text 5.95 (1-57232-178-4, 21473) Seymour Pubns.

— Variables & Patterns: Introducing Algebra. Anderson, Catherine et al, eds. (Connected Mathematics Ser.). (Illus.). 68p. (Orig.). (J). (gr. 7). 1996. pap., teacher ed. 16.50 (0-614-17412-0) Seymour Pubns.

— Variables & Patterns: Introducing Algebra. Anderson, Catherine et al, eds. (Connected Mathematics Ser.). (Illus.). 130p. (Orig.). 1996. teacher ed. 16.50 (1-57232-163-6, 21458) Seymour Pubns.

— Variables & Patterns: Introducing Algebra. Anderson,

L

Catherine et al, eds. (Connected Mathematics Ser.). (Illus.). 68p. (Orig.). (J). (gr. 7). 1996. student ed., wbk. ed. 5.95 (*1-57232-162-8*, 21457) Seymour Pubns.

— Variables & Patterns: Introducing Algebra. rev. ed. Anderson, Catherine et al, eds. (Connected Mathematics Ser.). (Illus.). 152p. (Orig.). (J). (gr. 7). 1997. pap. text, teacher ed. 16.50 (*1-57232-646-8*, 45841); pap. text, student ed. 5.95 (*1-57232-645-X*, 45840) Seymour Pubns.

— What Do You Expect? Probability & Expected Value. Anderson, Catherine et al, eds. (Connected Mathematics Ser.). (Illus.). 78p. (J). (gr. 7). 1996. wbk. ed. 5.95 (*1-57232-174-1*, 21469) Seymour Pubns.

— What Do You Expect? Probability & Expected Value. Anderson, Catherine et al, eds. (Connected Mathematics Ser.). (Illus.). 161p. 1996. teacher ed. 16.50 (*1-57232-175-X*, 21470) Seymour Pubns.

— What Do You Expect? Probability & Expected Value. rev. ed. Anderson, Catherine et al, eds. (Connected Mathematics Ser.). (Illus.). 84p. (YA). (gr. 7 up). 1997. pap. text, student ed. 5.95 (*1-57232-647-6*, 45842) Seymour Pubns.

— What Do You Expect? Probability & Expected Value. rev. ed. Anderson, Catherine et al, eds. (Connected Mathematics Ser.). (Illus.). 179p. (J). (gr. 7). 1997. pap. text, teacher ed. 16.50 (*1-57232-648-4*, 45843) Seymour Pubns.

Lappe, Claus O., jt. auth. see Daly, Peter M.

Lappe, Frances M. Diet for a Small Planet. 20th ed. 528p. 1991. pap. 15.00 (*0-345-37366-9*) Ballantine Pub Grp.

— Diet for a Small Planet: 10th Anniversary Edition. anniversary ed. 496p. 1985. mass mkt. 6.99 (*0-345-32120-0*) Ballantine Pub Grp.

Lappe, Frances M. & Du Bois, Paul M. The Quickening of America: Rebuilding Our Nation, Remaking Our Lives. LC 93-35547. (Nonprofit Ser.). 353p. 1994. pap. 21.00 (*1-55542-605-0*) Jossey-Bass.

Lappe, Frances M. & Schurman, Rachel. Taking Population Seriously. 96p. 1990. pap. 7.95 (*0-935028-53-6*) Inst Food & Develop.

Lappe, Frances Moore, et al. World Hunger: Twelve Myths. rev. ed. LC 98-29927. 288p. 1998. reprint ed. pap. 13.00 (*0-8021-3591-9*, Grove) Grove-Atltc.

Lappe, Marc. The Body's Edge: Our Cultural Obsession with the Skin. 88p. 1995. 22.50 (*0-8050-4208-3*) H Holt & Co.

— The Tao of Immunology: A Revolutionary New Understanding of Our Body's Defenses. LC 97-9707. (Illus.). 332p. (C). 1997. 27.95 (*0-306-45626-5*, Kluwer Plenum) Kluwer Academic.

— When Antibiotics Fail: Restoring the Ecology of the Body. rev. ed. 288p. (Orig.). 1987. reprint ed. pap. 14.95 (*0-938190-74-1*) North Atlantic.

— When Antibiotics Fail: Restoring the Ecology of the Body. 2nd ed. LC 94-48258. 320p. (Orig.). (C). 1995. pap. 14.95 (*1-55643-191-0*) North Atlantic.

Lappe, Marc & Bailey, Britt. Against the Grain: Biotechnology & the Corporate Takeover of Your Food. 163p. 1998. pap. 14.95 (*1-56751-150-3*) Common Courage.

Lappe, Marc, jt. ed. see Murphy, Timothy F.

Lappe, Mark & Bailey, Britt. Against the Grain: Biotechnology & the Corporate Takeover of Your Food. 163p. 1998. lib. bdg. 29.95 (*1-56751-151-1*) Common Courage.

***Lappe, Markus.** Neuronal Processing of Optic Flow. (International Review of Neurobiology Ser.: Vol. 44). (Illus.). 343p. 1999. 99.95 (*0-12-366844-1*) Acad Pr.

Lappe, Robert J., jt. auth. see McDonald, Hugh J.

Lappenkueper, Ulrich & Kosthorst, Daniel. The Federal Republic of Germany. (Illus.). 460p. 1999. 39.95 (*3-8290-2869-5*, 810167) Konemann.

Lapper, Richard. Honduras: State for Sale. (Latin America Bureau Ser.). 128p. (Orig.). 1985. pap. 12.00 (*0-85345-697-6*, Pub. by Lat Am Bur) Monthly Rev.

Lappies, Pamela, ed. see Bass, Ruth.

Lappies, Pamela, ed. see Costenbader, Carol W.

Lappies, Pamela, ed. see Damerow, Gail.

Lappies, Pamela, ed. see Fisher, Joe & Fisher, Dennis.

Lappies, Pamela, ed. see Pleasant, Barbara.

Lappies, Pamela, ed. see Vargas, Pattie & Gulling, Rich.

Lappies, Pamela, ed. see Zabarkes, Adriana & Zabarkes, Rochelle.

Lappin. Alpha Olefins Applications Handbook. Sauer, Joe D., ed. (Chemical Industries Ser.: Vol. 37). (Illus.). 480p. 1989. text 195.00 (*0-8247-7895-2*) Dekker.

Lappin, A. J., ed. & tr. see Vicente, Gil.

***Lappin, Anthony, ed.** Berceo's 'Vida de Santa Oria' Text, Translation & Commentary. (Legenda Ser.). 200p. (C). 2000. pap. 49.50 (*1-900755-17-3*, Pub. by E H R C) David Brown.

Lappin, Ben W. & Teicher, Morton I. Distant Partners: Community Change Through Project Renewal. 298p. (Orig.). (C). 1990. pap. text 25.50 (*0-8191-7761-X*); lib. bdg. 49.00 (*0-8191-7760-1*) U Pr of Amer.

***Lappin, Elena.** Foreign Brides. LC 99-18684. 176p. 1999. 22.00 (*0-374-15758-8*) FS&G.

— Foreign Brides: Stories. 2000. pap. 12.00 (*0-312-26737-1*, Picador USA) St Martin.

Lappin, Elena, ed. Daylight in Nightclub Inferno: Czech Fiction from the Post-Kundera Generation. LC 96-43674. 320p. 1997. pap. 15.95 (*0-945774-33-8*, PG5145.E8D39) Catbird Pr.

— Jewish Voices, German Words: Growing up Jewish in Postwar Germany & Austria. Winston, Krishna, tr. from GER. LC 93-39950. 304p. 1994. 23.95 (*0-945774-23-0*, PT405.J48) Catbird Pr.

Lappin, Greg, et al. Tennis Doubles No. 1: Winning Strategies for All Levels. (Illus.). 144p. (Orig.). 1985. pap. 9.95 (*0-930425-00-6*) KG Bks Co.

Lappin, Ivan M., jt. auth. see Blakely, Robert J.

Lappin, Kendall. Memoirs of a Translator of Poetry. 72p. 1999. pap. 10.00 (*1-878580-32-9*) Asylum Arts.

Lappin, Kendall, tr. from FRE. Dead French Poets Speak Plain English: An Anthology of Poems. 300p. (Orig.). 1997. pap. 16.00 (*1-878580-78-7*) Asylum Arts.

— The Muse Spoke French: Selected Poems. LC 94-70671. 128p. (Orig.). 1994. pap. 9.95 (*1-878580-59-0*) Asylum Arts.

Lappin, Kendall, tr. see Baudelaire, Charles.

Lappin, Kendall, tr. see Nerval, Gerard De.

Lappin, Kendall E. Baudelaire Revisited: Forty-One Poems. LC 81-90014. (Illus.). 196p. 1981. 11.95 (*0-9605710-1-9*) KEL Pubns.

Lappin, Kendall E., tr. see Baudelaire, Charles.

Lappin, Linda, tr. see Careri, Giovanni.

Lappin, Linda, tr. see Nieh, Hualing.

Lappin, Linda, tr. see Petrucci, Armando.

Lappin, Linda, tr. see Pollera, Alberto.

***Lappin, Peter.** Challenge & Change. LC 92-74770. 1999. write for info. (*0-932406-21-1*) AFC.

Lappin, Peter. First Lady of the World: A Popular History of Devotion to Mary. 192p. 1988. 14.95 (*0-89944-098-3*); pap. 9.95 (*0-89944-091-6*) Salesiana Pubs.

— Give Me Souls! Life of Don Bosco. rev. ed. 367p. 1986. reprint ed. pap. 13.00 (*0-89944-087-8*) Salesiana Pubs.

— Stories of Don Bosco. 2nd ed. LC 78-72525. (Illus.). 272p. (J). (gr. 5-12). 1979. pap. 9.50 (*0-89944-036-3*) Salesiana Pubs.

— Zatti! 77p. 1987. pap. 2.50 (*0-89944-090-8*) Salesiana Pubs.

Lappin-Scott, Hilary M. & Costerton, J. William, eds. Microbial Biofilms. (Plant & Microbiotechnology Research Ser.: No. 5). (Illus.). 324p. (C). 1995. text 110.00 (*0-521-45412-3*) Cambridge U Pr.

Lappin, Shalom. Sorts, Ontology, & Metaphor: The Semantics of Sortal Structure. (Foundations of Communication & Cognition Ser.). 173p. 1981. 65.40 (*3-11-008309-4*) De Gruyter.

Lappin, Shalom, ed. The Handbook of Contemporary Semantic Theory. (Handbooks in Linguistics). 670p. 1997. pap. text 44.95 (*0-631-20749-X*) Blackwell Pubs.

Lappin, Shalom & Benmamoun, Elabbas, eds. Fragments: Studies in Ellipsis & Gapping. LC 98-26311. 320p. 1999. text 60.00 (*0-19-512302-6*) OUP.

Lappin, Shalom, jt. auth. see Johnson, David.

Lappin, Terence R., jt. ed. see Rich, Ivan N.

Lappin, Zoe Von Ende, see Von Ende Lappin, Zoe.

Lapping, Brian & Radice, Giles. More Power to the People: Young Fabian Essays on Democracy in Britain. 1968. pap. 49.50 (*0-614-01798-X*) Elliots Bks.

Lapping, Mark, ed. & abr. see Russell, Howard S.

Lapping, Mark B., jt. ed. see Furuseth, Owen J.

Lapple, Alfred, jt. auth. see Hegering, Heinz-Gerd.

Lappo-Danilevskii, J. A. Systemes des Equations Differentielles, 3 Vols. in 1. LC 53-7110. 35.00 (*0-8284-0094-6*) Chelsea Pub.

Laprade, Armand, ed. see De Montherlant, Henry.

Laprade, B. N., jt. ed. see Johnson, C. B.

Laprade, William T. England & the French Revolution, 1789-1797. LC 77-109922. reprint ed. 32.50 (*0-404-03878-6*) AMS Pr.

Lapre, Don. Don Lapre's Making Money Package. unabridged ed. (Illus.). 300p. 1992. pap. 39.95 (*1-928788-00-9*) New Strategies.

Lapres, Daniel A. & Yuejiao, Zhang. Business Law in China: Trade, Investment & Finance. LC 98-112152. 474p. (C). 1997. pap. 125.00 (*92-842-1234-0*, 576) ICC Pub.

Laprie, J. C., et al, eds. Dependability: Basic Concepts & Terminology. (Dependable Computing & Fault-Tolerant Systems Ser.: Vol. 5). (Illus.). xii, 268p. 1992. 93.95 (*0-387-82296-8*) Spr-Verlag.

Laprie, J. C., jt. ed. see Avizienis, A.

Laprise, Susan, ed. see Parent-Child Nursing Department.

Lapsanski, Duane V. Evangelican Perfection: An Historical Examination of the Concept in the Early Franciscan Sources. (Theology Ser.). xii, 302p. 1977. pap. 15.00 (*1-57659-028-3*) Franciscan Inst.

Lapsansky, Phillip, contrib. by. An African American Miscellany: Selections from a Quarter Century of Collecting 1970-1995. (Illus.). 46p. 1996. pap. 5.00 (*0-914076-91-4*) Lib Co Phila.

Lapseritis, Jack. The Psychic Sasquatch: And Their UFO Connection. 300p. 1999. pap. 18.95 (*1-893183-14-9*, Pub. by Granite Pub) ACCESS Pubs Network.

— The Psychic Sasquatch: The UFO Connection. LC 98-13417. xxii, 225p. 1998. pap. 18.95 (*0-926524-17-8*) Granite WI.

Lapsley, Hilary. Margaret Mead & Ruth Benedict: The Kinship of Women. LC 98-54185. (Illus.). 376p. 1999. 34.95 (*1-55849-181-3*) U of Mass Pr.

Lapsley, D. K. & Power, F. Clark, eds. Self, Ego, & Identity. (Illus.). 280p. 1988. 79.95 (*0-387-96588-2*) Spr-Verlag.

Lapsley, Daniel K. Moral Psychology. (Developmental Psychology Ser.). (C). 1996. pap. 25.00 (*0-8133-3033-5*, Pub. by Westview) HarpC.

Lapsley, Daniel K., jt. ed. see Power, F. Clark.

Lapsley, Irvine & Mitchell, Falconer, eds. Accounting & Performance Management: Issues in the Private & Public Sectors. 224p. (Orig.). 1996. pap. text 39.95 (*1-55876-140-3*) Wiener Pubs Inc.

— Accounting & Performance Measurement: Issues in the Private & Public Sectors. 224p. 1996. pap. text 47.95 (*1-85396-324-0*, Pub. by P Chapman) Taylor & Francis.

Lapsley, Irvine & Wilson, Richard M., eds. Explorations in Financial Control: Essays in Honour of John Perrin. 240p. 1997. pap. 74.95 (*1-86152-001-8*) Thomson Learn.

Lapsley, Irvine, jt. ed. see Clark, Chris.

Lapsley, J. T., jt. auth. see Cooke, George M.

Lapsley, James N. Renewal in Late Life Through Pastoral Counseling. LC 92-19818. (Integration Bks.). viii, 118p. 1992. pap. 9.95 (*0-8091-3333-4*) Paulist Pr.

Lapsley, James T. Bottled Poetry: Napa Winemaking from Prohibition to the Modern Era. LC 96-7072. (Illus.). 301p. 1996. 29.95 (*0-520-20272-4*, Pub. by U CA Pr) Cal Prin Full Svc.

Lapsley, Phil. DSP Processor Fundamentals: Architectures & Features. LC 96-41738. 224p. 1997. pap. 59.95 (*0-7803-3405-1*, PP5386) Inst Electrical.

Lapsley, Robert & Westlake, Michael. Film Theory: An Introduction. (Images of Culture Ser.). 256p. 1989. text 24.95 (*0-7190-2602-4*, Pub. by Manchester Univ Pr) St Martin.

Lapuente, F. A., jt. auth. see Rogers, P. P.

LaPuma. Finding the Goddess Within, Vol. 1. 1995. 9.95 (*1-878203-01-0*) SoulSource.

LaPuma, John. Managed Care Ethics: Essays on the Impact of Managed Care on Traditional Medical Ethics. LC 97-41350. (Hatherligh CME Book Ser.). 224p. 1998. pap. 39.95 (*1-57826-012-4*, Pub. by Hatherleigh) Norton.

LaPuma, Karen & Runkis, Walt. Awakening Female Power: The Way of the Goddess Warrior. 4th rev. ed. LC 89-51331. (Illus.). 144p. (Orig.). 1991. reprint ed. pap. 12.95 (*1-878203-02-9*) SoulSource.

Lapunzina, Alejandro. Maison Curutchet. LC 97-4043. (Illus.). 176p. (Orig.). 1997. pap. 19.95 (*1-56898-095-7*) Princeton Arch.

Laqua, H., jt. auth. see Lucke, K.

LaQuatra. Nutrition: A Development Approach. (Nursing Education Ser.). 1990. pap., teacher ed. 12.00 (*0-8273-3076-6*) Delmar.

Laquatra, Idamarie. Nutrition in Clinical Nursing. (Nursing Education Ser.). 1990. pap. 31.50 (*0-8273-3075-8*) Delmar.

Laque, Carol F. The Fury of the Birds. (Orig.). 1992. pap. 12.95 (*0-9619532-1-7*) Circumference Pr.

— Jazzwork Quilt. 100p. (Orig.). 1996. pap. 15.00 (*0-9619532-3-3*) Circumference Pr.

— Midnight Noon. (Orig.). 1995. pap. 15.00 (*0-9619532-2-5*) Circumference Pr.

LaQue Center for Corrosion Technology, Inc. Staff. Optimizing Cleaning Techniques for Copper Alloy Condenser Tubing in Seawater Service. 48p. 1984. write for info. (*0-318-60405-1*) Intl Copper.

Laquer, Walter. The New Terrorism: Fanaticism & the Arms of Mass Destruction. LC HV6431.L35 1999. 320p. 1999. 30.00 (*0-19-511816-2*) OUP.

Laquer, Walter & Breitman, Richard. Breaking the Silence: The German Who Exposed the Final Solution. LC 93-33566. (Tauber Institute for the Study of European Jewry Ser.: No. 18). (Illus.). 320p. Date not set. reprint ed. pap. 99.20 (*0-608-20683-0*, 207179000002) Bks Demand.

Laqueur, Richard. Epigraphische Untersuchungen Zu Den Griechischen Volksbeschlussen. (GER.). iv, 211p. reprint ed. write for info. (*0-318-72099-X*) G Olms Pubs.

Laqueur, Thomas. Making Sex: Body & Gender from the Greeks to Freud. (Illus.). 352p. 1990. text 42.00 (*0-674-54349-1*) HUP.

— Making Sex: Body & Gender from the Greeks to Freud. (Illus.). 336p. 1992. pap. text 17.50 (*0-674-54355-6*) HUP.

Laqueur, Thomas, jt. ed. see Gallagher, Catherine.

Laqueur, Thomas W. Religion & Respectability: Sunday Schools & Working Class Culture, 1780-1850. LC 75-29728. 308p. reprint ed. pap. 95.50 (*0-8357-8302-2*, 203379700087) Bks Demand.

Laqueur, W. & Sloss, L. European Security in the 1990s: Deterrence & Defense after the INF Treaty. LC 89-49472. (Issues in International Security Ser.). (Illus.). 224p. (C). 1990. 45.00 (*0-306-43442-3*, Plenum Trade) Perseus Pubng.

Laqueur, Walter. The Age of Terrorism. 1988. pap. 12.95 (*0-316-51479-9*) Little.

— The Age of Terrorism. 385p. 1997. pap. text 24.95 (*1-56000-969-1*) Transaction Pubs.

— America, Europe, & the Soviet Union: Selected Essays. LC 82-19423. 234p. 1983. 44.95 (*0-87855-362-2*) Transaction Pubs.

— The Dream That Failed: Reflections on the Soviet Union. 248p. 1994. text 30.00 (*0-19-508978-2*) OUP.

— The Dream That Failed: Reflections on the Soviet Union. 256p. 1996. pap. 12.95 (*0-19-510282-7*) OUP.

— Europe in Our Time: A History, 1945-1992. 624p. 1993. pap. 17.95 (*0-14-013969-9*, Penguin Bks) Viking Penguin.

— Fascism: Past, Present, Future. (Illus.). 272p. (C). 1996. 30.00 (*0-19-509245-7*) OUP.

— Fascism: Past, Present, Future. 272p. 1997. reprint ed. pap. 13.95 (*0-19-511793-X*) OUP.

— Fin de Siecle & Other Essays on America & Europe. LC 96-33084. 287p. 1996. text 34.95 (*1-56000-261-1*) Transaction Pubs.

***Laqueur, Walter.** Guerilla Warfare: A Historical & Critical Study. LC 97-29417. xx, 462p. 1998. pap. 24.95 (*0-7658-0406-9*) Transaction Pubs.

Laqueur, Walter. A History of Zionism. LC 96-76469. (Illus.). 638p. 1996. reprint ed. 14.98 (*1-56731-100-8*, MJF Bks) Fine Comms.

— Looking Forward, Looking Backward, 100. LC 83-11038. 154p. 1983. pap. 9.95 (*0-275-91578-6*, B1578, Praeger Pubs) Greenwood.

— The Political Psychology of Appeasement: Finlandization & Other Unpopular Essays on World Affairs. LC 79-6854. 283p. 1980. text 34.95 (*0-87855-336-3*) Transaction Pubs.

— Russia & Germany: A Century of Conflict. 379p. (C). 1990. pap. 21.95 (*0-88738-349-1*) Transaction Pubs.

— Soviet Realities: Culture & Politics from Stalin to Gorbachev. 305p. 1989. 44.95 (*0-88738-302-5*) Transaction Pubs.

— Soviet Union, 2000: Reform or Revolution? 224p. 1999. pap. 10.95 (*0-312-06471-3*) St Martin.

— The Terrible Secret: Suppression of the Truth about Hitler's Final Solution. LC 98-27001. 304p. 1998. pap. 13.95 (*0-8050-5984-9*, Owl) H Holt & Co.

— U. S. Defense Posture. (Task Force on the Eighties Ser.). 24p. 1981. pap. 2.50 (*0-87495-036-8*) Am Jewish Comm.

— The Uses & Limits of Intelligence. rev. ed. LC 92-32932. 445p. (C). 1993. pap. 24.95 (*1-56000-594-7*) Transaction Pubs.

— Young Germany: A History of the German Youth Movement. 260p. 1984. 34.95 (*0-88738-002-6*); pap. 21.95 (*0-87855-960-4*) Transaction Pubs.

Laqueur, Walter, ed. Middle East in Transition: Studies in Contemporary History. LC 70-156676. (Essay Index Reprint Ser.). 1977. reprint ed. 31.95 (*0-8369-2367-7*) Ayer.

— The Second World War: Essays in Military & Political History. LC 81-86067. (Sage Readers in 20th Century History Ser.: No. 4). 413p. reprint ed. pap. 128.10 (*0-8357-8444-4*, 203470800091) Bks Demand.

Laqueur, Walter & Hunter, Robert, eds. European Peace Movements & the Future of the Western Alliance. 385p. (C). 1985. 44.95 (*0-88738-035-2*) Transaction Pubs.

Laqueur, Walter & Mosse, George L., eds. Historians in Politics. LC 74-78421. (Sage Readers in 20th Century History Ser.: Vol. 1). 360p. reprint ed. pap. 111.60 (*0-608-30160-4*, 202192000026) Bks Demand.

Laqueur, Walter & Rubin, Barry, eds. The Israel-Arab Reader: A Documentary History of the Middle East. rev. ed. 720p. 1995. pap. 16.95 (*0-14-024562-6*, Penguin Bks) Viking Penguin.

— The Israel-Arab Reader: A Documentary History of the Middle East Conflict. LC 84-8047. 720p. reprint ed. pap. 200.00 (*0-8357-5600-9*, 203524100093) Bks Demand.

Laqueur, Walter, ed. see Friend, Julius W.

Laqueur, Walter, ed. see George, Bruce, et al.

Laqueur, Walter, ed. see Hanson, Philip.

Laqueur, Walter, ed. see Lowenthal, Mark M.

Laqueur, Walter, ed. see Ratesh, Nestor.

Laqueur, Walter, ed. see Ter Haar, Barend.

Laquey, Tracy L. The Internet Companion: A Beginner's Guide to Global Networking. 2nd ed. 272p. (C). 1994. pap. text 12.95 (*0-201-40766-3*) Addison-Wesley.

— The Internet Companion Plus: A Beginner's Start-Up Kit for Global Networking. Set. 2nd ed. 272p. 1994. 19.95 incl. disk (*0-201-40837-6*) Addison-Wesley.

LaQuey, Tracy L., jt. auth. see Ryer, Jeanne C.

Laquian, E. & Sobrevinas, Irene. Filipino Cooking Abroad. 194p. 1977. 11.95 (*0-318-36289-9*) Asia Bk Corp.

Lara & Alfonso Castilla. Vuela A Tu Libertad. (SPA.). 1997. pap. text 11.98 (*968-13-1598-7*) Libros Fronteras.

Lara, A. Jimenez, see Amezcua Viedma, C. & Jimenez Lara, A.

***Lara, Adair.** The Best of Adair Lara: Award Winning Columns from the San Francisco Chronicle. (Illus.). 276p. 1999. pap. 14.95 (*0-942087-17-8*) Scottwall Assocs.

Lara, Adair. Slowing down in a Speeded-Up World. (Illus.). 171p. (Orig.). 1994. pap. 8.95 (*0-943233-57-7*) Conari Press.

***Lara, Brian.** Beating the Field. 2000. 26.95 (*1-85225-244-8*, Pub. by Transworld Publishers Ltd); pap. 9.95 (*0-552-14350-2*, Pub. by Transworld Publishers Ltd) Trafalgar.

Lara, Jan. Soulcatchers. 1990. mass mkt. 4.95 (*0-445-20918-6*, Pub. by Warner Bks) Little.

Lara, Jeff, jt. auth. see Isorena, Teresa.

Lara, Jesus. Diccionario de Qheshwa-Espanol, Espanol-Qheshwa. 3rd ed. (MIS & SPA.). 430p. 1990. pap. write for info. (*0-7859-4889-9*) Fr & Eur.

— Diccionario de Ro de Qheshwa-Espanol, Espanol-Qheshwa. (SPA.). 39.95 (*0-686-56703-X*) Fr & Eur.

— Quechua Peoples Poetry. Proser, Maria A. & Scully, James, eds. & trs. by. from QUE. LC 76-26704. Orig. Title: Poesia Popular Quechua. 68p. 1986. pap. 9.95 (*0-915306-09-3*) Curbstone.

Lara, Jorge S. Breve Historia Contemporanea del Ecuador. (Histories of Latin American Nations Ser.). (SPA.). 638p. 1994. pap. 12.99 (*968-16-4174-4*, Pub. by Fondo) Continental Bk.

Lara, Jose A. Jimmy Smits. 1999. mass mkt. 5.99 (*0-312-96812-4*) St Martin.

Lara, Juan, jt. auth. see Neuberger, Egon.

Lara, Karen, intro. Moderno Formulario de Hechiceria 157p. (Orig.). 1997. pap. text 11.98 (*968-409-588-0*) Edamex.

— Recetario De Magia Blanca. 166p. (Orig.). 1997. pap. text 11.98 (*968-409-379-9*) Edamex.

Lara, L. Gutierrez De, see De Lara, L. Gutierrez.

Lara, L. Gutierrez De, see Gutierrez De Lara, L.

Lara, Maria Pia. Moral Textures: Feminist Narratives in the Public Sphere. LC 99-200368. 280p. 1999. 45.00 (*0-520-21776-4*, Pub. by U CA Pr); pap. 19.95 (*0-520-21777-2*, Pub. by U CA Pr) Cal Prin Full Svc.

Lara, Silvia, et al. Inside Costa Rica. 176p. 1995. pap. text 11.95 (*0-911213-51-1*) Interhemisp Res Ctr.

Lara, Susan S. ExCet Study Sessions: Bilingual Education Endorsement Study Manual for the Texas Teacher ExCET Examination. (C). pap. text 20.00 (*1-893629-08-2*) ExCET.

— ExCet Study Sessions: Bilingual Elementary Comprehensive Study Manual for the Texas Teacher ExCET Examination. (C). pap. text 20.00 (*1-893629-04-X*) ExCET.

An Asterisk (*) at the beginning of an entry indicates that the title is appearing for the first time.

— ExCet Study Sessions: English as a Second Language (ESL) Endorsement Study Manual for the Texas Teacher ExCET Examination. (C). pap. text 20.00 (1-893629-19-8) ExCET.
— ExCet Study Sessions: English (Secondary) Study Manual for the Texas Teacher ExCET Examination. (C). pap. text 20.00 (1-893629-09-0) ExCET.
— ExCet Study Sessions: Practice Questions for the Bilingual Elementary Comprehensive Examination for the Texas Teachers ExCET Examination. (C). pap. text, teacher ed. 12.00 (1-893629-03-1) ExCET.
— ExCet Study Sessions: Practice Questions for the English as a Second Language (ESL) Examination for the Texas Teachers ExCET Examination. (C). pap. text, teacher ed. 12.00 (1-893629-12-0) ExCET.
— ExCet Study Sessions: Practice Questions for the Professional Development Examination for the Texas Teachers. (C). pap. text, teacher ed. 12.00 (1-893629-17-1) ExCET.
— ExCet Study Sessions: Professional Development Study Manual for the Texas Teacher ExCET Exam. (C). pap., teacher ed. 20.00 (1-893629-01-5) ExCET.
Lara, Susan S., jt. auth. see Cropper, Carolyn.
Larabee, Virginia Poole & Gracey, Edith M. Herbert William Larrabee, Sr., 1900-1968. LC 98-93018. 1998. write for info. (0-9644673-1-3) E M Gracey.
Larabee, Ann. Decade of Disaster. LC 99-6114. 208p. 1999. pap. 15.95 (0-252-06820-3) U of Ill Pr.
— Decade of Disaster. LC 99-6114. 208p. 1999. 42.50 (0-252-02483-4) U of Ill Pr.
Larabee, Ellen. Sermon Starters & Chancel Teasers: Four Short Interludes. (Christian Theatre Ser.). 33p. (Orig.). 1994. pap. 5.95 (1-57514-132-9, 1164) Encore Perform Pub.
Laraby, Larry, ed. see Haines, John, et al.
***Laracy, Marian A., tr.** The Years. (Illus.). 96p. 1999. per. 10.95 (0-9674098-0-2) The Years.
Laragh, John H., ed. Frontiers in Hypertension Research. (Illus.). 628p. 1981. 94.00 (0-387-90557-X) Spr-Verlag.
Laragh, John H. & Brenner, Barry M. Hypertension: Pathophysiology, Diagnosis, & Management, 2 vols. 2nd ed. (Illus.). 3219p. 1994. text 380.00 (0-7817-0157-0) Lppncott W & W.
Laragh, John H., jt. auth. see Blumenfeld, Jon D.
Laragh, John H., jt. ed. see Brenner, Barry M.
Laraia. Principles & Practices of Psychology Nursing I. (C). text. write for info. (981-4033-14-6) Harcourt Coll Pubs.
***Laraia, Anthony C., et al.** The Kaizen Blitz: Acclerating Breakthroughs in Productivity & Performance. LC 98-41478. (National Association of Manufacturers Ser.). 304p. 1999. 45.00 (0-471-24648-4) Wiley.
Laraia, Michele T. Quick Psychopharmacology Reference. 2nd ed. (Illus.). 64p. (C). (gr. 13). 1994. pap. text 8.95 (0-8016-8064-6, 08064) Mosby Inc.
Laraia, Michele T., jt. auth. see Stuart, Gail W.
***Laraja, Taryn & Kaplan, Farida.** Smart Start! Grade 3. (Illus.). 68p. (J). 2000. pap. text 5.95 (1-893110-14-1) Silver Moon.
Laraja, Taryn, jt. auth. see Lynch, Priscilla.
Laramee, Eve A. The Eroded Terrain of Memory. Ottmann, Klaus, ed. (Illus.). 4p. (Orig.). (C). 1990. pap. text 5.00 (0-929687-04-3) E & C Zilkha Gal.
***Laramie, Anthony J. & Mair, Douglas.** A Dynamic Theory of Taxation: Integrating Kalecki into Modern Public Finance. LC 99-59156. 208p. 2000. 80.00 (1-85898-668-0) E Elgar.
Laramore, Darryl, jt. auth. see Kennedy, Joyce L.
Laramore, Jon. A Guide for Social Security Advocates. 40p. 1984. pap. 4.00 (0-685-23187-9, 41,250) NCLS Inc.
Laramore, Robert D., jt. auth. see McPherson, George.
Larana, Enrique, et al, eds. New Social Movements: From Ideology to Identity. LC 93-37495. 384p. (C). 1994. text 59.95 (1-56639-186-5); pap. text 22.95 (1-56639-187-3) Temple U Pr.
Larance, Charles L. Miss Myrtle's Boy: A Collection of Southeast Arkansas Memories. LC 98-61619. 238p. 1998. 19.95 (0-9667665-0-4); pap. 12.95 (0-9667665-1-2) Windchimes MO.
Laraneta, M. & Peccei, Roberto D., eds. Trends in Astroparticle Physics. 600p. (C). 1991. text 130.00 (981-02-0825-1) World Scientific Pub.
***Larar, Allen M., ed.** Optical Spectroscopic Techniques & Instrumentation for Atmospheric & Space Research II. 1999. pap. text 111.00 (0-8194-3242-3) SPIE.
Larason, Lew. The Basket Collectors Book. (Illus.). 156p. (Orig.). 1978. pap. 6.95 (0-936099-00-3) Scorpio Pubns.
— Baskets - Baskets - Baskets: An Advisory for Collectors. (Illus.). 8p. (Orig.). 1988. pap. 1.95 (0-936099-01-1) Scorpio Pubns.
— Buying Antique Furniture: An Advisory. Guthrie, Pattie, ed. (Illus.). 174p. (Orig.). 1992. pap. text 14.95 (0-936099-02-X) Scorpio Pubns.
***Larason, Thomas C.** Spectroradiometric Detector Measurements. 118p. 1998. per. 9.50 (0-16-060877-5) USGPO.
Laraya-Cuasay, L. R. Interstitial Lung Diseases in Children, 3 vols., Vol. I. Hughes, W. T., ed. LC 87-18185. 224p. 1988. 119.00 (0-8493-4301-1, RJ436, CRC Reprint) Franklin.
— Interstitial Lung Diseases in Children, 3 vols., Vol. 2. Hughes, W. T., ed. LC 87-18185. 208p. 1988. 123.00 (0-8493-4302-X, RJ436, CRC Reprint) Franklin.
— Interstitial Lung Diseases in Children, 3 vols., Vol. III. Hughes, W. T., ed. LC 87-18185. 224p. 1988. 116.00 (0-8493-4303-8, RJ436, CRC Reprint) Franklin.
Laraya, L. R. & Hughes, W. T. Interstitial Lung Diseases in Children, 3 vols., Set. LC 87-18185. 1988. 357.00 (0-8493-4300-3, RJ436, CRC Reprint) Franklin.
Larayette Chamber Singers. Latin Music through the Ages. 87p. audio 15.00 (0-86516-249-2) Bolchazy-Carducci.
Larbalestier, Simon. The Art & Craft of Collage. LC 94-22236. (Illus.). 144p. 1995. pap. 19.95 (0-8118-0806-8) Chronicle Bks.
Larbalestier, Tiffany F., jt. auth. see Walker, Tim.
Larbalestrier, Deborah E. Paralegal Practice & Procedure: A Practical Guide for the Legal Assistant. 3rd ed. LC 94-28860. 576p. (C). 1994. pap. text 27.95 (0-13-108564-6) P-H.
— Paralegal's Handbook of Annotated Legal Forms, Clauses & Procedures. 384p. 1982. 39.50 (0-13-648642-8, Busn) P-H.
Larbaud, V. Oeuvres. (FRE.). 1957. lib. bdg. 110.00 (0-8288-3519-5, F10840) Fr & Eur.
— Les Poesies de A. O. Barnabooth: Poesies Divers. (FRE.). 1987. pap. 10.95 (0-8288-3863-1, F109090) Fr & Eur.
Larbaud, Valery. Childish Things. Wald, Catherine, tr. from FRE. (Sun & Moon Classics Ser.: No. 19). 208p. (Orig.). 1990. pap. 13.95 (1-55713-119-8) Sun & Moon CA.
— The Diary of A. O. Barnabooth. Cannan, Gilbert, tr. from FRE. LC 90-46619. (Recovered Classics Ser.). 336p. 1990. reprint ed. 18.00 (0-929701-14-3); reprint ed. pap. 10.00 (0-929701-15-1) McPherson & Co.
— An Homage to Jerome. Chezet, Jean-Paul de, tr. from FRE. LC 83-63447.Tr. of Le/Patron des traducteurs. 64p. (Orig.). 1984. pap. 8.95 (0-910395-09-8) Marlboro Pr.
Larbey, Bob. A Month of Sundays: A Comedy LC 88-142128. 99 p. 1988. write for info. (0-573-61870-4) S French Trade.
Larbig, Laura M. White Buffalo Poems. Sharenov, Evelyn, ed. 24p. (Orig.). 1994. pap. 5.50 (0-9627791-4-8) Willamette Bks OR.
***Larbulestier, Tiffany.** Words of Ages: Witnessing U. S. History Through Literature. 300p. 2000. pap. text 18.95 (0-932765-84-X) Close Up Fnd.
Larcada, Luis I. La Imagen Que No Se Deteriora. Editorial Arcos, Inc., Staff, ed. (Arcos Poetica Ser.: No. 1). (SPA., Illus.). 110p. (Orig.). 1989. lib. bdg. 10.00 (0-937509-04-3) Edit Arcos.
— El Piano de Cristal. Editorial Arcos, Inc., Staff, ed. LC 86-80617. (Coleccion Narrativa y Ensayo). (Illus.). 117p. (Orig.). 1986. 7.50 (0-937509-00-0) Edit Arcos.
— Tierra del Sur. Editorial Arcos, Inc., Staff, ed. (Arcos Poetica Ser.: No. 3). (SPA., Illus.). 44p. 1993. lib. bdg. 6.00 (0-937509-09-4) Edit Arcos.
Larcada, Luis I., ed. see Guerra, Pedro L.
Larcan, A., et al, eds. Consumption Coagulpathies. 176p. (gr. 13). 1987. 73.50 (2-225-80981-X, MA981) Mosby Inc.
***Larchar, Martha.** Bible Discovery Devotions. LC 99-89234. 2000. write for info. (0-570-05225-4) Concordia.
Larche. From the Heartland: Introduction to Speech Communication. 1995. pap. write for info. (0-8087-7522-7) Pearson Custom.
Larche, Doug. O Christmas Three! 1995. 5.50 (0-87129-535-0, O54) Dramatic Pub.
Larche, Douglas. Father Gander Nursery Rhymes. LC 85-72785. (Illus.). 47p. (J). (ps up). 1986. 15.95 (0-911655-12-3) Advocacy Pr.
Larche, Douglas W. Truth on Trial: The Ballad of Sojourner Truth. 1996. pap. 5.50 (0-87129-712-4, TA6) Dramatic Pub.
***Larche Lusk, Martha.** Fanball. 190p. 2000. pap. 12.95 (1-891929-47-X) Four Seasons.
Larcher, Fabian R., tr. see Aquinas, Thomas, Saint.
Larcher, Jean. Fantastic Alphabets. LC 76-24153. (Pictorial Archive Ser.). 72p. (Orig.). 1976. pap. 7.95 (0-486-23412-6) Dover.
— Geometrical Designs & Optical Art. LC 74-79464. (Pictorial Archive Ser.). (Illus.). 80p. 1974. 8.95 (0-486-23100-3) Dover.
— Optical & Geometrical Allover Patterns: 70 Original Drawings. LC 78-72985. (Pictorial Archive Ser.). (Illus.). 70p. 1979. pap. 7.95 (0-486-23758-3) Dover.
— Ready-to-Use News Announcements. 1981. pap. 4.95 (0-486-24173-4) Dover.
***Larcher, Paul.** Labour-Based Road Construction. 200p. 1998. pap. 22.95 (1-85339-416-5, Pub. by Intermed Tech) Stylus Pub VA.
Larcher, Walter. Physiological Plant Ecology: Ecophysiology & Stress Physiology of Function Groups. 3rd ed. LC 94-24405.Tr. of Okophysiologie der Pflanzen. 506p. 1995. 47.95 (0-387-58116-2) Spr-Verlag.
Larcher, Walter. Physiological Plant Ecology: Ecophysiology & Stress Physiology of Functional Groups. 3rd ed. 1997. 53.95 (3-540-58116-2) Spr-Verlag.
Larchey, Eitenne-Loredan. Dictionnaire de l'Argot Parisien. (FRE.). 252p. 1985. pap. 32.95 (0-7859-8233-7, 2905291036) Fr & Eur.
Larchey, Loredan. Dictionnaire de L'Argot Parisien. (FRE.). 240p. 1996. 59.95 (0-7859-9256-1) Fr & Eur.
Larchivolto. New Offices in the USA. 1997. 79.95 (88-7685-100-3) LArchivolto.
— Showroom & Art Galleries in the Usa. 1999. 79.95 (1-56970-531-3) Bks Nippan.
L'Archivolto Editorial Staff, ed. Disco Design in Italy. (Illus.). 260p. 1997. 79.95 (88-7685-085-6, Pub. by LArchivolto) Bks Nippan.
L'Archivolto Editorial Staff, ed. New Shops in Italy, Vol. 5. (Illus.). 240p. 79.95 (88-7685-101-1, Pub. by LArchivolto) Bks Nippan.
L'Archivolto Editorial Staff, ed. Showrooms & Art Galleries in the U. S. A. (Illus.). 240p. 1999. 79.95 (88-7685-102-X, Pub. by LArchivolto) Bks Nippan.
LArchivolto Editors. Industrial Design in Italy. 1998. 79.95 (88-7685-088-0) Bks Nippan.
— Lofts in Italy. 1998. 79.95 (1-56970-530-5) Bks Nippan.
— New American Houses: Country, Sea & Cities. LC 98-164354. 1998. 79.95 (88-7685-097-X, Pub. by LArchivolto) Bks Nippan.
— New Exhibits in Italy. (Illus.). 260p. 1997. 79.95 (88-7685-084-8, Pub. by LArchivolto) Bks Nippan.
— New Offices in the USA. 1998. 79.95 (1-56970-528-3) US Renditions.
— New Restaurants in U. S. A. & East Asia. LC 99-174810. 1998. 79.95 (88-7685-098-8, Pub. by LArchivolto) Bks Nippan.
— New Shops in Italy. 1998. 79.95 (1-56970-529-1) Bks Nippan.
LArchivolto Editors. New Shops in Italy, Vol. 4. 79.95 (88-7685-096-1, Pub. by LArchivolto) Bks Nippan.
LArchivolto Editors. Restaurant & Shop Facades: 301 Outstanding Restaurants, Cafes, Bars & Amusement Facilities. 1998. 69.95 (4-7858-0251-0, Pub. by Shotenkenchiku-Sha) Bks Nippan.
— Urban Interiors in New York & U. S. A. (Illus.). 260p. 1997. 79.95 (88-7685-086-4, Pub. by LArchivolto) Bks Nippan.
— Villas in Italy. (Illus.). 230p. 1996. 59.95 (88-7685-076-7, Pub. by LArchivolto) Bks Nippan.
***LArchivolto Editors, ed.** Lofts & Apartments in New York. (Illus.). 240p. 1999. 79.95 (88-7685-104-6, Pub. by LArchivolto) Bks Nippan.
LArchivolto Editors, ed. New Stores in the U. S. A. (Illus.). 240p. 1999. 79.95 (88-7685-105-4, Pub. by LArchivolto) Bks Nippan.
LArchivolto Editors, jt. auth. see Gallo, Paola.
Larco, Jorge L., jt. auth. see Henderson, Bruce A.
Larcom. March. (Illus.). 32p. (ps-3). 14.95 (0-06-024307-4); lib. bdg. 14.89 (0-06-024308-2) HarpC.
Larcom, Lucy. As It Is in Heaven. (Notable American Authors Ser.). 1999. reprint ed. lib. bdg. 125.00 (0-7812-3750-5) Rprt Serv.
— As It Is in Heaven (1898) 160p. 1998. reprint ed. pap. 17.95 (0-7661-0335-8) Kessinger Pub.
— At the Beautiful Gate & Other Songs of Faith. 1999. reprint ed. lib. bdg. 125.00 (0-7812-3752-1) Rprt Serv.
— Childhood Songs. (Notable American Authors Ser.). 1999. reprint ed. lib. bdg. 125.00 (0-7812-3747-5) Rprt Serv.
— Collected Poems. (Notable American Authors Ser.). 1999. reprint ed. lib. bdg. 125.00 (0-7812-3748-3) Rprt Serv.
— Easter Gleams. (Notable American Authors Ser.). 1999. reprint ed. lib. bdg. 125.00 (0-7812-3749-1) Rprt Serv.
— An Idyl of Work. LC 72-88503. 183p. 1970. reprint ed. lib. bdg. 59.50 (0-8371-4968-1, LAIW, Greenwood Pr) Greenwood.
— Leila Amoung the Mountains. (Notable American Authors Ser.). 1999. lib. bdg. 125.00 (0-7812-3745-9) Rprt Serv.
— A New England Girlhood. 1990. 16.50 (0-8446-2431-4) Peter Smith.
— A New England Girlhood. 274p. 1977. reprint ed. 24.95 (0-87928-078-6) Corner Hse.
— A New England Girlhood: Outlined from Memory. (Illus.). 300p. 1985. reprint ed. pap. text 16.95 (0-930350-82-0) NE U Pr.
— Poems. (Notable American Authors Ser.). 1999. reprint ed. lib. bdg. 125.00 (0-7812-3746-7) Rprt Serv.
— Ships in the Mist. (Notable American Authors Ser.). 1999. reprint ed. lib. bdg. 125.00 (0-7812-3743-2) Rprt Serv.
— Similitudes from Ocean & Prairie. (Notable American Authors Ser.). 1999. reprint ed. lib. bdg. 125.00 (0-7812-3742-4) Rprt Serv.
— The Sunbeam & Other Stories. (Notable American Authors Ser.). 1999. reprint ed. lib. bdg. 125.00 (0-7812-3744-0) Rprt Serv.
— The Unseen Friend. (Notable American Authors Ser.). 1999. reprint ed. lib. bdg. 125.00 (0-7812-3751-3) Rprt Serv.
Larcombe, Isobel. Reintegration to School after Hospital Treatment: Needs & Services. 137p. (C). 1995. 61.95 (1-85628-990-7, Pub. by Avebry) Ashgate Pub Co.
Larcombe, Jennifer Rees. The Baby in the Basket. LC 98-51207. (Best Bible Stories Ser.). (Illus.). 24p. (J). (ps-3). 1999. pap. 2.99 (1-58134-055-9) Crossway Bks.
***Larcombe, Jennifer Rees.** The Best Boat Ever Built. (Illus.). 24p. (J). (ps-3). 1999. pap. 2.99 (1-58134-148-2) Crossway Bks.
— Danger on the Lonely Road. (Illus.). 24p. (J). (ps-3). 1999. pap. 2.99 (1-58134-149-0) Crossway Bks.
Larcombe, Jennifer Rees. Giving Cards: No Hands by Ours. 192p. pap. 6.99 (0-551-02863-7) Zondervan.
— The Gospel According to Brodie: Lessons from a Blind Labrador. 160p. 1996. pap. 6.99 (0-551-02985-4) Zondervan.
***Larcombe, Jennifer Rees.** Lost in Jerusalem. (Illus.). 24p. (J). (gr. k-3). 1999. pap. 2.99 (1-58134-150-4) Crossway Bks.
Larcombe, Jennifer Rees. The Man Who Was Not Tall Enough. LC 98-51208. (Best Bible Stories Ser.). (Illus.). 24p. (J). (ps-3). 1999. pap. 2.99 (1-58134-052-4) Crossway Bks.
***Larcombe, Jennifer Rees.** The Terrible Giant. LC 98-51210. (Best Bible Stories Ser.). (Illus.). 24p. (J). (ps up). 1999. pap. 2.99 (1-58134-054-0) Crossway Bks.
— The Walls That Fell down Flat. (Illus.). 24p. (J). (ps-3). 1999. pap. 2.99 (1-58134-151-2) Crossway Bks.
Larcombe, Jennifer Rees & IEEE Communications Society Staff. The Boy Who Ran Away. LC 98-51209. (Best Bible Stories Ser.). (Illus.). 24p. (J). (ps-3). 1999. pap. 2.99 (1-58134-053-2) Crossway Bks.
***Larcon, Jean-Paul.** Entrepreneurship & Economic Transition in Central Europe. LC 98-39133. 1998. 89.95 (0-7923-8279-X) Kluwer Academic.
Lard, Melva S. A Bouquet from Heaven. LC 96-69681. (Illus.). 72p. 1997. boxed set 14.95 (0-89221-325-6) New Leaf.
Lardaro, Leonard. Applied Econometrics. (C). 1993. pap., student ed. 30.00 (0-06-501610-6) Addson-Wesley Educ.
Lardas, George, jt. tr. see Lambertsen, Isaac.
Lardas, George D., tr. & intro. see St. Tikhon of Zadonsk.
***Lardas, John.** The Bop Apocalypse: The Religious Visions of Kerouac, Ginsberg, & Burroughs. 376p. 2000. text 39.95 (0-252-02599-7) U of Ill Pr.
***Larden, Michael L.** Mas Oyama: The Legend, the Legacy. (Illus.). 184p. 2000. pap. 14.95 (1-892515-24-5, Pub. by Multi-Media Commns) Unique Pubns.
Lardent, Esther F. The Law Firm Pro Bono Resource Guide. (Illus.). 450p. 1998. pap. 149.95 (0-9659548-2-X) Pro Bono Inst.
— 1995 Challenge Report: Meeting the Challenge: The First Status Report on the Pro Bono Activities of America's Major Law Firms. 40p. (Orig.). 1997. pap. write for info. (0-9659548-0-3) Pro Bono Inst.
Lardet, Pierre. L' Apologie de Jerome Contre Rufin: Un Commentaire. LC 93-13086. (Supplements to Vigiliae Christianae Ser.: Vol. 15). (FRE.). xxxii, 564p. 1993. 182.50 (90-04-09457-1) Brill Academic Pubs.
Lardie, Debra. Dictionary of the Occult & New Age. 352p. 1997. 19.99 (0-8254-3090-9) Kregel.
***Lardinois, A. P. & McClure, Laura.** Making Silence Speak: Women's Voices in Greek Literature & Society. LC 00-33648. 2001. pap. write for info. (0-691-00466-8) Princeton U Pr.
Lardinois, A. P., jt. auth. see Oudemans, T. C.
Lardinois, Robert, et al. Deedo & Dido. LC 92-20879. (Our Feathered & Furry Friends Ser.). (Illus.). 42p. (J). (ps-2). 1992. lib. bdg. 21.95 incl. audio (0-9629715-2-9); audio 7.95 (0-9629715-3-7) Jewel Publishing.
— Deedo & Dido: Story. LC 92-20879. (Our Feathered & Furry Friends Ser.). (Illus.). 42p. (J). (ps-2). 1992. lib. bdg. 14.95 (0-9629715-1-0) Jewel Publishing.
Lardinois, Sandra. Patchy Pumpkin Finds Himself a Home. rev. ed. Gress, Jonna C., ed. (Illus.). 22p. (J). (ps-2). reprint ed. pap. 2.99 (0-944943-64-0) Current Inc.
Lardner. Mechanics of Solids. 1993. text, student ed. 31.25 (0-07-036404-4) McGraw.
— Mechanics of Solids. 1994. text 27.50 (0-07-036403-6) McGraw.
Lardner, D. Manufacturing of Porcelain & Glass. 320p. 1994. pap. 25.00 (0-87556-795-9) Saifer.
— Steam Engine, 1888. (Illus.). 135p. 1989. pap. 20.00 (0-87556-165-9) Saifer.
Lardner, D., jt. auth. see Kater, Henry.
Lardner, Dionysius. Railway Economy: A Treatise on the New Art of Transport. LC 67-29509. (Reprints of Economic Classics Ser.). xxiii, 442p. 1968. reprint ed. 49.50 (0-678-00361-0) Kelley.
Lardner, George. The Stalking of Kristin. 400p. 1997. mass mkt. 6.99 (0-451-40731-8, Onyx) NAL.
Lardner, James, jt. auth. see Reppetto, Thomas A.
Lardner, Janet. Balti Secrets of the Birmingham Balti Company: A Cross Between Wok & Casserole Cookery. (Illus.). 192p. (Orig.). 1996. pap. 17.95 (0-572-02298-0, Pub. by W Foulsham) Trans-Atl Phila.
Lardner, John. Strong Cigars & Lovely Women. 21.95 (0-8488-0124-5) Amereon Ltd.
Lardner, Kym. Arnold the Prickly Teddy. LC 92-31919. (Voyages Ser.). (Illus.). (J). 1993. 14.00 (0-383-03552-X) SRA McGraw.
Lardner, Nathaniel, jt. auth. see Wake, William.
Lardner, Ring. Annotated Baseball Stories of Ring W. Lardner 1914-1919. 1997. pap. text 24.95 (0-8047-2963-8) Stanford U Pr.
— The Best Short Stories of Ring Lardner. 352p. 1976. 40.00 (0-684-14743-2, Scribners Ref) Mac Lib Ref.
— The Best Short Stories of Ring Lardner. LC 57-13394. 346p. 1985. lib. bdg. 22.50 (0-685-04559-5, Scribners Ref) Mac Lib Ref.
Lardner, Ring, Jr. The Best Short Stories of Ring Lardner. 1976. 23.95 (0-89190-073-X) Amereon Ltd.
Lardner, Ring. Ecstacy of Owen Muir. LC 97-26668. (Literary Classics Ser.). 272p. 1997. pap. text 7.95 (1-57392-173-4) Prometheus Bks.
— Haircut & Other Stories. 190p. reprint ed. lib. bdg. 20.95 (0-88411-583-6) Amereon Ltd.
— How to Write Short Stories. 1971. reprint ed. 59.00 (0-403-01063-2) Scholarly.
***Lardner, Ring, Jr.** I'd Hate Myself in the Morning: A Memoir. 2000. 22.95 (1-56025-296-0, Thunders Mouth) Avalon NY.
Lardner, Ring, Jr. Letters from Ring. Caruthers, Clifford M., ed. 1979. 10.95 (0-685-05275-3); pap. 5.95 (0-911938-09-5) Walden Pr.
— Mathematical Theory of Dislocations & Fracture. LC 75-190346. (Mathematical Expositions Ser.: No. 17). 375p. reprint ed. pap. 116.30 (0-608-30067-5, 202049800018) Bks Demand.
— Ring Lardner: Selected Short Fiction. LC 96-44827. 384p. 1997. pap. 10.95 (0-14-118018-8) Viking Penguin.
Lardner, Ring. The Ring Lardner Reader. 1999. pap. 4.99 (0-451-52586-8, Sig Classics) NAL.
— Some Champions: Sketches & Fiction from a Humorist's Career. LC 75-38544. (Illus.). xv, 205 p. 1976. write for info. (0-684-14582-0) Free Pr.
— The Story of a Wonder Man: Being the Autobiography of Ring Lardner. LC 75-26216. (Illus.). 151p. 1975. reprint ed. lib. bdg. 45.00 (0-8371-8414-2, LAWOM, Greenwood Pr) Greenwood.
— Story of the Wonder Man. 1976. 22.95 (0-8488-1073-2) Amereon Ltd.
— You Know Me Al. 1987. 30.00 (0-02-568440-X) S&S Trade.
***Lardner, Ring, Jr.** You Know Me Al. 210p. 2000. text 25.95 (1-56000-443-6) Transaction Pubs.
Lardner, Ring, Jr. You Know Me Al. (Prairie State Bks.). 272p. 1992. pap. text 16.95 (0-252-06230-2) U of Ill Pr.
Lardner, Ring. You Know Me Al. 218p. reprint ed. lib. bdg. 21.95 (0-88411-584-4) Amereon Ltd.
— You Know Me Al. 1993. reprint ed. lib. bdg. 18.95 (1-56849-207-3) Buccaneer Bks.

L

— You Know Me Al. unabridged ed. 128p. 1995. pap. 1.00 (*0-486-28513-8*) Dover.

Lardner, Ring & Sheed, Wilfrid, intros. Haircut & Other Stories. LC 84-40002. 192p. 1984. pap. 6.95 (*0-394-72610-3*) Vin Bks.

Lardner, Robin W., jt. auth. see Arya, Jagdish C.

Lardner, T. & Trawick, Leonard M., eds. Voices of Cleveland. (Illus.). 170p. (Orig.). 1996. pap. 17.50 (*1-880834-21-9*) Cleveland St Univ Poetry Ctr.

***Lardner, Ted & Lundberg, Todd.** Exchanges: Reading & Writing about Consumer Culture. LC 00-28737. 2000. write for info. (*0-321-03799-5*) Longman.

Lardner, Thomas J. & Archer, R. R. Mechanics of Solids: An Introduction. LC 93-2372. 992p. (C). 1994. 100.31 (*0-07-833358-X*) McGraw.

***Lardo, Vincent.** The Hampton Affair. 352p. 2000. mass mkt. 6.99 (*0-425-17482-4*) Berkley Pub.

— The Hampton Affair. LC 98-33259. 320p. 1999. 23.95 (*0-399-14476-5*, G P Putnam) Peng Put Young Read.

— The Hampton Connection. 320p. 2000. 23.95 (*0-399-14631-8*) Putnam Pub Group.

Lardy, Nicholas R. Agriculture in China's Modern Economic Development. LC 82-23555. (Illus.). 304p. 1983. text 80.00 (*0-521-25246-6*) Cambridge U Pr.

— China in the World Economy. 156p. (Orig.). (C). 1994. pap. 16.95 (*0-88132-200-8*) Inst Intl Eco.

— China's Entry into the World Economy: Implicatioms for Northeast Asia & the U. S. (Asian Agenda Reports: No. 11). (Illus.). 76p. (Orig.). (C). 1987. pap. text 10.50 (*0-8191-6372-4*); lib. bdg. 27.00 (*0-8191-6371-6*) U Pr of Amer.

— China's Unfinished Economic Revolution. LC 98-19667. 240p. 1998. 44.95 (*0-8157-5134-6*); pap. 18.95 (*0-8157-5133-8*) Brookings.

— Economic Growth & Distribution in China. (Illus.). 256p. 1978. text 74.95 (*0-521-21904-3*) Cambridge U Pr.

— Foreign Trade & Economic Reform in China, 1978-1990. (Illus.). 209p. (C). 1991. text 59.95 (*0-521-41495-4*) Cambridge U Pr.

— Foreign Trade & Economic Reform in China, 1978-1990. (Illus.). 209p. (C). 1993. pap. text 17.95 (*0-521-45835-8*) Cambridge U Pr.

Lardy, Nicholas R., ed. Chinese Economic Planning: Transations from Chi-Hua Ching-Chi. LC 78-52292. 280p. reprint ed. pap. 86.80 (*0-608-14216-6*, 202185800024) Bks Demand.

Lardy, Nicholas R. & Lieberthal, Kenneth G., eds. Chen Yun's Strategy for China's Development: A Non-Maoist Alternative. LC 82-16776. (China Book Project Ser.). 250p. (C). (gr. 13). 1983. text 85.95 (*0-87332-225-8*) M E Sharpe.

Lare, Gary, jt. auth. see Schroeder, Don.

Lare, Gary A. Acquiring & Organizing Curriculum Materials: A Guide & Directory of Resources. LC 97-17597. 208p. 1997. pap. 32.00 (*0-8108-3347-6*) Scarecrow.

Lare, James, jt. ed. see Rossiter, Clinton.

Lareau, Alan. The Wild Stage: Literary Cabarets of the Weimar Republic. LC 94-48349. (Studies in German Literature, Linguistics & Culture). 215p. 1995. 55.00 (*1-879751-86-0*) Camden Hse.

***Lareau, Annette.** Home Advantage: Social Class & Parental Intervention in Elementary Education. 288p. 2000. 69.00 (*0-7425-0144-2*); pap. 21.95 (*0-7425-0145-0*) Rowman.

Lareau, Annette. Home Advantage: Social Class & Parental Intervention in Elementary Education. 220p. 1989. pap. 29.95 (*1-85000-317-3*, Falmer Pr) Taylor & Francis.

Lareau, Annette, ed. see Shultz, Jeffrey.

***Lareau, Gwen B.** The National Directory of Integrated Healthcare Delivery Systems. 2nd ed. Harris, Phyllis, ed. 557p. 1999. pap. text 395.00 (*1-882364-31-7*, Amer Busn Pub) Hlth Res Pub.

— The National Directory of Physician Organizations. 2nd ed. Harris, Phyllis, ed. 605p. 1999. pap. text 495.00 (*1-882364-18-X*, Amer Busn Pub) Hlth Res Pub.

— The Workers' Compensation Managed Care Directory & Reference Guide. Harris, Phyllis & Kerber, Beth, eds. 252p. 1999. pap. text 185.00 (*1-882364-38-4*, Amer Busn Pub) Hlth Res Pub.

Lareau, Gwen B., ed. What's Working in Eldercare. Orig. Title: What's Working in Adult Day Care. 431p. 1996. ring bd. 107.45 (*1-882364-05-8*, Amer Busn Pub) Hlth Res Pub.

***Lareau, Gwen B. & Harris, Phyllis, eds.** The National Directory of Managed Care Organizations. 2nd ed. 863p. 1998. pap. text 285.00 (*1-882364-28-7*, Amer Busn Pub) Hlth Res Pub.

***Lareau, Mark.** All Wired Up: Wire Techniques for the Beadworker & Jewelry Maker. 128p. 2000. pap. 21.95 (*1-883010-73-X*, Pub. by Interweave) IPG Chicago.

Lareau, Peter N. Drafting the Union Contract: A Handbook for the Management Negotiator. 1988. 160.00 (*0-8205-1494-2*) Bender.

Lareau, Thomas J. & Darmstadter, Joel. Energy & Household Expenditure Patterns. LC 83-17633. 161p. 1983. pap. 15.95 (*0-8018-3204-7*) Resources Future.

Lareau, William. The Businessuses of American't & Change. 128p. 1992. 12.95 (*0-8329-0501-1*) New Win Pub.

— Conduct Expected for the 21st Century: Rules for a Successful Career. LC 97-42117. 1996. pap. text 14.95 (*0-8329-0514-3*) New Win Pub.

— Dancing with the Dinosaur. LC 93-33922. 256p. 1993. 14.95 (*0-8329-0505-4*) New Win Pub.

— Where Am I Now? Where Am I Going? The Career Manual. LC 92-3981. 1992. pap. 12.95 (*0-8329-0500-3*) New Win Pub.

Laredo. Beginning & Intermediate Algebra. 608p. 1998. pap. text 50.75 (*0-536-01371-3*) Pearson Custom.

— Beginning & Intermediate Algebra. 2nd ed. 634p. 1999. pap. text 55.00 (*0-536-02258-5*) Pearson Custom.

Laredo, J. D., jt. ed. see Bard, M.

Laredo, Joseph, tr. see Camus, Albert.

Laredo, Miguel Carmena. Etica Para Pancho: Al Rescate de los Valores de los Jovenes. 2nd ed. (SPA.). 179p. (J). (gr. 4-7). 1997. pap. 14.98 (*968-13-2791-8*) Edit Diana.

Laredo Publishing Staff, ed. see Sultemeier, Annette.

Laredo, Ruth. The Ruth Laredo Becoming a Musician Book. (Illus.). 72p. 1992. pap. 11.95 (*0-913574-99-6*, EA00714) Eur-Am Music.

Laredo, Victor. Sephardic Spain. (Illus.). 1978. pap. 8.00 (*84-399-8381-6*) Edit Mensaje.

Laredu, tr. see Baichelor.

LaRegina, Marie, jt. auth. see Sharp, Patrick.

Laremont, Ricardo R. Islam & the Politics of Resistance in Algeria, 1783-1992. LC 99-26862. 1999. write for info. (*0-86543-753-X*) Africa World.

Larence, et al, eds. Introduction to Archival Science. 96p. 1996. 10.95 (*0-910653-21-6*) Archival Servs.

Larence, Anna. After Hours. 1996. mass mkt. 4.99 (*0-7860-0277-8*, Pinncle Kensgtn) Kensgtn Pub Corp.

— Give & Take. 1999. mass mkt. 4.99 (*1-58314-017-4*) BET Bks.

***Larence, Anna.** Give & Take. (Arabesque Ser.). 2000. mass mkt. 5.99 (*1-58314-111-1*) BET Bks.

Larence, Anna. Love Everlasting. (Arabesque Ser.). 256p. 1998. pap. 4.99 (*0-7860-0512-2*, Pinncle Kensgtn) Kensgtn Pub Corp.

— Second Time Around. 256p. 1997. mass mkt. 4.99 (*0-7860-0433-9*, Pinncle Kensgtn) Kensgtn Pub Corp.

Larence, Eileen R. Superfund: State Voluntary Programs Provide Incentives to Encourage Cleanups. (Illus.). 60p. 1998. pap. text 20.00 (*0-7881-4633-5*) DIANE Pub.

Larere, Philippe. Baptism in Water & Baptism in the Spirit: A Biblical, Liturgical & Theological Exposition. Madigan, Patrick, tr. 96p. (Orig.). 1993. pap. 7.95 (*0-8146-2225-9*) Liturgical Pr.

— The Lord's Supper: Toward an Ecumenical Understanding of the Eucharist. Madigan, Patrick, tr. 100p. (Orig.). 1993. pap. 7.95 (*0-8146-2226-7*) Liturgical Pr.

***Larew, Hiram.** Part Of. (Illus.). 32p. 1999. pap. 5.00 (*1-879457-62-8*) Norton Coker Pr.

Larew, Hiram & Capizzi, Joseph. Common Insect & Mite Galls of the Pacific Northwest. (Illus.). 80p. (Orig.). 1983. pap. 8.95 (*0-87071-055-9*) Oreg St U Pr.

Larew, James C. A Party Reborn: The Democrats of Iowa, 1950-1974. LC 80-51855. (Illus.). 216p. (C). 1980. 3.50 (*0-89033-002-6*); pap. 6.00 (*0-686-69969-6*) State Hist Iowa.

***Larew, Richard, ed.** Skills & Knowledge of Cost Engineering. 4th rev. ed. LC 99-228258. (Illus.). 125p. 1999. pap. 32.50 (*1-885517-13-0*) AACE Intl.

Larfeld, Wilhelm. Handbuch der Griechischen Epigraphik, 2 vols. in 3. xxii, 1561p. 1971. reprint ed. write for info. (*0-318-70953-8*); reprint ed. write for info. (*0-318-72100-7*) G Olms Pubs.

— Handbuch der Griechischen Epigraphik, 2 vols. in 3, Bd. I. xxii, 1561p. 1971. reprint ed. write for info. (*0-318-70954-6*) G Olms Pubs.

— Handbuch der Griechischen Epigraphik, 2 vols. in 3, Bd. II, 1: Die Attischen Inschriften. xxii, 1561p. 1971. reprint ed. write for info. (*0-318-70955-4*) G Olms Pubs.

— Handbuch der Griechischen Epigraphik, 2 vols. in 3, Bd. II, 2: Handbuch der Attischen Inschriften. xxii, 1561p. 1971. reprint ed. write for info. (*0-318-70956-2*) G Olms Pubs.

Larg, Alex. Beauty Shots. (Pro-Lighting Ser.). (Illus.). 160p. 1997. pap. 35.00 (*2-88046-323-8*, Rotovision) Watsn-Guptill.

— Black & White Shots. (Pro-Lighting Ser.). 160p. 1999. pap. 35.00 (*2-88046-462-5*) Watsn-Guptill.

— Erotica: A Guide to Professional Lighting Techniques. (Pro-Lighting Ser.). (Illus.). 160p. 1999. pap. 35.00 (*2-88046-373-4*, Rotovision) Watsn-Guptill.

— Fashion Shots: A Guide to Professional Lighting Techniques. (Pro-Lighting Ser.). (Illus.). 160p. 1999. pap. 35.00 (*2-88046-372-6*, Rotovision) Watsn-Guptill.

— New Glamour. (Pro-Lighting Ser.). (Illus.). 160p. 1997. pap. 35.00 (*2-88046-322-X*, Rotovision) Watsn-Guptill.

— New Product Shots: A Guide to Professional Lighting Techniques. (Pro-Lighting Ser.). 100p. 1999. pap. 35.00 (*2-88046-371-8*, Rotovision) Watsn-Guptill.

— Night Shots. (Pro-Lighting Ser.). (Illus.). 160p. 1997. pap. 35.00 (*2-88046-324-6*, Rotovision) Watsn-Guptill.

— Provocative Shots. (Pro-Lighting Ser.). 160p. 1999. pap. 35.00 (*2-88046-467-6*) Watsn-Guptill.

Larg, D. John Ruskin. LC 74-1447. (John Ruskin Ser.: No. 87). 1974. lib. bdg. 75.00 (*0-8383-2047-3*) M S G Haskell Hse.

Largan, Mark. Corporate Banking: Practice & Law. 1997. pap. 90.00 (*0-85297-418-3*, Pub. by Chartered Bank) St Mut.

***Largan, Mark.** Introduction to Law in the Financial Services. 208p. 1999. pap. 80.00 (*0-85297-522-8*, Pub. by Chartered Bank) St Mut.

Largan, Mark. Operating in a Regulated Environment. 2nd ed. 400p. 1999. pap. 120.00 (*0-85297-508-2*, Pub. by Chartered Bank) St Mut.

Largan, Mark & Colley, Allan. Banking Operations: Regulation, Market Practice & Treasury Management. 390p. 1999. pap., wbk. ed. 120.00 (*0-85297-417-5*, Pub. by Chartered Bank) St Mut.

Largan, Mark & Featherstone-Witty, Virginia Alexandra. Multinational Corporate Finance. 371p. 1999. pap. 120.00 (*0-85297-427-2*, Pub. by Chartered Bank) St Mut.

Largay, James A. & Livingston, John. Accounting for Changing Prices: Replacement Cost & General Price Level Adjustments. LC 76-7491. (Wiley Hamilton Publication). 317p. reprint ed. pap. 98.30 (*0-8357-5065-5*, 202517700042) Bks Demand.

Large. Berlin. 1993. write for info. (*0-201-62283-1*) Addison-Wesley.

Large, Andrew. The Future of Global Financial Regulation. (Occasional Paper Ser.: No. 57). 41p. 1998. pap. 10.00 (*1-56708-106-1*) Grp of Thirty.

***Large, Andrew, et al.** Information Seeking in the Online Age: Principles & Practice. LC 98-41496. 336p. 1999. 95.00 (*1-85739-260-4*) Bowker-Saur.

Large, Andrew, jt. ed. see Armstrong, C. J.

Large, Andy, jt. auth. see Armstrong, Chris.

Large, B. J. & Hughes, I. E. Learning Pharmacology Through MCQ. 2nd ed. LC 89-21548. 258p. 1990. pap. 78.50 (*0-471-92708-2*) Wiley.

Large, Brian. Martinu. LC 75-45082. (Illus.). 198p. 1976. 45.00 (*0-8419-0256-9*) Holmes & Meier.

— Smetana. LC 84-1825. (Music Reprint Ser.). (Illus.). 524p. 1985. reprint ed. lib. bdg. 52.50 (*0-306-76243-9*) Da Capo.

Large, Brian, ed. see Wagner, Richard.

Large, Char. The Clustering Approach to Better Essay Writing. 59p. 1987. pap., student ed. 14.99 (*0-89824-146-4*) Trillium Pr.

Large, Clay. Berlin. 1995. 25.00 (*0-689-12185-7*) S&S Trade.

Large, David C. Between Two Fires: Europe's Path in the 1930s. 1991. pap. 16.95 (*0-393-30757-3*) Norton.

— Germans to the Front: West German Rearmament in the Adenauer Era. LC 95-5401. 1995. pap. text 22.50 (*0-8078-4539-6*); lib. bdg. 59.95 (*0-8078-2235-3*) U of NC Pr.

— Where Ghosts Walked: Munich's Road to the Third Reich. LC 97-4263. 480p. 1997. 32.50 (*0-393-03836-X*) Norton.

Large, David C., ed. Contending with Hitler: Varieties of German Resistance in the Third Reich. (Publications of the German Historical Institute, Washington, D.C.). 207p. (C). 1994. pap. text 15.95 (*0-521-46668-7*) Cambridge U Pr.

Large, David Clay. Berlin. 40.00 (*0-465-02646-X*, Pub. by Basic) HarpC.

Large, David G. & Warren, Christopher D., eds. Glycopeptides & Related Compounds. LC 97-10206. (Illus.). 768p. 1997. text 225.00 (*0-8247-9531-8*) Dekker.

Large, Duncan, tr. & intro. see Nietzsche, Friedrich Wilhelm.

Large, E. C. Asleep in the Afternoon: A Novel. Reginald, R. & Melville, Douglas, eds. LC 77-84241. (Lost Race & Adult Fantasy Ser.). 1978. reprint ed. lib. bdg. 33.95 (*0-405-10991-1*) Ayer.

Large, George R. Battle of Gettysburg: The Official History by the Gettysburg National Military Park Commission. LC 99-19685. (Illus.). 342p. 1999. pap. 19.95 (*1-57249-171-X*, HE9356) White Mane Pub.

***Large, George R. & Swisher, Joe A.** Battle of Antietam: The Official History by the Antietam Battlefield Board. LC 98-19999. 224p. 1998. pap. 14.95 (*1-57249-102-7*, Burd St Pr) White Mane Pub.

Large Imprint Books Staff. Goalkeepers Are Crazy. Date not set. pap. text. write for info. (*0-582-23326-7*, Pub. by Addison-Wesley) Longman.

Large, J. A., jt. auth. see Armstrong, C. J.

Large, J. H. Abraham - Idolater to Friend of God. 1996. pap. 13.99 (*0-946351-04-X*, Pub. by John Ritchie) Loizeaux.

— Jacob - Supplanter to Prince with God. 1996. pap. 16.99 (*0-946351-14-7*, Pub. by John Ritchie) Loizeaux.

Large, James. Titles & Symbols of Christ: 280 Titles & Symbols. (World Classic Reference Library). 578p. 1995. reprint ed. 19.99 (*0-529-10335-4*, TSC) World Publng.

— Two Hundred & Eighty Titles & Symbols of Christ. (Bible Study Ser: Pulpit Legends Collection: Vol. 578). 578p. 1995. 19.99 (*0-89957-201-4*) AMG Pubs.

Large, Jean-Francoise & Laguerie, Claude, eds. Fluidization VIII. LC 96-85044. (Engineering Foundation - International Fluidization Conference Proceedings Ser.: Vol. 8). 718p. 1997. 120.00 (*0-939204-54-1*, P-80) Am Inst Chem Eng.

Large, Josaphat. Pe Set: Powem. Mafrou, Edisyon, ed. 1994. text. write for info. (*0-9641162-0-0*) Edit La Jeremienne.

Large, Judith. The War Next Door: A Study of Second Track Interventions During the War in Ex-Yugoslavia. LC 99-170736. (Political Science Ser.). (Illus.). 160p. 1998. pap. 21.95 (*1-869890-97-3*, Pub. by Hawthorn Press) Anthroposophic.

Large, Judy. Troll of Tree Hill. (Illus.). 72p. 1995. 18.95 (*1-869890-74-4*, Pub. by Hawthorn Press) Anthroposophic.

Large, Judy, jt. auth. see Carey, Diana.

Large, Peter. The Micro Revolution Revisited. LC 84-2164. 224p. 1984. 36.00 (*0-8476-7361-8*) Rowman.

Large, R. Passenger Tramways of Pontypridd. 52p. (C). 1985. 39.00 (*0-85361-208-0*) St Mut.

Large, Stephen S. Emperors of the Rising Sun: Three Biographies. 1997. 19.00 (*4-7700-1839-8*, Pub. by Kodansha Int) OUP.

Large, Stephen S., ed. Showa Japan: Political, Economic & Social History, 1926-1989, 4 vols. LC 97-39255. (Library of Modern Japan). (Illus.). 1440p. (C). 1998. reprint ed. 700.00 (*0-415-14319-5*, D5678) Routledge.

Largen, Velda L. & Bence, Deborah L. Guide to Good Food. LC 99-10565. 2000. 51.96 (*1-56637-624-6*) Goodheart.

Largent, Christopher, jt. auth. see Breton, Denise.

Largent, D. L. Leptonia & Related Genera of the West Coast. 1976. 52.00 (*3-7682-1114-2*) Lubrecht & Cramer.

Largent, David. How to Identify Mushrooms to Genus 1: Macroscopic Features. 2nd ed. (Illus.). 166p. 1986. pap. 14.95 (*0-916422-01-1*) Mad River.

Largent, David L. Agaricales of California 5: Hygrophoraceae. (Illus.). 220p. (Orig.). 1985. pap. text 67.95 (*0-916422-54-2*) Mad River.

— Entolomataceae of Western North America: Agaricales of California, Vol. 8. (Illus.). 550p. (Orig.). 1994. pap. 225.00 (*0-916422-81-X*) Mad River.

Largent, David L. & Baroni, Timothy J. How to Identify Mushrooms to Genus VI: The Modern Genera - Keys & Descriptions. 200p. (Orig.). 1987. pap. 23.95 (*0-916422-76-3*) Mad River.

Largent, David L. & Thiers, Harry D. How to Identify Mushrooms to Genus II: Field Identification of Genera. (Illus.). 32p. (C). 1977. pap. 6.95 (*0-916422-08-9*) Mad River.

Largent, David L., et al. How to Identify Mushrooms to Genus III Microscopic Features: Microscopic Features. (Illus.). 148p. (C). 1977. pap. 23.95 (*0-916422-09-7*) Mad River.

***Largent, R. Karl.** The Assassin. 368p. 2000. mass mkt. 5.50 (*0-8439-4684-9*, Leisure Bks) Dorchester Pub Co.

Largent, R. Karl. Get the Job You Want: Workbook for the Rotten Resume Writer. Clemens, Matthew V., ed. (Rotten Writer Ser.). (Illus.). 206p. (Orig.). 1995. student ed. 19.95 (*0-9644770-1-7*) Threadbare Pub.

— Getting Started. . . Handbook for the Beginning Novelist. 144p. 1992. pap. write for info. (*1-882214-00-5*) PowerHse Pr.

***Largent, R. Karl.** The Jakarta Plot. 368p. 1999. mass mkt. 5.99 (*0-8439-4568-0*, Pub. by Dorchester Pub Co) CMG.

Largent, R. Karl. Red Ice. 448p. (Orig.). 1995. pap. text 5.99 (*0-8439-3774-2*) Dorchester Pub Co.

***Largent, R. Karl.** Red Ice. 448p. (Orig.). 1999. reprint ed. mass mkt. 5.99 (*0-8439-4604-0*, Leisure Bks) Dorchester Pub Co.

Largent, R. Karl. Red Sand. 400p. (Orig.). 1997. mass mkt. 6.99 (*0-8439-4301-7*, Leisure Bks) Dorchester Pub Co.

Largent, R. Karl. Red Skies. 400p. (Orig.). 1996. mass mkt. 6.99 (*0-8439-4117-0*) Dorchester Pub Co.

Largent, R. Karl. Red Tide. 448p. (Orig.). 1992. mass mkt. 4.99 (*0-8439-3366-6*) Dorchester Pub Co.

***Largent, R. Karl.** Red Tide. 448p. (Orig.). 1999. reprint ed. mass mkt. 5.99 (*0-8439-4602-4*, Leisure Bks) Dorchester Pub Co.

Largent, R. Karl. Red Wind. 368p. 1998. mass mkt. 5.99 (*0-8439-4361-0*, Leisure Bks) Dorchester Pub Co.

***Largent, R. Karl.** Red Wind. 368p. 1999. reprint ed. mass mkt. 5.99 (*0-8439-4603-2*, Leisure Bks) Dorchester Pub Co.

Largent, R. Karl. The Sea. 368p. 1999. mass mkt. 5.99 (*0-8439-4495-1*) Dorchester Pub Co.

— Write Tight & Right: Workbook for the Rotten Business Writer. Clemens, Matthew V., ed. (Rotten Writer Ser.). (Illus.). 224p. (Orig.). 1995. student ed. 19.95 (*0-9644770-2-5*) Threadbare Pub.

Largent, Richard J. Preventing Substance Abuse in the Workplace: A Corporate Handbook. (Illus.). v, 189p. (Orig.). 1996. pap. text 49.95 (*0-9656503-0-8*) Target Investigations.

***Largent, Will.** RAF Wings over Florida. LC 99-59577. 2000. 24.95 (*1-55753-203-6*) Purdue U Pr.

Largeut, Vera, ed. see University of North Carolina Woman's College Facul.

Largier, Niklaus, jt. ed. see der Heyde, Claudia Brinker-von.

Largo, Frances De, see De Largo, Frances.

Largo, Hoskie R., Jr., jt. auth. see Sanderson, Priscilla Lansing.

Largo, Michael. Lies Within. LC 98-88028. 433p. 1999. pap. 14.95 (*0-9666173-0-4*) Tropical Pr.

***Largo, Michael.** Southern Comfort. 4th ed. 240p. 1999. pap. 14.95 (*0-9666173-1-2*) Tropical Pr.

— Welcome to Miami. (Illus.). 2000. pap. 14.95 (*0-9666173-4-7*) Tropical Pr.

Largus, Scribonius. Scribonius Largus - Concordantia in Scribonium Largum. Sconocchia, Sergio, ed. (Alpha-Omega, Reihe A Ser.: Bd. XCII). (GER.). xi, 390p. 1988. write for info. (*3-487-09116-X*) G Olms Pubs.

Lari, Suhail Z. A History of Sindh. (Illus.). 246p. 1995. text 16.95 (*0-19-577501-5*) OUP.

Lari, Suhail Zaheer & Lari, Yasmeen. The Jewel of Sindh: Samma Monuments on Makli Hill :with 326 Illustrations, 50 in Colour. LC 98-930126. (Illus.). 1997. write for info. (*0-19-577901-0*) OUP.

Lari, Yasmeen. The Dual City: Karachi During the Raj. (Illus.). 368p. 1997. 140.00 (*0-19-577735-2*) OUP.

Lari, Yasmeen, jt. see Lari, Suhail Zaheer.

Laribee, Ellen. I Am Native American. LC 97-2468. (Our American Family Ser.). (J). (gr. k-4). 1997. lib. bdg. 15.93 (*0-8239-5014-X*, PowerKids) Rosen Group.

Laric, Michael V. & Stiff, M. Ronald. Lotus 1-2-3 for Marketing & Sales. 256p. 1984. pap. 24.95 (*0-685-08556-2*) P-H.

— Marketing & Business Planning with the IBM PCs: A Guide to the Productive Use of Personal Computers for Business & Marketing Professionals. (Illus.). 224p. 1985. pap. 16.95 (*0-13-557067-0*) P-H.

Larichev, Oleg I. & Moshkovich, Helen M. Verbal Decision Analysis for Unstructured Problems. LC 97-20775. (Theory & Decision Library). 1997. lib. bdg. 121.00 (*0-7923-4578-9*) Kluwer Academic.

Laricino, Patricia. Opportunities in Speech-Language Pathology Careers. (Illus.). 160p. 1987. 13.95 (*0-8442-6013-4*, VGM Career) NTC Contemp Pub Co.

An Asterisk (*) at the beginning of an entry indicates that the title is appearing for the first time.

L

— Opportunities in Speech-Language Pathology Careers. (Illus.). 160p. 1993. pap. 10.95 (0-8442-6014-2, VGM Career) NTC Contemp Pub Co.

Larijani, L. Casey. GPS for Everyone: How the Global Positioning System Can Work for You. LC 97-77600. (Illus.). 384p. 1998. pap. 24.95 (0-9659667-5-5) Am Interface.

***Larimer, Charles F.** Love & Valor: Intimate Civil War Letters Between Captain Jacob & Emeline Ritner. LC 99-72882. (Illus.). 453p. 2000. 27.95 (0-9673863-1-4) Sigourney Pr Inc.

Larimer, George H. & Baldwin, Thomas O., eds. Methods in Enzymology Vol. 290: Molecular Chaperones, Vol. 290. (Illus.). 500p. 1998. text 99.95 (0-12-182191-9) Acad Pr.

Larimer, Louie V., Jr. The Legal Guide for Practicing Psychotherapy in Colorado. 1992. pap. 34.95 (0-9633550-0-7) Ctr Prof Develop.

Larimer, Olga, tr. see Zepeda, Adan.

***Larimer, Ruth E. & Schleicher, Leigh, eds.** New Ways in Using Authentic Materials in the Classroom. LC 98-61418. (New Ways in Tesol Ser.: Vol. II). 233p. 1999. pap. 29.95 (0-939791-80-3) Tchrs Eng Spkrs.

Larimer, Tamela. Buck. LC 86-90774. 176p. (Orig.). (J). (gr. 7 up). 1986. pap. 2.50 (0-380-75172-0, Avon Bks) Morrow Avon.

Larimore, Bertha B. Sprouting for All Seasons: How & What to Sprout, Including Delicious Easy-to-Prepare Recipes. LC 75-23564. (Illus.). 140p. (Orig.). 1993. reprint ed. pap. 11.98 (0-88290-055-2) Horizon Utah.

Larimore, Cindy. Painting Horses in Oil. (How to Draw & Paint Ser.). (Illus.). 32p. (Orig.). 1990. pap. 6.95 (1-56010-065-6, HT-228) W Foster Pub.

Larimore, Colleen, jt. ed. see Garrod, Andrew.

***Larimore, Walter L. & Peel, William C.** The Saline Solution Video Participant's Guide: Sharing Christ in a Busy Practice. (Illus.). 160p. 2000. 9.99 (0-9666809-4-4) Christ Med & Dental Soc.

Larin, Rafael M., jt. ed. see Tardanico, Richard.

Larin, Susan, photos by. Hollywood TV's, Vol. 1. (Illus.). 28p. 1998. pap. 19.95 (0-9666596-0-0, 1) Calendar Girl.

Larina, Anna. This I Cannot Forget: The Memoirs of Nikolai Bukharin's Widow. 408p. 1994. pap. 15.00 (0-393-31234-8) Norton.

Larios A, Pedro, tr. see Wagman, Richard J.

Larios, Julie Hofstrand. On the Stairs. LC 99-25625. (Illus.). 32p. (J). (ps-1). 1999. 15.95 (1-886910-34-0, Pub. by Front Str) Publishers Group.

Larios, Richard, jt. auth. see De Ruiz, Dana C.

Larios S, Maia & Sanz, Maria L., trs. Los Porques de Nuestro Mundo. (Explora y Aprende Ser.). (SPA., Illus.). 96p. (YA). (gr. 3-8). 1993. 15.00 (0-915741-48-2) C D Stampley Ent.

Larios S, Maia, tr. see Martin, Paul D.

Larios S, Maia, tr. see McGrath, Susan.

Larios S, Maia, tr. see O'Neill, Catherine.

Larios S, Maia, tr. see Rathbun, Elizabeth.

Larios S, Maia, jt. tr. see Sanz, Maria T.

Laris. This Is Fun Poems/fngrpls. 64p. (C). 1997. pap. text 13.16 (0-673-19188-5) Addson-Wesley Educ.

Larish, John J. Fun with Digital Photography. LC 96-70653. (Illus.). 78p. (Orig.). (YA). (gr. 7-12). 1998. pap. 9.95 (0-87985-786-2, AC-260, Kodak) Saunders Photo.

— Photo CD: Quality Photographs at Your Fingertips. 256p. 1994. pap. 27.95 (0-941845-09-5) Micro Pub Pr.

Larison, C. W. Silvia Dubois: A Biografy of the Slav Who Whipt Her Mistres & Gand Her Fredom. Lobdell, Jared C., tr. & intro. by. (Schomburg Library of Nineteenth-Century Black Women Writers). (Illus.). 168p. 1990. reprint ed. pap. 9.95 (0-19-506671-5) OUP.

Larison, Cindy, jt. auth. see Johnson, Robert A.

Larison, Cornelius W. Silvia Dubois: A Biography of the Slave Who Whipt Her Mistres & Gained Her Fredom. Lobdell, Jared C., tr. & intro. by. (Schomburg Library of Nineteenth-Century Black Women Writers). 288p. 1988. text 38.00 (0-19-505239-0) OUP.

Larison, Julie, jt. auth. see Sexton, Tom.

Laritz, Kenneth F. Attorney's Guide to Social Security Disability Claims. LC 86-10210. (Regulatory Manual Ser.). 451p. 1986. text 110.00 (0-07-008461-0) Shepards.

LaRiviere, Ann. The Development Council: Cornerstone for Success Considerations. 50p. (Orig.). 1993. pap. 8.00 (1-55833-091-7) Natl Cath Educ.

***Lariviere, Katherine & Audeh, Ida.** United Nations Resolutions on Palestine & the Arab-Israel Conflict 1992-1998, Vol. V. 1999. pap. 19.95 (0-88728-273-3) Inst Palestine.

***Lariviere, Katherine & Audeh, Ida, eds.** United Nations Resolutions on Palestine & the Arab Israili Conflict 1992-1998, Vol. V. 1999. 29.95 (0-88728-272-5) Inst Palestine.

***Lariviere, M. C.** Cixiida: (Insecta: Hemiptera: Auchenorrhyncha) (Fauna of New Zealand Ser.: No. 40). 93p. 1999. 37.50 (0-478-09334-9, Pub. by Manaaki Whenua) Balogh.

Lariviere, Richard W. The Divyatattva of Raghunandana Bhattacarya: Ordeals in Classical Hindu Law. 1982. 22.00 (0-8364-0854-3, Pub. by Manohar) S Asia.

Lariviere, Richard W., ed. from SAN. The Naradasmrti, Pt. 1. LC 89-37780. (Studies on South Asia: No. 4). xxx, 328p. 1989. 30.00 (0-936115-06-8) U Penn South Asia.

— The Naradasmrti, Pt. 2. LC 89-37780. (Studies on South Asia: No. 5). xxxii, 250p. 1989. 30.00 (0-685-48877-2) U Penn South Asia.

— The Naradasmrti, Set. LC 89-37780. (Studies on South Asia: No. 4). xxx, 328p. 1989. 20.00 (0-936115-04-1) U Penn South Asia.

— The Naradasmrti, Set. LC 89-37780. (Studies on South Asia: No. 5). xxxii, 250p. 1989. 20.00 (0-936115-05-X) U Penn South Asia.

Lark Books Staff. Creating with Polymer Clay Book & Kit. 1998. 48.00 (1-57990-034-8, Pub. by Lark Books) Random.

***Lark Books Staff.** A Gallery of Contemporary Work. (Illus.). 2000. pap. 24.95 (1-57990-176-X) Lark Books.

Lark Books Staff. Making Wire Jewelry Book & Kit. (Illus.). 1998. 50.00 (1-57990-033-X, Pub. by Lark Books) Random.

— Sock Doll Workshop Book & Kit. 1998. pap. text 29.95 (1-57990-079-8) Lark Books.

Lark Books Staff & Philbin, Marianne. The Ribbon: A Celebration of Life. LC 85-80922. (Illus.). 160p. 1985. pap. 5.00 (0-937274-24-0) Lark Books.

Lark Books Staff, tr. see Evers, Inge.

Lark, Jim. The Ultimate Lark: An Epicurean Adventure. LC 96-41204. (Illus.). 320p. 1996. 29.95 (1-879094-49-5) Momentum Bks.

***Lark, Liz.** Power Yoga: Connect to the Core with Astanga Yoga. (Illus.). 160p. 2000. pap. 19.95 (1-55209-502-9) Firefly Bks Ltd.

Lark, Liz, jt. auth. see Ansari, Mark.

Lark, Lolita, ed. see Mho Works Staff.

Lark, Madeline. All for a Lark. large type ed. (Ulverscroft). 208p. 1994. 27.99 (0-7089-3046-8) Ulverscroft.

Lark, Michael. Graphic Comic Book: Raymond Chandler's 'The Little Sister' LC 96-42005. 144p. 1997. per. 15.00 (0-684-82933-9) S&S Trade.

Lark, Susan, jt. auth. see Kollmer, Louise.

Lark, Susan M. Anxiety & Stress: A Self-Help Book. LC 95-37723. 288p. 1993. pap. 16.95 (0-89087-775-0) Celestial Arts.

— Chronic Fatigue: Self Help Book. 3rd ed. LC 95-10916. 240p. 1995. pap. 16.95 (0-89087-772-6) Celestial Arts.

— Menstrual Cramps: Self Help Book. 3rd ed. LC 95-14861. 224p. 1995. pap. 16.95 (0-89087-771-8) Celestial Arts.

— Easing Anxiety & Stress Naturally. Herman, Phyllis, ed. (Good Health Guides Ser.). 48p. 1996. pap. 3.95 (0-87983-728-4, 37284K, Keats Publng) NTC Contemp Pub Co.

— The Estrogen Decision: A Self-Help Program. (Women's Health Ser.). 316p. 1994. pap. 14.95 (0-917010-56-6) Celestial Arts.

— The Estrogen Decision: Self Help Book. 3rd ed. 320p. 1996. pap. 17.95 (0-89087-776-9) Celestial Arts.

— Fibroid Tumors & Endometriosis: A Self-Help Program. (Women's Health Ser.). 264p. 1993. pap. 12.95 (0-917010-54-X) Celestial Arts.

— Fibroid Tumors & Endometriosis: Self Help Book. rev. ed. LC 95-17689. 272p. 1995. pap. 16.95 (0-89087-773-4) Celestial Arts.

— Heavy Menstrual Flow & Anemia: Self Help Book. 184p. 1996. pap. 16.95 (0-89087-774-2) Celestial Arts.

— Making the Estrogen Decision. Herman, Phyllis, ed. (Good Health Guides Ser.). 48p. 1996. pap. 3.95 (0-87983-696-2, 36962K, Keats Publng) NTC Contemp Pub Co.

— Menopause: Self Help Book. rev. ed. LC 89-25292. 224p. 1995. pap. 16.95 (0-89087-592-8) Celestial Arts.

— The Menopause Self Help Book: A Woman's Guide to Feeling Wonderful for the Second Half of Her Life. rev. ed. (Illus.). 239p. 1999. pap. text 17.00 (0-7881-6074-5) DIANE Pub.

— Natural Treatment of Fibroid Tumors & Endometriosis. (Good Health Guides Ser.). 48p. 1995. pap. 3.95 (0-87983-690-3, 36903K, Keats Publng) NTC Contemp Pub Co.

— Overcoming Chronic Fatigue. (Good Health Guide Ser.). (Orig.). 1996. pap. 3.95 (0-87983-716-0, Keats Publng) NTC Contemp Pub Co.

— PMS: Self Help Book. LC 89-25292. 240p. 1995. pap. 16.95 (0-89087-587-1) Celestial Arts.

— The Women's Health Companion: Self Help Nutrition Guide & Cookbook. 350p. 1995. pap. 26.95 (0-89087-733-5) Celestial Arts.

— The Women's Health Companion: Self Help Nutrition Guide & Cookbook. 384p. 1996. pap. text 18.95 (0-89087-797-1) Celestial Arts.

Lark, Susan M. & Richards, James A. The Chemistry of Success: Six Secrets of Peak Performance. LC 99-35728. 464p. 1999. 24.95 (1-57959-501-4) BB&T Inc.

***Lark, Susan M. & Richards, James A.** The Chemistry of Success Action Plan: 180 Days to Peak Performance. 256p. 2000. spiral bd. 17.95 (1-57959-503-0, Pub. by BB&T Inc) Publishers Group.

Lark, Virginia, ed. see Maze, Carol M.

Larka, Robert. Television's Private Eye. Sterling, Christopher H., ed. LC 78-21724. (Dissertations in Broadcasting Ser.). (Illus.). 1980. lib. bdg. 23.95 (0-405-11763-9) Ayer.

Larkcom, Joy. Creative Vegetable Gardening. LC 97-187471. (Illus.). 204p. 1997. 35.00 (0-7892-0352-9) Abbeville Pr.

— Creative Vegetable Gardening: Accenting Your Vegetables with Flowers. (Illus.). 204p. 1999. 17.98 (0-89660-112-9, Artabras) Abbeville Pr.

— Oriental Vegetables: The Complete Guide for the Gardening Cook. (Illus.). 240p. 1994. pap. 17.00 (1-56836-017-7) Kodansha.

***Larke, J. R.** The Eye in Contact Lens Wear. 202p. 1999. 48.00 (0-7506-4438-9) Buttrwrth-Heinemann.

Larke, Joe. The Bullfrog & the Grasshopper & Other "Tails" (Illus.). 72p. (J). (gr. k-6). 1987. 10.00 (0-9620112-0-7) Grin A Bit.

— Can't Reach the Itch. (Illus.). 72p. (J). (gr. 1-6). 1988. 10.00 (0-9620112-1-5) Grin A Bit.

— Dopie Dope Goes to the Fair. (Illus.). 49p. (J). (gr. k-5). 1992. 13.95 (0-9620112-7-4) Grin A Bit.

— Dopie Dope Grin A Bit Poetry Series. (Illus.). (J). (gr. k-6). 1992. write for info. (0-9620112-9-0) Grin A Bit.

— Two Pigs in Wigs. (J). (ps-3). 1991. 11.95 (0-9620112-2-3) Grin A Bit.

Larke, John. The Eye in Contact Lens Wear. 2nd rev. ed. LC 96-38860. 224p. 1997. text 95.00 (0-7506-1518-4) Buttrwrth-Heinemann.

Larke, Stan. The Doodledipper Works. LC 96-71070. (Illus.). 72p. (Orig.). (J). (gr. 2-6). 1997. pap. 8.95 (1-57197-055-X) Pentland Pr.

Larken, Diarmuid. Art Learning & Teaching: A Seven Year Manual for the Primary Elementary Teacher. 256p. 1997. pap. 9.95 (0-86327-025-5, Pub. by Wolfhound Press) Irish Amer Bk.

Larken, H. W. Compositors Work in Printing. 3rd ed. 382p. 1969. 40.00 (0-905418-08-5) St Mut.

— Modern Type Setting Techniques: Electric Composition. 192p. 1984. 60.00 (0-946095-10-8, Pub. by Gresham Bks) St Mut.

— Type Composition in the Private Press. 128p. 1983. 40.00 (0-946095-11-6, Pub. by Gresham Bks) St Mut.

Larkey, Arieh. A Town House in Jerusalem. 376p. 1996. 19.95 (965-229-153-6) Gefen Bks.

Larkey, Betty B. Planting the Faith: A History of St. John's Episcopal Church-Memphis, Tennessee. (Illus.). 200p. 1996. write for info. (0-9654666-0-4) St Johns Episcopal.

Larkey, Edward. Pungent Sounds: Constructing Identity with Popular Music in Austria. LC 93-20113. (Austrian Culture Ser.: Vol. 9). (Illus.). XXII, 342p. (Orig.). (C). 1993. pap. text 35.95 (0-8204-2170-7) P Lang Pubng.

Larkey, Jan. Flatter Your Figure. (Illus.). 102p. 1991. per. 11.00 (0-671-76296-6) S&S Trade.

Larkey, Joann L. Winters: A Heritage of Horticulture, a Harmony of Purpose. (Illus.). viii, 126p. 1991. pap. 15.85 (1-892626-02-0) Yolo County.

Larkey, Patrick D. Evaluating Public Programs: The Impact of General Revenue Sharing on Municipal Government. LC 78-51176. 283p. 1979. reprint ed. pap. 87.80 (0-7837-9367-7, 206011000004) Bks Demand.

Larkham, P. J., jt. auth. see Harris, Richard.

Larkham, Peter J. Conservation & the Changing Urban Landscape. (Progress in Planning Ser.: No. 37). 88p. 1992. pap. 60.00 (0-08-041852-X, Pergamon Pr) Elsevier.

— Conservation & the City. LC 95-44402. (Illus.). 352p. (C). 1996. pap. 29.99 (0-415-07948-9) Routledge.

Larkides, Mike, ed. see Stern, Hal.

Larkin. James Larkin. 306p. (C). pap. 15.95 (0-7453-0304-8, Pub. by Pluto GBR) Stylus Pub VA.

— PPM Drafting & CAD. 2nd abr. ed. 64p. 1996. pap. text, student ed. 12.00 (0-8273-4625-5) Delmar.

Larkin, jt. auth. see Morris.

Larkin, A. I. & Zavaritsky, N. V. High Temperature Superconductivity from Russia. 320p. (C). 1989. text 137.00 (9971-5-0798-6) World Scientific Pub.

Larkin, A. I., ed. see Barone, Antonio.

***Larkin, Barbara, ed.** Country Reports on Human Rights Practices for 1998, Vol. 1 & 2. 3107p. 2000. pap. text 125.00 (0-7567-0054-X) DIANE Pub.

Larkin, Barbara, ed. Presidential Certification of Narcotics Producing & Transit Countries. 49p. (C). 1999. pap. text 20.00 (0-7881-7842-3) DIANE Pub.

Larkin, Bruce D. Nuclear Designs: Great Britain, France, & China in the Global Governance of Nuclear Arms. 354p. (C). 1996. text 39.95 (1-56000-239-5) Transaction Pubs.

Larkin, Chris. The Book of Candlemaking: Creating Scent, Beauty & Light. LC 97-41180. (Illus.). 128p. 1998. 24.95 (0-8069-0676-6) Sterling.

— The Book of Candlemaking: Creating Scent, Beauty & Light. (Illus.). 1999. pap. 14.95 (0-8069-7787-6) Sterling.

Larkin, Clarence. The Book of Revelation: A Study of the Last Prophetic Book of Holy Scripture. (Illus.). 210p. 1996. pap. 18.00 (0-89540-303-X, SB-303) Sun Pub.

Larkin, Clarence. Daniel. 1990. 14.36 (0-00-147293-3) Rev C E Harris.

Larkin, Clarence. Dispensational Truth: God's Plan & Purpose in the Ages, Including Copious Charts & Illustrations. 267p. 1998. pap. 45.00 (0-89540-388-9) Sun Pub.

Larkin, Clarence. Revelation. 1990. 16.60 (0-00-147312-3) Rev C E Harris.

Larkin, Clarence. Rightly Dividing the Word. 328p. 1997. pap. write for info. (0-89540-368-4) Sun Pub.

— The Second Coming of Christ. 71p. 1997. pap. 7.50 (0-89540-367-6) Sun Pub.

— The Spirit World. 158p. 1997. pap. write for info. (0-89540-379-X) Sun Pub.

— Why I Am a Baptist. 77p. 1998. pap. 7.50 (0-89540-407-9, SB-407) Sun Pub.

Larkin, Colin. The Billboard Illustrated Encyclopedia of Rock. (Illus.). 386p. 1998. 45.00 (0-8230-7697-0) Watsn-Guptill.

***Larkin, Colin.** Encyclopedia of Jazz. 1999. text 60.00 (1-85227-754-8) Virgin Bks.

— Encyclopedia of World & Folk Music. 1999. pap. text 26.95 (0-7535-0247-X) Virgin Bks.

Larkin, Colin. The Virgin Encyclopedia of Dance Music. 1998. pap. text 24.95 (0-7535-0252-6, Pub. by Virgin Bks) London Brdge.

— Virgin Encyclopedia of Heavy Rock. 1999. pap. text 26.95 (0-7535-0257-7) London Brdge.

— The Virgin Encyclopedia of R & B & Soul. 1998. text 24.95 (0-7535-0241-0, Pub. by Virgin Bks) London Brdge.

— The Virgin Encyclopedia of Reggae. 1998. pap. text 24.95 (0-7535-0242-9, Pub. by Virgin Bks) London Brdge.

— Virgin Encyclopedia of Stage & Film Musicals. 1999. pap. text 29.95 (0-7535-0375-1) Virgin Pubng.

— The Virgin Encyclopedia of the Blues. 1998. text 24.95 (0-7535-0226-7, Pub. by Virgin Bks) London Brdge.

***Larkin, Colin, ed.** All-Time Top 1000 Albums. (Illus.). 208p. 2000. mass mkt. 9.95 (0-7535-0354-9) Virgin Pubng.

Larkin, Colin, ed. The Encyclopedia of Popular Music, 8 vols. 3rd ed. LC 98-37439. Orig. Title: The Guinness Encyclopedia of Popular Music. 8000p. 1998. lib. bdg. 500.00 (1-56159-237-4, Pub. by Muze Ltd) Groves Dictionaries.

— Virgin All Time Top 1000 Albums. 1999. pap. text 24.95 (0-7535-0258-5, Pub. by Virgin Bks) London Brdge.

— The Virgin Encyclopedia of Country Music. 1998. text 24.95 (0-7535-0236-4, Pub. by Virgin Bks) London Brdge.

— The Virgin Encyclopedia of Eighties Music. 1997. pap. text 24.95 (0-7535-0159-7, Pub. by Virgin Bks) London Brdge.

— The Virgin Encyclopedia of Indie & New Wave. 512p. 1998. text 24.95 (0-7535-0231-3, Pub. by Virgin Bks) London Brdge.

— The Virgin Encyclopedia of Popular Music. 1344p. 1998. text 60.00 (1-85227-745-9, Pub. by Virgin Bks) London Brdge.

***Larkin, Colin, ed.** Virgin Encyclopedia of Popular Music. 3rd ed. (Illus.). 1408p. 2000. 60.00 (1-85227-832-3) Virgin Pubng.

Larkin, Colin, ed. The Virgin Encyclopedia of Seventies Music. 1997. pap. text 24.95 (0-7535-0154-6, Pub. by Virgin Bks) London Brdge.

— The Virgin Encyclopedia of Sixties Music. 1998. pap. text 24.95 (0-7535-0149-X, Pub. by Virgin Bks) London Brdge.

Larkin, David. Acres of Country Wisdom. LC 98-198519. 160p. 1998. 35.00 (0-395-77188-9) HM.

— Country Wild. LC 97-176039. (Illus.). 160p. 1998. 35.00 (0-395-77190-0) HM.

— Country Wisdom. LC 97-22925. (Illus.). 160p. 1997. 35.00 (0-395-77189-7) HM.

— Essential Barn: Discovering the Design, Function & Form. (Illus.). 96p. 1995. 17.95 (0-7893-0008-7, Pub. by Universe) St Martin.

— Essential Book of Rural America. (Illus.). 80p. 1996. text 18.95 (0-7893-0070-2) St Martin.

— Essential Shaker: Discovering the Designs, Building & Furniture. (Illus.). 96p. 1995. 17.95 (0-7893-0007-9, Pub. by Universe) St Martin.

— Farm: The Vernacular Tradition of Working Buildings. LC 95-24305. (Illus.). 240p. 1995. 60.00 (1-885254-08-3, Pub. by Monacelli Pr) Penguin Putnam.

— Farm: The Vernacular Tradition of Working Buildings. (Illus.). 240p. 1998. pap. 35.00 (1-58093-000-X, Pub. by Monacelli Pr) Penguin Putnam.

— Farm: The Vernacular Tradition of Working Buildings, 4 vols., Set. LC 95-24305. (Illus.). 240p. 1995. 240.00 (1-885254-20-2) Monacelli Pr.

***Larkin, David.** Mill: The History & Future of Naturally Powered Buildings. (Illus.). 2000. 50.00 (0-7893-0501-1) Universe.

Larkin, David, jt. auth. see Frampton, Kenneth.

Larkin, David, jt. auth. see Joels, Kerry M.

Larkin, David, jt. auth. see Roscoe, Gerald.

Larkin, David, jt. auth. see Sprigg, June.

Larkin, David, ed. see Garrett, Wendell.

Larkin, David, ed. see Pfeiffer, Bruce B.

Larkin, David, ed. see Rocheleau, Paul & Sprigg, June.

Larkin, David, ed. see Schulz, Charles M.

Larkin, David, ed. & des. see Beveridge, Charles E.

Larkin, David, ed. & des. see Beveridge, Charles & Rocheleau, Paul.

Larkin, David E., ed. Faeries. 192p. 1979. pap. 19.95 (0-553-34634-2) Bantam.

Larkin, Diana W., jt. auth. see Lesko, Barbara S.

Larkin, E. L. Dead Men Die. LC 98-97005. 192p. 1999. lib. bdg. 18.95 (0-8034-9348-7, Avalon Bks) Bouregy.

— Die & Die. LC 98-96617. 192p. 1998. 18.95 (0-8034-9328-2, Avalon Bks) Bouregy.

— Hear Me Die. LC 98-96231. 192p. 1998. 18.95 (0-8034-9309-6, Avalon Bks) Bouregy.

— Hear My Cry. LC 96-95478. 192p. 1997. 18.95 (0-8034-9229-4, Avalon Bks) Bouregy.

***Larkin, E. L.** The Swallow Murders. LC 99-90983. 192p. 1999. 18.95 (0-8034-9388-6, Avalon Bks) Bouregy.

Larkin, E. Martin De, see De Larkin, E. Martin, Jr.

Larkin, Edgar L. The Matchless Altar of the Soul: Symbolized As a Shining Cube of Diamond, One Cubit in Dimensions, & Set Within the Holy of Holies in All Grand Esoteric Temples of Antiquity (1917) 310p. 1996. reprint ed. pap. 24.95 (1-56459-525-0) Kessinger Pub.

Larkin, Edward T. War in Goethe's Writings: Representation & Assessment. LC 92-10192. 268p. 1992. lib. bdg. 69.95 (0-7734-9540-1) E Mellen.

Larkin, Elle & Maines, Leah, eds. Music & Mandrakes: Anthology of Contemporary American Poets. 40p. 2000. pap. 8.95 (0-9664324-5-2) Finishng Line.

— Mutant Mule Review: Anthology of Contemporary American Poets. 40p. 1999. pap. 7.95 (0-9664324-4-4) Finishng Line.

Larkin, Emmet & Fitzpatrick, David, eds. Memoirs of Joseph Prost C. SS. R: A Redemptorist Missionary in Ireland, 1851-1854. (Irish Narrative Ser.). 96p. 1998. pap. 12.95 (1-85918-160-0, Pub. by Cork Univ) Intl Spec Bk.

Larkin, Emmet J. The Consolidation of the Roman Catholic Church in Ireland, 1860-1870. LC 86-25059. xxii, 714p. 1987. 70.00 (0-8078-1725-2) U of NC Pr.

— The Consolidation of the Roman Catholic Church in Ireland, 1860-1870. LC 86-25059. (Illus.). 736p. reprint ed. pap. 200.00 (0-608-10495-7, 207112400009) Bks Demand.

— The Historical Dimensions of Irish Catholicism. LC 76-6350. (Irish Americans Ser.). 1976. 23.95 (0-405-09344-6) Ayer.

— The Making of the Roman Catholic Church in Ireland, 1850-1860. LC 79-19560. (Illus.). 544p. reprint ed. pap. 168.70 (*0-7837-6857-5*, 204668600003) Bks Demand.

— The Roman Catholic Church & the Creation of the Modern Irish State, 1878-1886. LC 75-7169. (American Philosophical Society, Memoirs Ser.: Vol. 108). 436p. reprint ed. pap. 135.20 (*0-608-14117-8*, 202429300036) Bks Demand.

— The Roman Catholic Church & the Emergence of the Modern Irish Political System, 1874-1878. 618p. 1996. text 74.95 (*0-8132-0873-4*) Cath U Pr.

Larkin, Ernest E. Silent Presence. 1984. pap. 11.95 (*0-87193-172-9*) Dimension Bks.

Larkin, Ernest F., ed. Proceedings of the Nineteen Eighty-Six Conference of the American Academy of Advertising. 1986. pap. 25.00 (*0-931030-09-9*) Am Acad Advert.

Larkin, Ernest F. & Larkin, Susan S. College Newspaper Advertising Managers Handbook. 60p. 1994. pap. text 25.00 (*0-9644192-0-3*) Assoc Collegiate Pr.

Larkin, F. Daniel. John B. Jervis: An American Engineering Pioneer. LC 89-26953. (History of Technology & Science Ser.). (Illus.). 212p. 1990. text 44.95 (*0-8138-0355-1*) Iowa St U Pr.

— New York State Canals: A Short History. LC 97-40532. (Illus.). 104p. 1998. pap. 12.00 (*0-935796-90-8*) Purple Mnt Pr.

— Pioneer American Railroads: The Mohawk & Hudson & the Saratoga & Schenectady. LC 95-41702. (Illus.). 96p. 1995. lib. bdg. 25.00 (*0-935796-71-1*) Purple Mnt Pr.

Larkin, Frank J. Basic Coastal Navigation: An Introduction to Piloting. 1996. text 29.95 (*0-07-036453-2*) McGraw.

— Basic Coastal Navigation: An Introduction to Piloting. 2nd ed. LC 98-13057. (Illus.). 288p. 1998. bds. 29.95 (*1-57409-052-6*) Sheridan.

Larkin, Frank L. God Said It, & You'd Better Believe It. 136p. 1996. pap. 10.50 (*0-8158-0519-5*) Chris Mass.

Larkin, Geraldine A. 12 Simple Steps to a Winning Marketing Plan. 210p. 1992. per. 17.95 (*1-55738-297-2*, Irwn Prfssnl) McGraw-Hill Prof.

— Woman to Woman: Street Smarts for Women Entrepreneurs. LC 93-4260. (Illus.). 265p. 1993. pap. 14.95 (*0-13-706658-9*) P-H.

Larkin, Geri. Bad Hair Days: A Memoir. 175p. 1995. pap. 10.95 (*0-9647963-1-7*) Strategic Think.

— Building a Business the Buddhist Way. 256p. (Orig.). 1999. pap. 12.95 (*0-89087-888-9*) Celestial Arts.

— Stumbling Toward Enlightenment. LC 97-21858. 244p. 1997. pap. 12.95 (*0-89087-849-8*) Celestial Arts.

— Tap Dancing in Zen. 160p. 1999. pap. 12.95 (*0-89087-889-7*) Celestial Arts.

Larkin, Gregory, jt. ed. see Kagan, Alfred.

Larkin, Henry. Carlyle & the Open Secret of His Life. LC 76-122621. (English Biography Ser.: No. 31). 1970. reprint ed. lib. bdg. 75.00 (*0-8383-0905-4*) M S G Haskell Hse.

Larkin, J. Practical Problems in Mathematics for Mechanical Drafting. LC 77-78236. (C). 1979. pap. 15.00 (*0-8273-1670-4*) Delmar.

Larkin, J. Donald & Larkin, Sue. The Larkin Guide: Enjoying the Riches of Retirement. LC 87-73134. 96p. 1988. spiral bd. 7.95 (*0-9619643-0-8*) Damike Pub.

Larkin, Jack. Children Everywhere. LC 87-22685. (Illus.). 47p. 1987. 6.95 (*0-913387-02-9*) Old Sturbridge.

— The Merriams of Brookfield: Printing in the Economy & Culture of Rural Massachusetts in the Early Nineteenth Century. 48p. 1986. pap. 5.00 (*0-912296-84-4*) Am Antiquarian.

***Larkin, Jack.** The New England Country Tavern. (Illus.). iv, 56p. 2000. pap. write for info. (*0-913387-05-3*) Old Sturbridge.

Larkin, Jack. The Reshaping of Everyday Life: 1790-1840. LC 87-46152. (Everyday Life in America Ser.). 384p. 1989. reprint ed. pap. 14.50 (*0-06-091606-0*, Perennial) HarperTrade.

Larkin, Jack & Bassett, Lynne Z. Northern Comfort: New England's Early Quilts 1780-1850. LC 98-5678. (Illus.). 128p. 1998. pap. 19.95 (*1-55853-655-8*) Rutledge Hill Pr.

Larkin, Jack, ed. see McCallum, Kent.

Larkin, James B., ed. see Martinez de Toledo, Alfonso.

Larkin, James F. & Hughes, Paul L., eds. Stuart Royal Proclamations: Royal Proclamations of King James I 1603-1625, Vol. 1. 1973. 125.00 (*0-19-822372-2*) OUP.

Larkin, James R. Reluctant Frontiersman: James Ross Larkin on the Sante Fe Trail, 1856-57. Barbour, Barton H., ed. & anno. by. LC 89-25073. (Illus.). 220p. 1990. reprint ed. pap. 68.20 (*0-608-04136-X*, 206486900011) Bks Demand.

Larkin, Jean, ed. see Deitering-Ancell, Carolyn.

Larkin, Jean, ed. see Dotterweich, Kass P.

Larkin, Jean, ed. see Fischer, Carl.

Larkin, Jean, ed. see O'Connor, Francine M.

Larkin, Jill, et al, eds. Computer Assisted Instruction & Intelligent Tutoring Systems: Establishing Communication & Collaboration. 288p. (C). 1992. pap. 34.50 (*0-8058-0233-9*); text 69.95 (*0-8058-0232-0*) L Erlbaum Assocs.

Larkin, Joan. Cold River. LC 97-20933. 1997. pap. 10.00 (*0-9651558-5-4*) Painted Leaf.

— Glad Day: Daily Affirmations for Gay, Lesbian, Bisexual, & Transgender People. LC 98-24698. 400p. 1998. 11.00 (*1-56838-189-1*) Hazelden.

— If You Want What We Have: Sponsorship Meditations. LC 97-48995. 400p. 1998. pap. 14.00 (*1-56838-192-1*) Hazelden.

***Larkin, Joan.** A Woman Like That: Lesbian & Bisexual Writers Tell Their Coming Out Stories. 352p. 2000. pap. 14.00 (*0-380-80247-3*, Perennial) HarperTrade.

***Larkin, Joan, ed.** A Woman Like That: Lesbian & Bisexual Writers Tell Their Coming Out Stories. LC 99-35286. 352p. 1999. 24.00 (*0-380-97698-6*, Avon Bks) Morrow Avon.

Larkin, Joan & Manrique, Jaime, trs. Sor Juana's Love Poems. LC 97-23522. (ENG & SPA.). 1997. pap. 10.00 (*0-9651558-6-2*) Painted Leaf.

Larkin, Joan, jt. ed. see Morse, Carl.

Larkin, John, ed. The Trial of William Drennan. 144p. 1991. 14.95 (*0-7165-2457-0*, Pub. by Irish Acad Pr) Intl Spec Bk.

Larkin, John, jt. auth. see Kramer, Kenneth P.

Larkin, John A. The Pampangans: Colonial Society in a Philippine Province. LC 74-165232. (Illus.). 358p. reprint ed. pap. 111.00 (*0-7837-4814-0*, 204446100003) Bks Demand.

— Sugar & the Origins of Modern Philippine Society. 339p. 1994. 55.00 (*0-520-07956-6*, Pub. by U CA Pr) Cal Prin Full Svc.

Larkin, John A., ed. Perspectives on Philippine Historiography: A Symposium. LC 78-59565. (Monographs: No. 21). iv, 74p. 1979. pap. 9.50 (*0-938692-09-7*) Yale U SE Asia.

Larkin, John C. Practical Problems in Mathematics for Drafting & CAD. 2nd ed. LC 95-22533. (Business/Vocational Math Ser.). 320p. (C). 1995. mass mkt. 21.95 (*0-8273-4624-7*) Delmar.

Larkin, John D. John D. Larkin: A Business Pioneer. LC 98-91231. (Illus.). 212p. 1998. pap. 14.95 (*0-9619697-1-7*) WNY Wares.

Larkin, Joseph M. & Sleeter, Christine E., eds. Developing Multicultural Teacher Education Curricula. LC 94-38173. (SUNY Series, The Social Context of Education & SUNY Series, Teacher Preparation & Development). 298p. (C). 1995. text 64.50 (*0-7914-2593-2*); pap. text 21.95 (*0-7914-2594-0*) State U NY Pr.

Larkin, Judy, jt. auth. see McFarland, Kathleen.

Larkin, June. Sexual Harassment: High School Girls Speak Out. 168p. 1994. pap. 14.95 (*0-929005-65-1*, Pub. by Sec Story Pr) LPC InBook.

Larkin, Kara. Home Ties. 1994. per. 2.75 (*0-373-19047-6*, 1-19047-9) Harlequin Bks.

Larkin, Katrina J. Ruth & Esther. LC 96-183325. (Old Testament Guides Ser.: Vol. 9). 106p. 1996. pap. 12.50 (*1-85075-755-0*, Pub. by Sheffield Acad) CUP Services.

Larkin, Kenneth D. Journey in the Spirit: Parables & Poems of Faith. 1996. pap. 9.95 (*0-7880-0902-8*, Fairway Pr) CSS OH.

Larkin, Kenneth J. Barron's Regents Exams & Answers: Comprehensive Latin. (LAT.). 1996. pap. 5.95 (*0-8120-3345-0*) Barron.

Larkin, Kevin, ed. The West Virginia Journal of Psychological Research & Practice: The Journal of the West Virginia Psychological Association. 1992. write for info. (*0-9634170-0-2*) WVa Psychol Assn.

— The West Virginia Journal of Psychological Research & Practice: The Journal of the West Virginia Psychological Association. (C). 1992. pap. text. write for info. (*0-9634170-4-5*) WVa Psychol Assn.

Larkin, LaRae. The Legitimacy in International Law of the Detention & Internment of Aliens & Minorities in the Interest of National Security. LC 96-41016. (Symposium Ser.: Vol. 40). 508p. 1996. text 119.95 (*0-7734-8755-7*) E Mellen.

Larkin, Larry. Full Speed Ahead. LC 72-80818. (Illus.). 146p. reprint ed. 14.00 (*0-686-36269-1*) Larkin.

Larkin, M. J., jt. auth. see Patrick, S.

Larkin, Margaret. The Theology of Meaning. LC 96-139046. (American Oriental Ser.: Vol. 79). ix, 220p. 1995. 35.00 (*0-940490-79-X*) Am Orient Soc.

Larkin, Marilyn. Redux: The Miracle Weight Loss Drug. (Orig.). 1997. mass mkt. 5.99 (*0-614-27709-4*, Avon Bks) Morrow Avon.

Larkin, Marilynn. Redux: The Miracle Weight-Loss Drug. LC 97-93006. 224p. (Orig.). 1997. mass mkt. 5.99 (*0-380-79218-4*, Avon Bks) Morrow Avon.

***Larkin, Marty.** The Rock & Roll Chef's "Halloween Decoration Kit" (Illus.). 2000. boxed set. write for info. (*0-9675649-3-X*, Hunt Corporation) R R C Prod.

Larkin, Mary A. For Better, For Worse. large type ed. (Magna Large Print Ser.). 592p. 1997. 27.99 (*0-7505-1168-0*, Pub. by Mgna Lrg Print) Ulverscroft.

***Larkin, Mary A.** Full Circle. large type ed. 576p. 2000. 31.99 (*0-7505-1472-8*, Pub. by Mgna Lrg Print) Ulverscroft.

Larkin, Mary A. White Clapboard. (Illus.). 12p. (Orig.). (C). 1988. pap. 7.00 (*0-9620840-0-X*) C O Allen.

Larkin, Mary A., jt. auth. see Papademetriou, Demetrios G.

Larkin, Mary Ann. The Coil of the Skin. LC 82-70066. (Series Seven). 50p. (Orig.). 1980. pap. 7.00 (*0-931846-20-X*) Wash Writers Pub.

Larkin, Mary C., jt. auth. see O'Brien, Edward L.

Larkin, Maureen, jt. auth. see Schneider, Meir.

Larkin, Maurice. France Since the Popular Front: Government & People, 1936-1996. 2nd ed. LC 98-138168. (Illus.). 522p. 1997. text 89.00 (*0-19-873152-3*); pap. text 24.00 (*0-19-873151-5*) OUP.

— Religion, Politics & Preferment in France since 1890: "La Belle Epoque" & Its Legacy. 263p. (C). 1995. text 49.95 (*0-521-41916-6*) Cambridge U Pr.

Larkin, Miriam T. Language in the Philosophy of Aristotle. LC 74-165145. (Janua Linguarum, Ser. Minor: No. 87). 113p. 1971. pap. text 34.65 (*90-279-1843-0*) Mouton.

Larkin, Molly & Heart, Bear. The Wind Is My Mother: The Life & Teachings of a Native American Shaman. 272p. 1996. 24.00 (*0-517-70283-5*) Random.

Larkin, Molly, jt. auth. see Heart, Bear.

Larkin, Murl. Civil Evidence Trial Manual for Texas Lawyers, 2 vols. 2nd ed. 1991. ring bd. 180.00 (*0-327-00943-8*, 82480, MICHIE) LEXIS Pub.

Larkin, Murl A. Civil Evidence Trial Manual for Texas Lawyers, 1986-93, 2 vols., Vol. 13. 2nd ed. 92p. 1997. ring bd. 180.00 (*0-409-25658-7*, 82480-10, MICHIE) LEXIS Pub.

— Criminal Evidence Trial Manual for Texas Lawyers. 2nd ed. 1300p. 1994. suppl. ed. 65.00 (*0-685-70861-6*, MICHIE) LEXIS Pub.

— Federal Testimonial Privileges. LC 82-12958. (Federal Court Rules Ser.). 1982. ring bd. 145.00 (*0-87632-319-0*) West Group.

— New Mexico Rules of Evidence. 480p. 1994. ring bd. 125.00 (*0-614-05925-9*, MICHIE) LEXIS Pub.

— New Mexico Rules of Evidence, 1983, 1986, 1991. rev. ed. 480p. 1991. ring bd. 125.00 (*0-409-25133-X*, MICHIE) LEXIS Pub.

— New Mexico Rules of Evidence, 1983, 1986, 1991. rev. ed. 1994. ring bd., suppl. ed. 65.00 (*0-685-49752-6*, MICHIE) LEXIS Pub.

Larkin, P. J. African Heritage. rev. ed. (Illus.). 64p. 1980. pap. 11.95 (*0-7175-0613-4*) Dufour.

— Age of Discovery. rev. ed. (Illus.). 64p. 1976. pap. 11.95 (*0-7175-0761-0*) Dufour.

— American Heritage. (Illus.). 64p. 1984. pap. 9.95 (*0-7175-0783-1*) Dufour.

— The Ancient World. (Illus.). 64p. 1971. reprint ed. pap. 11.95 (*0-7175-0588-X*) Dufour.

— European Heritage. (Illus.). 64p. 1981. pap. 9.95 (*0-7175-0882-X*) Dufour.

— Medieval World. (Illus.). 64p. 1974. pap. 11.95 (*0-7175-0663-0*) Dufour.

— U. S. A. & Russia. (World History in 20th Century Ser.). (Illus.). 158p. 1977. pap. 11.95 (*0-7175-0063-2*) Dufour.

Larkin, Patricia & Backer, Barbara. Problem-Oriented Nursing Assessment. (C). 1977. text 17.95 (*0-07-036450-8*) McGraw.

Larkin, Patricia, jt. auth. see Crudi.

***Larkin, Peter.** Dog Breeds of the World. (Illustrated Encyclopedias Ser.). (Illus.). 1999. pap. 10.95 (*0-7548-0021-0*, Lorenz Bks) Anness Pub.

Larkin, Peter. Dog Care. (Practical Handbook Ser.). 1999. pap. 8.95 (*0-7548-0031-8*, Lorenz Bks) Anness Pub.

Larkin, Peter A. Freshwater Pollution, Canadian Style. LC 73-94316. (Environmental Damage & Control in Canada Ser.: No. 3). 168p. reprint ed. pap. 52.10 (*0-7837-1032-1*, 204134300020) Bks Demand.

Larkin, Phil. Genes at Work: Biotechnology. 1995. pap. 26.95 (*0-643-05649-1*, Pub. by CSIRO) Accents Pubns.

Larkin, Philip. All What Jazz: A Record Diary, 1961-1971. rev. ed. 316p. 1985. pap. 9.95 (*0-374-51908-0*) FS&G.

— Collected Poems. 330p. 1993. pap. 15.00 (*0-374-52275-8*) FS&G.

— A Concordance to the Poetry of Philip Larkin. Watt, R. J., ed. LC 96-173549. (Alpha-Omega Series C. English Authors: Vol. 3). xxi, 660p. 1995. write for info. (*3-487-09801-6*) G Olms Pubs.

— A Girl in Winter. LC 75-27291. 256p. 1985. pap. 12.95 (*0-87951-217-2*, Pub. by Overlook Pr) Penguin Putnam.

— High Windows. LC 74-9800. 42p. 1983. pap. 9.00 (*0-374-51212-4*) FS&G.

— Jill: A Novel. LC 75-27292. (Tusk Bks.). 256p. 1984. 22.50 (*0-87951-038-2*, Pub. by Overlook Pr); pap. 12.95 (*0-87951-961-4*, Pub. by Overlook Pr) Penguin Putnam.

— Required Writing: Miscellaneous Pieces, 1955-1982. LC 98-53786. (Poets on Poetry Ser.). 328p. 1999. pap. 17.95 (*0-472-08584-0*, 08584) U of Mich Pr.

— Selected Letters of Philip Larkin, 1940-1985. Thwaite, Anthony, ed. 1993. 40.00 (*0-374-25829-5*) FS&G.

— Selected Letters of Philip Larkin, 1940-1985. (Illus.). 848p. 1999. pap. 20.00 (*0-571-17048-X*) Faber & Faber.

— The Whitsun Weddings. 46p. 1971. pap. 11.95 (*0-571-09710-3*) Faber & Faber.

Larkin, Philip, ed. The Oxford Book of Twentieth Century English Verse. 692p. 1973. 35.00 (*0-19-812137-7*) OUP.

***Larkin, Priscilla & King, Warrior.** Perceptions of Priscilla. 2nd ed. 52p. 1998. reprint ed. mass mkt. 7.95 (*0-9672329-0-2*) CGI Assocs.

Larkin, Ralph W. Suburban Youth in Cultural Crisis. LC 78-10742. (Illus.). 272p. 1979. pap. text 21.95 (*0-19-502523-7*) OUP.

Larkin, Ralph W., jt. auth. see Foss, Daniel A.

***Larkin, Richard F.** Financial Statement Presentation & Disclosure Practices for Not-for-Profit Organizations. Frohlich, Susan, ed. (Practice Aid Ser.). 185p. 1999. pap. 61.25 (*0-87051-289-7*, 006605) Am Inst CPA.

Larkin, Richard F. Wiley Not-for-Profit GAAP 1999: Interpretation & Application of Generally Accepted Accounting Standards for Not-for-Profit Organizations 1999. 99th ed. (Illus.). 536p. 1999. pap. 65.00 (*0-471-29596-5*) Wiley.

***Larkin, Richard F.** Wiley Not-for-Profit GAAP 2000 Interpretation & Application of Generally Accepted Accounting Standards. 522p. 2000. pap. 69.00 (*0-471-35111-3*) Wiley.

Larkin, Richard F. & DiTommaso, Marie. The Not-for-Profit Accounting Field Guide, 1999-2000. 248p. 1999. pap. 22.95 (*0-471-24637-9*) Wiley.

Larkin, Richard F., jt. auth. see Gross, Malvern J.

Larkin, Robert P. & Peters, Gary L. Biographical Dictionary of Geography. LC 92-18364. 384p. 1993. lib. bdg. 79.50 (*0-313-27622-6*, LBG, Greenwood Pr) Greenwood.

— Dictionary of Concepts in Human Geography, 2. LC 82-24258. (Reference Sources for the Social Sciences & Humanities Ser.: No. 2). 286p. 1983. lib. bdg. 65.00 (*0-313-22729-2*, LHG, Greenwood Pr) Greenwood.

Larkin, Robert P., jt. auth. see Peters, Gary L.

Larkin, Rochelle. My First Little 12 Story Book Set. (J). (ps-2). 1994. 29.95 (*1-886520-00-3*) Micro R&D.

Larkin, Sandar, jt. auth. see Larkin, T. J.

Larkin, Sharon, jt. auth. see Swain, Merrill.

Larkin, Stillman C. The Pioneer History of Meigs County, Ohio. 208p. 1995. reprint ed. lib. bdg. 31.00 (*0-8328-4479-9*) Higginson Bk Co.

Larkin, Sue, jt. auth. see Larkin, J. Donald.

Larkin, Susan S., jt. auth. see Larkin, Ernest F.

Larkin, T. J. & Larkin, Sandar. Communicating Change: Winning Employee Support for New Business Goals. 252p. 1994. 22.95 (*0-07-036452-4*) McGraw.

***Larkin, Tanya.** Christopher Columbus. LC 00-20249. (Famous Explorers Ser.). 2000. lib. bdg. write for info. (*0-8239-5554-0*) Rosen Group.

— John Cabot. LC 99-48793. (Famous Explorers Ser.). (J). 2000. lib. bdg. 18.60 (*0-8239-5553-2*, PowerKids) Rosen Group.

— What Was Cooking in Abigail Adam's White House? LC 00-28593. (Cooking Throughout American History Ser.). (Illus.). (J). 2000. write for info. (*0-8239-5607-5*, PowerKids) Rosen Group.

— What Was Cooking in Martha Jefferson's White House? LC 00-39167. (Cooking Throughout American History Ser.). (Illus.). 2000. write for info. (*0-8239-5610-5*, PowerKids) Rosen Group.

— What Was Cooking in Martha Washington's Presidential Mansions? LC 00-39168. (Cooking Throughout American History Ser.). (Illus.). 2000. write for info. (*0-8239-5606-7*, PowerKids) Rosen Group.

Larkin, Troy J. Tax Break: How to Reduce the Taxes on Your Home. Graviet, Lois, ed. 100p. (Orig.). 1992. pap. 29.95 (*0-9632424-0-7*) CITTA.

Larkin, William. Get Real about Yourself: Twenty-Five Ways to Grow Whole & Holy. LC 94-60341. 160p. (Orig.). 1995. pap. 9.95 (*0-89622-606-9*) Twenty-Third.

Larkin, William, ed. see Dixon, David R.

Larkin, William J., Jr. Culture & Biblical Hermeneutics: Interpreting & Applying the Authoritative Word in a Relativistic Age. 402p. (Orig.). (C). 1993. reprint ed. pap. text 37.50 (*0-8191-9219-8*) U Pr of Amer.

Larkin, William J., Jr. & Williams, Joel F., eds. Mission in the New Testament: An Evangelical Approach. LC 97-38902. (American Society of Missiology Ser.: No. 27). 176p. (Orig.). 1998. pap. 20.00 (*1-57075-169-2*) Orbis Bks.

Larking, Lambert B., ed. Proceedings Principally in the County of Kent, in Connection with the Parliaments Called in 1640, & Especially with the Committee of Religion Appointed in That Year. (Camden Society, London. Publications, First Ser.: No. 80a). reprint ed. 70.00 (*0-404-50180-X*) AMS Pr.

Larking, Lambert B., ed. see Philippus De Thame.

Larking, Peter & Stockman, Mike. The Complete Dog Book: A Comprehensive, Practical Care & Training Manual, & a Definitive Encyclopedia of World Breeds. (Illus.). 256p. 1997. 29.95 (*1-85967-326-0*, Lorenz Bks) Anness Pub.

Larkins, B. A., jt. ed. see Herrmann, R. G.

Larkins, Brian A. & Vasil, Indra K., eds. Cellular & Molecular Biology of Plant Seed Development. LC 97-24681. (Advances in Cellular & Molecular Biology of Plants Ser.: No. 4). 648p. 1997. text 368.00 (*0-7923-4645-9*) Kluwer Academic.

Larkins, D O. Happy Is the Man. pap. 4.95 (*0-9642909-6-0*) Spirit of Life Christian.

Larkins, Ernest R. The Impact of Taxes on U. S. Citizens Working Abroad. LC 83-9201. (Research for Business Decisions Ser.: No. 66). 143p. reprint ed. pap. 44.40 (*0-8357-1487-X*, 207039900088) Bks Demand.

Larkins, Jeremy, jt. ed. see Fawn, Rick.

Larkins, Peter L., jt. auth. see Payling, R.

Larkins, R. G. & Smallwood, R. A. Clinical Skills: The Medical Interview, Physical Examination & Assessment of the Patient's Problems. 396p. 1994. pap. 39.95 (*0-522-84467-7*, Pub. by Melbourne Univ Pr) Paul & Co Pubs.

Larkins, William T. Battleship & Cruiser Aircraft of the United States Navy, 1910-1949. (Illus.). 208p. 1996. 49.95 (*0-7643-0088-1*) Schiffer.

— The Ford Tri-Motor, 1926-1992. LC 92-60363. (Illus.). 288p. 1992. 49.95 (*0-88740-416-2*) Schiffer.

— U. S. Navy Aircraft, 1921-1941, U. S. Marine Corps Aircraft, 1914-1959: Two Classics in One Volume. LC 88-17753. (Illus.). 203p. 1995. 39.95 (*0-88740-742-0*) Schiffer.

***Larkspur, Penelope.** The Secret Life of Fairies. (Illus.). 32p. (YA). (gr. 3 up). 1999. 14.95 (*1-55074-547-6*) Kids Can Pr.

Larkum, A. W., et al, eds. Biology of Seagrasses: A Treatise of Seagrasses with Special Reference to the Australian Region. (Aquatic Plant Studies: No. 2). 842p. 1989. 240.75 (*0-444-87403-8*) Elsevier.

Larlee, Jennifer K., jt. auth. see Larlee, Melinda B.

***Larlee, Melinda B. & Larlee, Jennifer K.** The Autumn Almanac of Hillsborough County, NH: 1999 Edition. (Illus.). 88p. 1999. pap. 7.95 (*0-9673954-0-2*) Autumn Almanac.

Larlham, Peter F. Black Theater, Dance, & Ritual in South Africa. Brockett, Oscar G., ed. LC 85-8758. (Theater & Dramatic Studies: No. 29). 191p. 1985. reprint ed. pap. 59.30 (*0-8357-1658-9*, 207047300095) Bks Demand.

***Larman.** Supplement: Applying UML & Patterns Video Tapes - Applying UML & Patterns -The Complete Video Course 1/e: VIDEO TAPES. 1999. VHS 104.99 (*0-13-016880-7*) Pearson Custom.

Larman, Craig. Applying UML & Patterns: An Introduction to Object-Oriented Analysis & Design. LC 97-33977. 528p. 1998. 47.00 (*0-13-748880-7*) P-H.

***Larman, Craig.** Applying UML & Patterns: An Introduction to Object-Oriented Analysis & Design. 1999. pap. text 149.99 (*0-13-025559-9*) P-H.

Larman, Craig. Java 2 Performance & Idiom Guide. LC 99-45773. 299p. (C). 1999. 39.99 (0-13-014260-3) P-H.

***Larmer.** Ethics in the Workplace. 2nd ed. (Philosophy Ser.). 2001. 40.00 (0-534-54659-5) Wadsworth Pub.

Larmer, Larry. A Guide to Parliamentary Procedure for Local Government in WI. LC 99-188464. 98p. (C). 1998. per. 19.95 (0-7872-5533-5) Kendall-Hunt.

Larmer, Robert A. Water into Wine? An Investigation of the Concept of Miracle. 168p. 1988. 65.00 (0-7735-0615-2, Pub. by McG-Queens Univ Pr) CUP Services.

Larmer, Robert A., compiled by. Ethics in the Workplace: Selected Readings in Business Ethics. LC 95-45562. 600p. (C). 1995. pap. 55.95 (0-314-06802-3) West Pub.

Larmer, Robert A., ed. Questions of Miracle. LC 97-187330. 184p. (C). 1996. 65.00 (0-7735-1416-3); pap. 19.95 (0-7735-1501-1, Pub. by McG-Queens Univ Pr) CUP Services.

***Larminie.** Fuel Cell Systems Explained. 2000. text. write for info. (0-471-49026-1) Wiley.

Larminie, Vivienne. Wealth, Kinship & Culture: The 17th-Century Newdigates of Arbury & Their World. (Royal Historical Society Studies in History: No. 72). (Illus.). 259p. (C). 1995. 75.00 (0-86193-231-5, Royal Historical Soc) Boydell & Brewer.

Larminie, William, compiled by. West Irish Folk-Tales & Romances. LC 72-4191. (Select Bibliographies Reprint Ser.). 1977. reprint ed. 19.95 (0-8369-6888-3) Ayer.

***Larmony, Audrey Walwyn.** Giving Up Was Never an Option. LC 00-90440. 2000. pap. 10.95 (0-533-13508-7) Vantage.

Larmore, Charles. The Romantic Legacy. 120p. 1996. 21.00 (0-231-10134-1) Col U Pr.

Larmore, Charles E. The Morals of Modernity. (Modern European Philosophy Ser.). 236p. (C). 1996. pap. text 20.95 (0-521-49772-8) Cambridge U Pr.

— Patterns of Moral Complexity. 212p. 1987. pap. text 20.95 (0-521-33891-3) Cambridge U Pr.

Larmore, Lewis & Gervals, Robert L., eds. Space Stations & Space Shuttles & Interplanetary Missions 16th Annual AAS Meeting, Jun. 8-10, 1970, Anaheim, CA: 16th Annual AAS Meeting, Anaheim, CA, June 8-10, 1970. LC 57-43769. (Advances in the Astronautical Sciences Ser.: Vol. 27). 606p. 1970. 45.00 (0-87703-054-5, Am Astronaut Soc) Univelt Inc.

— Space Stations & Space Shuttles & Interplanetary Missions 16th Annual AAS Meeting, Jun. 8-10, 1970, Anaheim, CA: 16th Annual AAS Meeting, Anaheim, CA, June 8-10, 1970, Vol. 28. LC 57-43769. (Advances in the Astronautical Sciences Ser.: Vol. 27). 488p. 1970. 35.00 (0-87703-055-3, Am Astronaut Soc) Univelt Inc.

Larmoth, Jeanine, text. Victoria, at Home with White. LC 95-41343. 1996. 25.00 (0-688-14471-3, Hearst) Hearst Commns.

***Larmoth, Jeanine & The Peterboro Basket Company Staff.** Beautiful Baskets: Decorating, Entertaining & Collecting. 144p. 2000. 25.00 (1-928998-34-8, Pub. by Q V C Pubg) Client Dist Srvs.

Larmour, A. S. Step by Step. 211p. 1986. 50.00 (0-7212-0736-7, Pub. by Regency Pr GBR) St Mut.

Larmour, David H., et al. Rethinking Sexuality: Foucault & Classical Antiquity. LC 97-18650. 280p. 1997. text 55.00 (0-691-01680-1, Pub. by Princeton U Pr); pap. text 18.95 (0-691-01679-8, Pub. by Princeton U Pr) Cal Prin Full Svc.

Larmour, David H., jt. auth. see Georgiadou, Aristoula.

Larmour, Peter J. The French Radical Party in the, 1930's. viii, 328p. 1964. 42.50 (0-8047-0206-3) Stanford U Pr.

— The French Radical Party in the, 1930's. fac. ed. LC 64-14554. (Illus.). 337p. 1964. reprint ed. pap. 30.00 (0-7837-7916-X, 204767200008) Bks Demand.

Larmour, Peter J., et al, eds. Land, People & Government: Public Lands Policy in the South. LC 82-188428. 203p. reprint ed. pap. 63.00 (0-7837-3945-1, 204371000011) Bks Demand.

Larmour, Peter J. & Australian National University Press Staff. Governance & Reform in the South Pacific LC 98-200155. (Pacific Policy Papers). x, 326p. 1997. write for info. (0-7315-2347-4) Aust Nat Univ.

***Larmouth, John.** ASN.I Complete. 1999. 44.95 (0-12-233435-3) Morgan Kaufmann.

Larmouth, John. Understanding OSI. (Illus.). 320p. 1995. mass mkt. 41.95 (1-85032-176-0) ITCP.

Larmoyeux, Mary. My Heart's at Home. LC 98-31336. 224p. 1999. pap. 12.99 (0-8054-1658-7) Broadman.

Larn, Richard. Shipwrecks Around Land's End. (C). 1989. pap. 35.00 (0-85025-307-1, Pub. by Tor Mark Pr) St Mut.

— Shipwrecks Around the Lizard. (C). 1990. pap. 24.95 (0-85025-306-3, Pub. by Tor Mark Pr) St Mut.

— Shipwrecks North Coast: St. Ives to Bude. (C). 1990. pap. 35.00 (0-85025-324-1, Pub. by Tor Mark Pr) St Mut.

Larned, ed. Stone Soup for the World. 464p. 1999. 8.98 (1-56731-321-3, MJF Bks) Fine Comms.

Larned, Augusta. Old Tales Retold from Grecian Mythology in Talks Around the Fire (1876) 498p. 1998. reprint ed. pap. 36.00 (0-7661-0250-5) Kessinger Pub.

Larned, E. D. Church Records of Killingly, Connecticut. 56p. 1984. pap. 7.00 (0-912606-22-3) Hunterdon Hse.

Larned, Ellen D. Historic Gleanings in Windham County, Connecticut. 254p. 1992. reprint ed. pap. 19.50 (1-55613-659-5) Heritage Bk.

— Historic Gleanings in Windham County, Connecticut. 254p. 1997. reprint ed. lib. bdg. 32.50 (0-8328-5699-1) Higginson Bk Co.

— History of Windham County, 2 vols. (Illus.). 1181p. 1995. reprint ed. lib. bdg. 109.00 (0-8328-4488-8) Higginson Bk Co.

— History of Windham County, 2 vols. (Illus.). 1181p. 1998. reprint ed. lib. bdg. 109.00 (0-8328-7018-8) Higginson Bk Co.

— History of Windham County, CT, Vol. 1. (Illus.). 595p. 1998. pap. 41.00 (0-7884-0959-X, L065) Heritage Bk.

— History of Windham County, CT, Vol. 2. (Illus.). 632p. 1998. pap. 42.50 (0-7884-0960-3, L066) Heritage Bk.

Larned, J. N., ed. The Literature of American History: A Bibliographical Guide. 588p. 1995. reprint ed. lib. bdg. 59.95 (0-8328-4487-X) Higginson Bk Co.

— The Literature of American History: A Bibliographical Guide. 588p. 1995. reprint ed. lib. bdg. 64.50 (0-8328-4506-X) Higginson Bk Co.

Larned, Joseph N. Life & Work of William Pryor Letchworth, Student & Minister of Public Benevolence. LC 71-172592. (Criminology, Law Enforcement, & Social Problems Ser.: No. 182). (Illus.). 1974. reprint ed. 24.00 (0-87585-182-7) Patterson Smith.

Larned, Josephus N. Books, Culture & Character. LC 70-90650. (Essay Index Reprint Ser.). 1977. 19.95 (0-8369-1211-X) Ayer.

— Study of Greatness in Men. LC 73-156677. (Essay Index Reprint Ser.). 1977. reprint ed. 23.95 (0-8369-2557-2) Ayer.

Larned, Josephus N., et al. English Leadership. LC 70-93353. (Essay Index Reprint Ser.). 1977. 26.95 (0-8369-1416-3) Ayer.

Larned, Larry. Traveling the Merritt Parkway. (Images of America Ser.). (Illus.). 128p. 1998. pap. 16.99 (0-7524-0946-8) Arcadia Publng.

***Larned, Marianne.** The Leader's Guide to "Stone Soup for the World" Life Changing Stories of Kindness & Courageous Acts of Service. (Illus.). 186p. 1999. pap. text 15.00 (0-9700364-0-X) Stone Soup.

Larned, Marianne, ed. Stone Soup for the World: Life Changing Stories of Kindness & Courageous Acts of Service. LC 97-44692. 438p. (Orig.). 1998. pap. 15.95 (1-57324-118-0) Conari Press.

Larned, W. T. & Green, John. North American Indian Tales. LC 96-48788. (Children's Thrift Classics Ser.). (Illus.). 96p. 1997. reprint ed. pap. text 1.00 (0-486-29656-3) Dover.

Larner, Christina. Enemies of God: The Witch-Hunt in Scotland. LC 81-47605. 256p. reprint ed. pap. 79.40 (0-7837-2186-2, 204252400004) Bks Demand.

Larner, Gerald. Maurice Ravel. (20th Century Composers Ser.). (Illus.). 240p. (Orig.). 1996. pap. 19.95 (0-7148-3270-7, Pub. by Phaidon Press) Phaidon Pr.

***Larner, John.** Marco Polo & the Discovery of the World. LC 99-24887. (Illus.). 288p. 1999. 29.95 (0-300-07971-0) Yale U Pr.

Larner, John W., et al. The Papers of the Society of American Indians. LC 86-24843. 10p. 1987. 10.00 (0-8420-4005-6) Scholarly Res Inc.

Larner, Joseph, ed. see Brody, Harold J., et al.

Larner, Mary. In the Neighborhood: Programs That Strengthen Family Day Care for Low-Income Families. 96p. (Orig.). 1994. pap. 12.95 (0-926582-12-7) NCCP.

— Linking Family Support & Early Childhood Programs: Issues, Experience, Opportunities. Lalley, Jacqueline, ed. (Guidelines for Effective Practice Ser.). 40p. (Orig.). 1995. pap. 7.00 (1-885429-09-6) Family Resource.

Larner, Mary, et al, eds. Fair Start for Children: Lessons Learned from Seven Demonstration Programs. LC 92-10965. 288p. (C). 1993. 35.00 (0-300-05206-5) Yale U Pr.

Larner, Mary & Chaudry, Nina. Promoting Professionalism Through Family Day Care Networks: A Study of Child Care Inc.'s Neighborhood Child Care Initiatives Project, New York City. 39p. 1993. pap. 4.00 (0-926582-11-9) NCCP.

Larner, Monica, jt. auth. see Neighbor, Travis.

Larner, Robert A. Water into Wine? An Investigation of the Concept of Miracle. 168p. 1996. pap. text 19.95 (0-7735-1527-5, Pub. by McG-Queens Univ Pr) CUP Services.

Larner, Robert J. & Meehan, James W., Jr., eds. Economics & Antitrust Policy. LC 88 18515. 250p. 1989. 65.00 (0-89930-386-2, LRA/, Quorum Bks) Greenwood.

Larner, Robin. Laws Relating to the Department of Public Safety: Reprinted from the Code of Laws of South Carolina 1976. LC 96-77031. 1300p. 1996. pap. text. write for info. (0-7620-0077-5) West Group.

Laro, Julia. Second Language Learners & Middle School Reform. 48p. (Orig.). 1995. pap. 8.00 (1-884037-10-0) Coun Chief St Schl Offs.

LaRocca, Charles J., ed. see Crane, Stephen.

***Larocca, Danielle.** SAP Reporting Tools. (SAP Ser.). (Illus.). 528p. 1999. pap. 49.99 (0-07-212342-7) McGraw.

***Larocca, Donald J.** Academy of the Sword: Illustrated Fencing Books, 1500-1800. LC 98-50294. 1998. pap. write for info. (0-87099-894-3) Metro Mus Art.

Larocca, Donald J. & Metropolitan Museum of Art Staff (New York, N.Y.). The Gods of War: Sacred Imagery & the Decoration of Arms & Armor. LC 96-49662. 47p. 1996. pap. 6.95 (0-87099-779-3) Metro Mus Art.

Larocca, Felix E., jt. auth. see Cassell, Dana K.

Larocca, Joanne C. Pocket Guide to IV Therapy. 4th ed. (Illus.). 213p. (C). (gr. 13). 1993. spiral bd. 28.95 (0-8016-6910-3, 06910) Mosby Inc.

LaRocca, Joanne C. & Otto, Shirley E. Pocket Guide to Intravenous Therapy. 3rd ed. LC 96-14139. (Illus.). 464p. (C). (gr. 13). 1996. text 22.95 (0-8151-5298-1, 28205) Mosby Inc.

Larocce, jt. auth. see Johnson.

Larocco. The Art of Life & Work. 288p. 1997. mass mkt. 24.95 (0-538-68297-3) S-W Pub.

— The Art of Life & Work. 1998. pap. 13.95 (0-538-68298-1) S-W Pub.

— The Art of Work: An Anthology of WKP Life. (EC - HS Communication/English Ser.). 1995. mass mkt. 19.95 (0-538-63651-3) S-W Pub.

— Literature for Life & Work. 11th ed. (CA - Career Development Ser.). (YA). (gr. 9). Date not set. pap. write for info. (0-314-21768-1) S-W Pub.

— Literature for Life & Work. 11th ed. (EJ - Tech Prep Ser.). (YA). (gr. 10). Date not set. pap. write for info. (0-314-21769-X) S-W Pub.

Larocco & Johnson. Spanish Handbook, Literature. (Tech Prep Ser.). 1997. pap. text 18.75 (0-538-68040-7) Thomson Learn.

Larocco, jt. auth. see Johnson.

LaRocco, Christine & Coughlin, James. The Art of Work: An Anthology of Workplace Literature. (Illus.). 280p. 1997. pap. 19.95 (0-534-63654-3) S-W Pub.

LaRocco, Lesli, ed. see Zoshchenko, Mikhail.

LaRocco, Rich, ed. see Darner, Kirt I.

Larocea, Danielle. Teach Yourself SAP R/3 in 24 Hours. LC 99-61493. (Sams Teach Yourself ... in 24 Hours Ser.). 472p. 1999. pap. 24.99 (0-672-31624-2) Sams.

Laroche, Loretta. Happy Talk: Fun Ways to Talk to Yourself. 2nd ed. (Illus.). 133p. 1996. pap. 6.95 (0-9644014-9-5) Humor Potential.

— How Serious is This? (Illus.). 93p. 1995. pap. 6.95 (0-9644014-8-7) Humor Potential.

— Relax - You May Only Have a Few Minutes Left. LC 98-4936. 190p. 1998. 21.00 (0-375-50145-2) Villard Books.

***Laroche, Loretta.** Relax You May Only Have A Few Minutes Left. abr. ed. 1998. 18.00 incl. audio (0-375-40348-5) Random.

Laroche, Loretta & Donnelly, Laurie. The Joy Journal. (Illus.). 1997. 12.00 (0-9644014-7-9) Humor Potential.

Laroche, Michel, jt. auth. see Kirpalani, Vishnu H.

Larochelle. The Year-Round Book of Fun Stuff. (J). 15.95 (0-8126-0147-5) Open Court.

LaRochelle, David. Detective Dave: Space Case. (Mad Mysteries Ser.: Vol. 7). (Illus.). 48p. (J). (gr. 2-4). 1998. pap. 3.50 (0-8431-7850-7, Price Stern) Peng Put Young Read.

— A Dog Gone Dilemma. (Mad Mysteries Ser.). (Illus.). (J). (ps-3). 1996. pap. 3.50 (0-8431-3946-3, Price Stern) Peng Put Young Read.

— Miss Taken's Identity. (Mad Mysteries Ser.: Vol. 8). (Illus.). 48p. (J). (gr. 2-4). 1998. pap. 3.50 (0-8431-7849-3, Price Stern) Peng Put Young Read.

— The Pirate's Yo-Ho Hoax, Vol. 6. (Mad Mysteries Ser.: Vol. 6). (Illus.). 48p. (J). (gr. 2 up). 1997. pap. 2.95 (0-8431-7958-9, Price Stern) Peng Put Young Read.

— Trapped in Hill House. (Mad Mysteries Ser.). (Illus.). (J). (ps-3). 1996. pap. 3.50 (0-8431-3945-5, Price Stern) Peng Put Young Read.

Larochelle, Marie, et al, eds. Constructivism & Education. LC 97-46098. (Illus.). 336p. (C). 1998. text 54.95 (0-521-62135-6) Cambridge U Pr.

Larock, Bruce. Civil Engineering Hydraulics & Hydrology: Review for the Professional Engineer's Exam. (Illus.). 98p. (Orig.). 1999. pap. 19.95 (1-57645-044-9, 449) Engineering.

***Larock, Bruce E. & Jeppson, Roland W.** Hydraulics of Pipeline Systems. LC 99-32568. 552p. 1999. boxed set 89.95 (0-8493-1806-8) CRC Pr.

Larock, Bruce E., jt. auth. see Newman, Donald G.

Larock, R. C. Organomercury Compounds in Organic Synthesis. (Reactivity & Structure Ser.: Vol. 22). 420p. 1985. 299.95 (0-387-13749-1) Spr-Verlag.

Larock, Richard C. Comprehensive Organic Transformations: A Guide to Functional Group Preparations. LC 89-30333. 1160p. 1989. 75.00 (0-89573-710-8, Wiley-VCH) Wiley.

***Larock, Richard C.** Comprehensive Organic Transformations: A Guide to Functional Group Preparations. 2nd ed. LC 98-37314. 2583p. 1999. 150.00 (0-471-19031-4) Wiley.

LaRocque, L. E. Boiler Operator's Dictionary. LC 87-18417. 151p. 1988. pap. 6.95 (0-912524-41-3) Busn News.

— Starting in Heating & Air Conditioning Service. Turpin, Joanna, ed. LC 92-11928. (Illus.). 180p. (C). 1992. 24.95 (0-912524-63-4) Busn News.

LaRocque, Lionel. Boilers Simplified. LC 87-685. 240p. 1987. 24.95 (0-912524-40-5) Busn News.

Larocque, Thomas. Memories of an Ordinary Man. LC 98-86799. 192p. 1999. pap. 11.95 (1-56167-501-6) Am Literary Pr.

LaRoe, Diane. The Awakening. 256p. 1998. 22.50 (0-9653171-1-0) Light Pub Co.

LaRoe, Edward T. Our Living Resources: Report to the Nation on the Distribution, Abundance & Health of United States Plants, Animals & Ecosystems. 542p. 1995. boxed set 51.00 (0-16-061698-0) USGPO.

LaRoe, Ross M., jt. auth. see Pool, John Charles.

Larom, Mary, jt. auth. see Clegg, Helen.

Larom, Peter, jt. auth. see Rousmaniere, Leah R.

Laron, Z., ed. European Society for Pediatric Endocrinology (ESPE) & Lawson Wilkins Pediatric Endocrinology Society (LWPES) Abstracts: Third Joint Meeting, Jerusalem, October - November 1989. (Journal: Hormone Research Ser.: Vol. 31, Suppl. 1). viii, 84p. 1989. 40.00 (3-8055-5117-7) S Karger.

— Prognosis of Diabetes in Children. (Pediatric & Adolescent Endocrinology Ser.: Vol. 18). xiv, 304p. 1989. 216.75 (3-8055-4702-1) S Karger.

— Third Joint Meeting of the European Society for Pediatric Endocrinology (ESPE) & the Lawson Wilkins Pediatric Endocrine Society (LWPES) Proceedings of the Plenary Lectures & Symposia, Jerusalem, October - November 1989. (Journal: Hormone Research Ser.: Vol. 33, No. 2-4, 1990). (Illus.). 116p. 1990. pap. 118.50 (3-8055-5289-0) S Karger.

Laron, Z. & Butenandt, O., eds. Evaluation of Growth Hormone Secretion. (Pediatric & Adolescent Endocrinology Ser.: Vol. 12). (Illus.). viii, 200p. 1983. 132.25 (3-8055-3623-2) S Karger.

Laron, Z. & Galatzer, A., eds. Psychological Aspects of Diabetes in Children & Adolescents. (Pediatric & Adolescent Endocrinology Ser.: Vol. 10). xvi, 248p. 1983. 160.00 (3-8055-3575-9) S Karger.

— Recent Progress in Medico-Social Problems in Juvenile Diabetics, Pt. II. (Pediatric & Adolescent Endocrinology Ser.: Vol. 11). (Illus.). x, 210p. 1983. 133.25 (3-8055-3594-5) S Karger.

Laron, Z. & Karp, M., eds. Future Trends in Juvenile Diabetes. (Pediatric & Adolescent Endocrinology Ser.: Vol. 15). (Illus.). xiv, 410p. 1986. 304.50 (3-8055-3958-4) S Karger.

— Prediabetes - Are We Ready to Intervene? (Pediatric & Adolescent Endocrinology Ser.: Vol. 23). (Illus.). x, 192p. 1993. 213.25 (3-8055-5665-9) S Karger.

Laron, Z. & Parks, J. S., eds. Lessons from Laron Syndrome (LS), 1966-1992: A Model of GH & IGF-I Action & Interaction. (Pediatric & Adolescent Endocrinology Ser.: Vol. 24). (Illus.). x, 368p. 1993. 321.75 (3-8055-5671-3) S Karger.

Laron, Z., ed. see International Beilinson Symposium Staff.

Laron, Zvi, ed. The Adipose Child. (Pediatric & Adolescent Endocrinology Ser.: Vol.1). 250p. 1976. 77.50 (3-8055-2343-2) S Karger.

Laron, Zvi, ed. see International Beilinson Symposium Staff.

LaRonde, Philip H. Record of the Marriages of Saint Jean-Baptiste (1914-51) in Manchester, New Hampshire. (Illus.). 114p. 1997. reprint ed. pap. 18.00 (0-8328-7138-9) Higginson Bk Co.

LaRonde, Philip H., ed. Record of the Marriages of Saint Antoine (1900-50) in Manchester, New Hampshire. (Illus.). 77p. 1997. reprint ed. pap. 15.00 (0-8328-7139-7) Higginson Bk Co.

LaRondelle, Hans. How to Understand the End-Time Prophecies of the Bible: The Biblical-Contextual Approach. LC 97-90722. 1997. 29.90 (0-9659202-0-8) First Impr FL.

***LaRondelle, Hans K.** Assurance of Salvation. LC 99-16208. 1999. 8.99 (0-8163-1712-7) Pacific Pr Pub Assn.

LaRondelle, Hans K. The Israel of God in Prophecy: Principles of Prophetic Interpretation. LC 82-74358. 240p. 1983. pap. 15.99 (0-943872-14-6) Andrews Univ Pr.

***LaRondelle, Hans K.** Light for the Last Days: Jesus' End-Time Prophecies Made Plain in the Book of Revelation. James, David C., ed. LC 99-57497. 187p. 2000. pap. 12.99 (0-8163-1758-5) Pacific Pr Pub Assn.

Larone, Davise H., ed. Medically Important Fungi: A Guide to Identification. 3rd ed. LC 94-40202. 1995. 49.95 (1-55581-091-8) ASM Pr.

Larone, J. N. Two-over-One Game Force Bidding Problems No. 1: Responses When Responder Has Fit with Opener's One Heart or One Spade Bid. 88p. (Orig.). 1996. pap. 9.95 (0-89412-255-X, B-1) Aegean Park Pr.

Laroque, François. The Age of Shakespeare. Campbell, Alexandra, tr. (Discoveries Ser.). (Illus.). 192p. 1993. pap. 12.95 (0-8109-2890-6, Pub. by Abrams) Time Warner.

— The Journal of Francois Laroque. 102p. 1981. 16.95 (0-87770-262-4) Ye Galleon.

Laroque, P. The Social Institutions of France. xxii, 802p. 1983. text 984.00 (0-677-30970-8) Gordon & Breach.

Laros, Russell K., ed. Blood Disorders in Pregnancy. LC 85-24012. 257p. reprint ed. pap. 79.70 (0-7837-2724-0, 204310400006) Bks Demand.

LaRosa & Mora. Neighborly Adversaries. LC 99-25947. 368p. 1999. text 69.00 (0-8476-9396-1) Rowman.

LaRosa, A. Dictionnaire du Droit International Penal. (FRE.). 1998. 79.95 (0-320-00256-X) Fr & Eur.

LaRosa, Benedict D. Gun Control: A Historical Perspective. 2nd large type ed. 50p. (Orig.). 1996. lib. bdg. 40.00 (0-9627423-5-X, GCHP) Candlestick.

LaRosa, Dominic. How to Build Everything You Need for Your Birds, from Aviaries... to Nestboxes. 2nd rev. ed. LC AA529799. (Illus.). 57p. (YA). (gr. 7 up). 1973. pap. 15.00 (0-9672622-0-8) LaRosa Pubns.

LaRosa, John. The U. S. Billiard Parlors Industry. 12p. 1997. 59.00 (1-891084-12-7) Mktdata Ent.

Larosa, John C., ed. Medical Management of Atherosclerosis. LC 97-50182. (Illus.). 344p. 1998. text 135.00 (0-8247-0149-6) Dekker.

LaRosa, Judith H., et al, eds. Proceedings of the National Heart, Lung & Blood Institute Symposium on Rapid Identification & Treatment of Acute Myocardial Infarction: Issues & Answers. (Illus.). 157p. (Orig.). 1996. pap. text 25.00 (0-7881-2825-6) DIANE Pub.

LaRosa, Judith H., jt. auth. see Alexander, Linda L.

LaRosa, Judith H., jt. auth. see Alexander, Linda Lewis.

LaRosa, Michael & Mora, Frank O., eds. Neighborly Adversaries: Readings in U. S. - Latin American Relations. LC 99-25947. 368p. 1999. pap. 23.95 (0-8476-9397-X) Rowman.

Larosa, Sheila de, see De Larosa, Sheila.

LaRosa, Theodore, jt. auth. see Magnani, Loris.

***Larose & Straubhaar.** Electronic Media in the Information Age. 2001. pap. 43.75 (0-534-56047-4) Thomson Learn.

Larose, Daniel T. & Jin, Chun. Ready, Set, Run! A Student Guide to the SAS Software for Microsoft Windows. LC 97-43412. v, 96p. 1998. pap. text 15.95 (0-7674-0422-X, 0422-X) Mayfield Pub.

LaRose-Edwards, Paul, et al. Non-Traditional Military Training for Canadian Peacekeepers. 2nd ed. LC 98-179945. 125p. 1997. pap. 14.95 (0-660-16881-2, Pub. by Canadian Govt Pub) Accents Pubns.

LaRose, Lawrence, jt. auth. see Penn, Nate.

LaRose, Linda. Jessica Takes Charge. (Illus.). 24p. (J). (ps-2). 1999. pap. 5.95 (1-55037-562-8, Pub. by Annick Pr) Firefly Bks Ltd.

L

— Jessica Takes Charge. (Illus.). 24p. (J). (ps-1). 1999. lib. bdg. 15.95 (*1-55037-563-6*, Pub. by Annick Pr) Firefly Bks Ltd.

LaRose, Mary K., tr. see Descamps-Lequime, Sophie.

LaRose, Mary K., tr. see Descamps-Lequime, Sophie & Vernerey, Denise.

LaRose, Mary K., tr. see Guittard, Charles.

LaRose, Mary K., tr. see Koenig, Viviane.

LaRose, Mary K., tr. see Moktefi, Mokhtar.

LaRose, Robert & Straubhaar, Joseph D. Communications Media in the Information Society. LC 95-6379. 490p. 1995. pap. 34.50 (*0-534-21534-3*) Wadsworth Pub.

— Communications Media in the Information Society: Updated Edition. rev. ed. LC 96-23298. (Wadsworth Series in Mass Communication & Journalism). 490p. 1996. pap. 40.50 (*0-534-52128-2*) Course Tech.

LaRose-Weaver, Diane & Cusick, Dawn. Glorious Christmas Crafts: Celebrate the Holidays with More Than 120 Festive Projects to Make. (Illus.). 160p. 1993. pap. 14.95 (*0-8069-8379-5*) Sterling.

Larosi Ere, Jacques De, see De Larosi Ere, Jacques.

Larosiere, Jacques De, see De Larosiere, Jacques.

LaRossa, Maureen M., jt. auth. see LaRossa, Ralph.

LaRossa, Ralph. Becoming a Parent. LC 85-30246. (Family Studies Text: No. 3). 135p. (Orig.). 1986. reprint ed. pap. 41.90 (*0-7837-9906-3*, 206063200006) Bks Demand.

— Conflict & Power in Marriage: Expecting the First Child. LC 77-8566. (Sage Library of Social Research: No. 50). 176p. reprint ed. pap. 54.60 (*0-8357-8445-2*, 203470900091) Bks Demand.

— The Modernization of Fatherhood: A Social & Political History. (Illus.). 320p. 1999. lib. bdg. 55.00 (*0-226-46903-4*) U Ch Pr.

Larossa, Ralph. The Modernization of Fatherhood: A Social & Political History. (Illus.). 320p. 1996. pap. text 18.95 (*0-226-46904-2*) U Ch Pr.

LaRossa, Ralph, ed. Family Case Studies: A Sociological Perspective. 260p. (C). 1984. pap. 15.95 (*0-02-918010-4*) Free Pr.

LaRossa, Ralph & LaRossa, Maureen M. Transition to Parenthood: How Infants Change Families. LC 80-26766. (Sage Library of Social Research: Vol. 119). 263p. 1981. reprint ed. pap. 81.60 (*0-608-03381-2*, 205964500008) Bks Demand.

LaRossa, Robert A., ed. Bioluminescence Methods & Protocols. LC 97-44152. (Methods in Molecular Biology Ser.). 320p. 1998. 89.50 (*0-89603-520-4*) Humana.

LaRouche, Janice & Ryan, Regina. Janice LaRouche's Strategies for Women at Work. 400p. 1984. pap. 9.95 (*0-380-86744-3*, Avon Bks) Morrow Avon.

Larouche, L. & Pilon, J. Terminologie de la Gestion: Le Organigrammes: Management Terminology. Cote, M., ed. 223p. 1974. pap. 24.95 (*0-8288-6215-X*, M-9220) Fr & Eur.

LaRouche, Lois E. The Settee: A Novel. LC 98-83193. 365p. 1999. 25.00 (*0-7388-0349-9*); pap. 15.00 (*0-7388-0350-2*) Xlibris Corp.

LaRouche, Lyndon H., Jr. La Ciencia de la Economia Christiana. Small, Dennis & Lozano, Salvador, trs. LC 93-83889. (SPA., Illus.). 300p. (Orig.). 1993. pap. 10.00 (*1-882985-00-1*) Schiller Inst.

— Cold Fusion: A Challenge to United States Science Policy. Gallagher, Paul, ed. LC 92-60722. (Illus.). 173p. (Orig.). (C). 1992. pap. 20.00 (*0-9621095-7-6*) Schiller Inst.

— The Power of Reason - 1988: An Autobiography. LC 87-7894. (Illus.). 331p. (Orig.). 1987. pap. 10.00 (*0-943235-00-6*) Exec Intel Review.

— Selections from Lyndon H. LaRouche, Jr. Wei, Ray, ed. & tr. by. Chu, Andy, tr. LC 92-62931. (CHI.). 140p. (Orig.). 1992. pap. 7.00 (*0-9621095-9-2*) Schiller Inst.

— So, You Wish to Learn All about Economics? A Text on Elementary Mathematical Economics. 192p. (Orig.). 1995. pap. 10.00 (*0-933488-35-1*) Exec Intel Review.

Larouche, Lyndon H. & Spannaus, Nancy B. So, You Wish to Learn All about Economics? A Text on Elementary Mathematical Economics. 2nd ed. (Illus.). 192p. (Orig.). 1995. pap. 10.00 (*0-943235-13-8*) Exec Intel Review.

Larouche, Michael, ed. Le Cinema d'Aujourd'Hui. 266p. 1988. pap. write for info. (*2-89135-016-2*) Guernica Editions.

Larouche, Michel, ed. Films d'Afrique. 144p. 1991. pap. 15.00 (*2-89135-035-9*) Guernica Editions.

***Larouche, Pierre.** EC Telecommunications Law: Regulation & Market Liberalisation. 512p. 2000. 72.00 (*1-84113-144-X*, Pub. by Hart Pub) Intl Spec Bk.

LaRoue, Samuel D., Jr. & Uguccioni, Ellen J. Coral Gables in Postcards: Scenes from Florida's Yesterday. LC 88-71025. (Illus.). 56p. (Orig.). 1988. pap. 12.95 (*0-9620565-0-2*) Dade Heritage Trust.

Larousse. El Pegueno Larousse Ilustrado, 2000. (Illus.). 1794p. 1999. 39.95 (*970-607-910-6*, Larousse LKC) LKC.

Larousse, ed. Petit Dictionnaire Francais-Portugais/ Portugais-Francais. (FRE & POR.). 912p. 1997. 34.95 (*0-7859-9508-0*) Fr & Eur.

— Petit Larousse 1999. (FRE.). 1998. 95.00 (*0-7859-9724-5*) Fr & Eur.

Larousse, David P. Edible Art. (Professional Bks.). (Illus.). 232p. 1987. text 44.95 (*0-442-25832-1*, VNR) Wiley.

— Edible Art: Forty-Eight Garnishes for the Professional. 96p. 1986. 40.00 (*0-471-28935-3*, VNR) Wiley.

— The Hors D'Oervre Bible. 432p. 1995. 49.00 (*0-471-01312-9*) Wiley.

— The Professional Garde Manger: A Guide to the Arts of the Buffett. LC 95-41073. (Illus.). 440p. 1996. 65.00 (*0-471-10603-8*) Wiley.

— The Sauce Bible: A Guide to the Saucier's Craft. LC 92-37388. (Illus.). 400p. 1993. 54.95 (*0-471-57228-4*) Wiley.

— The Soup Bible. LC 96-25881. 340p. 1997. 49.95 (*0-471-13562-3*) Wiley.

— A Taste for All Seasons: A Celebration of American Food. LC 89-24688. (Illus.). 192p. 1990. 24.95 (*1-55832-020-2*) Harvard Common Pr.

***Larousse, David Paul.** More Edible Art: 75 Fresh Ideas for Garnishing. 2nd ed. LC 99-49568. (Illus.). 168p. 2000. 40.00 (*0-471-17639-7*) Wiley.

Larousse Editorial Staff. Grand Larousse Universel. 1995. 2995.00 (*0-7859-9474-2*) Fr & Eur.

Larousse Editorial Staff, ed. Gran Diccionario Enciclopedico Larousse, 15 vols. (SPA.). 1987. 1495.00 (*0-320-03698-7*) Fr & Eur.

— Gran Larousse Universel, 40 vols. (SPA.). 1996. 2495.00 (*0-320-03707-X*) Fr & Eur.

— Larousse Enciclopedia Alfabetica, 10 vols. (SPA.). 1994. 995.00 (*0-320-03699-5*) Fr & Eur.

— Pequeno Larousse Ilustrado 1999. annuals (SPA.). 49.95 (*0-320-03691-X*) Fr & Eur.

— Petit Larousse 2000. annuals (FRE.). 1999. 95.00 (*0-320-03690-1*) Fr & Eur.

Larousse Editors. Grand Usuel Larousse. (FRE.). 7616p. 1997. pap. 395.00 (*0-7859-9560-9*) Fr & Eur.

— Larousse Encyclopedique Illustre. (FRE., Illus.). 1824p. 1997. 195.00 (*0-7859-9552-8*) Fr & Eur.

— Larousse Gastronomique. 1215p. 1996. 295.00 (*0-7859-9475-0*) Fr & Eur.

Larousse Editors, ed. Dictionary Encyclopedique Larousse, 4 vols. (FRE.). 1732p. 1997. 395.00 (*0-7859-9563-3*) Fr & Eur.

Larousse, J., ed. Food Canning Technology. LC 96-22781. 500p. 1996. 150.00 (*1-56081-688-0*, Wiley-VCH) Wiley.

Larousse, Jean & Brown, Bruce E., eds. Food Canning Technology. LC 96-22781. 719p. 1997. 135.00 (*0-471-18610-4*) Wiley.

Larousse, Kingfischer Chambers. Fascinating Facts: About the Earth, Space, Wild Animals & People. LC 99-34907. 96p. (J). 1999. pap. 9.95 (*0-7534-5265-0*) LKC.

— Fun Finding Out: About Our World. LC 99-34908. 96p. (J). 1999. pap. 10.95 (*0-7534-5264-2*) LKC.

— Ha! Ha! Ha! Over 400 Very Funny Jokes. LC 99-34911. 192p. (J). 1999. pap. 5.95 (*0-7534-5266-9*) LKC.

***Larousse, Kingfischer Chambers.** The Kingfisher First Encyclopedia of Animals. 160p. (J). 1999. pap. 12.95 (*0-7534-5259-6*, Kingfisher) LKC.

Larousse, Kingfischer Chambers. Superschool: Art, Drama, Nature & Science All in One Book. LC 99-34909. 160p. (J). 1999. pap. 12.95 (*0-7534-5263-4*) LKC.

***Larousse, Kingfishers Chambers.** Best Book Assortment. 1999. pap. text 12.95 (*5-555-08886-8*) LKC.

Larousse LKC Publishing Staff. Diccionario Compact Larousse. 1997. pap. 13.98 (*970-607-421-X*, Larousse LKC) LKC.

Larousse, Pierre, jt. auth. see Clement, Felix.

Larousse, Pierre. Grand Dictionnaire Universel du XIX Siecle, 24 vols. fac. ed. (FRE.). 1990. write for info. (*0-7859-8661-8*, 286971193x) Fr & Eur.

Larousse Staff. Allemand: Guide de Conversation et Dictionnaire. (FRE.). 187p. 1991. pap. 16.95 (*0-7859-7656-6*, 2034035046) Fr & Eur.

— Anglais: Guide de Conversation et Dictionnaire. (ENG & FRE.). 175p. 1991. pap. 16.95 (*0-7859-7655-8*, 2034035011) Fr & Eur.

— Diccionario Enciclopedia Larousse, 12 vols., Set.Tr. of Larousse Encyclopaedia Dictionary (Spanish Edition). (SPA.). 995.00 (*0-8288-8245-2*) Fr & Eur.

— Diccionario Enciclopedico Larousse: Larousse Encyclopedia Dictionary: Spanish Edition, 12 vols. (SPA.). 1992. 995.00 (*0-7859-5231-4*) Fr & Eur.

— Diccionario Enciclopedico Larousse en Tres Volumenes, 3 vols. 1999. 49.95 (*970-607-107-5*) Larousse Eds.

— Diccionario Larousse del Espanol Moderno. (SPA.). 1983. mass mkt. 6.99 (*0-451-16809-7*) NAL.

— Diccionario Manual Ilustrado. 1999. 34.95 (*970-607-539-9*) Larousse Eds.

— Dictionnaire de la Langue Francaise: 35,000 Mots Avec Etymologies. (FRE.). 1092p. 1991. 49.95 (*0-7859-7640-X*, 2033202178) Fr & Eur.

— Dictionnaire de la Medecine Larousse. (FRE.). 1990. pap. 16.95 (*0-7859-7850-X*, 2253037842) Fr & Eur.

— Dictionnaire de la Peinture Allemande et d'Europe Centrale. (FRE.). 414p. 1990. pap. 79.95 (*0-7859-7693-0*, 2037400179) Fr & Eur.

— Dictionnaire de la Peinture Francaise. (FRE.). 520p. 1989. pap. 89.95 (*0-8288-2596-3*, 203740011X) Fr & Eur.

— Dictionnaire de la Peinture Italienne. (FRE.). 528p. 1989. pap. 79.95 (*0-7859-5540-2*, 2037400136) Fr & Eur.

— Dictionnaire des Difficultes de la Langue Francaise. (FRE.). 435p. 1992. 55.00 (*0-7859-0962-1*, 2033409023) Fr & Eur.

— Dictionnaire des Jeux de Lettres. (FRE.). 1088p. 1994. pap. 32.95 (*0-7859-7689-2*, 2037300913) Fr & Eur.

— Dictionnaire des Mots Croises. rev. ed. (FRE.). 904p. 1991. pap. 32.95 (*0-7859-7690-6*, 2037302150) Fr & Eur.

— Dictionnaire des Termes Techniques, l'Atelier du Peintre. (FRE.). 408p. 1990. pap. 79.95 (*0-7859-7696-5*, 2037400667) Fr & Eur.

— Dictionnaire du Francais Contemporain Manual et Travaux Pratiques. (FRE.). 29.95 (*0-317-45626-1*) Fr & Eur.

— Dictionnaire Encyclopedique Larousse L1. (FRE.). 1979. 250.00 (*0-7859-0127-2*, M7733) Fr & Eur.

— Dictionnaire Europa. (FRE.). 1959. write for info. (*0-7859-7649-3*, 2034010329) Fr & Eur.

— Dictionnaire General pour la Maitrise de la Langue Francaise. (FRE.). 1993. write for info. (*0-7859-7641-8*, 2033203026) Fr & Eur.

— Dictionnaire Larousse Bilingue de Poche. (FRE.). write for info. (*0-7859-8605-7*, 203401104X) Fr & Eur.

— Dictionnaire Moderne Larousse Saturne Francais-Anglais, Anglais-Francais. (FRE.). 49.95 (*0-317-45631-8*) Fr & Eur.

— Dictionnaire Moderne Larousse Saturne Francais-Anglais, Anglais-Francaise. (ENG & FRE.). write for info. (*0-8288-7839-0*) Fr & Eur.

— Dictionnaire Pratique des Medicaments. (FRE.). 1989. write for info. (*0-7859-8609-X*, 203510128X) Fr & Eur.

— Dictionnaire Sachs, No. 2. (FRE.). write for info. (*0-7859-7634-5*, 2030281034) Fr & Eur.

— Dictionnaire Sachs-Villate, Vol. 1. (FRE.). write for info. (*0-7859-7633-7*, 2030281034) Fr & Eur.

— Dictionnaire Sachs-Villate Francais-Allemand, Allemand-Francais. (FRE & GER.). 450.00 (*0-7859-7632-9*) Fr & Eur.

— Larousse Concise French English Dictionary. 1280p. 1999. 21.95 (*2-03-420302-X*) LKC.

***Larousse Staff.** Larousse French English Dictionary. unabridged ed. (FRE.). 2064p. 1999. 55.00 (*2-03-420101-9*) LKC.

Larousse Staff. French Collegiate Dictionary. (FRE.). 1092p. 1991. 39.95 (*0-8288-6960-X*, 2033202178) Fr & Eur.

— French-English, English-French Dictionary. 1984. mass mkt. 4.99 (*0-671-45851-5*) PB.

— Grammaire Anglaise. (ENG & FRE.). 256p. 1992. pap. 15.95 (*0-7859-0963-X*, 2034060024) Fr & Eur.

— Gran Enciclopedia Larousse, 24 vols., Set. (SPA.). 10740p. 2495.00 (*0-8288-8250-9*, S12308) Fr & Eur.

— Gran Enciclopedia Larousse: Atlas Historico: Larousse Historical Atlas. (SPA., Illus.). 125.00 (*0-8288-8248-7*) Fr & Eur.

— Gran Enciclopedia Larousse Atlas Geografico: Geographical Atlas. (SPA., Illus.). 125.00 (*0-8288-8247-9*) Fr & Eur.

— Gran Enciclopedia Larousse Color, 24 vols. (SPA.). 10740p. 1992. 3995.00 (*0-7859-5123-7*) Fr & Eur.

— Grand Dictionnaire Encyclopedique Larousse, 10 vols. 1250.00 (*0-685-13389-3*) Fr & Eur.

— Grand Dictionnaire Francais-Espagnol Espagnol-Francais. (FRE & SPA.). 1500p. 1992. 105.00 (*0-7859-7660-4*, 2034513282) Fr & Eur.

— Le Grand Larousse, Vol. 5. (FRE.). 3560p. 1992. 995.00 (*0-8288-1941-6*, M522) Fr & Eur.

— Grand Larousse Annuel 1993. 576p. 1993. 250.00 (*0-7859-5598-4*, 2031002937) Fr & Eur.

— Grand Larousse Encyclopedique. (FRE.). 1088p. 1975. suppl. ed. 89.50 (*0-8288-5893-4*, M6288) Fr & Eur.

— Grand Larousse Encyclopedique, 15 vols., Set. (FRE.). 11200p. 1985. 2995.00 (*0-8288-6775-5*, F42400) Fr & Eur.

— Grand Larousse Universel, 15 vols. (FRE.). 11130p. 1988. 2295.00 (*0-8288-1940-8*, F12840) Fr & Eur.

— La Grande Encyclopedie, 22 vols. 1995.00 (*0-317-45639-3*) Fr & Eur.

— La Grande Encyclopedie, 22 vols., Set. (FRE.). 2995.00 (*0-8288-7841-2*, M8689) Fr & Eur.

— La Grande Encyclopedie, Vol. 2: Amiens-Austen. 1976. 160.00 (*0-7859-5579-8*, 2030009024) Fr & Eur.

— Italien: Guide de Conversation et Dictionnaire. (FRE & ITA.). 174p. 1991. pap. 16.95 (*0-7859-8606-5*, 203403502x) Fr & Eur.

— Larousse: Pluridictionnaire. 45.00 (*0-317-45660-1*) Fr & Eur.

— Larousse Business Dictionary English-French - Francais-Anglais. 336p. 1990. pap. 59.95 (*0-8288-2394-4*, F137232) Fr & Eur.

— Larousse Concise Spanish/English Dictionary. rev. ed. LC 98-75570. 1280p. 1999. 21.95 (*2-03-420413-1*) LKC.

— Larousse de Poche. 8.95 (*0-317-45661-X*); 18.95 (*0-8288-7843-9*, M9357) Fr & Eur.

— Larousse de Poche: Dictionnaire des Noms Communs et des Noms Propres. (FRE.). 864p. 1993. pap. 19.95 (*0-7859-7638-8*, 2033201066) Fr & Eur.

— Larousse Diccionario Economico Comercial y Financiero. 1999. pap. text 9.95 (*970-607-450-3*) Larousse Eds.

— Larousse Diccionario School Pocket. 1999. pap. text 9.95 (*970-607-630-1*) Larousse Eds.

— Larousse Dictionary of Literature: Larousse Dictionnaire des Litteratures, 2 vols., Set. (FRE.). 1888p. 1986. 250.00 (*0-8288-1564-X*, F41450) Fr & Eur.

— Larousse Dictionary of Music: Larousse de la Musique, 2 vols., Set. 1803p. 1982. 295.00 (*0-8288-2169-0*, M14302) Fr & Eur.

— Larousse Dictionnaire Agricole. (FRE.). 195.00 (*0-320-00621-2*) Fr & Eur.

— Larousse Dictionnaire Analogique. 39.95 (*0-317-45643-1*) Fr & Eur.

— Larousse Dictionnaire Compact Francais-Anglais, Anglais-Francais. 1000p. 1993. pap. 49.95 (*0-7859-5599-2*, 2034016319) Fr & Eur.

— Larousse Dictionnaire Complet des Mots Croises. (FRE.). 55.00 (*0-7859-7643-4*, 2033402010) Fr & Eur.

— Larousse Dictionnaire de la Peinture Espagnole et Portugais du Moyen Age a nos Jours. (FRE.). 319p. 1989. pap. 69.95 (*0-7859-7692-2*, 2037400160) Fr & Eur.

— Larousse Dictionnaire de la Peinture Flamande et Hollandaise du Moyen Age a nos Jours. (FRE.). 493p. 1989. pap. 79.95 (*0-7859-7691-4*, 2037400152) Fr & Eur.

— Larousse Dictionnaire de la Prononciation. 37.50 (*0-317-45654-7*) Fr & Eur.

— Larousse Dictionnaire de la Sculpture. (FRE.). 624p. 1992. 195.00 (*0-7859-7671-X*, 2035113091) Fr & Eur.

— Larousse Dictionnaire de la Sociologie. (FRE.). 288p. 1993. pap. 29.95 (*0-7859-7728-7*, 2097202276) Fr & Eur.

— Larousse Dictionnaire de l'Ancien Francais. 39.95 (*0-317-45644-X*) Fr & Eur.

— Larousse Dictionnaire de Linguistique. (FRE.). 37.50 (*0-8288-7846-3*) Fr & Eur.

— Larousse Dictionnaire de Psychologie. (FRE.). 273p. 1991. pap. 28.95 (*0-7859-7684-1*, 2037202164) Fr & Eur.

— Larousse Dictionnaire des Anglicismes. 37.50 (*0-317-45645-8*); write for info. (*0-8288-7847-1*) Fr & Eur.

— Larousse Dictionnaire des Courants Picturaux Tendences, Mouvements, Ecoles, Genres, du Moyen Age a nos Jours. (FRE.). 448p. 1990. pap. 79.95 (*0-7859-7694-9*, 2037400616) Fr & Eur.

— Larousse Dictionnaire des Difficultes de la Langue Francaise. 37.50 (*0-317-45646-6*); write for info. (*0-8288-7848-X*) Fr & Eur.

— Larousse Dictionnaire des Locutions Francaises. 37.50 (*0-317-45651-2*) Fr & Eur.

— Larousse Dictionnaire des Mots Croises. 39.95 (*0-317-45652-0*) Fr & Eur.

— Larousse Dictionnaire des Mots Croises. (FRE.). 1956p. 1992. 59.95 (*0-8288-2339-1*, F136840) Fr & Eur.

— Larousse Dictionnaire des Noms de Famille et Prenoms de France. 37.50 (*0-317-45653-9*); write for info. (*0-8288-7851-X*) Fr & Eur.

— Larousse Dictionnaire des Proverbs, Sentences et Maximes. (FRE.). 37.50 (*0-8288-7852-8*) Fr & Eur.

— Larousse Dictionnaire des Rimes Orales et Ecrites. 37.50 (*0-317-45656-3*) Fr & Eur.

— Larousse Dictionnaire des Rimes Orales et Ecrites. (FRE.). 576p. 1992. 27.95 (*0-8288-7401-8*, F12341) Fr & Eur.

— Larousse Dictionnaire des Verbes Francais. (FRE.). 37.50 (*0-8288-7853-6*) Fr & Eur.

— Larousse Dictionnaire du Francais Classique. 39.95 (*0-317-45648-2*) Fr & Eur.

— Larousse Dictionnaire du Francais Contemporain Illustre. 29.95 (*0-317-45649-0*); write for info. (*0-8288-7855-2*) Fr & Eur.

— Larousse Dictionnaire Etymologique. 39.95 (*0-317-45647-4*) Fr & Eur.

— Larousse Dictionnaire Francais. (FRE.). 767p. 1991. 32.95 (*0-7859-7639-6*, 2033201392) Fr & Eur.

— Larousse Francais-Anglais - Anglais-Francais de Poche. 8.95 (*0-317-45658-X*); write for info. (*0-8288-7858-7*) Fr & Eur.

— Larousse Illustrated International Encyclopedia. 1975. text 11.50 (*0-07-036479-6*) McGraw.

— Larousse "L3", 3 vols. 495.00 (*0-317-45659-8*) Fr & Eur.

— Larousse L3, 3 vols., Set. 595.00 (*0-8288-7842-0*, M6473) Fr & Eur.

— Larousse Mercury French-Spanish, Spanish-French Dictionary: Dictionnaire Mercure Francais-Espagnol-Francais. (FRE & SPA.). 1981. 35.00 (*0-8288-0739-6*, S34571) Fr & Eur.

***Larousse Staff.** Larousse Mini German/English Dictionary. (GER.). 672p. 1999. pap. 5.95 (*2-03-420912-5*) LKC.

— Larousse Mini Italian/English Dictionary. (ITA.). 640p. 1999. pap. 5.95 (*2-03-420911-7*) LKC.

— Larousse Pocket Italian/English Dictionary. LC 98-75563. (ITA.). 576p. 1999. pap. 5.50 (*2-03-420715-7*) LKC.

Larousse Staff. Larousse pour Tous. 18.95 (*0-317-45662-8*) Fr & Eur.

— Larousse Practical English-Spanish Technical-Scientific Vocabulary: Vocabulario Pratico Larousse Tecnico-Cientifico Ingles-Espanol. (ENG & SPA.). 670p. 1984. 9.95 (*0-8288-0663-2*, F13910) Fr & Eur.

— Larousse Universel, 2 vols., Level 2. (FRE.). 1800p. 1969. 395.00 (*0-8288-6609-0*, F128509); 295.00 (*0-685-62924-4*, F12850) Fr & Eur.

— Mon Dictionnaire Francais - Anglais-Anglais - Anglais-Francais en Couleurs. 24.95 (*0-317-45756-X*) Fr & Eur.

— Nouveau Dictionnaire Larousse des Mots Croises. (FRE.). 1981. 24.95 (*0-8288-2340-5*, F 136830) Fr & Eur.

— Nouveau Larousse Elementaire. 35.00 (*0-317-45759-4*) Fr & Eur.

— Nouveau Petit Larousse. write for info. (*0-8288-7835-8*) Fr & Eur.

— Petit Larousse en Couleurs. 95.00 (*0-317-45760-8*) Fr & Eur.

— Petit Larousse Illustre. (Illus.). 1872p. write for info. (*0-7859-3734-X*) Fr & Eur.

— Le Petit Larousse Illustre. 39.95 (*0-317-45763-2*) Fr & Eur.

— Portugais: Guide de Conversation et Dictionnaire. (FRE & POR.). 192p. 1992. pap. 16.95 (*0-7859-7657-4*, 2034035054) Fr & Eur.

Larousse Staff, ed. L' Art de la Renaissance, le XVe Siecle Peinture, Sculpture, Architecture. (FRE.). 424p. 1991. 295.00 (*0-7859-9892-6*) Fr & Eur.

— Dictionaire des Litteratures Francaises et Etrangeres. (FRE.). 1876p. 1992. 250.00 (*0-7859-9842-X*) Fr & Eur.

— Dictionnaire Apollo Francais-Russe/Russe-Francais. (FRE & RUS.). 800p. 1976. 34.95 (*0-7859-9836-5*) Fr & Eur.

— Dictionnaire de la Langue Francaise: 35,000 Mots Avec Etymologies. 1995. 150.00 incl. audio compact disk (*0-7859-9546-3*) Fr & Eur.

— Dictionnaire des Films. (FRE.). 1440p. 1995. 75.00 (*0-7859-9915-9*) Fr & Eur.

— Dictionnaire du Cinema. (FRE.). 1280p. 1995. 110.00 (*0-7859-9916-7*) Fr & Eur.

— Dictionnaire Francais/Anglais-Anglais/Francais. (ENG & FRE.). 2100p. 1994. 59.95 (*0-7859-9755-5*) Fr & Eur.

— Dictionnaire Mars Francais-Russe/Russe-Francais. (FRE & RUS.). 800p. 69.95 (*0-7859-9837-3*) Fr & Eur.

— Dictionnaire Mondial de la Photographie. (FRE.). 704p. 1994. 195.00 (*0-7859-9841-1*) Fr & Eur.

— Encyclopedie de l'Univers en Couleurs, 8 vols. (FRE.). Date not set. 995.00 (*0-7859-9895-0*) Fr & Eur.

An Asterisk (*) at the beginning of an entry indicates that the title is appearing for the first time.

— Gran Diccionario Espanol-Ingles/Ingles-Espanol. (ENG & SPA.). 1600p. 1994. 59.95 (*0-7859-9757-1*) Fr & Eur.
— Grand Atlas Historique Larousse. 324p. 1995. 175.00 (*0-7859-9840-3*) Fr & Eur.
— Grand Dictionnaire Allemand-Francais/Francais-Allemand, 2 vols. (FRE & GER.). 1552p. 1995. 150.00 (*0-7859-9834-9*) Fr & Eur.
— Grand Dictionnaire Espanol-Francais/Francais-Espanol, 2 vols. (ENG & FRE.). 1552p. 1995. 150.00 (*0-7859-9835-7*) Fr & Eur.
— Grand Dictionnaire Francais-Anglais/Anglais-Francais, 2 vols. (ENG & FRE.). 2112p. 1993. 150.00 (*0-7859-9833-0*) Fr & Eur.
— Grand Dictionnaire Francais-Anglais/Anglais-Francais. (ENG & FRE.). 1995. 150.00 incl. audio compact disk (*0-7859-9545-5*) Fr & Eur.
— Grand Larousse Junior, 10 vols. (FRE.). 1995. 1495.00 (*0-7859-9248-0*) Fr & Eur.
— Grand Larousse Universel, 15 vols. (FRE.). 1995. 2995.00 (*0-7859-9246-4*) Fr & Eur.
— Histoire de la France en Bandes Dessinnees, 8 vols. (FRE.). 1980. 295.00 (*0-7859-9838-1*) Fr & Eur.
— Histoire de l'Art, 2 vols. (FRE.). 780p. 1985. 325.00 (*0-7859-9891-8*) Fr & Eur.
— Larousse, 10 vols. (FRE.). 1994. 1295.00 (*0-7859-9247-2*) Fr & Eur.
— Larousse Annuel: Le Livre de l'Annee, 1995. 576p. 1995. 95.00 (*0-7859-9803-9*) Fr & Eur.
— Larousse de la Cuisine. (FRE.). 800p. 1995. 150.00 (*0-7859-9844-6*) Fr & Eur.
— Larousse de Poche Francais-Espangol, Espangol-Francais. (FRE & SPA.). 768p. 1995. 19.95 (*0-7859-9917-5*) Fr & Eur.
— Larousse de Poche Francais-Italien, Italien-Francais. (FRE & ITA.). 832p. 1995. 19.95 (*0-7859-9920-5*) Fr & Eur.
— Larousse de Poche French-English, English-French. (FRE.). 768p. 1995. 19.95 (*0-7859-9918-3*) Fr & Eur.
— Larousse des Vins. (FRE.). 608p. 1994. 150.00 (*0-7859-9845-4*) Fr & Eur.
— Larousse Encyclopedique, 2 vols. (FRE.). 2200p. 1994. 195.00 (*0-7859-9303-7*) Fr & Eur.
— Larousse Gastronomique. 1152p. 1984. 195.00 (*0-7859-9800-4*) Fr & Eur.
— Larousse Medical. 1142p. 1995. 195.00 (*0-7859-9843-8*) Fr & Eur.
— Larousse Thesaurus. (FRE.). 1148p. 1995. 49.95 (*0-7859-9301-0*) Fr & Eur.
— Larousse's French-English Dictionary. LC 96-163295. 720p. 1996. per. 5.99 (*0-671-53407-6*) PB.
— Nouveau Larousse Encyclopedique, 2 vols. 1895p. Date not set. 395.00 (*0-7859-9802-0*) Fr & Eur.
— Nuevo Diccionario Enciclopedico Larousse, 9 vols. (SPA.). 2680p. 1995. 1495.00 (*0-7859-9772-5*) Fr & Eur.
— Paris Atlas - 1900. (FRE.). 310p. 1989. 150.00 (*0-7859-9839-X*) Fr & Eur.
— Pequeno Larousse Illustrado, 1996. 1776p. 1996. 49.95 (*0-7859-9804-7*) Fr & Eur.
— El Pequeno Larousse Ilustrado: 1999 Edition. (Illus.). 1998. 39.95 (*970-607-778-2*) LKC.
— Petit Larousse Grand Format, 1996. 1872p. 1996. 175.00 (*0-7859-9893-4*) Fr & Eur.
— Le Petit Larousse Illustre en Couleurs, 1996. 1784p. 1996. 95.00 (*0-7859-9894-2*) Fr & Eur.
— Le Petit Larousse Illustre, 1995. 1784p. 1994. 95.00 (*0-7859-8753-3*) Fr & Eur.
— Le Petit Larousse Illustre, 1994. (Illus.). 59.95 (*0-685-74790-5*) Schoenhof.
— Petit Larousse 1998. (FRE.). 1998. 95.00 incl. audio compact disk (*0-7859-9537-4*) Fr & Eur.
— Petit Larousse, 1997. (FRE.). 1997. 95.00 (*0-7859-9308-8*) Fr & Eur.
Larousse Staff & Dauzat, Albert. Larousse Dictionnaire Etymologique. (FRE.). 626p. 1985. pap. 27.95 (*0-7859-4539-3*) Fr & Eur.
Larousse Staff & Garcia-Pelayo, Ramon. Pequena Enciclopedia Tematica Larousse en Color. Small Thematic Larousse Encyclopedia in Color, 2 vols. 1096p. 1978. 175.00 (*0-8288-5260-X*, S30235) Fr & Eur.
Larousse Staff & Lange-Kowal, Ernst E. Mercury Larousse French-German, German-French Dictionary: Dictionnaire Mercure Francais-Allemand-Francais. 3rd ed. (FRE & GER.). 1206p. 1964. 55.00 (*0-7859-4826-0*) Fr & Eur.
Larousse Staff, ed. see Grappin, Pierre.
Larousse Staff, ed. see Margueron, Claude & Eolena, Gianfranco.
Larousse Stsff, ed. Larousse de Poche Francais-Allemand, Allemand-Francais. (FRE & GER.). 768p. 1995. 19.95 (*0-7859-9919-1*) Fr & Eur.
Laroussse Staff, ed. Dictionnaire du Cinema, 2 vols. (FRE.). 2160p. 1995. 125.00 (*0-7859-9847-0*) Fr & Eur.
LaRovere, Richard, ed. see Leach, Bob.
Laroy, C., jt. auth. see Cranmer, D.
Laroy, Clement. Pronunciation. 160p. 1995. pap. text 13.95 (*0-19-437087-9*) OUP.
Laroyster, Angela. Puppy. (See How They Grow Ser.). (Illus.). (J). 10.95 (*0-590-73805-4*) Scholastic Inc.
Laroze, Catherine. L'ame Parfumee Des Jardins. 1999. 65.00 (*2-909838-16-1*) A Gourcuff.
Laroze, Catherine, jt. auth. see Barile, Elizabeth.
***Larpent, Francis Seymour, ed.** The Private Journal of Judge-Advocate Larpent: Attached to the Head-Quarters of Lord Wellington During the Peninsular War from 1812 to Its Close. 608p. 2000. 120.00 (*1-86227-100-3*, Pub. by Spellmnt Pubs) St Mut.
Larpenter, Carl. Electricians' Pocket Reference & Record. 1964. 4.50 (*0-87511-071-1*) Claitors.
Larpenteur, Charles. Forty Years a Fur Trader on the Upper Missouri: The Personal Narrative of Charles Larpenteur, 1833-1872. LC 88-38637. (Illus.). xxvii, 388p. 1989. reprint ed. pap. 12.95 (*0-8032-7930-2*, Bison Books) U of Nebr Pr.
***Larra, M J De.** Articulos Escogidos. (SPA.). 1999. 13.00 (*84-481-0627-X*, McGrw-H College) McGrw-H Hghr Educ.
Larra, Mariano J. De, see De Larra, Mariano J.
Larrabee, Carroll B. How to Package for Profit: A Manual of Packaging. LC 75-39257. (Getting & Spending: Tthe Consumer's Dilemma Ser.). (Illus.). 1976. reprint ed. 20.95 (*0-405-08030-1*) Ayer.
Larrabee, Denise M. Anne Hampton Brewster: Nineteenth-Century Author & "Social Outlaw" 32p. (Orig.). 1992. pap. 5.00 (*0-914076-86-8*) Lib Co Phila.
Larrabee, E. Eugene, jt. auth. see Abzug, Malcolm J.
Larrabee, Elizabeth. Random Pieces: Vignettes from the Thirties. 96p. 1993. pap. 8.95 (*0-9636690-0-1*) Withee Pub.
Larrabee, Eric. Commander in Chief - Franklin Delano Roosevelt: His Lieutenants & Their War. 1988. pap. 18.00 (*0-671-66382-8*, Touchstone) S&S Trade Pap.
Larrabee, Eric, ed. see American Studies Association Staff.
Larrabee, F. Stephen. Eastern European Security After the Cold War. LC 93-38122. 1994. pap. text 15.00 (*0-8330-1471-4*, MR-254-USDP) Rand Corp.
Larrabee, F. Stephen, ed. The Volatile Powder Keg: Balkan Security after the Cold War. LC 94-12476. 346p. (Orig.). (C). 1994. pap. text 30.50 (*1-879383-23-3*) Am Univ Pr.
— The Volatile Powder Keg: Balkan Security after the Cold War. LC 94-12476. 346p. (Orig.). (C). 1994. lib. bdg. 69.50 (*1-879383-22-5*) Am Univ Pr.
Larrabee, F. Stephen & Karasik, Theodore W. Foreign & Security Policy Decisionmaking under Yeltsin. LC 96-6711. 67p. 1997. pap. 15.00 (*0-8330-2485-X*, MR-831-OSD) Rand Corp.
Larrabee, F. Stephen & Thorson, Carla. Mediterranean Security: New Issues & Challenges: Conference Proceedings. 50p. 1996. pap. text 9.00 (*0-8330-2384-5*, CF-122-NATO) Rand Corp.
Larrabee, F. Stephen, jt. auth. see Szayna, Thomas S.
Larrabee, F. Stephen, jt. ed. see Gompert, David C.
Larrabee, Graydon B., jt. ed. see Kane, Philip F.
Larrabee, James, ed. Philosophy, B-BJ. (LC Cumulative Classification Ser.). 300p. 1985. ring bd. 38.00 (*0-933949-14-6*); fiche 13.00 (*0-933949-18-9*) Livia Pr.
— Religion, BL-BX. LC 85-6863. (LC Cumulative Classification Ser.). 1000p. 1985. fiche. write for info. (*0-933949-15-4*) Livia Pr.
— Religion, BL-BX, Set. LC 85-6863. (LC Cumulative Classification Ser.). 1000p. 1985. ring bd. 105.00 (*0-933949-11-1*) Livia Pr.
— Religion, BL-BX, Vol. 1. LC 85-6863. (LC Cumulative Classification Ser.). 1000p. 1985. write for info. (*0-933949-12-X*); fiche. write for info. (*0-933949-16-2*) Livia Pr.
— Religion, BL-BX, Vol. 2. LC 85-6863. (LC Cumulative Classification Ser.). 1000p. 1985. write for info. (*0-933949-13-8*); fiche. write for info. (*0-933949-17-0*) Livia Pr.
Larrabee, Larry. Satisfaction in Parenting. Goc, Michael J., ed. 128p. (Orig.). 1995. pap. 12.00 (*0-938627-24-4*) New Past Pr.
Larrabee, Lisa. Grandmother Five Baskets. LC 93-10451. (Illus.). 64p. (J). (gr. 3-7). 1993. pap. 9.95 (*0-943173-90-6*) Roberts Rinehart.
Larrabee, Margery. All the Time in the World. 1971. pap. 2.00 (*0-911214-21-6*) Rational Isl.
Larrabee, Mary J., ed. An Ethic of Care: Feminist & Interdisciplinary Perspectives. LC 92-13206. (Thinking Gender Ser.). 288p. (C). (gr. 13). 1992. 70.00 (*0-415-90567-2*, A7152); pap. 23.99 (*0-415-90568-0*, A7156) Routledge.
Larrabee, Stephen, ed. Conventional Arms Control & East-West Security. LC 89-7685. (Duke Press Policy Studies). 491p. 1989. text 74.95 (*0-8223-0980-7*); pap. text 24.95 (*0-8223-0992-0*) Duke.
Larrabee, Stephen A. English Bards & Crecian Marbles: The Relationship Between Sculpture & Poetry Especially. 1988. reprint ed. lib. bdg. 69.00 (*0-7812-0062-8*) Rprt Serv.
— English Bards & Grecian Marbles: The Relationship Between Sculpture & Poetry Especially in the Romantic Period. reprint ed. 59.00 (*0-403-08621-3*) Somerset Pub.
Larrabee, Stephen F., et al. NATO's Mediterranean Initiative: Policy Issues & Dilemmas. LC 98-14140. (Illus.). 107p. 1998. pap. 15.00 (*0-8330-2605-4*, MR-957-IMD) Rand Corp.
Larrabee, Wayne, Jr. Principles of Facial Reconstruction. (Illus.). 272p. 1995. text 104.00 (*0-7817-0150-3*) Lppncott W & W.
Larrabee, Wayne F., Jr. & Makielski, Kathleen H. Surgical Anatomy of the Face. LC 92-21808. 240p. 1992. text 160.00 (*0-88167-945-3*) Lppncott W & W.
— Surgical Anatomy of the Face, Set. LC 92-21808. 240p. 1993. sl. 184.00 (*0-7817-0053-1*) Lppncott W & W.
Larrabee, William. Railroad Question. LC 76-150190. (Select Bibliographies Reprint Ser.). 1977. 25.95 (*0-8369-5703-2*) Ayer.
Larraga, Ricardo. Mariano Brull y la Poesia Pura en Cuba. (SPA.). 1994. pap. 19.00 (*0-89729-735-0*) Ediciones.
Larrain, B., jt. auth. see Sachs, Jeffrey.
Larrain, Carlos J. Struktur der Reden in der Odyssee 1-8. (Spudasmata Ser.: Bd. 41). (GER.). xi, 497p. 1987. write for info. (*3-487-07831-7*) G Olms Pubs.
Larrain, Felipe & Velasco, Andres. Can Swaps Solve the Debt Crisis? Lessons from the Chilean Experience. Riccardi, Margaret B., ed. LC 90-21355. (Studies in International Finance: No. 69). 50p. 1990. pap. text 13.50 (*0-88165-241-5*) Princeton U Int Finan Econ.
Larrain, Felipe B. Return of Private Capital to Latin America. (Development & Inequality in the Market Economy Ser.). 296p. 1999. text 57.50 (*0-472-11098-5*, 11098) U of Mich Pr.
Larrain, Jorge A. Ideology & Cultural Identity: Modernity & the Third World Presence. 220p. (C). 1994. pap. text 26.95 (*0-7456-1316-0*) Blackwell Pubs.
— Marxism & Ideology. (Modern Revivals in Philosophy Ser.). 272p. 1992. 58.95 (*0-7512-0013-1*, Pub. by Gregg Revivals) Ashgate Pub Co.
— A Reconstruction of Historical Materialism. Bottomore, Thomas B. & Mulkay, Michael, eds. LC 85-18699. (Controversies in Sociology Ser.: No. 19). 120p. 1986. text 44.95 (*0-04-301207-8*); pap. text 17.95 (*0-04-301208-6*) Routledge.
— A Reconstruction of Historical Materialism. (Modern Revivals in Philosophy Ser.). 138p. 1992. 49.95 (*0-7512-0048-4*, Pub. by Gregg Pub) Ashgate Pub Co.
— Theories of Development: Capitalism, Colonialism & Dependency. (Illus.). 220p. (C). 1989. pap. text 31.95 (*0-7456-0711-X*) Blackwell Pubs.
Larralde, Elsa. The Land & People of Mexico. rev. ed. LC 64-23213. (Portraits of the Nations Ser.). (Illus.). (J). (gr. 5-9). 1964. lib. bdg. 12.89 (*0-397-31552-X*) HarpC Child Bks.
Larralde, Signa, jt. auth. see Sebastian, Lynne.
***Larranaga, Ana M.** Animal Actions. (Copy Cat Bks.). (Illus.). 8p. (J). 2000. bds. 5.95 (*1-58646-005-6*) Polka Dot.
— Animal Noises. (Copy Cat Bks.). (Illus.). (J). 2000. 5.95 (*1-58646-004-8*) Polka Dot.
— Beautiful Bugs. (Ana's Animals Bks.). (Illus.). (J). 2000. 3.95 (*1-58646-002-1*) Polka Dot.
Larranaga, Ana M. The Big Wide-Mouthed Frog. LC 98-33873. (Illus.). 24p. (J). (ps up). 1999. 10.99 (*0-7636-0807-6*) Candlewick Pr.
***Larranaga, Ana M.** Family Farm. (Ana's Animals Bks.). (Illus.). (J). 2000. 3.95 (*1-58646-000-5*) Polka Dot.
— Jungle Jamboree. (Ana's Animals Bks.). (Illus.). (J). 2000. 3.95 (*1-58646-003-X*) Polka Dot.
— Playful Pets. (Ana's Animals Bks.). (Illus.). (J). 2000. 3.95 (*1-58646-001-3*) Polka Dot.
***Larranaga, Ignacio.** El Sentido De La Vida. 1999. pap. 19.95 (*84-270-2416-9*) E Martinez Roca.
Larranaga, Ignacio. The Silence of Mary. Gaudet, V., tr. LC 91-34526. 237p. (Orig.). 1991. pap. 15.95 (*0-8198-6911-2*) Pauline Bks.
***Larranaga, Jim.** The Dead Farmer's Almanac. LC 00-190944. 2000. 25.00 (*0-7388-2118-7*); pap. 18.00 (*0-7388-2117-9*) Xlibris Corp.
Larranaga, Osvaldo, jt. ed. see Aedo, Cristian.
Larrard, Francois De, see De Larrard, Francois.
Larrauri, Augustin. Dictionnaire d'Oto-Rhino-Laryngologie, 5 vols. (ENG, FRE, GER, ITA & SPA.). 1971. 95.00 (*0-8288-6442-X*, M-6338) Fr & Eur.
Larrazabal, J. M., et al, eds. Logic Colloquium '96: Proceedings of the Colloquium Held in San Sebastian, Spain, July 9-15, 1996. (Lecture Notes in Logic Ser.: Vol. 12). vii, 261p. 1998. pap. 115.00 (*3-540-64668-X*) Spr-Verlag.
Larrazabal, Jorge, tr. see Schmidt, Fran & Friedman, Alice.
Larrazabal, Mariana, tr. see Schmidt, Fran & Friedman, Alice.
Larre, Claude. Rooted in Spirit: The Heart of Chinese Medicine. De la Vallee, Elisabeth R., tr. from CHI. LC 93-33271. 224p. 1992. pap. 19.95 (*0-88268-120-6*) Station Hill Pr.
Larre, Claude, et al. Survey of Traditional Chinese Medicine. Stang, Sarah E., tr. (FRE., Illus.). 231p. (Orig.). 1986. pap. 24.00 (*0-912381-00-0*) Trad Acupuncture.
Larrea, Juan. Guernica: Pablo Picasso. LC 73-91376. (Contemporary Art Ser.). (Illus.). 1970. reprint ed. 18.95 (*0-405-00731-0*) Ayer.
Larreche, Jean-Claude. Market Strategy. 3rd ed. 1998. text 52.95 incl. 3.5 hd (*0-538-86759-0*) S-W Pub.
— Markops. 2nd ed. 180p. 1992. teacher ed. 32.50 incl. disk (*0-89426-204-1*); teacher ed. 32.50 incl. disk (*0-89426-205-X*); teacher ed. 32.50 incl. disk (*0-685-74392-6*); pap. 32.50 (*0-685-74391-8*) Course Tech.
Larreche, Jean-Claude & Gatignon, Hubert A. MARKSTRAT 2. 2nd ed. 240p. (C). 1990. pap. text, teacher ed. 38.50 (*0-89426-125-8*) Course Tech.
— MARKSTRAT 2. 2nd ed. 240p. (C). 1990. mass mkt. 40.25 incl. disk (*0-89426-164-9*) Course Tech.
Larreche, Jean-Claude, et al. Markstrat3: The Strategic Marketing Simulation. 3rd ed. 1997. pap. text 65.95 (*0-538-88089-9*) Sth-Wstrn College.
Larreche, Jean-Claude, jt. auth. see Cook, Victor J.
Larreche, Jean-Claude, jt. auth. see Weinstein, David.
Larremore, Thomas A. & Hopkins, Amy. The Marion Press: A Survey & a Checklist. LC 85-51272. 293p. 1981. reprint ed. 35.00 (*0-938768-04-2*) Oak Knoll.
Larrere, Catherine, jt. auth. see Mondot, Jean.
***Larres, Klaus & Meehan, Elizabeth M., eds.** Uneasy Allies: British-German Relations & European Integration since 1945. LC 99-57192. 360p. 2000. write for info. (*0-19-829383-6*) OUP.
Larres, Klaus & Panayi, Panikos, eds. Federal Republic Germany Since 1949. LC 96-346. 272p. (C). 1996. pap. text 17.75 (*0-582-23891-9*, Pub. by Addison-Wesley) Longman.
— Federal Republic Of Germany Since 1949. LC 96-346. 272p. (C). 1996. text 47.25 (*0-582-23890-0*) Addison-Wesley.
Larrick, Geary. Analytical & Biographical Writings in Percussion Music. (American University Studies: Fine Arts: Ser. XX, Vol. 10). XVI, 227p. (C). 1989. text 38.60 (*0-8204-0876-X*) P Lang Pubng.
***Larrick, Geary.** Bibliography, History, Pedagogy, & Philosophy in Music & Percussion LC 99-17041. (History & Interpretation of Music Studies). 1999. write for info. (*0-7734-8165-6*) E Mellen.
Larrick, Geary. Biographical Essays on Twentieth-Century Percussionists. LC 92-18731. 336p. 1992. lib. bdg. 99.95 (*0-7734-9559-2*) E Mellen.
— Musical References & Song Texts in the Bible. LC 90-13480. (Studies in the History & Interpretation of Music: Vol. 9). (Illus.). 172p. 1990. lib. bdg. 79.95 (*0-88946-492-8*) E Mellen.
Larrick, J. W. & Burck, K. B. Gene Therapy: Application of Molecular Biology. 3rd ed. 575p. (C). 1992. pap. text 45.00 (*0-8385-3104-0*, A3104-5, Apple Lange Med) McGraw.
Larrick, James N., jt. ed. see Siebert, Paul D.
Larrick, James W. The PCR Technique Quantitative PCR. LC 97-17660. (Update Ser.). (Illus.). 325p. 1997. pap. text 36.95 (*1-881299-06-6*, BioTechniques) Eaton Pub Co.
Larrick, Jon P., ed. see Pollack, Pamela D.
Larrick, Nancy. Piping down the Valleys Wild. (J). 1982. 10.60 (*0-606-03339-4*, Pub. by Turtleback) Demco.
— Piping down the Valleys Wild: Poetry for the Young of All Ages. 272p. (J). 1999. pap. 5.99 (*0-440-41582-9*) BDD Bks Young Read.
Larrick, Nancy, ed. Songs from Mother Goose: With the Traditional Melody for Each. LC 88-754466. (Illus.). 80p. (J). (ps up). 1989. 16.95 (*0-06-023713-9*) HarpC Child Bks.
Larrie, Reginald. Corners of Black History. (Illus.). 70p. 1986. reprint ed. 9.95 (*0-9615662-0-5*); reprint ed. teacher ed. write for info. (*0-9615662-1-3*) Olympian King Co.
***Larrier, Renee Brenda.** Francophone Women Writers of Africa & the Caribbean. LC 99-56589. 176p. 2000. 49.95 (*0-8130-1742-4*) U Press Fla.
LarRieu, Barry. Stoned Dead (Includes Right-Place Bookmark) LC 99-189133. (Illus.). vi, 245p. 1997. mass mkt. 5.50 (*0-9660373-0-8*, 11-97-500) Bench Press.
Larrieu, Robert. Dictionnaire Espagnol-Francais et Francais-Espagnol. (FRE.). 1978. pap. text 14.95 (*0-7859-8006-7*, 2-7370-0109-9) Fr & Eur.
Larrieu, Robert, jt. ed. see Salva, Vicente.
Larrigan, Tex. Buckmaster. large type ed. (Linford Western Library). 272p. 1993. pap. 16.99 (*0-7089-7443-0*, Linford) Ulverscroft.
— Buckmaster & the Cattlelifters. large type ed. (Linford Western Library). 272p. 1992. pap. 16.99 (*0-7089-7176-8*, Linford) Ulverscroft.
— Buscadero. large type ed. (Linford Western Library). 288p. 1994. pap. 16.99 (*0-7089-7496-1*, Linford) Ulverscroft.
***Larrigan, Tex.** The Chiseller. large type ed. 208p. 1999. pap. 18.99 (*0-7089-5496-0*, Linford) Ulverscroft.
Larrigan, Tex. Fyngal's Gold. large type ed. (Linford Western Library Ser.). 224p. 1997. pap. 16.99 (*0-7089-5089-2*, Linford) Ulverscroft.
***Larrigan, Tex.** New Sensations for Horse & Rider. 2000. 35.00 (*0-85131-767-7*, Pub. by J A Allen) Trafalgar.
Larrigan, Tex. Night Stalker. large type ed. (Linford Western Large Print Ser.). 224p. 1998. pap. 17.99 (*0-7089-5277-1*, Linford) Ulverscroft.
***Larrigan, Tex.** The Undertaker. large type ed. 224p. 1999. pap. 18.99 (*0-7089-5551-7*, Linford) Ulverscroft.
Larrimer, Don. Bio-Bibliography of Justice Tom C. Clark. (Legal Bibliography Ser.: No. 27). 37p. (Orig.). 1985. pap. 20.00 (*0-935630-10-4*) U of Tex Tarlton Law Lib.
Larrimore, Dale G. Pennsylvania Rules of the Road. LC 95-80822. 250p. 1995. pap. text. write for info. (*0-7620-0025-2*) West Group.
Larrimore, Don & Calder, Clare Evans, texts. Scotland Pocket Guide. LC 99-226246. 1999. pap. text 8.95 (*2-8315-6372-0*) Berlitz.
***Larrimore, Mark J.** The Problem of Evil: A Reader. LC 00-9180. 2001. write for info. (*0-631-22014-3*) Blackbirch.
Larrington, Carolyne. A Store of Common Sense: Gnomic Theme & Style in Old Icelandic & Old English Wisdom Poetry. LC 92-11139. (Oxford English Monographs). 254p. 1993. text 55.00 (*0-19-811982-8*) OUP.
— Women & Writing in Medieval Europe: A Sourcebook. LC 94-30485. 272p. (C). 1995. pap. 22.99 (*0-415-10685-0*, B3166) Routledge.
Larrington, Carolyne, ed. The Woman's Companion to Mythology. (Illus.). 500p. 1997. pap. 25.00 (*0-04-440992-3*) NYU Pr.
Larrington, Carolyne, tr. The Poetic Edda. LC 96-5465. 367p. 1999. pap. 12.95 (*0-19-283946-2*) OUP.
Larrison, Earl J. Mammals of the Northwest: Washington, Oregon, Idaho, & British Columbia. LC 73-94501. (Trailside Ser.). (Illus.). 1976. pap. 8.95 (*0-914516-04-3*) Seattle Audubon Soc.
Larrison, Earl J., jt. auth. see Higman, Harry W.
Larrison, Roxann. A Garden of Bitter Herbs. 304p. (Orig.). (YA). 1993. mass mkt. 3.95 (*0-87067-389-0*) Holloway.
Larrissy, Edward. W. B. Yeats. Armstrong, Isobel & Loughrey, Bryan, eds. (Writers & Their Work Ser.). 1998. pap. 17.00 (*0-7463-0830-2*, Pub. by Northcote House) U Pr of Miss.
— Yeats the Poet. 224p. (C). 1995. pap. text 24.95 (*0-13-320706-4*) P-H.

An Asterisk (*) at the beginning of an entry indicates that the title is appearing for the first time.

Larrissy, Edward, ed. Romanticism & Postmodernism. 250p. (C). 1999. 59.95 (*0-521-64272-8*) Cambridge U Pr.

Larrivee. Authentic Classroom Management. LC 99-483165. 368p. 1998. pap. text 41.00 (*0-205-29739-0*) Allyn.

Larrivee, Barbara. Moving into Balance: Creating Your Personal Pathway. unabridged ed. LC 96-92140. (Illus.). x, 202p. (Orig.). 1996. pap. 14.95 (*0-9651780-9-9*) Shoreline Publns.

Larrivee-Cohen, Donna, jt. ed. see Baird, Mary.

Larroche, Caroline. Corot from A to Z. Bedrick, Claudia Z., tr. from FRE. LC 96-32693. (Artists from A to Z Ser.). (Illus.). 60p. (YA). (ps-3). 1996. lib. bdg. 14.95 (*0-87226-477-7*, 64777B, P Bedrick Books) NTC Contemp Pub Co.

Larrondo, Rosi, jt. ed. see Glaeser, Phyllis S.

***Larroque, Charles.** Memoires de Lafayette. (FRE., Illus.). 32p. 1999. pap. 7.95 (*1-56554-644-X*) Pelican.

Larroque, Charles. Memoires de St Martinville. (FRE., Illus.). 32p. 1999. pap. 6.95 (*1-56554-398-X*) Pelican.

***Larroque, Charles.** Memories of Lafayette. LC 99-34823. (Illus.). 32p. (J). 1999. pap. 7.95 (*1-56554-664-4*) Pelican.

— Memories of St. Martinville. LC 99-10417. 32p. 1999. pap. 7.95 (*1-56554-660-1*) Pelican.

Larrouturou, Bernard, ed. Recent Advances in Combustion Modelling. (Series on Advances in Mathematics for Applied Sciences: Vol. 6). 240p. 1990. text 84.00 (*981-02-0380-2*) World Scientific Pub.

Larrouturou, Bernard, jt. auth. see Berestycki, Henri.

Larrouturou, Bernard, jt. ed. see Dervieux, A.

Larrouturou, Bernard, ed. see Temam, Roger, et al.

Larrowe, Charles P. Shape-Up & Hiring Hall. LC 75-46614. (Illus.). 250p. 1976. reprint ed. lib. bdg. 69.50 (*0-8371-8750-8*, LASU, Greenwood Pr) Greenwood.

Larrson, Borje, jt. ed. see Amaldi, Ugo.

Larrucea De Tovar, C., jt. auth. see Tovar, A.

Larry, Charles. Peboan & Seegwun. LC 93-10092. 32p. (J). (ps-3). 1993. 16.00 (*0-374-35773-0*) FS&G.

Larry, Charles. Peboan & Seegwun. LC 93-10092. 32p. (J). (ps-3). 1995. 4.95 (*0-374-45750-6*) FS&G.

— Peboan & Seegwun. LC 93-10092. (J). 1993. 10.15 (*0-606-09737-6*, Pub. by Turtleback) Demco.

Larrymore Brown, Sylvia A. Simply Phonics, Simply Reading: A Program Designed to Simplify the Process of Teaching Readings. (Illus.). 71p. (J). (gr. k-12). 1998. pap. 14.95 (*1-892818-00-0*) Majestic Scholar.

Lars, Melvin. Dare to Be Positive: A Non-Traditional Tutorial Program. Johnson, Sweettie A. & Brown, Ruby, eds. (Illus.). 48p. 1995. pap. 55.00 (*0-9638218-5-7*) M Lars.

— Painted Images. Johnson, Sweettie A., ed. LC 94-12045. (Illus.). 125p. (Orig.). (YA). (gr. 9 up). 1996. pap. 12.00 (*0-9638218-4-9*) M Lars.

— Reflections of Life. 55p. (Orig.). 1993. pap. 10.00 (*0-9638218-0-6*) M Lars.

Larschan, Edward J. & Larschan, Richard J. The Diagnosis Is Cancer: A Psychological & Legal Resource Handbook for Cancer Patients, Their Families & Helping Professionals. 144p. 1986. pap. 9.95 (*0-915950-77-4*) Bull Pub.

Larschan, Richard J., jt. auth. see Larschan, Edward J.

Larsen. Anatomy Review. 2000. pap. text. write for info. (*0-7216-4648-4*, W B Saunders Co) Harcrt Hlth Sci Grp.

— Dissector for Gross Anatomy. 1999. pap. text. write for info. (*0-7216-4647-6*, W B Saunders Co) Harcrt Hlth Sci Grp.

— Gross Anatomy. 1999. pap. text 29.95 (*0-7216-4646-8*, W B Saunders Co) Harcrt Hlth Sci Grp.

— Knocking on Heaven's Door. Date not set. pap. 10.00 (*0-06-250984-5*, Perennial) HarperTrade.

— Long Walk Home. 1981. pap. 10.00 (*0-06-250980-2*, Perennial) HarperTrade.

— Mathematical Statistics & Its Applications. 3rd ed. 640p. (C). 2000. 106.67 (*0-13-922303-7*, Macmillan Coll) P-H.

— Mayans, Aztecs & Incas: Thematic Unit. 80p. (J). (gr. 5-8). 1996. pap., wbk. ed. 9.95 (*1-55734-595-3*) Tchr Create Mat.

***Larsen.** Modern Advanced Accounting. 8th ed. LC 98-55220. 912p. 1999. 90.31 (*0-07-029991-9*) McGraw.

— Music Appreciation. 2000. student ed. 15.00 (*0-534-51635-1*) Wadsworth Pub.

Larsen. Space. Date not set. pap. 10.00 (*0-06-250979-9*, Perennial) HarperTrade.

— Vision Catcher. pap. 10.00 (*0-06-250978-0*, Perennial) HarperTrade.

***Larsen.** West's American Goverment. 2nd ed. 1999. pap., student ed. 19.95 (*0-538-43150-4*) Sth-Wstrn College.

Larsen & Marold, Kathryn A. Using Microsoft Works for Windows Version 4.0. (DF - Computer Applications Ser.). 1997. text 32.95 (*0-7895-0168-6*) Course Tech.

***Larsen & Marx.** Mathematical Statistics & Its Applications. 3rd ed. 2000. pap., student ed. write for info. (*0-13-031015-8*) P-H.

Larsen & Marx. Statistics for Decision Making. (Business Statistics Ser.). 1998. pap. 17.95 (*0-534-51730-7*) Wadsworth Pub.

Larsen & Stanchina, Carolyn. Grammar Dimensions L1-L4. (College ESL Ser.). (J). 1994. mass mkt., wbk. ed. 13.95 (*0-8384-4356-7*) Heinle & Heinle.

Larsen, jt. auth. see Hepworth.

***Larsen, A., et al, eds.** Wind Engineering into the 21st Century: Proceedings of the 10th International Conference on Wind Engineering, Copenhagen, Denmark, 21-24 June 1999, 3 vols. (Illus.). 2062p. (C). 1999. text 260.00 (*90-5809-059-0*, Pub. by A A Balkema) Ashgate Pub Co.

Larsen, A. & Esdahl, S., eds. Bridge Aerodynamics: Proceedings of the International Symposium on Advances in Bridge Aerodynamics, Copenhagen Denmark, 10-13 May 1998. (Illus.). 358p. (C). 1998. text 74.00 (*90-5410-961-0*, Pub. by A A Balkema) Ashgate Pub Co.

Larsen, Agnessa. Graffiti on My Heart. 416p. (Orig.). 1994. pap. text 15.95 (*0-89716-509-8*, Peanut Btr Pubng) Elton-Wolf Pub.

Larsen, Allan, ed. Aerodynamics of Large Bridges: Proceedings of the First International Symposium, Copenhagen, Denmark, 19-21 February 1992. (Illus.). 313p. (C). 1992. 110.00 (*90-5410-042-7*, Pub. by A A Balkema) Ashgate Pub Co.

Larsen, Andy, jt. auth. see Heon, Al.

Larsen, Anita. Amelia Earhart: Missing, Declared Dead. LC 91-19246. (History's Mysteries Ser.). (Illus.). 48p. (J). (gr. 5-6). 1992. text, lib. bdg. 11.95 (*0-89686-613-0*, Crstwood Hse) Silver Burdett Pr.

— Psychic Sleuths: How Psychic Information Is Used to Solve Crimes. LC 93-40593. (J). 1994. lib. bdg. 14.95 (*0-02-751645-8*, New Dscvry Bks) Silver Burdett Pr.

— True Crimes & How They Were Solved. 96p. (J). (gr. 7-9). 1993. pap. 2.99 (*0-590-46856-1*) Scholastic Inc.

Larsen, Anne R. & Winn, Colette H., eds. Renaissance Women Writers: French Texts - American Contexts. LC 93-26577. (Illus.). 242p. 1994. text 39.95 (*0-8143-2473-8*) Wayne St U Pr.

— Writings by Pre-Revolutionary French Women: From Marie de France to Elizabeth Vigee-Le Brun. LC 99-39116. (Women Writers of the World Ser.: No. 5). (Illus.). 500p. 1999. reprint ed. 95.00 (*0-8153-3190-8*, H2111) Garland.

Larsen, B. Microbiology. 2nd ed. LC 97-41309. 1997. pap. 45.00 (*0-915473-37-2*) Am Coll Obstetric.

Larsen, B., jt. ed. see Galask, R. P.

Larsen, Barbara. Tea Leaves: History & Delights of Tea Drinking. LC 99-62490. (Illus.). 64p. 1999. pap. 14.95 (*0-9671668-0-2*) Beach Road Pr.

Larsen, Barbara & McEwen, Charles, eds. Mass Spectrometry of Biological Materials. 2nd ed. LC 97-52814. (Illus.). 488p. 1998. text 195.00 (*0-8247-0157-7*) Dekker.

Larsen, Bev. Darla: Faith over Fire. 130p. (Orig.). 1991. pap. 12.00 (*0-929690-13-3*) Herit Pubs AZ.

***Larsen, Beverly Jean.** Bessy Bear at the Zoo. (Illus.). 34p. (J). (ps-2). 2000. 12.95 (*0-9649922-7-2*) Deforest Pr.

Larsen, Bryan, jt. auth. see Duffy, Kate.

Larsen, C. M. Floating Production Systems Research & Development Program. (C). 1989. 95.00 (*0-89771-722-8*, Pub. by Lorne & MacLean Marine) St Mut.

Larsen, C. M., et al. Structural Dynamics: Proceedings, 2nd European Conference, Eurodyn 93, Trondheim, Norway, June 1993. Kratzig, W. B. et al, eds. (Illus.). 1300p. 1993. text 220.00 (*90-5410-336-1*, Pub. by A A Balkema) Ashgate Pub Co.

Larsen, Carl. Even the Dog Won't Eat My Meat Loaf. LC 79-19887. 1980. pap. 5.95 (*0-89645-011-2*) Media Ventures.

Larsen, Carl M. Floating Production Systems Research & Development Program. 1989. 150.00 (*90-6314-580-2*, Pub. by Lorne & MacLean Marine) St Mut.

Larsen, Carolyn. God's World. (Wee Sing Bible Songs & Stories Ser.). (Illus.). 12p. (J). (ps-3). 1998. bds. 9.99 incl. audio (*0-8431-7852-3*, Price Stern) Peng Put Young Read.

— Heroes of the Bible. (Illus.). 400p. (J). (gr. k-7). 1998. pap. 12.99 (*0-8010-4408-1*, New Kids Media) Baker Bks.

— Jesus Loves Me. LC 96-65666. (Wee Sing Bible Songs & Stories Ser.). (Illus.). 12p. (J). (ps-3). 1998. bds. 9.99 incl. audio (*0-8431-7853-1*, Price Stern) Peng Put Young Read.

— Jonah & the Whale. (Wee Sing Bible Songs & Stories Ser.). (Illus.). 12p. (J). (ps-3). 1998. bds. 9.99 incl. audio (*0-8431-7968-6*, Price Stern) Peng Put Young Read.

— Life Is a Meatloaf Sandwich: A Devotional for Early Teens. LC 95-61689. 382p. (J). (gr. 5-9). 1995. pap. 11.99 (*0-529-10452-0*, LMS) World Publng.

***Larsen, Carolyn.** Little Boysu Book of Prayers. 192p. (J). (ps-7). 2000. 12.99 (*0-8010-4440-5*, New Kids Media) Baker Bks.

Larsen, Carolyn. Little Girls Bible Easter Storybook. (Illus.). 32p. (ps-2). 1999. 7.99 (*0-8010-4421-9*, New Kids Media) Baker Bks.

***Larsen, Carolyn.** Little Girlsu Devotional Storybook. 192p. (J). (ps-7). 2000. 16.99 (*0-8010-4446-4*, New Kids Media) Baker Bks.

Larsen, Carolyn. A Mother's Heartsong. LC 96-61532. (Illus.). 32p. 1997. 11.99 (*0-529-10727-9*) World Publng.

— My Bedtime Bible. LC 95-217315. (Illus.). 384p. (J). (ps). 1994. 19.99 (*0-529-10248-X*, MB1) World Publng.

— Noah's Big Boat. (Wee Sing Bible Songs & Stories Ser.). (Illus.). 12p. (J). (ps-3). 1998. bds. 9.99 incl. audio (*0-8431-7967-8*, Price Stern) Peng Put Young Read.

Larsen, Carolyn, adapted by. Heroes of the Bible: God's Word Illustrated in Comic. (Illus.). 416p. 1997. pap. 15.99 (*0-529-10761-9*, HTB1) World Publng.

***Larsen, Carolyn & Totel, Vicki.** Little Boysu Bible Activity Calendar. 368p. (J). (ps-8). 2000. spiral bd. 9.99 (*0-8010-4457-X*, New Kids Media) Baker Bks.

— Little Girlsu Bible Activity Calendar. 368p. (J). (ps-8). 2000. spiral bd. 9.99 (*0-8010-4456-1*, New Kids Media) Baker Bks.

Larsen, Carolyn C., jt. auth. see Rave, Elizabeth S.

Larsen, Carsten. Sites & Monuments. (Illus.). 250p. 1992. 49.50 (*87-89364-02-3*) David Brown.

Larsen, Chris, et al. National Summary Report on State Financial Incentives for Renewable Energy. (Illus.). 140p. (Orig.). 1997. pap. 50.00 (*0-9660039-0-X*) NC Solar Ctr.

— National Summary Report on State Regulatory Incentives for Renewable Energy. 170p. 1997. pap. 50.00 (*0-9660039-1-8*) NC Solar Ctr.

Larsen, Christine & Zaro, Ann. How to Survive the Sexual Abuse of Your Child. 4th rev. ed. 40p. 1994. 4.95 (*1-930489-02-1*) Act For Kids.

Larsen, Clark S. Native American Demography in the Spanish Borderlands. LC 90-22357. (Spanish Borderlands Sourcebooks Ser.: Vol. 2). 478p. 1991. reprint ed. text 30.00 (*0-8240-0781-6*) Garland.

Larsen, Clark S. & Milner, George R., eds. In the Wake of Contact: Biological Responses to Conquest. 206p. 1993. 147.50 (*0-471-30544-8*) Wiley.

Larsen, Clark S., et al. Human Origins: The Fossil Record. 3rd rev. ed. (Illus.). 225p. (C). 1998. pap. text 19.95 (*1-57766-002-1*) Waveland Pr.

***Larsen, Clark Spencer.** Bioarchaeology: Interpreting Behavior form the Human Skeleton. (Cambridge Studies in Biological Anthropology: Vol. 21). (Illus.). 473p. (C). 1999. pap. 39.95 (*0-521-65834-9*) Cambridge U Pr.

— Skeletons in Our Closet: Revealing Our Past Through Bioarchaeology. LC 99-53724. 2000. 35.00 (*0-691-00490-0*, Pub. by Princeton U Pr) Cal Prin Full Svc.

Larsen, Clark Spencer, jt. ed. see Hemphill, Brian E.

Larsen, Connie R. HIV & Communication Disorders: What Speech & Hearing Professionals Need to Know. LC 98-3471. (Illus.). 192p. 1998. pap. 35.00 (*1-56593-968-9*, 1916) Thomson Learn.

Larsen, Curtis E. Life & Land Use on the Bahrain Islands: The Geoarcheology of an Ancient Society. LC 83-5085. (Prehistoric Archeology & Ecology Ser.). (Illus.). 360p. 1984. pap. text 11.00 (*0-226-46906-9*) U Ch Pr.

— Life & Land Use on the Bahrain Islands: The Geoarcheology of an Ancient Society. LC 83-5085. (Prehistoric Archeology & Ecology Ser.). (Illus.). 320p. 1995. lib. bdg. 24.00 (*0-226-46905-0*) U Ch Pr.

Larsen, Cynthia & Shannon, Paul. The Synchronicity Guidebook . . . High-Tech Meditation. rev. ed. LC 93-74177. (Illus.). 109p. (Orig.). 1994. pap. write for info. (*1-884068-20-0*) Synch Found.

Larsen, Dale. Ultimate Hope for Changing Times. 80p. 1999. pap. 4.99 (*0-87788-842-6*, H Shaw Pubs) Waterbrook Pr.

Larsen, Dale & Larsen, Sandy. Discovering Myself: Who Am I Anyway? (Bible Discovery Guide Ser.). (Illus.). 32p. (Orig.). (YA). (gr. 7-10). 1987. teacher ed. 3.50 (*0-87788-179-0*, H Shaw Pubs); student ed. 1.50 (*0-87788-178-2*, H Shaw Pubs) Waterbrook Pr.

— Exodus: God Our Deliverer. 80p. 1998. pap. 4.99 (*0-87788-209-6*, H Shaw Pubs) Waterbrook Pr.

— Faith: Depending on God. (LifeGuide Bible Studies). 64p. 1997. pap. 4.99 (*0-8308-1081-1*, 1081) InterVarsity.

— Hosea: God's Persistent Love. (LifeGuide Bible Studies). 60p. (Orig.). 1996. pap., wbk. ed. 4.99 (*0-8308-1041-2*, 1041) InterVarsity.

— It's up to Me: Choosing God's Way. (Bible Discovery Guide Ser.). (Illus.). 32p. (J). (gr. 4-6). 1989. pap., teacher ed., student ed. 1.50 (*0-87788-405-6*, H Shaw Pubs) Waterbrook Pr.

— It's up to Me: Choosing God's Way. (Bible Discovery Guide Ser.). (Illus.). 32p. (J). (gr. 4-6). 1989. pap. 1.50 (*0-87788-404-8*, H Shaw Pubs) Waterbrook Pr.

— Joseph: From Pit to Pyramid. (Bible Discovery Guide Ser.). (Illus.). 32p. (J). (gr. 4-6). 1989. pap. text, teacher ed. 3.50 (*0-87788-436-6*, H Shaw Pubs); pap. text, student ed. 1.50 (*0-87788-435-8*, H Shaw Pubs) Waterbrook Pr.

— One Body, One Spirit: Building Relationships in the Church. (Fisherman Bible Studyguide Ser.). 64p. (Orig.). 1988. pap. text 4.99 (*0-87788-619-9*, H Shaw Pubs) Waterbrook Pr.

— Seven Myths about Christianity. LC 98-14178. 140p. 1998. pap. 9.99 (*0-8308-1909-6*, 1909) InterVarsity.

Larsen, Dale, jt. auth. see Larsen, Sandy.

Larsen, Dan. David Livingstone. (Young Reader's Christian Library). (Illus.). 224p. (J). (gr. 3 up). 1992. pap. 1.39 (*1-55748-259-4*) Barbour Pub.

Larsen, Dan, ed. see Bunyan, John.

Larsen, David. Jews, Gentiles & the Church: A New Perspective on History & Prophecy. LC 94-43624. 432p. 1995. 19.99 (*0-929239-42-3*) Discovery Hse Pubs.

Larsen, David C. Who Gets It When You Go? Wills, Probates, & Inheritance Taxes for the Hawaii Resident. 3rd rev. ed. 128p. 1997. pap. 14.95 (*0-8248-1940-3*, Latitude Twenty) UH Pr.

Larsen, David G., ed. see Berlin, Howard M.

***Larsen, David L.** The Anatomy of Preaching: Identifying the Issues in Preaching Today. LC 99-24710. 208p. 1999. pap. 11.99 (*0-8254-3098-4*) Kregel.

Larsen, David L. Caring for the Flock: Pastoral Ministry in the Local Congregation. LC 91-2175. 256p. 1991. pap. 10.99 (*0-89107-609-3*) Crossway Bks.

***Larsen, David L.** The Company of the Creative: A Christian's Guide to Great Literature & Its Themes. LC 99-36565. 656p. 1999. 29.99 (*0-8254-3097-6*) Kregel.

Larsen, David L. The Company of the Preachers: A History of Biblical Preaching from the Old Testament to the Modern Era. LC 97-10242. 896p. 1997. 34.99 (*0-8254-3128-X*) Kregel.

Larsen, Dawnie, ed. see Crane, Danford L.

Larsen, Deborah. Stitching Porcelain: After Matteo Ricci in Sixteenth-Century China. LC 90-21176. 80p. (Orig.). 1991. pap. 9.95 (*0-8112-1161-4*, NDP710, Pub. by New Directions) Norton.

Larsen, Dinah, ed. see Ray, Dorothy J.

Larsen, Don & Shaw, Mark. The Perfect Yankee: The Incredible Story of the Greatest Miracle in Baseball History. LC 96-68629. (Illus.). 272p. 1996. 22.95 (*1-57167-043-2*) Sports Pub.

Larsen, Donald E., jt. ed. see Staum, Martin S.

Larsen, Donna, ed. see Cadell, Ava.

Larsen, E. Secret to a Satisfied Life. 1996. 32.95 incl. VHS (*0-89486-817-9*, 5855) Hazelden.

Larsen, E. John. Modern Advanced Accounting. 6th ed. LC 93-27419. (C). 1994. text 70.25 (*0-07-036595-4*) McGraw.

— Modern Advanced Accounting. 7th ed. (C). 1996. pap., student ed. 31.88 (*0-07-036714-0*); text 97.75 (*0-07-036710-8*) McGraw.

— Modern Advanced Accounting: Working Papers. 7th ed. (C). 1996. pap. text 32.81 (*0-07-036715-9*) McGraw.

Larsen, Earnie. From Anger to Forgiveness. (Orig.). 1992. mass mkt. 5.99 (*0-345-37982-9*) Ballantine Pub Grp.

— I Should Be Happy...Why Do I Hurt? A Personal Growth Series for Adult Children of Alcoholic/Neurotic Families, 5 pamphlets, Set. 81p. 1986. pap. 5.00 (*0-936098-42-2*) Intl Marriage.

— Recovering Catholics & the God Who Loves Them: Practical Steps for Freeing Yourself from Negative Experiences in Your Religious Upbringing, 5 pamphlets. 64p. 1990. pap. 5.00 (*0-936098-61-9*) Intl Marriage.

— Something's Missing in My Life! A Close Look at Spirituality & Loving for Adult Children of Alcoholics & Disfunctional Families, 3 pamphlets, Set. 37p. 1987. pap. 3.00 (*0-936098-55-4*) Intl Marriage.

— Stage II Recovery: Life Beyond Addiction. LC 85-51017. 112p. 1984. pap. 13.00 (*0-86683-460-5*, Pub. by Harper SF) HarpC.

— Stage II Relationships: Love Beyond Addiction. LC 86-45815. 128p. 1987. pap. 12.00 (*0-06-254808-5*, PL-4199, Pub. by Harper SF) HarpC.

Larsen, Earnie & Hagarty, Carole L. From Anger to Forgiveness. (Orig.). 10.00 incl. audio (*0-89486-835-7*) Hazelden.

Larsen, Earnie & Hegarty, Carol. Como Creer en Mi Mismo: Believing in Myself.Tr. of Believing in Myself. 384p. 1996. per. 10.00 (*0-684-82359-4*, Libros) S&S Trade Pap.

Larsen, Earnie & Hegarty, Carol L. Days of Healing, Days of Joy: Daily Meditations for Adult Children. 400p. pap. 10.00 (*0-89486-455-6*, 5024A) Hazelden.

Larsen, Earnie & Macken, Cara A. Overcoming Depressive Living Syndrome: How to Enjoy Life, Not Just Endure It. LC 95-46964. 208p. (Orig.). 1996. pap. 13.95 (*0-89243-868-1*, Liguori Triumph) Liguori Pubns.

Larsen, Earnier & Heggerty, Carol L. Believing in Myself: Self-Esteem: Daily Meditations. 384p. 1991. per. 10.00 (*0-671-76616-3*, Fireside) S&S Trade Pap.

***Larsen, Eric.** Calvinistic Economy & 17th Century Dutch Art. LC 99-43390. 88p. 1999. pap. 21.50 (*0-7618-1517-1*) U Pr of Amer.

Larsen, Eric. Spider-Man: Revenge of Sinister Six. (Spider-Man Ser.). (Illus.). 128p. 1994. pap. 15.95 (*0-7851-0047-4*) Marvel Entrprs.

— A Walk in the Woods: A Great Grandpa Day Book. (Illus.). 32p. (J). (ps-3). 1997. pap. 4.95 (*1-879432-28-5*) Explorers Guide Pub.

Larsen, Eric, jt. auth. see Hill, Clifford.

Larsen, Erik. Savage Dragon: A Talk with God. (Illus.). 176p. (Orig.). 1997. pap. 17.95 (*1-887279-59-8*) Image Comics.

— Savage Dragon: A Talk with God. (Illus.). 176p. (Orig.). 1998. 74.95 (*1-887279-90-3*) Image Comics.

— Savage Dragon: Possessed. (Illus.). 148p. 1998. pap. 12.95 (*1-58240-031-8*, Pub. by Image Comics) Midpt Trade.

***Larsen, Erik.** Savage Dragon: Revenge. 128p. 1999. pap. 16.95 (*1-58240-101-2*, Pub. by Image Comics) Midpt Trade.

— Savage Dragon: Team Ups. (Illus.). 176p. 1998. pap. 21.95 (*1-58240-047-4*, Pub. by Image Comics) Midpt Trade.

Larsen, Erik. Savage Dragon: The Fallen. (Illus.). 128p. 1997. pap. 12.95 (*1-887279-83-0*) Image Comics.

— Savage Dragon: The Fallen. (Illus.). 128p. 1998. 29.95 (*1-887279-89-X*) Image Comics.

Larsen, Erik, jt. auth. see Eastman, Kevin.

Larsen, Erik, jt. ed. see Bunn, Derek W.

Larsen, Erling. James Agee. LC 78-633324. (University of Minnesota Pamphlets on American Writers Ser.: No. 95). 47p. (Orig.). reprint ed. pap. 30.00 (*0-7837-2877-8*, 205757800006) Bks Demand.

***Larsen, F., et al.** An Introduction to K-Theory for C*-Algebras. (London Mathematical Society Student Texts Ser.: Vol. 49). 250p. (C). 2000. text Price not set. (*0-521-78334-8*); pap. text Price not set. (*0-521-78944-3*) Cambridge U Pr.

Larsen, Freeman. Introduction to Language. (Teaching Methods Ser.). 2001. pap. 20.95 (*0-8384-6675-3*) Wadsworth Pub.

Larsen-Freeman, Diane. Techniques & Principles in Language Teaching. (Techniques in Teaching English As a Second Language Ser.). (Illus.). 160p. 1986. pap. text 13.50 (*0-19-434133-X*) OUP.

Larsen, Gwynne & Marold, Kathryn A. USING MICROSOFT WORKS 4.0 FOR. 516p. (C). 1997. pap. text 57.00 (*0-03-020614-6*) Dryden Pr.

Larsen, Gwynne & Shaw, Kenneth. Using WordPerfect 6.0 for Windows. LC 93-78737. (C). 1994. text 31.00 (*0-07-036602-0*) McGraw.

Larsen, Gwynne, et al. Using Microsoft Works 3.0 for Windows: An Introduction to Computing. LC 94-21639. 583p. (C). 1995. mass mkt. 36.00 (*0-87709-845-X*) Course Tech.

Larsen, Gwynne, jt. auth. see Leeburg, Verlene.

Larsen, Gywnne. Using WordPerfect 5.1, IBM PC. 1991. text 43.13 incl. disk (*0-07-911024-X*, Irwn McGrw-H) McGrw-H Hghr Educ.

Larsen, H. A. Knut Hamsun. 1971. 59.95 (*0-87968-385-6*) Gordon Pr.

Larsen, H. Hartvig, et al, eds. Marketing & Semiotics: Selected Papers from the Copenhagen Symposium. 240p. (Orig.). 1991. pap. 110.00 (*87-17-03591-0*) Coronet Bks.

Larsen, Hal S., jt. auth. see Rice-Spearman, Lori.

Larsen, Hanna A., ed. Norway's Best Stories: An Introduction to Modern Norwegian Fiction. Orbeck, Anders, tr. from NOR. LC 75-169557. (Short Story Index Reprint Ser.). 1977. reprint ed. 23.95 (*0-8369-4019-9*) Ayer.

— Sweden's Best Stories: An Introduction to Swedish Fiction. Stork, Charles W., tr. from SWE. LC 70-37276. (Short Story Index Reprint Ser.). 1977. reprint ed. 23.95 (*0-8369-4087-3*) Ayer.

— Told in Norway: An Introduction to Modern Norwegian Fiction. Orbeck, Anders, tr. LC 72-3366. (Short Story Index Reprint Ser.). 1977. reprint ed. 23.95 (*0-8369-4152-7*) Ayer.

Larsen, Hanne H., ed. Cases in Marketing. 256p. 1997. 79.95 (*0-7619-5569-0*); pap. 35.00 (*0-7619-5570-4*) Sage.

Larsen, Hans-Erik. The Aesthetics of the Elements: Imaginary Morphologies in Texts & Paintings. (Illus.). 112p. (C). 1997. pap. 19.95 (*87-7288-543-2*, Pub. by Aarhus Univ Pr) David Brown.

Larsen, Henning. An Old Icelandic Medical Miscellany. LC 75-23736. reprint ed. 40.00 (*0-404-13293-6*) AMS Pr.

Larsen, Henrik. Foreign Policy & Discourse Analysis. LC 97-5238. (Routledge Advances in International Political Economy Ser.). 256p. (C). 1997. 85.00 (*0-415-15976-8*) Routledge.

Larsen, Henry D. Nautical Knowledge. LC 92-27896. 1992. write for info. (*0-934523-05-3*) Middle Coast Pub.

Larsen, Hovis J. Telecommunications: Index of New Information with Authors, Subjects & References. 1994. 47.50 (*1-55914-994-9*); pap. 44.50 (*1-55914-995-7*) ABBE Pubs Assn.

— Telecommunications: Index of New Information with Authors, Subjects & References. 183p. 1997. 47.50 (*0-7883-1614-1*); pap. 44.50 (*0-7883-1615-X*) ABBE Pubs Assn.

Larsen, Ivind & Olsen, Bent O. The Shaping of a Profession: Physicians in Norway, Past & Present. LC 96-46645. 1996. write for info. (*0-88135-168-7*) Watson Pub Intl.

Larsen, J. A. The Northern Forest Border in Canada & Alaska. (Ecological Studies: Vol. 70). (Illus.). 260p. 1988. 175.00 (*0-387-96753-2*) Spr-Verlag.

Larsen, Jack L. Folk Art from the Global Village: The Girard Collection at the Museum of International Folk Art. (Illus.). 96p. 1995. bds. 19.95 (*0-89013-273-9*) Museum NM Pr.

— Jack Lenor Larsen . . . A Weaver's Memoir. LC 98-12989. (Illus.). 160p. 1998. 39.95 (*0-8109-3589-9*, Pub. by Abrams) Time Warner.

— Material Wealth: Living with Luxurious Fabrics. deluxe ed. (Illus.). 240p. 1989. 125.00 (*1-55859-112-5*) Abbeville Pr.

— The Tactile Vessel: New Basket Form. (Illus.). 100p. (Orig.). 1989. pap. 19.95 (*0-9616623-3-6*) Erie Art Mus.

Larsen, Jack L. & Weeks, Jeanne. Fabrics for Interiors. 1975. pap. 32.95 (*0-442-24684-6*, VNR) Wiley.

Larsen, Jack L. & Weeks, Jeanne. Fabrics for Interiors: A Guide to Architects, Designers, & Consumers. (Interior Design Ser.). 128p. 1975. pap. 44.95 (*0-471-28933-7*, VNR) Wiley.

Larsen, Jacob, jt. ed. see Patterson, David J.

Larsen, James. QuickSteps to Learning: Word 2.0 for Windows Beginners. (Quicksteps to Learning Ser.). 1993. spiral bd. 22.95 (*1-56951-003-2*) Sftware Trng.

Larsen, James & Sunny, Bethany. QuickSteps to Learning: Word 6.0 for Windows Beginning. 221p. 1994. spiral bd. 22.95 (*1-56951-020-2*) Sftware Trng.

Larsen, James, ed. see Shankar, Ravi.

Larsen, James M. & Allison, John E., eds. Small-Crack Test Methods. LC 92-10509. (STP Ser.: Vol. 1149). (Illus.). 230p. 1992. text 72.00 (*0-8031-1469-9*, STP1149) ASTM.

Larsen, Jeanne. Manchu Palaces. (Illus.). 88p. 1995. 19.95 (*0-8050-1111-0*) H Holt & Co.

Larsen, Jeanne, tr. & intro. see Hsueh, Tao.

Larsen, Jeffrey A. & Rattray, Gregory J., eds. Arms Control Toward the 21st Century. LC 95-26188. 348p. 1996. pap. text 22.95 (*1-55587-584-X*); lib. bdg. 55.00 (*1-55587-561-0*) L Rienner.

Larsen, Jens. Haydn. rev. ed. 1997. pap. 16.95 (*0-393-30359-4*) Norton.

Larsen, Jens P. Handel, Haydn, & the Viennese Classical Style. Krhamer, Ulrich, tr. LC 88-1206. (Studies in Musicology: No. 100). 344p. reprint ed. pap. 106.70 (*0-8357-1851-4*, 207065200013) Bks Demand.

— Handel's Messiah: Origins, Composition, Sources. 2nd ed. LC 88-10128. 336p. 1990. reprint ed. lib. bdg. 77.50 (*0-313-24426-X*, LAHM, Greenwood Pr) Greenwood.

Larsen, Jens P., et al, eds. Haydn Studies. (C). 1981. 39.00 (*0-393-01454-1*) Norton.

***Larsen, Jerry.** Religious Education & the Brain: A Practical Resource for Understanding How We Learn about God. LC 99-86126. 192p. 2000. pap. 19.95 (*0-8091-3934-0*) Paulist Pr.

Larsen, Jo A. How Do You Want Your Room...Plain or Padded? Sanity-Preserving Tactics for the 90's Woman. LC 95-19172. (Illus.). 1995. pap. 14.95 (*0-87579-972-8*, Shadow Mount) Deseret Bk.

Larsen, Jo A., jt. auth. see Hepworth, Dean H.

Larsen, Jo Ann. The Heart of Goodness: Kind Acts That Touch the Soul. LC 98-8495. 528p. 1999. pap. 19.95 (*1-57345-226-2*, Shadow Mount) Deseret Bk.

***Larsen, Jo Ann.** I'm a Day Late & a Dollar Short - And It's Okay! LC 99-23259. 324p. 1999. pap. 14.95 (*1-57345-539-3*, Shadow Mount) Deseret Bk.

Larsen, Joan S. Lovin' Dutch Ovens: A Cook Book for the Dutch Oven Enthusiast. Bessey, Carolyn & Ware, Julie, eds. LC 91-90722. (Illus.). 241p. 1991. 19.95 (*1-880415-03-8*) L F S Pubns.

Larsen, Jodie. Deadly Rescue. 1998. mass mkt. 5.99 (*0-451-40861-6*, Sig) NAL.

— Deadly Silence. 1997. mass mkt. 5.99 (*0-451-40786-5*, Onyx) NAL.

Larsen, John W., ed. Organic Chemistry of Coal. LC 78-8114. (ACS Symposium Ser.: Vol. 71). 335p. 1978. reprint ed. pap. 103.90 (*0-608-03930-6*, 206437700009) Bks Demand.

***Larsen, K., et al, eds.** Automata, Languages & Programming: 25th International Colloquium, ICALP '98, Aalborg, Denmark, July 13-17, 1998, Proceedings. (Lecture Notes in Computer Sciences Ser.: Vol. 1443). xvi, 932p. 1998. pap. 98.00 (*3-540-64781-3*) Spr-Verlag.

Larsen, K. G. & Skou, A., eds. Computer Aided Verification. (Lecture Notes in Computer Science Ser.: Vol. 575). 487p. 1992. 69.95 (*0-387-55179-4*) Spr-Verlag.

Larsen, Karen K. Make Your Own Decorative Boxes with Easy-to-Use Patterns. LC 94-44866. (Illus.). 32p. 1995. reprint ed. pap. text 3.50 (*0-486-27814-X*) Dover.

***Larsen, Karin.** Faces of Goa: A Journey Through the History & Cultural Revolution of Goa & Other Communities Influenced by the Portuguese LC 98-907236. 507p. 1998. write for info. (*81-212-0584-0*, Pub. by Gyan Publishing Hse) S Asia.

Larsen, Karl V. See & Draw. LC 91-73904. (Illus.). 152p. (YA). (gr. 9-12). 1993. text 25.95 (*0-87192-242-8*) Davis Mass.

Larsen, Kenneth J., ed. Edmund Spenser's Amoretti & Epithalamion: A Critical Edition. LC 96-53914. (Medieval & Renaissance Texts & Studies: Vol. 146). 304p. 1997. 25.00 (*0-86698-186-1*, MR146) MRTS.

Larsen, Kent P. A Touch of Larceny: The Insurance Agent's Survival Guide. LC 84-60877. 120p. (Orig.). 1984. pap. 7.95 (*0-913581-01-1*) Publitec.

***Larsen, Kevin S.** Cervantes & Galdos in Fortunata y Jacinta--Tales of Impertinent Curiosity. LC 99-41482. (Hispanic Literature Ser.: Vol. 49). 176p. 1999. text 79.95 (*0-7734-7927-9*) E Mellen.

Larsen, Knud, ed. Dialectics & Ideology in Psychology. LC 85-22991. (Publications for the Advancement of Theory & History in Psychology, the PATH Ser.). 296p. 1986. text 73.25 (*0-89391-222-0*) Ablx Pub.

Larsen, Knud S., ed. Conflict & Social Psychology. 272p. (C). 1993. text 65.00 (*0-8039-8745-5*) Sage.

***Larsen, Knut Einar & Marstein, Nils.** Conservation of Historic Timber Structures: An Ecological Approach. (Illus.). 160p. 2000. 74.95 (*0-7506-3434-0*) Buttrwrth-Heinemann.

Larsen, L. C., jt. ed. see Babovic, V.

Larsen, Larry. An Angler's Guide to Bass Patterns: Productive Methods, Places & Times. LC 89-92685. (Bass Series Library). (Illus.). 160p. (Orig.). 1990. pap. 11.95 (*0-936513-07-1*, BSL8) Larsens Outdoor.

— Bass Fishing Facts: Angler's Guide to Bass Lifestyles & Behavior. LC 88-91464. (Bass Series Library). (Illus.). 135p. (Orig.). 1989. pap. 11.95 (*0-936513-05-5*, BSL6) Larsens Outdoor.

— Bass Guide Tips: An Angler's Guide. LC 90-63531. (Bass Series Library). (Illus.). 160p. 1991. text 11.95 (*0-936513-10-1*) Larsens Outdoor.

— Bass Lures: Tricks & Techniques. LC 87-82758. (Illus.). 128p. (Orig.). 1988. pap. 9.95 (*0-936513-02-0*) Larsens Outdoor.

— Bass Pro Strategies. LC 87-82757. (Illus.). 128p. (Orig.). 1988. pap. 11.95 (*0-936513-01-2*) Larsens Outdoor.

— Crappie Tactics. LC 93-79800. (Freshwater Library). (Illus.). 160p. (Orig.). 1993. pap. text 9.95 (*0-936513-40-3*) Larsens Outdoor.

— Guide to Central Florida Bass Waters. LC 91-76768. (Illus.). 192p. (Orig.). 1991. pap. 12.95 (*0-936513-19-5*) Larsens Outdoor.

— Guide to South Florida Bass Waters. LC 92-71319. (Bass Water Ser.). (Illus.). 192p. (Orig.). 1992. pap. 12.95 (*0-936513-20-9*) Larsens Outdoor.

— Larry Larsen on Bass Tactics. LC 92-74325. (Larsen on Bass Ser.). (Illus.). 228p. (Orig.). (C). 1992. pap. text 12.95 (*0-936513-27-6*) Larsens Outdoor.

— Mastering Largemouth Bass. LC 89-63111. (Complete Angler's Library). 261p. 1989. write for info. (*0-914697-24-2*) N Amer Outdoor Grp.

— Peacock Bass Addiction: The Newest Spots & Latest Tactical Secrets. (Illus.). 192p. 1999. pap. 14.95 (*0-936513-49-7*) Larsens Outdoor.

— Peacock Bass & Other Fierce Exotics: Where, When & How to Catch Latin America's Most Exciting Freshwater Fish. LC 95-95343. (Illus.). 192p. (Orig.). 1996. pap. 13.95 (*0-936513-33-0*) Larsens Outdoor.

— Peacock Bass Explosions: Where, When & How to Catch America's Greatest Gamefish. LC 93-79801. (Illus.). 192p. (Orig.). 1993. pap. text 12.95 (*0-936513-35-7*) Larsens Outdoor.

— Shallow Water Bass. LC 85-82041. (Illus.). 160p. (Orig.). 1986. pap. 9.95 (*0-936513-00-4*) Larsens Outdoor.

Larsen, Larry & O'Keefe, M. Timothy. Fish & Dive Florida & the Keys: A Candid Destination Guide. Larsen, Lilliam M., ed. LC 92-90226. (Outdoor Travel Ser.). (Illus.). 192p. (Orig.). 1992. pap. 12.95 (*0-936513-26-8*) Larsens Outdoor.

— Fish & Dive the Caribbean: A Truthful Destination Guide from Cancun to the British Virgin Islands. Larsen, Lilliam M., ed. LC 91-76441. (Outdoor Travel Ser.). (Illus.). 192p. (Orig.). 1991. pap. 11.95 (*0-936513-17-9*) Larsens Outdoor.

Larsen, Larry L. The Winner Within: Habits of the Happy, Healthy, Wealthy, & Wise. French, Florence E., ed. LC 92-97556. (Illus.). 212p. (Orig.). 1993. pap. 18.00 (*0-9634716-0-0*) Achieve Bk.

***Larsen, Laurie.** Whispers of the Heart. 2000. pap. write for info. (*1-893162-85-0*) AmErica.

Larsen, Lawrence H. Federal Justice in Western Missouri: The Judges, the Cases, the Times. (Illus.). 304p. 1994. text 42.50 (*0-8262-0973-4*) U of Mo Pr.

— The President Wore Spats: A Biography of Glenn Frank. LC 65-63009. (Illus.). 198p. 1965. 4.50 (*0-87020-056-9*) State Hist Soc Wis.

— The Rise of the Urban South. LC 84-25596. 232p. 1985. 27.50 (*0-8131-1538-8*) U Pr of Ky.

— The Urban South: A History. LC 89-34162. 224p. 1990. text 27.50 (*0-8131-0309-6*) U Pr of Ky.

— Wall of Flames: The Minnesota Forest Fire of 1894. LC 84-61133. 187p. 1984. 9.85 (*0-911042-29-6*) NDSU Inst Reg.

Larsen, Lawrence H. & Cottrell, Barbara J. The Gate City: A History of Omaha. enl. rev. ed. LC 97-12743. (Illus.). xix, 356p. 1997. pap. text 18.95 (*0-8032-7967-1*) U of Nebr Pr.

Larsen, Lawrence H. & Hulston, Nancy J. Pendergast! LC 97-33391. (Biography Ser.). (Illus.). 256p. 1997. 29.95 (*0-8262-1145-3*) U of Mo Pr.

— The University of Kansas Medical Center: A Pictorial History. LC 91-44669. (Illus.). x, 222p. 1992. 35.00 (*0-7006-0539-8*) U Pr of KS.

Larsen, Lawrence H., jt. auth. see Glaab, Charles N.

Larsen, Lawrence P. Macro 86 Assembly Language Programming. LC 84-19295. (Macro-86 Software Design Ser.). (Illus.). 900p. 1984. ring bd. 59.95 (*0-87119-100-8*, EC-1201) Heathkit-Zenith Ed.

Larsen, Lilliam M., ed. see Larsen, Larry & O'Keefe, M. Timothy.

***Larsen, Linda.** True Power: Get It, Use It, Share It. 143p. 2000. pap. 12.95 (*0-9678084-0-5*) Brandywne FL.

Larsen, Linda J. Renaissance: A Thematic Unit. Coan, Sharon & Levin, Ina M., eds. (Thematic Units Ser.). (Illus.). 80p. (J). (gr. 5-8). 1994. student ed. 9.95 (*1-55734-580-5*) Tchr Create Mat.

— Wolves: A Thematic Unit. (Thematic Units Ser.). (Illus.). 80p. (Orig.). (J). (gr. 5-8). 1994. pap., student ed. 9.95 (*1-55734-583-X*) Tchr Create Mat.

Larsen, Lucretia. The Wholesome Ways of Our Olden Days. 116p. 1985. 16.95 (*0-87770-360-4*) Ye Galleon.

Larsen, Ludwig B. Key to the Bible & Heaven: The Mystery of the Ages Revealed (1919) 280p. 1996. reprint ed. pap. 24.95 (*1-56459-865-9*) Kessinger Pub.

— The Little Book: Key to the Bible & Heaven. 280p. 1996. reprint ed. spiral bd. 18.50 (*0-7873-0535-9*) Hlth Research.

Larsen, Lyle. Dr. Johnson's Household. LC 85-4056. (Illus.). xiii, 155p. (C). 1985. 29.50 (*0-208-02078-0*, Archon Bks) Shoe String.

Larsen, Lyle, ed. & intro. see Wilkinson, Tate.

Larsen, M. J. & Cobb-Poulle, L. A. Phellinus (Hymenochaetaceae) A Survey of the World Taxa, 1990. (Synopsis Fungorum Ser.: No. 3). 206p. 1990. pap. text 60.00 (*82-90724-07-1*, Pub. by Fungi-Flora) Lubrecht & Cramer.

Larsen, M. T., ed. see Copenhagen University, Center for Research in the.

Larsen, M. T., jt. ed. see Harbsmeier, Michael.

Larsen, Margie. Baby Bop Goes to the Doctor. (Barney's Go to Ser.). (Illus.). (J). (ps-k). 1996. pap. 2.95 (*0-614-15551-7*) BDD Bks Young Read.

— Barney & Baby Bop Go to the Doctor. LC 95-79188. (Barney's Go to Ser.). (Illus.). 24p. (J). (ps-3). 1996. pap. 3.25 (*1-57064-074-2*) Lyrick Pub.

— Barney Plays Nose to Toes. Dudko, Mary A., ed. LC 95-83155. (Barney Ser.). (Illus.). 22p. (J). (ps-k). 1996. bds. 4.95 (*1-57064-077-7*) Lyrick Pub.

— Barney y Baby Bop Van al Doctor. LC 96-86683. (Barney Go to Ser.). (SPA., Illus.). 24p. (J). (ps-k). 1997. pap. text 2.95 (*1-57064-166-8*, Barney Publ) Lyrick Pub.

— Barney's Halloween Box of Treats. (Barney Ser.). (Illus.). (J). (ps-k). 1998. 9.99 (*1-57064-515-9*) Lyrick Pub.

— Barney's Halloween Party. LC 96-83766. (Barney Ser.). (Illus.). 24p. (J). (ps-k). 1996. pap. 3.25 (*1-57064-046-7*) Lyrick Pub.

— Larsen's Shapes, Colors & Numbers. (Barney's Beginnings Ser.). (Illus.). (J). (ps-1). 1996. pap. 2.95 (*0-614-15552-5*) BDD Bks Young Read.

Larsen, Margie, ed. Barney's Friends. LC 95-79190. (Barney Ser.). (Illus.). 16p. (J). (ps-k). 1996. bds. 4.95 (*1-57064-114-5*) Lyrick Pub.

Larsen, Margie & Dudko, Mary A. Barney Says "Play Safely" LC 95-79185. (Barney Ser.). (Illus.). 24p. (J). (ps-3). 1996. pap. 2.95 (*1-57064-073-4*) Lyrick Pub.

— Colors: Barney's Balloons. (Barney's Beginnings Ser.). (Illus.). 16p. (J). (ps-k). 1996. pap. 2.95 (*1-57064-090-4*) Lyrick Pub.

— Numbers: Barney's Number Circus. (Barney's Beginnings Ser.). (Illus.). 16p. (J). (ps-k). 1996. pap., wbk. ed. 2.95 (*1-57064-092-0*) Lyrick Pub.

— Numbers: Barney's Number Circus. (Barney's Beginnings Ser.). (Illus.). 32p. (J). (ps-k). 1997. pap., wbk. ed. 2.95 (*1-57064-175-7*) Lyrick Pub.

— Same & Different: Barney Pretends. (Barney's Beginnings Ser.). (Illus.). 16p. (J). (ps-k). 1996. pap., wbk. ed. 2.95 (*1-57064-093-9*) Lyrick Pub.

— Same/Different: Barney Pretends. (Barney's Beginnings Ser.). 32p. (J). (ps-3). 1997. pap., wbk. ed. 2.95 (*1-57064-176-5*) Lyrick Pub.

— Shapes: Barney's Shape Picnic. (Barney's Beginnings Ser.). (Illus.). 16p. (J). (ps-k). 1996. pap., wbk. ed. 2.95 (*1-57064-091-2*) Lyrick Pub.

— Shapes: Barney's Shape Picnic. (Barney's Beginnings Ser.). (Illus.). 32p. (J). (ps-k). 1997. pap., wbk. ed. 2.95 (*1-57064-224-9*) Lyrick Pub.

Larsen, Margie & Dudko, Mary Ann. Barney's "Let's Learn" Boxed Set. (Barney Ser.). (Illus.). (J). (ps-k). 1998. 9.99 (*1-57064-517-5*) HarpC Child Bks.

Larsen, Margie, jt. auth. see Dudko, Mary A.

Larsen, Margie, jt. auth. see Dudko, Mary Ann.

Larsen, Margie, ed. see Bernthal, Mark S.

Larsen, Margie, ed. see Cooner, Donna.

Larsen, Margie, ed. see Dudko, Mary A.

Larsen, Margie, ed. see Leach, Sheryl.

Larsen, Margie, ed. see Leach, Sheryl & Leach, Patrick.

Larsen, Margie, ed. see Levy, Paul.

Larsen, Margie, ed. see Mody, Monica.

Larsen, Margie, ed. see White, Stephen.

Larsen, Marianne. Selected Poems. Christensen, Nadia, tr. LC 82-5083. 50p. 1982. pap. 7.95 (*0-915306-29-8*) Curbstone.

Larsen, Merlin D. Jackals in Iron. LC 99-60979. (Illus.). 448p. 1999. pap. 10.95 (*1-888106-83-2*) Agreka Bks.

Larsen, Michael. Dave Godfrey & His Works. (Canadian Author Studies). 55p. (C). 1989. pap. text 9.95 (*0-920763-87-1*, Pub. by ECW) Genl Dist Srvs.

— How to Write a Book Proposal. rev. ed. LC 97-18103. 224p. 1997. pap. 14.99 (*0-89879-771-3*, Wrtrs Digest Bks) F & W Pubns Inc.

— Literary Agents: What They Do, How They Do It, How to Find & Work with the Right One for You. rev. ed. LC 95-53093. 207p. 1996. pap. 15.95 (*0-471-13046-X*) Wiley.

— Uncertainty. LC 97-90646.Tr. of Uden Sikker Viden. 272p. 1998. pap. 12.00 (*0-449-91236-1*) Fawcett.

— Uncertainty. Blecher, Lone T. & Blecher, George, trs. from DAN. LC 96-7256.Tr. of Uden Sikker Viden. 272p. 1996. 22.00 (*0-15-100202-9*) Harcourt.

Larsen, Michael, jt. auth. see Pomada, Elizabeth.

Larsen, Michael J. A Contribution to the Taxonomy of the Genus Tomentella. (Mycologia Memoirs Ser.: No. 4). (Illus.). 145p. 1974. pap. text 12.50 (*0-945345-40-2*) Lubrecht & Cramer.

Larsen, Mogens T. The Conquest of Assyria: Excavations in an Antique Land, 1840-1860. LC 96-3606. (DAN & ENG., Illus.). 416p. (C). 1996. 65.00 (*0-415-14356-X*) Routledge.

Larsen, Naomi H. & Windham, Lisa A. Thoughts from My Rocking Chair. (Illus.). 39p. (Orig.). 1994. pap. 7.95 (*1-884498-00-0*) CompuVisuals.

Larsen, Neil. Modernism & Hegemony: A Materialistic Critique of Aesthetic Agencies. 150p. 1990. pap. 14.95 (*0-8166-1785-6*) U of Minn Pr.

— Reading North by South: On Latin American Literature, Culture & Politics. LC 94-43194. 1995. pap. 18.95 (*0-8166-2584-0*) U of Minn Pr.

— Reading North by South: On Latin American Literature, Culture & Politics. LC 94-43194. 1995. text 47.95 (*0-8166-2583-2*) U of Minn Pr.

Larsen, Nella. Passing. Davis, Thadious, ed. & intro. by. LC 97-9482. xxxiv, 122p. 1997. pap. 8.95 (*0-14-118025-0*) Penguin Putnam.

***Larsen, Nella.** Passing. 2000. 18.95 (*0-375-50446-X*) Random.

Larsen, Nella. Passing. LC 76-92233. (American Negro: His History & Literature. Series 3: His History & Literature, Ser. No. 3). 1970. reprint ed. 27.95 (*0-405-01930-0*) Ayer.

— Passing. LC 69-18567. 226p. 1990. reprint ed. pap. 19.95 (*0-88143-119-2*) Ayer.

— Passing. LC 73-82056. 215p. 1969. reprint ed. lib. bdg. 38.50 (*0-8371-1541-8*, LAP&, Greenwood Pr) Greenwood.

— Quicksand. LC 74-75553. 312p. 1970. reprint ed. lib. bdg. 49.50 (*0-8371-1127-7*, LAQ&, Greenwood Pr) Greenwood.

— Quicksand & Passing. McDowell, Deborah, ed. (American Women Writers Ser.). 300p. (C). 1986. pap. text 10.00 (*0-8135-1170-4*) Rutgers U Pr.

Larsen, Otto N. Milestones & Millstones: Social Science at the National Science Foundation, 1945-1991. 292p. (C). 1991. text 44.95 (*0-88738-441-2*) Transaction Pubs.

— Voicing Social Concern: The Mass Media, Violence, Pornography, Censorship, Organization, Social Science, the Ultramultiversity. 318p. lib. bdg. 39.00 (*0-8191-9437-9*) U Pr of Amer.

Larsen, Otto N., jt. auth. see De Fleur, Melvin L.

Larsen, Otto N., jt. auth. see Medalia, Nahum Z.

Larsen, P. G., ed. see First International Symposium of Formal Methods Eu.

Larsen, P. K. & Dobson, P. J. Reflection High-Energy Electron Diffraction & Reflection Electron Imaging of Surfaces. LC 88-28843. (NATO ASI Ser.: Vol. 188). (Illus.). 556p. (C). 1988. text 145.00 (*0-306-43035-5*, Kluwer Plenum) Kluwer Academic.

Larsen, Pamela, jt. auth. see Lubkin, Ilene.

Larsen, Patricia, jt. auth. see Joseph, John.

***Larsen, Paul.** Montana Entrepreneurs Guide How to Start & Manage a Business in Montana. 3rd ed. 1999. pap. 19.95 (*0-9624819-6-3*) University MT.

Larsen, Paul, jt. auth. see Coutts, Russell.

Larsen, Paul, tr. see Nissen, Hans J., et al.

Larsen, Paul L. Why Do We Wear Ashes? 1991. pap. 6.50 (*1-55673-284-8*, 9117) CSS OH.

Larsen, Paula B. Beauty at Dawn: Notes to My Sisters. LC 94-7824. (Women's Wisdom Ser.). (Illus.). 64p. (Orig.). 1994. 7.95 (*0-89243-692-1*, Liguori Triumph) Liguori Pubns.

— Gammaw...Gammaw... Thunder in an Infant's Voice. LC 94-7303. (Women's Wisdom Ser.). (Illus.). 48p. 1994. 7.95 (*0-89243-693-X*, Liguori Triumph) Liguori Pubns.

Larsen, Per W. Just a Minute. Rinden, David, ed. 90p. 1997. pap. 6.95 (*0-943167-35-3*) Faith & Fellowship Pr.

Larsen, Peter G., jt. auth. see Fitzgerald, John.

Larsen, Phyllis. Ghirardelli Original Chocolate Cookbook. 3rd rev. ed. Allen, Vera, ed. (Illus.). (Orig.). 6.00 (*0-9610218-0-2*) Ghirardelli Choc.

Larsen, Poul S., jt. auth. see Garby, Lars.

Larsen, R. M., et al, eds. Structural & Tectonic Modelling Had Its Application to Petroleum Geology. 550p. 1992. 219.75 (*0-444-88607-9*) Elsevier.

Larsen, Ray. Toolmaking for Woodworkers. 2nd ed. (Illus.). 160p. (Orig.). 1997. reprint ed. pap. 22.95 (*0-9643999-8-9*, Cambium) Cambium Pr.

Larsen, Ray R., jt. ed. see Chance, Michael R.

Larsen, Rayola C. Alphabet Talk: Gospel Rhymes for Each Letter of the Alphabet. LC 89-83429. (Illus.). 32p. (Orig.). (J). (gr. k-3). 1989. reprint ed. pap. 5.98 (*0-88290-147-8*) Horizon Utah.

Larsen, Rebecca. Franklin D. Roosevelt: Man of Destiny. (Non-Fiction Ser.). (Illus.). 160p. (YA). (gr. 9-12). 1991. lib. bdg. 24.00 (*0-531-11068-0*) Watts.

— Paul Robeson: Hero Before His Time. LC 89-8880. (Illus.). 160p. (J). (gr. 6-9). 1989. lib. bdg. 24.00 (*0-531-10779-5*) Watts.

— Richard Nixon: The Rise & Fall of a President. (Illus.). 160p. (YA). (gr. 9-12). 1991. lib. bdg. 24.00 (*0-531-10997-6*) Watts.

— Ronald Reagan. (Impact Biographies Ser.). (Illus.). 112p. (YA). (gr. 7-12). 1994. lib. bdg. 24.00 (*0-531-11191-1*) Watts.

Larsen, Richard. Ted Bundy: The Deliberate Stranger. 1990. mass mkt. 5.50 (*0-671-72866-0*) PB.

Larsen, Richard, et al. Statistics for Applied Problem Solving & Decision Making. LC 96-35368. (Business Statistics Ser.). (C). 1997. pap. 85.95 (*0-534-93084-0*) Wadsworth Pub.

Larsen, Richard J. & Marx, Morris L. An Introduction to Mathematical Statistics & Its Applications. 2nd ed. (Illus.). 640p. (C). 1985. 105.00 (*0-13-487174-X*) P-H.

— An Introduction to Probability & Its Applications. (Illus.). 480p. (C). 1985. text 52.60 (*0-13-493453-9*) P-H.

— Statistics. 800p. (C). 1990. text 66.80 (*0-13-844085-9*) P-H.

Larsen, Robin, et al, eds. Emanuel Swedenborg: A Continuing Vision. LC 87-51521. (Illus.). 576p. 1988. 39.95 (*0-87785-136-0*) Swedenborg.

Larsen, Robin, et al, eds. Emanuel Swedenborg: A Continuing Vision. LC 87-51521. (Illus.). 576p. 1988. pap. 29.95 (*0-87785-137-9*) Swedenborg.

***Larsen, Robin & Larsen, Stephen.** Fashioning of Angels: Partnership as Spiritual Practice. 248p. 2000. pap. 19.95 (*0-87785-390-8*, Chrysalis Books) Swedenborg.

***Larsen, Ron.** A Fisherman Passing Through. (Illus.). 86p. 2000. pap. 15.00 (*0-9679359-0-3*) Glacier Graph.

Larsen, Ronald. Banach Algebras: An Introduction. LC 73-84868. (Pure & Applied Mathematics Ser.: No. 24). 359p. reprint ed. pap. 111.30 (*0-8357-6032-4*, 203454500090) Bks Demand.

— Functional Analysis: An Introduction. LC 72-90375. (Pure & Applied Mathematics Ser.: Vol. 15). 515p. reprint ed. pap. 159.70 (*0-608-16936-6*, 202709900054) Bks Demand.

— Introduction to MathCAD. LC 99-12148. 150p. 1999. pap. 21.33 (*0-13-937493-0*) P-H.

— Introduction to the Theory of Multipliers. LC 78-134023. (Grundlehren der Mathematischen Wissenschaften Ser.: Vol. 175). 1971. 93.95 (*0-387-05120-1*) Spr-Verlag.

— A Potter's Companion: Imagination, Originality, & Craft. (Illus.). 192p. (Orig.). 1992. pap. 19.95 (*0-89281-445-4*, Park St Pr) Inner Tradit.

Larsen, Roy A., ed. Introduction to Floriculture. 2nd ed. (Illus.). 636p. 1992. text 62.00 (*0-12-437651-7*) Acad Pr.

***Larsen, S., et al.** Exchange & Transport of Air Pollutants over Complex Terrain & the Sea: Field Measurements & Numerical Modelling: Ship, Ocean Platform & Laboratory Measurements. LC 00-38813. (Transport & Chemical Transformation of Pollutants in the Troposphere Ser.). (Illus.). 2000. write for info. (*3-540-67438-1*) Spr-Verlag.

Larsen, Sally, photos by. Japlish. (Illus.). 82p. 1998. text 25.00 (*0-7881-5456-7*) DIANE Pub.

Larsen, Sandra A., et al, eds. Manual of Tests for Syphilis. 8th ed. 208p. 1990. 30.00 (*0-87553-174-1*) Am Pub Health.

***Larsen, Sandra A., et al, eds.** Manual of Tests for Syphilis. 9th ed. LC 98-72440. 361p. 1998. pap. 48.00 (*0-87553-234-9*) Am Pub Health.

Larsen, Sandy. Choosing: Which Way Do I Go? (Bible Discovery Guide for Campers Ser.). (Illus.). 32p. (J). (gr. 7-10). 1985. teacher ed. 3.50 (*0-87788-116-2*, H Shaw Pubs); student ed. 1.50 (*0-87788-115-4*, H Shaw Pubs) Waterbrook Pr.

***Larsen, Sandy.** The Dark Lighthouse. LC 99-66714. (Jackpine Point Adventure Ser.: Vol. 4). (Illus.). 128p. (YA). (gr. 5-9). 2000. pap. 5.99 (*0-9666677-3-5*) Merritt Park Pr.

Larsen, Sandy. Eye-Opening Bible Studies. (Bible Discovery Guide for Campers Ser.). 32p. (J). (gr. 6-10). 1986. student ed. 1.95 (*0-87788-247-9*, H Shaw Pubs) Waterbrook Pr.

— Forgiving: Lightening Your Load. (Bible Discovery Guide Ser.). (Illus.). 32p. (J). (gr. 6-8). 1985. teacher ed. 3.50 (*0-87788-280-0*, H Shaw Pubs); student ed. 1.50 (*0-87788-279-7*, H Shaw Pubs) Waterbrook Pr.

— Ice Festival. (Jackpine Point Adventure Ser.: Vol. 2). (Illus.). 126p. (J). (gr. 4-6). 1999. pap. 5.99 (*0-9666677-1-9*) Merritt Park Pr.

— The Re-Appearing Statue. LC 98-96504. (Jackpine Point Adventure Ser.: Vol. 1). (Illus.). 120p. (J). (gr. 6-9). 1998. pap. 5.99 (*0-9666677-0-0*) Merritt Park Pr.

***Larsen, Sandy.** Something's Fishy. (Jackpine Point Adventure Ser.: Vol. 3). (Illus.). 128p. (YA). (gr. 6-9). 1999. pap. 5.99 (*0-9666677-2-7*, Pub. by Merritt Park Pr) Bookmen Inc.

Larsen, Sandy. Standing Strong: Notes from Joseph's Journal. (Bible Discovery Guide Ser.). (Illus.). 32p. (Orig.). 1986. pap. text, teacher ed. 3.50 (*0-87788-785-3*, H Shaw Pubs); pap. text, student ed. 1.50 (*0-87788-784-5*, H Shaw Pubs) Waterbrook Pr.

— Sticking Together: Friendships for Life. (Bible Discovery Guide Ser.). (Illus.). 32p. (Orig.). 1987. pap. text, teacher ed. 3.50 (*0-87788-788-8*, H Shaw Pubs); pap. text, student ed. 1.50 (*0-87788-787-X*, H Shaw Pubs) Waterbrook Pr.

Larsen, Sandy & Larsen, Dale. Celebrating Creation: Exploring God's World. (Bible Discovery Guide Ser.). 32p. (YA). (gr. 7-10). 1988. 1.50 (*0-87788-109-X*, H Shaw Pubs) Waterbrook Pr.

— Celebrating Creation: Exploring God's World. (Bible Discovery Guide Ser.). 32p. (YA). (gr. 7-10). 1988. 3.50 (*0-87788-110-3*, H Shaw Pubs) Waterbrook Pr.

Larsen, Sandy, jt. auth. see Larsen, Dale.

Larsen, Scott & Humpherys, Gayle. Maximizing Corel WordPerfect Suite 8. LC 98-150466. 800p. 1997. pap. text 39.99 incl. cd-rom (*0-07-882451-6*) Osborne-McGraw.

Larsen, Sharon. Your Child's Medical Journal. 1999. 16.00 (*0-609-60434-1*) Random Hse Value.

Larsen, Shirley, ed. Translation: A Means to an End. (Dolphin Ser.: No. 18). (Illus.). 128p. (C). 1990. pap. 19.95 (*0-614-11377-6*, Pub. by Aarhus Univ Pr) David Brown.

Larsen, Sonja & Hoffman, G. L. Signs that Sell: The Handbook of Successful Merchandise Signing. (Illus.). 200p. (C). 1991. 29.95 (*0-9629666-0-6*); pap. text. write for info. (*0-9629666-1-4*) Insignia Systs.

Larsen, Sonja, jt. auth. see Bourdeau, John.

Larsen, Stein & Hagtvet, Bernt. Modern Europe after Fascism, 2 vols. LC 97-62081. 1900p. 1998. 250.00 (*0-88033-973-X*, Pub. by East Eur Monographs) Col U Pr.

Larsen, Stein U. Modern Europe after Fascism. (Social Science Monograph Ser.). 700p. 1996. 103.00 (*0-88033-970-5*, 414, Pub. by East Eur Monographs) Col U Pr.

***Larsen, Stein Ugelvik.** The Challenges of Theories on Democracy: Elaboration Over New Trends in Transitology. 500p. 2000. text 65.00 (*0-88033-986-1*) Col U Pr.

Larsen, Stephen. The Mythic Imagination: The Quest for Meaning Through Personal Mythology. LC 95-54017. (Illus.). 432p. 1996. pap. 16.95 (*0-89281-574-4*, Inner Trad) Inner Tradit.

— The Shaman's Doorway: Opening Imagination to Power & Myth. LC 97-49239. (Illus.). 272p. 1998. pap. 14.95 (*0-89281-672-4*) Inner Tradit.

— The Shaman's Doorway: Opening Imagination to Power & Myth. (Illus.). 260p. 1988. reprint ed. pap. 13.95 (*0-88268-072-2*) Station Hill Pr.

Larsen, Stephen, jt. auth. see Larsen, Robin.

Larsen, Stephen, ed. see Mutwa, Credo.

Larsen, Stephen, ed. & intro. see Blackmer, Carolyn.

Larsen, Susan. Boldstrokes & Quiet Gestures: Twentieth Century Drawings & Watercolors from the Santa Barbara Museum of Art. 1992. 25.00 (*1-882603-00-1*) Mid Am Arts.

Larsen, Susan, et al. Richard Diebenkorn: Works on Paper from the Harry W. & Margaret Anderson Collection. LC 92-73206. (Illus.). 96p. (Orig.). (C). 1993. pap. 15.00 (*0-945192-11-8*) USC Fisher Gallery.

Larsen, Susan C. Jean Arp Centenary Exhibition: Sculpture, Reliefs, & Graphic Work. Hunter, Sam & Matinko-Wald, Ruth A., eds. LC 87-60011. 64p. (Orig.). (C). 1987. pap. write for info. (*0-942461-01-0*) Mus Art Fl.

***Larsen, Susan C.** Maine & the Modern Spirit. (Illus.). 36p. 2000. 12.00 (*0-915171-55-4*) Katonah Gal.

Larsen, Susan C. Variations: Five Los Angeles Painters. LC 80-69334. (Illus.). 51p. (Orig.). 1980. pap. 7.50 (*0-911291-05-9*) Fellows Cont Art.

Larsen, Susan C., text. Sunshine & Shadow: Recent Painting in Southern California. LC 84-73006. (Illus.). 75p. 1985. pap. 10.00 (*0-911291-10-5*, Pub. by Fellows Cont Art) RAM Publications.

Larsen, Svend E., et al, eds. Nature: Literature & its Otherness la Litterature et Son Autre. 265p. pap. 30.75 (*87-7838-282-3*, Pub. by Odense Univ) Intl Spec Bk.

Larsen, T., jt. auth. see Engberg, J.

Larsen, Terry, jt. auth. see Landphair, Harlow.

Larsen, Thor. The Polar Bear Family Book. (Illus.). 64p. (J). (gr. 1-5). 1996. pap. 8.95 (*1-55858-613-X*, Pub. by North-South Bks NYC) Chronicle Bks.

Larsen, Timothy. Friends of Religious Equality: Nonconformist Politics in Mid-Victorian England. LC 98-43277. (Studies in Modern British Religious History). 256p. 1999. 60.00 (*0-85115-726-2*, Boydell Pr) Boydell & Brewer.

Larsen, Tom. Bench-Tested Circuits for Surveillance & Counter-Surveillance Technicians. (Illus.). 128p. 1997. pap. 22.00 (*0-87364-917-6*) Paladin Pr.

— More Bench-Tested Circuits: Innovative Designs for Surveillance & Countersurveillance Technicians. LC 99-160374. (Illus.). 72p. 1998. pap. 21.00 (*1-58160-007-0*) Paladin Pr.

Larsen, Ton. The Layman's Guide to Electronic Eavesdropping: How It's Done & Simple Ways to Prevent It. (Illus.). 112p. 1996. pap. 17.00 (*0-87364-879-X*) Paladin Pr.

Larsen, Tor J. & McGuire, Eugene, eds. Information Systems Innovation & Diffusion: Issues & Directions. LC 97-45778. (Illus.). 464p. (C). 1998. 64.95 (*1-878289-43-8*); pap. 49.95 (*1-878289-46-2*) Idea Group Pub.

Larsen, Torben B. The Butterflies of Kenya: And Their Natural History. (Illus.). 522p. 1996. reprint ed. pap. text 70.00 (*0-19-850005-X*) OUP.

— Butterflies of Saudi Arabia & Its Neighbors. (Illus.). 160p. 1984. 49.95 (*0-86685-542-4*, Pub. by Stacey Intl) Intl Bk Ctr.

Larsen, Vera J. With Every Goodbye: The Seasons of a Woman's Life. 150p. 1998. pap. 12.95 (*1-888106-34-4*) Agreka Bks.

Larsen, Walter G., et al, eds. Color Text of Contact Dermatitis. (Illus.). 252p. 1991. text 135.00 (*0-7216-3518-0*, W B Saunders Co) Harcrt Hlth Sci Grp.

Larsen, Wanwadee. Confessions of a Mail Order Bride: American Life Through Thai Eyes. LC 89-43331. 324p. 1989. pap. 18.95 (*0-88282-174-1*) New Horizon NJ.

Larsen, Wendy. After Dark. (Illus.). 19p. (J). (ps-3). 1999. pap. 10.99 (*0-9665699-0-3*) Chase Publications.

Larsen, Wendy U., jt. auth. see Babcock, Richard F.

Larsen, William J. Essentials of Human Embryology. LC 97-17953. 1997. pap. text 34.95 (*0-443-07514-X*) Church.

— Human Embryology. 2nd ed. LC 97-8214. 1997. pap. text 39.00 (*0-443-07989-7*) Church.

***Larsen, William J.** Human Embryology. 3rd ed. 2001. pap. text. write for info. (*0-443-06583-7*) Harcrt Hlth Sci Grp.

***Larsgaard, Chris.** The Heir Hunter: A Novel of Suspense. LC 99-56185. 356p. 2000. 23.95 (*0-385-33363-3*) Delacorte.

Larsgaard, Mary L. Map Librarianship: An Introduction. 3rd ed. LC 98-15451. (Illus.). 475p. 1998. 68.50 (*1-56308-474-0*) Libs Unl.

— Topographic Mapping of Africa, Antarctica, & Eurasia. LC 92-39327. (Occasional Papers: No. 14). (Illus.). 1992. 45.00 (*0-939112-29-9*) Western Assn Map.

Larsion, Holly, jt. auth. see Hunter, Brenda.

Larson. American Illustration, 1890-1925. 1986. pap. 24.95 (*0-226-28740-8*) U Ch Pr.

— Calculus. 6th ed. (C). 1997. text 97.16 (*0-395-86974-9*); text 97.16 (*0-395-88577-9*) HM.

***Larson.** Calculus , 1. 6th ed. 1999. text 43.17 (*0-618-03388-2*) HM.

— Calculus , 2. 6th ed. 1999. text 22.47 (*0-618-03389-0*) HM.

Larson. Calculus: An Applied Approach. 5th ed. 1998. pap. text 18.57 (*0-395-93345-5*) HM.

— Calculus: An Applied Approach. 5th ed. 1998. pap. text, student ed. 18.57 (*0-395-93344-7*) HM.

— Calculus: Vectors & Value Functions, 6 vols. 6th ed. (C). Date not set. pap. text 11.96 (*0-395-89554-5*) HM.

— Calculus Answer Key, 6 vols. (C). Date not set. pap. 11.96 (*0-395-89551-0*) HM.

***Larson.** College Algebra. 3rd ed. 1999. pap. text 17.07 (*0-395-97625-1*) HM.

Larson. Elementary/Intermediate Algebra. (C). 1997. pap. text 6.76 (*0-669-41852-8*) HM.

— Essential Financial Accounting. 7th ed. 1997. pap., student ed. 28.75 (*0-256-20917-0*) McGraw.

— Essential Intermediate Algebra. 2nd ed. (C). 1997. pap. text 55.16 (*0-395-87616-8*) HM.

Larson. Inspired by the Worlds End. 30.00 (*0-465-03810-7*, Pub. by Basic); pap. 17.00 (*0-465-03811-5*, Pub. by Basic) HarpC.

Larson. Intermediate Algebra, 2 vols. (C). Date not set. pap., teacher ed. write for info. (*0-395-89586-3*) HM.

— Math K: An Incremental Development. (J). (gr. k). 1991. 175.00 (*0-939798-90-5*); teacher ed. 125.00 (*0-939798-84-0*) Saxon Pubs OK.

— Math K: An Incremental Development, Manipulative kit. 1991. 340.00 (*1-56577-001-3*) Saxon Pubs OK.

— Math 1: An Incremental Development. (J). (gr. 1). 1991. 568.00 (*0-939798-26-3*); 465.00 (*0-939798-85-9*); teacher ed. 125.00 (*0-939798-27-1*); student ed. 22.75 (*0-939798-81-6*); 365.00 (*0-939798-68-9*); 468.00 (*0-939798-67-0*); 320.00 (*1-56577-002-1*) Saxon Pubs OK.

— Math 2: An Incremental Development. (J). (gr. 2). 1991. teacher ed. 125.00 (*0-939798-29-8*); student ed. 475.00 (*0-939798-86-7*); student ed. 584.00 (*0-939798-28-X*); student ed. 23.00 (*0-939798-82-4*); 375.00 (*0-939798-69-7*); 484.00 (*0-939798-88-3*); 360.00 (*1-56577-003-X*) Saxon Pubs OK.

— Math 3: An Incremental Development. (J). (gr. 3). 1991. 592.00 (*0-939798-30-1*); 480.00 (*0-939798-87-5*); teacher ed. 125.00 (*0-939798-31-X*); student ed. 23.50 (*0-939798-83-2*); 380.00 (*0-939798-70-0*); 492.00 (*0-939798-89-1*); 265.00 (*1-56577-004-8*) Saxon Pubs OK.

***Larson.** Music Appreciation. (Music Ser.). 2000. 33.00 incl. audio compact disk (*0-534-51634-3*) Wadsworth Pub.

Larson. Los Ovnis y la Agenda de Extraterrestres.Tr. of UFOs & the Alien Agenda. (SPA.). 1997. 9.99 (*0-88113-497-X*, B001-497X) Caribe Betania.

— Persuasion: Reception & Respons. 6th ed. (Speech & Theater Ser.). 1992. mass mkt., teacher ed. write for info. (*0-534-14983-9*) Wadsworth Pub.

— Persuasion: Reception & Responsibility. 7th ed. (Speech & Theater Ser.). 1994. pap., teacher ed. 49.00 (*0-534-23071-7*) Wadsworth Pub.

— Persuasion: Reception & Responsibility. 9th ed. (Speech & Theater Ser.). 2000. 34.75 (*0-534-52285-8*) Wadsworth Pub.

— Principle Study Guide to Fundamental Accounts. 14th ed. 1996. 84.00 (*0-256-23714-X*) McGraw.

— Surgery of the Lumbar Spine. LC 99-22441. (Illus.). 336p. 1999. 139.00 (*0-86577-758-6*) Thieme Med Pubs.

— World of Sports/Fundamental Accounting. 6th ed. 1990. 15.16 (*0-256-08621-4*) McGraw.

***Larson & Ovando.** The Color of Bureacracy. 2000. pap. 32.00 (*0-534-58212-5*) Wadsworth Pub.

Larson & Ponce, eds. Hymnal Companion Two. 1992. 29.95 (*0-87162-622-5*, D4711) Warner Pr.

Larson, et al. Introduction to Sociology: Order & Change in Society. 6th ed. 454p. (C). 1998. per. 42.95 (*0-7872-5233-6*, 41523301) Kendall-Hunt.

— Statistics: A Tool for the Social Sciences. 4th ed. (C). 1987. pap. 38.25 (*0-87150-034-5*, 36G0170) PWS Pubs.

***Larson, et al.** The Weird Western Adventures of Haakon Jones. (Other Door -- Science Fiction -- Macabre Ser.). 1999. text 28.00 (*1-55246-164-5*) Battered Silicon.

Larson, jt. auth. see Dunn, Susan.

Larson, jt. auth. see Pyle, William W.

***Larson, Amanda.** Healing from a Grandmother's Heart: Wisdom & Power to Heal Your Life. LC 00-190629. 120p. 2000. pap. 12.95 (*0-9679575-0-8*) Larson Inst Pr.

Larson, Richard P., et al, eds. The Return of Lake Agassiz: UND & the Flood of 1997. Penwarden, James F., tr. (Illus.). 160p. (Orig.). 1998. pap. 7.00 (*1-880400-00-6*) U NDak Pres.

Larson, A. Karl, ed. see Walker, Charles L.

***Larson, Aaron B.** Dads at a Distance: An Activities Handbook for Strengthening Long Distance Relationships. Larson, Elizabeth A., ed. 28p. 1999. pap. 6.95 (*0-9673599-0-2*) A E Family.

— Moms over Miles: An Activities Handbook for Strengthening Long Distance Relationships. Larson, Elizabeth A., ed. 28p. 1999. pap. 6.95 (*0-9673599-1-0*) A E Family.

Larson, Agnes M. History of the White Pine Industry in Minnesota. LC 72-2875. (Use & Abuse of America's Natural Resources Ser.). (Illus.). 468p. 1972. reprint ed. 35.95 (*0-405-04516-6*) Ayer.

— John A. Johnson: An Uncommon American. 312p. 1969. 15.00 (*0-87732-049-7*) Norwegian-Am Hist Assn.

Larson, Al. Your Electric Life-Science for a New Age: How to Use the Cosmic Internet, Collect Free Energy & Harmonize with Nature. Buckley, Wava, ed. (Illus.). 153p. 1998. pap. 29.95 (*0-9664860-0-5*, YEL) Micromedia.

Larson, Alicia. Stained Glass Anatomy. unabridged ed. 35p. 1992. pap. 9.95 (*1-892700-02-6*) Crystal Images.

— Stained Glass Design Secrets. unabridged ed. (Illus.). iii, 92p. 1991. pap. 12.95 (*1-892700-00-X*) Crystal Images.

— Stained Glass Secrets. 3rd rev. ed. (Illus.). v, 107p. 1990. pap. 12.95 (*1-892700-01-8*) Crystal Images.

Larson, Allan L. The Human Triad: An Introductory Essay on Politics, Society, & Culture. LC 87-30485. xii, 148p. 1988. pap. 12.95 (*0-88280-119-8*) ETC Pubns.

Larson, Andre, et al. Beethoven: Musical Treasures from the Age of Revolution & Romance. (Illus.). 48p. Date not set. pap. 17.95 (*0-9633959-8-X*) Bowers Mus.

Larson, Andrea & Freeman, R. Edward. Women's Studies & Business Ethics: Toward a New Conversation. (The Ruffin Series in Business Ethics). (Illus.). 208p. 1997. text 45.00 (*0-19-510758-6*) OUP.

Larson, Anne M., jt. auth. see Clarkson, Angela G.

Larson, Arthur. A Twentieth-Century Life: The Memoirs of Arthur Larson. LC 97-945. (Illus.). 200p. 1997. 16.95 (*0-931170-63-X*) Ctr Western Studies.

— Workers' Compensation Law. 1992. write for info. (*0-8205-0281-2*, 512); teacher ed. write for info. (*0-8205-0282-0*) Bender.

— Workmen's Compensation: Desk Edition, 3 vols., Set. 1972. ring bd. 650.00 (*0-8205-1347-4*) Bender.

Larson, Arthur & Larson, Lex K. Employment Discrimination, 9 vols. 1975. ring bd. 1260.00 (*0-8205-1626-0*) Bender.

Larson, Arthur, jt. auth. see Larson, Lex K.

Larson, B. Luke. (Mastering the Old & New Testament Ser.: Vol. 3). pap. 14.99 (*0-8499-3319-6*) Word Pub.

Larson, B. C., et al, eds. Characterization of the Structure & Chemistry of Defects in Materials Vol. 138: Materials Research Society Symposium Proceedings. 601p. 1989. text 17.50 (*1-55899-011-9*) Materials Res.

Larson, Barbara. The Prairie Collection Cookbook Centennial Edition. Gonzalez, Helga, ed. (Illus.). 224p. 1988. 17.95 (*0-318-35132-3*) Bismarck Mandan.

Larson, Beverly. New Baby's Bible. (Illus.). 98p. (J). (ps). 1998. bds. 9.99 (*0-7847-0790-1*, 03850) Standard Pub.

— The Whale's Tale: A Little Bible Playbook about Obedience. (Chunky Board Books). (Illus.). 18p. (J). (ps-k). 1999. 4.99 (*0-7847-0927-0*, 03500) Standard Pub.

Larson, Bob. Dead Air: A Novel. 352p. (Orig.). 1996. mass mkt. 5.99 (*0-7852-7526-6*) Nelson.

***Larson, Bob.** Extreme Evil: Kids Killing Kids, Study Guide. (EZ Lesson Plan Ser.). 1999. pap. 7.99 (*0-7852-9702-2*) Tommy Nelson.

Larson, Bob. In the Name of Satan: How the Forces of Evil Work & How You Can Defeat Them. 252p. 1996. pap. 11.99 (*0-7852-7881-8*, J Thoma Bks) Nelson.

— Larson's Book of Rock. 192p. 1987. pap. 7.99 (*0-8423-5687-8*) Tyndale Hse.

— Larson's Book of Spiritual Warfare. LC 98-51360. 504p. 1999. pap. 15.99 (*0-7852-6985-1*) Nelson.

— Larson's New Book of Cults. 499p. 1989. pap. 12.99 (*0-8423-2860-2*) Tyndale Hse.

— Satanism: The Seduction of America's Youth. LC 89-38105. 1989. pap. 10.99 (*0-8407-3034-9*) Nelson.

— The Senator's Agenda. LC 94-49019. 288p. 1995. 16.99 (*0-7852-7879-6*) Nelson.

— Straight Answers on the New Age. 1989. pap. 12.99 (*0-8407-3032-2*) Nelson.

— Sus Hijos y el Rock. (Serie Guia de Bolsillo - Pocket Guides Ser.).Tr. of Your Kids & Rock. (SPA.). 45p. 1990. pap. 2.79 (*0-945792-75-1*, 498047) Editorial Unilit.

— UFOs & the Alien Agenda: Uncovering the Mystery Behind UFOs & the Paranormal. LC 97-20782. 228p. (Orig.). 1997. pap. 12.99 (*0-7852-7182-1*, J Thoma Bks) Nelson.

Larson, Bob, jt. auth. see Gurley, Heather.

Larson, Brooke. Cochabamba, 1550-1900: Colonialism & Agrarian Transformation in Bolivia. LC 97-29926. 1998. write for info. (*0-8223-2061-4*) Duke.

— Cochabamba, 1550-1900: Colonialism & Agrarian Transformation in Bolivia. expanded ed. LC 97-29926. xxvii, 422p. 1998. pap. 19.95 (*0-8223-2088-6*) Duke.

Larson, Brooke, et al, eds. Ethnicity, Markets, & Migration in the Andes: At the Crossroads of History & Anthropology. LC 95-864. (Illus.). 432p. 1995. text 59.95 (*0-8223-1633-1*); pap. text 19.95 (*0-8223-1647-1*) Duke.

Larson, Bruce. Dare to Live Now! 112p. 1987. pap. 5.95 (*0-310-27201-7*, 10002P) Zondervan.

— Luke. (Communicator's Commentary Ser.: Vol. 3). 347p. 22.99 (*0-8499-0156-1*) Word Pub.

— There's a Lot More to Health Than Not Being Sick. 144p. 1991. write for info. (*1-879989-00-X*) New Hope Pub.

Larson, Bruce, jt. auth. see Henson, Sarah.

Larson, Bruce A., jt. ed. see Bluffstone, Randall.

Larson, Bruce C., jt. auth. see Oliver, Chadwick.

Larson, Bruce L., ed. Lactation. (Illus.). 276p. (C). 1985. 42.95 (*0-8138-1063-9*) Iowa St U Pr.

Larson, Bruce R., jt. auth. see Abrahams, Paul W.

Larson, C. F., jt. ed. see Smith, W. Novis.

Larson, C. Kay. Til I Come Marching Home: A Brief History of American Women in World War II. LC 95-81150. (Illus.). (Orig.). 1995. pap. 10.00 (*0-9634895-2-6*) Minerva Ctr.

Larson, C. Lindon, jt. contrib. by see Black, Donald W.

Larson, C. Lyn, jt. auth. see Kraizer, Sherryll.

Larson, C. Philip, Jr., jt. auth. see Cullen, Stuart C.

Larson, Calvin J. Sociological Theory: From the Enlightenment to the Present. LC 86-80124. 247p. (Orig.). 1987. pap. text 22.95 (*0-930390-71-7*); lib. bdg. 38.95 (*0-930390-72-5*) Gen Hall.

Larson, Calvin J. & Garrett, Gerald R. Crime, Justice, & Society. 2nd ed. LC 95-82131. (Illus.). 420p. 1996. text 46.95 (*1-882289-26-9*); pap. text 31.95 (*1-882289-25-0*) Gen Hall.

Larson, Carl E. & LaFasto, Frank M. Teamwork: What Must Go Right - What Can Go Wrong. (Series in Interpersonal Communication). 152p. (C). 1989. text 52.00 (*0-8039-3289-8*); pap. text 23.50 (*0-8039-3290-1*) Sage.

Larson, Carl E., jt. auth. see Chrislip, David D.

Larson, Carl V. Annals of the Mormon Battalion. Shawgo, Bob, ed. (Illus.). 650p. 1994. 75.00 (*0-910523-40-1*) Grandin Bk Co.

Larson, Carol. Forbidden Angel: Dark Romance - Passion in Cajun Country. 108p. 1995. pap. 9.95 (*1-881147-05-3*) Lowell Print.

Larson, Carol A. Sharing Time: A Guide to Quality Kindergarten Enrichment. 64p. 1990. 9.00 (*0-911943-22-6*) Leadership Pub.

Larson, Carole. Forgotten Frontier: The Story of Southeastern New Mexico. LC 93-3631. (Illus.). 316p. 1993. pap. 12.95 (*0-8263-1440-6*) U of NM Pr.

***Larson, Carolyn.** Little Girls Bible Christmas Storybook. 32p. (ps-2). 1999. 7.99 (*0-8010-4431-6*, New Kids Media) Baker Bks.

Larson, Carolyn. Little Girls Book of Prayers. (Illus.). 192p. (ps-2). 1999. 12.99 (*0-8010-4422-7*, New Kids Media) Baker Bks.

Larson, Carolyn, ed. & pref. see Old World Wisconsin Staff.

Larson, Catherine. Language & the Comedia: Theory & Practice. LC 89-46406. 1991. 35.00 (*0-8387-5180-6*) Bucknell U Pr.

***Larson, Catherine & Vargas, Margarita, eds.** Latin American Women Dramatists: Theater, Texts, & Theories. LC 98-34127. 320p. 1998. 39.95 (*0-253-33461-6*); pap. 19.95 (*0-253-21240-5*) Ind U Pr.

Larson, Catherine, tr. see Sotomayor, Maria de Zayas y.

Larson, Catherine A., jt. ed. see Kruger, Betsy.

Larson, Cedric. Who: Sixty Years of American Eminence. (Illus.). 1958. 25.00 (*0-8392-1131-7*) Astor-Honor.

Larson, Cedric, jt. auth. see Mock, James R.

Larson, Charles. Persuasion: Reception & Responsibility. 8th ed. LC 97-18841. (Speech & Theater Ser.). (C). 1997. 56.95 (*0-534-52281-5*) Wadsworth Pub.

Larson, Charles B. Innovative Billing & Collection Methods That Work. LC 94-15855. 192p. 1994. text 50.00 (*1-55623-032-X*, Irwn Prfssnl) McGraw-Hill Prof.

Larson, Charles F., jt. ed. see Smith, W. Novis.

Larson, Charles M. By His Own Hand Upon Papyrus: A New Look at the Joseph Smith Papyri. 240p. (Orig.). 1990. pap. text 11.95 (*0-9620963-2-6*) Inst Rel Rsch.

Larson, Charles R. The Emergence of African Fiction. rev. ed. LC 71-180489. 305p. 1972. 14.00 (*0-253-31945-5*); pap. 7.00 (*0-253-20149-7*) Ind U Pr.

— Invisible Darkness: Jean Toomer & Nella Larsen. LC 93-15637. (Illus.). 255p. 1993. pap. text 16.95 (*0-87745-437-X*) U of Iowa Pr.

— Under African Skies: Modern African Stories. LC 96-48601. 352p. 1997. 25.00 (*0-374-21178-7*) FS&G.

Larson, Charles R., ed. Under African Skies: Modern African Stories. 336p. 1998. pap. 14.00 (*0-374-52550-1*, Noonday) FS&G.

Larson, Charles R., jt. auth. see Rubenstein, Roberta.

Larson, Charles U. Persuasion: Reception & Responsibility. 4th ed. 349p. (C). 1985. pap. write for info. (*0-534-06162-1*) Wadsworth Pub.

— Persuasion: Reception & Responsibility. 5th ed. 434p. (C). 1989. pap. write for info. (*0-534-10134-8*) Wadsworth Pub.

— Persuasion: Reception & Responsibility. 6th ed. 422p. (C). 1991. pap. 32.95 (*0-534-14982-0*) Wadsworth Pub.

— Persuasion: Reception & Responsibility. 7th ed. LC 94-12354. 447p. 1994. mass mkt. 41.95 (*0-534-23070-9*) Wadsworth Pub.

Larson, Charles V. An Illustrated Glossary of Lava Tube Features. (Illus.). 56p. (Orig.). (C). 1993. pap. 9.00 (*1-886168-06-7*) ABC Pubng.

Larson, Charles V. & Larson, Josephine J. Caves of Oregon. (Illus.). 326p. 1996. pap. 25.00 (*1-886168-07-5*) ABC Pubng.

Larson, Charles V., jt. auth. see Halliday, William R.

Larson, Charlie & Larson, Jo. Central Oregon Caves. (Illus.). 44p. (Orig.). (C). 1987. pap. 2.95 (*1-886168-01-6*) ABC Pubng.

— Lava Beds Caves. (Illus.). 56p. (Orig.). (C). 1990. pap. 4.50 (*1-886168-04-0*) ABC Pubng.

— Lava River Caves. (Illus.). 24p. (Orig.). (C). 1987. pap. 1.95 (*1-886168-02-4*) ABC Pubng.

Larson, Cheryl. Low Fat Living Menu Planner: Time Saving Tips to Cook & Look Lean. (Illus.). 1995. 24.95 (*0-9648696-0-8*) Nutrilife.

Larson, Chiles T. Virginia's Past Today. LC 99-161063. (Illus.). 160p. 1998. 45.00 (*1-57427-067-2*) Howell Pr VA.

Larson, Christian D. Brains & How to Get Them. 233p. 1997. pap. 22.00 (*0-89540-382-X*) Sun Pub.

— Business Inspirations. 163p. 1997. pap. 15.00 (*0-89540-399-4*, SB-399) Sun Pub.

— The Great Within. 104p. 1996. reprint ed. pap. 9.95 (*0-87877-237-5*) Newcastle Pub.

— The Hidden Secret. 101p. 1997. pap. 9.00 (*0-89540-404-4*, SB-404) Sun Pub.

— How Great Men Succeed. 82p. 1997. pap. 8.00 (*0-89540-398-6*, SB-398) Sun Pub.

— Ideal Made Real: Applied Metaphysics for Beginners. 1995. pap. 12.95 (*0-87877-228-6*) Newcastle Pub.

— Leave It to God. 1940. pap. 4.50 (*0-87516-191-X*) DeVorss.

— The Ideal Made Real, or Applied Metaphysics for Beginners (1912) 264p. 1998. reprint ed. pap. 19.95 (*0-7661-0348-X*) Kessinger Pub.

— Mastery of Fate. 95p. 1997. pap. 35.00 (*0-89540-383-8*) Sun Pub.

— Mastery of Self. 87p. 1997. pap. 35.00 (*0-89540-384-6*) Sun Pub.

— Nothing Succeeds Like Success. 80p. 1997. pap. 35.00 (*0-89540-385-4*) Sun Pub.

— On the Heights (1908) 75p. 1998. reprint ed. pap. 16.95 (*0-7661-0312-9*) Kessinger Pub.

— The Pathway of Roses: Paths to the Life Beautiful. 368p. 1994. reprint ed. pap. 12.95 (*0-87877-187-5*) Newcastle Pub.

— Perfect Health. 78p. 1997. pap. 8.00 (*0-89540-397-8*, SB-397) Sun Pub.

— Practical Self-Help: or How to Make the Full & Effective Use of the Greatest & Best That Is in You. 223p. 1997. pap. 20.00 (*0-89540-400-1*, SB-400) Sun Pub.

— Thinking for Results. 132p. 1997. pap. 15.00 (*0-89540-381-1*) Sun Pub.

— What Right Thinking Will Do. 50p. 1997. pap. 15.00 (*0-89540-386-2*) Sun Pub.

— Your Forces & How to Use Them. 331p. 1997. pap. 30.00 (*0-89540-380-3*) Sun Pub.

— Your Forces & How to Use Them. 330p. 1998. reprint ed. pap. 24.95 (*0-7661-0183-5*) Kessinger Pub.

Larson, Colleen L. & Preskill, Hallie, eds. Organizations in Transition: Opportunities & Challenges for Evaluation. LC 85-644749. (New Directions for Evaluation Ser.: No. PE 49). 1991. pap. 22.00 (*1-55542-795-2*) Jossey-Bass.

Larson, Connie, jt. auth. see Eichelberger, Barbara.

Larson, Constant. History of Douglas & Grant Counties, Minnesota, Vol. 1. (Illus.). 509p. 1994. reprint ed. lib. bdg. 52.50 (*0-8328-3840-3*) Higginson Bk Co.

— History of Douglas & Grant Counties, Minnesota, Vol. 2. (Illus.). 693p. 1994. reprint ed. lib. bdg. 69.50 (*0-8328-3841-1*) Higginson Bk Co.

Larson, Craig B. Choice Contemporary Stories & Illustrations: For Preachers, Teachers, & Writers. (Illus.). 304p. 1998. 18.99 (*0-8010-9064-4*) Baker Bks.

— Pastoral Grit: The Strength to Stand & to Stay. Goetz, David L., ed. LC 97-45441. (Pastor's Soul Ser.). 176p. 1998. text 16.99 (*1-55661-969-3*) Bethany Hse.

Larson, Craig Brian. Contemporary Illustrations for Preachers, Teachers & Writers. LC 96-6790. 320p. 1996. 14.99 (*0-8010-9020-2*) Baker Bks.

— Hang in There...to the Better End. (Illus.). 192p. (YA). (gr. 10). 1996. mass mkt. 5.99 (*0-8007-8635-1*, Spire) Revell.

***Larson, Craig Brian.** Illustrations for Preaching & Teaching: From Leadership Journal. 288p. 1999. pap. 12.99 (*0-8010-5950-X*) Baker Bks.

***Larson, Craig Brian, ed.** Choice Contemporary Stories & Illustrations: For Preachers, Teachers & Writers. 320p. (gr. 13 up). 2000. pap. 14.99 (*0-8010-6332-9*) Baker Bks.

— Contemporary Illustrations for Preachers, Teachers, & Writers. 320p. (gr. 13 up). 2000. pap. 14.99 (*0-8010-6333-7*) Baker Bks.

Larson, D. H. & Fejer, M. Improving Glass Melting Furnace Operation Using Improved Combustion Control Methods. 66p. 1973. pap. 6.00 (*0-318-12639-7*, L10373) Am Gas Assn.

Larson, Dale G. The Helper's Journey: Working with People Facing Grief, Loss & Life-Threatening Illness. LC 93-84096. 292p. (Orig.). 1993. pap. text 17.95 (*0-87822-344-X*, 4668) Res Press.

Larson, Dale L. Connect Your Amiga! A Guide to the Internet, LANs, BBSs & Online Services. rev. ed. 256p. 1996. reprint ed. pap. 9.95 (*1-885876-02-5*) Intangible Assets.

Larson, Dale L., ed. see Mohanraj, Mary A.

Larson, Dale L., ed. see Siegel, Jules & Wexler, Virginia C.

Larson, Dana & Lowehndorf, Dan. Pot Puzzle Fun Book. (Illus.). 64p. 2000. pap. 12.95 (*0-932551-34-3*) Quick Am Pub.

***Larson, Darlene.** Library Explorations: Activities for International Students. (Illus.). 144p. (C). 2000. pap. text 16.95 (*0-472-08641-3*, 08641) U of Mich Pr.

Larson, David. Crosscountry Skier's Log. (Illus.). 72p. (Orig.). 1984. pap., spiral bd. 3.00 (*0-9613928-0-0*) Larson Joliet.

Larson, David, jt. auth. see Galuppi, Baldassare.

Larson, David E. (revised) Mayo Clinic Family Health Book. 2nd rev. ed. LC 96-23661. (Illus.). 1456p. 1996. 42.50 (*0-688-14478-0*, Wm Morrow) Morrow Avon.

Larson, David L. Security Issues & the Law of the Sea. LC 93-20257. 396p. (C). 1994. lib. bdg. 55.00 (*0-8191-9089-6*) U Pr of Amer.

Larson, David R., ed. Abortion: Ethical Issues & Options. LC 92-28584. (C). 1992. pap. 9.95 (*1-881127-00-1*) LLU Ctr Christ Bio.

Larson, David R., jt. auth. see Dai, Xingde.

Larson, David R., jt. auth. see Han, Deguang.

Larson, David Royal, ed. see AMS Special Session on the Functional & Harmonic Analysis of Wavelets Staff, et al.

***Larson, Deborah & Shevchenko, Alexei V.** Explaining Gorbachev's New Thinking: The Role of Economic Status Incentives. (New Ser.: Vol. 20). 41p. 1999. pap. 15.00 (*0-86682-106-6*) Ctr Intl Relations.

Larson, Deborah A. John Donne & Twentieth-Century Criticism. LC 87-46423. 208p. 1989. 36.50 (*0-8386-3338-2*) Fairleigh Dickinson.

Larson, Deborah W. Anatomy of Mistrust: U. S. - Soviet Relations During the Cold War. LC 96-49153. (Cornell Studies in Security Affairs). 320p. 1996. text 37.50 (*0-8014-3302-9*) Cornell U Pr.

— Negotiation the Austrian State Treaty, 1953-1955. (Pew Case Studies in International Affairs). 50p. (C). 1995. pap. text 3.50 (*1-56927-432-0*) Geo U Inst Dplmcy.

— Origins of Containment: A Psychological Explanation. LC 85-42691. 420p. 1985. pap. text 20.95 (*0-691-02303-4*, Pub. by Princeton U Pr) Cal Prin Full Svc.

***Larson, Deborah Welch.** Anatomy of Mistrust: U. S.-Soviet Relations During the Cold War. 2000. reprint ed. pap. 18.95 (*0-8014-8682-3*) Cornell U Pr.

Larson, Don W. Medical Cost Crisis! A Common-Sense Solution. 240p. 1993. 24.00 (*0-9635576-0-2*) Bond Pub MN.

Larson, Donald N. & Smalley, William A. Becoming Bilingual: A Guide to Language Learning. LC 84-15383. 450p. 1984. reprint ed. pap. text 34.00 (*0-8191-4246-8*) U Pr of Amer.

Larson, Donald R. The Honor Plays of Lope De Vega. 272p. 1978. 31.00 (*0-674-40628-1*) HUP.

Larson, Donald W., et al, eds. Structural Change & Performance of the U.S. Grain Marketing System. LC 98-61153. xiv, 305 p. 1998. write for info. (*0-9647738-4-8*) Scherer Communs.

Larson, Doran. Marginalia. 176p. 1997. 22.00 (*1-877946-90-7*) Permanent Pr.

Larson, Dorothy W. Bright Shadows. LC 92-81679. (Illus.). 96p. (J). (gr. 4-6). 1992. 14.95 (*0-9621779-0-3*) Sandstone Pub.

— Shadows. 50p. 1997. pap. 7.50 (*0-9621779-1-1*) Sandstone Pub.

***Larson, Douglas W., et al.** Cliff Ecology: Pattern & Process in Cliff Ecosystems. LC 99-12175. (Cambridge Studies in Ecology). (Illus.). 320p. (C). 2000. 69.95 (*0-521-55489-6*) Cambridge U Pr.

Larson, Duane H. Times of the Trinity: A Proposal for Theistic Cosmology. LC 94-37760. (Worcester Polytechnic Institute Studies in Science, Technology & Culture: Vol. 17). IX, 214p. (C). 1995. 45.95 (*0-8204-2706-3*) P Lang Pubng.

***Larson, Edward C.** Gaff-Rigged Remembrance: Writings from the Santa Cruz Harbor. LC 00-91095. (Illus.). 117p. 2000. pap. 16.95 (*0-9654376-1-2*) E Larson.

Larson, Edward C. Spring Tides: Memories of Alaskan Towboats. LC 96-94798. (Illus.). 130p. (Orig.). 1996. pap. 14.95 (*0-9654376-0-4*) E Larson.

Larson, Edward J. Sex, Race, & Science: Eugenics in the Deep South. 264p. 1996. reprint ed. pap. text 14.95 (*0-8018-5511-X*) Johns Hopkins.

Larson, Edward J. Summer for the Gods: The Scopes Trial & America's Continuing Debate over Science & Religion. LC 97-9648. 336p. 1997. 25.00 (*0-465-07509-6*, Pub. by Basic) HarpC.

Larson, Edward J. Summer for the Gods: The Scopes Trial & America's Continuing Debate over Science & Religion. LC 97-9648. (Illus.). 336p. 1998. pap. 14.95 (*0-674-85429-2*) HUP.

Larson, Edward J. & Amundsen, Darrel W. A Different Death: Euthanasia & the Christian Tradition. LC 98-9544. 288p. 1998. pap. 14.99 (*0-8308-1518-X*, 1518) InterVarsity.

Larson, Edwin E., jt. auth. see Birkeland, Peter W.

Larson, Elizabeth A., ed. see Larson, Aaron B.

Larson, Ellen. The Hatch & Brood of Time. LC 99-60140. 300p. 1999. pap. 14.95 (*0-9669877-0-5*) Savvy Pr.

Larson, Elsa, ed. see Dale, Bill.

Larson, Elsie. Bombus Creativity Book. LC 98-66647. 40p. (J). 1998. pap. 4.99 (*0-89051-241-8*) Master Bks.

— Bombus Finds a Friend. LC 98-66307. (Illus.). 40p. (J). 1998. boxed set 10.99 (*0-89051-231-0*) Master Bks.

— Bombus the Bumblebee: Created, Just Like You & Me. LC 97-70169. (Illus.). 40p. (J). 1997. boxed set 11.99 (*0-89051-177-2*) Master Bks.

Larson, Elsie J. Dawn's Early Light. LC 95-24380. (Tides of War Ser.: Bk. 1). 240p. 1996. pap. 10.99 (*0-7852-7688-2*) Nelson.

— Strength for the Journey: Daily Encouragement for Caregivers. LC 99-19006. 222p. 1999. pap. 12.99 (*0-87788-790-X*, H Shaw Pubs) Waterbrook Pr.

***Larson, Elyse.** For Such a Time. (Women of Valor Ser.). 352p. 2000. pap. 10.99 (*0-7642-2355-0*) Bethany Hse.

Larson, Emil L. One-Room & Consolidated Schools of Connecticut: A Comparative Study of Teachers, Costs & Holding Power. LC 78-176976. (Columbia University. Teachers College. Contributions to Education Ser.: No. 182). reprint ed. 37.50 (*0-404-55182-3*) AMS Pr.

***Larson, Eric & Stephenson, Brian.** Administering Web Servers, Security & Maintenance: Interactive Workbook. LC 99-57681. (Interactive Workbook Ser.). 592p. 1999. pap., wbk. ed. 40.00 (*0-13-022534-7*) P-H.

— The Complete Web Site Administration Interactive Training Course. 2000. 37.00 (*0-13-089456-7*) P-H.

— The Complete Web Site Administration Training Course. 2000. student ed. 78.00 (*0-13-089457-5*) P-H.

— The Complete Web Site Administration Training Course. 2000. pap. 109.99 (*0-13-089437-0*) P-H.

Larson, Eric, jt. auth. see Kantor, Herman I.

Larson, Eric B. & Lilies, W. Conrad, Jr. Manual of Admitting Orders & Therapeutics. 3rd ed. LC 93-26134. 1994. pap. text 31.95 (*0-7216-5268-9*, W B Saunders Co) Harcrt Hlth Sci Grp.

Larson, Eric B. & Ramsey, Paul G. Medical Therapeutics: A Pocket Companion. 3rd ed. Kersey, Ray, ed. (Illus.). 720p. 1997. pap. text 29.95 (*0-7216-5126-7*, W B Saunders Co) Harcrt Hlth Sci Grp.

Larson, Eric M. Immigration Statistics: Information Gaps, Quality Issues Limit Utility of Federal Data to Policymakers. (Illus.). 87p. (C). 1999. text 20.00 (*0-7881-7733-8*) DIANE Pub.

— Variations of the Smooth Bore H & R Handy-Gun: A Pocket Guide to Their Identification. LC 93-91518. (Illus.). 64p. (Orig.). 1993. pap. 10.00 (*0-9636465-0-8*) E M Larson.

Larson, Eric V. Casualties & Consensus: The Historical Role of Casualties in Domestic Support for U. S. Military Operations. LC 96-19852. 130p. 1996. pap. text 15.00 (*0-8330-2370-5*, MR-726-RC) Rand Corp.

Larson, Eric V. & Kent, Glenn A. A New Methodology for Assessing Multi-Layer Missile Defense Options. LC 94-32983. 1994. pap. 13.00 (*0-8330-1579-6*, MR-390-AF) Rand Corp.

Larson, Eric V. & Palmer, Adele R. The Decisionmaking Context in the Department of the Navy: A Primer for Cost Analysts. LC 93-48871. 189p. 1995. pap. text 15.00 (*0-8330-1502-8*, MR-255-PA&E) Rand Corp.

Larson, Eric V., jt. auth. see Palmer, Adele R.

Larson, Erik. Isaac's Storm: A Man, a Time & the Deadliest Hurricane in History. LC 99-25515. 323p. 1999. 25.00 (*0-609-60233-0*, Crown) Crown Pub Group.

***Larson, Erik.** Isaac's Storm: A Man, a Time & the Deadliest Hurricane in History. 336p. 2000. pap. 13.00 (*0-375-70827-8*) Vin Bks.

Larson, Erik. Lethal Passage. 1995. 22.95 (*0-8050-2531-6*) H Holt & Co.

— Lethal Passage: The Journey of a Gun. LC 97-189011. 1995. pap. 12.00 (*0-679-75927-1*) Vin Bks.

— Savage Dragon: A Force to Be Reckoned With. (Illus.). 160p. (YA). 1996. pap. 14.95 (*1-887279-12-1*, Pub. by Image Comics) Midpt Trade.

— Savage Dragon: Force to Be Reckoned With. (Illus.). 160p. (Orig.). (YA). 1996. 39.95 (*1-887279-13-X*) Image Comics.

***Larson, Erik & Cline, Isaac Monroe.** Isaac's Storm: A Man, a Time & the Deadliest Hurricane in History. LC 99-55835. 2000. pap. write for info. (*0-7838-8933-X*, G K Hall & Co) Mac Lib Ref.

— Isaac's Storm: A Man, a Time, & the Deadliest Hurricane in History. LC 99-55835. 2000. 30.95 (*0-7838-8932-1*, G K Hall & Co) Mac Lib Ref.

Larson, Erik W. The Translation of Enoch: From Aramaic into Greek. (Study of Judaism Ser.: No. 53). (Illus.). 376p. 1998. 124.50 (*90-04-10690-1*) Brill Academic Pubs.

Larson, Esther E. Swedish Commentators on America: Sixteen Thirty-Eight to Eighteen Sixty-Five. Scott, Franklyn D., ed. LC 78-15194. (Scandinavians in America Ser.). 1979. reprint ed. lib. bdg. 17.95 (*0-405-11647-0*) Ayer.

Larson, Eugene A. Gene's Great Grub & Gourmet Goodies for Gratifying Gastronomy. large type ed. Hamilton, James B. & Larson, Jessie M., eds. LC 97-93119. 175p. 1999. spiral bd. 29.95 (*0-9660961-0-X*) Select Merch.

Larson, Frank. Jackpine Savages: Skinny-Dipping for Fun & Profit. LC 96-92669. 172p. (Orig.). 1997. pap. 9.95 (*0-9654917-2-2*) Placer Pr.

Larson-Freeman, Diane. Introduction to Second Language Acquisition Research. (C). 1989. pap. text 35.64 (*0-582-55377-6*, Pub. by Addison-Wesley) Longman.

Larson, G. J. Classical Sankhya. 1979. 18.50 (*0-89684-058-1*, Pub. by Motilal Bnarsidass) S Asia.

Larson, G. J. & Bhattacharya, R. S. Encyclopaedia of Indian Philosophies, Ea., Vols. 1-4. 1987. 44.95 (*81-208-0311-6*) Asia Bk Corp.

Larson, Gale K., ed. see Shaw, George Bernard.

Larson, Gary. Beyond the Far Side. (Illus.). 104p. (Orig.). 1983. pap. text 7.95 (*0-8362-1149-9*) Andrews & McMeel.

— Bride of the Far Side. (Illus.). 104p. (Orig.). 1985. pap. 7.95 (*0-8362-2066-8*) Andrews & McMeel.

— The Chickens Are Restless. (Illus.). 112p. (Orig.). 1993. pap. 8.95 (*0-8362-1717-9*) Andrews & McMeel.

— Cows of Our Planet: A Far Side Collection. (Illus.). 112p. (Orig.). 1992. pap. 8.95 (*0-8362-1701-2*) Andrews & McMeel.

— Curse of Madame C: A Far Side Collection. (Illus.). 112p. 1994. pap. 8.95 (*0-8362-1763-2*) Andrews & McMeel.

— The Far Side. LC 82-72418. (Illus.). 104p. (Orig.). 1982. pap. 7.95 (*0-8362-1200-2*) Andrews & McMeel.

Larson, Gary. The Far Side Gallery. (Illus.). 192p. (Orig.). 1984. pap. 12.95 (*0-8362-2062-5*) Andrews & McMeel.

Larson, Gary. Far Side Gallery 4. (Illus.). 172p. 1993. 19.95 (*0-8362-1726-8*) Andrews & McMeel.

— The Far Side Gallery 4. LC 93-71009. (Illus.). 167p. 1993. pap. 12.95 (*0-8362-1724-1*) Andrews & McMeel.

— Far Side Gallery 2. (Illus.). 192p. (Orig.). 1986. pap. 12.95 (*0-8362-2085-4*) Andrews & McMeel.

L

An Asterisk (*) at the beginning of an entry indicates that the title is appearing for the first time.

— Far Side Gallery 3. (Illus.). 192p. 1988. 19.95 (*0-8362-1810-8*); pap. 12.95 (*0-8362-1831-0*) Andrews & McMeel.

— Far Side Gallery 5. (Illus.). 160p. 1995. 19.95 (*0-8362-0426-3*); pap. 12.95 (*0-8362-0425-5*) Andrews & McMeel.

— The Far Side Observer. (Illus.). 104p. (Orig.). 1987. pap. 7.95 (*0-8362-2098-6*) Andrews & McMeel.

— Hound of the Far Side. (Illus.). 104p. (Orig.). 1987. pap. 7.95 (*0-8362-2087-0*) Andrews & McMeel.

— In Search of the Far Side. (Illus.). 104p. (Orig.). 1984. pap. 7.95 (*0-8362-2060-9*) Andrews & McMeel.

— It Came from the Far Side. (Illus.). 104p. 1985. pap. 7.95 (*0-8362-2073-0*) Andrews & McMeel.

— Last Chapter & Worse. LC 96-83997. (Far Side Collection). (Illus.). 96p. (Orig.). 1996. pap. 9.95 (*0-8362-2131-1*) Andrews & McMeel.

— Night of the Crash-Test Dummies. (Illus.). 104p. 1988. pap. 7.95 (*0-8362-2049-8*) Andrews & McMeel.

— PreHistory of the Far Side: A Tenth Anniversary Exhibit. (Illus.). 288p. 1989. pap. 12.95 (*0-8362-1851-5*) Andrews & McMeel.

— Prehistory of the Far Side: A Tenth Anniversary Exhibit. (Illus.). 288p. 1989. 19.95 (*0-8362-1861-2*) Andrews & McMeel.

— There's a Hair in My Dirt! A Worm's Story. LC 98-11779. (Illus.). 64p. 1998. 15.95 (*0-06-019104-X*) HarpC.

***Larson, Gary.** There's a Hair in My Dirt! A Worm's Story. LC 98-11779. (Illus.). 64p. (J). 1999. pap. 9.95 (*0-06-093274-0*) HarpC Child Bks.

Larson, Gary. Unnatural Selections: A Far Side Collection. (Illus.). 112p. (Orig.). 1991. pap. 8.95 (*0-8362-1881-7*) Andrews & McMeel.

— Valley of the Far Side. (Illus.). 104p. (Orig.). 1985. pap. 6.95 (*0-8362-2067-6*) Andrews & McMeel.

— Wiener Dog Art: A Far Side Collection. (Illus.). 112p. 1990. pap. 7.95 (*0-8362-1865-5*) Andrews & McMeel.

— Wildlife Preserves: A Far Side Collection. (Illus.). 104p. (Orig.). 1989. pap. 7.95 (*0-8362-1842-6*) Andrews & McMeel.

***Larson, Gary E. & Johnson, James R.** Plants of the Black Hills & Bear Lodge Mountains. 608p. 1999. pap. 37.95 (*0-913062-05-7*) SD Agriculture.

Larson, Gary E., jt. auth. see Johnson, James R.

Larson, Gary L., et al, eds. Crater Lake: An Ecosystem Study. LC 89-63688. (Illus.). 221p. 1991. 27.95 (*0-934394-07-5*) AAASPD.

Larson, Gene & Snyder, Jeffrey B. Power Carving Birds, Fish & Penguins: Using Beautiful Hardwoods. LC 93-87058. (Illus.). 64p. (Orig.). 1994. pap. 12.95 (*0-88740-565-7*) Schiffer.

Larson, Geoff, jt. auth. see Daniels, Ray.

Larson, George A. & Pridmore, Jay. Chicago Architecture & Design. LC 93-18306. (Illus.). 256p. 1993. 49.50 (*0-8109-3192-3*, Pub. by Abrams) Time Warner.

Larson, Georgianna, ed. Managing the School Age Child with a Chronic Health Condition: A Practical Guide for Schools, Families & Organizations. (Illus.). 335p. 1988. pap. text 29.95 (*0-9624814-3-2*) Sunrise River Pr.

Larson, Gerald J. India's Agony over Religion. LC 94-18318. (SUNY Series in Religious Studies). 393p. (C). 1995. pap. text 23.95 (*0-7914-2412-X*) State U NY Pr.

Larson, Gerald J., et al, eds. Myth in Indo-European Antiquity. LC 72-93522. (Publications of the UCSR Institute of Religious Studies). 205p. reprint ed. pap. 63.60 (*0-608-18008-4*, 202904900058) Bks Demand.

Larson, Gerald J. & Bhattacharya, Ram S., eds. Samkhya: A Dualist Tradition in Indian Philosophy. LC 87-16892. (Encyclopedia of Indian Philosophy Ser.: No. 4). 689p. reprint ed. pap. 200.00 (*0-608-07151-X*, 206737600009) Bks Demand.

Larson, Gerald J. & Deutsch, Eliot, eds. Interpreting Across Boundaries: New Essays in Comparative Philosophy. LC 87-20611. 327p. reprint ed. pap. 101.40 (*0-608-06397-5*, 206675800008) Bks Demand.

Larson, Gerald L., ed. Advances in Silicon Chemistry, Vol. 1. 387p. 1991. 109.50 (*1-55938-176-0*) Jai Pr.

— Advances in Silicon Chemistry, Vol. 2. 195p. 1993. 109.50 (*1-55938-177-9*) Jai Pr.

— Advances in Silicon Chemistry, Vol. 3. 1996. 109.50 (*1-55938-831-5*) Jai Pr.

— Advances in Silicon Chemistry, Vol. 4. Date not set. 109.50 (*0-7623-0349-2*) Jai Pr.

Larson, Gloria, ed. Alaska My State. (Illus.). 39p. (J). (gr. 3-7). 1990. pap. 7.95 (*1-878051-11-3*) Circumpolar Pr.

Larson, Gregory W. & Shakespeare, Robert A. Rendering with Radiance. LC 98-12223. 600p. 1998. pap. text 79.95 (*1-55860-499-5*) Morgan Kaufmann.

Larson, H. M., jt. auth. see Gras, N. S.

Larson, Hal. If He Loves Me, Why Doesn't He Tell Me? LC 93-24300. 128p. 1994. pap. 12.95 (*1-879904-11-X*) Halo Bks.

— This Isn't Exactly What I Had in Mind, God: How to Get Your Life Back on Course. LC 97-3947. (Illus.). 228p. (Orig.). 1996. pap. 14.95 (*1-879904-17-9*) Halo Bks.

Larson, Hal & Larson, Susan. Suddenly Single! A Lifeline for Anyone Who Has Lost a Love. 2nd ed. LC 92-34631. 240p. (Orig.). 1993. pap. 15.95 (*1-879904-09-8*) Halo Bks.

Larson, Harold J. Introduction to Probability. (Illus.). 371p. (C). 1994. 97.00 (*0-201-51286-6*) Addison-Wesley.

Larson, Harold J. Introduction to Probability Theory & Statistical Inference. 3rd ed. LC 81-16246. 656p. (C). 1982. text 97.95 (*0-471-05909-9*) Wiley.

Larson, Harold J. & Shubert, Bruno O. Probabilistic Models in Engineering Science: Random Noise, Signals & Dynamic Systems. LC 89-2828. 750p. (C). 1989. reprint ed. lib. bdg. 82.50 (*0-89464-373-8*) Krieger.

***Larson, Harold V.** Bombs Away! A History of the 70th Bombardment Squadron (M) in Early World War II. unabridged ed. (Illus.). 174p. 1998. pap. 15.00 (*0-9668307-0-9*) SeaCliff Pr.

Larson, Helen. Kia Kayanguqau?Tr. of Whose Egg is This?. (ESK., Illus.). 8p. (J). (gr. k-3). 1998. pap. text 6.00 (*1-58084-040-X*) Lower Kuskokwim.

Larson, Helen, jt. auth. see Wassillie, Irene.

Larson, Helen C. Bird's Life. large type ed. (Illus.). 8p. (J). (gr. k-3). 1999. pap. text 14.50 (*1-58084-086-8*) Lower Kuskokwim.

— Tengmiam Cullra (Bird's Life) large type ed. (ESK., Illus.). 8p. (J). (gr. k-3). 1999. pap. text 14.50 (*1-58084-147-3*) Lower Kuskokwim.

— Yaqulgem Angliurallra (Bird's Life) large type ed. (ESK., Illus.). 8p. (J). (gr. k-3). 1999. pap. text 14.95 (*1-58084-087-6*) Lower Kuskokwim.

Larson, Henrietta M. Wheat Market & the Farmer in Minnesota, 1858-1900. LC 70-82232. (Columbia University. Studies in the Social Sciences: No. 269). reprint ed. 29.50 (*0-404-51269-0*) AMS Pr.

Larson, Henrietta M. & Porter, Kenneth W. History of Humble Oil & Refining Company: A Study in Industrial Growth. LC 75-41768. (Companies & Men: Business Enterprises in America Ser.). (Illus.). 1976. reprint ed. 82.95 (*0-405-08083-2*) Ayer.

***Larson, Ingrid Dana.** Herman & Hurby. (Illus.). 74p. 2000. pap. write for info. (*0-7541-0964-X*, Pub. by Minerva Pr) Unity Dist.

Larson, J. & Unger, C., eds. Engineering for Human-Computer Interaction: Proceedings of the Working Conference on Engineering for Human-Computer Interaction, Ellivuori, Finland, 10-14 August 1992. LC 92-40525. (IFIP Transactions A: Computer Science & Technology Ser.: Vol. A-18). 424p. 1992. 143.25 (*0-444-89904-9*, North Holland) Elsevier.

Larson, Jack L., jt. auth. see DeBruyn, Robert L.

Larson, James. Television's Window on the World: International Affairs Coverage on the U. S. Networks. Voigt, Melvin J., ed. LC 84-15859. (Communication & Information Science Ser.). 224p. 1984. pap. 39.50 (*0-89391-312-X*); text 73.25 (*0-89391-142-9*) Ablx Pub.

Larson, James, jt. tr. see Nathan, Leonard.

Larson, James A. Database Directions: Beyond Relational Introduction to Distributed Multimedia & Object. 288p. 1995. pap. 52.00 (*0-13-290867-0*) P-H.

— Treasury Auction Results As Interest Rate Predictors. rev. ed. LC 93-41567. (Financial Sector of the American Economy Ser.). 152p. 1994. text 15.00 (*0-8153-1682-8*) Garland.

Larson, James F. Global Television & Foreign Policy. LC 87-72369. (Headline Ser.: No. 283). (Illus.). 72p. (Orig.). 1988. pap. 5.95 (*0-87124-117-X*) Foreign Policy.

— The Telecommunications Revolution in Korea. (Illus.). 356p. 1995. text 59.00 (*0-19-586785-8*) OUP.

Larson, James L. Interpreting Nature: The Science of Living Form from Linnaeus to Kant. LC 94-2904. 256p. 1994. text 40.00 (*0-8018-4840-7*) Johns Hopkins.

Larson, James S. The Measurement of Health: Concepts & Indicators, 31. LC 90-44840. (Contributions in Medical Studies: No. 31). 192p. 1991. 52.95 (*0-313-27339-1*, LMH, Greenwood Pr) Greenwood.

— Why Government Programs Fail: Improving Policy Implementation. LC 79-26917. 124p. 1980. 45.00 (*0-275-90511-X*, C0511, Praeger Pubs) Greenwood.

Larson, Jane, jt. auth. see Hirshman, Linda.

Larson, Jane E., jt. auth. see Hirshman, Linda R.

Larson, Janet E. The Versatile Border Collie. 2nd ed. LC 98-37873. 288p. 1998. 39.95 (*0-931866-92-8*) Alpine Pubns.

Larson, Jay L. Earth Data & New Weapons. (Illus.). 133p. (Orig.). (C). 1994. pap. text 40.00 (*0-7881-1214-7*) DIANE Pub.

Larson, Jean A., ed. BST - Bovine Growth Hormone: Bibliography January 1991-December 1993. 98p. (Orig.). (C). 1995. pap. text 20.00 (*0-7881-2304-1*) DIANE Pub.

Larson, Jean A., jt. ed. see Smith, Cynthia P.

Larson, Jean Ann. Healthcare Redesign Tools & Techniques. LC 96-52973. 1997. 42.50 (*0-527-76322-5*) Productivity Inc.

Larson, Jean L., jt. auth. see Fontana, Marjorie A.

Larson, Jean R. The Fish Bride & Other Gypsy Tales. (Illus.). 128p. (YA). (gr. 5-12). 2000. 22.50 (*0-208-02474-3*, Linnet Bks) Shoe String.

Larson, Jeanette & Totten, Herman L. Model Policies for Small & Medium Public Libraries. LC 98-7917. 214p. 1998. pap. 40.00 (*1-55570-343-7*) Neal-Schuman.

***Larson, Jeffry H.** Should We Stay Together? The Compatibility Test. LC 99-50745. 2000. pap. 25.00 (*0-7879-5144-7*) Jossey-Bass.

Larson, Jenniece, jt. auth. see Baumgart, Alice J.

Larson, Jennifer. Greek Heroine Cults. LC 94-11044. (Wisconsin Studies in Classics). 1995. 37.00 (*0-299-14370-8*); pap. 18.95 (*0-299-14374-0*) U of Wis Pr.

Larson, Jennifer, jt. auth. see Goldstein, Margaret J.

Larson, Jennifer L. Greek Heroine Cults. LC 94-11044. (Wisconsin Studies in Classics). (Illus.). 255p. 1985. reprint ed. pap. 79.10 (*0-608-07452-7*, 206767900009) Bks Demand.

Larson, Jerry W., jt. auth. see Wilkins, Ernest J.

Larson, Jessie M., ed. see Larson, Eugene A.

Larson, Jim & Feldmeth, Joanne R. Your Spiritual Gifts Can Help Your Church Grow. 64p. 1985. pap. 3.95 (*0-8307-1008-6*, 6101951, Regal Bks) Gospel Lght.

Larson, Jo, jt. auth. see Larson, Charlie.

Larson, Joan. 2030 the Beginning. 1350p. 1997. 29.95 (*0-9661762-0-0*) Chislev.

Larson, Joan Mathews. Seven Weeks to Emotional Healing: Proven Natural Formulas for Eliminating Anxiety, Depression, Anger, & Fatigue from Your Life. LC 99-12489. 400p. 1999. 24.00 (*0-345-43686-5*) Ballantine Pub Grp.

Larson, Jody B., ed. see Vallangca, Caridad C.

Larson, John. How to Train a Guard Dog. LC 86-81033. (Illus.). 112p. (Orig.). 1987. pap. 10.00 (*0-918751-05-5*, 02) Delta Pr.

Larson, John & Rodriguez, Carol. Road Rage to Road-Wise. 1999. 71.70 (*0-312-89080-X*) Forge NYC.

— Road Rage to Road-Wise. 2nd ed. LC 99-21887. 1999. pap. 11.95 (*0-312-89058-3*, Pub. by Forge NYC) St Martin.

Larson, John, jt. auth. see Cooper, Martin.

Larson, John A. Steering Clear of Highway Madness: A Driver's Guide to Curbing Stress & Strain. LC 96-83183. (Illus.). 176p. (Orig.). 1996. pap. 14.95 (*1-885221-38-X*) BookPartners.

Larson, John A., et al. Lying & Its Detection: A Study of Deception & Deception Tests. LC 69-16241. (Criminology, Law Enforcement, & Social Problems Ser.: No. 78). 1969. reprint ed. 30.00 (*0-87585-078-2*) Patterson Smith.

Larson, John A., jt. auth. see Northrup, Herbert R.

Larson, John A., jt. ed. see Teeter, Emily.

Larson, John C., jt. auth. see Fleming, Jeff.

Larson, John L. Bonds of Enterprise: John Murray Forbes & Western Development in America's Railway Age. 1984. text 30.00 (*0-07-103279-7*) McGraw.

Larson, John L., ed. see Trollope, Frances M.

Larson, John W. South Dakota Evidence. 973p. 1991. 95.00 (*0-87473-748-6*, 64235-10, MICHIE) LEXIS Pub.

— South Dakota Evidence: 1998 Cumulative Supplement. 550p. 1998. pap., suppl. ed. write for info. (*0-327-00358-8*, 6423616) LEXIS Pub.

Larson, Jonathan. Rent. Giel, Kate, ed. LC 97-1171. (Illus.). 160p. 1997. 38.00 (*0-688-15437-9*, Wm Morrow) Morrow Avon.

Larson, Josephine J., jt. auth. see Larson, Charles V.

Larson, Joyce E., ed. New Foundations for Asian & Pacific Security. 330p. (C). 1980. text 39.95 (*0-87855-413-0*); pap. text 24.95 (*0-87855-845-4*) Transaction Pubs.

Larson, Judith, jt. auth. see Nolen-Hoeksema, Susan.

Larson, Judy L., et al. American Paintings at the High Museum of Art. LC 94-13850. (Illus.). 220p. 1994. 50.00 (*1-55595-094-9*) Hudson Hills.

Larson, Juliana. Water Dance: Water Fitness for Mind, Body & Soul. 1999. pap. text 14.95 (*1-879706-79-2*) Paper Chase.

Larson, Julie. Whatever You Do, Don't Go near That Canoe! (Illus.). 32p. 1996. write for info. (*0-590-24429-9*) Andrews & McMeel.

Larson, K. Oscar & American Occupational Therapy Association Staff. Rote: The/Role of Ot with the Elderly. 2nd ed. LC 97-118173. 930 p. 1996. 61.00 (*1-56900-054-9*) Am Occup Therapy.

***Larson, Karen.** Formula for Success: Business Leader's Guide to Supporting Math & Science Achievement. 32p. 1998. pap. 3.50 (*0-16-063658-2*) USGPO.

Larson, Karl, ed. see Elizabeth, Ann.

Larson, Katharine M., ed. see Walker, Charles L.

Larson, Kathy. 77 Secrets to Leadership Success. unabridged ed. Adams, Milton, ed. (Illus.). 168p. 1997. pap. 7.95 (*1-890676-06-3*) Beavers Pond.

Larson, Kay. Jennifer Bartlett. LC 98-87552. 46p. 1998. pap. 20.00 (*1-879173-39-5*) Locks Gallery.

— Nancy Graves: In Memoriam. (Illus.). 31p. (Orig.). 1996. pap. 20.00 (*1-879173-27-1*) Locks Gallery.

Larson, Kelli A. Ernest Hemingway: A Reference Guide, 1974-1989. 352p. 1990. 55.00 (*0-8161-8944-7*, Hall Reference) Macmillan.

— Guide to the Poetry of William Carlos Williams. LC 94-40682. (Guides to 20th Century Poets Ser.). 1995. 45.00 (*0-8161-1986-4*, G K Hall & Co) Mac Lib Ref.

Larson, Ken. Becoming Self-Reliant & Survival - How to Be Less Dependent of Society & Y2K with Disaster Prepardness & Food Storage Skills. 208p. 1997. pap. 12.95 (*0-9642497-1-5*) Rhema Pubng.

— God's Free Harvest - Successful Harvesting of Nature's Free Wild Foods & Wild Edibles for Your Survival & Y2K. 240p. 1997. reprint ed. pap. 12.95 (*0-9642497-0-7*) Rhema Pubng.

— Nature's Free Herbal Pharmacy - Herbal Healing Using Nature's Wild Foods & Wild Herbs. (Illus.). 160p. 1997. pap. 10.95 (*0-9642497-3-1*) Rhema Pubng.

— Nuclear Emergency - How to Protect Your Family from Nuclear Radiation, Fallout & Terrorism. 144p. 1997. pap. 10.95 (*0-9642497-2-3*) Rhema Pubng.

Larson, Kenneth H., jt. ed. see Krebs, Mary J.

Larson, Kent. Louis I. Kahn: Unbuilt Masterworks. LC 98-52140. (Illus.). 232p. 2000. 60.00 (*1-58093-014-X*, Pub. by Monacelli Pr) Penguin Putnam.

Larson, Kermit & Miller, Paul B. Fundamental Accounting Principles (Canadian), 1. 8th ed. LC 95-80682. 608p. (C). 1996. per. 29.95 (*0-256-17506-3*, Irwn McGrw-H) McGrw-H Hghr Educ.

— Fundamental Accounting Principles (Canadian), 2. 8th ed. 456p. (C). 1996. per. 39.95 (*0-256-17507-1*, Irwn McGrw-H) McGrw-H Hghr Educ.

— Fundamental Accounting Principles (Canadian), 2. 8th ed. 52p. (C). 1996. 35.95 (*0-256-24350-6*, Irwn McGrw-H) McGrw-H Hghr Educ.

Larson, Kermit & Nelson, Morton. Fundamental Accounting Principles, 1. 8th ed. 1168p. (C). 1996. per. 43.95 (*0-256-20964-2*, Irwn McGrw-H) McGrw-H Hghr Educ.

Larson, Kermit & Zin, Michael. Initiation a la Comptabilite Financiere Cinquiene. 5th ed. 400p. (C). 1992. per. 19.95 (*0-256-10601-0*, Irwn McGrw-H) McGrw-H Hghr Educ.

Larson, Kermit, et al. Financial Accounting & General Ledger Applications Software. 6th ed. (C). 1996. pap., text 54.95 incl. disk (*0-256-19409-2*, Irwn McGrw-H) McGrw-H Hghr Educ.

***Larson, Kermit, et al.** Fundamental Accounting Principles: Ch. 13-26, Vol. 2. 752p. (C). 1998. 46.56 (*0-07-366127-9*) McGrw-H Hghr Educ.

— Fundamental Accounting Principles: Chapters 1-12. 312p. (C). 1998. pap., student ed. 26.88 (*0-07-233914-4*) McGrw-H Hghr Educ.

— Fundamental Accounting Principles: Chapters 1-12, Vol. 1. 696p. (C). 1998. 59.69 (*0-07-366126-0*) McGrw-H Hghr Educ.

— Fundamental Accounting Principles: Chapters 1-18. 800p. (C). 1998. 83.75 (*0-07-366315-8*) McGrw-H Hghr Educ.

Larson, Kermit D. Essentials of Financial Accounting: Information for Business Decisions. 7th ed. LC 96-48062. (Irwin Series in Undergraduate Accounting). 768p. (C). 1997. text 49.95 (*0-256-20916-2*, Irwn Prfssnl) McGraw-Hill Prof.

— Essentials of Financial Accounting Working Papers. 7th ed. 512p. (C). 1997. text 26.25 (*0-256-20919-7*, Irwn McGrw-H) McGrw-H Hghr Educ.

— Fundamental Accounting Principles. 14th ed. 216p. (C). 1995. text, student ed. 31.25 (*0-256-17828-3*, Irwn McGrw-H) McGrw-H Hghr Educ.

— Fundamental Accounting Principles, 2. 14th ed. (C). 1996. text, student ed. 62.95 (*0-256-24356-5*, Irwn McGrw-H) McGrw-H Hghr Educ.

— Fundamental Accounting Principles, Chapters 1-13. 13th ed. (C). 1999. student ed. 48.95 (*0-256-17876-3*, Irwn McGrw-H) McGrw-H Hghr Educ.

— Fundamental Accounting Principles, Vol. 1. 14th ed. 240p. (C). 1996. text 25.62 (*0-256-20754-2*, Irwn McGrw-H) McGrw-H Hghr Educ.

— Fundamental Accounting Principles: Chapters 1-12, 1. 14th ed. 248p. (C). 1995. text, student ed. 31.25 (*0-256-16933-0*, Irwn McGrw-H) McGrw-H Hghr Educ.

— Fundamental Accounting Principles: Chapters 1-17. 14th abr. ed. 806p. (C). 1995. text 58.45 (*0-256-21983-4*, Irwn McGrw-H) McGrw-H Hghr Educ.

— Fundamental Accounting Principles: Chapters 1-17. 14th abr. ed. 320p. (C). 1996. text, student ed. 35.62 (*0-256-22273-8*, Irwn McGrw-H) McGrw-H Hghr Educ.

— Fundamental Accounting Principles: Fast Mart Inc. Practice Set. 14th ed. 64p. (C). 1995. text 20.95 (*0-256-20747-X*, Irwn McGrw-H) McGrw-H Hghr Educ.

— Fundamental Accounting Principles: Freewheel Corporation Practice Set. 14th ed. 64p. (C). 1995. text 20.95 (*0-256-17849-6*, Irwn McGrw-H) McGrw-H Hghr Educ.

— Fundamental Accounting Principles: KJC Manufacturing Practice Set. 14th ed. 80p. (C). 1995. text 20.95 (*0-256-17850-X*, Irwn McGrw-H) McGrw-H Hghr Educ.

— Fundamental Accounting Principles: Ready Notes - Chapters 13-25, Vol. 2. 14th ed. 272p. (C). 1995. text, suppl. ed. 23.12 (*0-256-21170-1*, Irwn McGrw-H) McGrw-H Hghr Educ.

— Fundamental Accounting Principles: Republic Lighting Company Practice Set. 14th ed. 56p. (C). 1995. text 20.95 (*0-256-17852-6*, Irwn McGrw-H) McGrw-H Hghr Educ.

— Fundamental Accounting Principles: Republic Lighting Company Practice Set, Extended Version. 14th ed. 80p. (C). 1995. text 20.95 (*0-256-19768-7*, Irwn McGrw-H) McGrw-H Hghr Educ.

— Fundamental Accounting Principles: With Working Papers & Ready Notes. 14th ed. (C). 1996. text 87.25 (*0-256-24852-4*, Irwn McGrw-H) McGrw-H Hghr Educ.

— Fundamental Accounting Principles: Working Papers - Chapters 1-17. 14th ed. 536p. (C). 1996. text, suppl. ed. 33.12 (*0-256-22275-4*, Irwn McGrw-H) McGrw-H Hghr Educ.

— Fundamental Accounting Principles: Working Papers Chapters 13-25, II. 14th ed. (C). 1995. text 23.43 (*0-256-16905-5*, Irwn McGrw-H) McGrw-H Hghr Educ.

— Fundamental Accounting Principles & Careers. 14th ed. (C). 1996. text 71.75 incl. cd-rom (*0-256-22171-5*, Irwn McGrw-H) McGrw-H Hghr Educ.

— Fundamental Accounting Principles with Working Papers, Vol. 1. 14th ed. (C). 1996. text, pap. text 44.95 incl. disk (*0-256-22006-9*, Irwn McGrw-H) McGrw-H Hghr Educ.

— Fundamental Accounting Principles With Working Papers: Volume I, Chapters 1 - 12, Vol. 1. 14th ed. 1018p. (C). 1995. text 50.00 (*0-256-19645-1*, Irwn McGrw-H) McGrw-H Hghr Educ.

— Fundamental Accounting Principles With Working Papers: Volume II, Chapters 13 - 25, Vol. 2. 14th ed. 928p. (C). 1995. text 44.95 (*0-256-19646-X*, Irwn McGrw-H) McGrw-H Hghr Educ.

— Fundamental Accounting Principles Working Papers: Chapters 1-12. 14th ed. 500p. (C). 1996. text 22.95 (*0-256-23000-5*, Irwn McGrw-H) McGrw-H Hghr Educ.

Larson, Kermit D. & Miller, Paul B. Financial Accounting. 6th ed. LC 94-22610. 714p. (C). 1994. text 49.95 (*0-256-13338-7*, Irwn McGrw-H) McGrw-H Hghr Educ.

— Financial Accounting: F.A.S.T. Edition. 6th ed. LC 94-22610. (C). 1994. write for info. (*0-256-13378-6*, Irwn McGrw-H) McGrw-H Hghr Educ.

— Fundamental Accounting Principles. 13th ed. LC 92-21073. 1600p. (C). 1992. text 72.00 (*0-256-10128-0*, Irwn McGrw-H) McGrw-H Hghr Educ.

— Fundamental Accounting Principles. 14th ed. LC 95-20806. (C). 1995. text 72.00 (*0-256-16449-5*, Irwn McGrw-H) McGrw-H Hghr Educ.

Larson, Kermit D. & Pyle, William E. Fundamental Accounting Principles, 1. 12th ed. (C). 1989. 18.95 (*0-256-08065-8*, Irwn McGrw-H); student ed. 20.95 (*0-256-08224-3*, Irwn McGrw-H) McGrw-H Hghr Educ.

An Asterisk (*) at the beginning of an entry indicates that the title is appearing for the first time.

— Fundamental Accounting Principles, 2. 12th ed. (C). 1989. student ed. 20.95 (*0-256-08225-1*, Irwn McGrw-H) McGrw-H Hghr Educ.

— Fundamental Accounting Principles, 3. 12th ed. (C). 1989. 18.95 (*0-256-08067-4*, Irwn McGrw-H) McGrw-H Hghr Educ.

Larson, Kermit D. & Spoede, Charlene W. Fundamentals of Financial Managerial Accounting Working Papers: Chapters 1-13, vol 1. 488p. (C). 1994. text 27.50 (*0-256-12593-7*, Irwn McGrw-H) McGrw-H Hghr Educ.

Larson, Kermit D., et al. Fundamentals of Accounting Principles. 15th ed. LC 99-192445. 1360p. 1998. 89.69 (*0-256-25534-2*) McGraw.

— Fundamentals of Financial & Managerial Accounting. LC 93-36781. 1993. teacher ed. write for info. (*0-256-15502-X*, Irwn McGrw-H) McGrw-H Hghr Educ.

— Fundamentals of Financial & Managerial Accounting. LC 93-36781. 1362p. (C). 1993. text 72.00 (*0-256-11023-9*, Irwn McGrw-H) McGrw-H Hghr Educ.

— Fundamentals of Financial & Managerial Accounting. 304p. (C). 1994. text 26.25 (*0-256-12591-0*, Irwn McGrw-H) McGrw-H Hghr Educ.

Larson, Kermit D., jt. auth. see Chiappetta, Barbara.

Larson, Kermit D., jt. auth. see Irwin Staff.

Larson, Kermit D., jt. auth. see Legare, Michel.

Larson, Kermit D., jt. auth. see Miller, Paul B.

Larson, Kermit D., jt. auth. see Saunders, Anthony.

Larson, Kermit D., jt. auth. see Spoede, Charlene W.

Larson, Kermit D., jt. auth. see Zin, Michael.

Larson, Kerry C. Whitman's Drama of Consensus. 296p. 1988. pap. text 18.95 (*0-226-46908-5*); lib. bdg. 54.00 (*0-226-46907-7*) U Ch Pr.

Larson, Kirby. Cody & Quinn, Sitting in a Tree. (Illus.). 96p. (J). (gr. 2-5). 1997. pap. 3.99 (*0-440-41378-8*) BDD Bks Young Read.

— Cody & Quinn, Sitting in a Tree. LC 95-25079. (Illus.). 64p. (J). (gr. k-3). 1996. 14.95 (*0-8234-1227-X*) Holiday.

***Larson, Kirby.** Cody & Quinn, Sitting in a Tree. (Picture Puffin Ser.). (J). 1998. 9.09 (*0-606-13287-2*, Pub. by Turtleback) Demco.

Larson, Kirby. The Magic Kerchief. LC 99-18846. (Illus.). 32p. (J). (ps-3). 2000. 15.95 (*0-8234-1473-6*) Holiday.

— Second-Grade Pig Pals. (Illus.). 96p. (J). (gr. 1-4). 1995. pap. 3.50 (*0-440-41104-1*, YB BDD) BDD Bks Young Read.

— Second-Grade Pig Pals. 1996. 8.70 (*0-606-09835-6*, Pub. by Turtleback) Demco.

***Larson, Knute.** 1 & 2 Thessalonians, 1 & 2 Timothy, Titus, Philemon. (Holman New Testament Commentary Ser.: Vol. 9). 2000. 16.99 (*0-8054-0209-8*) Broadman.

Larson, L. C. Problem-Solving Through Problems. Halmos, P. R., ed. (Problem Books in Mathematics). (Illus.). xi, 332p. 1997. reprint ed. 45.00 (*0-387-96171-2*) Spr-Verlag.

Larson, L. H., et al. An Unusual Wooden Rattle from the Etowah Site. (Missouri Archaeologist Ser.: Vol. 19, No. 4). 1957. pap. 1.00 (*0-943414-79-2*, 111904) MO Arch Soc.

Larson, L. L. National Avenue: Of Prohibition & Politics. unabridged ed. LC 96-92516. 269p. 1997. pap. 15.00 (*0-9654307-0-7*, 1) South Shore Pr.

Larson, Lane, jt. auth. see Larson, Peggy.

Larson, Larry & Lee, Levi. The Salvation of Iggy Scrooge: A Rock & Roll Christmas Carol LC 98-104345. 63p. 1997. write for info. (*0-573-69615-2*) S French Trade.

Larson, Larry & Lee, Levi. Some Things You Need to Know . . . 1986. pap. 5.25 (*0-8222-1056-8*) Dramatists Play.

Larson, Lars L., jt. ed. see Hunt, James G.

Larson, Laurence M. Canute the Great, Nine Ninety-Five to Ten Thirty-Five. LC 71-111764. (Heroes of the Nations Ser.). reprint ed. 30.00 (*0-404-03879-4*) AMS Pr.

— The Changing West: And other Essays. 180p. 1937. 15.00 (*0-87732-018-7*) Norwegian-Am Hist Assn.

— Changing West, & Other Essays. LC 68-16946. (Essay Index Reprint Ser.). (Illus.). 1977. reprint ed. 19.95 (*0-8369-0606-3*) Ayer.

— The King's Household in England Before the Norman Conquest. 1971. 7.00 (*0-403-00042-4*) Scholarly.

— The King's Household in England Before the Norman Conquest. LC 75-99885. reprint ed. 29.50 (*0-404-00617-5*) AMS Pr.

— The King's Household in England Before the Norman Conquest. LC 69-13967. 211p. 1970. reprint ed. lib. bdg. 59.50 (*0-8371-1805-0*, LAKH, Greenwood Pr) Greenwood.

— Log Book of a Young Immigrant. 318p. 1939. 15.00 (*0-87732-021-7*) Norwegian-Am Hist Assn.

Larson, Laurence M., tr. The King's Mirror (Speculum Regale--Konungs Skuggsja) LC 72-1542. 1917. pap. 12.95 (*0-685-02669-8*); lib. bdg. 7.50 (*0-8057-3328-0*) Irvington.

Larson, Lawrence A. RF & Microwave Circuit Design for Wireless Communications. LC 95-49987. 411p. 1996. 99.00 (*0-89006-818-6*) Artech Hse.

Larson, Lawrence R. The Spirit in Paradise: History of the Assemblies of God of Fiji, & Its Ministries to Other Countries of the South Pacific. LC 96-95442. (Illus.). 512p. 1996. 32.95 (*0-9656302-0-X*) L R Larson.

Larson, LeRoy. Reflections from the North Woods. LC 86-62069. (Orig.). 1986. write for info. (*0-9617181-0-2*) Banjar Pubns.

Larson, Lester. Farm Tractors, 1950-1975. LC 81-69655. (Illus.). 184p. (Orig.). 1981. pap. 17.95 (*0-916150-36-4*, HO981) Am Soc Ag Eng.

Larson, Lewis H. Aboriginal Subsistence Technology on the Southeastern Coastal Plain During the Late Prehistoric Period. LC 80-16279. (Ripley P. Bullen Monographs in Anthropology & History: No. 2). (Illus.). 1980. 32.95 (*0-8130-0675-9*) U Press Fla.

Larson, Lewis H., jt. auth. see Moore, Clarence Bloomfield.

Larson, Lex K. Employment Screening. 1988. 210.00 (*0-8205-1464-0*) Bender.

Larson, Lex K. & Borowsky, Philip. Unjust Dismissal, 3 vols. 1985. ring bd. 490.00 (*0-8205-1779-8*) Bender.

***Larson, Lex K. & Larson, Arthur.** Workers' Compensation Law: Cases, Materials & Text. 3rd ed. LC 00-27188. (Casebook Ser.). 2000. 58.00 (*0-8205-3013-1*) Bender.

Larson, Lex K., jt. auth. see Larson, Arthur.

Larson, Linda, jt. auth. see Baeckler, Virginia.

Larson, Linda, ed. see Rita, Suzanne, et al.

Larson, Linda S. & Kelly, Mona M. Conch Cats at Ernest Hemingway Home & Museum. (Illus.). 20p. (Orig.). 1993. pap. 5.95 (*0-9636896-0-6*) Conch Cats.

Larson, Loan M. Seven Weeks to Sobriety. LC 97-214438. 1997. pap. 12.95 (*0-449-00259-4*) Fawcett.

Larson, Loren C. Algebra & Trigonometry Refresher for Calculus Students. LC 79-20633. (Mathematical Sciences Ser.). (Illus.). 192p. (C). 1979. pap. text 22.95 (*0-7167-1110-9*) W H Freeman.

Larson, Louise L. Sweet Bamboo: A Saga of a Chinese American Family. LC 89-62055. (Illus.). viii, 227p. (Orig.). 1990. pap. 12.95 (*0-930377-02-8*) Chinese Hist CA.

Larson, Luther & Olsen, Warren. Ministerial Acts of the Church of the Lutheran Brethren. rev. ed. Rinden, David, ed. 145p. 1993. ring bd. 14.95 (*0-943167-28-0*) Faith & Fellowship Pr.

Larson, Magali S. Behind the Postmodern Facade: Architectural Change in Late Twentieth-Century America. (Illus.). 319p. 1995. pap. 17.95 (*0-520-20161-2*, Pub. by U CA Pr) Cal Prin Full Svc.

Larson, Marie & Kern, Christina. Saaskaaq Suulutaalek. (ESK., Illus.). 12p. (J). (gr. k-3). 1998. pap. text 6.00 (*1-58084-016-7*) Lower Kuskokwim.

Larson, Mark. Making Conversation. LC 97-3498. 126p. 1997. pap. text 18.50 (*0-86709-424-9*, 0424) Heinemann.

***Larson, Mark.** The Mullet: Hairstyle of the Gods. 2000. 14.95 (*1-58234-064-1*) Bloomsbury Pubg.

— Trade Stocks Online. LC 99-59988. (Online Trading for a Living Ser.). 224p. 2000. text 29.95 (*0-471-38473-9*) Wiley.

Larson, Mark K. Complete Guide to Baseball Memorabilia. 3rd ed. LC 92-71451. 480p. 1996. pap. 18.95 (*0-87341-455-1*) Krause Pubns.

— SCD Minor League Baseball Card Price Guide. LC 92-74798. (Illus.). 480p. (Orig.). 1993. pap. 14.95 (*0-87341-239-7*, SG01) Krause Pubns.

Larson, Mark K., jt. auth. see Amberg, Jay.

Larson, Mark K., jt. auth. see Wagner, Betty J.

Larson, Mark K., ed. see Sports Collectors Digest Staff.

Larson, Martin. How to Defend Yourself Against the Internal Revenue Service. rev. ed. 1985. 175.00 (*0-935036-08-3*) Liberty Lobby.

— Martin Larson's Best. 1982. 5.95 (*0-935036-02-4*) Liberty Lobby.

Larson, Martin A. The Continuing Tax Rebellion: What Millions of Americans Are Doing to Restore Constitutional Government. rev. ed. LC 79-89020. 1979. pap. 12.95 (*0-8159-5220-1*) Devin.

— The IRS vs. the Middle Class: or How the Average Citizen Can Protect Himself Against the Federal Tax Collector. LC 79-67271. (Orig.). 1980. 12.95 (*0-8159-5824-2*); pap. 6.95 (*0-8159-5827-7*) Devin.

— Modernity of Milton: A Theological & Philosophical Interpretation. LC 76-124764. reprint ed. 37.00 (*0-404-03880-8*) AMS Pr.

— Tax Revolt: The Battle for the Constitution. LC 84-14219. 304p. 1985. 16.95 (*0-8159-6922-8*) Devin.

Larson, Mary. Radar Rooster: Egg-Sploring Safety Activity Book. Altman, Brian A., ed. & illus. by. Prince, Karen D., illus. 68p. (J). (ps up). 1997. pap. 8.95 (*1-887050-26-4*) Meridian Creative.

Larson, Michael. Teach Yourself Web Publishing for Microsoft Office 97 in a Week. LC 96-71211. 454p. 1997. 39.99 (*1-57521-232-3*) Sams.

Larson, Mildred L. Meaning-Based Translation: A Guide to Cross-Language Equivalence. 548p. 1985. pap. text 36.00 (*0-8191-4301-4*) U Pr of Amer.

— Meaning-Based Translation: A Guide to Cross-Language Equivalence. 2nd ed. LC 97-44626. 596p. (C). 1997. text 69.00 (*0-7618-0970-8*); pap. text 38.50 (*0-7618-0971-6*) U Pr of Amer.

Larson, Mildred L., ed. Translation: Theory & Practice, Tension & Interdependence. (American Translators Association Scholarly Monograph Ser.: Vol. V). viii, 270p. 1991. lib. bdg. 45.00 (*0-614-16446-X*) J Benjamins Pubng Co.

Larson, Mildred L. & Davis, Patricia M. Bilingual Education: An Experience in Peruvian Amazonia. LC 81-51059. 435p. reprint ed. pap. 134.90 (*0-8357-3358-0*, 203959500013) Bks Demand.

Larson, Mildred L. & Davis, Patricia M., eds. Bilingual Education: An Experience in Peruvian Amazonia. LC 81-51059. 417p. 1981. pap. 12.00 (*0-88312-918-3*) S I L Intl.

Larson, Mildred L., et al. Meaning-Based Translation Workbook: Biblical Exercises. LC 97-41214. 328p. (C). 1997. pap., wbk. ed. 39.50 (*0-7618-0948-1*) U Pr of Amer.

Larson-Miller, Lizette, ed. see Salisbury, Joyce E.

Larson, Mobby. Prayers of a Christian Educator. (Greeting Book Line Ser.). 32p. (Orig.). 1985. pap. 1.95 (*0-89622-277-2*) Twenty-Third.

Larson, Muriel. Joy Every Morning. (Quiet Time Books for Women). pap. 4.99 (*0-8024-4396-6*, 410) Moody.

Larson, Nancy. Math 65 Teacher's Edition. 2nd ed. 1994. teacher ed. 85.00 (*1-56577-037-4*) Saxon Pubs OK.

— Math Three Home Study Kit. 1994. 90.00 (*1-56577-039-0*) Saxon Pubs OK.

— Math Two Home Study Kit. 1994. 87.50 (*1-56577-038-2*) Saxon Pubs OK.

Larson, Neal L., et al. Ammonites & Other Cephalopods of the Pierre Seaway: An Identification Guide. LC 96-78211. (Illus.). 144p. (Orig.). 1997. pap. 18.00 (*0-945005-25-3*) Geoscience Pr.

Larson, Noel R., jt. auth. see Maddock, James W.

Larson, Nola, et al. Transition Magician: Strategies for Guiding Your Children in Early Childhood Programs. (Illus.). 136p. (Orig.). 1994. pap. 18.95 (*0-934140-81-2*, 3029) Redleaf Pr.

***Larson, Nola, et al.** Transition Magician II: More Strategies for Guiding Young Children in Early Childhood Programs. 224p. 2000. pap. 24.95 (*1-884834-86-8*, 304901, Pub. by Redleaf Pr) Gryphon Hse.

Larson, Olaf F., et al. Sociology in Government: The Galpin-Taylor Years in the U. S. Department of Agriculture, 1919-1953. (Rural Studies). 300p. (C). 1999. 65.00 (*0-8133-8793-0*) Westview.

Larson, Orville K. Scene Design in the American Theatre from 1915-1960. LC 88-27628. (Illus.). 405p. (C). 1990. pap. 40.00 (*1-55728-065-7*); text 55.00 (*1-55728-064-9*) U of Ark Pr.

Larson, Orville K., ed. Scene Design for Stage & Screen. LC 76-10460. (Illus.). 334p. 1976. reprint ed. lib. bdg. 35.00 (*0-8371-8320-0*, LASS, Greenwood Pr) Greenwood.

— The Theatrical Writings of Fabrizio Carini Motta. LC 87-4296. (Illus.). 145p. (C). 1987. text 21.95 (*0-8093-1337-5*) S Ill U Pr.

Larson, Orvin. American Infidel: Robert G. Ingersoll. 2nd ed. LC 62-1223. (Illus.). 316p. 1993. reprint ed. pap. 15.00 (*1-877733-33-4*) Freedom Rel Found.

Larson, P. D. Boxwood: Its History, Cultivation, Propagation & Descriptions. Flanagan, Christine & Sacchi, Christopher F., eds. LC 96-86223. (Illus.). iv, 228p. (Orig.). 1996. pap. 24.95 (*0-9654150-0-7*) Foliar Pr.

Larson, Patricia, ed. see McKay, David O.

Larson, Patricia J., ed. Symptom Management Proceedings. (C). 1995. pap. 25.00 (*0-943671-13-2*) UCSF Schl Nursing.

Larson, Paul. Montana Entrepreneur's Guide: How to Start & Manage a Business in Montana. 2nd ed. 368p. 1995. pap. 19.95 incl. disk (*0-9624819-4-7*) University MT.

Larson, Paul C. Historic Quincy Architecture: Architectural Treasures of Quincy, Illinois. (Illus.). 128p. 1996. 35.00 (*0-917001-11-7*) Herring Pr.

— Icy Pleasures: Minnesota Celebrates Winter. Rubinstein, Sally, ed. LC 97-25217. (Illus.). 160p. 1998. 40.00 (*1-890434-01-9*) Afton Hist Soc.

— Municipal Monument: A Centennial History of the Municipal Building Serving Minneapolis & Hennepin County, Minnesota. 128p. 1991. 18.95 (*0-9630086-0-9*) Muni Bldg Comm.

— A Place at the Lake. LC 97-53072. (Illus.). 160p. 1998. 45.00 (*1-890434-05-1*) Afton Hist Soc.

Larson, Paul C., et al. The Spirit of H. H. Richardson on the Midland Prairies. (Illus.). 176p. 1988. pap. 24.95 (*0-938713-02-7*) Univ MN Art Mus.

Larson, Paul Clifford. Minnesota Architect: The Life & Work of Clarence H. Johnston. (Illus.). 224p. 1996. 35.00 (*1-890434-35-3*) Afton Hist Soc.

Larson, Paul F., et al, eds. Health Workforce Issues for the Twenty-First Century. LC 94-15952. (Health Policy Annual Ser.: No. 4). 206p. 1994. pap. 20.00 (*1-879694-08-5*) AAH Ctrs.

Larson, Paul W. Discipline by Design: A Handbook of Proven Steps to Operative Control. (Illus.). 302p. (Orig.). 1996. pap. 45.00 (*1-888355-06-9*) Renaiss Busn.

— Guidelines for a Visual Factory. (Illus.). 72p. (Orig.). 1996. pap. 20.00 (*0-614-11234-6*) Renaiss Busn.

— A Workbook for Action Teams. (Illus.). 102p. (Orig.). 1996. pap. text 24.50 (*1-888355-08-5*) Renaiss Busn.

Larson, Peggy. Complete Guide to Establishing a Professional Astrological Practice. 27p. 1990. pap. 4.95 (*0-935127-06-2*) ACS Pubns.

***Larson, Peggy.** The Deserts of the Southwest. 2nd ed. LC 99-56996. (Naturalist's Guides Ser.). (Illus.). 288p. 2000. pap. 16.00 (*1-57805-052-9*, Pub. by Sierra) Random.

Larson, Peggy & Larson, Lane. A Sierra Club Naturalist's Guide to the Deserts of the Southwest. LC 76-24835. (Naturalist's Guides Ser.). (Illus.). 288p. 1982. pap. 12.00 (*0-87156-186-7*, Pub. by Sierra) Random.

Larson, Per. Gay Money: Personal Finance for Gay Men & Lesbians. LC 97-570. 1997. pap. 12.95 (*0-440-50799-5*) Dell.

***Larson, Peter E. & Coe, Amanda, eds.** Managing Change Vol. 7: Changing the Role of Top Public Servants. (Managing the Public Service). 72p. 2000. pap. 16.95 (*0-85092-584-3*, Pub. by Comm Sec) Stylus Pub VA.

Larson, Philip R. The Vascular Cambium: Development & Structure. LC 94-7963. (Springer Series in Wood Science). 1994. write for info. (*3-540-57165-5*) Spr-Verlag.

— The Vascular Cambium: Development & Structure. LC 94-7963. (Springer Series in Wood Science). 1994. 343.95 (*0-387-57165-5*) Spr-Verlag.

***Larson, Pier M.** History & Memory in the Age of Enslavement. 440p. 2000. 24.95 (*0-325-00216-9*, Greenwood Pr); 65.00 (*0-325-00217-7*, Greenwood Pr) Greenwood.

Larson, R. L., et al. The Bedrock Geology of the World. (Illus.). (C). 1984. pap. text 36.80 (*0-7167-1702-6*) W H Freeman.

Larson, Ralph. The Word Was Made Flesh. LC 94-60461. 384p. 1995. per. 8.95 (*1-57258-032-1*) Teach Servs.

Larson, Randall D. Films into Books: An Analytical Bibliography of Film Novelization, Movie, & TV Tie-ins. LC 94-24274. 623p. 1995. 75.00 (*0-8108-2928-2*) Scarecrow.

— Music from the House of Hammer: Music in the Hammer Horror Films, 1950-1980. 234p. 1996. 32.50 (*0-8108-2975-4*) Scarecrow.

— Musique Fantastique: A Survey of Film Music in the Fantastic Cinema. LC 84-13954. 602p. 1984. 52.00 (*0-8108-1728-4*) Scarecrow.

— Robert Bloch. Schlobin, Roger C., ed. LC 86-5751. (Starmont Reader's Guide Ser.: Vol. 37). iv, 148p. 1986. pap. 19.00 (*0-930261-58-5*) Millefleurs.

***Larson, Randy.** Commas: Teaching Students to Use Commas Correctly, Without Boring Them to Tears. (Teaching the Boring Stuff Ser.). (Illus.). 79p. (YA). (gr. 5-9). 1999. pap. 14.95 (*1-877673-38-2*) Cottonwood Pr.

Larson, Randy. DownWrite Funny: Using Students' Love of the Ridiculous to Teach Serious Writing Skills. (Illus.). 128p. (YA). (gr. 5-12). 1997. pap. text 18.95 (*1-877673-31-5*, DWF) Cottonwood Pr.

— Hot Fudge Monday: Tasty Ways to Teach Parts of Speech to Students Who Have a Hard Time Swallowing Anything to Do with Grammar. 127p. 1993. pap. text 19.95 (*1-877673-17-X*, HOT) Cottonwood Pr.

— Short & Sweet: Quick Creative Writing Activities That Encourage Imagination, Humor & Enthusiasm about Writing. 36p. 1993. pap. text 10.95 (*1-877673-19-6*, SS) Cottonwood Pr.

Larson, Raymond, intro. The Apology & Crito of Plato & the Apology & Symposium of Xenophon. 122p. (C). 1980. pap. 10.50 (*0-87291-141-1*) Coronado Pr.

Larson, Raymond, ed. & tr. see Plato.

Larson, Rebecca. Daughters of Light: Quaker Women Preaching & Prophesying in the Colonies & Abroad, 1700-1775. LC 98-42459. 416p. 1999. 35.00 (*0-679-43762-2*) Knopf.

***Larson, Rebecca.** Daughters of Light: Quaker Women Preaching & Prophesying in the Colonies & Abroad, 1700-1775. LC 00-25221. 400p. 2000. pap. 17.95 (*0-8078-4897-2*) U of NC Pr.

Larson, Rebecca D. Blue & Gray Roses of Intrigue. (Illus.). 72p. (C). 1993. pap. text 6.95 (*0-939631-46-6*) Thomas Publications.

Larson, Reed, jt. auth. see Csikszentmihalyi, Mihaly.

Larson, Renae, ed. see Grein, Judith H.

Larson, Richard. Introduction to Sociology: Order & Change in Society. 5th ed. 456p. (C). 1996. per. 28.95 (*0-8403-9275-3*) Kendall-Hunt.

Larson, Richard & Segal, Gabriel. Knowledge of Meaning: An Introduction to Semantic Theory. LC 95-5324. (Illus.). 659p. 1995. pap. text 42.00 (*0-262-62100-2*, Bradford Bks) MIT Pr.

Larson, Richard A. Naturally Occurring Antioxidants. LC 97-8169. 224p. 1997. lib. bdg. 89.95 (*0-87371-957-3*) Lewis Pubs.

Larson, Richard A., ed. Biohazards of Drinking Water Treatment. (Illus.). 304p. 1988. lib. bdg. 99.95 (*0-87371-110-6*, L110) Lewis Pubs.

Larson, Richard A. & Weber, Eric J. Reaction Mechanisms in Environmental Organic Chemistry. 448p. 1994. lib. bdg. 85.00 (*0-87371-258-7*, L258) Lewis Pubs.

Larson, Richard K. Control & Grammar. (Studies in Linguistics & Philosophy). 352p. (C). 1992. lib. bdg. 189.00 (*0-7923-1692-4*, Pub. by Kluwer Academic) Kluwer Academic.

Larson, Richard K., et al. Semantica: Version 1.0 (for Nextstep) 200p. 1997. pap. text 25.00 (*0-262-62117-7*) MIT Pr.

— Syntactica: NeXStep Edition. (Illus.). 140p. 1996. pap. text 30.00 (*0-262-62106-1*) MIT Pr.

Larson, Robert. Changing Schools from the Inside Out. LC 91-68578. 170p. 1992. pap. text 39.95 (*0-87762-901-3*) Rowman.

Larson, Robert A. & Slosson, James E., eds. Storm-Induced Geologic Hazards: Case Histories from the 1992-1993 Winter in Southern California & Arizona. (Reviews in Engineering Geology Ser.: No. 11). (Illus.). 1997. 60.00 (*0-8137-4111-4*) Geol Soc.

Larson, Robert A. & Williams, Hiram. Hiram Williams: Images of Compassion. LC 98-25874. (Illus.). 156p. (C). 1998. 27.50 (*0-7618-1196-6*) U Pr of Amer.

Larson, Robert C. God's Best for Your Success. 144p. 1995. pap. 7.99 (*0-8499-5155-0*) Word Pub.

— God's Little Answer Book. 144p. 1995. 7.99 (*0-8499-5156-9*) Word Pub.

Larson, Robert C., jt. auth. see Engstrom, Ted W.

Larson, Robert C., jt. auth. see Pauley, Edward H.

Larson, Robert E. & Casti, John L. Principles of Dynamic Programming Pt.2: Advanced Theory & Applications. (Control & Systems Theory Ser.: Vol. 7). 512p. 1982. text 140.00 (*0-8247-6590-7*) Dekker.

Larson, Robert Edward & Casti. Principles of Dynamic Programming Pt. 1: Basic Analytical & Computational Methods. (Control & Systems Theory Ser.: Vol. 7). 344p. 1978. text 100.00 (*0-8247-6589-3*) Dekker.

Larson, Robert H. The British Army & the Theory of Armored Warfare 1918-1940. LC 83-47509. (Illus.). 272p. 1984. 45.00 (*0-87413-219-3*) U Delaware Pr.

Larson, Robert H., et al. Williamsport: Frontier Village to Regional Center. 2nd rev. ed. (Illus.). 176p. 1996. 34.95 (*0-89781-483-5*) Am Historical Pr.

Larson, Robert L. Changing Schools from the Inside Out. 2nd ed. LC 98-86721. 225p. 1998. pap. text 29.95 (*1-56676-698-2*) Scarecrow.

— Goal Setting in Planning: Myths & Realities. (Occasional Papers: No. 3). (Illus.). 41p. 1980. pap. text 5.00 (*0-944277-04-7*, L37) U VT Ctr Rsch VT.

Larson, Robert L. & Grana, William A. The Knee: Form, Function, Pathology & Treatment. (Illus.). 715p. 1992. text 155.00 (*0-7216-3495-8*, W B Saunders Co) Harcrt Hlth Sci Grp.

L

An Asterisk (*) at the beginning of an entry indicates that the title is appearing for the first time.

Larson, Robert L., jt. auth. see English, Fenwick W.

Larson, Robert W. New Mexico's Quest for Statehood, 1846-1912. LC 68-23022. 415p. reprint ed. pap. 128.70 (*0-608-15463-6*, 20293150060) Bks Demand.

— Populism in the Mountain West. LC 86-16160. 220p. reprint ed. pap. 68.20 (*0-7837-5854-5*, 204557300006) Bks Demand.

Larson, Robert W. Red Cloud: Warrior-Statesman of the Lakota Sioux. LC 96-30793. (Oklahoma Western Biographies Ser.: Vol. 13). 352p. 1997. 24.95 (*0-8061-2930-1*) U of Okla Pr.

***Larson, Robert W.** Red Cloud: Warrior-Statesman of the Lakota Sioux. (Illus.). 352p. 1999. pap. 12.95 (*0-8061-3189-6*) U of Okla Pr.

Larson, Rodger. What I Know Now. LC 96-36723. 96p. (J). (gr. 7-12). 1997. 15.95 (*0-8050-4869-3*) H Holt & Co.

Larson, Rodger, et al. Scars, Pleasure & Sacrifice: Argentina-Colombia Video Creations. LC 94-66181. (ENG & SPA., Illus.). 64p. (Orig.). 1994. pap. write for info. (*1-883592-08-9*) Perm Mission.

Larson, Roger. No Winners. 1979. pap. 3.95 (*0-9602468-0-0*) Ipse Dixit Pr.

Larson, Roland E. Algebra & Trigonometry. 2nd ed. 736p. (C). 1990. teacher ed. 2.66 (*0-669-16270-1*); text 72.36 (*0-669-16269-8*); student ed. 22.36 (*0-669-16272-8*) HM Trade Div.

— College Algebra. 2nd ed. 576p. (C). 1990. teacher ed. 22.36 (*0-669-16276-0*); teacher ed. 2.66 (*0-669-16274-4*); text 67.16 (*0-669-16273-6*) HM Trade Div.

— Precalculus. 2nd ed. 736p. (C). 1990. text 72.36 (*0-669-16277-9*); pap. text, student ed. 22.36 (*0-669-17345-2*); teacher ed. 2.00 (*0-685-67669-2*); student ed. 10.50 (*0-685-58267-1*); trans. 84.36 (*0-669-17346-0*) HM Trade Div.

— Trigonometry. 2nd ed. 400p. (C). 1990. teacher ed. 2.66 (*0-669-16267-1*); text 67.16 (*0-669-16266-3*); pap. text, teacher ed. 22.36 (*0-669-19540-5*); teacher ed. 22.36 (*0-669-16268-X*) HM Trade Div.

Larson, Roland E. & Edwards, Bruce H. Elementary Linear Algebra. LC 87-81233. 528p. (C). 1988. text 77.56 (*0-669-14583-1*) HM Trade Div.

— Elementary Linear Algebra. 2nd ed. LC 90-81475. 592p. (C). 1991. teacher ed. 24.36 (*0-669-27145-4*); student ed. 22.36 (*0-669-27143-8*); 2.76 (*0-669-27142-X*); 2.66 (*0-669-27146-2*) HM Trade Div.

— Finite Mathematics. LC 90-83169. 500p. (C). 1991. text 76.36 (*0-669-16801-7*); pap. text, student ed. 22.76 (*0-669-16803-3*); teacher ed. 2.66 (*0-669-16802-5*); teacher ed. 25.16 (*0-669-27154-3*); 2.66 (*0-669-27155-1*); trans. 84.36 (*0-669-27337-6*) HM Trade Div.

— Finite Mathematics with Calculus. 926p. (C). 1991. text 80.76 (*0-669-16804-1*); teacher ed. 2.66 (*0-669-16805-X*); teacher ed. 25.16 (*0-669-27156-X*); 2.66 (*0-669-27157-8*); trans. write for info. (*0-318-68395-4*) HM Trade Div.

Larson, Roland E. & Farber, Elizabeth. Elementary Statistics: Picturing the World. LC 99-23835. 641p. (C). 1999. 86.00 (*0-13-010734-4*) P-H.

Larson, Roland E. & Hostetler, Robert P. Algebra & Trigonometry. 3rd ed. 818p. (C). 1993. text 72.36 (*0-669-28298-7*); pap. text, student ed. 22.36 (*0-669-28300-2*); 22.36 (*0-669-28301-0*); 2.66 (*0-669-28302-9*); trans. write for info. (*0-318-70104-9*) HM Trade Div.

— Algebra & Trigonometry. 3rd annot. ed. 818p. (C). 1993. text, teacher ed. 73.56 (*0-669-33234-8*) HM Trade Div.

— Brief Calculus with Application. 2nd ed. LC 86-82096. 640p. (C). 1987. text 77.56 (*0-669-12060-X*); student ed. 22.36 (*0-669-12061-8*); 3.96 (*0-669-13013-3*); 2.66 (*0-669-12063-4*) HM Trade Div.

— Brief Calculus with Applications Alternate. 2nd ed. LC 86-82095. 512p. (C). 1990. text 74.76 (*0-669-12186-X*) HM Trade Div.

— Calculus with Analytic Geometry, 3 vols. 3rd ed. LC 85-80719. 1013p. (C). 1986. text 97.16 (*0-669-09568-0*); student ed. 27.56 (*0-669-10098-6*); 20.76 (*0-669-10099-4*); 20.76 (*0-669-10100-1*); 20.76 (*0-669-10101-X*); trans. 84.36 (*0-669-10102-8*) HM Trade Div.

— Calculus with Analytic Geometry. 5th alternate ed. 1123p. (C). 1994. text 97.16 (*0-669-34227-0*) HM Trade Div.

— Calculus with Analytic Geometry Alternate. 3rd ed. LC 85-80735. 1029p. (C). 1986. text 97.16 (*0-669-09569-9*) HM Trade Div.

— Calculus with Analytic Geometry, Alternate. 5th ed. 1123p. (C). 1994. text 97.16 (*0-669-35336-1*); text, teacher ed. 2.66 (*0-669-34228-9*) HM Trade Div.

— Calculus with Analytic Geometry, Alternate: Complete Solutions Guide, Vol. I, Chpts. 1-7. 5th ed. (C). 1994. text, student ed. 22.76 (*0-669-34230-0*) HM Trade Div.

— Calculus with Analytic Geometry, Alternate: Complete Solutions Guide, Vol. II, Chpts. 8-14. 5th ed. (C). 1994. text, student ed. 22.76 (*0-669-34232-7*) HM Trade Div.

— Calculus with Analytic Geometry, Alternate: Complete Solutions Guide, Vol. III, Chpts. 15-18. 5th ed. (C). 1994. text, student ed. 23.56 (*0-669-34233-5*) HM Trade Div.

— Calculus with Analytic Geometry, Alternate: Study & Solutions Guide. 5th ed. (C). 1994. text, student ed. 28.36 (*0-669-34229-7*) HM Trade Div.

— Calculus with Analytic Geometry Alternate with Late Trigonometry. 4th alternate ed. 1113p. (C). 1990. text 97.16 (*0-669-17843-8*); pap. text 27.56 (*0-669-17844-6*); teacher ed. 2.66 (*0-669-21738-7*); 20.76 (*0-669-17845-4*); 20.76 (*0-669-17846-2*); 20.76 (*0-669-17847-0*); 2.66 (*0-669-21817-0*); trans. 84.36 (*0-669-16412-7*) HM Trade Div.

— College Algebra. 3rd ed. 620p. (C). 1993. text 67.16 (*0-669-28304-5*); text, teacher ed. 22.36 (*0-669-28307-X*); text, student ed. 62.36 (*0-669-33235-6*); text, student ed. 22.76 (*0-669-28306-1*); 2.66 (*0-669-28309-6*); trans. 84.36 (*0-669-28322-3*); VHS 666.66 (*0-669-28580-3*) HM Trade Div.

— Elementary Algebra. 551p. (C). 1992. student ed. 22.36 (*0-669-18766-6*) HM Trade Div.

— Interactive College Algebra & Trignometry CD-ROM. 4th ed. 976p. (C). 1996. text 72.36 (*0-669-41746-7*) HM Trade Div.

— Interactive College Algebra & Trignometry CD-ROM. 4th annot. ed. LC 96-77322. xxvi, 878p. (C). 1996. pap. text, teacher ed. 70.76 incl. cd-rom (*0-669-41747-5*) HM Trade Div.

— Interactive College Algebra & Trignometry CD-ROM: Complete Solutions Guide. (C). 1997. pap. text 22.36 (*0-669-41749-1*) HM Trade Div.

— Interactive College Algebra CD-ROM. annot. ed. LC 96-76656. (C). 1996. text, teacher ed. 66.76 (*0-669-41752-1*) HM Trade Div.

— Interactive College Algebra CD-ROM. 4th ed. 848p. (C). 1996. text 67.16 (*0-669-41751-3*) HM Trade Div.

— Interactive College Algebra CD-ROM: Complete Solutions Guide. (C). 1997. pap. text 22.36 (*0-669-41754-8*) HM Trade Div.

— Interactive Precalculus CD-ROM. annot. ed. (C). 1996. text, teacher ed. 71.96 (*0-669-41742-4*) HM Trade Div.

— Interactive Precalculus CD-ROM. 4th ed. (C). 1996. text 72.36 (*0-669-41741-6*) HM Trade Div.

— Interactive Precalculus CD-ROM: Complete Solutions Guide. (C). 1997. pap. text 22.36 (*0-669-41744-0*) HM Trade Div.

— Interactive Trigonometry CD-ROM. annot. ed. (C). 1997. text, teacher ed. 63.16 (*0-669-41738-6*) HM Trade Div.

— Interactive Trigonometry CD-ROM. 4th ed. 448p. (C). 1997. text 67.16 (*0-669-41737-8*) HM Trade Div.

— Precalculus. 826p. (C). 1993. teacher ed. 22.36 (*0-669-28313-4*); 2.66 (*0-669-28314-2*) HM Trade Div.

— Precalculus. annot. ed. 826p. (C). 1993. text, teacher ed. 53.56 (*0-669-33236-4*) HM Trade Div.

— Precalculus. 3rd ed. 826p. (C). 1993. text 72.36 (*0-669-28310-X*); pap. text, student ed. 22.36 (*0-669-28312-6*) HM Trade Div.

— Precalculus. 4th ed. 826p. (C). 1993. pap. text 21.56 (*0-669-21885-5*) HM Trade Div.

— Trigonometry. 3rd ed. 592p. (C). 1993. text 67.16 (*0-669-28317-7*); teacher ed. write for info. (*0-669-28318-5*); 2.66 (*0-669-28321-5*); trans. write for info. (*0-318-70103-0*) HM Trade Div.

— Trigonometry. 3rd ed. 592p. (C). 2000. pap. text, student ed. 22.36 (*0-669-28319-3*) HM Trade Div.

— Trigonometry. 3rd annot. ed. 592p. (C). 1993. text, teacher ed. 68.36 (*0-669-33237-2*) HM Trade Div.

— Trigonometry: A Graphing Approach. 500p. (C). 1995. text 67.16 (*0-669-28296-0*) HM Trade Div.

Larson, Roland E., et al. Brief Calculus with Applications. 3rd ed. LC 89-81072. 812p. (C). 1991. text 77.56 (*0-669-21767-0*); pap. text, student ed. 22.36 (*0-669-24500-3*); pap. text, student ed. 22.36 (*0-669-21769-7*); teacher ed. 2.66 (*0-669-21768-9*); write for info. (*0-669-21770-0*); 24.36 (*0-669-27149-7*); 2.66 (*0-669-27150-0*); trans. 84.36 (*0-669-27336-8*) HM Trade Div.

— Brief Calculus with Applications. 4th ed. 736p. (C). 1994. text 77.56 (*0-669-35165-2*) HM Trade Div.

— Brief Calculus with Applications. 4th ed. (C). 1995. text, teacher ed. 2.66 incl. trans. (*0-669-35166-0*) HM Trade Div.

— Brief Calculus with Applications: Alternate Third Edition. 648p. (C). 1990. student ed. write for info. (*0-318-68032-7*) HM Trade Div.

— Brief Calculus with Applications: Solutions to Even-Numbered Exercises. 4th ed. (C). 1995. text 22.36 (*0-669-35168-7*) HM Trade Div.

— Calculus: Early Transcendental Functions. 1128p. (C). 2000. text 97.16 (*0-669-39349-5*) HM Trade Div.

— Calculus of a Single Variable. 4th ed. 707p. (C). 1990. text 75.16 (*0-669-24591-7*); pap. text 22.76 (*0-669-28905-1*); teacher ed. 2.66 (*0-669-21737-9*); 27.56 (*0-669-21676-3*); write for info. (*0-318-70107-3*) HM Trade Div.

— Calculus of a Single Variable. 5th ed. 713p. (C). 1994. text 75.16 (*0-669-35250-0*) HM Trade Div.

— Calculus of a Single Variable: Early Transcendental Functions. 714p. (C). 2000. text 75.16 (*0-669-39348-7*) HM Trade Div.

— Calculus with Analytic Geometry. 4th ed. 1083p. (C). 1993. text 97.16 (*0-669-16406-2*); pap. text 27.56 (*0-669-16407-0*); pap. text 7.96 (*0-669-28499-8*); 20.76 (*0-669-16408-9*); 20.76 (*0-669-16409-7*); 20.76 (*0-669-16411-9*); 2.66 (*0-669-21828-6*) HM Trade Div.

— Calculus with Analytic Geometry, 5 Vols. 5th ed. 1127p. (C). 1994. text 97.16 (*0-669-35335-3*) HM Trade Div.

— College Algebra: A Graphing Approach. 688p. (C). 1993. text 67.16 (*0-669-28294-4*); text, teacher ed. 2.66 (*0-669-33231-3*); pap. text 22.76 (*0-669-28295-2*); write for info. (*0-318-70105-7*) HM Trade Div.

— College Algebra: Concepts & Models. 678p. (C). 1992. trans. write for info. (*0-318-70102-2*) HM Trade Div.

— College Algebra: Concepts & Models. 2nd ed. 778p. (C). 1996. text 67.16 (*0-669-39617-6*) HM Trade Div.

— College Algebra: Concepts & Models. 2nd annot. ed. (C). 1996. text, teacher ed. 62.36 (*0-669-39618-4*) HM Trade Div.

— College Algebra: Concepts & Models: Complete Solutions Guide. 2nd ed. (C). 1996. text 22.76 (*0-669-41634-7*) HM Trade Div.

— College Algebra: Concepts & Models: Study & Solutions Guide. 2nd ed. (C). 1996. pap. text 22.36 (*0-669-41632-0*) HM Trade Div.

— Elementary Algebra. 2nd ed. 684p. (C). 1996. text 63.56 (*0-669-39613-3*); pap. text, student ed. 22.36 (*0-669-41636-3*) HM Trade Div.

— Elementary Algebra. 2nd annot. ed. (C). 1996. text, teacher ed. 58.36 (*0-669-39614-1*) HM Trade Div.

— Elementary Algebra: Concepts & Models. 792p. (C). 1993. text 57.16 (*0-669-36074-0*); text, teacher ed. 80.92 (*0-669-26752-X*); text, student ed. 18.16 (*0-669-38354-6*) HM Trade Div.

— Elementary Algebra: Concepts & Models: Applications Handbook. (C). 1993. text 14.08 (*0-669-29944-8*) HM Trade Div.

— Elementary Algebra: Concepts & Models: Complete Solutions Manual. (C). 1993. text 57.72 (*0-669-30026-8*) HM Trade Div.

— Elementary Algebra: Student Solutions Guide. 2nd ed. (C). 1996. pap. text 22.36 (*0-669-41635-5*) HM Trade Div.

— Elementary & Intermediate Algebra: A Combined Course. 2nd ed. 886p. (C). 1996. text 72.36 (*0-669-41764-5*) HM Trade Div.

— Interactive Algebra & Trigonometry: A Graphing Approach CD-ROM. 2nd ed. 794p. (C). 1996. text 72.36 (*0-669-41723-8*) HM Trade Div.

— Interactive Algebra & Trigonometry: A Graphing Approach CD-ROM: Even-Numbered Solutions Guide. 2nd ed. (C). 1997. text 22.36 (*0-669-41726-2*) HM Trade Div.

— Interactive Calculus: Early Transcendental Functions, CD-ROM for Windows. (C). 1995. text, teacher ed. 2.66 (*0-669-39350-9*) HM Trade Div.

— Interactive Calculus: Early Transcendental Functions, CD-ROM for Windows: Complete Solutions Guide, Vol. I. (C). 1995. text 22.76 (*0-669-39352-5*) HM Trade Div.

— Interactive Calculus: Early Transcendental Functions, CD-ROM for Windows: Complete Solutions Guide, Vol. II. (C). 1995. text 20.36 (*0-669-32713-1*) HM Trade Div.

— Interactive Calculus: Early Transcendental Functions, CD-ROM for Windows: Complete Solutions Guide, Vol. III. (C). 1995. text 21.16 (*0-669-32714-X*) HM Trade Div.

— Interactive Calculus: Early Transcendental Functions, CD-ROM for Windows: Study & Solutions Guide. (C). 1995. pap. text 26.36 (*0-669-39351-7*) HM Trade Div.

— Interactive Calculus CD-ROM for Windows with Mathcad Runtime Version: Complete Solutions Guide, Vol. I, Chpts. 0-6. (C). 1994. text 20.36 (*0-669-32712-3*) HM Trade Div.

— Interactive Calculus CD-ROM for Windows with Mathcad Runtime Version: Complete Solutions Guide, Vol. II, Chpts. 7-13. (C). 1994. text. write for info. (*0-614-25393-4*) HM Trade Div.

— Interactive College Algebra: A Graphing Approach CD-ROM. 2nd ed. LC 96-76660. 704p. (C). 1996. text 67.16 (*0-669-41732-7*) HM Trade Div.

— Interactive College Algebra: A Graphing Approach CD-ROM. 2nd annot. ed. (C). 1996. text, teacher ed. 66.76 (*0-669-41733-5*) HM Trade Div.

— Interactive College Algebra: A Graphing Approach: Even-Numbered Solutions Guide. 2nd ed. (C). 1997. pap. text 22.36 (*0-669-41735-1*) HM Trade Div.

— Interactive Precalculus: A Graphing Approach CD-ROM. 2nd ed. 794p. (C). 1996. text 72.36 (*0-669-41812-9*) HM Trade Div.

— Interactive Precalculus: A Graphing Approach CD-ROM. 2nd annot. ed. (C). 1996. text, teacher ed. 67.56 (*0-669-41724-6*) HM Trade Div.

— Interactive Precalculus: A Graphing Approach CD-ROM: Even-Numbered Solutions Guide. 2nd ed. (C). 1997. text. write for info. (*0-614-25398-5*) HM Trade Div.

— Interactive Precalculus: Functions & Graphs CD-ROM. 2nd ed. 992p. (C). 1996. text 72.36 (*0-669-41727-0*) HM Trade Div.

— Interactive Precalculus: Functions & Graphs CD-ROM. 2nd annot. ed. (C). 1996. text, teacher ed. 67.56 (*0-669-41728-9*) HM Trade Div.

— Interactive Precalculus: Functions & Graphs CD-ROM: Even-Numbered Solutions Guide. 2nd ed. (C). 1997. pap. text 22.36 (*0-669-41730-0*) HM Trade Div.

— Interactive Precalculus with Limits: A Graphing Approach CD-ROM. annot. ed. (C). 1997. text, teacher ed. 67.56 (*0-669-41759-9*) HM Trade Div.

— Interactive Precalculus with Limits: A Graphing Approach CD-ROM. 2nd ed. 1088p. (C). 1997. text 72.36 (*0-669-41758-0*) HM Trade Div.

— Interactive Precalculus with Limits: A Graphing Approach CD-ROM: Even-Numbered Solutions Guide. (C). 1997. text. write for info. (*0-614-25399-3*) HM Trade Div.

— Intermediate Algebra. 2nd ed. LC 95-75643. 694p. (C). 1996. text 63.56 (*0-669-39615-X*); pap. text, student ed. 22.36 (*0-669-41640-1*) HM Trade Div.

— Intermediate Algebra. 2nd annot. ed. (C). 1996. text, teacher ed. 58.36 (*0-669-39616-8*) HM Trade Div.

— Intermediate Algebra: Concepts & Models. 932p. (C). 1993. text 60.52 (*0-669-36075-9*); text, teacher ed. 83.96 (*0-669-26753-8*) HM Trade Div.

— Intermediate Algebra: Graphs & Functions. 800p. (C). 1994. text 63.56 (*0-669-33755-2*) HM Trade Div.

— Intermediate Algebra: Graphs & Functions. annot. ed. (C). 1994. text, teacher ed. 64.76 (*0-669-33756-0*) HM Trade Div.

— Intermediate Algebra: Graphs & Functions: Complete Solutions Guide & Transparency Masters. (C). 1994. text 24.36 (*0-669-33758-7*) HM Trade Div.

— Intermediate Algebra: Graphs & Functions: Student Study & Solutions Guide. (C). 1994. text 23.56 (*0-669-33757-9*) HM Trade Div.

— Intermediate Algebra: Student Solutions Guide. 2nd ed. (C). 1996. pap. text 22.36 (*0-669-41639-8*) HM Trade Div.

— Mathematics for Everyday Living: The Mathematics of Buying. (Illus.). 119p. (J). (gr. 9-12). 1996. pap. text 19.95 (*1-887050-21-3*) Meridian Creative.

— Mathematics for Everyday Living: The Mathematics of Investment. (Illus.). 135p. (J). (gr. 9 up). 1997. pap. text 19.95 (*1-887050-29-9*) Meridian Creative.

— Mathematics for Everyday Living: The Mathematics of Saving. (Illus.). 134p. (J). (gr. 9-12). 1997. pap. text 19.95 (*1-887050-24-8*) Meridian Creative.

— Mathematics of Everday Living: The Mathematics of Borrowing. (Illus.). 157p. (J). (gr. 9-12). 1997. pap. text 19.95 (*1-887050-27-2*) Meridian Creative.

— Multivariable Calculus. 5th ed. 413p. (C). 1994. text 67.16 (*0-669-39345-2*) HM Trade Div.

— Multivariable Calculus: Complete Solutions Guide, Vol. I, Chpts. 0-6. 5th ed. (C). 1994. text. write for info. (*0-614-25395-0*) HM Trade Div.

— Multivariable Calculus: Complete Solutions Guide, Vol. II, Chpts. 7-13. (C). 1994. text. write for info. (*0-614-25396-9*) HM Trade Div.

— Multivariable Calculus: Complete Solutions Guide, Vol. III, Chpts. 14-16. (C). 1994. text. write for info. (*0-614-25397-7*) HM Trade Div.

— Multivariable Calculus: Study & Solutions Guide. 5th ed. (C). 1994. pap. text 27.56 (*0-669-32711-5*) HM Trade Div.

— Precalculus: A Graphing Approach. 826p. (C). 1993. text 72.36 (*0-669-28500-5*); text, teacher ed. 2.66 (*0-669-33232-1*); pap. text, student ed. 22.36 (*0-669-28501-3*); write for info. (*0-318-70106-5*) HM Trade Div.

— Precalculus: Functions & Graphs: A Graphing Approach. 750p. (C). 1994. text 72.36 (*0-669-35206-3*) HM Trade Div.

— Precalculus: Functions & Graphs: A Graphing Approach. teacher ed. 1.99 (*0-669-35207-1*) Free Pr.

— Precalculus with Limits: A Graphing Approach. 932p. (C). 1994. text 72.36 (*0-669-35251-9*) HM Trade Div.

— Trigonometry with Technology Updates: A Graphing Approach. 688p. (C). 1997. text 67.16 (*0-669-41760-2*) HM Trade Div.

— Trigonometry with Technology Updates: A Graphing Approach: Study & Solutions Guide. (C). 2000. pap. text 22.36 (*0-669-28297-9*) HM Trade Div.

Larson, Roland S. Greet Those at Home. (Illus.). 64p. (Orig.). 1982. 8.95 (*0-86683-684-5*) Harper SF.

Larson, Ron. Brief Calculus: An Applied Worktext. 5th ed. LC 98-71517. 554p. 1999. pap. text 48.87 (*0-395-91686-0*) HM.

— Swamp Song: A Natural History of Florida's Swamps. LC 95-9806. (Illus.). 231p. 1995. pap. 19.95 (*0-8130-1355-0*) U Press Fla.

— Upper Mississippi River History: Fact - Fiction - Legend. 2nd rev. ed. (Illus.). 200p. 1998. pap. 18.70 (*0-9640937-2-3*) Steamboat Pr.

— Upper Mississippi River History: Fact-Fiction-Legend. limited ed. LC 94-92055. (Illus.). 122p. 1995. 45.00 (*0-9640937-0-7*) Steamboat Pr.

Larson, Ron & Edwards, Bruce H. Calculus: An Applied Approach. 5th ed. LC 98-71514. 1999. text 66.27 (*0-395-91683-6*) HM.

Larson, Ron, et al. Geometry: An Integrated Approach, 1 Vol. LC 98-232398. 1998. write for info. (*0-669-45531-8*) Free Pr.

Larson, Ronald & West, Ronald E., eds. Implementation of Solar Thermal Technology. (Solar Heat Technologies: Vol. 10). (Illus.). 1000p. 1996. 95.00 (*0-262-12187-5*) MIT Pr.

Larson, Ronald A. Calculus, Pt. 1. 3rd ed. LC 88-81166. 922p. (C). 1988. pap. text 72.36 (*0-669-19600-2*) HM Trade Div.

Larson, Ronald C., jt. ed. see Garrett, Jessie A.

Larson, Ronald G. The Structure & Rheology of Complex Fluids. (Topics in Chemical Engineering Ser.). (Illus.). 688p. (C). 1998. text 79.95 (*0-19-512197-X*) OUP.

Larson, Rory, tr. see Kappeler, Max.

Larson, Ross. Fantasy & Imagination in the Mexican Narrative. LC 77-3019. 154p. 1977. 20.00 (*0-87918-031-5*); pap. 10.00 (*0-87918-032-3*) ASU Lat Am St.

— Writing for Information Age. 256p. Date not set. text 23.95 (*0-393-04786-5*) Norton.

Larson, Roy A. Production of Florist Azaleas. Armitage, Allan M., ed. LC 92-41795. (Growers Handbook Ser.: Vol. 6). (Illus.). 160p. 1993. pap. 17.95 (*0-88192-230-7*) Timber.

Larson, Russ. N Scale Model Railroad Track Plans. LC 99-196095. (Illus.). 64p. 1969. pap. 10.95 (*0-89024-335-2*) Kalmbach.

Larson, Russ & Horowitz, Mark. Beginner's Guide to Large Scale Model Railroading. Miller, Allan & Johnson, Kent J., eds. (Illus.). 96p. (Orig.). 1995. pap. 19.95 (*0-89778-397-2*, 10-7940, Greenberg Books) Kalmbach.

Larson, Rustin. Loving the Good Driver: Poems. LC 95-39507. 64p. 1996. pap. 14.95 (*0-7734-2672-8*, Mellen Poetry Pr) E Mellen.

— Tiresias Strung Out on a Half Can of Pepsi. 25p. (Orig.). 1993. pap. 5.00 (*0-9619744-6-X*) Blue Light Pr.

Larson, Sarah. Making Meaning: A Guide for Passing the Regents' Essay. 3rd ed. 196p. (C). 1998. per. 29.95 (*0-7872-5063-5*, 41506301) Kendall-Hunt.

Larson, Scott. At Risk: Bringing Hope to Hurting Teenagers. LC 99-21809. 1999. 14.99 (*0-7644-2091-7*) Group Pub.

***Larson, Scott.** Risk in Our Midst. 2000. pap. 14.99 (*0-7644-2248-0*) Group Pub.

Larson, Sharon. Your Child's Medical Journal: Keeping Track of Your Child's Personal Health, History from Conceptions Through Adulthood. LC 98-8801. 1999. pap. 14.00 (*0-609-80244-5*) Crown Pub Group.

An Asterisk (*) at the beginning of an entry indicates that the title is appearing for the first time.

Larson, Sheryl A., et al. Staff Recruitment & Retention: Study Results & Intervention Strategies. LC 98-10508. 1998. pap. 31.95 (*0-940898-56-X*) Am Assn Mental.

Larson, Shirley. A Cowboy Is Forever. 1996. per. 3.99 (*0-373-24055-4*, 1-24055-5) Silhouette.

— Season of Loving. 400p. 1988. per. 3.95 (*0-373-97058-7*) Harlequin Bks.

— That Wild Stallion. 1997. per. 3.99 (*0-373-24109-7*, 1-24109-0) Silhouette.

***Larson, Sidner J.** Captured in the Middle: Tradition & Experience in Contemporary Native American Writing. LC 99-48431. 224p. 1999. 27.95 (*0-295-97904-6*) U of Wash Pr.

Larson, Sidner J. Catch Colt. LC 94-32267. (American Indian Lives Ser.). vii, 164p. 1995. text 25.00 (*0-8032-2908-9*) U of Nebr Pr.

Larson, Sidney, jt. auth. see Overby, Osmund.

Larson, Signe, jt. auth. see Osborn, Kevin.

Larson, Simeon & Nissen, Bruce, eds. Theories of the Labor Movement. LC 86-32414. 408p. (C). 1987. text 49.95 (*0-8143-1815-0*); pap. text 19.95 (*0-8143-1816-9*) Wayne St U Pr.

Larson, Stan. Quest for the Gold Plates: Thomas Stuart Ferguson's Archaeological Search for the Book of Mormon. LC 94-20959. (Illus.). 320p. Date not set. reprint ed. pap. 12.95 (*0-9634732-6-3*) Signature Bks.

Larson, Stan, ed. Prisoner for Polygamy: The Memoirs & Letters of Rudger Clawson at the Utah Territorial Penitentiary, 1884-87. (Illus.). 282p. (C). 1993. 29.95 (*0-252-01861-3*) U of Ill Pr.

Larson, Stan, ed. see Bertoch, Marvin J. & Bertoch, Julia B.

Larson, Stan, ed. see Canning, Ray R.

Larson, Stan, ed. see Clawson, Rudger.

Larson, Stan, ed. see McKay, David O.

Larson, Stan, ed. see Poll, Richard D.

Larson, Stan, ed. see Roberts, B. H.

Larson, Stan, ed. see Talmage, Sterling B., et al.

Larson, Stephanie G. Creating Consent of the Governed: A Member of Congress & the Local Media. LC 91-40750. 232p. (C). 1992. 31.95 (*0-8093-1787-7*) S Ill U Pr.

Larson, Steven B. Desktop Publishing: Essential Applications. 1990. teacher ed. write for info. (*0-318-66849-1*) McGraw.

— Desktop Publishing: Essential Applications. 1990. pap. 22.24 (*0-07-036491-5*) McGraw.

— Desktop Publishing Applications. 3rd ed. (C). 1995. pap. text 33.74 (*0-07-036484-2*) McGraw.

Larson, Steven B. & Nordenstam, Garry L. DATABASE APP IG D3.5: Instructor's guide with data disk, 3.5 IBM. text 69.00 (*1-56118-397-0*) EMC-Paradigm.

— DATABASE APP JOB-BASED TXT D3. Textbook with data disk, 3.5 IBM. 157p. text 15.95 (*1-56118-396-2*) EMC-Paradigm.

Larson, Steven J., et al. Pesticides in Surface Water: Distribution, Trends & Governing Factors. Gilliom, Robert J., ed. LC 97-22728. (Pesticides in the Hydrologic System: No. 3). 400p. (C). 1997. ring bd. 79.95 (*1-57504-006-9*) CRC Pr.

Larson, Steven M. & Kaplan, William. Nuclear Medicine in Oncology. (Illus.). 500p. 1997. text 135.00 (*0-397-51375-5*) Lppncott W & W.

Larson, Susan. Booklover's Guide to New Orleans. LC 99-37833. (Illus.). 272p. 1999. 34.95 (*0-8071-2415-X*); pap. 19.95 (*0-8071-2416-8*) La State U Pr.

Larson, Susan. You Are My Friend: A Celebration of Friendship. LC 90-3028. 156p. (Orig.). 1991. pap. 9.95 (*0-9622874-8-2*) Halo Bks.

Larson, Susan, jt. auth. see Larson, Hal.

Larson, Susan C., et al. William Kienbusch: A Retrospective Exhibition, 1946-1979. (Illus.). 80p. 1996. pap. 7.95 (*0-918749-05-0*) W A Farnsworth.

Larson, Suzanne. Children Everywhere LC 99-188458. 16 p. 1995. write for info. (*0-8136-7985-0*) Modern Curr.

Larson, Suzanne. I Am Japanese American. LC 96-53932. (Our American Family Ser.). (J). (gr. k-3). 1997. lib. bdg. 15.93 (*0-8239-5011-5*, PowerKids) Rosen Group.

— Little Red Riding Hood: Can You Tell If the Big Bad Wolf Is Lying? (Distinguished Faculty Lecture Ser.). 16p. 1993. pap. text. write for info. (*0-935615-09-1*) S Utah U Pr.

Larson Texts, Inc. (Meridian Creative Group) Staff. CBL Explorations in Calculus for the TI-82: Calculator-Based Laboratory. 112p. (C). 1995. pap. text 19.95 (*0-9639121-1-9*) Meridian Creative.

Larson, Verna. Bearables of Bernie Bear. Pappas, Debra S., ed. (Illus.). 20p. (Orig.). (J). 1994. pap. 6.95 (*1-56550-022-9*) Vis Bks Intl.

***Larson, Verna.** Bernie's Forest Adventure. 2nd rev. ed. Jones, Sharon, ed. LC 99-71334. (Bearables of Bernie Bear Ser.: No. 1). (Illus.). 24p. (ps-k). 1999. 8.95 (*1-56550-085-7*) Vis Bks Intl.

Larson, Vicki L. & McKinley, Nancy L. Communication Assessment & Intervention Strategies for Adolescents. LC 86-51418. 387p. 1987. text 23.00 (*0-930599-07-1*) Thinking Pubns.

— Language Disorders in Older Students: Preadolescents & Adolescents. LC 94-34928. 1995. pap. 42.00 (*0-930599-29-2*) Thinking Pubns.

Larson, Virginia. How to Write a Winning Proposal. Payne, Linda A., ed. LC 86-70729. (Illus.). 55p. (Orig.). 1998. pap. 14.95 (*0-931954-02-9*) Classic Hse.

— Thomas Holdup. Payne, Linda A., ed. (Illus.). 200p. 1998. pap. 20.00 (*0-931954-03-7*) Classic Hse.

Larson, W. E., et al, eds. Mechanics & Related Processes in Structured Agricultural Soils. (C). 1989. text 160.00 (*0-7923-0342-3*) Kluwer Academic.

Larson, W. E., ed. see Robert, P. C.

***Larson, Waldo N.** The Code That Counts: Bible Code Truth. LC 99-95198. (Illus.). 64p. 1999. pap. 8.95 (*0-9672877-0-7*) Illum Reflect.

Larson, Walt. From the Wilderness. Helms, E. Michael, ed. LC 96-78400. 288p. (Orig.). 1996. pap. 14.95 (*0-9653966-5-7*) Karmichael Pr.

Larson, Wanda Z. Bird Woman Vol. 1: Sacajawea, the Ballad of John Minto; Other Poems (3) (Illus.). 150p. (Orig.). 1999. pap. 15.00 (*0-9628584-8-X*) Blue Uncrn.

— Elisabeth - A Biography: From Bavarian Princess to Queen of the Belgians. (Illus.). 264p. 1997. 69.95 (*1-57309-093-X*); pap. 49.95 (*1-57309-092-1*) Intl Scholars.

— Glorious Destiny: The Spiritual Story of the Great Seal of These United States. (Illus.). 303p. 1999. pap. 16.99 (*0-9628584-7-1*) Blue Uncrn.

— Miracle at Blowing Rock. Bard, Ruth, ed. (Illus.). 20p. (Orig.). 1992. pap. 4.95 (*0-9628584-2-0*) Blue Uncrn.

— Our Flag: Born Through Valor. (Illus.). 75p. (J). (gr. 4-12). 1999. pap. 12.00 (*0-9628584-1-2*) Blue Uncrn.

— Portlandia. (Illus.). 1991. pap. 8.95 (*0-9628584-0-4*) Blue Uncrn.

— To Pick a Willow: Selected Non-Fiction Selected Poems. (Illus.). 64p. 1999. pap. 7.95 (*0-9628584-6-3*) Blue Uncrn.

Larson, Warren F. Islamic Ideology & Fundamentalism in Pakistan: Climate for Conversion to Christianity? LC 98-6064. 300p. (C). 1998. 42.00 (*0-7618-1094-3*) U Pr of Amer.

Larson, Wendy. Literary Authority & the Modern Chinese Writer: Ambivalence & Autobiography. LC 90-27835. 222p. 1991. text 42.95 (*0-8223-1113-5*) Duke.

— Women & Writing in Modern China. LC 97-50614. 280p. 1998. 49.50 (*0-8047-3129-2*); pap. 19.95 (*0-8047-3151-9*) Stanford U Pr.

Larson, Wendy & Wedell-Wedellsborg, Anne, eds. Inside Out: Modernism & Postmodernism in Chinese Literary Culture. 208p. (C). 1993. text 36.00 (*87-7288-427-4*, Pub. by Aarhus Univ Pr) David Brown.

Larson, Wendy, tr. see Wang, Meng.

Larson, Wendy A., ed. 1975-1997 Case Currents Index. Eveland, Sarah, tr. (Orig.). 1997. pap. 30.00 (*0-89964-327-2*, 22703) Coun Adv & Supp Ed.

— When Crisis Strikes on Campus. 254p. 1994. boxed set 79.95 incl. vdisk (*0-89964-297-7*, 24902S) Coun Adv & Supp Ed.

Larson, Wiley J. & Wertz, James R. Reducing Space Mission Cost. LC 96-16835. (Space Technology Library). 1996. text 198.00 (*0-7923-4021-3*, D Reidel) Kluwer Academic.

Larson, Wiley J. & Wertz, James R., eds. Space Mission Analysis & Design. 2nd ed. LC 92-64312. (Space Technology Library). 1992. text 177.00 (*0-7923-1998-2*) Kluwer Academic.

— Space Mission Analysis & Design. 2nd ed. LC 92-64312. (Space Technology Library). (Illus.). 904p. (C). 1992. pap. text 49.95 (*1-881883-01-9*) Microcosm.

Larson, Wiley J., jt. auth. see Boden, Daryl G.

Larson, Wiley J., jt. auth. see Sellers, Jerry.

Larson, Wiley J., ed. see Sarafin, Thomas P.

Larson, Wiley J., jt. ed. see Sarafin, Thomas P.

Larson, Wiley J., jt. ed. see Wertz, James R.

Larson, Wiley J., jt. ed. see Wetrz, James R.

Larson, William C., ed. see Society of Mining Engineers of AIME Staff.

Larsson, Agne, et al, eds. Functions of Glutathione: Biochemical, Physiological Toxicological, & Clinical Aspects. LC 83-11011. 423p. 1983. pap. 131.20 (*0-608-00410-3*, 206112400007) Bks Demand.

Larsson, Anita. Women Householders & Housing Strategies: The Case of Gaborone, Botswana. (Illus.). 180p. (Orig.). 1989. pap. 40.00 (*91-540-9339-2*) Coronet Bks.

Larsson, Birgitta. Conversion to Greater Freedom? Women, Church & Social Change in North-Western Tanzania under Colonial Rule. (Studia Historica Upsaliensia: No. 162). (Illus.). 230p. (Orig.). 1991. pap. 46.50 (*91-554-2684-0*) Coronet Bks.

Larsson, Bjorn. The Celtic Ring. Simpson, George, tr. from SWE. LC 97-202110. 388p. 1992. 22.95 (*1-57409-024-0*) Sheridan.

***Larsson, Bjorn.** Celtic Ring. Simpson, George, tr. 400p. 2000. reprint ed. pap. 14.95 (*1-57409-114-X*) Sheridan.

— Long John Silver. 1999. 26.00 (*1-86046-694-X*, Pub. by Harvill Press) FS&G.

***Larsson, Bjorn.** Long John Silver. 2000. pap. text 12.00 (*1-86046-538-2*) Harvill Press.

Larsson, Borje, et al. Advances in Neutron Capture Therapy: Proceedings of the 17th International Symposium on Neutron Capture Therapy for Cancer, Zurich, Switzerland, 4-7 September, 1996, 2 vols., Vol. 1132. LC 97-42036. 1356p. 1997. 359.00 (*0-444-82781-1*) Elsevier.

Larsson, Borje, jt. auth. see Kullander, Sven.

Larsson, C. & Moller, I. M., eds. The Plant Plasma Membrane. (Illus.). 432p. 1990. 227.95 (*0-387-50836-8*) Spr-Verlag.

Larsson, Carl. Carl Larsson. 1998. pap. 12.95 (*0-88138-142-X*) S&S Trade.

— Carl Larsson: The Autobiography of Sweden's Most Beloved Artist. (Illus.). 208p. 1992. pap. 16.95 (*0-941016-91-9*) Penfield.

Larsson, Carl, et al. Carl & Karin Larsson: Creators of the Swedish Style. LC 97-19666. (Illus.). 252p. 1998. 40.00 (*0-8212-2481-6*, Pub. by Bulfinch Pr) Little.

Larsson, Clarence. Identity Through the Other: Canadian Adventure Romance for Adolescents. LC 97-161941. (Umea Studies in the Humanities: No. 133). 148p. 1996. pap. 48.50 (*91-7191-231-2*, Pub. by Almqvist Wiksell) Coronet Bks.

Larsson, Clotye M., ed. Marriage Across the Color Line. LC 65-21549. 204p. 1965. 4.95 (*0-87485-014-2*) Johnson Chicago.

Larsson, G. Land Registration & Cadastral Systems: Tools for Land Information & Management. 1991. pap. 48.95 (*0-582-08952-2*, Pub. by Addison-Wesley) Longman.

Larsson, Gerhard. Land Management: Public Policy, Control & Participation. (Swedish Council for Building Research Ser.). (Illus.). 232p. 1997. pap. 72.50 (*91-540-5783-3*, Pub. by Almqvist Wiksell) Coronet Bks.

— Land Readjustment: A Modern Approach to Urbanization. LC 93-1214. 160p. 1993. 72.95 (*1-85628-507-3*, Pub. by Avebry) Ashgate Pub Co.

***Larsson, Goran.** Bound for Freedom: The Book of Exodus in Jewish & Christian Traditions. LC 98-52685. (SWE.). 334p. 1999. 24.95 (*1-56563-083-1*) Hendrickson MA.

Larsson, Goran. Den Storsta Lognen: Sions Vises Protokoll. (SWE., Illus.). 84p. 1995. 5.00 (*1-888235-12-8*) AMI-Jerusalem.

***Larsson, Goran.** Die Juden, Eure Majestat! 4th rev. ed. Orig. Title: Jews! Your Majesty. (GER., Illus.). 45p. 2000. pap. 4.00 (*1-888235-29-2*) AMI-Jerusalem.

Larsson, Goran. Fact or Fraud? The Protocols of the Elders of Zion. (Illus.). 79p. 1994. 5.00 (*1-888235-10-1*) AMI-Jerusalem.

— Fakten Oder Falschung? Die Protokolle der Weisen Von Zion. (GER., Illus.). 93p. 1995. 5.00 (*1-888235-11-X*) AMI-Jerusalem.

— The Jews! Your Majesty. 3rd rev. ed. (Illus.). 40p. 1996. 3.00 (*1-888235-20-9*) AMI-Jerusalem.

***Larsson, Goran.** The Jews! Your Majesty. 4th rev. ed. 38p. 2000. pap. 4.00 (*1-888235-28-4*) AMI-Jerusalem.

Larsson, Goran. De Joden, Majesteit! 2nd rev. ed. (DUT., Illus.). 37p. 1989. 5.00 (*1-888235-07-1*) AMI-Jerusalem.

— Judarna Ers Majestat!Tr. of Jews! Your Majesty. (SWE., Illus.). 45p. 1988. 5.00 (*1-888235-08-X*) AMI-Jerusalem.

***Larsson, Goran.** Judarna Ers Majestat! 3rd rev. ed.Tr. of Jews! Your Majesty. (SWE., Illus.). 46p. 2000. pap. 4.00 (*1-888235-27-6*) AMI-Jerusalem.

Larsson, Goran. Die Juden, Eure Majestat! 2nd rev. ed. (GER., Illus.). 38p. 1990. 5.00 (*1-888235-03-9*) AMI-Jerusalem.

— Les Juifs, Majeste! 2nd rev. ed. (Illus.). 36p. 1991. 5.00 (*1-888235-05-5*) AMI-Jerusalem.

— Les Juifs, Majeste! 3rd rev. ed. (FRE., Illus.). 40p. 1998. pap. 5.00 (*1-888235-25-X*) AMI-Jerusalem.

— Os Judeus, Vossa Majestade! 2nd rev. ed. Pereira, Paulo R. & Barros, Maria D., trs.Tr. of Jews! Your Majesty. (POR., Illus.). 40p. 1997. pap. 3.00 (*1-888235-23-3*) AMI-Jerusalem.

— Sua Majestade, Os Judeus. (POR., Illus.). 38p. 1996. 3.00 (*1-888235-21-7*) AMI-Jerusalem.

— Waarheid of Bedrog? (DUT., Illus.). 85p. 1996. 5.00 (*1-888235-22-5*) AMI-Jerusalem.

Larsson, Gunnar & Astrand, Hans, eds. Gustavian Opera: Swedish Opera, Dance & Theatre 1771-1809. (Royal Swedish Academy of Music Ser.: No. 66). (Illus.). 492p. 1991. 121.00 (*91-85428-64-7*) Coronet Bks.

Larsson, Hans, jt. auth. see Olsen, Klaus M.

Larsson, Jytte T. Catalogue of the Rischel & Birket-Smith Collection of Guitar Music in the Royal Library of Copenhagen. Danner, Peter, ed. LC 89-80417. 272p. 1989. 25.00 (*0-936186-20-8*); pap. 15.00 (*0-936186-33-X*) Edit Orphee.

Larsson, Kare. Lipids-Molecular Organization, Physical Function & Technical Applications. (Oily Press Lipid Library Ser.). (Illus.). 235p. (C). 1994. 60.00 (*0-9514171-4-2*, Pub. by Oily Pr) Matreya.

Larsson, Kare, jt. auth. see Eliasson, Ann-Charlotte.

Larsson, Kare, jt. ed. see Friberg, Stig E.

Larsson, L. H., jt. ed. see Herrmann, K. P.

Larsson, Lars. Principles of Yacht Design. 1995. 39.95 (*0-07-036492-3*) Intl Marine.

Principles of Yacht Design. 352p. 1999. 44.95 (*0-07-135393-3*) McGraw.

Larsson, Lars & Eliasson, Rolf E. Principles of Yacht Design. (Illus.). 302p. 1994. 85.00 (*0-7136-3855-9*, Pub. by A & C Blk) Lubrecht & Cramer.

Larsson, Lars & Stjernquist, Berta, eds. The World-View of Prehistoric Man: Papers Presented at a Symposium in Lund, 5-7 May, 1997, Arranged by the Royal Academy of Letters, History & Antiquities along with the Foundation Natur Och Kultur, Publishers. LC 98-192674. (Illus.). 274p. 1998. pap. 49.50 (*91-7402-279-2*) Coronet Bks.

Larsson, Lars-Gunnar. Proceedings of the 2nd Scandinavian Symposium on Aspectology. (Studia Uralica et Altaica Upsaliensia: No. 19). 130p. (Orig.). 1989. pap. 37.50 (*91-554-2412-0*) Coronet Bks.

Larsson, Lars-Gunnar, jt. auth. see Hardh, Birgittta.

Larsson, Lars Hannes. Elastic Plastic Fracture. 1985. text 220.00 (*90-277-2017-7*) Kluwer Academic.

Larsson, Lars-Inge. Immunocytochemistry: Theory & Practice. 256p. 1988. lib. bdg. 249.00 (*0-8493-6078-1*, QR187) CRC Pr.

Larsson, Mats. Transparent Market: Management Challenges in the Electronic Age. LC 98-34808. 288p. 1998. text 49.95 (*0-312-21888-5*) St Martin.

***Larsson, Mats & Mitchell, J. B., eds.** Dissociative Recombination. LC 99-50189. 260p. 2000. 58.00 (*981-02-4077-5*) World Scientific Pub.

Larsson, Olle & Major, James. World Cup Ski Technique: Learn & Improve. Smith, Doug, ed. LC 79-90395. (Illus.). (Orig.). 1979. pap. 18.95 (*0-935240-00-4*) Poudre Pr.

Larsson, Petter & Weider, Lawrence J., eds. Cladocera as Model Organisms in Biology. LC 95-13976. (Developments in Hydrobiology Ser.: No. 107). 1995. text 220.50 (*0-7923-3471-X*) Kluwer Academic.

Larsson, Thomas B. Bronze Age Metalwork in Southern Sweden: Aspects of Social & Spatial Organization 1800-500 B. C. (Illus.). xii, 200p. (Orig.). 1986. pap. text 70.00 (*91-7174-229-8*) Coronet Bks.

Lart, Charles E. Huguenot Pedigrees, 2 vols. in 1. 258p. 1997. reprint ed. pap. 27.50 (*0-8063-0207-0*, 3290) Clearfield Co.

Larter, Chris. Horses on Wings, Wheels & Waves. 192p. 1984. 39.00 (*0-7212-0654-9*, Pub. by Regency Pr GBR) St Mut.

Lartey, Emmanuel Y. In Living Colour: An Intercultural Approach to Pastoral Care & Counselling. LC 97-185471. 147p. 1997. pap. 25.00 (*0-304-33942-3*) Continuum.

Lartey, Emmanuel Y., et al, eds. The Church & Healing: Echoes from Africa. LC 94-26926. (African Pastoral Studies, Etudes Pastorales Africaines: 2). (ENG & FRE.). 157p. 1994. 29.95 (*3-631-47227-7*) P Lang Pubng.

Lartillot, Francoise. Le Lieu Commun du Moi: Identite Poetique dans l'Oeuvre d'Ernst Meister (1911-1979) (Etudes & Documents Serie III: Vol. 42). xx, 490p. 1998. 52.95 (*3-906759-57-1*) P Lang Pubng.

LaRue, Bob & Spangler, Steve. Bouncing Back: 50 New Routines & Presentation Ideas Using Bounce-No-Bounce Balls. Smith, Lindsay, ed. Sheets, John T., tr. (Illus.). 64p. 1997. pap. text 12.95 (*0-9649353-2-5*) Wren Pubng.

LaRue, C. Steven. Handel & His Singers: The Creation of the Royal Academy Operas, 1720-1728. (Oxford Monographs on Music). (Illus.). 228p. 1995. text 49.95 (*0-19-816315-0*) OUP.

LaRue, Charles. Basic Biology, Text 2. 1992. 31.95 (*0-88671-543-1*, 80190) Am Guidance.

LaRue, ChiChi & Erich, John. Making It Big: Sex Stars, Porn Films & Me. LC 97-23969. 250p. (Orig.). 1997. pap. 12.95 (*1-55583-392-6*) Alyson Pubns.

LaRue, Cleophus J. The Heart of Black Preaching. LC 99-43131. 250p. 1999. pap. 14.95 (*0-664-25847-6*) Westminster John Knox.

Larue, D. K. & Steel, R. J., eds. Cenozoic Marine Sedimentation, Pacific Margin U. S. A. (Illus.). 247p. (Orig.). 1983. pap. 8.00 (*1-878861-44-1*) Pac Section SEPM.

Larue, D. K., jt. auth. see Lidiak, Edward G.

LaRue, Debra. Dance with the Dark Poet. LC 97-173446. 1996. 5.95 (*0-9641606-3-3*) Easy Break.

LaRue, Debrah. CycloDrama. x, 134p. (Orig.). 1999. pap. 8.95 (*1-891571-03-6*) Easy Break.

Larue, Gerald A. Ancient Myth & Modern Life. rev. ed. (Illus.). 304p. 1988. pap. 16.95 (*0-913111-24-4*) Centerline.

— Freethought Across the Centuries: Toward a New Age of Enlightenment. LC 94-74348. 500p. 1995. pap. 15.00 (*0-931779-03-0*, Humanist Press) Am Humanist.

— Freethought Across the Centuries: Toward a New Age of Enlightenment. LC 94-74348. 527p. 1996. write for info. (*0-931779-04-9*, Humanist Press) Am Humanist.

— Geroethics: A New Vision of Growing Old in America. LC 92-15264. (Golden Age Books - Perspectives on Aging Ser.). 267p. (C). 1992. 26.95 (*0-87975-750-7*) Prometheus Bks.

— Sex & the Bible. LC 83-60201. 175p. 1983. 31.95 (*0-87975-206-8*); pap. 20.95 (*0-87975-229-7*) Prometheus Bks.

— The Supernatural, the Occult, & the Bible. LC 90-40144. 303p. (C). 1990. 27.95 (*0-87975-615-2*) Prometheus Bks.

— The Way of Ethical Humanism. 96p. 1989. pap. 10.95 (*0-913111-22-8*) Centerline.

— The Way of Positive Humanism. 96p. 1989. pap. 10.95 (*0-913111-25-2*) Centerline.

Larue, Gerald A. & Bayly, Rich, eds. Long-Term Care in an Aging Society: Choices & Challenges for the '90s. LC 91-18979. (Golden Age Books - Perspectives on Aging Ser.). 170p. (Orig.). 1992. 26.95 (*0-87975-695-0*); pap. 18.95 (*0-87975-712-4*) Prometheus Bks.

Larue, Gerald A. & Hoffman, R. Joseph, eds. Jesus in History & Myth. LC 86-5052. 217p. 1986. 32.95 (*0-87975-332-3*) Prometheus Bks.

Larue, Gerald A., jt. ed. see Hoffmann, R. Joseph.

***LaRue, Gloria T. & Pinkham, Myra, eds.** Metal Statistics 1999: The Statistical Guide to North American Metals. 91st ed. (Illus.). 375p. 1999. 250.00 (*0-910094-00-4*) AMM.

LaRue, James, ed. see McGinty, Patricia.

LaRue, James H. & Johnson, R. Scott, eds. Peaches, Plums & Nectarines: Growing & Handling for Fresh Market. LC 89-83832. (Illus.). 252p. (Orig.). 1989. pap. 45.00 (*0-931876-88-5*, 3331) ANR Pubns CA.

LaRue, Jan. A Catalogue of Eighteenth Century Symphonies Vol. I: Thematic Identifier. LC 86-46404. 368p. 1989. 14.95 (*0-253-31363-5*) Ind U Pr.

— A Catalogue of Eighteenth Century Symphonies Vol. I: Thematic Identifier. LC 86-46404. 368p. Date not set. reprint ed. pap. 114.10 (*0-608-20556-7*, 205447000001) Bks Demand.

— Guidelines for Style Analysis. 2nd ed. LC 92-25439. (Detroit Monographs in Musicology: No. 12). 1992. 35.00 (*0-89990-062-3*) Harmonie Park Pr.

LaRue, Jan, ed. see Oakland, Roger.

Larue, L. H. Constitutional Law as Fiction: Narrative in the Rhetoric of Authority. LC 94-15750. 176p. 1995. 32.50 (*0-271-01406-7*); pap. 16.95 (*0-271-01407-5*) Pa St U Pr.

LaRue, L. H. A Student's Guide to the Study of Law 1988: An Introduction. annuals 1988. text 24.00 (*0-8205-2779-3*) Bender.

LaRue, L. H., ed. see Ritz, Wilfred J.

LaRue, Steven, ed. The India Handbook. LC 98-122585. (Regional Handbooks of Economic Development Ser.: Vol. 2). 350p. 1997. lib. bdg. 55.00 (*1-884964-89-3*) Fitzroy Dearborn.

Larue, V. Passion Quest. 1997. mass mkt. 11.95 (*0-340-68483-6*, Pub. by Hodder & Stought Ltd) Trafalgar.

LaRue, Walt. Rodeo Cartoons from The Buckboard. LC 89-91854. (Illus.). x, 135p. 1989. 12.95 (0-9624489-0-7) G Logsdon Bks.

***LaRue, William D.** Collecting Simpsons! An Unofficial Guide to Merchandise from "The Simpsons" LC 99-73666. (Illus.). 152p. 1999. pap. 24.95 (0-9675421-0-3) K M L Enterp.

Laruelle, F. Dictionnaire de la Non-Philosophie. (FRE.). 1998. 69.95 (0-320-00300-0) Fr & Eur.

LaRuffa, A. L. Monte Carmelo: An Italian-American Community in the Bronx, Vol. 9. (Library of Anthropology). 192p. 1988. text 69.00 (2-88124-253-7) Gordon & Breach.

LaRuffa, Anthony L. San Cipriano: Life in a Puerto Rican Community, Vol. 1. LC 73-136765. (Library of Anthropology). (Illus.). xiv, 148p. 1971. text 106.00 (0-677-03470-9) Gordon & Breach.

Laruffa, Joseph P. Prayers for Peace of Mind & Heart. 60p. pap. 1.25 (0-8198-5866-8) Pauline Bks.

LaRune, T. D. LaRune's Rockpecker Notes: "A Mineral Prospector's Primer" unabridged ed. Worth, M. S., ed. LC 94-67809. (Illus.). 543p. (C). 1996. lib. bdg. 36.00 (1-886499-00-4, Skill Ware) Skill-Quest.

Larus, Joel, jt. ed. see Lawrence, Robert M.

LaRusch, Cynthia, jt. auth. see Reinard, R. Douglas.

LaRusso, Carol, ed. see Carden, Barbara.

Larusso, Nicholas F., ed. Gallbladder & Bile Ducts. LC 96-43739. (Gastroenterology & Hepatology Ser.: Vol. 6). 1997. text 105.00 (0-443-07858-0) Church.

Larvor, Brendan. Lakatos: An Introduction. LC 97-26569. 144p. (C). 1998. 65.00 (0-415-14275-X); pap. 19.99 (0-415-14276-8) Routledge.

Larwill, Jim, et al. Speak! Six OmniGothic NeoFuterists. LC 98-183738. 96p. 1997. pap. 10.50 (0-921411-67-7) Genl Dist Srvs.

Larwood, G. P., ed. Extinction & Survival in the Fossil Record. (Systematics Association Special Volume Ser.: Vol. 34). (Illus.). 376p. 1988. text 90.00 (0-19-857708-7) OUP.

Larwood, G. P., jt. ed. see Taylor, P. D.

Larwood, Laurie & Gattiker, Urs E., eds. Impact Analysis: How Research Can Enter Application & Make a Difference. LC 99-30893. (Applied Social Research Ser.). 312p. 1999. 69.95 (0-8058-2103-1); pap. 32.50 (0-8058-2104-X) L Erlbaum Assocs.

Larwood, Laurie, jt. ed. see Gattiker, Urs E.

Larwood, Laurie, jt. ed. see Gutek, Barbara A.

Larwood, Laurie, jt. ed. see Rose, Suzanna.

Larwood, Laurie, ed. see Women & Work: An Annual Review Staff.

Lary, Diana, jt. auth. see Gottschang, Thomas R.

Lary, Hal B. Imports of Manufactures from Less Developed Countries. (Studies in International Economic Relations: No. 4). 303p. 1968. 79.10 (0-87014-485-5) Natl Bur Econ Res.

— Imports of Manufactures from Less Developed Countries. LC 67-28434. (Studies in International Economic Relations: No. 4). (Illus.). 304p. reprint ed. pap. 94.30 (0-8357-7576-3, 205689700096) Bks Demand.

— Problems of the United States As World Trader & Banker. (Economic Relations Ser.: No. 1). 191p. 1963. reprint ed. 49.70 (0-87014-153-8) Natl Bur Econ Res.

Lary, Hal B., et al. The United States in the World Economy. LC 75-26859. (Economic Handbook Ser.: No. 23). 216p. 1975. reprint ed. lib. bdg. 59.50 (0-8371-8257-3, LAUS, Greenwood Pr) Greenwood.

Lary, N. M. Dostoevsky & Soviet Film: Visions of Demonic Realism. LC 86-47645. (Illus.). 280p. 1986. 37.50 (0-8014-1882-8) Cornell U Pr.

Lary, Nikita M. Dostoevsky & Soviet Film: Visions of Demonic Realism. LC 86-11561. (Illus.). 280p. reprint ed. pap. 86.80 (0-608-20917-1, 207201600003) Bks Demand.

Laryea, Tony, ed. 30 Designs for Small Gardens. LC 95-83719. (Illus.). 128p. 1996. pap. 16.95 (0-563-37122-6, BBC-Parkwest) Parkwest Pubns.

***Larzar, John.** La Strada. unabridged ed. White, Bradford, ed. LC 99-33485. 312p. 1999. 21.75 (0-9620016-1-9) Grt Lakes MI.

Larzelere, Alex. The Coast Guard at War: Vietnam, 1965-1975. LC 96-32130. (Illus.). 384p. 1997. 32.95 (1-55750-529-2) Naval Inst Pr.

Larzelere, Bob. The Harmony of Love. 3rd ed. LC 81-3189. 144p. (Orig.). 1982. pap. 15.00 (0-932654-03-7) Context Pubns.

Larzen, jt. auth. see Bloom, H. J. G.

Las Casas. Le Memorial de Sant-Helene, Chapitres 9-14. 1520p. 41.50 (0-686-56533-9) Fr & Eur.

Las Casas, Bartholomew. The Log of Christopher Columbus' First Voyage to America: In the Year 1492, As Copied Out in Brief by Bartholomew Las Casas. LC 88-32567. (Illus.). 84p. (J). (gr. 3 up). 1989. reprint ed. lib. bdg. 17.00 (0-208-02247-3, Linnet Bks) Shoe String.

las Casas, Bartolome de, see De Las Casas, Bartolome.

Las Casas, Cristobal De, see De Las Casas, Cristobal.

Las Casas, Walter M. De, see De Las Casas, Walter M.

Las Cases. Le Memorial de Saint-Helene, Vol. 1. (FRE.). 1978. lib. bdg. 95.00 (0-8288-3520-9, F13311) Fr & Eur.

— Le Memorial de Saint-Helene, Vol. 2. (FRE.). 1978. lib. bdg. 95.00 (0-8288-3521-7, F13312) Fr & Eur.

Las Vergnas, Raymond. W. M. Thackeray (1811-1863) L'Homme, le Penseur, le Romancier. LC 70-148810. reprint ed. 49.50 (0-404-08876-7) AMS Pr.

Lasa, Bernardo E. Diccionario Enciclopedica Vasco Vol. 11: Ento-Esubi. (SPA.). 624p. 1980. 195.00 (0-7859-6475-4) Fr & Eur.

— Diccionario Enciclopedica Vasco Vol. 14: Fortif-Gallet. 592p. 1982. 195.00 (0-7859-6070-8, 8470252143) Fr & Eur.

— Diccionario Enciclopedica Vasco Vol. 16: Geol-Gruzeta. (SPA.). 592p. 1984. 195.00 (0-7859-6477-0) Fr & Eur.

— Diccionario Enciclopedica Vasco Vol. 27: Mars-Mendix. (SPA.). 576p. 1989. 195.00 (0-7859-6478-9) Fr & Eur.

— Diccionario Espanol-Vasco, Vol. 3. (SPA.). 170p. 1965. pap. 19.95 (0-7859-6476-2) Fr & Eur.

Lasa, H. I. De, see De Lasa, H. I.

Lasa Heydebrand, Leopold Von U. D., see Von U. D. Lasa Heydebrand, Leopold.

Lasaga, A. C. Kinetic Theory & Applications to Geochemistry. LC 97-385. (Princeton Series in Geochemistry). 728p. 1998. text 99.50 (0-691-03748-5, Pub. by Princeton U Pr) Cal Prin Full Svc.

Lasaga, A. C. & Kirkpatrick, R. J., eds. Kinetics of Geochemical Processes. (Reviews in Mineralogy Ser.: Vol. 8). 398p. 1981. per. 20.00 (0-939950-08-1) Mineralogical Soc.

Lasaga, Jose I. Vidas Cubanas (Cuban Lives), 2 vols. Duran, Nelson, tr. LC 84-189243. (Coleccion Cuba y sus Jueces). (ENG & SPA., Illus.). (Orig.). 1988. pap. 12.00 (0-89729-407-6) Ediciones.

— Vidas Cubanas (Cuban Lives), 2 vols., 1. Duran, Nelson, tr. LC 84-189243. (Coleccion Cuba y sus Jueces). (ENG & SPA., Illus.). (Orig.). 1988. pap. 12.00 (0-89729-165-4) Ediciones.

Lasagabaster, Jesus M., ed. see Baroja, Y Nessi, Pio.

Lasagna, Louis. 1998 Year Book of Drug Therapy. (Illus.). 408p. (C). (gr. 13). 1998. text 79.95 (0-8151-5296-5, 24747) Mosby Inc.

— 1997 Year Book of Drug Therapy. (Illus.). 488p. (C). (gr. 13). 1997. text 79.95 (0-8151-5295-7, 24746) Mosby Inc.

— Phenylpropanolamine: A Review. LC 86-28963. 458p. reprint ed. pap. 142.00 (0-7837-2818-2, 205765400006) Bks Demand.

Lasagna, Louis & Bearn, Alexander G., eds. Innovation & Acceleration in Clinical Drug Development: Merck Sharp & Dohme International Medical Advisory Council, Siena, Italy, June 9-10, 1986. LC 87-12782. (MEDAC, Medical Advisory Council Ser.: 1986). 182p. 1987. reprint ed. pap. 56.50 (0-608-00355-7, 206107200007) Bks Demand.

Lasagna, Michele, jt. auth. see Faber, Gail.

Lasagne, Louis S. Doctor's Dilemmas. LC 70-105025. (Essay Index Reprint Ser.). 1977. 23.95 (0-8369-1669-7) Ayer.

Lasalamonie, A., jt. auth. see Khan, T.

Lasalle. Management Information System: Project Cases. (C). 1996. pap. text. write for info. (0-03-055752-6) Harcourt Coll Pubs.

— Management Information Systems. (C). 1997. text 49.00 (0-03-055749-6) Harcourt Coll Pubs.

LaSalle, Charles. Heads & Figures in Charcoal. (How to Draw & Paint Ser.). (Illus.). 32p. (Orig.). 1989. pap. 6.95 (1-56010-005-2, HT051) W Foster Pub.

LaSalle Genealogical Association Staff, ed. History of LaSalle Parish, Louisiana. (Illus.). 293p. 1989. reprint ed. text 60.00 (0-88107-141-2) Curtis Media.

LaSalle History Book Committee Staff. LaSalle County, Colorado. (Illus.). 178p. 1988. 30.00 (0-88107-108-0) Curtis Media.

Lasalle, J. P. The Stability & Control of Discrete Processes. (Applied Mathematical Sciences Ser.: Vol. 62). (Illus.). 610p. 1986. 58.95 (0-387-96411-8) Spr-Verlag.

LaSalle, J. P. The Stability of Dynamical Systems. (CBMS-NSF Regional Conference Ser.: No. 25). v, 76p. 1976. pap. text 24.50 (0-89871-022-7) Soc Indus-Appl Math.

LaSalle, J. P., jt. ed. see Gauld, Ian D.

***LaSalle, Mick.** Complicated Women. (Illus.). 304p. 2000. 24.95 (0-312-25207-2, Thomas Dunne) St Martin.

LaSalle, Patricia A. Gifts to the Future: What Planned Giving Can Do for Your Institution. 31p. 1995. pap. 16.00 (0-89964-284-5, 28902) Coun Adv & Supp Ed.

LaSalle, Peter. The Graves of Famous Writers & Other Stories. LC 79-3065. (Breakthrough Bks.). 96p. 1980. 19.95 (0-8262-0287-X) U of Mo Pr.

— Hockey Sur Glace: Stories. 224p. 1996. 20.00 (1-55821-505-0, Pub. by Breakaway Bks) Consort Bk Sales.

— Hockey Sur Glace: Stories. (FRE.). 224p. 1998. reprint ed. pap. 13.00 (1-891369-00-8, Pub. by Breakaway Bks) Consort Bk Sales.

Lasansky, Jeannette. Collecting Guide: Holiday Paper Honeycomb-Cards, Garlands, Centerpieces, & Other Tissue-Paper Fantasies of the 20th Century. Foster, Joseph G., ed. LC 92-44577. (Illus.). 48p. (Orig.). 1993. pap. 15.00 (0-917127-07-2) Oral Traditions.

— A Good Start: The Aussteier or Dowry. Foster, Joseph, ed. (Illus.). 88p. (Orig.). 1990. pap. 22.00 (0-917127-05-6) Oral Traditions.

— Made of Mud: Stoneware Potteries in Central Pennsylvania, 1831-1929. LC 79-2708. (Illus.). 1979. pap. 12.50 (0-271-00228-X, Keystone Bks) Pa St U Pr.

— Willow, Oak & Rye: Basket Traditions in Pennsylvania. LC 79-2709. (Illus.). 1979. pap. 15.00 (0-271-00229-8, Keystone Bks) Pa St U Pr.

Lasansky, Jeannette, et al, eds. On the Cutting Edge: Textile Collectors, Collections, & Traditions. LC 93-46431. (Illus.). 120p. 1994. pap. 24.00 (0-8122-1518-4) U of Pa Pr.

Lasansky, Jeannette, et al. The History & Magic of Honeycomb. LC 97-17173. 1997. 25.00 (0-917127-11-0) Oral Traditions.

— On the Cutting Edge: Textile Collectors, Collections, & Traditions. LC 93-46431. 1994. 24.95 (0-917127-08-0) Oral Traditions.

— Pieced by Mother: Symposium Papers. (Illus.). 104p. (Orig.). 1988. pap. 19.95 (0-917127-03-X) Oral Traditions.

Lasansky, Jeannette, jt. auth. see Blake, Jody.

Lasar, Matthew. Pacifica Radio: The Rise of an Alternative Network. LC 98-19096. (American Subjects Ser.). (Illus.). 304p. 1999. 49.95 (1-56639-660-3) Temple U Pr.

***Lasar, Matthew.** Pacifica Radio: The Rise of an Alternative Network. rev. ed. (American Subjects Ser.). (Illus.). 320p. 2000. pap. 19.95 (1-56639-777-4) Temple U Pr.

LaSarre, Zulu. La Palabra. LC 93-199226. (Colecciom Luz Ser.). (SPA., Illus.). 76p. 1991. pap. 12.50 (0-9634009-0-8) Luz Bilingual.

Lasarte, Pedro, ed. Satira Hecha Por Mateo Rosas De Oquendo a las Cosas Que Pasan En el Piru, Ano De 1598. (Colonial Spanish American Ser.: No. 2). cxx, 182p. 1990. 20.00 (0-940639-52-1) Hispanic Seminary.

Lasater, Ann. Affirming Miracles: (How to Use Affirmations to Change Your Life) 35p. 1998. mass mkt. 7.95 (0-9665988-1-4) Anns Bks.

— Journey of Gratitude: Writing a Gratitude Journal. (Illus.). 66p. 1998. mass mkt. 10.00 (0-9665988-2-2) Anns Bks.

***Lasater, Annette N. & Casey, Watt M., Jr.** Two to Mexico. 2nd ed. (Illus.). 180p. 2000. reprint ed. pap. text 20.00 (0-9672336-1-5, Santa Cruz Pr) Isa Cattle.

Lasater, Dale. Falfurrias: Ed C. Lasater & the Development of South Texas. LC 84-40130. (Illus.). 344p. 1998. pap. 16.95 (0-89096-830-6) Tex A&M Univ Pr.

***Lasater, Judith.** Living Your Yoga: Finding the Spiritual in Everyday Life. LC 99-75818. (Illus.). 192p. 2000. pap. 12.95 (0-9627138-8-0, Pub. by Rodmell Pr) SCB Distributors.

Lasater, Judith. Relax & Renew: Restful Yoga for Stressful Times. LC 95-68875. (Illus.). 240p. (Orig.). 1995. pap. 21.95 (0-9627138-4-8) Rodmell Pr.

Lasater, Kaye, ed. see Hill, Harriet T.

***Lasater, Laurence M.** The Lasater Philosophy of Cattle Raising. rev. ed. Zapiola, Marcos Gimenez, ed. (Illus.). 116-120p. 2000. pap. text 20.00 (0-9672336-2-3) Isa Cattle.

Lasater, Martin. The New Pacific Community: U. S. Strategic Options in Asia. LC 96-19487. 192p. (C). 1996. pap. 69.00 (0-8133-8869-4, Pub. by Westview) HarpC.

Lasater, Martin L. Changing of the Guard: President Clinton & the Security of Taiwan. 280p. (C). 1995. pap. 75.00 (0-8133-8806-6, Pub. by Westview) HarpC.

***Lasater, Martin L.** The Taiwan Conundrum in U. S. China Policy. 329p. 1999. 69.00 (0-8133-3696-1) Westview.

***Lasater, Martin L. & Yu, Peter Kien-Hong.** Taiwan's Security in the Post-Deng Xiaoping Era. LC 00-31562. 2000. write for info. (0-7146-5083-8, Pub. by F Cass Pubs) Intl Spec Bk.

Lasater, Martin L., jt. ed. see Chang, Parris H.

***Lasatowicz, Maria Katarzyna & Joachimsthaler, Jurgen.** Assimilation - Abgrenzung - Austausch: Interkulturalitat in Sprache und Literatur. (Oppelner Beitrage Zur Germanistik Ser.). 411p. 1999. 52.95 (3-631-34894-0) P Lang Pubng.

Lasby, Clarence G. Eisenhower's Heart Attack: How Ike Beat Heart Disease & Held on to the Presidency. LC 96-45407. (Illus.). 400p. 1997. 29.95 (0-7006-0822-2) U Pr of KS.

Lasca, N. P. & Donahue, J., eds. Archaeological Geology of North America. (DNAG Centennial Special Volumes Ser.: Vol. 4). (Illus.). 543p. 1990. 31.25 (0-8137-5304-X) Geol Soc.

Lascar, Daniel, jt. auth. see Cori, Rene.

***Lascardo, Rita.** Down on the Farm. (Green Light Readers Ser.). 24p. (J). 2000. 10.95 (0-15-202363-1) Harcourt.

Lascariges, V. Celia, jt. auth. see Hinitz, Blythe F.

Lascaro, Rita. Down on the Farm. LC 98-15567. (Green Light Readers Ser.). (Illus.). 20p. (J). 1999. pap. 3.95 (0-15-202000-4) Harcourt.

Lascaux, P., ed. see Destuynder, P. & Salaun, M.

Lascelle, Joan, jt. auth. see Brown, Howard Mayer.

Lascelle, Ruth. A Dwelling Place for God. 6th rev. ed. LC 97-71131. (Illus.). 300p. 1997. pap. text 15.00 (0-9654519-2-5) Bedrock Pub.

— Jewish Faith & the New Covenant. 2nd rev. ed. LC 98-70019. (Illus.). 380p. 1998. pap. 15.00 (0-9654519-6-8) Bedrock Pub.

— My Jewish People. LC 97-77833. (Illus.). 256p. 1998. pap. 13.00 (0-9654519-1-7) Bedrock Pub.

— New Covenant Passover Haggadah: Remembering the Exodus of Deliverance. LC 96-80197. (Illus.). 200p. (Orig.). 1997. pap. text 10.00 (0-9654519-3-3) Bedrock Pub.

— A New Look into the Old Book: A Look into the Bible to Be in Health. 230p. (C). 1998. pap. text 13.00 (0-9654519-0-9) Bedrock Pub.

— On What Day Did Christ Die? The Last Week of Christ. 2nd rev. ed. LC 96-80198. 162p. 1997. pap. text 10.00 (0-9654519-9-2) Bedrock Pub.

— Pictures of Messiah (In the Holy Scriptures) LC 97-71130. (Illus.). 255p. (Orig.). 1997. pap. text 13.00 (0-9654519-8-4) Bedrock Pub.

— We Have a Great High Priest: A Brief Study of the Book of Hebrews. LC 97-72359. 225p. 1997. pap. text 13.00 (0-9654519-7-6) Bedrock Pub.

Lascelles, ed. see Kennett-Barrington.

Lascelles, David & Peacock, Roy. Self Assessment for Business Excellence. LC 95-39122. (Quality in Action Ser.). 1996. pap. write for info. (0-07-709186-8) McGraw.

Lascelles, Mary. Jane Austen & Her Art. 240p. (C). 1995. pap. 22.50 (0-485-12113-1, Pub. by Athlone Pr) Humanities.

— The Story-Teller Retrieves the Past: Historical Fiction & Fictitious History in the Art of Scott, Stevenson, Kipling, & Some Others. 1980. 39.95 (0-19-812802-9) OUP.

Lascelles, Mary, ed. see Johnson, Samuel.

Lascelles, P. T. & Donaldson, D. Diagnostic Function Tests in Chemical Pathology. 224p. 1990. lib. bdg. 82.00 (0-7462-0108-7) Kluwer Academic.

— Diagnostic Function Tests in Chemical Pathology. (C). 1990. pap. text 73.50 (0-7462-0107-9) Kluwer Academic.

Lascelles, T. S. City & South London Railway. (C). 1985. 50.00 (0-85361-360-5) St Mut.

***Lasceve, Vincent.** Qualifying Paper for use on the AGFA Chromapress. (Research & Technology Reports Ser.: Vol. 20). (Illus.). 64p. (C). 2000. pap. 50.00 (0-88362-304-8) GATFPress.

Lasch, Callie & Hanlon, Grace. The Three R's for Special Education: Rights Resources & Results. abr. ed. 1997. pap. text 29.95 incl. audio (0-9646168-2-3) Edvantage Media.

Lasch, Christopher. The Culture of Narcissism. 1983. mass mkt. 5.95 (0-446-32104-4, Pub. by Warner Bks) Little.

— The Culture of Narcissism: American Life in an Age of Diminishing Expectations. 1991. pap. 13.95 (0-393-30738-7) Norton.

— Essays on Women & Family. Date not set. write for info. (0-393-03951-X) Norton.

— Haven in a Heartless World: The Family Besieged. 256p. 1995. pap. 12.95 (0-393-31303-4, Norton Paperbks) Norton.

— The Minimal Self: Psychic Survival in Troubled Times. LC 84-4103. 352p. 1985. reprint ed. pap. 12.95 (0-393-30263-6) Norton.

— The New Radicalism in America, 1889-1963: The Intellectual As a Social Type. 384p. 1997. pap. 14.95 (0-393-31696-3) Norton.

— The Revolt of the Elites & the Betrayal of Democracy. 276p. 1995. 22.00 (0-393-03699-5) Norton.

— The Revolt of the Elites & the Betrayal of Democracy. 256p. 1996. pap. 12.95 (0-393-31371-9, Norton Paperbks) Norton.

— The True & Only Heaven: Progress & Its Critics. 592p. 1991. pap. 16.95 (0-393-30795-6) Norton.

— Women & the Common Life: Love, Marriage, & Feminism. Lasch-Quinn, Elizabeth, ed. LC 96-15988. 192p. 1997. 23.00 (0-393-04018-6) Norton.

— Women & the Common Life: Love, Marriage & Feminism. 224p. 1997. pap. 12.95 (0-393-31697-1) Norton.

Lasch, Christopher, ed. see Addams, Jane.

Lasch-Quinn, Elisabeth. Black Neighbors: Race & the Limits of Reform in the American Settlement House Movement, 1890-1945. LC 93-18533. (Illus.). xiv, 226p. (C). 1993. 55.00 (0-8078-2114-4); pap. 18.95 (0-8078-4423-3) U of NC Pr.

Lasch-Quinn, Elizabeth, ed. see Lasch, Christopher.

Lascher, Edward L., Jr. The Politics of Automobile Insurance Reform: Ideas, Institutions & Public Policy in North America. LC 99-18215. (American Governance & Public Policy Ser.). 160p. 1999. 69.00 (0-87840-739-1) Georgetown U Pr.

Lascher, Edward L., Jr., jt. ed. see Williams, Shirley.

Laschever, Barnett D. & Fusco, Andi M. Connecticut: An Explorer's Guide. 3rd ed. LC 98-13751. (Explorer's Guide Ser.). (Illus.). 409p. 1999. pap. 18.00 (0-88150-415-7, Pub. by Countryman) Norton.

***Laschi, Giuliana.** L'agricoltura Italiana E l'Integrazione Europea. xi, 350p. 1999. 33.95 (3-906762-37-8) P Lang Pubng.

Lasco, Dianna. Developing a Successful Women's Track & Field Program. LC 85-21790. 228p. (C). 1986. text 27.95 (0-13-205261-X, Busn) P-H.

Lascoe, O. D. Handbook of Fabrication Processes. 456p. 1988. 155.00 (0-87170-302-5, 6401) ASM.

Lascoe, Orville D., et al. Machine Shop Operations & Setups. 4th ed. (Illus.). 582p. 1973. 25.96 (0-8269-1842-5) Am Technical.

LasCola, Amy, ed. see Eichel, Carol.

LaScola, Jane N., jt. auth. see Blanchette, Rick.

LaScolea, Len J., Jr. & Rangoonwala, Ramzan. Quinolones in Pulmonary Tuberculosis Management. LC 96-13283. (Illus.). 120p. 1996. text 55.00 (0-8247-9740-X) Dekker.

Lascombe, J., ed. see Societe de Chimie Physique Staff.

Lascombe, Jean, ed. see International Conference on Raman Spectroscopy Staff.

Lascombes, Andre, ed. Spectacle & Image in Renaissance Europe: Selected Papers of the 32nd Conference at the Centre d'Etudes Superieures de la Renaissance de Tours 29 June-8 July 1989. LC 92-44780. (Symbola et Emblemata, Studies in Renaissance & Baroque Symbolism: No. 4). (FRE., Illus.). viii, 367p. 1993. 119.50 (90-04-09774-0) Brill Academic Pubs.

Lasconi, Diego & Gutierez, Guillermo, trs. Los Cinco Patitos. LC 96-44511.Tr. of Five Little Ducks. (SPA., Illus.). 32p. (J). (gr. k-1). 1997. 15.95 (1-55858-716-0, Pub. by North-South Bks NYC) Chronicle Bks.

Lasconi, Diego & Gutierrez, Guillermo, trs. Los Cinco Patitos. LC 96-44511.Tr. of Five Little Ducks. (SPA., Illus.). 32p. (J). (gr. k-1). 1997. pap. 6.95 (1-55858-715-2, Pub. by North-South Bks NYC) Chronicle Bks.

Lasconi, Diego, tr. see Joosse, Barbara.

Lasconi, Diego, tr. see Masurel, Claire.

Lasconi, Diego, tr. see Reider, Katja.

Lascurain, Anna M., jt. auth. see McMahon, Joanne D.

***Lasdun, James.** Besieged. 256p. 2000. pap. 13.00 (0-393-32074-X, Norton Paperbks) Norton.

Lasdun, James. Three Evenings: Stories. 192p. 1992. 18.00 (0-374-20887-5) FS&G.

— Woman Police Officer in Elevator: Poems. 72p. 1998. pap. 11.00 (0-393-31838-9, Norton Paperbks) Norton.

Lasdun, James & Davis, Pia. Walking & Eating in Tuscany & Umbria. LC 97-142931. 1997. pap. write for info. (0-14-024476-X) Viking Penguin.

An Asterisk (*) at the beginning of an entry indicates that the title is appearing for the first time.

— Two by Two: The Story of Noah's Faith. (J). (ps-2). 1998. 5.95 (0-933657-66-8, 3000850) Rainbow Studies.
— Two Lads & a Dad: The Prodigal Son. (J). (gr. k-4). 1998. pap. 5.95 (0-933657-85-4) Rainbow Studies.
— The Wall That Did Not Fall: The Story of Rahab's Faith. (J). (ps-2). 1998. pap. 5.95 (0-933657-70-6) Rainbow Studies.
— The Wall That Did Not Fall: The Story of Rahab's Faith. LC 87-63420. (Me Too! Bks.). (Illus.). 32p. (J). (ps-k). 1988. 6.95 (0-86606-433-8, 3000885) Treasure Pub.
— The Weak Strongman: Samson. LC 90-60456. (Me Too! Bks.). (Illus.). 32p. (J). (gr. k-3). 1990. 6.95 (0-86606-442-7, 3000915) Treasure Pub.
— Weak Strongman: Samson. (J). (gr. k-4). 1998. pap. 5.95 (0-933657-81-1) Rainbow Studies.
— Who Needs a Boat: Moses. (J). (ps-2). 1998. pap. 5.95 (0-933657-64-1) Rainbow Studies.
— Who Needs a Boat? The Story of Moses. LC 87-83295. (Me Too! Bks.). (Illus.). 32p. (J). (ps-k). 1988. 6.95 (0-86606-431-1, 3000877) Treasure Pub.

Lashbrooke, E. C., Jr. Tax-Exempt Organizations. LC 84-22253. 364p. 1985. 75.00 (0-89930-083-9, LTE/, Quorum Bks) Greenwood.

Lashbrooke, E. C., Jr. & Swygert, Michael I. The Legal Handbook of Business Transactions: A Guide for Managers & Entrepreneurs. LC 86-30595. 599p. 1987. 95.00 (0-89930-179-7, LLH/, Quorum Bks) Greenwood.

***Lasher.** Practical Financial Management. 2nd ed. (SWC-Finance Ser.). (C). 2000. pap. 19.00 (0-324-05598-6) Sth-Wstrn College.

Lasher. Practical Financial Management. 2nd ed. LC 99-25138. (SWC-Finance). 650p. 1999. pap. 95.95 (0-324-00674-8) Thomson Learn.

***Lasher.** Survey of Finance. 2001. 66.50 (0-324-02034-1) Thomson Learn.

Lasher, Lawrence, ed. Conversations with Bernard Malamud. LC 90-49374. (Literary Conversations Ser.). xxiii, 156 p. 1991. pap. 15.95 (0-87805-490-1) U Pr of Miss.

Lasher, Marcia. Scrap Quilt, Strips & Spider Webs. (Illus.). 64p. 1991. 10.95 (0-922705-26-7) Quilt Day.

Lasher, Margot. And the Animals Will Teach You: Discovering Ourselves Through Our Relationships with Animals. LC 97-103387. 256p. 1996. pap. 13.00 (0-425-15458-0) Berkley Pub.

Lasher, Micah. The Magic of Micah Lasher. 256p. 1996. pap. 15.00 (0-684-81390-4) S&S Trade.
— Practical Financial Management. (FN - Financial Mangement Ser.). (C). 1996. mass mkt. 17.95 (0-314-20753-8) S-W Pub.
— Practical Financial Management. 2nd ed. (SWC-Finance Ser.). 1999. pap., student ed. 19.75 (0-324-00797-3) Thomson Learn.

Lasher, William. Practical Financial Management. LC 96-41519. 600p. 1996. mass mkt. 68.00 (0-314-20186-6) West Pub.

Lasher, William R. The Perfect Business Plan Made Simple. LC 93-35669. 288p. 1994. pap. 12.95 (0-385-46934-9) Doubleday.
— Strategic Thinking for Smaller Businesses & Divisions. LC 99-17509. 250p. 1999. 62.95 (0-631-20838-0); pap. 26.95 (0-631-20839-9) Blackwell Pubs.

Lashgari, Deirdre, ed. Violence, Silence & Anger: Women's Writing As Transgression. 384p. (C). 1995. pap. text 19.50 (0-8139-1493-0) U Pr of Va.

Lashgari, Dierdre, ed. Violence, Silence, & Anger: Women's Writing As Transgression. 384p. (C). 1995. text 55.00 (0-8139-1492-2) U Pr of Va.

Lashier, Jennifer L. College Memories 101: 101 Questions for the Graduate to Preserve Precious College Memories. large type ed. 108p. 1998. spiral bd. 9.99 (1-56383-077-9, 4501) G & R Pub.
— From This Day Forward: 101 Questions for the Bride to Preserve Precious Dating, Engagement & Wedding Memories. large type ed. 108p. 1998. spiral bd. 9.99 (1-56383-078-7, 4502) G & R Pub.
— Tassels & Tomorrows: 101 Questions for the Graduate to Preserve Precious High School Memories. large type ed. 114p. 1998. spiral bd. 9.99 (1-56383-076-0, 4500) G & R Pub.

Lashier, Kathleen. Dad, Share Your Life with Me... (Memory-a-Day Ser.). 366p. (Orig.). 1992. pap. 8.95 (1-56383-040-X, 5054) G & R Pub.
— Grandma, Tell Me Your Memories... (Memory-a-Day Ser.). 366p. (Orig.). 1992. pap. 8.95 (1-56383-037-X, 5051) G & R Pub.
— Grandpa, Tell Me Your Memories... (Memory-a-Day Ser.). 366p. (Orig.). 1992. pap. 8.95 (1-56383-038-8, 5052) G & R Pub.
— Heirloom Edition - "Grandma, Tell Me Your Memories..." A Daily Journal of Childhood Memories. (Memory-a-Day Ser.). 370p. (Orig.). 1997. pap., spiral bd. 18.95 (1-56383-067-1, 5060) G & R Pub.
— Heirloom Edition - "Mom, Share Your Life with Me..." A Daily Journal of Childhood Memories. (Memory-a-Day Ser.). (Illus.). 370p. (Orig.). 1997. pap. 18.95 (1-56383-068-X, 5061) G & R Pub.
— Heirloom Edition - "To the Best of My Recollection" A Daily Journal of Childhood Memories. (Memory-a-Day Ser.). 370p. (Orig.). 1997. pap. 18.95 (1-56383-069-8, 5062) G & R Pub.
— Mom, Share Your Life with Me . . . (Memory-a-Day Ser.). 366p. (Orig.). 1992. pap. 8.95 (1-56383-039-6, 5053) G & R Pub.
— My Days...My Pictures Vol. I: A Daily Drawing Journal for 4 to 6 Year Olds. (Memory Journals for Young Writers Ser.). 375p. (J). (ps-1). 1995. pap. text 9.99 (1-56383-054-X, 5055) G & R Pub.
— To My Dear Friend: Oh, the Memories We've Made. (Memory-a-Day Ser.). 366p. (Orig.). 1996. pap., spiral bd. 8.95 (1-56383-061-2, 5059) G & R Pub.
— To the Best of My Recollection: A Childhood Memory Journal for Adults. (Memory-a-Day Ser.). 366p. (Orig.). 1996. pap., spiral bd. 8.95 (1-56383-060-4, 5058) G & R Pub.

Lashier, Kathleen & Farrell, Joanne B. Sisters: A Daily Journal of Memories. 376p. 1998. spiral bd. 12.95 (1-56383-071-X, 5050) G & R Pub.

Lashings, Edwina G. Chocolate & Chortles. 64p. (Orig.). 1975. pap. 2.95 (0-938758-02-0) MTM Pub Co.

Lashinsky, Herbert, tr. see Leontovich, M. A., ed.

Lashley, Conard. Improving Study Skills: A Competence Approach. LC 95-14759. (Illus.). 192p. 1996. 29.95 (0-304-33336-0) Continuum.

***Lashley, Conrad.** Hospitality Retail Management: A Unit Manager's Guide. 256p. 2000. pap. 35.95 (0-7506-4616-0) Buttrwrth-Heinemann.

***Lashley, Conrad & Morrison, Alison, eds.** In Search of Hospitality: Theoretical Perspectives & Debates. 320p. 2000. 56.95 (0-7506-4562-8) Buttrwrth-Heinemann.

Lashley, Cynthia. Taking the "Sigh" Out of Science: A Handbook for Teachers & Parents of Young Children. (Illus.). 60p. (Orig.). 1992. pap., spiral bd. 7.95 (0-9623249-6-5) Intermountain.

Lashley, Felissa R. Clinical Genetics in Nursing Practice. 2nd ed. LC 98-12409. (Illus.). 543p. 1998. 79.95 (0-8261-1177-7) Springer Pub.

Lashley, Felissa R., jt. ed. see Durham, Jerry D.

Lashley, Marilyn E. Public Television: Panacea, Pork Barrel, or Public Trust?, 33. LC 91-34482. (Contributions to the Study of Mass Media & Communications Ser.: No. 33). 176p. 1992. 42.95 (0-313-27964-0, LPT/, Greenwood Pr) Greenwood.

Lashley, Marilyn E. & Jackson, Melanie N., eds. African Americans & the New Policy Consensus: Retreat of the Liberal State?, 347. LC 94-872. (Contributions in Political Science Ser.: No. 347). 264p. 1994. 59.95 (0-313-28880-1, Greenwood Pr) Greenwood.

Lashley, Mary E., et al. Being Called to Care. LC 93-7296. 215p. (C). 1994. pap. text 21.95 (0-7914-1840-5) State U NY Pr.
— Being Called to Care. LC 93-7296. 215p. (C). 1994. text 64.50 (0-7914-1839-1) State U NY Pr.

Lashley, Rickey D. Policework: The Need for a Noble Character. LC 94-32921. 144p. 1995. 55.00 (0-275-95013-1, Praeger Pubs) Greenwood.

***Lashley, Thomas.** Disdain. LC 99-66934. 192p. 2000. pap. 11.95 (1-56315-270-3, Pub. by SterlingHse) Natl Bk Netwk.

Lashley, Thomas. Malevolence. 184p. 1997. 19.95 (1-56315-080-8) SterlingHse.

Lashman, Rebekah, jt. auth. see McCarthy, Karin.

Lashmar, Paul. Spy Flights in the Cold War. (Illus.). 256p. 1998. pap. 24.95 (0-7509-1970-1, Pub. by Sutton Pub Ltd) Intl Pubs Mktg.

Lashmore-Davies, C. N., jt. auth. see Manheimer, Wallace M.

Lashner, William. Hostile Witness. 608p. 1996. mass mkt. 6.50 (0-06-100988-1) HarpC.
— Hostile Witness. large type ed. LC 95-34856. (Large Print Bks.). 1995. 25.95 (1-56895-248-1, Compass) Wheeler Pub.
— Veritas. 592p. 1997. mass mkt. 6.50 (0-06-101023-5, Harp PBks) HarpC.

Lashnits, Judi W., jt. auth. see Wright, John C., Jr.

Lashof, Daniel & Tirpak, Dennis A. Policy Options for Stabilizing Global Climate. 825p. 1990. 160.00 (1-56032-072-9) Hemisp Pub.

***Lashof, Daniel, et al.** Kingpens of Carbon: How Fossil Fuel Producers Contribute to Global Warming. 32p. 1999. pap. write for info. (1-893340-21-X) Natl Resources Defense Coun.

Lashomb, Audrey. Going Home: Grindstone Island. (Illus.). 150p. 1998. pap. 20.00 (0-9626898-5-8) Grindstone Pr.

Lashway, Larry. Leading with Vision. LC 97-27661. xii, 148p. 1997. pap. 13.50 (0-86552-138-7) U of Oreg ERIC.
— Measuring Leadership: A Guide to Assessment for Development of School Executives. LC 99-19446. 1999. pap. 9.75 (0-86552-140-9) U of Oreg ERIC.
— Multidimensional School Leadership. LC 97-69150. (Fastback Ser.: No. 424). 53p. 1997. pap. 3.00 (0-87367-624-6, FB#424) Phi Delta Kappa.

***Lashway, Mark.** The Blood Moon. LC 00-190072. 2000. 25.00 (0-7388-1472-5); pap. 18.00 (0-7388-1473-3) Xlibris Corp.

Lasic, D. D. & Papahadjopoulos, Demetrios. Medical Applications of Liposomes. LC 98-22644. 779p. 1998. 273.00 (0-444-82917-2) Elsevier.

Lasic, Danilo D. Liposomes: From Physics to Applications. LC 92-49031. 594p. 1993. 323.50 (0-444-89548-5) Elsevier.
— Liposomes in Gene Delivery. LC 96-35300. (Illus.). 320p. 1997. spiral bd. 74.95 (0-8493-3109-9) CRC Pr.

Lasic, Danilo D. & Barenholz, Yechezkel, eds. Handbook of Nonmedical Applications of Liposomes, 4 vols., Set. 1996. 695.00 (0-8493-4014-4) CRC Pr.
— Handbook of Nonmedical Applications of Liposomes, Vol. 1. 352p. 1996. boxed set 199.95 (0-8493-4731-9, 4731) CRC Pr.
— Handbook of Nonmedical Applications of Liposomes, Vol. 2. 400p. 1996. boxed set 209.95 (0-8493-4011-X, 4011) CRC Pr.
— Handbook of Nonmedical Applications of Liposomes, Vol. III. LC 95-426. 368p. 1996. boxed set 209.95 (0-8493-4012-8, 4012) CRC Pr.
— Handbook of Nonmedical Applications of Liposomes, Vol. 4. 352p. 1996. boxed set 209.95 (0-8493-4013-6, 4013) CRC Pr.

Lasic, Danilo D., jt. ed. see Martin, F. J.

Lasic, Vinko D. Pleterni Ukras Od Najstarijih Vremena Do Danas: Njegov Likovni Oblik I Nutarnje Znacenje - Supplement: The Principal Conclusions of This Research: The Twist or Guilloche As Ornament from Ancient Times to Present: Its Exterior Form & Inner Meaning. Ziral Staff, ed. Condic, Dusko, tr. from CRO. (CRO., Illus.). 920p. 1995. 100.00 (1-880829-02-9) Z I R A L.

Lasic, Vinko D., ed. see Coric, Simun S.

Lasic, Vinko D., ed. see Kordic, Lucijan.

Lasic, Vinko D., ed. see Pandzic, Bazilije.

Lasiecka, Irena & Morton, Blaise, eds. Control Problems in Industry: Proceedings of the SIAM Symposium on Control Problems, 1994. LC 95-36464. (Progress in Systems & Control Theory Ser.: Vol. 21). 349p. 1995. 98.50 (0-8176-3813-X) Birkhauser.
— Control Problems in Industry: Proceedings of the SIAM Symposium on Control Problems, 1994. LC 95-36464. (Progress in Systems & Control Theory Ser.: Vol. 21). 1995. write for info. (3-7643-3813-X) Birkhauser.

***Lasiecka, Irena & Triggiani, Roberto.** Control Theory for Partial Differential Equations - Continuous & Approximation Theories Vol. I: Abstract Parabolic Systems. LC 99-11617. (Encyclopedia of Mathematics & Its Applications Ser.: No. 74). 680p. (C). 1999. 120.00 (0-521-43408-4) Cambridge U Pr.
— Control Theory for Partial Differential Equations - Continuous & Approximation Theories Vol. II: Abstract Hyperbolic-Like Systems over a Finite Time Horizon. LC 99-11617. (Encyclopedia of Mathematics & Its Applications Ser.: No. 75). 464p. (C). 2000. 90.00 (0-521-58401-9) Cambridge U Pr.

Lasiecka, Irena, jt. auth. see Triggiani, R.

Lasiecka, Irena, jt. ed. see Cox, Steven.

Lasiecka, Irena, jt. ed. see Kurzhanski, Alexander B.

Lasiecka, Irena, jt. ed. see Triggiani, R.

Lasierra, Inigo Abbad Y, see Abbad y Lasierra, Inigo.

Lasilla, Dennis R. & Kilpatrick, Bob G. Compensation Tax Guide. 2nd ed. LC 94-191943. 504p. 1994. pap. 39.50 (0-8080-0008-X) CCH INC.

Lasinski, Thomas, jt. auth. see Levi-Setti, Riccardo.

Lasio. Professor Lasio's The Office Passalong: Round Tuits & Other Silliness. Sharp, F. J., ed. LC 91-71394. (Illus.). 50p. 1991. 5.00 (0-9629202-0-7) Co Called W.

Lasjaunias, P., et al, eds. Frontiers in European Radiology, Vol. 4. (Illus.). 165p. 1984. 69.95 (0-387-13410-7) Spr-Verlag.

Lasjaunias, P. & Berenstein, A. Surgical Neuroangiography, Vol. 1. (Functional Anatomy of Craniofacial Arteries Ser.). (Illus.). 450p. 1994. text 215.00 (0-387-16534-7) Spr-Verlag.
— Surgical Neuroangiography, Vol. 2. (Endovascular Treatment of Craniofacial Lesions Ser.). (Illus.). 450p. 1996. 199.00 (0-387-16535-5) Spr-Verlag.

Lasjaunias, P., jt. auth. see Berenstein, A.

Lasjaunias, Pierre & Berenstein, Alejandro. Endovascular Treatment of Cerebral Lesions. (Surgical Neuroangiography Ser.: Vol. 4). (Illus.). 344p. 1992. 198.00 (3-540-17500-8) Spr-Verlag.
— Endovascular Treatment of Craniofacial Lesions. (Surgical Neuroangiography Ser.: Vol. 2). 434p. 1996. 215.00 (3-540-16535-5) Spr-Verlag.
— Functional Anatomy of Craniofacial Arteries. (Surgical Neuroangiography Ser.: Vol. 1). 426p. 1987. 199.00 (3-540-16534-7) Spr-Verlag.
— Functional Vascular Anatomy of Brain, Spinal Cord & Spine. (Surgical Neuroangiography Ser.: Vol. 3). 337p. 1990. 198.00 (3-540-17501-6) Spr-Verlag.

Lasjaunias, Pierre L. Vascular Diseases in Neonates, Infants & Children: Interventional Neuroradiology Management: P. Lasjaunias. LC 96-29097. 1996. write for info. (0-387-60845-1) Spr-Verlag.
— Vascular Diseases in Neonates, Infants & Children: Interventional Neuroradiology Management: P. Lasjaunias. LC 96-29097. (Illus.). 400p. 1997. 239.00 (3-540-60845-1) Spr-Verlag.

Lask, Bryan. Anorexia Nervosa & Related Eating Disorders in Childhood & Adolescence. 2nd ed. 416p. 1999. 44.95 (0-86377-803-8) L Erlbaum Assocs.

Lask, Bryan & Fosson, Abe. Childhood Illness: The Psychosomatic Approach: Children Talking with Their Bodies. LC 89-4332. (Wiley Series in Family Psychology). 174p. 1989. reprint ed. pap. 54.00 (0-608-07295-8, 206752300009) Bks Demand.

***Lask, Emil.** The Logic of Philosophy & the Doctrine of Categories. Braun, Christian, tr. 400p. 1999. 55.00 (1-85343-474-4, Pub. by Free Assoc Bks); pap. 25.00 (1-85343-475-2, Pub. by Free Assoc Bks) Intl Spec Bk.

Lask, Gary P. & Lowe, Nicholas J. Lasers in Cutaneous & Cosmetic Surgery. Fletcher, Judy, ed. LC 98-7037. (Illus.). 285p. 1999. text. write for info. (0-443-07639-1, W B Saunders Co) Harcrt Hlth Sci Grp.

Lask, Gary P. & Moy, Ronald L., eds. Principles & Techniques of Cutaneous Surgery. 637p. 1995. text 179.00 (0-07-036471-0) McGraw-Hill HPD.

Lask, I. M., tr. see Ben-Amos, Dan, et al, eds.

Laska, Eugene M., et al, eds. Information Support to Mental Health Programs: An International Perspective. 301p. 1983. 40.95 (0-89885-083-5, Kluwer Acad Hman Sci) Kluwer Academic.

Laska, John A. & Juarez, Tina. Grading & Marking in American Schools: Two Centuries of Debate. LC 92-5612. 162p. 1992. pap. 25.95 (0-398-06223-4) C C Thomas.
— Grading & Marking in American Schools: Two Centuries of Debate. LC 92-5612. 162p. (C). 1992. text 38.95 (0-398-05806-7) C C Thomas.

Laska, Lewis L. Tennessee Legal Research Handbook. LC 77-71305. x, 203p. 1977. lib. bdg. 36.00 (0-930342-04-6, 300860) W S Hein.
— The Tennessee State Constitution: A Reference Guide, 2. LC 90-32454. (Reference Guides to the State Constitutions of the United States Ser.: No. 2). 216p. 1990. lib. bdg. 65.00 (0-313-26653-0, LTO/, Greenwood Pr) Greenwood.

Laska, Mark, jt. auth. see Winsor, Mari.

Laska, P. J. The Day the Eighties Began. LC 91-71452. 62p. (Orig.). 1991. pap. 8.00 (0-9627891-1-9) Igneus Pr.

Laska, Shirley. Floodproof Retrofitting: Homeowner Self-Help Behavior. (Monograph: No. 49). 280p. (Orig.). 1991. pap. 20.00 (1-877943-04-5) Natural Hazards.

Laska, Shirley & Puffer, Andrew, eds. Coastlines of the Gulf of Mexico. LC 93-14140. (Coastlines of the World Ser.). 264p. 1993. 29.00 (0-87262-960-0) Am Soc Civil Eng.

Laska, Vera. Nazism Resistance & Holocaust in World War II: A Bibliography. LC 84-23586. 205p. 1985. 21.00 (0-8108-1771-3) Scarecrow.

Laska, Vera, ed. Women in the Resistance & in the Holocaust: The Voices of Eyewitnesses, 37. LC 82-12018. (Contributions in Women's Studies: No. 37). 330p. 1983. 69.50 (0-313-23457-4, LWH/, Greenwood Pr) Greenwood.

Laskar, A. L., et al, eds. Diffusion in Materials. (C). 1990. text 325.00 (0-7923-0653-8) Kluwer Academic.
— Diffusion in Solids. (Material Science Forum Ser.: Vol. 1). 290p. (C). 1984. pap. text 92.00 (0-87849-533-9, Pub. by Trans T Pub) Enfield Pubs NH.

***Laskaris.** Color Atlas of Oral Diseases in Children & Adolescents. LC 99-36035. (Illus.). 352p. 1998. 129.00 (0-86577-789-6, L2371) Thieme Med Pubs.

Laskaris, G. Pocket Atlas of Oral Diseases. (Illus.). 444p. 1997. pap. text 22.00 (0-86577-635-0) Thieme Med Pubs.

Laskaris, George. Color Atlas of Oral Diseases. 2nd ed. LC 94-9767. (Illus.). 400p. 1994. 99.00 (0-86577-537-0) Thieme Med Pubs.

Laskas, Jeanne M. The Balloon Lady & Other People I Know. LC 95-50215. (Emerging Writers in Creative Nonfiction Ser.). 210p. 1996. 24.95 (0-8207-0271-4); pap. 16.95 (0-8207-0266-8) Duquesne.

***Laskas, Jeanne Marie.** Fifty Acres & a Poodle: A True Story of Love & Adventure. LC 00-36075. 288p. 2000. pap. 23.95 (0-553-10904-9) Bantam.

Laskas, Jeanne Marie. We Remember: Women Born at the Turn of the Century Tell the Stories of Their Lives in Words & Pictures. LC 98-21777. (Illus.). 112p. 1999. 25.00 (0-688-15863-3, Wm Morrow) Morrow Avon.

Laskaya, Anne. Chaucer's Approach to Gender in the Canterbury Tales. (Chaucer Studies: No. 23). 232p. (C). 1995. 75.00 (0-85991-481-X) Boydell & Brewer.

Laskaya, Anne & Salisbury, Eve, eds. The Middle English Breton Lays. (Middle English Texts Ser.). 1995. pap. 16.00 (1-879288-62-1) Medieval Inst.

Lasken, Thomas H. Hiker's Diary. (Illus.). i, 40p. 1998. pap. write for info. (0-9664886-0-1) Creative Jrnls.

Lasker. Common Sense in Chess. pap. 3.95 (0-679-14006-9) Fodors Travel.

Lasker. Knowledge Capital. 1999. 24.95 (0-07-134125-0) McGraw.

Lasker, Albert D. The Lasker Story. 128p. 1994. pap. 11.95 (0-8442-3099-5, NTC Business Bks) NTC Contemp Pub Co.

Lasker, Bruno. Filipino Immigration to the Continental United States & to Hawaii. LC 69-18783. (American Immigration Collection. Series 1). (Illus.). 1976. reprint ed. 26.95 (0-405-00531-8) Ayer.
— Human Bondage in Southeast Asia. LC 79-138155. 406p. (C). 1972. reprint ed. lib. bdg. 26.00 (0-8371-5612-2, LAHU, Greenwood Pr) Greenwood.
— Peoples of Southeast Asia. LC 74-161765. (Institute of Pacific Relations Ser.). reprint ed. 37.50 (0-404-09029-X) AMS Pr.

Lasker, Bruno & Roman, Agnes. Propaganda from China & Japan: A Case Study in Propaganda Analysis. LC 75-30126. (Institute of Pacific Relations Ser.). reprint ed. 39.50 (0-404-59537-5) AMS Pr.

Lasker, Carrol, tr. see Small, Adam.

Lasker, Daniel J., tr. see Crescas, Hasdai.

Lasker, Edward. Chess for Fun & Chess for Blood. 2nd ed. (Illus.). 224p. 1962. pap. 6.95 (0-486-20146-5) Dover.
— Chess Strategy. Du Mont, J., tr. (Illus.). 282p. 1959. pap. 7.95 (0-486-20528-2) Dover.
— Go & Go Moku. (Illus.). 215p. 1960. pap. 6.95 (0-486-20613-0) Dover.
— Modern Chess Strategy. rev. ed. 1979. pap. 15.00 (0-679-14022-0, 9, Tarten) McKay.

Lasker, Emanuel. Common Sense in Chess. 139p. 1965. pap. 5.95 (0-486-21440-0) Dover.
— The Community of the Future. 1976. lib. bdg. 59.95 (0-8490-1650-9) Gordon Pr.
— Lasker's Manual of Chess. 390p. (YA). (gr. 7-12). 1960. pap. 8.95 (0-486-20640-8) Dover.

Lasker, G. W. & Mascie-Taylor, C. G., eds. Atlas of British Surnames. LC 89-70574. 96p. 1990. pap. 14.95 (0-8143-2253-0) Wayne St U Pr.

***Lasker, Gabriel W.** Happenings & Hearsay: Experiences of a Biological Anthropologist. (Illus.). 256p. 1999. 30.00 (0-8143-2840-7) Wayne St U Pr.

Lasker, Gabriel W. Surnames & Genetic Structure. (Cambridge Studies in Biological Anthropology). 150p. 1985. text 44.95 (0-521-30285-4) Cambridge U Pr.

Lasker, Gabriel W., ed. The Processes of Ongoing Human Evolution. LC 60-12566. 113p. reprint ed. pap. 35.10 (0-7837-3783-1, 204360200010) Bks Demand.

Lasker, Gabriel W. & Mascie-Taylor, C. G., eds. Research Strategies in Human Biology: Field & Survey Studies. (Studies in Biological Anthropology: No. 14). (Illus.). 216p. (C). 1993. text 69.95 (0-521-43188-3) Cambridge U Pr.

Lasker, Gabriel W., jt. ed. see Mascie-Taylor, C. G.

An Asterisk (*) at the beginning of an entry indicates that the title is appearing for the first time.

Lasker, George E. The Relation Between Major World Problems & Systems Learning: Proceedings of the Society for General Systems Research, 1983. 800p. 1983. pap. text 66.00 (*0-914105-28-0*) Intersystems Pubns.
Lasker, J., et al, eds. HIV Infection in Women Conference '95: Program & Abstracts. 157p. (Orig.). 1995. pap. text 25.00 (*0-924236-09-4*) Phila Scis Group.
Lasker, J., jt. auth. see Wallace, B.
Lasker, Joe. He's My Brother. LC 73-7318. (Albert Whitman Concept Bks.). (Illus.). 40p. (J). (gr. 1-3). 1974. lib. bdg. 14.95 (*0-8075-3218-5*) A Whitman.
— Nick Joins In. Tucker, Kathleen, ed. LC 79-29637. (Albert Whitman Concept Bks.: Level 1). (Illus.). 32p. (J). (gr. 1-3). 1980. lib. bdg. 14.95 (*0-8075-5612-2*) A Whitman.
Lasker, Jonathan. Complete Essays 1984-1998. LC 98-72158. (Illus.). 64p. 1998. pap. 10.00 (*0-9646466-5-X*) Edgewise Pr.
— Telling the Tales of Painting. 1994. 55.00 (*3-89322-564-1*, Pub. by Edition Cantz) Dist Art Pubs.
Lasker, Judith & Borg, Susan. In Search of Parenthood: Coping with Infertility & High-Tech Conception. LC 86-47863. 346p. reprint ed. pap. 107.30 (*0-7837-1384-3*, 204156000021) Bks Demand.
Lasker, Judith N. & Borg, Susan O. In Search of Parenthood: Coping with Infertility & High-Tech Conception. enl. rev. ed. LC 94-12494. 1994. lib. bdg. 69.95 (*1-56639-258-6*) Temple U Pr.
— In Search of Parenthood: Coping with Infertility & High-Tech Conception. rev. ed. LC 94-12494. 1994. pap. text 22.95 (*1-56639-259-4*) Temple U Pr.
Lasker, Roz D. Medicine & Public Health: The Power of Collaboration. LC 97-42385. 176p. (C). 1997. pap. text. write for info. (*0-924143-05-3*) NY Acad Med.
Lasker, Roz D., et al. Medicine & Public Health: The Power of Collaboration. LC 98-51607. 178p. 1998. 26.00 (*1-56793-100-6*) Health Admin Pr.
— Pocket Guide to Cases of Medicine & Public Health Collaboration. LC 98-22071. 1998. write for info. (*0-924143-08-8*) NY Acad Med.
Lasker-Schuler, Else. Concert (Konzert) Snook, Jean M., tr. from GER. & intro. by. LC 93-45427. (European Women Writers Ser.). xvi, 164p. 1994. text 35.00 (*0-8032-2900-3*) U of Nebr Pr.
***Lasker-Schuler, Else.** Selected Poems. 152p. 2000. pap. 11.95 (*1-892295-86-5*) Green Integer.
Lasker-Schuler, Else. Star in my Forehead. LC 99-87465. (Illus.). 118p. 2000. pap. text 12.95 (*0-930100-88-3*, Pub. by Holy Cow) Consort Bk Sales.
— Your Diamond Dreams Cut Open My Arteries: Poems by Else Lasker-Schuler. LC 82-2656. (Germanic Languages & Literatures Ser.: No. 100). ix, 317p. 1983. 32.50 (*0-8078-8100-7*) U of NC Pr.
***Lasker-Wallfisch, Anita.** Inherit the Truth: A Memoir of Survival & the Holocaust. 176p. 2000. text 22.95 (*0-312-20897-9*) St Martin.
Lasker, William. The World of Musical Instrument Makers: A Guided Tour. (Illus.). 109p. 1993. 29.95 (*0-88962-349-X*) Mosaic.
Laskey, Brian, jt. auth. see Kreines, David C.
Laskey, Carolyn T. Nurturing the Nurse on the Path to Success. Rezvan, Jerena B., ed. LC 93-61664. 210p. 1994. pap. 16.95 (*1-880254-11-5*) Vista.
— Poetry to Heal Your Inner Self. Hutchings, Patty, ed. LC 94-62011. 136p. 1994. pap. 9.95 (*1-880254-29-8*) Vista.
Laskey, Marcia L. & Gibson, Paula W. College Study Strategies: Thinking & Learning. 276p. (C). 1996. pap. text, teacher ed. write for info. (*0-205-26462-X*, T6462-0) Allyn.
— College Study Strategies: Thinking & Learning. LC 96-34290. 276p. 1996. pap. 34.00 (*0-205-19152-5*) Allyn.
Laskey, R. A., jt. ed. see Friday, L. E.
Laski, H. El Liberalismo Europeo. (Breviarios Ser.). (SPA.). pap. 8.99 (*968-16-0931-X*, Pub. by Fondo) Continental Bk.
Laski, Harold J. American Democracy: A Commentary & an Interpretation. LC 74-122066. x, 785p. 1977. reprint ed. 57.50 (*0-678-03165-7*) Kelley.
— The American Presidency. LC 80-50104. (Social Science Classics Ser.). 278p. 1980. pap. 24.95 (*0-87855-821-7*) Transaction Pubs.
— The American Presidency: An Interpretation. LC 80-50104. (Social Science Classics Ser.). 278p. 1980. 39.95 (*0-87855-390-8*) Transaction Pubs.
— The American Presidency: An Interpretation, Vol. 1. vii, 278p. 1998. reprint ed. 86.00 (*1-56169-372-3*) Gaunt.
— Danger of Being a Gentleman: And Other Essays. LC 72-1154. (Essay Index Reprint Ser.). 1977. reprint ed. 20.95 (*0-8369-2849-0*) Ayer.
— Democracy in Crisis. LC 70-97892. reprint ed. 37.50 (*0-404-03882-4*) AMS Pr.
— The Dilemma of Our Times: An Historical Essay. LC 68-14930. 272p. 1968. reprint ed. 39.50 (*0-678-05062-7*) Kelley.
— Faith, Reason & Civilization: An Essay in Historical Analysis. LC 74-167375. (Essay Index Reprint Ser.). 1977. reprint ed. 18.95 (*0-8369-2662-5*) Ayer.
— Foundations of Sovereignty & Other Essays. LC 68-22105. (Essay Index Reprint Ser.). 1977. 20.95 (*0-8369-0607-1*) Ayer.
— Liberty in the Modern State. rev. ed. LC 77-122064. xi, 175p. 1972. reprint ed. 35.00 (*0-678-03166-5*) Kelley.
— Reflections on the Revolution of Our Time. 367p. 1968. reprint ed. 25.00 (*0-7146-1564-1*, Pub. by F Cass Pubs) Intl Spec Bk.
— Reflections on the Revolution of Our Time. LC 68-14931. 367p. 1968. reprint ed. 22.50 (*0-678-05063-5*) Kelley.
— The Rise of European Liberalism. LC 96-20337. 327p. (Orig.). 1996. pap. text 22.95 (*1-56000-845-8*) Transaction Pubs.
— The Rise of European Liberalism: An Essay in Interpretation. LC 83-45444. reprint ed. 31.50 (*0-404-20152-0*) AMS Pr.
— State in Theory & Practice. 336p. 1967. 49.50 (*0-614-01806-4*) Elliots Bks.
— Studies in Law & Politics. LC 68-22106. (Essay Index Reprint Ser.). 1977. 20.95 (*0-8369-0608-X*) Ayer.
Laski, Harold J., et al, eds. A Century of Municipal Progress, 1835-1935. LC 77-27362. 511p. 1978. reprint ed. lib. bdg. 75.00 (*0-313-20192-7*, LACE, Greenwood Pr) Greenwood.
Laski, Harold J. & Hirst, Paul Q. Harold Laski: Collected Works. LC 97-9256. 330p. (C). 1997. write for info. (*0-415-16119-3*); write for info. (*0-415-16122-3*); write for info. (*0-415-16123-1*); write for info. (*0-415-16124-X*); write for info. (*0-415-16125-8*); write for info. (*0-415-16126-6*); write for info. (*0-415-16127-4*) Routledge.
Laski, Harold J., et al. A Century of Municipal Progress, 1835-1935: From Self-Government to National Sovereignty. Jennings, W. Ivor, ed. LC 75-41171. reprint ed. 45.00 (*0-404-14561-2*) AMS Pr.
Laski, Kazimiera, jt. auth. see Brus, Wlodzimierz.
Laski, Marghanita. Jane Austen. LC 85-51361. (Literary Lives Ser.). (Illus.). 144p. 1998. reprint ed. pap. 12.95 (*0-500-26015-X*, Pub. by Thames Hudson) Norton.
— Jane Austen & Her World. LC 77-422962. 143 p. 1969. write for info. (*0-500-13023-X*) Thames Hudson.
— The Victorian Chaise Longue. 152p. 1984. pap. 5.00 (*0-89733-097-8*) Academy Chi Pubs.
Laskier, Michael M. The Alliance Israelite Universelle & the Jewish Communities of Morocco, 1862-1962. LC 82-5892. (SUNY Series in Modern Jewish History). 384p. (C). 1984. text 21.50 (*0-87395-656-7*); pap. text 21.95 (*0-87395-655-9*) State U NY Pr.
— The Jews of Egypt, 1920-1970: In the Midst of Zionism, Anti-Semitism, & the Middle East Conflict. 350p. (C). 1993. pap. text 19.50 (*0-8147-5078-8*) NYU Pr.
— North African Jewry in the Twentieth Century: The Jews of Morocco, Tunisia, & Algeria. LC 93-28377. (C). 1994. text 65.00 (*0-8147-5072-9*) NYU Pr.
— North African Jewry in the Twentieth Century: The Jews of Morocco, Tunisia, & Algeria. 1997. pap. text 20.00 (*0-8147-5129-6*) NYU Pr.
Laskin. Progress Notes. 1994. text 65.00 (*0-7216-5964-0*, W B Saunders Co) Harcrt Hlth Sci Grp.
Laskin. Spasibo za vnimanie: B Level. 8.95 (*0-88436-052-0*) EMC-Paradigm.
Laskin, jt. auth. see Sarnet.
Laskin, A. & Lechevalier, Hubert A. Handbook of Microbiology, 2 vols., Set. 2nd ed. LC 77-12460. 1981. 3128.00 (*0-8493-7200-3*) CRC Pr.
— Microbiak Composition Amino Acids, Proteins & Nucleic Acids. 2nd ed. LC 77-12460. (Handbook of Microbiology Ser.: Vol. 3). 1008p. 1981. 540.00 (*0-8493-7203-8*, CRC Reprint) Franklin.
Laskin, Allan I. & Lechevalier, Hubert A., eds. Handbook of Microbiology, Vol. VII. 2nd ed. 624p. 1984. lib. bdg. 162.95 (*0-8493-7207-0*, QR6, CRC Reprint) Franklin.
Laskin, Allen, jt. ed. see Sandford, Paul A.
Laskin, Allen I., et al, eds. Enzyme Engineering XIV. LC 98-41795. (Annals of the New York Academy of Sciences Ser.: Vol. 864). 665p. 1998. write for info. (*1-57331-149-9*); pap. write for info. (*1-57331-150-2*) NY Acad Sci.
Laskin, Allen I. & Last, Jerold A., eds. Nucleic Acid Biosynthesis. LC 72-89529. (Methods in Molecular Biology Ser.: No. 4). (Illus.). 288p. reprint ed. pap. 89.30 (*0-7837-0781-9*, 204109500019) Bks Demand.
Laskin, Allen I. & Lechevalier, Hubert. Handbook of Microbiology: Fungi, Algae, Protozoa & Viruses, Vol. II. 2nd ed. 888p. 1979. lib. bdg. 175.00 (*0-8493-7202-X*, QR6, CRC Reprint) Franklin.
Laskin, Allen I. & Lechevalier, Hubert A. Toxins & Enzymes: Microbial Composition: Amino Acids, Proteins & Nucleic Acids, Vol. 8. 2nd ed. LC 77-12460. (Handbook of Microbiology Ser.). 1000p. 1987. lib. bdg. 213.00 (*0-8493-7208-9*, QR6) Franklin.
Laskin, Allen I. & Lechevalier, Hubert A., eds. Handbook of Microbiology, Vol. V. 2nd ed. 936p. 1984. lib. bdg. 197.00 (*0-8493-7205-4*, QR6, CRC Reprint) Franklin.
— Handbook of Microbiology, Vol. IX, Pt. A. 2nd ed. 544p. 1988. lib. bdg. 359.00 (*0-8493-7210-0*, QR6) CRC Pr.
— Handbook of Microbiology, Vol. IX, Pt. B. 2nd ed. 224p. 1988. lib. bdg. 259.00 (*0-8493-7211-9*, QR6) CRC Pr.
— Handbook of Microbiology: Bacteria, Vol. I. 2nd ed. 770p. 1977. 418.00 (*0-8493-7201-1*, QR6, CRC Reprint) Franklin.
— Handbook of Microbiology: Growth & Metabolism, Vol. VI. 2nd ed. 392p. 1984. lib. bdg. 139.95 (*0-8493-7206-2*, QR6, CRC Reprint) Franklin.
— Handbook of Microbiology: Microbial Composition: Carbohydrates, Lipids & Minerals, Vol. IV. 2nd ed. 744p. 1982. 403.00 (*0-8493-7204-6*, QR6, CRC Reprint) Franklin.
— Handbook of Microbiology, CRC, Vol. 3: Microbial Metabolism, Genetics & Immunology. LC 72-88766. (Handbook Ser.). 800p. 1974. 53.95 (*0-87819-584-X*, CRC Reprint) Franklin.
Laskin, Allen I. & Meidleman, Saul L., eds. Advances in Applied Microbiology, Vol. 42. (Illus.). 312p. 1996. text 79.00 (*0-12-002642-2*) Acad Pr.
Laskin, Allen I., ed. see Last, Jerold A.
Laskin, Allen I., jt. ed. see Last, Jerold A.
Laskin, Allen I., jt. ed. see Neidleman, Saul L.
Laskin, Allen I., jt. ed. see Neidleman, Saul.
Laskin, Allen I., jt. ed. see Neidlleman, Saul L.
Laskin, Allen L., jt. ed. see Neidleman, Saul L.
Laskin, Amy. Maximizing Your Mac. 1995. pap. 24.95 (*1-55828-244-0*, MIS Pr) IDG Bks.
Laskin, Benjamin. When the Half Gods Go. LC 94-12045. 384p. 1997. pap. 14.95 (*0-9649600-0-1*) Phx Prime.
Laskin, Daniel M., jt. auth. see Kwon, Paul H.
Laskin, David. Braving the Elements. 256p. 1997. pap. 12.95 (*0-385-46956-X*, Anchor NY) Doubleday.
— Eastern Islands: Accessible Islands of the East Coast. LC 89-39390. (Illus.). 288p. reprint ed. pap. 89.30 (*0-7837-6692-0*, 204630900011) Bks Demand.
— Parents Book of Child Safety. (Parents Magazine Childcare Ser.). 320p. (Orig.). 1991. mass mkt. 4.99 (*0-345-35104-5*) Ballantine Pub Grp.
— Partisans: Marriage, Politics & Betrayal among the New York Intellectuals. LC 99-41977. 320p. 2000. 26.00 (*0-684-81565-6*) S&S Trade.
— Rains All the Time: A Connoisseur's History of Weather in the Pacific Northwest. LC 97-16051. 224p. (Orig.). 1997. pap. 16.95 (*1-57061-063-0*) Sasquatch Bks.
Laskin, David, ed. An Angel a Week. 1992. pap. 4.00 (*0-345-38075-4*) Ballantine Pub Grp.
Laskin, David & Hughes, Holly. The Reading Group Companion: Starting & Sustaining a Book Discussion Group. LC 94-30200. 1995. 11.95 (*0-452-27201-7*) Macmillan.
Laskin, David & Laskin, Kathleen O. The Little Girl Book. 304p. (Orig.). 1992. pap. 11.00 (*0-345-36802-9*) Ballantine Pub Grp.
Laskin, David & O'Neill, Kathleen. The Little Girl Book: Everything You Need to Know to Raise a Daughter Today. 1996. mass mkt. 5.99 (*0-345-38678-7*) Ballantine Pub Grp.
Laskin, Davis. Common Life: Four Generations of American Literary Friendship & Influence. LC 93-40588. 1994. 27.50 (*0-671-72419-3*) S&S Trade.
Laskin, Debra L. & Schook, Lawrence B., eds. Xenobiotics & Inflammation: Roles of Cytokines & Growth Factors. (Illus.). 361p. 1994. text 104.00 (*0-12-628930-1*) Acad Pr.
Laskin, Debra L., jt. auth. see Laskin, Jeffrey D.
Laskin, Franklin T., jt. auth. see Arkin, Michael B.
Laskin, Irving. Prediction of Gear Noise from Design Data. (Technical Papers: Vol. P299.03). (Illus.). 19p. (Orig.). 1968. pap. text 30.00 incl. audio compact disk (*1-55589-382-1*) AGMA.
Laskin, Irving & Lawson, Ed. Separation of Runout from Elemental Inspection Data. (Technical Papers: Vol. 95FTM2). (Illus.). 15p. 1995. pap. text 30.00 (*1-55589-650-2*) AGMA.
Laskin, Irving, et al. Effect of Radial Runout on Element Measurements. (Nineteen Ninety-Three Fall Technical Meeting Ser.: Vol. 93FTM6). (Illus.). 16p. 1993. pap. text 30.00 (*1-55589-599-9*) AGMA.
Laskin, Irving, jt. auth. see Smith, Robert E.
Laskin, Jeffrey D. & Laskin, Debra L. Cellular & Molecular Biology of Nitric Oxide. LC 99-17778. (Illus.). 400p. 1999. text 185.00 (*0-8247-1965-4*) Dekker.
Laskin, Kathleen O., jt. auth. see Laskin, David.
Laskin, Myron, Jr., ed. European & American Painting, Sculpture & Decorative Arts in the National Gallery of Canada, 1300-1800, Vol. 1. (Illus.). 475p. 1993. 97.50 (*0-226-56336-7*) U Ch Pr.
Laskin, Pamela L. & Moskowitz, Addie A. Wish upon a Star: A Story for Children with a Parent Who Is Mentally Ill. LC 91-211. (Illus.). 32p. (J). (ps-2). 1991. 16.95 (*0-945354-30-4*) Am Psychol.
Laskin, R. S., ed. Total Knee Replacement. (Illus.). xvi, 268p. 1991. 192.00 (*0-387-19644-7*) Spr-Verlag.
Laskin, Sidney & Goldstein, Bernard D., eds. Benzene Toxicity: A Critical Evaluation. LC 77-17128. 152p. reprint ed. pap. 47.20 (*0-8357-7133-4*, 205532900016) Bks Demand.
Lasko, Keith Alan. The Great Billion Dollar Medical Swindle. 1980. 10.95 (*0-672-52625-5*) Sams.
Lasko, Paul F. Molecular Genetics of Drosophilia Oogenesis. (Molecular Biology Intelligence Unit Ser.). 118p. 1994. 99.00 (*1-57059-032-X*, LN9032) Landes Bioscience.
Lasko, Peter. Ars Sacra, 800-1200. 2nd ed. (Pelican History of Art Ser.). (Illus.). 320p. 1995. 65.00 (*0-300-06048-3*) Yale U Pr.
Lasko, Peter. The Kingdom of the Franks: North-West Europe Before Charlemagne. LC 70-151498. (Library of Medieval Civilization). 141p. 1971. write for info. (*0-07-036498-2*) Gregg-McGraw.
***Laskody, Edward.** The Country Where Golf is King. (Illus.). 165p. 2000. 21.95 (*0-7541-1018-4*, Pub. by Minerva Pr) Unity Dist.
Laskow, Leonard. Healing with Love: A Breakthrough Mind/Body Medical Program for Healing Yourself & Others. LC 98-61230. 341p. 1998. reprint ed. pap. 18.00 (*0-9665195-0-7*) Wholeness Pr.
Laskowski. Kingsley Amis. LC 98-12893. 166p. 1998. 28.95 (*0-8057-1663-7*, Twyne) Mac Lib Ref.
Laskowski, Birgit. Piero Della Francesca. (Masters Of Italian Art Ser.). (Illus.). 140p. 1998. 19.95 (*3-8290-0247-5*, 520534) Konemann.
***Laskowski-Caujolle, Elvira.** Die Macht der Vier: Von der Pythagoreischen Zahl Zum Modernen Mathematischen Strukturbegriff in Jacques Roubauds Oulipotischer Erzahlung. (Artefakt. Schriften Zur Soziosemiotik und Komparatistik Ser.). 376p. 1999. 56.95 (*3-631-34872-X*) P Lang Pubng.
Laskowski, J. Magnetite Dense Medium, Its Rheology Effect on Separation Efficiency. 109p. 1990. text 384.00 (*2-88124-473-4*) Gordon & Breach.
Laskowski, J. S., ed. Frothing in Flotation: A Volume in Honor of Jan Leja. (Mineral Processing & Extractive Metallury Review Ser.: Vol. 5). viii, 338p. 1989. text 129.00 (*2-88124-297-9*) Gordon & Breach.
***Laskowski, J. S., ed.** Trace Elements in Coal. 196p. 1999. pap. text 35.00 (*90-5699-675-4*) Gordon & Breach.
Laskowski, J. S. & Ralston, J. K. Colloid Chemistry in Mineral Processing. (Developments in Mineral Processing Ser.: Vol. 12). 428p. 1992. 197.75 (*0-444-88284-7*) Elsevier.
Laskowski, Janusz S. & Woodburn, E. T., eds. Frothing in Flotation II. (Recent Advances in Coal Processing Ser.: Vol. 2). (Illus.). 336p. 1998. text 60.00 (*90-5699-631-2*, ECU86, Harwood Acad Pubs) Gordon & Breach.
Laskowski, Larry. Heinrich Schenker: An Annotated Index to His Analyses of Musical Works, No. 1, Harmonologia. LC 78-16997. 1978. lib. bdg. 48.00 (*0-918728-06-1*) Pendragon NY.
Laskowski, Lester P., jt. auth. see Tocci, Ronald J.
Laskowski, William E., Jr. Rupert Brooke. LC 93-40510. (Twayne's English Authors Ser.: No. 504). 1994. 32.00 (*0-8057-7025-9*, Twyne) Mac Lib Ref.
Lasky. The Dead Bird Page. (J). 1997. pap. 5.95 (*0-7868-1287-7*, Pub. by Hyperion) Time Warner.
— Grace. (J). 1997. pap. 3.95 (*0-7868-4241-5*, Pub. by Hyperion) Little.
— The Myth of Hercules, Vol. 1. (J). 1997. 15.95 (*0-7868-1278-8*, Pub. by Hyperion) Little.
— Sugaring Time. (J). 1998. pap. 4.95 (*0-87628-350-4*) Ctr Appl Res.
Lasky, Barry S., ed. The New Careers Directory: Internships & Professional Opportunities in Technology & Social Change. rev. ed. 325p. (Orig.). 1993. pap. 18.00 (*0-9639007-0-6*) Student Pugwash.
Lasky, Betty. Rko: The Biggest Little Major of Them All. (Illus.). 240p. 1984. pap. 9.95 (*0-13-781444-5*) P-H.
Lasky, Celeste. Ghost Stories of the Estes Valley, Vol. 1. 53p. 1998. pap. 4.99 (*0-9643331-3-9*) Write On Pubns.
— Hidden Vengeance. 400p. (Orig.). 1997. pap. 7.99 (*0-9643331-2-0*) Write On Pubns.
— More Ghost Stories of the Estes Valley. 53p. 1999. pap. 4.99 (*0-9643331-4-7*) Write On Pubns.
— Resurrection of a Woman. 465p. (Orig.). 1995. pap. 6.99 (*0-9643331-0-4*) Write On Pubns.
Lasky, David. Three Trumpet Tunes on Easter Hymns, Vol. 3. Tucker, Dale, ed. 16p. (C). 1997. pap. text 6.95 (*0-7692-1706-0*, GB9712) Wrner Bros.
Lasky, Herbert. Psychiatric Claims in Workers' Compensation & Civil Actions, 2, Vol. 2. (Personal Injury Library). 592p. 1993. boxed set 255.00 (*0-471-58490-8*) Wiley.
Lasky, Jane E. L. A. Woman. 240p. (Orig.). 1990. mass mkt. 12.95 (*0-446-38779-7*, Pub. by Warner Bks) Little.
— Passport Singapore: Your Pocket Guide to Singaporean Business, Customs & Etiquette. Szerlip, Barbara, ed. LC 97-22973. (Computer Science). (Illus.). 96p. (Orig.). 1996. pap. 6.95 (*1-885073-38-0*) Thomson Learn.
Lasky, Janet. Higher Choices: Life Enhancing Recipes. 2nd rev. ed. LC 98-92144. (Illus.). vi, 114p. 1999. pap. 15.95 (*0-9663603-1-1*) Higher Choices.
Lasky, Judith, et al, eds. Psychoanalytic Reflections on Current Issues. 228p. (C). 1991. text 45.00 (*0-8147-7909-3*) NYU Pr.
***Lasky, Julie & Chantry, Art.** Some People Can't Surf: The Graphic Design of Art Chantry. LC 00-29465. 2001. pap. 27.50 (*0-8118-2365-2*) Chronicle Bks.
Lasky, Julie, jt. auth. see Heller, Steven.
Lasky, Kathryn. Alice Rose & Sam. LC 97-40132. (Illus.). 208p. (J). (gr. 3-7). 1998. 15.95 (*0-7868-0336-3*, Pub. by Hyprn Child); lib. bdg. 16.49 (*0-7868-2277-5*, Pub. by Hyprn Child) Little.
— Alice Rose & Sam. LC 97-40132. 252p. (J). (gr. 3-7). 1999. pap. 4.50 (*0-7868-1222-2*, Pub. by Hyprn Ppbks) Little.
— A Baby for Max. LC 86-22131. (Illus.). 48p. (J). (ps-2). 1987. pap. 4.95 (*0-689-71118-2*) Aladdin.
— Beyond the Burning Time. 176p. (YA). (gr. 7-9). 1994. 14.95 (*0-590-47331-X*, Blue Sky Press) Scholastic Inc.
— Beyond the Burning Time. LC 94-5231. 288p. (YA). (gr. 7 up). 1996. 4.50 (*0-590-47332-8*) Scholastic Inc.
Lasky, Kathryn. Beyond the Burning Time. LC 94-5231. 1994. 10.09 (*0-606-09073-8*, Pub. by Turtleback) Demco.
Lasky, Kathryn. Beyond the Divide. LC 82-22867. 264p. (YA). (gr. 7 up). 1983. lib. bdg. 17.00 (*0-02-751670-9*, Mac Bks Young Read) S&S Childrens.
— A Brilliant Streak: The Story of Mark Twain. LC 95-18479. (Illus.). 41p. (J). (gr. 4-7). 1998. 18.00 (*0-15-252110-0*) Harcourt.
— Cloud Eyes. abr. ed. LC 93-37805. (Illus.). 32p. (J). (ps-5). 1994. 14.95 (*0-15-219168-2*) Harcourt.
— Days of the Dead. LC 93-47957. (Illus.). 48p. (J). (gr. 3-7). 1994. 15.95 (*0-7868-0022-4*, Pub. by Hyprn Child) Time Warner.
— Days of the Dead. LC 93-47957. (Illus.). 48p. (J). (gr. 4-7). 1994. lib. bdg. 15.89 (*0-7868-2018-7*, Pub. by Hyprn Child) Little.
— Days of the Dead. 1996. 11.15 (*0-606-11244-8*, Pub. by Turtleback) Demco.
— Double Trouble Squared: A Starbuck Family Adventure, Vol. 1. LC 91-10655. 240p. (J). (gr. 3-7). 1991. 14.95 (*0-15-224126-4*, Harcourt Child Bks) Harcourt.
— Double Trouble Squared: A Starbuck Family Adventure, Vol. 1. LC 91-10655. 240p. (J). (gr. 4-7). 1991. pap. 8.00 (*0-15-224127-2*) Harcourt.
— Dreams in the Golden Country: The Diary of Zipporah Feldman, a Jewish Immigrant Girl, New York City, 1903. LC 97-26213. (Dear America Ser.). (Illus.). 188p. (J). (gr. 4-7). 1998. pap. 11.95 (*0-590-02973-8*) Scholastic Inc.
— Elizabeth I: Red Rose of the House of Tudor, England 1544. LC 99-11178. (Royal Diaries Ser.). (Illus.). 192p. (J). (gr. 4-8). 1999. 10.95 (*0-590-68484-1*, Pub. by Scholastic Inc) Penguin Putnam.
— The Emperor's Old Clothes. LC 98-5502. (Illus.). 32p. (J). 1999. 16.00 (*0-15-200384-3*) Harcourt.

L

An Asterisk (*) at the beginning of an entry indicates that the title is appearing for the first time.

*Lasky, Kathryn. First Painter. LC 98-41154. (Illus.). 40p. (J). (ps-3). 1999. 16.95 (0-7894-2578-5) DK Pub Inc.

Lasky, Kathryn. The Gates of the Wind. abr. ed. LC 94-8390. (Illus.). 32p. (J). (ps-3). 1995. 15.00 (0-15-204264-4, Harcourt Child Bks) Harcourt.

— Grace the Pirate. LC 97-9947. (Hyperion Chapters Ser.). (Illus.). 64p. (J). (gr. 3-4). 1997. lib. bdg. 14.49 (0-7868-2236-8, Pub. by Hyprn Ppbks) Little.

— Grace the Pirate. LC 97-9947. (Hyperion Chapters Ser.). (Illus.). 64p. (J). (gr. 3-4). 1997. pap. 3.95 (0-7868-1147-1, Pub. by Hyprn Ppbks) Little.

— Grace the Pirate. (Hyperion Chapters Ser.). 1997. 9.15 (0-606-13448-4, Pub. by Turtleback) Demco.

— Hercules: The Man, the Myth, the Hero. LC 96-40208. (Illus.). 32p. (J). (gr. k-4). 1997. 15.95 (0-7868-0329-0, Pub. by Hyprn Child) Little.

Lasky, Kathryn. Hercules: The Man, the Myth, the Hero. LC 96-40208. (Illus.). 32p. (J). (gr. k-4). 1997. lib. bdg. 15.89 (0-7868-2274-0, Pub. by Hyprn Child) Little.

— Interrupted Journey. LC 99-57126. (Illus.). (J). 2001. 15.99 (0-7636-0635-9) Candlewick Pr.

— The Journal of Augustus Pelletier: The Lewis & Clark Expedition. LC 00-20201. (My Name Is America Ser.). (Illus.). 192p. (YA). (gr. 4-7). 2000. 10.95 (0-590-68489-2) Scholastic Inc.

Lasky, Kathryn. The Librarian Who Measured the Earth. LC 92-42656. (Illus.). 48p. (J). (gr. k-3). 1994. 16.95 (0-316-51526-4, Joy St Bks) Little.

— Lucille Sweats. LC 99-462101. (Illus.). 32p. (ps up). 2000. 14.95 (0-517-80037-3) Crown Pub Group.

— Lucille Sweats. LC 99-462102. (Illus.). 32p. (ps up). 2000. lib. bdg. 16.99 (0-517-80038-1) Random Hse Value.

— Lunch Bunnies. LC 92-31554. (Illus.). 32p. (J). (gr. k-3). 1996. 14.95 (0-316-51525-6, Joy St Bks) Little.

— Lunch Bunnies. (Illus.). 32p. (J). (ps-3). 1999. pap. 5.95 (0-316-51586-8) Little.

*Lasky, Kathryn. Marie Antoinette: Princess of Versailles, Austria-France 1544. LC 99-19804. (Royal Diaries Ser.). (Illus.). 240p. (J). (gr. 4-8). 2000. 10.95 (0-439-07666-8) Scholastic Inc.

Lasky, Kathryn. Marven of the Great North Woods. LC 96-2334. (Illus.). 48p. (J). (gr. 1-5). 1997. 16.00 (0-15-200104-2) Harcourt.

— Memoirs of a Bookbat. LC 93-36402. 192p. (YA). (gr. 7 up). 1994. 10.95 (0-15-215727-1) Harcourt.

— Memoirs of a Bookbat. 224p. (YA). (gr. 5 up). 1996. pap. 6.00 (0-15-201259-1) Harcourt.

Lasky, Kathryn. Mommy, I Love Your Hands. (J). Date not set. 14.99 (0-7868-0280-4, Pub. by Hyperion) Little.

— Mommy, I Love Your Hands. (J). 2005. lib. bdg. 15.49 (0-7868-2225-2, Pub. by Hyperion) Little.

— Mommy's Hands. 32p. (J). 2001. pap. 4.99 (0-7868-1437-3, Pub. by Hyperion) Time Warner.

— Monarchs. 1993. 15.20 (0-606-12426-8, Pub. by Turtleback) Demco.

Lasky, Kathryn. The Most Beautiful Roof: Exploring the Rainforest Canopy. LC 95-48193. (Illus.). 48p. 1997. pap. 8.00 (0-15-200897-7) Harcourt.

— The Most Beautiful Roof in the World. LC 95-48193. (Illus.). 48p. (J). 1997. 18.00 (0-15-200893-4) Harcourt.

— The Night Journey. (Novels Ser.). (Illus.). 152p. (J). (gr. 5-9). 1986. pap. 4.99 (0-14-032048-2, PuffinBks) Peng Put Young Read.

— Night Journey. 1986. 10.09 (0-606-00929-9, Pub. by Turtleback) Demco.

— Pond Year. LC 94-14834. (Illus.). 32p. (J). (ps-3). 1995. 14.99 (1-56402-187-4) Candlewick Pr.

— Pond Year. 1997. 11.19 (0-606-12794-1, Pub. by Turtleback) Demco.

— Pond Year. LC 94-14834. (Illus.). 32p. (J). (gr. k-3). 1997. reprint ed. pap. 5.99 (0-7636-0112-8) Candlewick Pr.

— Robin Hood: The Boy Who Became a Legend. LC 97-11769. (J). 1999. write for info. (0-590-25933-4, Blue Sky Press) Scholastic Inc.

*Lasky, Kathryn. Science Fair Bunnies. LC 99-46883. (Illus.). 32p. (J). 2000. 15.99 (0-7636-0729-0) Candlewick Pr.

Lasky, Kathryn. Searching for Laura Ingalls. 1998. 12.19 (0-606-13766-1, Pub. by Turtleback) Demco.

— Shadows in the Dawn: The Lemurs of Madagascar. LC 97-6055. (Illus.). 64p. (J). (gr. 5 up). 1997. 18.00 (0-15-200258-8) Harcourt.

— Shadows in the Dawn: The Lemurs of Madagascar. LC 97-6055. (Illus.). 64p. (J). (gr. 5 up). 1998. pap. 9.00 (0-15-200281-2) Harcourt.

— Shadows in the Water: A Starbuck Family Adventure, Vol. 2. LC 92-8139. 224p. (J). (gr. 3-7). 1992. pap. 8.00 (0-15-273534-8, Harcourt Child Bks) Harcourt.

— She's Wearing a Dead Bird on Her Head! LC 94-18204. (Illus.). 40p. (J). (ps-3). 1995. 14.95 (0-7868-0065-8, Pub. by Hyprn Child) Time Warner.

— She's Wearing a Dead Bird on Her Head! LC 94-18204. (Illus.). 40p. (J). (gr. k-4). 1997. pap. 5.95 (0-7868-1164-1, Pub. by Hyprn Ppbks) Little.

— She's Wearing a Dead Bird on Her Head! (J). 1997. 11.15 (0-606-11005-4, Pub. by Turtleback) Demco.

— Show & Tell Bunnies. LC 98-17484. (Illus.). 32p. (J). (ps-2). 1998. 15.99 (0-7636-0396-1) Candlewick Press.

— Sophie & Rose. LC 97-37126. (Illus.). 32p. (J). (ps-3). 1998. 15.99 (0-7636-0459-3) Candlewick Pr.

— Star Split. LC 98-43839. 192p. (YA). (gr. 5-9). 1999. 16.49 (0-7868-2401-8, Pub. by Hyprn Child) Little.

— Star Split. LC 98-43839. (Illus.). 203p. (YA). (gr. 5-9). 1999. 15.99 (0-7868-0459-9, Pub. by Hyprn Child) Time Warner.

— Sugaring Time. (J). 1986. 10.15 (0-606-03308-4, Pub. by Turtleback) Demco.

— Surtsey: The Newest Place on Earth. LC 92-52990. (Illus.). 64p. (J). (gr. 3-7). 1992. 15.95 (1-56282-300-0, Pub. by Hyprn Child); lib. bdg. 15.89 (1-56282-301-9, Pub. by Hyprn Child) Little.

— Surtsey: The Newest Place On Earth. 1994. 12.15 (0-606-06775-2, Pub. by Turtleback) Demco.

— The Tantrum. LC 92-3701. (Illus.). 32p. (J). (ps-1). 1993. lib. bdg. 13.95 (0-02-751661-X, Mac Bks Young Read) S&S Childrens.

— Think Like an Eagle: At Work with a Wildlife Photographer. (Illus.). 48p. (J). (gr. 3 up). 1992. 15.95 (0-316-51519-1, Joy St Bks) Little.

— True North: A Novel of the Underground Railroad. LC 95-2922. 208p. (YA). (gr. 7 up). 1996. 14.95 (0-590-20523-4, Blue Sky Press) Scholastic Inc.

— True North: A Novel of the Underground Railroad. (J). 1998. pap. text 4.99 (0-590-20524-2) Scholastic Inc.

— True North: A Novel of the Underground Railroad. (J). 1998. 10.09 (0-606-13874-9, Pub. by Turtleback) Demco.

*Lasky, Kathryn. Untitled Middle Grade Novel (J). 2000. lib. bdg. 15.49 (0-7868-2278-3, Pub. by Disney Pr) Little.

Lasky, Kathryn. Vision of Beauty: The Story of Sarah Breedlove Walker. LC 99-19594. (Illus.). 48p. (J). (ps-3). 2000. 16.99 (0-7636-0253-1) Candlewick Pr.

— Voice in the Wind: A Starbuck Family Adventure. LC 93-14883. (Illus.). 224p. (J). (gr. 3-7). 1993. 10.95 (0-15-294102-9, Harcourt Child Bks); pap. 6.00 (0-15-294103-7, Harcourt Child Bks) Harcourt.

Lasky, Kathryn & Gregory, Kristiana. A Journey to the New World: The Diary of Remember Patience Whipple, Mayflower, 1620. LC 95-25715. (Dear America Ser.: Vol. 3). (Illus.). 176p. (J). (gr. 4-7). 1996. 9.95 (0-590-50214-X) Scholastic Inc.

Lasky, Katryn. Beyond the Divide. LC 82-22867. 296p. (J). (gr. 7). 1995. mass mkt. 3.95 (0-689-80163-7) Aladdin.

Lasky, Larry C. & Warkentin, Phyllis, eds. Marrow & Stem Cell Processing for Transplantation. (Illus.). (C). 1995. text 35.00 (1-56395-042-1) Am Assn Blood.

Lasky, Lila & Mukerji, Rose. Art: Basic for Young Children. LC 80-82565. (Illus.). 164p. 1980. pap. text 6.00 (0-912674-73-3, NAEYC NO. 106) Natl Assn Child Ed.

Lasky, Mark A., jt. auth. see Landes, William-Alan.

*Lasky, Melvin J. The Language of Journalism Vol. 1: Newspaper Culture. (Newspaper Culture Ser.). 453p. 2000. 39.95 (0-7658-0001-2) Transaction Pubs.

Lasky, Melvin J. On the Barricades, & Off. 256p. (Orig.). 1989. pap. 24.95 (0-88738-726-8) Transaction Pubs.

— Utopia & Revolution: On the Origins of a Metaphor or Some Illustrations of Political Temperament & Intellectual Climate & How Ideas, Ideals & Ideologies Have Been Historically Related. LC 75-27893. xiv, 740p. 1998. pap. text 36.00 (0-226-46911-5) U Ch Pr.

Lasky, Melvin J., ed. The Hungarian Revolution: A White Book. LC 70-119936. (Select Bibliographies Reprint Ser.). 1977. reprint ed. 28.95 (0-8369-5379-7) Ayer.

Lasky, Melvin J. & Lasky, Michael S. Voices in a Revolution: The Collapse of East German Communism. 188p. (C). 1992. 34.95 (1-56000-030-9) Transaction Pubs.

Lasky, Meredith & Knight, Meribah. Searching for Laura Ingalls. (Illus.). 48p. (J). 1998. mass mkt. 6.99 (0-689-82029-1) S&S Childrens.

Lasky, Michael S., jt. auth. see Harris, Robert A.

Lasky, Michael S., jt. auth. see Lasky, Melvin J.

Lasky, Richard. Dynamics of Development & the Therapeutic Process. LC 92-17808. 488p. 1993. 60.00 (0-87668-565-3) Aronson.

Lasky, Ronald C., et al, eds. Optoelectronics for Data Communication. (Illus.). 338p. 1995. text 73.00 (0-12-437160-4) Acad Pr.

Lasky Schub, Joyce & Carr, Raymond, eds. Spain: Studies in Political Security, 117. LC 85-16948. (Washington Papers: No. 117). 125p. 1985. 49.95 (0-275-90192-0, C0192, Praeger Pubs) Greenwood.

Lasky, Tamar, jt. auth. see Stolley, Paul D.

Lasky, Vivienne, jt. auth. see Freeman, Robert.

Laslett, Barbara, et al, eds. Gender & Scientific Authority. 350p. 1996. lib. bdg. 30.00 (0-226-46917-4) U Ch Pr.

Laslett, Barbara & Thorne, Barrie, eds. Feminist Sociology: Life Histories of a Movement. LC 97-1778. 320p. (C). 1997. text 50.00 (0-8135-2428-8); pap. text 19.95 (0-8135-2429-6) Rutgers U Pr.

Laslett, Barbara, et al. Gender & Scientific Authority. 350p. (C). 1996. pap. 19.95 (0-226-46918-2) U Ch Pr.

Laslett, Barbara, jt. ed. see Joeres, Ruth-Ellen B.

Laslett, Betsy. Arts & 504: A Handbook for Accessible Arts Programming. 1992. (Illus.). 101p. 1992. pap. 6.50 (0-16-038201-7, 036000000554) USGPO.

Laslett, John & Tyler, Mary. International Ladies Garment Workers Union in Los Angeles, 1907-1988. LC 89-50435. (Illus.). 167p. (Orig.). 1989. pap. 10.00 (0-923145-02-8) Ten Star Pr.

*Laslett, John H. Colliers Across the Sea. LC 99-6466. (Illus.). 320p. 1999. 49.95 (0-252-02511-3) U of Ill Pr.

Laslett, John H. Nature's Noblemen: The Fortunes of the Independent Collier in Scotland & the American Midwest, 1855-1889. (Monograph & Research Ser.: No. 34). 87p. 1984. 6.00 (0-89215-120-X) U Cal LA Indus Rel.

Laslett, John H. M. Colliers Across the Sea: A Comparative Study of Class Formation in Scotland & the American Middle Class. LC 99-6466. 320p. 2000. pap. text 18.95 (0-252-06827-0) U of Ill Pr.

Laslett, John M., ed. The United Mine Workers of America: A Model of Industrial Solidarity? LC 95-39732. 1996. 65.00 (0-271-01537-3) Pa St U Pr.

Laslett, Peter. A Fresh Map of Life: The Emergence of the Third Age. LC 90-47101. 328p. 1991. pap. 18.00 (0-674-32327-0, LASFRX) HUP.

— The World We Have Lost. 3rd ed. (C). 1986. pap. text 12.95 (0-684-18079-0) S&S Trade.

Laslett, Peter, et al, eds. Bastardy & Its Comparative History: Studies in the History of Illegitimacy & Martial Nonconformism. (Studies in Social & Demographic History). (Illus.). 446p. 1980. 55.50 (0-674-06338-4) HUP.

Laslett, Peter & Fishkin, James S., eds. Justice Between Age Groups & Generations. (Philosophy, Politics, & Society Ser.: No. 6). 272p. (C). 1992. 40.00 (0-300-05073-9) Yale U Pr.

Laslett, Peter, jt. ed. see Kertzer, David I.

Laslett, Peter, ed. see Locke, John.

Lasley. California Criminal Justice. LC 97-147200. 96p. 1996. pap. text 17.20 (0-13-571522-9) Allyn.

— Classroom Management. 1997. pap. text 6.95 (0-534-51647-5) Brooks-Cole.

— Essential Criminal Justice & Criminology Research: Explanations Exercises. LC 98-207781. 191p. (C). 1998. pap. text, wbk. ed. 30.40 (0-13-080899-7) P-H.

*Lasley & Matczynski, Thomas J. Strategies for Teaching in a Diverse Society: Instructional Models. 2nd ed. (Education Ser.). (C). 2001. text 54.00 (0-534-52840-6) Wadsworth Pub.

Lasley, Mary. Do-It-Yourself Story Puzzle Book. (Illus.). 2p. (J). (ps). 1988. 9.95 (0-9622406-0-5) MOL Bks.

Lasley, Thomas J. Teaching Peace: Toward Cultural Selflessness. LC 93-43730. 216p. 1994. 55.00 (0-89789-371-9, Bergin & Garvey) Greenwood.

Lasley, Thomas J. & Matczynski, Thomas J. Strategies for Teaching in a Diverse Society: Instructional Models. LC 96-41180. 425p. (C). 1997. 75.95 (0-534-51645-9) Wadsworth Pub.

*Lasley, William Kerr, Jr. Alamance County, North Carolina. (Images of America Ser.). (Illus.). 128p. (C). 1999. pap. 18.99 (0-7385-0036-4) Arcadia Publng.

Laslie, Judy A. 9 Chances to Feel Good About Yourself. 128p. 1997. reprint ed. pap. 14.95 (0-9650218-3-1) Radnor Hse.

Laslier, Jean-Francois. Freedom in Economics: New Perspectives in Normative Analysis. LC 97-7493. 256p. (C). 1997. 85.00 (0-415-15468-5) Routledge.

— Tournament Solutions & Majority Voting. Aliprantis, C. D. & Yannelis, N. C., eds. LC 97-21690. (Studies in Economic Theory: No. 7). (Illus.). xiv, 255p. 1997. 83.00 (3-540-62897-5) Spr-Verlag.

Laslo, Alexander J. A Glossary of Terms Used in Phaleristics - the Science, Study, & Collecting of the Insignia of Orders, Decorations, & Medals. limited ed. LC 95-92439. (Illus.). 68p. 1995. 25.00 (0-9617320-2-4) Dorado Publishing.

— The Interallied Victory Medals of World War I. 2nd rev. ed. LC 91-76602. (Illus.). 130p. (Orig.). 1992. 29.95 (0-9617320-1-6) Dorado Publishing.

*Laslo, Cynthia. Brandy. (High Interest Bks.). (Illus.). (J). 2000. 19.00 (0-516-23320-3) Childrens.

— Brandy. LC 99-43191. (High Interest Bks.). (Illus.). 48p. (J). (gr. 4-7). 2000. pap. 6.95 (0-516-23520-6) Childrens.

— Brandy. LC 99-43191. (Celebrity Bios Ser.). 2000. pap. write for info. (0-531-17608-8) Watts.

— Lauryn Hill. (High Interest Bks.). (Illus.). (J). 2000. 19.00 (0-516-23322-X) Childrens.

— Lauryn Hill. LC 99-44798. (High Interest Bks.). (Illus.). 48p. (J). (gr. 4-7). 2000. pap. 6.95 (0-516-23522-2) Childrens.

— Lauryn Hill. LC 99-44798. (Celebrity Bios Ser.). 2000. pap. write for info. (0-531-17610-X) Watts.

— 'N Sync. (High Interest Bks.). (Illus.). (J). 2000. 19.00 (0-516-23324-6) Childrens.

— 'N Sync. LC 00-23321. (High Interest Bks.). (Illus.). 48p. (J). (gr. 4-7). 2000. pap. write for info. (0-516-23524-9) Childrens.

— Rat Attacks. LC 99-58300. (Animal Attacks Ser.). (Illus.). 48p. (J). (gr. 4-7). 2000. pap. 6.95 (0-516-23517-6) Childrens.

Laslo, Cynthia. The Rosen Photo Guide to a Career in the Circus. (Illus.). (YA). (gr. 7-12). 1988. lib. bdg. 12.95 (0-8239-0819-4) Rosen Group.

*Laslo, Cynthia. Sarah Michelle Gellar. (High Interest Bks.). (Illus.). (J). 2000. 19.00 (0-516-23326-2) Childrens.

— Sarah Michelle Gellar. (High Interest Bks.). (Illus.). 48p. (J). (gr. 4-7). 2000. pap. 6.95 (0-516-23526-5) Childrens.

— Sarah Michelle Gellar. LC 99-41086. (Celebrity Bios Ser.). (Illus.). (J). 2000. pap. write for info. (0-531-17614-2) Watts.

Laslof, Joyce C., et al, eds. Presidential Advisory Committee on Gulf War Veterans' Illnesses: Final Report. (Illus.). 174p. (Orig.). 1997. pap. text 40.00 (0-7881-4271-2) DIANE Pub.

Lasn, Kalle. Culture Jam: The Uncooling of America. LC 99-18409. 272p. 1999. 25.00 (0-688-15656-8, Wm Morrow) Morrow Avon.

*Lasn, Kalle. Culture Jam: The Uncooling of America (tm) 272p. 2000. pap. 13.00 (0-688-17805-7, Wm Morrow) Morrow Avon.

Lasne, John. Robbie Rabbit. (Littlebook Ser.). (Illus.). 18p. (J). (gr. k-4). 1996. 5.95 (0-9642815-4-6) Natl Fmly Prtnship.

— Stinky the Skunk. LC 97-208490. (Illus.). 16p. (J). (gr. k-3). 1997. 7.95 (0-9642815-5-4, STSKY) Natl Fmly Prtnship.

Lasner, Mark. William Allingham: A Bibliographical Study. (Illus.). 88p. 1999. 50.00 (0-9619693-4-2) Holmes Publishing Co.

Lasner, Mark S. A Selective Checklist of the Published Work of Aubrey Beardsley. 1994. text 75.00 (0-9644734-0-2) T G Boss.

Lasner, Mart S., jt. auth. see Stetz, Margaret D.

Lasnier, F. & Ang, T. Photovoltaic Engineering Handbook. (Illus.). 568p. 1990. 238.00 (0-85274-311-4) IOP Pub.

Lasnik, Howard. Essays on Anaphora. (C). 1989. lib. bdg. 106.00 (1-55608-090-5) Kluwer Academic.

— Essays on Anaphora. (C). 1989. pap. text 41.50 (1-55608-091-3) Kluwer Academic.

— Essays on Restrictiveness & Learnability. (C). 1990. lib. bdg. 129.00 (0-7923-0628-7) Kluwer Academic.

— Minimalist Analysis. LC 98-35453. (Generative Syntax Ser.). 224p. 1999. 64.95 (0-631-21093-8); pap. 29.95 (0-631-21094-6) Blackwell Pubs.

Lasnik, Howard & Saito, Mamoru. Move Alpha: Conditions on Its Application & Output. (Current Studies in Linguistics: No. 22). (Illus.). 234p. 1992. 36.00 (0-262-12161-1) MIT Pr.

— Move Alpha: Conditions on Its Application & Output. (Current Studies in Linguistics: No. 22). (Illus.). 240p. 1994. pap. text 18.00 (0-262-62091-X) MIT Pr.

Lasnik, Howard & Uriagereka, Juan. A Course in GB Syntax: Lectures on Binding & Empty Categories. 192p. (Orig.). (C). 1988. 40.00 (0-262-12130-1, Bradford Bks); pap. text 20.00 (0-262-62060-X, Bradford Bks) MIT Pr.

*Lasnik, Howard, et al. Syntactic Structures Revisited: Contemporary Lectures on Classic Transformational Theory. LC 99-39907. (Current Studies in Linguistics). (Illus.). 437p. 2000. 50.00 (0-262-12222-7) MIT Pr.

— Syntactic Structures Revisted: Contemporary Lectures on Classic Transformational Theory. (Current Studies in Linguistics). 224p. 2000. pap. 20.00 (0-262-62133-9) MIT Pr.

Lasobre, Jacques. Risk, Insurance, Reinsurance: Lexicon. (ENG & FRE.). 396p. 1981. 75.00 (0-8288-0968-2, M 6354) Fr & Eur.

Lasocki, David. Traverso, Historical Flute Newsletter Vols. 1-10: With a Bibliography of Publications on Historical Flutes, 1989-98. Powell, Ardal, ed. LC 99-72226. (Illus.). viii, 198p. (Orig.). 1999. pap. 24.95 (0-9670368-0-1) Folkers Flute.

Lasocki, David, compiled by. Fluting & Dancing: Articles & Reminiscences for Betty Bang Mather on Her 65th Birthday. LC 92-20693. (Illus.). 208p. (Orig.). 1992. pap. text 25.00 (0-941084-12-4) McGinnis & Marx.

Lasocki, David & Mather, Betty B. The Classical Woodwind Cadenza: A Workbook. 1978. 10.00 (0-941084-06-X) McGinnis & Marx.

Lasocki, David & Prior, Roger. The Bassanos: Venetian Musicians & Instrument Makers in England, 1531-1665. 324p. 1995. 78.95 (0-85967-943-8, Pub. by Scolar Pr) Ashgate Pub Co.

Lasocki, David, jt. auth. see Griscom, Richard.

Lasocki, David, jt. auth. see Mather, Betty B.

Lasocki, S., jt. ed. see Gibowicz, S. J.

Lasok. The Trade & Customs Law of the European Union. LC 97-39546. 1997. 175.00 (90-411-0688-X) Kluwer Law Intl.

Lasok, D., et al, eds. Fundamental Duties: A Volume of Essays by Present & Former Members of the Law Faculty of the University of Exeter to Commemorate the Silver Jubilee of the University. LC 80-40933. 269p. 1980. 129.00 (0-08-024048-8, Pub. by Pergamon Repr) Franklin.

Lasok, Dominik. The Customs Law of the European Economic Community. 2nd ed. 300p. 1991. pap. 108.00 (90-6544-483-1) Kluwer Law Intl.

— The Professions & Services in the European Economic Community. LC 86-15274. 396p. 1986. 133.00 (90-6544-253-7) Kluwer Law Intl.

Lasok, Dominik, jt. auth. see Stone, P. A.

Lasonsky, Joyce, jt. auth. see Lasonsky, Terry.

Lasonsky, Terry & Lasonsky, Joyce. McDonald's Happy Meal Toys: In the U. S. A. LC 95-9054. (Illus.). 224p. (Orig.). 1995. pap. 24.95 (0-88740-853-2) Schiffer.

LaSor, W. S., et al. Panorama del Antiguo Testamento: Mensaje, Forma y Trasfondo. (SPA., Illus.). 688p. 32.00 (1-55883-400-1, 6791-0007C) Libros Desafio.

LaSor, William S. Great Personalities of the Bible. 192p. 1997. reprint ed. 19.95 (1-56563-301-6) Hendrickson MA.

Lasorda, Tommy. Dodger Blue. (Illus.). 288p. 1999. 25.00 (0-06-019272-0) HarpC.

LaSorda, Tommy & Fisher, David. The Artful Dodger. (Illus.). 368p. 1986. pap. 3.95 (0-380-70085-9, Avon Bks) Morrow Avon.

*Lasorso, Vincent J., Jr. The Immortal's Gift: A Parable for the Soul. (Illus.). 200p. 2000. pap. 14.95 (0-9679867-1-0) White Willow Pub.

Lasota, J. P., jt. ed. see Marck, J. A.

LaSpina, James A. The Visual Turn & the Transformation of the Textbook. LC 97-44944. 180p. 1998. write for info. (0-8058-2701-3); pap. write for info. (0-8058-2702-1) L Erlbaum Assocs.

LaSpina, John J., jt. auth. see Edelman, Michael E.

Lasrgaard, Mary Lynette, jt. ed. see Andrew, Paige G.

Lasry, Benaim De, see De Lasry, Benaim.

Lasry, George. Valuing Common Stock: The Power of Prudence. LC 78-24023. 270p. reprint ed. pap. 83.70 (0-608-12973-9, 202393000034) Bks Demand.

*Lasry, Jean-Claude, et al, eds. Latest Contributions to Cross-Cultural Psychology: Selected Papers from the Thirteenth International Congress of the International Association for Cross-Cultural Psychology. LC 99-13929. (Conference Proceedings of the International Association for Cross-Cultural Psychology Ser.). 376p. 1999. 84.00 (90-265-1547-2) Swets.

Lass & Horwitz. Stories for Youth, 3 vols. (J). 30.00 (0-614-30540-3) NAVH.

Lass, A. H., jt. auth. see Flesch, Rudolf.

Lass, Abraham H. Business Spelling & Word Power. 2nd ed. 1961. teacher ed. 6.67 (0-672-96013-3, Bobbs) Macmillan.

— Business Spelling & Word Power. 7th ed. 1961. pap. text 9.95 (*0-672-96012-5*, Bobbs); student ed. 3.95 (*0-672-96015-X*, Bobbs) Macmillan.

— The Dictionary of Classical, Biblical & Literary Allusions. 288p. 1988. mass mkt. 5.99 (*0-449-14565-4*) Fawcett.

Lass, Abraham H. & Tasman, Norma L., eds. Twenty-One Great Stories. (Orig.). 1969. mass mkt. 6.99 (*0-451-62785-7*, Sig) NAL.

Lass, Bonnie, jt. auth. see Davis, Beth G.

Lass, Bonnie, jt. auth. see Sturges, Philemon.

Lass, Jonathan H., ed. see World Congress on the Cornea Staff.

Lass, Laure & Pike-Baky, Meredith. Mosaic I: A Writing Process Book, Vol. 1. 3rd ed. 430p. (C). 1995. pap. 23.13 (*0-07-005849-0*) McGraw.

Lass, Norman & Fucci, Donald. Fundamentals of Speech Science. LC 99-14316. (Illus.). 206p. (C). 1999. 53.00 (*0-13-345695-1*, Macmillan Coll) P-H.

Lass, Norman J., ed. Experimental Phonetics. 552p. 1974. pap. text 19.95 (*0-8422-0375-3*) Irvington.

— Principles of Experimental Phonetics. (Illus.). 600p. (C). (gr. 13). 1995. text 69.00 (*0-8016-7975-3*, 07975) Mosby Inc.

— Speech & Hearing Science: Selected Readings. 382p. 1974. text 52.50 (*0-8422-5154-5*); pap. text 17.50 (*0-8422-0377-X*) Irvington.

Lass, Roger. Historical Linguistics & Language Change. LC 96-12317. (Cambridge Studies in Linguistics: No. 81). 447p. (C). 1997. pap. text 29.95 (*0-521-45924-9*) Cambridge U Pr.

— Old English: A Historical Linguistic Companion. LC 93-18182. 320p. (C). 1994. pap. text 34.95 (*0-521-45848-X*) Cambridge U Pr.

— Old English: A Historical Linguistic Companion. LC 93-18182. 320p. (C). 1994. text 95.00 (*0-521-43087-9*) Cambridge U Pr.

— On Explaining Language Change. LC 79-51825. (Cambridge Studies in Linguistics: No. 27). 200p. reprint ed. pap. 57.00 (*0-608-12082-0*, 2024580) Bks Demand.

— Phonology: An Introduction to Basic Concepts. LC 83-23915. (Cambridge Textbooks in Linguistics Ser.). 384p. 1984. pap. text 27.95 (*0-521-28183-0*) Cambridge U Pr.

***Lass, Tristam.** Paradox: Introduction to a New Approach Towards Philosophical Investigation. LC 99-70722. 64p. 1999. pap. 9.95 (*1-57197-182-3*) Pentland Pr.

Lass, William E. From the Missouri to the Great Salt Lake: An Account of Overland Freighting. LC 75-183071. (Nebraska State Historical Publications: Vol. 26). (Illus.). 312p. 1972. 5.00 (*0-933307-07-1*) Nebraska Hist.

— A History of Steamboating on the Upper Missouri River. LC 62-14663. (Illus.). 247p. reprint ed. pap. 76.60 (*0-8357-8168-2*, 203416300088) Bks Demand.

***Lass, William E.** Minnesota. 2nd ed. (Illus.). 336p. 2000. pap. 15.95 (*0-393-31971-7*) Norton.

Lass, William E. Minnesota: A History. 2nd ed. LC 97-34650. (Illus.). 336p. 1998. 27.50 (*0-393-04628-1*) Norton.

Lassaigne, Jacques & Weelen, Guy. Vieira Da Silva. (Grandes Monografías). (SPA., Illus.). 340p. 1993. 175.00 (*84-343-0303-5*) Elliots Bks.

Lassakers, Karin. The Polish Debt Crises. (Pew Case Studies in International Affairs). 50p. (C). 1994. pap. text 3.50 (*1-56927-209-3*, GU Schl Foreign) Geo U Inst Dplmcy.

Lassaletta, Manuel C. Mensajes de Luz Profetica.Tr. of Messages of Prophetic Light. (SPA.). 1991. pap. 3.99 (*0-945792-71-9*, 498452) Editorial Unilit.

Lassalle, Ferdinand. Die Philosophie Herakleitos des Dunklen Von Ephesos, 2 vols. in 1. (Spudasmata Ser.: Bd. XLI). xxii, 858p. 1973. reprint ed. write for info. (*3-487-05004-8*) G Olms Pubs.

Lassan, N. A. Advances & Technical Standards in Neurosurgery, Vol. 4. LC 74-10499. 1977. 96.00 (*0-387-81423-X*) Spr-Verlag.

Lassanyi, Mary E. Agribusiness: 1980's & 1990's Perspective. Bibliography: January 1985-May 1991. 27p. 1996. reprint ed. pap. text 20.00 (*0-7881-3353-5*) DIANE Pub.

— Central & Eastern Europe: Going Global: A Bibliography & Directory. (Illus.). 95p. (Orig.). (C). 1995. pap. text 35.00 (*0-7881-1531-6*) DIANE Pub.

— North American Free Trade Agreement: Mexico - U. S. - Canada Trade Accord. 27p. (C). 1995. pap. text 15.00 (*0-7881-1843-9*) DIANE Pub.

Lassanyi, Mary E. & Olson, Wayne. Agricultural Marketing Directory for U. S. & Africa Trade. 215p. 1997. reprint ed. pap. text 50.00 (*0-7881-4479-0*) DIANE Pub.

Lassanyl, Mary E., ed. South America's Economic Development & Emerging Markets: A Bibliography. 57p. (Orig.). (C). 1994. pap. text 30.00 (*0-7881-1541-3*) DIANE Pub.

Lassar, Terry J. Carrots & Sticks: New Zoning Downtown. LC 89-51454. 196p. (Orig.). 1989. pap. text 56.95 (*0-87420-693-6*, C58) Urban Land.

— City Deal Making. LC 90-70877. 1990. 37.95 (*0-87420-704-5*, C41) Urban Land.

Lassarre, jt. auth. see Gaudry.

Lassau, Jean-Pierre. Atlas of Neonatal Anatomy. (Illus.). 180p. (gr. 13). 1982. 73.00 (*0-89352-139-6*, MA139) Mosby Inc.

Lasse, Antonsen. Per Kirkeby: Works from the 60's. (Illus.). 50p. 1995. 25.00 (*1-885013-08-6*) M Werner.

Lassegue, Pierre. Lexique de Comptabilite. 3rd ed. 404p. 1993. pap. 39.95 (*0-7859-5622-0*, 2247015328) Fr & Eur.

Lassell, Georgiou, jt. ed. see Lassell, Michael.

Lassell, Michael. Certain Ecstasies: Bedtime Stories. LC 98-50722. 1999. pap. text 15.00 (*1-891305-12-3*) Painted Leaf.

— Elton John & Tim Rice's Elaborate Lives: The Legend of Aida - The Making of the Broadway Show. (Illus.). 160p. 2000. trans. 40.00 (*0-7868-6484-2*, Pub. by Disney Pr) Time Warner.

— A Flame for the Touch That Matters: Poems. LC 97-41686. 1998. write for info. (*0-9651558-9-7*) Painted Leaf.

— The Hard Way. (Orig.). 1995. pap. 12.95 (*1-56333-231-0*, R Kasak Bks) Masquerade.

— The Name of Love: Great Gay Love Poems. LC 94-36026. 87p. 1994. text 10.00 (*0-312-11863-5*, Stonewall Inn) St Martin.

— Poems for Lost & Un-Lost Boys. LC 85-73772. (Amelia Chapbooks Ser.). (Illus.). 92p. (Orig.). 1985. pap. 10.95 (*0-936545-00-3*) Amelia.

Lassell, Michael, ed. Men Seeking Men: Adventures in Gay Personals. LC 98-27646. 248p. 1998. pap. 15.00 (*1-891305-02-6*) Painted Leaf.

***Lassell, Michael & Lassell, Georgiou, eds.** The World in Us: Lesbian & Gay Poetry of the Next Wave. 416p. 2000. text 27.50 (*0-312-20943-6*) St Martin.

Lassen, jt. auth. see Cahn.

***Lassen, Abraham.** Gersonidies Commentary on the Book of Job. 266p. 1999. reprint ed. pap. 14.95 (*0-8197-0682-5*) Bloch.

Lassen, Cheryl A. Reaching the Assetless Poor: Projects & Strategies for Their Self-Reliant Development. (Special Series on Landlessness & Near-Landlessness: No. 6). 68p. (Orig.). (C). 1980. pap. text 6.75 (*0-86731-073-1*) Cornell CIS RDC.

Lassen, Christian R. The Art of Christian Riese Lassen. 120p. 1993. pap. 21.95 (*1-55912-376-1*) CEDCO Pub.

***Lassen, Christian Riese.** Lassen Island. (Illus.). 88p. 1999. pap. 24.95 (*1-56931-382-2*) Viz Commns Inc.

Lassen, Coralou P., ed. see Pardington, John H.

Lassen, Inger, ed. Interactional Perspectives on LSP. (Language & Cultural Contact Ser.: Vol. 22). 94p. 1997. pap. 12.95 (*87-7307-602-3*, Pub. by Aalborg Univ) David Brown.

***Lassen, Jeremy, ed.** After Shocks: An Anthology of So-Cal Horror. 221p. 2000. 21.00 (*0-9700097-0-4*) Freak.

Lassen, Mary M. Community-Based Family Support in Public Housing. LC 95-76523. 172p. 1995. pap. text 15.00 (*0-9630627-5-1*) Harvard Fam.

Lassen, Maureen K., jt. auth. see Elliot, Charles H.

***Lassen, Maureen Kirby.** Why Are We Still Fighting? How to End Your Schema Wars & Start Connecting with the People You Love. 240p. 2000. pap. text 13.95 (*1-57224-186-1*) New Harbinger.

***Lassen, Tina.** Moon Handbooks: Michigan: Featuring the Great Lakes & the Upper Peninsula. LC 98-767. (Illus.). 360p. 1999. pap. 15.95 (*1-56691-134-6*, Moon Handbks) Avalon Travel.

Lasser. American Constitutional Law, Vol. 1. (C). 1900. pap. 46.67 (*0-205-29009-4*, Longwood Div) Allyn.

— American Constitutional Law, Vol. 2. (C). 1900. pap. 46.67 (*0-205-29010-8*, Longwood Div) Allyn.

Lasser, Bonnie. Let's Have a Sleepover. (Look-Look Bks.). (Illus.). 24p. (J). (ps-3). 1998. pap. 3.29 (*0-307-12963-2*, 12963, Goldn Books) Gldn Bks Pub Co Inc.

Lasser, Carol, ed. Educating Men & Women Together: Coeducation in a Changing World. LC 86-7126. (Illus.). 184p. 1987. text 24.95 (*0-252-01346-8*) U of Ill Pr.

Lasser, Carol & Merrill, Marlene D., eds. Friends & Sisters: Letters Between Lucy Stone & Antoinette Brown Blackwell, 1846-93. LC 86-24984. (Women in American History Ser.). (Illus.). 314p. 1987. text 29.95 (*0-252-01396-4*) U of Ill Pr.

Lasser, Dieter, jt. auth. see Hoschek, Josef.

Lasser Institute Staff. American Express Tax Guide & Financial Organizer Prior Year Plant. 1991. pap. 29.95 (*0-13-032335-7*) P-H

— Professional Edition JK Lasser Your Income Tax, 1995. 1994. pap. 40.00 (*0-671-89880-9*) S&S Trade.

Lasser, J. K. How to Pay Less Tax on Retirement. 192p. 1995. 15.95 (*0-02-860088-6*, Lasser) Macmillan Gen Ref.

— J. K. Lasser's How You Can Profit from the New Tax Laws: 1985 Edition. 160p. 1984. pap. 5.95 (*0-317-06509-2*) S&S Trade.

— J. K. Lasser's Your Income Tax Record Book. 144p. 1984. pap. 4.95 (*0-317-06480-0*) S&S Trade.

— Monthly Tax Service, 1986. 1985. pap. 12.00 (*0-671-31059-3*) PB.

— Monthly Tax Service, 1988. 1987. pap. 24.00 (*0-13-600800-3*) P-H.

Lasser, J. K., Tax Institute Staff. How to Run a Small Business. 7th ed. 352p. 1994. 27.95 (*0-07-036576-8*) McGraw.

— J. K. Lasser's Guide to Planning Your Successful Retirement. write for info. (*0-318-59619-9*) S&S Trade.

— J. K. Lasser's How to Avoid a Tax Audit of Your Return. rev. ed. write for info. (*0-318-59599-0*) S&S Trade.

— J. K. Lasser's 1986 Taxes Made Easy. 1986. pap. 3.95 (*0-317-40477-6*) P-H.

— J. K. Lasser's Professional Edition of Your Income Tax. write for info. (*0-318-59616-4*) S&S Trade.

— J. K. Lasser's Retirement Plan Handbook, 1989-1990. (IRAs, 401(k)s, Keoghs & Other Retirement Plans Ser.). 272p. 1988. pap. 8.95 (*0-318-37356-4*, Lasser) Macmillan Gen Ref.

— J. K. Lasser's Your Income Tax, 1981. 1980. pap. 5.95 (*0-686-72557-3*, Fireside) S&S Trade Pap.

— J. K. Lasser's Your Income Tax, 1988. 1988. pap. write for info. (*0-318-62741-8*) S&S Trade.

— Lasser's Your Income Tax, 1982. pap. 5.95 (*0-686-91635-2*) S&S Trade.

Lasser, J. K., Tax Institute Staff & Greisman, Bernard. Estate Tax Techniques, 3 vols. 1955. ring bd. 640.00 (*0-8205-1350-4*) Bender.

Lasser, J.K., Tax Institute Staff, jt. auth. see Greisman, Bernard.

Lasser, Joseph R., et al. The Coins of Colonial America: World Trade Coins of the Seventeenth & Eighteenth Centuries. LC 98-105629. (Illus.). 47p. 1997. pap. 9.95 (*0-87935-181-0*) Colonial Williamsburg.

Lasser, Mark R. & Machen, Eli. Faithful & True: Sexual Integrity in a Fallen World. 240p. 1996. pap. text 12.95 (*0-8054-9819-2*, LifeWy Press) LifeWay Christian.

Lasser, Rupert. Introduction to Fourier Series. LC 95-51808. (Monographs & Textbooks in Pure & Applied Mathematics: Vol. 199). (Illus.). 304p. 1996. text 145.00 (*0-8247-9610-1*) Dekker.

Lasser, Scott. Battle Creek. LC 99-12607. 288p. 1999. 24.00 (*0-688-16785-3*, Wm Morrow) Morrow Avon.

***Lasser, Scott.** Battle Creek: A Novel. 288p. 2000. pap. 14.00 (*0-688-17763-8*, Perennial) HarperTrade.

Lasser, William. American Politics. 2nd ed. LC 98-72057. 1998. pap. text 34.17 (*0-395-90207-X*) HM.

— American Politics: Institutions & Interconnections. 614p. (C). 1996. pap. text 41.96 (*0-669-32584-8*); pap. text, student ed. 21.16 (*0-669-32585-6*) HM Trade Div.

— American Politics: Institutions & Interconnections. (C). 1996. pap. text, teacher ed. 11.96 (*0-669-32586-4*) HM Trade Div.

— The Limits of Judicial Power: The Supreme Court in American Politics. LC 88-40141. xi, 354p. (C). 1988. 39.95 (*0-8078-1810-0*) U of NC Pr.

— The Limits of Judicial Power: The Supreme Court in American Politics. LC 88-40141. 366p. reprint ed. pap. 113.50 (*0-608-08600-2*, 206912300003) Bks Demand.

— Perspectives on American Government: A Comprehensive Reader. 775p. (C). 1992. teacher ed. 2.66 (*0-669-28289-8*) HM Trade Div.

— Perspectives on American Government: A Comprehensive Reader. 2nd ed. (C). 1996. text, teacher ed. 28.36 (*0-669-41643-6*) HM Trade Div.

— Perspectives on American Government: A Comprehensive Reader, 2 Vols. 2nd ed. 625p. (C). 2000. pap. text 29.16 (*0-669-41642-8*) HM Trade Div.

***Lassergard, Joseph Paul.** A Fine Mesh. (Illus.). 48p. 1999. pap. 8.95 (*1-58535-005-2*) In His Steps.

Lasserre, Guy. Synopse des Lois du Pentateuque. 242p. 1994. text 107.00 (*90-04-10202-7*) Brill Academic Pubs.

Lasserre, Jean. War & the Gospel. Coburn, O., tr. 248p. 1962. 10.00 (*0-227-67635-1*) Attic Pr.

***Lasserre, Jean.** War & the Gospel. 244p. 1998. pap. 23.00 (*1-57910-156-9*) Wipf & Stock.

Lasserre, Jean B., jt. auth. see Hernandez-Lerma, Onesimo.

Lasserre, Jean-Bernard, jt. auth. see Dauzere-Peres, Stephane.

Lasserre, Philippe & Schutte, Hellmut. Strategies for Asia Pacific. 400p. 1996. 59.95 (*0-7329-3664-0*, Pub. by Macmill Educ) Paul & Co Pubs.

Lasserre, Phillippe. Strategies for Asia Pacific: Beyond the Crisis. LC 98-54345. 1999. pap. text 22.50 (*0-8147-5156-3*) NYU Pr.

Lasserre, Phillippe & Schutte, Hellmut. Strategies for Asia Pacific. 400p. (C). 1995. text 55.00 (*0-8147-5109-1*) NYU Pr.

Lasserre, Pierre. Long Term Control of Exhaustable Resources, Vol. 13. (Fundamentals of Pure & Applied Economics Ser.). viii, 122p. 1991. pap. text 59.00 (*3-7186-5134-3*, Harwood Acad Pubs) Gordon & Breach.

***Lasserre, Pierre & Marzollo, Angelo, eds.** The Venice Lagoon Ecosystem: Inputs & Interactions Between Land & Sea. LC 99-31158. (Man & the Biosphere Ser.: Vol. 25). (Illus.). 533p. 2000. 98.00 (*1-85070-083-4*) Prthnon Pub.

Lassers, Eugene W. The Famous & the Infamous: Presidential Trivia, Book 1. (Illus.). 66p. (Orig.). 1990. pap. 3.00 (*0-9626129-0-1*) E W Lassers.

***Lasserson, Daniel.** Lo Esencial en Sistema Nervios. (C). 1998. text 14.09 (*84-8174-367-4*) Mosby Inc.

Lasseter, Don. Cold Storage. LC 99-185331. (Pinnacle True Crime Ser.). 400p. 1998. mass mkt. 5.99 (*0-7860-0583-1*, Pinncle Kensgtn) Kensgtn Pub Corp.

***Lasseter, Don.** Die for Me. 432p. 2000. mass mkt. 6.99 (*0-7860-1107-6*, Pinncle Kensgtn) Kensgtn Pub Corp.

Lasseter, Don. Going Postal. LC 97-217917. 320p. 1997. mass mkt. 5.99 (*0-7860-0439-8*, Pinncle Kensgtn) Kensgtn Pub Corp.

***Lasseter, Don.** Killer Kids. (Illus.). 2000. pap. 6.50 (*0-7860-1283-8*, Pinncle Kensgtn) Kensgtn Pub Corp.

Lasseter, Don. Property of the Folsom Wolf. 512p. 1995. mass mkt. 4.99 (*0-7860-0090-2*, Pinncle Kensgtn); mass mkt. 4.99 (*0-8217-0090-1*, Zebra Kensgtn) Kensgtn Pub Corp.

***Lasseter, Don.** Zodiac of Death. 1999. mass mkt. 6.99 (*0-425-17146-9*) Berkley Pub.

Lasseter, Donald, jt. auth. see King, Gary C.

Lasseter, John. Toy Story: The Art & Making of the Animated Film. (Disney Miniatures Ser.). (Illus.). 192p. (J). 1996. 10.95 (*0-7868-6254-8*, Pub. by Hyperion) Time Warner.

Lasseter, John & Daly, Steve. Toy Story: The Art & Making of the Animated Film. (Illus.). 136p. (J). 1995. 38.95 (*0-7868-6180-0*, Pub. by Hyperion) Time Warner.

***Lassetter, Stuart & Creek, Robert.** General Botany Laboratory Manual. 4th ed. 142p. 1998. pap. text 21.95 (*0-88725-255-9*) Hunter Textbks.

Lasseur, Michele. Egypt. (Evergreen Ser.). (Illus.). 160p. 1998. 19.99 (*3-8228-7643-7*) Taschen Amer.

Lassey, Peter. Developing a Learning Organisation. 160p. 1998. pap. 27.50 (*0-7494-2413-3*, Kogan Pg Educ) Stylus Pub VA.

Lassey, William R. Health Care Systems Around the World: Characteristics, Issues, Reforms. LC 96-10745. 370p. (C). 1996. pap. 53.00 (*0-13-104233-5*) P-H.

Lassey, William R., jt. auth. see Carlson, John E.

Lassez, Jean-Louis & Plotkin, Gordon, eds. Computational Logic: Essays in Honor of Alan Robinson. (Illus.). 752p. 1991. 82.50 (*0-262-12156-5*) MIT Pr.

***Lassieur, Allison.** Abortion. LC 00-9250. 2001. write for info. (*1-56006-818-3*) Lucent Bks.

— The Ancient Egyptians. LC 00-8655. 2000. lib. bdg. write for info. (*1-56006-755-1*) Lucent Bks.

Lassieur, Allison. Before the Storm: American Indians Before Columbus. LC 97-50072. (Library of American Indian History). (Illus.). 150p. (YA). (gr. 7 up). 1998. 19.95 (*0-8160-3651-9*) Facts on File.

***Lassieur, Allison.** Buses. 1999. 14.60 (*0-516-21871-9*) Capstone Pr.

Lassieur, Allison. Buses. LC 99-24249. (Transportation Library). 24p. (J). 2000. 14.60 (*0-7368-0360-2*, Bridgestone Bks) Capstone Pr.

***Lassieur, Allison.** Earthquakes. LC 00-20876. (Natural Disasters Ser.). 48p. (YA). (gr. 5 up). 2000. lib. bdg. 21.26 (*0-7368-0586-9*, Capstone Bks) Capstone Pr.

— Head Lice. (My Health Ser.). (Illus.). (YA). 2000. pap. 6.95 (*0-531-16450-0*) Watts.

— The Inuit. LC 99-52065. (Native Peoples Ser.). (Illus.). 24p. (J). (ps-3). 2000. lib. bdg. 15.93 (*0-7368-0498-6*, Bridgestone Bks) Capstone Pr.

— Leonardo da Vinci & the Renaissance in World History. LC 99-50571. (In World History Ser.). (Illus.). 128p. (YA). (gr. 5 up). 2000. lib. bdg. 20.95 (*0-7660-1401-0*) Enslow Pubs.

— The Nez Perce Tribe. LC 99-53167. (Native Peoples Ser.). 24p. (J). (ps-3). 2000. lib. bdg. 15.93 (*0-7368-0500-1*) Capstone Pr.

— Passenger Trains. 1999. 14.60 (*0-516-21874-3*) Capstone Pr.

— Serial Killers. LC 99-33814. (History Makers Ser.). (Illus.). 144p. (YA). (gr. 6-9). 2000. lib. bdg. 23.70 (*1-56006-650-4*) Lucent Bks.

— Subways. 1999. 14.60 (*0-516-21875-1*) Capstone Pr.

Lassieur, Allison. Subways. LC 99-14632. (Transportation Library). 24p. (J). 1999. 14.60 (*0-7368-0363-7*, Bridgestone Bks) Capstone Pr.

***Lassieur, Allison.** Taxis. 1999. 14.60 (*0-516-21876-X*) Capstone Pr.

Lassieur, Allison. Taxis. LC 99-24135. (Transportation Library). 24p. (J). 2000. 14.60 (*0-7368-0365-3*, Bridgestone Bks) Capstone Pr.

***Lassieur, Allison.** Unicorn. (Legend of the Five Rings Ser.: Vol. 2). 288p. 2000. mass mkt. 6.99 (*0-7869-1658-3*) Wizards Coast.

— Volcanoes. LC 00-21415. (Natural Disasters Ser.). (Illus.). 48p. (YA). (gr. 5 up). 2000. lib. bdg. 21.26 (*0-7368-0589-3*, Capstone Bks) Capstone Pr.

***Lassieur, Allison & Savage, Steve.** Scorpions, the Sneaky Stingers. LC 99-42709. (Animals in Order Ser.). (Illus.). (J). 2000. 23.00 (*0-531-11651-4*) Watts.

Lassig, Jurgen. Spiny. LC 94-40893. (Illus.). 64p. (J). (gr. 1-3). 1995. lib. bdg. 13.88 (*1-55858-402-1*, Pub. by North-South Bks NYC) Chronicle Bks.

— Spiny. LC 94-40893. (Illus.). 64p. (J). (gr. 1-3). 1996. pap. 5.95 (*1-55858-552-4*, Pub. by North-South Bks NYC) Chronicle Bks.

***Lassila, D. H., et al, eds.** Multiscale Phenomena in Materials--Experiments & Modeling Vol. 578: Materials Research Society Symposium Proceedings. 2000. text 93.00 (*1-55899-486-6*) Materials Res.

Lassila, Dennis. Bender's Payroll Tax Guide. Matthew Bender Tax Staff, ed. text 117.00 (*0-8205-4230-X*) Bender.

Lassila, Dennis R. & Kilpatrick, Bob. U. S. Master Compensation Tax Guide. Muzinic, Jason M., ed. LC 98-102816. 520p. 1997. pap. text 49.95 (*0-8080-0227-9*) CCH INC.

***Lassila, Dennis R. & Kilpatrick, Bob G.** U. S. Master Compensation Tax Guide. 2nd ed. 704p. 1999. pap. text 54.95 (*0-8080-0416-6*) CCH INC.

Lassila, J., jt. ed. see Broer, D. P.

Lassiter, Harry. A Guide to Advanced Mathematics. LC 98-85642. (Learning Tools That Work Ser.). 104p. 1998. write for info. (*1-57163-906-3*) Sofsource.

Lassiter, James & Gilbertie, James. Survey of Economics. 2nd ed. 530p. (C). 1992. pap. text 50.56 (*1-56226-118-5*) CAT Pub.

Lassiter, Karen. Algebra. (Mathematics Skill Bks.). 1997. pap., student ed. 3.00 (*0-8114-4321-3*) Raintree Steck-V.

— Decimals & Percents. (Math Skills for the Workforce Ser.). 1997. pap. text 10.64 (*0-8172-6377-2*) Raintree Steck-V.

— Measurement & Geometry. (Mathematics Skill Bks.). 1997. pap., student ed. 3.00 (*0-8114-4320-5*) Raintree Steck-V.

***Lassiter, Karl.** First Cherokee Rifles. 352p. 1999. mass mkt. 5.99 (*0-7860-1008-8*, Pinncle Kensgtn) Kensgtn Pub Corp.

Lassiter, Karl. The Long Walk. 416p. 1996. mass mkt. 5.99 (*0-7860-0305-7*, Pinncle Kensgtn) Kensgtn Pub Corp.

— The Warriors' Path. 352p. 1998. pap. 4.99 (*0-7860-0528-9*, Pinncle Kensgtn) Kensgtn Pub Corp.

Lassiter, Kenneth T., ed. see Society of Photographic Scientists & Engineers Sta.

Lassiter, Luke E. The Power of Kiowa Song: A Collaborative Ethnography. LC 98-8866. 270p. 1998. lib. bdg. 40.00 (*0-8165-1834-3*) U of Ariz Pr.

— The Power of Kiowa Song: A Collaborative Ethnography. LC 98-8866. (Illus.). 270p. 1998. pap. 17.95 (*0-8165-1835-1*) U of Ariz Pr.

Lassiter, Matthew D. & Lewis, Andrew B., eds. The Moderates' Dilemma: Massive Resistance to School Desegregation in Virginia. LC 98-13877. 304p. 1998. pap. 18.50 (*0-8139-1817-0*); text 49.50 (*0-8139-1816-2*) U Pr of Va.

***Lassiter, Patrice Shelton.** Generations of Black Life in Kennesaw & Marietta, Georgia. (Images of America Ser.). (Illus.). 1999. pap. 18.99 (*0-7524-1399-6*) Arcadia Publng.

***Lassiter, Rhiannon.** Psychic Phenomena. (Unexplained Ser.). 32p. (YA). (gr. 5 up). 1999. pap. 5.95 (*0-7641-1063-2*) Barron.

Lassiter, Sybil M. Cultures of Color in America: A Guide to Family, Religion & Health. LC 97-24550. 224p. 1998. lib. bdg. 65.00 (*0-313-30070-4*, Greenwood Pr) Greenwood.

— Multicultural Clients: Professional Handbook for Health Care Providers & Social Workers. LC 94-30927. 224p. 1995. lib. bdg. 69.50 (*0-313-29140-3*, Greenwood Pr) Greenwood.

Lassleur, Allison. Subways. LC 99-24132. 24p. (J). 1999. 14.60 (*0-7368-0364-5*) Capstone Pr.

***Lasslo, Andrew.** Molecules, Miracles & Medicine. 89p. 2000. pap. 12.99 (*0-87527-533-8*) Green.

Lasslo, Andrew. Travel at Your Own Risk: Reflections on Science, Research & Education. LC 98-29463. 1998. 23.95 (*0-915340-21-6*) PJD Pubns.

***Lasslo, Andrew & Quandt, Richard E.** Library Automation in Transitional Societies: Lessons from Eastern Europe. LC 98-50384. (Illus.). 468p. 2000. text 55.00 (*0-19-513262-9*) OUP.

Lassman, Janet. Daring to Care: Training Manual. 3rd ed. (Illus.). 506p. 1999. ring bd. 35.00 (*0-935890-27-0*) Emerg Nurses IL.

Lassman, P. & Buckler, S. Political Thinkers of the Twentieth Century. 240p. (C). 1999. 59.99 (*0-415-10876-4*, D4207) Routledge.

— Political Thinkers of the Twentieth Century. 240p. (C). 1999. pap. 17.99 (*0-415-10877-2*, D4211) Routledge.

Lassman, Peter, et al, eds. Max Weber's "Science As a Vocation" 240p. 1988. 55.00 (*0-04-301211-6*) Routledge.

Lassman, Peter, jt. auth. see Velody, Irving.

Lassman, Peter, ed. see Weber, Max.

Lassmann, Hersausgegeben Von Gert, see Schwark, Eberhard & Von Gert Lassmann, Hersausgegeben, eds.

Lassner, Dirk, et al, eds. Modern Applications of DNA Amplification Technqiues: Problems & New Tools: Proceedings of the Augustusburg Conference of Advanced Science on Problems of Quantitation of Nucleic Acids by Amplification Techniques Held in Augustusburg, Germany, September 23-26, 1996. LC 97-41939. 152p. 1998. 75.00 (*0-306-45801-2*, Kluwer Plenum) Kluwer Academic.

Lassner, E. & Schubert, W. Tungsten: Properties, Chemistry, Technology of the Element, Alloys & Chemical Compounds. LC 98-45787. (Illus.). 444p. (C). 1999. text 125.00 (*0-306-45053-4*, Kluwer Plenum) Kluwer Academic.

Lassner, Jacob. Demonizing the Queen of Sheba: Boundaries of Gender & Culture in Postbiblical Judaism & Medieval Islam. 360p. 1996. pap. 19.95 (*0-614-21386-X*, 195) Kazi Pubns.

— Demonizing the Queen of Sheba: Boundaries of Gender & Culture in Postbiblical Judaism & Medieval Islam. LC 93-7499. (Chicago Studies in the History of Judaism). 308p. 1993. pap. text 19.95 (*0-226-46915-8*); lib. bdg. 55.00 (*0-226-46913-1*) U Ch Pr.

— Islamic Revolution & Historical Memory: An Inquiry into the Art of Abbasid Apologetics. (American Oriental Ser.: Vol. 66). xv, 156p. 1986. 22.50 (*0-940490-66-8*) Am Orient Soc.

***Lassner, Jacob.** Middle East Remembered: Forged Identities, Competing Narratives, Contested Spaces. 430p. 1999. text 54.50 (*0-472-11083-7*, 11083) U of Mich Pr.

Lassner, Jacob. The Topography of Baghdad in the Early Middle Ages: Text & Studies. LC 69-11339. 325p. reprint ed. pap. 100.80 (*0-7837-3580-4*, 204343900009) Bks Demand.

Lassner, Jacob, jt. auth. see Goitein, S. D.

Lassner, Jacob, jt. ed. see Fields, Phillip.

Lassner, Joseph, et al, eds. Social Group Work: Competence & Values in Practice. LC 86-32012. (Social Work with Groups Supplement Ser.: No. 2). 230p. 1987. text 49.95 (*0-86656-643-0*) Haworth Pr.

Lassner, Phyllis. British Women Writers of World War II: Battlegrounds of Their Own. LC 97-40947. 304p. 1998. text 55.00 (*0-312-21241-0*) St Martin.

— Elizabeth Bowen. 204p. (C). 1989. pap. 19.00 (*0-389-20879-5*); text 46.00 (*0-389-20878-7*) B&N Imports.

— Elizabeth Bowen: A Study of Short Fiction. (Twayne's Studies in Short Fiction: No. 27). 216p. 1991. 23.95 (*0-8057-8336-9*) Macmillan.

Lasso de La Vega, Javier & Rubert Candau, Jose M., eds. Diccionario Enciclopedias Labor, 9 vols. 7th ed.Tr. of Encyclopaedia Dictionary of Labor. (ENG, FRE, GER, POR & SPA.). 6500p. 1978. 495.00 (*0-8288-5127-1*, S12269) Fr & Eur.

Lasso, Orlando di. Kompositionen Mit Deutschem Text I: 5 - Stimmige Deutsche Lieder (1567-1576) (Samtliche Werke (Alte Reihe) Ser.: Vol. 18). (Illus.). 1973. reprint ed. pap. 85.00 (*0-8450-1918-X*) Broude.

— Kompositionen Mit Deutschem Text II: Deutsche Lieder Aus Verschiedenen Drucken. (Samtliche Werke (Alte Reihe) Ser.: Vol. 20). (Illus.). 1973. reprint ed. pap. 85.00 (*0-8450-1920-1*) Broude.

— Kompositionen Mit Franzosischem Text I: Chansons Aus "Les Melanges de Lassus" (Samtliche Werke (Alte Reihe) Ser.: Vol. 12). 1973. reprint ed. pap. 85.00 (*0-8450-1912-0*) Broude.

— Kompositionen Mit Franzosischem Text III: Chansons Aus "Les Melanges de Lassus" (Samtliche Werke (Alte Reihe) Ser.: Vol. 16). (Illus.). 1973. reprint ed. pap. 85.00 (*0-8450-1916-3*) Broude.

— Kompositionen Mit Franzosischem Text II: Chason Aus "Les Meslanges de Lassus" (Samtliche Werke (Alte Reihe) Ser.: Vol. 14). (Illus.). 1973. reprint ed. pap. 85.00 (*0-8450-1914-7*) Broude.

— Madregale V: 6 & Mehrstimmige Madregale aus verschiedenen Drucken. (Samtliche Werke (Alte Reihe) Ser.: Vol. 10). (Illus.). 1973. reprint ed. pap. 85.00 (*0-8450-1910-4*) Broude.

— Madrigale IV: 4 & 5-Stimmige Madrigale aus Verschiedenen Drucken. (Samtliche Werke (Alte Reihe) Ser.: Vol. 8). (Illus.). 1973. reprint ed. pap. 85.00 (*0-8450-1908-2*) Broude.

— Madrigale I: Das 1 & 2 Buch 5-Stimmiger Madrigale (1555 & 1557) (Samtliche Werke (Alte Reihe) Ser.: Vol. 2). (Illus.). 1973. reprint ed. pap. 85.00 (*0-8450-1902-3*) Broude.

— Madrigale III: Die Beiden Madrigalsammlungen (1585 & 1587) (Samtliche Werke (Alte Reihe) Ser.: Vol. 6). (Illus.). 1973. reprint ed. pap. 85.00 (*0-8450-1906-6*) Broude.

— Madrigale II: Das 3 & 4, Buch 5-Stimmiger Madrigale (1562 & 1567) (Samtliche Werke (Alte Reihe) Ser.: Vol. 4). (Illus.). 1973. reprint ed. pap. 85.00 (*0-8450-1904-X*) Broude.

— Magnum Opus Musicum VIII: Motetten zu 6 Stimmen (Nr. 374-418) (Samtliche Werke (Alte Reihe) Ser.: Vol. 15). (Illus.). 1973. reprint ed. pap. 85.00 (*0-8450-1915-5*) Broude.

— Magnum Opus Musicum XI: Motetten fur 8, 9, 10 & 12 Stimmen (Nr. 493-516) (Samtliche Werke (Alte Reihe) Ser.: Vol. 21). (Illus.). 1973. reprint ed. pap. 85.00 (*0-8450-1921-X*) Broude.

— Magnum Opus Musicum V: Motetten fur 5 Stimmen (Nr. 249-289) (Samtliche Werke (Alte Reihe) Ser.: Vol. 9). (Illus.). 1973. reprint ed. pap. 85.00 (*0-8450-1909-0*) Broude.

— Magnum Opus Musicum IV: Motetten fur 5 Stimmen (Nr. 212-248) (Samtliche Werke (Alte Reihe) Ser.: Vol. 7). 1973. reprint ed. pap. 85.00 (*0-8450-1907-4*) Broude.

— Magnum Opus Musicum IX: Motetten fur 6 Stimmen (Nr. 419-456) (Samtliche Werke (Alte Reihe) Ser.: Vol. 17). (Illus.). 1973. reprint ed. pap. 85.00 (*0-8450-1917-1*) Broude.

— Magnum Opus Musicum I: Motetten fur 2, 3 & 4 Stimmen (Nr. 1-90) (Samtliche Werke (Alte Reihe) Ser.: Vol. 1). (Illus.). 1973. reprint ed. pap. 85.00 (*0-8450-1901-5*) Broude.

— Magnum Opus Musicum VII: Motetten zu 6 Stimmen (Nr. 336-373) (Samtliche Werke (Alte Reihe) Ser.: Vol. 13). (Illus.). 1973. reprint ed. pap. 85.00 (*0-8450-1913-9*) Broude.

— Magnum Opus Musicum VI: Motetten zu 5 & 6 Stimmen (Nr. 290-335) (Samtliche Werke (Alte Reihe) Ser.: Vol. 11). (Illus.). 1973. reprint ed. pap. 85.00 (*0-8450-1911-2*) Broude.

— Magnum Opus Musicum X: Motetten fur 6, 7 & 8 Stimmen (Nr. 457-492) (Samtliche Werke (Alte Reihe) Ser.: Vol. 19). (Illus.). 1973. reprint ed. pap. 85.00 (*0-8450-1919-8*) Broude.

— Magnum Opus Musicum III: Motetten fur 5 Stimmen (Nr. 161-211) (Samtliche Werke (Alte Reihe) Ser.: Vol. 5). (Illus.). 1973. reprint ed. pap. 85.00 (*0-8450-1905-8*) Broude.

— Magnum Opus Musicum II: Motetten fur 4 & 5 Stimmen (Nr. 91-160) (Samtliche Werke (Alte Reihe) Ser.: Vol. 3). (Illus.). 1973. reprint ed. pap. 85.00 (*0-8450-1903-1*) Broude.

— Samtliche Werke (Alte Reihe), 21. (Illus.). 1973. reprint ed. pap. 1500.00 (*0-8450-1900-7*) Broude.

Lasso, Orlando Di, see Di Lasso, Orlando.

Lassoie, James P., et al, eds. Forest Trees of the Northeast. (Illus.). 277p. (Orig.). 1996. pap. 18.95 (*1-57753-012-8*, 147IB235) Corn Coop Ext.

Lassoie, James P. & Hinckle. Techniques & Approaches in Forest Tree Ecophysiology. 616p. 1991. lib. bdg. 349.00 (*0-8493-6866-9*, QK938) CRC Pr.

Lassoie, James P., jt. auth. see Buck, Louise E.

Lassoie, James P., jt. ed. see McDonald, Peter.

Lasson, Frans. The Life & Destiny of Isak Dinesen. LC 75-40669. (Illus.). 232p. 1994. reprint ed. pap. 17.95 (*0-226-46916-6*, P686) U Ch Pr.

Lasson, Frans, ed. see Dinesen, Isak.

Lasson, Kenneth. Private Lives of Public Servants. LC 77-15758. 275p. reprint ed. pap. 85.30 (*0-608-17073-9*, 205623400056) Bks Demand.

Lasson, Kenneth, jt. auth. see Cohen, William S.

Lasson, Kenneth, jt. auth. see Margulies, Sheldon.

Lasson, Nelson B. The History & Development of the Fourth Amendment to the United States Constitution. LC 78-64166. (Johns Hopkins University. Studies in the Social Sciences. Thirtieth Ser. 1912: 2). reprint ed. 34.50 (*0-404-61276-8*) AMS Pr.

— History & Development of the Fourth Amendment to the United States Constitution. LC 75-87389. (American Constitutional & Legal History Ser.). 1970. reprint ed. lib. bdg. 27.50 (*0-306-71532-5*) Da Capo.

Lassonde, M. & Jeeves, M. A. Callosal Agenesis: A Natural Split Brain? LC 93-46518. (Advances in Behavioral Biology Ser.: Vol. 42). (Illus.). 318p. (C). 1994. text 95.00 (*0-306-44660-X*, Kluwer Plenum) Kluwer Academic.

Lassonde, Reid E. Thirty-Five Practical Ways to Improve Your Health: A Common Sense Approach for Wholesome Living. LC 91-68336. (Illus.). 142p. (Orig.). 1992. pap. 9.95 (*0-9631846-7-9*) Real-Life Pubns.

Lassqussios, J. World of Watches. 144p. 1996. 17.98 (*0-7858-0743-8*) Bk Sales Inc.

Lassure, C. Tech Vocabulary-Vocabulaire Anglais-Francais de la Haute Technologie. (ENG & FRE.). 223p. 1991. pap. 39.95 (*0-7859-7150-5*) Fr & Eur.

Lassus, Bernard. Landscape Approach. LC 98-26259. (Penn Studies in Landscape Architecture). (Illus.). 216p. 1998. 39.95 (*0-8122-3450-2*) U of Pa Pr.

Lassus, Jean. Antioch-on-the-Orontes Vol. 5: Les Portiques D'Antioche. LC 35-1197. (Publications of the Committee for the Excavation of Antioch & Its Vicinity). 226p. 1972. pap. 70.10 (*0-7837-9368-5*, 206011100005) Bks Demand.

Lassus, Patrick. Harmful Marine Algal Blooms. LC 95-208352. 170.00 (*1-898298-11-4*) Spr-Verlag.

Lasswell. Jurisprudence. 1997. pap. text, student ed. 75.00 (*90-411-0611-1*) Kluwer Academic.

Lasswell & Gillette. Marriage & the Family. 2nd ed. (Sociology - Introductory Level Ser.). 1987. pap., student ed. 10.00 (*0-534-07585-1*) Wadsworth Pub.

— Marriage & the Family. 2nd ed. (Sociology - Introductory Level Ser.). 1987. pap., teacher ed. write for info. (*0-534-07586-X*) Wadsworth Pub.

Lasswell, jt. auth. see Mitchell.

Lasswell, Harold. The Garrison State. LC 96-38936. 120p. 1997. text 29.95 (*1-56000-268-9*) Transaction Pubs.

Lasswell, Harold D. Harold D. Lasswell on Political Sociology. LC 76-22961. (Heritage of Sociology Ser.). 462p. 1977. lib. bdg. 33.00 (*0-226-46920-4*) U Ch Pr.

— Jurisprudence for a Free Society: Studies in Law, Science & Policy, 2 vols., Set. 1612p. (C). 1992. lib. bdg. 638.50 (*0-7923-0989-8*) Kluwer Academic.

— National Security & Individual Freedom. LC 71-139193. (Civil Liberties in American History Ser.). 1971. reprint ed. lib. bdg. 32.50 (*0-306-70085-9*) Da Capo.

— Politics: Who Gets What, When & How. 1990. 22.25 (*0-8446-1277-4*) Peter Smith.

— Power & Personality. LC 75-22644. 262p. 1976. reprint ed. lib. bdg. 59.75 (*0-8371-8374-X*, LAPOP, Greenwood Pr) Greenwood.

— A Pre-View of Policy Sciences. LC 78-165801. (Policy Sciences Book Ser.). 187p. reprint ed. pap. 58.00 (*0-608-16307-4*, 202625900049) Bks Demand.

— Psychopathology & Politics. xxvi, 368p. 1986. pap. text 23.00 (*0-226-46919-0*) U Ch Pr.

— The Signature of Power: Buildings, Communication, & Policy. 224p. (C). 1978. text 44.95 (*0-87855-289-8*) Transaction Pubs.

Lasswell, Harold D., ed. Pluralizing World in Formation. LC 79-21108. (Propaganda & Communication in World History Ser.: Vol. 3). 576p. reprint ed. pap. 178.60 (*0-608-09994-5*, 202958800003) Bks Demand.

Lasswell, Harold D., et al, eds. Emergence of Public Opinion in the West. LC 79-18790. (Propaganda & Communication in World History Ser.: Vol. 2). 576p. reprint ed. pap. 178.60 (*0-608-17225-1*, 202702700002) Bks Demand.

— Propaganda & Promotional Activities: An Annotated Bibliography. LC 75-77979. 474p. reprint ed. pap. 147.00 (*0-608-11161-9*, 202010000016) Bks Demand.

Lasswell, Harold D. & Blumenstock, Dorothy. World Revolutionary Propaganda. LC 78-114887. (Select Bibliographies Reprint Ser.). 1977. 29.95 (*0-8369-5291-X*) Ayer.

Lasswell, Harold D. & Lerner, Daniel, eds. World Revolutionary Elites: Studies in Coercive Ideological Movements. LC 80-21600. 478p. 1980. reprint ed. lib. bdg. 85.00 (*0-313-22572-9*, LAWE, Greenwood Pr) Greenwood.

Lasswell, Harold D., jt. auth. see Arens, Richard.

Lasswell, Marcia & Lasswell, Thomas E. Marriage & the Family. 2nd ed. 596p. (C). 1987. pap. write for info. (*0-534-07584-3*) Wadsworth Pub.

Lasswell, Mary. Bread for the Living. 1976. 20.95 (*0-8488-1405-3*) Amereon Ltd.

— Mrs. Rasmussen's Book of One-Arm Cookery. 17.95 (*0-8488-1406-1*) Amereon Ltd.

— Mrs. Rasmussen's Book of One-Arm Cookery. 1981. reprint ed. lib. bdg. 18.95 (*0-89966-437-7*) Buccaneer Bks.

Lasswell, Thomas E., jt. auth. see Lasswell, Marcia.

Lasswitz, Kurd. Geschichte der Atomistik Vom Mittelalter Bis Newton. (GER.). 1997. reprint ed. 278.00 (*3-487-00490-9*) G Olms Pubs.

Last, jt. auth. see Pratt, James.

Last, B. F. & Van Veldhuizen, A. M. Developments in Pediatric Psychosocial Oncology. 184p. 1992. pap. 37.50 (*90-265-1131-0*) Swets.

Last, B. F. & VanVeldhuizn. Children with Cancer. viii, 280p. 1991. 42.50 (*90-265-1038-1*) Swets.

Last, C. G. & Hersen, M. Adult Behavior Therapy Casebook. 324p. (C). 1994. pap. 41.00 (*0-306-44459-3*, Kluwer Plenum) Kluwer Academic.

— Issues in Diagnostic Research. LC 86-30575. (Illus.). 360p. (C). 1987. 75.00 (*0-306-42424-X*, Plenum Trade) Perseus Pubng.

Last, C. G., jt. auth. see Hersen, M.

Last, Cynthia G. Five Reasons Why We Overeat: How to Develop a Long-Term Weight-Control Plan That's Right for You. LC 98-34216. (Illus.). 208p. 1998. 19.95 (*1-55972-479-X*, Birch Ln Pr) Carol Pub Group.

Last, Cynthia G. & Herson, Michel, eds. Adult Behavior Therapy Casebook. LC 93-6252. (Illus.). 324p. (C). 1993. 65.00 (*0-306-44451-8*, Kluwer Plenum) Kluwer Academic.

Last, Cynthia G., jt. auth. see Klein, Rachel G.

Last, Dick Van Galen, see Wolfswinkel, Rolf & Van Galen Last, Dick.

Last, Ellen. Guide to Curriculum Planning in English Language Arts. 274p. (C). 1988. pap. text 33.00 (*1-57337-001-0*) WI Dept Pub Instruct.

***Last, Eugenia.** Eugenia Last's Horoscopes 2000. 560p. 1999. mass mkt. 6.99 (*0-440-23530-8*) Dell.

Last, F. T., et al, eds. Land & Its Uses-Actual & Potential: An Environmental Appraisal. LC 85-28111. (NATO ASI Conference Series I, Ecology: Vol. 10). 610p. 1986. 110.00 (*0-306-42214-X*, Plenum Trade) Perseus Pubng.

Last, G., jt. auth. see Brandt, A.

Last, George & Williams, Paul, compiled by. An Introduction to ROV Operations. (Illus.). 300p. (C). 1992. pap. 125.00 (*1-870945-23-9*) Oilfield Publns.

Last, Jay T., jt. auth. see McClelland, Gordon T.

Last, Jerold A. Subcellular Particles, Structures, & Organelles. Laskin, Allen I., ed. LC 73-90306. (Methods in Molecular Biology Ser.: No. 5). (Illus.). 325p. reprint ed. pap. 100.80 (*0-7837-0906-4*, 204121100019) Bks Demand.

Last, Jerold A., ed. Eukaryotes at the Subcellular Level: Development & Differentiation. LC 75-42541. (Methods in Molecular Biology Ser.: No. 8). (Illus.). 472p. reprint ed. pap. 146.40 (*0-7837-0838-6*, 204115200019) Bks Demand.

Last, Jerold A. & Laskin, Allen I., eds. Protein Biosynthesis in Bacterial Systems. LC 78-160517. (Methods in Molecular Biology Ser.: No. 1). 349p. reprint ed. pap. 108.20 (*0-7837-0745-2*, 204106500019) Bks Demand.

— Protein Biosynthesis in Nonbacterial Systems. LC 78-189798. (Methods in Molecular Biology Ser.: No. 2). (Illus.). 352p. reprint ed. pap. 109.20 (*0-7837-0740-1*, 204106200019) Bks Demand.

Last, Jerold A., jt. ed. see Laskin, Allen I.

Last, Joan. At the Keyboard, 4 bks., Bk. 1. 1954. pap. 6.95 (*0-19-322280-9*) OUP.

— At the Keyboard, 4 bks., Bk. 2. 1954. pap. 6.95 (*0-19-322281-7*) OUP.

— At the Keyboard, 4 bks., Bk. 3. 1954. pap. 6.95 (*0-19-322282-5*) OUP.

— At the Keyboard, 4 bks., Bk. 4. 1954. pap. 6.95 (*0-19-322283-3*) OUP.

— The Young Pianist: An Approach for Teachers & Students. 2nd ed. (Illus.). 168p. 1985. pap. 15.95 (*0-19-322287-6*) OUP.

Last, John M. Diccionario de Enfermeria. 15th ed. (SPA.). 400p. 1984. pap. 19.95 (*0-7859-5929-7*, 8434523728) Fr & Eur.

— Diccionario de Epidemiologia. (SPA.). 216p. 1989. 49.95 (*0-7859-3356-5*, 8434523728) Fr & Eur.

— A Dictionary of Epidemiology. 3rd ed. (Illus.). 208p. 1995. pap. text 22.95 (*0-19-509668-1*) OUP.

— Maxcy-Rosenau-Last Public Health & Preventive Medicine. 13th ed. (Illus.). 1257p. (C). 1991. pap. text 135.00 (*0-8385-6188-8*, A6188-5) Appleton & Lange.

— Public Health & Human Ecology. 2nd ed. LC 97-7896. 464p. (C). 1998. pap. 42.50 (*0-8385-8080-7*, A-8080-2, Apple Lange Med) McGraw.

***Last, John M., ed.** A Dictionary of Epidemiology. 4th ed. (Illus.). 224p. 2000. text 45.00 (*0-19-514168-7*); pap. text 24.95 (*0-19-514169-5*) OUP.

Last, Mary Z., jt. auth. see Pratt, Philip J.

Last, P. & Stevens, J. Sharks & Rays of Australia. (Illus.). 600p. 1993. 59.95 (*0-643-05143-0*, Pub. by CSIRO) Accents Pubns.

Last, P. R., et al. Fishes of Tasmania. (Illus.). 563p. 1983. pap. text 75.00 (*0-7246-1143-6*, Pub. by Tasmanian Govt Print) Lubrecht & Cramer.

Last, R. W. Artificial Intelligence Techniques in Language Learning. LC 08-933533. 1989. text 64.95 (*0-470-21503-8*) P-H.

Last, R. W., et al, eds. The Arthurian Bibliography II: Subject Index, No. II. (Arthurian Studies: Vol. VI). 137p. 1983. 75.00 (*0-85991-099-7*) Boydell & Brewer.

Last, Rex W., jt. auth. see Barker, Christine R.

***Last Unicorn Games Staff.** Arrakis: Center of the Universe. (Illus.). 1999. pap. 28.00 (*0-671-03507-X*) S&S Childrens.

— Core Game Book. (Star Trek Deep Space Nine Ser.). (Illus.). (J). 1999. 35.00 (*0-671-04014-6*) Simon & Schuster.

— Narrator's Toolkit. (Illus.). 1999. pap. 16.00 (*0-671-04015-4*) S&S Childrens.

— Planets of the UFP: A Guide to Federation Worlds. (Star Trek Next Generation Ser.). 1999. pap. 20.00 (*0-671-04006-5*) PB.

— Through a Glass Darkly: The Mirror Universe. (Illus.). (J). 1999. pap. 30.00 (*0-671-04018-9*) S&S Childrens.

Last, W. M., jt. ed. see Renaut, R. W.

Last, Walter. Heal Yourself: A Practical Self-Help Manual of Natural Healing. LC 88-1685. 1988. 14.95 (*0-943920-56-6*) Metamorphous Pr.

— Problem Foods. LC 86-18130. 1987. write for info. (*0-943920-54-X*) Metamorphous Pr.

Lastage, Donna, jt. auth. see Mallory, Randy.

***Lastarria-Cornhiel, Susana & Barnes, Grenville.** Formalizing Informality: The Praedial Registration System in Peru. (Research Paper Ser.: Vol. 131). (Illus.). v, 54p. 1999. pap. 7.00 (*0-934519-80-3*, RP131) U of Wis Land.

Lastarria, Jose Victorino. Literary Memoirs. Nunn, Frederick M., ed. Washbourne, R. Kelly, tr. from SPA. LC 99-55771. (Library of Latin America). 448p. 2000. 30.00 (*0-19-511685-2*); pap. 19.95 (*0-19-511686-0*) OUP.

Laster, Ann A. & Pickett, Nell A. Occupational English 85. 4th ed. 576p. (C). 1997. pap. text 70.00 (*0-06-043858-4*) Addson-Wesley Educ.

Laster, Ann A., jt. auth. see Pickett, Nell A.

Laster, Ann A., jt. auth. see Pickett, Nell Alan.

***Laster, Clay.** Beginner's Handbook of Amateur Radio. 4th ed. (Illus.). 2000. pap. 34.95 (*0-07-136187-1*) McGraw.

Laster, Clay. The Complete Handbook of Amateur Radio. 3rd ed. 416p. 1994. pap. 24.95 (*0-07-036594-6*) McGraw.

An Asterisk (*) at the beginning of an entry indicates that the title is appearing for the first time.

— The Complete Handbook of Amateur Radio. 3rd ed. LC 93-1556. 1993. pap. 19.60 (0-8306-4354-0) McGraw-Hill Prof.

Laster, J. Travis, jt. auth. see Finkelstein, Jesse A.

Laster, James H. Catalogue of Choral Music Arranged in Biblical Order. 2nd ed. LC 95-33461. 717p. 1996. 75.00 (0-8108-3071-X) Scarecrow.

Laster, James H., compiled by. A Discography of Treble Voice Recordings. LC 84-22179. 157p. 1984. 21.00 (0-8108-1760-8) Scarecrow.

Laster, Janet F. Toward Excellence in Secondary Vocational Education: Using Cognitive Psychology in Curriculum Planning. 65p. 1985. 7.25 (0-318-22221-3, IN297) Ctr Educ Trng Employ.

Laster, Jim. The Birthday Gift That Beeped. Knight, George, ed. LC 83-176266. (Illus.). 56p. (J). (gr. k-4). 1983. 10.95 (0-9612780-0-5) J Laster Pub Co.

Laster, Kathy & Taylor, Veronica. Interpreters & the Legal System. 280p. 1994. pap. 39.00 (1-86287-130-2, Pub. by Federation Pr) Gaunt.

— Law As Culture. 264p. 1997. pap. 49.00 (1-86287-226-0, Pub. by Federation Pr) Gaunt.

Laster, Leonard. Life after Medical School: Thirty-Two Doctors Describe How They Shaped Their Medical Careers. 320p. (C). 1996. 29.95 (0-393-71030-0) Norton.

Laster, Paul & Riccardo, Renee. Spiral of Artificiality. Bershad, Deborah, ed. (Illus.). 24p. (Orig.). 1987. pap. write for info. (0-936739-09-6) Hallwalls Inc.

Lastigzon, J. World Fertilizer Progress into the 1980s. (Technical Bulletin Ser.: No. T-22). (Illus.). 64p. (Orig.). 1981. pap. 4.00 (0-88090-021-0) Intl Fertilizer.

Lasting, Ingeborg & Singer, Heidi. Living Language German All the Way Cassette/Book: Learn at Home & on the Go. LC 93-22955. (ENG & GER.). 1994. 60.00 incl. audio (0-517-58378-X, Crown) Crown Pub Group.

— Living Language German All the Way Manual: Learn at Home & on the Go. LC 93-22955. (ENG & GER.). 1994. pap. 16.00 (0-517-58379-8, Crown) Crown Pub Group.

Lastiri, Santiago, jt. ed. see Ramirez, Bernardo.

***Lastmanout.** Soul Cries. vi, 160p. 2000. 12.95 (0-615-11239-0) Wind Whisper.

***Lastoka, Mariann.** A Part of Me. (Illus.). 47p. 1998. pap. 15.00 (1-892860-00-7, 001) MRL Inc.

Lastoka, Susan H. The Harney Lastoka Cookbook. unabridged ed. LC 98-88270. (Illus.). 227p. 1998. pap. 18.00 (1-892860-01-5) MRL Inc.

Lastovicka, J., et al. Coupling & Energetics in the Stratosphere-Mesosphere-Thermosphere-Ionosphere System. (Advances in Space Research Ser.: Vol. 20). 212p. 1997. pap. 100.50 (0-08-043303-0, Pergamon Pr) Elsevier.

Lastovka, M., ed. International Association of Logopedics & Phoniatrics, 21st Congress, Prague, August 1989: Main Reports. (Illus.). 96p. 1989. pap. 53.25 (3-8055-5053-7) S Karger.

***Lastra, James.** Sound Technology & the American Cinema: Perception, Representation, Modernity. LC 99-87737. (Sun Microsystems Press Java Ser.). 2000. 49.50 (0-231-11516-4); pap. text 18.50 (0-231-11517-2) Col U Pr.

Lastra, Yolanda. El Otomi de Ixtenxo. (SPA.). 453p. 1997. pap. 37.00 (968-36-6000-2, UN048, Pub. by Instit de Invest) UPLAAP.

Lastrapes, Marie. Mais Oui, Marie Creole Cookin: Life & Flavor in the Creole Tradition. (Illus.). 60p. 1999. pap. 9.95 (0-9672043-0-5) Maries Catering.

Lastrapes, Paul L. Looking Back at Washington, LA: The Memoirs of David Jasper McNicoll. LC 96-79501. (Illus.). xiv, 176p. 1997. reprint ed. 21.95 (0-9660421-0-7); reprint ed. pap. 11.95 (0-9660421-1-5) P L Lastrapes.

Lastres, Helena M. The Advance Materials Revolution & the Japanese System of Innovation. LC 94-16019. 1994. text 69.95 (0-312-12055-9) St Martin.

Lastrucci, Carlo. Scientific Approach. 257p. 1967. pap. 16.95 (0-87073-042-8) Schenkman Bks Inc.

Lastu, Daniele. All the World's 1/43 Scale Ferraris Vol. L: Sport, Prototype, 250GT & GTO Models. 1993. 60.00 (1-872727-37-9) Pincushion Pr.

Lastufka, Francine. Alaskan Eskimo Sculpture. Lynch, Kathleen, ed. & illus. by. 37p. 1994. reprint ed. pap. 6.95 (1-878051-42-3) Circumpolar Pr.

Lastz, L., ed. see Symposia Angiologica Santoriana Staff.

Lasure, Linda L., jt. ed. see Bennett, J. W.

Laswell, J. Verne. Poems by the End of the Oregon Trail. Stiltner, E., ed. & intro. by. 76p. (Orig.). 1990. 7.75 (1-878457-54-3); pap. 7.75 (0-685-30411-6) Skunk Creek Computing Servs.

Laswell, Magdalena. Las Matematicas/Mathematics: Grades 1-6 Mathematics Handbook for Bilingual Education Teachers. (SPA., Illus.). 114p. 1998. spiral bd. 25.00 (0-944551-33-5) Sundance Pr TX.

Laswell, Mary. Suds in Your Eye. adapted ed. 1944. pap. 5.25 (0-8222-1095-9) Dramatists Play.

Laszewski, Matthew & Sung, Marina H. The Most Useful Sentence Patterns in Mandarin Chinese: Shih yung Chung Ying wen Chu hsing. LC 98-154964. 1998. write for info. (0-9630354-2-8) Brave New Wrld.

Laszity, Radomir & Hidvegi, Mate, eds. Amino Acid Composition & Biological Value of Cereal Proteins. 1985. text 249.00 (90-277-1937-3) Kluwer Academic.

***Laszlo, Andrew & Quicke, Andrew.** Every Frame a Rembrandt: Art & Practice of Cinematography. LC 99-58083. (Illus.). 240p. 2000. pap. 34.95 (0-240-80399-X, Focal) Buttrwrth-Heinemann.

Laszlo, Christopher, jt. auth. see Bates, Norman.

Laszlo, Christopher, jt. auth. see Laszlo, Ervin.

Laszlo, E. Creative Evolution. 136p. 1991. pap. text 192.00 (2-88124-526-9) Gordon & Breach.

Laszlo, E., ed. The New Evolutionary Paradigm: Transdisciplinary Studies. xxvi, 204p. 1991. text 101.00 (2-88124-375-4) Gordon & Breach.

Laszlo, Ervin. Co-Operation for Development: Strategies for the 1980's. 107p. 1984. pap. 20.00 (0-86346-046-1, Tycooly Pub) Weidner & Sons.

— Co-Operation in the 1980s: Principles & Prospects, Vol. 1. 208p. 1984. pap. 20.00 (0-907567-73-8, Tycooly Pub) Weidner & Sons.

— The Communist Idealogy in Hungary: Handbook for Basic Research. (Sovietica Ser.: No. 23). 359p. 1966. text 173.50 (90-277-0056-7, D Reidel) Kluwer Academic.

— Creative Cosmos. 320p. 1997. pap. 34.95 (0-86315-172-8, 1899, Pub. by Floris Bks) Anthroposophic.

— Evolution: Foundations of a General Theory. Montuori, Alfonso, ed. (Advances in System Theory & Complexity Ser.). 208p. (C). 1996. pap. text 18.95 (1-57273-052-8) Hampton Pr NJ.

— The Inner Limits of Mankind. 160p. 1994. pap. 7.95 (1-85168-015-2, Pub. by Onewrld Pubns) Penguin Putnam.

— The Interconnected Universe: Conceptual Foundations of Transdisciplinary Unified Theory. LC 95-1807. 170p. 1995. text 32.00 (981-02-2202-5) World Scientific Pub.

— Introduction to Systems Philosophy - Toward a New Paradigm of Contemporary Thought. LC 76-156080. 328, xxiip. 1972. 108.00 (0-677-03850-X) Gordon & Breach.

— Multi-Cultural Planet: The Report of a UNESCO International Expert Group. 212p. 1994. pap. 17.95 (1-85168-042-X, Pub. by Onewrld Pubns) Penguin Putnam.

— System, Structure & Experience: Toward a Scientific Theory of Mind. (Current Topics of Contemporary Thought Ser.: Vol. 1). xii, 112p. 1969. text 132.00 (0-677-02360-X) Gordon & Breach.

— The Systems View of the World. LC 71-188357. 131p. 1972. pap. 7.95 (0-8076-0636-7) Braziller.

— The Systems View of the World: A Holistic Vision for Our Time. LC 96-711. (Advances in Systems Theory, Complexity & the Human Sciences Ser.). 112p. 1996. pap. 15.95 (1-57273-053-6) Hampton Pr NJ.

— Vision, 2020: Reordering Chaos for Global Survival. LC 93-30959. 160p. 1994. pap. text 16.00 (2-88124-612-5) Gordon & Breach.

— The Whispering Pond: A Personal Guide to the Emerging Vision of Science. 208p. 1996. pap. 24.95 (1-85230-899-0, Pub. by Element MA) Penguin Putnam.

— Whispering Pond: A Personal Guide to the Emerging Vision of Science. 224p. 1999. pap. 18.95 (1-86204-362-0, Pub. by Element MA) Penguin Putnam.

— The World Encyclopedia of Peace, 4 vols., Vols. 1-4. 1986. 250.00 (0-08-032686-2, Pergamon Pr) Elsevier.

Laszlo, Ervin, ed. Philosophy in the Soviet Union: A Survey of the Mid-Sixties. (Sovietica Ser.: No.25). 208p. 1967. lib. bdg. 68.50 (90-277-0057-5) Kluwer Academic.

— The Relevance of General Systems Theory. LC 72-81355. 213p. 1972. 8.95 (0-8076-0659-6) Braziller.

Laszlo, Ervin, et al, eds. The Evolution of Cognitive Maps: New Paradigms for the Twenty-First Century. LC 92-23607. (World Futures General Evolution Studies: Vol. 5). 288p. 1993. text 101.00 (2-88124-559-5) Gordon & Breach.

Laszlo, Ervin & Bierman, Judah, eds. Goals in a Global Community, Vol. II. 1978. text 130.00 (0-08-022973-5, Pergamon Pr) Elsevier.

Laszlo, Ervin & Kurtzman, Joel, eds. Political & Institutional Issues of the New International Economic Order. (Policy Studies on the New International Economic Order). 208p. 1981. 52.00 (0-08-025122-6, Pergamon Pr) Elsevier.

— The Structure of the World Economy & Prospects for a New International Economic Order. LC 79-23350. (Policy Studies on the New International Economic Order). 120p. 1980. 44.00 (0-08-025119-6, Pergamon Pr) Elsevier.

— The United States, Canada & the New International Economic Order. (Policy Studies). 1979. 52.00 (0-08-025113-7, Pergamon Pr) Elsevier.

Laszlo, Ervin & Laszlo, Christopher. The Insight Edge: An Introduction to the Theory & Practice of Evolutionary Management. LC 96-9049. 160p. 1997. 49.95 (1-56720-096-6, Quorum Bks) Greenwood.

Laszlo, Ervin & Wilbur, James B., eds. Value Theory in Philosophy & Social Science. LC 73-84239. (Current Topics of Contemporary Thought Ser.). x, 154p. 1973. text 132.00 (0-677-14160-2) Gordon & Breach.

Laszlo, Ervin & Yoo, Jong Y., eds. The World Encyclopedia of Peace, 4 vols. LC 86-25520. (Illus.). 1930p. 1986. 615.00 (0-08-032685-4, Pergamon Pr) Elsevier.

Laszlo, Ervin, et al. Changing Visions: Human Cognitive Maps: Past, Present & Future. LC 96-15309. (Praeger Studies on the 21st Century). 144p. 1996. 59.95 (0-275-95676-8, Praeger Pubs); pap. 18.95 (0-275-95677-6, Praeger Pubs) Greenwood.

— The Consciousness Revolution: A Transatlantic Dialogue. LC 99-15431. 192p. 1999. text 24.95 (1-86204-540-2, Pub. by Element MA) Penguin Putnam.

— RCDC (Regional Cooperation among Developing Countries) The New Imperative of Development in the 1980's. 75p. 1981. pap. 25.00 (0-08-027556-7, Pergamon Pr) Elsevier.

Laszlo, Ervin, jt. ed. see Gotesky, Rubin.

Laszlo, F. A. Renal Cortical Necrosis. (Contributions to Nephrology Ser.: Vol. 28). (Illus.). viii, 216p. 1981. pap. 29.75 (3-8055-2109-X) S Karger.

Laszlo, F. A. & Antoni, F. Biomedical Significance of Peptide Research. 278p. (C). 1984. 90.00 (963-05-3886-5, Pub. by Akade Kiado) St Mut.

Laszlo, Ferenc A. & Janaky, Tibor. Clinical Applications of Radioimmunoassay. 230p. 1992. pap. 325.00 (963-05-6219-7, Pub. by Akade Kiado) St Mut.

Laszlo, G. Dictionary of Technical Information: Power Electronics. 584p. (C). 1985. 125.00 (0-7855-6854-9, Pub. by Collets) St Mut.

Laszlo, G., ed. Dictionary of Technical Information: Power Electronics. 584p. (C). 1985. 125.00 (0-7855-6552-3, Pub. by Collets) St Mut.

Laszlo, Gabriel. Pulmonary Function: A Guide for Clinicians. (Illus.). 259p. (C). 1994. text 110.00 (0-521-43050-X); pap. text 42.95 (0-521-44679-1) Cambridge U Pr.

***Laszlo, Gyula.** The Magyars: Their Life & Civilization. 128p. 1999. 48.00 (963-13-4807-5, Pub. by Corvina Bks); pap. 21.00 (963-13-4226-3, Pub. by Corvina Bks) St Mut.

Laszlo, Illes, et al, eds. Hungarian Studies on Gyorgy Lukacs I-II. 1993. pap. 129.00 (963-05-6028-3, Pub. by Akade Kiado) St Mut.

Laszlo, Ivan. Malmond. LC 94-78724. 216p. (Orig.). 1995. pap. 12.95 (1-882897-00-5) Lost Coast.

Laszlo, J. A., jt. ed. see Dintzis, F. R.

***Laszlo, Janos.** Cognition & Representation in Literature: The Psychology of Literary Narratives. 272p. 1999. pap. 52.00 (963-05-7663-5, Pub. by Akade Kiado) Intl Spec Bk.

Laszlo, Janos, jt. ed. see Cupchik, Gerald C.

Laszlo, John. The Cure of Childhood Leukemia: Into the Age of Miracles. LC 94-47285. (Illus.). 300p. 1996. pap. 16.95 (0-8135-2385-0) Rutgers U Pr.

— The Cure of Childhood Leukemia: Into the Age of Miracles. (Illus.). 300p. (C). 1996. 29.95 (0-8135-2186-6) Rutgers U Pr.

Laszlo, John, ed. Physician's Guide to Cancer Care Complications: Prevention & Management. LC 85-29361. (Fundamentals of Cancer Management Ser.: No. 2). 359p. 1986. reprint ed. pap. 111.30 (0-608-01296-3, 206204200001) Bks Demand.

Laszlo, Judith I. & Bairstow, Phillip J. Perceptual Motor Behavior: Developmental Assessment & Therapy. 1985. 37.50 (0-275-91650-2, C1650, Praeger Pubs) Greenwood.

Laszlo, M. B., jt. auth. see Krompecher, I.

Laszlo, Marilyn. Mission Possible. LC 98-25029. 1998. 9.99 (0-8423-3881-0) Tyndale Hse.

Laszlo, Mary De, see De Laszlo, Mary.

Laszlo, Michael J. Computational Geometry & Computer Graphics in C++ LC 95-38141. 266p. 1995. 45.00 (0-13-290842-5) P-H.

— The Schemer's Guide to Solid Modeling. LC 98-60493. (Illus.). 230p. (C). 1998. pap. 44.95 (1-888579-14-5) Schemers.

Laszlo, Pierre. Organic Reactions: Simplicity & Logic. 716p. 1996. pap. 74.95 (0-471-95278-8) Wiley.

Laszlo, Pierre, jt. auth. see Balogh, M.

Laszlo, Veres & Woodman, Richard. The Story of Sail. (Illus.). 1999. 55.00 (1-55750-896-8) Naval Inst Pr.

Laszok, Anthony A., ed. see Appleyard, et al.

Laszt, L. & Schaad, R. Luftverunreinigung und Herz-Kreislauf-System. (Illus.). viii, 140p. 1980. pap. 24.50 (3-8055-3067-6) S Karger.

Laszt, L., ed. see Symposia Angiologica Santoriana Staff.

***Lasztity, Radomir.** Cereal Chemistry. 300p. 1999. 70.00 (963-05-7626-0, Pub. by Akade Kiado) Intl Spec Bk.

Lasztity, Radomir. The Chemistry of Cereal Proteins. 216p. 1984. 124.00 (0-8493-5140-5, TP453, CRC Reprint) Franklin.

— The Chemistry of Cereal Proteins. 2nd ed. 336p. 1995. boxed set 179.95 (0-8493-2763-6, 2763) CRC Pr.

Lasztity, Radomir, jt. ed. see Bekes, Ferec.

Lat-Kla, Loo-Wit. Gold Hunting in the Cascade Mountains. LC 91-72915. (Illus.). vi, 56p. 1991. reprint ed. 45.00 (0-9629954-0-1) Bk Club Wash.

Lat-kla, Loo-wit, jt. auth. see Heinzen, Steve.

Lata Bahadur, Om. Book of Hindu Festivals & Ceremonies. (C). 1997. pap. 14.00 (81-7476-163-2, Pub. by UBS Pubs Dist) S Asia.

***Lata, Jennifer & Rung, Mark.** The Pocket Idiot's Guide to Being a Groom. (Pocket Idiot's Guide Ser.). 200p. 1999. pap. 7.95 (0-02-863649-X) Macmillan.

***Lata, Leenco.** The Ethiopian State at the Crossroads: Decolonization & Democratization or Disintegration? LC 99-32715. 304p. 1999. pap. 21.95 (1-56902-121-X) Red Sea Pr.

Lata, Vidyu. Developing Rural Women. (C). 1990. text 29.50 (81-7141-083-9) S Asia.

Latacz, Joachim. Homer, His Art & His World. Holoka, James P., tr. LC 95-42481.Tr. of Erste Dichter des Abandlands. (Illus.). 192p. (C). 1998. pap. text 19.95 (0-472-08353-8, 08353) U of Mich Pr.

Latacz, Joachim, ed. Prolegomena. (GRE.). 100p. 1998. pap. 19.95 (3-519-04300-9, T4300, Pub. by B G Teubner) U of Mich Pr.

Latacz, Joachim, tr. Prolegomena Vol. I(A), Fascicle 1: Text with Critical Apparatus & Translation. (GRE.). 70p. 1998. pap. 15.95 (3-519-04301-7, T4301, Pub. by B G Teubner) U of Mich Pr.

Lataillade, Alix. Institutrice au Cceur du Siecle. large type ed. 458p. 1996. pap. 25.99 (2-84011-161-6) Ulverscroft.

Lataille, Jane I. Electrical Equipment in Hazardous (Classified) Locations. 1988. 5.35 (0-685-38091-2, TR 88-1) Society Fire Protect.

Latal, Heimo & Schweiger, Wolfgang, eds. Matter under Extreme Conditions: Proceedings of the 33th Internationale Universitat Atswochen fur Kern - und Teilchenphysik, Schladming, Austria, 27 February - 5 March 1994. (Lecture Notes in Physics Ser.: Vol. 440). 1995. 72.95 (3-540-58689-X) Spr-Verlag.

Latal, Heimo, jt. ed. see Mitter, H.

Latall, Roy. Murder Aboard Yorktown. 200p. 1998. pap. 23.95 (1-57502-830-1, P02230) Morris Pubng.

Latane, John H. America As a World Power, 1897-1907. (History - United States Ser.). 350p. 1992. reprint ed. lib. bdg. 89.00 (0-7812-6213-5) Rprt Serv.

— America As a World Power, 1897-1907. LC 79-145131. (Illus.). 1971. reprint ed. 49.00 (0-403-01064-0) Scholarly.

Latanision, R. M. & Fischer, T. E. Advances in Mechanics & Physics of Surfaces, Vol. 1. vii, 254p. 1981. text 335.00 (3-7186-0026-9) Gordon & Breach.

— Advances in the Mechanics & Physics of Surfaces, Vol. 3. xxi, 332p. 1986. text 365.00 (3-7186-0251-2) Gordon & Breach.

Latanision, R. M. & Fischer, T. E., eds. Advances in the Mechanics & Physics of Surfaces, Vol. 2. xii, 364p. 1983. text 358.00 (3-7186-0156-7) Gordon & Breach.

Latanision, R. M. & Jones, R. H., eds. Chemistry & Physics of Fracture. (C). 1987. text 326.50 (90-247-3580-7) Kluwer Academic.

Latanision, R. M., jt. auth. see Mansfeld, Florian.

***Latarche, Malcolm.** Port Agency. 200p. 1998. pap. 60.00 (1-85609-157-0, Pub. by Witherby & Co) St Mut.

Latas, Michael. Job Series Now: The Series. 336p. 1993. pap. 25.95 (1-882904-05-2) Job Srch Pubs.

— Job Series Now: The Series, 1. 336p. 1993. pap. 3.95 (1-882904-10-9) Job Srch Pubs.

Latash, Mark L. Control of Human Movement. LC 92-36991. (Illus.). 392p. 1993. text 49.00 (0-87322-455-8, BLAT0455) Human Kinetics.

— Neurophysiological Basis of Movement. LC 97-31920. (Illus.). 280p. 1998. text 45.00 (0-88011-756-7, BLAT0756) Human Kinetics.

Latash, Mark L., ed. Progress in Motor Control: Bernstein's Traditions in Movement Studies, Vol. 1. LC 97-44950. (Illus.). 408p. 1998. text 49.00 (0-88011-674-9, BLAT0674) Human Kinetics.

***Latash, Mark L. & Zatsiorsky, Vladimir M., eds.** Classical Papers in Movement Science. (Illus.). 416p. 2000. write for info. (0-7360-0028-3) Human Kinetics.

Latash, Mark L., jt. auth. see Bernstein, Nicolai A.

Latassa y Ortin, Felix D. Bibliotecas Antiguas y Nuevas, 3 vols. reprint ed. write for info. (0-318-71836-7) G Olms Pubs.

Latassa y Ortin, Felix De, see De Latassa y Ortin, Felix.

Lataste, Xavier. An Atlas of Migraine. (Encyclopedia of Visual Medicine Ser.). (Illus.). 96p. 2000. 85.00 (1-85070-001-X) Prthnon Pub.

Latch, Edward. The Great Pyramid of Egypt: Mosaic System of Chronology in the Elucidation of Mysteries Pertaining to the "Bible in Stone" 1987. reprint ed. pap. 6.95 (0-916411-71-0, Sure Fire) Holmes Pub.

***Latch, Ollie E.** History of the General Baptist. 210p. (C). 2000. write for info. (0-9642674-3-8) Stinson Pr.

Latcham, Jack, jt. auth. see Birch, Derek W.

Latcham, Michael, tr. see Locher, Hans.

***Latchaw, Bob.** Instant Christmas Pageant: Operation Baby King. LC 00-25635. 2000. 24.99 (0-7644-2230-8) Group Pub.

Latchaw, Bob, jt. auth. see Hansen, Cindy.

Latchem, C. R. & Lockwood, Fred. Staff Development in Open & Flexible Learning. LC 97-30930. (Routledge Studies in Distance Education). 320p. (C). 1998. 85.00 (0-415-17376-0); pap. 25.99 (0-415-17390-6) Routledge.

Latchem, Colin, et al, eds. Interactive Multimedia: Practice & Promise. 224p. 1992. 39.95 (0-7494-0815-4, Kogan Pg Educ) Stylus Pub VA.

Latchman. Eukaryotic Transcription Factors. 3rd ed. LC 98-87659. (C). 1999. pap. text 39.95 (0-12-437177-9) Acad Pr.

Latchman, D. Gene Regulation: A Eukaryotic Perspective. 3rd ed. 352p. 1998. pap. 42.50 (0-7487 3977 7) St Mut.

Latchman, D. S., ed. From Genetics to Gene Therapy. (University College, London, Molecular Pathology Ser.). 250p. 1994. 167.50 (1-872748-36-8, Pub. by Bios Sci) Coronet Bks.

Latchman, David, ed. Basic Molecular & Cell Biology. 3rd ed. 299p. 1997. pap. 27.00 (0-7279-1195-3, Pub. by BMJ Pub) Login Brothers Bk Co.

— Landmarks in Gene Regulation. (Landmarks in Science & Medicine Ser.: Vol. 1). (Illus.). 320p. (C). 1997. pap. text 34.00 (1-85578-109-3, Pub. by Portland Pr Ltd) Ashgate Pub Co.

— Transcription Factors: A Practical Approach. 2nd ed. LC 98-40981. (Practical Approach Ser.: No. 201). (Illus.). 325p. 1999. text 120.00 (0-19-963697-4); pap. text 60.00 (0-19-963696-6) OUP.

Latchman, David, jt. auth. see Abe, H.

Latchman, David S. Eukaryotic Transcription Factors. 2nd ed. (Illus.). 304p. 1995. text 58.00 (0-12-437172-8) Acad Pr.

— Eukaryotic Transcription Factors. 2nd ed. (Illus.). 304p. 1996. pap. text 29.95 (0-12-437173-6) Acad Pr.

— Eukaryotic Transcription Factors. 3rd ed. LC 98-87659. (Illus.). 352p. (C). 1998. text 59.95 (0-12-437176-0) Acad Pr.

— Gene Regulation: A Eukaryotic Perspective. (Illus.). 220p. (C). 1990. pap. 34.95 (0-04-445243-8) Thomson Learn.

Latchman, David S., ed. Genetic Manipulation of the Nervous System: Viral Approaches. (Neuroscience Perspectives Ser.). (Illus.). 336p. 1995. text 69.95 (0-12-437165-5) Acad Pr.

— PCR Applications in Pathology: Principles & Practice. (Modern Methods in Pathology Ser.). (Illus.). 288p. 1995. text 55.00 (0-19-854835-4) OUP.

Late, N. T. Bay of Pigs: Can of Worms. (Orig.). 1994. pap. 2.50 (0-9641448-9-1) N Late Pub.

— Biopsych Notes. 14p. (Orig.). 1994. pap. write for info. (0-9641448-7-5) N Late Pub.

— Intomorrow. 40p. (Orig.). 1995. pap. write for info. (0-9641448-6-7) N Late Pub.

L

— The Second Hand. 11p. (Orig.). (C). 1994. pap. write for info. (0-9641448-3-2) N Late Pub.

Late Night with David Letterman Writers Staff & Letterman, David. An Altogether New Book of Top Ten Lists: From "Late Night with David Letterman" Peters, Sally, ed. 160p. (Orig.). 1991. pap. 12.00 (0-671-74901-3) PB.

— The Late Night with David Letterman Book of Top Ten Lists. Wells, Leslie, ed. 160p. (Orig.). 1990. pap. 12.00 (0-671-72671-4) PB.

Late Show with David Letterman Writers Staff, jt. auth. see Letterman, David.

Latecki, Longin J. Discrete Representation of Spatial Objects in Computer Vision. LC 97-49831. 228p. 1998. lib. bdg. 112.00 (0-7923-4912-1) Kluwer Academic.

***Latecki, Longin J., et al, eds.** Vision Geometry VIII. 388p. 1999. pap. text 72.00 (0-8194-3297-0) SPIE.

Lateef, K. Sarwar, jt. ed. see Boughton, James M.

LaTeef, Nelda. Women of Lebanon: Interviews with Champions for Peace. LC 97-14088. (Illus.). 291p. 1997. pap. 39.95 (0-7864-0329-2) McFarland & Co.

Lateef, Noel V. Crisis in the Sahel. (Special Studies in Social, Political, & Economic Development). (Illus.). 285p. 1981. text 50.00 (0-89158-991-0) Westview.

Lateef, Sarwar, ed. The Evolving Role of the World Bank: Helping Meet the Challenge of Development. 240p. 1995. pap. 22.00 (0-8213-3234-1, 13234) World Bank.

Lateef, Shahida. Muslim Women in India: Political & Private Realities, 1890s-1980s. LC 90-39964. 240p. (C). 1990. text 62.50 (0-86232-954-X, Pub. by St Martin); text 19.95 (0-86232-955-8, Pub. by St Martin) St Martin.

Lategahn. Quickbasic 4.5. (C). 1989. text. write for info. (0-201-51469-9) Addison-Wesley.

Lategan, Hilda. South African Cookbook for Food Allergies & Food Intolerance. (Illus.). 145p. 1999. pap. 15.00 (0-627-02320-7, Pub. by J L Van Schaik) BHB Intl.

Lategan, Hilda, et al. Cooking the Diabetic Way. (Illus.). 244p. 1999. pap. 17.00 (0-627-01970-6, Pub. by J L Van Schaik) BHB Intl.

Lategan, T., jt. auth. see De Koker, A. P.

Lateiner, Alfred. Modern Techniques of Supervision. 16th rev. ed. LC 66-4182. 1988. pap. 10.00 (0-911722-00-9) Lateiner.

Lateiner, Donald. The Historical Method of Herodotus. (Phoenix Supplementary Volumes Ser.: No. 23). 333p. 1989. text 45.00 (0-8020-5793-4) U of Toronto Pr.

— The Historical Method of Herodotus. (Phoenix Supplementary Volumes Ser.: No. 23). 336p. 1992. pap. text 19.95 (0-8020-7684-X) U of Toronto Pr.

— Sardonic Smile: Nonverbal Behavior in Homeric Epic. 368p. (C). 1998. pap. text 24.95 (0-472-08490-9, 08490) U of Mich Pr.

Latela, Mary E. My Friend Is Dying: Prayers & Reflections. LC 92-75204. 64p. 1993. pap. 3.95 (0-89243-517-8) Liguori Pubns.

— Prepare Him Room: Advent for Busy Christians. LC 98-75662. 64p. 1999. pap. 5.95 (0-7648-0397-2) Liguori Pubns.

Latella, Lisa. A Song for the Prince. (Illus.). 36p. (Orig.). (J). (gr. k up). 1984. pap. write for info. (0-9608592-1-7) Gallery Arts.

***Lately, Thomas.** The Astor Orphans: A Pride of Lions. LC 99-44718. (Illus.). 421p. 1999. 33.00 (1-881324-03-6) Wash Park.

Laterrade, Remig. Dat Little Low-Sugar Cajun Cookbook: By Chef Remy. 144p. 1998. spiral bd. 5.95 (0-9632197-6-6) Relco Ent.

Laterrade, Remig E. Dat Little Louisianna "Out of the Ordinary" Cookbook: By Chef Remy. 180p. 1997. spiral bd. 5.95 (0-9632197-5-8) Relco Ent.

Laterrade, Remy. Dat Little Cajun Cookbook by Remy. 150p. 1993. spiral bd. 5.95 (0-9632197-1-5) Relco Ent.

— Dat Little New Orleans Cookbook. 150p. 1994. spiral bd. 5.95 (0-9632197-2-3) Relco Ent.

— I Want Dat Cajun Cookbook: A Collection of Cajun Cuisine. 2nd rev. ed. (Illus.). 218p. 1995. reprint ed. 16.95 (0-9632197-3-1) Relco Ent.

Laterrade, Remy & Arrigo, Joseph. Dat Little Louisiana Plantation Cookbook. (Illus.). 151p. 1995. pap. 5.95 (0-9632197-4-X) Relco Ent.

Latessa, Edward, ed. Strategic Solutions: The International Community Corrections Association Examines Substance Abuse. LC 99-13337. 1999. pap. 24.95 (1-56991-108-8) Am Correctional.

Latessa, Edward J. & Allen, Harry E. Corrections in the Community. LC 96-85370. (Illus.). 475p. (C). 1996. pap. 42.95 (0-87084-236-6) Anderson Pub Co.

— Corrections in the Community. LC 99-18634. 9p. 1999. 42.95 (0-87084-238-2) Anderson Pub Co.

Latessa, Edward J., jt. auth. see Vito, Gennaro F.

***Latessa, Shirley.** Dancing in the Fire. 2000. pap. 15.00 (0-9657922-1-8, Pub. by Waverly Pr) R Steiner Col.

Latessa, Shirley. Eighteen Days Till Home. LC 98-110932. 368p. (Orig.). 1997. pap. 12.00 (0-9657922-0-X, Pub. by Waverly Pr) R Steiner Col.

***Latford, Bob.** Nascar: A Celebration. 1999. 24.95 (1-85868-796-9, Pub. by Carlton Bks Ltd) Natl Bk Netwk.

Latge, J. P., et al, eds. Fungal Antigens: Isolation, Purification, & Detection. (Illus.). 486p. 1988. 125.00 (0-306-43115-7, Plenum Trade) Perseus Pubng.

Latge, J. P. & Boucias, D., eds. Fungal Cell Wall & Immune Response. (NATO ASI Series H: Cell Biology: Vol. 53). (Illus.). 472p. 1991. 217.95 (0-387-53147-5) Spr-Verlag.

Lath, Mukund. Dattilam. (C). 1988. 48.50 (81-208-0586-0, Pub. by Motilal Bnarsidass) S Asia.

Lath, Mukund, jt. auth. see Callewaert, Winand.

Latha, Digumarti Pushpa, jt. ed. see Rao, Digumarti Bhaskara.

Latham & Watkins Staff, jt. auth. see Environmental Law Institute Staff.

Latham, A. J. Old Calabor, 1600 to 1891: The Impact of the International Economy Upon a Traditional Society. 1973. 36.00 (0-19-821687-4) OUP.

Latham, A. J., jt. auth. see Miller, Sally M.

***Latham, A. J. H. & Kawakatsu, Heita.** Asia-Pacific Dynamism, 1550-2000. LC 99-88193. 280p. 2000. 110.00 (0-415-22778-X) Routledge.

Latham, Aaron. The Ballad of Gussie & Clyde: A True Story of True Love. large type ed. LC 97-35683. 232p. 1997. 24.95 (0-7862-1237-3) Thorndike Pr.

Latham, Agnes & Youings, Joyce, eds. The Letters of Sir Walter Ralegh. (Illus.). 464p. 1999. 89.95 (0-85989-527-0, Pub. by Univ Exeter Pr) Northwestern U Pr.

Latham, Agnes, ed. see Shakespeare, William.

Latham, Ajh. Rice: The Primary Commodity. LC 97-41056. (Studies in the Modern World Economy). 144p. (C). 1998. 65.00 (0-415-15153-8) Routledge.

Latham, Alison, jt. ed. see Sadie, Stanley.

Latham, Andrew, ed. see NATO Advanced Research Workshop on the Future.

***Latham, Angela J.** Posing a Threat: Flappers, Chorus Girls, & Other Brazen Performers of the American 1920s. LC 99-45571. (Illus.). 217p. 2000. pap. 19.95 (0-8195-6401-X, Wesleyan Univ Pr) U Pr of New Eng.

— Posing a Threat: Flappers, Chorus Girls & Other Brazen Performers of the American 1920s. LC 99-45571. (Illus.). 217p. 2000. text 50.00 (0-8195-6400-1, Wesleyan Univ Pr) U Pr of New Eng.

Latham, Art. Lost in the Land of Enchantment: Travels in New Mexico. LC 95-30909. (Illus.). 232p. (Orig.). 1995. pap. 14.95 (0-9623682-8-8) Arroyo Pr.

Latham, Barbara, jt. auth. see Carr, Harold.

Latham, Barbara, jt. auth. see Center for Disease Control Editors.

Latham, Betty S. Stamper Footprints: Eleven Generations. (Illus.). 154p. (Orig.). 1995. pap. 24.00 (0-7884-0320-6) Heritage Bk.

Latham, Bill, jt. auth. see Lea, Thomas D.

Latham, Bill, jt. auth. see Neighbor, Ralph W., Jr.

***Latham, Caroline.** The Heart of Healing Body, Mind & Spirit. LC 99-67787. 96p. 2000. pap. 10.95 (1-899171-28-2, Pub. by Findhorn Pr) Words Distrib.

Latham, Caroline. Michael Jackson: Thrill. 1984. mass mkt. 2.95 (0-8217-1430-9, Zebra Kensgtn) Kensgtn Pub Corp.

Latham, Caroline & Agresta, David. Dodge Dynasty: The Car & the Family That Rocked Detroit. (Illus.). 360p. 1989. 19.95 (0-15-125320-X) Harcourt.

Latham, Cathy. Measure Twice, Cut Once: Construction Debris & Nonhazardous Industrial Waste Report. (Illus.). 89p. (Orig.). (C). 1994. pap. text 35.00 (0-7881-1067-5) DIANE Pub.

Latham, Cathy, jt. auth. see Hickle, Garth.

Latham, Charles, Jr Dublin School, a New Beginning, 1970-1985. (Illus.). 1987. pap. 10.00 (0-87233-089-3) Bauhan.

Latham, Charles. William Fortune: A Hoosier Biography. (Illus.). 150p. 1994. 18.95 (0-87820-837-2); 18.95 (1-878208-37-3) Guild Pr IN.

Latham, Charles W. Lithographic Offset Press Operating. rev. ed. LC 57-22887. 273p. reprint ed. pap. 84.70 (0-7837-0365-1, 204068700018) Bks Demand.

Latham, Colin & Stobbs, Anne. Radar: A Wartime Miracle. (Illus.). 256p. 1996. 31.95 (0-7509-1114-X, Pub. by Sutton Pub Ltd) Intl Pubs Mktg.

Latham, Colin, et al. Radar: A Wartime Miracle. 238p. 1997. reprint ed. pap. 22.95 (0-7509-1643-5, Pub. by Sutton Pub Ltd) Intl Pubs Mktg.

Latham, D. & De Costa, L. A., eds. Large-Scale Structures & Peculiar Motions in the Universe. (ASP Conference Series Proceedings: Vol. 15). 406p. 1991. 34.00 (0-937707-34-1) Astron Soc Pacific.

Latham, D. W., jt. ed. see Davis Philip, A. G.

Latham, David. Sinclair Ross: An Annotated Bibliography. 395p. (C). 1981. pap. text 9.00 (0-920763-63-4, Pub. by ECW) Genl Dist Srvs.

Latham, David A., jt. ed. see Kolbert, June G.

Latham, Don, et al. Using Lightning Location in the Wildland Fire Assessment System. (Illus.). 10p. 1997. reprint ed. pap. 1.25 (0-89904-695-9, Ecosytems Resrch) Crumb Elbow Pub.

Latham, Don J. & Rothermel, Richard C. Probability of Fire-Stopping Precipitation Events. 10p. 1997. reprint ed. 7.00 (0-89904-604-5, Bear Meadows Resrch Grp); reprint ed. pap. 2.00 (0-89904-605-3, Bear Meadows Resrch Grp) Crumb Elbow Pub.

Latham, Donald C., jt. auth. see Martin, Thomas L., Jr.

Latham, Donald C., jt. ed. see Gold, Theodore S.

Latham, Earl. The Communist Controversy in Washington: From the New Deal to McCarthy. LC 66-14447. 460p. reprint ed. pap. 142.60 (0-608-16137-3, 200278500015) Bks Demand.

— The Group Basis of Politics: Notes for a Theory. (Reprint Series in Social Sciences). (C). 1993. reprint ed. pap. text 5.00 (0-8290-2753-X, PS-164) Irvington.

— Politics of Railroad Coordination, 1933-1936. LC 59-9279. 348p. 1959. 40.50 (0-674-68951-8) HUP.

Latham, Earl, ed. The Philosophy & Policies of Woodrow Wilson. LC 58-5620. (Midway Reprint Ser.: No. 15). 284p. reprint ed. pap. 88.10 (0-608-09461-7, 205426100005) Bks Demand.

Latham, Edward. A Dictionary of Names, Nicknames, & Surnames of Persons, Places & Things. LC 89-26513. 334p. 1990. reprint ed. lib. bdg. 48.00 (1-55888-901-9) Omnigraphics Inc.

Latham, Edward C. Chronological Tables of American Newspapers: 1690-1820. LC 70-185613. 140p. 1972. 40.00 (0-8271-7204-4) Am Antiquarian.

Latham, Elizabeth. Silences of the Heart. 232p. 1998. pap. 12.95 (0-7472-5640-3, Pub. by Headline Bk Pub) Trafalgar.

***Latham, Ernest H., Jr., ed.** Miorita: An Icon of Romanian Culture. (Illus.). 96p. 1999. 49.95 (973-9432-04-2, Pub. by Ctr Romanian Studies) Intl Spec Bk.

Latham, G. C., jt. auth. see Notcott, L. A.

Latham, Gary P. Increasing Productivity Through Performance Appraisal. 2nd ed. LC 93-26044. 250p. (C). 1993. pap. text 42.00 (0-201-51400-1) Addison-Wesley.

Latham, Gary P., jt. auth. see Mealiea, Laird W.

Latham, George H. Alleghany County North Carolina Marriages 1849-1900. 354p. (Orig.). 1996. pap. 29.00 (0-7884-0480-6, L075) Heritage Bk.

***Latham, Glenn.** Christlike Parenting: Taking the Pain Out of Parenting. LC 99-32778. 208p. 1999. 22.95 (1-882723-40-6, Pub. by Gold Leaf Pr) Origin Bk Sales.

Latham, Glenn. What's a Parent to Do? Solving Family Problems in a Christlike Way. LC 96-49406. 1997. 15.95 (1-57345-228-9) Deseret Bk.

Latham, Glenn I. Power of Positive Parenting. 1994. pap. text 19.95 (1-56713-175-1) APP.

Latham, Gwynneth. Kilimanjaro Tales: The Saga of a Medical Family in Africa. 1995. text 45.00 (1-85043-881-1, Pub. by I B T) St Martin.

Latham, Hugh, tr. see Sehlin, Gunhild.

Latham, Hugh, tr. see Streit, Jacob.

Latham, J. D., ed. see Paterson, W. F.

***Latham, J. E. M.** Search for a New Eden: James Pierrepont Greaves (1777-1842): The Sacred Socialist & His Followers. LC 99-24087. (Illus.). 296p. 2000. 47.50 (0-8386-3809-0) Fairleigh Dickinson.

Latham, Jacqueline E., ed. Critics on Virginia Woolf. LC 77-124653. (Readings in Literary Criticism Ser.: No. 8). 1979. pap. 19.95 (0-87024-170-2) U of Miami Pr.

***Latham, Jay.** Galaxy of Fire: Journey to an Ancient Spiritual World. (Illus.). 350p. 2000. pap. 17.95 (1-887472-77-0) Sunstar Pubng.

***Latham, Jean L.** Carry on, Mr. Bowditch. (gr. 4-7). 1999. pap. 14.50 (0-88103-752-4) Econo-Clad Bks.

Latham, Jean L. Carry on, Mr. Bowditch, 001. LC 55-5219. (Illus.). 256p. (YA). (gr. 6 up). 1955. pap. 6.95 (0-395-13713-6, Sandpiper) HM.

— Carry on, Mr. Bowditch, 001. (Illus.). 256p. (YA). (gr. 6 up). 1955. 16.00 (0-395-06881-9) HM.

— Carry on, Mr. Bowditch. 1955. 12.05 (0-606-00452-1, Pub. by Turtleback) Demco.

— Thanks, Awfully! 30p. (YA). 1929. pap. 3.50 (0-87129-654-3, T18) Dramatic Pub.

Latham, Jean L., compiled by. Do's & Don'ts of Drama. rev. ed. 1983. pap. 5.00 (0-87129-311-0, D22) Dramatic Pub.

Latham, John. Trench-Fever: Poems. LC 92-21182. 72p. 1996. pap. 14.95 (0-7734-2675-2, Mellen Poetry Pr) E Mellen.

Latham, John, jt. ed. see Ruhnke, Lothar H.

Latham, John-Paul, ed. Advances in Aggregates & Armourstone Evaluation. (Geological Society Engineering Geology Special Publication Ser.: No. 13). 216p. 1998. 99.00 (1-86239-000-2, Pub. by Geol Soc Pub Hse) AAPG.

Latham, Joy. Living & Learning with Nursery Children. 128p. 1975. pap. 7.99 (0-8341-0383-4) Beacon Hill.

Latham, Lance. Standard C Date/Time Library: Programming the World's Calendars & Clocks. (Illus.). 576p. 1998. pap. 49.95 incl. cd-rom (0-87930-496-0) C M P Books.

Latham, Linnet, ed. see Pepys, Samuel.

Latham, Linnet, tr. see Pepys, Samuel.

Latham, Marcia L., tr. see Descartes, Rene.

Latham, Mark. Civilising Global Capital: New Thinking for Australian Labor. LC 98-218756. xlii, 391p. 1998. pap. 24.95 (1-86448-668-6, Pub. by Allen & Unwin Pty) Paul & Co Pubs.

Latham, Maxwell E., Jr. Abortion in the Church. LC 89-85219. (Illus.). 216p. (Orig.). 1990. pap. 6.95 (1-878153-00-5) Light The World.

***Latham, Michael E.** Modernization As Ideology: American Social Science & "Nation-Building" in the Kennedy Era. LC 99-35517. (New Cold War History Ser.). 328p. 2000. pap. 18.95 (0-8078-4844-1) U of NC Pr.

— Modernization As Ideology: American Social Science & "Nation Building" in the Kennedy Era. LC 99-35517. (New Cold War History Ser.). 328p. 2000. lib. bdg. 45.00 (0-8078-2533-6) U of NC Pr.

Latham, Minor W. The Elizabethan Fairies: The Fairies of Folklore & the Fairies of Shakespeare. (BCL1-PR English Literature Ser.). 313p. 1992. reprint ed. lib. bdg. 89.00 (0-7812-7033-2) Rprt Serv.

Latham, Patricia H., et al. Tales from the Workplace. 102p. (Orig.). 1997. pap. 15.00 (1-883560-08-X) JKL Communs.

Latham, Patricia H., jt. auth. see Latham, Peter S.

Latham, Patricia Horan, jt. auth. see Latham, Peter S.

Latham, Peter. Brahms: Music Book Index. 230p. 1993. reprint ed. lib. bdg. 79.00 (0-7812-9574-2) Rprt Serv.

Latham, Peter, jt. auth. see Houseley, David.

Latham, Peter S. Government Contract Disputes & Supplement. 2nd ed. (Illus.). 1000p. 1986. ring bd. 175.00 (0-318-23582-X) Fed Pubns Inc.

Latham, Peter S. & Latham, Patricia H. Attention Deficit Disorder & the Law. 143p. 1993. pap. text 25.00 (1-883560-00-4) JKL Communs.

— Attention Deficit Disorder & the Law. 2nd ed. 230p. (C). 1997. pap. text 29.00 (1-883560-09-8) JKL Communs.

— Documentation & the Law: For Professionals Concerned with ADD/LD & Those They Serve. 182p. (Orig.). (C). 1996. pap. text 28.00 (1-883560-07-1) JKL Communs.

— Higher Education Services for Students with LD or ADD: A Legal Guide. 1999. pap. text 29.00 (1-883560-10-1) JKL Communs.

— Learning Disabilities & the Law. 178p. 1993. pap. text 28.00 (1-883560-02-0) JKL Communs.

***Latham, Peter S. & Latham, Patricia Horan.** Learning Disabilities & the Law. 2nd ed. 2000. pap. 29.00 (1-883560-11-X) JKL Communs.

Latham, R. E., tr. On the Nature of the Universe. 320p. 1994. pap. 13.95 (0-14-044610-9, Penguin Classics) Viking Penguin.

Latham, R. G. Two Dissertations on the Hamlet of Saxo Grammaticus & of Shakespeare. LC 71-171658. reprint ed. 39.50 (0-404-03883-2) AMS Pr.

Latham, Richard. The Account Book of Richard Latham, 1724-1767. Weatherrill, Lorna, ed. (Records of Social & Economic History, New Series British Academy: No. XV). 320p. 1990. 69.00 (0-19-726092-6) OUP.

Latham, Richard T. The Law & the Commonwealth. LC 70-104250. 632p. 1970. reprint ed. lib. bdg. 89.50 (0-8371-3974-0, LALC, Greenwood Pr) Greenwood.

Latham, Robert. Catalogue of the Pepys Library at Magdalene College, Cambridge Vol. 3, Pt. 1: Prints & Drawings (General) Aspital, A. W., ed. (Illus.). 396p. 1980. 205.50 (0-8476-3637-2) Rowman.

— The Liberal Moment: Modernity, Security & the Making of Postwar International Order. LC 96-53164. (New Directions in World Politics Ser.). (Illus.). 296p. 1997. pap. 19.50 (0-231-10757-9); lib. bdg. 52.00 (0-231-10756-0) Col U Pr.

Latham, Robert & Smith, N. A., eds. Catalogue of the Pepys Library, Vol. 1. (Printed Bks.). 201p. 1978. 136.50 (0-87471-819-8) Rowman.

Latham, Robert, jt. auth. see Collins, Robert A.

Latham, Robert, jt. ed. see Collins, Robert A.

Latham, Robert, ed. see Pepys, Samuel.

Latham, Robert, ed. & selected by see Pepys, Samuel.

Latham, Robert, tr. see Pepys, Samuel.

Latham, Robert A. & Collins, Robert A. Modes of the Fantastic: Selected Essays from the Twelfth International Conference on the Fantastic in the Arts, 66. LC 95-4661. (Contributions to the Study of Science Fiction & Fantasy: Vol. 66). 256p. 1995. 69.50 (0-313-29085-7, Greenwood Pr) Greenwood.

Latham, Robert C., ed. Samuel Pepys & the Second Dutch War: Pepys's Navy White Book & Brooke House Papers. (Navy Records Ser.: Vol. 133). 350p. 1995. 86.95 (1-85928-136-2) Ashgate Pub Co.

Latham, Robert G. The Ethnology of the British Colonies & Dependencies. LC 74-7976. reprint ed. 45.00 (0-404-11866-6) AMS Pr.

Latham, Rodney V. High Voltage Vacuum Insulation: Basic Concepts & Technological Practice. (Illus.). 568p. 1995. boxed set 105.00 (0-12-437175-2) Acad Pr.

Latham, Ronald, tr. see Polo, Marco.

Latham, Ronald, tr. & intro. see Polo, Marco.

Latham, Ronald E., compiled by. Dictionary of Medieval Latin from British Sources: Fascicule I, A-B. (LAT.). 280p. (C). 1975. pap. text 135.00 (0-19-725948-0) OUP.

— Dictionary of Medieval Latin from British Sources: Fascicule I, A-B. (LAT.). 332p. (C). 1981. pap. text 198.00 (0-19-725968-5) OUP.

Latham, Ronald E., ed. Revised Medieval Latin Word-List from British & Irish Sources. (British Academy Ser.). 548p. 1965. text 58.00 (0-19-725891-3) OUP.

Latham, Ronald E. & Howlett, D. R., eds. Dictionary of Medieval Latin from British Sources Fascicule D-E. 370p. 1986. pap. text 125.00 (0-19-726023-3) OUP.

Latham, Roy. The Dictionary of Computer Graphics Technology & Applications. 2nd ed. LC 94-36569. (Illus.). 169p. 1995. 21.95 (0-387-94405-2) Spr-Verlag.

Latham, Sheila. W. O. Mitchell: An Annotated Bibliography. 364p. (C). 1981. pap. text 9.00 (0-920763-59-6, Pub. by ECW) Genl Dist Srvs.

***Latham, Thomas W. & Zabronsky, Andrew.** California Trust & Probate Litigation: May 2000 Update. Tom, Janette, ed. LC 99-62300. 540p. 2000. 64.00 (0-7626-0422-0, ES-32851) Cont Ed Bar-CA.

Latham, Tony. BBC Microcomputer Disk Companion. 1984. pap. 12.95 (0-13-069311-1) P-H.

***Latham, William.** Mary's Monster. 298p. 1999. pap. 9.95 (0-9677280-0-2) Powys.

***Latham, William & Higgins, Cindy.** How to Find Your Family Roots & Write Your Family History. 2nd ed. LC 99-59931. 288p. 2000. pap. 14.95 (1-891661-12-4, Pub. by Snta Monica) IPG Chicago.

Latham, William R. Locational Behavior in Manufacturing Industries. (Studies in Applied Regional Science: No. 4). 1976. pap. text 48.00 (90-207-0638-1) Kluwer Academic.

Latham, Williams. Epitaphs in Old Bridgewater, Massachusetts. (Illus.). x, 260p. 1997. reprint ed. pap. 21.50 (0-917890-91-4, 1076) Heritage Bk.

***Lathan, Tamala.** Black Butterflies. 250p. (J). 2000. 7.99 (0-9700599-0-6) Sybrell Pubng.

Lathan, Virginia A. The Deposition Handbook: A Guide to Help You Give a Winning Deposition. rev. ed. LC 93-71190. 100p. (Orig.). 1995. pap. 14.95 (0-9636195-2-7) Curry-Co Pubns.

— Preventing Sexual Harassment: A Training Manual for the Workplace. rev. ed. 50p. 1997. spiral bd. 16.95 (0-9636195-4-3) Curry-Co Pubns.

Lathe, Robert, tr. see Steiner, Rudolf.

Lathe, Robert F. & Steiner, Rudolf. Education As a Force for Social Change. Whittaker, Nancy K., tr. LC 97-2781. (Foundations of Waldorf Education Ser.: Vol. 9). 256p. 1997. pap. 16.95 (0-88010-411-2) Anthroposophic.

Lathe, Robert F., tr. see Steiner, Rudolf.

Lathem, Edward C. Robert Frost Poetry & Prose. LC 74-188990. 496p. 1995. pap. 14.95 (0-8050-0245-6, Owl) H Holt & Co.

Lathem, Edward C., ed. A Concordance to the Poetry of Robert Frost. rev. ed. 640p. 1994. 65.00 (0-88432-742-6) Audio-Forum.

An Asterisk (*) at the beginning of an entry indicates that the title is appearing for the first time.

— Interviews with Robert Frost. 320p. 1997. 34.50 (*0-88432-888-0*, B28880) Audio-Forum.
— On the Teaching & Writing of History: Responses to a Series of Questions. LC 95-62168. 97p. 1994. pap. 9.95 (*0-87451-720-6*) U Pr of New Eng.
— The Poetry of Robert Frost. LC 68-24759. 632p. 1995. 27.50 (*0-8050-0502-1*) H Holt & Co.
— 76 United Statesiana. 165p. 1976. 25.00 (*0-918006-04-X*) Assn Res Lib.
— Seventy-Six United Statesiana: Seventy-Six Works of American Scholarship Relating to America as Published During Two Centuries from the Revolutionary Era of the United States Through the Nation's Bicentennial Year, 1776-1976. LC 76-151831. 170p. reprint ed. pap. 52.70 (*0-8357-2718-1*, 203983200013) Bks Demand.
— Thirteen Colonial Americana. 93p. 1977. write for info. (*0-918006-06-6*) Assn Res Lib.
— Your Son, Calvin Coolidge. 244p. 1968. pap. 7.50 (*0-914960-35-0*) Academy Bks.

Lathem, Edward C., ed. see Stegner, Wallace.

***Lathem, Edward Connery & Shribman, David M., eds.** Miraculously Builded in Our Hearts: A Dartmouth Reader. 422p. 1999. 35.00 (*1-58465-054-0*) U Pr of New Eng.

Lathem, Edward Connery, ed. see Frost, Robert.

Lathem, Maude A., jt. ed. see Holmes, Ernest.

Lathen, Emma. Accounting for Murder. 1995. pap. 7.00 (*0-684-80103-5*); pap. 7.00 (*0-684-80245-7*) S&S Trade.
— Accounting for Murder: A John Putnam Thatcher Mystery. 192p. 1995. per. 7.00 (*1-57283-000-X*) S&S Trade.
— Brewing up a Storm. large type ed. 368p. 1998. mass mkt. 5.99 (*0-06-104434-2*, Harp PBks) HarpC.
— East is East: East is East. 336p. 1994. mass mkt. 5.99 (*0-06-104296-X*) HarpC Child Bks.
— Right on the Money: Right on the Money. 288p. 1995. mass mkt. 4.99 (*0-06-104295-1*, Harp PBks) HarpC.
— A Shark out of Water. (John Putnam Thatcher Mystery Ser.). 336p. 1998. reprint ed. mass mkt. 5.99 (*0-06-104460-1*, Harp PBks) HarpC.

Lather, Patricia A. Troubling the Angels: Women Living with HIV/AIDS. LC 97-3989. (C). 1997. pap. 24.00 (*0-8133-9016-8*, Pub. by Westview) HarpC.

Lather, Patti. Feminist Research in Education: Within - Against. 116p. (C). 1991. pap. 60.00 (*0-7300-1256-5*, ESA846, Pub. by Deakin Univ) St Mut.
— Getting Smart: Feminist Research & Pedagogy within the Postmodern. (Critical Social Thought Ser.). 256p. (C). (gr. 13). 1991. pap. 19.99 (*0-415-90378-5*, A5173) Routledge.

Lathers, Marie. The Aesthetics of Artifice: Villiers' Future Eve. LC 91-58691. (AMS Studies in the Nineteenth Century: No. 13). 1992. 39.50 (*0-404-61493-0*) AMS Pr.
— The Aesthetics of Artifice: Villiers' L'Eve Future, Vol. 254. LC 96-14848. (North Carolina Studies in the Romance Languages & Literatures Ser.: No. 254). 141p. (C). 1996. 27.50 (*0-8078-9258-0*) U of NC Pr.

Lathers, Marie, jt. auth. see Schraeder.

Lathey, Gillian. The Impossible Legacy: Identity & Purpose in Autobiographical Children's Literature Set in the Third Reich & the Second World War. 258p. (C). 1999. pap. text 41.95 (*0-8204-4208-9*) P Lang Pubng.

Lathi, B. P. Linear Systems & Signals. LC 91-75492. 656p. (C). 1992. 79.95 (*0-941413-34-9*) Berkeley-Cambridge.
— Modern Digital & Analog Communication Systems. 3rd ed. (The Oxford Series in Electrical & Computer Engineering). (Illus.). 800p. (C). 1998. text 89.95 (*0-19-511009-9*) OUP.
— Signal Processing & Linear Systems. LC 98-10609. 850p. (C). 1998. 79.95 (*0-941413-35-7*) Berkeley-Cambridge.
— Signals & Systems. LC 86-72954. 531p. 1987. text 69.95 (*0-941413-33-0*) Berkeley-Cambridge.

Lathim, Marie. Seeds of Wisdom. Owens, Mig, ed. LC 98-87081. 52p. 1998. pap. 6.00 (*0-9666767-1-8*, EW002) Encourag Word.
— Women with a Vision. Owens, Mig, ed. LC 98-96503. (Illus.). 212p. 1998. pap. 12.00 (*0-9666767-2-6*, EW001) Encourag Word.

Lathouwers, L., jt. auth. see Broeckhove, J.

Lathrap, Donald, jt. auth. see Wallace, William.

Lathrap, Donald W., jt. auth. see Wallace, William J.

Lathrop. Index to How to Do It Information: 1996 Supplement. 198p. 1998. pap. 35.00 (*0-910868-96-4*) Lathrop.

Lathrop. Red Hat Linux Desktop. 49.99 (*0-07-212281-1*) McGraw.
— Red Hat Linux Desktop. LC 99-88660. 704p. 2000. pap. 49.99 (*0-07-212283-8*) McGraw.

Lathrop, Alan K., jt. ed. see Kelly, Richard J.

***Lathrop, Ann & Foss, Kathleen E.** Student Cheating & Plagiarism in the Internet Era: A Wake-Up Call for Educators & Parents. 230p. 2000. pap. 30.00 incl. disk (*1-56308-841-X*) Libs Unl.

Lathrop, Ann & Goodson, Bobby. Courseware in the Classroom: Selecting, Organizing, & Using Educational Software. 1983. text 12.95 (*0-201-20007-4*) Addison-Wesley.

Lathrop, Casey L. Pen Rose Poems: Personalized Wedding Theme Poems. 80p. (Orig.). 1997. pap. 14.95 (*1-57502-489-6*, PO1456) Morris Pubng.

Lathrop, Churchill & Elzea, Rowland, intros. Thomas George - A Retrospective: Paintings & Works on Paper. (Illus.). 32p. (Orig.). 1987. pap. 7.50 (*0-938766-04-X*) NJ State Mus.

Lathrop, Cornelia P. Black Rock: Seaport of Old Fairfield, 1644-1870. (Illus.). 214p. 1995. reprint ed. lib. bdg. 32.00 (*0-8328-4980-4*) Higginson Bk Co.

Lathrop, Donald, jt. auth. see Gibson, Karen.

Lathrop, Dorothy B. Animals of the Bible. LC 37-28415. 72p. (J). (ps-3). 1998. 17.95 (*0-397-31536-8*); lib. bdg. 16.89 (*0-397-30047-6*) HarpC Child Bks.

Lathrop, Elise L. Early American Inns & Taverns. LC 68-20234. (Illus.). 1972. reprint ed. 20.95 (*0-405-08734-9*, Pub. by Blom Pubns) Ayer.
— Early American Inns & Taverns. 365p. 1993. reprint ed. lib. bdg. 89.00 (*0-7812-5297-0*); reprint ed. lib. bdg. 89.00 (*0-7812-5479-5*) Rprt Serv.
— Historic Houses of Early America. 464p. 1993. reprint ed. lib. bdg. 99.00 (*0-7812-5298-9*) Rprt Serv.
— Where Shakespeare Set His Stage. LC 70-128571. (Studies in Shakespeare: No. 24). 1970. reprint ed. lib. bdg. 75.00 (*0-8383-0907-0*) M S G Haskell Hse.

Lathrop, G., ed. How Does Worship Evangelize? 1996. pap. 6.95 (*0-8066-2800-6*, 10-28006) Augsburg Fortress.
— What Are the Essentials of Christian Worship? 1996. pap. 7.25 (*0-8066-2797-2*, 10-27972) Augsburg Fortress.
— What Are the Ethical Implications of Worship? 1996. pap. 7.25 (*0-8066-2804-9*, 10-28049) Augsburg Fortress.
— What Does "Multicultural" Worship Look Like? LC 96-206125. 1996. pap. 7.25 (*0-8066-2799-9*, 10-27999) Augsburg Fortress.
— What Is Changing in Baptismal Practice? LC 96-121358. 1996. pap. 7.25 (*0-8066-2801-4*, 10-28014) Augsburg Fortress.
— What Is Changing in Eucharist Practice? LC 96-133584. 1996. pap. 7.25 (*0-8066-2802-2*, 10-28022) Augsburg Fortress.
— What Is "Contemporary" Worship? LC 96-121357. 1996. pap. 7.25 (*0-8066-2798-0*, 10-27980) Augsburg Fortress.

Lathrop, George P. A Masque of Poets. 1999. reprint ed. lib. bdg. 125.00 (*0-7812-3757-2*) Rprt Serv.
— Riverside Edition of Hawthorne's Works. (Notable American Authors Ser.). 1999. reprint ed. lib. bdg. 125.00 (*0-7812-3758-0*) Rprt Serv.
— Rose & Roof-Tree. (Notable American Authors Ser.). 1999. reprint ed. lib. bdg. 125.00 (*0-7812-3754-8*) Rprt Serv.
— Spanish Vistas. (Notable American Authors Ser.). 1999. reprint ed. lib. bdg. 125.00 (*0-7812-3756-4*) Rprt Serv.
— A Story of Courage. (Notable American Authors Ser.). 1999. reprint ed. lib. bdg. 125.00 (*0-7812-3759-9*) Rprt Serv.
— A Study of Hawthorne. (BCL1-PS American Literature Ser.). 350p. 1992. reprint ed. lib. bdg. 89.00 (*0-7812-6728-5*) Rprt Serv.
— A Study of Hawthorne. 1999. reprint ed. lib. bdg. 125.00 (*0-7812-3755-6*) Rprt Serv.
— A Study of Hawthorne. LC 78-107178. 1970. reprint ed. 16.00 (*0-403-00237-0*) Scholarly.
— Would You Kill Him? LC 73-104507. 388p. reprint ed. lib. bdg. 32.00 (*0-8398-1151-9*) Irvington.
— Would You Kill Him? 388p. (C). 1986. reprint ed. pap. text 6.95 (*0-8290-1959-6*) Irvington.

Lathrop, Gordon. Readings for the Assembly. pap. 19.95 (*0-8066-2333-0*, Augsburg) Augsburg Fortress.

Lathrop, Gordon & Ramshaw, Gail, eds. Lectionary for the Christian People, Cycle B. 273p. 1992. pap. 17.95 (*0-8146-6081-9*, Pueblo Bks) Liturgical Pr.
— Readings for the Assembly: Revised Common Lectionary-Year A. 1995. 19.95 (*0-8066-0434-4*, 3-389) Augsburg Fortress.
— Readings for the Assembly: Revised Common Lectionary-Year B. 1996. 19.95 (*0-8066-2332-2*, 3-397) Augsburg Fortress.

Lathrop, Gordon W. Holy People: A Liturgical Ecclesiology. LC 99-10520. 240p. 1999. 29.00 (*0-8006-3133-1*, 1-3133, Fortress Pr) Augsburg Fortress.
— Holy Things: A Liturgical Theology. 1998. pap. 20.00 (*0-8006-3131-5*, 1-3131, Fortress Pr) Augsburg Fortress.

Lathrop, Gordon W., ed. How Does the Liturgy Speak of God? (Open Questions Ser.: Vol. 8). 1996. pap. 6.95 (*0-8066-2803-0*, 10-28030) Augsburg Fortress.

Lathrop, Gordon W., jt. auth. see Ramshaw, Gail.

Lathrop, Irvin T., jt. auth. see La Cour, Marshall.

Lathrop, J. Philip. Restructuring Health Care: The Patient-Focused Paradigm. LC 93-29550. (Health Ser.). 272p. 1993. text 38.95 (*1-55542-594-1*) Jossey-Bass.

Lathrop, J. W., jt. auth. see IIASA International Workshop Staff.

***Lathrop, Jacqueline.** Ancient Mexico: Cultural Traditions in the Land of the Feathered. 6th ed. LC F1219.L36 1998. 308p. (C). 1998. per. 37.95 (*0-7872-4981-5*, 41498101) Kendall-Hunt.

Lathrop, James K., jt. auth. see Birk, David M.

Lathrop, JoAnna. Willa Cather: A Checklist of Her Published Writing. LC 74-82561. 132p. reprint ed. pap. 41.00 (*0-7837-6031-0*, 204584300008) Bks Demand.

Lathrop, Julia C. The United States Children's Bureau, 1912-1972. 1979. 26.95 (*0-405-05988-4*) Ayer.

Lathrop, Kathleen. Amy Angel Goes Home: A Spiritual Tale of Adoption. (Illus.). 32p. (J). (ps-3). 1996. 17.95 (*0-9642128-0-3*) Diotima Pr.

Lathrop, Lori. An Indexer's Guide to the Internet. 40p. 1995. pap. 15.00 (*0-936547-22-7*) Info Today Inc.
— An Indexer's Guide to the Internet. 2nd ed. 100p. 1999. pap. 31.25 (*1-57387-078-1*) Info Today Inc.

Lathrop, Mary Lou, jt. auth. see Tolpin, Jim.

***Lathrop, Michael L.** Environmental Insurance Coverage: State, Law & Regulation, Issue 12. 500p. 1999. ring bd. write for info. (*0-327-01678-7*, 8041517) LEXIS Pub.

Lathrop, Michael L. Insurance Coverage for Environmental Claims. 1992. 110.00 incl. cd-rom (*0-8205-1833-6*) Bender.

Lathrop, Mitchell L. Environmental Insurance Coverage: State Law & Regulation, 2 vols. 810p. 1991. suppl. ed. 60.00 (*1-56257-153-2*, MICHIE) LEXIS Pub.
— Environmental Insurance Coverage: State Law & Regulation, 2 vols. 810p. 1994. spiral bd. 195.00 (*0-88063-362-X*, 80411-10, MICHIE) LEXIS Pub.
— Environmental Insurance Coverage Issue 11: State, Law & Regulation. LC 90-23012. 500p. 1998. ring bd., suppl. ed. write for info. (*0-327-00558-0*, 8041516) LEXIS Pub.
— State Hazardous Waste Regulation, 1991-1992, 2 vols. 1992. ring bd., suppl. ed. 62.00 (*0-685-74334-9*, MICHIE); ring bd. 160.00 (*0-88063-361-1*, MICHIE) LEXIS Pub.

Lathrop, Norman M. Index to How to Do It Information: 1994 Supplement. 206p. (Orig.). 1995. pap. 35.00 (*0-910868-94-8*) Lathrop.

Lathrop, Olin. The Way Computer Graphics Works. LC 96-42688. 201p. 1997. pap. 32.95 (*0-471-13040-0*) Wiley.

Lathrop, Richard. Don't Use a Resume. 64p. 1981. pap. 3.95 (*0-89815-027-2*) Ten Speed Pr.
— The Job Market: What Ails It & What Needs to Be Done about It to Reduce Unemployment. (Illus.). (Orig.). 1978. pap. 4.85 (*0-935234-00-4*) Natl Ctr Job Mkt.
— Who's Hiring Who. rev. ed. (Illus.). 266p. 1989. pap. 11.95 (*0-89815-298-4*) Ten Speed Pr.

Lathrop, Rose H. Memories of Hawthorne. 1972. 59.95 (*0-8490-0606-6*) Gordon Pr.
— Memories of Hawthorne. (BCL1-PS American Literature Ser.). 482p. 1992. reprint ed. lib. bdg. 99.00 (*0-7812-6729-3*) Rprt Serv.
— Rose Hawthrone Lathrop: Selected Writings. LC 93-14622. (Sources of American Spirituality Ser.). 256p. 1993. 24.95 (*0-8091-0463-6*) Paulist Pr.

Lathrop-Smit, Hermine. Natural Dyes. 72p. 1978. 14.95 (*0-88862-227-9*, Pub. by J Lorimer) Formac Dist Ltd.

Lathrop, Tad & Pettigrew, Jim. This Business of Music Marketing & Promotion. LC 98-39920. (Illus.). 320p. 1999. text 21.95 (*0-8230-7711-X*, Billboard Bks) Watsn-Guptill.

Lathrop, Tad, ed. see Wolper, Andrea.

Lathrop, Thomas & Dias, Eduardo. Portugal: Lingua e Cultura: Writing & Langauage Lab Manual. (Illus.). 440p. (Orig.). 1995. pap. text, wbk. ed. 20.95 (*0-942566-20-3*) LinguaText.

Lathrop, Thomas, ed. see Barnell, Hal.

Lathrop, Thomas, ed. see De Vooght, Marian & Lefevere, Andre.

Lathrop, Thomas A. & Dias, Eduardo. Portugal! Lingua e Cultura. (Illus.). 510p. 1995. text 49.95 (*0-942566-19-X*) LinguaText.

***Lathrop, Thomas A. & Dias, Eduardo M.** Brasil! Lingua e Cultura. 2nd rev. ed. (POR., Illus.). 512p. (C). 1998. 49.95 (*0-942566-27-0*) LinguaText.
— Brasil! Lingua e Cultura: Writing & Language Lab Manual. rev. ed. (POR., Illus.). 390p. (C). 1998. pap. 20.95 (*0-942566-28-9*) LinguaText.

Lathrop, Thomas A., jt. auth. see Jensen, Frede.

Lathrop, Tom. The Evolution of Spanish. 3rd ed. (Estudios Linguisticos Ser.: Vol. 1). 240p. 1996. pap. 16.50 (*0-936388-58-7*) Juan de la Cuesta.

Lathrop, Tom, compiled by. Don Quijote Dictionary. (Documentacion Cervantina Ser.: No. 18). (SPA.). 1998. pap. 4.00 (*0-936388-88-9*) Juan de la Cuesta.

Lathrop, Tom, ed. see De Cervantes Saavedra, Miguel.

Lathrop, Wendy R., ed. Legal Topics in Boundary Surveying. 264p. 1990. pap. 65.00 (*0-614-06110-5*, S293) Am Congrs Survey.

Lathrop, William G. The Brass Industry in the U. S. A Study of the Origin & the Development of the Brass Industry in the Naugatuck Valley & Its Subsequent Extension over the Nation. LC 72-5060. (Technology & Society Ser.). (Illus.). 230p. 1972. reprint ed. 17.95 (*0-405-04711-8*) Ayer.

Lathrope, Daniel J. The Alternative Minimum Tax. 1993. ring bd. 155.00 (*0-685-69582-4*, ALMT) Warren Gorham & Lamont.
— Alternative Minimum Tax. 672p. 1994. 185.00 (*0-7913-1978-4*, AMT) Warren Gorham & Lamont.

Lathrope, Daniel J. & Rosenberg, Joshua D. Fundamentals of Partnership Taxation: Cases & Materials. 4th ed. (University Textbook Ser.). 232p. 1994. pap. text, teacher ed. write for info. (*1-56662-196-8*) Foundation Pr.

Lathrope, Daniel J., et al. Fundamentals of Corporate Taxation: Cases & Materials, 1994 Supplement. 3rd ed. (University Textbook Ser.). 43p. 1994. 4.50 (*1-56662-202-6*) Foundation Pr.
— 1995 Supplement to Cases & Materials on Fundamentals of Corporate Taxation. 3rd ed. (University Casebook Ser.). 59p. 1995. pap. text 4.95 (*1-56662-298-0*) Foundation Pr.

Lathrope, Daniel J., jt. auth. see Schwartz, Stephen.

Latia, Douglas C. Non-Destructive Testing for Aircraft. (Illus.). 1994. pap. text 26.95 (*0-89100-415-7*, JS312640) Jeppesen Sanderson.

Latif, A. Slavery: The African American Psychic Trauma. 1994. pap. 14.95 (*0-9640118-0-8*) Latif Communs.

Latif, Abdul M., jt. auth. see Khandker, Shahidur R.

Latif-Ansari, Farzana. Electrocyclic Reactions: Fundamentals to Research. LC 99-186705. 288p. 1999. pap. 69.95 (*3-527-29755-3*) Wiley.

***Latif, Bilkees I.** The Essential Andhra Cookbook with Hyderabadi Specialities. LC 99-937896. (Illus.). 1999. write for info. (*0-14-027184-8*) Penguin Books.

Latif, Rebecca C. IBM Displaywriter: Word Processing Production Techniques Made Easy. (Illus.). 25p. 15.94 (*0-317-13055-2*) P-H.

Latif, S. A. Basics of Islamic Culture. 1989. pap. 4.25 (*0-935782-45-1*) Kazi Pubns.
— The Mind Al-Quran Builds. 200p. 1983. 8.50 (*1-56744-330-3*) Kazi Pubns.

Latif, S. Abdul. Muslim Mystic Movement in Bengal, 1301-1550. (C). 1993. 14.00 (*81-7074-136-X*, Pub. by KP Bagchi) S Asia.

Latif, Syed A. Islamic Cultural Studies. 140p. 1996. pap. 3.00 (*0-614-21626-5*, 619) Kazi Pubns.

***Latifah, Queen.** Ladies First: Revelations of a Strong Woman. 208p. 2000. pap. 12.00 (*0-688-17583-X*) Morrow Avon.

Latifi. Snakes of Iran. LC 90-63908. 1991. write for info. (*0-916984-22-2*) SSAR.

***Latifi, Alma.** Effects of War on Property: Being Studies in International Law & Policy. xi, 155p. 2000. reprint ed. 60.00 (*1-56169-597-1*) Gaunt.

Latifi, M. L' Hotellerie en Francais. (FRE.). pap. 34.95 (*0-7859-7570-5*) Fr & Eur.

Latifi, Rifat, ed. Amino Acids in Critical Care & Cancer. 118p. 1994. 94.00 (*1-57059-027-3*, LN9027) CRC Pr.

***Latifi, Rifat, ed.** Intensive Care Procedures. 2001. 45.00 (*1-57059-596-8*) Landes Bioscience.

Latiko, Hubert, jt. ed. see Vom Brocke, Bernhard.

Latimer, Carole. Wilderness Cuisine: How to Prepare & Enjoy Fine Food on the Trail & in Camp. LC 91-9288. 240p. (Orig.). 1990. pap. 12.95 (*0-89997-114-8*) Wilderness Pr.

Latimer, Clare. The Comfort Food Cookbook. 192p. 1997. 35.00 (*1-85375-226-6*, Pub. by Prion) Trafalgar.

***Latimer, Clare.** The Comfort Food Cookbook. 192p. 1998. pap. 14.95 (*1-85375-288-6*, Pub. by Prion) Trafalgar.

Latimer, Clay. It's 3rd & Long So... 101 Ways to Improve the Game of Football. LC 98-27608. (Illus.). 144p. 1998. 9.95 (*1-886110-57-3*) Addax Pubng.
— John Elway: Armed & Dangerous. rev. ed. Kidson, Darcie, ed. LC 98-13487. (Illus.). 240p. 1998. pap. 14.95 (*1-886110-53-0*) Addax Pubng.

***Latimer, Clay.** Mia Hamm. (Sports Heroes Ser.). 48p. (YA). (gr. 5 up). 2000. lib. bdg. 21.26 (*0-7368-0579-6*, Capstone Bks) Capstone Pr.
— Muhammad Ali. LC 99-47617. (J). 2000. lib. bdg. write for info. (*1-56766-723-6*) Childs World.

Latimer, Clay. Relentless! The Long Journey of the Denver Broncos' Howard Griffith. 228p. 2000. 22.95 (*1-58261-060-6*, Pub. by Sprts Pubng) Partners-West.
— Special Delivery: The Amazing Basketball Career of Karl Malone. LC 98-43524. (Illus.). 224p. 1999. pap. 14.95 (*1-886110-64-6*) Addax Pubng.

Latimer, Dan. The Elegiac Mode in Milton & Rilke. (European University Studies: Comparative LIterature: Ser. 18, Vol. 10). 56p. 1977. pap. 18.00 (*3-261-02039-3*) P Lang Pubng.

Latimer, Dean. The High Times Guide on How to Pass a Drug Test. 1998. pap. text 14.95 (*0-9647858-2-X*) Trans-High Corp.

***Latimer, Deborah.** Fairy Secrets: A Magical Secret Envelope Book. LC 98-61387. (Secrets Ser.). (Illus.). 20p. (ps-3). 1999. 9.98 (*0-7651-0922-0*) Smithmark.

Latimer, Deborah & Ninham, Sue. The Tooth Fairy. (Illus.). 28p. (J). 1997. 6.98 (*0-7651-9122-9*) Smithmark.

Latimer, E. Spain in the 19th Century. 1976. lib. bdg. 59.95 (*0-8490-2643-1*) Gordon Pr.

Latimer, Frances B. The 1860 Census for Northampton County, Virginia. 104p. pap. text 13.50 (*1-886706-07-7*) Hickory Hse.

***Latimer, Frances Bibbins.** Mortality Schedule 1850-1880-1850 Census for Northampton Co., VA. 1999. 20.00 (*1-886706-12-3*) Hickory Hse.
— Remembering Cape Charles. 1996. 7.00 (*1-886706-11-5*) Hickory Hse.

Latimer, Gordon, jt. auth. see Latimer, Norma.

Latimer, Heather. Curse of the Painted Cats: A Romantic Suspense Novel. 250p. 1989. 18.95 (*0-943698-03-0*) Papyrus Letterbox.

***Latimer, Heather.** Hospitality Jill/Hospitality Jack: How to Approach, Greet & Win over Strangers in Groups, Twos & Ones. (Illus.). 60p. 2000. 25.00 (*0-943698-17-0*, COV.P10, Diff Subjects) Papyrus Letterbox.
— How to Approach & Greet a Stranger in Minutes Vol. II: How to: Enter a Roomful of Strangers, Work the Crowd, Seat Yourself Favorably, Go Solo Around the Corner or the World, Plus One Secret Crucial Element. (Illus.). 8p. 2000. 5.00 (*0-943698-19-7*, LFT2MEET, Diff Subjects) Papyrus Letterbox.
— How to Be Entertaining. What It Takes. You Don't Have to Be a Born Extrovert. How Others Produce Better Results. Make Others Happier by Being with You. Dealing with Couples. (Illus.). 8p. 2000. 5.00 (*0-943698-18-9*, LFTIINTR, Diff Subjects) Papyrus Letterbox.
— How to Become an Outstanding Tour Guide or Docent Vol. IV: How to: Conduct a Walking Tour, Handle Sightseers on a Moving Vehicle, Respond When You Don't Know the Answer, Encourage More People to Join Your Group. (Illus.). 8p. 2000. 5.00 (*0-943698-21-9*, LFT3AGUIDE, Diff Subjects) Papyrus Letterbox.
— How to Handle Disagreeable Situations in an Agreeable Manner Vol. VI: How to: Be More Tactful, Handle Demanding People & Win, Impress Others by the Way You Speak, Plus List of Words That Actually Work, Extra, How Cruise, Bridge & Social Directors Handle Their Problems. (Illus.). 8p. 2000. 5.00 (*0-943698-23-5*, LFTVITAL, Diff Subjects) Papyrus Letterbox.

Latimer, Heather. How to Win over the Stranger You've Just Met Vol. III: How to: Create the Right Image by Your Attire & Grooming, Small-Talk & Converse, Display Interest, Say "Hello" & "Goodbye" with Style, Plus Proxemics & Body Language. (Illus.). 8p. 2000. pap. 5.00 (*0-943698-20-0*, Diff Subjects) Papyrus Letterbox.

***Latimer, Heather.** Ignore Time Factors & You'll Be Gone! Vol. V: How to: Calculate Arrival & Departure Times, Overcome Irritations & Oversights, Know What Organizers Really Expect, Keep Audiences Alert, Plus Hints for Entertainers & Speakers. (Illus.). 8p. 2000. 5.00 (*0-943698-22-7*, LFTSTIMP2, Diff Subjects) Papyrus Letterbox.

L

Latimer, Heather. Is Forever Too Long? A Saga about the Dashing Wexford Males & the Women Who Love Them. Hutchison-Cleaves, Geoffrey, ed. 224p. 1998. reprint ed. pap. 15.00 (*0-943698-15-4*) Papyrus Letterbox.

— Louis Wain - King of the Cat Artists, 1860-1939: A Dramatized Biography. Hutchison-Cleaves, Geoffrey, ed. LC 82-82032. (Illus.). 172p. 1982. lib. bdg. 25.00 (*0-943698-01-4*) Papyrus Letterbox.

— Louis Wain - King of the Cat Artists, 1860-1939: A Dramatized Biography. limited ed. 1982. 25.00 (*0-943698-00-6*) Papyrus Letterbox.

— Louis Wain - King of the Cat Artists, 1860-1939: A Dramatized Biography. Hutchison-Cleaves, Geoffrey, ed. LC 82-82032. (Illus.). 172p. 1982. reprint ed. 25.00 (*0-943698-02-2*) Papyrus Letterbox.

Latimer, Hugh. Selected Sermons of Hugh Latimer. Chester, Allan G., ed. (Documents Ser.). 1978. 29.50 (*0-918016-43-6*) Folger Bks.

— Sermons. LC 76-172301. reprint ed. 45.00 (*0-404-03886-7*) AMS Pr.

— Seven Sermons Before Edward the Sixth, 1549. Arber, Edward, ed. 208p. 1993. pap. 20.00 (*0-87556-144-6*) Saifer.

Latimer, Ian, jt. auth. see Hawkes, John.

Latimer, James W. The Pits of Middle Texas: People of the Smoke Pits . . . & Their Barbecue. (Illus.). 144p. (Orig.). 1993. pap. 12.95 (*0-9635939-0-0*) Literary Serv.

Latimer, Jane E. Beyond the Food Game: A Spiritual & Psychological Approach to Healing Emotional Eating. LC 93-10052. (Illus.). 1993. pap. 9.95 (*1-882109-01-5*) LivingQuest.

— The Healing Power of Inner Light-Fire: Accessing Higher Consciousness to Heal Your Life. LC 90-5492. 160p. (Orig.). 1990. pap. 9.95 (*1-882109-05-8*) LivingQuest.

— Living Binge Free: A Personal Guide to Victory over Compulsive Eating. LC 88-15899. 1991. pap. 11.95 (*1-882109-00-7*) LivingQuest.

Latimer, Jim. Going the Moose Way Home. LC 87-9762. (Illus.). 32p. (J). (gr. 1-3). 1988. lib. bdg. 15.00 (*0-684-18890-2*) Scribner.

— The Irish Piper. LC 90-34550. (Illus.). 32p. (J). (gr. 1-3). 1991. 13.95 (*0-684-19130-X*) Scribner.

— James Bear & the Goose Gathering. LC 92-26190. (Illus.). 32p. (J). (gr. k-2). 1994. mass mkt. 14.95 (*0-684-19526-7*) Scribner.

— Moose & Friends. LC 91-14047. (Illus.). 32p. (J). (gr. 1-3). 1993. 14.95 (*0-684-19335-3*) Scribner.

***Latimer, Joanna.** The Conduct of Care: Understanding Nursing Practice. LC 00-36012. 2000. write for info. (*0-632-05575-8*) Blackwell Sci.

Latimer, Jon, ed. Applying to Colleges & Universities in the United States 1998: A Handbook for International Students. 560p. 1997. pap. write for info. (*1-56079-873-4*) Petersons.

— Peterson's Colleges & Universities in the U. S. A., 1998: A Handbook for International Students. 1997. pap. 24.95 (*1-56079-758-4*) Petersons.

— Peterson's Graduate & Professional Programs: An Overview. (Graduate & Professional Programs Ser.). 1412p. 1997. pap. 29.95 (*1-56079-791-6*) Petersons.

— Peterson's Graduate Programs in Biological Sciences, 1998. (Graduate & Professional Programs Ser.). 2924p. 1997. pap. 46.95 (*1-56079-793-2*) Petersons.

— Peterson's Graduate Programs in Business, Education, Health, Information Studies, Law & Social Work 1998. (Graduate & Professional Programs Ser.). 1986p. 1997. pap. 29.95 (*1-56079-796-7*) Petersons.

— Peterson's Graduate Programs in Engineering & Applied Sciences, 1998. (Graduate & Professional Programs Ser.). 1714p. 1997. pap. 39.95 (*1-56079-795-9*) Petersons.

— Peterson's Graduate Programs in Humanities, Arts & Social Sciences, 1998. (Graduate & Professional Programs Ser.). 1575p. 1997. pap. 39.95 (*1-56079-792-4*) Petersons.

— Peterson's Graduate Programs in the Physical Sciences, Mathematics & Agricultural Sciences, 1998. (Graduate & Professional Programs Ser.). 1038p. 1997. pap. 36.95 (*1-56079-794-0*) Petersons.

— Peterson's Graduate Schools in the U. S. & Canada. 800p. 1997. pap. 24.95 (*1-56079-765-7*) Petersons.

— Peterson's Guide to Adult Learning Opportunities. 600p. 1997. pap. 21.95 (*1-56079-807-6*) Petersons.

— Peterson's Guide to Graduate Computer Science & Electrical Engineering Programs. 2nd ed. 800p. 1997. pap. 24.95 (*1-56079-874-2*) Petersons.

— Peterson's Guide to MBA Programs, 1998. 4th ed. 1220p. 1997. pap. 24.95 (*1-56079-862-9*) Petersons.

— Peterson's Register of Higher Education, 1998. 11th ed. 1160p. 1997. pap. 49.95 (*1-56079-872-6*) Petersons.

— Peterson's Sports Scholarships & College Athletic Programs, 1998. 3rd ed. 864p. 1997. pap. 24.95 (*1-56079-830-0*) Petersons.

— Peterson's Vocational & Technical Schools & Programs - East: Accredited Institutions Offering Career Training Programs. 3rd ed. 660p. 1997. pap. 34.95 (*1-56079-864-5*) Petersons.

— Peterson's Vocational & Technical Schools & Programs - West: Accredited Institutions Offering Career Training Programs. 3rd ed. 660p. 1997. pap. 34.95 (*1-56079-865-3*) Petersons.

Latimer, Jon, ed. see Digby, Joan.

Latimer, Jon, ed. see Mangrum, Charles & Strichart, Stephen.

Latimer, Jon, ed. see Peterson's Guides Staff.

Latimer, Jonathan. The Dead Don't Care. (C). 1989. 35.00 (*0-948353-07-4*, Pub. by Oldcastle Bks) St Mut.

— Headed for a Hearse. LC 80-12148. 306p. 1980. 18.95 (*0-8398-2652-4*) Boulevard.

— Headed for a Hearse. LC 90-80763. 306p. 1990. pap. 7.95 (*1-55882-069-8*) Intl Polygonics.

— The Lady in the Morgue. 192p. 1988. pap. 4.95 (*0-930330-79-X*) Intl Polygonics.

— Murder in the Madhouse. LC 89-85727. 300p. 1989. reprint ed. pap. 7.95 (*1-55882-023-X*, Lib Crime Classics) Intl Polygonics.

— Red Gardenias. LC 91-70601. 280p. 1991. reprint ed. pap. 8.95 (*1-55882-094-9*, Lib Crime Classics) Intl Polygonics.

— The Search for My Great Uncle's Head. LC 89-85718. 294p. 1990. reprint ed. pap. 7.95 (*1-55882-052-3*, Lib Crime Classics) Intl Polygonics.

— Sinners & Shrouds. LC 82-21449. 1983. pap. 4.95 (*0-685-57776-7*) S&S Trade.

Latimer, Jonathan P. & Nolting, Karen S. Backyard Birds. LC 98-35509. (Peterson Field Guides for Young Naturalists Ser.). (Illus.). 48p. (J). (gr. 3-7). 1999. 15.00 (*0-395-95210-7*) HM.

***Latimer, Jonathan P. & Nolting, Karen S.** Caterpillars. LC 99-38944. (Peterson Field Guides for Young Naturalists Ser.). (Illus.). 48p. (J). (gr. 3-7). 2000. pap. 5.95 (*0-395-97945-5*) HM.

Latimer, Jonathan P. & Nolting, Karen S. Shorebirds. LC 98-35510. (Peterson Field Guides for Young Naturalists Ser.). (Illus.). 48p. (J). (gr. 3-7). 1999. pap. 5.95 (*0-395-92278-X*) HM.

Latimer, Jonathan P., et al. Birds of Prey. LC 98-35516. (Peterson Field Guides for Young Naturalists Ser.). (Illus.). 48p. (J). (gr. 3-7). 1999. 15.00 (*0-395-95211-5*); pap. 5.95 (*0-395-92277-1*) HM.

— Bizarre Birds. LC 98-35512. (Peterson Field Guides for Young Naturalists Ser.). (Illus.). 48p. (J). (gr. 3-7). 1999. 15.00 (*0-395-95213-1*); pap. 5.95 (*0-395-92279-8*) HM.

***Latimer, Jonathan P., et al.** Butterflies. LC 99-38605. (Peterson Field Guides for Young Naturalists Ser.). (Illus.). 48p. (J). (gr. 3-7). 2000. 5.95 (*0-395-97944-7*) HM.

Latimer, Jonathan P., et al. Shorebirds. LC 98-35510. (Peterson Field Guides for Young Naturalists Ser.). (Illus.). 48p. (J). (gr. 3-7). 1999. 15.00 (*0-395-95212-3*) HM.

***Latimer, Jonathan P., et al.** Songbirds. LC 99-38293. (Illus.). 48p. (J). (gr. 3-7). 2000. pap. 5.95 (*0-395-97946-3*) HM.

Latimer, Leah Y. Higher Ground: Preparing African-American Children for College. LC 99-208794. 320p. 1999. pap. 12.00 (*0-380-79919-7*, Eos) Morrow Avon.

Latimer, Mansfield. Never Too Old to Play Tennis . . . & Never Too Old to Start. (Illus.). 176p. (Orig.). 1993. pap. 12.95 (*1-55870-288-1*, Betrwy Bks) F & W Pubns Inc.

Latimer, Margery. Guardian Angel, & Other Stories. LC 75-157783. (Short Story Index Reprint Ser.). 1977. reprint ed. 20.95 (*0-8369-3895-X*) Ayer.

— Guardian Angel & Other Stories. LC 84-14175. 264p. 1984. reprint ed. pap. 8.95 (*0-935312-13-7*) Feminist Pr.

Latimer, Margery T., ed. see Toomer, Jean.

Latimer, Norma & Latimer, Gordon. Irish Country Cooking. (Traditional Cooking of Ireland Ser.). (Illus.). 108p. (Orig.). 1985. pap. 8.95 (*0-941869-03-2*) Latimers.

— Scottish Fare. (Traditional Cooking of Scotland Ser.). (Illus.). 105p. (Orig.). 1983. pap. 8.95 (*0-941869-02-4*) Latimers.

Latimer, Norma, et al. Eat, Sleep & Be Merrie in Britain. (Travel in Britain Ser.). (Illus.). 343p. (Orig.). 1985. pap. 14.95 (*0-941869-04-0*) Latimers.

— English Desserts, Puddings, Cakes & Scones. (Traditional Cooking of Great Britain Ser.). (Illus.). 123p. (Orig.). 1984. pap. 8.95 (*0-941869-01-6*) Latimers.

— Olde English Traditional Country Style Recipes. (Traditional Cooking of Great Britain Ser.). (Illus.). 105p. (Orig.). 1984. pap. 8.95 (*0-941869-00-8*) Latimers.

Latimer, Paul. Commercial Law Workbook. 350p. 1995. pap. 29.00 (*0-455-21290-2*, Pub. by LawBk Co) Gaunt.

Latimer, Paul, jt. auth. see Hardy Ivamy, E. R.

Latimer, Paul R., et al. Behavioral Medicine Vol. 3: International Perspectives. Caddy, Glenn R. et al, eds. (Developments in Clinical Psychology Ser.: Vol. 3). (Illus.). 464p. (C). 1995. text 78.50 (*0-89391-744-3*) Ablx Pub.

Latimer, Paula. Mediate Your Divorce & Save Attorneys' Fees. 52p. (Orig.). 1993. pap. write for info. (*0-9636555-0-7*) P Latimer.

Latimer, Ray, jt. auth. see Ghosh, Sunit.

Latimer, Rebecca. You're Not Old Until You're Ninety: Best to Be Prepared, However. LC 97-6720. 208p. 1997. pap. 12.95 (*1-57733-009-9*) B Dolphin Pub.

Latimer, Renate, jt. auth. see Merkel, Inge.

Latimer, Renate, tr. & afterword by see Eisenreich, Herbert.

Latimer, Sallie W. Narragansett. LC 97-208129. (Images of America Ser.). 1997. pap. 16.99 (*0-7524-0268-4*) Arcadia Publng.

***Latimer, Sallie W.** Narragansett AC. (Images of America Ser.). 128p. 2000. pap. 18.99 (*0-7385-0085-2*) Arcadia Publng.

— Narragansett Postcards. (Images of America Ser.). 128p. 1999. pap. 18.99 (*0-7385-0086-0*) Arcadia Publng.

Latimer, Tirza T. The Perfume Atomizer: An Object with Atmosphere. LC 91-67016. (Illus.). 168p. 1992. text 69.95 (*0-88740-382-4*) Schiffer.

Latimore, James. Weeding Out the Target Population: The Law of Accountability in a Manpower Program, 54. LC 84-8952. (Contributions in Sociology Ser.: No. 54). (Illus.). 176p. 1985. 49.95 (*0-313-24495-2*, LWT/, Greenwood Pr) Greenwood.

***Latimore, Sarah Briggs.** Arthur Rackham, a Bibliography. xiii, 112p. 1999. reprint ed. 35.00 (*1-57898-156-5*) Martino Pubng.

Latin American Conference Staff. Fiscal Policy for Industrialization & Development in Latin America. Geithman, David T., ed. LC 74-2231. 380p. reprint ed. pap. 117.80 (*0-7837-4954-6*, 204462000004) Bks Demand.

— Man in the Amazon. Wagley, Charles, ed. LC 74-10857. (Illus.). 346p. reprint ed. pap. 107.30 (*0-7837-5011-0*, 204467800004) Bks Demand.

— Universities in Transition: The U. S. Presence in Latin American Higher Education. Renner, Richard R., ed. LC 73-8234. 156p. reprint ed. pap. 48.40 (*0-7837-5085-4*, 204478300004) Bks Demand.

Latin American Economic Institute Staff. Economic Defense of the Western Hemisphere. LC 68-57328. (Essay Index Reprint Ser.). 1977. 19.95 (*0-8369-0609-8*) Ayer.

Latin American Institute Staff, tr. see Adams, Clinton, et al.

***Latin American Symposium on Theoretical Informatics Staff.** Latin 2000: Theoretical Informatics: Fourth Latin American Symposium Punta del Esk, Uruguay, April 10-14, 2000, Proceedings. Gonnet, G. H. et al, eds. LC 00-35819. (Lecture Notes in Computer Science Ser.: Vol. 1776). xiv, 484p. 2000. pap. 73.00 (*3-540-67306-7*) Spr-Verlag.

Latin American Workshop on Plasma Physics Staff, et al. Plasma Physics: Proceedings of the 1997 Latin American Workshop on Plasma Physics Held in Caracas, Venezuela, January 20-31, 1997. LC 98-32183. 14p. 1999. write for info. (*0-7923-5527-X*) Kluwer Academic.

Latin Culture Productions Staff, ed. see Lacoren, Nestor R.

Latin, Howard A. Privacy: A Selected Bibliography & Topical Index of Social Science Materials. iv, 94p. 1976. pap. 17.50 (*0-8377-0805-2*, Rothman) W S Hein.

Latin, Richard, jt. auth. see Berg, Kris.

Latin School of Physics Staff. Selected Topics in Physics: Astrophysics & Biophysics, Proceedings of the Latin School of Physics, 14th, Caracas, Venezuela, July 10-28, 1972. Abecassis De Laredo, E. & Jurisic, N. K., eds. LC 73-83563. 420p. 1973. text 211.50 (*90-277-0367-1*) Kluwer Academic.

***Latin Vulgate Staff.** Latin Vulgate Bible. (LAT.). 2000. 105.98 (*1-58516-085-7*) Am Bible.

Lating, J. M., jt. ed. see Everly, George S., Jr.

Latini, Brunetto. Brunetto Latini: The Book of the Treasure - Li Livres dou Treasure. Barrette, Paul & Baldwin, Spurgeon, trs. LC 92-21785. (Library of Medieval Literature: Series B, Vol. 90). 440p. 1992. text 20.00 (*0-8153-0763-2*) Garland.

— Libro del Tesoro: Version Castellana de Li Livres dou Tresor. Baldwin, Spurgeon, ed. & tr. by. (Spanish Ser.: No. 46). (SPA.). viii, 260p. 1989. 25.00 (*0-940639-31-9*) Hispanic Seminary.

Latini, MarySue P. At the Hearth: Early American Cooking. LC 95-77714. (Illus.). 176p. (Orig.). 1995. pap. 14.95 (*1-56167-215-7*) Am Literary Pr.

Latini, Roberto, jt. ed. see Tognoni, Gianni.

Latino, Frank. The Legend of Holly Boy. (Illus.). 38p. (J). (ps-12). 1993. 15.95 (*0-9640474-0-3*); pap. 7.95 (*0-9640474-1-1*) F Latino Pub Co.

Latinoamericana Editores, ed. see Castro-Urioste, Jose.

Latinopoulos, P., jt. ed. see Wrobel, L. C.

Latinus, Ioannes, et al. The First African Authors to Write in Latin, 3 wks. (B. E. Ser.: No. 1). 60.00 (*0-8115-2952-5*) Periodicals Srv.

Latiolais, P., et al, eds. Topology & Combinatorial Group Theory: Proceedings of the Fall Foliage Topology Seminars Held in New Hampshire, 1985-1988. (Lecture Notes in Mathematics Ser.: Vol. 1440). vi, 207p. 1990. 38.95 (*0-387-52990-X*) Spr-Verlag.

Latke, Vishnu. Nepal: Negendra Kr. Singh. 1997. pap. 54.00 (*0-7855-7451-4*, Pub. by Ratna Pustak Bhandar) St Mut.

Latkovich, V. J., ed. Proceedings of a Pressure Transducer-Packer Workshop. 48p. (Orig.). (C). 1994. pap. text 30.00 (*0-7881-0804-2*) DIANE Pub.

Latman, et al. Copyright of the 90s: 1990-1992 Cumulative Supplement. 386p. 1992. pap. text. write for info. (*0-87473-981-0*, 11984-10, MICHIE) LEXIS Pub.

Latman, Alan. Copyright of the 90s: Statistical Appendix. 1990. write for info. (*0-87473-505-X*, 11980-10, MICHIE) LEXIS Pub.

Latman, Alan & Lightstone, James F., eds. The Kaminstein Legislative History Project: A Compendium & Analytical Index of Materials Leading to the Copyright Act of 1976, 6 vols. (Illus.). 1985. text 625.00 (*0-8377-0732-3*, Rothman) W S Hein.

Latman, Alan, jt. auth. see Baumgarten, Jon A.

Latner, Connie J., ed. The 1900 Census of Carter County, Tennessee. vi, 304p. 1997. pap. 38.50 (*0-9659386-0-3*) C L Latner.

Latner, Helen. Everything Jewish Wedding Book. LC 97-43502. (Illus.). 304p. 1998. pap. 12.95 (*1-55850-801-5*) Adams Media.

Latner, Joel. The Gestalt Therapy Book. rev. ed. LC 73-82442. 240p. 1984. reprint ed. pap. 20.00 (*0-939266-04-0*) Gestalt Journal.

Latnie, Melvin D., Jr. School Bus Driver, the Inside Story. 112p. 1997. 16.95 (*0-9648599-0-4*) Mind Pwr.

Latombe, Jean-Claude. Robot Motion Planning. (International Series in Engineering & Computer Science, VLSI, Computer Architecture, & Digital Screen Processing). 672p. 1990. lib. bdg. 135.50 (*0-7923-9129-2*) Kluwer Academic.

— Robot Motion Planning. 672p. (C). 1991. pap. text 113.00 (*0-7923-9206-X*) Kluwer Academic.

***Latona, Jan & Stricklin, Gary J.** Love Is a Journey: Couples Facing Cancer. LC 99-66209. (Illus.). xv, 110p. 1999. pap. 14.95 (*0-9673715-0-3*) Greyrock.

Latona, John & Stirba, Dick. Tetherless Trucking: Mobile Data Opportunities in the Trucking Industry. LC 94-237735. xx, 327 p. 1994. write for info. (*1-56925-025-1*) Capitol VA.

Latona, Norey, jt. auth. see Young, Edwin M.

LaTorra, Michael. A Warrior Blends with Life: A Modern Tao. LC 93-12491. 170p. 1993. pap. 14.95 (*1-55643-160-0*) North Atlantic.

LaTorre. Calculator Enhanced Science/English Math. 5th ed. LC 93-85550. (C). 1994. pap. text 24.50 (*0-03-097000-8*) Harcourt Coll Pubs.

Latorre. Calculus Concepts. (C). 1997. pap. text 45.56 (*0-669-45205-X*) HM.

— Calculus Concepts Exam. (C). Date not set. text 50.76 (*0-669-45196-7*) HM.

LaTorre, D., et al. HP48G/GX Investigations in Mathematics. (Illus.). 700p. (Orig.). (C). 1996. pap. 29.95 (*1-886801-23-1*) Thomson Learn.

LaTorre, D. R. Calculus Concepts: An Informal Approach to the Mathematics of Change LC 97-72513. xxii, 468p. 1998. write for info. (*0-669-39859-4*) HM.

LaTorre, D. R., jt. auth. see Proctor, T.

Latorre, Dolores L. Cooking & Curing with Herbs in Mexico. (Illus.). 1977. 17.50 (*0-88426-051-8*) Encino Pr.

Latorre, Dolores L., ed. see McKellar, Margaret M.

LaTorre, Don, et al. Calculus Concepts: An Informal Approach, 1997 Preliminary Edition. (C). 1996. text, teacher ed. 20.76 (*0-669-39868-3*); pap. text 40.36 (*0-669-39865-9*) HM Trade Div.

LaTorre, Donald R. Calculus Investigations with the HP48G/GX. (Illus.). 206p. 1995. pap. 14.95 (*1-886801-18-5*) Thomson Learn.

— Linear Algebra with the HP-48G/GX. (Illus.). 226p. (C). 1995. pap. 15.95 (*1-886801-20-7*) Thomson Learn.

Latorre, Felipe. Mexican Kickapoo Indians. (Illus.). 416p. 1991. pap. 11.95 (*0-486-26742-3*) Dover.

Latorre, J. & Monreal, M., eds. Clinical Atlas of Vascular Disorders. 128p. 1988. 24.95 (*0-8151-5325-2*, CDA-1) Mosby Inc.

Latorre, Ramon, ed. Ionic Channels in Cells & Model Systems. LC 86-12265. (Centro de Estudios Cientificos de Santiago Ser.). (Illus.). 462p. (C). 1986. text 132.00 (*0-306-42194-1*, Kluwer Plenum) Kluwer Academic.

Latorre, Ramon & Saez, Juan C., eds. From Ion Channels to Cell to Cell Conversations. LC 97-13654. (Series of the Centro de Estudios Cientificos de Santiago). 532p. 1997. 135.00 (*0-306-45605-2*, Kluwer Plenum) Kluwer Academic.

Latorre, Robert, et al. Linear Simulation of Time Dependent Towing of Ocean Vehicles. LC VM0521.. (University of Michigan, Dept. of Naval Architecture & Marine Engineering, Report Ser.: No. 268). 82p. reprint ed. pap. 30.00 (*0-608-18656-2*, 202482500038) Bks Demand.

LaTouche, Bill, jt. auth. see Dropkin, Murray.

Latouche, C., jt. auth. see Jouanneau, J. M.

Latouche, Daniel, jt. auth. see Resnick, Philip.

Latouche, G. & Ramaswami, R. Introduction to Matrix Analytic Methods in Stochastic Modeling. LC 98-48647. (ASA-SIAM Series on Statistics & Applied Probability: Vol. 5). (Illus.). xix, 334p. 1999. pap. text 49.50 (*0-89871-425-7*, BKSA0005) Soc Indus-Appl Math.

Latouche, Serge. In the Wake of the Affluent Society: An Exploration of Post-Development. LC 93-13947. 224p. (C). 1993. text 65.00 (*1-85649-171-4*, Pub. by Zed Books) St Martin.

— The Westernization of the World: The Significance, Scope & Limits of the Drive Towards Global Uniformity. Morris, Rosemary, tr. from FRE. 160p. (C). 1996. text 52.95 (*0-7456-1428-0*, Pub. by Polity Pr); pap. text 27.95 (*0-7456-1429-9*, Pub. by Polity Pr) Blackwell Pubs.

Latour, Arsaene L., et al. Historical Memoir of the War in West Florida & Louisiana in 1814-15: With an Atlas. rev. ed. LC 98-44742. 1999. 49.95 (*0-8130-1675-4*) U Press Fla.

Latour, Bruno. Aramis, or the Love of Technology.Tr. of Aramis. (Illus.). 336p. 1996. 48.95 (*0-674-04322-7*) HUP.

— Aramis, or the Love of Technology. Porter, Catherine, tr. from FRE. LC 95-34920.Tr. of Aramis. (Illus.). 336p. 1996. pap. 19.95 (*0-674-04323-5*) HUP.

— Pandora's Hope: Essays on the Reality of Science Studies. LC 98-50061. 1999. 45.00 (*0-674-65335-1*); pap. 19.95 (*0-674-65336-X*) HUP.

— The Pasteurization of France. Sheridan, Alan & Law, John, trs. from FRE. LC 88-2670. (Illus.). 288p. 1988. 45.00 (*0-674-65760-8*) HUP.

— The Pasteurization of France. LC 88-2670. (Illus.). 288p. 1988. reprint ed. pap. 21.50 (*0-674-65761-6*) HUP.

— Science in Action: How to Follow Scientists & Engineers Through Society. (Illus.). 288p. 1987. reprint ed. pap. 18.95 (*0-674-79291-2*) HUP.

— We Have Never Been Modern. Porter, Catherine, tr. from FRE. LC 93-15226.Tr. of Nous N'Avons Jamais Ete Modernes. 168p. 1993. pap. 16.50 (*0-674-94839-4*) HUP.

— We Have Never Been Modern. Porter, Catherine, tr. from FRE. LC 93-15226.Tr. of Nous N'Avons Jamais Ete Modernes. 167p. 1993. 37.95 (*0-674-94838-6*) HUP.

Latour, Bruno & Woolgar, Steve. Laboratory Life: The Construction of Scientific Facts. LC 85-43378. 296p. 1986. pap. text 18.95 (*0-691-02832-X*, Pub. by Princeton U Pr) Cal Prin Full Svc.

Latour, C., jt. auth. see Nahas, Gabriel G.

Latour, Colette, ed. see Nahas, Gabriel G.

***Latour, Jose.** Outcast. LC 99-70482. 220p. 1999. pap. 13.95 (*1-888451-07-6*, AKB04, Pub. by Akashic Bks) SPD-Small Pr Dist.

LaTour, Kathy. Breast Cancer Compan Co. 512p. 1994. reprint ed. pap. 15.00 (*0-380-71996-7*, Avon Bks) Morrow Avon.

***LaTour, Pierre & Anges, Aux.** Up in Heaven. 272p. 2000. mass mkt. 7.95 (*1-56201-153-7*, Pub. by Blue Moon Bks) Publishers Group.

LaTour, Pierre, jt. auth. see LaTour, Susan.

LaTour, Susan & LaTour, Pierre. Dead Reckoning. 352p. 1995. text 21.95 (*0-312-13958-6*) St Martin.

***Latourelle, Rene.** Dictionary of Fundamental Theology. 2000. pap. 49.95 (*0-8245-1834-9*, Pub. by Crossroad NY) Natl Bk Netwk.

Latourelle, Rene. Dictionnaire de la Theologie Fondamentale. (FRE.). 1993. pap. 195.00 (*0-7859-3020-5*) Fr & Eur.

— The Miracle of Jesus & the Theology of Miracles. 1988. pap. 14.95 (*0-8091-2997-3*) Paulist Pr.

— Theology of Revelation. LC 65-15734. 1966. pap. 17.95 (*0-8189-0401-1*) Alba.

Latourelle, Rene, ed. Vatican II: Assessment & Prespectives, Twenty-Five Years After (1962-1987), Vol. III. 1988. 25.00 (*0-8091-0414-8*) Paulist Pr.

Latourelle, Rene & Fisichella, Rino. The Dictionary of Fundamental Theology. 1264p. 1994. 175.00 (*0-85439-395-1*, Pub. by St Paul Pubns) St Mut.

Latourette, Jane. Daniel in the Lions' Den: Daniel 6. (Arch Bks.). (Illus.). 24p. (J). (gr. k-4). 1970. pap. 1.99 (*0-570-06018-4*, 59-1127) Concordia.

— Story of Noah's Ark: Genesis 6: 5-9: 17. (Arch Bks.). (J). (ps-3). 1993. pap. 1.99 (*0-570-06009-5*, 59-1110) Concordia.

Latourette, Jane & Wind, Betty. Jon & the Little Lost Lamb: Luke 15:1-7. LC 65-15145. (Arch Bks.: Set 2). (Illus.). 24p. 1970. pap. 1.99 (*0-570-06008-7*, 59-1106) Concordia.

Latourette, Kenneth S. Historia del Cristianismo: A History of the Expansion of Christ, Tomo I. Quarles, Jaime C. & Quarles, Lemuel C., trs. from ENG. (Illus.). 819p. 1960. reprint ed. pap. 35.99 (*0-311-15010-1*) Casa Bautista.

— Historia del Cristianismo: A History of the Expansion of Christ, Tomo II. Quarles, Jaime C. & Quarles, Lemuel C., trs. (Desde el Siglo XVI Hasta el Siglo XX). 968p. 1966. reprint ed. pap. 35.99 (*0-311-15012-8*) Casa Bautista.

— A History of Christianity. rev. ed. Incl. Vol. 1. History of Christianity: Volume I, A: Beginnings to 1500:Revised Edition. rev. ed. LC 74-25692. 768p. 1975. pap. 24.00 (*0-06-064952-6*, RD-93, Pub. by Harper SF); Vol. 2. History of Christianity: Volume II, A: Reformation to the Present:Revised Edition. LC 74-25692. 928p. 1975. pap. 24.00 (*0-06-064953-4*, RD-94, Pub. by Harper SF); LC 74-25692. 1975. pap. write for info. (*0-318-52923-8*) Harper SF.

— The History of Early Relations Between the United States & China, 1784-1844. (Connecticut Academy of Arts & Sciences Ser., Trans.: Vol. 22). 1917. pap. 75.00 (*0-685-44362-0*) Elliots Bks.

— Voyages of American Ships to China, 1784-1844. (Connecticut Academy of Arts & Sciences Ser., Trans.: Vol. 28). 1927. pap. 49.50 (*0-685-22810-X*) Elliots Bks.

Latourette, Kenneth S., ed. Gospel, the Church & the World. LC 76-134107. (Essay Index Reprint Ser.). 1977. 20.95 (*0-8369-1972-6*) Ayer.

Latousek, Rob. Software Directory for the Classics. 95p. 1993. spiral bd. 10.00 (*0-939507-45-5*, W900) Amer Classical.

Latov, N., et al, eds. Immunological & Infectious Diseases of the Peripheral Nerves. (Illus.). 454p. (C). 1998. text 145.00 (*0-521-46265-7*) Cambridge U Pr.

Latow, Roberta. Acts of Love. 400p. (Orig.). 1995. mass mkt. 5.50 (*0-380-77415-1*, Avon Bks) Morrow Avon.

— Hungry Heart. 416p. (Orig.). 1994. mass mkt. 5.50 (*0-380-77414-3*, Avon Bks) Morrow Avon.

— The Pleasure Seekers. 320p. 1997. pap. 11.95 (*0-7472-5305-6*, Pub. by Headline Bk Pub) Trafalgar.

Latreille, Stan. Perjury. LC 97-40653. 352p. 1998. 24.00 (*0-609-60138-5*) Crown Pub Group.

— Perjury. 1999. reprint ed. mass mkt. 6.99 (*0-451-19687-2*, Onyx) NAL.

LaTrenta, Gregory S., jt. auth. see Rees, Thomas D.

Latrobe, Benjamin. The Virginia Journals of Benjamin Henry Latrobe, 1795-1798. Carter, Edward C., ed. LC 77-76301. (Illus.). 1977. 130.00 (*0-300-02198-4*) Yale U Pr.

Latrobe, Benjamin H. The Correspondence & Miscellaneous Papers of Benjamin Henry Latrobe. Van Horne, John C. & Formwalt, Lee W., eds. LC 83-27423. (Series No. IV: Vol. I). (Illus.). 640p. 1985. 85.00 (*0-300-02901-2*) Yale U Pr.

— The Correspondence & Miscellaneous Papers of Benjamin Henry Latrobe, Vol. 3. LC 83-27423. 1024p. (C). 1988. 145.00 (*0-300-03521-7*) Yale U Pr.

— The Engineering Drawings of Benjamin Henry Latrobe, Vol. 1. LC 78-15405. (Series II: Vol. 1). 256p. 1980. 115.00 (*0-300-02227-1*) Yale U Pr.

Latrobe, Benjamin H. Latrobe's View of America, 1795-1820: Selections from the Watercolors & Sketches. Carter, Edward C. et al, eds. LC 84-7580. (Papers of Benjamin Henry Latrobe: No. 3). (Illus.). 420p. 1985. 55.00 (*0-300-02949-7*) Yale U Pr.

Latrobe, Benjamin H., et al, eds. The Journals of Benjamin Henry Latrobe, 1799-1820: From Philadelphia to New Orleans. LC 79-19001. (Papers of Benjamin Henry Latrobe: Vol. 3). (Illus.). 432p. 1981. 95.00 (*0-300-02383-9*) Yale U Pr.

Latrobe, Benjamin H. & Van Horne, John C. The Correspondence & Miscellaneous Papers of Benjamin Henry Latrobe: 1805-1810, Ser. IV, Vol. II. Formwalt, Lee W. et al, eds. LC 83-27423. (Papers of Benjamin Henry Latrobe). 1018p. 1986. 100.00 (*0-300-03229-3*) Yale U Pr.

Latrobe, Kathy H., ed. The Emerging School Library Media Center: Historic Issues & Perspectives. LC 98-43715. 320p. 1998. 42.00 (*1-56308-389-2*) Teacher Ideas Pr.

— Exploring the Great Lakes States Through Literature. LC 93-2486. (Exploring the United States Through Literature Ser.). 168p. 1993. pap. 27.50 (*0-89774-731-3*) Oryx Pr.

Latrobe, Kathy H. & Laughlin, Mildred K. Multicultural Aspects of Library Media Programs. 217p. 1992. 27.50 (*0-87287-879-1*) Libs Unl.

— Readers Theatre for Young Adults: Scripts & Script Development. xi, 130p. 1989. pap. text 20.00 (*0-87287-743-4*) Teacher Ideas Pr.

Latrobe, Kathy H., jt. auth. see Laughlin, Mildred K.

Latruffe, N. & Bugaut, M., eds. Peroxisomes. 210p. 1994. student ed. 107.95 (*0-387-56860-3*) Spr-Verlag.

Latsha, Christiana B. Good. The Adam Good Family History. (Illus.). 150p. 1997. reprint ed. pap. 23.50 (*0-8328-8767-6*); reprint ed. lib. bdg. 33.50 (*0-8328-8766-8*) Higginson Bk Co.

***Latshaw, George.** The Complete Book of Puppetry. LC 99-89991. (Illus.). 160p. (YA). (gr. 6). 2000. pap. 8.95 (*0-486-40952-X*) Dover.

Latson, W. R. Secrets of Mental Supremacy. 138p. 1996. reprint ed. spiral bd. 14.00 (*0-7873-1047-6*) Hlth Research.

— Secrets of Mental Supremacy: How to Cultivate Mind, Memory, Perspective, Imagination & Ideas. 1991. lib. bdg. 75.00 (*0-8490-4185-6*) Gordon Pr.

— Secrets of Mental Supremacy (1913) 138p. 1996. reprint ed. pap. 13.95 (*1-56459-864-0*) Kessinger Pub.

Latt, A. English Commercial Correspondence: Correspondencia Commercial Inglesa. (ENG & SPA.). 399p. 1985. 19.95 (*0-8288-1547-X*, S14171) Fr & Eur.

Latt, David J. & Monk, Samuel H. John Dryden: A Survey & Bibliography of Critical Studies, 1895-1974. LC 75-36033. 215p. reprint ed. pap. 66.70 (*0-8357-8928-4*, 203326700085) Bks Demand.

Latt, Mimi. Powers of Attorney. Rubenstein, Julie, ed. 544p. 1994. reprint ed. per. 5.99 (*0-671-86916-7*) PB.

— Pursuit of Justice. 1999. per. 6.99 (*0-671-03411-1*, Pocket Star Bks) PB.

— Pursuit of Justice. LC 97-29855. 384p. 1998. 22.50 (*0-684-81184-7*) S&S Trade.

— Pursuit of Justice. LC 98-47823. (Large Print Bks). 1998. 23.95 (*1-56895-589-8*) Wheeler Pub.

***Latt, Mimi.** Ultimate Justice. 2000. mass mkt. 7.99 (*0-671-01461-7*, Pocket Star Bks) PB.

— Ultimate Justice: A Novel. LC 99-22206. 384p. 1999. 24.00 (*0-684-84382-X*) Simon & Schuster.

***Latt Wiatt, Carrie.** Eating by Design: The Individualized Food Personality Type Nutrition Plan. 436p. 2000. reprint ed. text 23.00 (*0-7881-6869-X*) DIANE Pub.

Latta, Ann, jt. auth. see Turner, Carol.

Latta, Estelle. Controversial Mark Hopkins. 2nd rev. ed. (Illus.). 254p. 1963. 10.00 (*0-910740-23-2*) Holmes.

***Latta, Frank F.** Handbook of Yokuts Indians: 50th Anniversary Edition. 2nd ed. (Illus.). 800p. 1999. reprint ed. 75.00 (*1-892622-09-2*) Brewers Hist.

Latta, Gordon, jt. auth. see Polya, Geroge.

Latta, Jim. Around the Drums with Syncopation. (Progressive Ser.). (Illus.). 1997. pap. text 14.95 (*0-947183-69-8*) Koala Pubns.

— Rock, Jazz, & Funk Drumming. 1997. pap. 16.95 (*0-947183-18-3*) Koala Pubns.

Latta, John. Rubbing Torsos. LC 79-465. 93p. 1979. 4.50 (*0-87886-101-7*, Greenfld Rev Pr) Greenfld Rev Lit.

Latta, Loren L., jt. auth. see Sarmiento, Augusto.

Latta, Raymond F. & Downey, Carolyn J. Tools for Achieving TQE. LC 94-9174. (Total Quality Education for the World's Best Schools Ser.: Vol. 10). 160p. 1994. pap. 22.95 (*0-8039-6178-2*) Corwin Pr.

Latta, Rich. The Old Train. (Books for Young Learners). (Illus.). 12p. (J). (gr. k-2). 1998. pap. text 5.00 (*1-57274-133-3*, A2487) R Owen Pubs.

— El Viejo Tren. Romo, Alberto, tr. (Books for Young Learners).Tr. of Old Train. (SPA., Illus.). 12p. (J). (gr. k-2). 1999. pap. text 5.00 (*1-57274-295-X*) R Owen Pubs.

Latta, Richard. Drawbridge. (Books for Young Learners). (Illus.). 8p. (J). (gr. k-2). 1997. pap. text 5.00 (*1-57274-082-5*, A2140) R Owen Pubs.

— Games for Travel. (Illus.). 48p. (J). (gr. 2 up). 1976. pap. 2.95 (*0-8431-0406-6*, Price Stern) Peng Put Young Read.

Latta, Robert. The Basic Humor Process: A Cognitive-Shift Theory & the Case Against Incongruity. LC 98-30868. (Humor Research Ser.). 257p. 1998. 114.85 (*3-11-016103-6*) De Gruyter.

Latta, Sara L. Allergies. LC 97-34156. (Diseases & People Ser.). (Illus.). 128p. (YA). (gr. 6 up). 1998. lib. bdg. 20.95 (*0-7660-1048-1*) Enslow Pubs.

— Food Poisoning & Foodborne Diseases. LC 98-36134. (Diseases & People Ser.). 128p. (YA). (gr. 6 up). 1999. lib. bdg. 20.95 (*0-7660-1183-6*) Enslow Pubs.

Latta, Virginia G., et al. Principles of Biology: Laboratory Investigations. 3rd ed. 218p. 1991. pap. text, teacher ed. 26.95 (*0-88725-150-1*) Hunter Textbks.

Lattacher, Siegbert, jt. auth. see Kronberger, Hans.

Lattal, Alice D., jt. auth. see Clark, Ralph W.

Lattal, K. A. & Perone, M. Handbook of Research Methods in Human Operant Behavior. LC 98-28963. (Applied Clinical Psychology Ser.). (Illus.). 654p. (C). 1998. 115.00 (*0-306-45668-0*, Plenum Trade) Perseus Pubng.

Lattal, K. A., jt. auth. see Iversen, I. H.

***Lattany, Kristin Hunter.** Do unto Others. LC 99-42406. 272p. 2000. 24.00 (*0-345-40708-3*) Ballantine Pub Grp.

— Do unto Others. 2000. pap. 14.00 (*0-345-43837-X*) Ballantine Pub Grp.

Lattany, Kristin Hunter. Kinfolks. LC 96-24557. 320p. 1996. 23.00 (*0-345-40706-7*) Ballantine Pub Grp.

— Kinfolks. 288p. 1997. pap. 10.95 (*0-345-41720-8*) Ballantine Pub Grp.

***Lattany, Kristin Hunter.** Kinfolks. 2000. mass mkt. 6.99 (*0-345-43805-1*) One Wrld.

Lattanzi-Licht, Marcia, et al. The Hospice Choice: In Pursuit of a Peaceful Death. LC 97-36948. 288p. 1998. per. 12.00 (*0-684-82269-5*, Fireside) S&S Trade Pap.

Lattas, Andrew. Cultures of Secrecy: Reinventing Race in Bush Kaliai Cargo Cults. LC 97-44008. (New Directions in Anthropological Writing Ser.). (Illus.). 320p. (Orig.). 1998. text 59.95 (*0-299-15800-4*); pap. text 24.95 (*0-299-15804-7*) U of Wis Pr.

Lattaye, Tim. How to Study the Bible for Yourself. expanded rev. ed. LC 97-29028. 200p. 1998. pap. 9.99 (*1-56507-631-1*) Harvest Hse.

Latte, K. & Erbse, H. Lexica Graeca Minora. xvii, 372p. 1965. write for info. (*0-318-72039-6*) G Olms Pubs.

Lattea, Karen, ed. see Myers, Ched, et al.

Latteier, Carolyn. Breasts: The Women's Perspective on an American Obsession. LC 98-9556. 200p. 1998. 49.95 (*0-7890-0422-4*, Harrington Park); pap. 14.95 (*1-56023-927-1*, Harrington Park) Haworth Pr.

Latter, Bill. Blacklegs: The 1911 Strike at the Scottish Colliery. LC 96-145699. (Staples South West Region Publications). 1995. pap. 16.95 (*1-875560-52-1*, Pub. by Staples) Intl Spec Bk.

Latter, J. H., ed. Volcanic Hazards: Assessment & Monitoring. (IAVECI Proceedings in Volcanology Ser.: Vol. 1). (Illus.). 625p. 1989. 162.95 (*0-387-19337-5*) Spr-Verlag.

Latter, Richard & Wilton Park (Conference Center). Russia, Its Neighbours & the Future of European Security. LC 96-138042. 29 p. 1995. 11.00 (*0-11-701892-9*, Pub. by Statnry Office) Bernan Associates.

Latter, Thomas. Grammar of the Language of Burma. (BUR & ENG.). 260p. 1991. 59.95 (*0-8288-8456-0*) Fr & Eur.

Latter, William B., ed. see International Astronomical Union Staff.

Latterman, Harry. Celebration of Life: Your Guide Book To Prosperity. Hawkins, Mary E., ed. LC 85-62792. (Illus.). 136p. 1986. pap. 8.95 (*0-934739-02-1*) Pussywillow Pub.

Latterman, Terry. Little Joe, a Hopi Indian Boy, Learns a Hopi Indian Secret. Hawkins, Mary E., ed. LC 85-61836. (Illus.). 32p. (J). (gr. 4-12). 1985. 12.95 (*0-934739-01-3*) Pussywillow Pub.

— The Watermelon Treat. Hawkins, Mary E., ed. LC 85-63266. (Illus.). 48p. (J). (gr. 1-4). 1987. 8.95 (*0-934739-03-X*); pap. 5.95 (*0-934739-04-8*) Pussywillow Pub.

Latterman, Terry, jt. auth. see Perez, Maya.

Lattey, Cuthbert, jt. auth. see Ozanam, Frederic.

Lattiboudeaine, Michael, ed. see Luster, Ivon.

Lattiboudeaire, Israel & Lattiboudeaire, Michael. People (Community) that Listens: The Listening Ears. LC 98-91105. (Illus.). 30p. (YA). (gr. 3 up). 1999. 14.95 (*1-889448-57-5*) NBN Publishers Group.

Lattiboudeaire, Michael. Entertainment Bible: Biblical Truths for Entertainers. LC 98-91108. 1999. write for info. (*1-889448-55-9*) NBN Publishers Group.

— The Evening after the Dawn. LC 98-91104. 250p. 1999. pap. 19.95 (*1-889448-56-7*) NBN Publishers Group.

— Jubilante: The Joys of Intercession. LC 98-91113. 100p. 1999. pap. 12.95 (*1-889448-12-5*) NBN Publishers Group.

— Maturation of the Prophetic Life. LC 98-91111. 100p. 1999. pap. 14.95 (*1-889448-51-6*) NBN Publishers Group.

— Prophetic Life: Powerful Truths for Powerful Leadership. LC 96-72018. 400p. 1998. 19.95 (*1-889448-08-7*); pap. 14.95 (*1-889448-05-2*); pap. 6.99 (*1-889448-04-4*); pap. 6.99 (*1-889448-09-5*); pap., wbk. ed. 15.95 (*1-889448-06-0*); lib. bdg. 19.95 (*1-889448-07-9*); lib. bdg. 19.95 (*1-889448-11-7*); mass mkt. 14.95 (*1-889448-10-9*) NBN Publishers Group.

— The Prophetic Life: Powerful Truths for Powerful Leadership. 14 vols., No. 1. LC 96-72018. 400p. 1998. 19.95 (*1-889448-03-6*) NBN Publishers Group.

***Lattiboudeaire, Michael.** Standard & Poor: Show Me the Money. LC 98-91109. 200p. 1998. pap. 85.00 incl. audio (*1-889448-19-2*) NBN Publishers Group.

Lattiboudeaire, Michael, jt. auth. see Lattiboudeaire, Israel.

Lattime, Edmund C. & Gerson, Stanton L., eds. Gene Therapy of Cancer: Translational Approaches from Preclinical Studies to Clinical Implementation. LC 98-85115. (Illus.). 406p. (C). 1998. boxed set 119.95 (*0-12-437190-6*) Acad Pr.

Lattimer, C., et al. Key Topics in General Surgery. (Key Topics Ser.). 304p. (Orig.). 1996. pap. 39.95 (*1-872748-02-3*, Pub. by Bios Sci) Bks Intl VA.

Lattimer, John K. Hitler & Nazi Leaders: Eyewitness Account at the Nuremburg Trials. (Illus.). 400p. 1999. 35.00 (*0-7818-0742-5*) Hippocrene Bks.

Lattimer, Pamela. A Family of Ginger Griffins. 112p. (C). 1988. 35.00 (*0-7212-0787-1*, Pub. by Regency Pr GBR) St Mut.

Lattimer, Robert P., jt. auth. see Montaudo, Giorgio.

Lattimore. Female Indiana Homes, No. 3. lib. bdg. 14.89 (*0-06-026208-7*) HarpC Child Bks.

— Female Indiana Jones, No. 2. lib. bdg. 14.89 (*0-06-026206-0*) HarpC Child Bks.

Lattimore. Female Indiana Jones: Book 1, No. 1. (Illus.). lib. bdg. 14.89 (*0-06-026204-4*) HarpC.

— I Wonder What's Under. LC 96-80504. (Illus.). 24p. (C). 1998. 15.95 (*0-15-276652-9*) Harcourt.

— Mystery at Midnight Museum. 32p. (J). lib. bdg. 14.89 (*0-06-026202-8*) HarpC Child Bks.

***Lattimore, Arthurine.** From Prison to the Palace: Walking with the Master. 32p. 1999. mass mkt. 3.00 (*0-927936-22-4*) Vincom Pubng Co.

Lattimore, Dan & Terry, Art. Desktop Study Guide. (Illus.). 208p. (C). 1990. pap. text 21.95 (*0-89582-209-1*) Morton Pub.

Lattimore, Dan & Windhauser, John. The Editorial Process. 2nd ed. 320p. (C). 1984. student ed. 21.95 (*0-89582-115-X*) Morton Pub.

Lattimore, David, tr. The Harmony of the World: Chinese Poems. enl. rev. ed. 1980. pap. 8.00 (*0-914278-31-2*) Copper Beech.

Lattimore, Deborah. Digging into the Past. (BrainBooster Ser.). (Illus.). 32p. (J). (gr. 3 up). 1986. 6.95 (*0-88679-460-9*) Educ Insights.

Lattimore, Deborah N. Cinderhazel. LC 95-13089. (Illus.). 32p. (J). (gr. 1-4). 1997. 15.95 (*0-590-20232-4*) Scholastic Inc.

— Dragons Robe. LC 89-34512. (Illus.). 32p. (J). (gr. 1-5). 1990. 15.00 (*0-06-023719-8*) HarpC Child Bks.

— The Flame of Peace: A Tale of the Aztecs. LC 86-26934. (Illus.). 48p. (J). (gr. k-3). 1987. lib. bdg. 14.89 (*0-06-023709-0*) HarpC Child Bks.

— The Flame of Peace: A Tale of the Aztecs. LC 86-26934. (Trophy Picture Bk.). (Illus.). 48p. (J). (ps-3). 1991. pap. 7.95 (*0-06-443272-6*, HarpTrophy) HarpC Child Bks.

— The Flame of Peace: A Tale of the Aztecs. (J). 1991. 11.15 (*0-606-01094-7*, Pub. by Turtleback) Demco.

— The Fool & the Phoenix: A Tale of Old Japan. LC 96-27329. (Joanna Cotler Bks.). (Illus.). 40p. (J). (gr. 1 up). 1997. 14.95 (*0-06-026209-5*) HarpC Child Bks.

— The Fool & the Phoenix: A Tale of Old Japan. LC 96-27329. (Joanna Cotler Bks.). (Illus.). 40p. (J). (gr. 1-6). 1997. lib. bdg. 14.89 (*0-06-026211-7*) HarpC Child Bks.

— Lady with the Ship on Her Head. LC 89-11218. (Illus.). 32p. (J). (ps-3). 1990. 14.95 (*0-15-243525-5*) Harcourt.

— Lady with the Ship on Her Head. LC 89-11218. (Illus.). 32p. (J). (ps-3). 1992. pap. 6.00 (*0-15-243526-3*) Harcourt.

— Punga: The Goddess of Ugly. LC 92-23191. (Illus.). 32p. (J). (ps-3). 1993. 14.95 (*0-15-292862-6*) Harcourt.

— The Winged Cat. LC 90-38441. (Trophy Picture Bk.). (Illus.). 80p. (J). (gr. 4-7). 1995. pap. 6.95 (*0-06-443424-9*, HarpTrophy) HarpC Child Bks.

— The Winged Cat: A Tale of Ancient Egypt. LC 90-38441. (Illus.). 40p. (J). (gr. 2-5). 1992. 15.00 (*0-06-023635-3*) HarpC Child Bks.

Lattimore, Deborah N. Arabian Nights: Three Tales. LC 94-9828. (Joanna Cotler Bks.). 64p. (J). (gr. k up). 1995. 16.95 (*0-06-024585-9*) HarpC Child Bks.

— Arabian Nights: Three Tales. LC 94-9828. (Joanna Cotler Bks.). 64p. (J). (gr. k up). 1995. lib. bdg. 16.89 (*0-06-024734-7*) HarpC Child Bks.

***Lattimore, Deborah Nourse.** Arabian Nights: Three Tales. LC 00-23959. (Chapter Bks.). 80p. (J). 2000. mass mkt. 4.25 (*0-06-442136-8*, HarpTrophy) HarpC Child Bks.

Lattimore, Deborah Nourse. Frida Maria: A Story of the Old Southwest. LC 93-17250. (Illus.). 32p. (J). (gr. k-3). 1997. pap. 6.00 (*0-15-201515-9*) Harcourt.

— Frida Maria: A Story of the Old Southwest. (J). 1997. 11.20 (*0-606-11354-1*, Pub. by Turtleback) Demco.

— Frida Maria: A Story of the Old Southwest. abr. ed. LC 93-17250. (Illus.). 28p. (J). (ps-3). 1994. 14.95 (*0-15-276636-7*, Harcourt Child Bks) Harcourt.

— Frida Maria: Un Cuento del Sudoeste de Antes. LC 96-18602. (SPA., Illus.). 32p. (J). (gr. k-3). 1997. pap. 6.00 (*0-15-201487-X*, Voyager Bks) Harcourt.

— Frida Maria: Un Cuento del Sudoeste de Antes. (J). 1997. 11.20 (*0-606-11355-X*, Pub. by Turtleback) Demco.

***Lattimore, Deborah Nourse.** I Wonder What's under There? A Brief History of Underwear: A Lift-the-Flap Book. (Illus.). 21p. (YA). (gr. 7-9). 2000. reprint ed. text 16.00 (*0-7881-9080-6*) DIANE Pub.

Lattimore, Deborah Nourse. The Lady with the Ship on Her Head. (Reading Rainbow Bks.). 1990. 11.20 (*0-606-01029-7*, Pub. by Turtleback) Demco.

— Medusa. LC 99-29244. (Illus.). 32p. (J). (gr. 2-5). 2000. 15.95 (*0-06-027904-4*); lib. bdg. 15.89 (*0-06-027905-2*) HarpC Child Bks.

— The Winged Cat a Tale of Ancient Egypt. (J). 1992. 11.15 (*0-606-08434-7*, Pub. by Turtleback) Demco.

Lattimore, Eleanor F. Little Pear. D'Andrade, Diane, ed. LC 90-45526. (Odyssey Ser.). (Illus.). 144p. (J). (gr. 2-5). 1991. pap. 6.00 (*0-15-246685-1*, Harcourt Child Bks) Harcourt.

— Little Pear. (Illus.). (J). 1992. reprint ed. lib. bdg. 14.95 (*0-89966-917-4*) Buccaneer Bks.

— Little Pear. LC 31-22069. (Illus.). (J). (gr. 2-5). 1968. reprint ed. pap. 3.95 (*0-15-652799-5*, Voyager Bks) Harcourt.

— Little Pear & His Friends. LC 90-45519. (Odyssey Ser.). (Illus.). 144p. (J). (gr. 3-7). 1991. pap. 4.95 (*0-15-246863-3*, Harcourt Child Bks) Harcourt.

Lattimore, Eleanor H. Turkestan Reunion. LC 72-4440. reprint ed. 37.50 (*0-404-10636-6*) AMS Pr.

— Turkestan Reunion. LC 94-40023. (Illus.). 329p. 1994. reprint ed. pap. 14.00 (*1-56836-053-3*, Kodansha Globe) Kodansha.

Lattimore, Eleanor H., jt. auth. see Lattimore, Owen.

Lattimore, Owen. China Memoirs. 1991. text 34.50 (*0-86008-468-X*, Pub. by U of Tokyo) Col U Pr.

— Desert Road to Turkestan. LC 70-112348. (Illus.). reprint ed. 35.00 (*0-404-03887-5*) AMS Pr.

— Gold Tribe Fishskin Tatars of the Lower Sungari. LC 34-3704. (American Anthropological Association Memoirs Ser.: No. 40). 1933. 25.00 (*0-527-00539-8*) Periodicals Srv.

— High Tartary. LC 72-4433. reprint ed. 37.50 (*0-404-10630-7*) AMS Pr.

— High Tartary. 384p. 1994. reprint ed. pap. 15.00 (*1-56836-054-1*) Kodansha.
— Inner Asian Frontiers of China. (Illus.). 610p. 1989. reprint ed. text 35.00 (*0-19-582781-3*) OUP.
— Manchuria: Cradle of Conflict. rev. ed. LC 72-4435. reprint ed. 37.50 (*0-404-10632-3*) AMS Pr.
— Mongol Journeys. LC 72-4436. reprint ed. 32.50 (*0-404-10633-1*) AMS Pr.
— Pivot of Asia. LC 72-4438. reprint ed. 32.50 (*0-404-10634-X*) AMS Pr.
— Solution in Asia. LC 72-4439. reprint ed. 31.50 (*0-404-10635-8*) AMS Pr.
Lattimore, Owen & Lattimore, Eleanor H. China: A Short History. LC 75-7663. reprint ed. 32.50 (*0-404-10646-3*) AMS Pr.
Lattimore, Pamela K. Homicide in Eight U. S. Cities: Trends, Context & Policy Implications. (Illus.). 143p. (C). 1999. pap. text 30.00 (*0-7881-7831-8*) DIANE Pub.
Lattimore, Pamela K. & Nahabedian, Cynthia A., eds. The Nature of Homicide: Trends & Changes - Proceedings of the 1996 Meeting of the Homicide Research Working Group. (Illus.). 261p. (C). 1999. pap. text 50.00 (*0-7881-7323-5*) DIANE Pub.
Lattimore, Ralston B. Fort Pulaski: National Monument, Georgia. (National Park Service Handbook Ser.: No. 18). (Illus.). 55p. 1985. reprint ed. pap. 4.00 (*0-16-003475-2*, S/N 024-005-00890-0) USGPO.
Lattimore, Richard. Poems from 3 Decades. LC 80-39709. xiv, 288p. 1999. pap. text 17.00 (*0-226-46946-8*) U Ch Pr.
Lattimore, Richard, ed. see Aeschylus.
Lattimore, Richmond. The New Testament. 608p. 1997. pap. text 16.00 (*0-86547-524-5*) N Point Pr.
— The Odyssey of Homer. (Perennial Classics Ser.). 384p. 1999. pap. 13.00 (*0-06-093195-7*) HarpC.
Lattimore, Richmond, tr. Alcestis. LC 55-5787. write for info. U Ch Pr.
— Greek Lyrics. rev. ed. LC 60-51619. 99p. (Orig.). 1960. pap. 6.95 (*0-226-46944-1*, P48) U Ch Pr.
— Helen. LC 56-6639. 8.95 U Ch Pr.
— The New Testament: King James Version. 592p. 1996. 35.00 (*0-86547-499-0*) N Point Pr.
— Rhesus. LC 55-5787. 1968. write for info. U Ch Pr.
— The Trojan Women. LC 55-5787. write for info. U Ch Pr.
— The Works & Days: Theogony & the Shield of Herakles, 2 vols. (Illus.). 256p. 1991. pap. text 13.95 (*0-472-08161-6*, 08161) U of Mich Pr.
Lattimore, Richmond, ed. see Euripides.
Lattimore, Richmond, jt. ed. see Grene, David.
Lattimore, Richmond, ed. see Sophocles.
Lattimore, Richmond, tr. see Homer.
Lattimore, Richmond, tr. see Pindar, Peter.
Lattimore, Richmond, tr. & intro. see Aeschylus.
Lattimore, Richmond A. Continuing Conclusions: New Poems & Translations. fac. ed. LC 83-727. 71p. 1983. reprint ed. pap. 30.00 (*0-7837-7743-4*, 204749900009) Bks Demand.
Lattimore, Steve. Circumnavigation. 224p. 1998. pap. 12.00 (*0-395-92621-1*) HM.
Lattimore, Steven. Sculpture II: Marble Sculpture, 1967-1980. (Isthmia Ser.: No. 6). xviii, 64p. 1996. 55.00 (*0-87661-936-7*) Am Sch Athens.
Lattimore, Steven, tr. & intro. see Thucydides.
Lattin. Corporations. 2nd ed. 1971. text 28.00 (*0-88277-411-5*) Foundation Pr.
Lattin & Green, Paul E. Analyzing Multivariate Data. (Career Planning Guide Ser.). 2000. pap. 80.95 (*0-534-34974-9*) Brooks-Cole.
Lattin, A. W. & Petersson, C., eds. Rheumatoid Arthritis Surgery of the Shoulder. (Rheumatology, the Interdisciplinary Concept Ser.: Vol. 12). (Illus.). xiv, 138p. 1989. 121.75 (*3-8055-4804-4*) S Karger.
Lattin, Don, jt. auth. see Cimino, Richard.
Lattin, Gerald W., et al. Introduction to the Hospitality Industry. 4th rev. ed. LC 99-231118. (Illus.). 395p. (C). 1998. pap. write for info. (*0-86612-170-6*) Educ Inst Am Hotel.
— The Lodging & Food Service Industry. 4th rev. ed. LC 98-6590. (Illus.). 395p. (C). 1998. pap. 60.95 (*0-86612-169-2*) Educ Inst Am Hotel.
Lattin, Vernon E., ed. Contemporary Chicano Fiction: A Critical Survey. LC 85-71528. (Studies in the Language & Literature of United States Hispanos). (ENG & SPA.). 336p. (C). 1986. pap. text 20.00 (*0-916950-57-3*); lib. bdg. 30.00 (*0-916950-56-5*) Biling Rev-Pr.
Lattin, Vernon E., et al, eds. Tomas Rivera, 1935-1984: The Man & His Work. LC 88-71440. (Illus.). xviii, 158p. 1988. pap. 20.00 (*0-916950-89-1*) Biling Rev-Pr.
Lattion, Emmanuelle. Goldilocks & the Three Bears. (Little Puppet Theaters Ser.). 1998. 19.95 (*1-57178-076-9*) Coun Oak Bks.
Lattis, James M. Between Copernicus & Galileo: Christoph Clavius & the Collapse of Ptolemaic Cosmology. LC 94-8675. 314p. 1994. pap. text 22.50 incl. 5.25 hd (*0-226-46929-8*); lib. bdg. 54.00 (*0-226-46927-1*) U Ch Pr.
Lattke, M. Die Oden Salomos in Ihrer Bedeutung fur Neues Testament und Ginosis: Forschungsgeschichtliche Bibliographie 1799-1984 mit Krit-Ischen Anmerkungen - Mit Einem Beitrag von Majella Franzmann - A Study of the Odes of Solomon with Reference to the French Scholarship 1909-1980. (Orbis Biblicus et Orientalis Ser.). (GER.). 1986. text 96.75 (*3-7278-0358-4*, Pub. by Presses Univ Fribourg) Eisenbrauns.
— Die Oden Salomos in Ihrer Bedeutung fur Neues Testament und Ginosis: Vollstandige Wortkonkordanz zur Handschriftlichen, Griech-Ischen, Loptischen, Lateinischen und Syrischen Uberlieferung der Oden Salomos. (Orbis Biblicus et Orientalis Ser.). (GER.). 1979. text 32.25 (*3-7278-0536-6*, Pub. by Presses Univ Fribourg) Eisenbrauns.
— Die Oden Salomos in Ihrer Bedeutung fur Neues Testament und Ginosis Vol. XI: Der Syrische Text der Edition in Estrangela Faksimile des Griechischen Papyrus Bodmer. (Orbis Biblicus et Orientalis Ser.). (GER.). 1980. text 10.50 (*3-7278-0219-7*, Pub. by Presses Univ Fribourg) Eisenbrauns.
Lattke, Michael. Hymnus: Materialien Zu Einer Geschichte der Antiken Hymnologie. (Novum Testamentum et Orbis Antiquus Ser.: Vol. 19). (GER.). 510p. 1991. text 100.25 (*3-7278-0751-2*, Pub. by Presses Univ Fribourg) Eisenbrauns.
***Lattke, Michael.** Oden Salomos: Text, Ubersetzung, Kommentar. (Novum Testamentum et Orbis Antiquus Ser.: Vol. 41/1). xii, 301p. 1999. text 63.00 (*3-7278-1245-1*, Pub. by Ed Univ Fri) Eisenbrauns.
Lattke, Michael. Die Oden Salomos in Ihrer Bedeutung fur Neues Testament und Gnosis. (Orbis Biblicus et Orientalis Ser.: Vol. 25/4). (GER.). xii, 272p. 1998. text 58.25 (*3-7278-1164-1*, Pub. by Ed Univ Fri) Eisenbrauns.
Lattman, Eaton, jt. ed. see Love, Warner.
Lattman, Laurence H., jt. auth. see Zillman, Donald N.
Latto, L. P. Difficulties in Tracheal Intubation. 2nd ed. (Illus.). 395p. (C). 1996. text 79.00 (*0-7020-2116-4*) Harcourt.
Lattu, Kristan R., ed. History of Rocketry & Astronautics. LC 57-43769. (AAS History Ser.: Vol. 8). (Illus.). 368p. 1989. 50.00 (*0-87703-307-2*, Am Astronaut Soc); pap. 35.00 (*0-87703-308-0*, Am Astronaut Soc) Univelt Inc.
Lattuca, Lisa R., jt. auth. see Stark, Joan S.
Latulipe, Celine. How to Use Microsoft Frontpage 97. 2nd ed. 1997. 24.99 (*1-56276-562-0*, Ziff-Davis Pr) Que.
— How to Use Microsoft Frontpage 97 for Windows. LC 97-170658. 1996. pap. text 24.99 (*1-56276-462-4*, Ziff-Davis Pr) Que.
Latulippe, Laura. Understanding Each Other. 1997. pap. text. write for info. (*0-201-84675-6*) Addison-Wesley.
Latulippe, Laura D. Developing Academic Reading Skills. (Illus.). 320p. (C). 1987. pap. text 34.60 (*0-13-204157-X*) P-H.
— Writing As a Personal Product. 240p. (C). 1992. pap. text 31.80 (*0-13-005869-6*) P-H.
Latus, Thomas, jt. ed. see Hehir, Thomas.
Latuselao, Rogelio A. Elsevier's Dictionary of Cummunicative Abbreviations. LC 98-47035. 372p. 1998. 158.00 (*0-444-82889-3*) Elsevier.
Latushkin, Yuri, jt. auth. see Chicone, Carmen Charles.
Latvian Evangelical Lutheran Church in America Sta. Vins Necinijas Pasauligi. Liepkalns, Arturs, ed.Tr. of He Did Not Wage Wordly War. (LAV., Illus.). 200p. 1997. 15.00 (*0-9660422-0-4*) Latvian Evang.
Latvus, Kari. God, Anger & Ideology: The Anger of God in Joshua & Judges in Relation to Deuteronomy & the Priestly Writings the Priestly Writing. LC 99-158754. (JSOTS Ser.: Vol. 279). 108p. 1998. 46.50 (*1-85075-922-7*, Pub. by Sheffield Acad) CUP Services.
Latymer, Francis B. Ventures in Thought. LC 67-23238. (Essay Index Reprint Ser.). 1977. 20.95 (*0-8369-0610-1*) Ayer.
Latymer, Hugo. The Mediterranean Gardener. (Illus.). 160p. 2000. 35.00 (*0-7112-0631-7*, Pub. by F Lincoln) Antique Collect.
Latynin, Leonid. The Face-Maker & the Muse. Bromfield, Andrew, tr. (Glas Ser.: Vol. 21). 240p. 1999. pap. 14.95 (*1-56663-275-7*, Pub. by I R Dee) Natl Bk Netwk.
— Sleeper at Harvest Time. Bromfield, Andrew, tr. from RUS. (Illus.). 288p. 1994. 21.00 (*0-939010-36-4*); pap. 11.00 (*0-939010-37-2*) Zephyr Pr.
Latynski, Maya, ed. Reappraising the Munich Pact: Continental Perspectives. LC 91-45734. (Woodrow Wilson Center Press Ser.). 120p. 1992. text 22.00 (*0-943875-38-2*); pap. text 10.95 (*0-943875-39-0*) Johns Hopkins.
Latynski, Maya, tr. see Michnik, Adam.
Latyon, David. WW II: A Global Perspective. 200p. (C). 1995. pap. text, per. 37.74 (*0-7872-0421-8*) Kendall-Hunt.
Latypov, T., jt. auth. see Khrutsky, V.
Latyschev, Basilius, ed. Inscriptiones Antiquae Orae Septentrionalis Ponti Euxini Graecae et Latinae, Vols. I, II & IV. 1965. reprint ed. write for info. (*0-318-72101-5*) G Olms Pubs.
Latyschev, Basillius. Inscriptiones Antiquae Orae Septentrionalis Ponti Euxini Graecae et Latinae, Vols. I, II & IV. (GER.). xii, 1359p. 1965. reprint ed. write for info. (*0-318-70445-5*) G Olms Pubs.
Latysev, K. P., ed. see Steklov Institute of Mathematics, Academy of Scien.
***Latz.** Early Modern Englishwoman Part 2, Vol. 9. LC 99-56944. 2000. 47.95 (*1-84014-222-7*) Ashgate Pub Co.
Latz, Dorothy L. Neglected English Literature. LC 98-101782. 130p. 1997. pap. 19.95 (*3-7052-0072-0*, Pub. by Poetry Salzburg) Intl Spec Bk.
Latz, Gil. Agricultural Development in Japan: The Land Improvement District in Concept & Practice. LC 89-943. (Research Papers: No. 225). (Illus.). 1989. pap. text 14.50 (*0-89065-129-9*) U Ch Pr.
— The Power of Place: World Regional Geography. 235p. 1997. pap., student ed. 28.95 (*0-471-12841-4*) Wiley.
Latz, Gottlieb. The Secret of the Emerald Tablet of Hermes. Holmes, J. D., ed. Hauck, D. William, tr. from GER. 1993. pap. 8.95 (*1-55818-203-9*) Holmes Pub.
***Latz, Peter.** Pocket Bushtucker. (Illus.). 240p. 1999. pap. 22.95 (*1-86465-023-0*, Pub. by IAD Pr) Intl Spec Bk.
***Latza, Greg.** Back on the Farm: A Celebration of South Dakota Farm & Ranch Families. Latza, Jodi Holley, ed. LC 99-64745. (Illus.). 160p. 1999. pap. 24.95 (*0-9673485-0-1*) PeopleScapes.
Latza, Jodi Holley, ed. see Latza, Greg.
Latzer, Barry. State Constitutional Criminal Law. LC 94-69102. 1995. ring bd. 135.00 (*0-614-07299-9*) West Group.
— State Constitutions & Criminal Justice, 65. LC 91-3249. (Contributions in Legal Studies). 232p. 1991. 62.95 (*0-313-26112-1*, LLF, Greenwood Pr) Greenwood.
Latzer, Barry & U. S. Supreme Court Staff. Death Penalty Cases: Leading U. S. Supreme Court Cases on Capital Punishment. LC 97-28267. 260p. 1998. pap. 26.95 (*0-7506-9939-6*) Buttrwrth-Heinemann.
Latzke, Deborah. Searching for the Accorn. (Illus.). 72p. (Orig.). 1995. pap. 12.95 (*0-9643956-2-2*) Legacy of Love.
— When the Last Acorn Is Found. 64p. 1993. 14.95 (*0-9643956-1-4*) Legacy of Love.
Latzko, Adolf A. Men in War. LC 71-116961. (Short Story Index Reprint Ser.). 1977. 20.95 (*0-8369-3465-2*) Ayer.
Latzko, D. G., et al, eds. Post-Yield Fracture Mechanics. 2nd ed. (Illus.). 512p. 1985. mass mkt. 221.50 (*0-85334-276-8*) Elsevier.
Latzko, Marian. I Can Do It: A Micropedia of Living on Your Own. LC 96-94294. (Illus.). 128p. (Orig.). 1996. pap. 15.95 (*0-9651826-0-6*) MicroLife.
Latzko, William. Quality & Productivity for Bankers & Financial Managers. (Qualtiy & Reliability Ser.: Vol. 10). (Illus.). 224p. 1986. text 75.00 (*0-8247-7682-8*) Dekker.
Latzko, William J. & Saunders, David M. Four Days with Dr. Deming: A Strategy for Modern Methods of Management. LC 94-29252. (Engineering Process Improvement Ser.). 256p. (C). 1995. pap. 34.00 (*0-201-63366-3*) Addison-Wesley.
Lau, jt. auth. see Ebenezer.
Lau, A., et al, eds. Time-Resolved Vibrational Spectroscopy VI: Proceedings of the Sixth International Conference on Time-Resolved Vibrational Spectroscopy, Berlin, Germany, May 23-28, 1993. LC 93-40610. (Proceedings in Physics Ser.: Vol. 74). 1994. 86.95 (*0-387-57573-1*) Spr-Verlag.
Lau A To-Ming. Topological Vector Spaces, Algebras & Related Areas. 1994. lib. bdg. 65.95 (*0-582-25777-8*) Addison-Wesley.
Lau, Alan C. Songs for Jadina. LC 80-66984. 94p. (Orig.). 1981. pap. 4.95 (*0-912678-46-1*, Greenfld Rev Pr) Greenfld Rev Lit.
***Lau, Alan Chong.** Blues & Greens: A Produce Worker's Journal. LC 99-57298. (Intersections Ser.). (Illus.). 136p. 2000. pap. 17.95 (*0-8248-2323-0*); text 36.00 (*0-8248-2210-2*) UH Pr.
Lau, Albert. The Malayan Union Controversy, 1942-1948. (South-East Asian Historical Monographs). 340p. 1991. 45.00 (*0-19-588964-9*) OUP.
— A Moment of Anguish: Singapore in Malaysia & the Politics of Disengagement. LC 98-945733. 312p. 1998. pap. 25.00 (*981-210-134-9*, Pub. by Times Academic) Intl Spec Bk.
— A Moment of Anguish: Singapore in Malaysia & the Politics of Disengagement LC 98-945733. viii, 312 p. 1998. write for info. (*981-210-130-6*) Times Academic.
Lau, Andrew Y. Manifest in Flesh: The Epiphany Christology of the Pastoral Epistles. LC 96-221067. (WissUnt Zum Neuen Testament Ser.: No. 2-86). 336p. (Orig.). 1996. pap. 82.50 (*3-16-146302-1*) Coronet Bks.
Lau, Barbara, jt. auth. see Edwards, Ted L., Jr.
Lau, Beth. Keats's Paradise Lost. LC 97-42542. (Illus.). 215p. 1998. 49.95 (*0-8130-1579-0*) U Press Fla.
Lau, Beth, jt. ed. see Hoeveler, Diane L.
Lau, C. K. Hong Kong's Colonial Legacy: A Hong Kong Chinese's View of the British Heritage. 224p. 1997. pap. text 18.95 (*962-201-793-2*, Pub. by Chinese Univ) U of Mich Pr.
Lau, Charles & Glossbrenner, Alfred. The Art of Hitting Three Hundred. rev. ed. 1992. pap. 24.95 (*0-14-015335-7*, Penguin Bks) Viking Penguin.
***Lau, Charley, Jr. & Flanagan, Jeff.** Lau's Laws on Hitting. (Illus.). 224p. 2000. pap. 21.95 (*1-886110-95-6*) Addax Pubng.
Lau, Chong-chor & Geng, Xiao, eds. China Review 1999. (Illus.). 500p. (C). pap. text 55.00 (*962-201-896-3*, Pub. by Chinese Univ) U of Mich Pr.
Lau, Christina. Building Distributed Applications with IBM Component Broker. 512p. 1998. pap. text 49.99 (*0-471-15661-2*) Wiley.
— Object-Oriented Programming Using SOM & DSOM. 288p. 1995. pap. text 44.95 incl. disk (*0-471-13123-7*) Wiley.
***Lau, Chung-Ming, et al.** Asian Management Matters: Regional Relevance & Global Impact. 300p. 2000. 58.00 (*1-86094-238-5*, Pub. by Imperial College) World Scientific Pub.
Lau, Clifford. Neural Networks: Theoretical Foundations & Analysis. LC 91-39114. (Illus.). 336p. (C). 1991. 69.95 (*0-87942-280-7*, PC0279-0) Inst Electrical.
Lau, Clifford, jt. ed. see Sanchez-Sinencio, Edgar.
Lau, D. C., tr. Tao Te Ching. LC 98-126698. (C). 1997. 35.00 (*962-201-467-4*, Pub. by Chinese Univ) U of Mich Pr.
Lau, D. C., tr. Lu Xun Xiao Shuo Ji: Vocabulary (Selected Short Stories) rev. ed. 220p. 1987. pap. 14.95 (*962-201-391-0*, Pub. by Chinese Univ) U of Mich Pr.
***Lau, D. C. & Ames, Roger T., trs.** Yuan Dao: Tracing Dao to Its Source. LC 97-52299. 160p. 1998. pap. 12.00 (*0-345-42568-5*) Ballantine Pub Grp.
Lau, D. C., tr. see Confucius.
Lau, D. C., tr. see Mencius.
Lau, D. C., tr. & intro. see Tza, Lao.
Lau, Deborah, tr. see Adames, Jay.
Lau-Dickinson, Aileen C., jt. auth. see Raymond, Gail.
Lau, Dicksen T. Engin Politism: A New Political Theory for Permanent World Peace. LC 83-62601. 396p. (Orig.). 1983. pap. 9.50 (*0-9612000-1-4*) Magnolia Bks.
— The New Religion & Relativity. LC 83-62038. 138p. (Orig.). 1983. pap. 5.95 (*0-9612000-0-6*) Magnolia Bks.
Lau, Edward. Poets & Gay Poets. 150p. 1996. pap. text 10.00 (*1-888065-09-5*) New Wrld Poetry.
Lau, Edwin J. Performance Improvement of Virtual Memory Systems. Stone, Harold, ed. LC 82-13393. (Computer Science: Systems Programming Ser.: No. 17). 228p. 1982. reprint ed. pap. 70.70 (*0-8357-1366-0*, 207007300063) Bks Demand.
Lau, Evelyn. Fresh Girls & Other Stories. LC 94-7565. 128p. (J). 1995. 17.45 (*0-7868-6058-8*, Pub. by Hyperion) Time Warner.
Lau, Grace. Adults in Wonderland: A Retrospective. LC 96-71370. 120p. 1997. pap. text 29.99 (*1-85242-552-0*) Serpents Tail.
Lau, Grace, et al. Chinese-American Food Practices, Customs, & Holidays. 2nd ed. LC 98-20458. (Ethnic & Regional Food Practices Ser.). 1998. 10.00 (*0-88091-166-2*) Am Dietetic Assn.
Lau, Grace S. Metabolic Activation of Drugs & Other Xenobiotics in Hapatocellular Carcinoma. 1998. pap. text 44.50 (*962-201-744-4*, Pub. by Chinese Univ) U of Mich Pr.
Lau, H. T. Algorithms on Graphs. 180p. 1989. 29.95 (*0-8306-3429-0*) McGraw-Hill Prof.
— Algorithms on Graphs. 1991. 24.95 (*0-8306-5429-1*) McGraw-Hill Prof.
— Chinese Chess. LC 84-52394. (Illus.). 248p. 1991. pap. 12.95 (*0-8048-1675-1*) Tuttle Pubng.
— Combinatorial Heuristic Algorithms with FORTRAN. (Lecture Notes in Economics & Mathematical Systems Ser.: Vol. 280). vii, 126p. 1986. 29.60 (*0-387-17161-4*) Spr-Verlag.
— A Numerical Library in C for Scientists & Engineers. 816p. 1994. boxed set 94.95 (*0-8493-7376-X*, 7376) CRC Pr.
Lau, J. Chip on Board Technology. 1994. text 69.95 (*0-442-01441-4*, VNR) Wiley.
Lau, James B., jt. auth. see Shani, Abraham B.
Lau, Jesus, ed. see Muro, Ernest A.
Lau, John H. Ball Grid Array Technology. 635p. 1994. 75.00 (*0-07-036608-X*) McGraw.
— Flip Chip Technologies. LC 95-44649. (Illus.). 560p. 1995. 89.00 (*0-07-036609-8*) McGraw.
***Lau, John H.** Low Cost Flip Chip Technologies: Direct Chip Attack. LC 99-88307. (Professional Engineering Ser.). (Illus.). 600p. 2000. 89.95 (*0-07-135141-8*) McGraw-Hill Prof.
— Microvias: Low Cost, High Density Interconnects. 2000. 89.95 (*0-07-136327-0*) McGraw.
Lau, John H., ed. Handbook of Fine Pitch Surface Mount Technology. LC 93-25289. 1994. text 99.95 (*0-442-01258-6*, VNR) Wiley.
— Handbook of Tape Automated Bonding. (Illus.). 650p. 1992. text 89.95 (*0-442-00427-3*, VNR) Wiley.
— Thermal Stress & Strain in Microelectronics Packaging. LC 92-43285. 1993. text 99.95 (*0-442-01058-3*, VNR) Wiley.
Lau, John H. & Lee, Ricky S. Chip Scale Packaging: Design, Materials, Processes, & Reliability. LC 98-53224. (Electronic Packaging & Interconnection Ser.). (Illus.). 400p. 1998. 127.95 (*0-07-038304-9*) McGraw-Hill Prof.
Lau, John H. & Pao, Yi-Hsin. Solder Joint Reliability of BGA, CSP, & Flip Chip Assemblies. LC 96-31361. (Illus.). 408p. 1996. 65.00 (*0-07-036648-9*) McGraw.
Lau, John H., et al. Electronic Packaging: Design, Materials, Process, & Reliability. (Electronic Packaging & Interconnection Ser.). (Illus.). 496p. 1998. 69.00 (*0-07-037135-0*) McGraw.
Lau, Johnson Y. N. Hepatitis C Protocols. LC 98-24896. (Methods in Molecular Medicine Ser.: No. 19). (Illus.). 648p. 1998. 99.50 (*0-89603-521-2*) Humana.
Lau, Joseph S., et al, eds. Modern Chinese Stories & Novellas, 1919-1949. LC 80-27572. (Modern Asian Literature Ser.). (ENG.). 608p. 1981. pap. text 32.50 (*0-231-04203-5*) Col U Pr.
Lau, Joseph S. & Goldblatt, Howard. The Columbia Anthology of Modern Chinese Literature. (Illus.). 736p. 1996. pap. 24.00 (*0-231-08003-4*) Col U Pr.
Lau, Joseph S. & Ross, Timothy A., eds. Chinese Stories from Taiwan, Nineteen Sixty to Nineteen Seventy. LC 75-4391. 359p. 1976. text 65.00 (*0-231-04007-5*) Col U Pr.
Lau, Joseph S., jt. ed. see Ma, Y. W.
Lau, Joseph S., jt. ed. see Minford, John.
Lau, Joseph S. M. & Goldblatt, Howard, eds. The Columbia Anthology of Modern Chinese Literature. LC 94-35304. (Modern Asian Literature Ser.). (CHI & ENG.). 720p. 1995. 46.50 (*0-231-08002-6*) Col U Pr.
Lau, Kam. Cantonese Phrasebook. 2nd ed. (Illus.). 224p. (Orig.). 1995. pap. 5.95 (*0-86442-340-3*) Lonely Planet.
— Japanese Phrasebook. 2nd ed. (JPN., Illus.). 224p. 1994. pap. 5.95 (*0-86442-230-X*) Lonely Planet.
Lau, Kenneth, jt. auth. see Lau, Theodora.
***Lau, Kimberly J.** New Age Capitalism: Making Money East of Eden. 192p. 2000. pap. text 19.95 (*0-8122-1729-2*) U of Pa Pr.
Lau, Kit-ching Chan. From Nothing to Nothing: The Chinese Communist Movement & Hong Kong, 1921-1936. LC 99-20746. 1999. text 59.95 (*0-312-22428-1*) St Martin.
Lau, Kung-Kiu & Clement, Tim P., eds. Logic Program Synthesis & Transformation: Proceedings of LOPSTR '92, International Workshop on Logic Program Synthesis & Transformation, University of Manchester, 2-3 July, 1992. LC 92-43296. (Workshops in Computing Ser.). 1993. 69.00 (*0-387-19806-7*) Spr-Verlag.
Lau, Kwan. Feng Shui for Today: Arranging Your Life for Health & Wealth. (Illus.). 112p. (Orig.). 1996. pap. 9.95 (*0-8348-0356-9*, Tengu Bks) Weatherhill.

An Asterisk (*) at the beginning of an entry indicates that the title is appearing for the first time.

93-10609. (Let's-Read-&-Find-Out Science Bks.). (Illus.). 32p. (J). (gr. 7-11). 1995. lib. bdg. 15.89 (*0-06-022982-9*) HarpC Child Bks.

— You're Aboard Spaceship Earth. LC 94-18704. (Let's-Read-&-Find-Out Science Bks.). (Illus.). 32p. (J). (gr. k-4). 1996. lib. bdg. 14.89 (*0-06-024408-9*) HarpC Child Bks.

— You're Aboard Spaceship Earth. LC 94-18704. (Trophy Let's-Read-&-Find-Out Bk., Stage 2). (Illus.). 32p. (J). (ps-3). 1996. pap. 4.95 (*0-06-445159-3*, HarpTrophy) HarpC Child Bks.

— You're Aboard Spaceship Earth. LC 94-18704. (Let's-Read-And-Find-Out Science. Stage 2 Ser.). 1996. 10.15 (*0-606-10099-7*, Pub. by Turtleback) Demco.

Lauber, Timothy J. Furniture Associations in North America. LC 94-1179. 80p. 1999. spiral bd. 450.00 (*0-921577-41-9*) AKTRIN.

— Furniture Exhibitions in North America: U. S. A., Canada, Mexico. LC 94-45364. 90p. 1995. spiral bd. 450.00 (*0-921577-49-4*) AKTRIN.

Lauber, Volkmar. The Politics of Economic Policy, 97. 128p. 1983. pap. 14.95 (*0-275-91579-4*, B1579, Praeger Pubs) Greenwood.

Lauber, William F., jt. auth. see Rector, Robert.

Laubereau, A. & Seilmeier, A., eds. Ultrafast Processes in Spectroscopy, 1991: Proceedings of the Seventh International Symposium, Bayreuth, 1991. (Illus.). 688p. 1992. 315.00 (*0-7503-0198-8*) IOP Pub.

Laubheim, Charles S. Just Writing. 4th ed. 328p. (C). 1994. pap. text, spiral bd. 34.95 (*0-8403-4517-8*) Kendall-Hunt.

Laubich, Arnold & Spencer, Ray. Art Tatum: A Guide to His Recorded Music. LC 82-10752. (Studies in Jazz: No. 2). 359p. 1982. 45.00 (*0-8108-1582-6*) Scarecrow.

Laubin, Gladys, jt. auth. see Laubin, Reginald.

Laubin, Reginald & Laubin, Gladys. American Indian Archery. LC 78-58108. (Civilization of the American Indian Ser.: Vol. 154). (Illus.). 192p. 1991. 27.95 (*0-8061-1467-3*); pap. 15.95 (*0-8061-2387-7*) U of Okla Pr.

— Indian Dances of North America: Their Importance to Indian Life. LC 76-40962. (Civilization of the American Indian Ser.: No.141). (Illus.). 576p. 1989. pap. 24.95 (*0-8061-2172-6*) U of Okla Pr.

Laubin, Reginald, et al. The Indian Tipi: Its History, Construction, & Use. LC 77-23039. (Illus.). 384p. 1989. pap. 19.95 (*0-8061-2236-6*) U of Okla Pr.

***Laubner, Ellie.** Collectible Fashions of the Turbulent 1930's. (Illus.). 244p. 1999. 49.95 (*0-7643-0867-X*) Schiffer.

Laubner, Ellie. Fashions of the Roaring '20s. LC 96-15436. (Illus.). 176p. 1996. pap. 29.95 (*0-7643-0017-2*) Schiffer.

Laubscher, B. J. Where Mystery Dwells: A Psychiatrist Studies Psychical Phenomena. 272p. 1972. 11.50 (*0-227-67801-X*) Attic Pr.

Laubscher, G. G. Syntactical Causes of Case Reduction in Old French. (Elliott Monographs: Vol. 7). 1921. 30.00 (*0-527-02611-5*) Periodicals Srv.

Laubscher, Michael R. Encounters with Difference: Student Perceptions of the Role of Out-of-Class Experiences in Education Abroad, 105. LC 93-37505. (Contributions to the Study of Education Ser.: No. 105). 152p. 1994. 55.00 (*0-313-28977-8*, Greenwood Pr) Greenwood.

***Lauby, Linda.** Insiders' Guide to North Carolina's Outer Banks, 21st ed. 21st ed. 584p. 2000. pap. text 16.95 (*1-57380-154-2*) IPBI.

Lauby, Paul T. Sailing on Winds of Change: Two Decades in the Life of the United Board for Christian Higher Education in Asia, 1969-1990. Ellis, Anne L., ed. 213p. (Orig.). (C). 1996. pap. write for info. (*0-9646943-1-X*) United Board CHE.

Laucella, Linda. Assassination! The Politics of Murder. LC 97-48721. 480p. 1998. 28.00 (*1-56565-628-8*, 06288W, Pub. by Lowell Hse) NTC Contemp Pub Co.

— Assassination! The Politics of Murder. 480p. 1999. pap. 19.95 (*0-7373-0132-5*, 01325W) NTC Contemp Pub Co.

— Hormone Replacement Therapy. 2nd rev. ed. 204p. 1997. pap. 16.00 (*1-56565-805-1*, Woman-Woman) Lowell Hse.

— Hormone Replacement Therapy: Conventional Medicine & Natural Alternates: Your Guide to Menopausal Health Care Choices. 204p. 1994. 22.95 (*1-56565-154-5*) Lowell Hse.

— Hormone Replacement Therapy: Conventional Medicine & Natural Alternatives. 204p. 1995. pap. 16.00 (*1-56565-343-2*) Lowell Hse.

— Hormone Replacement Therapy: Conventional Medicine & Natural Alternatives Your Guide to Menopause. 2nd ed. LC 99-39388. 256p. 1999. pap. 16.95 (*0-7373-0251-8*, 02518W) NTC Contemp Pub Co.

Lauchlan, Michael. Sudden Parade. 40p. (Orig.). 1997. pap. text 8.00 (*1-56439-057-8*) Ridgeway.

Lauchland, Henry. Touch Me Inside. LC 74-24548. 46p. (C). 1975. reprint ed. 9.95 (*0-931820-00-6*) High Q.

Lauchland, K. A. & Le Brun, M. J. Legal Interviewing: Theory, Tactics & Techniques. (Butterworths Skills Ser.). 200p. 1996. pap. write for info. (*0-409-30809-9*, MICHIE) LEXIS Pub.

Lauchli, Andre & Bieleski, R. L., eds. Inorganic Plant Nutrition. (Encyclopedia of Plant Physiology Ser.: Vol. 15, Part A & B). (Illus.). 900p. 1983. 398.95 (*0-387-12103-X*) Spr-Verlag.

Lauchli, Andre, jt. ed. see Tinker, Bernard.

Lauchli, Andre, jt. ed. see Tinker, P. B.

Lauchman, Richard. Plain Style: Techniques for Simple, Concise, Emphatic Business Writing. LC 93-4324. 144p. 1993. pap. 15.95 (*0-8144-7852-3*) AMACOM.

Lauck, Dave. The Tactical 1911: The Street Cop's & SWAT Operator's Guide to Employment & Maintenance. LC 98-228572. (Illus.). 152p. 1998. pap. 22.00 (*0-87364-985-0*) Paladin Pr.

Lauck, Dave M. The Tactical Marksman: A Complete Training Manual for Police & Practical Shooters. (Illus.). 176p. 1996. pap. 35.00 (*0-87364-881-1*) Paladin Pr.

***Lauck, Jennifer.** Blackbird: A Childhood Lost. 416p. 2000. 23.95 (*0-671-04255-6*) PB.

Lauck, Joanne E. The Voice of the Infinite in the Small: Revisioning the Insect-Human Connection. 358p. 1998. pap. 18.95 (*1-893183-10-6*, Pub. by Granite Pub) ACCESS Pubs Network.

— The Voice of the Infinite in the Small: Revisioning the Insect-Human Connection. Crissey, Brian L., ed. LC 98-7162. (Illus.). 378p. 1998. pap. 18.95 (*0-926524-49-6*) Granite WI.

Lauck, Johnny. Comic Book Index. 1997. pap. 29.95 (*0-9649515-0-9*) Alternate Concepts.

Lauck, Jon. American Agriculture & the Problem of Monopoly: The Political Economy of Grain Belt Farming, 1953-1980. LC 99-38710. 304p. 2000. text 45.00 (*0-8032-2932-1*) U of Nebr Pr.

Lauck, William J. & Sydenstricker, Edgar. Conditions of Labor in American Industries. LC 70-89746. (American Labor, from Conspiracy to Collective Bargaining Ser., No. 1). 404p. 1971. reprint ed. 26.95 (*0-405-02134-8*) Ayer.

Lauckner, Kurt. The Computer Continuum. 479p. (C). 1998. pap. text 76.00 (*1-58076-059-7*) Que Educ & Trng.

Lauckner, Kurt F. & Lintner, Mildred D. Computers: Inside & Out. 5th ed. (Illus.). 464p. 1996. pap. 37.00 (*1-880066-13-0*) Pippin Publishing.

***Lauckner, Nancy A. & Jokiniemi, Miriam, eds.** Shedding Light on Darkness: A Guide to Teaching the Holocaust. 224p. 2000. 39.95 (*1-57181-208-3*) Berghahn Bks.

Laucks, Eulah C. Saucer Eyes: A Story of Becoming in Hard Rock Mining Country. (Illus.). 96p. (Orig.). 1996. pap. 9.95 (*1-56474-153-2*) Fithian Pr.

Laud, Catherine, jt. auth. see Jackins, Harvey.

Laud, William. Articles Exhibited in Parliament Against William, Archbishop of Canterbury. LC 72-212. (English Experience Ser.: No. 333). 16p. 1971. reprint ed. 20.00 (*90-221-0333-1*) Walter J Johnson.

— A Speech Delivered in the Starr-Chamber, at the Censure of J. Bastwick. LC 79-171771. (English Experience Ser.: No. 396). 92p. 1971. reprint ed. 20.00 (*90-221-0396-X*) Walter J Johnson.

— The Works, 7 vols. in 5, Set. (Anglistica & Americana Ser.: No. 168). 1977. reprint ed. 518.70 (*3-487-06277-1*) G Olms Pubs.

— The Works of the Most Reverend Father in God, William Laud, D. D., 9 pts. LC 74-5373. (Library of Anglo-Catholic Theology: No. 11). reprint ed. 805.00 (*0-404-52120-7*) AMS Pr.

Laudahr, W. R., et al. The Human & Divine Universe. 125p. 1989. pap. 8.50 (*0-913004-66-9*, 353) Point Loma Pub.

Laudal, Olav A. & Jahren, Bjorn, eds. The Sophus Lie Memorial Conference: Oslo, 1992 - Proceedings. 381p. 1994. 18.00 (*82-00-21646-2*) Scandnvan Univ Pr.

Laudan, Larry. Beyond Positivism & Relativism: Theory, Method & Evidence. (C). 1996. pap. 27.00 (*0-8133-2469-6*, Pub. by Westview) HarpC.

— Danger Ahead: The Risks You Really Face on Life's Highway, Vol. II. LC 97-9920. 203p. 1997. pap. 14.95 (*0-471-13440-6*) Wiley.

— Progress & Its Problems: Towards a Theory of Scientific Growth. LC 76-24586. 1977. pap. 17.95 (*0-520-03721-9*, Pub. by U CA Pr) Cal Prin Full Svc.

— Science & Hypothesis: Historical Essays on Scientific Methodology. (University of Western Ontario Series in Philosophy of Science WONS: No. 19). 269p. 1981. lib. bdg. 93.00 (*90-277-1315-4*) Kluwer Academic.

— Science & Relativism: Some Key Controversies in the Philosophy of Science. LC 90-32112. (Science & Its Conceptual Foundations Ser.). 194p. 1990. pap. text 13.95 (*0-226-46949-2*) U Ch Pr.

— Science & Relativism: Some Key Controversies in the Philosophy of Science. LC 90-32112. (Science & Its Conceptual Foundations Ser.). 194p. 1996. lib. bdg. 37.50 (*0-226-46948-4*) U Ch Pr.

— Science & Values: An Essay on the Aims of Science & Their Role in Scientific Debate. LC 84-249. (Pittsburgh Series in Philosophy & History of Science: No. 3). 160p. 1984. pap. 17.95 (*0-520-05743-0*, Pub. by U CA Pr) Cal Prin Full Svc.

Laudan, Rachel. The Food of Paradise: Exploring Hawaii's Culinary Heritage. LC 95-46407. (Illus.). 384p. 1996. 38.95 (*0-8248-1708-7*, Kolowalu Bk); pap. 24.95 (*0-8248-1778-8*, Kolowalu Bk) UH Pr.

— From Mineralogy to Geology: The Foundations of a Science, 1650-1830. LC 86-30783. (Science & Its Conceptual Foundations Ser.). (Illus.). xii, 288p. (C). 1987. 33.00 (*0-226-46950-6*) U Ch Pr.

— From Mineralogy to Geology: The Foundations of a Science, 1650-1830. (Science & Its Conceptual Foundations Ser.). (Illus.). xii, 290p. 1994. pap. text 15.95 (*0-226-46947-6*) U Ch Pr.

Laudan, Rachel, ed. The Nature of Technological Knowledge: Are Models of Scientific Change Relevant? 1984. lib. bdg. 84.00 (*90-277-1716-8*) Kluwer Academic.

Laudan, Rtachel. Hunger for Life. 1996. 37.50 (*0-226-46965-4*) U Ch Pr.

Laudati. European Competition Forum. LC 97-211550. 1996. text 121.00 (*0-471-96668-1*) Wiley.

Laudati, Laraine, jt. ed. see Ehlermann, Claus D.

Laudati, Laraine L., jt. ed. see Ehlermann, Claus Dieter.

Laude, Jean. The Arts of Black Africa. Decock, Jean, tr. LC 71-125165. (African Studies Center, UCLA: No. 1). (Illus.). 1971. pap. 17.95 (*0-520-02358-7*, Pub. by U CA Pr) Cal Prin Full Svc.

— The Beaches of Thule. Cloutier, David, tr. from FRE. LC 84-48261. (Modern Poets in Translation Ser.: Vol. III). Orig. Title: Les Plages de Thule. ix, 57p. (C). 1985. 22.95 (*0-916426-09-2*); pap. 12.95 (*0-916426-10-6*) KOSMOS.

Laude, Jean, jt. auth. see De Romilly, Nicole.

Laude, Lucien D., ed. Cohesive Properties of Semi-Conductors under Laser Irradiation. 1983. text 282.00 (*90-247-2857-6*) Kluwer Academic.

— Excimer Lasers: Proceedings of the NATO Advanced Study Institute on 'Excimer Lasers: The Tools, Fundamental Processes & Applications', Elounda, Crete, Greece, September 6-17, 1993. 512p. (C). 1994. text 326.50 (*0-7923-2819-1*) Kluwer Academic.

Laude, Lucien D., et al, eds. Interfaces under Laser Irradiation. (C). 1987. text 237.50 (*90-247-3569-6*) Kluwer Academic.

Laude, Patrick. L' Eden Entredit Vol. 2: Lecture de La Chanson D'Eve de Charles Van Lerberghe. LC 93-40235. (Belgian Francophone Library: Vol. 2). (FRE.). 150p. (C). 1994. text 42.95 (*0-8204-2374-2*) P Lang Pubng.

Laudelot, Marc. Hommage a Ferdinand Celine. (Illus.). 1993. 450.00 (*0-914301-31-4*, Pub. by Marco) West-Art.

***Laudeman, William.** Sailboat Electrical Systems: Improvement, Wiring, & Repair. LC 98-53152. (International Marine Sailboat Library Ser.). (Illus.). 176p. 1999. 21.95 (*0-07-036649-7*) McGraw.

Laudemus, Leif. The History of Atomic Energy Collection at Oregon State University. Krishnamurthy, Ramesh S., ed. (Illus.). 433p. 1998. 75.00 (*1-882860-13-6*) J Cummins Bksell.

— The History of Atomic Energy Collection at Oregon State University. deluxe ed. Krishnamurthy, Ramesh S., ed. (Illus.). 433p. 1998. lthr. 750.00 (*1-882860-14-4*) J Cummins Bksell.

Laudenat, R. T., ed. Proceedings of the 1995 International Joint Power Generation Conference Vol. 2: October 8-12, 1995 Minneapolis, Minnesota, NE-Vol. 17. LC 95-80547. (NE Ser.: Vol. 17). 144p. 1995. 70.00 (*0-7918-1487-4*, G00982) ASME.

Laudenslager, Jeff. Jeff Laudenslager: Sculpture. (Illus.). 20p. 1989. pap. text 15.00 (*0-8150-0024-3*) Wittenborn Art.

Lauder. On the Deutie of Kings. Hall, F., ed. (EETS, OS Ser.: Nos. 3, 41). 1974. reprint ed. 20.00 (*0-8115-3957-1*) Periodicals Srv.

Lauder, Evelyn. The Seasons Observed: Photographs. LC 94-8418. (Illus.). 96p. 1994. 24.95 (*0-8109-4455-3*, Pub. by Abrams) Time Warner.

Lauder, George V., jt. ed. see Feder, Martin E.

Lauder, George V., jt. ed. see Rose, Michael R.

Lauder, I. J., jt. auth. see Aitchison, J.

Lauder, Jean M., et al, eds. Molecular Aspects of Development & Aging of the Nervous System. LC 89-70995. (Advances in Experimental Medicine & Biology Ser.: Vol. 265). (Illus.). 335p. 1989. 89.50 (*0-306-43408-3*, Plenum Trade) Perseus Pubng.

Lauder, John. Historical Notices of Scottish Affairs, 2 vols. LC 73-172303. (Bannatyne Club, Edinburgh. Publications: No. 87). reprint ed. 90.00 (*0-404-52828-7*) AMS Pr.

— Historical Observes of Memorable Occurents in Church & State. LC 77-172304. (Bannatyne Club, Edinburgh. Publications: No. 66). reprint ed. 34.50 (*0-404-52779-5*) AMS Pr.

Lauder, Robert. Walker Percy: Prophetic, Existentialist, Catholic Storyteller. (New Connections Ser.: Vol. 12). X, 127p. (C). 1996. pap. text 24.95 (*0-8204-3333-0*) P Lang Pubng.

Lauder, Robert E. Rediscovering Myself & Others in God: The Never-Ending Dialogue. LC 86-32171. 73p. (Orig.). 1987. pap. 4.95 (*0-8189-0517-4*) Alba.

Lauder, Robert S. Engraved Portrait of Thomas Thomson. (Bannatyne Club, Edinburgh. Publications: No. 95). reprint ed. 29.50 (*0-404-52839-2*) AMS Pr.

Lauder, William. Essay on Milton's Use & Imitation of the Moderns in Paradise Lost. LC 74-172306. reprint ed. 40.00 (*0-404-03888-3*) AMS Pr.

Lauder, William C. A Voyage Round the World in the Years 1785, 1786, 1787, & 1788. 150p. 1985. reprint ed. 19.95 (*0-87770-325-6*) Ye Galleon.

Lauderbaugh, J. J. Customer Service Management in a Telemarketing Environment: The Key to Corporate Survival. 160p. 1994. write for info. (*0-936840-15-3*) Tech Marketing.

Lauderbaugh, Richard A. American Steel Makers & the Coming of the Second World War. LC 80-39892. (Studies in American History & Culture: No. 20). 276p. reprint ed. pap. 85.60 (*0-8357-1150-1*, 207010100064) Bks Demand.

Lauderdale, Beverly. The Long Wind. LC 87-91110. 1988. 16.95 (*0-87212-211-5*) Libra.

Lauderdale, Clifford M. The Color to Be. Hwayer, David, ed. (Poetry Ser.). (Illus.). 39p. (Orig.). 1994. pap. text 8.00 (*1-882300-03-3*) Willo Trees.

Lauderdale, Clint A. History of the Lauderdales in America: 1714-1850. LC 98-212926. (Illus.). 237p. 1998. pap. 18.50 (*0-7884-0952-2*, Laud) Heritage Bk.

Lauderdale, David. Alexander Brest Museum & Gallery: A Guide to the Collections. Sowder, Cheryl, ed. LC 94-78736. 112p. (Orig.). 1994. pap. write for info. (*0-9643165-0-1*) Jacksnvl Univ.

Lauderdale Graham, Sandra. House & Street: The Domestic World of Servants & Masters in Nineteenth-Century Rio de Janeiro. LC 92-26226. (Illus.). 224p. 1992. pap. 12.95 (*0-292-72757-7*) U of Tex Pr.

Lauderdale, James M. An Inquiry into the Nature & Origin of Public Wealth & into the Means of Its Increase. 2nd ed. LC 66-24414. (Reprints of Economic Classics Ser.). xxvii, 482p. 1967. reprint ed. 49.50 (*0-678-00208-8*) Kelley.

— Lauderdale's Notes on Adam Smith's Wealth of Nations. Sugiyama, Chuhei, ed. LC 95-11820. 176p. (C). (gr. 13). 1995. 85.00 (*0-415-12284-8*) Routledge.

— Three Letters to the Duke of Wellington on the Fourth Report of the Select Committee of the House of Commons, Appointed in 1828 to Enquire into the Public Income & Expenditure of the United Kingdom. LC 64-7668. (Reprints of Economic Classics Ser.). 138p. 1965. reprint ed. 35.00 (*0-678-00089-1*) Kelley.

Lauderdale, John V., jt. auth. see Green, Jerry.

Lauderdale, Katherine, et al, eds. Addictive & Compulsive Disorders: A View from the Trenches. LC 98-75739. (Illus.). 142p. 1999. pap. 19.95 (*1-879774-18-6*) ICA Pub Co.

Lauderdale, Katherine, jt. ed. see Bonilla, C. F.

Lauderdale, Katherine, ed. see Bonilla, Carlos A.

Lauderdale, Kathi & Bonilla, Carlos A. Tending to the Emotional Needs of Teachers & Children: Tricks of the Trade. Roberson, Jerry L., ed. LC 98-71926. (Illus.). 106p. 1998. pap. 19.95 (*1-879774-15-1*) ICA Pub Co.

Lauderdale, Kathie L., et al. Minefields in the Way: Growing Up in America. LC 98-73820. (Illus.). 112p. 1998. pap. 19.95 (*1-879774-17-8*) ICA Pub Co.

Lauderdale, Michael L. Reinventing Texas Government. LC 98-25509. 240p. 1999. pap. 19.95 (*0-292-74711-X*) U of Tex Pr.

Lauderdale, Pat, ed. A Political Analysis of Deviance. LC 79-27057. 257p. 1980. reprint ed. pap. 79.70 (*0-608-00791-9*, 205934000010) Bks Demand.

Lauderdale, Pat & Amster, Randall. Lives in the Balance: Perspectives on Global Injustice & Inequality. LC 97-16211. (International Studies in Sociology & Social Anthropology). viii, 154p. 1997. 54.50 (*90-04-10875-0*) Brill Academic Pubs.

Lauderdale, Pat & Cruit, Michael. The Struggle for Control: A Study of Law, Disputes, & Deviance. LC 91-47942. (SUNY Series in Deviance & Social Control). 256p. (C). 1993. text 64.50 (*0-7914-1311-X*); pap. text 21.95 (*0-7914-1312-8*) State U NY Pr.

Laudermilk, Janet. Dimensions: A Youth Focus on Churches in Solidarity with Women. (Illus.). 32p. 1992. pap. 3.95 (*0-377-00245-3*) Friendship Pr.

Laudermilk, Sharon & Hamlin, Teresa. The Regency Companion. LC 88-28203. 368p. 1989. text 35.00 (*0-8240-2249-1*, H841) Garland.

Laudet, Claire & Cox, Richard. Le Peuple de France Aujourd'hui. (FRE., Illus.). 200p. 1995. text 19.95 (*0-7190-4216-X*) Manchester Univ Pr.

Laudet, Claire & Cox, Richard, eds. La Vie Politique en France Aujourd'hui. LC 94-29770. (Readers in Contemporary French Civilisation Ser.). (FRE.). 1995. text 19.95 (*0-7190-4218-6*) Manchester Univ Pr.

Laudici. App Pathology Radiographers. 1989. 600.00 (*0-7216-2988-1*) Harcourt.

Laudicina, Paul. Applied Pathology for Radiographies. 308p. 1989. text 52.00 (*0-7216-2143-0*, W B Saunders Co) Harcrt Hlth Sci Grp.

Laudicina, Paul & Wean, Douglas. Applied Angiography for Radiographers. LC 93-27002. 1994. text 52.50 (*0-7216-3283-1*, W B Saunders Co) Harcrt Hlth Sci Grp.

Laudon. Computer Access, 97. 1997. pap. 28.13 (*0-07-292969-3*) McGraw.

— Computer Excel, 97. 1997. pap. 28.13 (*0-07-292965-0*) McGraw.

— Computer Powerpoint 97. 1998. pap. 28.13 (*0-07-292959-6*) McGraw.

— Computer Window, 95. 1997. pap. 28.13 (*0-07-292967-7*) McGraw.

— Computer Word 97. 1997. 28.13 (*0-07-292961-8*) McGraw.

— Corp Information Systems Management TB. 1998. write for info. (*0-02-368133-0*) P-H.

— Essentials of Management Information Systems. 3rd ed. LC 99-175785. (Illus.). 545p. 1998. 82.67 (*0-13-081973-5*) P-H.

— Information System & the Internet. 4th ed. (C). 1997. pap. text 2.70 (*0-03-021138-7*) Harcourt Coll Pubs.

— Information Systems & Internet. 4th ed. 1998. pap. text 29.50 (*0-03-024841-8*) Harcourt Coll Pubs.

— Microsoft Windows 98. 2nd ed. 96p. 1999. pap. 15.31 (*0-07-228567-2*) McGraw.

— MS Access '97. 1998. text 23.25 incl. cd-rom (*0-07-013732-3*) McGraw.

— MS Excel '97. 1998. text 22.00 incl. cd-rom (*0-07-013727-7*) McGraw.

— MS Office '97. 1997. text 43.00 incl. cd-rom (*0-07-013735-8*) McGraw.

— MS Office 97. 1997. text 35.50 (*0-07-561614-9*) McGraw.

— MS Office Pro '97. 1997. text 56.50 incl. cd-rom (*0-07-013729-3*) McGraw.

— MS Powerpoint '97. 1998. text 17.50 incl. cd-rom (*0-07-013736-6*) McGraw.

— MS Windows '95. 1997. text 23.25 incl. cd-rom (*0-07-013738-2*) McGraw.

— MS Word '97. 1998. text 23.25 incl. cd-rom (*0-07-013739-0*) McGraw.

— Multimedia Education Management Information. 5th ed. 1998. text 43.50 (*0-13-888926-0*) P-H.

— Solving Classic Business Problems: An Introduction to Lotus 1-2-3 Release 2.3. (C). 1992. 23.50 incl. 5.25 hd (*0-201-50686-6*) Addison-Wesley.

— Teaching Notes. 960p. (C). 1998. write for info. (*0-02-368132-2*, Macmillan Coll) P-H.

***Laudon.** Website T/A Microsoft Office 2000. 1999. write for info. (*0-07-236855-1*, McGrw-H College) McGrw-H Hghr Educ.

Laudon, Bernard, tr. see Tre-Hardy, Gilles.

Laudon, Jane P. Business Information Systems. 3rd ed. (C). 1995. pap. text, teacher ed. 36.75 (*0-03-012727-0*) Harcourt Coll Pubs.

An Asterisk (*) at the beginning of an entry indicates that the title is appearing for the first time.

— Tut Guide Solvg Class Bus. (C). 1992. 32.00 (*0-201-60572-4*) Addison-Wesley.

*__Laudon, Jane P. & Laudon, Kenneth.__ Essentials of Management Information Systems. 4th ed. 576p. 2000. 82.67 (*0-13-019323-2*) P-H.

Laudon, Jane P., jt. auth. see Laudon, Kenneth C.

Laudon, Jane P., jt. auth. see Traver.

Laudon, Ken. Microsoft Windows 98. 2nd ed. (Interactive Computing Ser.). 200p. 1999. 20.00 incl. cd-rom (*0-07-228448-X*) McGraw.

— Solve It! Management Problem Solving with PC Software, Version 2.0. (Illus.). 200p. 1988. pap. text 14.00 (*0-945991-00-2*) Azimuth Corp.

— Solve It! Management Problem Solving with PC Software, Version 2.0. (Illus.). 250p. 1989. pap. text 14.00 (*0-945991-02-9*) Azimuth Corp.

— Solve It! Management Problem Solving with PC Software, Version 2.0. (Illus.). 300p. (C). 1990. pap. text 14.00 (*0-945991-03-7*) Azimuth Corp.

— Solve It! Management Problem Solving with PC Software, Version 2.0. (Illus.). 300p. (C). 1991. pap. text 14.00 (*0-945991-04-5*) Azimuth Corp.

— Solve It! Management Problem Solving with PC Software, Version 2.0. (Illus.). (C). 1992. pap. text 14.00 (*0-945991-05-3*) Azimuth Corp.

— Solve It! Management Problem Solving with PC Software, Version 2.0. (Illus.). (C). 1993. pap. text 14.00 (*0-945991-06-1*) Azimuth Corp.

— Solve It! Management Problem Solving with PC Software, Version 2.0. (Illus.). 350p. (C). 1994. pap. text 14.00 (*0-945991-08-8*) Azimuth Corp.

Laudon, Kenneth. Access 95 - 97. LC 97-46809. 120p. (C). 1998. pap. 14.69 (*0-07-038435-5*) McGraw.

— Excel 95 - 97. LC 97-46810. 160p. (C). 1998. pap. 14.69 (*0-07-038443-6*) McGraw.

— The Interactive Computer: Concepts & Skills: Text Plus Concepts. (C). 1996. pap. text 22.00 (*0-07-036618-7*) McGraw.

— Office 95 - 97 with Windows, Word, Excel, Access, Powerpoint. 1997. pap. text. write for info. (*0-07-038456-8*) McGraw.

— Office 95 - 97 with Windows, Word, Excel, Access. 1997. pap. text. write for info. (*0-07-038457-6*) McGraw.

— PowerPoint 9 - 97. LC 97-46808. 128p. (C). 1998. pap. 14.69 (*0-07-038439-8*) McGraw.

— Solving Classic Business Problems: An Introduction to Lotus 1-2-3, Release 2.2 User's Manual. (C). 1993. text 34.00 incl. 3.5 hd (*0-8053-1345-1*) Benjamin-Cummings.

— Windows 95 - 97. LC 97-5548. 128p. (C). 1997. pap. 14.69 (*0-07-038441-X*) McGraw.

— Word 95 - 97. LC 97-2210. 208p. (C). 1997. pap. 14.69 (*0-07-038437-1*) McGraw.

*__Laudon, Kenneth, et al.__ Microsoft Office 2000 in Brief. 528p. (C). 1999. pap. 44.69 (*0-07-234085-1*) McGrw-H Hghr Educ.

Laudon, Kenneth, jt. auth. see Laudon, Jane P.

Laudon, Kenneth C. Information Systems & the Internet. 4th ed. LC 98-116760. (Dryden Press Series in Information Systems). 1997. pap. text 81.00 (*0-03-024797-7*) Harcourt Coll Pubs.

— The Interactive Computer: Concepts & Skills: Text Plus Concepts. (C). 1996. pap. text 61.50 (*0-07-847133-8*) McGraw.

— The Interactive Computer Text Plus Concepts CD-ROM: Concepts & Skills: Text Plus Concepts. (C). 1996. pap. text 30.50 (*0-07-847134-6*) McGraw.

*__Laudon, Kenneth C. & Eiseman, Jason.__ Microsoft Access 2000. LC 99-62020. 1999. write for info. (*0-07-234075-4*) McGrw-H Hghr Educ.

Laudon, Kenneth C. & Laudon, Jane P. Management Information Systems: A Contemporary Perspective. 3rd ed. (Illus.). 818p. (C). 1993. write for info. (*0-318-69911-7*) Macmillan.

*__Laudon, Kenneth C. & Laudon, Jane P.__ Management Information Systems: Organization & Technology in the Networked Enterprise. 6th ed. LC 99-16968. 662p. 1999. 90.67 (*0-13-011732-3*) P-H.

*__Laudon, Kenneth C. & Rosenblatt, Kenneth.__ Microsoft Excel 2000. LC 99-62388. 1999. write for info. (*0-07-234076-2*) McGrw-H Hghr Educ.

— Microsoft PowerPoint 2000. LC 99-63168. (Illus.). 2000. write for info. (*0-07-234078-9*) McGrw-H Hghr Educ.

— Microsoft Word 2000. LC 99-62006. 1999. write for info. (*0-07-234087-8*) McGrw-H Hghr Educ.

Laudon, Kenneth C., et al. Information Technology: Concepts & Issues. LC 94-26935. 352p. 1994. pap. 34.95 (*0-534-24924-8*) Course Tech.

— Information Technology: Concepts & Issues. 312p. (C). 1997. teacher ed. 49.95 (*0-7600-4918-1*) Course Tech.

— Information Technology: Concepts & Issues. 2nd ed. 312p. (C). 1997. pap. 37.35 (*0-7600-4917-3*) Course Tech.

Laudon, Lowell R., jt. auth. see Moore, C. Raymond.

Laudon, Robert C. Principles of Petroleum Geology. LC 95-24201. (Petroleum Engineering Ser.). 224p. 1995. 105.00 (*0-13-649468-4*) P-H.

Laue. Named Organic Reactions. 298p. 1998. 79.95 (*0-471-97142-1*) Wiley.

Laue, Alice. Cooking from Denim to Lace. (Illus.). 400p. 1989. ring bd. write for info. (*0-9624351-0-4*) A Laue.

Laue, Angela Von, see Von Laue, Theodore H. & Von Laue, Angela.

Laue, Ingrid E. Pictorialism in the Fictional Miniatures of Albert Paris Guttersloh. (Austrian Culture Ser.: Vol. 22). XIV, 186p. (C). 1996. text 47.95 (*0-8204-3003-X*) P Lang Pubng.

Laue, Kurt & Stenger, Helmut. Extrusion. (Illus.). 457p. 1981. 208.00 (*0-87170-094-8*, 6457) ASM.

— Extrusion: Processes, Machinery, Tooling. Castle, A. F. & Lang, Gernot, trs. from GER. LC 80-23076. (Illus.). 471p. reprint ed. pap. 146.10 (*0-608-15943-3*, 203305700083) Bks Demand.

Laue, Thomas M., jt. ed. see Schuster, Todd M.

Lauen, Roger J. Positive Approaches to Corrections: Research, Policy & Practice. LC 96-50994. 256p. 1997. pap. 29.95 (*1-56991-065-0*) Am Correctional.

Lauener, L. A. The Introduction of Chinese Plants into Europe. Ferguson, D. K., ed. xii, 270p. 1996. 90.00 (*90-5103-130-0*, Pub. by SPB Acad Pub) Balogh.

Lauenroth, W. K. & Preston, E. M., eds. The Effects of SO2 on a Grassland: A Case Study in the Northern Great Plains of the United States. (Ecological Studies, Analysis & Synthesis: Vol. 45). (Illus.). 270p. 1984. 105.00 (*0-387-90943-5*) Spr-Verlag.

Lauer. Design Basics. 5th ed. LC 99-62330. (C). 2000. pap. 68.50 (*0-15-508377-5*) Harcourt Coll Pubs.

— Marriage & Family. 4th ed. 168p. 1999. pap., student ed. 19.38 (*0-07-234189-0*) McGraw.

— Marriage & Family. 4th ed. LC 99-30977. 1999. 37.50 (*0-07-231572-5*) McGraw.

— Personal Journal on Marriage. 3rd ed. 1996. pap. 14.69 (*0-697-34016-3*) McGraw.

— SC Marr Family Quest/Make Choices. 1994. 45.00 (*0-697-27712-7*, WCB McGr Hill) McGrw-H Hghr Educ.

— Social Problems. 6th ed. 1994. teacher ed. 14.37 (*0-697-21353-6*, WCB McGr Hill) McGrw-H Hghr Educ.

— Social Problems. 6th ed. 1994. 10.31 (*0-697-25715-0*, WCB McGr Hill) McGrw-H Hghr Educ.

Lauer, A. R., jt. auth. see Delaney, Connie White.

Lauer, A. Robert & Sullivan, Henry W., eds. Hispanic Essays in Honor of Frank P. Casa. 2nd ed. (Iberica Ser.: Vol. 20). (Illus.). XVI, 481p. 1999. pap. text 49.95 (*0-8204-4570-3*, 45703) P Lang Pubng.

Lauer, Alphonse M., ed. see Colombas, Garcia M.

Lauer, Alphonse M., ed. see Gruen, Anselm.

Lauer, Alphonse M., ed. see Gruen, Anselm & Dufner, Meinrad.

Lauer, Alphonse M., ed. see Gruen, Anselm & Roettger, Gregory J.

Lauer, Alphonse M., ed. see Gruen, Anselm & Scharper, Philip J.

Lauer, Alphonse M., ed. see Ruppert, Fidelis & Gruen, Anselm.

Lauer, Alphonse M., ed. see Stevens, Clifford J.

Lauer, Alphonse M., ed. see Uebler, Leonard.

Lauer, Alphonse M., ed. see Uhing, M. James.

Lauer, Carlo, ed. Family World Atlas: An Illustrated & Informative View of the Earth. (Illus.). 232p. 1998. reprint ed. text 35.00 (*0-7881-5601-2*) DIANE Pub.

Lauer, Charles. Auto Body Repair. LC 85-702615. 1985. student ed. 7.00 (*0-8064-0209-1*, 484) Bergwall.

Lauer, Charles D. Old West Adventures in Arizona. LC 88-24676. 176p. (Orig.). 1989. pap. 6.95 (*0-914846-39-6*) Golden West Pub.

— Tales of Arizona Territory. LC 90-3336. (Illus.). 160p. (Orig.). 1990. pap. 6.95 (*0-914846-47-7*) Golden West Pub.

Lauer, Charles S. Reach for the Stars: Pursuing Success Through Excellence. LC 96-85313. 224p. (Orig.). 1996. pap. 13.95 (*1-881802-33-7*) CCI Bks WA.

— Soar with the Eagles. LC 91-73259. 236p. 1991. 24.95 (*0-8163-1061-0*) CCI Bks WA.

— Soar with the Eagles: A Challenge to Excellence. LC 93-83849. 236p. 1993. pap. 11.95 (*1-881802-01-9*) CCI Bks WA.

Lauer, David. Design Basics. 4th ed. LC 93-80822. (C). 1994. pap. text 62.00 (*0-15-501184-7*, Pub. by Harcourt Coll Pubs) Harcourt.

Lauer, David, tr. see Pacheco, Jose E.

Lauer, David, tr. see Vicens, Josefina.

Lauer, Dorothy S. & Steiger, Brad. How to Use ESP: The Hidden Power of Your Mind. LC 98-10396. 192p. 1998. reprint ed. pap. 12.95 (*1-880090-51-1*) Galde Pr.

Lauer, Gary. Principles & Practices of the College-Based Radiography Program. Gardner, Alvin F., ed. (Allied Health Professions Monograph). 294p. (C). 1984. 37.50 (*0-87527-310-6*) Green.

Lauer, Gerhard. Die Verspaetete Revolution: Erich von Kahler Wissenschaftsgeschichte Zwischen Konservativer. (Revolution und Exil Philosophie und Wissenschaft Ser.: Bd. 6). (GER.). 566p. (C). 1994. pap. text 58.00 (*3-11-014397-6*) De Gruyter.

Lauer, Hans E. Aggression & Repression in the Individual & Society. Castelliz, K. & Davies, Saunders, trs. from GER.Tr. of Aggression und Repression im individuellen und Sozialen Berich. 111p. 1981. pap. 9.95 (*0-85440-359-0*, Pub. by R Steiner Pr) Anthroposophic.

Lauer, Helen. Changing Values, Changing Technologies: Ghanaian Philosophical Studies, II. LC 99-37506. (Cultural Heritage & Contemporary Change Ser.). write for info. (*1-56518-144-1*) Coun Res Values.

Lauer, J. L. Tribology for Practicing Engineers. (Mechanical Engineering Ser.). Date not set. write for info. (*0-8247-9565-2*) Dekker.

Lauer, Janice M. Four Worlds of Writing. 3rd ed. (C). 1991. pap. 40.31 (*0-06-043860-6*) Addson-Wesley Educ.

Lauer, Janice M. & Asher, J. William. Composition Research: Empirical Designs. (Illus.). 320p. 1988. pap. text 27.95 (*0-19-504172-0*) OUP.

Lauer, Jeanette C. & Lauer, Robert H. How to Survive & Thrive in an Empty Nest: Reclaiming Your Life When Your Children Have Grown. LC 98-68752. 192p. 1999. pap. 13.95 (*1-57224-137-3*) New Harbinger.

— Til Death Do Us Part: A Study & Guide to Long-Term Marriage. LC 86-22735. (Marriage & Family Review Ser.: Supp. No. 1). 192p. 1986. pap. text 14.95 (*0-918393-32-9*, Harrington Park) Haworth Pr.

— Til Death Do Us Part: How Couples Stay Together. LC 86-22735. (Supplement to Marriage & Family Review Ser.: No. 1). 192p. 1986. text 39.95 (*0-86656-601-5*) Haworth Pr.

Lauer, Jeanette C., jt. auth. see Lauer, Robert H.

Lauer, Jeanette C., jt. ed. see Lauer, Robert H.

Lauer, Kathy & Brozenec, Sally A. Pathophysiology: With Disk. LC 98-49667. (Notes Ser.). 320p. 1999. pap. 24.95 (*0-87434-964-8*) Springhouse Corp.

Lauer, Keith & Robinson, Julie. Celluloid: Collector's Reference & Value Guide. LC 99-196356. 224p. 1998. 24.95 (*1-57432-076-9*) Collector Bks.

Lauer, Kristin O., ed. see Wharton, Edith.

Lauer, Larry D. Communication Essentials for the Nonprofit Executive. LC 97-3284. 228p. 1997. pap. 49.00 (*0-8342-0893-8*, 08938) Aspen Pub.

Lauer, Mark T. Buying & Selling a Business. Franco, Debra L., ed. 272p. (Orig.). 1995. pap. 24.95 (*1-880539-33-0*) Garrett FL.

Lauer, Mark T., ed. see Goldstein, Arnold S.

Lauer, Mark T., ed. see Levinson, Robert E.

Lauer, Matthias B. Nachhaltige Entwicklung und Religion: Gesellschaftsvisionen unter Religionsverdacht und die Frage der Religiosen Bedingungen Okologischen Handelns. (GER.). 1998. text 24.00 (*3-927120-48-0*, 30) Ugarit-Verlag.

Lauer, O. Gary, et al. Evaluating Radiographic Quality: The Variables & Their Effects. (Illus.). 160p. (C). 1991. text 48.00 (*0-916973-04-2*) Burnell Co.

Lauer, P. E., ed. Functional Programming, Concurrency, Simulation & Automated Reasoning: International Lecture Series 1991-1992, MacMaster University, Hamilton, Ontario, Canada. (Lecture Notes in Computer Science Ser.: Vol. 693). xi, 397p. 1993. 61.95 (*0-387-56883-2*) Spr-Verlag.

Lauer, P. E., jt. auth. see Janicki, R.

Lauer, Paul E. Church & State in New England. LC 78-63809. (Johns Hopkins University. Studies in the Social Sciences. Thirtieth Ser. 1912: 2-3). reprint ed. 29.50 (*0-404-61072-2*) AMS Pr.

Lauer, Quentin. Essays in Hegelian Dialectic. LC 76-18465. 208p. 1977. 35.00 (*0-8232-1021-9*); pap. 17.50 (*0-8232-1022-7*) Fordham.

— G. K. Chesterton: Philosopher Without a Portfolio. LC 88-80057. viii, 191p. 1992. reprint ed. pap. 19.95 (*0-8232-1199-1*) Fordham.

— Hegel's Concept of God. LC 81-21452. (SUNY Series in Hegelian Studies). 339p. (C). 1983. text 21.50 (*0-87395-597-8*) State U NY Pr.

— Hegel's Idea of Philosophy. 2nd ed. LC 74-152244. 159p. (C). 1983. pap. 17.00 (*0-8232-0927-X*) Fordham.

— Nature of Philosophical Inquiry. LC 88-64165. (Aquinas Lectures). 1989. text 15.00 (*0-87462-156-9*, AQ-53) Marquette.

— A Reading of Hegel's "Phenomenology of Spirit" 3rd rev. ed. LC 92-9891. vii, 303p. 1993. 30.00 (*0-8232-1354-4*); pap. 18.95 (*0-8232-1355-2*) Fordham.

— The Triumph of Subjectivity: An Introduction to Transcendental Phenomenology. 2nd ed. LC 58-12363. xxiii, 182p. 1978. 30.00 (*0-8232-0336-0*) Fordham.

Lauer, Reinhard. Langenscheidt Universal German-Serbocroatian, Serbocroatian-German Dictionary: Langenscheidt Serbokroatisch-Deutsch-Serbokroatisch Universal Woerterbuch. 7th ed. (GER & SER.). 448p. 1981. 14.95 (*0-8288-1051-6*, F19620) Fr & Eur.

Lauer, Richard A., ed. see McBride, William E.

*__Lauer, Robert.__ Marriage & Family: The Quest for Intimacy. 4th ed. 532p. (C). 1999. pap. 47.81 (*0-07-236163-8*) McGrw-H Hghr Educ.

Lauer, Robert H. Perspectives on Social Change. 4th ed. 416p. 1991. text 42.00 (*0-205-12575-1*, H25752) Allyn.

— Social Problems & the Quality of Life. 7th ed. LC 97-70818. 688p. (C). 1997. text. write for info. (*0-697-24455-5*, WCB McGr Hill) McGrw-H Hghr Educ.

— Temporal Man: The Meaning & Uses of Social Time. LC 81-11917. 181p. 1981. 49.95 (*0-275-90666-3*, C0666, Praeger Pubs) Greenwood.

Lauer, Robert H. & Lauer, Jeanette C. Becoming Family: How to Build a Stepfamily That Really Works. LC 98-48892. 192p. 1999. pap. text 12.99 (*0-8066-3730-7*, 9-3730, Augsburg) Augsburg Fortress.

— For Better & Better: Building a Healthy Marriage for a Lifetime. LC 94-12861. 144p. (Orig.). 1995. pap. 9.00 (*0-687-23623-1*) Dimen for Liv.

— Intimacy on the Run. LC 96-19531. 160p. (Orig.). 1996. pap. 10.00 (*0-687-01770-X*) Dimen for Liv.

— Marriage & Family: The Quest for Intimacy. 3rd ed. LC 96-83188. 544p. (C). 1996. text. write for info. (*0-697-24452-0*, WCB McGr Hill) McGrw-H Hghr Educ.

— Sociology: Contours of Society. LC 97-13296. (Illus.). 530p. (C). 1998. pap. text. write for info. (*1-891487-01-9*) Roxbury Pub Co.

— True Intimacy: Fifty-Two Devotions for Married Couples. LC 95-41091. 144p. 1996. pap. 9.00 (*0-687-00806-9*) Dimen for Liv.

— Watersheds: Mastering Life's Unpredictable Crises. 272p. 1988. 16.95 (*0-316-51629-5*) Little.

Lauer, Robert H. & Lauer, Jeanette C., eds. Troubled Times: Readings in Social Problems. LC 98-44608. 280p. (C). 1999. pap. text. write for info. (*1-891487-19-1*) Roxbury Pub Co.

Lauer, Robert H., jt. auth. see Lauer, Jeanette C.

Lauer, Simon & Ernst, Hanspeter, eds. Tempelkult und Tempelzerstorung (70 N. Chr.) Festschrift Fur Clemens Thoma Zum 60. Geburtstag. (Judaica et Christiana Ser.: Bd. 15). (GER.). 265p. 1995. 38.95 (*3-906753-46-8*, Pub. by P Lang) P Lang Pubng.

Lauer, Steve, et al. Now Hiring: Finding & Keeping Good Help for Your Entry-Wage Jobs. LC 96-20824. 192p. (Orig.). 1996. 17.95 (*0-8144-7912-X*) AMACOM.

Lauer, Teresa. Years of Silence: My Soul Was the Scene of the Crime. LC 98-71676. 158p. 1998. per. 14.95 (*0-9662078-0-7*) Inst Inter Rels.

*__Lauer, Teresa M.__ The Truth about Rape: Emotional, Physical, Spiritual & Sexual Healing. 204p. 2000. pap. 14.95 (*0-9662078-1-5*) Inst Inter Rels.

Lauer, Thomas. Porting to Win32, No. 32. LC 95-23946. 504p. 1995. 43.95 (*0-387-94572-5*) Spr-Verlag.

Lauer, Thomas, et al, eds. Questions & Information Systems. 376p. 1992. pap. 45.00 (*0-8058-1019-6*); text 69.95 (*0-8058-1018-8*) L Erlbaum Assocs.

Lauer, Walter E. Battle Babies: The Story of the Ninety-Ninth Infantry Division. 28th ed. (Illus.). 353p. 1985. 49.95 (*0-89839-089-3*) Battery Pr.

Lauer, William. Prisoner Exchange: The Murder of Joshua Huddy. (Illus.). 72p. (Orig.). 1994. pap. 6.00 (*0-941965-07-4*) Ocean Cnty Hist.

*__Lauerach, Edward.__ The Setter. Hamilton, Lynn, ed. 100p. 1999. pap. 14.95 (*1-892937-04-2*) Spec Pubns.

Lauerer, John A. I Remember Fairbanks & Skibo. LC 94-61703. 96p. (Orig.). 1994. pap. 8.95 (*0-9636894-1-X*) Estrn Itascan.

Lauersdorf, Lynn R., jt. ed. see Melander, John M.

Lauersdorf, Richard E. Hebrews. (People's Bible Commentary Ser.). 185p. 1992. pap. 9.99 (*0-570-04595-9*, 12-8013) Concordia.

— Hebrews. LC 85-63195. (People's Bible Ser.). 192p. 1986. pap. 9.99 (*0-8100-0236-1*, 15N0423) Northwest Pub.

— Hebrews. Fischer, William E., ed. (The People's Bible Ser.). 48p. 1986. pap., student ed. 5.00 (*0-938272-56-X*, 22-2189) WELS Board.

Lauersen, Niels. Childbirth with Love. 1991. pap. 17.95 (*0-425-12618-8*) Berkley Pub.

— The Complete Book of Breast Care. 1998. pap. 14.95 (*0-449-91241-8*) Fawcett.

Lauersen, Niels H. It's Your Body. (J. Hook Ser.). 1992. mass mkt. 7.99 (*0-425-13920-4*) Berkley Pub.

Lauersen, Niels H. & Bouchez, Colette. Getting Pregnant: What Couples Need to Know Right Now. 368p. 1992. pap. 12.95 (*0-449-90667-1*, Columbine) Fawcett.

Lauersen, Niels H. & DeSwaan, Constance. The Endometriosis Answer Book: New Hope, New Help. 1989. pap. 12.00 (*0-449-90361-3*, Columbine) Fawcett.

Lauersen, Niels H. & Hendra, Judy. It's Your Pregnancy: Questions You Ask Yourself & Are Afraid to Ask Your Obstetrician. 480p. 1987. pap. 12.95 (*0-671-50211-5*, Fireside) S&S Trade Pap.

Lauersen, Niels H. & Stukane, Eileen. Listen to Your Body: A Gynecologist Answers Women's Most Intimate Questions. (Orig.). pap. 7.99 (*0-425-13921-2*) Berkley Pub.

— Listen to Your Body: A Gynecologist Answers Women's Most Intimate Questions. (Orig.). 2000. reprint ed. pap. 16.00 (*0-684-85411-2*, Fireside) S&S Trade Pap.

Lauersen, Niels H. & Whitney, Steven. It's Your Body: A Woman's Guide to Gynecology. LC 80-80994. (Illus.). 576p. 1986. mass mkt. 7.99 (*0-425-09917-2*) Berkley Pub.

Lauersen, Niels H., jt. ed. see Reyniak, J. Victor.

Lauf, Cornelia & Phillpot, Clive. Artist - Author: Contemporary Artists' Books. (Illus.). 184p. 1998. 45.00 (*1-881616-94-0*, 810431) Dist Art Pubs.

— Artist Author: Contemporary Artists' Books. LC 97-29911. 1998. pap. 35.00 (*1-885444-07-9*) Am Fed Arts.

Lauf, Cornelia, ed. see Dwyer, Nancy.

Lauf, Robert J., jt. ed. see McCarthy, Gregory J.

Laufe, Abe, ed. see FitzGerald, Emily M.

Laufenberg, Holger. Conceptual People Photography. 1998. pap. 29.95 (*1-887165-19-3*) Am Showcase.

— Conceptual Still Life Photography. 1998. pap. 24.95 (*1-887165-18-5*) Am Showcase.

Laufer, Alexander. Simultaneous Management: Managing Projects in a Dynamic Environment. LC 96-34247. 300p. 1996. 59.95 (*0-8144-0312-3*) AMACOM.

*__Laufer, Alexander & Hoffman, Edward J.__ Project Management Success Stories: Lessons of Project Leaders. 240p. 2000. text 44.95 (*0-471-36007-4*) Wiley.

Laufer, Berthold. The American Plant Migration Pt. 1: The Potato. LC 39-5394. (Field Museum of Natural History Anthropological Ser.: Vol. 28, No. 1). (Illus.). 134p. 1938. reprint ed. pap. 41.60 (*0-608-02715-4*, 206338000001) Bks Demand.

— The American Plant Migration Vol. 1: The Potato. (Field Museum of Natural History Ser.: Vol. 28). (Illus.). 1938. 25.00 (*0-527-01888-0*) Periodicals Srv.

— The Beginnings of Porcelain in China: Field Museum of Natural History, 3 vols. in 1. (Field Museum Monographs: Vol. 15). 1917. 50.00 (*0-527-01875-9*) Periodicals Srv.

— Chinese Baskets. LC 28-1443. (Illus.). 42p. 1925. boxed set 50.00 (*0-686-25961-0*) Rare Oriental Bk Co.

— Chinese Clay Figures Pt. 1: The Mrs. T. B. Blackstone Expedition: Prolegomena on the History of Defensive Armor. LC NB0159.C3L3. (Field Museum of Natural History, Publication 177, Anthropological Ser.: Vol. 13, No. 2). 485p. reprint ed. pap. 150.40 (*0-608-02119-9*, 206276800001) Bks Demand.

— Chinese Grave: Sculptures of the Han Period. (Illus.). 45p. 1911. 65.00 (*0-318-04695-4*) Rare Oriental Bk Co.

— The Decorative Art of the Amur Tribes. LC 73-3524. (Jesup North Pacific Expedition. Publications: No. 4). reprint ed. 57.50 (*0-404-58104-8*) AMS Pr.

— The Diamond: A Study in Chinese & Hellenistic Folk-Lore. LC GR0805.L3. (Field Museum of Natural History, Publication 184, Anthropological Ser.: Vol. 15, No. 1). 75p. 1915. reprint ed. pap. 30.00 (*0-608-02099-0*, 206275300004) Bks Demand.

— The Domestication of the Cormorant in China & Japan.

L

An Asterisk (*) at the beginning of an entry indicates that the title is appearing for the first time.

LC 31-33981. (Field Museum of Natural History Anthropological Ser.: Vol. 18, No. 3). (Illus.). 71p. 1931. reprint ed. pap. 30.00 (*0-608-02725-1*, 206339000004) Bks Demand.

— Geophagy. LC 31-35691. (Field Museum of Natural History Publication 280 Ser.: Vol. 18, No. 2). 102p. 1930. reprint ed. pap. 31.70 (*0-608-02704-9*, 206336900004) Bks Demand.

— Historical Jottings on Amber in Asia. LC 08-11467. (American Anthropological Association Memoirs Ser.). 1906. pap. 25.00 (*0-527-00502-9*) Periodicals Srv.

— Jade: A Study in Chinese Archaeology & Religion. (Field Museum of Natural History Ser.: Vol. 10). (Illus.). 50.00 (*0-527-01870-8*) Periodicals Srv.

— Notes on Turquois in the East, 1913-1914: Field Museum of Natural History. (Field Museum Monographs: Vol. 13). 1913. 50.00 (*0-527-01873-2*) Periodicals Srv.

— The Prehistory of Aviation. LC 28-30680. (Field Museum of Natural History, Publication 184, Anthropological Ser.: Vol. 18, No. 1). 120p. 1928. reprint ed. pap. 37.20 (*0-608-02114-8*, 206276300004) Bks Demand.

— Reindeer & Its Domestication. LC 18-12075. (American Anthropological Association Memoirs Ser.). 1917. pap. 25.00 (*0-527-00517-7*) Periodicals Srv.

— Sino-Iranica: Chinese Contributions to the History of Civilization in Ancient Iran, with Special Reference to the History of Cultivated Plants & Products. LC 20-5115. (Field Museum of Natural History, Publication 201). 436p. 1919. reprint ed. pap. 135.20 (*0-608-02108-3*, 206275700004) Bks Demand.

Laufer, Edward. Guide to the Study of Schenkerian Analysis. (Illus.). 1999. 49.95 (*0-02-871325-7*, Schirmer Books) Mac Lib Ref.

Laufer, Gabriel. Introduction to Optics & Lasers in Engineering. 550p. 1996. text 95.00 (*0-521-45233-3*) Cambridge U Pr.

Laufer, Geraldine A. Tussie-Mussies. LC 92-50927. (Illus.). 160p. 1993. 22.95 (*1-56305-106-0*, 3106) Workman Pub.

***Laufer, Geraldine A.** Tussie-Mussies: And the Language of Flowers. (Illus.). 160p. 2000. pap. 15.95 (*0-7611-2066-1*) Workman Pub.

Laufer, Greg, jt. auth. see Belsky, Walter.

Laufer, Henry B. Normal Two-Dimensional Singularities. LC 78-160261. (Annals of Mathematics Studies: No. 71). (Illus.). 173p. 1971. reprint ed. pap. 53.70 (*0-608-06633-8*, 206683000004) Bks Demand.

Laufer, Igor & Levine, Marc S., eds. Double Contrast Gastrointestinal Radiology. 2nd ed. (Illus.). 713p. 1992. text 179.00 (*0-7216-5649-8*, W B Saunders Co) Harcrt Hlth Sci Grp.

Laufer, Igor, et al. Double Contrast Gastrointestinal Radiology. 3rd ed. LC 99-29019. (Illus.). 605p. 2000. text. write for info. (*0-7216-8211-1*, W B Saunders Co) Harcrt Hlth Sci Grp.

Laufer, Judy E. Where Did Papa Go? Looking at Death from a Young Child's Perspective. (Illus.). 32p. (Orig.). (J). (ps-2). 1991. pap. 9.95 (*1-881669-00-9*) Little Egg Pub.

Laufer, Liora. Callirobics. unabridged ed. (J). (gr. 3-12). 1990. 26.95 incl. audio (*0-9630478-0-9*, CL500) Callirobics.

Laufer, Moses. Adolescence & Developmental Breakdown: A Psychoanalytic View. 240p. 1995. pap. text 25.00 (*1-85575-108-9*, Pub. by H Karnac Bks Ltd) Other Pr LLC.

Laufer, Moses. Adolescent Breakdown & Beyond. 168p. 1997. pap. 25.00 (*1-85575-149-6*, Pub. by H Karnac Bks Ltd) Other Pr LLC.

Laufer, Moses, ed. Adolescent Breakdown & Beyond. LC 97-28140. 168p. 1998. 27.50 (*0-8236-0063-7*, 00063) Intl Univs Pr.

— The Suicidal Adolescent. 168p. 1995. pap. text 25.00 (*1-85575-121-6*, Pub. by H Karnac Bks Ltd) Other Pr LLC.

— The Suicidal Adolescent. 162p. 1996. 28.50 (*0-8236-6697-2*, BN 06697) Intl Univs Pr.

***Laufer, Peter.** Hecho en Mexico. Reyes, Victor, tr. LC 99-38220. (SPA., Illus.). 32p. (J). (gr. 4-6). 2000. 16.95 (*0-7922-7925-5*, Pub. by Natl Geog) S&S Trade.

Laufer, Peter. Inside Talk Radio: America's Voice or Just Hot Air? (Illus.). 288p. 1995. 19.95 (*1-55972-278-9*, Birch Ln Pr) Carol Pub Group.

— Iron Curtain Rising: A Personal Journey Through the Changing Landscape of Eastern Europe. LC 91-11997. (Illus.). 248p. 1991. 19.50 (*1-56279-015-3*) Mercury Hse Inc.

***Laufer, Peter.** Mobile Phone Etiquette. 2000. pap. 8.95 (*1-873668-17-1*, Pub. by Take That Bks) Trafalgar.

Laufer, Peter. Nightmare Abroad: Stories of Americans Imprisoned in Foreign Lands. LC 92-15811. (Illus.). 208p. 1993. 20.00 (*1-56279-028-5*) Mercury Hse Inc.

***Laufer, Peter.** 101 Differences between Men & Women: From Closets Full of Shoes to Never Asking Directions. 1999. pap. text 12.95 (*0-8065-2158-9*) Carol Pub Group.

Laufer, Peter. A Question of Consent: Innocence & Complicity in the Glen Ridge Rape Case. LC 93-42464. 208p. 1994. 19.95 (*1-56279-059-5*) Mercury Hse Inc.

— Wireless Etiquette: A Guide to the Changing World of Instant Communication. LC 98-96554. (Illus.). 103p. 1999. 14.50 (*1-892918-00-5*, 101-WE) Omnipoint Bks.

***Laufer, Peter & Roth, Susan L.** Made in Mexico. LC 99-38220. 32p. (J). 2000. 16.95 (*0-7922-7118-1*) Natl Geog.

Laufer, Peter, jt. auth. see Lester, Gene.

Laufer, Peter, jt. auth. see Swan, Sheila.

Laufer, Robert, jt. auth. see Frey-Wouters, Ellen.

Laufer, Romain & Paradeise, Catherine. Marketing Democracy: Public Opinion & Media Formation in Democratic Societies. 347p. 1989. 49.95 (*0-88738-199-5*) Transaction Pubs.

Laufer, William, jt. ed. see Day, James M.

Laufer, William S. & Adler, Freda, eds. Advances in Criminological Theory, Vol. 1. 256p. 1988. 44.95 (*0-88738-182-0*) Transaction Pubs.

— Advances in Criminological Theory, Vol. 2. 256p. 1990. 44.95 (*0-88738-287-8*) Transaction Pubs.

— The Criminology of Criminal Law Vol. 8: Advances in Criminological Theory. 360p. 1999. 44.95 (*1-56000-329-4*) Transaction Pubs.

Laufer, William S., et al. Criminology. 2nd ed. LC 94-15931. (C). 1994. text 56.25 (*0-07-000471-4*); text 48.00 (*0-07-000498-6*) McGraw.

Laufer, William S., jt. ed. see Adler, Freda.

Laufer, William S., jt. ed. see Kagehiro, D.

Lauffenburger, Douglas A. & Linderman, Jennifer J. Receptors: Models for Binding, Trafficking, & Signaling. (Illus.). 376p. (C). 1996. pap. text 40.00 (*0-19-510663-6*) OUP.

Lauffer, Armand. The Aim of the Game. LC 73-84873. 132p. 1974. 9.95 (*0-88437-052-6*) Psych Dimensions.

— Assessment Tools: For Practitioners, Managers, & Trainers. LC 82-10552. (Sage Human Services Guides Ser.: No. 30). 192p. reprint ed. pap. 59.60 (*0-7837-6576-2*, 204614100011) Bks Demand.

— Careers, Colleagues, & Conflicts: Understanding Gender, Race, & Ethnicity in the Workplace. LC 85-14276. (Sage Human Services Guides Ser.: No. 43). 182p. reprint ed. pap. 56.50 (*0-7837-6580-0*, 204614500011) Bks Demand.

— Grants, Etc. 2nd ed. LC 97-4597. Orig. Title: Grantsmanship & Fund Raising. 384p. (C). 1997. 56.00 (*0-8039-5468-9*, 54689) Sage.

— Grants, Etc. 2nd rev. ed. LC 97-4597. Orig. Title: Grantsmanship & Fund Raising. 384p. (C). 1997. pap. 26.00 (*0-8039-5469-7*, 54697) Sage.

— Grantsmanship. 2nd ed. (Human Services Guides Ser.: Vol. 1). 120p. 1983. pap. 18.95 (*0-8039-2022-9*) Sage.

— Resources for Child Placement & Other Human Services: A Project CRAFT Publication. LC 78-26352. (Sage Human Services Guides Ser.: No. 6). 192p. 1979. reprint ed. pap. 59.60 (*0-608-01468-0*, 205951200001) Bks Demand.

— Strategic Marketing for Not-for-Profit Organizations: Program & Resource Development. LC 83-49509. 384p. (C). 1984. 40.00 (*0-02-918260-3*) Free Pr.

— Understanding Your Social Agency. 2nd ed. 168p. 1984. pap. 18.95 (*0-8039-2349-X*) Sage.

— Working in Social Work: Growing & Thriving in Human Services Practice. LC 86-29700. (Sage Sourcebooks for the Human Services Ser.: No. 6). 339p. reprint ed. pap. 105.10 (*0-7837-6582-7*, 204614700011) Bks Demand.

Lauffer, Armand & Gorodezky, Sarah. Volunteers. LC 77-9003. (Sage Human Services Guides Ser.: No. 5). 87p. 1977. reprint ed. pap. 30.00 (*0-608-01518-0*, 205956200002) Bks Demand.

Lauffer, Butch & Davie, Sandy. Soccer Coach's Guide to Practices, Drills & Skill Training. LC 92-44087. (Illus.). 160p. 1993. pap. 14.95 (*0-8069-8219-5*) Sterling.

Lauffer, Lisa B., jt. auth. see Parolini, Stephen.

Lauffer, Max A. Entropy-Driven Processes in Biology: Polymerization of Tobacco Mosaic Virus Protein & Similar Reactions. LC 74-18267. (Molecular Biology, Biochemistry & Biophysics Ser.: Vol. 20). (Illus.). x, 264p. 1975. 60.00 (*0-387-06933-X*) Spr-Verlag.

Lauffer, Randall B., ed. Iron & Human Disease. 534p. 1992. lib. bdg. 249.00 (*0-8493-6779-4*, RC632) CRC Pr.

Lauffer, Siegfried, ed. Diokletians Preisedikt. (Texte und Kommentare Ser.: Vol. 5). (C). 1971. 192.30 (*3-11-002282-6*) De Gruyter.

Laufman, Alan, ed. Organ Handbook, 1985. 100p. 1985. 5.00 (*0-913499-52-8*) Organ Hist Soc.

— Organ Handbook, 1984. 112p. 1984. 5.00 (*0-913499-51-X*) Organ Hist Soc.

— Organ Handbook, 1987. (Illus.). 100p. (Orig.). 1987. pap. 5.00 (*0-913499-54-4*) Organ Hist Soc.

— Organ Handbook, 1983. 136p. 1983. 5.00 (*0-913499-50-1*) Organ Hist Soc.

Laufman, Alan K. The Law of Medical Malpractice in Texas: A Primer for the Medical Community. LC 77-420. (Illus.). 136p. reprint ed. pap. 42.20 (*0-8357-7750-2*, 203610700002) Bks Demand.

Laufman, Dudley. An Orchard & a Garden. 1974. pap. 10.00 (*0-87233-026-5*) Bauhan.

Laufman, Judy, ed. see Hoefler, Patricia A.

Laufs, Adolf. Rechtsentwicklungen in Deutschland. 3rd ed. (Lehrbuch der Allgemeinen Geographie Ser. Vol. 12). 1984. 32.35 (*3-11-009758-3*) De Gruyter.

Laugen, Linda F. Paperwraps: A Collector's Guide to Paperbound Books. LC 97-92317. (Illus.). xii, 252p. 1999. pap. 17.95 (*0-9669296-0-8*) Shadowbend.

Laugesen, Richard W. Colorado Litigation Forms & Analysis. LC 95-80827. (Practitioner's Ser.). 3300p. 1995. text. write for info. (*0-7620-0021-X*) West Group.

Laugharne, P. Parliament & Specialist Advice. 1993. 75.00 (*1-873534-03-5*, Pub. by Manutius Pr) St Mut.

Laughbaum. Intermediate Algebra. rev. ed. LC 93-222208. (Mathematics Ser.). 1994. text 56.95 (*0-534-17216-4*) PWS Pubs.

— Intermediate Mathematics - Prelim Ed. (Math). 1992. mass mkt. 47.25 (*0-534-17215-6*) PWS Pubs.

— Modeling Projects For Math Before Calc. (Math). 1996. mass mkt. 28.95 (*0-534-94636-4*) PWS Pubs.

Laugher, Charles T. Thomas Bray's Grand Design: Libraries of the Church of England in America, 1695-1785. LC 73-16332. (ACRL Publications in Librarianship: No. 35). 125p. reprint ed. pap. 38.80 (*0-608-18643-0*, 202422400035) Bks Demand.

Laughery, Kenneth R., Sr., et al, eds. Human Factors Perspectives on Warnings: Selections from Human Factors & Ergonomics Society Annual Meetings 1980-1993. 296p. 1994. pap. 50.00 (*0-945289-02-2*) Human Factors.

Laughing, Elephant. Christmas Alphabet. (Illus.). 32p. (ps up). 1999. 20.00 (*1-883211-22-0*, Darling & Comp) Laughing Elephant.

Laughingwand, Sparrow. Hell Soup: The Collected Writings of Sparrow 13 LaughingWand. 96p. (Orig.). 1996. pap. 8.95 (*0-916397-43-2*) Manic D Pr.

Laughingwand, Sparrow T. Queen of Shade. (Orig.). 1993. pap. 3.00 (*0-929730-44-5*) Zeitgeist Pr.

— Seven Dollar Shoes. 20p. (Orig.). 1994. pap. 3.00 (*0-916397-24-6*) Manic D Pr.

Laughlin. Financial Accounting. 1989. pap., teacher ed. write for info. (*0-278-00026-6*) Thomson Learn.

Laughlin, Bonnie, ed. see O., Bill.

Laughlin, Brenda & Nason, Kelly. Cooking Low Carb. Date not set. pap. 17.95 (*0-9672271-0-0*) Two Ns Pubg.

Laughlin, Burgess. The Aristotle Adventure: A Guide to the Greek, Arabic, & Latin Scholars Who Transmitted Aristotle's Logic to the Renaissance. LC 94-73795. (Illus.). 243p. (Orig.). 1995. pap. 19.95 (*0-9644714-9-3*) A Hale Pub.

Laughlin, Charles D., Jr. & D'Aquili, Eugene G. Biogenetic Structuralism. LC 74-13245. (Illus.). 211p. 1974. text 48.50 (*0-231-03817-8*) Col U Pr.

Laughlin, Charlotte & Levack, Daniel J. De Camp: An L. Sprague de Camp Bibliography. 328p. 1983. lib. bdg. 65.00 (*0-313-27677-3*) Greenwood.

Laughlin, Chuck. Samurai Selling: The Ancient Art of Modern Service. 6th ed. 1994. pap. 8.95 (*0-312-11885-6*) St Martin.

Laughlin, Clara E. Work-a-Day Girl: A Study of Some Present-Day Conditions. LC 74-3956. (Women in America Ser.). (Illus.). 320p. 1974. reprint ed. 26.95 (*0-405-06105-6*) Ayer.

Laughlin, Clarence J., et al. Haunter of Ruins: The Photography of Clarence John Laughlin. LC 97-4077. (Illus.). 112p. (gr. 8). 1997. 40.00 (*0-8212-2361-5*) Little.

Laughlin, Erin. Culture Book: Hourani. 96p. 1996. pap. write for info. (*1-889312-25-8*) ForeverWrld.

— Culture Book: Neuonians. 192p. Date not set. pap. 18.00 (*1-889312-26-6*) ForeverWrld.

— The NeverWorld. 1996. boxed set 38.00 (*1-889312-01-0*) ForeverWrld.

— The NeverWorld: A Life-Time Experience. 304p. 1996. pap. write for info. (*1-889312-00-2*) ForeverWrld.

— The NeverWorld: GM's Screen. 6p. 1996. pap. write for info. (*1-889312-75-4*) ForeverWrld.

Laughlin, Greg, jt. auth. see Adams, Fred.

Laughlin, Haller & Wheeler, Randy. Producing the Musical: A Guide for School, College & Community Theatres. LC 83-22704. (Illus.). 151p. 1984. lib. bdg. 47.95 (*0-313-24100-7*, LPM/, Greenwood Pr) Greenwood.

Laughlin, Haller, jt. auth. see Wheeler, Jacque.

Laughlin, Harold E., ed. see Ranson, Nancy R.

Laughlin, J., ed. New Directions 17-55. LC 37-1751. 1971. 6.75 (*0-8112-0300-X*, Pub. by New Directions) Norton.

Laughlin, J. Laurence, Jr. Industrial America. LC 72-1245. (Select Bibliographies Reprint Ser.). 1977. reprint ed. 23.95 (*0-8369-6832-8*) Ayer.

Laughlin, J. Laurence, Jr. & Bruchey, Stuart, eds. Banking Reform. LC 80-1160. (Rise of Commercial Banking Ser.). 1981. reprint ed. lib. bdg. 38.95 (*0-405-13667-6*) Ayer.

Laughlin, James. The Bird of Endless Time. LC 88-63226. 128p. (Orig.). 1989. 15.00 (*1-55659-020-2*); pap. 9.00 (*1-55659-021-0*) Copper Canyon.

— Collected Poems of James Laughlin. 608p. 1995. pap. 19.95 (*1-55921-128-8*) Moyer Bell.

***Laughlin, James.** The Commmon Place Book of Pentastichs. LC 98-12968. 1998. 19.95 (*0-8112-1386-2*, Pub. by New Directions) Norton.

Laughlin, James. Ezra. deluxe ed. (Illus.). 16p. 1994. pap. 100.00 (*1-891472-03-8*) Dim Gray.

— Heart Island & Other Epigrams. limited ed. (Illus.). 1995. 325.00 (*0-918824-59-1*) Turkey Pr.

— James Laughlin: Selected Poems, 1935-1985. 208p. (Orig.). 1986. 25.95 (*0-87286-179-1*); pap. 9.95 (*0-87286-180-5*) City Lights.

— The Lost Fragments. LC 98-147172. 24p. 1998. pap. 10.95 (*1-901233-10-3*) Dufour.

— The Love Poems. LC 97-10980. 96p. 1998. pap. 7.95 (*0-8112-1387-0*, NDP865, Pub. by New Directions) Norton.

— The Man in the Wall: Poems. LC 92-45790. 128p. 1993. 19.95 (*0-8112-1236-X*, Pub. by New Directions) Norton.

— The Man in the Wall: Poems. LC 92-45790. Vol. 759. 128p. 1993. pap. 9.95 (*0-8112-1237-8*, NDP759, Pub. by New Directions) Norton.

— The Music of Ideas. 44p. 1995. 75.00 (*0-918116-88-0*) Brooding Heron Pr.

— The Music of Ideas. deluxe limited ed. 44p. 1995. 125.00 (*0-918116-87-2*) Brooding Heron Pr.

— The Owl of Minerva. LC 86-73198. 96p. (Orig.). 1987. 15.00 (*1-55659-005-9*); pap. 9.00 (*1-55659-004-0*) Copper Canyon.

— Phantoms: Poetry. LC 94-79649. (Illus.). 64p. 1995. 19.95 (*0-89381-613-2*) Aperture.

— Poems New & Selected. LC 97-52320. 294p. 1998. pap. 12.95 (*0-8112-1375-7*, NDP857, Pub. by New Directions) Norton.

— Remembering William Carlos Williams. LC 95-15719. 64p. (Orig.). 1995. pap. 7.95 (*0-8112-1307-2*, NDP811, Pub. by New Directions) Norton.

— The Secret Room: Poems. LC 96-26188. 192p. 1997. 22.95 (*0-8112-1343-9*, Pub. by New Directions); pap. 14.95 (*0-8112-1344-7*, NDP837, Pub. by New Directions) Norton.

— Stolen & Contaminated Poems. 60p. 1985. text 150.00 (*0-918824-47-8*) Turkey Pr.

Laughlin, James, jt. auth. see Miller, Henry.

Laughlin, James L. History of Bimetallism in the United States. LC 68-28639. 353p. 1968. reprint ed. lib. bdg. 38.50 (*0-8371-0138-7*, LAHB, Greenwood Pr) Greenwood.

Laughlin, Jeannine L. & Laughlin, Sherry, eds. Children's Authors Speak. (Illus.). viii, 256p. 1993. lib. bdg. 27.00 (*0-87287-921-6*) Libs Unl.

***Laughlin, Jennifer Bauer.** Roan Mountain: A Passage of Time. LC 99-462537. 220p. 1999. pap. 17.95 (*1-57072-100-9*) Overmountain Pr.

Laughlin, Jerry, ed. see Compton, Dennis.

Laughlin, Jim M. Travellers & Ireland: Whose History, Whose Country? 80p. 1995. pap. 7.50 (*1-85918-090-6*, Pub. by Cork Univ) Intl Spec Bk.

Laughlin, John C. H. Archaeology & the Bible. LC 99-19503. 1999. pap. 18.99 (*0-415-15994-6*) Routledge.

Laughlin, Karen & Schuler, Catherine, eds. Theatre & Feminist Aesthetics. LC 94-20057. 1995. 45.00 (*0-8386-3549-0*) Fairleigh Dickinson.

***Laughlin, Kathleen A.** Women's Work & Public Policy: A History of the Women's Bureau, U. S. Department of Labor, 1945-1970. LC 99-58664. 208p. 2000. text 40.00 (*1-55553-444-9*) NE U Pr.

Laughlin, Kay, et al. The Children's Song Index, 1978-1993. xii, 153p. 1995. lib. bdg. 37.50 (*1-56308-332-9*) Libs Unl.

Laughlin, Kit. Overcome Neck & Back Pain. (Illus.). 208p. 1998. pap. 15.00 (*0-684-85252-7*, Fireside) S&S Trade Pap.

***Laughlin, Kit.** Stretching & Flexibility. (Illus.). 280p. 2000. per. 18.00 (*0-7432-0069-1*) S&S Trade.

Laughlin, Lizette M., jt. auth. see Marinelli, Patti J.

Laughlin, Margaret A. Social Studies: Middle & High School. LC 95-136357. (C). 1994. text 77.50 (*0-15-500098-5*, Pub. by Harcourt Coll Pubs) Harcourt.

Laughlin, Margaret A., jt. ed. see Haas, Mary E.

Laughlin, Margaret A., ed. see Sanders, Norris M.

Laughlin, Mark A. & Pomerantz, Roger J., eds. Retroviral Latency. (Medical Intelligence Unit Ser.). 115p. 1994. 99.00 (*1-57059-034-6*, LN9034) Landes Bioscience.

Laughlin, Mary E. More Than Four: A Guide for Multiple Harness Weavers. 1992. pap. 16.50 (*1-56659-048-5*) Robin & Russ.

Laughlin, Mary M., jt. auth. see Ballington, Don A.

***Laughlin, Michael L.** The Legend of Thornbush. LC 99-37002. (Illus.). 32p. (J). (ps-2). 2000. 12.99 (*0-8499-5968-3*) Tommy Nelson.

Laughlin, Mildred K. & Kardaleff, Patricia P. Literature-Based Social Studies: Children's Books & Activities to Enrich the K-5 Curriculum. LC 90-46103. 160p. 1990. pap. 27.50 (*0-89774-605-8*) Oryx Pr.

Laughlin, Mildred K. & Latrobe, Kathy H. Readers Theatre for Children: Scripts & Script Development. xi, 131p. 1990. pap. text 17.50 (*0-87287-753-1*) Teacher Ideas Pr.

Laughlin, Mildred K. & Street, Terri P., eds. Literature-Based Art & Music: Children's Books & Activities to Enrich the K-5 Curriculum. LC 91-33662. 168p. 1991. pap. 29.95 (*0-89774-661-9*) Oryx Pr.

Laughlin, Mildred K. & Watt, Letty S. Developing Learning Skills Through Children's Literature: An Idea Book for K-5 Classrooms & Libraries, Vol. 1. LC 85-43470. 288p. 1986. pap. 30.00 (*0-89774-258-3*) Oryx Pr.

Laughlin, Mildred K., et al. Social Studies Readers Theatre for Children: Scripts & Script Development. xi, 189p. 1991. pap. text 22.50 (*0-87287-865-1*) Teacher Ideas Pr.

Laughlin, Mildred K., jt. auth. see Latrobe, Kathy H.

Laughlin, Minnabell, jt. ed. see Burton, Susan S.

Laughlin, Nancy M. Puppet Power. (Illus.). 128p. 1998. pap. 10.95 (*0-673-36389-9*, GoodYrBooks) Addson-Wesley Educ.

Laughlin-Porter, Jeannine. Exploring the Southeast States Through Literature. LC 93-40813. (Exploring the United States Through Literature Ser.). 224p. 1994. pap. 27.50 (*0-89774-770-4*) Oryx Pr.

Laughlin, Robert G., ed. The Aqueous Phase Behavior of Surfactants. (Colloid Science Ser.). (Illus.). 580p. 1996. reprint ed. pap. text 59.95 (*0-12-437760-2*) Acad Pr.

Laughlin, Robert M. The Great Tzotzil Dictionary of San Lorenzo Zinacantan. LC 74-32060. (Smithsonian Contributions to Anthropology Ser.: No. 19). 624p. reprint ed. pap. 193.50 (*0-608-13834-7*, 202031000016) Bks Demand.

— Of Cabbages & Kings: Tales from Zinacantan. LC 76-608180. (Smithsonian Contributions to Anthropology Ser.: No. 23). 437p. reprint ed. pap. 135.50 (*0-608-13833-9*, 202031100016) Bks Demand.

Laughlin, Robert M. & Haviland, John B. The Great Tzotzil Dictionary of Santo Domingo Zinacantan: With Grammatical Analysis & Historical Commentary, 3 vols., Vol. 1: Tzotzil-English. LC 87-600364. (Smithsonian Contributions to Anthropology Ser.: No. 31). (Illus.). 370p. reprint ed. pap. 114.70 (*0-8357-8153-4*, 203408000001) Bks Demand.

— The Great Tzotzil Dictionary of Santo Domingo Zinacantan: With Grammatical Analysis & Historical Commentary, 3 vols., Vol. 2: English-Tzotzil. LC 87-600364. (Smithsonian Contributions to Anthropology Ser.: No. 31). (Illus.). 305p. reprint ed. pap. 94.60 (*0-8357-8154-2*, 203408000002) Bks Demand.

— The Great Tzotzil Dictionary of Santo Domingo Zinacantan: With Grammatical Analysis & Historical Commentary, 3 vols., Vol. 3: Spanish-Tzotzil. LC 87-600364. (Smithsonian Contributions to Anthropology Ser.: No. 31). (Illus.). 472p. reprint ed. pap. 146.40 (*0-8357-8155-0*, 203408000003) Bks Demand.

Laughlin, Robert M., jt. auth. see Breedlove, Dennis E.

Laughlin, Robert M., tr. see Karasik, Carol, ed.

Laughlin, Robin K. Backyard Bugs. LC 95-21386. (Illus.). 80p. 1996. 12.95 (*0-8118-0907-2*) Chronicle Bks.

An Asterisk (*) at the beginning of an entry indicates that the title is appearing for the first time.

Laughlin, Rosemary. The Great Iron Link: The Building of the Central Pacific Railroad. LC 96-21722. (Great Events Ser.). (YA). (gr. 5 up). 1996. lib. bdg. 18.95 (*1-883846-14-5*) M Reynolds.
— The Pullman Strike of 1894: American Labor Comes of Age. LC 99-25695. (Great Events Ser.). 112p. (YA). (gr. 5 up). 1999. lib. bdg. 18.95 (*1-883846-28-5*) M Reynolds.
Laughlin, Ruth. The Wind Leaves No Shadow. LC 48-10425. 1951. pap. 8.95 (*0-87004-083-9*) Caxton.
Laughlin, Sara, jt. ed. see Puckett, Katharyn E.
Laughlin, Sherry, jt. ed. see Laughlin, Jeannine L.
Laughlin, Terry & Delves, John. Total Immersion: A Revolutionary Way to Swim Better & Faster. 288p. 1996. per. 13.00 (*0-684-81885-X*) S&S Trade.
Laughlin, William F., jt. auth. see Smith, Alexander.
Laughlin, William S. Aleuts: Survivors of the Bering Land Bridge. 160p. (C). 1981. pap. text 23.50 (*0-03-081269-0*) Harcourt Coll Pubs.
Laughon, Helen & Laughon, Nel. August Edouart - A Quaker Album: American & English Duplicate Silhouettes 1827-1845. (Illus.). 144p. 1987. text 29.95 (*0-9616686-0-1*) Cheswick Pr.
Laughon, Nel, jt. auth. see Laughon, Helen.
Laughrey, Christopher D. Petrology & Reservoir Characteristics of the Lower Silurian Medina Group Sandstones, Athens & Geneva Fields, Crawford County Pennsylvania. (Mineral Resource Reports: No. 85). (Illus.). 126p. 1984. pap. 6.35 (*0-8182-0054-5*) Commonweal PA.
Laughrey, John P. From Milk to Meat: A Guide to Christian Growth. 94p. 1998. pap. 6.95 (*1-890622-17-6*) Leathers Pub.
Laughridge, David. Dr. Tinker Repairs Toy Trains. (Illus.). 96p. 1997. per. 14.95 (*0-9650291-1-5*) O Gauge Railrd.
Laughridge, Eugene N. The Orient Out the Window: Places & Things Asian. 149p. (Orig.). 1993. pap. 7.95 (*0-9639455-0-5*) MLH Bks.
Laughridge, Pat. Let's Weave Color into Baskets. LC 85-63237. (Illus.). 58p. 1986. pap. 12.95 (*0-88740-056-6*) Schiffer.
Laughrin, M. Fidelia. Juan Pablo Forner As a Critic. LC 79-94173. (Catholic University of America. Studies in Romance Languages & Literatures: No. 26). reprint ed. 37.50 (*0-404-50326-8*) AMS Pr.
Laughter, John. Contemporary Saxophone. 56p. 1992. pap. text 17.95 incl. audio compact disk (*0-931759-58-7*) Centerstream Pub.
— Rock & Roll Saxophone. LC 96-124401. 64p. 1989. pap. text 17.95 incl. audio compact disk (*0-931759-36-6*) Centerstream Pub.
Laughton, Bruce. The Drawings of Daumier & Millet. (Illus.). 256p. (C). 1991. 70.00 (*0-300-04764-9*) Yale U Pr.
— The Euston Road School: A Study in Objective. 384p. 1986. text 144.95 (*0-85967-694-3*, Pub. by Scolar Pr) Ashgate Pub Co.
— Honore Daumier. LC 96-21441. (Illus.). 244p. 1996. 60.00 (*0-300-06945-6*) Yale U Pr.
Laughton, Charles, tr. see Brecht, Bertolt.
Laughton, J. K., ed. State Papers Relating to the Defeat of the Spanish Armada Anno, 1588. 418p. 1987. text 104.95 (*0-566-05540-6*, Pub. by Scolar Pr) Ashgate Pub Co.
Laughton, J. K. & Sulivan, J. Y. Journal of Rear-Admiral Bartholomew James, 1725-1828. (C). 1987. 100.00 (*0-7855-4015-6*) St Mut.
Laughton, John Knox, jt. auth. see Hamilton, R. Vesey.
***Laughton, Leonard.** Old Ship Figureheads & Sterns. 329p. 2000. reprint ed. lib. bdg. 79.00 (*0-7812-0011-3*) Rprt Serv.
Laughton, M. A. Renewable Energy Resources. (Illus.). 439p. (C). (gr. 13). 1986. pap. 39.99 (*0-419-12010-6*) Routledge.
Laughton, M. A., ed. Renewable Energy Sources: Watt Committee Report -- Published on Behalf of the Watt Committee on Energy, No. 22. 172p. 1990. mass mkt. 125.50 (*1-85166-500-5*) Elsevier.
Laughton, Robert, jt. auth. see Hayes, Cedric J.
Laughton, Rodney. Scarborough. (Images of America Ser.). 128p. 1996. pap. 16.99 (*0-7524-0262-5*) Arcadia Publng.
Laughton, Timothy. Maya: Life, Myth, & Art. (Illus.). 144p. 1998. 27.50 (*1-55670-823-8*) Stewart Tabori & Chang.
Laughy, Linwood. Getting the Best Bite of the Apple: How to Take Control of Your Child's Education in the Public Schools. LC 93-77570. 165p. 1993. pap. 11.95 (*0-945519-14-1*) Mountn Meadw Pr.
Laughy, Linwood, jt. auth. see Hendrickson, Borg.
Laugier, C., ed. Geometric Reasoning for Perception & Action: Proceedings of a Workshop, Grenoble, France, September 16-17, 1991. (Lecture Notes in Computer Science Ser.: Vol. 708). viii, 281p. 1993. pap. write for info. (*3-540-57132-9*) Spr-Verlag.
— Geometric Reasoning for Perception & Action: Selected Papers from the Workshop in Grenoble, France, September 16-17, 1991. (Lecture Notes in Computer Science Ser.: Vol. 708). viii, 281p. 1993. 44.95 (*0-387-57132-9*) Spr-Verlag.
Laugier, Marc-Antoine. An Essay on Architecture. Herrmann, Wolfgang & Herrmann, Anni, trs. from FRE. LC 75-28448. (Documents & Sources in Architecture Ser.: No. 1). 163p. 1985. reprint ed. pap. 14.95 (*0-912158-92-1*) Hennessey.
***Laugs, Martha.** America after Life. (Illus.). 120p. 2000. 45.00 (*3-929078-97-X*, Kehayoff) te Neues.
Laugwitz, Detlef. Bernhard Riemann, 1826-1866: Turning Points in the Conception of Mathematics. Shenitzer, Abe, tr. from GER. LC 98-17834. 1998. write for info. (*3-7643-4040-1*) Birkhauser.
Laugwitz, Detleff. Bernard Riemann, 1826-1866: Turning Points in the Conception of Mathematics. Shenitzer, Abe, tr. LC 98-17834. (Illus.). 350p. 1998. text 75.00 (*0-8176-4040-1*) Birkhauser.
Lauing, Daniel A. Manitou, Fountains of the Deep: The Crash of Flight 585, March 3, 1991, Widefield, Colorado. 320p. 1999. per. 13.50 (*0-9641269-0-7*) Benchmark Invest.
— Manitou, Fountains of the Deep: The Crash of Flight 585, March 3, 1991, Widefield, Colorado. 2000. boxed set 23.50 (*0-9641269-1-5*) Benchmark Invest.
***Laukel, Hans Gerold.** The Desert Fox Family Book. Lanning, Rosemary, tr. LC 95-52219. (Illus.). 64p. (J). (gr. 1-5). 1999. pap. 8.95 (*0-7358-1095-8*, Pub. by North-South Bks NYC) Chronicle Bks.
Laukien. Advanced Cobra Programming For C++ (C). 1999. 45.00 (*0-13-780453-9*, Macmillan Coll) P-H.
Laulajainen, Risto. Spatial Strategies in Retailing. (C). 1987. lib. bdg. 134.00 (*90-277-2595-0*) Kluwer Academic.
Laulajainen, Risto & Stafford, Howard A. Corporate Geography: Business Location Principles & Cases. LC 94-42236. 1995. lib. bdg. 228.00 (*0-7923-3326-8*) Kluwer Academic.
Laule, Bernhard. Schlob Madrid. (Studien Zur Kunstgeschichte Ser.: Bd. 19). (GER.). iv, 363p. 1983. write for info. (*3-487-07384-6*) G Olms Pubs.
Lauman, Carol. Prayerlike Poems. 2nd ed. LC 96-96992. (Illus.). ix, 55p. 1996. reprint ed. pap. 7.95 (*0-9654672-0-1*) Chriss Pub.
Laumann, Beverley. A Taste of the Good Life: A Cookbook for an Interstitial Cystitis Diet. LC 98-73062. (Illus.). x, 240p. 1998. pap. 24.00 (*0-9665706-0-X*) Freeman Family.
Laumann, Edward O. Prestige & Association in an Urban Community: An Analysis of an Urban Stratification System. LC 66-29709. (Orig.). 1966. pap. 4.95 (*0-672-60620-8*, Bobbs) Macmillan.
Laumann, Edward O. Sex Love & Health in America. 1997. 48.00 (*0-226-46967-0*) U Ch Pr.
Laumann, Edward O., ed. Social Stratification: Research & Theory for the 1970's. LC 77-135769. (Illus.). (Orig.). 1970. 8.50 (*0-672-51402-8*, Bobbs); pap. 6.95 (*0-672-61195-3*, Bobbs) Macmillan.
Laumann, Edward O. & Knoke, David. Organizational State: Social Change in National Policy Domains. LC 87-40142. (Illus.). 592p. 1987. pap. text 21.95 (*0-299-11194-6*) U of Wis Pr.
Laumann, Edward O., et al. The Social Organization of Sexuality: Sexual Practices in the United States. (Illus.). 742p. 1994. lib. bdg. 49.95 (*0-226-46957-3*) U Ch Pr.
Laumann, Edward O., jt. auth. see Heinz, John P.
Laumann, Maryta M. The Secret of Excellence in Ancient Chinese Silks: Factors Contributing to the Extraordinary Development of Textile Design & Technology Achieved in Ancient China. 1984. 35.00 (*0-89986-357-4*) Oriental Bk Store.
Laumann, Silken, jt. auth. see Cantwell, Susan.
Laumbach, Karl W., jt. ed. see Duran, Meliha S.
Laumeister, Shannah, jt. auth. see Haft, Jennifer.
Laumer. Purple Book. 1987. mass mkt. write for info. (*0-8125-3768-8*) Tor Bks.
Laumer, Frank. Dade's Last Command. LC 94-26086. (Illus.). 312p. 1995. 29.95 (*0-8130-1324-0*) U Press Fla.
— Massacre! LC 68-9812. (Illus.). 1968. pap. 15.95 (*0-8130-0479-9*) U Press Fla.
Laumer, Frank, ed. Amidst a Storm of Bullets: The Diary of Lt. Henry Prince in Florida, 1836-1842. LC 98-40151. (Seminole Wars Historic Foundation Ser.). 166p. 1998. 29.95 (*1-879852-59-4*) Univ Tampa.
Laumer, Keith. The Breaking Earth. 288p. 1988. pap. 3.50 (*0-8125-4387-4*, Pub. by Tor Bks) St Martin.
— The Compleat Bolo. 320p. (Orig.). 1990. per. 5.99 (*0-671-69879-6*) Baen Bks.
— Dangerous Vegetables. 1998. mass mkt. 5.99 (*0-671-57781-6*) Baen Bks.
— Earthblood. 1991. mass mkt. 4.50 (*0-671-72060-0*) Baen Bks.
— The Glory Game. 256p. (Orig.). 1985. pap. 2.95 (*0-8125-4383-1*, Pub. by Tor Bks) St Martin.
— The Other Sky & the House in November. 256p. 1985. pap. 2.95 (*0-8125-4377-7*, Pub. by Tor Bks) St Martin.
— The Return of Retief. 1984. pap. 2.95 (*0-685-09411-1*) PB.
— The Unconquerable. (Bolos Ser.). 288p. 2000. reprint ed. mass mkt. 5.99 (*0-671-87629-5*) PB.
— Worlds of the Imperium. 288p. 1986. 2.95 (*0-8125-4379-3*, Pub. by Tor Bks) St Martin.
Laumer, Keith, creator. Honor of the Regiment. (BOLOS Ser.: Vol. 1). 320p. (Orig.). 1993. mass mkt. 4.99 (*0-671-72184-4*) Baen Bks.
— Last Stand. (Bolos Ser.: Vol. 4). 384p. 1997. per. 5.99 (*0-671-87760-7*) Baen Bks.
— The Triumphant. LC 96-213166. (BOLOS Ser.: Vol. 3). 400p. 1995. per. 5.99 (*0-671-87683-X*) Baen Bks.
Laumeyer, Robert L. The Song of the Hunter. 1998. pap. write for info. (*1-57553-862-8*) Watermrk Pr.
***Laumon, G. & Moret-Bailly, L.** Champs Algebriques. (Ergebnisse der Mathematik & Ihrer Grenzgebiete: Vol. 39). (FRE.). 225p. 2000. 109.00 (*3-540-65761-4*) Spr-Verlag.
Laumon, Gerard. Cohomology of Drinfeld Modular Varieties Part 1: Geometry, Counting of Points & Local Harmonic Analysis. (Studies in Advanced Mathematics: No. 41). 358p. (C). 1996. text 69.95 (*0-521-47060-9*) Cambridge U Pr.
— Cohomology of Drinfeld Modular Varieties Pt. II: The Arthur-Selberg Trace Formula. (Studies in Advanced Mathematics: No. 56). 377p. (C). 1997. text 69.95 (*0-521-47061-7*) Cambridge U Pr.
Laumond, J. P., ed. Robot Motion Planning & Control. LC 97-40560. (Lecture Notes in Control & Information Sciences: Vol. 229). xii, 347p. 1997. pap. 63.00 (*3-540-76219-1*) Spr-Verlag.
Laumond, J. P., jt. ed. see Boissonnat, L. D.
Laumond, Jean-Paul & Overmars, Mark, eds. Algorithms for Robotic Motion & Manipulation. (Workshop on the Algorithmic Foundations of Robotics Ser.: Vol. 2). (Illus.). 480p. (C). 1997. text 55.00 (*1-56881-067-9*) AK Peters.
Laumonier, Yves. The Vegetation & Physiography of Sumatra. LC 95-40385. (Geobotany Ser.: Vol. 22). 1997. text 267.50 (*0-7923-3761-1*) Kluwer Academic.
Laun, Charles. Handbook of Nature & Scientific Photography. 472p. 1994. pap. 13.95 (*0-9640598-0-0*); lib. bdg. 17.95 (*0-9640598-1-9*) Alsace Bks.
Laun, Hellmut. How I Met God: An Unusual Conversion. Smith, David, tr. 154p. 1983. 5.00 (*0-8199-0871-1*, Frncscn Herld) Franciscan Pr.
Laun, Mary A., ed. Vocational & Technical Resources for Community College Libraries. 622p. (Orig.). (C). 1995. pap. 45.00 (*0-8389-7775-8*) Assn Coll & Res Libs.
Laun, Mary Ann, ed. Vocational & Technical Resources for Community College Libraries: Selected Materials. LC 94-46648. 1995. pap. 85.00 (*0-8389-7758-8*) ALA.
Launay, A. J. Dictionary of Contemporaries, Famous People & Events. 1970. 25.00 (*0-87556-145-4*) Saifer.
***Launay, Drew.** The Xenophobe's Guide to the Spanish. (Xenophobe's Guides Ser.). 64p. 1999. pap. 5.95 (*1-902825-43-8*) Oval Bks.
Launay, Michel, ed. see Rousseau, Jean-Jacques.
Launay, Robert. Beyond the Stream: Islam & Society in a West African Town. (Comparative Studies on Muslim Societies: No. 15). (C). 1992. 48.00 (*0-520-07718-0*, Pub. by U CA Pr) Cal Prin Full Svc.
Launchberry, Jane. At the Circus. 1988. 2.98 (*0-671-09596-X*) S&S Trade.
— In Nursery Rhyme Land. (J). 1988. 2.98 (*0-671-09597-8*) S&S Trade.
Launchbury, John. Project Factorisations in Partial Evaluation. (Distinguished Dissertations in Computer Science Ser.: No. 1). 175p. (C). 1991. text 52.95 (*0-521-41497-0*) Cambridge U Pr.
Launchbury, John & Sansom, Patrick M., eds. Functional Programming, Glasgow 1992: Proceedings of the 1992 Glasgow Workshop on Functional Programming, Ayr, Scotland, 6-8 July 1992. LC 93-3308. 1993. 71.95 (*0-387-19820-2*) Spr-Verlag.
Launchbury, John, et al. Advanced Functional Programming: Second International School, Olympia, WA, U. S. A., August 26-30, 1996: Tutorial Text. LC 96-3337. (Lecture Notes in Computer Science Ser.: Vol. 1129). 238p. 1996. 43.00 (*3-540-61628-4*) Spr-Verlag.
Launder, Elizabeth, jt. ed. see Legard, Hilary.
Launders, Michele & Spiegel, Penina. Don't Call Her Lisa Steinberg: The Story of Michele Launders & Her Daughter Lisa. 1991. mass mkt. 4.99 (*0-446-36110-0*, Pub. by Warner Bks) Little.
Laundon, Jack R. Lichens. 1989. pap. 25.00 (*0-85263-811-6*, Pub. by Shire Pubns) St Mut.
Laundrie, Amy C. Deliver Us from Evil: A Kayla Montgomery Mystery. 109p. (YA). 1997. pap. 9.99 (*0-88092-369-5*, 3695) Royal Fireworks.
— Eye of Truth: A Kayla Montgomery Mystery. 119p. (J). 1996. pap. 9.99 (*0-88092-304-0*) Royal Fireworks.
— Lead Us Not into Temptation. (Kayla Montgomery Mystery Ser.: No. 4). 188p. (YA). 1999. pap. 9.99 (*0-88092-454-3*, 4543) Royal Fireworks.
— Thirty Pieces of Silver: A Kayla Montgomery Mystery. 156p. (YA). (gr. 6 up). 1996. pap. 9.99 (*0-88092-364-4*) Royal Fireworks.
Laundy, Philip. Parliament & the People: The Reality & the Public Perception. LC 97-15772. 240p. 1997. text 72.95 (*1-85521-949-2*, JF1051.P316, Pub. by Dartmth Pub) Ashgate Pub Co.
— Parliaments in the Modern World. 250p. 1989. text 72.95 (*1-85521-042-8*, Pub. by Dartmth Pub); pap. text. write for info. (*1-85521-055-X*, Pub. by Dartmth Pub) Ashgate Pub Co.
Laune, Ferris F. Predicting Criminality: Forecasting Behavior on Parole. LC 73-10851. 163p. 1974. reprint ed. lib. bdg. 22.50 (*0-8371-7041-9*, LAPC, Greenwood Pr) Greenwood.
Laune, Seigniora R. Sand in My Eyes. LC 86-40089. (Illus.). 264p. 1986. pap. 9.95 (*0-8061-2016-9*) U of Okla Pr.
Launer, Donald. A Cruising Guide to New Jersey Waters. (Orig.). 1995. text 25.95 (*0-07-036677-2*) McGraw.
— A Cruising Guide to New Jersey Waters. LC 95-8590. (Illus.). 250p. (Orig.). (C). 1995. text 25.95 (*0-8135-2238-2*) Rutgers U Pr.
— A Cruising Guide to New Jersey Waters. LC 95-8590. (Illus.). 250p. (Orig.). 1997. pap. 17.95 (*0-8135-2386-9*) Rutgers U Pr.
Launer, L. J., et al, eds. European Studies on the Incidence of Dementing Diseases: A Report of the EURODEM Research Group - Neuroepidemiology Journal, 1992, Vol. 11, Suppl. 1. (Illus.). vi, 122p. 1992. pap. 39.25 (*3-8055-5593-8*) S Karger.
Launer, Louis J., ed. see Adamson, Bruce Campbell & Foley, William.
Launer, Michael K., jt. auth. see Young, Marilyn J.
Launert, E. Biologisches Woerterbuch. Deutsch-Englisch, Englisch-Deutsch (Biological Dictionary. German-English, English-German) (ENG & GER.). 720p. 1998. 71.00 (*3-8001-2577-3*, Pub. by Eugen Ulmer) Balogh.
Launert, Edmund. Dictionary of Biology, English-German/ German-English. 4th ed. (ENG & GER.). 700p. 1995. 175.00 (*0-7859-9938-8*) Fr & Eur.
Laungan, Pittu. It Shouldn't Happen to a Patient: A Survivor's Guide to Fighting Life-Threatening Illness. 192p. 1992. text 29.95 (*1-871177-14-6*, Pub. by Whiting & Birch) Paul & Co Pubs.
Laungani, Pittu. Death & Bereavement Across Cultures. LC 96-7558. 272p. (C). 1997. pap. 24.99 (*0-415-13137-5*) Routledge.
— It Shouldn't Happen to a Patient: A Survivor's Guide to Fighting Life-Threatening Illness. 192p. 1993. reprint ed. pap. 18.95 (*1-871177-15-4*, Pub. by Whiting & Birch) Paul & Co Pubs.
Laungani, Pittu, jt. ed. see Palmer, Stephen.
Launikonis, Rosemary. The Women's Victory Journal. 28p. 1994. 15.99 incl. audio (*0-9642143-0-X*) Launikonis & Assocs.
***Launius, Robert D.** Beyond Moon: A Golden Era of Planetary Exploration, 1971-1978. LC 00-26963. 2000. 34.95 (*1-56098-954-8*) Smithsonian.
Launius, Roger D. Alexander William Doniphan: Portrait of a Missouri Moderate. LC 97-15906. (Biography Ser.). (Illus.). 336p. 1997. 37.50 (*0-8262-1132-1*) U of Mo Pr.
— Father Figure: Joseph Smith III & Creation of the Reorganized Church. 275p. 1990. pap. text 5.00 (*0-8309-0576-6*) Herald Pub Hse.
— Frontiers of Space Exploration. LC 97-34788. (Greenwood Press Guides to Historic Events of the Twentieth Century Ser.). 256p. 1998. 39.95 (*0-313-29968-4*, Greenwood Pr) Greenwood.
— Illustrated History of Kirtland Temple. (Illus.). 1986. pap. 7.00 (*0-8309-0438-7*) Herald Pub Hse.
— Invisible Saints: A Study of Black Americans in the Reorganized Church. 1988. pap. 8.00 (*0-8309-0508-1*) Herald Pub Hse.
— Joseph Smith III: Pragmatic Prophet. (Illus.). 424p. (C). 1995. 15.95 (*0-252-06515-8*) U of Ill Pr.
— NASA: A History of the U. S. Civil Space Program. LC 93-35977. (Anvil Ser.). 286p. (C). 1994. pap. text 16.50 (*0-89464-727-X*) Krieger.
— NASA: A History of the U. S. Civil Space Program. LC 93-35977. 286p. 1994. 19.50 (*0-89464-878-0*) Krieger.
— NASA & the Exploration of Space: With Works from the NASA Art Collection. LC 98-17742. 224p. 1998. 60.00 (*1-55670-696-0*) Stewart Tabori & Chang.
— The U. S. Space Program. (Perspectives on History Ser.: Pt. III). Date not set. pap. 6.95 (*1-57960-008-5*) Disc Enter Ltd.
Launius, Roger D., ed. History of Rocketry & Astronautics. LC 57-43769. (AAS History Ser.: Vol. 11). (Illus.). 236p. 1994. 60.00 (*0-87703-382-X*, Am Astronaut Soc); pap. 40.00 (*0-87703-383-8*, Am Astronaut Soc) Univelt Inc.
— Innovation & the Development of Flight. LC 98-48723. (Illus.). 400p. 1998. 44.95 (*0-89096-876-4*) Tex A&M Univ Pr.
— Organizing for the Use of Space: Historical Perspectives on a Persistent Issue. LC 96-103619. (AAS History Ser.: Vol. 18). (Illus.). 234p. 1995. 60.00 (*0-87703-403-6*, Am Astronaut Soc); pap. 40.00 (*0-87703-404-4*, Am Astronaut Soc) Univelt Inc.
***Launius, Roger D., et al, eds.** Reconsidering Sputnik: Forty Years Since the Soviet Satellite. (Studies in the History of Science, Technology & Medicine Ser.). 432p. 2000. 55.00 (*90-5702-623-6*, Harwood Acad Pubs) Gordon & Breach.
Launius, Roger D. & Hallwas, John E., eds. Nauvoo in Mormon History: The Kingdom on the Mississippi Revisited. LC 95-14673. 280p. 1996. text 36.50 (*0-252-02197-5*); pap. text 16.95 (*0-252-06494-1*) U of Ill Pr.
Launius, Roger D. & McCurdy, Goward E. Spaceflight & the Myth of Presidential Leadership. LC 96-51213. 288p. 1997. text 36.95 (*0-252-02336-6*) U of Ill Pr.
Launius, Roger D. & McCurdy, Howard E. Spaceflight & the Myth of Presidential Leadership. LC 96-51213. 288p. 1997. pap. text 19.95 (*0-252-06632-4*) U of Ill Pr.
Launius, Roger D. & Spillman, W. B., eds. Let Contention Cease: The Dynamics of Dissent in the Reorganized Church of Jesus Christ of Latter Day Saints. 304p. (Orig.). 1991. pap. text 3.00 (*0-8309-0592-8*) Herald Pub Hse.
Launius, Roger D. & Thatcher, Linda, eds. Differing Visions: Dissenters in Mormon History. LC 93-5463. 414p. 1994. text 32.50 (*0-252-02069-3*) U of Ill Pr.
— Differing Visions: Dissenters in Mormon History. 424p. 1998. 18.95 (*0-252-06731-2*) U of Ill Pr.
Launius, Roger D., jt. ed. see McKiernan, F. Mark.
Launko, Okniba. Ma'mi. (Junior African Writers Ser.). (Illus.). 80p. (J). (gr. 3 up). 1995. pap. 4.95 (*0-7910-3164-0*) Chelsea Hse.
Launois, Bernard & Jamieson, Glyn G. Modern Operative Techniques in Liver Surgery. LC 92-49203. 160p. 1993. text 114.00 (*0-443-04616-6*) Church.
Launsby, Robert G. & Weese, Daniel L. Straight Talk on Designing Experiments. 150p. 1993. text 39.95 (*0-9636093-3-5*) Launsby Cnslting.
Launsby, Robert G., et al. Process Validation for Business Success. 150p. 1995. pap. text 49.95 (*0-9636093-4-3*) Launsby Cnslting.
Launsby, Robert G., jt. auth. see Schmidt, Stephen R.
Laur, Lewis, jt. auth. see Miller, Jamie C.
Laur, Timothy. Military Airlift Command. LC 91-23951. (Illus.). 325p. 1994. 26.95 (*1-877853-15-1*) Nautical & Aviation.
Laur, Timothy M. & Llanso, Steven L. Encyclopedia of Modern U. S. Military Weapons. Boyne, Walter J., ed. (Illus.). 544p. 1995. 39.95 (*0-425-14781-9*) Berkley Pub.
— Encyclopedia of Modern U. S. Military Weapons. Boyne, Walter J., ed. 1998. pap. 19.95 (*0-425-16437-3*) Berkley Pub.
Laura Ashley (Firm) Staff, jt. auth. see Berry, Susan.

Laura, Ellen M. The One-Minute Healing Experience. LC 97-14227. 120p. (Orig.). 1997. pap. 11.00 (*1-57733-012-9*) B Dolphin Pub.

Laura, Judith. Goddess Spirituality for the 21st Century: From Kabbalah to Quantum Physics. LC 97-65320. 200p. (Orig.). 1997. pap. 12.95 (*1-884570-64-X*) Research Triangle.

— She Lives! The Return of Our Great Mother: Myths, Rituals & Meditations. LC 99-61930. 365p. 1999. 25.00 (*0-7388-0358-8*); pap. 15.00 (*0-7388-0359-6*) Xlibris Corp.

Laura, P. A., jt. auth. see Schinzinger, R.

Laura, Ron, jt. auth. see Ashton, John.

Laura, Ronald S. Empathetic Education. 1998. pap. text 42.95 (*0-7507-0763-1*) Taylor & Francis.

— Twelve Weeks to a Better Body for Women. (Illus.). 144p. 1994. pap. 9.95 (*1-86373-483-X*) IPG Chicago.

Laura, Ronald S. & Ashman, Adrian F., eds. Moral Issues in Mental Retardation. LC 84-29329. 224p. 1985. 35.00 (*0-7099-1692-2*, Pub. by C Helm) Routldge.

Laura, Ronald S. & Dutton, Kenneth R. The Matrix Principle: Drug-Free Training for Sport & Bodybuilding a Revolutionary Approach to Muscle Development. McDermott, Richard J. & Gardner, Gai, eds. LC 92-60316. (Illus.). 238p. (Orig.). 1992. pap. 19.95 (*0-910944-02-4*) Magee.

Lauraitis, K. N., ed. Fatigue of Fibrous Composite Materials - STP 723. 311p. 1981. 30.00 (*0-8031-0719-6*, STP723) ASTM.

Laurance, B. F. Desperate Trail. Laurance, Claire, ed. LC 95-96175. 75p. (Orig.). (J). (gr. 3-7). 1996. pap. 7.95 (*0-9650660-0-2*) B&C Publns.

Laurance, Claire, ed. see Laurance, B. F.

Laurance, Ewa M. The Complete Idiot's Guide to Billiards. LC 98-88702. (Illus.). 445p. 1998. pap. text 18.95 (*0-02-862645-1*) Macmillan Gen Ref.

Laurance, Robert. Going Freelance: A Guide for Professionals. 218p. 1988. pap. 17.95 (*0-471-63255-4*) Wiley.

Laurance, Willaim F. & Bierregaard, Richard O. Tropical Forest Remnants: Ecology, Management & Conservation of Fragmented Communities. LC 96-38038. 1997. lib. bdg. 105.00 (*0-226-46898-4*) U Ch Pr.

***Laurance, William F.** Stinging Trees & Wait-a-Whiles: Confessions of a Rainforest Biologist. LC 00-20543. 1999. 25.00 (*0-226-46896-8*) U Ch Pr.

Laurance, William F. & Bierregaard, Richard O. Tropical Forest Remnants: Ecology, Management & Conservation of Fragmented Communities. LC 96-38038. 1997. pap. text 38.00 (*0-226-46899-2*) U Ch Pr.

Laure, ed. Writing in Context & Action. (C). 1983. text. write for info. (*0-321-01590-8*) Addson-Wesley Educ.

Laure, E. Laure: The Collected Writings. Herman, Jeanine, tr. from FRE. 240p. (Orig.). 1995. pap. 13.95 (*0-87286-293-3*) City Lights.

Laure, Jason, jt. auth. see Blauer, Ettagale.

Laureano, Judy. A New Owner's Guide to Golden Retrievers: AKC Rank #4. (New Owner's Guide to Ser.). (Illus.). 160p. 1996. 12.95 (*0-7938-2757-4*, JG-108) TFH Pubns.

***Laurel, Alicia Bay.** Living on the Earth. LC 99-49096. 224p. 2000. pap. 16.95 (*0-375-70881-2*) Villard Books.

Laurel, Brenda. Computers As Theatre. LC 93-17107. (Illus.). 256p. (C). 1993. pap. text 22.95 (*0-201-55060-1*) Addison-Wesley.

Laurel, Brenda, ed. The Art of Human-Computer Interface Design. 544p. (C). 1990. pap. text 39.95 (*0-201-51797-3*) Addison-Wesley.

Laurel, Chris. 3D Java. Date not set. pap. text 50.00 (*1-56205-597-6*) New Riders Pub.

Laurel, Lisa K. The Groom Maker: Wedding Month. 1995. per. 2.99 (*0-373-19107-3*) Harlequin Bks.

— The Irresistible Prince. 1998. per. 3.50 (*0-373-19293-2*, 1-19293-9) Silhouette.

— Mommy for the Moment. (Romance Ser.). 1996. per. 3.25 (*0-373-19173-1*, 1-19173-3) Silhouette.

— La Petite Princesse. (FRE.). 1998. mass mkt. 3.50 (*0-373-39479-9*, 1-39479-0) Harlequin Bks.

— Le Prince Exile. (Horizon Ser.: No. 483). (FRE.). 1998. mass mkt. 3.50 (*0-373-39483-7*, 1-39483-2) Harlequin Bks.

— The Prince's Baby. 1997. per. 3.25 (*0-373-19263-0*, 1-19263-2) Silhouette.

— The Prince's Bride. 1997. per. 3.25 (*0-373-19251-7*, 1-19251-7) Silhouette.

Laurel Technical Services. Experiencing Algebra. 680p. 1999. student ed. 29.33 (*0-13-799982-8*) P-H.

Laurel Technical Services Staff. Algebra & Trigonometry. 1995. pap. text, student ed. 18.80 (*0-13-393984-7*) P-H.

— Algebra & Trigonometry. 5th ed. 1995. pap. text, student ed. 29.33 (*0-13-311796-0*) P-H.

— Beginning Algebra. 2nd ed. 1996. pap. text, student ed. 29.33 (*0-13-568387-4*) P-H.

— College Algebra. 464p. 1998. pap. text, student ed. 30.80 (*0-13-746869-5*) P-H.

— College Algebra. 4th ed. 1995. pap. text, student ed. 28.00 (*0-13-311622-0*) P-H.

— Elementary Algebra College. 4th ed. 1995. pap. text, student ed. 29.33 (*0-13-367590-4*) P-H.

— Holder's Primer. 7th ed. (Mathematics Ser.). 1996. pap., teacher ed. 22.95 (*0-534-94832-4*) PWS Pubs.

— Intermediate Algebra. 2nd ed. 1996. pap. text, student ed. 29.33 (*0-13-258096-9*) P-H.

— Intermediate Algebra. 4th ed. 1996. pap. text, student ed. 29.33 (*0-13-235367-9*) P-H.

— Precalculus Math Solutions Manual. 5th ed. 1995. pap. text, student ed. 28.00 (*0-13-159626-8*) P-H.

Lauremberg, J. A. Description of Ancient Greece. (Illus.). 140p. 1969. 52.50 (*0-317-54451-9*, Pub. by AM Hakkert) Coronet Bks.

Lauren. There Is a Rainbow in the Moon. 80p. 1985. 8.95 (*0-911051-24-4*) Plain View.

Lauren, Christer & Nordman, Marianne. Wissenschaftliche Technolekte. 1996. 44.95 (*3-631-48435-6*) P Lang Pubng.

Lauren, Christer & Nordman, Marianne, eds. From Office to School: Special Language & Internalization. 164p. 1989. 99.00 (*1-85359-038-X*, Pub. by Multilingual Matters); pap. 39.95 (*1-85359-037-1*, Pub. by Multilingual Matters) Taylor & Francis.

— Special Language: From Human Thinking to Thinking Machines. 490p. 1989. 99.00 (*1-85359-034-7*, Pub. by Multilingual Matters); pap. 39.95 (*1-85359-033-9*, Pub. by Multilingual Matters) Taylor & Francis.

Lauren, Christer, jt. ed. see Herberts, Kjell.

Lauren, Covell K., jt. auth. see Covell, Stephen E.

Lauren, Jessica. She Died Twice. LC 91-10551. 192p. (Orig.). 1991. pap. 8.95 (*0-934678-34-0*) New Victoria Pubs.

Lauren, Jill. Succeeding with LD* 20 True Stories about Real People with LD* (*Learning Differences) Verdick, Elizabeth, ed. LC 96-47404. (Illus.). 160p. (YA). (gr. 5 up). 1997. pap. 14.95 (*1-57542-012-0*) Free Spirit Pub.

Lauren Myracle. Turtle Morning. LC 98-54139. (J). 1999. pap. 15.95 (*0-936389-64-8*) Tudor Pubs.

Lauren, Paul G. Evolution of International Human Rights: Visions Seen. LC 98-15215. (Pennsylvania Studies in Human Rights). (Illus.). 396p. 1998. 49.95 (*0-8122-3274-7*); pap. 29.95 (*0-8122-1521-4*) U of Pa Pr.

Lauren, Ricky A. My Island. (Illus.). 140p. 1994. 100.00 (*0-679-43711-8*) Random.

Lauren Rogers Museum of Art Staff. The Lauren Rogers Museum of Art: A Handbook of the Collections. LC 89-5451. (Illus.). 198p. (Orig.). 1989. pap. 19.95 (*0-685-45630-7*) Lauren Rogers.

Laurence. Election Intrigue: Read-Along. (Illus.). 32p. (J). (gr. 4-8). 1982. pap. 9.95 (*0-87386-293-7*) Jan Prods.

— MCQS in Clinical Pharmacology. 2nd ed. 1988. pap. text 27.95 (*0-443-03416-8*, W B Saunders Co) Harcrt Hlth Sci Grp.

— Pipeline at Sparrow Ridge: Read-Along. (Illus.). 32p. (J). (gr. 4-8). 1982. pap. 9.95 (*0-87386-307-0*) Jan Prods.

— South Shore Smugglers: Read-Along. (Illus.). 32p. (J). (gr. 4-8). 1983. pap. 9.95 (*0-87386-305-4*) Jan Prods.

— Where Is Bobby? Read-Along. (Illus.). 32p. (J). (gr. 4-8). 1983. pap. 9.95 (*0-87386-301-1*) Jan Prods.

Laurence, A., et al, eds. John Bunyan & His England, 1628-88. xxiii, 181p. 1990. 55.00 (*1-85285-027-2*) Hambledon Press.

Laurence, Amy R. Happy Birthday & Other Easy Songs. (Amateur Virtuoso Ser.). 1995. wbk. ed. 9.95 (*1-887445-06-4*) A R Laurence Music.

— How to Read Notes: A Basic Workbook. (Amateur Virtuoso Ser.). 1995. wbk. ed. 9.95 (*1-887445-05-6*) A R Laurence Music.

***Laurence, Anne.** Lady Mistress. (Zebra Splendor Historical Romances Ser.). 352p. 2000. mass mkt. 4.99 (*0-8217-6621-X*, Zebra Kensgtn) Kensgtn Pub Corp.

Laurence, Anne. Parliamentary Army Chaplains, 1642-1651. (Royal Historical Society: Studies in History: No. 59). 222p. (C). 1990. 75.00 (*0-86193-216-1*) Boydell & Brewer.

— Remember When. (Superromance Ser.). 1993. per. 3.39 (*0-373-70539-5*, 1-70539-1) Harlequin Bks.

Laurence, Bethany K., jt. auth. see Mancuso, Anthony.

Laurence, Charles. About Alice. LC 98-211962. 84p. 1998. write for info. (*0-573-62632-4*) S French Trade.

***Laurence, Cosmo.** I've Got Your Science & Religion Right Here Buddy! LC 98-91079. 2000. 19.95 (*0-533-13040-9*) Vantage.

Laurence, D. R., ed. A Dictionary of Pharmacology & Allied Topics. 2nd ed. LC 98-33476. 386p. 1998. 187.00 (*0-444-82591-6*, Excerpta Medica); pap. 46.00 (*0-444-50050-2*, Excerpta Medica) Elsevier.

Laurence, D. R., et al. Clinical Pharmacology. 8th ed. LC 96-26060. (C). 1998. pap. text 65.00 (*0-443-04990-4*) Church.

— Self-Assessment in Clinical Pharmacology. 3rd ed. LC 98-32448. 224p. 1999. pap. write for info. (*0-443-06125-4*, W B Saunders Co) Harcrt Hlth Sci Grp.

Laurence, Dan H. Bernard Shaw: A Bibliography, 2 vols., Set. (Illus.). 1058p. 1984. 215.00 (*0-19-818179-5*) OUP.

— A Portrait of the Author As a Bibliography. LC 83-600082. (Engelhard Lecture on the Book). 19p. 1983. 3.95 (*0-8444-0426-8*, 030-000-0241-5) Lib Congress.

— Shaw, Books & Libraries. LC 76-620048. (Bibliographical Monograph: No. 9). (Illus.). 1976. 8.00 (*0-87959-022-X*) U of Tex H Ransom Ctr.

Laurence, Dan H., compiled by. Shaw: An Exhibit. LC 76-620047. (Illus.). 1977. 20.00 (*0-87959-081-5*); pap. 15.00 (*0-87959-082-3*) U of Tex H Ransom Ctr.

Laurence, Dan H., jt. auth. see Edel, Leon.

Laurence, Dan H., ed. see Shaw, George Bernard.

Laurence, Dan H., ed. & intro. see Shaw, George Bernard.

Laurence, Daniel. Captain & Matey Set Sail. 64p. (ps-3). pap. 3.95 (*0-06-444285-3*) HarpC.

— Pirate: An I Can Read Book. (Illus.). 64p. (J). (ps-3). 14.95 (*0-06-028956-2*); 14.89 (*0-06-028957-0*) HarpC Child Bks.

Laurence, Desmond R. & Carpenter, John. A Dictionary of Pharmacology & Clinical Drug Evaluation. 200p. 1994. pap. 34.95 (*1-85728-113-6*, Pub. by UCL Pr Ltd) Taylor & Francis.

Laurence, Donna M. & Titus, Rosalyn J. Skeletons Without Bones: Dragging Recovered Memories of Sexual Abuse Out of the Closet. LC 97-62306. 240p. 1998. pap. 15.95 (*1-57921-077-5*) WinePress Pub.

Laurence, Edward, Jr. The Duty & Office of a Land Steward: Represented Several Plain & Distinct Articles. Chandler, Alfred D., ed. LC 79-7549. (History of Management Thought & Practice Ser.). 1980. reprint ed. lib. bdg. 30.95 (*0-405-12333-7*) Ayer.

Laurence, Edward J., et al. Arms Watch: SIPRI Report on the First Year of the UN Register of Conventional Arms. LC 93-36596. (SIPRI Research Reports: Vol. 6). (Illus.). 156p. (C). 1994. pap. text 28.00 (*0-19-829177-9*) OUP.

Laurence, Ester H. The Butterfly Bandit. LC 95-78162. (Illus.). (J). (gr. 1-4). 1995. 14.95 (*1-880851-19-9*) Greene Bark Pr.

Laurence, Frances. Maverick Women: 19th Century Women Who Kicked over the Traces. LC 97-74353. (Illus.). 290p. 1998. pap. 18.50 (*0-9627896-0-7*) Manifest Pubns.

Laurence, Frank M. Hemingway & the Movies. LC 79-56697. (Illus.). 349p. reprint ed. pap. 108.20 (*0-8357-4345-4*, 203714800007) Bks Demand.

***Laurence, Henry.** Money Rules: The New Politics of Finance in Britain & Japan. 2000. 29.95 (*0-8014-3773-3*) Cornell U Pr.

Laurence, Janet. Canaletto & the Case of the Westminster Bridge, Vol. 1. LC 98-6744. 400p. 1998. text 24.95 (*0-312-18551-0*) St Martin.

— Death at the Table. (Mystery Ser.: Bk. 316). 1999. per. 4.99 (*0-373-26316-3*, 1-26316-9, Wrldwide Lib) Harlequin Bks.

— Death at the Table. large type ed. LC 97-14759. (Paperback Ser.). 360p. 1997. lib. bdg. 21.95 (*0-7838-8255-6*, G K Hall Lrg Type) Mac Lib Ref.

— Death at the Table. large type ed. LC 96-48772. 224p. 1997. 20.95 (*0-312-15105-5*, Thomas Dunne) St Martin.

— Hotel Morgue. large type ed. (Magna Mystery Ser.). 431p. 1992. 27.99 (*0-7505-0298-3*) Ulverscroft.

— A Little Coffee Cookbook. (Illus.). 60p. 1995. 7.95 (*0-8118-1036-4*) Chronicle Bks.

— A Little French Cookbook. (Illus.). 60p. 1989. 7.95 (*0-87701-642-9*) Chronicle Bks.

— Recipe for Death. large type ed. LC 93-20595. 442p. 1993. lib. bdg. 17.95 (*1-56054-794-4*) Thorndike Pr.

— To Kill the Past. large type ed. 413p. 1996. 11.50 (*0-7505-0877-9*, Pub. by Mgna Lrg Print) Ulverscroft.

Laurence, Janice H. & Ramsberger, Peter F. Low-Aptitude Men in the Military: Who Profits, Who Pays? LC 91-20081. 200p. 1991. 52.95 (*0-275-94060-8*, C4060, Praeger Pubs) Greenwood.

Laurence, Jean-Roch & Perry, Campbell. Hypnosis, Will & Memory: A Psycho-Legal History. LC 87-19672. (Clinical & Experimental Hypnosis Ser.). 432p. 1988. pap. text 28.50 (*0-89862-504-1*) Guilford Pubns.

Laurence, Larry. Life of the Bones to Come. 70p. 1999. pap. 11.95 (*0-930773-57-8*, Pub. by Black Heron Pr) Midpt Trade.

— Scenes Beginning with the Footbridge at the Lake. (Illus.). 1992. 25.00 (*0-918116-68-6*); pap. 10.00 (*0-918116-69-4*) Brooding Heron Pr.

— Scenes Beginning with the Footbridge at the Lake. deluxe limited ed. (Illus.). 1992. 40.00 (*0-918116-67-8*) Brooding Heron Pr.

Laurence, Leslie & Weinhouse, Beth. Outrageous Practices: How Gender Bias Threatens Women's Health. LC 97-12096. xxi, 434p. (Orig.). 1997. pap. 18.95 (*0-8135-2448-2*) Rutgers U Pr.

— Outrageous Practices: The Alarming Truth about How Medicine Mistreats Women. 434p. 1998. text 22.00 (*0-7881-5948-8*) DIANE Pub.

Laurence, Louise, jt. auth. see Brechling, Frank.

Laurence, Louise, jt. auth. see Brechling, Frank P.

Laurence, Margaret. A Bird in the House: Stories. (Phoenix Fiction Ser.). 192p. (C). 1993. pap. 11.95 (*0-226-46934-4*) U Ch Pr.

— Crossing the River: Essays in Honour of Margaret Laurence. Gunnars, Kristjana, ed. 1997. pap. 12.95 (*0-88801-128-8*, Pub. by Turnstone Pr) Genl Dist Srvs.

— The Diviners. 480p. 1984. mass mkt. 4.95 (*0-7704-2176-8*) Bantam.

— The Diviners. (Phoenix Fiction Ser.). 392p. (C). 1993. pap. 12.95 (*0-226-46935-2*) U Ch Pr.

— The Fire-Dwellers. (Phoenix Fiction Ser.). viii, 288p. 1993. pap. 10.95 (*0-226-46951-4*) U Ch Pr.

— A Jest of God. LC 93-8034. (Phoenix Fiction Ser.). 224p. 1993. pap. 13.50 (*0-226-46952-2*) U Ch Pr.

— The Olden Days Coat. (Illus.). 40p. (J). (gr. k-5). pap. 14.95 (*0-7710-4743-6*) McCland & Stewart.

— The Olden Days Coat. rev. ed. LC 98-60285. (Illus.). 32p. 1998. 14.95 (*0-88776-455-X*) Tundra Bks.

— Selected Letters of Margaret Laurence & Adele Wiseman. Lennox, John & Panofsky, Ruth, eds. LC 97-228619. 528p. 1997. pap. 24.95 (*0-8020-8090-1*); text 60.00 (*0-8020-4247-3*) U of Toronto Pr.

— The Stone Angel. (Phoenix Fiction Ser.). 320p. (C). 1993. pap. 14.00 (*0-226-46936-0*) U Ch Pr.

— A Tree for Poverty. 160p. (C). 1993. pap. 16.00 (*1-55022-177-9*, Pub. by ECW) Genl Dist Srvs.

Laurence, Mary. All Kinds of Everything. 16p. 1986. pap. 35.00 (*0-7223-2058-2*, Pub. by A H S Ltd) St Mut.

***Laurence, Mary L.** Daughter of the Regiment: Memoirs of a Childhood in the Frontier Army, 1878-1898. Smith, Thomas T., ed. LC 95-24896. (Illus.). 220p. 1999. pap. 12.95 (*0-8032-7988-4*) U of Nebr Pr.

Laurence, Mary S. Best Loved Poems to Read Again & Again. 1989. 9.98 (*0-88365-714-7*) Galahad Bks.

— Best Loved Poems to Read Again & Again. (Second Ser.). 1989. 9.98 (*0-88365-726-0*) Galahad Bks.

— Best Loved Poems to Read Again & Again, 2 vols. 1990. boxed set 19.98 (*0-88365-760-0*) Galahad Bks.

— Treasured Poems That Touch the Heart. 256p. 1995. 12.00 (*0-88486-116-3*, Bristol Park Bks) Arrowood Pr.

***Laurence, Mary S.** Tresured Poems That Touch the Heart: Cherished Poems & Favorite Poets. 256p. 2000. 7.99 (*1-57866-099-8*) Galahad Bks.

Laurence, Mary S., compiled by. More Treasured Poems That Touch the Heart. 256p. 1997. 14.00 (*0-88486-171-6*, Bristol Park Bks) Arrowood Pr.

Laurence, Michael, et al. The 1982 Register. (Illus.). 124p. 1983. 30.00 (*0-9610384-0-3*) US Pict Res.

Laurence, Michael D., et al. Social Control of the Drinking Driver. (Studies in Crime & Justice). xxx, 482p. 1988. pap. text 24.00 (*0-226-46954-9*) U Ch Pr.

Laurence, Michael J. Lyricism & the Electric: Poems. (Illus.). 70p. (Orig.). 1996. pap. write for info. (*0-9649233-0-0*) Space Los Angeles.

Laurence, Murray. High Times in the Middle of Nowhere: The Misadventures of Murray Laurence, Compulsive Traveller. LC 86-11444. 317p. 1987. pap. 16.95 (*0-7022-2013-2*, Pub. by Univ Queensland Pr) Intl Spec Bk.

Laurence, P., jt. auth. see Avellaneda, Marco.

Laurence, Patricia O. The Reading of Silence: Virginia Woolf in the English Tradition. LC 90-23636. 253p. 1991. 39.50 (*0-8047-1831-8*) Stanford U Pr.

— The Reading of Silence: Virginia Woolf in the English Tradition. 253p. (C). 1993. pap. 13.95 (*0-8047-2179-3*) Stanford U Pr.

Laurence, R. & Wallace-Hadrill, A. Domestic Space in the Roman World: Pompeii & Beyond. (JRA Supplementary Ser.: Vol. 22). (Illus.). 240p. 1997. 79.50 (*1-887829-22-9*) Jour Roman Arch.

Laurence, R. V., ed. see Acton, John E.

Laurence, Rassophor-Monk, tr. from SLV. Divine Liturgy of St. Gregory. 52p. (Orig.). 1993. pap. 5.00 (*0-912927-22-4*, D001) St John Kronstadt.

Laurence, Ray. Roads of Roman Italy: Mobility & Cultural Change. LC 99-20446. 1999. text. write for info. (*0-415-16616-0*) Routledge.

— Roman Pompeii. 176p. 1996. pap. text 16.95 (*0-415-13816-7*) Routledge.

— Roman Pompeii: Space & Society. 176p. (C). 1996. pap. 19.99 (*0-415-14103-6*) Routledge.

Laurence, Ray & Berry, Joanne. Cultural Identity in the Roman Empire. LC 97-15373. (Illus.). 224p. (C). 1998. 70.00 (*0-415-13594-X*) Routledge.

Laurence, Reginald V., ed. see Acton, John E.

Laurence, Richard. The Book of Enoch. LC 72-95273. (Secret Doctrine Reference Ser.). xlvii, 192p. 1998. reprint ed. pap. 11.00 (*0-913510-67-X*) Wizards.

***Laurence, Richard, tr.** The Book of Enoch the Prophet. (Illus.). 224p. 2000. pap. 16.95 (*0-932813-85-2*, Pub. by Adventures Unltd) SCB Distributors.

— The Book of Enoch the Propht: From the Ethiopic. 96p. 1998. pap. 5.00 (*0-944379-21-4*) CPA Bk Pub.

Laurence, Richard H. Medals of Giovanni Cavino, the Paduan. 1981. reprint ed. pap. 6.00 (*0-915262-56-8*) S J Durst.

Laurence, Robert, jt. auth. see Leflar, Robert A.

Laurence, Robert, pseud & Minzner, Pamela B. Student's Guide to Estates in Land & Future Interests: Text, Examples, Problems, & Answers. 2nd ed. (Student Guide Ser.). 1981. teacher ed. write for info. (*0-8205-0352-5*) Bender.

Laurence, Sandy. South Shore Smugglers. LC 95-21090. (Mystery Ser.). (Illus.). (J). (gr. 4-8). 1983. 9.95 incl. audio (*0-934898-27-7*) Jan Prods.

Laurence, Stephen, jt. auth. see MacDonald, Cynthia.

Laurence, Stephen, jt. ed. see MacDonald, Cynthia.

Laurence, Stephen, jt. ed. see Margolis, Eric.

Laurence, William L. Dawn over Zero: The Story of the Atomic Bomb. LC 71-153156. (Illus.). 289p. 1972. reprint ed. lib. bdg. 35.00 (*0-8371-6064-2*, LADZ, Greenwood Pr) Greenwood.

Laurenceau, Jean. Speak to Us of Mary: Biblical Homilies As Aids to Prayer with the Blessed Virgin. 181p. (Orig.). 1987. pap. 3.95 (*0-8199-0802-9*, Frncscn Herld) Franciscan Pr.

Laurencich, Laura, jt. auth. see Howe, Henry V.

Laurencie, Lionel D. La, see La Laurencie, Lionel D.

Laurencin, Genevieve. Music! Bogard, Vicki, tr. from FRE. LC 89-8892. (Young Discovery Library). (Illus.). (J). (gr. k-5). 1989. 5.95 (*0-944589-25-1*, 025) Young Discovery Lib.

Laurencin, Michel. Dictionnaire Biographique de Touraine. (FRE.). 1990. write for info. (*0-7859-8654-5*, 285443210X) Fr & Eur.

Laurencio, Angel A. Blas Hernandez y la Revolucion de 1933: La Campana en los Campos de Cuba. LC 93-73414. (Coleccion Cuba y sus Jueces). (SPA., Illus.). 183p. (Orig.). 1994. pap. 19.95 (*0-89729-706-7*) Ediciones.

— Don Jose Maria Chacon y Calco en Su Correspondencia. (SPA.). 31p. 1987. pap. 5.00 (*0-89729-452-1*) Ediciones.

— Jose Antonio Saco y la Cuba de Hoy. (Coleccion Cuba y sus Jueces). (SPA.). 27p. (Orig.). 1989. pap. 5.00 (*0-89729-558-7*) Ediciones.

— Trabajos Desconocidos y Olvidados de Jose Maria Heredia. (SPA.). 1972. pap. 9.00 (*0-89729-140-9*) Ediciones.

Laurencot, Elizabeth, jt. ed. see Ciarcia, Steve.

Laurendeau, Monique & Pinard, Adrien. Causal Thinking in the Child. LC 62-21895. 293p. 1963. 42.50 (*0-8236-0680-5*) Intl Univs Pr.

Laurendon, G. Dictionnaire Portatif de Cuisine. (FRE.). 1995. 125.00 (*0-7859-9801-2*) Fr & Eur.

Laurene, Ruth. Bellringer: Angels in Woodcuts. LC 74-75851. (Illus.). 88p. 1974. 30.00 (*0-933652-08-9*) Domjan Studio.

Laurens, Henry. The Papers of Henry Laurens: July 7, 1778-December 9, 1778. Chesnutt, David R., et al, eds. LC 67-29381. (Papers of Henry Laurens Ser.: Vol. 14). 700p. 1994. text 49.95 (*1-57003-030-8*) U of SC Pr.

— The Papers of Henry Laurens: Vol. X, December 12,

An Asterisk (*) at the beginning of an entry indicates that the title is appearing for the first time.

1774-January 4, 1776, Vol. X. Chesnutt, David R. et al, eds. LC 67-29381. (Papers of Henry Laurens Ser.). 736p. 1985. text 49.95 (*0-87249-445-4*) U of SC Pr.

— Papers of Henry Laurens: Vol. 1, September 11, 1746-October 31, 1755. Hamer, Philip M. & Rogers, George C., eds. LC 67-29381. (Papers of Henry Laurens Ser.). (Illus.). xlii, 447p. 1968. text 49.95 (*0-87249-128-5*) U of SC Pr.

— Papers of Henry Laurens: Vol. 2, November 1, 1755-December 31, 1758. Hamer, Philip M. & Rogers, George C., Jr., eds. LC 67-29381. (Papers of Henry Laurens Ser.). (Illus.). xxviii, 608p. 1970. text 49.95 (*0-87249-141-2*) U of SC Pr.

— The Papers of Henry Laurens: Vol. 3, January 1, 1759-August 31, 1763. Hamer, Philip M. & Rogers, George C., Jr., eds. LC 67-29381. (Papers of Henry Laurens Ser.). xxviii, 625p. 1972. text 49.95 (*0-87249-228-1*) U of SC Pr.

— The Papers of Henry Laurens: Vol. 5, September 1, 1765-July 31, 1768. Rogers, George C., Jr. & Chesnutt, David R., eds. LC 67-29381. xxxii, 872p. 1974. text 49.95 (*0-87249-331-8*) U of SC Pr.

— The Papers of Henry Laurens Vol. 6: August 1, 1768-July 31, 1769. Rogers, George C., Jr. et al, eds. LC 67-29381. (Illus.). xxvi, 685p. 1978. text 49.95 (*0-87249-356-3*) U of SC Pr.

— The Papers of Henry Laurens Vol. 7: August 1, 1769 to October 9, 1771. Rogers, George C., Jr. et al, eds. LC 67-29381. xxx, 656p. 1979. text 49.95 (*0-87249-372-5*) U of SC Pr.

— The Papers of Henry Laurens Vol. 8: October 10, 1771 to April 19, 1773. Rogers, George C., Jr., ed. LC 67-29381. xxiv, 784p. 1980. text 49.95 (*0-87249-385-7*) U of SC Pr.

— The Papers of Henry Laurens Vol. 9: April 19, 1773 to December 12, 1774. Rogers, George C., Jr. & Chesnutt, David R., eds. LC 67-29381. (Illus.). 734p. 1981. text 49.95 (*0-87249-399-7*) U of SC Pr.

— The Papers of Henry Laurens Vol. 11: January 6, 1776-November 1, 1777, Vol. XI. Chesnutt, David R. et al, eds. LC 67-29381. (Papers of Henry Laurens Ser.: Vol. 11). 710p. 1988. text 49.95 (*0-87249-516-7*) U of SC Pr.

— The Papers of Henry Laurens Vol. 12: November 1, 1777-March 15, 1778. Chesnutt, David R. et al, eds. LC 67-29381. (Papers of Henry Laurens Ser.: Vol. 12). 684p. 1990. text 49.95 (*0-87249-664-3*) U of SC Pr.

Laurens, Jeannine, jt. auth. see Stallaerts, Robert.

Laurens, John. Army Correspondence of Colonel John Laurens in the Years 1777-1778. Decker, Peter, ed. LC 78-77106. (Eyewitness Accounts of the American Revolution Ser.). 1969. reprint ed. 18.95 (*0-405-01160-1*) Ayer.

Laurens, Kate, jt. auth. see Bulhof, Ilse N.

Laurens, R. C. Inleiding Tot Die Studie van Aktebesorging. (AFR.). 145p. 1988. pap. write for info. (*0-409-04010-X*, MICHIE) LEXIS Pub.

Laurens, Roy. Fully Alive. 252p. 1988. pap. 6.95 (*0-933071-21-3*) Saybrook Pub Co.

Laurens, Sidney. London's City: A Guide Through the Historic Square Mile. LC 94-75991. (Illus.). 344p. (Orig.). 1994. pap. 15.95 (*0-9641263-0-3*) Marmot Pubng.

Laurens, Stephanie. Captain Jack's Woman. 416p. 1997. mass mkt. 5.99 (*0-380-79455-1*, Avon Bks) Morrow Avon.

— A Comfortable Wife. large type ed. (Mills & Boon Large Print Ser.). 350p. 1997. 23.99 (*0-263-15148-4*, Pub. by Mills & Boon) Ulverscroft.

— A Convenient Marriage. 1996. per. 4.99 (*0-373-83321-0*, 1-83321-9) Harlequin Bks.

***Laurens, Stephanie.** Devil's Bride. 400p. 1998. mass mkt. 5.99 (*0-380-79456 X*, Avon Bks) Morrow Avon.

Laurens, Stephanie. Fair Juno. (Historical Ser.: No. 13). 1999. mass mkt. 4.99 (*0-373-30322-X*, 1-30322-1) Harlequin Bks.

— Impetuous Innocent. (Historical Ser.: No. 19). 1999. per. 4.99 (*0-373-30328-9*, 1-30328-8, Harlequin) Harlequin Bks.

— A Lady of Expectations. large type ed. 350p. 1996. 23.99 (*0-263-14646-4*, Pub. by Mills & Boon) Ulverscroft.

— A Rake's Vow. (Avon Romantic Treasure Ser.). 374p. 1998. mass mkt. 5.99 (*0-380-79457-8*, Avon Bks) Morrow Avon.

— The Reasons for Marriage. large type ed. 350p. 1995. 23.99 (*0-263-14190-X*, Pub. by Mills & Boon) Ulverscroft.

***Laurens, Stephanie.** A Rogue's Proposal, 1. 416p. 1999. mass mkt. 6.50 (*0-380-80569-3*, Avon Bks) Morrow Avon.

— Rogues' Reform: The Reasons for Marriage, A Lady of Expectations, An Unwilling Conquest. 2000. mass mkt. 6.99 (*0-373-83458-6*, 1-83458-9) Harlequin Bks.

Laurens, Stephanie. Scandal's Bride. LC 98-93541. (Avon Historical Romance Ser.). 416p. 1999. mass mkt. 5.99 (*0-380-80568-5*, Avon Bks) Morrow Avon.

***Laurens, Stephanie.** A Secret Love. 384p. 2000. mass mkt. 6.99 (*0-380-80570-7*) Morrow Avon.

— Secrets of a Perfect Night. 384p. 2000. mass mkt. 6.99 (*0-380-81805-1*, Avon Bks) Morrow Avon.

Laurens, Stephanie. Tangled Reins. (Historical Ser.: Vol. 3). 1998. mass mkt. 4.99 (*0-373-30312-2*, 1-30312-2) Harlequin Bks.

Laurensen, Niels H. & Bouchez, Colette. Getting Pregnant: What Couples Need to Know Right Now. rev. adapted ed. LC 99-59045. 592p. 2000. per. 16.00 (*0-684-86404-5*) S&S Trade.

Laurenson, Robert M., ed. see American Society of Mechanical Engineers Staff.

Laurent, Bertel. Introduction to Spacetime. 204p. 1995. text 32.00 (*981-02-1929-6*) World Scientific Pub.

Laurent, C., jt. ed. see Encrenaz, P.

Laurent, Christopher L., ed. Emergency Department Patient Classification Systems Manual. 2nd ed. 1995. ring bd. 48.00 (*0-935890-54-8*) Emerg Nurses IL.

Laurent, D., et al. La Gratte ou Ciguatera (Ciguatera Poisoning) Ses Remedes Traditionnels dans le Pacifique Sud (Traditional Remedies in the South Pacific)Tr. of Ciguatera Poisoning - Traditional Remedies in the South Pacific.. (FRE., Illus.). 152p. 1993. pap. 24.00 (*2-7099-1171-X*, Pub. by LInstitut Francais) Balogh.

Laurent, Francis W. The Business of a Trial Court: One Hundred Years of Cases; a Census of the Actions & Special Proceedings in the Circuit of Chippewa County, Wisconsin, 1855-1954. LC 59-5305. 348p. reprint ed. pap. 107.90 (*0-8357-7498-8*, 202113900021) Bks Demand.

Laurent, G. Dizionario Italiano-Francese, Francese-Italiano. deluxe ed. (FRE & ITA.). 413p. 1979. 14.95 (*0-8288-4731-2*, M9173) Fr & Eur.

Laurent, Gilles, et al, eds. Research Traditions in Marketing. LC 93-14432. (International Series in Quantitative Marketing). 464p. (C). 1993. lib. bdg. 148.50 (*0-7923-9388-0*) Kluwer Academic.

Laurent, J., et al. Hypoglycaemic Tumors. 1971. 30.50 (*90-219-2029-8*, Excerpta Medica) Elsevier.

Laurent, Janet St., see St. Laurent, Janet.

Laurent, John, ed. Tom Mann's Social & Economic Writings. 148p. 1988. pap. 22.50 (*0-85124-468-8*, Pub. by Spkesman) Coronet Bks.

Laurent, Leo. La Guitare par l'Image. Lefferts, Michael, ed. (FRE.). 48p. (Orig.). (C). 1997. pap. text 19.95 (*0-7692-1328-6*, 01010301) Wrner Bros.

Laurent, Linda. On the Interpretation of the Melodies of Claude Debussy: Bathori or Debussy. LC 98-19192. (Vox Musicae Ser.: No. 2). (Illus.). 101p. 1998. pap. text 27.00 (*1-57647-008-3*) Pendragon NY.

Laurent, M., jt. auth. see Deza, M. M.

Laurent, Monique. Rodin. LC 89-45937. (Illus.). 160p. 1995. pap. 19.95 (*0-8050-1363-6*) H Holt & Co.

***Laurent, Pauline.** Grief Denied: A Vietnam Widow's Story. LC 99-93155. 232p. 1999. pap. 14.95 (*0-9671424-0-7*, Pub. by Catalyst CA) Rayve Prodns.

Laurent, Pierre H., jt. ed. see Papacosma, S. Victor.

Laurent, Pierre-Henri, ed. The European Community: To Maastricht & Beyond. LC 93-85874. (Annals of the American Academy of Political & Social Science Ser.: Vol. 531). 1994. 28.00 (*0-8039-5584-7*); pap. 18.00 (*0-8039-5585-5*) Am Acad Pol Soc Sci.

Laurent, Pierre-Henri & Maresceau, Marc, eds. The State of the European Union Vol. 4: Deepening & Widening. LC 97-36618. (European Community Studies Association). 374p. 1998. 55.00 (*1-55587-720-6*) L Rienner.

Laurent, Pierre-Jean. Wavelets, Images & Surface Fitting. LeMehaute, Alain & Schumaker, Larry L., eds. LC 94-11330. (Illus.). 544p. (C). 1994. text 82.00 (*1-56881-040-7*) AK Peters.

***Laurent, Pierre-Jean, et al, eds.** Curve & Surface Design: Saint-Malo 1999. LC 99-86571. (Innovations in Applied Mathematics Ser.). (Illus.). 510p. 2000. 60.00 (*0-8265-1356-5*, Pub. by Vanderbilt U Pr) U of Okla Pr.

Laurent, Pierre-Joseph, jt. ed. see Bako-Arifari, Nassirou.

***Laurent, Richard.** Past Participles from Latin to Romance LC 99-36467. 598p. 1999. pap. 72.00 (*0-520-09832-3*, Pub. by U CA Pr) Cal Prin Full Svc.

Laurent, Simon & Biggar, Robert J. Inside XML DTDS: Scientific & Technical. 512p. 1999. 49.95 (*0-07-134621-X*) Osborne-McGraw.

Laurent, T. C., ed. The Chemistry, Biology & Medical Applications of Hyaluronan & Its Derivatives. (Wenner-Gren International Ser.: Vol. 72). 300p. 1998. 127.50 (*1-85578-119-0*, Pub. by Portland Pr Ltd) Ashgate Pub Co.

Laurent, Thomas De Saint, see De Saint Laurent, Thomas.

Laurent, Yves. Theorie de la Deuxieme Microlocalisation dans le Domaine Complex. (Progress in Mathematics Ser.: No. 53). 311p. (C). 1985. 63.00 (*0-8176-3287-5*) Birkhauser.

Laurent, Yves Saint. Yves Saint Laurent & the Photography of Fashion. (Illus.). 240p. 1999. 19.95 (*3-8238-9961-9*) te Neues.

***Laurent, Yves Saint & Pelle, Marie-Paule.** Love. (Illus.). 80p. 2000. 12.95 (*0-8109-3584-8*, Pub. by Abrams) Time Warner.

Laurenti, Joseph L. Bibliografia de la Literatura Picaresca: Desde Sus Origenes Hasta el Presente: A Bibliography of Picaresque Literature; from Its Origins to the Present. LC 79-6271. reprint ed. 42.50 (*0-404-18019-1*) AMS Pr.

— A Bibliography of Picaresque Literature: Supplement. LC 79-8635.Tr. of Bibliografia De la Literatura Picaresca Suplemento. 1981. 42.50 (*0-404-18018-3*) AMS Pr.

— A Catalog of Spanish Rare Books (1701-1974) in the Library of the University of Illinois & in Selected North American Libraries. LC 84-47693. (American University Studies: Romance Languages & Literature: Ser. II, Vol. 12). XVII, 215p. (Orig.). 1984. text 23.40 (*0-8204-0129-3*) P Lang Pubng.

— Hispanic Rare Books of the Golden Age (1470-1699) in the Newberry Library of Chicago & in Selected North American Libraries. (American University Studies: Romance Languages & Literature: Ser. II, Vol. 111). XXVIII, 229p. (C). 1989. text 29.95 (*0-8204-1066-7*) P Lang Pubng.

Laurenti, Luigi. Property Values & Race: Studies in Seven Cities. LC 76-5437. (Illus.). 256p. 1976. reprint ed. lib. bdg. 69.50 (*0-8371-8795-8*, LAPV, Greenwood Pr) Greenwood.

Laurentian Hormone Conferences Staff & Pincus, Gregory, eds. Recent Progress in Hormone Research: Proceedings, Vols. 1-43. Incl. Vols. 26-27. 1971. write for info. (*0-318-50355-7*) Acad Pr.

Laurentin, Rene. Apparitions of the Blessed Virgin Mary Today. 163p. (Orig.). 1990. pap. 13.95 (*1-85390-054-0*, Pub. by Veritas Pubns) St Mut.

***Laurentin, Rene.** Bernadette Speaks to You: A Life of Saint Bernadette Soubirous in Her Own Words. Lynch, John W. & DesRosiers, Ronald, trs. from FRE. LC 99-36942. Orig. Title: Bernadette vous parle. (Illus.). 608p. 1999. pap. 24.95 (*0-8198-1154-8*) Pauline Bks.

Laurentin, Rene. The Bible & the Fatima Message. (Queen of Apostles Ser.: No. XV). 13p. 1992. 0.65 (*1-56036-043-7*, 49746) AMI Pr.

— The Cause of Liberation in U. S. S. R. Turner, Leslie S., tr. LC 93-83222. 189p. 1993. pap. 9.95 (*1-882972-07-4*) Queenship Pub.

— The Meaning of Consecration Today: A Marian Model for a Secularized Age. LC 91-77302. 208p. (Orig.). 1992. pap. 11.95 (*0-89870-403-0*) Ignatius Pr.

— Our Lady of Argentina. 1993. pap. text 29.00 (*0-85597-538-5*) St Mut.

— A Short Treatise on the Virgin Mary. 391p. 1991. 7.95 (*1-56036-015-1*; 38347) AMI Pr.

— The Truth of Christmas Beyond the Myths: The Gospel of the Infancy of Christ. LC 85-1402. (Studies in Scripture: Vol. III). 1986. pap. 24.95 (*0-932506-34-8*) St Bedes Pubns.

— War Love Your Enemies: Medjugorje 12 Years Later. LC 94-65099. 145p. (Orig.). 1994. pap. 2.00 (*1-882972-26-0*, 3023) Queenship Pub.

— When God Gives a Sign: A Response to Objections Made Against Vassula's Testimony on True Life in God. 139p. (Orig.). 1993. pap. 7.00 (*1-883225-14-0*) Trinitas.

— A Year of Grace with Mary. 162p. 1989. pap. 30.00 (*0-86217-797-9*, Pub. by Veritas Pubns) St Mut.

— A Year of Grace with Mary: Rediscovering Her Presence. 161p. (Orig.). 1987. pap. 10.95 (*0-86217-279-9*) Ignatius Pr.

Laurents, Arthur. A Clearing in the Woods. 1960. pap. 5.25 (*0-8222-0215-8*) Dramatists Play.

— The Enclave. 1974. pap. 5.25 (*0-8222-0359-6*) Dramatists Play.

— Home of the Brave. 1949. pap. 5.25 (*0-8222-0529-7*) Dramatists Play.

— Invitation to a March. 1963. pap. 5.25 (*0-8222-0575-0*) Dramatists Play.

***Laurents, Arthur.** Original Story By: A Memoir of Broadway & Hollywood. LC 99-40733. (Illus.). 400p. 2000. 30.00 (*0-375-40055-9*) Knopf.

Laurents, Arthur. The Way We Were. 22.95 (*0-88411-446-5*) Amereon Ltd.

Laurents, Arthur, jt. auth. see Sondheim, Stephen.

***Laurents, David.** Feeling Frisky. 1999. pap. 9.99 (*1-902644-15-8*) Prowler Pr.

— Hard at Work. 2000. pap. 9.95 (*1-873741-39-1*) Millivres Bks.

— Rough & Ready. 2000. pap. 9.95 (*1-902644-21-2*) Prowler Pr.

Laurents, David, ed. The Badboy Book of Erotic Poetry. 1995. mass mkt. 5.95 (*1-56333-382-1*, Badboy) Masquerade.

— Southern Comfort. (Orig.). 1996. mass mkt. 6.50 (*1-56333-466-6*, Badboy) Masquerade.

— Wanderlust: Homoerotic Tales of Travel. (Orig.). 1996. mass mkt. 5.95 (*1-56333-395-3*, Badboy) Masquerade.

Laurenzi, Elise & Levinson, Gerald B. Portraits of Garden Bedfellows: The Gardeners Guide to Plants that Go - & Grow - Well Together. LC 86-92069. (Illus.). 24p. 1987. pap. 5.95 (*0-9617942-0-8*) Corydalis Pr.

Laures, John. Catholic Church in Japan: A Short History. LC 73-100165. 252p. 1970. reprint ed. lib. bdg. 38.50 (*0-8371-2974-5*, LACC, Greenwood Pr) Greenwood.

Lauret. Alice Walker LC 99-25773. 2000. text 35.00 (*0-312-22431-1*) St Martin.

Lauret, A., jt. auth. see Ginguay, Michel.

Lauret, Bernard. Nouveau Dictionnaire de Theologie. 2nd ed. (FRE.). 1136p. 1996. 250.00 (*0-7859-9493-9*) Fr & Eur.

Lauret, Maria. Liberating Literature: Feminist Fiction in America. LC 93-48839. 224p. (C). 1994. pap. 27.99 (*0-415-06516-X*, A7975) Routledge.

Lauretis, Teresa De, see De Lauretis, Teresa.

Laureys, ed. Caballini, Ioannis, de Cerronibus. (LAT.). 1995. 100.00 (*3-8154-1128-9*, T1128, Pub. by B G Teubner) U of Mich Pr.

Laurg, Jean R. Imagery on Fabric: A Complete Surface Design Handbook. 2nd expanded ed. Lanzarotti, Sally & Jonsson, Lee, eds. LC 97-23759. (Illus.). 176p. 1997. pap. text 27.95 (*1-57120-034-7*, 10158) C & T Pub.

Laurgaard, Rachel K. Patty Reed's Doll: The Story of the Donner Party. 1989. 13.05 (*0-606-00841-1*, Pub. by Turtleback) Demco.

— Patty Reed's Doll: The Story of the Donner Party. LC 89-51264. (Illus.). 144p. (J). (gr. 3-6). 1989. reprint ed. pap. 7.95 (*0-9617357-2-4*) Tomato Enter.

Laurgeau, Claude, jt. auth. see Parent, Michel.

Lauria, A. & Gandolfi, F., eds. Embryonic Development & Manipulation in Animal Production: Trends in Research & Applications. (Portland Press Proceedings Ser.: Vol. 2). (Illus.). 296p. 1992. 102.00 (*1-85578-033-X*, Pub. by Portland Pr Ltd) Ashgate Pub Co.

***Lauria, David C.** The Alphabet God's Way. (Illus.). 56p. (J). (ps-6). 1999. pap. text 12.00 (*0-9676600-0-9*) D C Lauria.

***Lauria, Frank.** Blue Limbo. 250p. (Orig.). 2000. pap. 15.95 (*1-58394-037-5*) Frog Ltd CA.

Lauria, Frank. Blue Limbo. 352p. (Orig.). 1991. pap. 3.95 (*0-380-76164-5*, Avon Bks) Morrow Avon.

— Dark City, Vol. 1. 1998. mass mkt. 5.99 (*0-312-96343-2*) St Martin.

— The Mask of Zorro. (J). (gr. 3-7). 1998. mass mkt. 4.50 (*0-671-51967-0*) PB.

***Lauria, Frank.** Pitch Black. 1999. 143.75 (*0-312-97529-5*) St Martin.

Lauria, Frank. Pitch Black, 1 Vol. 1999. mass mkt. 5.99 (*0-312-97088-9*, St Martins Paperbacks) St Martin.

— Skull & Crossbones. (Zorro Ser.: No. 2). 160p. (J). (gr. 3-7). 1999. pap. 3.99 (*0-671-51970-0*) PB.

Lauria, Jo, jt. auth. see Clark, Garth.

Lauria, M., jt. auth. see Sivasubramaniam, A.

Lauria, Mickey, ed. Reconstructing Urban Regime Theory: Regulating Urban Politics in a Global Economy. LC 96-25361. 278p. 1996. 52.00 (*0-7619-0150-7*); pap. 23.95 (*0-7619-0151-5*) Sage.

Lauria, Peter. New York's Strongest. 181p. 1992. pap. 3.50 (*0-9635713-0-3*) Longshot Prod.

— Shedding Light. 135p. 1992. pap. write for info. (*0-9635713-1-1*) Longshot Prod.

Lauria-Santiago, Aldo. An Agrarian Republic: Land, Commercial, Agriculture & Politics of Peasants in El Salvador, 1780-1929. LC 99-6343. (Pitt Latin American Ser.). (Illus.). 324p. 1999. pap. 19.95 (*0-8229-5700-0*); text 45.00 (*0-8229-4099-X*) U of Pittsburgh Pr.

Lauria-Santiago, Aldo & Chomsky, Aviva. At the Margins of the Nation State: Identity & Struggle in the Making of the Laboring Peoples of Central America & the Hispanic Caribbean. LC 97-44374. 1998. write for info. (*0-8223-2202-1*); pap. write for info. (*0-8223-2218-8*) Duke.

Laurian, C., jt. auth. see George, B.

Lauriat, Peter M., et al, eds. Massachusetts Deposition Practice Manual, 1996 Supplement. LC 92-64380. 330p. 1996. ring bd., suppl. ed. 39.50 (*0-944490-42-5*, 96-05.29-SP) Mass CLE.

Lauriat, Peter M. & Pomeroy, Toni L., eds. Massachusetts Jury Trial Benchbook. xii, 238p. (Orig.). 1996. pap. 100.00 (*1-889916-00-5*) F N Flaschner.

***Lauricella, John A.** Home Games: Essays on Baseball Fiction. LC 99-10933. 253p. 1999. lib. bdg. 28.50 (*0-7864-0625-9*) McFarland & Co.

Lauridsen, David. The Token Economy System. Langdon, Danny G., ed. LC 77-25897. (Instructional Design Library). (Illus.). 96p. 1978. 27.95 (*0-87778-123-0*) Educ Tech Pubns.

Lauridsen, Peter. Vitus Bering. LC 70-94274. (Select Bibliographies Reprint Ser.). 1977. 23.95 (*0-8369-5048-8*) Ayer.

Laurie, Alex. Introduction to Landscape Architecture. 2nd ed. (C). 1985. text 79.00 (*0-13-500752-6*) P-H.

Laurie, Alex, et al. Commercial Flower Forcing. 8th ed. (Illus.). 544p. (C). 1979. 98.75 (*0-07-036633-0*) McGraw.

Laurie, Alison J., jt. auth. see Glamuzina, Julie.

Laurie, Arthur P. Painter's Methods & Materials. (Illus.). 250p. 1967. reprint ed. pap. 8.95 (*0-486-21868-6*) Dover.

Laurie, Ben & Laurie, Peter. Apache: The Definitive Guide. Denn, Robert J., ed. LC 97-159229. (Illus.). 274p. 1997. pap. 34.95 (*1-56592-250-6*) Thomson Learn.

***Laurie, Ben & Laurie, Peter.** Apache: The Definitive Guide. 2nd ed. Denn, Robert J., ed. (Illus.). 369p. 1999. pap. 34.95 incl. cd-rom (*1-56592-528-9*) OReilly & Assocs.

Laurie, Bruce. Artisans into Workers: Labor in Nineteenth-Century America. LC 96-52553. 272p. 1997. pap. text 16.95 (*0-252-06660-X*) U of Ill Pr.

— The Life of Richard Kane: Britain's First Lieutenant-Governor of Minorca. LC 92-54650. 1994. 42.50 (*0-8386-3501-6*) Fairleigh Dickinson.

Laurie, Clayton D. Anzio: The United States Army Campaigns of World War II. 24p. 1994. pap. 1.75 (*0-16-042084-9*) USGPO.

Laurie, Clayton D. The Propaganda Warriors: America's Crusade Against Nazi Germany. LC 95-26321. (Modern War Studies). (Illus.). 321p. (C). 1996. 35.00 (*0-7006-0765-X*) U Pr of KS.

Laurie, Clayton D. & Cole, Ronald H. The Role of Federal Military Forces in Domestic Disorders, 1877-1945. (Illus.). 475p. 1999. text 50.00 (*0-7881-7747-8*) DIANE Pub.

Laurie, Clayton D. & Cole, Ronald H. The Role of Federal Military Forces in Domestic Disorders, 1877-1945. LC 94-13148. (Illus.). 491p. 1997. write for info. (*0-16-048983-0*) USGPO.

Laurie, David. Reminiscences of a Fiddle Dealer. (Illus.). 1977. reprint ed. text 22.00 (*0-918624-01-0*) Virtuoso.

Laurie, David R., jt. auth. see Corbin, Charles B.

Laurie, Dennis. Yankee Samurai: American Managers Speak Out about What It's Like to Work for Japanese Companies in the U. S. LC 91-58508. 288p. 1992. 23.00 (*0-88730-552-0*, HarpBusn) HarpInfo.

Laurie, Dirk P. Numerical Solution of Partial Differential Equations. (International Series of Numerical Mathematics: Vol. 66). 334p. (C). 1983. text 54.95 (*3-7643-1561-X*) Birkhauser.

***Laurie, Donald L.** The Real Work of Leaders: A Report from the Front Lines of Management. 272p. 2000. text 26.00 (*0-7382-0249-5*, Pub. by Perseus Pubng) HarpC.

Laurie, Erynn Rowan. A Circle of Stones: Journeys & Meditations for Modern Celts. (Illus.). 112p. 1995. pap. 9.95 (*1-57353-106-5*, Eschaton Bks) Eschaton Prods.

Laurie, G., et al, eds. Handbook on the Late Effects of Poliomyelitis for Physicians & Survivors. 48p. (Orig.). 1984. pap. 6.75 (*0-931301-00-9*) Gazette Intl.

Laurie, G. & Raymond, J., eds. Proceedings of G. I. N. I.'s Third International Polio & Independent Living Conference, May 10-12, 1985, St. Louis, Missouri. 68p. (Orig.). 1986. pap. 4.00 (*0-931301-02-5*) Gazette Intl.

— Proceedings of Rehabilitation Gazette's Second International Post-Polio Conference & Symposium on Living Independently with Severe Disability. 74p. (Orig.). 1984. pap. 4.00 (*0-931301-01-7*) Gazette Intl.

L

Laurie, Gini, et al, eds. Rehabilitation into Independent Living: 30th Anniversary of Rehabilitation Gazette. 128p. (Orig.). 1989. write for info. (*0-614-28390-6*) Gazette Intl.

Laurie, Gloria J., ed. see Ray, Brenda.

***Laurie, Greg.** Como Compartir So Fe. (SPA.). 2000. mass mkt. 2.99 (*0-7899-0784-4*) Spanish Hse Distributors.

Laurie, Greg. Discipleship: The Next Step in Following Jesus. 108p. 1998. mass mkt. 4.99 (*1-56507-953-1*) Harvest Hse.

— Every Day with Jesus. LC 93-19334. 350p. 1996. reprint ed. pap. 11.99 (*1-56507-309-6*) Harvest Hse.

— Experiencing Forgiveness. 1997. 18.99 (*0-8499-6263-3*) Word Pub.

— God's Design for Christian Dating. 2nd ed. LC 82-83836. 96p. (YA). (gr. 10-12). 1983. mass mkt. 3.99 (*0-89081-373-6*) Harvest Hse.

***Laurie, Greg.** How to Live Forever, 5 vols. 1999. pap. 5.99 (*0-8423-0372-3*) Tyndale Hse.

Laurie, Greg. How to Share Your Faith. LC 99-26275. 1999. pap. text 7.99 (*0-8423-3345-2*) Tyndale Hse.

— A Passion for God. LC 98-5936. 192p. 1998. pap. 8.99 (*1-56507-802-0*) Harvest Hse.

— The Upside-down Church. LC 98-51016. 222p. 1999. 11.99 (*0-8423-7847-2*) Tyndale Hse.

— La Vida: Que Quiere Saber?Tr. of Life: Any Questions?. 1996. pap. 8.99 (*0-88113-424-4*) Caribe Betania.

***Laurie, Greg & Kopp, David.** The Upside-Down Church. LC 98-51016. 222p. 1999. 165.97 (*0-8423-7812-X*) Focus Family.

Laurie, Haruko Urya, jt. auth. see Bowring, Richard.

***Laurie, Hilary.** Versus of the Poets Laureate: From John Dryden to Andrew Motion. (Illus.). 208p. 1999. pap. 17.95 (*0-7528-1859-7*, Pub. by Orion Pubng Grp) Trafalgar.

Laurie, Hilary, ed. Evergreen Verse, 1 vol. 128p. 1998. mass mkt. 3.50 (*0-460-87966-9*) J M Dent & Sons.

Laurie, Hilary, ed. see Moore, George Edward.

Laurie, Hugh. The Gun Seller. 368p. 1998. pap. 14.00 (*0-671-02082-X*) S&S Trade.

— The Gun Seller. LC 96-46813. 340p. 1997. 24.00 (*1-56947-087-1*) Soho Press.

Laurie, Ian C., ed. Nature in Cities: The Natural Environment in the Design & Development of Urban Green Space. LC 77-20987. 448p. reprint ed. pap. 138.90 (*0-608-14537-8*, 202480300038) Bks Demand.

Laurie, J. R. & Webby, Barry D., eds. Global Perspectives on Ordovician Geology: Proceedings of the Sixth International Symposium on the Ordovician System, University of Sydney, Australia, 15-19 July 1991. (Illus.). 524p. (C). 1992. text 142.00 (*90-5410-048-6*, Pub. by A A Balkema) Ashgate Pub Co.

Laurie, J. R., jt. ed. see Young, G. C.

***Laurie, James.** Earth Adventure. (Science Comic Bks.). (YA). (gr. 4-7). 1998. pap. text 8.95 (*957-8741-82-0*) Large Nature.

Laurie, James. Great Car Adventure. (Science Comic Bks.). (YA). (gr. 4-7). 1998. pap. text 8.95 (*957-8741-75-8*) Large Nature.

— Weather Genie. (Science Comic Bks.). (YA). (gr. 4-7). 1998. pap. text 8.95 (*957-8741-79-0*) Large Nature.

Laurie, Joe, Jr., jt. auth. see Green, Abel.

Laurie, Laurie & Pike-Bakey, Meredith. Mosaic II: A Writting Process Book, Vol. 3. 3rd ed. LC 95-82405. 254p. (C). 1996. pap. 24.38 (*0-07-005932-2*) McGraw.

Laurie, Lucy. A Day in the Country. (J). 1990. 29.00 (*0-85439-374-9*, Pub. by St Paul Pubns) St Mut.

— A Way of Living. 109p. (C). 1990. text 40.00 (*0-85439-348-X*, Pub. by St Paul Pubns) St Mut.

Laurie, Michael. Introduction to Landscape Architecture. 2nd ed. xii, 248p. 1985. 41.00 (*0-444-00970-1*) P-H.

Laurie, Murray & Bardon, Doris. Florida's Museums & Cultural Attractions. LC 98-38719. (Illus.). 192p. 1998. pap. 16.95 (*1-56164-162-6*) Pineapple Pr.

Laurie, Murray D. Guide to FSU & Tallahassee. LC 99-23103. (Illus.). 158p. 1999. pap. 12.95 (*1-56164-184-7*) Pineapple Pr.

Laurie, Murray D., jt. auth. see McCarthy, Kevin.

Laurie, Peggy. Season Pleasers, Vol. 2. (Illus.). 54p. 1999. pap. 10.95 (*1-57377-080-9*, 0-19884-2306) Easl Pubns.

Laurie, Peter, jt. auth. see Laurie, Ben.

Laurie, Rona. The Actor's Art & Craft. (Illus.). 164p. 1994. pap. 15.00 (*0-85343-595-2*, Pub. by J G Miller Ltd) Empire Pub Srvs.

— Auditioning: A Practical Guide for the Would-Be Actor & Drama Student. (Illus.). 64p. (YA). 1994. pap. 5.00 (*0-85343-585-5*, Pub. by J G Miller Ltd) Empire Pub Srvs.

— Festivals & Adjudication. 150p. 1975. pap. 22.00 (*0-8464-1464-3*) Beekman Pubs.

Laurie, S. S. Studies in the History of Educational Opinion from the Renaissance. 261p. 1968. reprint ed. 30.00 (*0-7146-1447-5*, Pub. by F Cass Pubs) Intl Spec Bk.

Laurie, Sanders G. Centering: A Guide to Inner Growth. 1994. pap. 9.95 incl. audio (*0-89281-521-3*) Inner Tradit.

Laurie, Sanders G. & Tucker, Melvin J. Centering: A Guide to Inner Growth. 2nd ed. LC 92-44726. 224p. 1993. pap. 9.95 (*0-89281-420-9*, Destiny Bks) Inner Tradit.

— Centrandose: Guia Para Crecimiento Interno. (SPA., Illus.). 288p. 1996. pap. 9.95 (*0-89281-579-5*, Inner Trad Espanol) Inner Tradit.

— Centrarse: Guia Para El Crecimiento Interior. (SPA., Illus.). 288p. 1996. pap. write for info. (*968-458-501-2*) Rowman.

Laurie, Simon S. Historical Survey of Pre-Christian Education. 1977. lib. bdg. 59.95 (*0-8490-1954-0*) Gordon Pr.

— Historical Survey of Pre-Christian Education. LC 76-108504. 1970. reprint ed. 25.00 (*0-403-00214-1*) Scholarly.

— Historical Survey of Pre-Christian Education. 2nd rev. ed. LC 79-124596. reprint ed. 55.00 (*0-404-03889-1*) AMS Pr.

— Studies in the History of Educational Opinion from the Renaissance. LC 72-93272. vi, 261p. 1969. reprint ed. 39.50 (*0-678-05086-4*) Kelley.

Laurikainen, K. V. & Montonen, C. Foundations of Modern Physics, 1992: Proceedings of the Symposium. 460p. 1993. text 116.00 (*981-02-1324-7*) World Scientific Pub.

Laurikainen, Kalervo V. The Message of the Atoms: Wolfgang Pauli & the Unspeakable. LC 96-43199. (Illus.). 216p. 1997. 49.00 (*3-540-61754-X*) Spr-Verlag.

Laurila, J. & Hattari, A. Paper Container Dictionary, English, Finnish, Russian, Swedish, French, Spanish: Paperi-Ja Kartonkisanakirja Englanti-Suomi-Ruotsi-Saksa-Ranska-Espanja. (ENG, FIN, FRE, GER & SPA.). 839p. 1986. 295.00 (*0-8288-0334-X*, F23020) Fr & Eur.

Laurila, Juha. Managing Technological Discontinuities: The Case of the Finnish Paper Industry. LC 98-3179. 208p. (C). 1998. 90.00 (*0-415-17853-3*) Routledge.

Laurila, Simo H. Electronic Surveying in Practice. LC 82-20127. 404p. 1983. reprint ed. pap. 125.30 (*0-7837-2817-4*, 205765500006) Bks Demand.

Laurillard, D. & Keynes, Milton, eds. Interactive Media: Working Methods & Practical Applications. (New Technology in Training Ser.). 241p. 1987. text 54.95 (*0-470-20885-6*) P-H.

Laurillard, Diana. Re-Thinking University Teaching: A Framework for the Effective Use of Educational Technology. LC 93-20258. 240p. (C). 1993. pap. 25.99 (*0-415-09289-2*, B2545) Routledge.

Laurimore. Dinosaur Days. LC 99-38695. 1999. text 24.95 (*0-312-20887-1*) St Martin.

Laurin, Carl, et al. Scandinavian Art. LC 69-13242. (Illus.). 1972. reprint ed. 52.95 (*0-405-08735-7*) Ayer.

Laurin-Lam, Lou. Wilfredo Lam - Catalogue Raisonne of the Painted Work Vol. 1: 1923-1960, Vol. 1. (Illus.). 1998. 295.00 (*2-940033-19-6*) Acatos Edit.

Laurin, Robert B. The Layperson's Introduction to the Old Testament. rev. ed. 173p. 1990. pap. 12.00 (*0-8170-1163-3*) Judson.

Laurin, Roy L. Colossians: Where Life Is Established. LC 88-12129. (Life Commentary Ser.). 192p. (C). 1988. reprint ed. pap. 10.99 (*0-8254-3135-2*) Kregel.

— Designed for Conquest: Biblical Models for Overcoming Life's Struggles. LC 90-36540. Orig. Title: Meet Yourself in the Bible. 192p. 1990. reprint ed. pap. 10.99 (*0-8254-3139-5*) Kregel.

— First Corinthians: Where Life Matures. LC 86-7163. (Life Commentary Ser.). 328p. 1987. reprint ed. pap. 13.99 (*0-8254-3132-8*) Kregel.

— First John: Life at its Best. LC 86-27394. (Life Commentary Ser.). 200p. (C). 1987. reprint ed. pap. 10.99 (*0-8254-3136-0*) Kregel.

— Philippians: Where Life Advances. LC 86-7177. (Life Commentary Ser.). 208p. 1987. reprint ed. pap. 10.99 (*0-8254-3134-4*) Kregel.

— Romans: Where Life Begins. LC 88-12130. (Life Commentary Ser.). 528p. 1988. pap. 18.99 (*0-8254-3130-1*) Kregel.

— Second Corinthians: Where Life Endures. LC 85-8154. 256p. 1985. pap. 12.99 (*0-8254-3129-8*) Kregel.

Laurincikas, A., et al, eds. Analytic & Probabilistic Methods in Number Theory: Proceedings of the 2nd International Conference in Honour of J. Kubilius, Lithuania, 23-27 September, 1996. LC 99-496388. (New Trends in Probability & Statistics Ser.: No. 4). (Illus.). 511p. 1997. 260.00 (*90-6764-255-X*, Pub. by VSP) Coronet Bks.

Laurincikas, Antanas. Limit Theorems for the Riemann Zeta-Function. (Mathematics & Its Applications Ser.: Vol. 352). 312p. (C). 1995. text 158.50 (*0-7923-3824-3*) Kluwer Academic.

Laurini, Robert & Thompson, Derek. Fundamentals of Spatial Information Systems. (APIC Ser.). (Illus.). 680p. 1992. text 59.95 (*0-12-438380-7*) Acad Pr.

***Laurino, Maria.** Were You Always an Italian? Ancestors & Other Icons of Life in Italian America. LC 00-26028. 192p. 2000. 23.95 (*0-393-04930-2*) Norton.

Laurisen, Craig. Drum Grooves. (Progressive Ser.). 1997. pap. 13.95 (*1-875726-31-4*) Koala Pubns.

— Drum Grooves in 4/4 Time. 1997. pap. write for info. (*1-875726-09-8*) Klappenbach Pubns.

— Progressive Drum Method. (Progressive Ser.). 1997. pap. 14.95 (*1-875726-18-7*) Koala Pubns.

***Laurisen, Peta.** Creating Grand Illusions: The Art Techniques of Trompe L'oeil. (Illus.). 156p. 1999. text 42.00 (*90-5703-971-0*) Craftsman House.

Lauriston, Andy. Bilingual Dictionary of International Telecommunications, Vol. 2: Transmission Equipment. (ENG & FRE.). 506p. 1985. 225.00 (*0-8288-9449-3*) Fr & Eur.

— Bilingual Dictionary of International Telecommunications, Vol. 3: Switching Equipment. (ENG & FRE.). 544p. 1988. 225.00 (*0-8288-9450-7*) Fr & Eur.

— Bilingual Dictionary of International Telecommunications, Vol. 4: Telecommunications Services. (ENG & FRE.). 547p. 225.00 (*0-8288-9451-5*) Fr & Eur.

Lauriston, Robert. The PC Bible. 3rd ed. (Bible Ser.). 960p. (C). 1998. pap. text 34.99 (*0-201-35382-2*, Pub. by Peachpit Pr) Addison-Wesley.

***Laurita, Jaime & McLachlan, Sarah.** Plenty: A Collection of Sarah McLachlan's Favorite Recipes. 1999. pap. text 24.95 (*1-894160-01-0*) MP Ltd.

Laurita, Raymond E. The Advanced Day-by-Day Way to Spelling Mastery. 103p. (Orig.). (J). (gr. 4-12). 1993. pap. 10.50 (*0-914051-33-4*) Leonardo Pr.

— Affixes & Their Role in English Spelling. 108p. 1998. pap. 14.95 (*0-914051-40-7*) Leonardo Pr.

— The Beginning Day-by-Day Way to Spelling Mastery. 107p. 1998. spiral bd. 10.50 (*0-914051-39-3*) Leonardo Pr.

— Building Word Power Through Spelling Mastery: Questions & Answers about Words & Their Origins. 64p. (Orig.). (YA). (gr. 6-12). 1991. pap. text 9.95 (*0-914051-25-3*) Leonardo Pr.

— The Complete & Simplified Spelling Book of Verbs. 2nd rev. ed. 84p. 1998. spiral bd. 10.95 (*0-914051-37-7*) Leonardo Pr.

— The Complete How to Book: One Hundred One Lessons about Language. 400p. (Orig.). (J). (gr. 1-12). 1995. pap. text 28.95 (*0-914051-34-2*) Leonardo Pr.

— Greek Roots & Their Modern English Spelling: A Dictionary of Roots Transliterated from Ancient Greek with Their Modern English Spellings. LC 89-63327. 296p. (Orig.). (C). 1989. pap. text 18.95 (*0-914051-10-5*) Leonardo Pr.

— A Handy Guide to Greek Derived Affixes. 70p. (Orig.). (YA). (gr. 9-12). 1994. pap. text 12.95 (*0-914051-35-0*) Leonardo Pr.

— Latin Roots & Their Modern English Spelling. 500p. 2000. pap. 24.95 (*0-914051-41-5*) Leonardo Pr.

— Lessons from the Spelling Doctor Pt. 1: Essays on the Way Words Work. 117p. (YA). (gr. 6-12). 1991. pap. 12.95 (*0-914051-19-9*) Leonardo Pr.

— More Lessons from the Spelling Doctor: Ten New Essays on the Way Words Work, Pt. 2. 117p. 1998. spiral bd. 12.95 (*0-914051-38-5*) Leonardo Pr.

— The New Spelling: Orthographic Structuralism. 192p. (Orig.). 1981. pap. 14.95 (*0-914051-00-8*) Leonardo Pr.

— One Thousand & One Affixes & Their Meanings: A Dictionary of Prefixes, Suffixes & Inflections. rev. ed. 154p. (YA). (gr. 9-12). 1995. pap. 14.95 (*0-914051-36-9*) Leonardo Pr.

— One Thousand & One Homonyms & Their Meanings: A Dictionary of Homonyms with Defining Sentences. 160p. (Orig.). (YA). (gr. 9-12). 1992. pap. 14.95 (*0-914051-29-6*) Leonardo Pr.

— Spelling Keys to 1000 Words from 10 Latin Based Roots. 64p. (Orig.). (YA). (gr. 9-12). 1991. pap. text 11.95 (*0-914051-24-5*) Leonardo Pr.

— Spelling Keys to Five Hundred One Words from 12 Old-Middle English Roots. 63p. (Orig.). (YA). (gr. 9-12). 1992. pap. text 11.95 (*0-914051-31-8*) Leonardo Pr.

— Spelling Keys to 1001 Words from Ten Greek Based Roots. 80p. (Orig.). (YA). (gr. 9-12). 1991. pap. text 11.95 (*0-914051-26-1*) Leonardo Pr.

— Spelling Keys to 2001 Words from 10 Indo-European Roots. 140p. (Orig.). (YA). (gr. 9-12). 1992. pap. text 11.95 (*0-914051-30-X*) Leonardo Pr.

— Student Test Lesson Books, Pt. 1 (Lessons 1-15) 55p. (Orig.). (J). (ps-8). 1980. pap., student ed. 8.50 (*0-914051-05-9*) Leonardo Pr.

— Student Test Lesson Books, Pt. 1 (Lessons 16-30) 52p. (Orig.). (J). (ps-8). 1980. pap., student ed. 8.50 (*0-914051-14-8*) Leonardo Pr.

— Student Test Lesson Books, Pt. 2 (Lessons 1-15) 66p. (Orig.). (YA). (gr. 6 up). 1989. pap., student ed. 8.50 (*0-914051-07-5*) Leonardo Pr.

— Student Test Lesson Books, Pt. 2 (Lessons 16-30) 43p. (Orig.). (YA). (gr. 6 up). 1989. pap., student ed. 8.50 (*0-914051-17-2*) Leonardo Pr.

— The Vowel Category Individual Spelling Set, Pt. 1. (Illus.). 112p. (J). (gr. 1-6). 1980. pap. 32.95 (*0-914051-08-3*) Leonardo Pr.

— The Vowel Category Individual Spelling Set, Pt. 2. (Illus.). 305p. (J). (gr. 6 up). 1982. pap. 36.95 (*0-914051-09-1*) Leonardo Pr.

— The Vowel Category Resource Lists, Pt. 1. 112p. (Orig.). (J). (ps-8). 1980. pap. 13.95 (*0-914051-04-0*) Leonardo Pr.

— The Vowel Category Resource Lists, Pt. II. 305p. (Orig.). (YA). (gr. 6 up). 1989. pap. 17.95 (*0-914051-06-7*) Leonardo Pr.

Lauritis, K. N., jt. ed. see Reifsnider, K. L.

Lauritsen, John. The AIDS War: Propaganda, Profiteering & Genocide from the Medical-Industrial Complex. LC 93-71717. (Illus.). 480p. (Orig.). 1993. pap. 20.00 (*0-943742-08-0*, Asklepios) Pagan Pr.

— A Freethinker's Primer of Male Love. LC 97-95099. (Illus.). 96p. 1998. pap. 6.95 (*0-943742-11-0*) Pagan Pr.

Lauritsen, John & Thorstad, David. The Early Homosexual Rights Movement (1864-1935) 2nd rev. ed. LC 95-33424. (Illus.). 121p. (Orig.). 1995. pap. 9.95 (*0-87810-041-5*, HQ76) Times Change.

Lauritsen, John & Young, Ian, eds. The AIDS Cult: Essays on the Gay Health Crisis. LC 96-79334. (Illus.). 224p. (Orig.). 1997. pap. 15.00 (*0-943742-10-2*, Asklepios) Pagan Pr.

Lauritsen, John, ed. see Thomson, Michael M.

Lauritzen, C., ed. see Estrogens in the Post-Menopause Workshop Staff.

Lauritzen, Carol & Jaeger, Michael. Integrating Learning Through Story: The Narrative Curriculum. LC 96-4765. 352p. (C). 1996. pap. 63.95 (*0-8273-7418-6*) Delmar.

Lauritzen, Cyndi. Create & Write. (Learning Works Creative Writing Ser.). (Illus.). 48p. (J). (gr. 4-6). 1982. pap. 6.95 (*0-88160-052-0*, LW238) Learning Wks.

Lauritzen, Erik K., ed. Demolition & Reuse of Concrete & Masonry: Proceedings of the Third International Rilem Symposium. (Rilem Proceedings Ser.). (Illus.). 552p. (C). 1994. 200.00 (*0-419-18400-7*, E & FN Spon) Routledge.

Lauritzen, Erik K., jt. auth. see De Pauw.

Lauritzen, Hal, photos by. Marin. (Illus.). 120p. 1996. pap. 18.95 (*0-8118-1424-6*) Chronicle Bks.

— Marin. (Illus.). 120p. 1993. 35.00 (*0-8118-0022-9*) Chronicle Bks.

Lauritzen-Jaeger. Integrating Learning Through Story: The Narrative Curriculum. 64p. 1996. teacher ed. 10.00 (*0-8273-7419-4*) Delmar.

Lauritzen, Paul. Religious Belief & Emotional Transformation: A Light in the Heart. LC 91-55509. 128p. 1992. 29.50 (*0-8387-5217-9*) Bucknell U Pr.

***Lauritzen, Paul, ed.** Cloning & the Future of Human Embryo Research. (Illus.). 275p. 2000. text 39.95 (*0-19-512858-3*) OUP.

Lauritzen, Phyllis, jt. auth. see Cecil, Nancy Lee.

Lauritzen, S. L. Extremal Families & Systems of Sufficient Statistics. (Lecture Notes in Statistics Ser.: Vol. 49). (Illus.). xv, 268p. 1988. 58.95 (*0-387-96872-5*) Spr-Verlag.

Lauritzen, Steffen L. Graphical Models. LC 97-109162. (Statistical Science Ser.: No. 17). (Illus.). 308p. 1996. text 65.00 (*0-19-852219-3*) OUP.

Laurmann, J. A., jt. auth. see Robinson, Abraham.

Lauro, Cathy W. The Inside Advantage: How Ordinary People Can Accomplish Extraordinary Things. 184p. 1999. pap. 17.95 (*1-890777-08-0*) Select Pr.

Lauro, Antonio. Venezuelan Waltz (for Guitar) Stang, Aaron, ed. 4p. (Orig.). (C). 1985. pap. text 5.00 (*0-7692-1335-9*, FCS02316) Wrner Bros.

Lauro, Estrada Inda. Por Que Deja de Amarnos Nuestra Pareja? 1997. pap. text 14.98 (*970-05-0636-3*) Grijalbo Edit.

Lauro, Shirley. The Coal Diamond. 1979. pap. 3.25 (*0-8222-0223-9*) Dramatists Play.

— Contest: A New Play. 96p. Date not set. pap. text 6.95 (*1-55783-368-0*) Applause Theatre Bk Pubs.

Laursen. Structural Analysis. 3rd ed. 1988. student ed. 27.50 (*0-07-036646-2*) McGraw.

— Variety of Rites. LC 99-12813. 1999. text 45.00 (*0-312-22233-5*) St Martin.

Laursen, Brett, ed. Close Friendships in Adolescence. LC 85-644581. (New Directions for Child Development Ser.: No. CD 60). 110p. (Orig.). 1993. pap. 25.00 (*1-55542-689-1*) Jossey-Bass.

Laursen, Brett, jt. ed. see Collins, W. Andrew.

Laursen, Byron, jt. auth. see Jack, Wolfman.

Laursen, Byron, jt. auth. see Leonard, Thomas J.

Laursen, Dan. Quarternary Shells Collected by the Fifth Thule Expedition, 1921-24. LC 76-21342. (Thule Expedition, 5th, 1921-1924 Ser.: Vol. 1, No. 7). (Illus.). reprint ed. 37.50 (*0-404-58307-5*) AMS Pr.

Laursen, Finn. Small Powers at Sea: Scandinavia & the New International Marine Order. LC 93-10952. 336p. (C). 1993. lib. bdg. 124.00 (*0-7923-2341-6*) Kluwer Academic.

— Superpower at Sea: U. S. Ocean Policy. LC 83-21222. 209p. 1983. 55.00 (*0-275-91033-4*, C1033, Praeger Pubs) Greenwood.

— Toward a New International Marine Order. 1982. lib. bdg. 101.00 (*90-247-2597-6*) Kluwer Academic.

Laursen, Finn, ed. The Intergovernmental Conference on Political Union: Institutional Reforms, New Policies & International Identity of the European Community. 250p. (C). 1992. lib. bdg. 155.50 (*0-7923-1670-3*) Kluwer Academic.

— The Political Economy of European Integration. LC 95-527. 1995. lib. bdg. 118.00 (*90-411-0086-5*) Kluwer Academic.

Laursen, Finn & Vanhoonacker, Sophie, eds. The Ratification of the Maastricht Treaty: Issues, Debates & Future Implications. LC 94-34814. 1994. lib. bdg. 155.50 (*0-7923-3125-7*) Kluwer Academic.

Laursen, Gary A. Proceedings of the 3rd & 4th International Symposium on Arctic & Alpine Mycology. Petrini, Orlando, ed. (Bibliotheca Mycologica: Vol. 150). (GER., Illus.). xiv, 270p. 1993. 53.00 (*3-443-59051-9*, Pub. by Gebruder Borntraeger) Balogh.

Laursen, Gary A., et al, eds. Arctic & Alpine Mycology II. LC 87-7814. (Environmental Science Research Ser.: Vol. 34). 374p. 1987. 89.50 (*0-306-42558-0*, Plenum Trade) Perseus Pubng.

Laursen, Gary A. & Ammirati, Joseph F. Arctic & Alpine Mycology: The First International Symposium on Arcto-Alpine Mycology. LC 81-51281. 502p. 1981. 60.00 (*0-295-95856-1*) U of Wash Pr.

Laursen, Harold I. Structural Analysis. 3rd ed. 475p. (C). 1988. 101.56 (*0-07-036645-4*) McGraw.

Laursen, John C. The Politics of Skepticism in the Ancients, Montaigne, Hume, & Kant. LC 92-28512. (Brill's Studies in Intellectual History: Vol. 35). vi, 253p. 1992. 99.00 (*90-04-09459-8*) Brill Academic Pubs.

Laursen, John C., ed. New Essays on the Political Thought of the Huguenots of the Refuge. LC 94-24939. (Brill's Studies in Intellectual History: Vol. 60). v, 222p. 1994. 75.00 (*90-04-09986-7*) Brill Academic Pubs.

Laursen, John C. & Nederman, Cary J., eds. Beyond the Persecuting Society: Religious Toleration Before the Enlightenment. LC 97-26795. 296p. 1997. pap. 19.95 (*0-8122-1567-2*) U of Pa Pr.

— Beyond the Persecuting Society: Religious Toleration Before the Enlightenment. LC 97-26795. 296p. (C). (gr. 13). 1997. 39.95 (*0-8122-3331-X*) U of Pa Pr.

Laursen, John C., jt. ed. see Nederman, Cary J.

Laursen, John Christian, tr. see Bahrdt, Carl Friedrich.

***Laursen, Keld.** Trade Specialisation, Technology & Economic Growth: Theory & Evidence from Advanced Countries. LC 00-39370. (New Horizons in the Economics of Innovation Ser.). 2000. write for info. (*1-84064-385-4*) E Elgar.

***Laursen, Kjeld & Neuman, Michael.** Introduction to Local Spectral Theory. LC 99-53780. (London Mathematical Society Monographs). 608p. 2000. text 125.00 (*0-19-852381-5*) OUP.

Laursen, Per M. Description of Various Leafcasters, 1956-1982: Translation of Selected Passages in Beschreibung verschiedener Anfaserungsgerate, 1983. McCrady, Ellen R., ed. Tonnies, Moya, tr. from GER. (Monograph to Abbey Newsletter: Suppl. 2). (Illus.). v, 23p. (Orig.). 1992. pap. 30.00 (*0-9622071-1-X*) Abbey Pubns.

An Asterisk (*) at the beginning of an entry indicates that the title is appearing for the first time.

L

Laursen, Virginia R., tr. see Kirmmse, Bruce H., ed.

Laury, Jean R. The Creative Woman's Getting-It-All-Together Handbook. 2nd ed. (Illus.). 144p. 1988. reprint ed. pap. 8.95 (0-9614804-0-8) Hot Fudge Pr.

— Incredible Quilts for Kids of All Ages. LC 93-7624. (Illus.). 192p. 1993. pap. 24.95 (0-8442-2640-8, Quilt Dgst Pr) NTC Contemp Pub Co.

— Keeping It All Together: The Not-Just-for-Quiltmakers Coping Book. 50p. (Orig.). 1983. pap. 5.95 (0-9602970-5-7) Leman Pubns.

***Laury, Jean R.** The Photo Transfer Handbook: Snap It, Print It, Stitch It! Aneloski, Liz & Tobin, Vera, eds. LC 98-38813. (Illus.). 80p. 1999. pap. text 21.95 (1-57120-064-9, 10189) C & T Pub.

Laury, Jean R. Sunbonnet Sue Gets It All Together at Home. LC 86-63601. (Adventures of Sunbonnet Sue Ser.). (Illus.). 24p. (Orig.). 1987. pap. 4.95 (0-8442-2611-4, Quilt Dgst Pr) NTC Contemp Pub Co.

— Sunbonnet Sue Goes to the Quilt Show. LC 86-63602. (Adventures of Sunbonnet Sue Ser.). (Illus.). 24p. (Orig.). 1987. pap. 4.95 (0-8442-2610-6, Quilt Dgst Pr) NTC Contemp Pub Co.

Laury, Ritva. Demonstratives in Interaction: The Emergence of a Definite Article in Finnish. LC 97-17249. (Studies in Discourse & Grammar: No. 7). viii, 294p. 1997. lib. bdg. 69.00 (1-55619-373-4) J Benjamins Pubng Co.

Laus, Universa. Growing in Church Music. 1985. 4.95 (0-9602378-1-X, Pastoral Press) OR Catholic.

Lausberg, Heinrich. Handbook of Literary Rhetoric: A Foundation for Literary Studies. LC 97-51646. 954p. 1997. 224.00 (90-04-10705-3) Brill Academic Pubs.

Lausch, David, Graphics Staff. U. S. Virgins Swimsuit Calendar, 1990. 8p. 1989. 9.95 (0-927400-00-6) Deaner Pub.

Lause, David B., jt. auth. see Colborn, Gene L.

Lause, Kevin, jt. ed. see Nachbar, Jack.

Laushey, David M. A Primer for American History. LC 95-77375. (Illus.). 240p. (Orig.). (C). 1995. pap. text 24.00 (0-15-502081-1, Pub. by Harcourt Coll Pubs) Harcourt.

Laussat, Anthony, Jr. An Essay on Equity in Pennsylvania. LC 76-37981. (American Law: The Formative Years). 164p. 1972. reprint ed. 16.95 (0-405-04024-5) Ayer.

Laussat, Pierre-Clement De, see De Laussat, Pierre-Clement.

Lauster, Jorg. Die Erlosungslehre Marsilio Ficinos. 280p. 1997. text 84.00 (3-11-015713-6) De Gruyter.

Laustsen, S., et al. Exploring the Southern Sky: A Pictorial Atlas from the European Southern Observatory. (Illus.). 274p. 1987. 99.95 (0-387-17735-3) Spr-Verlag.

Laut, Agnes C. Pathfinders of the West. LC 74-90651. (Essay Index Reprint Ser.). 1977. 30.95 (0-8369-1220-9) Ayer.

— The Romance of the Rails, 2 Vols. LC 75-37891. (Select Bibliographies Reprint Ser.). 1977. reprint ed. 48.95 (0-8369-6728-3) Ayer.

Laut, Phil. Money Is My Friend. LC 99-212901. 145p. 1999. pap. 5.99 (0-345-43279-7) Ballantine Pub Grp.

— Money Is My Friend. 160p. 1990. mass mkt. 5.99 (0-8041-0534-0) Ivy Books.

— Money Is My Friend. rev. ed. LC 79-51206. 150p. 1989. pap. 7.95 (0-9610132-2-2) Vivation Pub.

Laut, William, et al. Raising Multiple Birth Children: A Parents' Survival Guide - Birth to Age 3. 256p. 1999. 19.95 (1-886284-35-0, Pub. by Chandler Hse) Natl Bk Netwk.

Laute, Maureen, jt. auth. see Ravet, Serge.

Lautenbach, E. Zahn - Mund - Kiefer: Rezepte und Therapien. (Illus.). vi, 1266p. 1990. 141.75 (3-8055-5098-7) S Karger.

Lautenschlager, Michael, ed. Climate & Environmental Database Systems. LC 96-45099. (SECS Ser.). 208p. (C). 1996. text 115.00 (0-7923-9832-7) Kluwer Academic.

Lauter. Anthology of American Literature, 3 vols. (C). Date not set. pap. 11.96 (0-395-86824-6) HM.

Lauter, ed. see Meville, Herman.

Lauter, Estella. Women As Mythmakers: Poetry & Visual Art by Twentieth-Century Women. LC 83-48636. (Illus.). 288p. 1984. 35.00 (0-253-36606-2); pap. 8.95 (0-253-20325-2, MB-325) Ind U Pr.

Lauter, Estella & Rupprecht, Carol S., eds. Feminist Archetypal Theory: Interdisciplinary Re-Visions of Jungian Thought. LC 84-12007. (Illus.). 302p. 1985. reprint ed. pap. 93.70 (0-7837-9508-4, 206025800005) Bks Demand.

Lauter, G. Peter, jt. auth. see Higashi, Chikara.

Lauter, H. J., jt. ed. see Fedorov, V.

Lauter, H. J., jt. ed. see Wyatt, A. F.

Lauter, Ken. Before the Light. LC 87-70810. (Target Midwest Poetry Ser.). 64p. 1987. 6.95 (0-933532-66-0) BkMk.

Lauter-Klatell, Nancy. Readings in Child Development. LC 90-46200. 178p. (C). 1991. pap. text 27.95 (0-87484-942-X, 942) Mayfield Pub.

Lauter, Paul. Walden & Civil Disobedience: Henry David Thoreau. (Riverside Editions Ser.). 416p. 1999. pap. 7.64 (0-395-98077-1) HM.

Lauter, Paul, ed. The Heath Anthology of American Literature: Supplement to Vol. 2, 2 vols. & Supp. (C). 1997. 44.76 (0-669-35303-5) HM Trade Div.

Lauter, Paul, et al, eds. The Heath Anthology of American Literature, 2 vols. (C). 1990. pap. text 19.50 (0-685-74209-1); teacher ed. 2.66 (0-669-12066-9) HM Trade Div.

— The Heath Anthology of American Literature, 2 vols., Vol. 1. 2nd ed. LC 93-71044. 2965p. (C). 1994. pap. text 44.76 (0-669-32972-X) HM Trade Div.

Lauter, Paul & Yarborough, Richard, eds. The Heath Anthology of American Literature, 2 vols., Vol. 2. 2nd ed. 3156p. (C). 1994. pap. text 44.76 (0-669-32973-8) HM Trade Div.

Lauterbach, Ann. And, for Example: Poems. LC 94-5814. (Poets Ser.). 112p. 1994. pap. 14.95 (0-14-058715-2, Penguin Classics) Viking Penguin.

— Before Recollection. 80p. 1987. pap. 9.95 (0-691-01437-X, Pub. by Princeton U Pr) Cal Prin Full Svc.

— On a Stair. 1997. pap. 16.95 (0-614-29442-8) Penguin Putnam.

Lauterbach, Ann & Princenthal, Nancy. Ann Hamilton Whitecloth: The 1998 Larry Aldrich Foundation Award Exhibition. (Illus.). 71p. 1999. pap. 19.95 (1-888332-09-3) Aldrich Mus.

Lauterbach, Ann, et al. Jessica Stockholder: Your Skin in This Weather Bourne Eye-Threads & Swollen Perfume. Kelly, Karen, ed. LC 96-83107. (Illus.). 64p. 1996. 45.00 (0-944521-33-9, 620682) Dia Ctr Arts.

Lauterbach, Ann, jt. tr. see Salisbury, E.

Lauterbach, Anne. And for Example. 128p. 1999. text 22.95 (0-14-058738-1) NAL.

— On a Stair. LC 97-3564. 89p. 1997. pap. 14.95 (0-14-058793-4) Viking Penguin.

Lauterbach, Bernice, ed. see D'Angelo, Anthony J.

Lauterbach, C. A., jt. auth. see Schumann, K. M.

Lauterbach, Christiane. Atlanta Restaurant Guide. 3rd ed. LC 95-39910. (Marmac Guide Ser.). (Illus.). 352p. 1996. pap. 9.95 (1-56554-031-X) Pelican.

***Lauterbach, Edward C.** Psychiatric Management in Neurological Disease. LC 99-40517. (Clinical Practice Ser.). 2000. 39.00 (0-88048-786-0) Am Psychiatric.

Lauterbach, Eva, ed. Eurythmy: Essays & Anecdotes in Art, Education & Therapy. LC 80-22938. (Illus.). 256p. (Orig.). 1981. pap. 15.95 (0-935690-01-8) Schaumburg Pubns.

Lauterbach, Eva, tr. see Benesch, Friedrich & Wilde, Klaus.

Lauterbach, Jacob Z. Rabbinic Essays. LC 52-18170. 586p. reprint ed. pap. 181.70 (0-608-14972-1, 202569300045) Bks Demand.

Lauterbach, Jeffery R., jt. auth. see Gourgues, Harold W., Jr.

Lauterbach, William A. More Precious Than Gold: Quiet Times with God. LC 93-84930. 133p. (Orig.). 1993. pap. 8.99 (0-8100-0500-X, 06N0702) Northwest Pub.

— Prayers for the Sickroom. 64p. 1968. pap. 1.95 (0-570-03524-4, 14-1236) Concordia.

Lauterback, Ruth A. Intruder in the House. (Illus.). 75p. 1987. 10.95 (0-9618709-0-7) Leander Pub.

Lauterbeck, Georg. Regentenbuch: Darinn viel und Mancherley Nutzliche Anweisung... Zu Loblicher und Gluckhaffter Regierung/Anrichtung/... und Erhaltung Guter Policey/ in Friedens und Kriegzeiten. (GER.). xxviii, 626p. 1997. reprint ed. write for info. (3-487-10508-X) G Olms Pubs.

Lauterborn, W., ed. Cavitation & Inhomogeneities in Underwater Acoustics: Proceedings. (Electrophysics Ser.: Vol. 4). (Illus.). 319p. 1980. 50.95 (0-387-09939-5) Spr-Verlag.

Lauterborn, W., et al. Coherent Optics. (Illus.). 304p. 1995. 49.00 (0-387-58372-6) Spr-Verlag.

— Coherent Optics: Fundamentals & Applications. LC 95-9942.Tr. of Koharente Optik. 1995. 49.00 (3-540-58372-6) Spr-Verlag.

***Lauterborn, Werner & Kurz, Thomas, eds.** Nonlinear Acoustics at the Turn of the Millennium: ISNA 15, 15th International Symposium. LC 00-104855. (AIP Conference Proceedings Ser.: Vol. 524). (Illus.). xxii, 591p. 2000. 185.00 (1-56396-945-9) Am Inst Physics.

Lauterer, Jock. Community Journalism: A Personal Approach - Teacher's Manual. 1996. pap., teacher ed. write for info. (0-8138-2336-6) Iowa St U Pr.

— Community Journalism: The Personal Approach. LC 95-19990. 224p. 1995. pap. text 34.95 (0-8138-2309-9) Iowa St U Pr.

***Lauterer, Jock.** Community Journalism: The Personal Approach. (Illus.). 384p. 2000. pap. 36.95 (0-8138-0286-5) Iowa St U Pr.

Lauterer, Jock. Hogwild. (Illus.). (Orig.). 1993. pap. text 12.95 (0-913239-69-0) Appalach Consortium.

— Wouldn't Take Nothin' for My Journey Now. LC 80-13425. (Illus.). 186p. reprint ed. pap. 57.70 (0-8357-3888-4, 203662000004) Bks Demand.

***Lauterin, Rene.** Lourdes. (SPA.). 1999. 24.95 (84-08-02180-X) Planeta Edit.

Lautermilch, Steven. Grass Script. Sherman, Alana & DeGennaro, Lorraine, eds. 16p. (Orig.). 1991. pap. 4.95 (0-939689-14-6) Alms Hse Pr.

Lauterpacht, E. Aspects of the Administration of International Justice. 200p. (C). 1991. 140.00 (0-949009-90-3, Pub. by Grotius Pubns Ltd) St Mut.

Lauterpacht, E., compiled by. The United Nations Emergency Force: Basic Documents. (International & Comparative Law Quarterly Supplement Publication Ser.: No. 3). 1974. reprint ed. pap. 25.00 (0-8115-3194-5) Periodicals Srv.

Lauterpacht, E., et al, eds. International Law Reports, Vol. 103. 741p. 1996. text 150.00 (0-521-56311-9) Cambridge U Pr.

— International Law Reports, Vol. 104. 805p. (C). 1997. text 150.00 (0-521-58066-8) Cambridge U Pr.

— International Law Reports, Vol. 105. 730p. (C). 1997. text 150.00 (0-521-58067-6) Cambridge U Pr.

Lauterpacht, E. & Greenwood, C. J. International Law Reports, 80 vols. (C). 1989. text 11800.00 (0-7855-0123-1, Pub. by Grotius Pubns Ltd) St Mut.

— International Law Reports, 88 vols. (C). 1993. text 320.00 (0-7855-2637-4, Pub. by Grotius Pubns Ltd) St Mut.

— International Law Reports, 80 vols., 80. (C). 1989. text 270.00 (0-7855-6967-7, Pub. by Grotius Pubns Ltd) St Mut.

— International Law Reports, 88 vols., Set. (C). 1993. text 18134.00 (0-318-70313-0, Pub. by Grotius Pubns Ltd) St Mut.

— International Law Reports, 80 vols., Vols. 51-74. (C). 1989. text 234.00 (0-7855-2635-8, Pub. by Grotius Pubns Ltd) St Mut.

— International Law Reports, 80 vols., Vols. 75-79. (C). 1989. text 254.00 (0-318-70035-2, Pub. by Grotius Pubns Ltd) St Mut.

Lauterpacht, E. & Greenwood, C. J., eds. International Law Reports. 1994. text 3500.00 (0-521-46926-0) Cambridge U Pr.

— International Law Reports, No. 108. 762p. (C). 1998. text 150.00 (0-521-58070-6) Cambridge U Pr.

— International Law Reports, Vol. 102. (C). 1996. text 150.00 (0-521-55199-4) Cambridge U Pr.

— International Law Reports, Vol. 106. 832p. (C). 1998. text 150.00 (0-521-58068-4) Cambridge U Pr.

— International Law Reports, Vol. 107. 732p. (C). 1998. text 150.00 (0-521-58069-2) Cambridge U Pr.

— International Law Reports, Vol. 109. 736p. (C). 1998. text 150.00 (0-521-58071-4) Cambridge U Pr.

— International Law Reports, Vol. 110. 888p. (C). 1999. text 150.00 (0-521-58072-2) Cambridge U Pr.

— International Law Reports, Vol. 111. 752p. (C). 1999. text 150.00 (0-521-64214-0) Cambridge U Pr.

— International Law Reports, Vol. 112. 700p. (C). 1999. text 150.00 (0-521-64242-6) Cambridge U Pr.

— International Law Reports, Vol. 113. 3rd ed. 768p. (C). 1999. text 150.00 (0-521-64243-4) Cambridge U Pr.

— International Law Reports, Vol. 114. (Illus.). 700p. (C). 1999. 150.00 (0-521-64244-2) Cambridge U Pr.

***Lauterpacht, E. & Greenwood, C. J., eds.** International Law Reports, Vol. 115. 770p. (C). 2000. 150.00 (0-521-64245-0) Cambridge U Pr.

— International Law Reports, Vol. 116. (Illus.). 700p. (C). 2000. text Price not set. (0-521-66119-6) Cambridge U Pr.

— International Law Reports, Vol. 117. 672p. (C). 2000. text Price not set. (0-521-66120-X) Cambridge U Pr.

Lauterpacht, E. & Greenwood, C. J., eds. International Law Reports: Consolidated Tables of Cases & Treaties & Indexes, Vols. 81-100. 847p. (C). 1996. text 200.00 (0-521-56229-5) Cambridge U Pr.

Lauterpacht, E., et al. The Kuwait Crisis: Basic Documents. 330p. (C). 1991. pap. 140.00 (0-949009-86-5, Pub. by Grotius Pubns Ltd) St Mut.

Lauterpacht, E., jt. ed. see Bethlehem, Daniel L.

Lauterpacht, E., jt. ed. see Greenwood, C. J.

Lauterpacht, E., ed. see Lauterpacht, Hersh.

Lauterpacht, E., jt. ed. see Weller, Marc.

***Lauterpacht, Hersch.** The Function of Law in the International Community. fac. ed. LC 00-22124. 2000. write for info. (1-58477-090-2) Lawbk Exchange.

Lauterpacht, Hersch. The Development of International Law by the International Court. 427p. (C). 1982. 150.00 (0-906496-30-6, Pub. by Grotius Pubns Ltd) St Mut.

— The Function of Law in the International Community, No. 1. xxiv, 469p. 1999. reprint ed. 148.50 (1-56169-447-9) Gaunt.

— International Law Vol. 2, Pt. 1: The Law of Peace: International Law in General. Lauterpacht, E., ed. LC 70-92250. 612p. reprint ed. pap. 174.50 (0-608-17517-X, 2030603) Bks Demand.

Lauth, Thomas P., jt. auth. see Abney, Glenn.

Lauth, Thomas P., jt. ed. see Clynch, Edward J.

Lauther, Howard. Creating Characters: A Writer's Reference to the Personality Traits That Bring Fictional People to Life. LC 98-8073. 256p. 1998. lib. bdg. 35.00 (0-7864-0569-4) McFarland & Co.

— Punctuation Thesaurus of the English Language. 360p. 1991. 19.95 (0-8283-1945-6) Branden Bks.

Lautier, Jack. Forever Whalers, From Abrahamsson to Zuke: An Encyclopedia of Hockey's Icemen. 2nd ed. (Illus.). 190p. (Orig.). 1998. pap. 24.95 (0-9650315-3-5) Glacier Publng.

— Off Broadway: A Season with the Hartford Wolf Pack. (Illus.). 200p. 1999. pap. 19.95 (0-9650315-5-1) Glacier Publng.

— Pro Hockey Trivia Compendium. (Illus.). 97p. (Orig.). 1999. pap. 7.95 (0-9650315-2-7) Glacier Publng.

— Whalers Trivia Compendium. (Illus.). 72p. 1995. pap. 7.95 (0-9650315-0-0) Glacier Publng.

Lautier, Jack & Polnaszek, Frank. Same Game, Different Name: The World Hockey Association. 2nd ed. (Illus.). 206p. 1998. pap. 24.95 (0-9650315-1-9) Glacier Publng.

***Lautin, Andrew.** The Limbic Brain. LC 00-30936. 2000. write for info. (0-306-46086-6) Kluwer Academic.

Lautman, Kay P. & Goldstein, Henry, eds. Dear Friend: Mastering the Art of Direct-Mail Fund Raising. 2nd ed. 378p. 1991. 70.00 (0-930807-18-9, 600301) Fund Raising.

Lautman, Robert C. Thomas Jefferson's Monticello: A Photographic Portrait. (Illus.). 1997. 35.00 (0-614-28246-2) Monacelli Pr.

Lautman, Robert C., photos by. Thomas Jefferson's Monticello: A Photographic Portrait. LC 96-45704. (Illus.). 144p. 1997. 29.95 (1-885254-46-6, Pub. by Monacelli Pr) Penguin Putnam.

Lautman, Victoria. The New Tattoo. LC 94-5033. (Illus.). 128p. 1994. 35.00 (1-55859-785-9) Abbeville Pr.

— The New Tattoo. (Illus.). 128p. 1996. pap., bds. 24.95 (0-7892-0233-6) Abbeville Pr.

Lautner, Peter, tr. see Simplicius.

Lautreamont. Les Chants de Maldoror. unabridged ed. (FRE.). pap. 7.95 (2-87714-228-0, Pub. by Bookking Intl) Distribks Inc.

— Oeuvres Completes: Les Chants de Maldoror; Lettres; Poesies. (Poesie Ser.). (FRE.). 512p. 1973. pap. 12.95 (2-07-032000-6) Schoenhof.

Lautreamont, Comte De, see De Lautreamont, Comte.

Lautreamont, Comte D., pseud. Oeuvres Completes. deluxe ed. (Pleiade Ser.). (FRE.). 77.95 (2-07-010304-8) Schoenhof.

Lautreamont, Isidore de. Oeuvres Completes. 428p. 1970. 19.95 (0-686-54284-3) Fr & Eur.

Lautreamont, Isidore De, see De Lautreamont, Isidore.

Lautreamont-Nouveau. Oeuvres Completes. Walzer, Gerard, ed. (FRE.). 1488p. 1970. lib. bdg. 110.00 (0-7859-3763-3, 2070103048) Fr & Eur.

Lautrup, B., jt. auth. see Brunak, S.

Lautt, W. Wayne. Hepatic Circulation in Health & Disease. LC 80-5833. 392p. 1981. reprint ed. pap. 121.60 (0-608-00423-5, 206113800007) Bks Demand.

Lauture, Denize. Running the Road to ABC. LC 95-38290. (Illus.). 32p. (J). (gr. k-3). 1996. per. 16.00 (0-689-80507-1) S&S Bks Yung.

***Lauture, Denize.** Running the Road to ABC. (Illus.). 32p. (J). (gr. k-3). 2000. reprint ed. pap. 5.99 (0-689-83165-X) Aladdin.

Laut, Abraham D. Sha'ar Hakolel. 3rd ed. (HEB.). 476p. 1990. reprint ed. 17.00 (0-8266-5341-3) Kehot Pubn Soc.

Lauvand, Rhona P., jt. auth. see Thuries, Yves.

Lauvand, Rhonda P., jt. auth. see Thuries, Yves.

Lauvaux, Eric & Turton, Julian, eds. The Impact of Competition Law on the Music Industry: Reports Presented at the Meeting of the International Association of Entertainment Lawyers Midem 1997, Cannes. 196p. 1997. pap. 135.00 (90-6715-015-0, Pub. by Maklu Uitgev) Gaunt.

Lauve, Richard, ed. Physician Payment Reform: Its Impact on Payers & Providers. LC 92-81837. (Orig.). (C). 1992. pap. text 25.95 (0-924674-15-6) Am Coll Phys Execs.

Lauver, Gene. Survey of State Procedures Related to Firearm Sales. (Illus.). 62p. (C). 1998. reprint ed. pap. text 25.00 (0-7881-4346-8) DIANE Pub.

Lauver, Gene, ed. Survey of State Procedures Related to Firearm Sales, 1996. (Illus.). 70p. (C). 1998. pap. text 20.00 (0-7881-7433-9) DIANE Pub.

Lauver, Philip & Harvey, David R. The Practical Counselor: Elements of Effective Helping. LC 96-12007. 277p. (C). 1996. mass mkt. 45.95 (0-534-34349-X) Brooks-Cole.

Lauver, Philip, jt. auth. see Fogel.

***Lauvergne, J. J.** Mendelian Inheritance in Cattle. 450p. 2000. 85.00 (90-74134-75-0) Wageningen Pers.

Lauwerier, Hans. Fractals: Endlessly Repeated Geometrical Figures. Gill-Hoffstadt, Sophia, tr. (Illus.). 168p. 1991. text 69.50 (0-691-08551-X, Pub. by Princeton U Pr); pap. text 16.95 (0-691-02445-6, Pub. by Princeton U Pr) Cal Prin Full Svc.

Lauwers, Albert & Scharpe, Simon. Pharmaceutical Enzymes. LC 97-15723. (Drugs & the Pharmaceutical Sciences Ser.: Vol. 84). (Illus.). 408p. 1997. text 165.00 (0-8247-9375-7) Dekker.

Lauwers, Judith, et al. Counseling the Nursing Mother: A Lactation Consultant's Guide 3rd ed. LC 99-29436. 1999. write for info. (0-7637-0975-1) Jones & Bartlett.

Lauwers-Rech, Magda. Nazi Germany & the American Germanists: A Study of Periodicals, 1930-1946, Vol. 2. LC 94-12036. (Literature & the Sciences of Man Ser.: No. 2). X, 222p. (C). 1995. 46.95 (0-8204-1656-8) P Lang Pubng.

Lauwerys, Joseph A., jt. ed. see Bereday, George Z.

Lauwerys, Robert R. Industrial Chemical Exposure: Guidelines for Biological Monitoring. LC 82-70668. 162p. reprint ed. pap. 50.30 (0-8357-7861-4, 203627800002) Bks Demand.

Lauwerys, Robert T. & Hoet, Perrine, eds. Industrial Chemical Exposure: Guidelines for Biological Monitoring. 2nd ed. 336p. 1993. lib. bdg. 95.00 (0-87371-650-7, L650) Lewis Pubs.

Laux, Connie. Devil's Diamond. 352p. 1998. mass mkt. 5.99 (0-451-40837-3) NAL.

Laux, Constance. Diamond Rain. 320p. (Orig.). 1999. mass mkt. 5.99 (0-451-40813-6) NAL.

***Laux, Constance.** Diamonds & Desire. (Lords of Desire Ser.). 2000. mass mkt. 3.99 (0-451-20092-6) Signet.

Laux, Don, ed. see Moore, Andrea A.

Laux, Dorianne. Awake. (New Poets of America Ser.: No. 12). 63p. 1990. pap. 10.00 (0-918526-77-9) BOA Edns.

***Laux, Dorianne.** Smoke. (American Poets Continuum Ser.: Vol. 62). 65p. 2000. 20.00 (1-880238-85-3); pap. 12.50 (1-880238-86-1) BOA Edns.

Laux, Dorianne. What We Carry. LC 94-205339. (American Poets Continuum Ser.). 80p. 1994. pap. 12.50 (1-880238-07-1) BOA Edns.

Laux, Dorianne, jt. auth. see Addonizio, Kim.

Laux, E. Vernon. Bird News: Vagrants & Visitors on a Peculiar Island. LC 99-33176. (Illus.). 256p. 1999. 20.00 (1-56858-113-0) FWEW.

Laux, James M. The European Automobile Industry. 250p. (C). 1992. pap. 14.95 (0-8057-3801-0); text 26.95 (0-8057-3800-2) Macmillan.

— European Automobile Industry. (International Business History Ser.). 1991. pap. 12.95 (0-685-54772-8) Macmillan.

Laux, James M., jt. auth. see Kafker, Frank A.

Laux, James M., jt. ed. see Kafker, Frank A.

Laux, James M., tr. see Bardou, Jean P., et al.

Laux, Jeanne K. & Molot, Maureen A. State Capitalism: Public Enterprise in Canada. LC 86-47600. (Cornell Studies in Political Economy). (Illus.). 272p. (C). 1988. pap. 16.95 (0-8014-9469-9) Cornell U Pr.

Laux, John. Catholic Apologetics: God, Christianity & the Church. LC 90-70439. (Course in Religion for Catholic High Schools & Academies Ser.: Bk. IV). (Illus.). 134p. 1994. reprint ed. pap. text 10.00 (*0-89555-394-5*) TAN Bks Pubs.

— Catholic Morality: Sin, Virtue, Conscience, Duties to God, Neighbor, Etc. LC 90-70439. (Course in Religion for Catholic High Schools & Academies Ser.: Bk. III). (Illus.). 164p. 1994. reprint ed. pap. text 10.00 (*0-89555-393-7*) TAN Bks Pubs.

— Chief Truths of the Faith: Creation, Original Sin, Christ, Faith, Grace, Eternal Life, Etc. LC 90-70439. (Course in Religion for Catholic High Schools & Academies Ser.: Bk. I). (Illus.). 179p. 1994. reprint ed. pap. text 10.00 (*0-89555-391-0*) TAN Bks Pubs.

— Introduction to the Bible: The Nature, History, Authorship & Content of the Holy Bible with Selections from & Commentaries on the Various Books. LC 90-70241. (Illus.). 315p. 1992. reprint ed. pap. text 16.50 (*0-89555-396-1*) TAN Bks Pubs.

— Mass & the Sacraments: The Mass, Seven Sacraments, Indulgences, Sacramentals. LC 90-70439. (Course in Religion for Catholic High Schools & Academies Ser.: Bk. II). (Illus.). 199p. 1994. reprint ed. pap. text 10.00 (*0-89555-392-9*) TAN Bks Pubs.

Laux, John J. Church History: A Complete History of the Catholic Church to the Present Day - For High School, College & Adult Reading. LC 88-51074. (Illus.). 659p. 1989. reprint ed. pap. text 24.00 (*0-89555-349-X*) TAN Bks Pubs.

Laux, Keith R. The World's Greatest Paper Airplane & Toy Book. (Illus.). 120p. 1987. pap. 7.95 (*0-07-155079-8*) McGraw.

— The World's Greatest Paper Airplane & Toy Book. (Illus.). 120p. (YA). (gr. 5 up). 1987. pap. 7.95 (*0-8306-2846-0*) McGraw-Hill Prof.

Laux, Marcus. Natural Woman, Natural Menopause. 272p. 1998. pap. 13.00 (*0-06-092894-8*, Perennial) HarperTrade.

Laux, Marcus & Conrad, Christine. Natural Woman, Natural Menopause. LC 96-30096. (Illus.). 272p. 1997. 24.00 (*0-06-017341-6*) HarpC.

Lauxtermann, P. F. Constantin Frantz: Romantik und Realismus im Werk eines Politischen Aussenseiters. (Historische Studies: Bk. XXXV). vi, 217p. (Orig.). 1978. pap. 21.00 (*90-01-39021-8*) J Benjamins Pubng Co.

Lauzen, Elizabeth, ed. see Madison, Kathy.

Lauzen, Sara, jt. auth. see Armstrong, Missy.

Lauzon, June. The Birds Talk to God: 1995 Reprint Edition. (Illus.). 115p. 1995. reprint ed. pap. 11.00 (*0-9648082-7-7*) Crowell House.

Lava, Horacio C. Levels of Living in the Ilocos Region. LC 75-30066. (Institute of Pacific Relations Ser.). reprint ed. 29.50 (*0-404-59538-3*) AMS Pr.

Lavabre, Marcel. Aromaterapia: Libro Practico. (SPA.). 176p. 1995. pap. 12.95 (*0-89281-464-0*) Inner Tradit.

— Aromatherapy Workbook. LC 98-177975. 192p. 1996. reprint ed. pap. 16.95 (*0-89281-644-9*, Heal Arts VT) Inner Tradit.

Lavacic, Rosalind. Local Management of Schools: Analysis & Practice. LC 95-5855. 240p. 1995. 124.95 (*0-335-19376-5*) OpUniv Pr.

Lavaggi, Steven J. A State of the Heart. unabridged ed. (Illus.). 56p. 1997. 9.95 (*0-9660929-0-2*, LIAB6307) Glory Communs.

Lavagnino. Guatemala. 3578p. 1986. reprint ed. pap. 3.75 (*0-913129-15-1*) La Tienda.

Lavakare, P. J., et al, eds. Scientific Cooperation for Development: Search for New Directions. 216p. 1980. text 20.00 (*0-7069-0955-0*, Pub. by Vikas) S Asia.

Lavakare, P. J. & Waardenburg, J. G., eds. Science Policies in International Perspective: The Experience of India & the Netherlands. 280p. 1992. text 49.00 (*0-86187-826-4*, Pub. by P P Pubs) Cassell & Continuum.

Laval, J., jt. ed. see Lambert, M. W.

Laval, Pierre. The Diary of Pierre Laval. LC 72-6725. reprint ed. 22.50 (*0-404-10644-7*) AMS Pr.

LaVal, Richard K. & Fitch, Henry S. Structure, Movements & Reproduction in Three Costa Rican Bat Communities. (Occasional Papers: No. 69). 28p. 1977. pap. 1.00 (*0-317-04875-9*) U KS Nat Hist Mus.

Laval Staff. Dictionnaire Biographique du Canada Vol. 1: 1000-1700. (FRE.). 800p. 1966. 95.00 (*0-8288-9452-3*) Fr & Eur.

— Dictionnaire Biographique du Canada Vol. 2: 1701-1740. (FRE.). 834p. 1969. 95.00 (*0-8288-9453-1*) Fr & Eur.

— Dictionnaire Biographique du Canada Vol. 3: 1741-1770. (FRE.). 888p. 1974. 95.00 (*0-8288-9454-X*) Fr & Eur.

— Dictionnaire Biographique du Canada Vol. 4: 1771-1800. (FRE.). 1044p. 1980. 95.00 (*0-8288-9455-8*) Fr & Eur.

— Dictionnaire Biographique du Canada Vol. 6: 1801-1820. (FRE.). 1168p. 1983. 95.00 (*0-8288-9456-6*) Fr & Eur.

— Dictionnaire Biographique du Canada Vol. 6: 1821-1835. (FRE.). 1243p. 1987. 95.00 (*0-8288-9457-4*, 2763770983) Fr & Eur.

— Dictionnaire Biographique du Canada Vol. 8: 1851-1860. (FRE.). 1243p. 1985. 95.00 (*0-8288-9458-2*, 276377069X) Fr & Eur.

— Dictionnaire Biographique du Canada Vol. 9: 1861-1870. (FRE.). 1060p. 1977. 95.00 (*0-8288-9459-0*) Fr & Eur.

— Dictionnaire Biographique du Canada Vol. 10: 1871-1880. (FRE.). 926p. 1972. 95.00 (*0-8288-9460-4*, 2763766382) Fr & Eur.

— Dictionnaire Biographique du Canada Vol. 11: 1881-1890. (FRE.). 1212p. 1982. 95.00 (*0-8288-9461-2*) Fr & Eur.

Lavalette. A Thing of the Past? Child Labour in Britain in 1800 to the Present. LC 98-27172. 240p. 1999. text 65.00 (*0-312-21811-7*) St Martin.

Lavalette, Antoine M. Memoirs of Count Lavallette. 1977. 41.95 (*0-8369-7145-0*, 7978) Ayer.

Lavalette, Michael. Child Employment in the Capitalist Labour Market. 320p. 1994. 83.95 (*1-85628-600-2*, Pub. by Avebry) Ashgate Pub Co.

Lavalette, Michael, et al, eds. Anti-Racism & Social Welfare. LC 98-73763. 262p. 1998. text 63.95 (*1-84014-507-2*, Pub. by Ashgate Pub) Ashgate Pub Co.

***Lavalette, Michael & Mooney, Gerry.** Class Struggle & Social Welfare. LC 99-52995. (State of Welfare Ser.). 256p. 2000. pap. 25.99 (*0-415-20105-5*) Routledge.

***Lavalette, Michael & Mooney, Gerry, eds.** Class Struggle & Social Welfare. LC 99-52995. 288p. (C). 2000. text. write for info. (*0-415-20104-7*) Routledge.

Lavalette, Michael & Pratt, Alan, eds. Social Policy: A Conceptual & Theoretical Introduction. 304p. 1997. 75.00 (*0-8039-7532-5*); pap. 24.95 (*0-8039-7533-3*) Sage.

Lavall, Patrick & Stoffel, Robert C. Personnel Safety in Helicopter Operations: Helirescue Manual. (Illus.). 124p. 1988. ring bd. 8.50 (*0-913724-36-X*) Emerg Response Inst.

Lavalla, Patrick. Handbook: Living Life's Emergencies. (Illus.). 72p. 1981. pap. 4.00 (*0-913724-25-4*) Emerg Response Inst.

Lavalla, Patrick & Stoffel, Robert C. Instructor Guide for Managing Emergency Operations. 600p. 1992. ring bd. 40.00 (*0-913724-38-6*) Emerg Response Inst.

— Living Life's Emergencies: Text for Total Emergency Preparedness. rev. ed. (Illus.). (C). 1992. pap. 35.00 (*0-913724-40-8*) Emerg Response Inst.

— National Emergency Training & Information Guide. (Illus.). 350p. 1992. ring bd. 30.00 (*0-913724-35-1*) Emerg Response Inst.

Lavalla, Patrick, et al. Blueprint for Community Emergency Management: Managing Emergency Operations. (Illus.). 600p. 1991. 35.00 (*0-913724-33-5*) Emerg Response Inst.

— Community Emergency Management: Development & Strategies. (Illus.). 1987. ring bd. 25.00 (*0-913724-39-4*) Emerg Response Inst.

— Search Is an Emergency: Field Coordinator's Handbook. (Illus.). 154p. 1978. pap. 9.00 (*0-913724-30-0*) Emerg Response Inst.

Lavalle, James B. Black Cohosh: Nature's Versatile Healer. 192p. 2000. pap. text 9.95 (*0-89529-925-9*, Avery) Penguin Putnam.

Lavalle, James B., ed. see Pelton, Ross.

LaValle, John, jt. auth. see Bandler, Richard.

LaValle, Maria T., tr. see Robertson, Jenny.

LaValle, Patrick & Stoffel, Robert C. Survival Sense for Pilots & Passengers. LC 80-70906. (Illus.). 224p. 1987. pap. 9.95 (*0-913724-24-6*) Emerg Response Inst.

Lavallee, Barbara. Barbara Lavallee's Painted Ladies & Other Celebrations. 80p. 1995. 22.95 (*0-945397-36-4*) Epicenter Pr.

Lavallee, Barbara & Shtainmets, Leon. The Snow Child. 32p. (J). (gr. 2-5). 1989. pap. 2.50 (*0-590-42141-7*) Scholastic Inc.

Lavallee, Barbara, jt. auth. see Cobb, Vicki.

Lavallee, D. K. The Chemistry & Biochemistry of N-Substituted Porphyrins. 313p. 1987. 99.95 (*0-471-18693-7*) Wiley.

***Lavallee, Daniele.** The First South Americans: The Peopling of a Continent from the Earliest Evidence to High Culture. Bahn, Paul G., tr. 208p. 2000. pap. 25.00 (*0-87480-665-8*) U of Utah Pr.

Lavallee, David K. The Chemistry & Biochemistry of N-Substituted Porphyrins. LC 87-23206. 313p. 1988. 55.00 (*0-89573-147-9*, Wiley-VCH) Wiley.

Lavallee, Louis. La Prairie en Nouvelle-France, 1647-1760: Itude d'histoire sociale. (FRE.). 304p. 1992. 65.00 (*0-7735-0933-X*, Pub. by McG-Queens Univ Pr); pap. 29.95 (*0-7735-1108-3*, Pub. by McG-Queens Univ Pr) CUP Services.

Lavallee, Omer. Van Horne's Road: Construction & Early Operation of the Canadian Pacific Railway. (Illus.). 304p. 45.00 (*0-919130-22-4*, Pub. by Boston Mills) Genl Dist Srvs.

Lavallee, Omer, ed. Canadian Pacific Diagrams & Data: Steam Locomotives. (Illus.). 72p. 10.00 (*0-919130-45-3*, Pub. by Boston Mills) Genl Dist Srvs.

Lavallee, Ronald. Tchipayuk: or The Way of the Wolf. Claxton, Patricia, tr. LC 94-224322. 480p. 1994. pap. 26.95 (*0-88922-338-6*, Pub. by Talonbks) Genl Dist Srvs.

LaVallee, Timothy J., ed. see Goldstein, Jessica W.

Lavallet, Martha, jt. auth. see Varnum, Ann.

Lavallet, Martha, ed. see Varnum, Ann.

Lavalley, Al, ed. Invasion of the Body Snatchers. LC 89-30374. (Films in Print Ser.). (Illus.). 250p. (C). 1989. text 35.00 (*0-8135-1460-6*); pap. text 17.00 (*0-8135-1461-4*) Rutgers U Pr.

LaValley, Albert J., ed. see MacDougall, Ranald & Cain, James M.

Lavalley, Jack, et al. Mysteries from the Finger Lakes: Short Stories from In-Between Magazine. (Illus.). 128p. 1989. pap. 8.95 (*0-685-29418-8*) Six Lakes Arts.

LaValley, James F. Freedom Voyage. LC 97-185487. (Freedom Quest Ser.). 1997. pap. 9.99 (*0-911866-34-5*) LifeSprings Res.

LaValva, Rosamaria. The Eternal Child: The Poetry & Poetics of Giovanni Pascoli. LC 99-72079. (Annali D'Italianistica Ser.: No. 2). (ENG & ITA.). 232p. 1999. pap. 21.00 (*0-9657956-1-6*) Annali D.

Lavan, Bruce. The Spiritual Solution to America's Problems. 150p. 1998. pap. text 10.95 (*1-57532-090-8*) Press-Tige Pub.

Lavan, George, ed. see Cannon, James P.

***LaVan, Ken & Colbin, Kaila.** The Real People's Guide to the Internet. (Real People's Guide to Learning Ser.). (Illus.). 96p. 1999. pap. 29.95 incl. VHS (*0-9669483-3-5*) ThoughtSource.

— The Real People's Guide to the Internet. (Illus.). 96p. (YA). (gr. 5 up). 1999. pap. 19.95 (*0-9669483-2-7*) ThoughtSource.

Lavan, S. A. & Fletcher, B. G. Student's Guide to Structural Design. 105p. 1997. pap. text 39.95 (*0-7506-3803-6*, TA633, Pub. by Laxtons) Buttrwrth-Heinemann.

Lavan, Spencer. Unitarians & India: A Study in Encounter & Response. 3rd ed. LC 90-86029. (Illus.). 217p. 1991. reprint ed. pap. 18.95 (*0-913552-46-1*) Exploration Pr.

Lavanda, Violet, jt. auth. see Finocchiaro, Mary.

Lavandier, Jean-Pierre. Le Livre au Temps de Joseph II & de Leopold II Vol. 2: Code des Lois de Censure du Livre pour les Pays Austro-Bohemiens. (FRE.). 388p. 1995. 55.95 (*3-906753-73-5*) P Lang Pubng.

— Le Livre au Temps de Marie-Therese Vol. 1: Code des Lois de Censure du Livre pour les Pays Austro-Bohemiens (1740-1780) (FRE.). 168p. 1993. 27.80 (*3-906750-34-5*) P Lang Pubng.

Lavandier, Odile, jt. auth. see Howard, Janet L.

Lavanger, Denis P., jt. ed. see Hermann, Richard K.

Lavania, Shipra. Juvenile Delinquency. (C). 1993. 18.00 (*81-7033-207-9*, Pub. by Rawat Pubns) S Asia.

Lavapies, Steve. Sports Imitated: The Swimsuit Issue Parody. 80p. (Orig.). 1996. pap. 10.00 (*1-57297-071-5*) Blvd Books.

***Lavarack, Bill, et al.** Dendrobium & Its Relatives. LC 00-39226. (Illus.). 288p. 2000. 39.95 (*0-88192-490-3*) Timber.

Lavarch, Michael, jt. ed. see Stacy, Helen.

Lavardin, Jacques De, see Drysdall, Denis L. & De Lavardin, Jacques, eds.

***Lavaroni, Charles & Leisey, Donald E.** The Educational Entrepreneur: Making a Difference. 208p. 2000. pap. write for info. (*0-9677433-0-3*) Edupreneur.

Lavas, Ray. Tracking & Locating Systems. Berkel, Bob, ed. (CCS SecuritySource Library: Vol. X). (Illus.). 720p. 1995. 300.00 (*1-884674-10-0*) CCS Security.

Lavash, Donald R. A Journey Through New Mexico History: The Land of Enchantment. rev. ed. LC 92-27191. 1993. pap. 24.95 (*0-86534-194-X*) Sunstone Pr.

LaVash, Donald R. Sheriff William Brady: Tragic Hero of the Lincoln County War. LC 85-8025. (Illus.). 128p. (Orig.). 1986. pap. 10.95 (*0-86534-064-1*) Sunstone Pr.

Lavash, Donald R. Wilson & the Kid. LC 90-34762. (Illus.). 171p. 1990. 21.95 (*0-932702-49-X*) Creative Texas.

Lavash, Ted & Fremont, Victoria. Spooky Mazes. (Illus.). 64p. (J). 1998. pap. 1.00 (*0-486-29926-0*) Dover.

Lavash, Ted, jt. auth. see Fremont, Victoria.

LaVasque, Jeanne. Musings from the Menopause. LC 90-91722. (Illus.). 61p. (Orig.). 1990. pap. 9.95 (*0-9628454-0-X*) Polliwog Pr.

***Lavastida, Jose I.** Health Care & the Common Good: A Catholic Theory of Justice. LC 99-48697. 368p. 1999. 64.00 (*0-7618-1524-4*); pap. 39.50 (*0-7618-1525-2*) U Pr of Amer.

Lavater, J. C. Aphorisms on Man. LC 79-23298. 272p. 1980. reprint ed. 50.00 (*0-8201-1336-0*) Schol Facsimiles.

Lavater, Johann C. Nachgelassene Schriften, 4 vols. Gessner, George, ed. (GER.). lvi, 1652p. 1993. reprint ed. write for info. (*3-487-09697-8*) G Olms Pubs.

— Samtliche Kleinere Prosaische Schriften vom Jahre 1763-1783, 3 vols. in 1. (GER.). xvi, 1185p. 1987. reprint ed. write for info. (*3-487-07958-5*) G Olms Pubs.

— Vermische Schriften. (GER.). xxiv, 811p. 1988. reprint ed. write for info. (*3-487-09015-5*) G Olms Pubs.

Lavatori, Gerard P. Language & Money in Rabelais. (Renaissance & Baroque Studies & Texts: Vol. 18). 194p. (C). 1996. text 46.95 (*0-8204-2734-9*) P Lang Pubng.

Lavauzelle Staff. Dictionnaire des Communes. (FRE.). 1787p. 1984. 125.00 (*0-7859-7915-8*, 2702500757) Fr & Eur.

Lavay, Barry, jt. ed. see French, Ron.

Lavay, Barry W., et al. Positive Behavior Management Strategies for Physical Educators. LC 97-18733. (Illus.). 176p. (Orig.). 1997. pap. text 22.00 (*0-87322-880-4*, BLAV0880) Human Kinetics.

Lavay, Barry W., jt. auth. see Eichstaedt, Carl B.

Lavazzi, Thomas. Crossing-Borders. LC 93-6536. 64p. 1996. pap. 14.95 (*0-7734-2784-8*, Mellen Poetry Pr) E Mellen.

Lavdas, Kostas A. & Mendrinou, Maria M. Politics, Subsidies & Competition: The New Politics of State Intervention in the European Union. LC 98-53416. 200p. 1999. 80.00 (*1-85898-324-X*) E Elgar.

Lave, Charles A., ed. Automobile Choice & Its Energy Implications. (Illus.). 137p. 1981. pap. write for info. (*0-08-027397-1*, Pergamon Pr) Elsevier.

— Urban Transit: The Private Challenge to Public Transportation. LC 84-21529. (Illus.). 372p. 1985. 29.95 (*0-936488-62-X*); pap. 14.95 (*0-936488-63-8*) PRIPP.

Lave, Charles A. & March, James G. An Introduction to Models in the Social Sciences. 432p. (C). 1991. reprint ed. pap. 32.50 (*0-8191-8381-4*) U Pr of Amer.

Lave, E. & Sheilgold, N. Plays for the Actress. LC 96-53573. 1997. pap. 18.00 (*0-679-77281-2*) McKay.

— Take Ten: New 10-Minute Plays. LC 96-53571. 1997. pap. 14.00 (*0-679-77282-0*) McKay.

Lave, Jean. Cognition in Practice: Mind, Mathematics & Culture. (Illus.). 232p. 1988. pap. text 19.95 (*0-521-35734-9*) Cambridge U Pr.

Lave, Jean & Wenger, Etienne. Situated Learning: Legitimate Peripheral Participation. (Learning in Doing: Social, Cognitive & Computational Perspectives Ser.). 138p. (C). 1991. pap. text 13.95 (*0-521-42374-0*) Cambridge U Pr.

Lave, Jean, jt. ed. see Chaiklin, Seth.

Lave, Jean, jt. ed. see Rogoff, Barbara.

Lave, Lester B. The Strategy of Social Regulation: Decision Frameworks for Policy. LC 81-7685. (Studies in the Regulation of Economic Activity). 166p. 1981. 31.95 (*0-8157-5162-1*); pap. 12.95 (*0-8157-5161-3*) Brookings.

Lave, Lester B., ed. Quantitative Risk Assessment in Regulation. LC 82-22603. (Studies in the Regulation of Economic Activity). 264p. 1983. 34.95 (*0-8157-5164-8*); pap. 14.95 (*0-8157-5163-X*) Brookings.

— Risk Assessment & Management. LC 87-21288. (Advances in Risk Analysis Ser.: Vol. 5). (Illus.). 752p. (C). 1987. text 210.00 (*0-306-42683-8*, Kluwer Plenum) Kluwer Academic.

Lave, Lester B. & Covello, Vincent T., eds. Uncertainty in Risk Assessment, Risk Management & Decision Making. (Advances in Risk Analysis Ser.: Vol. 4). (Illus.). 548p. (C). 1987. 168.00 (*0-306-42557-2*, Plenum Trade) Perseus Pubng.

Lave, Lester B. & Omenn, Gilbert S. Clearing the Air: Reforming the Clean Air Act. LC 81-70469. (Studies in the Regulation of Economic Activity). 51p. 1981. pap. 7.95 (*0-8157-5159-1*) Brookings.

Lave, Lester B. & Seskin, Eugene P. Air Pollution & Human Health. LC 74-6830. 388p. reprint ed. pap. 120.30 (*0-8357-5282-8*, 203074000070) Bks Demand.

Lave, Lester B. & Upton, Arthur C., eds. Toxic Chemicals, Health & the Environment. LC 86-46276. (Johns Hopkins Series in Environmental Toxicology). 336p. 1987. pap. text 18.95 (*0-8018-3474-0*) Johns Hopkins.

Lave, Lester B., jt. ed. see Crandall, Robert W.

Lavean, Gilbert E. & Schmidt, William G., eds. Communication Satellite Developments: Systems. LC 75-45244. (PAAS Ser.: Vol. 41). (Illus.). 333p. 1976. 34.95 (*0-915928-05-1*, V-41) AIAA.

LaVeck, James J. Collage: A Shattered Story. Stein, Jenny, ed. LC 93-10083. (Illus.). 150p. (Orig.). 1993. pap. 9.00 (*1-882979-07-9*) Tribe Heart.

Laveissiere, Sylvain. Dictionnaire des Artistes et Ouvriers d'Art de Bourgogne Vol. 1: A-K. (FRE.). 290p. 1980. pap. 145.00 (*0-7859-8066-0*, 2851890069) Fr & Eur.

Laveissiere, Sylvain & Metropolitan Museum of Art (New York, N. Y.) Staff. Prud'Hon. LC 97-44759. (Illus.). 344p. 1998. 75.00 (*0-8109-6520-8*, Pub. by Abrams) Time Warner.

***Laveist, Thomas.** DayStar Guide to Colleges for African American Students: Get What You Need to Make the Right Choices. 464p. 2000. pap. 20.00 (*0-684-85954-8*) Kaplan.

Laveleye, Emile De, see De Laveleye, Emile.

Laveleye, Emile L. On the Causes of War. 1972. 59.95 (*0-8490-0763-1*) Gordon Pr.

Lavell, Cherry. Handbook for British & Irish Archaeology: Sources & Resources. LC 99-171055. 480p. 1997. pap. 45.00 (*0-7486-0764-1*, Pub. by Edinburgh U Pr) Col U Pr.

***Lavell, Kit.** Flying Black Ponies: The Navy's Close Air Support Squadron in Vietnam. LC 00-41136. (Illus.). 360p. 2000. 32.95 (*1-55750-521-7*) Naval Inst Pr.

LaVelle, Bob. Observations of a Short Cowboy. (Illus.). 1997. mass mkt. 12.95 (*0-9663247-0-6*) LaVelle.

Lavelle, Doris. Latin & American Dances. (Ballroom Dance Ser.). 1984. lib. bdg. 79.95 (*0-87700-512-5*) Revisionist Pr.

Lavelle, Geoffrey. An Expatriate's Sketchbook. limited ed. 1994. 10.00 (*1-884185-05-3*) O Zone.

Lavelle, J. The Role of Training Manager. 1996. pap. 129.00 (*1-85953-013-3*, Pub. by Tech Comm) St Mut.

Lavelle, Jerome P., jt. auth. see Newnan, Donald G.

Lavelle, Jon. The Role of the Training Manager. 1997. pap. 89.50 (*0-273-63198-5*) F T P-H.

Lavelle, Louis. The Dilemma of Narcissus. Gairdner, William T., tr. 230p. 1993. reprint ed. 22.95 (*0-943914-61-2*); reprint ed. pap. 15.95 (*0-943914-62-0*) Larson Pubns.

LaVelle, Louis, jt. auth. see Von Christian, Wolff.

Lavelle, M., tr. see Povh, B., et al.

Lavelle, Marianne & Fagin, Dan. Toxic Deception: How the Chemical Industry Manipulates Science, Subverts the Law & Threatens Your Health. LC 96-41045. (Illus.). 336p. 1996. 24.95 (*1-55972-385-8*, Birch Ln Pr) Carol Pub Group.

Lavelle, Martin, tr. see Povh, Bogdan, et al.

Lavelle, P., et al. Earthworm Management in Tropical Agroecosystems. LC 99-12081. 320p. 1999. text 90.00 (*0-85199-270-6*) OUP.

Lavelle, Robert, jt. ed. see Blackside, Inc. Staff.

Lavelle, S. M., jt. ed. see Beneken, J. E.

Lavelle, Sheila. The Best of the First Ten Years of the Siberian Quarterly. deluxe ed. (Illus.). 304p. 1995. 80.00 (*0-614-04552-5*) Donald R Hoflin.

LaVelle, Sheila. Calamity with the Fiend. (Illus.). 144p. (J). (gr. 3-6). pap. 7.95 (*0-14-036413-7*, Pub. by Pnguin Bks Ltd) Trafalgar.

Lavelle, Sheila. Fiend Next Door. (Illus.). (J). 1995. pap. 7.95 (*0-14-037183-4*, Pub. by Pnguin Bks Ltd) Trafalgar.

— My Best Fiend. (Illus.). 1998. pap. 9.95 (*0-14-037182-6*, Pub. by Pnguin Bks Ltd) Trafalgar.

Lavelle, Sheila. Snowy. (Illus.). 32p. (J). Date not set. write for info. (*0-19-279909-6*) OUP.

Lavelle, Sheila. Trouble with the Fiend. (Illus.). 128p. (J). (gr. 3-6). 1995. pap. 7.95 (*0-14-037184-2*, Pub. by Pnguin Bks Ltd) Trafalgar.

LaVelle, Steven. Just Passing Through. (Illus.). 32p. (Orig.). (J). (gr. k-3). 1980. pap. 6.95 (*0-87516-402-1*) DeVorss.

An Asterisk (*) at the beginning of an entry indicates that the title is appearing for the first time.

Lavely, Carolyn, et al. At-Risk Students & Their Families: What Teachers, Principals, Counselors, Psychologists, & Social Workers Can Do. 1993. pap. 15.95 (*1-55691-103-3*, 033) Learning Pubns.

Laven, David, jt. ed. see Riall, Lucy.

Laven, Edward E. The Nez Perce National Forest Story. rev. ed. Moore, Shirley T. & Zabinski, Mary, eds. (Illus.). 57p. 1991. pap. 4.95 (*0-914019-30-9*) NW Interpretive.

Laven, Richard D. Pattern & Process. (Illus.). pap. 0.00 (*0-691-02514-2*) Princeton U Pr.

Lavenberg, Robert J., jt. auth. see Grove, Jack S.

Lavenda, Beranrd H. Statistical Physics: A Probabilistic Approach. LC 91-15687. 384p. 1991. 149.00 (*0-471-54607-0*) Wiley.

Lavenda, Bernard H. Nonequilibrium Statistical Thermodynamics. LC 84-26992. 213p. reprint ed. pap. 66.10 (*0-7837-4010-7*, 204384000011) Bks Demand.

— Thermodynamics of Extremes. 256p. 1996. 65.00 (*1-898563-24-1*, Pub. by Horwood Pub) Paul & Co Pubs.

— Thermodynamics of Irreversible Processes. 6th ed. LC 93-3190. vii, 182p. 1993. reprint ed. pap. 7.95 (*0-486-67576-9*) Dover.

Lavenda, Robert H. Corn Fests & Water Carnivals: Celebrating Community in Minnesota. LC 96-41467. (Series in Ethnographic Inquiry). (Illus.). 192p. (Orig.). 1997. pap. 25.00 (*1-56098-711-1*) Smithsonian.

***Lavenda, Robert H. & Schultz, Emily A.** Core Concepts in Cultural Anthropology. LC 99-38501. vii, 216p. 1999. pap. text 22.95 (*0-7674-1169-2*) Mayfield Pub.

Lavenda, Robert H., jt. auth. see Schultz, Emily A.

Lavender. Economy & Built Environment. 1997. pap. text. write for info. (*0-582-04295-X*) Addison-Wesley.

— Management for Building. 1966. pap. text. write for info. (*0-582-26235-6*, Pub. by Addison-Wesley) Longman.

***Lavender, Abraham D.** Miami Beach Nineteen Hundred Twenty. (Illus.). 260p. 2000. 24.95 (*0-9677694-1-8*) Miami Beach Hist.

Lavender, Abraham D., ed. A Coat of Many Colors: Jewish Subcommunities in the United States, 1. LC 77-71865. (Contributions in Family Studies: No. 1). 324p. 1977. 59.95 (*0-8371-9539-X*, LCM/, Greenwood Pr) Greenwood.

Lavender, Abraham D. & Newson, Adele S., eds. Black Communities in Transition: Voices from South Florida. LC 96-9231. 254p. 1996. pap. text 29.50 (*0-7618-0447-1*); lib. bdg. 49.00 (*0-7618-0446-3*) U Pr of Amer.

Lavender, Abraham D. & Steinberg, Clarence. Jewish Farmers of the Catskills: A Century of Survival. (Illus.). 288p. 1995. 39.95 (*0-8130-1343-7*) U Press Fla.

***Lavender, Bill.** Guest Chain. (Illus.). 24p. 1999. pap. 4.00 (*0-9663846-6-0*, Video Press) Lavender Ink.

Lavender, C. Help! I'm a Substitute Music Teacher. 52p. 1987. pap. 12.95 (*0-7935-2759-7*) H Leonard.

— Music Listening Bingo. 1992. pap. text 29.95 incl. audio (*0-7935-2912-3*) H Leonard.

Lavender, Catherine J., jt. auth. see Schlissel, Lillian.

Lavender, Cheryl. Making Each Minute Count: Time-Savers, Tips, & Kid-Tested Strategies for the Music Class. Crocker, Emily, ed. 240p. (Orig.). 1991. per. 19.95 (*0-7935-0348-5*, HL44223055) H Leonard.

Lavender, Cheryl. Moans, Groans & Skeleton Bones: Fun Songs & Activities for Kids. (MusicTivity Ser.). (Illus.). 32p. (Orig.). (J). 1993. pap. 9.95 (*0-7935-2372-9*, HL00330605) H Leonard.

Lavender, David. The American Heritage History of the Great West. Josephy, Alvin M., Jr., ed. LC 65-23041. (Illus.). 416p. 1985. reprint ed. pap. 16.00 (*0-8281-0303-8*) Forb Custom Pub.

— Bent's Fort. 1990. 16.50 (*0-8446-1279-0*) Peter Smith.

— Bent's Fort. LC 54-7322. (Illus.). 479p. 1972. reprint ed. pap. 14.95 (*0-8032-5753-8*, Bison Books) U of Nebr Pr.

— California: Land of New Beginnings. LC 86-30929. x, 480p. 1987. reprint ed. pap. 19.95 (*0-8032-7924-8*, Bison Books) U of Nebr Pr.

— DeSoto, Coronado, Cabrillo: Explorers of the Northern Mystery. LC 91-47633. (Official National Park Handbook Ser.: No. 144). (Illus.). 112p. 1992. pap. 4.50 (*0-912627-48-4*, 024-005-01102-1) Natl Park Serv.

Lavender, David. Desoto, Coronado, Cabrillo: Explorers of the Northern Mystery. 112p. 1992. per. 4.50 (*0-16-061653-0*) USGPO.

Lavender, David. The First in the Wilderness. LC 97-51210. (Illus.). xxii, 498p. 1998. pap. 22.00 (*0-8032-7976-0*, Bison Books) U of Nebr Pr.

— Fort Laramie & the Changing Frontier. LC 82-600401. (Official National Park Handbook Ser.: No. 118). (Illus.). 160p. 1984. pap. 12.00 (*0-912627-20-4*) Natl Park Serv.

— Great Persuader: The Biography of Collis P. Huntington. LC 98-28484. 1998. pap. 24.95 (*0-87081-476-1*) Univ Pr Colo.

— The Great West. LC 85-13476. (American Heritage Library). (Illus.). 400p. 1985. pap. 8.95 (*0-8281-0481-6*) HM.

***Lavender, David.** The Great West. (Illus.). 480p. 1999. pap. 16.00 (*0-618-00189-1*, Mariner Bks) HM.

Lavender, David. The History of Arizona's Pipe Spring National Monument. 2nd ed. Orig. Title: Pipe Spring & the Arizona Strip. (Illus.). 57p. 1997. reprint ed. pap. 4.95 (*0-915630-20-6*) Zion.

— Mother Earth, Father Sky: The Pueblo Indians of the American Southwest. LC 97-38119. (Illus.). 96p. (J). (gr. 4-7). 1998. 16.95 (*0-8234-1365-9*) Holiday.

— One Man's West. LC 76-45450. (Illus.). iv, 316p. 1977. pap. 12.50 (*0-8032-5855-0*, Bison Books) U of Nebr Pr.

— Overland Migrations. LC 79-607769. (Official National Park Handbook Ser.: No. 105). 1980. pap. 7.50 (*0-912627-02-6*) Natl Park Serv.

Lavender, David. Overland Migrations: Settlers to Oregon, California & Utah. 111p. 1980. pap. 221.00 (*0-16-003439-6*); per. 7.50 (*0-16-003502-3*) USGPO.

— Red Mountain. 2nd ed. LC 63-7704. 540p. 2000. pap. 19.95 (*1-890437-35-2*) Western Reflections.

Lavender, David. Snowbound: The Tragic Story of the Donner Party. (Illus.). 96p. (J). (gr. 4-6). 1996. 18.95 (*0-8234-1231-8*) Holiday.

— The Southwest. LC 83-19740. 362p. 1984. pap. 16.95 (*0-8263-0736-1*) U of NM Pr.

— The Telluride Story. 68p. (Orig.). 1987. pap. 19.95 (*0-9608764-6-4*) Wayfinder Pr.

— The Way to the Western Sea: Lewis & Clark Across the Continent. 464p. 1990. pap. 14.95 (*0-385-41155-3*, Anchor NY) Doubleday.

— Westward Vision: The Story of the Oregon Trail. LC 84-20815. (Illus.). xx, 425p. 1985. reprint ed. pap. 16.95 (*0-8032-7915-9*, Bison Books) U of Nebr Pr.

Lavender, David S. The Santa Fe Trail. LC 94-16638. (Illus.). 64p. (J). (gr. 3-7). 1995. lib. bdg. 15.95 (*0-8234-1153-2*) Holiday.

***Lavender, David Sievert.** Let Me Be Free: The Nez Perce Tragedy. LC 99-24427. 432p. 1999. 17.95 (*0-8061-3190-X*) U of Okla Pr.

Lavender, Donald E. Nudge Blue: A Rifleman's Chronicle of World War II. 2nd rev. ed. (World War II Monograph: Vol. 222). (Illus.). 82p. 1997. reprint ed. 25.95 (*1-57638-096-3*, M222H); reprint ed. pap. 15.95 (*1-57638-095-5*, M222S) Merriam Pr.

Lavender, Kenneth & Stockton, Scott. Book Repair: A How-to-Do-It Manual for School & Public Librarians. (How-to-Do-It Ser.). 128p. 1992. 45.00 (*1-55570-103-5*) Neal-Schuman.

Lavender, Larry. Dancers Talking Dance: Critical Evaluation in the Choreography Class. LC 95-49233. (Illus.). 160p. (Orig.). 1996. pap. text 22.00 (*0-87322-667-4*, BLAV0667) Human Kinetics.

Lavender, Lucille. Los Pastores Tambien Lloran: They Cry Too! Smith, Josie H., tr. from ENG. 136p. (Orig.). 1988. reprint ed. pap. 8.99 (*0-311-42075-3*) Casa Bautista.

— They Cry, Too. 176p. 1986. pap. 7.99 (*0-310-41651-5*, 9970P) Zondervan.

Lavender, Michael R., ed. The Companion. 70p. 1996. pap. 9.95 (*0-9654164-0-2*) Emergence Inc.

Lavender, Neil J., jt. auth. see Cavalola, Alan A.

Lavender, Paul W. The Cry of the Humble: Vignettes from a Life Well Lived. (Illus.). 177p. 1998. 19.99 (*0-9666244-0-8*) Blackmore & Black.

Lavender, Peter. Songs & Dances of Ireland. (Illus.). 80p. 1982. pap. 14.95 (*0-7119-0099-X*, AM31402) Music Sales.

— Start Playing Keyboard: Omnibus Edition, 2 bks. in 1. (Illus.). 96p. 1987. pap. 14.95 (*0-8256-1187-3*, AM67588) Music Sales.

Lavender, Sharline. Lone Star Time Machine: Game & Activity Workbook for Texas History Students. (Illus.). 37p. 1986. pap. 7.95 (*0-937460-22-2*) Hendrick-Long.

Lavender, Susan & Franklin, Anna. Herb Craft: A Guide to Shamanic & Ritual Use of Herbs. (Illus.). 600p. (Orig.). 1995. pap. 39.95 (*1-898307-57-1*, Pub. by Capall Bann Pubng) Holmes Pub.

Lavender, William. The Invisible People. (J). (gr. 1-8). 2000. 7.00 (*0-87602-400-2*) Anchorage.

Lavendhomme, Rene. Basic Concepts of Synthetic Differential Geometry. LC 96-204. (Texts in the Mathematical Sciences Ser.: Vol. 13). 336p. (C). 1996. text 169.00 (*0-7923-3941-X*) Kluwer Academic.

Lavene, James, jt. auth. see Lavene, Joyce.

Lavene, Jim, jt. auth. see Lavene, Joyce.

***Lavene, Joyce & Lavene, James.** Flowers in the Night. ed. 1999. 4.50 (*1-928670-46-6*, Ennoble) Awe Struck E Bks.

***Lavene, Joyce & Lavene, Jim.** Last Dance. LC 99-90984. 192p. 1999. 18.95 (*0-8034-9389-4*, Avalon Bks) Bouregy.

Lavenex, Sandra. Safe Third Countries: Extending the EU Asylum & Immigration Policies to Central & Eastern Europe. LC 99-32712. 200p. (C). 1999. pap. 22.95 (*963-9116-44-0*) Ctrl Europ Univ.

***Lavenham, Clare.** Island Doctor. large type ed. 272p. 2000. 20.99 (*1-84137-010-X*, Pub. by Mgna Lrg Print) Ulverscroft.

Lavenham, Clare. Nurse Weston's New Job. large type ed. (Dales Large Print Ser.). 205p. 1997. pap. 18.99 (*1-85389-756-6*, Dales) Ulverscroft.

— Web of Memories. large type ed. (Magna Large Print Ser.). 248p. 1997. 27.99 (*0-7505-1060-9*) Ulverscroft.

Lavenhar, Paul. Women of the 20th Century. 384p. 1999. 6.95 (*1-928684-03-3*, Pub. by Affinity Pubg) BookWorld.

Lavenia, George P. What You Think Is What You Get: Realizing Your Creative Power & True Potential. Lavenia, Joe & Barkin, Anya, eds. LC 97-94136. 208p. 1998. pap. 12.95 (*0-9658679-0-0*) Earth Fnd.

Lavenia, Joe, ed. see Lavenia, George P.

Laventhol & Howarth. Uniform System of Accounts for Restaurants. rev. ed. 160p. 1996. pap. 39.95 (*0-317-57883-9*, MG936) Natl Restaurant Assn.

Laventiev, Alexander, ed. Rodchenko: Photography, 1924-1954. (Illus.). 344p. 1998. 39.95 (*3-89508-110-8*, 810056) Konemann.

Lavenue, Jean-Jacques. Dictionnaire de la Vie Politique et du Droit Constitutionnel Americains. (FRE.). 313p. 1995. 95.00 (*0-7859-9914-0*) Fr & Eur.

Laver, James. Costume & Fashion: A Concise History. 2nd rev. ed. LC 94-61062. (World of Art Ser.). (Illus.). 296p. 1995. pap. 16.95 (*0-500-20266-4*, Pub. by Thames Hudson) Norton.

Laver, James, jt. auth. see Brooke, Iris.

Laver, James, jt. auth. see Sheringham, George.

Laver, John. The Gift of Speech: Papers in the Analysis of Speech & Voice. (Illus.). 224p. 1992. 85.00 (*0-7486-0313-1*, Pub. by Edinburgh U Pr) Col U Pr.

— The Gift of Speech: Readings in the Analysis of Speech & Voice. 400p. 1997. pap. 35.00 (*0-7486-0875-3*, Pub. by Edinburgh U Pr) Col U Pr.

— Principles of Phonetics. LC 93-18183. (Textbooks in Linguistics Ser.). (Illus.). 735p. (C). 1994. pap. text 32.95 (*0-521-45655-X*) Cambridge U Pr.

— Voice Quality: A Classified Research Bibliography. (Library & Information Sources in Linguistics: No. 5). viii, 225p. 1979. 52.00 (*90-272-0996-0*) J Benjamins Pubng Co.

Laver, John, jt. ed. see Hardcastle, William J.

Laver, John, jt. ed. see Jack, Mervyn.

Laver, Lance, et al. Process in Architecture: A Documentation in Six Examples. LC 79-88539. (Illus.). 144p. (Orig.). 1979. pap. 4.00 (*0-938437-00-3*) MIT List Visual Arts.

Laver, Michael. Playing Politics: The Nightmare Continues. LC 97-7910. (Illus.). 182p. 1997. pap. 11.95 (*0-19-285321-X*) OUP.

— Private Desires, Political Action: An Invitation to the Politics of Rational Choice. 192p. 1997. 69.95 (*0-7619-5114-8*); pap. 24.95 (*0-7619-5115-6*) Sage.

Laver, Michael & Schofield, Norman. Multiparty Government: The Politics of Coalition in Europe. LC 98-33545. (Ann Arbor Paperbacks Ser.). 328p. 1998. pap. text 19.95 (*0-472-08562-X*, 08562) U of Mich Pr.

Laver, Michael J., jt. auth. see Shepsle, Kenneth A.

Laver, Michael J., jt. ed. see Shepsle, Kenneth A.

***Laver, Mimi, et al.** Foundations for Success: Strengthening Your Agency Attorney Office. LC 99-38558. 1999. write for info. (*1-57073-731-2*) Amer Bar Assn.

Laver, Murray. Information Technology: Agent of Change. (Illus.). 200p. (C). 1989. text 64.95 (*0-521-35035-2*); pap. text 22.95 (*0-521-35925-2*) Cambridge U Pr.

— Planning Successful Computing. 52p. (C). 1986. 70.00 (*0-86236-004-8*, Pub. by Granary) St Mut.

Laver, Ross, jt. auth. see Kaihla, Paul.

Laver, Sue, jt. ed. see Hjort, Mette.

Laver, W. G. & Bachmayer, H., eds. The Influenza Virus Haemagglutinin. LC 77-17581. (Topics in Infectious Diseases Ser.: Vol. 3). (Illus.). 1978. 47.95 (*0-387-81459-0*) Spr-Verlag.

Laver, W. Graeme & Air, Gillian M., eds. Immune Recognition of Protein Antigens. LC 85-232272. (Current Communications in Molecular Biology Ser.). (Illus.). 207p. Date not set. reprint ed. pap. 64.20 (*0-608-20712-8*, 207181000002) Bks Demand.

Laverack, M. S. & Kerkut, G. A. Physiology of Earthworms. (International Series of Monographs on Pure & Applied Mathematics: Vol. 15). 1963. 99.00 (*0-08-009812-6*, Pub. by Pergamon Repr) Franklin.

***Laverde, Arlene.** Alaska's Three Pigs. (Illus.). 32p. (J). (gr. k-4). 2000. pap. 9.95 (*1-57061-239-0*) Sasquatch Bks.

***Laverde, Arlene & Dwyer, Mindy.** Alaska's Three Pigs. LC 00-29664. (Illus.). (J). 2000. write for info. (*1-57061-229-3*) Sasquatch Bks.

***LaVerdiere, Eugene.** The Beginning of the Gospel: Introducing the Gospel According to Mark, 2 vols. 1999. pap. 44.95 (*0-8146-2575-4*, Liturg Pr Bks) Liturgical Pr.

LaVerdiere, Eugene. A Church for All Peoples: Missionary Issues in a World Church. 104p. (Orig.). 1992. pap. text 7.95 (*0-8146-2141-4*) Liturgical Pr.

— The Eucharist in the New Testament & the Early Church. LC 96-19721. 206p. (Orig.). 1996. pap. 17.95 (*0-8146-6152-1*, Pueblo Bks) Liturgical Pr.

***LaVerdiere, Eugene.** Fundamentalism: A Pastoral Concern. LC 99-39498. 24p. 2000. pap. 1.95 (*0-8146-2713-7*) Liturgical Pr.

LaVerdiere, Eugene. Luke. LC 80-65618. (New Testament Message Ser.: Vol. 5). 296p. 1980. pap. 16.95 (*0-8146-5128-3*) Liturgical Pr.

— Mark 8:22-16:20 Vol. 2: Introducing the Gospel According to Mark. (Beginning of the Gospel Ser.). 1999. pap. text 29.95 (*0-8146-2574-6*) Liturgical Pr.

Laverdiere, Eugene, jt. ed. see Casgrain.

LaVerdiere, Eugene A. Dining in the Kingdom of God: The Origins of the Eucharist According to Luke. LC 94-2940. 227p. (Orig.). 1994. pap. 12.00 (*1-56854-022-1*, DINING) Liturgy Tr Pubns.

***LaVerdiere, Eugene A.** Mark 1-8:21. LC 98-44957. 227p. 1999. pap. 24.95 (*0-8146-2478-2*, Liturg Pr Bks) Liturgical Pr.

Laverdiere, Suzanne & Ibenthal, Dianne. The Rose Cookbook: Featuring Pink Ribbon Recipes. 256p. 1996. write for info. (*0-9647648-0-6*) The Rose.

Laverdure, Paul, tr. see Rey-Meret, Theodule.

LaVere, Bill. Reclaiming Power: How to Take Back Our Government from Career Politicians. 215p. (Orig.). 1994. pap. 14.95 (*1-886335-02-8*) Bydand.

LaVere, William R. Social Security Disability: A Comprehensive & Practical Guide to the Effective Representation of Claimants. 1995. write for info. (*1-877663-01-8*) Bydand.

— Social Security Disability: A Comprehensive & Practical Guide to the Effective Representation of Claimants. 3rd ed. 357p. 1994. ring bd. 125.00 (*1-886335-00-1*) Bydand.

Laverghetta, Thomas S. Handbook of Microwave Testing. LC 81-67941. (Illus.). 536p. reprint ed. pap. 152.80 (*0-8357-3935-X*, 2036670) Bks Demand.

— Microwave Materials & Fabrication Techniques. LC 84-71819. (Artech House Microwave Library). (Illus.). 237p. reprint ed. pap. 73.50 (*0-608-16026-1*, 203312500083) Bks Demand.

***Laverghetta, Thomas S.** Microwave Materials & Fabrication Techniques. 3rd ed. (Microwave Library). 2000. 83.00 (*1-58053-064-8*) Artech Hse.

Laverghetta, Thomas S. Microwave Measurements & Techniques. LC 75-31383. (Illus.). 411p. reprint ed. pap. 127.50 (*0-8357-4233-4*, 203702000002) Bks Demand.

— Microwaves & Wireless Simplified. LC 97-40457. 266p. 1997. 55.00 (*0-89006-908-5*) Artech Hse.

— Practical Microwaves. LC 95-10971. 484p. (C). 1995. 63.80 (*0-13-186875-6*) P-H.

— Solid State Microwave Devices. LC 87-19319. (Artech House Microwave Library). (Illus.). 208p. reprint ed. pap. 64.50 (*0-8357-3938-4*, 203667300004) Bks Demand.

Lavergnat. Radiowave Propagation. text. write for info. (*0-471-49027-X*) Wiley.

Lavergne, Connie H. Self-Defense. 2nd ed. 102p. (C). 1995. pap. text 12.95 (*0-89641-244-X*) American Pr.

***Lavergne, Gary.** Bad Boy from Rosebud: The Murderous Life of Kenneth Allen McDuff. LC 99-22050. (Illus.). 366p. 1999. lib. bdg. 29.95 (*1-57441-072-5*, Pub. by UNTX Pr) Tex A&M Univ Pr.

***Lavergne, Gary M.** A Sniper in the Tower. 416p. 1998. mass mkt. 6.50 (*0-553-57959-2*) Bantam.

Lavergne, Gary M. A Sniper in the Tower: The Charles Whitman Murders. LC 96-50411. (Illus.). 324p. 1997. pap. 18.95 (*1-57441-029-6*) UNTX Pr.

Lavergne, Michel. Seismic Methods. (Illus.). 192p. (C). 1989. 375.00 (*2-7108-0552-9*, Pub. by Edits Technip) Enfield Pubs NH.

Lavergne-Peguilhen, Marietta Von, see Von Lavergne-Peguilhen, Marietta.

Lavergne, Real & Whyte, A. V. Integration et Cooperation Regionales en Afrique de L'Ouest. LC 98-77. (FRE.). 408p. 1996. pap. 20.00 (*0-88936-818-X*, Pub. by IDRC Bks) Stylus Pub VA.

Lavergne, Real, jt. prod. see Diop, Momar-Coumba.

Lavergne, Real P. Regional Integration & Cooperation in West Africa: A Multidimensional Perspective. LC 97-4957. 1997. write for info. (*0-86543-566-9*) Africa World.

— Regional Integration & Cooperation in West Africa: A Multidimensional Perspective. LC 97-4957. 1997. pap. text 21.95 (*0-86543-567-7*) Africa World.

Laverick, Charles. Buying Guide to Inexpensive Wines: More Than 1500 Wines Reviewed by the Beverage Testing Institu. 256p. 1999. pap. text 14.95 (*0-8069-2861-1*) Sterling.

***Laverick, Charles, ed.** Buying Guide to Imported Wines: More than 3000 Wines Reviewed by the Beverage Testing Institute. 512p. 1999. pap. text 19.95 (*0-8069-2859-X*) Sterling.

Laverick, Charles, ed. Buying Guide to Wines of North America: More Than 3000 Wines Reviewed by the Beverage Testing Institute. 512p. 1999. pap. text 19.95 (*0-8069-2857-3*) Sterling.

Laverick, Jack. Royalty & Their Jewels. Laverick, Mark, ed. LC 93-84490. (Illus.). 120p. (Orig.). 1993. per. 18.95 (*1-884054-99-4*) Printers Shopper.

Laverick, Mark, ed. see Laverick, Jack.

Laverick, Mark, ed. see Laverick, William.

Laverick, William. Animals in Funny Verses & Their Habits & Habitats. Laverick, Mark, ed. LC 95-72866. (Illus.). 123p. (Orig.). (J). 1996. pap. 11.95 (*1-884054-98-6*) Printers Shopper.

Laverne, Andy. Handbook of Chord Substitutions. 1992. pap. 12.95 (*0-943748-51-8*) Ekay Music.

Lavernia, E. J., jt. ed. see Srivatsan, T. S.

Lavernia, Enrique J., et al, eds. Synthesis & Analysis in Materials Processing: Characterization & Diagnostics of Ceramics & Metal Particulate Processing: Proceedings of a Symposium/Sponsored by the TMS Synthesis & Analysis in Materials Processing Committee, Held During the 1989 TMS Annual Meeting, Las Vegas, Nevada, February 28-March 3, 1989. LC 89-61036. (Illus.). 104p. 1989. pap. 32.30 (*0-608-04979-4*, 206559600004) Bks Demand.

Lavernia, Enrique J. & Wu, Yue. Spray Atomization & Deposition. LC 95-37441. 644p. 1997. 340.00 (*0-471-95477-2*) Wiley.

Lavernia, Enrique J., ed. see Minerals, Metals & Materials Society Staff.

Laverov, N. P. Concise Terminological Dictionary of Fossil Energy Resources. 224p. (C). 1985. 60.00 (*0-7855-6679-1*, Pub. by Collets) St Mut.

Lavers, Annette. Roland Barthes: Structuralism & After. LC 81-13447. 310p. 1982. 37.50 (*0-674-77721-2*) HUP.

Lavers, Annette, tr. see Barthes, Roland.

***Lavers, Anthony P.** Case Studies in Post Construction Liability & Insurance. LC 99-17528. 1999. 0.00 (*0-419-24570-7*, E & FN Spon) Routledge.

Lavers, Norman. Growing up in Berkeley with the Bomb. LC 97-62090. 185p. 1998. pap. 14.00 (*0-9638099-3-8*, 500) SPSHR.

— The Northwest Passage. LC 83-27484. 137p. 1984. 15.95 (*0-914590-86-3*); pap. 7.95 (*0-914590-87-1*) Fiction Coll.

— Pop Culture into Art: The Novels of Manuel Puig. LC 88-4807. 80p. 1988. pap. 12.95 (*0-8262-0685-9*) U of Mo Pr.

Laverty, J. R., ed. see Laverty, R. V.

Laverty, M. The Food & Beverage Container Market. 580p. 1998. 1295.00 (*0-318-00492-5*) Busn Trend.

— The Health & Natural Food Market: Past Performance, Current Trends & Strategies for the Future. 330p. 1998. 1995.00 (*0-317-55180-9*) Busn Trend.

— Processed Fruits & Vegetables Market. 800p. 1997. 1195.00 (*0-318-00496-8*) Busn Trend.

Laverty, Mike. Plug Fishing for Steelhead. 64p. 1994. pap. 8.95 (*1-878175-92-0*) F Amato Pubns.

Laverty, Paul. Carla's Song. 144p. 1997. pap. 13.95 (*0-571-19162-2*) Faber & Faber.

An Asterisk (*) at the beginning of an entry indicates that the title is appearing for the first time.

Laverty, Philip B. Disciplinary Tactics at Mission Santa Cruz: A Foucoultian Approach to California Missions. fac. ed. 48p. (C). 1995. reprint ed. pap. text 5.31 (*1-55567-785-1*) Coyote Press.

Laverty, R. V. Railroad Law Digest. 2nd ed. Laverty, J. R., ed. lib. bdg. 47.00 (*0-318-04011-5*) J R Laverty.

Lavery, Brian. The Arming & Fitting of English Ships of War, 1600-1815. LC 87-62011. (Illus.). 288p. 1988. 65.00 (*0-87021-009-2*) Naval Inst Pr.

***Lavery, Brian.** Maritime Scotland. (Historic Scotland Ser.). 1999. pap. 23.95 (*0-7134-8583-3*) B T B.

Lavery, Brian. Nelson & the Nile: The Naval War Against Bonaparte, 1798. (Classics of Naval Literature Ser.). (Illus.). 352p. 1998. 42.95 (*1-55750-640-X*) Naval Inst Pr.

— Nelson's Navy: Its Ships, Men & Organization, 1793-1815. LC 89-62380. (Illus.). 352p. 2000. 59.95 (*0-87021-258-3*) Naval Inst Pr.

— Ship of the Line: Design, Construction & Fittings. (Conway Classics Ser.). 1998. 49.95 (*0-85177-287-0*) Brasseys.

— Shipboard Life & Organization, 1731-1815. LC 97-34827. (Naval Records Ser.: No. 138). 682p. 1998. text 96.95 (*1-84014-228-6*, Pub. by Ashgate Pub) Ashgate Pub Co.

Lavery, Brian, intro. Marine Architecture: Directions for Carrying on a Ship (1739) LC 93-13766. (Scholars' Facsimiles & Reprints, Maritime History Ser.: Vol. 481). 102p. 1993. 75.00 (*0-8201-1481-2*) Schol Facsimiles.

Lavery, Brian & Stephens, Simon. Ship Models: Their Purposes & Development from 1650 to the Present. LC 95-71117. (Illus.). 256p. 1995. 80.00 (*0-302-00654-0*, Pub. by Zwemmer Bks) Intl Spec Bk.

***Lavery, Bryony.** More Light. (Connections Ser.). (Illus.). 112p. 2000. pap. 17.95 (*0-7487-4287-5*, Pub. by S Thornes Pubs) Trans-Atl Phila.

Lavery, Bryony. Tallulah Bankhead: Outlines. 128p. 1999. pap. text 9.95 (*1-899791-42-6*) Stewart Tabori & Chang.

***Lavery, Byrony.** Lavery Plays, No. 1. 1998. pap. 14.95 (*0-413-72340-2*) Methn.

Lavery, David. Late for the Sky: The Mentality of the Space Age. LC 91-24128. 272p. (C). 1992. 26.95 (*0-8093-1767-2*) S Ill U Pr.

Lavery, David, ed. Full of Secrets: Critical Approaches to Twin Peaks. LC 94-17604. (Contemporary Film & Television Ser.). 292p. 1994. pap. text 19.95 (*0-8143-2506-8*) Wayne St U Pr.

Lavery, David, et al, eds. Deny All Knowledge: Reading the X-Files. LC 96-28814. (Television Ser.). 233p. 1996. 49.95 (*0-8156-2717-3*, LATN); pap. 19.95 (*0-8156-0407-6*, LATNP) Syracuse U Pr.

Lavery, Dennis S. & Jordan, Mark H. Iron Brigade General: John Gibbon, a Rebel in Blue. LC 92-36516. 232p. 1993. 52.95 (*0-313-28576-4*, LIB, Greenwood Pr) Greenwood.

Lavery, Donald S., tr. see Lewin, Leif.

Lavery, Duncan. Meditations for Pregnancy. 1999. text. write for info. (*0-312-24558-0*) St Martin.

— Meditations for Your Pregnancy. LC 99-27620. 112p. 1999. pap. 17.95 (*1-58238-055-4*, Whitman Coin) St Martin.

Lavery, Hugh. Reflections on the Creed. (C). 1988. 39.00 (*0-85439-213-0*, Pub. by St Paul Pubns) St Mut.

Lavery, J. Patrick, jt. ed. see Sanfilippo, Joseph S.

***Lavery, John.** Very Good Butter. 150p. 2000. pap. 14.95 (*1-55022-411-5*, Pub. by ECW) LPC InBook.

Lavery, Kevin. Smart Contracting for Local Government Services: Processes & Experience. LC 98-33628. (Privatizing Government Ser.). 232p. 1999. 65.00 (*0-275-96428-0*, Praeger Pubs) Greenwood.

Lavery, P., jt. ed. see Pompl, W.

Lavery, Peter, photos by. Circus Work. (Illus.). 144p. 1997. 59.95 (*0-9529647-0-8*, Pub. by Art Bks Intl) Partners Pubs Grp.

Lavery, R. V. Shipboard Operations. 2nd ed. 296p. 1990. pap. 49.95 (*0-7506-1857-4*) Buttrwrth-Heinemann.

Lavery, R. V., jt. ed. see Beveridge, David L.

Lavery, Richard, et al, eds. Advances in Biomolecular Simulations. LC 91-58106. (AIP Conference Proceedings Ser.: No. 239). (Illus.). 392p. 1992. lib. bdg. 85.00 (*0-88318-940-2*) Am Inst Physics.

Lavery, Vincent J., ed. see Dewazien, Karl.

Laves, Walter H., jt. auth. see Thomson, Charles A.

Laves, Walter Herman. German Governmental Influence on Foreign Investment, 1871-1914. Wilkins, Mira, ed. LC 76-29742. (European Business Ser.). 1977. reprint ed. lib. bdg. 21.95 (*0-405-09759-X*) Ayer.

Lavett. Integrated Genetics. 2000. pap. text. write for info. (*0-7167-3606-3*) St Martin.

— Integrated Genetics. (Illus.). 2000. pap. text. write for info. (*0-7167-3443-5*) St Martin.

Lavett, Diane K., jt. auth. see Griffiths.

Lavett, Diane K., jt. auth. see Manheim, Carol J.

Lavetta, Gary. Civil War Angel. 128p. (Orig.). 1987. pap. 4.95 (*0-9618951-0-1*) Memory Ln Bks.

— Home in the Hills. LC 88-90882. (Illus.). 143p. (Orig.). 1988. pap. 4.95 (*0-9618951-1-X*) Memory Ln Bks.

— The Lily Trail. 144p. (YA). (gr. 7-12). 1990. pap. 4.95 (*0-9618951-2-8*) Memory Ln Bks.

Lavette, Lavaille. The Adventures of Roopster Roux: Escape from Vulture's Roost. LC 98-15426. (Illus.). 32p. (J). (ps-3). 1998. pap. text 5.95 (*1-56554-360-2*) Pelican.

— The Adventures of Roopster Roux: Slammin' Slime. LC 98-15425. (Illus.). 32p. (J). (ps-3). 1998. pap. 5.95 (*1-56554-359-9*) Pelican.

***Lavette, Lavaille.** The Adventures of Roopster Roux: Surfing the Net. LC 98-15433. (Illus.). 32p. (J). (ps-3). 1998. text 5.95 (*1-56554-361-0*) Pelican.

— The Adventures of Roopster Roux: The Monster All-Stars. LC 98-16366. (Illus.). 32p. (J). (ps-3). 1998. pap. text 5.95 (*1-56554-362-9*) Pelican.

Lavey, Anton, et al, contrib. by. Might Is Right: The Survival of the Fittest. deluxe ed. 230p. (C). 1996. pap. 13.00 (*1-929399-02-2*) M Hunt Pubg.

LaVey, Anton S. Satanic Rituals. 1976. mass mkt. 6.99 (*0-380-01392-4*, Avon Bks) Morrow Avon.

— The Satanic Rituals. (Illus.). 300p. 1991. reprint ed. lib. bdg. 23.95 (*0-89966-827-5*) Buccaneer Bks.

***Lavey, Elliott.** New Frontiers in Ultrasonic & Traditional Liposuction. 1998. 15.00 incl. audio (*1-58111-075-8*) Contemporary Medical.

Lavey, Elliott, jt. auth. see Fang, Erlinda.

Lavey, Kathleen, ed. see Galbraith, James D. & Galbraith, Susan S.

Lavi, A. Ocean Thermal Energy Conversion. 80p. 1981. pap. 36.00 (*0-08-026705-X*, Pergamon Pr) Elsevier.

Lavi, Abrahim, ed. see Recent Advances in Optimization Techniques Symposium Staff.

Lavi, Zvi, ed. Kibbutz Members Study Kibbutz Children. 1. LC 89-25872. (Kibbutz Study Ser.: No. 1). 248p. 1990. 62.95 (*0-313-27387-1*, LKB/, Greenwood Pr) Greenwood.

Lavia, L. A., ed. Cellular Signals Controlling Uterine Function. (Illus.). 198p. (C). 1991. text 102.00 (*0-306-43822-4*, Kluwer Plenum) Kluwer Academic.

Lavie, Arie & Kuhn, Robert L. Industrial Research & Development in Israel: Patterns & Portents. LC 87-32787. 160p. 1988. 47.95 (*0-275-92967-1*, C2967, Praeger Pubs) Greenwood.

Lavie, Arlette. Half a World Away. LC 90-49096. 32p. (J). (ps-3). 1990. 7.99 (*0-85953-335-2*); pap. 3.99 (*0-85953-334-4*) Childs Play.

— Tower. LC 90-1372. 32p. (J). (ps-3). 1990. 11.99 (*0-85953-392-1*); pap. 5.99 (*0-85953-393-X*) Childs Play.

Lavie, Peretz. The Enchanted World of Sleep. Berris, Anthony, tr. LC 95-41304. (Illus.). 286p. 1996. 32.50 (*0-300-06602-3*) Yale U Pr.

— The Enchanted World of Sleep. Berris, Anthony, tr. (Illus.). 286p. 1998. pap. 15.00 (*0-300-07436-0*) Yale U Pr.

Lavie, Smadar. The Poetics of Military Occupation: Mzeina Allegories of Bedouin Identity under Israeli & Egyptian Rule. 1990. 45.00 (*0-520-06880-7*, Pub. by U CA Pr) Cal Prin Full Svc.

Lavie, Smadar, et al, eds. Creativity - Anthropology. LC 92-52765. (Anthropology of Contemporary Issues Ser.). (Illus.). 368p. 1993. text 45.00 (*0-8014-2255-8*); pap. text 17.95 (*0-8014-9542-3*) Cornell U Pr.

Lavie, Smadar & Swedenburg, Ted, eds. Displacement, Diaspora, & Geographies of Identity. LC 95-39399. (Illus.). 344p. 1996. text 49.95 (*0-8223-1710-9*); pap. text 17.95 (*0-8223-1720-6*) Duke.

Lavielle, Gail. Carmen: Seduction of the Century. McGuire, Beverly & Caldwell, Robert, eds. LC 97-75711. (Illus.). 1999. pap. write for info. (*1-877761-91-5*) Pst.

Lavier, Bertrand. Bertrand Lavier. 1997. pap. 39.95 (*88-8158-103-5*, Pub. by Charta) Dist Art Pubs.

Laviera, Tato. La Carreta Made a U-Turn. 2nd ed. LC 92-38421. 74p. 1993. pap. 7.00 (*1-55885-064-3*) Arte Publico.

— Mainstream Ethics. LC 88-6377. 64p. (Orig.). 1988. pap. 7.00 (*0-934770-90-5*) Arte Publico.

Lavies, Bianca. Backyard Hunter: The Praying Mantis. (Illus.). 32p. (J). (gr. 2-5). 1995. pap. 4.99 (*0-14-055494-7*, PuffinBks) Peng Put Young Read.

Lavies, Bianca. Backyard Hunter: The Praying Mantis. 1995. 10.19 (*0-606-07257-8*, Pub. by Turtleback) Demco.

Lavies, Bianca. Compost Critters. LC 92-35651. (Illus.). 32p. (J). (gr. 2-6). 1993. 15.99 (*0-525-44763-6*, Dutton Child) Peng Put Young Read.

— A Gathering of Garter Snakes. (Illus.). 32p. (J). (gr. 3 up). 1993. 15.99 (*0-525-45099-8*, Dutton Child) Peng Put Young Read.

Lavies, Bianca. It's an Armadillo! (Picture Puffin Ser.). (Illus.). (J). 1994. 10.19 (*0-606-05890-7*, Pub. by Turtleback) Demco.

Lavies, Bianca. Monarch Butterflies, Mysterious Travelers. (Illus.). 32p. (J). (gr. 3-6). 1993. 15.99 (*0-525-44905-1*, Dutton Child) Peng Put Young Read.

Lavigna, Claire. Anna Kulisciloff: From Russian Populism to Italian Socialism. Noether, Emiliana P., ed. LC 91-12419. (Modern European History Ser.). 264p. 1991. text 20.00 (*0-8240-2542-3*) Garland.

LaVigna, Gary W. & Donnellan, Anne M. Alternatives to Punishment: Solving Behavior Problems with Non-Aversive Strategies. (Illus.). 274p. (C). 1996. reprint ed. pap. text 19.95 (*0-8290-5204-6*) Ardent Media.

LaVigna, Gary W., et al. The Periodic Service Review: A Total Quality Assurance System for Human Services & Education. LC 93-39241. 256p. 1994. spiral bd. 37.95 (*1-55766-142-1*) P H Brookes.

Lavignac, A. The Music Dramas of Richard Wagner & His Musical Theatre in Bayreuth. LC 68-25293. (Studies in Music: No. 42). 1969. reprint ed. lib. bdg. 75.00 (*0-8383-0284-X*) M S G Haskell Hse.

Lavignac, Albert. The Music Dramas of Richard Wagner. Singleton, Esther, tr. LC 77-121292. 1977. reprint ed. 22.75 (*0-404-03890-5*) AMS Pr.

— The Music Dramas of Richard Wagner & His Festival Theatre in Bayreuth. 515p. 1990. reprint ed. lib. bdg. 99.00 (*0-7812-9157-7*) Rprt Serv.

LaVigne, Duncan L. The Wine Inventory Book. 90p. 1990. 59.95 (*0-9625723-0-6*) Wine Bk Co.

Lavigne, Gilchrist, tr. see Dimier, Anselme.

Lavigne, Guy. Mourir Sur Fond Blanc. (Novels in the Roman Plus Ser.). (FRE.). 160p. (YA). (gr. 8 up). 1994. pap. 8.95 (*2-89021-209-2*, Pub. by La Courte Ech) Firefly Bks Ltd.

— L' Obsession de Jerome Delisle. (Novels in the Roman Plus Ser., (FRE., Illus.). 160p. (YA). (gr. 8 up). 1993. pap. 8.95 (*2-89021-190-8*, Pub. by La Courte Ech) Firefly Bks Ltd.

— Pas de Quartier pour les Poires. (Novels in the Roman Plus Ser., (FRE., Illus.). 160p. (YA). (gr. 8 up). 1996. pap. 8.95 (*2-89021-250-5*, Pub. by La Courte Ech) Firefly Bks Ltd.

LaVigne, James & Wechsler, Charles. Minnesota: State of Beauty. 2nd ed. (Illus.). 96p. 1992. pap. 6.98 (*0-931714-12-5*, Pub. by Nodin Pr) Bookmen Inc.

LaVigne, Jeanne M., jt. auth. see Sawner, Kathryn A.

Lavigne, John R. Instrumentation Applications for the Pulp & Paper Industry. LC 77-93837. (Illus.). 320p. 1979. 45.00 (*0-87930-074-4*) Miller Freeman.

— An Introduction to Paper Industry Instrumentation. rev. ed. LC 77-89603. (Pulp & Paper Book). (Illus.). 488p. 1977. 48.00 (*0-87930-069-8*) Miller Freeman.

— Pulp & Paper Dictionary. 480p. 1986. 75.00 (*0-8288-1428-7*, M15398) Fr & Eur.

— Pulp & Paper Dictionary. 2nd ed. 370p. 1993. 65.00 (*0-87930-303-4*) Miller Freeman.

***Lavigne, John R.** Pulp & Paper Dictionary. 3rd ed. 452p. 1999. 69.00 (*0-87930-579-7*) Miller Freeman.

Lavigne, Marie. The Economics of Transition: From Socialist Economy to Market Economy. 2nd ed. LC 98-47532. 304p. 1999. pap. 22.95 (*0-312-22089-8*); text 65.00 (*0-312-22088-X*) St Martin.

— International Political Economy & Socialism. Lambert, David, tr. (Illus.). 424p. (C). 1991. text 69.95 (*0-521-33427-6*); pap. text 24.95 (*0-521-33663-5*) Cambridge U Pr.

Lavigne, Marie, ed. The Soviet Union & Eastern Europe in the Global Economy. (International Council for Soviet & East European Studies). 236p. (C). 1992. text 69.95 (*0-521-41417-2*) Cambridge U Pr.

Lavigne, Michel, jt. auth. see Brown, George.

Lavigne, Nancy & Wartell, Julie, eds. Crime Mapping Case Studies: Success in the Field. 150p. 1998. pap. 20.00 (*1-878734-61-X*) Police Exec Res.

LaVigne, Ruth A. The Life of St. Claude de la Colombiere: Spiritual Director of St. Margaret Mary Alacoque. rev. ed. 127p. 1992. pap. 7.95 (*0-8198-4467-5*) Pauline Bks.

Lavigne, Shelly. Boy or Girl? Fifty Fun Ways to Find Out. (Illus.). 64p. (Orig.). 1992. pap. 6.95 (*0-440-50459-7*, Dell Trade Pbks) Dell.

***Lavigne, Yves.** Death Dealers: A Witness to the Drug Wars That Are Bleeding America. 1999. mass mkt. 7.50 (*0-00-638538-9*) HarpC.

Lavigne, Yves. Hell's Angels: Into the Abyss. 352p. 1997. mass mkt. 6.50 (*0-06-101104-5*, Harp PBks) HarpC.

— Hell's Angels: "Three Can Keep a Secret If Two Are Dead" (Illus.). 344p. 1989. reprint ed. pap. 13.95 (*0-8184-0514-7*) Carol Pub Group.

***Lavigne, Yves.** Hells Angels at War: Hells Angels & Their Violent Conspiracy to Supply Illegal Drugs to the World. 1999. 25.00 (*0-00-200024-5*) HarpC.

Lavik, Nils J., ed. Pain & Survival: Human Rights Violations & Mental Health. 244p. 1994. 33.00 (*82-00-21907-0*) Scandnvan Univ Pr.

LaVilla-Havelin, Lucia. The New Basket: A Vessel for the Future. (Illus.). 36p. 1984. pap. 10.00 (*0-942746-06-6*) SUNYP R Gibson.

Lavin, Audrey A. Aspects of the Novelist: E. M. Forster's Pattern & Rhythm. LC 93-12338. (AUS IV: Vol. 151). XI, 155p. (C). 1995. text 35.95 (*0-8204-1966-4*) P Lang Pubng.

Lavin, Bebe, jt. auth. see Haug, Marie R.

Lavin Camacho, Enrique. Diccionario de Verbos Ingleses con Particula. (ENG & SPA.). 240p. 1989. pap. 32.95 (*0-7859-5714-6*, 8420516724) Fr & Eur.

Lavin, Claire & Doka, Kenneth. Older Adults with Developmental Disabilities. LC 97-44006. (Society & Aging Ser.). 151p. 1999. 32.00 (*0-89503-188-4*) Baywood Pub.

Lavin, Claire, jt. auth. see Bagley, Michael.

Lavin, Claire, jt. auth. see Rothman, Rosalind.

Lavin, David E. & Hyllegard, David. Changing the Odds: Open Admissions & the Life Chances of the Disadvantaged. LC 95-31948. 292p. 1996. 37.50 (*0-300-06328-8*) Yale U Pr.

Lavin, David E., et al. Right vs. Privilege: The Open Admissions Experiment at the City University of New York. LC 80-69571. (Illus.). 1981. 35.00 (*0-02-918080-5*) Free Pr.

Lavin, Deborah. From Empire to International Commonwealth: A Biography of Lionel Curtis. (Illus.). 384p. (C). 1995. text 85.00 (*0-19-812616-6*) OUP.

Lavin, Edward. Reading Through Imagery: Grades K-5. 1989. pap. 15.00 (*0-89824-095-6*) Trillium Pr.

Lavin, Edward J. Everyday Meditations. 1997. 20.00 (*0-517-20072-4*) Random Hse Value.

— Life Meditations. (Illus.). 192p. 1993. 12.99 (*0-517-09374-X*) Random Hse Value.

***Lavin, Ellen R. & Wood, Samuel H.** Essential over 35 Pregna. LC 97-37542. 192p. 1998. pap. 11.00 (*0-380-78819-5*, Avon Bks) Morrow Avon.

Lavin, Enrique, jt. auth. see Boyarsky, Bill.

Lavin, Hank. Outsourcing to Industrial Sales RE for Manufacturers & Distributors. (Illus.). 40p. 1998. 14.95 (*0-941890-07-4*, B9) Lavin Assocs.

Lavin, Hank & Freeman, Priscilla. How to Get-& Keep!-A Profitable Rep Agency by Effective Marketing. 2nd ed. LC 98-100594. (Illus.). 216p. 1996. text 36.95 (*0-941890-06-6*, B45) Lavin Assocs.

Lavin, Henry. How to Get-& Keep!-Good Industrial Representatives. 4th ed. (Illus.). 252p. 1997. ring bd. 85.00 (*0-941890-02-3*, B8) Lavin Assocs.

— How to Get-& Keep!-Good Product Lines. 2nd ed. (Illus.). 95p. 1991. pap. 29.95 (*0-941890-03-1*, B4) Lavin Assocs.

Lavin, Irving. Past-Present: Essays on Historicism in Art from Donatello to Picasso. (Una's Lectures: No. 6). (C). 1992. 75.00 (*0-520-06816-5*, Pub. by U CA Pr) Cal Prin Full Svc.

Lavin, Irving, ed. Gianlorenzo Bernini: New Aspects of His Art & Thought. LC 84-43087. (College Art Association Monographs: Vol. 37). (Illus.). 234p. 1985. 39.50 (*0-271-00387-1*) Pa St U Pr.

— World Art: Themes of Unity in Diversity, Acts of the XXVIth International Congress of the History of Art, 3 vols. 906p. 1989. 95.00 (*0-271-00607-2*) Pa St U Pr.

Lavin, Irving, ed. see Panofsky, Erwin.

Lavin, J. A., ed. see Goldsmith, Oliver.

Lavin, J. A., ed. see Sheridan, Richard Brinsley.

Lavin, James D. The Art & Tradition of the Zuloagas: Spanish Damascene from the Khalili Collection. LC 99-193799. (Illus.). 216p. (C). 1999. text 90.00 (*1-874780-10-2*); pap. text 45.00 (*1-874780-11-0*) OUP.

***Lavin, Joe.** But I Digress... Humor Columns from the Web. 160p. 1999. pap. 15.95 (*0-9677771-0-0*, Redline Pr) A F Pubng.

Lavin, Lisa M. Radiography in Veterinary Technology. 2nd ed. Williams, Adrianne, ed. LC 98-3626. (Illus.). 440p. (C). 1998. text 44.00 (*0-7216-7552-2*, W B Saunders Co) Harcrt Hlth Sci Grp.

Lavin, Marilyn A. Piero Della Francesca. (Masters of Art Ser.). (Illus.). 128p. 1992. 24.95 (*0-8109-3210-5*, Pub. by Abrams) Time Warner.

— Piero Della Francesca: San Francesco, Arezzo. (Great Fresco Cycles of the Renaissance Ser.). (Illus.). 104p. 1994. 25.00 (*0-8076-1317-7*) Braziller.

— Piero Della Francesca: The Flagellation. (Illus.). 112p. 1990. pap. 14.95 (*0-226-46958-1*) U Ch Pr.

— The Place of Narrative: Mural Decoration in Italian Churches, 431-1600. LC 89-49474. (Illus.). 448p. 1993. 65.00 (*0-226-46956-5*) U Ch Pr.

— The Place of Narrative: Mural Decoration in Italian Churches, 431-1600. (Illus.). xx, 426p. 1994. pap. text 49.95 (*0-226-46960-3*) U Ch Pr.

— William Bostwick: Connecticut Yankee in Antebellum Georgia. LC 77-14787. (Dissertations in American Economic History Ser.). 1978. 37.95 (*0-405-11044-8*) Ayer.

Lavin, Marilyn A., ed. IL 60: Essays Honoring Irving Lavin on His Sixtieth Birthday. LC 89-85336. (Illus.). 303p. 1990. 45.00 (*0-934977-18-6*) Italica Pr.

— Piero Della Francesca & His Legacy. (Illus.). 1995. 60.00 (*0-300-07711-4*) Yale U Pr.

Lavin, Martin & Watters, Dianne, eds. Programmed Cell Death: The Cellular & Molecular Biology of Apoptosis. LC 93-27865. xviii, 331p. 1993. text 129.00 (*3-7186-5461-X*) Gordon & Breach.

Lavin, Martin, jt. ed. see Watters, Dianne.

Lavin, Mary. In a Cafe. 336p. (C). 1999. pap. 13.95 (*0-14-118040-4*, PuffinBks) Peng Put Young Read.

Lavin, Mary & Gault, Alison. A Likely Story. 56p. 1997. pap. 7.95 (*1-85371-104-7*, Pub. by Poolbeg Pr) Dufour.

Lavin, Matt. Biogeography & Systematics of Poitea (Leguminosae) Anderson, Christiane, ed. (Systematic Botany Monographs: Vol. 37). (Illus.). 87p. 1993. pap. 11.00 (*0-912861-37-1*) Am Soc Plant.

— Systematics of Coursetia (Leguminosae-Papilionoideae) Anderson, Christiane, ed. (Systematic Botany Monographs: Vol. 21). (Illus.). 167p. 1988. pap. 20.00 (*0-912861-21-5*) Am Soc Plant.

Lavin, Matt & Sousa, Mario. Phylogenetic Systematics & Biogeography of the Tribe Robinieae (Leguminosae) Anderson, Christiane, ed. (Systematic Botany Monographs: Vol. 45). (Illus.). 165p. 1995. pap. 22.00 (*0-912861-45-2*) Am Soc Plant.

Lavin, Matt, jt. auth. see Beyra M., Angela.

Lavin, Maud. Cut with the Kitchen Knife: The Weimar Photomontages of Hannah Hoch. (Illus.). 280p. 1994. pap. 25.00 (*0-300-06164-1*) Yale U Pr.

— Cut with the Kitchen Knife: The Weimer Photomontages of Hannah Hoch. LC 92-14332. (Illus.). 256p. (C). 1993. 50.00 (*0-300-04766-5*) Yale U Pr.

***Lavin, Michael.** Business Information: How to Find It, How to Use It. 3rd ed. (Illus.). 560p. 2001. pap. text 48.50 (*1-57356-213-0*) Oryx Pr.

Lavin, Michael. Business Information: How to Find It, How to Use It. 3rd ed. (Illus.). 560p. (C). 2001. text 61.00 (*1-57356-212-2*) Oryx Pr.

Lavin, Michael R. Business Information: How to Find It, How to Use It. 2nd ed. LC 91-28129. 512p. 1992. pap. 42.50 (*0-89774-643-0*) Oryx Pr.

— Understanding the Census: A Guide for Marketers, Planners, Grant Writers & Other Data Users. LC 92-74697. (Illus.). 535p. (Orig.). 1996. pap. 49.95 (*0-9629586-1-1*) Epoch Bks.

— Understanding the Census: A Guide for Marketers, Planners, Grant-Writers & Other Data Users. 560p. 1996. boxed set 62.00 (*0-89774-995-2*) Oryx Pr.

Lavin, Michael R., et al. Subject Index to the 1990 Census of Population & Housing. LC 98-201134. vi, 260p. 1997. pap. 39.95 (*0-9629586-2-X*) Epoch Bks.

Lavin, Norman. Manual of Endocrinology & Metabolism. 770p. 1986. pap. text 21.00 (*0-316-51651-1*, Little Brwn Med Div) Lppncott W & W.

Lavin, Norman. Manual of Endocrinology & Metabolism. 3rd ed. 720p. spiral bd. 39.95 (*0-7817-2014-1*) Lppncott W & W.

Lavin, Norman, ed. Manual of Endocrinology & Metabolism. 2nd ed. LC 93-874. (Illus.). 688p. 1993. spiral bd. 35.95 (*0-316-51657-0*, Little Brwn Med Div) Lppncott W & W.

Lavin, Paul. The Online Office: Get Wired with Microsoft. (Illus.). 208p. 2001. pap., mass mkt. 34.95 incl. cd-rom (*1-85032-269-4*) ITCP.

— The Online Office: Getting Wired with IBM. (Illus.). 208p. 2001. pap. 34.99 (*1-85032-292-9*) ITCP.

An Asterisk (*) at the beginning of an entry indicates that the title is appearing for the first time.

— Online Office to Get Wired with Oracle. (ITCP-UK Computer Science Ser.). (Illus.). 208p. 2001. pap. 34.95 (*1-85032-291-0*) ITCP.

— Parenting the Overactive Child: Alternatives to Drug Therapy. LC 89-2613. (Illus.). 160p. (Orig.). (C). 1989. 21.95 (*0-8191-7297-9*); pap. 10.95 (*0-8191-7315-0*) Madison Bks UPA.

Lavin, Paul & Parker, Cynthia. Despair Turned into Rage: Understanding & Helping Abused, Neglected & Abandoned Youth. LC 99-20810. 1999. 29.95 (*0-87868-745-9*, CWLA Pr) Child Welfare.

***Lavin, Robin.** Christian Ethics: An Essential Guide. 128p. 2000. pap. 15.00 (*0-687-05462-1*) Abingdon.

***Lavin, Ron.** The Advocate: Gospel Sermons for Sundays after Pentecost (First Third), Cycle B. LC 99-33002. 90p. 1999. pap. 9.25 (*0-7880-1397-1*) CSS OH.

— Turning Griping into Gratitude: A Study in the Psalms. LC 99-54635. 2000. pap. 18.50 (*0-7880-1576-1*) CSS OH.

Lavin, Ronald J. The Great I Am: Preaching the "I Am" Statements of Jesus. 1995. pap. 11.95 (*0-7880-0576-6*) CSS OH.

— Previews of Coming Attractions. 1991. pap. 8.25 (*1-55673-317-8*, 9138) CSS OH.

— Way to Grow: Dynamic Church Growth Through Small Groups. 208p. 1996. pap. 17.25 (*0-7880-0733-5*, Fairway Pr) CSS OH.

— You Can Grow in a Small Group. 144p. 1976. pap. 6.00 (*0-89536-273-2*, 2500, Fairway Pr) CSS OH.

Lavin, S. R. Let Myself Shine. 7.00 (*0-686-65484-6*); pap. 3.50 (*0-686-65485-4*) Kulchur Foun.

— The Stonecutters at War with the Cliffdwellers: 9 Poems. (Illus.). 1971. 95.00 (*0-685-47825-4*) Heron Pr.

— The Stonecutters at War with the Cliffdwellers: 9 Poems. deluxe ed. (Illus.). 1971. boxed set 200.00 (*0-685-47826-2*) Heron Pr.

Lavin, Sylvia. Quatremere de Quincy & the Invention of a Modern Language of Architecture. (Illus.). 352p. 1992. 55.00 (*0-262-12166-2*) MIT Pr.

Lavine, A. S., et al, eds. General Papers in Heat Transfer & Heat Transfer in Hazardous Waste Processing. (HTD Ser.: Vol. 212). 176p. 1992. 50.00 (*0-7918-1052-6*, G00696) ASME.

— Transport Phenomena in Materials Processing & Manufacturing: Proceedings, International Mechanical Engineering Congress & Exposition, Atlanta, GA, 1996. LC 96-78667. 331p. 1996. pap. 96.00 (*0-7918-1524-2*, TS183) ASME.

Lavine, Alan. The Complete Idiot's Guide to Making Money with Mutual Funds 2E. 2nd ed. 352p. 1998. pap. text 16.95 (*0-02-862413-0*) Macmillan Gen Ref.

— 50 Ways to Mutual Fund Profits. 1996. text 22.95 (*0-7863-1173-8*, Irwn Prfssnl) McGraw-Hill Prof.

— 50 Ways to Mutual Fund Profits: Market-Proven Techniques to Build Lasting Wealth. 1995. 22.95 (*0-614-15439-1*, Irwn Prfssnl) McGraw-Hill Prof.

— Your Life Insurance Options. LC 92-14939. (ICFP Personal Wealth Building Guides Ser.). 240p. 1993. pap. 12.95 (*0-471-54919-3*) Wiley.

***Lavine, Alan & Liberman, Gail.** Rags to Riches. 2000. pap. 18.95 (*0-7931-3392-0*) Dearborn.

Lavine, Alan, jt. auth. see Liberman, Gail.

Lavine, Alan, jt. auth. see Perritt, Gerald W.

Lavine, Harold & Wechsler, James. War Propaganda & the United States. 1972. 59.95 (*0-8490-1277-5*) Gordon Pr.

Lavine, Harold & Wechsler, James A. War Propaganda & the United States. LC 72-4668. (International Propaganda & Communications Ser.). (Illus.). 389p. 1972. reprint ed. 21.95 (*0-405-04753-3*) Ayer.

Lavine, Lance, et al. Five Degrees of Conservation: A Graphic Analysis of Energy Alternatives for a Northern Climate. LC 83-620711. 72p. reprint ed. pap. 30.00 (*0-7837-2939-1*, 205751500006) Bks Demand.

Lavine, Larry. Torts. (Quick Review Ser.). 222p. (Orig.) (C). 1993. pap. text 18.95 (*0-614-30137-8*) Sum & Substance.

Lavine, Richard I., jt. auth. see Wilson, Robert H.

Lavine, Robert, ed. Human Brain Function: An Introduction to Clinical Neurophysiology. 264p. (C). 1996. pap. text 42.00 (*0-536-59822-3*) Pearson Custom.

Lavine, Shaughan. Understanding the Infinite. LC 93-49697. (Illus.). 376p. 1994. text 46.50 (*0-674-92096-1*) HUP.

— Understanding the Infinite. (Illus.). 384p. 1998. pap. text 19.95 (*0-674-92117-8*) HUP.

Lavine, Steven D., jt. ed. see Karp, Ivan.

Lavine, Thelma Z. From Socrates to Sartre. 448p. 1985. mass mkt. 7.99 (*0-553-25161-9*) Bantam.

Lavine, Thelma Z., jt. auth. see Frankel, Charles.

Lavine, Thelma Z., jt. ed. see Tejera, Victorino.

Lavinga, N., jt. auth. see Westney, Richard E.

Lavinger, Bob. Programming Outlook 2000. 1999. 29.99 (*0-672-31549-1*) Sams.

Lavington, Camille & Losee, Stephanie. You've Only Got Three Seconds: How to Make the Right Impression in Your Business & Social Life. 240p. 1998. pap. 11.95 (*0-385-48455-0*) Doubleday.

Lavington, Frederick. The English Capital Market. LC 67-30469. (Reprints of Economic Classics Ser.). ix, 297p. 1968. reprint ed. 45.00 (*0-678-00345-9*) Kelley.

Lavington, Simon, jt. ed. see Abdelguerfi, Mahdi.

Lavington, Simon H., jt. auth. see Freitas, Alex A.

Lavinia, Alice S. Endocrinology: Index of New Information with Authors, Subjects & References. 150p. 1994. 47.50 (*1-55914-718-0*); pap. 44.50 (*1-55914-719-9*) ABBE Pubs Assn.

Lavinia, Stan, ed. Romania in Transition. LC 96-36537. (Illus.). 240p. 1997. text 72.95 (*1-85521-886-0*, Pub. by Dartmth Pub) Ashgate Pub Co.

Lavinio, Stefano. The Hedge Fund Handbook. LC 99-15642. 192p. 1999. 65.00 (*0-07-135030-6*) McGraw.

***Lavino, Patrick.** Celtic World: An Illustrated History. LC 99-37960. (Illus.). 191p. 1999. 14.95 (*0-7818-0731-X*) Hippocrene Bks.

Lavinthal, Hy. Defense Strategy in Bridge. Coffin, George, ed. 192p. 1974. reprint ed. pap. 4.95 (*0-486-23010-4*) Dover.

***LaViolette, Alyce D. & Barnett, Ola W.** It Could Happen to Anyone: Why Battered Women Stay. 2nd ed. LC 00-8737. 2000. write for info. (*0-7619-1995-3*) Sage.

LaViolette, Alyce D., jt. auth. see Barnett, Ola W.

LaViolette, Forrest E. Americans of Japanese Ancestry. Daniels, Roger, ed. LC 78-54822. (Asian Experience in North America Ser.). 1979. reprint ed. lib. bdg. 18.95 (*0-405-11278-5*) Ayer.

— The Canadian Japanese & World War II. LC 48-11190. 332p. reprint ed. pap. 103.00 (*0-608-30155-8*, 205547300022) Bks Demand.

— The Struggle for Survival: Indian Cultures & the Protestant Ethic in British Columbia. rev. ed. LC 73-84433. 215p. reprint ed. pap. 66.70 (*0-608-12883-X*, 202364300033) Bks Demand.

LaViolette, Paul A. Beyond the Big Bang: Ancient Myth & the Science of Continuous Creation. (Illus.). 384p. 1995. 29.95 (*0-89281-457-8*) Inner Tradit.

— Earth Under Fire: Humanity's Survival of the Apocalypse. LC 96-72264. (Illus.). 405p. 1997. 25.95 (*0-9642025-1-4*) Starlane Pubns.

— Subquantum Kinetics: The Alchemy of Creation. LC 94-224685. (Illus.). 208p. (Orig.). (C). 1994. pap. 15.00 (*0-9642025-0-6*) Starlane Pubns.

***LaViolette, Paul A.** The Talk of the Galaxy: An ET Message for Us? (Illus.). 200p. 2000. pap. 16.00 (*0-9642025-3-0*, Pub. by Starlane Pubns) New Leaf Dist.

***LaViolette, Paul E.** Waiting for the White Pelicans: And Other Tales of the Mississippi Gulf Coast. (Illus.). 183p. 2000. pap. 13.95 (*0-9673936-1-2*) Annabelle Pubg.

LaViolette, Paul E., ed. Seasonal & Interannual Variability of the Western Mediterranean Sea. LC 94-34453. (Coastal & Estuarine Studies: Vol. 46). 370p. 1994. 57.00 (*0-87590-260-X*) Am Geophysical.

LaViolette, Wesley. Wings Unfolding. LC 70-140225. 1971. pap. 5.95 (*0-87516-040-9*) DeVorss.

Lavis, D. A. & Bell, G. M. Statistical Mechanics of Lattice Systems Vol. 1: Closed-Form & Exact Solutions. Balian, R. et al, eds. LC 99-11692. (Texts & Monographs in Physics Ser.). (Illus.). xii, 363p. 1999. 69.95 (*3-540-64437-7*) Spr-Verlag.

— Statistical Mechanics of Lattice Systems Vol. 2: Exact, Series & Renormalization Group Methods. Balian, R. et al, eds. LC 99-11692. (Texts & Monographs in Physics Ser.). (Illus.). xii, 427p. 1999. 79.95 (*3-540-64436-9*) Spr-Verlag.

Lavis, Steve. Cock-a-Doodle-Doo: A Farmyard Counting Book. (J). (ps-1). 1997. 13.99 (*0-614-28849-5*, Dutton Child) Peng Put Young Read.

***Lavis, Steve.** Little Mouse Has a Busy Day. (Ready Readers Ser.). (Illus.). 24p. (J). (ps-1). 2000. 6.95 (*1-929927-10-X*) Ragged Bears NY.

— Little Mouse Has a Friend. (Ready Readers Ser.). (Illus.). 24p. (J). (ps-1). 2000. 6.95 (*1-929927-12-6*) Ragged Bears NY.

— Little Mouse Has a Party. (Ready Readers Ser.). (Illus.). 24p. (J). (ps-1). 2000. 6.95 (*1-929927-11-8*) Ragged Bears NY.

— Little Mouse Has an Adventure. (Ready Readers Ser.). (Illus.). 24p. (J). (ps-1). 2000. 6.95 (*1-929927-09-6*) Ragged Bears NY.

— Noisy Farm Animals: Mix & Match. (Illus.). 21p. (J). (gr. 13). 2000. 9.95 (*1-929927-08-8*) Ragged Bears NY.

— Noisy Wild Animals: Mix & Match. (Illus.). 21p. (J). (gr. 13). 2000. 9.95 (*1-929927-07-X*) Ragged Bears NY.

Lavisse, Emile C. Field Equipment of the European Foot Soldier, 1900-1914. Lawton, Edward P., tr. (Reference Ser.: No. 2). (Illus.). 256p. 1994. reprint ed. 39.95 (*0-89839-208-X*) Battery Pr.

Lavisse, Ernest. Youth of Frederick the Great. LC 71-172308. reprint ed. 45.00 (*0-404-03891-3*) AMS Pr.

Lavisse, Ernest, ed. Histoire de France Depuis les Origines Jusqu'a la Revolution Paris, 1900-1911, 9 vols. LC 73-89549. (Illus.). reprint ed. 1395.00 (*0-404-03900-6*) AMS Pr.

LaVita, J. A., ed. see NATO Advanced Study Institute Staff.

Lavitt, Ben, ed. & photos by see Bockwinkel, Susan R.

Lavitt, Edward & McDowell, Robert. In the Beginning Creation Stories. 156p. (J). (gr. 6-12). 1973. 18.95 (*0-89388-096-5*) Okpaku Communications.

— Nihancan's Feast of Beaver: Animal Tales of the North American Indians. (Illus.). 120p. 1990. pap. 12.95 (*0-89013-211-9*) Museum NM Pr.

Lavitt, Edward, ed. see Goodall, Jane.

Lavitt, Edward, ed. see Krantz, Judith.

Lavitt, Edward, jt. ed. see McDowell, Robert E.

Lavitt, Wendy, jt. auth. see Goddu, Krystyna P.

Lavitt, Wendy, jt. auth. see Weissman, Judith R.

Lavizzo-Mourey, Rise J., jt. ed. see Forciea, Mary A.

Lavle, Alice Richard. Diary of a Ghost. 161p. mass mkt. 4.99 (*1-55197-132-1*) Picasso Publ.

Lavlin. Moments: Poems. 80p. 1992. 10.00 (*0-7069-5892-6*, Pub. by Vikas) S Asia.

Lavo, Carl. Back from the Deep: The Strange Story of the Sister Subs, Squalus & Sculpin. LC 94-25853. (Illus.). 244p. 1994. 31.95 (*1-55750-507-1*) Naval Inst Pr.

LaVo, Carl. Back from the Deep: The Strange Story of the Sister Subs "Squalus" & "Sculpin" (Bluejacket Bks.). (Illus.). 256p. 1998. pap. 15.95 (*1-55750-530-6*) Naval Inst Pr.

Lavocat, Rene, jt. ed. see George, Wilma.

Lavoie, Alphee. Astro-Trading for a New Millennium No. 1: The Guide to Successful Financial Trading with Astrology. Lavoie, Carol, ed. (Illus.). 250p. 2000. pap. write for info. (*0-9645621-3-8*) AIR Soft.

— Horany Workbook: Perfecting Your Skills in Horany Astrology. Lavoie, Carol, ed. (Illus.). 1999. pap., wbk. ed. write for info. (*0-9645621-1-1*) AIR Soft.

— Lose This Book . . . And Find It Through Horary: A Practical Guide to Finding Lost Articles Through Horary Astrology. (Illus.). 140p. (Orig.). 1995. pap. 11.95 (*0-9645621-0-3*) AIR Soft.

Lavoie, Alphee & Lavoie, Carol. Life Lessons Through the Sun Signs. Date not set. pap. write for info. (*0-9645621-2-X*) AIR Soft.

Lavoie, Bob. Caterpillar D-2 & R-2 Photo Archive. LC 98-75275. (Photo Archive Ser.). (Illus.). 128p. 1999. pap. 29.95 (*1-882256-99-9*, 128283AE) Iconografix.

— Caterpillar Thirty Photo Archive: Including Best Thirty, 6G Thirty & R4. 2nd ed. (Illus.). 128p. 1999. pap. 29.95 (*1-58388-006-2*, Pub. by Iconografix) Motorbooks Intl.

LaVoie, Bob. Caterpillar D-8 1933-1974 Photo Archive: Including Diesel Seventy-Five & RD-8. LC 98-75276. (Photo Archive Ser.). (Illus.). 128p. 1999. pap. 29.95 (*1-882256-96-4*, 128282AE) Iconografix.

***LaVoie, Bob.** Caterpillar Pocket Book: The Track-Type Tractors, 1925-1957. LC 99-76044. (Illus.). 96p. 2000. pap. 19.95 (*1-58388-022-4*, 129951AE, Pub. by Iconografix) Motorbooks Intl.

— Caterpillar Ten Photo Archive: Including 7C Fifteen & High Fifteen. LC 99-76052. (Illus.). 128p. 2000. pap. 29.95 (*1-58388-011-9*, 129955AE, Pub. by Iconografix) Motorbooks Intl.

Lavoie, Carol, jt. auth. see Lavoie, Alphee.

Lavoie, Carol, ed. see Lavoie, Alphee.

Lavoie, D. L., jt. ed. see Rezak, Richard.

***Lavoie, Don & Chamlee-Wright, Emily.** Culture & Enterprise: The Development, Representation & Morality of Business. LC 00-42489. 2000. pap. write for info. (*0-415-23359-3*) Routledge.

Lavoie, Francine, et al, eds. Self-Help & Mutual Aid Groups: International & Multicultural Perspectives. LC 94-44762. (Prevention in Human Services Ser.). 363p. 1995. 49.95 (*1-56024-716-9*) Haworth Pr.

***Lavoie, Gilbert R.** Resurrected: Tangible Evidence Jesus Rose from the Dead... And Its Message Revealed 2,000 Years Later. 2nd rev. ed. LC 98-123581. (Illus.). 248p. 2000. pap. 14.95 (*0-88347-458-1*, Pub. by T More) BookWorld.

Lavoie, Kathleen H., ed. Cave Research Foundation Annual Report, 1983. (Illus.). 42p. (Orig.). 1984. pap. 5.00 (*0-939748-15-0*) Cave Bks MO.

Lavoie, Louis. Tides of History. LC 96-95301. (Illus.). 350p. (Orig.). 1997. pap. 14.95 (*1-57502-385-7*, P01220) Morris Pubng.

Lavoie, Marc. Foundations of Post-Keynesian Economic Analysis. (New Directions in Modern Economics Ser.). (Illus.). 480p. 1994. pap. 35.00 (*1-85278-816-X*) E Elgar.

Lavoie, Marc, ed. Foundations of Post-Keynesian Economic Analysis. (New Directions in Modern Economics Ser.). 480p. 1992. 120.00 (*1-85278-322-2*) E Elgar.

LaVoie, Nicole. Return to Harmony: Creating Harmony & Balance Through the Frequencies of Sound. Lawrence, Jill et al, eds. LC 96-92084. (Illus.). 260p. 1996. pap. 13.00 (*0-9650387-4-2*) Snd Wave Energy.

— Return to Harmony: Creating Harmony & Balance Through the Frequencies of Sound. 2nd ed. LC 96-92084. 1996. pap. text. write for info. (*0-9650387-1-8*) Snd Wave Energy.

Lavoie, P., tr. see Pikulik, Ivan I. & Leger, Francois, eds.

Lavoie, Richard H. Discovering Math. (Mathematics Ser.). 1993. pap., student ed. 16.75 (*0-534-93342-4*) PWS Pubs.

— Discovering Mathematics. LC 92-30662. (Math). 640p. 1993. text 54.50 (*0-534-93340-8*) PWS Pubs.

Lavoie, Roland E. Greenberg's Guide to Lionel Trains, 1970-97 Vol. III: Accessories. LC 97-179276. (Illus.). 160p. (Orig.). 1997. pap. 39.95 (*0-89778-419-7*, 10-8060, Greenberg Books) Kalmbach.

LaVoie, Roland E., et al. Greenberg's Guide to Lionel Trains, 1970-1991, Vol. 2. Kraszewski, Andrea L., ed. (Illus.). 192p. 1991. pap. 32.95 (*0-89778-272-0*, 10-7635, Greenberg Books) Kalmbach.

Lavoie-Sati, Helene. Les 1001 Questions de Jeu de Sati. rev. ed. (FRE.). 1994. 19.95 (*2-920083-78-3*) Edns Roseau.

LaVoie, Steven. Erosion Surface. (Morning Coffee Chapbook Ser.). (Illus.). 40p. (Orig.). 1984. pap. 10.00 (*0-915124-98-X*) Coffee Hse.

Lavoie, Steven. Harbor of Light: An Illustrated History of Greater Oakland. Parks, Lori, ed. LC 99-73077. (Illus.). 300p. 2000. 49.95 (*1-886483-36-1*, Pub. by Heritge Media) Sunbelt Pubns.

Lavoisier, A. L. & Laplace, P. S. Memoir on Heat. Guerlac, Henry, ed.Tr. of Memoire sur la Chaleur. 1981. 14.95 (*0-88202-195-8*) Watson Pub Intl.

Lavoisier, Antoine Laurent. Elements of Chemistry. 539p. 1984. reprint ed. pap. 15.95 (*0-486-64624-6*) Dover.

— Essays, Physical & Chemical. Thomas, H., tr. 511p. 1970. reprint ed. 45.00 (*0-7146-1604-4*, Pub. by F Cass Pubs) Intl Spec Bk.

***Lavold, Elsebeth.** Viking Patterns for Knitting: Inspiration & Projects for Today's Knitter. (Illus.). 2000. 22.95 (*1-57076-137-X*, Trafalgar Sq Pub) Trafalgar.

***Lavon, Yaakov, tr.** My Footsteps Echo: The Yemen Journal of Rabbi Yaakov Sapir. 1998. 17.95 (*1-56871-184-0*, Pub. by Targum Pr) Feldheim.

Lavon, Yaakov, tr. see Adler, Binyamin.

Lavon, Yaakov, tr. see Gold, Avie, ed.

LaVopa, Anthony J. Prussian Schoolteachers: Profession & Office, 1763-1848. LC 79-24873. 230p. 1980. reprint ed. pap. 71.30 (*0-7837-0312-0*, 204063400018) Bks Demand.

LaVor, Marty. No Borders. (Illus.). 1992. 35.00 (*0-9632680-0-7*) LaVor Grp.

Lavorgna, Gary. Environment. 240p. (C). 1995. pap. text, per. 47.95 (*0-7872-0597-4*) Kendall-Hunt.

— Environment: Issues & Alternatives. 2nd ed. 384p. (C). 1998. per. 49.95 (*0-7872-4738-3*) Kendall-Hunt.

***Lavoy, Peter R., et al, eds.** Planning the Unthinkable: How New Powers Will Use Nuclear, Biological, & Chemical Weapons. LC 00-37678. (Studies in Security Affairs). 2000. pap. 45.00 (*0-8014-3776-8*); pap. 19.95 (*0-8014-8704-8*) Cornell U Pr.

L

Lavrac. Intelligent Data Analysis. LC 97-27564. 1997. text 142.00 (*0-7923-8000-2*) Kluwer Academic.

Lavrac, Nada, et al, eds. Inductive Logic Programming: 7th International Workshop, ILP-97, Prague, Czech Republic, September 17-20, 1997, Proceedings, Vol. 129. LC 97-36662. (Lecture Notes in Artificial Intelligence: Vol. 1297). viii, 309p. 1997. pap. 55.00 (*3-540-63514-9*) Spr-Verlag.

Lavrac, Nada, ed. see Eighth European Conference on Machine Learning Sta.

Lavrac, Nada, ed. see European Conference on Machine Learning Staff.

Lavrac, Vladimir, jt. ed. see De Grauwe, Paul.

Lavrack, Kevin R., jt. auth. see Newell, Patricia J.

Lavrack-Newell. Developmental Algebra. 4th ed. 96p. (C). 1998. per. 14.95 (*0-7872-5436-3*, 41543601) Kendall-Hunt.

Lavrakas, Paul. The Princess & the Pea. (J). 1993. pap. 6.00 (*0-87602-321-9*) Anchorage.

Lavrakas, Paul J. Telephone Survey Methods: Sampling, Selection & Supervision. 2nd ed. (Applied Social Research Methods Ser.). (Illus.). 160p. 1993. 42.00 (*0-8039-5306-2*); pap. 18.95 (*0-8039-5307-0*) Sage.

Lavrakas, Paul J. & Holley, Jack K., eds. Polling & Presidential Election Coverage. (Focus Editions Ser.: Vol. 127). (Illus.). 264p. (C). 1990. text 59.95 (*0-8039-4073-4*); pap. text 26.00 (*0-8039-4074-2*) Sage.

— Polling & Presidential Election Coverage. LC 90-43950. (Sage Focus Editions Ser.: Vol. 127). (Illus.). 244p. reprint ed. pap. 75.70 (*0-608-09792-6*, 206996600007) Bks Demand.

Lavrakas, Paul J. & Traugott, Michael W., eds. Election Polls, the News Media & Democracy. LC 99-56614. (Illus.). 312p. (C). 1999. pap. text 24.95 (*1-889119-16-4*, Chatham House Pub) Seven Bridges.

Lavrakas, Paul J., jt. auth. see Traugott, Michael W.

Lavranos, Destini & Ritchie, Sheri. The Magical Tree. (Illus.). 2p. (J). (ps). 1993. 14.95 (*0-9638393-0-6*) Bedtime Bks.

Lavranos, Destini, jt. auth. see Ritchie, Sheri.

Lavrenko, V. A., jt. auth. see Gogotsi, Yu.

Lavrent, M. M., et al. Ill-Posed Problems of Mathematical Physics & Analysis. LC 86-3642. (Translations of Mathematical Monographs: 64). 290p. 1986. pap. 49.00 (*0-8218-0896-6*) Am Math.

Lavrentev, M. A. Variational Methods for Boundary Value Problems (Etc.) 160p. 1989. pap. 4.95 (*0-486-66170-9*) Dover.

Lavrent'ev, M. A., et al. One-Dimensional Inverse Problems of Mathematical Physics. LC 86-7917. (AMS Translations Ser.: Series 2, Vol. 130). 70p. 1986. text 47.00 (*0-8218-3099-6*, TRANS2/130) Am Math.

Lavrent'ev, M. M., ed. International Symposium on Computerized Tomography (CT-93) 396p. 1994. 215.00 (*90-6764-187-1*, Pub. by VSP) Coronet Bks.

Lavrent'ev, M. M. & Savel'ev, L. Ya. Linear Operators & Ill-Posed Problems. LC 95-22545. (Illus.). 396p. (C). 1995. text 120.00 (*0-306-11035-0*, Kluwer Plenum) Kluwer Academic.

Lavrent'ev, M. M., et al. Ill-Posed Problems of Mathematical Physics & Analysis. LC 86 3642. (Translations of Mathematical Monographs: Vol. 64). 290p. 1986. text 124.00 (*0-8218-4517-9*, MMONO/64) Am Math.

Lavrentev, V. V., jt. auth. see Bartenev, G. M.

Lavrentiev, Aleksander. Vavara Stepanova: The Complete Works. (Illus.). 1991. pap. text 21.95 (*0-262-62082-0*) MIT Pr.

Lavrentiev, Alexander, intro. Alexander Rodchenko Museum Series Portfolio. (Museum Series Portfolio: No. 1). 24p. 1994. write for info. (*1-882277-03-1*) Schickler-Lafaille.

Lavrentiev, Alexander, jt. ed. see Elliot, David.

***Lavrijsen, Ria, ed.** Global Encounters in the World of Art: Collisions of Tradition & Modernity. (Illus.). 168p. 1999. pap. 17.00 (*90-6832-281-8*) Royal Tropical.

Lavrik, O. I. Physicochemical Biology Reviews: Mechanisms of Enzyme Action, Vol. 9. Skulachev, V. P., ed. (Soviet Scientific Reviews Ser.: Vol. 9, Pt. 1). ii, 92p. 1989. text 87.00 (*3-7186-4918-7*) Gordon & Breach.

Lavrin, Asuncion. Women, Feminism & Social Change in Argentina, Chile, & Uruguay, 1890-1940. LC 95-2729. (Engendering Latin America Ser.). (Illus.). x, 491p. 1995. pap. text 25.00 (*0-8032-7973-6*) U of Nebr Pr.

— Women, Feminism & Social Change in Argentina, Chile, & Uruguay, 1890-1940. LC 95-2729. (Engendering Latin America Ser.). (Illus.). x, 491p. 1995. text 70.00 (*0-8032-2897-X*) U of Nebr Pr.

Lavrin, Asuncion, ed. Latin American Women: Historical Perspectives, 3. LC 77-94758. (Contributions in Women's Studies: No. 3). 343p. 1978. 67.95 (*0-313-20309-1*, LLA/, Greenwood Pr) Greenwood.

— Sexuality & Marriage in Colonial Latin America. LC 88-33980. (Latin American Studies). (Illus.). ix, 350p. 1989. reprint ed. text 50.00 (*0-8032-2885-6*) U of Nebr Pr.

— Sexuality & Marriage in Colonial Latin America. LC 88-33980. (Latin American Studies). (Illus.). ix, 350p. 1989. reprint ed. pap. text 22.00 (*0-8032-7940-X*, Bison Books) U of Nebr Pr.

L

Lavrin, Janko. Aspects of Modernism, from Wilde to Pirandello. LC 68-22107. (Essay Index Reprint Ser.). 1977. reprint ed. 18.95 (*0-8369-0611-X*) Ayer.

— From Pushkin to Mayakovsky: A Study in the Evolution of a Literature. LC 72-114540. 308p. 1971. reprint ed. lib. bdg. 59.75 (*0-8371-4741-7*, LAPM, Greenwood Pr) Greenwood.

— Gogol. LC 72-2123. (Studies in European Literature: No. 56). 1972. reprint ed. lib. bdg. 75.00 (*0-8383-1473-2*) M S G Haskell Hse.

— Ibsen & His Creation. LC 72-2140. (Studies in Scandinavian Life & Literature: No. 18). 1972. reprint ed. lib. bdg. 75.00 (*0-8383-1484-8*) M S G Haskell Hse.

— Nietzsche & Modern Consciousness. LC 72-2094. (Studies in German Literature: No. 13). 1972. reprint ed. lib. bdg. 75.00 (*0-8383-1481-3*) M S G Haskell Hse.

Lavrin, Janko, ed. A First Series of Representative Russian Stories, Pushkin to Gorky. LC 74-114539. (Illus.). 239p. 1975. reprint ed. lib. bdg. 59.50 (*0-8371-4740-9*, LARS, Greenwood Pr) Greenwood.

Lavroff, Ellen C., et al, eds. Mas Cuentos y Juegos. 2nd rev. ed. (SPA., Illus.). (C). 1982. pap. text 9.75 (*0-393-95108-1*) Norton.

Lavroff, Nicholas. Behind the Scenes at Sega: The Making of a Video Game. LC 93-87197. (Illus.). 128p. 1994. pap. 14.95 (*1-55958-525-0*) Prima Pub.

Lavrov. Years of Emigration, Vol. 1. (Russian Series on Social History). 1987. lib. bdg. 41.50 (*90-277-0384-1*) Kluwer Academic.

— Years of Emigration, Vol. 2. (Russian Series on Social History). 1987. lib. bdg. 41.50 (*90-277-0443-0*) Kluwer Academic.

Lavrov, S. & Sdasyuk, G., eds. Concepts of Regional Development. 268p. (C). 1988. 70.00 (*0-7855-3900-X*) St Mut.

Lavrova, Elisaveta, tr. see Chekhov, Anton.

Lavsky, Hagit. Before Catastrophe: The Distinctive Path of German Zionism. (Illus.). 304p. 1996. 34.95 (*0-8143-2673-0*) Wayne St U Pr.

Lavut, Avraham D., jt. auth. see M'Liadi, Schneur Z.

Lavy, Christopher & Barrett, David S. Questions & Answers on Apley's Concise System of Orthopedics. 192p. 1991. pap. text 30.00 (*0-7506-1170-7*) Buttrwrth-Heinemann.

Lavy, Christopher B., jt. ed. see Marks, Paul V.

Lavy, George. Germany & Israel: Moral Debt & National Interest. LC 95-12715. 240p. 1996. 49.50 (*0-7146-4626-1*, Pub. by F Cass Pubs); pap. 24.50 (*0-7146-4191-X*, Pub. by F Cass Pubs) Intl Spec Bk.

Lavy, J. Langenscheidts Handworterbucher: Deutsch-Hebraisch. 1997. pap. write for info. (*3-468-04165-9*) Langenscheidt.

— Langenscheidts Handworterbucher: Hebraisch. 639p. 1997. pap. write for info. (*3-468-04160-8*) Langenscheidt.

Lavy, Matthew M., jt. auth. see Meggitt, Ashley J.

Lavy, Victor. Investment in Human Capital: Schooling Supply Constraints in Rural Ghana. LC 92-41656. (Living Standards Measurement Study Working Papers: No. 93). 47p. 1992. pap. 22.00 (*0-8213-2321-0*, 12321) World Bank.

Lavy, Victor & Germain, Jean-Marc. Quality & Cost in Health Care Choice in Developing Countries. LC 94-12590. (LSMS Working Papers: No. 105). 48p. 1994. pap. 22.00 (*0-8213-2854-9*, 12854) World Bank.

Lavy, Victor & Sheffer, Eliezer. Foreign Aid & Economic Development in the Middle East: Egypt, Syria & Jordan. LC 90-27796. 184p. 1991. 45.00 (*0-275-93827-1*, C3827, Praeger Pubs) Greenwood.

Lavy, Victor, et al. Changing Patterns of Illiteracy in Morocco: Assessment Methods Compared. LC 95-12294. (LSMS Working Papers: No. 115). 52p. 1995. pap. 22.00 (*0-8213-3192-2*, 13192) World Bank.

— Health Care in Jamaica: Quality, Outcomes, & Labor Supply. LC 95-17080. (LSMS Working Papers: No. 116). 40p. 1995. pap. 22.00 (*0-8213-3243-0*, 13243) World Bank.

— The Impact of the Quality of Health Care on Children's Nutrition & Survival in Ghana. LC 94-41226. (LSMS Working Papers: No. 106). 62p. 1995. pap. 22.00 (*0-8213-2997-9*, 12997) World Bank.

Lavy, Victor, jt. auth. see Behrman, Jere R.

Lavy, Victor, jt. auth. see Hanushek, Eric A.

***Law.** Allyn & Bacon Guide to MLA Documentation of Electronic Sources. 32p. 1998. write for info. (*0-205-29790-0*) Allyn.

Law. The Early Identification of Language Impairment in Children. 214p. 1992. 42.50 (*1-56593-026-6*, 0270) Singular Publishing.

***Law.** Little Book of God's Love. (J). 1999. pap. 7.50 (*0-7459-4074-9*, Pub. by Lion Pubng) Trafalgar.

— Little Book of God's Promises. (J). 1999. pap. 7.50 (*0-7459-4075-7*, Pub. by Lion Pubng) Trafalgar.

— Little Book of Short Prayers. 1998. pap. 7.50 (*0-7459-4062-5*, Pub. by Lion Pubng) Trafalgar.

— Little Book of Spiritual Wisdom. 1998. pap. 7.50 (*0-7459-4063-3*, Pub. by Lion Pubng) Trafalgar.

Law. A Serious Call to a Devout & Holy Life. 1959. pap. 2.00 (*0-8358-0061-X*) Upper Room Bks.

— Suffrage & Power, 1918-1928. 224p. 1997. text 59.50 (*1-86064-201-2*, Pub. by I B T) St Martin.

Law, jt. auth. see DeWeese.

Law & Business Inc. Staff. Advising Corporations on Merger, Acquisition, & Takeover Situations. LC 85-242505. (Illus.). iv, 442p. 40.00 (*0-685-13426-1*) Harcourt.

Law & Business Inc. Staff, ed. Law & Business Directory of Corporate Counsel, 1982-1983. enl. rev. ed. 1496p. 1982. 110.00 (*0-686-89146-5*, H42787) Harcourt.

— Law & Business Directory of Corporate Counsel, 1984-1985. rev. ed. 1546p. 1984. 125.00 (*0-15-004278-7*) Harcourt.

— Law & Business Directory of Major U. S. Law Firms, 2 vols. 1800p. 1984. 200.00 (*0-15-004293-0*) Harcourt.

— The Lawyer's Almanac, 1984. 1984. 45.00 (*0-317-12324-6*) Harcourt.

— The Lawyer's Almanac, 1985: An Encyclopedia of Information about Law, Lawyers, & the Profession. 1018p. 1985. 60.00 (*0-317-29466-0*, #H4383X) Harcourt.

— Legal Times of Washington D.C. Circuit Handbook. 1061p. 1980. ring bd. 55.00 (*0-686-89148-1*, H39867) Harcourt.

— Legal Times of Washington D.C. Circuit Handbook. 1061p. 1982. suppl. ed. 35.00 (*0-686-89149-X*) Harcourt.

— Practical Guide to the Tax Act of 1984. LC 84-27795. 243p. 1985. 60.00 (*0-15-004375-9*) Harcourt.

Law & Business Inc. Staff & Annas, George J. American Health Law. 1990. 54.00 (*0-316-04309-5*, Aspen Law & Bus) Aspen Pub.

Law & Business Inc. Staff & Legal Business Seminars Staff, eds. Executive Compensation & Employee Benefits. (Seminar Course Handbks.). 1983. pap. 30.00 (*0-686-89369-7*, C01058) Harcourt.

Law & Business Inc. Staff & Legal Times Seminars Staff, eds. Age Discrimination. (Seminar Course Handbks.). 1983. pap. 30.00 (*0-686-89354-9*, C01139) Harcourt.

— Asbestos Litigation. (Seminar Course Handbks.). 1983. pap. 30.00 (*0-686-89355-7*, C01104) Harcourt.

— Contesting Computer Disputes. (Seminar Course Handbks.). 1983. pap. 30.00 (*0-686-89333-6*, C00957) Harcourt.

— Equipment Leasing & Leveraged Leasing under the Tax Equity & Fiscal Responsibility Act of 1982. (Seminar Course Handbks.). 1983. pap. 30.00 (*0-686-89368-9*, C01430) Harcourt.

— Foreign Investment in U. S. Real Estate. (Seminar Course Handbks.). 1983. pap. 30.00 (*0-686-89370-0*, C0071X) Harcourt.

— Hazardous Waste Update. (Seminar Course Handbks.). 1983. pap. 30.00 (*0-686-89376-X*, C00760) Harcourt.

— How to Practice Before the New Court of Appeals. (Seminar Course Handbks.). 1983. pap. 35.00 (*0-686-89356-5*, C01333) Harcourt.

— Lease Financing. LC 82-9507. (Seminar Course Handbks.). 1983. pap. 30.00 (*0-686-89371-9*, C01074) Harcourt.

— Litigating Against the U. S. Government. (Seminar Course Handbks.). 1983. pap. 30.00 (*0-686-89357-3*, C00906) Harcourt.

— New Directions at the Department of the Interior. (Seminar Course Handbks.). 1983. pap. 30.00 (*0-686-89377-8*, C00981) Harcourt.

— New Exemptions from SEC Regulations. (Seminar Course Handbks.). 1983. pap. 30.00 (*0-686-89348-4*, C01228) Harcourt.

— Pensions & Employee Benefits. (Seminar Course Handbks.). 1983. pap. 30.00 (*0-686-89372-7*, C01473) Harcourt.

— Regulatory Impact Analysis. (Seminar Course Handbks.). 1983. pap. 30.00 (*0-686-89378-6*, C00982) Harcourt.

— Rescuing & Revitalizing Thrift Institutions. (Seminar Course Handbks.). 1983. pap. 30.00 (*0-686-89349-2*, C00930) Harcourt.

— SEC Consent Decrees, 2 vol., Set. (Seminar Course Handbks.). 1983. pap. 30.00 (*0-686-89352-2*, S00161) Harcourt.

— Second Annual Securities Activities of Banks. (Seminar Course Handbks.). 1983. pap. 35.00 (*0-686-89350-6*, C01376) Harcourt.

— Securities Law & Enforcement, 1982. (Seminar Course Handbks.). 1983. pap. 30.00 (*0-686-89351-4*, C01147) Harcourt.

— Shared Appreciation Mortgages. (Seminar Course Handbks.). 1983. pap. 30.00 (*0-686-89373-5*, C00868) Harcourt.

— Tax Shelter Controversies. (Seminar Course Handbks.). 1983. pap. 35.00 (*0-686-89375-1*, C01384) Harcourt.

— Thrift Acquisitions: FDIC & FHLBB Speak. (Seminar Course Handbks.). 1983. pap. 35.00 (*0-686-89353-0*, C01198) Harcourt.

Law & Business Inc. Staff & Mathews, Arthur F. Civil RICO Litigation. 40.00 (*0-685-14422-4*) Harcourt.

— Rico: Expanding Uses in Civil Litigation. v, 649p. write for info. (*0-318-58374-7*) Harcourt.

Law & Business Inc. Staff & Sanders, Michael I. New Tactics for Real Estate Syndication under the 1984 Tax Act. (Illus.). write for info. (*0-318-59551-6*) Harcourt.

Law & Business Inc. Staff & Wallison, Peter J. State Banking Regulation & Deregulation. write for info. (*0-318-60227-X*) Harcourt.

Law & Business Inc. Staff, et al. Abbreviated New Drug Applications. (Illus.). iv, 122p. write for info. (*0-318-60198-2*) Harcourt.

— Entrepreneurial Health Care: How to Structure New Ventures. (Illus.). v, 316p. write for info. (*0-318-60199-0*) Harcourt.

— Municipal & Agency Securities after WPPSS. vi, 509p. write for info. (*0-318-58371-2*) Harcourt.

— New Patent Interference Rules Implementing Patent Law Amendments Act of 1984. (Illus.). xi, 299p. write for info. (*0-318-60203-2*) Harcourt.

— The New Telecommunications Landscape. iv, 199p. write for info. (*0-318-58373-9*) Harcourt.

— State Taxation of Multi-National Corporations after Container Corporation: Corporate Strategies to Deal with Worldwide Unitary Tax. (Illus.). v, 203p. write for info. (*0-318-57920-0*) Harcourt.

Law & Business Inc. Staff, ed. see Cooper, R. John & Sanford, Bruce W.

Law, Alexander, ed. Robert Fergusson: Scots Poems. 70p. 1986. 20.00 (*0-85411-022-4*, Pub. by Saltire Soc) St Mut.

Law, Alma. Meyerhold Speaks/Meyerhold Rehearses. (Russian Theatre Archive Ser.). (Illus.). 288p. 1998. text 53.00 (*90-5702-044-0*, Harwood Acad Pubs); pap. text 18.00 (*90-5702-045-9*, Harwood Acad Pubs) Gordon & Breach.

Law, Alma, ed. Aleksandr Vampilov: The Major Plays. (Russian Theatre Archive Ser.: Vol. 6). 363p. 1996. text 82.00 (*3-7186-5584-5*, ECU66, Harwood Acad Pubs); pap. text 18.00 (*3-7186-5585-3*, ECU22, Harwood Acad Pubs) Gordon & Breach.

Law, Alma & Gordon, Mel. Meyerhold, Eisenstein & Biomechanics: Actor Training in Revolutionary Russia. LC 95-42738. (Illus.). 294p. 1995. lib. bdg. 47.50 (*0-7864-0098-6*) McFarland & Co.

Law, Alma H., tr. see Vampilov, Aleksandr.

Law and Business, creator. Competition in Contracting. 35.00 (*0-317-29645-0*, #CO3557) Harcourt.

Law, Andy. Creative Company: How St. Luke's Became "The Ad Agency to End All Ad Agencies" LC 99-28937. (Adweek Ser.). 269p. 1999. 29.95 (*0-471-35026-5*) Wiley.

Law, Anne L., jt. auth. see Anselmi, Dina.

Law Associates of Philadelphia Staff. The Law Association of Philadelphia: Addresses Delivered March 13, 1902, & Papers Prepared or Republished to Commemorate the Centennial Celebration of the Law Association of Philadelphia, Pennsylvania, 1802-1902. xii, 462p. 1998. reprint ed. 158.00 (*1-56169-413-4*) Gaunt.

Law, Averill & Kelton, David M. Simulation Modeling & Analysis. 3rd ed. LC 99-52146. 784p. 1999. 95.63 (*0-07-059292-6*) McGraw.

Law, Averill M. & Kelton, W. David. Simulation Modeling & Analysis. 2nd ed. (Industrial Engineering & Management Science Ser.). (Illus.). 544p. (C). 1991. 103.44 (*0-07-036698-5*) McGraw.

Law, B. A., ed. Microbiology & Biochemistry of Cheese & Fermented Milk. 2nd ed. LC 96-86400. 365p. 1997. 169.00 (*0-7514-0346-6*) Chapman & Hall.

Law, B. C. A History of Pali Literature, 2 vols. 1972. lib. bdg. 600.00 (*0-87968-535-2*) Krishna Pr.

Law, B. C., tr. The Debates Commentary. (C). 1940. 31.90 (*0-86013-019-3*, Pub. by Pali Text) Elsevier.

— Designation of Human Types. (C). 1922. 17.90 (*0-86013-009-6*, Pub. by Pali Text) Elsevier.

— The Legend of the Topes. (C). 1986. 13.50 (*81-7069-000-5*, Pub. by M Manoharial) S Asia.

Law, B. W. & Law, R. G. From Reason to Romanticism. LC 72-4541. (Studies in French Literature: No. 45). 1972. reprint ed. lib. bdg. 75.00 (*0-8383-1595-X*) M S G Haskell Hse.

Law, Barbara & Eckes, Mary. Assessment & ESL: On the Yellow Big Road to the Withered of Oz. (Illus.). 328p. 1995. pap., teacher ed. 21.00 (*1-895411-77-7*) Peguis Pubs Ltd.

— The More Than Just Surviving Handbook: ESL for Every Classroom Teacher. (Illus.). 209p. (Orig.). (gr. k-12). 1990. pap., teacher ed. 19.00 (*0-920541-98-4*) Peguis Pubs Ltd.

***Law, Barry A.** Technology of Cheesemaking LC 99-28556. (Sheffield Food Technology Ser.). 1999. write for info. (*0-8493-9744-8*) CRC Pr.

Law, Barry A., jt. auth. see Tamime, A. Y.

Law, Ben E., et al, eds. Abnormal Pressures in Hydrocarbon Environments: An Outgrowth of the AAPG Hedberg Research Conference, Golden, Colorado, June 8-10, 1994. LC 98-202431. (Memoir Ser.: Vol. 70). (Illus.). xiii, 264p. 1998. 89.00 (*0-89181-350-0*, 554) AAPG.

Law, Ben E. & Rice, Dudley D., eds. Hydrocarbons from Coal. LC 94-122178. (AAPG Studies in Geology: No. 38). (Illus.). 408p. 1993. reprint ed. pap. 126.50 (*0-608-02950-5*, 206341500006) Bks Demand.

Law, Bill. The Pre-Vocational Franchise: Organising Community-Linked Education for Adult & Working Life. 224p. (C). 1986. pap. 50.00 (*0-06-318354-4*, Pub. by P Chapman) St Mut.

Law, Bill, ed. Uses & Abuses of Profiling: A Handbook on Reviewing & Recording Student Experience & Achievement. 192p. (C). 1984. 50.00 (*0-06-318300-5*, Pub. by P Chapman) St Mut.

***Law, Bimala C.** History of Pali Literature. 2000. 49.50 (*81-86569-18-9*, Pub. by Indica Bks) S Asia.

Law, Bimala C. The Buddhist Conception of Spirits. 2nd enl. rev. ed. LC 78-72462. reprint ed. 32.50 (*0-404-17334-9*) AMS Pr.

— The Life & Work of Buddhaghosa. LC 98-905010. xii, 183 p. 1997. write for info. (*81-206-1096-2*) Asian Educ Servs.

— Some Ksatriya Tribes of Ancient India. LC 78-72468. reprint ed. 42.00 (*0-404-17338-1*) AMS Pr.

Law, Bimala C. ed. Buddhistic Studies. LC 78-72463. reprint ed. 74.50 (*0-404-17335-7*) AMS Pr.

— Geography of Early Buddhism. LC 78-72464. reprint ed. 32.50 (*0-404-17336-5*) AMS Pr.

— Historical Gleanings. LC 78-72466. reprint ed. 20.00 (*0-404-17337-3*) AMS Pr.

— A History of Pali Literature, 2 vols. LC 78-72467. reprint ed. 75.00 (*0-404-17650-X*) AMS Pr.

— A Study of the Mahavastu. LC 78-72469. reprint ed. 32.50 (*0-404-17339-X*) AMS Pr.

Law, Bimala Churn, tr. see Dhamma-Kitti.

Law, Bimla C. Concept of Buddhism. 142p. 1986. 22.95 (*0-318-37011-5*) Asia Bk Corp.

— Concepts of Buddhism. (C). 1986. 9.00 (*0-8364-2830-7*, Pub. by Gian Publng Hse) S Asia.

Law, Bob. Voices from the Future: A Contemporary Look at African Wisdom That Provides a Blueprint for the Future. 110p. 1998. pap. 14.95 (*0-913543-57-8*) African Am Imag.

Law, Carolyn L., jt. ed. see Dews, C. L.

Law, Carolyn Leste, jt. ed. see Dews, Carlos L.

Law, Charles J. Tech Prep Education: A Total Quality Approach. LC 93-60982. 250p. 1995. 35.95 (*1-56676-086-0*) Scarecrow.

***Law, Cheryl.** Suffrage & Power: The Women's Movement 1918-1928. 2000. pap. 22.50 (*1-86064-478-3*, Pub. by I B T) St Martin.

— Women a Modern Political Dictionary. 2000. text 35.00 (*1-86064-502-X*, Pub. by I B T) St Martin.

Law, Christopher M. Tourism in Major Cities. (Tourism & Hospitality Management Ser.). 256p. 1996. pap. 47.00 (*0-415-08986-7*) Thomson Learn.

Law, Christopher M., et al. The Uncertain Future of the Urban Core. LC 89-101872. (Geography & Environment Ser.). (Illus.). 267p. reprint ed. pap. 82.80 (*0-608-20358-0*, 207161100002) Bks Demand.

***Law, Cortez R., III.** My Brother's Keeper. viii, 194p. 1999. pap. 10.99 (*0-9673478-0-7*) Issues of Blood.

Law, Daniel, tr. see Stibbs, Alan N.

Law, David, jt. auth. see Gill, Stephen.

Law, David A. From Samaria to Samarkand: The Ten Lost Tribes of Israel. 228p. (C). 1992. lib. bdg. 45.00 (*0-8191-8409-8*) U Pr of Amer.

— Russian Civilization. (Illus.). 490p. (C). 1975. 39.50 (*0-8422-5232-0*); pap. text 15.50 (*0-8422-0529-2*) Irvington.

Law, David B., jt. ed. see Carapezza, Edward M.

Law, David R. The Hiddenness of God: Negative Theology in the Pseudonymous Works of Kierkegaard. LC 92-24777. (Oxford Theological Monographs). 242p. (C). 1993. text 55.00 (*0-19-826336-8*, Clarendon Pr) OUP.

Law, David R., tr. see Thielicke, Helmut.

Law, Deborah. Growing Fuchsias. 2nd ed. (Growing Ser.). (Illus.). 96p. 1993. reprint ed. pap. 11.95 (*0-86417-297-4*, Pub. by Kangaroo Pr) Seven Hills Bk.

***Law, Deborah.** Growing Fuchsias. 3rd ed. (Growing Ser.). 1998. pap. 14.95 (*0-86417-870-0*, Pub. by Kangaroo Pr) Seven Hills Bk.

Law, Deborah, jt. auth. see Degnen, Lisa.

Law, Debra T. Expecting: Quick Reference Guide to Childbirth. rev. ed. (Illus.). 122p. (C). 1989. student ed. write for info. (*0-318-66610-3*); pap. text. write for info. (*0-318-66609-X*) Imprint Commns.

Law, Dennis L. Mined-Land Rehabilitation. 198p. (C). 1984. text 39.95 (*0-442-25987-5*) Krieger.

Law, Derek G., jt. auth. see Elkin, Judith.

Law, Donald, ed. see Burns, Robert.

Law, Donald F., jt. auth. see Hinkle, Joseph D.

Law, E., ed. see Freeman, Don.

Law, Elizabeth. Double Deception. 1989. mass mkt. 2.95 (*0-8217-2825-3*, Zebra Kensgtn) Kensgtn Pub Corp.

— Double Deception. 224p. 1987. 16.95 (*0-8027-0950-8*) Walker & Co.

***Law, Elizabeth.** Flower Fairies Gardener's Year. (Illus.). (J). 2000. text 12.00 (*0-7232-4492-8*) F Warne Pubs.

Law, Elizabeth. Regency Morning. 1990. mass mkt. 2.95 (*0-8217-3152-1*, Zebra Kensgtn) Kensgtn Pub Corp.

— Regency Morning. 224p. 1988. 17.95 (*0-8027-1043-3*) Walker & Co.

Law, Elizabeth. Scent of Lilac. 25.95 (*0-8027-1010-7*) Walker & Co.

— The Sealed Knot. 224p. 1989. 18.95 (*0-8027-1085-9*) Walker & Co.

Law, Ellen. Torn Pages. (Illus.). 16p. 1997. 14.95 (*0-9649922-5-6*) Deforest Pr.

***Law, Eric H. F.** Inclusion: Making Room for Grace. 2000. pap. 15.99 (*0-8272-1620-3*) Chalice Pr.

Law, Eric H. F. The Wolf Shall Dwell with the Lamb: A Spirituality for Leadership in a Multicultural Community. LC 93-9205. 152p. (Orig.). 1993. pap. 14.99 (*0-8272-4231-X*) Chalice Pr.

Law, Eric H.F. The Bush Was Blazing but Not Consumed: Developing a Multi Cultural Community Through Dialogue & Liturgy. LC 96-34936. 144p. (Orig.). 1997. pap. 16.99 (*0-8272-0222-9*) Chalice Pr.

Law Firm of Parsons, Behle & Latimer Staff. Utah Environmental Law Handbook. 2nd rev. ed. LC 98-120595. 209p. 1998. pap. text 89.00 (*0-86587-614-2*, 614) Gov Insts.

Law Firm of Sidley & Austin Staff. Illinois Environmental Law Handbook. 4th rev. ed. LC 98-155027. 371p. 1998. pap. text 95.00 (*0-86587-618-5*, 618) Gov Insts.

Law, Frank. Through the Eyes of an Adoptee Vol. 1: One Man's Compelling Search for His Beginnings. LC 96-94346. (Illus.). 130p. (Orig.). 1996. pap. 10.95 (*0-9652437-3-7*) Gann Pubng.

Law, Frederick H. Modern Great Americans. LC 72-99706. (Essay Index Reprint Ser.). 1977. 26.95 (*0-8369-1417-1*) Ayer.

Law, Frederick H., ed. Modern Plays, Short & Long. (Play Anthology Reprint Ser.). 1977. reprint ed. 29.95 (*0-8369-8250-9*) Ayer.

Law, Gordon T., Jr. & Reilly, Michael E. A Guide to Information on Closely Held Corporations. LC 86-32812. (Orig.). 1986. pap. text 4.00 (*0-9615917-1-4*) NY Ind Labor.

***Law, Graham.** Serializing Fiction in the Victorian Press. LC 00-31124. 2000. write for info. (*0-312-23574-7*) St Martin.

Law, Graham, ed. The Evil Genius: Wilkie Collins. 280p. 1994. pap. 12.95 (*1-55111-017-2*) Broadview Pr.

Law, Graham, jt. auth. see Poole, Trevor.

Law, Graham, ed. see Dickens, Charles.

An Asterisk (*) at the beginning of an entry indicates that the title is appearing for the first time.

***Law, Gwillim.** Administrative Subdivisions of Countries: A Comprehensive World Reference, 1900 Through 1998. LC 99-34429. (Illus.). 463p. 1999. lib. bdg. 95.00 (*0-7864-0729-8*) McFarland & Co.

Law, Hamish, jt. auth. see Lamb, Douglas W.

Law, Harriet, ed. see Shakespeare, William.

Law, Harry D. The Organic Chemistry of Peptides. LC 75-126888. 243p. reprint ed. pap. 75.40 (*0-608-14049-X*, 202401500035) Bks Demand.

Law, Helen M., tr. see De Paul, Vincent.

Law, Henry. The Gospel in Genesis. 188p. 1993. reprint ed. pap. text 6.99 (*0-85151-038-8*) Banner of Truth.

Law, Henry G., et al, eds. Research Methods for Multi-Mode Data Analysis. 272p. 1984. 95.00 (*0-275-91210-8*, C1210, Praeger Pubs) Greenwood.

Law, Hugh T. How to Trace Your Ancestors to Europe: 117 Stories, Procedures, Sources to Use for 24 countries, Vol. 1. (Illus.). 422p. (Orig.). 1987. 19.00 (*0-935775-01-3*) Cottonwood Bks.

***Law, I.** Harnessing Outsourcing for Business Advantage. (Management Briefings Ser.). (Illus.). 1999. pap. 127.50 (*0-273-63723-1*, Pub. by F T P-H) Trans-Atl Phila.

Law, Ian. Racism, Ethnicity, & Social Policy. LC 96-498. (Contemporary Social Policy Ser.). 208p. (C). 1996. pap. text 24.95 (*0-13-354093-6*) P-H.

Law in the Service of Man, Al Haq Staff. Punishing a Nation: Israeli Human Rights Violations During the Palestinian Uprising. 300p. (Orig.). (C). 1990. 40.00 (*0-89608-379-9*); pap. 16.00 (*0-89608-378-0*) South End Pr.

Law, Ivan. Gears & Gear Cutting. (Workshop Practice Ser.: No. 17). (Illus.). 136p. (Orig.). 1987. pap. 19.95 (*0-85242-911-8*, Pub. by Nexus Special Interests) Trans-Atl Phila.

— Measuring & Marking Metals. (Workshop Practice Ser.: No. 6). (Illus.). 110p. 1985. pap. 21.50 (*0-85242-841-3*, Pub. by Nexus Special Interests) Trans-Atl Phila.

Law, J. Midi. 1992. pap. text 24.95 (*0-7195-5081-5*, Pub. by John Murray) Trafalgar.

Law, James & Elias, Jane. Trouble Talking: A Guide for Parents of Children with Difficulties Communicating. 200p. 1995. pap. text 27.50 (*1-85302-253-5*) Taylor & Francis.

Law, James, jt. auth. see Johnston, Hank.

Law, Jane M. Puppets of Nostalgia: The Life, Death, & Rebirth of the Japanese Awaji Ningyo Tradition. LC 96-33487. 321p. 1997. text 35.00 (*0-691-02894-X*, Pub. by Princeton U Pr) Cal Prin Full Svc.

Law, Jane M., ed. Religious Reflections on the Human Body. LC 94-4436. 336p. 1995. 35.00 (*0-253-33263-X*); pap. 15.95 (*0-253-20902-1*) Ind U Pr.

Law, Jane M., ed. see Eliade, Mircea.

Law, Janice. Backfire. (Worldwide Library Mysteries). 1996. per. 4.99 (*0-373-26201-9*, 1-26201-3, Wrldwide Lib) Harlequin Bks.

— Cross-Check. 256p. 1998. per. 4.99 (*0-373-26291-4*, 1-26291-4, Wrldwide Lib) Harlequin Bks.

***Law, Janice.** The Night Bus. LC 00-23938. 352p. 2000. 24.95 (*0-312-84882-X*, Pub. by Forge NYC) St Martin.

— The Night Bus. 19.95 (*0-312-87599-1*) St Martin.

Law, Janice. A Safe Place to Die. 1995. per. 3.99 (*0-373-26179-9*, 1-26179-1) Harlequin Bks.

— Time Lapse: An Anna Peters Mystery. (WWL Mystery Ser.). 1998. per. 4.99 (*0-373-26267-1*, 1-26267-4, Wrldwide Lib) Harlequin Bks.

***Law, Jennifer.** Go Ye Therefore. (Illus.). 46p. 1999. pap. 8.99 (*1-56309-362-6*, New Hope) Womans Mission Union.

— Thank You God for My Bible. Reeves, Rhonda, ed. (Missions & Me Ser.). (Illus.). 16p. (J). (ps). 1999. 7.99 (*1-56309-284-0*) Womans Mission Union.

Law, Jennifer, ed. see Burroughs, Esther.

Law, Jennifer, ed. see George, Denise.

Law, Jennifer, ed. see Joiner, Barbara.

Law, Jennifer, ed. see Leininger, Gayle, et al.

Law, Jennifer, ed. see Reeves, Rhonda.

Law, Jennifer, ed. see Richardson, Dawn.

Law, Jennifer, ed. see Strawn, Kathy, et al.

Law, Joan, jt. auth. see Ward, Barbara E.

Law, Joe & Hughes, Linda K., eds. Biographical Passages: Essays on Victorian & Modernist Biography. LC 99-48271. (Illus.). 224p. 2000. 34.95 (*0-8262-1256-5*) U of Mo Pr.

Law, Joe, jt. ed. see Murphy, Christina.

***Law, Joe E.** Maneuvers in Terror. 173p. 1999. pap. 13.95 (*0-7414-0142-8*) Buy Books.

Law, John. Money & Trade Considered: With a Proposal for Supplying the Nation with Money. LC 65-19649. (Library of Money & Banking History). 120p. 1966. reprint ed. 35.00 (*0-678-00187-1*) Kelley.

— Out of Work. (Radical Fiction Ser.). 304p. 1990. reprint ed. lib. bdg. 25.00 (*0-929587-39-1*) I R Dee.

Law, John & Hassard, John, eds. Actor Network Theory & After. LC 99-21566. (Sociological Review Monographs). 264p. 1999. pap. 34.95 (*0-631-21194-2*) Blackwell Pubs.

Law, John, jt. ed. see Bijker, Wiebe E.

Law, John, tr. see Latour, Bruno.

Law, John A. Adger - Law Ancestral Notebook. 159p. 1997. reprint ed. pap. 26.00 (*0-8328-7219-9*); reprint ed. lib. bdg. 36.00 (*0-8328-7218-0*) Higginson Bk Co.

Law, John W. Curse of the Silver Screen: Tragedy & Disaster Behind the Movies. (Illus.). 145p. 1998. pap. 12.95 (*0-9665676-0-9*) Aplomb Pubg.

Law, Jonathan. The Mammoth Book of 1001 Great Lives. LC 96-152774. (Mammoth Book Ser.). 512p. 1996. pap. 9.95 (*0-7867-0298-2*) Carroll & Graf.

Law, Jonathan & Isaacs, Alan, eds. European Culture: A Contemporary Companion. (European Reference Ser.). 416p. 1996. pap. 18.95 (*0-304-32720-4*) Continuum.

***Law, Joy.** Guide to Dordogne. 420p. 1999. pap. 24.95 (*1-873429-28-2*) Cimino Pub Grp.

Law, Judge. Colonial History of Vincennes: Under the French, British & American Governments, from Its First Settlement to the Territorial Administration of General William Henry Harrison. (Illus.). 157p. 1997. reprint ed. pap. 21.50 (*0-8328-6669-5*); reprint ed. lib. bdg. 29.50 (*0-8328-6668-7*) Higginson Bk Co.

Law, Jules D. The Rhetoric of Empiricism: Language & Perception, from Locke to I. A. Richards. LC 92-44276. 280p. (C). 1993. text 39.95 (*0-8014-2706-1*) Cornell U Pr.

Law, Julian. The Parole Game: Know Your Rights! 37p. 1998. 12.00 (*0-9639452-1-1*) Lerner Pub.

Law, K. H., ed. Engineering Data Management & Emerging Technologies, Vol. 7. LC 95-81285. (1995 ASME International Mechanical Engineering Congress & Exposition Ser.: CED-Vol. 7). 124p. 1995. 56.00 (*0-7918-1748-2*, H01027) ASME.

Law, K. K., jt. auth. see Duncan, J. P.

Law, K. T., jt. auth. see Wang, J. G.

Law, Katheryn. Salish Folk Tales. (Indian Culture Ser.). (J). (gr. 2-8). 1972. pap. 1.95 (*0-89992-028-4*) Coun India Ed.

Law, Keith. Hockey Prospectus 1999. 1999. pap. text 19.95 (*1-57488-213-9*) Brasseys.

***Law, Kendra.** The Cello Activity Bk. I: Chelsea Cello & Buddy Bow. (Illus.). 50p. (J). (ps up). 1999. wbk. ed. 12.95 (*1-930031-01-7*) Music Magic CO.

— The Violin Activity: Freddy Fiddle & Betty Bow, Bk. 1. (Illus.). 50p. (J). (ps up). 1999. wbk. ed. 12.95 (*1-930031-00-9*) Music Magic CO.

— The Violin Activity: Freddy Fiddle & Betty Bow, Bk. 2. (Illus.). 50p. (J). (ps up). 1999. wbk. ed. 12.95 (*1-930031-02-5*) Music Magic CO.

Law, Kenneth S., jt. auth. see Behling, Orlando.

Law, Kevin, ed. see Bowden, Vicky R., et al.

Law, Kevin J. Millard Fillmore: Thirteenth President of the United States. Young, Richard G., ed. LC 89-25651. (Presidents of the United States Ser.). (Illus.). 128p. (J). (gr. 5-9). 1990. lib. bdg. 19.93 (*0-944483-61-5*) Garrett Ed Corp.

Law Librarians' Society of the District of Columbia Staff. Union of Legislative Histories: 47th Congress, 1881-101st Congress, 1990. 6th ed. LC 91-31271. xxix, 605p. 1991. ring bd., suppl. ed. 95.00 (*0-8377-2705-7*, Rothman) W S Hein.

Law, Lisa. Flashing on the Sixties. LC 97-17228. (Illus.). 144p. 1997. pap. text 18.95 (*0-8118-1814-4*) Chronicle Bks.

***Law, Lisa.** Flashing on the Sixties. 2000. pap. 19.95 (*0-916290-81-6*) Squarebooks.

Law, Lisa. Interviews with Icons: Flashing on the '60s. (Illus.). 285p. 1999. pap. 20.00 (*0-930829-44-1*, Pub. by Lumen Inc) Consort Bk Sales.

***Law, Lisa.** Sex Work in Southeast Asia: The Place of Desire in a Time of Aids. LC 99-87581. 224p. 2000. write for info. (*0-415-21805-5*) Routledge.

Law, Louise Darragh, jt. auth. see Darragh, Francis.

***Law, Mary.** Evidence Based Practice: A Primer. (Illus.). 250p. 2000. pap. text 30.00 (*1-55642-453-1*) SLACK Inc.

Law, Mary, ed. Family-Centered Assessment & Intervention in Pediatric Rehabilitation. LC 98-23945. 107p. 1998. 39.95 (*0-7890-0539-5*) Haworth Pr.

Law, Mary, et al. Measurement of Occupational Performance: A Guide to Best Practice. 250p. 2000. pap. 38.00 (*1-55642-298-9*, 32989) SLACK Inc.

Law, Mary C. Client-Centered Occupational Therapy. LC 98-17783. (Illus.). 192p. 1998. pap. text 30.00 (*1-55642-264-4*, 32644) SLACK Inc.

Law, Merry E. Checklist. (Moving Abroad Ser.). 45p. 1998. pap. 11.95 (*0-9644773-1-9*) WorldView Pubns.

— A Guide to International Measurements. (Illus.). 65p. (Orig.). 1994. pap. 19.95 (*0-9644773-0-0*) WorldView Pubns.

Law, Narendra N. Studies in Indian History & Culture. 1990. reprint ed. 17.50 (*0-8364-2516-2*, Pub. by Low Price) S Asia.

Law, Norman & Smith, David. Problem-Solving Geography Analysis in a Changing World: Analysis in a Changing World. (Illus.). 240p. (Orig.). 1993. pap. 36.50 (*0-7487-1355-7*, Pub. by S Thornes Pubs) Trans-Atl Phila.

Law of the Sea Institute Staff, et al. Sustainable Development & Preservation of the Oceans: The Challenges of UNCLOS & Agenda 21. LC 97-4222. 1997. write for info. (*0-911189-32-7*) Law Sea Inst.

Law, P. K., et al, eds. Nondestructive Evaluation & Material Properties III. LC 96-80437. (Illus.). 127p. 1997. 94.00 (*0-87339-343-0*, 3430) Minerals Metals.

***Law, Philip.** Saviour: The Life of Christ in Words & Paintings. (Illus.). 2000. 19.95 (*0-8294-1561-0*) Loyola Pr.

— Teachings of the Master: The Collected Sayings of Jesus Christ. 129p. 2000. 15.95 (*0-664-22282-X*) Westminster John Knox.

Law, Philip. Wisdom of the Apostles. LC 97-180455. (Wisdom Ser.). 48p. 1997. 8.00 (*0-8028-3852-9*) Eerdmans.

***Law, Philip.** The Wisdom of the Prophets. (Wisdom of Ser.). (Illus.). 48p. 2000. 6.95 (*0-664-22214-5*, Pub. by Westminster John Knox) Presbyterian Pub.

***Law, Philip, ed.** The Wisdom of Solomon. (Wisdom of Ser.). (Illus.). 48p. 2000. 6.95 (*0-664-22209-9*, Pub. by Westminster John Knox) Presbyterian Pub.

Law, Phillip. The Antarctic Voyage of HMAS Wyatt Earp. (Illus.). 158p. 1995. pap. 29.95 (*1-86373-803-7*) Paul & Co Pubs.

Law, Phlip. A Time to Pray: 365 Classical Prayers. 256p. 1998. boxed set 20.00 (*0-687-08574-8*) Abingdon.

Law, Preston E. Shipboard Antennas. LC 82-72892. (Illus.). 561p. reprint ed. pap. 159.90 (*0-608-16031-8*, 2033130) Bks Demand.

— Shipboard Antennas. 2nd ed. LC 86-70448. (Artech House Antenna Library). (Illus.). 566p. 1986. reprint ed. pap. 175.50 (*0-7837-4725-X*, 204429000004) Bks Demand.

Law, Preston E., Jr. Shipboard Electromagnetics. 320p. 1987. text. write for info. (*0-89006-247-1*) Artech Hse.

Law, Preston E. Shipboard Electromagnetics. LC 87-19293. (Artech House Antenna Library). (Illus.). 278p. reprint ed. pap. 86.20 (*0-8357-7926-2*, 203635200002) Bks Demand.

Law, R., et al, eds. The Exploitation of Evolving Resources: Proceedings of an International Conference Held at Julich, Germany, September 3-5, 1991. LC 93-32081. (Lecture Notes in Biomathematics Ser.: Vol. 99). 1993. 50.00 (*3-540-57242-2*) Spr-Verlag.

Law, R. G., jt. auth. see Law, B. W.

Law, R. J., jt. auth. see Owen, John.

Law, R. J., ed. see Owen, John.

Law, Rachel N. & Taylor, Cynthia W. Appalachian White Oak Basketmaking: Handing down the Basket. LC 90-12043. 328p. 1991. pap. 19.95 (*0-87049-672-7*) U of Tenn Pr.

Law Reform Commission of Canada Staff. Trial Within a Reasonable Time: Working Paper Prepared for the Law Reform Commission of Canada. 122p. (Orig.). 1994. pap. 38.95 (*0-660-59103-0*, Pub. by Canadian Govt Pub) Accents Pubns.

Law Reform Commission of Tasmania Staff. Report & Recommendations on Proposal for Drivers Who Have Been Disqualified for Drink/Driving Offences to Be Required to Undertake a Course Before Being Re-Issued with a Licence to Drive a Motor Vehicle LC 80-482760. (Report & Law Reform Commission Ser.), 6 p. 1978. write for info. (*0-7246-0604-1*, Pub. by Tasmanian Govt Print) Lubrecht & Cramer.

Law, Robin. The Horse in West African History: The Role of the Horse in the Societies of Pre-Colonial West Africa. LC 81-129421. (Illus.). 248p. reprint ed. pap. 76.90 (*0-8357-3012-3*, 205709800010) Bks Demand.

— The Oyo Empire, c. 1600-c. 1836: A West African Imperialism in the Era of the Atlantic. (Modern Revivals in History Ser.). 354p. 1992. 63.95 (*0-7512-0006-9*, Pub. by Gregg Revivals) Ashgate Pub Co.

Law, Robin, ed. Correspondence of the Royal African Company's Chief Merchants at Cabo Corso Castle with William's Ort, Whydah, & the Little Popo Factory, 1727-1728: An Annotated Transcription of Ms. Francklin 1055-1 in the Bedfordshire County Record Office. LC 91-15880. (African Primary Texts Ser.: No. 3). 53p. (Orig.). 1991. pap. 15.00 (*0-942615-08-5*) U Wis African Stud.

— The English in West Africa, 1681-1683 Pt. 1: The Local Correspondence of the Royal African Company of England, 1681-1699, Pt. 1. LC 98-145166. (Fontes Historiae Africanae Ser.: No. 1). 382p. 1998. text 95.00 (*0-19-726176-0*) OUP.

— From Slave Trade to 'Legitimate' Commerce: The Commercial Transition in Nineteenth-Century West Africa. (African Studies: No. 86). 291p. (C). 1995. text 69.95 (*0-521-48127-9*) Cambridge U Pr.

— Further Correspondence of the Royal African Company of England Relating to the 'Slave Coast', 1681-1699: Selected Documents from Ms. Rawlinson c.745-747 in the Bodleian Library, Oxford. LC 92-11701. (African Primary Texts Ser.: No. 5). 100p. (Orig.). 1992. 15.00 (*0-942615-13-1*) U Wis African Stud.

Law, Robin, ed. see Lovejoy, Paul E.

Law, Robin, jt. ed. see Lovejoy, Paul E.

Law, Rod. Rod, Write On: Pts. I-VIII, 1970-80, Pts. I-VIII. (Orig.). (C). text 19.95 (*0-9601730-2-1*); pap. text 12.50 (*0-9601730-3-X*) Rod Law.

Law Rules Editorial Staff. Easy Review for Federal Estate & Gift Tax: With 2000 Supplement. Hollander, M., ed. 168p. 1998. pap. text 16.95 (*1-887426-38-8*) Law Rules.

Law, Ruth. Dim Sum: Fast & Festive Chinese Cooking. Crossman, Nancy, ed. LC 82-45410. (Illus.). 256p. 1985. reprint ed. pap. 9.95 (*0-9614250-9-1*) Whats Cooking.

— Indian Light Cooking: Delicious & Healthy Food from One of the World's Great Cuisines. LC 93-72588. 464p. 1994. pap. 25.00 (*1-55611-389-7*, Pub. by D I Fine) Penguin Putnam.

— Pacific Light Cooking. 1998. 27.50 (*1-55611-519-9*, Pub. by D I Fine) Penguin Putnam.

— The Southeast Asia Cookbook. (Illus.). 1990. pap. 28.00 (*1-55611-214-9*, Pub. by D I Fine) Penguin Putnam.

Law, S. K. & Reid, K. B. Complement: In Focus. 2nd ed. (In Focus Ser.). (Illus.). 100p. 1995. pap. text 19.95 (*0-19-963356-8*) OUP.

Law School Adimisson Council. The Official Guide to U. S. Law Schools 2000. (Illus.). 448p. 1999. pap. 20.00 (*0-8129-9046-3*, Times Bks) Crown Pub Group.

Law School Admission Council Staff. The Official Guide to U. S. Law School, 1999. LC 98-14303. 448p. 1998. pap. 20.00 (*0-7679-0078-2*) Broadway BDD.

— So You Want to Be a Lawyer. LC 98-169647. 160p. 1998. pap. 13.00 (*0-7679-0160-6*) Broadway BDD.

***Law School Admission Staff.** Official LSAT Preptests; 10 Actual. (LSAT Ser.). 1999. mass mkt. write for info. (*0-942639-63-4*) Law Schl Admission.

Law School Admissions Council Staff & Mitchell, Carolyn B. So You Want to Be a Lawyer. 1997. pap. 13.95 (*0-553-06889-X*) Broadway BDD.

Law School Admissions Services Staff. LSAT: Triple Prep, Vol. 2. (Kaplan Source Ser.). 128p. 1994. pap. 14.95 (*0-553-06226-3*) Bantam.

— LSAT the Official Triple Prep, Vol. 1. LC 97-221989. (Kaplan Source Ser.). 128p. (C). 1994. pap. 15.95 (*0-553-06222-0*) Bantam.

Law Student Division Members. Energy Methods: Keeping Fresh Under the Pressure of Law Practice. LC 80-81336. 42p. 1981. 2.75 (*0-685-14377-5*, 213-0001) Amer Bar Assn.

Law, Sue, jt. auth. see Glover, Derek.

Law, Susan K. The Last Man in Town. 384p. 1999. mass mkt. 5.99 (*0-380-80496-4*, Avon Bks) Morrow Avon.

***Law, Susan K.** The Most Wanted Bachelor. 384p. 2000. mass mkt. 5.99 (*0-380-80497-2*) Morrow Avon.

Law, T. S. La Verdad Sobre los Angelea.Tr. of Truth about Angels. (SPA.). 9.99 (*958-9354-18-1*, 550056) Editorial Unilit.

Law, Terry. How to Enter the Presence of God. 1994. pap. 9.99 (*0-932081-40-1*) Victory Hse.

— The Power of Praise & Worship. (Illus.). 256p. (Orig.). 1985. pap. 9.99 (*0-932081-01-0*) Victory Hse.

— Praise Releases Faith. 252p. (Orig.). 1987. pap. 9.99 (*0-932081-15-0*) Victory Hse.

— The Truth about Angels. 1994. pap. 11.99 (*0-88419-368-3*) Creation House.

— Your Spiritual Weapons & How to Use Them. (Orig.). 1983. pap. write for info. (*0-88144-028-0*, CPS028) Christian Pub.

Law-Trac Staff. Divorce: Your Fault, My Fault, No Fault. 3rd rev. ed. 1992. pap. text 11.95 (*0-940722-04-6*) Law-Trac Pr.

Law Union of Ontario Staff. The Immigrant's Handbook: A Critical Guide. LC 82-162049. (Black Rose Bks.: No. K68). 272p. 1981. pap. 84.40 (*0-608-00465-0*, 206128400007) Bks Demand.

Law, Victor J. & Teck, Kah Lim. Pascal/Macpascal. (C). 1986. ring bd. 54.37 (*0-697-03145-4*, Irwn McGrw-H) McGrw-H Hghr Educ.

Law, Vivien. The Insular Latin Grammarians. (Studies in Celtic History: No. III). 145p. (C). 1987. 75.00 (*0-85115-147-7*) Boydell & Brewer.

— Origin & Development of the Study of Language in the West. (C). 1997. text 90.00 (*0-485-11498-4*) Humanities.

— Wisdom, Authority & Grammar in the Seventh Century: Decoding Virgilius Maro Grammaticus. 180p. (C). 1995. text 54.95 (*0-521-47113-3*) Cambridge U Pr.

Law, Vivien, ed. History of Linguistic Thought in the Early Middle Ages. LC 93-5696. (Studies in the History of the Language Sciences: No. 71). viii, 255p. 1993. 59.00 (*1-55619-366-1*) J Benjamins Pubng Co.

Law, William. The Absolute Unlawfulness of the Stage Entertainment Fully Demonstrated. LC 75-170493. (English Stage Ser.: Vol. 49). 1973. lib. bdg. 64.00 (*0-8240-0632-1*) Garland.

— Daily Readings with William Law. Llewelyn, Robert, ed. (Daily Readings Ser.). 96p. 1987. pap. 4.95 (*0-87243-153-3*) Templegate.

— A Devout & Holy Life. 303p. (Orig.). 1996. mass mkt. 6.99 (*0-88368-463-2*) Whitaker Hse.

— Extracts from the Writings of William Law. 60p. 1992. reprint ed. pap. 12.95 (*1-56459-121-2*) Kessinger Pub.

— God's Power in You. LC 98-10097. 176p. 1998. pap. 6.99 (*0-88368-513-2*) Whitaker Hse.

— The Power of the Spirit. Hunt, D., ed. 1993. pap. 5.99 (*0-87508-247-5*) Chr Lit.

— Remarks upon a Late Book Entitled, the Fable of the Bees: 1725 Edition. 108p. 1996. reprint ed. 48.00 (*1-85506-127-9*) Bks Intl VA.

— The Search for Holy Living. Hinten, Marvin D., ed. & intro. by. (Essential Christian Library Ser.). 287p. 1999. 9.97 (*1-57748-446-0*) Barbour Pub.

— A Serious Call to a Devout & Holy Life. Meister, John et al, eds. LC 55-5330. 156p. 1968. reprint ed. pap. 13.95 (*0-664-24833-0*) Westminster John Knox.

***Law, William.** Total Devotion to God: Selected Writings of William Law. Wilburn, Stephen S., ed. LC 99-37905. (Spiritual Classics). 95p. 2000. pap. 5.00 (*0-8358-0901-3*) Upper Room Bks.

Law, William. William Law: Selections on the Interior Life. Morrison, Mary C., ed. LC 62-15272. (Orig.). 1962. pap. 4.00 (*0-87574-120-7*) Pendle Hill.

— William Law & Eighteenth-Century Quakerism. Hobhouse, Stephen, ed. LC 77-175870. (Illus.). 1972. reprint ed. 26.95 (*0-405-08736-5*) Ayer.

— The Works, 9 vols. in 3, Set. (Anglistica & Americana Ser.: No. 146). 1974. reprint ed. 323.70 (*3-487-05100-1*) G Olms Pubs.

— You Will Receive Power. LC 97-36560. 204p. 1997. pap. 6.99 (*0-88368-476-4*) Whitaker Hse.

Law, William, tr. see Boehme, Jacob.

Law, William L. Heart of Freedom. unabridged ed. LC 97-92700. (Illus.). ix, 384p. 1998. 29.95 (*0-9660838-0-6*) W L Law.

Lawaetz, Gudie, ed. Spanish Short Stories Two. 216p. 1993. pap. 12.95 (*0-14-003378-5*, Penguin Bks) Viking Penguin.

Lawal. Gelede Spectacle: Art, Gender & Social Harmony in an African Culture. LC 96-47862. (Illus.). xxiv, 327p. 1997. pap. 35.00 (*0-295-97599-7*) U of Wash Pr.

Lawal, Ibironke O., ed. Metalworking in Africa South of the Sahara: An Annotated Bibliography. 19. LC 95-7485. (African Special Bibliographic Ser.: No. 19). 288p. 1995. lib. bdg. 89.50 (*0-313-29324-4*, Greenwood Pr) Greenwood.

Lawall, David B., ed. John Barber, 1893-1965: Selections from the Archive. LC 92-72648. (Illus.). 224p. 1992. reprint ed. pap. 69.50 (*0-608-04241-2*, 206499700012) Bks Demand.

Lawall, Gilbert. Carmina Catulli I-XI. (J). (gr. 10-12). 1983. pap. 5.95 (*0-88334-166-2*) Longman.

— Ecce Romani, Vol. 2. 2nd ed. 1995. text, teacher ed. 54.08 (*0-8013-1218-3*) Addison-Wesley.

— The Romans Speak for Themselves. 1989. teacher ed. 7.50 (*0-8013-0269-2*, 78040) Longman.

— The Romans Speak for Themselves, Bk. I. 1988. pap. text 7.80 (*0-8013-0267-6*, 75919) Longman.

— The Romans Speak for Themselves, Bk. II. 1987. pap. text 7.80 (*0-8013-0268-4*, 78041) Longman.

Lawall, Gilbert, ed. Petronius: Selections from the Satyricon. (Textbook Ser.). (Illus.). 260p. (Orig.). 1995. pap. text 18.00 (*0-86516-288-3*) Bolchazy-Carducci.

L

L

— Plautus' Aulularia: The Pot of Gold; An Adaptation for Production by High School Latin Students. (LAT.). 35p. 1992. spiral bd. 3.25 (*0-939507-30-7*, B724) Amer Classical.

— Teacher's Handbook to the Longman Latin Readers. 1988. pap. text 13.95 (*0-582-36770-0*, 72542) Longman.

Lawall, Gilbert & Kindel, Gerde. The Phaedra of Seneca. 238p. 1989. pap. text 16.00 (*0-86516-016-3*) Bolchazy-Carducci.

Lawall, Gilbert & Quinn, Betty N. The Aulularia of Plautus. 1988. pap. text 14.88 (*0-582-36753-0*, 72529) Longman.

Lawall, Gilbert & Quinn, Betty N., eds. Plautus' Menaechmi. (Textbook Ser.). (Illus.). 200p. (Orig.). 1981. pap. 15.00 (*0-86516-007-4*) Bolchazy-Carducci.

Lawall, Gilbert & Tafe, David M. Ecce Romani, Bk. 2. 1990. pap. text, teacher ed. 10.44 (*0-8013-0445-8*, 78255) Longman.

Lawall, Gilbert, et al. Ecce Romani, Bk. 1. 1984. pap. text, teacher ed. 8.28 (*0-582-36730-1*, 72519); pap. text, student ed. 7.29 (*0-582-36664-X*, 72458) Longman.

— Ecce Romani, Bk. 1. 1986. pap. text, student ed. 6.04 (*0-582-36654-2*, 72448) Longman.

— Ecce Romani, Bk. 1. 1990. pap. text, teacher ed. 10.44 (*0-8013-0444-X*, 78254) Longman.

— Ecce Romani, Bk. 2. 1984. pap. text 7.29 (*0-582-36665-8*, 72459); pap. text, teacher ed. 8.28 (*0-582-36731-X*, 72520) Longman.

— Ecce Romani, Bk. 2. 1986. pap. text, student ed. 4.53 (*0-582-36655-0*, 72449) Longman.

— Ecce Romani, Bk. 3. 1984. pap. text, teacher ed. 8.28 (*0-582-36732-8*, 72521); pap. text, student ed. 4.53 (*0-582-36656-9*, 72450); pap. text, student ed. 7.29 (*0-582-36666-6*, 72460) Longman.

— Ecce Romani, Bk. 3. 1990. pap. text, teacher ed. 10.44 (*0-8013-0446-6*, 78256) Longman.

— Ecce Romani, Bk. 4. 1984. pap. text, teacher ed. 8.28 (*0-582-36733-6*, 72522); pap. text, student ed. 4.53 (*0-582-36657-7*, 72451); pap. text, student ed. 7.29 (*0-582-36667-4*, 72461) Longman.

— Ecce Romani, Bk. 4. 1990. pap. text, teacher ed. 10.44 (*0-8013-0447-4*, 78257) Longman.

— Ecce Romani, Bk. 5. 1984. pap. text, teacher ed. 8.28 (*0-582-36734-4*, 72523); pap. text, student ed. 4.53 (*0-582-36658-5*, 72452) Longman.

— Ecce Romani, Bk. 5. 1990. pap. text, teacher ed. 10.44 (*0-8013-0448-2*, 78258); pap. text, student ed. 7.29 (*0-8013-0559-4*, 78463) Longman.

— Ecce Romani, Set, Vol. I, Bks. 1-3. 1990. pap. text 31.08 (*0-8013-0646-9*, 78588) Longman.

— Ecce Romani, Set, Vol. II, Bks. 3-4. 1990. text, student ed. 24.96 (*0-8013-0440-7*, 78250) Longman.

— Ecce Romani, Set, Vol. II, Bks. 4-5. 1990. pap. text 23.31 (*0-582-99857-3*, 78587) Longman.

— Ecce Romani, Test 1. 1988. pap. text, student ed. 23.25 (*0-8013-0241-2*, 75897) Longman.

— Ecce Romani, Test 2. 1988. student ed. 23.25 (*0-8013-0242-0*, 75898) Longman.

— Ecce Romani, Test 3. 1991. pap., student ed. 24.20 (*0-8013-0538-1*, 78415) Longman.

Lawall, Gilbert, jt. auth. see Balme, Maurice G.

Lawall, Gilbert, jt. auth. see Davis, Sally.

Lawall, Gilbert, jt. auth. see Lawall, S.

Lawall, Robert, et al. Ecce Romani, Set, Vol. I, Bks. 1-2. 1990. text 24.96 (*0-8013-0439-3*, 78249) Longman.

Lawall, S. & Lawall, Gilbert. Euripides' Hippolytus: A Companion with Translation. (Classics Companions Ser.). 166p. 1986. pap. 18.95 (*0-86292-212-7*, Pub. by Brist Class Pr) Focus Pub-R Pullins.

Lawall, Sarah, ed. Reading World Literature: Theory, History, Practice. LC 94-4041. (Illus.). 376p. (C). 1994. text 55.00 (*0-292-74679-2*) U of Tex Pr.

Lawall, Sarah N. Critics of Consciousness: The Existential Structures of Literature. LC 68-25614. 295p. reprint ed. pap. 91.50 (*0-7837-1519-6*, 204179600024) Bks Demand.

— Norton Anthology of World Masterpieces, Vol. 1. 7th ed. LC 98-35047. Vol. 1. 2500p. 1998. pap. 51.50 (*0-393-97289-5*) Norton.

— Norton Anthology of World Masterpieces, Vol. 2. 7th ed. LC 98-35047. Vol. 2. 2500p. 1998. pap. 51.50 (*0-393-97300-X*) Norton.

Lawalree, A. Flore Generale de Belgique - Spermatophytes, 5 vols. 1992. 350.00 (*1-878762-89-3*) Balogh.

Lawand, Jamile T. El Arte Epistolar en el Renacimiento Espanol. (SPA.). 146p. 1997. 53.00 (*1-85566-035-0*, Pub. by Tamesis Bks Ltd) Boydell & Brewer.

Lawania, Vinod K. Rural Development in India. (C). 1992. 15.00 (*81-7024-468-4*, Pub. by Ashish Pub Hse) S Asia.

Lawatsch, Anne & Storey, Judy. Hors d'Oeuvres & Desserts. (Illus.). 96p. 1988. pap. 8.95 (*0-89709-167-1*) Liberty Pub.

Lawatsch-Boomgaarden, Barbara, ed. see White, Andrew & Ijsewijn, Jozef.

Lawchek Limited, Staff. Intellectual Property Law. (Lawchek Personal Legal Sourcebooks Ser.). 160p. 1999. pap. text 24.95 (*0-02-861762-2*) Macmillan.

— Real Estate Law. (Lawchek Personal Legal Sourcebooks Ser.). 160p. 1999. pap. text 24.95 (*0-02-861763-0*) Macmillan.

Lawchek, Ltd. Staff. Contract Law. LC 96-68546. (Lawchek Personal Legal Sourcebooks Ser.). 160p. 1996. pap. 24.95 incl. disk (*0-02-861401-1*) Macmillan.

— Domestic & Family Law. LC 96-68545. (Lawchek Personal Legal Sourcebooks Ser.). 160p. 1996. pap. 24.95 incl. disk (*0-02-861404-6*) Macmillan.

— Wills & Estates Law. LC 96-68547. (Lawchek Personal Legal Sourcebooks Ser.). 160p. 1996. pap. 24.95 incl. disk (*0-02-861403-8*) Macmillan.

Lawden, D. F. Elliptic Functions & Applications. (Applied Mathematical Sciences Ser.: Vol. 80). (Illus.). xiv, 334p. 1989. 79.95 (*0-387-96965-9*, 2664) Spr-Verlag.

Lawder, Donald. Fishing in the Sky: The Education of Namory Keita. LC 96-32672. 207p. 1997. 24.00 (*1-877946-89-3*) Permanent Pr.

— The Wild Bird & Other Poems. Warren, Shirley, ed. 40p. (Orig.). 1992. pap. 5.00 (*1-877801-20-8*) Still Waters.

Lawenik, Libby. Anything Can Happen. 1993. 14.95 (*1-56871-017-8*, Pub. by Targum Pr) Feldheim.

Lawent, Louie. Gerty the Pig. LC 96-32098. (Illus.). (J). 1997. write for info. (*1-56763-279-3*); pap. write for info. (*1-56763-280-7*) Ozark Pub.

Lawer, Sarita M., ed. Diccionario Webster Universal Ingles-Espanol - Espanol-Ingles (Webster English-Spanish - Spanish-English Universal Dictionary. (ENG & SPA.). 384p. (YA). (gr. 7-12). 1995. pap. 1.60 (*0-8056-0139-2*, MV0497) Minerva Bks Ltd.

Lawerence, Frederick G., ed. see Lonergan, Bernard.

Lawerence, Paul R. Unsportsmanlike Conduct: The National Collegiate Athletic Association & the Business of College Football. LC 87-12496. 189p. 1987. 52.95 (*0-275-92725-3*, C2725, Praeger Pubs) Greenwood.

Lawerys, Roberts R. Industrial Chemical Exposure. 2nd ed. 1989. 20.00 (*0-88416-716-X*) Mosby Inc.

Lawes. Management Skills for the Information Manager. 1993. 65.95 (*1-85742-019-5*) Ashgate Pub Co.

***Lawes, Aidan.** Chancery Lane, 1377-1977. 1999. 12.00 (*1-873162-35-9*, Pub. by PRO Pubns) Midpt Trade.

***Lawes, Carolyn.** Women & Reform in a New England Community, 1815-1860. LC 99-28840. (Illus.). 288p. (C). 2000. 39.95 (*0-8131-2131-0*) U Pr of Ky.

Lawes, D. A. & Thomas, H., eds. The Second International Oat Conference - Proceedings: World Corps, Production, Utilization & Description. 1986. text 140.00 (*90-247-3335-9*) Kluwer Academic.

Lawes, Diane N. Bahamas 1985. Fisher, Robert C., ed. (Fisher Annotated Travel Guides Ser.). 258p. 1984. 11.95 (*0-8116-0070-X*) NAL.

***Lawes, Kim.** Paternalism & Politics: The Revival of Paternalism in Early Nineteenth-century Britain. LC 99-56310. 288p. 2000. 65.00 (*0-312-23116-4*) St Martin.

Lawes, Lewis E. Twenty Thousand Years in Sing Sing. LC 74-3830. (Criminal Justice in America Ser.). 1974. reprint ed. 37.95 (*0-405-06150-1*) Ayer.

Lawes, William G. Grammar & Vocabulary of Language Spoken by Motu Tribe (New Guinea) 3rd enl. ed. LC 75-35132. 1976. reprint ed. 39.50 (*0-404-14148-X*) AMS Pr.

Lawesson, J. E., et al. An Updated & Annotated Check List of the Vascular Plants of the Galapagos Islands. annot. ed. Ollgaard, Benjamin, ed. (Reports from the Botanical Institute, University of Aarhus: No. 16). 74p. (C). 1987. pap. 12.95 (*87-87600-23-4*, Pub. by Aarhus Univ Pr) David Brown.

Lawesson, Jonas, jt. ed. see Poulsen, Ebbe.

Lawford, Mary S. & Galon, Beauregard B. Bitch: The Autobiography of Lady Lawford. (Illus.). 178p. 17.95 (*0-8283-1995-2*) Branden Bks.

Lawford, R. G. & Mooney, Gavin A. High Latitude Rain Forests & Associated Ecosystems of the West Coast of the Americas: Climate, Hydrology, Ecology & Conservation. (Ecological Studies: Vol. 116). (Illus.). 352p. 1995. 107.00 (*0-387-94487-7*) Spr-Verlag.

Lawford, Richard G., et al, eds. High Altitude Rain Forests & Associated Ecosystems of the West Coast of the Americas: Climate, Hydrology, Ecology, & Conservation. LC 95-5547. (Ecological Studies: Vol. 116). (Illus.). xxiii, 409p. 1995. write for info. (*3-7879-4487-7*) Spr-Verlag.

***Lawhead.** The Ancient Voyage. 2000. pap. 15.00 (*0-534-56125-X*) Thomson Learn.

— The Contemporary Voyage. 2000. pap. 15.00 (*0-534-56126-8*) Thomson Learn.

— The Medieval Voyage. 2000. pap. 15.00 (*0-534-56157-8*) Thomson Learn.

— The Modern Voyage. 2000. pap. 15.00 (*0-534-56158-6*) Thomson Learn.

Lawhead. Voyage of Discovery: A History of Western Philosophy. 2nd ed. 2000. pap. text 46.25 (*0-534-52022-7*) Thomson Learn.

Lawhead, Alice & Lawhead, Stephen R. The Total Guide to College Life. rev. ed. LC 97-486. 1997. 10.99 (*0-87788-848-5*, H Shaw Pubs) Waterbrook Pr.

Lawhead, Alice S. Doing the Right Thing: Eleven Exercises for Your Ethical Mind. 160p. (Orig.). 1991. pap. 9.99 (*0-87788-183-9*, H Shaw Pubs) Waterbrook Pr.

Lawhead, Stephen R. Arthur. LC 95-49364. (Pendragon Cycle Ser.: Bk. 3). 448p. 1996. pap. 13.00 (*0-310-20507-7*) Zondervan.

— Arthur. (Pendragon Cycle Ser.: Bk. 3). 448p. 1990. reprint ed. mass mkt. 6.99 (*0-380-70890-6*, Avon Bks) Morrow Avon.

— Avalon: The Return of King Arthur. LC 99-25048. 448p. 1999. 25.00 (*0-380-97702-8*, Eos) Morrow Avon.

***Lawhead, Stephen R.** Avalon: The Return of King Arthur. 496p. 2000. mass mkt. 6.99 (*0-380-80297-X*) Morrow Avon.

Lawhead, Stephen R. Byzantium. 1997. mass mkt. write for info. (*0-614-27751-5*, HarperPrism) HarpC.

— Byzantium MM: Byzantium MM. 880p. 1997. mass mkt. 6.99 (*0-06-105754-1*) Zondervan.

***Lawhead, Stephen R.** The Celtic Crusades: The Black Rood. LC 00-28831. (Celtic Crusades Ser.: Bk. II). 448p. 2000. 25.00 (*0-06-105034-2*) HarpC.

Lawhead, Stephen R. Empyrion I: The Search for Fierra. (Empyrion Saga Ser.: Vol. 1). 432p. (Orig.). 1996. pap. 13.00 (*0-310-20509-3*) Zondervan.

— The Endless Knot. LC 92-44645. (Song of Albion Trilogy Ser.). 450p. 1993. 19.95 (*0-7459-2231-7*) Lion USA.

— The Endless Knot. (Song of Albion Ser.: Bk. 3). 416p. 1994. mass mkt. 5.99 (*0-380-71648-8*, Avon Bks) Morrow Avon.

— The Endless Knot, 3. LC 97-44610. (Song of Albion Ser.). 1998. pap. 12.99 (*0-310-21901-9*) Zondervan.

Lawhead, Stephen R. Grail. LC 96-6605. (Pendragon Cycle Ser.: Bk. 5). 464p. 1997. pap. 24.00 (*0-380-97526-2*, Avon Bks) Morrow Avon.

Lawhead, Stephen R. Grail. LC 96-6605. Vol. 5. 400p. 1998. mass mkt. 6.99 (*0-380-78104-2*, Eos) Morrow Avon.

— In the Hall of the Dragon King. (Dragon King Trilogy Ser.: Bk. 1). (YA). 1992. mass mkt. 6.50 (*0-380-71629-1*, Avon Bks) Morrow Avon.

— In the Hall of the Dragon King. (Dragon King Trilogy Ser.: Bk. 1). 352p. (YA). 1996. pap. 13.00 (*0-310-20502-6*) Zondervan.

— The Iron Lance, 1. LC 98-32360. (Celtic Crusades Ser.). 1999. pap. 16.99 (*0-310-21782-2*) Zondervan.

***Lawhead, Stephen R.** The Iron Lance: The Celtic Crusades:Book I. (Celtic Crusades Ser.: Bk. I). 656p. 2000. mass mkt. 6.99 (*0-06-105109-8*, Torch) HarpC.

Lawhead, Stephen R. Iron Lance: Volume One of The Celtic Crusades. LC 98-32360. (Celtic Crusades Ser.: Bk. 1). 512p. 1998. 24.00 (*0-06-105032-6*, HarperPrism) HarpC.

— Merlin. (Pendragon Cycle Ser.: Bk. 2). 448p. 1990. reprint ed. mass mkt. 6.99 (*0-380-70889-2*, Avon Bks) Morrow Avon.

— The Paradise War. (Song of Albion Ser.). 420p. 1992. pap. 11.95 (*0-7459-2242-2*) Lion USA.

— The Paradise War. (Song of Albion Ser.: Bk. 1). 432p. 1993. mass mkt. 5.99 (*0-380-71646-1*, Avon Bks) Morrow Avon.

Lawhead, Stephen R. Pc 4: Pendragon. (Pendragon Cycle Ser.: Bk. 4). 448p. 1995. reprint ed. mass mkt. 6.99 (*0-380-71757-3*, Avon Bks) Morrow Avon.

— Pendragon. 2000. 23.00 (*0-380-97242-5*) Morrow Avon.

Lawhead, Stephen R. Riverbank Stories: The Tale of Anabelle Hedgehog. (Riverbank Stories Ser.: Bk. 3). 112p. (J). 1994. pap. 3.50 (*0-380-72200-3*, Avon Bks) Morrow Avon.

— Riverbank Stories: The Tale of Jeremy Vole. 112p. (J). (gr. 4). 1993. pap. 3.50 (*0-380-72198-8*, Avon Bks) Morrow Avon.

— Riverbank Stories: The Tale of Timothy Mallard. 112p. (J). (gr. 4). 1993. pap. 3.50 (*0-380-72199-6*, Avon Bks) Morrow Avon.

— The Silver Hand. (Song of Albion Ser.: Bk. 2). 400p. 1993. mass mkt. 5.99 (*0-380-71647-X*, Avon Bks) Morrow Avon.

— The Sword & the Flame. (Dragon King Trilogy Ser.: Bk. 3). 384p. (YA). 1992. mass mkt. 5.99 (*0-380-71631-3*, Avon Bks) Morrow Avon.

— Taliesin. (Pendragon Cycle Ser.: Bk. 1). 486p. 1990. reprint ed. mass mkt. 6.99 (*0-380-70613-X*, Avon Bks) Morrow Avon.

— The Warlords of Nin. (Dragon King Trilogy Ser.: Bk. 2). 416p. (YA). 1992. mass mkt. 5.99 (*0-380-71630-5*, Avon Bks) Morrow Avon.

— The Warlords of Nin, Bk. 2. (Dragon King Trilogy Ser.: Vol. 2). 368p. (YA). 1996. pap. 13.00 (*0-310-20503-4*) Zondervan.

Lawhead, Stephen R., jt. auth. see Lawhead, Alice.

Lawhead, Stephen R., jt. auth. see Slaikeu, Karl.

***Lawhead, William F.** The Philosophical Journey: A Field Manual for Explorers. LC 99-37468. 1999. text 52.95 (*0-7674-0218-9*) Mayfield Pub.

Lawhead, William F. The Voyage of Discovery: A History of Western Philosophy. LC 95-30240. 614p. (C). 1995. pap. 67.95 (*0-534-23346-5*) Wadsworth Pub.

Lawhon, Catherine D., jt. auth. see Lawhon, John F.

Lawhon, John F. The Selling Bible: For People in the Business of Selling. 2nd ed. Harris, Sherwood, ed. LC 94-79522. (Illus.). 490p. 1996. 36.95 (*0-9616736-3-X*) J Franklin.

Lawhon, John F. & Lawhon, Catherine D. Selling Retail: All the Secrets of Many of the Highest Paid Retail Salespeople in America. LC 86-80853. (Illus.). 382p. 1986. 29.95 (*0-9616736-0-5*) J Franklin.

— La Vente Au Detail: Tous les Secrets Des Vendeurs Au Detail les Mieux Remuneres. (FRE., Illus.). 395p. (C). 1990. 29.95 (*0-9616736-2-1*) J Franklin.

Lawhon, M. L., jt. auth. see Smith, Dane F.

***Lawhorn, Juanita.** I Saw Him. 215p. 2000. pap. 10.95 (*0-9678455-0-5*, 2001) G & J Pub IN.

Lawhorne, Clifton O. & Long, Howard R. The Supreme Court & Libel. LC 80-21161. (New Horizons in Journalism Ser.). 176p. 1981. 21.95 (*0-8093-0998-X*) S Ill U Pr.

Lawing, Carolyn, jt. ed. see Lawing, Mike.

***Lawing, Mike & Lawing, Carolyn, eds.** My Dearest Friend: The Civil War Correspondence of Cornelia McGimsey & Lewis Warlick. LC 99-69190. 224p. 2000. pap. 20.00 (*0-89089-832-4*) Carolina Acad Pr.

Lawler. Advances in Group Processes, Vol. 16. 73.25 (*0-7623-0452-9*) Jai Pr.

Lawler. Design & Communication. Date not set. pap. text. write for info. (*0-582-00270-2*) Addison-Wesley.

Lawler, jt. auth. see Clement-O'Brien.

Lawler, Donald L., ed. see Wilde, Oscar.

Lawler, E. L., et al. Traveling Salesman Problem. LC 85-3158. (Discrete Mathematics Ser.). 476p. 1985. 245.00 (*0-471-90413-9*) Wiley.

***Lawler, Ed.** Charlie Trotter's. LC 99-59970. (Illus.). 160p. 2000. 27.95 (*0-86730-803-6*) Lebhar Friedman.

Lawler, Edmund O., jt. auth. see Walden, Gene.

Lawler, Edward. Advances in Group Processes, Vol. 15. 1998. 73.25 (*0-7623-0362-X*) Jai Pr.

Lawler, Edward E., III. Doing Research That Is Useful for Theory & Practice. LC 97-50468. 400p. 1999. pap. text 27.00 (*0-7879-4126-3*) Jossey-Bass.

Lawler, Edward E. From the Ground Up: Six Principles for Building the New Logic Corporation. LC 96-19552. (Business-Management Ser.). 1996. 27.00 (*0-7879-0241-1*) Jossey-Bass.

***Lawler, Edward E., III.** From the Ground Up: Six Principles for Building the New Logic Corporation. LC 96-19552. (Illus.). 336p. 2000. reprint ed. pap. 18.00 (*0-7879-5197-8*, Pfffr & Co) Jossey-Bass.

Lawler, Edward E., III. High-Involvement Management: Participative Strategies for Improving Organizational Performance. LC 85-45909. (Management Ser.). 269p. 1986. text 37.95 (*0-87589-686-3*) Jossey-Bass.

— High-Involvement Management: Participative Strategies for Improving Organizational Performance. LC 85-45909. (Management-Social & Behavioral Science Ser.). 272p. 1991. reprint ed. pap. text 24.00 (*1-55542-330-2*) Jossey-Bass.

Lawler, Edward E., 3rd. Motivation in Work Organizations. LC 93-50161. (Management Ser.). 336p. 1994. pap. 27.00 (*1-55542-661-1*) Jossey-Bass.

***Lawler, Edward E., III.** Rewarding Excellence: Pay Strategies for the New Economy. LC 99-47329. (Business & Management Ser.). 352p. 2000. 34.00 (*0-7879-5074-2*, Pfffr & Co) Jossey-Bass.

Lawler, Edward E., III. Strategic Pay: Aligning Organizational Strategies & Pay Systems. LC 90-37168. (Management Ser.). 328p. 1990. text 34.95 (*1-55542-262-4*) Jossey-Bass.

— The Ultimate Advantage: Creating the High-Involvement Organization. LC 91-41095. (Management Ser.). 392p. 1992. text 34.95 (*1-55542-414-7*) Jossey-Bass.

***Lawler, Edward E., III, et al.** Doing Research That Is Useful for Theory & Practice. LC 99-45573. 432p. 1999. pap. 27.00 (*0-7391-0100-5*) Lxngtn Bks.

Lawler, Edward E., et al. Strategies for High Performance Organizations: Employee Involvement, TQM, & Renegineering Programs in Fortune 1000 Corporations. (Business & Management Ser.). 256 p. 1998. pap. 75.00 (*0-7879-4397-5*) Jossey-Bass.

Lawler, Edward E., jt. auth. see Galbraith, Jay.

Lawler, Edward E., 3rd, jt. auth. see McMahan, Gary C.

Lawler, Edward J., ed. Advances in Group Processes, Vol. 14. 1997. 73.25 (*0-7623-0172-4*) Jai Pr.

Lawler, Edward J., et al, eds. Advances in Group Processes, Vol. 1. 255p. 1984. 73.25 (*0-89232-369-8*) Jai Pr.

— Advances in Group Processes, Vol. 2. 281p. 1985. 73.25 (*0-89232-524-0*) Jai Pr.

— Advances in Group Processes, Vol. 3. 246p. 1986. 73.25 (*0-89232-572-0*) Jai Pr.

— Advances in Group Processes, Vol. 4. 315p. 1987. 73.25 (*0-89232-733-2*) Jai Pr.

— Advances in Group Processes, Vol. 5. 279p. 1988. 73.25 (*0-89232-893-2*) Jai Pr.

— Advances in Group Processes, Vol. 6. 257p. 1989. 73.25 (*0-89232-995-5*) Jai Pr.

— Advances in Group Processes, Vol. 7. 234p. 1990. 73.25 (*1-55938-071-3*) Jai Pr.

— Advances in Group Processes, Vol. 9. 280p. 1992. 73.25 (*1-55938-516-2*) Jai Pr.

— Advances in Group Processes, Vol. 10. 304p. 1994. 73.25 (*1-55938-280-5*) Jai Pr.

— Advances in Group Processes, Vol. 11. 239p. 1994. 73.25 (*1-55938-857-9*) Jai Pr.

— Advances in Group Processes, Vol. 12. 300p. 1995. 73.25 (*1-55938-872-2*) Jai Pr.

— Advances in Group Processes, Vol. 13. 1996. 73.25 (*0-7623-0005-1*) Jai Pr.

Lawler, Edward J. & Markovsky, Barry, eds. Social Psychology of Groups: A Reader. LC 93-41124. 277p. 1991. pap. 25.75 (*1-55938-754-8*) Jai Pr.

Lawler, Edward J., jt. auth. see Bacharach, Samuel B.

Lawler, Edwina, tr. see Schlegel, Dorothea.

Lawler, Edwina, tr. see Schlegel, Dorothea M.

Lawler, Edwina, tr. see Schleiermacher, Friedrich Daniel Ernst.

Lawler, Edwina, jt. tr. see Tice, Terrence N.

Lawler, Eugene S. A Technique for Computing the Amount of New Aid Required for State Equalization Programs. LC 77-176981. (Columbia University. Teachers College. Contributions to Education Ser.: No. 547). reprint ed. 37.50 (*0-404-55547-0*) AMS Pr.

Lawler, G. F. Intersections of Random Walks: Probability & Its Applications. x, 209p. 1991. 52.00 (*0-8176-3557-2*) Birkhauser.

An Asterisk (*) at the beginning of an entry indicates that the title is appearing for the first time.

Lawler, Gary. Cultural Traditions Dictionary. LC 99-165860. 1999. pap. text 19.95 (*0-85640-636-8*) Blckstaff Pr.

Lawler, Gregory F. Intersections of Random Walks. LC 96-17863. (Probability & Its Applications Ser.). 230p. 1996. pap. 36.50 (*0-8176-3892-X*) Birkhauser.

— Introduction to Stochastic Processes. 192p. (gr. 13). 1995. boxed set 59.95 (*0-412-99511-5*, Chap & Hall CRC) CRC Pr.

***Lawler, Gregory F. & Coyle, Lester N.** Lectures on Contemporary Probability LC 99-23838. (Student Mathematical Library). 1999. pap. write for info. (*0-8218-2029-X*) Am Math.

Lawler, Howard E. Discover Deserts. (Discover Ser.). (Illus.). 48p. (J). (gr. 3-6). 1992. lib. bdg. 15.95 (*1-56674-029-0*, HTS Bks) Forest Hse.

***Lawler, J.** Qualitative Research in Nursing: Methods in Context. 176p. 1998. pap. write for info. (*0-443-05207-7*) Church.

Lawler, J., ed. The Body in Nursing: A Collection of Views. 240p. 1998. pap. write for info. (*0-443-05250-6*) Church.

Lawler, J. E., jt. ed. see Stewart, R. S.

Lawler, James. The Existentialist Marxism of Jean-Paul Sartre. (Philosophical Currents Ser.: No. 18). x, 291p. 1976. pap. write for info. (*90-6032-039-5*) B R Gruner.

Lawler, James M. IQ, Heritability & Racism. LC 78-14264. 204p. reprint ed. pap. 63.30 (*0-608-17490-4*, 202998900067) Bks Demand.

Lawler, James R. Poetry & Moral Dialectic: Baudelaire's "Secret Architecture" LC 97-19940. 224p. 1997. 36.00 (*0-8386-3758-2*) Fairleigh Dickinson.

— Rene Char: The Myth & the Poem. LC 77-85547. (Princeton Essays in Literature Ser.). 135p. 1978. reprint ed. pap. 41.90 (*0-7837-9369-3*, 206011200004) Bks Demand.

— Rimbaud's Theatre of the Self. 256p. (C). 1992. 46.95 (*0-674-77075-7*) HUP.

***Lawler, Jennifer.** Coaching Women in the Martial Arts. LC 98-42957. 128p. 1999. pap. 14.95 (*1-57028-211-0*, 82110H) NTC Contemp Pub Co.

Lawler, Jennifer. The Curmudgeon's Guide to Child-Free Travel: Exactly How & Precisely Where to Enjoy Idyllic, Grown-Up Getaways. LC 98-14736. (Curmudgeon's Guides Ser.). (Illus.). 248p. 1998. pap. 13.95 (*0-87576-218-2*) Pilot Bks.

***Lawler, Jennifer.** Cyberdanger & Internet Safety. LC 99-37013. (Hot Issues Ser.). (Illus.). 64p. (YA). (gr. 6 up). 2000. lib. bdg. 19.95 (*0-7660-1368-5*) Enslow Pubs.

Lawler, Jennifer. Drug Legalization: A Pro/Con Issue. LC 98-34043. (Hot Pro/Con Issues Ser.). 64p. (YA). (gr. 6 up). 1999. lib. bdg. 19.95 (*0-7660-1197-6*) Enslow Pubs.

***Lawler, Jennifer.** Drug Testing in Schools: A Pro/Con Issue. LC 99-41165. (Hot Pro/Con Issues Ser.). (Illus.). 64p. (gr. 6 up). 2000. lib. bdg. 19.95 (*0-7660-1367-7*) Enslow Pubs.

Lawler, Jennifer. Martial Arts Encyclopedia. (Illus.). 328p. (Orig.). 1996. pap. 19.95 (*1-57028-068-1*, 80681H, Mstrs Pr) NTC Contemp Pub Co.

— Martial Arts for Women: A Practical Guide. LC 97-27231. (Illus.). 256p. (Orig.). 1998. pap. 19.95 (*1-880336-16-2*) Turtle CT.

— The Secrets of Tae Kwon Do. (Illus.). 240p. 1998. pap. 17.95 (*1-57028-202-1*, 82021H, Mstrs Pr) NTC Contemp Pub Co.

***Lawler, Jennifer.** Small-Business Ownership for Creative People. 280p. 1999. pap. 19.95 (*0-9639260-9-8*) Aletheia.

Lawler, Jennifer. Songs of Life: The Meaning of Country Music. LC 96-69695. (Illus.). 160p. (Orig.). 1996. pap. 15.95 (*1-880654-09-1*) Pogo Pr.

— Weight Training for Martial Artists. LC 98-38644. (Illus.). 208p. 1999. pap. 16.95 (*1-880336-23-5*) Turtle CT.

Lawler, Jennifer, jt. auth. see Jung, Woo Jin.

Lawler, Jocalyn. Behind the Screens: Nursing Somology & the Problem of the Body. 264p. 1991. pap. 24.00 (*0-443-04444-9*) Church.

— Behind the Screens: Nursing, Somology, & the Problem of the Body. LC 93-9933. 1993. write for info. (*0-8053-4070-X*) Benjamin-Cummings.

— Behind the Screens: Nursing, Somology, & the Problem of the Body. LC 93-9933. (C). 1993. pap. text 24.50 (*0-8053-4090-4*) Benjamin-Cummings.

Lawler, John & Dry, Helen A. Using Computers in Linguistics: A Practical Guide. LC 97-23787. 304p. (C). 1998. pap. 22.99 (*0-415-16793-0*) Routledge.

— Using Computers in Linguistics: A Practical Guide. LC 97-23787. (Illus.). 320p. (C). 1998. 75.00 (*0-415-16792-2*) Routledge.

Lawler, John J. Unionization & Deunionization: Strategy, Tactics, & Outcomes. LC 89-21496. (Studies in Industrial Relations). 300p. (C). 1990. text 34.95 (*0-87249-662-7*) U of SC Pr.

Lawler, Joy. Bible People - Women: Cokesbury. pap. 5.95 (*0-687-07385-5*) Abingdon.

— People of the Bible: Women. (Bible People Ser.). 1996. pap. text 5.95 (*0-687-07395-2*) Abingdon.

Lawler, Joy, jt. auth. see Hambrick, Charles.

Lawler, Justus G. Celestial Pantomime: Poetic Structures of Transcendence. rev. ed. 300p. (C). 1994. pap. 19.95 (*0-8264-0679-3*) Continuum.

— Hopkins Re-Constructed: Life, Poetry, & the Tradition. LC 81-17505. 256p. 1997. 34.50 (*0-8264-1058-8*) Continuum.

Lawler, K. A. The Firm & Industrial Analysis. 1986. 100.00 (*0-946796-03-3*) St Mut.

Lawler, K. A. & Seddighi, H. A. Economic Theory & Modelling: An Integrated Approach. 1986. 140.00 (*0-946796-05-X*) St Mut.

— Problems & Solutions in Economic Theory. 1986. 100.00 (*0-7855-1834-7*) St Mut.

Lawler, Lillian B. The Dance in Ancient Greece. fac. ed. LC 65-13203. (Dance Ser.: No. 657). (Illus.). 160p. 1984. reprint ed. pap. 49.60 (*0-7837-8196-2*, 204790100008) Bks Demand.

— The Dance on the Ancient Greek Theatre. LC 64-65259. (University of Iowa Monographs). 143p. reprint ed. pap. 44.40 (*0-608-15049-5*, 202594200047) Bks Demand.

— Latin Club. 12th ed. 73p. (YA). (gr. 9-12). 4.95 (*0-939507-08-0*, B905) Amer Classical.

Lawler, Mary. Marcus Garvey: Black Nationalist Leader. Huggins, Nathan I., ed. (Black Americans of Achievement Ser.). (Illus.). 124p. (YA). (gr. 5 up). 1987. lib. bdg. 19.95 (*1-55546-587-0*) Chelsea Hse.

— Marcus Garvey: Black Nationalist Leader. Huggins, Nathan I., ed. (Black Americans of Achievement Ser.). (Illus.). 124p. (YA). (gr. 5 up). 1989. pap. 8.95 (*0-7910-0203-9*) Chelsea Hse.

— Marcus Garvey: Black Nationalist Leader. (Black American Ser.). 192p. (YA). 1990. mass mkt. 3.95 (*0-87067-568-0*, Melrose Sq) Holloway.

Lawler, Michael G. Family: American & Christian. LC 97-36981. 1997. 24.95 (*0-8294-0972-6*) Loyola Pr.

— Marriage & Sacrament: A Theology of Christian Marriage. LC 93-22619. 122p. (Orig.). 1993. pap. text 9.95 (*0-8146-5051-1*, M Glazier) Liturgical Pr.

— Symbol & Sacrament: A Contemporary Sacramental Theology. 2nd rev. ed. LC 95-69003. xii, 293p. 1994. reprint ed. 29.95 (*1-881871-11-8*); reprint ed. pap. 19.95 (*1-881871-10-X*) Creighton U Pr.

— Theology of Ministry. LC 89-61929. 152p. (Orig.). 1990. pap. 10.95 (*1-55612-310-8*) Sheed & Ward WI.

***Lawler, Michael G. & Risch, Gail S., eds.** Practical Theology: A View from the Plains. 440p. 2000. 25.00 (*1-881871-36-3*, Pub. by Creighton U Pr); pap. 17.00 (*1-881871-37-1*, Pub. by Creighton U Pr) BookMasters.

Lawler, Michael G. & Roberts, William P., eds. Christian Marriage & Family: Contemporary Theological & Pastoral Perspectives. 1996. pap. 22.95 (*0-8146-5021-X*, M Glazier) Liturgical Pr.

Lawler, Michael G. & Shanahan, Thomas J. Church: A Spirited Communion. LC 94-41758. (Theology & Life Ser.: Vol. 40). 192p. (Orig.). 1995. pap. 12.95 (*0-8146-5821-0*, M Glazier) Liturgical Pr.

Lawler, Mickey. Skydyes: A Visual Guide to Fabric Painting. Nelson, Annie & Koolish, Lynn, eds. LC 98-58154. (Illus.). 111p. 1999. pap. text 24.95 (*1-57120-072-X*, 10192) C & T Pub.

Lawler, Nan. Closing the Gap: The Coast Line & Its Bridges in Ventura & Santa Barbara Counties. (Illus.). 19p. (Orig.). 1984. reprint ed. pap. 2.00 (*0-911773-03-7*) Inst Am Res.

Lawler, Nancy, jt. ed. see Hunwick, John O.

Lawler, Nancy E. Soldiers of Misfortune: Invoirien Tirailleurs of World War II. LC 91-24369. (Illus.). 281p. (C). 1992. text 35.00 (*0-8214-1012-1*) Ohio U Pr.

Lawler, Patricia, jt. auth. see Kenet, Barney.

Lawler, Patricia A. The Keys to Adult Learning: Theory & Practical Strategies. 61p. 1991. pap. 19.95 (*1-56602-037-9*) Research Better.

Lawler, Patricia A. & King, Kathleen P. Planning for Effective Faculty Development: Using Adult Learning Strategies. LC 00-26717. (Illus.). (C). 2000. pap. text. write for info. (*1-57524-105-6*) Krieger.

Lawler, Patrick. A Drowning Man is Never Tall Enough. LC 89-4823. (Contemporary Poetry Ser.). 104p. 1990. pap. 15.95 (*0-8203-1158-8*) U of Ga Pr.

Lawler, Peter. American Political Rhetoric: A Reader. 2nd ed. 180p. 1990. pap. text 16.95 (*0-8476-7642-0*) Rowman.

— A Question of Values: Johan Galtung's Peace Research. LC 94-8624. (Critical Perspectives on World Politics Ser.). 280p. 1994. lib. bdg. 52.00 (*1-55587-507-6*) L Rienner.

Lawler, Peter, et al, eds. Active Duty: Public Administration As Democratic Statesmanship. LC 98-9907. 360p. 1997. 70.00 (*0-8476-8646-9*); pap. 24.95 (*0-8476-8647-7*) Rowman.

Lawler, Peter A. American Views of Liberty. LC 97-8545. (Major Concepts in Politics & Political Theory Ser.: Vol. 5). X, 183p. (C). 1997. pap. text 24.95 (*0-8204-2412-9*) P Lang Pubng.

— Postmodernism Rightly Understood: The Return to Realism in American Thought LC 99-13633. (American Intellectual Culture Ser.). 208p. 1999. 19.95 (*0-8476-9426-7*) Rowman.

— Postmodernism Rightly Understood: The Return to Reason in American Thought. LC 99-13633. 208p. 1999. pap. 60.00 (*0-8476-9425-9*) Rowman.

— The Restless Mind: Alexis de Tocqueville on the Origin & Perpetuation of Human Liberty. 210p. (Orig.). (C). 1993. pap. text 25.95 (*0-8476-7824-5*); lib. bdg. 65.00 (*0-8476-7823-7*) Rowman.

— Under God with Liberty: The Religious Dimension of American Liberty. LC 93-38666. 300p. 1994. text 35.00 (*0-89341-686-X*, Longwood Academic) Hollowbrook.

Lawler, Peter A., ed. Tocqueville's Political Science Vol. 1: Classic Essays. LC 91-35663. 422p. 1992. text 20.00 (*0-8153-0050-6*, H1491) Garland.

Lawler, Peter A. & Alulis, Joseph, eds. Tocqueville's Defense of Human Liberty: Current Essays. LC 92-22994. 384p. 1992. text 20.00 (*0-8153-0051-4*, 1492) Garland.

Lawler, Peter A. & Schaefer, Robert M., eds. The American Experiment: The Theory & Practice of Liberty. 538p. (C). 1994. pap. text 31.95 (*0-8476-7904-7*); lib. bdg. 72.00 (*0-8476-7903-9*) Rowman.

— American Political Rhetoric: A Reader. 3rd ed. LC 95-7428. 370p. (C). 1995. pap. text 24.95 (*0-8476-8047-9*) Rowman.

Lawler, Peter A., jt. ed. see Knippenberg, Joseph M.

Lawler, Peter Augustine & McConkey, Dale, eds. Community & Political Thought Today. LC 98-14906. 256p. 1998. 59.95 (*0-275-96096-X*, Praeger Pubs) Greenwood.

Lawler, Peter Augustine, jt. see McConkey, Dale.

Lawler-Prince, Dianne, et al. Moving Toward an Integrated Curriculum in Early Childhood Education. LC 95-42453. (Early Childhood Education Ser.). 1995. 14.95 (*0-8106-0367-5*) NEA.

Lawler, R. & May, W. Perspectives in Bioethics. Lescoe, F. & Liptak, D., eds. (Pope John Paul II Lecture Series in Bioethics: Vol. I). 66p. (Orig.). 1983. pap. 3.75 (*0-910919-00-3*) Mariel Pubns.

Lawler, Ray. Summer of the Seventeenth Doll. LC 58-7670. (Illus.). 142p. 1958. 16.95 (*0-910278-04-0*) Boulevard.

Lawler, Rick. How to Contact World Leaders: Write, Phone & Fax. 1998. pap. text 12.50 (*0-9624394-5-2*) MinRef Pr.

— How to Contact World Leaders - 1999 Edition: Write - Phone - Fax. annuals Orig. Title: How to Write to World Leaders. 76p. 1999. pap. 12.50 (*0-9624394-7-9*) MinRef Pr.

***Lawler, Rick.** How to Contact World Leaders 2000: Write - Phone - Fax - E-Mail. LC 89-27317. 224p. 2000. pap. 16.95 (*1-930322-00-3*, Pub. by MinRef Pr) Quality Bks IL.

Lawler, Rick. How to Write to World Leaders. 160p. (Orig.). 1992. pap. 7.00 (*0-380-76538-1*, Avon Bks) Morrow Avon.

— How to Write to World Leaders: 1997 Edition. LC 90-351003. 76p. (Orig.). 1996. pap. 12.50 (*0-9624394-4-4*) MinRef Pr.

— Myth: The Extinction Factor. 176p. (Orig.). 1994. pap. 8.50 (*0-9624394-2-8*) MinRef Pr.

***Lawler, Rick.** United Nations Representatives. 1999. pap. 6.75 (*0-9624394-8-7*) MinRef Pr.

Lawler, Rick, ed. Abortion Stories: Fiction on Fire. LC 92-61240. 248p. (Orig.). 1992. pap. 11.00 (*0-9624394-1-X*) MinRef Pr.

— United Nations Representatives, Foreign Ambassadors to the United States: Names, Addresses, Phone & FAX Numbers. rev. ed. 36p. (Orig.). 1996. pap. 6.75 (*0-9624394-3-6*) MinRef Pr.

Lawler, Robert W. Computer Experience & Cognitive Development: A Child's Learning in a Computer Culture. LC 85-5534. (Cognitive Science Ser.). 275p. 1985. pap. text 31.95 (*0-470-20194-0*) P-H.

Lawler, Robert W., et al. Cognition & Computers: Studies in Learning. LC 86-2928. (Cognitive Science Ser.). 1986. text 57.95 (*0-470-20324-2*); pap. text 29.95 (*0-470-20328-5*) P-H.

Lawler, Ronald D. Divine Faith, Private Revelation, Popular Devotion. (Queen of Apostles Ser.: Vol. II). 15p. 1989. 0.65 (*0-911988-78-5*, 49715) AMI Pr.

Lawler, Ronald D., et al. Catholic Sexual Ethics. 2nd ed. LC 84-62225. 336p. 1998. pap. 12.95 (*0-87973-952-5*) Our Sunday Visitor.

Lawler, S. Dianne. Parent-Teacher Conferencing in Early Childhood Education. 112p. 1991. pap. 11.95 (*0-8106-0356-X*) NEA.

Lawler, Susan & Graham, Katherine. Moms on the Move: The Complete Fitness Guide for Pregnancy & Postpartum. (Illus.). x, 225p. (Orig.). 1996. pap., mass mkt. 15.95 (*1-889152-02-1*) Logan Hse Publns.

Lawler, T. C., ed. see Gregory, Saint.

Lawler, T. C., ed. see Irenaeus, Saint.

Lawler, T. Josephine. Good News for Your Autumn Years: Leader's Guide. 48p. 1994. pap., teacher ed. 10.95 (*0-89390-305-1*) Resource Pubns.

— Good News for Your Autumn Years: Reflections on the Gospel of Luke. LC 94-21114. 160p. (Orig.). 1994. pap. 10.95 (*0-89390-303-5*) Resource Pubns.

Lawler, Thomas A. Iowa Legal Forms: Probate, 1984-1993. (Iowa Legal Forms Ser.). 250p. ring bd. 85.00 incl. disk (*0-685-49483-7*, MICHIE); suppl. ed. 37.50 (*0-86678-043-2*, MICHIE) LEXIS Pub.

— Iowa Legal Forms: Probate, 1984-1993. (Iowa Legal Forms Ser.). 250p. 1993. ring bd. 60.00 incl. disk (*0-86678-326-1*, 81025-10, MICHIE) LEXIS Pub.

Lawler, Thomas C. & Burghart, Johannes, eds. The Octavius of Marcus Minucius Felix. Clarke, G. W., tr. from LAT. (Ancient Christian Writers Ser.: No. 39). 1974. 26.95 (*0-8091-0189-0*) Paulist Pr.

Lawler, Thomas C., tr. see Augustine, Saint.

Lawler, Traugott. One & the Many in the Canterbury Tales. 209p. 1980. 69.50 (*0-208-01842-5*) Elliots Bks.

Lawler, Vinita. Tantalizing Thai Cuisine. LC 93-78019. 208p. (Orig.). 1993. pap. 12.95 (*1-878044-10-9*) Mayhaven Pub.

Lawler, William, et al. Essential Pathology for Dental Students. 160p. 1987. pap. text 35.00 (*0-443-02910-5*) Church.

Lawless. Lifetime Data. 2nd ed. text. write for info. (*0-471-37215-3*) Wiley.

Lawless, Agnes, jt. auth. see Goodboy, Eadie.

Lawless, Agnes C. & Lawless, John W. The Drift into Deception: The Eight Characteristics of Abusive Christianity. 240p. 1995. pap. 11.99 (*0-8254-3163-8*) Kregel.

Lawless, Brian. Fundamental Analog Electronics. LC 96-6774. 336p. 1996. pap. 74.00 (*0-13-534298-8*) P-H.

Lawless, Brian. Kathleen Mavourneen. Date not set. 25.00 (*0-9652387-1-7*) Brians Pub.

— Lord of the Andes. LC 96-96321. 220p. (Orig.). 1996. pap., per. 12.95 (*0-9652387-0-9*, PO791) Brians Pub.

Lawless, Donald I. A Flying Skull: The Chronicle of a Fighter Pilot Who Fought in Southern Europe During the Second World War. Dreinhofer, D. L., ed. 230p. 1993. write for info. (*0-9638453-0-6*) D I Lawless.

Lawless, Edward W. & Smith, Ivan C. Inorganic High-Energy Oxidizers: Synthesis, Structure, & Properties. LC 68-56023. 314p. reprint ed. pap. 97.40 (*0-608-30378-X*, 205504600008) Bks Demand.

Lawless, Elaine J. God's Peculiar People: Women's Voices & Folk Tradition in a Pentecostal Church. LC 88-4236. 152p. 1988. 20.00 (*0-8131-1628-7*) U Pr of Ky.

— Handmaidens of the Lord: Pentecostal Women & Traditional Religion. LC 88-4838. (Publications of the American Folklore Society, Bibliographical & Special Ser.). (Illus.). 294p. (Orig.). (C). 1988. pap. 19.95 (*0-8122-1265-7*); text 48.95 (*0-8122-8100-4*) U of Pa Pr.

— Holy Women, Wholly Women: Sharing Ministries Through Life Stories & Reciprocal Ethnography. (Publications of the American Folklore Society, Bibliographical & Special Ser.). 256p. (Orig.). (C). 1993. text 42.95 (*0-8122-8240-X*); pap. text 17.95 (*0-8122-1444-7*) U of Pa Pr.

***Lawless, Elaine J.** Women Escaping Violence: Empowerment through Narrative. 296p. 2000. 32.50 (*0-8262-1314-6*); pap. 17.50 (*0-8262-1319-7*) U of Mo Pr.

Lawless, Elaine J. Women Preaching Revolution: Calling for Connection in a Disconnected Time. 232p. 1996. text 36.50 (*0-8122-3198-8*) U of Pa Pr.

Lawless, Elinor R., jt. auth. see Ringer, Benjamin B.

Lawless, Gary. Caribouddhism: Sutras & the Holy Lands. 96p. 1998. pap. 9.95 (*0-942396-80-4*) Blackberry ME.

— First Sight of Land. 120p. (Orig.). 1990. pap. 7.50 (*92-64-13396-8*) Blackberry ME.

— Sitka Spring. (Illus.). 32p. (Orig.). 1991. pap. 5.00 (*0-942396-63-4*) Blackberry ME.

— Wolf Driving Sled: Sel Poems, 1970-1980. 1981. pap. 3.50 (*0-942396-28-6*) Blackberry ME.

Lawless, Gary, ed. Poems for the Wild Earth. 96p. (Orig.). 1995. pap. 8.95 (*0-942396-72-3*) Blackberry ME.

Lawless, Gary & Fox, S. Dark Moon-White Pine. 5.00 (*0-686-15298-0*) Great Raven Pr.

Lawless, Gary & Petrof, Stephen. Ice Tattoo. (Illus.). 32p. (Orig.). 1982. pap. 3.00 (*0-942396-30-8*) Blackberry ME.

Lawless, George. Augustine of Hippo & His Monastic Rule. 202p. 1990. reprint ed. pap. 18.95 (*0-19-826741-X*) OUP.

Lawless, George, jt. auth. see Dodaro, Robert.

Lawless, Harry, jt. auth. see Heymann, Hildegarde.

Lawless, Harry T. & Klein, Barbara P., eds. Sensory Science Theory & Applications in Foods. (IFT Basic Symposium Ser.: Vol. 6). (Illus.). 456p. 1991. text 125.00 (*0-8247-8537-1*) Dekker.

Lawless, Harry T., jt. auth. see Heymann, Hildegarde.

Lawless, J. F. Statistical Models & Methods for Lifetime Data. LC 81-11446. (Probability & Mathematical Statistics Ser.). 592p. 1982. 139.95 (*0-471-08544-8*) Wiley.

Lawless, Joanne A. Strange Stories of Life. (Great Unsolved Mysteries Ser.). 1997. pap. 4.95 (*0-8114-6865-8*) Raintree Steck-V.

Lawless, John W., jt. auth. see Lawless, Agnes C.

***Lawless, Joseph F., Jr.** Prosecutorial Misconduct. 2nd ed. 1219p. 1999. 120.00 (*0-327-04963-4*, 6424111) LEXIS Pub.

Lawless, Joseph F., Jr. Prosecutorial Misconduct: Law, Procedure, Forms. 812p. 1985. 120.00 (*0-930273-06-0*, 64241-10, MICHIE) LEXIS Pub.

Lawless, Julia. Aromatherapy & the Mind: An Exploration into the Psychological & Emotional Effects of Essential Oils. (Illus.). 240p. 1995. pap. 16.00 (*0-7225-2927-9*) Harper SF.

— The Complete Illustrated Guide to Aromatherapy: A Practical Approach to the Use of Essential Oils for Health & Well-Being. LC 97-34034. (Illustrated Health Bks.). (Illus.). 224p. 1997. pap. 24.95 (*1-85230-987-3*, Pub. by Element MA) Penguin Putnam.

— Encyclopaedia of Essential Oils: A Complete Guide to the Use of Aromatics in Aromatherapy, Herbalism, Health & Well-Being. 1992. pap. 16.95 (*1-85230-311-5*, Pub. by Element MA) Penguin Putnam.

***Lawless, Julia.** Heaven Scent: Aromatic Christmas Crafts, Recipes & Decorations. (Illus.). 125p. 2000. reprint ed. text 28.00 (*0-7881-9095-4*) DIANE Pub.

Lawless, Julia. Heaven Scent: Aromatic Christmas Gifts, Decorations & Gifts. LC 98-48458. (Illus.). 128p. 1998. 27.95 (*0-8069-7062-6*) Sterling.

— Illustrated Encyclopedia of Essential Oils: The Complete Guide to the Use of Oils in Akomatherapy & Herbalism. (Illus.). 256p. 1995. pap. 24.95 (*1-85230-721-8*, Pub. by Element MA) Penguin Putnam.

— The Illustrated Encyclopedia of Essential Oils: The Complete Guide to the Use of Oils in Aromatherapy & Herbalism. (Illus.). Date not set. write for info. (*0-614-17668-9*) Penguin Putnam.

— Tea Tree Oil: The New Guide to One of Nature's Most Remarkable Gifts. 96p. 1995. pap. 7.00 (*0-7225-3032-3*) Thorsons PA.

***Lawless, Julia & Allan, Judith.** Aloe Vera: Natural Wonder Cure. 2000. pap. 11.00 (*0-7225-3824-3*, Pub. by Thorsons PA) HarpC.

Lawless, Linda L. How to Build & Market Your Mental Health Practice. LC 96-35437. 224p. 1999. pap. 39.95 (*0-471-14760-5*) Wiley.

Lawless, Linda L. & Wright, Jean. How to Get Referrals: The Mental Health Professional's Guide to Strategic Marketing. LC 99-23933. 328p. 1999. pap. 39.95 (*0-471-29791-7*) Wiley.

Lawless, Michael W., et al, eds. Strategic Management in High Technology Firms. LC 90-33863. (Monographs in Organizational Behavior & Industrial Relations: Vol. 12). 245p. 1990. 78.50 (*1-55938-105-1*) Jai Pr.

Lawless, Michael W., jt. auth. see Goodman, Richard A.

Lawless, Michael W., jt. ed. see Gomez-Mejia, Luis R.

L

Lawless, Paul. Britain's Inner Cities: Problems & Policies. 304p. (C). 1982. pap. 50.00 (*0-06-318185-1*, Pub. by P Chapman) St Mut.

Lawless, Paul & Brown, Frank. Urban Growth & Change in Britain: An Introduction. 256p. (C). 1986. pap. 36.00 (*0-06-318336-6*, Pub. by P Chapman) St Mut.

Lawless, Paul & Raban, Colin, eds. The Contemporary British City. 192p. (C). 1986. pap. 60.00 (*0-06-318340-4*, Pub. by P Chapman) St Mut.

Lawless, Paul, et al. Unemployment & Social Exclusion: Landscapes of Labor Inequality. LC 98-113400. (Regional Policy & Development Ser.: No. 13). 280p. 1997. pap. 34.95 (*1-85302-341-8*, Pub. by Jessica Kingsley) Taylor & Francis.

Lawless, Paul, jt. auth. see Chandler, J. A.

Lawless, R. I., jt. ed. see Blake, G. H.

Lawless, Ray M. Folksingers & Folksongs in America: A Handbook of Biography, Bibliography & Discography. LC 81-6398. (Illus.). 750p. 1981. reprint ed. lib. bdg. 75.00 (*0-313-23104-4*, LAFO, Greenwood Pr) Greenwood.

Lawless, Richard, ed. The Middle Eastern Village. 320p. 1987. lib. bdg. 59.00 (*0-7099-1695-7*, Pub. by C Helm) Routldge.

Lawless, Richard & Manahan, Liala. War & Refugees. (Illus.). 280p. 1992. 47.50 (*0-86187-900-7*) St Martin.

Lawless, Richard I. Algeria. 2nd rev. ed. (World Bibliographical Ser.: No. 19). 384p. 1995. lib. bdg. 89.00 (*1-85109-130-0*) ABC-CLIO.

— Algeria, Vol. 19. (World Bibliographical Ser.). 249p. 1981. 55.00 (*0-903450-32-1*) ABC-CLIO.

— The Arab-Israeli Conflict: An Encyclopedia. 2001. lib. bdg. 55.00 (*0-87436-886-3*) ABC-CLIO.

— From Ta'izz to Tyneside: An Arab Community in the North-East of England in the Twentieth Century. LC 95-189884. (Illus.). 256p. 1995. text 60.00 (*0-85989-447-9*, Pub. by Univ Exeter Pr); pap. text 29.95 (*0-85989-460-6*, Pub. by Univ Exeter Pr) Northwestern U Pr.

— Libya. LC 88-149408. (World Bibliographical Ser.: No. 79). 268p. 1987. lib. bdg. 65.00 (*1-85109-033-9*) ABC-CLIO.

Lawless, Robert. Haiti's Bad Press. 261p. (Orig.). (C). 1992. 25.95 (*0-87047-060-4*); pap. 14.95 (*0-87047-061-2*) Schenkman Bks Inc.

Lawless, Robert, et al, eds. Fieldwork: The Human Experience, Vol. 7. (Library of Anthropology). xxii, 196p. 1983. text 90.00 (*0-677-16460-2*); pap. text 59.00 (*0-677-16465-3*) Gordon & Breach.

Lawless, Susan J., jt. ed. see Johnson, Eleanor L.

Lawley, Alan. Atomization: The Production of Metal Powders. LC 92-13307. (Monographs in P-M Ser.: No. 1). (Illus.). 1992. pap. 60.00 (*1-878954-15-6*) Metal Powder.

Lawley, Alan & Swanson, Armour, eds. Advances in Powder Metallurgy & Particulate Materials - 1993. (Illus.). 1953p. 1993. text 200.00 (*1-878954-34-2*) Metal Powder.

Lawley, David. A Nature & Hiking Guide to Cape Breton's Cabot Trail. LC 95-208023. (Illus.). 164p. 1995. pap. 14.95 (*1-55109-105-4*) Nimbus Publ.

Lawley, Elizabeth L. & Summerhill, Craig. An Internet Primer for Information Professionals: A Basic Guide to Internet Networking Technology. 175p. 1993. pap. 29.95 (*0-88736-831-X*) Mecklermedia.

Lawley, Francis E. The Growth of Collective Economy: The Growth of National Collective Eonomy & The Growth of International Collective Economy, 2 vols. LC 80-20904. (Studies in International Economics: No. 1). 1040p. 1980. reprint ed. lib. bdg. 95.00 (*0-87991-850-0*) Porcupine Pr.

Lawley, Joan L., jt. ed. see Bagwell, Philip S.

Lawley, K. P. Molecular Scattering: Physical & Chemical Applications. LC 74-23667. (Advances in Chemical Physics Ser.: Vol. 30). 549p. reprint ed. pap. 170.20 (*0-608-18640-6*, 202401200035) Bks Demand.

Lawley, K. P., ed. Ab Initio Methods in Quantum Chemistry, Pt. 1. LC 86-9168. (Advances in Chemical Physics Ser.: No. 67). (Illus.). 566p. 1987. reprint ed. pap. 175.50 (*0-8357-4619-4*, 203755100001) Bks Demand.

— Ab Initio Methods in Quantum Chemistry, Vol. 2. LC 86-9168. (Advances in Chemical Physics Ser.: Pt. 2). (Illus.). 598p. 1987. pap. 185.40 (*0-608-05164-0*, 203755100002) Bks Demand.

— Dynamics of the Excited State. LC QD0461.5. (Advances in Chemical Physics Ser.: No. 50). (Illus.). 675p. reprint ed. pap. 200.00 (*0-8357-3078-6*, 203933500012) Bks Demand.

— Potential Energy Surfaces. LC 81-466015. 618p. reprint ed. pap. 191.60 (*0-608-12466-4*, 202519600042) Bks Demand.

Lawley, Lisa. World of Elephants. LC 95-223115. 128p. 1994. pap. 11.95 (*1-56799-069-X*, Friedman-Fairfax) M Friedman Pub Grp Inc.

Lawley, Lisa, jt. auth. see Vitale, Gioietta.

Lawley, Sue. Desert Island Discussions. 331p. 1991. 24.95 (*1-85089-555-4*, Pub. by ISIS Lrg Prnt) Transaction Pubs.

Lawlis, Frank, jt. auth. see Achterberg, Jeanne.

Lawlis, G. Frank. The Cure: Caregiver's Guide. LC 93-29825. 51p. (C). 1994. pap. 9.95 (*0-89390-274-8*) Resource Pubns.

— The Cure: The Hero's Journey with Cancer. LC 93-29828. (Illus.). 51p. (Orig.). (C). 1994. pap. text 9.95 (*0-89390-273-X*) Resource Pubns.

Lawlis, G. Frank & Chatfield, Douglas. Multivariate Approaches for the Behavioral Sciences: A Brief Text. (Illus.). 153p. (Orig.). 1974. pap. text 5.00 (*0-89672-051-9*) Tex Tech Univ Pr.

Lawlis, Merritt E., ed. see Deloney, Thomas.

Lawliss, Charles. And God Cried. 175p. 1994. write for info. (*1-57215-036-X*) World Pubns.

— Jacqueline Kennedy Onassis. (Illus.). 128p. 1994. write for info. (*1-57215-040-8*) World Pubns.

— John Paul II, 1920-199? LC 95-30111. Date not set. write for info. (*0-8245-1600-1*) Crossroad NY.

Lawliss, Chuck. The Civil War: Unstilled Voices. LC 99-13047. 40p. 1999. 29.95 (*0-609-60255-1*, Crown) Crown.

— Civil War Sourcebook. (Illus.). 320p. 1991. 20.00 (*0-517-57767-4*) Harmony Bks.

***Lawliss, Chuck.** The Long & the Short & the Tall: Marines in Combat on Guam & Iwo Jima. 2000. pap. 16.95 (*1-58080-080-7*) Burford Bks.

Lawliss, Chuck. The Marine Book: A Portrait of America's Military Elite. rev. ed. LC 91-67311. (Illus.). 192p. 1992. pap. 19.95 (*0-500-27665-X*, Pub. by Thames Hudson) Norton.

— New York Theatre Sourcebook. 1990. pap. 12.95 (*0-671-69970-9*) S&S Trade.

***Lawliss, Chuck.** Retro NY: Rediscovering Old New York. (Illus.). 2000. pap. 16.95 (*0-87833-171-9*) Taylor Pub.

Lawliss, Chuck. Robert E. Lee Slept Here. LC 98-96013. 224p. 1998. pap. 10.00 (*0-345-42156-6*) Ballantine Pub Grp.

***Lawliss, Chuck.** The Submarine Book: An Illustrated History of the Attack Submarine. rev. ed. (Illus.). 16.95p. 2000. pap. 16.95 (*1-58080-078-5*) Burford Bks.

Lawlor. Computer Information System. 3rd ed. (C). 1994. suppl. ed. 20.50 incl. 3.5 ld (*0-03-098196-4*) Harcourt Coll Pubs.

Lawlor, Gretchen, et al, contrib. by. Llewellyn's 2000 Herbal Almanac. annuals (Illus.). 336p. 1999. pap. 6.95 (*1-56718-961-X*) Llewellyn Pubns.

Lawlor, Alan. Productivity Improvement Manual. LC 85-12194. (Illus.). 306p. 1986. 59.95 (*0-89930-148-7*, LPY/, Quorum Bks) Greenwood.

Lawlor, Anthony. A Home for the Soul. 1997. pap. 25.00 (*0-609-80129-5*) Random Hse Value.

— A Home for the Soul: Guide for Dwelling with Spirit & Imagination. LC 97-19702. 1997. 30.00 (*0-517-70400-5*, Carol Southern Bks) Crown.

Lawlor, Brian A., ed. Behavioral Complications in Alzheimer's Disease. (Clinical Practice Ser.: No. 31). 272p. 1995. text 38.50 (*0-88048-477-2*, 8477) Am Psychiatric.

***Lawlor, Chris.** Canon Frederick Donovan's Dunlavin, 1884-1896: A West Wicklow Village in the Late Nineteenth Century. (Maynooth Studies in Irish Local History Ser.). 72p. 2000. pap. 12.50 (*0-7165-2724-3*, Pub. by Irish Acad Pr) Intl Spec Bk.

Lawlor, David W., tr. see Mohr, Hans & Schopfer, Peter.

Lawlor, Deborah, tr. see Schwaller De Lubicz, R. A.

Lawlor, Edward E., III. Pay & Organization Development. 253p. (C). 1981. pap. text 42.00 (*0-201-03990-7*) Addison-Wesley.

Lawlor, Elizabeth P. Discover Nature at Sundown: Things to Know & Things to Do. (Illus.). 224p. 1995. pap. 14.95 (*0-8117-2527-8*) Stackpole.

— Discover Nature at the Seashore: Things to Know & Things to Do. LC 91-17260. (Discover Nature Ser.). (Illus.). 224p. (J). 1992. pap. 14.95 (*0-8117-3079-4*) Stackpole.

— Discover Nature Close to Home: Things to Know & Things to Do. (Discover Nature Ser.). (Illus.). 224p. (Orig.). (YA). (gr. 8 up). 1993. pap. 14.95 (*0-8117-3077-8*) Stackpole.

***Lawlor, Elizabeth P.** Discover Nature in Water & Wetlands: Things to Know & Things to Do. LC 99-44787. 1999. 14.95 (*0-8117-2731-9*) Stackpole.

Lawlor, Elizabeth P. Research in Science Education, 1953-1957. LC 69-12581. (Reviews of Research in Science Education Ser.). 120p. reprint ed. pap. 37.20 (*0-608-14864-4*, 202604000048) Bks Demand.

Lawlor, Elizabeth P., et al. Discover Nature in Winter. LC 98-17606. (Illus.). 208p. (J). 1998. pap. 14.95 (*0-8117-2719-X*) Stackpole.

***Lawlor, Florine.** Mojave Desert Trails. Zdon, Andy, ed. Orig. Title: Mojave OHV Trails. (Illus.). 80p. 2000. pap. 9.95 (*1-893343-03-0*, Pub. by Spotted Dog CA) Sunbelt Pubns.

Lawlor, Florine. Out from Las Vegas. LC 99-27088. (Illus.). 288p. 1999. mass mkt. 16.95 (*0-9647530-4-9*) Spotted Dog CA.

Lawlor, G. A Sufficient Criterion for a Cone to Be Area-Minimizing. LC 91-8060. (Memoirs Ser.: Vol. 91/446). 111p. 1991. pap. 22.00 (*0-8218-2512-7*, MEMO/91/446) Am Math.

Lawlor, Glenn J., Jr. Manual of Immunology Asia, No. 2. 1987. 10.95 (*0-316-51669-4*, Little Brwn Med Div) Lppncott W & W.

— Manual of Immunology ISE, No. 2. 1987. 15.95 (*0-316-51667-8*, Little Brwn Med Div) Lppncott W & W.

Lawlor, Glenn J., Jr., et al, eds. Manual of Allergy & Immunology. 3rd ed. LC 94-26782. 608p. 1995. spiral bd. 38.00 (*0-316-51681-3*, Little Brwn Med Div) Lppncott W & W.

Lawlor, Gudron, tr. see Mohr, Hans & Schopfer, Peter.

Lawlor, Gudrun, jt. auth. see Jones, Alan G.

Lawlor, Hugh, jt. ed. see Brock, Colin.

Lawlor, Jacques. Beauty Is an Inside Job: A Hair & Skin Care Alternative to Beauty Industry Bondage. LC 89-82692. (Illus.). 95p. (Orig.). 1990. pap. 8.95 (*1-878398-02-4*) Blue Note Pubns.

Lawlor, John. Auto Math Handbook. (Illus.). 144p. 1991. pap. 17.95 (*1-55788-020-4*, HP Books) Berkley Pub.

Lawlor, John & Hooper, Walter. C. S. Lewis: Memories & Reflections. LC 98-24265. (Illus.). 160p. 1998. 22.95 (*1-890626-08-2*) Spence Pub.

Lawlor, Laurie. Addie Across the Prairie. LC 85-115548. (Illus.). 128p. (J). (gr. 3-6). 1986. lib. bdg. 13.95 (*0-8075-0165-4*) A Whitman.

Lawlor, Laurie. Addie Across the Prairie. 1986. 9.09 (*0-606-04854-5*, Pub. by Turtleback) Demco.

Lawlor, Laurie. Addie Across the Prairie. MacDonald, Patricia, ed. (Illus.). 128p. (J). 1991. reprint ed. pap. 3.99 (*0-671-70147-9*, Minstrel Bks) PB.

— Addie's Dakota Winter. Tucker, Kathy, ed. Gowing, Toby, tr. LC 89-5564. (Illus.). 160p. (J). (gr. 2-6). 1989. lib. bdg. 13.95 (*0-8075-0171-9*) A Whitman.

— Addie's Dakota Winter. 1989. 9.09 (*0-606-00254-5*, Pub. by Turtleback) Demco.

— Addie's Dakota Winter. MacDonald, Patricia, ed. (Illus.). 160p. (J). (gr. 3-6). 1991. reprint ed. pap. 3.99 (*0-671-70148-7*, Minstrel Bks) PB.

— Addie's Forever Friend. LC 96-54016. (Illus.). 128p. (J). (gr. 2-5). 1997. lib. bdg. 13.95 (*0-8075-0164-6*) A Whitman.

— Addie's Long Summer. Tucker, Kathleen, ed. LC 91-34877. (Illus.). 176p. (J). (gr. 3-6). 1992. text 13.95 (*0-8075-0167-0*) A Whitman.

— Addie's Long Summer. 1995. 8.60 (*0-606-07178-4*, Pub. by Turtleback) Demco.

— Addie's Long Summer. (Illus.). 173p. (J). (gr. 3-7). 1995. reprint ed. pap. 3.50 (*0-671-52607-3*, Minstrel Bks) PB.

***Lawlor, Laurie.** Adventure on the Wilderness Road, 1775. (American Sisters Ser.). (J). (gr. 3-6). 2001. pap. 4.50 (*0-671-77568-5*, Minstrel Bks) PB.

Lawlor, Laurie. Adventure on the Wilderness Road, 1775: American Sisters 4. (American Sisters Ser.: Vol. 4). 186p. (YA). (gr. 3-6). 1999. 9.00 (*0-671-01553-2*, Minstrel Bks) PB.

— American Sisters: West along the Wagon Road, 1852. (American Sisters Ser.: Vol. 1). (J). (gr. 4-7). 1998. pap. 9.00 (*0-671-01551-6*, Minstrel Bks) PB.

Lawlor, Laurie. The Biggest Pest on Eighth Avenue. LC 97-2215. (Holiday House Reader Ser.). (Illus.). 48p. (J). (gr. k-3). 1997. lib. bdg. 14.95 (*0-8234-1321-7*) Holiday.

Lawlor, Laurie. Come Away with Me. (Heartland Ser.: ser. 1). 192p. (J). 1996. per. 3.99 (*0-671-53716-4*, Minstrel Bks) PB.

— Come Away with Me. (Heartland Ser.). 1996. 9.09 (*0-606-10163-2*, Pub. by Turtleback) Demco.

— Crossing the Colorado Rockies, 1814. (American Sisters Ser.: Vol. 5). (J). (gr. 3-7). 1999. 9.00 (*0-671-01554-0*, Minstrel Bks) PB.

***Lawlor, Laurie.** Crossing the Colorado Rockies, 1864. (American Sisters Ser.). (J). (gr. 3-6). 2001. pap. 4.50 (*0-671-77572-3*, Minstrel Bks) PB.

Lawlor, Laurie. George on His Own. (Illus.). 192p. (J). 1996. per. 3.50 (*0-671-52608-1*, Minstrel Bks) PB.

— George on His Own. LC 92-28166. 1996. 8.60 (*0-606-09313-3*, Pub. by Turtleback) Demco.

— Gold in the Hills. (J). 1997. per. 3.99 (*0-671-56833-7*, Minstrel Bks) PB.

Lawlor, Laurie. Gold in the Hills. 1997. 9.09 (*0-606-11399-1*, Pub. by Turtleback) Demco.

Lawlor, Laurie. Gold in the Hills. 196p. (J). (gr. 4-8). 1995. 15.95 (*0-8027-8371-6*) Walker & Co.

— Gold in the Hills. (J). (gr. 3-7). 1997. reprint ed. pap. 3.99 (*0-614-28887-8*, Minstrel Bks) PB.

***Lawlor, Laurie.** Horseback on the Old Post Road from Boston to New York 1704. (American Sisters Ser.: Vol. 7). (Illus.). 208p. 2000. 9.00 (*0-671-03923-7*, Minstrel Bks) PB.

Lawlor, Laurie. How to Survive Third Grade. Levine, Abby, ed. LC 87-25430. (Illus.). 80p. (J). (gr. 2-5). 1988. lib. bdg. 9.95 (*0-8075-3433-1*) A Whitman.

— How to Survive Third Grade. (Illus.). (J). (gr. 2-4). 1991. reprint ed. pap. 3.99 (*0-671-67713-6*, Minstrel Bks) PB.

— Luck Follows Me. (Heartland Ser.: No. 3). 176p. (J). (gr. 3-6). 1996. per. 3.99 (*0-671-53718-0*) PB.

— Luck Follows Me. (Heartland Ser.). 1996. 9.09 (*0-606-10862-9*, Pub. by Turtleback) Demco.

— The Real Johnny Appleseed. LC 94-22010. (Illus.). 64p. (J). (gr. 3-7). 1994. lib. bdg. 13.95 (*0-8075-6909-7*) A Whitman.

— Shadow Catcher: The Life & Work of Edward Sheriff Curtis. LC 93-40272. (YA). 1994. lib. bdg. 20.85 (*0-8027-8289-2*) Walker & Co.

— Shadow Catcher: The Life & Work of Edward Sheriff Curtis. LC 93-40272. (Illus.). 132p. (YA). 1994. 19.95 (*0-8027-8288-4*) Walker & Co.

— Take to the Sky. (Heartland Ser.: No. 2). 176p. (J). (gr. 3-6). 1996. per. 3.99 (*0-671-53717-2*) PB.

Lawlor, Laurie. Take to the Sky. LC 49-244400. (Heartland Ser.). 1996. 9.09 (*0-606-10949-8*, Pub. by Turtleback) Demco.

— 'Till They Loved You Big & Far: The Life & Times of Helen Keller. LC 00-36950. (Illus.). 2001. write for info. (*0-8234-1588-0*) Holiday.

Lawlor, Laurie. A Titanic Journey Across the Sea, 1912. LC 99-165369. (American Sisters Ser.: Vol. 2). (J). (gr. 3-6). 1998. 9.00 (*0-671-02718-2*, Minstrel Bks) PB.

***Lawlor, Laurie.** A Titanic Journey Across the Sea, 1912. rev. ed. (American Sisters Ser.). (Illus.). 224p. (J). 2000. pap. 4.50 (*0-671-77559-6*, Minstrel Bks) PB.

Lawlor, Laurie. Voyage to a Free Land 1630. (American Sisters Ser.). (J). (gr. 3-6). 2001. pap. 4.50 (*0-671-77562-6*, Minstrel Bks) PB.

— Voyage to a Free Land 1630: American Sisters, Vol. 3. LC 99-168700. (American Sisters Ser.: 03). 160p. (J). (gr. 3-7). 1998. per. 9.00 (*0-671-01552-4*, Minstrel Bks) PB.

Lawlor, Laurie. West Along the Wagon Road 1852. (American Sisters Ser.: Vol. 1). 160p. (J). (gr. 4-7). 1909. mass mkt. 4.50 (*0-671-77557-X*, Minstrel Bks) PB.

Lawlor, Laurie. Where Will This Shoe Take You? A Walk Through the History of Footwear. (Illus.). 132p. (YA). (gr. 5 up). 1996. 17.95 (*0-8027-8434-8*); lib. bdg. 18.85 (*0-8027-8435-6*) Walker & Co.

***Lawlor, Laurie.** Wind on the River: A Story of the Civil War. (Jamestown's American Portraits Ser.). (Illus.). 144p. (J). 2000. pap. 5.95 (*0-8092-0624-2*, 06242E, Jamestwn Pub) NTC Contemp Pub Co.

— Window on the West: The Frontier Photography of William Henry Jackson. LC 98-56083. (Illus.). 144p. (YA). (gr. 5 up). 1999. 18.95 (*0-8234-1380-2*) Holiday.

Lawlor, Laurie. The Worm Club. Clancy, Lisa, ed. 128p. (Orig.). (J). 1994. mass mkt. 2.99 (*0-671-78900-7*, Minstrel Bks) PB.

— The Worst Kid Who Ever Lived on Eighth Avenue: A Holiday House Reader. LC 97-28185. (Illus.). 45p. (J). (gr. k-3). 1998. lib. bdg. 14.95 (*0-8234-1350-0*) Holiday.

Lawlor, Leonard. Imagination & Chance: The Difference Between the Thought of Ricoeur & Derrida. LC 92-13359. (SUNY Series, Intersections: Philosophy & Critical Theory). 203p. (C). 1993. text 64.50 (*0-7914-1217-2*); pap. text 21.95 (*0-7914-1218-0*) State U NY Pr.

Lawlor, Leonard, jt. ed. see Evans, Frederick.

Lawlor, Leonard, tr. see Hyppolite, Jean.

Lawlor, Mark R. Brandywine Springs Amusement Park, (1886-1923) Echoes of the Past. (Illus.). 160p. (Orig.). 1993. pap. 20.00 (*0-9638422-0-X*) M & M Pub.

***Lawlor, Mary.** Recalling the Wild: Naturalism & the Closing of the American West. LC 99-56541. (Illus.). 208p. 2000. text 52.00 (*0-8135-2829-1*); pap. text 22.00 (*0-8135-2830-5*) Rutgers U Pr.

Lawlor, Mary A., jt. auth. see Foran, James.

Lawlor, Michael. Lawlor's Radio Values. (Orig.). 1991. pap. 12.50 (*0-9629640-0-X*) Bare Bones.

— Negotiating with Insight. (C). 1992. 36.00 incl. audio (*0-85171-089-1*, Pub. by IPM Hse) St Mut.

Lawlor, Michael S., jt. ed. see Cottrell, Allin F.

Lawlor, Michel & Handley, Peter. The Creative Trainer: Holistic Facilitation Skills for Accelerated Learning. LC 95-49800. (Training Ser.). (Illus.). 200p. 1997. pap. 29.95 (*0-07-709030-6*) McGraw.

Lawlor, Monica, ed. see Harding, D. W.

Lawlor, Patricia M. La Fonctionnement de la Metaphore dans les Chants de Maldoror. LC 83-26991. (Romance Monographs: No. 44). (FRE.). 174p. 1984. 23.00 (*84-499-7154-3*) Romance.

Lawlor, Patrick T., compiled by. Thomas Merton: The Poet & the Contemplative Life. 64p. 1990. pap. 12.50 (*0-9607862-2-8*) Columbia U Libs.

Lawlor, Peter. Windsocks & Lyrica. LC 94-90586. 55p. 1994. pap. write for info. (*0-9644104-0-0*) Full Moon CA.

Lawlor, Robert. Earth Honoring: The New Male Sexuality. 256p. 1989. 16.95 (*0-89281-254-0*, Destiny Bks) Inner Tradit.

— Earth Honoring: The New Male Sexuality. 224p. 1991. reprint ed. pap. 12.95 (*0-89281-428-4*, Park St Pr) Inner Tradit.

— Sacred Geometry: Philosophy & Practice. LC 88-51328. (Art & Imagination Ser.). (Illus.). 112p. 1989. reprint ed. pap. 15.95 (*0-500-81030-3*, Pub. by Thames Hudson) Norton.

— Voices of the First Day: Awakening in the Aboriginal Dreamtime. (Illus.). 352p. (Orig.). 1991. pap. 29.95 (*0-89281-355-5*) Inner Tradit.

Lawlor, Robert, tr. see Schwaller De Lubicz, R. A.

Lawlor, Robert, tr. see Theon of Smyrna.

Lawlor, Robert C. American Kang Duk Won Karate: Basic Principles & Techniques. 212p. 1995. pap. text 24.95 (*0-9649468-0-7*) Panther.

Lawlor, Sheila. Churchill & the Politics of War, 1940-1941. LC 93-28733. 286p. (C). 1994. pap. text 27.95 (*0-521-46685-7*) Cambridge U Pr.

Lawlor, Steven C. ANSI C Programming. LC 94-189251. 384p. (C). 1994. mass mkt. 65.95 (*0-314-02830-7*) West Pub.

— The Art of Programming: Computer Science with C. LC 95-38925. 450p. (C). 1996. mass mkt. 55.95 (*0-314-06814-7*) West Pub.

— Computer Information System. 2nd ed. (C). 1992. pap. text, student ed. 31.50 (*0-15-500222-8*) Harcourt Coll Pubs.

— Computer Information Systems. 3rd ed. LC 93-72826. (C). 1994. disk 29.75 (*0-03-098197-2*) Dryden Pr.

— PRESENT SFR(3.5 DSK&DOC)-COMP. 3rd ed. LC 93-72826. 266p. (C). 1994. pap. 102.00 incl. disk (*0-03-098201-4*) Dryden Pr.

Lawlor, Timothy E. Handbook to the Orders & Families of Living Mammals. 2nd ed. (Illus.). 327p. (C). 1976. pap. 22.95 (*0-916422-16-X*) Mad River.

Lawlor, Veronica. I Was Dreaming to Come to America: Memories from the Ellis Island Oral History Project. (Illus.). 40p. (J). 1997. pap. 6.99 (*0-14-055622-2*) Penguin Putnam.

Lawlor, Veronica. I Was Dreaming to Come to America: Memories from the Ellis Island Oral History Project. (J). 1997. 11.19 (*0-606-11501-3*, Pub. by Turtleback) Demco.

Lawlor, Veronica. I Was Dreaming to Come to America: Memories from the Ellis Island Oral History Project. 40p. (J). 1995. 15.99 (*0-670-86164-2*, Viking Child) Peng Put Young Read.

Lawlor, William. The Beat Generation: A Bibliographical Teaching Guide. LC 98-3157. (Magill Bibliographies Ser.). 376p. 1998. 42.00 (*0-8108-3387-5*) Scarecrow.

— Let's Go down to the Beach: Poems & Translations of Four Caribbean Writers. 128p. (Orig.). 1996. pap. text 13.95 (*0-9641986-9-X*) Poetry Harbor.

Lawman, jt. auth. see Wace.

Lawn, Beverly. The Short Story: Thirty Masterpieces. 2nd ed. LC 90-71633. 454p. (C). 1992. pap. text 16.95 (*0-312-04835-1*) St Martin.

— Throat of Feathers. 1979. 6.00 (*0-918870-07-0*); pap. 3.00 (*0-918870-08-9*) Pleasure Dome.

An Asterisk (*) at the beginning of an entry indicates that the title is appearing for the first time.

Lawn, Brian. Fracture of Brittle Solids. 2nd ed. (Solid State Science Ser.). (Illus.). 398p. (C). 1993. pap. text 45.00 (*0-521-40972-1*) Cambridge U Pr.
— The Rise & Decline of the Scholastic Quaestio Disputata: With Special Emphasis on Its Use in the Teaching of Medicine & Science. LC 92-42729. (Education & Society in the Middle Ages & Renaissance Ser.: No. 2). x, 176p. 1993. 71.00 (*90-04-09740-6*) Brill Academic Pubs.
Lawn, Brian R., jt. ed. see Blau, Peter J.
Lawn, G. R. Music in State Clothing: The Story of the Kettledrummers, Trumpeters & Band of the Life Guards. (Illus.). 194p. 1995. 31.95 (*0-85052-454-7*, Pub. by Leo Cooper) Trans-Atl Phila.
Lawn, John, jt. auth. see Chambers, Catherine E.
Lawn, Martin. Modern Times? Work, Professionalism & Citizenship in Teaching. 200p. 1996. 79.95 (*0-7507-0495-0*, Falmer Pr); pap. 27.95 (*0-7507-0496-9*, Falmer Pr) Taylor & Francis.
Lawn, Martin & Grace, G., eds. Teachers: The Culture & Politics of Work. 225p. 1987. 75.00 (*1-85000-216-9*, Falmer Pr) Taylor & Francis.
Lawn, Martin, jt. ed. see Grace, Gerald.
***Lawn, Philip A.** Toward Sustainable Development: An Ecological Economics Approach. LC 00-39082. (Ecological Economics Ser.). (Illus.). 2000. write for info. (*1-56670-411-1*) Lewis Pubs.
Lawn, R. E., et al, eds. Proficiency Testing in Analytical Chemistry. 122p. 1997. pap. 47.00 (*0-85404-432-9*) Am Chemical.
Lawn, Richard J., jt. auth. see Hellmer, Jeffrey L.
Lawn, Robert. The Instruction Book of the Rich & Famous: Helpful Hints for a Happy Life from 108 Celebrities. Carle, Cliff, ed. 184p. 1996. pap. 5.99 (*0-918259-96-7*) CCC Pubns.
Lawn, Sand, jt. auth. see Kinzey, Allen.
Lawne, Christopher. Brownisme Turned the In-Side Out-Ward. LC 76-6282. (English Experience Ser.: No. 74). 40p. 1968. reprint ed. 20.00 (*90-221-0074-X*) Walter J Johnson.
Lawner, Lynne. Harlequin on the Moon: Commedia dell'Arte & the Visual Arts. LC 97-35371. (Illus.). 208p. 1998. 60.00 (*0-8109-1194-9*, Pub. by Abrams) Time Warner.
Lawniczak, Anna T., jt. ed. see Kapral, Raymond.
LawPak Staff. Bankruptcy - Chapter 7: Bankruptcy for Individual. (Illus.). 288p. (Orig.). 1994. pap. 27.95 (*1-879421-00-3*) LawPak.
— Contracts & Promissory Notes. (Illus.). 190p. 1999. pap. 17.95 (*1-879421-08-9*) LawPak.
— Emergency Medical Consent: Medical Consent for a Minor. (Illus.). 72p. (Orig.). 1994. pap. 7.95 (*1-879421-03-8*) LawPak.
— Landlord - Tenant: Rights & Obligations. (Illus.). 181p. (Orig.). 1996. pap. 16.95 (*1-879421-04-6*) LawPak.
— Last Will & Testament: Simple Will. (Illus.). 140p. (Orig.). 1999. pap. 13.95 (*1-879421-01-1*) LawPak.
— Living Will: Power of Attorney for Health Care. (Illus.). 198p. (Orig.). 1994. pap. 18.95 (*1-879421-07-0*) LawPak.
— Name Change: Change Adult or Minors Name. 92p. (Orig.). 1994. pap. 15.95 (*1-879421-06-2*) LawPak.
— Power of Attorney: Durable & General. 120p. (Orig.). 1994. pap. 14.95 (*1-879421-02-X*) LawPak.
— Real Estate Contracts: Buy & Sell. (Illus.). 176p. 1998. pap. 17.75 (*1-879421-11-9*) LawPak.
Lawrance, Alan. Mao Zedong: A Bibliography, 3. LC 91-8424. (Bibliographies of World Leaders Ser.: No. 3). 232p. 1991. lib. bdg. 65.00 (*0-313-28222-6*, LMZ/, Greenwood Pr) Greenwood.
Lawrance, Alan & Dodd, Peter. Anthony Eden, 1897-1977: A Bibliography, Vol. 20. LC 95-7480. (Bibliographies of British Statesmen Ser.: 20). 240p. 1995. lib. bdg. 75.00 (*0-313-28286-2*, Greenwood Pr) Greenwood.
Lawrance, Allan. China under Communism. LC 98-17286. (Making of the Contemporary World Ser.). (Illus.). 160p. (C). 1998. 65.00 (*0-415-18692-7*) Routledge.
— China under Communism. LC 98-17286. (Making of the Contemporary World Ser.). (Illus.). 160p. (C). 1998. pap. 15.99 (*0-415-15045-0*) Routledge.
Lawrance, Gayford R. Demons or Lunatics? 108p. 1999. pap. 10.00 (*1-892477-16-5*) Barnabs Pub.
Lawrance, Jeremy, tr. & pref. see Vitoria, Francisco.
Lawren, Bill, jt. auth. see Cooney, Craig.
Lawren, Bill, jt. auth. see Sears, Barry.
Lawrence. Accounting Principles: Sonya McDowell-Essential Accounting. 8th ed. (C). 1994. mass mkt. 20.95 (*0-538-83216-9*) S-W Pub.
— America: The Politics of Diversity. (Political Science Ser.). 1998. pap. 44.95 (*0-534-54864-4*); pap. 16.00 (*0-534-54865-2*) Wadsworth Pub.
— Archaeological Findings on the Ark of the Covenant. 1999. 5.95 (*0-910653-20-8*, 8115W, Red River Pr) Archival Servs.
— Behind Factory Walls. 350p. 1990. 35.00 (*0-07-103247-9*) McGraw.
— Chiropractic Two Thousand. (Illus.). 350p. 2000. text 73.00 (*0-8151-2860-6*, 31806) Mosby Inc.
— Chiropractic Two Thousand & One. 2001. text 73.00 (*0-8151-2871-1*, 31807) Mosby Inc.
— Chiropractic Two Thousand & Three. 2002. text 73.00 (*0-8151-2880-0*, 31808) Mosby Inc.
***Lawrence.** CompaQ Visual Fortran: A Guide to Creating Windows Application. 600p. 2001. pap. 44.95 (*1-55558-249-4*, Digital DEC) Buttrwrth-Heinemann.
Lawrence. Creative Crafting with Recycled Greeting Cards. (Illus.). 112p. 1998. pap. 12.95 (*0-8069-9826-1*) Sterling.
— Falsecards. 9.95 (*0-910791-47-3*, 0636) Devyn Pr.
— Guide to Modern Biology. rev. ed. 1998. pap. text. write for info. (*0-582-22711-9*, Pub. by Addison-Wesley) Longman.
— Harriet & the Promise Land. (J). 1998. pap. 5.99 (*0-87628-392-X*) Ctr Appl Res.
Lawrence. International Accounting. 1996. pap. 21.99 (*1-86152-256-8*, Pub. by ITBP) Thomson Learn.
Lawrence. Internet Commerce. (C). 1998. pap. text 30.00 (*0-471-34027-8*) Wiley.
— Introduction to BASIC Astronomy with a PC. 1989. pap. 19.95 (*0-943396-23-9*) Willmann-Bell.
Lawrence. Lactancia Materna. 4th ed. (C). 1996. text 73.88 (*84-8174-176-0*) Mosby Inc.
Lawrence. Lawrence Kursk. 2000. 35.00 (*0-8133-3673-2*) HarpC.
— Modern Biology. 1996. 44.67 (*0-582-44272-9*) Addison-Wesley.
— Modernity & War. LC 96-52561. 206p. 1998. text 65.00 (*0-312-17402-0*) St Martin.
— 1999 Year Book of Chiropractic. (Illus.). 416p. 1998. text 78.00 (*0-8151-9603-2*, 24942) Mosby Inc.
— Organization & Environment. 296p. 1986. pap. 14.36 (*0-07-103246-0*) McGraw.
— Partnership Understandings. 4.95 (*0-910791-08-2*, 0634) Devyn Pr.
— Play Bridge with Mike Lawrence. 11.95 (*0-910791-09-0*, 0635) Devyn Pr.
— The Practice of the Presence of God. Demaray, Donald E., ed. LC 96-53201. 81p. 1997. mass mkt. 4.50 (*0-8189-0770-3*) Alba.
— The Practice of the Presence of God. LC 99-32606. (Nelson's Royal Classic Ser.: Vol 6). 320p. 1999. 18.99 (*0-7852-4227-9*) Nelson.
— Practicing the Presence of God: Conversations & Letters of Nicholas Herman of Lorraine. Coleman, Robert E., ed. (Collection of Classics Ser.). 56p. 1996. pap. text 2.95 (*1-879089-23-8*) B Graham Ctr.
— Racial Discrimination under the Law. 1996. pap. 26.74 (*0-07-218478-7*) McGraw.
— Selections from Brother Lawrence's the Practice of the Presence of God. 1959. pap. 2.00 (*0-8358-0051-2*) Upper Room Bks.
***Lawrence.** Small Animal Emergency. 2000. pap. text. write for info. (*0-7216-7773-8*, W B Saunders Co) Harcrt Hlth Sci Grp.
Lawrence. Strong on Music, Vol. 3. 1999. pap. text 25.00 (*0-226-47016-4*) U Ch Pr.
— Strong on Music, Vol. 3. LC 94-205956. Vol. 3. (Illus.). 488p. 1999. lib. bdg. 65.00 (*0-226-47015-6*) U Ch Pr.
— Vicki! The True - Life Adventures of Miss Fireball. 1995. 23.00 (*0-671-89204-5*) S&S Trade.
Lawrence, et al, eds. Archival Science. 256p. (C). 1999. 16.95 (*0-910653-17-8*, 8005S, Red River Pr) Archival Servs.
Lawrence & Bullen. The Complete Fortune Teller. 196p. 1997. reprint ed. pap. 19.95 (*0-7661-0053-7*) Kessinger Pub.
Lawrence & Leonard. Primer to California Politics. pap. text. write for info. (*0-312-13677-3*) St Martin.
Lawrence & Loudder. Financial Accounting: Critical Thinking Activities. 3rd ed. LC 97-68552. 1998. pap. 16.95 (*0-87393-744-9*) Dame Pubns.
***Lawrence, et al.** Essentials of Accounting. 9th ed. (AB - Accounting Principles Ser.). 336p. 1998. pap. 50.95 (*0-538-86352-8*) S-W Pub.
Lawrence, et al. Special Edition Using Turbo C Plus Plus for Windows. (Illus.). 800p. (Orig.). 1995. pap. 39.99 (*0-614-07261-1*) Que.
Lawrence, jt. auth. see Hubbard.
Lawrence, jt. auth. see McGovern.
Lawrence, jt. ed. see Case.
Lawrence & Wishart Ltd. Staff, ed. Documents of the First Council of the International Working Men's Association, 1864-1872, 5 vols. 705p. 1974. 115.00 (*0-8464-0340-4*) Beekman Pubs.
Lawrence, A. Modern Inertial Technology: Navigation, Guidance, & Control. 2nd ed. LC 98-13047. (Mechanical Engineering Ser.). (Illus.). 280p. 1998. 59.00 (*0-387-98507-7*) Spr-Verlag.
— Who's Who among Living Authors of Older Nations. 1973. 59.95 (*0-8490-1297-X*) Gordon Pr.
Lawrence, A. W. Greek Architecture. 5th rev. ed. LC 95-53785. (Illus.). 264p. 1996. 65.00 (*0-300-06491-8*); pap. 30.00 (*0-300-06492-6*) Yale U Pr.
Lawrence, A. W., ed. T. E. Lawrence by His Friends. 576p. 1980. reprint ed. 75.00 (*0-87752-196-4*) Gordian.
Lawrence, A. W. & Young, Jean, eds. Narratives of the Discovery of America. xiii, 300p. 1987. reprint ed. pap. 17.50 (*1-55613-086-4*) Heritage Bk.
***Lawrence, Aaron.** The Male Escort's Handbook: Your Guide to Getting Rich the Hard Way. 250p. 2000. pap. 14.95 (*0-9667691-1-2*) Late Night Pr.
Lawrence, Aaron. Suburban Hustler: Stories of a Hi-Tech Callboy. LC 98-96656. 230p. 1999. pap. 14.95 (*0-9667691-0-4*, Pub. by Late Night Pr) Bookazine Co Inc.
Lawrence, Al. Playing Computer Chess. LC 98-130578. (Illus.). 144p. 1998. 12.95 (*0-8069-0717-7*) Sterling.
Lawrence, Al, ed. see Alburt, Lev & Krogeur, Nikolai.
Lawrence, Albert, ed. see Alburt, Lev & Palatnik, Sam.
***Lawrence, Alexander.** Passage. 2000. mass mkt. 5.99 (*0-451-40944-2*, Onyx) NAL.
Lawrence, Alexander A. A Present for Mr. Lincoln: The Story of Savannah from Secession to Sherman. 1997. reprint ed. 25.00 (*1-891495-00-3*) Oglethorpe Pr.
Lawrence, Allan. Running & Racing after Thirty-Five. 242p. 1990. pap. 14.95 (*0-316-51675-9*) Little.
Lawrence, Althea. Unity Without Uniformity: History of the Rhinebeck, N. Y. Church Community, 1718-1918. LC 91-33508. 184p. 1992. 30.00 (*0-912526-54-8*) Lib Res.
Lawrence, Amy. Echo & Narcissus: Women's Voices in Classical Hollywood Cinema. LC 90-50903. (Illus.). 218p. 1991. 55.00 (*0-520-07071-2*, Pub. by U CA Pr); pap. 18.95 (*0-520-07082-8*, Pub. by U CA Pr) Cal Prin Full Svc.
— The Films of Peter Greenaway. (Film Classics Ser.). (Illus.). 236p. (C). 1997. text 54.95 (*0-521-47363-2*); pap. text 15.95 (*0-521-47919-3*) Cambridge U Pr.
Lawrence, Anita, ed. Comets to Cosmology. (Lecture Notes in Physics Ser.: Vol. 297). x, 415p. 1988. 59.95 (*0-387-19052-X*) Spr-Verlag.
— Inter-Noise, '91: Proceedings Held in Sydney, Australia on 1991 December 2-4, 2 vols., Set. (Inter-Noise Ser.). xxxiv, 1289p. 130.00 (*0-909882-12-6*) Noise Control.
Lawrence, Ann. Between the Forest & the Hills. LC 98-73488. (Adventure Library). 264p. (YA). (gr. 8 up). 1999. reprint ed. pap. text 12.95 (*1-883937-39-6*, 39-6) Bethlehem ND.
***Lawrence, Ann.** Lord of the Keep. 400p. (Orig.). 1999. mass mkt. 5.99 (*0-505-52351-5*, Love Spell) Dorchester Pub Co.
— Virtual Desire. (Perfect Heroes Ser.). 400p. 2000. mass mkt. 5.99 (*0-505-52393-0*, Love Spell) Dorchester Pub Co.
Lawrence, Ann. Virtual Heaven. (Love Spell Ser.). 400p. 1999. mass mkt. 5.99 (*0-505-52307-8*, Love Spell) Dorchester Pub Co.
Lawrence, Ann, tr. see Perrault, Charles.
Lawrence, Ann M., jt. auth. see Lawrence, Paul R.
Lawrence, Ann T., jt. auth. see Schattinger, Joan M.
Lawrence, Anthony. The Fragrant Chinese: A Portrait of Hong Kong & Its People. (Illus.). 233p. (C). 1997. 29.95 (*962-201-572-7*, Pub. by Chinese Univ) U of Mich Pr.
— Modern Inertial Technology: Navigation, Guidance, & Control. LC 92-16602. (Instrumentation & Systems Ser.). (Illus.). 328p. 1993. 74.95 (*0-387-97868-2*) Spr-Verlag.
— New & Selected Poems. LC 98-204375. 1998. pap. 24.95 (*0-7022-2980-6*, Pub. by Univ Queensland Pr) Intl Spec Bk.
— The Taipan Traders. (Illus.). 95p. 1994. 38.00 (*962-7283-07-X*, Pub. by FormAsia) Weatherhill.
Lawrence, Anthony G. Pricing & Planning in the U. S. Natural Gas Industry: An Econometric & Programming Study. Bruchey, Stuart, ed. LC 78-22693. (Energy in the American Economy Ser.). (Illus.). 1979. lib. bdg. 19.95 (*0-405-11996-8*) Ayer.
Lawrence, Ardi. A Daytripper's Guide to the Natural Wonders of Kentucky. LC 97-10060. (Daytripper's Guide to the Natural Wonder Ser.). (Illus.). 200p. 1997. pap. 12.95 (*1-56626-190-2*, Cntry Rds Pr) NTC Contemp Pub Co.
***Lawrence, Ardi.** Natural Wonders of Kentucky: Exploring Wild & Scenic Places. 2nd ed. LC 98-25114. (Natural Wonders of... Ser.). (Illus.). 400p. 1999. pap. 15.95 (*1-56626-139-2*, 61392) NTC Contemp Pub Co.
Lawrence, Ardi & Lawrence, H. Lea. Natural Wonders of Tennessee: Exploring Wild & Scenic Places. 2nd ed. LC 98-39698. (Natural Wonders of... Ser.). (Illus.). 304p. 1999. pap. 14.95 (*1-56626-196-1*, 61961, Cntry Rds Pr) NTC Contemp Pub Co.
Lawrence, Ardi, jt. auth. see Lawrence, H. Lea.
Lawrence, Ardi, ed. see Szepes, Maria.
Lawrence, Ardis. How to Eat an Elephant: One Bite at a Time. 60p. (Orig.). 1994. pap. 9.00 (*0-9644370-1-5*) Dryden Publ.
Lawrence, Arthur. The Management of Trade Marketing. 200p. 1983. text 78.95 (*0-566-02395-4*) Ashgate Pub Co.
— Sir Arthur Sullivan. LC 79-27876. (Music Reprint Ser.: 1980). (Illus.). 340p. 1980. reprint ed. lib. bdg. 39.50 (*0-306-76029-0*) Da Capo.
— Sir Arthur Sullivan. LC 72-3244. (English Biography Ser.: No. 31). 1972. reprint ed. lib. bdg. 75.00 (*0-8383-1522-4*) M S G Haskell Hse.
Lawrence, Ava. Wahili: The Waterboy. (Illus.). 32p. (J). (gr. 2-5). 1996. 14.95 (*0-9651048-0-X*) Papillon TX.
Lawrence, Barbara. Mammals Found at the Awatovi Site. (HU PMP Ser.: Vol. 35, No. 3). (Illus.). 1951. pap. 25.00 (*0-527-01290-4*) Periodicals Srv.
Lawrence, Barbara & Branz, Nedra, eds. The Flagg Correspondence: Selected Letters, 1816-1854. LC 85-27774. 289p. 1986. text 31.95 (*0-8093-1242-5*) S Ill U Pr.
Lawrence, Barbara Kent. Bitter Ice: A Memoir of Love, Food & Obsession. LC 99-16615. 352p. 1999. 25.00 (*0-688-16215-0*, Wm Morrow) Morrow Avon.
***Lawrence, Barbara Kent.** Pap Bitter Ice. 2000. pap. write for info. (*0-688-17777-8*, Wm Morrow) Morrow Avon.
Lawrence, Basil E. History of the Laws Affecting the Property of Married Women in England: Being an Essay Which Obtained the Yorke Prize of the University of Cambridge. xvi, 183p. 1986. reprint ed. 47.50 (*0-8377-2404-X*, Rothman) W S Hein.
Lawrence, Benjamin F. History of Jay, Franklin County. (Illus.). 93p. 1997. reprint ed. pap. 18.00 (*0-8328-5862-5*) Higginson Bk Co.
Lawrence, Berta. Discovering the Quantocks. 1989. pap. 25.00 (*0-85263-660-1*, Pub. by Shire Pubns) St Mut.
Lawrence, Betty. Unrevised History of the War for Southern Independence. 1996. 29.50 (*0-89896-431-8*) Larksdale.
Lawrence, Beverly H. Reviving the Spirit: A Generation of African Americans Goes Home to Church. 192p. 1997. reprint ed. pap. 11.00 (*0-8021-3499-8*, Grove) Grove-Atltic.
Lawrence, Beverly Hall. Home Design Workbook: A Design Guide for Every Room of the House. (Illus.). 159p. 1999. pap. 21.99 (*1-56496-513-9*) Rockport Pubs.
Lawrence, Bill. Early American Wilderness. 243p. 1994. 23.95 (*1-56924-870-2*) Marlowe & Co.
— Effective Pastor, 1. LC 99-41679. 1999. 24.99 (*0-8499-1353-5*) Word Pub.
— Effective Pastor: Supersaver Edition, 1. 1999. 19.97 (*0-8499-1584-8*) Word Pub.
— Using Netware 4.1: Special Edition. 2nd ed. LC 96-69613. 1488p. 1996. 59.99 incl. cd-rom (*0-7897-0810-8*) Que.
— Using Netware 3.12, Special Edition: Special Edition. LC 94-65885. 1118p. 1994. 39.99 (*1-56529-627-3*) Que.
Lawrence, Bill, et al. Special Edition Using NetWare 4.X. (Illus.). 1275p. (Orig.). 1995. 39.99 (*1-56529-894-2*) Que.
Lawrence, Bob. A Guide to College Resource & Financial Management. LC 95-7250. (Managing Colleges Effectively Ser.: Vol. 1). 1995. 85.00 (*0-7507-0445-4*, Falmer Pr); pap. 34.95 (*0-7507-0446-2*, Falmer Pr) Taylor & Francis.
Lawrence, Bobby E. Nashville's Tennessee Centennial, 1897. (Images of America Ser.). (Illus.). 128p. 1998. pap. 18.99 (*0-7524-1311-2*) Arcadia Publng.
Lawrence, Bonita. The Exclusion of Survivors' Voices in Feminist Discourse on Violence Against Women LC 98-104139. (Voix Feministes = Ser.). 43 p. 1996. write for info. (*0-919653-71-5*) CRIA.
Lawrence, Bonita & Solow, Daniel. Solutions Manual for the Keys to Linear Algebra: Applications, Theory & Reasoning. (Illus.). 1998. pap. text 10.00 (*0-9644519-3-X*) Books Unltd.
Lawrence, Bonnie M. The Credit Repair Handbook. rev. ed. Harris, Deborah F., ed. 60p. 1989. 29.95 (*0-685-29184-7*); pap. 19.95 (*0-9624059-0-6*) MoneyTree Enterprises.
***Lawrence, Brad.** Revelation Decoy. 100p. 1999. mass mkt. 10.00 (*0-9652528-8-4*, Pub. by Neshui Pubng) Booksource.
Lawrence, Bradley & Pardee Staff. Carriages & Sleighs: 200 Illustrations from the 1862s. LC 98-7047. (Illus.). 160p. 1998. pap. 10.95 (*0-486-40219-3*) Dover.
Lawrence, Brenda, jt. auth. see Murray, Louisa.
Lawrence, Brother. The Practice of the Presence of God. Helms, Hal M., ed. LC 84-61019. (Living Library). 158p. 1984. pap. 8.95 (*0-941478-29-7*, 930-008, Pub. by Paraclete MA) BookWorld.
— The Practice of the Presence of God. Attwater, Donald, tr. (Illus.). 128p. 1981. pap. 9.95 (*0-87243-104-5*) Templegate.
— The Practice of the Presence of God. 95p. 1982. mass mkt. 5.99 (*0-88368-105-6*) Whitaker Hse.
— The Practice of the Presence of God. large type ed. LC 85-61019. 144p. 1985. reprint ed. pap. 7.95 (*0-8027-2510-4*) Walker & Co.
— The Practice of the Presence of God. 60p. 1996. reprint ed. pap. 8.00 (*0-7873-1325-4*) Hlth Research.
— The Practice of the Presence of God. 114p. 1990. reprint ed. 9.95 (*0-910261-12-1*, Arcana Pubng) Lotus Pr.
— The Practice of the Presence of God: Conversations & Letters of Brother Lawrence. (Mystical Classics of the World Ser.). 112p. 1999. reprint ed. text 7.99 (*1-85168-198-1*, Pub. by Onewrld Pubns) Penguin Putnam.
— The Practice of the Presence of God: The Best Rule of a Holy Life. Epworth Press Staff, ed. 96p. 1996. pap. 4.95 (*1-888813-04-0*) Brghtside.
Lawrence, Bruce B. Defenders of God: The Fundamentalist Revolt Against the Modern Age. Denny, Frederick, ed. LC 95-23076. (Studies in Comparative Religion). 320p. 1995. reprint ed. pap. text 16.95 (*1-57003-091-X*) U of SC Pr.
Lawrence, Bruce B. Shattering the Myth: Islam Beyond Violence. LC 97-38776. (Comparative Studies in Muslim Politics). 229p. 1998. text 24.95 (*0-691-05769-9*, Pub. by Princeton U Pr) Cal Prin Full Svc.
***Lawrence, Bruce B.** Shattering the Myth: Islam Beyond Violence. (Studies in Muslim Politics). 2000. pap. text 15.95 (*0-691-00487-0*, Pub. by Princeton U Pr) Cal Prin Full Svc.
Lawrence, Bruce B., ed. Nizam Ad-Din Awliya: Morals for the Heart. (Classics of Western Spirituality Ser.). 1991. 26.95 (*0-8091-0451-2*); pap. 18.95 (*0-8091-3280-X*) Paulist Pr.
Lawrence, Bruce B., tr. see Awliya, Nizam A.
Lawrence, C., jt. auth. see McDaniel, E.
Lawrence, C. Edward & Vachon, Myra K. How to Handle Staff Misconduct: A Step-by-Step Guide. (Illus.). 160p. 1994. pap. 29.95 (*0-8039-6185-5*) Corwin Pr.
— How to Handle Staff Misconduct: A Step-by-Step Guide. 160p. 1994. pap., wbk. ed. 29.95 (*2-8106-6185-5*) NEA.
— The Incompetent Specialist: How to Evaluate, Document Performance, & Dismiss School Staff. (Illus.). 232p. 1996. 74.95 (*0-8039-6438-2*); pap. 34.95 (*0-8039-6439-0*) Corwin Pr.
— The Incompetent Specialist: How to Evaluate, Document Performance, & Dismiss School Staff. 232p. 1996. wbk. ed. 69.95 (*2-8106-6438-2*); pap., wbk. ed. 29.95 (*2-8106-6439-0*) NEA.
Lawrence, C. Edward, et al. The Marginal Teacher: A Step-by-Step Guide to Fair Procedures for Identification & Dismissal. 192p. 1993. pap., student ed. 32.95 (*0-8039-6048-4*) Corwin Pr.
— The Marginal Teacher: A Step-by-Step Guide to Fair Procedures for Identification & Dismissal. 192p. 1993. pap., wbk. ed. 29.95 (*2-8106-6048-4*) NEA.
Lawrence, C. H. English Church & the Papacy in the Middle Ages. 1999. pap. text 23.95 (*0-7509-1947-7*) A Sutton.
— The Friars: The Impact of the Early Mendicant Movement on Western Society. LC 93-25750. (Medieval World Ser.). 320p. (C). 1994. pap. text 30.00 (*0-582-05632-2*, Pub. by Addison-Wesley) Longman.
— Friars Impact Early Mend. LC 93-25750. (Medieval World Ser.). 320p. (C). 1994. text 63.50 (*0-582-05633-0*, Pub. by Addison-Wesley) Longman.

L

An Asterisk (*) at the beginning of an entry indicates that the title is appearing for the first time.

Lawrence, C. M., ed. see Witte, Karl.

Lawrence, Candida. Change of Circumstance. LC 94-41983. 222p. (Orig.). 1995. pap. 16.95 (*1-878448-63-3*) MacMurray & Beck.

— Reeling & Writhing. LC 93-80395. 346p. 1994. 22.95 (*1-878448-60-9*) MacMurray & Beck.

Lawrence, Carl. The Broken Letter. 130p. 1993. pap. 9.95 (*0-9638575-0-9*) Shannon Pubs.

***Lawrence, Carl.** The Broken Letter: Divorce Through the Eyes of a Child. 2nd rev. ed. Myers, Thomas & Lawrence, Sean, eds. (Illus.). 175p. 2000. pap. 10.00 (*0-9638575-2-5*) Shannon Pubs.

Lawrence, Carl. The Coming Influence of China. 1996. pap. 10.99 (*1-885305-50-8*) Multnomah Pubs.

***Lawrence, Carl.** The Cross & the Sword: The Rebellion & Revolution in Chiapas, Mexico. (Illus.). 255p. 1999. pap. 12.00 (*0-9638575-1-7*) Shannon Pubs.

Lawrence, Carol, et al. Storytelling for Teachers & School Library Media Specialists LC 81-65700. 56 p. 1981. write for info. (*0-513-01714-3*) Denison.

Lawrence, Catherine. Creative Crafting with Recycled Greeting Cards. LC 97-22141. (Illus.). 112p. 1997. 24.95 (*0-8069-9825-3*) Sterling.

Lawrence Center Staff. U. S. Immigration Made Easy. 1999. 44.95 (*0-87337-530-0*) Nolo com.

Lawrence, Charles. History of the Philadelphia Almshouses & Hospitals from the Beginning of the Eighteenth to the Ending of the Nineteenth Centuries, Covering a Period of Nearly Two Hundred Years. LC 75-17231. (Social Problems & Social Policy Ser.). (Illus.). 1976. reprint ed. 35.95 (*0-405-07500-6*) Ayer.

Lawrence, Charles, et al. Foundations of Physical Chemistry. (Oxford Chemistry Primers Ser.: No. 40). (Illus.). 96p. (C). 1996. pap. text 12.95 (*0-19-855904-6*) OUP.

***Lawrence, Charles B.** Jus' Family. 32p. 2000. 9.00 (*0-8059-4757-4*) Dorrance.

Lawrence, Charles R., III & Matsuda, Mari J. Affirmative Action. 1997. 23.95 (*0-614-20402-X*) HM.

— We Won't Go Back: Making the Case for Affirmative Action. LC 96-46158. 288p. 1997. 25.00 (*0-395-79125-1*) HM.

Lawrence, Charlotte. The Holographic Dollhouse. LC 95-43006. 464p. 1999. mass mkt. 6.99 (*1-56718-413-8*) Llewellyn Pubns.

— The Rag Bone Man. LC 94-26188. 336p. 1999. pap. 4.99 (*1-56718-412-X*) Llewellyn Pubns.

Lawrence, Chellaian. Jesus as Prophet in Christianity & Islam: A Model for Interfaith Dialogue. LC 98-906382. xxiv, 425 p. 1997. write for info. (*81-7214-352-4*) ISPCK.

Lawrence, Chris, jt. auth. see Connors, J. C.

Lawrence, Christine C. & Duncan, Phil, eds. Politics in America, 1998: The 105th Congress. LC 93-11559. (Illus.). 1647p. (C). (gr. 11). 1997. text 96.95 (*0-87187-909-3*) Congr Quarterly.

— Politics in America, 1998: The 105th Congress. LC 93-11559. (Illus.). 1647p. (YA). (gr. 11). 1997. pap. text 55.95 (*0-87187-917-4*) Congr Quarterly.

***Lawrence, Christopher.** Science Incarnate. LC 97-28762. (Illus.). 352p. 1998. lib. bdg. 55.00 (*0-226-47012-1*) U Ch Pr.

Lawrence, Christopher & Shapin, Steven, eds. Science Incarnate. LC 97-28762. (Illus.). 352p. 1998. pap. 19.00 (*0-226-47014-8*) U Ch Pr.

Lawrence, Christopher & Weisz, George, eds. Greater than the Parts: Holism in Biomedicine, 1920-1950. (Illus.). 384p. 1998. text 55.00 (*0-19-510904-X*) OUP.

Lawrence, Christopher J. Medicine in the Making of Modern Britain, 1700-1920. LC 93-33387. (Historical Connections Ser.). 112p. (Orig.). (C). 1994. pap. 16.99 (*0-415-09168-3*, B3713) Routledge.

Lawrence, Christopher J., jt. auth. see Fox, Daniel M.

Lawrence, Chuck. Tears of Blood: The Betrayal of America's Veterans. LC 97-80994. 338p. 1998. pap. 19.95 (*0-9659743-0-8*) Soar Eagle Pub.

— Tears of Blood: The Betrayal of America's Veterans. unabridged ed. LC 97-80994. 338p. 1998. 24.95 (*0-9659743-1-6*) Soar Eagle Pub.

Lawrence, Clifford H., ed. The English Church & the Papacy in the Middle Ages. LC 65-12529. 275p. reprint ed. pap. 85.30 (*0-7837-5610-0*, 204551600005) Bks Demand.

Lawrence, Clifford M. & Panting, Gerard. Introduction to Dermatological Surgery. LC 96-8184. (Illus.). 160p. (Orig.). 1996. pap. text 39.95 (*0-86542-964-2*) Blackwell Sci.

Lawrence, Clifford M., jt. auth. see Cox, Neil H.

Lawrence, Colin & Shay, Robert, eds. Technological Innovation, Regulation, & the Monetary Economy. LC 85-23310. 240p. 1986. text 34.95 (*0-88730-078-2*, HarpBusn) HarpInfo.

Lawrence, Colton. Camy/Your Secrets & Mine. 144p. 1999. pap. 4.50 (*0-553-48694-2*) Bantam.

Lawrence, Cynthia. Women & Ary in Early Modern Europe: Patrons, Collectors & Connoisseurs. 1999. pap. 25.00 (*0-271-01969-7*) Pa St U Pr.

Lawrence, Cynthia, ed. Patrons, Collectors, & Connoisseurs: Women & Art, 1350-1750. LC 95-25743. 1996. 42.50 (*0-271-01568-3*) Pa St U Pr.

***Lawrence, D. A.** Toxicology of the Immune System, 13 vols. (Comprehensive Toxicology Ser.: Vol. 5). 534p. 1999. 165.00 (*0-08-042970-X*) Elsevier.

Lawrence, D. H. Aaron's Rod. Kalnins, Mara, ed. (Cambridge Edition of the Works of D. H. Lawrence). 400p. 1988. text 105.00 (*0-521-25250-4*); pap. text 39.95 (*0-521-27246-7*) Cambridge U Pr.

— Aaron's Rod. Kalnins, Mara, ed. 324p. 1996. pap. 11.95 (*0-14-018814-2*) Penguin Putnam.

Lawrence, D. H. Aaron's Rod. 1990. pap. 9.95 (*0-14-018196-2*, Penguin Classics) Viking Penguin.

Lawrence, D. H. Aaron's Rod. large type ed. (Classics Ser.). 480p. 1982. 27.99 (*0-7089-8068-6*, Charnwood) Ulverscroft.

— El Amante de Lady Chatterley. 1998. pap. 8.95 (*84-08-00280-5*) Planeta.

— Apocalypse. 1976. 18.95 (*0-8488-0558-5*) Amereon Ltd.

— Apocalypse & The Writings on Revelation. LC 96-147951. 240p. 1996. pap. 11.95 (*0-14-018781-2*) Penguin Putnam.

— Apropos of Lady Chatterley's Lover. LC 73-8959. (English Literature Ser.: No. 33). 1973. reprint ed. lib. bdg. 75.00 (*0-8383-1702-2*) M S G Haskell Hse.

— Assorted Articles. LC 68-29223. (Essay Index Reprint Ser.). 1977. reprint ed. 21.95 (*0-8369-0612-8*) Ayer.

— Birds, Beasts & Flowers. LC 92-701. 213p. (Orig.). 1992. 20.00 (*0-87685-867-1*) Black Sparrow.

— Birds, Beasts & Flowers! LC 92-701. 213p. 1992. pap. 14.00 (*0-87685-866-3*) Black Sparrow.

— Birds, Beasts & Flowers: Poems. LC 74-7102. (Studies in D. H. Lawrence: No. 20). 1974. lib. bdg. 75.00 (*0-8383-1966-1*) M S G Haskell Hse.

— The Centaur Letters. Roberts, F. W., ed. LC 75-110977. 1970. 25.00 (*0-87959-060-2*) U of Tex H Ransom Ctr.

— Complete Poems. Roberts, F. Warren, ed. & intro. by. 1088p. 1994. pap. 24.95 (*0-14-018657-3*, Penguin Classics) Viking Penguin.

— D. H. Lawrence: The Complete Short Stories, 3 vols., Vol. 2. 586p. 1976. pap. 11.00 (*0-14-004255-5*, Penguin Bks) Viking Penguin.

— D. H. Lawrence & Italy. LC 97-178642. 512p. 1997. pap. 15.95 (*0-14-118030-7*) Penguin Putnam.

— David: A Play. LC 74-6380. (Studies in D. H. Lawrence: No. 20). (C). 1974. lib. bdg. 75.00 (*0-8383-1960-2*) M S G Haskell Hse.

— Divas & Lovers: The Erotic Art of Studio Manasse. (Illus.). 160p. 1998. 35.00 (*0-7893-0234-9*, Pub. by Universe) St Martin.

— England, My England. LC 72-3279. (Short Story Index Reprint Ser.). 1980. reprint ed. 21.95 (*0-8369-4153-5*) Ayer.

— England, My England & Other Stories. Steele, Bruce, ed. (Cambridge Edition of the Works of D. H. Lawrence). 340p. (C). 1990. text 105.00 (*0-521-35267-3*); pap. text 39.95 (*0-521-35814-0*) Cambridge U Pr.

***Lawrence, D. H.** The First & Second Lady Chatterley Novels. Mehl, Dieter & Jansohn, Christa, eds. LC 98-30352. (Works of D. H. Lawrence). (Illus.). 736p. (C). 1999. 130.00 (*0-521-47116-8*) Cambridge U Pr.

Lawrence, D. H. The First Women in Love. Worthen, John & Vasey, Lindeth, eds. LC 97-18195. (Edition of the Works of D. H. Lawrence). 579p. (C). 1998. 110.00 (*0-521-37326-3*) Cambridge U Pr.

— Four Short Novels. 1976. 32.95 (*0-8488-1074-0*) Amereon Ltd.

— The Fox: Penguin Reader Level 2. 1998. pap. 7.00 (*0-14-081486-8*) Viking Penguin.

— The Fox, The Captain's Doll, The Ladybird. Mehl, Dieter, ed. 272p. 1995. pap. 12.95 (*0-14-018779-0*, Penguin Classics) Viking Penguin.

— The Fox, the Captain's Doll, the Ladybird. Mehl, Dieter, ed. (Cambridge Edition of the Works of D. H. Lawrence). (Illus.). 355p. (C). 1992. text 95.00 (*0-521-35266-5*) Cambridge U Pr.

— Kangaroo. 26.95 (*0-89190-613-4*) Amereon Ltd.

— Kangaroo. Steele, Bruce, ed. LC 93-31877. (Letters & Works of D. H. Lawrence). (Illus.). 549p. (C). 1994. text 110.00 (*0-521-38455-9*) Cambridge U Pr.

— Kangaroo. LC 97-200900. 400p. 1997. pap. 13.95 (*0-14-018972-6*) Viking Penguin.

— Lady Chatterley's Lover. 1976. 20.95 (*0-8488-0559-3*) Amereon Ltd.

— Lady Chatterley's Lover. Durrell, Lawrence, ed. (Bantam Classics Ser.). 384p. 1983. mass mkt. 4.95 (*0-553-21262-1*) Bantam.

— Lady Chatterley's Lover. LC 92-39247. 384p. 1993. pap. 12.00 (*0-8021-3334-7*, Grove) Grove-Atltic.

— Lady Chatterley's Lover. 1959. mass mkt. 5.50 (*0-451-52498-5*, CE1787, Sig Classics) NAL.

— Lady Chatterley's Lover. LC 93-15337. 544p. 1993. 17.50 (*0-679-60065-5*) Random.

— Lady Chatterley's Lover. 1981. reprint ed. lib. bdg. 23.95 (*0-89966-375-3*) Buccaneer Bks.

— Lady Chatterley's Lover, Set. unabridged ed. Kay, Marilyn, ed. 1986. pap. 12.95 incl. audio (*1-882071-10-7*, 012) B&B Audio.

— Lady Chatterley's Lover: A Propos of "Lady Chatterley's Lover" Squires, Michael, ed. & intro. by. 400p. 1995. pap. 10.95 (*0-14-018786-3*) Viking Penguin.

— Lady Chatterley's Lover & a Propos of "Lady Chatterley's Lover" Squires, Michael, ed. (Cambridge Edition of the Works of D. H. Lawrence). 522p. (C). 1993. text 105.00 (*0-521-22266-4*) Cambridge U Pr.

— Last Poems. LC 74-6449. (Studies in D. H. Lawrence: No. 20). 1974. lib. bdg. 75.00 (*0-8383-1954-8*) M S G Haskell Hse.

— Last Poems. Aldington, Richard & Orioli, Giuseppe, eds. 1971. reprint ed. 49.00 (*0-403-01066-7*) Scholarly.

— The Letters of D. H. Lawrence, 7 vols., Vol. 1: 1901-1913. Boulton, James T., ed. LC 78-7531. (Cambridge Edition of the Works of D. H. Lawrence). (Illus.). 624p. 1979. text 105.00 (*0-521-22147-1*) Cambridge U Pr.

— The Letters of D. H. Lawrence, 7 vols., Vol. 2: 1913-1916. Boulton, James T., ed. LC 78-7531. (Cambridge Edition of the Works of D. H. Lawrence). (Illus.). 710p. 1982. text 105.00 (*0-521-23111-6*) Cambridge U Pr.

— The Letters of D. H. Lawrence, 7 vols., Vol. 5: March 1924-March 1927. Boulton, James T., ed. LC 78-7531. (Cambridge Edition of the Works of D. H. Lawrence). (Illus.). 736p. 1989. text 105.00 (*0-521-23114-0*) Cambridge U Pr.

— The Letters of D. H. Lawrence, 7 vols., Vol. 7: Nov. 1928-Feb. 1930. Boulton, James T., ed. LC 78-7531. (Cambridge Edition of the Works of D. H. Lawrence). (Illus.). 713p. 1993. text 105.00 (*0-521-23116-7*) Cambridge U Pr.

— Letters to Thomas & Adele Seltzer. Lacy, Gerald M., ed. LC 76-10782. (Illus.). 283p. (Orig.). 1976. pap. 9.00 (*0-87685-224-X*) Black Sparrow.

— The Lost Girl. 26.95 (*0-89190-611-8*) Amereon Ltd.

— The Lost Girl. Worthen, John, ed. LC 80-40457. (Cambridge Edition of the Works of D. H. Lawrence). (Illus.). 483p. 1981. pap. text 39.95 (*0-521-29423-1*) Cambridge U Pr.

— Love among the Haystacks. reprint ed. lib. bdg. 20.95 (*0-88411-676-X*) Amereon Ltd.

— Love among the Haystacks & Other Pieces. (Select Bibliographies Reprint Ser.). 1977. reprint ed. 18.95 (*0-518-19074-9*) Ayer.

— Lovely Lady. LC 77-38721. (Short Story Index Reprint Ser.). 1977. reprint ed. 15.95 (*0-8369-4134-9*) Ayer.

— The Man Who Died: A Story. LC 93-39307. (Illus.). 1994. 21.00 (*0-88001-353-2*) HarpC.

— The Man Who Died: A Story. (Illus.). 112p. 1995. pap. 12.00 (*0-88001-429-6*) HarpC.

— Memoir of Maurice Magnus. Cushman, Keith, ed. LC 87-22671. (Illus.). 158p. 1987. 30.00 (*0-87685-716-0*) Black Sparrow.

— Mr. Noon: Cambridge Lawrence Edition. Vasey, Lindeth, ed. LC 97-150723. 1997. pap. 12.95 (*0-14-018973-4*) Viking Penguin.

— A Modern Lover. LC 70-38722. (Short Story Index Reprint Ser.). 1977. reprint ed. 17.95 (*0-8369-4135-7*) Ayer.

— Movements in European History. Crumpton, Philip, ed. (Cambridge Edition of the Works of D. H. Lawrence). (Illus.). 400p. (C). 1990. text 95.00 (*0-521-26201-1*) Cambridge U Pr.

— New Poems. LC 74-6450. (Studies in D. H. Lawrence: No. 20). (C). 1974. lib. bdg. 75.00 (*0-8383-1967-X*) M S G Haskell Hse.

— The Plays. Schwarze, Hans-Wilhelm & Worthen, John, eds. LC 98-8068. (Edition of the Works of D. H. Lawrence). (Illus.). 900p. (C). 1999. 150.00 (*0-521-24277-0*) Cambridge U Pr.

— The Plumed Serpent. 480p. 1992. pap. 16.00 (*0-679-73493-7*) McKay.

— Prussian Officer. (Penguin Twentieth-Century Classics). 1995. 17.30 (*0-606-12491-8*) Turtleback.

— The Prussian Officer & Other Stories. Atkins, Antony, ed. (World's Classics Ser.). 308p. 1995. pap. 8.95 (*0-19-283181-X*) OUP.

— The Prussian Officer & Other Stories. Worthen, John, ed. LC 95-220738. (Twentieth-Century Classics Ser.). 304p. 1995. pap. 12.95 (*0-14-018780-4*, Penguin Classics) Viking Penguin.

— Prussian Officer & Other Stories. (Oxford World Classics Ser.). 2000. pap. text 8.95 (*0-19-283474-6*) OUP.

— The Prussian Officer & Other Stories. LC 72-160939. (Short Story Index Reprint Ser.). 1977. reprint ed. 23.95 (*0-8369-3918-2*) Ayer.

— Quetzalcoatl. Martz, Louis L., ed. & intro. by. LC 98-14094. 358p. 1998. pap. 14.95 (*0-8112-1385-4*, NDP864, Pub. by New Directions) Norton.

— The Rainbow. Kinkead-Weekes, Mark, ed. (Cambridge Edition of the Works of D. H. Lawrence). (Illus.). 752p. (C). 1989. text 125.00 (*0-521-22869-7*) Cambridge U Pr.

— The Rainbow. LC 93-1860. 1993. 20.00 (*0-679-42305-2*) Everymns Lib.

— The Rainbow. LC 90-64387. 544p. 1991. mass mkt. 5.95 (*0-451-52529-9*, Sig Classics) NAL.

— The Rainbow. Kinkead-Weekes, Mark, ed. (Twentieth-Century Classics Ser.). 528p. 1995. pap. 8.95 (*0-14-018813-4*, Penguin Classics) Viking Penguin.

— The Rainbow. (Classics Library). 548p. 1998. pap. 3.95 (*1-85326-250-1*, 2501WW, Pub. by Wrdsworth Edits) NTC Contemp Pub Co.

— The Rainbow. large type ed. (Large Print Ser.). 705p. 1993. reprint ed. lib. bdg. 25.00 (*0-939495-44-9*) North Bks.

— The Rainbow. 576p. 1989. reprint ed. lib. bdg. 35.95 (*0-89966-644-2*) Buccaneer Bks.

— The Rainbow. 550p. 1998. reprint ed. lib. bdg. 24.00 (*1-58287-061-6*) North Bks.

— Reflections on the Death of a Porcupine & Other Essays. Herbert, Michael, ed. (Cambridge Edition of the Works of D. H. Lawrence). 552p. 1988. text 115.00 (*0-521-26622-X*) Cambridge U Pr.

— The Rocking-Horse Winner. 36p. (YA). (gr. 10 up). 1966. pap. 3.50 (*0-87129-918-6*, R21) Dramatic Pub.

— St. Mawr. 1959. pap. 10.00 (*0-394-70071-6*) Vin Bks.

— St. Mawr & the Man Who Died. 1976. 21.95 (*0-8488-0560-7*) Amereon Ltd.

— Sea & Sardinia. Kalnins, Mara, ed. (Edition of the Works of D. H. Lawrence Ser.). 281p. (C). 1997. text 74.95 (*0-521-24275-4*) Cambridge U Pr.

***Lawrence, D. H.** Sea & Sardinia. Kalnins, Mara, ed. 256p. 1999. pap. 13.95 (*0-14-118076-5*, Penguin Classics) Viking Penguin.

Lawrence, D. H. The Selected Letters of D. H. Lawrence. Boulton, James T., ed. LC 96-24763. (Cambridge Edition of the Letters of D. H. Lawrence Ser.). (Illus.). 568p. (C). 1997. 39.95 (*0-521-40115-1*) Cambridge U Pr.

***Lawrence, D. H.** The Selected Letters of D. H. Lawrence. Boulton, James T., ed. (Cambridge Edition of the Works of D. H. Lawrence). (Illus.). 568p. (C). 1999. pap. 21.95 (*0-521-77799-2*) Cambridge U Pr.

Lawrence, D. H. Selected Poems. 272p. 1989. pap. 12.95 (*0-14-058540-0*, Penguin Bks) Viking Penguin.

— Selected Short Stories. Lockwood, Michael, ed. LC 98-139232. (Literature Ser.). 336p. (C). 1998. pap. text, student ed. 7.95 (*0-521-57505-2*) Cambridge U Pr.

— Selected Short Stories. 128p. 1993. reprint ed. pap. text 1.00 (*0-486-27794-1*) Dover.

— Selected Short Stories of D. H. Lawrence. Wood, James, ed. LC 99-17368. 1999. 21.95 (*0-679-60327-1*) Random.

— Sex, Literature & Censorship. 122p. 1953. 19.50 (*0-8290-0206-5*); pap. text 8.95 (*0-8290-2394-1*) Irvington.

— Sketches of Etruscan Places. 390p. 1999. pap. 14.95 (*0-14-118105-2*, PuffinBks) Peng Put Young Read.

***Lawrence, D. H.** Snake & Other Poems. Blaisdell, Bob, ed. LC 98-41016. 64p. 1999. pap. text 1.00 (*0-486-40647-4*) Dover.

Lawrence, D. H. Sons & Lovers. (Longman Simplified English Ser.). 124p. 1930. pap. text 5.95 (*0-582-52634-5*) Addison-Wesley.

— Sons & Lovers. 1976. 23.95 (*0-8488-0561-5*) Amereon Ltd.

— Sons & Lovers. (Classics Ser.). 432p. 1985. mass mkt. 5.95 (*0-553-21192-7*) Bantam.

— Sons & Lovers. (Barron's Book Notes Ser.). 1985. pap. 2.50 (*0-8120-3540-2*) Barron.

— Sons & Lovers. 432p. 1991. 17.00 (*0-679-40572-0*) Everymns Lib.

— Sons & Lovers. (Study Texts Ser.). 1988. pap. text 5.95 (*0-582-33166-8*, 72062) Longman.

— Sons & Lovers. LC 99-13055. 1999. pap. 8.95 (*0-375-75373-7*) Modern Lib NY.

— Sons & Lovers. 1985. mass mkt. 5.95 (*0-451-51882-9*, Sig Classics) NAL.

— Sons & Lovers. (Critical Editions Ser.). (C). 1997. pap. write for info. (*0-393-95758-6*, Norton Paperbks) Norton.

— Sons & Lovers. Trotter, David, ed. & intro. by. (Oxford World's Classics Ser.). 522p. 1998. pap. 9.95 (*0-19-283860-1*) OUP.

— Sons & Lovers. Baron, Helen & Baron, Carl, eds. 544p. 1995. pap. 10.95 (*0-14-018832-0*, Penguin Classics) Viking Penguin.

— Sons & Lovers. (Classics Library). 464p. 1997. pap. 3.95 (*1-85326-047-9*, 0479WW, Pub. by Wrdsworth Edits) NTC Contemp Pub Co.

— Sons & Lovers. large type ed. (Classics Ser.). 1988. 16.95 (*0-7089-8008-2*, Charnwood) Ulverscroft.

— Sons & Lovers. large type ed. 642p. 1997. reprint ed. lib. bdg. 25.00 (*0-939495-13-9*) North Bks.

— Sons & Lovers. 1982. reprint ed. lib. bdg. 28.95 (*0-89966-400-8*) Buccaneer Bks.

— Sons & Lovers. 463p. 1998. reprint ed. lib. bdg. 24.00 (*1-58287-072-1*) North Bks.

— Studies in Classic American Literature. 1976. 24.95 (*0-8488-1075-9*) Amereon Ltd.

— Studies in Classic American Literature. 190p. 1990. pap. 12.95 (*0-14-018377-9*, Penguin Classics) Viking Penguin.

— Study of Thomas Hardy & Other Essays. Steele, Bruce, ed. (Cambridge Edition of the Works of D. H. Lawrence). 384p. 1985. text 95.00 (*0-521-25252-0*) Cambridge U Pr.

— The Trespasser. Mansfield, Elizabeth, ed. LC 80-41663. (Cambridge Edition of the Works of D. H. Lawrence). 352p. 1982. pap. text 39.95 (*0-521-29424-X*) Cambridge U Pr.

— The Trespasser. 350p. 1989. reprint ed. lib. bdg. 29.95 (*0-89966-645-0*) Buccaneer Bks.

— The Trespasser. 1988. reprint ed. lib. bdg. 49.00 (*0-7812-0179-9*) Rprt Serv.

— The Trespasser. 1971. reprint ed. 49.00 (*0-403-01067-5*) Scholarly.

— Twilight in Italy & Other Essays. Eggert, Paul, ed. (Cambridge Edition of the Works of D. H. Lawrence). (Illus.). 403p. (C). 1994. text 95.00 (*0-521-26888-5*) Cambridge U Pr.

— Twilight in Italy & Other Essays. Eggert, Paul, ed. LC 97-200896. xlviii, 267p. 1997. reprint ed. pap. 12.95 (*0-14-018994-7*) Viking Penguin.

— The Virgin & the Gypsy. LC 84-50303. 128p. 1984. pap. 8.00 (*0-394-72666-9*) Vin Bks.

— The Virgin & the Gypsy. 192p. 1992. pap. 11.00 (*0-679-74077-5*) Vin Bks.

— We Need One Another. LC 74-1421. (Studies in D. H. Lawrence: No. 20). 1974. lib. bdg. 75.00 (*0-8383-2031-7*) M S G Haskell Hse.

— White Peacock. (Oxford World Classics Ser.). 410p. 2000. pap. 9.95 (*0-19-283639-0*) OUP.

— The Woman Who Rode Away & Other Stories. Mehl, Dieter & Jansohn, Christa, eds. (Cambridge Edition of the Works of D. H. Lawrence). 554p. (C). 1995. text 105.00 (*0-521-22270-2*) Cambridge U Pr.

— The Woman Who Rode Away & Other Stories. Mehl, Dieter & Jansohn, Christa, eds. LC 97-183654. 448p. 1997. pap. 12.95 (*0-14-018806-1*) Viking Penguin.

— Women in Love. 30.95 (*0-89190-612-6*) Amereon Ltd.

— Women in Love. 1992. 20.00 (*0-679-41326-X*) Everymns Lib.

— Women in Love. 1992. 20.00 (*0-679-40995-5*) Knopf.

— Women in Love. LC 99-16866. 520p. 1999. pap. 8.95 (*0-375-75488-1*) Modern Lib NY.

— Women in Love. 480p. 1995. mass mkt. 4.95 (*0-451-52591-4*, Sig) NAL.

— Women in Love. Bradshaw, David, ed. (Oxford World's Classics Ser.). 562p. 1998. pap. 8.95 (*0-19-282995-5*) OUP.

— Women in Love. Farmer, David H. et al, eds. 592p. 1995. pap. 10.95 (*0-14-018816-9*, Penguin Classics) Viking Penguin.

An Asterisk (*) at the beginning of an entry indicates that the title is appearing for the first time.

— Women in Love. pap. 3.95 (*1-85326-007-X*, 007XWW, Pub. by Wrdsworth Edits) NTC Contemp Pub Co.
— Women in Love. 560p. 1996. reprint ed. mass mkt. 4.95 (*0-553-21454-3*, Bantam Classics) Bantam.
— Women in Love. 421p. 1984. reprint ed. lib. bdg. 27.95 (*0-89966-496-2*) Buccaneer Bks.
— Women in Love: New York Public Library Collector's Edition. LC 99-24890. 640p. 1999. 19.95 (*0-385-48734-7*) Doubleday.
— Women in Love 1920. 512p. 2000. pap. 12.95 (*0-14-028337-4*) Viking Penguin.
— The Works of D. H. Lawrence. 800p. 1995. pap. write for info. (*1-57215-127-7*) World Pubns.
***Lawrence, D. H.** The Works of D. H. Lawrence. (Poetry Library). 576p. 1998. pap. 7.95 (*1-85326-417-2*, 4172WW, Pub. by Wrdsworth Edits) NTC Contemp Pub Co.
Lawrence, D. H. & Flint, Kate. The Rainbow. (Oxford World's Classics Ser.). 542p. 1998. pap. 7.95 (*0-19-283524-6*) OUP.
Lawrence, D. H. & Skinner, M. L. The Boy in the Bush. Eggert, Paul, ed. (Cambridge Edition of the Works of D. H. Lawrence). 561p. (C). 1990. text 110.00 (*0-521-30704-X*) Cambridge U Pr.
— The Boy in the Bush. Eggert, Paul, ed. LC 97-101107. 432p. 1996. pap. 12.95 (*0-14-018817-7*) Viking Penguin.
Lawrence, D. H., jt. auth. see Griffith, Trevor.
Lawrence, D. H., tr. see Gascar, Pierre.
Lawrence, D. H., tr. see Verga, Giovanni.
Lawrence, D. M., ed. see Deledda, Grazia.
Lawrence, Daisy Gordon & Schultz, G. D. Lady from Savannah: The Life of Juliette Low. (Illus.). 383p. 1988. reprint ed. pap. 6.50 (*0-88441-147-8*, 19-401) Girl Scouts USA.
***Lawrence, Dale.** The Hoosier Hysteria Road Book. 2000. pap. 19.95 (*1-888698-27-6*) Diamond Communications.
Lawrence, Dale, jt. auth. see Smith, Sean.
Lawrence, Dan H., jt. auth. see Edel, Leon.
Lawrence, Dana J. Advances in Chiropractic, 4. 4th ed. (Illus.). 688p. (C). (gr. 13). 1997. text 83.00 (*0-8151-5309-0*, 23097) Mosby Inc.
— Advances in Chiropractic, Vol. 5. 5th ed. (C). (gr. 13). 1998. text 79.95 (*0-8151-5310-4*) Mosby Inc.
— Fundamentals of Chiropractic Diagnosis & Management. (Illus.). 608p. 1990. 89.00 (*0-683-04902-X*) Lppncott W & W.
Lawrence, Dana J., ed. The Year Book of Chiropractic, 1996. LC 94-657513. (Illus.). 464p. 1996. reprint ed. pap. 143.90 (*0-608-04223-4*, 206496700012) Bks Demand.
Lawrence, Dana J., ed. see Beideman, Ronald P.
Lawrence, Dana J., ed. see Gaucher-Peslherbe, Pierre-Louis.
Lawrence, Daniel. Black Migrants: White Natives. (Modern Revivals in Sociology Ser.). 251p. 1992. 56.95 (*0-7512-0057-3*, Pub. by Gregg Revivals) Ashgate Pub Co.
***Lawrence, Daniel H.** The Great Mystery Explained: or The Indians of America Proved to Be the Ten Tribes of Israel. (LC History-America-E). 12p. 1999. reprint ed. lib. bdg. 69.00 (*0-7812-4346-7*) Rprt Serv.
Lawrence, David. California: The Politics of Diversity. LC 94-35221. 320p. (C). 1995. 24.50 (*0-314-04600-3*) West Pub.
— California: The Politics of Diversity. 2nd ed. LC 99-46725. (Political Science). (C). 1999. pap. text 38.95 (*0-534-53568-2*) Wadsworth Pub.
— The Complete Guide to Barber Half Dollars. (Illus.). 120p. pap. 25.00 (*1-880731-05-3*) S J Durst.
— The Complete Guide to Barber Quarters. LC 94-79248. 1995. pap. 29.95 (*1-880731-22-3*) DLRC Pr.
— The Complete Guide to Barber Quarters. 2nd ed. LC 94-79248. (Illus.). 1995. pap. 25.00 (*1-880731-21-5*) S J Durst.
***Lawrence, David.** Good Little Girl. (Illus.). (J). 2000. 12.44 (*0-606-18784-7*) Turtleback.
— Kakadu: The Making of a National Park. (Illus.). 300p. 2000. 49.95 (*0-522-84868-0*, Pub. by Melbourne Univ Pr) Paul & Co Pubs.
Lawrence, David. Measuring & Managing Derivative Market Risk. LC 96-38892. 208p. 1996. pap. 55.00 (*1-86152-006-9*) Thomson Learn.
— Steel Toe Boots. LC 96-6328. 80p. (Orig.). 1996. pap. 9.50 (*1-56474-188-5*) Fithian Pr.
— Stripping & Polishing Furniture. 1985. 39.00 (*0-7855-2952-7*, Pub. by Bishopsgate Pr Ltd) St Mut.
— Stripping & Polishing Furniture. 1985. pap. 21.00 (*0-7855-2953-5*) St Mut.
— Stripping & Polishing Furniture: A Practical Guide. (Illus.). 95p. 1987. pap. 11.95 (*0-900873-55-8*, Pub. by Bishopsgte Pr) Intl Spec Bk.
Lawrence, David & Mark, Dave. Learn HTML on the Macintosh Pages: Everything You Need to Create Your Own World Wide Web Pages. 304p. 1996. pap. 29.95 (*0-201-88793-2*) Pearson Custom.
Lawrence, David & Spencer, Henry. Managing Usenet. 508p. 1998. pap. 32.95 (*1-56592-198-4*) OReilly & Assocs.
Lawrence, David B. The Economic Value of Information. LC 98-51179. (Illus.). 380p. 1999. 69.95 (*0-387-98706-1*) Spr-Verlag.
***Lawrence, David M.** Economic Development Law for North Carolina Local Governments. (C). 2000. pap. write for info. (*1-56011-364-2*) Institute Government.
Lawrence, David M. Financing Capital Projects in North Carolina. 2nd ed. 176p. (C). 1994. text 15.00 (*1-56011-234-4*, 94.05HB); pap. text 12.50 (*1-56011-273-5*, 94.05) Institute Government.
— Incorporation of a North Carolina Town. 2nd ed. LC 98-231314. 35p. (C). 1998. pap. text 13.00 (*1-56011-334-0*, 98.14) Institute Government.
— The Local Government Budget & Fiscal Control Act. 3rd ed. 31p. 1988. pap. 6.00 (*1-56011-098-8*) Institute Government.
— Local Government Finance in North Carolina. rev. ed. 323p. (C). 1990. pap. text 12.00 (*1-56011-099-6*) Institute Government.
— Local Government Property Transactions in North Carolina. 124p. (Orig.). (C). 1987. pap. text 9.00 (*1-56011-100-3*, 87.13) Institute Government.
***Lawrence, David M.** Local Government Property Transactions in North Carolina. 2nd ed. (Orig.). (C). 2000. pap. write for info. (*1-56011-366-9*) Institute Government.
Lawrence, David M. North Carolina City Council Procedures. 2nd rev. ed. LC 97-192212. 38p. (Orig.). 1997. pap. text 13.00 (*1-56011-301-4*, 96.22) Institute Government.
— Open Meetings & Local Governments in North Carolina: Some Questions & Answers. 5th ed. LC 98-203566. vii, 61p. (C). 1998. pap. text 13.00 (*1-56011-326-X*) Institute Government.
— Property Interests in North Carolina City Streets. LC 86-621832. 59p. (C). 1985. 7.00 (*1-56011-131-3*) Institute Government.
— Public Records Law for North Carolina Local Government: 1997-1998 Supplement. 1999. pap. text, suppl. ed. 10.00 (*1-56011-343-X*, 97.02A) Institute Government.
— Public Records Law for North Carolina Local Governments. LC 97-151573. 207p. 1997. pap. text 34.00 (*1-56011-299-9*) Institute Government.
Lawrence, David M., compiled by. Form of Government of North Carolina Cities, 1998. 44p. (C). 1998. pap. text 16.00 (*1-56011-329-4*) Institute Government.
Lawrence, David M., jt. auth. see Wicker, Warren J.
Lawrence, David M., jt. ed. see Wicker, Warren J.
Lawrence, David P. The Algebra Skill Builder: Reproducible Masters for Review & Practice. 128p. 1997. teacher ed., ring bd. 22.95 (*1-881641-60-0*) Pencil Point.
Lawrence, David P. Algebra Using the TI-80. (Skill & Practice Masters Ser.). 50p. 1996. teacher ed. 12.95 (*1-881641-57-0*) Pencil Point.
— Algebra Using the TI-83. (Skill & Practice Masters Ser.). 50p. 1996. teacher ed. 12.95 (*1-881641-55-4*) Pencil Point.
— Algebra Using the TI-92. (Skill & Practice Masters Ser.). 50p. 1996. teacher ed. 12.95 (*1-881641-56-2*) Pencil Point.
Lawrence, David P. Algebra Using the TI-82. (Skill & Practice Masters Using the TI-82 Ser.). (YA). (gr. 8-12). 1994. pap. 12.95 (*1-881641-22-8*) Pencil Point.
— Algebra Using the TI-85. (Skill & Practice Masters Using the TI-85 Ser.). 1995. pap. 12.95 (*1-881641-36-8*) Pencil Point.
— Algebra Using the TI-86. (Skill & Practice Masters Ser.). 50p. 1998. teacher ed. 12.95 (*1-881641-93-7*) Pencil Point.
— Biology. (Graphing Calculator Approach Ser.). 64p. (YA). (gr. 9 up). 1995. pap. text, lab manual ed. 12.95 (*1-881641-26-0*) Pencil Point.
— Biology: Answer Key. (Graphing Calculator Approach Ser.). 4p. (YA). (gr. 9 up). 1995. pap. text 1.50 (*1-881641-35-X*) Pencil Point.
***Lawrence, David P.** Calculus Using the TI-86. (Skill & Practice Masters Ser.). 50p. 1998. teacher ed. 12.95 (*1-881641-94-5*) Pencil Point.
Lawrence, David P. Calculus Using the TI-80. (Skill & Practice Masters Ser.). Date not set. ring bd. 12.95 (*1-881641-96-1*) Pencil Point.
— Calculus Using the TI-82. (Skill & Practice Masters Using the TI-82 Ser.). (YA). (gr. 8-12). 1994. pap. 10.95 (*1-881641-21-X*) Pencil Point.
— Calculus Using the TI-83. (Skill & Practice Masters Ser.). 50p. 1997. 12.95 (*1-881641-89-9*) Pencil Point.
— Calculus Using the TI-85. 1995. pap. 12.95 (*1-881641-37-6*) Pencil Point.
— Calculus Using the TI-92. (Skill & Practice Masters Ser.). 50p. 1997. teacher ed. 12.95 (*1-881641-91-0*) Pencil Point.
— The Casio CFX-9800G. (Graphing Calculators Ser.). 22p. (YA). (gr. 8 up). 1995. pap. text 7.25 (*1-881641-32-5*) Pencil Point.
— The Casio CFX-9850G. (Graphing Calculators Ser.). (Illus.). 22p. 1997. pap. text, teacher ed. 7.25 (*1-881641-50-3*) Pencil Point.
— The Casio FX-7000. (Graphing Calculators Ser.). 22p. (YA). (gr. 8-12). 1993. pap. text 7.25 (*1-881641-11-2*) Pencil Point.
— The Casio FX-7700-8700. (Graphing Calculators Ser.). 22p. (YA). (gr. 8-12). 1993. pap. text 7.25 (*1-881641-10-4*) Pencil Point.
— The Casio FX-7700GE. (Graphing Calculators Ser.). 22p. (YA). (gr. 8-12). 1994. pap. text 7.25 (*1-881641-20-1*) Pencil Point.
— The Casio FX-9700GE. (Graphing Calculators Ser.). 22p. (YA). (gr. 8-12). 1994. pap. text 7.25 (*1-881641-19-8*) Pencil Point.
— Chemistry. (Graphing Calculator Approach Ser.). 64p. (YA). (gr. 9 up). 1995. pap. text, lab manual ed. 12.95 (*1-881641-24-4*) Pencil Point.
— Chemistry: Answer Key. (Graphing Calculator Approach Ser.). 4p. (YA). (gr. 9-12). 1995. pap. text 1.50 (*1-881641-33-3*) Pencil Point.
— Earth Science. (Graphing Calculator Approach Ser.). 60p. 1999. pap. text, teacher ed., lab manual ed. 12.95 (*1-58108-009-3*) Pencil Point.
— Earth Science Answer Key. (Graphing Calculator Approach Ser.). 4p. 1999. pap. text, teacher ed. 1.50 (*1-58108-011-5*) Pencil Point.
— Geometry Using the TI-92. (Skill & Practice Masters Ser.). 50p. 1999. 12.95 (*1-58108-020-4*) Pencil Point.
— Graphing Calculator Basics: For Introductory Courses & Laboratory Applications. 19p. (YA). (gr. 8 up). 1995. pap. text 3.95 (*1-881641-44-9*) Pencil Point.
— Hewlett Packard 48G-48GX. (Graphing Calculators Ser.). 22p. (YA). (gr. 8-12). 1994. pap. text 7.25 (*1-881641-16-3*) Pencil Point.
— Modeling & Applications. 2nd rev. ed. (Graphing Calculator Connection Ser.). (Illus.). 100p. 1998. spiral bd. 23.95 (*1-58108-008-5*) Pencil Point.
— Physics. (Graphing Calculator Approach Ser.). 64p. (YA). (gr. 9 up). 1995. pap. text, lab manual ed. 12.95 (*1-881641-25-2*) Pencil Point.
— Physics: Answer Key. (Graphing Calculator Approach Ser.). 4p. (YA). (gr. 9 up). 1995. pap. text 1.50 (*1-881641-34-1*) Pencil Point.
— Problem Solving & Investigations. (Graphing Calculator Connection Ser.). 102p. (YA). (gr. 6-12). 1995. spiral bd. 23.95 (*1-881641-31-7*) Pencil Point.
— Rediscovering God with Transcendental Argument: A Contemporary Interpretation of Monistic Kashmiri Salva Philosophy. LC 98-38219. (Suny Series Toward a Comparative Philosophy of Religions). 306p. (C). 1999. pap. text 21.95 (*0-7914-4058-3*) State U NY Pr.
— Rediscovering God with Transcendental Argument: A Contemporary Interpretation of Monistic Kashmiri Salva Philosophy. LC 98-38219. (SUNY Series, Toward a Comparative Philosophy of Religions). 288p. (C). 1999. text 65.50 (*0-7914-4057-5*) State U NY Pr.
— The Sharp EL9600. (Graphing Calculators Ser.). 24p. 1998. pap. text, teacher ed. 7.25 (*1-58108-003-4*) Pencil Point.
— The Sharp EL-9200-9300. (Graphing Calculators Ser.). 22p. (YA). (gr. 8-12). 1993. pap. text 7.25 (*1-881641-09-0*) Pencil Point.
— Skill & Practice Masters in Trigonometry Using the TI-83. (Skill & Practice Masters Ser.). 50p. 1999. 12.95 (*1-58108-019-0*) Pencil Point.
Lawrence, David P. Statistics Using the TI-83. (Skill & Practice Masters Ser.). 50p. 1997. teacher ed. 12.95 (*1-881641-90-2*) Pencil Point.
— Statistics Using the TI-83, Pt. 2. (Skill & Practice Masters Ser.). 50p. 1997. teacher ed. 12.95 (*1-881641-99-6*) Pencil Point.
Lawrence, David P. Statistics Using the TI-80. (Skill & Practice Masters Ser.). (Illus.). Date not set. ring bd. 10.95 (*1-881641-97-X*) Pencil Point.
— Statistics Using the TI-82. (Skill & Practice Masters Using the TI-82 Ser.). (YA). (gr. 8-12). 1994. pap. 12.95 (*1-881641-23-6*) Pencil Point.
— Statistics Using the TI-86. (Skill & Practice Masters Ser.). 50p. 1998. teacher ed. 12.95 (*1-881641-95-3*) Pencil Point.
— Statistics Using the TI-92. (Skill & Practice Masters Ser.). 50p. 1998. teacher ed. 12.95 (*1-881641-92-9*) Pencil Point.
— The TI-89. (Graphing Calculators Ser.). 24p. 1998. pap. text, teacher ed. 7.25 (*1-58108-033-6*) Pencil Point.
— TI-86. (Graphing Calculators Ser.). (Illus.). 24p. 1997. pap. text, teacher ed. 7.35 (*1-881641-98-8*) Pencil Point.
— TI-83 Easy Warm-Ups in Algebra Two. (Easy Warm-Ups Ser.). 32p. 1999. pap. 12.95 (*1-58108-016-6*) Pencil Point.
— TI-83 Easy Warm-Ups in Algebra One. (Easy Warm-Ups Ser.). 32p. 1999. pap. 12.95 (*1-58108-014-X*) Pencil Point.
— TI-83 Easy Warm-Ups in Pre-Algebra. (Easy Warm-Ups Ser.). 32p. 1998. pap., teacher ed. 12.95 (*1-58108-002-6*) Pencil Point.
— TI-82 Easy Warm-Ups in Algebra One. (Easy Warm-Ups Ser.). 32p. 1998. pap. 12.95 (*1-58108-013-1*) Pencil Point.
— TI-82 Easy Warm-Ups in Algebra Two. (Easy Warm-Ups Ser.). 32p. 1999. pap. 12.95 (*1-58108-015-8*) Pencil Point.
— TI-82 Easy Warm-Ups in Pre-Algebra. (Easy Warm-Ups Ser.). 32p. 1998. pap., teacher ed. 12.95 (*1-58108-000-X*) Pencil Point.
— TI-73. (Graphing Calculators Ser.). 24p. 1998. pap. text, teacher ed. 7.25 (*1-58108-004-2*) Pencil Point.
— TI-73 Easy Warm-Ups in Pre-Algebra. (Easy Warm-Ups Ser.). 32p. 1998. teacher ed. 12.95 (*1-58108-001-8*) Pencil Point.
— The TI-80. (Graphing Calculators Ser.). 22p. (YA). (gr. 8 up). 1995. pap. text 6.35 (*1-881641-43-0*) Pencil Point.
— The TI-81. (Graphing Calculators Ser.). 22p. (YA). (gr. 8-12). 1993. pap. text 7.25 (*1-881641-06-6*) Pencil Point.
— The TI-82. (Graphing Calculators Ser.). 22p. (YA). (gr. 8-12). 1993. pap. text 7.25 (*1-881641-07-4*) Pencil Point.
— The TI-83. (Graphing Calculators Ser.). 24p. (YA). (gr. 9 up). 1996. pap. text 7.25 (*1-881641-45-7*) Pencil Point.
— The TI-85. (Graphing Calculators Ser.). 22p. (YA). (gr. 8-12). 1993. pap. text 7.25 (*1-881641-08-2*) Pencil Point.
— The TI-92. (Graphing Calculators Ser.). 24p. (YA). (gr. 9 up). 1996. pap. text 7.25 (*1-881641-46-5*) Pencil Point.
— Trigonometry Using the TI-82. (Skill & Practice Masters Ser.). 50p. 1999. 12.95 (*1-58108-018-2*) Pencil Point.
Lawrence, David P. & Fetta, Iris B. Applying Pre-Algebra: Algebra Using the Sharp EL-9300 Graphing Calculators. (YA). (gr. 9-12). 1994. pap. text 16.95 (*1-881641-17-1*) Pencil Point.
— Applying Pre-Calculus: Calculus Using the Sharp EL-9200, EL-9300 Graphing Calculators. LC 94-227784. (YA). (gr. 9-12). 1994. pap. text 16.95 (*1-881641-18-X*) Pencil Point.
— Applying Statistics Using the Sharp EL-9200, EL-9300 Graphing Calculators. (YA). (gr. 9-12). 1994. pap. text 16.95 (*1-881641-15-5*) Pencil Point.
— Applying Trigonometry Using the Sharp EL-9200, EL-9300 Graphing Calculators. (YA). (gr. 9-12). 1994. pap. text 16.95 (*1-881641-14-7*) Pencil Point.
Lawrence, Dean S. Travels with Peppy: A Motorcycle Adventure Across the Country. LC 94-90172. 250p. 1994. pap. 12.95 (*0-9641348-0-2*) Triad Pubng.
Lawrence, Debbi, jt. auth. see Lawrence, Don.
***Lawrence, Debbie.** Complete Guide to Exercise in Water. unabridged ed. (Illus.). 160p. 1999. pap. 16.95 (*0-7136-4849-X*, Pub. by A & C Blk) Midpt Trade.
— The Complete Guide to Exercise to Music. 1999. pap. 14.95 (*0-7136-4995-X*) A & C Blk.
Lawrence, Deborah. Courting Sarah, Vol. 1. (Friends Romance Ser.). 1999. mass mkt. 5.99 (*0-515-12480-X*, Jove) Berkley Pub.
— The Hat Box. 288p. 1997. mass mkt. 5.99 (*0-515-12033-2*, Jove) Berkley Pub.
— Humble Pie. 272p. (Orig.). 1996. mass mkt. 5.99 (*0-515-11900-8*, Jove) Berkley Pub.
Lawrence, Denis. Enhancing Self-Esteem in the Classroom. 100p. (C). 1988. 55.00 (*1-85396-000-4*, Pub. by P Chapman) St Mut.
— Enhancing Self-Esteem in the Classroom, Second Edition. 2nd ed. (One-Off Ser.). (Illus.). 136p. 1996. pap. (*1-85396-351-8*) Corwin Pr.
Lawrence, Don & Lawrence, Debbi. Walk Log: Diary & Guide for the Exercise Walker. (SportsLog Ser.). (Illus.). 176p. 1995. reprint ed. spiral bd. 9.95 (*1-57028-053-3*, 80533H, Mstrs Pr) NTC Contemp Pub Co.
Lawrence, Don Harold, ed. see Todd, Virgil H.
Lawrence, E. Spiritualism among Civilized & Savage Races. 1972. lib. bdg. 250.00 (*0-87968-536-0*) Krishna Pr.
***Lawrence, E. & Loon, Bert.** Instant Guide to Weather. LC 99-50242. (Instant Guide Ser.). (Illus.). 2000. 4.99 (*0-517-20833-4*) Random Hse Value.
Lawrence, Ed. Frommer's Yellowstone & Grand Teton National Parks. 248p. 1998. pap. 9.95 (*0-02-862085-2*, Pub. by Macmillan) S&S Trade.
Lawrence, Ed, jt. auth. see Frommer's Staff.
Lawrence, Eddie. 57 Original Auditions for Actors: A Workbook of Monologs for Professional & Nonprofessional Actors. Zapel, Arthur L., ed. LC 83-62157. 112p. (Orig.). (YA). (gr. 9 up). 1983. pap. 12.95 (*0-916260-25-9*, B181) Meriwether Pub.
Lawrence, Edgar D. El Lenguaje por Senas Simplificado. LC 91-39463. (Illus.). 240p. 1992. kivar 13.95 (*0-88243-300-8*, 02-0300) Gospel Pub.
— Sign Language Made Simple. 2nd ed. LC 96-6501. (Illus.). 240p. 1997. 18.95 (*0-88243-500-0*) Gospel Pub.
Lawrence, Edith. The Wayfaring Princes: A Tale of Questing & Adventure. (Illus.). 136p. (Orig.). (J). (gr. 4-7). 1987. pap. 9.50 (*0-936132-86-8*) Merc Pr NY.
Lawrence, Edith C., jt. auth. see Waters, David B.
Lawrence, Edward. Complete Antique Shop Directory for Eastern Michigan, 1994-95. (Illus.). 260p. (Orig.). pap. 10.95 (*0-9634597-2-4*) Complete Antique.
Lawrence, Edward. Complete Antique Shop Directory for Illinois South of Chicago 96. Date not set. pap. 7.95 (*0-9634597-4-0*) Complete Antique.
Lawrence, Edward. Complete Antique Shop Directory for Indiana, 1994. (Illus.). 272p. (Orig.). 1993. pap. text 5.00 (*0-9634597-1-6*) Complete Antique.
Lawrence, Edward. Complete Antique Shop Directory for Indiana 96. Date not set. pap. 7.95 (*0-9634597-5-9*) Complete Antique.
Lawrence, Edward. Complete Antique Shop Directory for Western Michigan, 1993. (Illus.). 163p. (Orig.). 1992. pap. 5.00 (*0-9634597-0-8*) Complete Antique.
— Complete Antique Shop Directory for Western Michigan, 1995. rev. ed. (Illus.). 224p. 1994. pap. 10.95 (*0-9634597-3-2*) Complete Antique.
Lawrence, Edward. Spiritualism among Civilised & Savage Races: A Study in Anthropology. 1977. 19.95 (*0-8369-5848-9*, 6912) Ayer.
Lawrence, Eleanor. Henderson's Dictionary of Biological Terms. 693p. 1995. 54.95 (*0-470-23507-1*) Wiley.
Lawrence, Elizabeth. The Complete Caterer: A Practical Guide to the Craft & Business of Catering. rev. ed. 368p. 1992. pap. 15.00 (*0-385-23480-5*) Doubleday.
— The Complete Restaurateur: A Practical Guide to the Craft & Business of Restaurant Ownership. 240p. (Orig.). 1992. pap. 13.95 (*0-452-26752-8*, Plume) Dutton Plume.
— A Garden of One's Own: Writings of Elizabeth Lawrence. Scott, Barbara & Ward, Bobby J., eds. LC 96-39348. 1997. 27.50 (*0-8078-2349-X*) U of NC Pr.
— Gardening for Love: The Market Bulletins. Lacy, Allen, ed. LC 86-32896. (Illus.). 238p. (Orig.). 1987. pap. 16.95 (*0-8223-0887-8*); text 39.95 (*0-8223-0715-4*) Duke.
— Gardens in Winter. 1973. 15.95 (*1-57980-026-2*) Claitors.
— Gender & Trade Unions. LC 93-48358. (Gender & Society Ser.). 208p. 1994. 85.00 (*0-7484-0146-6*); pap. 29.95 (*0-7484-0147-4*) Taylor & Francis.
— The Little Bulbs: A Tale of Two Gardens. LC 57-6248. 261p. (Orig.). 1986. reprint ed. pap. 16.95 (*0-8223-0739-1*); reprint ed. text 39.95 (*0-8223-0671-9*) Duke.
— A Rock Garden in the South. Goodwin, Nancy & Lacy, Allen, eds. LC 89-49426. 239p. 1990. 22.95 (*0-8223-0986-6*) Duke.
— A Southern Garden: Fiftieth Anniversary Edition. rev. ed. LC 90-44658. (Illus.). 288p. (C). 1991. reprint ed. pap. 16.95 (*0-8078-4355-5*) U of NC Pr.
— A Southern Garden: Fiftieth Anniversary Edition. 4th rev. ed. LC 90-44658. (Illus.). 288p. (C). 1991. reprint ed. 29.95 (*0-8078-1962-X*) U of NC Pr.
— Through the Garden Gate. Neal, Bill, ed. LC 89-27890. xiv, 256p. (C). 1990. 29.95 (*0-8078-1907-7*) U of NC Pr.
— Through the Garden Gate. Neal, Bill, ed. LC 89-27890. (Chapel Hill Bks.). 256p. 1995. pap. 17.95 (*0-8078-4519-1*) U of NC Pr.

L

An Asterisk (*) at the beginning of an entry indicates that the title is appearing for the first time.

Lawrence, Elizabeth A. His Very Silence Speaks: Comanche, the Horse Who Survived Custer's Last Stand. LC 89-5612. (Illus.). 358p. (C). 1989. pap. 19.95 (*0-8143-2197-6*) Wayne St U Pr.

— Hunting the Wren: Transformation of Bird to Symbol. LC 96-25191. (Illus.). 256p. 1997. 30.00 (*0-87049-960-2*) U of Tenn Pr.

— Rodeo: An Anthropologist Looks at the Wild & the Tame. LC 83-18176. (Illus.). xvi, 304p. (C). 1984. reprint ed. pap. text 19.00 (*0-226-46955-7*) U Ch Pr.

— Rodeo, an Anthropologist Looks at the Wild & the Tame. LC 81-3330. (Illus.). 304p. reprint ed. pap. 94.30 (*0-8357-8604-8*, 203500100091) Bks Demand.

Lawrence, Elleanor, jt. ed. see Kendrew, John.

Lawrence, Elliot. Doctor Dolittle's Animals. LC 99-159266. (Illus.). 32p. (J). (ps-3). 1998. pap. 4.99 (*0-440-41556-X*) Dell.

Lawrence, Elwood P., et al. George & Democracy in the British Isles: The American Social Philosopher Helped Form Britain's Social Conscience, Inspired the People's Struggle That Overthrew the Lords' Political Power & Launched Ireland's March Toward Freedom. Lissner, Will & Lissner, Dorothy B., eds. LC 92-56462. (George Studies Program: Vol. 2). 386p. (Orig.). 1993. 18.00 (*0-911312-88-9*); pap. 12.00 (*0-911312-87-0*) Schalkenbach.

Lawrence, Emeric A. The Ministry of Believers. (Ministry Ser.). 28p. (Orig.). 1982. pap. text 1.95 (*0-8146-1276-8*) Liturgical Pr.

***Lawrence, Emily.** Beyond the Shadows. 59p. 2000. pap. 9.95 (*1-890307-29-7*) Boyd Pub Co.

Lawrence, Ernest O. Centennial of the Sheffield Scientific School. Baitsell, George A., ed. LC 70-107681. (Essay Index Reprint Ser.). 1977. 23.95 (*0-8369-1544-5*) Ayer.

— Science in Progress. Baitsell, George A., ed. LC 78-37534. (Essay Index Reprint Ser.: 1). 1977. reprint ed. 39.95 (*0-8369-2526-2*) Ayer.

Lawrence, Ethel V. Doty. Continuing the Line of Doty-Lawrence Family, As Found in "Doty-Doten Family", by Ethan Allen Doty. (Illus.). 78p. 1997. reprint ed. pap. 16.00 (*0-8328-8338-7*); reprint ed. lib. bdg. 26.00 (*0-8328-8337-9*) Higginson Bk Co.

Lawrence, Ethel V., compiled by. Doty: Continuing the Line of Doty-Lawrence Family As Found in Doty-Doten Family, by E. A. Coty. (Illus.). 74p. 1997. reprint ed. pap. 15.00 (*0-8328-8336-0*); reprint ed. lib. bdg. 25.00 (*0-8328-8335-2*) Higginson Bk Co.

Lawrence, Eugene. The Science of Palmistry. 138p. 1996. reprint ed. spiral bd. 13.00 (*0-7873-0538-3*) Hlth Research.

Lawrence, F. L. Moliere: The Comedy of Unreason, Vol. 2. 119p. 1968. pap. 7.00 (*0-912788-01-1*) Tulane Romance Lang.

Lawrence, Florence, ed. see Wirths, Wallace R.

Lawrence, Fred, jt. auth. see Auh, Yoon-il.

Lawrence, Fred, ed. see Jane Jacobs Conference Staff.

Lawrence, Frederick & Auh, Yoonil. A Guide to the Programming Process: A Complement to a Multi-Sensory Approach for Learning Programming Constructs & Problem Solving. (Illus.). 500p. 1995. text 85.00 (*0-9655063-0-4*) Frdrck Lawrence.

Lawrence, Frederick, tr. see Habermas, Jurgen.

Lawrence, Frederick G., ed. see Lonergan, Bernard.

Lawrence, Frederick G., tr. see Gadamer, Hans-Georg.

Lawrence, Frederick G., tr. see Habermas, Jurgen.

Lawrence, Frederick M. Punishing Hate: Bias Crimes under American Law. LC 98-49780. 1999. 39.95 (*0-674-73845-4*) HUP.

Lawrence, Frieda. Not I, but the Wind. 2000. reprint ed. lib. bdg. 79.00 (*0-7812-7713-2*) Rprt Serv.

***Lawrence, G.** Coyote: A Novel. LC 99-97513. 2000. pap. 11.95 (*0-533-13420-X*) Vantage.

Lawrence, G. H., compiled by. Catalogue of the 2nd International Exhibition of Botanical Art & Illustration. (Illus.). 267p. 1968. 7.00 (*0-913196-11-8*) Hunt Inst Botanical.

Lawrence, G. H., ed. Adanson: The Bicentennial of Michel Adanson's "Familles des Plantes", 2 vols., Pt. 1. (Illus.). 392p. 1964. pap. 5.00 (*0-913196-25-8*) Hunt Inst Botanical.

— Adanson: The Bicentennial of Michel Adanson's "Familles des Plantes", 2 vols., Pt. 2. (Illus.). 243p. 1964. 5.00 (*0-913196-24-X*) Hunt Inst Botanical.

Lawrence, G. R. Randstad, Holland. (Problem Regions of Europe Ser.). (Illus.). 1973. pap. 7.95 (*0-19-913101-5*) OUP.

Lawrence, G. R., jt. auth. see Gresswell, R. Kay.

Lawrence, Gabrielle A., jt. auth. see Campbell, Mary.

Lawrence, Gale. The Beginning Naturalist: Weekly Encounters with the Natural World. LC 79-89171. (Illus.). xii, 209p. 1979. pap. 12.95 (*0-933050-02-X*) New Eng Pr VT.

— A Field Guide to the Familiar: Learning to Observe the Natural World. LC 97-47151. (Illus.). 288p. 1998. reprint ed. pap. 17.95 (*0-87451-865-2*) U Pr of New Eng.

— Vermont Life's Guide to Fall Foliage. 2nd ed. 1993. pap. 4.95 (*0-936896-25-6*) VT Life Mag.

Lawrence, Gary L. Rejection Junkies. (Illus.). 187p. 1996. pap. 11.95 (*0-9649924-0-X*) Lawrence Seminars.

Lawrence, Gary M. Due Diligence in Business Transactions. LC 94-43241. 1994. write for info. (*0-614-32187-5*) Law Journal.

Lawrence, Geoffrey, jt. auth. see Vanclay, Frank.

Lawrence, George, tr. see De Tocqueville, Alexis.

Lawrence, George A. Guy Livingston: or Thorough. LC 79-8148. reprint ed. 44.50 (*0-404-61960-6*) AMS Pr.

Lawrence, Gerda & Hunter, Madeline C. Parent-Teacher Conferencing. LC 95-12896. 112p. (Orig.). 1978. pap. text 19.95 (*0-8039-6327-0*) Corwin Pr.

Lawrence, Glenwood A. A Broom to Fly: New Ways of Solving the Age-Old Problems of Self-Management. rev. ed. LC 90-82823. (Dance to the Music of Circumstances Ser.). (Illus.). 134p. 1997. pap. text 4.95 (*0-9624719-4-1*) Growth Pubs.

— Hurt: The Human Saga. (Illus.). 160p. (Orig.). 1989. pap. write for info. (*0-318-65941-7*) Growth Pubs.

Lawrence, Gordon. People Types & Tiger Stripes. 3rd ed. 256p. 1993. 15.00 (*0-935652-16-7*) Ctr Applications Psych.

Lawrence, Gordon, ed. see Crawshaw, Dale.

Lawrence, Gordon D. Looking at Type & Learning Styles. 72p. 1997. pap. 7.00 (*0-935652-33-7*) Ctr Applications Psych.

***Lawrence, Greer.** Elvis The King of Rock & Roll. 1998. pap. text 6.98 (*1-57717-021-0*) Todtri Prods.

— Elvis: The King of Rock & Roll. (Illus.). 45p. (YA). (gr. 8-10). 2000. 17.00 (*0-7881-9258-2*) DIANE Pub.

Lawrence, Greer. Prayers & Meditations for Children. 1998. pap. text 7.98 (*1-57717-061-X*) Todtri Prods.

Lawrence, Greg, jt. auth. see Costanza, Mike.

Lawrence, H. Lea. The Archer's & Bowhunter's Bible. LC 93-16901. 192p. 1993. pap. 12.95 (*0-385-42221-0*) Doubleday.

— Fly Fisherman's Guide to the Great Smoky Mountains National Park. LC 98-16426. (Illus.). 196p. 1998. pap. 18.95 (*1-888952-82-2*) Cumberland Hse.

***Lawrence, H. Lea.** A Hemingway Odyssey. LC 99-24090. (Illus.). 201p. 1999. pap. 12.95 (*1-58182-024-0*) Cumberland Hse.

Lawrence, H. Lea & Lawrence, Ardi. Natural Wonders of Tennessee: A Guide to Parks, Preserves & Wild Places. LC 94-20920. (Natural Wonders Ser.). (Illus.). 140p. 1994. pap. 9.95 (*1-56626-110-4*, Cntry Rds Pr) NTC Contemp Pub Co.

Lawrence, H. Lea & Watson, Aubrey. The Outdoor Photographer's Bible. LC 96-21940. (Illus.). 160p. 1997. pap. 12.00 (*0-385-48220-5*, Main St Bks) Doubleday.

Lawrence, H. Lea, jt. auth. see Lawrence, Ardi.

Lawrence, H. S. Addition: No Regrouping. (Puzzles & Practice Ser.). (ENG & SPA., Illus.). 30p. (Orig.). (J). (gr. 1-6). 1992. pap., wbk. ed. 3.95 (*0-931993-49-0*, GP-049) Garlic Pr OR.

— Addition & Subtraction: With Regrouping. (Puzzle & Practice Ser.). (ENG & SPA., Illus.). 30p. (Orig.). (J). (gr. 1-6). 1992. pap., wbk. ed. 3.95 (*0-931993-51-2*, GP-051) Garlic Pr OR.

— Advanced Multiplication. (Puzzles & Practice Ser.). (ENG & SPA., Illus.). 30p. (Orig.). (J). (gr. 1-6). 1993. pap., wbk. ed. 3.95 (*0-931993-62-8*, GP-062) Garlic Pr OR.

— Decimals. (Puzzles & Practice Ser.). (ENG & SPA., Illus.). 30p. (J). (gr. 1-6). 1993. pap. 3.95 (*0-931993-60-1*, GP-060) Garlic Pr OR.

— Division. (Puzzles & Practice Ser.). (ENG & SPA., Illus.). 30p. (J). (gr. 1-6). 1993. pap. 3.95 (*0-931993-59-8*, GP-059) Garlic Pr OR.

— Fractions. (Puzzles & Practice Ser.). (ENG & SPA., Illus.). 30p. (J). (gr. 1-6). 1993. pap. 3.95 (*0-931993-61-X*, GP-061) Garlic Pr OR.

— Multiplication: Factors 1-12. (Puzzles & Practice Ser.). (ENG & SPA., Illus.). 30p. (Orig.). (J). (gr. 1-6). 1992. pap., student ed. 3.95 (*0-931993-52-0*, GP-052) Garlic Pr OR.

— Subtraction: No Regrouping. (Puzzles & Practice Ser.). (ENG & SPA., Illus.). 30p. (Orig.). (J). (gr. 1-6). 1992. pap., student ed. 3.95 (*0-931993-50-4*, GP-050) Garlic Pr OR.

— Word Problems, Bk. 1. (Straight Forward Math Ser.). 40p. (J). (gr. 3-6). 1996. pap., wbk. ed. 3.95 (*0-931993-83-0*, GP-083) Garlic Pr OR.

***Lawrence, H. S.** Word Problems, Bk. 2. (Straight Forward Math Ser.). 39p. (J). (gr. 3-6). 1999. pap. 3.95 (*0-931993-42-3*, GP-042) Garlic Pr OR.

Lawrence, Hanson. Have I Got a Story for You. 1988. pap. 7.95 (*0-910791-15-5*) Devyn Pr.

Lawrence, Harold A. Asbury's South Carolina Visits. 115p. 1995. reprint ed. pap. 10.00 (*0-9644858-2-6*) Boyd Pub Co.

— Into the Presence. 136p. 1998. pap. 12.95 (*1-890307-07-6*) Boyd Pub Co.

***Lawrence, Harold A.** Seeing the Elephant. (Illus.). 213p. 1999. pap. 16.95 (*1-890307-28-9*) Boyd Pub Co.

Lawrence, Harold A. Southland: Poems of the South. (Illus.). 256p. (Orig.). 1992. pap. 14.95 (*0-87797-251-6*) Cherokee.

— The Voice of the Turtle. (Illus.). 97p. (Orig.). 1995. pap. 12.95 (*0-9644858-4-2*) Boyd Pub Co.

Lawrence, Harold A., ed. Methodist Preachers in Georgia, 1783-1900 Supplement. 224p. 1995. 20.00 (*0-9644858-0-X*) Boyd Pub Co.

Lawrence, Harold A. & Culberson, Nancy, eds. Darien Baptist Church Records, 1794-1863. 200p. 1995. 20.00 (*0-9644858-1-8*) Boyd Pub Co.

Lawrence, Heather, jt. auth. see Evans, Ifor M.

Lawrence, Helen. Career Search: A Personal Process. (Illus.). 140p. (C). 1993. pap. text. write for info. (*1-884155-05-7*) Day & Nite Pub.

— Taking Chances, Making Choices. 148p. (C). 1993. pap. text. write for info. (*1-884155-04-9*) Day & Nite Pub.

Lawrence, Helen, tr. see Pugnetti, Gino.

Lawrence Henry Gipson Institute Staff. Revisioning the British Empire in the Eighteenth Century: Essays from Twenty-Five Years of the Lawrence Henry Gipson Institute for Eighteenth-Century Studies. Shade, William G., ed. LC 98-22711. 304p. 1999. 38.50 (*0-934223-57-2*) Lehigh Univ Pr.

Lawrence, Hermano. La Practica de la Presencia de Dios.Tr. of Practice of the Presence of God. (SPA.). 96p. 1997. mass mkt. 5.99 (*0-88368-012-2*) Whitaker Hse.

Lawrence, Hilda. Pavilion. 1999. lib. bdg. 22.95 (*1-56723-147-0*, 156) Yestermorrow.

Lawrence, Hinman. Contemporary Moral Issues: Diversity & Consensus. 2nd ed. LC 99-44843. 619p. (C). 1999. pap. text 42.00 (*0-13-086219-3*) P-H.

Lawrence, Hoe R. & Hufeland, Otto. Valentine's Manuals: A General Index to the Manuals of the Corporation of the City of New York, 1841-1870. LC 81-6437. 157p. 1981. 15.00 (*0-916346-42-0*) NY Bound.

Lawrence, Iain. Far-Away Places: 50 Anchorages on the Northwest Coast. (Illus.). 192p. (Orig.). 1995. pap. 14.95 (*1-55143-033-9*) Orca Bk Pubs.

***Lawrence, Iain.** Ghost Boy. LC 00-25590. (Illus.). (J). 2000. pap. 15.95 (*0-385-32739-0*) Delacorte.

Lawrence, Iain. Sea Stories of the Inside Passage: In the Wake of the Nid. LC 98-11937. (Illus.). 164p. 1997. 13.95 (*0-938665-47-2*) Fine Edge Prods.

— The Smugglers. LC 98-41582. 192p. 1999. 15.95 (*0-385-32663-7*) BDD Bks Young Read.

***Lawrence, Iain.** The Smugglers. (Illus.). 208p. (J). 2000. pap. 4.99 (*0-440-41596-9*, Yearling) BDD Bks Young Read.

— The Wreckers. LC 97-31625. 256p. (YA). (gr. 5-9). 1998. 15.95 (*0-385-32535-5*) Delacorte.

— The Wreckers. large type ed. LC 99-42431. (Thorndike Young Adult Ser.). 241p. (YA). (gr. 7-12). 1999. 21.95 (*0-7862-2189-5*) Thorndike Pr.

Lawrence, Iain. The Wreckers. 224p. (YA). (gr. 4-7). 1999. reprint ed. pap. 4.99 (*0-440-41545-4*) BDD Bks Young Read.

Lawrence, Ian. Power & Politics at the Department of Education & Science. Sayer, John, ed. (Education Management Ser.). 192p. 1992. text 80.00 (*0-304-32624-0*); pap. text 37.95 (*0-304-32607-0*) Continuum.

Lawrence, Ian, ed. Education Tomorrow. (Education Management Ser.). 224p. 1994. 80.00 (*0-304-32927-4*) Continuum.

Lawrence, Ingrid. The Day Mama Played. LC 97-150945. 32p. (J). (ps-2). 1997. pap. 5.99 (*1-56476-525-3*, Chariot Bks) Chariot Victor.

***Lawrence, Irene.** Fifty Tips for Organizing Your Life. LC 00-100653. (Illus.). 70p. 2000. pap. 7.95 (*1-885003-53-6*, Pub. by R D Reed Pubs) Midpt Trade.

Lawrence, Irene. Linguistics & Theology: The Significance of Noam Chomsky for Theological Construction. LC 80-24210. (American Theological Library Association Monograph: No. 16). 214p. 1980. 29.00 (*0-8108-1347-5*) Scarecrow.

— Love's Last Barrier. large type ed. (Linford Romance Library). 1990. pap. 16.99 (*0-7089-6881-3*, Linford) Ulverscroft.

— No Escape from Love. large type ed. (Linford Romance Library). 1991. pap. 16.99 (*0-7089-7099-0*) Ulverscroft.

— Switch on to Love. large type ed. (Linford Romance Library). 224p. 1993. pap. 16.99 (*0-7089-7470-8*) Ulverscroft.

Lawrence, J. The Genealogy of the Family of John Lawrence of Wisset in Suffolk, England, & of Watertown & Groton, Mass. 332p. reprint ed. pap. 50.00 (*0-8328-0754-0*); reprint ed. lib. bdg. 58.00 (*0-8328-0753-2*) Higginson Bk Co.

— A Profit in Our Own Country. 139p. 1994. pap. 30.00 (*1-86320-119-X*, Pub. by ACIAR) St Mut.

Lawrence, J., jt. auth. see Crabb, Jr.

Lawrence, J., jt. auth. see Crabb, Lawrence J., Jr.

Lawrence, J., jt. ed. see Boundy, Ray H.

Lawrence, J. D. Furniture Makers' Designs. 1998. write for info. (*0-8069-9710-9*) Sterling.

— Furniture-Making from the Inside Out. LC 95-20391. (Illus.). 192p. 1996. pap. 18.95 (*0-8069-8566-6*) Sterling.

Lawrence, J. Dennis. Catalog of Special Plane Curves. LC 72-80280. (Illus.). 218p. 1972. pap. text 8.95 (*0-486-60288-5*) Dover.

Lawrence, J. F., jt. ed. see Frei, R. W.

Lawrence, J. H., et al. Radioisotopes & Radiation: Recent Advances in Medicine, Agriculture, & Industry. (Illus.). 1990. 16.00 (*0-8446-0765-7*) Peter Smith.

Lawrence, J. M., jt. ed. see Jangoux, Michel.

Lawrence, J. R. & Hunter, J. D., eds. MCQs in General Medicine. 216p. (Orig.). 1989. pap. text 26.00 (*0-443-03425-7*) Church.

Lawrence, J. R., jt. ed. see Whitworth, Judith A.

Lawrence, Jacob. The Great Migration. LC 93-16788. (Trophy Picture Bk.). (Illus.). 48p. (J). (gr. 3 up). 1995. reprint ed. pap. 8.95 (*0-06-443428-1*, HarpTrophy) HarpC Child Bks.

***Lawrence, Jacob.** The Great Migration: An American Story. (Illus.). (J). 1999. pap. text 16.90 (*0-7857-7628-1*) Econo-Clad Bks.

Lawrence, Jacob. The Great Migration: An American Story. (Illus.). 48p. (J). (gr. 3-7). 1993. 22.00 (*0-943044-20-0*); pap. write for info. (*0-943044-21-9*) Phillips Coll.

— Harriet & the Promised Land. LC 92-33740. (Illus.). 40p. (J). 1993. pap. 16.00 (*0-671-86673-7*) S&S Bks Yung.

— Harriet & the Promised Land. 1997. mass mkt. 5.99 (*0-689-80965-4*) S&S Bks Yung.

Lawrence, Jacob. Harriet & the Promised Land. 1997. 11.19 (*0-606-11440-8*, Pub. by Turtleback) Demco.

Lawrence, James. Station Break. LC 99-91267. 160p. 1997. 25.00 (*0-7388-0718-4*); pap. 18.00 (*0-7388-0719-2*) Xlibris Corp.

Lawrence, James, ed. see Paletta, Michael S.

Lawrence, James, ed. see Tullock, John H.

Lawrence, James, ed. see Wilkerson, Joyce D.

Lawrence, James F., ed. Food Constituents & Food Residues: Their Chromatographic Determination. LC 84-4267. (Food Science & Technology Ser.: Vol. 11). (Illus.). 629p. 1984. reprint ed. pap. 195.00 (*0-608-01647-0*, 206229900002) Bks Demand.

— Liquid Chromatography in Environmental Analysis. LC 83-10711. (Contemporary Instrumentation & Analysis Ser.). 385p. 1984. 99.50 (*0-89603-045-8*) Humana.

Lawrence, James F., ed. see Milosz, Czeslaw, et al.

Lawrence, James F., ed. see Swedenborg, Emanuel.

Lawrence, James H. Empire of the Nairs: Or, the Rights of Women, 4 vols. in 1. LC 76-21346. 1050p. 1976. reprint ed. 90.00 (*0-8201-1270-4*) Schol Facsimiles.

Lawrence, James K., jt. auth. see Atherton, M. A.

Lawrence, James M. & Martin, Rux. Sweet Maple: Life, Lore & Recipes from the Sugarbush. (Illus.). 223p. 1999. reprint ed. pap. text 20.00 (*0-7881-6296-9*) DIANE Pub.

Lawrence, Jan. America's Most Wanted Fifth-Graders. (J). (gr. 3-7). 1997. pap. 3.99 (*0-590-58295-X*, Apple Paperbacks) Scholastic Inc.

— Revenge of the Substitute Teacher. (J). 1998. pap. text 3.99 (*0-590-05902-5*, Apple Paperbacks) Scholastic Inc.

— Revenge of the Substitute Teacher. 1998. 9.09 (*0-606-13739-4*, Pub. by Turtleback) Demco.

Lawrence, Jan & Raskin, Linda. The Timeless Travels of J. J. & Kelly: The London Adventure. 78p. (Orig.). (J). (gr. 6-9). 1994. pap. 9.99 (*0-88092-085-8*) Royal Fireworks.

Lawrence, Jane F., jt. auth. see Marchese, Theodore J.

Lawrence, Janet. A Tasty Way to Die. large type ed. 464p. 1992. 27.99 (*0-7089-2613-4*) Ulverscroft.

Lawrence, Janet H., jt. auth. see Blackburn, Robert T.

Lawrence, Jeannette. Introduction to Neural Networks: Design, Theory, & Applications. 5th ed. Luedeking, Sylvia, ed. (Illus.). 348p. (C). 1994. pap. text 30.00 (*1-883157-00-5*) Calif Sci Sftware.

Lawrence, Jennie. Choosing a Canine Companion: A Lifetime of Love. LC 95-77064. 102p. 1995. pap. 10.95 (*0-9646463-0-7*) Heritage Concepts.

— Puppy Puppy . . . What Are You Doing Now? 180p. 1996. pap. 12.95 (*0-9646463-2-3*) Heritage Concepts.

Lawrence, Jerome. Actor - the Life & Times of Paul Muni. 380p. 1982. reprint ed. 9.45 (*0-573-69034-0*) French.

— Inherit the Wind. 1969. 10.09 (*0-606-00870-5*, Pub. by Turtleback) Demco.

— Live Spelled Backwards. 1970. pap. 3.25 (*0-8222-0681-1*) Dramatists Play.

— The Night Thoreau Spent in Jail. 1982. 11.09 (*0-606-12451-9*, Pub. by Turtleback) Demco.

Lawrence, Jerome & Lee, Robert E. The Croccodile Smile. 1972. pap. 5.25 (*0-8222-0253-0*) Dramatists Play.

— The Gang's All Here. LC 60-11223. (Illus.). 129p. 1960. 16.95 (*0-910278-33-4*) Boulevard.

— The Incomparable Max. 1972. pap. 5.25 (*0-8222-0566-1*) Dramatists Play.

— Inherit the Wind. 144p. 1982. mass mkt. 5.50 (*0-553-26915-1*) Bantam.

— Inherit the Wind. 1963. pap. 5.25 (*0-8222-0570-X*) Dramatists Play.

— The Night Thoreau Spent in Jail. 128p. (YA). (gr. 8-12). 1982. mass mkt. 5.99 (*0-553-27838-X*) Bantam.

— Sparks Fly Upward. 1967. pap. 5.25 (*0-8222-1064-9*) Dramatists Play.

Lawrence, Jill, ed. see LaVoie, Nicole.

Lawrence, Jill T. AS/400 Architecture & Application: The Database Machine. 320p. 1993. pap. 64.99 (*0-471-58141-0*) Wiley.

Lawrence, Jim, jt. auth. see Harmon, Renee.

Lawrence, Joan. The House on the Cliff. LC 89-81666. (Illus.). 160p. 1990. 28.00 (*0-7206-0763-9*, Pub. by P Owen Ltd) Dufour.

— Scapegoat: A Novel on the Life of Moses. 188p. 1988. 29.95 (*0-7206-0708-6*, Pub. by P Owen Ltd) Dufour.

Lawrence, Joe, Jr. & Brucker, Roger W. The Caves Beyond: The Story of the Floyd Collins' Crystal Cave Exploration. LC 75-34060. (Illus.). 320p. 1975. reprint ed. pap. 10.95 (*0-914264-18-4*) Cave Bks MO.

Lawrence, John. Argument for Action: Ethics & Professional Conduct. LC 98-74840. 1p. 1999. text 78.95 (*1-84014-998-1*) Ashgate Pub Co.

— Good Babies, Bad Babies: A Primer for Expectant Parents. (J). (ps). 1990. 10.95 (*0-87923-823-2*) Godine.

Lawrence, John, ed. Forests & Clearing: History of Stanstead County, Province of Quebec, with Sketches of More Than Five Hundred Families. (Illus.). 367p. 1996. reprint ed. lib. bdg. 42.00 (*0-8328-6532-X*) Higginson Bk Co.

Lawrence, John. A New Treasury of Poetry. LC 89-49089. 256p. 1990. 27.50 (*1-55670-145-4*) Stewart Tabori & Chang.

— Robin Hood. 89p. (J). (gr. 4-7). 1995. 15.95 (*0-8050-3397-1*) H Holt & Co.

Lawrence, John, photos by. Faulkner's Rowan Oak. LC 93-10719. (Illus.). 72p. 1993. pap. 14.95 (*0-87805-662-9*) U Pr of Miss.

Lawrence, John & Britton, E. B. Australian Beetles. LC 95-106663. (Illus.). 208p. 1994. 44.95 (*0-522-84519-3*, Pub. by Melbourne Univ Pr) Paul & Co Pubs.

Lawrence, John, jt. auth. see Martin, Bernice.

Lawrence, John, ed. see Hubbard, B. F.

Lawrence, John A. & Pasternack, Barry A. Applied Management Science: A Computer-Integrated Managerial Approach. LC 97-24497. 704p. 1997. text 102.95 incl. cd-rom (*0-471-13776-6*) Wiley.

Lawrence, John H. Preservation Guide No. 2: Photographs. LC 84-106237. (Illus.). ii, 14p. 1983. pap. 3.95 (*0-917860-17-9*) Historic New Orleans.

Lawrence, John H., intro. Guide to the Photographic Collections at the Historic New Orleans Collection. LC 89-81507. (Illus.). 24p. (Orig.). 1989. pap. 3.95 (*0-917860-29-2*) Historic New Orleans.

Lawrence, John H., ed. & intro. see Crawford, Ralston.

Lawrence, John, Interdisciplinary Symposium on the. Dissipative Structures & Spatiotemporal Organization Studies in Biomedical Research: Report of the First John Lawrence Interdisciplinary Symposium on the Physical

An Asterisk (*) at the beginning of an entry indicates that the title is appearing for the first time.

& Biomedical Sciences, Held January 17, 1979, Sioux Falls, SD. Scott, George P. & McMillin, J. Michael, eds. LC 80-148258. (Illus.). 281p. 1980. reprint ed. pap. 87.20 (*0-608-00122-8*, 206088700006) Bks Demand.

Lawrence, John M. Echinoderms: Proceedings of the International Echinoderms Conference, Tampa Bay, 14-17 September 1981. 552p. (C). 1982. text 233.00 (*90-6191-228-8*, Pub. by A A Balkema) Ashgate Pub Co.

— A Functional Biology of Echinoderms. LC 87-2843. 352p. 1987. reprint ed. pap. 109.20 (*0-608-03713-3*, 206453800009) Bks Demand.

Lawrence, John M., jt. ed. see Jangoux, Michel.

Lawrence, John S. Electronic Scholar: A Guide to Academic Microcomputing. Voigt, Melvin J., ed. LC 84-16952. (Communication & Information Science Ser.). 192p. (Orig.). 1985. pap. 39.50 (*0-89391-299-9*); text 73.25 (*0-89391-298-0*) Ablx Pub.

Lawrence, John S., et al, eds. Fair Use & Free Inquiry: Copyright Law & the New Media. 2nd ed. LC 89-213. (Communication & Information Science Ser.). 440p. (C). 1989. text 78.50 (*0-89391-484-3*) Ablx Pub.

Lawrence, John T. A Dictionary of Musical Biography. 1976. lib. bdg. 75.00 (*0-8490-1720-3*) Gordon Pr.

— A History of Russia. 7th rev. ed. 382p. 1993. pap. 15.95 (*0-452-01084-5*, Mer) NAL.

— Perfect Ashlar & Other Masonic Symbols. 376p. 1999. reprint ed. pap. 19.95 (*0-7661-0834-1*) Kessinger Pub.

— The Slavery Question. 1977. 18.95 (*0-8369-9168-0*, 9043) Ayer.

Lawrence, John W. The Seven Laws of the Harvest: Understanding the Realities of Sowing & Reaping. LC 95-13297. 128p. 1995. pap. 8.99 (*0-8254-3151-4*) Kregel.

— Las Siete Leyes de la Cosecha. (SPA.). 128p. 1996. pap. 5.99 (*0-8254-1444-X*, Edit Portavoz) Kregel.

— The Six Trials of Jesus. 240p. 1996. pap. 11.99 (*0-8254-3152-2*) Kregel.

Lawrence, Johnny & White, James. They Seek Me Early. 42p. 1993. pap. 5.00 (*0-916092-18-6*) Tex Ctr Writers.

Lawrence, Jon. Speaking for the People: Party, Language & Popular Politics in England, 1867-1914. LC 97-30166. 303p. (C). 1998. text 64.95 (*0-521-47034-X*) Cambridge U Pr.

Lawrence, Jon, jt. ed. see Taylor, Miles.

Lawrence, Joy E., jt. auth. see Anderson, William M.

Lawrence, Judy M. The Budget Kit: The Common Cents Money Management Workbook. 2nd rev. ed. LC 96-36019. 320p. 1997. pap. 15.95 (*0-7931-2343-7*, 5608-7402) Dearborn.

— Common Cents: The Complete Money Management Workbook. 84p. (Orig.). 1989. 10.95 (*0-9607096-6-5*) Lawrence & Co Pubs.

— The Family Chronicle: The Complete Family Memory Book. 96p. (Orig.). 1987. pap. 12.95 (*0-9607096-5-7*) Lawrence & Co Pubs.

— The Family Memory Book: Highlights of Our Times Together. 2nd ed. Spadaccini, Victor M. & Schreifels, Susan, eds. (Illus.). 96p. 1992. 9.95 (*0-911493-13-1*) Blue Sky.

— The Money Tracker: A Quick & Easy Way to Keep Tabs on Your Spending. 416p. 1996. 14.95 (*0-7931-1786-0*, 5680-3201) Dearborn.

— Our Family Memories: Highlights of Our Times Together. Spadaccini, Victor M. & Schreifels, Susan, eds. (Illus.). 96p. 1995. 9.95 (*0-911493-14-X*) Blue Sky.

Lawrence, Judy M., jt. auth. see Yurick, Clotilde.

Lawrence, K. J. Zebra Finches. (Colorguide Ser.). 1982. pap. 6.95 (*0-940842-12-2*) South Group.

Lawrence, K. O. A Question of Labour: Indentured Immigration into Trinidad & British Guiana, 1875-1917. LC 94-1159. 1994. text 55.00 (*0-312-12172-5*) St Martin.

Lawrence, Karen, et al, eds. The McGraw-Hill Guide to English Literature: Beowulf to Jane Austen, Vol. 1. 497p. (C). 1985. pap. 9.95 (*0-07-036704-3*) McGraw.

Lawrence, Karen R. Penelope Voyages: Women & Travel in the British Literary Tradition. (Reading Women Writing Ser.). 288p. 1994. text 42.50 (*0-8014-2610-3*); pap. text 16.95 (*0-8014-9913-5*) Cornell U Pr.

Lawrence, Karen R., ed. Decolonizing Tradition: New Views of Twentieth-Century "British" Literary Canons. 304p. 1991. text 42.50 (*0-252-01821-4*); pap. text 15.95 (*0-252-06193-4*) U of Ill Pr.

Lawrence, Karen R., ed. Transcultural Joyce. LC 97-27463. 259p. (C). 1998. text 59.95 (*0-521-62109-7*) Cambridge U Pr.

Lawrence, Kathy. Tin Angel. 352p. (Orig.). 1989. mass mkt. 3.95 (*0-380-75735-4*, Avon Bks) Morrow Avon.

Lawrence, Keith, ed. The Complete Guide to Boat Kits & Plans. 10th ed. 1996. pap. text. write for info. (*0-07-006072-X*) McGraw.

Lawrence, Ken. Photography for the Archivist. Gill, Rowland P., ed. (Collegiate Guide to Archival Science Ser.). 56p. (C). 1999. 7.95 (*0-910653-10-0*, 8334K, Red River Pr) Archival Servs.

— Sociological Aspects of the Church. Sauls, Dale & Hill, James, eds. 144p. (Orig.). (C). 1999. pap. 5.95 (*0-910653-25-9*, Red River Pr) Archival Servs.

— A Town on the Grow, the History of Blanchard, Louisiana. 1999. 3.50 (*0-910653-24-0*, 8332Q, Red River Pr) Archival Servs.

Lawrence, Ken & Hughes, Jeff. An Extensive Look at Museums in Louisiana. rev. ed. Sibley, James A., Jr., ed. & intro. by. 72p. 1999. 10.00 (*0-910653-15-1*, 8220H, Red River Pr) Archival Servs.

Lawrence, Ken & Sandifer, Kevin W., Jr. The Ark of the Covenant & Christianity. rev. ed. Sibley, J. Ashley, ed. 112p. 1998. 5.95 (*0-910653-13-5*, 8111G, Red River Pr) Archival Servs.

Lawrence, Kenneth. Korah's Travels: The Saga of an Israelite Family. (Illus.). 256p. (Orig.). (YA). 1999. pap. 19.95 (*0-910653-14-3*, 8123M, Red River Pr) Archival Servs.

Lawrence, Kenneth, ed. Classic Themes of Disciples Theology: Rethinking the Traditional Affirmations of the Christian Church (Disciples of Christ) LC 85-50712. 150p. 1986. text 20.00 (*0-87565-024-4*) Tex Christian.

Lawrence, Kenneth D., et al, eds. Advances in Business Management & Forecasting, Vol. 2. 1998. 73.25 (*0-7623-0002-7*) Jai Pr.

— Advances in Business Management & Forecasting: Forecasting Sales. LC 94-15832. (Advances in Business & Management Forecasting Ser.: Vol. 1). 298p. 1994. 73.25 (*1-55938-602-9*) Jai Pr.

— Advances in Mathematical Programming & Financial Planning, Vol. 1. 284p. 1986. 73.25 (*0-89232-582-8*) Jai Pr.

— Advances in Mathematical Programming & Financial Planning, Vol. 2. 258p. 1990. 73.25 (*0-89232-815-0*) Jai Pr.

— Advances in Mathematical Programming & Financial Planning, Vol. 3. 295p. 1993. 73.25 (*1-55938-251-1*) Jai Pr.

— Advances in Mathematical Programming & Financial Planning, Vol. 4. 1995. 73.25 (*1-55938-724-6*) Jai Pr.

— Advances in Mathematical Programming & Financial Planning, Vol. 5. 1999. 73.25 (*0-7623-0128-7*) Jai Pr.

— Applications of Management Science, Vol. 1. 400p. 1981. 78.50 (*0-89232-023-0*) Jai Pr.

— Applications of Management Science, Vol. 2. 231p. 1983. 78.50 (*0-89232-258-6*) Jai Pr.

— Applications of Management Science, Vol. 3. 291p. 1986. 78.50 (*0-89232-324-8*) Jai Pr.

— Applications of Management Science, Vol. 4. 234p. 1985. 78.50 (*0-89232-468-6*) Jai Pr.

— Applications of Management Science, Vol. 5. 303p. 1987. 78.50 (*0-89232-687-5*) Jai Pr.

— Applications of Management Science, Vol. 6. 276p. 1991. 78.50 (*0-89232-939-4*) Jai Pr.

— Applications of Management Science, Vol. 7. 191p. 1993. 78.50 (*1-55938-556-1*) Jai Pr.

— Applications of Management Science, Vol. 9. 1996. 78.50 (*0-7623-0012-4*) Jai Pr.

— Applications of Management Science: Network Optimization in Applications, Vol. 8. 280p. (Orig.). 1995. 78.50 (*1-55938-729-7*) Jai Pr.

— Applications of Management Science No. 1: Management Science Implementaiton. 182p. 1984. suppl. ed. 73.25 (*0-89232-509-7*) Jai Pr.

Lawrence, Kenneth D. & Arthur, Jeffrey L. Robust Regression: Analysis & Applications. (Statistics: Textbooks & Monographs: Vol. 108). (Illus.). 312p. 1989. text 137.50 (*0-8247-8129-5*) Dekker.

Lawrence, Kenneth D. & Reeves, Gary R., eds. Applications of Management Science, Vol. 10. Date not set. 78.50 (*0-7623-0365-4*) Jai Pr.

Lawrence, Kenneth E. & Painter, Sandra J., eds. Women's Health Patient Education Resource Manual. LC 93-33562. ring bd. 189.00 (*0-8342-0547-5*) Aspen Pub.

Lawrence, Kenneth E., jt. auth. see Aspen Reference Group Staff.

Lawrence, Kenneth E., ed. see Aspen Reference Group Staff.

Lawrence, Kenneth R. Public Relations Are an Asset for Archives & Museums. rev. ed. Joyner, Virginia, ed. 32p. (Orig.). (C). 1996. pap. 8.95 (*0-910653-26-7*, 8004L) Archival Servs.

Lawrence, Kent L., jt. auth. see Woods, Robert L.

Lawrence, Kevin. The Divine Liturgy: A Hymnal in Greek & English. Holly Cross Greek Orthodox School of Theology Staff, tr. 366p. 1998. pap. 10.00 (*0-9650957-2-X*) Southestrn Fed.

— The Divine Liturgy in Greek & English: Set to Traditional Byzantine Melodies. 242p. 1996. pap. write for info. (*0-9650957-0-3*) Southestrn Fed.

Lawrence, Kim. Accidental Baby: Expecting! (Presents Ser.: No. 2034). 1999. per. 3.75 (*0-373-12034-6*, 1-12034-4, Harlequin) Harlequin Bks.

— Un Bonheur Imprevisible. (Azur Ser.: Bk. 738). 1999. mass mkt. 3.50 (*0-373-34738-3*, 1-34738-4) Harlequin Bks.

— Esposa de Conveniencia (Wife of Convenience) (Bianca Ser.). (SPA.). 1998. per. 3.50 (*0-373-33451-6*, 1-33451-5) Harlequin Bks.

— Esposa de Nueve a Cinco. (Bianca Ser.).Tr. of Nine to Five Wife. (SPA.). 1999. per. 3.50 (*0-373-33528-8*, 1-33528-0) Harlequin Bks.

***Lawrence, Kim.** Hijo Del Amor. Vol. 210.Tr. of Son of Love. (SPA.). 2000. per. 3.50 (*0-373-33560-1*, 1-33560-3) Harlequin Bks.

Lawrence, Kim. Hijo Secreto: The Secret Father. (Bianca Ser.: No. 174).Tr. of Secret Son. (SPA.). 1999. per. 3.50 (*0-373-33524-5*, 1-33524-9) Harlequin Bks.

***Lawrence, Kim.** An Innocent Affair: Triplet Brides. (Presents Ser.: Bk. 2114). 2000. per. 3.99 (*0-373-12114-8*, 1-12114-4) Harlequin Bks.

Lawrence, Kim. Novio de Alquiler (Hiring Boyfriend), No. 135. (Harlequin Bianca Ser.). (SPA.). 1998. mass mkt. 3.50 (*0-373-33485-0*, 1-33485-3) Harlequin Bks.

— Salvajey Ardiente, 163. (Harlequin Bianca Ser.). 1999. per. 3.50 (*0-373-33513-X*) Harlequin Bks.

***Lawrence, Kim.** Secret Father. (Presents Ser.). 2000. per. 3.99 (*0-373-12096-6*) Harlequin Bks.

Lawrence, Kim. Wedding-Night Baby. (Romance Ser.). 1999. per. 3.75 (*0-373-12053-2*, 1-12053-4) Harlequin Bks.

***Lawrence, Kim.** Wife by Agreement. (Presents Ser.). 2000. mass mkt. 3.99 (*0-373-12147-4*, 1121474) Harlequin Bks.

Lawrence, Kim. Wild & Willing! (Presents Ser.: Bk. 2078). 187p. 2000. per. 3.75 (*0-373-12078-8*, 1-12078-1) Harlequin Bks.

***Lawrence, Kim & Williams, Cathy.** His Secretary Bride: Baby & the Boss - Assignment: Seduction, 2 vols. in 1. (Presents Ser.). 2000. mass mkt. 3.99 (*0-373-12123-7*, 1-12123-5) Harlequin Bks.

Lawrence, L. George. Galactic Life Unveiled: Interstellar Communications & Their Subliminal Effects on Man. (Illus.). 330p. 1997. spiral bd. 34.95 (*0-945685-24-6*) Borderland Sciences.

Lawrence, L. J., tr. see Strauss, Richard.

Lawrence, Lady. Indian Embers. LC 91-18463. 406p. 1991. reprint ed. pap. 13.95 (*1-879434-02-4*) Trackless Sands Pr.

Lawrence, Larry, ed. see American Motorcyclist Association Staff.

Lawrence, Lary. Introduction to Payment Systems. LC 99-36479. 592p. 1997. pap. text 28.95 (*1-56706-492-2*, 64922) Panel Pubs.

***Lawrence, Lary.** Payment Systems: Aspen Roadmap Law Course Outline. LC 99-36479. 432p. 1999. pap. text 21.95 (*0-7355-0638-8*) Panel Pubs.

***Lawrence, Lauren.** Dream Keys: Unlocking the Power of Your Unconscious. 320p. 1999. mass mkt. 6.50 (*0-440-23477-8*) Dell.

— Dream Keys for Love: Unlocking the Secrets of Your Own Heart. 336p. 1999. mass mkt. 5.99 (*0-440-23478-6*) Dell.

— Dream Keys for the Future: Unlocking the Secrets of Your Destiny. 304p. 2000. mass mkt. 6.50 (*0-440-23479-4*) Dell.

Lawrence, Laurie. Sink or Swim. 64p. (C). 1990. pap. 40.00 (*0-86439-092-0*, Pub. by Boolarong Pubns) St Mut.

Lawrence, Lea. The Small-Game & Varmint Hunter's Bible. LC 94-1637. 192p. 1994. pap. 12.00 (*0-385-46836-9*) Doubleday.

Lawrence, Lee E. The Wisconsin Ice Trade. (Wisconsin Stories Ser.). 12p. pap. 1.25 (*0-87020-197-2*) State Hist Soc Wis.

Lawrence, Les. Prophesy to the Land. LC 96-101189. 238p. (Orig.). 1994. pap. 10.99 (*1-56043-802-9*, Treasure Hse) Destiny Image.

Lawrence, Leslie, ed. Profile of 1994-95 State Assessment Systems & Reported Results National Education Goals Panel. (Illus.). 140p. (C). 1999. reprint ed. pap. text 30.00 (*0-7881-7695-1*) DIANE Pub.

Lawrence, Leslie & Price-Cohen, Cynthia. The National Education Goals Report: Building a Nation of Learners (1998) 78p. (C). 1999. pap. text 20.00 (*0-7881-7623-4*) DIANE Pub.

Lawrence, Leslie, jt. auth. see Prince, Cynthia.

Lawrence-Lightfoot, Sara. Art & Science of Portraiture. LC 97-4902. 1997. 29.95 (*0-7879-1064-3*) Jossey-Bass.

— Balm in Gilead: Journey of a Healer. (Illus.). 368p. 1995. pap. 13.95 (*0-14-024967-2*, Penguin Bks) Viking Penguin.

— I've Known Rivers: Lives of Loss & Liberation. 656p. 1994. 25.00 (*0-201-58120-5*) Addison-Wesley.

Lawrence-Lightfoot, Sara. Respect: An Exploration. LC 98-89427. (Merloyd Lawrence Book Ser.). 256p. 1999. 23.00 (*0-7382-0093-X*) Perseus Pubng.

***Lawrence-Lightfoot, Sara.** Respect: An Exploration. 256p. 2000. pap. text 15.00 (*0-7382-0318-1*) Perseus Pubng.

Lawrence, Linda & Thorne, Kate. Adventures in Arizona: An Illustrated History. Caillou, Aliza, ed. LC 91-65779. (Illus.). 48p. (Orig.). (J). (gr. 4 up). 1991. pap. 6.95 (*0-9628329-3-6*) Thorne Enterprises.

***Lawrence, Loretta N.** Cooking for My Family, from Catherine Pasculli's Hoboken Kitchen: Ethnic, Earthy, Easy & Italian Cooking. Arnesen, Anna M., ed. (Illus.). 1999. 15.00 (*0-9674919-0-8*) L Lawrence.

Lawrence, Lorna, jt. auth. see Taylor, Arlene.

Lawrence, Louis. Hirado--Prince of Porcelains. LC 97-31964. (Encyclopedia of Japanese Art Ser.). 1997. write for info. (*1-878529-30-7*) Art Media Resources.

Lawrence, Louis, jt. auth. see Schaefer, Jean.

Lawrence, Louise. Andra. LC 90-38595. 240p. (YA). (gr. 7 up). 1991. 14.95 (*0-06-023685-X*) HarpC Child Bks.

— Calling B for Butterfly. LC 81-48648. (Trophy Starwanderer Bk.). 224p. (YA). (gr. 7 up). 1988. mass mkt. 3.95 (*0-06-447036-9*, HarpTrophy) HarpC Child Bks.

— Dream-Weaver. LC 95-25856. 240p. (YA). (gr. 9). 1996. 15.00 (*0-395-71812-0*, Clarion Bks) HM.

— Dream-Weaver. (J). (gr. 9 up). 1998. pap. 6.95 (*0-395-92864-8*, Clarion Bks) HM.

— Moonwind. LC 85-45507. 192p. (YA). (gr. 7 up). 1986. 12.95 (*0-06-023733-3*) HarpC Child Bks.

— The Patchwork People. LC 93-40830. 240p. (J). 1994. 14.95 (*0-395-67892-7*, Clarion Bks) HM.

— The Warriors of Taan. LC 87-45291. 224p. (YA). (gr. 7 up). 1988. 12.95 (*0-06-023736-8*) HarpC Child Bks.

Lawrence, Lucy G., ed. see Medvedev, Zhores A.

***Lawrence, Lynn.** Frozen Moments in Time: A Treasury of Photographic Impressions. (Illus.). 330p. 1999. 75.00 (*1-888122-04-8*) Status Pubs.

Lawrence, Lynne. Montessori Read & Write: A Parents Guide for Teaching at Home. LC 98-26639. (Illus.). 160p. 1998. pap. 19.95 (*0-609-80335-2*, Crown) Crown Pub Group.

Lawrence, M. Hand Analysis. 1972. pap. 5.95 (*0-13-372466-2*, Reward) P-H.

Lawrence, M. & Pritchard, L., eds. General Practitioner Education: U. K. & Nordic Perspectives. 192p. 1992. 24.95 (*0-387-19741-9*) Spr-Verlag.

Lawrence, M. L. & Lombard, G. L. Murray - Conwell: Genealogy & Allied Families. (Illus.). 115p. 1992. reprint ed. pap. 19.50 (*0-8328-2697-9*); reprint ed. lib. bdg. 29.50 (*0-8328-2696-0*) Higginson Bk Co.

Lawrence, Madelaine. In a World of Their Own: Experiencing Unconsciousness. LC 96-25076. 200p. 1997. 55.00 (*0-275-95323-8*) Greenwood.

— In a World of Their Own: Experiencing Unconsciousness. LC 96-25076. 200p. 1998. pap. 19.95 (*0-89789-650-5*, Bergin & Garvey) Greenwood.

Lawrence, Maggie, et al. Christmas Plays for Young Audiences: 'Twas the Night Before Columbus Day. . . I Mean Christmas; The Angels' Greatest Message; How Santa Claus Discovered Christmas. (Illus.). 52p. (YA). (gr. 6-12). 1994. pap. 4.25 (*0-88680-391-8*) I E Clark.

Lawrence, Marc. Long Time No See: Confessions of a Hollywood Ganster. 240p. 1996. pap. text 18.95 (*1-880756-17-X*) Riverwood Pr.

— Long Time No See: Confessions of a Movie Gangster. (Illus.). 199p. (Orig.). (C). 1993. pap. text 19.95 (*0-9636700-0-X*) Ursus Pr CA.

Lawrence, Margaret. Blood Red Roses: A Novel of Historical Suspense. LC 97-15120. 368p. 1997. 23.00 (*0-380-97352-9*, Avon Bks) Morrow Avon.

— Blood Red Roses: A Novel of Historical Suspense. 400p. 1998. mass mkt. 6.50 (*0-380-78880-2*, Avon Bks) Morrow Avon.

— The Burning Bride. LC 98-4491. 400p. 1998. 23.00 (*0-380-97620-X*, Avon Bks) Morrow Avon.

***Lawrence, Margaret.** The Burning Bride. 400p. 1999. mass mkt. 6.99 (*0-380-79612-0*, Avon Bks) Morrow Avon.

— Hearts & Bones. LC 96-2394. 304p. 1996. 23.00 (*0-380-97351-0*, Avon Bks) Morrow Avon.

Lawrence, Margaret. Hearts & Bones. 336p. 1997. mass mkt. 6.50 (*0-380-78879-9*, Avon Bks) Morrow Avon.

***Lawrence, Margaret.** The Iceweaver. LC 99-58661. 416p. 2000. 24.00 (*0-380-97621-8*, Wm Morrow) Morrow Avon.

***Lawrence, Margery.** Nights of the Round Table. Dalby, Richard, ed. xx, 220p. 1998. 39.50 (*1-899562-63-X*) Ash-Tree.

— The Terraces of Night. Dalby, Richard, ed. xvi, 212p. 1999. 39.50 (*1-899562-78-8*) Ash-Tree.

Lawrence, Marie, ed. see Daniels, Patricia A.

Lawrence, Marilyn. The Anorexic Experience. 3rd rev. ed. 144p. 1997. pap. 13.95 (*0-7043-4441-6*, Pub. by Womens Press) Trafalgar.

Lawrence, Marilyn, ed. Fed up & Hungry: Women, Oppression & Food. pap. 15.95 (*0-7043-4008-9*, Pub. by Womens Press) Trafalgar.

Lawrence, Marilyn, et al. Psychotherapy with Women: Feminist Perspectives. LC 98-38228. 1999. pap. 24.99 (*0-415-92265-8*) Routledge.

Lawrence, Marjorie. Interrupted Melody: The Story of My Life: Music Book Index. 307p. 1993. reprint ed. lib. bdg. 89.00 (*0-7812-9632-3*) Rprt Serv.

— What? Me Teach Music? A Classroom Teacher's Guide to Music in Early Childhood. 140p. (Orig.). 1982. pap. text 24.95 (*0-88284-213-7*, 2075) Alfred Pub.

Lawrence, Mark. Old Testament Stories: The Kid's Translation. (Orig.). 1997. pap. 5.75 (*0-7880-0768-8*) CSS OH.

Lawrence, Martha. Lightship Baskets of Nantucket. Schiffer, Nancy N., ed. LC 90-60. (Illus.). 120p. (Orig.). 1990. pap. text 24.95 (*0-88740-256-9*) Schiffer.

***Lawrence, Martha.** Lightship Baskets of Nantucket. (Illus.). 120p. (Orig.). 2000. pap. 24.95 (*0-7643-0891-2*) Schiffer.

Lawrence, Martha. Scrimshaw, the Whaler's Legacy. LC 93-85225. (Illus.). 240p. 1993. 69.95 (*0-88740-455-3*) Schiffer.

Lawrence, Martha C. Aquarius Descending. LC 98-44604. 304p. 1998. text 23.95 (*0-312-19829-9*) St Martin.

***Lawrence, Martha C.** Aquarius Descending. 320p. 2000. mass mkt. 5.99 (*0-312-97284-9*) St Martin.

Aquarius Descending Newsletter Kit. 2000. pap. write for info. (*0-312-20695-X*) St Martin.

Lawrence, Martha C. The Cold Heart of Capricorn, Vol. 1. 1998. mass mkt. 5.99 (*0-312-96294-0*) St Martin.

— Murder in Scorpio. 1996. mass mkt. 5.50 (*0-312-95984-2*) St Martin.

***Lawrence, Martha C.** Pisces Rising. 240p. 2000. text 23.95 (*0-312-20298-9*, Minotaur) St Martin.

Lawrence, Martin. Clyde to Colonsay. 160p. 1994. pap. 125.00 (*0-85288-189-4*, Pub. by Laurie Norie & Wilson Ltd) St Mut.

— Crinan to Canna. (Illus.). 170p. 1994. pap. 125.00 (*0-85288-250-5*, Pub. by Laurie Norie & Wilson Ltd) St Mut.

***Lawrence, Martin.** The Yachtsman's Pilot to North & East Scotland. 160p. 2000. pap. 125.00 (*0-85288-430-3*, Pub. by Laurie Norie & Wilson Ltd) St Mut.

— The Yachtsman's Pilot to the Isle of Mull & Adjacent Coasts. rev. expanded ed. (Illus.). 170p. 1999. pap. 150.00 (*0-85288-404-4*, Pub. by Laurie Norie & Wilson Ltd) St Mut.

Lawrence, Martin. The Yachtsman's Pilot to the West Coast of Scotland: Clyde to Colonsay. (Illus.). 152p. (C). 1993. pap. 36.95 (*0-85288-132-0*, Pub. by Laurie Norie & Wilson Ltd) Bluewater Bks.

— The Yachtsman's Pilot to the West Coast of Scotland: Crinan to Canna. 170p. (C). 1987. 110.00 (*0-85288-107-X*, Pub. by Laurie Norie & Wilson Ltd) St Mut.

Lawrence, Martin. You So Crazy. (Illus.). 128p. (J). 1994. pap. 7.70 (*0-7868-8083-X*, Pub. by Hyperion) Time Warner.

Lawrence, Martin, jt. ed. see Grol, Richard.

Lawrence, Martin S. & Schofield, Theo, eds. Medical Audit in Primary Health Care. LC 92-48416. (Oxford Medical Pubns.). (Illus.). 270p. 1993. pap. text 34.50 (*0-19-262267-6*) OUP.

Lawrence, Marty. Vests to Dye For. (Illus.). 8p. 1990. 2.95 (*0-944588-14-X*) K Wood.

L

L

Lawrence, Mary. Little Book of Potpourri. 1994. 4.98 (1-55521-989-6) Bk Sales Inc.

Lawrence, Mary C. The Captain's Best Mate: The Journal of Mary Chipman Lawrence on the Whaler Addison, 1856-1860. Garner, Stanton, ed. LC 83-40018. (Illus.). 335p. 1986. reprint ed. pap. 19.95 (0-87451-366-9) U Pr of New Eng.

Lawrence, Mary Jo, jt. auth. see King, Laura Franklin.

Lawrence, Mary S. Reading, Thinking, Writing: A Text for Students of English As a Second Language. 254p. (C). 1975. pap. text 17.95 (0-472-08548-4, 08548) U of Mich Pr.

Lawrence, Mary S. Reading, Thinking, Writing: A Text for Students of English As a Second Language. 254p. (C). 1975. teacher ed. 2.00 (0-472-08549-2, 08549) U of Mich Pr.

Lawrence, Mary S. Writing As a Thinking Process. rev. ed. LC 78-185153. 272p. 1996. pap. text 18.95 (0-472-08368-6, 08368) U of Mich Pr.

Lawrence, Melinda. My Life, Melinda's Story. 15p. 1987. pap. 4.95 (0-317-61838-5) Child Hospice VA.

Lawrence, Merle, jt. auth. see Wever, Ernest G.

Lawrence, Merloyd, tr. see Flaubert, Gustave.

Lawrence, Michael. Baby Loves. LC 97-45858. (Illus.). 32p. (J). 1999. 9.95 (0-7894-3410-5) DK Pub Inc.

***Lawrence, Michael.** Baby Loves. LC 97-45858. (Toddlers Storybook Ser.). (Illus.). 32p. (J). (ps). 2000. pap. text 5.95 (0-7894-5744-X, D K Ink) DK Pub Inc.

— Baby Loves Hugs & Kisses. (Toddlers Storybook Ser.). (Illus.), 24p. (J). (ps-k). 2000. pap. 5.95 (0-7894-5649-4) DK Pub Inc.

— Caterpillar That Roared. (Share-a-Story Ser.). (Illus.). 995p. (ps-3). 2000. 9.95 (0-7894-6351-2) DK Pub Inc.

Lawrence, Michael. The Complete Book on Takeout Doubles. LC 94-77342. (Doubles Ser.). 256p. 1994. pap. text 12.95 (0-9637533-1-2) Magnus Bks.

— Lonely Planet Dominica. 128p. 1999. pap. 15.95 (0-86442-764-6) Lonely Planet.

— Major Suit Raises. 86p. (Orig.). 1987. pap. 4.95 (0-9628297-1-4) C & T Bridge.

***Lawrence, Michael.** The Poppykettle Papers. (Illus.). 128p. (J). (gr. 3-7). 1999. 22.95 (1-86205-282-4, Pub. by Pavilion Bks Ltd) Trafalgar.

***Lawrence, Michael & Bartlett, Alison.** The Caterpillar That Roared. LC 99-49689. (Share-a-Story Ser.). (Illus.). (J). (ps-3). 2000. 9.95 (0-7894-5618-4, D K Ink) DK Pub Inc.

Lawrence, Michael D. & Ryan, Joan S. Essentials of Accounting. 8th ed. LC 94-3885. (C). 1994. mass mkt. 36.95 (0-538-83213-4) S-W Pub.

Lawrence, Michael D., jt. auth. see Dansby, Robert L.

Lawrence, Mike. A to Z of Sports Cars, 1945-1990. (Illus.). 336p. 1996. pap. 26.95 (1-870979-81-8, Bay View Bks) MBI Pubg.

— Bathrooms. 1989. 30.00 (1-85368-004-4, Pub. by New5 Holland) St Mut.

— Bidding Quizzes, Vol. 1: The Uncontested Auction. LC 90-91520. 288p. (Orig.). 1990. pap. 13.95 (1-877908-02-9) Lawrence & Leong Pub.

***Lawrence, Mike.** Brabham Ralt Honda: The Ron Tauranac Story. (Illus.). 288p. 1999. 34.95 (1-899870-35-0, Pub. by Motor Racing) Motorbooks Intl.

Lawrence, Mike. The Complete Book on Balancing in Contract Bridge. LC 84-223527. 209p. 1981. 14.95 (0-939460-14-9); pap. 11.95 (0-939460-13-0) Devyn Pr.

— The Complete Book on Hand Evaluation in Contract Bridge. LC 84-223827. 194p. 1983. pap. 11.95 (0-939460-27-0) Devyn Pr.

— The Complete Book on Overcalls in Contract Bridge. LC 80-123383. 202p. 1979. 14.95 (0-939460-08-4); pap. 11.95 (0-939460-07-6) Devyn Pr.

***Lawrence, Mike.** The Complete Decorating & Home Improvement Book: Ideas & Techniques for Decorating Your Home - A Complete Step-by-Step Guide. (Illus.). 256p. 1999. 24.95 (1-85967-711-8, Lorenz Bks) Anness Pub.

Lawrence, Mike. The Complete Guide to Contested Auctions. LC 92-90023. 368p. (Orig.). 1992. text 14.95 (1-877908-04-5) Lawrence & Leong Pub.

— The Complete Guide to Passed Hand Bidding. LC 89-80899. 224p. 1989. pap. 12.95 (1-877908-01-0) Lawrence & Leong Pub.

***Lawrence, Mike.** Cooper. 160p. 2000. pap. 19.95 (0-7509-2344-X) Sutton Publng.

— Do-It-Yourself. (Practical Handbook Ser.). 1999. pap. 12.95 (0-7548-0022-9, Lorenz Bks) Anness Pub.

Lawrence, Mike. Dynamic Defense. 228p. 1991. pap. 11.95 (0-910791-01-5) Devyn Pr.

— Essential Austin-Healey 100 & 3000: The Cars & Their Story 1953-1967. (Essential Ser.). (Illus.). 80p. 1994. pap. 15.95 (1-870979-49-4, Bay View Bks) MBI Pubg.

— Essential Jaguar XK, XK120, 140, 150: The Cars & Their Story 1949-61. (Essential Ser.). (Illus.). 80p. 1995. pap. 15.95 (1-870979-61-3, Bay View Bks) MBI Pubg.

Lawrence, Mike. Floors & Tiling: Techniques & Ideas for Floor Coverings & Tiles: A Complete Step-by-Step Guide. (Illus.). 1997. 8.98 (1-901289-13-3) Hermes Hse.

— Glory of Goodwood: The Spiritual Home of British Motor Racing. 288p. 2000. 39.95 (1-85227-826-9) Virgin Pubng.

Lawrence, Mike. Grand Prix Cars, 1945-1965. (Illus.). 264p. 1998. 39.95 (1-899870-39-3, Pub. by Motor Racing) Motorbooks Intl.

— How to Play Card Combinations at Bridge: Unlocking the Secrets. 1989. pap. 11.95 (0-910791-63-5) Devyn Pr.

— How to Read Your Opponent's Cards: The Bridge Experts' Way to Locate Missing High Cards. 175p. 1991. pap. 9.95 (0-910791-48-1) Devyn Pr.

— Judgement at Bridge. LC 80-123381. 151p. 1976. pap. 9.95 (0-939460-02-5) Devyn Pr.

— Outdoor Woodwork. (Step-by-Step Ser.). (Illus.). 96p. 1998. pap. 15.95 (1-85368-225-X, Pub. by New5 Holland) Sterling.

— Play a Swiss Teams of 4 with Mike Lawrence. LC 84-223798. 99p. 1982. pap. 7.95 (0-939460-19-X) Devyn Pr.

— Play Equipment for Kids: Great Projects You Can Build. Steege, Gwen, ed. LC 95-24038. (Illus.). 96p. (Orig.). 1996. pap. 18.95 (0-88266-916-8, 916-8, Storey Pub) Storey Bks.

— The Reynard Story: From Formula Ford to Indy Champions. (Illus.). 192p. 1997. 39.95 (1-85260-576-6) Haynes Manuals.

Lawrence, Mike, ed. Backyard Brickwork: How to Build Walls, Paths, Patios, & Barbecues. LC 89-45218. (Illus.). 96p. 1989. 17.95 (0-88266-567-7, Garden Way Pub); pap. 14.95 (0-88266-562-6, Garden Way Pub) Storey Bks.

— Garden Brickwork: How to Build Walls, Paths, Patios & Barbecues. 96p. (C). 1988. 80.00 (1-85368-006-0, Pub. by New5 Holland) St Mut.

— Step-by-Step Outdoor Stonework: Over Twenty Easy-to-Build Projects for Your Patio & Garden. LC 94-23205. (Illus.). 96p. 1995. pap. 18.95 (0-88266-891-9, Garden Way Pub) Storey Bks.

Lawrence, Mike & Klinger, Ron. Opening Leads for ACOL Players. 1998. pap. 19.95 (0-575-06502-8, Pub. by V Gollancz) Trafalgar.

Lawrence, Mike & Milson, Fred. Walls & Woodwork. (Home Decorator Ser.). (Illus.). 96p. 1997. pap. 15.95 (1-85368-738-3, Pub. by New5 Holland) Sterling.

Lawrence, Mike, jt. auth. see Klinger, Ron.

Lawrence, Milo. The Next Dominant Species. LC 93-74163. 403p. 1994. 19.95 (0-9639372-5-1) Altos Pubng.

***Lawrence, Nancy.** Intimate Arrangement. (Regency Romance Ser.). 2000. mass mkt. 4.99 (0-8217-6740-2, Zebra Kensgtn) Kensgtn Pub Corp.

Lawrence, Nancy. Miss Hamilton's Hero. 224p. 1999. mass mkt. 4.99 (0-8217-6154-4) Kensgtn Pub Corp.

— A Noble Rogue. 224p. 1998. pap. 4.99 (0-8217-5994-9) Kensgtn Pub Corp.

— Once upon a Christmas. 1997. pap. 4.99 (0-8217-5791-1) Kensgtn Pub Corp.

— A Scandalous Season. 224p. 1996. mass mkt. 4.50 (0-8217-5466-1, Zebra Kensgtn) Kensgtn Pub Corp.

Lawrence, Naomi, jt. auth. see Coleman, William P., III.

***Lawrence, Nathan, et al.** Foundations of Physical Chemistry: Worked Examples. LC 98-31454. (Oxford Chemistry Primers Ser.: 68). (Illus.). 156p. (C). 1999. pap. text 12.95 (0-19-850462-4) OUP.

Lawrence, Nathaniel. Alfred North Whitehead: A Primer of His Philosophy. 192p. 1974. 59.50 (0-685-63209-1) Elliots Bks.

Lawrence, Nathaniel M. Whitehead's Philosophical Development. LC 68-23306. 370p. 1968. reprint ed. lib. bdg. 35.00 (0-8371-0139-5, LAWD, Greenwood Pr) Greenwood.

Lawrence, Neal H. Shining Moments: Tanka Poems in English. (Illus.). 140p. 1993. 12.00 (0-944676-39-1) AHA Bks.

Lawrence, Neil. Tribute: A Day on the Beat with America's Finest. 29.95 (0-7316-8126-6) Emperor Pub.

Lawrence, Norman, et al, eds. Handbook of Emergencies in General Practice. 2nd ed. (Illus.). 390p. 1996. pap. 39.95 (0-19-262545-4) OUP.

Lawrence, P. A. & Lee, R. Alton. Insight into Management. 2nd ed. (Illus.). 248p. 1989. 65.00 (0-19-856227-6); pap. 26.00 (0-19-856226-8) OUP.

Lawrence, Patricia, jt. auth. see Amyx, D. A.

Lawrence, Patricia B., ed. see Ladis, Andrew, et al.

Lawrence, Paul & Paul, Douglas J. Mastering the Math SAT 1 - PSAT. LC 98-203040. 512p. (YA). (gr. 10-12). 1997. text, teacher ed. 26.60 (0-669-45763-9) Great Source.

Lawrence, Paul R. The Changing of Organizational Behavior Patterns: A Case Study of Decentralization. 256p. (C). 1991. pap. 21.95 (0-88738-894-9) Transaction Pubs.

***Lawrence, Paul R. & Lawrence, Ann M.** Good Connections for Testing: Using Children's Books to Maximize Understanding & Achievement. (Illus.). 354p. 2000. 34.95 (0-9676545-0-5) L L Teach.

Lawrence, Paul R., et al. Human Resource Management: A General Manager's Perspective. LC 84-21080. 786p. 1985. 35.00 (0-02-902360-2) Free Pr.

Lawrence, Paul R., jt. ed. see Etzioni, Amitai.

Lawrence, Paul R., jt. ed. see Walton, Richard E.

***Lawrence, Peter.** Essentials of General Surgery. 3rd ed. LC 99-37812. 550p. 1999. 42.95 (0-683-30133-0) Lppncott W & W.

— Gensler Architecture: Form & Strategy. 48p. 1999. pap. 25.00 (0-9662230-3-9, Pub. by Edizioni Pr) Antique Collect.

Lawrence, Peter. Management in the U. S. A. 192p. 1996. 69.95 (0-8039-7832-4); pap. 24.95 (0-8039-7833-2) Sage.

— Road Belong Cargo: A Study of the Cargo Movement in the Southern Madang District New Guinea. (Illus.). 293p. (C). 1989. reprint ed. pap. text 13.50 (0-88133-458-8) Waveland Pr.

— Workflow Handbook, 1997. LC 97-159593. 532p. 1997. 110.00 (0-471-96947-8) Wiley.

Lawrence, Peter, ed. Essentials of Surgical Specialties. 2nd ed. LC 00-20778. 514p. 42.95 (0-683-30134-9) Lppncott W & W.

Lawrence, Peter, jt. auth. see Barsoux, Jean-Louis.

Lawrence, Peter, jt. auth. see Cason, Jeff.

Lawrence, Peter, jt. auth. see Edwards, Vincent.

Lawrence, Peter, jt. auth. see Hutton, Stanley.

Lawrence, Peter, jt. auth. see Lee, Bob.

Lawrence, Peter, jt. auth. see Whitman, Neal A.

Lawrence, Peter, jt. ed. see Calori, Roland.

Lawrence, Peter, ed. see Cason, Jeffrey.

Lawrence, Peter A. The Making of a Fly: The Genetics of Animal Design. (Illus.). 242p. 1992. pap. 49.95 (0-632-03048-8) Blackwell Sci.

***Lawrence, Peter A. & Edwards, Vincent.** Management in Western Europe. LC 99-45121. 2000. text 65.00 (0-312-22944-5) St Martin.

Lawrence, Peter A., jt. auth. see Edwards, Vincent.

Lawrence, Peter F. Essentials of General Surgery. 3rd ed. 664p. 75.00 (0-7817-2817-7) Lppncott W & W.

Lawrence, Peter F. Essentials of General Surgery Set: Textbook & the Essentials of Surgical Specialties, 2 bks. 2nd ed. 1994. write for info. (0-683-04838-4) Lppncott W & W.

Lawrence, Peter F., et al, eds. Essentials of Surgical Specialties. LC 92-21071. (Illus.). 448p. 1993. 35.00 (0-683-04871-6) Lppncott W & W.

Lawrence, Peter F. & Goldman, Mitchell H. Essentials of General Surgery: Oral Examinations. 2nd ed. (Illus.). 112p. 1992. pap. 35.00 (0-683-04870-8) Lppncott W & W.

Lawrence, Peter F., et al. Essentials of General Surgery. 2nd ed. (Illus.). 454p. 1992. pap. 37.00 (0-683-04869-4) Lppncott W & W.

Lawrence, Philip, et al, eds. Strategic Issues in the European Aerospace Industry. LC 98-41214. 250p. 1999. text 69.95 (1-84014-823-3, Pub. by Ashgate Pub) Ashgate Pub Co.

Lawrence, Philip K. Democracy & the Liberal State. 213p. 1989. text 69.95 (1-85521-019-3, Pub. by Dartmth Pub) Ashgate Pub Co.

Lawrence, Philip K., ed. Knowledge & Power: The Changing Role of European Intellectuals. (Perspectives on Europe Ser.). 192p. 1997. 68.95 (1-85972-266-0, Pub. by Avebry) Ashgate Pub Co.

Lawrence, Priscilla O. Before Disaster Strikes: Prevention, Planning, & Recovery: Caring for Your Personal Collections in the Event of Disaster. LC 92-37511. 1992. pap. 6.95 (0-917860-32-2) Historic New Orleans.

Lawrence, R. The Descendants of Major Samuel Lawrence of Groton, Mass., with Some Mention of Allied Family. (Illus.). 355p. reprint ed. pap. 44.00 (0-8328-0756-7); reprint ed. lib. bdg. 54.00 (0-8328-0755-9) Higginson Bk Co.

Lawrence, R., jt. auth. see Nair, P. K.

Lawrence, R. D. Cry Wild. 224p. 1992. mass mkt. 3.99 (1-55817-636-5, Pinncle Kensgtn) Kensgtn Pub Corp.

— The Green Trees Beyond: A Memoir. LC 93-11961. 318p. 1995. 25.00 (0-8050-1297-4) H Holt & Co.

— In Praise of Wolves. 1997. pap. 11.00 (0-345-41802-6) Ballantine Pub Grp.

— Owls: The Silent Fliers. (Illus.). 176p. 1997. 29.95 (1-55209-146-5) Firefly Bks Ltd.

— Paddy. LC 99-158602. (Illus.). 240p. 1998. reprint ed. pap. 14.95 (1-55821-573-5, 15735) Lyons Pr.

— A Shriek in the Forest Night. 224p. 1997. pap. 13.95 (0-7737-5917-4) Stoddart Publ.

— A Shriek in the Forest Night: Wilderness Encounters. 224p. 1996. 25.95 (0-7737-2941-0) Stoddart Publ.

— The Study of Life: A Naturalist's View. (Illus.). 43p. (gr. 7-12). 1980. pap. 1.50 (0-913098-37-X) Orion Society.

— Trail of the Wolf. (Illus.). 160p. 1997. pap. 19.95 (1-55209-186-4) Firefly Bks Ltd.

— Trail of the Wolf. LC 92-44404. (Illus.). 160p. 1993. 35.00 (0-87596-594-6) Rodale Pr Inc.

— The White Puma. 1991. mass mkt. 4.95 (1-55817-532-6, Pinncle Kensgtn) Kensgtn Pub Corp.

— Wolves. (Sierra Club Bks.). (Illus.). 64p. (J). (gr. 3-6). 1994. pap. 9.95 (0-316-51677-5) Little.

Lawrence, R. F. The Centipedes & Millipedes of Southern Africa: A Guide. 168p. (C). 1984. text 91.00 (0-86961-142-9, Pub. by A A Balkema) Ashgate Pub Co.

Lawrence, R. S., jt. ed. see Goldbloom, R. B.

***Lawrence, Race G.** Feedback for Better Building Service Design. 72p. 1998. pap. 100.00 (0-86022-520-8, Pub. by Build Servs Info Assn) St Mut.

***Lawrence, Ray.** Jacqueline Susann's Shadow. 2001. 25.00 (0-609-60585-2) Crown Pub Group.

Lawrence, Ray. Muscle Art. 1995. per. 35.00 (0-85449-198-8, Pub. by Gay Mens Pr) LPC InBook.

Lawrence, Raymond J., Jr. The Poisoning of Eros: Sexual Values in Conflict. LC 89-92038. 281p. (C). 1989. 19.95 (0-9623310-0-7) Augustine Moore.

Lawrence, R.D. Wolves. (Sierra Club Wildlife Library). 1990. 15.15 (0-606-06890-2, Pub. by Turtleback) Demco.

Lawrence, Rebecca, ed. Drawing Your Own Conclusions: Government & the Arts: New Hampshire's Story. LC 95-72868. (Illus.). 64p. 1996. per. write for info. (0-9621915-2-3) NH SCA.

Lawrence, Rebecca L. & Sylvester, Audrey V., eds. Art in Unexpected Places. LC 88-64115. (Illus.). 96p. (Orig.). 1989. pap. 10.00 (0-9621915-0-7) NH SCA.

***Lawrence, Regina G.** The Politics of Force. LC 99-53115. (Illus.). 279p. 2000. pap. 17.95 (0-520-22192-3, Pub. by U CA Pr) Cal Prin Full Svc.

— The Politics of Force: Media, Policy Discourse, & the Construction of Police Brutality. LC 99-53115. (Illus.). 279p. 2000. 45.00 (0-520-22191-5, Pub. by U CA Pr) Cal Prin Full Svc.

Lawrence, Rhonda K., jt. auth. see Lembke, Melody B.

Lawrence, Richard. Journey into Supermind: A Step by Step Guide to Unlocking Your Inner Potential. 208p. 1996. pap. text 12.95 (0-285-63252-3, Pub. by Souvenir Pr Ltd) IPG Chicago.

— School Crime & Juvenile Justice. LC 96-34162. (Illus.). 288p. (C). 1997. text 50.00 (0-19-510164-2); pap. text 21.95 (0-19-510165-0) OUP.

Lawrence, Richard, tr. The Book of Enoch. LC 80-65736. 96p. 1980. reprint ed. pap. 7.00 (0-934666-06-7) Artisan Pubs.

***Lawrence, Richard, tr.** The Books of Enoch the Prophet: Translated by Richard Lawrence. 150p. 1999. 10.95 (1-930097-04-2) Lushena Bks.

Lawrence, Richard, jt. auth. see Blake, Nicholas.

Lawrence, Richard, jt. auth. see King, George.

Lawrence, Richard D. & Record, Jeffrey. United States Force Structure in NATO: An Alternative: A Staff Paper. LC 74-1436. (Studies in Defense Policy). (Illus.). 148p. reprint ed. pap. 45.90 (0-608-18067-X, 202796800057) Bks Demand.

Lawrence, Richard H. The Paduans, Medals by Giovanni Cavino. (Illus.). 1980. pap. 5.00 (0-916710-74-2) Obol Intl.

Lawrence, Richard R. & Chris, Teresa. The Period House: Style, Detail & Decoration, 1774-1914. (Illus.). 192p. 1998. pap. 24.95 (0-7538-0119-1) Phoenix Hse.

***Lawrence, Rick.** Trendwatch: Insights That Fuel Authentic Youth Ministry. 2000. pap. 16.99 (0-7644-2187-5) Group Pub.

Lawrence, Rick, jt. auth. see Freudenburg, Ben.

Lawrence, Robb. Heathcliff's Night Before Christmas. 1989. pap. 1.95 (0-8167-1559-9) Troll Communs.

Lawrence, Robert. High Tech Austin. (Illus.). 144p. 1998. 32.95 (0-9666346-1-6); pap. 24.95 (0-9666346-0-8) Best Pubg.

— The Impact of Trade on OECD Labor Markets. (Occasional Paper Ser.: No. 45). 28p. (Orig.). 1994. pap. text 10.00 (1-56708-041-3) Grp of Thirty.

— The World of Opera. LC 77-2268. (Illus.). 208p. 1977. reprint ed. lib. bdg. 59.50 (0-8371-9551-9, LAWO, Greenwood Pr) Greenwood.

Lawrence, Robert, ed. Energy Policy Issues. (C). 1978. pap. 15.00 (0-918592-28-3) Pol Studies.

— New Dimensions to Energy Policy. (Organization Ser.). 233p. 1979. 15.00 (0-317-35630-5) Pol Studies.

Lawrence, Robert & Case, Deborah A., eds. Rembrances. LC 94-69864. (Illus.). 312p. 1995. text 49.95 (1-885206-12-7, Iliad Pr) Cader Pubng.

Lawrence, Robert, jt. auth. see Hart, Frederick.

Lawrence, Robert C., 3rd. International Tax & Estate Planning: A Practical Guide for Multinational Investors. 3rd ed. 800p. 1995. ring bd. 145.00 (0-685-46013-4, J1-1472) PLI.

Lawrence, Robert C. The State of Robeson County, North Carolina. 279p. 1994. reprint ed. lib. bdg. 32.50 (0-8328-4154-4) Higginson Bk Co.

Lawrence, Robert C., III, ed. International Personal Tax Planning Encyclopedia, 2 vols. 1994. ring bd., suppl. ed. 69.00 (0-318-72491-X, MICHIE) LEXIS Pub.

Lawrence, Robert C., ed. Lawrence: International Personal Tax Planning Encyclopaedia. 1990. ring bd. write for info. (0-406-99831-0, LIPTASET, MICHIE) LEXIS Pub.

Lawrence, Robert D. Burba, Burbee, Burby: Descendants of Peter Burbee, Sr. & Others Who Share These Surnames. LC 94-77401. 500p. 1994. 30.00 (0-9617907-4-1) Lawrence KS.

— The Graying of My Guardian Angel. 112p. (Orig.). 1991. pap. 3.00 (0-9617907-3-3) Lawrence KS.

— The Many Generations of Davis Dimock Cheever, 1851-1920, Lest We Forget. (Illus.). 64p. 1983. pap. text 5.00 (0-9617907-0-9) Lawrence KS.

Lawrence, Robert De Treville, see De Treville Lawrence, Robert, III.

Lawrence, Robert G. U. S. Policy in Southwest Asia: A Failure in Perspective. 65p. (C). 1997. reprint ed. pap. text 20.00 (0-7881-4827-3) DIANE Pub.

Lawrence, Robert L., jt. auth. see Rapalje, Stewart.

Lawrence, Robert M. & Larus, Joel, eds. Nuclear Proliferation: Phase II. LC 74-11724. viii, 256p. (Orig.). (C). 1974. pap. 12.95 (0-7006-0128-7) U Pr of KS.

Lawrence, Robert S., jt. ed. see Feasley, Jill C.

Lawrence, Robert Z. Can America Compete? LC 84-9401. 156p. 1984. 28.95 (0-8157-5176-1); pap. 10.95 (0-8157-5175-3) Brookings.

— Regionalism, Multilateralism & Deeper Integration. LC 95-26205. (Integrating National Economies: Promise & Pitfalls Ser.). 158p. 1996. 34.95 (0-8157-5182-6); pap. 14.95 (0-8157-5181-8) Brookings.

— Single World, Divided Nations? International Trade & the OECD Labor Markets. LC 96-25252. 146p. 1996. pap. 14.95 (0-8157-5185-0) Brookings.

Lawrence, Robert Z., ed. Brookings Trade Forum, 1998. 350p. 1998. pap. text 24.95 (0-8157-1187-5) Brookings.

Lawrence, Robert Z. & Litan, Robert E. Saving Free Trade: A Pragmatic Approach. LC 86-14705. 132p. 1986. 29.95 (0-8157-5178-8); pap. 11.95 (0-8157-5177-X) Brookings.

Lawrence, Robert Z. & Schultze, Charles L., eds. American Trade Strategy: Options for the 1990's. 234p. 1990. pap. 16.95 (0-8157-5179-6) Brookings.

— Barriers to European Growth: A Transatlantic View. LC 87-26900. 619p. 1987. 44.95 (0-8157-7770-1); pap. 22.95 (0-8157-7769-8) Brookings.

Lawrence, Robert Z., et al. Emerging Agenda for Global Trade: High Stakes for Developing Countries. LC 96-41368. (Overseas Development Council Ser.: Vol. 20). 112p. (Orig.). 1996. pap. text 13.95 (1-56517-014-8) Overseas Dev Council.

— A Vision for the World Economy: Openness, Diversity, & Cohesion. LC 95-21051. (Integrating National Economies Ser.). 124p. (C). 1996. 34.95 (0-8157-5184-2); pap. 14.95 (0-8157-5183-4) Brookings.

Lawrence, Robert Z., jt. auth. see Bosworth, Barry P.

Lawrence, Robert Z., jt. ed. see Galal, Ahmed.

Lawrence, Robert Z., jt. ed. see Litan, Robert E.

An Asterisk (*) at the beginning of an entry indicates that the title is appearing for the first time.

Lawrence, Rod. Painting Wildlife Textures Step by Step. LC 96-46457. (Illus.). 144p. 1997. 29.99 (*0-89134-669-4*, North Lght Bks) F & W Pubns Inc.

Lawrence, Roderick. Better Understanding Our Cities: The Role of Urban Indicators. LC 97-223928. 96p. (Orig.). 1997. pap. 24.00 (*92-64-15454-X*, 04-97-01-1, Pub. by Org for Econ) OECD.

Lawrence, Ronald & Rosch, Paul J. Magnet Therapy: The Pain Cure Alternative. LC 98-12167. 272p. 1998. per. 15.00 (*0-7615-1547-X*) Prima Pub.

Lawrence, Ronald M. Goodbye Pain! Two Dozen Ways You Can Prevent & Relieve Pain. LC 88-28001. (Illus.). 112p. 1988. pap. 5.95 (*0-88007-169-9*) Woodbridge Pr.

Lawrence, Rosemary, jt. auth. see Mason, John.

Lawrence, Roy. How to Pray When Life Hurts: Experiencing the Power of Healing Prayer. LC 92-35136. 129p. (Orig.). 1993. pap. 8.99 (*0-8308-1384-5*, 1384, Saltshaker Bk) InterVarsity.

— Motive & Intention: An Essay in the Appreciation of Action. LC 72-186548. (Publications in Analytical Philosophy). 146p. reprint ed. pap. 45.30 (*0-8357-9465-2*, 201530100094) Bks Demand.

***Lawrence, Russell.** Montana's Bitterroot Valley. LC 99-75625. 158p. 1999. pap. 19.95 (*0-912299-89-4*) Stoneydale Pr Pub.

— Montana's Bitterroot Valley. LC 99-75625. (Illus.). 158p. 1999. 29.95 (*0-912299-88-6*) Stoneydale Pr Pub.

Lawrence, Ruth A. Breastfeeding: A Guide to the Medical Profession. 5th ed. (Illus.). 981p. (C). (gr. 13). 1998. text 54.95 (*0-8151-2615-8*, 31637) Mosby Inc.

Lawrence, Ruth A., et al. Breastfeeding Care: Setting the Environment, Supporting the Process. LC 94-29660. 1994. write for info. (*0-86525-058-8*) March of Dimes.

Lawrence, S. Method for the Harp. (ENG & FRE.). 80p. 1986. pap. 13.95 (*0-7935-4531-5*, 50328070) H Leonard.

Lawrence, Sandra. Rapture's Voyage. (Bedroom Adventures Ser.). 1993. write for info. (*1-884057-00-4*) Trivial Development Corp.

Lawrence, Sean, ed. see Lawrence, Carl.

Lawrence, Sheila D. The Girls from the Basement. unabridged ed. 197p. 1998. pap. 14.95 (*1-892896-21-4*) Buy Books.

Lawrence, Shirley B. Behind Numerology: Complete Details on the Hidden Meaning of Letters & Numbers. 285p. 1989. pap. 14.95 (*0-87877-145-X*) Newcastle Pub.

— Numerology & the English Cabalah: Translating Numbers into Words & Words into Numbers. Lammey, William L. & Misiroglu, Gina, eds. (Illus.). 224p. (Orig.). 1994. pap. 18.95 (*0-87877-188-3*) Newcastle Pub.

Lawrence, Sidney, ed. see Alarid, William M.

Lawrence, Sidney R. Shrinking the Globe into Your Company's Hands: The Step-by-Step International Trade Guide for Small Businesses. 192p. (Orig.). 1997. pap. 24.95 (*1-877810-46-0*, SHRI) Rayve Prodns.

Lawrence, Starling. Legacies. 243p. 1996. text 20.00 (*0-374-18474-7*) FS&G.

— Legacies: Stories. 256p. 1998. pap. 13.00 (*0-393-31869-9*, Norton Paperbks) Norton.

— Montenegro. LC 96-52424. 320p. 1997. 23.00 (*0-374-21407-7*) FS&G.

— Montenegro. 350p. 1998. reprint ed. mass mkt. 6.99 (*0-425-16446-2*) Berkley Pub.

***Lawrence, Starling R.** The Lightning Keeper. 2002. text. write for info. (*0-374-18745-2*) FS&G.

Lawrence, Stephen. Rescue Swine 1-1: True Stories & Poems about Life at an Animal Sanctuary. Wrolstad, Jay & Johnson, Emily R., eds. LC 95-82167. (Illus.). 88p. (Orig.). (J). (gr. 3-9). 1996. pap. 9.95 (*0-9650379-0-8*) Msty Valley NY.

Lawrence, Stephen S., jt. auth. see Hulan, Richard.

Lawrence, Steve. International Accounting. (Illus.). 320p. 1995. mass mkt. 32.95 (*0-412-60830-8*) Chapman & Hall.

Lawrence, Steven C. Day of the Comancheros. large type ed. (Linford Western Library). 272p. 1985. pap. 16.99 (*0-7089-6080-4*) Ulverscroft.

— The Lynchers. large type ed. LC 98-21238. (Western Ser.). 162 p. 1998. pap. write for info. (*0-7540-3437-2*) Chivers N Amer.

— The Lynchers. large type ed. LC 98-21238. (Nightingale Western Ser.). 172p. 1998. pap. 19.95 (*0-7838-0246-3*, G K Hall Lrg Type) Mac Lib Ref.

— A Northern Saga. large type ed. LC 97-38877. 1997. 21.95 (*0-7838-8367-6*, G K Hall & Co) Mac Lib Ref.

— Slattery Stands Alone. large type ed. LC 96-20885. (Orig.). 1996. pap. 17.95 (*0-7838-1848-3*, G K Hall Lrg Type) Mac Lib Ref.

Lawrence, Stewart, jt. auth. see Hilsman, Roger.

Lawrence, Sue. Feasting on Herbs. (Illus.). 182p. 1996. 29.95 (*1-85626-176-X*, Pub. by Cathie Kyle) Trafalgar.

— Feasting on Herbs. (Illus.). 224p. 1998. pap. 19.95 (*1-85626-233-2*, Pub. by Cathie Kyle) Trafalgar.

— Food with Flair. (Illus.). 208p. 1994. 34.95 (*1-85158-559-1*, Pub. by Mainstream Pubng) Trafalgar.

***Lawrence, Sue.** On Salads: Sensation on a Plate. (Illus.). 160p. 2000. 29.95 (*1-85626-323-1*, Pub. by Cathie Kyle) Trafalgar.

***Lawrence, Susan.** Dolly's Creek: An Archaeology of a Goldfields Community. (Illus.). 250p. 2000. pap. 29.95 (*0-522-84912-1*, Pub. by Melbourne Univ Pr) Paul & Co Pubs.

Lawrence, Susan. A Family Garden of Christian Virtues. LC 96-19022. 112p. 1997. 9.99 (*0-570-04875-3*, 12-3300) Concordia.

Lawrence, Susan. Law & Politics of the Supreme Court: Cases & Readings. 2nd ed. 592p. (C). per. write for info. (*0-7872-6732-5*) Kendall-Hunt.

Lawrence, Susan. A Young Child's Garden of Christian Virtues. LC 97-31705. 1998. 9.99 (*0-570-05314-5*, 12-3364) Concordia.

Lawrence, Susan C. Charitable Knowledge: Hospital Pupils & Practitioners in Eighteenth-Century London. (History of Medicine Ser.). (Illus.). 399p. (C). 1996. text 69.95 (*0-521-36355-1*) Cambridge U Pr.

Lawrence, T. C. Fatal Paradise. (Sandwich Islands Quintet Ser.). Date not set. pap. 12.95 (*0-9663004-0-8*) Dark Matter.

Lawrence, T. E. Crusader Castles. 224p. (C). 1990. pap. 125.00 (*0-907151-67-1*, Pub. by IMMEL Pubng) St Mut.

— Crusader Castles. (Illus.). 224p. (C). 1995. 90.00 (*0-907151-68-X*, Pub. by IMMEL Pubng) St Mut.

— Crusader Castles. Pringle, Denys, ed. (Illus.). 192p. 1989. text 69.00 (*0-19-822964-X*) OUP.

— Lawrence of Arabia, Strange Man of Letters: The Literary Criticism of T. E. Lawrence. Orlans, Harold, ed. LC 92-53456. 1993. 47.50 (*0-8386-3508-3*) Fairleigh Dickinson.

— Revolt in the Desert. (Wordsworth Collection). 448p. 1998. pap. 11.95 (*1-85326-680-9*, Pub. by Wrdsworth Edits) Combined Pub.

— Revolt in the Desert. large type ed. 438p. 1990. 22.95 (*1-85089-401-9*, Pub. by ISIS Lrg Prnt) Transaction Pubs.

— Seven Pillars of Wisdom. 1976. 36.95 (*0-8488-0562-3*) Amereon Ltd.

— Seven Pillars of Wisdom: A Triumph. 784p. 1991. pap. 16.95 (*0-385-41895-7*) Doubleday.

Lawrence, T. E. & Clarke, Angela. Bahrain Oil & Development 1929-1989. 224p. (C). 1995. 81.00 (*0-907151-51-5*, Pub. by IMMEL Pubng) St Mut.

Lawrence, T. E., tr. see Homer.

Lawrence, T. J. Essays on Some Disputed Questions in Modern International Law. 2nd enl. rev. ed. xiii, 313p. 1990. reprint ed. 48.50 (*0-8377-2412-0*, Rothman) W S Hein.

— Principles of International Law. xxi, 645p. 1987. reprint ed. 65.00 (*0-8377-2405-8*, Rothman) W S Hein.

— The Principles of International Law. 4th rev. ed. xxi, 745p. 1999. reprint ed. 192.50 (*1-56169-500-9*) Gaunt.

Lawrence, T. L. & Fowler, V. R. Growth of Farm Animals. LC 96-48880. 344p. 1997. pap. text 45.00 (*0-85198-849-0*) OUP.

Lawrence, Tammi A. Lost Souls: A Cry to Recapture What's Disappearing in American Education. x, 231p. 1996. 22.00 (*1-889934-01-1*) Bs Hive Pub.

Lawrence, Thea. Unity Without Uniformity: The Story of Rhinebeck Churches. (Illus.). (Orig.). (C). 1990. pap. write for info. (*0-318-65920-4*) Dawn Treader.

Lawrence, Theodor. The Sexual Key to the Tarot. (Illus.). 1971. 5.95 (*0-8065-0242-8*, Citadel Pr) Carol Pub Group.

Lawrence, Thomas & Sheppeck, Michael A. The Game Called Industry. LC 93-73954. 96p. (C). 1993. pap. 6.95 (*0-9639245-0-8*) Black Collegiate.

Lawrence, Thomas E. Afstand In der Wuste. (Illus.). 402p. 1988. reprint ed. write for info. (*3-487-08300-0*) G Olms Pubs.

***Lawrence, Thomas H., et al.** ERISA Subrogation: Enforcing Recoupment Provisions in ERISA-covered Health & Disability Plans. LC 99-39755. 1999. write for info. (*1-57073-686-3*) Amer Bar Assn.

Lawrence, Trevor & Norquay, Paul. Practical Tree Management: An Arborists Handbook. 132p. 1997. pap. 44.95 (*0-909605-72-6*) Buttrwrth-Heinemann.

Lawrence, Tyrone. The Official Dumper's Handbook. 120p. 1996. pap. 9.95 (*0-9658676-1-7*) Dataway Inc.

— Treasures of the Throne. (Illus.). 70p. 1997. pap. 9.95 (*0-9658676-0-9*) Dataway Inc.

Lawrence, V. Public Enemy. 1996. pap., mass mkt. 5.99 (*0-671-89561-3*) PB.

Lawrence, V. L., jt. auth. see Gould, W. J.

Lawrence, Vera B. The Piano Works of Louis Moreau Gottschalk, 5 vols. 1970. 247.95 (*0-405-02401-0*) Ayer.

— Strong on Music: The New York Music Scene in the Days of George Templeton Strong. 886p. 1995. lib. bdg. 90.00 (*0-226-47010-5*) U Ch Pr.

— Strong on Music: The New York Music Scene in the Days of George Templeton Strong. (Illus.). xxii, 864p. 1995. pap. text 27.50 (*0-226-47011-3*) U Ch Pr.

— Strong on Music - The New York Music Scene in the Days of George Templeton Strong, 1836-1850 Vol. 1: Resonances, 1836-1850. LC 94-205956. (Illus.). lvi, 686p. 1995. pap. text 27.50 (*0-226-47009-1*) U Ch Pr.

— Wa-Wan Press, 1901-1911, 5 vols. LC 74-97068. (American Music Ser.). 1970. reprint ed. 269.95 (*0-405-02407-X*) Ayer.

Lawrence, Vera B., ed. see Joplin, Scott.

Lawrence, Vicki & Eliot, Marc. Vicki! The True-Life Adventures of Miss Fireball. LC 94-46710. (Illus.). 237p. 1995. 23.00 (*0-684-80286-4*) S&S Trade.

Lawrence, Victor B., jt. auth. see Ahamed, Syed V.

Lawrence, Victor J. Elementary Guitar Method. 1943. 5.95 (*0-913650-30-7*) Wrner Bros.

Lawrence, W. Dwayne & Abdul-Karim, Fadi W. Gynecologic & Obstetrical Disorders, Vol. I. LC 97-50435. (Differential Diagnosis in Pathology Ser.). 180p. 1998. 69.00 (*0-683-30339-2*) Lppncott W & W.

Lawrence, W. Dwayne & Abdul-Karim, Fadi W., eds. Gynecologic & Obstetrical Disorders, Vol. 1. (Differential Diagnosis in Pathology Ser.). (Illus.). 192p. 1998. write for info. (*0-89640-304-1*) Igaku-Shoin.

Lawrence, W. G., jt. auth. see Tichane, Robert.

***Lawrence, W. Gordon.** Exploring Individual & Organizational Boundaries. 278p. 1999. reprint ed. pap. 50.00 (*1-85575-232-8*, Pub. by H Karnac Bks Ltd) Other Pr LLC.

Lawrence, W. Gordon. Roots in a Northern Landscape: Celebrations of Childhood in the NE of Scotland. 160p. 1990. pap. 24.00 (*1-898218-79-X*) St Mut.

***Lawrence, W. Gordon.** Social Dreaming @ Work. 224p. 1998. pap. 32.00 (*1-85575-209-3*, Pub. by H Karnac Bks Ltd) Other Pr LLC.

Lawrence, W. Gordon. To Surprise the Soul: Psychoanalytic Explorations of Groups, Institutions & Society in the Bion-Tavistock Tradition. 1998. pap. 28.95 (*1-899209-08-5*, Pub. by Process Pr) Intl Spec Bk.

***Lawrence, W. Gordon.** Tongued with Fire: Groups in Experience. 300p. 2000. pap. 37.00 (*1-85575-224-7*, Pub. by H Karnac Bks Ltd) Other Pr LLC.

Lawrence, W. Gordon, ed. Exploring Individual & Organizational Boundaries: A Tavistock Open Systems Approach. LC 78-8603. (Wiley Series on Individuals, Groups & Organizations). 274p. reprint ed. pap. 85.00 (*0-608-16315-5*, 202667500051) Bks Demand.

Lawrence, W. Gordon & Gosling, Robert, eds. Dwell in Possibility: Selected Writings of Pierre Turquet. 1998. pap. 28.95 (*1-899209-05-0*, Pub. by Process Pr) Intl Spec Bk.

Lawrence, W. J. Shakespeare's Workshop. 161p. (C). 1966. lib. bdg. 75.00 (*0-8383-0580-6*) M S G Haskell Hse.

— Those Nut-Cracking Elizabethans. LC 74-98684. (Studies in Drama: No. 39). 1970. reprint ed. lib. bdg. 49.95 (*0-8383-0988-7*) M S G Haskell Hse.

Lawrence, William. The Pyramid & the Urn: The Life in Letters of a Restoration Squire: William Lawrence of Shurdington. LC 95-148922. 1998. 30.95 (*0-7509-0765-7*, Pub. by Sutton Pub Ltd) Intl Pubs Mktg.

Lawrence, William B. Painting Light & Shadow in Watercolor. LC 94-21078. (Illus.). 144p. 1995. 27.99 (*0-89134-577-9*, North Lght Bks) F & W Pubns Inc.

— Sundays in New York: Pulpit Theology at the Crest of the Protestant Mainstream, 1930-1955. (ATLA Monographs: Vol. 41). 400p. 1996. 49.50 (*0-8108-3079-5*) Scarecrow.

Lawrence, William B., et al, eds. The People(s) Called Methodist: Forms & Reforms of Their Life. LC 97-42781. (United Methodism & American Culture Ser.: Vol. 2). 320p. 1997. pap. 19.95 (*0-687-02199-5*) Abingdon.

Lawrence, William H. Commercial Paper & Payment Systems, 2 vols., Set. 880p. 1990. ring bd. 150.00 (*0-88063-325-5*, MICHIE) LEXIS Pub.

Lawrence, William H. Understanding Secured Transactions 1999. annuals 2nd ed. text 30.00 (*0-8205-4060-9*) Bender.

Lawrence, William J. Life of Amos A. Lawrence. LC 70-154158. (Select Bibliographies Reprint Ser.). 1977. reprint ed. 23.95 (*0-8369-5774-1*) Ayer.

— Old Theatre Days & Ways. LC 68-20236. 255p. 1972. reprint ed. 20.95 (*0-405-08737-3*, Pub. by Blom Pubns) Ayer.

— Pre-Restoration Stage Studies. LC 67-23857. 1972. reprint ed. 30.95 (*0-405-08738-1*, Pub. by Blom Pubns) Ayer.

— Shakespeare's Workshop. (BCL1-PR English Literature Ser.). 161p. 1992. reprint ed. lib. bdg. 69.00 (*0-7812-7296-3*) Rprt Serv.

— Speeding up Shakespeare. LC 68-20235. 1972. reprint ed. 20.95 (*0-405-08739-X*) Ayer.

Lawrence, William J. & Leeds, Stephen. An Inventory of Federal Income Transfer Programs, Fiscal Year 1977. LC 77-92998. 219p. 1978. 12.00 (*0-915312-07-7*) Inst Socioecon.

— An Inventory of State & Local Income Transfer Programs: Fiscal Year 1977. LC 80-82153. 301p. 1980. 12.00 (*0-915312-09-3*) Inst Socioecon.

Lawrence-Wynn, Elaine. Parenting with Ease: It Doesn't Have to Be Difficult. 243p. 1996. pap. 14.95 (*0-9649665-0-6*) E Lawrence-Wynn.

Lawrence-Zuniga, Denise, jt. ed. see Birdwell-Pheasant, Donna.

Lawrencee, Robert G., ed. Restoration Plays. 704p. 1994. 14.95 (*0-460-87432-2*, Everyman's Classic Lib) Tuttle Pubng.

Lawrenceson, Derek. The Long Game. (Golf Basics Ser.). (Illus.). 112p. (Orig.). 1996. pap. 14.95 (*1-57243-121-0*) Triumph Bks.

— The Short Game. (Golf Basic Ser.). (Illus.). 112p. (Orig.). 1996. pap. 14.95 (*1-57243-120-2*) Triumph Bks.

***Lawrenson, D.** The Moonbathers. 330p. 1998. 27.00 (*0-434-00462-6*, Pub. by Random) Trafalgar.

— The Moonbathers. 330p. 1998. pap. 11.95 (*0-7493-2434-1*, Pub. by Random) Trafalgar.

Lawrenson, Deborah. Hot Gossip. 350p. 1996. mass mkt. 6.99 (*0-7493-2400-7*) Buttrwrth-Heinemann.

— Idol Chatter. 1996. mass mkt. 6.99 (*0-7493-2405-8*) Buttrwrth-Heinemann.

***Lawrenson, Derek.** Complete Encyclopedia of Golf. 1999. text 45.00 (*1-85868-752-7*, Pub. by Carlton Bks Ltd) Natl Bk Netwk.

Lawrenson, Thomas E. The French Stage & Playhouse in the Seventeenth Century. 2nd rev. ed. LC 79-3697. (Studies in the Seventeenth Century: No. 1). 1986. 47.50 (*0-404-61721-2*) AMS Pr.

Lawreny, John C. Judges - Ruth. LC 97-69199. (People's Bible Ser.). 260p. 1998. pap. text 11.99 (*0-8100-0789-4*, 15N0580) Northwest Pub.

***Lawrenz, Mel.** Dynamics of Spiritual Formation. LC 99-55497. (Ministry Dynamics for a New Century Ser.). 176p. 2000. pap. 10.99 (*0-8010-9097-0*) Baker Bks.

Lawrenz, Mel, jt. auth. see Green, Daniel R.

Lawrenz, Melvin E., 3rd. The Christology of John Chrysostom. LC 96-36777. 184p. 1997. text 79.95 (*0-7734-2272-2*) E Mellen.

Lawrenz, W. CAM System Engineering: From Theory to Practical Applications. LC 96-39961. 520p. 1997. 69.95 incl. disk (*0-387-94939-9*) Spr-Verlag.

Lawrey, David M., ed. Calculation of Precision Data: Petroleum Test Methods, D2PP, Vol. 2. ((MNL) Manual Ser.). 16p. 1996. pap. text 99.00 (*0-8031-2071-0*, MNL2) ASTM.

Lawrey, James D. & Hale, Mason E., Jr. Biology of Lichenized Fungi. LC 84-9908. 416p. 1984. 42.95 (*0-275-91211-6*, C1211, Praeger Pubs) Greenwood.

Lawrie. Lawrie's Meat Science. 6th ed. 352p. 1998. pap. 84.95 (*1-85573-395-1*) Technomic.

Lawrie, A., et al. Glimmer of Cold Brine: A Scottish Sea Anthology. (Illus.). 250p. 1988. pap. 18.00 (*0-08-036579-5*, Pergamon Pr) Elsevier.

Lawrie, Christine. Ask about Animals. LC 94-28180. (Read All about It Ser.). (Illus.). 32p. (J). 1995. lib. bdg. 5.00 (*0-8114-5729-X*) Raintree Steck-V.

Lawrie, I. D. A Unified Grand Tour of Theoretical Physics. LC 89-24740. (Illus.). 392p. 1990. pap. 60.00 (*0-85274-015-8*) IOP Pub.

— A Unified Grand Tour of Theoretical Physics. LC 89-24740. (Illus.). 392p. 1990. 180.00 (*0-85274-014-X*) IOP Pub.

Lawrie, Laura, ed. see Williams, Robert A.

Lawrie, Peggie. Season Pleasers. (Illus.). 56p. Date not set. pap. 10.95 (*1-57377-053-1*, 01988402250) Easl Pubns.

Lawrie, R. A. Meat Science. (C). 1985. text 74.00 (*0-08-030790-6*, Pergamon Pr); pap. text 42.00 (*0-08-030789-2*, Pergamon Pr) Elsevier.

— Meat Science. 5th ed. (Food Science Ser.). (Illus.). 312p. (C). 1991. text 66.95 (*0-08-040824-9*, Prgamon Press); pap. text 62.95 (*0-08-040825-7*, Prgamon Press) Buttrwrth-Heinemann.

Lawrie, R. A., ed. see Easter School in Agricultural Science (14th 1967,.

Lawrie, R. A., ed. see Easter School in Agricultural Science (21st: 1974:.

Lawrie, Richard A., jt. auth. see Heins, Conrad P.

Lawrie, Robert J., jt. ed. see Berutti, Alfred.

Lawrie, Robin. Magic Tales Beauty. (J). Date not set. pap. 3.95 (*0-448-11255-8*) Putnam Pub Group.

— Magic Tales Jack. Date not set. pap. 3.95 (*0-448-11253-1*) Putnam Pub Group.

— Magic Tales Rumpel. (J). Date not set. pap. 3.95 (*0-448-11254-X*) Putnam Pub Group.

— Magic Tales Snow. (J). Date not set. pap. 3.95 (*0-448-11252-3*) Putnam Pub Group.

— Magic Tales Wild. (J). Date not set. pap. 3.95 (*0-448-11251-5*) Putnam Pub Group.

Lawrie, Robin. Fantasy Stories. LC 94-2338. 260p. (J). (gr. 1 up). 1994. pap. 7.95 (*1-85697-982-2*) LKC.

Lawrie, Robin, jt. auth. see Lewis, C. S.

Lawrie, Steven W. Erich Fried Vol. 24: A Writer Without a Country. (Austrian Culture Ser.). X, 407p. (C). 1996. text 55.95 (*0-8204-3035-8*) P Lang Pubng.

Lawrie, T. D., jt. ed. see Macfarlane, Peter W.

Lawrinowicz, Julian, ed. Deformations of Mathematical Structures II: Hurwitz-Type Structures & Applications to Surface Physics: Selected Papers from the Seminar on Deformations, Lodz'-Malinka 1988-92. LC 93-33466. 480p. (C). 1994. text 313.00 (*0-7923-2576-1*) Kluwer Academic.

Lawruszczuk, R., jt. ed. see Heldt, J.

Lawry, Antje, tr. see Von Balthasar, Hans U.

Lawry, Ed, ed. Study Guide Electrical General: Electrical Inspector Certification Program. 6th ed. (Illus.). iv, 174p. 1996. pap., spiral bd. 22.50 (*1-890659-09-6*, 360016) Intl Assn Elec Inspect.

— Study Guide Electrical 1- & 2-Family: Electrical Inspector Certification Program. 6th ed. (Illus.). iv, 142p. 1996. pap., spiral bd. 22.50 (*1-890659-08-8*, 360014) Intl Assn Elec Inspect.

— Study Guide Electrical Plan Review: Electrical Inspector Certification Program. 6th ed. (Illus.). iv, 156p. 1996. pap., spiral bd. 22.50 (*1-890659-10-X*, 360018) Intl Assn Elec Inspect.

Lawry, John D. College 101: A First-Year Reader. 2nd ed. LC 98-13918. 294p. 1998. pap. 24.43 (*0-07-303159-3*) McGraw.

— Guide to the History of Psychology. LC 90-41777. 128p. (C). 1990. reprint ed. pap. text 17.50 (*0-8191-7851-9*) U Pr of Amer.

— May You Never Stop Dancing: A Professor's Letters to His Daughter. LC 98-230569. 136p. (C). 1998. pap. 13.95 (*0-88489-535-1*) St Marys.

Lawry, Mark H. College 101: A Freshman Reader. 450p. (C). 1992. pap. 24.43 (*0-07-036733-7*) McGraw.

— I-DEAS Student Guide. (Master Ser.: No. 5). (Illus.). 476p. (C). Date not set. pap. text, student ed. 34.95 (*0-9638178-2-5*, P-50002) Structrl Dynmcs.

— I-DEAS Student Guide. 650p. (C). 1993. pap. text 19.50 (*0-9638178-0-9*) Structrl Dynmcs.

— I-DEAS Student Guide. (Master Ser.: No. 6). (Illus.). 476p. (C). 1998. pap. text, student ed. 39.95 (*0-9638178-3-3*, P-60002) Structrl Dynmcs.

— I-DEAS Student Guide. (Illus.). 476p. (C). 1999. pap., student ed. 39.95 (*0-9638178-4-1*) Structrl Dynmcs.

— I-DEAS Student Guide: Master Series 2.0. 500p. (C). pap. text 25.00 (*0-9638178-1-7*) Structrl Dynmcs.

Lawry, Robert P., jt. ed. see Clarke, Robert W.

Lawry, Steven W. Politiques de Tenure et Gestion des Ressources Naturelles en Afrique de l'Ouest Sahelienne. (LTC Paper Ser.: Vol. 130-F). (FRE.). v, 24p. (C). 1990. pap. 4.00 (*0-934519-46-3*, LTC130-F) U of Wis Land.

— Tenure Policy & Natural Resource Management in Sahelian West Africa. (LTC Paper Ser.: Vol. 130). vi, 24p. (C). 1989. pap. 4.00 (*0-934519-45-5*, LTC130) U of Wis Land.

— Tenure Policy Toward Common Property Natural Resources. (LTC Paper Ser.: Vol. 134). 22p. (C). 1989. pap. 4.00 (*0-934519-50-1*, LTC134) U of Wis Land.

Lawry, Steven W. & Stienbarger, Douglas M. Tenure & Alley Farming in the Humid Zone of West Africa: Final Report of Research in Cameroon, Nigeria, & Togo. (Research Paper Ser.: Vol. 105). xi, 63p. (C). 1991. pap. 7.00 (*0-934519-15-3*, RP105) U of Wis Land.

Lawrynowicz, Julian, ed. Deformations of Mathematical Structures: Complex Analysis with Physical Applications. (C). 1988. text 237.50 (*0-7923-0023-8*) Kluwer Academic.
— Seminar on Deformations. (Lecture Notes in Mathematics Ser.: Vol. 1165). ix, 331p. 1985. 46.95 (*0-387-16050-7*) Spr-Verlag.
Lawrynowicz, Julian & Lodz, J., eds. Analytic Functions, Blazejewko 1982. (Lecture Notes in Mathematics Ser.: Vol. 1039). (ENG & FRE.). 494p. 1984. 57.95 (*0-387-12712-7*) Spr-Verlag.
***Laws.** Aquatic Pollution: An Introductory Text. 3rd ed. 700p. 2000. pap. 99.00 (*0-471-34875-9*) Wiley.
Laws. Workshop Physics Activity Guide: Core Volume with Module 2. 224p. 1996. ring bd. 23.95 (*0-471-15594-2*) Wiley.
— Workshop Physics Activity Guide: Core Volume with Module 3. 128p. 1996. ring bd. 18.95 (*0-471-15595-0*) Wiley.
— Workshop Physics Activity Guide: Core Volume with Module 4. 272p. 1996. pap. 25.95 (*0-471-15596-9*) Wiley.
Laws, Ami, jt. ed. see Reaven, Gerald M.
Laws, Anna C. Author Notation in the Library of Congress. 1976. lib. bdg. 59.95 (*0-8490-1463-8*) Gordon Pr.
Laws, B. Irish Country Style. 1999. text 29.95 (*1-85410-523-X*) Aurum Pub.
Laws, Bill. Artists' Gardens. LC 98-89408. (Illus.). 192p. 1999. 35.00 (*1-57076-147-7*, Trafalgar Sq Pub) Trafalgar.
— Old English Farmhouses. (Illus.). 160p. 1992. 29.95 (*1-55859-407-8*) Abbeville Pr.
— Perfect Country Cottage. (Illus.). 144p. 1994. 35.00 (*1-55859-784-0*) Abbeville Pr.
— Traditional Houses of Rural France. (Illus.). 160p. 1991. 27.50 (*1-55859-222-9*) Abbeville Pr.
— Traditional Houses of Rural France. (Traditional Houses Ser.). (Illus.). 160p. 1997. pap. 17.95 (*0-7892-0474-6*) Abbeville Pr.
— Traditional Houses of Rural Spain. (Illus.). 160p. 1995. 27.50 (*0-7892-0057-0*) Abbeville Pr.
Laws, D. Richard, ed. Relapse Prevention with Sex Offenders. LC 88-36840. 338p. 1989. lib. bdg. 44.00 (*0-89862-381-2*) Guilford Pubns.
Laws, D. Richard & O'Donohue, William, eds. Sexual Deviance: Theory, Assessment & Treatment. LC 97-25929. 514p. 1997. lib. bdg. 63.00 (*1-57230-241-0*, 0241) Guilford Pubns.
Laws, Diane M., ed. see Laws, James E., 3rd.
Laws, E. R., jt. ed. see Karim, A. B.
Laws, Edward. Mathematical Methods for Oceanographers: An Introduction. LC 96-31998. 343p. 1997. 90.00 (*0-471-16221-3*) Wiley.
Laws, Edward A. El Nino & the Peruvian Anchovy Fishery: Mac Version. LC 95-61065. (Illus.). 80p. (C). 1997. pap. text 30.00 (*0-935702-79-2*) Univ Sci Bks.
— El Nino & the Peruvian Anchovy Fishery: Windows Version. LC 95-61065. (Illus.). 80p. (Orig.). (C). 1997. pap. text 30.00 (*0-935702-80-6*) Univ Sci Bks.
Laws, Edward R., Jr. & Fox, William L. Dandy of Johns Hopkins. (Illus.). 291p. 1984. lib. bdg. 21.00 (*0-683-04903-8*) Lppncott W & W.
Laws, Edward R., Jr. & Udvarhelyi, George B., eds. The Genesis of Neuroscience by A. Earl Walker, M. D. 371p. 65.00 (*1-879284-62-6*) Am Assn Neuro.
Laws, Edward R., ed. see Hayes, Wayland J.
Laws, Edward R., Jr., jt. ed. see Hayes, Wayland J., Jr.
Laws, Edward R., jt. ed. see Kaye, Andrew H.
Laws, Edward S. Aquatic Pollution: An Introductory Text. 2nd ed. (Environmental Science & Technology Ser.). 624p. 1993. pap. 90.00 (*0-471-58883-0*, Wiley-Interscience) Wiley.
Laws, Eleanor J., jt. auth. see Hadley, Ernest C.
Laws, Eric. Managing Packaged Tourism. (Topics in Tourism Ser.). 248p. 1997. pap. 15.99 (*0-415-11347-4*) Thomson Learn.
— Tourism Marketing: Service & Quality Management Perspectives. 288p. (Orig.). 1991. pap. 39.50 (*0-7487-0428-0*, Pub. by S Thornes Pubs) Trans-Atl Phila.
— Tourism Marketing Service & Quality Management Perspectives. 288p. (C). 1991. 62.00 (*0-7478-0428-1*, Pub. by S Thornes Pubs) Trans-Atl Phila.
— Tourist Destination Management: Issues, Analysis & Policies. LC 94-32453. (Topics in Tourism Ser.). 224p. (C). 1995. pap. 16.99 (*0-415-10591-9*, C0385) Thomson Learn.
Laws, Eric & Moscardo, Gianna, eds. Embracing & Managing Change in Tourism: Casebook. LC 97-35290. (Illus.). 472p. (C). 1998. 115.00 (*0-415-15998-9*) Routledge.
Laws, James E., 3rd. Let the Ancestors Speak: Removing the Veil of Mysticism from Medu Netcher. Laws, Diane M. & Grimball, Gilberta D., eds. (Illus.). 288p. (Orig.). (C). 1995. pap. text 19.95 (*0-9640661-1-4*) J E Laws.
Laws, Jim, ed. The Book of Mark: Jesus - The Servant of Jehovah Fourteenth Annual Spiritual Sword Lectureship. 457p. 1989. 20.00 (*0-9615751-5-8*) Getwell Church.
— God's Amazing Grace: The Twentieth Annual Spiritual Sword Lectureship. 1995. 24.00 (*1-886220-01-8*) Getwell Church.
— The Restoration: the Winds of Change: Eighteenth Annual Spiritual Sword Lectureship. 1993. 24.00 (*0-9615751-9-0*) Getwell Church.
— The Scheme of Redemption: Fifteenth Annual Spiritual Sword Lectureship. (Illus.). 618p. 1990. 24.00 (*0-9615751-7-4*) Getwell Church.
— There Was a Man Named Job: Sixteenth Annual Spiritual Sword Lectureship. (Illus.). 416p. 1991. 24.00 (*0-9615751-6-6*) Getwell Church.
***Laws, John, et al.** Sydney: World-Class Jewel. LC 99-29198. (Urban Tapesty Ser.). (Illus.). 320p. 1999. write for info. (*1-881096-68-8*) Towery Pub.
Laws, Kenneth & Harvey, Cynthia. Physics, Dance & the Pas de Deux. (Illus.). 224p. 1994. 22.00 (*0-02-871326-5*, Schirmer Books) Mac Lib Ref.
— Physics, Dance & the Pas de Deux. 1994. 35.00 incl. VHS (*0-02-871327-3*, Schirmer Books) Mac Lib Ref.
— Physics, Dance & the Pas de Deux. (Illus.). 227p. 1994. text 50.00 incl. VHS (*0-02-871329-X*, Schirmer Books) Mac Lib Ref.
Laws, Kyle & Moffeit, Tony. Tanqo. Kempher, Ruth M., ed. (Illus.). 80p. 1997. pap. 14.95 (*1-888832-05-3*) Kings Estate.
Laws, Lynda, ed. see Brown, John F.
Laws, P., jt. auth. see Baxter-Hastings, N.
Laws, Priscilla, jt. auth. see Hastings, Nancy B.
Laws, Priscilla W. Workshop Physics Activity Guide, Set of 4 Modeules. LC 95-37038. 896p. 1995. pap. text 28.00 (*0-471-10957-6*) Wiley.
— Workshop Physics Activity Guide Core Volume. 304p. 1996. pap. 37.95 (*0-471-15593-4*) Wiley.
Laws, Richard. Antarctica the Last Frontier. 192p. (C). 1990. 60.00 (*1-85283-247-9*, Pub. by Boxtree) St Mut.
Laws, Richard M. Antarctic Seals: Research Methods & Techniques. LC 92-47467. (Illus.). 412p. (C). 1993. text 90.00 (*0-521-44302-4*) Cambridge U Pr.
Laws, Richard M., ed. Antarctic Ecology, 1. 1984. text 157.00 (*0-12-439501-5*) Acad Pr.
Laws, Richard M., jt. ed. see Le Boeuf, Burney J.
Laws, Rita & O'Hanlon, Tim. Adoption Assistance: Tools for Navigating the Bureaucracy. LC 98-55901. 288p. 1999. 35.00 (*0-89789-668-8*, Bergin & Garvey) Greenwood.
Laws, Rita, jt. auth. see Babb, L. Anne.
Laws, Robin D. The Cut-Ups Project. (On the Edge Ser.). 1995. 1.95 (*1-887801-23-5*, Atlas Games) Trident MN.
***Laws, Robin D.** Feng Shui: Action Movie Roleplaying. rev. ed. (Illus.). 256p. 1999. 30.00 (*1-887801-76-6*) Trident MN.
Laws, Robin D. Pierced Heart. Nephew, John, ed. (Over the Edge Ser.). 207p. (Orig.). 1996. pap. 14.95 (*1-887801-54-5*) Trident MN.
— Unauthorized Broadcast: An Adventure Resource for Over the Edge. (Over the Edge Ser.). 16p. 1993. pap. 4.95 (*1-887801-06-5*, Atlas Games) Trident MN.
— Weather the Cuckoo Likes: The Sourcebook of the Cut-Ups Project. (Over the Edge Ser.). 96p. 1994. pap. 12.95 (*1-887801-12-X*, Atlas Games) Trident MN.
Laws, Robin D., et al. Wildest Dreams: The Sourcebook of Nightmare. (Over the Edge Ser.). 64p. 1993. pap. 10.95 (*1-887801-11-1*, Atlas Games) Trident MN.
Laws, Robin D., jt. auth. see Tweet, Jonathan.
Laws, Sophie. The Epistle of James. (Black's New Testament Commentary Ser.: No. 16). 274p. 1993. 22.95 (*1-56563-017-3*) Hendrickson MA.
***Laws, Stephen.** The Midnight Man. 264p. 2000. 35.00 (*0-9675157-1-8*); pap. write for info. (*0-9675157-2-6*, Silver Salamander Pr) Darkside.
Lawson. Casebook in Family Therapy. (Counseling Ser.). 358p. 1998. pap. 36.95 (*0-534-34415-1*) Wadsworth Pub.
— Current Medicine. 2nd ed. 1990. pap. text 41.00 (*0-443-04254-3*, W B Saunders Co) Harcrt Hlth Sci Grp.
— Differential Geometry. 1991. 84.95 (*0-582-05590-3*, Pub. by Addison-Wesley) Longman.
Lawson. Directors Duties. 87.95 (*0-7546-2009-3*) Ashgate Pub Co.
— Domestic Goddess. text 35.00 (*0-471-35971-8*) Wiley.
Lawson. Engineering & Industrial Statistics. (Statistics Ser.). 2000. pap. 47.95 (*0-534-19050-2*) Wadsworth Pub.
— Human Policy, 3 vols. (C). 1993. pap., teacher ed. 3.16 (*0-395-64009-1*) HM.
— Human Polity, 4 vols. (C). 1997. pap., teacher ed. 11.96 (*0-395-74357-5*) HM.
— Human Polity, 4 vols. 4th ed. LC 96-76922. (C). 1997. text 57.96 (*0-395-74356-7*) HM.
— Interactive Speaking. LC 99-226230. 208p. 1998. pap. text 14.95 (*0-205-26811-0*) P-H.
— Leisure & Entertainment Facilities. 1999. pap. 79.95 (*0-7506-3377-8*) Buttrwrth-Heinemann.
Lawson. Linear Algebra: Maple Labs. 112p. 1996. pap. text, suppl. ed. 21.95 (*0-471-13594-1*) Wiley.
Lawson. Linear Algebra, Mat Labs. 83p. 1996. pap., lab manual ed. 23.95 (*0-471-14953-5*) Wiley.
— Linear Algebra, Students Solutions Manual. 112p. 1996. pap., student ed. 23.95 (*0-471-14954-3*) Wiley.
Lawson. Perspective Charts. Ep. 1940. pap. 44.95 (*0-471-28852-7*, VNR) Wiley.
Lawson. Practice Using Word 6 for Windows. 1995. pap. text, teacher ed. 39.99 (*1-56529-814-4*) Que Educ & Trng.
Lawson & Smith. Business Law for Students. 384p. 1997. pap. 34.95 (*0-7506-2570-8*) Buttrwrth-Heinemann.
Lawson, A. California Earthquake of April 18, 1906: Report of the State Earthquake Commission. (Illus.). 721p. 1970. reprint ed. 35.00 (*0-87279-086-X*, 87) Carnegie Inst.
***Lawson, A.** Disease Mapping & Risk Assessment for Public Health. LC 98-40964. 502p. 1999. 275.00 (*0-471-98634-8*) Wiley.
Lawson, A. Star Baby. LC 90-36806. (Illus.). 72p. (J). 1992. 15.95 (*0-15-200905-1*, Harcourt Child Bks) Harcourt.
Lawson, A. M., jt. auth. see Chalmers, R. A.
Lawson, Alan. Michael Douglas. large type ed. 347p. 1994. 27.99 (*0-7505-0596-6*, Pub. by Mgna Lrg Print) Ulverscroft.
Lawson, Alan, et al. Post Colonial Literatures in English: General Theoretical Comparative, 1970-1993. LC 97-3559. 1997. 65.00 (*0-8161-7358-3*) Mac Lib Ref.
Lawson, Alan, jt. auth. see Lock, Fred.
Lawson, Alan, ed. see Baynton, Barbara.
Lawson, Alan, jt. ed. see Tiffin, Chris.
Lawson, Alexander. The Compositor As Artist, Craftsman, & Tradesman. (Illus.). 40p. 1990. 40.00 (*0-912960-17-5*) Nightowl.
Lawson, Alexander, ed. see James First King of Scotland.
Lawson, Alexander S. Anatomy of a Typeface. (Illus.). 2000. reprint ed. pap. 24.95 (*0-87923-333-8*) Godine.
Lawson, Alexander S. & Agner, Dwight. Printing Types: An Introduction. rev. ed. LC 70-136232. 160p. 1974. pap. 14.00 (*0-8070-6661-3*) Beacon Pr.
Lawson, Alice, ed. see Parce, Mead.
Lawson, Amelia, jt. auth. see Lawson, James S.
Lawson, Andrew. The Gardener's Book of Color: Creating Contrasts, Harmonies & Multicolor Themes in Your Garden. LC 95-39686. (Illus.). 407p. 1996. 32.95 (*0-89577-858-0*, Pub. by RD Assn) Penguin Putnam.
— Plants for All Season: Creating a Garden with Year-Round Beauty. LC 98-139483. 168p. 1998. pap. 19.95 (*0-14-027057-4*) Viking Penguin.
***Lawson, Andrew & Taylor, Jane.** Great English Gardens. (Illus.). 160p. 2000. pap. 24.95 (*0-7538-0498-0*) Phoenix Hse.
Lawson, Andrew & Taylor, Jane. Great English Gardens. (Illus.). 192p. 1997. 45.00 (*0-297-83622-6*, Pub. by Weidenfeld & Nicolson) Trafalgar.
Lawson, Andrew, jt. auth. see Evans, Bill.
Lawson, Andrew, jt. auth. see Taylor, Jane.
Lawson, Andrew J. Cave Art. (Archaeology Ser.: No. 64). (Illus.). 64p. 1989. pap. 10.50 (*0-7478-0120-7*, Pub. by Shire Pubns) Parkwest Pubns.
Lawson, Andrew J., jt. auth. see Coles, John M.
Lawson, Anita. Girl! Serenity Courage & Wisdom. 74p. 1995. pap. text 13.95 (*0-9647410-3-2*) After Words Ink.
— Irvin S. Cobb: Humorist & Newspaperman. LC 83-73108. 1984. 25.95 (*0-87972-275-4*); pap. 13.95 (*0-87972-300-9*) Bowling Green Univ Popular Press.
Lawson, Anita. The Mating Game. 360p. pap. 13.95 (*0-9647410-4-0*) After Words Ink.
Lawson, Ann. Kids & Gangs: What Parents & Educators Need to Know. LC 93-48373. 60p. 1994. pap. 5.50 (*1-56246-091-9*, 3056, HazeldenJohnson Inst) Hazelden.
Lawson, Ann W., jt. auth. see Lawson, Gary.
Lawson, Ann W., jt. auth. see Lawson, Gary W.
Lawson, Annette. Politics of Pregnancy: Adolescent Sexuality & Public Policy. 1993. pap. 19.00 (*0-300-06548-5*) Yale U Pr.
Lawson, Annette & Rhode, Deborah L., eds. The Politics of Pregnancy: Adolescent Sexuality & Public Policy. LC 92-38539. (Illus.). 360p. 1993. reprint ed. pap. 111.60 (*0-608-07830-1*, 205400600010) Bks Demand.
Lawson, Anton E. The Nature of Life: Exploring the Living World. (C). 1995. pap. text, lab manual ed. 23.00 (*0-07-036791-4*) McGraw.
— Science Teaching & the Development of Thinking. LC 94-6339. 593p. 1994. 72.95 (*0-534-23994-3*) Wadsworth Pub.
Lawson, Anton E. & Smith, Brenda D. Studying for Biology. 4th ed. 325p. (C). 1997. pap. text 17.81 (*0-06-500650-X*) Addson-Wesley Educ.
***Lawson, Arvest N.** The Holy Spirit in John Wesley's Theology. 130p. 1999. pap. write for info. (*0-7392-0449-1*, PO3742) Morris Pubng.
Lawson, Barbara. Collected Curios: Missionary Tales from the South Seas. (Illus.). 334p. 1995. text 49.95 (*0-7735-1382-5*) McG-Queens Univ Pr.
— Collected Curios: Missionary Tales from the South Seas. LC 95-153311. (Fontanus Monograph Ser.: No. 3). (Illus.). 313p. 1995. 49.95 (*0-7717-0436-4*, Pub. by McG-Queens Univ Pr) CUP Services.
Lawson, Barbara, jt. auth. see Harman, Thomas L.
Lawson, Barbara, ed. see Grinder, Michael.
Lawson, Benjamin S. Joaquin Miller. LC 80-69014. (Western Writers Ser.: No. 43). (Illus.). 52p. (Orig.). 1980. pap. 4.95 (*0-88430-067-6*) Boise St U W Writ Ser.
Lawson, Benjamin S. Rereading the Revolution: The Turn-of-the-Century American Revolutionary War Novel. 248p. 25.95 (*0-87972-817-5*) Bowling Green Univ Popular Press.
— Rereading the Revolution: The Turn-of-the-Century American Revolutionary War Novel. LC 00-25233. 248p. 2000. pap. 25.95 (*0-87972-818-3*) Bowling Green Univ Popular Press.
Lawson, Betty. Shelling San Sal. (Illus.). 63p. (Orig.). 1993. pap. text 12.00 (*0-935909-44-3*) Bahamian.
Lawson, Bill E., ed. The Underclass Question. 350p. (C). 1992. 59.95 (*0-87722-922-8*) Temple U Pr.
Lawson, Bill E. & Kirkland, Frank M. Frederick Douglass: A Critical Reader. LC 98-24582. (Critical Readers Ser.). 356p. (C). 1998. 59.95 (*0-631-20577-2*); pap. 26.95 (*0-631-20578-0*) Blackwell Pubs.
Lawson, Bill E. & Wilson, William Julius, intros. The Underclass Question. 232p. 1992. pap. 22.95 (*1-56639-062-1*) Temple U Pr.
Lawson, Bill E, jt. auth. see McGary, Howard.
Lawson, Brian, jt. auth. see Howath, Jan.
Lawson, Bryan. Design in Mind. LC 93-50198. (Illus.). 160p. 1994. pap. text 41.95 (*0-7506-1211-8*, Butterwrth Archit) Buttrwrth-Heinemann.
— How Designers Think: The Design Process Demystified. 3rd ed. LC 98-116953. 352p. 2000. pap. text 36.95 (*0-7506-3073-6*) Buttrwrth-Heinemann.
Lawson, Byran. How Designers Think. (Illus.). 212p. 20.00 (*0-89860-047-2*) Eastview.
***Lawson, Carol & Lawson, Robert F., eds.** Decisions! Decisions! The Dynamics of Choice. LC 99-38429. (Chrysalis Reader Ser.: Vol. 6). (Illus.). 160p. 1999. pap. 13.95 (*0-87785-230-8*, Chrysalis Books) Swedenborg.
Lawson, Carol S., ed. Going for It! Thirty-Six Views on the Good Life. LC 97-18274. (Chrysalis Reader Ser.: Vol. 4). (Illus.). 160p. 1997. pap. 13.95 (*0-87785-228-6*, Pub. by Swedenborg) Words Distrib.
— Gold from Aspirin: Spiritual Views on Chaos & Order. (Chrysalis Reader Ser.: Vol. 1). 192p. 1995. pap. 7.95 (*0-87785-225-1*) Swedenborg.
— The Power of Play: New Visions of Creativity. (Chrysalis Reader Ser.: Vol. 3). 160p. (Orig.). 1996. pap. 12.95 (*0-87785-227-8*) Swedenborg.
— Twelve Gates to the City: Spiritual Views on the Journey from 30 Authors. (Chrysalis Reader Ser.: Vol. 2). (Illus.). 160p. (Orig.). 1996. pap. 7.95 (*0-87785-226-X*) Swedenborg.
***Lawson, Carol S. & Lawson, Robert F., eds.** Rocking the Ages: The Pulse of Continuity & Change. (Chrysalis Reader Ser.: Vol. 7). (Illus.). 192p. 2000. pap. 13.95 (*0-87785-231-6*, Pub. by Swedenborg) Words Distrib.
Lawson, Carol S. & Lawson, Robert F., eds. Seeing Through Symbols: Insights on Our World. LC 98-28707. (Chrysalis Reader Ser.: Vol. 5). (Illus.). 192p. 1998. pap. 13.95 (*0-87785-229-4*, Chrysalis Books) Swedenborg.
Lawson, Carolina D. Nuove Letture di Cultura. (SPA.). 296p. 1990. pap. 20.95 (*0-8442-8000-3*) NTC Contemp Pub Co.
Lawson, Charles L. & Hanson, Richard J. Solving Least Squares Problems. LC 95-35178. (Classics in Applied Mathematics Ser.: Vol. 15). xii, 337p. 1995. pap. 35.50 (*0-89871-356-0*, CL15) Soc Indus-Appl Math.
Lawson, Cheryl A., jt. auth. see Goodman, George J.
Lawson, Chris. 330 Reasons to Love the Corps: Silly, Serious & Revealing Reasons to Love the U. S. Marine Corps. LC 96-78537. 160p. (Orig.). 1996. pap. 7.95 (*9964-79-241-7*) Army Times Pubng.
***Lawson, Christine.** Understanding the Borderline Mother (A1) Helping Her Childresn Transcend the Intense, Unpredictable, & Volatile Relationship. 2001. 40.00 (*0-7657-0288-6*) Aronson.
Lawson, Christopher M., ed. Nonlinear Optical Liquids, Vol. 2853. 218p. 1996. 56.00 (*0-8194-2241-X*) SPIE.
— Nonlinear Optical Liquids & Power Limiters, Vol. 3146. LC 98-122019. 194p. 1997. 59.00 (*0-8194-2568-0*) SPIE.
— Nonlinear Optical Liquids for Power Limiting & Imaging, Vol. 3472. 1998. 59.00 (*0-8194-2927-9*) SPIE.
Lawson, Cliff. A Traveler's Guide to Death Valley National Park. (Illus.). 40p. (Orig.). 1996. pap. 7.95 (*1-878900-30-7*) DVNH Assn.
Lawson, Colin. Brahms: Clarinet Quintet. LC 97-5990. (Music Handbks.). (Illus.). 312p. (C). 1998. text 39.95 (*0-521-58193-1*); pap. text 13.95 (*0-521-58831-6*) Cambridge U Pr.
***Lawson, Colin.** The Early Clarinet: A Practical Guide. (Cambridge Handbooks to the Historical Performance of Music Ser.). (Illus.). 138p. 2000. 49.95 (*0-521-62459-2*); pap. 17.95 (*0-521-62466-5*) Cambridge U Pr.
***Lawson, Colin & Stowell, Robin.** The Historical Performance of Music: An Introduction. LC 98-42731. (Cambridge Handbooks to the Historical Performance of Music Ser.). (Illus.). 212p. (C). 1999. 54.95 (*0-521-62193-3*); pap. 19.95 (*0-521-62738-9*) Cambridge U Pr.
Lawson, Colin J. The Cambridge Companion to the Clarinet. (Cambridge Companions to Music Ser.). (Illus.). 256p. (C). 1996. text 64.95 (*0-521-47066-8*) Cambridge U Pr.
— The Cambridge Companion to the Clarinet. (Cambridge Companions to Music Ser.). (Illus.). 256p. (C). 1996. pap. text 19.95 (*0-521-47668-2*) Cambridge U Pr.
— The Chalumeau in Eighteenth-Century Music. LC 81-15961. (Studies in British Musicology: No. 6). (Illus.). 218p. reprint ed. pap. 67.60 (*0-8357-1246-X*, 207022100064) Bks Demand.
— Mozart: Clarinet Concerto. (Cambridge Music Handbks.). (Illus.). 222p. (C). 1996. text 39.95 (*0-521-47384-5*); pap. text 13.95 (*0-521-47929-0*) Cambridge U Pr.
Lawson-Cruttenden, Timothy & Addison, Neil. Blackstone's Guide to the Protection from Harassment Act, 1997. 93p. 1997. pap. 34.00 (*1-85431-695-8*, Pub. by Blackstone Pr) Gaunt.
Lawson, D. H., ed. Current Medicine 4: Royal College of Physicians of Edinburgh. (Illus.). 330p. 1994. pap. write for info. (*0-443-05040-6*) Church.
Lawson, Daniel D. Handbook of Solubility Parameters for Inorganic Substances. 2000. 125.00 (*0-8493-2510-2*) CRC Pr.
Lawson, David. A Company of Angels. (Illus.). (Orig.). 1997. pap. 11.95 (*1-899171-02-9*, Pub. by Findhorn Pr) Words Distrib.
— Principles of Your Psychic Pot. 1998. pap. 11.00 (*1-85538-487-6*) Thorsons PA.
***Lawson, David.** So You Want to Be a Shaman: A Creative & Practical Guide to the History, Wisdom & Rituals of This Ancient Tradition. (Illus.). 64p. 1999. reprint ed. text 9.00 (*0-7881-6564-X*) DIANE Pub.
Lawson, David. Wellness: Safety & Accident Prevention. 128p. (C). 1991. text 13.50 (*0-87967-864-X*, Dshkn McG-Hill) McGrw-H Hghr Educ.
Lawson, David & Griffiths, Jennifer. Star Healing: Your Sun Sign, Your Health & Your Success. 352p. 1995. pap. 11.95 (*0-340-60646-0*, Pub. by Hodder & Stought Ltd) Trafalgar.
Lawson, David, jt. auth. see Arthur, Kay.
Lawson, David A., ed. Current Medicine Three. 3rd ed. (Illus.). 300p. (Orig.). 1991. pap. text 47.00 (*0-443-04598-4*) Church.
Lawson, David J. Hungering for the Future: Whispers of Hope for a Church in Mission. 160p. (Orig.). 1996. pap. 9.95 (*0-687-01592-8*) Abingdon.
Lawson, Dawn, tr. see Oshima, Nagisa.

*Lawson, Denis & Daniels, Anthony. The Thrawn Trilogy Boxed Set: Heir to the Empire; Dark Force Rising; The Last Command, Set. abr. ed. (Star Wars). (YA). (gr. 5 up). 2000. boxed set 29.95 incl. audio (0-553-52699-5) BDD Aud Pub.

Lawson, Denise, ed. see Dienstfrey, Patricia.

Lawson, Denise, ed. see Gevirtz, Susan.

*Lawson, Denise Liddell. Even the Smallest Act. 16p. 1998. pap. 15.00 (1-889589-01-2, Pub. by Em Pr) SPD-Small Pr Dist.

Lawson, Don. F D R's New Deal. LC 78-4775. (Illus.). (YA). (gr. 7 up). 1979. 12.95 (0-690-03953-0) HarpC Child Bks.

— Long March. (J). 1983. 12.95 (0-690-04271-X) HarpC Child Bks.

— The United States in the Indian Wars. LC 75-6684. (Young People's History of America's Wars Ser.). (Illus.). (J). (gr. 7 up). 1950. 12.95 (0-200-00158-2) HarpC Child Bks.

— The United States in the Indian Wars. LC 75-6684. (Young People's History of America's Wars Ser.). (Illus.). 145p. (YA). (gr. 7 up). 1989. lib. bdg. 12.89 (0-690-04713-4) HarpC Child Bks.

Lawson, Don & Barish, Wendy. The French Resistance. (Spyshelf Ser.). 192p. (J). (gr. 3-7). 1984. lib. bdg. 8.79 (0-671-50832-6) S&S Trade.

*Lawson, Dorothea V. S. Laughter Wasn't Rationed: Remembering the War Years in Germany. LC 99-71359. (Illus.). vi, 538p. 1999. pap. 24.95 (0-9673830-3-X) Tricor Pr.

Lawson, Dorris M. Nathan Roberts: Erie Canal Engineer. Lawson, Eric W., ed. (Illus.). 96p. 1997. pap. 15.00 (0-925168-57-2) North Country.

Lawson, Doug. A Patrimony of Fishes. LC 97-67764. 128p. 1997. pap. 10.95 (1-888996-04-8, Red Hen Press) Valentine CA.

Lawson, Douglas. Give to Live Program Manual: Letterhead. 8.00 (0-687-01243-0) Abingdon.

— Give to Live Program Manual: Pledge Card. 9.00 (0-687-01233-3) Abingdon.

— Give to Live Program Manual: Poster Set 7.00 (0-687-01253-8) Abingdon.

Lawson, Douglas M. Give to Live: How Giving Can Change Your Life. LC 91-72216. 208p. 1991. pap. 11.95 (0-9625399-9-6) ALTI Pub.

— More Give to Live: How Giving Can Change Your Life. rev. expanded ed. 304p. 1998. pap. 16.95 (1-883051-22-3, Pub. by ALTI Pub) Natl Bk Netwk.

— Volunteering: 101 Ways to Improve the World & Your Life. LC 98-13475. 1998. pap. 47.70 (1-883051-18-5) ALTI Pub.

— Volunteering: 101 Ways You Can Improve the World & Your Life. LC 98-13475. 144p. 1998. pap. 7.95 (1-883051-17-7) ALTI Pub.

Lawson, E. Thomas. Religions of Africa: Traditions in Transformation. (Illus.). 106p. (C). 1998. reprint ed. pap. 9.95 (1-57766-012-9) Waveland Pr.

Lawson, Ed, jt. auth. see Laskin, Irving.

Lawson, Edward, ed. Encyclopedia of Human Rights. 2nd ed. LC 96-21852. 1715p. 1996. text 392.00 (1-56032-362-0) Taylor & Francis.

Lawson, Edwin D., compiled by. More Names & Naming: An Annotated Bibliography, 9. LC 95-31626. (Bibliographies & Indexes in Anthropology Ser.: No. 9). 320p. 1995. lib. bdg. 75.00 (0-313-28582-9, Greenwood Pr) Greenwood.

— Personal Names & Naming: An Annotated Bibliography, 3. LC 86-31789. (Bibliographies & Indexes in Anthropology Ser.: No. 3). 198p. 1987. lib. bdg. 59.95 (0-313-23817-0, LNN/, Greenwood Pr) Greenwood.

Lawson, Eileen, ed. see Hanson, Frances E.

Lawson, Elizabeth. The Natural Art of Louisa Atkinson. (Illus.). 144p. 1995. 65.00 (0-7305-8927-7, Pub. by Univ Queensland Pr) Intl Spec Bk.

Lawson, Elizabeth, ed. see Atkinson, Louisa.

Lawson, Ellen N. The Three Sarahs: Documents of Antebellum Black College Women. LC 84-18914. (Studies in Women & Religion: Vol. 13). (Illus.). 350p. 1984. lib. bdg. 99.95 (0-88946-536-3) E Mellen.

Lawson, Eric & Lawson, Jane. The First Air Campaign: August,1914-November,1918. (Great Campaigns Ser.). (Illus.). 256p. 1995. 24.95 (0-938289-44-6, 289446) Combined Pub.

Lawson, Eric W., ed. see Lawson, Dorris M.

Lawson, Erma J. & Rodgers-Rose, LaFrancis, eds. Black Women's Health Vol. 1: Research & Social Policy. unabridged ed. 262p. (Orig.). 1997. pap. text 15.95 (0-934185-03-4) Traces Inst.

Lawson, Erma J. & Thompson, Aaron. Black Men & Divorce. LC 98-40251. (Understanding Families Ser.). 2000. write for info. (0-8039-5955-9) Sage.

Lawson, Erma Jean & Thompson, Aaron. Black Men & Divorce. LC 98-40251. (Understanding Families Ser.: Vol. 15). 259p. 1999. 47.50 (0-8039-5954-0) Sage.

Lawson, Eugene K. The Sino-Vietnamese Conflict. LC 84-8329. 321p. 1984. 55.00 (0-275-91212-4, C1212, Praeger Pubs) Greenwood.

Lawson, Eugene K., ed. U. S. - China Trade: Problems & Prospects. LC 88-3214. 345p. 1988. 75.00 (0-275-92494-7, C2494, Praeger Pubs) Greenwood.

Lawson, Evald B., jt. auth. see Olson, Ernest W.

Lawson, Evald R. Two Primary Sources for a Study of the Life of Jonas Swensson. (Augustana Historical Society Publications: Vol. 17). 39p. 1957. pap. 3.00 (0-910184-17-8) Augustana.

Lawson, F. H. A Common Lawyer Looks at the Civil Law. LC 88-61807. (Michigan Legal Publications). xvii, 238p. 1988. reprint ed. lib. bdg. 39.00 (0-89941-661-6, 305680) W S Hein.

— Rational Strength of English Law. (Hamlyn Lectures, Third Ser.). viii, 147p. 1988. reprint ed. 35.00 (0-8377-2410-4, Rothman) W S Hein.

Lawson Fall Limited Staff. Kittens. 1996. 5.99 (1-895911-30-3) LAW.

Lawson, Falle. Fox. (Illus.). 1996. 5.99 (0-9693994-9-9) Image Craft Inc.

Lawson Falle Limited Company Staff. Peach Roses. (Illus.). 1996. (1-895911-29-X) LAW.

— Peaches. (Illus.). 1997. pap. 5.99 (1-895911-51-6) LAW.

— Stripe. 1996. pap. 5.99 (1-895911-13-3) LAW.

*Lawson, Fred. Conference, Convention & Exhibition Facilities: Planning, Design & Management. (Illus.). 300p. 2000. pap. text 74.95 (0-7506-2790-5) Buttrwrth-Heinemann.

Lawson, Fred. Restaurants, Clubs & Bars: Planning, Design Investment for Food Service Facilities. rev. ed. (Illus.). 338p. 1995. pap. text 66.95 (0-7506-2076-5, Butterwrth Archit) Buttrwrth-Heinemann.

Lawson, Fred, jt. auth. see Baud-Bovy, Manuel.

Lawson, Fred H. Why Syria Goes to War: Thirty Years of Confrontation. LC 96-17769. (Studies in Political Economy). (Illus.). 224p. 1996. text 29.95 (0-8014-2373-2) Cornell U Pr.

Lawson, Frederick H. A Common Lawyer Looks at the Civil Law: Five Lectures Delivered at the University of Michigan, November 16, 17, 18, 19, & 20, 1953, 5th Series--5. LC 77-23760. (Thomas M. Cooley Lecture: No. 5). 238p. 1977. reprint ed. lib. bdg. 35.00 (0-8371-9778-3, LACO) Greenwood.

Lawson, Frederick H. & Rudden, Bernard. The Law of Property. 2nd ed. (Clarendon Law Ser.). (Illus.). 256p. (C). 1982. pap. text 24.95 (0-19-876129-5) OUP.

Lawson, Frederick H., jt. auth. see Keir, David L.

Lawson, G. H., ed. Studies in Cash Flow Accounting & Analysis: Aspects of Interface Between Managerial Planning, Reporting & Control & External Performance Measurement. LC 92-5927. (New Works in Accounting History). 328p. 1992. text 20.00 (0-8153-0687-3) Garland.

Lawson, G. W. & John, David M. The Marine Algae & Coastal Environment of Tropical West Africa. 2nd ed. (Nova Hedwigia Beihefte Ser.: Vol. 93). (Illus.). vi, 415p. 1987. pap. 130.00 (3-443-51015-9, Pub. by Gebruder Borntraeger) Balogh.

*Lawson, Gary & Lawson, Ann W. Alcoholism & the Family: A Guide to Treatment & Prevention. 2nd ed. LC 97-51270. 400p. 1998. 42.00 (0-8342-1058-4) Aspen Pub.

Lawson, Gary M. The Perfect Paradox. LC 93-30580. (Lewiston Poetry Ser.: Vol. 20). 64p. 1993. pap. 14.95 (0-7734-2789-9, Mellen Poetry Pr) E Mellen.

Lawson, Gary S. Federal Administrative Law. LC 97-48501. (Paralegal). 900p. (C). 1998. text 44.25 (0-314-21132-2) West Pub.

*Lawson, Gary W. Essentials of Chemical Dependency Counseling. 3rd ed. 2000. 49.00 (0-8342-1824-0) Aspen Pub.

Lawson, Gary W. & Cooperrider, Craig C. Clinical Psychopharmacology: A Practical Reference for Nonmedical Psychotherapists. LC 87-33480. 398p. (C). 1988. 75.00 (0-87189-751-2) Aspen Pub.

Lawson, Gary W. & Lawson, Ann W. Adolescent Substance Abuse: Etiology, Treatment & Prevention. LC 92-11363. 576p. 1992. pap. 47.00 (0-8342-0254-9) Aspen Pub.

— Alcoholism & Substance Abuse in Special Populations. LC 88-7600. 390p. (C). 1989. 67.00 (0-8342-0007-4) Aspen Pub.

Lawson, Gary W., et al. Alcoholism & the Family: A Guide to Treatment & Prevention. LC 82-24352. 296p. (C). 1983. 42.00 (0-87189-606-0) Aspen Pub.

— Essentials of Chemical Dependency Counseling. 2nd ed. LC 96-2427. 227p. 1995. 41.00 (0-8342-0683-8) Aspen Pub.

Lawson, George. Politica Sacra et Civilis. Condren, Conal, ed. (Cambridge Texts in the History of Political Thought Ser.). 336p. (C). 1993. text 23.95 (0-521-39248-9) Cambridge U Pr.

Lawson, George W., ed. Plant Ecology in West Africa: Systems & Processes. LC 84-17347. (Illus.). 376p. 1986. reprint ed. pap. 116.60 (0-608-05276-0, 206581400001) Bks Demand.

Lawson, Gerald. World Record Breakers in Track & Field Athletics. LC 96-54043. (Illus.). 480p. (Orig.). 1997. pap. 24.95 (0-88011-679-X, PLAW0679) Human Kinetics.

Lawson, Gerald H. Aspects of the Economic Implications of Accounting. LC 97-25940. (New Works in Accounting History). (Illus.). 404p. 1997. text 76.00 (0-8153-3025-1) Garland.

Lawson, Glenn. BayKeeper. 340p. (Orig.). 1993. pap. 12.95 (0-9620439-5-8) ZAK Bks.

— The Story of Lem Ward As Told by Ida Ward to Glenn Lawson. LC 84-72621. (Illus.). 128p. 1984. 35.00 (0-88740-028-0) Schiffer.

Lawson, Gloria. Caring Kitchen Recipes. LC 93-61485. 229p. (Orig.). 1989. otabind 12.95 (0-945383-63-0) Teach Servs.

Lawson, Greg. Palm Springs Oasis: Photographic Portfolio of the Coachella Valley Region. LC 89-85067. (Pictorial Bks.). (Illus.). 1990. 19.95 (0-916251-40-3) Sunbelt Pubns.

Lawson, Greg C. Race, Racism & Rhyme. (Illus.). (Orig.). 1990. 8.00 (0-9623750-0-4) SunLaw Pubns.

Lawson, H. Blaine. The Quantitative Theory of Foliations. LC 76-51339. (Regional Conference Series in Mathematics: Vol. 27). (Illus.). 78p. 1977. reprint ed. pap. 30.00 (0-7837-8856-8, 204956600001) Bks Demand.

Lawson, H. Blaine, Jr. The Quantitative Theory of Foliations. LC 76-51339. (CBMS Regional Conference Series in Mathematics: No. 27). 65p. 1977. reprint ed. pap. 22.00 (0-8218-1677-2, CBMS/27) Am Math.

— The Theory of Gauge Fields in Four Dimensions. LC 85-441. (CBMS Regional Conference Series in Mathematics: No. 58). 101p. 1985. pap. 24.00 (0-8218-0708-0, CBMS/58) Am Math.

Lawson, H. Blaine, Jr. & Michelsohn, Marie-Louise. Spin Geometry. 450p. 1990. text 85.00 (0-691-08542-0, Pub. by Princeton U Pr) Cal Prin Full Svc.

Lawson, H. Blaine, ed. see Tenenblat, Keti.

Lawson, H. H. Corrosion Testing Made Easy Vol. 4: Atmospheric Corrosion Test Methods. LC 94-74062. (Illus.). 80p. 1994. 85.00 (1-877914-82-7) NACE Intl.

Lawson, H. M. History & Genealogy of the Descendants of Clement Corbin of Muddy River (Brookline), Mass. & Woodstock, Conn., with Other Lines of Corbins. (Illus.). 378p. 1989. reprint ed. pap. 56.50 (0-8328-0423-1); reprint ed. lib. bdg. 64.50 (0-8328-0422-3) Higginson Bk Co.

Lawson, Hal A. Invitation to Physical Education. LC 83-81454. (Illus.). 255p. 1984. reprint ed. pap. 79.10 (0-608-07090-4, 206731700009) Bks Demand.

Lawson, Hal A., ed. Undergraduate Physical Education Programs: Issues & Approaches. LC GV0361.U5. 112p. reprint ed. pap. 34.80 (0-608-16601-4, 202662200050) Bks Demand.

Lawson, Hal A., jt. ed. see Hooper-Briar, Katharine.

Lawson-Hall, Toni & Rotheva, Brian. Hydrangeas: A Gardeners' Guide. (Illus.). 160p. 1995. 34.95 (0-88192-327-3) Timber.

Lawson, Harry. College Bound Blacks: How to Succeed in College. 3rd rev. ed. LC 96-95293. (Illus.). 189p. 1997. pap. 14.95 (0-9611668-1-9) Lawsons Psych.

— The History of African Americans in Tucson Vol. I from 1860 to 1960: An Afrocentric Perspective. LC 96-80110. (Illus.). 201p. (Orig.). 1997. pap. 19.95 (0-9611668-2-7) Lawsons Psych.

Lawson, Harry D. Dynamic Muscular Relaxation. LC 86-17410. (Illus.). 1991. 150.00 (0-87949-270-8) Ashley Bks.

Lawson, Harry W. Standards for Fats & Oils. 2nd ed. 1992. text. write for info. (0-442-01053-2) Chapman & Hall.

Lawson, Harvey & Blazucki, Joan. Bench-Top Orthodontics. (Illus.). 140p. 1990. ring bd. 42.00 (0-86715-233-8) Quint Pub Co.

Lawson, Harvey M., et al. History of Union: Founded on Material Gathered by Rev. Charles Hammond. (Illus.). 509p. 1995. reprint ed. lib. bdg. 53.00 (0-8328-4991-X) Higginson Bk Co.

*Lawson, Helene M. Ladies on the Lost: Women, Car Sales, & the Pursuit of the American Dream. LC 99-57385. 175p. 2000. text 55.00 (0-8476-9862-9) Rowman.

— Ladies on the Lost: Women, Car Sales, & the Pursuit of the American Dream. LC 99-57385. 175p. 2000. pap. 15.95 (0-8476-9863-7) Rowman.

Lawson, Herbert H., jt. ed. see Kirk, W. W.

Lawson, J. D., jt. ed. see Boucot, A. J.

Lawson, J. Gilchrist. Deeper Experiences of Famous Christians. LC 98-19190. 267p. 1998. pap. 6.99 (0-88368-517-5) Whitaker Hse.

Lawson, J. H. A Synopsis of Fevers & Their Treatment. 12th ed. 1977. pap. 15.95 (0-8151-5335-X) Mosby Inc.

Lawson, J. Randall. Firefighter Thermal Exposure Workshop: Protective Clothing, Tactics, & Fire Service Ppe Training Procedures, Gaithersburg, Maryland, June 25-26, 1996. 45p. 1997. pap. 4.25 (0-16-054526-9) USGPO.

Lawson, J. Randall & Jason, Nora H., eds. Firefighter Thermal Exposure Workshop: Protective Clothing, Tactics, & Fire Service PPE Training Procedures. (Illus.). 68p. (C). 1998. pap. text 25.00 (0-7881-7475-4) DIANE Pub.

Lawson, J. Richard. The Language of Success: How to Join the Inner Circle. 256p. (Orig.). 1989. pap. 19.95 (0-945071-10-8) Lawco.

Lawson, Jack. Andro, This Is Crazy. 96p. (Orig.). (J). 1991. pap. 2.95 (0-380-76234-X, Avon Bks) Morrow Avon.

— Carl Nielsen. (Twentieth Century Composers Ser.). (Illus.). 240p. 1997. pap. 19.95 (0-7148-3507-2, Pub. by Phaidon Press) Phaidon Pr.

Lawson, Jacqueline. Cerrillos: Yesterday, Today & Tomorrow. LC 88-34578. (Illus.). 96p. (Orig.). 1989. pap. 8.95 (0-86534-130-3) Sunstone Pr.

Lawson, Jacqueline, ed. Gender & the War: Men, Women & Viet Nam. 280p. pap. write for info. (1-885215-03-7, Viet Nam Gnrtn) Burning Cities Pr.

Lawson, Jacqueline A. An Index of African Americans Identified in Select Records of the Bureau of Refugees, Freedmen, & Abandoned Lands. 101p. (Orig.). 1995. pap. 12.00 (0-7884-0291-9) Heritage Bk.

Lawson, Jacqueline E. Domestic Misconduct in the Novels of Defoe, Richardson & Fielding. LC 93-26975. 200p. 1993. text 79.95 (0-7734-9978-4) E Mellen.

Lawson, James. Drama - Giordana. (Notable American Authors Ser.). 1999. reprint ed. lib. bdg. 125.00 (0-7812-3760-2) Rprt Serv.

— Liddesdale: or The Border Chief. (Notable American Authors Ser.). 1999. reprint ed. lib. bdg. 125.00 (0-7812-3761-0) Rprt Serv.

— The Maiden's Oath. (Notable American Authors Ser.). 1999. reprint ed. lib. bdg. 125.00 (0-7812-3762-9) Rprt Serv.

— Poems: Glenings from Spare Hours of a Business Life. (Notable American Authors Ser.). 1999. reprint ed. lib. bdg. 125.00 (0-7812-3764-5) Rprt Serv.

— Poetry - Ontwa: The Son of the Forest. (Notable American Authors Ser.). 1999. reprint ed. lib. bdg. 125.00 (0-7812-3763-7) Rprt Serv.

— Sacred & Profane: New Works by Calum Colvin. (Illus.). 48p. 1998. pap. 19.95 (0-903598-82-5) Natl Galleries.

— Stories - Tales & Sketches, by a Cosmopolite. (Notable American Authors Ser.). 1999. reprint ed. lib. bdg. 125.00 (0-7812-3765-3) Rprt Serv.

Lawson, James & Rotem, A. From Clinician to Manager: An Introduction to Hospital & Health Services Management. (Illus.). 256p. 1995. text 44.00 (0-07-470153-3) McGraw-Hill HPD.

Lawson, James, jt. auth. see Saint, Steven.

Lawson, James, jt. ed. see Welter, Volker M.

Lawson, James B., ed. & tr. see Zimmer, Heinrich R.

Lawson, James B., tr. see Frischmuth, Barbara.

*Lawson, James G. Deeper Experiences of Famous Christians. (Essential Christian Library Ser.). 320p. 1999. 9.97 (1-57748-523-8) Barbour Pub.

Lawson, James G. Deeper Experiences of Famous Christians. 1981. pap. 3.99 (0-87162-069-3, D3349) Warner Pr.

*Lawson, James Gilchrist. Deeper Experiences of Famous Christians. (Christian Classics). 320p. 2000. pap. 4.97 (1-57748-790-7) Barbour Pub.

Lawson, James R. The Advanced Pool Player's Handbook. Thompson, Bill, ed. 124p. (Orig.). 1994. pap. 18.95 (0-945071-91-4) Lawco.

Lawson, James R., ed. Pocket Billiard Guidebook for Pool Players, Tournament Directors & Spectators. 192p. (Orig.). 1994. pap. 39.95 (0-945071-55-8) Lawco.

— The Pool Player's Road Atlas. 200p. (Orig.). 1994. pap. 34.95 (0-945071-80-9) Lawco.

Lawson, James S. Public Health Australia: An Introduction. (Illus.). 225p. 1991. pap. text 24.00 (0-07-452913-7) McGraw-Hill HPD.

Lawson, James S. & Lawson, Amelia. Breast Cancer: Can You Prevent It? 230p. 1999. pap. write for info. (0-07-470723-X) McGraw-Hill HPD.

Lawson, Jane, jt. auth. see Lawson, Eric.

Lawson, Jennifer. Hands-on Science: Early Childhood. (Illus.). 122p. (gr. k). 1991. teacher ed., ring bd. 85.00 (1-895411-02-5) Peguis Pubs Ltd.

— Hands-on Science: Level Four. (Illus.). 240p. (J). (gr. 4). 1991. teacher ed., ring bd. 85.00 (1-895411-10-6) Peguis Pubs Ltd.

— Hands-on Science: Level One. (Illus.). 216p. (gr. 1). 1991. teacher ed., ring bd. 85.00 (1-895411-04-1) Peguis Pubs Ltd.

— Hands-on Science: Level Three. (Illus.). 240p. (gr. 3). 1991. teacher ed., ring bd. 85.00 (1-895411-08-4) Peguis Pubs Ltd.

— Hands-on Science: Level Two. (Illus.). 204p. (gr. 2). 1991. teacher ed., ring bd. 85.00 (1-895411-06-8) Peguis Pubs Ltd.

*Lawson, Jennifer. Violent Weather Predictions, 2000-2001. LC 99-40795. 192p. 1999. 9.95 (1-56718-414-6) Llewellyn Pubns.

*Lawson, Jerry. The Complete Internet Handbk for Lawyers. LC 98-74962. 1999. pap. text 49.95 (1-57073-640-5, Pub. by Amer Bar Assn) IPG Chicago.

Lawson, Jerry. Not Always the Winter: The Human Side of Racial Prejudice. 223p. 1996. 16.00 (0-9652034-0-9) J Lawson.

Lawson, Jim & Laird, Peter. Planet Racers: Life Cycle. LC 99-176320. (Illus.). 300p. 1997. pap. 14.95 (0-9661985-0-6) Zeromayo Studios.

— Planet Racers: Off-Season. (Illus.). 175p. 1998. pap. 7.95 (0-9661985-1-4) Zeromayo Studios.

Lawson, Jimmie D. The Physics of Charged-Particle Beams. 2nd ed. (International Series of Monographs on Physics: No. 75). (Illus.). 472p. 1988. 135.00 (0-19-851719-X) OUP.

Lawson, Joan. Ballet Class. (Illus.). 126p. 1988. pap. 18.95 (0-87830-989-6, A2130, Thtre Arts Bks) Routledge.

— Beginning Ballet: From the Classroom to the Stage. 2nd ed. (Illus.). 96p. (J). (gr. 13). 1994. pap. 17.99 (0-87830-056-2, B4551) Routledge.

— European Folk Dance. LC 79-7773. (Dance Ser.). 1980. reprint ed. lib. bdg. 42.95 (0-8369-9300-4) Ayer.

— Teaching of Classical Ballet. 1985. 19.95 (0-87830-143-7) Routledge.

— The Teaching of Classical Ballet. 2nd ed. LC 73-83997. (Illus.). 1974. 19.95 (0-87830-583-1, Thtre Arts Bks) Routledge.

— Teaching Young Dancers: Muscular Coordination in Classical Ballet. LC 75-15369. (Illus.). 1975. 19.95 (0-87830-144-5, Thtre Arts Bks) Routledge.

Lawson, JoAnne, jt. auth. see Carter, Louise.

Lawson, John. The Affirmation of Life: A Reichian Energetic Perspective. LC 91-75113. 128p. 1991. pap. 7.95 (0-9630338-1-6) Ardengrove.

— The High Hills. LC 80-53537. (Illus.). 220p. (Orig.). 1981. pap. 4.95 (0-938658-01-8) West SW Pub Co.

— Introduction to Christian Doctrine. 1986. 18.95 (0-310-75020-2, 17026) Zondervan.

— A New Voyage to Carolina. Lefler, Hugh T., ed. LC 67-23498. liv, 305p. 1984. pap. 19.95 (0-8078-4126-9) U of NC Pr.

— The Spring Rider. LC 68-17079. (Illus.). 160p. (J). (gr. 3-7). 1990. lib. bdg. 12.89 (0-690-04785-1) HarpC Child Bks.

— The Spring Rider. LC 68-17079. (Trophy Bk.). 160p. (J). (gr. 3-7). 1990. reprint ed. pap. 3.50 (0-06-440349-1, HarpTrophy) HarpC Child Bks.

— A Vocabulary of Tuscarora, Vol. 6. LC 98-6752. (American Language Reprints Ser.: 6). (ENG & IRO.). 33p. 1998. 16.00 (0-9644234-9-9) Evol Pubng & Manuf.

— A Vocabulary of Woccon. LC 98-6750. (American Language Reprints Ser.: No. 7). 33p. 1998. 16.00 (1-889758-00-0) Evol Pubng & Manuf.

— The Wesley Hymns: As a Guide to Scriptural Teaching. 224p. 1988. reprint ed. 14.95 (0-310-75290-6, 17184) Zondervan.

L

An Asterisk (*) at the beginning of an entry indicates that the title is appearing for the first time.

L

— You Better Come Home with Me. LC 66-10059. 136p. (J). (gr. 3-7). 1990. lib. bdg. 12.89 (*0-690-04781-9*) HarpC Child Bks.

— You Better Come Home with Me. LC 66-10059. (Trophy Bk.). 136p. (J). (gr. 3-7). 1990. reprint ed. pap. 3.50 (*0-06-440350-5*, HarpTrophy) HarpC Child Bks.

Lawson, John D. Law of Expert & Opinion Evidence Reduced to Rules: With Illustrations from Adjudged Cases. lxxii, 595p. 1982. reprint ed. 55.00 (*0-8377-0813-3*, Rothman) W S Hein.

— Law of Presumptive Evidence: Including Presumptions Both of Law & of Fact & the Burden of Proof Both in Civil & Criminal Cases, Reduced to Rules. lxxxix, 648p. 1982. reprint ed. 52.00 (*0-8377-0812-5*, Rothman) W S Hein.

— Leading Cases Simplified: A Collection of the Leading Cases of the Common Law. (Illus.). xxvi, 327p. 1987. reprint ed. 42.00 (*0-8377-2406-6*, Rothman) W S Hein.

Lawson, John D., ed. American State Trials: Sixteen Fifty-Nine to Nineteen Twenty, 17 vols., Set. LC 74-182150. 1972. reprint ed. lib. bdg. 400.00 (*0-8420-0510-2*) Scholarly Res Inc.

Lawson, Jonathan N., ed. & intro. see Bloomfield, Robert.

Lawson, Joseph W., II. How to Develop an Employee Handbook. 2nd ed. LC 97-33531. 392p. 1997. spiral bd. 75.00 (*0-8144-7964-2*) AMACOM.

Lawson, Jospeh W., II. How to Develop a Personnel Policy Manual. 6th ed. 540p. 1998. 75.00 (*0-8144-7963-4*) AMACOM.

Lawson, Julie. Bear on the Train. (Illus.). 32p. (J). (ps-3). 1999. 15.95 (*1-55074-560-3*) Kids Can Pr.

— Blown Away. (Northern Lights Books for Children Ser.). (Illus.). 32p. (J). (ps-3). 1995. pap. 15.95 (*0-88995-119-5*, Pub. by Red Deer) Genl Dist Srvs.

— Cougar Cove. (Illus.). 144p. (J). (gr. 3-6). 1996. pap. 6.95 (*1-55143-072-X*) Orca Bk Pubs.

— The Dragon's Pearl. (Illus.). 32p. (J). (gr. k-3). 1993. 15.95 (*0-395-63623-X*, Clarion Bks) HM.

Lawson, Julie. Emma & the Silk Train. (J). 1997. pap. 5.95 (*1-55074-651-0*) Kids Can Pr.

Lawson, Julie. Emma & the Silk Train. (Illus.). 32p. (J). (gr. k-3). 1998. 15.95 (*1-55074-388-0*, Pub. by Kids Can Pr) Genl Dist Srvs.

***Lawson, Julie.** Goldstone. unabridged ed. 170p. (J). (gr. 5-9). 1998. pap. 6.95 (*0-7737-5891-7*) STDK.

Lawson, Julie. Kate's Castle. LC 98-226798. (Illus.). (ps-3). 1997. pap. text. write for info. (*0-7737-5899-2*) STDK.

— Kate's Castle. unabridged ed. (Illus.). 32p. (J). (gr. 1 up). 1994. pap. write for info. (*0-19-541001-7*) STDK.

— Midnight in the Mountains. LC 98-85282. (Illus.). 32p. (J). (gr. k-3). 1998. 14.95 (*1-55143-113-0*) Orca Bk Pubs.

— A Morning to Polish & Keep. (Illus.). 32p. (J). (ps-3). 1998. pap. 7.95 (*0-88995-179-9*, Pub. by Red Deer) Genl Dist Srvs.

— Too Many Suns. unabridged ed. (Illus.). 32p. (J). (gr. 1 up). 1997. 18.95 (*0-7737-2897-X*) STDK.

***Lawson, Julie.** Turns on a Dime. LC 97-930656. (Goldstone Trilogy Ser.). 173p. 1999. pap. 6.95 (*0-7737-5942-5*) Stoddart Publ.

Lawson, Julie & McKenzie, Ray, eds. Photography, 1900. (Illus.). 111p. 1992. pap. text 22.50 (*0-903598-45-0*, 8450, Pub. by Ashmolean Mus) A Schwartz & Co.

Lawson, Julie & Morin, Paul. The Dragon's Pearl. 32p. 1992. write for info. (*0-19-540843-8*) OUP.

Lawson, K. H. Analysis & Ideology: Conceptual Essays on the Education of Adults. 100p. (C). 1983. text 75.00 (*0-7855-3190-4*, Pub. by Univ Nottingham) St Mut.

— Philosophical Issues in the Education of Adults. 150p. 1997. 29.95 (*1-85041-085-2*, Pub. by U of Nottingham) St Mut.

Lawson, Karen. The Art of Influencing. LC 96-78301. 164p. 1996. per., boxed set 23.95 (*0-7872-2990-3*) Kendall-Hunt.

— Improving Workplace Performance Through Coaching. Miller, Karen M., ed. LC 96-79982. (How-To Book Ser.). 95p. (Orig.). 1996. pap. 12.95 (*1-884926-39-8*, COACH) Amer Media.

— Train the Trainer: Instructor's Guide. 192p. 1998. teacher ed., ring bd. 99.95 (*0-7879-3990-0*) Jossey-Bass.

— The Trainer's Handbook. LC 98-5369. 256p. 1998. pap. 39.95 (*0-7879-3991-9*) Jossey-Bass.

Lawson, Karen, jt. auth. see Silberman, Melvin L.

Lawson, Karol & Foley, Brigitte. The Art of Teaching: Regional Faculty Invitational. Young, Becky, ed. (Illus.). 32p. 1998. pap. 5.00 (*1-882650-08-5*) Colmbs Mus GA.

Lawson, Kate, ed. see Heller, Ann.

Lawson, Kay. The Human Polity: An Introduction to Political Science. 2nd ed. 1988. teacher ed. write for info. (*0-318-63319-1*) HM.

Lawson, Kay, ed. How Political Parties Work: Perspectives from Within. LC 93-23674. 336p. 1994. 67.95 (*0-275-94393-3*, Praeger Pubs) Greenwood.

— Political Parties & Linkage: A Comparative Perspective. LC 79-26751. 416p. reprint ed. pap. 129.00 (*0-7837-4532-X*, 208021600003) Bks Demand.

Lawson, Kay & Merkl, Peter H., eds. When Parties Fail: Emerging Alternative Organizations. LC 87-22566. 605p. 1988. reprint ed. pap. 187.60 (*0-608-03755-9*, 206457800009) Bks Demand.

Lawson, Kay, ed. see Karasimeonov, Georgi.

***Lawson, Ken.** KISS Guide to Managing Your Career. (Illus.). 352p. 2000. pap. 18.95 (*0-7894-6138-2*) DK Pub Inc.

Lawson, Ken, jt. auth. see Matthew, Stewart.

Lawson, Ken, jt. auth. see Matthews, Stewart.

Lawson, Kenneth. Analysis & Idealogy. (C). 1982. 110.00 (*0-902031-77-5*, Pub. by Univ Nottingham) St Mut.

***Lawson, Kristan.** California Babylon: A Guide to Sites of Scandal, Mayhem & Celluloid in the Golden State. (Illus.). 272p. 2000. pap. 15.95 (*0-312-26385-6*) St Martin.

Lawson, Kristan. The Rules of Speed Chess. LC 92-73541. (Illus.). 56p. (Orig.). 1992. pap. 5.95 (*0-9634205-7-7*) J Roger Pr.

Lawson, Kristan & Rufus, Anneli. Weird Europe: A Guide to Bizarre, Macabre & Just Plain Weird Sights. 2nd ed. LC 99-10047. 2000. pap. 14.95 (*0-312-19873-6*, Pub. by Tor Bks) St Martin.

Lawson, L. & Hardy, H. The Town They Called the World Charters Towers. Roderick, Don, ed. 64p. (C). 1990. 69.00 (*0-908175-94-9*, Pub. by Boolarong Pubns) St Mut.

Lawson, L., jt. auth. see Redmond, R.

Lawson, L. L. & Rushforth, S. R. The Diatom Flora of the Provo River, Utah, U. S. A. 1975. 40.00 (*3-7682-0955-5*) Lubrecht & Cramer.

Lawson, Larry D. & Bauer, Rudolph, eds. Phytomedicines of Europe: Chemistry & Biological Activity. (ACS Symposium Ser.: No. 691). (Illus.). 336p. 1998. text 125.00 (*0-8412-3559-7*) OUP.

Lawson, Larry D., jt. auth. see Koch, Heinrich P.

Lawson, Laura. Lamb Problems: Detecting, Diagnosing, Treating. rev. ed. LC 92-7300. (Illus.). 264p. (Orig.). 1996. pap. 29.95 (*0-9633923-0-1*) LDF Pubns.

— Managing Your Ewe: And Her Newborn Lambs. rev. ed. LC 93-79480. (Illus.). 352p. (Orig.). 1997. pap. 34.95 (*0-9633923-1-X*) LDF Pubns.

— Showing Sheep: Select, Feed, Fit & Show. rev. ed. LC 94-78838. (Illus.). 224p. (Orig.). 1996. pap. 12.95 (*0-9633923-2-8*) LDF Pubns.

Lawson, Laurie. Down the Rio Grande 1829. (American Sisters Ser.: Vol. 6). 208p. (J). (gr. 4-7). 1909. 9.00 (*0-671-03922-9*, Minstrel Bks) PB.

***Lawson, Lee.** Visitations from the Afterlife: True Stories of Love & Healing. LC 00-26196. 2000. pap. write for info. (*0-06-251654-X*) Harper SF.

— Visitations From the Afterlife: True Stories of Love & Healing. 224p. 2000. 22.00 (*0-06-251653-1*) HarpC.

Lawson, Leonard. Down 25 Walks. Smith, Roger, ed. (Twenty-Five Walks Ser.). (Illus.). 112p. 1997. pap. 16.95 (*0-11-495773-8*, Pub. by Statnry Office) Seven Hills Bk.

Lawson, Leroy. Family of God: The Meaning of Church Membership. 1997. pap. text 4.99 incl. VHS (*0-89900-703-1*, GN-260) College Pr Pub.

Lawson, LeRoy. Questions for God. 146p. (C). 1990. pap. 6.99 (*0-89900-414-8*) College Pr Pub.

***Lawson, LeRoy.** Roadworthy: Gearing up for the Race. Hayes, Theresa, ed. 160p. 2000. 7.99 (*0-7847-7099-9*, 09019) Standard Pub.

Lawson, Lewis A. Following Percy: Essays on Walker Percy's Work. LC 87-61269. viii, 245p. 1988. 35.00 (*0-87875-345-1*) Whitston Pub.

Lawson, Lewis A. Still Following Percy. LC 95-16820. 256p. 1995. 37.50 (*0-87805-826-5*) U Pr of Miss.

Lawson, Lewis A. & Kramer, Victor A., eds. Conversations with Walker Percy. LC 84-40715. (Literary Conversations Ser.). 240p. 1985. pap. 15.95 (*0-87805-252-6*) U Pr of Miss.

— More Conservations with Walker Percy. LC 92-44968. (Literary Conversations Ser.). 288p. 1993. pap. 16.95 (*0-87805-624-6*); text 39.50 (*0-87805-623-8*) U Pr of Miss.

Lawson, Lewis A. & Oleksy, Elzbieta, eds. Walker Percy's Feminine Characters. vi, 141p. 1995. 35.00 (*0-87875-456-3*) Whitston Pub.

Lawson, Lewis A., jt. ed. see Friedman, Melvin J.

Lawson, Linda. Truth in Publishing: Federal Regulation of the Press's Business Practices, 1880-1920. LC 92-34828. 224p. (C). 1993. 31.95 (*0-8093-1829-6*) S Ill U Pr.

***Lawson, Lori & Johnson, Rob.** Green Flash. 2000. pap. 14.95 (*0-939837-36-6*) Paradise Cay Pubns.

Lawson, Lynda. Staying Ahead Activity Book. 72p. 1997. pap. text 10.95 (*0-521-57817-5*) Cambridge U Pr.

Lawson, Lynn. Staying Well in a Toxic World: Understanding Environmental Illness, Multiple Chemical Sensitivities, Chemical Injuries, & Sick Building Syndrome. LC 96-94641. 488p. (Orig.). 1996. pap. 15.95 (*0-9653659-0-5*) Lynnwrd Pr.

Lawson, M. Maths & Statistics for Business. 1995. pap. 18.95 (*0-582-23187-6*) Addison-Wesley.

Lawson, M. & Skip, D. Sexo y Mas.Tr. of Sex & That. (SPA.). 1988. 3.99 (*0-8423-6521-4*, 490249) Editorial Unilit.

Lawson, M. & Skipp, D. Sexo y Mas.Tr. of Sex & That. (SPA.). 112p. 1988. pap. write for info. (*0-614-27139-8*) Editorial Unilit.

Lawson, M. K. Cnut. LC 92-12808. (Medieval World Ser.). (C). 1992. text 53.75 (*0-582-05969-0*, 79461) Longman.

— CNUT:Danes England Early 11 Century. LC 92-12808. (Medieval World Ser.). (C). 1995. pap. text 30.00 (*0-582-05970-4*, 79460) Addson-Wesley Educ.

Lawson, Margaret. Macro Cafe Cookbook: Macrobiotic Cooking Made Easy. 1997. pap. 12.95 (*0-9660712-0-4*) Lawson Pubns.

Lawson, Margaret & Monte, Tom. Naturally Healthy Gourmet: Secrets of Quick, Tasty, & Wholesome Cooking. Ruggles, Laurel, ed. LC 94-76116. 232p. (Orig.). 1994. pap. 14.95 (*0-918860-53-9*) G Ohsawa.

Lawson, Mark. Bloody Margaret: Three Political Fantasies LC 93-157348. 374 p. 1992. write for info. (*0-330-32387-3*) Mcm Child Bks.

— John Keane. (Illus.). 120p. 1996. 40.00 (*1-85158-752-7*, Pub. by Mainstream Pubng) Trafalgar.

Lawson, Mark V. Inverse Semigroups: The Theory of Partial Symmetries. 250p. 1998. 38.00 (*981-02-3316-7*) World Scientific Pub.

Lawson, Mattie. From Colored Water till Now. 176p. (Orig.). 1994. mass mkt. 3.95 (*0-87067-394-7*) Holloway.

Lawson, Merlin P. & Baker, Maurice E., eds. The Great Plains: Perspectives & Prospects. LC 80-10962. 294p. reprint ed. pap. 91.20 (*0-8357-3805-1*, 203653300003) Bks Demand.

Lawson, Merlin P., jt. ed. see Blouet, Brian W.

***Lawson, Michael.** Conflict: How It Happens, How to Stop It. 1999. pap. text 7.99 (*1-85792-528-9*) Christian Focus.

Lawson, Michael. Damned Indians: The Pick-Sloan Plan & the Missouri River Sioux, 1944-1980. LC 81-19721. (Illus.). 300p. 1994. pap. 15.95 (*0-8061-2672-8*) U of Okla Pr.

— How to Make More Profit. 200p. 1996. pap. 29.95 (*0-566-07762-0*, Pub. by Gower) Ashgate Pub Co.

Lawson, Michael & Skipp, David. Sexo y Mas: Guia Para la Juventud. (SPA., Illus.). 110p. (Orig.). (YA). (gr. 10-12). 1988. pap. 2.95 (*0-945792-02-6*) Editorial Unilit.

Lawson, Michael S. & Choun, Robert J., Jr. Christian Education for the Twenty-First Century. 416p. 2000. pap. 13.99 (*0-8254-2348-1*) Kregel.

— Directing Christian Education: The Changing Role of the Christian Education Specialist. pap. 19.99 (*0-8024-1702-7*, 128) Moody.

Lawson, Michael S., jt. auth. see Choun, Robert J.

***Lawson, Mike.** Fly Fishing the Henry's Fork. LC 00-29406. (River Book Ser.: Vol. 2). (Illus.). 2000. pap. write for info. (*1-890373-09-5*, Pub. by Greycliff Pub) Baker & Taylor.

Lawson, Myldred. Big Black Buzzard & Little Rabbit. Rowden, Thomas, tr. (Illus.). 32p. (Orig.). (J). (ps-5). 1994. pap. text, per. 5.95 (*0-9642481-1-5*) NE Texas Pub.

***Lawson, Nigella.** How to Eat: The Pleasures & Principles of Good Food. LC 99-57439. 496p. 2000. pap. 35.00 (*0-471-34830-9*) Wiley.

Lawson, Nigella. Il Museo Immaginario Della Pasta: The "musee Imaginaire" of Pasta. LC 96-160542. (ITA., Illus.). 170p. 1998. 75.00 (*88-422-0544-3*) Allemandi.

Lawson, P. V. Fleming Family & Allied Lines: Baird, Blair, Butler, Cook, Childs, Clark, Cole, Crane, et al. 304p. 1992. reprint ed. pap. 46.50 (*0-8328-2316-3*); reprint ed. lib. bdg. 56.50 (*0-8328-2315-5*) Higginson Bk Co.

Lawson, Patricia. The Tangled Garden. large type ed. 608p. 1986. 27.99 (*0-7089-8357-X*) Ulverscroft.

***Lawson, Paul D.** Old Wine in New Skins: Centering Prayer & Systems Theory - Congregational Leadership for the Next Millennium. 2000. pap. 20.00 (*1-930051-29-8*) Lantern Books.

Lawson, Paul E. Solving Somebody Else's Blues: A Study of Police Mediation Activities. LC 81-40881. (Illus.). 246p. (Orig.). 1982. pap. text 23.00 (*0-8191-2174-6*) U Pr of Amer.

Lawson-Peebles, R., jt. ed. see Gidley, M.

Lawson-Peebles, Robert, ed. Approaches to the American Musical. 192p. 1995. pap. 19.95 (*0-85989-405-3*, Pub. by Univ Exeter Pr) Northwestern U Pr.

Lawson-Peebles, Robert, jt. ed. see Gidley, Mick.

Lawson, Peter R. Selected Papers on Long Baseline Stellar Interferometry. LC 97-26616. (Milestone Ser.). 1997. write for info. (*0-8194-2672-5*) SPIE.

Lawson, Peter W., et al. Potential Effects of Selective Fishing on Stock Composition Estimates from the Mixed-Stock Model: Application of a High-Dimension Selective Fisheries Model. 26p. 1997. reprint ed. pap. 3.60 (*0-89904-588-X*, Cascade Geog Soc) Crumb Elbow Pub.

Lawson, Philip. East India Company. LC 92-44920. (Studies in Modern History). (C). 1993. text 58.50 (*0-582-07386-3*, 79776, Pub. by Addison-Wesley) Longman.

— East India Company: A History. LC 92-44920. (Studies in Modern History). 188p. (C). 1995. pap. 39.06 (*0-582-07385-5*, 79775) Longman.

— The Imperial Challenge: Quebec & Britain in the Age of the American Revolution. 208p. (C). 1989. text 65.00 (*0-7735-0698-5*, Pub. by McG-Queens Univ Pr) CUP Services.

— The Imperial Challenge: Quebec & Britain in the Age of the American Revolution. 208p. (C). 1994. pap. text 24.95 (*0-7735-1205-5*, Pub. by McG-Queens Univ Pr) CUP Services.

***Lawson, Philip.** Muskrat Courage. LC 00-24756. 288p. 2000. text 23.95 (*0-312-26207-8*, Minotaur) St Martin.

Lawson, Philip. Would It Kill You to Smile? LC 98-66372. 208p. 1998. 22.00 (*1-56352-511-9*) Longstreet.

Lawson, Philip, ed. Parliament & the Atlantic Empire. 130p. 1996. pap. 23.00 (*0-7486-0628-9*, Pub. by Edinburgh U Pr) Col U Pr.

Lawson, Philip, et al. A Taste for Empire & Glory: Studies in British Overseas Expansion, 1600-1800. LC 96-37233. (Collected Studies: No. CS563). 320p. 1997. text 97.95 (*0-86078-636-6*, Pub. by Variorum) Ashgate Pub Co.

Lawson, Philip J. Lawson Perspective Charts. rev. ed. 1940. text 39.95 (*0-442-13053-8*, VNR) Wiley.

Lawson, Polly. Sam Luckless. (J). pap. 14.95 (*0-86315-126-4*, 1470, Pub. by Floris Bks) Anthroposophic.

Lawson, Polly, tr. see Berger, Thomas.

Lawson, Polly, tr. see Leeuwen, M. & Moeskops, J.

Lawson, Polly, tr. see Lesch, Christiane.

Lawson, Publius V., et al, eds. History of Winnebago County: Its Cities, Towns, Resources, People, 2 vols. (Illus.). 1208p. 1997. reprint ed. lib. bdg. 124.00 (*0-8328-6988-0*) Higginson Bk Co.

Lawson, R. Exclusion Clauses. (C). 1983. 230.00 (*0-7855-4173-X*, Pub. by Witherby & Co) St Mut.

Lawson, R. Measuring 6 Sigma & Beyond. 1997. pap. 10.00 (*1-56946-023-X*) Motorola Univ.

Lawson, R. A. & Schermers, H. G., eds. Leading Cases of the European Court of Human Rights. annot. ed. xv, 788p. 1997. pap. 55.50 (*90-6215-555-9*, Pub. by Maklu Uitgev) Gaunt.

Lawson, R. C. An Open Letter to a Southern White Minister on Prejudice: The Eating Cancer of the Soul. 24p. 1995. pap. 3.50 (*1-887939-01-6*, Ohio Minist) VisionQuest Media.

Lawson, R. D. Theory of the Nuclear Shell Model. (OSNP). (Illus.). 546p. (C). 1980. text 125.00 (*0-19-851516-2*) OUP.

Lawson, R. G. & Smith, D. Business Law. 2nd ed. 208p. 1992. pap. 34.95 (*0-7506-0375-5*) Buttrwrth-Heinemann.

Lawson, Richard. Bills of Health. LC 96-13782. 1996. write for info. (*1-85775-101-9*, Radcliffe Med Pr) Scovill Paterson.

Lawson, Richard A. & Mavigliano, George J. Fred E. Myers, Wood-Carver. LC 80-14243. (Illus.). 167p. 1980. 16.95 (*0-8093-0974-2*) S Ill U Pr.

Lawson, Richard A., jt. auth. see Mavigliano, George J.

Lawson, Richard H., ed. New Anthology of Contemporary Austrian Folk Plays. (Studies in Austrian Literature, Culture, & Thought). 364p. (Orig.). 1996. pap. 26.50 (*1-57241-020-5*) Ariadne CA.

— Seven Contemporary Austrian Plays. LC 95-14086. (Studies in Austrian Literature, Culture, & Thought). 284p. 1995. pap. 24.50 (*1-57241-017-5*) Ariadne CA.

Lawson, Richard H., jt. ed. see Berlin, Jeffrey B.

Lawson, Richard H., tr. & intro. see Hermann, Brother.

Lawson, Rick, ed. The Dynamics of the Protection of Human Rights in Europe: Essays in Honour of Henry G. Schermers, Vol. III. 440p. (C). 1994. lib. bdg. 169.50 (*0-7923-3161-3*, Pub. by M Nijhoff) Kluwer Academic.

Lawson, Robert. Ben & Me: A New & Astonishing Life of Benjamin Franklin as Written by His Good Mouse Amos. LC 87-33549. (J). 1988. 11.05 (*0-606-03968-6*, Pub. by Turtleback) Demco.

— Ben & Me An Astonishing Life of Benjamin Franklin as Written by His Good Mouse... (J). 1999. pap. write for info. (*0-316-52520-0*) Little.

— Ben & Me An Astonishing Life of Benjamin Franklin as Written by His Mouse... (J). 1999. write for info. (*0-316-52533-2*) Little.

— Ben & Me: An Astonishing Life of Benjamin Franklin by His Good Mouse Amos. (Illus.). 114p. (J). (gr. 7-10). 1939. 16.95 (*0-316-51732-1*) Little.

— Ben & Me: An Astonishing Life of Benjamin Franklin by His Good Mouse Amos. (Illus.). 114p. (J). (gr. 3-7). 1988. pap. 5.95 (*0-316-51730-5*) Little.

— Captain Kidd's Cat. (Illus.). (J). (gr. 2-4). 1984. mass mkt. 7.95 (*0-316-51735-6*) Little.

***Lawson, Robert.** Carrier Air Group Commanders: Men & Their Machines. (Illus.). 208p. 2000. 45.00 (*0-7643-1035-6*) Schiffer.

Lawson, Robert. The Fabulous Flight. (Illus.). 152p. (J). (gr. 4-8). 1984. mass mkt. 5.95 (*0-316-51731-3*) Little.

— The Great Wheel. LC 92-19992. (Illus.). 180p. (J). (gr. 4-7). 1993. pap. 7.95 (*0-8027-7392-3*) Walker & Co.

— Great Wheel. (Newbery Honor Roll Ser.). (J). 1993. 13.05 (*0-606-02657-6*, Pub. by Turtleback) Demco.

— The Kentucky Evidence Handbook. 3rd ed. 744p. 1993. text 95.00 (*0-327-03915-9*, 64252-10, MICHIE) LEXIS Pub.

— Mr. Revere & I. (Illus.). 152p. (J). (gr. 3-6). 1988. pap. 5.95 (*0-316-51729-1*) Little.

— Rabbit Hill. (Illus.). (J). (ps-3). 1944. 16.99 (*0-670-58675-7*, Viking Child) Peng Put Young Read.

— Rabbit Hill. (Illus.). (J). (gr. 1-3). 1977. pap. 4.99 (*0-14-031010-X*, PuffinBks) Peng Put Young Read.

— Rabbit Hill. (J). 1977. 9.60 (*0-606-02235-X*, Pub. by Turtleback) Demco.

— Rabbit Hill. large type ed. (J). (gr. 4-6). reprint ed. 10.00 (*0-89064-076-9*) NAVH.

— Upton-on-Severn Words & Phrases. (English Dialect Society Publications: No. 42). 1974. reprint ed. pap. 25.00 (*0-8115-0468-9*) Periodicals Srv.

Lawson, Robert & Murphy, Gene. The Black Pursuit Study Guide. LC 85-73098. 281p. 1985. pap. 19.95 (*0-935979-00-X*) Prof Dynamics.

— Yes We Can! Black Achievement. 320p. 1995. boxed set 49.95 (*0-7872-0575-3*) Kendall-Hunt.

Lawson, Robert & Shen, Zheng. Organizational Psychology: Foundations & Applications. LC 96-29599. (Illus.). 288p. (C). 1997. text 57.95 (*0-19-511069-2*) OUP.

Lawson, Robert & Tillman, Barrett. Carrier Air War: U. S. Navy Air Combat 1939-1946. LC 96-718. (Illus.). 176p. 1996. 29.95 (*0-87938-983-4*) MBI Pubg.

Lawson, Robert, jt. auth. see Leaf, Munro.

Lawson, Robert, ed. & intro. see Buckman, Repha.

Lawson, Robert F., jt. ed. see Lawson, Carol S.

Lawson, Robert F., jt. ed. see Lawson, Carol.

Lawson, Robert G. The Kentucky Evidence Law Handbook. 3rd ed. 744p. 95.00 (*0-327-10695-6*) LEXIS Pub.

Lawson, Robert G. The Kentucky Evidence Law Handbook. 3rd ed. (Kluwer Litigation Library). 744p. 1993. 95.00 (*1-55834-009-2*, MICHIE) LEXIS Pub.

— The Kentucky Evidence Law Handbook: With 1989 Supplement. 2nd ed. (State Practice Publications). 470p. 1993. pap., suppl. ed. 25.00 (*0-87473-476-2*, 64251-10, MICHIE) LEXIS Pub.

— The Kentucky Evidence Law Handbook, 1998 Cumulative Supplement. 3rd ed. 150p. 1998. suppl. ed. 45.00 (*0-327-00496-7*, 6425115) LEXIS Pub.

Lawson, Robert G., jt. auth. see Fortune, William H.

Lawson, Robert L. Destined for Greatness: Getting the Results You Desire from Yourself & Others. 160p. (Orig.). reprint ed. pap. text 9.95 (*0-935979-01-8*) Prof Dynamics.

Lawson, Robert N., ed. see Sadowski, Larry R., et al.

An Asterisk (*) at the beginning of an entry indicates that the title is appearing for the first time.

Lawson, Robert W. Teletraffic Concepts in Corporate Communications. (Traffic Ser.). (Illus.). 220p. 1989. pap. 39.95 (*1-56016-042-X*) ABC TeleTraining.

Lawson, Robert W., tr. see Einstein, Albert.

Lawson, Rose Mary. Shaker Paper Dolls. (Illus.). 16p. (Orig.). (J). (gr. 2-5). 1998. pap. 5.00 (*0-9655018-2-5*) Knot Grdn Pr.

Lawson, Rowena. Allen County, Kentucky, Censuses, 1820-1840. iii, 51p. (Orig.). 1987. pap. 8.00 (*1-55613-031-7*) Heritage Bk.

— Bath County Kentucky: 1820-1840 Censuses. iv, 67p. (Orig.). 1986. pap. 10.00 (*0-917890-88-4*) Heritage Bk.

— Boone County Kentucky: 1810-1840 Censuses. iv, 68p. (Orig.). 1986. pap. 10.00 (*0-917890-79-5*) Heritage Bk.

— Boone County Kentucky: 1850 Census. iv, 93p. (Orig.). 1986. pap. 12.50 (*0-917890-80-9*) Heritage Bk.

— The Economics of Fisheries Development. LC 84-15074. 296p. 1984. 52.95 (*0-275-91213-2*, C1213, Praeger Pubs) Greenwood.

— Nelson County, Kentucky, 1850 Census. iv, 88p. (Orig.). 1985. pap. 12.50 (*0-917890-60-4*) Heritage Bk.

— Nicholas County Kentucky, 1850 Census: 1850 Census. iv, 92p. (Orig.). 1983. pap. 12.50 (*0-917890-34-5*) Heritage Bk.

— Ohio County Kentucky: 1850 Census. iv, 87p. (Orig.). 1984. pap. 12.50 (*0-917890-40-X*) Heritage Bk.

Lawson, Rowena, jt. auth. see Crutchfield, James A.

Lawson, Rowena M. The Changing Economy of the Lower Volta, 1954-1967: A Study in the Dynamics of Rural Economic Growth. LC 72-177589. 139p. reprint ed. pap. 43.10 (*0-8357-3013-1*, 205709900010) Bks Demand.

Lawson, Russell K., jt. ed. see Lepor, Herbert.

Lawson, Russell M. The American Plutarch: Jeremy Belknap & the Historian's Dialogue with the Past. LC 98-12155. 184p. 1998. 55.00 (*0-275-96336-5*, Praeger Pubs) Greenwood.

Lawson, Ruth C., compiled by. Homelessness - A Journey Down Homeless Avenue. 66p. 1991. pap. write for info. (*0-9632210-0-0*) R C Lawson.

Lawson, Sarah, tr. & intro. see De Pisan, Christine.

Lawson, Sheryl D., jt. auth. see Adams, Peter B.

Lawson, Stephanie. The Failure of Democratic Politics in Fiji. (Illus.). 322p. 1991. text 75.00 (*0-19-827322-3*) OUP.

— Tradition Versus Democracy in the South Pacific: Fiji, Tonga & Western Samoa. (Asia-Pacific Studies: No. 2). (Illus.). 240p. (C). 1996. text 64.95 (*0-521-49638-1*) Cambridge U Pr.

Lawson, Stephanie, ed. New Agenda for Global Security: The Cooperating for Peace & Beyond. LC 96-154501. 217p. 1996. pap. 24.95 (*1-86373-974-2*, Pub. by Allen & Unwin Pty) Paul & Co Pubs.

Lawson, Steve. The Legacy. LC 97-36396. (What Every Father Wants to Leave His Child Ser.). 216p. 1998. 12.99 (*1-57673-329-7*) Multnomah Pubs.

***Lawson, Steven F.** Black Ballots: Voting Rights in the South, 1944-1969. LC 99-46219. 496p. 1999. pap. 26.95 (*0-7391-0087-4*) Lxngtn Bks.

Lawson, Steven F. In Pursuit of Power: Southern Blacks & Electoral Politics 1965-1982. LC 84-17036. (Contemporary American History Ser.). 391p. 1987. pap. text 21.00 (*0-231-04627-8*) Col U Pr.

— Running for Freedom: Black Politics in White America. 2nd ed. LC 96-25931. 336p. (C). 1996. pap. 26.25 (*0-07-036801-5*) McGraw.

— Running for Freedom: Civil Rights & Black Politics in America. (C). 1991. pap. text 15.75 (*0-07-556975-2*) McGraw.

Lawson, Steven F. & Payne, Charles. Debating the Civil Rights Movement, 1945-1968. LC 98-39053. 160p. 1998. pap. 9.95 (*0-8476-9054-7*) Rowman.

— Debating the Civil Rights Movement, 1945-1968. LC 98-39033. 160p. 1999. 19.95 (*0-8476-9053-9*, Pub. by Rowman) Natl Bk Netwk.

Lawson, Steven J. Absolutely Sure: Settle the Question of Eternal Life. LC 99-12145. 1999. pap. 12.99 (*1-57673-409-9*) Multnomah Pubs.

— Cuando el Infierno Se Nos Viene Encima.Tr. of When All Hell Breaks Loose. (SPA.). 288p. 1996. 10.99 (*0-88113-428-7*, B031-4287) Caribe Betania.

— Faith under Fire: Standing Strong When Satan Attacks. LC 95-17308. 224p. 1995. 17.99 (*0-89107-847-9*) Crossway Bks.

— Final Call: It's Time for the Church to Wake up & Answer the Call! LC 94-7174. 224p. 1994. 15.99 (*0-89107-796-0*) Crossway Bks.

***Lawson, Steven J.** Made in Our Image: The Fallacy of the User-Friendly God. LC 00-8519. 220p. 2000. pap. 10.99 (*1-57673-610-5*, Pub. by Multnomah Pubs) GL Services.

Lawson, Suzy. Amish Patchwork: Full-Size Patterns for 46 Authentic Designs. (Illus.). 144p. 1988. reprint ed. pap. 7.95 (*0-486-25701-0*) Dover.

Lawson, T. V. Wind Effects on Buildings, Vol. 2: Statistics & Meteorology. (Illus.). 1980. pap. 74.50 (*0-85334-893-6*) Thomson Learn.

— Wind Loading Handbook: Guide to the Use of BS 6399, Pt. 2. LC 95-37496. 1996. text 59.95 (*0-7506-1094-8*) Buttrwrth-Heinemann.

Lawson-Tancred, Hugh, tr. The Art of Rhetoric. LC 92-208185. 304p. 1992. pap. 13.95 (*0-14-044510-2*, Penguin Classics) Viking Penguin.

Lawson-Tancred, Hugh, tr. & intro. see Aristotle.

Lawson, Ted. Understanding Alcoholism: A Starting Point for Families. LC 90-64269. 64p. 1991. pap. 3.95 (*0-89243-341-8*) Liguori Pubns.

Lawson, Ted W. Thirty Seconds over Tokyo. 290p. 1992. reprint ed. 35.95 (*0-89966-886-0*) Buccaneer Bks.

Lawson, Terry. How to Study the Word. LC 96-150526. 256p. 1994. 9.99 (*0-89274-695-5*, HH-695) Harrison Hse.

— Linear Algebra. LC 95-49808. 432p. 1996. text 92.95 (*0-471-30897-8*) Wiley.

Lawson, Terry & Emerson, William D. Mathematica Labs for Linear Algebra. LC 97-104051. 161p. 1996. pap., lab manual ed. 23.95 (*0-471-14952-7*) Wiley.

Lawson, Thomas, Jr. Logging Railroads of Alabama. LC 96-92823. (Illus.). 296p. 1997. 59.95 (*0-9666247-0-X*) Cabbage Stack Pub.

***Lawson, Thomas, Jr.** Logging Railroads of the Florida Panhandle. (Illus.). x, 175p. 2000. 50.00 (*0-9666247-2-6*) Cabbage Stack Pub.

Lawson, Thomas, Jr. Shay-the-Supplement. LC 98-93112. (Illus.). 96p. 1998. pap. 23.95 (*0-9666247-1-8*) Cabbage Stack Pub.

Lawson, Thomas, jt. auth. see McCollum, Allan.

Lawson, Thomas B. Fundamentals of Aquacultural Engineering. LC 93-38073. 1994. 59.95 (*0-442-23772-3*) Chapman & Hall.

Lawson, Thomas L., et al. Diagnostic Ultrasonography (Second Series) Test & Syllabus. LC 94-16701. (Professional Self-Evaluation Program Ser.: Vol. 38). (Illus.). 940p. 1994. 220.00 (*1-55903-038-0*) Am Coll Radiology.

Lawson, Thomas L., jt. auth. see Wagner, Marvin.

Lawson, Thomas L., jt. ed. see Middleton, William D.

Lawson, Tom. Building Aerodynamics. 300p. 1999. 68.00 (*1-86094-187-7*) World Scientific Pub.

Lawson, Tom, contrib. by. A Fatal Attraction: Art & the Media. (Illus.). 20p. 1982. 10.00 (*0-941548-03-1*) Ren Soc U Chi.

Lawson, Tom, ed. see Rotherham, J. B., et al.

Lawson, Tom E. Formative Instructional Product Evaluation: Instruments & Strategies. LC 73-22336. 132p. 1974. pap. 34.95 (*0-87778-068-4*) Educ Tech Pubns.

Lawson, Tony. Economics & Reality. LC 96-16352. (Economics as Social Theory Ser.). 384p. (C). 1997. write for info. (*0-415-15420-0*); pap. 27.99 (*0-415-15421-9*) Routledge.

Lawson, Tony, et al, eds. Kaldor's Political Economy. 283p. 1989. text 48.00 (*0-12-439640-2*) Acad Pr.

Lawson, Tony & Pesaran, Hashem, eds. Keynes' Economics: Methodological Issues. LC 85-1722. 271p. 1985. reprint ed. pap. 84.10 (*0-7837-9983-7*, 206071000006) Bks Demand.

Lawson, V. Paul Laurence Dunbar, Critically Examined. 1972. 59.95 (*0-8490-0808-5*) Gordon Pr.

Lawson, V. K. Thinking Is a Basic Skill: Creating Humanities Materials for the Adult New Reader. 55p. 1988. pap. text 5.00 (*0-930713-33-8*) Lit Vol Am.

Lawson, V. K., ed. Read On! Two. 60p. 1987. pap. text 10.00 (*0-930713-01-X*); pap. text, teacher ed. 5.50 (*0-930713-20-6*); pap. text, teacher ed. 2.00 (*0-930713-21-4*) Lit Vol Am.

— Read On! Two, Set. 60p. 1987. pap. text 45.00 (*0-930713-00-1*); 50.00 (*0-930713-46-X*) Lit Vol Am.

— READ Trainer's Kit. 1982. 20.00 incl. audio (*0-930713-40-0*) Lit Vol Am.

Lawson, V. K. & MacDonald, Barbara J., eds. Core Library for Literacy - Conversational English Programs: A Bibliography. 34p. 1984. pap. text 5.00 (*0-930713-35-4*) Lit Vol Am.

Lawson, V. K., et al. Read All About It - Tutor Adults with Daily Newspaper: Tutor Handbook. 95p. 1984. pap. text 4.00 (*0-930713-31-1*) Lit Vol Am.

Lawson, V. K., ed. see Colvin, Ruth J. & Root, Jane.

Lawson, V. K., ed. see Coville, Bruce & Lee, Artis.

Lawson, V. K., ed. see Lee, Artis.

Lawson, V. K., ed. see Lee, Artis & Elmore, Fred.

Lawson, V. K., ed. see Lee, Artis & Simmons, Judy D.

Lawson, V. K., ed. see Lee, Artis, et al.

Lawson, V. K., ed. see Literacy Volunteers Computer Task Force Staff.

Lawson, V. K., ed. see LVA Basic Reading Task Force Staff.

Lawson, V. K., ed. see Price, Margaret, et al.

Lawson, V. K., ed. see Simmons, Judy D. & Lee, Artis.

Lawson, V. K., ed. see Trabert, Judith A. & McKallip, Jonathan.

Lawson, V. K., ed. see Williams, Margaret, et al.

Lawson, Victoria, jt. auth. see Hilbert, Sarah.

Lawson, Victoria, jt. auth. see Hillbert, Sarah.

Lawson, W., jt. auth. see Mayergoyz, I. D.

Lawson, W., jt. auth. see Zak, F. G.

***Lawson, Wendy.** Life Behind Glass: A Personal Account of Autism Spectrum Disorder. LC 00-40567. 2000. write for info. (*1-85302-911-4*, Pub. by Jessica Kingsley) Taylor & Francis.

Lawson, Wes, ed. Advanced Accelerator Concepts: Eighth Workshop. (AIP Conference Proceedings Ser.: Vol. 472). (Illus.). 1052p. 1999. 250.00 (*1-56396-889-4*) Am Inst Physics.

Lawson, Will. Pacific Steamers. (C). 1987. 96.00 (*0-85174-245-9*) St Mut.

Lawson, William, et al. Diseases of the External Ear. 3rd ed. (Illus.). 352p. 1995. text 90.00 (*0-7216-5667-6*, W B Saunders Co) Harcrt Hlth Sci Grp.

Lawson, Winston. Religion & Race: African & European Roots in Conflict - a Jamaican Testament. (Research in Religion & Family Ser.: Vol. 4). 240p. (C). 1996. pap. text 29.95 (*0-8204-3093-5*) P Lang Pubng.

Lawston, Lisa. Can You Hop? LC 98-67079. (Illus.). 22p. (J). (ps). 1999. 5.95 (*0-531-30131-1*) Orchard Bks Watts.

— Can You Sing? LC 98-67080. (Illus.). 22p. (J). (ps). 1999. 5.95 (*0-531-30132-X*) Orchard Bks Watts.

— A Pair of Red Sneakers. LC 98-10481. (Illus.). 32p. (J). (ps-2). 1998. 15.95 (*0-531-30104-4*); lib. bdg. 16.99 (*0-531-33104-0*) Orchard Bks Watts.

Lawther, Betty C. Woman - Aware & Choosing: Keys to Healthy Relationships. 2nd rev. ed. LC 98-215447. 262p. 1998. pap. 12.95 (*0-9665115-2-2*) Minmar Press.

Lawther, Christopher, jt. auth. see Lawther, Gail.

Lawther, Gail. Celtic Cross Stitch: 30 Alphabet, Animal, & Knotwork Projects. LC 95-25749. (Illus.). 128p. 1996. 26.95 (*0-89577-859-9*, Pub. by RD Assn) Penguin Putnam.

— Inspirational Ideas for Embroidery. 96p. 1997. pap. 24.95 (*0-85532-711-1*, Pub. by Srch Pr) A Schwartz & Co.

***Lawther, Gail & Lawther, Christopher.** Introducing Cross Stitch. 1999. pap. 24.00 (*1-85608-389-6*, Pub. by Hunt GBR) St Mut.

Lawther, P., et al. Epidemiology of Air Pollution: Report on a Symposium. (Public Health Papers: No. 15). 31p. 1962. pap. text 1.00 (*92-4-130015-9*, 1110015) World Health.

***Lawther, Wendell C.** Privatizing Toll Roads: A Public-Private Partnership. LC 99-54744. (Privatizing Government). 232p. 2000. 67.50 (*0-275-96900-2*, C6900, Praeger Pubs) Greenwood.

***Lawton.** The Built Environment. 208p. 2000. pap. text 34.95 (*0-7506-4085-5*) Buttrwrth-Heinemann.

Lawton. Essentials of Gynaecological Care. 392p. 1999. pap. text 49.50 (*0-412-79290-7*, Pub. by E A) OUP.

— Judaism. 1991. pap. text. write for info. (*0-582-02969-4*, Pub. by Addison-Wesley) Longman.

— A Lovely Country. 1996. pap. 12.00 (*0-15-600466-6*) Harcourt.

Lawton, ed. Judaism. 1990. pap. write for info. (*0-582-31790-8*) Addison-Wesley.

Lawton, jt. auth. see Kelly.

Lawton, jt. auth. see Lawton, William.

Lawton, Alan. Ethical Management for the Public Services. LC 98-9696. (Managing the Public Services Ser.). 167p. 1998. 92.00 (*0-335-19920-8*); pap. 29.95 (*0-335-19919-4*) OpUniv Pr.

Lawton, Alan & McKevitt, David, eds. Case Studies in Public Services Management. (Illus.). 200p. (Orig.). (C). 1996. pap. 40.95 (*0-631-19579-3*) Blackwell Pubs.

Lawton, Alan, jt. auth. see Rose, Aidan.

Lawton, Alan, jt. ed. see McKevitt, David.

Lawton, Anna. Kinoglasnost: Soviet Cinema in Our Time. (Cambridge Soviet Paperbacks Ser.: No. 9). (Illus.). 304p. (C). 1992. pap. text 22.95 (*0-521-38814-7*) Cambridge U Pr.

— Kinoglasnost: Soviet Cinema in Our Time. (Cambridge Soviet Paperbacks Ser.: No. 9). (Illus.). 304p. (C). 1993. text 59.95 (*0-521-38117-7*) Cambridge U Pr.

Lawton, Anna, ed. The Red Screen: Politics, Society, Art in Soviet Cinema. LC 91-33268. 352p. 1992. 67.50 (*0-415-07818-0*, A8196) Routledge.

Lawton, Anna & Eagle, Herbert, eds. Russian Futurism Through Its Manifestos, 1912-1928. LC 88-47733. 320p. 1988. 49.95 (*0-8014-1883-6*); pap. text 18.95 (*0-8014-9492-3*) Cornell U Pr.

Lawton, B., jt. auth. see Klingenberg, G.

Lawton, Barbara P. The Magic of Irises. LC 97-40543. (Illus.). 192p. 1998. 39.95 (*1-55591-267-2*) Fulcrum Pub.

— Seasonal Guide to the Natural Year: Illinois, Missouri & Arkansas. LC 94-4158. (Illus.). 320p. (Orig.). 1994. pap. 16.95 (*1-55591-156-0*) Fulcrum Pub.

Lawton, Barbara P. & Van Patten, George F. Organic Gardener's Basics. Daniels, Stevie O., ed. (Organic Gardener's Ser.). (Illus.). 208p. (Orig.). 1993. pap. 12.95 (*1-878823-01-9*) Van Patten Pub.

Lawton Barrett, Karren. Cheated Hearts. large type ed. (Black Satin Romance Ser.). 255p. 1997. 27.99 (*1-86110-036-1*) Ulverscroft.

***Lawton, Blythe.** Breaking Free. 304p. 2000. 31.95 (*0-7541-1207-1*, Pub. by Minerva Pr) Unity Dist.

Lawton, Carl W., ed. see American Society of Mechanical Engineers Staff.

Lawton, Carol L. Attic Document Reliefs: Art & Politics in Ancient Athens. (Oxford Monographs on Classical Archaeology). (Illus.). 190p. 1995. text 110.00 (*0-19-814955-7*) OUP.

Lawton, Carol L., ed. Bearers of Meaning: The Ottilia Buerger Collection of Ancient & Byzantine Coins at Lawrence University. 1995. 35.00 (*0-9613429-3-5*) Lawrence Univ.

***Lawton, Clive.** The Story of the Holocaust LC 99-29047. 2000. 9.95 (*0-531-15376-2*) Watts.

Lawton, Clive, jt. ed. see Morgan, Peggy.

Lawton, David. Blasphemy. LC 93-19145. 228p. (Orig.). (C). 1993. pap. 17.95 (*0-8122-1503-6*); text 42.50 (*0-8122-3219-4*) U of Pa Pr.

— Faith, Text & History: The Bible in English. (C). 1991. pap. text 16.50 (*0-8139-1326-8*) U Pr of Va.

— A Lovely Country: A Novel. 288p. 1995. 22.00 (*0-15-100171-5*) Harcourt.

***Lawton, David, et al, eds.** New Medieval Literatures Volume Iii. (Illus.). 344p. 2000. text 74.00 (*0-19-818680-0*) OUP.

Lawton, David, ed. see Verdi, Giuseppe.

Lawton, David A. Faith, Text & History: The Bible in English. LC 90-47688. (Studies in Religion & Culture). 213p. reprint ed. pap. 66.10 (*0-608-20050-6*, 207132200011) Bks Demand.

Lawton, Deborah L., jt. auth. see Kelly, William J.

Lawton, Denis. Education & Politics for the Nineteen Nineties: Conflict or Consensus? LC 92-13828. 224p. 1992. 85.00 (*0-7507-0078-5*, Falmer Pr); pap. 29.95 (*0-7507-0079-3*, Falmer Pr) Taylor & Francis.

— Education & Social Justice. LC 74-31568. (Sage Studies in Social & Educational Change: Vol. 7). 206p. reprint ed. pap. 63.90 (*0-608-30500-6*, 202192100026) Bks Demand.

— The Tory Mind on Education. LC 94-28780. 168p. 1994. 85.00 (*0-7507-0350-4*, Falmer Pr); pap. 29.95 (*0-7507-0351-2*, Falmer Pr) Taylor & Francis.

Lawton, Denis, jt. auth. see Gordon, Peter.

***Lawton, Dennis, et al.** Education for Values: Morals, Ethics & Citizenship in Contemporary Teaching. 192p. 1999. 59.95 (*0-7494-3065-6*, Kogan Pg Educ) Stylus Pub VA.

Lawton, Dot, jt. auth. see Parker, Gillian.

Lawton, Edward P., tr. see Lavisse, Emile C.

Lawton, Elise T. Swimming: Gift for Life, Vol. I. (Illus.). 64p. 1986. pap. text 3.00 (*0-9617193-0-3*) Lawton E T.

Lawton, Eric, jt. auth. see Cousineau, Phil.

Lawton, Fay G. Ringing Changes. LC 98-94228. 65p. 1999. 10.00 (*0-9669331-0-9*) Hillside PA.

Lawton, George. Anatomy of the Network Computer. (Illus.). 1997. pap. text 29.95 incl. cd-rom (*0-07-036878-3*) McGraw.

***Lawton, George.** Real-Time Internet Protocols Clearly Explained. (Clearly Explained Ser.). (Illus.). 400p. (C). 1999. pap. 44.95 (*0-12-439840-5*) Acad Pr.

Lawton, George, ed. New Goals for Old Age. LC 76-169390. (Family in America Ser.). 230p. 1972. reprint ed. 17.95 (*0-405-03868-2*) Ayer.

Lawton, George, jt. auth. see Schneider, Herbert W.

Lawton, H., et al. The Journal of California Anthropology. fac. ed. (Malki Museum, Journal of California Anthropology Ser.: Vol. 3:1). 164p. (C). 1976. reprint ed. pap. text 17.50 (*1-55567-766-5*) Coyote Press.

Lawton, H. W., ed. see Hall, M. C. & Barker, J. P.

Lawton, Harry, ed. see McCawley, William.

Lawton, Harry, tr. see Marotti, Giorgio.

Lawton, Harry W. Willie Boy: A Desert Manhunt. 1995. 22.00 (*0-939046-27-X*); pap. 16.00 (*0-939046-28-8*) Malki Mus Pr.

Lawton, Harry W., jt. auth. see Bean, L. John.

Lawton, Helen. The Diary of Helen Lawton: 1909-1911. Shurtleff, William R., ed. 59p. (Orig.). 1987. spiral bd. 19.95 (*0-942515-00-5*) Pine Hill CA.

— Moggy the Mouser. LC 93-6571. (Voyages Ser.). (Illus.). (J). 1994. write for info. (*0-383-03702-6*) SRA McGraw.

Lawton, James, ed. see Singer, Jonathan M. & Deitch, Samuel L.

Lawton, Jeffery. Bally's Bingo Pinball Machines. (Illus.). 144p. 1999. 39.95 (*0-7643-0874-2*) Schiffer.

Lawton, John. D. H. Lawrence. 1998. pap. text 4.95 (*0-460-87962-6*, Everyman's Classic Lib) Tuttle Pubng.

— 1963 Five Hundred Days. (Illus.). 407p. 1993. text 45.00 (*0-340-50846-9*, Pub. by Headline Bk Pub) Trafalgar.

— Samarkand & Bukhara. (Travel to Landmarks Ser.). 1992. 24.95 (*1-85043-178-7*, Pub. by I B T) St Martin.

Lawton, John, intro. When the Sleeper Wakes. 352p. 1994. pap. 7.95 (*0-460-87499-3*, Everyman's Classic Lib) Tuttle Pubng.

Lawton, John E. Mom & Her Nineteen. Wightman, Christina C. & Wightman, Heather, eds. (Illus.). 250p. 1998. pap. write for info. (*1-888911-05-0*) Benson Smythe.

Lawton, John H. & May, Robert M., eds. Extinction Rates. (Illus.). 246p. 1995. pap. text 40.00 (*0-19-854829-X*) OUP.

Lawton, Jorge A., ed. Privatization Amidst Poverty: Contemporary Challenges in Latin American Political Economy. 336p. (C). 1995. pap. 22.95 (*0-935501-95-9*, Pub. by U Miami N-S Ctr) L Rienner.

***Lawton, Julia.** Disintegrating Selves: A Study of Dying Patients in Palliative Care Settings. LC 99-87378. 2000. pap. write for info. (*0-415-22679-1*) Routledge.

Lawton, Laura Connerat, jt. auth. see Cooper, Polly Wylly.

Lawton, M. P. & Herzog, A. R., eds. Special Research Methods for Gerontology. (Society & Aging Ser.: Vol. 2). 257p. 1989. text 43.95 (*0-89503-061-6*); pap. text 32.97 (*0-89503-053-5*) Baywood Pub.

Lawton, M. Powell. Environment & Aging. 2nd ed. LC 86-9665. 1986. 14.95 (*0-937829-00-5*) Ctr Study Aging.

Lawton, M. Powell, ed. Annual Review of Gerontology & Geriatrics: Geriatrics & Psychological Interventions, Vol. 9. 416p. 1989. 46.00 (*0-8261-6491-9*) Springer Pub.

Lawton, M. Powell, et al, eds. Measurement in Elderly Chronic Care Populations. LC 97-28766. (Illus.). 272p. 1997. 43.95 (*0-8261-9990-9*) Springer Pub.

Lawton, M. Powell & Maddox, George L. Annual Review of Gerontology & Geriatrics: Social & Psychological Aspects of Aging, Vol. 5. 352p. 1985. 46.00 (*0-8261-3084-4*) Springer Pub.

***Lawton, M. Powell & Rubinstein, Robert L.** Interventions in Dementia: Toward Improving Quality of Life. LC 99-59273. 2000. write for info. (*0-8261-1325-7*) Springer Pub.

Lawton, M. Powell & Salthouse, Timothy A., eds. Essential Papers on the Psychology of Aging. LC 98-12220. (Essential Papers in Psychoanalysis Ser.). 500p. 1998. text 75.00 (*0-8147-5125-3*); pap. text 29.50 (*0-8147-5126-1*) NYU Pr.

Lawton, M. Powell, et al. Respite for Caregivers of Alzheimer's Patients: Research & Practice. 176p. 1991. 27.95 (*0-8261-6610-5*) Springer Pub.

Lawton, M. Powell, jt. auth. see Rubinstein, Robert L.

Lawton, M. Powell, jt. ed. see Maddox, George L.

Lawton, M. Powell, jt. ed. see Schaie, K. Warner.

Lawton, M. Powell, jt. ed. see Teresi, Jeanne.

Lawton, Mary. A Lifetime with Mark Twain. LC 72-3627. (American Literature Ser.: No. 49). (Illus.). 1972. reprint ed. lib. bdg. 75.00 (*0-8383-1562-3*) M S G Haskell Hse.

— Schumann-Heink: The Last of the Titans. Farkas, Andrew, ed. LC 76-29945. (Opera Biographies Ser.). (Illus.). 1977. reprint ed. lib. bdg. 41.95 (*0-405-09687-9*) Ayer.

Lawton, Mary, jt. auth. see Paderewski, Jan I.

Lawton, Mary S. Hsieh Shih-ch'en: A Ming Dynasty Painter Reinterprets the Past. LC 77-18637. (Illus.). 55p. (Orig.). 1978. pap. 3.00 (*0-935573-04-6*) D & A Smart Museum.

Lawton, Mortimer P. Planning & Managing Housing for the Elderly. LC 74-28099. (Illus.). 350p. reprint ed. pap. 108.50 (*0-608-30696-7*, 202248800027) Bks Demand.

Lawton, Moyra F. Before the Face of the Sun. large type ed. 368p. 1994. 27.99 (*0-7089-3096-4*) Ulverscroft.

Lawton, Philip. The Kernel of Truth in Freud. 154p. (Orig.). (C). 1991. pap. text 19.50 (*0-8191-8035-1*); lib. bdg. 39.50 (*0-8191-8034-3*) U Pr of Amer.

Lawton, R., jt. ed. see Gould, W. T.

Lawton, R. M. Construction & the Natural Enviornment. LC 97-145459. 1997. pap. text 28.95 (*0-7506-2302-0*) Buttrwrth-Heinemann.

Lawton, Rebecca. Discover Nature in the Rocks. LC 97-6064. (Illus.). 224p. 1997. pap. 14.95 (*0-8117-2720-3*) Stackpole.

Lawton, Richard, ed. Census & Social Structure: An Interpretative Guide to Nineteenth-Century Censuses for England & Wales. 330p. 1978. 35.00 (*0-7146-2965-0*, Pub. by F Cass Pubs) Intl Spec Bk.

Lawton, Richard & Pooley, Colin G. Britain 1740-1950: An Historical Geography. (Illus.). 288p. (Orig.). 1992. pap. text 22.50 (*0-7131-6550-2*, A6105, Pub. by E A) Routldge.

Lawton, Robin L. Creating a Customer-Centered Culture: Leadership in Quality, Innovation & Speed. LC 93-15572. 180p. 1993. text 21.95 (*0-87389-151-1*, H0689) ASQ Qual Pr.

***Lawton, Russell A., et al, eds.** MEMS Reliability for Critical & Space Applications. 182p. 1999. pap. text 62.00 (*0-8194-3477-9*) SPIE.

Lawton, Samuel. Municipal Legal Forms, 1964-1992, 10 vols. LC 76-49998. 900.00 (*0-685-09237-2*) West Group.

Lawton-Smith, Helen & Woodward, Nick, eds. Energy & Environment Regulation. (Studies in Regulation). 336p. 1997. text 75.00 (*0-312-15951-X*) St Martin.

Lawton-Smith, Helen, jt. ed. see Jasinski, Piotr.

Lawton, Stephen. Santa Barbara's Flying a Studio. LC 96-39089. (Illus.). 160p. (Orig.). 1997. pap. 12.95 (*1-56474-210-5*) Fithian Pr.

Lawton, Stephen B., et al. Busting Bureaucracy to Reclaim Our Schools. 158p. 1995. pap. 15.95 (*0-88645-161-2*, Pub. by Inst Res Pub) Ashgate Pub Co.

Lawton, Thomas. Chinese Art of the Warring States Period: Change & Continuity, 480-222 B.C. LC 82-600184. (Illus.). 204p. (Orig.). 1982. 35.00 (*0-934686-39-4*); pap. 20.00 (*0-934686-50-5*) Freer.

Lawton, Thomas, ed. New Perspectives on Chu Culture During the Eastern Zhou Period. (Illus.). 230p. 1991. text 52.50 (*0-691-04095-8*, Pub. by Princeton U Pr) Cal Prin Full Svc.

***Lawton, Thomas & Lentz, Thomas W.** Beyond the Legacy: Anniversary Acquisitions for the Freer Gallery of Art & the Arthur M. Sakle Gallery. LC 98-38878. (Illus.). 352p. 1999. pap. 60.00 (*0-295-97908-9*) U of Wash Pr.

Lawton, Thomas & Murphy, Franklin D. A Time of Transition: Two Collectors of Chinese Art. 1991. 18.00 (*0-913689-30-0*) Spencer Muse Art.

Lawton, Thomas, et al. Ancient Chinese Bronzes in the Saint Louis Art Museum. Steiner, Mary A., ed. LC 97-66604. (Illus.). 160p. 1997. write for info. (*0-89178-045-9*); pap. 24.95 (*0-89178-049-1*) St Louis Art Mus.

***Lawton, Thomas C.** European Industrial Policy & Competitiveness: Concepts & Instruments. LC 99-11255. 1999. text 59.95 (*0-312-22333-1*) St Martin.

Lawton, Thomas C. Technology & the New Diplomacy: The Creation & Control of EC Industrial Policy for Semiconductors. LC 97-70638. (Illus.). 296p. 1997. text 73.95 (*1-85972-523-6*, Pub. by Ashgate Pub) Ashgate Pub Co.

***Lawton, Thomas C., et al.** Strange Power: Shaping the Parameters of International Relations & International Political Economy. LC 00-36348. 2000. write for info. (*0-7546-1324-0*, Pub. by Ashgate Pub) Ashgate Pub Co.

***Lawton, Timothy F. & Weiss, Malcolm P.** Geologic Map of the Wales Quadrangle, Juab & Sanpete Counties, Utah. (Miscellaneous Publication Ser.: Vol. 99-2). (Illus.). 29p. 1999. pap. 9.60 (*1-55791-635-7*, MP-99-2) Utah Geological Survey.

***Lawton, Tom.** Walking Ireland. (Illus.). 176p. 2000. pap. 25.95 (*0-7171-2963-2*, Pub. by Gill & MacMill) Irish Bks Media.

Lawton, William & Lawton. Spanish on the Road, Level 2. (Languages on the Road Ser.). (ENG & SPA.). 1992. pap. 11.95 incl. audio (*0-8120-7934-5*) Barron.

Lawton, William C. New England Poets: A Study of Emerson, Hawthorne, Longfellow, Whittier, Lowell, Holmes. LC 72-6941. (Essay Index Reprint Ser.). 1977. reprint ed. 23.95 (*0-8369-7245-7*) Ayer.

Lawton, William J. The Better Time to Be: Utopian Attitudes to Society among Sydney Anglicans, 1885 to 1914. (Modern History Ser.). 220p. 1990. pap. 24.95 (*0-86840-076-9*, Pub. by New South Wales Univ Pr) Intl Spec Bk.

Lawver, David E., jt. auth. see Johnson, Donald M.

Lawvere, F. William. Algebra Step by Step. (Illus.). 363p. 1997. spiral bd., wbk. ed. 25.00 (*0-9631805-2-5*) Buffalo Wksp.

Lawvere, F. William & Schanuel, Stephen H. Conceptual Mathematics: A First Introduction to Categories. (Illus.). 376p. (C). 1997. pap. text 34.95 (*0-521-47817-0*) Cambridge U Pr.

Lawvere, F. William & Schanuel, Stephen H., eds. Categories in Continuum Physics. (Lecture Notes in Mathematics Ser.: Vol. 1174). v, 126p. 1986. 30.95 (*0-387-16096-5*) Spr-Verlag.

Lawvere, F. William & Schanuel, Stephen R. Conceptual Mathematics: A First Introduction to Categories. (Illus.). 376p. (C). 1997. text 90.00 (*0-521-47249-0*) Cambridge U Pr.

Lawwill, Theodore. Erg, Ver & Psychophysics. (Documenta Ophthalmologica Proceedings Ser.: Vol. 13). 1977. text 191.50 (*90-6193-153-3*) Kluwer Academic.

Lawwill, Theodore, jt. ed. see Heckenlively, John R.

***Lawyer-Brook, Dianna.** Shifting Focus: A Handbook for ITV Educators. 192p. 2000. pap. 27.95 (*0-8108-3756-0*) Scarecrow.

***Lawyer, Eunice L. & Miller, Roy L., Sr.** From Kibler's Bridge to Miller Road: 65 Years of Christian Service in the African Methodist Episcopal Church. Graham, Nicole E., ed. (Illus.). 200p. 2000. 29.95 (*0-9700136-0-4*) Stay-In-Touch.

Lawyer, John, jt. auth. see Meyers, J. Gordon.

Lawyer, John W., jt. auth. see Katz, Neil.

Lawyer, John W., jt. auth. see Katz, Neil H.

***Lawyer, L. C., et al.** Geophysics in the Affairs of Mankind: A Personalized History of Exploration Geophysics. 2nd ed. LC 00-27649. (Geophysical References Ser.). (Illus.). 2000. write for info. (*1-56080-087-9*) Soc Expl Geophys.

Lawyer, Sarah R. Steelman: Jonathan & Hannah Steelman Family. (Illus.). 106p. 1996. reprint ed. pap. 18.50 (*0-8328-5607-X*); reprint ed. lib. bdg. 28.50 (*0-8328-5606-1*) Higginson Bk Co.

Lawyer, William S., ed. Binghamton: Settlement, Growth & Development & the Factors in Its History, 1800-1900, Together with a History of the Villages & Towns of the County. (Illus.). 1035p. 1997. reprint ed. lib. bdg. 99.50 (*0-8328-6101-4*) Higginson Bk Co.

Lawyer's Association of G. D. R. Staff. Law & Legislation in the German Democratic Republic, 1959-1989, 11 vols., Set. 1982. reprint ed. lib. bdg. 675.00 (*0-89941-281-5*, 108410) W S Hein.

Lawyers Committee for Human Rights. Critique of the U. S. Department of State's Country Reports on Human Rights Practices for 1994: Review of the U.S. Department of State's Country Reports on Human Rights Practices for 1994. Black, George, ed. 302p. (Orig.). (C). 1995. pap. text 19.50 (*0-934143-75-7*) Lawyers Comm Human.

Lawyers Committee for Human Rights. In Defense of Rights: Attacks on Judges & Lawyers in 1991. Masih, Jeneen, ed. (Illus.). 200p. (Orig.). 1992. pap. text 19.95 (*0-934143-50-1*) Lawyers Comm Human.

— Seeking Shelter: Cambodian Refugees in Thailand. 118p. (Orig.). 1986. pap. 8.00 (*0-934143-14-5*) Lawyers Comm Human.

Lawyers Committee for Human Rights (LCHR) Staff & Institute for Policy Research & Advocacy (ELSAM) S. In the Name of Development: Human Rights & the World Bank in Indonesia. LC 96-113411. 142p. (Orig.). (C). 1995. pap. text 12.00 (*0-934143-74-9*) Lawyers Comm Human.

Lawyers Committee for Human Rights Staff. Abandoning the Victims: The U.N. Advisory Service Program in Guatemala. 101p. 1990. lib. bdg. 10.00 (*0-934143-31-5*) Lawyers Comm Human.

— Critique: Review of the U. S. Department of State's Country Reports on Human Rights Practices, 1996. Black, George, ed. 284p. (C). 1997. pap. 18.00 (*0-934143-88-9*) Lawyers Comm Human.

— Critique: Review of the U. S. Dept of State's Country Reports on Human Rights Practices, 1995. Black, George, ed. LC 97-153085. 256p. (Orig.). 1996. pap. 19.50 (*0-934143-82-X*) Lawyers Comm Human.

— Human Rights & U. S. Foreign Policy Reports & Recommendations, 1992. 86p. (Orig.). 1992. pap. 10.00 (*0-934143-51-X*) Lawyers Comm Human.

— In Defense of Rights: Attacks on Judges & Lawyers in 1992. (Illus.). 210p. (Orig.). 1993. pap. text 19.95 (*0-934143-61-7*) Lawyers Comm Human.

— In Defense of Rights: Attacks on Lawyers & Judges in 1989. 118p. 1990. lib. bdg. 12.00 (*0-934143-33-1*) Lawyers Comm Human.

— In Defense of Rights: Attacks on Lawyers & Judges in 1990. 174p. (Orig.). 1991. pap. 12.00 (*0-934143-40-4*) Lawyers Comm Human.

— Kampuchea: After the Worst. 161p. 1990. reprint ed. 10.00 (*0-934143-29-3*) Lawyers Comm Human.

— Kuwait Building the Rule of Law. 53p. (Orig.). 1992. pap. 10.00 (*0-934143-49-8*) Lawyers Comm Human.

— Out of Control: Militia Abuses in the Philippines. 149p. (Orig.). 1990. pap. 8.00 (*0-934143-37-4*) Lawyers Comm Human.

— Refugee Refoulement: The Forced Return of Haitians under the U. S. - Haitian Interdiction Agreement. 64p. 1990. lib. bdg. 8.00 (*0-934143-30-7*) Lawyers Comm Human.

— Repression As Policy. 230p. 1990. pap. text 12.00 (*0-934143-35-8*) Lawyers Comm Human.

— Summary Injustice: Military Tribunals in Burma. 63p. (Orig.). 1991. pap. 8.00 (*0-934143-41-2*) Lawyers Comm Human.

Lawyers Committee for Human Rights Staff, ed. see Turnbull, Bruce H. & Naftalin, Ethan S.

Lawyers Cooperative Publishing Staff. ALR Index: Covering ALR 2d, ALR3d, ALR 4th, ALR Fed. LC 92-75797. 1993. suppl. ed. 285.00 (*0-318-62121-5*) West Group.

— ALR Medical Malpractice, 13 vols. LC 87-80380. 1987. 914.00 (*0-686-14517-8*) West Group.

— ALR Medical Malpractice, 13 vols. LC 70-1405. 1993. suppl. ed. 113.00 (*0-317-03150-3*) West Group.

— Americans with Disabilities Decisions, 8 vols. LC 92-75431. 1993. 970.00 (*0-317-05365-5*) West Group.

— Decisions of the United States Supreme Court: 1963-64, 1964-65, 1965-66, 1966-67, 1967-68, 1968-69, 1969-70, 1970-71, 1971-72, 1972-73, 1973-74, 1974-75, 1975-76, 1976-77, 1977-78, 1978-79, 1979-80, 1980-81, 1981-82, 1982-83, 1983-84, 1984-85, 1985-86, 1986-87, 1987-88, 1988-89, 1989-90, 1990-91, 29 vols. 1100.00 (*0-317-00149-3*) West Group.

— Decisions of the United States Supreme Court: 1963-64, 1964-65, 1965-66, 1966-67, 1967-68, 1968-69, 1969-70, 1970-71, 1971-72, 1972-73, 1973-74, 1974-75, 1975-76, 1976-77, 1977-78, 1978-79, 1979-80, 1980-81, 1981-82, 1982-83, 1983-84, 1984-85, 1985-86, 1986-87, 1987-88, 1988-89, 1989-90, 1990-91, 29 vols., Set. LC 64-17924. 1575.00 (*0-317-00147-7*) West Group.

— Employee Dismissal - Critical Issues & Proofs, 3 vols., Set. LC 92-71657. 1993. ring bd. 315.00 (*0-317-05361-2*) West Group.

— Employment Law in Illinois. LC 96-75686. 3000p. 1996. text. write for info. (*0-7620-0048-1*) West Group.

— Federal Trial Handbook. 3rd ed. LC 92-75424. 1993. 180.00 (*0-318-04258-4*) West Group.

— Florida Uniform Commercial Code, 4 vols., Set. LC 92-71380. 1992. ring bd. 300.00 (*0-317-05368-X*) West Group.

— Georgia Code Research Guide. LC 87-82576. 1988. 95.00 (*0-318-43159-9*) West Group.

— Georgia Code Research Guide. 1991. suppl. ed. 32.50 (*0-317-03345-X*) West Group.

— Handling Sexual Harassment Cases: Practice Guide. LC 92-74952. 1993. ring bd. 120.00 (*0-317-05380-9*) West Group.

— Hedonic Damages: Critical Issues & Proofs Regarding Damages for Loss of Enjoyment of Life, 2 vols., Set. LC 92-72989. 1992. ring bd. 156.00 (*0-317-05362-0*) West Group.

— Illinois Family Law & Practice. LC 95-80928. 2600p. 1995. text. write for info. (*0-7620-0014-7*) West Group.

— Louisiana Code Research Guide. 1988. 95.00 (*0-318-43161-0*) West Group.

— Michigan Research Guide, 2 vols. 1991. 87.50 (*0-318-43162-9*) West Group.

— Michigan Research Guide, 2 vols. 1993. suppl. ed. 40.00 (*0-317-03347-6*) West Group.

— New York Litigation Checklists, 2 vols., Set. LC 92-73799. 1992. ring bd. 150.00 (*0-317-05372-8*) West Group.

— New York Uniform Commercial Code, 4 vols., Set. LC 92-74149. 1993. ring bd. 375.00 (*0-317-05379-5*) West Group.

— Pre-Natal Injuries & Wrongful Life: Practice Guide. LC 92-74951. 1993. ring bd. 105.00 (*0-317-05381-7*) West Group.

— United States District Court for the Northern District of Ohio Rules. 1993. ring bd. 39.50 (*0-317-05383-3*) West Group.

Lawyers Cooperative Publishing Staff, ed. Age Discrimination: Critical Issues & Proofs. LC 92-72111. 1992. ring bd. 120.00 (*0-317-05359-0*) West Group.

— Age Discrimination: Critical Issues & Proofs. 1993. suppl. ed. 45.00 (*0-317-05707-3*) West Group.

— Federal Rules of Evidence: Annotations from the ALR System. LC 90-63684. (Critical Issues Ser.). 1990. 90.00 (*0-317-03034-5*) West Group.

— Trademarks: Annotations from the ALR System. LC 90-63738. (Critical Issues Ser.). 1991. ring bd. 112.50 (*0-317-03033-7*) West Group.

Lawyers Cooperative Publishing Staff, ed. see Dwyer, John P. & Bergsund, Marika F.

Lax, Anneli. Modern Algebra&Discr Struct 91. 384p. (C). 1997. 95.00 (*0-06-043878-9*) Addson-Wesley Educ.

Lax, David A. & Sebenius, James K. The Manager As Negotiator: Bargaining for Cooperation & Competitive Gain. 304p. 1987. 35.00 (*0-02-918770-2*) Free Pr.

Lax, Doris, ed. see Tillich, Paul Johannes.

Lax, Edward S. Summit: Treaty of Peace. 90p. (C). 1988. lib. bdg. 30.00 (*0-9620530-0-7*) Hist Bks Ltd.

Lax, Eric. Newman: Paul Newman - A Celebration. (Illus.). 1999. pap. 24.95 (*1-85793-955-7*, Pub. by Pavilion Bks Ltd) Trafalgar.

— Woody Allen. 1991. 24.00 (*0-394-58349-3*) Knopf.

Lax, Eric. Woody Allen: A Biography. (Illus.). 396p. 1998. pap. text 13.00 (*0-7881-5744-2*) DIANE Pub.

***Lax, Eric.** Woody Allen: A Biography. 2000. pap. 16.00 (*0-306-80985-0*, Pub. by Da Capo) HarpC.

Lax, Eric, jt. auth. see Sperber, A. M.

Lax, Howard L. States & Companies: Political Risks in the International Oil Industry. LC 88-15227. (Illus.). 209p. 1988. 55.00 (*0-275-93074-2*, C3074, Praeger Pubs) Greenwood.

Lax, Ken, photos by. Dogon Sculpture: Symbols of a Mythical Universe: January 15-March 24, 1997. (Illus.). 72p. (Orig.). 1997. pap. write for info. (*0-614-29352-9*) Hillwood Art.

Lax, M., et al, eds. Frontiers in Condensed Matter Theory: Proceedings of a U. S. - U. S. S. R. Conference Held in New York City, December 4-8 1989. (AIP Conference Proceedings Ser.: No. 213). 220p. 1990. 70.00 (*0-88318-771-X*); pap. 30.00 (*0-88318-772-8*) Am Inst Physics.

Lax, Marc D. Selected Strategic Minerals: The Impending Crisis. 356p. (C). 1991. lib. bdg. 57.50 (*0-8191-8300-8*) U Pr of Amer.

Lax, Martin H. & Lax, Michael B. Caraseu: A Holocaust Remembrance. LC 96-30889. 264p. (Orig.). 1996. pap. 16.95 (*0-8298-1139-7*) Pilgrim OH.

Lax, Michael B., jt. auth. see Lax, Martin H.

Lax, P. D. Hyperbolic Systems of Conservation Laws & the Mathematical Theory of Shock Waves. (CBMS-NSF Regional Conference Ser.: No. 11). v, 48p. 1973. reprint ed. pap. text 19.00 (*0-89871-177-0*) Soc Indus-Appl Math.

Lax, Peter. Linear Algebra. LC 96-36417. (Pure & Applied Mathematics: A Wiley-Interscience Series of Texts, Monographs & Tracts). 272p. 1996. 79.95 (*0-471-11111-2*) Wiley.

Lax, Peter D., ed. Mathematical Aspects of Production & Distribution of Energy. LC 77-7174. (Proceedings of Symposia in Applied Mathematics Ser.: No. 21). 137p. 1977. reprint ed. pap. 26.00 (*0-8218-0121-X*, PSAPM/21) Am Math.

Lax, Peter D. & Phillips, Ralph S., eds. Scattering Theory. rev. ed. (Pure & Applied Mathematics Ser.: Vol. 26). 309p. 1990. text 86.00 (*0-12-440051-5*) Acad Pr.

Lax, Peter D., et al. Calculus with Applications & Computing, Vol. 1. (Illus.). 600p. 1983. 51.00 (*0-387-90179-5*) Spr-Verlag.

— Recent Advances in Partial Differential Equations, Venice, 1996: Proceedings of a Conference in Honor of the 70th Birthdays of Peter D. Lax & Louis Nirenberg : June 10-14, 1996, Venice, Italy. LC 97-29150. (Proceedings Of Symposia In Applied Mathematics ;). 1997. write for info. (*0-8218-0657-2*) Am Math.

Lax, Peter D., jt. auth. see Glimm, James.

***Lax, Robert.** Circus Poems. 2000. 26.95 (*1-58567-041-3*, Pub. by Overlook Pr) Penguin Putnam.

Lax, Robert. Circus/Zirkus/Cirque/Circo: Circus of the Sun. Kuoni, Alfred et al, trs. (Illus.). 120p. (Orig.). 1981. pap. text 20.00 (*3-85842-033-6*) Franciscan Inst.

— Dialogues/Dialoge. Kuoni, Alfred, tr. from GER. (Illus.). 127p. (Orig.). 1994. pap. text 15.00 (*3-85842-284-3*) Franciscan Inst.

— Episodes/Episoden. Kuoni, Alfred, tr. from GER. 142p. (Orig.). 1983. pap. text 15.00 (*3-85842-073-5*) Franciscan Inst.

— Fables/Fabeln. Kuoni, Alfred, tr. from GER. (Illus.). 103p. (Orig.). 1983. pap. text 15.00 (*3-85842-074-3*) Franciscan Inst.

— Journal/Tagebuch A. Kuoni, Alfred, tr. from GER. 136p. (Orig.). 1986. pap. text 15.00 (*3-85842-107-3*) Franciscan Inst.

— Journal/Tagebuch B. Kuoni, Alfred, tr. from GER. 127p. (Orig.). 1988. pap. text 15.00 (*3-85842-156-1*) Franciscan Inst.

— Journal/Tagebuch C. Kuoni, Alfred, tr. from GER. (ENG & GER.). 167p. 1990. pap. text 15.00 (*3-85842-182-0*, Pub. by Pendo-Verlag) Franciscan Inst.

— Journal/Tagebuch D. Kuoni, Alfred, tr. from GER. 103p. (Orig.). 1993. pap. text 15.00 (*3-85842-249-5*) Franciscan Inst.

— The Light the Shade. (Illus.). 96p. (Orig.). 1989. pap. text 15.00 (*3-85842-166-9*, Pub. by Pendo-Verlag) Franciscan Inst.

— Love Had a Compass: Journals & Poetry. Uebbing, Jim, ed. 272p. 1996. 22.00 (*0-8021-1587-X*, Grove) Grove-Atltic.

— Mogador's Book - Fur Mogador. Spaeth, Paul J., ed. Kuoni, Alfred, tr. from GER. 80p. (Orig.). 1992. pap. text 15.00 (*3-85842-237-1*) Franciscan Inst.

— Notes/Notizen. Kuoni, Alfred, tr. from GER. 93p. (Orig.). 1995. pap. text 15.00 (*3-85842-295-9*) Franciscan Inst.

— Psalm & Homage to Winngenstein. Kuoni, Alfred, tr. from GER. 91p. (Orig.). 1991. pap. text 15.00 (*3-85842-193-6*) Franciscan Inst.

— A Thing That Is: New Poems. Spaeth, Paul, ed. LC 96-29264. 96p. 1997. 19.95 (*0-87951-699-2*, Pub. by Overlook Pr) Penguin Putnam.

— A Thing That Is: New Poems. 96p. 1998. pap. 14.95 (*0-87951-885-5*, Pub. by Overlook Pr) Penguin Putnam.

— 21 Pages/21 Seiten. Kuoni, Alfred, tr. from GER. 84p. (Orig.). 1984. pap. text 15.00 (*3-85842-090-5*) Franciscan Inst.

Lax, Robert, jt. auth. see Merton, Thomas.

Lax, Roger & Smith, Frederick. The Great Song Thesaurus. 2nd enl. rev. ed. 792p. (C). 1989. text 95.00 (*0-19-505408-3*) OUP.

Lax, Ruth, et al. Rapprochement: The Critical Subphase of Separation-Individuation. LC 80-66351. 528p. 1980. 45.00 (*0-87668-409-6*) Aronson.

Lax, Ruth F. Becoming & Being a Woman: Development, Theory, & Therapeutic Considerations. LC 96-46470. 1997. pap. 45.00 (*0-7657-0050-6*) Aronson.

Lax, Ruth F., ed. Essential Papers on Character Neurosis & Treatment. (Essential Papers in Psychoanalysis). 384p. (C). 1989. text 75.00 (*0-8147-5041-9*); pap. text 27.50 (*0-8147-5042-7*) NYU Pr.

Lax, Ruth F., et al, eds. Rapprochment: The Critical Subphase of Separation-Individuation. LC 80-66351. 528p. 1994. pap. 50.00 (*1-56821-103-1*) Aronson.

— Self & Object Constancy: Clinical & Theoretical Perspectives. LC 85-27365. (Psychiatry Ser.). 355p. 1985. lib. bdg. 47.00 (*0-89862-226-3*) Guilford Pubns.

Lax, Scott. The Year That Trembled: A Novel. LC 98-12845. 192p. 1998. 21.95 (*0-8397-8660-3*) Eriksson.

Lax, Stephen. Beyond the Horizon. 1997. 32.00 (*1-86020-514-3*, Pub. by U of Luton Pr) Bks Intl VA.

***Laxalt, Paul.** Nevada's Paul Laxalt: A Memoir. 425p. 2000. 27.50 (*0-930083-09-1*) J Bacon Co.

Laxalt, Robert. Basque Family Trilogy, 3 vols. 1997. boxed set 50.00 (*0-87417-309-4*) U of Nev Pr.

— The Basque Hotel. LC 89-4953. (Basque Ser.). 136p. 1993. pap. 18.00 (*0-87417-216-0*) U of Nev Pr.

— Child of the Holy Ghost. LC 92-7216. (Basque Ser.). 168p. 1992. reprint ed. pap. 18.00 (*0-87417-307-8*) U of Nev Pr.

— Child of the Holy Ghost. LC 92-7216. (Basque Ser.). 168p. 1997. reprint ed. 20.00 (*0-87417-196-2*) U of Nev Pr.

— A Cup of Tea in Pamplona. LC 85-16371. (Basque Ser.). (Illus.). 96p. 1993. pap. 12.00 (*0-87417-192-X*) U of Nev Pr.

— Dust Devils. LC 97-15224. (Western Literature Ser.). 120p. (YA). 1997. pap. 16.00 (*0-87417-300-0*) U of Nev Pr.

— The Governor's Mansion. LC 94-4858. (Basque Ser.). 240p. 1997. reprint ed. 23.00 (*0-87417-251-9*); reprint ed. pap. 18.00 (*0-87417-308-6*) U of Nev Pr.

— The Land of My Fathers: A Son's Return to the Basque Country. LC 99-34731. (Basque Ser.). (Illus.). 136p. 2000. 21.00 (*0-87417-338-8*) U of Nev Pr.

An Asterisk (*) at the beginning of an entry indicates that the title is appearing for the first time.

— A Lean Year & Other Stories. LC 93-33529. (Western Literature Ser.). 208p. 1994. 21.00 (0-87417-241-1) U of Nev Pr.
— A Man in the Wheatfield. LC 87-10774. 192p. 1987. reprint ed. 18.00 (0-87417-130-X) U of Nev Pr.
— Nevada: A Bicentennial History. LC 91-31281. (Illus.). 176p. 1991. reprint ed. pap. 14.95 (0-87417-179-2) U of Nev Pr.
— A Private War: An American Code Officer in the Belgian Congo. limited ed. LC 98-11581. 96p. 1998. 25.00 (0-87417-323-X) U of Nev Pr.
***Laxalt, Robert.** A Private War: An American Code Officer in the Belgian Congo. limited ed. LC 98-11581. x, 103p. 1998. pap. 14.00 (0-87417-324-8) U of Nev Pr.
Laxalt, Robert. Sweet Promised Land. (Basque Ser.). (Illus.). 200p. 1988. reprint ed. pap. 18.00 (0-87417-137-7) U of Nev Pr.
***Laxalt, Robert.** Time of the Rabies: A Novella. LC 00-8546. (Basque Ser.). 104p. 2000. pap. 16.00 (0-87417-350-7) U of Nev Pr.
Laxdal, Vivienne. Karla & Griff. 96p. (Orig.). 1999. pap. 13.95 (0-88754-570-X, Pub. by Theatre Comm) Consort Bk Sales.
Laxer, Gordon. Open for Business: The Roots of Foreign Ownership in Canada. (Illus.). 256p. 1989. pap. text 17.95 (0-19-540734-2) OUP.
Laxer, Gordon & Harrison, Trevor. The Trojan Horse: Alberta & the Future of Canada. LC 95-79349. 335p. 1995. 48.99 (1-55164-035-X, Pub. by Black Rose); pap. 19.99 (1-55164-034-1, Pub. by Black Rose) Consort Bk Sales.
Laxer, James. Canada's Energy Crisis. 136p. 1974. 30.00 (0-88862-088-8, Pub. by J Lorimer); pap. 14.95 (0-88862-087-X, Pub. by J Lorimer) Formac Dist Ltd.
Laxer, Mark E. Take Me for a Ride: Coming of Age in a Destructive Cult. 200p. 1993. pap. 14.00 (0-9638108-3-9) Outer Rim Pr.
Laxer, Robert M. Canada's Unions. 341p. 1976. pap. 16.95 (0-88862-096-9, Pub. by J Lorimer) Formac Dist Ltd.
Laxman, Kamala. The Thama Stories. LC 95-904675. (Illus.). (J). pap. write for info. (0-14-037812-X, PuffinBks) Peng Put Young Read.
Laxmanan, V., et al, eds. Materials Processing in Space. (Materials Science Forum Ser.). 450p. 1989. text 106.00 (0-87849-592-4, Pub. by Trans T Pub) Enfield Pubs NH.
Laxness, Halldor Kiljan. Atom Station. 1976. 20.95 (0-8488-0177-6) Amereon Ltd.
— The Atom Station. LC 81-85725. 206p. (C). 1982. reprint ed. pap. 16.95 (0-933256-31-0) Second Chance.
— Independent People. 1998. 25.50 (0-8446-6949-0) Peter Smith.
— Independent People: An Epic. Thompson, J. A., tr. 1997. pap. 14.00 (0-679-76792-4) Vin Bks.
Laxson, Ruth. HO Plus GO (Squared) Equals It. 1986. pap. 30.00 (0-932526-10-1) Nexus Pr.
Laxton, Douglas. Multimod Mark III: The Core Dynamic & Steady-State Models, Vol. 164. LC 98-20633. (Occasional Paper Ser.). 1998. write for info. (1-55775-722-4) Intl Monetary.
Laxton, Edward. Famine Ships: The Irish Exodus to America. 1998. pap. 14.95 (0-8050-5844-3, Owl) H Holt & Co.
Lay. Instructor's Edition Contigo: Essentials of Spanish. 1994. 74.33 (0-201-52032-X) Addison-Wesley.
— Linear Algebra Applications 97. 2nd ed. 1997. text (0-201-30121-0) Addison-Wesley.
— Supplement: Linear Algebra & Its Applications. 2nd ed. 1997. teacher ed. 23.67 (0-201-87491-1) Addison-Wesley.
Lay, jt. auth. see Bartlett, Sy.
Lay, Arthur H. Brief Sketch of the History of Political Parties in Japan. LC 78-78387. 462p. 1979. reprint ed. lib. bdg. 79.50 (0-313-26997-1, U6997, Greenwood Pr) Greenwood.
Lay, Artie K. & Runnels, Gayle S. Amigo, the Friendly Gray Whale. LC 91-65227. (Blubber Buddy Adventure Ser.). (Illus.). 140p. (J). (gr. 2-6). 1991. 24.95 incl. audio (0-9628626-0-6) Blubber Budd.
Lay, Beirne, Jr. & Bartlett, Sy. Twelve O'Clock High! Gilbert, James B., ed. LC 79-7278. (Flight: Its First Seventy-Five Years Ser.). (Illus.). 1980. reprint ed. lib. bdg. 25.95 (0-405-12187-3) Ayer.
Lay, Benjamin. All Slave-Keepers That Keep the Innocent in Bondage, Apostates Pretending to Lay Claim to the Pure & Holy Christian Religion. LC 72-82203. (Anti-Slavery Crusade in America Ser.). 1970. reprint ed. 15.95 (0-405-00642-X) Ayer.
Lay, Carol. Joyride. (Illus.). 112p. (Orig.). 1996. pap. 11.95 (0-87816-398-0) Kitchen Sink.
— Strip Joint. LC 98-35925. 105p. 1998. pap. 11.95 (0-87816-578-9) Kitchen Sink.
Lay, Carol & Brown, M. K. Twisted Sisters Vol. 2: Drawing the Line. Noomin, Diane, ed. (Illus.). 176p. 1995. 24.95 (0-87816-344-1) Kitchen Sink.
Lay Commission on Catholic Social Teaching & the U. Toward the Future: Catholic Social Thought & the U. S. Economy, a Lay Letter. 120p. 1985. reprint ed. pap. text 15.00 (0-8191-4860-1) U Pr of Amer.
Lay, Daniel W., jt. auth. see Truett, Joe C.
Lay, David C. Getting Your Job in the Middle East. 200p. 1992. pap. 19.95 (0-9631540-0-1) DCL Pub.
— Instructor's Hp-48g Graphing Calculator Manual to Accompany Linear Algebra & its Applications. 2nd ed. 76p. (C). 2000. pap. text 21.00 (0-201-64851-2) Addison-Wesley.
— Instructor's Maple Manual to Accompany Linear Algebra & its Applications. 2nd ed. 56p. (C). 1999. pap. text 21.00 (0-201-64849-0) Addison-Wesley.
***Lay, David C.** Instructor's Math lab Manual to Accompany Linear Algebra & its Applications. 2nd ed. 108p. (C). 2000. pap. text 21.00 (0-201-64848-2) Addison-Wesley.
Lay, David C. Instructor's Ti-85/86 Graphing Calculator Manual to Accompany Linear Algebra & its Applications. 2nd ed. (C). 2000. pap. text 21.00 (0-201-64850-4) Addison-Wesley.
— Linear Algebra. 2nd ed. 304p. (C). 1999. pap. text, student ed. write for info. (0-201-64847-4) Addison-Wesley.
— Linear Algebra & Applications. (C). 1994. pap. text. write for info. (0-201-84556-3) Addison-Wesley.
— Linear Algebra & Its Applications. 2nd ed. Guardino, Karen, ed. LC 96-9417. 560p. (C). 1996. 97.00 (0-201-82478-7) Addison-Wesley.
— Linear Algebra & Its Applications. 2nd ed. (C). 1997. pap. text. write for info. (0-201-76717-1) Addison-Wesley.
— Linear Algebra & Its Applications. 2nd ed. 272p. (C). 1997. pap. text, student ed. 15.00 (0-201-82477-9) Addison-Wesley.
— Linear Algebra & its Applications Updated. 2nd ed. LC 99-37547. 576p. (C). 1999. 86.00 incl. cd-rom (0-201-34774-1) S&S Trade.
Lay, Donald P. Law: A Human Process. LC 96-22825. (Paralegal). 200p. 1996. pap. text 14.95 (0-314-20058-4) West Pub.
Lay-Dopyera, Margaret Z. Becoming a Teacher of Young Children. 5th ed. 1993. 26.87 (0-07-036778-7) McGraw.
Lay-Dopyera, Margaret Z., jt. auth. see Dopyera, John.
Lay, Eldonna, jt. auth. see Massie, Shirley.
Lay, Eldonna, ed. see De Bac Vacher, Eugene.
Lay, Eldonna, ed. see Paul, George.
Lay, Eldonna, ed. see Schorsch, Harry.
Lay, Eldonna, ed. see Vacher, Josephine A. & De Bac Vacher, Eugene.
Lay, Graeme. Motu Tapu: Short Stories of the South Pacific. 172p. (C). 1991. pap. text 20.00 (0-908597-06-1) UH Pr.
Lay, Graeme, jt. auth. see Leue, Holger.
Lay, Gunter, et al. Innovation in Production: The Adoption & Impacts of New Manufacturing Concepts in German Industry. LC 98-47865. (Technology, Innovation & Policy Ser.). 1998. pap. 63.00 (3-7908-1140-8) Spr-Verlag.
***Lay, Humberto.** Discipulado. (SPA.). 2000. pap. 10.99 (0-8297-2884-8) Vida Pubs.
Lay, J. E., ed. see Midwestern Mechanics Conference.
Lay, J. O. Colitis & Irritable Bowel Syndrome. 1998. mass mkt. 7.00 (0-7225-3199-0, 902693Q) Thorsons PA.
***Lay, Joan.** Hiatus Hernia: Safe Alternatives Without Drugs. rev. ed. 1998. pap. 7.00 (0-7225-3558-9) Thorsons PA.
***Lay, K. Edward.** The Architecture of Jefferson Country: Charlottesville & Albermarle County, Virginia. LC 99-39178. 2000. 49.95 (0-8139-1885-5) U Pr of Va.
Lay, K. W., ed. see AIME, Metallurgical Society Staff.
Lay, M. G. Handbook of Road Technology. 3rd ed. (Transportation Studies: Vol. 8). 1304p. 1999. text 230.00 (90-5699-159-0) Gordon & Breach.
— Handbook of Road Technology, 1. (Transportation Studies: Vol. 8). 712p. 1986. text 90.00 (2-88124-159-X) Gordon & Breach.
— Handbook of Road Technology, 2. (Transportation Studies: Vol. 8). 712p. 1986. text 90.00 (2-88124-160-3) Gordon & Breach.
— Handbook of Road Technology, 2 vols., Set. (Transportation Studies: Vol. 8). 712p. 1986. text 145.00 (2-88124-161-1) Gordon & Breach.
— Handbook of Road Technology, 2 vols., Vol. 2. 2nd ed. 1990. text 252.00 (2-88124-775-X) Gordon & Breach.
— Handbook of Road Technology, Planning & Pavements, Pt. 1. 2nd ed. (Transportation Studies). xvii, 337p. 1990. text 160.00 (2-88124-776-8) Gordon & Breach.
— Handbook of Road Technology, Traffic & Transport, Vol. 2. 2nd ed. xvii, 431p. 1990. text 160.00 (2-88124-777-6) Gordon & Breach.
Lay, Ma M. Not Out of Hate: A Novel of Burma. Frederick, William, ed. Aung-Thwin, Margaret, tr. from BUR. LC 90-28553. (Monographs in International Studies, Southeast Asia Ser.: No. 88). 260p. (Orig.). 1991. pap. text 20.00 (0-89680-167-5) Ohio U Pr.
***Lay, Marilyn, ed.** International Oil & Gas Development Yearbook (Review of 1997) Vol. 68: Production. 912p. 1999. ring bd. 300.00 (1-928601-03-0, Intl Oil Scouts) Mason Map Serv.
Lay, Marilyn, ed. International Oil & Gas Development Yearbook (Review of 1996) Vol. 67: Exploration. 200p. 1998. ring bd. 150.00 (1-928601-00-6, Intl Oil Scouts) Mason Map Serv.
— International Oil & Gas Development Yearbook (Review of 1996) Vol. 67: Production. 955p. 1998. ring bd. 350.00 (1-928601-01-4, Intl Oil Scouts) Mason Map Serv.
***Lay, Marilyn, ed.** International Oil & Gas Development Yearbook (Review of 1997) Vol. 68: Exploration. 241p. 1999. ring bd. 150.00 (1-928601-02-2, Intl Oil Scouts) Mason Map Serv.
Lay, Marilyn, ed. see International Oil Scouts.
***Lay, Mary M.** The Rhetoric of Midwifery: Gender, Knowledge, & Power. LC 99-43562. 256p. 2000. pap. 24.00 (0-8135-2779-1); text 55.00 (0-8135-2778-3) Rutgers U Pr.
Lay, Mary M. Technical Communication. LC 94-29205. 784p. (C). 1994. text 56.75 (0-256-11985-6, Irwn McGrw-H) McGrw-H Hghr Educ.
***Lay, Mary M., et al, eds.** Body Talk: Rhetoric, Technology, Reproduction. LC 99-6903. (Rhetoric of the Human Sciences Ser.). 2000. pap. 24.95 (0-299-16794-1) U of Wis Pr.
Lay, Mary M. & Karis, William M., eds. Collaborative Writing in Industry: Investigations in Theory & Practice. (Technical Communications Ser.). 284p. 1991. text 38.95 (0-89503-071-3); pap. text 29.22 (0-89503-070-5) Baywood Pub.
Lay, Max. Handbook of Road Technology, 2 Vol. 3rd ed. Vol. 1. 576p. 1999. text 125.00 (90-5699-157-4) Gordon & Breach.
— Handbook of Road Technology, 2 Vol. 3rd ed. Vol. 2. 728p. 1999. text 155.00 (90-5699-158-2) Gordon & Breach.
Lay, Maxwell G. Ways of the World: A History of the World's Roads & of the Vehicles That Used Them. LC 91-23148. (Illus.). 500p. (C). 1992. text 50.00 (0-8135-1758-3) Rutgers U Pr.
Lay Miller, Esther. A Potpourri of Life's Challenges. 1998. pap. write for info. (1-57553-835-0) Watermrk Pr.
***Lay, Molly.** The Art of Temping: Use Your Expertise, Flexibility & Objectivity in the Workplace. (Illus.). 134p. 1999. pap. 10.95 (1-883707-41-2) Protea Publng GA.
Lay, Nancy. No Film in the Camera. 64p. (Orig.). 1992. pap. 8.00 (0-912449-21-7) Floating Island.
Lay, Nancy D. Say It in Chinese. (Say It Ser.). (Orig.). 1980. pap. 4.95 (0-486-23325-1) Dover.
Lay, Norman. Linear Algebra for John Abbott College. (C). 1998. pap. text. write for info. (0-201-45673-7) Addison-Wesley.
Lay, Peter W. Zyzyskqa's War & Other Stories. 69p. (Orig.). 1992. pap. 7.50 (971-10-0491-7, Pub. by New Day Pub) Cellar.
Lay, Richard, ed. see Schorsch, Harry.
Lay, Richard A. Measuring the Metric Way. (Illus.). 76p. 1975. pap. text 2.50 (0-88323-123-9, 211) Pendergrass Pub.
Lay, Shawn. Hooded Knights on the Niagara: The Ku Klux Klan in Buffalo, New York. 208p. (C). 1995. text 45.00 (0-8147-5101-6); pap. text 18.50 (0-8147-5102-4) NYU Pr.
Lay, Shawn, ed. The Invisible Empire in the West: Toward a New Historical Appraisal of the Ku Klux Klan of the 1920s. (Illus.). 240p. 1992. text 32.50 (0-252-01832-X) U of Ill Pr.
Lay, Stephen G. De, see De Lay, Stephen G.
Lay, Steven R. Analysis. 2nd ed. 304p. (C). 1990. 82.67 (0-13-033267-4) P-H.
— Convex Sets & Their Applications. rev. ed. LC 90-49488. 262p. (C). 1992. reprint ed. 49.95 (0-89464-537-4) Krieger.
Lay, Thorne, ed. Structure & Fate of Subducting Slabs. LC 97-107931. Orig. Title: Advances in Geophysics, Vol. 35. (Illus.). 185p. 1996. reprint ed. pap. text 34.95 (0-12-439860-X) Morgan Kaufmann.
Lay, Thorne & Wallace, Terry C. Modern Global Seismology. LC 94-33101. (International Geophysics Ser.: Vol. 58). (Illus.). xii, 521p. 1995. text 61.00 (0-12-732870-X) Acad Pr.
Lay, U Ko. Essence of Tipitaka. 221p. 1995. pap. 7.95 (81-7414-021-2) Vipassana Res Pubns.
Lay-Wahlstrom. Technical Communication. 2nd ed. 768p. (C). 1999. pap. 56.88 (0-256-22058-1) McGraw.
Lay, Wilfrid. Man's Unconscious Passion (1920) 254p. 1999. reprint ed. pap. 19.95 (0-7661-0774-4) Kessinger Pub.
— Man's Unconscious Spirit: The Psychoanalysis of Spiritism (1921) 338p. 1998. reprint ed. pap. 27.95 (0-7661-0559-8) Kessinger Pub.
Lay, William O. A Naturalist Afield: J. Alden Loring. Davis, Joan, ed. (Illus.). 200p. 1998. pap. 20.00 (0-9639651-2-3) Tioga Cnty.
Lay, Wolfgang, jt. auth. see Slavyanov, Sergei Yuryevitsh.
Layachi, Azzedine. State, Society & Democracy in Morocco: The Limits Of Associative Life. LC 98-73092. 120 p. 1998. write for info. (0-932568-25-4) GU Ctr CAS.
— The United States & North Africa: A Cognitive Approach to Foreign Policy. LC 89-22962. 217p. 1990. 57.95 (0-275-93365-2, C3365, Greenwood Pr) Greenwood.
Layachi, Azzedine, ed. Economic Crisis & Political Change in North America. LC 97-50039. 192p. 1998. 55.00 (0-275-96142-7, Praeger Pubs) Greenwood.
Layachi, Larbi. The Jealous Lover. 140p. (Orig.). 1986. 13.95 (0-939180-41-3); pap. 7.50 (0-939180-30-8) Tombouctou.
— Yesterday & Today. LC 85-3912. 189p. (Orig.). 1985. 14.00 (0-87685-632-6) Black Sparrow.
— Yesterday & Today. limited ed. LC 85-3912. 189p. (Orig.). 1985. pap. 8.50 (0-87685-631-8) Black Sparrow.
— Yesterday & Today, signed ed. deluxe ed. LC 85-3912. 189p. (Orig.). 1985. 25.00 (0-87685-633-4) Black Sparrow.
Layamon. Layamon's Brut: Selections. (BCL1-PR English Literature Ser.). 150p. 1992. reprint ed. lib. bdg. 69.00 (0-7812-7184-3) Rprt Serv.
— Layamon's Brut: or Chronicle of Britain, 3 vols. Madden, Frederic, tr. LC 72-137262. reprint ed. 195.00 (0-404-03910-3) AMS Pr.
Layard. Education & Equality. LC 98-16544. 1999. text 79.95 (0-312-21576-2) St Martin.
Layard, G. G., jt. auth. see Spielmann, Marion H.
Layard, John. A Celtic Quest: Sexuality & Soul in Individuation. LC 87-34569. (Seminar Ser.: No. 10). (Illus.). 254p. 2001. reprint ed. pap. 19.50 (0-88214-110-4, Pub. by Spring Pubns) Continuum.
Layard, P., jt. ed. see Ashenfelter, Orley C.
Layard, Richard, ed. Cost - Benefit Analysis. (Education Ser.). 1999. mass mkt. 10.95 (0-14-086458-X) Viking Penguin.
Layard, Richard, et al, eds. Britain's Training Deficit: A Centre for Economic Performance Report. 384p. 1994. 72.95 (1-85628-878-1, Pub. by Avebry) Ashgate Pub Co.
Layard, Richard & Calmfors, Lars, eds. The Fight Against Unemployment: Macroeconomic Analysis from the Centre for European Policy Studies. (CEPS Annual Ser.: No. 2). 240p. 1987. 32.50 (0-262-12122-0) MIT Pr.
Layard, Richard & Glaister, Stephen, eds. Cost Benefit Analysis. LC 93-37740. (Illus.). 507p. (C). 1994. pap. text 26.95 (0-521-46674-1) Cambridge U Pr.
— Cost Benefit Analysis. 2nd ed. LC 93-37740. (Illus.). 507p. (C). 1994. text 74.95 (0-521-46128-6) Cambridge U Pr.
Layard, Richard, et al. East-West Migration: The Alternatives. (Illus.). 76p. 1992. 22.00 (0-262-12168-9) MIT Pr.
— East-West Migration: The Alternatives. 104p. 1994. pap. text 11.00 (0-262-62092-8) MIT Pr.
— Unemployment: Macroeconomic Performance & the Labour Market. Jackman, Richard, ed. (Illus.). 634p. 1991. pap. text 35.00 (0-19-828434-9) OUP.
— The Unemployment Crisis. (Illus.). 176p. 1994. text 35.00 (0-19-877395-1); pap. text 14.95 (0-19-877394-3) OUP.
Layard, Richard, jt. ed. see Dornbusch, Rudiger.
Layberry, Ross A. The Butterflies of Canada. (Illus.). 376p. 1998. pap. 29.95 (0-8020-7881-8); text 75.00 (0-8020-0898-4) U of Toronto Pr.
Laybourn, Ann, et al. Hurting on the Inside: Children's Experiences of Parental Alcohol Abuse. LC 96-84598. 163p. 1996. 63.95 (1-85972-319-5, Pub. by Avebry) Ashgate Pub Co.
***Laybourn, Emma.** Monster Shoes. (J). 2000. pap. 6.95 (0-552-54634-8, Pub. by Transworld Publishers Ltd) Trafalgar.
Laybourn, Keith. Britain on the Breadline: A Social & Political History of Britain Between the Wars. (Illus.). 240p. (C). 1990. 30.95 (0-86299-490-X, Pub. by Sutton Pub Ltd) Intl Pubs Mktg.
— Britain on the Breadline: A Social & Political History of Britain, 1918-1939. (Illus.). 256p. 1998. pap. 27.95 (0-7509-1752-0, Pub. by Sutton Pub Ltd) Intl Pubs Mktg.
***Laybourn, Keith.** British Political Leaders: A Biographical Dictionary of British Prime Ministers & Great Officers of State. 2001. lib. bdg. 55.00 (1-57607-043-3) ABC-CLIO.
Laybourn, Keith. General Strike Day By Day. 1999. pap. text 19.95 (0-7509-2254-0) Sutton Pub Ltd.
— The General Strike Day by Day. (Illus.). 192p. 1996. 33.95 (0-7509-1058-5, Pub. by Sutton Pub Ltd) Intl Pubs Mktg.
— The General Strike of 1926. LC 93-28180. (New Frontiers in History Ser.). 1993. text 27.95 (0-7190-3865-0, Pub. by Manchester Univ Pr) St Martin.
— The Guild of Help & the Changing Face of Edwardian Philanthropy: The Guild of Help, Voluntary Work & the State, 1904-1919. LC 93-51035. 236p. 1994. text 89.95 (0-7734-9144-9) E Mellen.
— A History of British Trade Unionism. (History Paperbacks Ser.). 256p. (Orig.). 1997. pap. 26.95 (0-7509-1478-5, Pub. by Sutton Pub Ltd) Intl Pubs Mktg.
— The History of British Trade Unionism c. 1770-1990. (Illus.). 256p. 1992. 42.95 (0-86299-785-2, Pub. by Sutton Pub Ltd) Intl Pubs Mktg.
***Laybourn, Keith.** Modern Britain Since 1906: A Reader. 2000. pap. 24.50 (1-86064-237-3, Pub. by I B T); text 59.50 (1-86064-298-5, Pub. by I B T) St Martin.
Laybourn, Keith. Rise of Labour: The British Labour Party, 1890-1979. 192p. 1991. 34.95 (0-7131-6600-2, A3045, Pub. by E A) Routldge.
— The Rise of Socialism in Britain. LC 97-157652. 224p. 1997. pap. 22.95 (0-7509-1341-X, Pub. by Sutton Pub Ltd) Intl Pubs Mktg.
— The Rise of Socialism in Britian. LC 97-157652. 224p. 1997. 72.00 (0-7509-1340-1) Bks Intl VA.
— Under the Red Flag A History of Communism in Britain. 1999. 34.95 (0-7509-1485-8) Bks Intl VA.
Laybourn, Keith, ed. Social Conditions, Status & Community c. 1860-1920. (Studies in Modern British History). 224p. 1997. 72.00 (0-7509-1070-4, Pub. by Sutton Pub Ltd); pap. 23.50 (0-7509-1501-3, Pub. by Sutton Pub Ltd) Intl Pubs Mktg.
Laybourne, Harry. Springfield. (Images of America Ser.). (Illus.). 128p. 1998. pap. 16.99 (0-7524-0566-7) Arcadia Publng.
***Laybourne, Harry C.** Springfield, Ohio Revisited. (Images of America Ser.). (Illus.). 128p. 2000. pap. 18.99 (0-7385-0708-3) Arcadia Publng.
Laybourne, Kit. The Animation Book. LC 97-32774. 1998. pap. 24.95 (0-517-88602-2, Crown) Crown Pub Group.
Laychock, Suzanne, jt. auth. see Rubin, Ronald P.
Laycock. Wild Bears. 1988. pap. 19.95 (1-55654-038-8) Times Mir Mag Bk Div.
Laycock, David. Populism & Democratic Thought in the Canadian Prairies, 1910-1945. (State & Economic Life Ser.). 369p. 1990. pap. 19.95 (0-8020-6681-X); text 45.00 (0-8020-2637-0) U of Toronto Pr.
Laycock, David H. & Howlett, Michael. The Puzzles of Power: An Introduction to Political Science. 2nd ed. LC 99-176185. 440p. 1998. pap. text 35.00 (0-19-541377-6) OUP.
Laycock, Don, tr. see Beier, Ulli, ed.
Laycock, Donald C. The Complete Enochian Dictionary: A Dictionary of the Angelic Language As Revealed to John Dee & Edward Kelley. LC 94-20716. (Illus.). 288p. (Orig.). 1994. pap. 16.95 (0-87728-817-8) Weiser.
Laycock, Douglas. The Death of the Irreparable Injury Rule. 382p. 1991. text 65.00 (0-19-506356-2) OUP.
— Modern American Remedies. 2nd ed. LC 94-223935. 1184p. 1994. lib. bdg. 55.00 (0-316-51759-3) Little.
— Modern American Remedies: Cases & Materials. 1184p. 1994. teacher ed. write for info. (0-316-51377-6, 13776) Aspen Law.
— Modern American Remedies: Cases & Materials. LC 84-82267. (C). 1985. 46.00 (0-316-51749-6) Aspen Pub.
***Laycock, Douglas.** Modern American Remedies: Cases & Materials, 1999 Supplement. 2nd rev. ed. 250p. 1999. pap. text, suppl. ed. 17.95 (0-7355-0254-4, 02544) Panel Pubs.
Laycock, Douglas. Supplement Modern America '89. 1989. 9.95 (0-316-51757-7, Aspen Law & Bus) Aspen Pub.

L

— Supplement Modern America '91. 1991. 12.95 (*0-316-51761-5*) Aspen Pub.

Laycock, Ellen, jt. auth. see Laycock, George.

Laycock, George. Birdwatcher's Bible. 1996. pap. 15.95 (*0-385-42729-8*) Doubleday.

— Deer Hunter's Bible. 4th ed. LC 85-29215. (Illus.). 176p. 1986. pap. 12.95 (*0-385-19985-6*) Doubleday.

— Grizzly: Wilderness Legend. LC 96-37144. (Wildlife Ser.). (Illus.). 144p. (Orig.). 1997. pap. 14.95 (*1-55971-588-X*, NorthWord Pr) Creat Pub Intl.

— The Hunters & the Hunted: The Pursuit of Game in America from Indian Times to the Present. (Illus.). 280p. 1997. reprint ed. text 25.00 (*0-7881-5092-8*) DIANE Pub.

— John Ruthven, in the Audobon Tradition. (Illus.). 196p. 1994. text 75.00 (*1-882151-01-1*) Cin Mus Ctr.

— The Mountain Men. (Illus.). 288p. 1996. pap. 16.95 (*1-55821-454-2*, 14542) Lyons Pr.

— Shotgunner's Bible. LC 86-29156. (Illus.). 176p. 1987. pap. 12.00 (*0-385-23907-6*) Doubleday.

Laycock, George & Laycock, Ellen. The Ohio Valley. LC 81-43579. 1983. pap. 10.95 (*0-385-17591-4*) Doubleday.

Laycock, John & Wise, Peter. Endocrinology: Key Questions Answered. LC 98-107373. (Illus.). 332p. 1997. pap. text 35.00 (*0-19-262846-1*) OUP.

Laycock, John F. & Wise, Peter H. Essential Endocrinology. 3rd ed. (Illus.). 418p. 1996. pap. text 37.95 (*0-19-262471-7*) OUP.

Laycock, Larry R. & Laycock, Lisa G. Evergreen Miracles. (Illus.). 95p. (Orig.). 1995. pap. 5.95 (*0-9648178-1-0*) Moon Water Prodns.

— Gathering Christmas. (Illus.). 95p. (Orig.). 1995. pap. 5.95 (*0-9648178-0-2*) Moon Water Prodns.

Laycock, Lisa G., jt. auth. see Laycock, Larry R.

Laycock, Mary. Base Ten Mathematics. (Illus.). 60p. (J). (gr. k-8). 1976. pap. 8.50 (*0-918932-03-3*, A-1333) Activity Resources.

— Bucky for Beginners. (Illus.). 64p. (Orig.). (J). (gr. 4-12). 1984. pap. text 8.50 (*0-918932-82-3*, A-1676) Activity Resources.

— Straw Polyhedra. (Illus.). 39p. (Orig.). (J). (gr. 4-12). 1992. pap. 6.50 (*0-918932-99-8*) Activity Resources.

Laycock, Mary & Dominques, Manuel. Discover It! (Illus.). 32p. (Orig.). (J). (gr. 4-9). 1986. pap. 7.50 (*0-918932-87-4*, A-5555) Activity Resources.

Laycock, Mary & McLean, Peggy. Magician's Castle Fantasy. Smart, Margaret, ed. (Illus.). 80p. (Orig.). (J). (gr. 5-10). 1996. pap. 9.95 (*1-882293-05-3*, A-1700) Activity Resources.

— Skateboard Practice: Multiplication & Division. (Illus.). 64p. (J). (gr. 2-6). 1979. pap. text 8.50 (*0-918932-65-3*, A-1596) Activity Resources.

Laycock, Mary & Schadler, Reuben. Algebra in Concrete. rev. ed. (Illus.). 40p. (J). (gr. 4-9). 1987. pap. 8.50 (*0-918932-00-9*, A-1110) Activity Resources.

Laycock, Mary & Smaer, Margaret. Hands-on Math for Secondary Teachers. (Illus.). 64p. (Orig.). (YA). (gr. 7-12). 1984. pap. 8.50 (*0-918932-83-1*, A-1675) Activity Resources.

Laycock, Mary, et al. Skateboard Practice: Addition & Subtraction. (Illus.). 63p. (J). (gr. 1-3). 1978. pap. text 8.50 (*0-918932-55-6*, A-1570) Activity Resources.

Laycock, Mary, jt. auth. see Smart, Margaret A.

Laycock, Mary, ed. see Brownlee, Juanita.

Laycock, Mary, ed. see Jenkins, Lee & McLean, Peggy.

Laycock, Mary, ed. see Lund, Charles.

Laycock, Mary, ed. see Nicosia, Mary E. & Brandes, Louis G.

Laycock, Mary, ed. see Smart, Margaret.

Laycock, Rebecca A., ed. Ascended Masters Write the Book of Life. 2nd rev. ed. (Illus.). 300p. 1996. write for info. (*0-614-16421-4*) Brdge To Spiritual.

Laycock, Steven W. Foundations for a Phenomenological Theology. LC 87-37233. (Problems in Contemporary Philosophy Ser.: Vol. 8). 258p. 1988. lib. bdg. 89.95 (*0-88946-335-2*) E Mellen.

— Mind As Mirror & the Mirroring of Mind: Buddhist Reflections on Western Phenomenology. LC 93-41539. 337p. (C). 1994. text 64.50 (*0-7914-1997-5*); pap. text 21.95 (*0-7914-1998-3*) State U NY Pr.

***Laycock, Steven W.** Nothingness & Emptiness: A Buddhist Engagement with the Ontology of Jean-Paul Sartre. (C). 2001. pap. text. write for info. (*0-7914-4910-6*) State U NY Pr.

— Nothingness & Emptiness: A Buddhist Engagement with the Ontology of Jean-Paul Sartre. (C). 2001. text. write for info. (*0-7914-4909-2*) State U NY Pr.

Laycock, Steven W. & Hart, James G., eds. Essays in Phenomenological Theology. LC 85-14674. 219p. (C). 1986. pap. text 21.95 (*0-88706-165-6*) State U NY Pr.

Laycock, T., tr. see Prochaska, Georg.

Laycock, Thomas. Mind & Brain: or The Correlation of Consciousness, 2 vols. LC 75-16715. (Classics in Psychiatry Ser.). (Illus.). 1976. reprint ed. 75.95 (*0-405-07443-3*) Ayer.

Laycook, Mary & McLean, Peggy. Weaving Your Way from Arithmetic to Mathematics with Manipulatives. Smart, Margaret, ed. & illus. by. 133p. (J). (gr. k-8). 1993. pap. text 18.95 (*1-882293-00-2*, A-1680) Activity Resources.

Layden, Joe. Against the Odds. (Fast Breaks Ser.: Vol. 4). (Illus.). (J). (gr. 2-5). 1998. pap. 3.99 (*0-590-12082-4*) Scholastic Inc.

***Layden, Joe.** Against the Odds. (Fast Breaks Ser.). 1998. 9.09 (*0-606-13377-1*, Pub. by Turtleback) Demco.

— Double Play. (Moffatts on the Road Ser.: Vol. 2). (Illus.). 144p. (J). (gr. 3-9). 2000. pap. 5.99 (*0-439-13687-3*) Scholastic Inc.

Layden, Joe. Dream Team 1996 Scrapbook. (J). 1996. mass mkt. 3.99 (*0-590-89660-1*) Scholastic Inc.

— Dribble Shoot Score. LC 97-133589. (J). (gr. 5-7). 1997. mass mkt. 3.50 (*0-590-13767-0*) Scholastic Inc.

— Fast Breaks No. 1. (gr. 5-7). 1997. mass mkt. 3.50 (*0-590-13771-9*) Scholastic Inc.

— The Great American Baseball Strike. LC 95-14292, (Headliners Ser.). (Illus.). 64p. (J). (gr. 5-8). 1995. lib. bdg. 23.40 (*1-56294-930-6*) Millbrook Pr.

— Heroe del Jonron: La Historia de Sammy Sosa, 1 vol. (SPA., Illus.). 58p. (J). (gr. 2-9). 1998. pap. 3.99 (*0-439-07758-3*) Scholastic Inc.

— Home Run Heroes: Mark McGwire & Sammy Sosa. (Illus.). 118p. (gr. 2-9). 1998. mass mkt. 5.99 (*0-439-05746-9*) Scholastic Inc.

***Layden, Joe.** Inside The WNBA: A Behind The Scenes Photo Scrapbook. LC 99-217185. (Illus.). 48p. (gr. 2-7). 1999. pap. text 5.99 (*0-439-07803-2*) Scholastic Inc.

Layden, Joe. Kobe: The Story of the NBA's Rising Young Star. LC 98-216547. (Illus.). 192p. 1998. mass mkt. 4.50 (*0-06-101377-3*) HarpC.

— Meet the Los Angeles Lakers. LC 98-137436. 32p. (J). (gr. 2-5). 1997. pap. text 4.99 (*0-590-38382-5*) Scholastic Inc.

Layden, Joe. Meet the Los Angeles Lakers. (J). 1997. 10.19 (*0-606-12992-8*, Pub. by Turtleback) Demco.

Layden, Joe. NBA Hot Shots, 1 vol. LC 99-207568. (Illus.). 24p. (ps-2). 1999. 3.50 (*0-590-06056-2*) Scholastic Inc.

— NBA Slam Dunk Champ. (J). (gr. 5-7). 1997. mass mkt. 7.99 (*0-590-13770-0*) Scholastic Inc.

***Layden, Joe.** NBA Up & Coming: Stars of the New Millennium. (NBA Ser.). (Illus.). 32p. (J). (gr. 2-5). 2000. pap. 7.99 (*0-439-14069-2*) Scholastic Inc.

— Superstars of U. S. A. Women's Basketball 2000. (Illus.). 32p. 2000. 5.99 (*0-689-83570-1*) Aladdin.

— Superstars of U. S. A. Women's Gymnastics 2000. (Illus.). 32p. 2000. 5.99 (*0-689-83526-4*) Aladdin.

— Superstars of U. S. A. Women's Soccer 2000. (Illus.). 32p. 2000. 5.99 (*0-689-83593-0*) Aladdin.

Layden, Joe & Preller, James. NBA Game Day: An Inside Look at the NBA. (Illus.). 48p. (J). (gr. 2-7). 1997. pap. 10.95 (*0-590-76742-9*) Scholastic Inc.

— NBA Slam & Jam Map Skills for Grades 7-8. (NBA Game Day Ser.). (J). (gr. 7-8). 1997. pap. 3.50 (*0-590-06382-0*) Scholastic Inc.

— NBA Slam & Jam Study Skills for Grades 7-8. (NBA Game Day Ser.). (J). (gr. 7-8). 1997. pap. 3.50 (*0-590-29968-9*) Scholastic Inc.

Layden, Joe, jt. auth. see The Rock.

Layden, John J. Through the Eyes of a Poet: A Collection of Philosophical Poems. LC 95-94677. 80p. (Orig.). 1995. pap. write for info. (*1-57502-028-9*, P00431) Morris Pubng.

Layden, Joseph. Return of a Champion: The Monica Seles Story. 1996. mass mkt. 5.99 (*0-312-96002-6*) St Martin.

— Team U. S. A., 1996 Scrapbook. (J). 1996. mass mkt. 4.50 (*0-590-89661-X*) Scholastic Inc.

Layden, Mary A., et al. Cognitive Therapy of Borderline Personality Disorder. LC 93-16298. (Practitioner Guidebook Ser.). 256p. (C). 1993. 49.00 (*0-205-14807-7*, 48077, Longwood Div) Allyn.

Layder, Derek. Modern Social Theory: Key Debates & New Directions. LC 97-171393. 256p. 1997. 65.00 (*1-85728-385-6*, Pub. by UCL Pr Ltd); pap. 19.95 (*1-85728-386-4*, Pub. by UCL Pr Ltd) Taylor & Francis.

— New Strategies in Social Research: An Introduction & Guide. LC 92-30551. 1992. pap. 26.95 (*0-7456-0881-7*) Blackwell Pubs.

— Sociological Practice: Linking Theory & Social Research. LC 98-60952. vi, 191 p. 1998. write for info. (*0-7619-5430-9*) Sage.

— Understanding Social Theory. 240p. (C). 1994. text 69.95 (*0-8039-8448-0*); pap. text 22.95 (*0-8039-8449-9*) Sage.

Layder, Derek & Davidson, Julia O. Methods, Sex & Madness. LC 94-5596. (Illus.). 240p. (C). 1994. pap. 24.99 (*0-415-09764-9*, B4626) Routledge.

Laye, Camara. Dramouss. (FRE.). 1991. pap. 8.95 (*0-7859-3236-4*, 2266040243) Fr & Eur.

— L' Enfant Noir. (FRE.). 1976. pap. 9.95 (*0-7859-3219-4*, 2266023128) Fr & Eur.

— Le Maitre de la Parole - Kouma Lafolo Kouma. (FRE.). 1980. pap. 11.95 (*0-7859-3231-3*, 2266033891) Fr & Eur.

— Le Regard du Roi. (FRE.). 1975. pap. 8.95 (*0-7859-3251-8*, 2266046705) Fr & Eur.

Layefsky, Virginia. Impossible Things. LC 98-11459. 208p. (J). (gr. 5-8). 1998. 14.95 (*0-7614-5038-6*) Marshall Cavendish.

Layer, Harold A. ZByte High Tech Playing Cards. (Illus.). 32p. 1992. boxed set. write for info. (*1-882569-00-8*) ZByte Games Co.

Layers, Ralph, jt. auth. see Grant, Joan M.

Layfield, Eleanor N., jt. auth. see Newman, Gerald.

Layfield, Lester J., et al. Cytopathology of the Head & Neck. LC 96-36586. (ASCP Theory & Practice of Cytopathology Ser.). 1996. 115.00 (*0-89189-421-7*) Am Soc Clinical.

Layhe, Robert W., ed. Archaeological Investigations at AZ U-14-75(ASM), a Turn-of-the-Century Pima Household. (Archaeological Ser.: Vol. 172). (Illus.). 173p. 1986. pap. 12.95 (*1-889747-43-2*) Ariz St Mus.

— The 1985 Excavations at the Hodges Site, Pima County, Arizona. (Archaeological Ser.: No. 170). (Illus.). 436p. 1986. pap. 19.95 (*1-889747-42-4*) Ariz St Mus.

Layhe, Robert W., jt. auth. see Tagg, Martyn D.

Layish, Aharon. Women & Islamic Law in a Non-Muslim State. 352p. 1975. boxed set 34.95 (*0-87855-170-0*) Transaction Pubs.

***Layiwola, Dele, ed.** African Theatre in Performance: A Festschrift in Honour of Martin Banham. (Contemporary Theatre Studies: Vol. 35). (Illus.). 153p. 2000. text 44.00 (*90-5755-108-X*, Harwood Acad Pubs) Gordon & Breach.

Layland, Don, et al. Contributions to the Linguistic Prehistory of Central & Baja California. (Archives of California Prehistory Ser.: No. 44). (Illus.). 146p. (C). 1997. pap. text 16.25 (*1-55567-625-1*) Coyote Press.

Layland, Robin. LAN Internetworking: Building the Corporate Network for the 90's. 1996. 39.75 (*0-201-63360-4*) Addison-Wesley.

Layman. Medical Language. 1994. audio 107.25 (*0-8273-6923-9*) Delmar.

Layman, Bruccoli-Clark. American Poets since World War II: 5th Series. (Dictionary of Literary Biography Ser.: Vol. 169). 1996. 146.00 (*0-8103-9364-6*) Gale.

Layman, Bruccoli-Clark. DLB 156: The Romantic Tradition. Naufftus, William F., ed. LC 95-22179. (Dictionary of Literary Biography Ser.: Vol. 156). 400p. 1995. text 155.00 (*0-8103-5717-8*, 007491) Gale.

Layman, Bruccoli-Clark, ed. Dictionary of Literary Biography Vol. 13: Documentary Series: House of Scribner, Vol. 13. LC 95-81422. 400p. 1995. text 146.00 (*0-8103-5706-2*, 006487) Gale.

Layman, Bruccoli-Clark, et al. Dictionary of Literary Biography, Vol. 136. 400p. 1994. text 155.00 (*0-8103-5395-4*, 007471) Gale.

— Dictionary of Literary Biography Vol. 14: Documentary Series. 400p. 1996. text 146.00 (*0-8103-9365-4*) Gale.

Layman, C. H., ed. Man of Letters. 1991. text 60.00 (*0-7486-0164-3*, Pub. by Edinburgh U Pr) Col U Pr.

— Man of Letters: The Early Life & Love-Letters of Robert Chambers. (Illus.). 204p. 1994. pap. 22.00 (*0-7486-0193-7*, Pub. by Edinburgh U Pr) Col U Pr.

Layman, C. H. & Cameron, Jane. The Falklands & HMS Dwarf. LC 96-212417. 176p. 1990. 100.00 (*0-948251-76-X*, Pub. by Picton) St Mut.

Layman, C. Stephen. The Shape of the Good: Christian Reflections on the Foundation of Ethics. LC 90-50977. (Library of Religious Philosophy: Vol. 7). (C). 1994. reprint ed. pap. text 15.00 (*0-268-01752-2*) U of Notre Dame Pr.

***Layman, C. Stephen & Martin, Edwin.** The Power of Logic Test Bank. 92p. (C). 1999. pap. text. write for info. (*0-7674-1363-6*, 1363-6) Mayfield Pub.

Layman, C. Stephen, et al. The Power of Logic: Study Guide. vi, 164p. (C). 1999. pap. text, student ed. 17.95 (*0-7674-0690-7*, 0690-7) Mayfield Pub.

Layman, Carol S. Growing up Rich in Vernon, Indiana: A Celebration of American Small-Town Life in the 1940s & '50s. LC 92-80229. (Illus.). 288p. 1992. 19.95 (*0-9631855-7-8*) Still Waters Pr.

Layman, Charles S. The Power of Logic. LC 98-13617. ix, 566p. 1998. text 51.95 (*1-55934-955-7*, 1955) Mayfield Pub.

***Layman, Charles S.** The Power of Logic: Alternate Printing. LC 99-51536. ix, 566p. 1999. pap. text. write for info. (*0-7674-1773-9*, 1773-9) Mayfield Pub.

Layman, Dale P. Essentials of Anatomy & Physiology. (Allied Health Ser.). 1998. pap. 37.95 (*0-8273-6116-5*) Delmar.

— The Medical Language. (Medical Terminology Ser.). 1995. 62.95 (*0-8273-6924-7*) Delmar.

Layman, Dale P. The Medical Language: A Programmed Body-System Approach. LC 93-37629. 513p. (C). 1994. pap. 52.95 (*0-8273-5612-9*) Delmar.

Layman, Dale P. The Medical Language: A Programmed Body-System Approach. 544p. (C). 1994. text 46.00 incl. digital audio (*0-8273-6922-0*) Delmar.

— The Medical Language: A Programmed Body-System Approach. 544p. 1995. text 42.95 incl. digital audio (*0-8273-6925-5*) Delmar.

— Medical Terminology: Self-Directed Approach. 1998. pap. 29.95 (*0-8273-5611-0*) Delmar.

Layman, Donald K., ed. Nutrition & Aerobic Exercise. LC 85-26872. (ACS Symposium Ser.: No. 294). 160p. reprint ed. pap. 49.60 (*0-7837-1967-1*, 205244500001) Bks Demand.

Layman, Gary. Touchstone Art Magic. (Illus.). 153p. 1985. pap. 19.95 (*0-9616550-0-3*) Touch Art Magic.

Layman, George J. A Guide to Maynard Breech-Loader Top. 1995. pap. 11.95 (*1-877704-18-0*) Pioneer Pr.

— A Guide to the Ballard Breechloader. (Illus.). 216p. (Orig.). 1997. pap. 19.95 (*1-877704-26-1*) Pioneer Pr.

— The Military Remongton Rolling Block Rifle. 4th rev. ed. (Illus.). 148p. 2001. reprint ed. pap. 24.95 (*1-877704-32-6*) Pioneer Pr.

Layman, John, ed. see Mariotte, Jeff & Cassady, John.

Layman, John W. Inquiry & Learning: Realizing Science Standards in the Classroom. LC 96-84400. (Thinking Ser.). 60p. 1996. pap. 14.95 (*0-87447-547-3*) College Bd.

Layman, Katie. KTs QuickClicks Microsoft Access 97. 14p. 1999. pap. 12.99 (*1-893532-03-8*, 98-504) Compute Made.

— KTs QuickClicks Microsoft Access 2000. 12p. 1999. pap. 12.99 (*1-893532-07-0*, 98-504) Compute Made.

— KTs QuickClicks Microsoft Excel 2000. 12p. 1999. pap. 10.99 (*1-893532-05-4*, 99-502) Compute Made.

— KTs QuickClicks Microsoft PowerPoint 97. 12p. 1999. pap. 10.99 (*1-893532-02-X*) Compute Made.

— KTs QuickClicks Microsoft PowerPoint 2000. 12p. 1999. pap. 10.99 (*1-893532-06-2*, 99-503) Compute Made.

— KTs QuickClicks Microsoft Word 97. 12p. 1999. pap. 10.99 (*1-893532-00-3*, 98-501) Compute Made.

— KTs QuickClicks Microsoft Word 2000. 12p. 1999. pap. 10.99 (*1-893532-04-6*) Compute Made.

***Layman, Katie.** Microsoft Access 2000 in Layman's Terms: The Reference Guide for the Rest of Us. (Illus.). 60p. 1999. pap. write for info. (*1-893532-11-9*) Compute Made.

— Microsoft Excel 2000 in Layman's Terms: The Reference Guide for the Rest of Us. (Illus.). 50p. 1999. pap. write for info. (*1-893532-10-0*) Compute Made.

— Microsoft PowerPoint 2000 in Layman's Terms: The Reference Guide for the Rest of Us. 1999. pap. write for info. (*1-893532-12-7*) Compute Made.

— Microsoft Word 2000 in Layman's Terms: The Reference Guide for the Rest of Us. (Illus.). 60p. 1999. pap. write for info. (*1-893532-09-7*) Compute Made.

— WordPerfect 5.1 Made Easy. 320p. (C). 1991. pap. text 56.00 (*0-13-963125-9*) P-H.

Layman, Katie. WordPerfect 6.0 Made Easy. 562p. (C). 1993. pap. 53.33 (*0-13-953829-1*) P-H.

Layman, Katie & Hart, Lavaugh. Microsoft Word for Windows 97 Made Easy Easy Short Course: Version 7.0. LC 97-23744. 429p. (C). 1997. pap. text 51.00 (*0-13-676818-0*) P-H.

Layman, Katie & Hart, Lavaughn. Corel Wordperfect 7.0 Made Easy: Extended Course. LC 97-156798. 575p. (C). 1997. spiral bd. 67.20 (*0-13-456351-4*) P-H.

— Microsoft Word 97 Made Easy: Extended Course. LC 97-29748. 528p. (C). 1997. pap. text 65.00 (*0-13-676826-1*) P-H.

***Layman, Katie & Hart, LaVaughn.** Microsoft Word 2000 Made Easy: Extended Course. LC 99-16574. (Illus.). 694p. 1999. pap. 59.00 incl. disk (*0-13-012951-8*) P-H.

Layman, Katie & Hart, LaVaughn. Wordperfect 7.0 for Windows 95 Made Easy: Short Course, Vol. 1. LC 97-156752. 414p. (C). 1997. spiral bd. 52.00 (*0-13-456369-7*) P-H.

Layman, Katie & Renner, Adrienne G. Learn Apple Writer IIe the Easy Way. 1986. 17.95 (*0-13-527060-X*) S&S Trade.

Layman, Katie, et al. Corel WordPerfect 8 Made Easy: Extended Course. LC 97-43381. (Layman & Hart's Word Processing Made Easy Ser.). 601p. (C). 1998. pap. text 65.00 (*0-13-080080-5*) P-H.

Layman, Kim F. Poems for Everyday People. 57p. (Orig.). 1993. pap. 9.95 (*0-9639836-0-1*) K F Layman.

Layman, Nancy S. Sexual Harassment in American Secondary Schools: A Legal Guide for Administrators, Teachers, & Students. LC 93-11323. 207p. 1993. pap. 18.95 (*0-935061-52-5*) Contemp Res.

Layman, R. D. Naval Aviation in the First World War: Its Impact & Influence. LC 96-69149. (Illus.). 256p. 1996. 37.95 (*1-55750-617-5*) Naval Inst Pr.

Layman, R. D. & McLaughlin, Stephen. The Hybrid Warship: The Amalgamation of Big Guns & Aircraft. LC 90-62897. (Illus.). 192p. 1991. 44.95 (*1-55750-374-5*) Naval Inst Pr.

Layman, Richard. Current Issues: Child Abuse, Vol. 1. 122p. 1990. lib. bdg. 45.00 (*1-55888-271-5*) Omnigraphics Inc.

***Layman, Richard.** Dashiell Hammett. (Literary Masters Ser.: Vol. 3). 217p. 2000. 49.95 (*0-7876-3964-8*) Gale.

Layman, Richard. Dashiell Hammett: A Descriptive Bibliography. LC 78-53600. (Pittsburgh Series in Bibliography). (Illus.). 200p. 1979. text 100.00 (*0-8229-3394-2*) U of Pittsburgh Pr.

***Layman, Richard.** The Maltese Falcon. Gale Group Publishing Staff, ed. (Literary Masterpieces Ser.: Vol. 3). (Illus.). 192p. 2000. 49.95 (*0-7876-3965-6*) Gale.

***Layman, Richard & Rivett, Julie M., eds.** The Selected Letters of Dashiell Hammett. 2000. 30.00 (*1-58243-081-0*, Pub. by Counterpt DC) HarpC.

Layman, Richard, jt. auth. see Bruccoli, Matthew J.

Layman, Richard, jt. ed. see Bruccoli, Mary.

Layman, Richard, ed. see Bruccoli, Matthew J.

Layman, Richard, jt. ed. see Bruccoli, Matthew J.

Layman, Richard, ed. see Dos Passos, John.

Layman, Sue, jt. auth. see Porter, Gail.

Layman, Teresa. Gingerbread for All Seasons. LC 97-5132. (Illus.). 128p. 1997. 24.95 (*0-8109-3395-0*, Pub. by Abrams) Time Warner.

— Handmade Baby Gifts LC 99-11061. 128p. 1999. 24.95 (*0-8109-4151-1*, Pub. by Abrams) Time Warner.

Layman, Teresa & Morgenroth, Barbara. Gingerbread: Things to Make & Bake. (Illus.). 144p. 1992. 29.95 (*0-8109-3367-5*, Pub. by Abrams) Time Warner.

Layman, Thomas A., ed. The Pocket Webster School & Office Dictionary. 888p. 1990. per. 4.99 (*0-671-70016-2*) PB.

Laymon, Charles M., ed. Interpreter's One-Volume Commentary on the Bible. (Illus.). 1971. 39.95 (*0-687-19299-4*); 33.95 (*0-687-19300-1*) Abingdon.

Laymon, Heather & Yasenchack, Mark. Nothing but theworldtheworldtheworld & Family Practice. 44p. (Orig.). 1989. pap. text 3.00 (*0-9623107-0-0*) Mybrothers Pr.

***Laymon, R.** Allhallow's Eve. 1998. mass mkt. 11.95 (*0-7472-4783-8*, Pub. by Headline Bk Pub) Trafalgar.

— Body Rides. 1998. mass mkt. 11.95 (*0-7472-5100-2*, Pub. by Headline Bk Pub) Trafalgar.

— Endless Night. 1998. mass mkt. 11.95 (*0-7472-4367-0*, Pub. by Headline Bk Pub) Trafalgar.

— Fiends. 1998. mass mkt. 13.95 (*0-7472-5525-3*, Pub. by Headline Bk Pub) Trafalgar.

— In the Dark. 1998. mass mkt. 13.95 (*0-7472-4509-6*, Pub. by Headline Bk Pub) Trafalgar.

— Island. mass mkt. 13.95 (*0-7472-5099-5*, Pub. by Headline Bk Pub) Trafalgar.

— Night Show. 1998. mass mkt. 13.95 (*0-7472-4782-X*, Pub. by Headline Bk Pub) Trafalgar.

***Laymon, Richard.** Beast House. 1998. 50.00 (*1-881475-39-5*) Cemetery Dance.

Laymon, Richard. Bite. (Love Spell Ser.). 384p. 1999. mass mkt. 5.50 (*0-8439-4550-8*, Leisure Bks) Dorchester Pub Co.

***Laymon, Richard.** Bite. 1998. mass mkt. 11.95 (*0-7472-5101-0*, Pub. by Headline Bk Pub) Trafalgar.

— Come out Tonight. 440p. 1999. 40.00 (*1-881475-62-X*) Cemetery Dance.

— Cuts. (Illus.). 1999. 40.00 (*1-881475-64-6*) Cemetery Dance.

An Asterisk (*) at the beginning of an entry indicates that the title is appearing for the first time.

Laymon, Richard. A Good & Secret Place: Short Fiction by Richard Laymon. (Illus.). 224p. 1992. 35.00 (*0-9631367-4-7*) Deadline Pr.

— The Midnight Tour: Cemetery Dance. 600p. 40.00 (*1-881475-40-9*) Cemetery Dance.

***Laymon, Richard.** One Rainy Night. 416p. 2000. mass mkt. 5.99 (*0-8439-4690-3*, Leisure Bks) Dorchester Pub Co.

Laymon, Richard. Out Are the Lights. 224p. (Orig.). 1983. mass mkt. 2.75 (*0-446-90519-4*, Pub. by Warner Bks) Little.

***Laymon, Richard.** Stake. 2000. mass mkt. 5.99 (*0-7860-1258-7*, Pinncle Kensgtn) Kensgtn Pub Corp.

— The Traveling Vampire Show. 540p. 2000. 40.00 (*1-58767-000-3*) Cemetery Dance.

— Wilds. 1998. 30.00 (*1-881475-37-9*) Cemetery Dance.

Laymon, Richard. A Writer's Tale. 350p. 1998. 35.00 (*0-9631367-7-1*) Deadline Pr.

Layne, jt. auth. see Eichhorn.

Layne, Charles A., jt. auth. see Veconi, Gilbert J.

Layne, Christopher & Lynn-Jones, Sean M. Should America Promote Democracy? A Debate. (Illus.). 225p. 1999. pap. text 15.00 (*0-262-62122-3*) MIT Pr.

Layne, F. B. Lane: Layne - Lain - Lane Genealogy, Being a Compilation of Names & Historical Information of Male Descendants of 16 Branches of the Layne - Lain - Lane Family in the U. S. 336p. 1992. reprint ed. pap. 52.00 (*0-8328-2320-1*); reprint ed. lib. bdg. 62.00 (*0-8328-2319-8*) Higginson Bk Co.

— Layne Genealogy. (Illus.). 251p. 1993. reprint ed. pap. 39.00 (*0-8328-2807-6*); reprint ed. lib. bdg. 49.00 (*0-8328-2806-8*) Higginson Bk Co.

— Layne Genealogy. (Illus.). 251p. 1993. reprint ed. pap. 39.00 (*0-8328-3694-X*); reprint ed. lib. bdg. 49.00 (*0-8328-3693-1*) Higginson Bk Co.

Layne, Gwendolyn, tr. see Banabhatta.

Layne, Helen, ed. see Dixon, Ramon T. & Deanes, Charles.

Layne, James N., jt. ed. see Kirkland, Gordon L., Jr.

Layne, Joann G. The Champagne Slipper. LC 97-91224. 1998. pap. 13.95 (*0-533-12597-9*) Vantage.

Layne, Ken. Automotive Chassis Electronic System. 1989. text 23.00 (*0-13-053265-7*, Macmillan Coll) P-H.

— Automotive Engine Performance, Vol. I. 3rd ed. 300p. (C). 2001. pap. 59.33 (*0-13-758962-X*, Macmillan Coll) P-H.

— Automotive Engine Performance: Tune-Up, Testing, & Service. 2nd ed. 1993. write for info. (*0-318-69518-9*) P-H.

— Automotive Engine Performance: Tune-Up, Testing & Service, Vol. 1. 2nd ed. LC 92-24357. Vol. 1. 534p. 1992. pap. text 73.00 (*0-13-059775-9*) P-H.

— Automotive Engine Performance: Tune-Up, Testing & Service Volume II, Practice Manual, Vol. 2. 2nd ed. LC 92-24357. Vol. 2. 562p. 1992. pap. text 73.00 (*0-13-061177-8*) P-H.

Layne, Larry J., jt. auth. see Griffith, Daniel A.

Layne, Leah, jt. auth. see Dey, Dena.

Layne, Libby. The Sound of the Dolphin's Psalm. Jenkins, Molly R., ed. LC 97-60211. (Illus.). 255p. (Orig.). 1997. pap. 12.00 (*1-890306-01-0*) Warwick Hse.

Layne, Linda L. Home & Homeland: The Dialogics of Tribal & National Identities in Jordan. LC 93-23878. 158p. 1994. text 35.00 (*0-691-09478-0*, Pub. by Princeton U Pr) Cal Prin Full Svc.

***Layne, Linda L.** Transformative Motherhood: On Giving & Getting in a Consumer Culture. LC 99-6661. 222p. 1999. pap. text 18.50 (*0-8147-5155-5*) NYU Pr.

Layne, Linda L., ed. Transformative Motherhood: On Giving & Getting in a Consumer Culture. LC 99-6661. 240p. 1999. text 55.00 (*0-8147-5154-7*) NYU Pr.

Layne, Linda L., jt. ed. see Hess, David J.

Layne, Linda L., ed. see Kuklick, Henrika & Long, E.

Layne, Ron L., jt. auth. see Wall, Allie P.

Layne, Sara S., jt. auth. see Yee, Martha M.

Layne, Steven L. Thomas' Sheep & the Great Geography Test. LC 97-15816. (Illus.). 32p. (J). (ps-3). 1998. 14.95 (*1-56554-274-6*) Pelican.

Layng, Charles. The Game Is Afoot! 190p. 1995. text 24.00 (*1-896032-68-0*) Battered Silicon.

Layng, Judith, ed. see Barton, Andrew & Adler, Samuel.

***Layng, Ruth D.** Letters from James. 352p. 2000. pap. write for info. (*1-887905-23-5*) Pkway Pubs.

***Layoun, Mary N.** Wedded to the Land? Gender, Boundaries, & Nationalism in Crisis. (Illus.). 248p. 2000. pap. 18.95 (*0-8223-2545-4*); lib. bdg. 54.95 (*0-8223-2507-1*) Duke.

Layoun, Mary N., ed. Modernism in Greece? Essays on the Critical & Literary Margins of a Movement. LC 90-62251. 234p. (Orig.). 1990. pap. text 12.00 (*0-918618-43-6*) Pella Pub.

Layrock, George. An Eye on Nature: A Photographer's Introduction to Familiar Wildlife. (Illus.). 160p. 1986. 19.95 (*0-668-06536-2*) P-H.

Layte, Richard. Divided Time: Gender, Paid Employment & Domestic Labour. LC 98-73762. 8p. 1999. text 59.95 (*1-84014-397-5*, Pub. by Ashgate Pub) Ashgate Pub Co.

Laythorpe, Mark. The Penny Pincher's Profit Portfolio. How to Make Dollars in Cents. (Illus.). 80p. 1981. pap. 19.95 (*0-939230-00-3*) SNOWCO.

Laytin, Peter. Creative Camera Control. rev. ed. (Illus.). 128p. 1996. pap. 15.95 (*0-240-80268-3*, Focal) Buttrwrth-Heinemann.

***Laytin, Peter.** Creative Camera Control. 3rd ed. (Illus.). 160p. 2000. pap. 16.95 (*0-240-80426-0*, Focal) Buttrwrth-Heinemann.

Laytner, Anson. Arguing with God: A Jewish Tradition. LC 89-28654. 336p. 1990. 27.50 (*0-87668-817-2*) Aronson.

— Arguing with God: A Jewish Tradition. 336p. 1998. pap. 30.00 (*0-7657-6025-8*) Aronson.

Layton. Early Language Impairments in Children. (Early Childhood Education Ser.). 1998. 41.95 (*0-8273-7523-9*) Delmar.

— God's Plan for You. 1995. pap. 8.00 (*0-927936-41-0*) Vincom Pubng Co.

— A Northern Childhood. (Longman Literature Ser.). 1995. pap. text. write for info. (*0-582-25404-3*, Pub. by Addison-Wesley) Longman.

— Sibelius. (Dent Master Musicians Ser.). (Illus.). (C). pap. write for info. (*0-19-816482-3*) OUP.

Layton-Anderson, Laurie. The Art of William Alexander & Lowell Speers, Ser. 1. (Illus.). 76p. 1987. pap. text. write for info. (*1-883576-00-8*) Alexander Art.

— The Art of William Alexander & Lowell Speers, Series 2. (Illus.). 80p. 1987. pap. text. write for info. (*1-883576-01-6*) Alexander Art.

Layton, Arthur. Maine: Cruising the Coast by Car. LC 94-40886. (Illus.). 180p. (Orig.). 1994. pap. 9.95 (*1-56626-087-6*, Cntry Rds Pr) NTC Contemp Pub Co.

— Maine: Cruising the Coast by Car. 2nd rev. ed. LC 97-2221. (Illus.). 140p. (Orig.). 1997. pap. 10.95 (*1-56626-182-1*, Cntry Rds Pr) NTC Contemp Pub Co.

— Relocation Tax Advisor. 36p. 1997. pap. 7.00 (*0-9636296-5-4*) Hessel Group.

***Layton, Arthur, ed.** Relocation Tax Advisor. rev. ed. 36p. 2000. pap. 7.00 (*0-9636296-0-3*) Hessel Group.

Layton, Aviva, jt. auth. see Mansouri, Lofti.

Layton, Aviva, jt. auth. see Mark, Bonnie S.

***Layton, Azza Salama.** International Politics & Civil Rights Policies in the United States, 1941-1960. LC 99-24439. 232p. (C). 2000. 49.95 (*0-521-66002-5*); pap. 17.95 (*0-521-66976-6*) Cambridge U Pr.

Layton, B. Cooking for One Cookbook. LC 96-146305. (Illus.). 212p. 1994. spiral bd. 11.95 (*1-57166-011-9*) Hearts N Tummies.

— Off-to-College Cookbook. (Illus.). 176p. 1994. spiral bd. 5.95 (*1-57166-013-5*) Hearts N Tummies.

— Super Simple Cooking. (Illus.). 192p. 1994. spiral bd. 5.95 (*1-57166-012-7*) Hearts N Tummies.

Layton, Bentley. The Gnostic Scriptures: A New Translation with Annotations. LC 85-25234. (Illus.). 800p. 1987. 35.00 (*0-385-17447-0*) Doubleday.

— Gnostic Scriptures: A New Translation with Introduction & Notes. 576p. 1995. pap. 22.95 (*0-385-47843-7*) Doubleday.

Layton, Bob. Hercules: Prince of Power. (Illus.). 192p. 1997. pap. text 19.99 (*0-7851-0555-7*) Marvel Entrprs.

***Layton, Bruce D. & Musselwhite, James C., Jr.** VA Healthcare: More Veterans Are Being Served, But Better Oversight Is Needed. (Illus.). 58p. (C). 2000. reprint ed. pap. text 20.00 (*0-7881-8716-3*) DIANE Pub.

Layton, C. Bradley, jt. auth. see Wertz, Keith.

Layton, C. D. Hansen's Improved Ex-Meridian Tables. (C). 1987. 50.00 (*0-85174-093-6*) St Mut.

Layton, C. W. Dictionary of Nautical Words & Terms. 4th ed. 395p. 1994. text 45.00 (*0-85174-618-7*) Sheridan.

Layton, Carol, jt. ed. see Marini, Tara.

Layton, Daphne, ed. Integrated Planning for Campus Information Systems. (Library, Information, & Computer Science Ser.: No. 12). (Illus.). 130p. (Orig.). 1989. pap. 13.00 (*1-55653-071-4*) OCLC Online Comp.

Layton, Daphne N. Philanthropy & Voluntarism: An Annotated Bibliography. LC 87-12032. 308p. 1987. 18.50 (*0-87954-198-9*) Foundation Ctr.

Layton, David. German Shorthaired Pointers Today. LC 93-39078. (Illus.). 176p. 1994. 27.95 (*0-87605-181-6*) Howell Bks.

***Layton, David.** Motion Sickness: A Memoir. (Illus.). 240p. 2000. 21.95 (*1-55199-039-3*) MW&R.

Layton, David. Technology's Challenge to Science Education: Cathedral, Quarry, or Company Store? LC 92 30287. (Developing Science & Technology Education Ser.). 1993. pap. 31.95 (*0-335-09958-0*) OpUniv Pr.

Layton, David, ed. Innovations in Science & Technology. (Science & Technology of Teacher Training Ser.: No. 5). 258p. 1994. pap. 25.00 (*92-3-102975-4*, U9754, Pub. by UNESCO) Bernan Associates.

— Innovations in Science & Technology Education, Vol. 6. 258p. (Orig.). 1997. pap. 25.00 (*92-3-103278-X*, U3278, Pub. by UNESCO) Bernan Associates.

Layton, Deborah. Seductive Poison: A Jonestown Survivor's Story of Life & Death in the People's Temple. LC 98-18009. (Illus.). 336p. 1998. 23.95 (*0-385-48983-8*) Doubleday.

***Layton, Deborah.** Seductive Poison: A Jonestown Survivor's Story of Life & Death in the People's Temple. 368p. 1999. pap. 14.00 (*0-385-48984-6*, Anchor NY) Doubleday.

Layton, Dian. Mommy, Why Can't I Watch That TV Show? (Mommy, Why...Ser.). (Illus.). 24p. (Orig.). (J). 1995. pap. 3.99 (*1-56043-148-2*) Destiny Image.

— Mommy, Why Did Jesus Have to Die? (Mommy, Why...Ser.). (Illus.). 24p. (Orig.). (J). 1995. pap. 3.99 (*1-56043-146-6*) Destiny Image.

— Soldiers with Little Feet. 182p. (Orig.). 1989. pap. 10.99 (*0-914903-86-1*) Destiny Image.

Layton, Diane C. Hind's Feet on High Places. 1998. pap. 12.99 (*0-7684-2021-0*) Destiny Image.

Layton, Donald. Aircraft Performance. 224p. 1988. 39.95 (*0-916460-40-1*) Weber Systems.

— System Safety: Including Department of Defense Standards. 200p. 1989. text 39.95 (*0-938862-64-2*) Weber Systems.

— World War II: A Global Perspective. 2nd ed. 208p. (C). 1998. per. 34.95 (*0-7872-1942-8*) Kendall-Hunt.

Layton, Donald H. & Scribner, Jay D., eds. Teaching Educational Politics & Policy. 102p. 1989. 4.50 (*0-922971-04-8*) Univ Council Educ Admin.

Layton, Donald H., jt. ed. see Scribner, Jay D.

Layton, Donald M. Helicopter Performance. 170p. 1984. 49.95 (*0-916460-39-8*, Matrix Pubs Inc) Weber Systems.

Layton, E. T., et al, eds. The Dynamics of Science & Technology. (Sociology of the Sciences Yearbook Ser.: No. 2). 1978. pap. text 73.50 (*90-277-0881-9*) Kluwer Academic.

Layton, Edith. Bound by Love. 1996. mass mkt. 5.99 (*0-671-53531-5*) PB.

— Captured Hearts: Five Favorite Love Stories. 345p. 1999. mass mkt. 6.99 (*0-451-40883-7*, Topaz) NAL.

***Layton, Edith.** The Challenge. 400p. 2000. mass mkt. 5.99 (*0-06-101433-8*) HarpC.

— The Chance. 384p. 2000. mass mkt. 6.99 (*0-06-101434-6*, Torch) HarpC.

Layton, Edith. The Choice. 352p. 1999. mass mkt. 5.99 (*0-06-101392-7*) HarpC.

***Layton, Edith.** Duke's Wager & Lord of Dishonor. 2000. mass mkt. 5.50 (*0-451-20139-6*) Signet.

Layton, Edith. A True Lady. 1995. mass mkt. 5.99 (*0-671-88301-1*) PB.

— The Wedding. 1995. mass mkt. 5.50 (*0-671-88300-3*) PB.

Layton, Edwin T. The Revolt of the Engineers: Social Responsibility & the American Engineering Profession. LC 85-23981. 310p. reprint ed. pap. 96.10 (*0-608-06105-0*, 206643700008) Bks Demand.

Layton, Eunice & Layton, Felix. Life Your Great Adventure: A Theosophical View. rev. ed. LC 88-40136. Orig. Title: Theosophy: Key to Understanding. 194p. 1988. reprint ed. pap. 7.25 (*0-8356-0635-X*, Quest) Theos Pub Hse.

Layton, Felix, jt. auth. see Layton, Eunice.

Layton, George. The Swap. LC 96-40447. 192p. (YA). (gr. 4 up). 1997. 16.95 (*0-399-23148-X*, G P Putnam) Peng Put Young Read.

Layton-Henry, Zig, ed. The Political Rights of Migrant Workers in Western Europe. (Modern Politics Ser.: Vol. 25). 256p. (C). 1990. text 45.00 (*0-8039-8271-2*) Sage.

Layton-Henry, Zig, jt. ed. see Cohen, Robin.

Layton, Irving. Dance with Desire: The Love Poems of Irving layton. 176p. 1992. pap. write for info. (*0-88984-135-7*) Porcup Quill.

— Fornalutx: Selected Poems, 1928-1990. 208p. 1991. pap. 19.95 (*0-7735-0963-1*, Pub. by McG-Queens Univ Pr) CUP Services.

— Fornalutx: Selected Poems, 1928-1990. 208p. 1992. 60.00 (*0-7735-0952-6*, Pub. by McG-Queens Univ Pr) CUP Services.

— The Improved Binoculars. 128p. 1991. pap. write for info. (*0-88984-101-2*) Porcup Quill.

— The Selected Poems of Irving Layton. LC 76-54704. 1977. 8.50 (*0-8112-0641-6*, Pub. by New Directions); pap. 2.25 (*0-8112-0642-4*, NDP431, Pub. by New Directions) Norton.

— The Uncollected Poems of Irving Layton, 1936-1959. limited ed. 153p. 1988. 150.00 (*0-88962-042-3*) Mosaic.

— Wild Peculiar Joy. 1990. audio 4.98 (*0-7710-4950-1*) McCland & Stewart.

Layton, Irving & Creeley, Robert. Irving Layton & Robert Creeley: The Complete Correspondence, 1953-1978. Faas, Ekbert & Reed, Sabrina, eds. (Illus.). 288p. (C). 1990. 60.00 (*0-7735-0657-8*, Pub. by McG-Queens Univ Pr) CUP Services.

Layton, Jeffrey. Blowout. 400p. (Orig.). 1995. mass mkt. 4.99 (*0-380-78066-6*, Avon Bks) Morrow Avon.

— Warhead. 448p. (Orig.). 1997. mass mkt. 5.99 (*0-380-79154-4*, Avon Bks) Morrow Avon.

Layton, John M. Multivariable Control Theory. LC 77-360712. (IEE Control Engineering Ser.: Vol. 1). (Illus.). 246p. reprint ed. pap. 76.30 (*0-608-17788-1*, 203225200079) Bks Demand.

Layton, L. & Steinwall, R. Butterworths Annotated Acts: Trade Practices Act. 550p. 1994. pap. 30.00 (*0-409-30968-0*, Austral, MICHIE) LEXIS Pub.

Layton, Lesley. Songbirds in Singapore: The Growth of a Pastime. (Images of Asia Ser.). (Illus.). 120p. 1991. 21.00 (*0-19-588999-1*) OUP.

Layton, Lyn, et al. Sound Practice: Phonological Awareness in the Classroom. LC 97-196882. 112p. 1997. pap. 24.95 (*1-85346-456-2*, Pub. by David Fulton) Taylor & Francis.

Layton, Lynne. Who's That Girl? Who's That Boy? Clinical Practice Meets Postmodern Gender Theory. LC 97-40089. 288p. 1999. pap. text 30.00 (*0-7657-0182-0*) Aronson.

— Who's That Girl? Who's That Boy? Clinical Practice Meets Postmodern Gender Theory. LC 97-40089. 288p. Date not set. 40.00 (*0-7657-0140-5*) Aronson.

Layton, Marcia. New Rider's Official World Wide Web Yellow Pages. abr. ed. LC 98-85921. 1998. pap. 19.99 (*0-7357-0005-2*) Que.

— Official World Wide Web Directory & Internet Directory, 1 Vol. LC 98-86521. 1998. pap. text 19.99 (*0-7357-0015-X*) New Riders Pub.

— Successful Fine Art Marketing. 256p. 1993. 39.95 (*0-913069-45-0*); pap. 19.95 (*0-913069-39-6*) Consultant Pr.

Layton, Marcia, jt. auth. see Paulson, Ed.

Layton, Marilyn S. Choosing to Emerge As Readers & Writers: A Multicultural Reader. LC 92-25113. 432p. (C). 1997. pap. text 47.00 (*0-06-500727-1*) Addson-Wesley Educ.

— Intercultural Journeys Through Reading & Writing. 672p. (C). 1997. pap. text 50.00 (*0-06-046437-2*) Addson-Wesley Educ.

Layton, Mary J. Advancing the Message: Tips & Suggestions for Communications People in Child Welfare Agencies. LC 98-111023. (Illus.). 28p. (Orig.). 1997. pap. 12.95 (*0-87868-659-2*, CWLA Pr) Child Welfare.

Layton, Max. Objects in Mirror Are Closer Than They Appear. 200p. 1994. pap. 14.95 (*0-88962-541-7*) Mosaic.

Layton, Meredith. Baby's First Words: A Sign & Say Interactive Language Book. LC 99-61431. (Sign & Say Interactive Language Ser.). (Illus.). 32p. (J). 1999. 16.95 (*0-9670821-0-2*) Peek-A-Boo Pubg.

Layton, Mike. Easy Blood: Ronald Reagan's Proxy Wars in Central America. LC 96-96996. (Illus.). 320p. (Orig.). 1996. pap. 15.00 (*0-9654533-0-8*) DragonRed Pr.

— My Very Worst Friend: A Survivor's Report on the Twentieth Century. LC 97-94775. (Illus.). 311p. 1998. pap. 16.00 (*0-9654533-1-6*) DragonRed Pr.

Layton, Monique, tr. see Levi-Strauss, Claude.

Layton, Neal. Smile If You're Human. Sherry, Toby & Goyette, Cecile, eds. LC 98-11482. (Illus.). 32p. (J). (ps-2). 1999. 14.99 (*0-8037-2381-4*, Dial Yng Read) Peng Put Young Read.

***Layton, Peggy & Tate, Vicki.** Cooking with Home Storage. 304p. 1999. pap. 16.95 (*1-882723-39-2*, Pub. by Gold Leaf Pr) Origin Bk Sales.

Layton, Peter. Glass Art. (Illus.). 216p. 1996. text. write for info. (*90-5703-181-7*, Harwood Acad Pubs) Gordon & Breach.

Layton, Peter. Glass Art. LC 96-15718. (Illus.). 224p. 1996. 49.95 (*0-295-97565-2*) U of Wash Pr.

Layton, R., ed. Conflict in the Archaeology of Living Traditions. (One World Archaeology Ser.). (Illus.). 272p. (C). 1994. pap. 34.99 (*0-415-09559-X*, B4610) Routledge.

— Who Needs the Past? Indigenous Values in Archaeology. (One World Archaeology Ser.). 240p. (C). 1994. pap. 19.95 (*0-415-09558-1*, B4706) Routledge.

Layton, R. B. The Purple Martin. LC 71-92883. (Illus.). 192p. 1969. reprint ed. pap. 9.95 (*0-912542-01-2*) Nature Bks Pubs.

Layton, R. B. Thirty Birds That Will Build in Bird Houses. LC 77-81805. 1977. pap. 10.95 (*0-912542-05-5*) Nature Bks Pubs.

Layton, Richard A. Principles of Analytical System Dynamics. LC 97-45237. (Mechanical Engineering Ser.). (Illus.). 158p. 1998. text 49.00 (*0-387-98405-4*) Spr-Verlag.

Layton, Robert. The Anthropology of Art. 2nd ed. (Illus.). 272p. (C). 1991. pap. text 19.95 (*0-521-36894-4*) Cambridge U Pr.

— The Illustrated Lives of the Great Composers: Greig. 157p. 1998. pap. text 17.95 (*0-7119-4811-9*, OP47745) Omnibus NY.

— An Introduction to Theory in Anthropology. LC 97-10237. 254p. (C). 1998. text 54.95 (*0-521-62018-X*); pap. text 18.95 (*0-521-62982-9*) Cambridge U Pr.

Layton, Robert, ed. A Guide to the Symphony. (Illus.). 510p. 1995. pap. 19.95 (*0-19-288005-5*) OUP.

Layton, Robert, ed. Who Needs the Past? Indigenous Values in Archaeology. LC 88-15598. (One World Archaeology Ser.: No. 5). 256p. (C). 1988. text 62.95 (*0-04-445020-6*) Routledge.

Layton, Robert, jt. auth. see Ucko, Peter J.

Layton, Roger, jt. auth. see Lazer, William.

Layton, Sarah, et al. Competitive Strategy: Planning Your Organization's Success. Paris, Janis, ed. LC 95-67038. (Fifty-Minute Ser.). (Illus.). 103p. (Orig.). 1995. pap. 10.95 (*1-56052-350-6*) Crisp Pubns.

Layton, Susan. Russian Literature & Empire: The Conquest of the Caucasus from Pushkin to Tolstoy. LC 93-47121. (Studies in Russian Literature). 370p. (C). 1995. text 69.95 (*0-521-44443-8*) Cambridge U Pr.

Layton, T. A. The Cheese Handbook: A Guide to the World's Best Cheeses. rev. ed. 160p. 1973. reprint ed. pap. 4.50 (*0-486-22955-6*) Dover.

***Layton, Thomas N.** Voyage of Frolic: New England Merchants & The Opium Trade. 1999. pap. text 14.95 (*0-8047-3849-1*) Stanford U Pr.

Layton, Thomas N. Voyage of the Frolic: New England Merchants & the Opium Trade. LC 96-44320. 1997. 24.95 (*0-8047-2909-3*) Stanford U Pr.

Layton, W. T., rev. Harbord's Glossary of Navigation. rev. ed. (C). 1987. 100.00 (*0-85174-277-7*) St Mut.

Layton, William I. College Arithmetic. LC 73-155121. 244p. reprint ed. pap. 75.70 (*0-608-30885-4*, 205510800008) Bks Demand.

Layton, William W. Layton Looks at Life: Timely Essays on the Past, Present & Future by a Virginia Octogenarian. 160p. 1995. pap. 9.50 (*0-9649806-3-0*) W W Layton.

Laywine, Alison. Kant's Early Metaphysics & the Origins of the Critical Philosophy. (North American Kant Society Studies in Philosophy: Vol. 3). (Orig.). 1994. pap. text 20.00 (*0-924922-20-6*); lib. bdg. 39.00 (*0-924922-70-2*) Ridgeview.

Laywine, Charles F. & Mullen, Gary L. Discrete Mathematics Using Latin Squares. LC 97-52401. (Wiley-Interscience Series in Discrete Mathematics & Optimization). 328p. 1998. 79.95 (*0-471-24064-8*, Wiley-Interscience) Wiley.

Layzell, Daniel T. & Lyddon, Jan W. Budgeting for Higher Education at the State Level: Enigma, Paradox, & Ritual. Fife, Jonathan D., ed. LC 90-63845. (ASHE-ERIC Higher Education Reports: No. 90-4). 110p. 1990. pap. 20.75 (*1-878380-01-X*) GWU Grad Schl E&HD.

Layzell, Daniel T., jt. auth. see Jordan, Stephen M.

Layzell, Paul, jt. ed. see Spurr, Kathy.

Layzer, David. Cosmogenesis: The Growth of Order in the Universe. (Illus.). 336p. 1991. reprint ed. pap. 14.95 (*0-19-506908-0*) OUP.

Layzer, David, jt. ed. see Dalgarno, A.

Laz, Bob. Epic of Wonderland Park: So We Build a Resort. large type unabridged ed. (Illus.). 369p. (Orig.). 1990. pap. 16.90 (*0-9625861-0-2*) R & L Enterprise.

L

Laz, Medard. Coping When Your Spouse Dies. LC 98-65698. 80p. 1998. pap. 4.95 (*0-7648-0226-7*, Liguori Lifespan) Liguori Pubns.

— Life after the Divorce: Practical Guidance for Starting Over. LC 97-75382. 80p. 1998. pap. 4.95 (*0-7648-0191-0*) Liguori Pubns.

— Love Adds a Little Chocolate: 100 Stories to Brighten Your Day & Sweeten Your Life. 224p. 1998. 14.00 (*0-446-52424-7*, Pub. by Warner Bks) Little.

— Making Parish Meetings Work: Planning, Leading, Listening, Running, Evaluating. LC 96-52317. 128p. 1997. pap. 5.95 (*0-87793-597-1*) Ave Maria.

Laz, Thom, jt. illus. see Southcott, Marrin.

Lazaar, Milan. Chemical Reactions of Natural & Synthetic Polymers. LC 08-813424. (Polymer Science & Technology Ser.). 1989. text 69.95 (*0-470-21231-4*) P-H.

Lazan, B. Damping of Materials & Members in Structural Mechanics. LC 66-27370. 1968. 144.00 (*0-08-013221-9*, Pub. by Pergamon Repr) Franklin.

Lazan, Marian Blumenthal, jt. auth. see Perl, Lila.

Lazandes, M., et al. CSIRO Handbook of Australian Weeds. (Illus.). 272p. 1997. pap. 49.95 (*0-643-05981-4*, Pub. by CSIRO) Accents Pubns.

Lazano, Ed, ed. Alternative Sessions for Guitar. (Illus.). 6p. 1998. pap. text 12.95 (*0-8256-1630-1*, AM945208) Music Sales.

***Lazano, Ed, ed.** Eddie Money: His Greatest Hits. 160p. 2000. pap. text 24.95 (*0-8256-1764-2*, AM961433) Music Sales.

Lazano, Ed, ed. Grunge Rock Sessions for Guitar. (Illus.). 6p. 1998. pap. text 12.95 (*0-8256-1627-1*, AM945175) Music Sales.

— Modern Blues Sessions for Guitar. 6p. 1998. pap. 12.95 (*0-8256-1625-5*, AM945153) Music Sales.

— Modern Rock Sessions for Guitar. 5p. 1998. pap. text 12.95 (*0-8256-1626-3*, AM945164) Music Sales.

— Nineties Rock Sessions for Guitar. 6p. 1998. pap. text 12.95 (*0-8256-1629-8*, AM945197) Music Sales.

— Sixties Rock Sessions for Guitar. (Illus.). 6p. 1998. pap. text 12.95 (*0-8256-1628-X*, AM945186) Music Sales.

***Lazano, Ed, ed.** Woody Mann: Lisboa. 112p. 2000. pap. text 24.95 (*0-8256-0338-2*, OK65004) Music Sales.

Lazar, A. L. & Taylor, D. C. Multipliers of Pedersen's Ideal. LC 75-44302. (Memoirs Ser.: No. 5/169). 111p. 1976. pap. 22.00 (*0-8218-1869-4*, MEMO/5/169) Am Math.

Lazar, Arthur. Intimate Landscapes. LC 93-80036. (Illus.). 96p. 1994. 60.00 (*0-9638189-5-3*) Lke Forest Coll.

LaZar, Arthur, photos by. Of Earth & Timbers Made: New Mexico Architecture. LC 73-91766. (Illus.). 93p. 1974. reprint ed. pap. 30.00 (*0-608-04132-7*, 206486500011) Bks Demand.

Lazar, Aurel A. & IEEE Staff. 1998 IEEE Open Architectures & Network Programming: Openarch'98: 3-4 April 1998, San Francisco, Ca, USA. LC 98-84565. v, 145p. 1998. pap. write for info. (*0-7803-4784-6*) IEEE Standards.

Lazar, Barry & Douglas, Tamsin. The Guide to Ethnic Montreal. rev. expanded ed. (Illus.). 360p. (Orig.). 1993. pap. 13.95 (*1-55065-030-0*, Pub. by Vehicule Pr) Genl Dist Srvs.

Lazar, Clifford W. Ten Minutes to MS-DOS Word Perfect, WordStar, Lotus BASIC. (Illus.). 210p. 1989. teacher ed. 24.95 (*0-685-30761-1*, TM01); pap. 24.95 (*0-685-30759-X*, TM01); pap. text 24.95 (*0-685-30760-3*, TM01); lib. bdg. 29.95 (*0-9624618-0-6*, TM01) Systems Express.

— Ten Minutes to MS-DOS, WordPerfect, WordStar, Lotus, BASIC. (Illus.). 210p. 1989. pap. 24.95 (*0-685-29337-8*, TM01); pap. text 24.95 (*0-685-29338-6*, TM01); lib. bdg. 24.95 (*0-685-29336-X*, TM01) Systems Express.

Lazar-Curatolo, Linda. Are You Green Yet? 72p. (YA). (gr. 5-12). 1992. pap. 6.95 (*1-57515-013-1*) PPI Pubng.

Lazar, David, ed. Conversations with M. F. K. Fisher. LC 92-28485. (Literary Conversations Ser.). 184p. 1993. text 39.50 (*0-87805-595-9*) U Pr of Miss.

Lazar, Ed, ed. Tibet: The Issue Is Independence. 92p. 1994. pap. 7.00 (*0-938077-75-9*) Parallax Pr.

Lazar, Edward. Thoughts: Reflections in the Search for Meaning. Tobin, Sheilah & Banwarth, Francine, eds. 144p. 1989. write for info. (*0-318-64896-2*) JZ Redman Pubs.

— Thoughts: Reflections in the Search for Meaning. Banwarth, Francine & Lembeck, Michael, eds. LC 89-91041. (Illus.). 138p. 1989. pap. 6.00 (*0-9622548-0-0*) JZ Redman Pubs.

Lazar, Elysa. Museum Shop Report: A Guide to Museum Shop Catalogs. 1992. pap. 14.95 (*1-881642-02-X*) Lazar Comms.

— Outlet Report. 1992. pap. 9.95 (*1-881642-01-1*) Lazar Comms.

— Shop-by-Mail: The Mail Order Bible. 1992. pap. 9.95 (*1-881642-00-3*) Lazar Comms.

Lazar, Elysa & Miceli, Eve. Elysa Lazar's Smart Shopping: An Amateur's Guide to Shopping Like a Pro. (Illus.). 320p. (Orig.). 1993. pap. 14.95 (*1-881642-03-8*) Lazar Comms.

— Lazar's Museum Shop Treasures: The Exclusive Guide to Museum Catalog Shopping. 2nd ed. (Illus.). 300p. 1994. pap. 14.95 (*1-881642-05-4*) Lazar Comms.

— Lazar's Outlet Shopper's Guide: A Field Guide to Factory Outlet Shopping. 2nd ed. 250p. 1994. pap. 12.95 (*1-881642-06-2*) Lazar Comms.

— Lazar's Shop by Mail: A Field Guide to Shopping by Mail. 2nd ed. (Illus.). 350p. 1993. pap. 14.95 (*1-881642-04-6*) Lazar Comms.

Lazar, Gillian. Using Literature in Language Teaching: A Guide for Teachers & Trainers. LC 92-8942. (Teacher Training & Development Ser.). 281p. (C). 1993. text 54.95 (*0-521-40480-0*); pap. text 22.95 (*0-521-40651-X*) Cambridge U Pr.

Lazar, H. P. Human Digestive System. (Perspectives in Medicine Ser.: Vol. 4). (Illus.). 1972. pap. 16.75 (*3-8055-1429-8*) S Karger.

Lazar, Harold L., ed. Current Therapy for Acute Coronary Ischemia. LC 93-14925. (Illus.). 320p. 1993. 65.00 (*0-87993-555-3*) Futura Pub.

***Lazar, Harvey.** Canada: State of the Federation 1999-2000: Rebalancing & Decentralizing Fiscal Federation. (Institute of Intergovernmental Relations Ser.). 350p. 2000. pap. 24.95 (*0-88911-843-4*, Pub. by Queens U Inst Intergov) CUP Services.

— Canada: The State of the Federation, 1999-2000: Rebalancing & Decentralizing Fiscal Federation. 350p. 2000. text 55.00 (*0-88911-839-6*, Pub. by Queens U Inst Intergov) CUP Services.

Lazar, I. Hungary. (Illus.). 143p. (C). 1988. pap. 100.00 (*0-7855-5212-X*, Pub. by Collets) St Mut.

— Hungary: A View from the Air. (C). 1991. 68.00 (*0-89771-851-8*, Pub. by Collets) St Mut.

Lazar, Irving, frwd. Sex, Kids & Politics: Health Services in Schools. LC 97-16422. 256p. 1997. 46.00 (*0-8077-3636-8*); pap. 21.95 (*0-8077-3635-X*) Tchrs Coll.

Lazar, Irving & Tapert, Annette. Swifty: My Life & Good Times. LC 94-47215. 1995. 24.00 (*0-684-80418-2*) S&S Trade.

Lazar, Israel. The New Dictionary: Hebrew-English English-Hebrew. (HEB & ENG.). 762p. 1998. pap. 6.99 (*1-880880-31-8*) Israeli Trad.

Lazar, Istvan. Hungary: A Brief History. 248p. 1989. pap. 50.00 (*963-13-3861-4*, Pub. by Corvina Bks) St Mut.

***Lazar, Istvan.** Hungary: A Brief History. 248p. 1999. pap. 21.00 (*963-13-4850-4*, Pub. by Corvina Bks) St Mut.

Lazar, Istvan. An Illustrated History of Hungary. (Illus.). 132p. 1989. 140.00 (*963-13-4054-6*, Pub. by Corvina Bks) St Mut.

***Lazar, Istvan.** An Illustrated History of Hungary. (Illus.). 132p. 1999. 46.00 (*963-13-4542-4*, Pub. by Corvina Bks) St Mut.

Lazar, Istvan. Transylvania: A Short History. LC 98-138539. 248p. 1999. pap. 21.00 (*963-13-4333-2*, Pub. by Corvina Bks) St Mut.

***Lazar, John.** The Foot Book. (Illus.). 130p. (Orig.). 2000. pap. 16.95 (*1-883938-55-4*) Dry Bones Pr.

Lazar, Larry, ed. New Jersey's Distinguished Restaurants, 1995. 160p. 1994. pap. 9.95 (*0-9634765-3-X*) Qual Restaurants.

— New Jersey's Distinguished Restaurants, 1996. pap. 9.95 (*0-9634765-4-8*) Qual Restaurants.

— New Jersey's Distinguished Restaurants, 1997. 1997. pap. text 9.95 (*0-9634765-5-6*) Qual Restaurants.

Lazar, Liliane, jt. auth. see Dormay, Nadine.

Lazar, Mashe. Biblia Ladinada: Escorial I. J. 3, 2 vols. 888p. 1995. 60.00 (*1-56954-047-0*) Hispanic Seminary.

Lazar, Mike, jt. auth. see Colvin, Geoffrey.

Lazar, Milan, et al. Free Radicals in Chemistry & Biology. (Illus.). 304p. 1989. lib. bdg. 225.00 (*0-8493-5387-4*, QD471) CRC Pr.

Lazar, Miriam A. Let's Review Physics. 1996. pap. text 11.95 (*0-8120-9606-1*) Barron.

Lazar, Moshe. Biblia Romanceada: MS. RAH 87. lxx, 354p. 1994. 50.00 (*1-56954-029-2*) Hispanic Seminary.

Lazar, Moshe, ed. The Anxious Subject: Nightmares & Daymares in Literature & Film. LC 82-70791. (Interplay Ser.: Vol. 2). 208p. 1983. pap. 21.00 (*0-89003-116-9*) Undena Pubns.

— The Dream & the Play: Ionesco's Theatrical Quest. LC 81-71734. (Interplay Ser.: Vol. 1). 184p. 1982. pap. 21.00 (*0-89003-108-8*) Undena Pubns.

— Play Durrenmatt. (Interplay Ser.: Vol. 3). 219p. (C). 1983. pap. text 21.00 (*0-89003-129-0*, 82-50986) Undena Pubns.

***Lazar, Moshe, ed.** Sefarad in My Heart: A Ladino Reader. 984p. 1999. pap. 36.00 (*0-911437-83-5*) Labyrinthos.

Lazar, Moshe, ed. Text & Concordance of Biblioteca Nacional, Madrid, MS10289: Moses Maimonides, Mostrador e Ensennador de los Turbados. Toledo, Pedro, tr. (Spanish-Jewish Ser.: No. 1). (SPA.). 12p. 1987. 10.00 incl. fiche (*0-942260-84-8*) Hispanic Seminary.

Lazar, Moshe, tr. The Ladino Bible of Ferrara (1553) LC 92-70756. (Sephardic Classical Library). (LAD.). 766p. 1992. 100.00 (*0-911437-56-8*) Labyrinthos.

— Ladino Pentateuch: (Constantinople, 1547) LC 88-82628. (Sephardic Classical Library). (HEB & LAD., Illus.). 560p. 1988. lib. bdg. 90.00 (*0-911437-46-0*) Labyrinthos.

Lazar, Moshe & Dilligan, Robert, eds. The Ladino Five Scrolls: Abraham Asa's Versions of the Hebrew & Aramaic Texts. LC 92-73523. (Sephardic Classical Library). (HEB & LAD.). 304p. 1992. text 65.00 (*0-911437-58-4*) Labyrinthos.

— The Ladino Mahzor of Ferrara (1553) LC 93-77908. (Sephardic Classical Library). (HEB & LAD.). 320p. 1993. text 55.00 (*0-911437-60-6*) Labyrinthos.

— Libro de las Generaciones & The Book of Yashar. LC 89-85090. (Sephardic Classical Library: No. 3). (ENG & SPA.). 515p. (C). 1990. lib. bdg. 90.00 (*0-911437-51-7*) Labyrinthos.

— Libro de Oracyones: Ferrara Ladino Siddur. LC 95-80477. (Sephardic Classical Library: Vol. 11). (LAD., Illus.). 612p. (C). 1995. 95.00 (*0-911437-64-9*) Labyrinthos.

— Sefer Ha-Yasar: First Ladino Translation. LC 97-76086. (Sephardic Classical Library: Vol. 12). (Illus.). 562p. 1998. 95.00 (*0-911437-79-7*) Labyrinthos.

— Sefer Tesubah: Book on Repentance. LC 93-85953. (Sephardic Classical Library). (LAD.). 304p. (C). 1993. text 65.00 (*0-911437-62-2*) Labyrinthos.

— Siddur Tefillot: A Woman's Ladino Prayer Book (Paris B. N., Esp. 668; 15th C.) LC 95-81321. (Sephardic Classical Library: Vol. 10). (HEB & LAD., Illus.). 302p. (C). 1995. 55.00 (*0-911437-67-3*) Labyrinthos.

Lazar, Moshe & Gottesman, Ronald, eds. The Dove & the Mole: Kafka's Journey into Darkness & Creativity. (Interplay Ser.: Vol. 5). 276p. 1987. 32.00 (*0-89003-251-3*); pap. 21.00 (*0-89003-250-5*) Undena Pubns.

Lazar, Moshe & Haliczer, Stephen, eds. The Jews of Spain & the Expulsion of 1492. LC 96-78910. (Illus.). 352p. (C). 1997. pap. 27.00 (*0-911437-68-1*) Labyrinthos.

Lazar, Moshe, ed. see Halevi, Yehuda.

Lazar, Moshe, ed. & tr. see Halevi, Yehudah.

Lazar, Moshe, ed. & tr. see Maimonides.

Lazar, Moshe, tr. & intro. see Dilligan, Robert, ed.

Lazar, Paul, jt. auth. see Schoen, Linda Allen.

Lazar, Rande H. Pediatric Sinus Disease. (Illus.). 224p. 1998. 59.00 (*0-86577-615-6*) Thieme Med Pubs.

Lazar, Richard B., ed. Principles of Neurologic Rehabilitation. (Illus.). 752p. 1997. text 85.00 (*0-07-036794-9*) McGraw-Hill HPD.

Lazar, Shelley F. Oriental Collection: 20 Original Needlepoint Designs. 1992. 24.95 (*0-316-88902-4*) Little.

— Pictures in Needlework: Twenty Miniature Designs for All Occasions. (Illus.). 96p. 1990. text 15.95 (*0-02-569510-X*) Macmillan.

Lazar, Susan G., ed. Extended Dynamic Psychotherapy: Making the Case in an Era of Managed Care. (Special Supplement to Psychoanalytic Inquiry 1997 Ser.). 184p. 1997. 28.50 (*0-88163-928-1*) Analytic Pr.

Lazar, Swifty. Swifty: The Autobiography of Irving Lazar. 1995. 24.00 (*0-671-52505-0*) S&S Trade.

Lazar, Y. The New Dictionary: Hebrew English - English Hebrew. 778p. 1995. pap. 4.95 (*1-888162-00-7*) Kuperand USA.

— Practical Hebrew to English Dictionary. (ENG & HEB.). 538p. 1997. 95.00 (*0-320-00694-8*) Fr & Eur.

Lazar, Zachary. Aaron, Approximately. LC 97-19540. 352p. 1998. 22.00 (*0-06-039211-8*, ReganBks) HarperTrade.

— Aaron, Approximately. LC 97-19540. 352p. 1999. pap. 13.50 (*0-380-73213-0*, Avon Bks) Morrow Avon.

Lazaravich, Gordana, ed. Livietta e Tracollo: La Contadina Astuta: Intermezzi. LC 85-753856. (Complete Works of Pergolesi: No. 2, Vol. VI). (Illus.). 132p. 1991. lib. bdg. 112.00 (*0-918728-45-2*) Pendragon NY.

Lazard, Naomi. The Moonlit Upper Deckerina. LC 76-57519. 77p. 1977. pap. 12.95 (*0-8180-1540-3*, Pub. by Sheep Meadow) U Pr of New Eng.

— Ordinances. (Poetry Chapbook Ser.). 58p. (Orig.). 1984. pap. 12.00 (*0-937669-11-3*) Owl Creek Pr.

— Ordinances. 60p. (Orig.). 1995. pap. 12.00 (*1-887478-04-3*, WiseAcre) Red Sea NY.

Lazard, Naomi, tr. see Faiz, Faiz A.

Lazardfeld, Paul & Reitz, Jeffery G. An Introduction to Applied Sociology. LC 75-8274. 196p. 1981. lib. bdg. 25.00 (*0-444-99006-2*, LAP/) Greenwood.

Lazare, Aaron. Outpatient Psychiatry. 2nd ed. (Illus.). 752p. 1988. lib. bdg. 79.00 (*0-683-04851-1*) Lppncott W & W.

Lazare, Bernard. Antisemitism, Its History & Causes. LC 95-5651. xxiii, 200p. 1995. pap. 10.00 (*0-8032-7954-X*, Bison Books) U of Nebr Pr.

Lazare, Daniel. The Frozen Republic. 408p. 1997. pap. 14.00 (*0-15-600494-1*) Harcourt.

— The Frozen Republic: How the Constituiton Is Paralyzing Democracy. LC 95-22354. 378p. 1996. 25.00 (*0-15-100085-9*) Harcourt.

Lazare, Felix. Dictionnaire Administratif et Historique des Rues et des Monuments de Paris. (FRE.). 796p. 1993. 350.00 (*0-7859-9282-0*) Fr & Eur.

Lazare, Lucien. Rescue as Resistance: How Jewish Organizations Fought the Holocaust in France. Green, J. M., tr. LC 95-50615. (ENG & FRE.). 353p. 1996. 36.00 (*0-231-10124-4*) Col U Pr.

Lazare, S., jt. ed. see Fogarassy, E.

***Lazares, John.** Please Don't Call My Mother: An Administrative Philosophy & Parental Intervention Plan That Works. 1999. pap. text 12.95 (*1-886021-33-3*) J W Wood.

Lazarescu-Zobian, Maria M. Kipchak Turkik Lexical Traces of Ottoman Heritage in Rumanian & Balkan Languages. 320p. 1995. 36.50 (*0-88033-323-5*, 426, Pub. by East Eur Monographs) Col U Pr.

Lazareski, Vladimir, tr. see Spiridovich, Alexander I.

Lazareth, William H., jt. ed. see Forell, George W.

Lazarev, Adrian N. Molecular Approach to Solids. LC 98-28915. (Vibrational Spectra & Structure Ser.). 350p. 1998. 244.00 (*0-444-50039-1*) Elsevier.

Lazarev, Nikolai I. Dyshormonal Tumors: The Theory of Prophylaxis & Treatment. Haigh, Basil, tr. LC 65-27347. 146p. reprint ed. pap. 45.30 (*0-608-30226-0*, 202067100018) Bks Demand.

Lazarev, P. I., ed. Molecular Electronics: Materials & Methods. (C). 1991. text 191.00 (*0-7923-1196-5*) Kluwer Academic.

Lazarev, Sergey D. & Meilikhov, Evgenii Z. Electrophysical Properties of Semiconductors: In Tables & Figures. 184p. 1995. 97.50 (*1-56700-043-6*) Begell Hse.

Lazarev, V. N. Novgorodian Icon-Painting. (Illus.). 210p. (C). 1976. text 180.00 (*0-569-08320-6*, Pub. by Collets) St Mut.

— Russian Icon Painting: Russkaia Ikonopis'. Ot Istokov Do Nachala XVI Veka. (ENG & RUS.). 538p. 1984. 305.00 (*0-7855-1667-0*) St Mut.

Lazarev, Viktor Nikitich. The Russian Icon: From Its Origins to the Sixteenth Century. McDarby, Nancy, ed. Dees, Colette Joly, tr. LC 97-25470. (Illus.). 404p. 1997. 99.95 (*0-8146-2452-9*, Liturg Pr Bks) Liturgical Pr.

Lazarevich, Gordana. The Musical World of Frances James & Murray Adaskin. 331p. 1988. text 40.00 (*0-8020-5738-1*) U of Toronto Pr.

Lazarevich, Gordana, ed. see Hasse, Johann A.

Lazaric, Nathalie & Lorenz, Edward, eds. Trust & Economic Learning. LC 97-31187. 304p. 1998. 90.00 (*1-85898-460-2*) E Elgar.

Lazarides, Linda. The Nutritional Health Bible. 336p. 1998. pap. 16.00 (*0-7225-3424-8*) Thorsons PA.

Lazarides, M. The Tropical Grasses of Southeast Asia: Excluding Bamboos. 350p. 1980. lib. bdg. 50.00 (*3-7682-1255-6*) Lubrecht & Cramer.

Lazaridis, Gabriella, jt. ed. see Anthias, Flora.

Lazaridis, Gabriella, jt. ed. see Anthias, Floya.

Lazaris. The Sacred Journey: You & Your Higher Self. 2nd ed. 220p. 1987. reprint ed. pap. 14.95 (*1-55638-080-1*, NPN Pub) Concept Synergy.

— The Sirius Connection. 144p. (Orig.). 1996. pap. 12.95 (*1-55638-301-0*, NPN Pub) Concept Synergy.

— Working with Your Shadow: An Imperative on the Spiritual Path. 144p. (Orig.). 1995. pap. 12.95 (*1-55638-289-8*, NPN Pub) Concept Synergy.

Lazaris & Pursel, Jach. Lazaris Interviews. LC 88-70670. 1988. write for info. (*1-55638-072-0*) Concept Synergy.

Lazaris Johnston, Willis. Developmental Math: Exambuiler QuizBook. 4th ed. 1995. (*0-534-28204-0*) Intrepid Travel.

Lazarkiewi, S. & Troskolanski, A. T. Impeller Pumps. LC 65-14226. 1965. 344.00 (*0-08-011172-6*, Pub. by Pergamon Repr) Franklin.

Lazarnick, George. Netsuke & Inro Artists, & How to Read Their Signatures, 2 vols. deluxe ed. LC 81-51945. (Illus.). 1376p. 1982. lthr. 950.00 (*0-686-79507-5*) Reed Pubs.

Lazaro Carreter, Fernando, jt. auth. see Garcia Lorca, Federico.

Lazaro, Iciaro. Diccionario de Quimica. 130p. 1988. 32.95 (*0-7859-6030-9*, 8439712693) Fr & Eur.

Lazaro, Jose M. El Pensar Logico. 321p. 1988. 6.50 (*0-8477-2825-0*) U of PR Pr.

Lazaro, Judith, jt. auth. see Marshad, David S.

Lazaro, Olga J. QuickCheck Spanish. Luft, Kathleen, tr. from ENG. LC 97-31024. (Barron's Quickcheck Language Ser.). (ENG & SPA.). 160p. 1998. pap. 8.95 (*0-7641-0310-5*) Barron.

Lazaro, Pedro, jt. auth. see Danowski, Debbie.

Lazaro, Platon, tr. see Febres, Mayra S.

Lazaro, Roberto & Waterman, Floyd T. A Comparison of the Corporate Structures & Delivery of City Services in Omaha & Manila. 104p. (Orig.). 1984. pap. 6.50 (*1-55719-075-5*) U NE CPAR.

Lazaro, Timothy. Urban Hydrology. rev. ed. LC 89-51913. 260p. 1990. 99.95 (*0-87762-547-6*) Technomic.

***Lazaroff, Catherine.** Teaching Children about Backyard Birds. 64p. 2000. pap. 7.95 (*0-7938-3579-8*) TFH Pubns.

Lazaroff, David W. Sabino Canyon: The Life of a Southwestern Oasis. LC 92-18057. (Illus.). 119p. (Orig.). 1993. pap. 17.95 (*0-8165-1344-9*) U of Ariz Pr.

— The Secret Lives of Hummingbirds. (Illus.). 24p. (Orig.). 1995. pap. 4.95 (*1-886679-00-2*) Ariz-Sonora Des Mus.

Lazaroff, David W. & Arizona-Sonora Desert Museum (Tucson, Ariz.) Staff. Arizona-Sonora Desert Museum Book of Answers. LC 97-31829. (Illus.). 198p. 1998. pap. 14.95 (*1-886679-09-6*) Ariz-Sonora Des Mus.

Lazaron, Hilda. Gabriel Marcel the Dramatist. 186p. 1978. 40.00 (*0-901072-77-X*, Pub. by Smyth) Dufour.

Lazarony, jt. auth. see Olinzock, Anthony A.

***Lazaroo, Simone.** The World Waiting to be Made. 2745p. 2000. pap. 17.95 (*1-86368-302-X*, Pub. by Fremantle Arts) Intl Spec Bk.

Lazarov, Conner & Wasserman, Arthur. Complex Actions of Lie Groups. LC 73-18039. (Memoirs Ser.: No. 1/137). 82p. 1973. pap. 17.00 (*0-8218-1837-6*, MEMO/1/137) Am Math.

***Lazarov, N. E.** The Mesencephalic Trigeminal Nucleus in the Cat. LC QL801.E67 vol. 153. (Advances in Anatomy, Embryology & Cell Biology Ser.: Vol. 153). (Illus.). 85p. 2000. pap. 72.00 (*3-540-66524-2*) Spr-Verlag.

Lazarov, R., jt. ed. see Petkov, V.

Lazarovici, Philip, et al, eds. Biochemical Aspects of Marine Pharmacology. (Illus.). 227p. (C). 1996. text 84.00 (*1-880293-07-2*) Alaken.

Lazarovici, Philip, jt. ed. see Gutman, Yehuda.

Lazarow. Harvey Lectures, 1996-97, Vol. 92. 145p. 1998. 89.95 (*0-471-28326-6*) Wiley.

Lazarow, Paul, ed. The Harvey Lectures Series 91. (Harvey Lectures: No. 91). 164p. 1997. 99.95 (*0-471-17885-3*) Wiley.

Lazarowich, N. Michael. Granny Flats As Housing for the Elderly: International Perspectives. (Journal of Housing for the Elderly: Vol. 7 No. 2). (Illus.). 82p. 1991. text 4.95 (*1-56024-124-1*) Haworth Pr.

Lazarowitz, Arlene. Years in Exile: The Liberal Democrats, 1950-1959. LC 88-25978. (Modern American History Ser.). 200p. 1988. 25.00 (*0-8240-4333-2*) Garland.

Lazarre, Jacob. Beating Sea & Changeless Bar. LC 79-86149. (Short Story Index Reprint Ser.). 1977. 17.95 (*0-8369-3053-3*) Ayer.

Lazarre, Jane. Beyond the Whiteness of Whiteness: Memoir of a White Mother of Black Sons. LC 96-452. 168p. 1996. 17.95 (*0-8223-1826-1*) Duke.

— Beyond the Whiteness of Whiteness: Memoir of a White Mother of Black Sons. LC 96-452. 168p. 1997. pap. 12.95 (*0-8223-2044-4*) Duke.

— The Mother Knot. LC 97-13516. 176p. 1997. pap. 14.95 (*0-8223-2039-8*) Duke.

***Lazarre, Jane.** The Powers of Charlotte. LC 00-21649. (Orig.). 2000. write for info. (*1-891305-53-0*) Painted Leaf.

Lazarre, Jane. Wet Earth & Dreams: A Narrative of Grief & Recovery. LC 98-10116. 128p. 1998. 17.95 (*0-8223-2206-4*) Duke.

An Asterisk (*) at the beginning of an entry indicates that the title is appearing for the first time.

***Lazarre, Jane.** Wet Earth & Dreams: A Narrative of Grief & Recovery. 136p. 2000. reprint ed. pap. 12.95 (*0-8223-2543-8*) Duke.

— Worlds Beyond My Control. LC 00-21648. 2000. write for info. (*1-891305-54-9*) Painted Leaf.

Lazarro-Carreter, Fernando. Diccionario de Terminos Filologicos. 3rd ed. 444p. 1990. pap. 29.95 (*0-7859-5787-1*) Fr & Eur.

Lazarsfeld, P. F. & Van de Ven, eds. Topics in the Geometry of Projective Space: Recent Work of F. L. Zak. (DMV Seminar Ser.: No. 4). 52p. 1985. 29.00 (*0-8176-1660-8*) Birkhauser.

Lazarsfeld, Patricia K., ed. The Varied Sociology of Paul Lazarsfeld. LC 81-24205. 400p. 1982. text 80.00 (*0-231-05122-0*); pap. text 29.00 (*0-231-05123-9*) Col U Pr.

Lazarsfeld, Paul F. On Social Research & Its Language. LC 93-12748. (Heritage of Sociology Ser.). (Illus.). 344p. 1993. pap. text 19.95 (*0-226-46963-8*); lib. bdg. 49.95 (*0-226-46961-1*) U Ch Pr.

— Radio & the Printed Page: An Introduction to the Study of Radio & Its Role in the Communication of Ideas. LC 70-161161. (History of Broadcasting: Radio to Television Ser.). 1976. reprint ed. 28.95 (*0-405-03575-6*) Ayer.

Lazarsfeld, Paul F., et al, eds. Communications Research, Nineteen Forty-Eight to Nineteen Forty-Nine. LC 79-7005. (Perennial Works in Sociology). (Illus.). 1980. reprint ed. lib. bdg. 29.95 (*0-405-12103-2*) Ayer.

— Radio Research, 1941. LC 79-7003. (Perennial Works in Sociology Ser.). (Illus.). 1980. reprint ed. lib. bdg. 29.95 (*0-405-12101-6*) Ayer.

— Radio Research, Nineteen Hundred Forty-Two to Nineteen Hundred Forty-Three. LC 79-7004. (Perennial Works in Sociology). (Illus.). 1980. reprint ed. lib. bdg. 49.95 (*0-405-12102-4*) Ayer.

Lazarsfeld, Paul F. & Kendall, Patricia L. Radio Listening in America: The People Look at Radio - Again. Coser, Lewis A. & Powell, Walter W., eds. LC 79-7002. (Perennial Works in Sociology). (Illus.). 1980. reprint ed. lib. bdg. 18.95 (*0-405-12100-8*) Ayer.

Lazarsfeld, Paul F. & Reitz, Jeffrey G. An Introduction to Applied Sociology. LC 75-8274. 203p. reprint ed. pap. 63.00 (*0-608-16260-4*, 205609900049) Bks Demand.

Lazarsfeld, Paul F. & Thielens, Wagner P., Jr. The Academic Mind: Social Scientists in Time of Crisis. Metzger, Walter P., ed. LC 76-55178. (Academic Profession Ser.). (Illus.). 1977. reprint ed. 39.95 (*0-405-10006-X*) Ayer.

Lazarsfeld, Paul F., et al. Jugend und Beruf: Youth & Job. LC 74-25762. (European Sociology Ser.). 206p. 1975. reprint ed. 24.95 (*0-405-06516-7*) Ayer.

— The People's Choice: How the Voter Makes up His Mind in a Presidential Campaign. 3rd ed. LC 68-20443. 224p. reprint ed. pap. 69.50 (*0-608-17713-X*, 203010900067) Bks Demand.

Lazarsfeld, Paul F., jt. auth. see Stouffer, Samuel A.

Lazarsfeld, Paul F., jt. ed. see Merton, Robert K.

Lazarski, Christopher & Siekierski, Maciej, compiled by. Polish Independent Publications, 1976-1990: Guide to the Collection in the Hoover Institution Archives. LC 98-44721. (Bibliography Ser.: Vol. 77). 510p. 1998. pap. 25.95 (*0-8179-2772-7*) Hoover Inst Pr.

Lazarus. Opera Handbook. 1987. text. write for info. (*0-582-00107-2*, Pub. by Addison-Wesley) Longman.

Lazarus, A. L., ed. A George Jean Nathan Reader. LC 88-45873. (Illus.). 408p. 1990. 45.00 (*0-8386-3369-2*) Fairleigh Dickinson.

Lazarus, Alan, jt. auth. see Funes, Marilyn.

Lazarus, Arnold. In the Mind's Eye: The Power of Imagery for Personal Enrichment. LC 84-9016. 208p. 1984. reprint ed. pap. text 21.00 (*0-89862-641-2*) Guilford Pubns.

Lazarus, Arnold & Fay, Allen. I Can If I Want To. 118p. 1975. reprint ed. pap. 12.95 (*0-9659818-1-9*) FMC.

Lazarus, Arnold A. Behavior Therapy & Beyond. LC 96-16611. (Master Works). 320p. 1996. pap. 50.00 (*1-56821-839-7*, RA1) Aronson.

— Brief But Comprehensive Psychotherapy: The Multimodal Way. LC 96-39552. (Behavior Therapy & Behavioral Medicine Ser.). (Illus.). 192p. 1997. 35.95 (*0-8261-9640-3*) Springer Pub.

Lazarus, Arnold A., ed. Casebook of Multimodal Therapy. LC 84-19835. (Illus.). 224p. 1985. reprint ed. pap. 69.50 (*0-608-07817-4*, 205988600010) Bks Demand.

Lazarus, Arnold A. & Colman, Andrew M., eds. Abnormal Psychology. LC 95-18120. (Essential Psychology Ser.). 108p. (C). 1995. pap. text 14.06 (*0-582-27807-4*, Pub. by Addison-Wesley) Longman.

Lazarus, Arnold A. & Lazarus, Clifford N. The 60-Second Shrink: 101 Strategies for Staying Sane in a Crazy World. LC 96-53590. 176p. 1997. pap. 14.95 (*1-886230-04-8*) Impact Pubs CA.

Lazarus, Arnold A., et al. Don't Believe It for a Minute: Forty Toxic Ideas That Are Driving You Crazy. LC 93-4934. 192p. (Orig.). 1993. pap. 9.95 (*0-915166-80-1*) Impact Pubs CA.

Lazarus, Arnold L., ed. The Indiana Experience: An Anthology. LC 76-50528. 444p. 1977. reprint ed. pap. 137.70 (*0-7837-6103-1*, 205914900008) Bks Demand.

Lazarus, Arthur, ed. Career Pathways in Psychiatry: Transition in Changing Times. 216p. 1996. 36.00 (*0-88163-217-1*) Analytic Pr.

— Controversies in Managed Mental Health Care. 480p. 1996. text 62.95 (*0-88048-115-3*, 8115) Am Psychiatric.

— MD-MBA: Physicians on the New Frontier of Medical Management. LC 97-78156. 240p. 1998. pap. 45.00 (*0-924674-61-X*) Am Coll Phys Execs.

Lazarus, Bernice N., jt. auth. see Lazarus, Richard S.

Lazarus-Black, Mindie. Legitimate Acts & Illegal Encounters: Law & Society in Antigua & Barbuda. LC 93-11005. (Series in Ethnographic Inquiry). 424p. (C). 1994. pap. text 24.95 (*1-56098-326-4*) Smithsonian.

Lazarus-Black, Mindie & Hirsch, Susan F., eds. Contested States: Law, Hegemony, & Resistance. LC 93-47569. (After the Law Ser.). 320p. (C). 1994. 85.00 (*0-415-90779-9*) Routledge.

Lazarus, Carole. Glorafilia. LC 96-84779. (Illus.). 192p. 1996. 29.95 (*0-8212-2330-5*, Pub. by Bulfinch Pr) Little.

Lazarus, Clifford N., jt. auth. see Lazarus, Arnold A.

Lazarus, David & Raether, Manfred. Practical Physics: How Things Work. (Illus.). 1984. pap. text 15.80 (*0-87563-167-3*) Stipes.

Lazarus, Deborah. Big Machines. 32p. (Orig.). (J). (gr. 1-4). 1997. pap. text, wbk. ed. 2.25 (*1-56762-076-0*) Modern Learn Pr.

— Dinosaurs & Other Creatures. (Illus.). 32p. (Orig.). (J). (gr. 1-4). 1997. pap., wbk. ed. 2.25 (*1-56762-073-6*) Modern Learn Pr.

— Exploring the Kitchen. (Illus.). 32p. (Orig.). (J). (gr. 1-4). 1997. pap., wbk. ed. 2.25 (*1-56762-075-2*) Modern Learn Pr.

— Insects Around Us. (Illus.). 32p. (Orig.). (J). (gr. 1-4). 1997. pap., wbk. ed. 2.25 (*1-56762-074-4*) Modern Learn Pr.

Lazarus, Edward. Black Hills - White Justice: The Sioux Nation vs. the United States, 1775 to the Present. LC 99-17707. (Illus.). 520p. 1999. pap. 22.00 (*0-8032-7987-6*, Bison Books) U of Nebr Pr.

— Closed Chambers: The Rise, Fall & Future of the Modern Supreme Court. LC 99-462636. (Illus.). 592p. 1999. pap. 15.95 (*0-14-028356-0*) Viking Penguin.

Lazarus, Edward P. Closed Chambers: The First Eyewitness Account of the Epic Struggles Inside the Supreme Court. LC 97-35708. 576p. 1998. 27.50 (*0-8129-2402-9*, Times Bks) Crown Pub Group.

Lazarus, Emma. Admetus. LC 77-104508. reprint ed. lib. bdg. 39.00 (*0-8398-1152-7*) Irvington.

— Admetus & Other Poems. (Notable American Authors Ser.). 1999. reprint ed. lib. bdg. 125.00 (*0-7812-3767-X*) Rprt Serv.

— Alide: An Episode in Goethe's Life. 1999. reprint ed. lib. bdg. 125.00 (*0-7812-3768-8*) Rprt Serv.

— By the Waters of Babylon. (Notable American Authors Ser.). 1999. reprint ed. lib. bdg. 125.00 (*0-7812-3772-6*) Rprt Serv.

— Letters to Emma Lazarus in the Columbia University Library. Rusk, Ralph L., ed. LC 39-14112. 1984. reprint ed. 20.00 (*0-404-05459-5*) AMS Pr.

— Poems. (Notable American Authors Ser.). 1999. reprint ed. lib. bdg. 125.00 (*0-7812-3773-4*) Rprt Serv.

— Poems & Balads of Heinrich Heine. (Notable American Authors Ser.). 1999. reprint ed. lib. bdg. 125.00 (*0-7812-3770-X*) Rprt Serv.

— Poems & Translations. (Notable American Authors Ser.). 1999. reprint ed. lib. bdg. 125.00 (*0-7812-3766-1*) Rprt Serv.

— Songs of a Semite (Including the Dance to Death) (Notable American Authors Ser.). 1999. reprint ed. lib. bdg. 125.00 (*0-7812-3771-8*) Rprt Serv.

— The Spagnoletto: A Drama in Verse. (Notable American Authors Ser.). 1999. reprint ed. lib. bdg. 125.00 (*0-7812-3769-6*) Rprt Serv.

Lazarus, Eve, jt. auth. see Newman, Peter C.

Lazarus, H. Method for Clarinet, 2 pts., Pt. 1. Bellison, Simeon, ed. (Illus.). 140p. 1946. pap. 15.95 (*0-8258-0206-7*, 0-327) Fischer Inc NY.

— Method for Clarinet, 2 pts., Pt. 2. Bellison, Simeon, ed. (Illus.). 142p. 1946. pap. 17.95 (*0-8258-0207-5*, 0-328) Fischer Inc NY.

Lazarus, J. H., jt. auth. see Wheeler, M. H.

Lazarus, J. Michael, jt. auth. see Brenner, Barry M.

Lazarus, J. Michael, jt. ed. see Brenner, Barry M.

Lazarus, Jeremy A. & Sharfstein, Steven S., eds. New Roles for Psychiatrists in Organized Systems of Care. LC RC465.5.N49 1998. 271p. 1998. pap. text 38.00 (*0-88048-758-5*, 8758) Am Psychiatric.

***Lazarus, John.** Not So Dumb: "Secrets," "Schoolyard Games," "Not So Dumb" & "Night Light" 208p. (gr. 7-12). 2000. pap. 17.95 (*0-88754-578-5*) Theatre Comm.

Lazarus, John. Village of Idiots LC 98-182146. 76p. 1997. write for info. (*1-55173-468-0*) PUC.

Lazarus, John, et al. YP Three: Three Plays from Young People's Theatre. LC 95-152246. 300p. (J). 1997. pap. 17.95 (*0-88754-475-4*) Theatre Comm.

Lazarus, John, jt. auth. see Cockburn, Andrew.

Lazarus, John H. Endocrine & Metabolic Effects of Lithium. LC 85-28308. (Illus.). 220p. (C). 1986. text 90.00 (*0-306-42057-0*, Kluwer Plenum) Kluwer Academic.

Lazarus, Joseph. In Praise of the King Without a Face. LC 77-82728. (Scene Award Ser.). 80p. 1978. pap. 8.00 (*0-912292-45-8*) Smith.

Lazarus, Josephine. Spirit of Judaism. LC 77-38031. (Essay Index Reprint Ser.). 1977. reprint ed. 18.95 (*0-8369-2602-1*) Ayer.

***Lazarus, Joyce B.** Strangers & Sojourners: Jewish Identity in Contemporary Francophone Fiction. LC 98-12262. (Francophone Cultures & Literatures Ser.: Vol. 26). 141p. (C). 1999. text 41.95 (*0-8204-4020-5*) P Lang Pubng.

***Lazarus, Judith.** The Spa Sourcebook. (Roxbury Park Bks.). 272p. 2000. pap. 16.95 (*0-7373-0390-5*, 03905W, Pub. by Lowell Hse) NTC Contemp Pub Co.

— Stress Relief & Relaxation Techniques. LC 00-28697. (Illus.). 160p. 2000. pap. 11.95 (*0-658-00385-2*, 003852, Keats Publng) NTC Contemp Pub Co.

Lazarus, Ken. Conquering Kids Cancer: Triumphs & Tragedies of a Children's Cancer Doctor. LC 98-40258. 240p. 1999. pap. 19.95 (*1-885373-22-8*) Emerald Ink.

Lazarus, Lawrence W., et al, eds. Essentials of Geriatric Psychiatry: A Guide for Health Professionals. 272p. 1988. 38.95 (*0-8261-5990-7*) Springer Pub.

Lazarus, Lois. Country Is My Music! (J). 15.00 (*0-671-86773-3*) S&S Bks Yung.

Lazarus, M., et al. Die Ethnik des Judenthums, 2 vols., Set. LC 79-7146. (Jewish Philosophy, Mysticism & History of Ideas Ser.). 1980. reprint ed. lib. bdg. 88.95 (*0-405-12276-4*) Ayer.

Lazarus, Neil. Nationalism & Cultural Practice in the Postcolonial World. LC 98-38084. (Cultural Margins Ser.: No. 6). 240p. (C). 1999. text 57.95 (*0-521-62410-X*); pap. text 19.95 (*0-521-62493-2*) Cambridge U Pr.

Lazarus, Pat. Keep Your Cat Healthy. LC 98-34704. 1999. pap. 12.95 (*0-449-00513-5*) Fawcett.

— Keep Your Pet Healthy the Natural Way. LC 82-17846. 228p. 1983. write for info. (*0-672-52726-X*) Macmillan.

— Keeping Your Dog Healthy the Natural Way. LC 99-10801. 1999. pap. 12.95 (*0-449-00514-3*) Fawcett.

Lazarus, Paul N., III. The Film Producer: A Handbook for Producing. (Illus.). 224p. 1992. pap. 14.95 (*0-312-06969-3*) St Martin.

— Working in Film: The Marketplace in the '90s. LC 93-677. 224p. (Orig.). 1993. pap. 15.95 (*0-312-09418-3*) St Martin.

Lazarus, Rachel M. The Education of the Heart: The Correspondence of Rachel Mordecai Lazarus & Maria Edgeworth. MacDonald, Edgar E., ed. LC 76-29062. 364p. reprint ed. pap. 112.90 (*0-8357-3880-9*, 203661200004) Bks Demand.

Lazarus, Richard S. Emotion & Adaptation. (Illus.). 576p. 1991. text 75.00 (*0-19-506994-3*) OUP.

— Emotion & Adaptation. (Illus.). 576p. 1994. reprint ed. pap. text 35.00 (*0-19-509266-X*) OUP.

— Fifty Years of Research & Theory by R. S. Lazarus: Historical & Perennial Arguments. LC 97-9632. 350p. 1997. text. write for info. (*0-8058-2657-2*) L Erlbaum Assocs.

— The Life & Work of an Eminent Psychologist: Autobiography of Richard S. Lazarus. LC 98-10419. 1998. 39.95 (*0-8261-1179-3*) Springer Pub.

***Lazarus, Richard S.** Stress & Emotion: A New Synthesis. LC 98-45782. xiv, 342 p. 1999. 44.95 (*0-8261-1250-1*) Springer Pub.

Lazarus, Richard S. & Folkman, Susan. Stress, Appraisal, & Coping. 464p. (C). 1984. pap. 46.95 (*0-8261-4191-9*) Springer Pub.

Lazarus, Richard S. & Lazarus, Bernice N. Passion & Reason: Making Sense of Our Emotions. LC 94-9320. 336p. 1994. text 30.00 (*0-19-508757-7*) OUP.

— Passion & Reason: Making Sense of Our Emotions. 336p. 1996. reprint ed. pap. 15.95 (*0-19-510461-7*) OUP.

Lazarus, Richard S., jt. auth. see Monat, Alan.

Lazarus, Simon, jt. auth. see Juster, Kenneth I.

Lazarus, Sophia. Inspirational Words. 82p. Date not set. pap. text 5.95 (*0-9638300-0-7*) S Lazarus.

Lazarus, Stephen C. & Lofholm, Paul W., eds. Asthma Management. (Illus.). 43p. 1996. pap. write for info. (*0-614-04577-0*) Bimark.

Lazarus, Wayne H. & Stokes, Marion B. The Seller's Credit Guide, Vol. 1. (Illus.). 250p. 1996. 29.95 (*0-9651931-0-1*) Busn Pathways.

Lazarus, William, jt. auth. see Cornesky, Robert.

***Lazarus-Yafeh, Hava.** Intertwined Worlds: Medieval Islam & Bible Criticism. (HEB.). 255p. 1998. text 47.00 (*965-342-715-6*, Pub. by Bialik) Eisenbrauns.

Lazarus-Yafeh, Hava. Intertwined Worlds: Medieval Islam & Bible Criticism. 200p. 1992. text 37.50 (*0-691-07398-8*, Pub. by Princeton U Pr) Cal Prin Full Svc.

Lazdinis, Audrius & Hey, Jeanne. From Russia to Kaliningrad: The Case of Russian Transit Rights Through Lithuania. (Pew Case Studies in International Affairs). 50p. (C). 1996. text 3.50 (*1-56927-370-7*) Geo U Inst Dplmcy.

***Lazear, David.** Pathways of Learning: Teaching Students & Parents about Multiple Intelligences. (Illus.). 260p. 2000. pap. 37.00 (*1-56976-118-3*, 1115) Zephyr Pr AZ.

Lazear, David. Intelligence Builders for Every Student: 44 Exercises to Expand MI in Your Classroom. (Illus.). 142p. 1997. 25.00 (*1-56976-069-1*, 1086-F3) Zephyr Pr AZ.

— Pathways of Learning: Teaching Students & Parents about Multiple Intelligences. LC 93-33054. 256p. 1999. pap. 37.00 (*0-913705-92-6*) Zephyr Pr AZ.

— Seven Ways of Knowing: Teaching for Multiple Intelligences. 2nd ed. LC 91-67598. (Illus.). 256p. (Orig.). 1991. pap. text 41.95 (*0-932935-39-7*) SkyLght.

— Seven Ways of Teaching: The Artistry of Teaching with Multiple Intelligences. LC 91-65666. (Illus.). 192p. (Orig.). 1991. pap. text 35.95 (*0-932935-32-X*) SkyLght.

Lazear, David G. 8 Ways of Teaching. LC 98-61254. 1998. pap. text 38.95 (*1-57517-119-8*) SkyLght.

***Lazear, David G.** The Intelligent Curriculum: Using MI to Develop Your Students' Full Potential. LC 99-34599. (J). (gr. k-12). 1999. 39.00 (*1-56976-099-3*) Zephyr Pr AZ.

Lazear, David G. Multiple Intelligence Approaches to Assessment: Solving the Assessment Conundrum. rev. ed. LC 94-216. (Illus.). 108p. 1998. pap. 39.00 (*0-913705-95-0*, 1029-F3) Zephyr Pr AZ.

— The Rubrics Way: Using MI to Assess Student Understanding. LC 98-35241. 1998. 39.00 (*1-56976-087-X*) Zephyr Pr AZ.

Lazear, Edward P. Culture Wars In America. LC 96-24448. (Essays in Public Policy Ser.: Vol. 71). 1996. pap. 5.00 (*0-8179-5762-6*) Hoover Inst Pr.

— Personnel. LC 97-7933. 560p. 1998. text 89.95 (*0-471-59466-0*) Wiley.

— Personnel Economics. (Wicksell Lectures). (Illus.). 184p. 1995. 27.50 (*0-262-12188-3*) MIT Pr.

Lazear, Edward P., ed. Economic Transition Eastern Europe & Russia: Realities of Reform. (Publication Ser.: No. 425). 448p. (C). 1995. pap. 24.95 (*0-8179-9332-0*) Hoover Inst Pr.

Lazear, Edward P. & Michael, Robert T. Allocation of Income Within the Household. (Illus.). 228p. 1988. 41.95 (*0-226-46966-2*) U Ch Pr.

Lazear, Edward P., jt. ed. see Krauss, Melvyn B.

Lazear, Edward P., jt. ed. see Ricardo-Campbell, Rita.

Lazear, Jonathon. Meditations for Men Who Do Too Much. LC 92-20030. (Fireside - Parkside Recovery Bk.). 400p. 1992. pap. 9.00 (*0-671-75908-6*, Fireside) S&S Trade Pap.

Lazear, Jonathon & Lazear, Wendy. Meditations for Parents Who Do Too Much. LC 93-12432. (Meditation Bk.). 400p. (Orig.). 1993. pap. 10.00 (*0-671-79635-6*, Fireside) S&S Trade Pap.

Lazear, Wendy, jt. auth. see Lazear, Jonathon.

Lazega, Emmanuel. The Micropolitics of Knowledge: Communication & Indirect Control in Workgroups. (Communication & Social Order Ser.). 156p. 1992. lib. bdg. 44.95 (*0-202-30426-4*) Aldine de Gruyter.

Lazega, Emmanuel. The Micropolitics of Knowledge: Communication & Indirect Control in Workgroups. (Communication & Social Order Ser.). 156p. 1992. pap. text 21.95 (*0-202-30427-2*) Aldine de Gruyter.

Lazega, Jay S., jt. auth. see Sellers, Tonia C.

Lazell, Barry. Bob Marley: The Illustrated Legend. (Illus.). 80p. 1994. pap. 14.95 (*0-7935-4034-8*, HL00330008) H Leonard.

— Bob Marley: The Illustrated Legend. LC 97-215460. (Illus.). 160p. 1998. pap. 14.95 (*0-600-58221-3*) Hamlyn Publishing Group Ltd.

Lazell, James D., jt. auth. see Alexander, John R.

Lazell, T. S. Nathaniel Whiting of Dedham MA, 1641, & Five Generations of His Descendants. 80p. 1990. reprint ed. pap. 16.00 (*0-8328-1561-6*); reprint ed. lib. bdg. 24.00 (*0-8328-1560-8*) Higginson Bk Co.

Lazenby, A., jt. auth. see Jones, M. B.

Lazenby, A., jt. ed. see Tow, P.

***Lazenby, Carl, ed.** McComb City Moments: Selections from the Newspaper of McComb, Mississippi over the Past 125 Years. 206p. 1999. pap. 10.00 (*0-9677048-0-4*) LazArt.

Lazenby, Edith P. Tabernacle in the Wilderness: As It Relates to Jesus Christ. LC 97-215170. xv, 160p. 1997. pap. 12.00 (*1-56043-209-8*, Companion Pr) Destiny Image.

Lazenby, Gina. The Feng Shui House Book: Change Your Home, Transform Your Life. LC 97-62240. (Illus.). 160p. 1998. pap. 29.95 (*0-8230-1654-4*) Watsn-Guptill.

***Lazenby, Gina.** Healthy House Book: Using Feng Shui to Organize Your Home & Transform Your Life. 2000. 35.00 (*1-58574-111-6*) Lyon Press.

— Simple Feng Shui. (Illus.). 96p. 2000. write for info. (*0-8230-4835-7*) Watsn-Guptill.

Lazenby, J. F. Hannibal's War: A Military History of the Second Punic War. LC 97-38302. (Illus.). 368p. 1998. pap. 17.95 (*0-8061-3004-0*) U of Okla Pr.

Lazenby, John. The Defence of Greece 490-479 B.C. 1993. pap. 40.00 (*0-85668-591-7*, Pub. by Aris & Phillips) David Brown.

— The First Punic War. LC 95-78817. 224p. (Orig.). 1996. 45.00 (*0-8047-2673-6*); pap. 17.95 (*0-8047-2674-4*) Stanford U Pr.

— Hannibal's War. 1978. pap. 40.00 (*0-85668-080-X*, Pub. by Aris & Phillips) David Brown.

Lazenby, Kathryn W. My Patchwork Spirit. (Illus.). 96p. 1998. 22.95 (*1-57736-089-3*) Providence Hse.

Lazenby, Lucy M. One-Person Puppets: A Guide to Writing, Producing & Surviving the One-Person Puppet-Play. 65p. (Orig.). 1996. pap. 12.00 (*0-9648744-0-7*) Southshore Pr.

Lazenby, Norman A. Dead Sinners. large type ed. (Linford Mystery Library). 256p. 1993. pap. 16.99 (*0-7089-7422-8*) Ulverscroft.

— Death in the Stars. large type ed. (Linford Mystery Library). 224p. 1993. pap. 16.99 (*0-7089-7419-8*) Ulverscroft.

— A Fightin' Hombre. large type ed. (Linford Western Library). 1990. pap. 16.99 (*0-7089-6810-4*) Ulverscroft.

— Gunplay over Laredo. large type ed. (Linford Western Library). 1991. pap. 16.99 (*0-7089-7091-5*) Ulverscroft.

— I Never Killed. large type ed. (Linford Mystery Library). 240p. 1992. pap. 16.99 (*0-7089-7220-9*) Ulverscroft.

— Singing Lead. large type ed. (Linford Western Library). 240p. 1989. pap. 16.99 (*0-7089-6678-0*, Linford) Ulverscroft.

— We the Condemned. large type ed. (Linford Mystery Library). 272p. 1992. pap. 16.99 (*0-7089-7229-2*) Ulverscroft.

Lazenby, Roland. And Now, Your Chicago Bulls: A 30-Year Celebration. (Illus.). 240p. 1995. 39.95 (*0-87833-113-1*) Taylor Pub.

— And Now, Your Chicago Bulls: A 30-Year Celebration. limited ed. 1995. 75.00 (*0-87833-114-X*) Taylor Pub.

— Bird: Portrait of a Competitor. LC 98-12221. (Illus.). 112p. 1998. pap. 25.00 (*1-886110-39-5*) Addax Pubng.

— Blood on the Horns: The Long Strange Ride of Michael Jordan's Chicago Bulls. LC 98-27534. (Illus.). 240p. 1998. 22.95 (*1-886110-59-X*) Addax Pubng.

— Bull Run! Vol. 1: The Story of the 1995-96 Chicago Bulls: The Greatest Team in Basketball History. Cameron, Steve, ed. LC 96-85190. (Illus.). 160p. 1996. pap. 16.95 (*1-886110-10-7*, Pub. by Addax Pubng) Midpt Trade.

— The Bulls A Pocket Primer. LC 98-17576. 96p. 1998. pap. 8.95 (*1-886110-41-7*) Addax Pubng.

— Championship Basketball. (Illus.). 176p. (Orig.). 1986. pap. 12.95 (*0-8092-4874-3*, 487430, Contemporary Bks) NTC Contemp Pub Co.

An Asterisk (*) at the beginning of an entry indicates that the title is appearing for the first time.

— The Lakers: A Basketball Journey. rev. ed. (Illus.). 320p. 1995. reprint ed. pap. 14.95 (*1-57028-062-2*, 80622H, Mstrs Pr) NTC Contemp Pub Co.

***Lazenby, Roland.** Mad Game. LC 99-45112. 256p. 1999. 21.95 (*1-57028-225-0*, 82250H, Mstrs Pr) NTC Contemp Pub Co.

— Mad Game: The NBA Education of Kobe Bryant. (Illus.). 2000. pap. 14.95 (*0-8092-9605-5*, Contemporary Bks) NTC Contemp Pub Co.

— Mindgames: Phil Jackson's Long Strange Journey. 256p. 2000. 23.95 (*0-8092-9707-8*, Contemporary Bks) NTC Contemp Pub Co.

Lazenby, Roland. Chicago Bulls: Authorized Pictorial. LC 97-21212. (Illus.). 120p. 1997. 39.99 (*1-56530-270-2*); pap. 24.99 (*1-56530-271-0*) Summit TX.

— Smashmouth: Attitude Between the Lines. Storey, Susan, ed. LC 97-35121. 144p. 1997. pap. 14.95 (*1-886110-26-3*, Pub. by Addax Pubng) Midpt Trade.

— Stockton to Malone: The Rise of the Utah Jazz. LC 98-6540. (Illus.). 96p. 1998. pap. 8.95 (*1-886110-43-3*) Addax Pubng.

— Yo Baby It's Attitude! The New Bad Boyz of the NBA, Take the Jordan Test. Storey, Susan, ed. LC 97-8587. 144p. 1997. pap. 14.95 (*1-886110-15-8*, Pub. by Addax Pubng) Midpt Trade.

Lazenby, Roland & Doughty, Doug. Hoos 'n' Hokies, the Rivalry: 100 Years of Virginia Tech-Virginia Football. (Illus.). 192p. 1995. 29.95 (*0-87833-116-6*) Taylor Pub.

Lazenby, Roland, jt. auth. see Packer, Billy.

Lazenby, Roland, ed. see Chicago Sun-Times Staff.

***Lazendorf, John.** Dinosaur Imagery. (Illus.). 200p. 2000. 49.95 (*0-12-436590-6*) Acad Pr.

***Lazer, Dianne.** Adding Value to Long-Term Care: An Administrator's Guide to Improving Staff Performance, Patient Care. 2000. 69.95 (*0-7879-5170-6*) Jossey-Bass.

Lazer, Hank. Doublespace. LC 91-66723. (Segue Bks.). 192p. (Orig.). 1992. pap. 12.00 (*0-937804-44-4*) Segue NYC.

— Inter (ir) ruptions. (Chapbook Ser.). 22p. 1992. pap. 5.00 (*0-945112-14-9*) Generator Pr.

— Opposing Poetries: Issues & Institutions. (Avant-Garde & Modernism Studies: Pt. 1). 296p. 1996. text 69.95 (*0-8101-1264-7*); pap. text 16.95 (*0-8101-1265-5*) Northwestern U Pr.

— Opposing Poetries: Readings. (Avant-Garde & Modernism Studies: Pt. 2). 296p. 1996. text 69.95 (*0-8101-1413-5*) Northwestern U Pr.

— Opposing Poetries Pt. 2: Readings. 296p. 1996. pap. text 16.95 (*0-8101-1414-3*) Northwestern U Pr.

— 3 of 10: Poems. LC 96-3079. 1996. write for info. (*0-925904-18-X*) Chax Pr.

Lazer, Hank, ed. On Louis Simpson: Depths Beyond Happiness. (Under Discussion Ser.). 408p. (Orig.). 1988. pap. text 17.95 (*0-472-06382-0*, 06382) U of Mich Pr.

— What Is a Poet? LC 86-19234. 296p. 1987. text 32.50 (*0-8173-0325-1*) U of Ala Pr.

Lazer, Harriet L., jt. auth. see Walker, James W.

Lazer, Lou. Effie's Bytes. 52p. 1987. pap. 14.00 (*0-937953-04-0*) Tiptoe Lit Serv.

Lazer, William. Handbook of Demographics for Marketing & Advertising: New Trends in the American Marketplace. 325p. 1994. 47.00 (*0-02-918175-5*) Jossey-Bass.

— Marketing 2000 & Beyond: Future Perspectives in Marketing. LC 89-29851. 246p. 1990. 25.00 (*0-87757-204-6*) Am Mktg.

Lazer, William & Layton, Roger. Contemporary Hospitality Marketing. LC 98-50023. (Illus.). (C). 1998. pap. 72.95 (*0-86612-158-7*) Educ Inst Am Hotel.

— Marketing of Hospitality Services. LC 99-217175. (Illus.). (C). 1998. pap. 77.95 (*0-86612-157-9*) Educ Inst Am Hotel.

Lazer, William, ed. see Academy of Marketing Science Staff.

Lazere. Reading & Writing for Citizenship. pap. text. write for info. (*0-312-13797-4*) St Martin.

Lazere, Cathy, jt. auth. see Shasha, Dennis.

Lazere, Cathy, jt. auth. see Shasha, Dennis E.

Lazere, Donald, ed. American Media & Mass Culture: Left Perspectives. (Illus.). 560p. 1987. pap. 19.95 (*0-520-04496-7*, Pub. by U CA Pr) Cal Prin Full Svc.

— American Media & Mass Culture: Left Perspectives. LC 87-22182. (Illus.). 630p. reprint ed. pap. 195.30 (*0-7837-4819-1*, 204446600003) Bks Demand.

Lazere, Monroe R., ed. Commercial Financing. LC 67-30356. 317p. reprint ed. pap. 98.30 (*0-608-13692-1*, 205510700008) Bks Demand.

Lazerow, Jama. Religion & the Working Class in Antebellum America. LC 95-8600. 354p. 1995. text 45.00 (*1-56098-544-5*) Smithsonian.

Lazerowitz, M. & Ambrose, A. Philosophical Theories. 1976. text 42.35 (*90-279-7501-9*) Mouton.

Lazerowitz, Morris. The Language of Philosophy. LC 77-23068. (Boston Studies in the Philosophy of Science: No. 55). 224p. 1977. pap. text 70.50 (*90-277-0862-2*, D Reidel); lib. bdg. 82.50 (*90-277-0826-6*, D Reidel) Kluwer Academic.

Lazerowitz, Morris & Ambrose, Alice. Essays in the Unknown Wittgenstein. LC 83-62923. 233p. 1984. 40.95 (*0-87975-234-3*) Prometheus Bks.

— Necessity & Language. LC 85-22201. 272p. 1986. text 39.95 (*0-312-56259-4*) St Martin.

Lazerowitz, Morris, jt. ed. see Ambrose, Alice.

Lazerowitz, Morris, jt. ed. see Hanly, Charles.

Lazerson, Arlyne, jt. auth. see Bloom, Floyd E.

Lazerson, Arlyne, jt. auth. see Hayes, Floyd.

Lazerson, David B. Skullcaps n Switchblades. (Illus.). 204p. (C). 1988. 14.95 (*0-935063-30-7*, Bristol Rhein) CIS Comm.

Lazerson, Jeffrey M. How to Make a Fortune in Loans Without Leaving Your Desk. 2nd ed. 120p. 1996. reprint ed. per. 99.00 (*0-9665023-0-2*) Portfolio Mort.

Lazerson, Marvin. Origins of the Urban School: Public Education in Massachusetts, 1870-1915. LC 77-168433. (Joint Center for Urban Studies Publications). 302p. reprint ed. pap. 93.70 (*0-608-16109-8*, 201768600007) Bks Demand.

Lazerson, Marvin, ed. American Education in the Twentieth Century: A Documentary History. (Classics in Education Ser.). 224p. (C). 1987. pap. text 12.00 (*0-8077-2851-9*) Tchrs Coll.

Lazerson, Marvin & Grubb, W. Norton, eds. American Education & Vocationalism: A Documentary History, 1870-1970. LC 73-87511. (Classics in Education Ser.: Vol. 48). 189p. 1974. pap. 58.60 (*0-7837-8951-3*, 204966300002) Bks Demand.

Lazerson, Marvin, jt. auth. see Grubb, W. Norton.

Lazerwitz, Bernard, et al. Jewish Choices: American Jewish Denominationalism. LC 97-3079. (SUNY Series in American Jewish Society in the 1990s). 209p. (C). 1997. text 59.50 (*0-7914-3581-4*); pap. text 19.95 (*0-7914-3582-2*) State U NY Pr.

Lazewark, Libby. The Second Secret: A Shraga Morgenstern - Pinny Katz Mystery Trilogy. 178p. (J). (gr. k-4). 1995. 11.95 (*1-56871-088-7*) Targum Pr.

Lazewnik, Baruch. Handwriting Analysis: A Guide to Understanding Personalities. LC 90-70970. 208p. 1991. pap. 14.95 (*0-924608-06-4*, Whitford) Schiffer.

Lazewnik, Libby. Baker's Dozen: Baker's Best. 150p. (J). (gr. 4-8). 1996. pap. 9.95 (*1-56871-107-7*) Targum Pr.

— Baker's Dozen No. 1: On Our Own. 144p. (J). 1993. pap. 8.95 (*0-944070-34-5*) Targum Pr.

— Baker's Dozen No. 5: The Inside Story. (J). 1993. pap. 8.95 (*0-944070-93-0*) Targum Pr.

***Lazewnik, Libby.** Buried Treasure & Other Stories. 192p. 1998. 14.95 (*1-56871-146-8*, Pub. by Targum Pr) Feldheim.

Lazewnik, Libby. Give Me the Moon. 423p. 1996. 22.95 (*1-56871-102-6*) Targum Pr.

— Top Secret: A Shraga Morgenstern-Pinny Katz Mystery Trilogy. (Little Black Box Ser.: Pt. 1). 165p. (J). (gr. 5-9). 1995. 11.95 (*1-56871-078-X*) Targum Pr.

Lazewnik, Libby, et al. Baker's Dozen Bk. 6: Trapped! 172p. (J). 1993. pap. 8.95 (*0-944070-94-9*) Targum Pr.

Lazewnik, Libby, jt. ed. see Zakon, Miriam S.

Lazic, Mladen, ed. Protest in Belgrade: Winter of Discontent. LC 99-35900. (Illus.). 200p. 1999. pap. 22.95 (*963-9116-45-9*) Ctrl Europ Univ.

***Lazic, Mladen, ed.** Protest in Belgrade: Winter of Discontent. LC 99-35900. (Illus.). 200p. (C). 1999. 49.95 (*963-9116-72-6*) Ctrl Europ Univ.

Lazic, Vesna. Insolvency Proceedings & Commercial Arbitration. LC 98-49926. (International Arbitration Law Library). 1999. 95.00 (*90-411-1115-8*) Kluwer Law Intl.

***Lazich, Michael C.** E.C. Bridgman, 1801-1861: America's First Missionary to China. LC 00-36121. (Studies in the History of Missions : Vol. 19). 396p. 2000. 99.95 (*0-7734-7733-0*) E Mellen.

Lazich, Robert S., jt. ed. see Darnay, Arsen J.

Lazich, Robert S., jt. ed. see Reddy, Marlita A.

Lazicki, Ted. Do You Mean Me Lord? (Illus.). 120p. (Orig.). 1993. pap. 7.95 (*0-943167-24-8*) Faith & Fellowship Pr.

— Something for the Kids: Fifty-two Children's Sermons for Worship. Zapel, Arthur L., ed. LC 85-62468. (Illus.). 96p. (Orig.). 1985. pap. 9.95 (*0-916260-34-8*, B192) Meriwether Pub.

— Where Does God Live? Fifty Eight More "Something for the Kids" Children's Sermons for Worship. Zapel, Arthur L. & Wray, Rhonda, eds. LC 91-8734. (Illus.). 144p. (Orig.). (J). (ps-5). 1991. pap. 9.95 (*0-916260-77-1*, B189) Meriwether Pub.

Lazier, Audrey, jt. auth. see Mann.

Lazier, Christine. Exotic Wildlife. Royston, Angela et al, trs. LC 97-27530. Orig. Title: Animals of the Wild. (Illus.). 80p. (J). (gr. 2-9). 1998. lib. bdg. 23.95 (*0-88682-956-9*, Creat Educ) Creative Co.

— Seashore Life. Bogard, Vicki, tr. from FRE. LC 90-50781. (Young Discovery Library). (Illus.). 38p. (J). (gr. k-5). 1991. 5.95 (*0-944589-39-1*, 391) Young Discovery Lib.

Lazier, John R., jt. auth. see Mann, Kenneth H.

Lazier, William C., jt. auth. see Collins, James C.

Lazin, Fred, et al, eds. Developing Areas, Universities, & Public Policy. 184p. (Orig.). 1986. pap. 15.00 (*0-918592-86-0*) Pol Studies.

Lazin, Fred, jt. auth. see Nagel, Stuart.

Lazin, Frederick A. Policy Implementation & Social Welfare in the 1980s: Israel & the United States. 145p. (Orig.). 1986. 34.95 (*0-88738-084-0*) Transaction Pubs.

— Politics & Policy Implementation: Project Renewal in Israel. LC 92-40308. (SUNY Series in Israeli Studies). 201p. (C). 1993. pap. text 21.95 (*0-7914-1692-5*) State U NY Pr.

— Politics & Policy Implementation: Project Renewal in Israel. LC 92-40308. (SUNY Series in Israeli Studies). 201p. (C). 1993. text 59.50 (*0-7914-1691-7*) State U NY Pr.

Lazin, Frederick A. & Mahler, Gregory S. Israel in the Nineties: Development & Conflict. LC 96-12042. (Illus.). 256p. 1996. 49.95 (*0-8130-1452-2*) U Press Fla.

Lazinger, Susan S. & Shoval, Peretz. Prototyping a Microcomputer-Based Online Library Catalog. (Occasional Papers: No. 177). 1987. pap. 2.50 (*0-317-59035-9*) U of Ill Grad Sch.

Lazinger, Susan S., et al. Cataloging Hebrew Materials in the Online Environment: A Comparative Study of American & Israeli Approaches. LC 97-35508. 1998. 85.00 (*1-56308-358-2*) Libs Unl.

Lazio, Rick, ed. Crime & Community Opportunity: Field Hearing Before the Subcommittee on Housing & Community Opportunity. 136p. (C). 1999. reprint ed. text 30.00 (*0-7881-4541-X*) DIANE Pub.

Lazitch, Branko & Drachkovitch, Milorad M. Biographical Dictionary of the Comintern. rev. ed. (Publication Ser.: No. 340). 532p. (C). 1986. text 44.95 (*0-8179-8401-1*) Hoover Inst Pr.

Laznicka, P. Breccias & Coarse Fragmentites: Petrology, Environments, Associations, Ores. (Developments in Economic Geology Ser.: Vol. 25). 832p. 1988. 295.25 (*0-444-42938-7*) Elsevier.

— Precambrian Empirical Metallogeny: Precambrian Lithologic Associations & Metallic Ores. (Developments in Economic Geology Ser.: Vol. 29). 1640p. 1993. 408.25 (*0-444-89953-7*) Elsevier.

Lazo, Lucita. Practical Actions for the Social Protection of Homeworkers in Indonesia LC 98-949262. (Out of the Shadows Ser.). iii, 109 p. 1996. write for info. (*92-2-110193-2*) Intl Labour Office.

— Practical Actions for the Social Protection of Homeworkers in Thailand LC 98-949260. (Out of the Shadows Ser.). iii, 139p. 1996. write for info. (*92-2-110195-9*) Intl Labour Office.

Lazo, Lucita & ILO Regional Office for Asia & the Pacific Staff. Homeworkers of Southeast Asia. LC 98-947401. 1992. write for info. (*92-2-108490-6*) Intl Labour Office.

Lazo, Lucita & ILO Regional Office for Asia & the Pacific Staff. Practical Actions for the Social Protection of Homeworkers in Indonesia. LC 98-947402. (From the Shadows to the Fore Ser.). ii, 86p. 1993. write for info. (*92-2-109068-X*) Intl Labour Office.

Lazo, Caroline. Eleanor Roosevelt. LC 93-6610. (Peacemakers Ser.). (Illus.). 64p. (J). (gr. 4 up). 1993. text 13.95 (*0-87518-594-0*, Dillon Silver Burdett) Silver Burdett Pr.

— Elie Wiesel. LC 93-44473. (J). 1994. pap. 7.95 (*0-382-24715-9*, Dillon Silver Burdett) Silver Burdett Pr.

— Jimmy Carter: On the Road to Peace. (People in Focus Ser.). (Illus.). 160p. (J). (gr. 5 up). 1996. lib. bdg. 13.95 (*0-382-39262-0*, Dillon Silver Burdett) Silver Burdett Pr.

— Jimmy Carter: On the Road to Peace. (People in Focus Ser.). (Illus.). 160p. (YA). (gr. 5 up). 1996. pap. 7.95 (*0-382-39263-9*) Silver Burdett Pr.

— Mahatma Gandhi. LC 92-14314. (Peacemakers Ser.). (Illus.). 64p. (J). (gr. 4 up). 1993. lib. bdg. 13.95 (*0-87518-526-6*, Dillon Silver Burdett) Silver Burdett Pr.

— Martin Luther King, Jr. LC 93-9069. (Peacemakers Ser.). (Illus.). 64p. (J). (gr. 4 up). 1994. lib. bdg. 13.95 (*0-87518-618-1*, Dillon Silver Burdett) Silver Burdett Pr.

— Mother Teresa. LC 92-23765. (Peacemakers Ser.). (Illus.). 64p. (J). (gr. 4 up). 1993. lib. bdg. 13.95 (*0-87518-559-2*, Dillon Silver Burdett) Silver Burdett Pr.

— Rigoberta Menchu. LC 93-8381. (Peacemakers Ser.). (Illus.). 64p. (J). (gr. 4 up). 1994. lib. bdg. 13.95 (*0-87518-619-X*, Dillon Silver Burdett) Silver Burdett Pr.

— The Terra Cotta Army of Emperor Qin. LC 92-26189. (Illus.). 80p. (YA). (gr. 6 up). 1993. lib. bdg. 14.95 (*0-02-754631-4*, Mac Bks Young Read) S&S Childrens.

— Wilma Mankiller. LC 94-1229. (Peacemakers Ser.). (J). (gr. 4 up). 1994. pap. 7.95 (*0-382-24716-7*, Dillon Silver Burdett) Silver Burdett Pr.

***Lazo, Caroline E.** Alice Walker: Freedom Writer. LC 99-34469. (Biographies Ser.). (Illus.). 112p. (YA). (gr. 6-12). 2000. lib. bdg. 25.26 (*0-8225-4960-3*, Lerner Publctns) Lerner Pub.

Lazo, Caroline E. Arthur Ashe. LC 97-38737. 128p. (J). (gr. 6-9). 1998. 25.26 (*0-8225-4932-8*, Lerner Publctns) Lerner Pub.

— Gloria Steinem. LC 97-16831. (J). (gr. 5 up). 1997. lib. bdg. 17.95 (*0-8225-4934-4*) Lerner Pub.

— Lech Walesa. LC 92-39959. (Peacemakers Ser.). (Illus.). 64p. (J). (gr. 4 up). 1993. lib. bdg. 13.95 (*0-87518-525-8*, Dillon Silver Burdett) Silver Burdett Pr.

— Walt Disney. LC 98-18772. (People in Focus Book Ser.). (J). 1999. 13.95 (*0-382-39856-4*, Dillon Silver Burdett); pap. 7.95 (*0-382-39857-2*, Dillon Silver Burdett) Silver Burdett Pr.

Lazo, Donald M. Let Your Alcoholic Suffer! A Battle Plan for Families of Alcoholics. Fair, Erik, ed. (Illus.). 128p. (Orig.). 1999. pap. 11.95 (*0-913581-12-7*) Publitec.

Lazo, Guillermo. Bathers of the Med Sea & Other Stories. 174p. 1997. pap. 12.95 (*1-880046-03-2*) Baculite Pub.

Lazo, John, jt. ed. see Hacker, Miles P.

Lazo, John A., ed. Directory of the APA, 1993. 1952p. 1993. 70.00 (*1-55798-210-4*) Am Psychol.

Lazo, John S., et al. Review for USMILE Step 1: United States Medical Licensing Examination, Step 1. 5th ed. LC 98-33988. (National Medical Series for Independent Study). 380p. 1998. pap. 35.95 (*0-683-30490-9*) Lppncott W & W.

— Review for USMLE: United States Medical Licensing Examination, Step 1. 3rd ed. LC 93-41661. (National Medical Series for Independent Study). (Illus.). 300p. 1994. 29.95 (*0-683-06265-4*) Lppncott W & W.

Lazo, Julia A., tr. see Rice, Wayne & Yaconelli, Mike.

Lazo, William. Augustine's Trick. (Augustine Detective Ser.). 64p. (Orig.). (C). 1991. pap. 4.00 (*1-880046-05-9*) Baculite Pub.

Lazo, William J. The Ching Poems. (Minority Poet Ser.). (ENG & SPA., Illus.). 38p. 1990. pap. 5.00 (*1-880046-02-4*) Baculite Pub.

Lazonick, William. Business Organization & the Myth of the Market Economy. (Illus.). 388p. (C). 1993. pap. text 18.95 (*0-521-44788-7*) Cambridge U Pr.

— The Competitive Advantage on the Shop Floor. LC 90-32203. (Illus.). 464p. 1990. 54.50 (*0-674-15416-9*) HUP.

— Japanese Corporate Governance & Strategy. (Public Policy Brief Highlights Ser.: Vol. 48A). 6p. 1998. pap. write for info. (*0-941276-64-3*) J Levy.

— Japanese Corporate Governance & Strategy: Adapting to Financial Pressures for Change. (Public Policy Briefs Ser.: Vol. 48). 55p. 1998. pap. write for info. (*0-941276-63-5*) J Levy.

— Organization & Technology in Capitalist Development. LC 92-2430. (Economists of the Twentieth Century Ser.). 320p. 1992. 110.00 (*1-85278-742-2*) E Elgar.

Lazonick, William & Mass, William, eds. Organizational Capability & Competitive Advantage. LC 94-44343. (International Library of Critical Writings in Economics: Vol. 11). 672p. 1995. 265.00 (*1-85278-776-7*) E Elgar.

Lazonick, William & O'Sullivan, Mary. Investment in Innovation. (Public Policy Brief Ser.: Vol. 37A). 6p. 1997. pap. write for info. (*0-941276-37-6*) J Levy.

— Investment in Innovation: Corporate Governance & Employment: Is Prosperity Sustainable in the United States? (Public Policy Brief Ser.: Vol. 37). 52p. 1997. pap. write for info. (*0-941276-36-8*) J Levy.

Lazonick, William, et al. The Corporate Triangle: The Structure & Performance of Corporate Systems in a Global Economy. Admiraal, P. H., ed. LC 97-20351. (DeVries Lecture Ser.). 100p. (C). 1997. text 55.95 (*0-631-20715-5*) Blackwell Pubs.

Lazor, Mark & Institute of International Education (New York, N. Y.) Staff. Fortifying the Foundations: U. S. Support for Developing & Strengthening Democracy in East Central Europe. LC 97-195864. iii, 112 p. 1996. write for info. (*0-87206-236-8*) Inst Intl Educ.

Lazor-Bahr, Beverly. Fievel Saves the Day. LC 90-85174. (American Tail: Fievel Goes West Ser.). 14p. (J). (ps). 1991. 5.95 (*0-448-41075-3*, G & D) Peng Put Young Read.

Lazor-Bahr, Beverly, jt. auth. see Carlson, Dolley.

Lazor, Paul, tr. & pref. see Uspensky, Nicholas.

Lazoritz, Stephen, jt. auth. see Shelman, Eric A.

Lazou, Christopher. Supercomputers & Their Use. rev. ed. (Illus.). 276p. 1988. pap. 29.95 (*0-19-853759-X*) OUP.

***Lazourenko, S.** Bee. (Babies Bks.). (Illus.). 8p. (J). 2000. 11.95 (*0-7641-5264-5*) Barron.

— Bee. (Babies Bks.). (Illus.). 8p. (J). (ps-k). 2000. 10.95 (*0-7641-5234-3*) Barron.

— Penguin. (Babies Bks.). (Illus.). 8p. (J). 2000. 10.95 (*0-7641-5235-1*); 11.95 (*0-7641-5265-3*) Barron.

Lazowska, Ed, jt. ed. see Jones, Michael B.

Lazreg, Marnia. The Eloquence of Silence: Algerian Women in Question. LC 94-6193. 288p. (C). (gr. 13). 1994. pap. 25.99 (*0-415-90731-4*) Routledge.

Lazreg, N. Ben & Mattingly, D. J. Leptiminus (Lamta). A Roman Port City in Tunisia, No. 1. (JRA Supplementary Ser.: No. 4). (ENG, FRE & ITA., Illus.). 334p. 1992. 79.50 (*1-887829-04-0*) Jour Roman Arch.

Lazur, Louise, et al. Beauty & the Breast - The Cost of Living. 96p. 1998. 30.00 (*1-57833-034-3*) Todd Commns.

Lazure, Denis, ed. On Equal Terms: The Social Integration of Handicapped Persons in Canada: A Challenge for Everyone. (Illus.). 328p. 1999. reprint ed. pap. text 40.00 (*0-7881-8017-7*) DIANE Pub.

Lazure, Noel. Dictionnaire d'Intelligence Artificielle, Anglais-Francais. (ENG & FRE.). 216p. 1993. pap. 115.00 (*0-7859-5617-4*, 2225840288) Fr & Eur.

Lazurus, Francis M., intro. Faith, Discovery, Service: Perspectives on Jesuit Education. LC 92-82566. 105p. (C). 1992. pap. 10.00 (*0-87462-000-7*) Marquette.

Lazurus, John, ed. The Opera Handbook. (Monograph Ser.). 242p. 1990. 30.00 (*0-8161-9094-1*, Hall Reference); 18.95 (*0-8161-1827-2*, Hall Reference) Macmillan.

Lazutkin, Vladimir F. KAM Theory & Semiclassical Approximations to Eigenfunctions. LC 93-17491. (Ergebnisse der Mathematik und Ihrer Grenzgebiete Ser.: Vol. 24). (Illus.). ix, 389p. 1993. 158.95 (*0-387-53389-3*) Spr-Verlag.

Lazutkin, Y. Socialism & Wealth: The Creation & Distribution of Socialist Wealth. 217p. 1975. 22.95 (*0-8464-0859-7*) Beekman Pubs.

Lazzara, Judy, jt. auth. see Olson, Beverly.

***Lazzara, Margo Valentine.** The Healing Aromatherapy Bath: Therapeutic Treatments Using Meditation, Visualization & Essential Oils. LC 99-29330. (Illus.). 144p. 1999. pap. 16.95 (*1-58017-197-4*) Storey Bks.

Lazzara, Ralph, jt. ed. see Aliot, Etienne.

Lazzarelli, Ludovico. A Critical Edition of "De Gentilium Deorum Imaginibus" by Ludovico Lazzarelli: First Edited Text with Introduction & Translation. O'Neal, William J., ed. LC 97-27181. (Studies in Classics: Vol. 4). (ENG & LAT.). 144p. 1997. text 69.95 (*0-7734-8579-1*) E Mellen.

Lazzari. KIT: DA CAPO 4E-TEXT + STUDENT. 4th ed. (SPA.). (C). 1995. 51.50 incl. audio (*0-03-016273-4*) Harcourt.

— The Transition Sourcebook. 1998. pap. text 33.50 (*0-12-784561-5*) Acad Pr.

— Why Art? (C). Date not set. pap. text 43.00 (*0-15-505796-0*) Harcourt Coll Pubs.

Lazzari, Andrea M. & Peters, Patricia M. HELP 5: Handbook of Exercises for Language Processing. 190p. 1991. spiral bd. 39.95 (*1-55999-181-X*) LinguiSystems.

— HELP 4 (Handbook of Exercises for Language Processing) 190p. 1989. spiral bd. 39.95 (*1-55999-048-1*) LinguiSystems.

Lazzari, Andrea M., jt. auth. see Peters, Patricia.

Lazzari, Andrea M., jt. auth. see Peters, Patricia M.

Lazzari, Andrea M., jt. auth. see Wood, Judy W.

Lazzari, Eugene P., ed. CRC Handbook of Experimental Aspects of Oral Biochemistry. 384p. 1983. 145.00 (*0-8493-3162-5*, QP146, CRC Reprint) Franklin.

Lazzari, Margaret R. The Practical Handbook for the Emerging Artist. 302p. (C). 1995. pap. text 24.00 (*0-15-501498-6*, Pub. by Harcourt Coll Pubs) Harcourt.

Lazzari, Marie. Nineteenth Century Literary Criticism, Vol. 53. 500p. 1996. text 150.00 (*0-8103-9299-2*) Gale.

An Asterisk (*) at the beginning of an entry indicates that the title is appearing for the first time.

— Nineteenth Century Literary Criticism Vol. 48: Excerpts from Criticism of the Works of Novelists, Poets, Playwrights, Short Story Writers, Philosophers & Other Creative Writers Who Died Between 1800 & 1899, from the First Published Critical Appraisals to Current Evaluations. 460p. 1995. text 150.00 (*0-8103-8939-8*) Gale.

— Nineteenth Century Literature, Vol. 51. 500p. 1995. text 150.00 (*0-8103-9297-6*) Gale.

Lazzari, Marie, ed. Environmental Viewpoints, Vol. 2. 2nd ed. 453p. (C). 1993. 65.00 (*0-8103-8932-0*, 101632) Gale.

Lazzari, Marie, ed. Nineteenth Century Literary Criticism: Criticism of the Works of Novelists, Poets, Playwrights, Short Story Writers, Philosophers, & Other Creative Writers Who Died Between 1800 & 1899, from the First Published Critical Appraisals to Current Evaluations, Vol. 4. 450p. 1995. text 150.00 (*0-8103-8940-1*, 002314) Gale.

— Nineteenth Century Literary Criticism Vol. 47: Excerpts from Criticism of the Works of Novelists, Poets, Playwrights, Short Story Writers, Philosophers & Other Creative Writers Who Died Between 1800 & 1899, from the First Published Critical Appraisals to Current Evaluations. 460p. 1995. text 150.00 (*0-8103-8938-X*) Gale.

— Twentieth Century Criticism Vol. 55 & Index: Excerpts from Criticism of the Works of Novelists, Poets, Playwrights, Short Story Writers & Other Creative Writers who Lived Between 1900 & 1960, from the First Published Critical Appraisals to Current Evaluations. 532p. 1994. text 150.00 (*0-8103-2435-0*) Gale.

Lazzari, Marie, ed. Twentieth-Century Literary Criticism Vol. 55: Excerpts from Criticism of the Works of Novelists, Poets, Playwrights, Short Story Writers, & Other Creative Writers Who Lived Between 1900 & 1960, from the First Published Critical Appraisals to Current Evaluations. 532p. 1994. text 150.00 (*0-8103-2436-9*) Gale.

Lazzari, Marie & Dominic, Catherine C., eds. Epics for Students: Presenting Analysis, Context & Criticism on Commonly Studied Epics. LC 97-27859. 440p. (YA). 1997. text 70.00 (*0-7876-1685-0*, GML00198-111086) Gale.

Lazzari, Marie, jt. ed. see Cerrito, Joann.

Lazzarini, Roberta. Maximova & Vasiliev at the Bolshoi. (Illus.). 176p. 1995. 45.00 (*0-903102-62-5*, Pub. by Dance Bks) Princeton Bk Co.

Lazzarini, Tony. Never Trust a Man in Curlers. xix, 105p. 1997. 14.95 (*1-891555-00-6*); pap. 9.95 (*1-891555-01-4*) Voyager Pub.

Lazzarini, Zita, jt. auth. see Gostin, Lawrence O.

Lazzarino, Graziana. Da Capo. 4th ed. (C). 1995. wbk. ed. 34.00 (*0-03-016178-9*) Harcourt Coll Pubs.

***Lazzarino, Graziana.** Prego! An Invitation to Italian. LC 00-23140. 2000. write for info. (*0-07-365513-9*) McGraw.

Lazzarino, Graziana. Prego! An Invitation to Italian. 1990. student ed. write for info. (*0-07-909486-4*) McGraw.

— Prego! An Invitation to Italian. 3rd ed. (C). 1990. text 63.75 (*0-07-557426-8*) McGraw.

— Prego! An Invitation to Italian. 3rd ed. 1990. write for info. (*0-07-540866-X*) McGraw.

Lazzarino, Graziana & Moneti, Annamaria. Attualita Video. 3rd ed. (ITA.). 404p. (C). 1990. 241.50 (*0-03-053792-4*) Harcourt Coll Pubs.

— Attualita Video. 3rd ed. (ITA.). 404p. (C). 1991. pap. text, student ed. 26.50 (*0-03-053898-X*) Harcourt Coll Pubs.

— Da Capo: An Italian Review Grammar, Level II. 3rd ed. (ITA.). 404p. (C). 1991. write for info. (*0-318-69164-7*) Harcourt Coll Pubs.

— Da Capo, 4/E. 4th ed. (C). 1996. pap. text 50.00 (*0-03-009522-0*) Holt R&W.

Lazzarino, Graziana, et al. Prego! An Invitation to Italian. 4th ed. LC 94-42536. 544p. (C). 1995. 68.13 (*0-07-037722-7*) McGraw.

***Lazzarino, Graziana, et al.** Prego! An Invitation to Italian. 5th ed. (ITA & ENG.). (C). 2000. pap., student ed. 66.56 (*0-07-234221-8*) McGrw-H Hghr Educ.

Lazzarino, Luciano, tr. see McCall, Barbara A.

Lazzaro, Bea, jt. auth. see Mendelsohn, Lotte.

Lazzaro-Bruno, Claudia. Seventeenth-Century Italian Prints from the Collection of Mr. & Mrs. Marcus S. Sopher. LC 78-61801. (Illus.). 1978. pap. 10.00 (*0-937031-11-9*) Stanford Art.

Lazzaro-Bruno, Claudia, jt. auth. see Sopher, Marcus S.

Lazzaro, Claudia. The Italian Renaissance Garden: From the Conventions of Planting, Design, & Ornament to the Grand Gardens of Sixteenth-Century Central Italy. LC 89-78473. (Illus.). 354p. 1990. reprint ed. pap. 109.80 (*0-608-07831-X*, 205400700010) Bks Demand.

Lazzaro, D., et al, eds. Solar System Formation & Evolution. LC 98-72563. (Conference Series Proceedings: Vol. 149). 194p. 1998. 52.00 (*1-886733-69-4*) Astron Soc Pacific.

Lazzaro, Joseph J. Adapting PCs for Disabilities. LC 95-24982. 320p. (C). 1995. pap., pap. text 39.95 incl. cd-rom (*0-201-48354-8*) Addison-Wesley.

Lazzaro, Joseph J. Adaptive Technologies for Learning & Work Environments. LC 92-46993. (Illus.). 250p. 1993. pap. 45.00 (*0-8389-0615-X*) ALA.

Lazzaro, Paolo D., et al, eds. Second GR-I International Conference on New Laser Technologies & Applications. LC 99-159851. (Proceedings of SPIE Ser.: Vol. 3423). 480p. 1998. 89.00 (*0-8194-2878-7*) SPIE.

Lazzaro, Sam. More Than a Ball Game: An Inside Look at Minor League Baseball. LC 97-18355. (Illus.). (Orig.). 1997. pap. 18.95 (*0-936015-71-3*) Pocahontas Pr.

Lazzaro-Weis, Carol M. Confused Epiphanies: L'Abbe Prevost & the Romance Tradition. LC 90-24446. (American University Studies: Romance Languages & Literature: Ser. II, Vol. 161). 195p. (C). 1991. text 34.95 (*0-8204-1459-X*) P Lang Pubng.

— From Margins to Mainstream: Feminism & Fictional Modes in Italian Women's Writing, 1968-1990. LC 93-10867. 240p. (Orig.). (C). 1993. text 37.50 (*0-8122-3195-3*); pap. text 16.95 (*0-8122-1438-2*) U of Pa Pr.

Lazzati, Santiago. Diccionario del Verbo Castellano.Tr. of Dictionary of Castilian Verbs. (SPA.). 438p. 1977. pap. 24.95 (*0-8288-5332-0*, S12049) Fr & Eur.

Lazzerini, Beatrice, jt. auth. see Jain, L. C.

***Lazzerini, Edward J.** The Chinese Revolution, 1911-1998. LC 99-10141. (Guides to Historic Events of the Twentieth Century Ser.). 224p. 1999. 39.95 (*0-313-30110-7*) Greenwood.

Lazzerini, Edward J., jt. auth. see Yang, Richard.

Lazzerini, Edward J., jt. ed. see Brower, Daniel R.

Lbevitt, Albert, et al. The Albert Lbevitt Papers. LC 89-955813. (American Legal Manuscripts from the Harvard). 42p. 1985. write for info. (*0-89093-807-5*) U Pubns Amer.

LBJ School of Public Affairs Staff. Alternative Care for the Elderly: An Annotated Bibliography. (Policy Research Project Report Ser.: No. 22). 1977. pap. 3.00 (*0-89940-615-7*) LBJ Sch Pub Aff.

L.B.K.C. Staff. Recent Nepal: An Analysis of Recent Democratic Upsurge & Its Aftermath. (C). 1993. 85.00 (*0-7855-0212-2*, Pub. by Ratna Pustak Bhandar) St Mut.

***Lbopez-Alves, Fernando.** State Formation & Democracy in Latin America, 1810-1900. LC 99-45624. 272p. 2000. pap. 17.95 (*0-8223-2474-1*) Duke.

***Lbopez-Claros, Augusto & Alexashenko, Sergei V.** Fiscal Policy Issues During the Transition in Russia. LC 98-169274. (Occasional Papers). v, 58 p. 1998. write for info. (*1-55775-703-8*) Intl Monetary.

LC Marc Tapes Staff & New York Public Library Staff. Bibliographic Guide to Microform Publications: 1990. (Bibliographic Guides Ser.). 600p. (C). 1991. 265.00 (*0-8161-7144-0*, G K Hall & Co) Mac Lib Ref.

LC Marc Tapes Staff & Oriental Division of the New York Public Library S. Bibliographic Guide to East Asian Studies, 1990. (Bibliographic Guides Ser.). 350p. (C). 1991. 185.00 (*0-8161-7137-8*, G K Hall & Co) Mac Lib Ref.

LC Van Savage. LC's Take: Poetry I. LC 98-36371. (Illus.). 128p. 1998. pap. 11.95 (*1-892168-03-0*) Custom Communs.

Lcakey, Mercedes. Winds of Change. (Mage Winds Ser.: Bk. 2). 480p. 1993. mass mkt. 6.99 (*0-88677-563-9*, Pub. by DAW Bks) Penguin Putnam.

LCC-ST Staff. Directory of Certified Surgical Technologists & Certified First Assistants, 1995. Davis, Nadine A., ed. 1995. pap. text. write for info. (*0-9622332-5-0*) Liaison Coun.

LCE, Inc. Staff. Finding Legal Help: An Older Person's Guide. 25p. 1995. pap. text 3.00 (*0-933945-12-4*) Legal Coun Elderly.

LCPS Staff. The Legislative Elections in 1996 & the Democratic Crisis in Lebanon. (ARA., Illus.). 680p. 1998. pap. write for info. (*1-886604-16-9*) Lebanese Ctr.

— The National Dialogue Conference on National Agenda, 1996. 18th ed. 136p. 1998. pap. write for info. (*1-886604-13-4*) Lebanese Ctr.

— The Situation of Municipalities in Lebanon: And the Obstacles Towards Local Participation & Equiliberal Growth. (ARA., Illus.). 554p. 1998. pap. write for info. (*1-886604-18-5*) Lebanese Ctr.

LCPS Staff, et al. Decentralization in Lebanon. Saab, Fares A., ed. (ARA., Illus.). 382p. (Orig.). 1996. pap. 14.00 (*1-886604-00-2*) Lebanese Ctr.

L.C.W. Staff. The Autobiography of a Magdalen. reprint ed. 9.75 (*0-87651-208-2*) Southern U Pr.

Ldekker, John W. Faithful Mohawks. 312p. 1993. reprint ed. lib. bdg. 89.00 (*0-7812-5159-1*) Rprt Serv.

Le-Ba-Khanh. Vietnamese-English - English-Vietnamese Standard Dictionary: With a Supplement of New Words. 501p. 1992. pap. 19.95 (*0-87052-924-2*) Hippocrene Bks.

Le-Ba-Khanh & Le-Ba-Kong. Vietnamese-English-Vietnamese Dictionary. 9th ed. (ENG & VIE.). 501p. 1980. 69.95 (*0-8288-1085-0*, M 9502) Fr & Eur.

Le-Ba-Kong, jt. auth. see Le-Ba-Khanh.

Le Bailly, Pamela. Pressed Flowers. (Illus.). 76p. 1996. 18.95 (*1-870586-14-X*, D Porteous-Parkwest) Parkwest Pubns.

***Le Bailly, Pamela.** Pressed Flowers. (Illus.). 1999. pap. 15.95 (*1-870586-37-9*, D Porteous-Parkwest) Parkwest Pubns.

***Le Ban, Karen, et al.** African Women Gain Leadership Skills to Guide Agricultural Development: Lessons Learned & Best Practices First 10 Years, 1989-1999. LC 00-38163. (Professionals & Farmers Ser.). 2000. pap. write for info. (*1-57360-030-X*) Winrock Intl.

Le Baron Stockwell, M. Descendants of Francis LeBaron of Plymouth, Mass. (Illus.). 521p. reprint ed. pap. 81.50 (*0-8328-0758-3*); reprint ed. lib. bdg. 91.50 (*0-8328-0757-5*) Higginson Bk Co.

Le Barz, Patrick, jt. auth. see Dias, Danielle.

Le Bas, Elizabeth, tr. see LeFebvre, Henri.

Le Bas, M. J., ed. Milestones in Geology. (Geological Society Memoir Ser.: No. 16). 272p. 1995. 49.00 (*1-897799-24-1*, 247, Pub. by Geol Soc Pub Hse) AAPG.

Le Bas, Michael J. Carbonatite-Nephelinite Volcanism: An African Case History. LC 76-21090. (Illus.). 401p. reprint ed. pap. 124.40 (*0-608-18364-4*, 203304900083) Bks Demand.

Le Bas, Philippe & Waddington, William H. Inscriptions Grecques et Latines Recueillies en Grece et Asie Mineure, 2 vols., Set. (Subsidia Epigraphica Ser.: Vols. I-II). (GER.). xi, 884p. 1972. reprint ed. write for info. (*3-487-04396-3*) G Olms Pubs.

— Inscriptions Grecques et Latines Recueillies en Grece et Asie Mineure, Vol. I: Textes en Majuscules. (GER.). xi, 884p. 1972. reprint ed. write for info. (*0-318-71362-4*) G Olms Pubs.

— Inscriptions Grecques et Latines Recueillies en Grece et Asie Mineure, Vol. II: Textes en Minuscules et Explications. (GER.). xi, 884p. 1972. reprint ed. write for info. (*0-318-71363-2*) G Olms Pubs.

***Le Bas, Tom, ed.** Insight Guide Korea. 8th rev. ed. (Insight Guides Ser.). 297p. 2000. pap. 23.95 (*1-58573-002-5*) Langenscheidt.

— Insight Guide Nepal. 4th rev. ed. (Insight Guides Ser.). (Illus.). 362p. 2000. pap. 23.95 (*1-58573-004-1*, Insight Guides) Langenscheidt.

Le Beau, Bryan F. Frederic Henry Hedge: Nineteenth Century American Transcendentalist: Intellectually Radical, Ecclesiastically Conservative. LC 85-570. (Pittsburgh Theological Monographs, New Ser.: No. 16). (Orig.). 1985. pap. 10.00 (*0-915138-71-9*) Pickwick.

— Jonathan Dickinson & the Formative Years of American Presbyterianism. LC 97-1321. 256p. 1997. text 39.95 (*0-8131-2026-8*) U Pr of Ky.

***Le Beau, Bryan F., et al, eds.** The Historical Jesus Through Catholic & Jewish Eyes. 2000. pap. 18.00 (*1-56338-322-5*) TPI PA.

Le Beau, Bryan F. & Mor, Menachem, eds. Pilgrims & Travelers to the Holy Land. (Studies in Jewish Civilization: Vol. 7). xix, 284p. 1995. 30.00 (*1-881871-15-0*) Creighton U Pr.

— Religion in the Age of Exploration: The Case of Spain & New Spain. (Studies in Jewish Civilization: Vol. 5). xvi, 161p. 1996. 30.00 (*1-881871-21-5*) Creighton U Pr.

Le Beau, Bryan F., jt. ed. see Greenspoon, Leonard J.

Le Beau, Claude. Avantures Du Sr. C. Le Beau, Avocat En Parlement, Ou Voyage Curieux et Nouveau Parmi les Sauvages De L'amerique Septentrionale, 2 vols., Set. (Canadiana Avant 1867 Ser.: No. 16). 1966. 83.10 (*3-10-800086-1*) Mouton.

Le Bel, Pauline. Song Spinner. (Northern Lights Young Novels Ser.). 108p. (J). (gr. 3-9). 1994. pap. 7.95 (*0-88995-120-9*, Pub. by Red Deer) Genl Dist Srvs.

Le Bellac, Michel. Quantum & Statistical Field Theory. Barton, Gabriel, tr. (Illus.). 608p. 1992. pap. text 55.00 (*0-19-853964-9*) OUP.

— Thermal Field Theory. (Monographs on Mathematical Physics). (Illus.). 270p. (C). 1999. pap. text 37.95 (*0-521-65477-7*) Cambridge U Pr.

Le Beouf, Burney J. Elephant Seals. 1985. pap. 1.98 (*0-910286-98-1*) Boxwood.

Le Berre, Aline. Criminalite et Justice dans les "Contes Nocturnes" d'E. T. A. Hoffmann: Une Image Noire de l'Homme. (Publications Universitaires Europeennes Ser.: Series 1, Vol. 1547). (FRE.). 480p. 1996. 60.95 (*3-906754-38-3*, Pub. by P Lang) P Lang Pubng.

Le Berre, Francois. The New Chameleons Handbook. (Illus.). 160p. (Orig.). 1995. pap. 9.95 (*0-8120-1805-2*) Barron.

Le Bert, Joseph J. CICS Essentials for Application Developers & Programmers. LC 92-25967. 440p. 1993. 55.00 (*0-07-035869-9*) McGraw.

***Le Bertre, T., et al, eds.** Asymptotic Giant Branch Stars: Symposium No.191. (International Astronomical Union Ser.: Vol. 191). 632p. 1999. text 95.00 (*1-886733-90-2*) Astron Soc Pacific.

Le Bidois. Syntaxe du Francais Moderne, 2 tomes, Set. 35.90 (*0-685-36655-3*); 60.95 (*0-8288-7865-X*, F135480) Fr & Eur.

Le Bihan, Denis, ed. Diffusion & Perfusion Magnetic Resonance Imaging. LC 94-24643. 408p. 1995. text 172.00 (*0-7817-0244-5*) Lppncott W & W.

Le Blanc, Charles. Huai-nan Tzu: Philosophical Synthesis in Early Han Thought. 268p. (C). 1985. pap. 42.50 (*962-209-169-5*, Pub. by HK Univ Pr) Coronet Bks.

Le Blanc, Charles & Blader, Susan, eds. Chinese Ideas about Nature & Society Studies in Honour of Derk Bodde. 360p. (C). 1987. 77.50 (*962-209-189-X*, Pub. by HK Univ Pr); pap. 46.50 (*962-209-188-1*, Pub. by HK Univ Pr) Coronet Bks.

Le Blanc, Daird, ed. see Calvet, Koala.

Le Blanc, Elaine, jt. auth. see Fredericks, Anthony.

Le Blanc, H., jt. auth. see Wyatt, J.

Le Blanc, Jill. Thinking Clearly: A Guide to Critical Reasoning. LC 97-24969. (C). 1998. pap. text 22.00 (*0-393-97218-6*) Norton.

Le Blanc, L. Little Frog Learns to Sing. LC 68-16394. (Illus.). 32p. (J). (ps-2). 1967. lib. bdg. 9.95 (*0-87783-022-3*); audio 7.94 (*0-87783-191-2*) Oddo.

Le Blanc, Marcel & Frechette, M. Male Criminal Activity from Childhood Through Youth. (Research in Criminology Ser.). (Illus.). xi, 228p. 1989. 123.95 (*0-387-96859-8*) Spr-Verlag.

Le Blanc, Michelle, jt. auth. see Odell, Colin.

Le Blanc, Paul. Lenin & the Revolutionary Party. LC 88-18067. 456p. (C). 1993. pap. 25.00 (*0-391-03742-0*) Humanities.

— Rosa Luxemburg: Writings & Reflections. LC 99-42498. 275p. 1999. 59.95 (*1-57392-728-7*, Humanity Bks) Prometheus Bks.

— A Short History of the U. S. Working Class: From Colonial Times to the Twenty-First Century. 160p. 1998. 45.00 (*0-391-04088-X*); pap. 15.00 (*0-391-04089-8*) Humanities.

— A Short History of the U. S. Working Class: From Colonial Times to the Twenty-First Century. LC 99-24426. 160p. 1999. 45.95 (*1-57392-665-5*, Humanity Bks); pap. 17.95 (*1-57392-664-7*, Humanity Bks) Prometheus Bks.

— U. S. Labor in the Twentieth Century: Studies in Working Class Fragmentation & Insurgency. (C). Date not set. pap. write for info. (*0-391-04040-5*); text. write for info. (*0-391-04039-1*) Humanities.

Le Blanc, Paul, contrib. by. From Marx to Gramsci: A Reader in Revolutionary Marxist Politics. LC 95-44966. 512p. (C). 1996. pap. 22.50 (*0-391-03960-1*) Humanities.

***Le Blanc, Paul, ed.** Rosa Luxemburg: Writings & Reflections. LC 99-42498. (Revolutionary Studies). 275p. 1999. pap. 21.95 (*1-57392-729-5*, Humanity Bks) Prometheus Bks.

Le Blanc, Paul, jt. ed. see McLemee, Scott.

Le Blanc, Paul, ed. & intro. see Marx, Eleanor & Aveling, Edward.

Le Blanc, Rufus J. & Breeding, Julia G., eds. Regional Aspects of Carbonate Deposition: A Symposium. LC 57-2837. (Society of Economic Paleontologists & Mineralogists, Special Publication Ser.: No. 5). 215p. reprint ed. pap. 66.70 (*0-608-12926-7*, 202473200038) Bks Demand.

Le Blanc Staff. Thinking Clearly. Date not set. pap. text. write for info. (*0-393-97250-X*) Norton.

— Thinking Clearly with Lemur. Date not set. pap. text. write for info. (*0-393-97248-8*) Norton.

Le Blanc, Sydney. Whitney Guide to Twentieth Century American Architecture: Two Hundred Key Buildings. 2nd rev. ed. (Illus.). 256p. 1996. pap. text 19.95 (*0-8230-2173-4*) Watsn-Guptill.

Le Blant, Edmont F. Inscriptions Chretiennes de la Gaule Anterieure au Huitieme Siecle, 2 vols. clvi, 1142p. reprint ed. write for info. (*0-318-71364-0*) G Olms Pubs.

— Inscriptions Chretiennes de la Gaule Anterieure au VIIIe Siecle, 2 vols. reprint ed. write for info. (*0-318-72102-3*) G Olms Pubs.

Le Bloas, Renbee, jt. auth. see Julienne, Jbercome.

Le Bloas, Renee, et al. The Shark: Silent Hunter. LC 97-43254. (Animal Close-Ups Ser.). (Illus.). 28p. (J). (ps-3). 1998. pap. 6.95 (*0-88106-258-8*) Charlesbridge Pub.

Le Boeuf, Burney J. & Laws, Richard M., eds. Elephant Seals: Population Ecology, Behavior, & Physiology. LC 93-38142. 1994. 65.00 (*0-520-08364-4*, Pub. by U CA Pr) Cal Prin Full Svc.

Le Boeuf, Michael. How to Win Customers & Keep Them for Life. 192p. 1989. pap. 12.00 (*0-425-11468-6*) Berkley Pub.

— The Perfect Business. 224p. 1997. per. 11.00 (*0-684-83345-X*) S&S Trade Pap.

Le Bohec, Yann. The Imperial Roman Army. (Illus.). 400p. 1994. 35.00 (*0-7818-0259-8*) Hippocrene Bks.

***Le Bohec, Yann.** Imperial Roman Army. (Illus.). 2000. pap. 27.99 (*0-415-22295-8*) Routledge.

Le Bon, Daniel, tr. see Jackins, Harvey.

Le Bon, Gustav. The Crowd. rev. ed. 224p. (C). 1994. pap. 24.95 (*1-56000-788-5*) Transaction Pubs.

Le Bon, Gustave. The Evolution of Forces. 1991. lib. bdg. 75.95 (*0-8490-4812-5*) Gordon Pr.

— The Evolution of Matter. 1991. lib. bdg. 79.95 (*0-8490-4809-5*) Gordon Pr.

— The Psychology of Peoples. LC 73-14164. (Perspectives in Social Inquiry Ser.). 252p. 1979. reprint ed. 19.95 (*0-405-05509-9*) Ayer.

— The Psychology of Revolution. LC 68-29699. 1968. reprint ed. pap. 19.00 (*0-87034-026-3*) Fraser Pub Co.

Le Bon, Leo. Where Mountains Live: Twelve Great Treks of the World. (Illus.). 144p. 1987. 60.00 (*0-89381-242-0*) Aperture.

Le Bon, S., ed. see Sartre, Jean-Paul.

Le Bonheur, Albert. Of Gods, Kings, & Men: Bas-Reliefs of Angkor Wat & Bayon. (Illus.). 112p. (Orig.). 1996. pap. 39.95 (*0-906026-37-7*, Pub. by Serindia) Weatherhill.

Le Book Publishing Inc Staff. Le Book New York, 2. 1999. 150.00 (*2-905190-27-2*) Bk Assoc.

Le Bossu, Adam. Jeu de la Feuille. (FRE.). 181p. 1970. 19.95 (*0-8288-7471-9*) Fr & Eur.

— Le Jeu de Robin et Marion. (FRE.). 91p. 1968. 9.95 (*0-8288-7494-8*) Fr & Eur.

Le Bossu, Rene. Traite du Poeme Epique, 2 vols. 646p. reprint ed. write for info. (*0-318-71365-9*) G Olms Pubs.

Le Bot, Yvon. La Guerra en Tierras Mayas (War in Maya Lands) (SPA.). 1997. pap. 7.95 (*968-16-4537-5*, Pub. by Fondo) Continental Bk.

Le Bourdais, Donat M. Stefansson: Ambassador of the North. LC 63-17243. (Emulation Bks.). 206p. reprint ed. pap. 63.90 (*0-608-13594-1*, 202230700026) Bks Demand.

Le Bourgeois, Helen, jt. auth. see Ward, Ola M.

Le Boursicaud, Henri. Rags to Riches: The Story of the Companions of Emmaus. 144p. 1989. pap. 22.00 (*1-85390-053-2*, Pub. by Veritas Pubns) St Mut.

Le Bras, Gabriel. Etudes De Sociologie Religieuse: Studies in Religious Sociology, 2 vols. LC 74-25763. (European Sociology Ser.). 824p. 1975. reprint ed. 65.95 (*0-405-06517-5*) Ayer.

Le Bras, Georges. Chemical Processes in Atmospheric Oxidation: Laboratory Studies of Chemistry Related to Tropospheric Ozone. LC 96-41132. (Transport & Chemical Transformation of Pollutants in the Troposphere Ser.). (Illus.). xiv, 320p. 1997. 99.50 (*3-540-60998-9*) Spr-Verlag.

Le Bras, M., ed. Fire Retardancy of Polymers: The Use of Intumescence. 482p. 1999. 145.00 (*0-85404-738-7*) Royal Soc Chem.

Le Bras, Yvon, jt. auth. see Dengler, William.

Le Bras, Yvon, jt. auth. see Quiring, James P.

Le Bras, Yvon, jt. auth. see Scharf, Janet.

Le Bras, Yvon, tr. see Black, Susan E.

Le Bras, Yvon, tr. see Borglum, Lincoln.

Le Bras, Yvon, tr. see Bowman, Lori & Bowman, Carl.

Le Bras, Yvon, tr. see Colclazer, Susan.

L

An Asterisk (*) at the beginning of an entry indicates that the title is appearing for the first time.

Le Bras, Yvon, tr. see Cook, Kayci.

Le Bras, Yvon, tr. see Cox, W. Eugene.

Le Bras, Yvon, tr. see Davies, Denny.

Le Bras, Yvon, tr. see Den Dooven, K. C.

Le Bras, Yvon, tr. see Gilmore, Jackie.

Le Bras, Yvon, tr. see Hunter, Wilson, Jr.

Le Bras, Yvon, tr. see Jackson, Victor L.

Le Bras, Yvon, tr. see Ladd, Gary.

Le Bras, Yvon, tr. see Mack, James A.

Le Bras, Yvon, tr. see Martin, Linda.

Le Bras, Yvon, tr. see McKenzie, Leonard.

Le Bras, Yvon, tr. see Nielsen, Cindy.

Le Bras, Yvon, tr. see Palmer, John J.

Le Bras, Yvon, tr. see Rasp, Richard A.

Le Bras, Yvon, tr. see Robinson, Sandra C. & Robinson, George B.

Le Bras, Yvon, tr. see Rohde, Katherine M.

Le Bras, Yvon, tr. see Rudd, Connie.

Le Braz, Anatole. Dealings with the Dead: Narratives from "La Legende de la mort en Basse Bretagne" Whitehead, E. A., tr. from FRE. LC 77-87695. reprint ed. 37.50 (*0-404-16491-9*) AMS Pr.

— The Night of Fires & Other Breton Studies. Gostling, Frances M., tr. from FRE. LC 77-87696. (Illus.). reprint ed. 45.00 (*0-404-16492-7*) AMS Pr.

Le Breton, Anna L. Memoir of Mrs. Barbauld, Including Letters & Notices of Her Family & Friends. LC 73-172311. reprint ed. 39.50 (*0-404-07397-2*) AMS Pr.

Le Breton, Binka. A Land to Die For. (Illus.). 167p. (Orig.). 1997. pap. 12.95 (*0-932863-24-8*) Clarity Pr.

— Voices from the Amazon. LC 93-16349. (Books for a World That Works). (Illus.). xiv, 165p. 1993. pap. 14.95 (*1-56549-021-5*) Kumarian Pr.

Le Breton, F. Vocabulaire Francais-Islandais. (FRE & ICE.). 119p. 1996. 27.95 (*0-320-00943-2*) Fr & Eur.

Le Breton, Kenny. Lovebirds As a Hobby. (TT Ser.). (Illus.). 96p. 1992. pap. 8.95 (*0-86622-411-4*, TT011) TFH Pubns.

Le Bris, Annie. Phraseological Dictionary of Economics & & Business Terms French-Italian--Italian-French. (FRE & ITA.). 1152p. 125.00 (*0-7859-8864-5*) Fr & Eur.

Le Bris, Michel. Victor Hugo a Guernsey. (FRE., Illus.). 180p. 1996. pap. 59.95 (*2-86808-098-7*) Intl Scholars.

Le Bris, Pierre & Prost, Andre. Dictionnaire Bobo-Francais. 1981. write for info. (*0-7859-8653-7*, 285297102X) Fr & Eur.

Le Brizault, Jean-Louis. Dictionnaires des Sigles Anglais Utilises en Electronique et en Informatique. (FRE.). 240p. 1990. pap. 125.00 (*0-8288-2587-4*, 2852065835) Fr & Eur.

Le Brocquy, Sybil. Swift's Most Valuable Friend. LC 68-26028. 128p. 1968. 18.95 (*0-8023-1165-2*) Dufour.

Le Brun, Annie. Sade: A Sudden Abyss. Naish, Camille, tr. from FRE. 232p. (Orig.). 1991. pap. 12.95 (*0-87286-250-X*) City Lights.

Le Brun, Charles. A Method to Learn to Design the Passions, Proposed in a Conference on Their General & Particular Expression. Williams, John, tr. from FRE. LC 92-24907. (Augustan Reprints Ser.: Nos. 200-201). 1980. reprint ed. 21.50 (*0-404-70200-7*, NC825) AMS Pr.

— Methode pour Apprendre a Dessiner les Passions. vi, 63p. 1982. reprint ed. write for info. (*3-487-06717-X*) G Olms Pubs.

Le Brun, M. J., jt. auth. see Lauchland, K. A.

Le Brun, Marlene & Johnstone, Richard. The Quiet (R)evolution: Improving Student Learning in Law. LC 95-102827. 412p. 1994. pap. 65.00 (*0-455-21279-1*, Pub. by LawBk Co) Gaunt.

Le Bruyn, Lieven, et al. Graded Orders. 250p. 1988. 40.50 (*0-8176-3360-X*) Birkhauser.

Le Bruyn, Lieven, jt. ed. see Van Oystaeyen, Freddy.

Le Cain, George, jt. auth. see Donaldson, Cyril.

***Le Calvez, Patrice.** Dynamical Properties of Diffeomorphisms of the Annulus & of the Torus. LC 99-87060. (SMFAMS Ser.: Vol. 4). 105p. 2000. 21.00 (*0-8218-1943-7*) Am Math.

Le Cam, Lucien M. Asymptotic Methods in Statistical Decision Theory. (Series in Statistics). 770p. 1986. 74.95 (*0-387-96307-3*) Spr-Verlag.

— Festschrift for Lucien Le Cam: Research Papers in Probability & Statistics. Pollard, David et al, eds. LC 96-52745. 464p. 1997. 59.95 (*0-387-94952-6*) Spr-Verlag.

Le Cam, Lucien M. & Lo Yang, G. Asymptotics in Statistics: Some Basic Concepts. Berger, J. O. et al, eds. (Series in Statistics). (Illus.). viii, 180p. 1990. 47.95 (*0-387-97372-9*) Spr-Verlag.

***Le Cam, Lucien M. & Yang, Grace L.** Asymptotics in Statistics: Some Basic Concepts. 2nd ed. LC 00-30759. (Series in Statistics). 304p. 2000. 69.95 (*0-387-95036-2*) Spr-Verlag.

Le Camus de Mezieres, Nicolas. The Genius of Architecture: or The Analogy of That Art with Our Sensations. Britt, David, tr. LC 92-875. (Texts & Documents Ser.). (Illus.). 238p. 1992. pap. 19.95 (*0-89236-235-9*, Pub. by J P Getty Trust) OUP.

— The Genius of Architecture: or The Analogy of That Art with Our Sensations. Britt, David, tr. LC 92-875. (Texts & Documents Ser.). (Illus.). 238p. 1992. 29.95 (*0-89236-234-0*, Pub. by J P Getty Trust) OUP.

Le Camus, Sebastien. Sebastien le Camus: Airs a Deux et Trois Parties. Green, Robert A., ed. (Recent Researches in Music of the Baroque Era Ser.: No. RRB89). (Illus.). xxi, 55p. 1998. pap. 35.00 (*0-89579-407-1*) A-R Eds.

***Le Carre, John, pseud.** La Casa Rusia. Orig. Title: Russia House. 1999. 14.95 (*84-01-49981-X*) Plaza.

— The Honourable Schoolboy. 688p. 2000. reprint ed. per. 7.99 (*0-671-04274-2*) PB.

— The Little Drummer Girl. 672p. 2000. reprint ed. per. 7.99 (*0-671-04278-5*, Pocket Books) PB.

Le Carre, John, pseud. The Looking Glass War. 1997. pap. 12.00 (*0-345-41829-8*) Ballantine Pub Grp.

***Le Carre, John, pseud.** The Naive & Sentimental Lover. 528p. 2000. reprint ed. per. 7.99 (*0-671-04277-7*) PB.

Le Carre, John, pseud. The Night Manager: A Novel. 1994. mass mkt. 6.99 (*0-345-38576-4*) Ballantine Pub Grp.

— The Night Manager: A Novel. 1997. pap. 12.00 (*0-345-41830-1*) Ballantine Pub Grp.

— The Night Manager: A Novel. LC 92-55070. 1993. 24.00 (*0-679-42513-6*) Knopf.

— Our Game. 1996. mass mkt. 6.99 (*0-345-40000-3*) Ballantine Pub Grp.

— Our Game. 1997. pap. 12.00 (*0-345-41831-X*) Ballantine Pub Grp.

— Our Game: A Novel. 1995. 24.00 (*0-679-44189-1*) Knopf.

***Le Carre, John, pseud.** A Perfect Spy. 688p. 2000. reprint ed. per. 7.99 (*0-671-04275-0*, Pocket Books) PB.

Le Carre, John, pseud. The Russia House. 1989. 19.95 (*0-394-57789-2*) Knopf.

***Le Carre, John, pseud.** The Russia House. 448p. 2000. reprint ed. per. 7.99 (*0-671-04279-3*) PB.

Le Carre, John, pseud. The Secret Pilgrim. 1992. mass mkt. 5.99 (*0-345-37476-2*) Ballantine Pub Grp.

— The Secret Pilgrim. 1990. 27.50 (*0-394-58842-8*) Knopf.

— Single & Single. LC 98-47174. 347p. 1999. 26.00 (*0-684-85926-2*) Scribner.

— Single & Single. LC 99-31995. 1999. write for info. (*1-56895-748-3*) Wheeler Pub.

***Le Carre, John, pseud.** Single & Single. large type ed. 2000. pap. 11.95 (*1-56895-969-9*) Wheeler Pub.

— Single & Single. 400p. 2000. reprint ed. per. 7.99 (*0-671-02797-2*, Pocket Star Bks) PB.

Le Carre, John, pseud. A Small Town in Germany. 1969. mass mkt. 3.25 (*0-440-18036-8*) Dell.

***Le Carre, John, pseud.** Smiley's People. 448p. 2000. reprint ed. per. 7.99 (*0-671-04276-9*, Pocket Books) PB.

Le Carre, John, pseud. The Spy Who Came in from the Cold. (Read-Along Ser.). (YA). 1985. pap., student ed. 34.95 incl. audio (*0-88432-970-4*, S23911) Audio-Forum.

— The Spy Who Came in from the Cold, 2 vols., Set. large type ed. (YA). (gr. 10-12). reprint ed. 10.00 (*0-89064-058-0*) NAVH.

— The Tailor of Panama. 1997. mass mkt. 6.99 (*0-345-42043-8*) Ballantine Pub Grp.

— The Tailor of Panama. LC 96-34802. 1996. 25.00 (*0-679-45446-2*); 25.00 (*0-679-45480-2*) Knopf.

— Tinker, Tailor, Soldier, Spy. 384p. 1984. mass mkt. 6.99 (*0-553-26778-7*) Bantam.

— Tinker, Tailor, Soldier, Spy. Date not set. 14.95 (*0-559-35018-X*) Putnam Pub Group.

***Le Carre, John, pseud.** Tinker, Tailor, Soldier, Spy. 448p. 2000. reprint ed. per. 7.99 (*0-671-04273-4*) PB.

Le Cato, Nathaniel J. The Curse of Caste. LC 75-39092. (Black Heritage Library Collection). 1977. reprint ed. 24.95 (*0-8369-9030-7*) Ayer.

***Le, Chap T.** Applied Categorical Data Analysis. LC 98-14782. (Probability & Statistics Ser.). 312p. 1998. pap. 69.95 (*0-471-24060-5*) Wiley.

Le, Chap T. Applied Survival Analysis. LC 97-6506. 257p. 1997. pap. 64.95 (*0-471-17085-2*) Wiley.

— Health & Numbers: Basic Biostatistical Methods. LC 94-25553. 260p. 1994. pap. 54.95 (*0-471-01248-3*) Wiley.

Le, Chap T., ed. Fundamentals of Biostatistical Inference. (Statistics: Textbooks & Monographs: Vol. 124). (Illus.). 272p. 1991. text 75.00 (*0-8247-8674-2*) Dekker.

Le, Charles T. The Most Paradoxist Mathematician of the World. LC PC0840.29.M2. 58p. reprint ed. pap. 30.00 (*0-608-20021-2*, 207114300010) Bks Demand.

Le Charlier, B., ed. Static Analysis: Proceedings of the First International Static Analysis Symposium, SAS '94, Namur, Belgium, September 28-30, 1994. (Lecture Notes in Computer Science Ser.: Vol. 864). xii, 465p. 1994. 65.95 (*3-540-58485-4*) Spr-Verlag.

Le Charlier, Baudouin, ed. see SAS Staff.

Le Chevalier, T., jt. ed. see Arriagada, R.

Le Clair, Charles. The Art of Watercolor. rev. ed. LC 93-38097. (Illus.). 144p. 1994. 29.95 (*0-8230-0291-8*) Watsn-Guptill.

— The Art of Watercolor: Revised Edition. expanded rev. ed. LC 99-12869. (Illus.). 176p. 1999. pap. text 29.95 (*0-8230-0292-6*) Watsn-Guptill.

Le Clair, Mary & Fortune, Peter. A Lazy Man's Guide to Public Speaking. 139p. (C). 1986. text 100.00 (*0-9588155-0-X*, Pub. by Peter Fortune) St Mut.

Le Clair, Robert C. Three American Travellers in England. (BCL1-PS American Literature Ser.). 223p. 1993. reprint ed. lib. bdg. 79.00 (*0-7812-6571-1*) Rprt Serv.

— Three American Travellers in England: James Russell Lowell, Henry Adams, Henry James. LC 77-19341. 222p. 1978. reprint ed. lib. bdg. 59.50 (*0-313-20190-0*, LETA, Greenwood Pr) Greenwood.

— Young Henry James, 1813-1876. LC 77-153337. reprint ed. 39.50 (*0-404-03897-2*) AMS Pr.

Le Clair, Robert C., ed. see James, William.

***Le Claire, Chris.** Worlds to Conquer: An Authorized Biography of Steve Reeves. (Illus.). 256p. 1999. pap. 29.95 (*0-9676754-1-3*) Monomoy.

Le Clercq, Chretien. First Establishment of the Faith in New France. 2 vols., Set. LC 77-172312. reprint ed. 87.50 (*0-404-03914-6*) AMS Pr.

— New Relation of Gaspesia: With the Customs & Religion of the Gaspesian Indian, Vol. 5. Ganong, William F., ed. LC 68-28600. 452p. 1969. reprint ed. lib. bdg. 75.00 (*0-8371-5044-2*, LERG, Greenwood Pr) Greenwood.

Le Clercq, Jacques, tr. see Dumas, Alexandre.

Le Clerq, Jacques, tr. see Reyles, Carlos.

Le Clezia, J. M. El Sueno Mexicano (The Mexican Dream) O el Pensamiento Interrumpido (Or the Interrupted Thought) (SPA.). 278p. 1992. pap. 8.99 (*968-16-3699-6*, Pub. by Fondo) Continental Bk.

Le Clezio, Alexandrina. Effective Team Management. 120p. 1993. 26.00 (*1-85431-209-X*, Pub. by Blackstone Pr) Gaunt.

Le Clezio, J. M. Celui Qui N'Avait Jamais vu la Mer. (Folio - Junior Ser.: No. 492). (FRE., Illus.). 107p. (J). (gr. 5-10). 1988. pap. 6.95 (*2-07-033492-9*) Schoenhof.

— Chercheir D'Or. (Folio Ser.: No. 2000). (FRE.). pap. 10.95 (*2-07-038082-3*) Schoenhof.

— Le Chercheur D'Or. (FRE.). 1988. pap. 13.95 (*0-8288-3706-6*) Fr & Eur.

— Desert. (FRE.). 1985. pap. 13.95 (*0-7859-0646-0*, F113320) Fr & Eur.

— Desert. (Folio Ser.: No. 1670). (FRE.). pap. 10.95 (*2-07-037670-2*) Schoenhof.

Le Clezio, J. M. Diego y Frida. LC 96-133117. (SPA.). 207p. 1997. pap. 18.98 (*968-13-2856-6*) Edit Diana.

Le Clezio, J. M. L' Extase Materielle. (FRE.). 1971. pap. 10.95 (*0-7859-2838-3*) Fr & Eur.

— Fievre. (Imaginaire Ser.). (FRE.). pap. 13.95 (*2-07-072257-0*) Schoenhof.

— La Fievre. (FRE.). 1991. pap. 16.95 (*0-7859-2946-0*) Fr & Eur.

— Guerre. (Imaginaire Ser.). (FRE.). 1992. pap. 12.95 (*2-07-072546-4*) Schoenhof.

— La Guerre. (FRE.). 1992. pap. 15.95 (*0-7859-2952-5*) Fr & Eur.

— Le Livre des Fuites. (FRE.). 1989. pap. 16.95 (*0-7859-2941-X*, 2070718204) Fr & Eur.

— Le Livre des Fuites. (Imaginaire Ser.). (FRE.). 1990. pap. 13.95 (*2-07-071820-4*) Schoenhof.

— Lullaby. (Folio - Junior Ser.: No. 448). (FRE., Illus.). (J). (gr. 5-10). 1995. pap. 6.95 (*2-07-033448-1*) Schoenhof.

— The Mexican Dream: or The Interrupted Thought of Amerindian Civilizations. Fagan, Teresa L., tr. (Illus.). 232p. 1993. 22.50 (*0-226-11002-8*) U Ch Pr.

— Mondo et Autres Histoires. (FRE.). 1982. pap. 11.95 (*0-8288-3704-X*, M1262) Fr & Eur.

— Mondo et Autres Histoires. (Folio Ser.: No. 1365). (FRE.). pap. 9.95 (*2-07-037365-7*) Schoenhof.

— Onitsha. (Folio Ser.: No. 2472). (FRE.). 1991. pap. 29.95 (*2-07-038726-7*) Schoenhof.

— Onitsha. Anderson, Alison, tr. LC 96-32612. (Illus.). vii, 206p. 1997. pap. 15.00 (*0-8032-7966-3*); text 40.00 (*0-8032-2915-1*) U of Nebr Pr.

— Printemps et Autres Saisons. (Folio Ser.: No. 2264). (FRE.). pap. 8.95 (*0-685-65407-9*) Schoenhof.

— Le Proces-Verbal. (FRE.). 1973. pap. 11.95 (*0-8288-3707-4*) Fr & Eur.

— Le Proces-Verbal. (Folio Ser.: No. 353). (FRE.). pap. 9.95 (*2-07-036353-8*) Schoenhof.

— Reve Mexicain. (Folio Essais Ser.: No. 178). (FRE.). pap. 11.95 (*2-07-032680-2*) Schoenhof.

— La Ronde et Autres Faits Divers. (FRE.). 1990. pap. 10.95 (*0-8288-3708-2*) Fr & Eur.

— La Ronde et Autres Faits Divers. (Folio Ser.: No. 2148). (FRE.). pap. 8.95 (*2-07-038237-0*) Schoenhof.

— Villa Aurore. (Folio - Junior Ser.: No. 603). (FRE., Illus.). 112p. (J). (gr. 5-10). 1990. pap. 7.95 (*2-07-033603-4*) Schoenhof.

— Voyage au Pays des Arbres. (Folio - Cadet Rouge Ser.: No. 187). (FRE., Illus.). 48p. (J). (gr. 3-7). 1990. pap. 8.95 (*2-07-031187-2*) Schoenhof.

Le Clezio, J. M. G. The Prospector. Marks, Carol, tr. from FRE. (Verba Mundi Ser.). 352p. 1993. 22.95 (*0-87923-976-X*) Godine.

Le, Clezio J.M.G. Diego y Frida. 1998. pap. 22.95 (*84-7880-399-8*) Planeta.

Le Coeur, C. Le Culte de la Generation et l'Evolution Religieuse et Sociale en Guinee. (B. E. Ser.: No. 150). (FRE.). 1932. 25.00 (*0-8115-3070-1*) Periodicals Srv.

Le Comte, Edward. Milton Re-Viewed: Ten Essays. LC 91-1083. 160p. 1991. text 10.00 (*0-8153-0306-8*, 1446) Garland.

Le Comte, Edward S. Dictionary of Puns in Milton's English Poetry. LC 80-15500. xx, 238 p. 1981. text 76.00 (*0-231-05102-6*) Col U Pr.

Le Conte, John E. Le Conte's Report of East Florida. LC 77-9286. (FTU Monograph Ser.: No. 1). 90p. reprint ed. pap. 30.00 (*0-7837-5025-0*, 204469300004) Bks Demand.

Le Conte, Joseph. Race Problem in the South. LC 78-81123. (Black Heritage Library Collection). 1977. 11.95 (*0-8369-8619-9*) Ayer.

Le Corbeiller, Clare. Eighteenth-Century Italian Porcelain. (Illus.). 32p. 1985. pap. 1.95 (*0-87099-421-2*) Metro Mus Art.

— Gold Boxes: The Wrightsman Collection. LC 77-23592. (Illus.). 1977. pap. 1.00 (*0-87099-166-3*) Metro Mus Art.

Le Corbeiller, Philippe. Dimensional Analysis. (C). 1966. pap. text 16.95 (*0-89197-126-2*) Irvington.

Le Corbusier. City of Tomorrow. 301p. 1975. pap. text 41.95 (*0-7506-1604-0*); pap. text 39.95 (*0-85139-124-9*) Buttrwrth-Heinemann.

— City of Tomorrow & Its Planning. (Illus.). 352p. 1987. reprint ed. pap. 10.95 (*0-486-25332-5*) Dover.

— Essential Le Corbusier: Liesprit Nouveau Articles. LC 99-169886. 377p. 1998. pap. 49.95 (*0-7506-4138-X*) Buttrwrth-Heinemann.

— Etude Sur Le Mouvement D'art Decoratif En Allemagne. LC 68-26652. (Architecture & Decorative Art Ser.). 1968. reprint ed. lib. bdg. 27.50 (*0-306-71147-8*) Da Capo.

— Le Corbusier Album. LC 96-52593. 1997. 250.00 (*1-885254-58-X*, Pub. by Monacelli Pr) Penguin Putnam.

— Une Petite Maison. (Illus.). 84p. 1923. pap. 16.95 (*3-7643-5512-3*, Pub. by Birkhauser) Princeton Arch.

— Towards a New Architecture. (Illus.). 312p. 1970. pap. text 38.95 (*0-7506-0627-4*) Buttrwrth-Heinemann.

— Towards a New Architecture. (Illus.). 320p. 1985. reprint ed. pap. 9.95 (*0-486-25023-7*) Dover.

Le Corbusier Staff. Journey to the East. Zaknic, Ivan, ed. & tr. by. Pertuiset, Nicole, tr. (Illus.). 296p. 1989. pap. text 17.95 (*0-262-62068-5*) MIT Pr.

***Le Corbusier Staff.** Le Modulor, Modulor 2, 2 vols. LC 99-53635. (Illus.). 580p. 2000. pap. 38.00 (*3-7643-6188-3*, Pub. by Birkhauser) Princeton Arch.

— Le Modulor, Modulor 2, 2 vols. (FRE., Illus.). 580p. 2000. pap. 35.00 (*3-7643-6187-5*, Pub. by Birkhauser) Princeton Arch.

Le Cordeur, Basil A. The Politics of Eastern Cape Separatism, 1820-1854. (Illus.). 1981. 45.00 (*0-19-570196-8*) OUP.

Le Cordon Bleu Staff. Chicken. LC 98-65443. (Cordon Bleu Home Collection: Vol. 3). 64p. 1998. 12.00 (*962-593-435-9*, Periplus Eds) Tuttle Pubng.

— Chocolate. LC 98-65972. (Le Cordon Bleu Home Collection Ser.: Vol. 8). 64p. 1998. 12.00 (*962-593-431-6*, Periplus Eds) Tuttle Pubng.

— Cordon Bleu Complete Cooking Techniques, Le. LC 97-7952. 352p. 1997. 40.00 (*0-688-15206-6*, Wm Morrow) Morrow Avon.

— Desserts. LC 98-65442. (Cordon Bleu Home Collection: Vol. 4). 64p. 1998. 12.00 (*962-593-432-4*, Periplus Eds) Tuttle Pubng.

— Potatoes. LC 98-65969. (Cordon Bleu Home Collection: Vol. 5). 64p. 1998. 12.00 (*962-593-428-6*, Periplus Eds) Tuttle Pubng.

— Regional French. LC 98-65970. (Cordon Bleu Home Collection: Vol. 6). (Illus.). 64p. 1998. 12.00 (*962-593-429-4*, Periplus Eds) Tuttle Pubng.

— Sauces. LC 98-65971. (Cordon Bleu Home Collection: Vol. 7). 64p. 1998. 12.00 (*962-593-430-8*, Periplus Eds) Tuttle Pubng.

— Soups. LC 98-65440. (Cordon Bleu Home Collection: Vol. 1). 64p. 1998. 12.00 (*962-593-434-0*, Periplus Eds) Tuttle Pubng.

— Tarts & Pastries, Vol. 9. LC 98-65973. (Cordon Bleu Home Collection). 64p. 1998. 12.00 (*962-593-436-7*) Periplus.

— Vegetables. LC 98-65441. (Cordon Bleu Home Collection: Vol. 2). 64p. 1998. 12.00 (*962-593-433-2*, Periplus Eds) Tuttle Pubng.

— Winter. LC 98-65974. (Cordon Bleu Home Collection: Vol. 10). 64p. 1998. 12.00 (*962-593-437-5*, Periplus Eds) Tuttle Pubng.

Le Count, Cynthia G. Andean Folk Knitting. 2nd ed. LC 87-72565. 1990. pap. 29.95 (*0-685-66216-0*) Dos Tejedoras.

Le Coze, Maguy & Ripert, Eric. Le Bernardin Cookbook: Four Star Simplicity. LC 98-14704. (Illus.). 384p. 1998. 35.00 (*0-385-48841-6*) Doubleday.

Le Crom, Reverend. Mother of a Family: The Life of Mme Gabrielle Lefebvre, 1880-1938.Tr. of Une Mere de Famille. 35p. 1994. pap. 3.25 (*0-935952-55-1*) Angelus Pr.

Le Dantec, ed. see Baudelaire, Charles.

Le Dantec, ed. see Verlaine, Paul.

Le Dantec, Denise & Le Dantec, Jean-Pierre. Reading the French Gardens: Story & History. Levine, Jessica, tr. (Illus.). 288p. (C). 1993. pap. text 16.95 (*0-262-62087-1*) MIT Pr.

Le Dantec, Jean-Pierre, jt. auth. see Le Dantec, Denise.

Le Dimet, F. X. & Navon, I. M. Variational Methods in Atmospheric Sciences. 450p. 1994. text 68.00 (*981-02-0890-1*) World Scientific Pub.

Le Dimet, Francois-Xavier. High Performance Computing in the Geosciences: Proceedings of the Workshop Held at the Centre de Physique, Les Houches, France, 21-25 June 1993. LC 95-12569. (NATO ASI Ser.: Series C, Mathematical & Physical Sciences: No. 462). 1995. text 140.00 (*0-7923-3488-4*) Kluwer Academic.

Le Docte, Edgard. Diccionario de Terminos Juridicos en Cuatro Idiomas. (SPA.). 760p. 1987. 295.00 (*0-7859-6220-4*, 8473984692) Fr & Eur.

— Legal Dictionary in Four Languages French-Dutch-English-German. 800p. 1988. 150.00 (*90-6215-163-9*, Pub. by Maklu Uitgev) Gaunt.

— Legal Dictionary in Four Languages. 3rd ed. (DUT, ENG, FRE & GER.). 758p. 1982. 195.00 (*0-8288-1532-1*, M6349) Fr & Eur.

— Legal Dictionary in Four Languages. 4th ed. (DUT, ENG, FRE & GER.). 822p. 1987. 295.00 (*0-8288-0412-5*, M15088) Fr & Eur.

— Quadralingual Legal Dictionary. (ENG, FRE, GER & SPA.). 822p. 1992. 295.00 (*0-8288-9433-7*) Fr & Eur.

Le Doeuff, Michele. The Philosophical Imaginary. Gordon, Colin, tr. LC 88-63325. 222p. 1990. 35.00 (*0-8047-1619-6*) Stanford U Pr.

Le Doeuff, R. & Robert, J. Modelling & Control of Electrical Machines: New Trends. (Illus.). x,312p. 1991. 140.00 (*0-444-88732-6*) Elsevier.

Le Doran, Serge. Dictionnaire San-Antonio. (FRE.). 638p. 1993. text 65.00 (*0-7859-7871-2*, 2265049646) Fr & Eur.

Le Douarin, Nicole & McLaren, Anne, eds. Chimaeras in Development Biology. 1984. text 104.00 (*0-12-440580-0*) Acad Pr.

***Le Douarin, Nicole M. & Kalcheim, Chaya.** The Neural Crest. 2nd ed. LC 98-53256. (Developmental & Cell Biology Ser.: No. 36). (Illus.). 480p. (C). 1999. 95.00 (*0-521-62010-4*) Cambridge U Pr.

Le Doux, Joan. Come Sing, Jimmy Jo: A Study Guide. (Novel-Ties Ser.). (J). (gr. 6-8). 1988. pap. text, teacher ed., student ed. 15.95 (*0-88122-109-0*) Lrn Links.

Le Drean, Laura T., jt. auth. see Fellag, Linda Robinson.

An Asterisk (*) at the beginning of an entry indicates that the title is appearing for the first time.

Le, Duan. The Vietnamese Revolution: Fundamental Problems & Essential Tasks. LC 71-171528. 159p. reprint ed. pap. 49.30 (*0-608-13356-6*, 202554900044) Bks Demand.

Le Duc, Don R., jt. auth. see Teeter, Dwight L., Jr.

Le Duc, Thomas. Piety & Intellect at Amherst College, 1865-1912. LC 77-89196. (American Education: Its Men, Institutions, & Ideas. Series 1). 1977. reprint ed. 17.95 (*0-405-01434-1*) Ayer.

***Le Duc, Tony, photos by.** The Blue Elephant Cookbook: Royal Thai Cuisine. (Illus.). 160p. 2000. 35.00 (*1-86205-144-5*, Pub. by Pavilion Bks Ltd) Trafalgar.

Le-Falle-Collins, Lizzetta. Betye Saar: Personal Icons. Gladsky, Kristen, ed. 28p. (Orig.). (C). 1995. 10.00 (*1-882603-01-X*) Mid Am Arts.

Le Fanu, James. The Rise & Fall of Modern Medicine. (Illus.). 512p. 2000. 26.00 (*0-7867-0732-1*, Pub. by Carroll & Graf) Publishers Group.

Le Fanu, Joseph Sheridan. All in the Dark, 2 vols. LC 76-4046. (Collected Works). 1977. reprint ed. 53.95 (*0-405-09191-5*) Ayer.

— All in the Dark, 2 vols., Vol. 1. Varma, Devendra P., ed. LC 76-4046. (Collected Works). 1977. reprint ed. 26.95 (*0-405-09192-3*) Ayer.

— All in the Dark, 2 vols., Vol. 2. Varma, Devendra P., ed. LC 76-4046. (Collected Works). 1977. reprint ed. 26.95 (*0-405-09193-1*) Ayer.

— Best Ghost Stories. Bleiler, Everett F., ed. (Illus.). 467p. 1964. pap. 9.95 (*0-486-20415-4*) Dover.

— Checkmate. LC 97-175676. (Pocket Classics Ser.). 288p. 1997. pap. 12.95 (*0-7509-1469-6*, Pub. by Sutton Pub Ltd) Intl Pubs Mktg.

— Checkmate, 3 vols., Set. LC 76-4184. (Collected Works). 1977. reprint ed. 90.95 (*0-405-09194-X*) Ayer.

— Checkmate, 3 vols., Vol. 1. Varma, Devendra P., ed. LC 76-4184. (Collected Works). 1977. reprint ed. 30.95 (*0-405-09195-8*) Ayer.

— Checkmate, 3 vols., Vol. 2. Varma, Devendra P., ed. LC 76-4184. (Collected Works). 1977. reprint ed. 30.95 (*0-405-09196-6*) Ayer.

— Checkmate, 3 vols., Vol. 3. Varma, Devendra P., ed. LC 76-4184. (Collected Works). 1977. reprint ed. 30.95 (*0-405-09197-4*) Ayer.

— Chronicles of Golden Friars, 3 vols., Set. LC 76-4178. (Collected Works). 1977. reprint ed. 87.95 (*0-405-09198-2*) Ayer.

— Chronicles of Golden Friars, 3 vols., Vol. 1. Varma, Devendra P., ed. LC 76-4178. (Collected Works). 1977. reprint ed. 29.95 (*0-405-09199-0*) Ayer.

— Chronicles of Golden Friars, 3 vols., Vol. 2. Varma, Devendra P., ed. LC 76-4178. (Collected Works). 1977. reprint ed. 29.95 (*0-405-09200-8*) Ayer.

— Chronicles of Golden Friars, 3 vols., Vol. 3. Varma, Devendra P., ed. LC 76-4178. (Collected Works). 1977. reprint ed. 29.95 (*0-405-09201-6*) Ayer.

— The Cock & Anchor: Being a Chronicle of Old Dublin City, 3 vols., Set. LC 76-4606. (Collected Works). 1977. reprint ed. 90.95 (*0-405-09202-4*) Ayer.

— The Cock & Anchor: Being a Chronicle of Old Dublin City, 3 vols., Vol. 1. Varma, Devendra P., ed. LC 76-4606. (Collected Works). 1977. reprint ed. 30.95 (*0-405-09203-2*) Ayer.

— The Cock & Anchor: Being a Chronicle of Old Dublin City, 3 vols., Vol. 2. Varma, Devendra P., ed. LC 76-4606. (Collected Works). 1977. reprint ed. 30.95 (*0-405-09204-0*) Ayer.

— The Cock & Anchor: Being a Chronicle of Old Dublin City, 3 Vols., Vol. 3. Varma, Devendra P., ed. LC 76-4606. (Collected Works). 1977. reprint ed. 30.95 (*0-405-09205-9*) Ayer.

— The Collected Works of Joseph Sheridan Le Fanu. Varma, Devendra P., ed. (Illus.). 1977. 1327.50 (*0-405-09190-7*) Ayer.

— The Evil Guest. LC 76-4605. (Collected Works). (Illus.). 1977. reprint ed. lib. bdg. 25.95 (*0-405-09206-7*) Ayer.

— The Fortunes of Colonial Torlogh O'Brien: A Tale of the Wars of King James. LC 76-4603. (Collected Works). (Illus.). 1977. reprint ed. 39.95 (*0-405-09207-5*) Ayer.

— Ghost Stories & Mysteries. Bleiler, Everett F., ed. LC 74-75845. 372p. 1975. pap. 8.95 (*0-486-20715-3*) Dover.

— Ghost Stories & Tales of Mystery. LC 76-6013. (Collected Works). (Illus.). 1977. reprint ed. 27.95 (*0-405-09254-7*) Ayer.

— Green Tea & Other Ghost Stories, Vol. 100. LC 93-11037. (Thrift Editions Ser.). 96p. 1998. pap. 1.00 (*0-486-27795-X*) Dover.

— Guy Deverell, 3 vols., Set. Varma, Devendra P., ed. LC 76-6015. (Collected Works). 1977. reprint ed. 78.95 (*0-405-09255-5*) Ayer.

— Guy Deverell, 3 vols., Vol. 1. Varma, Devendra P., ed. LC 76-6015. (Collected Works). 1977. reprint ed. 25.95 (*0-405-09256-3*) Ayer.

— Guy Deverell, 3 vols., Vol. 2. Varma, Devendra P., ed. LC 76-6015. (Collected Works). 1977. reprint ed. 26.95 (*0-405-09257-1*) Ayer.

— Guy Deverell, 3 vols., Vol. 3. Varma, Devendra P., ed. LC 76-6015. (Collected Works). 1977. reprint ed. 26.95 (*0-405-09258-X*) Ayer.

— Haunted Lives. 525p. 1998. reprint ed. lib. bdg. 24.00 (*1-58287-002-0*) North Bks.

— Haunted Lives: A Novel, 3 vols., Set. Varma, Devendra P., ed. LC 76-5268. (Collected Works). 1977. reprint ed. 80.95 (*0-405-09208-3*) Ayer.

— Haunted Lives: A Novel, 3 vols., Vol. 1. Varma, Devendra P., ed. LC 76-5268. (Collected Works). 1977. reprint ed. 26.95 (*0-405-09209-1*) Ayer.

— Haunted Lives: A Novel, 3 Vols., Vol. 2. Varma, Devendra P., ed. LC 76-5268. (Collected Works). 1977. reprint ed. 26.95 (*0-405-09210-5*) Ayer.

— Haunted Lives: A Novel, 3 vols., Vol. 3. Varma, Devendra P., ed. LC 76-5268. (Collected Works). 1977. reprint ed. 26.95 (*0-405-09211-3*) Ayer.

— The House by the Church-Yard. 500p. 1992. reprint ed. lib. bdg. 43.95 (*0-89968-312-6*, Lghtyr Pr) Buccaneer Bks.

— The House by the Church-Yard, 3 vols., Set. LC 76-5270. (Collected Works). 1977. reprint ed. 87.95 (*0-405-09212-1*) Ayer.

— The House by the Church-Yard, 3 vols., Vol. 1. Varma, Devendra P., ed. LC 76-5270. (Collected Works). 1977. reprint ed. 29.95 (*0-405-09213-X*) Ayer.

— The House by the Church-Yard, 3 vols., Vol. 2. Varma, Devendra P., ed. LC 76-5270. (Collected Works). 1977. reprint ed. 29.95 (*0-405-09214-8*) Ayer.

— The House by the Church-Yard, 3 vols., Vol. 3. Varma, Devendra P., ed. LC 76-5270. (Collected Works). 1977. reprint ed. 29.95 (*0-405-09215-6*) Ayer.

— The House by the Church-Yard: A Novel, 3 vols. in 1. LC 74-148811. reprint ed. 57.50 (*0-404-08877-5*) AMS Pr.

***Le Fanu, Joseph Sheridan.** In a Glass Darkly. Tracy, Robert, ed. (Oxford World's Classics Ser.). 382p. 1999. pap. 11.95 (*0-19-283947-0*) OUP.

Le Fanu, Joseph Sheridan. In a Glass Darkly. (Classics Library). 320p. 1998. pap. 3.95 (*1-85326-265-X*, 265XWW, Pub. by Wrdsworth Edits) NTC Contemp Pub Co.

— In a Glass Darkly, 3 vols., Set. LC 76-5271. (Collected Works). 1977. reprint ed. 80.95 (*0-405-09216-4*) Ayer.

— In a Glass Darkly, 3 vols., Vol. 1. Varma, Devendra P., ed. LC 76-5271. (Collected Works). 1977. reprint ed. 26.95 (*0-405-09217-2*) Ayer.

— In a Glass Darkly, 3 vols., Vol. 2. Varma, Devendra P., ed. LC 76-5271. (Collected Works). 1977. reprint ed. 26.95 (*0-405-09218-0*) Ayer.

— In a Glass Darkly, 3 vols., Vol. 3. Varma, Devendra P., ed. LC 76-5271. (Collected Works). 1977. reprint ed. 26.95 (*0-405-09219-9*) Ayer.

— A Lost Name, 3 vols., 1. Varma, Devendra P., ed. LC 76-5272. (Collected Works). (Illus.). 1977. reprint ed. 29.95 (*0-405-09221-0*) Ayer.

— A Lost Name, 3 vols., Set. LC 76-5272. (Collected Works). (Illus.). 1977. reprint ed. 87.95 (*0-405-09220-2*) Ayer.

— A Lost Name, 3 vols., Vol. 2. Varma, Devendra P., ed. LC 76-5272. (Collected Works). (Illus.). 1977. reprint ed. 29.95 (*0-405-09222-9*) Ayer.

— A Lost Name, 3 vols., Vol. 3. Varma, Devendra P., ed. LC 76-5272. (Collected Works). (Illus.). 1977. reprint ed. 29.95 (*0-405-09223-7*) Ayer.

— Madame Crowl's Ghost & Other Tales of Mystery. James, Montague R., ed. LC 72-167459. (Short Story Index Reprint Ser.). 1977. reprint ed. 18.95 (*0-8369-3985-9*) Ayer.

— The Poems of Joseph Sheridan Le Fanu. Graves, Alfred P., ed. LC 78-148812. reprint ed. 32.50 (*0-404-08878-3*) AMS Pr.

— The Poems of Joseph Sheridan Le Fanu. Graves, Alfred P., ed. LC 76-5273. (Collected Works). 1977. reprint ed. 23.95 (*0-405-09224-5*) Ayer.

— The Purcell Papers. LC 75-2524. 1975. 12.95 (*0-87054-072-6*) Arkham.

— The Purcell Papers, 3 vols. LC 71-148813. reprint ed. 145.00 (*0-404-08880-5*) AMS Pr.

— The Purcell Papers: With a Memoir by Alfred Perceval Graves, 3 vols., Set. LC 76-5274. (Collected Works). 1977. reprint ed. 76.95 (*0-405-09225-3*) Ayer.

— The Purcell Papers: With a Memoir by Alfred Perceval Graves, 3 vols., Vol. 1. Varma, Devendra P., ed. LC 76-5274. (Collected Works). 1977. reprint ed. 25.95 (*0-405-09226-1*) Ayer.

— The Purcell Papers: With a Memoir by Alfred Perceval Graves, 3 vols., Vol. 2. Varma, Devendra P., ed. LC 76-5274. (Collected Works). 1977. reprint ed. 25.95 (*0-405-09227-X*) Ayer.

— The Purcell Papers: With a Memoir by Alfred Perceval Graves, 3 vols., Vol. 3. Varma, Devendra P., ed. LC 76-5274. (Collected Works). 1977. reprint ed. 25.95 (*0-405-09228-8*) Ayer.

— The Rose & the Key, 3 vols., 1. Varma, Devendra P., ed. LC 76-5275. (Collected Works). 1977. reprint ed. 29.95 (*0-405-09230-X*) Ayer.

— The Rose & the Key, 3 vols., Set. LC 76-5275. (Collected Works). 1977. reprint ed. 87.95 (*0-405-09229-6*) Ayer.

— The Rose & the Key, 3 vols., Vol. 2. Varma, Devendra P., ed. LC 76-5275. (Collected Works). 1977. reprint ed. 29.95 (*0-405-09231-8*) Ayer.

— The Rose & the Key, 3 vols., Vol. 3. Varma, Devendra P., ed. LC 76-5275. (Collected Works). 1977. reprint ed. 29.95 (*0-405-09232-6*) Ayer.

— A Stable for Nightmares or Weird Tales: Anthology. LC 75-46286. (Supernatural & Occult Fiction Ser.). (Illus.). 256 p. 1976. reprint ed. lib. bdg. 23.95 (*0-405-08147-2*) Ayer.

— The Tenants of Malory: A Novel, 3 vols., 1. Varma, Devendra P., ed. LC 76-5276. (Collected Works). 1977. reprint ed. 25.95 (*0-405-09234-2*) Ayer.

— The Tenants of Malory: A Novel, 3 vols., Set. LC 76-5276. (Collected Works). 1977. reprint ed. 76.95 (*0-405-09233-4*) Ayer.

— The Tenants of Malory: A Novel, 3 vols., Vol. 2. Varma, Devendra P., ed. LC 76-5276. (Collected Works). 1977. reprint ed. 25.95 (*0-405-09235-0*) Ayer.

— The Tenants of Malory: A Novel, 3 vols., Vol. 3. Varma, Devendra P., ed. LC 76-5276. (Collected Works). 1977. reprint ed. 25.95 (*0-405-09236-9*) Ayer.

— Uncle Silas. McCormack, W. J., ed. & intro. by. (Oxford World's Classics Ser.). 432p. 2000. pap. 10.95 (*0-19-283564-5*) OUP.

— Uncle Silas. large type ed. (Large Print Ser.). 655p. 1992. reprint ed. lib. bdg. 25.00 (*0-939495-37-6*) North Bks.

— Uncle Silas. 436p. 1966. reprint ed. pap. 8.95 (*0-486-21715-9*) Dover.

— Uncle Silas. 515p. 1998. reprint ed. lib. bdg. 24.00 (*1-58287-001-2*) North Bks.

— Uncle Silas: A Tale of Bartram-Haugh, 3 vols. LC 76-5278. (Collected Works). 1977. reprint ed. 90.95 (*0-405-09237-7*) Ayer.

— Uncle Silas: A Tale of Bartram-Haugh. 400p. 1992. reprint ed. lib. bdg. 34.95 (*0-89968-311-8*, Lghtyr Pr) Buccaneer Bks.

— Uncle Silas: A Tale of Bartram-Haugh, 3 vols., 1. Varma, Devendra P., ed. LC 76-5278. (Collected Works). 1977. reprint ed. 30.95 (*0-405-09238-5*) Ayer.

— Uncle Silas: A Tale of Bartram-Haugh, 3 vols., Vol. 2. Varma, Devendra P., ed. LC 76-5278. (Collected Works). 1977. reprint ed. 30.95 (*0-405-09239-3*) Ayer.

— Uncle Silas: A Tale of Bartram-Haugh, 3 vols., Vol. 3. Varma, Devendra P., ed. LC 76-5278. (Collected Works). 1977. reprint ed. 30.95 (*0-405-09240-7*) Ayer.

— The Watcher & other weird stories. LC 74-189003. 157 p. (J). 1974. write for info. (*0-450-01880-6*) New Eng Lib.

— The Watcher & Other Weird Stories. LC 76-5279. (Collected Works). (Illus.). 1977. reprint ed. 26.95 (*0-405-09241-5*) Ayer.

— Willing to Die, 3 vols., Set. LC 76-5280. (Collected Works). 1977. reprint ed. 87.95 (*0-405-09242-3*) Ayer.

— Willing to Die, 3 vols., Vol. 1. Varma, Devendra P., ed. LC 76-5280. (Collected Works). 1977. reprint ed. 29.95 (*0-405-09243-1*) Ayer.

— Willing to Die, 3 vols., Vol. 2. Varma, Devendra P., ed. LC 76-5280. (Collected Works). 1977. reprint ed. 29.95 (*0-405-09244-X*) Ayer.

— Willing to Die, 3 vols., Vol. 3. Varma, Devendra P., ed. LC 76-5280. (Collected Works). 1977. reprint ed. 29.95 (*0-405-09245-8*) Ayer.

— Wylder's Hand: A Novel, 3 vols., Set. Varma, Devendra P., ed. LC 76-5281. (Collected Works). 1977. reprint ed. 87.95 (*0-405-09246-6*) Ayer.

— Wylder's Hand: A Novel, 3 vols., Vol. 1. Varma, Devendra P., ed. LC 76-5281. (Collected Works). 1977. reprint ed. 29.95 (*0-405-09247-4*) Ayer.

— Wylder's Hand: A Novel, 3 vols., Vol. 2. Varma, Devendra P., ed. LC 76-5281. (Collected Works). 1977. reprint ed. 29.95 (*0-405-09248-2*) Ayer.

— Wylder's Hand: A Novel, 3 vols., Vol. 3. Varma, Devendra P., ed. LC 76-5281. (Collected Works). 1977. reprint ed. 29.95 (*0-405-09249-0*) Ayer.

***Le Fanu, Joseph Sheridan.** Wyvern Mysteries. 2000. reprint ed. pap. 10.95 (*0-7509-0687-1*, Pub. by Sutton Publng) Intl Pubs Mktg.

Le Fanu, Joseph Sheridan. The Wyvern Mystery: A Novel, 3 vols., Set. LC 76-5282. (Collected Works). 1977. reprint ed. 76.95 (*0-405-09250-4*) Ayer.

— The Wyvern Mystery: A Novel, 3 vols., Vol. 1. Varma, Devendra P., ed. LC 76-5282. (Collected Works). 1977. reprint ed. 25.95 (*0-405-09251-2*) Ayer.

— The Wyvern Mystery: A Novel, 3 vols., Vol. 2. Varma, Devendra P., ed. LC 76-5282. (Collected Works). 1977. reprint ed. 25.95 (*0-405-09252-0*) Ayer.

— The Wyvern Mystery: A Novel, 3 vols., Vol. 3. Varma, Devendra P., ed. LC 76-5282. (Collected Works). 1977. reprint ed. 25.95 (*0-405-09253-9*) Ayer.

Le Fanu, Joseph Sheridan, et al. Three Short Novels of Mystery & Suspense. large type ed. (Large Print Ser.). 542p. 1992. reprint ed. lib. bdg. 24.00 (*0-939495-41-4*) North Bks.

Le Fanu, Mark, ed. & intro. see James, Henry.

Le Fanu, William, jt. ed. see Sheridan, Betsy.

Le Faye, Deirdre. Jane Austen. LC 99-176677. (British Library Writers' Lives). (Illus.). 124p. (J). 1998. 22.95 (*0-19-521440-4*) OUP.

***Le Faye, Deirdre.** Jane Austen. (British Library Writers' Lives Ser.). (Illus.). 128p. 2000. pap. 15.95 (*0-19-521654-7*) OUP.

Le Faye, Deirdre. Jane Austen: A Family Record. (Reference Guides to Literature Ser.). 332p. 1989. 40.00 (*0-8161-9092-5*, Hall Reference) Macmillan.

Le Faye, Deirdre, ed. see Austen, Jane.

Le Febvre, G. La Revolucion Francesa y el Imperio. (Breviarios Ser.). (SPA.). pap. 8.99 (*968-16-0191-2*, Pub. by Fondo) Continental Bk.

Le Fevers, Stephen & Marshall, Loren. Prehospital Care for the EMT-Intermediate: Assessment & Intervention. 288p. 1983. pap. 18.95 (*0-317-58949-0*) P-H.

Le Fleming, S. & Kay, S. Colloquial Russian: The Complete Course for Beginners. 2nd ed. 288p. 1997. pap. 29.95 incl. audio (*0-415-16142-8*) Routledge.

***Le Fleming, Stephen & Harrison, William.** Intermediate Russian Grammar. 352p. 2000. 70.00 (*0-7083-1577-1*, Pub. by U Wales Pr) Paul & Co Pubs.

Le Fleming, Svetlana & Kay, Susan E. Colloquial Russian: Complete Course for Beginners. 2nd ed. (Colloquials Ser.). 320p. 1997. pap. 19.99 (*0-415-16140-1*) Routledge.

Le Fort, Gertrud F. Von, see Von Le Fort, Gertrud F.

Le Freuvre, Amy. Probable Sons. LC 96-46432. (Golden Inheritance Ser.). (J). 1996. pap. 5.90 (*0-921100-81-7*) Inhtce Pubns.

Le Gac, Y., ed. Les Inscriptions d'Assur-Nasir-Aplu III, roi d'Assyrie. LC 78-72728. (Ancient Mesopotamian Texts & Studies). reprint ed. 37.50 (*0-404-18164-3*) AMS Pr.

Le Gai Eaton, Charles. Islam & the Destiny of Man. 242p. 1996. pap. 19.95 (*0-614-21421-1*, 556) Kazi Pubns.

— Islam & the Destiny of Man. LC 85-14877. (SUNY Series in Islam). 242p. (C). 1985. pap. text 21.95 (*0-88706-163-X*) State U NY Pr.

— The Richest Vein: The Eastern Tradition & Modern Thought. 1996. pap. 18.95 (*0-614-21334-7*, 1079) Kazi Pubns.

Le Gal, M. Recherches sur les Ornementations Sporales des Discomycetes Opercules. 1970. reprint ed. 40.00 (*3-7682-0694-7*) Lubrecht & Cramer.

Le Gales, Patrick, jt. ed. see Bagnasco, Arnaldo.

Le Gall, Guillaume. Atget, Life in Paris. 1998. pap. 12.95 (*2-85025-641-2*) Hazan.

***Le Gall, J. F.** Spatial Branching Processes, Random Snakes & Partial Differential Equations LC 99-37606. (Lectures in Mathematics Eth Zhurich). 1999. write for info. (*0-8176-6126-3*) Birkhauser.

— Spatial Branching Processes, Random Snakes & Partial Differential Equations. LC 99-37606. (Lectures in Mathematics ETH Zurich). 176p. 1999. pap. text 29.95 (*3-7643-6126-3*, Pub. by Birkhauser) Spr-Verlag.

Le Gall, J. F., jt. auth. see Freidlin, M. I.

Le Gall, Michel & Perkins, Kenneth J., eds. The Maghrib in Question: Essays in History & Historiography. LC 96-44825. (Illus.). 304p. 1997. 40.00 (*0-292-76576-2*) U of Tex Pr.

Le Gall, Robert. Dictionnaire de Liturgie. (FRE.). 279p. 1987. pap. 38.95 (*0-7859-8089-X*, 2854431359) Fr & Eur.

Le Gallienne, Eva. The Mystic in the Theatre: Eleonora Duse. LC 72-11975. (Arcturus Books Paperbacks). 189p. 1973. pap. 14.95 (*0-8093-0631-X*) S Ill U Pr.

Le Gallienne, Eva, tr. see Andersen, Hans Christian.

Le Gallienne, Eva, tr. see Ibsen, Henrik.

Le Gallienne, Eve, tr. see Ibsen, Henrik.

Le Gallienne, Richard. Attitudes & Avowals with Some Retrospective Reviews. LC 71-99640. (Essay Index Reprint Ser.). 1977. 28.95 (*0-8369-1418-X*) Ayer.

— Little Dinners with the Sphinx, & Other Prose Fancies. LC 72-11932. (Short Story Index Reprint Ser.). 1977. reprint ed. 26.95 (*0-8369-4239-6*) Ayer.

— Maker of Rainbows, & Other Fairy-Tales & Fables. LC 77-167460. (Short Story Index Reprint Ser.). (Illus.). 1977. reprint ed. 18.95 (*0-8369-3986-7*) Ayer.

— Painted Shadows. LC 77-94738. (Short Story Index Reprint Ser.). 1977. 21.95 (*0-8369-3118-1*) Ayer.

— Romances of Old France. LC 75-81271. (Short Story Index Reprint Ser.). 1977. 20.95 (*0-8369-3023-1*) Ayer.

Le Gallienne, Richard, ed. see Hallam, Arthur H.

Le Garff, B. Dictionnaire Etymologique de Zoologie. (FRE.). 1998. 69.95 (*0-320-00294-2*) Fr & Eur.

Le Garsmeur, Alain, photos by. James Joyce: Reflections of Ireland. LC 93-21770. (Illus.). 160p. 1993. 35.00 (*0-02-559895-3*) Macmillan.

Le Gassick, Trevor, tr. see Barakat, Halim.

Le Gassick, Trevor, tr. see Kathir, Ibn.

Le Gear, Clara E. United States Atlases: A List of National, State, County, City & Regional Atlases in the Library of Congress, 2 vols. 766p. 1997. reprint ed. 85.00 (*1-57898-016-X*) Martino Pubng.

Le Gear, Clara E., ed. United States Atlases. LC 71-154058. (Library of Congress Publications in Reprint). 1971. reprint ed. 23.95 (*0-405-03424-5*) Ayer.

Le Gear, Clara Egli, compiled by. A List of Geographical Atlases in the Library of Congress, 5 vols. 2535p. 1996. reprint ed. 350.00 (*1-888262-94-X*) Martino Pubng.

Le Glay, Marcel, et al. A History of Rome. Nevill, Antonia, tr. (Illus.). 484p. 1996. pap. 36.95 (*0-631-19458-4*) Blackwell Pubs.

— A History of Rome. Nevill, Antonia, tr. (Illus.). 484p. (C). 1996. 66.95 (*0-631-19457-6*) Blackwell Pubs.

Le Gleau, Rene. Dictionnaire Classique Francais-Breton, Vol. 6. (BRE & FRE.). 384p. 1987. pap. 55.00 (*0-7859-8001-6*, 2736800184) Fr & Eur.

— Dictionnaire Classique Francais-Breton, Vol. 6. (BRE & FRE.). 384p. 1988. pap. 45.00 (*0-7859-8002-4*, 2736800206) Fr & Eur.

— Dictionnaire Classique Francais-Breton, Vol. 6. (BRE & FRE.). 348p. 1989. pap. 45.00 (*0-7859-8003-2*, 2736800265) Fr & Eur.

— Dictionnaire Classique Francais-Breton Vol. 2: C-Debla. (BRE & FRE.). 352p. 1984. pap. 45.00 (*0-7859-7999-9*, 2736800087) Fr & Eur.

— Dictionnaire Classique Francais-Breton Vol. 3: Deblo-Embeg. (BRE & FRE.). 352p. 1986. pap. 45.00 (*0-7859-8000-8*, 2736800141) Fr & Eur.

Le Goff, Claude. French for Business: Le Francais des Affaires. 160p. 1989. pap. 32.95 (*2-218-02469-1*) Schoenhof.

— Le Nouveau French for Business: Le Francais des Affaires. (FRE.). 191p. 1994. teacher ed. 37.95 (*2-278-04408-7*, U0975) Hatier Pub.

— Le Nouveau French for Business: Teacher's Guide, Answer Key. (FRE.). 47p. 1995. pap., teacher ed. 14.95 (*2-278-04410-9*, Pub. by Edns Didier) Hatier Pub.

Le Goff, Denise-Claude. Peter Neagoe: L'Homme et l'Oeuvre. (American University Studies: General Literature: Ser. XIX, Vol. 16). 423p. (C). 1988. text 51.50 (*0-8204-0658-9*) P Lang Pubng.

Le Goff, Jacques. The Birth of Purgatory. Goldhammer, Arthur, tr. from FRE. LC 83-1108. (Illus.). 448p. 1984. 25.00 (*0-226-47082-2*) U Ch Pr.

— The Birth of Purgatory. Goldhammer, Arthur, tr. from FRE. LC 83-1108. (Illus.). 440p. 1986. pap. text 22.00 (*0-226-47083-0*) U Ch Pr.

— History & Memory. Rendall, Stephen & Claman, Elizabeth, trs. from FRE. (European Perspectives Ser.). 320p. (C). 1992. text 38.50 (*0-231-07590-1*) Col U Pr.

— History & Memory. Randall, Steven & Claman, Elizabeth, trs. 288p. 1996. pap. 18.50 (*0-231-07591-X*) Col U Pr.

— Intellectuals in the Middle Ages. Fagan, Teresa L., tr. (Illus.). 256p. 1992. pap. 22.95 (*0-631-18519-4*) Blackwell Pubs.

— Medieval Callings. Cochrane, Lydia G., tr. from FRE. xiii, 400p. 1995. pap. text 18.00 (*0-226-47087-3*) U Ch Pr.

— Medieval Civilization, 400-1500. Barrow, Julia, tr. 1991. pap. 31.95 (*0-631-17566-0*) Blackwell Pubs.

L

— The Medieval Imagination. Goldhammer, Arthur, tr. LC 88-4787. 302p. 1992. pap. text 14.95 (*0-226-47085-7*) U Ch Pr.
— The Medieval Imagination. Goldhammer, Arthur, tr. 302p. 1998. 35.95 (*0-226-47084-9*) U Ch Pr.
— Time, Work, & Culture in the Middle Ages. Goldhammer, Arthur, tr. LC 79-25400. xvi, 400p. (C). 1982. pap. 22.50 (*0-226-47081-4*) U Ch Pr.
— Your Money or Your Life: Economy & Religion in the Middle Ages. Ranum, Patricia M., tr. from FRE. LC 87-25248. 116p. 1988. 24.95 (*0-942299-14-0*); pap. 10.95 (*0-942299-15-9*) Zone Bks.
Le Goff, Jacques, ed. Medieval Callings. Cochrane, Lydia G., tr. x, 400p. 1990. 47.50 (*0-226-47086-5*) U Ch Pr.
— The Medieval World: The History of European Society. Cochrane, Lydia G., tr. from ITA. 392p. (C). 1998. pap. text 15.00 (*0-7881-5535-0*) DIANE Pub.
Le Goff, Jacques, ed. see Brown, Peter.
Le Goff, Jacques, ed. see Eco, Umberto.
Le Goff, Jacques, ed. see Montanari, Massimo.
Le Goff, T. J. France, 1661-1789. 288p. 1999. pap. 19.95 (*0-7131-6527-8*, A9527, Pub. by E A); text 75.00 (*0-340-64532-6*, Pub. by E A) OUP.
Le Golvan, Yves. Dictionnaire Marketing. (FRE.). 1988. write for info. (*0-7859-7704-X*, 2040169962) Fr & Eur.
***Le Goueff, Stephan.** Satellite Regulation in Europe: Legal Texts & Materials. LC 99-86510. 704p. 2000. 200.00 (*90-411-1346-0*) Kluwer Law Intl.
***Le Goues, Thierry, photos by.** Popular. (Illus.). 2000. 75.00 (*1-57687-075-8*, pwerHse Bks) pwerHse Cultrl.
Le Goues, Thierry, photos by. Soul. LC 97-34501. (Illus.). 104p. 1999. pap. 49.95 (*1-57687-041-3*, pwerHse Bks) pwerHse Cultrl.
Le Grand, H. E., ed. Experimental Inquiries: Historical, Philosophical & Social Studies of Experimentation in Science. 296p. (C). 1990. lib. bdg. 144.00 (*0-7923-0790-9*, Pub. by Kluwer Academic) Kluwer Academic.
Le Grand, Julia, jt. auth. see Robinson, Ray.
Le Grand, Julian & Robinson, Ray, eds. Privatisation & the Welfare State. 256p. (C). 1984. pap. text 17.95 (*0-04-336080-7*) Routledge.
Le Grand, Julian, jt. ed. see Mossialos, Elias.
Le Grand, Scott M., jt. ed. see Merz, Kenneth M., Jr.
le Grange, Lesley & Reddy, Chris. Continuous Assessment: An Introduction & Guidelines to Implementation. LC 98-188174. 41p. 1998. write for info. (*0-7021-4383-9*) Juta & Co.
Le Gray, Gustave, jt. auth. see Croucher, J. H.
Le Gros, Clark F. & Dunne, Agnes C. Ageing in Industry: An Inquiry, Based on Figures Derived from Census Reports. LC 75-136890. (Illus.). 146p. 1971. reprint ed. lib. bdg. 55.00 (*0-8371-5332-8*, CLAI, Greenwood Pr) Greenwood.
Le, Grys Alan. Preaching to the Nations: Origins of Mission in the Early Church. 1999. pap. text 28.95 (*0-281-05148-8*) Society Prom Christ Know.
Le Guerer, Annick. Scent: The Mysterious & Essential Powers of Smell. Turner, Philip, ed. Miller, Richard, tr. LC 94-2370. 272p. 1994. pap. 13.00 (*1-56836-024-X*) Kodansha.
Le Guillou, J. C. & Zinn-Justin, J., eds. Large-Order Behaviour of Perturbation Theory. (Current Physics Sources & Comments Ser.: Vol. 7). 560p. 1990. 145.00 (*0-685-45103-8*, North Holland); pap. 75.50 (*0-444-88597-8*, North Holland) Elsevier.
Le Guillou, Philippe. Chateaubriand. (FRE., Illus.). 152p. 1997. pap. write for info. (*2-86808-111-8*) Intl Scholars.
Le Guilloux, Isabelle, jt. auth. see Beeching, Kate.
Le Guin, Charles A., ed. A Home-Concealed Woman: The Diaries of Magnolia Wynn Le Guin, 1901-1913. LC 90-34163. (Illus.). 416p. 1990. 30.00 (*0-8203-1236-3*) U of Ga Pr.
Le Guin, Ursula K. The Altered I: Ursula K. Le Guin's Science Fiction Writing Workshop. Harding, Lee, ed. 1978. pap. 7.50 (*0-425-03849-1*) Ultramarine Pub.
— Blue Moon over Thurman Street. (Illus.). 128p. 1993. pap. 16.95 (*0-939165-22-8*) NewSage Press.
— Buffalo Gals, Won't You Come Out Tonight. LC 94-18443. (Illus.). 80p. 1994. 19.95 (*0-87654-071-X*) Pomegranate Calif.
— Catwings. LC 87-33104. (Illus.). 48p. (J). (gr. 2-5). 1988. 14.95 (*0-531-05759-3*) Orchard Bks Watts.
— Catwings. LC 87-33104. (Illus.). 39p. (J). (gr. 1-4). 1999. pap. 3.95 (*0-531-07110-3*) Orchard Bks Watts.
— Catwings. (Illus.). 40p. (J). (gr. 1-4). 1990. pap. 3.50 (*0-590-42833-0*, Little Apple) Scholastic Inc.
— Catwings. (Illus.). 48p. (J). (gr. 1-4). 1992. pap. 2.95 (*0-590-46072-2*) Scholastic Inc.
— Catwings. (J). 1988. 8.19 (*0-606-00536-6*, Pub. by Turtleback) Demco.
— Catwings Return. LC 88-17902. (Illus.). 56p. (J). (gr. 1-4). 1989. pap. 3.95 (*0-531-07111-1*) Orchard Bks Watts.
— Catwings Return. LC 88-17902. (Illus.). 56p. (J). (gr. 2-5). 1989. 14.95 (*0-531-05803-4*) Orchard Bks Watts.
— Catwings Return. LC 88-17902. (J). 1991. 8.15 (*0-606-04888-X*, Pub. by Turtleback) Demco.
— Catwing's Return. 64p. (J). (ps-3). 1991. pap. 3.50 (*0-590-42832-2*) Scholastic Inc.
— Compass Rose Reissue. 1995. mass mkt. 4.99 (*0-06-105607-3*, Harp PBks) HarpC.
— Dancing at the Edge of the World: Thoughts on Words, Women, Places. LC 88-11266. 320p. 1997. reprint ed. pap. 12.00 (*0-8021-3529-3*, Grove) Grove-Atltic.
— The Dispossessed: An Ambiguous Utopia. 400p. 1994. mass mkt. 5.99 (*0-06-105488-7*, Harp PBks) HarpC.
— The Dispossessed: An Ambiguous Utopia. 1976. pap. 3.95 (*0-380-00382-1*, Avon Bks) Morrow Avon.
***Le Guin, Ursula K.** The Eye of the Heron. large type ed. LC 99-48477. 2000. 25.95 (*0-7838-8843-0*, G K Hall Lrg Type) Mac Lib Ref.
Le Guin, Ursula K. The Farthest Shore. (Earthsea Trilogy Ser.). 1975. 11.60 (*0-606-00601-X*, Pub. by Turtleback) Demco.
— The Farthest Shore. rev. ed. LC 72-75273. (Illus.). 240p. (YA). (gr. 6 up). 1990. 17.00 (*0-689-31683-6*) Atheneum Yung Read.
— The Farthest Shore, No. 3. 208p. (YA). (gr. 6 up). 1984. mass mkt. 6.99 (*0-553-26847-3*) Bantam.
— A Fisherman of the Inland Sea. 224p. 1995. mass mkt. 4.99 (*0-06-105491-7*, HarperPrism) HarpC.
— Four Ways to Forgiveness. 320p. 1996. mass mkt. 5.99 (*0-06-105401-1*, HarperPrism) HarpC.
— Gwilan's Harp. deluxe limited ed. 1981. 35.00 (*0-935716-11-4*) Lord John.
— In the Red Zone. deluxe limited ed. (Illus.). 50p. 1983. 75.00 (*0-935716-21-1*) Lord John.
— Jane on Her Own: A Catwings Tale. LC 98-30100. (Illus.). 48p. (J). (gr. 1-4). 1999. 14.95 (*0-531-30133-8*); lib. bdg. 15.99 (*0-531-33133-4*) Orchard Bks Watts.
— The Language of the Night: Essays on Fantasy & Science Fiction. Wood, Susan, ed. LC 78-24350. 270p. 1979. 25.00 (*0-399-12325-3*) Ultramarine Pub.
— Lao Tzu: Tao Te Ching, a Book about the Way & the Power of the Way. 1998. pap. 12.00 (*1-57062-395-3*, Pub. by Shambhala Pubns) Random.
— The Lathe of Heaven. 176p. 1976. mass mkt. 5.50 (*0-380-01320-7*, Avon Bks) Morrow Avon.
— Lathe of Heaven. 176p. 1997. pap. 12.50 (*0-380-79185-4*, Avon Bks) Morrow Avon.
— The Lathe of Heaven. LC 81-18093. 192p. 1982. reprint ed. 14.00 (*0-8376-0464-8*) Bentley Pubs.
— The Left Hand of Darkness. 304p. 1982. mass mkt. 6.99 (*0-441-47812-3*) Ace Bks.
***Le Guin, Ursula K.** The Left Hand of Darkness. 320p. 2000. pap. 12.95 (*0-441-00731-7*) Ace Bks.
Le Guin, Ursula K. The Left Hand of Darkness. 25th anniversary ed. LC 94-27147. 325p. 1994. 27.50 (*0-8027-1302-5*) Walker & Co.
— Love Stories. write for info. (*0-06-105201-9*, HarperPrism) HarpC.
— Orsinian Tales. 6.99 (*0-06-105606-5*) HarpC.
— Orsinian Tales. 224p. 1991. mass mkt. 4.50 (*0-06-100182-1*, Harp PBks) HarpC.
— A Ride on the Red Mare's Back. LC 91-21677. (Illus.). 48p. (J). (gr. 1-4). 1992. 16.95 (*0-531-05991-X*); lib. bdg. 17.99 (*0-531-08591-0*) Orchard Bks Watts.
— A Ride on the Red Mare's Back. LC 91-21677. (Illus.). 48p. (J). (gr. 1-4). 1996. pap. 6.95 (*0-531-07079-4*) Orchard Bks Watts.
— A Ride on the Red Mare's Back. LC 91-21677. 1996. 12.15 (*0-606-10910-2*, Pub. by Turtleback) Demco.
— Science Fiction Stories. 2000. write for info. (*0-06-105202-7*, HarperPrism) HarpC.
— Sixty Odd: New Poems. LC 98-37084. 160p. 1999. pap. 14.00 (*1-57062 388 0*, Pub. by Shambhala Pubns) Random.
— Steering the Craft: Exercises & Discussions on Story Writing for the Lone Navigator or the Mutinous Crew. LC 97-32587. 176p. 1998. pap. 14.95 (*0-933377-46-0*) Eighth Mount Pr.
— Steering the Craft: Exercises & Discussions on Story Writing for the Lone Navigator or the Mutinous Crew. LC 97-32587. 176p. 1998. lib. bdg. 22.95 (*0-933377-47-9*) Eighth Mount Pr.
— Tehanu: The Last Book of Earthsea. LC 89-32780. 240p. (J). (ps up). 1990. 16.95 (*0-689-31595-3*) Atheneum Yung Read.
— Tehanu: The Last Book of Earthsea. (Earthsea Cycle Ser.). (J). 1991. 11.60 (*0-606-04825-1*, Pub. by Turtleback) Demco.
— Tehanu: The Last Book of Earthsea, No. 4. 288p. 1997. mass mkt. 6.99 (*0-553-28873-3*, Spectra) Bantam.
***Le Guin, Ursula K.** Telling. LC 00-29574. 272p. 2000. 24.00 (*0-15-100567-2*) Harcourt.
Le Guin, Ursula K. Tom Mouse & Ms. Howe. LC 98-16601. (Illus.). (J). 1999. write for info. (*0-7894-2554-8*) DK Pub Inc.
— The Tombs of Atuan. LC 70-154753. (Illus.). 176p. (J). (gr. 6-9). 1990. 18.00 (*0-689-31684-4*) Atheneum Yung Read.
— The Tombs of Atuan. (Earthsea Trilogy Ser.). (J). 1975. 11.60 (*0-606-00442-4*, Pub. by Turtleback) Demco.
— The Tombs of Atuan, No. 2. 160p. (J). 1984. mass mkt. 6.99 (*0-553-27331-0*, Bantam Classics) Bantam.
— Unlocking the Air & Other Stories. 224p. 1997. pap. 12.00 (*0-06-092803-4*, Perennial) HarperTrade.
— The Visionary, 2 vols. in 1. (Back-to-Back Ser.: Vol. 1). (YA). 7.50 (*0-685-10479-6*) McGraw.
— The Wind's Twelve Quarters. 400p. 1995. mass mkt. 4.99 (*0-06-105605-7*) HarpC.
— A Wizard of Earthsea. LC 68-21992. 208p. (YA). 1991. 16.95 (*0-689-31720-4*) Atheneum Yung Read.
— A Wizard of Earthsea. 192p. (YA). (gr. 9-12). 1984. mass mkt. 6.99 (*0-553-26250-5*) Bantam.
— A Wizard of Earthsea. (Earthsea Trilogy Ser.). (YA). 1975. 11.60 (*0-606-00573-0*, Pub. by Turtleback) Demco.
— Wonderful Alexander & the Catwings. LC 93-49397. (Illus.). 48p. (J). (gr. k-3). 1994. 14.95 (*0-531-06851-X*); lib. bdg. 15.99 (*0-531-08701-8*) Orchard Bks Watts.
— Wonderful Alexander & the Catwings. LC 93-49397. (Illus.). 48p. (J). (gr. 1-4). 1994. pap. 3.95 (*0-531-07112-X*) Orchard Bks Watts.
— Wonderful Alexander & the Catwings. (Illus.). (J). (gr. 2-5). 1996. pap. text 2.99 (*0-590-54336-9*) Scholastic Inc.
— Wonderful Alexander & the Catwings. LC 93-49397. 1996. 8.19 (*0-606-10083-0*, Pub. by Turtleback) Demco.
— World of Exile & Illusion. LC 96-26194. 384p. 1996. pap. 15.95 (*0-312-86211-3*) St Martin.
Le Guin, Ursula K. & Attebery, Brian, eds. The Norton Book of Science Fiction. 1997. pap. text. write for info. (*0-393-97241-0*) Norton.
— The Norton Book of Science Fiction: North American science fiction, 1960-1990. LC 93-16130. 869p. 1993. 29.95 (*0-393-03546-8*) Norton.
Le Guin, Ursula K. & Gallagher, Tess. King Dog: A Screenplay. LC 85-7872. (Back-to-Back Bks.). 208p. (Orig.). 1985. pap. 9.50 (*0-88496-236-9*) Capra Pr.
Le Guin, Ursula K. & Sanders, Scott Russell. The Visionary: The Life Story of Flicker of the Serpentine. LC 84-7656. (Back-to-Back Ser.). 128p. (Orig.). 1984. pap. 7.50 (*0-88496-219-9*) Capra Pr.
Le Guin, Ursula K. & Shevelev, Raphael. Wynn Bullock: The Enchanted Landscape, Photographs 1940-1975. 120p. 1999. pap. 29.95 (*0-89381-867-4*) Aperture.
Le Guin, Ursula K. & Tzu, Lao. Tao Te Ching: A Book about the Way & the Power of the Way. LC 97-18942. 1997. 20.00 (*1-57062-333-3*, Pub. by Shambhala Pubns) Random.
***Le Guin, Ursula K., et al.** Always Coming Home. LC 00-23409. (California Fiction Ser.). 2000. write for info. (*0-520-22735-2*) U CA Pr.
Le Guin, Ursula K., jt. auth. see Bellessi, Diana.
Le Harivel, Adrian. Irish Watercolours & Drawings. (Illus.). 176p. 1991. pap. 40.00 (*0-903162-56-3*, Pub. by Art Bks Intl) Partners Pubs Grp.
— Nathaniel Hone the Elder. (Lives of Irish Artists Ser.). (Illus.). 36p. 1995. 7.95 (*0-948524-36-7*, Pub. by Town Hse) Roberts Rinehart.
Le Hellaye, Catherine & Barzotti, Dominique. Farandole, No. 1. (FRE., Illus.). 91p. 1992. pap. text 17.95 (*2-278-04196-7*, Pub. by Edns Didier) Hatier Pub.
— Farandole, No. 2. (FRE., Illus.). 93p. 1993. pap. text 18.95 (*2-278-04276-9*, Pub. by Edns Didier) Hatier Pub.
***Le Heron, Richard, et al, eds.** Explorations in Human Geography: Encountering Place. (Illus.). 448p. 2000. pap. text 45.00 (*0-19-558420-1*) OUP.
Le Heron, Richard, jt. ed. see Van Der Knaap, Bert.
Le Hir, Marie-Pierre. Le Romantisme aux Encheres: Ducange, Pixerecourt, Hugo. LC 92-3694. (Purdue University Monographs in Romance Languages: Vol. 42). x, 225p. 1992. 65.00 (*1-55619-312-2*); pap. 27.95 (*1-55619-313-0*) J Benjamins Pubng Co.
***Le Hir, Marie-Pierre & Strand, Dana, eds.** French Cultural Studies: Criticism at the Crossroads. LC 99-89485. (C). 2000. text 59.50 (*0-7914-4585-2*) State U NY Pr.
— French Cultural Studies: Criticism at the Crossroads. LC 99-89485. 2000. pap. 19.95 (*0-7914-4586-0*) State U NY Pr.
Le Hir, Yves. Analyses Stylistiques. 302p. 1965. 9.95 (*0-8288-7489-1*) Fr & Eur.
Le, Ho P. Angels Postcard Book. 30p. 1996. pap. 6.95 (*0-87588-434-2*) Hobby Hse.
Le, Ho Phi. Angels from the Heart. LC 95-143924. (Illus.). 64p. 1995. 14.95 (*0-87588-431-8*, 4828) Hobby Hse.
— Dolls for Sentimental Reasons. (Illus.). 64p. 1999. 16.95 (*0-87588-516-0*, H5459) Hobby Hse.
— Forget Me Not: Teddy Bears, Dolls & Memories. LC 95-146720. (Illus.). 64p. 1994. 14.95 (*0-87588-425-3*, 4740) Hobby Hse.
— Romance of Dolls & Teddy Bears. LC 93-110176. (Illus.). 176p. 1992. 39.95 (*0-87588-390-7*) Hobby Hse.
Le Houerou, H. N. The Grazing Land Ecosystems of the African Sahel. (Ecological Studies: Vol. 75). (Illus.). 290p. 1989. 155.95 (*0-387-50791-4*) Spr-Verlag.
Le Houerou, Philippe H. Investment Policy in Russia. (Studies of Economies in Transformation). 88p. 1995. pap. 22.00 (*0-8213-3202-3*, 13202) World Bank.
— Investment Policy in Russia. (RUS.). 104p. 1996. pap. 22.00 (*0-8213-3564-2*, 13564) World Bank.
Le-Huong, Pham T., et al, trs. The ALA Glossary of Library & Information Science - Vietnamese/English: First English-Vietnamese Edition. (ENG & VIE.). 270p. 1996. pap. text. write for info. (*1-883620-15-5*) Galen AZ.
Le Huray, Peter. Music & the Reformation in England, 1549-1660. LC 77-87383. (Cambridge Studies in Music). 484p. reprint ed. pap. 138.00 (*0-608-16450-X*, 2026344) Bks Demand.
Le Huray, Peter, ed. Anthems for Men's Voices Vol. 1: Altos, Tenors & Basses. 96p. 1985. pap. 17.95 (*0-19-353234-4*) OUP.
Le Janu, Richard, tr. see Gouverneur, Jacques.
Le Jaouen, Jean-Claude. The Fabrication of Farmstead Goat Cheese. 206p. 1990. pap. 22.95 (*0-9607404-3-0*) Cheesemakers Jrnl.
Le Jeune, Claude. Claude le Jeune: Dodecacorde. Heider, Anne H., ed. (Recent Researches in Music of the Renaissance Ser.: Vol. RRR74). (Illus.). xxx, 92p. 1989. pap. 40.00 (*0-89579-346-6*) A-R Eds.
— Claude le Jeune: Dodecacorde. Heider, Anne H., ed. (Recent Researches in Music of the Renaissance Ser.: Vol. RRR75). (Illus.). xi, 99p. 1989. pap. 35.00 (*0-89579-347-4*) A-R Eds.
— Claude le Jeune: Dodecacorde. Heider, Anne H., ed. (Recent Researches in Music of the Renaissance Ser.: Vol. RRR76). (Illus.). xii, 118p. 1989. pap. 45.00 (*0-89579-348-2*) A-R Eds.
— Claude Le Jeune - Les Cent Cinquante Pseaumes de David: Misen Musique a Quatre et Cinq Parties. Heider, Anne H., ed. LC 94-45128. (Recent Researches in Music of the Renaissance Ser.: Vol. RRR98). (Illus.). lii, 268p. 1995. pap. 100.00 (*0-89579-312-1*) A-R Eds.
***Le Joly, Edward.** We Do It for Jesus: Mother Teresa & Her Missionaries of Charity. 2nd ed. (Illus.). 202p. 1998. pap. 14.50 (*0-19-564561-8*) OUP.
***Le Joly, Edward & Chaliha, Jaya.** Reaching Out in love: Stories Told by Mother Teresa. LC 99-55586. 224p. 2000. pap. 12.95 (*0-8264-1219-X*) Continuum.
Le, Juan, jt. auth. see Chia, Mantak.
Le Juez, Brigitte, jt. ed. see Gratton, Johnnie.
***Le, K. C.** Vibrations of Shells & Rods. LC 99-28999. (Illus.). iv, 423p. 1999. 112.00 (*3-540-64516-0*) Spr-Verlag.
Le Kernec, Bill. Alaskan Malamutes. (Illus.). 128p. 1991. 11.95 (*0-87666-711-6*, KW-094) TFH Pubns.
— Alaskan Malamutes. (Illus.). 128p. 1994. 9.95 (*0-7938-1059-0*, KW-094) TFH Pubns.
— Alaskan Malamutes: AKC Rank #44. (Illus.). 1997. pap. 9.95 (*0-7938-2368-4*, KW-094S) TFH Pubns.
Le Landgren. A Touch of Magic: A Fantasy Adventure. LC 90-8183. (Orig.). (J). (gr. 2-7). 1990. pap. 7.95 (*0-943367-03-4*) Princess Pub.
Le Lay, G., et al. Semiconductor Interfaces: Formation & Properties. (Proceedings in Physics Ser.: Vol. 22). (Illus.). 420p. 1987. 75.00 (*0-387-18328-0*) Spr-Verlag.
Le Letty, L., ed. see IFAC Symposium Staff & Babary, J. P.
Le, Linda. Slander. Allen, Esther, tr. & afterword by by. LC 96-33816. (European Women Writers Ser.). v, 160p. 1996. pap. 14.00 (*0-8032-7963-9*, Bison Books); text 35.00 (*0-8032-2913-5*) U of Nebr Pr.
Le Lionnais, Francois. Dictionary of Mathematics. 3rd ed. (ENG & FRE.). 848p. 1992. 150.00 (*0-7859-4704-3*, F70764) Fr & Eur.
Le Lionnais, Francois & Maget, E. Dictionnaire des Echecs. 2nd ed. (FRE.). 1984. 115.00 (*0-8288-2341-3*, F60500) Fr & Eur.
Le Luc, Don R. Beyond Broadcasting: Patterns in Policy & Law. LC 87-2654. 1987. text 39.16 (*0-582-29039-2*, 71737) Longman.
Le Maire De Belges, Jean. Oeuvres, 4 vols., Set. 1790p. 1972. reprint ed. write for info. (*3-487-04348-3*) G Olms Pubs.
Le Maire, M., et al. Laboratory Guide to Biochemistry, Enzymology, & Protein Physical Chemistry: A Study of Aspartate Transcarbamylase. (Illus.). 182p. (C). 1991. spiral bd. 39.50 (*0-306-43639-6*, Plenum Trade) Perseus Pubng.
Le Maistre. Dictionnaire Jersais-Francais, 2 tomes, Set. (FRE.). 150.00 (*0-685-57713-9*, F136580) Fr & Eur.
Le Maistre, Christopher & El-Sawy, Ahmed. Computer Integrated Manufacturing: A Systems Approach. (Illus.). 160p. 1987. pap. 19.95 (*0-527-91624-2*, 916242) Productivity Inc.
Le Mao, Sophie, jt. auth. see Fallon, Steve.
Le Marchant, C. M., jt. auth. see Johns, Richard A.
Le Marchant, Denis. Memoirs of the Late General Le Marchant, 1766-1812. 1997. 37.95 (*1-885119-47-X*) Sarpedon.
Le Marchant, Denis. Memoirs of the Late Major-General Le Marchant. 336p. 1997. 100.00 (*1-873376-94-4*, Pub. by Spellmnt Pubs) St Mut.
Le Mare, Karina. Great Danes: An Owner's Companion. (Illus.). 224p. 1993. 39.95 (*1-85223-316-8*, Pub. by Crolwood) Trafalgar.
Le Marechal, J. F. & Soulle, L. Dictionnaire Pratique de la Chimie. (FRE.). 158p. 1984. pap. 16.95 (*0-7859-7790-2*, 2218056070) Fr & Eur.
Le Marque, Tina. Coyote Woman Vol. 2: A Continuing Journey of My Life As an Artist. LC 97-72381. (Illus.). 216p. 1998. pap. 18.95 (*0-9630131-1-4*) Artists & Writers.
— Warrior Woman: A Journal of My Life As an Artist. 2nd ed. LC 91-73200. (Illus.). 160p. 1991. pap. 18.95 (*0-9630131-0-6*) Artists & Writers.
Le Massena, Robert A. Lackawanna - Superpower Railroad of the Northeast. (Illus.). 112p. 1998. pap. 26.95 (*1-883089-32-8*) TLC VA.
Le Massena, Robert A. & Yanosey, Robert J. Union Pacific Official Color Photography. (Illus.). 128p. 1993. 49.95 (*1-878887-25-4*) Morning NJ.
Le Master, Dennis C. & Towell, William E., frwds. Decade of Change: The Remaking of Forest Service Statutory Authority During the 1970s, 113. LC 83-22641. (Contributions in Political Science Ser.: No. 113). (Illus.). 290p. 1984. 37.50 (*0-313-24341-7*, LDC/) Greenwood.
***Le May, Alan.** Cattle Kingdom. large type ed. LC 00-40277. 2000. write for info. (*1-57490-285-7*, Sagebrush LP West) T T Beeler.
Le May, G. H. The Afrikaners: A Political History. (Illus.). 320p. (C). 1995. 34.95 (*0-631-18204-7*) Blackwell Pubs.
Le May, I., ed. Advances in Materials Technology in the Americas, 2 vols. Incl. Vol. 1. Materials Recovery & Utilization: Bk. H00161, MD1. 168p. 1980. Vol. 2. Materials Processing & Performance: Bk. H00162, MD2. 220p. 1980. 1980. 30.00 (*0-686-70426-6*) ASME.
Le May, Iain, ed. see Interamerican Conference on Materials Technology S.
Le May, Malcolm M., jt. ed. see Hillman, Jeffrey S.
Le May, Reginald S. An Asian Arcady: The Land & Peoples of Northern Siam. LC 77-87041. reprint ed. 27.00 (*0-404-16833-7*) AMS Pr.
— The Culture of South-East Asia: The Heritage of India. LC 77-87065. reprint ed. 30.00 (*0-404-16834-5*) AMS Pr.
Le May, Thomastine. Les Pecheurs. (Fropse Ser.: No. 5). write for info. (*0-918728-87-8*) Pendragon NY.
Le Meal, Joselyne. English-French Dictionary of Fibre-Optic Cables: Dictionnaire Anglais-Francais de Cables a Fibres Optiques. (ENG & FRE.). 1984. 39.95 (*0-8288-2232-8*, F107570) Fr & Eur.
Le Mehaute, Alain. Fractal Geometrics: Theory & Applications. 1991. 49.95 (*0-8493-7722-6*) CRC Pr.
Le Mehaute, Alain, et al, eds. Curves & Surfaces with Applications in CAGD & Surfaces & Multiresolution Methods, 2 vols. Incl. Vol. 1. Curves & Surfaces with Applications in CAGD. LC 97-9342. (Illus.). 496p.

An Asterisk (*) at the beginning of an entry indicates that the title is appearing for the first time.

1997. text 50.00 (*0-8265-1293-3*); Vol. 2. Surface Fitting & Multiresolution Methods. LC 97-9472. (Illus.). 368p. 1997. text 45.00 (*0-8265-1294-1*); 1997. 90.00 (*0-8265-1292-5*) Vanderbilt U Pr.

Le Mehaute, Bernard & Wang, Shen. Water Waves Generated by Underwater Explosion. LC 94-45506. (Advanced Series in Ocean Engineering). 400p. 1996. text 74.00 (*981-02-2083-9*); pap. text 43.00 (*981-02-2132-0*) World Scientific Pub.

Le Messurier, Brian. South West Coast Path: Falmouth to Exmouth. (National Trail Guides Ser.). (Illus.). 168p. 1995. pap. 19.95 (*1-85410-096-3*, Pub. by Aurum Pr) London Brdge.

***Le Mesurier, Peter.** Gods of the Dawn: The Message of the Pyramids & the True Stargate Mystery. (Illus.). 256p. 1998. 24.95 (*0-7225-3549-X*) Thorsons PA.

Le Metayer, Daniel, jt. ed. see Garlan, David.

Le Meur, Pierre-Yves, jt. ed. see Bierschenk, Thomas.

Le Moal. Cinema & Video Dictionary, French-English/ English-French. (ENG & FRE.). Date not set. pap. 60.00 (*0-7859-9565-X*) Fr & Eur.

— Dopamine & the Brain: From Neurons to Networks. 1999. 1.00 (*0-12-443460-6*) Acad Pr.

Le Moal, P. Lexique Cinema Video Francais-Anglais/ Anglais-Francais - Cinema & Video Dictionary French-English/English-French. (ENG & FRE.). 1995. spiral bd. 60.00 (*2-85608-074-X*, Pub. by La Maison Du Dict) IBD Ltd.

Le Moignan, Luke. Jersey on the Move: A Glimpse at Luke le Moignans Historic Photographs. (Jersey Heritage Editions Ser.). 1991. 40.00 (*0-86120-022-5*, Pub. by Aris & Phillips) David Brown.

Le Moigne, Guy J. Developing & Improving Irrigation & Drainage Systems: Selected Papers from World Bank Seminars. Barghouti, Shawki et al, eds. LC 92-17888. (Technical Papers: No. 178). 177p. 1992. pap. 22.00 (*0-8213-2165-X*, 12165) World Bank.

Le Moigne, Guy J., ed. A Guide to the Formulation of Water Resources Strategy. LC 94-37850. (Technical Papers: No. 263). 122p. 1994. pap. 22.00 (*0-8213-3038-1*, 13038) World Bank.

Le Moigne, Guy J., et al, eds. Dam Safety & the Environment. (Technical Papers: No. 115). 196p. 1990. pap. 22.00 (*0-8213-1438-6*, 11438) World Bank.

— Water Policy & Water Markets: Selected Papers & Proceedings from the World Bank's Ninth Annual Irrigation & Drainage Seminar Held in Annapolis, Maryland, December 8-10, 1992. LC 94-18954. (Technical Papers: Vol. 249). 128p. 1994. pap. 22.00 (*0-8213-2861-1*) World Bank.

Le Moigne, Guy J., et al. Using Water Efficiently: Technological Options. LC 93-15614. (Technical Papers: Vol. 205). 61p. 1993. pap. 22.00 (*0-8213-2455-1*, 12455) World Bank.

Le Moigne, Guy J., jt. auth. see Kirmani, Syed S.

Le Moine, Roger. L' Amerique & les Poetes Francais de la Renaissance. LC 72-354710. (Collection les Isles Fortunees: Vol. 1). (FRE.). 358p. 1972. reprint ed. pap. 111.00 (*0-608-02202-0*, 206287200004) Bks Demand.

— Napoleon Bourassa, l'Homme & l'Artiste. LC 75-3958. (Cahiers du Centre de Recherce en Civilisation Canadienne-Francaise Ser.: Vol. 8). (FRE.). 259p. 1974. reprint ed. pap. 80.30 (*0-608-02186-5*, 206285500003) Bks Demand.

Le Mouel, J. L., et al, eds. Dynamics of Earth's Deep Interior & Earth Rotation. LC 93-7784. (Geophysical Monograph Ser.: No. 72). 1993. 30.00 (*0-87590-463-7*) Am Geophysical.

Le Nard, M., jt. ed. see De Hertogh, A.

Le Navenec, Carole-Lynne. One Day at a Time: How Families Manage the Experience of Dementia. LC 95-24263. 240p. 1996. 57.95 (*0-86569-257-2*, Auburn Hse) Greenwood.

Le Nay, Louise. The Hero: A Story of Family & Belonging. 252p. (Orig.). 1997. pap. 12.95 (*1-86448-157-9*, Pub. by Allen & Unwin Pty) IPG Chicago.

Le Nevelon, Jean. Venjance Alixandre. Ham, Edward B., ed. (Elliott Monographs: Vol. 27). 1931. 25.00 (*0-527-02630-1*) Periodicals Srv.

Le-Ngoc, Tho, jt. auth. see Jamali, S. Hamidreza.

Le Ninan, Claude. Le Francais des Affaires Par la Video. (FRE.). 190p. 1993. pap. text 23.95 (*2-278-04272-6*) Hatier Pub.

— Le Francais des Affaires Par la Video, 2 vols., Set. (FRE.). 1993. VHS 172.95 (*0-87774-002-X*) Schoenhof.

Le Noble, William J. Highlights of Organic Chemistry: An Advanced Textbook. (Studies in Organic Chemistry: Vol. 3). (Illus.). 1000p. 1974. text 175.00 (*0-8247-6210-X*) Dekker.

***Le Noel, Christian.** On Target: History & Hunting in Central Africa. limited ed. LC 99-66167. (Illus.). 263p. 1999. 85.00 (*1-882458-24-9*) Trophy Rm Bks.

Le Page, Bill. The Turning of the Key: Meher Baba in Australia. (Illus.). 428p. (Orig.). 1993. pap. 12.00 (*0-913078-70-0*) Sheriar Pr.

Le Page, Jean-Francois. Applied Heterogeneous Catalysis: Design, Manufacture & the Use of Solid Catalysis. (Illus.). 552p. (C). 1987. 960.00 (*2-7108-0531-6*, Pub. by Edits Technip) Enfield Pubs NH.

Le Page, Jean-Francois, et al. Resid & Heavy Oil Processing. 188p. (C). 1992. 340.00 (*2-7108-0621-5*, Pub. by Edits Technip) Enfield Pubs NH.

Le Page, Victoria. Shambhala: The Fascinating Truth Behind the Myth of Shangri-la. LC 96-18045. 1996. pap. 16.00 (*0-8356-0750-X*, Quest) Theos Pub Hse.

Le Pan, Don. Common Errors in English. 3rd ed. 260p. 1998. pap. 9.95 (*1-55111-205-1*) Broadview Pr.

Le Patourel, John. Feudal Empires: Norman & Plantagenet. 385p. (C). 1984. 60.00 (*0-907628-22-2*) Hambledon Press.

***Le Peau, Andrew T. & Le Peau, Phyllis J.** Ephesians: Wholeness for a Broken World. 2nd rev. ed. (LifeGuide Bible Studies). 64p. 2000. pap. 4.99 (*0-8308-3012-X*) InterVarsity.

Le Peau, Phyllis J. Acts: Seeing God's Power in Action. (LifeGuide Bible Studies). 112p. (Orig.). 1992. pap., wbk. ed. 4.99 (*0-8308-1007-2*, 1007) InterVarsity.

— Caring for Physical Needs. (Caring People Bible Studies). 96p. (Orig.). 1991. pap. 4.99 (*0-8308-1196-6*, 1196) InterVarsity.

— Caring for Spiritual Needs. (Caring People Bible Studies). 96p. (Orig.). 1991. pap. 4.99 (*0-8308-1194-X*, 1194) InterVarsity.

— Love: The Greatest Gift of All. (LifeGuide Bible Studies). 64p. 1997. pap. 4.99 (*0-8308-1083-8*, 1083) InterVarsity.

Le Peau, Phyllis J., jt. auth. see Le Peau, Andrew T.

Le Pelletier, Louis. Etymological Dictionary of the Breton Language: Dictionnaire Etymologique de la Langue Bretonne. (BRE & FRE.). 1716p. 1973. reprint ed. pap. write for info. (*0-7859-4912-7*) Fr & Eur.

Le Pelley, Nicolette & Knorr, Cheryl. The House & Garden Book of Essential Addresses. 288p. 1997. pap. 24.95 (*0-9530079-0-1*, Pub. by Art Bks Intl) Partners Pubs Grp.

Le Penven, Yves. Dictionnaire des Signes et des Symptomes en Homeopathie et des Remedes Correspondent. (FRE.). 412p. 1986. 95.00 (*0-7859-7818-6*, 2224011733) Fr & Eur.

Le Pera, George, ed. Stray. (Illus.). 66p. (Orig.). 1989. pap. text 7.95 (*0-9624466-0-2*) United Action.

Le Petit, Jean Francois. The Low Country Commonwealth. Grimeston, E., tr. LC 72-25634. (English Experience Ser.: No. 208). 1969. reprint ed. 45.00 (*90-221-0208-4*) Walter J Johnson.

Le Petit, Jules. Bibliographie Des Principales Editions Originales D'Ecrivains Francaise Du Fifteenth Au Eighteenth Siecle. viii, 583p. 1969. reprint ed. write for info. (*3-487-04174-X*) G Olms Pubs.

Le Play, Frederic. Frederic Le Play on Family, Work, & Social Change. Silver, Catherine, ed. LC 81-23125. (Heritage of Sociology Ser.). (C). 1992. lib. bdg. 33.00 (*0-226-47266-3*) U Ch Pr.

Le Play, Frederick. La Reforme Sociale en France Deduite de l'Observation Comparee des Peuples Europeens: Social Reform in France Deduced from the Comparative Observation of the European Peoples, 2 vols. LC 74-25766. (European Sociology Ser.). 936p. 1975. reprint ed. 74.95 (*0-405-06520-5*) Ayer.

Le Plongeon, Alice D. Queen Moo's Talisman: The Fall of the Maya Empire. 90p. 1994. reprint ed. pap. 15.95 (*1-56459-426-2*) Kessinger Pub.

Le Plongeon, Augustus. Maya/Atlantis: Queen Moo & the Egyptian Sphinx. 418p. 1997. reprint ed. pap. 29.95 (*0-7661-0102-9*) Kessinger Pub.

— Origin of the Egyptians. 1985. 18.50 (*0-89314-418-5*) Philos Res.

— Queen Moo & the Egyptian Sphinx. 2nd ed. 277p. 1996. reprint ed. 32.50 (*0-7873-0539-1*) Hlth Research.

— Sacred Mysteries among the Mayas & Quiches. LC 73-76094. (Secret Doctrine Reference Ser.). (Illus.). 200p. 1997. reprint ed. 15.00 (*0-913510-02-5*) Wizards.

Le Poidevin, Robin. Arguing for Atheism: An Introduction to the Philosophy of Religion. LC 96-3431. 184p. (C). 1996. 70.00 (*0-415-09337-6*); pap. 20.99 (*0-415-09338-4*) Routledge.

Le Poidevin, Robin, ed. Questions of Time & Tense. LC 98-28486. 306p. 1998. text 65.00 (*0-19-823695-6*) OUP.

Le Poidevin, Robin, ed. see MacBeath, Murray.

Le Poitier, Joseph, jt. ed. see Verdier, Jean-Louis.

Le Poncin Lafitte, M., et al, eds. Functions of the Aging Brain from Physiological Ageing to Dementia. (Journal: Gerontology: Vol. 32, Suppl. 1, 1986). (Illus.). iv, 128p. 1986. pap. 41.75 (*3-8055-4386-7*) S Karger.

Le Poncin-Lafitte, M. & Rapin, J. R., eds. Deoxyglucose Uptake & Oxygen Consumption: A Metabolic Approach to Cerebral Function. (Journal: European Neurology: Vol. 20, No. 3). (Illus.). 170p. 1981. pap. 43.50 (*3-8055-3412-4*) S Karger.

Le Potier, J. Lectures on Vector Bundles. (Studies in Advanced Mathematics: No. 54). (Illus.). 259p. (C). 1997. text 64.95 (*0-521-48182-1*) Cambridge U Pr.

Le Poullioun, Maria-Luisa. Lexi-Tourisme Espagnol-Francais. 144p. 1993. pap. 22.95 (*0-7859-5636-0*, 2713512433) Fr & Eur.

Le Prestre, Philippe. The World Bank & the Environmental Challenge. LC 88-42825. 264p. 1989. 40.00 (*0-941664-98-8*) Susquehanna U Pr.

Le Prestre, Philippe G., ed. Role Quests in the Post-Cold War Era: Foreign Policies in Transition. 336p. 1997. 65.00 (*0-7735-1532-1*, Pub. by McG-Queens Univ Pr); pap. 22.95 (*0-7735-1533-X*, Pub. by McG-Queens Univ Pr) CUP Services.

Le Prestre, Philippe G., et al. Protecting the Ozone Layer: Lessons, Models, & Prospects. LC 98-30071. 1998. 99.95 (*0-7923-8245-5*) Kluwer Academic.

Le Proust, Ange. Treatise on the Rule of Saint Augustine. Rotelle, John E., ed. 290p. (Orig.). 1996. pap. 25.00 (*0-941491-99-4*) Augustinian Pr.

Le Queux, William. Spies of the Kaiser: Plotting the Downfall of England. 2nd ed. (Classics of Espionage Ser.). (Illus.). 219p. 1997. reprint ed. 39.50 (*0-7146-4728-4*, Pub. by F Cass Pubs); reprint ed. pap. 16.95 (*0-7146-4278-9*, Pub. by F Cass Pubs) Intl Spec Bk.

Le Queux, William T. The Eye of Istar: A Romance of the Land of No Return. Reginald, R. & Melville, Douglas, eds. LC 77-84247. (Lost Race & Adult Fantasy Ser.). (Illus.). 1978. reprint ed. lib. bdg. 36.95 (*0-405-10993-8*) Ayer.

— The Great White Queen: A Tale of Treasure & Treason. LC 74-16505. (Science Fiction Ser.). (Illus.). 322p. 1975. reprint ed. 26.95 (*0-405-06303-2*) Ayer.

***Le Rendu, Raymond.** Winds of Remembrance. LC 99-70516. 1999. write for info. (*0-89002-346-8*) Northwoods Pr.

Le Riche, Edith. Combating Truancy in Schools: Listening to the Voice of the Pupil. LC 96-127671. 144p. 1995. pap. 24.95 (*1-85346-337-X*, Pub. by David Fulton) Taylor & Francis.

Le Riche, William Harding. A Chemical Feast. LC 82-2442. 216p. 1982. reprint ed. pap. 67.00 (*0-7837-8155-5*, 204786000008) Bks Demand.

Le Roith, Derek & Bondy, Carolyn, eds. Growth Factors & Cytokines in Health & Disease, Set, Vols. 1A & 1B. 600p. 1996. 257.00 (*0-7623-0091-4*) Jai Pr.

Le Roith, Derek, jt. ed. see Draznin, Boris.

Le Rond D'Alembert, Jean. Preliminary Discourse to the Encyclopedia of Diderot. Schwab, Richard N., tr. 224p. 1995. pap. text 10.95 (*0-226-13476-8*) U Ch Pr.

Le Rossignol, James E. Backgrounds to Communist Thought. 1979. 12.50 (*0-8446-2454-3*) Peter Smith.

Le Rougetel, Hazel. A Little Book of Old Roses. (Illus.). 60p. 1998. 9.95 (*0-86281-333-6*, Pub. by Appletree Pr) Irish Bks Media.

Le Roux de Lincy, Antoine J. Recherches sur Jean Grolier, sur Sa Vie et Sa Bibliotheque. (In Zusammenarbeit Mit Dem Verlag B. de Graaf, Nieuwkoop Ser.). lix, 491p. 1971. reprint ed. write for info. (*3-487-04035-2*) G Olms Pubs.

Le-Roux De Lincy, M., ed. see Philippe De Remi.

Le Roux, Pak & Van Niekerk, Andre. South African Law of Unfair Dismissal. 380p. 1994. pap. 52.00 (*0-7021-3162-8*, Pub. by Juta & Co) Gaunt.

Le Rouzic, Pierre. Compatibility of Names: A Companion to the Name Book. 1989. pap. 7.95 (*0-9622069-1-1*) Topos Pr.

— The Name Book. rev. ed. Charles, Rodney, ed. LC 94-67155. (Illus.). 646p. 1995. pap. 15.95 (*0-9638502-1-0*) Sunstar Pubng.

— The Name Book: A Name for a Lifetime. rev. ed. LC 89-50198. 570p. reprint ed. pap. text 14.95 (*0-9622069-0-3*) Topos Pr.

***Le Rouzic, Pierre.** The Secret Meaning of Names: Personality Profiles for over 9,000 Names. rev. ed. Charles, Rodney, ed. LC 99-63470. (Illus.). 650p. 1999. pap. 18.95 (*1-887472-66-5*, Pub. by Sunstar Pubng) Midpt Trade.

Le Roy. Jacquou le Croquant. unabridged ed. (FRE.). 1996. pap. 5.95 (*2-87714-335-X*, Pub. by Bookking Intl) Distribks Inc.

Le Roy, Bruce, ed. see Chittenden, Hiram Martin.

Le Roy, Gaylord C. Perplexed Prophets: Six Nineteenth Century British Authors. LC 78-147220. 205p. 1971. reprint ed. lib. bdg. 59.50 (*0-8371-5985-7*, LEPR, Greenwood Pr) Greenwood.

Le Roy, James A. Americans in the Philippines, 2 vols. LC 73-126681. reprint ed. 165.00 (*0-404-03974-X*) AMS Pr.

Le Roy-Ladurie, Emmanuel. The Mind & Method of the Historian. Reynolds, Sian & Reynolds, Ben, trs. LC 81-449. (Illus.). vi, 310p. (C). 1984. pap. 12.95 (*0-226-47325-2*) U Ch Pr.

— The Mind & Method of the Historian. Reynolds, Sian & Reynolds, Ben, trs. LC 81-449. 320p. (C). 1997. lib. bdg. 31.50 (*0-226-47326-0*) U Ch Pr.

— Montaillou, Village Occitan de 1294 a 1324. (Folio-Histoire Ser.: No. 9). (FRE.). 640p. 1982. pap. 14.95 (*2-07-032328-5*) Schoenhof.

Le Roy Ladurie, Emmanuel. The Royal French State, 1460-1610: Louis XI-Henri IV, 1460-1610. Vale, Juliet, tr. from FRE. (History of France Ser.). (Illus.). 384p. 1994. 62.95 (*0-631-17027-8*) Blackwell Pubs.

Le Roy-Ladurie, Emmanuel. The Territory of the Historian. Reynolds, Ben & Reynolds, Sian, trs. LC 78-31362. viii, 346p. 1982. reprint ed. pap. 11.95 (*0-226-47328-7*) U Ch Pr.

Le Sage, Alain R. The Devil on Two Sticks. LC 75-46287. (Supernatural & Occult Fiction Ser.). (Illus.). 1976. reprint ed. lib. bdg. 25.95 (*0-405-08148-0*) Ayer.

Le Sann, Alain. A Livelihood from Fishing: Globalization & Sustainable Fisheries Policies. 112p. 1998. pap. 17.50 (*1-85339-398-3*, Pub. by Intermed Tech) Stylus Pub VA.

Le Saux, Francoise H., ed. Amys & Amylion. 157p. 1993. pap. text 19.95 (*0-85989-411-8*, Pub. by Univ Exeter Pr) Northwestern U Pr.

Le Saux, Henri. The Eyes of Light. 1983. pap. 12.95 (*0-87193-202-4*) Dimension Bks.

Le Scrope, Richard. De Controversia in Curia Militari inter Ricardum le Scrope et Robertum Grosvenor Milites, 2 vols., Set. LC 78-63514. reprint ed. 115.00 (*0-404-17220-2*) AMS Pr.

Le Sourd, Howard M. The University Work of the United Lutheran Church in America: A Study of the Work among Lutheran Students at Non-Lutheran Institutions. LC 70-176990. (Columbia University. Teachers College. Contributions to Education Ser.: No. 377). reprint ed. 37.50 (*0-404-55377-X*) AMS Pr.

Le Strange, Guy. Don Juan of Persia. LC 73-6288. (Middle East Ser.). 1973. reprint ed. 28.95 (*0-405-05333-9*) Ayer.

— The Lands of the Eastern Caliphate. LC 77-180355. (Cambridge Geographical Ser.). reprint ed. 55.00 (*0-404-56287-6*) AMS Pr.

Le Strange, Guy, ed. Don Juan of Persia: A Shi'ah Catholic (1560-1604) 360p. (C). 1996. text 70.00 (*0-7007-0347-0*, Pub. by Curzon Pr Ltd) Paul & Co Pubs.

Le Strange, Guy, tr. Palestine under the Moslems. LC 70-180356. reprint ed. 84.50 (*0-404-56288-4*) AMS Pr.

Le Sueur, A. P. & Herberg, J. W. Constitutional & Administrative Law. LC 96-143979. (Lecture Notes Ser.). 303p. 1995. pap. 25.50 (*1-874241-67-8*, Pub. by Cavendish Pubng) Gaunt.

***Le Sueur, Alec.** Running a Hotel on the Roof of the World. large type unabridged ed. 318p. 1999. 25.95 (*0-7531-5205-3*, 152053, Pub. by ISIS Lg Prnt) ISIS Pub.

Le Sueur, Alec. Running a Hotel on the Roof of the World: Five Years in Tibet. 1999. pap. 12.99 (*1-873475-93-4*, Pub. by Summers) Seven Hills Bk.

***Le Sueur, Andrew, et al.** Principles of Public Law. 2nd ed. 584p. 1999. pap. 34.50 (*1-85941-381-1*, Pub. by Cavendish Pubng) Gaunt.

Le Sueur, James D., ed. see Feraoun, Mouloud.

Le Sueur, Jean-Francois & Dercy, Palat dit. La Caverne. Mongredien, Jean, ed. LC 85-750828. (French Opera in the 17th & 18th Centuries Ser.: No. 2, Vol. LXXIV). (Illus.). 1985. lib. bdg. 94.00 (*0-918728-33-9*) Pendragon NY.

Le Sueur, Meridel. Chanticleer of Wilderness Road: A Story of Davy Crockett. annuals (Illus.). 153p. (gr. 7-12). 1998. pap. text 10.95 (*0-930100-87-5*, Pub. by Holy Cow) Consort Bk Sales.

— Chanticleer of Wilderness Road: A Story of Davy Crockett. LC 88-45372. (Meridel Le Sueur Wilderness Bk.). (Illus.). 160p. 1990. reprint ed. 13.95 (*0-930100-35-2*) Holy Cow.

— Crusaders: The Radical Legacy of Marian & Arthur Lesueur. LC 84-14696. (Illus.). xxix, 109p. 1984. reprint ed. 11.95 (*0-87351-174-3*, Borealis Book); reprint ed. pap. 6.95 (*0-87351-178-6*, Borealis Book) Minn Hist.

— The Dread Road. (Illus.). 65p. (Orig.). 1991. pap. 11.95 (*0-931122-63-5*) West End.

— The Girl. 158p. 1990. pap. 10.95 (*0-931122-56-2*) West End.

***Le Sueur, Meridel.** Girl. rev. ed. (Illus.). 2000. pap. 12.95 (*0-931122-97-X*) West End.

Le Sueur, Meridel. Harvest Song: Collected Stories & Essays, 1926-58. rev. ed. 244p. 1990. pap. 12.95 (*0-931122-60-0*) West End.

— I Hear Men Talking & Other Stories. 243p. (Orig.). 1984. pap. 5.95 (*0-931122-37-6*) West End.

— Little Brother of the Wilderness: The Story of Johnny Appleseed. (Illus.). 80p. 1996. pap. text 7.95 (*0-930100-71-9*) Holy Cow.

— Nancy Hanks of Wilderness Road: A Story of Abraham Lincoln's Mother. 80p. (J). 1997. pap. text 7.95 (*0-930100-73-5*) Holy Cow.

— North Star Country. LC 98-21093. (Fesler-Lampert Minnesota Heritage Book Ser.). 352p. 1998. 15.95 (*0-8166-3252-9*) U of Minn Pr.

— Ripening: Selected Work. 2nd ed. Hedges, Elaine, ed. & intro. by. LC 86-18308. (Illus.). 312p. (C). 1990. pap. 10.95 (*0-935312-41-2*) Feminist Pr.

— River Road: A Story of Abraham Lincoln. (Illus.). 176p. 1991. 14.95 (*0-930100-37-9*) Holy Cow.

— River Road: A Story of Abraham Lincoln. 152p. 1999. pap. text 10.95 (*0-930100-77-8*) Holy Cow.

— Salute to Spring. LC 75-38588. 192p. (Orig.). 1989. pap. 3.95 (*0-7178-0463-1*) Intl Pubs Co.

— Sparrow Hawk. (Illus.). 176p. (gr. 7-12). 1998. pap. text 10.95 (*0-930100-86-7*, Pub. by Holy Cow) Consort Bk Sales.

— Sparrow Hawk. LC 87-80573. (Illus.). 192p. (YA). (gr. 7 up). 1987. reprint ed. 13.95 (*0-930100-22-0*) Holy Cow.

— Winter Prairie Woman. 2nd ed. LC 91-60707. (Illus.). 31p. 1990. reprint ed. pap. 6.00 (*0-935697-05-5*) Midwest Villages.

— Women on the Breadlines. LC 78-108080. (Worker Writer Ser.). (Illus.). 1978. pap. text 2.00 (*0-931122-34-1*) West End.

— Word Is Movement: Journal Notes from Atlanta to Tulsa to Wounded Knee. 74p. 1984. pap. 6.00 (*0-943594-07-3*) Cardinal Pr.

Le, T. U. Van, see Van Le, T. U.

Le Tallec, P. V. Numerical Analysis of Viscoelastic Problems. Ciarlet, P. G. & Lions, J. L., eds. (Recherches en Mathematiques Appliquees Ser.: Vol. 15). iv, 136p. 1990. 44.95 (*0-387-52450-9*) Spr-Verlag.

Le Tallec, Patrick, jt. auth. see Glowinski, Roland.

***Le-Tan, Pierre.** What the Dormouse Said: Lessons for Grown-Ups from Children's Books. LC 99-28423. 160p. 1999. 14.95 (*1-56512-241-0*) Algonquin Bks.

Le, Tang T. Trai, see Trai Le, Tang T.

Le, Tao, et al. First Aid for the Match: Insider Advice From Students & Residency Directors. 2nd ed. (Illus.). 162p. (C). 1999. pap. text 27.95 (*0-8385-2607-1*) McGraw.

Le Targat, Francois. Chagall. LC 85-42875. (Illus.). 128p. 1991. 27.50 (*0-8478-0624-3*, Pub. by Rizzoli Intl) St Martin.

— Kandinsky. LC 86-43201. (Illus.). 128p. 1990. 27.50 (*0-8478-0810-6*, Pub. by Rizzoli Intl) St Martin.

Le Targat, P. Kandinsky. (C). 1990. 215.00 (*0-7855-4465-8*, Pub. by Collets) St Mut.

Le Targat, P., ed. Chagall. (C). 1990. 100.00 (*0-7855-4473-9*, Pub. by Collets) St Mut.

Le Target, Francois. Toulouse-Lautrec. (Grandes Monografias). (SPA., Illus.). 200p. 1993. 200.00 (*84-343-0541-0*) Elliots Bks.

Le Tellier, Robert Ignatius, jt. auth. see Meyerbeer, Giacomo.

***Le Tendre, Brenda G. & Lipka, Richard P.** An Elementary School Educator's Guide to Program Evaluation: Getting Answers to Your Questions. (Illus.). 320p. 2000. pap. text, teacher ed. 42.95 (*1-929024-08-8*, 2011) CG Pubs Inc.

Le Tirant, Pierre. Seabed Reconnaissance & Offshore Soil Mechanics for the Installation of Petroleum Structures. 512p. 1979. 685.00 (*2-7108-0333-X*, Pub. by Edits Technip) Enfield Pubs NH.

Le Tirant, Pierre, jt. auth. see CLAROM Staff.

Le Tirant, Pierre, ed. see ARGEMA Staff.

Le Tirant, Pierre, ed. see CLAROM Staff.

L

Le Tissier, Tony. Farewell to Spandau. LC 96-138791. 1995. 20.00 (1-85253-287-4, Pub. by Quiller Pr) St Mut.

— Race for the Reichstag: The 1945 Battle for Berlin. LC 99-13500. (Series on Soviet (Russian) Military Experience). 1999. write for info. (0-7146-4489-7, Pub. by F Cass Pubs) Intl Spec Bk.

*__Le Tissier, Tony.__ Race for the Reichstag: The 1945 Battle for Berlin. LC 99-13500. (Soviet (Russian) Military Experience Ser.: No. 5). (Illus.). 304p. 1999. 39.50 (0-7146-4929-5, Pub. by F Cass Pubs) Intl Spec Bk.

Le Tissier, Tony. Zukov at the Oder: The Decisive Battle for Berlin. LC 95-10099. 360p. 1996. 65.00 (0-275-95230-4, Praeger Pubs) Greenwood.

Le, Tony, jt. auth. see Brown, G. S.

*__Le Tord, Bijou.__ A Bird or Two: A Story about Henri Matisse. LC 98-55108. (Illus.). 32p. (J). (ps-3). 1999. 17.00 (0-8028-5184-3, Eerdmans Bks) Eerdmans.

Le Tord, Bijou. A Blue Butterfly. 1995. 21.95 (0-385-44640-3) Bantam.

— A Blue Butterfly: A Story about Claude Monet. LC 94-38779. (Illus.). 32p. (J). (ps up). 1995. 16.95 (0-385-31102-8, DD Bks Yng Read) BDD Bks Young Read.

— God's Little Seeds: A Book of Parables. LC 98-12161. (Illus.). 32p. (J). (ps-1). 1998. 15.00 (0-8028-5169-X, Eerdmans Bks) Eerdmans.

— Good Wood Bear. 1995. 10.19 (0-606-07587-9, Pub. by Turtleback) Demco.

— Little Shepherd. 1992. 14.95 (0-385-30707-1) Doubleday.

— The Little Shepherd: The 23rd Psalm. (J). 1995. 10.44 (0-606-07800-2) Turtleback.

Le, Tord Bijou. A Mountain Is to Climb. (Illus.). 40p. 5.95 (0-06-443591-1) HarpC.

Le Tord, Bijou. A Mountain Is to Climb. 40p. (J). 2001. 15.95 (0-06-028514-1) HarpC Child Bks.

— Noah's Trees. LC 98-53468. (Illus.). 40p. (J). (ps-1). 1999. 15.95 (0-06-028235-5); lib. bdg. 15.89 (0-06-028527-3) HarpC Child Bks.

*__Le Tord, Bijou.__ Noah's Trees. LC 98-53468. 40p. (J). (ps-1). 1999. pap. 5.95 (0-06-443540-7) HarpC Child Bks.

Le Tord, Bijou. The Little Shepherd: The 23rd Psalm. 32p. (J). (gr. 1 up). 1995. pap. 4.99 (0-440-40961-6, Yearling) BDD Bks Young Read.

Le Tourneau, Peter. Illustrated Buyer's Guide: Case Tractors. 2nd ed. LC 99-34757. (Illus.). 160p. 1999. pap. 17.95 (0-7603-0472-6, Pub. by MBI Pubg) Motorbooks Intl.

Le Tourneau, Roger. Fes avant le Protectorat: Etude economique et sociale d'une fille de l'occident musulman. LC 74-15063. (Illus.). reprint ed. 95.00 (0-404-12104-7) AMS Pr.

Le Treut, Herve, ed. Climate Sensitivity to Radiative Perturbations: Physical Mechanisms & Their Validation. LC 95-44957. (NATO ASI Ser.: Ser. 1, Vol. 34). 335p. 1995. 173.95 (3-540-60434-0) Spr-Verlag.

Le, Trong Cuc & Rambo, A. Terry, eds. Too Many People, Too Little Land: The Human Ecology of a Wet Rice-Growing Village in the Red River Delta of Vietnam. LC 93-23834. (Occasional Paper: Vol. 15). 1993. write for info. (0-86638-157-0) EW Ctr HI.

Le Trosne, Guillaume F. De l'Ordre Social. (Economistes Francais du XVIIIe Siecle Ser.). 1990. reprint ed. pap. 70.00 (3-601-00155-1) Periodicals Srv.

*__Le Va, Britta, photos by.__ The Cairo of Naguib Mahfouz. (Illus.). 96p. 1999. pap. 19.50 (977-424-526-1, Pub. by Am Univ Cairo Pr) Col U Pr.

Le Va, Britta & Ikram, Salima. Egyptian Pyramids. 60p. 1998. pap. 12.95 (977-424-464-8, Pub. by Am Univ Cairo Pr) Col U Pr.

Le Van, Gerald. Transforming Business Families. 4th ed. Marchuk, Margaret, ed. LC 96-95206. Orig. Title: Getting to Win - Win in Family Business. 320p. 1996. reprint ed. pap. 17.95 (0-9655448-0-X) Le Van Co.

Le Van, Leon C., ed. Poems from Swedenborg. LC 87-60469. 178p. (Orig.). 1987. pap. 5.95 (0-87785-134-4, Pub. by Swedenborg) Words Distrib.

Le Vasseur, Guillaume & De Beauplan, Sieur. A Description of Ukraine. LC 92-54347. (Harvard Series in Ukrainian Studies). (UKR., Illus.). 256p. 1990. text 5.00 (0-916458-40-7) Harvard Ukrainian.

— A Description of Ukraine. fac. ed. LC 92-54347. (Harvard Series in Ukrainian Studies). (FRE., Illus.). 112p. 1990. text 5.00 (0-916458-39-3) Harvard Ukrainian.

— A Description of Ukraine: Guillaume le Vasseur & Sieur de Beauplan. Pernal, Andrew B. & Essar, Dennis F., trs. LC 92-54347. (Harvard Series in Ukrainian Studies). (Illus.). cxiv, 243p. (C). 1993. text 75.00 (0-916458-44-X) Harvard Ukrainian.

*__Le Vay, Benedict.__ Eccentric Britain: The Bradt Guide to Britain's Follies & Foibles. LC 99-88559. (Illus.). 2000. pap. 18.95 (1-84162-011-4) Globe Pequot.

Le Vay, David. The History of Orthopedics. (History of Medicine Ser.). (Illus.). 693p. 1990. 125.00 (1-85070-145-8) Prthnon Pub.

— Teach Yourself Human Anatomy & Physiology. (Illus.). 384p. 1995. pap. 12.95 (0-8442-3924-0, Teach Yrslf) NTC Contemp Pub Co.

Le Vay, David, tr. see LeBlanc, Andre.

Le Vay, David, tr. see Roth, Joseph.

Le Vay, David, tr. see Wittig, Monique.

Le Vay, Simon. Albrick's Gold. LC 96-53108. 1997. 20.95 (1-56333-518-2, R Kasak Bks) Masquerade.

— Albrick's Gold. 1998. mass mkt. 7.95 (1-56333-644-8, Hard Candy) Masquerade.

Le Veque, R. J. Numerical Methods for Conservation Laws. 2nd ed. (Lectures in Mathematics ETH Zurich). 232p. 1996. 34.50 (0-8176-2723-5) Birkhauser.

Le Verdier, Zoe. Black Lace: Undercover Secrets. 1998. mass mkt. 6.95 (0-352-33285-9) BLA4.

— Black Lace Seven Year List. mass mkt. 5.95 (0-352-33254-9, Pub. by BLA4) London Brdge.

*__Le Verdier, Zoe.__ Insomnia. (Black Lace Ser.). 1999. pap. 9.99 (0-352-33345-6) Virgin Bks.

Le Verdier, Zoe. The Succubus. 1998. mass mkt. 5.95 (0-352-33230-1, Pub. by BLA4) London Brdge.

Le Vert, Suzanne. Huey Long: The Kingfish of Louisiana. LC 94-19439. (Makers of America Ser.). 144p. (J). (gr. 5-12). 1995. 19.95 (0-8160-2880-X) Facts on File.

Le Vey, David, tr. see Colette, Sidonie-Gabrielle.

Le Vine, Robert, et al, eds. Parental Behavior in Diverse Societies, No. 40. LC 85-644581. (New Directions for Child Development Ser.: No. CD 40). 1988. pap. 25.00 (1-55542-915-7) Jossey-Bass.

*__Le Vitus, Robert.__ Mac OS X for Dummies. (For Dummies Ser.). (Illus.). 424p. 2000. pap. 19.95 (0-7645-0706-0) IDG Bks.

*__Le Vot, Valerie.__ Des Livres a la Vie. (Contacts: Vol. 45). (Illus.). xiv, 451p. 1999. 56.95 (3-906760-62-6, Pub. by P Lang) P Lang Pubng.

Le Voy, David. Alexis Carrel: The Perfectibility of Man. unabridged ed. (Illus.). 402p. 1996. 79.50 (1-57529-022-7) Kabel Pubs.

Le Vrier, Philip. The Racing Kinsers: America's First Family of Sprint Car Racing. (Illus.). 205p. 1989. lib. bdg. 39.95 (0-915088-48-7) C Hungness.

Le Yaouanc, A., et al. Hadron Transitions of the Quark Model. xii, 312p. 1987. text 264.00 (2-88124-214-6) Gordon & Breach.

Le Zotte, Pam. Cahier d'Activites: Paralleles-Communication et Culture. 1994. pap. text, wbk. ed. 34.80 (0-13-249897-9) P-H.

Lea. Physics: The Nature of Things. (Physics Ser.). 1997. student ed. 18.50 (0-314-20731-7) Brooks-Cole.

— Physics: The Nature of Things. LC 99-194107. (Physics Ser.). 1997. mass mkt., student ed. 25.95 (0-314-20933-6) Wadsworth Pub.

— Physics: The Nature of Things, Vol. 1. (Physics Ser.). 1997. 68.95 (0-534-35734-2) Brooks-Cole.

— Physics: The Nature of Things, Vol. 2. (Physics Ser.). 1997. 58.95 (0-534-35735-0) Brooks-Cole.

— Understanding & Using Autocad. (West Engineering Ser.). 1989. text 44.95 (0-534-93831-0) PWS Pubs.

— What Can Be Done about Law & Order? Crisis in the '90s. 2nd ed. 284p. (C). pap. 29.95 (0-7453-0398-6, Pub. by Pluto GBR) Stylus Pub VA.

— What Done about Law & Order? Crisis in the '90s. (C). 95.95 (0-7453-0735-3, Pub. by Pluto GBR) Stylus Pub VA.

Lea & Burke. Physics: The Nature of Things. 1100p. 1997. write for info. (0-314-07012-5) West Pub.

Lea, A. P., tr. see Rosenius, Carl Olof.

Lea, Ani. Altura: Fusion of the Soul. 64p. (Orig.). 1995. pap. text 7.95 (0-9645725-2-4) Numina.

Lea, C. After CFCS? Options for Cleaning Electronics Assemblies. 395p. 1997. pap. 348.00 (0-901150-25-8) St Mut.

— A Scientific Guide to Surface Mount Technology. 569p. 1997. pap. 352.00 (0-901150-22-3) St Mut.

Lea, C. A. On Trek in Kordofan: The Diaries of a British District Officer in the Sudan, 1931-1933. Daly, Martin W., ed. (Oriental & African Archives Ser.: No. 2). (Illus.). 314p. 1994. text 49.95 (0-19-726128-0) OUP.

Lea, Carole A. Guess What, Mrs. Lea? 58p. (Orig.). 1990. pap. 10.00 (0-9625906-0-6) C A Lea.

Lea, Charles. Lee Papers. (Notable American Authors Ser.). 1999. reprint ed. lib. bdg. 125.00 (0-7812-3785-8) Rprt Serv.

— Strictures on a Pamphlet Entitled "A Friendly Address to All Reasonable Americans" (Notable American Authors Ser.). 1999. reprint ed. lib. bdg. 125.00 (0-7812-3784-X) Rprt Serv.

Lea, Christine. The Oxford Spanish Dictionary: Spanish-English, English-Spanish. (ENG & SPA.). 512p. 1997. mass mkt. 4.99 (0-425-16009-2) Berkley Pub.

Lea, Christine, compiled by. The Oxford Color Spanish Dictionary: Spanish-English, English-Spanish; Espanol-Ingles, Ingles-Espanol. 2nd rev. ed. 528p. 1998. pap. 7.95 (0-19-860214-6) OUP.

Lea, Christine, et al, eds. The Oxford Paperback Spanish Dictionary & Grammar. LC 98-112179. (SPA.). 864p. 1997. pap. 13.95 (0-19-860079-8) OUP.

Lea, Dale H., et al. Genetics in Nursing. LC 98-10873. (Nursing Ser.). 300p. 1998. pap. 41.25 (0-7637-0542-X) Jones & Bartlett.

Lea, David, ed. Melanesian Land Tenure in a Contemporary & Philosophical Context. LC 96-28822. 204p. 1996. lib. bdg. 34.50 (0-7618-0456-0) U Pr of Amer.

Lea, David A. & Chaudhri, D. P., eds. Rural Development & the State: Contradictions & Dilemmas in Developing Countries. 338p. 1984. pap. 22.50 (0-416-31320-5, NO. 3955) Routledge.

Lea, Doug. Concurrent Programming in Java: Design Principles & Patterns. 2nd ed. (The/Java Ser.). 448p. (C). 1999. pap. text 39.95 (0-201-31009-0) Addison-Wesley.

Lea, F. Shelley & the Romantic Revolution. LC 71-164028. (Studies in Shelley: No. 25). 1971. reprint ed. lib. bdg. 75.00 (0-8383-1328-0) M S G Haskell Hse.

Lea, F. A. The Tragic Philosopher: Friedrich Nietzsche. LC 93-9875. 354p. (C). 1993. reprint ed. pap. 29.95 (0-485-12095-X, Pub. by Athlone Pr) Humanities.

Lea, F. M. & Hewlett, P. C. Lea's Chemistry of Cement & Concrete. 4th ed. LC 98-126331. xxi, 1053 p. 1998. write for info. (0-340-56589-6) Arnld Pub.

Lea, Fannie H. Jaconetta Stories. LC 76-130061. (Short Story Index Reprint Ser.). (Illus.). 1977. 17.95 (0-8369-3647-7) Ayer.

Lea, Henry. Moriscos of Spain: Their Conversion & Expulsion. LC 68-26358. (Studies in Spanish Literature: No. 36). 1969. reprint ed. lib. bdg. 75.00 (0-8383-0266-1) M S G Haskell Hse.

Lea, Henry C. Chapters from the Religious History of Spain Connected with the Inquisition. LC 83-48778. 1988. reprint ed. 54.00 (0-404-19156-8) AMS Pr.

— Chapters from the Religious History of Spain Connected with the Inquisition. (Notable American Authors Ser.). 1999. reprint ed. lib. bdg. 125.00 (0-7812-3779-3) Rprt Serv.

— An Historical Sketch of Sacerdotal Celibacy. (Notable American Authors Ser.). 1999. reprint ed. lib. bdg. 125.00 (0-7812-3775-0) Rprt Serv.

— A History of Auricular Confession & Indulgence. (Notable American Authors Ser.). 1999. reprint ed. lib. bdg. 125.00 (0-7812-3780-7) Rprt Serv.

— History of Auricular Confession & Indulgences in the Latin Church, 3 Vols. LC 68-19287. 1968. reprint ed. lib. bdg. 67.25 (0-8371-0140-9, LEHC, Greenwood Pr) Greenwood.

— History of Sacerdotal Celibacy in the Christian Church. LC 83-48779. 1988. reprint ed. 84.50 (0-404-19115-0) AMS Pr.

— A History of the Inquisition in the Middle Ages. (Notable American Authors Ser.). 1999. reprint ed. lib. bdg. 125.00 (0-7812-3778-5) Rprt Serv.

— A History of the Inquisition of Spain. (Notable American Authors Ser.). 1999. reprint ed. lib. bdg. 125.00 (0-7812-3782-3) Rprt Serv.

— History of the Inquisition of Spain, 4 vols., Set. LC 83-45968. 1988. reprint ed. 275.00 (0-404-03920-0) AMS Pr.

— A History of the Inquisition of the Middle Ages. LC 83-48776. 1988. reprint ed. 97.50 (0-404-19157-6) AMS Pr.

— The Inquisition in the Spanish Dependencies. LC 83-48777. 1988. reprint ed. 57.50 (0-404-19158-4) AMS Pr.

— The Inquisition in the Spanish Dependencies. (Notable American Authors Ser.). 1999. reprint ed. lib. bdg. 125.00 (0-7812-3783-1) Rprt Serv.

— Moriscos of Spain: Their Conversion & Expulsion. LC 68-19286. 463p. 1968. reprint ed. lib. bdg. 75.00 (0-8371-0141-7, LEMS, Greenwood Pr) Greenwood.

— The Moroscos of Spain: Their Conversion & Expulsion. (Notable American Authors Ser.). 1999. reprint ed. lib. bdg. 125.00 (0-7812-3781-5) Rprt Serv.

— Studies in Church History. LC 83-48780. 1988. reprint ed. 57.50 (0-404-19154-1) AMS Pr.

— Studies in Church History. (Notable American Authors Ser.). 1999. reprint ed. lib. bdg. 125.00 (0-7812-3776-9) Rprt Serv.

— Superstition & Force. LC 79-148823. (World History Ser.: No. 48). 1971. reprint ed. lib. bdg. 75.00 (0-8383-1228-4) M S G Haskell Hse.

— Superstition & Force. (Notable American Authors Ser.). 1999. reprint ed. lib. bdg. 125.00 (0-7812-3774-2) Rprt Serv.

— Translations & Other Rhymes. (Notable American Authors Ser.). 1999. reprint ed. lib. bdg. 125.00 (0-7812-3777-7) Rprt Serv.

Lea, Henry C. & Burr, George L., eds. Materials Toward a History of Witchcraft, 3 vols. LC 79-8109. reprint ed. 265.00 (0-404-18420-0) AMS Pr.

Lea, Homer. Homer Lea: Prophet of the West. 1991. lib. bdg. 65.95 (0-8490-4434-0) Gordon Pr.

Lea, Hugh, jt. auth. see Dea, Don.

Lea, J., tr. An Answer to the Untruthes Published in Spaine, in Glorie of Their Supposed Victorie Against Our English Navie. LC 72-25756. (English Experience Ser.: No. 189). 56p. 1969. reprint ed. 20.00 (90-221-0189-4) Walter J Johnson.

Lea, J. H. & Hutchinson, J. R. Lincoln: The Ancestry of Abraham Lincoln. (Illus.). 310p. 1991. reprint ed. pap. 40.00 (0-8328-1819-4); reprint ed. lib. bdg. 50.00 (0-8328-1818-6) Higginson Bk Co.

Lea, James F. Political Consciousness & American Democracy. LC 81-13133. 218p. 1982. pap. text 16.95 (0-87805-151-1) U Pr of Miss.

Lea, James Milton. You Have My Word on It. (Illus.). 60p. 1998. pap. 12.95 (0-938041-35-5) Arc Pr AR.

Lea, James W. Keeping It in the Family: Successful Succession of the Family Business. LC 90-26862. 224p. 1991. 29.95 (0-471-53913-9) Wiley.

Lea, John & Pilling, Geoff. The Condition of Britain: Essays on Frederick Engels. 182p. 1996. pap. 19.95 (0-7453-0961-5, Pub. by Pluto GBR) Stylus Pub VA.

— The Condition of Britain: Essays on Frederick Engels. LC 95-37975. 182p. (C). 1996. text 54.95 (0-7453-0962-3, Pub. by Pluto GBR) Stylus Pub VA.

Lea, John, tr. see Pitch, Tamar.

Lea, John P. Tourism & Development in the Third World. (Introductions to Development Ser.). 80p. (C). 1988. pap. 16.99 (0-415-00671-6) Routledge.

Lea, John P. & Australian National University Staff. Government & the Community in Tennant Creek, 1947-78. LC 92-208853. x, 122 p. 1989. write for info. (0-7315-0540-9, Pub. by Aust Nat Univ) UH Pr.

Lea, John P., jt. auth. see Connell, John.

Lea, Judy, ed. see McCann, Yvette B.

Lea, Katherine. Careers Encyclopedia. 14th rev. ed. 736p. 1997. text 99.50 (0-304-33740-4) Continuum.

Lea, Katherine, ed. see Segal, Audrey.

Lea, Kathleen, ed. see Fairfax, Edward.

Lea, L. J., ed. Compendium of the Scriptures. 1951. pap. 20.00 (0-8309-0253-8) Herald Pub Hse.

Lea, Larry. Armas para la Lucha Espiritual.Tr. of Weapons of Warfare. (SPA.). 240p. 1990. pap. 6.99 (0-8297-0366-7) Vida Pubs.

— Could You Not Tarry One Hour? Learning the Joy of Prayer; Our Threefold Blessings in Christ. 1990. pap. 12.99 (0-88419-210-5) Creation House.

— Llamado Supremo.Tr. of Highest Calling. (SPA.). 1992. pap. 8.99 (0-88113-105-9) Caribe Betania.

— Ni Tan Solo Una Hora.Tr. of Could You Not Tarry One Hour. (SPA.). 176p. (Orig.). 1992. pap. 7.99 (0-88113-053-2) Caribe Betania.

— Releasing the Prayer Anointing. 288p. 1996. 19.99 (0-7852-7712-9) Nelson.

— Wisdom: The Gift Worth Seeking. 1997. pap. 12.99 (0-7852-7350-6) Nelson.

*__Lea, Mary R. & Stierer, Barry.__ Student Writing in Higher Education: New Contexts LC 99-40895. 2000. pap. 37.95 (0-335-20407-4) OpUniv Pr.

Lea, Mary R., jt. auth. see Creme, Phyllis.

Lea, P. D., jt. ed. see Clark, P. U.

Lea, Per, et al. Analysis of Variance for Sensory Data. LC 96-36112. 116p. 1997. 78.00 (0-471-96750-5) Wiley.

Lea, Peter J., ed. The Genetic Manipulation of Plants & Its Application to Agriculture. (Annual Proceedings of the Phytochemical Society of Europe: Vol. 23). 400p. 1985. 30.00 (0-19-854152-X) OUP.

Lea, Peter J, ed. Methods in Plant Biochemistry Vol. 9: Enzymes of Secondary Metabolism. (Illus.). 478p. 1993. text 104.00 (0-12-461019-6) Acad Pr.

Lea, Peter J., et al, eds. Methods in Plant Biochemistry Vol. 3: Enzymes of Primary Metabolism. 414p. 1990. text 104.00 (0-12-461013-7) Acad Pr.

Lea, Peter J. & Leegood, Richard C. Plant Biochemistry & Molecular Biology. 2nd ed. LC 98-29156. 384p. 1999. pap. 54.95 (0-471-97683-0) Wiley.

*__Lea, Peter J. & Leegood, Richard C.__ Plant Biochemistry & Molecular Biology. 2nd ed. LC 98-29156. 384p. 1999. 129.95 (0-471-97682-2) Wiley.

Lea, Peter J., ed. see Hostettmann, K.

Lea, Rob. Flying the RAF's Combat Aircraft: Display Pilot. (Color Library). (Illus.). 128p. 1994. pap. 15.95 (1-85532-445-8, Pub. by Ospry) Motorbooks Intl.

Lea, Robert N., jt. auth. see Miller, Daniel J.

Lea, Rosemary. Zagat Survey: Miss Lea's Bible Stories for Children. 244p. (J). 1994. 14.95 (1-57006-003-7) Zagat.

*__Lea, Sandie.__ Encyclopedia of Candlemaking Techniques A Step-by-Step Visual Directory. 1999. 24.95 (0-7624-0601-1) Running Pr.

Lea, Sidney. No Sign. LC 86-19160. (Contemporary Poetry Ser.). 112p. 1987. 14.95 (0-8203-0916-8) U of Ga Pr.

Lea, Sperry & Webley, Simon. Multinational Corporations in Developed Countries: A Review of Recent Research & Policy Thinking. LC 73-77813. (British-North American Committee Ser.). 88p. 1973. 2.00 (0-902594-07-9) Natl Planning.

Lea, Stephen. Instinct, Environment & Behavior. Herriot, Peter, ed. LC 83-17308. (New Essential Psychology Ser.). 160p. 1984. pap. 8.95 (0-416-33640-X, NO. 4042) Routledge.

Lea, Stephen E., et al. New Directions in Economic Psychology: Theory, Experiment & Application. 304p. 1992. text 95.00 (1-85278-462-8) E Elgar.

Lea, Susan. Perspectives on Mental Handicap in South Africa. Foster, Don, ed. 1990. pap. text 45.00 (0-409-10919-3) Buttrwrth-Heinemann.

Lea, Susan M. & Burke, John R. Physics: The Nature of Things. LC 96-13354. (C). 1996. mass mkt. 116.95 (0-314-05273-9) West Pub.

Lea, Sydney. The Blaineville Testament. 96p. 1992. pap. 11.95 (0-934257-80-9) Story Line.

— Hunting the Whole Way Home. LC 94-20491. (Illus.). 211p. 1994. pap. 15.95 (0-87451-737-0) U Pr of New Eng.

— A Place in Mind. LC 97-921. (Fiction Ser.). 240p. 1997. reprint ed. pap. 12.95 (1-885266-39-1) Story Line.

*__Lea, Sydney.__ Pursuit of a Wound. LC 99-6987. 2000. pap. 14.95 (0-252-06817-3) U of Ill Pr.

Lea, Sydney. Searching the Drowned Man: Poems. LC 79-26565. 86p. 1980. 9.95 (0-252-00798-0); text 14.95 (0-252-00796-4) U of Ill Pr.

— Searching the Drowned Man: Poems. fac. ed. LC 79-26565. 84p. 1980. reprint ed. pap. 30.00 (0-7837-8075-3, 204782800008) Bks Demand.

— To the Bone: New & Selected Poems. LC 95-50189. 232p. (C). 1996. 17.95 (0-252-06519-0); text 29.95 (0-252-02223-8) U of Ill Pr.

Lea, Sydney, et al, eds. Richard Eberhart: A Celebration. 76p. (Orig.). (C). 1980. pap. 6.00 (0-917241-00-2) Kenyon Hill.

Lea, Sydney L. Gothic to Fantastic: Readings in Supernatural Fiction. Varma, Devendra P., ed. LC 79-8463. (Gothic Studies & Dissertations). 1980. lib. bdg. 28.95 (0-405-12653-0) Ayer.

Lea, T. & Trollope, B. W. A Guide to Factoring & Invoice Discounting: The New Bankers. 232p. 1995. mass mkt. 74.95 (0-412-61370-0) Chapman & Hall.

Lea, Thomas, jt. auth. see Vaughn, Curtis.

Lea, Thomas D. The New Testament: Its Background & Message. LC 93-46945. 640p. 1995. pap. 34.99 (0-8054-1078-3, 4210-78) Broadman.

Lea, Thomas D. & Griffin, Hayne P. I, II Timothy, Titus. (New American Commentary Ser.: Vol. 34). 1992. 27.99 (0-8054-0134-2) Broadman.

Lea, Thomas D. & Hudson, Tom. Step by Step Through the New Testament. 228p. 1992. pap. text 12.95 (0-8054-9946-6, LifeWy Press) LifeWay Christian.

Lea, Thomas D. & Latham, Bill. Sigueme 3: Survival Kit III. Martinez, Mario, tr. from ENG. (SPA.). 128p. (Orig.). (YA). (gr. 5 up). 1989. pap. 7.50 (0-311-13847-0) Casa Bautista.

Lea, Thomas D., jt. auth. see Vaughan, Curtis.

Lea, Thomas S., et al. Materials for the Study of the Apostolic Gnosis. 130p. 1997. reprint ed. pap. 19.95 (0-7661-0098-7) Kessinger Pub.

An Asterisk (*) at the beginning of an entry indicates that the title is appearing for the first time.

Lea, Tom. The King Ranch, 2 vols., Set. (Illus.). 1957. boxed set 125.00 (*0-316-51745-3*) Little.

Lea, Wayne A. Selecting, Designing, & Using Speech Recognizers. (Speech Technology Ser.). (Illus.). 400p. 1982. 74.00 (*0-686-37644-7*); student ed. 49.00 (*0-686-37645-5*) Speech Science.

***Leab, Daniel J.** I Was a Communist for the F. B. I. The Unhappy Life & Times of Matt Cvetic. LC 00-35660. 2000. write for info. (*0-271-02053-9*) Pa St U Pr.

Leab, Daniel J. & Mason, Philip P., eds. Labor History Archives in the United States. LC 91-38550. 286p. 1992. pap. 18.95 (*0-8143-2389-8*) Wayne St U Pr.

— Labor History Archives in the United States: A Guide for Researching & Teaching. LC 91-38550. 286p. reprint ed. pap. 88.70 (*0-608-10580-5*, 2071201) Bks Demand.

Leab, Daniel J. & Morris, Richard B., eds. Labor History Reader. (Working Class in American History Ser.). 496p. 1985. text 39.95 (*0-252-01197-X*); pap. text 19.95 (*0-252-01198-8*) U of Ill Pr.

Leab, Katharine K., ed. American Book Prices Current, Vol. 101. rev. ed. 1100p. 1996. 140.00 (*0-914022-30-X*) Bancroft Parkman.

— American Book Prices Current, Vol. 102, 1996. 1050p. 1997. 131.95 (*0-914022-32-6*) Bancroft Parkman.

— American Book Prices Current, Vol. 103. 1100p. 1998. 143.00 (*0-914022-33-4*) Bancroft Parkman.

Leabeater, C. W. Inner Life (1911) 412p. 1998. reprint ed. pap. 17.95 (*0-7661-0557-1*) Kessinger Pub.

— The Perfume of Egypt & Other Stories. 270p. 1993. reprint ed. pap. 16.95 (*1-56459-381-9*) Kessinger Pub.

Leabhart, E. Thomas, et al, eds. Words on Decroux 2: Mime Journal - 1997. (Illus.). 120p. 1997. pap. 20.00 (*1-887482-02-4*) Mime Jour.

Leabhart, Thomas. Modern & Post-Modern Mime. 184p. 1998. pap. 18.95 (*0-312-17451-9*) St Martin.

Leabhart, Thomas, et al, eds. Theatre & Sport: Mime Journal - 1996. (Illus.). 112p. (Orig.). 1996. pap. 20.00 (*1-887482-01-6*) Mime Jour.

Leabhart, Thomas, ed. see Abdoh, et al.

Leabhart, Thomas, ed. see Bu, Peter.

Leabhart, Thomas, ed. see Decroux, Etienne.

Leabhart, Thomas, ed. see Moore, Jim, et al.

Leabhart, Thomas, ed. see Shank.

Leabo, Karen. Beach Baby. (Desire Ser.). 1995. per. 3.25 (*0-373-05922-1*, 1-05922-9) Silhouette.

— A Changed Man. large type ed. 224p. 1993. reprint ed. lib. bdg. 13.95 (*1-56054-612-3*) Thorndike Pr.

— Etroite Surveillance. (Amours d'Aujourd'Hui Ser.: Vol. 298). 1998. mass mkt. 4.99 (*0-373-38298-7*, 1-28298-5) Harlequin Bks.

— Feathers & Lace. (Desire Ser.). 1993. per. 2.99 (*0-373-05824-1*, 5-05824-3) Silhouette.

— Framed. (Intimate Moments Ser.). 1997. per. 3.99 (*0-373-07772-6*, 1-07772-6) Silhouette.

— The Housewarming. (Romance Ser.: No. 848). 1992. per. 2.59 (*0-373-08848-5*, 5-08848-9) Silhouette.

— L' Innocence en Danger. (Amours d'Aujourd'Hui Ser.: No. 337). (FRE.). 1999. mass mkt. 5.50 (*0-373-38337-1*, 1-38337-1) Harlequin Bks.

— Into Thin Air. (Intimate Moments Ser.). 1995. per. 3.75 (*0-373-07619-3*, 1-07619-9) Silhouette.

— Le Magicien des Bayous. (Rouge Passion Ser.). (FRE.). 1994. pap. 3.50 (*0-373-37292-2*, 1-37292-9) Harlequin Bks.

— Man Overboard. (Desire Ser.). 1995. per. 3.25 (*0-373-05946-9*, 1-05946-8) Silhouette.

— Megan's Miracle. (Desire Ser.). 1994. per. 2.99 (*0-373-05880-2*, 1-05880-9) Silhouette.

— Midnight Confessions. (Intimate Moments Ser.). 1996. per. 3.99 (*0-373-07734-3*, 1-07734-6) Silhouette.

— El Novio Perdido: The Prodigal Groom. (SPA.). 1997. per. 3.50 (*0-373-35175-5*, 1-35175-8) Harlequin Bks.

— The Prodigal Groom: The Wedding Night. (Desire Ser.). 1996. per. 3.50 (*0-373-76007-8*, 1-76007-3) Silhouette.

— Ryan's Rescue. (Intimate Moments Ser.: No. 832). 1998. per. 3.99 (*0-373-07832-3*, 1-07832-8) Silhouette.

— Twilight Man. (Desire Ser.). 1994. mass mkt. 2.99 (*0-373-05838-1*, 5-05838-3) Silhouette.

Leabo, Karl, ed. Tragical Comedy or Comical Tragedy of Punch & Judy. LC 83-70096. (Illus.). 1983. pap. 2.50 (*0-87830-582-3*, Thtre Arts Bks) Routledge.

Leacacos, John P. Fires in the In-Basket: The ABC's of the State Department. LC 75-36097. 1977. reprint ed. lib. bdg. 85.00 (*0-8371-8623-4*, LEFI, Greenwood Pr) Greenwood.

***Leach.** Advanced Java Networking. 2nd ed. (Illus.). 424p. 2000. pap. 44.99 (*0-13-084466-7*) P-H.

— AutoCAD 2000 Instructor. LC 99-16021. 1200p. 1999. pap. 62.50 (*0-07-234761-9*) McGraw.

Leach. Cadkey Companion for Windows. LC 97-40529. 1997. pap. text 29.56 (*0-256-26693-X*, Irwn McGrw-H) McGrw-H Hghr Educ.

— Discrete & Integral Circuit Electricity. (C). 1992. pap. text, lab manual ed. 35.50 (*0-03-020848-3*, Pub. by Harcourt Coll Pubs) Harcourt.

— Entrepreneurial Finance. 2001. 51.00 (*0-07-235604-9*) McGraw.

Leach & Logan. Future Interests & Estate Planning. 1961 text 32.00 (*0-88277-512-X*) Foundation Pr.

— 1962 Supplement to Future Interests & Estate Planning. 1962. pap. text 6.25 (*0-88277-389-5*) Foundation Pr.

Leach, A. F. Schools of Medieval England. LC 68-56478. (Illus.). 1972. reprint ed. 23.95 (*0-405-08740-3*) Ayer.

Leach, A. J. History of Antelope County: From Its First Settlement in 1868 to the Close of the Year 1883. (Illus.). 262p. 1997. reprint ed. lib. bdg. 35.00 (*0-8328-6863-9*) Higginson Bk Co.

Leach, Alice, jt. auth. see Jenkins, Lindsay.

Leach, Andrew R. Molecual Modelling. 585p. (C). 1996. pap. 69.00 (*0-582-23933-8*) Addison-Wesley.

Leach, Andy & Lumby, Ted. Christmas Balloons. (Henderson Activity Packs Ser.). 1998. pap. 4.95 (*0-7894-3718-X*) DK Pub Inc.

— Spooky Balloons. (Activity Fun Packs Ser.). 8p. 1998. pap. 4.95 (*0-7894-3719-8*) DK Pub Inc.

Leach, Ann. Oh, Doug! A Dragonfly's Day. (Illus.). 26p. (J). (gr. k-3). 1999. pap. 10.95 (*1-929150-00-8*) Take Flight.

Leach, Anne, ed. Marketing Your Indexing Services. LC 94-46408. 1995. 15.00 (*0-936547-28-6*) Am Soc Index.

— Marketing Your Indexing Services. 2nd ed. LC 98-21547. 70p. 1998. pap. 20.00 (*1-57387-054-4*) Info Today Inc.

Leach, Arthur F. Educational Charters & Documents, 598-1909. LC 76-137263. reprint ed. 54.00 (*0-404-03893-X*) AMS Pr.

Leach, Bernadette. 4 Ever Friends. (Bright Sparks Ser.). 176p. (YA). (gr. 8 up). 1998. pap. 4.95 (*1-85594-189-9*, Pub. by Attic Press) Intl Spec Bk.

Leach, Bernard. Bernard Leach. 1966. boxed set 400.00 (*0-685-45126-7*) R S Barnes.

— An Exhibition of the Art of Bernard Leach: His Masterpieces Loaned by British Museums & Collectors. (Illus.). 192p. 1980. pap. 100.00 (*0-685-45125-9*) R S Barnes.

— Hamada, Potter. (Illus.). 232p. 1997. reprint ed. pap. 35.00 (*0-87011-828-5*) Kodansha.

— My Faith. (Illus.). 1966. pap. 40.00 (*0-685-45124-0*) R S Barnes.

— Potter's Book. (J). 1946. pap. 14.00 (*0-693-01157-2*) Transatl Arts.

Leach, Bernard. Potters Book. 1988. pap. 29.95 (*0-571-10973-X*) Faber & Faber.

Leach, Billie A., jt. auth. see Leach, Dan.

***Leach, Bob.** Saloon Stories. LaRovere, Richard, ed. 115p. 1999. pap. 12.00 (*0-9674607-0-0*) Jersey City Libr.

Leach, Catherine, tr. see Harasymowicz, Jerzy.

Leach, Catherine S., ed. see Pasek, Jan Chryzostom.

Leach, Catherine S., tr. see Lem, Stanislaw.

Leach, Catherine S., tr. see Milosz, Czeslaw.

Leach, Charles. The Primordial Field. 24p. 1996. reprint ed. spiral bd. 10.50 (*0-7873-0540-5*) Hlth Research.

Leach, Charles D., ed. & frwd. see Hermansen, Knud E.

Leach, Charles R. In Tornado's Wake, a History of the 8th Armored Division. (Divisional Ser.: No. 42). (Illus.). 240p. reprint ed. 39.95 (*0-89839-176-8*) Battery Pr.

Leach, Chris. Introduction to Statistics: A Nonparametric Approach for the Social Sciences. LC 78-10194. (Illus.). 363p. reprint ed. pap. 112.60 (*0-8357-4320-9*, 203711900007) Bks Demand.

Leach, Cliff. NT: A Strategic Review. 400p. (C). 1993. pap. text 75.00 (*0-13-045261-0*) P-H.

Leach, Corl A. Aids to Goatkeeping. 15.00 (*0-686-26686-2*) Dairy Goat.

Leach, D. Genetic Recombination. 1996. pap. 39.95 (*0-632-03861-6*) Blackwell Sci.

Leach, D. & Schamhardt, H. C., eds. Animal Locomotion. (Journal: Acta Anatomica: Vol. 146, No. 2-3, 1993). (Illus.). 124p. 1993. pap. 214.00 (*3-8055-5777-9*) S Karger.

Leach, Dan & Leach, Billie A. Johnson County, Texas: A Pictorial History. LC 97-27971. 1997. write for info. (*1-57864-005-9*) Donning Co.

Leach, Dawn. Richard Hamilton: The Beginnings of His Art. LC 93-12559. (European University Studies: History of Art: Ser. 28, Vol. 159). (Illus.). 201p. 1993. 38.00 (*3-631-45755-3*) P Lang Pubng.

Leach, Donald P. Basic Electric Circuits. 3rd ed. LC 83-21794. 834p. (C). 1984. text 49.50 (*0-471-05421-6*) P-H.

— Basic Electric Circuits. 3rd ed. LC 83-21794. 834p. (C). 1984. pap. text 19.50 (*0-471-88496-0*) P-H.

— Basic Electric Circuits. 3rd ed. LC 83-21794. 834p. (C). 1984. pap. text 6.00 (*0-471-88497-9*) P-H.

— Discrete & Integrated Circuit Electronics. 790p. (C). 1992. text 85.00 (*0-03-020844-0*) SCP.

— Mathematics for Electronics. 2nd ed. (Illus.). 448p. (C). 1987. text. write for info. (*0-318-61354-9*) P-H.

Leach, Donald P. & Malvino, Albert P. Digital Principles & Applications. 5th ed. LC 93-29589. 1993. 83.95 (*0-02-801821-4*) Glencoe.

Leach, Douglas E. Flintlock & Tomahawk: New England in King Philip's War. LC 58-5467. 320p. (YA). 1992. reprint ed. pap. 12.95 (*0-940160-55-2*) Parnassus Imprints.

— Now Hear This: The Memoir of a Junior Naval Officer in the Great Pacific War. fac. ed. LC 87-3905. (Illus.). 202p. 1987. pap. 62.70 (*0-7837-7630-6*, 204738200007) Bks Demand.

— Roots of Conflict: British Armed Forces & Colonial Americans, 1677-1763. LC 85-24492. xv, 232p. (C). 1989. reprint ed. pap. 18.95 (*0-8078-4258-3*) U of NC Pr.

***Leach, Edmund.** Anthropology & Society, Vol. 1. Hugh-Jones, Stephen & Laidlaw, James, eds. 384p. 2000. 40.00 (*0-300-08124-3*) Yale U Pr.

— Culture & Human Nature, Vol. 2. Hugh-Jones, Stephen & Laidlaw, James, eds. 384p. 2000. 40.00 (*0-300-08508-7*) Yale U Pr.

Leach, Edmund. Pul Eliya, A Village in Ceylon: A Study of Land Tenure & Kinship. LC 61-1517. 375p. reprint ed. pap. 106.90 (*0-608-12064-2*, 2024486) Bks Demand.

Leach, Edmund R. Claude Levi-Strauss. 160p. 1989. pap. 11.95 (*0-226-46968-9*) U Ch Pr.

— Culture & Communication. LC 75-30439. (Themes in the Social Sciences Ser.). (Illus.). 105p. 1976. pap. text 18.95 (*0-521-29052-X*) Cambridge U Pr.

— Political Systems of Highlands Burma: A Study of Kachin Social Structure. 4th ed. (Monographs on Social Anthropology: No.44). (Illus.). 324p. (C). 1954. pap. 25.00 (*0-485-19644-1*, Pub. by Athlone Pr) Humanities.

— Rethinking Anthropology. 5th ed. (London School of Economics Monographs on Social Anthropology: No. 22). 146p. (C). 1961. pap. 18.50 (*0-485-19622-0*, Pub. by Athlone Pr) Humanities.

Leach, Edmund R., ed. Structural Study of Myth & Totemism. (Orig.). 1968. pap. 13.95 (*0-422-72530-7*, NO.2287, Pub. by Tavistock) Routldge.

Leach, Eleanor W. The Rhetoric of Space: Literary & Artistic Representations of Landscape in Republican & Augustan Rome. LC 88-19668. (Illus.). 537p. 1988. reprint ed. pap. 166.50 (*0-608-02500-3*, 206314400004) Bks Demand.

— Vergil's Eclogues: Landscapes of Experience. LC 73-17699. (Illus.). 288p. 1974. text 47.50 (*0-8014-0820-2*) Cornell U Pr.

Leach, Elizabeth, jt. auth. see Klinkersberg, Marty.

Leach, Eugene W. Racine/Civil War Racine County Militant: Illustrated Narrative of War Times, Also a Soldiers' Roster, a Pioneer Publication. (Illus.). 394p. 1997. reprint ed. lib. bdg. 41.50 (*0-8328-6984-8*) Higginson Bk Co.

Leach, Fiona E., jt. ed. see Little, Angela W.

Leach, Frank A. Recollections of a Newspaperman: A Record of Life & Events in California. (American Biography Ser.). 146p. 1991. reprint ed. lib. bdg. 59.00 (*0-7812-8239-X*) Rprt Serv.

Leach, Frank A. & Bowers, David Q. Recollections of a Mint Director. (Illus.). 136p. (Orig.). 1987. pap. 9.95 (*0-943161-01-0*) Bowers & Merena.

Leach, G. E., et al. The American Urological Association Female Stress Urinary Incontinence Clinical Guidelines Panel: Report on the Surgical Management of Female Stress Urinary Incontinence. 80p. 1997. pap. text 49.00 (*0-9649702-3-6*) Am Urological.

Leach, George W. UNIX: Self Teaching Guide. 272p. 1992. pap. 22.95 (*0-471-57924-6*) Wiley.

Leach, George W. & Topham, Douglas W. UNIX: Self-Teaching Guide & Portable UNIX, 2 vols., Set. 560p. 1993. pap. text 34.90 (*0-471-59678-7*) Wiley.

Leach, Graham. South Africa: No Easy Path to Peace. (Illus.). 312p. 1987. pap. 8.95 (*0-413-15330-4*, A0168) Routledge.

Leach, Hamish A. The Founding of Fort Amherstburg (Malden) along the Detroit Frontier-1796: A Political, Military, & Legal Frontier Study, with Computer Applications. LC 74-20147. (Veldt Protea International Study, An Official American Bicentennial Heritage Project, Registered As Part of the Nederland-Amerika Bicentennial). (Illus.). xxxii, 593p. 1984. 32.50 (*0-917538-01-3*) Veldt Protea Inst.

Leach, Henry G., ed. Pageant of Old Scandinavia. LC 68-57061. (Granger Index Reprint Ser.). 1977. 21.95 (*0-8369-6025-4*) Ayer.

Leach, J. G. Bringhurst: History of the Bringhurst Family with Notes on the Clarkson, de Peyster & Boude Families. (Illus.). 152p. 1992. reprint ed. pap. 24.00 (*0-8328-2646-4*); reprint ed. lib. bdg. 34.00 (*0-8328-2645-6*) Higginson Bk Co.

Leach, J. G., ed. see Carter, C. M.

Leach, J. J., et al, eds. Science, Decision & Value. LC 72-77877. (Western Ontario Ser.: Vol. 1). 220p. 1973. lib. bdg. 80.00 (*90-277-0239-X*, D Reidel) Kluwer Academic.

Leach, J. W. Two Tickets to the Revolution, Please. LC 94-66621. 105p. (Orig.). Date not set. pap. write for info. (*0-9641752-4-X*) J L Loving.

Leach, James, et al, contrib. by. Global Derivatives: Public Sector Responses. (Occasional Paper Ser.: No. 44). 46p. (Orig.). 1994. pap. 10.00 (*1-56708-040-5*) Grp of Thirty.

Leach, James & McKenzie, William P., eds. A Newer World: The Progressive Republican Vision of America. LC 88-21529. 172p. 1988. 16.95 (*0-8191-6827-0*) Madison Bks UPA.

Leach, James, jt. auth. see Giannetti, Louis D.

Leach, James A. AutoCAD Companion. 448p. (C). 1995. text 26.95 (*0-256-18296-5*, Irwn McGrw-H) McGrw-H Hghr Educ.

— AutoCAD Companion. LC 94-48563. (Graphics Ser.). 1995. write for info. (*0-256-16137-2*, Irwn McGrw-H) McGrw-H Hghr Educ.

— AutoCAD 14 Companion. LC 98-5483. 650p. 1998. pap. 30.50 (*0-256-26692-1*) McGraw-Hill Prof.

— AutoCAD 14 Instructor. LC 97-49114. 850p. 1997. pap. 36.74 (*0-256-26602-6*) McGraw-Hill Prof.

— AutoCAD Instructor: Release 12. LC 95-22409. 892p. (C). 1995. text 41.95 (*0-256-20223-0*, Irwn Prfssnl) McGraw-Hill Prof.

— AutoCAD 13 Companion. 496p. (C). 1995. text 25.95 (*0-256-19446-7*, Irwn Prfssnl) McGraw-Hill Prof.

— AutoCAD 13 Instructor. LC 95-45018. (Irwin Graphics Ser.). 896p. (C). 1995. text 43.95 (*0-256-19445-9*, Irwn McGrw-H) McGrw-H Hghr Educ.

***Leach, James A.** Autocad 2000 Companion. LC 99-56121. (Irwin Graphics Ser.). 2000. write for info. (*0-07-236298-7*) McGraw.

— AutoCAD 2000 Companion. LC 99-56121. 2000. write for info. (*0-07-234973-5*) McGrw-H Hghr Educ.

***Leach, James A., ed.** The Eizenstat Report & Related Issues Concerning United States & Allied Efforts to Restore Gold & Other Assets Looted by Nazis During World War II: Congressional Hearing. 313p. (C). 1999. reprint ed. pap. text 40.00 (*0-7881-8231-5*) DIANE Pub.

Leach, James A., ed. H. R. 607 - The Homeowners Insurance Protection Act: Congressional Hearing. (Illus.). 167p. (C). 1999. reprint ed. pap. text 30.00 (*0-7881-7522-X*) DIANE Pub.

— International Monetary Fund Reform & Authorizaiton Act of 1998. 53p. (C). 1999. pap. text 20.00 (*0-7881-7845-8*) DIANE Pub.

— Millennium Bug: Banking & the Year 2000 Computer Problem. 167p. (C). 1999. pap. text 25.00 (*0-7881-7840-7*) DIANE Pub.

***Leach, James A., ed.** Personal Banking Fraud: Hearings Before the Committee on Banking & Financial Services, U. S. House of Representatives. 144p. 2000. reprint ed. pap. text 25.00 (*0-7881-4538-X*) DIANE Pub.

— Sumitomo Corp: Hearing Before the Committee on Banking & Financial Services, U.S. House of Representatives. 134p. 1999. reprint ed. pap. text 25.00 (*0-7881-7269-7*) DIANE Pub.

Leach, James M. They Called Me Slim. 1998. pap. write for info. (*1-57532-044-4*) Press-Tige Pub.

***Leach, Jim.** Claude Jutra: Filmmaker. (Illus.). 320p. 1999. pap. 24.95 (*0-7735-2005-8*) McG-Queens Univ Pr.

Leach, Jim. A Possible Cinema: The Films of Alain Tanner. LC 84-10610. 220p. 1984. 25.00 (*0-8108-1714-4*) Scarecrow.

Leach, Joel. Earthquake Prepared: Securing Your Home, Protecting Your Family. 2nd ed. LC 94-69682. (Illus.). 102p. (Orig.). 1994. pap. 10.95 (*1-882349-42-3*) Studio Four Prods.

***Leach, Joel & Christensen, Carey.** Airfare Secrets Exposed: How to Find the Lowest Fares Available Anywhere! 3rd ed. LC 99-72794. 191p. 2000. pap. 14.95 (*1-882349-18-0*, Pub. by Studio Four Prods) ACCESS Pubs Network.

Leach, John. Pompey the Great. (Classical Lives Ser.). 256p. (Orig.). 1986. reprint ed. pap. 14.95 (*0-7099-4127-7*, Pub. by C Helm) Routldge.

— Running Applied Psychology Experiments. (Open Guides to Psychology Ser.). 160p. 1991. pap. 34.95 (*0-335-09482-1*) OpUniv Pr.

— Survival Psychology. 232p. (C). 1994. text 45.00 (*0-8147-5090-7*) NYU Pr.

***Leach, John & Paulsen, Albert Chr.** Practical Work in Science Education: Recent Research Studies. 331p. 1999. pap. 96.00 (*87-7867-079-9*) Kluwer Academic.

Leach, John B. The Muse from the Bridge. LC 97-91125. 1998. pap. 8.95 (*0-533-12565-0*) Vantage.

Leach, Joseph. Bright Particular Star: The Life & Times of Charlotte Cushman. LC 76-99829. 469p. reprint ed. pap. 145.40 (*0-8357-8048-1*, 203379800087) Bks Demand.

— Reconstruction of Nasal Tissue Deficits. LC 98-4650. (Self-Instructional Package Ser.). (Illus.). 88p. 1998. pap. text 25.00 (*1-56772-061-7*, 5506325) AAO-HNS.

Leach, Joseph & Close, Lanny. Open Rhinoplasty. LC 96-14951. (Self-Instructional Package Ser.). 1996. pap. text 25.00 (*1-56772-021-8*) AAO-HNS.

Leach, Joseph H., jt. ed. see Claudi, Renata.

Leach, Joseph L., jt. auth. see Howard, Brian K.

Leach, Joseph L., jt. auth. see Schaefer, Steven D.

Leach, Josiah G. History of the Bringhurst Family: With Notes on the Clarkson, De Peyster & Boude Families. With a Partial Listing of 20th Century Bringhurst Descendents by Robert Taylor. 2nd ed. LC 89-85223. (Illus.). 200p. 1989. reprint ed. lib. bdg. 24.75 (*0-944419-11-9*) Everett Inc.

Leach, Joy. A Practical Guide to Working with Diversity: The Process, the Tools, the Resources. LC 94-44293. 320p. 1995. 55.00 (*0-8144-0244-5*) AMACOM.

Leach, Karoline. In the Shadow of the Dream Child: A New Understanding of Lewis Carroll. LC 00-502453. (Illus.). 294p. 1999. 34.95 (*0-7206-1044-3*, Pub. by P Owen Ltd) Dufour.

— The Mysterious Mr Love: A Play LC 98-232331. 51 p. 1997. write for info. (*0-573-01830-8*) French.

Leach, Kristine. Walking Common Ground: Nineteenth & Twentieth Century Immigrant Women in America. 112p. 1996. 69.95 (*1-57292-021-1*); pap. text 49.95 (*1-57292-020-3*) Austin & Winfield.

Leach, L. York. Indian Miniature Paintings & Drawings, Pt. One. LC 85-7740. (Illus.). 334p. 1986. 50.00 (*0-910386-78-1*) Cleveland Mus Art.

An Asterisk (*) at the beginning of an entry indicates that the title is appearing for the first time.

L

Leach, Linda. Paintings from India. LC 99-214280. (The Nasser D. Khanlili Collection of Islamic Art: No. VIII). (Illus.). 260p. 1999. text 280.00 (*0-19-727629-6*) OUP.

Leach, M., ed. Paris & Vienne Translated from the French & Printed by William Caxton. (EETS Original Ser.: No. 234). 1970. reprint ed. 30.00 (*0-19-722234-X*, Pub. by EETS) Boydell & Brewer.

Leach, MacEdward & Glassie, Henry H. A Guide for Collectors of Oral Traditions & Folk Cultural Material in Pennsylvania. LC 72-650605. (Illus.). 70p. (Orig.). (C). 1973. pap. 3.95 (*0-911124-60-8*) Pa Hist & Mus.

Leach, Maria. The Lion Sneezed: Folktales & Myths of the Cat. LC 77-3665. (J). (gr. 3-5). 1977. 12.95 (*0-690-01364-7*) HarpC Child Bks.

Leach, Maria, ed. The Ultimate Insult. LC 97-27584. 256p. 1997. pap. 11.95 (*0-7867-0487-X*) Carroll & Graf.

Leach, Maria, ed. see Wilde, Oscar.

Leach, Marianne, compiled by. Newspaper Holdings of the California State Library. 396p. 1986. pap. 40.00 (*0-929722-09-4*) CA State Library Fndtn.

Leach, Marjorie. A Guide to the Gods: A Dictionary of the Functions & Aspects of Deities. LC 91-35820. (Mythology & Religion Ser.). 995p. 1991. lib. bdg. 150.00 (*0-87436-591-0*) ABC-CLIO.

Leach, Mark, contrib. by. Inside Out: Contemporary Japanese Photography. LC 94-78582. (Illus.). 57p. 1994. pap. 20.00 (*0-9642772-0-4*, Pub. by Light Factory) RAM Publications.

Leach, Mark C & Morse, Peter, eds. The Illustrated Bartsch Vol. 2: Netherlandish Artists. LC 79-50679. 1978. lib. bdg. 149.00 (*0-89835-002-6*) Abaris Bks.

Leach, Mark C., jt. ed. see Bellini, Paolo.

Leach, Mark R., contrib. by. Structure & Surface: Beads in Contemporary American Art. (Illus.). 48p. 1990. pap. 15.95 (*0-932718-28-0*) Kohler Arts.

Leach, Mark Richard, et al. Michael Lucero: Sculpture 1976-1995. LC 95-43867. (Illus.). 160p. 1996. 45.00 (*1-55595-126-0*, Pub. by Hudson Hills) Natl Bk Netwk.

Leach, Martha L. The Attributes of Lent: Repentance, Sacrifice, Commitment, Humility, Faith, Service. 55p. (Orig.). 1996. pap. 6.95 (*0-7880-0568-5*) CSS OH.

Leach, Maureen, jt. auth. see Schreck, Nancy.

Leach, Melissa & Mearns, Robin. The Lie of the Land: Challenging Received Wisdom on the African Environment. LC 96-49147. (African Issues Ser.). 1996. 80.00 (*0-435-07407-5*); pap. 24.00 (*0-435-07408-3*) Heinemann.

Leach, Melissa, jt. auth. see Fairhead, James.

Leach, Michael. Great Apes. (Illus.). 176p. 1998. pap. 19.95 (*0-7137-2614-8*, Pub. by Blandford Pr) Sterling.

— Mice of the British Isles. (Natural History Ser.: No. 54). (Illus.). 24p. 1989. pap. 5.25 (*0-7478-0056-1*, Pub. by Shire Pubns) Parkwest Pubns.

— The Rabbit. (Natural History Ser.: No. 39). (Illus.). 24p. pap. 5.25 (*0-7478-0021-9*, Pub. by Shire Pubns) Parkwest Pubns.

***Leach, Michael, et al, eds.** The Rise & Fall of One Nation. 2000. pap. 29.95 (*0-7022-3136-3*, Pub. by Univ Queensland Pr) Intl Spec Bk.

***Leach, Michael & Borchard, Therese Johnson.** I Like Being Catholic: Treasured Traditions, Rituals & Stories. LC 00-38424. 176p. 2000. 19.95 (*0-385-49951-5*) Doubleday.

Leach, Michael, jt. ed. see Borchard, Therese.

Leach, Mortimer. Lettering for Advertising. LC 56-10596. 244p. reprint ed. pap. 75.70 (*0-608-11285-2*, 200578900060) Bks Demand.

Leach, Neil. The Anaesthetics of Architecture. LC 98-37597. (Illus.). 120p. 1999. pap. text 16.50 (*0-262-62126-6*) MIT Pr.

— Architecture & Revolution: Contemporary Perspectives on Central & Eastern Europe. LC 98-26183. 16p. 1999. write for info. (*0-415-13914-7*); pap. write for info. (*0-415-13915-5*) Routledge.

— Rethinking Architecture: A Reader in Cultural Theory. LC 96-19406. 416p. 1997. pap. 24.99 (*0-415-12826-9*) Routledge.

— Rethinking Architecture: A Reader in Cultural Theory. LC 96-19406. 432p. (C). 1997. 85.00 (*0-415-12825-0*) Routledge.

Leach, Nell. Millennium Culture. pap. 12.00 (*1-84166-025-6*, Pub. by Ellipsis) Norton.

Leach, Nicholas. Lifeboats. (Album Ser.: No. 336). (Illus.). 32p. 1998. pap. 6.25 (*0-7478-0366-8*, Pub. by Shire Pubns) Parkwest Pubns.

Leach, Nicky. Arches & Canyonlands National Parks. (Pocket Portfolio Ser.: Vol. 1). (ENG & FRE., Illus.). 32p. (Orig.). 1997. pap. 6.95 (*0-939365-70-7*); pap. 6.95 (*0-939365-69-3*); pap. 6.95 (*0-939365-71-5*); pap. 6.95 (*0-939365-72-3*) Panorama Intl.

— Arches & Canyonlands National Parks. (Pocket Portfolio Ser.: Vol.1). (Illus.). 32p. (Orig.). 1997. pap. 5.95 (*0-939365-53-7*) Panorama Intl.

— Bryce Canyon National Park. Houk, Rose & Nicholas, Jeff, eds. (Visual Interpretation Ser.). (Illus.). 48p. (Orig.). 1995. pap. 7.95 (*0-939365-42-1*) Panorama Intl.

— Cedar Breaks National Monument. Houk, Rose, ed. (Illus.). 24p. (Orig.). 1994. pap. 5.95 (*0-915630-34-6*) Zion.

***Leach, Nicky.** Columbia River Gorge National Scenic Area. Nicholas, Jeff & Bohn, Cynthia N., eds. (Pocket Portfolio Ser.: Vol. 9). (Illus.). 32p. 1998. pap. 5.95 (*0-939365-62-6*) Panorama Intl.

Leach, Nicky. Kolob Canyons: Zion National Park. Houk, Rose, ed. (Illus.). 24p. (Orig.). 1994. pap. 5.95 (*0-915630-35-4*) Zion.

— Zion National Park. Houck, Rose, ed. (Visual Interpretation Ser.). 64p. 1994. pap. 9.95 (*0-939365-36-7*) Panorama Intl.

Leach, Nicky, ed. Hawaiian National Parks: The Site-by-Site Guide. (Illus.). 48p. 1989. pap. 5.95 (*0-917859-11-1*) Sunrise SBCA.

Leach, Nicky, ed. see Aitchison, Stewart & Yazzie, Susie.

Leach, Nicky, ed. see Gilmore, Jackie.

Leach, Nicky, ed. see Lister, Florence & Wilson, Lynn.

Leach, Nicky, ed. see Nicholas, Jeff.

Leach, Nicky, ed. see Robinson, George B.

Leach, Nicky, ed. see Warfield, Ron.

Leach, Nicky, ed. see Warneke, Al.

Leach, Nicky, ed. see Wilson, Lynn.

Leach, Nicky, ed. see Wilson, Lynn, et al.

Leach, Nicky, ed. see Wuerthner, George.

Leach, Nicky J. The Guide to National Parks of the Southwest. Houk, Rose et al, eds. LC 91-68245. (Illus.). 80p. 1992. pap. 9.95 (*1-877856-14-2*) SW Pks Mnmts.

***Leach, Nicky J.** Whale Watching LC 99-36005. (Insight Guides Ser.). 1999. 19.95 (*1-56331-836-9*) Discovery.

Leach, Nicky J. Wild West. LC 99-26078. (Travel Adventures Ser.). 1999. write for info. (*1-56331-833-4*) Discovery.

Leach, Noel J. Modern Wood Finishing Techniques. LC 92-37402. (Illus.). 256p. 1993. pap. 29.95 (*0-941936-24-4*) Linden Pub Fresno.

Leach, Norman. My Wicked Stepmother. LC 92-19674. (Illus.). 32p. (J). (ps-3). 1993. lib. bdg. 13.95 (*0-02-754700-0*, Mac Bks Young Read) S&S Childrens.

— The Seventh Door. (Illus.). (J). 1995. 13.99 (*0-85953-947-4*) Childs Play.

— The Seventh Door. (Children's Stories Published in Other Lands Ser.: Vol. 4). (Illus.). 32p. (J). (gr. k-3). 1997. lib. bdg. 16.95 (*1-56674-211-0*) Forest Hse.

Leach, P. G., et al, eds. Dynamical Systems, Plasmas & Gravitation: Selected Papers from a Conference Held in Orleans la Source, France 22-24 June, 1997. LC 99-13370. (Lecture Notes in Physics Ser.: Vol. 518). xii, 405p. 1999. 95.00 (*3-540-65467-4*) Spr-Verlag.

Leach, P. G. & Steeb, W. H., eds. Finite Dimensional Integrable Nonlinear Dynamical Systems: Proceedings of the Workshop on Finite Dimensional Integrable Nonlinear Dynamical Systems. 356p. 1988. text 84.00 (*9971-5-0541-X*) World Scientific Pub.

Leach, Patricia E. Because I Love You. 193p. 1994. 19.95 (*0-9642323-0-8*) Garnet Hse Pub.

Leach, Patrick, jt. auth. see Leach, Sheryl.

Leach, Penelope. Babyhood. 2nd enl. rev. ed. LC 82-48881. 1983. pap. 19.00 (*0-394-71436-9*) Knopf.

— Children First: What Our Society Must Do--& Is Doing--for Our Children Today. 1994. 22.00 (*0-679-42133-5*) Random.

— Children First: What Society Must Do - & Is Not Doing - for Children Today. 1995. pap. 13.00 (*0-679-75466-0*) Vin Bks.

— Your Baby & Child: From Birth to Age Five. LC 97-29325. 560p. 1997. 35.00 (*0-375-40007-9*) Knopf.

— Your Baby & Child: From Birth to Age Five. 3rd rev. ed. LC 97-29325. (Illus.). 559p. 1997. pap. 20.00 (*0-375-70000-5*) Knopf.

— Your Growing Child: From Babyhood Through Adolescence. 1986. pap. 19.95 (*0-394-71066-5*) Knopf.

Leach, Peter. James Paine. Harris, John & Laing, Alastair, eds. LC 87-50752. (Studies in Architecture). (Illus.). 240p. 1988. 95.00 (*0-302-00602-8*, Pub. by Zwemmer Bks) Intl Spec Bk.

***Leach, Peter.** Tales of Resistance. LC 99-27190. 1999. pap. text 15.00 (*1-881515-21-4*) TX Review Pr.

Leach, R. J. International Schools & Their Role in the Field of International Education. (C). 1969. 130.00 (*0-08-013037-2*, Pub. by Pergamon Repr) Franklin.

Leach, R. M., jt. auth. see Jeffrey, Hugh C.

***Leach, Richard E. & Ory, Steven J.** Management of Ectopic Pregnancy. LC 99-16453. (Illus.). 1999. 65.00 (*0-632-04469-1*) Blackwell Sci.

Leach, Richard H., ed. Contemporary Canada. LC 68-17411. (Duke University Commonwealth Studies Center: No. 32). 340p. reprint ed. 105.40 (*0-608-16105-5*, 201790900010) Bks Demand.

— Intergovernmental Relations in the 1980's. (Annals of Public Administration Ser.: Vol. 4). (Illus.). 120p. 1983. text 99.75 (*0-8247-1742-2*) Dekker.

Leach, Richard H., jt. auth. see Connery, Robert H.

Leach, Richard M. & Utera, Catherine. Gadabouts Cookbook & Travel Guide: Hanover - New London - Killington - Woodstock - Quechee. 288p. 1992. pap. 19.95 (*0-9633069-3-6*) Garlic NH.

— Gadabouts Cookbook & Travel Guide: Woodstock - Quechee - Killington - Hanover - New London. 288p. 1992. pap. 19.95 (*0-9633069-2-8*) Garlic NH.

Leach, Robert. British Political Ideologies. 2nd ed. LC 95-48445. (Contemporary Political Studies). 252p. (C). 1996. pap. text 34.95 (*0-13-518176-3*) P-H.

— Political Ideologies: An Australian Introduction. 2nd ed. 260p. 1994. 64.95 (*0-7329-2002-7*, Pub. by Macmill Educ); pap. 32.95 (*0-7329-2001-9*, Pub. by Macmill Educ) Paul & Co Pubs.

— Turncoats: Changing Party Allegiance by British Politicians. (Illus.). 304p. 1995. text 77.95 (*1-85521-617-5*, Pub. by Dartmth Pub) Ashgate Pub Co.

Leach, Robert & Borovsky, Victor, eds. A History of Russian Theatre. (Illus.). 425p. (C). 2000. text 90.00 (*0-521-43220-0*) Cambridge U Pr.

Leach, Robert & Gow, Peter. Quaker Nantucket. LC 97-70901. (Illus.). 224p. 1998. 29.95 (*0-9638910-7-3*) Mill Hill Pr.

Leach, Robert A. The Chiropractic Theories. 3rd ed. LC 93-17891. (Illus.). 288p. 1983. 50.00 (*0-683-04904-6*) Lppncott W & W.

Leach, Robert E., ed. Alpine Skiing. 2nd ed. LC 93-26993. (Handbook of Sports Medicine & Science Ser.). (Illus.). 144p. (Orig.). 1994. pap. text 32.00 (*0-632-03033-X*, BLEA3033, Pub. by Blckwll Scitfc UK) Human Kinetics.

Leach, Robert E., jt. auth. see Yacenda, John.

Leach, Robert J. Women Ministers: A Quaker Contribution. Blattenberger, Ruth, ed. LC 79-84922. 1979. pap. 4.00 (*0-87574-227-0*) Pendle Hill.

Leach, Robert J., ed. see Penington, Isaac.

Leach, Robert L. The Magic Cantina. 128p. 1999. pap. 9.95 (*0-9668580-0-X*) Vast Sky.

Leach, Robert P., Jr. Riggers Bible Handbook of Heavy Rigging. 1983. reprint ed. 39.95 (*0-9600992-1-2*) Riggers Bible.

Leach, Robin & Rozas, Diane. The Lifestyles of the Rich & Famous Cookbook: Recipes & Entertaining Secrets from the Most Extraordinary People in the World LC 91-45173. 280 p. 1992. 24.95 (*0-06-708445-1*) HarpC.

Leach, Ronald J. Advanced Topics in UNIX. 368p. 1994. pap. write for info. (*0-471-03663-3*); pap. text 59.95 incl. disk (*0-471-03685-4*) Wiley.

***Leach, Ronald J.** Introduction to Software Engineering. LC 99-46521. 428p. 1999. boxed set 79.95 (*0-8493-1445-3*) CRC Pr.

Leach, Sally. The Scholar at Work: An Exhibit. 53p. 1975. 12.00 (*0-87959-119-6*); pap. 6.00 (*0-87959-120-X*) U of Tex H Ransom Ctr.

Leach, Sally, compiled by. Lord Byron: A Sesquicentennial Exhibition Catalogue. (Illus.). 40p. 1975. pap. 7.00 (*0-87959-017-3*) U of Tex H Ransom Ctr.

Leach, Sally, jt. ed. see Henderson, Cathy.

***Leach, Samuel.** The Explosive Birth of the Beatles. 240p. 1999. pap. 19.95 (*1-901442-30-6*, Pub. by Pharaoh Pr) Seven Hills Bk.

Leach, Sarah S. Subgeometric Pottery from Southern Etruria. (Studies in Mediterranean Archaeology & Literature: No. 54). (Illus.). 213p. (Orig.). 1987. pap. 42.50 (*91-86098-60-8*, Pub. by P Astroms) Coronet Bks.

Leach, Sheryl. What Would Barney Say? Larsen, Margie, ed. LC 96-86262. (Barney Ser.). (Illus.). 22p. (J). (ps-k). 1996. pap. 3.25 (*1-57064-121-8*) Lyrick Pub.

Leach, Sheryl & Leach, Patrick. Barney's Book of Hugs. Larsen, Margie, ed. LC 96-86257. (Barney Ser.). (Illus.). 24p. (J). (ps-k). 1996. pap. 3.25 (*1-57064-120-X*) Lyrick Pub.

Leach, Steve. Perspectives on Local Government Reorganization. LC 97-29368. 1997. pap. write for info. (*0-7146-4416-1*, Pub. by F Cass Pubs) Intl Spec Bk.

Leach, Steve, ed. Local Government Reorganisation: The Review & Its Aftermath. LC 97-29368. 160p. 1998. 39.50 (*0-7146-4859-0*, Pub. by F Cass Pubs) Intl Spec Bk.

Leach, Steve & Davis, Howard. Enabling or Disabling Local Government: Choices for the Future. LC 95-36217. (Public Policy & Management Ser.). 325p. 1996. 107.95 (*0-335-19545-8*); pap. 34.95 (*0-335-19348-X*) OpUniv Pr.

Leach, Susan, ed. see Shakespeare, William.

Leach, T. M., jt. auth. see Mitchell, A. H.

***Leach, Terry & Clark, Tom.** Things Happen for a Reason: The True Story of an Itinerant Life in Baseball. LC 99-86103. (Illus.). 220p. 2000. pap. 14.95 (*1-58394-050-2*, Pub. by Frog Ltd CA) Publishers Group.

Leach, Thomas. How to Prepare, Stage, & Deliver Winning Presentations. LC 81-69351. (Illus.). 425p. reprint ed. pap. 131.80 (*0-7837-4236-3*, 204392500012) Bks Demand.

Leach, Virgil. Attitudes I. 1979. pap. 6.15 (*0-89137-803-0*) Quality Pubns.

— Attitudes II. 1979. pap. 6.15 (*0-89137-804-9*) Quality Pubns.

— Get Behind Me Satan. 1977. 10.95 (*0-89137-521-X*); pap. 8.25 (*0-89137-520-1*) Quality Pubns.

***Leach, W., Jr. & Brewer, Thomas.** Experiments in Modern Electronics. 496p. (C). 1999. pap. text 57.95 (*0-7872-6521-7*) Kendall-Hunt.

Leach, W. Barton. Perpetuities in a Nutshell & The Nutshell Revisited, 2 vols., Set. 1983. reprint ed. pap. 5.00 (*0-686-89066-3*, MICHIE) LEXIS Pub.

Leach, W. Barton & Logan, James K. Future Interests & Estate Planning, Teacher's Manual to Accompany Cases & Text On. 272p. 1992. reprint ed. pap. text. write for info. (*0-88277-511-1*) Foundation Pr.

Leach, W. Barton, jt. auth. see Casner, A. James.

Leach, William. Country of Exiles: The Destruction of Place in American Life. LC 98-29599. 288p. 1999. 24.00 (*0-679-44219-7*) Pantheon.

— Country of Exiles: The Destruction of Place in American Life. 288p. 2000. pap. 14.00 (*0-679-75865-8*) Random.

— Land of Desire: Merchants, Power & the Rise of a New American Culture. (Illus.). 560p. 1994. pap. 18.00 (*0-679-75411-3*) Vin Bks.

— True Love & Perfect Union: The Feminist Reform of Sex & Society. 2nd ed. LC 89-35791. 474p. reprint ed. pap. 147.00 (*0-608-09087-5*, 206972100005) Bks Demand.

Leache, Allen & Colbert, J. M. World Series Trivia: 75 Quizzes from A to Z. 176p. (Orig.). 2000. pap. 14.95 (*0-9653182-2-2*) Tuff Turtle.

Leachman, R. D. & Raineri, Angelo A., eds. The Big Heart: Proceedings of the International School of Medical Sciences, Ettore Majorana Centre for Scientific Culture 1990, Italy. LC 93-46071. (Ettore Majorana International Life Sciences Ser.: Vol. 14). (Illus.). 214p. 1994. text 61.00 (*3-7186-5510-1*) Gordon & Breach.

Leachman, Robert B. & Althoff, Philip, eds. Preventing Nuclear Theft: Guidelines for Industry & Government. LC 72-76452. (Special Studies in U. S. Economic, Social & Political Issues). 1972. 52.50 (*0-275-28618-5*) Irvington.

Leacock, Claudia, jt. ed. see Ravin, Yael.

Leacock, Cynthia Perry, see Perry Leacock, Cynthia.

Leacock, E. G., ed. see Morgan, L. H.

Leacock, Eleanor B. Myths of Male Dominance: Collected Articles on Women Cross-Culturally. LC 79-3870. 352p. reprint ed. pap. 109.20 (*0-7837-6993-8*, 204680500004) Bks Demand.

Leacock, Eleanor B. & Lee, Richard B., eds. Politics & History in Band Societies. (Illus.). 512p. 1982. pap. text 35.95 (*0-521-28412-0*) Cambridge U Pr.

Leacock, Eleanor B. & Lurie, Nancy O., eds. North American Indians in Historical Perspective. (Illus.). 498p. (C). 1988. reprint ed. pap. text 22.95 (*0-88133-377-8*) Waveland Pr.

Leacock, Eleanor B. & Safa, Helen I. Women's Work: Development & the Division of Labor by Gender. LC 85-26674. 311p. 1986. 62.95 (*0-89789-035-3*, Bergin & Garvey) Greenwood.

— Women's Work: Development & the Division of Labor by Gender. LC 85-26674. 311p. 1988. pap. 22.95 (*0-89789-036-1*, Bergin & Garvey) Greenwood.

Leacock, Eleanor B., ed. see Engels, Friedrich.

Leacock, Eleanor B., ed. see Strong, William D.

Leacock, Elspeth. Brain Quest Be a Know-It-All, Geography. (Illus.). 150p. 1997. pap. 10.95 (*0-7611-0805-X*, 10805) Workman Pub.

Leacock, John. The First Book of the American Chronicles of the Times, 1774-1775. LC 86-40594. 128p. 1988. 28.50 (*0-87413-305-X*) U Delaware Pr.

Leacock, Raymond. My Financial Career & Other Follies. 208p. 1996. pap. text 5.95 (*0-7710-9892-8*) McCland & Stewart.

— My Remarkable Uncle. 248p. 1996. pap. text 6.95 (*0-7710-9965-7*) McCland & Stewart.

Leacock, Robert J., jt. ed. see Eichhorn, Heinrich K.

Leacock, Ruth. Requiem for Revolution: The United States & Brazil, 1961-1969. LC 89-20054. (American Diplomatic History Ser.: No. 3). 329p. 1990. pap. 19.00 (*0-87338-402-4*) Kent St U Pr.

— Requiem for Revolution: The United States & Brazil, 1961-1969. LC 89-20054. (American Diplomatic History Ser.: No. 3). (Illus.). 329p. 1990. 30.00 (*0-87338-401-6*) Kent St U Pr.

Leacock, Stephen. Arcadian Adventures with the Idle Rich. (New Canadian Library). 216p. 1989. mass mkt. 6.95 (*0-7710-9966-5*) McCland & Stewart.

— Cuentecitos Risuenos. Ventura, Liliana, tr. from ENG. (SPA., Illus.). 46p. 1987. pap. text 5.00 (*0-9619890-0-9*) L Ventura.

— Frenzied Fiction. LC 78-125227. (Short Story Index Reprint Ser.). 1977. 30.95 (*0-8369-3594-2*) Ayer.

— Here Are My Lectures & Stories. LC 72-14188. (Essay Index Reprint Ser.). 1977. reprint ed. 20.95 (*0-518-10017-0*) Ayer.

— Literary Lapses. LC 70-122728. (Short Story Index Reprint Ser.). 1980. 18.95 (*0-8369-3561-6*) Ayer.

— Literary Lapses. 160p. 1996. pap. text 5.95 (*0-7710-9983-5*) McCland & Stewart.

— Mark Twain. LC 73-21633. (Mark Twain Ser.: No. 76). 1974. lib. bdg. 75.00 (*0-8383-1789-8*) M S G Haskell Hse.

— Model Memoirs: And Other Sketches from Simple to Serious. LC 77-156678. (Essay Index Reprint Ser.). 1977. reprint ed. 32.95 (*0-8369-2434-7*) Ayer.

— My Recollection of Chicago & the Doctrine of Laissez Faire. LC 99-172372. (Illus.). 160p. 1998. text 35.00 (*0-8020-4286-4*); pap. text 14.95 (*0-8020-8121-5*) U of Toronto Pr.

— The Social Criticism of Stephen Leacock: The Unsolved Riddle of Social Justice & Other Essays. LC 73-79860. (Social History of Canada Ser.). 193p. reprint ed. pap. 59.90 (*0-8357-3766-7*, 203649500003) Bks Demand.

— Sunshine Sketches of a Little Town. LC 71-125228. (Short Story Index Reprint Ser.). 1980. 24.95 (*0-8369-3595-0*) Ayer.

— Sunshine Sketches of a Little Town. 200p. 1996. pap. text 6.95 (*0-7710-9984-3*) McCland & Stewart.

— Sunshine Sketches of a Little Town. LC 6--931406. (Illus.). 192p. 1997. 26.95 (*0-7710-5001-1*) McCland & Stewart.

***Leacock, Stephen.** Sunshine Sketches of a Little Town. (Humour Classics Ser.). 224p. 2000. 13.95 (*1-85375-367-X*, Pub. by Prion) Trafalgar.

Leacock, Stephen. Winsome Winnie, & Other New Nonsense Novels. LC 74-140333. (Short Story Index Reprint Ser.). 1977. 16.95 (*0-8369-3725-2*) Ayer.

Leacox, Gloria, jt. auth. see Tatcove, Woody.

Leacox, Gloria, jt. auth. see Totcove, Woody.

Leacox, Gloria, jt. auth. see Tutcove, Woody.

Leacroft, Helen & Leacroft, Richard. The Buildings of Ancient Man. LC 73-159571. 40 p. 1973. write for info. (*0-340-15920-0*) St Martin.

Leacroft, Richard. The Development of the English Playhouse. 2nd ed. 354p. (C). 1988. pap. 19.95 (*0-413-60600-7*, A0076) Heinemann.

Leacroft, Richard, jt. auth. see Leacroft, Helen.

Lead, Edward. The Shadow Chasers: The Allies & the Nazi Atomic Threat. 1999. 29.95 (*0-85052-630-2*, 526302, Pub. by Leo Cooper) Combined Pub.

Lead, Jane. A Fountain of Gardens. 356p. 1997. reprint ed. pap. 24.95 (*0-7661-0109-6*) Kessinger Pub.

Leadabrand, Russ. California Ghost Town Trails. LC 85-71228. (Illus.). 128p. 1985. pap. 7.95 (*0-935182-21-7*) Gem Guides Bk.

Leadam, I. S. History of England from the Accession of Anne to the Death of George Second: Seventeen Hundred Two to Seventeen Sixty. (Political History of England Ser.). reprint ed. 39.00 (*0-685-02854-2*, Dutton Child) Peng Put Young Read.

An Asterisk (*) at the beginning of an entry indicates that the title is appearing for the first time.

Leadam, Issac S. History of England from the Accession of Anne to the Death of George the Second. LC 76-5628. (Political History of England Ser.: No. 9). reprint ed. 45.00 (*0-404-50779-4*) AMS Pr.

Leadbeater, B. S., jt. ed. see Green, J. C.

Leadbeater, Barry S. & Riding, Robvert, eds. Biomineralization in Lower Plants & Animals. (Illus.). 400p. 1986. text 85.00 (*0-19-857702-8*) OUP.

***Leadbeater, Barry S. C. & Green, J. C.** The Flagellates: Unity, Diversity & Evolution. LC 00-37778. (Systematics Association Special Volume Ser.). 2000. pap. write for info. (*0-7484-0914-9*) Taylor & Francis.

***Leadbeater, Bonnie J. & Way, Niobe.** Growing up Fast: Transitions to Early Adulthood for Inner City Adolescent Mothers. (Research Mongraphs in Adolescence). 280p. 2000. write for info. (*0-8058-3736-1*) L Erlbaum Assocs.

Leadbeater, Bonnie J. & Way, Niobe, eds. Urban Girls: Resisting Stereotypes, Creating Identities. 408p. (C). 1996. text 60.00 (*0-8147-5107-5*); pap. text 26.00 (*0-8147-5108-3*) NYU Pr.

Leadbeater, C. W. The Astral Plane. 100p. 1996. reprint ed. spiral bd. 12.00 (*0-7873-1122-7*) Hlth Research.

— The Astral Plane: Its Scenery, Inhabitants & Phenomena. 104p. 1996. reprint ed. pap. 11.95 (*1-56459-674-5*) Kessinger Pub.

— Australia & New Zealand As the Home of a New Sub-Race (1915) 64p. 1998. reprint ed. pap. 14.95 (*0-7661-0261-0*) Kessinger Pub.

— The Christian Creed: Its Origin & Signification. 172p. 1992. reprint ed. pap. 9.00 (*1-56459-238-3*) Kessinger Pub.

— The Christian Creed, Its Origin & Signification. 109p. 1996. reprint ed. spiral bd. 9.50 (*0-7873-0541-3*) Hlth Research.

— Clairvoyance. 61p. 1997. reprint ed. spiral bd. 9.00 (*0-7873-1244-4*) Hlth Research.

— Clairvoyance (1903) 186p. 1999. reprint ed. pap. 14.95 (*0-7661-0755-8*) Kessinger Pub.

— The Devachanic Plane. 102p. 1996. reprint ed. spiral bd. 9.50 (*0-7873-1247-9*) Hlth Research.

— Dreams. 4th ed. 32p. 1996. reprint ed. spiral bd. 9.00 (*0-7873-1248-7*) Hlth Research.

— Dreams: What They Are & How They Are Caused. 72p. 1997. reprint ed. pap. 12.95 (*0-7661-0075-8*) Kessinger Pub.

— Glimpses of Masonic History. 380p. 1996. reprint ed. spiral bd. 24.50 (*0-7873-0543-X*) Hlth Research.

— Glimpses of Masonic History. 418p. 1996. reprint ed. pap. 23.95 (*1-56459-613-3*) Kessinger Pub.

— Hidden Life in Freemasonry. 375p. 1992. reprint ed. pap. 23.95 (*1-56459-026-7*) Kessinger Pub.

— The Hidden Life in Freemasonry. 3rd ed. 374p. 1996. reprint ed. spiral bd. 24.50 (*0-7873-0544-8*) Hlth Research.

***Leadbeater, C. W.** The Hidden Side of Things: A Classic Work of Clairvoyant Investigation. 560p. 1999. 21.95 (*81-7059-337-9*) Theos Pub Hse.

Leadbeater, C. W. Hidden Side of Things (1913) 125p. 1998. reprint ed. pap. 17.95 (*0-7661-0604-7*) Kessinger Pub.

— How Theosophy Came to Me. 1986. 7.50 (*81-7059-010-8*, 7100, Quest) Theos Pub Hse.

— The Inner Life. 265p. 1996. reprint ed. spiral bd. 18.50 (*0-7873-0542-1*) Hlth Research.

— Invisible Helpers. 45p. 1996. reprint ed. spiral bd. 8.00 (*0-7873-1190-1*) Hlth Research.

— Invisible Helpers (1912) 120p. 1998. reprint ed. pap. 17.95 (*0-7661-0375-7*) Kessinger Pub.

— The Life after Death & How Theosophy Unveils It. 58p. 1996. reprint ed. spiral bd. 9.00 (*0-7873-1246-0*) Hlth Research.

— The Life after Death & How Theosophy Unveils It. 73p. 1992. reprint ed. pap. 8.00 (*1-56459-156-5*) Kessinger Pub.

— Man Visible & Invisible: Examples of Different Types of Men As Seen by Means of Trained Clairvoyance (1909) 144p. 1998. reprint ed. pap. 17.95 (*0-7661-0255-6*) Kessinger Pub.

— The Masters & the Path. 1998. pap. 24.95 (*81-7059-199-6*, Quest) Theos Pub Hse.

— The Masters & the Path. 354p. 1998. reprint ed. pap. 27.50 (*0-7873-0545-6*) Hlth Research.

— The Masters & the Path. 356p. 1996. reprint ed. pap. 24.95 (*1-56459-686-9*) Kessinger Pub.

— The Monad & Other Essays upon the Higher Consciousness. 140p. 1997. reprint ed. pap. 19.95 (*0-7661-0052-9*) Kessinger Pub.

— An Occult View of the War. 24p. 1997. reprint ed. pap. 9.95 (*0-7661-0057-X*) Kessinger Pub.

— The Other Side of Death: Scientifically Examined & Carefully Described. 864p. 1996. reprint ed. pap. 45.00 (*1-56459-624-9*) Kessinger Pub.

— An Outline of Theosophy (1915) 100p. 1996. reprint ed. pap. 14.95 (*1-56459-940-X*) Kessinger Pub.

— The Perfume of Egypt & Other Weird Stories. 306p. 1996. reprint ed. spiral bd. 18.50 (*0-7873-1070-0*) Hlth Research.

— The Rationale of Telepathy & Mind Cure. 26p. 1997. reprint ed. pap. 9.95 (*0-7661-0063-4*) Kessinger Pub.

— The Science of the Sacraments. 610p. 1997. reprint ed. pap. 28.95 (*0-7661-0116-9*) Kessinger Pub.

— The Soul & Its Vestures. 24p. 1983. pap. 1.50 (*0-918980-12-7*) St Alban Pr.

— The Soul's Growth Through Reincarnation Vols. I & II: The Lives of Erato & Spica. 1990. pap. 6.75 (*81-7059-140-6*, 7260, Quest) Theos Pub Hse.

— Starlight: Seven Address Given for Love of the Star. 104p. 1996. reprint ed. spiral bd. 15.00 (*0-7873-1245-2*) Hlth Research.

— Starlight: Seven Addresses Given for Love of the Star. 104p. 1992. reprint ed. pap. 9.95 (*1-56459-244-8*) Kessinger Pub.

***Leadbeater, C. W.** Talks On: At the Feet of the Master (1923) 524p. 1999. reprint ed. pap. 29.95 (*0-7661-0767-1*) Kessinger Pub.

— Textbook of Theosophy (1925) 154p. 1999. reprint ed. pap. 14.95 (*0-7661-0777-9*) Kessinger Pub.

Leadbeater, C. W. Vegetarianism & Occultism. 50p. 1995. reprint ed. pap. 7.95 (*1-56459-490-4*) Kessinger Pub.

Leadbeater, C. W., jt. auth. see Besant, A.

Leadbeater, C. W., jt. auth. see Besant, Annie W.

Leadbeater, Charles. Invisible Helpers. 1997. 11.50 (*81-7059-245-3*, Quest) Theos Pub Hse.

***Leadbeater, Charles.** Weightless Society. 256p. 2000. 27.95 (*1-58799-001-6*) Texere.

Leadbeater, Charles W. Ancient Mystic Rites. LC 86-40125. Orig. Title: Glimpses of Masonic History. (Illus.). 270p. 1995. reprint ed. pap. 14.00 (*0-8356-0609-0*, Quest) Theos Pub Hse.

— Chakras. LC 73-147976. (Illus.). 152p. 1997. pap. 14.00 (*0-8356-0422-5*, Quest) Theos Pub Hse.

— Clairvoyance. 10th ed. 1998. 8.95 (*81-7059-142-2*) Theos Pub Hse.

— Devachanic Plane. 1984. 7.50 (*81-7059-068-X*) Theos Pub Hse.

— Dreams: What They Are & How They Are Caused. 1997. pap. 4.25 (*81-7059-095-7*) Theos Pub Hse.

— The Inner Life. LC 77-17044. 383p. 1978. reprint ed. pap. 15.00 (*0-8356-0502-7*, Quest) Theos Pub Hse.

***Leadbeater, Charles W.** The Life after Death. 94p. 1998. 6.95 (*81-7059-254-2*, Quest) Theos Pub Hse.

Leadbeater, Charles W. Monad: And Other Essays on the Higher Consciousness. 1997. 10.95 (*81-7059-287-9*) Theos Pub Hse.

— An Outline of Theosophy. 1994. pap. 6.50 (*81-7059-073-6*) Theos Pub Hse.

— The Science of the Sacraments. 1999. 38.95 (*81-7059-181-3*, 7126, Quest) Theos Pub Hse.

— A Textbook of Theosophy. 1997. 12.95 (*81-7059-246-1*) Theos Pub Hse.

***Leadbeater, Charles W. & Besant, Annie W.** Talks on the Path of Occultism Vol. 3: Light on the Path. 472p. 1998. 17.95 (*81-7059-285-2*) Theos Pub Hse.

Leadbeater, Charles W., jt. auth. see Besant, Annie W.

Leadbeater, Simon R. The Politics of Textiles: The Indian Cotton-Mill Industry & the Legacy of Swadeshi, 1900-1985. LC 92-17600. (Illus.). 312p. (C). 1993. text 36.00 (*0-8039-9440-0*) Sage.

Leadbeater, W. W. Freemasonry & Other Mystic Rites. LC 98-10836. 256p. 1998. 6.99 (*0-517-20267-0*) Random Hse Value.

***Leadbeter, Paul, et al, eds.** Environmental Outlook No. 3: Law & Policy. 292p. 1999. pap. 49.95 (*1-86287-315-1*, Pub. by Federation Pr) Gaunt.

Leadbetter, D. Galerius. (Illus.). (C). text. write for info. (*0-472-10668-6*) U of Mich Pr.

Leadbetter, David. David Leadbetter's Positive Practice. LC 97-36840. (Illus.). 160p. 1998. 28.00 (*0-06-271607-7*, Harper Ref) HarpC.

— The Fundamentals of Hogan. LC 98-56193. (Illus.). 224p. 2000. 24.95 (*1-886947-50-3*) Sleepng Bear.

Leadbetter, David & Huggan, John. David Leadbetter's Faults & Fixes: How to Correct the 80 Most Common Problems in Golf. (Illus.). 192p. 1996. pap. 20.95 (*0-06-272005-8*, Harper Ref) HarpC.

Leadbetter, David & Simmons, Richard. David Leadbetter's Lessons from Golf Greats. LC 95-25302. (Illus.). 160p. 1997. 20.00 (*0-06-270147-9*, Harper Ref) HarpC.

Leadbetter, E. R. & Poindexter, J. S. Bacteria in Nature Vol. 1: Bacterial Activities in Perspective, Vol. 1. LC 85-3433. (Illus.). 282p. (C). 1985. text 85.00 (*0-306-41944-0*, Kluwer Plenum) Kluwer Academic.

— Bacteria in Nature Vol. 2: Methods & Special Applications in Bacterial Ecology, Vol. 2. LC 85-3433. (Illus.). 404p. (C). 1986. text 110.00 (*0-306-42346-4*, Kluwer Plenum) Kluwer Academic.

— Bacteria in Nature Vol. 3: Structure, Physiology & Genetic Adaptability, Vol. 3. LC 85-3433. (Illus.). 406p. (C). 1989. text 110.00 (*0-306-43173-4*, Kluwer Plenum) Kluwer Academic.

Leadbetter, Jane. Applying Psychology in the Classroom, Vol. 1. 1999. pap. 18.95 (*1-85346-584-4*) David Fulton.

Leadbetter, Laurie & Barrows, William, eds. Women in Development: Status, Issues, Information: APLIC Proceedings of the 23rd Annual Conference. 86p. (Orig.). 1991. pap. text 20.00 (*0-933438-17-6*) APLIC Intl.

Leadbetter, Ron, et al. Journey to Noah's Ark. Weems, Martha L., ed. LC 98-66467. (Illus.). 101p. 1998. 19.95 (*0-9651848-3-8*) Lakemoor.

Leadbetter, Russell. You Don't Have to Be in Harlem: The Story of the Glasgow Apollo. (Illus.). 160p. 1996. 35.00 (*1-85158-746-2*, Pub. by Mainstream Pubng) Trafalgar.

Leadbetter, Wayne B., et al, eds. Sports-Induced Inflammation: Clinical & Basic Science Concepts. LC 90-1055. 799p. 1990. 95.00 (*0-89203-037-2*) Amer Acad Ortho Surg.

Leadem, Christopher. Highland Ballad. LC 94-74988. 184p. (Orig.). 1995. pap. 7.95 (*0-88100-086-8*) Natl Writ Pr.

Leadem, Paul J. Christopher's Light. LC 86-60839. 100p. (Orig.). 1986. pap. 7.95 (*0-88100-053-1*) Natl Writ Pr.

Leadem, Tim. The West Coast Trail & Other Great Hikes. 8th ed. LC 98-16302. 112p. 1998. pap. 10.95 (*0-89886-536-0*) Mountaineers.

Leadenham, Carol A., compiled by. Guide to the Collections in the Hoover Institution Archives Relating to Imperial Russia, the Russian Revolutions & Civil War, & the First Emigration. (Bibliographical Ser.: No. 68). 208p. (C). 1986. 18.95 (*0-8179-2681-X*) Hoover Inst Pr.

Leader, Allison. Reinventing the Emblem. 1995. pap. 7.50 (*0-89467-069-7*) Yale Art Gallery.

Leader, Charles. Cargo to Saigon. large type ed. (Linford Mystery Library). 352p. 1998. pap. 17.99 (*0-7089-5213-5*) Ulverscroft.

— Death of a Marine. large type ed. (Linford Mystery Library). 352p. 1997. pap. 16.99 (*0-7089-5023-X*, Linford) Ulverscroft.

— The Double M Man. large type ed. (Linford Mystery Library). 368p. 1996. pap. 16.99 (*0-7089-7940-8*) Ulverscroft.

— The Dragon Roars. large type ed. (Linford Mystery Library). 304p. 1997. pap. 16.99 (*0-7089-5074-4*, Linford) Ulverscroft.

— Frontier of Violence. large type ed. (Linford Mystery Large Print Ser.). 384p. 1998. pap. 17.99 (*0-7089-5266-6*, Linford) Ulverscroft.

— The Golden Lure. large type ed. (Linford Mystery Library). 384p. 1997. pap. 16.99 (*0-7089-5164-3*) Ulverscroft.

— Kingdom of Darkness. large type ed. (Linford Mystery Library). 400p. 1996. pap. 16.99 (*0-7089-7979-3*) Ulverscroft.

— Murder in Marrakech. large type ed. (Linford Mystery Large Print Ser.). 368p. 1998. pap. 17.99 (*0-7089-5289-5*, Linford) Ulverscroft.

— Nightmare on the Nile. large type ed. (Linford Mystery Large Print Ser.). 384p. 1998. pap. 17.99 (*0-7089-5296-8*, Linford) Ulverscroft.

— Salesman of Death. large type ed. (Linford Mystery Library). 384p. 1997. pap. 16.99 (*0-7089-5062-0*, Linford) Ulverscroft.

— Scavengers at War. large type ed. (Linford Mystery Library). 352p. 1997. pap. 16.99 (*0-7089-5068-X*) Ulverscroft.

— Strangler's Moon. large type ed. (Linford Mystery Library). 368p. 1998. pap. 17.99 (*0-7089-5224-0*, Linford) Ulverscroft.

— A Wreath for Miss Wong. large type ed. (Linford Mystery Library). 352p. 1996. pap. 16.99 (*0-7089-7869-X*, Linford) Ulverscroft.

— A Wreath from Bangkok. large type ed. (Linford Mystery Library). 352p. 1996. pap. 16.99 (*0-7089-7907-6*) Ulverscroft.

— A Wreath of Cherry Blossom. large type ed. (Linford Mystery Library). 352p. 1996. pap. 16.99 (*0-7089-7933-5*) Ulverscroft.

— A Wreath of Poppies. large type ed. (Linford Mystery Library). 1996. pap. 16.99 (*0-7089-7862-2*, Linford) Ulverscroft.

Leader, Damian R. A History of the University of Cambridge, Vol. 1: The University to 1546. (Illus.). 424p. 1989. text 85.00 (*0-521-32882-9*) Cambridge U Pr.

Leader, Daniel & Blahnik, Judith. Bread Alone: Bold Fresh Loaves from Your Own Hands. LC 92-47236. 332p. 1993. 25.00 (*0-688-09261-6*, Wm Morrow) Morrow Avon.

Leader, Darian. Introducing Lacan. LC 96-60482. (Illus.). 176p. 1996. pap. text 9.95 (*1-874166-31-5*, Pub. by Totem Bks) Natl Bk Netwk.

Leader, Elliot. An Introduction to Gauge Theories & Modern Particle Physics Vol. 1: Electroweak Interactions, the "New Particles" & the Parton Model. (Monographs on Particle Physics, Nuclear Physics & Cosmology: No. 3). 1001p. 1996. pap. text 90.00 (*0-521-57742-X*) Cambridge U Pr.

Leader, Elliot & Predazzi, Enrico. An Introduction to Gauge Theories & Modern Particle Physics, 2 vols., Set. (Monographs on Particle Physics, Nuclear Physics & Cosmology: No. 3). 1001p. 1996. text 245.00 (*0-521-57780-2*) Cambridge U Pr.

— An Introduction to Gauge Theories & Modern Particle Physics Vol. 1: Electroweak Interactions, the "New Particles" & the Parton Model. (Cambridge Monographs on Particle Physics, Nuclear Physics & Cosmology: No. 3). (Illus.). 542p. (C). 1996. pap. text 52.95 (*0-521-46840-X*) Cambridge U Pr.

— An Introduction to Gauge Theories & Modern Particle Physics Vol. 1: Electroweak Interactions, the "New Particles" & the Parton Model. (Cambridge Monographs on Particle Physics, Nuclear Physics & Cosmology: No. 3). (Illus.). 542p. (C). 1996. text 150.00 (*0-521-46468-4*) Cambridge U Pr.

— An Introduction to Gauge Theories & Modern Particle Physics Vol. 2: CP-Violation, QCD & Hard Processes. (Cambridge Monographs on Particle Physics, Nuclear Physics & Cosmology: No. 3). (Illus.). 463p. (C). 1996. pap. text 47.95 (*0-521-49951-8*) Cambridge U Pr.

— An Introduction to Gauge Theories & Modern Particle Physics Vol. 2: CP-Violation, QCD & Hard Processes. (Cambridge Monographs on Particle Physics, Nuclear Physics & Cosmology: No. 3). (Illus.). 463p. (C). 1996. text 135.00 (*0-521-49617-9*) Cambridge U Pr.

Leader, Janice, ed. see Weber, Rosalind.

Leader, John P., jt. ed. see Macknight, Anthony D.

Leader, L., jt. auth. see Lender, W. G.

Leader, Laurie E. Employment Law: Wage-Hour Law & Practice. 1990. 140.00 (*0-8205-1629-5*, 629) Bender.

Leader, Lawrence. Drafting Employment & Termination Agreements. LC 93-15610. 1993. 120.00 (*0-8205-1274-5*) Bender.

Leader, Leonard J. Los Angeles & the Great Depression. LC 91-25485. (Modern American History: New Studies & Outstanding Dissertations). 344p. 1991. text 25.00 (*0-8240-1903-2*) Garland.

Leader, Mary. Red Signature. LC 96-78741. 72p. (Orig.). 1997. pap. 12.95 (*1-55597-255-1*) Graywolf.

Leader, Miriam. Second Chance to Dance. (Illus.). 50p. (Orig.). 1991. pap. text 10.00 (*0-9620092-6-1*) Pine Isl Pr.

Leader-Post Carrier Foundation Inc. Staff. Money & Time Saving Household Hints. LC 92-73856. (Illus.). 128p. (Orig.). 1992. pap. 6.95 (*0-911493-15-8*) Blue Sky.

Leader, R. W., ed. Blind Reading vs. Open Examination. 48p. 1988. pap. text 52.00 (*2-88124-415-7*) Gordon & Breach.

Leader, Ray. Colors & Markings Vol. 7: Special Purpose, C-130 Hercules. (Illus.). 64p. (Orig.). 1987. pap. 12.95 (*0-8306-8531-6*, 24531) McGraw-Hill Prof.

Leader, Ray, jt. auth. see Kinzey, Bert.

Leader, W. G. & Kyritsis, N. Fundamentals of Marketing. 296p. 1999. pap. 100.00 (*0-7487-0388-8*, Pub. by S Thornes Pubs) Trans-Atl Phila.

— Marketing in Practice. Thornes, Stanley, ed. 256p. (C). 1999. pap. 67.50 (*0-7487-0512-0*, Pub. by S Thornes Pubs) Trans-Atl Phila.

Leader-Williams, N., et al. Tourist Hunting in Tanzania: Proceedings of a Workshop Held in July 1993 LC 97-184660. (Occasional Paper of the IUCN Species Survival Commission Ser.). viii, 138 p. 1996. write for info. (*2-8317-0315-8*) IUCN.

Leader, Zachary. Revision & Romantic Authorship. 366p. 1999. pap. text 24.95 (*0-19-818634-7*) OUP.

Leader, Zachary, jt. auth. see Haywood, Ian.

***Leaderer, S.** Nothing Risque Nothing Gained. 1998. pap. 100.00 (*81-86982-61-2*, Pub. by Business Pubns) St Mut.

Leadership Council for Inter-American Summitry Staff. From Talk to Action: How Summits Can Help Forge A Western Hemisphere Community of Prosperous Democracies : A Policy Report. LC 99-175943. 27 p. 1998. 10.00 (*1-57454-059-9*) U Miami N-S Ctr.

***Leadership Magazine Editors.** Best Cartoons from Leadership Journal Vol. 5: It's Showtime, Baby! (Leadership Cartoon Treasury Bks.). 2000. pap. 8.99 (*0-8054-2156-4*) Broadman.

— Best Cartoons from Leadership Journal Vol. 6: They're Dividing Again! (Leadership Cartoon Treasury Bks.). (Illus.). 2000. pap. 8.99 (*0-8054-2157-2*) Broadman.

***Leadership Ministries Worldwide Staff.** Manual Personal del Obrero Cristiano. (SPA.). 272p. 1999. pap. 9.99 (*0-8254-1019-3*, Edit Portavoz) Kregel.

***Leadership Press Staff.** Leadership Bible. 2000. pap. 18.74 (*0-310-91244-X*) Zondervan.

***Leadership Press Staff, et al.** The Mindful Corporation. 224p. 2000. 25.00 (*0-9648466-7-5*, Pub. by Leadrship Pr) Gulf Pub.

Leadholm, Barbara J. & Miller, Jon F. Language Sample Analysis: The Wisconsin Guide. 187p. (C). 1992. pap. text 21.00 (*1-57337-011-8*) WI Dept Pub Instruct.

Leadingham, Everett. A Christian Attitude Toward Attitudes. (Dialog Ser.). 136p. 1995. pap. 6.50 (*0-8341-1526-3*); pap., teacher ed. 5.50 (*0-8341-1527-1*) Beacon Hill.

— I Believe, Now Tell Me Why. 48p. 1994. pap., teacher ed. 5.50 (*0-8341-1517-4*) Beacon Hill.

Leadingham, Everett, ed. Dear God . . . Help Me Understand: Real Questions from Real People. (Dialog Ser.). 144p. 1995. pap. text 6.50 (*0-8341-1541-7*) Beacon Hill.

— Dear God Help Me Understand: Real Questions from Real People. 48p. 1995. pap., teacher ed. 5.50 (*0-8341-1542-5*) Beacon Hill.

— The End. (Dialog Ser.). 136p. 1996. pap., student ed. 6.50 (*0-8341-1579-4*) Beacon Hill.

— I Believe, Now Tell Me Why. 156p. 1994. pap., student ed. 6.50 (*0-8341-1518-2*) Beacon Hill.

— The Me I See. 128p. 1994. pap., student ed. 6.50 (*0-8341-1520-4*) Beacon Hill.

***Leadingham, Everette.** Who's on First: Finding True Fulfillment in the Crush of Life. (Dialog Ser.). 128p. 1999. pap. 6.50 (*0-8341-1811-4*) Beacon Hill.

Leadingham, Everette, ed. The Me I See: A Christian Approach to Self-Esteem. (Dialog Ser.). 48p. 1994. pap., teacher ed. 5.50 (*0-8341-1519-0*) Beacon Hill.

Leadley, P. F. Introduction to Enzyme Chemistry, No. 32. 82p. 1989. 9.00 (*0-85186-599-2*) CRC Pr.

Leadley, Robert, jt. auth. see Johns, Helen.

Leadley, Robert A., jt. auth. see Johns, Helen.

Leaf, Alexander, et al, eds. Renal Pathophysiology: Recent Advances. fac. ed. LC 79-63038. (Illus.). 299p. pap. 92.70 (*0-7837-7290-4*, 204701600005) Bks Demand.

Leaf, Alexander & Cotran, Ramzi. Renal Pathophysiology. 3rd ed. (Illus.). 432p. 1985. pap. text 26.95 (*0-19-503488-0*) OUP.

Leaf, Alexander & Weber, Peter C. Prevention & Noninvasive Therapy of Atherosclerosis. LC 90-8445. (Atherosclerosis Reviews Ser.: No. 21). (Illus.). 220p. 1990. reprint ed. pap. 68.20 (*0-608-00603-3*, 206119000007) Bks Demand.

Leaf, Alexander, jt. ed. see Weber, Peter C.

Leaf, Alexandra. A Painter's Garden. 1998. write for info. (*0-609-60040-0*) C Potter.

Leaf, Claudia. Radical Will. unabridged ed. 28p. 1999. pap. 6.00 (*0-85343-614-2*, Pub. by J G Miller Ltd) Empire Pub Srvs.

Leaf, David A. Cholesterol Treatment: A Guide to Lipid Disorder Management. 4th rev. ed. LC 78-51737. (Illus.). 255p. 1999. pap. 17.95 (*0-917634-02-0*) EMIS.

— Exercise & Nutrition in Preventative Cardiology. 296p. (C). 1991. text. write for info. (*0-697-14839-4*) Brown & Benchmark.

Leaf, David A. & Glassman, Peter A. The Oxidative Balance: How to Lead the Antioxidant Lifestyle. LC 99-51361. (Illus.). 174p. 2000. pap. 14.95 (*0-917634-01-2*) EMIS.

An Asterisk (*) at the beginning of an entry indicates that the title is appearing for the first time.

L

Leaf, Edward. Above All Unseen: The Royal Air Force Photographic Reconnaissance Operations 1939-1945. (Illus.). 224p. 1997. 42.95 (*1-85260-528-6*) Haynes Manuals.

Leaf, Edwin B. Ship Modeling from Scratch: Tips & Techniques for Building Without Kits. (Illus.). 176p. 1993. pap. 18.95 (*0-87742-389-X*) Intl Marine.

— Ship Modeling from Scratch: Tips & Techniques for Building Without Kits. (Illus.). 184p. 1994. pap. 18.95 (*0-07-036817-1*) McGraw.

Leaf, June. People. (Illus.). 62p. 1994. pap. 19.95 (*1-879886-36-7*) Addison Gallery.

Leaf, Mindy. Things That Count: Sometimes Dogs Know Better. 1999. pap. 4.99 (*0-9662137-2-6*) InterMedia Pub.

— The Working Mom's Handbook. 1999. pap. 4.99 (*0-9662137-1-8*) InterMedia Pub.

Leaf, Munro. El Cuento de Ferdinando.Tr. of Story of Ferdinand. (SPA.). (J). 1990. 11.19 (*0-606-03254-1*, Pub. by Turtleback) Demco.

— El Cuento de Ferdinando. unabridged ed.Tr. of Story of Ferdinand. (SPA., Illus.). (J). (gr. k-3). 1990. pap. 15.95 incl. audio (*0-87499-216-8*) Live Oak Media.

— El Cuento De Ferdinando, 4 bks., Set. unabridged ed.Tr. of Story of Ferdinand. (Illus.). (J). (gr. k-3). 1990. pap., teacher ed. 33.95 incl. audio (*0-87499-218-4*) Live Oak Media.

— El Cuento de Ferdinando: The Story of Ferdinand. Belpre, Pura, tr. (SPA., Illus.). 72p. (J). (ps-3). 1990. pap. 6.99 (*0-14-054253-1*, PuffinBks) Peng Put Young Read.

***Leaf, Munro.** Ferdinandus Taurus. Hadas, Elizabeth, tr. (LAT., Illus.). 80p. 2000. reprint ed. pap. 15.95 (*1-56792-127-2*) Godine.

Leaf, Munro. Manners Can Be Fun. 2nd rev. ed. LC 84-48459. (Trophy Picture Bk.). (Illus.). 48p. (J). (gr. k-3). 1985. pap. 4.95 (*0-06-443053-7*, HarpTrophy) HarpC Child Bks.

— Manners Can Be Fun. 3rd ed. LC 84-48459. (Illus.). 48p. (J). (gr. k-3). 1985. lib. bdg. 12.89 (*0-397-32118-X*) HarpC Child Bks.

— Metric Can Be Fun. LC 75-29223. (Illus.). (J). (gr. 1-3). 1976. lib. bdg. 12.89 (*0-397-31679-8*) HarpC Child Bks.

— Safety Can Be Fun. rev. ed. LC 61-14579. (Illus.). (J). (gr. k-3). 1961. lib. bdg. 12.89 (*0-397-31593-7*) HarpC Child Bks.

— The Story of Ferdinand. (Illus.). (J). 1977. pap. 5.99 (*0-14-050234-3*, PuffinBks) Peng Put Young Read.

— The Story of Ferdinand. (Illus.). (J). (ps-3). 1988. 9.95 (*0-318-37105-7*, PuffinBks); audio 6.95 (*0-318-37106-5*, PuffinBks) Peng Put Young Read.

— The Story of Ferdinand. (J). 1977. 11.19 (*0-606-05026-4*, Pub. by Turtleback) Demco.

***Leaf, Munro.** Story of Ferdinand. (Illus.). 32p. (J). (ps-3). 2000. pap. 3.49 (*0-448-42190-9*, Planet Dexter) Peng Put Young Read.

Leaf, Munro. The Story of Ferdinand. (Illus.). 72p. (J). 1989. reprint ed. lib. bdg. 17.95 (*0-89966-590-X*) Buccaneer Bks.

***Leaf, Munro, ed.** The Story of Ferdinand; El Cuento De Ferdinando, Set. unabridged ed. Belpre, Pura, tr. (Illus.). (J). 1999. pap. 29.95 incl. audio (*0-87499-567-1*) Live Oak Media.

Leaf, Munro & Lawson, Robert. The Story of Ferdinand. unabridged ed. (J). 1985. pap. 15.95 (*0-670-67431-1*, Viking Child) Peng Put Young Read.

Leaf, Murray J. Pragmatism & Development: The Prospect for Pluralist Transformation in the Third World. LC 98-9534. 256p. 1998. 59.95 (*0-89789-573-8*, Bergin & Garvey) Greenwood.

Leaf, Reuben. Hebrew Alphabets: 400 B.C.E. to Our Times. LC 87-15820. 125p. 1987. 35.00 (*0-8197-0518-7*); spiral bd. 17.95 (*0-8197-0521-7*) Bloch.

Leaf, Ruth. Etching, Engraving & Other Intaglio Printmaking Techniques. (Illus.). 232p. 1984. pap. 12.95 (*0-486-24721-X*) Dover.

Leaf, Vadonna J. A Father for Jason: The Story of God's Love for a Child Without a Father. LC 94-78746. 32p. (J). (ps-3). 1994. pap. 6.99 (*0-8066-2733-6*, 9-2733, Augsburg) Augsburg Fortress.

Leaf, Walter. Troy: A Study in Homeric Geography. LC 70-150191. (Select Bibliographies Reprint Ser.). 1977. reprint ed. 39.95 (*0-8369-5704-0*) Ayer.

Leaf, Walter, tr. see Solovyoff, Vsevolod S.

Leafe, David, ed. Film & Television Handbook, 1992. (Illus.). 332p. 1992. pap. 28.95 (*0-85170-317-8*, Pub. by British Film Inst) Ind U Pr.

— Film & Television Handbook, 1994. (Illus.). 336p. 1994. pap. 28.95 (*0-85170-411-5*, Pub. by British Film Inst) Ind U Pr.

Leafe, G. Harry. Running to Win! A Positive Biblical Approach to Rewards & Inheritance. 108p. (Orig.). 1992. pap. 5.00 (*0-9635128-0-3*) Scriptel Pubs.

Leaffer, Marshall. Understanding Copyright Law. 2nd ed. 1995. write for info. (*0-8205-2747-5*, 839) Bender.

Leaffer, Marshall A. International Treaties on Intellectual Property. 2nd ed. LC 96-35181. 1997. 125.00 (*1-57018-056-3*) BNA Books.

***Leaffer, Marshall A.** Understanding Copyright Law 3rd ed. LC 99-22240. (Legal Text Ser.). 1999. 30.00 (*0-8205-4062-5*) Bender.

Leafgren, Fred. Leadership, Management & Career Development for Corporations & Organizations: Facilitator Guide. (Illus.). 113p. 1997. 175.00 (*1-929112-19-X*) Personality Res.

— True Colors Communicator. 103p. 1999. 125.00 (*1-929112-18-1*) Personality Res.

Leafgren, Fred, jt. auth. see Sullivan, Joseph R.

Leaflet Missal Company Staff. A Holy Card Prayer Book I & II: A Compilation of Saints & Holy People. (Illus.). 230p. 1994. 29.95 (*1-885845-02-2*) Leaflet Missal.

— A Holy Card Prayer Book II: A Compilation of Saints & Holy People. (Illus.). 115p. 1994. 19.95 (*1-885845-01-4*) Leaflet Missal.

Leafstedt, Carl S. Inside Bluebeard's Castle: Music & Drama in Bela Bartok's Opera. LC 98-40668. (Illus.). 254p. 1999. text 45.00 (*0-19-510999-6*) OUP.

Leagans, J. Paul, et al. Selected Concepts from Educational Psychology & Adult Education for Extension & Continuing Educators. LC 74-171881. (Notes & Essays Ser.: No. 71). 1971. pap. text 3.50 (*0-87060-046-X*, NES 71) Syracuse U Cont Ed.

Leage, R. W. Roman Private Law: Founded on the 'Institutes' of Gaius & Justinian. LC 93-79711. 450p. 1994. reprint ed. 110.00 (*1-56169-069-4*, Pub. by Juta & Co) Gaunt.

Leage, R. W., jt. auth. see Ziegler, C. H.

Leagjeld, Ted. Voyageur the Moose. (Illus.). (Orig.). (J). (gr. 4-8). 1992. pap. write for info. (*0-9616127-0-3*) T Leagjeld.

League of Nations, Economic, Financial & Transit D. The Course & Control of Inflation. Wilkins, Mira, ed. LC 78-3928. (International Finance Ser.). (Illus.). 1979. reprint ed. lib. bdg. 18.95 (*0-405-11231-9*) Ayer.

League of Nations, Financial Committee, Gold Deleg. Report & Interim Report, 2 vols. Wilkins, Mira, ed. LC 78-3929. (International Finance Ser.). 1979. reprint ed. lib. bdg. 23.95 (*0-405-11232-7*) Ayer.

League of Nations, Secretariat, Economic, Financia. International Currency Experience, Lessons of the Inter-War Period. Wilkins, Mira, ed. LC 78-3932. (International Finance Ser.). 1979. reprint ed. lib. bdg. 24.95 (*0-405-11235-1*) Ayer.

League of Nations, Secretariat Staff. Memorandum on Currency & Central Banks, 1913-1924, 2 vols. Wilkins, Mira, ed. LC 78-3931. (International Finance Ser.). (Illus.). 1979. reprint ed. lib. bdg. 53.95 (*0-405-11234-3*) Ayer.

— Memorandum on Currency & Central Banks, 1913-1925, 2 vols. Wilkins, Mira, ed. LC 78-3930. (International Finance Ser.). (Illus.). 1979. reprint ed. lib. bdg. 34.95 (*0-405-11233-5*) Ayer.

League of Nations Staff. European Conference on Rural Life, 29 parts in 3 vols., Set. LC 77-87670. reprint ed. 134.00 (*0-404-16550-8*) AMS Pr.

League of Saint Gerard Staff. Gerard Majella: The Mother's Saint. 16p. (Orig.). 1994. pap. 2.95 (*0-89243-706-5*) Liguori Pubns.

League of Vermont Writers Members. Vermont Voices: An Anthology. 288p. 1991. pap. 13.95 (*0-9630872-0-7*) League VT Writs.

League of Women Voters Education Fund Staff. Coping with Conflict: Reproductive Choices & Community Controversy. 36p. (Orig.). 1986. pap. 2.50 (*0-89959-367-4*, 802) LWVUS.

— Crosscurrents: The Water We Drink. 17p. 1989. 4.95 (*0-89959-413-1*, 880) LWVUS.

— Face to Face: A Guide to Candidate Debates. 10.00 (*0-89959-425-5*, 830) LWVUS.

— Going to Court in the Public Interest: A Guide for Community Groups. 1983. 0.85 (*0-89959-339-9*, 244) LWVUS.

— Know Your Community. 48p. 1972. pap. 1.50 (*0-89959-056-X*, 288) LWVUS.

— Plastic Waste Primer: A Handbook for Citizens. (Illus.). 152p. 1993. 10.95 (*1-55821-229-9*, 954) Lyons Pr.

— Protect Your Groundwater: Educating for Action. 64p. 1994. 6.95 (*0-89959-384-4*, 980) LWVUS.

— Public Policy on Reproductive Choice: A Community Action Guide. 1992. 5.00 (*0-89959-379-8*, 953) LWVUS.

— Re-Envisioning Medicare: Facts on Medicare & Congressional Proposals to Change It. 15p. 1995. 3.99 (*0-89959-398-4*, 1037) LWVUS.

— Recycling Is More Than Collections: Questions & Concerns from the Ground Up. 1992. 5.95 (*0-89959-421-2*, 926) LWVUS.

— Safety on Tap: A Citizen's Drinking Water Handbook. 68p. 1987. pap. 7.95 (*0-89959-402-6*, 840) LWVUS.

— Targeting Tomorrow: Washington's Economy Adjusts to the '90s. 42p. 1991. pap. text 4.95 (*1-878170-02-3*) LWV WA.

— Tell It to Washington. 36p. 1993. 2.75 (*0-89959-426-3*) LWVUS.

— Thinking Globally . . . Acting Locally. 87p. 1988. pap. 5.00 (*0-89959-406-9*, 849) LWVUS.

— Transforming Medicaid. 19p. 1996. 3.99 (*0-89959-399-2*, 1047) LWVUS.

— Transporting Radioactive Spent Fuel: An Issue Brief. 1996. 5.95 (*0-89959-394-1*, 1052) LWVUS.

— You & Your National Government. rev. ed. (Illus.). 32p. 1985. pap. 1.75 (*0-89959-027-6*, 273) LWVUS.

League of Women Voters Members. Choosing the President. LC 99-23839. 1999. 25.00 (*1-55821-958-7*) Lyons Pr.

***League of Women Voters Members.** Choosing the President: The Citizen's Guide to the 2000 Election. 1999. pap. 12.95 (*1-55821-959-5*) Lyons Pr.

League of Women Voters of California Staff, ed. Guide to California Government. rev. ed. 197p. 1992. pap. 8.95 (*0-9632465-0-X*) Leag Women Voters.

League of Women Voters of Cleveland Educational Fu. From Ordinance to Constitution: Government of & by the People. 73p. (YA). (gr. 9-12). 1987. pap. text 10.00 (*1-880746-05-0*) LOWV Cleve Educ.

— New Voter's Guide to Practical Politics. 61p. (YA). (gr. 7-12). 1982. reprint ed. pap. 2.00 (*1-880746-02-6*) LOWV Cleve Educ.

— Ohio: From Territory to Statehood - From Ordinance to Constitution. 99p. (J). (gr. 7-8). 1987. pap. text 10.00 (*1-880746-04-2*) LOWV Cleve Educ.

— Ohio: From Wilderness to Territory - The Law of the Land. (J). (gr. 3-6). 1987. pap. text 10.00 (*1-880746-03-4*) LOWV Cleve Educ.

League of Women Voters of Minnesota Education Fund. Child Care in Minnesota: Public Issues. 1987. write for info. (*0-9613566-4-2*) League Wmn Voters MN.

— A Citizen's Guide to State Finance: An Overview of Minnesota Governement Revenues & Expenditures. 1994. 7.00 (*1-877889-09-1*) LWV MN.

— Health Care for Minnesota's Children: Investing in the Future. 1987. write for info. (*0-9613566-3-4*) League Wmn Voters MN.

— How to Make a Difference: A Citizen's Guide to State Government. 1995. 10.00 (*1-877889-11-3*) LWV MN.

— Protecting Minnesota's Children: Public Issues. (Illus.). 29p. 1986. pap. 2.50 (*0-9613566-2-6*) League Wmn Voters MN.

— Seving Minnesota's Mentally Ill: An Introduction. 1988. write for info. (*0-9613566-6-9*) League Wmn Voters MN.

League of Women Voters of New York State Staff. Seeds of Failure: A Political Review of New York State's 1967 Constitutional Convention. reprint ed. pap. write for info. (*0-938588-14-1*) LWV NYS.

League of Women Voters of New York State Staff, jt. ed. see Fairbanks, Mary Jo.

League of Women Voters of Newtown Staff. Newtown, Connecticut: Directions & Images. Telfair, Carol & Greene, Carolyn, eds. (Illus.). 1989. text 30.00 (*0-9623444-0-0*) LWV Newtown.

***League of Women Voters of Ohio Staff.** Know Your Ohio Government. 8th ed. Moran, Chris & Wenig, Deborah, eds. (Illus.). 136p. (C). 1999. pap. 18.00 (*0-9618279-0-4*) Leag Wom Voters.

League of Women Voters of Pennsylvania Education F. Key to the Keystone State: Pennsylvania. Brandt, Susan E. & Piccoli, Terese S., eds. LC 87-43184. 1989. pap. 12.95 (*0-271-00635-8*) Pa St U Pr.

League of Women Voters of Seattle Staff. Seattle, the City We're In: A Citizen's Guide to Seattle City Government. 70p. 1996. pap. text 9.00 (*0-9648851-1-5*) LOWVS.

League of Women Voters Staff. The Garbage Primer: A Handbook for Citizens. (Illus.). 192p. 1993. pap. 12.95 (*1-55821-250-7*, 958) Lyons Pr.

— Know Your County. 36p. 1974. pap. 1.25 (*0-89959-058-6*) LWVUS.

— Know Your Schools. 31p. 1974. pap. 1.50 (*0-89959-057-8*) LWVUS.

— The Nuclear Waste Primer: A Handbook for Citizens. rev. ed. (Illus.). 176p. 1994. pap. 10.95 (*1-55821-226-4*, 448) Lyons Pr.

— Strategies for Effective Public Involvement: Drinking Water Source Assessment & Protection. (Illus.). 50p. 1998. pap. 10.00 (*0-89959-429-8*) LWVUS.

— Tools for Drinking - Water Protection Community Outreach Kit. 1997. pap. 25.00 incl. VHS (*0-89959-427-1*) LWVUS.

League of Women Voters Staff, ed. see Woodwell, William H., Jr.

League, Richard. Psycholinguistic Matrices Investigation into Osgood & Morris. (Approaches to Semiotics Ser.: Vol. 47). (Illus.). 1977. 51.55 (*90-279-3116-X*) Mouton.

League, V. C. The Proposal Writers Workshop. Bethea, Odessa, ed. LC 98-93880. 350p. 1998. pap. 24.95 (*0-9636195-5-1*) Curry-Co Pubns.

Leah Komaiko & Kids. A Million Moms & Mine. (Illus.). 28p. (J). 1992. 11.95 (*0-9634893-0-5*); pap. 5.95 (*0-9634893-1-3*) L Claiborne.

Leahey, Maureen, jt. auth. see Wright, Lorraine M.

***Leahey, Michael.** Broken Machines. 304p. 2000. 23.95 (*0-312-26130-6*, Thomas Dunne) St Martin.

Leahey, Thomas H. A History of Modern Psychology. 2nd ed. LC 93-34463. 400p. (C). 1993. 78.00 (*0-13-501271-6*) P-H.

***Leahey, Thomas H.** A History of Modern Psychology. 3rd ed. 400p. 2000. 70.67 (*0-13-017573-0*) P-H.

— A History of Psychology: Main Currents in Psychological Thought. 5th ed. LC 99-29097. 572p. 1999. 73.00 (*0-13-011286-0*) P-H.

Leahey, Thomas H., jt. auth. see Harris, Richard J.

Leahigh, David J. A Pocket Guide to Finance. 176p. (C). 1995. pap. text 23.00 (*0-03-015718-8*) Dryden Pr.

Leahy. Brian Lamb & C-Span. 1999. text. write for info. (*0-312-16794-6*) St Martin.

— Clinical Nursing Procedures. 1998. pap. text 42.50 (*0-7216-5004-X*) Harcourt.

— The Development of the Worcester Police Department. pap. 6.00 (*0-914206-13-3*) Clark U Pr.

— Excavations at Malkata & the Birket Habu, 1971-1974: The Inscriptions. (Egyptology Today Ser.: Vol. 4). 1978. pap. 32.50 (*0-85668-121-0*, Pub. by Aris & Phillips) David Brown.

Leahy, et al. Essentials of Map Interpretation. 3rd ed. 196p. (C). 1997. spiral bd., wbk. ed. 38.95 (*0-7872-4171-7*, 41417101) Kendall-Hunt.

Leahy, A. The Insect Workbook. (Illus.). 80p. (J). 1994. pap. 3.96 (*0-938522-51-5*, ESAWB) Entomol Soc.

Leahy, Alice & Dempsey, Anne. Not Just a Bed for the Night: The Story of Trust. 192p. 1997. pap. 12.95 (*1-86023-024-5*, Pub. by Martello Bks) Irish Amer Bk.

Leahy, Alice M. The Measurement of Urban Home Environments: Validation & Standardization of the Minnesota Home Status Index, Vol. 11. LC 79-142314. (Monograph: No. 11). (Illus.). 70p. 1975. reprint ed. lib. bdg. 45.00 (*0-8371-5902-4*, CWLM) Greenwood.

Leahy, Anthony. Libya & Egypt in the First Millennium BC. 224p. 1988. lib. bdg. 39.95 (*0-415-00478-0*) Routledge.

Leahy, Barbara H. Marijuana: A Dangerous "High" Way. rev. ed. Farrell, Lee et al, eds. LC 82-62440. (Illus.). 173p. (Orig.). (J). (gr. 4-9). 1983. pap. 6.95 (*0-9610312-1-2*) B Leahy.

***Leahy, Brendan.** Marian Profile: In the Ecclesiology of Hans Urs von Balthasar. (Illus.). 2000. pap. 14.95 (*1-56548-139-9*) New City.

Leahy, Christopher. Discovering Art: A Museum Guide for Girl Scouts in the Arts. McNamee, Harriet, ed. LC 97-121037. (Illus.). (Orig.). (J). (gr. 1-6). 1996. pap. text 1.65 (*0-940979-35-7*) Natl Museum Women.

— An Introduction to New England Birds. 2nd ed. (Illus.). 32p. 1989. reprint ed. pap. 3.00 (*0-932691-09-9*) MA Audubon Soc.

— Peterson First Guide to Insects of North America. 1987. 10.05 (*0-606-04507-4*, Pub. by Turtleback) Demco.

Leahy, Christopher, ed. Whalewatchers Guide to the North Atlantic. (Habitat Ser.). (Illus.). 8p. 1988. 3.95 (*0-932691-06-4*) MA Audubon Soc.

Leahy, Christopher, ed. see Colburn, Betsy & Tyning, Tom.

Leahy, Christopher, ed. see Perkins, Simon.

Leahy, Christopher, ed. see Zuchowski, Willow.

Leahy, D. G. Foundation: Matter the Body Itself. LC 93-36975. 696p. (C). 1995. text 89.50 (*0-7914-2021-3*); pap. text 29.95 (*0-7914-2022-1*) State U NY Pr.

Leahy, David G. Novitas Mundi: Perception of the History of Being. LC 93-45673. 422p. (C). 1994. text 59.50 (*0-7914-2137-6*); pap. text 19.95 (*0-7914-2138-4*) State U NY Pr.

Leahy, Diane, ed. see Hellstrom, Bill.

Leahy, Donna & Wallach, Louis. Morning Glories: Recipes for Breakfast, Brunch & Beyond from an American Country Inn. LC 95-49832. (Illus.). 208p. 1996. 30.00 (*0-8478-1923-X*, Pub. by Rizzoli Intl) St Martin.

Leahy, Frederick S. The Cross He Bore: Meditations on the Sufferings of the Redeemer. 82p. 1996. pap. 6.99 (*0-85151-693-9*) Banner of Truth.

***Leahy, Frederick S.** Great Conversions. 2nd rev. ed. 142p. (Orig.). 1999. reprint ed. pap. 9.99 (*1-84030-031-0*) Ambassador Prodns Ltd.

Leahy, Frederick S. Satan Cast Out. 200p. 1990. reprint ed. pap. 7.99 (*0-85151-234-8*) Banner of Truth.

Leahy, Gerald, ed. Managing Banking Relationships. 160p. 1997. 135.00 (*1-85573-326-9*, Pub. by Woodhead Pubng) Am Educ Systs.

***Leahy, Jack L., ed.** Medical Management of Diabetes Mellitus. (Clinical Guides to Medical Management Ser.). 738p. 2000. 99.75 (*0-8247-8857-5*) Dekker.

Leahy, James E. The First Amendment, 1791-1991: Two Hundred Years of Freedom. LC 90-53502. 320p. 1991. lib. bdg. 39.95 (*0-89950-573-2*) McFarland & Co.

— Freedom Fighters of the United States Supreme Court: Nine Who Championed Individual Liberty. LC 96-2815. (Illus.). 431p. 1996. lib. bdg. 52.50 (*0-7864-0206-7*) McFarland & Co.

— Supreme Court Justices Who Voted with the Government: Nine Who Favored the State over Individual Rights. (Illus.). 381p. 1998. lib. bdg. 52.50 (*0-7864-0547-3*) McFarland & Co.

Leahy, John A. Eagle's Chase: The Agony of Success. LC 85-21644. (Illus.). 192p. 1986. 19.95 (*0-88280-114-7*) ETC Pubns.

Leahy, John J., jt. auth. see Kristiansen, Rolf H.

Leahy, Julia M. & Kizilay, Patrica E., eds. Foundations of Nursing Practice: A Nursing Process Approach. (Illus.). 1215p. 1998. write for info. (*0-7216-3895-3*, W B Saunders Co) Harcrt Hlth Sci Grp.

Leahy, Julia M. & Kizilay, Patricia E. Foundations of Nursing Practice: A Nursing Process Approach. Eoyang, Thomas, ed. LC 97-9768. (Illus.). 1216p. 1998. text 57.95 (*0-7216-3881-3*, W B Saunders Co) Harcrt Hlth Sci Grp.

Leahy, Kathleen M., et al. Community Health Nursing. 4th ed. 432p. 1982. text 25.95 (*0-07-036834-1*) McGraw.

Leahy, Margaret, ed. Disorders of Communication. 2nd ed. (Illus.). 346p. (C). 1995. pap. text 49.95 (*1-56593-515-2*, 1188) Thomson Learn.

Leahy, Margaret M., jt. ed. see Rouseff, Russell L.

Leahy, Michael. Privileged Class: Senior Year at Beverly Hills High School. 320p. 1988. 17.95 (*0-316-51815-8*) Little.

Leahy, Michael & Cohn-Sherbok, Dan, eds. The Liberation Debate: Rights at Issue. LC 95-35993. 320p. (C). 1996. 70.00 (*0-415-11693-7*); pap. 25.99 (*0-415-11694-5*) Routledge.

Leahy, Michael J. Explorations into Highland New Guinea, 1930-1935. Jones, Douglas E., ed. LC 91-9027. 272p. 1991. pap. text 29.95 (*0-8173-0446-0*) U of Ala Pr.

Leahy, Michael J., jt. auth. see Fong Chan.

Leahy, Michael P. Against Liberation: Putting Animals in Perspective. 2nd ed. LC 94-168821. 304p. (C). 1993. pap. 27.99 (*0-415-10316-9*) Routledge.

— How to Overcome Your Fears. 1978. pap. 3.00 (*0-87980-062-3*) Wilshire.

Leahy, Monique C., ed. Indiana Real Estate Transactions. LC 96-75731. 2000p. 1996. text. write for info. (*0-7620-0052-X*) West Group.

Leahy, Monique C. & Kenter, Jerry. Missouri Worker's Compensation, 2 vols. 2nd ed. LC 96-78600. (Lawyers Cooperative Practice Guide Ser.). 1996. write for info. (*0-7620-0113-5*) West Group.

Leahy, Monique C., ed. see Dierker, Robert H. & Mehan, Richard J.

Leahy, Noreen M. Quick Reference to Neurological Critical Care Nursing. LC 89-18022. 248p. (C). 1990. 58.00 (*0-8342-0127-5*, 20127) Aspen Pub.

Leahy, P. Patrick, et al, eds. United States Geological Survey's National Water Quality Assessment Program (NAWQA) fac. ed. LC TD0223.A1A87. (AWRA Monograph: No. 19). 186p. 1993. reprint ed. pap. 57.70 (*0-608-01000-6*, 206185800012) Bks Demand.

Leahy, Patrick. To the Dead Already. 1984. pap. text 7.95 (*0-88982-076-7*, Pub. by Oolichan Bks) Genl Dist Srvs.

An Asterisk (*) at the beginning of an entry indicates that the title is appearing for the first time.

Leahy, Patrick J. Foundations of Nursing. (C). 1998. pap. text, student ed. 19.95 (*0-7216-5251-4*) Harcourt.

Leahy, Philippa. Spain. LC 93-2663. (Discovering Our Universe Ser.). (Illus.). 32p. (J). (gr. 5). 1993. lib. bdg. 13.95 (*0-89686-772-2*, Crstwood Hse) Silver Burdett Pr.

Leahy, Rita B. & Von Quintus, Harold. Validation of Relationships Between Specification Properties & Performance. (SHRP Ser.: A-409). (Illus.). 104p. (C). 1994. pap. text 15.00 (*0-309-05813-9*, PA409) Natl Res Coun.

Leahy, Robert L. Cognitive Therapy: Basic Principles & Applications. LC 96-11691. 1996. 50.00 (*1-56821-850-8*) Aronson.

Leahy, Robert L., ed. Practicing Cognitive Therapy: A Guide to Interventions. LC 97-5689. 504p. 1997. text 60.00 (*1-56821-824-9*) Aronson.

***Leahy, Robert L. & Holland, Stephen J.** Treatment Plans & Interventions for Depression & Anxiety Disorders. LC 99-59385. (Clinician's Toolbox Ser.). 320p. 2000. pap. text 55.00 (*1-57230-514-2*, CO514) Guilford Pubns.

Leahy, Syrell. The Good Friday Murder. large type ed. 400p. 1995. 27.99 (*0-7089-3417-X*) Ulverscroft.

Leahy, Syrell R. Family Truths. large type ed. 496p. 1986. 27.99 (*0-7089-8345-6*, Charnwood) Ulverscroft.

— Only Yesterday. large type ed. 1991. 27.99 (*0-7089-2448-4*) Ulverscroft.

***Leahy, T. M.** Sharron's Song. LC 99-91618. 1999. 25.00 (*0-7388-1132-7*); pap. 18.00 (*0-7388-1133-5*) Xlibris Corp.

Leahy, William. Providing Home Care: A Textbook for Home Care Aides. Fuzy, Jetta & Grafe, Julie, eds. (Illus.). 368p. (C). 1998. pap. text 34.95 (*1-888343-22-2*, TEXT22-2) Hartman Pub.

Leahy, William D. I Was There. Kohn, Richard H., ed. LC 78-22382. (American Military Experience Ser.). (Illus.). 1980. reprint ed. lib. bdg. 42.95 (*0-405-11859-7*) Ayer.

Leahy, William P. Adapting to America: Catholics, Jesuits, & Higher Education in the Twentieth Century. LC 90-40505. 210p. 1991. pap. 27.50 (*0-87840-504-6*) Georgetown U Pr.

Leaird, James T. Acoustic Emission Training Guide: How To Ensure An Accurate & Valid Acoustic Emission Test. Green, Allen T., ed. (Illus.). 179p. 1997. pap. 125.00 (*1-890545-00-7*) Greensland Pub.

Leak, Alexander. How to Sell to the U. S. Department of Commerce. Black, Breanda, ed. 42p. (Orig.). (C). 1995. pap. text 25.00 (*0-7881-2110-3*) DIANE Pub.

Leak, Andrew, tr. see Perec, Georges.

***Leak, Andrew N. & Paizis, George.** The Holocaust & the Text: Speaking the Unspeakable. LC 99-43178. 2000. text 39.95 (*0-312-22866-X*) St Martin.

***Leak, Anna Maxine.** Red Roses & Praise for My Lord. 2000. write for info. (*1-58235-495-2*) Watermrk Pr.

Leak, Colette, jt. auth. see Leak, John.

Leak, Jean, jt. auth. see Saunders, Donna.

Leak, John & Leak, Colette. Sri Lanka. (Travellers Survival Kit Ser.). 1999. pap. 18.95 (*1-85458-222-4*) Seven Hills Bk.

***Leak, S. G.** Tsetse Biology & Ecology: Their Role in the Epidemiology & Control of Trypanosomosis. LC 98-25951. 592p. 1999. text 120.00 (*0-85199-300-1*) OUP.

Leake. The Sixth Sense. (Longman Tutorial Resources Ser.). 1993. pap. text. write for info. (*0-582-22510-8*, Pub. by Addison-Wesley) Longman.

Leake, jt. auth. see Robottom.

Leake, Brenda, jt. ed. see Strahan, David.

Leake, Chauncey D. The Old Egyptian Medical Papyri: The Hearst Papyrus. 108p. (C). 1994. pap. text 15.00 (*0-89005-271-9*) Ares.

— Some Founders of Physiology: Contributors to the Growth of Functional Biology. LC 58-622. 132p. pap. 41.00 (*0-608-16755-X*, 202639500049) Bks Demand.

— What Are We Living For? A Practical Philosophy, 3 vols., Set. Incl. Vol. 1. What Are We Living For? A Practical Philosophy Vol. 1: Ethics. LC 72-95448. 1973. 19.95 (*0-9600290-2-8*); Vol. 2. What Are We Living For? A Practical Philosophy Vol. 2: Logics. LC 72-95448. 1974. 19.95 (*0-9600290-5-2*); Vol. 3. What Are We Living For? A Practical Philosophy Vol. 3: Esthetics. LC 72-95448. 1976. 19.95 (*0-9600290-6-0*); LC 72-95448. (C). 40.00 (*0-685-73414-5*) PJD Pubns.

— What Are We Living For? Vols. 1-3: A Practical Philosophy, Set. Date not set. 50.00 (*0-685-76504-0*) PJD Pubns.

Leake, Chauncey D., ed. see Percival, Thomas.

Leake, Chauncey D., tr. see Harvey, William.

Leake, David. Evaluating Explanations: A Content Theory. (Roger Schank's Artificial Intelligence Ser.). 280p. 1992. text 49.95 (*0-8058-1064-1*) L Erlbaum Assocs.

Leake, David, ed. Case-Based Reasoning: Papers from the 1993 Workshop. (Technical Reports). (Illus.). 171p. 1993. spiral bd. 25.00 (*0-929280-48-2*) AAAI Pr.

Leake, David B., ed. Case-Based Reasoning: Experiences, Lessons, & Future Directions. LC 96-18794. (AAAI Press Ser.). (Illus.). 525p. 1996. pap. text 42.00 (*0-262-62110-X*) MIT Pr.

Leake, David B. & Plaza, Enric. Case-Based Reasoning: Research & Development : Second International Conference, ICCBR-97, Providence, RI, U. S. A., July 25-27, 1997 : Proceedings, Vol. 126. LC 97-18145. (Lecture Notes in Artificial Intelligence). xiii, 648p. 1997. text. write for info. (*3-540-63233-6*) Spr-Verlag.

Leake, David B., jt. ed. see Ram, Ashwin.

Leake, Dorothy, jt. auth. see Leake, Henderson.

Leake, Dorothy V., et al. Desert & Mountain Plants of the Southwest. LC 92-50716. (Illus.). 1993. pap. 18.95 (*0-8061-2489-X*) U of Okla Pr.

Leake, Earnie, jt. auth. see Stanley, John L.

Leake, Henderson & Leake, Dorothy. Wildflowers of the Ozarks. LC 81-50400. (Illus.). vi, 170p. (Orig.). 1989. pap. 9.95 (*0-912456-04-3*) Ozark Soc Bks.

Leake, Percy D. Commercial Goodwill: Its History, Value & Treatment in Accounts. Brief, Richard P., ed. LC 80-1507. (Dimensions of Accounting Theory & Practice Ser.). 1980. reprint ed. lib. bdg. 30.95 (*0-405-13532-7*) Ayer.

— Depreciation & Wasting Assets & Their Treatment in Assessing Annual Profit & Loss. LC 75-18474. (History of Accounting Ser.). (Illus.). 1979. 20.95 (*0-405-07556-1*) Ayer.

Leake, William M. Journal of a Tour in Asia Minor with Comparative Remarks on the Ancient & Modern Geography of That Country. (GER.). xxvii, 362p. 1976. reprint ed. lib. bdg. 44.20 (*3-487-06055-8*) G Olms Pubs.

Leakey, F. W. Baudelaire: Collected Essays, 1953-1988. (Cambridge Studies in French: No. 30). (Illus.). 346p. (C). 1990. text 74.95 (*0-521-32335-5*) Cambridge U Pr.

— Baudelaire: "Les Fleurs du Mal" (Landmarks of World Literature Ser.). 142p. (C). 1992. text 34.95 (*0-521-36116-8*); pap. text 11.95 (*0-521-36937-1*) Cambridge U Pr.

Leakey, L. S., et al, eds. Adam or Ape: A Sourcebook of Discoveries about Early Man. LC 67-29326. 450p. 1982. 26.95 (*0-87073-700-7*); pap. text 19.95 (*0-87073-701-5*) Schenkman Bks Inc.

Leakey, Louis S. Defeating Mau Mau. LC 74-15061. reprint ed. 27.50 (*0-404-12102-0*) AMS Pr.

— White African: An Early Autobiography. LC 67-7042. (Illus.). 320p. (Orig.). 1966. reprint ed. pap. 99.20 (*0-608-05349-X*, 206505400012) Bks Demand.

Leakey, Louis S. & Goodall, Vanne M. Unveiling Man's Origins: Ten Decades of Thought about Human Evolution. LC 68-24269. (Illus.). 239p. 1969. reprint ed. pap. 74.10 (*0-608-05332-5*, 206503700012) Bks Demand.

Leakey, Mary. Olduvai Gorge Vol. 5: Excavations in Beds III, IV & the Masek Beds. (Illus.). 341p. (C). 1995. text 199.95 (*0-521-33403-9*) Cambridge U Pr.

Leakey, Meave G. & Leakey, Richard E., eds. Koobi Fora: Research Projects, Vol. 1. (Illus.). 208p. 1977. text 115.00 (*0-19-857392-8*) OUP.

Leakey, R. Introduction to Physical Anthropolgy. 448p. (C). 1995. pap. text 37.00 (*0-13-474446-2*, Macmillan Coll) P-H.

Leakey, R. R. & Newton, A. C., eds. Tropical Trees: The Potential for Domestication & the Rebuilding of Forest Resources. 284p. 1994. pap. 80.00 (*0-11-701562-8*, Pub. by Statnry Office) Balogh.

Leakey, R. R. B., et al, eds. Domestication & Commercialization of Non-Timber Forest Products in Agroforestry. LC 98-106430. (Non-Wood Forest Products Ser.: No. 9). 297p. 1997. pap. 31.00 (*92-5-103935-6*, F39356, Pub. by FAO) Bernan Associates.

Leakey, Richard. The Origin of Humankind. LC 94-3617. (Science Masters Ser.). (Illus.). 171p. 1994. 20.00 (*0-465-03135-8*, Pub. by Basic) HarpC.

— The Origin of Humankind. 192p. 1996. pap. 12.00 (*0-465-05313-0*) HarpC.

Leakey, Richard & Lewin, Roger. Origins Reconsidered: In Search of What Makes Us Human. 400p. 1993. pap. 16.95 (*0-385-46792-3*, Anchor NY) Doubleday.

— The Sixth Extinction: Patterns of Life & the Future of Humankind. (Illus.). 288p. 1996. pap. 14.00 (*0-385-46809-1*, Anchor NY) Doubleday.

Leakey, Richard E. & Lewin, Roger. People of the Lakes. 272p. 1979. mass mkt. 4.95 (*0-380-45575-7*, Avon Bks) Morrow Avon.

Leakey, Richard E. & Slikkerveer, Leendert J., eds. Origins & Development of Agriculture in East Africa: The Ethnosystems Approach to the Study of Early Food Production in Kenya. (Studies in Technology & Social Change: No. 19). (Illus.). 302p. (Orig.). (C). 1991. pap. 20.00 (*0-945271-28-X*) ISU-CIKARD.

Leakey, Richard E., jt. ed. see Leakey, Meave G.

Leakey, Richard E., jt. ed. see Walker, Alan.

Leal, Brigitte. Picasso: Les Demoiselles de Avignon - Album de Dibujos. (Ediciones Especiales y de Bibliofilo Ser.). (SPA., Illus.). 116p. 1993. 375.00 (*84-343-0533-X*) Elliots Bks.

***Leal, Brigitte, et al.** The Ultimate Picasso. Stevens, Molly & De Jager, Marjolijn, trs. (Illus.). 504p. 2000. 95.00 (*0-8109-3940-1*, Pub. by Abrams) Time Warner.

Leal, Dolores Y. & Hubbard, Elizabeth. Litigating Sexual Harassment & Sex Discrimination Cases. 500p. 1997. ring bd. 99.00 (*0-938065-99-8*) James Pub Santa Ana.

Leal, Donald E., jt. ed. see Baden, John A.

***Leal, Donald R. & Grewell, J. Bishop.** Hunting for Habitat: A Practical Guide to State-Landowner Partnerships. (Illus.). 72p. 1999. pap. 5.00i (*0-9668243-2-6*) Pol Econo Res.

Leal, Donald R., jt. auth. see Anderson, Terry L.

Leal Filho, Walter, ed. Lifelong Learning & Environmental Education. LC 97-18417. (GER.). 201p. 1997. pap. 31.95 (*3-631-32258-5*) P Lang Pubng.

Leal, Gilbert, jt. auth. see Salyer, Monica.

Leal-Idrogo, Anita, et al. Pak: Multicultural Women: Health, Disability & Rehabilitation. 446p. (C). 1996. pap. text, student ed., wbk. ed. 66.95 (*0-7872-1998-3*, 41199801) Kendall-Hunt.

Leal, J. H. Marine Prosobranch Gastropods from Oceanic Islands off Brazil. (Illus.). 419p. 1991. pap. 99.00 (*90-73348-11-0*, Pub. by Backhuys Pubs) Balogh.

Leal-Khouri, Susana, et al. Manual of Dermatologic Surgery Techniques. 320p. 1998. spiral bd. write for info. (*0-397-51497-2*) Lppncott W & W.

Leal-Khouri, Susana, jt. auth. see Mallory, Susan B.

Leal, L. Gary. Laminar Flow & Convective Transport Processes: Scaling Principles & Asymptotic Analysis. (Illus.). 592p. 1992. text 120.00 (*0-7506-9117-4*) Buttrwrth-Heinemann.

Leal, Linda. A Family-Centered Approach to People with Mental Retardation. LC 98-50474. (Innovations Ser.). 53p. 1999. write for info. (*0-940898-59-4*) Am Assn Mental.

Leal, Luis. Aztlan y Mexico: Perfiles Literarios e Historicos. LC 83-71984. (SPA.). 260p. 1985. lib. bdg. 28.00 (*0-916950-46-8*) Biling Rev-Pr.

— Don Luis Leal, una Vida y Dos Culturas. (SPA., Illus.). 152p. 1998. pap. 16.00 (*0-927534-77-0*) Biling Rev-Pr.

— No Longer Voiceless. (Illus.). 195p. (Orig.). (C). 1995. pap. 22.00 (*0-927065-16-9*) Marin Chula Vista.

— Spanish-English, English-Spanish Naval Dictionary. 3rd enl. rev. ed. (ENG & SPA.). 232p. 1987. pap. 24.25 (*84-283-1089-0*, Pub. by Paraninfo) IBD Ltd.

Leal, Luis L. Diccionario Naval: Ingles-Espanol, Espanol-Ingles. 4th ed. (ENG & SPA.). 232p. 1987. pap. 39.95 (*0-7859-3679-3*, S38405) Fr & Eur.

Leal, Magdalena L. De, see Deere, Carmen & De Leal, Magdalena L.

Leal, Maria T., tr. see Veiga, Jose C., et al.

Leal-McBride, Maria-Odilia. Narratives e Narradores em a Pedra do Reino: Estruturas e Perpectivas Cambiantes. (American University Studies: Romance Languages & Literature: Ser. II, Vol. 110). IX, 199p. (C). 1989. text 36.50 (*0-8204-1049-7*) P Lang Pubng.

Leal, Victor N. Coronelismo: The Municipality & Representative Government in Brazil. LC 76-46044. (Cambridge Latin American Studies: No. 28). 254p. reprint ed. pap. 72.40 (*0-608-13576-3*, 2022459) Bks Demand.

Leale, Judy. Three-Minute Bible Stories. (Illus.). 32p. (J). 1992. 9.95 (*1-56156-152-5*) Kidsbks.

Leaman, Christine, ed. see Yates, Elizabeth.

Leaman, Frank, jt. auth. see Puippe, Jean-Claude.

Leaman, James R. Faith Roots: Learning from & Sharing Witness with Jewish People. LC 92-75500. (Illus.). 171p. (Orig.). (C). 1993. pap. 12.95 (*0-916035-57-3*) Evangel Indiana.

Leaman, Jeremy, jt. ed. see Hargreaves, Alec G.

Leaman, Oliver. Averroes & His Philosophy. 220p. 1997. pap. 29.95 (*0-7007-0675-5*, Pub. by Curzon Pr Ltd) Paul & Co Pubs.

***Leaman, Oliver.** A Brief Introduction to Islamic Philosophy. LC 99-45343. 224p. 2000. text 59.95 (*0-7456-1960-6*, Pub. by Polity Pr); pap. text 24.95 (*0-7456-1961-4*, Pub. by Polity Pr) Blackwell Pubs.

Leaman, Oliver. Death & Loss: Compassionate Approaches in the Classroom. (Cassell Studies in Pastoral Care & PSE). (Illus.). 160p. 1995. 100.00 (*0-304-33087-6*); pap. 33.95 (*0-304-33089-2*) Continuum.

***Leaman, Oliver.** Eastern Philosophy: The Key Readings. 256p. 2000. 60.00 (*0-415-17357-4*); pap. 17.99 (*0-415-17358-2*) Routledge.

— Encyclopedia of Asian Philosophy. LC 00-32836. (Illus.). 2001. write for info. (*0-415-17281-0*) Routledge.

Leaman, Oliver. Evil & Suffering in Jewish Philosophy. (Cambridge Studies in Religious Traditions: No. 6). 272p. 1995. pap. text 22.95 (*0-521-42722-3*) Cambridge U Pr.

— The Future of Philosophy: Towards the Twenty-First Century. LC 97-18304. 192p. (C). 1998. 65.00 (*0-415-14928-2*); pap. 20.99 (*0-415-14929-0*) Routledge.

***Leaman, Oliver.** Key Concepts in Eastern Philosophy. 336p. 1999. 60.00 (*0-415-17362-0*) Routledge.

Leaman, Oliver. Key Concepts in Eastern Philosophy. (Key Concepts Ser.). 1999. pap. 17.99 (*0-415-17363-9*) Routledge.

— Moses Maimonides. 212p. 1997. pap. 29.95 (*0-7007-0676-3*, Pub. by Curzon Pr Ltd) Paul & Co Pubs.

Leaman, Oliver, ed. Friendship East & West: Philosophical Perspectives. (Curzon Studies in Asian Philosophy). 260p. (C). 1996. text 45.00 (*0-7007-0358-6*, Pub. by Curzon Pr Ltd) UH Pr.

Leaman, Oliver, jt. ed. see Frank, Daniel.

Leaman, Oliver, jt. ed. see Nasr, Seyyed Hossein.

Leaman, T. L. Healing the Anxiety Diseases. (Illus.). 304p. (C). 1992. 23.95 (*0-306-44128-4*, Plenum Trade) Perseus Pubng.

Leaman, T. L. & Saxton, J. W. Preventing Malpractice: The Co-Active Solution. (Illus.). 254p. (C). 1993. text 39.50 (*0-306-44441-0*, Kluwer Plenum) Kluwer Academic.

Leaman, Thomas L., jt. auth. see Saxton, James W.

Leamaster, A. James. Superwrite Vol. 2: An Alphabetic Writing System, Vol. 2. (KB - Notemaking Ser.). 1990. mass mkt. 22.50 (*0-538-60803-X*) S-W Pub.

Leamer. International Trade. write for info. (*1-57259-820-4*) Worth.

Leamer, E. E., jt. auth. see Heckman, J. J.

Leamer, Edward E. The Heckscher-Ohlin Model in Theory & Practice. LC 94-49591. (Studies in International Finance: No. 77). 77p. 1995. pap. 13.50 (*0-88165-249-0*) Princeton U Int Finan Econ.

— Specification Searches: Ad Hoc Inference with Nonexperimental Data. LC 77-26855. 383p. reprint ed. pap. 118.80 (*0-7837-2816-6*, 205765600006) Bks Demand.

— Sturdy Econometrics. LC 94-4208. (Economists of the Twentieth Century Ser.). 392p. 1994. 95.00 (*1-85278-802-X*) E Elgar.

***Leamer, Laurence.** Ascent: The Spiritual & Physical Quest of Legendary Mountaineer Willi Unsoeld. LC 99-12031. 400p. 1999. pap. 14.00 (*0-688-16543-5*, Quil) HarperTrade.

Leamer, Laurence. The Kennedy Men. 1924. write for info. (*0-688-16315-7*, Wm Morrow) Morrow Avon.

— Three Chords & the Truth. 1997. 26.00 (*0-614-27995-X*) HarpC.

Leaming, Barbara. Katharine Hepburn. (Illus.). 549p. 1998. text 30.00 (*0-7881-5915-1*) DIANE Pub.

***Leaming, Barbara.** Katharine Hepburn. (Illus.). 560p. 2000. pap. 23.95 (*0-87910-293-4*) Limelight Edns.

Leaming, Barbara. Katharine Hepburn. 592p. 1996. mass mkt. 7.50 (*0-380-72717-X*, Avon Bks) Morrow Avon.

— Katharine Hepburn. LC 94-46303. 1996. 12.60 (*0-606-09509-8*, Pub. by Turtleback) Demco.

— Marilyn Monroe. LC 98-18738. (Illus.). 448p. 1998. 27.50 (*0-517-70260-6*) Crown Pub Group.

***Leaming, Barbara.** Marilyn Monroe. 464p. 2000. pap. 15.00 (*0-609-80553-3*, Three Riv Pr) Crown Pub Group.

Leaming, Barbara. Orson Welles: A Biography. (Illus.). 592p. 1995. reprint ed. pap. 20.00 (*0-87910-199-7*) Limelight Edns.

— Rita Hayworth: Her Story. write for info. (*0-318-62112-6*) Viking Penguin.

Leaming, Chris, jt. auth. see Leaming, Stan.

Leaming, Deryl R. Academic Leadership: A Practical Guide to Chairing the Department. 300p. 1998. 35.95 (*1-882982-22-3*) Anker Pub.

Leaming, Hugo P. Hidden Americans: Maroons of Virginia & the Carolinas. rev. ed. LC 94-34177. (Studies in African American History & Culture). 505p. 1995. text 99.00 (*0-8153-1543-0*) Garland.

Leaming, Stan & Leaming, Chris. Western Rocks & Minerals. (Illus.). 33p. (Orig.). 1980. pap. 4.95 (*0-88839-053-X*) Hancock House.

Leaming, Thomas. Philadelphia Lawyer in the London Courts. (Illus.). xiii, 199p. 1987. reprint ed. 38.00 (*0-8377-2408-2*, Rothman) W S Hein.

— A Philadelphia Lawyer in the London Courts. 2nd rev. ed. xv, 199p. 1997. reprint ed. 65.00 (*1-56169-252-2*) Gaunt.

Leamnson, Robert. Thinking about Teaching: Developing Habits of Learning with First Year College & University Students. LC 98-39114. 1999. pap. 22.50 (*1-57922-013-4*) Stylus Pub VA.

Leamnson, Robert N. Learning Your Way Through College. LC 94-24778. 121p. 1994. 29.95 (*0-534-24504-8*) Wadsworth Pub.

— Thinking about Teaching: Developing Habits of Learning with First Year College & University Studies. LC 98-39114. 1999. 45.00 (*1-57922-012-6*) Stylus Pub VA.

Leamon, James S. Revolution Downeast: The War for American Independence in Maine. LC 92-17757. (Illus.). 320p. (Orig.). 1995. pap. 18.95 (*0-87023-959-7*) U of Mass Pr.

Leamon, Warren. Harry Mathews. LC 93-929. (United States Authors Ser.: No. 628). 144p. 1993. 22.95 (*0-8057-4008-2*) Macmillan.

Leamy, Edmund. Fairy Minstrel of Glenmalure & Other Stories for Children. LC 76-9901. (Children's Literature Reprint Ser.). (Illus.). (J). (gr. 4-6). 1976. reprint ed. 20.00 (*0-8486-0210-2*) Roth Pub Inc.

— Golden Spears & Other Fairy Tales. LC 76-9902. (Children's Literature Reprint Ser.). (Illus.). (J). (gr. 4-6). 1976. reprint ed. 20.00 (*0-8486-0211-0*) Roth Pub Inc.

Lean, jt. auth. see Kamm.

Lean, Arthur E. & Eaton, William E. Education or Catastrophe? LC 89-37671. 125p. (Orig.). (C). 1989. 25.00 (*0-89341-588-X*, Longwood Academic); pap. 14.95 (*0-89341-589-8*, Longwood Academic) Hollowbrook.

Lean, David, jt. auth. see Kemp, Richard.

Lean, Eric G., et al, eds. Display Devices & Systems, Vol. 2892. 292p. 1996. 46.00 (*0-8194-2293-2*) SPIE.

Lean, Garth. God's Politician: William Wilberforce's Struggle. LC 87-23705. 200p. (Orig.). (C). 1988. pap. 15.95 (*0-939443-03-1*) Helmers Howard Pub.

— Good God, It Works! 1974. 2.95 (*0-7137-0719-4*) Grosvenor USA.

— On the Tail of a Comet: The Life of Frank Buchman. LC 87-32740. (Illus.). 632p. 1988. 39.95 (*0-939443-06-6*); pap. 22.95 (*0-939443-07-4*) Helmers Howard Pub.

Lean, Geoffrey. Atlas of the Environment. 3rd ed. 192p. 1996. lib. bdg. 39.50 (*0-87436-849-9*) ABC-CLIO.

— Rich World, Poor World. 1979. pap. 13.50 (*0-04-309012-5*) Routledge.

Lean, Mary. Bread, Bricks & Belief: Communities in Charge of Their Future. LC 95-14670. (Kumarian Press Books for a World That Works). (Illus.). 192p. 1995. pap. 15.95 (*1-56549-046-0*) Kumarian Pr.

Lean, Vincent S. Lean's Collecteana, 5 vols., Set. 1969. reprint ed. 210.00 (*1-55888-181-6*) Omnigraphics Inc.

Leana, Carrie R. & Rouseau, Denise M. Relational Wealth: The Advantages of Stability in a Changing Economy. write for info. (*0-19-513447-8*) OUP.

Leana, Frank. The Best Private High Schools & How to Get In. 2nd ed. (Princeton Review Ser.). 1998. pap. 20.00 (*0-375-75208-0*) Villard Books.

Leander, Kristine, ed. Family Sagas: Stories of Scandinavian Immigrants. LC 98-124333. (Illus.). xi, 226p. 1997. pap. 39.95 (*0-9661693-1-X*) Scan Lang Inst.

Leander, Pontus, jt. auth. see Bauer, Hans.

***Leander, Richard.** Building Application Servers. (Advances in Object Technology Ser.: No. 24). 400p. 2000. pap. 39.95 (*0-521-77849-2*) Cambridge U Pr.

Leander, William J., et al. Patients First: Experiences of a Patient-Focused Pioneer. LC 95-46555. 1996. pap. 44.00 (*1-56793-039-5*, 0974) Health Admin Pr.

Leaner, Laurence. The Kennedy Women. 1996. pap. 16.00 (*0-449-91171-3*) Fawcett.

Leaning, Jennifer & Keyes, Langley C., eds. The Counterfeit Ark: Crisis Relocation for Nuclear War. LC 83-15519. 368p. 1983. pap. 14.95 (*0-88410-941-0*, HarpBusn) HarpInfo.

L

An Asterisk (*) at the beginning of an entry indicates that the title is appearing for the first time.

Leaning, Jennifer, et al. Humanitarian Crises: The Medical & Public Health Response. LC 98-41838. 1999. 45.00 (*0-674-15515-7*) HUP.

Leante, Cesar. Calembour. (SPA.). 189p. (Orig.). 1988. pap. 9.95 (*84-86214-41-6*) Ediciones.

Leanza, Umberto, jt. ed. see Pharand, Donat.

Leap. Principles of Management. (C). 1996. text. write for info. (*0-03-096375-3*) Harcourt Coll Pubs.

Leap Foundation Staff, jt. auth. see Mitchell, Patti.

Leap, Jackson. Rhyme & Reason: Pages from the Heart of a Songwriter. LC 96-70038. 160p. (Orig.). 1996. pap. 22.95 (*1-881576-91-4*) Providence Hse.

Leap, Nicky & Hunter, Billie. The Midwife's Tale: An Oral History from Handywoman to Professional Midwife. (Illus.). 238p. 1993. pap. 20.95 (*1-85727-041-X*, Pub. by Scarlet Pr) LPC InBook.

Leap, Terry L. Tenure, Discrimination, & the Courts. 2nd ed. LC 95-8943. 1995. pap. 16.95 (*0-87546-348-7*, ILR Press) Cornell U Pr.

Leap, William L. American Indian English. 352p. 1993. 37.50 (*0-87480-416-7*) U of Utah Pr.

***Leap, William L.** Public Sex/Gay Space. LC 98-26490. (Between Men - Between Women Ser.). 304p. 1998. 49.50 (*0-231-10690-4*) Col U Pr.

Leap, William L. Public Sex/Gay Space. LC 98-26490. (Illus.). 304p. 1999. pap. 17.50 (*0-231-10691-2*) Col U Pr.

— Word's Out: Gay Men's English. LC 95-35967. 216p. 1996. pap. 17.95 (*0-8166-2253-1*); text 44.95 (*0-8166-2252-3*) U of Minn Pr.

Leap, William L., ed. Beyond the Lavender Lexicon. 426p. 1995. text 76.00 (*2-88449-180-5*) Gordon & Breach.

— Beyond the Lavender Lexicon. 426p. 1996. pap. text 15.00 (*2-88449-181-3*) Gordon & Breach.

Leap, William L., jt. ed. see Lewin, Ellen.

Leapard, Dave. Making a Dream Come True. (C). 1993. student ed. 14.00 (*1-881592-33-2*) Hayden-McNeil.

Leape, Lucian L. Patient Care in Pediatric Surgery. 448p. 1987. 52.95 (*0-316-51821-2*, Little Brwn Med Div) Lppncott W & W.

Leape, Lucian L., et al. Coronary Angiography: Ratings of Appropriateness & Necessity by a Canadian Panel. LC 93-34519. 1993. pap. text 15.00 (*0-8330-1453-6*, MR-129-CWF/PCT) Rand Corp.

— Hysterectomy: Clinical Recommendations & Indications for Use. LC 97 11334. 1998. pap. 15.00 (*0-8330-2501-5*) Rand Corp.

Leape, Martha P. Harvard GT Careers. (Illus.). 1983. pap. 6.95 (*0-674-37375-8*) HUP.

Leape, Martha P. The Harvard Guide to Careers. 5th ed. LC 95-23202. 223p. 1995. pap. 13.00 (*0-943747-16-3*) Harvard OCS.

Leape, Martha P. & Vacca, Susan M. The Harvard Guide to Careers. 3rd ed. 232p. (C). 1991. pap. 12.95 (*0-674-37565-3*) HUP.

Leaper, Campbell, ed. Childhood Gender Segregation: Causes & Consequences. LC 85-644751. (New Directions for Child Development Ser.: No. CD 65). 104p. (Orig.). 1994. pap. 25.00 (*0-7879-9985-7*) Jossey-Bass.

Leaper, D. J., ed. Selected Papers & Discussion from the Second Annual Meeting of the SISE June 2-3, 1989, Geneva, Switzerland. (Surgical Research Communications Ser.). ii, 138p. 1990. pap. text 130.00 (*3-7186-5023-1*) Gordon & Breach.

— Selected Papers from the 1st Meeting of the SISE, Vol. 5, No. 1. (Surgical Research Communications Ser.). ii, 94p. 1989. pap. text 74.00 (*3-7186-4894-6*) Gordon & Breach.

Leaper, D. J. & Harding, K. G. Wounds: Biology & Management. (Illus.). 210p. 1998. text 149.50 (*0-19-262332-X*) OUP.

Leaper, David J. & Branicki, Frank J., eds. International Surgical Practice. (Illus.). 432p. 1992. 125.00 (*0-19-261999-3*); pap. 59.00 (*0-19-262252-8*) OUP.

Leaper, David J., jt. ed. see McLatchie, G.

Leaper, Mary J., ed. see Mills, Kenneth G.

Leaphart, C. Mark & Leaphart, J. Kirk, Jr. How to Build Your Net Worth: Buying Residential Real Estate with None of Your Own Money. (Workbook Ser.). 56p. 1994. pap., wbk. ed. 9.95 (*1-890646-02-4*) Leaphart Prodns.

— How to Build Your Net Worth: Buying Residential Real Estate with None of Your Own Money. (Guide Ser.: Vol. 2). 178p. 1994. pap. 19.95 (*1-890646-04-0*) Leaphart Prodns.

— How to Build Your Net Worth: Buying Residential Real Estate with None of Your Own Money. (Forms Library). (Illus.). 180p. 1994. pap. 29.95 (*1-890646-05-9*) Leaphart Prodns.

— How to Build Your Net Worth: Buying Residential Real Estate with None of Your Own Money. (Guide Ser.: Vol. 1). (Illus.). 160p. 1994. pap. 19.95 (*1-890646-03-2*) Leaphart Prodns.

Leaphart, C. Mark & Leaphart, J. Kirk. The Seventy Percent Factor: Accumulating Savings Through Residential Real Estate Buying. 2nd ed. (Forms Library). 62p. (Orig.). 1994. pap. write for info. (*0-9644909-1-9*) VCI Invest.

Leaphart, C. Mark, jt. auth. see Leaphart, J. Kirk, Jr.

Leaphart, J. Kirk, Jr. & Leaphart, C. Mark. The Seventy Percent Factor: Accumulating Savings Through Residential Real Estate Buying. 2nd ed. 233p. (Orig.). 1994. pap. write for info. (*0-9644909-0-0*) VCI Invest.

Leaphart, J. Kirk, jt. auth. see Leaphart, C. Mark.

***Leapman, Melissa.** Close-Knit Family: Sweaters for Everyone You Love. LC 99-14825. (Illus.). 153p. 1999. 24.95 (*1-56158-251-4*) Taunton.

— Crochet with Style: Fun-to-Make Sweaters for Every Occasion. (Illus.). 2000. pap. 19.95 (*1-56158-339-1*) Taunton.

Leapman, Michael. Arrogant Aussie: The Rupert Murdoch Story. LC 84-24093. (Illus.). 288p. 1985. 14.95 (*0-8184-0370-5*) Carol Pub Group.

— Companion Guide to New York. (Companion Guide Ser.). (Illus.). 350p. 1991. pap. 18.95 (*0-685-48925-6*, Harper Ref) HarpC.

— The Companion Guide to New York. rev. ed. (Illus.). 356p. 1996. 24.95 (*1-900639-09-2*) Boydell & Brewer.

***Leapman, Michael.** The Guide to New York. 2nd rev. ed. (Illus.). 352p. 2000. pap. 24.95 (*1-900639-32-7*) Boydell & Brewer.

Leapman, Michael. London. LC 92-53470. (Eyewitness Travel Guides Ser.). (Illus.). 432p. 1993. pap. 24.95 (*1-56458-183-7*) DK Pub Inc.

***Leapman, Michael.** Witnesses to War. (Illus.). 128p. (J). (gr. 5 up). 2000. pap. 7.99 (*0-14-130841-9*, PuffinBks) Peng Put Young Read.

Leapman, Michael. Witnesses to War: Eight True-Life Stories of Nazi Persecution. LC 98-208868. (Illus.). 127p. (YA). (gr. 5 up). 1998. 16.99 (*0-670-87386-1*) Viking Penguin.

Leaptrott & Company Staff. Domestic Protocol. (GI - Organizational Behavior Ser.). 1996. pap. 28.95 (*0-538-85456-1*) S-W Pub.

— Rules of the Game Resource Guide. (GC - Principles of Management Ser.). 1996. text 19.95 (*0-538-86199-1*) S-W Pub.

Lear, jt. auth. see Sowerby.

Lear, Amy C., jt. auth. see Bane, Adele F.

Lear, Dana. Sex & Sexuality: Risk & Relationships in the Age of AIDS. LC 97-4596. 157p. 1997. 42.00 (*0-7619-0477-8*); pap. 19.95 (*0-7619-0478-6*) Sage.

Lear, Edward. A Was Once an Apple Pie. LC 91-71865. (Illus.). 32p. (J). (ps-2). 1997. reprint ed. pap. 5.99 (*0-7636-0103-9*); reprint ed. pap. 5.99 (*0-614-28642-5*) Candlewick Pr.

— A Book of Learned Nonsense. Haining, Peter, ed. (Pocket Classics Ser.). (Illus.). 192p. 1992. reprint ed. pap. 8.95 (*0-7509-0087-3*, Pub. by Sutton Pub Ltd) Intl Pubs Mktg.

— A Book of Nonsense. LC 92-53176. (Everyman's Library of Children's Classics). (Illus.). 240p. (J). 1992. 13.95 (*0-679-41798-2*, Evrymans Lib Childs) Knopf.

— Complete Nonsense Book of Edward Lear. 1994. 8.98 (*0-7858-0168-5*) Bk Sales Inc.

— The Complete Nonsense of Edward Lear. 24.95 (*0-89190-090-X*) Amereon Ltd.

— The Complete Nonsense of Edward Lear. (Illus.). 320p. (J). (gr. 4-6). 1951. pap. 6.95 (*0-486-20167-8*) Dover.

— The Complete Nonsense of Edward Lear. Jackson, Holdrook, ed. (Illus.). 1990. 22.50 (*0-8446-0722-3*) Peter Smith.

— Daffy down Dillies: Silly Limericks. LC 91-72986. (Illus.). 32p. (J). 1992. 14.95 (*1-56397-007-4*) Boyds Mills Pr.

— The Dong with a Luminous Nose. LC 86-1143. (Illus.). 1986. 6.95 (*0-915361-46-9*) Lambda Pubs.

— An Edward Lear Alphabet. LC 98-27496. (Illus.). 32p. (J). (ps-2). 1999. 14.95 (*0-06-028113-8*); lib. bdg. 14.89 (*0-06-028114-6*) HarpC Child Bks.

— Edward Lear's Book of Nonsense. Shtull, Simcha, ed. & afterword by by. LC 96-150503. (Illus.). 46p. (J). (gr. 3-9). 1995. 18.95 (*1-888297-01-8*, LEAR-01) Maxima New Media.

— The Jumblies. LC 86-1147. (Illus.). 1986. 6.95 (*0-915361-34-5*) Lambda Pubs.

— The Jumblies & Other Nonsense Verse. (Classic Verse Ser.). 56p. (J). text 3.50 (*0-7214-1756-6*, Ladybrd) Penguin Putnam.

— Later Letters of Edward Lear. Strachey, Lady, ed. LC 75-175702. (Select Bibliographies Reprint Ser.). 1977. reprint ed. 27.95 (*0-8369-6617-1*) Ayer.

— Letters of Edward Lear to Chichester Fortescue & Frances Countess Waldegrave. LC 70-107812. (Select Bibliographies Reprint Ser.). 1977. 27.95 (*0-8369-5208-1*) Ayer.

— Nonsense Books. (BCL1-PR English Literature Ser.). 1992. reprint ed. lib. bdg. 139.00 (*0-7812-7589-X*) Rprt Serv.

— Nonsense Poems. LC 93-39193. (Illus.). 96p. (Orig.). (J). 1998. reprint ed. pap. 1.00 (*0-486-28031-4*) Dover.

— Nonsense Songs. LC 96-77401. (Illus.). 40p. (J). 1997. 16.00 (*0-689-81369-4*) McElderry Bks.

— Nonsense Verse. (Illus.). 32p. 1999. 12.95 (*1-85149-704-8*) Antique Collect.

— The Owl & the Pussy Cat. LC 95-83849. (Illus.). 32p. (J). (ps-2). 1996. 13.00 (*0-689-81032-6*) S&S Childrens.

— The Owl & the Pussy-Cat, & Other Nonsense Poems. LC 95-13076. (Illus.). 64p. (J). (gr. k-3). 1995. 18.95 (*1-55858-467-6*, Pub. by North-South Bks NYC) Chronicle Bks.

— The Owl & the Pussycat. (Illus.). (J). (ps-2). Date not set. 13.00 (*0-614-19209-9*) Atheneum Yung Read.

— The Owl & the Pussycat. LC 97-2131. (Illus.). 32p. (J). (ps-3). 1997. pap. 5.99 (*0-7636-0336-8*) Candlewick Pr.

— The Owl & the Pussycat. 32p. (J). (ps-1). 1989. pap. 6.95 (*0-89919-854-6*, Clarion Bks) HM.

— The Owl & the Pussycat. (Illus.). 16p. (J). (ps-2). 1993. 12.95 (*0-8249-8571-0*, Ideals Child) Hambleton-Hill.

— The Owl & the Pussycat. LC 86-46115. (Poetry Pop-Up Bk.). (Illus.). 14p. (J). (ps-3). 1987. 6.95 (*0-694-00193-7*) HarpC Child Bks.

— The Owl & the Pussycat. LC 92-52640. (Michael di Capua Bks.). (Illus.). 32p. (J). (gr. k up). 1998. lib. bdg. 15.89 (*0-06-205011-7*) HarpC Child Bks.

— The Owl & the Pussycat. LC 92-52640. (Michael di Capua Bks.). (Illus.). 32p. (J). (gr. k up). 1998. 15.95 (*0-06-205010-9*) HarpC Child Bks.

— The Owl & the Pussycat. LC 90-32244. (Illus.). 32p. (J). (ps-3). 1996. pap. 6.99 (*0-698-11367-5*, PapStar) Peng Put Young Read.

— The Owl & the Pussycat. LC 97-196479. (Illus.). 32p. 1997. bds. 7.95 (*0-399-23193-5*, G P Putnam) Peng Put Young Read.

— The Pelican Chorus: And Other Nonsense. LC 94-78570. (Illus.). 40p. (J). (gr. k up). 1995. 14.95 (*0-06-205062-1*) HarpC.

— The Quangle Wangle's Hat. LC 87-29616. (Illus.). 32p. (J). (ps-3). 1988. 12.95 (*0-15-264450-4*) Harcourt.

— The Quangle Wangle's Hat. LC 87-29616. (Illus.). 32p. (J). 1997. pap. 6.00 (*0-15-201478-0*) Harcourt.

— The Quangle Wangle's Hat. (J). 1997. 11.20 (*0-606-11774-1*, Pub. by Turtleback) Demco.

— The Table & the Chair. LC 91-45538. (Illus.). 32p. (J). (ps-3). 1993. 15.00 (*0-06-020804-X*); lib. bdg. 14.89 (*0-06-020805-8*) HarpC Child Bks.

Lear, Edward. There Was an Old Man... A Collection of Limericks. (Illus.). 80p. (J). 1994. 16.95 (*1-55074-213-2*) Kids Can Pr.

Lear, Edward. Two Nonsense Stories. (Illus.). 64p. 1993. 130.00 (*0-907664-19-9*, Pub. by Old Stiles) St Mut.

— Two Nonsense Stories. limited ed. (Illus.). 64p. 1993. 500.00 (*0-907664-18-0*, Pub. by Old Stiles) St Mut.

Lear, Edward & Allen, Jonathan. Nonsense Songs. (Illus.). 208p. (J). (gr. 4-8). 1995. 14.95 (*0-8050-2774-2*, Bks Young Read) H Holt & Co.

Lear, Edward & Carroll, Lewis. The Owl & the Pussycat. (Illus.). 64p. (J). write for info. (*0-19-276102-1*) OUP.

— Owls & Pussycats: Nonsense Verse. LC 93-2714. (Illus.). 64p. (J). (gr. 2 up). 1993. 16.95 (*0-87226-366-5*, 63665B, P Bedrick Books) NTC Contemp Pub Co.

Lear, Edward & Nash, Ogden. Scroobious Pip. LC 68-10373. (Illus.). (J). (gr. 3 up). 1968. 14.95 (*0-06-023764-3*) HarpC Child Bks.

Lear, Edward, jt. auth. see Brett, Jan.

Lear, Edward, jt. auth. see De Paola, Tomie.

Lear, Floyd S., jt. ed. see Drew, Katherine F.

Lear, G. M. Abramos la Biblia: Antiguo Testamento. Orig. Title: Let's Open the Bible. (SPA.). 200p. 1992. pap. 4.99 (*0-8254-1438-5*, Edit Portavoz) Kregel.

Lear, John. Skilful Weight Lifting. (Skilful Ser.). (Illus.). 96p. 1991. pap. write for info. (*0-7136-3396-4*, Pub. by A & C Blk) Midpt Trade.

— Weight Training & Lifting. pap. write for info. (*0-7136-5674-3*, 91804, Pub. by A & C Blk) Midpt Trade.

***Lear, John.** Workers, Neighbors & Citizens: The Revolution in Mexico City. (Illus.). 432p. 2001. text 60.00 (*0-8032-2936-4*); pap. text 29.95 (*0-8032-7997-3*, Bison Books) U of Nebr Pr.

Lear, John, jt. auth. see Collins, Joseph.

Lear, Jonathan. Aristotle: The Desire to Understand. 352p. 1988. pap. text 22.95 (*0-521-34762-9*) Cambridge U Pr.

***Lear, Jonathan.** Happiness, Death & the Remainder of Life. 224p. 2000. 24.00 (*0-674-00329-2*) HUP.

Lear, Jonathan. Love & Its Place in Nature: A Philosophical Interpretation of Freudian Psychoanalysis. 243p. 1991. pap. 10.00 (*0-374-52320-7*) FS&G.

— Love & Its Place in Nature: A Philosophical Interpretation of Freudian Psychoanalysis. 243p. 1999. reprint ed. text 19.00 (*0-7881-6269-1*) DIANE Pub.

— Open Minded: Working Out the Logic of the Soul. LC 97-41055. 368p. 1999. text 35.00 (*0-674-45533-9*) HUP.

— Open Minded: Working Out the Logic of the Soul. 345p. 1999. pap. 15.95 (*0-674-45534-7*) HUP.

Lear, Jonathan, pref. Love & Its Place in Nature: A Philosophical Interpretation of Freudian Psychoanalysis. LC 98-28023. 256p. 1998. pap. 12.50 (*0-300-07467-0*) Yale U Pr.

Lear, Linda. Rachel Carson: Witness for Nature. LC 97-8324. 634p. 1995. 35.00 (*0-8050-3427-7*) H Holt & Co.

***Lear, Linda.** Rachel Carson: Witness for Nature. (Illus.). 656p. 1998. pap. 17.95 (*0-8050-3428-5*, Owl) H Holt & Co.

Lear, Linda, ed. see Carson, Rachel Louise.

Lear, Linda J., jt. auth. see Fisher, Perry G.

Lear, Pat. The New Carbohydrate Diet Counter. 64p. 1982. pap. 4.95 (*0-941990-00-1*) Lear.

***Lear, Roma.** Fingers & Thumbs: Toys & Activities for Children with Hand-Function Problems. 134p. 1999. pap. text 25.00 (*0-7506-2524-4*) Buttrwrth-Heinemann.

Lear, Roma. Look at It This Way: Toys & Activities for Children with Visual Impairment. LC 99-164788. (Illus.). 144p. 1998. pap. text 25.00 (*0-7506-3895-8*) Buttrwrth-Heinemann.

Lear, W. H., jt. ed. see Parsons, L. S.

Leard, A. Morocco & the Moors. 416p. 1985. 280.00 (*1-85077-026-3*, Pub. by Darf Pubs Ltd) St Mut.

Leard, James R. Cascades East: A Closer Look. unabridged ed. (Illus.). 64p. 1997. 35.00 (*0-9659434-0-2*) Schwansee Pub.

Leardi, Lois. The Red Shirt. 137p. 1991. 19.00 (*1-883285-07-0*) Delphinium.

— The Red Shirt. 1994. pap. 9.95 (*1-883285-12-7*) Delphinium.

***Leardo, Roxanna.** A Silent Whisper. 2000. pap. write for info. (*1-58235-436-7*) Watermrk Pr.

Learl, ed. Chicago. (Discover America Ser.). 1989. 6.99 (*0-8442-7470-4*) NTC Contemp Pub Co.

Learmont, David, ed. The Visual Dictionary of Flight. (Eyewitness Visual Dictionaries Ser.). (Illus.). 64p. (J). (gr. 4 up). 1993. 16.95 (*1-56458-101-2*) DK Pub Inc.

Learmonth, A. T., jt. auth. see Spate, O. H.

Learmonth, Andrew, ed. The Geography of Health. (Social Science & Medicine Ser.: No. 15). (Illus.). 268p. 1981. 33.00 (*0-08-027434-X*, Pergamon Pr) Elsevier.

Learmonth, Bob, et al. The First Croydon Airport Nineteen Fifteen to Nineteen Twenty-Eight. (Illus.). 1985. pap. 35.00 (*0-9503224-3-1*, Pub. by Sutton Libs & Arts) St Mut.

***Learmouth, Ian D.** Interfaces in Total Hip Arthroplasty. LC 99-40676. xii, 172p. 2000. 106.00 (*1-85233-205-0*) Spr-Verlag.

Learmouth, John. Soccer Fundamentals. LC 94-12571. 1994. pap. 8.95 (*0-312-11532-6*) St Martin.

— Soccer Fundamentals: Basic Techniques & Training for Beginning Players. LC 78-19415. (Illus.). 1979. pap. 4.95 (*0-312-73133-7*) St Martin.

Learn Foundation Translation Committee, tr. The New Testament--International Standard Version: Preview Release Edition. LC 98-84061. 624p. 1998. pap. 15.95 (*1-891833-02-2*) Davidson Pr.

Learn Founderation Staff. International Standard Version. 1999. pap. 29.95 (*1-891833-11-1*) Davidson Pr.

Learn Inc. Staff. High Efficiency Meetings. 64p. pap. text 49.95 incl. audio (*1-55678-010-9*, 3007) Learn Inc.

— Speed Learning: Science & Engineering Edition. 39p. student ed. 154.00 incl. audio (*1-55678-035-4*, 3083) Learn Inc.

***Learn Incorporated Staff.** Smart Reading, Set. (Smart Tapes Ser.). 28p. 1999. pap. 19.95 incl. audio (*1-55678-067-2*, 3350) Learn Inc.

Learned, E. Old Portuguese Vocalic Finals, Phonology & Orthography of Accented -Ou, -Eu, Iu, & -Ao, Eo, -Io. (LD Ser.: No. 44). 1950. pap. 25.00 (*0-527-00790-0*) Periodicals Srv.

Learned, J. G., jt. auth. see Learned, W. L.

Learned, M. D., ed. Guide to Manuscript Materials Relating to American History in the German State Archives. (Carnegie Institute Ser.: Vol. 11). 1912. 40.00 (*0-527-00691-2*) Periodicals Srv.

Learned, Marion D. Life of Francis Daniel Pastorius. 1993. reprint ed. lib. bdg. 89.00 (*0-7812-5480-9*) Rprt Serv.

— The Saga of Walther of Aquitaine. (BCL1-PR English Literature Ser.). 208p. 1992. reprint ed. lib. bdg. 79.00 (*0-7812-7165-7*) Rprt Serv.

Learned, Marion D., ed. The Saga of Walther of Aquitaine. LC 76-98848. 225p. 1970. reprint ed. lib. bdg. 59.50 (*0-8371-3903-1*, LEWA, Greenwood Pr) Greenwood.

Learned, W. L. & Learned, J. G. Learned Family (Learned, Larned, Learnard, Lannard & Lerned) Being Descendants of William Learned Who Was of Charlestown, Mass., in 1632. 2nd ed. (Illus.). 510p. 1989. reprint ed. pap. 75.00 (*0-8328-0760-5*); reprint ed. lib. bdg. 83.00 (*0-8328-0759-1*) Higginson Bk Co.

Learned, Walter. Treasury of American Verse. LC 74-86799. (Granger Index Reprint Ser.). 1977. 29.95 (*0-8369-6081-5*) Ayer.

Learned, Walter, ed. see Coppee, Francois.

Learned, William S. Quality of the Educational Process in the United States & Europe. LC 75-165740. (American Education Ser, No. 2). 1972. reprint ed. 13.95 (*0-405-03610-8*) Ayer.

Learner, Joanna M. Dinosaur Songs & Other Museum Music: An Anthology of Museum Poetry...Set to Music. ix, 31p. (Orig.). (J). 1997. pap. 10.95 incl. audio (*0-9657488-1-2*) Kalamazoo River.

— Dinosaur Songs & Other Museum Music: An Anthology of Museum Poetry...Set to Music. ix, 31p. (Orig.). (YA). (gr. 4 up). 1997. pap. 19.95 incl. audio (*0-9657488-0-4*) Kalamazoo River.

Learner, Marsha. Meeting Strangers. LC 91-91842. 185p. 1991. pap. 12.95 (*0-9628968-0-2*) M Brandsdorfer.

Learner, Tobsha. Miracles. (Orig.). pap. 14.95 (*0-86819-557-X*, Pub. by Currency Pr) Accents Pubns.

Learner, Tobsha. Quiver: A Book of Erotic Tales. LC 98-10972. 198p. 1998. pap. 12.95 (*0-452-27984-4*, Plume) Dutton Plume.

Learner, Tom, jt. auth. see Crook, Jo.

Learnet. Business Link Financial Accounting: Video Student Guide. (Am-Financial Accounting Ser.). 1999. pap., wbk. ed. 5.95 (*0-538-87336-1*) S-W Pub.

***Learney, Rosalie, et al.** Whose Hand Is This? Our Story of Stroke, Recovery & Love. 164p. 1999. pap. 19.95 (*1-86368-273-2*, Pub. by Fremantle Arts) Intl Spec Bk.

Learning Achievement Corp. Staff. Learning Achievements: Proofamatics Instructors Guide Binder. 1983. 40.00 (*0-07-054530-8*) McGraw.

— Number Systems, Addition & Personal Communication: Subtraction & Recreation. (MATCH Ser.: Bk. 1). (Illus.). 128p. 1981. text 13.96 (*0-07-037111-3*) McGraw.

Learning Achievement Corporation Staff. Decimals, Percent & Money: Measurement & Transportation. Zak, Therese A., ed. (MATCH Ser.: Bk. 4). (Illus.). 144p. 1981. text 13.96 (*0-07-037114-8*) McGraw.

— Fractions & Food: Fractions, Decimals & Electronic Communications. Zak, Therese A., ed. (MATCH Ser.: Bk. 3). (Illus.). 144p. 1981. text 13.96 (*0-07-037113-X*) McGraw.

— Geometry & Design & Maintenance: Ratio, Proportion, Reading Graphs & Data. Zak, Therese A., ed. (MATCH Ser.: Bk. 5). (Illus.). 128p. 1981. text 13.96 (*0-07-037115-6*) McGraw.

— Multiplication & Energy & Construction: Division & Medicine. Zak, Therese A., ed. (MATCH Ser.: Bk. 2). (Illus.). 144p. 1981. text 13.96 (*0-07-037112-1*) McGraw.

Learning Business Staff. Competent Administrator Level. 1997. pap. 19.99 (*0-7506-3160-0*) Buttrwrth-Heinemann.

— Competent Administrator Level 3 User Guide. 1997. pap. 16.00 (*0-7506-3159-7*) Buttrwrth-Heinemann.

— Competent Administrator Level 3 Workbook, No. 5. 60p. 1997. pap., wbk. ed. 29.99 (*0-7506-3152-X*) Buttrwrth-Heinemann.

— Competent Administrator Level 3 Workbook, No. 7. 60p. 1997. pap., wbk. ed. 29.99 (*0-7506-3154-6*) Buttrwrth-Heinemann.

— Contributing to Health, Safety & Security. 1997. 26.95 (*0-7506-3149-X*) Buttrwrth-Heinemann.

— Handling Procedures. 1997. 26.95 (*0-7506-3155-4*) Buttrwrth-Heinemann.

An Asterisk (*) at the beginning of an entry indicates that the title is appearing for the first time.

— Maintaining Working Relationships. 1997. 26.95 (*0-7506-3151-1*) Buttrwrth-Heinemann.
— Open Learning: Improving Team Performances. 1997. 29.95 (*0-7506-3146-5*) Buttrwrth-Heinemann.
— Organizing & Managing Resources. 1997. 32.95 (*0-7506-3156-2*) Buttrwrth-Heinemann.
— Organizing Travel, Accommodation & Meetings. 1997. 32.95 (*0-7506-3157-0*) Buttrwrth-Heinemann.
— Planning & Organizing Work. 1997. 26.95 (*0-7506-3150-3*) Buttrwrth-Heinemann.
— Preparing & Producing Business Documents. 1997. 32.95 (*0-7506-3158-9*) Buttrwrth-Heinemann.
— Presenting Information & Data Level 3 Workbook. 1997. wbk. ed. 26.95 (*0-7506-3153-8*) Buttrwrth-Heinemann.

Learning Community Staff. A Journey to the Heart: Capturing the Spirit of Global Education. 136p. (Orig.). 1991. pap. 9.95 (*0-9615210-1-5*) Rainbow Bdg.

Learning Curve Series Staff. French: Beginning, Intermediate, Advanced. (Learning Curve). (ENG & FRE.). pap. 19.99 incl. audio (*0-88676-145-X*, 49782) Metacom Inc.

Learning Disabilities Council, Inc. Staff. Understanding Learning Disabilities: A Parent Guide & Workbook. 181p. 1991. pap. 19.95 (*0-9636305-0-4*) Lrning Disabil Coun.

Learning Exchange Staff. Free & Inexpensive Teaching Tools to Make & Use. (Illus.). 112p. 1986. student ed. 8.99 (*0-86653-388-5*, GA 1004) Good Apple.
— Seasonal Learning Activities. 112p. (J). (gr. 2-6). 1988. student ed. 6.99 (*0-86653-435-0*, GA1045) Good Apple.

***Learning Express Organization Staff.** Texas Real Estate Sales Exam. 2nd ed. LC 00-8928. 2000. pap. 34.95 (*1-57685-333-0*) LrningExprss.

Learning Express Staff. Allied Health California. LC 97-3651. (Health Care Library). 1997. pap. 35.00 (*1-57685-064-1*) LrningExprss.
— Allied Health Entrance Exams. LC 97-43306. (Health Care Library). 1998. pap. 20.00 (*1-57685-100-1*) LrningExprss.
— Allied Health New Jersey. LC 97-876. (Health Care Library). 1997. pap. 35.00 (*1-57685-068-4*) LrningExprss.
— AMP Real Estate Sales Exam. LC 98-37857. 256p. 1998. pap. 29.95 (*1-57685-150-8*) LrningExprss.
— ASI Real Estate Sales Exam. LC 98-37854. 256p. 1998. pap. 29.95 (*1-57685-152-4*) LrningExprss.
— ASVAB Core Review: Just What You Need to Get into the Military. LC 98-23942. 208p. 1998. pap. 12.95 (*1-57685-155-9*) LrningExprss.
— California Real Estate Sales Exam. LC 98-47906. 256p. 1999. pap. 34.95 (*1-57685-208-3*) LrningExprss.
— Catholic High School Entrance Exams. LC 99-28891. 1999. pap. 14.95 (*1-57685-232-6*) LrningExprss.

***Learning Express Staff.** Civil Service Career Starter. 2nd ed. LC 00-38436. 224p. 2000. pap. 15.95 (*1-57685-302-0*) LrningExprss.

Learning Express Staff. Civil Service Career Starter: Entry-Level Government Jobs for High School & College Graduates. Gish, Jim, ed. LC 97-8771. (Civil Service Library). 192p. (Orig.). 1997. pap. 14.00 (*1-57685-120-6*) LrningExprss.

***Learning Express Staff.** Corrections Officer: The Complete Preparation Guide. 304p. 2000. pap. 14.95 (*1-57685-295-4*) Random.

Learning Express Staff. Cosmetology Licensing Exam. LC 98-33729. 224p. 1998. pap. 20.00 (*1-57685-147-8*) LrningExprss.
— CUNY Skills Assessment Tests. LC 98-47877. 1999. pap. 15.95 (*1-57685-215-6*) LrningExprss.
— Federal Clerical Exam. (National Standards Ser.). 240p. 1998. pap. 14.95 (*1-57685-101-X*) LrningExprss.

***Learning Express Staff.** Firefighter Exam: The Complete Preparation Guide. 304p. 2000. pap. 14.95 (*1-57685-294-6*) Random.

Learning Express Staff. Firefighter Exam Midwest. Gish, Jim, ed. LC 97-12309. (Civil Service Library). 320p. (Orig.). 1997. pap. 30.00 (*1-57685-103-6*) LrningExprss.

***Learning Express Staff.** 501 Grammar & Writing Questions: Fast, Focused Practice to Help You Improve Your Grammer & Writing. LC 99-38373. 192p. 1999. pap. 14.95 (*1-57685-265-2*, Pub. by LrningExprss) Random.
— 501 Challenging Logic & Reasoning Problems. 192p. 2000. pap. 14.95 (*1-57685-285-7*) Random.

Learning Express Staff. 501 Reading Comprehension Questions. LC 98-47904. 1999. pap. 14.95 (*1-57685-201-6*) LrningExprss.

***Learning Express Staff.** Geometry Success in 20 minutes a Day. 208p. 2000. pap. 16.00 (*1-57685-277-6*) Random.

Learning Express Staff. Health Care Career Starter: Finding & Getting a Great Job. LC 98-4827. (Career Starters Ser.). 165p. 1998. pap. 14.95 (*1-57685-095-1*) LrningExprss.
— Job Hunting Made Easy. Gish, Jim, ed. LC 97-11420. 160p. (Orig.). 1997. pap. 12.95 (*1-57685-119-2*) LrningExprss.
— Law Enforcement Career Guide Texas. LC 96-76058. (Law Enforcement Library). 1996. pap. 20.00 (*1-57685-009-9*) LrningExprss.
— Office Basics Made Easy. Gish, Jim, ed. LC 97-11421. 160p. 1997. pap. 12.95 (*1-57685-118-4*) LrningExprss.
— 1001 Math Problems. LC 98-49074. 1999. pap. 14.95 (*1-57685-200-8*) LrningExprss.

***Learning Express Staff.** 1001 Vocabulary & Spelling Questions: Fast, Focused Practice to Help You Improve Your Vocabulary. LC 99-38375. 192p. 1999. pap. 14.95 (*1-57685-264-4*, Pub. by LrningExprss) Random.

Learning Express Staff. Paralegal Career Starter. LC 98-10846. (Career Starters Ser.). 1998. pap. 14.95 (*1-57685-098-6*) LrningExprss.
— Parent's Homework Helper: 4th Grade. 4th ed. pap. 14.95 (*1-57685-227-X*) Random.

***Learning Express Staff.** Pass the U. S. Citizenship Exam, Vol. 1. LC 99-20290. 1999. pap. 14.95 (*1-57685-222-9*) LrningExprss.
— Police Officer Exam: The Complete Preparation Guide. LC 98-44289. 384p. 1999. pap. 14.95 (*1-57685-207-5*) LrningExprss.

Learning Express Staff. Police Officer Exam, California. LC 95-51010. (Law Enforcement Library). 352p. 1996. pap. 35.00 (*1-57685-002-1*) LrningExprss.
— Police Officer Exam New York City & Nassau County. 2nd ed. LC 98-9243. 322p. 1998. pap. 25.00 (*1-57685-159-1*) LrningExprss.
— Police Officer Exam the South. Gish, Jim, ed. LC 97-22391. (Law Enforcement Library). 304p. (Orig.). 1997. pap. 25.00 (*1-57685-033-1*) LrningExprss.
— Policy Officer Exam, Midwest. Gish, Jim, ed. LC 97-8772. (Law Enforcement Library). 320p. (Orig.). 1997. pap. 30.00 (*1-57685-097-8*) LrningExprss.
— Postal Worker Florida. LC 96-32721. (Civil Service Library). 1996. pap. 30.00 (*1-57685-063-3*) LrningExprss.

***Learning Express Staff.** PPST: Praxis 1-Pre-Professional Skills Test. LC 98-24093. 272p. 1998. pap. 18.95 (*1-57685-136-2*) LrningExprss.

Learning Express Staff. PSI Real Estate Sales Exam. LC 98-37856. 256p. 1998. pap. 29.95 (*1-57685-151-6*) LrningExprss.
— Sanitation Worker Exam New York City. LC 96-48976. (Civil Service Library). 192p. 1997. pap. 25.00 (*1-57685-092-7*) LrningExprss.
— Treasury Enforcement Agent Exam: Secret Service Customs, IRS, U. S. Deputy Marshal, Alcohol Tobacco Firearms. LC 98-26817. 272p. 1998. pap. 17.95 (*1-57685-139-7*) LrningExprss.
— Postal Worker Exam. Gish, Jim, ed. LC 97-22384. (Civil Service Library Ser.). 192p. (Orig.). 1997. pap. 12.95 (*1-57685-045-5*) LrningExprss.

***Learning Express Staff, ed.** Great Interview! Master the Art of Self-Confidence. (Illus.). 128p. 2000. pap. text 12.95 (*1-57685-304-7*) LrningExprss.
— Great Resume! How to Stand Out from the Crowd. (Illus.). 128p. 2000. pap. text 12.95 (*1-57685-303-9*) LrningExprss.

Learning Express Staff & Weaver, Marcia. Visual Literacy: How to Read Information in Graphic Form. LC 99-28919. 1999. pap. 16.00 (*1-57685-223-7*) LrningExprss.

Learning Express Staff, jt. auth. see Chesla, Elizabeth L.

***Learning, George F.** The Story of Mining in Bisbee. (Illus.). 32p. 1998. 9.30 (*0-9675602-0-9*) Free Geos.

Learning Letter Staff. Parent Letters for the Intermediate Grades, Vol. 3337. Hall, Karen, ed. (Parent Letters Ser.: Vol. 2). (Illus.). 128p. 1997. pap. 12.98 (*1-57471-233-0*, 3337) Creat Teach Pr.
— Parent Letters for the Primary Grades, Vol. 3336. Cicciarelli, Joellyn T., ed. (Parent Letters Ser.). (Illus.). 128p. 1997. pap. 12.98 (*1-57471-232-2*, 3336) Creat Teach Pr.

Learning Place Cuisenaire Staff. Connecting People With Feathers & Otto: Activities for Learning: Sorting, Classifying & Addition, 1. 1997. pap. write for info. (*1-57452-130-6*) Cuisenaire.
— Cuisenaire Jumbo Rod With Feathers & Otto: Activities for Learning: Counting, & Comparing Numbers, 1. 1997. pap. write for info. (*1-57452-128-4*) Cuisenaire.
— Inchworm With Feathers & Otto: Activities for Learning: Measuring, Counting , Addition, & Estimating, 1. 1997. pap. write for info. (*1-57452-124-1*) Cuisenaire.
— Quilting Tile With Feathers & Otto: Activities for Learning: Shape Recognition, & Spatial Skills, 1. 1997. pap. write for info. (*1-57452-126-8*) Cuisenaire.

Learning Resources Staff. Balance with Weights. (C). 1998. 44.95 (*0-87628-167-6*) S&S Trade.

Learning Systems Ltd., Staff, ed. Elements of Injection Moulding of Thermoplastics. (Illus.). (Orig.). (gr. 10 up). 1969. pap. text 7.95 (*0-85334-043-9*) Transatl Arts.

Learning the Art of Pyrography, jt. auth. see Chapman, Al.

Learning Through Entertainment Staff. It's Potty Time. Finman, Ed, ed. (Illus.). 32p. (J). (ps-1). 1996. pap. 9.95 (*1-883681-06-5*) Lrning Thrgh Ent.

Learning to Teach Task Force. Learning to Teach: Workshops on Instruction. 86p. 1992. pap. 25.00 (*0-8389-7627-1*) Assn Coll & Res Libs.

Learning, Walter, ed. Gifts to Last: Christmas Stories from the Maritimes & Newfoundland. 212p. 1996. pap. 14.95 (*0-86492-206-X*) Goose Ln Edits.

Learning, Walter, jt. auth. see Nowlan, Alden.

Learning Works Staff & Schwartz, Linda. Squeeky Clean Hygiene. Clark Editorial & Design Staff, ed. (Illus.). 56p. (J). (gr. 1-3). 1999. pap. text 8.95 (*0-88160-308-2*, LW377) Learning Wks.

LearningExpress Staff. Border Patrol Exam. LC 98-26820. 1998. pap. 18.95 (*1-57685-140-0*, Pub. by LrningExprss) Natl Bk Netwk.
— Bus Operator Exam New York City. LC 96-48986. (Civil Service Library). 192p. 1997. pap. 25.00 (*1-57685-093-5*) LrningExprss.

***LearningExpress Staff.** CBEST: California Basic Educational Skills Test. LC 98-3560. 1998. pap. 17.95 (*1-57685-115-X*, Pub. by LrningExprss) Natl Bk Netwk.

LearningExpress Staff. Computer Technician Career Starter. LC 98-10799. (Career Starters Ser.). 208p. 1998. pap. 14.95 (*1-57685-096-X*) LrningExprss.

Learningexpress Staff. Firefighter Exam New Jersey. LC 96-32737. (Civil Service Library). 1996. pap. 35.00 (*1-57685-069-2*) LrningExprss.

LearningExpress Staff. Paramedic Licensing Exam. LC 98-26285. 256p. 1998. pap. 20.00 (*1-57685-148-6*) LrningExprss.
— Postal Worker New Jersey. LC 96-32256. (Civil Service Library). 1996. pap. 30.00 (*1-57685-070-6*) LrningExprss.
— Tasp: Texas Academic Skills Program. LC 98-24094. 1998. pap. 18.95 (*1-57685-114-1*) LrningExprss.
— Texas Real Estate Sales Exam. LC 98-37855. 256p. 1998. pap. 29.95 (*1-57685-153-2*) LrningExprss.

***Learnit Corporation Staff.** Microsoft Office 2000 Step-By-Step Interactive. (SPA.). 2000. pap. 29.99 incl. cd-rom (*0-7356-0659-5*) Microsoft Pr.
— Microsoft Office 2000 Step-By-Step Interactive. (JPN.). 2000. pap. 41.67 incl. cd-rom (*0-7356-0657-9*) Microsoft Pr.
— Microsoft Office 2000 Step-By-Step Interactive, Brazilian. 2000. pap. 29.99 incl. cd-rom (*0-7356-0827-X*) Microsoft Pr.
— Microsoft Word 2000 & Excel 2000 Step By Step Interactive. (gr. 8). 1999. cd-rom 29.99 (*0-7356-0507-6*) Microsoft Pr.
— Microsoft Word 2000 Learning Kit. 1999. pap. text 29.99 (*0-7356-0913-6*) Microsoft.

LearnQuick.com Staff, jt. auth. see Martin, Herb.

Lears, Jackson. Fables of Abundance: A Cultural History of Advertising in America. 512p. 1995. pap. 18.00 (*0-465-09075-3*, Pub. by Basic) HarpC.

Lears, Jackson T. No Place of Grace: Antimodernism & the Transformation of American Culture, 1880-1920. LC 93-39767. 400p. 1994. pap. text 16.95 (*0-226-46970-0*) U Ch Pr.

Lears, Jackson T., jt. ed. see Fox, Richard W.

***Lears, Laurie.** Ben Has Something to Say: A Story about Stuttering. LC 99-50866. (Illus.). (J). (gr. k-4). 2000. lib. bdg. 14.95 (*0-8075-0633-8*) A Whitman.

Lears, Laurie. Ian's Walk: A Story about Autism. LC 97-27873. (Illus.). 32p. (J). (gr. 1-4). 1998. lib. bdg. 14.95 (*0-8075-3480-3*) A Whitman.

***Lears, Laurie.** Waiting for Mr. Goose. LC 99-10698. (Illus.). 32p. (J). (gr. k-3). 1999. lib. bdg. 14.95 (*0-8075-8628-5*) A Whitman.

Lears, T. J., jt. ed. see Fox, Richard W.

Learsi, Rufus, tr. see Asch, Sholem.

Learst, Allen & Phillis, Randy, eds. Starting Rumors: America's Next Generation of Writers. 150p. 1999. pap. 12.95 (*0-9671216-0-4*) Pinyon Pr CO.

***Leartha, Mukunda.** Transformation As Creation: Essays in the History, Theory & Aesthetics of Indian Music, Dance & Theatre LC 98-901459. (ENG & SAN.). 1998. write for info. (*81-86471-16-2*, Pub. by Aditya Prakashan) S Asia.

Leartyeayana, et al. Leartyeayanabsrautaseutram = Leartyeayana-bsrauta-seutra, 3 Vol. LC 98-915308. (Kaleameulabseastra-granthamealea Ser.). xxxiii, 1266 p. 1998. write for info. (*81-208-1565-3*, Pub. by Motilal Bnarsidass) S Asia.

Leary. Introduction to Behavioral Research Methods. (Adaptable Courseware Ser.). 1996. 19.75 (*0-534-49703-9*) Brooks-Cole.

Leary, jt. auth. see Boydell.

Leary, Anna A. AndeLear Nail Care. LC 86-73045. (Illus.). 78p. 1987. 9.95 (*0-9617600-0-1*) AndeLear Pub.

Leary, Brian. Reengineering Handbook: A Step-by-Step Guide to Business Transformation. 2nd rev. ed. Carlisle, Patti, ed. (AT&T Quality Library). (Illus.). 146p. (Orig.). 1992. pap. 24.95 (*0-932764-36-3*, 500-449) AT&T Customer Info.

Leary, Brian & MacDorman, John. Quality Manager's Handbook. 2nd rev. ed. Carlisle, Patti, ed. (AT&T Quality Library). (Illus.). 146p. (Orig.). 1992. reprint ed. pap. 24.95 (*0-932764-35-5*, 500-442) AT&T Customer Info.

Leary, Daniel, ed. see Shakespeare, William.

Leary, Daniel J. Shaw's Plays in Performance. LC 83-2188. (Annual of Bernard Shaw Studies: Vol. 3). 268p. 1983. 40.00 (*0-271-00346-4*) Pa St U Pr.

Leary, Daniel J., ed. see Shaw, George Bernard.

Leary, David E., ed. Metaphors in the History of Psychology. (Studies in the History of Psychology). (Illus.). 397p. (C). 1990. text 69.95 (*0-521-37166-X*) Cambridge U Pr.
— Metaphors in the History of Psychology. (Cambridge Studies in the History of Psychology). (Illus.). 397p. (C). 1994. pap. text 19.95 (*0-521-42152-7*) Cambridge U Pr.

Leary, David E., jt. ed. see Koch, Sigmund.

Leary, Dennis. No Cure for Cancer. LC 92-16820. 160p. 1992. pap. 8.95 (*0-385-42581-3*, Anchor NY) Doubleday.

Leary, Edward J. Privacy Powerpak. unabridged ed. O'Neill, Karen, ed. LC 97-137669. 164p. 1996. spiral bd. 35.00 (*0-9654949-0-X*) Privacy Group.

Leary, Elizabeth D. Space Dreams. LC 84-80867. 168p. (Orig.). 1984. pap. 7.95 (*0-937884-08-1*, Bennington Bks) Hystry Mystry.

Leary, Emmeline, jt. auth. see Fairclough, Oliver.

Leary, Helen F. North Carolina Research: Genealogy & Local History. 2nd rev. ed. (Illus.). 600p. 1996. 48.00 (*0-936370-10-6*) N C Genealogical.

Leary, James P. Wisconsin Folklore: A Reader. LC 98-16371. 1999. 69.95 (*0-299-16030-0*); pap. 27.95 (*0-299-16034-3*) U of Wis Pr.

Leary, James R., et al. Cross-Cultural Studies of Factors Related to Differential Food Consumption. (Cross-Cultural Research Ser.). 1984. 22.00 (*0-317-37054-5*) HRAFP.

Leary, John. Prepare for the Great Tribulation. 11th ed. 1998. pap. text 3.95 (*1-57918-096-5*) Queenship Pub.
— Prepare for the Great Tribulation, Vol. 9. 1998. pap. 3.95 (*1-57918-073-6*) Queenship Pub.

***Leary, John.** Prepare for the Great Tribulation & Era of Peace, Vol. XIV. (Illus.). 108p. 1999. pap. 3.95 (*1-57918-115-5*, 3474) Queenship Pub.

Leary, John. Prepare for the Great Tribulation & the Era of Peace, Vol. I. LC 96-68181. 244p. (Orig.). 1996. pap. text 7.95 (*1-882972-69-4*, 3461) Queenship Pub.
— Prepare for the Great Tribulation & the Era of Peace, Vol. II. LC 96-68181. 344p. (Orig.). 1996. pap. 8.95 (*1-882972-77-5*, 3462) Queenship Pub.
— Prepare for the Great Tribulation & the Era of Peace, Vol. III. 2nd ed. LC 96-68181. 371p. (Orig.). 1996. pap. 8.95 (*1-882972-72-4*, 3463) Queenship Pub.
— Prepare for the Great Tribulation & the Era of Peace, Vol. IV. LC 96-68181. (Illus.). 89p. (Orig.). 1996. pap. 3.95 (*1-882972-91-0*, 3464) Queenship Pub.
— Prepare for the Great Tribulation & the Era of Peace, Vol. V. LC 96-68181. (Illus.). (Orig.). 1997. pap. text 2.95 (*1-882972-97-X*, 3465) Queenship Pub.
— Prepare for the Great Tribulation & the Era of Peace, Vol. VI. LC 97-68596. (Illus.). 94p. (Orig.). 1997. pap. 2.95 (*1-57918-002-7*, 3466) Queenship Pub.
— Prepare for the Great Tribulation & the Era of Peace, Vol. VII. (Illus.). 122p. (Orig.). 1997. pap. 2.95 (*1-57918-010-8*, 3467) Queenship Pub.
— Prepare for the Great Tribulation & the Era of Peace, Vol. VIII. LC 97-68596. (Illus.). 100p. (Orig.). 1997. pap. 3.95 (*1-57918-053-1*, 3468) Queenship Pub.
— Prepare for the Great Tribulation & the Era of Peace, Vol. IX. LC 95-73237. (Illus.). 152p. (Orig.). 1998. pap. 3.95 (*1-57918-066-3*, 3469) Queenship Pub.

***Leary, John.** Prepare for the Great Tribulation & the Era of Peace, Vol. 15. LC 95-73237. (Illus.). 114p. (Orig.). 2000. pap. 3.95 (*1-57918-122-8*) Queenship Pub.
— Prepare for the Great Tribulation & the Era of Peace, Vol. 16. LC 95-73237. (Prepare for the Great Tribulation Ser.). (Illus.). 119p. (Orig.). 2000. pap. text 3.95 (*1-57918-126-0*) Queenship Pub.

Leary, John. Violence & the Dream People: The Orang Asli in the Malayan Emergency, 1948-1960. LC 95-10758. (Monographs in International Studies, Southeast Asia Ser.: No. 95). (Illus.). 254p. (Orig.). (C). 1995. pap. 22.00 (*0-89680-186-1*) Ohio U Pr.

Leary, John, jt. auth. see Queenship Publishing Company Staff.

Leary, John E., Jr. Francis Bacon & the Politics of Science. LC 93-31898. 310p. (C). 1994. text 49.95 (*0-8138-1407-3*) Iowa St U Pr.

Leary, Katherine, tr. see Lejeune, Philippe.

Leary, L., ed. see Chopin, Kate.

Leary, Lani. Healing Hands: Meditations for Healing Through the Human Energy Field. Set. 18.95 incl. audio (*1-56455-630-1*, W116) Sounds True.

Leary, Lewis. John Lathrop, Jr. The Quiet Poet of Federalist Boston. 51p. 1981. pap. 6.00 (*0-912296-51-8*) Am Antiquarian.
— Literary Career of Nathaniel Tucker. LC 78-115998. (Duke University. Trinity College Historical Society. Historical Papers: No. 29). 1970. reprint ed. 30.00 (*0-404-51779-X*) AMS Pr.

Leary, Lewis, ed. Articles on American Literature: 1950-1967. LC 70-132027. xxxi, 751p. 1970. text 69.95 (*0-8223-0239-X*) Duke.
— Contemporary Literary Scholarship: A Critical Review. LC 58-6939. 1958. 52.50 (*0-89197-107-6*) Irvington.

Leary, Lewis, intro. American Literature to Nineteen Hundred. (Great Writers Library). 340p. pap. 6.00 (*0-312-34711-1*) Academy Chi Pubs.

Leary, Lewis, jt. auth. see Freneau, Philip M.

Leary, Lewis, ed. see Brackenridge, Hugh H.

Leary, Lewis, ed. see Thoreau, Henry David.

Leary, Lewis, ed. see Twain, Mark, pseud.

Leary, Lory B. An Alaskan Child's Garden of Verse. (Illus.). 40p. (Orig.). (J). (gr. 6 up). 1989. pap. 6.95 (*0-924663-02-2*) Alaskan Viewpoint.

Leary, Lory B., ed. Alaska Women: Yesterday, Today & Tomorrow. (Illus.). 60p. (Orig.). 1990. pap. 6.95 (*0-924663-10-3*) Alaskan Viewpoint.

Leary, Malcolm, jt. auth. see Boydell, Tom.

Leary, Margaret M., ed. see Hull, Dan.

Leary, Margaret M., ed. see Parnell, Dale P.

Leary, Margaret M., ed. see Teaff, Grant.

Leary, Mark, ed. see Amore, Dom.

Leary, Mark, ed. see Hartford Courant Staff, et al.

Leary, Mark R. Introduction to Behavioral Research Methods. 360p. (C). 1990. text 50.95 (*0-534-13818-7*) Brooks-Cole.

Leary, Mark R. Introduction to Behavioral Research Methods. 2nd ed. LC 94-32272. 422p. 1994. pap. 92.95 (*0-534-20490-2*) Brooks-Cole.
— Introduction to Behavioral Research Methods. 3rd ed. 464p. 2000. 76.00 (*0-205-32204-2*) Allyn.

Leary, Mark R. Introduction to Behavioral Research Methods: Instructor's Manual with Test Items. 2nd ed. 1994. mass mkt., teacher ed. 48.50 (*0-534-20491-0*) Brooks-Cole.
— Self-Presentation: Impression Management & Interpersonal Behavior. LC 96-1276. (Social Psychology Ser.). (C). 1996. pap. 24.00 (*0-8133-3004-1*, Pub. by Westview) HarpC.
— Social Anxiety. (Emotions & Social Behavior Ser.). 244p. 1997. pap. text 23.00 (*1-57230-263-1*) Guilford Pubns.
— The State of Social Psychology: Issues, Themes, & Controversies. 152p. (C). 1989. text 36.00 (*0-8039-3621-4*); pap. text 16.95 (*0-8039-3622-2*) Sage.

Leary, Mark R. & Kowalski, Robin M. Social Anxiety. LC 95-32612. (Emotions & Social Behavior Ser.). 244p. 1995. lib. bdg. 39.95 (*1-57230-007-8*) Guilford Pubns.

Leary, Mark R. & Miller, R. S. Social Psychology & Dysfunctional Behavior. (Social Psychology Ser.). (Illus.). 250p. 1986. 59.00 (*0-387-96325-1*) Spr-Verlag.

Leary, Mark R., jt. ed. see Kowalski, Robin M.

L

Leary, Martha R., jt. auth. see Donnellan, Anne M.

Leary, Mary. Karate Untitled. Date not set. text. write for info. (0-374-33977-5) FS&G.

Leary, Mary B., jt. ed. see Ellis, John S.

Leary, Michael. Web Designer's Guide to Typography. LC 96-78593. 384p. 1997. 39.99 (1-56830-337-8) Hayden.

Leary, Michael & Galapagos Design Group Staff. Web Designer's Guide to Typography. 1997. pap. 39.99 (0-614-28471-6, Hayden Sftwre) MCP SW Interactive.

Leary, Michael E. Photography: From Theory to Practice. 2nd ed. (Illus.). 176p. (C). 1988. pap. 34.95 (0-89863-124-6) Star Pub CA.

Leary, Patty, et al. Nurse Aide Test Study Guide. Balkema, Sandra et al, eds. (Illus.). 200p. (Orig.). 1989. pap. 10.00 (0-685-44697-2) Matthew Scott.

Leary, Paul M., ed. Virgin Islands of the United States Major Political Documents, 1666-1991. 450p. (Orig.). (C). 1992. pap. text 19.95 (0-9628909-2-8) U VI CES.

Leary, Penn. The Second Cryptographic Shakespeare. rev. ed. (Illus.). 313p. 1990. pap. 15.00 (0-9617917-1-3) Westchester Hse.

Leary, Richard L. Early Pennsylvanian Geology & Paleobotany of the Rock Island County, Illinois Area. (Reports of Investigations: No. 37). (Illus.). 100p. 1981. pap. 3.50 (0-89792-089-9) Ill St Museum.

Leary, Rolfe A. Interaction Theory in Forest Ecology & Management. LC 85-18146. (Forestry Sciences Ser.). 1985. text 147.00 (90-247-3220-4) Kluwer Academic.

Leary, Rosemary. Chemistry 130. (C). 1998. text 17.34 (1-56870-292-2) RonJon Pub.

Leary, Sheelagh. Activities for Personal Growth: A Comprehensive Handbook of Activities for Therapists. (Illus.). 1994. pap. 48.00 (0-86433-076-6) MacLennan & Petty.

Leary, Steven L., jt. auth. see Hawk, C. Terrance.

Leary, T. Acts of the Apostles: Passages for Translation. (LAT.). 104p. 1995. pap. 18.95 (1-85399-476-6, Pub. by Brist Class Pr) Focus Pub-R Pullins.

— Giger. 1994. pap. 12.99 (3-8228-9642-X) Taschen Amer.

Leary, Thomas & Sholes, Elizabeth C. The Pan American Exposition, Buffalo. (Images of America Ser.). (Illus.). 128p. 1998. pap. 16.99 (0-7524-0981-6) Arcadia Publng.

Leary, Thomas, et al. Buffalo's Waterfront. (Images of America Ser.). 1999. pap. 16.99 (0-7524-0829-1) Arcadia Publng.

Leary, Thomas E. & Sholes, Elizabeth C. From Fire to Rust: Business, Technology & Work at the Lackawana Steel Plant, 1899-1983. (Illus.). 134p. 1987. pap. 17.75 (0-939032-00-7) Buffalo Erie.

***Leary, Timothy.** Change Your Brain. (Self-Mastery Ser.: Vol. 1). 112p. 2000. pap. 12.95 (1-57951-017-5, Pub. by Ronin Pub) Publishers Group.

Leary, Timothy. Chaos & Cyber Culture. (Illus.). 292p. 1994. pap. 19.95 (0-914171-77-1) Ronin Pub.

— The Delicious Grace of Moving One's Hand: The Collected Sex Writings. LC 98-37028. 224p. 2000. pap. text 13.95 (1-56025-181-6, Thunders Mouth) Avalon NY.

— Flashbacks: A Personal & Cultural History of an Era. rev. ed. 416p. 1997. pap. 16.95 (0-87477-870-0, Tarcher Putnam) Putnam Pub Group.

— The Game of Life. LC 79-2283. (Future History Ser.). (Illus.). 304p. (Orig.). 1993. pap. 14.95 (1-56184-050-5) New Falcon Pubns.

— High Priest. 1976. 34.95 (0-8488-1408-8) Amereon Ltd.

— High Priest. 500p. 1991. reprint ed. lib. bdg. 33.95 (0-89966-801-1) Buccaneer Bks.

— High Priest. 2nd aut. limited ed. Orfali, Sebastian J., ed. (Illus.). 347p. 1995. 100.00 (0-914171-87-9) Ronin Pub.

— High Priest. 2nd ed. Orfali, Sebastian J., ed. (Illus.). 347p. 1995. reprint ed. pap. 19.95 (0-914171-80-1) Ronin Pub.

— Info-Psychology: A Re-Vision of Exo-Psychology. 2nd ed. LC 76-56056. (Future History Ser.). (Illus.). 160p. 1987. reprint ed. pap. 14.95 (1-56184-105-6) New Falcon Pubns.

— The Intelligence Agents. (Future History Ser.). (Illus.). 224p. 1996. pap. 14.95 (1-56184-038-6) New Falcon Pubns.

— Neuropolitique: A New Vision of Neuropolitics. rev. ed. LC 88-81431. (Future History Ser.). 208p. 1991. pap. 14.95 (1-56184-012-2) New Falcon Pubns.

— Politics of Ecstasy. 6th ed. 230p. 1998. reprint ed. pap. 14.95 (1-57951-031-0) Ronin Pub.

***Leary, Timothy.** The Politics of Self-Determination. LC 99-68418. (Self-Mastery Ser.). (Illus.). 112p. 2000. pap. 12.95 (1-57951-015-9) Ronin Pub.

Leary, Timothy. Psychedelic Prayers: And Other Meditations. 2nd ed. (Illus.). 128p. 1997. 20.00 (0-914171-96-8); pap. 12.95 (0-914171-84-4) Ronin Pub.

— Surfing the Consciousness Net: The Adventures of Dani Mellon Du Pont. 160p. 1995. pap. 12.95 (0-86719-410-3) Last Gasp.

— Turn on, Tune in, Drop Out. 6th ed. Orig. Title: Politics of Ecstasy. (Illus.). 160p. 1999. reprint ed. pap. 14.95 (1-57951-009-4) Ronin Pub.

— What Does Woman Want? 2nd ed. LC 87-83574. (Future History Ser.). 288p. 1998. pap. 14.95 (1-56184-086-6) New Falcon Pubns.

Leary, Timothy, et al, eds. The Psychedelic Reader: Classic Selections from the Psychedelic Review, the Revolutionary 1960s Forum of Psychopharmacological Substances. (Illus.). 272p. 1993. pap. 12.95 (0-8065-1451-5, Citadel Pr) Carol Pub Group.

Leary, Timothy & Sirius, R. U. Design for Dying. 239p. 1998. pap. text 12.00 (0-7881-5822-8) DIANE Pub.

Leary, Timothy & Weissman, Benjamin. Concrete & Buckshot: William S. Burroughs Paintings 1987-1996. (Illus.). 50p. (Orig.). 1996. pap. 15.00 (1-889195-01-4) Smart Art Pr.

Leary, Timothy, et al. The Psychedelic Experience: A Manual Based on the Tibetan Book of the Dead. 160p. 1995. pap. 10.95 (0-8065-1652-6, Citadel Pr) Carol Pub Group.

Leary, Virginia A. Ethnic Conflict & Violence in Sri Lanka: Report of a Mission to Sri Lanka in July-August 1981 on Behalf of the International Commission of Jurists: with a Supplement by the ICJ Staff for the Period 1981-1983. LC 84-172852. 92p. reprint ed. pap. 30.00 (0-608-18109-9, 203270800081) Bks Demand.

— International Labour & National Law. 1982. lib. bdg. 121.50 (90-247-2551-8) Kluwer Academic.

— The Philippines: Human Rights after Martial Law: Report of a Mission. fac. ed. LC 85-207205. (Illus.). 126p. 1984. reprint ed. pap. 39.10 (0-608-00956-3, 206180200011) Bks Demand.

Leary, William. Methodism in the Town of Boston. (C). 1989. text 35.00 (0-902662-55-4, Pub. by R K Pubns); pap. text 35.00 (0-7855-6993-6, Pub. by R K Pubns) St Mut.

Leary, William M. Fueling the Fires of Resistance: Army Air Forces Special Operations in the Balkans During World War 2. 47p. 1995. pap. 3.25 (0-16-061364-7) USGPO.

Leary, William M. Perilous Missions: Civil Air Transport & CIA Covert Operations in Asia. LC 83-3554. (Illus.). 294p. 1984. pap. 91.20 (0-608-05135-7, 206569600005) Bks Demand.

Leary, William M., Jr. The Progressive Era & the Great War, 1896-1920. 2nd ed. LC 78-70030. (Goldentree Bibliographies Series in American History). (C). 1978. text 24.95 (0-88295-574-8); pap. text 14.95 (0-88295-575-6) Harlan Davidson.

Leary, William M. Under Ice: Waldo Lyon & the Development of the Arctic Submarine. LC 98-19137. (Military History Ser.: Vol. 62). (Illus.). 320p. 1998. 32.95 (0-89096-845-4) Tex A&M Univ Pr.

Leary, William M., ed. The Airline Industry. (Encyclopedia of American Business History & Biography Ser.). (Illus.). 352p. 1992. lib. bdg. 85.00 (0-8160-2675-0) Facts on File.

Leary, William M., ed. Aviation's Golden Age: Portraits from the 1920s & 1930s. LC 89-4753. (Illus.). 232p. 1989. text 28.95 (0-87745-242-3) U of Iowa Pr.

Leary, William M., ed. From Airships to Airbus Vol. 1: The History of Civil & Commercial Aviation: Infrastructure & Environment. LC 94-26006. 256p. 1995. 33.00 (1-56098-467-8) Smithsonian.

***Leary, William M., ed.** MacArthur & the American Century: A Reader. (Illus.). 480p. 2000. 40.00 (0-8032-2930-5) U of Nebr Pr.

Leary, William M., ed. Pilots' Directions: The Transcontinental Airway & Its History. LC 89-20479. (American Land & Life Ser.). (Illus.). 112p. 1990. reprint ed. text 19.95 (0-87745-278-4) U of Iowa Pr.

— We Shall Return! MacArthur's Commanders & the Defeat of Japan, 1942-1945. LC 88-2731. 320p. 1988. 34.95 (0-8131-1654-6) U Pr of Ky.

Leary, William M. & LeSchack, Leonard A. Project Coldfeet: Secret Mission to a Soviet Ice Station. LC 96-38262. (Special Warfare Ser.). (Illus.). 240p. 1996. 28.95 (1-55750-514-4) Naval Inst Pr.

Leas, Ann. The Complete Idiot's Travel Guide to Hawaii. LC 99-226257. (Complete Idiot's Travel Guide Ser.). 1998. pap. 18.95 (0-02-862417-3) Macmillan Gen Ref.

Leas, Lyle S. Amish Country Cookbook. LC 81-14972. (Illus.). 1988. 22.95 (0-87949-200-7) Ashley Bks.

***Leas, Sara.** California for Dummies. (For Dummies Ser.). 2000. pap. 16.99 (0-7645-6158-8) IDG Bks.

Leas, Speed B. Discover Your Conflict Management Style. rev. ed. LC 97-73981. 49p. 1997. pap. 6.95 (1-56699-184-6, AL183) Alban Inst.

— Leadership & Conflict. (Creative Leadership Ser.). 128p. (Orig.). 1982. pap. 12.95 (0-687-21264-2) Abingdon.

— Moving Your Church Through Conflict. 84p. (Orig.). 1985. pap. 13.25 (1-56699-012-2, AL82) Alban Inst.

Leas, Speed B., jt. auth. see Oswald, Roy M.

Leas, Speed B., jt. auth. see Parsons, George D.

Lease, Benjamin. That Wild Fellow John Neal & the American Literary Revolution. LC 72-81630. 255p. reprint ed. pap. 79.10 (0-608-12562-8, 202405400035) Bks Demand.

Lease, Benjamin, et al, eds. The Genius of John Neal: Selections from His Writings. (Studien und Texte zur Amerikanistik: Vol. 1). XXVII, 297p. 1978. pap. 26.00 (3-261-02382-1) P Lang Pubng.

Lease, Gary. Odd Fellows in the Politics of Religion: Modernism, National Socialism, & German Judaism. LC 94-23869. (Religion & Society Ser.: No. 35). 325p. (C). 1994. lib. bdg. 121.55 (3-11-014323-2) Mouton.

Lease, Gary & Soule, Michael E., eds. Reinventing Nature? Responses to Postmodern Deconstruction. LC 94-22631. (Illus.). 176p. (C). 1995. text 40.00 (1-55963-310-7); pap. text 19.95 (1-55963-311-5) Island Pr.

Lease, John R. Cecil. Core, Graham, ed. LC 92-61877. (Illus.). 47p. 1992. 16.95 (1-880439-01-8) PERQ Pubns.

Lease, Joseph. Human Rights. LC 97-45793. 128p. 1998. pap. 13.00 (0-944072-85-2) Zoland Bks.

— The Room. LC 94-71039. (Series of Poetry & Verse Translation). 48p. 1994. pap. 12.00 (1-882509-01-3) Alef Bks.

Lease, Nicholas, tr. see Melanchthon, Philip.

***Lease, Ronald C.** Dividend Policy. LC 99-28695. (Financial Management Association Survey & Synthesis Ser.). 256p. 1999. 35.00 (0-87584-497-9) Harvard Busn.

Leash, Moroni. Death Notification: A Practical Guide to the Process. (Orig.). 1994. pap. 19.95 (0-942679-08-3) Upper Access.

***Leash, Neil H.** Prophetic Statements on Food Storage for Latter-Day Saints. 192p. 1999. pap. 13.98 (0-88290-665-8, 1255) Horizon Utah.

Leasher, Evelyn, compiled by. Oregon Women: A Bio-Bibliography. (Bibliographic Ser.: No. 18). 64p. 1981. pap. 9.95 (0-87071-138-5) Oreg St U Pr.

Leasher, Evelyn, ed. see Bailey, Margaret J.

***Leasher, Evelynn M.** Letter from Washington, 1863-1865. LC 98-46253. 1999. 39.95 (0-8143-2798-2) Wayne St U Pr.

Leashore, Bogart R., ed. see Everett, Joyce E., et al.

Leasia, Shelly. A Practical Guide to Health Assessment. Cullen, Barbara N., ed. LC 96-41703. (Illus.). 464p. 1997. pap. text 24.95 (0-7216-1468-X, W B Saunders Co) Harcrt Hlth Sci Grp.

Leask, Anna & Yeoman, Ian. Heritage Visitor Attractions: An Operations Management Perspective. LC 98-6740. 320p. 1999. 74.50 (0-304-70291-9); pap. 28.00 (0-304-70292-7) Continuum.

Leask, Harold G. Irish Castles. (Illus.). 170p. 1977. reprint ed. 30.00 (0-85221-010-8) Dufour.

— Irish Churches & Monastic Buildings: Gothic up to 1400, 3 vols., Vol. II: Gothic to A.D. 1400. 162p. 1967. 49.95 (0-85221-011-6) Dufour.

— Irish Churches & Monastic Buildings: Medieval Gothic, the Last Phases, 3 vols., Vol. III: Medieval Gothic, the Last Phases. 190p. 1960. 49.95 (0-85221-012-4) Dufour.

— Irish Churches & Monastic Buildings: The First Phases & the Romanesque, 3 vols., Vol. I: First Phases & Romanesque. 173p. 1987. 49.95 (0-85221-016-7) Dufour.

Leask, Marilyn & Goddard, Del. The Search for Quality: Planning for Improvement & Managing Change. 160p. 1992. pap. 37.50 (1-85396-190-6, Pub. by P Chapman) Taylor & Francis.

***Leask, Marilyn & Meadows, John.** Teaching & Learning with ICT in the Primary School. LC 99-40326. 256p. 2000. pap. write for info. (0-415-21505-6) Routledge.

***Leask, Marilyn & Pachler, Norbert.** Learning to Teach Using ICT in Secondary School. LC 98-48881. (Learning to Teach Subjects in the Secondary School Ser.). 264p. (C). 1999. pap. write for info. (0-415-19432-6) Routledge.

Leask, Marilyn & Terrill, Ian. Development Planning & School Improvement for Middle Managers. 192p. 1997. pap. 29.95 (0-7494-2038-3, Kogan Pg Educ) Stylus Pub VA.

Leask, R. A., jt. ed. see Kocurek, Michael J.

***Leaska, Mitchell.** Granite & Rainbow: The Hidden Life of Virginia Woolf. 2000. pap. 19.95 (0-8154-1047-6) Cooper Sq.

Leaska, Mitchell. Granite & Rainbow: The Life of Virginia Woolf. LC 97-18031. 656p. 1998. text 35.00 (0-374-16659-5) FS&G.

Leaska, Mitchell A., ed. A Passionate Apprentice: The Early Journals, 1897-1909. 512p. 1992. pap. 14.95 (0-15-671160-5, Harvest Bks) Harcourt.

Leaska, Mitchell A., ed. see Woolf, Virginia.

Leasman. Elvis. 156p. (C). 1998. pap. text 22.50 (0-536-01211-3) Pearson Custom.

***Leason.** Fine Old Imperial. 1999. mass mkt. 5.99 (0-8125-7634-9) Tor Bks.

***Leason, Barney.** Grand Cru. 2001. mass mkt. write for info. (0-312-87198-8, Pub. by Forge NYC) St Martin.

Leason, Barney. Rodeo Drive. 416p. 1988. mass mkt. 3.95 (1-55817-093-6, Pinncle Kensgtn) Kensgtn Pub Corp.

Leasor, James. Boarding Party: The Last Action of the Calcutta Light Horse. LC 95-32380. (Bluejacket Bks.). (Illus.). 228p. 1995. pap. 14.95 (1-55750-512-8) Naval Inst Pr.

— Follow the Drum. large type ed. 632p. 1982. 27.99 (0-7089-8033-3) Ulverscroft.

— Love down Under. large type ed. (Adventure Suspense Ser.). 512p. 1993. 27.99 (0-7089-2969-9) Ulverscroft.

— Open Secret. large type ed. 480p. 1983. 27.99 (0-7089-8141-0, Charnwood) Ulverscroft.

— Passport for a Pilgrim. large type ed. 381p. 1982. 27.99 (0-7089-0837-3) Ulverscroft.

— Passport to Oblivion. 1964th ed. (Spies & Intrigues Ser.: No. 5). 220p. pap. 5.95 (0-918172-18-7) Leetes Isl.

— Passport to Peril. large type ed. 1980. 27.99 (0-7089-0428-9) Ulverscroft.

— Passport to Peril. (Spies & Intrigues Ser.: No. 6). 240p. reprint ed. pap. 5.95 (0-918172-19-5) Leetes Isl.

— Tank of Serpents. large type ed. 528p. 1987. 11.50 (0-7089-1712-7) Ulverscroft.

***Leat, Mike.** Exploring Employee Relations. 2000. pap. 32.95 (0-7506-4396-X) Buttrwrth-Heinemann.

Leat, Mike. Human Resource Issues of the European Union. LC 99-220502. 320p. 1998. pap. 54.50 (0-273-62508-X, Pub. by Pitman Pub) Trans-Atl Phila.

Leat, Mike, jt. auth. see Hollinshead, Graham.

Leatart, Dennis, jt. auth. see Jandorf, Harold.

Leath, Carol B. The Big Book of Bible Word Search. 144p. 1997. 9.99 (0-88486-164-3, Bristol Park Bks) Arrowood Pr.

Leatham, Gary, et al. Polymers from Renewable Resources. (ACS Symposium Ser.). 110.00 (0-8412-3647-X, Pub. by Am Chemical) OUP.

Leatham, Gary F & Himmel, Michael E., eds. Enzymes in Biomass Conversion. LC 91-11798. (ACS Symposium Ser.: No. 460). (Illus.). 536p. 1991. text 110.00 (0-8412-1995-8, Pub. by Am Chemical) OUP.

Leatham, James. William Morris: Master of Many Crafts, 1900 Edition. Faulkner, Peter, ed. (William Morris Library). 150p. 1996. reprint ed. 48.00 (1-85506-257-7) Bks Intl VA.

Leatham-Jones, Barry. Introduction to Computer Numerical Control. (C). 1986. pap. text. write for info. (0-582-29040-6, Pub. by Addison-Wesley) Longman.

Leatham, Louis S. Letham or Leatham Family Book of Remembrance: The Story of Robert Letham & His Wife J net Urquhart with Historical-Genealogical & Biographical Data on Their Ancestry & Descendants. (Illus.). 1072p. 1995. reprint ed. lib. bdg. 145.00 (0-8328-4921-9) Higginson Bk Co.

— Letham or Leatham Family Book of Remembrance: The Story of Robert Letham & His Wife Janet Urquhart with Historical-Genealogical & Biographical Data on Their Ancestry & Descendants. (Illus.). 1072p. 1995. reprint ed. pap. 135.00 (0-8328-4922-7) Higginson Bk Co.

Leatham, W. Britt. Legacy of Life: Readings & Exercises. 438p. (C). 1997. pap. text, per. 59.95 (0-7872-2750-1) Kendall-Hunt.

Leathar, D. S. Health Education & the Media. 1985. pap. 22.75 (0-08-031996-3, Pergamon Pr) Elsevier.

***Leathard, Audrey.** Health Care Provision: Past, Present & into the 21st Century. 2nd ed. (Illus.). 352p. 2000. pap. 34.95 (0-7487-3354-X, Pub. by S Thornes Pubs) Intl Spec Bk.

Leathem, Cecilia, jt. ed. see Christiansen, Christine.

Leathem, Sherrill. Fantastic Fun Face Painting. LC 97-203449. (Illus.). 64p. 1997. 14.95 (0-8069-9850-4) Sterling.

Leather, Bob, jt. auth. see Martin, Tony.

Leather, J., jt. ed. see James, A.

Leather, John. Clinker Boatbuilding. (Illus.). 224p. 1996. pap. 24.50 (0-7136-3643-2) Sheridan.

— The Northseamen: The Story of the Fishermen, Yachtsmen & Shipbuilders of the Colne & Blackwater Rivers. 336p. 1990. 45.00 (0-900963-22-0, Pub. by T Dalton) St Mut.

— The Salty Shore: The Story of the River Blackwater. 216p. 1990. 36.00 (0-900963-52-2, Pub. by T Dalton) St Mut.

— Smacks & Bawleys. 160p. (C). 1990. 45.00 (0-86138-079-7, Pub. by T Dalton) St Mut.

Leather, Jonathan, ed. Language Learning, No. 49, Suppl. I. (Best of Language Learning Ser.: Vol. III). 300p. 1999. pap. 32.95 (0-631-21609-X) Blackwell Pubs.

Leather, Jonathan, jt. ed. see James, Allan.

Leather, Margaret, ed. Saltwater Village. 140p. 1990. pap. 21.00 (0-86138-022-3, Pub. by T Dalton) St Mut.

Leather, Phil, et al, eds. Work Related Violence: Assessment & Intervention. LC 98-25640. (Illus.). 224p. (C). (gr. 13). 1999. 95.00 (0-415-19414-8, D6383) Routledge.

— Work Related Violence: Assessment & Intervention. LC 98-25640. (World Encyclopedia of Contemporary Theatre Ser.: Vo). (Illus.). 224p. (C). (gr. 13). 1999. pap. 29.99 (0-415-19415-6, D6387) Routledge.

Leather, Simon R., et al, eds. Insect Overwintering. (Illus.). 400p. 1991. 49.95 (0-7131-2940-9, A2932, Pub. by E A) Routldge.

Leather, Simon R. & Hardie, R. Jim, eds. Insect Reproduction. 288p. 1995. 244.00 (0-8493-6695-X, 6695, CRC Reprint) Franklin.

Leather, Simon R., et al. The Ecology of Insect Overwintering. (Illus.). 265p. (C). 1993. text 74.95 (0-521-41758-9) Cambridge U Pr.

— The Ecology of Insect Overwintering. 265p. 1996. pap. text 30.95 (0-521-55670-8) Cambridge U Pr.

Leather, Simon R., jt. auth. see Burdon, J.

Leather, Stephen. The Chinaman. Grose, Bill, ed. 368p. 1993. mass mkt. 5.99 (0-671-74302-3) PB.

— Hungry Ghost. 384p. 1993. mass mkt. 5.50 (0-671-75300-2) PB.

— The Vets. Grose, Bill, ed. 512p. 1994. reprint ed. mass mkt. 5.99 (0-671-74304-X) PB.

***Leatherbarrow, David.** Uncommon Ground: Architecture, Technology & Topography. (Illus.). 335p. (C). 2000. 37.95 (0-262-12230-8) MIT Pr.

Leatherbarrow, David, jt. auth. see Mostafavi, Mohsen.

***Leatherbarrow, Liesbeth & Reynolds, Lesley.** 101 Best Plants for the Prairies. (Illus.). 264p. 1999. pap. 14.95 (1-894004-30-2) Fifth Hse Publ.

Leatherbarrow, Margaret. Gold in the Grass. Bargyla & Rateaver, Gylver, eds. LC 75-23179. (Conservation Gardening & Farming Ser.: Ser. C). (C). 1975. reprint ed. pap. 35.00 (0-9600698-8-7) Rateavers.

Leatherbarrow, W. J., ed. Dostoevskii & Britain. LC 94-32406. 1995. 46.00 (0-85496-784-2) Berg Pubs.

— Dostoevsky: Dream of a Ridiculous Man (Son Smeshnogo Cheloveka) (Bristol Russian Texts Ser.). (RUS.). 64p. 1994. pap. 18.95 (1-85399-364-6, Pub. by Brist Class Pr) Focus Pub-R Pullins.

Leatherbarrow, William J. Dostoevsky's the Devils: A Critical Companion. LC 99-27505. 136p. 1999. pap. text 17.95 (0-8101-1444-5) Northwestern U Pr.

— Dostoyevsky: "The Brothers Karamazov" (Landmarks of World Literature Ser.). (Illus.). 129p. (C). 1992. text 34.95 (0-521-38424-9); pap. text 11.95 (0-521-38601-2) Cambridge U Pr.

— Feodor Dostoevsky: A Reference Guide. (Reference Guides to Literature Ser.). 429p. (C). 1990. 45.00 (0-8161-8941-2, Hall Reference) Macmillan.

Leatherbarrow, William J. & Offord, Derek C., eds. A Documentary of Russian Thought: From the Enlightenment to Marxism. (RUS.). 316p. 1987. pap. 18.95 (0-87501-019-9) Ardis Pubs.

Leatherbury, Leven C., ed. see Dean, Wayne.

***Leatherdale.** Money is a Kid's Best Friend. 2000. pap. 22.95 (0-13-018878-6) P-H.

Leatherdale, Clive. Britain & Saudi Arabia, 1925-1939: The Imperial Oasis. 414p. 1983. text 52.50 (0-7146-3220-1, Pub. by F Cass Pubs) Intl Spec Bk.

— Dracula: The Novel & Legend: A Study of Bram Stoker's Gothic Masterpiece. rev. ed. 256p. 1993. 29.95 (1-874287-04-X, Pub. by Desert Island Bks) Firebird Dist.

— The Origins of Dracula: The Background to Bram Stoker's Gothic Masterpiece. LC 95-220634. 239p. 1995. 29.95 (1-874287-07-4, Pub. by Desert Island Bks) Firebird Dist.

— To Dream of Pigs: Travels in South & North Korea. 256p. 1995. 24.50 (1-874287-02-3, Pub. by Desert Island Bks) Hollym Intl.

An Asterisk (*) at the beginning of an entry indicates that the title is appearing for the first time.

*Leatherdale, Clive. The Virgin, Whore, & Other Chinese Characters: Tiananmen, Travels & Traumas. 256p. 1999. pap. 14.95 (1-874287-23-6, Pub. by Desert Island Bks) Firebird Dist.

Leatherdale, Clive, ed. see Calmet, Dom A.

Leatherdale, Clive, ed. & anno. see Stoker, Bram.

Leatherdale, Frank & Leatherdale, Paul. Successful Pistol Shooting. (Illus.). 160p. 1995. 35.00 (1-85223-883-6, Pub. by Cro1wood) Trafalgar.

Leatherdale, Paul, jt. auth. see Leatherdale, Frank.

Leatherman, Carroll S. Old Man & the Dog. 1991. 16.95 (1-879034-01-8) MS River Pub.

Leatherman, David, et al. Aspen: A Guide to Common Problems in Colorado. 2nd rev. ed. (Illus.). 40p. (Orig.). 1996. 5.00 (1-889143-01-4, 559a) CO St U Coop.

Leatherman, Diane. Crossing Kansas. 168p. 1998. pap. 10.75 (0-9665861-0-7) Diane Leatherman.

*Leatherman, Dick. Quality Leadership Skills: Standards of Leadership Behavior. 2nd rev. ed. 466p. 2000. pap. 29.95 (0-9674325-1-0) Intl Training.

Leatherman, Dick. The Training Trilogy: Assessing Needs. 72p. 1990. 10.00 (0-87425-141-9) HRD Press.

— The Training Trilogy: Designing Programs. 136p. 1990. 15.00 (0-87425-142-7) HRD Press.

— The Training Trilogy: Facilitation Skills. 96p. 1990. 10.00 (0-87425-143-5) HRD Press.

Leatherman, Janie, et al. Breaking Cycles of Violence: Conflict Prevention in Intrastate Crises. LC 98-52833. 272p. 1999. pap. 23.95 (1-56549-091-6) Kumarian Pr.

*Leatherman, Janie, et al. Breaking Cycles of Violence: Conflict Prevention in Intrastate Crises. LC 98-52833. 272p. 1999. 65.00 (1-56549-092-4) Kumarian Pr.

Leatherman, Richard W. The Supervisor's Complete Guide to Leadership Behavior. rev. ed. (Illus.). 102p. 1981. 17.50 (0-9603702-1-8) Intl Training.

Leatherman, Robin R. Rhymes of a Bluejacket: Verses of a World War II Navy Vet. LC 86-82065. (Illus.). 112p. (Orig.). 1986. pap. 6.95 (0-939127-00-8) Gulf Coast Pub.

Leatherman, Stephen P. America's Best Beaches. LC 99-227403. (Illus.). 112p. 1998. pap. 19.99 (0-9663451-0-X) S P Leatherman.

— Island States at Risk: Global Climate Change, Development & Population. LC 97-31358. (Journal of Coastal Research Special Issue Ser.). 1997. write for info. (0-938415-08-5) Coastal Res.

Leatherman, Thomas L., jt. ed. see Goodman, Alan H.

Leathers, Charles G., jt. auth. see Rayes, Patrick J.

Leathers, Dale. Successful Nonverbal Communication: Principles & Applications. 3rd ed. (C). 1996. pap. text, teacher ed. write for info. (0-205-26420-4, T6420-8) Allyn.

Leathers, Dale G. Successful Nonverbal Communication: Principles & Applications. 3rd ed. LC 96-33007. 436p. 1996. pap. text 50.00 (0-205-26230-9) Allyn.

Leathers, Howard D., jt. auth. see Foster, Phillips.

Leatherwood, Stephen. The Sierra Club Handbook of Seals & Sirenians. pap. text 18.00 (0-87156-560-9) Sierra.

Leatherwood, Stephen & Reeves, Randall R. The Handbook of Whales & Dolphins. LC 83-388. (Illus.). 320p. 1983. 25.00 (0-87156-341-X, Pub. by Sierra) Random.

— The Sierra Club Handbook of Whales & Dolphins. LC 83-388. (Illus.). 320p. 1983. pap. 18.00 (0-87156-340-1, Pub. by Sierra) Random.

Leatherwood, Stephen, et al. Whales, Dolphins, & Porpoises of the Eastern North Pacific & Adjacent Arctic Waters: A Guide to Their Identification. (Illus.). 258p. 1998. 32.00 (0-89904-715-7, Seascape Res Alliance); spiral bd. 26.80 (0-89904-716-5, Seascape Res Alliance) Crumb Elbow Pub.

— Whales, Dolphins, & Porpoises of the Eastern North Pacific & Adjacent Arctic Waters: A Guide to Their Identification. (Illus.). 256p. 1988. reprint ed. pap. 15.95 (0-486-25651-0) Dover.

Leatherwood, Stephen, jt. auth. see Jefferson, T.

Leatherwood, Stephen P. & Reeves, Randall R. The Sea World Book of Dolphins. LC 86-46212. (Illus.). 96p. (J). (gr. 4-7). 1987. pap. 9.95 (0-15-271957-1, Voyager Bks) Harcourt.

Leatherwood, Stephen P. & Reeves, Randall R., eds. The Bottlenose Dolphin: Tursiops Truncatus. LC 96-2750. (Illus.). 653p. 1989. text 87.00 (0-12-440280-1) Acad Pr.

Leathery, Sharon, ed. see Lovejoy, T. E., 3rd, et al.

Leathwood, J. Light Foods: An Assessment of Their Psychological, Sociocultural, Physiological, Nutritional, & Safety Aspects. LC 95-75553. (Illus.). 98p. 1995. pap. 22.50 (0-944398-44-8) ILSI.

Leathwood, Peter, et al, eds. For a Better Nutrition in the 21st Century. LC 92-49782. (Nestle Nutrition Workshop Ser.: Vol. 27). (Illus.). 272p. 1993. reprint ed. pap. 84.40 (0-608-07193-5, 206741800009) Bks Demand.

Leatt, James, et al, eds. Contending Ideologies in South Africa. LC 86-531. 328p. (Orig.). reprint ed. pap. 101.70 (0-608-17881-0, 203273600080) Bks Demand.

Leatz, Axel. A Swedish Officer in the American Civil War: The Diary of Axel Leatz of the 5th New York Veteran Volunteer Infantry Duryee's Zouaves (1863-1865) unabridged ed. Schroeder, Patrick, ed. & tr. by. from SWE. (Illus.). 60p. 2000. pap. 8.00 (1-889246-06-9) P A Schroeder.

Leatz, Christine A. & Stolar, Mark W. Career Success - Personal Stress: How to Stay Healthy in a High-Stress Environment. 356p. 1993. pap. 14.95 (0-07-036977-1) McGraw.

Leau, Leopold, jt. auth. see Couturat, Louis.

Leautaud, Paul. Amours. (FRE.). 1973. pap. 8.95 (0-7859-4019-7) Fr & Eur.

— Journal Litteraire. Pia & Guyot-Clement, Christine, eds. 65.00 (0-685-34264-6) Fr & Eur.

Leautey, Eugene & Guilbaut, Adolfe. La Science des Conptes Mise a la Portee de Tous: The Science of Accounting Put Within Reach of Us All. Brief, Richard P., ed. LC 80-1508. (Dimensions of Accounting Theory & Practice Ser.). (FRE.). 1980. reprint ed. lib. bdg. 50.95 (0-405-13533-5) Ayer.

Leavell. Criminal Procedures. (Criminal Justice Ser.). 400p. (C). 1919. pap. 52.95 (0-314-20489-X) Wadsworth Pub.

Leavell, Carol A., jt. auth. see Lewandowski, Lawrence J.

Leavell, Hugh R. The One-Minute Therapist: Collected Columns. 110p. 1999. pap. 12.95 (0-9668000-0-1) H R Leavell.

Leavell, Jo A. Joy in the Journey. LC 93-47619. 224p. 1994. 15.95 (1-56554-021-2) Pelican.

Leavell, Jo Ann P. Don't Miss the Blessing. LC 89-38308. 216p. 1990. 15.95 (0-88289-747-0) Pelican.

Leavell, L. P., jt. auth. see Bunyan, John.

*Leavell, Landrum P. Angels, Angels, Angels. 2nd ed. 1999. pap. text 9.95 (0-9671696-0-7) Journey Pub LA.

Leavell, Linda. Marianne Moore & the Visual Arts: Prismatic Color. (Illus.). 232p. 1995. text 32.50 (0-8071-1986-5) La State U Pr.

Leavell, Robert N., et al. Equitable Remedies, Restitution & Damages. 5th ed. (American Casebook Ser.). 190p. (C). 1994. pap. text, teacher ed. write for info. (0-314-04838-3) West Pub.

Leavell, Ronald P., jt. auth. see Girard, James A.

Leavell, Ronald Q. Mateo: El Rey y el Reino. Quezada, Alfredo, tr. from ENG. (Estudios Biblicos Basicos Ser.).Tr. of Matthew: the King & the Kingdom. (SPA.). 160p. 1988. pap. 7.99 (0-311-04363-1) Casa Bautista.

*Leaven in the World Editorial Team. Leaven in the World: Growing in Community Life. LC 00-8663. 2000. write for info. (0-88489-447-9) St Marys.

Leavengood, Betty. Faraway Ranch: Chiricahua National Monument. Scott, Sandra, ed. LC 94-67913. (Illus.). 16p. 1995. pap. 3.95 (1-877856-51-7) SW Pks Mnmts.

— Grand Canyon Women: Lives Shaped by Landscape. LC 99-12238. (Illus.). 248p. 1999. pap. 18.95 (0-87108-867-3) Pruett.

— Tucson ABC Coloring & Activity Book. (Illus.). 32p. (J). (gr. 1-3). 1995. pap. 4.95 (0-9645487-0-4) MP Pub AZ.

— Tucson Hiking Guide. 2nd ed. LC 97-1805. (Illus.). 213p. 1997. pap. 15.95 (0-87108-865-7) Pruett.

Leavens, Alex. Designing GUI Applications for Windows. LC 94-30874. 1994. pap. 39.95 incl. disk (1-55851-328-0, M&T Bks) IDG Bks.

— Visual C++ A Developer's Guide. 1995. pap. 39.95 incl. disk (1-55851-339-6, M&T Bks) IDG Bks.

— Visual C++ 2.0: A Developer's Guide. 1995. pap. 39.95 incl. disk (1-55851-416-3, M&T Bks) IDG Bks.

Leavens, C. R. & Taylor, R., eds. Interfaces, Quantum Wells, & Superlattices. LC 88-19476. (NATO ASI Series B, Physics: Vol. 179). (Illus.). 412p. 1988. 120.00 (0-306-42983-7, Plenum Trade) Perseus Pubng.

Leavens, Donald C., jt. auth. see Murray, Helen.

*Leavens, Gary T. & Sitaraman, Murali, eds. Foundations for Component-Based Systems. LC 99-49686. (Illus.). 320p. (C). 2000. 44.95 (0-521-77164-1) Cambridge U Pr.

Leavens, Ileana B. & Bruce, Chris. No! Contemporary American Dada. Vols. 1 & 2. Newland, Joseph N., ed. LC 85-81311. (Illus.). (Orig.). 1986. pap. 35.00 (0-935558-17-9) Henry Art.

Leavens, John M. The Catboat Book. 160p. 1991. pap. 19.95 (0-87742-314-8) Intl Marine.

Leavens, John M., ed. The Catboat Book. 160p. 1991. pap. 19.95 (0-07-010442-5) McGraw.

Leavenworth, Carol. Family Living. 1993. 30.00 (0-13-301961-6) P-H.

Leavenworth, E. W. A Genealogy of the Leavenworth Family in the United States. (Illus.). 376p. 1989. reprint ed. pap. 56.50 (0-8328-0762-1); reprint ed. lib. bdg. 64.50 (0-8328-0761-3) Higginson Bk Co.

Leavenworth, Richard S., jt. auth. see Grant, Eugene L.

Leavenworth, Russ, jt. auth. see Brengelman, Fred.

Leaver, Alan. Investigating Crime: A Guide to the Powers of Agencies Involved in the Investigation of Crime. LC 98-160516. 473p. 1997. pap. 55.00 (0-455-21501-4, Pub. by LawBk Co) Gaunt.

Leaver, Betty L. Teaching the Whole Class. 4th ed. LC 97-21131. 256p. 1997. 69.95 (0-8039-6645-8, 81669); pap. 32.95 (0-8039-6646-6, 81670) Corwin Pr.

Leaver, Betty L. & AGSI Staff. Teaching the Whole Class. 5th ed. LC 98-11037. 256p. 1998. per. 19.95 (0-7872-4777-4) Kendall-Hunt.

Leaver, Betty L., jt. ed. see Stryker, Stephen B.

Leaver-Cooper, Sheila & Smith, Ian S. Janet Frame's Kingdom by the Sea--Oamaru. LC 98-142709. (Illus.). 1997. write for info. (0-909049-05-X) Lincoln Univ Pr.

Leaver, Darren, jt. auth. see Lee, Gregory.

Leaver, Dennis T., jt. auth. see Washington, Charles M.

Leaver, Erik, jt. auth. see Barry, Tom.

Leaver, K. D., et al. Thin Films. LC 75-153871. (Wykeham Science Ser.: No. 17). 120p. (C). 1971. 18.00 (0-8448-1119-X, Crane Russak) Taylor & Francis.

— Thin Films. (Wykeham Science Ser.: No.17). 120p. 1971. pap. 18.00 (0-85109-230-6) Taylor & Francis.

Leaver, Keith. Microelectronic Devices. 2nd ed. 200p. 1997. 36.00 (1-86094-013-7); pap. 18.00 (1-86094-020-X) World Scientific Pub.

Leaver, Richard & Cox, David, eds. Middling, Meddling, Muddling: Issues in Australian Foreign Policy. LC 97-192774. 304p. 1997. pap. 24.95 (1-86448-305-9, Pub. by Allen & Unwin Pty) Paul & Co Pubs.

Leaver, Richard & Richardson, Jim. Post Cold War Order. 192p. 1994. pap. 24.95 (1-86373-399-X, Pub. by Allen & Unwin Pty) Paul & Co Pubs.

Leaver, Robin A. Music in the Service of the Church: The Funeral Sermon for Heinrich Schuetz. 68p. (Orig.). 1985. pap. 6.75 (0-570-01331-3, 99-1261) Concordia.

Leaver, Robin A. & Zimmerman, Joyce A. Liturgy & Music: Lifetime Learning. LC 98-12229. 464p. 1998. pap. 34.95 (0-8146-2501-0) Liturgical Pr.

Leaver, Robin A., jt. ed. see Brouwer, Frans.

Leaver, Robin A., ed. see Micklem, Caryl, et al.

Leaver, Robin A., ed. see Stiller, Gunther.

Leavers, V. F. Shape Detection in Computer Vision Using the Hough Transform. LC 92-23019. xiv, 201p. 1992. 58.95 (0-387-19723-0) Spr-Verlag.

Leaverton, Paul E. Environmental Epidemiology. Masse, Louis et al, eds. LC 82-5335. 176p. 1982. 57.95 (0-275-91369-4, C1369, Praeger Pubs) Greenwood.

— A Review of Biostatistics. 3rd ed. 128p. 1986. pap. 16.50 (0-316-51853-0, Little Brwn Med Div) Lppncott W & W.

— A Review of Biostatistics: A Program for Self-Instruction. 3rd ed. 1986. spiral bd. 12.00 (0-316-51852-2, Little Brwn Med Div) Lppncott W & W.

— A Review of Biostatistics: A Program for Self-Instruction. 5th ed. LC 94-22888. 144p. 1995. spiral bd. 25.00 (0-316-51883-2) Lppncott W & W.

Leaverton, Paul E. & Masse, Louis, eds. Health Information Systems. LC 84-3480. 220p. 1984. 45.00 (0-275-91440-2, C1440, Praeger Pubs) Greenwood.

Leavey, James. Forest Guide to Smoking in London. 1997. pap. text 12.95 (1-899163-29-8, Pub. by Quiller Pr) St Mut.

Leavey, John P., Jr. Glassary. LC 85-30902. iv, 320p. 1986. text 70.00 (0-8032-2871-6) U of Nebr Pr.

Leavey, John P., Jr., tr. see Derrida, Jacques.

Leavey, Peggy D. A Circle in Time. 104p. (J). (gr. 4-6). 1997. pap. 5.95 (0-929141-55-5) Napoleon Publ.

— Help Wanted: Wednesdays Only. 120p. 1994. pap. 5.95 (0-929141-23-7) Napoleon Publ.

Leavey, Peggy Dymond. Sky Lake Summer. 184p. (J). (gr. 4-7). 1999. pap. 6.95 (0-929141-64-4) Napoleon Publ.

Leavis, F. R. The Critic As Anti-Philosopher. Singh, G., ed. LC 97-17239. 211p. 1998. pap. 16.95 (1-56663-173-4, Elephant Paperbacks) I R Dee.

— Education & the University: A Sketch for an "English School" 139p. 1972. 15.95 (0-8369-2956-X) Ayer.

— The Living Principle: "English" As a Discipline of Thought. LC 97-17238. 266p. 1998. pap. 16.95 (1-56663-172-6, Elephant Paperbacks) I R Dee.

— Revaluation: Tradition & Development in English Poetry. LC 97-17240. 279p. 1998. pap. 16.95 (1-56663-171-8, Elephant Paperbacks) I R Dee.

Leavis, F. R. & Leavis, Q. D. Dickens: The Novelist. LC 77-541404. xviii, 371p. 1970. write for info. (0-7011-1644-7) Chatto & Windus.

Leavis, Frank R. D. H. Lawrence. LC 72-3172. (Studies in D. H. Lawrence: No. 20). 1972. reprint ed. lib. bdg. 75.00 (0-8383-1541-0) M S G Haskell Hse.

— D. H. Lawrence: Novelist. 1994. pap. 6.95 (0-226-46971-9, P805) U Ch Pr.

— Determinations: Critical Essays. LC 70-119085. (English Literature Ser.: No. 33). 1970. reprint ed. lib. bdg. 75.00 (0-8383-1081-8) M S G Haskell Hse.

— For Continuity. LC 68-54355. (Essay Index Reprint Ser.). 1977. 23.95 (0-8369-0613-6) Ayer.

— New Bearings in English Poetry: A Study of the Contemporary Situation. LC 75-30032. reprint ed. 32.50 (0-404-14035-1) AMS Pr.

— Revaluation: Tradition & Development in English Poetry. LC 75-17192. 275p. 1975. reprint ed. lib. bdg. 65.00 (0-8371-8297-2, LEREV, Greenwood Pr) Greenwood.

Leavis, Frank R. & Leavis, Q. D. Dickens, the Novelist. LC 77-135367. 391p. 1979. reprint ed. pap. 121.30 (0-7837-9211-5, 204996100004) Bks Demand.

Leavis, Frank R. & Thompson, Denys. Culture & Environment: The Training of Critical Awareness. LC 77-23346. 150p. 1977. reprint ed. lib. bdg. 52.50 (0-8371-9696-5, LECU, Greenwood Pr) Greenwood.

Leavis, Q. D. Collected Essays Vol. 3: The Novel of Religious Controversy. Singh, G., ed. 356p. (C). 1989. text 85.00 (0-521-26703-X) Cambridge U Pr.

Leavis, Q. D., jt. auth. see Leavis, F. R.

Leavis, Q. D., jt. auth. see Leavis, Frank R.

Leavitt. Cross-Cultral Rehabilitation: An International Perspective. LC 99-233555. (C). 1999. pap. text 31.00 (0-7020-2245-4, Pub. by W B Saunders) Saunders.

*Leavitt. Podere Fiume. 2000. 24.00 (1-58243-061-6, Pub. by Counterpt DC) HarpC.

Leavitt, Alga W., ed. Stories & Poems from the Old North State. LC 71-163039. (Short Story Index Reprint Ser.). (Illus.). 1977. reprint ed. 23.95 (0-8369-3953-0) Ayer.

Leavitt, Anne O. Southern Utah University: A Heritage History. LC 97-66545. 480p. 1997. 30.00 (0-935615-10-5) S Utah U Pr.

Leavitt, Caroline. The Haunted Clubhouse. (Wishbone Mysteries Ser.: Vol. 2). (Illus.). 142p. (J). (gr. 3-7). 1997. pap. 3.99 (1-57064-280-X, Big Red) Lyrick Pub.

— The Haunted Clubhouse, 2. (Wishbone Mysteries Ser.). (J). 1997. 9.09 (0-606-12856-5, Pub. by Turtleback) Demco.

— Into Thin Air. (Fresh Voices Ser.). pap. write for info. (0-446-36542-4) Warner Bks.

— The Prince & the Pooch. LC 97-72877. (Adventures of Wishbone Ser.: Vol. 3). (Illus.). 128p. (J). (gr. 3-7). 1997. mass mkt. 3.99 (1-57064-196-X, Big Red) Lyrick Pub.

Leavitt, Caroline. Prince & the Pooch. (Adventures of Wishbone Ser.). (Illus.). (J). 1997. 10.34 (0-606-18272-1) Turtleback.

Leavitt, Caroline. Robinhound Crusoe. LC 97-72878. (Adventures of Wishbone Ser.: Vol. 4). (Illus.). 144p. (J). (gr. 3-7). 1997. mass mkt. 3.99 (1-57064-271-0, Big Red) Lyrick Pub.

Leavitt, Caroline. Salty Dog. (Adventures of Wishbone Ser.). (Illus.). (J). 1997. 10.34 (0-606-18271-3) Turtleback.

Leavitt, Caroline. Tale of the Missing Head, 4. (Wishbone Mysteries Ser.). (J). 1998. 9.09 (0-606-12858-1, Pub. by Turtleback) Demco.

*Leavitt, Caroline, et al. The Wishbone High Seas Adventure. (Wishbone Super Special Ser.: Vol. 1). (Illus.). 448p. (J). (gr. 3-7). 2000. mass mkt. 5.99 (1-57064-942-1, Big Red) Lyrick Pub.

Leavitt, Cathie, ed. see Rowe, Jeremy.

Leavitt, Charles. Monarch Notes on Cooper's Last of the Mohicans. (C). 3.95 (0-671-00659-2, Arco) Macmillan Gen Ref.

— Monarch Notes on Hardy's Return of the Native. (C). 3.95 (0-671-00618-5, Arco) Macmillan Gen Ref.

— Monarch Notes on Hawthorne's House of the Seven Gables, Marble Faun. (C). 3.95 (0-671-00670-3, Arco) Macmillan Gen Ref.

— Monarch Notes on Twain's A Connecticut Yankee in King Arthur's Court. (Orig.). (C). 3.95 (0-671-00879-X, Arco) Macmillan Gen Ref.

Leavitt, Charles A. Monarch Notes on Hawthorne's Scarlet Letter. (C). 3.95 (0-671-00620-7, Arco) Macmillan Gen Ref.

*Leavitt, Charles Henry. Crook: An American Family. 254p. 1999. reprint ed. pap. 34.00 (0-7404-0009-6) Higginson Bk Co.

— Crook: An American Family, 1698-1955, Documented Genealogy. 254p. 1999. reprint ed. 44.00 (0-7404-0008-8) Higginson Bk Co.

Leavitt, Christine & McCarron, Robert J. Solid Waste Management in Minnesota: Economic Status & Outlook. (Illus.). 101p. (Orig.). (C). 1994. pap. text 35.00 (0-7881-0222-2) DIANE Pub.

Leavitt, David. Arkansas: Three Novellas. 1997. 22.95 (0-614-27881-3) HM.

— Arkansas: Three Novellas. 208p. 1998. pap. 12.00 (0-395-90128-6, Mariner Bks) HM.

— Equal Affections. 288p. 1997. pap. 12.00 (0-8021-3531-5, Grove) Grove-Atltic.

— Family Dancing. LC 97-35021. 224p. 1997. pap. 12.00 (0-395-87732-6, Mariner Bks) HM.

— Lost Language of Cranes. LC 97-18297. 352p. 1997. pap. 12.00 (0-395-87733-4) HM.

*Leavitt, David. Martin Bauman: or A Sure Thing: A Novel. LC 00-27589. 352p. 2000. 26.00 (0-395-90243-6) HM.

Leavitt, David. The Page Turner. LC 97-44864. 192p. 1998. 24.00 (0-395-75285-X) HM.

— The Page Turner. 192p. 1999. pap. 12.00 (0-395-95787-7, Mariner Bks) HM.

— A Place I've Never Been: Stories. (Contemporay American Fiction Ser.). 224p. 1991. reprint ed. pap. 12.95 (0-14-010959-5, Penguin Bks) Viking Penguin.

— While England Sleeps. rev. ed. 304p. 1995. pap. 11.95 (0-395-75286-8) HM.

Leavitt, David & Mitchell, Mark, eds. Pages Passed from Hand to Hand: Stories from the Hidden Tradition of Homosexual Literature from the Eighteenth Century to the Great War. LC 97-25631. 576p. 1998. 30.00 (0-395-83706-5, Mariner Bks); pap. 18.00 (0-395-83705-7, Mariner Bks) HM.

— The Penguin Book of Gay Short Stories. 688p. 1994. reprint ed. pap. 16.95 (0-14-024249-X, Penguin Bks) Viking Penguin.

Leavitt, Edward D., jt. auth. see Cummings, O. R.

Leavitt, Emily W. The Blair Family of New England. 197p. 1988. reprint ed. pap. 40.00 (0-8328-0261-1); reprint ed. lib. bdg. 50.00 (0-8328-0260-3) Higginson Bk Co.

Leavitt, Emily W., jt. auth. see Morse, J. H.

Leavitt, Fred. Drugs & Behavior. 3rd ed. 424p. 1994. 62.00 (0-8039-4783-6) Sage.

*Leavitt, Fred. Evaluating Scientific Research: Separating Fact from Fiction. LC 00-28480. 288p. 2000. pap. 26.67 (0-13-012845-7) P-H.

Leavitt, Fred. Unloosing Monsters: Plunging to the Depths of Human Wisdom. LC 84-90338. 1984. 10.00 (0-87212-179-8) Libra.

*Leavitt, Harold J. Hot Groups: Seeding Them, Feeding Them & Using Them to Ignite Your Organization. LC 98-8524. (Illus.). 320p. 1999. 25.00 (0-19-512686-6) OUP.

Leavitt, Harold J. Managerial Psychology. 4th ed. LC 77-13852. 1997. lib. bdg. 19.00 (0-226-46974-3) U Ch Pr.

Leavitt, Harold J. & Bahrami, Homa. Managerial Psychology: Managing Behavior in Organizations. 5th ed. (Illus.). 364p. 1988. 29.95 (0-226-46973-5) U Ch Pr.

Leavitt, Harold J., et al. Readings in Managerial Psychology. (Illus.). 784p. 1988. pap. text 28.00 (0-226-46992-1) U Ch Pr.

— Readings in Managerial Psychology. 4th ed. (Illus.). 784p. 1988. lib. bdg. 72.00 (0-226-46991-3) U Ch Pr.

Leavitt, Howard B., ed. Issues & Problems in Teacher Education: An International Handbook. LC 91-33503. 312p. 1992. lib. bdg. 75.00 (0-313-25991-7, LTC, Greenwood Pr) Greenwood.

Leavitt, Howard S. Looking for Angels & Answers. LC 94-38175. 1995. pap. 12.95 (1-883911-04-4) Brandylane.

Leavitt, Jacqueline. Defining Cultural Differences in Space: Public Housing As a Microcosm. (Urban Studies: No. 11). 84p. 1994. pap. 7.50 (0-913749-21-4) U MD Urban Stud.

Leavitt, Jay, tr. & photos by see Harding, Martha.

Leavitt, Jerome E. Easy Carpentry Projects for Children. Orig. Title: Carpentry for Children. (Illus.). 96p. (J). (gr. 2 up). 1986. reprint ed. pap. 3.95 (0-486-25057-1) Dover.

Leavitt, Jerome E., ed. Child Abuse & Neglect: Research & Innovation. 1983. lib. bdg. 162.50 (90-247-2862-2) Kluwer Academic.

L

Leavitt, John. UNIX Web Server Administration. Mui, Linda, ed. (Illus.). 325p. (Orig.). 1997. pap. 32.95 (*1-56592-217-4*) Thomson Learn.

Leavitt, John, tr. see Izard, Michel.

Leavitt, John, tr. see Izard, Michel & Smith, Pierre, eds.

Leavitt, John F. Wake of the Coasters. rev. ed. LC 75-120265. (American Maritime Library: Vol. 2). (Illus.). xvii, 201p. 1984. pap. 21.95 (*0-913372-34-X*) Mystic Seaport.

Leavitt, John H. Poetry & Prophecy: The Anthropology of Inspiration. LC 97-25223. 224p. (C). 1997. text 44.50 (*0-472-10688-0*, 10688) U of Mich Pr.

Leavitt, Joy. The Adventures of Huckleberry Finn: A Study Guide. (Novel-Ties Ser.). (YA). (gr. 10-12). 1983. pap. text, teacher ed., wbk. ed. 15.95 (*0-88122-020-5*) Lrn Links.

— The Adventures of Tom Sawyer: A Study Guide. (Novel-Ties Ser.). (YA). (gr. 7-12). 1984. pap. text, teacher ed., wbk. ed. 15.95 (*0-88122-103-1*) Lrn Links.

— All Quiet on the Western Front. (Novel-Ties Ser.). (YA). (gr. 9-12). 1983. pap. text, teacher ed., student ed. 15.95 (*0-88122-035-3*) Lrn Links.

— Catcher in the Rye: A Study Guide. (Novel-Ties Ser.). (YA). (gr. 7-12). 1985. pap. text, teacher ed., student ed. 15.95 (*0-88122-107-4*) Lrn Links.

— Death of a Salesman: A Study Guide. (Novel-Ties Ser.). (YA). (gr. 9-12). 1984. pap. text, teacher ed., student ed. 15.95 (*0-88122-113-9*) Lrn Links.

— The Red Pony: A Study Guide. (Novel-Ties Ser.). (J). (gr. 6-8). 1985. pap. text, teacher ed., student ed. 15.95 (*0-88122-125-2*) Lrn Links.

Leavitt, Judith A. American Women Managers & Administrators: A Selective Biographical Dictionary of Twentieth Century Leaders in Business, Education, & Government. LC 84-12814. 317p. 1985. lib. bdg. 75.00 (*0-313-23748-4*, LAO/, Greenwood Pr) Greenwood.

Leavitt, Judith K., jt. auth. see Mason, Diana J.

Leavitt, Judith W. Brought to Bed: Childbearing in America, 1750-1950. (Illus.). 304p. 1988. pap. text 13.95 (*0-19-505690-6*) OUP.

— The Healthiest City: Milwaukee & the Politics of Health Reform. rev. ed. LC 96-5117. (Illus.). 318p. 1996. pap. 19.95 (*0-299-15164-6*) U of Wis Pr.

— Typhoid Mary: Captive to the Public's Health. LC 95-46486. 352p. 1997. pap. 17.50 (*0-8070-2103-2*) Beacon Pr.

— Women & Health in America: Historical Readings. 2nd ed. LC 98-14446. 1999. 65.00 (*0-299-15960-4*); pap. 29.95 (*0-299-15964-7*) U of Wis Pr.

Leavitt, Judith W. & Numbers, Ronald L., eds. Sickness & Health in America: Readings in the History of Medicine & Public Health. LC 78-53288. (Illus.). 475p. reprint ed. pap. 147.30 (*0-608-07004-1*, 206721200009) Bks Demand.

— Sickness & Health in America: Readings in the History of Medicine & Public Health. 3rd rev. ed. LC 96-44916. (Illus.). 600p. 1997. 65.00 (*0-299-15320-7*); pap. 29.95 (*0-299-15324-X*) U of Wis Pr.

Leavitt, Judith W., jt. auth. see Numbers, Ronald L.

Leavitt, Lewis A. & Fox, Nathan A., eds. Psychological Effects of War & Violence on Children. 392p. 1993. pap. 36.00 (*0-8058-1172-9*); text 89.95 (*0-8058-1171-0*) L Erlbaum Assocs.

Leavitt, Mel, et al. The Court of Two Sisters Cookbook: With a History of the French Quarter & the Restaurant by Mel Leavitt. LC 91-17110. (Illus.). 112p. 1996. reprint ed. 14.95 (*0-88289-866-3*) Pelican.

Leavitt, Melvin J. A Snow Story. LC 94-21532. (Illus.). (J). (gr. k-3). 1995. 15.00 (*0-02-754633-0*) S&S Bks Yung.

Leavitt, Michael, jt. auth. see Shokek, Shimon.

Leavitt, Mort, ed. see Giusi, Nadya.

Leavitt, Moses A. Handicapped Wage Earners As Studied by A Family Welfare Agency. Phillips, William R. & Rosenberg, Janet, eds. LC 79-6913. (Physically Handicapped in Society Ser.). 1980. reprint ed. lib. bdg. 15.95 (*0-405-13122-4*) Ayer.

Leavitt, Paul & Vaughan, Jennifer, eds. Avoiding Liability in Hospital Security. 80p. 1998. pap. 97.00 (*1-887986-08-1*) Strafford Pubns.

— Avoiding Liability in Hotel/Motel Security. 313p. 1998. pap. 97.00 (*1-887986-06-5*) Strafford Pubns.

— Avoiding Liability in Retail Security. 2nd ed. 600p. 1998. pap. 97.00 (*1-887986-07-3*) Strafford Pubns.

Leavitt, Paul & Vaughan, Jennifer F., eds. Avoiding Liability in Premises Security. 3rd ed. 700p. 1997. pap. 149.00 (*1-887986-02-2*) Strafford Pubns.

Leavitt, Randy. Home Climbing Gyms: How to Build & Use. 1998. pap. 9.95 (*1-887216-11-1*) Elk Mtn Pr.

Leavitt, Robert H. Lebanon, New Hampshire in Pictures, Vol. 1. LC 97-61675. (Illus.). x, 899p. 1997. write for info. (*0-9660069-0-9*) Whitman Communs.

Leavitt, Robin L. Power & Emotion in Infant-Toddler Day Care. LC 93-28222. (SUNY Series, Early Childhood Education). 140p. (C). 1994. pap. text 17.95 (*0-7914-1886-3*) State U NY Pr.

Leavitt, Ronnie L. Disability & Rehabilitation in Rural Jamaica: An Ethnographic Study. LC 90-56172. (Illus.). 256p. 1992. 39.50 (*0-685-54895-3*) Fairleigh Dickinson.

Leavitt, Sarah. Slater Mill. LC 97-158775. (Images of America Ser.). 1997. pap. 16.99 (*0-7524-0567-5*) Arcadia Publng.

Leavitt, Shelley E. Active Parenting: A Trainer's Manual. 150p. (Orig.). 1982. pap. 6.95 (*0-938510-02-9*, 81-001) Boys Town Pr.

Leavitt, Stephen C., jt. ed. see Herdt, Gilbert H.

Leavitt, Thad W. History of Leeds & Grenville, Ontario: From 1749 to 1879, with Illustrations & Biographical Sketches of Some of Its Prominent Men & Pioneers. (Illus.). 200p. 1996. reprint ed. lib. bdg. 32.00 (*0-8328-5155-8*) Higginson Bk Co.

Leavitt, W. Guitar Duets Vol. 1: Set of Parts. 20p. 1986. pap. 8.95 (*0-7935-3900-5*, 50449430) H Leonard.

— The Guitar Phase I. 64p. 1988. pap., pap. text 14.95 incl. audio (*0-7935-4996-5*, 50449462) H Leonard.

— The Guitar Phase 2. 64p. 1986. pap. 7.95 (*0-7935-5526-4*, 50449470) H Leonard.

— Modern Method for Guitar, Vol. 1. (Berklee Ser.). 128p. 1986. otabind 14.95 (*0-7935-2545-4*, 50449400) H Leonard.

— Modern Method for Guitar, Vol. 2. (Berklee Ser.). 128p. 1986. otabind 14.95 (*0-7935-2572-1*, 50449410) H Leonard.

— Modern Method for Guitar, Vol. 3. (Berklee Ser.). 168p. 1987. otabind 14.95 (*0-7935-2598-5*, 50449420) H Leonard.

Leavitt, W. W., ed. Cell & Molecular Biology of the Uterus. LC 88-5793. (Advances in Experimental Medicine & Biology Ser.: Vol. 230). (Illus.). 254p. 1988. 75.00 (*0-306-42836-9*, Plenum Trade) Perseus Pubng.

***Leavitt, William.** A Modern Method for Guitar, 1&2. 432p. 1999. otabind 29.95 (*0-634-01233-9*) H Leonard.

Leavy, Barbara F. In Search of the Swan Maiden: A Narrative on Folklore & Gender. 374p. (C). 1995. pap. text 19.50 (*0-8147-5100-8*) NYU Pr.

— To Blight with Plague: Studies in a Literary Theme. 300p. (C). 1993. pap. text 19.00 (*0-8147-5083-4*) NYU Pr.

Leavy, Brain & Wilson, David. Strategy & Leadership. LC 93-23853. 224p. (C). 1994. pap. 26.95 (*0-415-07092-9*) Thomson Learn.

— Strategy & Leadership. LC 93-23853. 224p. (C). (gr. 13). 1994. pap. 64.95 (*0-415-07091-0*) Thomson Learn.

Leavy, Brian. Key Processes in Strategy: Themes & Theories. LC 95-20857. 224p. 1996. pap. 45.00 (*0-415-11466-7*); pap. 15.99 (*0-415-11467-5*) Thomson Learn.

Leavy-Ells, Jean. Hot Shots with Any Camera. LC 91-71095. (Illus.). 48p. (Orig.). (YA). (gr. 7-12). 1995. pap. 1.98 (*0-87985-745-5*, AC-210, Kodak) Saunders Photo.

Leavy, Margaret R. Looking for the Armenians: Eli Smith's Missionary Adventure, 1830-1831. (Transactions Ser.: Vol. 50, Pt. 4). (Illus.). 84p. 1992. pap. 16.00 (*1-878508-07-5*) CT Acad Arts & Sciences.

Leavy, Stanley A. In the Image of God: A Psychoanalyst's View. 128p. 1997. reprint ed. pap. 24.95 (*0-88163-276-7*) Analytic Pr.

— The Psychoanalytic Dialogue. LC 79-21796. 141p. 1987. pap. 15.00 (*0-300-04037-7*, Y-683) Yale U Pr.

Leavy, Una. Irish Fairy Tales & Legends. (Illus.). 96p. (J). (gr. 3-5). 1997. 18.95 (*1-57098-177-9*) Roberts Rinehart.

— Irish Fairy Tales & Legends, 1. 1998. audio 9.95 (*1-57098-240-6*) Roberts Rinehart.

***Leavy, Una.** Irish Fairy Tales & Legends. 1999. 9.95 (*1-57098-292-9*, TomiCo) Roberts Rinehart.

Leax, John. Country Labors. 96p. 1991. pap. 5.99 (*0-310-53281-7*) Zondervan.

— Grace Is Where I Live: Writing As a Christian Vocation. 152p. (YA). (gr. 10). 1996. pap. 9.99 (*0-8010-5714-0*, Ravens Ridge) Baker Bks.

— In Season & Out: A Steward's Journal. 1985. 7.95 (*0-310-45480-8*, 9373) Zondervan.

— Nightwatch: A Novel. 144p. 1990. pap. 6.99 (*0-310-21861-6*) Zondervan.

***Leax, John.** Out Walking: Reflections on Our Place in the Natural World. LC 99-58138. 144p. 2000. pap. 14.99 (*0-8010-1197-3*) Baker Bks.

— Out Walking: Reflections on Our Place in the Natural World. 176p. (gr. 13 up). 2000. pap. 13.99 (*0-8010-6175-X*, Ravens Ridge) Baker Bks.

Leax, John. Standing Ground. 176p. 1991. pap. 7.99 (*0-310-53791-6*) Zondervan.

— The Task of Adam. 1985. 7.95 (*0-310-45490-5*, 9374) Zondervan.

Leazer, Gary. Fundamentalism & Freemasonry: The Southern Baptist Investigation of the Fraternal Order. LC 94-49038. 256p. 1995. 19.95 (*0-87131-775-3*) M Evans.

Leazes, Francis J., Jr. Accountability & the Business State: The Structure of Federal Corporation. LC 86-25244. 160p. 1987. 55.00 (*0-275-92495-5*, C2495, Praeger Pubs) Greenwood.

Leb, G., ed. see Passath, A. & Hoefler, H.

Leba, John K., et al. The Vietnamese Entrepreneurs in the U. S. A. The First Decade. 276p. 1985. 14.50 (*0-936675-00-4*) Zieleks Co.

Lebacqz, Karen. Six Theories of Justice: Perspectives from Philosophical & Theological Ethics. LC 86-26457. 144p. (Orig.). (C). 1986. pap. 15.99 (*0-8066-2245-8*, 10-5820, Augsburg) Augsburg Fortress.

— Word, Worship, World & Wonder: Reflections on Christian Living. LC 97-13817. 128p. (Orig.). 1996. pap. 14.95 (*0-687-02089-1*) Abingdon.

Lebacqz, Karen & Barton, Ronald. Sex in the Parish. 256p. (Orig.). 1991. pap. 24.95 (*0-664-25087-4*) Westminster John Knox.

***Lebacqz, Karen & Driskill, Joseph D.** Ethics & Spiritual Care: A Guide for Pastors & Spiritual Directors. LC 00-32287. 2000. write for info. (*0-687-07156-9*) Abingdon.

Lebacqz, Karen & Sinacore-Guinn, David, eds. Sexuality: A Reader. LC 98-37851. (Pilgrim Library of Ethics). 480p. (Orig.). pap. 26.95 (*0-8298-1210-5*) Pilgrim OH.

Lebaigue, Charles. Dictionnaire Latin-Francais. (FRE & LAT.). 1382p. 59.95 (*0-7859-0744-0*, M-6340) Fr & Eur.

***Lebain, Frederic.** Mediterranean Cooking. (Illus.). 143p. 1999. 12.99 (*1-84100-126-0*) Quadrillion Media.

Lebano, Edoardo A. Italian: A Self-Teaching Guide. 296p. 1988. pap. 17.95 (*0-471-01143-6*); pap. 17.95 (*0-471-63838-2*) Wiley.

***Lebano, Edoardo A.** Italian: A Self-Teaching Guide. 2nd ed. LC 99-42195. 304p. 2000. pap. 17.95 (*0-471-35961-0*) Wiley.

Lebano, Edoardo A. & Baldini, Pier R. Buon Giorno a Tutti: First Year Italian. 2nd ed. LC 88-33973. 448p. 1989. 78.95 (*0-471-63129-9*) Wiley.

— Buon Giorno a Tutti: First Year Italian. 2nd ed. Ep. 1989. cd-rom 133.95 (*0-471-50250-2*) Wiley.

— Buon Giorno a Tutti! First Year Italian Workbook. 2nd ed. 208p. 1989. pap., student ed. 34.95 (*0-471-63128-0*) Wiley.

Lebanon, Abraham. Colored Pearls. 1997. 40.00 (*965-229-161-7*, Pub. by Gefen Pub Hse) Gefen Bks.

Lebans, Gertrude. Implementation Guide for the Standards of School Nursing Practice. 1991. 13.75 (*0-614-06295-0*) Am Sch Health.

LeBar, Frank M., ed. Ethnic Groups of Insular Southeast Asia Vol. 1: Indonesia. LC 72-90940. (Area & Country Surveys Ser.). 244p. 1972. 30.00 (*0-87536-403-9*) HRAFP.

— Ethnic Groups of Insular Southeast Asia Vol. 2: Philippines & Formosa. LC 74-19513. (Area & Country Surveys Ser.). 200p. 1975. 30.00 (*0-87536-405-5*) HRAFP.

LeBar, Frank M. & Suddard, Adrienne, eds. Laos. LC 60-7381. (Area & Country Surveys Ser.). 312p. 1967. 15.00 (*0-87536-915-4*) HRAFP.

LeBar, Frank M., et al. Ethnic Groups of Mainland Southeast Asia. LC 64-25414. 302p. reprint ed. 93.70 (*0-608-16110-1*, 201925800011) Bks Demand.

LeBar, John, jt. auth. see Wright, Harold Bell.

LeBar, Lois E. Education That Is Christian. Plueddemann, James E., ed. 324p. (Orig.). (C). 1995. pap. 13.99 (*1-56476-412-5*, 6-3412, Victor Bks) Chariot Victor.

Lebar, Lois E. Education that Is Christian. 1998. pap. 14.99 (*1-56476-749-3*, Victor Bks) Chariot Victor.

LeBaron, Anthony. Chamber Music. (Illus.). 48p. 1988. 9.95 (*0-921254-04-0*, Pub. by Penumbra Pr) U of Toronto Pr.

Lebaron, Dean. A Capitalist in Red Square. 1999. write for info. (*0-316-51864-6*) Little.

LeBaron, Dean. The Ultimate Book of Investment Quotations. (Orig.). 1999. pap. 19.95 (*1-84112-008-1*) Capstone Pub NH.

— The Ultimate Investor: The People & Ideas That Make Modern Investment. 1999. 19.95 (*1-84112-006-5*) Capstone Pub NH.

LeBaron, Gaye & Mitchell, Joann. Santa Rosa, a Twentieth Century Town, Vol. II. LC 93-79227. (Illus.). 352p. 1993. 59.95 (*0-9615010-2-2*) Historia Ltd.

LeBaron, Gaye, et al. Santa Rosa, a Nineteenth Century Town. LC 86-109023. (Illus.). 224p. 1992. reprint ed. pap. 24.95 (*0-9615010-1-4*) Historia Ltd.

LeBaron, Homer M., et al, eds. Biotechnology in Agricultural Chemistry. LC 87-1803. (Symposium Ser.: No. 334). (Illus.). xxii, 354p. 1987. 71.95 (*0-8412-1019-5*) Am Chemical.

— Biotechnology in Agricultural Chemistry. LC 87-1803. (ACS Symposium Ser.: Vol. 334). 392p. 1987. reprint ed. pap. 121.60 (*0-608-03546-7*, 206426500008) Bks Demand.

LeBaron, Jeff. Shed Antler Records of North American Big Game: A Record Book for the Recognition of North America's Big Game Shed Antlers. Falck, Sandi, ed. 210p. 1994. text 29.95 (*0-9644514-4-1*) NAm Shed Hunt.

LeBaron, Jeffery K. Shed Antler Records of North American Big Game: A Record Book for the Recognition of North America's Big Game Shed Antlers. 2nd ed. Leistico, Cathy R., ed. (Illus.). 240p. 1998. text 32.95 (*0-9644514-0-9*) NAm Shed Hunt.

LeBaron, John. Making Television: A Video Production Guide for Teachers. LC 81-703. (Illus.). 352p. (Orig.). reprint ed. pap. 109.20 (*0-7837-0989-7*, 204129500020) Bks Demand.

LeBaron, John F., et al. A Travel Agent in Cyber School: The Internet & the Library Media Program. LC 96-31826. 200p. 1996. pap. text 25.00 (*1-56308-333-7*) Libs Unl.

LeBaron, Melvin J. Workable Workplace: Excellence at Work for You. LC 87-83597. 200p. (C). 1988. text 18.95 (*0-944329-01-2*) KOBO Ent.

LeBaron, Melvin J., jt. auth. see Graham, Morris A.

LeBaron, Samuel, jt. auth. see Hilgard, Josephine R.

LeBaron, Wayne. America's Nuclear Legacy. 320p. 1998. 39.00 (*1-56072-556-7*) Nova Sci Pubs.

— Preparation for Nuclear Disaster. 387p. 1998. 38.00 (*1-56072-557-5*) Nova Sci Pubs.

Lebart, Ludovic, et al. Exploring Textual Data. LC 97-31927. (Text, Speech, & Language Technology). 280p. 1998. text 127.00 (*0-7923-4840-0*) Kluwer Academic.

LeBarz, P. & Hervier, Y., eds. Enumerative Geometry & Classical Algebra. (Progress in Mathematics Ser.: Vol. 24). 246p. 1982. 51.50 (*0-8176-3106-2*) Birkhauser.

Lebas, Elizabeth, jt. ed. see Harloe, Michael.

LeBauer. Journeys Reading, 2 vols. 1998. pap. text, teacher ed. write for info. (*0-13-409772-6*) P-H.

— Journeys Reading, Vol. 2. 1999. pap. text 9.95 (*0-13-409715-7*) P-H.

***Lebauer.** Learn to Listen Listen to Learn. 2nd ed. LC 99-47758. 2000. pap. text 26.00 (*0-13-919432-0*) P-H.

Lebauer, Roni. Journeys Reading, No. 1. 1997. pap. text 26.40 (*0-13-171448-1*) P-H.

Lebauer, Roni S. Learn to Listen, Listen to Learn. (Illus.). 256p. (C). 1988. pap. text 33.20 (*0-13-527128-2*) P-H.

Lebauer, Roni S. & Scarcella, Robin C. Reactions: Multi-Cultural Reading Based Writing Modules. 384p. (C). 1992. pap. text 33.00 (*0-13-756214-4*) P-H.

Lebay, Charles, jt. auth. see Gnann, Pearl R.

Lebbad, M. J. The Intelligent Buyer's Guide to New & Used Vehicles. (Illus.). 64p. (Orig.). 1990. pap. 1.25 (*0-9627718-0-5*) M J Lebbad.

Lebbe, L. C. Hydraulic Parameter Identification: Interpretation Method for Single & Multiple Pumping Tests. LC 99-19840. xvi, 376p. 1999. 129.00 (*3-540-65603-0*) Spr-Verlag.

***Lebbon, Tim.** Faith in the Flesh. 142p. 1998. pap. 9.00 (*0-9531468-4-7*, Pub. by RazorBlade Pr) Firebird Dist.

Lebeau, Andre, jt. auth. see Salomon, Jean-Jacques.

***LeBeau, Bryan F.** Religion in America to 1865. LC 99-56488. 2000. text 50.00 (*0-8147-5163-6*) NYU Pr.

LeBeau, Bryan F. The Story of the Salem Witch Trials. LC 97-5456. 308p. 1997. pap. text 31.80 (*0-13-442542-1*) P-H.

Lebeau, C., et al. Fabrics: The Decorative Art of Textiles. 1994. 58.00 (*0-500-01631-3*) Thames Hudson.

Lebeau, Caroline. Fabrics. LC 94-2604. (Illus.). 224p. 1994. 55.00 (*0-517-57434-9*) C Potter.

LeBeau, Charles & Lucas, David. Day Trading Systems & Methods. 90p. 1999. pap. 19.95 (*1-883272-27-0*) Traders Lib.

LeBeau, Charles & Lucas, David W. Technical Traders Guide to Computer Analysis of the Futures Market. 312p. 1991. text 70.00 (*1-55623-468-6*, Irwn Prfssnl) McGraw-Hill Prof.

LeBeau, Chris. The Healthy Heart Cookbook. LC 90-71663. (Illus.). xii, 310p. 1991. 19.95 (*0-934955-19-0*) Watercress Pr.

LeBeau, Dennis. The Brookfields from the Collection of William Bullard. LC 96-169606. (Images of America Ser.). 128p. 1996. pap. 16.99 (*0-7524-0294-3*) Arcadia Publng.

LeBeau, Gilles, jt. auth. see Croisille, Jean-Pierre.

Lebeau, Michael, jt. auth. see Cameron-Bandler, Leslie.

***LeBeau, Patrick Russell.** Stands Alone, Faces & Other Poems. LC 99-6504. 88p. 1999. pap. 15.95 (*0-87013-533-3*) Mich St U Pr.

LeBeau, Sinclair. Glory of Love. LC 98-156042. 1997. pap. 10.95 (*1-885478-19-4*, Pub. by Genesis Press) BookWorld.

***LeBeau, Sinclair.** So Amazing. 2000. pap. 8.95 (*1-58571-038-5*, 909-102, Pub. by Genesis Press) BookWorld.

LeBeau, Sinclair. Somebody's Someone. (Indigo Ser.). 162p. 1999. pap. 8.95 (*1-885478-57-7*, Pub. by Genesis Press) BookWorld.

Lebeau, T. K. The Crystal Skull Destiny's Courier. (Orig.). 1988. pap. 8.95 (*0-945680-00-7*) Harmony AZ.

— The Crystal Tunnel. 188p. (Orig.). 1989. pap. 9.95 (*0-945680-01-5*) Harmony AZ.

Lebeau, Vicky. Lost Angels: Psychoanalysis & Cinema. 168p. (C). 1994. pap. 22.99 (*0-415-10721-0*, B4795) Routledge.

***Lebeaux, David.** Language Acquisition & the Form of the Grammar. LC 00-39775. 2000. write for info. (*1-55619-858-2*) J Benjamins Pubng Co.

Lebeaux, Richard. Thoreau's Seasons. LC 83-17982. 432p. 1984. 40.00 (*0-87023-401-3*) U of Mass Pr.

— Young Man Thoreau. LC 76-44851. 272p. 1977. reprint ed. pap. 84.40 (*0-608-04440-7*, 206497200012) Bks Demand.

Lebeck, A. O., jt. auth. see Brown, Franklin L.

Lebeck, Alan O. Principles & Design of Mechanical Face Seals. LC 90-24783. 800p. 1991. 250.00 (*0-471-51533-7*) Wiley.

LeBeck, Eliane, tr. see Hemphill, MaryAnn.

Lebeck, Michael, tr. see Hesse, Hermann.

Lebeck, Robert. Robert Lebeck: The Mystery of Life. 1999. pap. text 19.95 (*3-570-19197-4*) Gruner & Jahr AG &.

Lebed, Alexander. My Life & My Country. LC 97-33323. 399p. 1997. 29.95 (*0-89526-422-6*) Regnery Pub.

Lebeda, Guy & Neibaur, Alexander. Writing Between the Lines: A Selection of Poetry Inspired by Notations in Alexander Neibaur's Journal, 1841 to 1862. Cole, W. Roger & Ostler, Rosalyn, eds. (Illus.). 96p. 1997. 10.50 (*0-9661741-0-0*) T L Bassett.

Lebedev, A. Soviet Paintings in the Tretyakov Gallery. 136p. 1976. 50.00 (*0-569-08318-4*) St Mut.

***Lebedev, A. V.** Transistorized Power Sources for Arc Welding. (Welding & Surfacing Reviews Ser.: Vol. 10, Part 2). 180p. 1998. pap. text 106.00 (*90-5702-357-1*, Harwood Acad Pubs) Gordon & Breach.

Lebedev, A. V. Welding & Surfacing Reviews: Automatic Control of Arc Welding Process, 6, Vol. 6. (Welding & Surfacing Reviews Ser.). 178p. 1997. pap. text 69.00 (*90-5702-097-1*, Harwood Acad Pubs) Gordon & Breach.

Lebedev, A. V. & Antonevich, Anatolij. Functional Differential Equations: Theory. LC 92-26873. (Pitman Monographs & Surveys in Pure & Applied Mathematics). 1993. 160.00 (*0-582-07251-4*) Longman.

Lebedev, I. P. Aviation Lend Lease to Russia. 278p. (C). 1997. lib. bdg. 85.00 (*1-56072-417-X*) Nova Sci Pubs.

Lebedev, K. A. Russian-Pashto-Dari Dictionary. (PUS & RUS.). 768p. 1983. 59.95 (*0-8288-1738-3*, F 47690) Fr & Eur.

Lebedev, K. A., et al. Immunology Reviews: Immune Monitoring: Its Principles & Application in Natural & Model Clinical Systems, Vol. 2. Petrov, R. V., ed. (Soviet Medical Reviews Ser.: Vol. 2, Pt. 1). x, 124p. 1989. pap. text 156.00 (*3-7186-4922-5*) Gordon & Breach.

Lebedev, L. P., et al. Functional Analysis: Applications in Mechanics & Inverse Problems. LC 95-47427. (Solid Mechanics & Its Applications Ser.: Vol. 45). 248p. (C). 1996. lib. bdg. 134.00 (*0-7923-3849-9*) Kluwer Academic.

Lebedev, N. A., jt. auth. see Smirnov, Vladimir I.

An Asterisk (*) at the beginning of an entry indicates that the title is appearing for the first time.

Lebedev, N. N. Special Functions & Their Applications. rev. ed. Silverman, Richard A., tr. from RUS. LC 72-86228. 308p. 1972. reprint ed. pap. 9.95 (*0-486-60624-4*) Dover.

Lebedev, N. N., et al. Worked Problems in Applied Mathematics. LC 78-67857. 429p. 1979. pap. text 11.95 (*0-486-63730-1*) Dover.

Lebedev, P. N. & Skalskaya, I. P. Problems in Mathematical Physics. LC 65-14785. (International Series of Monographs on Pure & Applied Mathematics: Vol. 84). 1966. 183.00 (*0-08-011134-3*, Pub. by Pergamon Repr) Franklin.

Lebedev, P. N., jt. ed. see Feinberg, E. L.

Lebedev, V. I., jt. auth. see Marchuk, Gurii I.

Lebedev, V. S., et al. Physics of Highly Excited Atoms & Ions. LC 98-35427. (Springer Series on Atoms & Plasmas: Vol. 22). (Illus.). 370p. 1998. 99.00 (*3-540-64234-X*) Spr-Verlag.

Lebedev, V. V., jt. auth. see Kats, Efim I.

Lebedev, Viacheslav I. An Introduction to Functional Analysis in Computational Mathematics. LC 96-33412. 255p. 1996. 59.95 (*0-8176-3888-1*) Birkhauser.

— An Introduction to Functional Analysis in Computational Mathematics. LC 96-33412. 266p. 1996. write for info. (*3-7643-3888-1*) Birkhauser.

Lebedev, Yu A., jt. ed. see Polak, L. S.

Lebedeva, Victoria. Boris Kustodiev. (Illus.). 212p. (C). 1981. text 150.00 (*0-7855-5834-9*, Pub. by Collets) St Mut.

— Boris Kustodiev: The Artist & His Work. (Illus.). 212p. 1981. 132.00 (*0-7855-1574-7*) St Mut.

Lebedinskaya, N. B., tr. see Ishkhanov, V. V., et al.

Lebedoff, David. Cleaning Up: The Exxon Valdez Case, from 3 Drinks to 5 Billion Dollars. LC 97-28385. 321p. 1997. 24.50 (*0-684-83706-4*) Free Pr.

Lebedun, Jean. Managing Workplace Conflict. Miller, Karen M., ed. LC 98-72097. (How-to Book Ser.). 104p. 1998. pap. 12.95 (*1-884926-93-2*, SOLV2) Amer Media.

Lebel, Gerard. Our French-Canadian Ancestors. LaForest, Thomas J., ed. & tr. by. from FRE. LC 83-81941. (Illus.). 1997. pap. 20.00 (*0-914163-25-6*) L I S I Pr.

Lebel, Gerard. Our French Canadian Ancestors, Vol. I. rev. ed. Leforest, Thomas J., ed. & tr. by. from FRE. LC 83-81941. (Illus.). 300p. 1983. reprint ed. pap. 20.00 (*0-914163-01-9*) L I S I Pr.

— Our French Canadian Ancestors, Vol. II. rev. ed. Laforest, Thomas J., ed. & tr. by. LC 83-81941. (Illus.). 290p. 1984. pap. 20.00 (*0-914163-02-7*) L I S I Pr.

— Our French Canadian Ancestors, Vol. III. rev. ed. Laforest, Thomas J., ed. & tr. by. LC 83-81941. (Illus.). 296p. 1985. pap. 20.00 (*0-914163-03-5*) L I S I Pr.

— Our French Canadian Ancestors, Vol. IX. Laforest, Thomas J., ed. & tr. by. LC 83-81941. (Illus.). 321p. 1986. pap. 20.00 (*0-914163-09-4*) L I S I Pr.

— Our French Canadian Ancestors, Vol. X. rev. ed. Laforest, Thomas J., ed. & tr. by. LC 83-81941. (Illus.). 312p. 1990. pap. 20.00 (*0-914163-10-8*) L I S I Pr.

— Our French Canadian Ancestors, Vol. XI. Laforest, Thomas J., ed. & tr. by. from FRE. LC 83-81941. (Illus.). 310p. 1990. pap. 20.00 (*0-914163-11-6*) L I S I Pr.

— Our French Canadian Ancestors, Vol. XII. Laforest, Thomas J., ed. & tr. by. LC 83-81941. (Illus.). 300p. 1991. pap. 20.00 (*0-914163-12-4*) L I S I Pr.

— Our French Canadian Ancestors, Vol. XIV. Leforest, Thomas J., ed. & tr. by. LC 83-81941. (Illus.). 310p. 1992. pap. 20.00 (*0-914163-14-0*) L I S I Pr.

— Our French Canadian Ancestors, Vol. XV. Laforest, Thomas J., ed. & tr. by. LC 83-81941. (Illus.). 284p. 1992. pap. 20.00 (*0-914163-15-9*) L I S I Pr.

— Our French Canadian Ancestors, Vol. XVI. Laforest, Thomas J., ed. & tr. by. LC 83-81941. (Illus.). 280p. 1993. pap. 20.00 (*0-914163-16-7*) L I S I Pr.

— Our French Canadian Ancestors, Vol. XVIII. Laforest, Thomas J., ed. & tr. by. LC 83-81941. (Illus.). 290p. 1994. pap. 20.00 (*0-914163-18-3*) L I S I Pr.

— Our French Canadian Ancestors, Vol. XIX. Laforest, Thomas J., ed. & tr. by. LC 83-81941. (Illus.). 270p. 1994. pap. text 20.00 (*0-914163-19-1*) L I S I Pr.

— Our French Canadian Ancestors, Vol. XX. Laforest, Thomas J., ed. & tr. by. from FRE. LC 83-81941. (Illus.). 249p. 1995. pap. 20.00 (*0-914163-20-5*) L I S I Pr.

— Our French Canadian Ancestors, Vol. XXI. Laforest, Thomas J., ed. & tr. by. from FRE. LC 83-81941. (Illus.). 285p. 1995. pap. 20.00 (*0-914163-21-3*) L I S I Pr.

***Lebel, Gerard & Saintonge, Jacques.** Our French Canadian Ancestors. LaForest, Thomas J., tr. from FRE. LC 83-81941. 1999. pap. 20.00 (*0-914163-28-0*) L I S I Pr.

— Our French-Canadian Ancestors. LaForest, Thomas J., tr. from FRE. LC 83-81941. 1999. pap. 20.00 (*0-914163-29-9*) L I S I Pr.

— Our French-Canadian Ancestors. LaForest, Thomas J., tr. from FRE. LC 83-81941. 2000. pap. 20.00 (*0-914163-30-2*) L I S I Pr.

— Our French-Canadian Ancestors: Index of Names. LaForest, Thomas J., tr. from FRE. LC 83-81941. 2000. pap. 20.00 (*0-914163-31-0*) L I S I Pr.

— Our French-Canadian Ancestors: 1 Aug 98. LaForest, Thomas J., tr. from FRE. LC 83-81941. 1998. pap. 20.00 (*0-914163-27-2*) L I S I Pr.

Lebel, Gerard & Saintonge, Jacques. Our French-Canadian Ancestors: 1 May 98. LaForest, Thomas J., tr. from FRE. LC 83-81941. 1998. pap. 20.00 (*0-914163-26-4*) L I S I Pr.

Lebel, Marc, tr. see Bessette, Gerard.

LeBel, Paul A. John Barleycorn Must Pay: Compensating the Victims of Drinking Drivers. 360p. 1992. text 39.95 (*0-252-01792-7*) U of Ill Pr.

— Products Liability Problems 1995 Edition for Use in Conjunction with Products Liability & Safety, Cases & Materials. 2nd ed. 171p. 1995. pap. text 10.95 (*1-56662-260-3*) Foundation Pr.

— Teacher's Manual for Products Liability Problems: 1995 Edition for Use in Conjunction with Products Liability & Safety, Cases & Materials. 2nd ed. (University Casebook Ser.). 241p. 1995. pap. text, teacher ed. write for info. (*1-56662-263-8*) Foundation Pr.

LeBel, Paul A., ed. see Owen, Montgomery & Owen, Keeton.

LeBel, Phillip. Economic Choices for Sustainable Agriculture in Africa. 97p. 1988. pap. 7.00 (*0-944572-01-4*) MSU Ctr Econ Res Africa.

— Promoting Human Resource Development in Africa. (Illus.). 104p. (Orig.). 1993. pap. 9.50 (*0-944572-06-5*) MSU Ctr Econ Res Africa.

LeBel, Phillip, ed. Europe, Africa, & the U. S. Nineteen Ninety-Two. 110p. (Orig.). 1990. pap. 8.50 (*0-944572-03-0*) MSU Ctr Econ Res Africa.

— New Initiatives for Africa's Debt. 104p. (Orig.). 1989. pap. 9.00 (*0-944572-02-2*) MSU Ctr Econ Res Africa.

— Privatization Strategies in Africa. 108p. (Orig.). 1992. pap. 9.00 (*0-944572-05-7*) MSU Ctr Econ Res Africa.

LeBel, Phillip, ed. Managing Africa's Economic Recovery. 72p. 1987. pap. 7.00 (*0-944572-00-6*) MSU Ctr Econ Res Africa.

LeBel, Phillip, intro. Environmental Policies for Sustainable Growth in Africa. 101p. (Orig.). 1991. pap. 9.00 (*0-944572-04-9*) MSU Ctr Econ Res Africa.

LeBel, Phillip, jt. ed. see Anyanwu, Longy.

LeBel, Phillip G. Energy Economics & Technology. LC 82-15183. (Illus.). 573p. reprint ed. pap. 177.70 (*0-608-06286-3*, 206661500008) Bks Demand.

Lebel, R. P. Our French Canadian Ancestors. LC 83-81941.Tr. of Now Ancetres. (FRE., Illus.). 288p. 1996. pap. write for info. (*0-914163-23-X*) L I S I Pr.

Lebel, R. P. Our French Canadian Ancestors, Vol. XXIV. LaForest, Thomas J., ed. & tr. by. from FRE. LC 83-81941.Tr. of Now Ancetres. 275p. 1997. pap. 20.00 (*0-914163-24-8*) L I S I Pr.

***LeBell, Gene.** Gene LeBell's Grappling World: Encyclopedia of Finishing Holds. (Illus.). 520p. 1999. pap. 39.95 (*0-86568-171-6*) Unique Pubns.

Lebell, Gene. Grappling & Self-Defense: For the Young Adult. rev. ed. Sobel, Stuart, ed. LC 95-71804. (Illus.). 130p. (YA). 1971. reprint ed. pap. 12.95 (*0-9615126-5-2*) Pro Action Pub.

LeBell, Gene. Grappling Master: Combat for Street Defense & Competition. Pimenta, Wendy, ed. LC 91-90363. (Illus.). 160p. (Orig.). 1992. pap. 16.95 (*0-9615126-2-8*) Pro Action Pub.

Lebell, Gene. Handbook of Judo: A Step-by-Step Guide to Winning in Sport Judo. rev. ed. Sobel, Stuart, ed. LC 95-72481. (Illus.). 186p. (YA). 1962. reprint ed. pap. 12.95 (*0-9615126-6-0*) Pro Action Pub.

— Handbook of Self-Defense. rev. ed. Sobel, Stuart, ed. LC 95-72482. (Illus.). 144p. 1964. reprint ed. pap. 12.95 (*0-9615126-7-9*) Pro Action Pub.

Lebell, Sharon, photos by. The Art of Living: The Classical Mannual on Virtue, Happiness, & Effectiveness. LC 95-14398. (Illus.). 128p. 1995. 16.00 (*0-06-251322-2*, Pub. by Harper SF) HarpC.

Lebell, Sharon, tr. Epictetus: The Art of Living: The Classic Manual on Virtue, Happiness & Effectiveness. abr. ed. text 11.95 incl. audio (*1-57453-088-7*) Audio Lit.

Lebell, Sharon, jt. auth. see Boorstein, Sylvia.

Lebell, Sharon, jt. auth. see Steindl-Rast, David.

Lebell, Sharon, ed. see Epictetus.

Leben, Joe. Asynchronous Transfer: ATM Architecture & Implementation. 272p. 1996. 46.60 (*0-13-567918-4*) P-H.

Leben, Joe, jt. auth. see Martin, James.

Leben, Joseph, jt. auth. see Martin, James.

Leben, Steve. Practitioner's Guide to Kansas Family Law, 2 vols. 1400p. 1997. write for info. (*1-890452-03-3*) KS Bar.

Leben, Ulrich. Ebeniste, Bernard Molitor: The Ancient Regime to the Bourbon Restoration, with a Complete Catalog of the Furniture. (Illus.). 352p. 1992. 145.00 (*0-85667-407-9*) Sothebys Pubns.

Leben, William R., et al. Hausar yau Da Kullum: Intermediate & Advanced Lessons in Hausa Language & Culture. LC 91-3933. (Illus.). 153p. (Orig.). (C). 1991. pap. text 19.95 (*0-937073-68-7*) CSLI.

— Hausar yau Da Kullum Workbook: Intermediate & Advanced Lessons in Hausa Language & Culture. LC 91-3933. (Illus.). 153p. (C). 1991. student ed. 7.50 (*0-937073-69-5*) CSLI.

Leben, William R., jt. auth. see Denning, Keith.

Lebenson, Richard & Creighton, Kathleen. Rsvp: The Directory of Illustration & Design. (Illus.). 320p. 1992. pap. 21.00 (*1-878118-01-3*) RSVP NY.

Lebenson, Richard & Creighton, Kathleen, eds. RSVP24: The Directory of Illustration & Design. (Illus.). 304p. 1999. pap. 21.00 (*1-878118-08-0*) RSVP NY.

— RSVP18: The Directory of Illustration & Design. (Directory of Illustration & Design Ser.). (Illus.). 304p. 1993. pap. 21.00 (*1-878118-02-1*) RSVP NY.

— RSVP19: The Directory of Illustration & Design. (Illus.). 304p. 1994. pap. 21.00 (*1-878118-03-X*) RSVP NY.

— RSVP16: The Directory of Illustration & Design. (Illus.). 320p. (Orig.). 1991. pap. 20.00 (*1-878118-00-5*) RSVP NY.

— RSVP20: The Directory of Illustration & Design. 320p. 1995. pap. 24.00 (*1-878118-04-8*) RSVP NY.

***Lebenson, Richard & Creighton, Kathleen, eds.** RSVP25: The Directory of Illustration & Design. (Illus.). 304p. 2000. pap. 21.00 (*1-878118-09-9*) RSVP NY.

Lebenson, Richard & Creighton, Kathleen, eds. RSVP21: The Directory of Illustration & Design. (Illus.). 308p. 1996. pap. 24.00 (*1-878118-05-6*) RSVP NY.

— RSVP22: The Directory of Illustration & Design. (Illus.). 304p. (Orig.). 1997. pap. 21.00 (*1-878118-06-4*) RSVP NY.

— RSVP23: The Directory of Illustration & Design. 304p. 1998. pap. 21.00 (*1-878118-07-2*) RSVP NY.

Lebensztejn, Jean-Claude, et al, texts. Parkett No. 52: Karen Kilimnick, Malcolm Morley & Ugo Rondinone. (Illus.). 250p. 1998. pap. 32.00 (*3-907582-01-2*, 811142, Pub. by Parkett Verlag AG) Dist Art Pubs.

Lebenthal, Emanuel. Human Gastrointestinal Development. LC 89-8383. 844p. 1989. reprint ed. pap. 200.00 (*0-608-04677-9*, 206539800004) Bks Demand.

Lebenthal, Emanuel, ed. Textbook of Gastroenterology & Nutrition in Infancy. LC 84-42947. (Illus.). 1407p. 1989. reprint ed. pap. 200.00 (*0-608-07258-3*, 206748600009) Bks Demand.

— Total Parenteral Nutrition: Indications, Utilization, Complications, & Pathophysiological Considerations. LC 85-23239. 528p. 1986. reprint ed. pap. 163.70 (*0-608-00412-X*, 206112600007) Bks Demand.

Lebenthal, Emanuel & Duffey, Michael E., eds. Textbook of Secretory Diarrhea. LC 90-8463. 456p. 1990. reprint ed. pap. 141.40 (*0-608-03426-6*, 206412500008) Bks Demand.

Lebeque, A., jt. auth. see Kaibel, George.

Leber, Hermann. Sehen Lernen Durch Kunstbetrachtung. (Hildesheimer Beitraege Zu Den Erziehungs und Sozial Wissenschaften Ser.: Bd. 14). (GER.). 153p. 1980. 20.00 (*3-487-07007-3*) G Olms Pubs.

Leber, Jody. Windows NT Backup & Restore. 336p. 1998. pap. 29.95 (*1-56592-272-7*) OReilly & Assocs.

Leber, Manfred. Vom Modernen Roman zur Antiken Tragodie: Interpretation von Max Frischs "HomoFaber" (Quellen und Forschungen zur Sprach und Kulturgeschichte der Germanischen Voelker). xii, 201p. (C). 1990. lib. bdg. 80.00 (*3-11-012240-5*) De Gruyter.

Leber, Max, et al. The Handbook of Over-the-Counter Drugs. 464p. (Orig.). 1995. pap. 14.95 (*0-89087-734-3*) Celestial Arts.

— Handbook of Over-the-Counter Drugs & Pharmacy Products. (C). (gr. 13). 1992. text 22.95 (*1-878060-01-5*) GW Medical.

Leber, Michael & Sandling, Judith. L. S. Lowry. (Illus.). 144p. (C). 1995. pap. 19.95 (*0-7148-3244-8*, Pub. by Phaidon Press) Phaidon Pr.

— L. S. Lowry: A Definitive Study of the Artist's Life & Work. (Illus.). 144p. 1990. text 29.95 (*0-7148-2475-5*) Phaidon Pr.

***Leber, Nancy J.** 25 Super-Fun Spelling Games: Easy, Reproducible Games That Help Kids Learn the Words on Their Spelling Lists. (Illus.). 64p. (J). 1999. pap. 10.95 (*0-590-52211-6*) Scholastic Inc.

Leber, Stefan, ed. & intro. see Steiner, Rudolf.

Leber, William R., jt. ed. see Beckham, E. Edward.

Leber, William R., jt. ed. see Beckham, Edward E.

***Leberer, Sigrid.** Farm Animals. (Funny Fingers Books Ser.). (Illus.). (J). 2000. 6.95 (*0-7892-0670-6*) Abbeville Pr.

Leberg, Eric. Understanding Child Molesters: Taking Charge. LC 97-4754. 264p. 1997. 47.00 (*0-7619-0186-8*); pap. 21.95 (*0-7619-0187-6*) Sage.

Leberge, Albert. Bitter Bread. Dion, Conrad, tr. LC 78-305999. (French Writers of Canada Ser.). 128p. reprint ed. pap. 39.70 (*0-8357-7281-0*, 202611900048) Bks Demand.

Lebergott, Stanley. The American Economy: Income, Wealth, & Want. LC 75-4461. 391p. 1976. reprint ed. pap. 121.30 (*0-7837-9371-5*, 206011500004) Bks Demand.

— The Americans: An Economic Record. 526p. (C). 1984. pap. 22.25 (*0-393-95311-4*) Norton.

— Consumer Expenditures: New Measures & Old Motives. LC 95-2852. 320p. 1996. text 57.50 (*0-691-04321-3*, Pub. by Princeton U Pr) Cal Prin Full Svc.

— Pursuing Happiness: American Consumers in the Twentieth Century. LC 92-40491. 208p. 1993. text 42.50 (*0-691-04322-1*, Pub. by Princeton U Pr); pap. text 15.95 (*0-691-02599-1*, Pub. by Princeton U Pr) Cal Prin Full Svc.

— Pursuing Happiness: American Consumers in the Twentieth Century. (C). 1996. pap. 14.95 (*0-614-12621-5*) Princeton U Pr.

— Wealth & Want. LC 75-4460. 229p. reprint ed. pap. 71.00 (*0-7837-6773-0*, 204660300003) Bks Demand.

Leberl, Franz W. Radargrammetric Image Processing. (Remote Sensing Library). (Illus.). 595p. 1989. text. write for info. (*0-89006-273-0*) Artech Hse.

— Radargrammetric Image Processing. LC 89-7033. (Artech House Remote Sensing Library). (Illus.). 621p. 1990. reprint ed. pap. 192.60 (*0-608-02495-3*, 206313900004) Bks Demand.

Leberman, Robert C. The Birds of the Ligonier Valley. (Special Publications: No. 3). (Illus.). 77p. (Orig.). 1976. pap. 6.00 (*0-911239-07-3*) Carnegie Mus.

— Birds of Western Pennsylvania & Adjacent Regions. (Special Publications: No. 13). 52p. 1988. pap. 3.95 (*0-911239-29-4*) Carnegie Mus.

***Leberre, Jacques.** Chameleon Handbook. LC 99-86072. (Pet Handbks.). (Illus.). 144p. 2000. pap. 9.95 (*0-7641-1242-2*) Barron.

Lebert. Celebration of Christian Mystery. LC 96-840023. 1995. pap. 4.95 (*0-8091-9444-9*) Paulist Pr.

— Profession of Faith. 1995. pap. 4.95 (*0-8091-9443-0*) Paulist Pr.

***Lebert, Benjamin.** Crazy: A Novel. Janeway, Carol Brown, tr. from GER. LC 99-49258. 192p. 2000. 17.95 (*0-375-40913-0*) Knopf.

LeBert, Margo A. Christian Prayer. LC 96-132178. (Breaking Open the Catechism of the Catholic Church Ser.). 64p. 1995. pap. 4.95 (*0-8091-9446-5*) Paulist Pr.

— Life in Christ. (Breaking Open the Catechism of the Catholic Church for Small Groups Ser.). 48p. (C). 1995. pap. 3.95 (*0-8091-9445-7*) Paulist Pr.

Lebesgue, Henri. Lecons sur l'Integration et la Recherche des Fonctions Primitives. 3rd ed. LC 73-921. (FRE.). 340p. (gr. 12 up). 1973. text 24.95 (*0-8284-0267-1*) Chelsea Pub.

Lebesque, Sabine & Van Vlissingen, Helene Fentener, eds. Yona Friedman: Between Structure & Coincidence. LC 99-496079. (Illus.). 112p. 1999. 35.00 (*90-5662-108-4*, Pub. by NAi Uitgevers) Dist Art Pubs.

Lebet, Philip E. & Perry, David J. Vocabula et Sermones (Basic Vocabulary & Sample Conversations) (LAT.). 25p. (YA). (gr. 6-12). 1991. spiral bd. 3.50 (*0-939507-19-6*, B4) Amer Classical.

Lebewohl, Sharon, et al. The Second Avenue Deli Cookbook: Recipes & Memories from Abe Lebewohl's Legendary New York Kitchen. LC 99-14156. 225p. 1999. 24.95 (*0-375-50267-X*) Random.

***Lebhar-Friedman Books Staff.** Great Restaurants of the World. (Illus.). 2000. 139.75 (*0-86730-800-1*) Lebhar Friedman.

Lebiere, Christian J., jt. auth. see Anderson, John R.

LeBihan, Jill, jt. auth. see Green, Keith.

Lebl, M., jt. auth. see Jost.

Leblanc. The OAS & the Promotion & Protection of Human Rights. 1977. pap. text 70.50 (*90-247-1943-7*) Kluwer Academic.

Leblanc, A. Anatomy & Imaging of the Cranial Nerves: Investigative Technique for the Imaging by Magnetic Resonance Imaging (MRI) & Computed Tomography (CT) (Illus.). xv, 277p. 1992. 248.00 (*0-387-18240-3*) Spr-Verlag.

LeBlanc, A. The Cranial Nerves. 2nd ed. (Illus.). 312p. 1996. 289.00 (*3-540-58702-0*) Spr-Verlag.

Leblanc, Andre. Atlas of Hearing & Balance Organs. LC 98-29337. (Illus.). 70p. 1998. pap. 55.00 (*2-287-59648-8*, Pub. by Spl France Editions) Spr-Verlag.

— Atlas of Hearing & Balance Organs. LC 98-29337. 1998. 55.00 (*3-540-59648-8*) Spr-Verlag.

LeBlanc, Andre. The Cranial Nerves: Anatomy, Imaging, Vascularisation. 2nd enl. rev. ed. Le Vay, David, tr. from FRE. LC 95-8410. Orig. Title: Anatomy & Imaging of the Cranial Nerves. (Illus.). 1995. write for info. (*0-387-58702-0*) Spr-Verlag.

LeBlanc, Anne. Benjamin Finds a Friend. 20p. (J). (ps-k). 1999. 4.95 (*0-8069-1923-X*) Sterling.

— Benjamin in the Snow. 20p. (J). (ps-k). 1999. 4.95 (*0-8069-1931-0*) Sterling.

— Benjamin Takes Care of Mommy. 20p. (J). (ps-k). 1999. 4.95 (*0-8069-1933-7*) Sterling.

— Benjamin's Busy Day. 20p. (J). (ps-k). 1999. 4.95 (*0-8069-1935-3*) Sterling.

Leblanc, B. The Complete Caribbean Cookbook. 160p. 1996. 15.98 (*0-7858-0556-7*) Bk Sales Inc.

Leblanc, Beverly. Spicy, Fresh, & Stir-Fried. 160p. 1996. 15.98 (*0-7858-0557-5*) Bk Sales Inc.

LeBlanc, Bryan J. Big Bob Does Bands. LeBlanc, Jamis L., ed. (Illus.). 81p. 1997. 19.90 (*0-9656666-2-X*) Knowledge Shoppe.

— Big Bob's Body Basic Workout, Bk. II. LeBlanc, Jamis L., ed. (Illus.). 81p. 1997. 19.90 (*0-9656666-1-1*) Knowledge Shoppe.

— Big Bob's Body Basic Workout Book. LeBlanc, Jamis L., ed. (Illus.). 81p. 1996. 19.90 (*0-9656666-0-3*) Knowledge Shoppe.

LeBlanc, D. The Acadian Miracle. 1966. 13.95 (*0-614-06315-9*) Claitors.

Leblanc, David. Hacking Windows 2000. 456p. 1999. 39.99 (*0-7357-0908-4*) New Riders Pub.

***LeBlanc, David E.** Slugging: The Commuting Alternative for Washington, DC. LC 99-90678. (Illus.). 128p. 1999. pap. 8.95 (*0-9673211-0-7*) Forel Pubg.

***LeBlanc, Dee-Ann.** Linux Exam Prep. (Exam Prep Ser.). (Illus.). 695p. 1999. pap. 49.99 (*1-57610-567-9*) Coriolis Grp.

LeBlanc, Dee-Ann. Linux Install & Configuration Little Black Book. LC 99-43504. 1999. pap. text 24.99 (*1-57610-489-3*) Coriolis Grp.

***LeBlanc, Dee Ann.** Word 2000 Introduction. Freeman, Holly et al, eds. (Illus.). 242p. 2000. pap. 20.00 (*1-58264-107-2*) ActiveEd.

***LeBlanc, Destin A.** Validated Cleaning Techniques for Pharmaceutical Manufacturing. LC 99-85697. 2000. write for info. (*1-57491-116-3*) Interpharm.

LeBlanc, Donald J., et al, eds. Microbial Pathogenesis: Current & Emerging Issues: Proceedings of the 2nd Annual Indiana Conference. LC 98-73482. (Illus.). 179p. 1998. text. write for info. (*0-9655149-1-9*) IN Univ Schl Dentstry.

LeBlanc, Donna. You Can't Quit Until You Know What's Eating You: Overcoming Compulsive Eating. 144p. 1990. pap. 7.95 (*1-55874-103-8*) Health Comm.

Leblanc, Georgette. Souvenirs, 1895 to 1918: My Life with Maeterlinck. Flanner, Janet, tr. from FRE. LC 76-22154. (Music Reprint Ser.). 352p. 1976. reprint ed. lib. bdg. 39.50 (*0-306-70841-8*) Da Capo.

Leblanc, Gerald, tr. see Villemaire, Yolande.

LeBlanc, H. Paul, 3rd. Student Perceptions of Rules for Classroom Interaction. 160p. (C). 1997. pap. text 19.95 (*0-9658564-8-8*) Dissertation.

Leblanc, Hugues, et al, eds. Foundations: Logic, Language & Mathematics. 288p. 1984. text 156.00 (*90-277-1841-5*, D Reidel) Kluwer Academic.

An Asterisk (*) at the beginning of an entry indicates that the title is appearing for the first time.

LeBlanc, Hugues & Gumb, Raymond D., eds. Essays in Epistemology & Semantics. LC 83-83298. (Language, Logic & Linguistics Ser.). 300p. 1983. pap. 24.00 (*0-930586-16-6*) Haven Pubns.

LeBlanc, J. Dudley. The Acadian Miracle. 1966. 20.00 (*1-57980-017-3*) Claitors.

LeBlanc, Jamis L., ed. see LeBlanc, Bryan J.

LeBlanc, Janet & Dickson, Louise. Straight Talk about Children & Sport. LC 97-11748. (Illus.). 135p. 1998. pap. 8.95 (*0-88962-630-8*) Mosaic.

Leblanc, John F., et al. Graphs Picturing Information. (Mathematics Ser.). (Illus.). 160p. (C). 1976. pap. text 4.75 (*0-201-14622-3*) Addison-Wesley.

— Math Method Programming Number. (Mathematics Ser.). (Illus.). 128p. (C). 1976. pap. text 4.00 (*0-201-14624-X*) Addison-Wesley.

LeBlanc, John F., et al. Mathematics Methods Program: Rational Numbers with Integers & Reals. (Mathematics Ser.). (Illus.). 240p. 1976. write for info. (*0-201-14613-4*) Addison-Wesley.

— Rational Numbers Integer. (Mathematics Ser.). (Illus.). 240p. 1976. pap. text 11.25 (*0-201-14612-6*) Addison-Wesley.

***LeBlanc, Joseph.** Associate Safety Professional Home Study Workbook, Safety Fundamentals (Core), 2 vols. rev. ed. Becker, Marvin & Watts, James, eds. Incl. Vol. I. Associate Safety Professional Home Study Workbook, Safety Fundamentals (Core) rev. ed. (Illus.). 444p. 2000. Not sold separately (*1-891017-26-8*); Vol. II. Associate Safety Professional Home Study Workbook, Safety Fundamentals (Core) rev. ed. 436p. 2000. Not sold separately (*1-891017-27-6*); (Illus.). 880p. 2000. Set wbk. ed. 160.00 (*1-891017-25-X*) SRS Safety Wrkshops.

— Certified Safety Professional Home Study Workbook, Comprehensive Practice, 2 vols. rev. ed. Watts, James, ed. Incl. Vol. I. Certified Safety Professional Home Study Workbook, Comprehensive Practice. rev. ed. Becker, Martin, ed. (Illus.). 448p. 2000. Not sold separately (*1-891017-29-2*); Vol. II. Certified Safety Professional Home Study Workbook, Comprehensive Practice. rev. ed. Becker, Marvin, ed. (Illus.). 370p. 2000. Not sold separately (*1-891017-30-6*); (Illus.). 818p. 2000. 165.00 (*1-891017-28-4*) SRS Safety Wrkshops.

LeBlanc, Joseph. Construction Health & Safety Technician Home Study Workbook, 2 vols. rev. ed. Watts, James & Becker, Marvin, eds. Incl. Construction Health & Safety Technician Home Study Workbook. rev. ed. (Illus.). 294p. 2000. Not sold separately (*1-891017-35-7*); Vol. II. Construction Health & Safety Technician Home Study Workbook. rev. ed. (Illus.). 2922p. 2000. Not sold separately (*1-891017-36-5*); wbk. ed. write for info. (*1-891017-21-7*) SRS Safety Wrkshops.

— Construction Health & Safety Technician Home Study Workbook, 2 vols. rev. ed. Watts, James & Becker, Marvin, eds. (Illus.). 600p. 1999. 170.00 (*1-891017-11-X*) SRS Safety Wrkshops.

***LeBlanc, Joseph.** Construction Health & Safety Technician Home Study Workbook, 2 vols. rev. ed. Watts, James & Becker, Marvin, eds. Incl. Construction Health & Safety Technician Home Study Workbook. rev. ed. (Illus.). 294p. 2000. Not sold separately (*1-891017-35-7*); Vol. II. Construction Health & Safety Technician Home Study Workbook. rev. ed. (Illus.). 2922p. 2000. Not sold separately (*1-891017-36-5*); (Illus.). 586p. 2000. 170.00 (*1-891017-34-9*) SRS Safety Wrkshops.

LeBlanc, Joseph. Construction Health & Safety Technician Home Study Workbook, Vol. I. rev. ed. Watts, James & Becker, Marvin, eds. (Illus.). 305p. 1999. write for info. (*1-891017-09-8*) SRS Safety Wrkshops.

— Construction Health & Safety Technician Home Study Workbook, Vol. II. rev. ed. Watts, James & Becker, Marvin, eds. (Illus.). 295p. 1999. write for info. (*1-891017-10-1*) SRS Safety Wrkshops.

— Occupational Health & Safety Technologist Home Study Workbook, 2 vols. rev. ed. Becker, Marvin, ed. Incl. Vol. I. Occupational Health & Safety Technologist Home Study Workbook. rev. ed. Watts, James W., ed. 352p. 2000. Not sold separately (*1-891017-32-2*); Vol. II. Occupational Health & Safety Technologist Home Study Workbook. rev. ed. Watts, James, ed. (Illus.). 244p. 2000. Not sold separately (*1-891017-33-0*); wbk. ed. write for info. (*1-891017-18-7*) SRS Safety Wrkshops.

— Occupational Health & Safety Technologist Home Study Workbook, 2 vols. rev. ed. Watts, James & Becker, Marvin, eds. (Illus.). 590p. 1999. 155.00 (*1-891017-08-X*) SRS Safety Wrkshops.

***LeBlanc, Joseph.** Occupational Health & Safety Technologist Home Study Workbook, 2 vols. rev. ed. Becker, Marvin, ed. Incl. Vol. I. Occupational Health & Safety Technologist Home Study Workbook. rev. ed. Watts, James W., ed. 352p. 2000. Not sold separately (*1-891017-32-2*); Vol. II. Occupational Health & Safety Technologist Home Study Workbook. rev. ed. Watts, James, ed. (Illus.). 244p. 2000. Not sold separately (*1-891017-33-0*); (Illus.). 596p. 2000. 155.00 (*1-891017-31-4*) SRS Safety Wrkshops.

LeBlanc, Joseph. Occupational Health & Safety Technologist Home Study Workbook, Vol. I. rev. ed. Watts, James & Becker, Marvin, eds. (Illus.). 355p. 1999. write for info. (*1-891017-06-3*) SRS Safety Wrkshops.

— Occupational Health & Safety Technologist Home Study Workbook, Vol. II. rev. ed. Watts, James & Becker, Marvin, eds. (Illus.). 235p. 1999. write for info. (*1-891017-07-1*) SRS Safety Wrkshops.

LeBlanc, Joseph, ed. see Watts, James.

LeBlanc, Joyce Y. Pelican Guide to Gardens of Louisiana. 2nd ed. (Pelican Guide Ser.). (Illus.). 80p. 1989. reprint ed. pap. 7.95 (*0-88289-729-2*) Pelican.

LeBlanc, Judy, ed. see Shazryl, Eskay & Hanks, Jarrod.

LeBlanc, Judy A. The Compromise. LC 96-91044. 1997. 14.95 (*0-533-12257-0*) Vantage.

— Things My Father Never Taught Me. 1994. 12.95 (*0-533-10817-9*) Vantage.

***LeBlanc, Judy A.** The Unveiling. LC 98-90668. 2000. 13.95 (*0-533-12878-1*) Vantage.

Leblanc, Lauraine. Pretty in Punk: Girls' Gender Resistance in a Boys' Subculture. LC 98-51532. (Illus.). 288p. (C). 1999. text 50.00 (*0-8135-2650-7*); pap. text 20.00 (*0-8135-2651-5*) Rutgers U Pr.

LeBlanc, Lawrence J. The Convention on the Rights of the Child: United Nations Lawmaking on Human Rights. LC 94-11887. (Human Rights in International Perspective Ser.: Vol. 3). xxvi, 338p. 1995. text 55.00 (*0-8032-2909-7*) U of Nebr Pr.

— The United States & the Genocide Convention. LC 90-45572. 303p. 1991. text 49.95 (*0-8223-1109-7*) Duke.

LeBlanc, Leslie, jt. auth. see Moscato, Michael.

Leblanc, Liz. Cheap Entertainment. 1986. pap. 5.00 (*0-941240-04-5*) Ommation Pr.

LeBlanc, Liz. No Mean Feet. (Dialogues on Dance Ser.: No. 4). 13p. 1985. pap. 4.00 (*0-941240-01-0*) Ommation Pr.

Leblanc, Louise. Ca Suffit, Sophie! (Novels in the Premier Roman Ser.). (FRE.). 64p. (J). (gr. 2-5). 1990. pap. 8.95 (*2-89021-131-2*, Pub. by La Courte Ech) Firefly Bks Ltd.

— Ca Va Mal Pour Sophie. (Novels in the Premier Roman Ser.). (FRE.). 64p. (J). (gr. 2-5). 1992. pap. 8.95 (*2-89021-177-0*, Pub. by La Courte Ech) Firefly Bks Ltd.

— Deux Amis Dans la Nuit. (Novels in the Premier Roman Ser.). (FRE., Illus.). 64p. (J). (gr. 2-5). 1996. pap. 8.95 (*2-89021-247-5*, Pub. by La Courte Ech) Firefly Bks Ltd.

— Leo & Julio. (First Novels Ser.). (Illus.). 64p. (J). (gr. 1-4). 1999. mass mkt. 3.99 (*0-88780-478-0*, Pub. by Formac Publ Co) Orca Bk Pubs.

***LeBlanc, Louise.** Leo & Julio. (First Novels). (Illus.). 62p. (J). 2000. bds. write for info. (*0-88780-479-9*, Pub. by Formac Publ Co) Formac Dist Ltd.

Leblanc, Louise. Maddie Goes to Paris. (First Novels Ser.). (Illus.). 61p. (J). (gr. 1-4). 1995. mass mkt. 3.99 (*0-88780-278-8*, Pub. by Formac Publ Co); bds. 14.95 (*0-88780-279-6*, Pub. by Formac Publ Co) Formac Dist Ltd.

— Maddie in Danger. (First Novels Ser.). (Illus.). 62p. (J). (gr. 1-4). 1995. mass mkt. 3.99 (*0-88780-306-7*, Pub. by Formac Publ Co); bds. 14.95 (*0-88780-307-5*, Pub. by Formac Publ Co) Formac Dist Ltd.

— Maddie in Goal. (First Novels Ser.). (Illus.). 62p. (J). (gr. 1-4). 1995. mass mkt. 3.99 (*0-88780-202-8*, Pub. by Formac Publ Co); bds. 14.95 (*0-88780-203-6*, Pub. by Formac Publ Co) Formac Dist Ltd.

Leblanc, Louise. Maddie in Hospital. (First Novels). (Illus.). 58p. (J). 1996. bds. 14.95 (*0-88780-375-X*, Pub. by Formac Publ Co) Formac Dist Ltd.

— Maddie in Hospital. Cummins, Sarah, tr. (First Novels Ser.). (Illus.). 58p. (J). 1996. mass mkt. 3.99 (*0-88780-374-1*, Pub. by Formac Publ Co) Formac Dist Ltd.

LeBlanc, Louise. Maddie in Trouble. (First Novels). 58p. (J). (gr. 1-4). 1998. text 3.99 (*0-88780-428-4*, Pub. by Formac Publ Co) Formac Dist Ltd.

***LeBlanc, Louise.** Maddie in Trouble. (First Novels). (Illus.). 58p. (J). 1998. bds. 14.95 (*0-88780-429-2*, Pub. by Formac Publ Co) Formac Dist Ltd.

***Leblanc, Louise.** Maddie Tries to Be Good. (Illus.). 64p. (J). (gr. 1-4). 1999. mass mkt. 3.99 (*0-88780-482-9*) Formac Publ Co.

Leblanc, Louise. Maddie Wants Music! (First Novels Ser.). (Illus.). 61p. (J). (gr. 1-4). 1995. mass mkt. 3.99 (*0-88780-219-2*, Pub. by Formac Publ Co); bds. 14.95 (*0-88780-220-6*, Pub. by Formac Publ Co) Formac Dist Ltd.

— Sophie Est en Danger. (Novels in the Premier Roman Ser.). (FRE.). 64p. (J). (gr. 2-5). 1994. pap. 8.95 (*2-89021-212-2*, Pub. by La Courte Ech) Firefly Bks Ltd.

— Sophie Lance et Compte. (Novels in the Premier Roman Ser.). (FRE.). 64p. (J). (gr. 2-5). 1991. pap. 8.95 (*2-89021-158-4*, Pub. by La Courte Ech) Firefly Bks Ltd.

— Sophie Part en Voyage. (Novels in the Premier Roman Ser.). (FRE.). 64p. (J). (gr. 2-5). 1993. pap. 8.95 (*2-89021-195-9*, Pub. by La Courte Ech) Firefly Bks Ltd.

— That's Enough, Maddie! (First Novels Ser.). (Illus.). 57p. (J). (gr. 1-4). 1995. mass mkt. 3.99 (*0-88780-090-4*, Pub. by Formac Publ Co); bds. 14.95 (*0-88780-091-2*, Pub. by Formac Publ Co) Formac Dist Ltd.

— Le Tombeau Mysterieux. (Novels in the Premier Roman Ser.). (FRE.). 64p. (J). (gr. 2-5). 1994. pap. 8.95 (*2-89021-222-X*, Pub. by La Courte Ech) Firefly Bks Ltd.

— Ya Basta, Sofia. (SPA., Illus.). 60p. (YA). (gr. 5 up). 1994. pap. 5.95 (*958-07-0080-X*) Firefly Bks Ltd.

***LeBlanc, Louise & Cummins, Sarah.** Maddie Tries to Be Good. (First Novels). (Illus.). 62p. (J). 2000. bds. write for info. (*0-88780-483-7*, Pub. by Formac Publ Co) Formac Dist Ltd.

***LeBlanc, Mark.** Growing Your Business. LC 99-63182. 96p. 1999. 14.95 (*1-890676-39-X*, Pub. by Beavers Pond) Bookman Bks.

— Growing Your Business: What You Need to Know What You Need to Do. LC 99-63182. (Illus.). 96p. 1999. pap. 7.95 (*1-890676-38-1*, Pub. by Beavers Pond) Bookman Bks.

LeBlanc, Maurice. Arsene Lupin: Gentleman Burglar. 18.95 (*0-89190-091-8*) Amereon Ltd.

— The Confessions of Arsene Lupin. 327p. 1980. reprint ed. lib. bdg. 15.50 (*0-89968-202-2*, Lghtyr Pr) Buccaneer Bks.

— The Crystal Stopper. 287p. 1980. reprint ed. lib. bdg. 14.25 (*0-89968-201-4*, Lghtyr Pr) Buccaneer Bks.

Leblanc, Maurice. The Exploits of Arsene Lupin. De Mattos, Alexander T., tr. LC 75-32758. (Literature of Mystery & Detection Ser.). 1976. reprint ed. 26.95 (*0-405-07881-1*) Ayer.

— The Extraordinary Adventures of Arsene Lupin, Gentleman-Burgler. Morehead, George, tr. from FRE. LC 76-163040. (Short Story Index Reprint Ser.). 1977. reprint ed. 19.95 (*0-8369-3954-9*) Ayer.

LeBlanc, Maurice. The Hollow Needle. 325p. 1980. reprint ed. lib. bdg. 15.50 (*0-89968-203-0*, Lghtyr Pr) Buccaneer Bks.

— Teeth of the Tiger. 490p. 1980. reprint ed. lib. bdg. 17.95 (*0-89968-204-9*, Lghtyr Pr) Buccaneer Bks.

***LeBlanc, Patty & Harper, Dennis O.** Generation www.Y: Curriculum Kit, Set. 1999. pap. 245.00 incl. VHS, cd-rom (*1-56484-147-2*) Intl Society Tech Educ.

LeBlanc, Patty, jt. auth. see Harper, Dennis O.

LeBlanc, Paul, jt. ed. see Hinshaw, John.

LeBlanc, Paul J., jt. ed. see Hawisher, Gail.

LeBlanc, Raymond J. The Crane Site & the Palaeoeskimo Period in the Western Canadian Arctic. (Mercury Ser.: ASC No. 148). (Illus.). 144p. 1994. pap. 18.95 (*0-660-14019-5*, Pub. by CN Mus Civilization) U of Wash Pr.

LeBlanc, Richard, jt. auth. see Fischer, Charles N.

LeBlanc, Richard J., jt. auth. see Fischer, Charles N.

LeBlanc, Robin M. Bicycle Citizens: The Political World of the Japanese Housewife. LC 98-46632. 263p. 1999. 40.00 (*0-520-21290-8*, Pub. by U CA Pr) Cal Prin Full Svc.

***LeBlanc, Robin M.** Bicycle Citizens: The Political World of the Japanese Housewife. LC 98-46632. (Asia--Local Studies). 263p. 1999. pap. 14.95 (*0-520-21291-6*, Pub. by U CA Pr) Cal Prin Full Svc.

Leblanc, Roger. Relativism as Religion. 143p. 1998. pap. text 10.70 (*0-536-01360-8*) Pearson Custom.

LeBlanc, Ronald D. The Russianization of Gil Blas: A Study in Literary Appropriation. 292p. (Orig.). 1986. pap. 22.95 (*0-89357-159-8*) Slavica.

LeBlanc, Steven, jt. auth. see Folger, H.

LeBlanc, Steven A. Prehistoric Warfare in the American Southwest. LC 98-42327. 1999. 34.95 (*0-87480-581-3*) U of Utah Pr.

***LeBlanc, Sydney.** The Architecture Traveler: A Guide to 250 Key 20th Century American Buildings. LC 99-88789. (Illus.). 256p. 2000. pap. text 21.95 (*0-393-73050-6*) Norton.

LeBlanc, Sydney. Secret Gardens of Santa Fe. LC 97-11858. (Illus.). 192p. 1997. 45.00 (*0-8478-2034-3*, Pub. by Rizzoli Intl) St Martin.

LeBlanc, Sydney, jt. auth. see Fahy, Charles L.

LeBlanc, Thomas. The General Radio-Telephone Operator's License Study Guide. 2nd ed. (Illus.). 230p. 1990. 23.95 (*0-8306-9518-4*, 3118); pap. 16.95 (*0-8306-3118-6*, 3118) McGraw-Hill Prof.

— General Radiotelephone Operator's License Study Guide. 3rd ed. 344p. 1992. 27.95 (*0-8306-3555-6*, 4075); pap. 17.95 (*0-8306-3554-8*, 4075) McGraw-Hill Prof.

— General Radiotelephone Operator's License Study Guide. 4th ed. LC 94-37458. 1995. 29.95 (*0-07-036936-4*) McGraw-Hill Prof.

LeBlanc, Yvonne. Va Lettre Va: The French Verse Epistle (1400-1550) LC 94-74076. 268p. 1995. lib. bdg. 41.95 (*1-883479-04-5*) Summa Pubns.

LeBlang, Theodore R., et al. Law of Medical Practice in Illinois. LC 86-83023. 1986. 125.00 (*0-317-03805-2*) West Group.

— Law of Medical Practice in Illinois. LC 86-83023. 1993. suppl. ed. 59.95 (*0-317-03806-0*) West Group.

Leble, S. B. Nonlinear Waves in Waveguides: With Stratification. (Research Reports in Physics). (Illus.). ix, 163p. 1991. pap. 69.00 (*0-387-52149-6*) Spr-Verlag.

Leblebici, Yusuf & Kang, Sung-Mo. Hot-Carrier Reliability of MOS VLSI Circuits. LC 93-15447. (International Series in Engineering & Computer Science, VLSI, Computer Architecture, & Digital Screen Processing: Vol. 227). 240p. (C). 1993. text 149.00 (*0-7923-9352-X*) Kluwer Academic.

Leblebici, Yusuf, jt. auth. see Kang, Sung-Mo.

Lebleu, Bernard, jt. ed. see Crooke, Stanley T.

Lebling, Robert W., Jr., ed. Gas Daily's Natural Gas Marketing Pipeline Guide. 900p. 1990. reprint ed. 567.00 (*0-935453-35-0*) Pasha Pubns.

LeBloas, Renee & Julienne, Jerome. The Dolphin: Prince of the Waves. LC 96-47064. (Animal Close-Ups Ser.). (Illus.). 28p. (J). (ps-3). 1997. pap. 6.95 (*0-88106-440-8*) Charlesbridge Pub.

Leblon, Bernard. Gypsies & Flamenco: The Emergence of the Art of Flamenco in Adalusia. (Interface Collection). 116p. 1995. pap. 19.95 (*0-900458-59-3*, Pub. by Univ of Herfordshire) Bold Strummer Ltd.

Leblon, Bernard. Gypsies & Flamenco: The Emergence of the Art of Flamenco in Andalusia. Shuineer, Sinead N., tr. from FRE. & illus. by. 116p. 1995. pap. 24.95 (*0-933224-91-5*, 1411) Bold Strummer Ltd.

Leblon, Jean M., ed. see Perec, Georges.

Leblon, Jean M., tr. see Zola, Emile.

Leblond, A. & Cosse, Rene. Basics of Reservoir Engineering. 3772p. (C). 1993. 420.00 (*2-7108-0630-4*, Pub. by Edits Technip) Enfield Pubs NH.

LeBlond, Bill, ed. see Della Croce, Julia.

LeBlond, Bill, ed. see Hosler, Ray.

LeBlond, Bill, ed. see Kagel, Katharine.

LeBlond, Bill, ed. see Perry, Sarah.

LeBlond, Geoffrey T. Using UNIX System V Release 3. 1989. text 27.95 (*0-07-881556-8*) Osborne-McGraw.

Leblond, Gerard F. The Hip-Pocket Guide to Basic Drum Beats. LC 82-70339. 60p. 1982. pap. 4.95 (*0-942836-00-6*) West Gate Pr.

Leblond Group Staff. PC Magazine Guide to Quattro Pro for Windows. (Guide to...Ser.). (Illus.). 1221p. (Orig.). 1992. pap. 27.95 (*1-56276-044-0*, Ziff-Davis Pr) Que.

— PC Magazine Guide to Using Quattro Pro 3.0. (Guide to...Ser.). (Illus.). 1040p. (Orig.). 1991. pap. 27.95 (*1-56276-003-3*, Ziff-Davis Pr) Que.

— PC Magazine Guide to Using Quattro Pro 3.0 - 4.0. (Guide to...Ser.). 1064p. (Orig.). 1992. pap. 27.95 (*1-56276-071-8*, Ziff-Davis Pr) Que.

Leblond, Marius-Ary. Peintres de Races: Reprint of the 1909 Edition. (FRE., Illus.). 238p. 1981. reprint ed. 50.00 (*0-8150-0006-5*) Wittenborn Art.

Lebmann, Rosamond, tr. see Cocteau, Jean.

Lebo, Charles P. Truth about Sinusitis. 1995. 12.95 (*1-880688-01-8*) New Life Opt.

Lebo, Fern. Mastering the Diversity Challenge: Easy On-the-Job Applications for Measurable Results. LC 95-226112. 176p. 1995. boxed set 49.95 (*1-884015-35-2*) St Lucie Pr.

— Your Outplacement Handbook: Redesigning Your Career. (Illus.). 200p. (Orig.). 1996. lib. bdg. 19.95 (*1-57444-029-2*) St Lucie Pr.

Lebo, Harlan. The Godfather Legacy. LC 96-49984. (Illus.). 288p. 1997. per. 15.00 (*0-684-83647-5*) S&S Trade Pap.

Leboas, Renee. The Dolphin: Prince of the Waves. (Animal Close-Ups Ser.). 1997. 12.15 (*0-606-13337-2*, Pub. by Turtleback) Demco.

LeBoeuf, Burney & Kaza, Stephanie, eds. The Natural History of Ano Nuevo. (Illus.). (Orig.). 1985. reprint ed. pap. 14.95 (*0-910286-77-9*) Otter B Bks.

Leboeuf, Daniel. The Wolf: Ghost Hunter. (Illus.). 144p. 1996. pap. text 19.95 (*1-895565-98-7*) Firefly Bks Ltd.

LeBoeuf, Gene. LeBoeuf's Home Health Care Handbook: All You Need to Become a Caregiver in Your Home. (Illus.). 1996. pap. 24.95 (*0-9648852-0-4*) LeBoeuf & Assocs.

Leboeuf, Michael. Fast Forward: How to Win a Lot More Business in a Lot Less Time. 224p. (Orig.). 1995. pap. 12.00 (*0-425-14613-8*) Berkley Pub.

— Getting Results! The Secret of Motivating Yourself & Others. 176p. 1986. pap. 10.00 (*0-425-08776-X*) Berkley Pub.

LeBoeuf, Michael. The Greatest Management Principle in the World. 1989. mass mkt. 5.50 (*0-425-11397-3*) Berkley Pub.

***LeBoeuf, Michael.** How to Win Customers & Keep Them for Life: Revised & Updated for the Digital Age. 256p. 2000. pap. 13.00 (*0-425-17501-4*) Berkley Pub.

Leboeuf, Michael. Working Smart: How to Accomplish More in Half the Time. 272p. 1988. mass mkt. 5.99 (*0-446-35356-6*, Pub. by Warner Bks) Little.

Leboeuff, Randall, Jr. Some Notes on the Life of Robert Fulton. (Illus.). 1971. 0.50 (*0-913344-11-7*) South St Sea Mus.

Leboffe, Michael & Pierce, Burton. A Photographic Atlas for the Microbiology Laboratory. (Illus.). 144p. (C). 1999. pap. text 15.95 (*0-89582-308-X*) Morton Pub.

LeBoit, Philip E. Inflammatory Skin Lesions. (Illus.). 250p. 2000. text 150.00 (*1-56053-357-9*) Hanley & Belfus.

LeBoit, Philip E., et al. Atlas of Cutaneous Surgery. LC 94-25752. (Illus.). 432p. 1995. text 158.00 (*0-7216-5404-5*, W B Saunders Co) Harcrt Hlth Sci Grp.

— Cantaneous Medicine & Surgery: Self Assessment & Review, Vol. 1. LC 94-21584. (Illus.). 304p. 1995. pap. text 42.00 (*0-7216-5408-8*, W B Saunders Co) Harcrt Hlth Sci Grp.

— Pocket Guide to Cutaneous Medicine & Surgery. (Illus.). 416p. 1995. pap. text 39.00 (*0-7216-5409-6*, W B Saunders Co) Harcrt Hlth Sci Grp.

Lebolt, Gladys. D. H. Lawrence: The True Redeemer? 1985. 15.00 (*0-916620-63-8*) Portals Pr.

Lebon, G., jt. ed. see Vazquez, J. C.

LeBon, Gustav, jt. auth. see Mackay, Charles.

LeBon, Gustave. The Crowd: A Study of the Popular Mind. LC 26-6009. 240p. 1982. reprint ed. pap. 13.95 (*0-87797-168-4*) Cherokee.

— The French Revolution & the Psychology of Revolution. LC 78-62691. (Social Science Classics Ser.). 337p. 1980. 44.95 (*0-87855-310-X*); pap. 24.95 (*0-87855-697-4*) Transaction Pubs.

— Gustave Lebon: The Man & His Works. 1991. lib. bdg. 74.95 (*0-8490-4435-9*) Gordon Pr.

— Psychology of Socialism. LC 81-1973. 415p. (C). 1982. reprint ed. pap. 24.95 (*0-87855-703-2*) Transaction Pubs.

— Psychology of the Great War: The First World War & Its Origins. LC 98-27088. 505p. 1999. pap. 29.95 (*0-7658-0479-4*) Transaction Pubs.

Lebon, Jean. How to Understand the Liturgy. (Adult Christian Formation Program Ser.). 164p. (Orig.). (C). 1988. pap. 15.95 (*0-8245-0867-X*) Crossroad NY.

— How to Understand the Liturgy - Participant Guide. (Adult Christian Formation Program Ser.). 1997. pap. 5.95 (*0-8245-7011-1*) Crossroad NY.

Lebon, Joseph. Le Monophysisme Severien: Etude Historique, Litteraire et Theologique sur la Resistance Monophysite au Concile de Chalcedoine Jusqu'a la Constitution de l'Eglise Jacobite. LC 77-84704. reprint ed. 72.50 (*0-404-16111-1*) AMS Pr.

***LeBon, Paul.** Escape from Voicemail Hell: Boost Your Productivity by Making Voicemail Work for You. Karam, Sara, ed. LC 99-90799. 88p. 1999. pap. 11.95 (*1-929398-00-X*) Parleau Pubng.

Lebon, Rachel L. The Professional Vocalist: A Handbook for Commercial Singers & Teachers. LC 98-30718. 144p. 1999. text 39.50 (*0-8108-3565-7*) Scarecrow.

***Lebon, Rachel L.** The Professional Vocalist: A Handbook for Commercial Singers & Teachers. LC 98-30718. 144p. 1999. pap. 29.50 (*0-8108-3566-5*) Scarecrow.

Lebor, Adam. Heart Turned East. LC 98-204426. 336p. 1997. text 23.95 (*0-312-18109-4*) St Martin.

An Asterisk (*) at the beginning of an entry indicates that the title is appearing for the first time.

— Hitler's Secret Bankers: The Myth of Swiss Neutrality During the Holocaust. LC 97-14196. 256p. 1997. 21.95 (*1-55972-421-8*, Birch Ln Pr) Carol Pub Group.
— Hitler's Secret Bankers The Myth of Swiss Neutrality During the Holocaust. rev. ed. 1999. pap. text 15.95 (*0-8065-2121-X*) Carol Pub Group.
LeBorg, Reginald. The Films of Reginald LeBorg: Interviews, Essays, & Filmography. Dixon, Wheeler W., ed. LC 92-14668. (Filmmakers Ser.: No. 31). (Illus.). 203p. 1992. 28.50 (*0-8108-2550-3*) Scarecrow.
Leborgne, Leon J. The Bull's-Eye of Life. LC 94-96685. 76p. (Orig.). (YA). 1995. pap. text 4.95 (*1-886707-01-4*) L & L Enter.
LeBorgne, Leon J. Study Guide for the Bull's-Eye of Life. LC 94-96684. 76p. (YA). 1995. pap. text 4.95 (*1-886707-02-2*) L & L Enter.
Leborgne, Leon J. You Can't Legislate Attitudes. LC 94-96686. 68p. (Orig.). 1995. pap. text 4.95 (*1-886707-00-6*) L & L Enter.
Lebot, Vincent, et al. Kava: The Pacific Elixir: The Definitive Guide to Its Ethnobotany, History, & Chemistry. LC 97-1057. (Illus.). 272p. 1997. pap. 19.95 (*0-89281-726-7*) Inner Tradit.
Lebouc, F. & Perthuis, E. Principles of Turbulent Fired Heat. (Illus.). 320p. (C). 1985. 590.00 (*2-7108-0457-3*, Pub. by Edits Technip) Enfield Pubs NH.
Lebouc, G. Dictionary Belgicismes: Belge Tout Ses Etats. (FRE.). 1998. 27.95 (*0-320-00283-7*) Fr & Eur.
LeBouef, Lilah. Baby E. D. the Enriched Development Program: Enriching the Lives of Children from Birth to Age Two. (Illus.). 208p. 1999. pap. 39.95 (*0-9670253-0-3*) Baby ED.
Leboutillier, John. Coming to Terms with Vietnam: The Case for Normalizing Relations with Hanoi. LC 89-3670. 134p. 1989. 32.95 (*0-275-93278-8*, C3278, Praeger Pubs) Greenwood.
LeBoutillier, Megan. Little Miss Perfect. 140p. (Orig.). 1987. pap. 8.95 (*0-910223-10-6*) MAC Pub.
— No is a Complete Sentence: Learning the Sacredness of Personal Boundaries. (Orig.). 1995. mass mkt. 5.99 (*0-345-37647-1*) Ballantine Pub Grp.
LeBouton, Albert V., ed. Molecular & Cell Biology of the Liver. 560p. 1993. lib. bdg. 229.00 (*0-8493-8891-0*, QP185) CRC Pr.
***Leboutte, Rene, ed.** Migrations et Migrants dans une Perspective Historique/Migrations & Migrants in Historical Perspective: Permanences et Innovations/Permanancies & Innovations. (FRE.). 313p. 2000. pap. text 34.95 (*0-8204-4660-2*) P Lang Pubng.
Lebov, Myrna. Practical Tools & Techniques for Managing Time. 1981. pap. 5.95 (*0-917386-38-8*) Exec Ent Pubns.
Lebov, Myrna, jt. auth. see Morrow, Jodie B.
Lebovic, James H. Foregone Conclusions: U. S. Weapons Acquisition in the Post-Cold War Transition. 197p. (C). 1996. pap. 65.00 (*0-8133-8985-2*, Pub. by Westview) HarpC.
Lebovici, Serge & Widlocher, K., eds. Psychoanalysis in France. Diamanti, J., tr. from FRE. LC 79-2483. 620p. 1980. 70.00 (*0-8236-5210-6*) Intl Univs Pr.
Lebovici, Serge, ed. see Esman, Aaron H.
Lebovics, Adel. What Will the World Be Like? (RUS., Illus.). 32p. (J). (ps-1). 1993. 9.95 (*0-922613-58-3*); pap. 6.95 (*0-922613-57-5*) Hachai Pubng.
Lebovics, Aydel. The Teeny Tiny Yarmulka. (Illus.). 32p. (J). 1982. reprint ed. 11.00 (*0-8266-0360-2*, Merkos LInyonei Chinuch) Kehot Pubn Soc.
— The Wind & the Sukkah. (Illus.). 32p. (J). 1982. reprint ed. 11.00 (*0-8266-0361-0*, Merkos LInyonei Chinuch) Kehot Pubn Soc.
— Zaydie's Special Esrogim. (Illus.). 28p. (J). 1991. reprint ed. 12.00 (*0-8266-0357-2*, Merkos LInyonei Chinuch) Kehot Pubn Soc.
***Lebovics, Dania.** Baby Chronicles: My Very Own Story: From Pre-Natal to Pre-School. (Illus.). 72p. 2000. 19.95 (*0-9699203-7-7*, Pub. by Kiddy Kronicles) Firefly Bks Ltd.
Lebovics, Dania. Kiddy Chronicles: My Very First Biography, from Pre-Natal to Pre-School. (Illus.). 64p. 1997. pap. text 14.95 (*0-9699203-2-6*) Kidd Kron.
Lebovics, Herman. Alliance of Iron & Wheat in the Third French Republic, 1860-1914: Origins of the New Conservatism. LC 87-21386. 240p. 1988. text 35.00 (*0-8071-1350-6*) La State U Pr.
— Mona Lisa's Escort: Andre Malraux & the Reinvention of French Culture. LC 98-30461. 1999. 29.95 (*0-8014-3565-X*, ILR Press) Cornell U Pr.
— True France: The Wars over Cultural Identity, 1900-1945. LC 91-44697. (Wilder House Series in Politics, History, & Culture). (Illus.). 248p. 1992. text 39.95 (*0-8014-2687-1*) Cornell U Pr.
— True France: The Wars over Cultural Identity, 1900-1945. (Wilder House Series in Politics, History, & Culture). (Illus.). 248p. 1994. pap. text 15.95 (*0-8014-8193-7*) Cornell U Pr.
Lebovitch, William L. Design for Dignity: Accessible Environments for People with Disabilities. LC 93-3310. 272p. 1993. 90.00 (*0-471-56910-0*) Wiley.
Lebovits, Allen H., et al. Exposure to Hazardous Substances: Psychological Parameters. fac. ed. LC 85-31163. (Advances in Environmental Psychology Ser.: No. 6). (Illus.). 151p. 1986. reprint ed. pap. 46.90 (*0-7837-7831-7*, 204758700007) Bks Demand.
Lebovits, Yehudah. Shidduchim & Zivugim: The Torah's Perspective on Finding Your Mate. 176p. 1988. 17.95 (*0-944070-01-9*, Pub. by Targum Pr) Feldheim.
Lebovits, Yehudah & Rosenstein, Mordechai. With an Eye on Eternity. 112p. 1995. 11.95 (*1-58330-021-X*) Feldheim.
Lebovitz. Ordinary Differential Equations. (Mathematics Ser.). 2002. pap. 60.00 (*0-534-36552-3*) Brooks-Cole.
Lebovitz, David. Room For Dessert: 110 Recipes for Cakes, Custards, Souffles, Tarts, Pies, Cobblers, Sorbets, Sherbets, Ice Creams, Cookies, Candies, & Cordials. LC 99-17078. 240p. 1999. 30.00 (*0-06-019185-6*) HarpC.
Lebovitz, Harold E., ed. Therapy for Diabetes Mellitus & Related Disorders. 3rd rev. ed. LC 98-4106. (Clinical Education Ser.). (Illus.). 487p. 1998. pap. 49.95 (*0-945448-94-5*) Am Diabetes.
Lebovitz, Norman, ed. Fluid Dynamics in Astrophysics & Geophysics. LC 83-2705. (Lectures in Applied Mathematics: Vol. 20). 269p. 1983. text 70.00 (*0-8218-1120-7*, LAM/20) Am Math.
Lebovitz, Norman, et al. Theoretical Principles in Astrophysics & Relativity. Reid, William H. & Vandervoort, Peter O., eds. LC 76-25636. 272p. 1981. pap. text 12.95 (*0-226-46990-5*) U Ch Pr.
Lebow. Lasting Change: The Shared Values Process That Makes Companies Great. 272p. 1999. pap. 17.95 (*0-471-32847-2*) Wiley.
— Oceanus: The Marine Environment. 5th ed. (Biology Ser.). 1993. mass mkt., student ed. 14.25 (*0-534-20562-3*) Wadsworth Pub.
Lebow, Barbara. The Keepers. 1995. pap. 5.25 (*0-8222-1459-8*) Dramatists Play.
— Little Joe Monaghan. 1995. pap. 5.25 (*0-8222-1414-8*) Dramatists Play.
— A Shayna Maidel. 1988. pap. 5.25 (*0-8222-1019-3*) Dramatists Play.
— Tiny Tim Is Dead. 1993. pap. 5.25 (*0-8222-1363-X*) Dramatists Play.
***Lebow, Cynthia C., et al.** Safety in the Skies: Personnel & Parties in NTSP Aviation Accident Investigations. LC 99-59279. (Illus.). xix, 65p. 1999. pap. 15.00 (*0-8330-2806-5*, MR-1122-ICJ) Rand Corp.
Lebow, Edward. Kenneth Ferguson Ceramics Retrospective: From the Nelson-Atkins Museum of Art. (Illus.). 120p. 1995. pap. text 29.95 (*0-942614-23-2*) Nelson-Atkins.
Lebow, Edward, jt. contrib. by see Hopps, Walter.
***Lebow, Eileen F.** The Bright Boys: A History of Townsend Harris High School, 80. LC 99-88492. (Contributions to the Study of Education Ser.: Vol. 80). 245p. 2000. 61.00 (*0-313-31479-9*, GM1479, Greenwood Pr) Greenwood.
Lebow, Eileen F. A Grandstand Seat: The American Balloon Service in World War I. LC 98-5240. 240p. 1998. 55.00 (*0-275-96255-5*, Praeger Pubs) Greenwood.
Lebow, Grace, et al. Coping with Your Difficult Older Parent: A Guide for Stressed Out Children. LC 98-47289. 224p. 1999. pap. 12.00 (*0-380-79750-X*, Avon Bks) Morrow Avon.
Lebow, Irwin. Information Highways & Byways: From the Telegraph to the Twenty-First Century. LC 94-45457. 348p. 1995. pap. 34.95 (*0-7803-1073-X*, PP4275) Inst Electrical.
— Understanding Digital Transmission & Recording. LC 97-34940. 248p. 1997. pap. text 34.95 (*0-7803-3418-3*, PP5387) Inst Electrical.
Lebow, Jeanne. The Outlaw James Copeland & the Champion-Belted Empress. LC 90-36868. (Contemporary Poetry Ser.). 72p. 1991. pap. 14.95 (*0-8203-1281-9*) U of Ga Pr.
LeBow, Michael D. Overweight Teenagers: Don't Bear the Burden Alone. (Illus.). 270p. (C). 1995. 23.95 (*0-306-45047-X*, Plenum Trade) Perseus Pubng.
— The Thin Plan. LC 87-35282. (Illus.). 181p. (Orig.). 1988. reprint ed. pap. 56.20 (*0-608-07100-5*, 206732700009) Bks Demand.
— Weight Control: The Behavioural Strategies. LC 79-41728. (Illus.). 358p. reprint ed. pap. 111.00 (*0-608-17547-1*, 203052700069) Bks Demand.
Lebow, Richard N. The Art of Bargaining. 192p. (C). 1996. 24.95 (*0-8018-5198-X*) Johns Hopkins.
— Nuclear Crisis Management: A Dangerous Illusion. LC 86-16767. (Cornell Studies in Security Affairs). 232p. 1987. 35.00 (*0-8014-1989-1*); pap. 14.95 (*0-8014-9531-8*) Cornell U Pr.
— Nuclear Crisis Management: A Dangerous Illusion. LC 86-16767. (Cornell Studies in Security Affairs). 227p. reprint ed. pap. 70.40 (*0-608-20918-X*, 207201700003) Bks Demand.
— We All Lost the Cold War. 566p. (C). 1993. pap. text 21.95 (*0-691-01941-X*, Pub. by Princeton U Pr) Cal Prin Full Svc.
Lebow, Richard N. & Risse-Kappen, Thomas. International Relations Theory & the End of the Cold War. LC 94-42569. 320p. 1995. 52.50 (*0-231-10194-5*); pap. 20.50 (*0-231-10195-3*) Col U Pr.
Lebow, Richard N. & Stein, Janice G. We All Lost the Cold War. (Studies in International History & Politics). 552p. 1993. text 60.00 (*0-691-03308-0*, Pub. by Princeton U Pr) Cal Prin Full Svc.
Lebow, Rob. A Journey into the Heroic Environment: Eight Principles That Lead to Greater Productivity. 1995. pap. 11.00 (*1-55958-688-5*) Prima Pub.
— A Journey into the Heroic Environment: Eight Principles That Lead to Greater Productivity, Quality, Job Satisfaction & Profits. 144p. 1990. 16.95 (*1-55958-047-X*) Prima Pub.
Lebow, Rob & Simon, William L. Lasting Change: Building the Shared Values That Make Companies Great. LC 97-208503. (Business Technology Ser.). 320p. 1997. 24.95 (*0-442-02585-8*, VNR) Wiley.
Lebow, Rob & Simon, William L. Lasting Change: The Shared Values Process That Makes Companies Great. 304p. 1997. 24.95 (*0-471-29264-8*, VNR) Wiley.
Lebow, Robert. Journey into Heroic Enviroment Study Guide Workbook. 1998. pap. write for info. (*0-7615-0964-X*) Prima Pub.
— Journey into the Heroic Environment: A Personal Guide for Creating a Work Environment. expanded rev. ed. LC 96-42039. 224p. 2000. pap. 14.00 (*0-7615-0904-6*) Prima Pub.
Lebow, Susan, ed. see Tarr, Mary A.
Lebowitz, Andrea, ed. Living in Harmony: Nature Writing by Women in Canada. 240p. (Orig.). 1996. pap. 15.95 (*1-55143-060-6*) Orca Bk Pubs.
Lebowitz, Arieh & Malmgreen, Gail, eds. Robert F. Wagner Labor Archives, New York University: The Papers of the Jewish Labor Committee. LC 89-16915. (Archives of the Holocaust Ser.: Vol. 14). 528p. 1993. text 138.00 (*0-8240-5496-2*) Garland.
Lebowitz, Barry D., jt. ed. see Light, Enid.
Lebowitz, Barry D., jt. ed. see Salzman, Carl.
Lebowitz, Clara. Tuvia & the Tiny Teacher. (Illus.). 100p. (J). (gr. 3-4). 1991. 12.95 (*1-56062-105-2*) CIS Comm.
Lebowitz, Fran. Exterior Signs: Health. 2000. mass mkt. write for info. (*0-8041-1264-9*) Ivy Books.
— The Fran Lebowitz Reader. 1994. pap. 14.00 (*0-679-76180-2*) Knopf.
Lebowitz, Fran & Lifson, Ben. The Man in the Crowd: The Uneasy Streets of Garry Winogrand. Fraenkel, Jeffrey, ed. 168p. 1999. 45.00 (*1-881337-05-7*) Fraenkel Gal.
Lebowitz, Gary N. Autovisor: The Ultimate Log Book & Maintenance Guide. (Illus.). 64p. (Orig.). 1995. pap. 6.95 (*0-9638788-3-2*) Autoviser.
Lebowitz, Harvey M. Bankruptcy Deskbook. 2nd ed. 836p. 1990. text 80.00 (*0-87224-004-5*, A1-1411) PLI.
Lebowitz, Holly, jt. auth. see Orfield, Gary.
Lebowitz, Joel L., jt. ed. see Domb, Cyril M.
Lebowitz, Joel L., jt. ed. see Montroll, E. W.
Lebowitz, Leon C., jt. ed. see Mazzagatti, Frank A.
Lebowitz, Marcia L. I Think Divorce Stinks. 3rd rev. ed. (Illus.). 32p. (J). (gr. 1-8). 1999. pap. 9.95 (*0-935769-05-6*) CDC Pr.
Lebowitz, Martin. Martin Lebowitz: His Thought & Writings. Jones, Robert E., ed. LC 97-34876. 496p. (C). 1997. text 29.95 (*0-7618-0933-3*) U Pr of Amer.
Lebowitz, Max, ed. see Nobel, Sylvia.
Lebowitz, Michael D., ed. Proceedings of the International Conference on Environmental Epidemiology & Exposure Analysis: I, Health Hazards from Toxic Pollutants & Biological Monitoring; II, Ethics & Law in Environmental Epidemiology. (Journal of Exposure Analysis & Environmental Epidemiology Ser.: Vol. 1, No. 1). (Illus.). 1993. pap. text 60.00 (*0-911131-71-X*) Specialist Journals.
Lebowitz, Milton M., ed. Practice Issues in Social Welfare Administration, Policy & Planning. LC 82-6269. (Administration in Social Work Ser.: Vol. 6, Nos. 2 & 3). 157p. 1982. text 49.95 (*0-86656-142-0*, B142); pap. text 17.95 (*0-86656-166-8*) Haworth Pr.
Lebowitz, Naomi. Ibsen & the Great World. LC 89-12988. 272p. 1990. text 37.50 (*0-8071-1543-6*) La State U Pr.
— The Imagination of Loving: Henry James's Legacy to the Novel. LC 65-14595. 184p. reprint ed. pap. 57.10 (*0-7837-3807-2*, 204362700010) Bks Demand.
— The Philosophy of Literary Amateurism. 152p. 1994. text 29.95 (*0-8262-0970-X*) U of Mo Pr.
Lebowitz, Naomi, jt. auth. see Newton, Ruth.
Lebowitz, Robert. Plant Biotechnology: A Laboratory Course. 160p. (C). 1994. text. write for info. (*0-697-15119-0*, WCB McGr Hill) McGrw-H Hghr Educ.
Lebowitz, Sally E. Friend of the Family: A Hospice Volunteer's Experience. 128p. (Orig.). 1989. pap. 12.95 (*0-9619155-1-X*) Laurel & Herbert.
LeBox, Annette. Miracle at Willowcreek. (Illus.). 172p. 1998. pap. 7.95 (*1-896764-04-5*, Pub. by Sec Story Pr) LPC InBook.
— The Princess Who Danced with Cranes. (J). 1998. pap. 5.95 (*0-929005-87-2*, Pub. by Sec Story Pr) LPC InBook.
— The Princess Who Danced with Cranes. (Illus.). (J). 1998. 13.95 (*0-929005-88-0*, Pub. by Sec Story Pr) LPC InBook.
Leboyer, Frederick. Birth Without Violence: The Book that Revolutionized the Way We Bring Our Children into the World. LC 95-13382.Tr. of Pour une Naissance sans Violence. (Illus.). 128p. 1995. pap. 14.95 (*0-89281-545-0*, Heal Arts VT) Inner Tradit.
— Inner Beauty, Inner Light: Yoga for Pregnant Women. LC 76-47945. (Illus.). 1997. pap. 18.95 (*1-55704-315-9*, Pub. by Newmarket) Norton.
— Loving Hands: The Traditional Art of Baby Massage. LC 97-25335. (Illus.). 1997. pap. 16.95 (*1-55704-314-0*, Pub. by Newmarket) Norton.
Lebra, Joyce C. Shaping Hawaii: The Voices of Women. 2nd ed. Chapman, Joyce, ed. (Illus.). 303p. 1999. pap. 19.95 (*0-9662945-2-1*) Goodale HI.
Lebra, Takie S. Above the Clouds: Status Culture of the Modern Japanese Nobility. (C). 1992. 55.00 (*0-520-07600-1*, Pub. by U CA Pr) Cal Prin Full Svc.
— Above the Clouds: Status Culture of the Modern Japanese Nobility. 1995. pap. 17.95 (*0-520-07602-8*, Pub. by U CA Pr) Cal Prin Full Svc.
— Japanese Patterns of Behavior. LC 76-110392. 312p. (C). 1976. pap. text 15.00 (*0-8248-0460-0*) EW Ctr HI.
— Japanese Women: Constraint & Fulfillment. LC 83-18029. 358p. (C). 1984. pap. text 15.00 (*0-8248-1025-2*) UH Pr.
Lebra, Takie S., ed. Japanese Social Organization. LC 92-3835. 256p. (C). 1992. pap. text 16.00 (*0 8248 1420 7*) UH Pr.
Lebra, Takie S. & Lebra, William P., eds. Japanese Culture & Behavior: Selected Readings. rev. ed. LC 86-4367. 448p. 1986. pap. text 18.00 (*0-8248-1055-4*) UH Pr.
Lebra, William P., ed. see Conference on Culture & Mental Health Research in.
Lebra, William P., jt. ed. see Lebra, Takie S.
LeBras, Yvon, tr. see Reed, Allen C.
Lebrat, Jean, jt. auth. see Biasini, Emile.
LeBrecht, James & Kaye, Deena. Sound & Music for the Theater: The Art & Technique of Design. 2nd ed. LC 99-27911. 240p. 1999. pap. 26.95 (*0-240-80371-X*, Focal) Buttrwrth-Heinemann.
Lebrecht, Norman. The Book of Musical Anecdotes: Hundreds of Classic & Little-Known Stories about the World's Greatest Composers & Performers. LC 85-16809. 480p. 1985. 27.95 (*0-02-918710-9*) Free Pr.
— A Companion to Twentieth-Century Music. (Illus.). 288p. 1993. 30.00 (*0-671-66654-1*) S&S Trade.
— The Companion to 20th-Century Music. (Illus.). 440p. 1996. reprint ed. pap. 16.95 (*0-306-80734-3*) Da Capo.
— The Maestro Myth: Great Conductors in Pursuit of Power. (Illus.). 402p. 1999. reprint ed. 42.95 (*0-7351-0093-4*) Replica Bks.
— The Maestro Myth: Great Conductors in Pursuit of Power. rev. ed. (Illus.). 400p. 1999. pap. 15.95 (*0-8065-2088-4*, Citadel Pr) Carol Pub Group.
— The Maestro Myth: Great Conductors in Pursuit of Power. (Illus.). 384p. 1992. 22.50 (*1-55972-108-1*, Birch Ln Pr) Carol Pub Group.
— The Maestro Myth: Great Conductors in the Pursuit of Power. (Illus.). 384p. 1993. pap. 15.95 (*0-8065-1450-7*, Citadel Pr) Carol Pub Group.
***Lebrecht, Norman.** Mahler Remembered. (Illus.). 336p. 2001. pap. 16.00 (*0-571-14692-9*) Faber & Faber.
Lebrecht, Norman. Who Killed Classical Music? Maestros, Managers & Corporate Politics. LC 97-9667. 448p. 1997. 24.95 (*1-55972-415-3*, Birch Ln Pr) Carol Pub Group.
***Lebrecht, Sue.** Hiking in Ontario. 2000. pap. 16.95 (*2-89464-306-3*, Pub. by Ulysses Travel) Globe Pequot.
— I Hate Winter: A Guide to Winter Outings in Ontario. (Illus.). 168p. 1999. pap. text. write for info. (*1-55046-318-7*) Bomporto.
Lebrecht, Sue. Mountain Bike Here: Ontario & Central & Western New York. (Illus.). 168p. 1999. pap. 13.95 (*1-55046-292-X*, Pub. by Boston Mills) Genl Dist Srvs.
Lebredo, Raquel, jt. auth. see Jarvis.
Lebredo, Raquel, jt. auth. see Jarvis, Ana C.
Lebret, Elizabeth. Allegro: Music for the Eurythmy Curriculum. Mitchell, David, ed. 50p. 1997. pap. 10.00 (*1-888365-08-0*) Assn Waldorf Schls.
LeBreton, J. The White Magic Book: The Correct Answers to Your Problems. 1991. lib. bdg. 79.95 (*0-8490-4553-3*) Gordon Pr.
Lebreton, J. D. & North, Ph. M., eds. Marked Individuals in the Study of Bird Population. LC 93-3400. (Advances in Life Sciences Ser.). xviii, 397p. 1993. 109.00 (*0-8176-2780-4*, Pub. by Birkhauser) Princeton Arch.
LeBreton, John. The White Magic Book. 100p. 1996. reprint ed. pap. 13.00 (*0-7873-0546-4*) Hlth Research.
LeBreton, Jonathan, compiled by. Library Buildings Consultant List 1999. 100p. 1999. pap. 12.50 (*0-8389-8016-3*) Library Admin.
Lebreton, Jules. Etudes Sur la Langue et la Grammaire de Ciceron. xxvii, 471p. 1979. reprint ed. write for info. (*3-487-00994-3*) G Olms Pubs.
LeBreton, Laurie W., et al. Building Equal Opportunity: Six Affirmative Action Programs for Women Construction Workers. (Illus.). 40p. 1998. pap. text 20.00 (*0-7881-4945-8*) DIANE Pub.
LeBreton, Marietta M. Northwestern State University of Louisiana, 1884-1948: A History. LC 85-61932. (Illus.). 320p. 1985. 30.00 (*0-917898-10-9*) NSU Pr LA.
Lebrich, Julie. Straight to the Point: Angles on Giving up Crime. 310p. 1993. pap. 34.95 (*0-908569-78-5*, Pub. by Univ Otago Pr) Intl Spec Bk.
LeBrie, Isolde. Joyous Feasts: A Cookbook for Easy Entertaining. LC 93-71135. (Illus.). 254p. 1993. 14.95 (*0-9637567-0-2*) Daniels OH.
Lebris, P. Dictionnaire Bobo-Francais. (FRE.). 416p. 1981. 69.95 (*0-8288-1599-2*, F37450) Fr & Eur.
Lebroke, Jody. Memories Forever. 218p. mass mkt. 4.99 (*1-55197-017-1*) Picasso Publ.
Lebron, Mariano M. How to Avoid Federal Income Tax Complications. Tools & Sources. LC 97-2884. 1997. 21.95 (*0-9626291-2-X*) U Cinn Law.
Lebrun. Mutism. 1990. 65.00 (*1-56593-539-X*, 0042) Singular Publishing.
Lebrun, Claude. Little Brown Bear Does Not Want to Eat. LC 95-1134. (Little Brown Bear Ser.). (Illus.). 16p. (J). (gr. k-2). 1996. 3.95 (*0-516-17823-7*) Childrens.
— Little Brown Bear Is Afraid of the Dark. LC 95-1133. (Little Brown Bear Ser.). (Illus.). 16p. (J). (ps-2). 1995. pap. 3.95 (*0-516-17825-3*) Childrens.
— Little Brown Bear Is Sick. LC 95-1138. (Little Brown Bear Ser.). (Illus.). 16p. (J). (ps-2). 1995. pap. 3.95 (*0-516-17821-0*) Childrens.
— Little Brown Bear Plays in the Snow. LC 95-26330. (Little Brown Bear Ser.). 16p. (J). 1997. 3.95 (*0-516-17847-4*) Childrens.
— Little Brown Bear Says "No" to Everything. LC 95-5732. (Little Brown Bear Ser.). (Illus.). 16p. (J). (ps-2). 1995. 3.95 (*0-516-17828-8*) Childrens.
— Little Brown Bear 3, 4 vols., Set. (J). 1996. boxed set 15.80 (*0-516-17804-0*) Childrens.
— Little Brown Bear Wants to Be Read To. LC 95-5733. (Little Brown Bear Ser.).Tr. of Petit Ours Brun Vent des Histoires. (Illus.). 16p. (J). (gr. k-3). 1996. 3.95 (*0-516-17829-6*) Childrens.
— Little Brown Bear Wants to Go to School. LC 95-5734. (Little Brown Bear Ser.). (Illus.). 16p. (J). (ps-2). 1995. pap. 3.95 (*0-516-17830-X*) Childrens.
Lebrun, David, ed. see Lebrun, Rico.
Lebrun, Francesca & Bayon, Mlle. Keyboard Sonatas: Six Sonatas for Harpsichord or Pianoforte with Accompaniment for Violin; Six Sonatas pour le Clavecin ou le Piano Forte dont 3 avec Accompagnement de Violon Oblige. Hayes, Deborah, ed. (Women Composers Ser.: No. 23). 90p. 1990. reprint ed. lib. bdg. 39.50 (*0-306-76285-4*) Da Capo.
Lebrun, Francoise, jt. auth. see Lena, Pierre.
LeBrun, Hope. All about Jesus. (Illus.). 48p. (Orig.). 1996. pap. 12.95 (*1-879099-25-X*) Thy Word.

L

LeBrun, J. Dictionnaire des Services Publics Relevant de l'Etat.Tr. of Dictionary of Public Services Related to Government. (FRE.). 1020p. 1978. 175.00 (*0-8288-5187-5*, M6341) Fr & Eur.

LeBrun, Ken. The Earthly Life of Jesus. LC 91-65760. 277p. (Orig.). 1991. boxed set 14.95 (*0-945383-24-X*, 945-5814) Teach Servs.

— The Earthly Life of Jesus. LC 91-65760. 277p. (Orig.). 1991. pap. 9.95 (*0-945383-25-8*, 945-5815) Teach Servs.

Lebrun, Richard A. Joseph de Maistre: An Intellectual Militant. 384p. (C). 1988. text 65.00 (*0-7735-0645-4*, Pub. by McG-Queens Univ Pr) CUP Services.

Lebrun, Richard A., ed. Maistre Studies. LC 88-26147. 318p. (C). 1988. lib. bdg. 49.00 (*0-8191-7201-4*) U Pr of Amer.

Lebrun, Richard A., ed. see De Maistre, Joseph.

Lebrun, Richard A., ed. & tr. see De Maistre, Joseph.

Lebrun, Richard A., ed. & tr. see DeMaistre, Joseph.

Lebrun, Richard A., tr. see Maistre, Joseph.

***Lebrun, Rico.** In the Meridian of the Heart: Selected Letters of Rico Lebrun. Lebrun, David & Renner, James, eds. (Illus.). 112p. 2000. 30.00 (*1-56792-112-4*) Godine.

Lebrun, Y. The Artificial Larynx. (Neurolinguistics Ser.: Vol. 1). 90p. 1973. pap. 18.50 (*90-265-0173-0*) Swets.

Lebrun, Y. & Hoops, R., eds. The Management of Aphasia. (Neurolinguistics Ser.: Vol. 8). 124p. 1978. 31.00 (*90-265-0280-X*) Swets.

— Recovery in Aphasics. (Neurolinguistics Ser.: Vol. 4). 270p. 1976. 41.50 (*90-265-0228-1*) Swets.

Lebrun, Y. & Zangwill, O. L., eds. Lateralisation of Language in the Child. (Neurolinguistics Ser.: Vol. 10). 175p. 1982. 37.25 (*90-265-0337-7*) Swets.

Lebrun, Y., ed. see International Symposium on Stuttering Staff.

Lebrun, Yvan, ed. From the Brain to the Mouth: Acquired Dysarthria & Dysfluency in Adults. LC 96-6578. (Neuropsychology & Cognition Ser.). 196p. (C). 1997. text 93.50 (*0-7923-4427-8*) Kluwer Academic.

LeBruyn, Lieven. Trace Rings of Generic Two by Two Matrices. LC 87-1810. (Memoirs of the American Mathematical Society Ser.: Vol. 363). 100p. 1987. pap. 18.00 (*0-8218-2425-2*, MEMO/66/363C) Am Math.

Lebsock, Suzanne. The Free Women of Petersburg: Status & Culture in a Southern Town, 1784-1860. (Illus.). 320p. 1985. reprint ed. pap. 12.95 (*0-393-95264-9*) Norton.

Lebsock, Suzanne, jt. auth. see Scott, Anne F.

Lebsock, Suzanne, jt. ed. see Hewitt, Nancy A.

LeBuff, Charles. Sanybel Light: An Historical Autobiography. LC 96-95126. (Illus.). 304p. 1997. pap. 19.95 (*0-9625013-1-X*) Amber Pubng FL.

LeBuff, Charles R., Jr. The Loggerhead Turtle: In the Eastern Gulf of Mexico. LC 89-81763. (Illus.). 236p. 1990. 24.95 (*0-9625013-0-1*, Pub. by Amber Pubng FL) Chelsea Green Pub.

LeBuffe, Claire, ed. International Directory of Engineering Societies & Related Organizations (1999-2000) 16th ed. 370p. 1998. pap. 204.00 (*0-87615-008-3*) AAES.

***LeBuffe, James R. & Hargreaves, Sherran A.** School-Age Child Care. (Fastback Ser.: No. 454). 50p. 1999. pap. 3.00 (*0-87367-654-8*, FB# 454) Phi Delta Kappa.

LeBuffe, Michael & Pierce, Burton. A Photographic Atlas for the Microbiology Laboratory. 2nd ed. (Illus.). 192p. 1998. pap. text 17.95 (*0-89582-461-2*) Morton Pub.

LeBuffe, Michael, jt. auth. see Pierce, Burton.

Leburton, J. P., et al, eds. Quantum Confinement: Nanoscale Materials, Devices & Systems: 4th International Symposium. LC 97-229055. (Proceedings Ser.: Vol. 97-11). 494p. 1997. 75.00 (*1-56677-138-2*) Electrochem Soc.

Leburton, Jean-Pierre, et al, eds. Phonons in Semiconductor Nanostructures. LC 93-17083. (NATO Advanced Study Institutes Series E, Applied Sciences: Vol. 236). 1993. text 276.50 (*0-7923-2277-0*) Kluwer Academic.

Leburton, Jean-Pierre, et al. Hot Carriers in Semiconductors. Hess, Karl & Ravaioli, Umberto, eds. LC 96-28770. (Illus.). 635p. (C). 1996. text 179.00 (*0-306-45366-5*, Kluwer Plenum) Kluwer Academic.

Lebwohl, M. Handbook of the Skin & Systemic Disease. (Illus.). 288p. 1997. pap. write for info. (*0-443-05793-1*) Church.

Lebwohl, Mark G. The Skin & Systemic Disease. (Illus.). 239p. 1995. text 110.00 (*0-443-08739-3*) Church.

Lebwohl, Mark G., ed. Difficult Diagnoses in Dermatology. LC 87-25675. (Illus.). 466p. reprint ed. pap. 144.50 (*0-7837-6226-7*, 204594000010) Bks Demand.

Lebzelter, Gisela C. Political Anti-Semitism in England, 1918-1939. LC 78-16795. 222p. 1979. 49.50 (*0-8419-0426-X*) Holmes & Meier.

Leca, Jean, jt. ed. see Birnbaum, Pierre.

Lecaillon, J., et al. Income Distribution & Economic Development: An Analytical Survey. (WEP Study). ix, 211p. 1986. 36.00 (*92-2-103559-X*); pap. 27.00 (*92-2-103366-X*) Intl Labour Office.

Lecam, Lucien M. Convergence in Distribution of Stochastic Processes. LC 57-9424. (University of California Publications in Social Welfare: Vol. 2, No. 11). 32p. reprint ed. pap. 30.00 (*0-608-30742-4*, 202118300022) Bks Demand.

Lecanuet, Jacqueline. Taking French Further. (Hugo's Language Courses Ser.). 192p. 1994. pap. 7.95 (*0-85285-211-8*) Hunter NJ.

Lecanuet, Jacqueline, jt. auth. see Overy, Ronald.

Lecanuet, Jean-Pierre, et al, eds. Fetal Development: A Psychobiological Perspective. LC 94-44324. 524p. 1995. text 99.95 (*0-8058-1485-X*) L Erlbaum Assocs.

Lecar, Harold, jt. auth. see Nossal, Ralph.

Lecar, M., ed. see International Astronomical Union Staff.

***Lecarme, Jacqueline, et al, eds.** Research in Afroasiatic Grammar: Papers from the Third Conference on Afroasiatic Languages, Sophia Antipolis, 1996. LC 99-89842. (Current Issues in Linguistic Theory Ser.: Vol. 202). vi, 378p. 2000. 95.00 (*1-55619-980-5*) J Benjamins Pubng Co.

Lecca, Pedro J. & McNeill, John S., eds. Interdisciplinary Team Practice: Issues & Trends. LC 85-3612. 256p. 1985. 62.95 (*0-275-90134-3*, C0134, Praeger Pubs) Greenwood.

Lecca, Pedro J. & Watts, Thomas D. Pathways for Minorities into the Health Professions. 98p. 1989. 33.00 (*0-8191-7552-8*) U Pr of Amer.

— Preschoolers & Substance Abuse: Strategies for Prevention & Intervention. LC 91-35921. 112p. 1993. pap. 14.95 (*1-56024-235-3*); lib. bdg. 39.95 (*1-56024-234-5*) Haworth Pr.

Lecca, Pedro J., et al. Cultural Competency in Health, Social & Human Services: Directions for the 21st Century. LC 97-52279. (Social-Psychology Reference Ser.). (Illus.). 320p. 1998. text 60.00 (*0-8153-2205-4*, SS1085); pap. text 24.95 (*0-8153-2206-2*, SS1085) Garland.

Leccabue, F. & Pasrici, C., eds. Crystal Growth & Characterization of Advanced Materials. 560p. (C). 1988. text 138.00 (*9971-5-0730-7*) World Scientific Pub.

***Leccese, Michael.** American Eden: Landscape Architecture of the Pacific Coast. (Illus.). 2000. 35.00 (*2-84576-005-1*) Vilo Intl.

— Contemporary Parks & Gardens: United States, The West Coast. (Illus.). 160p. 1999. 27.50 (*2-7450-0046-2*) Telleri Edit.

Leccese, Michael. Robert Murase: Stone & Water. (Landmarks Ser.: Vol. 3). (Illus.). 66p. 1997. pap. 24.95 (*1-888931-04-3*) Spacemkr Pr.

— Short Bike Rides in & Around Washington, DC. 4th ed. LC 98-27572. (Short Bike Rides Ser.). (Illus.). 224p. 1998. pap. 11.95 (*0-7627-0335-0*) Globe Pequot.

Leccesse, Michael. Short Bike Rides in Colorado. LC 95-13956. (Short Bike Rides Ser.). (Illus.). 160p. (Orig.). 1995. pap. 10.95 (*1-56440-640-7*) Globe Pequot.

Lecercle, Jean-Jacques. Interpretation as Pragmatics. LC 98-50634. (Language, Discourse, Society Ser.). 272p. 1999. pap. 24.95 (*0-312-22153-3*); text 69.95 (*0-312-22152-5*) St Martin.

— Philosophy of Nonsense: The Intuitions of Victorian Nonsense Literature. LC 93-5384. 288p. (C). 1994. pap. 24.99 (*0-415-07653-6*) Routledge.

Lecercq. Legal Writing. 3024p. 1993. suppl. ed. 695.00 (*0-316-16136-5*, Aspen Law & Bus) Aspen Pub.

***Lech, Raymond B.** Broken Soldiers. LC 00-8208. 320p. 2000. 27.95 (*0-252-02541-5*) U of Ill Pr.

Lech, Raymond B. Broken Soldiers: American Prisoners of War in North Korea. LC 91-20179. 1991. 23.95 (*0-8128-4016-X*) Madison Bks UPA.

Lech, Rob. Laughter, Grabber & Power: A Prophetic Revelation of the Current & Coming Move of God. Good News Fellowship Min. Staff, ed. 64p. (Orig.). 1997. pap. 4.99 (*1-888081-52-X*) Good News Min.

Lechaczynski, Jean & Lechaczynski, Serge. Verre Contemporain. (FRE.). 154p. 1993. lib. bdg. 150.00 (*0-7859-3649-1*, 2859171320); lib. bdg. 150.00 (*0-7859-3650-5*, 2859171339) Fr & Eur.

Lechaczynski, Serge, jt. auth. see Lechaczynski, Jean.

Lechago, Juan & Gould, Victor E. Bloodworth's Endocrine Pathology. 3rd ed. 709p. 1996. 139.00 (*0-614-26948-2*) Lppncott W & W.

Lechat, Lagier. Dictionary of Principal Medications: Dictionnaire des Medicaments Principaux. (FRE & SPA.). 528p. 1982. 110.00 (*0-8288-1815-0*, M15386) Fr & Eur.

Lecher, Doris. Angelita's Magic Yarn. (Illus.). 32p. (J). (ps-3). 1992. 14.00 (*0-374-30332-0*) FS&G.

Lecher, Wolfgang, ed. Trade Unions in the European Union: A Handbook. 288p. (C). 1994. pap. 32.50 (*0-85315-766-9*, Pub. by Lawrence & Wishart) NYU Pr.

Lecher, Wolfgang & Platzer, Hans-Wolfgang. European Union-European Industrial Relations? Global Challenges, National Developments & Transnational Dynamics. Burgess, Pete, tr. LC 97-16510. 312p. (C). 1997. 85.00 (*0-415-15872-9*) Routledge.

Lecher, Wolfgang & Platzer, Hans-Wolfgang. The Establishment of European Works Councils: From Information Committee to Social Actor. LC 98-73886. 5p. 1999. text 69.95 (*1-84014-886-1*) Ashgate Pub Co.

Lechevalier, Hubert, jt. auth. see Laskin, Allen I.

Lechevalier, Hubert A., jt. auth. see Laskin, A.

Lechevalier, Hubert A., jt. auth. see Laskin, Allen I.

Lechevalier, Hubert A., jt. ed. see Laskin, Allan I.

Lechevalier, Hubert A., jt. ed. see Laskin, Allen I.

LeChevalier, Patricia. Hard-Core Barbecue Book & Kit: Mastering America's Regional Traditions. 1998. 34.95 (*1-57990-072-0*, Pub. by Lark Books) Random.

— Hard-Core Chili Book & Kit: Mastering America's Regional Themes. 1998. 34.95 (*1-57990-071-2*, Pub. by Lark Books) Random.

LeChevalier, Patricia, ed. Atlantean Press Review, 1992. (Illus.). 230p. 1992. pap. 12.00 (*0-9626854-4-5*) Atlantean Pr.

LeChevalier, Patricia, ed. see Hugo, Victor.

Lechevallier-Chevignard, Edmond. European Costumes of the Sixteenth through Eighteenth Centuries: In Full Color. LC 95-5988. (Illus.). 96p. 1995. 17.95 (*0-486-28519-7*) Dover.

Lechevallier, Mark W. & AWWA Research Foundation Staff. Microbial Impact of Biological Filtration. LC 97-31912. 1998. write for info. (*0-89867-939-7*) Am Water Wks Assn.

LeChevallier, Mark W., et al. Factors Limiting Microbial Growth in the Distribution System Pt. II: Full-Scale Experiments. LC 97-139841. (Illus.). 172p. 1996. pap. 195.00 (*0-89867-875-7*, 90709) Am Water Wks Assn.

Lechevallier, Y., jt. ed. see Diday, E.

Lechford, Thomas. Note-Book Kept by Thomas Lechford, Esq., in Boston, Massachusetts Bay, from June 27, 1638 to July 29, 1641. 460p. 1998. reprint ed. pap. 34.50 (*0-7884-0926-3*, L113) Heritage Bk.

— Note-Book Kept by Thomas Lechford, Esq., in Boston, Massachusetts Bay, from June 27, 1638, to July 29, 1641. rev. ed. Hale, Edward E., Jr. et al, eds. LC 88-30732. 512p. 1989. reprint ed. 49.50 (*0-929539-06-0*, 1106) Picton Pr.

— Plain Dealings: or News from New England. 1972. reprint ed. lib. bdg. 20.50 (*0-8422-8140-1*) Irvington.

Lechich, Whitney, ed. see Lee, Soon C.

LeChien, Paul. The Tattooed Loverboy & Other Drawings. (Illus.). 62p. (Orig.). 1992. pap. 25.00 (*1-873741-03-0*, Pub. by Millvres Bks) LPC InBook.

Lechin, Fuad & Van der Dijs, Bertha, eds. Neurochemistry & Clinical Disorders Circuitry of Some Psychiatric & Psychosomatic Syndromes. LC 88-19263. 208p. 1989. 139.00 (*0-8493-6595-3*, RC483, CRC Reprint) Franklin.

Lechler. Handbook of HLA & Disease. 2nd ed. 600p. 1999. 136.00 (*0-12-440315-8*) Acad Pr.

Lechler, Doris A. English Toy China. (Illus.). 240p. 1990. pap. 24.95 (*0-915410-61-3*, 3041) Antique Pubns.

— French & German Dolls, Dishes & Accessories. (Illus.). 184p. 1991. pap. 29.95 (*0-915410-70-2*, 3075) Antique Pubns.

Lechler, Gotthard V. John Wycliffe & His English Precursors. LC 78-63197. (Heresies of the Early Christian & Medieval Era Ser.: Second Ser.). reprint ed. 49.50 (*0-404-16235-5*) AMS Pr.

Lechler, Paul. Gold from Water: And Other Mining Scams. (Special Publications: Vol. 22). (Illus.). 18p. 1997. pap. 2.00 (*1-888035-02-1*) Nev Bureau Mines & Geol.

Lechler, Robert. HLA & Disease. (Illus.). 320p. (C). 1994. text 39.95 (*0-12-440320-4*) Acad Pr.

Lechlitner, Laurie. Love Is . . . 80p. 1988. pap. 3.95 (*0-88144-125-2*) Christian Pub.

Lechmere, Adam. Mozambique. (Travellers Survival Kit Ser.). 1999. pap. 18.95 (*1-85458-223-2*) Seven Hills Bk.

Lechmere, Adam & Catto, Susan. Live & Work in the U. S. A. & Canada. (Live & Work Ser.). 288p. 1999. pap. 19.95 (*1-85458-211-9*, Pub. by Vac Wrk Pubns) Seven Hills Bk.

Lechmere, Edmund, jt. auth. see Wright, William.

Lechner, Benjamin, ed. Lechner's Comprehensive 4 Language Dictionary: Paper - Plastics - Aluminum Foil - Converting Terms. (FRE, GER & SPA.). 240p. 1994. 49.95 (*1-56676-265-0*, 762650) Technomic.

Lechner, Cathy. Couldn't We Just Kill 'Em & Tell God They Died? Overcoming Difficult Relationships with Your Family & Friends. LC 95-83903. 1999. pap. 12.99 (*0-88419-433-7*) Dake Pub.

***Lechner, Cathy.** Espero Que Sus Promesas Se Cumplan: Antes de Que Mi Cuerpo Se Arrugue! (SPA.). 1998. pap. 9.99 (*0-88419-554-6*) Casa Creacion.

Lechner, Cathy. Estoy Tratando de Sentarme a Sus Pies, pero Quien Cocina?Tr. of I'm Trying to Sit at His Feet, but Who's Going to Cook Dinner?. (SPA.). 1997. pap. 7.99 (*0-88419-515-5*) Creation House.

— I Hope God's Promises Come to Pass Before My Body Parts Go South. LC 98-5144. 1998. pap. 11.99 (*0-88419-529-5*) Creation House.

— I'm Trying to Sit at His Feet: But Who's Going to Cook Dinner. LC 95-68310. 1995. pap. 12.99 (*0-88419-409-4*) Creation House.

— You've Got to Be Kidding, I Thought This Was the Great Tribulation! Finding Strength When Life Disappoints You, Vol. 1. 1999. pap. 12.99 (*0-88419-667-4*) Creation House.

Lechner, Diane, et al, texts. Jesus Comes to Us. 143p. (J). pap. 6.50 (*0-8198-3921-3*) Pauline Bks.

Lechner, Diane, et al. Jesus Comes to Us. 268p. teacher ed., spiral bd. 16.95 (*0-8198-3923-X*) Pauline Bks.

Lechner, Elmar. Padagogische Grenzganger in Europa. 451p. 1997. 76.95 (*3-631-30798-5*) P Lang Pubng.

***Lechner, Frank & Boli, John, eds.** The Globalization Reader. LC 99-39722. 400p. 1999. 64.95 (*0-631-21476-3*); pap. 29.95 (*0-631-21477-1*) Blackwell Pubs.

***Lechner, G. & Naunheimer, H.** Automotive Transmissions: Foundations, Selection, Design & Application. Day, S., tr. from GER. LC 99-23781. (GER., Illus.). 450p. 1999. 125.00 (*3-540-65903-X*) Spr-Verlag.

Lechner, G., jt. ed. see Pokierser, Herbert.

Lechner, H. Epilepsy State of the Art, 1993. Scollo-Lavizzari, G., ed. (Journal: European Neurology: Vol. 34, Suppl. 1, 1994). (Illus.). iv, 90p. 1994. pap. 41.00 (*3-8055-6038-9*) S Karger.

Lechner, H., ed. Importance of Haemorheologic Aspects in the Diagnosis & Treatment of Ischaemic Cerebrovascular Disease. (Journal: European Neurology: Vol. 22, Suppl. 1). (Illus.). iv, 132p. 1983. pap. 34.00 (*3-8055-3731-X*) S Karger.

Lechner, H., et al, eds. Progress in Cerebrovascular Disease: Papers Presented at the XIVth World Congress of Neurology, New Delhi, 22-27 Oct., 1989. 142p. 1990. 108.75 (*0-444-81421-3*) Elsevier.

Lechner, H., ed. see Agnoli, A., et al.

***Lechner, Jack.** Can't Take My Eyes off of You: One Man, Seven Days, Twelve Televisions. 288p. 2000. 23.95 (*0-609-60681-6*, Crown) Crown Pub Group.

Lechner, Joan M. Renaissance Concepts of the Commonplaces. LC 74-6153. 268p. 1974. reprint ed. lib. bdg. 87.50 (*0-8371-7491-0*, LERC, Greenwood Pr) Greenwood.

Lechner, Jochen. Analyse, Rekonstruktion, Kritik: Logisch-Philosophische Abhandlungen. (Illus.). X, 296p. 1997. 51.95 (*3-631-31469-8*) P Lang Pubng.

Lechner, Judith. Struggling Toward Civil Rights: A Study Guide. Friedland, J. & Kessler, R., eds. (Novel-Ties Ser.). 1993. pap. text, student ed. 20.95 (*1-56982-024-4*) Lrn Links.

Lechner, M. Training the East German Labour Force: Microeconometric Evaluations of Continuous Vocational Training after Unification. LC 98-18414. (Studies in Contemporary Economics). (Illus.). x, 204p. 1998. pap. 63.00 (*3-7908-1091-6*) Spr-Verlag.

Lechner, M. D. Ultracentrifugation, 94. Kremer, F. et al, eds. (Progress in Colloid & Polymer Science Ser.). 120p. 1994. 68.95 (*0-387-91483-8*) Spr-Verlag.

Lechner, M. D., jt. auth. see Wohlfarth, C.

Lechner, M. D., jt. ed. see Gupta, R. R.

Lechner, Martin, jt. auth. see Keppler, Michael.

Lechner, Mildred. World of Salt Shakers. 2nd ed. 1996. 24.95 (*0-89145-467-5*, 2224) Collector Bks.

***Lechner, Norbert.** Heating, Cooling & Lighting: Design Methods for Architects. 2nd ed. 560p. 2000. 80.00 (*0-471-24143-1*) Wiley.

Lechner, Norbert. Heating, Cooling, Lighting: Design Methods for Architects. LC 90-31743. 544p. 1991. 99.95 (*0-471-62887-5*) Wiley.

Lechner, Ralph. World of Salt Shakers Vol. III: Antique & Art Glass Value Guide. LC 98-215820. 1998. 29.95 (*1-57432-065-3*, 5062) Collector Bks.

Lechner, Sheryl, jt. auth. see Lowenstein, Frank W.

Lechner, Sybille K., jt. auth. see MacGregory, Alastair R.

Lechner, Tammy. In the Cal: Pastime Goes Primetime in California's Minor League. LC 94-96164. (Illus.). 114p. (Orig.). 1994. pap. 15.00 (*0-9641987-0-3*) Still Prods.

***Lechner, Viola M.** Working & Caring for the Elderly: International Perspectives. 1999. pap. text, boxed set 24.95 (*0-87630-997-X*) Brunner-Mazel.

Lechner, Viola M. & Creedon, Michael. Managing Work & Family Life: The U. S. Response. (Social Work Ser.). (Illus.). 200p. 1994. 34.95 (*0-8261-8470-7*) Springer Pub.

***Lechner, Viola M. & Neal, Margaret B., eds.** Work & Caring for the Elderly: International Perspectives. LC 99-33102. 246p. 1999. 34.95 (*0-87630-996-1*) Brunner-Mazel.

Lechner, W. Europaworterbucher Business & Law: 1991. (DUT, ENG, FRE, GER & SPA.). 1991. lib. bdg. 195.00 (*0-8288-3898-4*, F63838) Fr & Eur.

Lecht, Leonard A. Experience Under Railway Labor Legislation. LC 68-59260. (Columbia University. Studies in the Social Sciences: No. 587). reprint ed. 31.00 (*0-404-51587-8*) AMS Pr.

— Priorities for Planning in Vocational Education: Alternatives for the 1970s. LC 75-37419. 68p. 1975. 3.00 (*0-89068-006-X*) Natl Planning.

Lechtanski, Valerie L. Inquiry-Based Experiments in Chemistry. LC 98-53217. (An American Chemical Society Publication). 320p. 2000. write for info. (*0-8412-3570-8*, Pub. by Am Chemical) OUP.

Lechte, John. Fifty Key Contemporary Thinkers: From Structuralism to Postmodernity. LC 94-996. 272p. (gr. 13). 1994. pap. 17.99 (*0-415-07408-8*, B4722) Routledge.

Lechte, John & Zournazi, Mary, eds. After the Revolution: On Kristeva. (Illus.). 182p. 1998. pap. write for info. (*1-876017-37-6*) Artspace.

Lechtenberg & Schutta, eds. Neurology Practical Guidelines. LC 97-36796. (Neurological Disease & Therapy Ser.). (Illus.). 544p. 1997. text 150.00 (*0-8247-0104-6*) Dekker.

Lechtenberg, Richard. Epilepsy & the Family. (Illus.). 240p. 1984. 29.00 (*0-674-25888-6*) HUP.

— Epilepsy & the Family. (Illus.). 240p. 1986. pap. text 16.00 (*0-674-25889-4*) HUP.

— Epilepsy & the Family: A New Guide. LC 98-42636. 240p. 1999. 24.95 (*0-674-25897-5*) HUP.

— Handbook of Cerebellar Diseases. (Neurological Disease & Therapy Ser.: Vol. 16). (Illus.). 600p. 1993. text 245.00 (*0-8247-8776-5*) Dekker.

— Multiple Sclerosis Fact Book. 2nd ed. LC 94-25306. (Illus.). 235p. (C). 1995. pap. text 23.95 (*0-8036-0074-7*) Davis Co.

Lechtenberg, Richard, ed. Neurology: Pretest Self-Assessment & Review. 3rd ed. LC 97-5463. (Pretest Clinical Science Ser.). (Illus.). 200p. 1997. pap. text 18.95 (*0-07-052528-5*) McGraw-Hill HPD.

Lechtenberg, Richard & Ohl, Dana A. Sexual Dysfunction: Neurologic, Urologic & Gynecologic Aspects. LC 94-450. 345p. 1994. 69.50 (*0-8121-1496-5*) Lppncott W & W.

Lechtenberg, Richard & Sher, Joan H. AIDS in the Nervous System. (Illus.). 136p. 1988. text 73.00 (*0-443-08616-8*) Church.

Lechter, Michael A. Intellectual Property Handbook. LC 94-61489. 164p. 1994. pap. text 19.95 (*0-9643856-0-0*) TechPress.

Lechter, Michael A., et al, eds. Successful Patents & Patenting for Engineers & Scientists. LC 94-46193. 432p. 1995. pap. 44.95 (*0-7803-1086-1*, PP4478) Inst Electrical.

Lechter, Sharon L., jt. auth. see Kiyosaki, Robert T.

Lechtman, Heather, et al. Seven Matched Hollow Gold Jaguars from Peru's Early Horizon. LC 75-21192. (Studies in Pre-Columbian Art & Archaeology: No. 16). (Illus.). 49p. 1975. pap. 6.00 (*0-88402-060-6*) Dumbarton Oaks.

Lechtman, Jay, ed. see Fazen, Marianne F.

Lechtman, Jay, ed. see Monea, Michael J.

Lechtman, Max D., et al. The Games Cells Play. 160p. (C). 1996. per. 17.95 (*0-8403-8382-7*) Kendall-Hunt.

Lechtman, Michael. Shapiro's Plan. 248p. mass mkt. 4.99 (*1-55197-282-4*) Picasso Publ.

Lechtman, Pam, jt. auth. see Fraser, Laura K.

Lechtman, Pamela Price, jt. auth. see Fraser, Laura Kath.

An Asterisk (*) at the beginning of an entry indicates that the title is appearing for the first time.

Lechuga, Carlos. In the Eye of the Storm: Castro, Khrushchev, Kennedy & the Missile Crisis. Muniz, Mirta, ed. Todd, Mary, tr. from SPA. (Illus.). 217p. (Orig.). 1995. pap. 15.95 (*1-875284-87-7*) Ocean Pr NJ.

Lechuga, Ruth D. & Sayer, Chloe. Mask Arts of Mexico. (Illus.). 96p. 1995. pap. 17.95 (*0-8118-0811-4*) Chronicle Bks.

Lechunere, Adam & Catto, Susan. Live & Work in the U. S. A. & Canada. (Live & Work Abroad Guides Ser.). 272p. (Orig.). 1997. pap. 16.95 (*1-85458-119-8*, Pub. by Vac Wrk Pubns) Seven Hills Bk.

***Leck, Charles E.** Why Catholics Don't Give... And What Can Be Done about It. LC 99-75033. (Illus.). 176p. 2000. 19.95 (*0-87973-706-9*) Our Sunday Visitor.

Leck, Charles F. The Status & Distribution of New Jersey's Birds. LC 83-17655. 210p. 1984. text 30.00 (*0-8135-1033-3*) Rutgers U Pr.

Leck, Charles F., jt. auth. see Norton, Robert L.

Leck, Ian, jt. ed. see Wald, Nicholas J.

***Leck, Ralph.** Georg Simmel & Avant-Garde Sociology: The Birth of Modernity, 1880-1920. 240p. 2000. pap. 24.95 (*1-57392-867-4*) Prometheus Bks.

***Lecke, Bodo.** Literatur und Medien in Studium und Deutschunterricht. (Illus.). 373p. 1998. 56.95 (*3-631-31742-5*) P Lang Pubng.

Leckel, Dave. Buying & Selling Softwood Lumber: A Guide to the Lumber Market of North America. Evans, David S., ed. LC 98-86031. Orig. Title: Trading Western Softwood Lumber. 228p. 1998. pap. text 39.95 (*1-884311-04-0*) Random Lgths Pubns.

Leckel, John L., jt. auth. see Feeney, Agnes M.

Lecker, Martin J. Multicultural Readings in Business & Industry. 272p. (C). 1995. text 38.20 (*0-536-59000-1*) Pearson Custom.

***Lecker, Michael.** Jews & Arabs in Pre- & Early Islamic Arabia. LC 98-42703. (Variorum Collected Studies Ser.: Vol. CS639). (Illus.). 368p. 1999. text 106.95 (*0-86078-784-2*, Pub. by Ashgate Pub) Ashgate Pub Co.

Lecker, Michael. Muslim, Jews & Pagans: Studies on Early Islamic Medina. 160p. 1996. 51.50 (*0-614-21164-6*, 1364) Kazi Pubns.

— Muslims, Jews, & Pagans: Studies on Early Islamic Medina. LC 95-9833. (Islamic History & Civilization, Studies & Text Ser.: Vol. 13). xviii, 180p. 1995. 68.50 (*90-04-10247-7*) Brill Academic Pubs.

Lecker, Robert. The Annotated Bibliography of Canada's Major Authors, Vol. 8. 1994. 55.00 (*0-8161-1635-0*, G K Hall & Co) Mac Lib Ref.

— On the Line: Readings in the Short Fiction of Clark Blaise, John Metcalf & Hugh Hood. 130p. (C). 1982. pap. 8.95 (*0-920802-31-1*, Pub. by ECW) Genl Dist Srvs.

— An Other I: The Fictions of Clark Blaise. 246p. (C). 1988. text 28.00 (*1-55022-083-7*, Pub. by ECW); pap. text 16.00 (*1-55022-082-9*, Pub. by ECW) Genl Dist Srvs.

Lecker, Robert, ed. Canadian Canons: Essays in Literary Value. 288p. 1992. pap. 16.95 (*0-8020-6700-X*); text 35.00 (*0-8020-5826-4*) U of Toronto Pr.

Lecker, Robert, et al, eds. Canadian Writers & Their Works: Essays on Form, Context, & Development. (Poetry Ser.: Vol. 10). (Illus.). 412p. (C). 1992. 45.00 (*1-55022-069-1*, Pub. by ECW) Genl Dist Srvs.

— Canadian Writers & Their Works: Fiction. (Illus.). 256p. (C). 1983. text 45.00 (*0-920802-45-1*, Pub. by ECW) Genl Dist Srvs.

— Canadian Writers & Their Works: Poetry. (Illus.). 250p. (C). 1988. text 45.00 (*0-920763-69-3*, Pub. by ECW) Genl Dist Srvs.

— Canadian Writers & Their Works Vol. 2: Fiction. (Illus.). 270p. (C). 1989. text 45.00 (*1-55022-046-2*, Pub. by ECW) Genl Dist Srvs.

— Canadian Writers & Their Works Vol. 2: Poetry. (Illus.). 289p. (C). 1983. text 45.00 (*0-920802-46-X*, Pub. by ECW) Genl Dist Srvs.

— Canadian Writers & Their Works Vol. 3: Fiction. (Illus.). 276p. (C). 1988. text 45.00 (*0-920763-74-X*, Pub. by ECW) Genl Dist Srvs.

— Canadian Writers & Their Works Vol. 3: Poetry. (Illus.). 200p. (C). 1987. text 45.00 (*0-920763-19-7*, Pub. by ECW) Genl Dist Srvs.

— Canadian Writers & Their Works Vol. 4: Fiction. (Illus.). 298p. (C). 1991. text 45.00 (*1-55022-052-7*, Pub. by ECW) Genl Dist Srvs.

— Canadian Writers & Their Works Vol. 4: Poetry. (Illus.). 286p. (C). 1990. text 45.00 (*1-55022-021-7*, Pub. by ECW) Genl Dist Srvs.

— Canadian Writers & Their Works Vol. 5: Fiction. (Illus.). 257p. (C). 1990. text 45.00 (*1-55022-027-6*, Pub. by ECW) Genl Dist Srvs.

— Canadian Writers & Their Works Vol. 5: Poetry. (Illus.). 329p. (C). 1985. text 45.00 (*0-920802-90-7*, Pub. by ECW) Genl Dist Srvs.

— Canadian Writers & Their Works Vol. 6: Fiction. (Illus.). 272p. (C). 1985. text 45.00 (*0-920802-86-9*, Pub. by ECW) Genl Dist Srvs.

— Canadian Writers & Their Works Vol. 6: Poetry. (Illus.). 316p. (C). 1991. text 45.00 (*1-55022-007-1*, Pub. by ECW) Genl Dist Srvs.

— Canadian Writers & Their Works Vol. 7: Fiction. (Illus.). 310p. (C). 1985. text 45.00 (*0-920802-88-5*, Pub. by ECW) Genl Dist Srvs.

— Canadian Writers & Their Works Vol. 7: Poetry. (Illus.). 316p. (C). 1990. text 45.00 (*1-55022-057-8*, Pub. by ECW) Genl Dist Srvs.

— Canadian Writers & Their Works Vol. 8: Fiction. (Illus.). 283p. (C). 1989. text 45.00 (*1-55022-032-2*, Pub. by ECW) Genl Dist Srvs.

— Canadian Writers & Their Works Vol. 8: Poetry. (Illus.). 412p. (C). 1992. text 45.00 (*1-55022-063-2*, Pub. by ECW) Genl Dist Srvs.

— Canadian Writers & Their Works Vol. 9: Fiction. (Illus.). 373p. (C). 1987. text 45.00 (*0-920763-79-0*, Pub. by ECW) Genl Dist Srvs.

— Canadian Writers & Their Works Vol. 9: Poetry. (Illus.). 271p. (C). 1985. text 45.00 (*0-920802-47-8*, Pub. by ECW) Genl Dist Srvs.

— Canadian Writers & Their Works Vol. 10: Fiction. (Illus.). 294p. (C). 1989. text 45.00 (*0-920763-85-5*, Pub. by ECW) Genl Dist Srvs.

— Canadian Writers & Their Works Vol. XI: Neil Bissoondath, Austin Clarke, Joy Kogawa, Rohinton Mistry, & Josef Skvorecky, Vol. 11. (Illus.). 300p. 50.00 (*1-55022-213-9*, Pub. by ECW) Genl Dist Srvs.

— Canadian Writers & Their Works Vol. XI: Roo Borson, Lorna Crozier, Mary di Michele, Erin Moure, & Sharon Thesen. (Illus.). 340p. 50.00 (*1-55022-217-1*, Pub. by ECW) Genl Dist Srvs.

— Canadian Writers & Their Works Vol. XII: Dennis Cooley, Christopher Dewdney, Steve McCaffery, Fred Wah, & Tom Wayman. (Illus.). 300p. 50.00 (*1-55022-219-8*, Pub. by ECW) Genl Dist Srvs.

— Canadian Writers & Their Works Vol. XII: Sandra Birdsell, Timothy Findley, W. P. Kinsella, & David Adams Richards. (Illus.). 350p. 50.00 (*1-55022-215-5*, Pub. by ECW) Genl Dist Srvs.

Lecker, Robert & David, Jack, eds. The Annotated Bibliography of Canada's Major Authors, Vol. I. 263p. (C). 1979. text 45.00 (*0-920802-02-8*) Genl Dist Srvs.

— The Annotated Bibliography of Canada's Major Authors, Vol. 2. 277p. (C). 1980. text 45.00 (*0-920802-38-9*) Genl Dist Srvs.

— The Annotated Bibliography of Canada's Major Authors, Vol. 3. 395p. (C). 1981. text 45.00 (*0-920802-23-0*) Genl Dist Srvs.

— The Annotated Bibliography of Canada's Major Authors, Vol. 4. 370p. (C). 1983. text 45.00 (*0-920802-52-4*); pap. text 28.00 (*0-920802-54-0*) Genl Dist Srvs.

— The Annotated Bibliography of Canada's Major Authors, Vol. 5. 480p. (C). 1984. text 45.00 (*0-920802-68-0*) Genl Dist Srvs.

— The Annotated Bibliography of Canada's Major Authors, Vol. 6. 448p. (C). 1985. text 45.00 (*0-920802-93-1*); pap. text 28.00 (*0-920802-95-8*) Genl Dist Srvs.

— The Annotated Bibliography of Canada's Major Authors, Vol. 7. 477p. (C). 1987. text 45.00 (*0-920763-11-1*); pap. text 28.00 (*0-920763-12-X*) Genl Dist Srvs.

— The Annotated Bibliography of Canada's Major Authors, Vol. 8. 576p. (C). 1993. text 50.00 (*1-55022-044-6*, Pub. by ECW) Genl Dist Srvs.

— The Annotated Bibliography of Canada's Major Authors, Vol. 8. 576p. (C). 1993. pap. text 28.00 (*1-55022-043-8*) Genl Dist Srvs.

— The Annotated Bibliography of Canada's Major Authors: Marian Engel, Anne Hebert, Robert Kroetsch, Stephen Leacock & Thomas Raddall, Vol. 7. (G. K. Hall Reference Ser.). 450p. 1988. 55.00 (*0-8161-8796-7*, Hall Reference) Macmillan.

Lecker, Robert, ed. see Artibise, A.

Lecker, Robert, jt. ed. see David, Jack.

Lecker, Robert, ed. see Donovan, Josephine.

Lecker, Robert, ed. see Lyons, Charles R.

Lecker, Robert, ed. see Matthews, John T.

Lecker, Robert, ed. see Page, Norman.

Lecker, Robert, ed. see Seidel, Michael.

Lecker, Robert, ed. see Vivante, Paolo.

Lecker, Seymour. Homemade Semtex: C-4's Ugly Sister. (Illus.). 40p. 1991. pap. 12.00 (*0-87364-617-7*) Paladin Pr.

Lecker, Sidney. The Success Factor. LC 85-16135. 111p. reprint ed. pap. 34.50 (*0-8357-4245-8*, 203703300007) Bks Demand.

Leckey, Andrew. Global Investing, 1999 Edition: A Guide to the 50 Best Stocks in the World. 384p. 1999. mass mkt. 14.99 (*0-446-67495-8*, Pub. by Warner Bks) Little.

— Global Investing 2000 Edition: A Guide to the 50 Best Stocks in the World. 384p. 2000. mass mkt. 15.95 (*0-446-67496-6*, Pub. by Warner Bks) Little.

***Leckey, Andrew.** Lack of Money Is the Root of All Evil: Mark Twain's Common Sense Guide to Investing. 2001. 22.00 (*0-7352-0219-2*) PH Pr.

Leckey, Andrew. The 20 Hottest Investments for the 21st Century. LC 95-32764. (Illus.). 320p. 1995. pap. 14.95 (*0-8092-3339-8*) NTC Contemp Pub Co.

Leckey, Dave. Trading Western Softwood Lumber: The Basics. 192p. (Orig.). 1989. pap. 24.95 (*0-9621022-0-2*) Highland Oregon.

Leckey, Dolores. Blessings All Around Us: Savoring God's Gifts. 128p. 1999. pap. 8.95 (*1-878718-50-9*, Resurrection Pr) Catholic Bk Pub.

— Winter Music: A Life of Jessica Powers. LC 92-27486. 180p. (Orig.). 1992. pap. 12.95 (*1-55612-559-3*, LL1559) Sheed & Ward WI.

— Women & Creativity. (Madeleva Lectures, 1991). 1991. pap. 3.95 (*0-8091-3259-1*) Paulist Pr.

***Leckey, Dolores R.** Seven Essentials for the Spiritual Journey. LC 98-46774. 1999. pap. 11.95 (*0-8245-1783-0*) Crossroad NY.

Leckey, Dolores R., intro. One Body - Different Gifts, Many Roles: Reflections on the American Catholic Laity. 64p. (Orig.). 1987. pap. 4.95 (*1-55586-162-8*) US Catholic.

Leckey, Howard L. Tenmile Country & Its Pioneer Family Vols. I-VI: Genealogical History of the Upper Monongahela Valley, Pennsylvania. (Illus.). 399p. 1997. reprint ed. lib. bdg. 43.00 (*0-8328-7165-6*) Higginson Bk Co.

Leckey, Hugo. Set for Edwin Honig. (First Edition Ser.: Vol. 2, No. 3). (Illus.). (Orig.). 1973. pap. 1.50 (*0-916912-07-8*) Hellcoal Pr.

***Leckie, Barbara.** Culture & Adultery: The Novel, the News & the Law, 1857-1914. LC 99-17837. 1999. 37.50 (*0-8122-3498-7*) U of Pa Pr.

Leckie, Barbara. Robinton Mistry & His Works. (Canadian Author Studies). 55p. 1997. pap. 9.95 (*1-55022-329-1*, Pub. by ECW) LPC InBook.

Leckie, Dale A., jt. ed. see MacQueen, Roger W.

Leckie, David. The 1998 Human Rights Act Explained. LC 99-210009. (Point of Law Ser.). 1999. 50.00 (*0-11-702684-0*, Pub. by Statnry Office) Balogh.

Leckie, George C., ed. see Korschelt, Oscar.

Leckie, Jacqueline. To Labour with the State: The Fiji Public Service Association. LC 98-106423. 230p. 1997. pap. 29.95 (*1-877133-32-9*, Pub. by Univ Otago Pr) Intl Spec Bk.

Leckie, James O., jt. ed. see Kavanaugh, Michael C.

***Leckie, R. William, Jr. & Yuretich, Richard.** Investigating the Ocean: An Interactive Guide to the Science of Oceanography. (C). 1999. pap. 17.50 (*0-07-239094-8*) McGrw-H Hghr Educ.

***Leckie, Robert.** Challenge for the Pacific: The Bloody Six-Month Battle of Guadalcanal. LC 98-47407. (Illus.). 392p. 1999. reprint ed. pap. 15.95 (*0-306-80911-7*, Pub. by Da Capo) HarpC.

Leckie, Robert. Conflict: The History of the Korean War, 1950-1953. LC 96-15600. (Illus.). 480p. 1996. reprint ed. pap. 16.95 (*0-306-80716-5*) Da Capo.

— Delivered from Evil: The Saga of World War II - The First Complete One-Volume History. LC 86-46305. 1024p. 1988. reprint ed. pap. 22.00 (*0-06-091535-8*, PL 1535, Perennial) HarperTrade.

***Leckie, Robert.** Few Acres of Snow: The Saga of the French & Indian Wars. (Illus.). 2000. pap. text 18.95 (*0-471-39020-8*) Wiley.

Leckie, Robert. A Few Acres of Snow: The Saga of the French & Indian Wars, Vol. 103. Prigogine, I., ed. LC 98-31023. 388p. 1999. 30.00 (*0-471-24690-5*) Wiley.

— From Sea to Shining Sea: From the War of 1812 to the Mexican War; The Saga of America's Expansion. 60th ed. LC 92-56243. 672p. 1994. pap. 20.00 (*0-06-092254-0*) HarpC.

— George Washington's War: The Saga of the American Revolution. LC 92-52607. (Illus.). 688p. 1993. reprint ed. pap. 18.00 (*0-06-092215-X*, Perennial) HarperTrade.

— None Died in Vain: The Saga of the American Civil War. LC 89-45832. 704p. 1991. reprint ed. pap. 19.00 (*0-06-092116-1*, Perennial) HarperTrade.

— Okinawa: The Last Battle of World War II. 256p. 1996. pap. 13.95 (*0-14-017389-7*, Penguin Bks) Viking Penguin.

— Strong Men Armed: The United States Marines vs. Japan. LC 97-11830. (Illus.). 561p. 1997. reprint ed. pap. 20.00 (*0-306-80785-8*) Da Capo.

— Wars of America. 1998. 17.99 (*0-7858-0914-7*) Bk Sales Inc.

— The Wars of America: From 1600 to 1900, Vol. 1. LC 92-54863. (Illus.). 640p. 1993. pap. 17.00 (*0-06-092409-8*, Perennial) HarperTrade.

Leckie, Ross. The Authority of Roses. LC 97-203849. 112p. 1997. pap. 12.95 (*0-919626-90-4*, Pub. by Brick Bks) Genl Dist Srvs.

***Leckie, Ross.** The Bluffer's Guide to The Classics: Bluff Your Way in The Classics. (Bluffer's Guides Ser.). 64p. 1999. pap. 5.95 (*1-902825-48-9*) Oval Bks.

— Carthage. 2000. 27.00 (*0-86241-944-1*, Pub. by Canongate Books) Interlink Pub.

Leckie, Ross. Hannibal: The Novel. 245p. 1998. pap. 14.95 (*0-89526-385-8*) Regnery Pub.

— Scipio Africanus: The Man Who Defeated Hannibal. LC 98-10948. 304p. 1998. 19.95 (*0-89526-412-9*) Regnery Pub.

***Leckie, Shirley A.** Angie Debo: Pioneering Historian. LC 00-26210. (Oklahoma Western Biographies Ser.: Vol. 18). (Illus.). 256p. 2000. 26.95 (*0-8061-3256-6*) U of Okla Pr.

Leckie, Shirley A. Elizabeth Bacon Custer & the Making of a Myth. LC 92-50717. 1993. 27.95 (*0-8061-2501-2*) U of Okla Pr.

— Elizabeth Bacon Custer & the Making of a Myth. LC 92-50717. (Illus.). 416p. 1998. pap. 17.95 (*0-8061-3096-2*) U of Okla Pr.

Leckie, Shirley A., jt. auth. see Leckie, William H.

Leckie, Shirley A., ed. & intro. see Grierson, Alice K.

Leckie-Tarry, Helen. Language & Context: A Functional Linguistic Theory of Register. Birch, David, ed. LC 95-3907. 1995. pap. 22.95 (*1-85567-272-3*) St Martin.

Leckie, William H. The Buffalo Soldiers: A Narrative of the Negro Cavalry in the West. LC 67-15571. (Illus.). 1975. pap. 14.95 (*0-8061-1244-1*) U of Okla Pr.

— The Military Conquest of the Southern Plains. LC 63-17160. (Illus.). 295p. reprint ed. 91.50 (*0-8357-9736-8*, 201623600002) Bks Demand.

Leckie, William H. & Leckie, Shirley A. Unlikely Warriors: General Benjamin H. Grierson & His Family. LC 84-40275. (Illus.). xv, 384p. 1998. per. 18.95 (*0-8061-3027-X*) U of Okla Pr.

Lecklider, G. Robert & Lund, John W. Road Design Handbook. 3rd ed. (Illus.). 151p. (C). 1976. pap. text 15.00 (*0-9619389-0-0*) J W Lund.

Lecklider, Jane K. Cleanness: Structure & Meaning. LC 97-15602. 292p. 1997. 75.00 (*0-85991-519-0*) Boydell & Brewer.

Leckman, James F. & Cohen, Donald J., eds. Tourette's Syndrome--Tics, Obsessions, Compulsions: Developmental Psychopathology & Clinical Care. 2nd ed. LC 98-9988. 600p. 1998. 125.00 (*0-471-16037-7*) Wiley.

Leckridge, Bob. Homeopathy in Primary Care. LC 96-37984. 1997. pap. text 29.95 (*0-443-05521-1*) Church.

Lecky, Prescott. Self-Consistency: A Theory of Personality. LC 82-82238. 144p. 1982. pap. 6.95 (*0-87208-221-0*) Shoeless Pub.

— Self-Consistency: A Theory of Personality. rev. ed. LC 93-81260. 176p. (C). 1994. pap. 12.95 (*0-87208-310-1*) Shoeless Pub.

***Lecky-Thompson, Roy.** Constructive Appraisals. LC 99-37538. (Self-Development for Success Ser.: Vol. 12). 96p. 1999. pap. 12.95 (*0-8144-7058-0*) AMACOM.

Lecky, William E. Democracy & Liberty, Set. LC 80-82371. 1981. reprint ed. 20.00 (*0-913966-80-0*); reprint ed. pap. 10.00 (*0-913966-81-9*) Liberty Fund.

— Historical & Political Essays. LC 76-99707. (Essay Index Reprint Ser.). 1977. 23.95 (*0-8369-1973-4*) Ayer.

— History of England in the Eighteenth Century, 7 vols. rev. ed. LC 68-57226. reprint ed. 540.00 (*0-404-03930-8*) AMS Pr.

— History of European Morals: From Augustus to Charlemagne, 2 vols. unabridged ed. 200p. 1998. reprint ed. 90.00 (*0-936128-86-0*) De Young Pr.

— History of European Morals from Augustus to Charlemagne, 2 vols., 1 bk. 3rd ed. LC 74-25764. (European Sociology Ser.). 912p. 1975. reprint ed. 59.95 (*0-405-06518-3*) Ayer.

— History of Ireland in the Eighteenth Century, 5 vols. LC 70-77896. reprint ed. 385.00 (*0-404-03940-5*) AMS Pr.

— A History of Ireland in the Eighteenth Century. LC 78-184286. (Classics of British Historical Literature Ser.). 565p. reprint ed. pap. 175.20 (*0-8357-8907-1*, 205677200085) Bks Demand.

— A History of Ireland in the Eighteenth Century, 5 vols., Set. 1972. reprint ed. 55.00 (*0-403-03601-1*) Scholarly.

Leclair. Clinical Laboratory Science: Exam Review. (C). 1999. pap. text 31.95 (*0-7216-4957-2*, W B Saunders Co) Harcrt Hlth Sci Grp.

LeClair, Allen K. The Home Storage Checklist. 2nd rev. ed. 72p. 1996. wbk. ed. 11.95 (*0-9653078-1-6*) Griffin Publng.

Leclair, Charles. Color in Contemporary Painting: Integrating Practice & Theory. (Illus.). 224p. 1997. pap. text 27.50 (*0-8230-0741-3*) Watsn-Guptill.

Leclair, Debbie T., et al. Integrity Management: A Guide to Managing Legal & Ethical Issues in the Workplace. LC 97-21063. 181p. 1998. write for info. (*1-879852-55-1*) Univ Tampa.

Leclair, Jean-Marie. Jean-Marie LeClair: Sonatas for Violin & Basso Continuo, Opus 1. Preston, Robert E., ed. (Recent Researches in Music of the Baroque Era Ser.: Vol. RRB76). (Illus.). xxvi, 177p. 1995. pap. 60.00 (*0-89579-324-5*) A-R Eds.

— Jean-Marie LeClair: Sonatas for Violin & Basso Continuo, Opus 2. Preston, Robert E., ed. (Recent Researches in Music of the Baroque Era Ser.: Vol. RRB58). (Illus.). xxi, 134p. 1988. pap. 50.00 (*0-89579-220-6*) A-R Eds.

— Jean-Marie Leclair: Sonatas for Violin & Basso Continuo, Opus 5. Preston, Robert E., ed. (Recent Researches in Music of the Baroque Era Ser.: Vol. RRB4). (Illus.). xxix, 77p. 1968. pap. 35.00 (*0-89579-008-4*) A-R Eds.

— Jean-Marie Leclair: Sonatas for Violin & Basso Continuo, Opus 5. Preston, Robert E., ed. (Recent Researches in Music of the Baroque Era Ser.: Vol. RRB5). (Illus.). 108p. 1968. pap. 40.00 (*0-89579-011-4*) A-R Eds.

— Jean-Marie Leclair Pt. 1: Sonatas for Violin & Basso Continuo, Op. 9. Preston, Robert, ed. (Recent Researches in Music of the Baroque Era Ser.: Vol. RRB10). (Illus.). 104p. 1970. pap. 40.00 (*0-89579-030-0*) A-R Eds.

— Jean-Marie Leclair Pt. 2: Sonatas for Violin & Basso Continuo, Op. 9; Op. 15. Preston, Robert, ed. (Recent Researches in Music of the Baroque Era Ser.: Vol. RRB11). (Illus.). 112p. 1971. pap. 40.00 (*0-89579-033-5*) A-R Eds.

***LeClair, Mark S.** International Commodity Markets & the Role of Cartels. (Illus.). 208p. 2000. text 64.95 (*0-7656-0516-3*) M E Sharpe.

LeClair, Mark S. Regional Integration & Global Free Trade: Addressing the Fundamental Conflicts. LC 96-79374. 128p. 1997. text 59.95 (*1-85972-571-0*, Pub. by Avebry) Ashgate Pub Co.

Leclair, Norman J. Chicken Expressions. (Illus.). 68p. 1992. spiral bd. 11.00 (*0-317-89539-7*) Normand Pub.

Leclair, Normand J. Chicken Expressions. 1991. pap. 9.95 (*0-9620331-0-3*) Normand Pub.

— Seafood Expressions. (Illus.). 312p. (Orig.). 1991. pap. 12.95 (*0-9620331-2-X*) Normand Pub.

LeClair, S. R., jt. auth. see Pao, Y. H.

LeClair, Tom. The Art of Excess: Mastery in Contemporary American Fiction. LC 88-31582. 256p. 1989. pap. text 15.95 (*0-252-06102-0*) U of Ill Pr.

— In the Loop: Don DeLillo & the Systems Novel. LC 87-10783. 260p. 1988. text 29.95 (*0-252-01483-9*) U of Ill Pr.

— Passing Off. LC 95-22746. 176p. 1996. 22.00 (*1-877946-77-X*) Permanent Pr.

LeClair, Tom & McCaffery, Larry, eds. Anything Can Happen: Interviews with Contemporary American Novelists. LC 82-2867. (Illus.). 320p. 1988. 9.95 (*0-252-00971-1*) U of Ill Pr.

LeClair, W. Forbes, jt. auth. see Hammond, Ruth.

LeClaire, David. Bridges to a Passionate Partnership: A Realistic Approach for Couples Who Want to Become Better Friends & Lovers. LC 96-76383. 232p. (Orig.). 1996. per. 12.95 (*0-9651055-3-9*) Equestrian Pr.

— How to Train Your Man: From the Mouths of Men Themselves. 232p. 1998. pap. 12.95 (*0-9651055-4-7*) Equestrian Pr.

Leclaire, Day. Accidental Wife. 1996. per. 3.25 (*0-373-03438-5*, 1-03438-8) Harlequin Bks.

— Accidental Wife. large type ed. (Fairytale Weddings Trilogy Ser.). 1996. per. 3.25 (*0-373-15684-7*) Harlequin Bks.

***Leclaire, Day.** The Baby Gift. (Romance Ser.). 2000. mass mkt. 3.50 (*0-373-03631-0*, 1036318) Harlequin Bks.

— The Baby Gift. large type ed. (Larger Print Ser.). 2000. mass mkt. 3.50 (*0-373-15877-7*, 1158773) Harlequin Bks.

Leclaire, Day. The Boss, the Baby & the Bride. (Romance Ser.). 1998. per. 3.50 (*0-373-03508-X*, 1-03508-8) Harlequin Bks.

— The Boss, the Baby & the Bride. large type ed. (Larger Print Ser.). 1998. per. 3.50 (*0-373-15754-1*, 1-15754-4) Harlequin Bks.

***Leclaire, Day.** The Boss, the Baby & the Bride. large type ed. 1999. 25.99 (*0-263-15925-6*) Mills & Boon.

— Bridegroom on Approval. (Romance Ser.: No. 3575). 1999. per. 3.50 (*0-373-03575-6*, 1-03575-7) Harlequin Bks.

— Bridegroom on Approval. large type ed. (Larger Print Ser.: No. 421). 1999. per. 3.50 (*0-373-15821-1*, 1-15821-1) Harlequin Bks.

— Bridegroom on Approval. large type ed. (Thorndike Harlequin Romance Ser.). 2000. 22.95 (*0-263-16371-7*) Mills & Boon.

— The Bride's Proposition. 2000. mass mkt. 3.50 (*0-373-03611-6*, 1-03611-0) Harlequin Bks.

Leclaire, Day. Un Defi Audacieux. (Horizon Ser.: No. 485). (FRE.). 1998. mass mkt. 3.50 (*0-373-39485-3*, 1-39485-7) Harlequin Bks.

***Leclaire, Day.** Her Secret Bodyguard. (Romance Ser.). 2000. mass mkt. 3.50 (*0-373-03591-8*) Harlequin Bks.

— Her Secret Bodyguard. large type ed. Vol. 437. 253p. 2000. per. 3.50 (*0-373-15837-8*) Harlequin Bks.

Leclaire, Day. Her Secret Santa. (Romance Ser.: No. 3486). 1997. per. 3.25 (*0-373-03486-5*, 1-03486-7) Harlequin Bks.

— Her Secret Santa. large type ed. 1997. per. 3.25 (*0-373-15732-0*) Harlequin Bks.

— In the Market. (Romance Ser.: No. 183). 1992. pap. 2.89 (*0-373-03183-1*, 1-03183-0) Harlequin Bks.

***Leclaire, Day.** Long-Lost Bride. large type ed. 1999. per. 3.50 (*0-373-15825-4*, Harlequin) Harlequin Bks.

— Long-Lost Bride. large type ed. (Harlequin Romance Ser.). 2000. 22.95 (*0-263-16408-X*) Mills & Boon.

— Long-Lost Bride: Fairytale Weddings. (Harlequin Romance Ser.). 1999. per. 3.50 (*0-373-03579-9*, Harlequin) Harlequin Bks.

Leclaire, Day. Mail-Order Bridegroom. LC 95-7056. (Romance Ser.). 185p. 1995. per. 2.99 (*0-373-03361-3*, 1-03361-2) Harlequin Bks.

— Mail-Order Bridegroom. (Promo Ser.). 1999. per. 4.50 (*0-373-21968-7*) Harlequin Bks.

— Make Believe Engagement (Bride's Bay) LC 96-2363. (Romance Ser.). 185p. 1996. per. 3.25 (*0-373-03404-0*, 1-03404-0) Harlequin Bks.

— Un Mariage de Conte de Fees. (Horizon Ser.: No. 518). (FRE.). 1999. mass mkt. 3.99 (*0-373-39518-3*, 1-39518-5) Harlequin Bks.

— The Miracle Wife: Kids & Kisses. (Romance Ser.: Vol. 3523). 1998. per. 3.50 (*0-373-03523-3*, 1-03523-7) Harlequin Bks.

— The Miracle Wife: Kids & Kisses. large type ed. (Larger Print Ser.: Vol. 369). 1998. per. 3.50 (*0-373-15769-X*, 1-15769-2) Harlequin Bks.

***Leclaire, Day.** The Miracle Wife: Kids & Kisses. large type ed. (Harlequin Ser.). 1999. 21.95 (*0-263-16079-3*) Mills & Boon.

Leclaire, Day. The Nine-Dollar Daddy: Texas Grooms Wanted! (Romance Ser.: No. 3543). 1999. per. 3.50 (*0-373-03543-8*, 1-03543-5) Harlequin Bks.

— The Nine-Dollar Daddy: Texas Grooms Wanted! large type ed. (Larger Print Ser.: No. 389). 1999. mass mkt. 3.50 (*0-373-15789-4*, 1-15789-0) Harlequin Bks.

***Leclaire, Day.** The Nine-Dollar Daddy: Texas Grooms Wanted! large type ed. 288p. 1999. 25.99 (*0-263-16139-0*, Pub. by Mills & Boon) Ulverscroft.

Leclaire, Day. Once a Cowboy . . . Back to the Ranch. (Romance Ser.). 1994. mass mkt. 2.99 (*0-373-03301-X*, 1-03301-8) Harlequin Bks.

— One Night Wife. 1995. per. 2.99 (*0-373-03376-1*) Harlequin Bks.

***Leclaire, Day.** The Perfect Solution: Heart of the West. 2000. per. 4.50 (*0-373-82594-3*) Harlequin Bks.

— Le Plus Beau Noel de Jackie. (Horizon Ser.: No. 537). (FRE.). 2000. mass mkt. 3.99 (*0-373-39537-X*, 1-39537-5, Harlequin French) Harlequin Bks.

— Une Seconde Chance pour Anna. (FRE.). 2000. mass mkt. 3.99 (*0-373-39544-2*) Harlequin Bks.

Leclaire, Day. The Secret Baby. (Baby Boom Ser.). 1997. per. 3.25 (*0-373-03457-1*, 1-03457-8) Harlequin Bks.

— The Secret Baby. large type ed. (Baby Boom Ser.). 1997. per. 3.25 (*0-373-15703-7*, 1-15703-1) Harlequin Bks.

***Leclaire, Day.** Shotgun Bridegroom. large type ed. (Romance Ser.). 1999. 21.95 (*0-263-16245-1*) Mills & Boon.

Leclaire, Day. Shotgun Bridegroom: White Weddings. 1999. per. 3.50 (*0-373-15810-6*, 1-15810-4) Harlequin Bks.

— Shotgun Bridegroom: White Weddings. 1999. per. 3.50 (*0-373-03564-0*, 1-03564-1) Harlequin Bks.

— Shotgun Marriage. 1997. per. 3.25 (*0-373-03440-7*, 1-03440-4) Silhouette.

— Shotgun Marriage. large type ed. (Fairytale Weddings Trilogy Ser.). 1997. per. 3.25 (*0-373-15686-3*) Harlequin Bks.

— Temporary Husband. 1996. per. 3.25 (*0-373-03433-4*, 1-03433-9) Harlequin Bks.

— Temporary Husband. large type ed. (Fairytale Weddings Trilogy Ser.). 1996. per. 3.25 (*0-373-15679-0*) Harlequin Bks.

— To Catch a Ghost. (Romance Ser.). 1993. per. 2.99 (*0-373-03285-4*, 1-03285-3) Harlequin Bks.

***Leclaire, Day.** To Marry a Sheikh. (Romance Ser.: Bk. 3623). 2000. mass mkt. 3.50 (*0-373-03623-X*, 1-03623-5) Harlequin Bks.

Leclaire, Day. The Twenty-Four-Hour Bride. (Romance Ser.). 1998. per. 3.50 (*0-373-03495-4*, 1-03495-8) Harlequin Bks.

— The Twenty-Four-Hour Bride. large type ed. (Whirlwind Weddings Ser.). 1998. per. 3.50 (*0-373-15741-X*, Harlequin) Harlequin Bks.

— Where There's a Will. (Family Continuity Program Ser.: No. 6). 1999. mass mkt. 4.50 (*0-373-82154-9*, 1-82154-5) Harlequin Bks.

— A Wholesale Arrangement. large type ed. LC 93-20048. 247p. 1993. reprint ed. 13.95 (*1-56054-681-6*) Thorndike Pr.

— Who's Holding the Baby? 1994. per. 2.99 (*0-373-03338-9*, 1-03338-0) Harlequin Bks.

Leclaire, Day, jt. auth. see Jordan, Penny.

Leclaire, Day, jt. auth. see Lewis Thompson, Vickie.

LeClaire, Linda. Yes, God Speaks to Women, Too! A Message of--Health, Healing & Hope. LC 98-61249. 254p. 1998. write for info. (*0-9665696-0-1*) Visual Eyes.

LeClaire, Serge. A Child Is Being Killed: On Primary Narcissism & the Death Drive. LC 97-23343. (Meridian, Crossing Aesthetics Ser.). 1998. write for info. (*0-8047-3140-3*) Stanford U Pr.

— A Child Is Being Killed: On Primary Narcissism & the Death Drive. Hays, Marie-Claude, tr. LC 97-23343. (Meridian, Crossing Aesthetics Ser.). 85p. 1998. pap. 12.95 (*0-8047-3141-1*) Stanford U Pr.

Leclaire, Serge. Psychoanalyzing: On the Order of the Unconscious & the Practice of the Letter. Kamauf, Peggy, tr. from ENG. LC 97-21856. (Meridian, Crossing Aesthetics Ser.). 125p. 1998. 32.50 (*0-8047-2910-7*) Stanford U Pr.

— Psychoanalyzing: On the Order of the Unconscious & the Practice of the Letter. Kamuf, Peggy, tr. from ENG. LC 97-21856. (Meridian, Crossing Aesthetics Ser.). 125p. 1998. pap. 12.95 (*0-8047-2911-5*) Stanford U Pr.

Leclant, J. & Clerc, G. Inventaire Bibliographique des Isiaca (IBIS), Vol. 4, R-Z. LC 72-340099. (Études Preliminaires aux Religions Orientales dans l'Empire Romain Ser.: Vol. 18). (FRE.). ix, 374p. 1990. 134.00 (*90-04-09247-1*) Brill Academic Pubs.

Leclerc, Annette, et al. Dictionnaire d'Epidemiologie. (FRE.). 143p. 1990. write for info. (*0-7859-0506-5*, 2876710382) Fr & Eur.

***LeClerc, Charles.** Bibliotheca Americana, 2 vols. 1999. reprint ed. 95.00 (*1-57898-147-6*) Martino Pubng.

Leclerc, Denise, ed. The Crisis of Abstraction in Canada: The 1950s. (Illus.). 272p. 1996. pap. text 39.95 (*0-88884-624-X*, Pub. by Natl Gallery) U Ch Pr.

Leclerc, Eloi. Francis of Assisi: Return to the Gospel. Arnandez, Richard, tr. 1983. 15.95 (*0-8199-0854-1*, Frncscn Herld) Franciscan Pr.

— The Wisdom of the Poor One of Assisi. Johnson, Marie-Louise, tr. from FRE. LC 91-27207. 118p. 1992. reprint ed. pap. 8.95 (*0-932727-45-X*); reprint ed. lib. bdg. 15.95 (*0-932727-47-6*) Hope Pub Hse.

— The Wisdom of the Poverello. Johnson, Marie-Louise, tr. 126p. 1989. reprint ed. pap. 6.95 (*0-8199-0147-4*, Frncscn Herld) Franciscan Pr.

Leclerc, Felix. The Madman, the Kite & the Island. 153p. 1983. pap. 3.95 (*0-7736-7054-8*) Genl Dist Srvs.

Leclerc, Gustavo. Urban Latino Cultures La Vida Latina in L.A. LC 98-58087. 1999. pap. write for info. (*0-7619-1620-2*) Sage.

— Urban Latino Cultures: La Vida Latina in L.A. LC 98-58087. 3p. 1999. 65.00 (*0-7619-1619-9*) Sage.

Leclerc, Ivor. The Nature of Physical Existence. 382p. 1986. reprint ed. pap. text 25.50 (*0-8191-4853-9*) U Pr of Amer.

— The Philosophy of Nature. LC 85-9607. (Studies in Philosophy & the History of Philosophy: No. 14). 234p. 1986. reprint ed. pap. 72.60 (*0-7837-9112-7*, 204991400004) Bks Demand.

Leclerc, Ivor, ed. The Philosophy of Leibniz & the Modern World. LC 72-1346. 322p. 1973. reprint ed. pap. 99.90 (*0-7837-9882-2*, 206060800006) Bks Demand.

Leclerc, J. C. & Cornu, A. Neutron Activation Analysis Tables: Analyses per Activation. LC 74-77710. 72p. reprint ed. pap. 30.00 (*0-608-14048-1*, 202401400035) Bks Demand.

Leclerc, Jacinthe, tr. see Juillard, Andre.

LeClerc, Jacinthe, tr. see Pichard, Georges & Von Sacher-Masoch, Leopold.

Leclerc, Jacinthe, tr. see Pratt, Hugo.

LeClerc, Paul O., jt. ed. see Graubard, Stephen R.

LeClercq, Anne S. An Antebellum Plantation Household: Including the South Carolina Low Country Receipts & Remedies of Emily Wharton Sinkler. LC 96-9970. (Illus.). 120p. 1996. 19.95 (*1-57003-129-0*) U of SC Pr.

Leclercq, D. & Bruno, J., eds. Item Banking: Interactive Testing & Self-Assessment. (NATO ASI Series F: Computer & Systems Sciences, Special Programme AET: Vol. 112). viii, 263p. 1993. 71.95 (*0-387-56653-8*) Spr-Verlag.

Leclercq, Dom H. & Marron, Henri. Dictionnaire d'Archeologie Chretienne et de Liturgie, 28 vols., Set. (FRE.). 1903. 2995.00 (*0-8288-6892-1*, M-6342) Fr & Eur.

Leclercq, Jacques, tr. see Verlaine, Paul M.

***Leclercq, Jean.** From Grace to Grace: Memoirs. LC 00-28083. 2000. pap. write for info. (*1-879007-26-6*) St Bedes Pubns.

Leclercq, Jean. Love of Learning & Desire for God: A Study of Monastic Culture. 3rd ed. LC 60-53004. viii, 282p. 1982. pap. 18.00 (*0-8232-0407-3*) Fordham.

— A Second Look at Saint Bernard. Said, Marie-Bernard, tr. from FRE. (Cistercian Studies: No. 105).Tr. of Nouveau Visage de Saint Bernard. 150p. 1991. 35.95 (*0-87907-605-4*); pap. 19.95 (*0-87907-405-1*) Cistercian Pubns.

— St. Bernard on Women. 1989. 34.95 (*0-318-41660-3*); pap. 16.95 (*0-318-41661-1*) Cistercian Pubns.

— Women & St. Bernard of Clairvaux. Said, Marie-Bernard, tr. from FRE. (Cistercian Studies: No. 104).Tr. of La/Femmes et les Femmes Daus l'Oeuvre de Saint Bernard. 171p. 1990. 34.95 (*0-87907-604-6*); pap. 16.95 (*0-87907-404-3*) Cistercian Pubns.

LeClercq, Jean, et al. The Spirituality of the Middle Ages. (History of Christian Spirituality Ser.: Vol. 2). 616p. 1982. reprint ed. 19.95 (*0-8164-2373-3*) Harper SF.

Leclercq, Jean, tr. see Bernard of Clairvaux.

Leclercq-k, Jacques & Albertazzi, Liliana. La Riviaere de Lin et Autres Fictions. LC 98-130997. (GER.). 119 p. 1997. write for info. (*2-86234-249-1*) Marval.

LeClercq, Terri. Expert Legal Writing. (Illus.). 184p. (Orig.). 1995. pap. 14.95 (*0-292-74688-1*); text 27.50 (*0-292-74687-3*) U of Tex Pr.

— Guide to Legal Writing Style. LC 95-76102. 244p. 1995. pap. write for info. (*0-316-16302-3*, 163023) Aspen Law.

Leclere, Adhemard. Le Buddhisme au Cambodge. LC 76-179215. reprint ed. 72.00 (*0-404-54843-1*) AMS Pr.

— Cambodge: Fetes Civiles et Religieuses. LC 77-87040. reprint ed. 47.50 (*0-404-16832-9*) AMS Pr.

— Contes Laotiens et Contes Cambodgiens: Recueillis, Traduits et Annotes. LC 70-179216. reprint ed. 49.50 (*0-404-54844-X*) AMS Pr.

— Histoire du Cambodge Depuis le Premier Siecle De Notre Ere. LC 73-179217. (FRE.). reprint ed. 82.50 (*0-404-54845-8*) AMS Pr.

LeClere, Christian, jt. ed. see Labelle, Jacques.

LeClere, Felicia B., jt. ed. see Hendershot, Gerry E.

Leclerq, Patricia R., tr. see Berlandier, Jean L.

LeCocq, Tracey, jt. auth. see Huber, Holly.

LeCocque, Andre, ed. Commitment & Commemoration: Jews, Christians, Muslims in Dialogue. LC 93-72787. 151p. 1994. text 25.95 (*0-913552-54-2*) Exploration Pr.

LeCoff, Albert, et al. Curators Focus: Turning in Context. LC 97-34004. (Illus.). 1997. pap. write for info. (*0-9624385-8-8*) Wood Turn Ctr.

LeCoff, Albert B. International Lathe-Turned Objects: Challenge IV. Silver, Eileen J. et al, eds. (Illus.). 68p. (Orig.). 1991. pap. text 16.00 (*0-9624385-3-7*) Wood Turn Ctr.

Lecoff, Albert B. Lathe-Turned Objects: An International Exhibition. Field, Carol & Silver, Eileen J., eds. LC 88-20688. (Illus.). 168p. 1988. text 40.00 (*0-9624385-1-0*); boxed set 40.00 (*0-9624385-0-2*) Wood Turn Ctr.

LeCoff, Albert B. Revolving Techniques: Clay - Glass - Metal - Wood. LeCoff, Tina C. et al, eds. (Illus.). 24p. (Orig.). 1992. pap. 6.00 (*0-9624385-4-5*) Wood Turn Ctr.

LeCoff, Albert B., ed. Challenge V: International Lathe-Turned Objects. (Illus.). 74p. (Orig.). 1994. pap. 20.00 (*0-9624385-7-X*) Wood Turn Ctr.

Lecoff, Albert B., ed. International Lathe-Turning: A Sampling of Papers from the 1993 World Turning Conference. 1997. pap. 20.00 (*0-9624385-5-3*) Wood Turn Ctr.

— Lathe-Turned Objects: An International Exhibition. 168p. 1988. pap. 29.95 (*0-9624385-2-9*) Wood Turn Ctr.

LeCoff, Tina C., ed. see LeCoff, Albert B.

Lecoffre, Yves. Cavitation: Bubble Trackers. (Illus.). 416p. (C). 1999. text 88.00 (*90-5410-783-9*, Pub. by A A Balkema) Ashgate Pub Co.

Lecointe, Jean. Dictionnaire des Synonymes et des Equivalences. (FRE.). 354p. 1993. pap. 19.95 (*0-7859-5625-5*, 2253061417) Fr & Eur.

Lecomber, Richard, jt. auth. see Barker, Terrence S.

LeCompte, Andrew. Creating Harmonious Relationships: A Practical Guide to the Power of True Empathy. LC 99-90511. 256p. 2000. pap. 16.95 (*0-9672741-6-8*) Atlantic Bks NH.

LeCompte, Brett A. Southwest Circle Quest: A Walkabout in the American Outback. LC 97-74934. (Illus.). 192p. 1998. pap. 12.00 (*0-925685-34-8*, Swallow Heart) Canyon Country Pubns.

LeCompte, I. C., ed. Roman des Romans. (Elliott Monographs: Vol. 14). 1974. reprint ed. 25.00 (*0-527-02617-4*) Periodicals Srv.

Lecompte, Janet, ed. see French, Emily.

LeCompte, Margaret D., et al, eds. The Handbook of Qualitative Research in Education. (Illus.). 881p. 1992. text 59.95 (*0-12-440570-3*) Acad Pr.

LeCompte, Margaret D. & Preissle, Judith. Ethnography & Qualitative Design in Educational Research. 2nd ed. (Illus.). 425p. 1993. text 55.00 (*0-12-440575-4*) Acad Pr.

LeCompte, Margaret D. & Schensul, Jean J. Analyzing & Interpreting Ethnographic Data. LC 99-6243. (Ethnographer's Toolkit Ser.: Vol. 5). (Illus.). 264p. 1999. pap. 19.95 (*0-7619-8974-9*) AltaMira Pr.

***LeCompte, Margaret D. & Schensul, Jean J.** Designing & Conducting Ethnographic Research. LC 98-40070. (Ethnographer's Toolkit Ser.: Vol. 1). (Illus.). 240p. 1999. pap. 19.95 (*0-7619-8975-7*) AltaMira Pr.

LeCompte, Margaret D., et al. Giving up on School: Student Dropouts & Teacher Burnouts. LC 91-28760. 312p. 1991. text 65.95 (*0-8039-3490-4*, D1478) Corwin Pr.

— Researcher Roles & Research Partnerships. LC 99-6349. (Ethnographer's Toolkit Ser.: Vol. 6). (Illus.). 192p. 1999. pap. 18.95 (*0-7619-8973-0*) AltaMira Pr.

LeCompte, Margaret D., jt. auth. see Bennett, Kathleen P.

LeCompte, Margaret D., jt. auth. see Schensul, Jean J.

***Lecompte, Mary Lou.** Cowgirls of the Rodeo: Pioneer Professional Athletes. 2000. pap. 16.95 (*0-252-06874-2*) U of Ill Pr.

Lecomte, A., et al, eds. Logical Aspects of Computational Linguistics: Second International Conference, LACL '97, Nancy, France, September 22-24, 1997, Selected Papers. LC 99-14930. (Lecture Notes in Computer Science Ser.: Vol. 1582). xi, 251p. 1999. pap. 52.00 (*3-540-65751-7*) Spr-Verlag.

Lecomte, Barbara J. Aphasia: What Is It? 16p. 1995. 14.95 (*0-937857-04-1*, 1550) Speech Bin.

Lecomte, Bernard, jt. auth. see Lesourne, Jacques.

Lecomte, Eva. Paula.Tr. of Paula la Pequena Valdense. (SPA.). 200p. 1987. pap. 5.20 (*0-7399-0295-4*, 2339.1) Rod & Staff.

Lecomte, Eva. Paula, the Waldensian. 191p. (J). (gr. 3-7). 1997. pap. 6.95 (*1-881545-76-8*) Angelas Bkshelf.

— Paula, the Waldensian. Strong, W. M., tr. 433p. (J). (gr. 3-7). 1942. pap. 7.99 (*0-87213-511-X*) Loizeaux.

Lecomte, Monia, jt. ed. see Scriven, Michael.

***Lecomte, Paul.** Polluted Sites: Remediation of Soils & Groundwater. (Illus.). 220p. 1999. 58.50 (*90-5410-784-7*, Pub. by A A Balkema) Ashgate Pub Co.

Lecomte, Paul & Mariotti, Claudio, eds. Handbook of Diagnostic Procedures for Petroleum-Contaminated Sites. LC 96-39429. 210p. 1997. 130.00 (*0-471-97108-1*) Wiley.

Lecomte, Serge. Crimson Rice. limited ed. 14.95 (*0-685-40173-1*) Librado Pr.

LeComte, Serge, tr. see Alekseev, A. I.

Lecomte, Serge, tr. see Khlebnikov, Kirill T.

Leconte De Lisle, Charles-Rene-Marie. Poemes Barbares. (Poesie Ser.). (FRE.). pap. 16.95 (*2-07-032326-9*) Schoenhof.

Leconte, Emile & Clerget, Charles E. Sourcebook of Elegant Historic Ornament. LC 95-32794. (Pictorial Archive Ser.). (Illus.). 80p. 1995. pap. 7.95 (*0-486-28709-2*) Dover.

LeConte, Emma. When the World Ended: The Diary of Emma LeConte. Miers, Earl S., ed. LC 87-5937. xxxii, 124p. 1987. reprint ed. pap. 8.95 (*0-8032-8151-X*, Bison Books) U of Nebr Pr.

LeConte, Frantz. La Tradition de l'Ennui Splenetique en France de Christine de Pisan a Baudelaire, Vol. 16. (Reading Plus Ser.). (FRE.). VII, 267p. (C). 1996. text 51.95 (*0-8204-2498-6*) P Lang Pubng.

LeConte, John L. & Horn, George H. Classification of the Coleoptera of North America: Smithsonian Miscellaneous Collections, Vol. 507. Sterling, Keir B., ed. LC 77-81103. (Biologists & Their World Ser.). 1978. reprint ed. lib. bdg. 51.95 (*0-405-10689-0*) Ayer.

Leconte, John L., ed. see Say, Thomas.

LeConte, Joseph. A Journal of Ramblings Through the High Sierras of California. LC 93-43686. (High Sierra Classics Ser.). (Illus.). 140p. 1994. pap. 7.95 (*0-939666-70-7*) Yosemite Assn.

***LeConte, Joseph.** Ware Sherman: A Journal of Three Months' Personal Experience in the Last Days of the Confederacy. LC 98-50885. 184p. 1999. pap. 12.95 (*0-8071-2395-1*) La State U Pr.

LeConte, Walter, jt. auth. see Gallagher, Mark.

Lecorche, P. P., jt. ed. see Dallmeyer, R. D.

LeCorgne, Margaret, jt. auth. see Martinez, Elsie.

Lecorne, Martin. Uptown Downtown Growing Up. 1987. pap. 10.00 (*0-940984-32-6*) Univ LA Lafayette.

LeCornu, Hilary, jt. auth. see Shulam, Joseph.

Lecorre, Emille, jt. auth. see Parma, Art.

Lecot, K., jt. compiled by see Balbin, I.

l'Ecotais, Emmanuelle De, see De l'Ecotais, Emmanuelle.

***Lecourt, Dominique.** The Mediocracy: French Philosophy since the Mid-1970's. Elliott, Gregory, tr. 240p. 2001. 27.00 (*1-85984-793-5*, Pub. by Verso) Norton.

Lecourtier, J. & Cartalos, M. V., eds. Cementing Technology & Procedures. (Illus.). 128p. (C). 1993. 265.00 (*2-7108-0649-5*, Pub. by Edits Technip) Enfield Pubs NH.

Lecourtier, J., jt. ed. see Toulhoat, H.

Lecouteux, Claude. Petit Dictionnaire de Mythologie Allemande. (FRE.). 286p. 1991. pap. 49.95 (*0-7859-7971-9*, 2726601014) Fr & Eur.

LeCouturier, Jacques. Intercession. Anomalous Publications Staff, ed. 170p. 1999. pap. 11.95 (*0-7392-0303-7*, PO3425) Morris Pubng.

Lecq, Fieke Van der, see Van der Lecq, Fieke.

Lecraw, Dan, jt. auth. see Conklin, David.

Lecraw, Donald J. & Morrison, Allen J., eds. Transnational Corporations & Business Strategy. (Readings in Transnational Corporations Ser.). 402p. 1996. pap. 29.95 (*0-415-14109-5*) Routledge.

Lecroix, Paul. Medieval Warrior, 1. 1999. 19.95 (*1-885440-48-0*) First Glance.

Lecrompe, Rene, ed. Caesar: De Bello Gallico - Index Verborum. xvi, 373p. 1968. write for info. (*0-318-71972-X*) G Olms Pubs.

— Caesar - De Bello Gallico - Index Verborum. xvi, 373p. 1968. write for info. (*0-318-71084-6*) G Olms Pubs.

— Caesar - De Bello Gallico. Index Verborum. xvi, 373p. 1968. write for info. (*0-318-70657-1*) G Olms Pubs.

LeCron, Leslie M. Magic Mind Power: Make It Work for You! 2nd ed. 176p. 1982. reprint ed. pap. 8.95 (*0-87516-496-X*) DeVorss.

— Self Hypnotism: The Technique & Its Use in Daily Living. 1970. mass mkt. 5.99 (*0-451-15984-5*, Sig) NAL.

Lecron, Leslie M. Self-Hypnotism: The Technique & Its Use in Daily Living. pap. 4.95 (*0-13-803486-9*, Reward) P-H.

LeCross, Christopher. Christopher LeCross' Rules for Winning Casino Blackjack. (Illus.). 50p. (Orig.). 1997. pap. 19.95 (*0-937408-74-3*) GMI Pubns Inc.

LeCross, Herman. LeCross' How to Play & Win at Blackjack. 50p. (Orig.). 1996. 20.00 (*0-937408-75-1*) GMI Pubns Inc.

An Asterisk (*) at the beginning of an entry indicates that the title is appearing for the first time.

L

LeCroy, Barbara & Holder, Bonnie. Bookwebs: A Brainstorm of Ideas for the Primary Classroom. (Illus.). 193p. 1994. pap. text 23.00 (*1-56308-109-1*) Teacher Ideas Pr.

LeCroy, C. Michael, jt. auth. see Dirschi, Douglas R.

LeCroy, Craig W. Case Studies in Social Work Practice. 296p. (C). 1992. pap. 38.50 (*0-534-15138-8*) Brooks-Cole.

Lecroy, Craig W. Case Studies in Social Work Practice. 2nd ed. LC 98-7745. 1998. 56.95 (*0-534-35656-7*) Brooks-Cole.

LeCroy, Craig W. Handbook of Child & Adolescent Treatment Manuals. LC 93-40136. 432p. 1994. 40.00 (*0-02-918485-1*) Free Pr.

LeCroy, Craig W., ed. Social Skills Training for Children & Youth. LC 83-228. (Child & Youth Services Ser.: Vol. 5, Nos. 3 & 4). 152p. 1983. text 39.95 (*0-86656-184-6*) Haworth Pr.

— Social Skills Training for Children & Youth. 152p. 1993. pap. 19.95 (*0-86656-229-X*) Haworth Pr.

***LeCroy, Dori & Moller, Peter.** Evolutionary Perspectives on Human Reproductive Behavior. LC 00-26920. 2000. pap. write for info. (*1-57331-254-1*) NY Acad Sci.

Lectorium Rosicrucianum Staff, ed. see De Petri, Catharose.

Lectorium Rosicrucianum Staff, tr. see De Petri, Catharose.

Lectorum Publications Staff. Deuda de Honor. 1995. pap. 153.95 (*84-01-00924-3*) Plaza.

— Enciclopedia de los Paises del Mundo, 10 vols. (SPA., Illus.). (gr. 7-12). 1999. 125.00 (*84-241-1980-0*) Everest SP.

— La Novia de Ultramar. 1997. pap. text 10.50 (*84-01-50801-0*) Lectorum Pubns.

— Tom Sawyer. (Illus.). (J). 1997. 15.95 (*84-241-5777-X*) Everest SP.

Lectorum Staff. Ceguera Asesina. 1998. pap. text 10.95 (*84-01-49288-2*) Lectorum Pubns.

— El Poder De la Espada. 1998. 24.95 (*84-01-49624-1*) Lectorum Pubns.

***Lecumberri, M. Luisa Garcia & Maidment, John A.** English Transcription Course. (An Arnold Publication). 192p. 2000. pap. 18.95 (*0-340-75978-X*, Pub. by E A) OUP.

Lecuona, E. Andalucia Suite Espagnole. 32p. 1984. pap. 7.95 (*0-7935-2515-2*, 00009231) H Leonard.

— Lecuona's Best Made Easier for You. 32p. 1984. pap. 5.95 (*0-7935-2401-6*, 00009281) H Leonard.

***Lecuona, Ernesto.** Suite Andaluca. 48p. 1998. pap. 9.95 (*0-7935-7971-6*) H Leonard.

LeCuyer, Annette W., ed. Mecanoo: Map 6. (Illus.). 1999. pap. 16.50 (*1-891197-05-3*) U Mich Arch.

— Studio Granda: Dreams & Other Realities. (John Dinkeloo Memorial Lectures). (Illus.). 48p. 1998. pap. 16.50 (*1-891197-03-7*) U Mich Arch.

LeCuyer, Annette W., jt. auth. see Libeskind, Daniel.

LeCuyer, Annette W., ed. see Sennett, Richard.

LeCuyer, Annette W., ed. see Vinoly, Rafael.

LeCuyer, E. J. College Mathematics with a Programming Language. (Undergraduate Texts in Mathematics Ser.). 1978. 35.00 (*0-387-90280-5*) Spr-Verlag.

LeCuyer, James M. A Brick for Offissa Pupp. (Illus.). 64p. (Orig.). 1989. pap. 8.00 (*0-912449-31-4*) Floating Island.

Lecuyer, Raymond. Historie de la Photographie. Bunnell, Peter C. & Sobieszek, Robert A., eds. LC 76-23050. (Sources of Modern Photography Ser.). (FRE., Illus.). 1979. reprint ed. lib. bdg. 40.00 (*0-405-09609-7*) Ayer.

L'Ecuyer, Rosalie E., ed. see Anders, Joyce J.

Ledbetter. Introductory Chemistry. 234p. (C). 1997. text, student ed. 19.37 (*0-8151-5691-X*, WCB McGr Hill) McGrw-H Hghr Educ.

Ledbetter, Bonnie, jt. auth. see Ainslie, Tom.

Ledbetter, Calvin R., Jr. Carpenter from Conway: George Washington Donaghey As Governor of Arkansas, 1909-1913. LC 92-29038. (Illus.). 320p. 1994. pap. text 18.00 (*1-55728-374-5*) U of Ark Pr.

Ledbetter, Cathy, jt. auth. see Dickler, Howard.

Ledbetter, Cynthia E. & Jones, Richard C. John Muir. LC 92-46763. (Pioneers Ser.). 112p. (J). 1993. lib. bdg. 25.27 (*0-86625-494-3*) Rourke Pubns.

Ledbetter, Cynthia E., jt. auth. see Fifer, Fred L.

Ledbetter, Dale. From Mother, with Love: Reflections on Achieving Sales Success. Gage, Randy, ed. (Sales Mastery Ser.). (Orig.). 1994. pap. 11.95 (*1-884667-01-5*) Prime Concepts Grp.

— Success Yearbook: Three Hundred Sixty-Five Days to Mastery. (Sales Mastery Ser.). 425p. 1994. pap. 15.95 (*1-884667-00-7*) Prime Concepts Grp.

— The Ultimate Sales Professional. Gaye, Randy, ed. (Sales Mastery Ser.). (Orig.). 1994. pap. 11.95 (*1-884667-02-3*) Prime Concepts Grp.

***Ledbetter, Darriel & Graham, Leland.** Graduation Exit Exam Preparation for Writing & Language Arts. Reiner, Angela, ed. 96p. (YA). (gr. 8-12). 2000. pap. text 10.95 (*0-86530-450-5*, IP 450-5) Incentive Pubns.

Ledbetter, Darriel, jt. auth. see Graham, Leland.

***Ledbetter, Darril & Graham, Leland.** Reading Bridge: 6th Grade. Willie, Kirsten et al, eds. (Illus.). 96p. (J). (gr. 6). 1999. pap., wbk. ed. 9.95 (*1-887923-13-6*, Pub. by Rainbow UT) Midpt Trade.

— Reading Bridge: 7th Grade. Willie, Kirsten et al, eds. (Illus.). 96p. (YA). (gr. 7). 1999. pap., wbk. ed. 9.95 (*1-887923-14-4*, Pub. by Rainbow UT) Midpt Trade.

— Reading Bridge: 8th Grade. Willie, Kirsten et al, eds. (Illus.). 96p. (YA). (gr. 8). 1999. pap., wbk. ed. 9.95 (*1-887923-15-2*, Pub. by Rainbow UT) Midpt Trade.

Ledbetter, David. Continuo Playing According to Handel. (Early Music Ser.: No. 12). (Illus.). 112p. 1990. pap. text 35.95 (*0-19-318433-8*) OUP.

— Harpsichord & Lute Music in Seventeenth Century France. LC 87-17041. (Illus.). 214p. 1988. 42.50 (*0-253-32707-5*) Ind U Pr.

Ledbetter, Frances M., jt. auth. see Melton, Dana D.

Ledbetter, Gail, jt. auth. see Ledbetter, Otis.

Ledbetter, H. & Lomax, John A. Buenas Noches, Irene: Black & White Nellie Edge I Can Read & Sing Big Book. Pike, D., ed. Pichardo, Hector, tr. from ENG. (SPA., Illus.). (J). (ps-2). 1993. pap. text 21.00 (*0-922053-27-8*) N Edge Res.

— Goodnight Irene Big Book: Black & White Nellie Edge I Can Read & Sing Big Book. Pike, D., ed. (Illus.). (J). (ps-2). 1988. pap. text 21.00 (*0-922053-08-1*) N Edge Res.

***Ledbetter, J. Otis.** Extending Your Heritage: Practical, Intentional Ways to Influence Your Family & Beyond. LC 99-59257. (Heritage Builders Ser.). 276p. 2000. pap. 10.99 (*1-56476-783-3*, Victor Bks) Chariot Victor.

— Family Fragrance: Practical, Intentional Ways to Fill Your Home with the Aroma of Love. (Heritage Builders Ser.). 276p. 2000. pap. 10.99 (*0-7814-3375-4*) Chariot Victor.

Ledbetter, J. Otis. Family Traditions. LC 98-34149. 1998. pap. 9.99 (*1-56476-753-1*, Victor Bks) Chariot Victor.

***Ledbetter, J. Otis.** Family Traditions: Practical, Interntional Ways to Strengthen Your Family Identity. (Heritage Builders Ser.). 276p. 2000. pap. 10.99 (*0-7814-3376-2*) Chariot Victor.

Ledbetter, J. Otis & Bruner, Kurt. The Heritage: How to Be Intentional about the Legacy You Leave. 272p. 1997. pap. 10.99 (*1-56476-694-2*, Victor Bks) Chariot Victor.

Ledbetter, J. Otis, jt. auth. see Bruner, Kurt D.

Ledbetter, J. T. Mark Van Doren. LC 96-7124. (American University Studies XXIV: Vol. 67). XII, 175p. (C). 1997. 35.95 (*0-8204-3334-9*) P Lang Pubng.

Ledbetter, James. Made Possible By ... The Death of Public Broadcasting in the United States. LC 97-38229. 280p. 1997. 25.00 (*1-85984-904-0*, Pub. by Verso) Norton.

— Made Possible By . . . The Death of Public Broadcasting in the United States. 288p. 1998. pap. 15.00 (*1-85984-029-9*, Pub. by Verso) Norton.

Ledbetter, Jim. First-Class Cricket: A Complete Record 1937. 251p. 1993. pap. 59.00 (*1-874524-04-1*, Pub. by Limlow Bks) St Mut.

Ledbetter, Jim & Wynne-Thomas, Peter. First-Class Cricket: A Complete Record 1939. 252p. 1992. 59.00 (*1-874524-00-9*, Pub. by Limlow Bks) St Mut.

Ledbetter, Joe O. Air Pollution Pt. 1: Analysis. LC 77-160112. (Environmental Health Engineering Textbooks Ser.: Vol. 2). (Illus.). 440p. reprint ed. pap. 136.40 (*0-8357-5284-4*, 202900100058) Bks Demand.

— Air Pollution Pt. 2: Prevention & Control. LC 77-160112. (Environmental Health Engineering Textbooks Ser.: Vol. 2). 304p. pap. 94.30 (*0-7837-0024-5*, 202900100059) Bks Demand.

Ledbetter, Joe O., jt. auth. see Gloyna, Earnest F.

Ledbetter, Kathryn & Hoagwood, Terence Allan, intros. Keepsake for MDCCCXXIX. LC 99-28755. (Scholars' Facsimiles & Reprints Ser.: Vol. 525). 1999. reprint ed. 50.00 (*0-8201-1525-8*) Schol Facsimiles.

Ledbetter, Kenneth W., jt. auth. see Wall, Stephen D.

Ledbetter Lusk Gallery Staff, jt. auth. see Umbreit, Jeane.

Ledbetter, M. L. General Biology. 81p. (C). 1993. teacher ed. 16.11 (*1-56870-056-3*) RonJon Pub.

Ledbetter, Marie, jt. auth. see Thiel, Linda.

Ledbetter, Mark. Victims & the Postmodern Narrative: or Doing Violence to the Body: An Ethic of Reading & Writing. LC 95-17626. (Studies in Literature & Religion). 172p. 1996. text 49.95 (*0-312-12863-0*) St Martin.

— Virtuous Intentions: The Religious Dimension of Narrative. 100p. 1989. 20.95 (*1-55540-394-8*, 01 01 66); pap. 13.95 (*1-55540-395-6*, 01 01 66) OUP.

Ledbetter, Mary E. Writing Portfolio Activities Kit: Ready to Use Management Techniques & Writing Activities for Grades 7-12. LC 97-40860. 400p. 1997. spiral bd. 29.95 (*0-87628-938-3*) Ctr Appl Res.

***Ledbetter, Mary Ellen.** Writing Research Projects Activities Kit: Ready-to-use Lessons & Activities to Build Research & Writing Skills for Grades 7-12. LC 99-39211. 2000. write for info. (*0-13-022816-8*) P-H.

Ledbetter, Mary L. Cell Biology. 98p. (C). 1993. student ed. 16.11 (*1-56870-042-3*) RonJon Pub.

Ledbetter, Otis & Ledbetter, Gail. The Family Fragrance. LC 98-4469. 272p. 1998. pap. 9.99 (*1-56476-696-9*, Victor Bks) Chariot Victor.

Ledbetter, Richard & Dwyer, William. Investigating Lake Iluko: Classroom Edition. (Illus.). 91p. (YA). (gr. 6-12). 1997. teacher ed., ring bd. 49.95 (*1-888573-03-1*, LI501) Learning Team.

Ledbetter, Steven, ed. see Marenzio, Luca.

Ledbetter, Steven, ed. see Sullivan, Arthur & Gilbert, William S.

***Ledbetter, Suzann.** East of Peculiar. 2000. per. 5.99 (*1-55166-597-2*, Mira Bks) Harlequin Bks.

Ledbetter, Suzann. Pure Justice. 1997. mass mkt. 5.99 (*0-451-19194-3*, Sig) NAL.

Ledbetter, William B., jt. auth. see Collier, Courtland.

Ledbetter, William B., ed. see National Research Council Staff.

Ledbury, Ron, ed. DuBay's LUBA Digest, Vol. 2. 550p. 1995. 285.00 (*1-888181-03-6*) NW Law Pubng.

Ledd, Paul. Shelter: Hanging Moon, No. 2. 256p. (Orig.). 1980. mass mkt. 1.95 (*0-89083-637-X*, Zebra Kensgtn) Kensgtn Pub Corp.

— Shelter: Savage Night, No. 15. 1983. mass mkt. 2.25 (*0-685-07875-2*, Zebra Kensgtn) Kensgtn Pub Corp.

— Shelter: Wichita Gunman, No. 16. 1983. pap. 2.25 (*0-8217-1299-3*, Zebra Kensgtn) Kensgtn Pub Corp.

Ledda, A., ed. Vascular Andrology: Erectile Dysfunction/Priapism Varicocele. (Illus.). 88p. 1996. pap. 49.50 (*3-540-59472-8*) Spr-Verlag.

Ledden, Carol. The Snack Sneak: Logic Games, Mysteries & Quests. (Illus.). 72p. 1993. pap. 9.95 (*1-55037-332-3*, Pub. by Annick) Firefly Bks Ltd.

***Ledderose, Lothar.** Ten Thousand Things: Module & Mass Production in Chinese Art. LC 99-34118. 2000. 60.00 (*0-691-00669-5*, Pub. by Princeton U Pr) Cal Prin Full Svc.

***Leddick, David.** George Platt Lynes. 2000. 39.99 (*3-8228-6403-X*) Taschen Amer.

— Homoerotic Art of Pavel Tchelitchev. (Illus.). 134p. 1999. 85.00 (*1-893450-04-X*) Elysium Pr.

Leddick, David. Intimate Companions: A Triography of George Platt Lynes, Paul Cadmus, Lincoln kirstein, & Their Circle. LC 99-34004. 336p. 1999. text 29.95 (*0-312-20898-7*) St Martin.

— The Male Nude. (Klotz Ser.). (Illus.). 1998. pap. 29.99 (*3-8228-7966-5*) Taschen Amer.

***Leddick, David.** Male Nude. 1998. 38.99 (*3-8228-7655-0*) Benedikt Taschen.

Leddick, David. Men in the Sun: A Beach Companion. (Illus.). 96p. 1999. pap. 16.95 (*0-7893-0266-7*, Pub. by Universe) St Martin.

— My Worst Date. 3rd ed. 272p. 1998. pap. 12.95 (*0-312-18138-8*) St Martin.

— Naked Men: Pioneering Male Nudes. (Illus.). 1997. 35.00 (*0-614-28247-0*) Universe.

***Leddick, David.** Naked Men, Too: Liberating the Male Nude, 1950-2000. (Illus.). 144p. 2000. text 35.00 (*0-7893-0396-5*, Pub. by Universe) St Martin.

— Never Eat In. 2000. 24.00 (*1-85242-655-1*) Serpents Tail.

— Sex Squad. LC 98-35891. 304p. 1998. text 22.95 (*0-312-18174-4*) St Martin.

***Leddick, David.** Sex Squad. 256p. 2000. pap. 12.95 (*0-312-24326-X*) St Martin.

Leddick, George R., jt. auth. see Borders, L. D.

Leddy, jt. auth. see Roach.

Leddy, J. & Wightman, R. M., eds. New Directions in Electroanalytical Chemistry. LC 95-83755. (Proceedings Ser.: Vol. 96-9). (Illus.). 408p. 1996. 59.00 (*1-56677-161-7*) Electrochem Soc.

Leddy, Johna, ed. see Symposium on New Directions in Electroanalytical Chemistry II, et al.

Leddy, Susan & Pepper, Mae J. Conceptual Bases of Professional Nursing. 4th ed. LC 97-42746. 528p. 1998. pap. text 33.95 (*0-397-55277-7*) Lppncott W & W.

Leddy, Tracy. Allison's Shadow. LC 82-61020. 124p. (Orig.). 1982. pap. 12.00 (*0-89142-040-1*) Sant Bani Ash.

— The Song of Everything. 2nd ed. (Illus.). 160p. 1995. pap. 16.00 (*0-9649601-5-X*) Quail Hill.

Lede, Naomi W. Mary Allen College: Its Rich History, Pioneering Spirit, & Continuing Tradition. 104p. (YA). 1995. 24.95 (*0-9646839-0-3*) NAAMAC.

— Precious Memories of a Black Socialite: A Narrative of the Life & Times of Constance Houston Thompson. LC 91-65957. 300p. (Orig.). 1991. 24.95 (*0-9630007-0-5*) Lede Consult.

— Samuel W. Houston & His Contemporaries: A Documentary History of Education. 348p. (Orig.). 1991. pap. 16.00 (*0-9630007-1-3*) Lede Consult.

Ledeboer, Suzanne, ed. see Griffin Printing Staff.

Ledebour, K. F. Icones Plantarum Novarum Vel Imperfecte Cognitarum Floram Rossicam. (C). 1988. text 1200.00 (*0-7855-3155-6*, Pub. by Scientific) St Mut.

— Icones Plantarum Novarum Vel Imperfecte Cognitarum Floram Rossicam, 5 Vols. in 1. 1968. 495.00 (*3-7682-0567-3*) Lubrecht & Cramer.

Ledebur, Larry C., et al, eds. Revitalizing the U. S. Economy. LC 85-30166. 242p. 1986. 59.95 (*0-275-92101-8*, C2101, Praeger Pubs) Greenwood.

Ledebur, Larry C., jt. auth. see Barnes, William R.

Ledeen, Jenny. Prophecy in the Christian Era: A Study of Bob Dylan's Work from 1961 to 1967 Emphasizing His Use of Enigma to Teach Ethics & Comparing Him to Dante Alighieri & Other Poets. LC 95-92819. (Illus.). 250p. (Orig.). (C). 1996. pap. text 18.00 (*0-9650542-0-9*) Peaceberry Pr.

***Ledeen, Michael.** Tocqueville on American Character. 240p. 2000. text 23.95 (*0-312-25231-5*) St Martin.

Ledeen, Michael A. The First Duce: D'Annunzio at Fiume. LC 76-47376. 240p. reprint ed. pap. 74.40 (*0-8357-6746-9*, 203540100095) Bks Demand.

— Freedom Betrayed: How American Led a Global Democratic Revolution, Won the Cold War, & Walked Away. (Illus.). 250p. 1996. 24.95 (*0-8447-3992-8*, AEI Pr) Am Enterprise.

— Machiavelli on Modern Leadership: Why Machiavelli's Iron Rules Are As Timely & Important Today As Five Centuries Ago. LC 99-19366. 240p. 2000. text 22.95 (*0-312-20471-X*) St Martin.

***Ledeen, Michael A.** Machiavelli on Modern Leadership: Why Machiavelli's Iron Rules Are as Timely & Important Today as Five Centuries Ago. 224p. 2000. pap. 13.95 (*0-312-26356-2*, St Martin Griffin) St Martin.

Ledeen, Michael A. Superpower Dilemmas: The U. S. & U. S. S. R. at Century's End. 264p. (C). 1991. pap. 24.95 (*0-88738-891-4*) Transaction Pubs.

— West European Communism & American Foreign Policy. 310p. 1987. 39.95 (*0-88738-140-5*) Transaction Pubs.

Ledeen, Robert W., et al, eds. New Trends in Ganglioside Research: Neurochemical & Neuroregenerative Aspects. (FIDIA Research Ser.: Vol. 14). xiv, 660p. 1988. 189.00 (*0-387-96797-4*) Spr-Verlag.

Ledek, Ronald. The Nature of Conscience & Its Religious Significance with Special Reference to John Henry Newman. 130p. 1996. 69.95 (*1-57309-043-3*); pap. 49.95 (*1-57309-042-5*) Intl Scholars.

Ledell, Marjorie. How to Avoid Crossfire & Seek Common Ground. 32p. 1995. 3.50 (*0-87652-217-7*, 021-0500) Am Assn Sch Admin.

Ledell, Marjorie & Arnsparger, Arleen. How to Deal with Community Criticism of School Change. LC 93-22715. 39p. (Orig.). 1993. pap. 8.95 (*0-87120-205-0*) ASCD.

Leden, Judy. Flying with Condors. (Illus.). 320p. 1997. 35.00 (*0-7528-0133-3*, Pub. by Orion Pubng Grp) Trafalgar.

Ledeneva, Alena. Russia's Economy of Favours: Blat, Networking & Informal Exchanges. LC 97-29949. (Russian, Soviet & Post-Soviet Studies: No. 102). (Illus.). 248p. (C). 1998. text 59.95 (*0-521-62174-7*) Cambridge U Pr.

***Ledeneva, Alena V. & Kurkchiyan, Marina.** Economic Crime in Russia. LC 00-29635. 2000. write for info. (*90-411-9782-6*) Kluwer Academic.

***Ledentsov, Nikolai N.** Growth Processes & Surface Phase Equilibria in Molecular Beam Epitaxy. LC 99-30928. (Tracts in Modern Physics Ser.: Vol. 156). (Illus.). viii, 84p. 1999. 75.00 (*3-540-65794-0*) Spr-Verlag.

Leder, Arie C. Reading & Hearing the Word: From Text to Sermon. LC 98-36775. 260p. 1998. 14.95 (*1-56212-373-4*, 1704-2520) CRC Pubns.

Leder, Drew. The Absent Body. 224p. 1990. pap. text 17.95 (*0-226-47000-8*); lib. bdg. 42.00 (*0-226-46999-9*) U Ch Pr.

***Leder, Drew.** Games for the Soul: 40 Playful Ways to Find Fun & Fulfillment in a Stressful World. LC 98-3798. 256p. (J). 1998. pap. 11.45 (*0-7868-8331-6*, Pub. by Hyperion) Time Warner.

— Soul Knows No Bars: Inmates Reflect on Life, Death & Hope. LC 99-45670. 176p. 2000. 23.95 (*0-8476-9290-6*, Pub. by Rowman) Natl Bk Netwk.

Leder, Drew, ed. The Body in Medical Thought & Practice. (Philosophy & Medicine Ser.). 266p. (C). 1992. lib. bdg. 166.50 (*0-7923-1657-6*, Pub. by Kluwer Academic) Kluwer Academic.

Leder, Gilah C., ed. Assessment & Learning of Mathematics. (C). 1992. pap. 29.95 (*0-86431-122-2*, Pub. by Aust Council Educ Res) Stylus Pub VA.

Leder, Gilah C., jt. auth. see Gunstone, Richard F.

Leder, Gilah C., jt. ed. see Fennema, Elizabeth.

Leder, Gottfried, ed. Zur Sache: Grundwerte. (Hildesheimer Beitrage Zu Den Erziehungs und Sozial Wissenschaften Ser.: Bd. 12). (GER.). 222p. 1979. write for info. (*3-487-06921-0*) G Olms Pubs.

Leder, Gottfried & Friedrich, W. U. Kommunalpolitik und Kommunalwahlen in Niedersachsen. 160p. 1989. write for info. (*3-487-09078-3*) G Olms Pubs.

Leder, Gottfried & Wichard, Rudolf. Institutionen und Probleme der Parlamentarischen Demokratie. (Hildesheimer Beitrage Zu Den Erziehungs und Sozial Wissenschaften Ser.: Bd. 1). (GER.). iv, 194p. 1976. 16.00 (*3-487-05991-6*) G Olms Pubs.

Leder, Hans-Claus. Frauen- und Madchenkriminalitat: Kritische Bestandsaufnahme aus Devianzsoziologischer und Wissenschaftstheoretischer Sicht. 3rd ed. (GER., Illus.). XV, 282p. 1997. 57.95 (*3-631-31337-3*) P Lang Pubng.

Leder, Hans H. Cultural Persistence in a Portuguese-American Community. Cordasco, Francesco, ed. LC 80-874. (American Ethnic Groups Ser.). 1981. lib. bdg. 20.95 (*0-405-13435-5*) Ayer.

Leder, Jan. Women in Jazz: A Discography of Instrumental Music, Nineteen Thirteen to Nineteen Sixty-Eight, 19. LC 85-17657. (Discographies Ser.: No. 19). 311p. 1985. lib. bdg. 45.00 (*0-313-24790-0*, LMI/, Greenwood Pr) Greenwood.

Leder, Jane M. Dead Serious: A Book for Teenagers about Teenage Suicide. 160p. (YA). (gr. 7 up). 1989. pap. 3.50 (*0-380-70661-X*, Avon Bks) Morrow Avon.

— Learning How: Gymnastics. James, Jody, ed. (Learning How Sports Ser.). (Illus.). 48p. (J). (gr. 4-7). 1992. pap. 5.95 (*0-944280-40-4*); lib. bdg. 14.95 (*0-944280-35-8*) Bancroft-Sage.

— Learning How: Karate. James, Jody, ed. (Learning How Sports Ser.). (Illus.). 48p. (J). (gr. 4-7). 1992. pap. 5.95 (*0-944280-39-0*); lib. bdg. 14.95 (*0-944280-34-X*) Bancroft-Sage.

— Learning How: Skateboarding. James, Jody, ed. (Learning How Sports Ser.). (Illus.). 48p. (J). (gr. 4-7). 1992. pap. 5.95 (*0-944280-42-0*); lib. bdg. 14.95 (*0-944280-33-1*) Bancroft-Sage.

— Learning How: Soccer. James, Jody, ed. (Learning How Sports Ser.). (Illus.). 48p. (J). (gr. 4-7). 1992. pap. 5.95 (*0-944280-38-2*); lib. bdg. 14.95 (*0-944280-32-3*) Bancroft-Sage.

— The Russian Jewish Experience. LC 95-38544. (Journey Between Two Worlds Ser.). (J). 1996. lib. bdg. 22.60 (*0-8225-3401-0*, Lerner Publctns) Lerner Pub.

— Russian Jewish Family. (J). 1996. pap. text 8.95 (*0-8225-9744-6*) Lerner Pub.

Leder, Sharon & Abbott, Andrea. The Language of Exclusion: The Poetry of Emily Dickinson & Christina Rossetti, 83. LC 87-7519. (Contributions in Women's Studies: No. 83). (Illus.). 250p. 1987. 59.95 (*0-313-25629-2*, LLE/, Greenwood Pr) Greenwood.

Leder, Sharon, jt. ed. see Teichman, Milton.

Leder, Steven Z. The Extraordinary Nature of Ordinary Things. LC 98-43113. 160p. 1999. pap. 14.00 (*0-87441-647-7*) Behrman.

Lederach, John, jt. auth. see Lederach, Naomi.

Lederach, John P. Building Peace: Sustainable Reconciliation in Divided Societies. LC 97-35584. 208p. 1997. 32.50 (*1-878379-74-7*); pap. 14.95 (*1-878379-73-9*) US Inst Peace.

— The Journey Toward Reconciliation. LC 98-31845. 204p. 1999. pap. 12.99 (*0-8361-9082-3*) Herald Pr.

— Preparing for Peace: Conflict Transformation Across Cultures. 1996. pap. text 15.95 (*0-8156-2725-4*) Syracuse U Pr.

Lederach, Naomi & Lederach, John. Recovery of Hope. LC 91-74057. 169p. 1991. pap. 11.95 (*1-56148-046-0*) Good Bks PA.

L

Lederach, Paul M. Daniel. LC 94-19516. (Believers Church Bible Commentary Ser.: Vol. 6). 328p. (Orig.). (C). 1995. pap. 21.99 (*0-8361-3663-2*) Herald Pr.
— A Third Way. LC 80-18041. 160p. 1980. pap. 9.99 (*0-8361-1934-7*) Herald Pr.
Lederberg, Joshua. Encyclopedia of Microbiology, 4 vols. 2nd ed. (Illus.). 3000p. 2000. 750.00 (*0-12-226800-8*) Acad Pr.
Lederberg, Joshua, compiled by. The Excitement & Fascination of Science, 3 vols. (Illus.). 1990. pap. 90.00 (*0-8243-2603-2*) Annual Reviews.
Lederberg, Joshua, ed. Encyclopedia of Microbiology, 1. (Illus.). 1992. text 209.00 (*0-12-226891-1*) Acad Pr.
— Encyclopedia of Microbiology, 2. (Illus.). 1992. text 209.00 (*0-12-226892-X*) Acad Pr.
— Encyclopedia of Microbiology, 3. (Illus.). 1992. text 209.00 (*0-12-226893-8*) Acad Pr.
— Encyclopedia of Microbiology, 4. (Illus.). 1992. text 209.00 (*0-12-226894-6*) Acad Pr.
— Encyclopedia of Microbiology, Set. (Illus.). 2650p. 1992. text 771.00 (*0-12-226890-3*) Acad Pr.
Lederberg, Joshua, et al, eds. Emerging Infections: Microbial Threats to Health in the United States. LC 92-26480. 312p. (C). 1992. pap. text 34.95 (*0-309-04741-2*) Natl Acad Pr.
Lederberg, Joshua, jt. auth. see Harrison, Polly.
Lederberg, Joshua, jt. ed. see Harrison, Polly F.
Lederberg, Joshua S., ed. Biological Weapons: Limiting the Threat. LC 98-52950. (BCSIA Ser.). (Illus.). 300p. 1999. 40.00 (*0-262-12216-2*); pap. 20.00 (*0-262-62128-2*) MIT Pr.
Lederer, jt. auth. see Cohen.
Lederer, Bill, et al, eds. Art Print Index. 750p. 1999. pap. 129.00 (*1-893835-00-6*); pap. 169.00 (*1-893835-01-4*); pap. 199.00 (*1-893835-02-2*); pap. 89.00 (*1-893835-03-0*); pap. 99.00 (*1-893835-04-9*); pap. 149.00 (*1-893835-05-7*); pap. 199.00 (*1-893835-06-5*); pap. 70.00 (*1-893835-07-3*) artcom.
Lederer & Posey Staff & Kelley, Gibbs & Reynolds Staff. Basic Virginia Law for Non-Lawyers: Legal Survival in the Commonwealth of Virginia. Lederer, Fredric, ed. 96p. 1993. pap. 8.95 (*0-9615670-3-1*, King & Queen Pr) Soc Alu Wm.
Lederer, Cohen. ABCs of Contract Bridge. (Illus.). 1993. 11.95 (*0-00-218442-7*, Pub. by HarpC) Trafalgar.
— All about ACOL. 1991. 11.95 (*0-00-218443-5*, Pub. by HarpC) Trafalgar.
Lederer, David, tr. see Behringer, Wolfgang.
***Lederer, Debra & Hall, Michael.** Instant Relaxation: How to Reduce Stress at Work, at Home & in Your Daily Life. 125p. 1999. pap. 12.95 (*1-899836-36-5*, Pub. by Crown Hse) LPC Group.
Lederer, Dolores P. The "Perfectionist's" How To: "Custom Draperies" 3rd ed. LC 88-91302. ("Perfectionist's" How To Bks.: Bk. 1). (Illus.). 104p. (Orig.). 1982. reprint ed. pap. text 35.00 (*0-9608040-0-5*) Lederer Enterprises.
— The "Perfectionist's" How To: "Drapery Top Treatments" ("Perfectionist's" How To Bks.: Bk. II). (Illus.). 108p. (Orig.). 1983. reprint ed. pap. text 35.00 (*0-9608040-1-3*) Lederer Enterprises.
— The "Perfectionist's" How To: "Window Specialties" ("Perfectionist's" How To Bks.: Bk. III). (Illus.). 112p. (Orig.). 1985. reprint ed. pap. text 35.00 (*0-9608040-2-1*) Lederer Enterprises.
— The "Perfectionist's" How to Books, 3 vols. (Illus.). (Orig.). 1992. reprint ed. pap. text 90.00 (*0-9608040-3-X*) Lederer Enterprises.
Lederer, Emil. Die Privatangestellten in der Modernen Wirtschaftsentwicklung: White Collar Workers in Modern Economic Development. LC 74-25765. (European Sociology Ser.). 300p. 1975. reprint ed. 28.95 (*0-405-06519-1*) Ayer.
Lederer, Eric M., ed. Calculus One Exam File. (Exam File Ser.). 250p. 1986. pap. 18.50 (*0-910554-61-7*) Engineering.
Lederer, Florence, tr. see Shabistari, Mahmud.
Lederer, Frederic, jt. auth. see Moliterno, James E.
Lederer, Fredric, ed. see Lederer & Posey Staff & Kelley, Gibbs & Reynolds Staff.
Lederer, Fredric I., jt. auth. see Gilligan, Francis A.
Lederer, Herbert. Die Neuen Leiden des Jungen Werther (The New Sorrows of Young Werther) (GER.). 58p. 1997. pap. 11.00 (*0-942017-53-6*, 04-64381) Amer Assn Teach German.
— Handbook of East German Drama 1945-1985: DDR Drama Handbuch. 2nd ed. (DDR-Studien - East German Studies: Vol. 1). 280p. (C). 1991. text 40.00 (*0-8204-0367-9*) P Lang Pubng.
— Reference Grammar of German. 1981. 22.50 (*0-684-41329-9*) S&S Trade.
Lederer, Herbert, et al, eds. A Reference Grammar of the German Language. LC 69-17352. 709p. (C). 1969. pap. text 42.80 (*0-13-033705-6*) P-H.
Lederer, Herbert, jt. adapted by see Hall, Douglas.
Lederer, Herbert, jt. auth. see Hall, Douglas.
Lederer-Homan, Andrew, tr. see Muller, Vanessa Y., et al.
Lederer, Ivo. Russian Foreign Policy: Essays in Historical Perspective. 1962. 97.50 (*0-685-26675-3*) Elliots Bks.
Lederer, Ivo John, jt. auth. see Sugar, Peter F.
Lederer, Janet R. Care Planning Pocket Guide. 4th ed. 288p. (C). 1991. pap. text 19.95 (*0-8053-4103-X*) Addison-Wesley.
— Care Planning Pocket Guide: A Nursing Diagnosis Approach. 3rd ed. 1990. spiral bd. 13.56 (*0-201-58298-8*) Addison-Wesley.
— Care Planning Pocket Guide: A Nursing Diagnosis Approach. 22nd ed. LC 87-28987. 1988. pap. 17.50 (*0-201-16399-3*) Addison-Wesley.
Lederer, Jean. Encyclopedie Moderne de l'Hygiene Alimentaire Vol. 1: Exigences Alimentaires de l'Homme Normal. (FRE.). 198p. 1978. pap. 65.00 (*0-7859-5076-1*) Fr & Eur.
— Encyclopedie Modern de L'hygiene Alimentaire, 4 vols. (FRE.). 95.00 (*0-686-57003-0*, M-6344) Fr & Eur.
— Encyclopedie Moderne de l'Hygiene Alimentaire: Vol. 2, Hygiene des Aliments. (FRE.). 282p. 1977. 55.00 (*0-8288-5421-1*, M6346) Fr & Eur.
— Encyclopedie Moderne de l'Hygiene Alimentaire Vol. 3: Technologie et Hygiene Alimentaire. (FRE.). 138p. 1978. pap. 65.00 (*0-7859-5077-X*) Fr & Eur.
— Encyclopedie Moderne de l'Hygiene Alimentaire Vol. 4: Les Intoxications Alimentaire. (FRE.). 164p. 1978. pap. 65.00 (*0-7859-5078-8*) Fr & Eur.
Lederer, Katherine. Lillian Hellman. (United States Authors Ser.: No. 338). 176p. 1979. 22.95 (*0-8057-7275-8*, Twyne) Mac Lib Ref.
Lederer, Katy. Music, No Staves. 22p. 1998. 6.00 (*0-937013-80-5*) Potes Poets.
Lederer, Laura. Price We Pay the Case Against Racist Speech, Hate Propaganda, & Pornography. 384p. 1995. 30.00 (*0-8090-7883-X*); pap. 15.00 (*0-8090-1577-3*) Hill & Wang.
Lederer, Laura J., ed. Speech, Equality & Harm: New Legal Paradigms. 1998. pap. 55.00 (*0-8133-2928-0*) Westview.
— Speech, Equality & Harm: New Legal Paradigms. (C). 1999. pap. 21.95 (*0-8133-2929-9*) Westview.
Lederer, Marianne, jt. auth. see Seleskovitch, Danica.
Lederer, Michael. Chromatography for Organic Chemistry. LC 93-31657. 1994. pap. text 45.00 (*0-471-94286-3*) Wiley.
Lederer, Phillip J., ed. see Karmarkar, Uday S.
Lederer, Richard. Anguished English. 192p. 1989. mass mkt. 6.99 (*0-440-20352-X*, LLL BDD) BDD Bks Young Read.
— Anguished English: An Anthology of Accidental Assaults upon Our Language. LC 87-40532. (Illus.). 117p. 1987. pap. 11.95 (*0-941711-04-8*) Wyrick & Co.
***Lederer, Richard.** Bride of Anguished English. 2000. text 23.95 (*0-312-26223-X*) St Martin.
Lederer, Richard. Crazy English. rev. ed. LC 99-182202. 160p. 1998. per. 12.00 (*0-671-02323-3*, Pocket Books) PB.
— Fractured English. LC 97-138005. 208p. 1996. per. 12.00 (*0-671-00036-5*) PB.
— Get Thee to a Punnery. (Illus.). 149p. 1988. pap. 11.95 (*0-941711-08-0*) Wyrick & Co.
— Literary Trivia: Fun & Games for Book Lovers. (Illus.). 208p. 1994. pap. 12.00 (*0-679-75380-X*) Vin Bks.
— The Miracle Language. 272p. 1999. pap. 12.00 (*0-671-02811-1*, PB Trade Paper) PB.
— The Miracle of Language. Rosenman, Jane, ed. 272p. 1992. reprint ed. mass mkt. 5.99 (*0-671-70940-2*) PB.
— More Anguished English. 208p. 1994. mass mkt. 6.50 (*0-440-21577-3*) Dell.
— Nothing Risque, Nothing Gained: Ribald Riddles, Lascivious Limericks, Carnal Corn & Other Good, Clean, Dirty Fun. LC 95-12959. (Illus.). 294p. (Orig.). 1995. pap. 12.00 (*1-55652-243-6*) Chicago Review.
— The Play of Words. Pfefferblit, Elaine, ed. 288p. 1991. reprint ed. pap. 12.00 (*0-671-68909-6*) PB.
— Pun & Games: Jokes, Riddles, Rhymes, Daffynitions, Tairy Fales, & More Wordplay for Kids. LC 96-11609. (Illus.). 112p. (Orig.). (YA). (gr. 5 up). 1996. pap. 9.95 (*1-55652-264-9*) Chicago Review.
— The Word Circus: A Letter-Perfect Book. LC 98-27000. (Illus.). 288p. 1998. 14.95 (*0-87779-354-9*) Merriam-Webster Inc.
Lederer, Richard & Ammer, Christine. Intrepid Linguist Library, 4 vols. 1990. boxed set 17.85 (*0-440-36023-4*) Dell.
Lederer, Richard & Burnham, Philip. Basic Verbal Skills. 4th rev. ed. 241p. (YA). (gr. 9-12). 1995. pap. text 13.34 (*1-877653-31-4*) Wayside Pub.
— Workbook for Basic Verbal Skills. 2nd ed. 75p. (YA). (gr. 9-12). 1980. reprint ed. pap. text 6.67 (*1-877653-58-6*) Wayside Pub.
Lederer, Richard & Dowis, Richard. Sleeping Dogs Don't Lay: Practical Advice for the Grammatically Challenged. LC 99-27231. 224p. 1999. text 22.95 (*0-312-20363-2*) St Martin.
— The Write Way: The Spell Guide to Good Grammar & Usage. Ng, Donna, ed. LC 95-17060. 256p. 1995. pap. 12.00 (*0-671-52670-7*, PB Trade Paper) PB.
Lederer, Richard, jt. auth. see Burnham, Phillip.
Lederer, Richard M., Jr. Colonial American English: A Glossary. LC 85-50954. 267p. 1985. 24.95 (*0-930454-19-7*) Verbatim Bks.
Lederer, Roger J. Bird Finder: A Guide to Common Birds of Eastern North America. (Illus.). 64p. 1990. pap. 3.00 (*0-912550-18-X*, T) Nature Study.
— Pacific Coast Bird Finder: A Manual for Identifying 61 Common Birds of Pacific Coast, Vol. 1. (Illus.). 62p. 1977. pap. 3.00 (*0-912550-04-X*) Nature Study.
Lederer, Susan E. Subjected to Science: Human Experimentation in America Before the Second World War. (Henry E. Siegrist Series in the History of Medicine). (Illus.). 192p. 1995. text 32.95 (*0-8018-4820-2*) Johns Hopkins.
— Subjected to Science: Human Experimentation in America Before the Second World War. 1997. pap. text 15.95 (*0-8018-5709-0*) Johns Hopkins.
Lederer, William H., jt. auth. see Keleti, Georg.
Lederer, William J. Creating a Good Relationship. 272p. 1984. reprint ed. pap. 12.00 (*0-393-30155-9*) Norton.
— Our Own Worst Enemy. LC 68-13847. 1968. 4.95 (*0-393-05357-1*) Norton.
Lederer, William J. & Burdick, Eugene. The Ugly American. LC 58-7388. 285p. 1999. pap. 13.00 (*0-393-31867-2*, Norton Paperbks) Norton.
Lederer, William J. & Jackson, Don D. The Mirages of Marriage. LC 67-16608. 1968. 21.95 (*0-393-08400-0*) Norton.
— The Mirages of Marriage. 1990. pap. 14.95 (*0-393-30632-1*) Norton.
Lederer, Wolfgang. Dragons, Delinquents & Destiny: An Essay on Positive Superego Functions. LC 64-23955. (Psychological Issues Monographs: No. 15, Vol. 4, No. 3). 83p. (Orig.). 1964. 27.50 (*0-8236-1420-4*) Intl Univs Pr.
Lederhandler, Sarah, tr. see Shulman, Eliezer.
Lederhendl, Eli. Jewish Responses to Modernity. 1997. pap. text 20.00 (*0-8147-5138-5*) NYU Pr.
Lederhendlender, Eli. Jewish Response to Modernity: New Voices in America & Eastern Europe. LC 94-2486. (Illus.). 250p. (C). 1994. text 50.00 (*0-8147-5084-2*) NYU Pr.
Lederis, K. & Veale, W. L., eds. Current Studies of Hypothalamic Function 1978. Incl. Pt. I. Hormones. 1978. 85.25 (*3-8055-2860-4*); Pt. II. Metabolism & Behaviour. 1978. 85.25 (*3-8055-2861-2*); (Illus.). 1978. 153.25 (*3-8055-2969-4*) S Karger.
Lederis, K., ed. see Symposium, Calgary, Alberta Staff.
***Lederkremer, Javier.** 1500 Sonidos para la PC: Los Mejores WAVs en 25 Categorias. (SPA.). 30p. 1999. pap. 12.90 incl. cd-rom (*987-526-007-X*, Pub. by MP Ediciones) Am Wholesale.
***Lederkremer, Javier & Baretto, Alina.** Guia de Cocina en Internet en Espanol: Internet Cooking Guide in Spanish. deluxe ed. (Guias Web PC Users Ser.). (SPA., Illus.). 224p. 2000. pap. 15.90 incl. cd-rom (*987-526-032-0*, Pub. by MP Ediciones) Downtown Bk.
***Lederkremer, Miguel.** La Biblia de Internet en Espanol/Spanish con CDROM. (SPA.). 327p. 1999. pap. 19.90 incl. cd-rom (*987-97441-0-1*, Pub. by MP Ediciones) Am Wholesale.
Lederleitner, Elaine M. Radiant Echoes. LC 97-90160. 1997. 24.95 (*0-533-12311-9*) Vantage.
Lederleitner, Joseph B. Lighting the Darkness. 1995. 13.95 (*0-533-11523-X*) Vantage.
Lederman. Anthropology & Feminism. 1995. 26.95 (*0-8057-9752-1*, Twyne) Mac Lib Ref.
***Lederman.** Harmonic Technique. 1999. text 79.00 (*0-443-06160-2*) Harcrt Hlth Sci Grp.
Lederman. How to Be a Truly Excellent Junior Medical Student. 1997. pap. 12.00 (*1-883205-18-2*) Intl Med Pub.
— Introduction to Group Theory. 1976. pap. text. write for info. (*0-582-44180-3*, Pub. by Addison-Wesley) Longman.
Lederman, Daniel, jt. auth. see Perry, Guillermo.
Lederman, Daniel, jt. auth. see Perry, Guillermo E.
Lederman, David. Multiple Choice & Free-Response Questions in Preparation for AP Calculus (AB) Examination. 7th ed. 1998. pap. 21.95 (*1-878621-49-1*) D & S Mktg Syst.
— Multiple-Choice & Free Response Questions in Preparation for the AP Calculus (BC) Examination. 6th ed. 1998. pap. 21.95 (*1-878621-51-3*) D & S Mktg Syst.
— Multiple Choice Questions in Preparation for the AP Calculus (AB) Examination. 90p. 1991. student ed. 15.95 (*1-878621-01-7*) D & S Mktg Syst.
— Multiple Choice Questions in Preparation for the AP Calculus (AB) Examination. 5th ed. 127p. 1991. student ed. 15.95 (*1-878621-00-9*) D & S Mktg Syst.
— Multiple Choice Questions in Preparation for the AP Calculus (AB) Examination. 6th ed. 1994. pap. 16.95 (*1-878621-23-8*) D & S Mktg Syst.
— Multiple Choice Questions in Preparation for the AP Calculus (BC) Examination. 90p. 1991. student ed. 15.95 (*1-878621-03-3*) D & S Mktg Syst.
— Multiple Choice Questions in Preparation for the AP Calculus (BC) Examination. 4th ed. 121p. 1991. student ed. 15.95 (*1-878621-02-5*) D & S Mktg Syst.
— Multiple Choice Questions in Preparation for the AP Calculus (BC) Examination. 5th ed. 1994. pap. 16.95 (*1-878621-33-5*) D & S Mktg Syst.
— Student's Solutions Manual to Accompany Multiple Choice & Free Response Questions in Preparation for the AP Calculus (AB) Examination. 7th ed. 1998. pap., student ed. 14.95 (*1-878621-50-5*) D & S Mktg Syst.
— Student's Solutions Manual to Accompany Multiple-Choice & Free-Response Questions in Preparation for the AP Calculus (BC) Examination. 6th ed. 1998. pap., student ed. 14.95 (*1-878621-52-1*) D & S Mktg Syst.
— Student's Solutions Manual to Accompany Multiple Choice Questions in Preparation for the AP Calculus (AB) Examination. 1994. pap., student ed. 13.95 (*1-878621-24-6*) D & S Mktg Syst.
— Student's Solutions Manual to Accompany Multiple Choice Questions in Preparation for the AP Calculus (BC) Examination. 5th ed. 1994. pap., student ed. 13.95 (*1-878621-34-3*) D & S Mktg Syst.
Lederman, Diana. Make-Me-a-Match - Hanukah. (ENG, FRE & HEB.). 1994. spiral bd. 4.95 (*965-229-118-8*, Pub. by Gefen Pub Hse) Gefen Bks.
— Make-Me-a-Match - Israel. (ENG, FRE & HEB., Illus.). 1994. spiral bd. 4.95 (*965-229-120-X*, Pub. by Gefen Pub Hse) Gefen Bks.
— Make-Me-a-Match - Les Fetes des Tishri. (ENG, FRE & HEB., Illus.). 1994. spiral bd. 4.95 (*965-229-119-6*, Pub. by Gefen Pub Hse) Gefen Bks.
— Make-Me-a-Match - Pesach. (ENG, FRE & HEB., Illus.). 1994. spiral bd. 4.95 (*965-229-116-1*, Pub. by Gefen Pub Hse) Gefen Bks.
— Make-Me-a-Match - Purim. (ENG, FRE & HEB., Illus.). 1994. spiral bd. 4.95 (*965-229-117-X*, Pub. by Gefen Pub Hse) Gefen Bks.
— Make-Me-a-Match - Shabbat. (ENG, FRE & HEB., Illus.). 1994. spiral bd. 4.95 (*965-229-115-3*, Pub. by Gefen Pub Hse) Gefen Bks.
Lederman, Diana. Make-Me-a-Match. (ENG, FRE & HEB.). (J). 1992. spiral bd. 4.95 (*965-229-025-4*, Pub. by Gefen Pub Hse) Gefen Bks.
Lederman, Dov B., tr. see Soloukhin, R. I., ed.
Lederman, Dov B., tr. see Styrikovich, M. A., et al.
Lederman, Dov B., tr. see Sychev, V. V., et al, eds.
Lederman, Dov B., tr. see Vilemas, Jurgis, et al.
Lederman, Dov B., tr. see Zukauskas, A. A., et al.
***Lederman, Ed.** A Tangled Web: Restraining Order, Domestic Violence & Hard Wired Therapy. 1999. pap. write for info. (*1-57655-184-9*) Independ Inst.
Lederman, Ed & DeRaad, Carolyn. The End of History: Colorado & Jefferson County's "Content Standards" (Issue Paper #6-96 Ser.). 11p. 1996. pap. text 8.00 (*1-57655-150-4*) Independ Inst.
Lederman, Edward L. Education Standards Proposal Will Harm Education: Academic Standards Could Fall While Political Correctness Standards Rise. (Issue Papers: No. 10-93). 4p. 1993. pap. text 8.00 (*1-57655-074-5*) Independ Inst.
— How Union Contracts Block School Reform: A Denver Case Study. (Issue Papers). 12p. 1990. pap. text 8.00 (*1-57655-034-6*) Independ Inst.
— Parent Control of Schools: Denver Flunks the Chicago Test: Will CDM Mean 'Can't Do Much' or 'Consumers Demand More'? (Issue Papers: No. 6-91). 18p. 1991. pap. text 8.00 (*1-57655-039-7*) Independ Inst.
Lederman, Ellen. The Best Places to Meet Good Men. 256p. (Orig.). 1991. pap. 12.95 (*1-55958-106-9*) Prima Pub.
— College Majors: A Complete Guide from Accounting to Zoology. LC 89-29540. 140p. (C). 1990. lib. bdg. 28.50 (*0-89950-462-0*) McFarland & Co.
— Health Career Planning: A Realistic Guide. 224p. 1988. 35.95 (*0-89885-397-4*, Kluwer Acad Hman Sci); pap. 18.95 (*0-89885-401-6*, Kluwer Acad Hman Sci) Kluwer Academic.
— Vacations That Can Change Your Life: Adventures, Retreats & Workshops for the Mind, Body & Spirit. 2nd rev. ed. 448p. 1998. pap. 16.95 (*1-57071-391-X*) Sourcebks.
Lederman, Eva. Careers in Advertising. 1998. pap. 17.95 (*0-375-75091-6*) Random.
Lederman, Eva, jt. auth. see Sanborn, Robert.
Lederman, Eyal. The Fundamentals of Manual Therapy: Physiology, Neurology & Psychology. LC 97-705. 1997. text 45.00 (*0-443-05275-1*) Church.
Lederman, Gordon Nathaniel. Reorganizing the Joint Chiefs of Staff: The Goldwater-Nichols Act of 1986, 182. LC 99-22874. (Contributions in Military Studies Ser.: No. 182). 232p. 1999. 59.95 (*0-313-31085-8*, Greenwood Pr) Greenwood.
***Lederman, Jacqueline.** Joy Ride! Faith-Filled Fun & Games for Drivetime. LC 00-20638. (Heritage Builders Ser.). (Illus.). 96p. (J). (gr. k-7). 2000. pap. 7.99 (*1-56179-798-7*) Tyndale Hse.
Lederman, Jeff. Cries of the Wild: A Wildlife Rehabilitator's Journal. 1997. pap. 19.95 (*1-895811-46-5*) Heritage Hse.
Lederman, Jess. Global Asset Allocation: Techniques for Optimizing Portfolio Management. 400p. 1994. 69.95 (*0-471-59373-7*) Wiley.
— Market Neutral: Long & Short Strategies for Every Market Environment. 288p. 1996. 65.00 (*0-7863-0733-1*, Irwn McGrw-H) McGrw-H Hghr Educ.
— The Secondary Mortgage Market: Strategies for Surviving & Thriving in Today's Challenging Markets. rev. ed. 675p. 1992. text 70.00 (*1-55738-288-3*, Irwn Prfssnl) McGraw-Hill Prof.
Lederman, Jess, ed. Breakthroughs in Mortgage Banking: Looking Toward the Future. (Distinguished Writers Ser.). 345p. 1996. pap. 65.00 (*1-57599-016-4*, Real Est Fin Pr) Mortgage Bankers.
— Handbook of Commercial Underwriting. (Mortgage Lending Handbook Ser.). 303p. 1998. 75.00 (*1-57599-019-9*, Real Est Fin Pr) Mortgage Bankers.
— Handbook of Secondary Marketing. (Mortgage Lending Handbook Ser.). 388p. 1997. 85.00 (*1-57599-013-X*, Real Est Fin Pr) Mortgage Bankers.
— Housing America: Mobilizing Bankers, Builders & Communities to Solve the Nation's Affordable-Housing Crisis. 400p. 1993. 32.50 (*1-55738-435-5*, Irwn Prfssnl) McGraw-Hill Prof.
Lederman, Jess, ed. Handbook of Mortgage Lending. (Mortgage Lending Handbook Ser.). 300p. 75.00 (*0-945359-43-8*) Mortgage Bankers.
Lederman, Jess & Klein, Richard A. Small Cap Stocks: Investment & Portfolio Strategies for the Institutional Investor. 450p. 1993. text 70.00 (*1-55738-518-1*, Irwn Prfssnl) McGraw-Hill Prof.
Lederman, Jess & Klein, Robert. Hedge Funds: Investment & Portfolio Strategies for the Institutional Investor. 250p. 1995. text 65.00 (*1-55738-861-X*, Irwn Prfssnl) McGraw-Hill Prof.
Lederman, Jess & Klein, Robert, eds. Financial Engineering with Derivatives: Cutting-Edge Innovations & Real-World Applications. 300p. 1995. text 70.00 (*1-55738-854-7*, Irwn Prfssnl) McGraw-Hill Prof.
Lederman, Jess & Klein, Robert A. Equity Style Management: Evaluating & Selecting Investment Styles. 250p. 1995. text 65.00 (*1-55738-860-1*, Irwn Prfssnl) McGraw-Hill Prof.
— Virtual Trading: How Any Trader with a PC Can Use the Power of Neural Nets & Expert Systems to Boost Trading Profits. 300p. 1994. text 45.00 (*1-55738-812-1*, Irwn Prfssnl) McGraw-Hill Prof.

An Asterisk (*) at the beginning of an entry indicates that the title is appearing for the first time.

Lederman, Jess & Park, Keith K., eds. Global Bond Markets: State-of-the-Art Research, Analysis & Investment Strategies. (Guide to World Markets Ser.). 1990. 70.00 (*1-55738-153-4*, Irwn Prfssnl) McGraw-Hill Prof.
— The Global Equity Markets: State-of-the-Art Research, Analysis & Investment Strategies. (Guide to World Markets Ser.). 1991. text 75.00 (*1-55738-152-6*, Irwn Prfssnl) McGraw-Hill Prof.
Lederman, Jess & Sullivan, Michael P., eds. The New High-Yield Bond Market: Investment Opportunities. 400p. 1993. 55.00 (*1-55738-436-3*, Irwn Prfssnl) McGraw-Hill Prof.
Lederman, Jess & Swoyer, G. Benjamin, eds. Handbook of Commercial Real Estate Finance. (Mortgage Lending Handbook Ser.). 450p. 1995. 85.00 (*0-945359-42-X*) Mortgage Bankers.
Lederman, Jess, jt. auth. see Klein, Robert A.
Lederman, Jess, ed. see Freedman, Roy S. & Klein, Robert A.
***Lederman, Lawrence.** Tombstones. LC 99-54848. 1999. write for info. (*1-893122-55-7*) Beard Bks.
Lederman, Leon & Teresi, Dick. God Particle: If the Universe Is the Answer, What is the Question. 448p. 1994. pap. 14.95 (*0-385-31211-3*, Delta Trade) Dell.
Lederman, Leon M. & Schramm, David N. From Quarks to the Cosmos: Tools of Discovery. (Illus.). 242p. 1995. pap. text 19.95 (*0-7167-6012-6*) W H Freeman.
Lederman, Linda C. Asking Questions & Listening. 80p. (C). 1995. per. 19.95 (*0-7872-1693-3*, 41169301) Kendall-Hunt.
Lederman, Linda C. & Dervin, Brenda, eds. Communication Pedagogy: Approaches to Teaching Undergraduate Courses in Communication. (Communication & Information Science Ser.). 352p. (C). 1992. text 78.50 (*0-89391-893-8*) Ablx Pub.
Lederman Mandell, Sherri L. Writers of the Holocaust. annot. ed. LC 98-23601. (Global Profiles Ser.). (Illus.). 160p. (J). 1999. 19.95 (*0-8160-3729-9*) Facts on File.
Lederman, Minna. The Life & Death of a Small Magazine (Modern Music, 1924-1946) LC 83-80057. (I.S.A.M. Monographs: No. 18). (Illus.). 211p. (Orig.). 1983. pap. 20.00 (*0-914678-20-5*) Inst Am Music.
Lederman, Nancy M., jt. auth. see Strauss, Peter J.
Lederman, Norman G., jt. ed. see Gess-Newsome, Julie.
Lederman, Raizel, jt. auth. see Teitelbaum, Chaya S.
Lederman, Regina P. Psychosocial Adaptation in Pregnancy: Assessment of Seven Dimensions of Maternal Development. 2nd rev. ed. (Illus.). 1996. 49.95 (*0-8261-6710-1*) Springer Pub.
***Lederman, Robert.** Freedom is about Authority: How Mayor Giuliani Is Turning New York City Into a Police State. (Illus.). 2000. pap. 13.00 (*1-887128-62-X*) Soft Skull Pr.
Lederman, Robert. Internal Medicine & Critical Care Pocketbook, Vol. 1. 124p. (Orig.). 1997. pap. 9.95 (*1-882742-07-9*) Tarascon Pub.
Lederman, S. & Scheiderman, Patricia. Smoking Cessation: HP 609 Study Guide. 15p. (C). 1989. student ed., spiral bd. write for info. (*0-931657-18-0*) Learning Proc Ctr.
Lederman, Stan & Scheiderman, Patricia. If You Smoke, Please Try...Quitting. (Illus.). 100p. (Orig.). 1986. pap. text 18.00 (*0-931657-02-4*) Learning Proc Ctr.
Ledermann. Handbook of Applicable Mathematics, 6 vols., Set. 5026p. 1999. text 2558.00 (*0-471-93053-9*) Wiley.
Ledermann, E. K. Philosophy & Medicine. (Avebury Series in the Philosophy of Science). 196p. 1986. text 78.95 (*0-566-05062-5*, Pub. by Avebry) Ashgate Pub Co.
Ledermann, Erich K. Medicine for the Whole Person: A Critique of Scientific Medicine. LC 97-16364. 192p. 1997. pap. 16.95 (*1-86204-056-7*, Pub. by Element MA) Penguin Putnam.
Ledermann, Isaac. Dicionario Tecnico de Electronica Ingles - Portugues. (ENG & POR.). 1986. pap. 39.95 (*0-8288-3966-2*, F92230) Fr & Eur.
Ledermann, Jess, ed. The New Dynamics of Emerging Markets Investment: Managing Sub-Investment-Grade Sovereign Risk. 1997. 270.00 (*1-85564-546-7*, Pub. by Euromoney) Am Educ Systs.
Ledermann, W. Introduction Group Theories. 2nd ed. LC 97-106162. (C). 1996. pap. text 60.95 (*0-582-25954-1*, Pub. by Addison-Wesley) Longman.
Ledermann, Walter. Introduction to Group Theory. 2nd ed. (C). 1996. pap. text. write for info. (*0-201-40378-1*) Addison-Wesley.
Ledermann, Walter, et al. , 2 pts., Pt. 6B. LC 79-42724. (Handbook of Applicable Mathematics Ser.). 450p. 1984. text 199.95 Wiley.
— Handbook of Applicable Mathematics, 6 vols. LC 79-42724. (Handbook of Applicable Mathematics Ser.). 500p. 1990. suppl. ed. 299.95 (*0-471-91825-3*) Wiley.
Ledermann, Walter, et al. Handbook of Applicable Mathematics, 6 vols., Vol. 6. Incl. Vol. 1. LC 79-42724. 544p. 1980. 425.00 (*0-471-27704-5*); Vol. 2. LC 79-42724. 470p. 1981. 450.00 (*0-471-27821-1*); Vol. 3. LC 79-42724. 584p. 1981. 450.00 (*0-471-27947-1*); Vol. 4. LC 79-42724. 890p. 1982. 450.00 (*0-471-10141-9*); Vol. 6, Pt. A, Statistics., 2 pts. LC 79-42724. 580p. 1984. 450.00 (*0-471-90274-8*); Vol. 6, Pt. B, Statistics., 2 pts. LC 79-42724. 522p. 1984. 450.00 (*0-471-90272-1*); Vol. 6, Pts. A & B, Statistics., 2 pts. LC 79-42724. 1102p. 1984. 650.00 (*0-471-90024-9*); LC 79-42724. (Handbook of Applicable Mathematics Ser.). 4390p. 1985. 1496.00 (*0-471-90804-5*) Wiley.
Ledermann, Walter, et al. Handbook of Applicable Mathematics: Contents & General Index, 6 vols. LC 79-42724. (Handbook of Applicable Mathematics Ser.). 136p. 1991. 129.95 (*0-471-92792-9*) Wiley.
***Ledesma, John.** Golf School. LC 99-58731. (Illus.). 1500p. 2000. 24.98 (*1-57145-226-5*, Thunder Bay) Advantage Pubs.
— Golf School: Everything You Need to Know about the Game & How to Play It. 2000. pap. 24.95 (*1-85585-868-1*, Pub. by Collins & Br) Sterling.
Ledesma, Ron. PC Hardware Guide for DOS Solaris. 352p. 1994. pap. 49.00 (*0-13-124678-X*) P-H.
Ledet, David A. Oboe Reed Styles: Theory & Practice. LC 80-8152. (Illus.). 224p. 1981. 36.95 (*0-253-37891-5*) Ind U Pr.
***Ledet, David A.** Oboe Reed Styles: Theory & Practice. (Illus.). 224p. 2000. pap. 21.95 (*0-253-21392-4*) Ind U Pr.
Ledet, David A., jt. auth. see Sprenkle, Robert.
Ledetti, Soren C. Phonetics - Research & Results: Index of New Information. 160p. Date not set. 47.50 (*0-7883-1886-1*); pap. 44.50 (*0-7883-1887-X*) ABBE Pubs Assn.
Ledford. Sharpening Your Writing Skills for English Competency Exams. 2nd ed. 180p. (C). 1994. per. 37.95 (*0-8403-9783-6*) Kendall-Hunt.
Ledford, Cawood, jt. auth. see Cameron, Chris.
Ledford, Dan. Cash in a Flash! Vol. 1: How to Make a Fortune in Photography. 150p. (Orig.). 1990. 19.95 (*1-879497-00-X*) Natl Crdt Ctr.
Ledford, Ibbie. Hill Country Cookin' & Memoirs. LC 91-12217. (Illus.). 224p. 1991. 15.95 (*0-88289-848-5*) Pelican.
— Y'All Come Back, Now: Recipes & Memories. LC 93-6074. (Illus.). 224p. 1994. 15.95 (*1-56554-015-8*) Pelican.
Ledford, James, jt. auth. see Grasso, Mary E.
Ledford, Jan Roadarmel, jt. auth. see Gayton, Johnny L.
Ledford, Janice K. Certified Opthalmic Assistant Exam Review Manual. LC 96-44190. (Basic Bookshelf for Eyecare Professionals Ser.). (Illus.). 240p. 1996. pap. text 33.00 (*1-55642-333-0*, 63330) SLACK Inc.
— Certified Ophthalmic Technician Exam Review Manual. LC 97-10166. (Basic Bookshelf for Eyecare Professionals Ser.). (Illus.). 256p. (Orig.). 1997. pap. text 33.00 (*1-55642-324-1*, 63241) SLACK Inc.
***Ledford, Janice K.** Certified Opthalmic Medical Technologist Exam Review Manual. (Illus.). 240p. 1999. pap. text 36.00 (*1-55642-422-1*) SLACK Inc.
Ledford, Janice K. The Complete Guide to Ocular History Taking. LC 98-36725. (Illus.). 144p. 1998. pap. text 30.00 (*1-55642-369-1*, 63691) SLACK Inc.
***Ledford, Janice K.** Ophthalmic Technical Skills Handbook. 200p. (C). 2000. pap. text 33.00 (*1-55642-464-7*) SLACK Inc.
Ledford, Janice K. & Sanders, Valerie. The Slit Lamp Primer. LC 97-30912. (Basic Bookshelf for Eyecare Professionals Ser.). 160p. 1997. pap. text 30.00 (*1-55642-330-6*, 63306) SLACK Inc.
Ledford, Kenneth F. From General Estate to Special Interest: German Lawyers, 1878-1933. (Illus.). 391p. (C). 1996. text 57.95 (*0-521-56031-4*) Cambridge U Pr.
Ledgard, Edna, compiled by. The Snake Prince & Other Stories: Burmese Folk Tales. LC 99-30328. 1999. pap. 15.00 (*1-56656-313-5*) Interlink Pub.
Ledgard, Henry. The Little Book of Object-Oriented Programming. LC 95-22671. 224p. (C). 1995. pap. 16.20 (*0-13-396342-X*) P-H.
Ledgard, Henry F. ADA: An Introduction. 2nd ed. (Illus.). 135p. 1987. pap. text 30.00 (*0-387-90814-5*) Spr-Verlag.
— ANSI-IEEE Pascal Standard: The American Pascal Standard. 1984. 58.95 (*0-387-91248-7*) Spr-Verlag.
— Professional Software: Programming Practice, Vol. 2. (C). 1987. pap. text 18.36 (*0-201-12232-4*) Addison-Wesley.
— Professional Software: Software Engineering Concepts, Vol. 1. LC 87-1760. (C). 1987. pap. text 24.75 (*0-201-12231-6*) Addison-Wesley.
— Programming Proverbs LC 74-22058. (Hayden Computer Programming Ser.). 134p. 1975. write for info. (*0-8104-5522-6*) Sams.
— Programming Proverbs for FORTRAN Programmers LC 74-22074. (Hayden Computer Programming Ser.). 130p. 1975. write for info. (*0-8104-5820-9*) Sams.
Ledgard, Henry F., jt. auth. see Singer, Andrew.
Ledger. New Woman. LC 96-29804. 272p. 1997. pap. 27.95 (*0-7190-4093-0*) St Martin.
Ledger, Allison C. Sex & Psychosexual Development: Index of New Information with Authors, Subjects & Bibliography. 180p. 1993. 47.50 (*1-55914-824-1*); pap. 44.50 (*1-55914-825-X*) ABBE Pubs Assn.
— Vulvar Disease. (C). 1995. text. write for info. (*0-7216-5317-0*, W B Saunders Co) Harcrt Hlth Sci Grp.
Ledger, David. Shifting Sands: The British in South Arabia. 232p. (C). 1995. 51.00 (*0-907151-08-6*, Pub. by IMMEL Pubng) St Mut.
Ledger, Frank & Sallis, Howard. Crisis Management in the Power Industry: An Inside Story. LC 94-12501. (Illus.). 360p. (C). (gr. 13). 1994. pap. 45.00 (*0-415-11876-X*, C0109) Thomson Learn.
Ledger, G. R. Re-Counting Plato: A Computer Analysis of Plato's Style. (Illus.). 272p. 1990. 85.00 (*0-19-814681-7*) OUP.
Ledger, Gillian & Roe, Michael. East European Change & Shipping Policy. LC 96-84611. 256p. 1996. 68.95 (*1-85972-384-5*, Pub. by Avebury) Ashgate Pub Co.
***Ledger, J.** Power Generation Conference, 1998: Power, Proceedings. LC TK101.I62 1998. 972p. 1998. 200.00 (*0-7918-1878-0*) ASME.
Ledger, Marshall A., jt. auth. see Cooper, David Y.
Ledger, Marshall A., jt. auth. see Ledger, Martha.
Ledger, Martha & Ledger, Marshall A. Dear Old Penn in Postcards: The University of Pennsylvania, 1900-1923. (Illus.). 60p. (Orig.). 1989. pap. write for info. (*0-318-65907-7*) M & M Ledger.
Ledger, Philip. Promised Messiah. 96p. 1998. pap. 8.00 (*0-89328-144-1*, 65/1867R) Lorenz Corp.
Ledger, Philip, ed. Anthems for Choirs Three: Twenty-Four Anthems for Sopranos & Altos, Three or More Parts. 110p. 1974. pap. 16.95 (*0-19-353242-5*) OUP.
— Anthems for Choirs Two: Twenty-Four Anthems for Sopranos & Altos, Unison & Two-Part. 112p. 1974. pap. 16.95 (*0-19-353240-9*) OUP.
— The Oxford Book of English Madrigals. 408p. 1979. pap. text 17.95 (*0-19-343664-7*) OUP.
Ledger, Richard T. Of Birds & Beasties: Or Conversations with the Animals. (Illus.). 145p. 1999. pap. 10.95 (*0-9668538-0-6*, P03119) Siskiyou.
***Ledger, Sally.** Henrik Ibsen. (Writers & Their Works Ser.). 96p. 1999. pap. text 19.00 (*0-7463-0842-6*, Pub. by Northcote House) U Pr of Miss.
Ledger, Sally & Kee Yong Lim. Cultural Politics at the'Fin de Siecle' McCracken, Scott, ed. (Illus.). 345p. (C). 1995. pap. text 22.95 (*0-521-48499-5*) Cambridge U Pr.
***Ledger, Sally & Luckhurst, Roger, eds.** The Fin De Siecle: A Reader in Cultural History, C.1880-1900. 340p. 2000. pap. 19.95 (*0-19-874279-7*); text 60.00 (*0-19-874278-9*) OUP.
Ledger, Sally & Swain, Stella, eds. Legal Fictions No. 32: Fall 1997. 192p. 1998. pap. 19.50 (*0-85315-847-9*, Pub. by Lawrence & Wishart) NYU Pr.
Ledger Stem Book Co. Staff. Tacoma: Western Terminus of the Northern Pacific Railroad. (Illus.). 32p. 1986. reprint ed. pap. 10.00 (*0-8466-0311-X*, S-311, Shorey Pubns) Shoreys Bkstore.
Ledger, William, jt. ed. see Muttukrishna, Shanti.
Ledger, William J. Antibiotics in Obstetrics & Gynecology: Developments in Perinatal Medicine, No. 2. 320p. 1982. text 171.00 (*90-247-2529-1*) Kluwer Academic.
Ledgerwood, Byron K., ed. Control Engineering Conference: Proceedings of the First Annual Control Engineering Conference. 239p. 1982. 75.00 (*0-914331-50-7*, Control Engrng) Cahners Busn Des Plaines.
— Control Engineering Conference: Proceedings of the Second Annual Control Engineering Conference. 347p. 1983. 75.00 (*0-914331-51-5*, Control Engrng) Cahners Busn Des Plaines.
— Control Engineering Conference: Proceedings of the Third Annual Control Engineering Conference. 486p. 1984. 85.00 (*0-914331-52-3*, Control Engrng) Cahners Busn Des Plaines.
— Proceedings of the 4th Annual Control Engineering Conference. 528p. 1985. 85.00 (*0-914331-54-X*, Control Engrng) Cahners Busn Des Plaines.
Ledgerwood, Byron K., ed. Proceedings of the 5th Annual Control Engineering Conference. (Control Engineering Conference Ser.). 478p. 1986. 85.00 (*0-914331-55-8*, Control Engrng) Cahners Busn Des Plaines.
— Proceedings of the 6th Annual Control Engineering Conference, 1987. (Control Engineering Conference Ser.). 703p. 1987. pap. 100.00 (*0-914331-56-6*, Control Engrng) Cahners Busn Des Plaines.
Ledgerwood, Byron K., intro. Proceeding of the 8th Annual Control Engineer Conference: Held As Part of the Control Engineering Conference & Exposition, O'Hare Exposition Center, Rosemont, IL, May 23-25, 1989. (Illus.). (Orig.). 1989. pap. 105.00 (*0-914331-58-2*, Control Engrng) Cahners Busn Des Plaines.
— Proceedings of the 7th Annual Control Engineering Conference: Held as Part of the Control Engineering Conference & Exposition Center, Rosemont, IL June 7-9, 1988. (Illus.). (Orig.). (C). 1988. pap. 100.00 (*0-914331-57-4*, Control Engrng) Cahners Busn Des Plaines.
Ledgerwood, Graham V. Keys to Higher Consciousness: How to Contact Your Inner Self. Kubis, Pat, ed. (Illus.). 512p. 1989. 24.95 (*0-9623840-0-3*) Everest Costa.
Ledgerwood, Grant. Implementing an Environmental Audit: How to Gain a Competitive Advantage Using Quality & Environmental Responsibility. 228p. 1994. text 45.00 (*0-7863-0142-2*, Irwn Prfssnl) McGraw-Hill Prof.
***Ledgerwood, Grant & Broadhurst, Arlene Idol.** Environment, Ethics & the Corporation. LC 99-49280. 2000. text 45.00 (*0-312-23010-9*) St Martin.
Ledgerwood, Joanna. Microfinance Handbook: An Institutional & Financial Perspective. LC 98-21754. 302p. 1998. 30.00 (*0-8213-4306-8*, 14306) World Bank.
Ledgerwood, Judy, et al. Why Paint? 24p. 1992. pap. 15.00 (*0-941548-24-4*) Ren Soc U Chi.
Ledgerwood, Judy, jt. ed. see Heder, Steve.
Ledgerwood, Mikle D. Images of the "Indian" in Four New-World Literatures. LC 97-38499. (Native American Studies: Vol. 4). 232p. 1997. 89.95 (*0-7734-8462-0*) E Mellen.
Ledgerwood, Mikle D., ed. New Approaches to Medieval Textuality. LC 95-40414. (Studies on Themes & Motifs in Literature: Vol. 28). VIII, 151p. (C). 1998. text 39.95 (*0-8204-3026-9*) P Lang Pubng.
Ledges, John, jt. auth. see Beatty, Chris.
***Ledgeway, Adam.** A Comparative Syntax of the Dialects of Southern Italy: A Minimalist Approach. (Publications of the Philological Society). 300p. 2000. pap. 29.95 (*0-631-22166-2*) Blackwell Pubs.
Ledgister, F. S. Class Alliances & the Liberal Authoritarian State. LC 97-22587. 220p. 1997. pap. text 21.95 (*0-86543-547-2*) Africa World.
— Class Alliances & the Liberal Authoritarian State: The Roots of Post-Colonial Democracy in Jamaica, Trinidad & Tobago, & Surinam. LC 97-22587. 220p. 1997. write for info. (*0-86543-546-4*) Africa World.
Ledig, F. Thomas & Neale, David B., eds. World Directory of Forest Geneticists & Tree Breeders. 191p. (C). 1999. pap. text 35.00 (*0-7881-7013-9*) DIANE Pub.
Ledingham, J. G., ed. see Advanced Medicine Symposia Staff & Royal College of Physicians Staff.
***Ledingham, J. G. G. & Warrell, D. A., eds.** Concise Oxford Textbook of Medicine. (Illus.). 2016p. 2000. 79.95 (*0-19-262870-4*) OUP.
Ledingham, John A. & Bruning, Stephen D., eds. Public Relations As Relationship Management: A Relational Approach to the Study & Practice of Public Relations. LC 99-13642. (LEA's Communication Ser.). 240p. 1999. write for info. (*0-8058-3050-2*) L Erlbaum Assocs.
Leditman, Jay, ed. St. Anthony's Guide to Chiropractic Managed Care. 150p. (C). Date not set. 149.00 (*1-56329-326-9*) St Anthony Pub.
Ledkovsky, Marina, et al, eds. Dictionary of Russian Women Writers. LC 93-13012. 960p. 1994. text 155.00 (*0-313-26265-9*, ASV/, Greenwood Pr) Greenwood.
Ledkovsky, Marina, intro. Russia According to Women. LC 91-11292. (Illus.). 172p. (Orig.). (C). 1991. pap. text 9.50 (*1-55779-023-X*) Hermitage Pubs.
Ledl, Arthur. Studien Zur Alteren Athenischen Verfassungsgeschichte. LC 72-7898. (Greek History Ser.). (GER.). 1973. reprint ed. 31.95 (*0-405-04797-5*) Ayer.
Ledlie, James C., tr. see Sohm, Rudolph.
Ledner, Caryl. The Bondswoman. LC 76-62782. 298p. (J). 1977. write for info. (*0-312-08767-5*) St Martin.
Ledney, G. D., jt. ed. see Baum, S. J.
Lednicer, Daniel. Strategies for Organic Drug Synthesis & Design. LC 97-11813. 500p. 1997. 89.95 (*0-471-19657-6*) Wiley.
Lednicer, Daniel, ed. Chronicles of Drug Discovery, Vol. 3. LC 81-11471. (ACS Professional Reference Bk.). (Illus.). 350p. 1993. text 95.00 (*0-8412-2523-0*, Pub. by Am Chemical); pap. text 38.00 (*0-8412-2733-0*, Pub. by Am Chemical) OUP.
— Contraception: The Chemical Control of Fertility. LC 79-99957. (Illus.). 285p. reprint ed. pap. 88.40 (*0-7837-0957-9*, 204126200019) Bks Demand.
***Lednicer, Daniel & Mitscher, Lester A.** The Organic Chemistry of Drug Synthesis., 6 Vol.Set. 2120p. 1998. 699.00 (*0-471-33370-0*) Wiley.
Lednicer, Daniel & Mitscher, Lester A. Organic Chemistry of Drug Synthesis, 4 vols., Set. 1616p. 1990. 349.00 (*0-471-53176-6*) Wiley.
— Organic Chemistry of Drug Synthesis, 4 vols., Vol. 1. LC 76-28387. 496p. 1977. 165.00 (*0-471-52141-8*) Wiley.
— Organic Chemistry of Drug Synthesis, 4 vols., Vol. 2. LC 76-28387. 544p. 1980. 165.00 (*0-471-04392-3*) Wiley.
— Organic Chemistry of Drug Synthesis, 4 vols., Vol. 3. 304p. 1984. 165.00 (*0-471-09250-9*) Wiley.
— Organic Chemistry of Drug Synthesis, 4 vols., Vol. 4. 272p. 1990. 165.00 (*0-471-85548-0*) Wiley.
— The Organic Chemistry of Drug Synthesis, Vol. 5. 240p. 1994. 165.00 (*0-471-58959-4*) Wiley.
— The Organic Chemistry of Drug Synthesis, 5 vols., Vol. 5. 1856p. 1996. 430.00 (*0-471-16990-0*) Wiley.
***Lednicer, Daniel & Mitscher, Lester A.** The Organic Chemistry of Drug Synthesis, Vol. 6. LC 76-28387. 264p. 1998. 98.95 (*0-471-24510-0*) Wiley.
Lednicki, Waclaw. Pushkin's Bronze Horseman: The Story of a Masterpiece, Vol. 1--1. LC 78-5547. (Univ. of California Publications Slavis Studies: Vol. 1). 163p. 1978. lib. bdg. 35.00 (*0-313-20482-9*, LEPB, Greenwood Pr) Greenwood.
Lednicki, Waclaw, ed. Zygmunt Krasinski, Romantic Universalist: An International Tribute. 227p. 1964. 6.00 (*0-940962-47-0*) Polish Inst Art & Sci.
Lednicky, H. Maurice. The Scriptures Applied: Insights from the Word - Relevant Scriptural Truth for Today's Believer. 130p. 1999. pap. write for info. (*0-7392-0155-7*, PO3102) Morris Pubng.
Lednicky, H. Maurice. The Scriptures Applied Vol. II: Insights from the Word - Relevant Scriptural Truth for Today's Believer. 118p. Date not set. pap. write for info. (*0-7392-0435-1*) Morris Pubng.
Lednor, P. W., et al, eds. Advanced Catalytic Materials--1996. LC 97-30412. (Materials Research Society Symposium Proceedings Ser.: No. 454). 306p. 1997. text 75.00 (*1-55899-358-4*) Materials Res.
Lednor, Peter W., et al, eds. Advanced Catalytic Materials 1998 Vol. 549. LC 99-33673. (Symposium Proceedings Ser.). 270p. 1999. 80.00 (*1-55899-455-6*) Materials Res.
Ledo, Michael. Bible Bloopers: Evidence That Demands a Verdict Too! A Skeptic Examines Josh McDowell. Wilson, Jim, ed. (Orig.). 1997. pap. 14.95 (*1-887392-06-8*) Atl Freethought Soc.
LeDocte, E. Legal Dictionary in Four Languages. (ENG, FRE, GER & SPA.). 822p. 1987. 195.00 (*3-7890-3961-6*) IBD Ltd.
Ledolter. Quality. 192p. (C). 1998. pap. text, teacher ed. 17.50 (*0-471-09278-9*) Wiley.
***Ledolter, Johannes & Burrill, Claude S.** Statistical Quality Control: Strategies & Tools for Continual Improvement. LC 98-27290. 544p. 1998. text 95.95 (*0-471-18378-4*) Wiley.
Ledolter, Johannes, jt. auth. see Abraham, Bovas.
Ledolter, Johannes, jt. auth. see Burrill, Claude W.
Ledolter, Johannes, jt. auth. see Hogg, Robert V.
LeDonne, John P. Absolutism & Ruling Class: The Formation of the Russian Political Order, 1700-1825. 400p. 1991. text 70.00 (*0-19-506805-X*) OUP.
— Ruling Russia: Politics & Administration in the Age of Absolutism, 1762-1796. LC 84-2168. (Studies of the Harriman Institute). 427p. 1984. reprint ed. pap. 132.40 (*0-608-03332-4*, 206404400008) Bks Demand.
— The Russian Empire & the World, 1700-1917: The Geopolitics of Expansion & Containment. (Illus.). 416p. (C). 1996. text 57.00 (*0-19-510926-0*); pap. text 27.95 (*0-19-510927-9*) OUP.
LeDonne, Patricia, jt. ed. see McAlpine, Jan C.
Ledour, Denis, jt. auth. see Schawlow, A. L.
LeDoux, Chris B., jt. auth. see Huyler, Neil K.
Ledoux, Claude N. L' Architecture. (FRE., Illus.). 328p. 1982. reprint ed. 65.00 (*0-910413-03-7*) Princeton Arch.

An Asterisk (*) at the beginning of an entry indicates that the title is appearing for the first time.

— L' Architecture Consideree sous le Rapport de l'Art, des Moeurs et de la Legislation. 250p. 1980. reprint ed. write for info. (3-487-07010-3) G Olms Pubs.

Ledoux, Denis. Mountain Dance: And Other Stories. 55p. 1990. pap. 7.95 (0-9626857-0-4) Maine Writers.

— The Photo Scriber's Memory Binder. Blowen, Martha, ed. 90p. 1999. ring bd. 21.95 (0-9619373-6-X) Soleil Pr.

— Turning Memories into Memoirs: A Handbook for Writing Lifestories. (Illus.). 208p. (Orig.). (C). 1993. pap. 19.95 (0-9619373-2-7) Soleil Pr.

— Turning Memories into Memoirs Memory Binder. Blowen, Martha, ed. (Illus.). 65p. 1998. ring bd. 21.95 (0-9619373-5-1) Soleil Pr.

Ledoux, Denis, intro. Lives in Translation: An Anthology of Contemporary Franco-American Writings. 144p. (Orig.). 1990. pap. 12.95 (0-9619373-1-9) Soleil Pr.

LeDoux, Joseph. The Emotional Brain. 384p. 1998. per. 14.00 (0-684-83659-9) S&S Trade.

LeDoux, Joseph E., jt. auth. see Gazzaniga, Michael S.

Ledoux-Lebard, Denise. Dictionary of French Furniture Makers of the 19th Century - Dictionnaire Des Ebenistes et Des Menuisiers. (ENG & FRE., Illus.). 736p. 250.00 (1-55660-195-6) A Wofsy Fine Arts.

— Mobilier Francais de XVIIIe Siecle: Dictionnaire des Ebenistes et des Menusiers. (FRE.). 736p. 1991. 450.00 (0-8288-7315-1, 285917088X) Fr & Eur.

— Versailles, le Petit Trianon: Le Mobilier des Inventaires de 1807-1810. (FRE.). 248p. 1993. lib. bdg. 225.00 (0-7859-3646-7, 2859170863) Fr & Eur.

LeDoux, Louis & Haynes, John Harold. Ford Laser & Mazda 323 Automotive Repair Manual. LC 97-73892. (Haynes Automotive Repair Manual Ser.). 1997. write for info. (1-56392-265-7) Haynes Manuals.

Ledoux, Louis V. & Haynes, John H. Hyundai Excel: Automotive Repair Manual, 86-94. LC 97-80266. (Haynes Automotive Repair Manual Ser.). 1997. write for info. (1-56392-282-7) Haynes Manuals.

Ledoux, M. & Talagrand, M. Probability in Banach Spaces: Isoperimetry & Processes. (Ergebnisse der Mathematik und Ihrer Grenzgebiete Ser.: Vol. 23). (Illus.). 490p. 1991. 171.95 (0-387-52013-9) Spr-Verlag.

Ledoux, P., ed. see International Astronomical Union Staff.

***Ledoux, Paul.** Anne. 1999. pap. 14.95 (0-88754-576-9) Theatre Comm.

Ledoux, Paul & Smythe, David. Cheatin' Hearts. LC 95-219052. 126p. (Orig.). 1997. pap. 11.95 (0-88754-536-X) Playwrights.

Ledoux, Stephen F. Origins & Components of Behaviorology. LC 96-84449. 368p. 1997. 50.00 (1-882508-07-6) ABCs.

Ledoux, Stephen F., jt. auth. see Case, Nelly M.

Ledoux, Steve. How to Win Lotteries, Sweepstakes & Contests in the 21st Century. LC 99-37841. 240p. 1999. pap. 14.95 (1-891661-07-8, 1078) Snta Monica.

LeDoux, T. James, jt. auth. see Smith, Larry W.

Ledoux, Trish & Ranney, Doug. The Complete ANIME Guide: Japanese Animation Film Directory & Resource Guide. 2nd rev. ed. Patten, Fred, ed. (Illus.). viii, 214p. (Orig.). 1997. pap. 19.95 (0-9649542-5-7) Tiger Mtn.

Ledray, Linda E. Recovering from Rape. 2nd ed. 1995. pap. 12.95 (0-8050-2928-1) H Holt & Co.

Ledrew, Ellsworth, ed. Canadian Sea Ice Atlas from Microwave Remotely Sensed Imagery, July 1987-June 1990. (Climatological Studies: No. 44). (Illus.). 80p. (Orig.). 1993. pap. 32.45 (0-660-57966-9, Pub. by Canadian Govt Pub) Accents Pubns.

Ledrick, David. Homoerotic Art of Pavel Tchelitchev. (Illus.). 144p. 1999. 150.00 (1-893450-05-8) Elysium Pr.

Ledsham, Ian. A Catalogue of the Shaw-Hellier Collection in the Music Library, Barbar Institute of Fine Arts, the University of Birmington. LC 98-45683. 500p. 1999. text 91.95 (1-85928-386-1) Ashgate Pub Co.

Ledson, Sidney. Raising Brighter Children. (Illus.). 256p. 1987. 17.95 (0-8027-0924-9); pap. 9.95 (0-8027-7299-4) Walker & Co.

— Raising Brighter Children: A Program for Busy Parents. 1994. pap. text 16.95 (0-7737-5490-3) Genl Dist Srvs.

— Teach Your Child to Read in Sixty Days. 3rd ed. 1994. pap. 12.95 (0-7737-5445-8) Genl Dist Srvs.

— Teach Your Child to Read in Ten Minutes a Day. 1999. pap. text 15.95 (0-7737-6035-0) Genl Dist Srvs.

Leduc, Blake, Sr. Euclid Beach Yearbook. (Illus.). 192p. (Orig.). 1996. pap. 24.95 (0-9654588-0-6) Duke Graphics.

LeDuc, Bob. The Guitar Coach: An Ensemble Guitar Method. Stang, Aaron, ed. 72p. (C). 1996. pap. text 9.95 (0-7692-1296-4, EL9684) Wrner Bros.

LeDuc, Don R., jt. auth. see Teeter, Dwight L., Jr.

LeDuc, Don R., jt. auth. see Tetter, Dwight L., Jr.

Leduc, Herman. Dictionnaire d'Homeopathie Pediatrique a l'Usage des Familles et des Medecins de Famille. (FRE.). 494p. 1990. pap. 79.95 (0-7859-7910-7, 2700211057) Fr & Eur.

Leduc, Jean-Pierre. Digital Moving Pictures: Coding & Transmission on ATM Networks. LC 94-27698. 588p. 1994. 191.50 (0-444-81786-7) Elsevier.

Leduc, Joanne, ed. Overland from Canada to British Columbia: By Mr. Thomas McMicking of Queenston, Canada West. (Pioneers of British Columbia Ser.). (Illus.). 169p. 1981. pap. 15.95 (0-7748-0393-2) U of Wash Pr.

LeDuc, Lawrence, et al, eds. Comparing Democracies: Elections & Voting in Global Perspective. LC 96-10055. 352p. 1996. 56.00 (0-8039-5835-8); pap. 26.95 (0-8039-5836-6) Sage.

Leduc, Lucien. Motivating Correctional Staff Course, 3 bks., Set. Geiman, Diane et al, eds. 1992. pap. 70.00 (0-929310-67-5, 174) Am Correctional.

Leduc, M. R. Reflections of a Frog. 23p. 1995. pap. text 3.00 (0-921411-40-5) Genl Dist Srvs.

***Leduc, Steven A.** Cracking the GRE Math. (Illus.). 450p. 2000. pap. 16.00 (0-375-75399-0, Pub. by PRP NY) Random.

Leduc, Steven A. Differential Equations Quick Review. (Cliffs Quick Reviews Ser.). (Illus.). 188p. (Orig.). (C). 1995. pap. text 9.95 (0-8220-5320-9, Cliff) IDG Bks.

— Linear Algebra Quick Review. (Cliffs Quick Reviews Ser.). (Illus.). 101p. (Orig.). 1996. pap. text 9.95 (0-8220-5331-4, Cliff) IDG Bks.

Leduc, Sylva, jt. auth. see Smith, Nancy J.

Leduc, Violette. La Batarde. Coltman, Derek, tr. from FRE. LC 96-52580. 448p. 1997. pap. 14.00 (1-57322-609-2, Riverhd Trade) Berkley Pub.

— La Batarde. (FRE.). 1964. pap. 49.95 (0-7859-3960-1) Fr & Eur.

— La Femme au Petit Renard. (FRE.). 1976. pap. 8.95 (0-7859-4052-9) Fr & Eur.

***Leduc, Violette.** Mad in Pursuit. LC 99-29869. 1999. pap. text 14.00 (1-57322-740-4, Riverhead Books) Putnam Pub Group.

Leduc, Violette. Tresors a Prendre. (FRE.). 1978. pap. 10.95 (0-7859-4101-0) Fr & Eur.

Ledvinka, James. Federal Reg Personnel Human Res Mgt. LC 81-20826. (SWC-Management). 274p. 1982. 18.50 (0-534-01160-8) PWS Pubs.

Ledvinka, James, jt. auth. see Scarpello, Vida G.

Ledward, D. A., et al, eds. High Pressure Processing of Foods. 206p. 1999. 160.00 (1-897676-50-6, Pub. by Nottingham Univ Pr) St Mut.

Ledward, Daphne. The Idiot Gardeners Handbook. (Illus.). 388p. 1996. pap. 14.95 (0-86051-899-X, Pub. by Robson Bks) Parkwest Pubns.

***Ledward, Daphne.** Kitchen Garden Yearbook: A Month by Month Guide to Growing Your Own Vegetables. (Illus.). 178p. 1999. 29.95 (1-86105-167-0) Robson.

Ledwidge, Asher. The Black Family: Towards More Self-Love. (Orig.). 1993. pap. 8.00 (0-9636109-0-2) Nuf-Love Pub.

Ledwidge, Francis. Francis Ledwidge: Selected Poems. Bolger, Dermot, ed. 80p. (Orig.). 1992. reprint ed. 19.95 (1-874597-30-8, Pub. by New Island Books); reprint ed. pap. 9.95 (1-874597-10-3, Pub. by New Island Books) Irish Bks Media.

Ledwidge, Michael S. The Narrowback. LC 98-25649. 240p. 1999. 23.00 (0-87113-716-X) Grove-Atltic.

***Ledwith & Walker.** The Politics of Health Care: Towards a Holistic Approach. 224p. 2000. pap. text 36.00 (0-7506-4310-2) Buttrwrth-Heinemann.

Ledwith, A., jt. ed. see Jenkins, A. D.

Ledwith, A., jt. ed. see Moss, S. J.

Ledwith, Irene. The Dog Bite. 1988. pap. 10.00 (0-932526-20-9) Nexus Pr.

— R. B. Schueller. (Illus.). 48p. (Orig.). 1992. pap. 12.00 (0-89822-101-3) Visual Studies.

Ledwith, Nettie H. A Rorschach Study of Child Development. LC 75-26632. 336p. 1975. reprint ed. lib. bdg. 59.75 (0-8371-8365-0, LERS, Greenwood Pr) Greenwood.

Ledwith, Stuart. Mary Magdalene: The Disciple Jesus Loved. J, Kathlyn, ed. LC 90-91795. (Illus.). 122p. (Orig.). 1990. pap. 6.95 (0-9627250-0-5) Soul Works Intl.

***Ledwith, Sue, et al.** Women & the City: Visibility & Voice in Urban Space. LC 00-31115. 2000. write for info. (0-312-23563-1) St Martin.

Ledwith, Tim, ed. see Hayes, Roger, et al.

Ledwon, Lenora, ed. Law & Literature: Text & Theory. LC 95-35321. 520p. 1995. reprint ed. pap. text 26.95 (0-8153-2046-9) Garland.

— Law & Literature: Text & Theory. LC 95-35321. (Garland Reference Library of the Humanities: Vol. 1784). xv, 501p. 1995. reprint ed. text 80.00 (0-8153-1472-8, H1784) Garland.

***Ledwon, Peter & Mets, Marilyn.** Midnight Math. LC 99-37167. 32p. (J). (gr. 1-5). 2001. 15.95 (0-8234-1530-9) Holiday.

Ledyaev, Valeri. Power: A Conceptual Analysis. LC 98-11746. 1998. 65.00 (1-56072-536-2) Nova Sci Pubs.

Ledyard, Gleason H. Eskimos: Now the World. (Illus.). 256p. 1958. pap. text 6.00 (0-913201-26-X) Christian Lit.

— His Life. (Illus.). 224p. 1991. pap. text 6.00 (0-913201-22-7) Christian Lit.

— Teacher's Manual: Companion to Gleason H. Ledyard's Topical Study Outlines. 80p. 1975. pap. text 5.00 (0-913201-18-9) Christian Lit.

— Topical Study Outlines. 160p. 1970. pap. text 5.00 (0-913201-34-0) Christian Lit.

— Topical Study Outlines Workbook. 112p. 1988. 3.00 (0-913201-35-9) Christian Lit.

Ledyard, John. Journey Through Russia & Siberia, 1787-1788: The Journals & Selected Letters. LC 66-22855. (Illus.). 316p. reprint ed. pap. 98.00 (0-608-30170-1, 201097400072) Bks Demand.

Ledyard, John O., ed. The Economics of Informational Decentralization: Commplexity, Efficiency & Stability: Essays in Honor of Stanley Reiter. LC 94-32947. 456p. (C). 1995. lib. bdg. 230.00 (0-7923-9502-6) Kluwer Academic.

Lee. Abortion Law & Politics Today. LC 98-16151. 304p. 1998. text 49.95 (0-312-21574-6) St Martin.

Lee. Advances in Quantitive Analysis of Finance & Accounting, Vol. 7. 78.50 (0-7623-0564-9) Jai Pr.

Lee. Angela Carter. LC 96-39867. 1997. 32.00 (0-8057-7823-3, Twyne) Mac Lib Ref.

— Apprentice C++ Program. LC 97-101475. (Computer Science Ser.). 1996. pap. 44.95 (1-85032-160-4) ITCP.

— Apprentice C++ Program: Touch of Class. (ITCP-UK Computer Science Ser.). 1996. mass mkt. 12.95 (1-85032-161-2) ITCP.

— At the Centre of Whitehall: Advising the Prime Minister & the Cabinet. LC 97-21583. 1998. text 65.00 (0-312-17730-5) St Martin.

— The Backyard Berry Book: A Hands-On Guide to Growing Berries, Brambles, & Vine Fruit in the Home Garden. LC 94-93935. (Illus.). 288p. 1995. pap. 15.95 (0-9634520-6-1, Pub. by OttoGraphics) Chelsea Green Pub.

— Ballet in Western Culture: A History of Its Origins & Evolution. LC 98-37110. 368p. 1998. pap. 31.00 (0-205-27439-0, Longwood Div) Allyn.

— The Basic Newbury House Dictionary. (Global ESL/ELT Ser.). 1997. pap. 15.95 (0-8384-7916-2) Heinle & Heinle.

— The Basic Newbury House Dictionary. (Global ESL/ELT Ser.). (J). 1997. mass mkt. 15.95 (0-8384-7917-0) Heinle & Heinle.

***Lee.** Chemical Engineering, Vol. 4. 4th ed. 2000. pap. text 56.95 (0-7506-4140-1) Buttrwrth-Heinemann.

Lee. Contract Programming for DP. 1987. pap. 19.95 (0-9611810-8-7) CCD Online Syst.

— Creating Internet Application Using Vb Script: An Introduction. (Programming Ser.). (C). 2000. pap. 29.25 (0-619-01523-3) Course Tech.

— Creating Internet Applications Using Vb Script: Comprehensive. (Programming Ser.). (C). 2000. pap. 36.50 (0-619-01524-1) Course Tech.

— Crime, Punishment & Protest. 1994. pap. text. write for info. (0-582-23931-1, Pub. by Addison-Wesley) Longman.

***Lee.** A Diagnostic Atlas of Ear, Nose & Throat Diseases. 400p. 2001. pap. 59.00 (0-86577-851-5) Thieme Med Pubs.

— Discovering the Leader in You: A Guide for Realizing Your Personal Leadership Potential. 2000. 27.00 (0-7879-0951-3) Jossey-Bass.

Lee. Energy Aftermath. 288p. 1990. 29.95 (0-07-103248-7) McGraw.

— English Connections, Bk. 2. 1994. pap. 42.33 incl. audio (0-8092-3540-4) NTC Contemp Pub Co.

— Essential Otolaryngology. 7th ed. LC 98-29768. 1232p. 1998. pap. text 75.00 (0-8385-2270-X, Apple Lange Med) McGraw.

— Essentials of Corporate Finance. (C). 1996. text. write for info. (0-03-097002-4) Harcourt Coll Pubs.

Lee. Ethnicity Education & Empowerment. 65.95 (0-7546-1138-8) Ashgate Pub Co.

Lee. Family Secrets: The Best of the Delta. 1990. 14.95 (0-9626151-0-2) Lee Acad Parents.

— Foundations of Financial Management. LC 96-19547. 750p. 1996. pap. 95.95 (0-314-09572-1) West Pub.

— Fundamentals of Mammography. 1995. pap. text 57.95 (0-7020-1797-3, W B Saunders Co) Harcrt Hlth Sci Grp.

Lee. Gettysburg of the West: The Battle of Westport, October 21-23, 1864. pap. 17.95 (0-9636780-7-8, Pub. by Two Trails Pubg) Booksource.

Lee. God Suffers for Us. 1974. pap. text 57.00 (90-247-1614-4, Pub. by M Nijhoff) Kluwer Academic.

— Grand Piano Came by Camel: Arthur C. Mace, the Neglected Egyptologist. 34.95 (1-85158-434-X, Pub. by Mainstream Pubng) Trafalgar.

— Growth & Development of Children. 1990. pap. text. write for info. (0-582-05934-8, Pub. by Addison-Wesley) Longman.

— H. Pylori: Techniques for Clinical Diagnosis. 1995. text 55.00 (0-7020-1999-2, W B Saunders Co) Harcrt Hlth Sci Grp.

— Income & Value Measurement. 3rd ed. 1986. pap. 27.95 (0-442-30615-6) Chapman & Hall.

— Information Technology Social Scientist. LC 94-39456. (Social Research Today Ser.: Vol. 7). 1995. 65.00 (1-85728-280-9, Pub. by UCL Pr Ltd); pap. 27.50 (1-85728-281-7, Pub. by UCL Pr Ltd) Taylor & Francis.

— Introduction to the Design & Analysis of Algorithms. (C). 1991. pap. 53.33 (0-13-480773-1) P-H.

***Lee.** Journey Through Astronomy. (Astronomy). 2000. pap. 68.95 (0-534-57240-5) Brooks-Cole.

Lee. Law of the Lawless. LC 98-48524. Date not set. 30.00 (0-7838-0442-3, G K Hall Lrg Type) Mac Lib Ref.

***Lee.** Legal Concepts & Issues in Emergency Care. 2000. pap. write for info. (0-7216-8324-X, W B Saunders Co) Harcrt Hlth Sci Grp.

Lee. Making Communicative. 1995. pap., wbk. ed. 22.19 (0-07-037694-8) McGraw.

— Managing Your College Experince. 2nd ed. 226p. (C). 1998. pap. text 16.90 (0-536-01288-1) Pearson Custom.

— Mobile Communications Design Fundamentals. 2nd ed. 372p. 1993. pap. text 98.95 (0-471-00747-1) Wiley.

— Multicultural Workshop Box. (College ESL Ser.). 1995. mass mkt., teacher ed. 6.95 (0-8384-5027-X) Heinle & Heinle.

— Multicultural Workshop Box-answer Key. (College ESL). 1995. mass mkt., suppl. ed. 6.95 (0-8384-5026-1) Heinle & Heinle.

***Lee.** Nutritional Assessment. 3rd ed. 2001. 18.74 (0-07-292731-3) McGraw.

— Online Journey Through Astronomy. (Astronomy). 2000. pap. 64.95 (0-534-37410-7) Brooks-Cole.

Lee. Oral Interpretation, 9 vols. 9th ed. LC 96-76923. (C). 1996. pap. text 36.76 (0-395-79485-4) HM.

— Other Britain, Other British: Essays in Contemporary Multicultural Fiction. 1996. pap. 18.95 (0-7453-0646-2, Pub. by Pluto GBR) Stylus Pub VA.

— Permanent Etcetera: Cross-cultural Perspectives on Post-War America. LC 93-24953. 199p. (C). 49.95 (0-7453-0640-3, Pub. by Pluto GBR); pap. 19.95 (0-7453-0641-1, Pub. by Pluto GBR) Stylus Pub VA.

— Production & Operations Management. LC 93-78633. (C). 1993. pap. text 77.56 (0-395-56084-5) HM.

— Production & Operations Management. (C). 1993. pap. 9.96 (0-395-69233-4) HM.

— Production & Operations Management. (C). 1994. pap. text, student ed. 20.76 (0-395-56085-3) HM.

— Red Unicorn. (Tor Fantasy Ser.). 192p. 1998. mass mkt. 4.99 (0-8125-3938-9, Pub. by Tor Bks) St Martin.

— Regulation of Banks & Other Depository Institutions in Malaysia - A Study in Monetary, Prudential & Other Controls. 385p. 1992. boxed set 171.00 (0-409-99601-7, MICHIE) LEXIS Pub.

— Revolution & Reflection. 1974. pap. text 71.50 (90-247-1638-1, Pub. by M Nijhoff) Kluwer Academic.

— Sewing Beautiful Pillows. (Illus.). 128p. 1998. pap. 14.95 (0-8069-9809-1) Sterling.

— Shanghai Modern: The Flowering of a New Urban Culture in China, 1930-1945 LC 98-32318. 1999. 49.95 (0-674-80550-X) HUP.

— Smuggling Armageddon: Nuclear Black Market in the Former Soviet Union & Europe. 224p. 2000. pap. 16.95 (0-312-22456-7) St Martin.

***Lee.** Tasks Community Language Classrooms. LC 99-30902. 184p. 1999. pap. 38.13 (0-07-231054-5) McGraw.

— Thoughts & Notions. (C). 1999. pap., teacher ed. 10.50 (0-8384-0022-1) Heinle & Heinle.

— Transitions Workbook 2: Integrated English Program. (Illus.). 1999. pap. 6.95 (0-19-434632-3) OUP.

Lee. The Underground Blue Book: A Guide to Buying & Selling New & Used Cars, Trucks & R. V.'s. 136p. (Orig.). 1987. pap. 9.95 (0-9617946-0-7) Diamond S Pub.

— Wireless Communications. (Illus.). 320p. 2000. pap. 49.95 (0-07-134542-6) McGraw.

— York Notes on Lee's Cider with Rosie. 1992. pap. text. write for info. (0-582-03365-9) Addison-Wesley.

Lee, ed. English Connections, Vol. 2. 1994. pap., teacher ed. 10.55 (0-8092-3702-4); pap., wbk. ed. 2.50 (0-8092-3705-9) NTC Contemp Pub Co.

***Lee, ed.** Manage Your College Experience. 3rd ed. 180p. 1999. pap. text 18.70 (0-536-02623-8) P-H.

Lee, ed. Remote Sensing in Exploration Geology. (IGC Field Trip Guidebooks Ser.). 64p. 1989. 21.00 (0-87590-564-1, T182) Am Geophysical.

Lee & Bushby, Alex. Thoughts & Notions. LC 99-34946. (J). 1999. pap. text 26.95 (0-8384-8222-8) Heinle & Heinle.

Lee & Gaskin. Word Processing Applications. 1997. teacher ed. write for info. (0-256-23166-4) McGrw-H Hghr Educ.

Lee & Olson. Introduction to Management Science. rev. ed. 1997. 78.95 (0-87393-589-6) Dame Pubns.

— Introduction to Management Science: Study Guide. rev. ed. 1997. pap. 28.95 (0-87393-449-0) Dame Pubns.

Lee & Palmer. Government by the People Study Guide, 16. 16th ed. 224p. 1995. pap. text, student ed. 20.00 (0-13-303991-9) P-H.

Lee & Progris. I Want to Play Alto Recorder. 1990. 3.95 (0-685-32168-1, N234) Hansen Ed Mus.

— I Want to Play Alto Saxophone. 1990. 3.95 (0-685-32217-3, N228) Hansen Ed Mus.

— I Want to Play Clarinet. 1990. 3.95 (0-685-32202-5, N230) Hansen Ed Mus.

— I Want to Play Flute. 1990. 3.95 (0-685-32114-2, N225) Hansen Ed Mus.

— I Want to Play Harmonica. 1990. 3.95 (0-685-32196-7, N235) Hansen Ed Mus.

— I Want to Play Soprano Recorder. 1990. 3.95 (0-685-32167-3, N233) Hansen Ed Mus.

— I Want to Play Tenor Saxophone. 1990. 3.95 (0-685-32218-1, N229) Hansen Ed Mus.

— I Want to Play Trombone. 1990. 3.95 (0-685-32234-3, N227) Hansen Ed Mus.

— I Want to Play Trumpet. 1990. 3.95 (0-685-32184-3, N226) Hansen Ed Mus.

— Top Score Solo Songbook. 1990. 1.95 (0-685-32120-7, N245); 1.95 (0-685-32198-3, N258); 1.95 (0-685-47133-0, N250); 1.95 (0-685-47134-9, N247) Hansen Ed Mus.

— Top Score Solo Songbook: Alto Saxophone. 1990. 1.95 (0-685-32212-2, N248) Hansen Ed Mus.

Lee & Wood, L. J. Adjustment in the Urban System: The Tasman Bridge Collapse & Its Effects on Metropolitan Hobart. (Progress in Planning Ser.: Vol. 15, Pt. 2). 85p. 1981. pap. 16.25 (0-08-026810-2) Elsevier.

Lee, et al. Business Statistics: Quality Information for Decision Analysis. LC 96-71827. (Illus.). 1998. 81.95 (0-87393-472-5) Dame Pubns.

— Guided Weapons. (Brassey's Battlefield Weapons Systems & Technology Ser.: Vol. 8). 160p. 1983. text 33.00 (0-08-028336-5, Pergamon Pr); pap. text 14.25 (0-08-028337-3, Pergamon Pr) Elsevier.

— Perspectives 2000: Intermediate English, Level 1. 3rd ed. 180p. (J). 1991. mass mkt. 13.00 (0-8384-2003-6); mass mkt., student ed. 9.95 (0-8384-2005-2) Heinle & Heinle.

— Perspectives 2000: Intermediate English, Level 1. 3rd ed. (J). 1991. mass mkt., teacher ed. 21.95 (0-8384-2052-4) Heinle & Heinle.

— Perspectives 2000: Intermediate English, Level 1. 3rd ed. (J). 1991. audio 60.95 (0-8384-2004-4) Heinle & Heinle.

— Perspectives 2000: Intermediate English, Level 1. 3rd ed. (YA). (gr. 8-12). 1991. mass mkt., lab manual ed. 38.95 (0-8384-2222-5) Heinle & Heinle.

— Perspectives 2000: Intermediate English, Level 1. 3rd ed. (J). 1992. audio 23.95 (0-8384-4233-1) Heinle & Heinle.

— Perspectives 2000: Intermediate English, Level 1. 3rd ed. (J). 1993. audio 42.95 (0-8384-4199-8) Heinle & Heinle.

Lee, jt. auth. see Aufmann.

Lee, jt. auth. see Huang.

Lee, jt. auth. see Jarrett.

Lee, jt. auth. see Johnson, Bernard.

Lee, jt. auth. see Johnston, Bernard.

Lee, jt. auth. see Lee, John.

An Asterisk (*) at the beginning of an entry indicates that the title is appearing for the first time.

Lee, jt. auth. see Lerner.

Lee, jt. auth. see Turner, Diana L.

Lee, jt. auth. see Watson.

Lee, jt. ed. see VanPatten, Bill.

Lee, Lam T. As I Was Saying: Viewpoints, Thoughts, & Aspirations of-- LC 98-944611. 248p. 1998. write for info. (*967-978-643-9*) Pelanduk.

Lee, A. Collingwood. Decameron: Its Sources & Analogues. LC 68-814. (Studies in Comparative Literature: No. 35). 1909. lib. bdg. 75.00 (*0-8383-0581-4*) M S G Haskell Hse.

***Lee, A. D.** Pagans & Christians in Late Antiquity: A Sourcebook. LC 00-21697. 2000. pap. write for info. (*0-415-13893-0*) Routledge.

Lee, A. G., ed. Biomembranes Vol. 3: Receptors of Cell Adhesion & Cellular Recognition. 336p. 1996. 128.50 (*1-55938-660-6*) Jai Pr.

— Biomembranes Vol. 4: Endocytosis & Exocytosis. 312p. 1996. 128.50 (*1-55938-661-4*) Jai Pr.

— Ovid: Metamorphoses I, Vol. I. (Bristol Latin Texts Ser.). (LAT.). 168p. 1992. pap. 20.95 (*0-86292-144-9*, Pub. by Brist Class Pr) Focus Pub-R Pullins.

— Ovid - Metamorphoses, Bk. 1. 1985. 14.00 (*0-86516-040-6*) Bolchazy-Carducci.

Lee, A. G., ed. see Ovid.

Lee, A. H., jt. ed. see Nicholson, D. H.

Lee, A. J. U-Statistics: Theory & Practice. (Statistics: Textbooks & Monographs: Vol. 110). (Illus.). 320p. 1990. text 125.00 (*0-8247-8253-4*) Dekker.

Lee, A. J., ed. see European Conference on Biomaterials Staff.

Lee, A. K., et al, eds. Biology of the Koala. 346p. (C). 1999. pap. 320.00 (*0-949324-34-5*, Pub. by Surrey Beatty & Sons) St Mut.

Lee, A. K. & Cockburn, Andrew. Evolutionary Ecology of Marsupials. (Monographs on Marsupial Biology). (Illus.). 288p. 1985. text 85.00 (*0-521-25292-X*) Cambridge U Pr.

Lee, A. Robert. Beat Generation Writers. LC 95-7723. 232p. (C). 1995. text 60.00 (*0-7453-0660-8*, Pub. by Pluto GBR) Stylus Pub VA.

— Beat Generation Writers. LC 95-7723. 232p. (C). 1996. pap. text 19.95 (*0-7453-0661-6*, Pub. by Pluto GBR) Stylus Pub VA.

— Designs of Blackness: Studies in the Literature of African-America. 192p. 1998. pap. 19.95 (*0-7453-0644-6*, Pub. by Pluto GBR) Stylus Pub VA.

— Designs of Blackness: Studies in the Literature of African-America. LC 98-19975. 192p. (C). 1998. text 59.95 (*0-7453-0643-8*, Pub. by Pluto GBR) Stylus Pub VA.

***Lee, A. Robert.** Loosening the Seams: Interpretations of Gerald Vizenor. LC 99-58862. (Illus.). 321p. 2000. pap. 29.95 (*0-87972-802-7*) Bowling Green Univ Popular Press.

Lee, A. Robert, ed. Herman Melville: Reassessments. LC 83-22340. 222p. 1984. 44.00 (*0-389-20376-9*, 07248); pap. 16.00 (*0-389-20471-4*, 08033) B&N Imports.

***Lee, A. Robert, ed.** Loosening the Seams: Interpretations of Gerald Vizenor. LC 99-58862. (Illus.). 321p. 2000. 59.95 (*0-87972-801-9*) Bowling Green Univ Popular Press.

Lee, A. Robert, ed. The Modern American Novella. LC 89-5876. 224p. 1989. text 39.95 (*0-312-02424-X*) St Martin.

— The Nineteenth-Century American Short Story. LC 85-15707. (Critical Studies). 224p. 1986. 56.50 (*0-389-20593-1*, N8151) B&N Imports.

— William Faulkner: The Yoknapatawpha Fiction. LC 84-6274. (Critical Studies). 224p. (C). 1986. 28.50 (*0-389-20489-7*, BNB-08051) B&N Imports.

Lee, A. Robert, jt. auth. see Vicenor, Gerald.

Lee, A. Robert, ed. see Melville, Herman.

Lee, Abigail, ed. & tr. see Galdos, Benito P.

Lee, Adam. The Dark Shore. LC 96-27286. (Dominions of Irth Ser.). 432p. 1997. pap. 13.00 (*0-380-79071-8*, Avon Bks); mass mkt. 24.00 (*0-380-97441-X*, Avon Bks) Morrow Avon.

— Dark Shore. (Dominions of Irth Ser.). 512p. 1998. mass mkt. 5.99 (*0-380-79617-1*, Avon Bks) Morrow Avon.

***Lee, Adam.** Octoberland. LC 99-11213. (Dominions of Irth Ser.: Vol. 3). 320p. 2000. mass mkt. 6.50 (*0-380-80628-2*, Avon Bks) Morrow Avon.

— Octoberland: Book Three of the Dominions of Irth. LC 99-11213. (Dominions of Irth Ser.: Bk. 3). 320p. 1999. pap. 13.50 (*0-380-79072-6*, Eos) Morrow Avon.

Lee, Adam. The Shadow Eater Bk. II: The Dominions of Irth. 352p. 1999. mass mkt. 5.99 (*0-380-80627-4*, Eos) Morrow Avon.

Lee, Addie. Crack Baby & Other Poems. LC 89-90581. (Illus.). 64p. (Orig.). 1990. per. 5.95 (*0-9625139-0-3*) White Dogwood Pr.

Lee, Adrianne. Alias: Daddy. (Intrigue Ser.: No. 422). 1997. per. 3.75 (*0-373-22422-2*, 1-22422-9) Harlequin Bks.

***Lee, Adrianne.** Au Risque de Lui Plaire. (Rouge Passion Ser.: No. 538). (FRE.). 2000. mass mkt. 3.99 (*0-373-37538-7*, 1-37538-7, Harlequin French) Harlequin Bks.

Lee, Adrianne. The Best-Kept Secret. (Intrigue Ser.: No. 496). 1998. per. 3.99 (*0-373-22496-6*, 1-22496-3) Harlequin Bks.

— The Bride's Secret. (Intrigue Ser.: Bk. 524). 1999. per. 3.99 (*0-373-22524-5*, 1-22524-2) Harlequin Bks.

— Eden's Baby. (Intrigue Ser.). 1996. per. 3.75 (*0-373-22383-8*, 1-22383-3) Harlequin Bks.

— Endless Fear. 320p. 1992. mass mkt. 4.50 (*0-8217-3852-6*, Zebra Kensgtn) Kensgtn Pub Corp.

***Lee, Adrianne.** Little Boy Lost. (Intrigue Ser.). 2000. mass mkt. 4.25 (*0-373-22580-6*, 1-22580-4) Harlequin Bks.

Lee, Adrianne. Little Girl Lost. 1997. per. 3.75 (*0-373-22438-9*, 1-22438-5) Harlequin Bks.

— Midnight Cowboy. LC 96-3539. (Intrigue Ser.). 250p. 1996. per. 3.50 (*0-373-22354-4*, 1-22354-4) Harlequin Bks.

— The Runaway Bride. (Intrigue Ser.: Vol. 479). 1998. per. 3.99 (*0-373-22479-6*, 1-22479-9) Harlequin Bks.

— Something Borrowed, Something Blue. LC 03-732229. 251p. 1994. per. 2.99 (*0-373-22296-3*, 1-22296-7) Harlequin Bks.

Lee, Alan. Lord Ted: The Dexter Enigma. (Illus.). 256p. 1996. pap. 13.95 (*0-575-60040-3*, Pub. by V Gollancz) Trafalgar.

Lee, Alan J., jt. ed. see Harris, Michael.

***Lee, Albert.** Thrilling Escapes by Night. 336p. 1998. pap. 6.65 (*0-7399-0311-X*, 2430.1) Rod & Staff.

— Thrilling Escapes by Night. 296p. (YA). (gr. 11). 1998. 10.75 (*0-7399-0310-1*, 2430) Rod & Staff.

Lee, Alex. Force Recon Command: A Special Marine Unit in Vietnam, 1969-1970. LC 95-15533. (Naval Institute Special Warfare Ser.). (Illus.). 308p. 1995. 31.95 (*1-55750-513-6*) Naval Inst Pr.

— Force Recon Command: 3rd Force Recon Company in Vietnam, 1969-70. 1996. mass mkt. 6.99 (*0-8041-1023-9*) Ivy Books.

***Lee, Alex.** Utter's Battalion: 2/7 Marines in Vietnam, 1965-66. 2000. mass mkt. 6.99 (*0-8041-1638-5*) Ivy Books.

***Lee, Alfonso Silva.** Coqui y Sus Amigos (Coqui & His Friends) Los Animales de Puerto Rico (The Animals of Puerto Rico) Hayskar, Bonnie J., ed. (SPA & ENG., Illus.). 100p. (J). (gr. 3-6). 2000. pap. 12.95 (*1-929165-03-X*) Pangaea Pub.

Lee, Alfonso Silva. Natural Puerto Rico - Puerto Rico Natural. LC 97-28419. (ENG & SPA., Illus.). 128p. 1998. pap. 18.95 (*0-9630180-6-X*) Pangaea Pub.

Lee, Alfonso Silva, see Silva Lee, Alfonso.

Lee, Alfred E. History of the City of Columbus, 2 vols. (Illus.). 1799p. 1997. reprint ed. lib. bdg. 169.00 (*0-8328-6308-4*) Higginson Bk Co.

Lee, Alfred M. Terrorism in Northern Ireland. LC 83-80158. 253p. 1983. lib. bdg. 38.95 (*0-930390-51-2*) Gen Hall.

Lee, Alfred M., ed. see Bowers, Raymond.

Lee, Alfred T. Handbook for the Executive As a Witness. LC 74-80504. 54p. 1980. pap. 10.00 (*0-939190-00-1*) Intl Trademark.

***Lee, Alison.** Culture & Text: Discourse & Methodology in Social Research & Cultural Studies. 240p. 2000. pap. 24.00 (*0-7425-0059-4*) Rowman.

Lee, Alison. Gender, Literacy, Curriculum: Rewriting School Geography. 240p. 1996. 79.95 (*0-7484-0297-7*); pap. 27.95 (*0-7484-0298-5*) Taylor & Francis.

***Lee, Alison & Poynton, Cate, eds.** Culture & Text: Discourse & Methodology in Social Research & Cultural Studies. 240p. 2000. text 65.00 (*0-7425-0058-6*) Rowman.

Lee, Alison, jt. ed. see Carmichael, Thomas.

Lee, Allan. American Transportation: History & Museums. (Illus.). 224p. 1993. pap. 17.95 (*0-943231-57-4*) Howell Pr VA.

Lee, Alton, compiled by. Dwight David Eisenhower: A Bibliography of His Times & Presidency. LC 90-23694. (Twentieth-Century Presidential Bibliography Ser.). 240p. 1991. 85.00 (*0-8420-2288-0*) Scholarly Res Inc.

Lee, Alvin. Gold-Hall & Earth-Dragon: 'Beowulf' as Metaphor. LC 99-19724. 328p. 1999. text 50.00 (*0-8020-4378-X*) U of Toronto Pr.

Lee, Alvin A. The Guest-Hall of Eden: Four Essays on the Design of Old English Poetry. LC 76-151581. 254p. reprint ed. pap. 78.80 (*0-608-14017-1*, 202201200024) Bks Demand.

Lee, Alvin A. & Denham, Robert D., eds. The Legacy of Northrop Frye. 354p. 1994. text 55.00 (*0-8020-0632-9*); pap. text 24.95 (*0-8020-7588-6*) U of Toronto Pr.

***Lee, Amelia M., et al.** Physical Education for Children: Daily Lesson Plans for Middle School. 2nd ed. LC 99-44613. (Illus.). 368p. 2000. 29.00 (*0-87322-683-6*) Human Kinetics.

***Lee, Amy.** Composing Critical Pedagogies: Teaching Writing as Revision. (Refiguring English Studies). 359p. (C). 2000. pap. write for info. (*0-8141-3040-2*, 30402) NCTE.

Lee, Amy. I Am Chinese American. LC 96-51076. (Our American Family Ser.: Set 1). (Illus.). 24p. (J). (gr. k-4). 1997. lib. bdg. 15.93 (*0-8239-5012-3*, PowerKids) Rosen Group.

Lee, Andrea. Sarah Phillips. (Northeastern Library of Black Literature). 144p. 1993. reprint ed. pap. text 14.95 (*1-55553-158-X*) NE U Pr.

Lee, Andrew C., jt. ed. see Henson, Lindsey C.

Lee, Andrew G. & Brazis, Paul W. Clinical Pathways in Neuro-Ophthalmology. LC 97-51525. 398p. 1998. 69.00 (*0-86577-755-1*); 69.00 (*3-13-108641-6*) Thieme Med Pubs.

Lee, Andy. Backyard Market Gardening: The Entrepreneur's Guide to Selling What You Grow. LC 90-84585. (Illus.). 352p. (Orig.). 1999. pap. 19.95 (*0-9624648-0-5*, Pub. by Good Earth Pubns) Chelsea Green Pub.

Lee, Andy & Foreman, Patricia. Chicken Tractor: The Permaculture Guide to Happy Hens & Healthy Soil. 2nd rev. ed. LC 92-76194. (Illus.). 320p. 1999. pap. 19.95 (*0-9624648-6-4*, Pub. by Good Earth Pubns) Chelsea Green Pub.

Lee, Angela. Burke County. LC 97-158777. (Images of America Ser.). (Illus.). 128p. 1999. pap. 16.99 (*0-7524-0514-4*) Arcadia Publng.

Lee, Anita. Knowledge-Based Flexible Manufacturing Systems (FMS) Scheduling. LC 93-43003. (Studies on Industrial Productivity). 136p. 1994. text 15.00 (*0-8153-1627-5*) Garland.

Lee, Anita J. Keys to Understanding Securities. (Barron's Business Keys Ser.). 160p. 1989. pap. 4.95 (*0-8120-4229-8*) Barron.

Lee, Anna C. From the Editor's Desk - Chinese Edition. (CHI.). 107p. 1989. pap. 5.50 (*1-56582-089-4*) Christ Renew Min.

Lee, Anna C., tr. see Schaeffer, Francis A.

Lee, Annabel & Levaar, Liz. Lost Poet. LC 96-61964. 416p. 1997. 25.95 (*1-890171-15-8*); pap. 16.95 (*1-890171-16-6*) Unicorn Recs & Pub.

Lee, Anne F. Hawaii State Constitution: A Reference Guide, 14. LC 92-35920. (Reference Guides to the State Constitutions of the United States Ser.: No. 14). 272p. 1993. lib. bdg. 75.00 (*0-313-27950-0*, LHI/) Greenwood.

Lee, Anne M. Children in Lent: A Resource Book for Home, School & Parish. (Illus.). 96p. (Orig.). 1996. pap. 9.95 (*1-85607-160-X*, Pub. by Columba Press) Whitecap Bks.

Lee, Anne M. & Wisdom, Elaine. Stories, Symbols, Songs & Skits for Lively Children's Liturgies. LC 94-61925. 88p. (Orig.). 1995. pap. 9.95 (*0-89622-640-9*) Twenty-Third.

Lee, Anne R., jt. auth. see Hoffman, Judith B.

Lee, Anthony & Martin, Roger. The Koala: A Natural History. 104p. 1996. reprint ed. pap. 19.95 (*0-86840-354-7*, Pub. by New South Wales Univ Pr) Intl Spec Bk.

Lee, Anthony A. The Unfriendly Governor. (Stories about 'Abdu'l-Baha Ser.). (Illus.). 24p. (J). (gr. k-5). 1980. pap. 3.00 (*0-933770-02-2*) Kalimat.

Lee, Anthony A., ed. Circle of Peace: Reflections on the Baha'i Teachings. 214p. (Orig.). 1986. pap. 14.95 (*0-933770-48-0*) Kalimat.

— Circle of Unity: Baha'i Approaches to Current Social Issues. 268p. (Orig.). 1984. pap. 14.95 (*0-933770-28-6*) Kalimat.

Lee, Anthony G., ed. Biomembranes: ATPases, Vol. 6A. 432p. 1997. 128.50 (*1-55938-663-0*) Jai Pr.

— Biomembranes: ATPases, Vol. 6B. 128.50 (*1-55938-664-9*) Jai Pr.

— Biomembranes: Endocytosis & Exocytosis, Vol. 5. 440p. 1996. 128.50 (*1-55938-662-2*) Jai Pr.

— Biomembranes: General Principles, Vol. 1. 279p. 1995. 128.50 (*1-55938-658-4*) Jai Pr.

— Biomembranes Vols. 2A & B: Rhodopsin & G-Protein Linked Receptors. 524p. 1996. 257.00 (*1-55938-659-2*) Jai Pr.

***Lee, Anthony M.** The Zen Gift Set. 96p. 2000. boxed set 24.95 (*0-7641-7405-3*) Barron.

Lee, Anthony W. Painting on the Left: Diego Rivera, Radical Politics & San Francisco's Public Murals. LC 98-18740. 1999. 50.00 (*0-520-21133-2*, Pub. by U CA Pr) Cal Prin Full Svc.

***Lee, Anthony W.** Painting on the Left: Diego Rivera, Radical Politics & San Francisco's Public Murals. 290p. 1999. pap. 24.95 (*0-520-21977-5*, Pub. by U CA Pr) Cal Prin Full Svc.

Lee, Antoinette J. Architects to the Nation: The Rise & Decline of the Supervising Architect's Office. LC 99-13565. (Illus.). 352p. 2000. 45.00 (*0-19-512822-2*) OUP.

Lee, Antoinette J., ed. Historical Perspectives on Urban Design Vol. O1: Washington, D. C. 1890-1910. 1983. 4.00 (*1-888028-14-9*) GWU Ctr WAS.

— Past Meets Future: Saving America's Historic Environment. (Illus.). 384p. 1995. 25.95 (*0-471-14412-6*) Wiley.

Lee, Antoinette J., jt. auth. see Scott, Pamela.

Lee, Antoinette J., ed. see Stipe, Robert E.

Lee, Arlee. Lafayette, Colorado: Treeless Plain to Thriving City. (Illus.). 382p. Date not set. reprint ed. text 60.00 (*0-88107-154-4*) Curtis Media.

Lee, Arnie. Building Your Own PC: Buying & Assembling with Confidence. LC 97-128661. 1996. pap. text 24.95 (*1-55755-320-3*) Abacus MI.

— Building Your Own PC: Buying & Assembling with Confidence. 2nd ed. (Illus.). 130p. 1998. pap. 32.95 (*1-55755-355-6*) Abacus MI.

— Upgrading Your 486: Buying & Replacing with Confidence. 1997. pap. text 24.95 (*1-55755-323-8*) Abacus MI.

Lee, Art. Fishing Dry Flies for Trout on Rivers & Streams. rev. ed. LC 97-26114. (Illus.). 320p. 1997. 24.95 (*0-88011-777-X*, PLEE0777) Human Kinetics.

— Leftover Lefse. (Illus.). 224p. (Orig.). 1987. pap. 7.95 (*0-934860-48-3*) Adventure Pubns.

— Leftover Lutefisk. 224p. 1984. pap. 7.95 (*0-934860-32-7*) Adventure Pubns.

— Lore of Trout Fishing. LC 98-47330. 264p. 1999. pap. 26.95 (*0-88011-790-7*) Human Kinetics.

— On Blue Water: A Limited Edition in Recognition of the Ernest Hemingway Centennial. limited ed. LC 99-94721. (Illus.). 60p. 1999. 50.00 (*0-9670639-0-6*) Beaverkill Prods.

***Lee, Art.** A Real Scandinavian Never Asks Directions: Scandinavian America, Then & Now. 102p. 2000. pap. 8.95 (*1-885061-78-1*) Adventure Pubns.

Lee, Art. Tying & Fishing the Riffling Hitch. LC 97-39318. (Illus.). 120p. 1998. 21.95 (*0-88011-782-6*, PLEE0782) Human Kinetics.

Lee, Art, ed. The Lutefisk Ghetto. 224p. 1978. pap. 7.95 (*0-934860-02-5*) Adventure Pubns.

Lee, Arthur B. The Microtomist's Vade-Mecum. (History of Microscopy Ser.). 448p. 1987. reprint ed. 33.00 (*0-940095-04-1*) Sci Heritage Ltd.

Lee, Artis. Read On! Two, Bk. 5. Lawson, V. K., ed. (Illus.). 78p. 1987. pap. text 3.75 (*0-930713-06-0*); audio 10.00 (*0-318-41218-7*) Lit Vol Am.

— Read On! Two, Wkbk. 5. Lawson, V. K., ed. (Illus.). 84p. 1987. pap. text 2.75 (*0-930713-15-X*) Lit Vol Am.

Lee, Artis & Elmore, Fred. Read On! Two, Bk. 3. Lawson, V. K., ed. (Illus.). 48p. 1987. pap. text 3.75 (*0-930713-04-4*); audio 8.00 (*0-930713-17-6*) Lit Vol Am.

— Read On! Two, Wkbk. 3. Lawson, V. K., ed. (Illus.). 48p. 1987. pap. text 2.75 (*0-930713-13-3*) Lit Vol Am.

Lee, Artis & Simmons, Judy D. Read On! Two, Bk. 2. Lawson, V. K., ed. (Illus.). 1987. audio 8.00 (*0-930713-09-5*) Lit Vol Am.

Lee, Artis, et al. Read On! Two, Bk. 1. Lawson, V. K., ed. (Illus.). 68p. 1987. pap. 3.75 (*0-930713-02-8*); audio 8.00 (*0-930713-08-7*) Lit Vol Am.

— Read On! Two, Wkbk. 1. Lawson, V. K., ed. (Illus.). 68p. 1987. 2.75 (*0-930713-11-7*) Lit Vol Am.

Lee, Artis, jt. auth. see Coville, Bruce.

Lee, Artis, jt. auth. see Simmons, Judy D.

Lee, Asher, ed. The Soviet Air & Rocket Forces. LC 75-27682. (Illus.). 311p. 1976. reprint ed. lib. bdg. 69.50 (*0-8371-8456-8*, LESAR, Greenwood Pr) Greenwood.

Lee, Ashley. Relationships: How to Have Relationships, God's Way. 96p. 1995. pap. 7.95 (*0-9643797-0-8*) Ashley Lee.

Lee, B. Chiral Dynamics. xii, 118p. (C). 1972. pap. text 195.00 (*0-677-01385-X*) Gordon & Breach.

— Escaping from Hunger. 1993. pap. 75.00 (*1-86320-093-2*, Pub. by ACIAR) St Mut.

— Music Made Easy, Pt. 1. (Made Easy Ser.). 1990. 7.95 (*0-685-32064-2*, 8413) Hansen Ed Mus.

Lee, B. B., jt. auth. see Valberg, A.

Lee, B. H. Food Biotechnology. (Food Science & Technology Ser.). (Illus.). 350p. 1995. 65.00 (*1-56081-694-5*, Wiley-VCH) Wiley.

Lee, B. H. Fundamentals of Food Biotechnology. 431p. 1996. 155.00 (*0-471-18616-3*) Wiley.

Lee, B. L., jt. auth. see Cleghorn, J. M.

Lee, Bang W. & Sheu, Bing J. Hardware Annealing in Analog VLSI Neurocomputing. (International Series in Engineering & Computer Science, VLSI, Computer Architecture, & Digital Screen Processing). 256p. 1990. text 103.50 (*0-7923-9132-2*) Kluwer Academic.

***Lee, Barbara.** Dead Man's Fingers. 2001. mass mkt. 5.99 (*0-373-26369-4*, 1-26369-8) Harlequin Bks.

Lee, Barbara. Final Closing. (Worldwide Library Mysteries: No. 304). 1999. per. 4.99 (*0-373-26304-X*, 1-26304-5, Wrldwide Lib) Harlequin Bks.

— Final Closing: An Eve Elliot Mystery. LC 97-16242. 304p. 1997. text 22.95 (*0-312-16762-8*) St Martin.

— Financially Independent Woman. 144p. 1996. 16.95 (*1-55972-366-1*, Birch Ln Pr) Carol Pub Group.

— Financially Independent Woman: A Step-By-Step Guide to Successful Living. LC 98-11169. 176p. 1998. pap. 12.95 (*0-8065-1977-0*, Citadel Pr) Carol Pub Group.

— Working in Health Care & Wellness. LC 95-49876. (Exploring Careers Ser.). (Illus.). (J). (gr. 6-8). 1996. lib. bdg. 23.93 (*0-8225-1760-4*, Lerner Publctns) Lerner Pub.

— Working in Music. LC 96-4694. (Exploring Careers Ser.). (J). 1996. 23.93 (*0-8225-1761-2*, Lerner Publctns) Lerner Pub.

— Working in Sports & Recreation. LC 95-46030. (Exploring Careers Ser.). (Illus.). (J). (gr. 6-8). 1996. lib. bdg. 23.93 (*0-8225-1762-0*, Lerner Publctns) Lerner Pub.

— Working with Animals. LC 95-25657. (Exploring Careers Ser.). (J). 1996. lib. bdg. 23.93 (*0-8225-1759-0*, Lerner Publctns) Lerner Pub.

Lee, Barbara, et al. Dead Man's Fingers. LC 99-19878. 276p. 1999. text 22.95 (*0-312-20524-4*) St Martin.

Lee, Barbara, jt. auth. see Nellis, John R.

Lee, Barbara, ed. see Roberson, William H.

Lee, Barbara A. Reasonable Accommodation under the Americans with Disabilities Act. (ADA Practice Ser.). 47p. 1994. pap. 16.00 (*0-934753-92-X*) LRP Pubns.

Lee, Barbara A., jt. auth. see Hendrickson, Robert M.

Lee, Barbara A., jt. auth. see Kaplan, William A.

Lee, Barbara A., jt. auth. see Kaplin, William A.

Lee, Barbara A., jt. auth. see Olswang, Steven G.

Lee, Barbara W. Productivity & Employee Ownership: The Case of Sweden. (Studia Oeconomiae Upsaliensia: No. 16). 110p. (Orig.). 1989. pap. 36.00 (*91-554-2424-4*, Pub. by Umea U Bibl) Coronet Bks.

***Lee, Barbie.** A Change of Heart - Passion of the Soul. Loftiss, Gary, ed. (Illus.). 560p. 2000. pap. text 19.95 (*0-9642120-8-0*) Chiffon Pubs.

Lee, Barry. A Clear & Present Danger to Society. 24p. 1981. pap. 4.00 (*0-939622-10-6*) Four Zoas Night Ltd.

Lee, Barry, ed. see Jones, Alan.

Lee, Ben, jt. auth. see Jolliffe, Norm.

Lee, Benjamin. Psychosocial Theories of the Self. (PATH in Psychology Ser.). 230p. 1982. 55.00 (*0-306-41117-2*, Plenum Trade) Perseus Pubng.

— Talking Heads: Language, Metalanguage, & the Semiotics of Subjectivity. LC 97-25393. (Illus.). 360p. 1997. pap. text 18.95 (*0-8223-2015-0*); lib. bdg. 54.95 (*0-8223-2006-1*) Duke.

Lee, Benjamin & Urban, Greg, eds. Semiotics, Self & Society. (Approaches to Semiotics Ser.: No. 84). xviii, 311p. (C). 1989. lib. bdg. 87.35 (*0-89925-560-4*) Mouton.

Lee-Benner. Physicians' Guide to Free Radicals, Immunity & Aging. 1986. lib. bdg. 125.00 (*0-944213-00-6*) World Hlth Found.

— Turning Back the Aging Clock: Dr. Lee-Benners' Scientifically Designed & Medically Based Longevity Program. (Illus.). 230p. (Orig.). 1991. pap. 25.00 (*0-944213-05-7*) World Hlth Found.

Lee-Benner, Lord. Physician's Guide to Free Radicals, Immunity & Aging. deluxe ed. LC 90-71564. (Illus.). 301p. (C). 1991. write for info. (*0-944213-27-8*) World Hlth Found.

— Physician's Guide to Free Radicals, Immunity & Aging. rev. ed. LC 90-71564. (Illus.). 301p. (C). 1991. lib. bdg. 150.00 (*0-944213-26-X*) World Hlth Found.

— Physician's Guide to Free Radicals, Immunity & Aging. 2nd rev. ed. LC 90-71564. (Illus.). 301p. (C). 1991. 125.00 (*0-944213-25-1*) World Hlth Found.

Lee, Bennett & Wong-Chu, Jim, eds. Many Mouthed Birds: Contemporary Writings by Chinese Canadians. LC 91-19664. 250p. 1991. 26.95 (*0-295-97149-5*) U of Wash Pr.

Lee, Benny K. & Facciola, Elena. Living Well with Seated Massage & Chi Kung. LC 97-93911. (Illus.). v, 96p. 1997. pap. text 13.95 (*0-9658485-0-7*) Lees Acupressure.

Lee, Bernard J. The Future Church of 140 BCE. 180p. 1995. pap. 17.95 (*0-8245-1529-3*) Crossroad NY.

— The Galilean Jewishness of Jesus: Retrieving the Jewish Origins of Christianity. 1988. pap. 12.95 (*0-8091-3021-1*) Paulist Pr.

— Jesus & the Metaphors of God Vol. 2: Conversation on the Road Not Taken. LC 93-14256. (Stimulus Bks.). 224p. (Orig.). 1993. pap. 10.95 (*0-8091-3429-2*) Paulist Pr.

Lee, Bernard J., ed. Alternative Futures for Worship Vol. III: The Eucharist. 176p. 1997. pap. 9.95 (*0-8146-1495-7*) Liturgical Pr.

Lee, Bernard J. & Cowan, Michael. Dangerous Memories: House Churches & Our American Story. LC 86-62123. 208p. (Orig.). 1986. pap. 9.95 (*0-934134-70-7*) Sheed & Ward WI.

***Lee, Bernard J. & D'Antonio, William V.** The Catholic Experience of Small Christian Communities. 194p. 2000. pap. 19.95 (*0-8091-3937-5*) Paulist Pr.

Lee, Bernard J., jt. auth. see Cowan, Michael A.

***Lee, Bernice.** The Security Implications if the New Taiwan. (Adelphi Papers: No. 331). (Illus.). 88p. 2000. pap. 26.00 (*0-19-922479-X*) OUP.

Lee, Bernie. Murder Takes Two. 1993. per. 3.99 (*0-373-26127-6*, 1-26127-0) Harlequin Bks.

— Murder Without Reservation. (Worldwide Library Mysteries: No. 96). 1992. mass mkt. 3.99 (*0-373-26096-2*, 1-26096-7) Harlequin Bks.

Lee, Bertram T., ed. see Carvajal, Gaspar de.

Lee, Betsy. Mother Teresa: Caring for All God's Children. LC 80-20286. 1985. 8.95 (*0-87518-205-4*, Dillon Silver Burdett) Silver Burdett Pr.

— Prayer Is a Welcome Place: A User-Friendly Guide to Prayer. McDowell, Terry, ed. LC 99-93354. (Illus.). 120p. 1999. pap. 10.00 (*0-9673557-0-2*) Prayer Vent.

Lee, Betsy & Harvey, Jim. The Best of Blue Moon Press. (Illus.). 144p. 1998. pap. 10.00 (*0-9667532-0-8*) Blue Moon.

Lee, Betsy, ed. see Peeples, Mary G. & Peeples, Sam L., Jr.

***Lee, Betsy Blizzard.** A Basic Guide to Writing, Selling & Promoting Children's Books: Plus Information about Self-Publishing. 40p. (C). 2000. pap. 3.95 (*0-9658853-3-X*) Learning Abil.

Lee, Betsy Blizzard. Little Lemon: Activities for Developing Motivation & Memory Skills. (Illus.). 32p. (J). (gr. k-3). 1997. pap., wbk. ed. 8.99 (*0-9658853-2-1*) Learning Abil.

***Lee, Betsy Blizzard.** A Purple Cow. (Illus.). (J). (ps-4). 2000. pap. write for info. (*0-9658853-4-8*) Learning Abil.

Lee, Betty. Marie Dressler: The Unlikeliest Star. LC 97-15244. (Illus.). 336p. 1997. 27.50 (*0-8131-2036-5*) U Pr of Ky.

Lee, Bibbi, tr. see Nedreaas, Torborg.

Lee, Bill. Accounting & Technological Change. 59.95 (*1-85972-594-5*) Ashgate Pub Co.

Lee, Bill. Bi-Ranchers, Bi-Mates. (Illus.). 176p. (Orig.). 1991. pap. 9.95 (*1-879194-02-3*) GLB Pubs.

— Chinese Playground: A Memoir. 277p. 1999. 28.00 (*0-9670023-0-3*) B Lee.

— Different Slopes. 213p. (Orig.). 1996. pap. 13.95 (*1-879194-21-X*) GLB Pubs.

— Newcomer's Guide to North Carolina: Everything You Need to Know to Be a Tar Heel. 2nd rev. ed. (Illus.). 286p. 1999. pap. 15.95 (*1-878086-73-1*, Pub. by Down Home NC) Blair.

— People in Jazz. 1984. 19.95 (*0-89898-358-4*, SB258) Wrner Bros.

— Rogues to Remember. (Rogues Ser.: No. 1). (Illus.). 168p. (Orig.). 1991. pap. 10.95 (*1-879194-00-7*) GLB Pubs.

Lee, Bill, ed. Country Rogues: Short Story Anthology. (Rogues Ser.: No. 4). 211p. 1995. pap. 12.95 (*1-879194-19-8*) GLB Pubs.

— Rogues of San Francisco. (Rogues Ser.: No. 3). 230p. (Orig.). 1993. pap. 11.95 (*1-879194-15-5*) GLB Pubs.

Lee, Billi. Get Savvy: Thirty Days to a Different Perspective. (Illus.). 71p. (Orig.). 1992. pap. 10.00 (*1-883330-69-6*); pap. 45.00 incl. audio (*1-883330-68-8*); pap. 300.00 incl. audio, VHS (*1-883330-67-X*) Alliance CO.

Lee, Billie W. Rainshine & Sundrops: Language Fun for Young Children. (Illus.). 40p. (Orig.). 1987. 6.95 (*0-9619675-0-1*) P & M Bear Pubns.

Lee, Billy, jt. auth. see Craze, Richard.

Lee, Blaine. Power Principle. LC 97-9793. 1997. 24.50 (*0-684-81058-1*) S&S Trade.

— The Power Principle. 384p. 1998. per. 14.00 (*0-684-84616-0*, Fireside) S&S Trade Pap.

Lee, Bob. Back to the Future: Tokheim. (Gas Pump Ser.: No. 5). (Illus.). 172p. 1993. text 44.95 (*0-9638220-0-4*) Bob Lee.

— The Black Hills after Custer. LC 97-5209. 1997. write for info. (*0-89865-996-5*) Donning Co.

Lee, Bob & Lawrence, Peter. Politics at Work. 208p. 1999. pap. 67.50 (*0-7487-1113-9*, Pub. by S Thornes Pubs) Trans-Atl Phila.

Lee, Bob, jt. auth. see Arnold, Henri.

Lee, Bob, jt. auth. see Wallington, Peter.

Lee, Bok Y. & Herz, Burton L. Surgical Management of Cutaneous Ulcers & Pressure Sores. LC 96-8950. 250p. 1997. text 95.00 (*0-412-99421-6*, Pub. by E A) OUP.

Lee, Brenda. The Abused & the Abuser. rev. ed. Pin, Hired, ed. LC 95-929785. (Illus.). 256p. (Orig.). 1996. 21.00 (*0-9649571-6-7*) Princess Lee.

— The Abused & the Abuser Vol. 1: Self Help - Guidance. LC 95-92785. 239p. (Orig.). 1996. lib. bdg. 25.95 (*0-9649571-1-6*) Princess Lee.

— A Klans Man Love: Human Biography. Pen, Hired, ed. (Illus.). 300p. (Orig.). Date not set. pap. 21.00 (*0-9649571-8-3*) Princess Lee.

— Manipulation of the Young Mind: Human Biography. Pen, Hired, ed. (Illus.). 400p. 1997. 21.00 (*0-9649571-9-1*) Princess Lee.

— The Roommates Vol. 1: Human Biography. Pen, Hired, ed. (Illus.). 200p. (Orig.). 1997. pap. 21.00 (*0-9649571-3-2*) Princess Lee.

***Lee, Brent.** Gangs of Pitch. 425p. 1999. pap. 19.95 (*0-7414-0246-7*) Buy Books.

Lee, Brian. American Fiction 1865-1940. (Literature in English Ser.). 288p. (C). 1987. text 41.95 (*0-582-49317-X*, 73574) Longman.

— AMERICAN FICTN 1865 1940. (Literature in English Ser.). 288p. (C). 1987. pap. text 28.50 (*0-582-49316-1*, 73575) Longman.

— The Novels of Henry James: A Study of Culture & Consciousness. LC 78-323943. viii, 123p. 1978. write for info. (*0-7131-6115-9*) Arnld Pub.

— Poetry & the System. (C). 1989. 30.00 (*0-907839-05-3*, Pub. by Brynmill Pr Ltd) St Mut.

Lee, Brian, ed. The Bookplate Designs of Claude Lovat Fraser. (Illus.). 88p. 1988. 75.00 (*0-933861-00-1*) H Berliner.

— Byron: Don Juan (Eighteen Nineteen) 2nd ed. (Annotated Student Texts Ser.). 192p. (Orig.). 1988. pap. text 20.00 (*1-85373-015-7*, Pub. by Northcote House) Trans-Atl Phila.

— An English Miscellany: Essays Presented to W. S. Mackie. 1977. 9.75 (*0-19-570101-1*) OUP.

***Lee, Brian.** Ghost Hunters. (J). (gr. 2-7). 1999. 15.99 (*0-7636-0889-0*) Candlewick Pr.

Lee, Brian, ed. & intro. see James, Henry.

Lee, Brian N. Bookplates of Robert Hancock, James Ross & William Bache. (Illus.). 58p. 1986. pap. 25.00 (*1-884718-75-2*, 33638) Oak Knoll.

— British Royal Bookplates: And Ex-Libris of Related Families. 259p. 1992. text 119.95 (*0-85967-883-0*, Pub. by Scolar Pr) Ashgate Pub Co.

— Early Printed Book Labels. (Illus.). 207p. 1976. 28.00 (*0-900002-72-7*, Pub. by Priv Lib Assn) Oak Knoll.

Lee, Briant H. European Post-Baroque Neoclassical Theatre Architecture. LC 95-41058. (Studies in Theatre Arts: Vol. 3). (Illus.). 248p. 1996. write for info. (*0-7734-8845-6*) E Mellen.

— Theatre Primer: A Manual for Success in Early College or University Theatre Courses. 192p. (C). 1991. pap. text, per. 15.95 (*0-8403-6910-7*) Kendall-Hunt.

Lee, Briant H. & Wedwick, Daryl M. Corrugated Cardboard Scenery. 2nd ed. LC 93-15777. (Illus.). 164p. 1993. pap. 20.00 (*0-88734-628-6*) Players Pr.

Lee, Bruce. The Art of Expressing the Human Body. LC 98-37849. (Bruce Lee Library Ser.: Vol. 4). (Illus.). 256p. 1998. pap. 18.95 (*0-8048-3129-7*) Tuttle Pubng.

***Lee, Bruce.** Bruce Lee: Artist of Life, Vol. 6. Little, John, ed. LC 99-33401. (Bruce Lee Library Ser.). (Illus.). 240p. 1999. pap. 24.95 (*0-8048-3131-9*) Tuttle Pubng.

— Bruce Lee's Fighting Method: Self-Defense Techniques. 1999. pap. text 33.95 (*1-58133-136-3*) Black Belt Mag.

Lee, Bruce. Bruce Lee's One & Three Inch Power Punch. 1989. pap. 4.95 (*0-86568-112-0*) Unique Pubns.

***Lee, Bruce.** Bruce Lee's Striking Thoughts: Wisdom of Daily Living. Little, John, ed. & anno. by. LC 99-55240. (Illus.). 228p. 2000. 21.95 (*0-8048-3221-8*) Tuttle Pubng.

Lee, Bruce. Chinese Gung Fu. LC 86-43242. (Specialties Ser.: No. 451). 112p. 1987. reprint ed. pap. 8.50 (*0-89750-112-8*) Ohara Pubns.

— Jeet Dune Do: Bruce Lee's Commentaries on the Martial Way. Little, John, ed. & contrib. by. by. LC 97-61948. (Bruce Lee Library: Vol. 3). (Illus.). 399p. 1997. pap. 16.95 (*0-8048-3132-7*) Tuttle Pubng.

— Letters of the Dragon: AN Anthology of Bruce Lee's Correspondence with Family, Friends & Fans, 1958-1973. Little, John, ed. LC 98-36553. (Bruce Lee Library: Vol. 5). (Illus.). 190p. 1998. pap. 14.95 (*0-8048-3111-4*) Tuttle Pubng.

— Tao of Gung Fu. (Bruce Lee Library). 1997. pap. text 16.95 (*0-8048-3110-6*) Tuttle Pubng.

— Tao of Jeet Kune Do. LC 75-13803. (Specialties Ser.). (Illus.). 1975. pap. 14.50 (*0-89750-048-2*, 401) Ohara Pubns.

Lee, Bruce & Uyehara, Mitoshi. Bruce Lee's Fighting Method: Advanced Techniques, Vol. 4 405. LC 77-92737. (Specialties Ser.). (Illus.). 126p. 1989. pap. 8.95 (*0-89750-053-9*) Ohara Pubns.

— Bruce Lee's Fighting Method: Basic Training, Vol. II, No. 403. Shelrud, Doris, ed. LC 77-79057. (Specialties Ser.). (Illus.). 1977. pap. text 8.95 (*0-89750-051-2*) Ohara Pubns.

— Bruce Lee's Fighting Method: Self-Defense Techniques, Vol. 1, No. 402. LC 76-51476. (Specialties Ser.). (Illus.). 1976. pap. text 8.95 (*0-89750-050-4*) Ohara Pubns.

— Bruce Lee's Fighting Method: Skill in Techniques, Vol. 3, No. 404. LC 77-81831. (Specialties Ser.). (Illus.). 127p. 1988. pap. 8.95 (*0-89750-052-0*) Ohara Pubns.

Lee, Bunny, ed. see Dolinger, James A.

Lee, Burton W., et al. Quick-Consult Manual of Evidence Based Medicine. LC 97-3306. (Illus.). 500p. 1997. pap. text 44.95 (*0-316-51887-5*) Lppncott W & W.

Lee, Burtrand I. & Pope, Edward J., eds. Chemical Processing of Ceramics. LC 94-25396. (Engineering Materials Ser.: Vol. 8). (Illus.). 568p. 1994. text 195.00 (*0-8247-9244-0*) Dekker.

Lee, Butch & Rover, Red. Night-Vision: Illuminating War & Class on the Neo-Colonial Terrain. 188p. (Orig.). 1993. pap. 14.95 (*1-883780-00-4*) Vagabond NY.

Lee, Byeong G. Scrambling Techniques for Digital Transmission. LC 94-37999. 445p. 1995. 59.95 (*0-387-19863-6*) Spr-Verlag.

— Scrambling Techniques for Digital Transmission: Telecommunications Networks & Computer. LC 94-37999. 1994. 59.00 (*3-540-19863-6*) Spr-Verlag.

Lee, Byung I., jt. auth. see Edmister, Wayne C.

***Lee, Byung Jin.** Kunst Als Korrelat und Korrektiv der Wirklichkeit: Dialektik der Kunstautonomie im Verhaltnis Zur Aufklarungskritik und Negativen Dialektik Bei Theodor W. Adorno. (Europaische Hochschulschriften Ser.). 323p. 1999. 48.95 (*3-631-35426-6*) P Lang Pubng.

Lee, C. Allyson & Silvera, Makeda, eds. Pearls of Passion. 208p. 1994. pap. 12.95 (*0-920813-99-2*) LPC InBook.

Lee, C. C. Dictionary of Enviromental Legal Terms. 818p. 1996. 79.95 (*0-07-038113-5*) McGraw.

— Environmental Engineering Dictionary. 3rd ed. 682p. 1998. text 89.00 (*0-86587-620-7*, 620) Gov Insts.

***Lee, C. C.** Environmental Law Index to Chemicals. 3rd rev. ed. 867p. 1999. pap. text 99.00 (*0-86587-670-3*, 670) Gov Insts.

Lee, C. C. Handbook of Environmental Engineering Calculations. LC 99-16746. 1504p. 2000. 125.00 (*0-07-038183-6*) McGraw.

***Lee, C. C.** Sampling, Analysis, & Monitoring Methods: A Guide to EPA & OSHA Requirements. 2nd ed. 500p. 2000. pap. text 99.00 (*0-86587-698-3*, 698) Gov Insts.

Lee, C. C. Sampling, Analysis & Monitoring Methods: A Guide to EPA Requirements. 272p. 1995. pap. text 79.00 (*0-86587-477-8*) Gov Insts.

Lee, C. C. & Lee, Eming. Chemical Guide to the Internet. 2nd ed. LC 99-20372. 340p. 1999. pap. text 69.00 (*0-86587-655-X*) Gov Insts.

Lee, C. F. Advances in Investment Analysis & Portfolio Management, Vol. 6. 301p. 1999. 78.50 (*0-7623-0356-5*) Jai Pr.

— Advances in Pacific Basin Business, Economics & Finance, Vol. 3. 1998. 78.50 (*0-7623-0191-0*) Jai Pr.

— Statistics for Business & Financial Economics. 864p. (C). 1993. text 80.36 (*0-669-24598-4*); teacher ed. 2.66 (*0-669-24600-X*); student ed. 25.96 (*0-669-24599-2*); student ed. 16.76 (*0-669-32684-4*) HM Trade Div.

Lee, C. F., ed. Advances in Pacific Basin Business, Economics & Finance, Vol. 1. 370p. 1995. 78.50 (*1-55938-737-8*) Jai Pr.

Lee, C. F., et al. Security Analysis & Portfolio Management. (C). 1990. text 87.33 (*0-673-38635-X*) Addson-Wesley Educ.

Lee, C. J. Caldwell Lee: The Poet to Be: The Forthright Omnipotence Era. 56p. 1994. pap. 7.95 (*0-8059-3526-6*) Dorrance.

— Forgiven. (Orig.). Date not set. pap. write for info. (*1-887939-28-8*) VisionQuest Media.

***Lee, C. J.** The Metaphysics of Mass Art Vol. 1: Cultural Ontology: Mysticism, Mexico & English Literature. LC 99-13416. (Studies in Art & Religious Interpretation: Vol. 24A). 168p. 1999. lib. bdg. 79.95 (*0-7734-8182-6*) E Mellen.

— The Metaphysics of Mass Art Vol. II: Cultural Ontology:Madness & the Savage Indigenous Peoples of the Americas & the Psychology of the Observer in U. S. Film. LC 99-13416. (Studies in Art & Religious Interpretation: Vol. 24B). 284p. 1999. lib. bdg. 89.95 (*0-7734-8184-2*) E Mellen.

***Lee, C. P.** Like a Bullet of Night: The Films of Bob Dylan. 2000. pap. 18.95 (*1-900924-06-4*, Pub. by Helter Skelter) Interlink Pub.

Lee, C. P., ed. Current Topics in Bioenergetics Vol. 17: Molecular Aspects of Mitochondrial Pathology. (Illus.). 254p. 1994. text. write for info. (*0-12-152517-1*) Acad Pr.

Lee, C. S., ed. Sensor-Based Robots: Algorithms & Architectures. (NATO ASI Series F: Computer & Systems Sciences, Special Programme AET: Vol. 66). x, 285p. 1991. 82.95 (*0-387-52298-0*) Spr-Verlag.

Lee, Cameron. Beyond Family Values: A Call to Christian Virtue. LC 98-21900. 240p. 1998. pap. 16.99 (*0-8308-1509-0*, 1509) InterVarsity.

— PK: Helping Pastors' Kids Through Their Identity Crisis. LC 92-12684. 256p. 1992. pap. 14.99 (*0-310-58451-5*) Zondervan.

Lee, Cameron & Balswick, Jack. Life in a Glass House: The Minister's Family in Its Unique Social Context. 304p. 1989. 16.95 (*0-310-28750-2*) Zondervan.

Lee, Cara. West Rock to the Barndoor Hills: The Traprock Ridges of Connecticut. (Illus.). 60p. 1985. pap. 5.00 (*0-942081-00-5*) CT DEP CGNHS.

Lee, Carl H. We Worship As We Live: A Devotional Journey Through the Years. 96p. 1996. pap. 21.95 (*0-9630111-1-1*) Concordia Coll.

Lee, Carla A. Fluids & Electrolytes: A Practical Approach. 4th ed. 360p. 1996. pap. 28.95 (*0-8036-5531-2*) Davis Co.

Lee, Carol. Early Records of Calhoun City (Miss.) Baptist Church. LC 99-214324. 83p. (Orig.). 1996. pap. 8.50 (*1-885480-08-3*) Pioneer Pubng.

— Good Grief: Experiencing Loss. 256p. 1995. pap. 15.95 (*1-85702-184-3*, Pub. by Fourth Estate) Trafalgar.

— In Your Own Voice. LC 99-63915. 300p. 1999. pap. write for info. (*1-893181-22-7*) Le Gesse Stevens.

— Legacy of the Land: 250 Years of Agriculture in Carroll County, Maryland. LC 82-83567. (Illus.). 177p. 1982. 6.00 (*0-685-33351-5*) Hist Soc Carroll.

— The Ostrich Position. pap. 5.95 (*0-86316-057-3*) Writers & Readers.

***Lee, Carol Ann.** La Biografia de Ana Frank.Tr. of Biography of Anne Frank. (SPA.). 368p. 1999. pap. 18.95 (*0-553-06102-X*) Bantam.

***Lee, Carol D. & Smagorinsky, Peter.** Vygotskian Perspectives on Literacy Research: Constructing Meaning Through Collaborative Inquiry. LC 99-12568. (Learning in Doing Ser.). 300p. 1999. pap. 19.95 (*0-521-63878-X*) Cambridge U Pr.

Lee, Carol D. & Smagorinsky, Peter, eds. Vygotskian Perspectives on Literacy Research: Constructing Meaning Through Collaborative Inquiry. LC 99-12568. (Learning in Doing Ser.). (Illus.). 320p. 1999. text 59.95 (*0-521-63095-9*) Cambridge U Pr.

Lee, Carol K. & Edwards, Fay. 57 Games to Play in the Library or Classroom. LC 97-27786. 128p. (J). 1997. pap. 15.95 (*1-57950-014-5*, Alleyside) Highsmith Pr.

***Lee, Carol K. & Langford, Janet.** Learning about Books & Libraries: A Gold Mine of Games. (Illus.). 80p. (J). (gr. k-6). 2000. pap. 15.95 (*1-57950-051-X*, Alleyside) Highsmith Pr.

Lee, Carol K. & Langford, Janet. Storytime Companion: Learning Games & Activities for Schools & Libraries. LC 98-20793. (Illus.). 100p. (ps-3). 1998. pap. 15.95 (*1-57950-019-6*, Alleyside) Highsmith Pr.

Lee, Carol M., jt. auth. see Olk, R. Joseph.

Lee, Carol W. Blue Garter Club: Ties That Bind Fourteen Christian Women for 40 Years. Hermanson, Renee, ed. LC 92-4563. (Illus.). 260p. (Orig.). 1992. pap. 11.95 (*1-880292-20-3*) LangMarc.

Lee, Carole. Early Records of College Hill Church, Lafayette County, Mississippi, with Cemetery Inscriptions. LC 99-214336. 131p. (Orig.). 1997. pap. 15.00 (*1-885480-13-X*) Pioneer Pubng.

Lee, Carolyn. The Promised God-Man Is Here: The Extraordinary Life-Story, the Crazy Teaching Work & the Divinely Emerging World-Blessing Work of the Divine World-Teacher of the Late-Time, Ruchira Avatar Adi Da Samraj. LC 98-89626. (Illus.). 856p. 1998. pap. 9.95 (*1-57097-059-9*) Dawn Horse Pr.

Lee, Catherine, photos by. Catherine Lee: The Alphabet Series & Other Works. LC 99-222220. (Illus.). 78p. 1997. pap. 24.95 (*0-9659746-0-X*, Pub. by P A Arts Mgmt) U of Wash Pr.

Lee, Catherine T., jt. auth. see Lee, Warren F.

Lee, Cathy H., ed. see Mailer, Stan.

Lee, Cazenove Gardner. Lee Chronicle: Studies of the Early Generations of the Lees of Virginia. Parker, Dorothy Mills, ed. LC 56-10782. 468p. reprint ed. pap. 145.10 (*0-608-10224-5*, 205025800058) Bks Demand.

Lee, Cecilia C., tr. see Rojas, Carlos.

Lee, Celeste. Understanding the Body Organs: And the Eight Laws of Health. LC 94-60068. 128p. (YA). 1994. reprint ed. per. 8.95 (*0-945383-44-4*) Teach Servs.

Lee, Chae-Jin. China & Japan: New Economic Diplomacy. LC 84-6602. (Publication Ser.: No. 297). (Illus.). xviii, 174p. (C). 1984. pap. 9.95 (*0-8179-7972-7*); lib. bdg. 19.95 (*0-8179-7971-9*) Hoover Inst Pr.

— China & Korea: Dynamic Relations. (Publication Ser.: No. 434). 218p. 1996. pap. 19.95 (*0-8179-9422-X*) Hoover Inst Pr.

— Japan Faces China: Political & Economic Relations in the Postwar Era. LC 75-40408. (Illus.). 256p. reprint ed. pap. 79.40 (*0-608-06076-3*, 206640800008) Bks Demand.

— Zhou Enlai: The Early Years. LC 93-33525. xiv, 241p. 1994. 35.00 (*0-8047-2302-8*) Stanford U Pr.

— Zhou Enlai: The Early Years. xiv, 241p. 1996. pap. 13.95 (*0-8047-2700-7*) Stanford U Pr.

Lee, Chae-Jin & Sato, Hideo, eds. U. S.-Japan Partnership in Conflict Management: The Case of Korea. LC 93-34391. (Keck Center for International & Strategic Studies: No. 5). viii, 174p. 1993. pap. 10.95 (*0-930607-16-3*) Keck Ctr.

Lee, Chae-Jin, jt. auth. see Rosenbaum, Arthur L.

Lee, Chae-Jin, jt. ed. see Speakman, Jay.

Lee, Chae-Jin, jt. ed. see Suh, Dae-Sook.

Lee, Chana Kai. For Freedom's Sake: The Life of Fannie Lou Hamer. LC 98-58017. 240p. 1999. 29.95 (*0-252-02151-7*) U of Ill Pr.

***Lee, Chana Kai.** For Freedom's Sake: The Life of Fannie Lou Hamer. (Women in American History Ser.). 288p. 2000. reprint ed. pap. 14.95 (*0-252-06936-6*) U of Ill Pr.

Lee, Chang-Rae. A Gesture Life. LC 99-28382. 356p. 1999. 23.95 (*1-57322-146-5*, Riverhead Books) Putnam Pub Group.

***Lee, Chang-Rae.** Gesture of Life. 2000. pap. 13.00 (*1-57322-828-1*, Riverhd Trade) Berkley Pub.

Lee, Chang-Rae. Native Speaker. 384p. 1996. pap. 12.95 (*1-57322-531-2*, Riverhd Trade) Berkley Pub.

Lee, Chang Y. & Whitaker, John R., eds. Enzymatic Browning & Its Prevention. LC 95-23301. (ACS Symposium Ser.: No. 600). (Illus.). 352p. 1995. text 98.00 (*0-8412-3249-0*, Pub. by Am Chemical) OUP.

Lee, Charles. The Hidden Public: The Story of the Book-of-the-Month Club. LC 73-724. 236p. 1973. reprint ed. lib. bdg. 59.50 (*0-8371-6785-X*, LEHI, Greenwood Pr) Greenwood.

— Love, Life, & Laughter. Harris, Paul N., ed. 180p. 1990. 12.50 (*0-915180-32-4*) Harrowood Bks.

— Love, Life, & Laughter. Harris, Paul N., ed. 180p. 1991. pap. 9.95 (*0-915180-34-0*) Harrowood Bks.

— Ten Sevens. LC 82-15771. 80p. 1983. 12.50 (*0-915180-23-5*) Harrowood Bks.

Lee, Charles, ed. The Vale of Lanherne. (C). 1989. 30.00 (*0-907566-45-6*, Pub. by Dyllansow Truran) St Mut.

Lee, Charles, jt. ed. see Kerr, Mary L.

Lee, Charles, jt. ed. see Lewis, Dominic B.

Lee, Charles A. & Dalman, G. Conrad. Microwave Devices, Circuits & Their Interaction. (Microwave & Optical Engineering Ser.). 384p. 1994. 98.50 (*0-471-55216-X*) Wiley.

Lee, Charles E., jt. auth. see Richardson, Katherine H.

An Asterisk (*) at the beginning of an entry indicates that the title is appearing for the first time.

Lee, Charles R., Jr. The Confederate Constitutions. LC 73-16628. 225p. 1974. reprint ed. lib. bdg. 52.50 (*0-8371-7201-2*, LECC, Greenwood Pr) Greenwood.

Lee, Charlotte A. In Touch with the Infinite. 2nd ed. 145p. 1972. pap. 4.50 (*0-87516-169-3*) DeVorss.

Lee, Charlotte I. & Gura, Timothy. Oral Interpretation, 8 vols. 8th ed. (C). 1991. text 62.76 (*0-395-59329-8*) HM.

Lee, Charmaine, jt. auth. see Moss, Ellen Feinman.

Lee, Charmaine, tr. see Orlando, Francesco.

Lee, Chas. Totally Trusting. LC 92-61475. (Illus.). 222p. (YA). (gr. 6-12). 1992. 19.95 (*1-878044-09-5*) Mayhaven Pub.

Lee, Chauncey. The American Accountant. LC 82-48375. (Accountancy in Transition Ser.). 318p. 1982. text 10.00 (*0-8240-5324-9*) Garland.

Lee, Chaur-Shyan. Production & Marketing of Milkfish in Taiwan: An Economic Analysis. (ICLARM Technical Reports: No. 6). (Illus.). 41p. (Orig.). 1983. pap. text 9.50 (*0-89955-390-7*, Pub. by ICLARM) Intl Spec Bk.

Lee, Cheng F. & Hong-Chang Chang, eds. Collected Papers of "Pacific Basin Financial Markets & Policies" Date not set. pap. 100.00 (*0-9651643-2-2*) Ctr Pac Basin.

Lee, Cheng-Few. Advances in Financial Planning & Forecasting, Vol. 8. 1998. 92.50 (*0-7623-0333-6*) Jai Pr.

— Advances in Quantitative Analysis & Financial Accounting, Vol. 6. 237p. 1998. 78.50 (*0-7623-0327-1*) Jai Pr.

— Statistics for Business & Financial Economics. 2nd rev. ed. 1112p. (C). 1998. 78.00 (*981-02-3485-6*) World Scientific Pub.

Lee, Cheng-Few, ed. Advances in Financial Planning & Forecasting, Vol. 6. 216p. 1995. 92.50 (*1-55938-976-1*) Jai Pr.

— Advances in Financial Planning & Forecasting: In Preparation, Fall, 1997, Vol. 7. 216p. 1997. 92.50 (*0-7623-0124-4*) Jai Pr.

— Advances in Investment Analysis & Portfolio Management: I, Vol. 4. 301p. 1997. 78.50 (*0-7623-0126-0*) Jai Pr.

— Advances in Quantitative Analysis of Finance & Accounting, Vol. 5. 237p. 1997. 78.50 (*0-7623-0197-X*) Jai Pr.

Lee, Cheng-Few, et al, eds. Advances in Financial Planning & Forecasting, Vol. 1. 323p. 1985. 92.50 (*0-89232-355-8*) Jai Pr.

— Advances in Financial Planning & Forecasting, Vol. 2. 302p. 1987. 92.50 (*0-89232-624-7*) Jai Pr.

— Advances in Financial Planning & Forecasting, Vol. 3. 393p. 1989. 92.50 (*0-89232-651-4*) Jai Pr.

— Advances in Financial Planning & Forecasting, Vol. 5. 1995. 92.50 (*1-55938-421-2*) Jai Pr.

— Advances in Financial Planning & Forecasting: International Dimension of Secondary & Current Markets, Vol. 4, Pt. A. 256p. 1991. 92.50 (*1-55938-202-3*) Jai Pr.

— Advances in Financial Planning & Forecasting: International Dimensions, 2 vols., Vol. 4. 1991. 157.00 (*1-55938-001-2*) Jai Pr.

— Advances in Financial Planning & Forecasting No. 1: Taiwan's Foreign Exchange, Exports & Financial Analysis. 276p. 1989. suppl. ed. 92.50 (*1-55938-049-7*) Jai Pr.

— Advances in Quantitative Analysis of Finance & Accounting, Vol. 1, Pt. A. 249p. 1991. 78.50 (*1-55938-026-8*) Jai Pr.

— Advances in Quantitative Analysis of Finance & Accounting, Vol. 2, Pt. B. 226p. 1993. 78.50 (*1-55938-565-0*) Jai Pr.

— Advances in Quantitative Analysis of Finance & Accounting, Vol. 4. 336p. 1996. 78.50 (*1-55938-988-5*) Jai Pr.

— Advances in Quantitative Analysis of Finance & Accounting: Applications, Vol. 1, Pt. B. 214p. 1991. 78.50 (*1-55938-138-8*) Jai Pr.

— Advances in Quantitative Analysis of Finance & Accounting: Methodologies, 2 vols., Set, Vol. 1. 1991. 157.00 (*1-55938-129-9*) Jai Pr.

— Advances in Quantitative Analysis of Finance & Accouting, Vol. 2, Pt. A. 250p. 1993. 78.50 (*1-55938-564-2*) Jai Pr.

— Advances in Quantitative Anlysis of Finance & Accounting, 2 vols., Set, Vol. 2. 1993. 157.00 (*1-55938-431-X*) Jai Pr.

— Advances in Quantitive Analysis of Finance & Accounting, 2 vols., Set, Vol. 3. 1995. 157.00 (*1-55938-847-1*) Jai Pr.

— Advances in Quantitive Analysis of Finance & Accounting, Vol. 3, Pt. A. 220p. 1995. 78.50 (*1-55938-848-X*) Jai Pr.

— Advances in Quantitive Analysis of Finance & Accounting, Vol. 3, Pt. B. 212p. 1995. 78.50 (*1-55938-849-8*) Jai Pr.

Lee, Cheng-Few, jt. ed. see Chen, Son-Nan.

Lee, Cheng-Sheng & Liao, I-Chiu, eds. Reproduction & Culture of Milkfish. (Illus.). 226p. (Orig.). 1985. pap. write for info. (*0-9617016-1-7*) Oceanic Inst.

Lee, Cheng-Sheng, et al. Aquaculture of Milkfish Chanos Chanos: State of the Art. (Illus.). 284p. (Orig.). 1986. pap. write for info. (*0-9617016-0-9*) Oceanic Inst.

Lee, Cheryl K., ed. see Faranda, Thomas W.

Lee, Chester M., ed. Apollo Soyuz Mission Report. LC 57-43769. (Advances in the Astronautical Sciences Ser.: Vol. 34). (Illus.). 336p. 1977. 35.00 (*0-87703-089-8*, Am Astronaut Soc) Univelt Inc.

Lee, Chi-Jen. Development - Evaluation - Drugs: From Laboratory Through Licensure to Market. 240p. 1993. boxed set 131.95 (*0-8493-4447-6*, RM301) CRC Pr.

— Managing Biotechnology in Drug Development. 192p. 1996. boxed set 119.95 (*0-8493-9466-X*) CRC Pr.

Lee, Chi-Ming, tr. see Kraft, Charles H.

Lee, Chin-Hui, et al, eds. Automatic Speech & Speaker Recognition: Advanced Topics. LC 96-1588. (International Series in Engineering & Computer Science, Natural Language Processing & Machine Translation: No. SECS 355). 536p. (C). 1996. text 159.50 (*0-7923-9706-1*) Kluwer Academic.

Lee, Ching K. Unravelling the South China Miracle: Two Worlds of Factory Women. LC 97-25832. 221p. 1998. 45.00 (*0-520-21125-1*, Pub. by U CA Pr); pap. 16.95 (*0-520-21127-8*, Pub. by U CA Pr) Cal Prin Full Svc.

Lee, Chong. Advanced Explosive Kicks. LC 78-61152. (Specialties Ser.). (Illus.). 1978. pap. 14.95 (*0-89750-060-1*, 133) Ohara Pubns.

— Dynamic Kicks: Essentials for Free Fighting. Johnson, Gilbert, ed. LC 75-36052. (Specialties Ser.). (Illus.). 1975. pap. text 11.95 (*0-89750-017-2*, 122) Ohara Pubns.

— Super Dynamic Kicks. LC 80-84496. (Korean Arts Ser.). (Illus.). 1980. pap. 9.95 (*0-89750-072-5*, 409) Ohara Pubns.

Lee, Chong M., jt. ed. see Lanier, Tyre C.

***Lee, Chong-Moon, et al.** The Silicon Valley Edge: A Habitat for Innovation & Entrepreneurship. 2000. pap. 19.95 (*0-8047-4063-1*) Stanford U Pr.

Lee, Chong-Sik. Japan & Korea: The Political Dimension. LC 85-5455. (Publication Ser.: No. 318). (Illus.). xiv, 234p. 1985. 24.95 (*0-8179-8181-0*) Hoover Inst Pr.

— Korean Workers' Party: A Short History. Staar, Richard F., ed. LC 77-2427. (Publication Series: Histories of Ruling Communist Parties: No. 185). (Illus.). 1978. pap. 7.95 (*0-8179-6852-0*) Hoover Inst Pr.

Lee, Chong-Sik & Yoo, Se-Hee, eds. North Korea in Transition. LC 90-85946. (Korea Research Monographs: No. 16). xx, 156p. (Orig.). 1991. pap. 12.00 (*1-55729-024-5*) IEAS.

Lee, Christina. Alternatives to Cognition: A New Look at Explaining Human Social Behavior. LC 97-12615. 1997. write for info. (*0-8058-2654-8*) L Erlbaum Assocs.

***Lee, Christine.** Northern California Events Calendar 2001: The Definitive Events Calendar for the Adventurous & Curious Minded. 28p. 2000. pap. 12.95 (*0-9661987-4-3*, Pub. by LT Comm) SCB Distributors.

— Southern California Events Calendar 2001: The Definitive Events Calendar for the Adventurous & Curious-Minded. 28p. 2000. pap. 12.95 (*0-9661987-5-1*, Pub. by LT Comm) SCB Distributors.

***Lee, Christine E.** 2000 Events Calendar for Northern California: The Definitive Events Calendar for the Adventurous. 1999. 12.95 (*0-9661987-2-7*) LT Comm.

— 2000 Events Calendar for Southern California: The Definitve Events Calendar for the Adventurous. 1999. 12.95 (*0-9661987-3-5*) LT Comm.

Lee, Christopher. Fish for Australian Freshwater Aquariums. LC 76-378811. 144p. 1975. write for info. (*0-600-07343-2*, Pub. by Hamlyn Publishing Group Ltd) Sterling.

— The Killing of Cinderella. large type unabridged ed. (Bath Detective Mystery Ser.). 2000. 26.95 (*0-7531-6030-7*, 160307, Pub. by ISIS Lrg Prnt) ISIS Pub.

Lee, Christopher. Learning Disabilities & Assistive Technology. 2nd ed. (Illus.). 1999. pap. 49.95 (*1-928752-13-6*) Mc Gowan Pubns.

— Tall, Dark, & Gruesome LC 98-201465. 320 p. 1997. write for info. (*0-575-06497-8*) V Gollancz.

— Tall, Dark & Gruesome: Christopher Lee. (Illus.). 320p. 1999. pap. 20.00 (*1-887664-25-4*) Midnght Marquee Pr.

— This Sceptred Isle. LC 98-196140. xix, 616p. 1997. 35.00 (*0-563-38384-4*, BBC Bks) BBC Worldwide.

***Lee, Christopher, ed.** Turning the Century: Writing of the 1890s. 390p. 1999. pap. 29.95 (*0-7022-3054-5*, Pub. by Univ Queensland Pr) Intl Spec Bk.

***Lee, Christopher & Jackson, Rosemary.** Making it: Tips for Teachers from a Successful Adult with Learning Disabilities. 2001. pap. text. write for info. (*0-86709-474-5*, Pub. by Boynton Cook Pubs) Heinemann.

Lee, Christopher & Jackson, Rosemary F. Faking It: A Look into the Mind of a Creative Learner. LC 91-23844. 181p. (C). 1992. pap. 14.95 (*0-86709-296-3*, 0296, Pub. by Boynton Cook Pubs) Heinemann.

Lee, Christopher, jt. auth. see Mackie-Mason, Jeffrey K.

Lee, Chun-Jean, jt. ed. see Yang, Wen-Jei.

Lee, Chung H. The Economic Transformation of South Korea: Lessons for the Transition Economies. 52p. (Orig.). 1995. pap. 17.00 (*92-64-14325-4*, Pub. by Org for Econ) OECD.

Lee, Chung H., jt. auth. see Haggard, Stephan.

Lee, Chung Min, jt. auth. see Pollack, Jonathan D.

Lee, Chung-Nim & Wasserman, Arthur G. On the Groups JO(G) (Memoirs Ser.: No. 2/159). 62p. 1975. pap. 17.00 (*0-8218-1859-7*, MEMO/2/159) Am Math.

Lee, Chung-Shing & Pecht, Michael. Electronics Industry in Taiwan. LC 97-147. (Electronics Industry Research Ser.). 176p. 1997. lib. bdg. 39.95 (*0-8493-3170-6*) CRC Pr.

Lee, Cindy. Waterloo & Byram Township. (Images of America Ser.). 1999. pap. 16.99 (*0-7524-0852-6*) Arcadia Publng.

Lee, Clara. Pet Owner's Guide to the Staffordshire Bull Terrier. (Pet Owner's Guide Ser.). 1998. 8.00 (*1-86054-082-1*, Pub. by Ringpr Bks) Seven Hills Bk.

***Lee, Cleta B.** Sing above the Pain, Bk. 1. 3rd ed. LC 99-95103. (Illus.). 244p. (Orig.). 1999. pap. 14.95 (*0-9654818-4-0*) Tanglewood Hill.

— Sing above the Pain, Bk. 2. 2nd ed. LC 99-95118. (Illus.). 292p. (Orig.). 1999. pap. 14.95 (*0-9654818-5-9*) Tanglewood Press.

Lee, Cleta B. Therapeutic Journaling Cleta Style: Cleta Style. 2nd large type ed. LC 97-90987. 53p. 1998. reprint ed. pap. 7.95 (*0-9654818-2-4*) Tanglewood Hill.

— The Unheard Cry. Tresidder, Caroline, ed. (Cleta's Story Ser.: Vol. 3). (Illus.). 240p. (Orig.). 1995. pap. 12.95 (*0-9649047-3-X*) Cletas Desk Top.

Lee, Clive. Scotland & the United Kingdom: The Economy & the Union in the Twentieth Century. LC 95-5482. (Insights from Economic History Ser.). 1995. text 69.95 (*0-7190-4100-7*, Pub. by Manchester Univ Pr); text 24.95 (*0-7190-4101-5*, Pub. by Manchester Univ Pr) St Martin.

Lee, Colin. Music at the Edge: Music Therapy with an AIDS Patient. LC 95-25782. 192p. (C). 1996. pap. 32.99 incl. audio compact disk (*0-415-12464-6*) Routledge.

— Music at the Edge: Music Therapy with an AIDS Patient. LC 95-25782. (Illus.). 192p. (C). 1996. text 85.00 incl. audio compact disk (*0-415-12463-8*) Routledge.

Lee, Colin, jt. ed. see Gilroy, Andrea.

Lee-Cooper, Catherine & Gilbert-Ouahib, Kristi. Understanding & Using Corel Office Suite 8. 432p. 1997. spiral bd. 46.95 (*0-538-71962-1*) Sth-Wstrn College.

Lee County Committee, ed. History of Lee County, Arkansas. (Illus.). 383p. 1987. reprint ed. text 60.00 (*0-88107-101-3*) Curtis Media.

***Lee County Historical Commission.** Lee County, Texas. (Images of America Ser.). (Illus.). 128p. 1999. pap. 18.99 (*0-7385-0296-0*) Arcadia Publng.

Lee, Courtland C. Saving the Native Son: Empowerment Strategies for Young Black Males. 170p. 1995. pap. text 17.95 (*1-56109-063-8*, EC 204R) CAPS Inc.

Lee, Courtland C., ed. Counseling for Diversity: A Guide for School Counselors & Related Professionals. 208p. (C). 1994. pap. text 51.50 (*0-205-15321-6*, Longwood Div) Allyn.

— Multicultural Issues in Counseling: New Approaches to Diversity. 2nd rev. ed. LC 96-48042. 368p. (Orig.). 1997. pap. text 40.95 (*1-55620-156-7*, 72627) Am Coun Assn.

Lee, Courtland C. & Ford, Allison B. School Counseling. (C). 1998. 52.00 (*0-205-18863-X*, Macmillan Coll) P-H.

Lee, Courtland C. & Walz, Garry R., eds. Social Action: A Mandate for Counseling. LC 97-43987. 336p. 1998. pap. text 27.95 (*1-55620-213-X*, 72683) Am Coun Assn.

Lee, Cyrus. Soldat: Equiping the German Army Foot Soldier in Europe, 1939-42, Vol. I. (Illus.). 302p. 1995. reprint ed. pap. 15.95 (*0-929521-94-3*) Pictorial Hist.

Lee, Cyrus A. Soldat: The World War II German Army Combat Uniform: Collections Handbook 1939-1942, Vol. 1. LC 92-61981. (Illus.). 232p. (Orig.). 1992. pap. 12.95 (*0-929521-59-5*) Pictorial Hist.

— Soldat: The WW II German Army Combat Uniform Collector's Handbook, Equipping the German Army Foot Soldier in Europe 1943, Vol. 2. LC 88-90959. (Illus.). 88p. 1988. pap. 7.95 (*0-929521-01-3*) Pictorial Hist.

— Soldat Vol. 3: Equipping the German Foot Soldier in Europe 1944-1945. LC 90-64461. (Illus.). 196p. 1991. pap. 10.95 (*0-929521-46-3*) Pictorial Hist.

— Soldat Vol. 5: The WW Two German Army Combat Uniform Collector's Handbook. LC 88-90959. (Illus.). 218p. 1993. pap. 12.95 (*0-929521-76-5*) Pictorial Hist.

Lee, D. C. I. I. Marine Law, No. 180M/063. (C). 1986. suppl. ed. 230.00 (*0-7855-4275-2*, Pub. by Witherby & Co) St Mut.

— Magic Methods of Screenwriting. 2nd ed. (C). 1995. pap. text 52.00 (*0-07-037097-4*) McGraw.

Lee, D. & McDaniel, S. T. Ocean Acoustic Propagation by Finite Difference Methods. (International Series in Modern Applied Mathematics & Computer Science: No. 15). 121p. 1988. 36.00 (*0-08-034871-8*, Pergamon Pr) Elsevier.

Lee, D., et al. Theoretical & Computational Acoustics, 2 Vols. 1024p. 1994. text 213.00 (*981-02-1695-5*) World Scientific Pub.

Lee, D., tr. see Scholz, Erhard.

Lee, D. B., ed. Intestinal Absorption of Minerals: Experimental & Clinical. (Journal: Mineral & Electrolyte Metabolism Ser.: Vol. 16, Nos. 2-3, 1990). (Illus.). 100p. 1990. pap. 156.75 (*3-8055-5212-2*) S Karger.

Lee, D. C. The Map-Building & Exploration Strategies of a Simple Sonar-Equipped Mobile Robot: An Experimental, Quantitative Evaluation. LC 96-15187. (Distinguished Dissertations in Computer Science Ser.: No. 13). (Illus.). 239p. 1996. text 64.95 (*0-521-57331-9*) Cambridge U Pr.

Lee, D. E., jt. auth. see Amrhein, James E.

Lee, D. John, ed. Life & Story: Autobiographies for a Narrative Psychology. LC 93-19093. 304p. 1993. 69.50 (*0-275-94095-0*, C4095, Praeger Pubs) Greenwood.

Lee, D. John & Stronks, Gloria G., eds. Assessment in Christian Higher Education: Rhetoric & Reality. LC 94-9171. (Calvin College Ser.: Vol. II). 270p. (Orig.). 1994. pap. text 27.50 (*0-8191-9409-3*); lib. bdg. 58.50 (*0-8191-9408-5*) U Pr of Amer.

Lee, D. S., et al. Atlas of North American Freshwater Fishes: 1983 Supplement. LC 98-115161. (Occasional Papers of the North Carolina Biological Survey: 1983-6). (Illus.). 67p. 1991. reprint ed. pap. 5.00 (*0-917134-06-0*) NC Natl Sci.

Lee, D. T., jt. auth. see Sarrafzadeh, M.

Lee, D. Y. & Shah, S. P., eds. New Horizons in Construction Materials. (Session Proceedings Ser.). 96p. 1988. 5.00 (*0-87262-677-6*) Am Soc Civil Eng.

Lee, Daborah, et al, eds. Unfaithing U. S. Colonialism. (Illus.). 183p. 1999. pap. 15.00 (*0-9623086-5-X*) Dharma Cloud Pubs.

Lee, Dalton S. The Basis of Management in Public Organizations. LC 89-13360. (American University Studies: Political Science: Ser. X, Vol. 24). (Illus.). XV, 240p. 1990. text 47.95 (*0-8204-1111-6*) P Lang Pubng.

Lee, Dalton S., et al. Supervision for Success in Government: Issues for the Changing Public Service. LC 93-43177. (Public Administration Ser.). 316p. 1994. 28.95 (*1-55542-632-8*) Jossey-Bass.

Lee, Daniel & Frost, Joseph H. Ten Years in Oregon. LC 72-9457. (Far Western Frontier Ser.). (Illus.). 348p. 1973. reprint ed. 26.95 (*0-405-04985-4*) Ayer.

***Lee, Daniel B.** Old Order Mennonites in New York State: Rituals, Beliefs & Community. LC 00-33739. (Illus.). 2000. pap. write for info. (*0-8304-1573-4*) Burnham Inc.

Lee, Daniel E. Generations: And the Challenge of Justice. LC 96-10434. 302p. 1996. pap. text 36.00 (*0-7618-0303-3*); lib. bdg. 56.00 (*0-7618-0302-5*) U Pr of Amer.

— Hope Is Where We Least Expect to Find It. 100p. (Orig.). (C). 1993. pap. 18.50 (*0-8191-9056-X*); lib. bdg. 39.50 (*0-8191-9055-1*) U Pr of Amer.

Lee, Daniel O. & Wickins, John F. Crustacean Farming. 392p. 1992. text 129.95 (*0-470-21850-9*) Halsted Pr.

Lee, Dao T., jt. ed. see Jiang, T.

Lee, David. Boeing from Peashooter to Jumbo. (Illus.). 128p. 1999. 17.99 (*0-7858-1044-7*) Bk Sales Inc.

— Competing Discourses: Perspective & Ideology in Language. (Real Language Ser.). 216p. (C). 1992. pap. text 30.12 (*0-582-07850-4*) Longman.

***Lee, David.** David Lee: A Listener's Guide. (Listener's Guide to Poetry Ser.). 32p. 1999. pap. 12.00 incl. cd-rom (*1-55659-137-3*) Copper Canyon.

Lee, David. The Fish. 24p. 1997. pap. 7.50 (*1-890654-04-3*) Wood Work.

— Identifying Commercial Airplanes. 1998. pap. text 7.99 (*0-7858-1019-6*) Bk Sales Inc.

— Identifying World War II Airplanes. 1998. 7.99 (*0-7858-0883-3*) Bk Sales Inc.

— IMS-VS DL 1 Programming with Cobol Examples. 1985. pap. 34.95 (*0-9611810-4-4*) CCD Online Syst.

— A Legacy of Shadows: Selected Poems. LC 99-6401. 440p. 1999. 28.00 (*1-55659-098-9*, Pub. by Copper Canyon); pap. 16.00 (*1-55659-097-0*, Pub. by Copper Canyon) SPD-Small Pr Dist.

***Lee, David.** Luke's Stories of Jesus: Theological Reading of Gospel Narrative & the Legacy of Hans Frei. (Journal for the Study of the New Testament, Supplement Ser.: No. 185). 408p. 1999. 85.00 (*1-84127-013-X*, Pub. by Sheffield Acad) CUP Services.

Lee, David. My Town. LC 95-17053. 132p. 1995. pap. 12.00 (*1-55659-074-1*) Copper Canyon.

— News from down to the Cafe: New Poems. LC 99-6576. 145p. 1999. pap. 14.00 (*1-55659-132-2*, Pub. by Copper Canyon) SPD-Small Pr Dist.

— Paragonah Canyon. deluxe limited ed. 1991. 40.00 (*0-918116-52-X*) Brooding Heron Pr.

— The Porcine Canticles. LC 84-71252. 120p. (Orig.). 1984. pap. 10.00 (*0-914742-83-3*) Copper Canyon.

— Search for Security: The Political Economy of Australia's Post War Foreign & Defense Policy. LC 96-146438. 200p. 1996. pap. 24.95 (*1-86373-607-7*) Paul & Co Pubs.

— The 21 Gun Salute. 31p. 1999. pap. 11.95 (*0-9652272-9-4*) Grey Spider.

Lee, David. Wayburne Pig. LC 98-174912. 1997. write for info. (*0-918116-94-5*) Brooding Heron Pr.

Lee, David. Wayburne Pig. LC 98-174912. (Illus.). 28p. 1997. pap. 11.95 (*0-918116-96-1*) Brooding Heron Pr.

Lee, David, contrib. by. Wayburne Pig. LC 98-174912. 1997. 29.95 (*0-918116-95-3*) Brooding Heron Pr.

Lee, David & Newby, Howard. The Problem of Sociology: An Introduction to the Discipline. 379p. (C). 1990. pap. text 21.95 (*0-04-445641-7*) Routledge.

Lee, David & Turner, Bryan S., eds. Conflicts about Class: Debating Inequality in Late Industrialism: a Selection of Readings. LC 95-12106. 304p. (C). 1996. pap. text 30.75 (*0-582-27567-9*, Pub. by Addison-Wesley) Longman.

Lee, David & Waters, Christopher, eds. Evatt to Evans: The Labor Tradition in Australian Foreign Policy. LC 97-184514. 200p. 1997. pap. 24.95 (*1-86373-979-3*, Pub. by Allen & Unwin Pty) Paul & Co Pubs.

***Lee, David, et al.** Decision Making in Organisations. 256p. (Orig.). 1999. pap. 45.00 (*0-273-63113-6*, Pub. by F T P-H) Trans-Atl Phila.

Lee, David, jt. auth. see Bley, Paul.

Lee, David, jt. auth. see Evans, Arthur S.

Lee, David, jt. auth. see Kloefkorn, William.

Lee, David, jt. ed. see Collins, Peter.

Lee, David, jt. ed. see Goebel, Ulrich.

Lee, David, jt. ed. see Quah, Euston.

Lee, David A. The Cost Analyst's Companion. LC 97-76098. (Illus.). 150p. 1997. text 59.95 (*0-9661916-0-9*) Logistics Mgmt.

Lee, David A. & Higginbotham, Eve J. Clinical Guide to Comprehensive Ophthalmology. LC 98-30784. 1998. write for info. (*3-13-111461-4*) Thieme Med Pubs.

— Clinical Guide to Comprehensive Ophthalmology. LC 98-30784. (Illus.). 744p. 1998. 159.00 (*0-86577-766-7*) Thieme Med Pubs.

Lee, David A., jt. auth. see Dyer, John A.

Lee, David C. Gravity Golf: The Evolution & Revolution of Golf Instruction. (Illus.). 184p. 1995. 18.75 (*0-9645478-7-2*) Gravty Sports.

— The People's Universities of the U. S. S. R., 29. LC 88-15486. (Contributions to the Study of Education Ser.: No. 29). (Illus.). 279p. 1988. 55.00 (*0-313-26344-2*, LPU/, Greenwood Pr) Greenwood.

Lee, David D. Sergeant York: An American Hero. LC 84-10465. (Illus.). 184p. 1985. 22.50 (*0-8131-1517-5*) U Pr of Ky.

***Lee, David Dodd.** Wilderness (Poems by David Dodd Lee) 33p. 2000. pap. 6.00 (*1-882983-47-5*) March Street Pr.

L

Lee, David J. Bridge Bearings & Expansion Joints. 2nd ed. LC 93-32192. (Illus.). 224p. (C). 1990. 110.00 (*0-419-14570-2*, E & FN Spon) Routledge.

*__Lee, David J.__ Who Stole the American Dream & How Black America Will Get It Back! Changing the Economy Destiny of Black America Through the Black Church. Wright-Lee, Linda D., ed. (Illus.). 100p. 1999. pap. 24.95 (*0-9673754-0-1*) Wright On Time.

Lee, David J., ed. see Wright-Lee, Linda D.

*__Lee, David Jon & Haman, Edward A.__ How to File for Divorce in California. 2nd rev. ed. LC 99-86140. (Legal Survival Guides Ser.). 304p. 2000. pap. 19.95 (*1-57248-126-9*, Sphinx Pubng) Sourcebks.

Lee, David L. Merchant Marine Days: My Life in World War II. LC 98-65033. (Illus.). 192p. 1998. 29.95 (*1-886391-20-3*); pap. 19.95 (*1-886391-21-1*) Narwhal Pr.

Lee, David M., ed. Liability in Construction Management. 89p. 1983. pap. 5.00 (*0-87262-383-1*) Am Soc Civil Eng.

Lee, David S. & Parnell, James F. Endangered, Threatened & Rare Fauna of North Carolina Pt. 3: A Re-evaluation of the Birds. (Occasional Papers of the North Carolina Biological Survey). 52p. (Orig.). 1990. pap. 8.00 (*0-917134-19-2*) NC Natl Sci.

Lee, David S. & Socci, Mary C. Potential Effects of Oil Spills on Seabirds & Selected Other Oceanic Vertebrates Off the North Carolina Coast. (Occasional Papers of the North Carolina Biological Survey). (Illus.). 64p. (Orig.). 1989. pap. text 8.00 (*0-917134-18-4*) NC Natl Sci.

Lee, David S., et al. A Distributional Survey of North Carolina Mammals. (Occasional Papers of the North Carolina Biological Survey: 1982-10). (Illus.). 70p. 1982. 5.00 (*0-917134-04-4*) NC Natl Sci.

Lee, David S., ed. see Schreiber, E. G.

Lee, David T. & Pfaltzgraff, Robert L., Jr. Taiwan in a Transformed Global Setting. (Institute for Foreign Policy Anaylsis Ser.). 147p. 1995. pap. 11.95 (*0-02-881138-0*) Brasseys.

*__Lee, David Tawei.__ The Making of the Taiwan Relations Act: Twenty Years in Retrospect. (Studies on Contemporary Taiwan). 228p. 2000. text 45.00 (*0-19-592209-3*) OUP.

Lee, Dean & Lerner, Lawrence. Physics, Science & Engineering. (Physics Ser.). 272p. 1996. pap. 50.00 (*0-7637-0205-6*) Jones & Bartlett.

Lee, Debbie, jt. ed. see Kitson, Peter.

Lee, Deborah. Cancer: The Positive Approach: A No-Nonsense Prevention &Treatment Guide. 1999. pap. text 14.95 (*1-58054-045-7*) Woodland UT.

— Exploring Nature's Uncultivated Garden. rev. ed. (Illus.). 195p. 1989. reprint ed. 12.50 (*0-925909-00-9*) Havelin Comns.

Lee, Debra. Heartbeat. LC 87-31823. 1989. pap. 13.95 (*0-87949-274-0*) Ashley Bks.

Lee, Debra S., et al. American Legal English: Using Language in Legal Contexts. (Series in English for Academic & Professional Purposes). 296p. 1999. pap. text 21.95 (*0-472-08586-7*, 08586); pap. text, teacher ed. 13.95 (*0-472-08587-5*, 08587) U of Mich Pr.

Lee, Dee. Let's Talk Money: Your Complete Personal Finance Guide. (Illus.). 411p. 1999. pap. 16.95 (*1-886284-40-7*, Pub. by Chandler Hse) Natl Bk Netwk.

Lee, Dee, jt. auth. see Bogosian, Wayne G.

Lee, Deemer. Esther's Town. LC 89-24440. (Iowa Heritage Collection). (Illus.). 276p. 1989. reprint ed. pap. 10.95 (*0-8138-0459-0*) Iowa St U Pr.

Lee, Delene W. & Lee, Jasper S. Agribusiness Procedures & Practices. (Career Preparation for Agriculture-Agribusiness Ser.). (Illus.). 1980. text 20.51 (*0-07-036737-X*) McGraw.

Lee, Denise K. Global Telecommunications Regulation: A Political Economy Perspective. LC 96-142106. 224p. 1995. 75.00 (*1-85567-223-5*) Bks Intl VA.

— Global Telecommunications Regulation: A Political Economy Perspective. LC 95-19057. 1995. 42.50 (*0-8386-3619-5*) Fairleigh Dickinson.

Lee, Dennis. Body Music. 242p. 1999. pap. 15.95 (*0-88784-627-0*) Genl Dist Srvs.

— Dinosaur Dinner. 1999. pap. 6.99 (*0-375-80053-0*) Knopf.

— Dinosaur Dinner: With a Slice of Aligator Pie. (Illus.). 32p. (J). 1997. lib. bdg. 18.99 (*0-679-97009-6*, Pub. by Random Bks Yng Read) Random.

— Dinosaur Dinner with a Slice of Alligator Pie. LC 96-31100. (Illus.). (J). 1997. 17.00 (*0-679-87009-1*) Random.

— The Ice Cream Store: Poems. (Illus.). 64p. (J). 1992. 14.95 (*0-590-45861-2*, 002) Scholastic Inc.

*__Lee, Dennis.__ The Ice Cream Store: Poems. 2nd ed. (Illus.). (YA). 1999. pap. 7.50 (*0-00-648507-3*) HarpC.

Lee, Dennis. Lizzy's Lion. (Illus.). 32p. (J). (gr. k-3). 1993. pap. write for info. (*0-614-17732-4*) Stoddart Publ.

— Lizzy's Lion. unabridged ed. (Illus.). 32p. (J). (ps-3). 1985. 7.95 (*0-7737-0078-1*) STDK.

— Lord Lyndhurst: The Flexible Tory. (Illus.). 288p. 1994. 35.00 (*0-87081-358-7*) Univ Pr Colo.

— Nightwatch: New & Selected Poems 1968-1996. 208p. 1996. pap. 15.99 (*0-7710-5215-4*) McCland & Stewart.

— Riffs. 64p. 1993. pap. 11.95 (*0-919626-65-3*, Pub. by Brick Bks) Genl Dist Srvs.

— Riffs. large type ed. 64p. 1995. pap. 14.00 (*0-919626-81-5*, Pub. by Brick Bks) Genl Dist Srvs.

Lee, Dennis & Gay, Marie-Louise. Lizzy's Lion. 2nd unabridged ed. (Illus.). 32p. (J). (gr. k up). 1984. pap. 5.50 (*0-7736-7397-0*) STDK.

Lee, Desmond, ed. see Wittgenstein, Ludwig Josef Johann.

Lee, Desmond, tr. & intro. see Plato.

Lee, Diane. The Pelvic Girdle. (Illus.). 149p. 1989. text 49.95 (*0-443-03795-7*) Church.

— The Pelvic Girdle: An Approach to the Examination & Treatment of the Lumbo-Pelvic-Hip Region. LC 88-25690. (Illus.). 159p. 1989. reprint ed. pap. 49.30 (*0-7837-9748-6*, 206047600005) Bks Demand.

— The Pelvic Girdle: An Approach to the Examination & Treatment of the Lumbo-Pelvic-Hip Region. 2nd ed. LC 98-40027. 1999. text. write for info. (*0-443-05814-8*) Church.

Lee, Dick. The Sales Automation Survival Guide: Everything You Need to Know, Before You Need to Know It. Ellis, Kristine, ed. LC 97-78125. 200p. 1998. pap. 23.00 (*1-886656-07-X*) Better Books.

Lee, Dik Lun, ed. see International Computer Science Conference.

Lee, Ding & Schultz, Martin H. Numerical Ocean Acoustic Propagation in Three Dimensions. LC 95-32946. 250p. 1995. 54.00 (*981-02-2303-X*) World Scientific Pub.

*__Lee, Dominic S. F.__ The American Missionaries, the Mandarins & the Opium War, Canton, China (Circa 1839) LC TXU 915-24. (Illus.). 362p. 2000. 35.00 (*0-9673708-0-9*, LSP #1) Little Susitna.

Lee, Don & Daniel, David, eds. Ploughshares Winter, 1994-95: Regrets Only. (Ploughshares Ser.). 230p. (Orig.). (C). 1994. pap. text 8.95 (*0-933277-12-1*) Ploughshares.

Lee, Don, ed. see Armstrong, Ruth M.

Lee, Don, ed. see Eann, Chris.

Lee, Don L. Think Black. 3rd ed. LC 70-882333. (YA). (gr. 12 up). 1969. pap. 3.00 (*0-910296-03-0*) Broadside Pr.

— We Walk the Way of the New World. LC 70-121885. (YA). (gr. 12 up). 1970. 6.00 (*0-910296-26-X*) Broadside Pr.

Lee, Don Y. An Annotated Archaeological Bibliography of Selected Works on Northern & Central Asia. LC 83-81570. 94p. (C). 1983. 33.00 (*0-939758-05-9*) Eastern Pr.

— An Annotated Bibliography of Selected Works on China. LC 81-67771. 270p. (C). 1990. reprint ed. 46.50 (*0-939758-02-4*) Eastern Pr.

— An Annotated Bibliography on Inner Asia. LC 83-80529. 183p. (C). 1983. 45.50 (*0-939758-04-0*) Eastern Pr.

— An Annotated Prehistoric Bibliography on Northern Asia: Research. 110p. (C). 1997. text 39.50 (*0-939758-36-9*) Eastern Pr.

— An Annotated Prehistoric Bibliography on South Asia. 170p. (C). 1995. 47.50 (*0-939758-32-6*) Eastern Pr.

— Arabic Verb Frequency: Analytic & Synthetic Observations. (C). 1991. text 49.00 (*0-939758-22-9*) Eastern Pr.

— Art in Korea: Historical. (C). 1990. 59.00 (*0-939758-20-2*) Eastern Pr.

— Autohaiku: Japanese Poetry. LC 95-96228. (ENG & JPN.). 170p. 1996. 39.50 (*0-939758-33-4*) Eastern Pr.

— Chinese Eulogy & the Textual Variation. LC 83-82652. 96p. (C). 1983. 32.50 (*0-939758-06-7*) Eastern Pr.

— East Asian Languages & Linguistics. LC 85-81335. (C). 1986. 47.00 (*0-939758-13-X*) Eastern Pr.

— Haiku: Short Japanese Poetry. (ENG & JPN.). 125p. 1996. 34.50 (*0-939758-35-0*) Eastern Pr.

— The History of Early Relations Between China & Tibet. LC 81-147860. 267p. (C). 1981. 43.50 (*0-939758-00-8*) Eastern Pr.

— An Introduction to East Asian & Tibetan Linguistics & Cultures. LC 81-67770. 339p. (C). 1981. 43.50 (*0-939758-01-6*) Eastern Pr.

— Learning Standard Arabic: Root & Pattern Reference. LC 86-82210. (C). 1988. 69.00 (*0-939758-15-6*) Eastern Pr.

— Light Literature & Philosophy of East Asia. LC 82-90698. 220p. (C). 1982. 36.50 (*0-939758-03-2*) Eastern Pr.

— An Outline of Confucianism. LC 85-80477. 113p. (C). 1984. 29.50 (*0-939758-10-5*) Eastern Pr.

— An Outline of Confucianism. rev. ed. LC 85-80477. (C). 1988. 33.50 (*0-939758-16-4*) Eastern Pr.

— Traditional Chinese Thought: The Four Schools. (C). 1990. 43.50 (*0-939758-17-2*) Eastern Pr.

— Western Asia: An Annotated Historical Bibliography. LC 84-70884. 213p. (C). 1984. 43.50 (*0-939758-07-5*) Eastern Pr.

— Written & Spoken Arabic: Based on Modern Standard Arabic. (ARA & ENG.). (C). 1993. text 57.50 (*0-939758-26-1*) Eastern Pr.

Lee, Don Y., ed. The Poet As Mythmaker: A Study of Edwin Muir. 121p. (C). 1990. 34.50 (*0-939758-21-0*) Eastern Pr.

Lee, Don Y., et al, eds. An Annotated Bibliography on South Asia: Research. LC 94-78180. 200p. (C). 1995. 49.00 (*0-939758-29-6*) Eastern Pr.

Lee, Don Y., tr. from KOR. Korean Literature: Sijo. abr. ed. 200p. (C). 1994. 43.50 (*0-939758-27-X*) Eastern Pr.

Lee, Don Y., ed. see Aung Chin Win Aung.

Lee, Don Y., ed. see Bernett, Donna L.

Lee, Don Y., ed. see Eann, Chris.

Lee, Don Y., ed. see Fields, Brian A.

Lee, Don Y., ed. see Goehlert, Robert.

Lee, Don Y., ed. see Notzon, Mark.

Lee, Don Y., ed. see Payne, David C.

Lee, Don Y., ed. see Traylor, Kenneth L.

Lee, Don Y., ed. see Young, Margaret H.

Lee, Donald C. Toward a Sound World Order: A Multidimensional, Hierarchical Ethical Theory, 49. LC 91-40942. (Contributions in Philosophy Ser.: No. 49). 240p. 1992. 49.95 (*0-313-27903-9*, LTA, Greenwood Pr) Greenwood.

Lee, Donald G., jt. auth. see Way, Robert F.

Lee, Donald J. Polyarchy: The Political Theory of Robert A. Dahl. LC 91-32764. (Political Theory & Political Philosophy Ser.). 224p. 1991. text 10.00 (*0-8153-0202-9*) Garland.

Lee, Donald L. Electromagnetic Principles of Integrated Optics. 348p. 1986. text 58.50 (*0-471-87978-9*) Krieger.

Lee, Donald W. Harbrace Vocabulary Guide. 2nd ed. 184p. (Orig.). (C). 1970. pap. text, student ed. 3.00 (*0-15-534472-2*, Pub. by Harcourt Coll Pubs) Harcourt.

Lee, Dorothy. Freedom & Culture. 179p. (C). 1987. reprint ed. pap. text 11.95 (*0-88133-303-4*) Waveland Pr.

— Valuing the Self: What We Can Learn from Other Cultures. (Illus.). 1986. reprint ed. pap. text 8.95 (*0-88133-229-1*) Waveland Pr.

Lee, Dorothy A. The Symbolic Narratives of the Fourth Gospel: The Interplay of Form & Meaning. (JSNT Supplement Ser.: No. 95). 263p. 1994. 75.00 (*1-85075-468-3*, Pub. by Sheffield Acad) CUP Services.

Lee, Dorothy S. Native North American Music & Oral Data: A Catalogue of Sound Recordings, 1893-1976. LC 78-20337. 477p. 1979. reprint ed. pap. 147.90 (*0-7837-9656-0*, 205928900005) Bks Demand.

Lee, Dorris M. The Importance of Reading for Achieving in Grades Four, Five, & Six. LC 75-176978. (No. 556). reprint ed. 37.50 (*0-404-55556-X*) AMS Pr.

— Rapidreader! Manual. (Illus.). 160p. (Orig.). 1988. 99.95 incl. VHS (*0-317-89789-6*) Norman Leslie.

Lee, Douglas. T'ai Chi Ch'uan the Philosophy of Yin & Yang & Its Applications. Lucas, Charles, ed. LC 76-6249. (Chinese Arts Ser.). (Illus.). 1976. pap. text 11.95 (*0-89750-044-X*, 317) Ohara Pubns.

Lee, Douglas A., jt. auth. see Benda, Franz.

Lee, Douglas A., ed. see Benda, Franz.

Lee, Douglas A., ed. see Nichelmann, Christoph.

Lee, Douglas B. Effects of the Eruptions of Mount St. Helens on Physical, Chemical, & Biological Characteristics of Surface Water, Ground Water, & Precipitation in the Western United States. (Illus.). 123p. (C). 1998. pap. text 45.00 (*0-7881-7444-4*) DIANE Pub.

Lee, Douglas B., et al. Stage for a Nation: The Story of the National Theatre. LC 85-22761. (Illus.). 152p. (C). 1986. 30.75 (*0-8191-5021-5*) U Pr of Amer.

Lee, Douglas H. Climate & Economic Development in the Tropics. LC 76-56184. 182p. 1977. reprint ed. lib. bdg. 55.00 (*0-8371-9410-5*, LECE, Greenwood Pr) Greenwood.

Lee, Douglas H., et al, eds. Handbook of Physiology: Section 9, Reactions to Environmental Agents. (American Physiological Society Book). (Illus.). 667p. 1988. text 100.00 (*0-19-520684-3*) OUP.

Lee, Douglas K., jt. auth. see Snow, Ralph L.

Lee, Dwight. The Next Environmental Battleground: Indoor Air. 1992. pap. 10.00 (*0-943802-78-4*, 174) Natl Ctr Pol.

Lee, Dwight & McKenzie, Richard. Failure & Progress: The Bright Side of the Dismal Science. 163p. 1993. 5.00 (*1-882577-03-5*); pap. 3.00 (*1-882577-02-7*) Cato Inst.

Lee, Dwight E. Europe's Crucial Years: The Diplomatic Background of World War I, 1902-1914. LC 73-91315. (Illus.). 496p. reprint ed. pap. 153.80 (*0-608-18420-9*, 203003100067) Bks Demand.

— Great Britain & the Cyprus Convention Policy of 1878. LC 35-2422. (Historical Studies: No. 38). (Illus.). 240p. 1934. 16.50 (*0-674-36100-8*) HUP.

*__Lee, Dwight R.__ Getting Rich In America: Eight Simple Rules for Bulding A Fortune--And A Satisfying LifeConger,&Eric, Set. 1999. audio 18.00 (*0-694-52159-0*) HarperAudio.

Lee, Dwight R. Getting Rich Is a Choice in America. 1997. pap. 5.00 (*1-883969-03-4*) CSU Smith Ctr.

— The Inflationary Impact of Labor Unions. 24p. 1979. 1.00 (*0-86599-006-9*) PERC.

Lee, Dwight R., ed. Taxation & the Deficit Economy: Fiscal Policy & Capital Formation in the United States. LC 85-63549. (Illus.). 554p. (C). 1986. 34.95 (*0-936488-13-1*); pap. 15.95 (*0-936488-03-4*) PRIPP.

Lee, Dwight R. & McKenzie, Richard B. Getting Rich In America: Eight Simple Rules for Building a Fortune--And a Satisfying LifeConger,&Eric. 240p. 2000. pap. 14.00 (*0-06-661983-1*) HarpC.

— Getting Rich in America: 8 Simple Rules for Building a Fortune & a Satisfying Life. LC 98-46232. 221p. 1998. 25.00 (*0-06-661982-3*, HarpBusn) HarpInfo.

Lee, Dwight R., jt. auth. see McKenzie, Richard B.

Lee, Dwight R., jt. ed. see Doti, James L.

Lee, E. & Nolan. Surgery of Inflammatory Bowel Disorders Vol. 14: CSI. (Illus.). 1987. pap. 15.00 (*0-443-03439-7*) Church.

Lee, E., ed. see Brezzi, Paolo & Lee, Egmont.

Lee, E. H., ed. see Joint National & Western Applied Mechanics Conference Staff.

Lee, E. Lawrence. Indian Wars in North Carolina, 1663-1763. (Illus.). viii, 94p. 1968. reprint ed. pap. 8.00 (*0-86526-084-2*) NC Archives.

— New Hanover County: A Brief History. (Illus.). xiv, 124p. 1984. pap. 6.00 (*0-86526-128-8*) NC Archives.

Lee, E. M. An Introduction to Pension Schemes. (C). 1986. 250.00 (*0-7855-4115-2*, Pub. by Witherby & Co) St Mut.

Lee, E. S. & Zhu, Q. G. Fuzzy & Evidence Reasoning. Kacprzyk, J., ed. (Studies in Fuzziness: Vol. 6). (Illus.). xii, 360p. 1995. 115.00 (*3-7908-0880-6*) Spr-Verlag.

Lee, E. Stewart. Data & Algorithms. (Math-Computers Ser.). (C). 1992. 45.00 (*0-86720-219-X*) Jones & Bartlett.

Lee, E. W. Magnetism: An Introductory Survey. (Illus.). 281p. 1984. reprint ed. pap. 8.95 (*0-486-24689-2*) Dover.

Lee, E. W., et al, eds. Light Weight Alloys for Aerospace Applications III. LC 95-78393. (Illus.). 466p. 1995. 20.00 (*0-87339-302-3*, 3023) Minerals Metals.

— Light Weight Alloys for Aerospace Applications IV. LC 97-71552. (Illus.). 491p. 1997. 146.00 (*0-87339-328-7*, 3287) Minerals Metals.

Lee, Earl. Libraries in the Age of Mediocrity. LC 98-24669. 159p. 1998. pap. 28.50 (*0-7864-0548-1*) McFarland & Co.

Lee, Earl, jt. ed. see Wallace, Patricia D.

Lee, Earl G. & Lee, Hazel. Committed to Grace. 79p. (Orig.). 1993. pap. 6.99 (*0-8341-1500-X*, 55705) Beacon Hill.

— The Cycle of Victorious Living: Commit, Trust, Delight & Rest in Jesus Christ--the Center of Victorious Living. rev. ed. 64p. 1971. pap. 5.99 (*0-8341-0275-7*) Beacon Hill.

— The Cycle of Victorious Living: Leader's Guide. 24p. 1995. pap. 4.99 (*0-8341-1567-0*) Beacon Hill.

Lee, Eddy. The Asian Financial Crisis: The Challenge for Social Policy. LC 99-166761. 100p. 1998. pap. 12.95 (*92-2-110850-3*) Century Foundation.

Lee, Edgar. Crazy 8's. 272p. (Orig.). 1996. pap. 9.95 (*0-9655249-0-6*) Cafe Reading Inc.

Lee, Edward. The Chosen. 384p. 1993. mass mkt. 4.50 (*0-8217-4372-4*, Zebra Kensgtn) Kensgtn Pub Corp.

— Musical London. 192p. pap. 19.95 (*0-7119-3083-X*, OP 47094) Omnibus NY.

*__Lee, Edward.__ Operator "B" 150p. 1999. 30.00 (*1-881475-73-5*) Cemetery Dance.

— The Stickmen. 240p. 2000. 40.00 (*1-881475-91-3*) Cemetery Dance.

— The Ushers: Stories by Edward Lee. (Illus.). 350p. 1999. 45.00 (*1-891480-04-9*) Obsidian Bks.

— The Ushers: Stories by Edward Lee. (Illus.). 330p. 1999. pap. 16.00 (*1-891480-03-0*) Obsidian Bks.

Lee, Edward & Pelan, John. Shifters, Vol. 1. 15th ed. 20p. 1997. 45.00 (*1-891480-00-6*) Obsidian Bks.

*__Lee, Edward & Steffen, Elizabeth.__ Dahmer's Not Dead. 288p. 1999. 40.00 (*1-881475-93-X*) Cemetery Dance.

Lee, Edward & Steffen, Elizabeth. Portrait of the Psychopath As a Young Woman. 1998. pap. 12.95 (*1-889186-09-0*) Necro Publns.

Lee, Edward A. Digital Communication. 2nd ed. LC 93-26197. 912p. (C). 1993. lib. bdg. 134.50 (*0-7923-9391-0*) Kluwer Academic.

Lee, Edward A. & Messerschmitt, David G. Digital Communication. 736p. (C). 1988. text 124.50 (*0-89838-274-2*) Kluwer Academic.

Lee, Edward G. & Nelson, W. M. Soldiers' National Cemetery - Gettysburg: Revised Report of the Select Committee Relative to the Soldiers' National Cemetery. Slack, Alfred, ed. (Illus.). 212p. (C). 1988. reprint ed. pap. 11.95 (*0-939631-08-3*) Thomas Publications.

Lee, Edward N. & Mandelbaum, Maurice, eds. Phenomenology & Existentialism. LC 67-15598. (Johns Hopkins Paperbacks Ser.: Vol. JH-57). 279p. 1969. reprint ed. pap. 86.50 (*0-608-03714-1*, 206453900009) Bks Demand.

Lee, Edwin. The British As Rulers: Governing Multiracial Singapore. 313p. 1991. pap. 42.50 (*9971-69-139-6*, Pub. by Sngapore Univ Pr) Coronet Bks.

— The British As Rulers Governing Multi-Racial Singapore, 1867-1914. 336p. 1991. 67.50 (*9971-69-159-0*, Pub. by Sngapore Univ Pr) Coronet Bks.

Lee, Egmont, jt. auth. see Brezzi, Paolo.

Lee, Elaine. Starstruck: The Expanding Universe, Vol. 1. 2nd ed. (Illus.). 256p. 1996. 22.95 (*1-56924-769-2*) Marlowe & Co.

Lee, Elaine. Vamps. Kahan, Bob, ed. LC 96-159726. (Illus.). 160p. 1996. pap. 9.95 (*1-56389-220-0*, Pub. by DC Comics) Time Warner.

Lee, Elaine, ed. Go Girl: The Black Woman's Book of Travel & Adventure. LC 97-25233. 288p. (Orig.). 1997. pap. 16.95 (*0-933377-42-8*) Eighth Mount Pr.

— Go Girl: The Black Woman's Book of Travel & Adventure. LC 97-25233. 288p. (Orig.). 1998. lib. bdg. 24.95 (*0-933377-43-6*) Eighth Mount Pr.

Lee, Elaine & Kaluta, Michael W. Starstruck: The Expanding Universe. 2nd ed. (Illus.). 256p. 1996. pap. 16.95 (*1-56924-795-1*) Marlowe & Co.

— Starstruck Vol. 1: The Expanding Universe. 2nd limited ed. (Illus.). 256p. 1997. 50.00 (*1-56924-794-3*) Marlowe & Co.

Lee, Elaine, et al. Skin Tight Orbit. 52p. 1995. pap. 9.95 (*1-56163-118-3*, Amerotica) NBM.

— Skin Tight Orbit. deluxe ed. 52p. 1995. 45.00 (*1-56163-119-1*, Amerotica) NBM.

— Skin Tight Orbit, 2. 52p. 1995. pap. 10.95 (*1-56163-132-9*, Amerotica) NBM.

— Skin Tight Orbit, Vol. 2. 52p. 1995. 50.00 (*1-56163-137-X*, Amerotica) NBM.

— Starstruck. 85p. (Orig.). 1985. pap. 11.95 (*0-88145-023-5*) Broadway Play.

Lee, Eldon. A Western Doctor's Odyssey: From Cariboo to Kos. (Illus.). 192p. 1996. pap. 11.95 (*1-895811-21-X*) Heritage Hse.

Lee, Elisa T. Statistical Methods for Survival Data Analysis. 2nd ed. LC 91-27926. (Probability & Mathematical Statistics: Applied Probability & Statistics Section Ser.). 496p. 1992. 94.95 (*0-471-61592-7*) Wiley.

Lee, Elizabeth, jt. auth. see Carty, Winthrop P.

Lee, Elizabeth, ed. see Bortolazzo, Paul.

Lee, Elizabeth, tr. see Jusserand, Jean J.

Lee, Elizabeth M. He Wears Orchids & Other Latin American Stories. LC 76-117327. (Biography Index Reprint Ser.). 1977. 21.95 (*0-8369-8019-0*) Ayer.

Lee, Elizabeth N. King George County, Virginia, Death Records, 1853-1896. LC 95-163200. 425p. (Orig.). 1995. pap. text 50.50 (*0-7884-0169-6*) Heritage Bk.

Lee, Ellen W. Seurat at Gravelines: The Last Landscapes. LC 90-83128. (Illus.). 80p. 1990. 32.50 (*0-936260-56-4*); pap. 22.50 (*0-936260-55-6*) Ind Mus Art.

Lee, Eming, jt. auth. see Lee, C. C.

*__Lee, Emma.__ Rice & Noodles: Over 75 Delicious Recipes Featuring Starters, Main Courses & Desserts. (Illus.). 2000. 14.95 (*0-7548-0272-8*, Lorenz Bks) Anness Pub.

Lee, Enid, et al, eds. Beyond Heroes & Holidays: A Practical Guide to K-12 Anti-Racist, Multicultural Education & Staff Development. LC 97-76289. 480p. 1998. pap. 27.00 (*1-878554-11-5*) Netwrk of Educ.

An Asterisk (*) at the beginning of an entry indicates that the title is appearing for the first time.

Lee, Eric. Ill Conceived. LC 97-90941. 1998. 24.95 (*0-533-12513-8*) Vantage.
— The Labour Movement & the Internet: The New Internationalism. 256p. 1996. pap. 19.95 (*0-7453-1114-8*, Pub. by Pluto GBR) Stylus Pub VA.
— The Labour Movement & the Internet: The New Internationalism. LC 96-28838. 256p. 1996. 55.00 (*0-7453-1119-9*, Pub. by Pluto GBR) Stylus Pub VA.
Lee, Eric M. Translations: Turner & Printmaking. LC 93-60992. (Illus.). 48p. (Orig.). 1993. pap. 8.95 (*0-930606-71-X*) Yale Ctr Brit Art.
Lee, Ernest M. Brahms, the Man & His Music. LC 74-24138. (Illus.). reprint ed. 37.50 (*0-404-13001-1*) AMS Pr.
Lee, Ernest W. Pidgin Phrasebook: Pidgin Language of Oceania. 2nd ed. 250p. 1999. pap. 5.95 (*0-86442-587-2*) Lonely Planet.
***Lee, Essie E.** Nurturing Success: Successful Women of Color & Their Daughters. LC 99-37530. 312p. 2000. write for info. (*0-275-96033-1*, Praeger Pubs) Greenwood.
Lee, Etrulia R. Phonics Is My Way Series, 21 bks. Incl. Blake the Duck. (Illus.). 24p. (J). (ps-2). 1994. pap. text (*1-884876-09-9*); Dill. (Illus.). 20p. (J). (ps-2). 1995. pap. text (*1-884876-03-X*); Footprints in the Sand. (Illus.). 32p. (J). (gr. k-2). 1994. pap. text (*1-884876-19-6*); Horse on a Porch. (Illus.). 36p. (J). (gr. k-2). 1994. pap. text (*1-884876-15-3*); I Can Jump. (Illus.). 16p. (J). (ps-2). 1994. pap. text (*1-884876-01-3*); I Like to Dream. (Illus.). 32p. (J). (gr. k-2). 1994. pap. text (*1-884876-11-0*); Jam, Ham & Yams. (Illus.). 20p. (J). (ps-2). 1994. pap. text (*1-884876-02-1*); Mel. (Illus.). 20p. (J). (ps-2). 1994. pap. text (*1-884876-07-2*); Mel Is Back. (Illus.). 32p. (J). (gr. k-2). 1994. pap. text (*1-884876-13-7*); Mel's Store. (Illus.). 36p. (J). (gr. k-2). 1994. pap. text (*1-884876-21-8*); Red Beans & Rice. (Illus.). 32p. (J). (gr. k-2). 1994. pap. text (*1-884876-20-X*); Skates & Grapes. (Illus.). 24p. (J). (gr. k-2). 1994. pap. text (*1-884876-12-9*); Space Trip. (Illus.). 24p. (J). (gr. k-2). 1994. pap. text (*1-884876-18-8*); Stuff. (Illus.). 20p. (J). (gr. k-2). 1994. pap. text (*1-884876-17-X*); Team. (Illus.). 24p. (J). (ps-2). 1994. pap. text (*1-884876-08-0*); Tiff & His Bone. (Illus.). 28p. (J). (ps-2). 1994. pap. text (*1-884876-04-8*); Train Ride. (Illus.). 20p. (J). (ps-2). 1994. pap. text (*1-884876-10-2*); Wake up Time. (Illus.). 20p. (J). (ps-2). 1994. pap. text What Would You Say? (Illus.). 24p. (J). (gr. k-2). 1994. pap. text (*1-884876-14-5*); Zip-a-Zap Zing. (Illus.). 32p. (J). (gr. k-2). 1994. pap. text (*1-884876-16-1*); 149.95 (*1-884876-00-5*) Chamike Pubs.
Lee, Eugene C. Managing Multicampus Systems: Effective Administration in an Unsteady State: A Report for the Carnegie Council on Policy Studies in Higher Education. LC 75-24012. (Carnegie Council Ser.). 192p. reprint ed. pap. 59.60 (*0-608-14788-5*, 202566100045) Bks Demand.
— The Origins of the Chancellorship: The Buried Report of 1948. LC 94-24409. (Chapters in the History of the University of California Ser.). 77p. (Orig.). 1995. pap. 10.00 (*0-87772-360-5*) UCB IGS.
Lee, Eui W. & Kim, Nack J., eds. Light-Weight Alloys for Aerospace Applications No. 2: Proceedings of a Symposium Sponsored by the TMS Nonferrous Metals Committee, Held During the 1991 TMS Annual Meeting, New Orleans, Louisiana, February 17-21, 1991. LC 91-62555. 516p. 1991. reprint ed. pap. 160.00 (*0-7837-9127-5*, 204992700004) Bks Demand.
Lee, Eui W., ed. see Minerals, Metals & Materials Society Staff.
Lee, Eun S., et al. Analyzing Complex Survey Data. (Quantitative Applications in the Social Sciences Ser.: Vol. 71). 80p. (C). 1989. pap. text 10.95 (*0-8039-3014-3*) Sage.
Lee, Eun S., jt. auth. see Forthofer, Ronald N.
Lee, Evelyn. Bluestem Horizon: A Story of a Tallgrass Prairie. LC 98-13739. (Habitat Ser.: Vol. 10). (Illus.). 36p. (J). (gr. 1-4). 1998. 15.95 (*1-56899-595-4*); 19.95 incl. audio (*1-56899-597-0*, BC7010); pap. 5.95 (*1-56899-596-2*); pap. 10.95 incl. audio (*1-56899-598-9*) Soundprints.
— Bluestem Horizon: A Story of a Tallgrass Prairie, Incl. toy. (Habitat Ser.: Vol. 10). (Illus.). 36p. (J). (gr. 1-4). 1998. 26.95 (*1-56899-599-7*); 31.95 incl. audio (*1-56899-601-2*); pap. 16.95 (*1-56899-600-4*); pap. 19.95 incl. audio (*1-56899-602-0*) Soundprints.
— Mountain Mists: A Story of the Virungas. LC 99-19981. (Habitat Ser.: No. 14). (Illus.). 36p. (J). (gr. 1-4). 1999. 19.95 incl. audio (*1-56899-787-6*, BC7014) Soundprints.
— Mountain Mists: A Story of the Virungas. (Habitat Ser.: No. 14). (Illus.). 36p. (J). (gr. 1-4). 1999. 26.95 (*1-56899-789-2*); pap. 5.95 (*1-56899-786-8*); pap. 16.95 (*1-56899-790-6*) Soundprints.
— Mountain Mists: A Story of the Virungas. LC 99-19981. (Habitat Ser.: No. 14). (Illus.). 36p. (J). (ps-3). 1999. 15.95 (*1-56899-785-X*) Soundprints.
— Ten Principles on Raising Chinese-American Teens. (Illus.). 69p. (Orig.). 1988. pap., student ed. 10.65 (*0-9621298-0-1*); 7.50 (*0-9621298-1-X*) Chinatown Youth Ctr.
Lee, Evelyn, ed. Working with Asian Americans: A Guide for Clinicians. LC 97-25930. 504p. 1997. lib. bdg. 47.95 (*1-57230-244-5*, C0244) Guilford Pubns.
***Lee, Evelyn, ed.** Working with Asian Americans: A Guide for Clinicians. 504p. 2000. pap. text 27.95 (*1-57230-570-3*, C0570) Guilford Pubns.
Lee, Everett S. & Goldsmith, Harold F., eds. Population Estimates: Methods for Small Area Analysis. LC 82-648. 248p. reprint ed. pap. 76.90 (*0-8357-8446-0*, 203471000091) Bks Demand.
Lee, F. & Dyke, C. Surgical Attending Rounds. 393p. 1992. pap. 29.50 (*0-8121-1470-1*) Lppncott W & W.
Lee, F. D. & Agnew, J. L. Historical Record of the City of Savannah. (Illus.). 248p. 1997. reprint ed. lib. bdg. 32.00 (*0-8328-6630-X*) Higginson Bk Co.
***Lee, Faye.** Is Measurement Disempowering? 14p. 1999. pap. 10.00 (*0-929556-17-8*) Ind Sector.
Lee, Fitzhugh. General Lee. (Illus.). 433p. 1989. reprint ed. 35.00 (*0-916107-91-4*) Broadfoot.
— General Lee: A Biography of Robert E. Lee. LC 94-11564. (Illus.). 478p. 1994. reprint ed. pap. 15.95 (*0-306-80589-8*) Da Capo.
Lee, Florence & Lee, H. Ten Lessons in Chinese Cooking. 1989. 18.95 (*0-930878-62-0*) Hollym Intl.
Lee, Florence C. Facts about Ginseng: The Elixir of Life. (Illus.). 104p. 1996. 27.95 (*0-930878-83-3*) Hollym Intl.
— Ten Lessons in Japanese Cooking. (Illus.). 80p. 1996. 16.95 (*1-56591-061-3*, Pub. by Hollym Bks) Weatherhill.
Lee, Florence C. & Lee, Helen C. Kimchi: A Natural Health Food. LC 88-83284. (Illus.). 64p. 1999. 16.95 (*0-930878-59-0*) Hollym Intl.
Lee Fook Hong. Company Secretarial Practice Manual. 396p. 1993. boxed set 115.00 (*0-409-99649-1*, SI, MICHIE) LEXIS Pub.
Lee-Ford, Angela. Screven & Jenkins Counties, GA. (Images of America Ser.). (Illus.). 128p. 1998. pap. 18.99 (*0-7385-0300-2*) Arcadia Publng.
Lee, Frances E. & Oppenheimer, Bruce I. Sizing up the Senate: The Unequal Consequences of Equal Representation. LC 99-20500. 288p. 1999. pap. 17.00 (*0-226-47006-7*); lib. bdg. 48.00 (*0-226-47005-9*) U Ch Pr.
Lee, Frances Y., tr. see Colclazer, Susan.
Lee, Frances Y., tr. see Davies, Denny.
Lee, Frances Y., tr. see Jackson, Victor L.
Lee, Frances Y., tr. see Maxon, James C.
Lee, Frances Y., tr. see McKenzie, Leonard.
Lee, Frances Y., tr. see Robinson, Sandra C. & Robinson, George B.
Lee, Frances Y., tr. see Rudd, Connie.
Lee, Frances Y., tr. see Smith, John L.
Lee, Francis A., jt. auth. see Eng, Maximo V.
***Lee, Francis Bazley, ed.** Genealogical & Memorial History of the State of New Jersey: A Record of the Achievements of Her People in the Making of a Commonwealth & the Founding of a Nation, 4 vols., Set. 1694p. 2000. reprint ed. pap. 165.00 (*0-8063-4955-7*, Pub. by Clearfield Co) ACCESS Pubs Network.
Lee, Francis G. Wall of Controversy. LC 85-19697. 132p. 1986. pap. 11.50 (*0-89874-828-3*) Krieger.
Lee, Francis G., ed. All Imaginable Liberty: The Religious Liberty Clauses & the First Amendment. 191p. (C). 1995. pap. text 24.50 (*0-8191-9886-2*) U Pr of Amer.
— All Imaginable Liberty - The Religious Liberty Clauses of the First Amendment. 191p. 1990. write for info. (*0-916101-08-8*) St Joseph.
Lee, Frank. My Bedtime Book of the Saints. rev. ed. LC 93-78437. (Illus.). 64p. (J). 1993. pap. 3.95 (*0-89243-585-2*) Liguori Pubns.
Lee, Frank. P.A.S.S. C.A.L.F. 8 Behaviors of Sales Success in an Agricultural Dealership. xiii, 95p. 1997. pap. text 10.95 (*0-9701399-0-X*) Sales Acdmy.
Lee, Frank E. Central Office Plant. 2nd ed. LC 73-85629. (ABC of the Telephone Ser.: Vol. 3). (Illus.). 58p. (C). 1985. pap. text 17.95 (*1-56016-002-0*) ABC TeleTraining.
— Outside Plant. rev. ed. LC 73-85629. (ABC of the Telephone Ser.: Vol. 4). (Illus.). 128p. (C). 1987. spiral bd. 19.95 (*1-56016-056-X*) ABC TeleTraining.
— Station Installation & Maintenance. rev. ed. LC 73-85629. (ABC of the Telephone Ser.: Vol. 2). (Illus.). 97p. (C). 1986. spiral bd. 19.95 (*1-56016-055-1*) ABC TeleTraining.
— Telephone Theory, Principles & Practice. rev. ed. LC 73-85629. (ABC of the Telephone Ser.: Vol. 1). (Illus.). 160p. (C). 1995. pap. text 19.95 (*1-56016-000-4*) ABC TeleTraining.
Lee, Frank F. Negro & White in a Connecticut Town: A Study in Race Relations. 1961. pap. 15.95 (*0-8084-0404-0*) NCUP.
Lee, Frankie. Diamonds Can Cut Glass & Unrepeatable Miracle. LC 88-22564. 286p. 1988. 17.75 (*0-930950-28-3*); pap. 10.75 (*0-930950-29-1*) Nopoly Pr.
Lee, Franklyn E. Maxwell Macmillan Preparing the 1040 Return. 1991. pap. 49.50 (*0-02-081143-8*) Macmillan.
Lee, Franklyn E. & Berkowitz, Lawrence B. Preparing the 1040 Return, 1992. 650p. 1992. 54.95 (*0-7811-0001-1*, Maxwell Macmillan) Macmillan.
— Preparing the 1040 Return, 1993. rev. ed. LC 78-71966. (Professional Tax Advisor's Guide Ser.). (Illus.). 650p. 1992. pap. text 56.00 (*0-7811-0058-5*) Res Inst Am.
Lee, Fred. The Computer Book. LC 78-17450. 381p. reprint ed. pap. 118.20 (*0-608-13082-6*, 202505800041) Bks Demand.
Lee, Frederic S. The Foundation of Post Keynesian Price Theory. LC 97-49242. 290p. (C). 1999. text 59.95 (*0-521-32870-5*) Cambridge U Pr.
Lee, Frederic S. & Samuels, Warren J., eds. The Heterodox Economics of Gardiner C. Means: A Collection. LC 90-8836. (Studies in Institutional Economics). 432p. (C). (gr. 13). 1992. text 93.95 (*0-87332-717-9*) M E Sharpe.
Lee, Frederic S., ed. see Means, Gardiner C.
Lee, Frederick S., jt. ed. see Earl, Peter E.
Lee, G. Avery. Affirmations of a Skeptical Believer. (C). 1993. pap. text 14.95 (*0-86554-395-X*, MUP-P093) Mercer Univ Pr.
— Living in the Meantime: Nine-Tenths of the 20th Century. 192p. 1993. 19.00 (*1-880837-38-2*); pap. 14.00 (*1-880837-39-0*) Smyth & Helwys.
Lee, G. K., ed. Computer Applications in Design, Simulation & Analysis (CADSA-92), 5th International Conference March 11-13, 1992, Orlando, Florida, USA: 5th International Conference on March 11-13, 1992, Orlando, FL. (Conference Proceedings Ser.). 250p. (C). write for info. (*1-880843-00-5*) Int Soc Comp App.
— Computer Applications in Industry & Engineering (CAINE-96), 9th International Conference, December 11-13, 1996, Orlando, Florida, U.S.A: CAINE-96, Dec. 11-13, 1996, Orlando, FL. (C). 1996. write for info. (*1-880843-18-8*) Int Soc Comp App.
— Software & Hardware Applications of Microcomputers: Proceedings IASTED Symposium, Fort Collins, U. S. A., February 4-6, 1987. 127p. 1987. 58.00 (*0-88986-102-1*, 108) Acta Pr.
Lee, G. K., jt. ed. see Hamza, M. H.
Lee, G. L., et al. The Sampling & Analysis of Compressed Air to Be Used for Breathing Purposes. (C). 1985. 45.00 (*0-905927-17-6*, Pub. by H&H Sci Cnslts) St Mut.
Lee, G. Richard, et al. Wintrobe's Clinical Hematology, 2 vols. 10th ed. LC 96-52799. (Illus.). 2837p. 1998. 179.00 (*0-683-18242-0*) Lppncott W & W.
— Wintrobe's Clinical Hematology, 2 vols., Set. 9th ed. LC 90-6194. (Illus.). 2320p. 1992. 175.00 (*0-8121-1188-5*) Lppncott W & W.
Lee, Garrison. Paralegal Guide to Qualifed Pension Benefit Plans under ERISA, 1. LC 97-3367. 568p. 1998. pap. text 75.00 (*0-471-08664-9*) Wiley.
Lee, Gary C., jt. auth. see Wong, Alice K.
Lee, Gaylen D. Walking Where We Lived: Memoirs of a Mono Indian Family. LC 98-13492. (Illus.). 224p. 1998. 23.95 (*0-8061-3087-3*) U of Okla Pr.
***Lee, Gaylen D.** Walking Where We Lived: Memoirs of a Mono Indian Family. 224p. 1999. pap. text 10.95 (*0-8061-3168-3*) U of Okla Pr.
Lee, Gennell. Quick Emergency Care Reference. (Illus.). 60p. (C). (gr. 13). 1991. pap. text 8.95 (*0-8016-6584-1*, 06584) Mosby Inc.
Lee, Gentry. Bright Messengers. 464p. 1996. mass mkt. 6.50 (*0-553-57329-2*, Spectra) Bantam.
— Double Full Moon Night. LC 98-31411. 320p. 1999. 23.95 (*0-553-09007-0*) Bantam.
***Lee, Gentry.** Double Full Moon Night. 416p. 2000. reprint ed. mass mkt. 6.99 (*0-553-57336-5*) Bantam.
Lee, Gentry, jt. auth. see Clarke, Arthur C.
Lee, Geoffrey & McAdam, Peter. Formwork: Practical Guide. LC 98-116359. (Illus.). 200p. (C). (gr. 13). 1997. pap. 55.00 (*0-419-22820-9*, E & FN Spon) Routledge.
Lee, Geoffrey, ed. see Grace, Charles S.
Lee, George. The American Revolution. (Illus.). 144p. (YA). (gr. 5). 1996. pap. text 12.95 (*1-58037-010-1*, Pub. by M Twain Media) Carson-Dellos.
— American Women. (Illus.). 176p. (YA). (gr. 5). 1993. pap. text 14.95 (*1-58037-103-5*, Pub. by M Twain Media) Carson-Dellos.
— Decisions That Shaped America, 1607-1865. (Illus.). 176p. (YA). (gr. 5-8). 1993. pap. text (*1-58037-019-5*) M Twain Media.
— Decisions That Shaped America, 1865-1976. (Illus.). 176p. (YA). (gr. 5-8). 1993. pap. text 14.95 (*1-58037-048-9*, Pub. by M Twain Media) Carson-Dellos.
— Elections. (Illus.). 80p. (YA). (gr. 5). 1998. pap. text 9.95 (*1-58037-036-5*, Pub. by M Twain Media) Carson-Dellos.
— Holocaust. (Illus.). 80p. 1998. pap. text 9.95 (*1-58037-070-5*, Pub. by M Twain Media) Carson-Dellos.
— U. S. Constitution: Preparing for the Test. (Illus.). 80p. 2000. pap. text 9.95 (*1-58037-138-8*, Pub. by M Twain Media) Carson-Dellos.
— World War II. (Illus.). 176p. (YA). (gr. 5-8). 1995. pap. 14.95 (*1-58037-083-7*, Pub. by M Twain Media) Carson-Dellos.
Lee, George & Gaston, Roger. Civil War. (Illus.). 176p. (YA). (gr. 5-8). 1994. pap. text 14.95 (*1-58037-007-1*, Pub. by M Twain Media) Carson-Dellos.
Lee, George, jt. auth. see Edgar, Frank.
***Lee, George B.** A Certain Feeling. 2000. pap. 18.00 (*0-7388-2153-5*) Xlibris Corp.
Lee, George L. Inspiring African Americans: Black History Makers in the United States, 1750-1980. LC 90-53503. (Illus.). 144p. 1991. lib. bdg. 25.00 (*0-89950-576-7*) McFarland & Co.
— Interesting People: Black American History Makers. LC 88-43542. (Illus.). 224p. 1989. lib. bdg. 15.95 (*0-89950-403-5*) McFarland & Co.
— Worldwide Interesting People: 162 History Makers of African Descent. LC 91-50939. (Illus.). 144p. (J). 1992. lib. bdg. 25.00 (*0-89950-670-4*) McFarland & Co.
***Lee, George Oscar.** Goat for Azazel: A World War II Story. LC 99-90832. 640p. 1999. 25.00 (*0-7388-0544-0*); pap. 18.00 (*0-7388-0545-9*) Xlibris Corp.
Lee, George W. River George. LC 73-18590. reprint ed. 36.00 (*0-404-11401-6*) AMS Pr.
Lee, Georgia. A Day with a Chumash. LC 98-35161. (Day with Ser.). (Illus.). 48p. (J). (gr. 5-7). 1999. lib. bdg. 22.60 (*0-8225-1918-6*, Runestone Pr) Lerner Pub.
— Rock Art & Cultural Resource Management. LC 91-33681. (Illus.). 72p. (Orig.). (C). 1991. pap. text 6.95 (*0-937523-04-6*) Wormwood Pr.
— Rock Art of Easter Island: Symbols of Power, Prayers to the Gods. LC 92-47034. (UCLA Institute of Archaeology Publications: No. 17). (Illus.). 225p. (C). 1992. 35.00 (*0-917956-74-5*) UCLA Arch.
— Spirit of Place: Petroglyphs of Hawaii. (Illus.). 212p. 1999. pap. write for info. (*1-880636-14-X*) Easter Isl Fnd.
— An Uncommon Guide to Easter Island: Exploring Archaeological Mysteries of Rapa Nui. (Illus.). 128p. 1989. 18.95 (*0-937480-17-7*) Intl Resources.
Lee, Georgia, ed. see Charola, A. Alena.
Lee, Georgia, ed. see Kurze, Joan S.
Lee, Georgia, ed. see Stevenson, Christopher M.
Lee, Georgia, ed. & illus. see Drake, Alan.
Lee, Gerald. Eating Dog: Travel Stories. 200p. 1994. pap. 16.95 (*0-7022-2184-8*, Pub. by Univ Queensland Pr) Intl Spec Bk.
— True Love & How to Get It. (Paperbacks Ser.). 204p. 1985. pap. 14.95 (*0-7022-1778-6*, Pub. by Univ Queensland Pr) Intl Spec Bk.
Lee, Gerald J. Dancing at Ground Zero. 48p. 1985. pap. 9.95 (*0-917658-21-3*) BPW & P.
Lee, Gerard. Leper Hospitals in Medieval Ireland. 72p. 1996. 15.00 (*1-85182-271-2*, Pub. by Four Cts Pr) Intl Spec Bk.
— Leper Hospitals in Medieval Ireland. limited ed. 72p. 1996. 75.00 (*1-85182-285-2*, Pub. by Four Cts Pr) Intl Spec Bk.
— Troppo Man. 1990. pap. 14.95 (*0-7022-2299-2*, Pub. by Univ Queensland Pr) Intl Spec Bk.
Lee, Gerard & Campion, Jane. Sweetie: The Screenplay. 1991. pap. 12.95 (*0-7022-2371-9*, Pub. by Univ Queensland Pr) Intl Spec Bk.
Lee, Geri, ed. see Mini, Anna M.
Lee, Gi-eun, ed. see Nahm, Andrew C.
Lee, Gilda. Flowers Can Heal Vol. 1: Essences Vibrational Therapy. (Illus.). (Orig.). 1997. pap. 11.00 (*0-9695954-0-9*) In The Pink.
— Flowers Can Heal Vol. 1: Essences Vibrational Therapy. LC 97-211078. (Illus.). 100p. (Orig.). 1997. per. 11.00 (*0-9659154-0-9*) In The Pink.
Lee, Gim, jt. auth. see Lim, Ching S.
Lee, Glenda. One Hundred One Bright Bulletin Board Ideas. 1991. pap. 8.00 (*0-89137-626-7*) Quality Pubns.
— One Hundred Two Bright Bulletin Board Ideas. 1992. pap. 8.00 (*0-89137-627-5*) Quality Pubns.
Lee, Gloria. Why We Are Here. 183p. 1996. reprint ed. spiral bd. 15.50 (*0-7873-0547-2*) Hlth Research.
Lee, Gonzales. Literature Express Level 2: Text. 2002. pap. text 30.00 (*0-8384-0122-8*) Heinle & Heinle.
— Literature Express: Text. 2002. pap. text 30.00 (*0-8384-0112-0*) Heinle & Heinle.
— Literature Express Level 2: Assessment. 2002. pap. 32.50 (*0-8384-0134-1*) Heinle & Heinle.
— Literature Express Level 2: Workbook. 2002. pap. 9.50 (*0-8384-0124-4*) Heinle & Heinle.
— Literature Express Level 1: Assessment. 2002. pap. text 32.50 (*0-8384-0115-5*) Heinle & Heinle.
— Literature Express Level 1: Workbook. 2002. pap. text 9.50 (*0-8384-0114-7*) Heinle & Heinle.
Lee, Gordon C. The Struggle for Federal Aid, First Phase: A History of the Attempts to Obtain Federal Aid for the Common Schools. LC 79-176979. (Columbia University. Teachers College. Contributions to Education Ser.: No. 957). reprint ed. 37.50 (*0-404-55957-3*) AMS Pr.
Lee-Gosselin, Martin, jt. ed. see Stopher, Peter.
Lee, Grace. On the Way to over the Hill: A Guide for Aging Gracefully. O'Mahony, Kieran, ed. 150p. (Orig.). 1997. pap. 12.95 (*0-944638-11-2*) EduCare Pr.
***Lee, Grace Lawless.** The Huguenot Settlements in Ireland. 281p. 1999. pap. 26.50 (*0-8063-4929-8*) Clearfield Co.
Lee, Grace O., ed. see Huque, Ahmed S.
Lee, Greg. Chris Burke: He Overcame Down Syndrome, Set III. LC 93-18213. (Reaching Your Goal Ser.). (Illus.). 24p. (J). (gr. 1-4). 1993. lib. bdg. 13.95 (*0-86593-263-8*) Rourke Corp.
— Food: Wacky Words. LC 92-41730. (Little Jokester Ser.). 24p. (J). (gr. k-4). 1993. lib. bdg. 10.95 (*0-86593-265-4*) Rourke Corp.
— Jim Abbott, Set III. LC 92-43251. (Reaching Your Goal Ser.). (Illus.). 24p. (J). (gr. 1-4). 1993. lib. bdg. 13.95 (*0-86593-258-1*) Rourke Corp.
— Money. LC 92-44074. (J). 1993. 9.50 (*0-685-66360-4*) Rourke Corp.
— Money. LC 92-44074. (Little Jokester Ser.). 24p. (J). (gr. k-4). 1993. lib. bdg. 10.95 (*0-86593-268-9*) Rourke Corp.
— Outer Space: Wacky Words. LC 92-43965. (Little Jokester Ser.). 24p. (J). (gr. k-4). 1993. lib. bdg. 10.95 (*0-86593-267-0*) Rourke Corp.
— Outer Space: Wacky Words. LC 92-43965. (Little Jokester Ser.). (J). (gr. 3 up). 1993. 9.50 (*0-685-66292-6*) Rourke Corp.
— Pets: Wacky Words. LC 92-43964. (Little Jokester Ser.). (J). (gr. 3 up). 1993. 9.50 (*0-685-66291-8*) Rourke Corp.
— Pets: Wacky Words. LC 92-43964. (Little Jokester Ser.). 24p. (J). (gr. k-4). 1996. lib. bdg. 10.95 (*0-86593-266-2*) Rourke Corp.
— School. LC 92-44073. (Little Jokester Ser.). 24p. (J). (gr. k-4). 1993. lib. bdg. 10.95 (*0-86593-269-7*) Rourke Corp.
— School. LC 92-44073. (J). (gr. 3 up). 1993. 9.50 (*0-685-66359-0*) Rourke Corp.
— Vacation. LC 92-45692. (Little Jokester Ser.). (J). 1993. 9.50 (*0-685-66420-1*) Rourke Corp.
— Vacation. LC 92-45692. (Little Jokester Ser.). 24p. (J). (gr. k-4). 1993. lib. bdg. 10.95 (*0-86593-270-0*) Rourke Corp.
Lee, Greglon, ed. see Demura, Fumio.
Lee, Gregory. Animal Rights. (Troubled Society Ser.: Set II). 64p. (J). 1991. lib. bdg. 17.95 (*0-86593-112-7*) Rourke Corp.
***Lee, Gregory.** Best of Orange County: A Guide to Scenic, Recreational & Historical Attractions. 2nd ed. (Illus.). 2000. pap. 14.95 (*1-881409-26-0*) Jhnstn Assocs.
Lee, Gregory. California Traveler: California Missions - A Guide to the State's Spanish Heritage. LC 92-200534. (American Traveler Ser.: Vol. 17). (Illus.). 48p. 1999. pap. 6.95 (*1-55838-122-8*) R H Pub.
— California Traveler: Whale Watching & Tidepools - A

L

Guide to California Marine Life. LC 92-199831. (American Traveler Ser.: Vol. 18). (Illus.). 48p. 1992. pap. 6.95 (*1-55838-123-6*) R H Pub.

— Discrimination. (Troubled Society Ser.: Set II). 64p. (J). 1991. lib. bdg. 17.95 (*0-86593-113-5*) Rourke Corp.

— Troubadours, Trumpeters & Troubled Makers: Lyricism, Nationalism & Hybridity in China & Its Others. LC 95-5193. (Asia-Pacific Ser.). 296p. 1996. text 49.95 (*0-8223-1659-5*) Duke.

Lee, Gregory & Leaver, Darren. Physical Geography Study Guide. 3rd ed. 176p. 1996. pap. text, per. 21.95 (*0-7872-2777-3*, 41277701) Kendall-Hunt.

Lee, Gregory B. Troubadours, Trumpeters & Troubled Makers: Lyricism, Nationalism & Hybridity in China & Its Others. LC 95-5193. (Asia-Pacific Ser.). 296p. 1996. pap. text 17.95 (*0-8223-1671-4*) Duke.

Lee, Grem. The Rounders 3. LC 97-23476. 304p. 1997. 24.95 (*0-87081-455-9*) Univ Pr Colo.

Lee, Gus. China Boy. LC 93-27236. 336p. 1994. pap. 12.95 (*0-452-27158-4*, Plume) Dutton Plume.

— No Physical Evidence. LC 98-15860. 400p. 1998. 24.95 (*0-449-91139-X*) Fawcett.

— No Physical Evidence: A Courtroom Novel. LC 99-94420. 372p. 2000. mass mkt. 6.99 (*0-8041-1779-9*) Ivy Books.

— Tiger's Tail. (Illus.). 1997. mass mkt. 6.99 (*0-8041-1326-2*) Ivy Books.

— Tiger's Tail. 288p. 1996. 24.00 (*0-679-43855-6*) Knopf.

***Lee, Guy.** Ovid in Love. (Illus.). 208p. 2000. 17.95 (*0-312-26891-2*, Thomas Dunne) St Martin.

Lee, Guy, tr. The Poems. LC 96-164134. (World's Classics WC Ser.). 230p. (Orig.). (C). 1996. pap. 8.95 (*0-19-283198-4*) OUP.

Lee, Guy, jt. auth. see Booth, Joan.

Lee, Guy, jt. auth. see Ovid.

Lee, Guy, tr. see Propertius.

Lee, Guy, tr. & intro. see Virgil.

Lee, Guy C. Historical Jurisprudence: An Introduction to the Systematic Study of the Development of Law, Vol. 1. LC 90-55181. xv, 517p. 1990. reprint ed. 120.00 (*0-912004-81-9*) Gaunt.

***Lee, Gwen & Sauter, Elaine.** What If Our World Is Their Heaven? The Final Conversations of Philip K. Dick. 256p. 2000. 26.95 (*1-58567-009-X*, Pub. by Overlook Pr) Penguin Putnam.

Lee, Gypsy Rose. The G-String Murders. 24.95 (*0-89190-147-7*) Amereon Ltd.

— Gypsy: Memoirs of America's Most Celebrated Stripper. LC 98-43226. (Illus.). 350p. 1999. pap. 18.95 (*1-883319-95-1*) Frog Ltd CA.

***Lee, H.** Dates in Cardiology. LC 99-54489. (Landmarks in Medicine Ser.). (Illus.). 100p. 2000. 29.00 (*1-85070-498-8*) Prthnon Pub.

— Dates in Gastroenterology. (Landmarks in Medicine Ser.). (Illus.). 100p. 2000. 29.00 (*1-85070-502-X*) Prthnon Pub.

— Dates in Neurology. (Landmarks in Medicine Ser.). (Illus.). 100p. 2000. 29.00 (*1-85070-529-1*) Prthnon Pub.

— Dates in Obstetrics & Gynecology. LC 99-57140. (Landmarks in Medicine Ser.). (Illus.). 100p. 2000. 29.00 (*1-85070-516-X*) Prthnon Pub.

— Dates in Oncology. (Landmarks in Medicine Ser.). (Illus.). 100p. 2000. 29.00 (*1-85070-499-6*) Prthnon Pub.

— Dates in Urology. LC 99-55487. (Landmarks in Medicine Ser.). (Illus.). 100p. 2000. 29.00 (*1-85070-496-1*) Prthnon Pub.

***Lee, H., ed.** The Medical Millennium. (Illus.). 100p. 2000. 45.00 (*1-85070-466-X*) Prthnon Pub.

Lee, H., et al, eds. Nucleic Acid Amplification Technologies: Application to Disease Diagnosis. (Molecular & Laboratory Medicine Ser.). (Illus.). 300p. 1997. pap. text 39.95 (*1-881299-04-X*, BioTechniques) Eaton Pub Co.

Lee, H. & Wade, Glen, eds. Acoustical Imaging, Vol. 18. (Illus.). 576p. (C). 1991. text 162.00 (*0-306-43900-X*, Kluwer Plenum) Kluwer Academic.

Lee, H., et al. Nucleic Acid Amplification Technologies. write for info. (*0-8176-3921-7*) Birkhauser.

Lee, H., jt. auth. see Lee, Florence.

Lee, H. A. & Raman, G. Venkat. Handbook of Parenteral Nutrition: Hospital & Home Applications. 180p. 1990. pap. 25.50 (*0-412-28030-2*, A4435) Chapman & Hall.

Lee, H. B. & Park, H. C., eds. International Society of Blood Purification. (Journal Ser.: Vol. 13, Suppl. 1, 1995). (Illus.). 70p. 1995. pap. 21.75 (*3-8055-6239-X*) S Karger.

Lee, H. C. An Introduction to Kaluza-Klein Theories: Proceedings of the Workshop on Kaluza-Klein Theories, Chalk River, Canada, Aug. 11-16, 1983. 380p. (C). 1984. 67.00 (*9971-966-19-0*); pap. 33.00 (*9971-966-20-4*) World Scientific Pub.

Lee, H. C. & Gaensslen, R. E., eds. Advanced Fingerprint Technology. (Series in Forensic & Police Science). (Illus.). 401p. 1991. 44.95 (*0-444-01579-5*, CRC Reprint) Franklin.

Lee, H. D., tr. Meteorologica. (Loeb Classical Library: No. 337). 468p. 1952. 18.95 (*0-674-99436-1*) HUP.

Lee, H. L. Vincent. Peptide & Protein Drug Delivery. (Advances in Parenteral Sciences Ser.: Vol. 4). (Illus.). 912p. 1990. text 250.00 (*0-8247-7896-0*) Dekker.

Lee, H. L. Vincent, jt. auth. see Robinson, Joseph R.

Lee, H. P. Constitutional Conflicts in Contemporary Malaysia. 180p. 1996. text 45.00 (*967-65-3095-6*) OUP.

Lee, H. P. & Winterton, George, eds. Australian Constitutional Perspectives. 347p. 1992. 82.00 (*0-455-21084-5*, Pub. by LawBk Co); pap. 63.00 (*0-455-21085-3*, Pub. by LawBk Co) Gaunt.

Lee, H. P., et al. In the Name of National Security: The Legal Dimensions. LC 96-128283. 260p. 1995. pap. 69.00 (*0-455-21323-2*, Pub. by LawBk Co) Gaunt.

Lee, H. P., jt. ed. see Trindade, Francis A.

***Lee, Hae-Geon.** Chemical Thermodynamics For Metals & Materials. 1999. pap. text 22.00 (*1-86094-178-8*) World Scientific Pub.

— Chemical Thermodynamics for Metals & Materials. 324p. 1999. 37.00 (*1-86094-177-X*) Imperial College.

***Lee, Hae-Yun.** Ellipsen in Satzkoordinationen: Syntaktische und Semantische Untersuchungen in Einer Unifikationsbasierten Grammatik. (Illus.). 198p. 1998. 37.95 (*3-631-34204-7*) P Lang Pubng.

Lee, Haeduck & Bobadilla, Jose-Luis. Health Statistics for the Americas. LC 94-36261. (Technical Papers: No. 262). 64p. 1994. pap. 22.00 (*0-8213-3037-3*, 13037) World Bank.

Lee, Hai-In, tr. see Stokes, Penelope J.

Lee, Hak C., jt. ed. see Chung, Kae H.

***Lee, Hang J. & Delisa, Joel A.** Surface Anatomy for Clinical Needle Electromyography. (Illus.). 233p. 1999. pap. text 42.95 (*1-888799-41-2*) Demos Medical.

Lee, Hannah S. Memoir of Pierre Toussaint: Born a Slave in St. Domingo. LC 91-68114. (Illus.). 93p. (Orig.). 1992. reprint ed. pap. 9.95 (*1-881008-02-9*) Am Soc Defense TFP.

Lee, Hansol H. Korean Grammar. (Illus.). 230p. (C). 1989. text 65.00 (*0-19-713606-0*) OUP.

Lee, Hansoon. Kunsttheorie in der Kunst. (Europaische Hochschulschriften Ser.: Reihe 28, Bd. 247). (Illus.). 232p. 1996. pap. 51.95 (*3-631-48841-6*) P Lang Pubng.

Lee, Harold. Roswell Garst: A Biography. LC 83-26452. (Henry A. Wallace Series on Agricultural History & Rural Studies). (Illus.). 351p. reprint ed. pap. 108.90 (*0-8357-6756-6*, 203541300095) Bks Demand.

Lee, Harold, ed. see Garst, Roswell.

Lee, Harold B. Be Loyal to the Royal Within You & to Ease the Aching Heart LC 98-72595. (Classic Talk Ser.). 58 p. 1998. write for info. (*0-87579-982-5*) Deseret Bk.

***Lee, Harper.** Kill a Mockingbird, To. 40th anniversary large type ed. 416p. 1999. pap. 20.00 (*0-06-093327-5*) HarpC.

Lee, Harper. Matar Un Ruisenor. 1986. 16.60 (*0-606-10483-6*, Pub. by Turtleback) Demco.

Lee, Harper. To Kill a Mockingbird. 80p. 1970. pap. 5.95 (*0-87129-920-8*, T91) Dramatic Pub.

Lee, Harper. To Kill a Mockingbird. 1989. pap., student ed. 11.00 (*0-03-023447-6*) Holt R&W.

— To Kill a Mockingbird. LC 60-7847. 1961. 23.00 (*0-397-00151-7*, Lippnctt) Lppncott W & W.

— To Kill a Mockingbird. 1969. text 12.99 (*0-7710-5234-0*) McClelland & Stewart.

— To Kill a Mockingbird. 1960. 10.09 (*0-606-00105-0*, Pub. by Turtleback) Demco.

— To Kill a Mockingbird. 300p. 1991. reprint ed. lib. bdg. 22.95 (*0-89966-858-5*) Buccaneer Bks.

— To Kill a Mockingbird. 288p. 1988. reprint ed. mass mkt. 6.99 (*0-446-31078-6*, Pub. by Warner Bks) Little.

— To Kill a Mockingbird. 35th anniversary ed. 336p. 1995. 18.00 (*0-06-017322-X*) HarperTrade.

***Lee, Harper.** To Kill a Mockingbird: The 40th Anniversary Edition of the Pulitzer Prize-Winning Novel. 40th anniversary ed. 336p. 1999. 18.00 (*0-06-019499-5*) HarpC.

***Lee, Harper & Hartley, Mary M.** To Kill a Mockingbird. (Literature Made Easy Ser.). (Illus.). 96p. (YA). 1999. pap. 4.95 (*0-7641-0822-0*) Barron.

Lee, Harper, jt. auth. see Center for Learning Network Staff.

Lee, Harris W. Effective Church Leadership: A Practical Sourcebook. LC 89-6486. 208p. (Orig.). 1989. pap. 15.99 (*0-8066-2423-X*, 9-2423) Augsburg Fortress.

Lee, Harry O. & Nagy, Jill. Review & Reduction of Real Property Assessments in New York-1994 Supplement. 68p. 1994. pap. text 25.00 (*0-942954-70-X*) NYS Bar.

Lee, Harry O., et al. Review & Reduction of Real Property Assessments in New York. 3rd ed. Nagy, Jill, ed. LC 88-43298. 600p. 1988. 95.00 (*0-942954-22-X*, 4A1264) NYS Bar.

Lee, Hazel, jt. auth. see Lee, Earl G.

Lee, Hector. 20 Tales of California: A Rare Collection of Western Stories. LC 97-28925. (Illus.). 176p. 1998. pap. 9.95 (*1-877810-62-2*) Rayve Prodns.

Lee, Hector V. I Had a Hippopotamus. LC 95-21730. (Illus.). 32p. (J). (ps-1). 1996. 14.95 (*1-880000-28-8*) Lee & Low Bks.

— I Had a Hippopotamus. LC 95-21730. (Illus.). 32p. (J). (ps-1). 1998. pap. 6.95 (*1-880000-62-8*) Lee & Low Bks.

***Lee, Hector Viveros.** I Had a Hippopotamus. (Illus.). 34p. (J). (gr. k-1). 1999. bds. 6.95 (*1-880000-96-2*, Pub. by Lee & Low Bks) Publishers Group.

— Yo Tenia un Hipopotamo.Tr. of I Had a Hippopotamus. (SPA., Illus.). 34p. (J). (ps-1). 1999. bds. 6.95 (*1-880000-97-0*, Pub. by Lee & Low Bks) Publishers Group.

Lee, Hector Viveros, see Viveros Lee, Hector.

Lee, Helen. The Tao of Beauty: Chinese Herbal Secrets to Feeling Good & Looking Great. (Illus.). 224p. 1999. pap. 18.00 (*0-7679-0256-4*) Broadway BDD.

— This Is My Home, Lord. 128p. 1983. reprint ed. 4.95 (*0-86683-683-7*) Harper SF.

Lee, Helen, jt. auth. see Clarke, Ian.

Lee, Helen C., jt. auth. see Lee, Florence C.

Lee, Helen E. The Serpent's Gift. 374p. 1994. 21.00 (*0-689-12193-8*, Scribner Pap Fic) S&S Trade Pap.

— The Serpent's Gift. 384p. 1995. per. 12.00 (*0-684-80160-4*, Scribner Pap Fic) S&S Trade Pap.

— Water Marked. LC 98-32204. 320p. 1999. 23.00 (*0-684-83843-5*) Scribner.

Lee, Helen J. Conceptual Basis for Rural Nursing. (Illus.). 520p. 1998. 48.95 (*0-8261-1189-0*) Springer Pub.

Lee, Helen J., et al. Watch Hill Hurricane September 21, 1938. (Illus.). 24p. 1996. pap. 10.00 (*0-910258-16-3*) Book & Tackle.

Lee, Helie. Still Life with Rice: A Young American Woman Discovers the Life & Legacy of Her Korean Grandmother. (Illus.). 320p. 1996. 24.00 (*0-684-80270-8*) S&S Trade.

Lee, Henry. Anti-Scepticism, or Notes upon Each Chapter of Mr. Lock's Essay Concerning Human Understanding. (Anglistica & Americana Ser.: No. 115). xxx, 342p. 1973. reprint ed. 115.70 (*3-487-04753-5*) G Olms Pubs.

— The Campaign of 1781 in the Carolinas. (Notable American Authors Ser.). 1999. reprint ed. lib. bdg. 125.00 (*0-7812-3786-6*) Rprt Serv.

— Cyanoacrylate Resins: The Instant Adhesives. 245p. (C). 1991. reprint ed. pap. 55.00 (*0-938648-27-6*) T-C Pr CA.

— The Life of the Emperor Napoleon. (Notable American Authors Ser.). 1999. reprint ed. lib. bdg. 125.00 (*0-7812-3788-2*) Rprt Serv.

— Memoirs of the War in the Southern Department of the U. S. Decker, Peter, ed. LC 75-76561. (Eyewitness Accounts of the American Revolution Ser.). 1969. reprint ed. 36.95 (*0-405-01161-X*) Ayer.

— Observations on the Writings of Thomas Jefferson. (Notable American Authors Ser.). 1999. reprint ed. lib. bdg. 125.00 (*0-7812-3787-4*) Rprt Serv.

— The Revolutionary War Memoirs of General Henry Lee. 3rd ed. Lee, Robert E., ed. LC 97-34561. Orig. Title: Memoirs of the War in the Southern Department of the United States. (Illus.). 647p. 1998. pap. 18.95 (*0-306-80841-2*) Da Capo.

Lee, Henry, ed. Shaping National Responses to Climate Change: A Post-Rio Policy Guide. 352p. 1995. text 55.00 (*1-55963-343-3*); pap. text 27.00 (*1-55963-344-1*) Island Pr.

***Lee, Henry, et al.** The Public Garden, Boston. rev. ed. Moore, Barbara W. & Weesner, Gail, eds. (Illus.). 88p. 2000. 25.00 (*0-9676835-0-5*); pap. 15.00 (*0-9676835-1-3*) Friends of Garden.

Lee, Henry, jt. auth. see Forbes, H. A.

Lee, Henry, jt. auth. see Piggin, Stuart.

Lee, Henry C., ed. Physics, Geometry & Topology. (NATO ASI Ser.: Vol. 232). (Illus.). 690p. (C). 1990. text 198.00 (*0-306-43693-0*, Kluwer Plenum) Kluwer Academic.

Lee, Henry C., et al, eds. Super Field Theories. LC 87-14159. (NATO ASI Series B, Physics: Vol. 160). (Illus.). 608p. 1987. 135.00 (*0-306-42660-9*, Plenum Trade) Perseus Pubng.

Lee, Henry C. & Gaensslen, R. E., eds. Advances in Fingerprint Technology. LC 93-46614. (CRC Series in Forensic & Police Science). 296p. 1992. boxed set 83.95 (*0-8493-9513-5*) CRC Pr.

***Lee, Henry C. & Harris, Howard A.** Physical Evidence in Forensic Science. 297p. 2000. 70.00 (*1-930056-00-1*, 5564-N); pap. 45.00 (*1-930056-01-X*, 5563-N) Lawyers & Judges.

Lee, Henry S. A Civil War Diary: January 1, 1863-May 31, 1864. Davis, John D., ed. xvi, 144p. 1997. pap. 18.00 (*0-9661946-0-8*) Craggy Mtn.

Lee, Hermione. Willa Cather: A Life Saved Up. (Illus.). 432p. 2000. pap. 15.95 (*1-86049-292-4*, Pub. by Virago) Trafalgar.

— Willa Cather: Double Lives. LC 91-50018. (Illus.). 432p. 1991. pap. 15.00 (*0-679-73649-2*) Vin Bks.

Lee, Hermione, ed. The Secret Self: Short Stories by Women. 384p. 1993. pap. 6.95 (*0-460-87348-2*, Everyman's Classic Lib) Tuttle Pubng.

Lee, Hermione, ed. see Bowen, Elizabeth.

Lee, Hermione, ed. see Woolf, Virginia.

Lee, Hermione, ed. & intro. see Trollope, Anthony.

Lee, Hermoine. Virginia Woolf. (Illus.). 944p. 1999. pap. 18.00 (*0-375-70136-2*) Vin Bks.

— Willa Cather: Double Lives. 1998. pap. write for info. (*0-316-55998-9*) Little.

Lee, Hetie. Still Life with Rice. 320p. 1997. per. 13.00 (*0-684-82711-5*, Touchstone) S&S Trade Pap.

Lee, Hi-Keun, et al, eds. Environmental & Safety Concerns in Underground: Proceedings of the 1st ARMS'97/A Regional Conference of ISRM, Seoul, 13-15.10.97, 2 vols. LC 99-496427. 1000p. 1997. 162.00 (*90-5410-910-6*, Pub. by A A Balkema) Ashgate Pub Co.

Lee, Hian K., ed. Fourth Symposium on Our Environment. (C). 1992. text 287.50 (*0-7923-1562-6*) Kluwer Academic.

Lee, Hing- Yan, jt. ed. see Motoda, Hiroshi.

Lee, Hiro, et al, eds. Economic Development & Cooperation in the Pacific Basin: Trade, Investment, & Environmental Issues. LC 97-40982. (Illus.). 350p. (C). 1998. 59.95 (*0-521-58366-7*) Cambridge U Pr.

Lee, Hong Y. The Politics of the Chinese Cultural Revolution: A Case Study. LC 76-19993. (Center for Chinese Studies, UC Berkeley: No. 17). 1978. pap. 17.95 (*0-520-04065-1*, Pub. by U CA Pr) Cal Prin Full Svc.

Lee, Hong Y., ed. Korean Options in a Changing International Order. LC 93-28487. (Korea Research Monographs: No. 18). 1993. pap. 17.00 (*1-55729-040-7*) IEAS.

Lee, Hongkoo, jt. ed. see Scalapino, Robert A.

Lee, Howard B. Bloodletting in Appalachia: The Story of West Virginia's Four Major Mine Wars & Other Thrilling Incidents of Its Coal Fields. annot. ed. (Illus.). 224p. 1969. reprint ed. pap. 9.95 (*0-87012-041-7*) McClain.
The author records the history of the "mine wars" in West Virginia during the early years of the twentieth century. Twelfth Printing, 1997. *Publisher Paid Annotation.*

–The Burning Springs & Other Tales of the Little Kanawha. annot. ed. (Illus.). 160p. 1968. reprint ed. pap. 9.95 (*0-87012-016-6*) McClain.
Historians say that the Burning Springs petroleum deposits was the richest shallow well oil pool the world has ever known. Third Printing, 1991. *Publisher Paid Annotation.*

Lee, Howard B., jt. auth. see Comrey, Andrew L.

Lee, Hsiao-Hung. Possibilities of Hidden Things: Narrative Transgression in Victorian Fictional Autobiographies. (Studies in Nineteenth-Century British Literature: Vol. 5). XIII, 178p. (C). 1996. text 42.95 (*0-8204-2872-8*) P Lang Pubng.

Lee, Hubert. Option Fool: Hundreds & Hundreds of Real World Answers from the Online Option Forum. LC 97-9621. 1997. 24.95 (*0-7863-1212-2*, Irwn Prfssnl) McGraw-Hill Prof.

Lee, Hugh, ed. A Cezanne in the Hedge & Other Memories of Charleston & Bloomsbury. LC 92-7268. (Illus.). 192p. 1992. 27.50 (*0-226-47003-2*) U Ch Pr.

— A Cezanne in the Hedge & Other Memories of Charleston & Bloomsbury. LC 92-7268. 192p. 1993. pap. 11.95 (*0-226-47004-0*) U Ch Pr.

Lee, Huy V. At the Beach. 32p. 1998. pap. 6.95 (*0-8050-5822-2*) H Holt & Co.

— In the Park. LC 97-24430. (Illus.). 32p. (J). 1998. 15.95 (*0-8050-4128-1*) H Holt & Co.

Lee, Huy-Voun. At the Beach. LC 93-25462. (Illus.). 32p. (J). (ps-3). 1995. 14.95 (*0-8050-2768-8*) H Holt & Co.

— In the Snow. LC 94-48807. (Illus.). (J). (ps-3). 1995. 15.95 (*0-8050-3172-3*) H Holt & Co.

***Lee, Huy Voun.** In the Snow. (Illus.). 32p. (ps-2). 2000. pap. 6.95 (*0-8050-6579-2*) H Holt & Co.

***Lee, Huyvoun.** One, Two, Three, Go. LC 99-48326. (Illus.). 32p. (ps-4). 2000. pap. text 15.95 (*0-8050-6205-X*) St Martin.

Lee Hwa Lin & Wei-Chuan Cultural Educational Foundation. Chinese Cuisine, Shanghai Style. Wolhardt, Connie, tr. (CHI., Illus.). 96p. (Orig.). 1994. pap. 19.95 (*0-941676-55-2*) Wei-Chuan Pub.

Lee, Hwa-Wei & Hunt, Gary A. Fundraising for the Nineteen Nineties: The Challenge Ahead. vi, 177p. (Orig.). 1992. pap. 39.95 (*0-943970-08-3*) Genaway.

***Lee, Hwain Chang.** The Korean American YWCA & the Church: Dialogue Face-to-Face, Partnership Hand-in-Hand. LC 00-36418. 2000. write for info. (*0-7618-1705-0*) U Pr of Amer.

***Lee, Hy-Sang.** North Korea: A Strange Socialist Fortress. LC 00-29838. 2000. write for info. (*0-275-96917-7*) Greenwood.

Lee, Hyung-Koo. The Korean Economy: Perspectives for the 21st Century. LC 95-39691. (SUNY Series in Korean Studies). 270p. (C). 1996. text 44.50 (*0-7914-2887-7*); pap. text 14.95 (*0-7914-2888-5*) State U NY Pr.

Lee, I. & Smolka, Scott A., eds. CONCUR '95 Concurrency Theory: 6th International Conference, Philadelphia, PA, August 21-24, 1995, Proceedings, Vol. X. (Lecture Notes in Computer Science Ser.: Vol. 962). 547p. 1995. pap. 87.00 (*3-540-60218-6*) Spr-Verlag.

Lee, I-Der & Amidon, Gordon L. Pharmacokinetic Analysis: A Practical Approach. LC 96-60272. 562p. 1996. text 179.95 (*1-56676-425-4*) Technomic.

Lee, Ian, ed. see Barnett, Lynn.

Lee, Ida J. Lancaster County, Virginia, Marriage Bonds, 1652-1850. 71p. 1997. reprint ed. pap. 10.00 (*0-8063-0500-2*, 3335) Clearfield Co.

***Lee, Iksop & Ramsey, S. Robert.** The Korean Language. (C). 2000. text 71.50 (*0-7914-4831-2*); pap. text 23.95 (*0-7914-4832-0*) State U NY Pr.

***Lee, Iris.** Fabric Etching: Creative Surface Texture & Design Using Fiber Etch. Teufez, Linda Chang, ed. (Illus.). 112p. 2000. pap. 25.00 (*0-9641201-1-9*) Dragon Threads.

Lee, Irving J. Language Habits in Human Affairs: An Introduction to General Semantics. LC 78-31179. (Illus.). 278p. 1979. reprint ed. lib. bdg. 72.50 (*0-313-20962-6*, LELH, Greenwood Pr) Greenwood.

— Language Habits in Human Affairs: An Introduction to General Semantics. 2nd ed. Berman, Sanford I., ed. LC 94-36138. 1994. pap. 21.95 (*0-918970-41-5*) Intl Gen Semantics.

Lee, Iva H. Data Entry: Concepts & Exercises. LC 81-11403. 355p. (C). 1982. pap. text 35.50 (*0-471-08605-3*) P-H.

— Data Entry: Concepts & Exercises. LC 81-11403. 355p. (C). 1982. pap. text 26.25 (*0-471-86584-2*) P-H.

— Data Entry for Microcomputers & Terminals with Business Applications. 2nd ed. 336p. (C). 1991. pap. text 22.60 (*0-13-201138-7*, 250101) P-H.

Lee, Ivy & Maykovich, Minako. Statistics: A Tool for Understanding Society. LC 94-4804. 560p. 1994. 85.00 (*0-205-13961-2*) Allyn.

Lee, Ivy & Maykovich, Minako K. Statistics: A Tool for Understanding Society. (C). 1994. teacher ed. write for info. incl. disk (*0-205-15455-7*, H5455-4) Allyn.

Lee, J., jt. ed. see Holland, Jerome H., Laboratory Staff.

Lee, J. A. N., ed. International Biographical Dictionary of Computer Pioneers. LC 94-40232. 830p. 1995. lib. bdg. 85.00 (*1-884964-47-8*, QA76) Fitzroy Dearborn.

Lee, J. D., ed. Simulation Software for Robotics. (Robotics & Computer Integrated Manufacturing Ser.). 116p. 1989. 36.50 (*0-08-037196-5*, Pergamon Pr) Elsevier.

Lee, J. D. & Lindahl, Barry A. Modern Tort Law, 4 vols. rev. ed. LC 88-2910. 1988. ring bd. 500.00 (*0-685-34582-3*) West Group.

***Lee, J. Edward & Chepesiuk, Ron, eds.** South Carolina in the Civil War: The Confederate Experience in Letters & Diaries. (Illus.). 192p. 2000. 28.50 (*0-7864-0794-8*) McFarland & Co.

An Asterisk (*) at the beginning of an entry indicates that the title is appearing for the first time.

***Lee, J. Edward & Haynsworth, Toby, eds.** White Christmas in April: The Collapse of South Vietnam, 1975. LC 99-30262. (Illus.). 256p. (C). 1999. pap. 28.00 (*0-8204-4538-X*) P Lang Pubng.

Lee, J. G. Automatic Control in Aerospace 1998. LC 99-31200. 468p. 1999. pap. 89.50 (*0-08-043041-4*, Pergamon Pr) Elsevier.

Lee, J. H., et al, eds. Environmental Hydraulics: Proceedings of the 2nd International Symposium on Environmental Hydraulics, Hong Kong, China, 15-18 December, 1998. 979p. (C). 1998. text 119.00 (*90-5809-035-3*) Ashgate Pub Co.

Lee, J. H. & Cheung, Y. K., eds. Environmental Hydraulics: Proceedings of the International Symposium on, Hong Kong, 16-18 December 1991, 2 vols., Set. (Illus.). 1500p. (C). 1991. text 246.00 (*90-5410-038-9*, Pub. by A A Balkema) Ashgate Pub Co.

Lee, J. H., jt. ed. see Wronkiewicz, D. J.

Lee, J. J. Divorce in Ireland: Who Should Bear the Cost? (Undercurrents Ser.). 1993. pap. 7.50 (*0-902561-69-3*, Pub. by Cork Univ) Intl Spec Bk.

— Facing the Unemployment Crisis in Ireland. (Undercurrents Ser.). 1994. pap. 7.50 (*0-902561-67-7*, Pub. by Cork Univ) Intl Spec Bk.

— Ireland, 1912-1985: Politics & Society. (Illus.). 776p. (C). 1990. pap. text 39.95 (*0-521-37741-2*) Cambridge U Pr.

***Lee, J. K.** Spiritual Warfare, Vol. 1. 2000. mass mkt. 10.95 (*0-89228-082-4*) Impact Christian.

Lee, J. L. The Ancient Supremacy: Bukhara, Afghanistan, & the Battle for Balkh, 1731-1901. LC 95-49300. (Islamic History & Civilization, Studies & Texts Ser.: Vol. 15). l, 695p. 1996. 214.00 (*90-04-10399-6*) Brill Academic Pubs.

Lee, J. M. Riemannian Manifolds: An Introduction to Curvature. LC 97-14537. (Graduate Tests in Mathematics Ser.: Vol. 176). (Illus.). 240p. (C). 1997. text 32.95 (*0-387-98322-8*) Spr-Verlag.

Lee, J. Marvin, ed. Centre County Heritage 1956-1975. (Illus.). 233p. (Orig.). 1975. pap. 5.00 (*1-887315-02-0*) Centre Cty Hist Soc.

Lee, J. P. & Grinstein, George G., eds. Database Issues for Data Visualization: Proceedings of the IEEE Visualization '93 Workshop, San Jose, California, USA, October 26, 1993. (Lecture Notes in Computer Science Ser.: Vol. 871). xiv, 229p. 1994. 39.95 (*3-540-58519-2*) Spr-Verlag.

Lee, J. S. Abstraction & Aging: A Social Psychological Analysis. (Recent Research in Psychology Ser.). (Illus.). 136p. 1990. 71.95 (*0-387-97433-4*) Spr-Verlag.

Lee, J. S., et al, eds. Mechanics of Electromagnetic Materials & Structures. LC 93-71575. (AMD Series, Vol. 161; MD: Vol. 42). 209p. 1993. pap. 50.00 (*0-7918-1140-9*, G00784) ASME.

Lee, J. S. & Newman, Michael E. Aquaculture: An Introduction. LC 96-75864. (Illus.). 526p. 1997. 62.50 (*0-8134-3084-4*); teacher ed. 12.95 (*0-8134-3085-2*) Interstate.

Lee, J. S. & Skalak, T. C., eds. Microvascular Mechanics. (Illus.). xv, 222p. 1989. 130.00 (*0-387-97038-X*) Spr-Verlag.

Lee, J. S., jt. ed. see Sancaktar, E.

Lee, J. Scott, ed. see Association for Core Texts & Courses Staff.

Lee, J. W., jt. ed. see Pollak, J. K.

Lee, J. Yimm. Wing Chun Kung-Fu. LC 72-87863. (Chinese Arts Ser.). (Illus.). 1972. pap. 14.95 (*0-89750-037-7*, 309) Ohara Pubns.

Lee, Jackson F., Jr. & Pruitt, K. Wayne. Providing for Individual Differences in Student Learning: A Mastery Learning Approach. (Illus.). 130p. 1984. pap. 20.95 (*0-398-06225-0*) C C Thomas.

— Providing for Individual Differences in Student Learning: A Mastery Learning Approach. (Illus.). 130p. (C). 1984. 33.95 (*0-398-05028-7*) C C Thomas.

Lee, Jackson F., jt. auth. see Rinehart, James R.

***Lee, Jae-eui, et al.** Kwangju Diary: Beyond Death, Beyond the Darkness of the Age. LC 99-26861. 1999. write for info. (*1-883191-03-3*) U CA Ctr Pac Rim.

Lee, Jae H. The Exploration of the Inner Wounds - Han. LC 94-2375. (AAR Academy Ser.: Vol. 86). 198p. 1994. pap. 19.95 (*1-55540-962-8*, 010186) OUP.

— The Exploration of the Inner Wounds - Han, Monograph. LC 94-2375. (AAR Academy Ser.: Vol. 86). 198p. 1994. 29.95 (*1-55540-961-X*, 010186) OUP.

Lee, Jae-Hyup. Dynamics of Ethnic Identity: Three Asian American Communities in Philadelphia. LC 98-27455. (Asian Americans). (Illus.). 200p. 1998. 53.00 (*0-8153-3118-5*) Garland.

Lee, Jae K., jt. auth. see Liang, Ting-Peng.

Lee, Jae K., jt. auth. see Trippi, Robert R.

Lee, Jae Num. Swift & Scatological Satire. LC 76-129807. 158p. 1976. text 29.95 (*0-8263-0196-7*) Irvington.

Lee, Jai Eui, jt. ed. see Scott-Stokes, Henry.

Lee, James. Electronics for the Radio Amateur. Stone, Jack L., ed. (Illus.). 1989. write for info. (*0-318-65728-7*) Franklin-Belle.

***Lee, James.** Housing, Home Ownership & Social Change in Hong Kong. (Social & Political Studies from Hong Kong). 246p. 1999. text 69.95 (*1-84014-562-5*, Pub. by Ashgate Pub) Ashgate Pub Co.

Lee, James. Speechreading in Context: A Guide to Practice in Everyday Settings. rev. ed. Mahshie, Shawn N., ed. (Sharing Ideas Ser.). 39p. 1997. pap. text 2.00 (*0-88095-216-4*) Gallaudet U Pre Coll.

Lee, James & Campbell, Cameron. Fate & Fortune in Rural China: Social Stratification & Population Behavior in Liaoning 1774-1873. (Cambridge Studies in Population, Economy & Society in Past Time: No. 31). 301p. (C). 1997. text 49.95 (*0-521-58119-2*) Cambridge U Pr.

Lee, James A. The Gold & the Garbage in Management Theories & Prescriptions. LC 80-12758. (Illus.). 490p. 1980. pap. 19.95 (*0-8214-0578-0*) Ohio U Pr.

Lee, James A. & Martin, Phillip. Contemporary Labor Relations. 3rd ed. 208p. (C). 1996. pap. text 21.35 (*1-56226-328-5*) CAT Pub.

Lee, James F. Que Te Parece? (C). 1996. pap. text, wbk. ed. 14.06 (*0-07-038074-0*) McGraw.

***Lee, James F.** Que Te Parece? Intermediate Spanish. 2nd ed. LC 99-47956. 1999. write for info. (*0-07-365519-8*) McGrw-H Hghr Educ.

Lee, James F. & Vanpatten, Bill. Directions for Language Learning & Teaching, Vol. 1. (Foreign Language Professional Ser.). 250p. (C). 1995. pap. 42.81 (*0-07-037693-X*) McGraw.

Lee, James F. & Wolf Darlene, F. Que Te Parece? 512p. (C). 1995. pap. 50.00 (*0-07-540891-0*) McGraw.

— Que Te Parece?, Vol. 2. (C). 1996. pap., wbk. ed., lab manual ed. 26.88 (*0-07-037707-3*) McGraw.

Lee, James F., et al. Form & Meaning: Multiple Perspectives (1999 Aausc Volume) 250p. pap. 24.95 (*0-8384-0846-X*, Pub. by Heinle & Heinle) Thomson Learn.

Lee, James F., et al. Que Te Parece? (C). 1996. pap. text, suppl. ed. 26.87 (*0-07-540900-3*) McGraw.

***Lee, James F., et al.** Que Te Parece? 2nd ed. 288p. (C). 1999. pap. 24.06 (*0-07-230855-9*) McGrw-H Hghr Educ.

— Que Te Parece? 2nd ed. 288p. (C). 2000. pap., wbk. ed. 24.06 (*0-07-230862-1*) McGrw-H Hghr Educ.

Lee, James F., et al. Que Te Parece?, Vol. 1. (C). 1996. pap., wbk. ed., lab manual ed. 26.88 (*0-07-540892-9*) McGraw.

***Lee, James H.** Prudent Day Trader: Balancing Risk & Reward for Long-Term Success. 2000. 34.95 (*0-7615-2019-8*) Prima Pub.

Lee, James L. & Pulvino, Charles J. Self-Exploration Inventories: Sixteen Reproducible Self-Scoring Instruments. 2nd ed. 32p. 1993. pap. text 12.95 (*0-932796-58-3*) Ed Media Corp.

Lee, James L., et al. Dynamic Counseling. 3rd ed. LC 94-72559. 288p. (C). 1994. pap. text 21.95 (*0-932796-66-4*) Ed Media Corp.

— Restoring Harmony: A Guide for Managing Conflicts in Schools. LC 96-53393. 194p. 1997. pap. text 26.00 (*0-13-470313-8*, Merrill Coll) P-H.

— Structured Activities for Dynamic Counseling. LC 94-72560. 248p. (Orig.). (C). 1994. pap. text 21.95 (*0-932796-67-2*) Ed Media Corp.

Lee, James M. The Content of Religious Instruction: A Social Science Approach. LC 84-18255. 815p. (Orig.). 1985. pap. 29.95 (*0-89135-050-0*) Religious Educ.

— The Flow of Religious Instruction: A Social-Science Approach. LC 74-29824. (Illus.). 379p. (Orig.). 1975. reprint ed. pap. 23.95 (*0-89135-003-9*) Religious Educ.

— The Flow of Religious Instruction: A Social-Science Approach. LC 74-29824. (Illus.). 379p. (Orig.). 1975. reprint ed. lib. bdg. 24.95 (*0-89135-001-2*) Religious Educ.

— The Sacrament of Teaching: A Social Science Approach. LC 98-23812. (Explorations in Religious Instruction Ser.: Vol. 1). 312p. 1999. 32.95 (*0-89135-100-0*) Religious Educ.

— The Shape of Religious Instruction: A Social-Science Approach. LC 74-29823. 330p. (Orig.). 1971. reprint ed. pap. 32.95 (*0-89135-002-0*); reprint ed. lib. bdg. 24.95 (*0-89135-000-4*) Religious Educ.

— Verilog Quickstart. LC 97-5202. 1997. text 89.50 (*0-7923-9927-7*) Kluwer Academic.

***Lee, James M.** Verilog Quickstart: A Practical Guide to Simulation & Synthesis in Verilog. 2nd ed. LC 99-20750. 1999. write for info. (*0-7923-8515-2*) Kluwer Academic.

Lee, James M., ed. Handbook of Faith. LC 90-31685. 328p. 1990. 34.95 (*0-89135-075-6*) Religious Educ.

— The Spirituality of the Religious Educator. LC 85-2250. 209p. (Orig.). 1985. pap. 19.95 (*0-89135-045-4*) Religious Educ.

Lee, James Michael, ed. Forging a Better Future for Religious Education in the Third Millennium. Date not set. pap. 24.95 (*0-89135-113-2*) Religious Educ.

***Lee, James R.** Exploring the Gaps: Vital Links Between Trade, Environment & Culture. (Illus.). 272p. 2000. 59.00 (*1-56549-115-7*); pap. 24.95 (*1-56549-114-9*) Kumarian Pr.

Lee, James R. & Walters, David. International Trade in Construction, Design & Engineering Services. LC 88-31240. (American Enterprise Institute Trade in Services Ser.). 164p. 1989. text 34.95 (*0-88730-235-1*, HarpBusn) HarpInfo.

***Lee, James S.** Underworld of the East. 192p. 2000. pap. 16.95 (*0-9536631-1-6*, Pub. by Green Magic) SCB Distributors.

Lee, James V. Nine Years in the Saddle. LC 98-161436. (Illus.). 138p. 1998. pap. 14.95 (*0-9663870-0-7*) Salado Pr.

Lee, James W. Classics of Texas Fiction. 200p. (Orig.). (C). 1987. pap. 9.95 (*0-935014-10-1*) E-Heart Pr.

— John Braine. LC 67-25191. (Twayne's English Authors Ser.). (C). 1968. lib. bdg. 20.95 (*0-8057-1056-6*) Irvington.

— Texas, My Texas. LC 92-38219. 102p. 1993. pap. 9.95 (*0-929398-54-8*) UNTX Pr.

Lee, James Z. One Quarter of Humanity: Malthusian Mythology & Chinese Realities, 1700-2000. LC 99-11863. 288p. 1999. 47.50 (*0-674-63908-1*) HUP.

***Lee, James Z.** Political Economy of a Frontier: Southwest China, 1250-1850. (Harvard East Asian Monographs: Vol. 190). 2000. text 49.50 (*0-674-00241-5*) HUP.

Lee, Jane. Derain, to Accompany the Exhibition Derain: The Late Work. 144p. 1993. pap. 100.00 (*0-7148-2649-9*, Pub. by Museum Modern Art) St Mut.

Lee, Jane C. & Cheung, Anthony B., eds. Public Sector Reform in Hong Kong: Key Concepts, Progress-to-Date & Future Directions. LC 96-118897. 338p. (C). 1997. pap. text 27.50 (*962-201-655-3*, Pub. by Chinese Univ) U of Mich Pr.

Lee, Jane R. From the Heart. 1998. pap. write for info. (*1-57553-746-X*) Watermrk Pr.

***Lee, Janet.** Comrades & Partners: The Shared Lives of Grace Hutchins & Anna Rochester. LC 99-15412. 290p. 2000. 29.95 (*0-8476-9620-0*, Pub. by Rowman) Natl Bk Netwk.

Lee, Janet, ed. With Special Distinction: A Collection of Recipes from the Mississippi College Family. LC 93-77090. (Illus.). 384p. 1993. 19.95 (*0-685-65593-8*) MS Coll Ckbk.

Lee, Janet & Sasser-Coen, Jennifer. Blood Stories: Menarche & the Politics of the Female Body in Contemporary U. S. Society. 208p. (C). 1996. 65.00 (*0-415-91546-5*); pap. 17.99 (*0-415-91547-3*) Routledge.

Lee, Janet, jt. auth. see Malecki, Joseph.

Lee, Janet, ed. & photos by see Henderson, Richard A., Jr.

Lee, Janice, et al, eds. A Legacy of Design: An Historical Survey of the Kansas City, Missouri, Parks & Boulevards System, 1893-1940. (Illus.). 296p. 1995. write for info. (*0-9648063-0-4*) KCC Design Educ.

Lee, Janie, ed. see Weckbaugh, Ernest L.

Lee, Janie C. Brice Marden: The Whitney Museum of American Art Collection. (Illus.). 84p. 1999. 19.95 (*0-8109-6828-2*, Pub. by Abrams) Time Warner.

***Lee, Jared.** Talk to the Hoof: Cartoons for People Who Love Horses. (Illus.). 2000. pap. 9.95 (*0-9677378-0-X*) Red Pony.

Lee, Jared. Incredible Fishing Stories. LC 94-1329. 176p. (Orig.). 1994. pap. 8.95 (*1-56305-637-2*, 3637) Workman Pub.

Lee, Jarene Frances & Catagnus, Julia M. What We Learned (The Hard Way) about Supervising Volunteers: An Action Guide for Making Your Job Easier. Ellis, Susan J., ed. (Collective Wisdom Ser.). (Illus.). 180p. 1999. pap. 21.95 (*0-940576-20-1*) Energize.

Lee, Jarita Ador, jt. auth. see Brooke, Jerome.

Lee, Jasper S. Agricultural Education: Review & Synthesis of the Research. 4th ed. 38p. 1985. text 4.75 (*0-318-20330-8*, IN298) Ctr Educ Trng Employ.

— Aquaculture: An Introduction: Activity Manual. 1996. text 19.95 (*0-8134-3105-0*) Interstate.

— Aquaculture: An Introduction: Activity Manual. 1996. text, teacher ed. 14.95 (*0-8134-3106-9*) Interstate.

— Program Planning Guide for AgriScience & Technology Education. 2nd rev. ed. LC 99-175508. 106p. 1998. pap. 29.95 (*0-8134-2999-4*, 2999) Interstate.

— Working in Agricultural Industry. (Illus.). (J). (gr. 9-10). 1978. text 17.96 (*0-07-000831-0*) McGraw.

Lee, Jasper S. & Newman, Michael E. The Earth & Agri Science. 1995. text, teacher ed. 14.95 (*0-8134-3075-5*) Interstate.

Lee, Jasper S., et al. AgriMarketing Technology: Selling & Distribution in the Agricultural Industry. LC 94-77465. 526p. 1998. 58.75 (*0-8134-2962-5*, 2962); teacher ed. 9.95 (*0-8134-2963-3*, 2963) Interstate.

— The Earth & Agri Science. 1995. text 17.95 (*0-8134-3074-7*) Interstate.

— The Earth & AgriScience. 384p. 1995. 58.75 (*0-8134-3015-1*); text, teacher ed. 9.95 (*0-8134-3016-X*) Interstate.

***Lee, Jasper S., et al.** Introduction to Livestock & Companion Animals. 2nd ed. 2000. teacher ed. 12.95 (*0-8134-3178-6*) Interstate.

— Introduction to Livestock & Companion Animals. 2nd ed. LC 99-71698. (Illus.). x, 629p. 2000. 74.95 (*0-8134-3177-8*) Interstate.

— Introduction to Livestock & Companion Animals: Activity Manual. 2nd ed. 2000. 19.95 (*0-8134-3200-6*) Interstate.

— Introduction to Livestock & Companion Animals: Instructional Resource Guide. 2nd ed. 2000. 89.95 (*0-8134-3202-2*) Interstate.

— Introduction to Livestock & Companion Animals: Instructor's Guide for Activity Manual. 2nd ed. 2000. teacher ed. 14.95 (*0-8134-3201-4*) Interstate.

Lee, Jasper S., jt. auth. see Biondo, Ronald J.

Lee, Jasper S., jt. auth. see Lee, Delene W.

Lee, Jasper S., jt. auth. see McGuire, James E.

Lee, Jasper S., ed. see Brown, Ronald & Oren, John W.

Lee, Jasper S., ed. see Long, Don L., et al.

Lee, Jasper S., ed. see Miller, Larry.

Lee, Jay, ed. Manufacturing Science & Engineering. LC 99-191723. 965p. 1998. pap. text 240.00 (*0-7918-1606-0*) ASME.

Lee, Jay & Schafrik, Robert. Manufacturing Engineering & System Handbook. (Mechanical Engineering Ser.). 1999. 125.00 (*0-8493-9582-8*) CRC Pr.

***Lee, Jay & Wong, David Wing-Shun.** GIS & Statistical Analysis with Arcview. LC 00-32090. (Illus.). 2000. write for info. (*0-471-34874-0*) Wiley.

Lee, Jay K., et al, eds. Critical Technology: Proceedings of the Third World Congress on Expert Systems, 2 vols., Set. LC 95-43907. (Illus.). 1,400p. (Orig.). (C). 1996. 185.00 (*1-882345-07-X*, 1-882345) Cognizant Comm.

Lee, Jean B. The Price of Nationhood: American Revolution in Charles County. (C). 1996. pap. text. write for info. (*0-393-96847-2*) Norton.

— The Price of Nationhood: The American Revolution in Charles County. LC 93-42536. 1994. write for info. (*0-393-36958-7*) Norton.

— The Price of Nationhood: The American Revolution in Charles County. 1994. 29.95 (*0-393-03658-8*) Norton.

Lee, Jeanette. The Ibsen Secret. LC 75-30877. (Studies in Scandinavian Life & Literature: No. 18). 1975. lib. bdg. 75.00 (*0-8383-2092-9*) M S G Haskell Hse.

***Lee, Jeanette & Gershenson, Adam Scott.** The Black Widow's Guide to Killer Pool: Become the Player to Beat. LC 99-46062. (Illus.). 160p. 2000. pap. 12.95 (*0-609-80506-1*, Three Riv Pr) Crown Pub Group.

Lee, Jeanne. Silent Lotus. LC 96-30895. (Illus.). 32p. (J). (ps-3). 1991. 14.95 (*0-374-36911-9*) FS&G.

Lee, Jeanne M. I Once Was a Monkey: Stories Buddha Told. LC 98-17651. (Illus.). 40p. (YA). (gr. k up). 1999. pap. text 16.00 (*0-374-33548-6*) FS&G.

— The Legend of the Milky Way. LC 81-6906. (Illus.). 32p. (J). (ps-2). 1995. pap. 5.95 (*0-8050-1361-X*, Owlet BYR) H Holt & Co.

— Silent Lotus. 32p. (J). (ps-3). 1994. pap. 5.95 (*0-374-46646-7*, Sunburst Bks) FS&G.

— Silent Lotus. 1994. 11.40 (*0-606-08163-1*) Turtleback.

— The Song of Mu Lan. LC 95-9594.Tr. of Mu-Lan Shih. (Illus.). 36p. (J). (gr. k-5). 1995. 15.95 (*1-886910-00-6*, Front Street) Front Str.

Lee, Jeanne M. Toad Is the Uncle of Heaven: A Vietnamese Folk Tale. LC 85-5639. 32p. (J). (ps-2). 1995. pap. 5.95 (*0-8050-1147-1*, Owlet BYR) H Holt & Co.

Lee, Jeffrey & Guill, Sandra. Vulnerability & Adaptation Assessment: An International Handbook. Benioff, Ron, ed. LC 96-26719. (Environmental Science & Technology Library). 564p. (C). 1996. text 235.50 (*0-7923-4140-6*) Kluwer Academic.

***Lee, Jeffrey A.** The Scientific Endeavor. LC 99-35623. 186p. (C). 1999. pap. text 27.80 (*0-8053-4596-5*) Benjamin-Cummings.

***Lee, Jeffrey D.** Opening the Prayer Book. LC 99-34805. (New Church's Teaching Ser.: Vol. 7). xv, 195p. 1999. pap. 11.95 (*1-56101-166-5*) Cowley Pubns.

Lee, Jei-In, tr. see Frangipane, Francis.

Lee, Jennifer. Talking Germany. (C). 1990. pap. text 32.00 (*0-948032-78-2*, Pub. by Rosters Ltd) St Mut.

Lee, Jennifer, jt. ed. see Cuevas, Antonio.

***Lee, Jennifer B. & Mandelbaum, Miriam.** Seeing is Believing: 700 Years of Scientific & Medical Illustration. LC 99-46587. 1999. write for info. (*0-87104-449-8*) NY Pub Lib.

Lee, Jennifer M., ed. Aids to Physiotherapy. 2nd ed. (Illus.). 216p. 1988. pap. text 15.00 (*0-443-03438-9*) Church.

Lee, Jenny. Meanjin: New Critical Essays, Fiction & Poetry. 846p. (C). 1990. 50.00 (*0-7855-6618-X*, Pub. by Pascoe Pub) St Mut.

Lee, Jenny, ed. see Tarikh.

Lee, Jeremy. Upon the Millenium: What Will We Tell Our Children?: Dispossessing the World's Richest Nations. unabridged ed. 240p. 1997. reprint ed. pap. 18.00 (*0-945001-64-9*) GSG & Assocs.

Lee, Jerri. A Fresh Look at God, from the End of the Twentieth Century. LC 99-182789. 303p. 1998. pap. 9.95 (*0-9660948-0-8*) Lee Pub CA.

Lee, Jesse. Live . . . from Golgotha: A One-Act Drama. 20p. 1987. pap. 3.25 (*0-88680-272-5*) I E Clark.

Lee, Jesse & Thrift, Minton. Memoir of the Reverend Jesse Lee, with Extracts from His Journals. LC 72-83428. (Religion in America, Ser. 1). 1977. reprint ed. 21.95 (*0-405-00253-X*) Ayer.

Lee, Jessie. Tell Me, Lord. 96p. Date not set. pap. 7.95 (*1-887150-00-5*) Millennia Bks.

Lee, Jhong S. CDMA System Engineering Handbook. LC 98-33846. 1998. 135.00 (*0-89006-990-5*) Artech Hse.

Lee, Jid. From the Promised Land to Home: Trajectories of Selfhood in Asian-American Women's Autobiography. LC 98-14371. (Woman in History Ser.). 1998. 40.00 (*0-86663-220-4*) Ide Hse.

Lee, Jik-Joen. Development, Delivery, & Utilization of Services under the Older Americans Act: A Perspective of Asian-American Elderly. LC 91-40937. (Studies on the Elderly in America). 199p. 1992. text 30.00 (*0-8153-0527-3*) Garland.

***Lee, Jill, et al.** Memories Forever: A Collection of Poems & Stories from Bereaved Parents Siblings, Friends & Young Cancer Patients. LC 99-75571. 80p. 1999. pap. 9.95 (*1-58597-002-6*) Leathers Pub.

Lee, Jim. Divine Right, the Adventures of Max Faraday No. 2: Collected Edition. (Illus.). 56p. 1998. pap. 5.95 (*1-58240-038-5*) Image Comics.

***Lee, Jim.** Fantastic Four: Heroes Reborn. (Marvels Finest Ser.). (Illus.). 160p. 2000. pap. 17.95 (*0-7851-0744-4*, Pub. by Marvel Entrprs) LPC Group.

Lee, Jim, ed. WildStorm Fine Arts: The Gallery Collection. (Illus.). 192p. 1998. pap. 19.95 (*1-58240-040-7*) Image Comics.

Lee, Jim, ed. Fast Forward: A Focus on the Rapidly Changing Media from Your Hometown Paper to Hands-on TV. (Southern Exposure Ser.). (Illus.). 64p. (Orig.). (C). 1992. pap. 5.00 (*0-943810-55-8*) Inst Southern Studies.

Lee, Jim, jt. auth. see Brandon, Choi.

Lee, Jim, jt. auth. see Choi, Brandon.

Lee, Jimmy R. Concerned Persons Group Facilitator's Guide: Because We Need Each Other. 89p. 1995. pap., teacher ed. 10.00 (*1-58119-004-2*) T P Min.

— Concerned Persons Group Member Guide: Because We Need Each Other. 46p. 1995. pap., student ed. 8.00 (*1-58119-003-4*) T P Min.

— Godly Heroes Facilitator's Guide (Youth Edition) A Small Group Study of Hebrews 11. 80p. (YA). (gr. 7-12). 1997. pap. 11.00 (*1-58119-025-5*) T P Min.

— Godly Heroes Group Member Guide (Youth Edition) A Small Group Study of Hebrews 11. 59p. (YA). (gr. 7-12). 1997. pap. 9.00 (*1-58119-024-7*) T P Min.

— Insight Group Facilitator's Guide: Discover the Path to Christian Character. 86p. 1995. pap., teacher ed. 10.00 (*1-58119-002-6*) T P Min.

— Insight Group Facilitator's Guide: Youth Edition. 3rd rev. ed. 103p. (J). 1997. pap. 10.00 (*1-58119-023-9*) T P Min.

L

L

— Insight Group Member's Guide: Discover the Path to Christian Character. 62p. 1995. pap., student ed. 8.00 (*1-58119-001-8*) T P Min.

— Insight Group Members Guide: Path to Christian Character, Youth Edition. 3rd rev. ed. 81p. (J). 1997. pap. text 8.00 (*1-58119-022-0*) T P Min.

***Lee, Jimmy R.** Knowing God My Father Facilitator's Guide: Applying the Names of God to My Personal Life. 2nd rev. ed. 50p. 1998. pap. 10.00 (*1-58119-008-5*) T P Min.

— Knowing God My Father Group Member Guide: Applying the Names of God to My Personal Life. 2nd rev. ed. 38p. 1998. pap. 8.00 (*1-58119-007-7*) T P Min.

Lee, Jimmy R. The Ten Commandments Facilitator's Guide: Applying the Foundations of Living to My Personal Life. 101p. 1994. pap., teacher ed. 11.00 (*1-58119-010-7*) T P Min.

— The Ten Commandments Group Member Guide: Applying the Foundations of Living to My Personal Life. 80p. 1994. pap., student ed. 9.00 (*1-58119-009-3*) T P Min.

— Understanding the Times & Knowing What to Do: Biblical Strategies for Contemporary Issues & Needs. 219p. 1997. pap. 11.99 (*1-58119-030-1*) T P Min.

***Lee, Jimmy Ray.** Stepping into Freedom Facilitator's Guide: A Christ-Centered Twelve-Step Program. 88p. 1999. pap. 12.00 (*1-58119-039-5*) T P Min.

— Stepping into Freedom Group Member Guide: A Christ-Centered Twelve-Step Program. 87p. 1999. pap. 10.00 (*1-58119-040-9*) T P Min.

***Lee, Jimmy Ray & Strickland, Dan.** Living Free: Discovering God's Path to Freedom. 90p. 1999. pap., wbk. ed. 12.99 (*1-58119-043-3*); teacher ed. 299.95 incl. VHS (*1-58119-041-7*) T P Min.

— Living Free: Discovering God's Path to Freedom. 98p. 1999. pap. 15.99 (*1-58119-042-5*) T P Min.

Lee, Jin-Woo. Politische Philosophie des Nihilismus: Neitzsches Neubestimmung des Verhaeltnisses von Politik & Metaphysik. (Monographien und Texte zur Nietzscge-Forschung Ser.: Bd. 26). (GER.). xi, 441p. (C). 1992. lib. bdg. 166.15 (*3-11-012908-6*) De Gruyter.

***Lee, Jinkook & Kelly, William A., Jr.** Who Uses Credit Unions? 48p. 1999. pap. 100.00 (*1-880572-37-0*, 1752-47) Filene Res.

Lee, Jo A. First Hunger. LC 73-76638. (Hip-Pocket Ser.: No. 2). 1973. pap. 2.50 (*0-87922-017-1*) Christophers Bks.

— Proofreading for Word Processing. 2nd ed. LC 93-43962. 248p. (C). 1994. pap. text 31.00 (*0-03-098011-9*) Dryden Pr.

— Proofreading for Word Processing. 2nd ed. LC 93-43962. 68p. (C). 1994. pap. text, teacher ed. 34.00 (*0-03-098012-7*) Dryden Pr.

— Proofreading for Wordprocessing. 184p. (C). 1988. pap. text 29.50 (*0-15-572260-3*); pap. text, teacher ed. 3.00 (*0-15-572261-1*) Dryden Pr.

Lee, Jo A. & Gaskin, Shelley. Word Processing Applications, Basic Activities. 304p. (C). 1996. text 17.50 (*0-256-22037-9*, Irwn McGrw-H) McGrw-H Hghr Educ.

Lee, Jo A. & Satterwhite, Marilyn. CPS - The Irwin Office Reference Manual: The Miami Jacobs College Office Reference Manual. (C). 1995. text 16.00 (*0-256-19904-3*, Irwn McGrw-H) McGrw-H Hghr Educ.

Lee, Jo A. & Satterwhite, Marilyn L. The Irwin Law Office Reference Manual. LC 95-12105. 568p. (C). 1995. text 16.40 (*0-256-18747-9*, Irwn McGrw-H) McGrw-H Hghr Educ.

— The Irwin Office Reference Manual. LC 93-14435. 440p. (C). 1993. text 16.00 (*0-256-15639-5*, Irwn McGrw-H) McGrw-H Hghr Educ.

Lee, Jo A., jt. auth. see Satterwhite, Mairlyn L.

Lee, Jo A., jt. auth. see Satterwhite, Marilyn L.

Lee, Joann. The Irwin Office Reference Manual. 136p. (C). 1993. text, suppl. ed. 6.00 (*0-256-15707-3*, Irwn McGrw-H) McGrw-H Hghr Educ.

Lee, Joann F. Asian American Experiences in the United States: Oral Histories of First to Fourth Generation Americans from China, the Philippines, Japan, India, the Pacific Islands, Vietnam & Cambodia. LC 90-53504. (Illus.). 240p. 1991. lib. bdg. 36.50 (*0-89950-585-6*) McFarland & Co.

— Asian Americans: Oral Histories of First to Fourth Generation Americans from China, Korea, the Philippines, Japan, India, the Pacific Islands, Vietnam, & Cambodia. LC 92-53730. (Illus.). 256p. 1992. pap. 11.95 (*1-56584-023-2*, Pub. by New Press NY) Norton.

***Lee, Joann Faung Jean.** Asian American Actors: Oral Histories from Stage, Screen & Television. (Illus.). 240p. 2000. per. 32.50 (*0-7864-0730-1*) McFarland & Co.

***Lee, Joanna.** A Difficult Woman in Hollywood. LC 98-90377. 1999. 21.95 (*0-533-12778-5*) Vantage.

Lee, Joe. Bankruptcy Practice Systems PSL. LC 79-92367. 1993. ring bd. 112.00 (*0-685-59823-3*) West Group.

— Dante for Beginners. (Illus.). 192p. 1999. pap. 11.95 (*0-86316-280-0*) Writers & Readers.

Lee, Joe. The History of Clowns for Beginners. 160p. 1995. pap. 11.00 (*0-86316-199-5*) Writers & Readers.

Lee, Joe, jt. auth. see Platania, Jon.

Lee, Joe W., tr. see Urabe, Kuniyoshi.

Lee, Joel M. & Hamilton, Beth A., eds. As Much to Learn As to Teach: Essays in Honor of Lester Asheim. LC 78-11313. 239p. 1979. 59.50 (*0-208-01751-8*) Elliots Bks.

Lee, Johannes M. When You Pray. 80p. (Orig.). 1995. pap. 5.99 (*0-89274-970-9*, HH-970) Harrison Hse.

Lee, John. Chinese Odyssey. 164p. 1997. 18.95 (*1-887269-21-5*); pap. text 12.95 (*1-887269-36-3*) J Culler & Sons.

— The Dragon's Letters. 16p. (Orig.). 1994. pap. 6.00 (*0-915408-54-6*) Ally Pr.

— The Flying Boy: Healing the Wounded Man. 120p. (Orig.). 1989. pap. 7.95 (*1-55874-006-6*) Health Comm.

***Lee, John.** The Flying Boy Bk. II: The Journey Continues. 131p. 1999. reprint ed. 12.95 (*1-888461-09-8*) Islewest Pub.

Lee, John. Generic Volunteer Orientation Manual: Your Guide to Developing an Orientation Manual for Volunteers. 70p. 1995. 25.00 (*1-887555-00-5*) Essential Pr.

***Lee, John.** Growing Yourself Back Up: Avoiding the Emotional Regression Trap & Healing the Wounds of Your Past. 2001. pap. 14.00 (*0-609-80641-6*, Three Riv Pr) Crown Pub Group.

— Shakespeare's Hamlet & the Controversies of Self. 256p. 2000. text 72.00 (*0-19-818504-9*) OUP.

— Spenser Shorter Poems: A Selection. 288p. 1998. pap. 9.95 (*0-460-87683-X*, Everyman's Classic Lib) Tuttle Pubng.

Lee, John. The Unicorn Dilemma. (Unicorn Ser.: No. 2). 384p. 1992. mass mkt. 4.99 (*0-8125-2092-0*, Pub. by Tor Bks) St Martin.

— Unicorn Peace. 352p. 1993. mass mkt. 4.99 (*0-8125-1981-7*, Pub. by Tor Bks) St Martin.

— The Unicorn Quest. (Unicorn Ser.: No. 1). (Orig.). 1992. mass mkt. 3.99 (*0-8125-2055-6*, Pub. by Tor Bks) St Martin.

— Unicorn Solution. 1991. pap. 3.95 (*0-8125-0346-5*, Pub. by Tor Bks) St Martin.

— Unicorn War. 1996. mass mkt. 5.99 (*0-8125-3639-8*, Pub. by Tor Bks) St Martin.

— Well Testing. 150p. 1982. 40.00 (*0-89520-317-0*, FETEXT001) Soc Petrol Engineers.

— The Wounded Lover: A Book for Women Raising Sons & Men Coming to Terms with Their Fathers. Orig. Title: At My Father's Wedding. 195p. 1995. pap. 12.00 (*0-915408-53-8*) Ally Pr.

Lee, John & Button, Graham. Talk & Social Organization. 290p. 1987. 99.00 (*0-905028-75-9*, Pub. by Multilingual Matters); pap. 39.95 (*0-905028-74-0*, Pub. by Multilingual Matters) Taylor & Francis.

Lee, John & Lee. Dads & Daughters - Fathers & Sons. unabridged ed. 140p. 1994. pap. text 16.95 incl. audio (*1-879323-12-5*) Sound Horizons AV.

Lee, John & Lee. Men in Balance: The Mid-Life Male & the Healthy Psyche. 142p. 1995. 16.95 incl. audio (*1-879323-13-3*) Sound Horizons AV.

Lee, John & Miller-Kritsberg, Ceci. Writing from the Body. 160p. 1994. pap. 10.95 (*0-312-11536-9*) St Martin.

Lee, John & Stott, Bill. Facing the Fire: Experiencing Expressing Anger Appropriately. LC 92-46216. 256p. 1993. pap. 13.95 (*0-553-37240-8*) Bantam.

Lee, John, jt. auth. see Armitage, Katie.

Lee, John, jt. auth. see Payne-Jackson, Arvilla.

Lee, John, jt. ed. see Ashcroft, Kate.

Lee, John, ed. see Robertson, George & Charteris, Henry.

Lee, John, tr. see Dovaz, Michel.

Lee, John A. Civilian into Soldier. (New Zealand Classics Ser.). 288p. 1986. pap. 9.95 (*0-19-558141-5*) OUP.

— Computer Pioneers. LC 94-40232. 816p. 1995. 58.00 (*0-8186-6357-X*, BP06357) IEEE Comp Soc.

— Gay Midlife & Maturity. LC 90-5285. (Journal of Homosexuality). 246p. 1991. text 39.95 (*1-56024-028-8*) Haworth Pr.

— Gay Midlife & Maturity. LC 90-5285. (Journal of Homosexuality). 246p. 1994. pap. text 14.95 (*0-918393-80-9*) Haworth Pr.

Lee, John A. & Allen, David G., eds. Modulation of Cardiac Calcium Sensitivity: A New Approach to Increasing the Strength of the Heart. LC 92-43149. (Illus.). 368p. (C). 1993. text 69.50 (*0-19-262347-8*) OUP.

Lee, John B. Hired Hands. 1986. pap. 9.95 (*0-919626-30-0*, Pub. by Brick Bks) Genl Dist Srvs.

Lee, John B. Institutional Aid, 1992-93. LC 97-219989. 80p. 1997. pap. 8.50 (*0-16-049290-4*) USGPO.

Lee, John B. Poems Only a Dog Could Love. 1979. pap. 3.95 (*0-919910-06-8*) Genl Dist Srvs.

— Rediscovered Sheep. 76p. 1989. pap. 9.95 (*0-919626-41-6*, Pub. by Brick Bks) Genl Dist Srvs.

— To Kill a White Dog. 30p. 1982. pap. 5.95 (*0-919626-19-X*, Pub. by Brick Bks) Genl Dist Srvs.

— Variations on Herb. (Illus.). 112p. 1993. pap. 11.95 (*0-919626-62-9*, Pub. by Brick Bks) Genl Dist Srvs.

— When Shaving Seems Like Suicide. 101p. 1992. pap. 10.95 (*0-86492-138-1*, Pub. by Goose Ln Edits) Genl Dist Srvs.

Lee, John B. & Merisotis, Jamie P. Proprietary Schools: Programs, Policies, & Prospects. Fife, Jonathan D., ed. LC 91-60263. (ASHE-ERIC Higher Education Reports: No. 90-5). 90p. 1990. pap. 24.00 (*1-878380-02-8*) GWU Grad Schl E&HD.

***Lee, John B., et al.** Employer Aid for Postsecondary Education. LC 99-224768. (Illus.). 124p. 1999. write for info. (*0-16-050058-3*) USGPO.

***Lee, John C.** Business & Financial Statistics Using Minitab 12 & Microsoft Excel 97. 1999. 38.00 (*981-02-3879-7*) WSC Inst MA Studies.

Lee, John C., jt. auth. see Snider, Ray S.

Lee, John D. Concise Inorganic Chemistry. 4th enl. rev. ed. (Illus.). 950p. (gr. 13). 1991. pap. text 48.95 (*0-412-40290-4*, A5898) Chapman & Hall.

***Lee, John D.** Concise Inorganic Chemistry. 5th ed. (Illus.). 1999. pap. 48.95 (*0-632-05293-7*) Blackwell Sci.

Lee, John D. Journals of John D. Lee, 1846-47 & 1859. Kelly, Charles, ed. LC 84-234912. 292p. reprint ed. pap. 90.60 (*0-8357-3270-3*, 203949100013) Bks Demand.

— Wordstar & CP-M Made Easy. LC 83-5939. (Illus.). 235p. reprint ed. pap. 72.90 (*0-8357-4600-3*, 203753300008) Bks Demand.

***Lee, John David.** Doomsday-Survivors' Guide. 1999. pap. 14.95 (*0-00-274039-7*, Pub. by HarpC) Trafalgar.

Lee, John E., tr. see Keller, Ferdinand.

Lee, John H. Flying Boy III: Stepping into the Mystery. Stot, Bill, ed. 1997. pap. 12.95 (*0-9654436-1-2*) Honey Creek WI.

Lee, John H., Jr. Management: A Study of Industrial Organization. Chandler, Alfred D., ed. LC 79-7550. (History of Management Thought & Practice Ser.). 1980. reprint ed. lib. bdg. 15.95 (*0-405-12334-5*) Ayer.

Lee, John H. The Origin & Progress of the American Party in Politics: Embracing a Complete History of the Philadelphia Riots in May & July of 1844. LC 79-117881. (Select Bibliographies Reprint Ser.). 1977. reprint ed. 26.95 (*0-8369-5334-7*) Ayer.

Lee, John H., Jr. & Chandler, Alfred D., eds. Pitman's Dictionary of Industrial Administration: A Comprehensive Encyclopedia of the Organization, Administration, & Management of Modern Industry, 2 vols. LC 79-7552. (History of Management Thought & Practice Ser.). 1980. reprint ed. lib. bdg. 158.95 (*0-405-12336-1*) Ayer.

— Pitman's Dictionary of Industrial Administration: A Comprehensive Encyclopedia of the Organization, Administration, & Management of Modern Industry, 2 vols., Vol. 1. LC 79-7552. (History of Management Thought & Practice Ser.). 1980. reprint ed. lib. bdg. 79.95 (*0-405-12337-X*) Ayer.

— Pitman's Dictionary of Industrial Administration: A Comprehensive Encyclopedia of the Organization, Administration, & Management of Modern Industry, 2 vols., Vol. 2. LC 79-7552. (History of Management Thought & Practice Ser.). 1980. reprint ed. lib. bdg. 79.95 (*0-405-12338-8*) Ayer.

***Lee, John J., Jr.** The Producer's Business Handbook. LC 99-87181. 210p. 2000. pap. 39.95 (*0-240-80396-5*, Focal) Buttrwrth-Heinemann.

Lee, John J., et al, eds. Illustrated Guide to the Protozoa. (Illus.). 629p. 1985. 80.00 (*0-914023-25-X*) Allen Pr.

Lee, John J. & Anderson, O. Roger, eds. Biology of Foraminifera. (Illus.). 384p. (C). 1991. text 146.00 (*0-12-440670-X*) Acad Pr.

Lee, John M. Counter-Clockwise. LC 73-18591. reprint ed. 29.50 (*0-404-11402-4*) AMS Pr.

— Custom Auto Upholstery: How to Design & Create Custom or Repro Interiors. (Illus.). 160p. 1988. pap. 19.95 (*0-87938-323-2*) MBI Pubg.

— How to Restore Auto Upholstery. (Illus.). 160p. 1994. pap. 17.95 (*0-87938-948-6*) MBI Pubg.

***Lee, John M.** Introduction to Topological Manifolds. Axler, S. et al. eds. LC 00-26156. (Graduate Texts in Mathematics Ser.: 202). (Illus.). 400p. 1999. 39.95 (*0-387-98759-2*) Spr-Verlag.

— Introduction to Topological Manifolds. LC 00-26156. (Graduate Texts in Mathematics Ser.: Vol. 202). (Illus.). 400p. (C). 2000. pap. text 34.95 (*0-387-95026-5*) Spr-Verlag.

Lee, John M. MSC - Nastran Linear Static Analysis User's Guide. rev. ed. (Illus.). 650p. 1997. pap. text 55.00 (*1-58524-001-X*) MacNeal-Schwendler.

— Riemannian Manifolds: An Introduction to Curvature, Vol. 176. LC 97-14537. (Graduate Texts in Mathematics Ser.). 1997. text. write for info. (*0-387-98271-X*) Spr-Verlag.

Lee, John M., ed. MSC - Nastran Common Questions & Answers. 3rd rev. ed. (Illus.). 194p. 1993. pap. text 35.00 (*1-58524-002-8*) MacNeal-Schwendler.

Lee, John M., et al. To Unite Our Strength: Enhancing United Nations Peace & Security. LC 92-26899. 180p. (Orig.). (C). 1992. pap. text 22.50 (*0-8191-8866-2*) U Pr of Amer.

Lee, John N., ed. Design Issues in Optical Processing. (Cambridge Studies in Modern Optics: 16). (Illus.). 292p. (C). 1995. text 69.95 (*0-521-43048-8*) Cambridge U Pr.

Lee, John P. & Grinstein, Georges G., eds. Database Issues for Data Visualization: Proceedings of the IEEE Visualization '93 Workshop, San Jose, California, USA, October 26, 1993. LC 94-34257. (Lecture Notes in Computer Science Ser.: Vol. 871). 1994. write for info. (*0-387-58519-2*) Spr-Verlag.

***Lee, John R.** Natural Progesterone: The Multiple Roles of a Remarkable Hormone. 4th rev. ed. (Illus.). VIII, 156p. 2000. pap. 12.00 (*0-9643737-3-4*) BLL Pubng.

— Optimal Health Guidelines. 4th rev. ed. (Illus.). xv, 211p. 1999. pap. 14.00 (*0-9643737-0-X*) BLL Pubng.

Lee, John R. & Hopkins, Virginia L. What Your Doctor May Not Tell You About Menopause: The Breakthrough Book on Natural Progesterone. 320p. (Orig.). 1996. mass mkt. 14.95 (*0-446-67144-4*, Pub. by Warner Bks) Little.

Lee, John R., et al. What Your Doctor May Not Tell You about Premenopause: Balance Your Hormones & Your Life from Thirty to Sixty. LC 98-29496. 395p. 1999. mass mkt. 14.99 (*0-446-67380-3*, Pub. by Warner Bks) Little.

Lee, John W., jt. auth. see Anselone, Philip M.

Lee, John W., jt. auth. see Guenther, Ronald B.

Lee, John Y. Managerial Accounting. LC 99-234141. (Illus.). 760p. (C). 1998. text 89.95 (*1-891666-00-2*) Hampton Hse.

***Lee, Johnathaun.** Implementing TMN. (Professional Telecom Ser.). 2000. pap. text 65.00 (*0-07-135791-2*) McGraw.

Lee, Johnny, ed. see Kahla, Bob.

***Lee, Jonathan & Krappe, Kirk.** The ASP Revolution: Winning Business Strategies Using Application Service Providers. 2000. pap. 29.99 (*0-07-212713-9*) Osborne-McGraw.

Lee, Jonathan, jt. ed. see Chiang, Weiling.

Lee, Jonathan S. Jacques Lacan. (Twayne's World Authors Ser.: No. 817). 272p. (C). 1990. 26.95 (*0-8057-8256-7*) Macmillan.

— Jacques Lacan. LC 90-21076. 264p. 1991. pap. 18.95 (*0-87023-737-3*) U of Mass Pr.

Lee, Jonathan S., ed. see Hord, Frederick L.

Lee, Jonathan S., jt. ed. see Hord, Frederick L.

Lee, Jonathan U., jt. auth. see Schimbor, Patricia S.

***Lee, Jonathaun.** Implementing Voice-Over IP: Using Intelligent Internet Protocol (IP) (Telecommunications Ser.). (Illus.). 450p. 2000. pap. text 60.00 (*0-07-135879-X*) McGraw-Hill Prof.

Lee, Jonghee, et al. Broadband Telecommunications Technology. 2nd ed. LC 96-24105. 672p. 1996. 95.00 (*0-89006-866-6*) Artech Hse.

***Lee, Jongsook, tr.** Paekpom Ilchi: The Autobiography of Kim Ku. (Illus.). 464p. 2000. 62.50 (*0-7618-1685-2*) U Pr of Amer.

Lee, Joon S., et al. Transport Phenomena in Thermal Engineering, 2 vols., Set. LC 93-39130. 1544p. 1995. 225.00 (*1-56700-015-0*) Begell Hse.

Lee, Jordan. Coping with Anxiety & Panic Attacks. LC 97-14367. (Coping Ser.). 105p. (YA). (gr. 7-12). 1997. lib. bdg. 17.95 (*0-8239-2548-X*) Rosen Group.

— Coping with Self-Mutilation. 1999. pap. text 6.95 (*1-56838-253-7*) Hazelden.

Lee, Jordan, jt. ed. see Kiyota, Minoru.

Lee, Joseph. The Modernization of Irish Society. 2nd ed. 181p. (C). 1989. reprint ed. pap. 17.95 (*0-7171-1693-X*, Pub. by Gill & MacMill) Irish Bks Media.

— The Normal Course in Play. LC 72-143067. 1982. 23.95 (*0-8434-0436-1*, Pub. by McGrath NH) Ayer.

— Play in Education. LC 74-143062. Date not set. 35.95 (*0-8434-0426-4*, Pub. by McGrath NH) Ayer.

Lee, Joseph & Tuathaigh, Gearboid. Age of de Valera. LC 82-231649. 216 p. 1982. 4.95 (*0-907085-34-2*) Poolbeg Pr.

Lee, Joseph J. Europe in Transition: Political, Economic, & Security Prospects for the 1990s. (Tom Slick World Peace Ser.). 339p. 1991. pap. 15.50 (*0-89940-425-1*) LBJ Sch Pub Aff.

Lee, Joseph K., et al, eds. Computed Body Tomography with MRI Correlation. 3rd ed. LC 96-17612. 2,000p. 1997. text 245.00 (*0-7817-0291-7*) Lppncott W & W.

***Lee, Joseph M., III.** Augusta: A Postcard History. (Postcard History Ser.). (Illus.). 128p. 1998. pap. 16.99 (*0-7524-0942-5*) Arcadia Publng.

Lee, Josephine. Performing Asian America: Race & Ethnicity on the Contemporary Stage. (Asian American History & Culture Ser.). (Illus.). 256p. (C). 1998. pap. text 19.95 (*1-56639-637-9*) Temple U Pr.

Lee, Josephine D. Performing Asian America: Race & Ethnicity on the Contemporary Stage. LC 96-31621. (Asian American History & Culture Ser.). (Illus.). 256p. 1997. 34.95 (*1-56639-502-X*) Temple U Pr.

Lee, Joy E. Further Collective Thoughts. 32p. 1986. pap. 35.00 (*0-7223-2027-2*, Pub. by A H S Ltd) St Mut.

Lee, Joyce, jt. auth. see Warner, Wayne.

Lee, Joyce G. Rolando Hinojosa & the American Dream. LC 96-50027. (Texas Writers Ser.: Vol. 5). 221p. 1997. 19.95 (*1-57441-023-7*) UNTX Pr.

Lee, Juanita E., jt. auth. see Shortridge, Lillie M.

Lee, Judith A. Group Work with the Poor & Oppressed. LC 88-32009. (Social Work with Groups Ser.: Vol. 11, No. 4). (Illus.). 138p. 1989. text 39.95 (*0-86656-884-0*) Haworth Pr.

— The Invisible Child: Healing the Damage of Childhood Sexual Abuse. xix, 297p. 1998. pap. 14.95 (*0-9668888-0-4*, PO2930) Heart Whisps.

Lee, Judith A. & Nisiroccia, Daniella. Walk a Mile in My Shoes: A Book about Biological Parents for Foster Parents & Social Workers. 1989. pap. 9.95 (*0-87868-349-6*) Child Welfare.

Lee, Judith A. B. The Empowerment Approach to Social Work Practice. LC 94-16601. 352p. 1994. 43.50 (*0-231-08026-3*); write for info. (*0-231-09997-5*) Col U Pr.

***Lee, Judith A. B.** The Empowerment Approach to Social Work Practice: Second Edition. 2nd ed. 400p. 2000. text 42.00 (*0-231-11548-2*) Col U Pr.

Lee, Judith Y. Defining 'New Yorker' Humor. LC 99-48347. (Studies in Popular Culture). (Illus.). 399p. 2000. 48.00 (*1-57806-197-0*); pap. 20.00 (*1-57806-198-9*) U Pr of Miss.

— Garrison Keillor: A Voice of America. LC 90-24702. 1991. pap. 15.95 (*0-87805-473-1*) U Pr of Miss.

Lee, Judith Y., jt. ed. see Slade, Joseph W.

Lee, Julian C. The Amphibians & Reptiles of the Yucatan Peninsula. (Comstock Bk.). (Illus.). 512p. 1996. text 175.00 (*0-8014-2450-X*) Cornell U Pr.

***Lee, Julian C.** A Field Guide to Amphibians & Reptiles of the Maya World: The Lowlands of Mexico, Northern Guatemala & Belize. LC 99-86709. 2000. pap. 35.00 (*0-8014-8587-8*) Cornell U Pr.

— Field Guide to the Amphibians & Reptiles of the Maya World: The Lowlands of Mexico. LC 99-86709. 2000. 59.95 (*0-8014-3624-9*) Cornell U Pr.

Lee, Julie & Northard, Jackie. Animals A to Zoo. (Illus.). 32p. (J). (gr. k-2). 1995. 14.95 (*0-9649808-0-0*) MN Zoo.

Lee, Jung Y. Korean Shamanistic Rituals. (Religion & Society Ser.: No. 12). 250p. 1980. 57.50 (*90-279-3378-2*) Mouton.

— The Theology of Change: A Christian Concept of God in an Eastern Perspective. LC 78-16745. 160p. reprint ed. pap. 49.60 (*0-8357-7054-0*, 203354700086) Bks Demand.

— The Trinity in Asian Perspective. 1996. pap. 19.95 (*0-687-42637-5*) Abingdon.

Lee, Jung Y., ed. Ancestor Worship & Christianity in Korea. LC 88-39988. (Studies in Asian Thought & Religion). 112p. 1989. lib. bdg. 59.95 (*0-88946-059-0*) E Mellen.

Lee, Jung-Young. Korean Preaching: An Interpretation. LC 96-42571. 144p. 1997. pap. 14.95 (*0-687-00442-X*) Abingdon.

An Asterisk (*) at the beginning of an entry indicates that the title is appearing for the first time.

— Marginality: The Key to Multicultural Theology. LC 94-31475. 224p. 1995. pap. 22.00 (*0-8006-2810-1*, 1-2810, Fortress Pr) Augsburg Fortress.

Lee, Jung Young, jt. ed. see Phan, Peter C.

***Lee-Junker, Laura.** Raiding, Trading & Feasting: The Political Economy. LC 98-54831. 512p. 1999. text 59.00 (*0-8248-2035-5*) UH Pr.

***Lee, Justin.** The Respiratory System. LC 00-9101. (Insider's Guide to the Body Ser.). (Illus.). 2000. lib. bdg. write for info. (*0-8239-3321-0*) Rosen Group.

Lee, K., jt. ed. see Vidyadhar, I.

Lee, K. C. Diplomacy of a Tiny State. 2nd ed. 364p. 1993. pap. text 29.00 (*981-02-1219-4*) World Scientific Pub.

Lee, K. C., et al, eds. Optical Properties of Solids. 350p. (C). 1991. text 104.00 (*981-02-0596-1*) World Scientific Pub.

Lee, K. Francis & Dyke, Cornelius M. Surgical Attending Rounds. LC 98-45984. 1999. 34.95 (*0-683-30585-9*) Lppncott W & W.

Lee, K-Fu, jt. ed. see Whel, Alexander.

Lee, K. J. Essential Otolaryngology. 6th ed. LC 94-34211. (Illus.). 1209p. (C). 1994. pap. text 75.00 (*0-8385-2214-9*, A2214-3) Appleton & Lange.

Lee, K. K., ed. Lectures on Dynamical Systems, Structural Stability & Their Application. 420p. (C). 1992. text 74.00 (*9971-5-0965-2*) World Scientific Pub.

Lee, K. M., jt. ed. see Nagar, Munari L.

Lee, K. W., jt. ed. see Mittal, K. L.

Lee, K. Y. & Takahashi, H., eds. Fracture & Strength, '90. 576p. 1991. text 233.00 (*0-87849-618-1*, Pub. by Trans T Pub) Enfield Pubs NH.

Lee, Kai. Computers in Nuclear Medicine: A Practical Approach. LC 91-4859. (Illus.). 290p. (Orig.). 1992. 42.00 (*0-932004-36-9*) Soc Nuclear Med.

Lee, Kai F. & Chen, Wei. Advances in Microstrip & Printed Antennas. LC 96-39032. (Wiley Series in Microwave & Optical Engineering). 624p. 1997. 110.00 (*0-471-04421-0*) Wiley.

Lee, Kai-Fu. Automatic Speech Recognition: The Development of the SPHINX Recognition System. (International Series in Engineering & Computer Science, VLSI, Computer Architecture, & Digital Screen Processing). 224p. (C). 1988. text 127.50 (*0-89838-296-3*) Kluwer Academic.

Lee, Kai N. Compass & Gyroscope: Integrating Science & Politics for the Environment. LC 92-38824. 243p. (C). 1994. reprint ed. pap. 19.95 (*1-55963-198-8*) Island Pr.

Lee, Kaiman. Air Pollution: Its Effect on the Urban Man & His Adaptive Strategies. LC 74-182905. 52p. 1974. 12.00 (*0-915250-13-6*) Environ Design.

— Comparison of Doctoral Programs in Architecture - U. S. A. 1976. pap. text 30.00 (*0-915250-22-5*) Environ Design.

— Computer Aided Architectural Design: 16 ARK-2 Articles. LC 74-160961. 1973. 30.00 (*0-915250-04-7*) Environ Design.

— Computer-Aided Building Code Checking: A Demonstration. 2nd ed. LC 74-308127. 34p. 1974. 12.00 (*0-915250-08-X*) Environ Design.

— Computer Aided Space Planning. LC 76-366704. 1976. 30.00 (*0-915250-20-9*) Environ Design.

— The Computer As an Architectural Design Tool: An Exploration into Certain Multi-Story Building Plan Layouts. 190p. 1979. 25.00 (*0-915250-00-4*) Environ Design.

— Computer Programs in Environmental Design, 5 vols., Set. LC 74-169212. (Illus.). 1308p. 1974. 210.00 (*0-915250-05-5*) Environ Design.

— Encyclopedia of Energy-Efficient Building Design: 391 Practical Case Studies, 2 vols., Set. LC 77-150686. 1977. 150.00 (*0-915250-18-7*) Environ Design.

— Evaluation of Computer Graphic Terminals. 2nd ed. LC 74-184824. 92p. 1974. 12.00 (*0-915250-11-X*) Environ Design.

— Evaluation, Syntheses & Development of an Interactive Approach to Space Allocation. 2nd ed. LC 74-187884. 50p. 1975. 15.00 (*0-915250-10-1*) Environ Design.

— Federal Environmental Impact Statements Related to Buildings. LC 75-323048. 102p. 1975. 30.00 (*0-915250-16-0*) Environ Design.

— Inevitability: Strategic Basis for Investing. LC 82-125420. 93p. 1982. 14.95 (*0-915250-39-X*) Environ Design.

— Integrated Municipal Information System. LC 74-184835. 52p. 1974. 12.00 (*0-915250-12-8*) Environ Design.

— Interactive Computer Aided Architectural Design: Four Applications. 1976. pap. text 12.00 (*0-915250-26-8*) Environ Design.

— Interactive Computer Graphics in Architecture. LC 76-366950. 100p. 1976. 30.00 (*0-915250-21-7*) Environ Design.

— Performance Specification of Computer Aided Environmental Design, 2 vols. LC 75-309149. (Illus.). 554p. 1975. 150.00 (*0-915250-15-2*) Environ Design.

— State of the Art of Computer Aided Environmental Design. LC 76-358975. (Illus.). 309p. 1975. 50.00 (*0-915250-14-4*) Environ Design.

***Lee, Kaiman.** Technology Revolution: Ramifications & Opportunities, 2 vols. (Illus.). 365p. 2000. 296.00 (*0-915250-88-8*) Environ Design.

Lee, Kaiman, ed. Bibliography of the Computer in Environmental Design, 3 Vols., Set. 2nd ed. LC 73-158197. 650p. 1973. 110.00 (*0-915250-03-9*) Environ Design.

— Energy Film List. 1977. pap. text 4.50 (*0-915250-25-X*) Environ Design.

Lee, Kaiman & Donnelly, Linda. Solar Failure. LC 80-130467. (Illus.). 1980. 30.00 (*0-915250-36-5*) Environ Design.

Lee, Kaiman & Koumjian, Lauren. Environmental Court Cases Related to Buildings. LC 79-105955. 1979. 30.00 (*0-915250-28-4*) Environ Design.

— Environmental Impact Statement: A Reference Manual for the Architect Planner. 2nd ed. 1978. 30.00 (*0-915250-27-6*) Environ Design.

Lee, Kaiman & Masloff, Jacqueline. Energy-Oriented Computer Programs for the Design & Monitoring of Buildings, 2 vols., Set. LC 79-104533. (Illus.). 400p. 1979. 150.00 (*0-915250-29-2*) Environ Design.

— Kaiman's Encyclopedia of Energy Topics, 2 vols., Set. LC 79-104541. (Illus.). 1979. 150.00 (*0-915250-31-4*) Environ Design.

Lee, Kaiman & Moberg, John. Environmental Design Evaluation: A Matrix Method. LC 75-330795. 190p. 1975. 30.00 (*0-915250-17-9*) Environ Design.

Lee, Kaiman & Rehr, Stuart. Energy Conservation & Building Codes: The Legislative & Planning Processes. LC 77-362518. 1977. 30.00 (*0-915250-23-3*) Environ Design.

Lee, Kaiman & Silverstein, Michael. The Buyer's Book of Solar Water Heaters. 4th ed. LC 79-104450. (Illus.). 1979. 50.00 (*0-915250-30-6*) Environ Design.

Lee, Kaiman & Yang, Rita. Encyclopedia of Financial & Personal Survival: Six Hundred Fifty Coping Strategies. LC 80-130472. 1980. 210.00 (*0-915250-34-9*) Environ Design.

Lee Kam Hing. The Sultanate of Aceh: Relations with the British, 1760-1824. (South-East Asian Historical Monographs). (Illus.). 362p. 1995. text 59.00 (*967-65-3055-7*) OUP.

***Lee, Kam-Lun Edwin.** Augustine, Manichaeism & the Good. LC 98-30634. (Patristic Studies: Vol. 2). 139p. 1999. 43.95 (*0-8204-4278-X*) P Lang Pubng.

Lee, Kang, ed. Childhood Cognitive Development: The Essential Readings. LC 99-58485. (Essential Readings in Developmental Psychology Ser.). 256p. 1999. 59.95 (*0-631-21655-3*); pap. 24.95 (*0-631-21656-1*) Blackwell Pubs.

Lee Kang Hoe, et al, eds. Survival Guide to Acute Medicine. (Illus.). 226p. 1998. pap. 27.50 (*9971-69-220-1*, Pub. by Sngapore Univ Pr) Coronet Bks.

Lee, Kang U. Tang Soo Do: The Ultimate Guide to the Korean Martial Art. (Illus.). 1998. 35.95 (*0-7136-4531-8*, Pub. by A & C Blk) Midpt Trade.

— Tang Soo Do: The Ultimate Guide to the Korean Martial Art. (Illus.). 256p. 1999. pap. text 16.95 (*0-86568-170-8*) Sakura Dragon Corp.

Lee, Karen. Dreams Have Wings: A Survival Kit for Dreamers. (Illus.). 48p. 1997. 24.95 (*0-9662128-0-0*) Quixote Proj.

Lee, Karen & Porter, Diana. The Occasional Vegetarian: More Than 200 Robust Dishes to Satisfy Both Full & Part-time Vegetarians. 272p. 1995. 24.95 (*0-446-51792-5*, Pub. by Warner Bks) Little.

***Lee, Karen & Porter, Diane.** The Occasional Vegetarian. 272p. 1998. mass mkt. 15.99 (*0-446-67452-4*, Pub. by Warner Bks) Little.

Lee, Karen K., jt. auth. see Lee, Ronald.

Lee, Karin. Halloween Tarot. LC 96-60917. 1997. pap. text 9.95 (*0-88079-989-7*, BK161) US Games Syst.

— Halloween Tarot Deck - Book Set. (Illus.). 148p. 1997. pap. 26.00 (*1-57281-034-3*, HAS99) US Games Syst.

Lee, Kate. Snappy Little Numbers. LC 98-19345. (Illus.). 20p. (J). (ps-1). 1998. 12.95 (*0-7613-0437-1*, Copper Beech Bks) Millbrook Pr.

Lee, Kate & Repchuk, Caroline. Snappy Little Colors. LC 98-36183. (Illus.). 20p. (J). (ps-1). 1999. 12.95 (*0-7613-0442-8*, Copper Beech Bks) Millbrook Pr.

Lee, Kathleen. Tracing Our Italian Roots. LC 93-5149. (American Origins Ser.). (Illus.). 48p. (J). (gr. 4-7). 1993. text 12.95 (*1-56261-149-6*, J Muir) Avalon Travel.

Lee, Kathleen, jt. auth. see Kappeler, Max.

Lee, Kathleen M., jt. auth. see Oliner, Samuel P.

Lee, Kathy, jt. auth. see Dibble, Carole H.

Lee, Kathy H., jt. auth. see Dibble, Carole H.

Lee, Kathy S. & Thomas, Debra J. Selecting Access Systems for Individuals with Physical Disabilities. 310p. 1990. pap. text 50.00 (*0-8020-6695-X*) U of Toronto Pr.

Lee, Katie. All My Rivers Are Gone: A Journey of Discovery Through Glen Canyon. LC 98-25872. 288p. 1998. pap. 18.00 (*1-55566-229-3*) Johnson Bks.

— Ten Thousand Goddam Cattle: A History of the American Cowboy in Song, Story & Verse. limited rev. ed. (Illus.). 257p. 1985. reprint ed. pap. 25.00 (*0-934573-68-9*) Katyd Bks & Music.

***Lee, Katie & Moyers, William.** Ten Thousand Goddam Cattle: A History of the American Cowboy in Song, Story & Verse. LC 00-42313. 2001. pap. write for info. (*0-8263-2335-9*) U of NM Pr.

Lee, Katie, jt. illus. see Nash, Ogden.

Lee, Kay & Marcus, Shirley. Home Rehabilitation Exercises: Hand. (Illus.). 16p. (Orig.). (C). 1990. pap. text 6.00 (*0-910317-58-5*) Am Occup Therapy.

— Home Rehabilitation Exercises: Shoulder, Elbow, Forearm, Wrist. (Illus.). 16p. (Orig.). (C). 1990. pap. text 6.00 (*0-910317-57-7*) Am Occup Therapy.

Lee, Keatjin. Otolaryngology: Head & Neck Surgery. 951p. (C). 1992. pap. text 155.00 (*0-8385-9067-5*, A9067-8, Apple Lange Med) McGraw.

Lee, Keekok. The Natural & the Artefactual: The Implications of Deep Science & Deep Technology for Environmental Philosophy. LC 99-20325. 288p. 1999. 49.00 (*0-7391-0061-0*) Lxngtn Bks.

— A New Basis for Moral Philosophy. (International Library of Philosophy). 288p. 1985. 42.50 (*0-7102-0445-0*, Routledge Thoemms) Routledge.

— The Positivist Science of Law. 224p. 1989. text 82.95 (*0-566-07032-4*, Pub. by Avebury) Ashgate Pub Co.

Lee, Keenan & Fetter, Charles W., Jr. Hydrogeology Laboratory Manual with Disk. 136p. (C). 1993. pap. text 43.00, lab manual ed. 43.00 incl. audio compact disk (*0-02-369201-4*, Macmillan Coll) P-H.

Lee, Kelley. Historical Dictionary of the World Health Organization. LC 97-26820. (Historical Dictionaries of International Organizations Ser.: No. 15). 333p. 1998. 75.00 (*0-8108-3371-9*) Scarecrow.

Lee, Kenneth. Huddled Masses, Muddled Laws: Why Contemporary Immigration Policy Fails to Reflect Public Opinion. LC 98-11126. 184p. 1998. 35.00 (*0-275-96272-5*, Praeger Pubs) Greenwood.

— Trouncing the Dow: A Value-Based Method for Making Huge Profits. LC 98-8619. (Illus.). 284p. 1998. 24.95 (*0-07-038301-4*) McGraw.

Lee, Kenneth & Mills, Anne, eds. The Economics of Health in Developing Countries. (Illus.). 256p. 1983. 39.95 (*0-19-261385-5*) OUP.

Lee, Kenneth, jt. ed. see Mills, Anne.

Lee, Kenneth B. Korea & East Asia: The Story of a Phoenix. LC 96-44693. 312p. 1997. 59.95 (*0-275-95823-X*, Praeger Pubs) Greenwood.

Lee, Kent D. Strategy & History. (EWS Occasional Papers). (C). 1996. pap. text 12.85 (*0-8133-8133-9*) Westview.

Lee, Kent D., ed. see Svechin, Aleksandra.

Lee, Kent D., tr. see Arbatov, Alexei G.

Lee, Kent D., tr. see Svechin, Aleksandr A.

Lee, Keun. Chinese Firms & the State in Transition: Property Rights & Agency Problems in the Reform Era. LC 91-2075. (Studies on Contemporary China). 224p. (C). (gr. 13). 1991. text 79.95 (*0-87332-850-7*, East Gate Bk) M E Sharpe.

— New East Asian Economic Development: The Interaction of Capitalism & Socialism. LC 93-19555. 224p. (C). (gr. 13). 1993. text 85.95 (*1-56324-218-4*, East Gate Bk) M E Sharpe.

Lee, Keun. New East Asian Economic Development: The Interaction of Capitalism & Socialism. LC 93-19555. 224p. (C). (gr. 13). 1993. pap. text 34.95 (*1-56324-219-2*, East Gate Bk) M E Sharpe.

Lee, Kevin, jt. auth. see James, Alan.

Lee, Kevin H., ed. see Euripides.

Lee, Kevin H., tr. see Euripides.

Lee, Khoon Choy. A Fragile Nation: The Indonesian Crisis. LC 99-34706. 350p. 1999. pap. text 18.00 (*981-02-4003-1*) World Scientific Pub.

Lee, Ki-baik. A New History of Korea. Wagner, Edward W. & Schultz, Edward J., trs. from KOR. LC 83-246. (Harvard-Yenching Institute Studies). (Illus.). 472p. 1985. 25.00 (*0-674-61575-1*) HUP.

— A New History of Korea. Wagner, Edward W. & Schultz, Edward J., trs. from KOR. LC 83-246. (Harvard-Yenching Institute Publications). (Illus.). 472p. 1985. reprint ed. pap. 14.95 (*0-674-61576-X*) HUP.

Lee, Kip. Eon: Evolution & Opinions of a Newjack. 135p. (Orig.). 1996. pap. 11.95 (*0-9649734-0-5*) Aframedia.

Lee, Kiyoung. Southeast Asian Families & Pooled Labor: Multiple Wage-Earner Strategies for Refugee Households in the U. S. rev. ed. (Studies in the History of American Labor). (Illus.). 174p. 1998. 45.00 (*0-8153-3216-5*) Garland.

Lee, Knute. Survivor. LC 84-81767. 224p. 1984. pap. 9.95 (*0-8187-0057-2*) Harlo Press.

Lee, Kou L. The Owl & Mrs. Wren: Correct Behavior. (ENG & LAO.). 36p. (Orig.). (J). 1995. pap. text 10.95 (*0-9645686-1-6*) NKL Multicult Educ.

Lee, Kristie, compiled by. Images of the Ozarks. LC 98-23153. (Illus.). 128p. 1998. 24.95 (*0-8262-1191-7*) U of Mo Pr.

***Lee, Kuan Yew.** From Third World to First: Singapore & the Asian Economic Boom. 752p. 2000. 35.00 (*0-06-019776-5*) HarpC.

Lee, Kuen H. Calculus: A Step-by-Step Approach, Vol. 1. (Illus.). 472p. 1997. per. 39.75 (*0-9618665-8-6*) Edmund Pub.

— Calculus: A Step-by-Step Approach, Vol. 2. (Illus.). 522p. 1998. per. 39.75 (*0-9618665-9-4*) Edmund Pub.

— College Algebra: A Step-by-Step Approach. (Illus.). 658p. 1992. pap. text 45.75 (*0-9618665-3-5*) Edmund Pub.

— Elementary Algebra: A Step-by-Step Approach (Brief Version) 2nd ed. (Illus.). 346p. (C). 1988. reprint ed. pap. text 37.00 (*0-9618665-2-7*) Edmund Pub.

— Essential Mathematics: A Step by Step Approach. 1994. pap. text 37.50 (*0-9618665-7-8*) Edmund Pub.

— Fundamental Arithmetic: A Step by Step Approach. 1986. pap. text 40.25 (*0-9618665-6-X*) Edmund Pub.

— Student's Solution Manual for Elementary Algebra: A Step-by-Step Approach. 3rd expanded ed. (Illus.). 524p. Date not set. pap. text, student ed. 40.25 (*0-9618665-5-1*) Edmund Pub.

Lee, Kunwoo. Principles of Cad Cam Cae Systems. 608p. (C). 1998. text Price not set. (*0-201-38043-9*) Addison-Wesley.

— Principles of CAD/CAM/CAE. LC 98-18040. 640p. (C). 1999. 97.00 (*0-201-38036-6*, Prentice Hall) P-H.

Lee, Kwan-Jo. Search for Nirvana: Korean Monks' Life. (Illus.). 128p. 1984. 24.00 (*0-8048-1417-1*, Pub. by Seoul Intl Tourist) Tuttle Pubng.

Lee, Kwang-Bok. Rezeption - Vermittlung - Reflexion. (Europaische Hochschulschriften Ser.: Reihe 1, vol. 1669). IX, 214p. 1998. pap. 37.95 (*3-631-33182-7*) P Lang Pubng.

Lee, Kwangsu. Buddhist Ideas & Rituals in Early India & Korea '. LC 98-915252. 196 p. 1998. write for info. (*81-7304-221-7*, Pub. by Manohar) St Mut.

Lee, Kyong M. Dynamic Taekwondo: A Martial Art & Olympic Sport. LC 95-76493. (Illus.). 170p. 1995. 18.95 (*1-56591-062-1*, Pub. by Hollym Bks) Weatherhill.

Lee, Kyu S. The Location of Jobs in a Developing Metropolis: Patterns of Growth in Bogota & Cali, Colombia. (World Bank Research Publications Ser.). (Illus.). 192p. 1989. text 24.95 (*0-19-520786-6*) OUP.

Lee, Kyung-Og. Antagonismen in den Dramen Von Max Frisch. (Europaische Hochschulschriften Ser.: Reihe 1, Bd. 1661). 166p. 1998. pap. 31.95 (*3-631-33023-5*) P Lang Pubng.

Lee, L. Basic Systems Analysis. (C). 1989. pap. 100.00 (*0-09-154091-7*, Pub. by S Thornes Pubs) St Mut.

Lee, L. & Lee, S. F. Lee: John Lee of Farmington, Hartford County, CT, & His Descendants, 1634-1897. (Illus.). 572p. 1993. reprint ed. pap. 87.00 (*0-8328-3698-2*); reprint ed. lib. bdg. 97.00 (*0-8328-3697-4*) Higginson Bk Co.

Lee, L., et al. Purchasing & Materials Management. Burt, B., ed. 796p. (C). 1984. 540.00 (*0-7855-5759-8*, Pub. by Inst Pur & Supply); student ed. 170.00 (*0-7855-5760-1*, Pub. by Inst Pur & Supply) St Mut.

Lee, L. H. Fundamentals of Adhesion. (Illus.). 472p. (C). 1991. text 110.00 (*0-306-43470-9*, Kluwer Plenum) Kluwer Academic.

Lee, L. H., ed. Adhesion & Adsorption of Polymers, 2 vols., Set. Incl. Pt. A. LC 80-262. 504p. 1980. 89.50 (*0-306-40427-3*, Kluwer Plenum); Pt. B. LC 80-262. 456p. 1980. 89.50 (*0-306-40428-1*, Kluwer Plenum); LC 80-262. (Polymer Science & Technology Ser.: Vols. 12A & B). 1980. 145.00 (*0-685-04067-4*, Plenum Trade) Perseus Pubng.

— Adhesive Bonding. (Illus.). 496p. (C). 1991. text 125.00 (*0-306-43471-7*, Kluwer Plenum) Kluwer Academic.

— New Trends in Physics & Physical Chemistry of Polymers. LC 89-22965. (Illus.). 672p. 1989. 155.00 (*0-306-43383-4*, Plenum Trade) Perseus Pubng.

***Lee, L. H. Charles.** Error-Control Block Codes for Communications Engineers. (Illus.). 2000. 93.00 (*1-58053-032-X*) Artech Hse.

Lee, L. L. Vladimir Nabokov. Bowman, Sylvia E., ed. LC 76-128. (Twayne's United States Authors Ser.). 166p. (C). 1976. lib. bdg. 20.95 (*0-8057-7166-2*) Irvington.

— Walter Van Tilburg Clark. LC 73-8337. (Western Writers Ser.: No. 8). 50p. 1973. pap. 4.95 (*0-88430-007-2*) Boise St U W Writ Ser.

Lee, L. L. & Johnson, Ellwood. A Directory of Scholarly Journals in English & American Literature. vi, 186p. 1990. 45.00 (*0-87875-401-6*) Whitston Pub.

Lee, L. L. & Lee, Sylvia. Virginia Sorensen. LC 78-52559. (Western Writers Ser.: No. 31). 50p. 1978. pap. 4.95 (*0-88430-055-2*) Boise St U W Writ Ser.

Lee, L. L., jt. ed. see Lewis, Merrill.

Lee, L. P. History of the Spirit Lake Massacre! LC 96-18804. 1996. 14.95 (*0-87770-592-5*); pap. 9.95 (*0-87770-591-7*) Ye Galleon.

Lee, Lai T. The Reunification of China: Pro-Taiwan Relations in Flux. LC 90-44388. 200p. 1991. 52.95 (*0-275-93772-0*, C3772, Praeger Pubs) Greenwood.

Lee-Lampshire. On Marx. (Philosophy Ser.). 2000. pap. text 13.95 (*0-534-57602-8*) Brooks-Cole.

***Lee, Lance.** A Poetics for Screenwriters. LC 00-36415. 160p. 2001. 30.00 (*0-292-74718-7*); pap. 15.95 (*0-292-74719-5*) U of Tex Pr.

Lee, Lance. Wrestling with the Angel. 92p. 1990. pap. 9.95 (*0-912292-86-5*) Smith.

Lee, Lance, jt. auth. see Brady, Ben.

***Lee, Lance R.** Twice Round the Loggerhead. 2000. 35.00 (*0-918172-22-5*) Leetes Isl.

***Lee, Lance R. & Halibisky, Bruce.** Twice Round the Loggerhead: The Culture of Whaling in the Azores. 2000. 35.00 (*0-918172-47-0*) Leetes Isl.

***Lee, Lanny E., III.** Virtual Memory for Humans: How to Develop a Photographic Memory. Carroll, Joe, ed. 179p. 2000. per. 11.95 (*0-9664386-1-2*) Triad Grp.

Lee, Larry. American Eagle: The Story of a Navajo Vietnam Veteran. (C). 1977. pap. text 6.00 (*0-686-12227-5*) Packrat Pr.

***Lee, Laura.** Arlo, Alice & Anglicans: The Lives of a New England Church. LC 99-41883. (Illus.). 240p. 2000. pap. 16.95 (*1-58157-010-4*) Berkshire Hse.

— Bad Predictions. 2000. pap. 15.95 (*0-9657345-9-5*) Elsewhere Pr MI.

Lee, Laura. The Name's Familiar: Mr. Leotard, Barbie, & Chef Boy-ar-dee. LC 98-56131. 312p. 1999. pap. 14.95 (*1-56554-394-7*) Pelican.

Lee, Laura & Lee, Martyn. Absent Friend: Coping with the Loss of a Treasured Pet. 142p. (Orig.). 1997. pap. 6.95 (*1-86054-037-6*, Pub. by Ringpr Bks) Seven Hills Bk.

Lee, Lauren. Stella: On the Edge of Popularity. LC 93-43917. (J). 1994. 10.95 (*1-879965-08-9*) Polychrome Pub.

Lee, Lauren K., et al, eds. The Elementary School Library Collection: A Guide to Books & Other Media, Phases 1-2-3. 19th ed. LC 93-24494. 1994. 99.95 (*0-87272-096-9*) Brodart.

Lee, Lauren K. & Hoyle, Gary D., eds. Elementary School Library Collection: A Guide to Books & Other Media. 18th ed. 1992. 99.95 (*0-87272-095-0*) Brodart.

Lee, Laurie. Cider with Rosie. Date not set. pap. text. write for info. (*0-582-23359-3*, Pub. by Addison-Wesley) Longman.

— Cider with Rosie. 1980. pap. text. write for info. (*0-582-53678-2*, Drumbeat) Longman.

— The Firstborn. 16p. 1998. 14.95 (*1-86105-101-8*, Pub. by Robson Bks) Parkwest Pubns.

— A Moment of War: A Memoir of the Spanish Civil War. 192p. 1994. pap. 9.95 (*1-56584-173-5*, Pub. by New Press NY) Norton.

Lee, Lawrence. Cockcrow at Night, the Heroic Journey, & 18 Other Stories. (Illus.). 250p. (Orig.). 1973. 6.00 (*0-910286-35-3*) Boxwood.

Lee, Lawrence & Gifford, Barry. Saroyan: A Biography. LC 97-31389. 345p. 1998. 17.95 (*0-520-21399-8*, Pub. by U CA Pr) Cal Prin Full Svc.

Lee, Lawrence, jt. auth. see Gifford, Barry.

L

Lee, Lawrence B. Kansas & the Homestead Act, 1862 to 1905, 2 vols. Bruchey, Stuart, ed. LC 78-36703. (Management of Public Lands in the U. S. Ser.). (Illus.). 1979. lib. bdg. 50.95 (*0-405-11341-2*) Ayer.

Lee, Lawrence D., tr. see Oldman, Oliver S., et al.

Lee, Leathea, jt. ed. see Leydon, Michael.

Lee, Lee C. & Zane, Nolan W. Handbook of Asian American Psychology. LC 98-8967. 1998. 78.95 (*0-8039-4963-4*) Sage.

Lee, Lenora H., jt. auth. see Pietsch, James H.

Lee, Leo O. The Romantic Generation of Modern Chinese Writers. LC 73-75058. (Harvard East Asian Ser.: No. 71). (Illus.). 383p. reprint ed. pap. 118.80 (*0-7837-4166-9*, 205901400012) Bks Demand.

— Voices from the Iron House: A Study of Lu Xun. LC 85-46049. (Studies in Chinese Literature & Society). 266p. 1987. 34.95 (*0-253-36263-6*) Ind U Pr.

— Voices from the Iron House: A Study of Lu Xun. LC 85-16049. (Studies in Chinese Literature & Society). 264p. Date not set. reprint ed. pap. 81.90 (*0-608-20557-5*, 2054471) Bks Demand.

Lee, Leo O., jt. ed. see Arkush, R. David.

***Lee, Leona Lipari.** How to Survive Menopause - Without Going Crazy. 185p. 1998. pap. 10.00 (*1-888315-04-0*) Power NY.

Lee, Leonard. The Complete Guide to Sharpening. LC 94-37677. (Illus.). 245p. 1995. 34.95 (*1-56158-067-8*, 70197) Taunton.

— The Complete Guide to Sharpening. (Illus.). 245p. 1996. pap. 22.95 (*1-56158-125-9*, 070256) Taunton.

Lee, Leonard, jt. auth. see Perch, David.

Lee, Leslie. Backcountry Ranger: In Glacier National Park 1910-1913 the Diaries & Photographs of Norton Pearl. LC 94-75921. (Illus.). 264p. 1994. write for info. (*0-9641250-0-5*); pap. write for info. (*0-9641250-3-X*); text. write for info. (*0-9641250-2-1*); pap. text. write for info. (*0-9641250-4-8*); lib. bdg. write for info. (*0-9641250-1-3*) L Lee Pub.

Lee, Leslie & Comte, Robert. Management Procedures. LC 74-18677. (Allied Health Ser.). 1975. pap. 6.35 (*0-672-61397-2*, Bobbs) Macmillan.

Lee, Leslie Enders. Horseplay. LC 00-90107. (Illus.). 96p. 2000. pap. 25.00 (0-9678367-0-0) Fethra Pr. Artist Leslie Lee presents her stable of horses from history, legend, literature, art, language, sport & popular culture. These mask-like horse heads in iron, copper, bronze & wood have been cut from a single template, the Workhouse. Each horse, however, has an individual identity, expression & accompanying narrative. Among the thirty-four horses are St. Jerome's Gift Horse; Australia's celebrated race horse, Phar Lap; the Chinese silk-worm goddess Lady Horse-head; Virgil's Trojan Horse; a Hobby Horse; the Iron Horse; a Horse of a Different Color; & "of course", television's talking horse, Mr. Ed. IN HORSEPLAY the sculpture & drawings point to the profound presence of the horse in our everyday language. With the head of the horse as the visual thread, Lee weaves together fact & myth with prose & verse to create a book that will delight horse enthusiasts & word play lovers alike. *Publisher Paid Annotation.

Lee, Levi, et al. Tent Meeting. 1987. pap. 5.25 (*0-8222-1121-1*) Dramatists Play.

Lee, Levi, jt. auth. see Larson, Larry.

Lee, Li-Young. The City in Which I Love You. (American Poets Continuum Ser.: No. 20). 89p. 1991. 18.00 (*0-918526-82-5*) BOA Edns.

— The City in Which I Love You. (American Poets Continuum Ser.: No. 20). 89p. 1998. pap. 10.00 (*0-918526-83-3*) BOA Edns.

— Rose. (New Poets of America Ser.: No. 9). 71p. 1986. pap. 10.00 (*0-918526-53-1*) BOA Edns.

— The Winged Seed: A Remembrance. LC 99-71484. 205p. 1999. pap. 13.00 (*1-886913-28-5*, Pub. by Ruminator Bks) Consort Bk Sales.

— The Winged Seed: A Remembrance. 1995. 20.00 (*0-671-70708-6*) S&S Trade.

Lee, Lieng-Huang. Adhesion Science & Technology. Incl. Pt. A. LC 75-35744. 470p. 1975. (*0-306-36493-X*, Kluwer Plenum); Pt. B. LC 75-35744. 456p. 1975. (*0-306-36494-8*, Kluwer Plenum); LC 75-35744. (Polymer Science & Technology Ser.: Vols. 9A & 9B). 1975. write for info. (*0-318-55304-X*, Plenum Trade) Perseus Pubng.

Lee, Lilian. Farewell My Concubine: Novel, A. LC 94-9785. 272p. 1994. pap. 13.00 (*0-06-097644-6*) HarpC.

Lee, Lily S. The Virtue of Yin: Essays on Chinese Women. LC 94-221833. 128p. (C). 1994. pap. text 14.00 (*0-646-14925-3*, Pub. by Wild Peony Pty) UH Pr.

Lee, Lily X., et al, eds. Biographical Dictionary of Chinese Women Vol. 1: The Qing Period, 1644-1911, Vol. I. LC 98-11262. Vol. 1. 424p. (C). (gr. 13). 1998. text 87.95 (*0-7656-0043-9*, East Gate Bk) M E Sharpe.

***Lee, Lily Xiao Hong & Wiles, Sue.** Women of the Long March. 328p. 2000. pap. 17.95 (*1-86448-569-8*, Pub. by Allen & Unwin Pty) IPG Chicago.

Lee, Linda. The Bruce Lee Story. Vaughan, Jack, ed. LC 88-63487. 192p. 1988. pap. text 19.95 (*0-89750-121-7*, 460) Ohara Pubns.

***Lee, Linda.** Edges & Corners: Decorative Techniques for Your Home & Wardrobe. (Illus.). 2000. 19.95 (*1-56158-418-5*) Taunton.

Lee, Linda. English Connections, Bk. 2. LC 93-22804. 182p. 1994. pap. 11.93 (*0-8092-4206-0*) NTC Contemp Pub Co.

— How to Write & Sell Romance Novels: A Step-by-Step Guide. LC 88-81232. 164p. (Orig.). 1988. pap. 9.95 (*0-929195-00-0*) Heartsong Pr.

— Scarves to Make. LC 98-3972. (Illus.). 160p. 1998. pap. 24.95 (*1-56158-256-5*, 070378) Taunton.

— Sewing Luxurious Pillows: Artistic Designs for Home Decor. LC 96-37103. (Illus.). 128p. 1997. 27.95 (*0-8069-9808-3*) Sterling.

***Lee, Linda.** Sewing Luxurious Pillows: Creative Designs for the Home Decor. (Illus.). 128p. 1999. 0.00 (*1-886884-08-0*) Sewing Info Res.

— Success Without College. LC 99-59364. 336p. 2000. 19.95 (*0-385-49669-9*) Doubleday.

Lee, Linda. Transitions, Vol. 1. LC 97-9680. (Illus.). 110p. 1997. pap. text, student ed. 11.50 (*0-19-434622-6*) OUP.

— Transitions, Vol. 1. (Illus.). 152p. 1998. pap. text, teacher ed. 12.95 (*0-19-434623-4*) OUP.

— Transitions, Vol. 2. LC 98-33869. (Illus.). 112p. 1999. student ed. 11.50 (*0-19-434630-7*) OUP.

— Transitions: Integrated English Program, No. 2. (Illus.). 160p. 1999. pap. text, teacher ed. 12.95 (*0-19-434631-5*) OUP.

***Lee, Linda & Brockman, Terra.** Explorations 1: Student Book. LC 99-41361. 2000. write for info. (*0-19-435032-0*) OUP.

Lee, Linda, jt. auth. see Blanton, Linda L.

Lee, Linda, jt. auth. see Winans, Ruthann.

Lee, Linda, ed. see Rodin, Cuia & Rodin, Tibor S.

Lee, Linda, ed. see Savage, Audrey.

Lee, Linda D. Safety Management for Health Care Facilities. (Management & Compliance Ser.: Vol. 5). (Illus.). 275p. 1989. ring bd. 110.00 (*0-87258-512-3*, 055204) Am Hospital.

— Waste Management for Health Care Facilities. rev. ed. (Management & Compliance Ser.: Vol. 1). (Illus.). 300p. 1992. ring bd. 110.00 (*0-87258-585-9*, 055401) Am Hospital.

Lee, Linda F. Blue Waltz. 352p. (Orig.). 1996. mass mkt. 5.99 (*0-515-11791-9*, Jove) Berkley Pub.

— Crimson Lace. 320p. 1997. mass mkt. 5.99 (*0-515-12187-8*, Jove) Berkley Pub.

— Emerald Rain. 1996. mass mkt. 5.99 (*0-515-11979-2*, Jove) Berkley Pub.

— The Wallflower. 272p. (Orig.). 1995. mass mkt. 4.99 (*0-515-11683-1*, Jove) Berkley Pub.

***Lee, Linda Francis.** Dove's Way. 2000. mass mkt. 6.50 (*0-449-00205-5*) Ballantine Pub Grp.

— Swan's Grace. 320p. 2000. mass mkt. 6.99 (*0-449-00206-3*) Ivy Books.

Lee, Linda H. Maggie Rose. LC 96-95475. 192p. 1997. 18.95 (*0-8034-9226-X*, Avalon Bks) Bouregy.

***Lee, Lisa.** Easy Ibook: See It Done, Do It Yourself. 269p. 1999. pap. 19.99 (*0-7897-2272-0*) Que.

— Easy iMac. 2nd ed. (Easy Ser.). 312p. 2000. pap. 19.99 (*0-7897-2339-5*) Que.

— Easy iMac: See It Done, Do It Yourself. LC 98-89540. (Easy ... / Que Ser.). (Illus.). 304p. 1999. pap. 19.99 (*0-7897-1992-4*) Que.

Lee, Lisa. Mac OS 8 Unleashed. 1997. pap. text 39.99 incl. cd-rom (*1-56830-419-6*) Hayden.

— MacWEEK Upgrading & Repairing Your Mac. 750p. 1995. 35.00 (*1-56830-249-5*) Hayden.

Lee, Lisa, jt. auth. see Good, Jim.

Lee, Lisa, ed. see Link, Geoffrey & Beggs, Marjorie.

Lee, Lissa, tr. see Hannah, Valerie.

Lee, Lita. Radiation Protection Manual. 3rd rev. ed. (Illus.). 150p. 1991. pap. 6.95 (*1-880358-00-X*) Lita Lee.

Lee, Lita, jt. auth. see Goldberg, Burton.

Lee, Liz. How to Have a Radical Attitude! Toward God (& Really Believe It) (Spending Prime Time with God Ser.). 208p. (J). (gr. 5-7). 1994. pap. 7.99 (*0-8054-4009-7*, 4240-09) Broadman.

Lee, Liz, jt. auth. see Nally, Susan.

Lee, Lloyd E. The Politics of Harmony: Civil Service, & Social Reform in Baden, 1800-1850. LC 77-92569. 272p. 1980. 38.50 (*0-87413-143-X*) U Delaware Pr.

— The War Years: A Global History of the Second World War. 496p. 1989. 55.00 (*0-04-445266-7*) Routledge.

Lee, Lois B. Rhymes for Talking Time. 1973. text 2.50 (*0-686-09389-5*) Expression.

Lee, Lorraine. The Magic Dulcimer. LC 83-17125. (Illus.). 130p. 1983. pap. 12.95 (*0-938756-09-5*) Yellow Moon.

Lee, Loyd E. World War II. LC 98-22903. (Guides to Historic Events of the Twentieth Century Ser.). 272p. 1999. 39.95 (*0-313-29998-6*) Greenwood.

Lee, Loyd E., ed. World War II in Asia & the Pacific & the War's Aftermath, with General Themes: A Handbook of Literature & Research. LC 98-5348. 528p. 1998. lib. bdg. 95.00 (*0-313-29326-0*, Greenwood Pr) Greenwood.

— World War II: Crucible of the Contemporary World: Commentary & Readings. LC 90-25544. 444p. (C). (gr. 13). 1991. text 81.95 (*0-87332-731-4*) M E Sharpe.

Lee, Loyd E., ed. World War II: Crucible of the Contemporary World: Commentary & Readings. LC 90-25544. 444p. (C). (gr. 13). 1991. pap. text 32.95 (*0-87332-732-2*) M E Sharpe.

Lee, Loyd E., ed. World War II in Europe, Africa & the Americas, with General Sources: A Handbook of Literature & Research. LC 96-37044. 544p. 1997. lib. bdg. 95.00 (*0-313-29325-2*, Greenwood Pr) Greenwood.

Lee, Luke T. Consular Law & Practice. 2nd ed. 772p. 1991. text 190.00 (*0-19-825601-9*) OUP.

Lee, Luther. Slavery Examined in the Light of the Bible. 1988. reprint ed. lib. bdg. 75.00 (*0-7812-0277-9*) Rprt Serv.

— Slavery Examined in the Light of the Bible. LC 76-92434. 185p. 1855. reprint ed. 39.00 (*0-403-00166-8*) Scholarly.

Lee, Lydia. The Kat's Meow. (Romance Ser.: No. 844). 1992. per. 2.59 (*0-373-08844-2*, 5-08844-8) Silhouette.

Lee, Lyle. Words of the Metis Poet. 1977. pap. 3.00 (*0-935350-96-9*) Luna Bisonte.

Lee, Lynn, jt. auth. see Lee, William H.

Lee, M. A., jt. ed. see Koch-Miramond, L.

Lee, M. L., ed. see Ling, W. & Ram, S.

Lee, M. Owen. Death & Rebirth in Virgil's Arcadia. LC 88-24824. (SUNY Series in Classical Studies). 140p. (C). 1989. pap. text 19.95 (*0-7914-0017-4*) State U NY Pr.

— Fathers & Sons in Virgil's Aeneid: Tum Genitor Natum. LC 79-15157. 200p. (C). 1982. text 59.50 (*0-87395-402-5*); pap. text 19.95 (*0-87395-451-3*) State U NY Pr.

— First Intermissions: Twenty-One Great Operas Explored, Explained, & Brought to Life from the Met. (Illus.). 272p. 1996. pap. 12.95 (*0-19-510649-0*) OUP.

— The Olive-Tree Bed & Other Quests. (Robson Classical Lectures). 175p. 1997. text 50.00 (*0-8020-4138-8*) U of Toronto Pr.

— The Olive-Tree Bed & Other Quests, Vol. 4. (Robson Classical Lectures). 186p. 1997. pap. text 16.95 (*0-8020-7984-9*) U of Toronto Pr.

— A Season of Opera: From Orpheus to Ariadne. LC 99-197740. 264p. 1998. text 30.00 (*0-8020-4296-1*) U of Toronto Pr.

— Virgil As Orpheus: A Study of the Georgics. LC 95-7687. (SUNY Series in Classical Studies). 171p. (C). 1996. text 44.50 (*0-7914-2783-8*); pap. text 14.95 (*0-7914-2784-6*) State U NY Pr.

***Lee, M. Owen.** Wagner: The Terrible Man & His Truthful Art. (Illus.). 96p. 1999. pap. 12.95 (*0-8020-8291-2*) U of Toronto Pr.

Lee, M. Owen. Wagner's Ring: Turning the Sky Around. LC 94-29968. 120p. 1994. reprint ed. pap. 10.00 (*0-87910-186-5*) Limelight Edns.

Lee, Mabel & Hua, Meng, eds. Cultural Dialogue & Misreading. (University of Sydney World Literature Ser.: No. 1). 500p. (C). 1996. pap. text 35.00 (*0-9586526-1-9*, Pub. by Wild Peony Pty) UH Pr.

Lee, Mabel & Syrokomia-Stefanowska, A. D., eds. Literacy Intercrossings: East Asia & the West. (University of Sydney World Literature Ser.: Vol. 2). 226p. (C). 1998. pap. text 27.00 (*0-9586526-5-1*) UH Pr.

Lee, Mabel & Syrokomia-Stefanowska, A. D., eds. Modernization of the Chinese Past. (University of Sydney Asian Studies Ser.: No. 1). 195p. (C). 1993. text 20.00 (*0-86758-658-3*, Pub. by Wild Peony Pty) UH Pr.

Lee, Mabel & Wagner, Miriam M. Fundamentals of Body Mechanics & Conditioning: An Illustrated Teaching Manual. LC 75-91765. 377p. 1969. reprint ed. lib. bdg. 65.00 (*0-8371-2417-4*, LEBM, Greenwood Pr) Greenwood.

Lee, Mabel & Wilding, Michael, eds. History, Literature & Society: Essays in Honour of S. N. Mukherjee. LC 97-906481. (C). 1997. 36.00 (*81-7304-201-2*, Pub. by Manohar) S Asia.

Lee, Mabel & Zhang Wu-Ai. Putonghua: A Practical Course in Spoken Chinese. 110p. 1991. pap. text 14.00 (*0-9590735-0-7*, Pub. by Wild Peony Pty) UH Pr.

Lee, Mabel, jt. auth. see Syrokomla-Stefanowska, A. D.

Lee, Mabel, tr. see Lian, Yang.

Lee, Mabel B. Cripple Creek Days. LC 84-5204. (Illus.). xvii, 288p. 1984. reprint ed. pap. 12.95 (*0-8032-7912-4*, Bison Books) U of Nebr Pr.

Lee, Mabel P. Economic History of China. LC 70-78006. (Columbia University. Studies in the Social Sciences: No. 225). reprint ed. 39.50 (*0-404-51225-9*) AMS Pr.

— The Economic History of China with Special Reference to Agriculture. 1976. lib. bdg. 59.95 (*0-8490-1746-7*) Gordon Pr.

Lee, Maggy. Youth, Crime & Police Work. LC 97-26515. 1998. text 65.00 (*0-312-17762-3*) St Martin.

Lee, Manwoo. The Odyssey of Korean Democracy: Korean Politics, 1987-1990. LC 90-7393. 184p. 1990. 52.95 (*0-275-93660-0*, C3660, Praeger Pubs) Greenwood.

Lee, Margaret, jt. auth. see Kim, Kumja P.

Lee, Margaret, tr. see Maisel, John.

Lee, Margaret E. Memories of Nauvoo: Walker County, Alabama. (Illus.). 272p. 1992. 35.00 (*0-9634326-1-3*); pap. 25.00 (*0-9634326-0-5*) Treasured Mem.

Lee, Marian. J. P. Landerz Solve a Mystery, Bk. 1. unabridged ed. (Illus.). 46p. (J). (gr. 3-5). 1982. reprint ed. pap. 5.95 (*1-928632-15-7*) Writers Mrktpl.

— J. P. Landerz Solve a Mystery, Bk. 2. unabridged ed. (Illus.). (J). (gr. 3-5). 1982. reprint ed. pap. 5.95 (*1-928632-19-X*) Writers Mrktpl.

— J. P. Landerz Solve a Mystery, Bk. 2. unabridged ed. (Illus.). (J). (gr. 3-5). 1999. reprint ed. 10.95 (*0-516-01992-9*) Writers Mrktpl.

Lee, Marie. The Curious Cape Cod Skull. LC 94-96731. (Cape Cod Mystery Ser.: Bk. 1). 224p. 1995. 18.95 (*0-8034-9109-3*, Avalon Bks) Bouregy.

— The Fatal Cape Cod Funeral. LC 96-96155. (Cape Cod Mystery Ser.: Bk. 2). 192p. 1996. 18.95 (*0-8034-9204-9*, Avalon Bks) Bouregy.

Lee, Marie. Finding My Voice. 176p. (gr. 7 up). mass mkt. 4.95 (*0-06-447245-0*) HarpC.

Lee, Marie. The Mysterious Cape Cod Manuscript. LC 97-93460. (Cape Cod Mystery Ser.: Bk. 3). 192p. 1997. 18.95 (*0-8034-9238-3*, Avalon Bks) Bouregy.

— Necessary Roughness. LC 96-34185. 176p. (YA). (gr. 7 up). 1996. lib. bdg. 14.89 (*0-06-025130-1*) HarpC Child Bks.

— Necessary Roughness. LC 96-34185. (Illus.). 240p. (YA). (gr. 7 up). 1996. 15.95 (*0-06-025124-7*) HarpC Child Bks.

Lee, Marie G. F Is for Fabuloso. LC 98-56288. 192p. (J). (gr. 5-9). 1999. 15.00 (*0-380-97648-X*, Avon Bks) Morrow Avon.

— Finding My Voice. 1994. 9.09 (*0-606-06979-8*, Pub. by Turtleback) Demco.

— If It Hadn't Been for Yoon Jun. 144p. (J). (gr. 5-9). 1995. mass mkt. 3.99 (*0-380-72347-6*, Avon Bks) Morrow Avon.

Lee, Marie G. If It Hadn't Been for Yoon Jun. 1995. 8.60 (*0-606-07695-6*, Pub. by Turtleback) Demco.

Lee, Marie G. Necessary Roughness. LC 96-34185. 240p. (J). (gr. 12 up). 1998. pap. 4.95 (*0-06-447169-1*) HarpC Child Bks.

— Necessary Roughness. (J). 1998. 10.05 (*0-606-13000-4*, Pub. by Turtleback) Demco.

— Night of the Chupacabras. LC 98-7996. (Avon Camelot Bks.). 144p. (J). (gr. 3-7). 1998. 14.00 (*0-380-97706-0*, Avon Bks) Morrow Avon.

***Lee, Marie G.** Night of the Chupacabras. 128p. 1999. 3.99 (*0-380-79773-9*, Avon Bks) Morrow Avon.

Lee, Marie G. Saying Goodbye. LC 93-26092. 240p. (J). 1994. 16.00 (*0-395-67066-7*) HM.

Lee, Mark. Lost Tribe. LC 98-6905. 256p. 1998. text 22.00 (*0-312-18695-9*) St Martin.

— The Lost Tribe. 288p. 1999. pap. 13.00 (*0-312-20420-5*, Picador USA) St Martin.

— Rebel Armies Deep into Chad. 1989. pap. 5.25 (*0-8222-0934-9*) Dramatists Play.

Lee, Mark R. Antitrust Law & Local Government. LC 84-23722. (Illus.). 220p. 1985. 49.95 (*0-89930-090-1*, LNL/, Quorum Bks) Greenwood.

Lee, Mark W. Finishing Well: Winning in the Race of Faith. LC 95-70932. 208p. 1996. pap. 10.99 (*0-87509-585-2*) Chr Pubns.

Lee, Marshall. Bookmaking: The Illustrated Guide to Editing/Design/Production. 3rd ed. (Illus.). 512p. (C). 1997. 60.00 (*0-393-73018-2*) Norton.

Lee, Marshall, ed. see Howard, Richard.

Lee, Marshall, ed. see McCormack, Edward.

Lee, Marshall, ed. see Theuerkauf, Heike & Fazzino, Charles.

Lee, Marshall M. & Michalka, Wolfgang. German Foreign Policy Nineteen Seventeen to Nineteen Thirty-Three: Continuity or Break? LC 85-22833. 180p. 1987. 19.95 (*0-907582-52-4*) Berg Pubs.

Lee, Martha. A Nation of Islam: An American Millenarian Movement. (Studies in Religion & Society: Vol. 21). 163p. 1989. 79.95 (*0-88946-853-2*) E Mellen.

Lee, Martha F. Earth First! Environmental Apocalypse. (Illus.). 200p. 1995. 44.95 (*0-8156-2677-0*); pap. 19.95 (*0-8156-0365-7*) Syracuse U Pr.

— The Nation of Islam: An American Millenarian Movement. (C). 1996. pap. 17.95 (*0-8156-0375-4*, LENIP) Syracuse U Pr.

***Lee, Martha F., ed.** Millennial Visions: Essays on Twentieth-Century Millenarianism. LC 99-88489. 240p. 2000. 64.00 (*0-275-96690-9*, C6690, Praeger Pubs) Greenwood.

Lee, Martha J., jt. auth. see Bates, Craig D.

***Lee, Martin.** 5-Minute Math Problem of the Day: 250 Fun, Multi-Step Problems That Sharpen Math Reasoning, Numbering. (Illus.). 64p. 2000. pap. text 10.95 (*0-439-17539-9*) Scholastic Inc.

Lee, Martin. Great Graphing. 1993. pap. 12.95 (*0-590-49470-8*) Scholastic Inc.

— Mega-Fun Multiplication Facts Activity Book: Easy Games, Poems, Mini-Books, Reproducibles. 72p. (J). 1998. pap. text 9.95 (*0-590-37350-1*) Scholastic Inc.

— Real Life Math Investigations: 30 Activities That Apply Mathematical Thinking to Real-Life Situa. 96p. (J). 1997. pap. text 10.95 (*0-590-96384-8*) Scholastic Inc.

— The Seminoles. LC 89-8900. (First Bks.). (Illus.). 64p. (J). (gr. 4-7). 1989. lib. bdg. 22.00 (*0-531-10752-3*) Watts.

— The Seminoles. (First Bks.). (Illus.). 64p. (J). (gr. 5-8). 1991. pap. 6.95 (*0-531-15604-4*) Watts.

— Seminoles. (First Bks.). (J). 1991. 11.15 (*0-606-05014-0*, Pub. by Turtleback) Demco.

***Lee, Martin.** Vocabulary Word of the Day: 180 Wonderful Words with Quick & Creative Activities That Expand Kids. (Illus.). 80p. Date not set. 11.95 (*0-439-07749-4*) Scholastic Inc.

***Lee, Martin & Miller, Marcia.** 50 Fabulous Measurement Activities: Hands-On Activities for Exploring Length, Perimeter, Weight, Volume, & Time That Will Make Kids' Measurement Ski. 64p. 2000. pap. 10.95 (*0-590-64406-8*) Scholastic Inc.

Lee, Martin, et al. The Healing Art of Tai Chi: Becoming One with Nature. LC 96-24179. (Illus.). 144p. 1996. pap. 14.95 (*0-8069-4297-5*) Sterling.

— Ride the Tiger to the Mountain: Tai Chi for Health. 1989. pap. 14.00 (*0-201-18077-4*) Addison-Wesley.

Lee, Martin, jt. auth. see Afifi, Abdelmonem.

Lee, Martin, jt. auth. see Miller, Marcia.

Lee, Martin A. The Beast Reawakens: Fascism's Resurgence from Hitler's Spymasters to Today's Neo-Nazi Games & Right-Wing Extremists. LC 96-50023. 560p. (gr. 8). 1997. 24.95 (*0-316-51959-6*) Little.

***Lee, Martin A.** The Beast Reawakens: Fascism's Resurgence from Hitler's Spymasters to Today's Neo-Nazi Games & Right-Wing Extremists. 560p. 1999. pap. 15.95 (*0-415-92546-0*) Routledge.

Lee, Martin A. Unreliable Sources: A Guide to Detecting Bias in News Media. 320p. 1990. 19.95 (*0-8184-0521-X*) Carol Pub Group.

Lee, Martin A. & Shlain, Bruce. Acid Dreams: The CIA, LSD & the Sixties Rebellion. LC 92-1238. 384p. (Orig.). 1987. pap. 14.00 (*0-8021-3062-3*, Grove) Grove-Atltic.

Lee, Martin L. & Strand, Vibeke, eds. Intravenous Immunoglobins in Clinical Practice. LC 97-25515. (Illus.). 536p. 1997. text 165.00 (*0-8247-9881-3*) Dekker.

An Asterisk (*) at the beginning of an entry indicates that the title is appearing for the first time.

An Asterisk (*) at the beginning of an entry indicates that the title is appearing for the first time.

Lee, Mo-Young. Wahrnehmungsdynamik und Ausdruckswahrnehmung: Das Moderne Westliche Konzept der Wahrnehmungsdynamik und seine Entsprechungen im Ostasiatischen Kulturkreis. (Europaische Hochschulschriften, Reihe 6: Bd. 563). (GER., Illus.). IX, 159p. 1996. 42.95 (3-631-30572-9) P Lang Pubng.

Lee, Molly. Bakeen Basketry of the North Alaskan Eskimo. LC 97-35482. (Illus.). 96p. 1998. pap. text 17.95 (0-295-97685-3) U of Wash Pr.

***Lee, Molly C.** Not Just a Pretty Face: Dolls & Human Figurines in Alaska Native Cultures. (Illus.). 2000. pap. 17.95 (0-931163-18-8) U Alaska Museum.

Lee, Mona. Alien Child. LC 98-54879. 288p. 1999. pap. 12.95 (0-940880-62-8) Open Hand.

Lee, Monika. Rousseau's Impact on Shelley: Figuring the Written Self. LC 99-15809. (Salzburger Studies in English Literature Romantic Reassessment: Vol. 154). 212p. 1999. text 89.95 (0-7734-7969-4) E Mellen.

Lee, Monle & Johnson, Carla. Principles of Advertising: A Global Perspective. LC 99-15065. (Illus.). 355p. 1999. lib. bdg. 69.95 (0-7890-0615-4) Haworth Pr.

Lee, Moon H. Purchasing Power Parity. LC 76-22815. (Business Economics & Finance Ser.: No. 9). 144p. reprint ed. pap. 44.70 (0-7837-0965-X, 204127000019) Bks Demand.

Lee, Moses. Identifying an Unknown Compound by Infrared Spectroscopy. Jeffers, J., ed. (Modular Laboratory Program in Chemistry Ser.). 12p. (C). 1997. pap. text 1.75 (0-87540-710-2) Chem Educ Res.

Lee, Motoko, ed. Needs of Foreign Students from Developing Nations at U. S. College & Universities. 179p. 1989. reprint ed. 15.00 (0-912207-27-2) NAFSA Washington.

Lee, Mu-Tsun. Shellfish: Chinese Style Made Easy. (SPA, ENG & CHI., Illus.). 96p. 1998. pap. 15.95 (0-941676-73-0, 11SF9) Wei-Chuan Pub.

Lee, Mu-Tsun & Chen, Hsueh-Hsia. Fish: Chinese Style Made Easy. (SPA & CHI., Illus.). 96p. 1998. pap. 15.95 (0-941676-72-2, 11FS9) Wei-Chuan Pub.

Lee, Muna, ed. Art in Review: Puerto Rico. (Puerto Rico Ser.). 1979. lib. bdg. 59.95 (0-8490-2868-X) Gordon Pr.

***Lee, Muriel.** Guide to Owning a Bull Terrier. (Illus.). 1999. pap. 6.95 (0-7938-2012-X) TFH Pubns.

Lee, Muriel P. The Complete Guide to Whelping & Rearing Puppies. (Illus.). 128p. Date not set. 19.95 (0-7938-0497-3, TS-288) TFH Pubns.

***Lee, Muriel P.** Guide to Owning a Fox Terrier. 1999. pap. 7.95 (0-7938-2013-8) TFH Pubns.

Lee, Muriel P. The Official Book of the Boston Terrier. 176p. 1998. 35.95 (0-7938-0507-4) TFH Pubns.

— The Whelping & Rearing of Puppies: A Complete & Practical Guide. 4th ed. LC 84-60962. (Illus.). 126p. 1984. pap. 11.95 (0-9612546-0-2) Plantin Pr.

Lee, Myoung-Jae. Methods of Moments & Semiparametric Methods for Limited Dependent & Variable Models. LC 95-44882. 256p. 1996. 54.95 (0-387-94626-8) Spr-Verlag.

Lee, Myrtle M. Branches of Poetry. 64p. 1993. pap. 9.95 (1-57087-009-8) Prof Pr NC.

Lee, Nam-In. Edmund Husserl's Phanomenologie der Instinkte. LC 92-36931. (Phaenomenologica Ser.: No. 128). 288p. (C). 1993. lib. bdg. 188.00 (0-7923-2041-7, Pub. by Kluwer Academic) Kluwer Academic.

Lee, Nanci. Self-paced Business Math. 3rd ed. (Math). 448p. (YA). (gr. 11-12). 1986. mass mkt. 32.50 (0-534-06222-9) PWS Pubs.

Lee, Nanci & Kelley, Jane. Accounting: An Introduction, Pt. I. 960p. (C). 1988. student ed. 7.00 (0-15-500449-2) Dryden Pr.

— Accounting: An Introduction, Pt. II. 960p. (C). 1989. write for info. (0-318-67134-4) Dryden Pr.

— Accounting: An Introduction, Pts. I & II. 960p. (C). 1989. trans. write for info. (0-318-67135-2) Dryden Pr.

Lee, Nancy. My Turn. (Illus.). 150p. 1982. pap. 10.95 (0-933704-23-2) Dawn Pr.

Lee, Nancy & Oldham, Linda. Hands on Heritage. LC 78-52312. 320p. 1978. 14.95 (0-931178-01-0) Hands on Pubns.

— Tacos, Tempura & Teem Gok. LC 78-75120. 80p. (J). (ps-8). 1979. 3.95 (0-931178-02-9) Hands on Pubns.

Lee, Nancy H. Search for an Abortionist. LC 74-75135. 1993. lib. bdg. 13.00 (0-226-47001-6) U Ch Pr.

Lee, Natalie H., jt. auth. see Brettell, Richard R.

Lee, Nathaniel. Lucius Junius Brutus. Loftis, John, ed. LC 67-12644. (Regents Restoration Drama Ser.). xxiv, 107p. 1967. pap. text 8.95 (0-8032-5362-1) U of Nebr Pr.

— The Rival Queens. Vernon, P. F., ed. LC 72-91330. (Regents Restoration Drama Ser.). 140p. 1970. pap. 43.40 (0-608-04823-2, 206548000004) Bks Demand.

Lee, Neil M. Patriot above Profit. LC 88-12032. (Illus.). 704p. 1988. 29.95 (0-934395-68-3) Rutledge Hill Pr.

Lee, Nell M. The Role of Tennessee in the War Between the States. (Illus.). 72p. 1995. pap. 10.00 (1-888366-01-X) Dixie Pr.

***Lee, Nella.** Crime & Culture in Yup'ik Villages: An Exploratory Study. LC 00-20255. (Criminology Studies: Vol. 10). 156p. 2000. pap. 69.95 (0-7734-7801-9) E Mellen.

Lee, Nelson. Three Years among the Comanches: The Narrative of Nelson Lee, the Texas Ranger. LC 57-11197. (Western Frontier Library: Vol. 9). 200p. 1991. pap. 11.95 (0-8061-2339-7) U of Okla Pr.

Lee, Newton S. The Nightmares of a Journalist. (Orig.). 1991. pap. 4.79 (0-9627016-1-0) VTLS.

***Lee, Nicholas, ed.** The Catholic Question in Ireland, 1762-1829, 8 vols. 3420p. 2000. 950.00 (1-85506-854-0) Thoemmes Pr.

Lee, Nicholas & Millman, Andrew, eds. ABC of Medical Computing. 85p. 1996. pap. text 42.00 (0-7279-1046-9, Pub. by BMJ Pub) Login Brothers Bk Co.

***Lee, Ning-Cheng.** Reflow Soldering Processes & Troubleshooting: SMT, BGA, CSP & Flip Chip Technologies. 384p. 2000. pap. 49.95 (0-7506-7218-8, Newnes) Buttrwrth-Heinemann.

***Lee, Norman & George, Clive.** Environmental Assessment in Developing Countries & Countries in Transition: Principles, Methods & Practice. LC 99-45846. 300p. 2000. pap. 39.95 (0-471-98557-0); text 95.00 (0-471-98556-2) Wiley.

***Lee, Norman & Kirkpatrick, Colin H., eds.** Sustainable Development & Integrated Appraisal in a Developing World. LC 99-39625. 272p. 2000. 95.00 (1-84064-162-2) E Elgar.

Lee, Norman, jt. ed. see Artis, Mike J.

Lee, Norman, jt. ed. see Kirkpatrick, Colin H.

Lee, Norman C. Blow Molding Design Guide. LC 97-43193. 212p. 1998. 68.00 (1-56990-227-5) Hanser-Gardner.

***Lee, Norman C.** Understanding Blow Molding. LC 00-39696. (Hanser Understanding Bks.). (Illus.). 2000. pap. write for info. (1-56990-301-8) Hanser-Gardner.

Lee, O-Young. The Compact Culture: The Japanese Tradition of "Smaller Is Better" Huey, Robert N., tr. from JPN. (Illus.). 192p. 1992. reprint ed. pap. 6.95 (4-7700-1643-3) Kodansha.

— Things Korean. Holstein, John, tr. (Illus.). 1999. 34.95 (0-8048-2129-1) Tuttle Pubng.

***Lee, Orlan.** Hong Kong Business Law in a Nutshell. 269p. 1999. 40.00 (1-57823-021-7) Juris Pubng.

Lee, Ou-Fan Leo. Shanghai Modern: The Flowering of a New Urban Culture in China, 1930-1945 LC 98-32318. 1999. 24.95 (0-674-80551-8) HUP.

Lee, P. A., ed. Optical & Electrical Properties. (Physics & Chemistry of Materials with Layered Structures Ser.: No. 4). 1976. text 211.50 (90-277-0676-X) Kluwer Academic.

Lee, P. A., et al, eds. Theories of Heavy-Electron Systems. (Journal Comments on Condensed Matter Physics). 65p. 1986. pap. text 58.00 (0-677-21460-X) Gordon & Breach.

Lee, P. A. & Anderson, T. Fault Tolerance: Principles & Practice. 2nd rev. ed. Avizienis, A. et al, eds. (Dependable Computing & Fault-Tolerant Systems Ser.: Vol. 3). xv, 320p. 1990. reprint ed. 94.00 (0-387-82077-9) Spr-Verlag.

Lee, P. A., jt. ed. see Plant, T. M.

Lee, P. C., ed. Comparative Primate Socioecology. LC 98-36457. (Studies in Biological Anthropology: Vol. 22). (Illus.). 370p. (C). 1999. 74.95 (0-521-59336-0) Cambridge U Pr.

Lee, P. K., ed. Structures in the New Millenium: Proceedings of the 4th International Kerensky Conference, Hong Kong, 3-5 September 1997. LC 99-496425. (Illus.). 688p. (C). 1997. 162.00 (90-5410-898-3, Pub. by A A Balkema) Ashgate Pub Co.

Lee, P. L., et al. Process Control & Management. LC 97-77204. 752p. 1997. write for info. (0-7514-0457-8) Kluwer Academic.

Lee, P. N. Environmental Tobacco Smoke & Mortality: A Detailed Review of Epidemiological Evidence Relating Environmental Tobacco Smoke to the Risk of Cancer, Heart Disease & Other Causes of Death in Adults Who Have Never Smoked. (Illus.). xx, 224p. 1992. 155.00 (3-8055-5529-6) S Karger.

Lee, P. S. Mountain Biking in South-Central Colorado. LC 95-90662. (Illus.). 140p. (Orig.). 1995. pap. 12.00 (0-9648169-0-3) Wherever Guidebks.

Lee, P. Y. Lanzhou Lectures on Henstork Integration. (Series in Real Analysis: Vol. 2). 192p. (C). 1989. text 61.00 (9971-5-0891-5); pap. text 28.00 (9971-5-0892-3) World Scientific Pub.

Lee, Pamela, et al. Drawing Is Another Kind of Language: Recent American Drawings from a New York Private Collection. LC 97-42830.Tr. of Zeichnen Ist Eine Andere Art von Sprache. (Illus.). 230p. (Orig.). 1997. pap. 40.00 (0-916724-96-4) Harvard Art Mus.

Lee, Pamela A. Etruscan Chariot. 1991. pap. 5.95 (0-88388-079-2) Bellerophon Bks.

Lee, Pamela A. & Gold, Todd. Pamdemonium. 1998. mass mkt. 24.00 (0-446-60668-5, Warner Vision) Warner Bks.

Lee, Pamela Anderson, see Anderson Lee, Pamela.

Lee, Pamela M. & Matta-Clark, Gordon. Object to Be Destroyed: The Work of Gordon Matta-Clark. LC 99-17978. (Illus.). 240p. 1999. 35.00 (0-262-12220-0) MIT Pr.

Lee, Pao-Chen. Read about China. 1953. 9.95 (0-88710-061-9) Yale Far Eastern Pubns.

Lee, Pao-Chen. Read About China. 1953. audio 8.95 (0-88710-062-7) Yale Far Eastern Pubns.

Lee, Pat, jt. auth. see Van Loan, Sharon.

Lee, Patricia. The Complete Guide to Job Sharing. 192p. 1983. 13.95 (0-8027-0740-8); pap. 6.95 (0-8027-7213-7) Walker & Co.

Lee, Patricia, jt. auth. see Van Loan, Sharon.

Lee, Patricia, jt. ed. see Lee, Ronald S.

Lee, Patrick. Abortion & Unborn Human Life. LC 95-34535. 167p. 1996. pap. text 14.95 (0-8132-0846-7) Cath U Pr.

Lee, Patrick, tr. see Iotti, Paolo.

***Lee, Patrick J.** We Borrow the Earth: An Intimate Portrait of the Gypsy Shamanic Tradition & Culture. 2000. pap. 16.00 (0-7225-3994-0) Thorsons PA.

Lee, Patrick W., jt. auth. see Black, Bert.

Lee, Patty A. Collaborative Practices for Educators: Strategies for Effective Communication. LC 99-70196. 84p. 1999. per. 19.95 (1-890455-26-1) Peytral Pubns.

Lee, Paul. My Heart a Hiding Place. 1986. pap. 7.95 (0-87508-316-1) Chr Lit.

Lee, Paul, ed. Telecommunications & Development in China. LC 97-20064. (Hampton Press Communication Ser.). 288p. (Orig.). 1997. text 69.50 (1-57273-060-9); pap. text 29.50 (1-57273-061-7) Hampton Pr NJ.

Lee, Paul, ed. see Kim, Yong-Jae.

Lee, Paul A. Florence the Goose: A True Story for Children of All Ages. (Illus.). 47p. (J). 1992. 12.95 (0-937011-51-7) Platonic Acad Pr.

— The Quality of Mercy: Homelessness in Santa Cruz 1985-1992. 141p. 1992. pap. 7.95 (0-937011-50-9) Platonic Acad Pr.

Lee, Paul A. & Ryan, Mark. Managing Stress Through Positive Christian Living. 112p. 1998. pap. 9.95 (0-88243-225-7); pap., student ed. 4.95 (0-88243-125-0) Gospel Pub.

Lee, Paul H. The Amateur Radio Vertical Antenna Handbook. 2nd ed. LC 74-83411. (Illus.). 142p. 1984. reprint ed. pap. 9.95 (0-943016-14-2) CQ Commns Inc.

Lee, Paul P., et al. Cataract Surgery: A Literature Review & Ratings of Appropriateness & Cruciality. LC 93-25076. 1993. pap. text 20.00 (0-8330-1405-6, JRA-06) Rand Corp.

— Estimating Eye Care Provider Supply & Workforce Requirements. LC 95-18056. 164p. 1995. pap. 9.00 (0-8330-1652-0, MR-516-AAO) Rand Corp.

Lee, Paul S. A Computerized Demonstration of the Central Limit Theorem in Statistics. 37p. (Orig.). 1978. pap. 3.00 (1-55719-041-0) U NE CPAR.

Lee, Paul S. & Chen, Yeshen. A Study of Boat Ownership in the Omaha-Council Bluffs Metropolitan Area. 26p. (Orig.). 1978. pap. 2.50 (1-55719-079-8) U NE CPAR.

Lee, Paula M., ed. see Massie, Brigid M. & Waters, John.

***Lee, Paulette Moore.** Helping Your Child Succeed in School: Discussion Leader Guide. 120p. 1999. ring bd. 11.00 (0-16-049854-6) USGPO.

***Lee Peng Yee & Vyborny, Rudolf.** The Integral: An Easy Approach after Kurzweil & Henstock. LC 99-24023. (Australian Mathematical Society Lecture Ser.: No. 14). 2000. 39.95 (0-521-77968-5) Cambridge U Pr.

Lee Peng Yee, tr. see Orlicz, W.

Lee, Penny. The Whorf Theory Complex: A Critical Reconstruction. LC 96-21119. (Studies in the History of the Language Sciences: No. 81). x, 324p. 1996. pap. 29.95 (1-55619-619-9); lib. bdg. 79.00 (1-55619-618-0) J Benjamins Pubng Co.

Lee, Peter, ed. Topics in Advanced Language Implementation. 350p. 1991. 46.50 (0-262-12151-4) MIT Pr.

Lee, Peter & Philips, Chris. The Apprentice C++ Programmer: A Touch of Class. LC 97-101475. (Computer Science Ser.). 672p. 1996. pap. 59.95 incl. disk (0-534-95339-5) PWS Pubs.

Lee, Peter A., jt. ed. see Banatre, Michel.

Lee, Peter H. Celebration of Continuity: Themes in Classic East Asian Poetry. LC 78-26145. 276p. reprint ed. pap. 85.60 (0-7837-1520-X, 204179700024) Bks Demand.

— Korean Literature: Topics & Themes. LC 64-19167. (Association for Asian Studies, Monographs & Papers: No. 16). 151p. reprint ed. pap. 46.90 (0-608-18580-9, 200344300028) Bks Demand.

— Songs of Flying Dragons: A Critical Reading. LC 73-92866. (Harvard-Yenching Institute Monographs: No. 22). 352p. 1975. 25.00 (0-674-82075-4) HUP.

Lee, Peter H., ed. Anthology of Korean Literature: From Early Times to the Nineteenth Century. LC 81-69567. 342p. 1981. pap. text 17.00 (0-8248-0756-1) UH Pr.

Lee, Peter H., et al, eds. Sourcebook of Korean Civilization, 2 vols. (Introduction to Asian Civilizations Ser.). 1996. 89.50 (0-231-10444-8) Col U Pr.

— Sourcebook of Korean Civilization: From Early Times to the Sixteenth Century. (Introduction to Asian Civilizations Ser.: Vol. 1). 576p. 1993. text 61.00 (0-231-07912-5) Col U Pr.

— Sourcebook of Korean Civilization: From the Seventeenth Century to the Modern Period. (Introduction to Asian Civilizations Ser.: Vol. 2). 576p. 1996. 52.00 (0-231-07914-1) Col U Pr.

Lee, Peter H., tr. from KOR. Pine River & Lone Peak: An Anthology of 3 Choson Dynasty Poets. LC 90-44433. 208p. 1991. text 21.50 (0-8248-1298-0) UH Pr.

Lee, Peter H. & De Bary, W. Theodore, eds. Sources of Korean Tradition Vol. I: From Early Times Through the 16th Century. LC 96-17701. 480p. 1996. pap. 24.00 (0-231-10567-3) Col U Pr.

Lee, Peter H., ed. see De Bary, William T.

Lee, Peter H., tr. see Kakhun.

Lee, Peter H., tr. see Sukkwon, O.

Lee, Peter K., ed. Confucian-Christian Encounters in Historical & Contemporary Perspective. LC 91-40387. (Religions in Dialogue Ser.: Vol. 5). 500p. 1992. lib. bdg. 109.95 (0-88946-521-5) E Mellen.

Lee, Peter L. Nonlinear Process Control: Applications of Generic Model Control. LC 93-21311. (Advances in Industrial Control Ser.). 1993. 64.95 (0-387-19856-3) Spr-Verlag.

Lee, Peter M. Bayesian Statistics: An Introduction. 2nd ed. (An Arnold Publication). (Illus.). 360p. 1997. pap. text 39.95 (0-340-67785-6) OUP.

Lee, Peter N. Industrial Management & Economic Reform in China, 1949-1984. (Illus.). 344p. 1988. text 38.00 (0-19-584118-2) OUP.

***Lee, Peter Nan-Shong & Lo, Carlos Wing-Hung, eds.** Remaking China's Public Management. LC 00-37270. 200p. 2000. 65.00 (1-56720-337-X, Q337, Quorum Bks) Greenwood.

Lee, Peter W. & Corbonars, Robert S., eds. Rapidly Solidified Materials: Proceedings of an International Conference, San Diego, CA, U. S. A., 3-5 February 1985 i.e. 1986. LC 85-73692. (Illus.). 446p. reprint ed. pap. 138.30 (0-608-16003-2, 203307800083) Bks Demand.

Lee, Phil & Raban, Colin. Welfare Theory & Social Policy: Reform or Revolution? 224p. (C). 1988. text 45.00 (0-8039-8130-9); pap. text 22.00 (0-8039-8131-7) Sage.

***Lee, Phil & Warne, Jeff.** Shrink Your Handicap. LC 99-55798. 256p. 2000. 23.95 (0-7868-6632-2, Pub. by Hyperion) Time Warner.

— Shrink Your Handicap. 256p. 2001. pap. 14.95 (0-7868-8554-8) Little.

Lee, Phil, jt. auth. see Dunford, Martin.

Lee, Phil, jt. auth. see Jepson, Tim.

Lee, Phil, jt. ed. see Langan, Mary.

Lee, Philip. The Democratization of Communication. 223p. 1996. pap. 25.00 (0-7083-1323-X, Pub. by Univ Wales Pr) Paul & Co Pubs.

— Home Pool: Fight to Save the Atlantic Salmon. LC 96-950159. (Illus.). 284p. 1997. pap. 24.95 (0-86492-200-0, Pub. by Goose Ln Edits) Genl Dist Srvs.

Lee, Philip J. Against the Protestant Gnostics. 368p. 1993. reprint ed. pap. text 21.00 (0-19-508436-5) OUP.

***Lee, Philip R. & Estes, Carroll L.** The Nation's Health. LC 00-22254. 2000. write for info. (0-7637-1286-8) Jones & Bartlett.

Lee, Philip R. & Estes, Carroll L. The Nation's Health. 3rd ed. 576p. 1990. pap. 37.50 (0-86720-428-1) Jones & Bartlett.

Lee, Philip R. & Estes, Carroll L., eds. The Nation's Health. 4th ed. LC 93-41200. 432p. 1994. pap. 46.25 (0-86720-840-6) Jones & Bartlett.

Lee, Philip R., et al. The Nation's Health. 5th ed. LC 97-5162. (Health Science Ser.). 448p. 1997. pap. 52.00 (0-7637-0405-9) Jones & Bartlett.

Lee, Philip R., jt. auth. see Lipton, Helene L.

Lee, Phyllis C., jt. ed. see Else, James G.

Lee, Ping, jt. auth. see Robinson, Allan R.

Lee, Ping I. & Good, William R. Controlled-Release Technology: Pharmaceutical Applications. LC 87-17447. (ACS Symposium Ser.: No. 348). (Illus.). 376p. 1987. 76.95 (0-8412-1413-1) Am Chemical.

Lee, Ping I. & Good, William R., eds. Controlled-Release Technology: Pharmaceutical Applications. LC 87-17447. (ACS Symposium Ser.: Vol. 348). 376p. 1987. reprint ed. pap. 116.60 (0-608-03871-7, 206431800008) Bks Demand.

Lee, Ping I., jt. auth. see Amidon, Gordon.

Lee, Pong K. & Ryu, Chi S. Easy Way to Korean Conversation. 3rd rev. ed. (Illus.). 78p. 1997. pap. 18.95 incl. audio (0-930878-17-5) Hollym Intl.

— Let's Talk in Korean. LC 78-72953. 312p. 1998. 14.95 (0-930878-10-8) Hollym Intl.

Lee, Pongsoon & Um, Young A. Libraries & Librarianship in Korea. LC 93-47094. (Guides to Asian Librarianship Ser.). 192p. 1994. lib. bdg. 59.95 (0-313-28743-0, Greenwood Pr) Greenwood.

Lee-Potter, Charlie, jt. auth. see Probert, Christina.

Lee-Potter, Jeremy. A Damn Bad Business: The NHS Deformed. 288p. 1997. 45.00 (0-575-06310-6, Pub. by V Gollancz) Trafalgar.

Lee, Preston. Research in Corporate Social Performance & Policy, Vol. 6. Post, James E. et al, eds. 252p. 1984. 78.50 (0-89232-499-6) Jai Pr.

***Lee, Priscilla.** Wishbone. (California Poetry Ser.: Vol. 5). 88p. 2000. pap. 12.50 (0-9666691-4-2, Pub. by Heyday Bks) SPD-Small Pr Dist.

Lee, Quarterman, et al. Facilities & Workplace Design: An Illustrated Guide. LC 96-22972. (Engineers in Business Ser.). 1996. pap. 25.00 (0-89806-166-0, FACDGN) Eng Mgmt Pr.

Lee, Quarterman, jt. ed. see Wrenall, William.

Lee, R. Chord Dictionary for Guitar Complete Reference with Photos Diagrams & Musical Notation Ron. (Illus.). 48p. 1986. pap. 4.95 (0-7935-5518-3, 50394260) H Leonard.

— Fundamental Guitar Chords with Photo Diagram & Musical Notation Each Chord. (Illus.). 32p. 1986. pap. 3.95 (0-7935-5536-1, 50394250) H Leonard.

Lee, R., ed. Blood Vessel Changes in Hypertension, II. 192p. 1989. lib. bdg. 149.00 (0-8493-4884-6, RC685) CRC Pr.

Lee, R., jt. auth. see Almenas, K.

Lee, R. Alton. Eisenhower & Landrum-Griffin: A Study in Labor-Management Politics. LC 89-35961. 216p. 1990. text 26.00 (0-8131-1683-X) U Pr of Ky.

— Harry S. Truman: Where Did the Buck Stop? Hendrickson, Kenneth E., Jr., ed. (Recent American History Ser.: Vol. 4). XII, 331p. 1991. 52.95 (0-8204-1422-0) P Lang Pubng.

— Truman & Taft-Hartley: A Question of Mandate. LC 80-17251. 254p. 1980. reprint ed. lib. bdg. 45.00 (0-313-22618-0, LETT, Greenwood Pr) Greenwood.

Lee, R. Alton, jt. auth. see Lawrence, P. A.

Lee, R. C., et al, eds. Electrical Trauma: The Pathophysiology, Manifestations, & Clinical Management. (Illus.). 456p. (C). 1992. text 130.00 (0-521-38345-5) Cambridge U Pr.

Lee, R. C., jt. ed. see Hsu, W. L.

Lee, R. F., et al. The Citrus Tristeza Virus. (CAB International Publication). (Illus.). 200p. 1994. pap. text 60.00 (0-85198-848-2) OUP.

Lee, R. G. Co-Unity & Forestry. 315p. 1990. pap. 200.00 (0-7855-2718-4, Pub. by Intl Bk Distr) St Mut.

— Community & Forestry. 315p. 1990. 98.00 (81-7089-430-1, Pub. by Intl Bk Distr) St Mut.

— Community & Forestry. 315p. (C). 1990. 295.00 (0-685-61468-9, Pub. by Intl Bk Distr) St Mut.

— Community & Forestry. 301p. (C). 1990. pap. 375.00 (81-7089-130-2, Pub. by Intl Bk Distr) St Mut.

— An Introduction to Battlefield Weapons Systems & Technology. (Illus.). 160p. 1981. text 29.50 (0-08-027043-3, Pergamon Pr); pap. text 15.00 (0-08-027044-1, Pergamon Pr) Elsevier.

— An Introduction to Battlefield Weapons Systems &

An Asterisk (*) at the beginning of an entry indicates that the title is appearing for the first time.

Technology. (Battlefield Weapons Systems & Technology Ser.: No. 12). (Illus.). 276p. 1985. 28.00 (*0-08-031199-7*, Pergamon Pr); pap. text 24.00 (*0-08-031198-9*, Pergamon Pr) Elsevier.

— Payday Someday & Other Sermons. (Library of Baptist Classics). 1999. pap. 9.99 (*0-8054-1865-2*) Broadman.

Lee, R. G., ed. Battlefield Weapons Systems & Technology Series, 12 vols., Set. 2540p. 1985. text 350.00 (*0-08-030003-0*, Pergamon Pr); pap. text 187.00 (*0-08-030526-1*, Pergamon Pr) Elsevier.

— Defence Terminology. 200p. 1991. 39.00 (*0-08-041320-X*, Pub. by Brasseys); pap. 18.95 (*0-08-041334-X*, Pub. by Brasseys) Brasseys.

Lee, R. G. & International Workshop on Nitric Acid-Based Fertil. Nitric Acid-Based Fertilizers & the Environment: Proceedings: International Workshop Nitric Acid-Based Fertilizers & the Environment (1993: Brussels, Belgium) LC 94-23796. (Special Publications: No. SP-21). 443p. 1994. pap. 40.00 (*0-88090-108-X*) Intl Fertilizer.

Lee, R. G., et al. Guided Weapons. 3rd rev. ed. LC 97-26425. (Land Warfare: Brassey's New Battlefield Weapons & Technology Ser.). (Illus.). 228p. 1998. 39.95 (*1-85753-152-3*, Pub. by Brasseys) Brasseys.

Lee, R. G., ed. see Courtney-Green, P. R.

Lee, R. G., ed. see Everett-Heath, E. J., et al.

Lee, R. G., ed. see Hall, P. S., et al.

Lee, R. G., ed. see Rice, M. A. & Sammes, A. J.

***Lee, R. R.** Pocket Guide to Electrical Equipment. LC 99-39142. (Illus.). 1999. 30.00 (*0-88415-305-3*) Gulf Pub.

Lee, R. R. Pocket Guide to Electrical Equipment & Instrumentation. 2nd ed. (Illus.). 340p. (Orig.). 1991. pap. 30.00 (*0-87201-234-4*, 1234) Gulf Pub.

— Pocket Guide to Flanges, Fittings, & Piping Data. 2nd ed. (Illus.). 176p. (Orig.). 1992. pap. 30.00 (*0-88415-023-2*, 5023) Gulf Pub.

***Lee, R. R.** Pocket Guide to Flanges, Fittings & Piping Data. 3rd ed. LC 99-38352. 1999. 30.00 (*0-88415-310-X*) Gulf Pub.

— Pocket Guide to Instrumentation. LC 99-41792. 1999. 30.00 (*0-88415-308-8*) Gulf Pub.

Lee, R. S., et al, eds. Aerothermodynamics in Combustors: IUTAM Symposium, Taipei, Taiwan, 1991. LC 92-13620. (International Union of Theoretical & Applied Mechanics Symposia Ser.). ix, 353p. 1992. 149.95 (*0-387-55404-1*) Spr-Verlag.

Lee, R. W., ed. see Macdonnell, John.

Lee, R. Wayne. Federal Prisons: Fact & Fiction. 1987. pap. text 34.95 (*0-685-20105-8*) Cambridge Law.

— Federal Prisons: Fact & Fiction, 1987. LC 87-90764. 219p. (Orig.). (C). 1987. pap. text 34.95 (*0-685-54307-2*, Chicago Law Bk) Cambridge Law.

***Lee, R. Y.** Damage Progression Model Theory: SCDAP/RELAP5/MOD 3.2 Code Manual. 216p. 1998. per. 18.00 (*0-16-062935-7*) USGPO.

— Developmental Assessment: SCDAP/RELAP5/MOD 3.2 Code Manual. 376p. 1998. per. 22.00 (*0-16-062938-1*) USGPO.

— Guide & Input Manual: SCDAP/RELAP5/MOD 3.2 Code Manual. 340p. 1998. per. 27.00 (*0-16-062936-5*) USGPO.

— Interface Theory: SCDAP/RELAP5/MOD 3.2 Code Manuall. 66p. 1998. pap. 5.50 (*0-16-062939-X*) USGPO.

— Matpro, a Library of Materials Properties for Light-Water-Reactor Accident Analysis: SCDAP/RELAP5/MOD 3.2 Code Manual. 736p. 1998. per. 61.00 (*0-16-062937-3*) USGPO.

Lee, R. Y., ed. 14th International Conference on Computers & Their Applications: Proceedings - CATA-99, April 7-9, 1999, Cancun, Mexico. 397p. (C). 1999. write for info. (*1-880843-27-7*) Int Soc Comp App.

***Lee, Rachel.** After I Dream. LC 00-36017. 2000. write for info. (*1-57490-278-4*, Beeler LP Bks) T T Beeler.

— After I Dream. 400p. 2000. mass mkt. 6.50 (*0-446-60654-5*) Warner Bks.

Lee, Rachel. Before I Sleep. 390p. 1999. mass mkt. 6.50 (*0-446-60653-7*, Pub. by Warner Bks) Little.

— The Catch of Conard County. (Harlequin World's Most Eligible Ser.). 1998. per. 4.50 (*0-373-65018-3*) Harlequin Bks.

— Caught. 1997. per. 5.99 (*1-55166-298-1*) Harlequin Bks.

— Le Coeur Mis a Nu. (Amours d'Aujourd'Hui Ser.: Vol. 293). (FRE.). 1998. mass mkt. 4.99 (*0-373-38293-6*, 1-38294-4) Harlequin Bks.

— Conard County. (Silhouette Promo Ser.). 1999. per. 5.99 (*0-373-48383-X*, 1-48383-3) Harlequin Bks.

— A Conard County Homecoming. (By Request Ser.). 1999. per. 4.99 (*0-373-48394-5*, 1-48394-0) Harlequin Bks.

— A Conard County Reckoning. (Silhouette Promo Ser.). 1996. per. 4.99 (*0-373-48317-1*, 1-48317-1, Wrldwide Lib) Harlequin Bks.

— Cowboy Comes Home. (Intimate Moments Ser.). 1998. per. 4.25 (*0-373-07865-X*, 1-07865-8) Silhouette.

— Cowboy Cop. (Montana Mavericks Ser.). 1995. per. 3.99 (*0-373-50176-5*, 1-50176-6) Harlequin Bks.

— Defying Gravity. (Intimate Moments Ser.: No. 430). 1992. mass mkt. 3.39 (*0-373-07430-1*, 5-07430-7) Harlequin Bks.

— Defying Gravity. (Men at Work Ser.). 1998. per. 4.50 (*0-373-81021-0*) Harlequin Bks.

— Destination: Conard County. 1996. per. 5.99 (*0-373-20121-4*, 1-20121-9) Harlequin Bks.

— A Fateful Choice. 1996. per. 5.99 (*1-55166-173-X*, 1-66173-5, Mira Bks) Harlequin Bks.

— Involuntary Daddy: Conard County. (Intimate Moments Ser.: No. 955). 1999. per. 4.25 (*0-373-07955-9*, 1-07955-7) Silhouette.

— Ironheart. (Intimate Moments Ser.). 1993. per. 3.39 (*0-373-07494-8*, 5-07494-3) Silhouette.

— Lost Warriors. (And the Winner Is...Ser.). 1997. mass mkt. 3.99 (*0-373-48347-3*, 1-48347-8) Harlequin Bks.

— Lost Warriors: American Hero, Conard County. (Intimate Moments Ser.). 1993. per. 3.50 (*0-373-07535-9*, 5-07535-3) Silhouette.

— Miss Emmaline & the Archangel. (Intimate Moments Ser.). 1993. mass mkt. 3.39 (*0-373-07482-4*, 5-07482-8) Silhouette.

— Nighthawk. (Conard County Ser.). 1997. per. 3.99 (*0-373-07781-5*, 1-07781-7) Silhouette.

***Lee, Rachel.** Nighthawk. large type ed. (Silhouette Romance Ser.). 1999. 21.95 (*0-373-59650-2*) Harlequin Bks.

Lee, Rachel. Point of No Return. 1994. per. 3.50 (*0-373-07566-9*) Silhouette.

— A Question of Justice. (Intimate Moments Ser.). 1995. per. 3.50 (*0-373-07613-4*, 1-07613-2) Silhouette.

— Snow in September. 2000. per. 5.99 (*1-55166-554-9*, Mira Bks) Harlequin Bks.

***Lee, Rachel.** When I Wake. 2000. mass mkt. 6.99 (*0-446-60655-3*) Warner Bks.

***Lee, Rachel C.** The Americas of Asian American Literature: Gendered Fictions of Nation & Transnation. LC 99-14575. 208p. 1999. 49.50 (*0-691-05960-8*, Pub. by Princeton U Pr) Cal Prin Full Svc.

— The Americas of Asian American Literature: Gendered Fictions of Nation & Transnation. LC 99-14575. 208p. (C). 1999. pap. text 16.95 (*0-691-05961-6*, Pub. by Princeton U Pr) Cal Prin Full Svc.

Lee, Ralph E. Nine Ways to Buy a House. 100p. (Orig.). 1981. pap. 6.95 (*0-9606268-0-8*) ProPress Pub.

Lee, Ranae. Heaven's Helpers. (Illus.). 28p. 1998. 8.99 (*1-58050-028-5*, 40-6157) Provo Craft.

Lee, Rand B. Pleasures of the Cottage Garden. LC 98-43511. (Illus.). 144p. 1998. 27.50 (*1-56799-695-7*, Friedman-Fairfax) M Friedman Pub Grp Inc.

Lee, Randal. A Gift for Santa. LC 97-61002. (Illus.). 64p. 1997. pap. 7.99 (*1-57921-036-8*) WinePress Pub.

Lee, Randall B., ed. Model Railroading's Guide to Modeling & Detailing Diesels, Vol. 1. (Illus.). 88p. 1991. pap. 9.95 (*0-9612692-4-3*) Rocky Mntn Pub Co.

— Model Railroading's Guide to Modeling & Detailing Diesels, Vol. II. (Illus.). 128p. 1993. pap. 14.95 (*0-9612692-7-8*) Rocky Mntn Pub Co.

Lee, Randall B., ed. see Nall, Bruce N.

Lee, Randy. Diesel Modelers Guide, Vol. 2. (Illus.). 112p. 1997. pap. 14.95 (*0-9655365-3-X*, Model Railroading) Highlands Station.

— Diesel Modeler's Guide: Photos, Drawings & Projects for the Diesel Modeler, Vol. 1. (Illus.). 112p. 1997. pap. 14.95 (*0-9655365-0-5*, Model Railroading) Highlands Station.

— Intermodal Modeler's Guide, Vol. 1. 112p. 1997. pap. 14.95 (*0-9655365-1-3*, Model Railroading) Highlands Station.

— Intermodal Modeler's Guide, Vol. 2. (Illus.). 112p. 1997. pap. 14.95 (*0-9655365-2-1*, Model Railroading) Highlands Station.

Lee, Raphael C., et al, eds. Electrical Injury: A Multidisciplinary Approach to Therapy, Prevention, & Rehabilitation. LC 94-9282. (Annals Ser.: Vol. 720). 299p. 1994. 95.00 (*0-89766-864-2*); pap. 95.00 (*0-89766-865-0*) NY Acad Sci.

***Lee, Raymond L.** The Tao of Representation: Postmodernity, Asia, & the West. LC 99-31578. 1999. lib. bdg. 59.00 (*1-56072-695-4*) Nova Sci Pubs.

Lee, Raymond L. & Ackerman, Susan E. Sacred Tensions: Modernity & Religious Transformation in Malaysia. LC 97-4725. (Studies in Comparative Religion). (Illus.). 190p. 1997. 29.95 (*1-57003-167-3*) U of SC Pr.

***Lee, Raymond L. & Fraser, Alistair B.** The Rainbow Bridge: Rainbows in Art, Myth & Science. LC 99-39847. (Illus.). 2001. pap. write for info. (*0-271-01977-8*) Pa St U Pr.

Lee, Raymond L. & Palmer, Dorothy A. Guide to Government by the People: National. 12th ed. 208p. (C). 1984. student ed. 8.95 (*0-685-08771-9*) P-H.

Lee, Raymond M. Dangerous Fieldwork. (Qualitative Research Methods Ser.: Vol. 34). 96p. 1994. 24.00 (*0-8039-5660-6*); pap. 10.50 (*0-8039-5661-4*) Sage.

— Doing Research on Sensitive Topics. (Illus.). 240p. 1993. 55.00 (*0-8039-8860-5*); pap. 18.95 (*0-8039-8861-3*) Sage.

— Mixed & Matched: Interreligious Courtship & Marriage in Northern Ireland. (Class, Ethnicity, Gender, & the Democratic Nation Ser.: Vol. 2). 154p. (C). 1992. lib. bdg. 39.50 (*0-8191-8480-2*) U Pr of Amer.

***Lee, Raymond M.** Unobtrusive Methods in Social Research. LC 99-56325. (Understanding Social Research Ser.). 2000. pap. 27.95 (*0-335-20051-6*) OpUniv Pr.

Lee, Raymond M., ed. Redundancy, Layoffs & Plant Closures: Their Nature & Social Impact. 352p. 1986. 59.95 (*0-7099-4129-3*, Pub. by C Helm) Routldge.

Lee, Raymond M., jt. auth. see Fielding, Nigel.

Lee, Raymond M., jt. auth. see Renzetti, Claire M.

Lee, Raymond M., jt. ed. see Fielding, Nigel G.

Lee, Rebecca H. Gossamer. 1999. mass mkt. 5.99 (*0-515-12430-3*, Jove) Berkley Pub.

***Lee, Rebecca Hagan.** Hint of Heather. (Seduction Romance Ser.). 2000. mass mkt. 5.99 (*0-515-12905-4*, Jove) Berkley Pub.

Lee, Rebecca Hagan. Whisper Always. 1999. mass mkt. 6.50 (*0-515-12712-4*, Jove) Berkley Pub.

Lee, Rebecca L. Concha: My Dancing Saint. LC 97-534. (Illus.). 240p. (YA). (gr. 7-12). 1997. pap. 12.95 (*1-56474-215-6*) Fithian Pr.

Lee, Rebecca S. An Alphabet about Families Living with HIV/AIDS. (Illus.). 120p. 1998. student ed. 11.97 (*0-9629365-5-3*) Childrens Lgcy.

— Mary Austin Holley: A Biography. (Elma Dill Russell Spencer Foundation Ser.: No. 2). (Illus.). 480p. 1987. reprint ed. pap. 14.95 (*0-292-75098-6*) U of Tex Pr.

Lee, Regina. Anatomical Gift: Whole Body Donation Guide. unabridged ed. (Illus.). 144p. 1997. per. 24.50 (*0-9657966-0-4*) Consumer Ed Serv.

Lee, Reiko T., jt. ed. see Lee, Y. C.

Lee, Rensselaer W. Names on Trees: Ariosto into Art. LC 76-3270. (Princeton Essays on the Arts Ser.: No. 3). (Illus.). 125p. reprint ed. pap. 38.80 (*0-608-06422-X*, 206663500008) Bks Demand.

Lee, Rensselaer W., III. Smuggling Armageddon: The Nuclear Black Market in the Former Soviet Union & Europe, Vol. 1. LC 98-3793. (Illus.). 224p. 1998. text 26.95 (*0-312-21156-2*) St Martin.

Lee, Rensselaer W. The White Labyrinth: Cocaine & Political Power. 256p. 1989. 39.95 (*0-88738-285-1*) Transaction Pubs.

Lee, Rensselaer W., III. The White Labyrinth: Cocaine & Political Power. 262p. (C). 1991. pap. text 24.95 (*1-56000-565-3*) Transaction Pubs.

Lee, Reta. The Ingredient Called Love. (Illus.). 520p. 1997. pap. 10.99 (*1-57502-578-7*, PO1662) Morris Pubng.

Lee, Reuben, et al. Electronic Transformers & Circuits. 3rd ed. LC 87-34062. 432p. 1988. 162.50 (*0-471-81976-X*) Wiley.

Lee, Rex E. The Case for Federalism. (Grace A. Tanner Lecture in Human Values Ser.). 11p. 1985. 7.50 (*0-910153-03-5*) E T Woolf.

— A Lawyer Looks at the Constitution. LC 81-1571. (Illus.). xii, 229p. 1981. pap. 12.95 (*0-8425-1904-1*, Friends of the Library) Brigham.

— What Do Mormons Believe? LC 92-36087. vii, 118p. 1992. 12.95 (*0-87579-639-7*) Deseret Bk.

Lee, Rex E., et al. A Marathon of Faith. LC 96-10450. xiii, 194p. 1996. 15.95 (*1-57345-163-0*) Deseret Bk.

Lee, Ricardo. Salome: Filmscript by Richard Lee. Brion, Rofel, tr. LC 92-72850. (Illus.). (Orig.). (C). 1992. pap. text 8.95 (*1-881261-07-7*); lib. bdg. 27.95 (*1-881261-06-9*) U Wisc Ctr SE Asian.

Lee, Richard. 1101 Water Gardening Questions & Answers. (Illus.). 335p. 1999. pap. 24.95 (*0-9649814-1-6*) W Tricker.

— Forest Microclimatology. LC 77-21961. (Illus.). 276p. 1978. text 69.50 (*0-231-04156-X*) Col U Pr.

***Lee, Richard.** The Healing Touch of Jesus: God's Passion & Power to Make You Whole. 208p. 2000. 17.99 (*1-58229-126-8*) Howard Pub LA.

Lee, Richard. Windows NT Microsoft Cluster Server. LC 99-218919. (Illus.). 375p. 1999. pap. 49.99 incl. cd-rom (*0-07-882500-8*) McGraw.

— You Can Tell Your Kid Will Grow up to Be a Librarian When: Cartoons about the Profession. LC 92-50309. (Illus.). 128p. 1992. pap. 23.00 (*0-89950-743-3*) McFarland & Co.

Lee, Richard, ed. & illus. see Rubin, Rhea J. & Suvak, Daniel.

***Lee, Richard A., II & Schell, Roger R.** 15 Top Level Security Points for Global Electronic Commerce. 63p. 1999. spiral bd. 37.00 (*0-89258-363-0*, D089) Assn Inform & Image Mgmt.

Lee, Richard B. The Dobe Ju-'hoansi. 2nd ed. (Case Studies in Cultural Anthropology). (Illus.). 224p. (C). 1993. pap. text 23.50 (*0-03-032284-7*) Harcourt Coll Pubs.

***Lee, Richard B. & Daly, Richard H., eds.** The Cambridge Encyclopedia of Hunters & Gatherers. LC 98-38671. (Illus.). 531p. (C). 2000. 125.00 (*0-521-57109-X*) Cambridge U Pr.

Lee, Richard B. & DeVore, Irven, eds. Kalahari Hunter-Gatherers: Studies of the Kung San & Their Neighbors. (Illus.). 390p. 1976. pap. 18.95 (*0-674-49985-9*) HUP.

— Man the Hunter. LC 67-17603. 431p. 1968. pap. text 31.95 (*0-202-33032-X*) Aldine de Gruyter.

Lee, Richard B., jt. ed. see Leacock, Eleanor B.

Lee, Richard C. UML & C++ A Practical Guide to Object-Oriented Development. LC 97-7688. 512p. (C). 1997. pap. 49.00 (*0-13-619719-1*) P-H.

Lee, Richard D. California Expert Witness Guide: June 1993 Update. 2nd ed. Chapin, John K., ed. LC 91-71424. 254p. 1993. 40.00 (*0-88124-658-1*, CP-31682) Cont Ed Bar-CA.

Lee, Richard D. & Matos, Paula C. California Decedent Estate Practice: June 1993 Update, Vol. 3. Tom, Janette, ed. LC 86-70193. 436p. 1993. 40.00 (*0-88124-661-1*, ES-30865) Cont Ed Bar-CA.

Lee, Richard E., Jr., et al, eds. Biological Ice Nucleation & Its Applications. LC 95-75812. (Illus.). ix, 370p. 1995. 89.00 (*0-89054-172-8*) Am Phytopathol Soc.

Lee, Richard H. Bioelectric Vitality: Exploring the Science of Human Energy. LC 96-92923. (Illus.). 80p. 1997. 24.95 (*1-889983-04-7*) China Hlthways.

— Life of Arthur Lee, 2 Vols., Set. LC 69-18528. (Select Bibliographies Reprint Ser.). 1977. 54.95 (*0-8369-5010-0*) Ayer.

Lee, Richard M. Mr. Lincoln's City: An Illustrated Guide to the Civil War Sites of Washington. LC 81-3267. (Illus.). 176p. 1981. pap. 17.95 (*0-914440-48-9*, EPM) Howell Pr VA.

Lee, Richard S. & Lee, Mary P. Caffeine & Nicotine. (Drug Abuse Prevention Library). 64p. (gr. 7-12). 1997. pap. 6.95 (*1-56838-168-9*, 1760 A) Hazelden.

— Careers for Car Buffs & Other Mechanical Types. LC 96-48286. (Illus.). 162p. 1997. 14.95 (*0-8442-4338-8*, 43388, VGM Career); pap. 9.95 (*0-8442-4339-6*, 43396, VGM Career) NTC Contemp Pub Co.

— Coping Through Effective Time Management. (Coping Ser.). 192p. (YA). (gr. 7-12). 1991. lib. bdg. 17.95 (*0-8239-1234-5*) Rosen Group.

— Everything You Need to Know about Natural Disasters & Post-Traumatic Stress Disorder. LC 95-13665. (Need to Know Library). (Illus.). 64p. (YA). (gr. 7-12). 1996. lib. bdg. 17.95 (*0-8239-2053-4*) Rosen Group.

Lee, Richard S. & Lee, Mary Price. Nicotine & Caffeine, 8 vols. LC 94-2279. (Drug Abuse Prevention Library). (Illus.). 64p. (YA). (gr. 7-12). 1998. lib. bdg. 17.95 (*0-8239-2745-8*) Rosen Group.

Lee, Richard S., jt. auth. see Lee, Mary P.

Lee, Richard T., et al, eds. Overview of Cardiac Surgery for the Cardiologist. LC 93-3832. 1993. 64.00 (*0-387-94066-9*) Spr-Verlag.

Lee, Richard T. & Braunwald, Eugene, eds. Atlas of Cardiac Imaging. LC 97-36794. 1998. text 115.00 (*0-443-07567-0*) Church.

Lee, Richard T., et al. Overview of Cardiac Surgery for the Cardiologist. (Illus.). 190p. 1993. write for info. (*3-540-94066-9*) Spr-Verlag.

Lee, Richard V. Current Obstetric Medicine, 5. 270p. 1999. text 69.95 (*0-8151-5553-0*) Mosby Inc.

***Lee, Richard V. & Davidoff, Frank, eds.** Annals of Internal Medicine: Time & Medicine. (Illus.). 91p. 2000. pap. text 16.00 (*0-943126-96-7*, 330301890) Amer Coll Phys.

Lee, Richard V., et al. Medical Care of the Pregnant Patient. LC 99-12514. (Women's Health Ser.). 2000. pap. 55.00 (*0-943126-81-9*, 330301190) Amer Coll Phys.

Lee, Ricky S., jt. auth. see Lau, John H.

***Lee, Robert.** The Clash of Civilizations: An Intrusive Gospel in Japanese Civilization. LC 99-52806. 144p. 2000. 12.00 (*1-56338-304-7*, Pub. by TPI PA) Morehouse Pub.

Lee, Robert. Death Rites. 324p. (C). 1996. pap. 25.99 (*0-415-14026-9*) Routledge.

— Fort Meade & the Black Hills. LC 91-4362. (Illus.). xii, 321p. (C). 1991. pap. 14.95 (*0-8032-7961-2*, Bison Books) U of Nebr Pr.

— Guide to Chinese American Philanthropy & Charitable Giving Patterns. 165p. (Orig.). 1990. pap. 25.00 (*0-9627474-0-8*) Pathway CA.

— Guiding Elliott. LC 97-3121. 192p. 1997. 22.95 (*1-55821-603-0*) Lyons Pr.

— Outline Studies in Acts. LC 87-3083. 128p. 1987. reprint ed. pap. 5.99 (*0-8254-3141-7*) Kregel.

— Outline Studies in Galatians. LC 87-3096. 128p. 1987. reprint ed. pap. 5.99 (*0-8254-3143-3*) Kregel.

— Outline Studies in John. LC 87-3623. 144p. 1987. reprint ed. pap. 5.99 (*0-8254-3140-9*) Kregel.

— Outline Studies in Romans. LC 87-3094. 112p. 1987. reprint ed. pap. 5.99 (*0-8254-3142-5*) Kregel.

Lee, Robert. The Outlined Bible. 1982. mass mkt. 14.99 (*0-310-44821-2*, 10465P) Zondervan.

Lee, Robert. Persistent Seraching for the True Light: Life & Spiritual Journal of a Taiwanese Immigrant. 103p. 1993. pap. 4.95 (*0-9631789-4-6*) Evan Formosan.

Lee, Robert, ed. Landlord & Tenant. (C). 1991. text 22.00 (*1-85431-137-9*, Pub. by Blackstone Pr) Gaunt.

Lee, Robert A. Alistair MacLean: The Key Is Fear. LC 76-29047. (Milford Series: Popular Writers of Today: Vol. 2). 60p. 1976. pap. 13.00 (*0-89370-203-X*) Millefleurs.

— First Impressions: How to Present an Inviting Church Facility. Miller, Herb, ed. LC 93-12891. (Effective Church Ser.). 144p. (Orig.). 1993. pap. 12.95 (*0-687-07855-5*) Abingdon.

Lee, Robert D. Overcoming Tradition & Modernity: The Search for Islamic Authenticity. LC 97-7391. 224p. (C). 1997. pap. text 23.00 (*0-8133-2798-9*, Pub. by Westview) HarpC.

Lee, Robert D., Jr. Public Personnel Systems. 3rd ed. 448p. 1993. 57.00 (*0-8342-0392-8*, 20392) Aspen Pub.

Lee, Robert D. & Johnson, Ronald W. Public Budgeting Systems. 6th ed. LC 97-47677. 540p. 1998. 49.00 (*0-8342-1044-4*) Aspen Pub.

Lee, Robert E. AIDS in America: Our Chances, Our Choices. LC 87-51105. vi, 208p. 1987. 49.50 (*0-87875-355-9*); pap. 25.00 (*0-87875-357-5*) Whitston Pub.

Lee, Robert E. Blackbeard the Pirate: A Reappraisal of His Life & Times. LC 74-75752. 264p. 1984. pap. 10.95 (*0-89587-032-0*) Blair.

— Colonel Noah Lee of Salisbury, Conn. & Castleton, Vt. & His Descendants: A 1990 Supplement to the 1897 Edition of John Lee of Farmington, Conn., & His Descendants - Thomas Branch. (Illus.). 171p. (Orig.). 1990. pap., per. 20.00 (*0-9625530-0-X*) R E Lee.

— A Copyright Guide for Authors. LC 96-181604. 250p. 1996. pap. 15.95 (*0-9627106-8-7*) Kent Communs.

— The Dialogues of Lewis & Clark: A Narrative Poem. LC 78-67631. (Illus.). 87p. reprint ed. pap. 30.00 (*0-8357-5504-5*, 203511900093) Bks Demand.

— ISDN Consultant: A Guide to Stressfree Telecommunications. 272p. (C). 1996. pap. text 29.95 (*0-13-259052-2*) P-H.

— The Library Sponsored Discussion Group. LC 57-4833. 87p. reprint ed. pap. 30.00 (*0-608-12799-X*, 202421000035) Bks Demand.

— North Carolina Family Law Vol. 1: 1989 Cumulative Supplement. 1989. pap. write for info. (*0-87215-893-4*, 64277-10, MICHIE) LEXIS Pub.

— Phycology. 2nd ed. (Illus.). 661p. (C). 1989. text 125.00 (*0-521-36502-3*); pap. text 44.95 (*0-521-36744-1*) Cambridge U Pr.

***Lee, Robert E.** Phycology. 3rd ed. LC 98-53255. (Illus.). 600p. (C). 1999. 100.00 (*0-521-63090-8*); pap. 44.95 (*0-521-63883-6*) Cambridge U Pr.

Lee, Robert E. The Recollections & Letters of General Robert E. Lee. (Civil War Ser.). 471p. 1993. 12.95 (*0-914427-66-0*) W S Konecky Assocs.

***Lee, Robert E.** The Recollections & Letters of General Robert E. Lee. Lee, Robert E., Jr., ed. 471p. 2000. reprint ed. 40.00 (*0-7881-9225-6*) DIANE Pub.

L

L

Lee, Robert E. Trademake Guide for Entrepreneurs. 200p. 1996. 29.95 (*1-888206-04-7*) Kent Communs.

— Trademaker Guide for Entrepreneurs. 200p. 1996. pap. text 15.95 (*1-888206-05-5*) Kent Communs.

— Victory at Guadalcanal. (World at War Ser.). 1983. mass mkt. 3.50 (*0-8217-1198-9*, Zebra Kensgtn) Kensgtn Pub Corp.

Lee, Robert E. & Emerson, Shirley, eds. The Eclectic Trainer. (C). 1999. pap. text 29.95 (*1-884228-28-3*) Geist & Russell.

Lee, Robert E. & Shosky, John. In the Public Interest: The Life of Robert Emmet Lee from the FIB to FCC. 284p. 1995. pap. 24.50 (*0-7618-0752-7*) U Pr of Amer.

— In the Public Interest: The Life of Robert Emmet Lee from the FIB to FCC. LC 95-43823. (Illus.). 284p. (C). 1995. 32.50 (*0-7618-0193-6*) U Pr of Amer.

Lee, Robert E., et al. North Carolina Family Law with 1991 Cumulative Supplements, 4 vols., Set. 4th ed. 1987. 240.00 (*0-87215-473-4*, 64270-10, MICHIE) LEXIS Pub.

Lee, Robert E., jt. auth. see Lawrence, Jerome.

Lee, Robert E., ed. see Lee, Henry.

Lee, Robert E., Jr., ed. see Lee, Robert E.

***Lee, Robert E. A.** Mathilda's Journey: The Life of Clara Mathilda Glasrud Lee. LC 99-76009. (Illus.). 288p. 2000. pap. 16.95 (*0-9675900-0-0*, Pub. by Real World Comm) ACCESS Pubs Network.

Lee, Robert F. Conrad's Colonialism. LC 68-30868. (Studies in English Literature: No. 54). 1969. text 52.35 (*3-11-000273-6*) Mouton.

Lee, Robert G. Broken Trust, Broken Land: Freeing Ourselves from the War over the Environment. LC 94-72358. 220p. (Orig.). 1994. pap. 14.95 (*1-885221-02-9*) BookPartners.

— Orientals: Asian Americans in Popular Culture. LC 98-25853. (Asian American History & Culture Ser.). (Illus.). 288p. 2000. text 59.50 (*1-56639-658-1*) Temple U Pr.

***Lee, Robert G.** Orientals: Asian Americans in Popular Culture. (Asian American History & Culture Ser.). (Illus.). 288p. 2000. pap. 19.95 (*1-56639-753-7*) Temple U Pr.

Lee, Robert G. SWOT Constitutional & Administrative Law. 204p. (C). 1990. 80.00 (*1-85431-030-5*, Pub. by Blackstone Pr) St Mut.

Lee, Robert G. & Stallworthy, Mark. SWOT Constitutional & Administrative Law. 4th ed. 252p. 1995. pap. 22.00 (*1-85431-337-1*, Pub. by Blackstone Pr) Gaunt.

Lee, Robert G. & Wheeler, Gordon, eds. The Voice of Shame: Silence & Connection in Psychotherapy. (Gestalt Institute of Cleveland Book Ser.). 416p. 1996. 38.95 (*0-88163-282-1*) Analytic Pr.

Lee, Robert G., jt. auth. see Wallington, Peter.

Lee, Robert G., jt. ed. see Morgan, Derek.

Lee, Robert G., jt. ed. see Wallington, Peter.

***Lee, Robert H.** Economics for Healthcare Managers. LC 00-39699. 2000. write for info. (*1-56793-130-8*) Health Admin Pr.

Lee, Robert J. & Freedman, Arthur M., eds. Consultation Skills Readings. 148p. (Orig.). 1984. pap. 18.95 (*0-9610392-1-3*) NTL Inst.

Lee, Robert L. Everything about Theatre! A Comprehensive Survey about the Arts & Crafts of the Stage. Zapel, Theodore O., ed. LC 96-6742. 224p. (YA). (gr. 9 up). 1996. pap. 17.95 (*1-56608-019-3*, B200) Meriwether Pub.

— Fever Saga. (Illus.). 160p. (Orig.). 1985. pap. 6.95 (*0-9615377-0-1*) Heirloom Pr.

Lee, Robert M. K. W., ed. Blood Vessel Changes in Hypertension, I. 216p. 1989. lib. bdg. 141.00 (*0-8493-4883-8*, RC685) CRC Pr.

Lee, Robert R. Pocket Guide to Flanges, Fittings, & Piping Data. LC 84-669. 151p. 1984. reprint ed. pap. 46.90 (*0-608-00831-1*, 206162100010) Bks Demand.

***Lee, Robert W. & Ford, Steven W.** Alabama Workers' Compensation Law & Handbook. 500p. 1999. 95.00 (*0-327-01763-5*, 6455810) LEXIS Pub.

Lee, Robin, ed. Manual of Small Animal Diagnostic Imaging. 200p. 1995. pap. 69.95 (*0-905214-26-9*, Pub. by BSAVA) Iowa St U Pr.

***Lee, Rochunda.** For Love's Sake, Vol. 1. 1999. mass mkt. 4.99 (*1-58314-052-2*) BET Bks.

Lee, Rodney. The Good Times, Hard Times & Other Times. (Illus.). 220p. (Orig.). 1995. pap. 8.99 (*0-9649495-0-4*) Commun Assocs.

***Lee, Roger.** Hospitality & Restaurant Design, No. 2. (Illus.). 320p. 2000. 49.95 (*1-58471-019-5*, Pub. by Visual Refer) Watsn-Guptill.

Lee, Roger & Wills, Jane, eds. Geographies of Economics. (Arnold Publications). (Illus.). 424p. 1997. pap. text 29.95 (*0-340-67716-3*) OUP.

Lee, Roger, jt. ed. see Daniels, Stephen.

***Lee, Roger Y., ed.** Association of Management/International Association of Management (AOM/IAOM) Vol. 17, No. 1: Proceedings Computer Science. 153p. (C). 1999. pap. 24.95 (*0-9668650-4-9*) Maximilian Pr.

— Association of Management/International Association of Management (AOM/IAOM) Vol. 17, No. 3: Computer Science Proceedings. 140p. 1999. pap. text 24.95 (*0-9668650-6-5*) Maximilian Pr.

Lee, Roland, ed. Commercial Real Estate Loan Administration. 171p. (Orig.). 1993. pap. 60.00 (*0-945359-20-9*) Mortgage Bankers.

Lee, Ron & Oliver, Gary J. Trust Builders: True Stories of Marriages Strengthened by Trials. LC 99-42804. 192p. 1999. pap. 10.99 (*1-56955-178-2*, Vine Bks) Servant.

Lee, Ronald & Lee, Karen K. Arguing Persuasively. 432p. (C). 1989. text 32.25 (*0-582-28670-0*, 71686) Longman.

Lee, Ronald, jt. auth. see Hicks, Richard.

Lee, Ronald, jt. ed. see Hing, Bill O.

Lee, Ronald, ed. see National Research Council Staff.

Lee, Ronald D. Econometric Studies of Topics in Demographic History. LC 77-14749. (Dissertations in American Economic History Ser.). 1978. 30.95 (*0-405-11045-6*) Ayer.

— Working with Sidekick. 150p. (Orig.). 1988. pap. 14.95 (*0-938862-82-0*) Weber Systems.

Lee, Ronald D., et al, eds. Population, Food & Rural Development. (International Studies in Demography). (Illus.). 224p. 1992. pap. text 22.00 (*0-19-828391-1*) OUP.

Lee, Ronald D., et al. Economics of Changing Age Distributions in Developed Countries. (International Studies in Demography). (Illus.). 232p. 1995. reprint ed. pap. text 21.00 (*0-19-828887-5*) OUP.

Lee, Ronald D., jt. ed. see Auerbach, Alan J.

Lee, Ronald D., jt. ed. see Johnson, D. Gale.

Lee, Ronald R. & Martin, J. Colby. Psychotherapy after Kohut: A Textbook of Self Psychology. 352p. 1991. 45.00 (*0-88163-129-9*) Analytic Pr.

Lee, Ronald S. & Lee, Patricia, eds. Stubs: The Seating Plan Guide for New York Theaters, Music Halls & Sports Stadia, 1986 Edition. (Illus.). 1986. pap. 6.95 (*0-911458-06-9*, MNYE9) Stubs.

Lee, Ronnie, et al. The Siegel Modular Variety of Degree Two & Level Four/Cohomology of the Siegel Modular Group of Degree Two & Level Four. LC 98-2692. (Memoirs of the American Mathematical Society Ser.: Vol. 133, No. 631). 75p. 1998. pap. 38.00 (*0-8218-0620-3*, MEMO/133/631) Am Math.

Lee, Ronny. Jazz Guitar Method, Vols. 1 & 2. 112p. 1962. spiral bd. 14.95 (*0-7866-0036-5*, 93240) Mel Bay.

— Learn to Sing Step by Step. 144p. (J). 1984. pap. 14.95 (*0-934401-00-4*) Sunrise Pub NY.

Lee, Ronny. The Ronny Lee Beginner's Chord Book for Guitar: A Guide to Popular & Folk Accompaniments. 48p. 1996. pap. 7.50 (*0-7390-0838-2*, 438) Alfred Pub.

***Lee, Rosanna & Seligman, Scott.** Jndi Tutorial & Reference Guide. 592p. 2000. pap. text 42.95 (*0-201-70502-8*) Addison-Wesley.

Lee, Rosanna, jt. auth. see Chan, Patrick.

Lee, Rose. The Healthful Gourmet Chinese Cookbook. LC 98-31191. 320p. 1999. pap. 16.95 (*1-55788-299-1*, HP Books) Berkley Pub.

***Lee, Rose Bente.** An American Dream. LC 99-76958. (Illus.). 186p. 2000. 24.95 (*0-9660597-3-5*, Pub. by Morley Bks) Midpt Trade.

Lee, Rose H. The Growth & Decline of Chinese Communities in the Rocky Mountain Region. Daniels, Roger, ed. LC 78-54823. (Asian Experience in North America Ser.). (Illus.). 1979. lib. bdg. 25.95 (*0-405-11279-3*) Ayer.

***Lee, Rose J. & Clark, Cal, eds.** Democracy & the Status of Women in East Asia. LC 99-48191. 213p. 2000. lib. bdg. 55.00 (*1-55587-888-1*) L Rienner.

Lee, Rosemary, tr. see Soler, Nike.

Lee-Ross, Darren, jt. auth. see Johns, Nick.

Lee, Roy S. & Hayashi, Moritaka. New Directions in the Law of the Sea: Regional & National Developments, 2 binders. 1995. ring bd. 222.00 (*0-379-16551-1*) Oceana.

Lee, Roy S. & Hayashi, Moritaka, eds. New Directions in the Law of the Sea: Global Developments, 2 vols. LC 96-36221. 1996. ring bd. 325.00 (*0-379-16552-X*, 7910061) Oceana.

Lee, Roy S., jt. auth. see Peck, Connie, Colloquium on Increasing the Effecti.

Lee, Ruben. What Is an Exchange? Automation, Management, & Regulation of Financial Markets. LC 98-20655. 424p. 1999. text 49.95 (*0-19-828840-9*) OUP.

***Lee, Ruben.** What Is an Exchange? The Automation, Management, & Regulation of Financial Markets. 424p. 2000. pap. 19.95 (*0-19-829704-1*) OUP.

Lee-Ruff, Edward, et al, eds. Strained Organic Molecules. 128p. 1991. pap. 35.00 (*1-56081-509-4*, Wiley-VCH) Wiley.

Lee, Rupert. How to Find Information - Medicine & Biology: A Guide to Searching in Published Sources. (How to Find Ser.). 20p. 1996. pap. 8.00 (*0-7123-0837-5*, Pub. by SRIS) L Erlbaum Assocs.

Lee, Russell, et al. Far from Main Street: Three Photographers in Depression-Era New Mexico. (Illus.). 88p. (Orig.). 1994. pap. 27.50 (*0-89013-259-3*) Museum NM Pr.

Lee, Ruth. It's about Time: Work for a New You. (Illus.). 151p. 1996. spiral bd., wbk. ed. 24.95 (*1-888988-00-2*) LeeWay.

— Within the Veil: An Adventure in Time. LC 96-94779. 1997. pap. 14.95 (*1-888988-05-3*, SAN 299-3228) LeeWay.

Lee, Ruth M. Orientation to Health Services. LC 77-15094. 1978. teacher ed. write for info. (*0-672-61435-9*); pap. write for info. (*0-672-61434-0*) Macmillan.

Lee, Ruthie, ed. see Grennell, Jim, et al.

Lee, S. Counseling in Male Infertility. 224p. 1996. pap. text 29.95 (*0-632-03906-X*) Blackwell Sci.

— Forty Melodic Progressive Etudes Opus 31 Nos. 23-40, Bk. 2. 24p. 1986. pap. 7.95 (*0-7935-4871-3*) H Leonard.

***Lee, S.** Love Is the Answer. 1998. pap. text 14.95 (*0-575-60246-5*, Pub. by V Gollancz) Trafalgar.

Lee, S. The Travels of Ibn Batuta. 264p. 1985. 210.00 (*1-85077-035-2*, Pub. by Darf Pubs Ltd) St Mut.

Lee, S., ed. Laser & Plasma Technology: Proceedings of the Second Tropical College on Applied Physics, University of Malaya, 17 March - 5 April 1986. 592p. 1989. text 133.00 (*9971-5-0767-6*) World Scientific Pub.

Lee, S., et al, eds. Laser & Plasma Technology: Proceedings of the First Tropical College on Applied Physics. 696p. 1985. text 159.00 (*9971-978-27-X*) World Scientific Pub.

Lee, S. & Sakanaka, Paulo H., eds. Small Plasma Physics Experiments: Proceedings of Symposium on Small Scale Lab Plasma Number Exp. Spring College. 396p. 1988. text 89.00 (*9971-5-0768-4*) World Scientific Pub.

— Small Plasma Physics Experiments II: Proceedings of the Symposium on Small Scale Laboratory Plasma Physics Experiments. 384p. (C). 1990. text 101.00 (*981-02-0285-7*) World Scientific Pub.

Lee, S. E., ed. Water Quality Conservation in Asia: Selected Proceedings of Asian Waterqual '97, the 6th IAWQ Asia-Pacific Regional Conference, Held in Seoul, Korea, 20-23 May 1997. 386p. 1997. pap. write for info. (*0-08-043378-2*) Elsevier.

Lee, S. F., jt. auth. see Lee, L.

Lee, S. H. Selected Papers on Optical Interconnects & Packaging. LC 97-44549. (Milestone Ser.). 1997. write for info. (*0-8194-2766-7*) SPIE.

Lee, S. Howard, et al, eds. Cranial MRI & CT. 4th ed. LC 97-28648. (Illus.). 816p. 1999. text 175.00 (*0-07-037689-1*) McGraw-Hill HPD.

Lee, S. J. Aspects of European History. 2nd ed. (Illus.). 320p. (C). 1984. pap. 20.99 (*0-415-02784-5*) Routledge.

Lee, S. K. & Shanmugan, N. E., eds. Proceedings of the Icsas 91: Recent Research & Development, 3 vols., Set. (Illus.). 1381p. (C). (gr. 13). 1991. text 470.00 (*1-85166-636-2*) Elsevier Applied Sci.

***Lee, S. L.** Muon Science: Proceedings of the 51st Scottish Universities Summer School in Physics, 17-28 August. LC 99-39147. (Physics Ser.: Vol. 51). (Illus.). 482p. 1999. 240.00 (*0-7503-0630-0*) IOP Pub.

Lee, S. L., ed. Charlemagne Romances Nos. 7 & 8, Pts. 1-2. Bourchier, John, tr. (EETS, ES Ser.: Nos. 40-41). 1972. reprint ed. 75.00 (*0-527-00249-6*) Periodicals Srv.

— Durability of Building Materials & Components: Proceedings of the International Conference, 4-6 November 1987, 2 vols., Set. 1048p. 1987. pap. 469.00 (*0-08-035914-0*, Pub. by Pergamon Repr) Franklin.

Lee, S. L. & Shanmugan, N. E., eds. Aluminium Structures: Recent Research & Developments. (Illus.). (C). (gr. 13). 1991. text 110.00 (*1-85166-641-9*) Elsevier Applied Sci.

— Composite Steel Structures: Recent Research & Developments. (Illus.). 500p. (C). (gr. 13). 1991. text 110.00 (*1-85166-642-7*) Elsevier Applied Sci.

Lee, S. M., ed. Handbook of Composite Reinforcements. 715p. 1992. 210.00 (*0-471-18861-1*) Wiley.

Lee, S. M., et al. Network Analysis for Management Decisions. (International Series in Management Science-Operations Research). 1981. lib. bdg. 73.50 (*0-89838-077-4*) Kluwer Academic.

***Lee, S. W., ed.** Cervical Spinal Disorders: A Textbook for Rehabilitation Sciences Students. LC 99-10460. (Illus.). 400p. 1999. pap. 39.00 (*981-4021-29-6*, Pub. by U Auckland) Spr-Verlag.

***Lee, S. W., et al, eds.** Document Analysis Systems: Theory & Practice: 3rd IAPR Workshop, DAS'98, Nagano, Japan, November 4-6, 1998, Selected Papers. LC 99-47215. (Lecture Notes in Computer Science Ser.: Vol. 1655). xi, 377p. 1999. pap. 62.00 (*3-540-66507-2*) Spr-Verlag.

***Lee, S. W., et al.** Biologically Motivated Computer Vision: Proceedings of the First IEEE/CS International Workshop BMCV 2000, Seoul, Korea, May 2000. LC 00-32965. 2000. pap. write for info. (*3-540-67560-4*) Spr-Verlag.

Lee, S. W., jt. ed. see Lo, Y. T.

Lee, S. Y. Accelerator Physics. LC 98-53244. 1999. 64.00 (*981-02-3709-X*); pap. 32.00 (*981-02-3710-3*) World Scientific Pub.

Lee, Saalih. Culture of Clothing Among Taiwan Aborigines: Tradition, Meaning, Images, 1. (Illus.). 434p. 1999. 150.00 (*957-638-487-7*) SMC Pub.

Lee, Sabine, jt. auth. see Aldous, Richard.

Lee, Sabine, jt. ed. see Aldous, Richard.

Lee, Salley & Harris-Charity, Liz. The Highway to Welfare Reform Recovery. Tanguman, Samuel, ed. & illus. by. 9p. 1995. pap. 4.95 (*0-9651866-5-2*) Youth Corp.

Lee, Sally. San Antonio. LC 91-34303. (Downtown America Ser.). (Illus.). 60p. (J). (gr. 4 up). 1992. lib. bdg. 13.95 (*0-87518-510-X*, Dillon Silver Burdett) Silver Burdett Pr.

Lee, Sam. The Perfect War. 2nd ed. Valentine, Margaret, ed. 186p. 1990. 15.95 (*0-9621667-1-5*) Chengalera Pr.

***Lee, Samantha.** Angel's Gold. 320p. 2000. pap. 4.99 (*0-8439-4765-9*, Leisure Bks) Dorchester Pub Co.

— Images In Scarlet. 320p. 1999. mass mkt. 4.99 (*0-8439-4578-8*, Pub. by Dorchester Pub Co) CMG.

***Lee, Samuel.** World Apart? Attitudes toward Traditional Chinese Medicine & Endangered Species in Hong Kong & the United States. LC 98-44688. 1998. pap. write for info. (*0-89164-156-4*) World Wildlife Fund.

Lee, Sander H. Woody Allen's Angst: Philosophical Commentaries on His Serious Films. LC 96-33403. (Illus.). 414p. 1996. lib. bdg. 49.95 (*0-7864-0207-5*) McFarland & Co.

Lee, Sander H., ed. Inquiries into Values: The Inaugural Session of the International Society for Value Inquiry. LC 91-40171. (Problems in Contemporary Philosophy Ser.: Vol. 11). 776p. 1991. reprint ed. lib. bdg. 139.95 (*0-88946-338-7*) E Mellen.

Lee, Sandra. Anteaters. LC 97-48259. (Illus.). 32p. (J). 1998. lib. bdg. 22.79 (*1-56766-498-9*) Childs World.

— Bald Eagles. (Nature Books Ser.). (Illus.). 32p. (J). (gr. 2-6). 1991. lib. bdg. 22.79 (*0-89565-706-6*) Childs World.

— Coyotes. (Nature Books Ser.). (Illus.). 32p. (J). (gr. 2-6). 1992. lib. bdg. 22.79 (*0-89565-843-7*) Childs World.

***Lee, Sandra.** Falling for Her. 2000. mass mkt. 5.50 (*0-553-58011-6*) Bantam.

Lee, Sandra. Giant Pandas. LC 92-35066. (Nature Books Ser.). (Illus.). 32p. (J). (gr. 2-6). 1994. lib. bdg. 22.79 (*1-56766-009-6*) Childs World.

— Koalas. LC 97-30410. (Nature Books Ser.). (Illus.). 32p. (J). (gr. 2-6). 1998. lib. bdg. 22.79 (*1-56766-396-6*) Childs World.

— Love at First Sight. 336p. 1999. mass mkt. 5.50 (*0-553-58008-6*) Bantam.

— Opossums. LC 97-35222. (Illus.). 32p. (J). 1998. lib. bdg. 22.79 (*1-56766-480-6*) Childs World.

— Rattlesnakes. (Nature Books Ser.). (Illus.). 32p. (J). (gr. 2-6). 1992. lib. bdg. 22.79 (*0-89565-842-9*) Childs World.

***Lee, Sandra.** Skunks. LC 97-43375. (Illus.). 32p. (J). 1998. lib. bdg. 22.79 (*1-56766-503-9*) Childs World.

Lee, Sandra & Hunt, Tom. At The Ballet: On Stage, Back Stage. (Illus.). 160p. 1998. pap. 27.50 (*0-7893-0232-2*, Pub. by Universe) St Martin.

— At the Ballet: Onstage, Backstage. (Illus.). 160p. 2000. 45.00 (*0-7893-0225-X*, Pub. by Universe) St Martin.

Lee, Sanford & Nyhoff, Larry. FORTRAN 77 for Engineers & Scientists with an Introduction to FORTRAN 90. 4th ed. LC 95-35426. 884p. 1995. pap. 68.00 (*0-13-363003-X*) P-H.

— Introduction to FORTRAN 90 for Engineers & Scientists. LC 96-23141. (Prentice Hall Modular Series for Engineering). 411p. (C). 1996. pap. 36.20 (*0-13-505215-7*) P-H.

— Pascal Programming & Problem Solving. 4th ed. (Illus.). 800p. (C). 1993. pap. 68.00 (*0-02-388731-1*, Macmillan Coll) P-H.

— Turbo Pascal: Programming & Problem Solving. 2nd ed. (Illus.). 1008p. (C). 1993. pap. 64.00 (*0-02-388701-X*, Macmillan Coll) P-H.

Lee, Sanford, jt. auth. see Nyhoff, Larry.

Lee, Sang-Bok. A Comparative Study Between Minjung Theology & Reformed Theology from a Missiological Perspective. (Asian Thought & Culture Ser.: Vol. 22). XV, 183p. (Orig.). (C). 1996. pap. text 29.95 (*0-8204-2702-0*) P Lang Pubng.

Lee, Sang-Gon & Ruffini, Pierre-Bruno. The Global Integration of Europe & East Asia: Studies of International Trade & Investment. LC 99-13611. (New Horizons in International Business Ser.). 288p. (C). 1999. 95.00 (*1-84064-058-8*) E Elgar.

Lee, Sang H. The End of Communism. 459p. (C). 1985. 25.00 (*0-9606480-1-1*); pap. text 18.00 (*0-9606480-2-X*) Unificat Thght.

— Explaining Unification Thought. 357p. (Orig.). (C). 1981. pap. text 15.00 (*0-9606480-0-3*) Unificat Thght.

***Lee, Sang H.** Die Realistische Perspektive: Die Rehabilitation Unserer Common-Sense-Weltanschauung in der Realismusdebatte. 214p. 1999. 37.95 (*3-631-34649-2*) P Lang Pubng.

Lee, Sang M. Japanese Management: Cultural & Environmental. Schwendiman, Gary, ed. LC 82-10116. 299p. 1982. 69.50 (*0-275-91709-6*, C1709, Praeger Pubs) Greenwood.

— Management by Japanese Systems. Schwendiman, Gary, ed. LC 82-7612. 562p. 1982. 105.00 (*0-275-91710-X*, C1710, Praeger Pubs) Greenwood.

Lee, Sang M. & Van Horn, James C. Academic Administration: Planning, Budgeting, & Decision Making with Multiple Objectives. LC 81-24061. (Illus.). 266p. reprint ed. pap. 82.50 (*0-8357-4102-8*, 203686800005) Bks Demand.

Lee, Sang M., et al. Management Science. 3rd ed. 900p. 1989. text 59.00 (*0-205-12145-4*, H21454) Allyn.

— Management Science. 3rd ed. 900p. 1989. write for info. (*0-318-66337-6*, H21462); write for info. (*0-318-66338-4*, H21470) P-H.

Lee, Sang M., ed. see Thorp, Cary.

Lee, Sang-Oak, ed. Basic Korean-English, English-Korean Dictionary. (ENG & KOR.). 436p. 1997. pap. text 13.95 (*1-56591-076-1*, Pub. by Hollym Bks) Weatherhill.

Lee, Sang-Oak & Duk-Soo Park, eds. Perspectives on Korea. 640p. (C). 1998. text 60.00 (*0-9586526-6-X*) UH Pr.

Lee, Sang S., ed. see Ryu, Dewey D.

Lee, Sang T. Religion & Social Formation in Korea: Minjung & Millenarianism. xv, 246p. 1996. lib. bdg. 109.65 (*3-11-014797-1*) Mouton.

Lee, Sang W., jt. ed. see Kim, Sung J.

***Lee, Sang Yup & Papoutsakis, E. Terry.** Metabolic Engineering. LC 99-38508. (Bioprocess Technology Ser.). (Illus.). 423p. 1999. text 165.00 (*0-8247-7390-X*) Dekker.

Lee, Sara, et al, eds. A Congregation of Learners: Transforming the Synagogue into a Learning Community. 1995. pap. text 12.95 (*0-8074-0538-8*, 243873) UAHC.

Lee, Sara S., et al. Communities of Learning: A Vision for the Jewish Future. 60p. 1997. pap. 10.00 (*0-9661523-0-1*) Hebrew Union.

Lee, Sarah. Who's Afraid of Freedom? Korean-American Artists in California. Price, Lorna, ed. (Illus.). 56p. (Orig.). 1996. pap. 14.95 (*0-917493-22-2*) Orange Cnty Mus.

Lee, Sarah H., jt. auth. see Velvel, Lawrence R.

Lee, Scout & Lane, Suzie W. Basic Terminology for Therapeutic Recreation & Other Action Therapies. 3rd ed. 67p. 1997. pap. text 7.20 (*0-87563-709-4*) Stipes.

Lee, Scout, et al. Challenge of Excellence: Learning the Ropes of Change. rev. ed. (Skill Builder Ser.). (Illus.). 192p. 1990. pap. 16.95 (*1-55552-004-9*) Metamorphous Pr.

Lee, Scout C. The Circle Is Sacred: A Medicine Book for Women. LC 94-37045. 256p. (Orig.). 1995. pap. 17.95 (*0-933031-97-1*) Coun Oak Bks.

Lee, Seong-Whan. Frontiers in Handwriting Recognition. 1999. 124.00 (*981-02-3715-4*) World Scientific Pub.

***Lee, Seong-Whan, et al, eds.** Advances in Oriental Document Analysis & Recognition Techniques. Vol. 33. 270p. 1999. 58.00 (*981-02-3744-8*) World Scientific Pub.

Lee, Seong-Woo. Das Wesen der Religion und Ihr Verhaltnis Zu Wissenschaft und Sittlichkeit Bei Wilhelm Herrmann. (Europaische Hochschulschriften Ser.: Reihe 23, Bd. 522). (GER.). 289p. 1995. 49.95 (*3-631-48141-1*) P Lang Pubng.

An Asterisk (*) at the beginning of an entry indicates that the title is appearing for the first time.

Lee, Seung H. Brain Respiration Vol. 1: An Introduction to the Brain Respiration. Paek, Seung M., ed. Huh, Yun K., tr. from KOR. (Illus.). 100p. (Orig.). 1997. pap. 14.95 (*0-9658848-0-5*) Bell Rock Dev.

***Lee, Seung Heun.** Healing Society: A Prescription for Global Enlightenment. 2000. pap. 14.95 (*1-57174-189-5*) Hampton Roads Pub Co.

***Lee, Seung-Youl.** Die Geschichte der Diakonie in Den Protestantischen Kirchen Koreas und Perspektiven Fur die Erneuerung Ihrer Diakonischen Arbeit: Eine Fallstudie Innerhalb der Presbyterian Church of Korea. (Europaische Hochschulschriften Ser.: Bd. 680). Xvi, 350p. 1999. 52.95 (*3-631-35694-3*) P Lang Pubng.

Lee, Shao C., jt. auth. see Inn, Henry.

Lee, Sharice A. The Survivor's Guide: A Guide for Teenage Girls Who Are Survivors of Sexual Abuse. LC 94-45028. 1995. 25.00 (*0-8039-5780-7*); pap. text 12.95 (*0-8039-5781-5*) Sage.

Lee, Sharon & Miller, Steve. Partners in Necessity: A Liaden Adventure, 4 vols. 648p. 2000. reprint ed. pap. 18.00 (*1-892065-01-0*) Meisha Merlin.

— Plan B: A Liaden Adventure, 4 vols. 336p. 1999. pap. 14.00 (*1-892065-00-2*) Meisha Merlin.

Lee, Sharon, jt. auth. see Stopsky, Fred.

Lee, Shelley A., jt. auth. see Anderson, Lester W.

Lee, Sherman E. The Colors of Ink: Chinese Paintings & Related Ceramics from the Cleveland Museum of Art. LC 74-27415. (Asia Society Ser.). (Illus.). 1976. reprint ed. lib. bdg. 33.95 (*0-405-06564-7*) Ayer.

— A History of Far Eastern Art. 5th ed. Richard, Naomi N., ed. LC 93-7267. 576p. (C). 1993. text 73.33 (*0-13-393398-9*) P-H.

— History of Far Eastern Art. 5th ed. (Illus.). 576p. 1994. 65.00 (*0-8109-3414-0*, Pub. by Abrams) Time Warner.

— Tea Taste in Japanese Art. LC 74-27416. (Asia Society Ser.). (Illus.). 1976. reprint ed. lib. bdg. 31.95 (*0-405-06565-5*) Ayer.

Lee, Sherman E., ed. On Understanding Art Museums. 1975. pap. 2.95 (*0-13-936278-9*) Am Assembly.

Lee, Sherman E., et al, eds. Eight Dynasties of Chinese Painting: The Collections of the Nelson Gallery-Atkins Museum, Kansas City, & The Cleveland Museum of Art. LC 80-66110. (Illus.). 472p. 1981. 30.00 (*0-910386-53-6*) Cleveland Mus Art.

Lee, Sherman E., frwd. Tuti Nama. fac. ed. (Codices Selecti D Ser.: Vol. LV). 1976. 57.00 (*3-201-00959-8*, Pub. by Akademische Druck-und); lthr. 741.00 (*3-201-00958-X*, Pub. by Akademische Druck-und) Balogh.

Lee, Sherman E. & Ho, Wai-Kam. Chinese Art under the Mongols: The Yuan Dynasty 1279-1368. LC 68-9276. (Illus.). 415p. reprint ed. pap. 128.70 (*0-608-11078-7*, 200510800049) Bks Demand.

Lee, Sherman E. & Indiana University Staff. Reflections of Reality in Japanese Art. LC 82-45940. (Illus.). 304p. 1983. 35.00 (*0-910386-70-6*) Cleveland Mus Art.

Lee, Sherman E., jt. auth. see Rogers, Howard.

***Lee, Shing Yip, ed.** The Mangrove Ecosystem of Deep Bay & the Mai Po Marshes, Hong Kong. 196p. 1999. pap. (*962-209-485-6*) HK Univ Pr.

Lee, Shirley. How to Outwit & Outsell Your Competition Before They Know What Hit Them: Avoiding Costly & Common Marketing Mistakes. 100p. 1999. pap. 19.95 (*1-891689-76-2*) Gabriel Pubns.

Lee, Sidney. Elizabethan & Other Essays. Boas, Frederick S., ed. LC 68-22108. (Essay Index Reprint Ser.). 1977. 23.95 (*0-8369-0614-4*) Ayer.

— Elizabethan & Other Essays. Boas, F. S., ed. LC 78-133811. reprint ed. 29.50 (*0-404-03928-6*) AMS Pr.

— The French Renaissance in England: An Account of the Literary Relations of England & France in the Sixteenth Century. (BCL1-PR English Literature Ser.). 494p. 1992. reprint ed. lib. bdg. 99.00 (*0-7812-7025-1*) Rprt Serv.

— Great Englishmen of the Sixteenth Century. LC 77-128269. (Essay Index Reprint Ser.). 1977. 23.95 (*0-8369-1885-1*) Ayer.

— A Life of William Shakespeare. (BCL1-PR English Literature Ser.). 476p. 1992. reprint ed. lib. bdg. 99.00 (*0-7812-7282-3*) Rprt Serv.

— A Life of William Shakespeare. LC 70-145137. (Illus.). 1971. reprint ed. 59.00 (*0-403-01069-1*) Scholarly.

— Shakespeare & the Modern Stage. LC 74-172042. reprint ed. 29.50 (*0-404-03929-4*) AMS Pr.

— Stratford-on-Avon from the Earliest Times to the Death of Shakespeare. LC 71-109654. (Select Bibliographics Reprint Ser.). 1977. 26.95 (*0-8369-5263-4*) Ayer.

— Stratford-on-Avon from the Earliest Times to the Death of Shakespeare. (BCL1-PR English Literature Ser.). 327p. 1992. reprint ed. lib. bdg. 89.00 (*0-7812-7286-6*) Rprt Serv.

Lee, Sidney, ed. see Smith, George.

Lee, Simon. David. LC 99-233997. (Illus.). 448p. 1998. pap. 19.95 (*0-7148-3804-7*) Phaidon Pr.

— Play the Game: Tennis. (Illus.). 80p. 1998. pap. 10.95 (*0-7063-7715-X*, Pub. by WrLock) Sterling.

Lee, Simon, ed. French Short Stories Two. 256p. 1993. pap. 10.95 (*0-14-003414-5*, Penguin Bks) Viking Penguin.

Lee, Simon & Fox, Marie. Learning Legal Skills. 224p. (C). 1991. text 24.00 (*1-85431-112-3*, Pub. by Blackstone Pr) Gaunt.

Lee, Simon, jt. ed. see Mullard, Maurice.

Lee, Simon, ed. see Petrie, Brian.

Lee, Sin H., jt. ed. see Perschuk, Louis P.

Lee, Sin H., jt. ed. see Pertschuk, Louis P.

Lee, Sing H., ed. Diffractive & Miniaturized Optics: Proceedings of a Conference Held 12-13 July 1993, San Diego, California. LC 93-47390. (Critical Reviews of Optical Science & Technology Ser.: Vol. CR49). 1993. 40.00 (*0-8194-1292-9*); 40.00 (*0-8194-1291-0*) SPIE.

Lee, Sing H., jt. ed. see Cindrich, Ivan.

Lee, Siu-Lam, jt. auth. see Lyon, John F.

Lee, Sky. Bellydancer. LC PR9199.3.L393B45 199. 224p. 1994. pap. 14.95 (*0-88974-039-9*, Pub. by Press Gang Pubs) LPC InBook.

Lee, Soon C. The Fifth Wheel. Lechich, Whitney, ed. LC 94-61952. 80p. 1994. 24.00 (*1-884740-01-4*) Whys World Pubns.

***Lee, Sophia.** The Recess: Or, A Tale of Other Times. Alliston, April, ed. LC 99-23224. (Eighteenth-Century Novels by Women Ser.). 400p. 2000. 47.50 (*0-8131-2146-9*) U Pr of Ky.

Lee, Sophia. Recess: or A Tale of Other Times, 3 vols., Set. LC 77-131325. (Gothic Novels Ser.). 1979. reprint ed. 54.95 (*0-405-00806-6*) Ayer.

***Lee, Sophia & Alliston, April.** The Recess: Or, a Tale of Other Times. LC 99-23224. (Eighteenth-Century Novels by Women Ser.). 400p. 2000. pap. 17.95 (*0-8131-0978-7*) U Pr of Ky.

Lee, Sophia, ed. see Chaucer, Geoffrey.

Lee, Spike. Inside Guerrilla Filmmaking. 1987. pap. write for info. (*0-318-62087-1*, Fireside) S&S Trade Pap.

***Lee, Spike & Lee, Tonya Lewis.** Please, Baby, Please. LC 99-462286. (Illus.). (J). 2001. write for info. (*0-689-83233-8*) S&S Childrens.

Lee, Spike & Reid, Calvin, intros. Michael Ray Charles. (Illus.). 80p. 1998. pap. 29.95 (*1-891475-10-X*, 810531) T Shafrazi.

Lee, Stacey J. Unraveling the "Model Minority" Stereotype: Listening to Asian American Youth. 160p. (C). 1996. text 39.00 (*0-8077-3510-8*); pap. text 17.95 (*0-8077-3509-4*) Tchrs Coll.

Lee, Stan. The Amazing Spider-Man. 128p. (Orig.). 1995. pap. 3.99 (*0-8125-1019-4*, Pub. by Tor Bks) St Martin.

— Avengers. (Marvel Essentials Ser.). 1998. pap. 14.95 (*0-7851-0701-0*) Marvel Entrprs.

— The Best of the World's Worst. 192p. 2000. 6.99 (*0-517-20620-X*) Random Hse Value.

— Bring Back the Bad Guys. (Origins of Marvel Ser.: No. V). (Illus.). 256p. (YA). (gr. 5-12). 1998. pap. 24.99 (*0-7851-0597-2*) Marvel Entrprs.

— Bring on the Bad Guys. (Illus.). 256p. (YA). (gr. 5-12). 1998. pap. 24.99 (*0-7851-0591-3*) Marvel Entrprs.

— Bring on the Bad Guys. 253p. 1976. 10.95 (*0-671-22354-2*) S&S Trade.

***Lee, Stan.** Essential Avengers, Vol. II. (Essential Collection). (Illus.). 528p. 2000. pap. 14.95 (*0-7851-0741-X*, Pub. by Marvel Entrprs) LPC Group.

— Essential Captain America. (Essential Collection). (Illus.). 528p. 2000. pap. 14.95 (*0-7851-0740-1*, Pub. by Marvel Entrprs) LPC Group.

— Essential Fantastic Four, Vol. II. (Illus.). 528p. 1999. pap. 14.95 (*0-7851-0731-2*, Pub. by Marvel Entrprs) LPC Group.

Lee, Stan. Essential Incredible Hulk. (Marvel Essentials Ser.). (Illus.). 528p. 1999. pap. 14.95 (*0-7851-0712-6*) Marvel Entrprs.

— The Essential Silver Surfer, Vol. 1. (Illus.). 528p. (J). (gr. 5-12). 1998. pap. 12.99 (*0-7851-0271-X*) Marvel Entrprs.

— Essential Spider-Man. (Illus.). 528p. 1997. pap. text 12.95 (*0-7851-0286-8*) Marvel Entrprs.

— The Essential Spider-Man, Vol. 2. (Illus.). 528p. 1998. pap. 12.99 (*0-7851-0299-X*) Marvel Entrprs.

— Essential Spider-Man, Vol. III. (Essential Ser.). (Illus.). 528p. 1998. pap. 12.95 (*0-7851-0658-8*) Marvel Entrprs.

***Lee, Stan.** Essential Uncanny X-Men. (Illus.). 528p. 1999. pap. 14.95 (*0-7851-0730-4*, Pub. by Marvel Entrprs) LPC Group.

Lee, Stan. Greatest Spider-Man & Daredevil Team-Ups. (Illus.). 176p. 1996. pap. text 16.95 (*0-7851-0223-X*) Marvel Entrprs.

— Here Comes Daredevil: The Man Without Fear! 1999. 34.95 (*0-7851-0714-2*) Marvel Entrprs.

— Marvel Massterworks: Thor. (Illus.). 272p. 1999. 34.95 (*0-7851-0733-9*, Pub. by Marvel Entrprs) LPC Group.

— Origins of Marvel Comics. (Illus.). 240p. 1997. pap. text 24.95 (*0-7851-0551-4*) Marvel Entrprs.

Lee, Stan. Origins of Marvel Comics. LC 74-11141. 254p. 1974. write for info. (*0-671-21864-6*) S&S Trade.

Lee, Stan. Son of Origins of Marvel Comics. (Illus.). 240p. 1997. pap. text 24.95 (*0-7851-0559-X*) Marvel Entrprs.

— Spider-Man. (Masterworks Ser.). (Illus.). 256p. 1994. 34.95 (*0-7851-0051-2*) Marvel Entrprs.

— Spider-Man Greatest Villians. (Illus.). 176p. 1995. pap. 15.95 (*0-7851-0136-5*) Marvel Entrprs.

***Lee, Stan.** Spider-Man vs. Doctor Octopus. (From the House of Ideas Ser.). (Illus.). 176p. 1999. pap. 17.95 (*0-7851-0742-8*, Pub. by Marvel Entrprs) LPC Group.

Lee, Stan. Spider-Man's Greatest Team-Ups. (Illus.). 176p. 1996. pap. text 16.95 (*0-7851-0203-5*) Marvel Entrprs.

— Thunderbolts: Marvel's Most Wanted. (Illus.). 176p. 1998. pap. text 16.95 (*0-7851-0592-1*) Marvel Entrprs.

— Ultimate Spider-Man. 1996. mass mkt. 6.99 (*0-425-17000-4*) Berkley Pub.

— The Ultimate Spiderman. 352p. (Orig.). 1994. pap. 12.00 (*0-425-14610-3*) Berkley Pub.

— The Ultimate Spiderman. 352p. (Orig.). 1996. mass mkt. 5.99 (*1-57297-103-7*) Blvd Books.

— The Very Best of Spider-Man. (Illus.). 176p. 1994. pap. 16.95 (*0-7851-0045-8*) Marvel Entrprs.

— The X-Men. (Masterworks Collection). (Illus.). 240p. 1998. 29.95 (*0-7851-0664-2*) Marvel Entrprs.

— X-Men, Vol. 3. (Masterworks Ser.). (Illus.). 224p. 1994. pap. 34.95 (*0-7851-0052-0*) Marvel Entrprs.

Lee, Stan, ed. The Ultimate Silver Surfer. 352p. (Orig.). 1995. pap. 12.00 (*1-57297-029-4*) Blvd Books.

— The Ultimate Silver Surfer. (Orig.). 1997. mass mkt. 6.50 (*1-57297-299-8*) Blvd Books.

— The Ultimate Super-Villains. LC 96-180332. 352p. 1996. pap. 14.00 (*1-57297-113-4*) Blvd Books.

— The Ultimate X-Men. LC 96-209722. 352p. (YA). 1996. pap. 14.00 (*1-57297-217-3*) Blvd Books.

***Lee, Stan, ed.** X-Men: Legends. 272p. 1999. pap. 12.00 (*0-425-17082-9*) Berkley Pub.

Lee, Stan & Buscema, John. How to Draw Comics the Marvel Way. (Illus.). 160p. 1984. pap. 15.00 (*0-671-53077-1*, Fireside) S&S Trade Pap.

Lee, Stan & Busiek, Kurt, eds. Untold Tales of Spider-Man. 320p. 1997. pap. 13.00 (*1-57297-294-7*) Blvd Books.

Lee, Stan & Byrne, John. Villainy of Doctor Doom. (Illus.). 176p. 1999. reprint ed. pap. 17.95 (*0-7851-0732-0*, Pub. by Marvel Entrprs) LPC Group.

Lee, Stan & David, Peter, eds. The Ultimate Hulk. LC 98-218557. 352p. 1998. pap. 14.00 (*0-425-16513-2*) Blvd Books.

Lee, Stan & Ditko, Steve. Amazing Spider-Man. (Marvel Masterworks Ser.: Vol. 10). 264p. 1989. 34.95 (*0-87135-596-5*) Marvel Entrprs.

— Spider-Man. (Marvel Masterworks Ser.: Vol. 5). 232p. 1988. 34.95 (*0-87135-480-2*) Marvel Entrprs.

— Spider-Man: Masterworks. (Illus.). 144p. 1992. pap. 12.95 (*0-87135-902-2*) Marvel Entrprs.

Lee, Stan & Kirby, Jack. Avengers. (Marvel Masterworks Ser.: Vol. 4). 240p. 1998. 29.99 (*0-87135-479-9*) Marvel Entrprs.

— Essential Fantastic Four. (Essential Ser.). 528p. Date not set. pap. 12.95 (*0-7851-0666-9*) Marvel Entrprs.

— Fantastic Four. (Marvel Masterworks Ser.: Vol. 2). 248p. 1998. 29.99 (*0-87135-307-5*) Marvel Entrprs.

— The Fantastic Four. (Masterworks Collection). (Illus.). Date not set. pap. 29.95 (*0-7851-0589-1*) Marvel Entrprs.

— Marvel Masterworks: The X-Men. (Marvel Masterworks Ser.: Vol. 3). (Illus.). 232p. (YA). 1987. 34.95 (*0-87135-308-3*) Marvel Entrprs.

— X-Men. (Marvel Masterworks Ser.: Vol. 7). 232p. 1988. 34.95 (*0-87135-482-9*) Marvel Entrprs.

Lee, Stan & McCay, Bill. Stan Lee's Riftworld, Odyssey. 432p. 1996. mass mkt. 5.99 (*1-57297-069-3*) Blvd Books.

Lee, Stan & Robinson, Graham. Process Development: Fine Chemicals from Grams to Kilograms. (Oxford Chemistry Primers Ser.: No. 30). (Illus.). 92p. (C). 1995. pap. text 12.95 (*0-19-855824-4*) OUP.

Lee, Stan, et al. Grandson of Origins. (Origins of Marvel Ser.: No. IV). (Illus.). 256p. (YA). (gr. 6-12). 1998. pap. 24.99 (*0-7851-0593-X*) Marvel Entrprs.

Lee, Stan, jt. auth. see Golden, Christopher.

Lee, Stan, jt. auth. see Wein, Len.

Lee-Stecum, Parshia. Powerplay in Tibullus: Reading Elegies, Bk. 1. LC 99-161355. (Cambridge Classical Studies). 330p. (C). 1998. 64.95 (*0-521-63083-5*) Cambridge U Pr.

***Lee, Stellasue.** Crossing the Double Yellow Line. 95p. 2000. pap. 12.95 (*0-941017-04-4*, Pub. by Bombshelter Pr) SPD-Small Pr Dist.

Lee, Stellasue, jt. auth. see Widup, Dave.

Lee, Stephen. Creation & Redemption in Isaiah 40-55. (Jian Dao Dissertation Ser.: No. 2). 219p. 1995. 65.00 (*962-7997-11-0*, Pub. by Sheffield Acad); pap. 23.75 (*962-7997-12-9*, Pub. by Sheffield Acad) CUP Services.

Lee, Stephen C., jt. ed. see Hu, Jerome P.

Lee, Stephen J. Aspects of British Political History, 1815-1914. LC 94-432. (Aspects of History Ser.). (Illus.). 368p. (C). 1994. pap. 22.99 (*0-415-09007-5*, B3981) Routledge.

— Aspects of British Political History, 1914-1995. LC 96-30548. (Aspects of History Ser.). 440p. (C). 1996. pap. 22.99 (*0-415-13103-0*) Routledge.

— Aspects of British Political History, 1914-1995. LC 96-30548. (Aspects of History Ser.). (Illus.). 448p. (C). 1996. 75.00 (*0-415-13102-2*) Routledge.

— Aspects of European History 1494-1789. 2nd ed. 336p. 1984. pap. 14.95 (*0-416-37490-5*, NO. 9079) Routledge.

— The European Dictatorships, 1918-1945. 400p. (C). 1987. pap. 22.99 (*0-415-02785-3*) Routledge.

— The European Dictatorships, 1918-1945. 352p. 1987. pap. 15.95 (*0-416-42280-2*) Routledge.

***Lee, Stephen J.** The European Dictatorships, 1918-1945. 2nd ed. LC 99-59922. 2000. pap. write for info. (*0-415-23046-2*) Routledge.

Lee, Stephen J. Hitler & Nazi Germany. LC 97-30891. 112p. (C). 1998. pap. 11.99 (*0-415-17988-2*) Routledge.

— Imperial Germany, 1871-1918. LC 98-21784. (Questions & Analysis in History Ser.). (Illus.). 112p. (C). (gr. 13). 1998. pap. 12.99 (*0-415-18574-2*, D5447) Routledge.

— Russia, 1924-1953. LC 99-11755. (Questions & Analysis in History Ser.). (Illus.). 112p. (C). 1999. pap. 11.99 (*0-415-18573-4*) Routledge.

— The Weimar Republic. LC 97-39300. (Questions & Analysis in History Ser.). 112p. (C). 1988. pap. 11.99 (*0-415-17178-4*) Routledge.

Lee, Steve A. & Stagner, Lloyd E. Illinois Central Steam Finale: 1936-1960. (Illus.). 108p. 1995. reprint ed. pap. 24.95 (*0-942035-35-6*) South Platte.

Lee, Steve S., jt. auth. see Schuler-Maloney, Doris L.

Lee, Steven, jt. auth. see Fine, Marvin J.

Lee, Steven, jt. ed. see Cohen, Avner.

Lee, Steven H. Outposts of Empire: Korea, Vietnam, & the Origins of the Cold War in Asia, 1949-1954. 320p. 1996. pap. text 19.95 (*0-7735-1420-1*, Pub. by McG-Queens Univ Pr) CUP Services.

— Outposts of Empire: Korea, Vietnam & the Origins of the Cold War in Asia, 1949-1954. LC 97-135057. 312p. 1995. 55.00 (*0-7735-1326-4*, Pub. by McG-Queens Univ Pr) CUP Services.

Lee, Steven P. Morality, Prudence & Nuclear Weapons. LC 92-30904. (Cambridge Studies in Philosophy & Public Policy). 432p. (C). 1993. text 80.00 (*0-521-38272-6*) Cambridge U Pr.

— Morality, Prudence & Nuclear Weapons. (Cambridge Studies in Philosophy & Public Policy). 432p. 1996. pap. text 25.95 (*0-521-56772-6*) Cambridge U Pr.

Lee, Stuart M. Dictionary of Composite Materials Technology. LC 89-50813. 171p. 1989. 99.95 (*0-87762-600-6*) Technomic.

Lee, Stuart M. International Encyclopedia of Composites, Vol. 1. 563p. 1989. 330.00 (*0-471-18749-6*) Wiley.

— International Encyclopedia of Composites, Vol. 2. 524p. 1990. 330.00 (*0-471-18750-X*) Wiley.

— International Encyclopedia of Composites, Vol. 3. 526p. 1990. 330.00 (*0-471-18751-8*) Wiley.

— International Encyclopedia of Composites, Vol. 4. 532p. 1990. 330.00 (*0-471-18759-3*) Wiley.

— International Encyclopedia of Composites, Vol. 5. 548p. 1991. 330.00 (*0-471-18760-7*) Wiley.

— International Encyclopedia of Composites, Vol. 6. 600p. 1991. 330.00 (*0-471-18761-5*) Wiley.

Lee, Stuart M. Reference Book for Composite Technology, Vol. 1. LC 89-50073. 334p. 1989. 49.95 (*0-87762-564-6*) Technomic.

— Reference Book for Composite Technology, Vol. 2. LC 89-50073. 203p. 1989. 49.95 (*0-87762-565-4*) Technomic.

Lee, Stuart M., ed. Advances in Biomaterials I. LC 86-72347. 292p. 1986. 36.95 (*0-87762-504-2*) Technomic.

— Handbook of Composite Reinforcements. LC 92-38661. 715p. 1992. 145.00 (*1-56081-632-5*, Wiley-VCH) Wiley.

Lee, Stuart M., ed. International Encyclopedia of Composites, 4 vols., Vol. 4. 3293p. 1989. 1755.00 (*0-471-18706-2*, Wiley-VCH) Wiley.

***Lee, Sue.** High Dependency Nursing Practice: Clinical Scenarios & Patient Problems. (Illus.). 192p. 2000. pap. 32.00 (*0-7506-4311-0*) Buttrwrth-Heinemann.

Lee, Suk C. New Drug Approval in South Korea. (Worldwide Pharmaceutical Regulation Ser.). 92p. (Orig.). 1995. pap. 100.00 (*1-882615-22-0*) Parexel Intl.

Lee, Sukhan, jt. ed. see Homen De Mello, Luiz S.

***Lee, Sul H.** Collection Development in a Digital Environment- Shifting Priorities. LC 99-39118. (Journal of Library Administration: Vol. 28, No. 1). 118p. 1999. pap. text 19.95 (*0-7890-0827-0*) Haworth Pr.

Lee, Sul H., ed. Access, Ownership, & Resource Sharing. LC 95-4208. (Journal of Library Administration: Vol. 20, No. 1). 125p. 1995. 39.95 (*1-56024-727-4*) Haworth Pr.

— Access, Resource Sharing, & Collection Development. LC 96-23321. (Journal of Library Administration: Vol. 22, No. 4). 133p. 1996. 24.95 (*1-56024-811-4*) Haworth Pr.

— Access to Scholarly Information: Issues & Strategies. LC 85-60595. (Library Management Ser.: No. 9). 130p. 1985. 30.00 (*0-87650-189-7*) Pierian.

— Acquisitions, Budgets, & Material Costs: Issues & Approaches. LC 87-29867. (Journal of Library Administration & Supplement: No. 2). (Illus.). 162p. 1988. 49.95 (*0-86656-690-2*) Haworth Pr.

— Budgets for Acquisitions: Strategies for Serials, Monographs, & Electronic Formats. LC 91-12603. (Journal of Library Administration: Vol. 14, No. 3). (Illus.). 134p. 1991. lib. bdg. 39.95 (*1-56024-158-6*) Haworth Pr.

— A Challenge for Academic Libraries: How to Motivate Students to Use the Library. LC 73-78295. (Library Orientation Ser.: No. 2). 100p. 1973. 25.00 (*0-87650-039-4*) Pierian.

***Lee, Sul H., ed.** Collection Development in a Digital Environment- Shifting Priorities. LC 99-39118. (Journal of Library Administration: Vol. 28, No. 1). 118p. (C). 1999. 49.95 (*0-7890-0794-0*) Haworth Pr.

— Collection Development in the Electronic Environment: Shifting Priorities. LC 99-57822. 125p. 2000. 49.95 (*0-7890-0964-1*); pap. text 19.95 (*0-7890-0982-X*) Haworth Pr.

Lee, Sul H., ed. Declining Acquisitions Budgets: Allocation, Collection Development & Impact Communication. LC 93-39258. (Illus.). 138p. 1994. lib. bdg. 39.95 (*1-56024-613-8*) Haworth Pr.

— Declining Acquisitions Budgets: Allocation, Collection Development & Impact Communication. LC 93-39258. (Illus.). 138p. 1994. pap. text 19.95 (*1-56024-614-6*) Haworth Pr.

— Economics of Digital Information: Collection, Storage, & Delivery. LC 97-41774. 117p. 1997. 29.95 (*0-7890-0369-4*) Haworth Pr.

— Emerging Patterns of Collection Development in Expanding Resource Sharing, Electronic Information, & Network Environment. LC 96-52926. (Journal of Library Administration Monographs: Vol. 24, Nos. 1-2). 156p. (C). 1997. 39.95 (*0-7890-0033-4*) Haworth Pr.

— Emerging Trends in Library Organization: What Influences Change. LC 78-56102. (Library Management Ser.: No. 4). 121p. 1978. 24.50 (*0-87650-093-9*) Pierian.

— The Impact of Rising Costs of Serials & Monographs on Library Services & Programs. LC 88-36774. (Journal of Library Administration: Vol. 10, No. 1). (Illus.). 125p. 1989. text 39.95 (*0-86656-885-9*) Haworth Pr.

— Issues in Acquisitions: Programs & Evaluation. LC 84-61226. (Library Management Ser.: No. 8). 144p. 1984. 30.00 (*0-87650-188-9*) Pierian.

— Library Budgeting: Critical Challenges for the Future. LC 77-85231. (Library Management Ser.: No. 3). 111p. 1977. 24.50 (*0-87650-083-1*) Pierian.

— Library Materials Costs & Access to Information. LC 91-12604. (Journal of Library Administration: Vol. 12, No. 3). (Illus.). 114p. 1991. lib. bdg. 39.95 (*1-56024-146-2*) Haworth Pr.

— Planning-Programming-Budgeting System: Implications for Library Management. LC 73-78314. (Library Management Ser.: No. 1). 112p. 1973. 24.50 (*0-87650-040-8*) Pierian.

— Pricing & Costs of Monographs & Serials: National & International Issues. LC 86-33653. (Journal of Library Administration Supplement: No. 1). 109p. 1987. text 39.95 (*0-86656-620-1*) Haworth Pr.

L

— Reference Service: A Perspective. LC 83-60917. (Library Management Ser.: No. 6). 140p. 1983. 30.00 (*0-87650-150-1*) Pierian.

— The Role & Future of Special Collections in Research Libraries: British & American Perspectives. LC 93-30716. (Journal of Library Administration: Vol. 19, No. 1). 98p. 1993. lib. bdg. 29.95 (*1-56024-479-8*) Haworth Pr.

— Serials Collection Development: Choices & Strategies. LC 81-84645. (Library Management Ser.: No. 5). x, 89p. 1981. 30.00 (*0-87650-136-6*) Pierian.

— Vendor Evaluation & Acquisition Budgets. LC 92-10146. (Journal of Library Administration: Vol. 16, No. 3). (Illus.). 143p. 1992. 39.95 (*1-56024-253-1*) Haworth Pr.

— Vendor Evaluation & Acquisition Budgets. LC 92-10146. (Journal of Library Administration: Vol. 16, No. 3). 143p. 1996. pap. 14.95 (*0-7890-0051-2*) Haworth Pr.

Lee, Sul H., intro. Collection Assessment & Acquisitions Budgets. LC 92-28676. (Journal of Library Administration: Vol. 17, No. 2). (Illus.). 148p. 1993. 39.95 (*1-56024-390-2*) Haworth Pr.

Lee, Sul H., jt. ed. see Woodrum, Pat.

Lee, Sun, ed. Manual of Microsurgery. (Illus.). 160p. 1985. 92.00 (*0-8493-0726-0*, RD33, CRC Reprint) Franklin.

Lee, Sun-Jae. Der Aufstieg der Industrie Koreas in der Weltwirtschaft: Die "Skalenertraege-Politik" und Ihre Konsequenzen Fuer den Handel mit der EG. Baltzarek, Franz, ed. (Forschungen zur Wirtschafts-, Finanz- und Sozialgeschichte Ser.: Vol. 6). (GER., Illus.). 506p. 1998. pap. 73.95 (*3-631-32436-7*) P Lang Pubng.

Lee, Sun O. & Heyman, Alan. Zen Dance: Meditation in Movement. (Illus.). 108p. 1985. 24.00 (*0-8048-1428-7*, Pub. by Seoul Intl Tourist) Tuttle Pubng.

Lee, Sung J., ed. Operator Methods for Optimal Control Problems. (Lecture Notes in Pure & Applied Mathematics Ser.: Vol. 108). (Illus.). 344p. 1987. pap. text 155.00 (*0-8247-7811-1*) Dekker.

***Lee, Sunggu.** Design of Computers & Other Complex Digital Devices: An Example of Advanced Digital Logic Design. LC 99-49967. 418p. 1999. 99.00 (*0-13-040267-2*) P-H.

Lee, Sunggyu. Alternative Fuels. (Applied Energy Technology Ser.). 650p. 1996. text 95.00 (*1-56032-361-2*) Taylor & Francis.

— Methane & Its Derivatives. LC 96-41107. (Chemical Industries Ser.: Vol. 70). (Illus.). 424p. 1996. text 180.00 (*0-8247-9754-X*) Dekker.

Lee, Sunggyu & Iredell, Robert. Methanol Synthesis Technology. 240p. 1989. lib. bdg. 195.00 (*0-8493-4610-X*, TP594) CRC Pr.

Lee, Sungkee, jt. auth. see Bhanu, Bir.

***Lee, Sungnack.** Behpcet's Disease: Textbook & Atlas. LC 00-30057. (Illus.). 2000. write for info. (*3-540-66761-X*) Spr-Verlag.

Lee, Sungyu, ed. Oil Shale Technology. 280p. 1990. lib. bdg. 225.00 (*0-8493-4615-0*, TP699) CRC Pr.

Lee, Sunhee. Die Minjung-Theologie Ahn Byungmus von Ihren Voraussetzungen Her Dargestellt. (Europaische Hochschulschriften Ser.: Reihe 23, Bd. 443). (GER.). XVII, 266p. 1991. 55.80 (*3-631-44459-1*) P Lang Pubng.

Lee, Sunngyu, jt. auth. see Speight, J. G.

Lee, Sunny. Sunny Lee's Eclectic Poetry: Love, Life & Destiny. 1998. pap. write for info. (*1-57553-979-9*) Watermrk Pr.

Lee, Susan. Hands Off: Why the Government Is a Menace to Economic Health. 272p. 1996. 22.50 (*0-684-81442-0*) S&S Trade.

— Unintended Consequences. 1999. pap. 12.95 (*0-14-016774-9*); pap. 23.95 (*0-670-84358-X*) Viking Penguin.

Lee, Susan, ed. The New Library Legacy. (New Library Ser.: Vol. 2). 200p. 1998. pap. 59.95 (*1-55570-294-5*) Neal-Schuman.

Lee, Susan & Libana, Susanaha. You Said, Why This Interest in Goddesses. (Fastbook 1985 Ser.). 20p. 1985. 6.00 (*0-911051-17-1*) Plain View.

Lee, Susan, jt. auth. see Flowers, Nancy.

Lee, Susan A., jt. ed. see Cytrynbaum, Solomon.

Lee, Susan D., ed. Ohio Records & Pioneer Families, Vol. 33. 1992. 9.00 (*0-935057-69-2*) OH Genealogical.

— Ohio Records & Pioneer Families, Vol. 34. 1993. 18.00 (*0-935057-72-2*) OH Genealogical.

— Ohio Records & Pioneer Families, Vol. 35. 1994. 18.00 (*0-935057-75-7*) OH Genealogical.

— Ohio Records & Pioneer Families, Vol. 36. 1995. 18.00 (*0-935057-78-1*) OH Genealogical.

— Ohio Records & Pioneer Families, Vol. 37. 1996. 18.00 (*0-935057-80-3*) OH Genealogical.

— Ohio Records & Pioneer Families: Surname Index, Vol. 27. 1986. 15.00 (*0-935057-44-7*) OH Genealogical.

— Ohio Records & Pioneer Families: Topical Index, Vols. I-XXV. 1986. 1.00 (*0-935057-43-9*) OH Genealogical.

***Lee, Susan E.** Stage Notes: A Field Guide for Teachers: The Music Man. (Illus.). 44p. (YA). (gr. 5-12). 2000. pap. text 12.95 (*1-930504-02-0*) Camp Broadway.

Lee, Susan P. The Westward Movement of the Cotton Economy, 1840-1860: Perceived Interests & Economic Realities. Bruchey, Stuart, ed. LC 76-39832. (Nineteen Seventy-Seven Dissertations Ser.). (Illus.). 1977. lib. bdg. 24.95 (*0-405-09912-6*) Ayer.

Lee, Susan P., et al. A New Economic View of American History. 2nd ed. (C). 1994. pap. 34.75 (*0-393-96315-2*) Norton.

Lee, Susan R. Lee's New School History of the United States. (Johnson Ser.). (Illus.). 422p. 1996. pap. 17.95 (*0-9627989-0-8*) Grapevine ID.

Lee, Suzanne. Bicycling Japan: A Touring Handbook. LC 90-83529. (Illus.). 168p. (Orig.). 1991. pap. 6.95 (*0-9627458-0-4*) Zievid Pr.

Lee, Sylvain A. The Practice of Hypnotic Suggestion. 160p. 1996. reprint ed. spiral bd. 13.50 (*0-7873-0548-0*) Hlth Research.

Lee, Sylvester, jt. auth. see Ros, Pablo R.

Lee, Sylvia, ed. The Holy Spirit in Christian Education. LC 88-80549. (Sunday School Staff Training Ser.). 141p. (J). (gr. k up). 1988. pap., teacher ed. 2.95 (*0-88243-854-9*, 02-0854) Gospel Pub.

Lee, Sylvia, jt. auth. see Lee, L. L.

Lee, T. Advanced Industrial Hygiene. 1990. text. write for info. (*0-442-23532-1*, VNR) Wiley.

— Company Financial Reporting U. K. 2nd ed. 1982. pap. 46.95 (*0-442-30707-1*) Chapman & Hall.

— Imaging of Surgical Diseases: A Practical Guide. (C). 2000. 85.00 (*0-8385-4071-6*, Medical Exam) Appleton & Lange.

Lee, T. Queen's Flight. text 35.00 (*0-340-67247-1*, Pub. by Hodder & Stought Ltd); mass mkt. 13.95 (*0-340-67248-X*, Pub. by Hodder & Stought Ltd) Trafalgar.

— Reap the Whirlwind. 1997. mass mkt. 13.95 (*0-340-67246-3*, Pub. by Hodder & Stought Ltd) Trafalgar.

Lee, T., et al. Revisiting the Americas: Teaching & Learning the Geography of the Western Hemisphere. Martinson, T. L. & Brooker-Gross, Susan, eds. (Pathways in Geography Ser.: No. 4). (Illus.). 260p. (Orig.). 1992. pap. text 25.00 (*0-9627379-2-5*) NCFGE.

Lee, T. A., et al, eds. Accounting History from the Renaissance to the Present: A Remembrance of Luca Pacioli. LC 95-51120. (New Works in Accounting History). (Illus.). 320p. 1996. reprint ed. text 66.00 (*0-8153-2271-2*) Garland.

Lee, T. A. & Tweedie, D. P. Shareholder Use & Understanding Financial Information. (Accounting History & Thought Ser.). 400p. 1990. reprint ed. text 10.00 (*0-8240-3321-3*) Garland.

Lee, T. A., jt. auth. see Walker, Stephen P.

Lee, T. C. The Wu Style of Tai Chi Chuan. LC 81-50511. (Illus.). 120p. (Orig.). 1981. pap. 9.95 (*0-86568-022-1*, 211) Unique Pubns.

Lee, T. D. Lee: Selected Papers, 1. Feinberg, Gerald, ed. (Contemporary Physicists Ser.). 1986. 109.50 (*0-8176-3341-3*) Birkhauser.

— Lee: Selected Papers, 2. Feinberg, Gerald, ed. (Contemporary Physicists Ser.). 1986. 109.50 (*0-8176-3342-1*) Birkhauser.

— Lee: Selected Papers, 3. Feinberg, Gerald, ed. (Contemporary Physicists Ser.). 1986. 109.50 (*0-8176-3343-X*) Birkhauser.

— Lee: Selected Papers, Set. Feinberg, Gerald, ed. (Contemporary Physicists Ser.). 1986. 273.50 (*0-8176-3344-8*) Birkhauser.

— Symmetries Asymmetries. (Illus.). 80p. 1987. pap. 15.00 (*0-295-96519-3*) U of Wash Pr.

Lee, T. D., ed. Particle Physics & Introduction to Field Theory. (Contemporary Concepts in Physics Ser.: Vol. 1). xvii, 866p. 1981. text 229.00 (*3-7186-0032-3*); pap. text 68.00 (*3-7186-0033-1*) Gordon & Breach.

Lee, T. H., et al, eds. The Methane Age. (C). 1988. text 153.00 (*90-277-2745-7*) Kluwer Academic.

***Lee, T. J.** T. J. Lee & Lee Hudspeth Teach PC Upgrades. (Illus.). 608p. 2000. pap. 19.99 (*0-7897-2417-0*) Que.

Lee, T. J., ed. Neurohumoral Control of Blood Vessel Tone: Springfield Blood Vessel Symposium. (Journal: Blood Vessels: Vol. 24, No. 3). (Illus.). 80p. 1987. pap. 42.75 (*3-8055-4604-1*) S Karger.

Lee, T. J., et al. The Unofficial Guide to PCs. LC 98-86230. (Illus.). 489p. 1999. pap. 17.99 (*0-7897-1797-2*) Que.

Lee, T. P. Current Trends in Integrated Optoelectronics. LC 95-135356. (Current Topics in Electronics & Systems Ser.). 148p. 1994. text 61.00 (*981-02-1862-1*) World Scientific Pub.

— Current Trends in Vertical Cavity Surface Emitting Lasers. 200p. 1995. text 58.00 (*981-02-2288-2*) World Scientific Pub.

Lee, T. S., jt. ed. see Dean, Sheldon W.

Lee, T. S., jt. ed. see Francis, P. E.

Lee, Ta-Ling & Copper, John Franklin. Reform in Reverse: Human Rights in the People's Republic of China, No. 6. 150p. 1987. 8.00 (*0-942182-86-3*, 83) Occasional Papers.

Lee, Ta-ling, jt. auth. see Cooper, John F.

Lee, Ta-ling, jt. auth. see Copper, John Franklin.

Lee, Tae-Woo. Shipping Developments in Far Eastern: The Korean Experience. LC 96-86686. (Plymouth Studies in Contemporary Shipping). 272p. 1996. text 81.95 (*1-85972-493-0*, Pub. by Avebry) Ashgate Pub Co.

Lee, Tahirih V., ed. Basic Concepts of Chinese Law. LC 96-47414. (Chinese Law Ser.: Vol. 1). 448p. 1997. text 88.00 (*0-8153-2481-2*) Garland.

— Contract, Guanxi, & Dispute Resolution in China. LC 96-44071. (Chinese Law Ser.: Vol. 3). 448p. 1997. text 88.00 (*0-8153-2483-9*) Garland.

— Foreigners in Chinese Law. LC 96-44070. (Chinese Law Ser.: Vol. 4). 488p. 1997. text 94.00 (*0-8153-2484-7*) Garland.

Lee, Tahirih V., ed. Law, the State & Society in China. LC 96-47413. (Chinese Law Ser.). 432p. 1997. text 88.00 (*0-8153-2482-0*) Garland.

Lee, Tanith. Biting the Sun. 384p. 1999. mass mkt. 5.99 (*0-553-58130-9*) Bantam.

— Black Unicorn. 192p. (J). 1993. mass mkt. 3.99 (*0-8125-2459-4*, Pub. by Tor Bks) St Martin.

— The Book of the Beast. (Secret Books of Paradys: Vol. 2). 240p. 1991. 19.95 (*0-87951-417-5*, Pub. by Overlook Pr) Penguin Putnam.

— The Book of the Beast, Vol. 2. LC 90-48488. (Secret Books of Paradys). 196p. 1997. reprint ed. pap. 13.95 (*0-87951-698-4*, Pub. by Overlook Pr) Penguin Putnam.

— The Book of the Damned. (Secret Books of Paradys: Vol. 2). 240p. 1990. 19.95 (*0-87951-408-6*, Pub. by Overlook Pr) Penguin Putnam.

— The Book of the Damned. LC 90-43843. (Secret Books of Paradys: Vol. 1). 229p. 1997. reprint ed. pap. 13.95 (*0-87951-697-6*, Pub. by Overlook Pr) Penguin Putnam.

— The Book of the Dead. (Secret Books of Paradys: Vol. III). 208p. 1997. pap. 13.95 (*0-87951-798-0*, Pub. by Overlook Pr) Penguin Putnam.

— The Book of the Dead: The Secret Books of Paradys III. 196p. 1991. 19.95 (*0-87951-440-X*, Pub. by Overlook Pr) Penguin Putnam.

— The Book of the Mad. (Secret Books of Paradys: Vol. IV). 222p. 1997. pap. 13.95 (*0-87951-799-9*, Pub. by Overlook Pr) Penguin Putnam.

— The Book of the Mad: The Secret Books of Paradys IV. LC 92-36788. 1993. 19.95 (*0-87951-481-7*, Pub. by Overlook Pr) Penguin Putnam.

— Darkness, I: Third in the Blood Opera Sequence. 416p. 1995. 24.95 (*0-312-13956-X*) St Martin.

— Faces under Water, Vol. 1. LC 98-4789. (Secret Books of Venus: Bk. I). 288p. 1998. 23.95 (*0-87951-835-9*, Pub. by Overlook Pr) Penguin Putnam.

— The Gods Are Thirsty. LC 96-22765. 528p. 1996. 26.95 (*0-87951-672-0*, Pub. by Overlook Pr) Penguin Putnam.

— Gold Unicorn. (Illus.). 160p. (J). (gr. 7 up). 1994. 15.95 (*0-689-31814-6*) Atheneum Yung Read.

— Gold Unicorn. 256p. 1996. pap., mass mkt. 5.99 (*0-8125-4320-3*, Pub. by Tor Bks); mass mkt. write for info. (*0-614-08669-8*) Tor Bks.

Lee, Tanith. Gold Unicorn. 1996. 11.09 (*0-606-11401-7*, Pub. by Turtleback) Demco.

Lee, Tanith. Island in the Sky. LC 99-23981. (Voyage of the Basset Ser.: Bk. 1). 249p. (J). (gr. 4-7). 1999. pap. 3.99 (*0-679-89127-7*) Random.

— Saint Fire, Vol. 2. 336p. 1999. text 25.95 (*0-87951-735-2*, Pub. by Overlook Pr) Penguin Putnam.

— The Silver Metal Lover. 304p. 1999. mass mkt. 5.99 (*0-553-58127-9*) Bantam.

***Lee, Tanith.** White as Snow. 2000. text 23.95 (*0-312-86993-2*) St Martin.

— Wolf Tower. LC 99-98192. (Claidi Journals). (Illus.). 240p. (J). (gr. 6-12). 2000. 15.99 (*0-525-46394-1*, Dutton Child) Peng Put Young Read.

Lee, Tarwith. Women As Demons. pap. 9.95 (*0-7043-4132-8*, Pub. by Womens Press) Trafalgar.

Lee, Te-Won. Independent Component Analysis: Theory & Applications. LC 98-38829. 210p. 1998. 118.00 (*0-7923-8261-7*) Kluwer Academic.

***Lee, Teng-Hui.** Road to Democracy: Taiwan's Pursuit of Identity. 1999. 30.00 (*4-569-60651-2*) PHP Kenkyujo.

***Lee, Terence Richard.** Water Management in the 21st Century: The Allocation Imperative. LC 99-42179. (New Horizons in Environmental Economics Ser.). 224p. 2000. 80.00 (*1-84064-080-4*) E Elgar.

Lee, Teresa. Legal Research Guide to Television Broadcasting & Program Syndication. LC 95-33965. (Legal Research Guides Ser.: Vol. 22). vi, iii, 42p. 1995. 35.00 (*0-89941-978-X*, 308650) W S Hein.

Lee, Teri, ed. see Lackey, Mercedes.

Lee, Terrence A. A Beginner's Guide to Mass Spectral Interpretation. LC 97-28548. 200p. 1998. 98.00 (*0-471-97628-8*) Wiley.

***Lee, Terrence A.** A Beginner's Guide to Mass Spectral Interpretation. LC 97-28548. 200p. 1998. pap. 49.95 (*0-471-97629-6*) Wiley.

Lee, Terri. Aquacises: Terri Lee's Water Workout Book. (Illus.). 240p. 1990. reprint ed. pap. text 15.00 (*0-9627703-0-2*) Lee Pub AZ.

Lee, Theresa M. Politics & Truth: Political Theory & the Postmodernist Challenge. LC 97-3267. (SUNY Series in Political Theory). 243p. (C). 1997. pap. text 17.95 (*0-7914-3504-0*) State U NY Pr.

— The Secret of the Tooth Fairy. LC 98-96244. 30p. (J). 1998. write for info. (*0-9664625-0-5*) Twinkle Toes.

Lee, Thomas. 20th Century First Edition Fiction: A Price & Identification Guide. LC 96-228480. 188p. (Orig.). 1996. pap. 24.95 (*0-9653429-1-3*) Bk Emporium.

***Lee, Thomas.** 20th Century First Edition Fiction - 2000: A Price & Identification Guide. 252p. 2000. pap. 24.95 (*0-9653429-3-X*, Pub. by Bk Emporium) IPG Chicago.

Lee, Thomas. 20th Century First Edition Fiction: A Price & Identification Guide. 98th ed. 225p. (Orig.). 1997. pap. 24.95 (*0-9653429-2-1*) Bk Emporium.

— 20th Century First Edition Fiction: A Price & Identification Guide 1996. 139p. (Orig.). 1995. pap. 19.95 (*0-9653429-0-5*) Bk Emporium.

***Lee, Thomas & Davies, Joseph E.** Microsoft Windows 2000 TCP/IP Protocols & Services Technical Reference. LC 99-56120. 800p. (gr. 8). 2000. pap. 49.99 (*0-7356-0556-4*) Microsoft.

Lee, Thomas, ed. see Maple Summer Workshop & Symposium Staff.

Lee, Thomas A. The Quest for a Science of Accounting: An Anthology of the Research of Robert R. Sterling. Wolnizer, Peter W. & Brief, Richard P., eds. LC 97-26158. (New Works in Accounting History Ser.). 854p. 1997. reprint ed. text 149.00 (*0-8153-3026-X*) Garland.

— Stalking the Wild Golf Ball: A Guide to Finding, & Not Losing, Golf Balls. 128p. 1994. pap. 16.95 (*0-9638807-4-8*) Fairway Pubng.

Lee, Thomas A., ed. Cash Flow Reporting: A Recent History of an Accounting Practice. LC 93-607. (New Works in Accounting History). 424p. 1993. reprint ed. text 25.00 (*0-8153-1217-2*) Garland.

— Shaping the Accountancy Profession: The Story of Three Scottish Pioneers. LC 95-49826. (New Works in Accounting History). (Illus.). 264p. 1996. reprint ed. text 57.00 (*0-8153-2269-0*) Garland.

Lee, Thomas F. Gene Future: The Promise & Perils of the New Biology. (Illus.). 350p. (C). 1993. 24.95 (*0-306-44509-3*, Plenum Trade) Perseus Pubng.

— The Human Genome Project: Cracking the Genetic Code of Life. (Illus.). 332p. (C). 1991. 24.50 (*0-306-43965-4*, Plenum Trade) Perseus Pubng.

Lee, Thomas H. The Design of CMOS Radio-Frequency Integrated Circuits. LC 97-34158. (Illus.). 614p. (C). 1998. pap. text 54.95 (*0-521-63922-0*) Cambridge U Pr.

Lee, Thomas H., compiled by. A Guide to East Asian Collections in North America, 25. LC 91-46698. (Bibliographies & Indexes in World History Ser.: No. 25). 184p. 1992. lib. bdg. 55.00 (*0-313-27397-9*, LGA, Greenwood Pr) Greenwood.

Lee, Thomas H., et al. Integrated Management Systems: A Practical Approach to Transforming Organizations. LC 99-23516. (Wiley Operationed Management Series for Professionals). 336p. 1999. 55.00 (*0-471-34595-4*) Wiley.

Lee, Thomas H., jt. auth. see Hajimiri, Ali.

Lee, Thomas H., jt. auth. see Shaeffer, Derek K.

Lee, Thomas H., ed. see National Academy of Engineering, Committee on Engi.

***Lee, Thomas H.C.** Education in Traditional China: A History. LC 99-52700. (Handbook of Oriental Studies: 13). 600p. 2000. 300.00 (*90-04-10363-5*) Brill Academic Pubs.

Lee, Thomas R. Rock Island Westward. LC 97-95053. 1998. write for info. (*0-916244-04-0*) T Lee Pubns.

— Turbines Westward. 1975. 16.95 (*0-686-00363-2*) AG Pr.

Lee, Thomas W. Using Qualitative Methods in Organizational Research. LC 98-9083. (Organizational Research Methods Ser.). 192p. 1998. 32.00 (*0-7619-0806-4*); pap. 14.99 (*0-7619-0807-2*) Sage.

Lee, Thomas W. & Pabbisetty, Seshu V., eds. Microelectronic Failure Analysis: Desk Reference. 3rd ed. LC 93-7792. 425p. 1993. 163.00 (*0-87170-479-X*, 9103) ASM.

Lee-Thorp, Karen. Exploring the Essentials. (Thinking Through Discipleship Ser.). 80p. (Orig.). 1993. pap. 5.00 (*0-89109-736-8*) NavPress.

— How to Ask Great Questions. LC 97-47657. 1997. pap. text 7.00 (*1-57683-078-0*) NavPress.

Lee-Thorp, Karen & Hicks, Cynthia. Why Beauty Matters. LC 96-36906. 264p. 1997. pap. 14.00 (*0-89109-979-4*) NavPress.

Lee-Thorp, Karen, ed. see Navigators Staff.

Lee, Tien-Chang. Applied Mathematics in Hydrogeology. LC 98-40039. 350p. 1998. 69.95 (*1-56670-375-1*) Lewis Pubs.

Lee, Tien-Pei, jt. auth. see Chi, Sien.

Lee, Tim. A Christian Contract with America: For the Soul of Our Nation. 1996. pap. 9.95 (*1-888684-01-1*) Liberty House.

— Economics for Professional Investors. 2nd ed. 224p. 1998. 63.00 (*0-13-792912-9*) P-H.

— The Search for Equity: The Funding of Additional Educational Needs under LMS. 151p. 1996. text 63.95 (*1-85972-413-2*, Pub. by Avebry) Ashgate Pub Co.

Lee, Timothy D., jt. auth. see Schmidt, Richard A.

Lee, Timothy-James, jt. auth. see Hudspeth, Lee.

Lee, Ting W. Call to Ministry - Chinese Edition: From Dream to Reality. (CHI.). 137p. 1996. pap. 6.50 (*1-56582-023-1*) Christ Renew Min.

— Equipping the Saints No. 1: Teacher's Hand Book - Chinese Edition. (CHI.). 75p. 1992. pap., teacher ed. 9.50 (*1-56582-046-0*) Christ Renew Min.

— Equipping the Saints No. 2: Teacher's Hand Book - Chinese Edition. (CHI.). 119p. 1995. pap., teacher ed. 9.50 (*1-56582-047-9*) Christ Renew Min.

— Kingdom & Little People - Chinese Edition. (CHI.). 169p. 1989. pap. 6.50 (*1-56582-022-3*) Christ Renew Min.

***Lee, Ting W.** A Renewed Approach to Bible Study: How to Use NIV Study Bible with All Its Worth - Chinese Edition. (CHI.). 108p. 1998. pap. 6.00 (*1-56582-123-8*) Christ Renew Min.

Lee, Ting W., tr. see Dawson, David.

Lee, Tish & Harris, Deborah. Food Stamp Advocacy Guide, 1998 Edition. 4th rev. ed. LC 97-76044. 70p. 1998. pap. text 7.95 (*1-57589-082-8*, 98-23.02-BK) Mass CLE.

Lee, Tish, jt. auth. see Harris, Deborah.

Lee, Tisha. My Image Is My Choice: How to Create the Perfect Haircut for Your Lifestyle. (Illus.). 260p. (Orig.). 1988. pap. text 24.95 (*0-9620833-0-5*) Castle Pubn.

Lee, Todd. The Snoring Log Mystery: Wilderness Adventures of a Young Naturalist. (Illus.). 96p. (Orig.). (J). (gr. 4-8). 1993. pap. write for info. (*0-919591-76-0*) Polstar Bk.

— The Twilight Marsh: And Other Wilderness Adventures. (Illus.). 96p. (Orig.). (J). (gr. 1-11). 1995. pap. 8.95 (*1-896095-07-0*) Polstar Bk.

Lee, Tom. Corporate Audit Theory. LC 92-36202. 224p. 1993. pap. 28.95 (*0-412-45220-0*) Chapman & Hall.

— Income & Value Measurement. 3rd ed. 196p. 1992. mass mkt. 29.95 (*0-412-38180-X*) Chapman & Hall.

— Income & Value Measurement: Theory & Practice. 3rd rev. ed. 187p. 1997. pap. 20.99 (*1-86152-051-4*) Thomson Learn.

Lee, Tom, jt. auth. see Vickers, Roderic.

Lee, Tom L. Lawyer Advertising: Consumer Attitudes, Response Patterns & Motivation Factors. LC 85-11699. 207p. (Orig.). 1985. pap. 325.00 (*0-934547-00-9*) CRI-Comm Res.

— Lawyers Direct Mail Advertising Handbook. 1989. write for info. (*0-934547-06-8*) CRI-Comm Res.

— Lawyers Publicity Handbook. 145p. 1986. ring bd. 68.00 (*0-934547-02-5*) CRI-Comm Res.

Lee, Tommy, et al. The Dirt: The Autobiography of Motley Crue. (Illus.). 304p. 2000. 24.95 (*0-06-039288-6*) HarpC.

An Asterisk (*) at the beginning of an entry indicates that the title is appearing for the first time.

Lee, Tonia R. Slavery Without Chains, & Other Selected Poems. LC 87-9058. (Orig.). 1988. pap. 5.00 (*0-942029-00-3*) Lee Price.

Lee, Tony. Collectible Card Games. 1999. pap. 17.95 (*0-676-60145-6*) Hse Collectbls.

— Maximum Damage. Maxwell, Duane, ed. 32p. 1998. pap. write for info. (*1-892519-08-9*, AAE-1020) Archangel Ent.

Lee, Tony & Miller, Steve. Die & Die Again. 32p. 1997. pap. 8.00 (*1-892519-07-0*, AEE-1010) Archangel Ent.

— Extreme Vengeance. 80p. 1997. pap. 10.00 (*1-892519-06-2*, AAE-1000) Archangel Ent.

Lee, Tony, jt. auth. see Brown, Timothy.

Lee, Tony, jt. auth. see Ghosh, Sumit.

Lee, Tony, jt. auth. see Koen, Deb.

Lee, Tony, ed. see Miller, Marc & Smith, Lester.

Lee, Tonya Lewis, jt. auth. see Lee, Spike.

***Lee, Tracy.** Extremities: A Story. 2000. pap. 11.95 (*0-533-13407-2*) Vantage.

***Lee-Treweek, Geraldine & Linkogle, Stephanie.** Danger in the Field: Risk & Ethics in Social Research. LC 00-35278. 2000. pap. write for info. (*0-415-19322-2*) Routledge.

Lee, Tsao Yuan, jt. see Mahizhnan, Arun.

Lee, Tsu-Chang. Structure Level Adaptation for Artificial Neural Networks. (C). 1991. text 91.00 (*0-7923-9151-9*) Kluwer Academic.

Lee, Tung-Ching & Kim, Hie-Joon, eds. Chemical Markers for Processed & Stored Foods. LC 96-19198. (ACS Symposium Ser.: No. 631). (Illus.). 304p. 1996. text 105.00 (*0-8412-3404-3*, Pub. by Am Chemical) OUP.

Lee, Tyrone, jt. ed. see Sen, Amartya K.

Lee, Tzexa C., jt. auth. see Coburn, Jewell R.

Lee, Uk-Bae. Sori's Harvest Moon Day: A Story of Korea. LC 98-51871. Orig. Title: Sori's Chu-Suk. (Illus.). 32p. (J). (gr. k-3). 1999. 15.95 (*1-56899-687-X*); pap. 5.95 (*1-56899-688-8*) Soundprints.

— Sori's Harvest Moon Day: A Story of Korea - Including Doll. Orig. Title: Sori's Chu-Suk. (Illus.). 32p. (J). (gr. k-3). 1999. 25.95 (*1-56899-690-X*) Soundprints.

— Sori's Harvest Moon Day: A Story of Korea - Including Doll. Orig. Title: Sori's Chu-Suk. (Illus.). 32p. (J). (ps-3). 1999. pap. 15.95 (*1-56899-691-8*) Soundprints.

Lee, Ulysses. United States Army in World War 2 (Paperbound) Special Studies of Negro Troops. 758p. 1994. per. 45.00 (*0-16-042951-X*) USGPO.

Lee, Ulysses, ed. see Locke, Alain L.

Lee, Umphrey. Historical Backgrounds of Early Methodist Enthusiasm. LC 31-18047. (Columbia University. Studies in the Social Sciences: No. 339). reprint ed. 20.00 (*0-404-51339-5*) AMS Pr.

Lee, V., ed. Trends & Future Perspectives in Peptide & Protein Drug Delivery. (Drug Targeting & Delivery Ser.). 340p. 1995. text 132.00 (*3-7186-5641-8*, Harwood Acad Pubs) Gordon & Breach.

***Lee, V., et al, eds.** Fatal Attractions: Protein Aggregates in Neurodegenerative Disorders. (Research & Perspectives in Alzheimer's Disease Ser.). (Illus.). 175p. 2000. 95.00 (*3-540-67172-2*) Spr-Verlag.

Lee, Valerie. Dysfunctional Families. (The Family Ser.). (Illus.). 64p. (J). (gr. 7 up). 1990. lib. bdg. 17.95 (*0-86593-077-5*) Rourke Corp.

— Granny Midwives & Black Women Writers: Double-Dutched Readings. LC 96-31239. (Illus.). 224p. (C). 1996. 65.00 (*0-415-91507-4*); pap. 17.99 (*0-415-91508-2*) Routledge.

— Pregnancy in the Executive Suite. LC 87-61045. 224p. (C). 1988. 19.95 (*0-944315-00-3*) Success Pubns.

— Www.sex.net. LC 97-76147. 200p. 1998. 18.95 (*0-9653524-8-X*) Russn Hill Pr.

Lee, Valeska. The Colors of Passion. 150p. 1997. mass mkt. 5.00 (*0-9634431-1-9*) C Y Pub Grp.

Lee Valley Tools Staff. The Gardeners Kalendar: The Works of Each Month in the English Garden, 1777. LC 97-900611. (Illus.). 390p. 1997. reprint ed. 16.95 (*0-921335-05-9*, Pub. by LVTL) Veritas Tools.

Lee Valley Tools Staff, contrib. by. The Gardeners Calendar: The Works of Each Month in the English Garden. 1777. limited ed. (Illus.). 390p. 1997. reprint ed. text 29.95 (*0-921335-07-5*, Pub. by LVTL) Veritas Tools.

Lee, Vera. How to Flirt Outrageously: A Step-by-Step Guide to Bewitching a Man. (Illus.). 144p. 1998. pap. 12.95 (*0-9663065-0-3*) Olympia Pr.

— Love & Strategy in the Eighteenth Century French Novel. 150p. (Orig.). 1986. pap. 14.95 (*0-87047-019-1*); text 19.95 (*0-87047-018-3*) Schenkman Bks Inc.

— Quest for a Public: French Popular Theatre Since 1945. 200p. 1976. text 18.95 (*0-87073-180-7*) Schenkman Bks Inc.

— Reign of Women in Eighteenth Century France. (Illus.). 140p. 1976. 18.95 (*0-87073-990-5*); pap. 14.95 (*0-87073-991-3*) Schenkman Bks Inc.

— Something Old, Something New: What You Didn't Know about Wedding Ceremonies, Celebrations & Customs. 224p. 1997. reprint ed. pap. 9.95 (*1-57071-148-8*, Casablanca) Sourcebks.

Lee, Vernell, ed. see Gall-Clayton, Nancy.

Lee, Vernon. The Handling of Words & Other Studies in Literary Psychology. LC 92-38266. 1993. reprint ed. text. write for info. (*0-7734-9174-0*) E Mellen.

— Supernatural Tales: Excursions into Fantasy. LC 87-60976. 222p. 1987. 27.00 (*0-7206-0680-2*, Pub. by P Owen Ltd) Dufour.

***Lee, Veronica.** Princess June: A Novel. LC 00-8261. 288p. 2001. pap. 14.95 (*1-56474-346-2*) Fithian Pr.

***Lee, Vicki.** The Tranny Guide. 8th ed. (Illus.). 336p. 2000. pap. 22.95 (*0-9526880-5-0*, Pub. by WayOut Pub Co) SCB Distributors.

Lee, Vicki E., ed. see Gano, Dean L.

Lee, Vicki L. Beyond Behaviorism. 216p. 1988. 39.95 (*0-8058-0115-4*) L Erlbaum Assocs.

Lee, Victor & Das Gupta, Prajna, eds. Children's Cognitive & Language Development. (Child Development Ser.). (Illus.). 344p. (C). 1995. pap. 27.95 (*0-631-19428-2*) Blackwell Pubs.

Lee, Victoria. Best Friends. Date not set. pap. write for info. (*1-888225-03-3*) A Touch of Heart.

— Grandparents Hall of Fame. Date not set. pap. write for info. (*1-888225-04-1*) A Touch of Heart.

— The Heart of a Coach. Date not set. pap. write for info. (*1-888225-02-5*) A Touch of Heart.

— Soulful Sex. 320p. 1997. 9.98 (*1-56731-198-9*, MJF Bks) Fine Comms.

— Soulful Sex: Opening Your Heart, Body & Spirit to Lifelong Passion. (Illus.). 350p. 1996. pap. 16.95 (*1-57324-006-0*) Conari Press.

— Unforgettable Grady. Date not set. pap. write for info. (*1-888225-05-X*) A Touch of Heart.

— A Way Out, 2 vols. 250p. 1997. pap. write for info. (*1-888225-01-7*) A Touch of Heart.

Lee, Victoria, jt. auth. see Shaw, Michael.

Lee, Victory & Zarif, Farid. Animating the Desire of Achievement: Developing Your Career. (Illus.). 178p. (Orig.). 1996. pap. 24.95 (*1-888611-03-0*, 88864) Victry Pub.

Lee, Victory, ed. see Zarif, Farid.

Lee, Victory, ed. & illus. see Zarif, Farid.

Lee, Vinny. Bathrooms. (Illus.). 96p. 1998. pap. 13.95 (*1-85793-957-3*, Pub. by Pavilion Bks Ltd) Trafalgar.

***Lee, Vinny.** Bathrooms: A Design Sourcebook. LC 00-29141. (Illus.). 2000. write for info. (*1-58479-023-7*) Stewart Tabori & Chang.

Lee, Vinny. Kitchens. (Library of Interiors). (Illus.). 96p. 1998. pap. 13.95 (*1-86205-101-1*, Pub. by Pavilion Bks Ltd) Trafalgar.

— Kitchens: A Design Source Book. LC 98-17171. 192p. 1998. 40.00 (*1-55670-697-9*) Stewart Tabori & Chang.

— Quiet Places: How to Create Peaceful Havens in Your Home, Garden & Workplace. LC 98-5092. (Simple Life Bks.). (Illus.). 160p. 1998. 15.95 (*0-7621-0060-5*, Pub. by RD Assn) Penguin Putnam.

***Lee, Vinny.** Recycled Spaces: Converting Buildings into Homes. LC 00-27991. (Illus.). 144p. 2000. 35.00 (*1-57959-055-1*, Pub. by BB&T Inc) Publishers Group.

Lee, Vinny. Zen Interiors. LC 99-14106. (Illus.). 160p. 1999. text 30.00 (*1-55670-930-7*) Stewart Tabori & Chang.

Lee, Virginia. Country Comforts. 336p. 1997. mass mkt. 5.99 (*0-515-12064-2*, Jove) Berkley Pub.

— Rivals, 1vol., Vol. 6. (Friends Ser.). 361p. 1999. mass mkt. 5.99 (*0-515-12432-X*, Jove) Berkley Pub.

Lee, Virginia, jt. auth. see Elliot, Elaine.

Lee, Virginia, jt. auth. see Pogue, Pamela.

Lee, Vivian W., jt. auth. see Sing, Rachel N.

Lee, W. John Lee of Aganam (Ipswich), Mass., 1634-1671, & His Descendants of the Name of Lee. (Illus.). 506p. 1989. reprint ed. pap. 75.00 (*0-8328-0764-8*); reprint ed. lib. bdg. 83.00 (*0-8328-0763-X*) Higginson Bk Co.

— Mobile Cellular Telecommunications Systems. 2nd ed. (Illus.). 664p. 1995. 69.95 (*0-07-038089-9*) McGraw.

Lee, W. A. Manual of Queensland Succession Law. 3rd ed. xlviii, 295p. 1991. pap. 49.00 (*0-455-21034-9*, Pub. by LawBk Co) Gaunt.

Lee, W. A., jt. auth. see Ford, H. A.

Lee, W. E. Overcoming Life. 191p. 1997. per. 8.75 (*1-57593-909-6*, 07-061-002) Living Stream Ministry.

Lee, W. E., ed. Ceramic Films & Coatings No. 54: Proceedings of Papers at the Ceramic Films & Coatings Meeting Held at Sheffield University on December 19-20, 1994, No. 54. 268p. 1995. 150.00 (*0-901716-79-0*, Pub. by Inst Materials) Ashgate Pub Co.

Lee, W. E. & Bell, A., eds. Electroceramics: Production, Properties & Microstructures. (British Ceramics Proceedings Ser.: No. 52). 342p. 1994. 150.00 (*0-901716-42-1*, Pub. by Inst Materials) Ashgate Pub Co.

***Lee, W. E. & Derby, B., eds.** Engineering with Ceramics. (British Ceramics Proceedings Ser.: No. 59). 320p. 1999. 150.00 (*1-86125-087-8*, Pub. by Inst Materials) Ashgate Pub Co.

Lee, W. H. & Dodge, D. A., eds. A Course on PC-Based Seismic Networks. (Illus.). 535p. (C). 1994. pap. text 145.00 (*0-7881-1247-3*) DIANE Pub.

Lee, W. Melville. History of Police in England. LC 70-108236. (Criminology, Law Enforcement, & Social Problems Ser.: No. 119). 1970. reprint ed. 24.00 (*0-87585-119-3*) Patterson Smith.

Lee, W. R. Ophthalmic Histopathology. (Illus.). 352p. 1993. 255.00 (*0-387-19686-2*) Spr-Verlag.

— Population Growth, Economic Development & Social Change in Bavaria, 1750-1850. Bruchey, Stuart, ed. LC 77-77194. (Dissertations in European Economic History Ser.). (Illus.). 1978. lib. bdg. 47.95 (*0-405-10806-0*) Ayer.

Lee, W. R., jt. ed. see Rosenhaft, Eve.

Lee, W. W. Cannon's Revenge. large type ed. 1996. 20.00 (*0-7838-1628-6*, G K Hall Lrg Type) Mac Lib Ref.

— Outlaw's Fortune. LC 92-44495. 154p. 1993. 19.95 (*0-8027-1270-3*) Walker & Co.

Lee, W. W., et al, eds. Plasma Deposition & Treatment of Polymers Vol. 544: Materials Research Society Symposium Proceedings. LC 99-40522. 300p. 1999. text 94.00 (*1-55899-450-5*) Materials Res.

***Lee, Wai.** Advanced Theory & Methodology. 2000. 60.00 (*1-883249-72-4*) F J Fabozzi.

Lee, Walt, ed. Reference Guide to Fantastic Films: Science Fiction, Fantasy, Horror. (Illus.). 750p. 1995. lib. bdg. 279.00 (*0-913616-30-3*) Hollywd Film Arch.

— Reference Guide to Fantastic Films: Science Fiction, Fantasy, Horror. (Illus.). 1995. reprint ed. lib. bdg. 149.00 (*0-913616-32-X*); reprint ed. lib. bdg. 179.00 (*0-913616-31-1*) Hollywd Film Arch.

— Reference Guide to Fantastic Films, Science Fiction, Fantasy, & Horror. LC 72-88775. (Illus.). 742p. (Orig.). 1974. lib. bdg. 169.00 (*0-913974-04-8*) Chelsea-Lee Bks.

— Reference Guide to Fantastic Films, Science Fiction, Fantasy, & Horror, Vol. 3: P-Z. LC 72-88775. (Illus.). 270p. (Orig.). 1974. pap. 29.95 (*0-913974-03-X*) Chelsea-Lee Bks.

Lee, Walter. AH. 240p. 1996. 27.95 (*1-887409-01-7*); pap. 14.95 (*1-887409-00-9*) Faun Pub Co.

— Computer Mirror Image. (Illus.). 1997. pap. 6.95 (*1-887409-09-2*) Faun Pub Co.

— Poems & Prayers. (Illus.). 54p. 1995. pap. 6.95 (*1-887409-06-8*) Faun Pub Co.

— Poems & Prayers. (Illus.). 54p. 1996. 11.95 (*1-887409-07-6*) Faun Pub Co.

— Radiation in Our Environment. 170p. 1995. 24.95 (*1-887409-04-1*); pap. 14.95 (*1-887409-03-3*) Faun Pub Co.

Lee, Walton, tr. see Murray, Andrew, ed.

Lee, Wanda. Angels in the Trees: A Poetry Collection. (Spiritual Growth & Awareness Ser.). 96p. (Orig.). 1993. pap. 7.95 (*1-883855-03-9*) St Georges Pr.

Lee, Wanda M. L. Introduction to Multicultural Counseling. LC 99-17941. 325p. 1999. 59.95 (*1-56032-567-4*); pap. 24.95 (*1-56032-568-2*) Hemisp Pub.

Lee, Warner. Night Sounds. Tobias, Eric, ed. 288p. (Orig.). 1992. mass mkt. 4.99 (*0-671-70426-5*) PB.

Lee, Warren. Sand Island Lighthouse Chronicles. Hurley, Neil, ed. (Illus.). 86p. 1998. spiral bd. 19.95 (*0-9661083-0-2*, 0398) Beacon Publ.

***Lee-Warren, Annabelle.** Guideline for Implementing Cryptography in the Federal Government. 139p. 2000. per. 15.00 (*0-16-058991-6*) USGPO.

Lee-Warren, Annabelle & Willard, Jo. A Blueprint for Health. LC 95-14339. 1995. pap. 9.95 (*0-8329-0512-7*) New Win Pub.

Lee, Warren F. Down along the Old Bel-Del: The History of the Belvidere Delaware Railroad Company. LC 86-61285. (Illus.). 350p. 1987. 34.95 (*0-9616893-0-7*) Bel-Del Ent.

Lee, Warren F. & Lee, Catherine T. A Chronology of the Belvidere Delaware Railroad & the Region Through Which It Operated. (Illus.). 325p. (Orig.). 1988. pap. 19.95 (*0-9616893-1-5*) Bel-Del Ent.

Lee, Warren F., et al. Agricultural Finance. 8th rev. ed. LC 87-31081. (Illus.). 480p. (C). 1988. text 44.95 (*0-8138-0051-X*) Iowa St U Pr.

Lee, Warren W. A Dream for South Central: The Autobiography of an Afro-Americanized Korean Christian Minister. LC 93-80837. 114p. (Orig.). 1993. pap. 6.95 (*0-9639920-0-7*) W W Lee.

***Lee, Watchman.** Table in the Wilderness. rev. ed. 224p. 2000. pap. 10.99 (*0-87508-707-8*, 707) Chr Lit.

Lee, Wayne. Deadly Days of Kansas. Cornell, Wayne, ed. LC 97-18894. (Illus.). 1997. pap. 14.95 (*0-87004-379-X*) Caxton.

— To Rise from Earth: An Easy-to-Understand Guide to Space Flight. LC 95-38941. (Illus.). 320p. 1996. 35.00 (*0-8160-3353-6*) Facts on File.

***Lee, Wayne.** To Rise from Earth: An Easy-to-Understand Guide to Space Flight. 2nd ed. LC 99-15971. (Illus.). 336p. 1999. 45.00 (*0-8160-4091-5*, Checkmark) Facts on File.

— To Rise from Earth: An Easy-to-Understand Guide to Spaceflight. 2nd ed. LC 99-15971. 1999. pap. 65.00 (*0-8160-4092-3*, Checkmark) Facts on File.

Lee, Wayne C. Bad Men & Bad Towns. LC 92-17951. (Orig.). 1993. pap. 14.95 (*0-87004-349-8*) Caxton.

— Ghost of a Gunfighter. (Orig.). 1979. mass mkt. 1.95 (*0-89083-559-4*, Zebra Kensgtn) Kensgtn Pub Corp.

***Lee, Wayne C.** Killer's Range. large type ed. LC 99-44239. 1999. 19.95 (*1-57490-237-7*) T T Beeler.

— Law of the Lawless LC 98-48524. 207 p. 1999. write for info. (*0-7540-3653-7*) Chivers N Amer.

Lee, Wayne C. Prairie Vengeance. large type ed. LC 97-44867. (Nightingale Ser.). 199p. 1998. pap. 18.95 (*0-7838-8379-X*, G K Hall & Co) Mac Lib Ref.

— Trail of the Skulls. large type ed. LC 97-36732. (Western Ser.). 200p. 1997. lib. bdg. 19.95 (*0-7862-1197-0*) Thorndike Pr.

— Trails of the Smoky Hill. LC 79-67199. (Illus.). 235p. (Orig.). 1980. pap. 12.95 (*0-87004-276-9*) Caxton.

— The Violent Man. large type ed. LC 97-40230. (Sagebrush Large Print Westerns Ser.). 1997. lib. bdg. 18.95 (*1-57490-098-6*) T T Beeler.

— War at Nugget Creek. large type ed. (Sagebrush Large Print Westerns Ser.). 179p. 1995. lib. bdg. 17.95 (*1-57490-004-8*) T T Beeler.

***Lee, Wayne C.** Warpath West. large type ed. (Nightingale Ser.). 2000. pap. 20.95 (*0-7838-8731-0*, G K Hall Lrg Type) Mac Lib Ref.

Lee, Wayne C. Wild Towns of Nebraska. LC 88-20227. (Illus.). 147p. (Orig.). 1988. pap. 14.95 (*0-87004-325-0*) Caxton.

— Wind over Rimfire. large type ed. LC 96-42252. (Sagebrush Large Print Westerns Ser.). 1996. lib. bdg. 17.95 (*1-57490-046-3*) T T Beeler.

Lee-Webb, Virginia, jt. ed. see Geary, Christrand M.

Lee, Wei-Chin, ed. Taiwan. annot. ed. LC 90-206517. (World Bibliographical Ser.: No. 113). 284p. 1990. lib. bdg. 69.00 (*1-85109-091-6*) ABC-CLIO.

***Lee, Wei-Chin, ed.** Taiwan in Perspective. 196p. 2000. 73.00 (*90-04-11849-7*) Brill Academic Pubs.

Lee, Weldon. A Guide to Photographing Rocky Mountain Wildlife. (Illus.). 340p. 1996. pap. text 7.98 (*1-56579-155-X*) Westcliffe Pubs.

Lee, Welton L., et al, eds. Guidelines to Acquisition & Management of Biological Specimens. 44p. 1982. pap. 7.00 (*0-942924-02-9*) Assn Syst Coll.

Lee, Welton L., ed. see Light, William J.

Lee, Welton L., ed. see Lindberg, David R.

***Lee, Wendi.** Deadbeat. 256p. 2000. per. 4.99 (*0-373-26339-2*) Harlequin Bks.

Lee, Wendi. Deadbeat. LC 98-37609. (Angela Matelli Mystery Ser.). 256p. 1999. text 22.95 (*0-312-16812-8*) St Martin.

— The Good Daughter. 1996. mass mkt. 4.99 (*0-312-95696-7*, Pub. by Tor Bks) St Martin.

***Lee, Wendi.** He Who Dies: An Angela Matelli Mystery. LC 99-86618. 256p. 2000. 22.95 (*0-312-20894-4*, Minotaur) St Martin.

Lee, Wendi. Missing Eden. 1999. per. 4.99 (*0-373-26301-5*) Harlequin Bks.

— Wendi Lee's Overland Trail. (Women of the West Ser.). 1997. mass mkt. 5.99 (*0-8125-5528-7*, Pub. by Forge NYC) St Martin.

Lee, Wendy, jt. auth. see Cousin, Pierre.

***Lee, Weng F.** Guide to Synthesizable VHDL Coding & Logic Synthesis with Synopsis. 550p. 2000. 79.95 (*0-12-440651-3*) Acad Pr.

Lee-Whiting, Brenda. Harvest of Stones: The German Settlement in Renfrew County. 336p. 1985. text 27.50 (*0-8020-2562-5*) U of Toronto Pr.

Lee, Wilford D. Control of Children Through Love & Counseling. 128p. (Orig.). 1975. pap. 2.95 (*0-89036-047-2*) Liahona Pub Trust.

Lee, Will. Cobalt. LC 95-90793. 1999. 16.95 (*0-533-11715-1*) Vantage.

Lee, William. Belwin Dictionary of Music. Bullock, Jack, ed. (Illus.). 152p. (YA). 1994. pap. text 9.95 (*0-89898-818-7*, EL03945) Wrner Bros.

— Belwin Dictionary of Music. rev. ed. Bullock, Jack, ed. (Illus.). 152p. (J). (gr. 2 up). 1994. pap. text 14.95 incl. disk (*0-89898-919-1*, EL03945IBM) Wrner Bros.

— Belwin Dictionary of Music. rev. ed. Bullock, Jack, ed. (Illus.). 152p. (J). (gr. 3 up). 1995. pap. text 14.95 incl. disk (*0-89898-920-5*, EL03945MAC) Wrner Bros.

— Belwin Pocket Dictionary of Music. Bullock, Jack, ed. (Illus.). 250p. (Orig.). (YA). 1994. pap. text 4.95 (*0-89898-817-9*, EL03946) Wrner Bros.

— Daniel Defoe: His Life, & Recently Discovered Writings: Extending from 1716 to 1729, 3 vols., Set. 1968. reprint ed. 219.70 incl. 3.5 hd (*0-685-66489-9*, 05101846) G Olms Pubs.

— Education in France: Contemporary Perspectives. Beauchamp, Edward R., ed. (Reference Books in International Education). 350p. Date not set. text 52.50 (*0-8153-1574-0*) Garland.

— John Leigh: Of Agawam (Ipswich), Massachusetts, 1634-1671, & His Descendants of the Name of Lee. 1998. reprint ed. pap. 36.00 (*0-7884-1056-3*, L111) Heritage Bk.

— Letters of William Lee, 1766-1783, 3 vols., Set. Ford, Worthington, ed. LC 70-140863. (Eyewitness Accounts of the American Revolution Ser.). (Illus.). 1971. reprint ed. 69.95 (*0-405-01254-3*) Ayer.

— Music in the 21st Century: The New Language. Bullock, Jack, ed. 84p. (Orig.). 1995. 14.95 incl. disk (*0-7604-0067-9*, EL03947IBM); 14.95 (*0-7604-0068-7*, EL03947MAC) Wrner Bros.

— Music in the 21st Century: The New Language. Bullock, Jack, ed. (Orig.). (C). 1995. pap. text 4.95 (*0-7604-0065-2*, EL03948) Wrner Bros.

— Music in the 21st Century: The New Language. Bullock, Jack, ed. 84p. (Orig.). 1995. pap. text 9.95 (*1-57623-841-5*, EL03947) Wrner Bros.

— Saps R-3 System Administrators Handbook. 1997. pap. text 79.99 (*0-7821-2051-2*) Sybex.

***Lee, William & Owens, Diana.** Multimedia-Based Instructional Design: Computer-Based Training, Web-Based Training, & Distance Learning. LC 99-51003. 350p. 2000. pap. 59.95 (*0-7879-5159-5*, Pfffr & Co) Jossey-Bass.

Lee, William, ed. see Somerville, Thomas.

***Lee, William B. & Sivell, John.** French Elementary Education & the Ecole Moderne. 140p. 2000. pap. 9.50 (*0-87367-823-0*) Phi Delta Kappa.

Lee, William B. & Steinberg, Earle. Service Parts Management: Principles & Practices. LC 84-70976. 129p. 1984. pap. 20.00 (*0-935406-47-6*) Am Prod & Inventory.

Lee, William C. Digital Cellular Systems. (Series in Telecommunications). 400p. 1997. write for info. (*0-471-52430-1*) Wiley.

— Mobile Communications Design Fundamentals. 2nd ed. LC 92-21130. (Series in Telecommunications). 400p. 1993. 98.95 (*0-471-57446-5*) Wiley.

— Mobile Communications Engineering. (Illus.). 480p. 1982. 70.00 (*0-07-037039-7*) McGraw.

— Mobile Communications Engineering. 2nd ed. LC 97-30668. (Telecommunications Ser.). (Illus.). 689p. 1997. 65.00 (*0-07-037103-2*) McGraw.

Lee, William F. M F Horn: Maynard Ferguson's Life in Music. LC 98-130080. (Illus.). 1997. write for info. (*0-89745-982-2*) Sunflower U Pr.

Lee, William G. Mavericks in the Workplace: Harnessing the Genius of American Workers. LC 98-23710. 208p. 1998. 25.00 (*0-19-511656-9*) OUP.

Lee, William H. Coenzyme Q-10. (Good Health Guides Ser.). 32p. pap. 3.95 (*0-87983-427-7*) NTC Contemp Pub Co.

Lee, William H. Friendly Bacteria. (Good Health Guide Ser.). 32p. (Orig.). 1988. pap. 3.95 (*0-87983-491-9*, 34919K, Keats Publng) NTC Contemp Pub Co.

— Getting the Best Out of Your Juicer. 176p. 1992. pap. 10.95 (*0-87983-586-9*, 35869K, Keats Publng) NTC Contemp Pub Co.

Lee, William H. Herbs & Herbal Medicine. Passwater, Richard A. & Mindell, Earl R., eds. (Good Health Guide Ser.). 31p. 1982. pap. 3.95 (*0-87983-294-0*, 32940K, Keats Publng) NTC Contemp Pub Co.

L

An Asterisk (*) at the beginning of an entry indicates that the title is appearing for the first time.

L

Lee, William H. Raw Fruit & Vegetable Juices & Drinks. LC 82-82323. 176p. (Orig.). 1982. pap. 4.95 (*0-87983-306-8*, 33068X, Keats Publng) NTC Contemp Pub Co.

Lee, William H. & Lee, Lynn. Book of Practical Aromatherapy. 200p. (Orig.). 1990. pap. 4.95 (*0-87983-539-7*, 35397K, Keats Publng) NTC Contemp Pub Co.

— Concentrated Youth-Restoring Foods. LC 93-50191. 315p. 1994. 29.98 (*0-941683-10-9*) Instant Improve.

— The Encyclopedia of Concentrated Aphrodisiacs. 300p. 1994. 29.98 (*0-941683-29-X*) Instant Improve.

Lee, William H. & Rosenbaum, Michael. Chlorella. (Good Health Guide Ser.). 32p. (Orig.). 1987. pap. 3.95 (*0-87983-464-1*, 34641K, Keats Publng) NTC Contemp Pub Co.

Lee, William M. & Williams, Roger, eds. Acute Liver Failure. (Illus.). 324p. (C). 1996. text 105.00 (*0-521-55381-4*) Cambridge U Pr.

Lee, William O., compiled by. Personal & Historical Sketches & Facial History of & by Members of the Seventh Regiment Michigan Volunteer Cavalry, 1862-1865. LC 89-83404. (Illus.). 313p. 1990. reprint ed. 25.00 (*0-914905-50-3*) Detroit Bk Pr.

Lee, William R. Kelp, Dulse & Other Supplements from the Sea. (Good Health Guide Ser.). 30p. 1983. pap. 2.95 (*0-87983-313-0*, 33130K, Keats Publng) NTC Contemp Pub Co.

— Language Teaching Games & Contests. 2nd ed. (Illus.). 214p. 1979. pap. text 13.50 (*0-19-432716-7*) OUP.

— Ophthalmic Histopathology. (Illus.). 352p. 1993. 250.00 (*3-540-19686-2*) Spr-Verlag.

Lee, William R., jt. auth. see James, C. Vaughan.

Lee, William S. & Brown, Derrick C. Advances in Telecommunications Networks. LC 94-44499. 204p. 1995. 83.00 (*0-89006-606-X*) Artech Hse.

Lee, William T. The ABM Treaty Charade: A Study in Elite Illusion & Delusion. LC 99-187491. (Journal of Social Political & Economic Studies Monographs: No. 25). 166p. 1997. pap. 24.00 (*0-930690-54-0*) Coun Soc Econ.

Lee, William W. Barkhamsted, Connecticut & Its Centennial, 1879. 178p. 1994. reprint ed. lib. bdg. 29.50 (*0-8328-4260-5*) Higginson Bk Co.

— Catalog of Barkhamsted Men Who Served in the Various Wars, 1775-1865. 100p. 1997. reprint ed. pap. 17.50 (*0-8328-5623-1*) Higginson Bk Co.

Lee, William W. & Mamone, Robert A. The Computer Based Training Handbook: Assessment, Design, Development, Evaluation. LC 94-46482. 283p. 1995. pap. 42.95 (*0-87778-286-5*) Educ Tech Pubns.

Lee, Winnie, jt. auth. see Lewis, Daniel I.

***Lee, Witness.** Abraham... Called by God. 342p. 1998. per. 16.00 (*0-7363-0359-6*, 07-070-901) Living Stream Ministry.

Lee, Witness. All Ages for the Lord's Testimony. 48p. 1987. pap. 3.50 (*0-87083-270-0*, 14-001-001) Living Stream Ministry.

— The All-Inclusive Christ. 192p. 1993. per. 8.00 (*0-87083-020-1*, 06-001-001) Living Stream Ministry.

— The All-Inclusive Spirit of Christ. 30p. 1969. pap. 2.00 (*0-87083-008-2*, 06-002-001) Living Stream Ministry.

— The Apostle's Teaching. 147p. 1994. per. 6.75 (*0-87083-550-5*, 04-012-001) Living Stream Ministry.

— An Autobiography Of A Person In Spirit. 88p. 1994. per. 5.50 (*0-87083-261-1*, 07-002-001) Living Stream Ministry.

— The Baptism in the Holy Spirit. 16p. 1969. pap. 2.25 (*0-87083-009-0*, 07-003-001) Living Stream Ministry.

— Basic Lessons on Life. 159p. 1993. per. 7.75 (*0-87083-729-X*, 07-037-001) Living Stream Ministry.

— Basic Lessons on Service. 158p. 1993. per. 7.75 (*0-87083-733-8*, 14-012-001) Living Stream Ministry.

— Being Desperate & Living Uniquely for the Gospel. 47p. 1987. pap. 3.75 (*0-87083-272-7*, 12-003-001) Living Stream Ministry.

— Being Desperate & Living Uniquely for the Gospel Small. 47p. 1987. pap. 2.50 (*0-87083-273-5*, 12-002-001) Living Stream Ministry.

— Being Renewed Day By Day. 29p. 1989. pap. 3.00 (*0-87083-478-9*, 13-001-001) Living Stream Ministry.

— The Body Of Christ. 56p. 1995. pap. 3.75 (*0-87083-395-2*, 08-001-001) Living Stream Ministry.

— A Brief Definition of the Kingdom of the Heavens. 56p. 1986. per. 3.75 (*0-87083-246-8*, 09-001-001) Living Stream Ministry.

— A Brief Presentation of the Lord's Recovery. 56p. 1993. pap. 3.75 (*0-87083-537-8*, 08-032-001) Living Stream Ministry.

— The Building Up Of The Body Of Christ. 61p. 1988. pap. 3.75 (*0-87083-400-2*, 08-002-001) Living Stream Ministry.

— El Caos Satanico En La Vieja Creacion Y La Economia Divina Para La Nueva Creacion.Tr. of SATANIC CHAOS IN THE OLD CREATION AND THE DIVINE ECONOMY FOR THE NEW CREATION. (SPA.). 127p. 1992. per. 6.25 (*0-87083-667-6*, 04-016-002) Living Stream Ministry.

— La Carne y El Espiritu.Tr. of FLESH AND THE SPIRIT. (SPA.). 57p. 1994. pap. 3.75 (*0-87083-793-1*, 07-039-002) Living Stream Ministry.

— The Centrality & Universality Of Christ. 53p. 1994. pap. 3.75 (*0-87083-750-8*, 06-016-001) Living Stream Ministry.

— Character. 67p. 1987. per. 4.00 (*0-87083-322-7*, 13-003-001) Living Stream Ministry.

— Christ & the Church Revealed & Typified in the Psalms. 239p. 1972. per. 9.25 (*0-87083-021-X*, 06-003-001) Living Stream Ministry.

— Christ as the Content of the Church & the Church as the Expression of Christ. 52p. 1997. pap. 4.25 (*0-87083-859-8*, 06-017-001) Living Stream Ministry.

— Christ As the Reality. 212p. 1981. per. 8.50 (*0-87083-047-3*, 06-004-001) Living Stream Ministry.

— Christ Our Portion. 37p. 1987. pap. 3.25 (*0-87083-373-1*, 06-005-001) Living Stream Ministry.

— Christ Revealed in the New Testament. 59p. 1989. pap. 3.75 (*0-87083-469-X*, 06-006-001) Living Stream Ministry.

— Christ vs. Religion. 194p. 1971. per. 8.50 (*0-87083-010-4*, 06-007-001) Living Stream Ministry.

— The Christian Life. 182p. 1994. per. 7.50 (*0-87083-820-2*, 07-046-001) Living Stream Ministry.

— The Church, The Reprint Of The Spirit. 29p. 1987. pap. 3.00 (*0-87083-374-X*, 08-004-001) Living Stream Ministry.

— The Completing Ministry of Paul. 107p. 1989. per. 5.75 (*0-87083-453-3*, 04-002-001) Living Stream Ministry.

— Concerning the Lord's Recovery. 88p. 1983. per. 5.50 (*0-87083-119-4*, 08-006-001) Living Stream Ministry.

— Concerning the Person of Christ. 47p. 1981. pap. 2.50 (*0-87083-088-0*, 06-008-001) Living Stream Ministry.

— Concerning the Triune God: The Father, the Son & the Spirit. 36p. 1980. pap. 2.50 (*0-87083-040-6*, 05-001-001) Living Stream Ministry.

— Conclusion Of The New Testament, 16. 2751p. 1991. per. 104.50 (*0-87083-215-8*, 10-073-001) Living Stream Ministry.

— Conformation To The Image Of The Son Of God. 22p. 1990. pap. 2.75 (*0-87083-529-7*, 07-026-001) Living Stream Ministry.

— El Conocimiento De La Vida.Tr. of KNOWLEDGE OF LIFE. (SPA.). 237p. 1995. per. 11.00 (*0-87083-917-9*, 07-010-002) Living Stream Ministry.

— La Constitucion Y La Edificacion Del Cuerpo De Cristo.Tr. of CONSTITUION AND THE BUILDING UP OF THE BODY OF CHRIST. (SPA.). 110p. 1995. per. 5.50 (*0-87083-858-X*, 08-038-002) Living Stream Ministry.

— The Constitution & the Building Up of the Body of Christ. 102p. 1992. pap. 5.50 (*0-87083-692-7*, 08-038-001) Living Stream Ministry.

— El Cristo Todo-Inclusivo.Tr. of ALL-INCLUSIVE CHRIST. (SPA.). 202p. 1991. per. 8.00 (*0-87083-626-9*, 06-001-002) Living Stream Ministry.

— The Crucial Points Of The Major Items Of The Lord's Recovery. 23p. 1993. pap. 3.00 (*0-87083-732-X*, 04-021-001) Living Stream Ministry.

— The Crucial Revelation of Life in the Scriptures. 150p. 1987. per. 7.00 (*0-87083-372-3*, 07-004-001) Living Stream Ministry.

— The Crystallization-Study Of The Book Of James. 96p. 1995. per. 6.50 (*0-87083-875-X*, 10-148-001) Living Stream Ministry.

— El Cuerpo De Cristo.Tr. of BODY OF CHRIST. (SPA.). 60p. 1989. pap. 3.75 (*0-87083-396-0*, 08-001-002) Living Stream Ministry.

— La Cumbre De La Vision Y La Realidad Del Cuerpo De Cristo.Tr. of HIGH PEAK OF THE VISION AND REALITY OF THE BODY OF CHRIST. (SPA.). 61p. 1995. pap. 4.25 (*0-87083-948-9*, 04-041-002) Living Stream Ministry.

— A Deeper Study Of The Divine Dispensing. 206p. 1990. per. 8.75 (*0-87083-562-9*, 04-015-001) Living Stream Ministry.

— Los Dios-Hombres.Tr. of GOD-MEN. (SPA.). 102p. 1995. per. 6.00 (*0-87083-877-6*, 04-039-002) Living Stream Ministry.

— La Dispensacion, La Transformacion Y La Edificacion Que La Trinidad Divina Procesada Efectua En Los Creyentes.Tr. of Dispensing, Transformation & Building of the Processed Divine Trinity in the Believers. (SPA.). 43p. 1995. pap. 4.00 (*0-87083-946-2*, 04-042-002) Living Stream Ministry.

— The Dispensing, Transformation & Building Of The Processed Divine Trinity In The Believers. 40p. 1995. pap. 4.00 (*0-87083-936-5*, 04-042-001) Living Stream Ministry.

— The Divine Dispensing For The Divine Economy. 51p. 1990. pap. 3.75 (*0-87083-558-0*, 04-014-001) Living Stream Ministry.

— The Divine Dispensing Of The Divine Trinity. 405p. 1990. per. 13.25 (*0-87083-519-X*, 05-002-001) Living Stream Ministry.

— The Divine Economy. 137p. 1986. per. 9.00 (*0-87083-268-9*, 04-003-001) Living Stream Ministry.

— The Divine Speaking. 67p. 1985. per. 4.75 (*0-87083-111-9*, 13-004-001) Living Stream Ministry.

— The Divine Stream. 17p. 1976. pap. 3.25 (*0-87083-000-7*, 07-005-001) Living Stream Ministry.

— La Dos Oraciones Mas Grandes del Apostol Pablo.Tr. of Two Greatest Prayers of the Apostle Paul. (SPA.). 49p. 1994. pap. 3.50 (*0-87083-795-8*, 08-026-002) Living Stream Ministry.

— La Economia De Dios.Tr. of Economy of God. (SPA.). 225p. 1990. per. 8.75 (*0-87083-536-X*, 04-005-002) Living Stream Ministry.

— La Economia Divina.Tr. of The/Divine Economy. (SPA.). 149p. 1989. per. 9.00 (*0-87083-443-6*, 04-003-002) Living Stream Ministry.

— La Economia Neotestamentaria De Dios.Tr. of God's New Testament Economy. (SPA.). 500p. 1989. per. 15.75 (*0-87083-252-2*, 04-006-002) Living Stream Ministry.

— The Economy & Dispensing of God. 114p. 1990. per. 8.75 (*0-87083-545-9*, 04-013-001) Living Stream Ministry.

— The Economy of God. 212p. 1968. per. 8.00 (*0-87083-001-5*, 04005001) Living Stream Ministry.

Lee, Witness. The Economy of God. 212p. 1968. per. 11.00 (*0-87083-415-0*) Living Stream Ministry.

Lee, Witness. The Economy of God & the Building Up of the Body of Christ. 72p. 1989. per. 7.50 (*0-87083-442-8*, 04-004-001) Living Stream Ministry.

— La Edificacion Del Cuerpo De Cristo.Tr. of BUILDING UP OF THE BODY OF CHRIST, THE. (SPA.). 68p. 1989. pap. 3.75 (*0-87083-435-5*, 08-002-002) Living Stream Ministry.

— The Enjoyment of Christ. 39p. 1995. pap. 4.00 (*0-87083-919-5*, 07-049-001) Living Stream Ministry.

— La Ensenanza de los Apostoles.Tr. of Apostles Teaching. (SPA.). 148p. 1990. per. 6.75 (*0-87083-554-8*, 04-012-002) Living Stream Ministry.

— Especialidad, La Generalidad y El Sentido Practico de La Vida de La Iglesia.Tr. of SPECIALITY, GENERALITY, AND PRACTICALITY OF THE CHURCH LIFE, THE. (SPA.). 77p. 1983. per. 4.75 (*0-87083-123-2*, 08-025-002) Living Stream Ministry.

— Estudio-Vida De Galatas, 2.Tr. of LIFE-STUDY OF GALATIANS. (SPA.). 435p. 1992. per. 20.00 (*0-87083-671-4*, 10-076-002) Living Stream Ministry.

— Estudio-Vida De Genesis: 1-17, 1.Tr. of LIFE-STUDY OF GENESIS. (SPA.). 234p. 1995. per. 11.50 (*0-87083-870-9*, 10-137-002) Living Stream Ministry.

— Estudio-Vida De Genesis: #18-36, 2.Tr. of LIFE-STUDY OF GENESIS. (SPA.). 277p. 1995. per. 12.50 (*0-87083-907-1*, 10-139-002) Living Stream Ministry.

— Estudio-Vida De Genesis: #37-55, 3.Tr. of LIFE-STUDY OF GENESIS. (SPA.). 243p. 1995. per. 12.00 (*0-87083-931-4*, 10-138-002) Living Stream Ministry.

Lee, Witness. Estudio-Vida de Ginesis, Mensajes 56-77.Tr. of Life-study of Genesis. (SPA.). 264p. 1995. per. 12.25 (*0-87083-949-7*) Living Stream Ministry.

— Estudio-Vida de Ginesis, Mensajes 92-109.Tr. of Life-study of Genesis. (SPA.). 238p. 1996. per. 11.50 (*0-87083-995-0*) Living Stream Ministry.

— Estudio-Vida de Ginesis, Mensajes 78-91.Tr. of Life-study of Genesis. (SPA.). 188p. 1996. per. 10.25 (*0-87083-967-5*) Living Stream Ministry.

— Estudio-Vida de Ginesis, Mensajes 110-120.Tr. of Life-study of Genesis. (SPA.). 130p. 1996. per. 9.00 (*1-57593-326-8*) Living Stream Ministry.

Lee, Witness. Estudio-Vida De Hebreos: Mensajes 1-17.Tr. of LIFE-STUDY OF HEBREWS. (SPA.). 205p. 1983. per. 10.75 (*0-87083-863-6*, 10-094-002) Living Stream Ministry.

— Estudio-Vida De Hebreos: Mensajes 18-33.Tr. of LIFE-STUDY OF HEBREWS. (SPA.). 202p. 1983. per. 10.75 (*0-87083-864-4*, 10-095-002) Living Stream Ministry.

— Estudio-Vida De Hebreos: Mensajes 34-52.Tr. of LIFE-STUDY OF HEBREWS. (SPA.). 218p. 1983. per. 11.00 (*0-87083-865-2*, 10-096-002) Living Stream Ministry.

— Estudio-Vida De Hebreos: Mensajes 53-69.Tr. of LIFE-STUDY OF HEBREWS. (SPA.). 190p. 1983. per. 10.00 (*0-87083-866-0*, 10-097-002) Living Stream Ministry.

— Estudio-Vida De Juan, 4.Tr. of LIFE-STUDY OF JOHN (4 VOLUME SET). (SPA.). 649p. 1986. per. 30.75 (*0-87083-237-9*, 10-123-002) Living Stream Ministry.

— Estudio-Vida De Romanos, Vol. 1, No. 1-16.Tr. of LIFE-STUDY OF ROMANS, VOLUME 1. (SPA.). 219p. 1985. per. 11.00 (*0-87083-190-9*, 10-029-002) Living Stream Ministry.

— Estudio-Vida De Romanos, Vol. 2, No. 17-31.Tr. of LIFE-STUDY OF ROMANS, VOLUME 1. (SPA.). 192p. 1986. per. 10.00 (*0-87083-191-7*, 10-030-002) Living Stream Ministry.

— Estudio-Vida De Romanos, Vol. 3, No. 32-50.Tr. of LIFE-STUDY OF ROMANS, VOLUME 1. (SPA.). 171p. 1986. per. 10.00 (*0-87083-192-5*, 10-031-002) Living Stream Ministry.

— Estudio-Vida De Romanos, Vol. 4, No. 51-69.Tr. of LIFE-STUDY OF ROMANS, VOLUME 1. (SPA.). 192p. 1986. per. 10.25 (*0-87083-193-3*, 10-032-002) Living Stream Ministry.

— Everyone Speaking The Word Of God. 68p. 1987. per. 4.75 (*0-87083-293-X*, 13-005-001) Living Stream Ministry.

— Excelling Gift For The Building Up Of The Church, The. 85p. 1989. per. 5.25 (*0-87083-437-1*, 08-007-001) Living Stream Ministry.

— The Exercise & Practice of the God-Ordained Way. 310p. 1990. per. 11.00 (*0-87083-509-2*, 12-004-001) Living Stream Ministry.

— The Exercise Of The Kingdom For The Building Of The Church. 82p. 1978. per. 5.25 (*0-87083-476-2*, 08-008-001) Living Stream Ministry.

— Experiementar A Cristo Comon Vida Para La Edificacion de La Iglesia.Tr. of EXPERIENCE OF CHRIST AS LIFE FOR THE BUILDING UP OF THE CHURCH, THE. (SPA.). 136p. 1994. per. 7.00 (*0-87083-824-5*, 07-041-002) Living Stream Ministry.

— The Experience & Growth In Life. 220p. 1990. per. 8.75 (*0-87083-508-4*, 07-006-001) Living Stream Ministry.

— The Experience of Christ. 216p. 1978. per. 9.00 (*0-87083-797-4*, 07-008-001) Living Stream Ministry.

— The Experience of Christ As Life for the Building Up of the Church. 128p. 1994. per. 7.00 (*0-87083-780-X*, 07-041-001) Living Stream Ministry.

— The Experience of Life. 386p. 1973. per. 15.50 (*0-87083-417-7*, 07-009-001) Living Stream Ministry.

— La Experiencia De Vida.Tr. of EXPERIENCE OF LIFE. (SPA.). 386p. 1992. per. 15.50 (*0-87083-632-3*, 07-009-002) Living Stream Ministry.

— La Experiencia y El Crecimiento en Vida.Tr. of EXPERIENCE AND GROWTH IN LIFE, THE. (SPA.). 246p. 1990. per. 8.75 (*0-87083-808-3*, 07-006-002) Living Stream Ministry.

— Experiencing Christ As the Offerings for The Church Meetings. 168p. 1983. per. 7.50 (*0-87083-117-8*, 06-009-001) Living Stream Ministry.

— Finding Christ by the Living Star. 29p. 1970. pap. 2.00 (*0-87083-012-0*, 06-010-001) Living Stream Ministry.

— Five Emphases In The Lord's Recovery. 67p. 1991. pap. 4.00 (*0-87083-631-5*, 08-021-001) Living Stream Ministry.

— The Flesh & The Spirit. 54p. 1994. pap. 3.75 (*0-87083-749-4*, 07-039-001) Living Stream Ministry.

— The Four Major Steps of Christ. 46p. 1969. pap. 2.50 (*0-87083-013-9*, 06-011-001) Living Stream Ministry.

— Fulfillment Of God's Purpose By The Growth Of Christ In Us. 80p. 1994. pap. 5.00 (*0-87083-826-1*, 07-047-001) Living Stream Ministry.

— The Fulfillment of the Tabernacle & the Offerings in the Writings of John. 590p. 1991. per. 17.75 (*0-87083-535-1*, 10-072-001) Living Stream Ministry.

— The Full Knowledge of the Word of God. 78p. 1987. per. 5.00 (*0-87083-289-1*, 10-018-001) Living Stream Ministry.

— Further Light Concerning The Building Up Of The Body Of Christ. 70p. 1988. pap. 4.50 (*0-87083-405-3*, 08-009-001) Living Stream Ministry.

— A Genuine Church. 18p. 1990. pap. 2.00 (*0-87083-530-0*, 08-031-001) Living Stream Ministry.

— The Genuine Ground of Oneness. 147p. 1979. per. 6.75 (*0-87083-022-8*, 08-011-001) Living Stream Ministry.

— Glad Tidings to Fallen Man. 21p. 1980. pap. 2.00 (*0-87083-041-4*, 11-001-001) Living Stream Ministry.

— The Glorious Vision & the Way of the Cross. 58p. 1989. pap. 3.75 (*0-87083-479-7*, 14-003-001) Living Stream Ministry.

— The God-Men. 105p. 1995. per. 6.00 (*0-87083-871-7*, 04-039-001) Living Stream Ministry.

— The God-Ordained Way To Practice The New Testament Economy. 173p. 1987. per. 8.00 (*0-87083-326-X*, 12-006-001) Living Stream Ministry.

— God's New Testament Economy. 466p. 1995. per. 19.25 (*0-87083-199-2*, 04-006-001) Living Stream Ministry.

— God's Way in Life. 44p. 1990. pap. 3.50 (*0-87083-546-7*, 07-028-001) Living Stream Ministry.

— Gospel Outlines. 380p. 1980. per. 13.75 (*0-87083-039-2*, 11-002-001) Living Stream Ministry.

— The Greatest Prophecy in the Bible & Its Fulfillment. 77p. 1994. pap. 4.75 (*0-87083-799-0*, 08-042-001) Living Stream Ministry.

— Hablando Poemas En Las Reuniones De La Iglesia Para La Edificacion Organica De La Iglesia Como El Cuerpo De Cristo (Bosq.Tr. of SPEAKING POEMS IN THE CHURCH MEETINGS FOR THE ORGANIC BUILDING UP OF THE CHURCH AS THE BODY OF CHRIST (OUTLINES). (SPA.). 24p. 1989. pap. 2.50 (*0-87083-485-1*, 12-020-002) Living Stream Ministry.

— The Heavenly Ministry of Christ. 81p. 1989. per. 5.25 (*0-87083-447-9*, 06-012-001) Living Stream Ministry.

— The Heavenly Vision. 64p. 1995. pap. 5.25 (*0-87083-852-0*, 04-036-001) Living Stream Ministry.

— The High Peak of the Vision & the Reality of the Body of Christ. 58p. 1995. pap. 4.25 (*0-87083-935-7*, 04-041-001) Living Stream Ministry.

— Historia De Dios En Su Union Con El Hombre.Tr. of HISTORY OF GOD IN HIS UNION WITH MAN. (SPA.). 188p. 1995. per. 7.50 (*0-87083-854-7*, 04-019-002) Living Stream Ministry.

— La Historia De La Iglesia Y Las Iglesias Locales.Tr. of HISTORY OF THE CHURCH AND THE LOCAL CHURCHES. (SPA.). 151p. 1991. per. 6.50 (*0-87083-585-8*, 08-033-002) Living Stream Ministry.

— The History of God in His Union With Man. 180p. 1993. per. 7.50 (*0-87083-721-4*, 04-019-001) Living Stream Ministry.

— The History of the Church & the Local Churches. 140p. 1991. per. 6.50 (*0-87083-578-5*, 08-033-001) Living Stream Ministry.

— The Holy Word for Morning Revival: Chronicles, Ezra, Nehemiah, Esther. 43p. 1995. pap. 4.25 (*0-87083-828-8*, 13-051-001) Living Stream Ministry.

— The Holy Word for Morning Revival: Colossians. 71p. 1991. pap. 4.75 (*0-87083-572-6*, 13-029-001) Living Stream Ministry.

— The Holy Word for Morning Revival: Constitution & the Building Up of the Body of Christ - One Body & One Spirit. 79p. 1992. pap. 5.00 (*0-87083-693-5*, 13-043-001) Living Stream Ministry.

— The Holy Word for Morning Revival: Daniel & Zechariah. 87p. 1991. pap. 5.25 (*0-87083-610-2*, 13-030-001) Living Stream Ministry.

— The Holy Word for Morning Revival: Ephesians, 2. 173p. 1990. pap. 10.50 (*0-87083-556-4*, 13025001) Living Stream Ministry.

— The Holy Word for Morning Revival: Galatians. 99p. 1990. pap. 5.50 (*0-87083-539-4*, 13-023-001) Living Stream Ministry.

— The Holy Word for Morning Revival: Hebrews, 4. 287p. 1993. pap. 19.00 (*0-87083-670-6*, 13040001) Living Stream Ministry.

— The Holy Word for Morning Revival: Isaiah. 71p. 1991. pap. 4.25 (*0-87083-565-3*, 13-026-001) Living Stream Ministry.

— The Holy Word for Morning Revival: James. 80p. 1993. pap. 4.75 (*0-87083-738-9*, 13-045-001) Living Stream Ministry.

— The Holy Word for Morning Revival: Jeremiah & Lamentations. 71p. 1992. pap. 4.75 (*0-87083-637-4*, 13-033-001) Living Stream Ministry.

— The Holy Word for Morning Revival: Job. 71p. 1993. pap. 4.75 (*0-87083-695-1*, 13-041-001) Living Stream Ministry.

— The Holy Word for Morning Revival: John, 4 vols. 295p. 1990. pap. 19.00 (*0-87083-491-6*, 13014001) Living Stream Ministry.

— The Holy Word for Morning Revival: Joshua, Judges & Ruth. 75p. 1993. pap. 5.00 (*0-87083-728-1*, 13-042-001) Living Stream Ministry.

An Asterisk (*) at the beginning of an entry indicates that the title is appearing for the first time.

— The Holy Word for Morning Revival: Minor Prophets. 71p. 1992. pap. 4.75 (*0-87083-664-1*, 13-036-001) Living Stream Ministry.
— The Holy Word for Morning Revival: Philippians. 85p. 1991. pap. 5.25 (*0-87083-568-8*, 13-028-001) Living Stream Ministry.
— The Holy Word for Morning Revival: Proverbs, Ecclesiastes, Song of Songs. 61p. 1995. pap. 4.25 (*0-87083-885-7*, 13-053-001) Living Stream Ministry.
— The Holy Word for Morning Revival: Romans, 3 vols. 217p. 1990. pap. 14.25 (*0-87083-482-7*, 13008001) Living Stream Ministry.
— The Holy Word for Morning Revival: Thessalonians. 92p. 1991. pap. 5.25 (*0-87083-612-9*, 13-031-001) Living Stream Ministry.
— The Holy Word for Morning Revival: Titus & Philemon. 57p. 1992. pap. 4.25 (*0-87083-641-2*, 13-035-001) Living Stream Ministry.
— The Holy Word for Morning Revival: 1 & 2 Kings. 71p. 1994. pap. 4.75 (*0-87083-787-7*, 13-048-001) Living Stream Ministry.
— The Holy Word for Morning Revival: 1 & 2 Samuel. 80p. 1994. pap. 4.75 (*0-87083-746-X*, 13-044-001) Living Stream Ministry.
— The Holy Word for Morning Revival: 1 Corinthians, 3 vols. 219p. 1990. pap. 14.25 (*0-87083-503-3*, 13020001) Living Stream Ministry.
— The Holy Word for Morning Revival: 1 John, 2 vols. 117p. 1995. pap. 8.50 (*0-87083-862-8*, 13052001) Living Stream Ministry.
— The Holy Word for Morning Revival: 1 Peter, 2. 115p. 1994. pap. 8.50 (*0-87083-777-X*, 13047001) Living Stream Ministry.
— The Holy Word for Morning Revival: 1 Timothy. 71p. 1991. pap. 4.75 (*0-87083-629-3*, 13-032-001) Living Stream Ministry.
— The Holy Word for Morning Revival: 2 Corinthians, 2. 143p. 1990. pap. 9.50 (*0-87083-520-3*, 13022001) Living Stream Ministry.
— The Holy Word for Morning Revival: 2 John, 3 John, Jude. 47p. 1995. pap. 4.25 (*0-87083-904-7*, 13-054-001) Living Stream Ministry.
— The Holy Word for Morning Revival: 2 Peter. 60p. 1994. pap. 4.50 (*0-87083-822-9*, 13-050-001) Living Stream Ministry.
— The Holy Word for Morning Revival: 2 Timothy. 57p. 1992. pap. 4.25 (*0-87083-634-X*, 13-034-001) Living Stream Ministry.
— The Home Meetings. 95p. 1986. per. 5.50 (*0-87083-231-X*, 12-007-001) Living Stream Ministry.
— How to Meet. 253p. 1979. per. 8.25 (*0-87083-023-6*, 14-004-001) Living Stream Ministry.
— The Indwelling Christ in the Canons of the New Testament. 145p. 1989. per. 6.75 (*0-87083-451-7*, 06-013-001) Living Stream Ministry.
— The Intrinsic View of the Body of Christ. 101p. 1991. per. 5.50 (*0-87083-636-6*, 08-035-001) Living Stream Ministry.
— Issue of the Dispensing of the Processed Trinity & Transmitting of the Transcending Christ. 99p. 1993. per. 5.50 (*0-87083-741-9*, 04-023-001) Living Stream Ministry.
— The Issue of the Union of the Consummated Spirit of the Triune God & the Regenerated Spirit of the Believers. 90p. 1995. per. 6.00 (*0-87083-857-1*, 04-037-001) Living Stream Ministry.
— The Kernel of the Bible. 216p. (J). (gr. k). 1977. per. 8.50 (*0-87083-464-9*, 04-007-001) Living Stream Ministry.
— Key Points on the Home Meetings. 88p. 1986. per. 5.50 (*0-87083-239-5*, 12-009-001) Living Stream Ministry.
— The Kingdom. 547p. 1980. per. 17.25 (*0-87083-038-4*, 09-002-001) Living Stream Ministry.
— The Kingdom & the Church. 41p. 1980. pap. 3.50 (*0-87083-042-2*, 09-003-001) Living Stream Ministry.
— The King's Antecedents & Status. 91p. 1977. pap. 5.50 (*0-87083-806-7*, 06-014-001) Living Stream Ministry.
— The Knowledge of Life. 216p. per. 8.25 (*0-87083-014-7*, 07010001) Living Stream Ministry.
— Lecciones de la Verdad, Nivel Uno, 1.Tr. of TRUTH LESSONS, LEVEL ONE, VOLUME 3. (SPA.). 184p. 1986. per. 7.25 (*0-87083-242-5*, 15-032-002) Living Stream Ministry.
— Lecciones de la Verdad, Nivel Uno, 2.Tr. of TRUTH LESSONS, LEVEL ONE, VOLUME 3. (SPA.). 215p. 1987. per. 8.00 (*0-87083-281-6*, 15033002) Living Stream Ministry.
— Lecciones de la Verdad, Nivel Uno, 3.Tr. of TRUTH LESSONS, LEVEL ONE, VOLUME 3. (SPA.). 140p. 1988. per. 6.50 (*0-87083-297-2*, 15-034-002) Living Stream Ministry.

Lee, Witness. Lecciones de la verdad, nivel uno, Vol. 2.Tr. of Truth Lessons, Level One, Volume 2. (SPA.). 215p. 1987. per. 8.50 (*0-87083-280-8*) Living Stream Ministry.

Lee, Witness. Lecciones de Vida, 2.Tr. of Life Lessons. (SPA.). 111p. 1987. per. 5.75 (*0-87083-294-8*, 15-011-002) Living Stream Ministry.
— Lecciones de Vida, 3.Tr. of Life Lessons. (SPA.). 95p. 1987. per. 5.50 (*0-87083-295-6*, 15-012-002) Living Stream Ministry.
— Lecciones de Vida, 4.Tr. of Life Lessons. (SPA.). 91p. 1987. per. 5.50 (*0-87083-296-4*, 15-013-002) Living Stream Ministry.
— Lecciones de Vida, Vol. 1.Tr. of Life Lessons. (SPA.). 85p. 1987. per. 5.25 (*0-87083-285-9*, 15-010-002) Living Stream Ministry.
— Lessons on Prayer. 247p. 1981. per. 10.00 (*0-87083-045-7*, 07-011-001) Living Stream Ministry.
— Life & Building As Portrayed in the Song of Songs. 171p. 1979. per. 7.50 (*0-87083-024-4*, 07-012-001) Living Stream Ministry.
— The Life & Way for the Practice of the Church Life. 151p. 1994. per. 7.50 (*0-87083-785-0*, 07-042-001) Living Stream Ministry.
— The Life for the Preaching of the High Gospel. 68p. 1994. pap. 4.00 (*0-87083-776-1*, 11-004-001) Living Stream Ministry.
— Life Lessons, 1. 83p. 1987. per. 5.25 (*0-87083-276-X*, 15-010-001) Living Stream Ministry.
— Life Lessons, 2. 109p. 1987. per. 5.75 (*0-87083-277-8*, 15-011-001) Living Stream Ministry.
— Life Lessons, 3. 93p. 1987. per. 5.50 (*0-87083-278-6*, 15-012-001) Living Stream Ministry.
— Life Lessons, 4. 89p. 1987. per. 5.50 (*0-87083-279-4*, 15-013-001) Living Stream Ministry.
— Life Lessons, Pocket Size. 361p. 1987. boxed set 18.00 (*0-87083-413-4*, 15-024-901) Living Stream Ministry.
— Life Messages, 2. 669p. 1992. per. 22.25 (*0-87083-659-5*, 07-036-001) Living Stream Ministry.
— Life-Study of Acts: Messages 1-18, 1. 150p. 1985. per. 9.50 (*0-87083-184-4*, 10-067-001) Living Stream Ministry.
— Life-Study of Acts: Messages 19-34, 2. 144p. 1985. per. 9.25 (*0-87083-185-2*, 10-068-001) Living Stream Ministry.
— Life-Study of Acts: Messages 35-55, 3. 187p. 1985. per. 10.25 (*0-87083-186-0*, 10-069-001) Living Stream Ministry.
— Life-Study of Acts: Messages 56-72, 4. 334p. 1985. per. 10.25 (*0-87083-187-9*, 10-070-001) Living Stream Ministry.
— Life-Study of Daniel. 114p. 1991. per. 8.75 (*0-87083-633-1*, 10-089-001) Living Stream Ministry.
— Life-Study of Deuteronomy. 214p. 1991. per. 11.25 (*0-87083-567-X*, 10-071-001) Living Stream Ministry.
— Life-Study of Ephesians: Messages 1-28, 1. 248p. 1991. per. 12.25 (*0-87083-147-X*, 10-033-001) Living Stream Ministry.
— Life-Study of Ephesians: Messages 29-63, 2. 287p. 1991. per. 13.00 (*0-87083-148-8*, 10-034-001) Living Stream Ministry.
— Life-Study of Ephesians: Messages 64-97, 3. 286p. 1991. per. 13.00 (*0-87083-149-6*, 10-035-001) Living Stream Ministry.
— Life-Study of 1 & 2 Chronicles, Ezra, Nehemiah, Esther. 201p. 1995. per. 10.75 (*0-87083-873-3*, 10-132-001) Living Stream Ministry.
— Life-Study of 1 & 2 Kings. 160p. 1994. per. 10.00 (*0-87083-809-1*, 10-113-001) Living Stream Ministry.
— Life-Study of 1 & 2 Samuel. 271p. 1994. per. 12.50 (*0-87083-805-9*, 10-112-001) Living Stream Ministry.
— Life-Study of 1 Corinthians: Messages 1-23, 1. 210p. 1990. per. 11.00 (*0-87083-140-2*, 10-052-001) Living Stream Ministry.
— Life-Study of 1 Corinthians: Messages 24-47, 2. 215p. 1990. per. 11.25 (*0-87083-141-0*, 10-053-001) Living Stream Ministry.
— Life-Study of 1 Corinthians: Messages 48-69, 3. 207p. 1990. per. 11.00 (*0-87083-142-9*, 10-054-001) Living Stream Ministry.
— Life-Study of Galatians: Messages 1-24, 1. 218p. 1990. per. 11.50 (*0-87083-145-3*, 10-063-001) Living Stream Ministry.
— Life-Study of Galatians: Messages 25-46, 2. 199p. 1990. per. 11.00 (*0-87083-146-1*, 10-064-001) Living Stream Ministry.
— Life-Study of Hebrews: Messages 1-17, 1. 190p. 1992. per. 10.75 (*0-87083-156-9*, 10-094-001) Living Stream Ministry.
— Life-Study of Hebrews: Messages 18-33, 2. 190p. 1993. per. 10.75 (*0-87083-157-7*, 10-095-001) Living Stream Ministry.
— Life-Study of Hebrews: Messages 34-52, 3. 206p. 1993. per. 11.00 (*0-87083-158-5*, 10-096-001) Living Stream Ministry.
— Life-Study of Hebrews: Messages 53-69. 186p. 1993. per. 10.00 (*0-87083-672-2*, 10-097-001) Living Stream Ministry.
— Life-Study of Isaiah: Messages 1-16, 1. 110p. 1991. per. 8.75 (*0-87083-580-7*, 10-065-001) Living Stream Ministry.
— Life-Study of Isaiah: Messages 17-32, 2. 111p. 1991. per. 8.75 (*0-87083-596-3*, 10-066-001) Living Stream Ministry.
— Life-Study of Isaiah Vol. 3: Messages 33-54. 226p. 1994. per. 11.25 (*0-87083-823-7*, 10-136-001) Living Stream Ministry.
— Life-Study of Jeremiah & Lamentations. 281p. 1992. per. 13.50 (*0-87083-666-8*, 10-045-001) Living Stream Ministry.
— Life-Study of Job. 209p. 1993. per. 11.50 (*0-87083-699-4*, 10-098-001) Living Stream Ministry.
— Life-Study of Joshua, Judges & Ruth. 305p. 1993. per. 11.25 (*0-87083-743-5*, 10-109-001) Living Stream Ministry.
— Life-Study of Leviticus, Pt. 2, Vol. 2. 127p. 1989. per. 9.00 (*0-87083-465-7*, 10-024-001) Living Stream Ministry.
— Life-Study of Leviticus, Vol. 1, Pt. 1. 160p. 1989. per. 12.50 (*0-87083-489-4*, 10-021-001) Living Stream Ministry.
— Life-Study of Leviticus, Vol. 1, Pt. 2. 134p. 1989. per. 9.25 (*0-87083-439-8*, 10-023-001) Living Stream Ministry.
— Life-Study of Leviticus, Vol. 2, Pt. 1. 149p. 1990. per. 9.75 (*0-87083-504-1*, 10-022-001) Living Stream Ministry.
— Life-Study of Leviticus: Numbers & Deuteronomy, 2. 1162p. 1991. boxed set 70.00 (*0-87083-599-8*, 10-080-901) Living Stream Ministry.

Lee, Witness. Life-study of Matthew: John, Acts, James, Revelation, 8 vols. 4811p. 1985. boxed set 350.00 (*0-7363-0113-5*) Living Stream Ministry.

Lee, Witness. Life-Study of Matthew-John, Acts, James-Revelation, 8. 4811p. 1985. 350.00 (*0-87083-160-7*, 10025901) Living Stream Ministry.
— Life-Study of Minor Prophets. 225p. 1993. per. 11.75 (*0-87083-691-9*, 10-105-001) Living Stream Ministry.
— Life-Study of Numbers: Messages 1-15, 1. 113p. 1990. per. 11.00 (*0-87083-513-0*, 10-048-001) Living Stream Ministry.
— Life-Study of Numbers: Messages 16-28, 2. 95p. 1990. per. 8.00 (*0-87083-514-9*, 10-049-001) Living Stream Ministry.
— Life-Study of Numbers: Messages 29-41, 3. 116p. 1990. per. 8.75 (*0-87083-538-6*, 10-050-001) Living Stream Ministry.
— Life-Study of Numbers: Messages 42-53, 4. 212p. 1990. per. 8.00 (*0-87083-549-1*, 10-051-001) Living Stream Ministry.
— Life-Study of of Genesis & Exodus, 7. 3495p. 1987. boxed set 240.00 (*0-87083-356-1*, 10-020-901) Living Stream Ministry.
— Life-Study of Pentateuch: Genesis & Deuteronomy, 9. 4657p. 1991. boxed set 310.00 (*0-87083-598-X*, 10-081-901) Living Stream Ministry.
— Life-Study of Romans: Messages 1-16, 9, 1. 202p. 1989. per. 11.00 (*0-87083-137-2*, 10-029-001) Living Stream Ministry.
— Life-Study of Romans: Messages 17-31, 9, 2. 174p. 1989. per. 10.00 (*0-87083-138-0*, 10-030-001) Living Stream Ministry.
— Life-Study of Romans: Messages 32-50, 9, 3. 162p. 1989. per. 10.00 (*0-87083-139-9*, 10-031-001) Living Stream Ministry.
— Life-Study of Romans: Messages 51-69, 9, 4. 178p. 1989. per. 10.25 (*0-87083-136-4*, 10-032-001) Living Stream Ministry.
— Life-Study of Romans - Hebrews, 9. 5551p. 1984. 350.00 (*0-87083-128-3*, 10026901) Living Stream Ministry.
— Life-Study of 2 Corinthians: Messages 1-29, 1. 262p. 1990. per. 12.50 (*0-87083-143-7*, 10-055-001) Living Stream Ministry.
— Life-Study of 2 Corinthians: Messages 30-59, 2. 257p. 1990. per. 12.50 (*0-87083-144-5*, 10-056-001) Living Stream Ministry.
— Life-Study of the Psalms Vol. 1: Messages 1-23. 284p. 1993. per. 13.00 (*0-87083-726-5*, 10-101-001) Living Stream Ministry.
— Life-Study of The Psalms Vol. 2: Messages 24-45. 228p. 1993. per. 12.00 (*0-87083-727-3*, 10-102-001) Living Stream Ministry.
— Life-Study of Zechariah. 97p. 1992. per. 8.25 (*0-87083-639-0*, 10-090-001) Living Stream Ministry.
— Living a Life According to the High Peak of God's Revelation. 41p. 1994. pap. 4.00 (*0-87083-791-5*, 04-032-001) Living Stream Ministry.
— The Living & Practical Way to Enjoy Christ. 59p. 1994. pap. 3.75 (*0-87083-775-3*, 07-040-001) Living Stream Ministry.
— Living in & with the Divine Trinity. 138p. 1990. per. 6.50 (*0-87083-560-2*, 05-003-001) Living Stream Ministry.
— The Living Needed for Building up the Small Group Meetings. 114p. 1986. per. 6.00 (*0-87083-222-0*, 12-010-001) Living Stream Ministry.
— Luz Adicional con Respecto a la Edificacion del Cuerpo de Cristo.Tr. of FURTHER LIGHT CONCERNING THE BUILDING UP OF THE BODY OF CHRIST. (SPA.). 81p. 1988. pap. 4.50 (*0-87083-426-6*, 08-009-002) Living Stream Ministry.
— La Manera Biblica de Reunirse y de Servir para la Edificacion del Cuerpo De Cristo.Tr. of SCRIPTURAL WAY TO MEET AND TO SERVE FOR THE BUILDING UP OF THE BODY OF CHRIST. (SPA.). 315p. 1988. per. 10.25 (*0-87083-423-1*, 12-018-002) Living Stream Ministry.
— La Manera de Practicar el Recobro Actual Del Senor.Tr. of Way to Practice the Lord's Present Recovery. (SPA.). 54p. 1989. pap. 3.75 (*0-87083-472-X*, 12-026-002) Living Stream Ministry.
— La Manera Ordenada Por Dios de Practicar la Economia Neotestamentaria.Tr. of God-Ordained Way to Practice the New Testament Economy. (SPA.). 183p. 1987. per. 8.00 (*0-87083-329-4*, 12-006-002) Living Stream Ministry.
— Manera Practica de Llevar una Vida Conforme a la Cumbre de la Revelacion Divinae Contenida En Las Santas Escrituras.Tr. of PRACTICAL WAY TO LIVE A LIFE ACCORDING TO THE HIGH PEAK OF THE DIVINE REVELATION IN THE HOLY SCRIPTURES. (SPA.). 50p. 1994. pap. 4.50 (*0-87083-825-3*, 04-033-002) Living Stream Ministry.
— La Manera Viva y Practica de Disfrutar a Cristo.Tr. of Living & Practical Way to Enjoy Christ. (SPA.). 72p. 1994. pap. 3.75 (*0-87083-790-7*, 07-040-002) Living Stream Ministry.
— Meeting to Speak the Word of God. 60p. 1987. per. 4.50 (*0-87083-291-3*, 12-011-001) Living Stream Ministry.
— Men Who Turn the Age. 30p. 1991. pap. 3.00 (*0-87083-604-8*, 16-025-001) Living Stream Ministry.
— The Mending Ministry of John. 154p. 1989. per. 7.00 (*0-87083-455-X*, 04-008-001) Living Stream Ministry.
— Messages Given to the Working Saints. 92p. 1989. per. 5.50 (*0-87083-480-0*, 13-009-001) Living Stream Ministry.
— The Ministry of the New Testament & the Teaching & Fellowship of the Apostles. 33p. 1993. pap. 3.25 (*0-87083-722-2*, 15-047-001) Living Stream Ministry.
— The Move of God in Man. 126p. 1994. per. 6.25 (*0-87083-807-5*, 04-020-001) Living Stream Ministry.
— The Mysteries in God's New Testament Economy. 83p. 1990. pap. 4.50 (*0-87083-527-0*, 04-011-001) Living Stream Ministry.
— The New Testament Priests of the Gospel. 145p. 1989. per. 6.75 (*0-87083-471-1*, 13-010-001) Living Stream Ministry.
— The New Testament Service. 158p. 1986. per. 7.00 (*0-87083-229-8*, 13-011-001) Living Stream Ministry.
— Nuestro Espiritu Humano.Tr. of OUR HUMAN SPIRIT. (SPA.). 82p. 1986. per. 4.50 (*0-87083-259-X*, 07-013-002) Living Stream Ministry.
— La Nueva Manera de Llevar a Cabo el Aumento y la Extension de la Iglesia.Tr. of NEW WAY TO CARRY OUT THE INCREASE AND SPREAD OF THE CHURCH. (SPA.). 67p. 1987. per. 5.25 (*0-87083-368-5*, 12-013-002) Living Stream Ministry.
— On Home Meetings. 64p. 1986. per. 4.75 (*0-87083-257-3*, 12-014-001) Living Stream Ministry.
— On Knowing The Bible. 64p. 1990. pap. 4.00 (*0-87083-561-0*, 10-059-001) Living Stream Ministry.
— One Body & One Spirit. 30p. 1992. pap. 3.50 (*0-87083-816-4*, 15-046-001) Living Stream Ministry.
— The One New Man. 77p. 1986. per. 5.00 (*0-87083-266-2*, 08-014-001) Living Stream Ministry.
— Oneness & The One Accord According to The Lord's Aspiration & The Body Life & Service According to His Pleasure. 53p. 1990. pap. 3.75 (*0-87083-511-4*, 08-029-001) Living Stream Ministry.
— Organic Building up of the Church As the Body of Christ to Be the Organism of the Processed & Dispensing Triune God. 82p. 1989. per. 5.25 (*0-87083-497-5*, 08-015-001) Living Stream Ministry.
— The Organic Practice of the New Way. 80p. 1989. per. 4.25 (*0-87083-477-0*, 12 015-001) Living Stream Ministry.
— The Organic Union in God's Relationship with Man. 94p. 1993. pap. 4.50 (*0-87083-736-2*, 04-022-001) Living Stream Ministry.
— The Organism of the Triune God in the Organic Union of the Divine Trinity. 64p. 1988. pap. 4.00 (*0-87083-399-5*, 08-016-001) Living Stream Ministry.
— El Organismo del Dios Triuno en la Union Organica de Su Trinidad Divina.Tr. of Organism of the triune God in the Organic Union of His Divine Trinity. (SPA.). 65p. 1989. pap. 4.00 (*0-87083-432-0*, 08-016-002) Living Stream Ministry.
— Our Human Spirit. 82p. 1984. per. 4.50 (*0-87083-124-0*, 07-013-001) Living Stream Ministry.
— Our Urgent Need - Spirit & Life. 37p. 1988. pap. 3.50 (*0-87083-394-4*, 07-014-001) Living Stream Ministry.
— The Overcomers. 109p. 1992. per. 6.25 (*0-87083-674-9*, 08-037-001) Living Stream Ministry.
— La Palabra Santa para el Avivamiento Matutino: Colosenses.Tr. of The/Holy Word for Morning Revival:Colossians. (SPA.). 71p. 1991. pap. 4.75 (*0-87083-574-2*, 13-029-002) Living Stream Ministry.
— La Palabra Santa para el Avivamiento Matutino: Cronicas, Esdras, Nehemias, Esther.Tr. of Holy Word For Morning Revival: Chronicles, Ezra, Nehemiah, Esther. (SPA.). 43p. 2001. pap. 4.25 (*0-87083-850-4*, 13-051-002) Living Stream Ministry.
— La Palabra Santa para el Avivamiento Matutino: Daniel y Zacarias.Tr. of The/Holy Word for Morning Revival: Daniel & Zechariah. (SPA.). 87p. 1991. pap. 5.25 (*0-87083-611-0*, 13-030-002) Living Stream Ministry.
— La Palabra Santa para el Avivamiento Matutino: Efesios, 2 vols.Tr. of The/Holy Word for Morning Revival:Ephesians. (SPA.). 173p. 1990. pap. 10.50 (*0-87083-537-2*, 13024002) Living Stream Ministry.
— La Palabra Santa para el Avivamiento Matutino: Filipenses.Tr. of The/Holy Word for Morning Revival: Philippians. (SPA.). 85p. 1991. pap. 5.25 (*0-87083-569-6*, 13-028-002) Living Stream Ministry.
— La Palabra Santa para el Avivamiento Matutino: Galatas.Tr. of The/Holy Word for Morning Revival: Galatians. (SPA.). 99p. 1990. pap. 5.50 (*0-87083-540-8*, 13-023-002) Living Stream Ministry.
— La Palabra Santa para el Avivamiento Matutino: Hebreos, 4.Tr. of The/Holy Word for Morning Revival: Hebrews. (SPA.). 287p. 1993. pap. 14.25 (*0-87083-675-7*, 13037002) Living Stream Ministry.
— La Palabra Santa para el Avivamiento Matutino: Isaias.Tr. of The/Holy Word for Morning Revival: Isaiah. (SPA.). 71p. 1991. pap. 4.25 (*0-87083-566-1*, 13-026-002) Living Stream Ministry.
— La Palabra Santa para el Avivamiento Matutino: Jacobo.Tr. of The/Holy Word for Morning Revival: James. (SPA.). 74p. 1993. pap. 4.75 (*0-87083-744-3*, 13-045-002) Living Stream Ministry.
— La Palabra Santa para el Avivamiento Matutino: Jeremias y Lamentaciones.Tr. of The/Holy Word for Morning Revival: Jeremiah & Lamentations. (SPA.). 71p. 1992. pap. 4.75 (*0-87083-638-2*, 13-033-002) Living Stream Ministry.
— La Palabra Santa para el Avivamiento Matutino: Job.Tr. of The/Holy Word for Morning Revival: Job. (SPA.). 57p. 1993. pap. 4.75 (*0-87083-696-X*, 13-041-002) Living Stream Ministry.
— La Palabra Santa para el Avivamiento Matutino: Josue, Jueces y Ruth.Tr. of The/Holy Word for Morning Revival: Joshua, Judges, & Ruth. (SPA.). 75p. 1993. pap. 5.00 (*0-87083-731-1*, 13-042-002) Living Stream Ministry.
— La Palabra Santa para el Avivamiento Matutino: Profetas Menores.Tr. of The/Holy Word for Morning Revival: Minor Prophets. (SPA.). 71p. 1992. pap. 4.75 (*0-87083-665-X*, 13-036-002) Living Stream Ministry.
— La Palabra Santa Para El Avivamiento Matutino: Proverbios, Eclesiastes, Cantar De Los Cantares.Tr. of

L

The/Holy Word for Morning Revival: Proverbs, Ecclesiastes, Song of Songs. (SPA.). 61p. 1995. pap. 4.25 (*0-87083-903-9*, 13-053-002) Living Stream Ministry.
— La Palabra Santa para el Avivamiento Matutino: Romamos, 3 vols.Tr. of The/Holy Word for Morning Revival: Romans 1:1--5:11. (SPA.). 217p. 1990. pap. 14.25 (*0-87083-484-3*, 13006002) Living Stream Ministry.
— La Palabra Santa para el Avivamiento Matutino: Tesalonicenses.Tr. of The/Holy Word for Morning Revival: Thessalonians. (SPA.). 87p. 1991. pap. 5.25 (*0-87083-615-3*, 13-031-002) Living Stream Ministry.
— La Palabra Santa para el Avivamiento Matutino: Tito y Filemon.Tr. of The/Holy Word for Morning Revival: Titus & Philemon. (SPA.). 57p. 1992. pap. 4.25 (*0-87083-645-5*, 13-035-002) Living Stream Ministry.
— La Palabra Santa para el Avivamiento Matutino: 1 Corintios, 3 vols.Tr. of The/Holy Word for Morning Revival: 1 Corinthians. (SPA.). 219p. 1990. pap. 14.25 (*0-87083-505-X*, 13020002) Living Stream Ministry.
— La Palabra Santa para el Avivamiento Matutino: 1 Juan, 2.Tr. of The/Holy Word for Morning Revival:1 John. (SPA.). 117p. 1995. pap. 8.50 (*0-87083-867-9*, 13049002) Living Stream Ministry.
— La Palabra Santa para el Avivamiento Matutino: 1 Pedro, 2.Tr. of The/Holy Word for Morning Revival:1 Peter. (SPA.). 115p. 1994. pap. 8.50 (*0-87083-800-8*, 13047002) Living Stream Ministry.
— La Palabra Santa para el Avivamiento Matutino: 1 Timoteo.Tr. of The/Holy Word for Morning Revival: 1 Timothy. (SPA.). 76p. 1991. pap. 4.75 (*0-87083-630-7*, 13-032-002) Living Stream Ministry.
— La Palabra Santa para el Avivamiento Matutino: 1 y 2 Reyes.Tr. of The/Holy Word for Morning Revival: 1 & 2 Kings. (SPA.). 71p. 1994. pap. 4.75 (*0-87083-789-3*, 13-048-002) Living Stream Ministry.
— La Palabra Santa para el Avivamiento Matutino: 1 y 2 Samuel.Tr. of The/Holy Word for Morning Revival: 1 & 2 Samuel. (SPA.). 71p. 1994. pap. 4.75 (*0-87083-747-8*, 13-044-002) Living Stream Ministry.
— La Palabra Santa para el Avivamiento Matutino: 2 Corintios, 2.Tr. of The/Holy Word for Morning Revival: 2 Corinthians. (SPA.). 143p. 1990. pap. 9.50 (*0-87083-534-3*, 13021002) Living Stream Ministry.
— La Palabra Santa para el Avivamiento Matutino: 2 Juan, 3 Juan, Judas.Tr. of The/Holy Word for Morning Revival: 2 John, 3 John, Jude. (SPA.). 47p. 1995. pap. 4.25 (*0-87083-906-3*, 13-054-002) Living Stream Ministry.
— La Palabra Santa para el Avivamiento Matutino: 2 Pedro, Vol. 2.Tr. of HOLY WORD FOR MORNING REVIVAL, THE: 2 PETER. (SPA.). 60p. 1994. pap. 4.50 (*0-87083-821-0*, 13-050-002) Living Stream Ministry.
— La Palabra Santa para el Avivamiento Matutino: 2 Timoteo.Tr. of The/Holy Word for Morning Revival: 2 Timothy. (SPA.). 57p. 1992. pap. 4.25 (*0-87083-640-4*, 13-034-002) Living Stream Ministry.
— La Palabra Santa Para El Avivamiento Matutino Cuerpo De Cristo: Constitucion Y La Edificacion Del Cuerpo De Cristo...Tr. of The/Holy Word for Morning Revival: Constitution & Building up of the Body of Christ . . . . (SPA.). 79p. 1992. pap. 5.00 (*0-87083-694-3*, 13-043-002) Living Stream Ministry.
— The Parts of Man. 49p. 1969. pap. 2.50 (*0-87083-002-3*, 04-024-001) Living Stream Ministry.
— The Passover. 58p. 1980. per. 3.00 (*0-87083-043-0*, 07-015-001) Living Stream Ministry.
— The Perfecting of the Saints & the Building up of the Body of Christ. 51p. 1989. pap. 3.75 (*0-87083-468-1*, 08-018-001) Living Stream Ministry.
— The Practical & Organic Building Up of the Church. 100p. 1989. per. 5.50 (*0-87083-462-2*, 08-019-001) Living Stream Ministry.
— The Practical Expression of the Church. 188p. 1970. per. 8.25 (*0-87083-015-5*, 08-020-001) Living Stream Ministry.
— Practical Points Concerning Blending. 47p. 1994. pap. 4.25 (*0-87083-783-4*, 08-040-001) Living Stream Ministry.
— Practical Way To Live a Life According to the High Peak of the Divine Revelation in the Holy Scriptures. 50p. 1994. pap. 4.50 (*0-87083-818-0*, 04-033-001) Living Stream Ministry.
— The Practice of Prophesying. 46p. 1990. pap. 3.50 (*0-87083-543-2*, 12-028-001) Living Stream Ministry.
— The Practice Of The Group Meetings. 68p. 1990. pap. 4.00 (*0-87083-551-3*, 12-027-001) Living Stream Ministry.
— Una Presentacion Breve de Lo Que es el Recobro Del Senor.Tr. of BRIEF PRESENTATION OF THE LORD'S RECOVERY. (SPA.). 59p. 1991. pap. 3.75 (*0-87083-570-X*, 08-032-002) Living Stream Ministry.
— The Priesthood. 202p. 1980. per. 8.25 (*0-87083-033-3*, 14-005-001) Living Stream Ministry.
— Profecia de los Cuatro "Sietes" en la Biblia.Tr. of Prophecy of the Four "Sevens" in the Bible, The. (SPA.). 97p. 1995. per. 5.50 (*0-87083-856-3*, 10-060-002) Living Stream Ministry.
— Profetizar En Las Reuniones De La Iglesia Para La Edificacion Organica De La Iglesia Como El Cuerpo De Cristo, El (Bosqu.Tr. of PROPHESYING IN THE CHURCH MEETINGS FOR THE ORGANIC BUILDING UP OF THE CHURCH AS THE BODY OF CHRIST (OUTLINES). (SPA.). 71p. 1989. pap. 4.50 (*0-87083-487-8*, 12-017-002) Living Stream Ministry.
— The Prophecy of the Four "Sevens" in the Bible. 96p. 1990. per. 5.50 (*0-87083-548-3*, 10-060-001) Living Stream Ministry.
— Puntos Claves Sobre las Reuniones en Casa.Tr. of KEY POINTS ON THE HOME MEETINGS. (SPA.). 91p. 1986. per. 5.50 (*0-87083-250-6*, 12-009-002) Living Stream Ministry.
— Puntos Practicos en Cuanto a la Compenetracion.Tr. of PRACTICAL POINTS CONCERNING THE BLENDING. (SPA.). 48p. 1994. pap. 4.25 (*0-87083-786-9*, 08-040-002) Living Stream Ministry.
— The Recovery of God's House & God's City. 84p. 1980. per. 5.25 (*0-87083-034-1*, 08-023-001) Living Stream Ministry.
— Renovados de Dia en Dia.Tr. of Being Renewed Day by Day. (SPA.). 30p. 1989. pap. 3.00 (*0-87083-490-8*, 13-001-002) Living Stream Ministry.
— El Resultado De La Dispensacion De La Trinidad Procesada Y La Transmision Del Cristo Que Lo Transciende Todo.Tr. of ISSUE OF THE DISPENSING OF THE PROCESSED TRINITY AND THE TRANSMITTING OF THE TRANSCENDING CHRIST. (SPA.). 106p. 1994. per. 5.50 (*0-87083-788-5*, 04-023-002) Living Stream Ministry.
— Las Reuniones en Casa.Tr. of HOME MEETINGS, THE. (SPA.). 102p. 1986. per. 5.50 (*0-87083-235-2*, 12-007-002) Living Stream Ministry.
— Salvation in Life in the Book of Romans. 57p. 1990. pap. 4.25 (*0-87083-526-2*, 07-025-001) Living Stream Ministry.
— The Satanic Chaos In The Old Creation & The Divine Economy For The New Creation. 122p. 1992. per. 6.25 (*0-87083-661-7*, 04-016-001) Living Stream Ministry.
— The Scriptural Way to Meet & to Serve for the Building Up of the Body of Christ. 285p. 1988. per. 10.25 (*0-87083-379-0*, 12-018-001) Living Stream Ministry.
— The Secret of Experiencing Christ. 125p. 1986. per. 6.75 (*0-87083-227-1*, 07-016-001) Living Stream Ministry.
— Seven Mysteries in the First Epistle of John. 79p. 1992. pap. 4.50 (*0-87083-089-9*, 10-086-001) Living Stream Ministry.
— La Situacion Mundial y la Direccion del Mover del Senor.Tr. of World Situation & the Direction of the Lord's Move. (SPA.). 65p. 1991. pap. 4.25 (*0-87083-593-9*, 04-017-002) Living Stream Ministry.
— Speaking Christ for the Building up of the Body of Christ. 143p. 1988. per. 6.75 (*0-87083-422-3*, 12-019-001) Living Stream Ministry.
— Speciality, Generality, & Practicality of the Church Life. 70p. 1984. per. 4.75 (*0-87083-121-6*, 08-025-001) Living Stream Ministry.
— The Spirit. 122p. 1990. per. 6.25 (*0-87083-553-X*, 07-027-001) Living Stream Ministry.
— The Spirit & the Body. 230p. 1976. per. 9.00 (*0-87083-459-2*, 07-017-001) Living Stream Ministry.
— The Spirit with Our Spirit. 144p. 1994. per. 6.75 (*0-87083-798-2*, 07-038-001) Living Stream Ministry.
— Spiritual Applications of the Tabernacle. 98p. 1987. per. 5.50 (*0-87083-376-6*, 14-007-001) Living Stream Ministry.
— The Stream Magazine, Bks. 1 & 2. 816p. 1980. per. 42.00 (*0-87083-036-8*, 20-004-001) Living Stream Ministry.
— A Summary of the Study of the New Testament Way of Christian Service. 50p. 1990. pap. 3.50 (*0-87083-515-7*, 14-009-001) Living Stream Ministry.
— The Ten Great Critical Ones. 64p. 1995. pap. 4.50 (*0-87083-937-3*, 04-043-001) Living Stream Ministry.
— A Thorough View of the Body of Christ. 57p. 1990. pap. 3.75 (*0-87083-512-2*, 08-030-001) Living Stream Ministry.
— To Be Saved in the Life of Christ As Revealed in Romans. 45p. 1990. pap. 4.00 (*0-87083-528-9*, 07-024-001) Living Stream Ministry.
— To Serve in the Human Spirit. 112p. 1984. per. 6.00 (*0-87083-102-X*, 14-008-001) Living Stream Ministry.
— The Tree Of Life. 156p. 1987. per. 7.50 (*0-87083-300-6*, 07-018-001) Living Stream Ministry.
— Tree of Life-Spanish. 162p. 1999. per. 8.25 (*1-57593-813-8*, 07-018-402) Living Stream Ministry.
— The Triune God to Be Life to the Tripartite Man. 163p. 1990. per. 7.25 (*0-87083-552-1*, 15-043-001) Living Stream Ministry.
— The Truth Concerning the Trinity. 37p. 1994. pap. 2.75 (*0-87083-751-6*, 20-101-001) Living Stream Ministry.
— Truth Lessons, Level 1, Level 1. 158p. 1985. per. 7.25 (*0-87083-205-0*, 15-032-001) Living Stream Ministry.
— Truth Lessons, Level 1, Level 1. 134p. 1986. per. 6.50 (*0-87083-209-3*, 15-034-001) Living Stream Ministry.
— Truth Lessons, Level 1, Level 1. 135p. 1987. per. 6.50 (*0-87083-211-5*, 15-035-001) Living Stream Ministry.
— Truth Lessons, Level 1, Level 2. 213p. 1986. per. 8.50 (*0-87083-207-7*, 15-033-001) Living Stream Ministry.
— Truth Lessons, Level 2, 1. 164p. 1988. per. 7.25 (*0-87083-357-X*, 15-036-001) Living Stream Ministry.
— Truth Lessons, Level 2, Level 2. 116p. 1990. per. 6.25 (*0-87083-359-6*, 15-041-001) Living Stream Ministry.
— Truth Lessons, Level 2, Level 2. 125p. 1994. per. 6.25 (*0-87083-361-8*, 15-057-001) Living Stream Ministry.
— Truth Messages. 112p. 1992. per. 6.50 (*0-87083-658-7*, 08-036-001) Living Stream Ministry.
— The Two Great Mysteries in God's Economy. 48p. 1989. pap. 3.75 (*0-87083-492-4*, 04-009-001) Living Stream Ministry.
— The Two Greatest Prayers of the Apostle Paul. 47p. 1989. pap. 3.50 (*0-87083-430-4*, 08-026-001) Living Stream Ministry.
— La Unidad Y La Unanimidad Segun La Aspiracion Del Senor Y La Vida Y El Servicio Del Cuerpo Segun Su Deleite.Tr. of The/Lord's Aspiration & the Body Life & Service According to His Pleasure. (SPA.). 54p. 1990. pap. 3.75 (*0-87083-516-5*, 08-029-002) Living Stream Ministry.
— Los Vencedores.Tr. of OVERCOMERS, THE. (SPA.). 111p. 1993. per. 6.25 (*0-87083-724-9*, 08-037-002) Living Stream Ministry.
— Una Vida Conforme a la Cumbre de la Revelacion de Dios.Tr. of Living a Life According to the Peak of God's Elevation. (SPA.). 41p. 1994. pap. 4.00 (*0-87083-792-3*, 04-032-002) Living Stream Ministry.
— Una Vision Completa del Cuerpo de Cristo.Tr. of THOROUGH VIEW OF THE BODY OF CHRIST. (SPA.). 62p. 1990. pap. 3.75 (*0-87083-531-9*, 08-030-002) Living Stream Ministry.
— The Vision of God's Building. 227p. 1968. per. 9.75 (*0-87083-025-2*, 08-027-001) Living Stream Ministry.
— The Vision of the Divine Dispensing & Guidelines for the Practice of the New Way. 94p. 1990. per. 5.50 (*0-87083-559-9*, 12-031-001) Living Stream Ministry.
— The Visions of Ezekiel. 242p. 1980. per. 9.25 (*0-87083-035-X*, 10-044-001) Living Stream Ministry.
— Vital Factors for the Recovery of the Church Life. 85p. 1986. per. 5.25 (*0-87083-228-X*, 08-028-001) Living Stream Ministry.
— El Vivir Necesario Para La Edificacion De Las Reuniones De Grupos Pequenos.Tr. of Living Needed for Building up the Small Group Meetings. (SPA.). 132p. 1986. per. 6.00 (*0-87083-251-4*, 12-010-002) Living Stream Ministry.
— Watchman Nee: A Seer Of The Divine Revelation In The Present Age. 348p. 1991. 17.25 (*0-87083-625-0*, 20-001-901) Living Stream Ministry.
— The Way to Practice the Lord's Present Move. 156p. 1986. per. 7.00 (*0-87083-233-6*, 12-025-001) Living Stream Ministry.
— The Way to Practice the Lord's Present Recovery. 50p. 1989. pap. 3.75 (*0-87083-433-9*, 12-026-001) Living Stream Ministry.
— The Wonderful Christ in the Canons of the New Testament. 270p. 1989. per. 9.75 (*0-87083-457-6*, 06-015-001) Living Stream Ministry.
— The World Situation & God's Move. 85p. 1982. per. 5.25 (*0-87083-092-9*, 04-010-001) Living Stream Ministry.
— The World Situation & the Direction of the Lord's Move. 59p. 1991. pap. 4.25 (*0-87083-586-6*, 04-017-001) Living Stream Ministry.
— A Young Man In God's Plan. 37p. 1986. pap. 3.25 (*0-87083-264-6*, 16-009-001) Living Stream Ministry.
— Young People's Training. 212p. 1989. per. 8.50 (*0-87083-467-3*, 16-010-001) Living Stream Ministry.

Lee, Witness, jt. auth. see Nee, Watchman.

Lee, Wo-Yen, jt. auth. see Geping, Qu.

***Lee-Wong, Song Mei.** Politeness & Face in Chinese Culture. 2000. 48.95 (*3-631-32022-1*) P Lang Pubng.
— Politeness & Face in Chinese Culture. LC 99-89976. (Cross Cultural Communication Ser.: Vol. 6). 344p. 2000. pap. text 48.95 (*0-8204-3295-4*) P Lang Pubng.

Lee, Wright. Not As Briefed. (Illus.). 240p. (Orig.). 1996. pap. text 14.95 (*1-885354-01-0*) Honoribus Pr.

Lee, Y. C. Evolution, Learning & Cognition. 600p. (Orig.). (C). 1989. pap. 48.00 (*9971-5-0530-4*); text 105.00 (*9971-5-0529-0*) World Scientific Pub.

***Lee, Y. C., ed.** Micro-Electro-Mechanical Systems, 1999. (MEMS Ser.). 611p. 1999. 170.00 (*0-7918-1638-9*) ASME Pr.

Lee, Y. C., et al, eds. Manufacturing Aspects in Electronic Packaging, 1993. LC 93-73267. 125p. pap. 40.00 (*0-7918-1032-1*) ASME.
— Neoglycoconjugates Pt. A: Synthesis. (Methods in Enzymology Ser.: Vol. 242). (Illus.). 328p. 1994. text 84.00 (*0-12-182143-9*) Acad Pr.

Lee, Y. C. & Bennett, T. J., eds. Manufacturing Aspects in Electronic Packaging. (EEP Series, Vol. 2: PED: Vol. 60). 220p. 1992. 57.50 (*0-7918-1112-3*, G00756) ASME.

Lee, Y. C. & Lee, Reiko T., eds. Neoglycoconjugates: Preparation & Applications. (Illus.). 549p. 1994. text 136.00 (*0-12-440585-1*) Acad Pr.

Lee, Y. C., ed. see Simon, Melvin I.

Lee, Y. K., et al. Application of Microbes in Biotechnology. LC 99-18302. 1999. 39.95 (*981-4021-40-7*) Spr-Verlag.

Lee, Y. K., jt. ed. see Nga, B. H.

Lee, Y. T. Interviews & Speeches. 244p. 1994. pap. text 13.00 (*1-879771-12-8*) Global Pub NJ.

***Lee Yang Chung.** Environmental & Safety Concerns in Undergroun, Vol. 1. LC 99-496427. 544p. 1998. 91.00 (*90-5410-911-4*) Ashgate Pub Co.
— Environmental & Safety Concerns in Underground, Vol. 2. LC 99-496427. 410p. 1998. 91.00 (*90-5410-912-2*) Ashgate Pub Co.

Lee Yao, Esther S. Chinese Women: Past & Present. LC 83-300. (Woman in History Ser.: Vol. 82). (Illus.). 271p. (Orig.). 1983. pap. text 15.00 (*0-86663-098-8*) Ide Hse.

Lee, Yeon-Ho. The State, Society & Big Business in South Korea. LC 96-28932. (Routledge Studies in the Growth Economies of Asia Ser.). 224p. (C). 1997. 75.00 (*0-415-14583-X*) Routledge.

Lee, Yeong H. Vertical Integration & Technological Innovation: A Transaction Cost Approach. LC 93-38432. (Studies on Industrial Productivity). 144p. 1994. text 15.00 (*0-8153-1569-4*) Garland.

Lee, Yim-Shu. Computer-Aided Analysis & Design of Switch-Mode Power Supplies. (Electrical Engineering & Electronics Ser.: Vol. 81). (Illus.). 544p. 1993. text 185.00 Dekker.

Lee Ying Ho. Antique Ceramics. Goh Beng Choo, tr. 125p. 1996. 19.95 (*981-3029-86-2*, Pub. by Asiapac) China Bks.
— Jadeite. 126p. 1996. 19.95 (*981-3029-87-0*, Pub. by Asiapac) China Bks.

Lee, Yo An, jt. auth. see Samimy, Keiko.

***Lee, Yok-Shiu F. & So, Alvin Y.** Asia's Environmental Movements: Comparative Perspectives. LC 99-12310. (Asia & the Pacific Ser.). (Illus.). 328p. 1999. pap. text 27.95 (*1-56324-909-X*, East Gate Bk) M E Sharpe.

Lee, Yok-Shiu F. & So, Alvin Y., eds. Asia's Environmental Movements: Comparative Perspectives. LC 99-12310. (Asia & the Pacific Ser.). (Illus.). 328p. 1999. text 77.95 (*1-56324-908-1*, East Gate Bk) M E Sharpe.

Lee, Yong S. Public Personnel Administration & Constitutional Values. LC 92-8404. 184p. 1992. 55.00 (*0-89930-610-1*, LCS, Quorum Bks) Greenwood.

Lee, Yong S., ed. Technology Transfer & Public Policy. LC 97-1699. 328p. 1997. 72.95 (*1-56720-084-2*, Quorum Bks) Greenwood.
— Technology Transfer & Public Policy: Preparing for the Twenty-First Century. 236p. (Orig.). 1994. pap. 15.00 (*0-944285-38-4*) Pol Studies.

Lee, Yongwoo. Information & Reality: Korean Contemporary Art. (Illus.). 91p. 1997. pap. 24.95 (*0-947912-27-4*) Dist Art Pubs.

***Lee, Yoonmi.** Modern Education, Textbooks & Image of the Nation: Politics of Modernization & Nationalism in Korean Education. LC 00-34725. (East Asia Ser.). 2000. write for info. (*0-8153-3874-0*) Garland.

Lee, Young C., et al. Across the Pacific: Contemporary Korean & Korean American Art. Kim, Su G. & Kang, Myung Y., trs. from KOR. (Illus.). 102p. (Orig.). (C). 1993. pap. text 26.00 (*0-9604514-4-7*) Queens Mus.

Lee, Young J., tr. see Kim, Dae-Jung.

Lee, Young Ki, jt. auth. see Judd, Kenneth L.

Lee, Young-Sook C., jt. auth. see Martin, Samuel E.

***Lee, Yuan-Kun, et al.** Handbook of Probiotics. LC 98-27805. 211p. 1999. 99.95 (*0-471-19025-X*) Wiley.

Lee, Yuan-Yuan & Shen, Sinyan. Chinese Musical Instruments. LC 99-31752. (Chinese Music Monograph Ser.). (Illus.). 208p. 1999. pap. text 22.95 (*1-880464-03-9*) Chinese Mus Soc.

Lee, Yuan-Yuan, ed. see Shen, Sin-yan.

Lee, Yuan-Yuan, ed. see Shen, Sinyan.

Lee, Yueh-Ting, et al, eds. Stereotype Accuracy: Toward Appreciating Group Differences. LC 95-16845. 330p. 1995. text 24.95 (*1-55798-307-0*) Am Psychol.
— Through the Looking-Glass: Personality in Culture. LC 98-16383. 265p. 1998. 69.95 (*0-8058-2813-3*) L Erlbaum Assocs.

Lee, Yung-Cheng, et al, eds. Optoelectronic Packaging. LC 96-44716. (Microwave & Optical Engineering Ser.). 261p. 1997. 87.95 (*0-471-11188-0*) Wiley.

Lee, Yung-Cheng, jt. ed. see Feldman, Michael R.

Lee, Yur-Bok & Patterson, Wayne, eds. Korean-American Relations, 1866-1997. LC 98-3401. (SUNY Series in Korean Studies). 256p. (C). 1998. text 65.50 (*0-7914-4025-7*); pap. text 21.95 (*0-7914-4026-5*) State U NY Pr.

Lee, Z., jt. auth. see Rand, W.

***Leeb, Carolyn S.** Away from the Father's House: The Social Location of the Na'ar & Na'arah in Ancient Israel. (Journal for the Study of the Old Testament Supplement Ser.: No. 301). 225p. 2000. 65.00 (*1-84127-105-5*, Pub. by Sheffield Acad) CUP Services.

Leeb, Donna, jt. auth. see Leeb, Stephen.

Leeb, Johannes, jt. auth. see Heydecker, Joe.

Leeb-Lundberg, Kristina. Mathematics is More Than Counting. LC 85-5967. 23p. 1985. 5.00 (*0-87173-110-X*) ACEI.

Leeb, Olli. Ausgewaehlte Desserts. (GER., Illus.). 197p. 1985. 20.50 (*3-921799-84-8*, Pub. by Olli Leeb) Lubrecht & Cramer.
— Bavarian Cooking. (Illus.). 176p. 1997. 25.00 (*0-7818-0561-9*, 659) Hippocrene Bks.
— Bavarian Cooking. Assembled by O. L. (Illus.). 171p. 1992. 20.50 (*3-921799-85-6*, Pub. by Olli Leeb) Lubrecht & Cramer.
— Bayerische Leibspeisen. Zusammengetragen von O. L. (GER., Illus.). 171p. 1991. 20.50 (*3-921799-80-5*, Pub. by Olli Leeb) Lubrecht & Cramer.
— Eva Kocht Fuer Adam, Natuerlich Collwertig - Adam Kocht Fuer Eva. (GER., Illus.). 180p. 1989. 20.50 (*3-921799-78-3*, Pub. by Olli Leeb) Lubrecht & Cramer.
— Die Feinsten Plaetzchen Rezepte: Gesammel von E. L. (GER., Illus.). 189p. 1991. 20.50 (*3-921799-98-8*, Pub. by Olli Leeb) Lubrecht & Cramer.
— Der Fleck Muss Weg. Pflege, Waesche und Reinigung Edler Textilien & Leder. (GER., Illus.). 83p. 1986. 17.25 (*3-921799-86-4*, Pub. by Olli Leeb) Lubrecht & Cramer.
— Garment Care - Stain Removal Made Easy - Laundering & Cleaning of Exclusive Fabrics & Leather. (Illus.). 84p. 1988. 17.95 (*3-921799-83-X*, Pub. by Olli Leeb) Lubrecht & Cramer.
— Koestlich Frische Salate. (GER., Illus.). 192p. 1984. 20.50 (*3-921799-88-0*, Pub. by Olli Leeb) Lubrecht & Cramer.
— Kuchen (Cakes) (GER., Illus.). 155p. 1992. 22.95 (*3-921799-70-8*, Pub. by Olli Leeb) Lubrecht & Cramer.
— My Favorite Cookies from the Old Country: Loved Recipes Assembled by . . . (Illus.). 189p. 1985. 20.50 (*3-921799-97-X*, Pub. by Olli Leeb) Lubrecht & Cramer.
— Schnell Was Feines, Natuerlich Frisch fuer Dich und Mich. (GER., Illus.). 209p. 1989. 20.50 (*3-921799-81-3*, Pub. by Olli Leeb) Lubrecht & Cramer.
— Von Frueh an Fit Mit Nico's Kinderkueche. 2nd ed. (GER., Illus.). 77p. (J). 1990. 17.25 (*3-921799-87-2*, Pub. by Olli Leeb) Lubrecht & Cramer.

Leeb, Olli, jt. auth. see Windisch, W. W.

Leeb, Ritter Von, see Von Leeb, Ritter.

Leeb, Rudolph. Konstantin und Christus: Die Verchristlichung der Imperialen Repraesentations Unter Konstantin Dem Grossen Als Spiegel Seiner Kirchenpolitik und Seines Selbstverstaendnisses Als Christlicher Kaiser. (Arbeiten zur Kirchengeschichte Ser.: Bd. 58). (GER.). xiv, 225p. (C). 1992. lib. bdg. 110.80 (*3-11-013544-2*) De Gruyter.

Leeb, Stephen & Conrad, Roger S. The Agile Investor: Profiting from the End of Buy & Hold. LC 96-33128. (Illus.). 192p. 1996. 23.00 (*0-88730-760-4*, HarpBusn) HarpInfo.

An Asterisk (*) at the beginning of an entry indicates that the title is appearing for the first time.

— Market Timing for the Nineties: The Five Key Signals for When to Buy, Hold, & Sell. LC 92-5433. 256p. 1993. reprint ed. 22.00 (0-88730-641-1, HarpBusn) HarpInfo.

***Leeb, Stephen & Leeb, Donna.** Defying the Market: Profiting in the Turbulent Post-Technology Boom. LC 99-24141. (Illus.). 267p. 1999. 24.95 (0-07-134110-2) McGraw.

Leebaert, Derek. The Fifty Year Wound: Assessing the Costs of the Cold War. 1999. write for info. (0-316-51847-6) Little.

Leebaert, Derek, ed. The Future of Software. (Illus.). 300p. 1995. 30.00 (0-262-12184-0) MIT Pr.

— The Future of Software. (Illus.). 320p. 1996. pap. text 15.00 (0-262-62109-6) MIT Pr.

***Leebaert, Derek, ed.** The Future of the Electronic Marketplace. LC 97-46856. (Illus.). 392p. 1998. 35.00 (0-262-12209-X) MIT Pr.

Leebaert, Derek, ed. The Future of the Electronic Marketplace. (Illus.). 400p. 1999. reprint ed. pap. 17.50 (0-262-62132-0) MIT Pr.

— Soviet Military Thinking. 304p. (C). 1981. pap. text 16.95 (0-04-355016-9) Routledge.

— Technology 2001: The Future of Computing & Communications. (Illus.). 416p. 1992. reprint ed. pap. text 18.50 (0-262-62084-7) MIT Pr.

Leebaert, Derek & Dickinson, Timothy, eds. Soviet Strategy & the New Military Thinking. 298p. (C). 1992. pap. text 24.95 (0-521-40769-9) Cambridge U Pr.

— Soviet Strategy & the New Military Thinking. 298p. (C). 1992. text 69.95 (0-521-40429-0) Cambridge U Pr.

Leebaert, Derek, jt. ed. see Zeckhauser, Richard F.

Leebov, Wendy & Scott, Gail. Health Care Managers in Transition: Shifting Roles & Changing Organizations. LC 90-38789. (Health-Management Ser.). 288p. 1990. text 36.95 (1-55542-248-9) Jossey-Bass.

— Service Quality Improvement: The Customer Satisfaction Strategy for Health Care. LC 93-32889. 378p. 1993. pap. 52.00 (1-55648-110-1, 136107) AHPI.

Leebov, Wendy, et al. Patient Satisfaction: A Guide to Practice Enhancement. LC 89-8255. (Illus.). 380p. 1990. 49.95 (0-87489-546-4, ME003) Practice Mgmt Info.

— Service Savvy Health Care: One Goal at a Time. LC 97-50160. 1998. pap. 30.00 (1-55648-225-6) AHPI.

— Seven Service Strategies That Work: The Health Care Manager's Guide to Customer Service. LC 97-51922. 1998. 36.95 (1-55648-230-2) American Host.

Leebow, Ken. 300 Incredible Things for Golfers on the Internet. Joffe, Paul, ed. LC 99-482798. (Illus.). 128p. 1999. pap. 8.95 (0-9658668-3-1) VIP Pub.

— 300 Incredible Things for Kids on the Internet. Joffe, Paul, ed. (Illus.). 120p. (YA). (gr. 5-12). 1999. pap. 8.95 (0-9658668-1-5, 97-02) VIP Pub.

— 300 Incredible Things for Sports Fans on the Internet. Joffe, Paul, ed. LC 99-483166. (Illus.). 128p. 1999. pap. 8.95 (0-9658668-2-3, 97-03) VIP Pub.

***Leebow, Ken.** 300 Incredible Things for Travelers on the Internet. (Illus.). 1999. pap. text 8.95 (0-9658668-6-6) VIP Pub.

Leebow, Ken. 300 Incredible Things to Do on the Internet, Vol. II. 5th rev. ed. Joffe, Paul, ed. (Illus.). 106p. 1998. pap. 8.95 (0-9658668-0-7, 97-01) VIP Pub.

***Leebow, Ken & Bolton, Janet.** 300 Incredible Things for Beanie Lovers on the Internet. Joffe, Paul, ed. (Illus.). 128p. 1999. pap. 8.95 (0-9658668-5-8) VIP Pub.

***Leebow, Ken & Lupus, Peter.** 300 Incredible Things for Health, Fitness & Diet on the Internet. Joffe, Paul & Bolton, Janet, eds. (Illus.). 128p. 1999. pap. 8.95 (0-9658668-7-4) VIP Pub.

Leebrick, Kristal. Imagine You Are a Crime Detective. LC 98-26364. (Career Achievement Library). 2002. lib. bdg. 21.35 (1-57765-206-1) ABDO Pub Co.

— Imagine You Are a Pro Baseball Player. LC 98-26361. (Professional Sports Library). (J). 2002. lib. bdg. 21.35 (1-57765-197-9) ABDO Pub Co.

Leebron. Creative Fiction Writers Companion. LC 94-78050. (C). 1994. pap. text 39.00 (0-15-501414-5, Pub. by Harcourt Coll Pubs) Harcourt.

Leebron, Fred G. Out West. LC 97-25492. 256p. 1997. pap. 12.00 (0-15-600546-8) Harcourt.

***Leebron, Fred G.** Six Figures. LC 99-57602. 208p. 2000. 22.00 (0-375-40640-9) Knopf.

Leeburg. Using Wordperfect Windows. 1993. teacher ed. 24.00 (0-07-037587-9) McGraw.

Leeburg, Verlene & Larsen, Gwynne. Using WordPerfect for Windows. 532p. (C). 1993. text 27.95 (0-07-037586-0) McGraw.

Leeburg, Verlene & Purvis, Peggy. Using WordPerfect 6.0 for DOS. (C). 1994. pap. text 25.00 (0-07-037625-5) McGraw.

Leech, Beth L., jt. auth. see Baumgartner, Frank R.

Leech, Bryan J. A Joyous Wedding Celebration Vocal Collection (Wedding) 1997. pap. 9.95 (0-634-00346-1) H Leonard.

— A Walk with the Spirit. 105p. 2000. pap. 12.00 (1-893774-17-1) Star Rising.

Leech, Bryan J., jt. ed. see Bock, Fred.

Leech, Clifford. Christopher Marlowe: Poet for the Stage. Lancashire, Anne, ed. LC 83-45278. (Studies in the Renaissance: No. 11). 1986. 39.50 (0-404-62281-X) AMS Pr.

— The Dramatist's Experience, with Other Essays in Literary Theory. LC 79-21161. 248 p. 1970. write for info. (0-389-03993-4) B&N Imports.

— John Webster. LC 78-143481. (English Biography Ser.: No. 31). 1969. reprint ed. lib. bdg. 75.00 (0-8383-0690-X) M S G Haskell Hse.

— Shakespeare - The Tragedies: A Collection of Critical Essays. LC 65-17295. (Midway Reprint Ser.). xxxii, 256p. 1994. reprint ed. pap. text 15.00 (0-226-47018-0) U Ch Pr.

— Shakespeare's Tragedies & Other Studies in Seventeenth Century Drama. LC 75-16846. 232p. 1975. reprint ed. lib. bdg. 49.75 (0-8371-8266-2, LESTO, Greenwood Pr) Greenwood.

— Tragedy. (Critical Idiom Ser.: Vol. 1). (C). 1969. pap. 8.50 (0-416-15720-3, NO. 2291) Routledge.

Leech, Clifford, et al, eds. The Revels History of Drama, 8 vols. LC 97-224912. 3342p. (C). 1997. 825.00 (0-415-14379-9) Routledge.

Leech, Clifford, ed. see Shakespeare, William.

Leech, Daniel D. The Post Office Department of the United States of America. LC 75-22825. (America in Two Centuries Ser.). 1976. reprint ed. 18.95 (0-405-07696-7) Ayer.

Leech, David P., et al. The Economics of a Technology-Based Service Sector. (Illus.). 177p. (C). 1998. pap. text 35.00 (0-7881-7315-4) DIANE Pub.

Leech, F. B. & Sellers, K. C. Statistical Epidemiology in Veterinary Science. 1979. 30.00 (0-85264-211-3) Lubrecht & Cramer.

Leech, Geoffrey. A-Z of English Grammar & Usage. 1991. pap. text. write for info. (0-17-556021-8) Addison-Wesley.

Leech, Geoffrey. Semantics. 1990. pap. 19.95 (0-14-013487-5, Pub. by Pnguin Bks Ltd) Trafalgar.

Leech, Geoffrey N. Linguistic Guide to English Poetry. (English Language Ser.). 240p. 1973. pap. text 13.95 (0-582-55013-0) Longman.

Leech, Geoffrey N. & Candlin, Christopher N., eds. Computers in English Language Teaching & Research: Applied Linguistics & Language Study. (Applied Linguistics & Language Ser.). 320p. (C). 1986. pap. text 27.95 (0-582-55069-6, 74300) Longman.

— Computers in English Language Teaching & Research: Selected Papers from the 1984 Lancaster Symposium Computers in English Language Education & Research. LC 85-17405. (Applied Linguistics & Language Studies). 248p. 1986. reprint ed. pap. 76.90 (0-608-03581-5, 206440400009) Bks Demand.

Leech, Geoffrey N. & Svartvik, Jan. A Communicative Grammar of English. 2nd ed. LC 93-45811. 1994. text. write for info. (0-582-23827-7, Pub. by Addison-Wesley) Longman.

— Communicative Grammar of English. 2nd ed. LC 93-45811. 1995. pap. text 23.73 (0-582-08573-X, Pub. by Addison-Wesley) Longman.

Leech, Harper & Carroll, John C. Armour & His Times. LC 79-179528. (Select Bibliographies Reprint Ser.). 1977. reprint ed. 29.95 (0-8369-6657-0) Ayer.

Leech, J. Two Papers: Eta-Coextensions of Monoids & the Structure of a Band of Groups. (Memoirs Ser.: No. 2/157). 95p. 1975. pap. 18.00 (0-8218-1857-0, MEMO/2/157) Am Math.

Leech, James H., et al, eds. Parasitic Infections. (Contemporary Issues in Infectious Diseases Ser.: Vol. 7). (Illus.). 364p. 1988. text 83.00 (0-443-08561-7) Church.

Leech, Jay & Spencer, Zane. Moon of the Big-Dog. LC 79-7893. (Illus.). 64p. (J). (gr. 2-6). 1980. 6.95 (0-690-04001-6) HarpC Child Bks.

Leech, John. Halt! Who Goes Where? The Future of NATO in the New Europe. (Illus.). 156p. 1991. 21.95 (0-08-040978-4, Pub. by Brasseys) Brasseys.

Leech, Ken. Dark Providence Bright Promise. 2nd ed. 166p. 1995. reprint ed. pap. 4.99 (0-89367-196-7) Light & Life Comm.

Leech, Kenneth. Soul Friend: An Invitation to Spiritual Direction. LC 91-58136. 272p. 1992. reprint ed. pap. 14.00 (0-06-065214-4, Pub. by Harper SF) HarpC.

— Spirituality & Pastoral Care. LC 89-22141. 149p. 1989. pap. 10.95 (0-936384-84-0) Cowley Pubns.

— Subversive Orthodoxy: Traditional Faith & Radical Commitment. 62p. 1992. pap. 6.95 (0-921846-49-5) Forward Movement.

— True Prayer: An Invitation to Christian Spirituality. LC 95-9588. 208p. 1995. reprint ed. pap. 12.95 (0-8192-1646-1) Morehouse Pub.

— We Preach Christ Crucified: Cowley's Lent Book for 1995. 105p. 1995. pap. 9.95 (1-56101-105-3) Cowley Pubns.

***Leech, Margaret.** In the Days of McKinley. unabridged ed. (Signature Ser.). (Illus.). 686p. 1999. reprint ed. 37.50 (0-945707-24-X) Amer Political.

Leech, Margaret. Reveille in Washington, 1860-1865. 496p. 1991. pap. 12.95 (0-88184-732-1) Carroll & Graf.

Leech, Mark. The Prisoners' Handbook. 424p. 1995. text 55.00 (0-19-825960-3) OUP.

***Leech, Mark.** The Prisons Handbook. 3rd ed. LC 99-205145. 507p. 1999. pap. 80.00 (1-872870-72-4, Pub. by Waterside Pr) Gaunt.

***Leech, Mark & Cheney, Deborah.** The Prisons Handbook 2000. 4th ed. 528p. 1999. pap. 95.00 (1-872870-82-1, Pub. by Waterside Pr) Gaunt.

Leech, Michael. Essential Kenya. LC 95-68322. (Essential Travel Guides Ser.). (Illus.). 128p. 1995. pap. text 7.95 (0-8442-8955-8, Passprt Bks) NTC Contemp Pub Co.

Leech, Michael T., jt. auth. see Holloway, William J.

Leech, Noyes E., et al. International Legal System, Documentary Supplement: Cases & Materials. 3rd ed. (University Casebook Ser.). 574p. 1991. reprint ed. pap. text 15.95 (0-88277-674-6) Foundation Pr.

Leech, Richard W., jt. ed. see Brumback, Roger A.

***Leech, Samuel.** Voice from the Main Deck: Being a Record of the Thirty Years Adventures of Samuel Leech. 1999. pap. 21.95 (1-86176-113-9, Chatham Pubg) G Duckworth.

— Voice from the Main Deck: Being a Record of the Thirty Years Adventures of Samuel Leech. LC 99-10617. 1999. 34.95 (1-55750-192-0) Naval Inst Pr.

Leech, Thomas, jt. auth. see Flenley, William.

Leech, Thomas F. How to Prepare, Stage, & Deliver Winning Presentations. 2nd ed. LC 92-29518. 400p. 1992. pap. 27.95 (0-8144-7813-1) AMACOM.

Leech, Tim J. Control Design & Assessment: A Shared Responsibility. Campbell, Lee A., ed. (Video Ser.). 1995. pap., teacher ed. 495.00 incl. VHS (0-89413-340-3, A6731) Inst Inter Aud.

— Control Design & Assessment: A Shared Responsibility Work Team Guide. Campbell, Lee A., ed. 1995. pap. 20.00 incl. VHS (0-89413-341-1, A7948) Inst Inter Aud.

Leech-Wilkinson, Daniel. Machaut's Mass: An Introduction. (Illus.). 224p. 1992. reprint ed. pap. text 19.95 (0-19-816306-1) OUP.

Leech-Wilkinson, Daniel & Wilhelm, James J., eds. Guillaume de Machaut, "Le Livre dou Voir Dit" ("The Book of the True Poem") Palmer, R. Barton, tr. from FRE. LC 98-5738. (Library of Medieval Literature: Vol. 106A). (Illus.). 892p. 1998. text 135.00 (0-8153-1327-6, H1732) Garland.

Leech, Wolfgang. Die Deutschen Archivare 1500 to 1945 Vol. 2: Biographisches Lexikon. (GER.). 737p. 1992. lib. bdg. 28.50 (3-598-10605-X) K G Saur Verlag.

Leecraft, Jodie, ed. The Blocks & Drilling Line. Albornoz, Fernando, tr. (Rotary Drilling Ser.: Unit I, Lesson 5). (SPA., Illus.). 67p. (Orig.). 1982. pap. text 14.00 (0-88698-033-X, 2.10522) PETEX.

— Field Handling of Natural Gas. 4th rev. ed. (Illus.). 177p. 1987. pap. text 25.00 (0-88698-127-1, 3.10040) PETEX.

Leecraft, Jodie, ed. see Donnelly, Richard W.

Leecraft, Jodie, ed. see Eubank, Judith.

Leecraft, Jodie, ed. see Hall, Lewis W.

Leecraft, Jodie, ed. see Longley, Mark.

Leecraft, Jodie, ed. see McCann-Baker, Annes & Whalen, Bruce.

Leecraft, Jodie, ed. see Morris, Jeff, et al.

Leed, Eric. Shores of Discovery: How Expeditionaries Have Constructed the World. 322p. 1998. text 25.00 (0-7881-5585-7) DIANE Pub.

***Leed, Maren.** Keeping the Warfighting Edge: An Empirical Analysis of Army Officers' Tactical Expertise. vii, 38p. 2000. pap. 6.00 (0-8330-2865-0) Rand Corp.

Leed, Richard L. Beginning Russian: Teacher's Manual. 2nd rev. ed. (RUS.). 78p. (C). 1991. pap. text, teacher ed. 5.95 (0-89357-222-5) Slavica.

Leed, Richard L. & Paperno, Slava. Five Thousand Russian Words with All Their Inflected Forms: A Russian-English Dictionary. xiv, 322p. (Orig.). (C). 1987. pap. text 19.95 (0-89357-170-9) Slavica.

Leed, Richard L., jt. auth. see Nakhimovsky, Alexander D.

Leed, Richard L., ed. see Iordanskaja, Lidija & Paperno, Slava.

Leed, Richard L., ed. & anno. see Zhitkov, Boris.

Leed, Theodore W., jt. auth. see German, Gene A.

Leedahl, Shelley A. The Bone Talker. (Northern Lights Books for Children Ser.). (Illus.). 32p. (J). (ps-3). 2000. text 15.95 (0-88995-214-0, Pub. by Red Deer) Genl Dist Srvs.

— Riding Planet Earth. 148p. (J). (gr. 5-7). 1997. pap. 7.95 (1-896184-26-X) Roussan Pubs.

Leedale, Mark. Intervention & the East London Clothing Industry. (C). 1988. 29.00 (0-7855-3820-8, Pub. by Oxford Polytechnic) St Mut.

Leeden, Frits Van Der, see Van Der Leeden, Frits.

Leeden, Ivy D. A Crime of Two Cities. (Ghostwriter Ser.). (J). 1995. 8.60 (0-606-08525-4, Pub. by Turtleback) Demco.

Leeden, Ivy D. & Frazier, Kermit, contrib. by. A Crime of Two Cities. (Ghostwriter Ser.). 128p. (J). (gr. 4-7). 1995. mass mkt. 3.50 (0-553-48279-3) BDD Bks Young Read.

Leeden, Robert W., et al, eds. Sphingolipids As Signaling Modulators in the Nervous System. LC 98-15146. (Annals of the New York Academy of Sciences Ser.: No. 845). 435p. 1998. 140.00 (1-57331-137-5); pap. 140.00 (1-57331-138-3) NY Acad Sci.

***Leeder.** We are Family. 2001. pap. text 19.75 (0-07-239284-3) McGraw.

Leeder, A. L. & Smith, Oswald J. Exiled from Russia: Life Story of Pastor Basil Malox. 1956. pap. 0.79 (1-56632-010-0) Revival Lit.

Leeder, Elaine. The Gentle General: Rose Pesotta, Anarchist & Labor Organizer. LC 92-43028. (SUNY Series in American Labor History). 212p. (C). 1993. pap. text 21.95 (0-7914-1672-0) State U NY Pr.

— The Gentle General: Rose Pesotta, Anarchist & Labor Organizer. LC 92-43028. (SUNY Series in American Labor History). 212p. (C). 1993. text 64.50 (0-7914-1671-2) State U NY Pr.

— Treating Abuse in Families: A Feminist & Community Approach. LC 94-15849. 232p. 1994. 41.95 (0-8261-8530-4) Springer Pub.

Leeder, Ellen L. El Desarraigo En las Novelas De Angel Maria De Lera. LC 77-82359. 1978. pap. 8.00 (0-89729-176-X) Ediciones.

— Justo Sierra y el Mar. LC 78-58669. (SPA.). 83p. (Orig.). 1979. pap. 7.00 (0-89729-202-2) Ediciones.

Leeder, Ellen L. & McCalley, Vivian. Here We Go, Level 1. 3rd ed. (Illus.). 64p. (J). (gr. k). 1994. pap. text, student ed. 14.20 (0-13-186032-1) P-H.

— Here We Go, Level 3. 3rd ed. (Illus.). 112p. 1995. pap. text, student ed. 14.20 (0-13-186057-7) P-H.

— Here We Go, Pre-Primary Book. 3rd ed. (Illus.). 48p. (J). (gr. k). 1994. pap. text, student ed. 14.20 (0-13-186024-0) P-H.

Leeder, Ellen L., jt. ed. see Jimenez, Luis A.

Leeder, Karen. Breaking Boundaries: A New Generation of Poets in the German Democratic Republic. (Oxford Modern Languages & Literature Monographs). 382p. (C). 1996. text 80.00 (0-19-815910-2) OUP.

Leeder, M. R. Sedimentology: Process & Product. (Illus.). 528p. (C). 1982. pap. text 34.95 (0-04-551054-7) Routledge.

Leeder, Mike R. Sedimentology & Sedimentary Basins: From Turbulence to Tectonics. LC 98-53090. (Illus.). 1999. pap. 69.50 (0-632-04976-6) Blackwell Sci.

Leeder, Ninon A. Hungarian Classical Ballads & Their Folklore. LC 67-11526. 379p. reprint ed. pap. 108.10 (0-608-10697-6, 2022460) Bks Demand.

Leeder, S., jt. auth. see Florey, C.

Leeder, S. H. Modern Sons of the Pharaohs. LC 73-6288. (Middle East Ser.). 1973. reprint ed. 31.95 (0-405-05346-0) Ayer.

***Leeder, Stephen R.** Healthy Medicine: Challenges Facing Australia's Health Services. 176p. 2000. pap. 24.95 (1-86508-054-3, Pub. by Allen & Unwin Pty) Paul & Co Pubs.

Leedham, jt. auth. see Hanke.

Leedham, Craig S., jt. auth. see Eitzen, D. Stanley.

Leedham, Craig S., ed. see Eitzen.

Leedham, G., jt. auth. see Plamondon, R.

Leedham-Green, E. S. Archives of the Cambridge University Press 1696-1902: A Guide to the Archives of the Cambridge University Press. (Archives of British & American Publishers Ser.). 36p. 1973. pap. write for info. (0-85964-001-9) Chadwyck-Healey.

Leedham-Green, E. S., jt. ed. see Fehrenbach, R. J.

Leedham-Green, Elisabeth. A Concise History of the University of Cambridge. LC 96-6469. (Illus.). 288p. (C). 1996. text 59.95 (0-521-43370-3); pap. text 18.95 (0-521-43978-7) Cambridge U Pr.

Leedham-Green, Elizabeth, jt. ed. see Fehrenbach, Robert J.

Leedom, Joe, jt. auth. see Drake, Hal.

Leedom, John H. The Group & You. 250p. 1994. 17.95 (1-884363-05-9) Odenwald Pr.

Leedom, Tim C., ed. Book Your Church Doesn't Want You to Read. 3rd ed. (Illus.). 446p. 1993. reprint ed. pap. 19.95 (0-939040-15-8) Truth Seeker.

Leedom, Tim C. & Carpenter, Harry W. The Main Man. 449p. 1999. mass mkt. 9.95 (0-939040-17-4) Truth Seeker.

Leeds. Nutrition & Healthy Living. 2nd ed. 2001. 40.50 (0-07-230078-7) McGraw.

Leeds, Anthony. Cities, Classes, & the Social Order. Sanjek, Roger, ed. (Anthropology of Contemporary Issues Ser.). (Illus.). 288p. 1994. text 45.00 (0-8014-2957-9); pap. text 17.95 (0-8014-8168-6) Cornell U Pr.

Leeds, Barbara. Fairy Tale Rap No. 2: The Fisherman & His Wife & Other Stories. (Illus.). 40p. (Orig.). (J). (ps-6). 1992. pap. 6.95 (0-9624932-4-4) Miramonte Pr.

Leeds, Bruce. Prompts: Readings for ESL Composition. (Illus.). 78p. (Orig.). (C). 1990. pap. text 9.95 (0-916177-68-8) Am Eng Pubns.

Leeds, David J., ed. see Brandow, Gregg.

Leeds, Dorothy. Powerspeak. 1991. mass mkt. 6.99 (0-425-12489-4) Berkley Pub.

***Leeds, Dorothy.** 7 Powers of Questions: Secrets to Successful Communication in Life & at Work. 2000. pap. 13.95 (0-399-52614-5, Perigee Bks) Berkley Pub.

Leeds, Dorothy. Smart Questions. 1988. mass mkt. 5.99 (0-425-11132-6) Berkley Pub.

Leeds, Edward T. Early Anglo-Saxon Art & Archaeology. LC 77-109764. (Illus.). 130p. 1971. reprint ed. lib. bdg. 55.00 (0-8371-4254-7, LEEA, Greenwood Pr) Greenwood.

Leeds, Geoffrey. Smoke. 368p. (Orig.). 1986. mass mkt. 3.95 (0-446-32716-6, Pub. by Warner Bks) Little.

Leeds-Hurwitz, Wendy. Communication in Everyday Life. A Social Interpretation. Thayer, Lee, ed. LC 89-282. (Communication: The Human Context Ser.: Vol. 3). 224p. (C). 1989. text 73.25 (0-89391-524-6) Ablx Pub.

— Communication in Everyday Life: A Social Interpretation. Thayer, Lee, ed. LC 89-282. (Communication: The Human Context Ser.: Vol. 3). 224p. (C). 1992. pap. 39.50 (0-89391-812-1) Ablx Pub.

— Semiotics & Communication: Signs, Codes, & Cultures. (Communication Ser.). 232p. (C). 1993. pap. 24.50 (0-8058-1140-0); text 49.95 (0-8058-1139-7) L Erlbaum Assocs.

Leeds-Hurwitz, Wendy, ed. Social Approaches to Communication. LC 95-18761. (Communication Ser.). 260p. 1995. pap. text 23.00 (0-89862-873-3); lib. bdg. 42.50 (0-89862-867-9) Guilford Pubns.

Leeds, Jeffery. The Spice of Life: A World of Healthy & Zesty Chicken Recipes. LC 99-19169. 200p. 1999. pap. 19.95 (1-879094-60-6) Momentum Bks.

***Leeds, Joshua.** The Power of Sound: Using Psychoacoustics for Improved Learning & Performance. 272p. 2001. pap. 19.95 incl. audio compact disk (0-89281-768-2) Inner Tradit.

***Leeds-Lyon Symposium on Tribology Staff, et al.** Lubrication at the Frontier: The Role of the Interface & Surface Layers in the Thin Film & Boundary Regime: Proceedings of the 25th Leeds Lyon Symposium on Tribology: Held in the Institut National des Science Appliqubees des Lyon, France, 8th-11th September, 1998. LC 99-34741. (Tribology Ser.). 908p. 1999. 276.50 (0-444-50267-X) Elsevier.

Leeds-Lyons Symposium on Tribology Staff. Lubricants & Lubrication: Proceedings of the 21st Leeds-Lyon Symposium on Tribology, University of Leeds, Institute of Tribology, Leeds, U. K., 6-9 September, 1994. Dowson, D. et al, eds. LC 95-20695. (Tribology Ser.: Vol. 30). 708p. 1995. 263.00 (0-444-82263-1) Elsevier.

Leeds, Marc. The Vonnegut Encyclopedia: An Authorized Compendium. LC 94-16122. 712p. 1994. lib. bdg. 89.50 (0-313-29230-2, Greenwood Pr) Greenwood.

Leeds, Marc, jt. ed. see Reed, Peter.

An Asterisk (*) at the beginning of an entry indicates that the title is appearing for the first time.

Leeds, Marc J. & Reed, Peter, eds. Kurt Vonnegut: Images & Representations, 83. LC 99-16096. Vol. 83. 216p. 2000. 55.00 (0-313-30975-2) Greenwood.

Leeds, Mark. Passport's Guide to Ethnic New York: A Complete Guide to the Many Faces & Cultures of New York. 2nd ed. LC 95-38970. (Illus.). 528p. 1995. pap. 14.95 (0-8442-9633-3, 96333, Passprt Bks) NTC Contemp Pub Co.

Leeds, Mathew J. & Practising Law Institute Staff. Residential Real Estate Contracts & Closings 1998. LC 98-178627. 880 p. 1998. 129.00 (0-87224-446-6) PLI.

Leeds, Michael & Burke, Johnny. Swinging on a Star: Musical. 1996. pap. 6.00 (0-8222-1523-3) Dramatists Play.

Leeds, Michelle S. Perchloroethylene.(Carbon Dichloride, Tetrachloroethylene, Drycleaner, Fumigant) - Effects on Health & Work: Index of New Information. 146p. 1995. 47.50 (0-7883-0352-X); pap. 44.50 (0-7883-0353-8) ABBE Pubs Assn.

Leeds, Mike. Passports Guide to Ethnic New York. (Illus.). 408p. 1994. pap. 14.95 (0-8442-9542-6, Passprt Bks) NTC Contemp Pub Co.

Leeds, Norman E., jt. auth. see Burrows, Edmund H.

Leeds, Rachel L., et al. What to Say When: A Guide to More Effective Communication. 2nd ed. 192p. (C). 1996. per. 17.95 (0-8403-9315-6) Kendall-Hunt.

***Leeds, Robert X.** Doctor Leeds' Selection of Popular Epic Recitations: For Minstrel & Stage Use. 1999. 24.95 (0-9674025-0-6) EPIC Pubg Co.

***Leeds, Rod.** The Plantfinder's Guide to Early Bulbs. LC 99-41603. (Illus.). 192p. 2000. 34.95 (0-88192-443-1) Timber.

Leeds, Roger S. & Thompson, Gale. The 1982 Mexican Debt Negotiations. (Pew Case Studies in International Affairs). 50p. (C). 1993. pap. text 3.50 (1-56927-201-8) Geo U Inst Dplmcy.

Leeds, Salvatore L. Hernia-Simple & Complex: Index of New Information & Medical Research Bible. 150p. 1994. 47.50 (0-7883-0136-5); pap. 44.50 (0-7883-0137-3) ABBE Pubs Assn.

Leeds, Stephen, jt. auth. see Lawrence, William J.

Leeds, Valerie A. Hidden Treasures: American Paintings from Florida Private Collections. 80p. 1992. pap. write for info. (1-880699-00-1) Orlando Mus Art.

— Seeking the Sublime: Neo-Romanticism in Landscape Photography. (Illus.). 24p. 1995. pap. text 12.00 (1-887040-13-7) SE Mus Photo.

Leeds, William M., jt. auth. see Masser, Barry Z.

Leedskalnin, Edward. Magnetic Current. 26p. 1997. reprint ed. pap. 11.50 (0-7873-0549-9) Hlth Research.

***Leedy.** Practical Research. 7th ed. 352p. 2000. pap. text. write for info. (0-13-960360-3) P-H.

Leedy, Daniel L., jt. ed. see Adams, Lowell W.

Leedy, G. Frank. Check List for Marriage. LC 72-181367. 1971. 10.00 (0-87212-023-6) Libra.

Leedy, Jack J. Poetry, the Healer. 1973. 12.75i (0-397-59057-1, Lippnctt) Lppncott W & W.

Leedy, Jack J. & Wynbrandt, James. Executive Retirement Management: A Manager's Guide to the Planning & Implementation of a Successful Retirement. LC 86-24010. 272p. reprint ed. pap. 84.40 (0-8357-4244-X, 203703200007) Bks Demand.

***Leedy, Jason.** Implementing Biztalk for E-commerce. 350p. 2001. pap. 44.99 (0-13-019612-6) P-H.

Leedy, Kay. Life Never Ends. 141p. pap. 7.95 (0-942494-41-5) Coleman Pub.

Leedy, Loreen. Blast off to Earth! A Look at Geography. LC 92-2567. (Illus.). 32p. (J). (gr. k-3). 1992. lib. bdg. 16.95 (0-8234-0973-2) Holiday.

— Blast off to Earth! A Look at Geography. (J). (ps-3). 1998. pap. text 6.95 (0-8234-1409-4) Holiday.

— Celebrate the 50 States. LC 99-10986. (J). (gr. 3-7). 1999. 16.95 (0-8234-1431-0) Holiday.

***Leedy, Loreen.** Celebrate the 50 States. (Illus.). (gr. 4-7). 2000. 6.95 (0-8234-1631-3) Holiday.

Leedy, Loreen. The Dragon Halloween Party. LC 86-286. (Illus.). 32p. (J). (gr. k-3). 1986. pap. 5.95 (0-8234-0765-9) Holiday.

— The Edible Pyramid. LC 94-2122. (Illus.). 32p. (J). (gr. k-3). 1994. lib. bdg. 16.95 (0-8234-1126-5) Holiday.

— The Edible Pyramid: Good Eating Every Day. (Illus.). 32p. (J). (ps-3). 1994. reprint ed. pap. 6.95 (0-8234-1233-4) Holiday.

— Fraction Action. LC 93-22800. (Illus.). 32p. (J). (gr. k-3). 1994. lib. bdg. 16.95 (0-8234-1109-5) Holiday.

— Fraction Action. (Illus.). 32p. (J). (gr. k-3). 1996. pap. 6.95 (0-8234-1244-X) Holiday.

— The Furry News: How to Make a Newspaper. LC 89-20094. (Illus.). 32p. (J). (gr. k-3). 1990. lib. bdg. 16.95 (0-8234-0793-4) Holiday.

— The Furry News - How to Make a Newspaper: A Reading Rainbow Feature Book. (Illus.). (J). (ps-3). 1990. reprint ed. pap. 6.95 (0-8234-1026-9) Holiday.

— The Great Trash Bash. LC 90-46554. (Illus.). 32p. (J). (gr. k-3). 1991. lib. bdg. 16.95 (0-8234-0869-8) Holiday.

***Leedy, Loreen.** The Great Trash Bash. (Illus.). (gr. 4-7). 2000. 6.95 (0-8234-1634-8) Holiday.

Leedy, Loreen. How Humans Make Friends. 3rd ed. LC 95-35633. (Illus.). 32p. (J). (gr. k-3). 1996. 15.95 (0-8234-1223-7) Holiday.

***Leedy, Loreen.** Mapping Penny's World. LC 99-48327. (Illus.). 32p. (gr. k-3). 2000. text 17.00 (0-8050-6178-9) St Martin.

Leedy, Loreen. Measuring Penny. LC 97-19108. (Illus.). 32p. (J). (gr. 1-4). 1998. 16.95 (0-8050-5360-3) H Holt & Co.

***Leedy, Loreen.** Measuring Penny. (Illus.). 32p. (gr. 2-4). 2000. pap. 6.95 (0-8050-6572-5) H Holt & Co.

Leedy, Loreen. Messages in the Mailbox: How to Write a Letter. (Illus.). (J). (gr. k-3). 1991. pap. 6.95 (0-8234-1079-X) Holiday.

— Messages in the Mailbox: How to Write a Letter. LC 91-8718. (Illus.). 32p. (J). (gr. k-3). 1991. lib. bdg. 16.95 (0-8234-0889-2) Holiday.

— Mission: Addition. (Illus.). (J). (gr. k-3). 1997. pap. 6.95 (0-8234-1412-4) Holiday.

— Mission-Addition. LC 96-37149. (Illus.). 32p. (J). (gr. k-3). 1997. lib. bdg. 16.95 (0-8234-1307-1) Holiday.

— The Monster Money Book. LC 91-18168. (Illus.). 32p. (J). (gr. k-3). 1992. lib. bdg. 16.95 (0-8234-0922-8) Holiday.

***Leedy, Loreen.** Monster Money Book. (Illus.). 2000. pap. 6.95 (0-8234-1558-9) Holiday.

Leedy, Loreen. Pingo the Plaid Panda. LC 88-17005. (Illus.). 32p. (J). (gr. k-3). 1989. lib. bdg. 13.95 (0-8234-0727-6) Holiday.

— Postcards from Pluto: A Tour of the Solar System. (Illus.). 32p. (J). (gr. k-3). 1993. pap. 6.95 (0-8234-1237-7); lib. bdg. 16.95 (0-8234-1000-5) Holiday.

— The Potato Party & Other Troll Tales. LC 89-1746. (Illus.). 32p. (J). (gr. k-3). 1989. lib. bdg. 14.95 (0-8234-0761-6) Holiday.

— The Race. (Let Me Read Ser.). (Illus.). 16p. (J). (ps-k). 1995. 2.95 (0-673-36277-9, GoodYrBooks) Addson-Wesley Educ.

***Leedy, Loreen.** Subtraction Action. LC 99-49803. (Illus.). 32p. (J). (ps-3). 2000. 16.95 (0-8234-1454-X) Holiday.

Leedy, Loreen. 2 x 2 = BOO! A Set of Spooky Multiplication Stories. LC 94-46711. (Illus.). 32p. (J). (gr. k-3). 1995. lib. bdg. 16.95 (0-8234-1190-7) Holiday.

— 2 x 2 = BOO! A Set of Spooky Multiplication Stories. (Illus.). 32p. (J). (gr. k-3). 1996. pap. 6.95 (0-8234-1272-5) Holiday.

— Who's Who in My Family. LC 94-16611. (Illus.). 32p. (J). (gr. k-3). 1995. lib. bdg. 16.95 (0-8234-1151-6) Holiday.

— Who's Who in My Family. (Illus.). (J). 1995. pap. 6.95 (0-8234-1478-7) Holiday.

Leedy, Paul D. Practical Research: Planning & Designing. 6th ed. LC 96-9917. 304p. (C). 1996. pap. 53.00 (0-13-241407-4) P-H.

Leedy, Walter C., Jr. Cleveland Builds an Art Museum: Patronage, Politics, & Architecture, 1884-1916. LC 91-3424. (Illus.). 104p. 1991. pap. 14.50 (0-940717-09-3) Cleveland Mus Art.

Leefe, Richard K. Louisiana Code of Evidence Practice Guide. 2nd ed. LC 98-87232. 640p. 1998. 130.00 (0-327-00303-0, 6878011) LEXIS Pub.

— Louisiana Code of Evidence Practice Guide. 2nd ed. 30p. 1999. 35.00 (0-327-01155-6, 6878512) LEXIS Pub.

Leefeldt, Christine, jt. auth. see Callenbach, Ernest.

Leefeldt, Ed. In Search of the Paper Children. 1982. 6.00 (0-943136-00-8) Ctr Analysis Public Issues.

***Leefeldt, Ed.** Lighter Than Air: A New Report on the Aero-Nautical Adventures Now Taking Place... LC 00-191013. (Illus.). 312p. 2000. pap. 9.95 (0-9679535-0-2) Lighter Than Air.

Leeflang, P. S. Mathematical Models in Marketing. lib. bdg. 24.00 (0-685-02820-8) Kluwer Academic.

— Mathematical Models in Marketing. 1974. pap. text 78.50 (90-207-0436-2, Pub. by Kluwer Academic) Kluwer Academic.

Leeflang, P. S., jt. auth. see Naert, P. A.

***Leeflang, P. S. H.** Building Models for Marketing Decisions. LC 00-24988. (International Series in Quantitative Marketing). 2000. write for info. (0-7923-7772-9) Kluwer Academic.

***Leeflang, Peter.S. H., et al.** Building Models for Marketing Decisions. 664p. 2000. pap. 59.95 (0-7923-7813-X) Kluwer Academic.

Leegard, Marj. Give Us This Day / LC 99-22496. 1999. 6.99 (0-8066-3866-4, Augsburg) Augsburg Fortress.

Leege, David C. & Kellstedt, Lyman A. Rediscovering the Religious Factor in American Politics. LC 92-34293. 320p. (C). (gr. 13). 1993. text 70.95 (1-56324-133-1) M E Sharpe.

Leege, David C. & Kellstedt, Lyman A. Rediscovering the Religious Factor in American Politics. LC 92-34293. 320p. (C). (gr. 13). 1993. pap. text 34.95 (1-56324-134-X) M E Sharpe.

***Leeger, John W.** One in a Hundred. LC 99-91435. 1999. 25.00 (0-7388-0772-9); pap. 18.00 (0-7388-0773-7) Xlibris Corp.

Leegood, Richard C., jt. auth. see Lea, Peter J.

Leehan, James. Defiant Hope: Spirituality for Survivors of Family Abuse. 176p. (Orig.). 1993. pap. 16.95 (0-664-25463-2) Westminster John Knox.

— Pastoral Care for Survivors of Family Abuse. 156p. (Orig.). 1989. pap. 15.95 (0-664-25025-4) Westminster John Knox.

Leehan, James, jt. auth. see Webb, Laura P.

Leehey, Patrick M. What Was the Name of Paul Revere's Horse? Twenty Questions about Paul Revere - Asked & Answered. (Illus.). 35p. 1997. pap. 6.50 (0-9619999-2-6) Paul Revere Mem Assn.

Leek. The Human Remains from the Tomb of Tutankhamun Vol. 5: Tutankhamun's Tomb. 104p. 1972. 30.00 (0-900416-02-5, Pub. by Aris & Phillips) David Brown.

Leek, James C., et al, eds. Principles of Physical Medicine & Rehabilitation in the Musculoskeletal Diseases. 544p. 1986. text 129.00 (0-8089-1773-0, 792502, Grune & Strat) Harcrt Hlth Sci Grp.

Leek, Janet, et al. Made in Africa: Learning from Carpentry Hand Tool Projects. 72p. 1993. pap. 12.00 (1-85339-209-X, Pub. by Intermed Tech) Stylus Pub VA.

***Leek, K. Mark, et al.** Cultural Attitudes about the Environment & Ecology, & Their Connection to Regional Political Stability: Proceedings of the Conference on Environmental Security, January 16-17, 1998 University of Washington, Seattle; Co-Sponsored by the University of Washington & the Pacific Northwest National Laboratory. LC 98-30077. 196p. 1998. pap. 35.00 (1-57477-065-9) Battelle.

Leek, Leslie. Heart of a Western Woman. 2nd ed. 72p. 1993. reprint ed. per. 9.00 (0-937179-09-4) Blue Scarab.

Leek, Michael. Art of Nautical Illustration. 1991. 29.98 (1-55521-737-0) Bk Sales Inc.

Leek, Michael E. The Art of Nautical Illustration. (Illus.). 192p. 1998. pap. 25.95 (1-57715-032-5) Knckerbocker.

Leek, Peter & Daniel, Sergei. Russian Painting: From Sacred Art to Avant-Garde. (Schools & Movements Ser.). (Illus.). 208p. 2000. 55.00 (1-85995-355-7) Parkstone Pr.

Leek, Sybil. Complete Art of Witchcraft. 208p. 1997. pap. 11.95 (0-452-27886-4, Plume) Dutton Plume.

— How to Be Your Own Astrologer. 1980. mass mkt. 4.95 (0-451-16546-2, E9426, Sig) NAL.

Leeke, Jim. Sudden Ice. LC 87-26771. (Illus.). 188p. (Orig.). 1988. pap. 8.95 (0-89407-073-8) Strawberry Hill.

Leeke, Jim, ed. A Hundred Days to Richmond: Ohio's "Hundred Days" Men in the Civil War. LC 99-20005. 1999. text 29.95 (0-253-33537-X) Ind U Pr.

Leeke, Jim, ed. see Wallace, Lew.

Leeke, John, jt. auth. see Ball, John E.

Leekley, John. Bruce Catton's Reflections on the Civil War. 1998. pap. text 9.99 (0-88394-101-5) Promntory Pr.

Leekley, John, ed. see Catton, Bruce.

Leekung Yu, M. Yu Study Bible, Chinese Study Bible. 2nd ed. (CHI., Illus.). 2000p. 1985. reprint ed. 45.00 (1-890610-03-8) Hymnody & Bible.

Leekung Yu, M., ed. Chinese-English Bible: Classic Edition. 9th ed. 1549p. 1989. reprint ed. 25.00 (1-890610-02-X) Hymnody & Bible.

— Chinese-English Bible: Deluxe Edition - Black. 9th deluxe ed. 1549p. 1989. reprint ed. bond lthr. 35.00 (1-890610-00-3) Hymnody & Bible.

— Chinese-English Bible: Personal Edition. 9th ed. 1549p. 1989. reprint ed. 30.00 (1-890610-01-1) Hymnody & Bible.

— Hymnody: Chinese-English Hymnbook. 8th ed. 610p. 1965. reprint ed. 9.00 (1-890610-04-6) Hymnody & Bible.

Leela, S., jt. auth. see Lakshmikantham, V.

Leelakrishnan, P. Law & Environment. (C). 1992. 130.00 (0-89771-782-1, Pub. by Eastern Book) St Mut.

Leelakrishnan, P., ed. Consumer Protection & Legal Control, Essays & Papers. (C). 1989. 75.00 (0-89771-762-7, Pub. by Eastern Book) St Mut.

Leelanan Historical Museum Staff. Hans W. Anderson: His Life & Art. (Illus.). 80p. 1988. 20.00 (0-930095-10-3) Signal Bks.

***Leeland, Jeff.** One Small Sparrow: The Remarkable True-Life Drama of One Community's Compassionate Response to Save a Little Boy's Life. (Illus.). 250p. 2000. pap. 9.99 (1-57673-693-8, Pub. by Multnomah Pubs) GL Services.

Leeman, Fred. Museum Mesdag: Catalogue of Paintings & Drawings. LC 97-191988. (Illus.). 460p. 1998. 100.00 (90-400-9868-9, Pub. by Waandrs) Consort Bk Sales.

Leeman, I., jt. ed. see Taitz, J.

Leeman, Leonard. In a Nutshell: Reflections by Leonard Leeman. LC 84-90418. (Illus.). 76p. (Orig.). 1984. pap. 5.95 (0-9613628-0-4) G Leeman.

Leeman, Richard W. Do Everything Reform: The Reform Oratory of Frances E. Willard, 15. LC 91-35714. (Great American Orators: Critical Studies, Speeches & Sources: No. 15). 232p. 1992. lib. bdg. 59.95 (0-313-27487-8, LEE/, Greenwood Pr) Greenwood.

— The Rhetoric of Terrorism & Counterterrorism, 29. LC 90-47522. (Contributions to the Study of Mass Media & Communications Ser.: No. 29). 232p. 1991. 59.95 (0-313-27587-4, LRT/, Greenwood Pr) Greenwood.

Leeman, Richard W., ed. African-American Orators: A Bio-Critical Sourcebook. LC 95-37338. 480p. 1996. lib. bdg. 95.00 (0-313-29014-8, Greenwood Pr) Greenwood.

Leeman, Richard W., jt. auth. see Hill, Bill.

Leeman, Wayne A. Oregon Land, Rural or Urban? LC 96-94975. xiv, 178p. 1997. pap. 12.95 (0-9654913-2-3) Millwright Pr.

Leemann, Sergio. Robert Wise on His Films: From Editing Room to Director's Chair. LC 95-10963. (Illus.). 224p. (Orig.). 1995. pap. 24.95 (1-879505-24-X) Silman James Pr.

Leemans. Management of Change in Government. (Development of Societies Ser.: No. 1). 1976. pap. text 152.50 (90-247-1817-1) Kluwer Academic.

Leemans, Rik, et al, eds. Theory & Models in Vegetation Science: Abstracts. (Illus.). 112p. (Orig.). 1985. pap. text 33.00 (91-7210-816-9) Coronet Bks.

Leemans, W. F. Ishtar of Lagaba & Her Dress. vi, 41p. 1952. pap. text 14.00 (0-614-04001-9, Pub. by Netherlands Inst) Eisenbrauns.

— Legal & Administrative Documents of the Time of Hammurabi & the Samsuiluna (Mainly from Lagaba) vi, 120p. 1960. pap. text 28.00 (0-614-04002-7, Pub. by Netherlands Inst) Eisenbrauns.

— Legal & Economic Records from the Kingdom of Larsa. viii, 103p. 1954. pap. text 28.00 (0-614-03986-X, Pub. by Netherlands Inst) Eisenbrauns.

LeeMaster, Marilyn R., ed. see Hasty, Ruth E.

Leemburg-Den Hollander, Jolanda, ed. European Directory of South-East Asian Studies. LC 98-234159. 628p. 1998. pap. 30.00 (90-6718-135-8, Pub. by KITLV Pr) Cellar.

Leemhuis, F., et al, eds. Scripta Signa Vocis: Studies about Scripts, Scriptures Scribes & Languages in the Near East, Presented to H. Hospers. (Illus.): 336p. (Orig.). 1986. pap. 46.00 (90-6980-008-X, Pub. by Egbert Forsten) Hod1der & Stoughton.

Leemhuis, F., et al. The Arabic Text of the Apocalypse of Baruch: Edited & Translated with a Parallel Translation of the Syriac Text. viii, 154p. 1986. 58.00 (90-04-07608-5) Brill Academic Pubs.

Leeming. Bank Equity. Date not set. text 79.95 (0-471-84331-8) Wiley.

— Stephen Spender: A Life in Modernism. LC 99-20425. 1999. text 27.50 (0-8050-4249-0) St Martin.

Leeming, A., et al. Lone Mothers. (DSS Research Report Ser.). 1994. 35.00 (0-11-762228-1, Pub. by Statnry Office) Bernan Associates.

Leeming, Andrew. The Super Analysis. 228p. 2000. 29.95 (0-471-84310-5) Wiley.

***Leeming, Andrew.** The Super Analysts: Conversations with the World's Leading Stock Market Investors & Analysts. LC 00-40811. 2000. boxed set. write for info. (0-471-47904-7) Wiley.

Leeming, Bruce. An Anger Bequeathed. 288p. (C). 1994. pap. write for info. (1-874640-70-X, Pub. by Argyll Pubng) St Mut.

— How You Must Dance. 228p. 1990. pap. 21.00 (1-898218-71-4) St Mut.

Leeming, D. & Hartley, R. Heavy Vehicle Technology. 2nd ed. (Illus.). 260p. 1981. pap. 39.50 (0-7487-0275-X, Pub. by S Thornes Pubs) Trans-Atl Phila.

Leeming, D. W., jt. auth. see Farrar, C. L.

Leeming, David. Amazing Grace: A Life of Beauford Delaney. LC 97-1645. (Illus.). 256p. 1998. 30.00 (0-19-509784-X) OUP.

— James Baldwin: A Biography. LC 94-43198. 1995. pap. 15.95 (0-8050-3835-3) H Holt & Co.

***Leeming, David.** Mythology of Native America. 224p. 2000. pap. text 11.95 (0-8061-3239-6) U of Okla Pr.

Leeming, David. The Peter Brook - Jean-Claude Carriere Mahabharata: The History of Mankind. 69p. 1986. 49.95 (0-88946-005-1) E Mellen.

***Leeming, David.** Stephen Spender. 2000. pap. write for info. (0-8050-6508-3) St Martin.

Leeming, David & Page, Jake. God: Myths of the Male Divine. (Illus.). 208p. 1996. 25.00 (0-19-509306-2) OUP.

— God: Myths of the Male Divine. (Illus.). 208p. 1997. reprint ed. pap. 12.95 (0-19-511387-X) OUP.

— Goddess: Myths of the Female Divine. (Illus.). 208p. (C). 1996. pap. 13.95 (0-19-510462-5) OUP.

— The Mythology of Native North America. LC 97-18451. 224p. 1998. 22.95 (0-8061-3012-1) U of Okla Pr.

***Leeming, David & Page, Jake.** Myths, Legends & Folktales of America: An Anthology. (Illus.). 240p. 2000. pap. 15.95 (0-19-511784-0) OUP.

Leeming, David & Page, Jake. Outlaws & Blues Queens, Tricksters & Gods: The Melting Pot of Myth, Legend & Folklore in America. LC 97-48607. (Illus.). 240p. 1999. 25.00 (0-19-511783-2) OUP.

Leeming, David A. Encyclopedia of Allegorical Literature. LC 96-31909. 326p. 1996. lib. bdg. 75.00 (0-87436-781-6) ABC-CLIO.

— Mythology: The Voyage of the Hero. 3rd ed. (Illus.). 288p. 1998. 30.00 (0-19-512153-8); pap. 16.95 (0-19-511957-6) OUP.

— The World of Myth: An Anthology. (Illus.). 384p. 1991. 35.00 (0-19-505601-9) OUP.

— The World of Myth: An Anthology. (Illus.). 384p. 1992. pap. 16.95 (0-19-507475-0) OUP.

Leeming, David A. & Leeming, Margaret A. A Dictionary of Creation Myths. (Illus.). 344p. 1996. pap. 18.95 (0-19-510275-4) OUP.

— Encyclopedia of Creation Myths. LC 94-7169. 330p. 1994. lib. bdg. 60.00 (0-87436-739-5) ABC-CLIO.

Leeming, David A., ed. see Book Builders, Inc. Staff.

***Leeming, David Adams.** Watts Children's Dictionary of Mythology. LC 99-25034. 128p. (J). (gr. 4-7). 1999. 32.00 (0-531-11708-1) Watts.

Leeming, Donald, jt. auth. see Tidy, Michael.

Leeming, E. Janice & Tripp, Cynthia F. Segmenting the Women's Market: Using Niche Marketing to Understand & Meet the Divers Needs. 300p. 1994. text 32.50 (1-55738-561-0, Irwn Prfssnl) McGraw-Hill Prof.

Leeming, Frank C. & Dwyer, William O. Issues in Adolescent Sexuality. LC 96-104771. 400p. 1995. pap. 31.00 (0-205-17444-2) Allyn.

Leeming, Glenda. Christopher Fry. (Twayne's English Authors Ser.: No. 479). 200p. (C). 1990. 23.95 (0-8057-6998-6, Twyne) Mac Lib Ref.

— Wesker the Playwright. 224p. (C). 1988. pap. write for info. (0-413-49240-0, A0315, Methuen Drama) Methn.

Leeming, Glenda, jt. compiled by see Trussler, Simon.

Leeming, Joseph. Brave Ships of England & America. LC 68-58801. (Essay Index Reprint Ser.). 1977. 24.95 (0-8369-0024-3) Ayer.

— Fun with String. LC 74-75260. (Illus.). 192p. 1999. reprint ed. pap. 4.95 (0-486-23063-5) Dover.

— Games & Fun with Playing Cards. (Illus.). 188p. 1980. reprint ed. pap. 4.95 (0-486-23977-2) Dover.

Leeming, M., jt. auth. see Hollaway, L.

Leeming, M. B. & Topping, B. H. V. Innovation in Civil & Construction Engineering. 372p. 1997. pap. (0-948749-51-2, Pub. by Civil-Comp) St Mut.

— Innovation in Composite Materials & Structure. 124p. 1997. pap. (0-948749-48-2, Pub. by Civil-Comp) St Mut.

— Innovation in Engineering for Seismic Regions. 115p. 1997. pap. 245.00 (0-948749-49-0, Pub. by Civil-Comp) St Mut.

Leeming, M. B., jt. auth. see Topping, B. H. V.

Leeming, M. B., ed. see Topping, B. H. V.

Leeming, Margaret A., jt. auth. see Leeming, David A.

Leeming, P. R., ed. Topics in Medicinal Chemistry, No. 65. 1988. 143.00 (0-85186-726-X) CRC Pr.

Leemis, Lawrence M. Reliability: Probabilistic Models & Statistical Methods. LC 94-23068. (International Series in Industrial & Systems Engineering). 288p. 1994. 92.00 (0-13-720517-1) P-H.

Leemis, Ralph. Smart Dog. LC 92-71274. (Illus.). 32p. (J). (ps-3). 1993. 14.95 (1-56397-109-7) Boyds Mills Pr.

Leen, Catherine, jt. auth. see Sturgess, Brian.

Leen, Daniel. The Freighthopper's Manual for North America: Hoboing in the 21st Century. 112p. (C). 1992. pap. 7.95 (*0-9632912-7-0*) Ecodesigns NW.

Leen, Edie. Complete Women's Weight Training Guide. LC 78-64384. (Illus.). 160p. 1980. pap. 6.95 (*0-89037-161-X*) Anderson World.

— Strength Training for Beauty. 160p. 1983. pap. 7.95 (*0-89037-266-7*) Anderson World.

Leen, Edie & Bertling, Ed. The Bodybuilder's Training Diary. 160p. 1983. spiral bd. 7.95 (*0-89037-258-6*) Anderson World.

Leen, Ediee. Strength Training for Beauty. 1983. 7.95 (*0-02-499810-9*, Macmillan Coll) P-H.

Leen, Edward. The Holy Spirit. 288p. 1998. reprint ed. pap. 9.95 (*1-889334-08-1*) Scepter Pubs.

Leen, Jason. The Death of the Prophet. rev. ed. LC 88-32021. 96p. 1988. reprint ed. pap. 7.95 (*0-935699-02-3*) Illum Arts.
The instructions The Death of the Prophet is a book, "channeled" by Jason Leen, which completes Kahlil Gibran's immortal trilogy that started with The Prophet. Gibran stated before his death, "I go, but if I go with a truth not yet voiced, that very truth will again see me & gather me, though my elements be scattered throughout the silences of eternity; & again shall I come before you that I may speak with a voice born anew." This powerful & poetic presentation tells the dramatic story of the prophet Almustafa as the priests of Orphalese challenge the prophet's teachings about the love of God. He tells them, "And so I did speak of unity with God, a unity which is not an idle promise, but an ever present reality. For where else does God dwell if not also within our very being?" The priests stone him for this blasphemy & Almustafa's spirit is released to "dance upon the wind." "Anybody who loved Kahlil Gibran's book The Prophet and/or The Garden of the Prophet will like this new addition. It is truly Gibran's masterful writing, & I love it!"--Elisabeth Kubler-Ross.
Publisher Paid Annotation.

— Peace at Last: The After-Death Experiences of John Lennon. Thompson, John M. et al, eds. LC 89-2223. (Illus.). 152p. 1989. pap. 11.95 (*0-935699-00-7*) Illum Arts.

Leen, Nina. Images of Sound. (Illus.). 1977. pap. 3.95 (*0-393-08800-6*) Norton.

Leen, Sarah, jt. auth. see Fisher, Ron.

Leenaars, Antoon A. Suicide in Canada. (Illus.). 624p. 1997. text 60.00 (*0-8020-0738-4*); pap. text 31.95 (*0-8020-7791-9*) U of Toronto Pr.

— Suicide Notes: Predictive Clues & Patterns. 272p. 1988. 42.95 (*0-89885-399-0*, Kluwer Acad Hman Sci) Kluwer Academic.

Leenaars, Antoon A., ed. Life Span Perspectives of Suicide: Time-Lines in the Suicide Process. LC 96-2679. (Illus.). 342p. (C). 1991. text 59.50 (*0-306-43620-5*, Kluwer Plenum) Kluwer Academic.

— Suicidology: Essays in Honor of Edwin Shneidman. LC 93-12028. 440p. 1993. 60.00 (*0-87668-571-8*) Aronson.

Leenaars, Antoon A., et al, eds. Suicide & the Older Adult. 160p. 1992. lib. bdg. 26.95 (*0-89862-587-4*) Guilford Pubns.

Leenaars, Antoon A. & Lester, David, eds. Suicide & the Unconscious. LC 95-30948. 312p. 1996. 60.00 (*1 56821 721 2*) Aronson.

Leenaars, Antoon A. & Wenkstern, Susanne. Suicide Prevention in Schools. 1990. 89.95 (*0-89116-954-7*); pap. 39.95 (*1-56032-081-8*) Hemisp Pub.

Leenaars, Antoon A., et al. Suicide: Individual, Cultural, International Perspectives. LC 98-155040. 152p. 1997. lib. bdg. 30.00 (*1-57230-240-2*, 0240) Guilford Pubns.

Leenaars, Antoon A., jt. auth. see Shneidman, Edwin S.

Leenaerts, Domine M. & Van Bokhoven, Wim M. Piecewise Linear Modeling & Analysis. LC 98-8186. 208p. 1998. 112.50 (*0-7923-8190-4*) Kluwer Academic.

Leenbouts, Keith J. Father, Son, 3-Mile Run: The Essence of Fatherhood. 3rd rev. ed. Doiron, Lynn & Boisclaire, Larry, eds. 128p. (YA). (gr. 10-12). 1999. pap. 9.95 (*0-9649997-4-9*) Clearwood Pubs.

Leenders. Purchase Supply Management. 11th ed. 1997. teacher ed. 36.25 (*0-256-24628-9*) McGraw.

Leenders, K., jt. auth. see Taube, M.

Leenders, Michael R. & Fearon, Harold. Purchasing & Materials Management. 11th ed. 736p. (C). 1996. text 71.75 (*0-256-14144-4*, Irwn Prfssnl) McGraw-Hill Prof.

Leenders, Michael R. & Fearon, Harold E. Purchasing & Materials Management. 10th ed. LC 92-20079. 704p. (C). 1992. text 71.75 (*0-256-10334-8*, Irwn McGrw-H) McGrw-H Hghr Educ.

Leenders, Michael R., et al. Purchasing & Materials Management. 9th ed. 672p. (C). 1989. text 61.95 (*0-256-06984-0*, Irwn McGrw-H) McGrw-H Hghr Educ.

Leenders, Michael R., jt. auth. see England, Wilbur B.

Leenders, Michiel R. & Blenkhorn, David L. Reverse Marketing. 1987. 45.00 (*0-02-918381-2*) Free Pr.

Leenders, Michiel R. & Flynn, Anna E. Value-Driven Purchasing: Managing the Key Steps in the Acquisition Process. LC 94-21172. (NAPM Professional Development Ser.: 13). 264p. 1994. text 45.00 (*0-7863-0236-4*, Irwn McGrw-H) McGrw-H Hghr Educ.

Leenders, Michiel R., jt. auth. see Fearon, Harold E.

***Leendertse, Jeannet.** Best of Business Card Design, 1vol. 4th ed. 2000. 45.00 (*1-56496-667-4*) Rockport Pubs.

Leene, Jentina E., ed. Textile Conservation. LC 74-179287. (Illus.). 285p. reprint ed. pap. 88.40 (*0-608-11292-5*, 2004628000045) Bks Demand.

Leenen, Frans H., et al, eds. Controlling High Blood Pressure. 176p. 1990. reprint ed. pap. 8.95 (*1-55958-087-9*) Prima Pub.

Leenen, Frans H. H., jt. auth. see Haynes, R. Bryan.

Leenen, H. J., et al. The Rights of Patients in Europe: A Comparative Study. LC 92-37647. 1992. 55.00 (*90-6544-671-0*) Kluwer Law Intl.

Leener, Philippe De, see Ndione, Emmanuel.

Leenhardt, Maurice. Do Kamo: La Personne et le Mythe Dans le Monde Melanesien. Bolle, Kees W., ed. LC 77-79137. (Mythology Ser.). (FRE.). 1978. reprint ed. lib. bdg. 26.95 (*0-405-10547-9*) Ayer.

— Do Kamo: Person & Myth in the Melanesian World. Gulati, Basia M. & Crapanzano, Vincent, trs. from FRE. LC 78-10826. 1979. lib. bdg. 18.00 (*0-226-47039-3*) U Ch Pr.

Leenheer, A. P. De, see De Leenheer, A. P.

Leenhouts, H. P., jt. auth. see Chadwick, K. H.

Leenhouts, P. W. Genus Canarium in the Pacific. (BMB Ser.: No. 216). 1969. reprint ed. pap. 25.00 (*0-527-02324-8*) Periodicals Srv.

Leep, Lisa. Number the Stars Study Guide. 54p. (J). (gr. 5-7). 1996. student ed., ring bd. 12.99 (*1-58609-146-8*) Progeny Pr WI.

— The Sign of the Beaver Study Guide. 54p. (J). (gr. 5-7). 1995. student ed., ring bd. 12.99 (*1-58609-143-3*) Progeny Pr WI.

Leeper, Alexander W. A History of Medieval Austria. Seton-Watson, Robert W., ed. LC 76-29416. reprint ed. 57.50 (*0-404-15347-X*) AMS Pr.

Leeper Buss, Fran. Journey of the Sparrows - a Play with Music. 66p. 1999. pap. 5.50 (*0-87129-795-7*, J32) Dramatic Pub.

Leeper, Doris, et al. The First Decade: Atlantic Center for the Arts. 82p. (Orig.). (C). 1987. pap. 12.00 (*1-882070-00-3*) Atlantic Ctr Arts.

Leeper, Ethel M., jt. ed. see Crowell, Nancy A.

***Leeper, F. J., et al, eds.** Biosynthesis: Aromatic Polyketides, Isoprenoids, Alkaloids. (Topics in Current Chemistry: 209). x, 244p. 2000. 159.00 (*3-540-66573-0*) Spr-Verlag.

***Leeper, F. J. & Vederas, J. C.** Biosynthesis: Polyketides & Vitamins. LC 00-20461. (Desktop Editions in Chemistry Ser.: 195). x, 193p. 2000. pap. text 42.95 (*3-540-66969-8*) Spr-Verlag.

Leeper, F. J. & Vederas, J. C., eds. Biosynthesis: Polyketides & Vitamins. (Topics in Current Chemistry Ser.: Vol. 195). (Illus.). 200p. 1997. 119.00 (*3-540-63418-5*) Spr-Verlag.

Leeper, G. W. & Uren, N. C. Soil Science: An Introduction. (Illus.). 260p. (Orig.). 1993. pap. 34.95 (*0-522-84464-2*, Pub. by Melbourne Univ Pr) Paul & Co Pubs.

Leeper, G. W., jt. auth. see Attiwill, P. M.

Leeper, Geoffrey W. Managing the Heavy Metals on the Land. LC 77-20934. (Pollution Engineering & Technology Ser.: Vol. 6). (Illus.). 143p. reprint ed. pap. 44.40 (*0-608-08949-4*, 206958400005) Bks Demand.

Leeper, John. The Brothers of the Sled. (Illus.). 130p. (Orig.). (J). (gr. 1-8). 1996. pap. 7.99 (*1-889893-01-3*) Emerald House Group Inc.

— The Riddle of the Outlaw Bear. (Illus.). 130p. (Orig.). (J). (gr. 1-8). 1996. pap. 7.99 (*1-889893-02-1*) Emerald House Group Inc.

Leeper, John H. & Tomassoni, Mark, eds. Coal Exports & Port Development. 2nd ed. LC 81-71245. (Illus.). 116p. 1982. pap. text 10.00 (*0-87033-286-4*) Cornell Maritime.

***Leeper, Linda.** Allyn & Bacon Quick Guide to the Internet 2000 Edition: For Speech-language Pathology & Audiology. 3rd ed. 1999. pap. 8.00 (*0-205-30970-4*) Allyn.

Leeper, Merton D. Colorado Trout Fishing Pt. 2: Prime Fishing Locations - Find Out Where 10 Percent of the Fishermen Catch 90 Percent of the Fish. 2nd ed. (Illus.). 100p. (Orig.). 1988. pap. text, per. 9.95 (*0-9617325-1-2*) ML Pubns.

— Colorado Trout Fishing Methods & Techniques. 2nd ed. (Illus.). 91p. (Orig.). 1989. pap. 9.95 (*0-9617325-2-0*) ML Pubns.

— Rocky Mountain Trout Fishing. (Illus.). (Orig.). 1991. pap. text 9.95 (*0-9617325-3-9*) ML Pubns.

Leeper, Robert. The Brindle Mule. LC 83-15521. 1983. 11.95 (*0-913239-09-7*); pap. 7.95 (*0-913239-08-9*) Appalach Consortium.

Leeper, Steven L., tr. see Nasu, Masamoto.

Leer, Anne C. It's a Wired World: The New Networked Economy. (Illus.). 188p. (Orig.). 1996. pap. 37.00 (*82-00-42310-7*) Scandnvan Univ Pr.

***Leer, Anne C.** Welcome to the Wired World: Key Strategic Agendas for Commerce in the Digital Age. (Illus.). 240p. 1999. pap. text 35.95 (*0-273-63560-3*, Pub. by F T P-H) Trans-Atl Phila.

Leer, Dustin, ed. see Chamberlin, Jane.

Leer, Jeff, jt. auth. see Krauss, Michael.

Leer, Jeff, jt. auth. see Nyman, Elizabeth.

Leer, Loreeta. Ascension at Midnight. Date not set. write for info. (*0-9659632-4-1*) Verda Publ.

Leer, Norman. I Dream My Father in a Song: Poems. LC 93-15647. (Illus.). 52p. 1993. reprint ed. pap. 14.95 (*0-7734-9453-7*) E Mellen.

— Second Lining: Poems. LC 97-11765. (Illus.). 80p. 1997. pap. 14.95 (*0-7734-2824-0*, Mellen Poetry Pr) E Mellen.

Leer, Steven F. & Anderson, Girard F. Vision 2020. (Illus.). 173p. (C). 1998. pap. text 35.00 (*0-7881-7040-6*) DIANE Pub.

Leerburger, Benedict A. Marketing the Library. LC 81-18132. (Professional Librarian Ser.). 124p. 1982. pap. 26.50 (*0-914236-89-X*, Hall Reference) Macmillan.

— Promoting & Marketing the Library. rev. ed. (Professional Librarian Ser.). 300p. 1989. 40.00 (*0-8161-1926-0*, Hall Reference); 30.00 (*0-8161-1895-7*, Hall Reference) Macmillan.

Leerhsen, Charles, jt. auth. see Trump, Donald J.

Leerhsen, Charles, jt. auth. see Yeager, Chuck.

Leermakers, Rene. The Functional Treatment of Parsing. LC 93-22799. 176p. (C). 1993. text 120.00 (*0-7923-9376-7*) Kluwer Academic.

Leers, Bernardino, jt. auth. see Moser, Antonio.

Leerssen, Joep & Rigney, Ann, eds. Historians & Social Values. (Illus.). 312p. (C). text 49.75 (*90-5356-458-6*, Pub. by Amsterdam U Pr); pap. text 28.75 (*90-5356-451-9*, Pub. by Amsterdam U Pr) U of Mich Pr.

Leerssen, Joep, jt. ed. see Jourdan, Annie.

Leerssen, Joseph T. Mere Irish & Fior-Ghael: Studies in the Idea of Irish Nationality, Its Development & Literary Expression Prior to the Nineteenth Century. LC 96-42498. (Critical Conditions Ser.). 1997. pap. text 20.00 (*0-268-01427-2*) U of Notre Dame Pr.

— Remembrance & Imagination: Patterns in the Historical & Literary Representation of Ireland in the Nineteenth Century. LC 96-42459. (Critical Conditions Ser.). 321p. 1997. pap. text 20.00 (*0-268-01655-0*) U of Notre Dame Pr.

Leerssen, Joseph Theodoor. Mere Irish & Fior-Ghael: Studies in the Idea of Irish Nationality, It's Literary Expression & Development. LC 86-6879. (Utrecht Publications in General & Comparative Literature: Vol. 22). xv, 543p. 1986. 124.00 (*90-272-2198-7*) J Benjamins Pubng Co.

Lees. Bill Evans: A Biography. 400p. 2000. per. 30.00 (*0-02-864923-0*) Mac Lib Ref.

***Lees.** Cats of Any Color. 2000. mass mkt. 18.00 (*0-306-80950-8*, Pub. by Da Capo) HarpC.

Lees. Children with Acquired Aphasias. 164p. 1993. pap. 38.95 (*1-56593-252-8*, 0545) Thomson Learn.

***Lees.** Skin Care: Beyond the Basics. (Milady - Cosmetology). 2000. pap. 42.75 (*1-56253-625-7*); pap., wbk. ed. 19.50 (*1-56253-626-5*) Thomson Learn.

Lees & Karel. Omega-Three Fatty Acids in Health & Disease. (Food Science & Technology Ser.: Vol. 37). (Illus.). 328p. 1990. text 165.00 (*0-8247-8292-5*) Dekker.

Lees, jt. auth. see Willis.

Lees, A. Science & Racket Sports 2. LC 98-16459. (Science & Racket Sports Ser.). (Illus.). 304p. (C). 1998. 85.00 (*0-419-23030-0*, E & FN Spon) Routledge.

Lees, Alfred & Heyn, Ernest V. Popular Science Decks & Sun Spaces. LC 90-10380. (Illus.). 256p. 1991. pap. 19.95 (*0-8069-7448-6*) Sterling.

Lees, Alfred & Nelson, Ronald, eds. Longtime Companions: Autobiographies of Gay Male Fidelity. LC 98-46138. 225p. 1999. pap. 17.95 (*1-56023-957-3*, Harrington Park); lib. bdg. 39.95 (*0-7890-0641-3*, Harrington Park) Haworth Pr.

Lees, Bill. Is It a Sacrifice? Experiencing Mission & Revival in Borneo. 1987. pap. 4.95 (*9971-972-53-0*) OMF Bks.

Lees, Brian. A Handbook of the Al Sa'ud Ruling Family of Saudi Arabia. 64p. 1979. boxed set 39.95 (*0-905743-17-2*, Pub. by Stacey Intl) Intl Bk Ctr.

Lees, Carlton B., jt. auth. see Johnson, Lady Bird.

Lees, Christopher C., et al. Pregnancy & Birth: Your Questions Answered. LC 96-33518. 240p. 1997. 19.95 (*0-7894-1470-8*) DK Pub Inc.

Lees, Clare A. Tradition & Belief: Religious Writing in Late Anglo-Saxon England. LC 99-38778. (Medieval Cultures Ser.: Vol. 19). 232p. 1999. lib. bdg. 49.95 (*0-8166-3002-X*, Pub. by U of Minn Pr) Chicago Distribution Ctr.

***Lees, Clare A.** Tradition & Belief: Religious Writing in Late Anglo-Saxon England. LC 99-38778. (Medieval Cultures Ser.: Vol. 19). 232p. 1999. pap. 19.95 (*0-8166-3003-8*, Pub. by U of Minn Pr) Chicago Distribution Ctr.

Lees, Clare A., ed. Medieval Masculinities: Regarding Men in the Middle Ages. LC 93-37311. 1994. pap. 17.95 (*0-8166-2426-7*); text 44.95 (*0-8166-2425-9*) U of Minn Pr.

***Lees, D. R. & Barrett, C. B., eds.** Tradeoffs or Synergies? Agricultural Intensification, Economic Development & The Environment. (CABI Publishing Ser.). (Illus.). 450p. 2000. text 90.00 (*0-85199-435-0*) OUP.

Lees, D. R. & Edwards, D., eds. Evolutionary Patterns & Processes. (Linnean Society Symposium Ser.: No. 14). (Illus.). 325p. 1993. text 83.00 (*0-12-440895-8*) Acad Pr.

***Lees, David H. & Steisel, Mark D.** Understanding Managed Care Contracts: A Practical Guide for Dental Professionals. LC 99-44719. (Illus.). 1999. pap. 64.95 (*0-87814-772-1*) PennWell Bks.

Lees, Dennis S. & University of Nottingham Staff. 1966 & All That. LC 78-476829. (Inaugural Lecture Ser.). 14 p. 1970. write for info. (*0-900572-16-7*) Univ Nottingham.

Lees, Diane, ed. Museums & Interactive Multimedia: Selected Papers from ICHIM 93. 1993. pap. text 20.00 (*0-905963-89-X*) Archives & Mus.

Lees, F. P. & Ang, M. L. Safety Cases. 363p. 1990. text 170.00 (*0-408-02708-8*) Buttrwrth-Heinemann.

Lees, Francis A. & Liaw, K. Thomas. Foreign Participation in China's Banking & Securities Markets. LC 95-34542. 208p. 1996. 59.95 (*1-56720-022-2*, Quorum Bks) Greenwood.

Lees, Francis A., et al. Global Finance. (C). 1997. text 83.00 (*0-673-46948-4*) Addson-Wesley Educ.

Lees, Francis A., jt. auth. see Gordon, Sara L.

Lees, Frank P. Loss Prevention in Process Industries, 2 vols. (C). 1980. 1160.00 (*0-7855-4098-9*, Pub. by Witherby & Co) St Mut.

Lees, G. D. & Williamson, W. G. Handbook for Marine Radio Communication. 383p. 1993. 40.00 (*1-85044-472-2*) LLP.

***Lees, Gene.** Arranging the Score: Portraits of the Great Arrangers. LC 99-42120. (Illus.). 1999. 34.95 (*0-304-70488-1*) Continuum.

Lees, Gene. Leader of the Band: The Life of Woody Herman. (Illus.). 432p. 1997. reprint ed. pap. 15.95 (*0-19-511574-0*) OUP.

— Meet Me at Jim & Andy's: Jazz Musicians & Their World. 288p. 1990. reprint ed. pap. 10.95 (*0-19-506580-8*) OUP.

— The Modern Rhyming Dictionary. 364p. (Orig.). (YA). (gr. 8 up). 1986. 19.95 (*0-89524-129-3*, 8649); pap. 14.95 (*0-89524-317-2*, Pub. by Cherry Lane) H Leonard.

***Lees, Gene.** Modern Rhyming Dictionary. rev. ed. 2000. pap. text 14.95 (*1-57560-196-6*) Cherry Lane.

Lees, Gene. Oscar Peterson: The Will to Swing. (Illus.). 304p. 1991. pap. 14.95 (*1-55958-111-5*) Prima Pub.

***Lees, Gene.** Oscar Peterson: The Will to Swing. rev. ed. (Illus.). 2000. pap. 18.95 (*0-8154-1021-2*) Cooper Sq.

Lees, Gene. Singers & the Song II. LC 97-29823. 272p. (C). 1998. 30.00 (*0-19-511556-2*) OUP.

— Singers & the Song II. 272p. 1999. pap. 15.95 (*0-19-512208-9*) OUP.

***Lees, Gene.** Waiting for Dizzy: Fourteen Jazz Portraits. (Illus.). 2000. pap. 17.95 (*0-8154-1037-9*) Cooper Sq.

Lees, Graham & Myers, Ben. The Encyclopedia of World Beers. (Illus.). 180p. 1997. 17.98 (*0-7858-0799-3*) Bk Sales Inc.

Lees-Haley, Paul R. Psychological & Neuropsychological Testing Terms: A Glossary in Nontechnical Language Version 1.0. 1998. 19.95 (*0-9668410-0-X*) Lees-Haley Psych.

Lees-Haley, Paul R., jt. ed. see Price, David R.

***Lees, Hilary.** English Churchyard Memorials. (Illus.). 176p. 2000. 29.99 (*0-7524-1441-0*, Pub. by Tempus Pubng) Arcadia Publng.

Lees, J. D. & Cerasini, M. The Official Godzilla Compendium: A 40 Year Retrospective. LC 97-75898. 1998. pap. 16.00 (*0-679-88822-5*) Random.

Lees, James. The Masting & Rigging of English Ships of War, 1625-1860. 2nd ed. (Illus.). 212p. 1984. 59.95 (*0-87021-948-0*) Naval Inst Pr.

Lees, Janet & Urwin, Shelagh. Children with Language Disorders. 2nd ed. LC 97-180304. (Illus.). 250p. 1997. pap. 48.95 (*1-56593-881-X*, 1726) Thomson Learn.

Lees, Jay T. Anselm of Havelberg: Deeds into Words in the Twelfth Century. LC 97-40019. (Studies in the History of Christian Thought, 0081-8607: No. 79). xiv, 317p. 1997. 115.50 (*90-04-10906-4*) Brill Academic Pubs.

Lees, Jennie R. Franquin: Master Showman. (Illus.). 1997. pap. 29.95 (*0-86819-519-7*, Pub. by Currency Pr) Accents Pubns.

Lees, John. Clinical Counselling in Context: An Introduction. LC 98-29006. (Clinical Counselling in Context Ser.). 1999. 75.00 (*0-415-17955-6*); pap. 24.99 (*0-415-17956-4*) Routledge.

***Lees, John.** Clinical Counselling in Further & Higher Education. LC 98-31368. (Clinical Counselling in Context Ser.). 1999. 65.00 (*0-415-19280-3*); pap. 20.99 (*0-415-19281-1*) Routledge.

Lees, John. Clinical Counselling in Primary Care. LC 98-29005. (Clinical Counselling in Context Ser.). 1999. 75.00 (*0-415-17953-X*); pap. 24.99 (*0-415-17954-8*) Routledge.

Lees, John & Rosenhaum, Stephanie. A Programmer's Guide to C. write for info. (*0-318-58252-X*) P-H.

Lees, Judi, jt. auth. see Wershler, Terri.

Lees, Kirsten. Votes for Women: The Australian Story. LC 95-130230. (Illus.). 224p. 1996. pap. 24.95 (*1-86373-630-1*, Pub. by Allen & Unwin Pty) Paul & Co Pubs.

***Lees, Laura & Mason, Kris.** Memory Folding: Tea Bag Paper Folding for Your Scrapbook. Durant, Judith, ed. (Illus.). 36p. 1999. pap. 9.50 (*1-892127-06-7*) Satellite Publ.

Lees, Lorraine M. Keeping Tito Afloat: The United States, Yugoslavia, & the Cold War. LC 96-9159. 1997. 40.00 (*0-271-01629-9*) Pa St U Pr.

Lees, Lynn H. The Solidarities of Strangers: The English Poor Laws & the People, 1700-1948. LC 97-613. (Illus.). 388p. (C). 1998. text 64.95 (*0-521-57261-4*) Cambridge U Pr.

Lees, Lynn H., jt. auth. see Hohenberg, Paul M.

Lees, Lynne S., tr. see Duncker, Karl.

Lees, Mark. Milady's Skin Care Reference Guide. LC 93-28236. (SKIN). 384p. 1993. pap. 39.95 (*1-56253-071-2*) Thomson Learn.

Lees, Michael. Rape of Serbia. 1990. 29.95 (*0-15-195910-2*) Harcourt.

***Lees, Miline J.** Through Wood & Dale. 1998. text 45.00 (*0-7195-5599-X*, Pub. by John Murray) Trafalgar.

Lees-Milne, James. The Age of Adam. 1988. reprint ed. lib. bdg. 59.00 (*0-7812-0146-2*) Rprt Serv.

— Ancient As the Hills: Diaries, 1973-1974. 240p. 1998. 40.00 (*0-7195-5596-5*, Pub. by John Murray) Trafalgar.

— Another Self. 92p. 1998. 35.00 (*0-7195-5598-1*, Pub. by John Murray) Trafalgar.

— The Bachelor Duke: A Life of William Spencer Cavendish, 6th Duke of Devonshire, 1790-1858. (Illus.). 256p. 1998. pap. 24.95 (*0-7195-5600-7*, Pub. by John Murray) Trafalgar.

— Diaries 1942-1945: Ancestral Voices & Prophesying Peace. 504p. 1996. 45.00 (*0-7195-5590-6*, Pub. by John Murray) Trafalgar.

— Diaries 1946-1949: Caves of Ice & Midway on the Waves. 450p. 1996. 45.00 (*0-7195-5591-4*, Pub. by John Murray) Trafalgar.

— Fourteen Friends. (Illus.). 256p. 1997. 40.00 (*0-7195-5594-9*, Pub. by John Murray) Trafalgar.

— A Mingled Measure Diaries, 1953-1972. 325p. 1996. 45.00 (*0-7195-5362-8*, Pub. by John Murray) Trafalgar.

An Asterisk (*) at the beginning of an entry indicates that the title is appearing for the first time.

L

— Roman Mornings. 148p. (Orig.). 1992. pap. 14.95 (*1-56131-011-5*, NAB) I R Dee.

Lees, Nick, jt. auth. see Stanton, John.

Lees, Nigel. How to Find Information - Chemistry: A Guide to Searching in Published Sources. (How to Find Ser.). 32p. 1995. pap. 8.00 (*0-7123-0806-7*, Pub. by SRIS) L Erlbaum Assocs.

Lees, Nigel & British Library Staff. Hazardous Materials: Sources of Information on their Transportation LC 98-105708. 70p. 1990. pap. write for info. (*0-7123-0773-7*) B23tish Library.

Lees, Nigel & Woolston, Helen. Environmental Information: A Guide to Sources. 2nd ed. 180p. 1997. pap. 52.00 (*0-7123-0825-3*, Pub. by SRIS) L Erlbaum Assocs.

Lees, Paul. The Dive Sites of Thailand. LC 97-67401. (Dive Sites of . . . Ser.). (Illus.). 176p. 1997. pap. 24.95 (*0-8442-4849-5*, 48495, Natl Textbk Co) NTC Contemp Pub Co.

Lees, Peter, ed. Navigating the NHS: Core Issues for Clinicians. 1996. write for info. (*1-85775-106-X*, Radcliffe Med Pr) Scovill Paterson.

Lees, R. & Smith, A. F., eds. Design, Construction & Refurbishment of Laboratories. LC 84-15788. (Chemical Science Ser.). 375p. 1984. text 119.00 (*0-470-20133-9*) P-H.

Lees, Robert B. English for Turks. (English for Foreigners Ser.).Tr. of Konusulan Ingilizce. (ENG & TUR.). 353p. 1980. pap., student ed. 20.00 (*0-87950-309-2*); digital audio 110.00 (*0-87950-615-6*) Spoken Lang Serv.

Lees, Robert B. English for Turks. (Spoken English As a Foreign Language Ser.).Tr. of Konusulan Ingilizce. (ENG & TUR.). 1980. audio 90.00 (*0-87950-614-8*) Spoken Lang Serv.

Lees, Russell. Nixon's Nixon. LC 98-178110. 1996. pap. 5.25 (*0-8222-1556-X*) Dramatists Play.

Lees, Sidney & Ferrari, Leonard A., eds. Acoustical Imaging Vol. 23: Proceedings of the 23rd International Symposium Held in Boston, Massachusetts, April 13-16, 1997. (Illus.). 670p. (C). 1998. text 198.00 (*0-306-45768-7*, Kluwer Plenum) Kluwer Academic.

Lees, Smith, Osborne. Proffessionally Speaking: Managing Your English in Bussiness. 1995. disk 121.00 (*0-471-95410-1*) Wiley.

Lees, Stella, ed. A Track to Unknown Water: Proceedings of the Second Pacific Rim Conference on Children's Literature. LC 87-12852. (Illus.). 420p. 1987. reprint ed. 39.50 (*0-8108-2006-4*) Scarecrow.

Lees, Stella & Macintyre, Pamela. The Oxford Companion to Australian Children's Literature. (Illus.). 494p. 1994. text 49.95 (*0-19-553284-8*) OUP.

Lees, Stewart. My First Word Book. 48p. (J). (ps-1). 1997. 7.98 (*1-85854-519-6*) Brimax Bks.

Lees, Sue. Carnal Knowledge: Rape on Trial. 320p. 1997. pap. 17.95 (*0-14-023915-4*, Pub. by Pnguin Bks Ltd) Trafalgar.

Lees, Sue. Losing Out: Sexuality & Adolescent Girls. LC 86-3137. pap. 12.50 (*0-09-164101-2*) Hutchinson UK.

— Ruling Passions: Sexual Violence, Reputation & the Law. LC 96-19876. 192p. 1996. pap. 26.99 (*0-335-19613-6*) OpUniv Pr.

Lees, Sue, jt. auth. see Gregory, Jeanne.

Lees, Susan, jt. ed. see Ortiz, Sutti.

Lees, Susan H. The Political Ecology of the Water Crisis in Israel. 208p. (C). 1997. 36.00 (*0-7618-0969-4*) U Pr of Amer.

Lees, Susan H., jt. ed. see Bates, Daniel G.

Lees, Thomas. A Glossary of the Dialect of Almondbury & Huddersfield. (English Dialect Society Publications: No. 39). 1969. reprint ed. pap. 25.00 (*0-8115-0464-6*) Periodicals Srv.

Lees, Virginia & Einspahr, Edith, eds. The Olson Family Recipe Book. (Illus.). 1997. spiral bd. 45.00 (*0-9625714-6-6*) Spruce Gulch Pr.

Lees, W. A. Adhesives in Engineering Design. 156p. (C). 1984. text 110.00 (*0-85072-150-4*) St Mut.

Lees, W. A., et al, eds. High Pressure Technology - 1995: Proceedings. LC 94-71662. (Proceedings of the 1995 ASME/JSME Pressure Vessels & Piping Conference Ser.: PVP-Vol. 297). 200p. 1995. 120.00 (*0-7918-1328-2*, H00960) ASME.

Leesch, Wolfgang. Die Deutschen Archivare, 1500 to 1945,, Vol. 1 & 2. rev. ed. (GER.). 1005p. 1992. lib. bdg. 58.00 (*3-598-10606-8*) K G Saur Verlag.

— Die Deutschen Archivare, 1500 to 1945 Vol. 1: Verzeichnis nach ihren Wirkungsstatten. (GER.). 268p. 1985. lib. bdg. 28.50 (*3-598-10530-4*) K G Saur Verlag.

Leesch, Wolfgang, jt. auth. see Brenneke, Adolf.

Leese, A. Agriculture & the Banking System. 1991. lib. bdg. 61.75 (*0-8490-4442-1*) Gordon Pr.

Leese, Brenda, jt. auth. see Bosanquet, Nick.

Leese, C. Leonard, tr. see Bobillier, Marie.

Leese, Charles. Leese: The Lawrence Leese Family: Two Centuries in America (1741-1941) (Illus.). 214p. 1993. reprint ed. pap. 34.00 (*0-8328-3362-2*); reprint ed. lib. bdg. 44.00 (*0-8328-3361-4*) Higginson Bk Co.

Leese, Elizabeth. Costume Design in the Movies: An Illustrated Guide to the Work of 158 Great Designers. (Illus.). 176p. 1991. pap. 14.95 (*0-486-26548-X*) Dover.

***Leese, Joan, et al.** Three Plays for Women. LC 99-52090. 44p. (YA). (gr. 8-12). 1999. pap. 6.00 (*0-88734-932-3*) Players Pr.

Leese, Marianne, ed. see Beman, Lynn S.

Leese, T. Anna. Blood Royal: Issue of the Kings & Queens of Medieval England 1066-1399. 467p. (Orig.). 1996. pap. 39.00 (*0-7884-0525-X*, L117) Heritage Bk.

Leeser, Isaac. The Holy Scriptures Holy Bible Commentary. 32.50 (*0-87559-196-5*) Shalom.

Leeser, M. & Brown, G., eds. Hardware Specification, Verification & Synthesis: Mathematical Aspects. (Lecture Notes in Computer Science Ser.: Vol. 408). (Illus.). vi, 402p. 1990. 58.95 (*0-387-97226-9*) Spr-Verlag.

Leeser, Robert C. Engineer's Procurement Manual for Major Plant Equipment: A Guide to Principles & Procedures. 368p. (C). 1996. 79.00 (*0-13-294711-0*) P-H.

Leesley, Michael E. Freshman Chemical Engineering. LC 79-18418. 200p. 1979. reprint ed. pap. 62.00 (*0-608-00829-X*, 206161900010) Bks Demand.

Leesley, Michael E., ed. Computer-Aided Process Plant Design. LC 81-20335. 1394p. 1982. reprint ed. pap. 200.00 (*0-608-01335-8*, 206207900001) Bks Demand.

Leeson. Constitutional Law. 1995. pap. text, suppl. ed. 10.00 (*0-312-14233-1*) St Martin.

— Constitutional Law, Vol. 1. 2nd ed. 2000. text. write for info. (*0-312-11723-X*) St Martin.

Leeson, Alan, tr. Manual of Sheep Production in the Humid Tropics of Africa. 250p. (Orig.). 1992. pap. 35.00 (*0-85198-795-8*) OUP.

***Leeson, Andrea & Alleman, Bruce C., eds.** In Situ & On-Site Bioremediation Symposium: San Diego, California. 2772p. 1999. 350.00 (*1-57477-073-X*) Battelle.

Leeson, Andrea, jt. auth. see Alleman, Bruce C.

Leeson, Andrea, jt. ed. see Alleman, Bruce C.

Leeson, Andrea, ed. see Hinchee, Robert F.

Leeson, C. Roland, et al. Text-Atlas of Histology. (Illus.). 768p. 1988. text 78.00 (*0-7216-2386-7*, W B Saunders Co) Harcrt Hlth Sci Grp.

— Text-Atlas of Histology Slide Set. 1989. 410.00 (*0-7216-2824-9*, W B Saunders Co) Harcrt Hlth Sci Grp.

Leeson, Edward, ed. The New Golden Treasury of English Verse. 506p. (Orig.). 1994. pap. 32.50 (*0-333-61649-9*, Pub. by Papermac) Trans-Atl Phila.

Leeson, Francis L. A Directory of British Peerages. LC 85-70013. 174p. 1986. reprint ed. pap. 12.50 (*0-8063-1121-5*) Genealog Pub.

Leeson, Fred. Rose City Justice: A Legal History of Portland, Oregon. LC 98-40991. 264p. 1999. pap. 15.95 (*0-87595-269-0*) Oregon Hist.

Leeson, George, tr. see Martin-Santos, Luis.

Leeson, Kenneth W., jt. auth. see Machlup, Fritz.

Leeson, Lynn H., ed. Clicking In: Hot Links to a Digital Culture. LC 96-14615. (Illus.). 385p. 1996. pap. 24.95 incl. cd-rom (*0-941920-42-9*) Bay Pr.

Leeson, M. A. Documents & Biography Pertaining to the Settlement & Progress of Stark County, Containing an Authentic Summary of Records, Documents, Historical Works & Newspapers. (Illus.). 708p. 1989. reprint ed. lib. bdg. 76.00 (*0-8328-0559-9*) Higginson Bk Co.

Leeson, Marjorie. Computing Fundamentals. 1993. teacher ed. 18.47 (*0-02-800345-4*) Glencoe.

Leeson, Marjorie. Programming Logic LC 82-16790. x, 358p. 1983. write for info. (*0-574-21420-8*) SRA.

Leeson, Muriel. Journey to Freedom. LC 89-83735. (Illus.). 128p. (Orig.). (J). (gr. 4-8). 1989. pap. 5.99 (*0-8361-3498-2*) Herald Pr.

Leeson, Pat, jt. auth. see Leeson, Tom.

Leeson, Richard. Voyage a Paris. (Illus.). 1971. pap. text 5.25 (*0-582-36036-6*); audio 12.50 (*0-582-37175-9*) Longman.

Leeson, Richard M. Lorraine Hansberry: A Research & Production Sourcebook, 13. LC 97-12283. (Modern Dramatists Research & Production Sourcebooks: Vol. 13). 192p. 1997. lib. bdg. 65.00 (*0-313-29312-0*, Greenwood Pr) Greenwood.

— William Inge: A Research & Production Sourcebook, 5. LC 93-46360. (Modern Dramatists Research & Production Sourcebooks Ser.: Vol. 5). 240p. 1994. lib. bdg. 65.00 (*0-313-27407-X*, Greenwood Pr) Greenwood.

***Leeson, Robert.** The Eclipse of Keynesianism: The Political Economy of the Chicago Counter-Revolution. LC 00-31118. 2000. write for info. (*0-312-23575-5*) St Martin.

— Geraldine Gets Lucky. (Illus.). 32p. (J). pap. 7.95 (*0-14-038615-7*, Pub. by Pnguin Bks Ltd) Trafalgar.

Leeson, Robert. Lucky LAD-LP. 1999. pap. text 16.95 (*0-7540-6042-X*) Chivers N Amer.

— Nunca Bese a los Sapos! (Never Kiss Frogs!) Mansour, Monica, tr. (SPA., Illus.). (J). (gr. 3-4). 1993. pap. 5.99 (*968-16-4235-X*, Pub. by Fondo) Continental Bk.

— Reading & Righting: The Past, Present & Future of Fiction for the Young LC 86-156602. 256p. 1985. write for info. (*0-00-184415-6*) Collins SF.

Leeson, Robert. Tom's Private War. (Illus.). 96p. (J). pap. 7.95 (*0-14-038427-8*, Pub. by Pnguin Bks Ltd) Trafalgar.

Leeson, Robert, jt. ed. see Phillips, A. W. H.

Leeson, Ruth K. Medical Psychology of Breast Cancer: Index of New Information. 153p. 1997. 47.50 (*0-7883-1500-5*); pap. 44.50 (*0-7883-1501-3*) ABBE Pubs Assn.

Leeson, Steven & Summers, John D. Commercial Poultry Nutrition. 370p. 1997. pap. 90.00 (*0-9695600-2-8*, Pub. by Univ Nottingham) St Mut.

Leeson, Susan & Johnston, Bryan M. Ending It: Dispute Resolution in America. LC 88-22027. 164p. (C). 1988. pap. 29.00 (*0-87084-404-0*) Anderson Pub Co.

Leeson, Susan M. & Foster, James C. Constitutional Law: Cases in Context. LC 90-63560. 912p. (C). 1992. pap. text 71.95 (*0-312-02512-2*) St Martin.

Leeson, Susan M., jt. auth. see Foster, James C.

Leeson, Ted. The Habit of Rivers: Reflections on Trout Streams & Fly Fishing. 192p. 1994. 22.95 (*1-55821-300-7*) Lyons Pr.

Leeson, Ted, ed. The Gift of Trout. LC 96-11356. (Illus.). 224p. 1996. 25.00 (*1-55821-477-1*) Lyons Pr.

Leeson, Ted & Schollmeyer, Jim. The Fly Tier's Benchside Reference: To Techniques & Dressing Styles. LC 99-462673. (Illus.). 464p. 1999. 100.00 (*1-57188-126-3*) F Amato Pubns.

Leeson, Ted, jt. auth. see Schollmeyer, Jim.

Leeson, Tom & Leeson, Pat. The American Eagle. Black, Cynthia, ed. (Earthsong Collection). (Illus.). 128p. (C). 1990. 39.95 (*0-941831-30-2*) Beyond Words Pub.

— The American Eagle. (EarthSong Collection). (Illus.). 128p. 1991. 69.95 (*0-941831-35-3*) Beyond Words Pub.

— The American Eagle. LC 88-71833. (Illus.). 128p. 1994. pap. 24.95 (*1-885223-25-0*) Beyond Words Pub.

— The American Eagle. limited ed. (EarthSong Collection). (Illus.). 128p. 1991. 1200.00 (*0-941831-31-0*) Beyond Words Pub.

***Leeson, Tom & Leeson, Pat.** Black Bear. (Wild Bears! Ser.). (Illus.). 24p. (ps-3). 2000. 16.95 (*1-56711-343-5*) Blackbirch.

— Giant Panda. LC 99-59464. (Wild Bears! Ser.). (Illus.). 24p. (ps-3). 2000. 16.95 (*1-56711-341-9*) Blackbirch.

Leestma, Robert & Walberg, Herbert J., eds. Japanese Educational Productivity. LC 91-32032. (Michigan Papers in Japanese Studies: No. 22). xi, 425p. (Orig.). 1992. pap. 24.95 (*0-939512-55-6*) U MI Japan.

Leet. Reinforced Concrete Design. 2nd ed. 1991. pap. text, student ed. 18.75 (*0-07-037053-2*) McGraw.

Leet, Don R. Population Pressure & Human Fertility Response: Ohio, 1810-1860. LC 77-14754. (Dissertations in American Economic History Ser.). 1978. 33.95 (*0-405-11046-4*) Ayer.

Leet, Don R. & Driggers, Joann. Economic Decisions for Consumers. 2nd ed. (Illus.). 1143p. (C). 1990. text 52.60 (*0-02-369491-2*, Macmillan Coll) P-H.

***Leet, Duane.** Gangs, Graffiti & Violence. 2nd ed. 268p. 2000. pap. text 21.00 (*1-928916-02-3*) Copperhouse.

Leet, Frank R. When Santa Was Late. (Illus.). 24p. (J). (ps-2). 1990. pap. 3.95 (*0-8249-8483-8*, Ideals Child) Hambleton-Hill.

***Leet, Frank R.** When Santa Was Late. (Illus.). 24p. (J). 2000. 7.95 (*1-57102-172-8*, Ideals Child) Hambleton-Hill.

Leet, John. Winning Backgammon. LC 97-46176. (Illus.). 128p. 1998. pap. 9.95 (*0-8069-0459-3*) Sterling.

Leet, Judith. Good Sports: Anthology of Great Sports Writing. large type ed. 1990. 21.95 (*0-8161-4735-3*, G K Hall & Co) Mac Lib Ref.

— Pleasure Seeker's Guide. (New Poetry Ser.). 1976. 6.95 (*0-395-24313-0*) HM.

Leet, Judith, jt. auth. see Flemming, Laraine M.

Leet, Kenneth M. Reinforced Concrete Design. (Illus.). 544p. (C). 1982. 36.00 (*0-07-037024-9*) McGraw.

— Reinforced Concrete Design. 3rd ed. LC 96-31173. 560p. (C). 1996. 95.94 (*0-07-037100-8*) McGraw.

Leet, Kenneth M. & Bernal, Dionisio. Reinforced Concrete Design: Conforms to 1995 ACI Codes. 3rd ed. LC 96-31173. 1997. 30.62 (*0-07-037101-6*) McGraw.

Leet, Leonora. Renewing the Covenant: A Kabbalistic Guide to Jewish Spirituality. LC 98-47553. 256p. 1999. pap. 16.95 (*0-89281-713-5*) Inner Tradit.

Leet, Leonora, et al. The Secret Doctrine of the Kabbalah: Recovering the Key to Hebraic Sacred Science. LC 99-24385. (Illus.). 384p. 1999. 19.95 (*0-89281-724-0*) Inner Tradit.

Leet, Lewis D. Vibrations from Blasting Rock. LC 60-10037. 150p. reprint ed. 46.50 (*0-8357-9183-1*, 201774700007) Bks Demand.

Leet, Rebecca K. Marketing for Mission. 24p. 1998. pap. text 12.00 (*0-925299-82-0*) Natl Ctr Nonprofit.

Leet, Richard E. Bil Baird...He Pulled Lots of Strings. LC 88-61658. (Illus.). 72p. (Orig.). 1988. pap. 12.50 (*0-9628930-1-3*) C H MacNider Mus.

— Twenty-Five Selections American Art: Charles H. MacNider Museum. LC 91-70433. (Illus.). 72p. (Orig.). 1991. pap. 12.50 (*0-9628930-0-5*) C H MacNider Mus.

Leetch, John M. AutoCAD Release 13: Manual. rev. ed. 120p. (C). 2005. pap. 26.67 (*0-13-568767-5*) P-H.

— Introduction to Proengineer. (C). 2001. 47.00 (*0-13-259359-9*, Macmillan Coll) P-H.

Leetch, Robert N., jt. auth. see Matthews, William R.

Leete, Burt A. & Fox, Karla H. Business Law & the Legal Environment. 3rd ed. 1216p. 1989. teacher ed. write for info. (*0-318-63874-6*, H1842-9); teacher ed. write for info. (*0-318-63878-9*, H88016); write for info. (*0-318-63875-4*, H18658); write for info. (*0-318-63876-2*, H1843-7); trans. write for info. (*0-318-63877-0*, H88008) P-H.

Leete, E. Leete: The Family of William Leete. (Illus.). 168p. 1990. reprint ed. pap. 26.00 (*0-8328-1487-3*); reprint ed. lib. bdg. 34.00 (*0-8328-1486-5*) Higginson Bk Co.

Leete, Elisabeth. Learn French the Fast & Fun Way. 2nd ed. (Barron's Fast & Fun Way Ser.). (FRE.). 300p. 1997. pap. text 14.95 (*0-7641-0199-4*) Barron.

Leete, Elisabeth B. & Wald, Heywood. Learn French the Fast & Fun Way. 2nd ed. LC 97-1365. (Fast & Fun Way Language Bks.). (FRE.). 300p. 1997. 39.95 incl. audio (*0-7641-7027-9*) Barron.

Leete, Richard, ed. The Dynamics of Values in Fertility Change. LC 98-26345. (International Studies in Demography). (Illus.). 400p. 1999. text 85.00 (*0-19-829439-5*) OUP.

Leete, Richard. Maylasia's Demographic Transition: Rapid Development, Culture, & Politics. (South-East Asian Social Science Monographs). (Illus.). 246p. 1996. text 39.95 (*967-65-3109-X*) OUP.

Leeth, John. A Short Biography of John Leeth: With an Account of His Life among the Indians. (American Biography Ser.). 90p. 1991. reprint ed. lib. bdg. 59.00 (*0-7812-8240-3*) Rprt Serv.

Leeth, John D., jt. ed. see Kniesner, Thomas J.

Leetham, Helen. Sir Percy & the Dragon. (Illus.). 32p. (J). (ps-1). 1994. 17.95 (*0-86264-273-6*) Random.

Leetz, Thomas. Snakes As a Hobby. (Illus.). 96p. 1991. pap. 8.95 (*0-86622-415-7*, TT001) TFH Pubns.

Leeuw, Adele De, see De Leeuw, Adele.

Leeuw, Ben De, see De Leeuw, Ben.

Leeuw, Charles Van Der, see Van Der Leeuw, Charles.

Leeuw, Eric De, see De Leeuw, Eric.

Leeuw, Frans L., et al, eds. Can Governments Learn? Comparative Perspectives on Evaluation & Organizational Learning. viii, 212p. (C). 1994. text 39.95 (*1-56000-130-5*) Transaction Pubs.

— Can Governments Learn? Comparative Perspectives on Evaluation & Organizational Learning. 212p. 1999. pap. 24.95 (*0-7658-0658-4*) Transaction Pubs.

Leeuw, Gerardus Van der, see Van der Leeuw, Gerardus.

Leeuw, Hendrik De, see De Leeuw, Hendrik.

Leeuw, J. J. Van Der, see Van Der Leeuw, J. J.

Leeuw, Jan de, see Kreft, Ita G. & de Leeuw, Jan.

Leeuw, Johanna E. Van Lohuizen-De, see Van Lohuizen-De Leeuw, Johanna E.

Leeuw, Manya De, see De Leeuw, Eric & De Leeuw, Manya.

Leeuw, P. W. De, see De Leeuw, P. W., ed.

Leeuwen, F. W. Van, see Van Leeuwen, F. W.

Leeuwen, Gerard Van, see Van Leeuwen, Gerard.

Leeuwen, J. Information Processing, 3 vols. 373.00 (*0-444-89750-X*, North Holland) Elsevier.

Leeuwen, J. Van, see Van Leeuwen, J.

Leeuwen, J. Van, see Dorr, Heiko & Van Leeuwen, J.

Leeuwen, J. Van, see Van Leeuwen, J.

Leeuwen, Jean Van. A Fourth of July on the Plains. LC 94-33172. (Illus.). 32p. 1997. 15.99 (*0-8037-1771-7*, Dial Yng Read) Peng Put Young Read.

— Oliver & Amanda & the Big Snow. (Puffin Easy-to-Read Program Ser.). 48p. (J). (gr. k-3). 1998. pap. 3.99 (*0-14-038250-X*, PuffinBks) Peng Put Young Read.

Leeuwen, Jean Van, see Van Leeuwen, Jean.

Leeuwen, M. & Moeskops, J. The Nature Corner: Celebrating the Year's Cycle with a Seasonal Tableau. Lawson, Polly, tr. (DUT., Illus.). 88p. (J). (ps-3). 1990. reprint ed. pap. 12.95 (*0-86315-111-6*, Pub. by Floris Bks) Gryphon Hse.

***Leeuwen, Marco H. van.** The Logic of Charity. LC 99-40411. 260p. 1999. text 69.95 (*0-312-22853-8*) St Martin.

Leeuwen, Mary S. Van, see Van Leeuwen, Mary S.

Leeuwen, Mary S. Van, see Carr, Anne E. & Van Leeuwen, Mary S., eds.

Leeuwen, Mary S. Van, see Van Leeuwen, Mary S.

Leeuwen, Teho Van, see Kress, Gunther & Van Leeuwen, Teho.

Leeuwen, Theo Van, see Kress, Gunther & Van Leeuwen, Theo.

Leeuwen, Theo Van, jt. auth. see Kress, Gunther.

Leeuwenberg, A. J. A Revision of Tabernaemontana Vol. 1: The Old World Species. (Illus.). xii, 211p. 1991. pap. 40.00 (*0-947643-30-3*, Pub. by Royal Botnic Grdns) Balogh.

— A Revision of Tabernaemontana Vol. 2: The New World Species & Stemmadenia. (Illus.). xvii, 237p. 1994. pap. 40.00 (*0-947643-74-5*, Pub. by Royal Botnic Grdns) Balogh.

Leeuwenberg, A. J. Revisions of Apocynaceae: Craspidospermum Boj. Ex A. DC., Gonioma E. Mey., Mascarenhasia A. DC., Petchia Livera, Plectaneia Thou. & Stephanostegia Baill, Vol. 17. LC 98-206464. (Papers). 124 p. 1997. 38.00 (*90-73348-76-5*) Balogh.

Leeuwenberg, A. J. Series of Revisions of Apocynaceae, Vol. XVI-XVIII. (Wageningen Agricultural University Papers: No. 85-2). 83p. 1985. pap. 22.00 (*90-6754-064-1*, Pub. by Backhuys Pubs) Balogh.

— Series of Revisions of Apocynaceae: The Genus Cerbera, No. XLVII. LC 99-198121. (Wageningen Agricultural University Papers). (Illus.). 64p. 1998. pap. 32.00 (*90-5782-019-6*, Pub. by Backhuys Pubs) Balogh.

Leeuwenberg, A. J., ed. Series of Revisions of Apocynaceae Vols. XXXVII, XXXVIII: Pollination of Apocynaceae. LC 96-224108. (Wageningen Agricultural University Papers: No. 94-3). (Illus.). 81p. 1994. pap. 21.00 (*90-6754-361-6*, Pub. by Backhuys Pubs) Balogh.

Leeuwenberg, A. J. M. Medicinal & Poisonous Plants of the Tropics. 152p. 1988. pap. 250.00 (*81-7089-098-5*, Pub. by Intl Bk Distr) St Mut.

Leeuwenberg, E. L. & Buffart, H. F., eds. Formal Theories of Visual Perception. LC 77-12441. (Illus.). 357p. reprint ed. pap. 110.70 (*0-8357-3109-X*, 203936500012) Bks Demand.

Leeuwenhoek, Antoni Van. The Collected Letters of Antoni Van Leeuwenhoek, Vol. 1. Palm, L. C., ed. 522p. 1939. text 233.00 (*90-265-0040-8*) Swets.

— The Collected Letters of Antoni Van Leeuwenhoek, Vol. 2. 506p. 1941. text 233.00 (*90-265-0041-6*) Swets.

— The Collected Letters of Antoni Van Leeuwenhoek, Vol. 3. 560p. 1948. text 233.00 (*90-265-0042-4*) Swets.

— The Collected Letters of Antoni Van Leeuwenhoek, Vol. 4. 383p. 1952. text 233.00 (*90-265-0043-2*) Swets.

— The Collected Letters of Antoni Van Leeuwenhoek, Vol. 5. 457p. 1958. text 233.00 (*90-265-0044-0*) Swets.

— The Collected Letters of Antoni Van Leeuwenhoek, Vol. 6. 425p. 1961. text 233.00 (*90-265-0045-9*) Swets.

— The Collected Letters of Antoni Van Leeuwenhoek, Vol. 7. 427p. 1965. text 233.00 (*90-265-0046-7*) Swets.

— The Collected Letters of Antoni Van Leeuwenhoek, Vol. 8. 383p. 1967. text 233.00 (*90-265-0047-5*) Swets.

— The Collected Letters of Antoni Van Leeuwenhoek, Vol. 9. 482p. 1976. text 233.00 (*90-265-0220-6*) Swets.

— The Collected Letters of Antoni Van Leeuwenhoek, Vol. 10. 362p. 1979. text 233.00 (*90-265-0285-0*) Swets.

— The Collected Letters of Antoni Van Leeuwenhoek, Vol. 11. 383p. 1983. text 233.00 (*90-265-0446-2*) Swets.

An Asterisk (*) at the beginning of an entry indicates that the title is appearing for the first time.

Leeuwenhoek, Antoni Van. The Collected Letters of Antoni Van Leeuwenhoek, Vol. 13. xviii, 344p. 1994. text 233.00 (*90-265-1239-2*) Swets.

Leeuwenhoek, Antoni Van. On the Circulation of the Blood: Latin Text of His Sixty-Fifth Letter to the Royal Society, 1688. (Illus.). 33p. 1962. reprint ed. text 47.50 (*90-6004-098-8*, Pub. by B De Graaf) Coronet Bks.

— Opera Omnia. (GER.). 1997. reprint ed. 698.00 (*3-487-04183-9*) G Olms Pubs.

— The Select Works of Antoni Van Leeuwenhoek: His Microscopical Discoveries in Many Works of Nature, 2 vols., 1 bk. Egerton, Frank N., ed. Hoole, Samuel, tr. LC 77-74236. (History of Ecology Ser.). (Illus.). 1978. reprint ed. lib. bdg. 59.95 (*0-405-10405-7*) Ayer.

Leeves, Juliet, et al. Library Systems in Europe: A Directory & Guide. LC 94-222321. (Publication No. Eur 15494 En of the European Commission, Dissemination of Scientific & Technical Knowledge Unit, Directorate-General Telecommunications, Information Market & Exploitation of Research). v, 401p. 1994. write for info. (*1-870889-47-9*) TFPL.

Leevw, Adolph L. De, see De Leevw, Adolph L.

Leevy, Carroll M., et al. Diseases of the Liver & Biliary Tract: Standardization of Nomenclature, Diagnostic Criteria, & Prognosis. LC 94-2183. 224p. 1994. text 53.00 (*0-7817-0211-9*) Lppncott W & W.

Leevy, Carroll M., ed. see International Association for the Study of Pain, T.

***Leevy, Maria.** Dangerous Passageways. LC 00-190851. 283p. 2000. 25.00 (*0-7388-1952-2*); pap. 18.00 (*0-7388-1953-0*) Xlibris Corp.

Lefafa Sedek. The Bandlet of Righteousness, An Ethiopian Book of the Dead: The Ethiopic text of the [Lefafa sedeq] : in facsimile from two manuscripts in the British Museum. Budge, E. A. Wallis, tr. LC 77-87667. (Luzac's Semitic Text & Translation Ser.: No. 19). reprint ed. 32.50 (*0-404-11349-4*) AMS Pr.

Lefaivre, Liane. Leon Battista Alberti's Hypnerotomachia Poliphili: Eros, Furore, & Humanism in the Early Italian Renaissance. LC 96-40960. (Illus.). 340p. 1997. 49.50 (*0-262-12204-9*) MIT Pr.

***Lefaivre, Liane.** Santiago Calatrava's Creative Process: Fundamentals & Sketchbooks. (Illus.). 500p. 2000. 125.00 (*3-7643-6323-1*, Pub. by Birkhauser) Princeton Arch.

Lefaivre, Liane, jt. auth. see Tzonis, Alexander.

LeFalle-Collins, Lizetta, et al, texts. In the Spirit of Resistance: African-American Modernists & the Mexican Muralist School. LC 95-52666. (Illus.). 192p. 1996. pap. 35.00 (*1-885444-01-X*, 620171) Am Fed Arts.

***LeFalle-Collins, Lizzetta.** Betye Saar: In Service: A Version of Survival. Harrisburg, Halley K., ed. (Illus.). 24p. 2000. pap. 12.00 (*1-930416-01-6*) M Rosenfeld.

LeFalle-Collins, Lizzetta, jt. auth. see Henderson, Robbin.

LeFan, Micheal. Patience My Foot: Learning God's Patience Through Life's Difficulties. 2nd ed. 155p. (Orig.). 1994. pap. 8.99 (*0-89900-619-1*) College Pr Pub.

LeFanu, Nicola & Fuller, Sophie, eds. Reclaiming the Muse. (Contemporary Music Review Ser.: Vol. 2). 349p. 1995. pap. text 44.00 (*3-7186-5528-4*, ECU56, Harwood Acad Pubs) Gordon & Breach.

LeFanu, Sarah. In the Chinks of the World Machine: Feminism & Science Fiction LC 88-162597. 231p. 1988. write for info. (*0-7043-4092-5*, Pub. by Womens Press) Trafalgar.

Lefanu, Sarah. Sex, Drugs, Rock n'Roll: Stories to End the Century. LC 97-67085. 1998. pap. 13.99 (*1-85242-538-5*) Serpents Tail.

LeFanu, Sarah. Writing Fantasy Fiction. pap. write for info. (*0-7136-4260-2*, Pub. by A & C Blk) Midpt Trade.

LeFanu, William. Nehemiah Grew: A Study & Bibliography of His Writings. 199p. 1990. 36.00 (*0-906795-43-5*) Oak Knoll.

LeFanu, William R. Notable Medical Books: From the Lilly Library Indiana University. Waife, S. O. et al, eds. (Illus.). 275p. (C). 1976. 20.00 (*0-685-20051-5*) IN Univ Lilly Library.

LeFar, Mable F. & Wilson, Caroline P. Abstract of Wills Catham County, Georgia, 1773-1817. 160p. 1985. 8.50 (*0-915156-06-7*, SP 6) Natl Genealogical.

Lefave, jt. auth. see Fitch, S.

Lefave, Linda. Mammography: Self-Assessment & Review. LC 93-3913. (Pretest Specialty Level Ser.). (Illus.). 160p. 1993. pap. text 25.00 (*0-07-052017-8*) McGraw-Hill HPD.

— Medical Radiography: Self-Assessment & Review. (Specialty Level PreTest Ser.). (Illus.). 304p. 1995. pap. text 28.00 (*0-07-052078-X*) McGraw-Hill HPD.

Lefavi, Robert. Reasons to Believe: A Journey of Spiritual Awareness in the Modern World. LC 99-21587. 176p. 1999. 22.00 (*0-932727-44-1*) Hope Pub Hse.

Lefavor, Marshall. Locals Only. 64p. 1993. pap. 4.95 (*1-880365-51-0*) Prof Pr NC.

LeFavour, Bruce. France on Foot: Village to Village, Hotel to Hotel: How to Walk the French Trail System on Your Own. LC 98-85117. (Illus.). 256p. 1999. pap. 24.95 (*0-9663448-0-4*) Attis Pr.

Lefcoe, George. Real Estate Transactions. 2nd ed. LC 97-71588. (Illus.). 1545p. 1997. text 55.00 (*1-55834-502-7*, 12077-11, MICHIE) LEXIS Pub.

Lefcoe, George, ed. Urban Land Policy for the 1980s: The Message for State & Local Government. LC 82-48492. (Lincoln Institute of Land Policy Bk.). 233p. reprint ed. pap. 72.30 (*0-7837-3269-4*, 204328800007) Bks Demand.

Lefcoe, George, ed. see Conference on Local Governments' Decisions & the L.

Lefcourt, Carol H. Women & the Law. LC 84-11150. (Civil Rights Ser.). 1984. ring bd. 140.00 (*0-87632-441-3*) West Group.

***Lefcourt, Herbert M.** Humor: The Psychology of Living Buoyantly. LC 00-33112. (Plenum Series in Social-Clinical Psychology). 2000. write for info. (*0-306-46407-1*) Kluwer Academic.

Lefcourt, Herbert M. Locus of Control: Current Trends in Theory & Research. 2nd ed. 288p. (C). 1982. text 55.00 (*0-89859-222-4*) L Erlbaum Assocs.

Lefcourt, Peter. The Dreyfus Affair: A Love Story. LC 92-54926. 304p. 1993. pap. 14.00 (*0-06-097559-8*, Perennial) HarperTrade.

— The Woody: A Novel. 352p. 1999. per. 14.00 (*0-671-03855-9*, PB Trade Paper) PB.

Lefcourt, Peter. The Woody: A Novel. LC 98-33816. 1998. write for info. (*0-684-85744-8*) S&S Trade.

— The Woody: A Novel. LC 98-33816. 320p. 1998. 23.00 (*0-684-85393-0*) Simon & Schuster.

***Lefcourt, Peter & Shapiro, Laura, eds.** The First Time I Got Paid for It: And Other Tales from the Hollywood Trenches. 2000. 24.00 (*1-58648-013-8*) PublicAffairs NY.

Lefcowitz, Allan B., jt. auth. see Jason, Philip K.

Lefcowitz, Barbara. Minarets of Vienna. Harriss, Clarinda, ed. 80p. 1996. pap. 10.00 (*0-932616-54-2*) Brick Hse Bks.

— The Queen of Lost Baggage. LC 85-52078. (Series Ten). 72p. (Orig.). 1986. pap. 7.00 (*0-931846-29-3*) Wash Writers Pub.

Lefcowitz, Barbara F. A Hand of Stars. 106p. 1999. pap. 10.00 (*1-892076-09-8*) Dancing Moon.

— Red Lies & White Lies. LC 93-85470. 270p. (Orig.). 1994. pap. 9.00 (*0-9637290-0-4*) East Coast Bks.

Lefcowitz, Eric. Buy American: Buy This Book. LC 92-18554. 96p. 1992. pap. 5.95 (*0-89815-495-2*) Ten Speed Pr.

— Monkees Tale. rev. ed. 120p. 1990. pap. 11.95 (*0-86719-378-6*) Last Gasp.

— Tomorrow Never Knows: The Beatles' Last Concert. Sethi, Anita, ed. LC 87-80730. (Illus.). 104p. (Orig.). 1987. pap. 12.95 (*0-943249-02-3*) Terra Firma Bks.

— Tomorrow Never Knows: The Beatles' Last Concert. 2nd ed. (Illus.). 104p. (Orig.). 1991. 24.95 (*0-943249-04-X*) Terra Firma Bks.

— The United States Immigration History Timeline. (Illus.). 1990. 5.95 (*0-943249-03-1*) Terra Firma Bks.

Lefeber, Louis, et al. Regional Development: Experiences & Prospects in South & Southeast Asia. LC 72-152080. (Regional Planning Ser.: No. 1). 278p. 1971. text 33.85 (*90-279-6914-0*) Mouton.

Lefeber, Rene. Transboundary Environmental Interference & the Origin of State Liability. LC 96-20679. (Developments in International Law Ser.). 365p. 1996. 195.00 (*90-411-0275-2*) Kluwer Law Intl.

Lefeber, Rene, ed. The Changing Political Structure of Europe: Aspects of International Law. 298p. (C). 1991. lib. bdg. 107.50 (*0-7923-1379-8*) Kluwer Academic.

Lefeber, Rene, jt. ed. see Klabbers, Jan.

Lefeber, Rosalind, jt. auth. see Goldman, Robert P., ed.

***Lefebure, Leo D.** Revelation, the Religions, & Violence. LC 00-28564. 240p. 2000. pap. 20.00 (*1-57075-300-8*) Orbis Bks.

Lefebure, Leo D. Toward a Contemporary Wisdom Christology: A Study of Karl Rahner & Norman Pittenger. LC 88-22798. 298p. (Orig.). (C). 1988. pap. text 25.00 (*0-8191-7152-2*); lib. bdg. 45.00 (*0-8191-7151-4*) U Pr of Amer.

Lefebure, Marcus & Schauder, Hans. Conversations on Counselling: Between a Doctor & a Priest. 3rd ed. 288p. 1990. pap. 29.95 (*0-567-29164-2*, Pub. by T & T Clark) Bks Intl VA.

Lefebure, Molly. Thomas Hardy's World. 1997. 22.95 (*1-57715-015-5*) Knckerbocker.

— Thomas Hardy's World: The Life, Work & Times of the Great Novelist & Poet. (Illus.). 144p. (YA). 1999. 24.95 (*1-85868-245-2*, Pub. by Carlton Bks Ltd) Natl Bk Netwk.

Lefebvre. Legal & Tax Guide. 1992. pap. text 102.50 (*90-6544-624-9*) Kluwer Academic.

— Monaco Tax Guide. 1991. lib. bdg. 68.50 (*90-6544-595-1*) Kluwer Academic.

Lefebvre, Alain. Kinship, Honour, & Money in Rural Pakistan: Subsistence Economy & the Effects of International Migration. (Nordic Institute for Asian Studies Monographs: Vol. 78). 288p. 1998. text 48.00 (*0-7007-0984-3*, Pub. by Curzon Pr Ltd) UH Pr.

Lefebvre, Andre. Dictionnaire Pratique des Collectivites Territoriales. (FRE.). 1988. write for info. (*0-7859-8176-4*, 2-87603-010-1) Fr & Eur.

— Glossaire de la Finance. (ENG & FRE.). 284p. 1976. 39.95 (*0-8288-5699-0*, M6350) Fr & Eur.

Lefebvre, Anny, tr. see Beaud, Michel.

Lefebvre, Arthur H. Gas Turbine Combustion. 2nd ed. LC 98-21946. 400p. 1998. pap. 80.00 (*1-56032-673-5*) Taylor & Francis.

Lefebvre, Christian. Belgium. LC 93-34971. (European Financial Reporting Ser.). (Illus.). 240p. (C). (gr. 13). 1994. pap. 109.95 (*0-415-06776-6*, B0272) Thomson Learn.

Lefebvre, Claire. Creole Genesis & the Acquisition of Grammar: The Case for Haitian Creole. LC 98-12930. (Cambridge Studies in Linguistics: No. 88). (Illus.). 480p. (C). 1999. text 74.95 (*0-521-59382-4*) Cambridge U Pr.

Lefebvre, Claire, ed. Serial Verbs: Grammatical, Comparative & Cognitive Approaches. LC 91-7128. (Studies in the Sciences of Languages: No. 8). viii, 210p. 1991. pap. 50.00 (*1-55619-384-X*) J Benjamins Pubng Co.

Lefebvre, Claire & Muysken, Pieter. Mixed Categories. (C). 1988. lib. bdg. 127.00 (*1-55608-050-6*) Kluwer Academic.

Lefebvre, Elizabeth & Lefebvre, Louis A. Information & Telecommunication Technologies: The Impact of Their Adoption on Small & Medium-Sized Enterprises. LC 97-700057. 133p. 1996. pap. 17.95 (*0-88936-807-4*, Pub. by IDRC Bks) Stylus Pub VA.

Lefebvre, Elizabeth, jt. ed. see Lefebvre, Louis.

Lefebvre, G., ed. Inscriptiones Graecae Aegypti, No. 5: Christian Inscriptions. xlii, 173p. 1978. 30.00 (*0-89005-248-4*) Ares.

Lefebvre, G., jt. ed. see Pedrizet, P.

LeFebvre, George, jt. auth. see Bloom, Anthony.

Lefebvre, Georges. Coming of the French Revolution. Palmer, Robert R., tr. 256p. 1989. pap. text 12.95 (*0-691-00751-9*, Pub. by Princeton U Pr) Cal Prin Full Svc.

***Lefebvre, Gilles & Lefebvre, Marcia.** Unto Caesar... Unto God: Political Analysis, Relationship Between Church & State. Sharp, Gladys & Sarricino, Rocco, eds. 360p. 1999. pap. 16.99 (*0-9672172-0-2*) Philadelphians.

Lefebvre, Gilles, jt. auth. see Chauvel, Alain.

Lefebvre, Henri. Critique of Everyday Life. LC 91-20747. 312p. (C). (gr. 13). 1991. 65.00 (*0-86091-340-6*, Pub. by Verso) Norton.

— Critique of Everyday Life, Vol. 1. Moore, John, tr. 312p. (C). 1992. pap. 22.00 (*0-86091-587-5*, A9726, Pub. by Verso) Norton.

— Everyday Life in the Modern World. Rabinovitch, Sacha, tr. 226p. 1994. pap. 21.95 (*0-87855-972-8*) Transaction Pubs.

— The Explosion: Marxism & the French Revolution. LC 69-19790. 157p. reprint ed. pap. 48.70 (*0-608-13126-1*, 201947500012) Bks Demand.

— Introduction to Modernity: Twelves Preludes, September 1959-May 1961. Moore, John, tr. 400p. (C). 1995. pap. 23.00 (*1-85984-056-6*, C0499, Pub. by Verso) Norton.

— The Production of Space. Nicholson-Smith, Donald, tr. 500p. 1991. pap. text 31.95 (*0-631-18177-6*) Blackwell Pubs.

— The Sociology of Marx. LC 82-9539. (Morningside Bk.). 218p. 1982. pap. text 19.00 (*0-231-05581-1*) Col U Pr.

LeFebvre, Henri. Writings on Cities. Kofman, Eleonore & Le Bas, Elizabeth, trs. from FRE. 272p. 1995. 66.95 (*0-631-19187-9*); pap. 28.95 (*0-631-19188-7*) Blackwell Pubs.

Lefebvre, Jeffrey. Arms for the Horn: U. S. Security Policy in Ethiopia & Somalia, 1953-1991. LC 90-28360. (Policy & Institutional Studies). (Illus.). 360p. (C). 1992. text 49.95 (*0-8229-3680-1*) U of Pittsburgh Pr.

Lefebvre, L. A., et al. Management of Technology, Sustainable Development & Eco-Efficiency. LC 97-44026. 1998. 176.75 (*0-08-043363-4*) Elsevier.

Lefebvre, Louis & Lefebvre, Elizabeth, eds. Management of Technology & Regional Development in a Global Environment: An International Perspective. 192p. 1995. text 69.95 (*1-85396-297-X*, Pub. by P Chapman) Taylor & Francis.

Lefebvre, Louis A., jt. auth. see Lefebvre, Elizabeth.

Lefebvre, M. N., jt. auth. see Ginns, J. H.

Lefebvre, Marcel. Against the Heresies: Archbishop Lefebvre Comments on the Papal Encyclicals Condemning Modern Errors Infecting the Catholic Church. Angelus Press Editors, ed. SSPX Staff, tr. from FRE. LC 98-118521. 384p. 1997. pap. 13.45 (*0-935952-28-4*) Angelus Pr.

***Lefebvre, Marcel.** I Accuse the Council. 2nd ed. LC 98-35488. 1998. pap. 7.95 (*0-935952-68-3*) Angelus Pr.

— The Mystery of Our Lord Jesus Christ. LC 00-29324. 2000. pap. write for info. (*1-892331-02-0*) Angelus Pr.

Lefebvre, Marcel. Open Letter to Confused Catholics. 3rd ed. Society of St. Pius X Staff, tr. from FRE. LC 99-19535. 163p. 1992. reprint ed. pap. 8.95 (*0-935952-13-6*) Angelus Pr.

— Pastoral Letters. Society of St. Pius X Staff, tr. from FRE. 148p. (Orig.). 1992. pap. text 8.95 (*0-935952-99-3*) Angelus Pr.

— Spiritual Journey. Society of St. Pius X Staff, tr. LC 98-27937. 73p. (Orig.). 1991. pap. text 8.45 (*0-935952-16-0*) Angelus Pr.

— They Have Uncrowned Him. 3rd ed. Society of St. Pius X Staff, tr. from FRE. 261p. 1992. reprint ed. pap. text 10.45 (*0-935952-05-5*) Angelus Pr.

— While the Meter Was Running. LC 97-199965. 69 p. 1995. pap. text. write for info. (*1-896243-04-5*) Providence Rd.

Lefebvre, Marcel & Laisney, Francois. Archbishop Lefebvre & the Vatican, 1987-1988. 2nd ed. LC 98-30197. iii, 239 p. 1999. 12.45 (*0-935952-69-1*) Angelus Pr.

Lefebvre, Marcia, jt. auth. see Lefebvre, Gilles.

Lefebvre, Mark. Wisconsin. (Illus.). 144p. 1993. 39.95 (*1-55868-362-3*) Gr Arts Ctr Pub.

— Wisconsin. 2nd ed. LC 97-80274. 1997. 42.50 (*1-55868-404-2*) Gr Arts Ctr Pub.

Lefebvre, P. J. Glucagon III: Handbook of Experimental Pharmacology. (Illus.). 400p. 1996. 369.00 (*3-540-60989-X*) Spr-Verlag.

Lefebvre, P. J. & Standl, E., eds. New Aspects in Diabetes: Treatment Strategies with Alphaglucosidase Inhibitors. (Illus.). xii, 306p. (C). 1993. lib. bdg. 98.50 (*3-11-013469-1*) De Gruyter.

Lefebvre, Philip, jt. auth. see Miller, Susan J.

Lefebvre, Pierre J., ed. Glucagon I. (Handbook of Experimental Pharmacology Ser.: Vol. 66, I). (Illus.). 535p. 1983. 287.00 (*0-387-12068-8*) Spr-Verlag.

Lefebvre, Pierre J., jt. ed. see Creutzfeldt, W.

Lefebvre, R. & Mukamel, S., eds. Stochasticity & Intramolecular Redistribution of Energy. (C). 1987. text 172.00 (*90-277-2462-8*) Kluwer Academic.

Lefebvre, Sue. Hermosillo from A to Z. LC 82-60112. (ENG & SPA., Illus.). 193p. (gr. 5-12). 1982. pap. 13.50 (*0-9608702-0-2*) Shared Care.

Lefebvre, Vladimir A. Algebra of Conscience. 224p. 1982. text 126.50 (*90-277-1301-4*, D Reidel) Kluwer Academic.

— A Psychological Theory of Bipolarity & Reflexivity. LC 92-21158. 120p. 1992. text 59.95 (*0-7734-9226-7*) E Mellen.

Lefebvre, Yolaine, ed. see Dunner, David L.

Lefebvre, Yolaine, jt. illus. see Chase, Edith N.

Lefenseld, Mark, jt. auth. see Curpisin, Jim.

Lefeowitz, Eric. The Rhino History of Rock 'n Roll the 70s: The '70s. 1997. 24.95 (*0-671-01175-8*, PB Hardcover) PB.

Lefer, Diane. The Circles I Move in: Short Stories. LC 94-14562. (Illus.). 192p. 1994. 19.95 (*0-944072-41-0*) Zoland Bks.

***Lefer, Diane.** Very Much Like Desire. 2000. pap. text 15.95 (*0-88748-330-5*) Carnegie-Mellon.

Lefer, W. & Grave, M., eds. Visualization in Scientific Computing, '97: Proceedings of the Eurographics Workshop in Boulogne-sur-Mer France, April 28-30, 1997. (Illus.). 180p. 1997. pap. 59.00 (*3-211-83049-9*) Spr-Verlag.

Lefever, Alan J. Fighting the Good Fight: The Life & Work of Benajah Harvey Carroll. LC 93-44797. 194p. 1994. 19.95 (*0-89015-943-2*) Sunbelt Media.

LeFever, Chuck, jt. auth. see Rodgers, J. Buddy.

Lefever, Ernest W. America's Imperial Burden: Is the Past Prologue? LC 98-26650. 208p. 1998. 24.00 (*0-8133-9999-8*, Pub. by Westview) HarpC.

— Nairobi to Vancouver: The World Council of Churches & the World, 1975-87. LC 87-30302. 166p. (Orig.). (C). 1988. pap. text 12.75 (*0-89633-118-0*); lib. bdg. 31.50 (*0-89633-117-2*) Ethics & Public Policy.

— Nuclear Arms in the Third World: U. S. Policy Dilemma. LC 78-24810. 168p. reprint ed. pap. 52.10 (*0-608-12715-9*, 202538800043) Bks Demand.

— Uncertain Mandate: Politics of the U. N. Congo Operation. LC 67-22890. 270p. reprint ed. pap. 83.70 (*0-608-13774-X*, 202054000018) Bks Demand.

Lefever, Ernest W., ed. Reinvigorating Our Schools: A Challenge to Parents, Teachers, & Policymakers. 56p. 1985. pap. 10.50 (*0-89633-094-X*) Ethics & Public Policy.

Lefever, Ernest W. & Kalb, Marvin. Ethics & United States Foreign Policy. 236p. 1986. reprint ed. pap. text 22.00 (*0-8191-5168-8*) U Pr of Amer.

Lefever, Ernest W. & Vander Lugt, Robert D., eds. Perestroika: How New Is Gorbachev's New Thinking? LC 88-21855. 259p. 1989. 29.95 (*0-89633-133-4*); pap. 12.95 (*0-89633-134-2*) Ethics & Public Policy.

Lefever, Ernest W., ed. see Niebuhr, Reinhold.

LeFever, F. Frank, jt. ed. see Bilder, Robert M.

Lefever, Harry G. Turtle Bogue: Afro-Caribbean Life & Culture in a Costa Rican Village. LC 90-50792. (Illus.). 256p. 1992. 39.50 (*0-945636-23-7*) Susquehanna U Pr.

LeFever, Marlene. 50 Days to Welcome Jesus to My Church: Children's Journal for the 50-Day Adventure Series. (1991 50-Day Spiritual Adventure Ser.). (Illus.). 64p. (Orig.). (J). (gr. 3-6). 1990. pap. text, student ed. 3.95 (*1-879050-02-1*) Chapel of Air.

— God's Special Creation--Me! (Bible Discovery Guide for Junior Campers Ser.). (Illus.). 48p. (Orig.). (J). (gr. 4-6). 1987. pap., teacher ed. 3.50 (*0-87788-314-9*, H Shaw Pubs); pap., student ed. 1.50 (*0-87788-313-0*, H Shaw Pubs) Waterbrook Pr.

— Survival Kit for Growing Christians. (Bible Discovery Guide Ser.). 32p. (J). (gr. 4-6). 1988. 1.50 (*0-87788-796-9*, H Shaw Pubs); pap. text, teacher ed. 3.50 (*0-87788-797-7*, H Shaw Pubs) Waterbrook Pr.

Lefever, Marlene D. Creative Teaching Methods. 1996. pap. text 21.99 (*0-7814-5256-2*, 14977) Cook.

Lefever, Michael. Hospitality Review. 560p. (C). 1995. pap. text 62.95 (*0-7872-0251-7*) Kendall-Hunt.

Lefever, Michael, jt. auth. see Brymer, Robert A.

Lefever, Michael M. Restaurant Reality: A Manager's Guide. 256p. 1988. pap. 44.95 (*0-471-28938-8*, VNR) Wiley.

— Restaurant Reality: A Manager's Guide. (Illus.). 304p. (C). 1989. pap. 34.95 (*0-442-25938-7*, VNR) Wiley.

Lefever, R., jt. auth. see Horsthemke, W.

***Lefever, Robert A.** Kick the Habit: Overcoming Addiction Using the Twelve-Step Programme. 256p. 2000. pap. 14.95 (*1-85868-965-1*, Pub. by Carlton Bks Ltd) Natl Bk Netwk.

Lefever, Robert A., ed. Preparation & Properties of Solid State Materials: Aspects of Crystal Growth, Vol. 1. LC 78-155744. (Illus.). 292p. reprint ed. pap. 90.60 (*0-608-30578-2*, 201785600009) Bks Demand.

Lefever, Robert A., jt. ed. see Wilcox, William R.

Lefevere, Andre. Translating Literature: Translational Practice, Literary Theory, Comparative Literature. LC 92-20469. vii, 165p. (C). 1992. pap. 15.50 (*0-87352-394-6*, S760P); lib. bdg. 37.50 (*0-87352-393-8*, S760C) Modern Lang.

Lefevere, Andre, jt. auth. see Bassnett, Susan.

Lefevere, Andre, jt. auth. see De Vooght, Marian.

Lefevere, Andre, ed. see Von Eschenbach, Wolfram.

Lefevere, Andre, tr. see Gilliams, Maurice.

Lefevere, Andre, tr. see Jaccottet, Philippe.

Lefevere, Andre, tr. see Muller, Herta.

Lefevere, Andre, tr. see Verdeyen, Paul.

Lefevere, Andre, tr. see Vuyk, Beb & Friedericy, H. J.

LeFevour, Edward. Western Enterprise in Late Ch'ing China: A Selective Survey of Jardine, Matheson & Company's Operations, 1842-1895. LC 73-386. (East Asian Monographs: No. 26). 222p. 1968. pap. 11.00 (*0-674-95010-0*) HUP.

Lefevre. Reminiscences of a Stock Operator. 75th anniversary ed. (Investment Classics Ser.). 298p. 1997. 100.00 (*0-471-24606-9*) Wiley.

Lefevre, jt. auth. see Schrock, Edward M.

Lefevre, Andre, jt. ed. see Bassnett, Susan.

L

L

LeFevre, Dale, jt. auth. see Strong, Todd.

LeFevre, Dale N. New Games for the Whole Family. 160p. 1988. pap. 9.95 (*0-399-51448-1*, Perigee Bks) Berkley Pub.

Lefevre, Edwin. The Golden Flood. LC 90-81218. 199p. 1990. reprint ed. pap. 15.00 (*0-87034-096-4*) Fraser Pub Co.

— The Making of a Stockbroker. LC 75-2645. (Wall Street & the Security Market Ser.). 1975. reprint ed. 28.95 (*0-405-06970-7*) Ayer.

— The Making of a Stockbroker. LC 84-80693. 341p. 1999. reprint ed. pap. 16.00 (*0-87034-072-7*) Fraser Pub Co.

— The Plunderers. LC 83-80981. (Illus.). 334p. 1983. reprint ed. pap. 19.00 (*0-87034-067-0*) Fraser Pub Co.

— The Plunderers: A Novel. LC 75-152945. (Short Story Index Reprint Ser.). 1977. reprint ed. 23.95 (*0-8369-3804-6*) Ayer.

— Reminiscences of a Stock Operator. 304p. 1994. 49.95 (*0-471-05968-4*); pap. 19.95 (*0-471-05970-6*) Wiley.

Lefevre, Edwin. Sampson Rock of Wall Street. LC 85-70939. 394p. 1985. reprint ed. pap. 21.00 (*0-87034-076-X*) Fraser Pub Co.

Lefevre, Edwin. Wall Street Stories. LC 75-150478. (Short Story Index Reprint Ser.). 1977. reprint ed. 19.95 (*0-8369-3819-4*) Ayer.

***Lefevre, Eric.** Brandenburg Division: Commandos of the Reich. (Special Operations Ser.). 1999. pap. text 24.95 (*2-908182-73-4*) Histoire.

Lefevre, Frances, tr. see Moro, Cesar.

Lefevre, Henry L. Quality Service Pays: Six Keys to Success. (Illus.). 375p. 1989. 32.95 (*0-527-91629-3*, 916293) Productivity Inc.

Lefevre, Herve C. The Fiber-Optic Gyroscope. LC 92-28194. (Artech House Optoelectronics Library). 329p. 1993. reprint ed. pap. 102.00 (*0-608-02079-6*, 206273200003) Bks Demand.

Lefevre, Holly & Cudanes, Christine. How to "I Do" Planning the Ultimate Wedding in Six Weekends or Less. 254p. 2000. pap. 20.00 (*0-06-098816-9*, ReganBks) HarperTrade.

Lefevre, J. P., jt. auth. see Pfleger, S.

Lefevre, Jean-Francois, jt. auth. see Lafaurie, Andre-Jean.

Lefevre, Jean-Francois, jt. ed. see Jardetzky, Oleg.

LeFevre, Joseph E. Reducing Benzil Using Sodium Borohydride. Jeffers, J., ed. (Modular Laboratory Program in Chemistry Ser.). 16p. (C). 1998. pap. text 1.75 (*0-87540-715-3*, REAC 715) Chem Educ Res.

LeFevre, Joseph W. Isolating Clove Oil from Cloves Using Steam Distillation. Jeffers, J., ed. (Modular Laboratory Program in Chemistry Ser.). 16p. (C). 1998. pap. text 1.75 (*0-87540-722-6*, TECH 722) Chem Educ Res.

— Measuring the Melting Points of Compounds & Mixtures. Jeffers, J., ed. (Modular Laboratory Program in Chemistry Ser.). 12p. (C). 1997. pap. text 1.75 (*0-87540-701-3*) Chem Educ Res.

***LeFevre, Joseph W.** Oxidizing Methoxybenzyl Alcohol to Methoxybenzaldehyde Using Phase-Transfer Catalysis. Jeffers, Joe, ed. (Modular Laboratory Program in Chemistry Ser.). 16p. (C). 1999. pap. text 1.75 (*0-87540-725-0*, SYNT 725-0) Chem Educ Res.

LeFevre, Joseph W. Separating Camphor from Beta-Carotene by Sublimation. Jeffers, J., ed. (Modular Laboratory Program in Chemistry Ser.). 12p. (C). 1997. pap. text 1.75 (*0-87540-706-4*) Chem Educ Res.

LeFevre, Karen B. Invention As a Social Act. LC 86-15437. (Studies in Writing & Rhetoric). 187p. (Orig.). 1986. pap. text 12.95 (*0-8093-1328-6*) S Ill U Pr.

Lefevre, Ken, ed. see Parnau, Jeffery R.

Lefevre, Marc J. First Aid Manual for Chemical Accidents. 2nd ed. 272p. 1989. pap. 60.95 (*0-442-20490-6*, VNR) Wiley.

Lefevre, Marc J. First Aid Manual for Chemical Accidents. 2nd ed. 272p. 1989. pap. 76.95 (*0-471-28855-1*, VNR) Wiley.

***Lefevre, Pascal & Dierick, Charles, eds.** Forging a New Medium: The Comic Strip in the Nineteenth Century. LC 99-229040. (Illus.). 200p. 1999. 16.95 (*90-5487-206-3*, Pub. by VUB Univ Pr) Paul & Co Pubs.

LeFevre, Perry D. Challenge & Response: The Chicago Theological Seminary Story, 1960-1980. LC 98-73880. (Studies in Ministry & Parish Life). 249p. 1999. 29.95 (*0-913552-62-3*) Exploration Pr.

— Modern Theologies of Prayer. LC 95-60692. 376p. 1995. text 32.95 (*0-913552-56-9*); pap. text 19.95 (*0-913552-57-7*) Exploration Pr.

LeFevre, Perry D., ed. Conflict in a Voluntary Association: A Case Study of a Classic Suburban Church Fight. LC 75-12388. (Studies in Ministry & Parish Life). 1975. pap. 12.95 (*0-913552-09-7*) Exploration Pr.

— Prayers of Kierkegaard. LC 56-11000. (Midway Reprint Ser.). 246p. 1996. pap. text 20.50 (*0-226-47059-8*) U Ch Pr.

LeFevre, Perry D. & Schroeder, W. Widick, eds. Creative Ministries in Contemporary Christianity. LC 90-86031. (Studies in Ministry & Parish Life). 280p. 1991. 32.95 (*0-913552-44-5*) Exploration Pr.

— Pastoral Care & Liberation Praxis: Studies in Personal & Social Transformation. (Studies in Ministry & Parish Life). 112p. 1986. text 19.95 (*0-913552-31-3*); pap. text 12.95 (*0-913552-32-1*) Exploration Pr.

Lefevre, Perry D. & Schroeder, W. Widick, eds. Spiritual Nurture & Congregational Development. (Studies in Ministry & Parish Life). 186p. 1984. text 21.95 (*0-913552-20-8*) Exploration Pr.

LeFevre, Perry D., ed. see Tillich, Paul.

LeFevre, Perry D., ed. see Williams, Daniel D.

LeFevre, Perry D., ed. & intro. see Meland, Bernard E.

Lefevre, Pierre, ed. One Hundred Stories to Change Your Life: Small Tales in Answer to Large Questions. 150p. (C). 1996. pap. 39.95 (*0-85439-382-X*, Pub. by St Paul Pubns) St Mut.

LeFevre, R. James. Redirecting Boards: A New Vision of Governance for Planned Parenthood. LC 92-46519. 134p. 1993. 11.95 (*0-934586-73-X*) Plan Parent.

LeFevre, Ralph. History of New Paltz, New York & Its Old Families, from 1678 to 1820. 2nd ed. LC 70-105530. (Illus.). 607p. 1996. reprint ed. pap. 55.00 (*0-8063-0551-7*) Clearfield Co.

Lefevre, Ralph. History of New Paltz, New York, & Its Old Families from 1678 to 1820: Including the Huguenot Pioneers & Others Who Settled in New Paltz Previous to the Revolution. (Illus.). 594p. 1903. reprint ed. pap. 38.50 (*1-55613-629-3*) Heritage Bk.

Lefevre, Raoul. The Recuyell of the Historyes of Troye, 2 vols. in 1. Caxton, William, tr. LC 70-178542. clxiii, 855 p. 1973. reprint ed. 115.00 (*0-404-56624-3*) AMS Pr.

LeFevre, Robert. The Fundamentals of Liberty. (Illus.). 487p. (C). 1988. 24.95 (*0-9620480-0-3*) Rampart Inst.

Leff, ed. Receptor - Based Drug Design. LC 98-13320. (Illus.). 408p. 1998. text 175.00 (*0-8247-0162-3*) Dekker.

Leff, jt. see Simmons.

Leff, Alan R., ed. Pulmonary & Critical Care Pharmacology & Therapeutics. (Illus.). 1200p. 1996. text 149.00 (*0-07-037096-6*) McGraw-Hill HPD.

Leff, Alan R. & Schumacker, Paul T. Respiratory Physiology: Basics & Applications. (Illus.). 224p. 1993. pap. text 27.00 (*0-7216-3952-6*, W B Saunders Co) Harcrt Hlth Sci Grp.

Leff, Carol. The Czech & Slovak Republics: Nation Versus State. LC 96-12080. (Nations of the Modern World Ser.). (C). 1996. pap. 30.00 (*0-8133-2922-1*, Pub. by Westview) HarpC.

Leff, Carol S. National Conflict in Czechoslovakia: The Making & Remaking of a State, 1918-1987. LC 87-29034. 315p. 1988. reprint ed. pap. 97.70 (*0-608-07646-5*, 205996300010) Bks Demand.

Leff, Edward, jt. auth. see Emanuel, Pericles J.

Leff, Enrique. Green Production: Toward an Environmental Rationality. LC 94-10841. (Democracy & Ecology Ser.). 168p. 1995. pap. text 16.95 (*0-89862-410-X*, C2410); lib. bdg. 40.00 (*0-89862-411-8*, C2411) Guilford Pubns.

Leff, Herbert L. Playful Perception: Choosing How to Experience Your World. LC 83-19876. (Illus.). 172p. (Orig.). 1984. 15.95 (*0-914525-01-8*); pap. 9.95 (*0-914525-00-X*) Waterfront Bks.

Leff, Jay C. Near Eastern & Far Eastern Art. 1966. pap. 4.50 (*0-8079-0092-3*) October.

Leff, Jim. The Eclectic Gourmet Guide to Greater New York City. LC 98-41637. 300p. 1998. pap. 11.95 (*0-89732-279-7*) Menasha Ridge.

Leff, Julian. Psychiatry Around the Globe: A Transcultural View. LC 89-43755. (Gaskell Psychiatry Ser.). 240p. reprint ed. pap. 74.40 (*0-7837-6211-9*, 204593500009) Bks Demand.

— Psychiatry Around the Globe: A Transcultural View. 5. LC 81-12577. (Experimental & Clinical Psychiatry Ser.: Vol. 5). 222p. reprint ed. pap. 68.90 (*0-608-08950-8*, 206958500005) Bks Demand.

Leff, Julian & Vaughn, Christine. Expressed Emotion in Families: Its Significance for Mental Illness. LC 84-549. 241p. 1985. lib. bdg. 34.50 (*0-89862-058-9*) Guilford Pubns.

Leff, Julian P. Care in the Community: Illusion or Reality. LC 96-3425. 230p. 1997. 135.00 (*0-471-96981-8*) Wiley.

— Care in the Community: Illusion or Reality. LC 96-3425. 230p. 1998. pap. 49.95 (*0-471-96982-6*) Wiley.

Leff, Julian P., jt. auth. see Bhugra, Dinesh K. L.

Leff, Larry. The Power of Pascal. 1986. text 39.95 (*0-13-687450-9*, Busn) P-H.

Leff, Lawrence S. Barron's Power Pack: Sequential Math, Course II. 2nd ed. 1996. pap. 13.95 (*0-8120-8416-0*) Barron.

***Leff, Lawrence S.** Barron's Regents Exams & Answers: Mathematics A. (Illus.). 2000. pap. 5.95 (*0-7641-1552-9*) Barron.

Leff, Lawrence S. College Algebra. LC 94-26836. (Barron's EZ-101 Study Keys Ser.). (C). 1995. pap. 6.95 (*0-8120-1940-7*) Barron.

— Geometry the Easy Way. 3rd ed. LC 97-482. (Barron's Easy Way Ser.). (Illus.). 368p. (J). 1997. pap. 12.95 (*0-7641-0110-2*) Barron.

***Leff, Lawrence S.** Let's Review: Math A. LC 99-53233. (Review Course Ser.). (Illus.). 624p. 2000. pap. 11.95 (*0-7641-1202-3*) Barron.

Leff, Lawrence S. Let's Review: Sequential Mathematics, Course I. 2nd ed. LC 95-2341. (Review Course Ser.). 464p. 1995. pap. 10.95 (*0-8120-9036-5*) Barron.

— Let's Review: Sequential Mathematics, Course II. 2nd ed. (Barron's Review Course Ser.). 480p. 1996. pap. 10.95 (*0-8120-9051-9*) Barron.

***Leff, Lawrence S.** Math Workbook for the SAT I. 2nd ed. 432p. 2000. pap. text 13.95 (*0-7641-0768-2*) Barron.

Leff, Lawrence S. New Math Workbook for SAT I. 7th ed. 1996. pap. 12.95 (*0-8120-9285-6*) Barron.

— Sequential Mathematics, Course III, No. III. 2nd ed. LC 96-35975. (Barron's Review Course Ser.). 280p. 1997. pap. 9.95 (*0-8120-9917-6*) Barron.

Leff, Leonard J. Film Plots: Scene-by-Scene Narrative Outlines for Feature Film Study, Vol. 1. LC 83-60916. 402p. 1983. 65.00 (*0-87650-149-8*) Pierian.

— Film Plots: Scene-by-Scene Narrative Outlines for Feature Film Study, Vol. 2. LC 83-60916. 483p. 1988. 65.00 (*0-87650-241-9*) Pierian.

— Hemingway & His Conspirators: Hollywood, Scribners, & the Making of American Celebrity Culture. LC 97-11766. (Illus.). 224p. 1997. 22.95 (*0-8476-8544-6*, Pub. by Rowman) Natl Bk Netwk.

— Hemingway & His Conspirators: Hollywood, Scribners, & the Making of American Celebrity Culture. (Illus.). 224p. 1999. pap. 16.95 (*0-8476-8545-4*, Pub. by Rowman) Natl Bk Netwk.

— Hitchcock & Selznick: The Rich & Strange Collaboration of Alfred Hitchcock & David O. Selznick in Hollywood. LC 98-34412. 398p. 1999. pap. 24.95 (*0-520-21781-0*, Pub. by U CA Pr) Cal Prin Full Svc.

Leff, Michael C. & Kauffeld, Fred J., eds. Texts in Context: Critical Dialogues on Significant Episodes in American Political Rhetoric. 225p. (Orig.). (C). 1989. 29.95 (*0-9611800-5-6*, Hermagoras); pap. 16.50 (*0-9611800-4-8*, Hermagoras) L Erlbaum Assocs.

Leff, Michael C., jt. ed. see Horner, Winifred B.

Leff, Nathaniel H. Brazilian Capital Goods Industry, 1929 to 1964. LC 68-21976. (Center for International Affairs Ser.). (Illus.). 198p. 1968. 25.95 (*0-674-08090-4*) HUP.

Leff, Richard D. & Roberts, Robert J. Practical Aspects of Intravenous Drug Administration: Principles for Nurses, Pharmacists, & Physicians. 64p. (C). 1992. pap. text 15.00 (*1-879907-23-2*) Am Soc Hlth-Syst.

Leff, Walli F. & Haft, Marilyn G. Time Without Work: People Who Are Not Working Tell Their Stories, How They Feel, What They Do, How They Survive. LC 83-61477. 403p. 1983. pap. 9.00 (*0-89608-185-0*) South End Pr.

Leff, Z. Outlooks & Insights. 1993. 15.99 (*0-89906-531-7*) Mesorah Pubns.

— Outlooks & Insights. 1993. 18.99 (*0-89906-530-9*) Mesorah Pubns.

Leffel, John C., ed. History of Posey County, Indiana. (Illus.). 401p. 1992. reprint ed. lib. bdg. 41.00 (*0-8328-2569-7*) Higginson Bk Co.

Leffel, Katherine & Bouchard, Denis. Views on Phrase Structure. (Studies in Natural Language & Linguistic Theory). 240p. (C). 1991. text 146.50 (*0-7923-1295-3*) Kluwer Academic.

Leffelaar, P. A. On Systems Analysis & Simulation of Ecological Processes. 2nd ed. LC 98-49744. (Current Issues in Production Ecology Ser.). 16p. 1999. write for info. (*0-7923-5525-3*) Kluwer Academic.

Leffelaar, P. A., ed. On Systems Analysis & Simulation of Ecological Processes with Examples in CSMP & FORTRAN. (Current Issues in Production Ecology Ser.). 308p. (C). 1993. pap. text 67.00 (*0-7923-2435-8*); lib. bdg. 137.00 (*0-7923-2434-X*) Kluwer Academic.

Leffell, David J. Total Skin: The Definitive Guide to Whole Skin Care for Life. LC 99-47396. (Illus.). 464p. 2000. 27.95 (*0-7868-6504-0*, Pub. by Hyperion) Time Warner.

Leffell, David J. & Brown, Marc D. Manual of Skin Surgery: A Practical Guide to Dermatologic Procedures. LC 96-30884. 250p. 1997. pap. 69.95 (*0-471-13411-2*) Wiley.

Leffell, Mary S., et al. CRC Handbook of Human Immunology. LC 96-45395. 656p. 1997. boxed set 119.95 (*0-8493-0134-3*) CRC Pr.

Leffers, Laura L. Dance on the Water. large type ed. 270p. (Orig.). 1996. pap. 12.95 (*1-881542-10-6*) Blue Star Prodns.

Leffers, Laura L. Out of the Blue. 4.80 (*0-9671113-5-8*) Electric Umb OR.

Leffert, Charles B. Evolution of Our Universe: Via Spatial Condensation. (Illus.). 280p. 1999. 49.95 (*0-9647745-9-3*) Anoka Pubng.

— Time & Cosmology: Creation & Expansion of Our Universe. LC 95-78202. (Illus.). 275p. 2000. 49.95 (*0-9647745-6-9*) Anoka Pubng.

***Leffert, Nancy.** Shema: Listening to Jewish Youth: Study Highlights. LC 99-181597. 20 p. 1998. 3.95 (*1-57482-174-1*) Search Inst.

Leffert, Nancy & Herring, Hayim. Shema: Listening to the Voices of Jewish Youth in Minneapolis. Tyler, Kate, ed. LC 99-174750. 1998. pap. 9.95 (*1-57482-124-5*) Search Inst.

Leffert, Nancy, jt. auth. see Roehlkepartain, Jolene L.

Leffert, Nancy, jt. auth. see Scales, Peter.

Leffert, Robert. Brachial Plexus Injuries. LC 85-13319. (Illus.). 235p. 1986. text 85.00 (*0-443-08026-7*) Church.

Lefferts, Michael. Cole Porter - Musical Anthology. 256p. (Orig.). (C). 1981. per. 17.95 (*0-88188-184-8*, 00312332) H Leonard.

Lefferts, Michael, ed. Ain't Misbehavin' Vocal Selections. 104p. (Orig.). (C). 1983. per. 12.95 (*0-88188-534-7*, 00359040) H Leonard.

— Anne of Green Gables: Vocal Selections. 32p. (Orig.). (C). 1997. pap. text 8.95 (*0-7692-0217-9*, CCC009) Wrner Bros.

Lefferts, Michael, ed. Anyone Can Whistle: Vocal Score. (Vocal Score Ser.). 244p. (Orig.). (C). 1981. per. 45.00 (*0-88188-002-7*, 00312012) H Leonard.

— Anyone Can Whistle: Vocal Selections. 40p. (Orig.). (C). 1981. pap. 8.95 (*0-88188-058-2*, 003112010) H Leonard.

Lefferts, Michael, ed. Babes in Arms: Vocal Score. (Vocal Score Ser.). 144p. (Orig.). (C). 1981. per. 45.00 (*0-88188-003-5*, 00312015) H Leonard.

— Babes in Arms: Vocal Selections. 32p. (Orig.). (C). 1981. pap. 7.95 (*0-88188-059-0*, 00312014) H Leonard.

— Backstreet Boys. 80p. (Orig.). (C). 1997. pap. text 17.95 (*0-7119-6340-1*, AM942403) Wrner Bros.

— The Ballad of Baby Doe: Vocal Score. (Vocal Score Ser.). 256p. (Orig.). (C). 1981. per. 40.00 (*0-88188-004-3*, 00312019) H Leonard.

— Barenaked Ladies/Born on a Pirate Ship. 140p. (Orig.). (C). 1997. pap. text 19.95 (*0-7692-0199-7*, CCC124) Wrner Bros.

— The Best of Cole Porter: Piano Solo. 144p. (Orig.). (C). 1992. otabind 14.95 (*0-7935-1518-1*, 00221012) H Leonard.

Lefferts, Michael, ed. The Best of U2: Includes Tablature. (Bass Recorded Versions Ser.). 112p. (C). 1992. per. 26.95 (*0-7935-0795-2*, 00694783) H Leonard.

— The Best of U2: With Notes & Tablature. (Guitar Recorded Versions Ser.). 136p. (C). 1987. per. 27.95 (*0-88188-763-3*, 00694410) H Leonard.

Lefferts, Michael, ed. Call Me Madam: Vocal Score. 140p. (Orig.). (C). 1997. pap. text 55.95 (*0-7692-0249-7*, 00005578) Wrner Bros.

— Can Can: Vocal Score. 124p. (Orig.). (C). 1997. pap. text 55.95 (*0-7692-0248-9*, 00312066) Wrner Bros.

— Celebration: Vocal Score. 180p. (Orig.). (C). 1997. pap. text 55.95 (*0-7692-0245-4*, 00312071) Wrner Bros.

— Chansons a Boire. 24p. (Orig.). (C). 1997. pap. text 16.95 (*0-7692-0246-2*, 01020683) Wrner Bros.

— Chansons Paillardes. 32p. (Orig.). (C). 1997. pap. text 12.95 (*0-7692-0247-0*, 01020510) Wrner Bros.

— Daho Songbook. 88p. (Orig.). (C). 1997. pap. text 34.95 (*0-7692-0282-9*, 07028598) Wrner Bros.

— The David Foster Collection. 100p. (Orig.). (C). 1995. pap. text 18.95 (*0-7692-0288-8*, CCC111) Wrner Bros.

— Do I Hear a Waltz? Vocal Selections. 32p. (Orig.). (C). 1997. pap. text 12.95 (*0-7692-0296-9*, 00312115) Wrner Bros.

— Do Re Mi: Vocal Selections. 32p. (Orig.). (C). 1997. pap. text 12.95 (*0-7692-0295-0*, 00312093) Wrner Bros.

— Edith Piaf/Album Commemoratif. 66p. (Orig.). (C). 1979. pap. text 12.95 (*0-7692-0291-8*, A0052OPX) Wrner Bros.

— Edith Piaf/10 Succes. 44p. (Orig.). (C). 1997. pap. text 25.95 (*0-7692-0294-2*, 01020686) Wrner Bros.

— Elton John - Greatest Hits Updated. 96p. (Orig.). (C). 1991. otabind 14.95 (*0-7935-1063-5*, 00308114) H Leonard.

— Elton John - The One. 72p. (Orig.). (C). 1997. pap. text 20.95 (*0-86359-926-5*, 00308167) Wrner Bros.

— Elton John - To Be Continued. (Piano-Vocal-Guitar Ser.). 264p. (Orig.). (C). 1991. otabind 27.95 (*0-7935-0375-2*, 00308086) H Leonard.

— Elton John Anthology. (EZ Play Today Ser.). 224p. (Orig.). (C). 1997. pap. text 17.95 (*0-7692-0297-7*, 00290104); pap. text 17.95 (*0-7692-0298-5*, 00290102) Wrner Bros.

— Elton John Anthology: For Easy Piano. 136p. (Orig.). (C). 1997. pap. text 20.95 (*0-7692-0302-7*, 00357102) Wrner Bros.

— Emerson, Lake & Palmer/Elp. 68p. (Orig.). (C). 1977. pap. text 7.95 (*0-7692-0299-3*, VF0392) Wrner Bros.

— Eric Clapton for Fingerstyle Guitar: Fingerstyle Guitar Collection. 40p. (Orig.). (C). 1994. pap. 14.95 (*0-7935-3657-X*, 00699411) H Leonard.

— Florent Pagny. 72p. (Orig.). (C). 1997. pap. text 22.95 (*0-7692-0453-8*, 07028628) Wrner Bros.

— Funk Bass Guitar - Slap Style. (FRE.). 40p. (Orig.). (C). 1997. pap. text 19.95 (*0-7692-1322-7*, 01010347) Wrner Bros.

— George Gershwin: 14 of His Greatest Compositions. (Piano Solos Ser.). 56p. (Orig.). (C). 1985. pap. 7.95 (*0-7935-0701-4*, 00009070) H Leonard.

— Gigi: Vocal Score. (Vocal Score Ser.). 200p. (Orig.). (C). 1981. per. 45.00 (*0-88188-022-1*, 00312175) H Leonard.

— Gigi: Vocal Selections. (Illus.). 56p. (Orig.). (C). 1981. pap. 8.95 (*0-88188-080-9*, 00312174) H Leonard.

— Great Balls of Fire & Other Classics of the Rock Era. 60p. (Orig.). (C). 1997. pap. text 13.95 (*0-7692-0742-1*, CCC102) Wrner Bros.

— The Greatest Songs of Rodgers & Hart. 128p. (Orig.). (C). 1997. pap. text 20.95 (*0-88188-180-5*, 00312354) H Leonard.

— La Guitare Basse par l'Image. (FRE.). 56p. (Orig.). (C). 1997. pap. text 19.95 (*0-7692-1324-3*, 01010311) Wrner Bros.

— Gypsy: Vocal Score. (Vocal Score Ser.). 192p. (Orig.). (C). 1981. per. 45.00 (*0-88188-024-8*, 00312188) H Leonard.

— Gypsy: Vocal Selections. 40p. (Orig.). (C). 1981. pap. 9.95 (*0-7935-3233-7*, 00312187) H Leonard.

— Les Hits de la Cie Creole. 52p. (Orig.). (C). 1997. pap. text 29.95 (*0-7692-0712-X*, 07028632) Wrner Bros.

— James Brown: 20 All Time Greatest Hits. 80p. (Orig.). (C). 1996. otabind 16.95 (*0-7935-3911-0*, 00306004) H Leonard.

— Jann Arden - Living under June. 64p. (Orig.). (C). 1996. otabind 16.95 (*0-7935-7201-0*, 00306132) H Leonard.

— Je Chante Edith Piaf. 56p. (Orig.). (C). 1997. pap. text 12.95 (*0-7692-0750-2*, 01020526) Wrner Bros.

— Je Chante Johnny Hallyday. 56p. (Orig.). (C). 1997. pap. text 12.95 (*0-7692-0748-0*, 01020541) Wrner Bros.

— Je Chante Michel Fugain. 60p. (Orig.). (C). 1997. pap. text 12.95 (*0-7692-0747-2*, 01020537) Wrner Bros.

— Je Chante Nino Ferrer. 56p. (Orig.). (C). 1997. pap. text 12.95 (*0-7692-0749-9*, 01020527) Wrner Bros.

— Je Chante Yves Duteil. 56p. (Orig.). (C). 1997. pap. text 12.95 (*0-7692-0751-0*, 01020522) Wrner Bros.

— Kiss Me Kate: Vocal Score. (Vocal Score Ser.). 216p. (Orig.). (C). 1981. per. 45.00 (*0-88188-029-9*, 00312232) H Leonard.

— Kiss Me Kate: Vocal Selections. 80p. (Orig.). (C). 1981. pap. 14.95 (*0-88188-090-6*, 00312230) H Leonard.

— Lady in the Dark: Vocal Score. (Vocal Score Ser.). 136p. (Orig.). (C). 1981. per. 45.00 (*0-88188-030-2*, 00312238) H Leonard.

— Lost in the Stars: Vocal Score. 184p. (Orig.). (C). 1981. per. 45.00 (*0-88188-031-0*, 00312251) H Leonard.

— Methode de Banjo Americain. (FRE.). 44p. (Orig.). (C). 1997. pap. text 19.95 (*0-7692-1312-X*, 01010402) Wrner Bros.

— My Fair Lady: Vocal Score. (Vocal Score Ser.). 256p. (Orig.). (C). 1981. per. 45.00 (*0-88188-036-1*, 00312266) H Leonard.

— Once upon a Mattress: Vocal Score. (Vocal Score Ser.). 160p. (Orig.). (C). 1981. per. 45.00 (*0-88188-041-8*, 00312301) H Leonard.

An Asterisk (*) at the beginning of an entry indicates that the title is appearing for the first time.

Lefferts, Michael, ed. Once upon a Mattress: Vocal Selections. (Illus.). 32p. (Orig.). (C). 1981. pap. 8.95 (*0-88188-101-5*, 00312300) H Leonard.
Lefferts, Michael, ed. Paint Your Wagon: Vocal Selections. (Illus.). 44p. (Orig.). (C). 1981. pap. 8.95 (*0-88188-103-1*, 00312310) H Leonard.
— Pal Joey: Vocal Score. (Vocal Score Ser.). 184p. (Orig.). (C). 1981. per. 45.00 (*0-88188-044-2*, 00312314) H Leonard.
— Pal Joey: Vocal Selections. (Illus.). 32p. (Orig.). (C). 1981. pap. 8.95 (*0-88188-104-X*, 00312313) H Leonard.
— Les Plus Belles Melodies de Schubert: For Guitar. (FRE.). 12p. (Orig.). (C). 1997. pap. text 11.95 (*0-7692-1310-3*, 01020302) Wrner Bros.
— The Rankin Family Album. 88p. (Orig.). (C). 1996. pap. text 19.95 (*0-7692-0472-4*, CCC112) Wrner Bros.
— Rem - Out of Time: Out of Time. 72p. (Orig.). (C). 1994. per. 16.95 (*0-7935-2748-1*, 00308202) H Leonard.
— Richard Cocciante. 72p. (Orig.). (C). 1997. pap. text 34.95 (*0-7692-0838-X*, 01020631) Wrner Bros.
— Rita MacNeil - Joyful Sounds: A Seasonal Collection. 96p. (Orig.). (C). 1996. pap. text 19.95 (*0-7692-0692-1*, CCC122) Wrner Bros.
— The Runaways: A Musical Play for Children. 48p. (Orig.). (C). 1997. pap. text 7.95 (*0-7692-0836-3*, 00312358) Wrner Bros.
— Snoopy: Vocal Selections. (Illus.). 64p. (Orig.). (C). 1981. pap. 8.95 (*0-88188-111-2*, 00312382) H Leonard.
— Spirit of the West - Open Heart Symphony. 68p. (Orig.). (C). 1996. pap. text 18.95 (*0-7692-0473-2*, CCC129) Wrner Bros.
— Spirit of the West Songbook. 80p. (Orig.). (C). 1997. pap. text 19.95 (*0-7692-0494-5*, CCC127) Wrner Bros.
— The Tragically Hip - Trouble at the Henhouse. 116p. (Orig.). (C). 1996. pap. text 19.95 (*0-7692-0826-6*, CCC118) Wrner Bros.
— 12 Songs by Jacques Brel. (Illus.). 64p. (Orig.). (C). 1997. pap. text 12.95 (*0-8256-1291-8*, AM80342) Music Sales.
— U2: Achtung Baby. 96p. (Orig.). (C). 1997. pap. text 18.95 (*0-7935-2071-1*, 00308174) H Leonard.
— U2: Joshua Tree with Notes & Tablature. (Guitar Recorded Versions Ser.). 120p. (C). 1987. otabind 19.95 (*0-88188-769-2*, 00694411) H Leonard.
— U2: The Joshua Tree. 32p. (Orig.). (C). 1987. pap. 12.95 (*0-7935-1937-3*, 00308525) H Leonard.
— Wham - Make It Big. 40p. (Orig.). (C). 1997. pap. text 13.95 (*0-88188-397-2*, 00308571) H Leonard.
— Yves Duteil - Ton Absence. 84p. (Orig.). (C). 1997. pap. text 25.95 (*0-7692-0837-1*, 01020684) Wrner Bros.
Lefferts, Michael & Bryan, Colgan, eds. Van Halen - Diver down & 1984. (Illus.). 160p. (Orig.). (C). 1997. pap. text 24.95 (*0-7692-0026-5*, 0062B) Wrner Bros.
Lefferts, Michael, ed. see Blitzstein, M.
Lefferts, Michael, ed. see Bonal, Jean.
Lefferts, Michael, ed. see Borello, Pierre.
Lefferts, Michael, ed. see Chierci, F.
Lefferts, Michael, ed. see Dadi, Marcel.
Lefferts, Michael, ed. see Darizcuren, Francis.
Lefferts, Michael, ed. see De Valencia, Jose.
Lefferts, Michael, ed. see Laurent, Leo.
Lefferts, Michael, ed. see Liebman, John.
Lefferts, Michael, ed. see March, Tony.
Lefferts, Michael, ed. see Moulou, Patrick.
Lefferts, Michael, ed. see Sokolow, Fred.
Lefferts, Peter. The Motet in England in the Fourteenth Century. LC 86-6900. (Studies in Musicology: No. 94). (Illus.). 391p. reprint ed. pap. 121.30 (*0-8357-1722-4*, 207059400004) Bks Demand.
Lefferts, Peter M., ed. & tr. see De Handlo, Robertus & Hanboys, Johannes.
Lefferts, Vena & Kelsey, John. Floral Style: The Art of Arranging Flowers. 1999. 40.00 (*0-88363-099-0*) H L Levin.
Leffin, Walter W., et al. Introduction to Technical Mathematics: With Problem Solving. 3rd rev. ed. (Illus.). 462p. (C). 1998. pap. text 30.95 (*1-57766-023-4*) Waveland Pr.
Leffingwell, Albert. Illegitimacy & the Influence of Seasons Upon Conduct: Two Studies in Demography. LC 75-38134. (Demography Ser.). (Illus.). 1976. reprint ed. 19.95 (*0-405-07987-7*) Ayer.
***Leffingwell, Dean & Widrig, Don.** Managing Software Requirements: A Unified Approach. LC 99-46571. (Object Technology Ser.). 544p. 1999. 49.95 (*0-201-61593-2*) Addison-Wesley.
Leffingwell, E., ed. see Smith, Jack.
Leffingwell, Ed, ed. see Smith, Jack.
Leffingwell, Edward. Earthly Paradise. (Illus.). 1994. 40.00 (*0-9642964-0-3*) Earthly Paradise.
Leffingwell, Edward, ed. Yamagata: The Car Series. (Illus.). 96p. (Orig.). 1993. pap. 25.95 (*1-882299-02-7*) Minic Art Gall.
Leffingwell, Georgia W. Social & Private Life at Rome in the Time of Plautus & Terence. LC 18-17902. (Columbia University. Studies in the Social Sciences: No. 188). reprint ed. 20.00 (*0-404-51188-0*) AMS Pr.
Leffingwell, Randy. The American Barn. LC 96-52378. (Illus.). 192p. 1997. 29.95 (*0-7603-0109-3*) MBI Pubg.
— The American Farm Tractor. (Illus.). 192p. 1991. 29.95 (*0-87938-532-4*) MBI Pubg.
— American Muscle: Muscle Cars from the Otis Chandler Collection. (Illus.). 192p. 1990. reprint ed. 29.95 (*0-87938-465-4*) MBI Pubg.
***Leffingwell, Randy.** Americas Classic Farm Tractor: The Illustrated History of the American Farm Tractor. LC 99-50182. 432p. 1999. 29.98 (*0-7603-0822-5*) MBI Pubg.
Leffingwell, Randy. Caterpillar: Farm Tractors, Bulldozers & Heavy Machinery. (Illus.). 192p. 1999. pap. 19.95 (*0-7603-0744-X*, 128643AP, Pub. by MBI Pubg) Motorbooks Intl.
— Classic Farm Tractors: History of the Farm Tractor. LC 95-45023. (Illus.). 192p. 1996. pap. 15.98 (*0-7603-0246-4*) MBI Pubg.
— Classic John Deere Tractors. LC 93-48651. (Enthusiast Color Ser.). (Illus.). 96p. 1994. pap. 13.95 (*0-87938-865-X*) MBI Pubg.
— Corvette: America's Sports Car. LC 97-15494. (Illus.). 192p. 1997. 29.95 (*0-7603-0135-2*) MBI Pubg.
***Leffingwell, Randy.** Farm Tractor Milestones. (Illus.). 160p. 2000. 29.95 (*0-7603-0730-X*, 130126AP, Pub. by MBI Pubg) Motorbooks Intl.
Leffingwell, Randy. Farm Tractors: A Living History. LC 95-5976. (Illus.). 240p. 1995. 24.98 (*0-7603-0030-5*) MBI Pubg.
— Ford Farm Tractors. LC 97-52220. 192p. 1998. 29.95 (*0-7603-0337-1*) MBI Pubg.
— Harley-Davidson: Myth & Mystique. (Illus.). 192p. 1995. 19.98 (*0-7603-0031-3*) MBI Pubg.
— International Harvester Tractors. LC 99-33376. (Illus.). 192p. 1999. 29.95 (*0-7603-0423-8*, Pub. by MBI Pubg) Motorbooks Intl.
— John Deere Farm Tractors. LC 93-1158. (Illus.). 192p. 1993. 29.95 (*0-87938-755-6*) MBI Pubg.
— Mustang. (Illus.). 192p. 1995. 29.95 (*0-7603-0048-8*) MBI Pubg.
— Porsche. LC 94-44211. (Enthusiast Color Ser.). (Illus.). 96p. 1995. pap. 13.95 (*0-87938-992-3*) MBI Pubg.
***Leffingwell, Randy, photos by.** Lighthouses of the Pacific Coast: Your Guide to the Lighthouses of California, Oregon, & Washington. LC 00-26342. (Pictorial Discovery Guide Ser.). (Illus.). 176p. 2000. 29.95 (*0-89658-429-1*) Voyageur Pr.
Leffingwell, Russell C., jt. auth. see Bogart, Ernest L.
Leffkowitz, M. & Steinitz, H., eds. Life Assurance Medicine Congress, 9th, Tel Aviv, March 1967: Proceedings. vi, 368p. 1968. pap. 99.25 (*3-8055-0910-3*) S Karger.
***Leffland, Ella.** Breath & Shadows. 320p. 2000. pap. 14.00 (*0-345-43923-6*) Ballantine Pub Grp.
— Breath & Shadows. 2000. pap. write for info. (*0-688-17588-0*, Quil) HarperTrade.
Leffland, Ella. Breath & Shadows. LC 98-8830. 320p. 1999. 24.00 (*0-688-14271-0*, Wm Morrow) Morrow Avon.
— Rumors of Peace. LC 78-20209. 400p. 1920. pap. 15.00 (*0-06-091301-0*, PL 1301, Perennial) HarperTrade.
Leffler, Adrienne Karel. California Traveler: Wine Country - Discover the Essence of California. (American Traveler Ser.: Vol. 47). (Illus.). 48p. 1992. pap. 4.95 (*1-55838-125-2*) R H Pub.
Leffler, John E. An Introduction to Free Radicals. LC 92-35288. 304p. 1993. 98.95 (*0-471-59406-7*) Wiley.
Leffler, John E. & Grunwald, Ernest. Rates & Equilbria of Organic Reactions. 474p. 1989. pap. 11.95 (*0-486-66068-0*) Dover.
Leffler, Keith B. Explanations in Search of Facts, a Critique of "A Study of Physicians' Fees" (LEC Occasional Paper). 1978. pap. text 2.50 (*0-916770-08-7*) Law & Econ U Miami.
Leffler, Lisa M., jt. auth. see Wesnousky, Steven G.
Leffler, Maryann. Mommy Love Hugs. (Illus.). 14p. (J). (ps-k). 1997. 5.99 (*0-689-80981-6*) S&S Bks Yung.
Leffler, Melvyn P. The Elusive Guest: America's Pursuit of European Stability & French Security, 1919-1933. LC 78-9782. 426p. reprint ed. pap. 132.10 (*0-8357-3890-6*, 203662200004) Bks Demand.
— A Preponderance of Power: National Security, the Truman Administration, & the Cold War. (Nuclear Age Ser.). (Illus.). 711p. 1992. 69.50 (*0-8047-1924-1*) Stanford U Pr.
— A Preponderance of Power: National Security, the Truman Administration, & the Cold War. (Illus.). 711p. (C). 1993. pap. 24.95 (*0-8047-2218-8*) Stanford U Pr.
— The Specter of Communism: The United States & the Origins of the Cold War, 1917-1953. Foner, Eric, ed. LC 94-13419. 144p. 1994. pap. 8.00 (*0-8090-1574-9*) Hill & Wang.
Leffler, Melvyn P. & Painter, David S., eds. Origins of the Cold War: An International History. LC 93-23298. (Illus.). 336p. (C). 1994. pap. 24.99 (*0-415-09694-4*) Routledge.
Leffler, Merrill. Take Hold. 1997. 7.50 (*0-931848-95-4*) Dryad Pr.
***Leffler, Mick.** Christmas Medleys. (Illus.). 96p. 1998. pap. 11.95 (*1-56922-196-0*, 07-2067) Creat Cncpts.
Leffler, Mick, contrib. by. Angel Music for Piano & All Keyboards. LC 00-511182. 1998. 11.95 (*1-56922-178-2*, 07-2062) Creat Cncpts.
Leffler, Phyllis K. & Brent, Joseph, III. Public & Academic History: Philosophy & Pardism. LC 89-2628. 108p. (Orig.). (C). 1990. 16.00 (*0-89464-298-7*) Krieger.
— Public & Academic History: Philosophy & Pardism. LC 89-2628. 108p. (Orig.). (C). 1990. pap. 12.50 (*0-89464-299-5*) Krieger.
— Public History Readings: A Book of Readings. 552p. (C). 1992. 31.50 (*0-89464-433-5*) Krieger.
Leffler, Richard, ed. The Response to the Federalist: Contemporary Commentaries on a Political Masterwork, 1787-1788. (Constitutional Heritage Ser.). 200p. Date not set. write for info. (*0-945612-03-6*) Madison Hse.
Leffler, Richard, jt. auth. see Kaminski, John P.
Leffler, Richard, jt. ed. see Kaminski, John P.
Leffler, Richard E. Where Are All the Angels? Heavenly Host Handbook. (Illus.). 192p. 1994. pap. 8.95 (*0-9640465-1-2*) Del King Pubng.
Leffler, Sam. The Design of Implementation of 4.3BSD UNIX. (C). 1989. text. write for info. (*0-201-50373-5*) Addison-Wesley.
Leffler, William L. Petroleum Refining for the Nontechnical Person. 2nd ed. 184p. 1985. 64.95 (*0-87814-280-0*) PennWell Bks.
***Leffler, William L.** Petroleum Refining in Nontechnical Language. 3rd ed. LC 00-21021. 2000. write for info. (*0-87814-776-4*) PennWell Bks.
Leffler, William L. & Burdick, Donald L. Petrochemicals in Nontechnical Language. 2nd ed. 360p. 1990. 64.95 (*0-87814-344-0*) PennWell Bks.
Lefgren & Jackson. Power Tools for Teaching. 1988. pap. 6.95 (*0-88494-660-6*) Bookcraft Inc.
Lefgren, Beth & Jackson, Jennifer. Amazing Achievement Days. 1995. pap. 9.95 (*1-57008-221-9*) Bookcraft Inc.
— More Amazing Achievement Days. LC 97-74878. 1997. pap. 9.95 (*1-57008-334-7*) Bookcraft Inc.
— More Power Tools for Teaching. 1991. pap. 6.95 (*0-88494-780-7*) Bookcraft Inc.
— Prophets & Pioneers. 1996. pap. 8.95 (*1-57008-280-4*) Bookcraft Inc.
— Sharing Time, Family Time, Anytime. 1992. pap. 8.95 (*0-88494-846-3*) Bookcraft Inc.
— Young Women Activities. LC 96-79581. 1997. pap. 7.95 (*1-57008-298-7*) Bookcraft Inc.
Lefgren, Beth, jt. auth. see Jackson, Jennifer.
Lefko, Linda C. & Knickerbocker, Barbara. The Art of Theorem Painting: A History & Complete Instruction Manual. LC 94-60775. (Illus.). 112p. 1994. pap. 21.95 (*0-525-48596-1*) Studio Bks.
Lefko, Perry, jt. auth. see Flutie, Doug.
Lefko, Pery, jt. auth. see Hart, Bret 'Hitman'.
Lefkoe, Morty. Re-Create Your Life: Transforming Yourself & Your World with the Decision Maker Process. LC 96-43406. 256p. 1997. 22.95 (*0-8362-2167-2*) Andrews & McMeel.
Lefkof, Amy, jt. auth. see Schorr, Kenneth L.
Lefkoff, Gerald. Analyzed Examples of Four-Part Harmony: For the Study of Harmonic Dictation, Part Singing & Keyboard Reading. LC 79-92507. 140p. 1980. pap. text 29.95 (*0-935964-00-2*) Glyphic Pr.
— The Elements of Tonal Harmony. LC 84-81074. 150p. (C). 1984. pap. text 35.95 (*0-935964-02-9*) Glyphic Pr.
— Reading & Writing Intervals: A Self-Instruction Book. 130p. 1980. pap. text 21.95 (*0-935964-01-0*) Glyphic Pr.
Lefkoff, Gerald, ed. Computer Application in Music. LC 67-24519. 105p. 1967. 7.50 (*0-937058-40-8*) West Va U Pr.
Lefkoff, Gerald, jt. auth. see Horacek, Leo.
Lefkovitch, L. P. Optimal Set Covering for Biological Classification: Theory of Conditional Clustering & Its Use in Biological Classification & Identification. (Illus.). 454p. (Orig.). 1993. pap. 32.50 (*0-660-14821-8*, Pub. by Canadian Govt Pub) Accents Pubns.
Lefkovits, Ivan. Portrait of the Immune System: Scientific Publications of Niels Kaj Jerne. 1996. pap. text 48.00 (*981-02-2614-4*) World Scientific Pub.
Lefkovits, Ivan, ed. Immunology Methods Manual: The Comprehensive Sourcebook of Techniques, 4 vols., Set. LC 96-44884. (Illus.). 2176p. 1996. boxed set 149.95 (*0-12-442710-3*) Morgan Kaufmann.
Lefkovits, Ivan, et al, eds. Immunology Methods Manual: The Comprehensive Sourcebook of Techniques, 4 vols. 2495p. 1997. 269.95 incl. cd-rom (*0-12-442716-2*) Acad Pr.
***Lefkovits, Ivan & Waldmann, Herman.** Limiting Dilution Analysis of Cells in the Immune System. 2nd ed. LC 98-50046. (Illus.). 320p. 1999. text 149.50 (*0-19-850128-5*) OUP.
Lefkovits, Ivan, jt. ed. see Steinberg, C. M.
Lefkovits, Judah K. The Copper Scroll - 3Q15: A Reevaluation: A New Reading, Translation, & Commentary. (Studies on the Texts of the Desert of Judah: No. 25). (Illus.). 500p. 1997. 162.50 (*90-04-10685-5*) Brill Academic Pubs.
Lefkovitz, Lori H., ed. Textual Bodies: Changing Boundaries of Literary Representation. LC 96-21758. (SUNY Series, The Body in Culture, History, & Religion). 292p. (C). 1997. text 65.50 (*0-7914-3161-4*); pap. text 21.95 (*0-7914-3162-2*) State U NY Pr.
Lefkowitch, Jay H. Histopathology of Disease. (Illus.). 234p. 1989. text 61.00 (*0-443-08566-8*) Church.
Lefkowith, Christie M. The Art of Perfume: Discovering & Collecting Perfume Bottles. LC 94-60270. (Illus.). 208p. 1994. 60.00 (*0-500-23686-0*, Pub. by Thames Hudson) Norton.
— The Art of Perfume: Discovery & Collecting Perfume Bottles. LC 94-60270. (Illus.). 208p. 1998. pap. 29.95 (*0-500-28044-4*, Pub. by Thames Hudson) Norton.
Lefkowith, Christie M., jt. auth. see Monsen, Randall B.
Lefkowitz, Arthur S. The Long Retreat: The Calamitous Defense of New Jersey, 1776. LC 99-29035. 190p. 1999. text 25.00 (*0-8135-2759-7*) Rutgers U Pr.
***Lefkowitz, Bernard.** In the Company of Women. 2002. text 27.50 (*0-8050-6358-7*) St Martin.
Lefkowitz, Bernard. Our Guys: The Glen Ridge Rape & the Secret Life of the Perfect Suburb. LC 94-48276. (Men & Masculinity Ser.). (Illus.). 454p. 1997. 29.95 (*0-520-20596-0*, Pub. by U CA Pr) Cal Prin Full Svc.
— Our Guys: The Glen Ridge Rape & the Secret Life of the Perfect Suburb. LC 98-5131. 1998. pap. 15.00 (*0-375-70269-5*) Vin Bks.
— Tough Changes: Growing up on Your Own in America. 1987. 29.95 (*0-02-918490-8*) Free Pr.
Lefkowitz, David & Siegel, Robert. A Patient's Journey. 99p. (Orig.). 1995. pap. 7.95 (*0-9637668-0-5*) Irving Pr.
Lefkowitz, Elliot B. A Passion for Life: The Story of Herman & Maurice Spertus. 70p. 1994. pap. 8.95 (*0-935982-48-5*) Spertus Coll.
Lefkowitz, Eric. Monkees Tale. 1986. pap. 9.95 (*0-86719-338-7*) Last Gasp.
Lefkowitz, Frances. David Letterman. (Pop Culture Legends Ser.). 120p. (YA). (gr. 5 up). 1996. pap. 8.95 (*0-7910-3253-1*) Chelsea Hse.
Lefkowitz, Howard N. New York Limited Liability Company Forms & Practice Manual, 2 vols. 3rd ed. LC 97-51696. 790p. 1998. ring bd. 239.90 (*1-57400-035-7*) Data Trace Pubng.
Lefkowitz, I. & Sakr, M. F., eds. Computer Applications in Industry: Proceedings of IASTED Symposium, Cairo, Egypt, February 1-3, 1988. 156p. 1988. 50.00 (*0-88986-095-5*, 139) Acta Pr.
Lefkowitz, I. & Taylor, G. Proceedings of the 5th International Meeting on Ferroelectricity, 5 pts. 1370p. 1981. 1238.00 (*0-685-27100-5*) Gordon & Breach.
Lefkowitz, Jerome. Public Employee Unionism in Israel. LC 78-634400. (Comparative Studies in Public Employment Labor Relations Ser.). 1971. 10.00 (*0-87736-017-0*); pap. 5.00 (*0-87736-018-9*) U of Mich Inst Labor.
— Public Sector Labor & Employment Law. LC 87-62965. 1100p. 1987. text 90.00 (*0-942954-18-1*) NYS Bar.
Lefkowitz, Jerome, ed. Evolving Process - Collective Negotiations in Public Employment. LC 85-80621. 553p. 1985. 35.00 (*0-934753-00-8*) LRP Pubns.
Lefkowitz, M. M., et al. Growing up to Be Violent: A Longitudinal Study of the Development of Aggression. 1977. 111.00 (*0-08-019515-6*, Pub. by Pergamon Repr) Franklin.
Lefkowitz, Mary. Not Out of Africa: How Afrocentrism Became an Excuse to Teach Myth As History. LC 97-183099. 256p. 1997. pap. 13.00 (*0-465-09838-X*, Pub. by Basic) HarpC.
Lefkowitz, Mary R. First-Person Fictions: Pindar's Poetic "I" 238p. 1991. text 75.00 (*0-19-814686-8*) OUP.
— Women in Greek Myth. LC 86-7146. 160p. 1990. reprint ed. pap. text 13.95 (*0-8018-4108-9*) Johns Hopkins.
Lefkowitz, Mary R. & Fant, Maureen B., eds. Women's Life in Greece & Rome: A Source Book in Translation. rev. ed. 376p. 1992. pap. text 16.95 (*0-8018-4475-4*) Johns Hopkins.
— Women's Life in Greece & Rome: A Source Book in Translation. 2nd rev. ed. 376p. 1992. text 38.50 (*0-8018-4474-6*) Johns Hopkins.
Lefkowitz, Mary R. & Rogers, Guy, eds. Black Athena Revisited. LC 95-8903. 560p. (C). 1996. pap. 19.95 (*0-8078-4555-8*) U of NC Pr.
Lefkowitz, Mathew, et al, eds. A Practical Approach to Pain Management. 310p. 1996. pap. text 40.00 (*0-316-51958-8*, Little Brwn Med Div) Lppncott W & W.
***Lefkowitz, Murray, et al.** The Varieties of Musicology: Essays in Honor of Murray Lefkowitz. LC 00-39666. (Detroit Monographs in Musicology/Studies in Music). 2000. pap. write for info. (*0-89990-093-3*) Harmonie Park Pr.
Lefkowitz, Natalie, jt. auth. see Gass, Susan M.
Lefkowitz, Patricia S. & Zimmer, Joy S. New York Part-Ease. 1982. pap. 7.95 (*0-9607664-0-5*) Part-Ease.
Lefkowitz, Rachel. Wow! Resumes for Administrative Careers: How to Put Together a Winning Resume. LC 96-38146. 192p. 1997. pap. 10.95 (*0-07-037102-4*) McGraw.
Leflar, Robert. American Conflict Law: 1991 Supplement. 2nd ed. 59p. 1996. pap. text 4.50 (*0-87473-804-0*, 12056-10, MICHIE) LEXIS Pub.
Leflar, Robert A. & Laurence, Robert. A Student's Guide to Estates in Land & Future Interests, Second Edition. 1993. text 24.00 (*0-8205-2718-1*) Bender.
LeFleming, Stephen, jt. auth. see LeFleming, Svetlana.
LeFleming, Svetlana & LeFleming, Stephen. Guide to Essay Writing in Russian. (Russian Language Ser.). 228p. 1996. pap. text 29.95 (*1-85399-493-6*, Pub. by Brist Class Pr) Focus Pub-R Pullins.
LeFlemming, Svetlana, jt. auth. see Harrison, W.
Lefler, Dan & Seredian, Dina. The Stability Enhancement Reductions Index: A Metric for Arms Control. (CISA Research Note Ser.: No. 16). 14p. 1986. pap. 10.00 (*0-86682-068-X*) Ctr Intl Relations.
Lefler, Hugh T. & Newsome, Albert R. North Carolina: The History of a Southern State. LC 72-81330. (Illus.). 825p. reprint ed. pap. 200.00 (*0-8357-3869-8*, 203660100004) Bks Demand.
Lefler, Hugh T., jt. auth. see Barck, Oscar T., Jr.
Lefler, Hugh T., ed. see Clark, Walter.
Lefler, Hugh T., ed. see Lawson, John.
Lefley, Harriet P. Family Caregiving in Mental Illness. (Family Caregiver Applications Ser.: Vol. 7). 288p. 1996. 48.00 (*0-8039-5720-3*) Sage.
— Family Caregiving in Mental Illness, No. 7. (Family Caregivers Applications Ser.: Vol. 7). 1996. pap. 23.50 (*0-8039-5721-1*) Sage.
Lefley, Harriet P. & Johnson, Dale L., eds. Families as Allies in Treatment of the Mentally Ill: New Directions for Mental Health Professionals. LC 89-17778. 284p. 1990. text 14.95 (*0-88048-298-2*, 8298) Am Psychiatric.
Lefley, Harriet P. & Pedersen, Paul B., eds. Cross-Cultural Training for Mental Health Professionals. (Illus.). 360p. 1986. pap. 44.95 (*0-398-06226-9*) C C Thomas.
— Cross-Cultural Training for Mental Health Professionals. (Illus.). 360p. (C). 1986. 57.95 (*0-398-05257-3*) C C Thomas.
Lefley, Harriet P. & Wasow, Mona, eds. Helping Families Cope with Mental Illness. (Chronic Mental Illness Ser.: Vol. 2). 336p. 1994. text 48.00 (*3-7186-0580-5*, Harwood Acad Pubs) Gordon & Breach.
Lefley, Harriet P., jt. auth. see Hatfield, Agnes B.
Lefley, Harriet P., jt. ed. see Hatfield, Agnes B.
Leflon, Jean. Eugene de Mazenod: Bishop of Marseilles, Founder of the Oblates of Mary Immaculate, 1782-1861, Vol. 1. LC 61-13025. 537p. reprint ed. pap. 166.50 (*0-7837-5710-7*, 204537500001) Bks Demand.
— Eugene de Mazenod: Bishop of Marseilles, Founder of the

L

Oblates of Mary Immaculate, 1782-1861. Vol. 2. LC 61-13025. 716p. reprint ed. pap. 200.00 (*0-7837-5711-5*, 204537500002) Bks Demand.

— De Mazenod, 1782-1864: Founder of the Oblates of Mary Immaculate. Flanagan, Francis D., tr. from FRE. LC 94-11821. 394p. (Orig.). 1994. pap. 17.50 (*1-56518-062-3*) Coun Res Values.

Lefohn, A. S. Surface-Level Ozone Exposures & Their Effects on Vegetation. 384p. 1991. lib. bdg. 119.00 (*0-87371-169-6*, L169) Lewis Pubs.

Lefond, Stanley J. Handbook of World Salt Resources. LC 68-13391. (Monographs in Geoscience). (Illus.). 408p. 1969. reprint ed. pap. 126.50 (*0-608-05558-1*, 206602600006) Bks Demand.

Lefond, Stanley J., ed. Industrial Minerals & Rocks: (Nonmetallics Other Than Fuels) 4th rev. ed. LC 73-85689. (Seeley W. Mudd Ser.). 1372p. reprint ed. pap. 200.00 (*0-608-14281-6*, 201742100005) Bks Demand.

— Industrial Minerals & Rocks (Nonmetallics Other Than Fuels), Vol. 1. 5th ed. LC 82-971993. (Illus.). 763p. 1983. reprint ed. pap. 200.00 (*0-7837-9168-2*, 204986900001) Bks Demand.

— Industrial Minerals & Rocks (Nonmetallics Other Than Fuels), Vol. 2. 5th ed. LC 82-971993. (Illus.). 764p. 1983. reprint ed. pap. 200.00 (*0-7837-9169-0*, 204986900002) Bks Demand.

Lefond, Stanley J., jt. ed. see Barker, James M.

LeFontaine, Joseph R. The Collector's Bookshelf: A Comprehensive Listing of Authors, Their Pseudonyms, & Their Books. LC 90-45897. 333p. (C). 1990. 79.95 (*0-87975-605-5*) Prometheus Bks.

— The Collector's Bookshelf Value Guide. LC 90-63999. 113p. (Orig.). (C). 1990. pap. 23.95 (*0-87975-606-3*) Prometheus Bks.

— A Handbook for Booklovers. LC 88-15128. 612p. 1988. 61.95 (*0-87975-491-5*) Prometheus Bks.

Lefor, Alan T., ed. Surgical Problems Affecting the Patient with Cancer: Interdisciplinary Management. 424p. 1995. text 86.00 (*0-397-51402-6*) Lppncott W & W.

Leforest, Thomas J., ed. & tr. see Lebel, Gerard.

LeForge, P. V. The Principle of Interchange & Other Stories. LC 89-92412. 179p. (Orig.). 1990. pap. 7.95 (*0-9624878-0-5*) Paperback Rack Bks.

— The Secret Life of Moles. LC 91-78124. 72p. (Orig.). (C). 1992. pap. 8.00 (*0-938078-35-6*) Anhinga Pr.

Leforge, Thomas H. & Marquis, Thomas B. Memoirs of a White Crow Indian. LC 74-6222. xxiv, 356p. 1974. reprint ed. pap. 10.95 (*0-8032-5800-3*, Bison Books) U of Nebr Pr.

LeFors, Rufe. Facts As I Remember Them: The Autobiography of Rufe LeFors. Peterson, John A., ed. (M. K. Brown Range Life Ser.: No. 16). (Illus.). 192p. 1986. text 20.95 (*0-292-70379-1*) U of Tex Pr.

Lefort, Claude. The Political Forms of Modern Society Bureaucracy: Democracy, Totalitarianism. Thompson, John B., ed. 352p. (Orig.). 1986. pap. text 18.50 (*0-262-62054-5*) MIT Pr.

***Lefort, Claude.** Writing, the Political Test. LC 99-51699. (Post-Contemporary Interventions Ser.). 328p. 2000. pap. 18.95 (*0-8223-2520-9*) Duke.

Lefort, Claude, ed. see Merleau-Ponty, Maurice.

Lefort, Gertrud F. Von, see Von Lefort, Gertrud F.

Lefort, Rafael. The Teachers of Gurdjieff. 2nd ed. LC 98-38564. 173p. (Orig.). 1998. reprint ed. pap. 17.00 (*1-883536-16-2*, Malor Bks) ISHK.

Lefort, Rosine. Birth of the Other. Du Ry, Marc et al, trs. LC 93-40386. 344p. (C). 1994. text 49.95 (*0-252-01900-8*); pap. text 18.95 (*0-252-06393-7*) U of Ill Pr.

Lefrak, Babs, jt. auth. see Mark, Lisbeth.

LeFrak, Samuel J., et al. A Passion for Art: The LeFrak Family Collection. (Illus.). 120p. text. write for info. (*0-9620593-1-5*) Lefrak Organization.

Lefranc, Abel. Under the Mask of William Shakespeare. Cragg, Cecil, tr. (C). 1989. 45.00 (*0-86303-352-0*, Pub. by Merlin Bks) St Mut.

LeFranc, Elsie, jt. ed. see Blustain, Harvey.

LeFranc, G., jt. auth. see LeFranc, Marie-Paule.

LeFranc, Marie-Paule & LeFranc, G. Restriction Fragment Length Polymorphism. (Experimental & Clinical Immunogenetics Ser.: Vol. 7, No. 1, 1990). (Illus.). 88p. 1989. pap. 41.00 (*3-8055-5113-4*) S Karger.

Lefranc, Norbert. Shrikes: A Guide to the Shrikes of the World. LC 97-60716. (Illus.). 192p. 1997. 35.00 (*0-300-07336-4*) Yale U Pr.

Lefrancois. Of Children. 2nd ed. (Psychology Ser.). 1977. pap. 18.25 (*0-534-00483-0*) Brooks-Cole.

LeFrancois. Of Children. 5th ed. (Education Ser.). 1985. pap., teacher ed. write for info. (*0-534-05504-4*); pap., student ed. 8.50 (*0-534-05503-6*) Wadsworth Pub.

Lefrancois. Of Children. 7th ed. (Education Ser.). 1992. teacher ed. write for info. (*0-534-16826-4*) Wadsworth Pub.

— Of Children. 8th ed. (Education Ser.). 1994. student ed. 17.25 (*0-534-21938-1*) Wadsworth Pub.

— Psychological Theories on Human Learning. (Psychology Ser.). 1971. mass mkt. 18.50 (*0-8185-0014-X*) Brooks-Cole.

LeFrancois. Psychology for Teaching. 2nd ed. (Education Ser.). 1975. pap. 9.00 (*0-534-00368-0*) Wadsworth Pub.

Lefrancois. Psychology for Teaching. 7th ed. (Education Ser.). 1991. mass mkt., teacher ed. write for info. (*0-534-14413-6*) Wadsworth Pub.

LeFrancois. Psychology for Teaching. 9th ed. (Education Ser.). 1996. student ed. 15.25 (*0-534-50679-8*) Wadsworth Pub.

***Lefrancois.** Psychology for Teaching. 10th ed. (Education Ser.). (C). 1999. text 19.00 (*0-534-57454-8*) Wadsworth Pub.

Lefrancois. Theories of Human Learning: What the Old Man Said. 4th ed. LC 99-25724. (Psychology Ser.). 1999. pap. text 89.95 (*0-534-36220-6*) Wadsworth Pub.

Lefrancois, Guy R. The Lifespan. 1996. teacher ed. write for info. (*0-534-25485-3*) Brooks-Cole.

— The Lifespan. (Education Ser.). 1984. pap., student ed. 8.25 (*0-534-02970-1*) Wadsworth Pub.

— The Lifespan. LC 96-37204. (Illus.). 640p. (C). 1984. pap. write for info. (*0-534-02969-8*) Wadsworth Pub.

— The Lifespan. 2nd ed. 664p. (C). 1987. pap. write for info. (*0-534-07470-7*) Wadsworth Pub.

— The Lifespan. 2nd ed. (Education Ser.). 1987. pap., teacher ed. write for info. (*0-534-07472-3*); pap., student ed. 11.00 (*0-534-07471-5*) Wadsworth Pub.

— The Lifespan. 3rd ed. (Education Ser.). 1990. pap., student ed. 12.75 (*0-534-11755-4*); mass mkt., teacher ed. write for info. (*0-534-11756-2*) Wadsworth Pub.

— The Lifespan. 3rd ed. 714p. (C). 1990. pap. write for info. (*0-534-11754-6*) Wadsworth Pub.

— The Lifespan. 4th ed. 739p. (C). 1993. mass mkt. 48.95 (*0-534-17778-6*) Wadsworth Pub.

— The Lifespan. 5th ed. LC 95-17026. (C). 1995. 49.25 (*0-534-25482-9*) Wadsworth Pub.

— The Lifespan. 5th ed. (Education Ser.). 1995. student ed. 17.25 (*0-534-25484-5*) Wadsworth Pub.

— The Lifespan. 6th ed. LC 98-47232. (Education Ser.). 1998. pap. 75.95 (*0-534-55692-2*) Wadsworth Pub.

— The Lifespan. 6th ed. (Education Ser.). 1999. pap., student ed. 17.25 (*0-534-55693-0*) Wadsworth Pub.

— Of Children. 4th ed. 192p. (C). 1983. pap. write for info. (*0-534-01308-2*) Wadsworth Pub.

— Of Children: An Introduction to Child Development. 5th ed. 606p. (C). 1985. pap. write for info. (*0-534-05502-8*) Wadsworth Pub.

— Of Children: An Introduction to Child Development. 6th ed. 698p. (C). 1988. pap. write for info. (*0-534-09990-4*) Wadsworth Pub.

— Of Children: An Introduction to Child Development. 7th ed. 762p. (C). 1991. pap. 39.25 (*0-534-16824-8*) Wadsworth Pub.

— Of Children: An Introduction to Child Development. 7th ed. 762p. (C). 1992. pap., student ed. 15.95 (*0-534-16825-6*) Wadsworth Pub.

— Of Children: An Introduction to Child Development. 8th ed. LC 94-30151. 688p. 1994. pap. 83.95 (*0-534-21936-5*) Wadsworth Pub.

LeFrancois, Guy R. Of Children: An Introduction to Child Development. 8th ed. 1995. teacher ed. write for info. (*0-534-21939-X*) Brooks-Cole.

Lefrancois, Guy R. Psychological Theories of Human Learning. 2nd ed. LC 81-15511. (Psychology Ser.). 348p. (C). 1982. boxed set 39.95 (*0-8185-0501-X*) Brooks-Cole.

Lefrancois, Guy R. Psychological Theories of Learning. 3rd rev. ed. LC 94-30411. (Illus.). 380p. 1994. pap. 54.75 (*0-534-23202-7*) Brooks-Cole.

Lefrancois, Guy R. Psychology for Teaching. 9th ed. LC 96-8707. (Education Ser.). 592p. (C). 1996. 53.25 (*0-534-50678-X*) Wadsworth Pub.

— Psychology for Teaching. 10th ed. LC 99-44849. (Education Ser.). 1999. 79.95 (*0-534-57447-5*) Thomson Learn.

— Psychology for Teaching: A Bear Always Faces the Front. 6th ed. 411p. (C). 1987. pap. write for info. (*0-534-08634-9*) Wadsworth Pub.

— Psychology for Teaching: A Bear Never Faces the Front. 5th ed. (C). 1984. pap. write for info. (*0-534-04464-6*) Wadsworth Pub.

— Psychology for Teaching: A Bear Will Not Commit Himself Just Now. 7th ed. 448p. (C). 1990. pap. 45.95 (*0-534-14412-8*) Wadsworth Pub.

LeFrancois, Guy R. Theories of Human Learning: Kro's Report, Test Items. 3rd ed. 1995. pap. write for info. (*0-534-23203-5*) Brooks-Cole.

Lefrancois, Guy R., et al. The Lifespan. 4th ed. (Education Ser.). 1993. mass mkt., student ed. 13.50 (*0-534-17779-4*) Wadsworth Pub.

Lefrant, Serge, jt. auth. see Bernier, Patrick.

Lefroy, Augustus H., tr. see Girard, Paul F.

Lefroy, Augustus Henry, tr. see Girard, Paul Frederic.

Lefroy, H. Maxwell. Indian Insect Pest. 2nd ed. xii, 318p. 1990. reprint ed. 25.00 (*1-55528-214-8*) Scholarly Pubns.

Lefroy, Helen. Jane Austen. (Get a Life...Pocket Biographies Ser.). (Illus.). 128p. 1997. pap. 9.95 (*0-7509-1580-3*, Pub. by Sutton Pub Ltd) Intl Pubs Mktg.

***LeFroy, Rod.** Agriculture as a Mimic of Natural Ecosystems. LC 99-44182. (Current Plant Science & Biotechnology in Agriculture Ser.). 1999. write for info. (*0-7923-5965-8*) Kluwer Academic.

LeFroy, Rod, jt. ed. see Blair, Graeme.

Lefroy, William. Church Leaders in Primitive Times. 1977. lib. bdg. 69.95 (*0-8490-1628-2*) Gordon Pr.

Lefschetz, Solomon. Algebraic Topology. LC 41-6147. (Colloquium Publications: Vol. 27). 389p. 1942. reprint ed. pap. 29.00 (*0-8218-1027-8*, COLL/27) Am Math.

— Contributions to the Theory of Nonlinear Oscillations, Vol. 4. LC 50-2400. (Annals of Mathematics Studies: No. 41). 222p. 1958. reprint ed. pap. 68.90 (*0-608-06636-2*, 206683300004) Bks Demand.

— Contributions to the Theory of Nonlinear Oscillations, Vols. 1, 1950. (Annals of Mathematics Studies). 1972. 26.00 (*0-527-02736-7*); 25.00 (*0-527-02745-6*); 25.00 (*0-527-02753-7*); 25.00 (*0-527-02761-8*) Periodicals Srv.

— Differential Equations: Geometric Theory. 390p. 1977. reprint ed. pap. text 11.95 (*0-486-63463-9*) Dover.

— Lectures on Differential Equations. LC 46-5010. (Annals of Mathematics Studies: No. 14). 216p. reprint ed. pap. 67.00 (*0-608-06640-0*, 206683700009) Bks Demand.

— Selected Papers. LC 73-113137. 639p. (C). 1990. text 59.50 (*0-8284-0234-5*, 234) Chelsea Pub.

— Topology. 2nd rev. ed. LC 56-11513. (Illus.). 410p. (C). 1990. text 23.95 (*0-8284-0116-0*, 116) Chelsea Pub.

Left Hand Bull, Jacqueline, jt. auth. see Haldane, Suzanne.

Left Handed. Left Handed, Son of Old Man Hat: A Navaho Autobiography. LC 95-37149. 378p. 1967. pap. 14.95 (*0-8032-7958-2*, Bison Books) U of Nebr Pr.

Lefter, James & Bergin, Thomas J. A Microcomputer Based Primer on Structural Behavior. (Illus.). 448p. (C). 1986. disk. write for info. (*0-318-60165-6*) P-H.

Leftheris, B., jt. ed. see Brebbia, C. A.

Lefton. Psychology. 7th ed. 1999. pap. text, student ed. 15.00 (*0-205-29671-8*) Allyn.

Lefton, Alice, jt. auth. see Rishel, Joseph J.

Lefton-Greif, Maureen A., jt. auth. see Arvedson, Joan C.

***Lefton, Lester A.** Interactive Psychology. 608p. 2000. pap. 33.33 (*0-205-32286-7*) Allyn.

Lefton, Lester A. Lefton Learning Community: An Interactive Site for Users. (C). 1996. write for info. (*0-205-26859-5*, T6859-7) Allyn.

— Mastering Psychology. 3rd ed. 680p. (C). 1988. pap. text 34.00 (*0-205-10626-9*, H0626-5) Allyn.

***Lefton, Lester A.** Psychology. 7th ed. LC 99-29523. 728p. (C). 1999. 83.00 (*0-205-28529-5*, Macmillan Coll) P-H.

***Lefton, Lester A. & Boyes, Michael C.** Psychology. 1999. pap., student ed. 26.60 (*0-205-30740-X*) P-H.

Lefton, Lester A. & Valvatne, Laura. Mastering Psychology. 4th ed. (C). 1992. teacher ed. write for info. (*0-205-13191-3*, H3191-7) Allyn.

Lefton, Phillip. Barron's Regents Exams & Answers: Global Studies. 160p. 1996. pap. 5.95 (*0-8120-4344-8*) Barron.

Lefton, Phillip, jt. auth. see Midgley, David A.

Lefton, Robert E., et al. Improving Productivity Through People Skills: Dimensional Management Strategies. LC 80-21691. 498p. 1991. reprint ed. text 25.00 (*0-9630421-1-4*) Psy Assocs.

Leftow, Brian. Time & Eternity. LC 90-55890. (Cornell Studies in the Philosophy of Religion). 352p. 1991. text 49.95 (*0-8014-2459-3*) Cornell U Pr.

Leftschatz, William. The Death of Tutankhamen. 220p. (Orig.). 1989. pap. 10.95 (*0-933753-07-1*) Canterbury.

Leftwich. Redefining Politics. 1986. 32.00 (*0-416-68150-6*) Routledge.

Leftwich, A. W. A Dictionary of Entomology. LC 75-27143. 368p. pap. 114.10 (*0-608-15680-9*, 203199600077) Bks Demand.

Leftwich, Adrian, ed. Democracy & Development: Theory & Practice. LC 95-25326. 304p. (C). Date not set. 60.95 (*0-7456-1266-0*) Blackwell Pubs.

— Democracy & Development: Theory & Practice. LC 95-25326. 304p. (C). 1996. pap. 27.95 (*0-7456-1267-9*) Blackwell Pubs.

***Leftwich, Brad.** Round Peak Style Clawhammer Banjo. 104p. 1999. pap. 22.95 incl. audio compact disk (*0-7866-2902-9*, 96660BCD) Mel Bay.

Leftwich, Howard, et al. The Executive Simulation. 170p. (C). 1996. per. 24.95 (*0-8403-9462-4*) Kendall-Hunt.

Leftwich, Jim. Dirt. 14p. (Orig.). 1995. pap. 4.00 (*0-935350-56-X*) Luna Bisonte.

— Improvisations/Transformations. 45p. 1998. 7.00 (*0-937013-76-5*) Potes Poets.

— Khawatir. 43p. 1995. pap. 3.00 (*1-57141-016-3*) Runaway Spoon.

— Sample Example: Visual Lyrics. (Illus.). 27p. 1998. pap. 7.00 (*1-892280-01-9*) Luna Bisonte.

Leftwich, Jim & Little, Jeffrey B. Gnommonclature. 22p. (Orig.). 1996. pap. 6.00 (*0-935350-63-2*) Luna Bisonte.

Leftwich, Joseph. Years at the Ending. LC 83-45131. 72p. 1984. 11.95 (*0-8453-4767-5*, Cornwall Bks) Assoc Univ Prs.

Leftwich, Joseph, ed. An Anthology of Modern Yiddish Literature. LC 74-82386. (Anthology Ser: No. 1). 346p. (C). 1974. pap. text 26.15 (*90-279-3496-7*) Mouton.

Leftwich, Joseph, tr. from YID. Distant Voice. LC 95-46694. 1997. write for info. (*0-8453-4854-X*) Assoc Univ Prs.

Leftwich, Joseph, tr. see Aleichem, Sholem.

Leftwich, Joseph, tr. see Lewin, Samuel.

Leftwich, Joseph, tr. see Morevski, Abraham.

Leftwich, Richard H. & Gay, David. A Basic Framework for Economics. 3rd ed. 408p. (C). 1987. pap. 28.50 (*0-256-03702-7*, Irwn McGrw-H) McGrw-H Hghr Educ.

Leftwich, Rodney. Arts & Crafts of the Cherokee. 160p. 1986. pap. 9.95 (*0-935741-11-9*, Pub. by Cherokee Pubns) Book Pub Co.

Leftwich, Samuel E., intro. Proceedings of the National Communications Forum, 1990, Vol. XXXXIV. (Illus.). 1042p. 1990. 139.00 (*0-933217-06-4*) Prof Educ Intl.

Lega, Leonor, jt. ed. see Dimattia, Dominic.

Lega Navale Italiana. Dizionario Enciclopedico Marinaresco. (ITA.). 1991. 195.00 (*0-8288-8457-9*) Fr & Eur.

Legacy Classroom Teachers Staff, et al. Legacy: Challenging Lessons in Civics & Citizenship. LC 95-69628. 258p. (Orig.). 1995. pap. 18.00 (*1-879953-07-2*) CRD Law-Related.

Legacy, Esther. Where the Snowman Lives. (Illus.). 15p. (J). (ps). 1998. pap. 3.95 (*0-9667332-0-7*) E Legacy.

***Legacy, Mary Ann Fleck.** Life & It's Poetry. 48p. 2000. pap. 9.99 (*1-892668-17-3*) Prospect Pr.

Legacy Press Staff. Gobble up the Bible: Cookbook for Kids. 192p. (J). (gr. k-7). spiral bd. 14.99 (*1-885358-59-8*, LP46811) Rainbow CA.

— God & Me: Devotions for Girls. 240p. (J). (gr. k-k). spiral bd. 11.99 (*1-885358-61-X*, LP46821) Rainbow CA.

— God & Me: Devotions for Girls. 232p. (J). (gr. 1-4). spiral bd. 11.99 (*1-885358-60-1*, LP46822) Rainbow CA.

***Legacy Press Staff.** God's Girls! Fun & Faith for Ages 9-12. 2000. pap. 12.99 (*1-58411-020-1*, Lgacy Pr); pap. 12.99 (*1-58411-021-X*, Lgacy Pr) Rainbow CA.

Legacy Press Staff. Gotta Have God! Devotions for Boys. (Gotta Have God Ser.). (J). (gr. 1-4). 1999. pap. 11.99 (*1-885358-97-0*, Lgacy Pr) Rainbow CA.

— Gotta Have God! Devotions for Boys. (Gotta Have God Ser.). (J). (gr. 5-7). 1999. pap. 11.99 (*1-885358-98-9*, Lgacy Pr) Rainbow CA.

— Gotta Have God! Devotions for Boys. (J). (ps-k). 1999. pap. 11.99 (*1-885358-96-2*, Lgacy Pr) Rainbow CA.

***Legacy Press Staff & Davis, Mary J.** My Praise Journal: A Celebration of Psalms for Kids. (Illus.). 144p. (J). (gr. 4-7). 1999. pap. 9.99 (*1-885358-71-7*, Lgacy Pr) Rainbow CA.

Legacy Press Staff, et al. God & Me Vol. 3: Devotions for Girls. 248p. (J). (gr. 5). 1998. pap. 11.99 (*1-885358-54-7*, Lgacy Pr) Rainbow CA.

Legacy, Sean. Point Zero Bliss: A Prisoner's Quest for Freedom. 292p. 1997. pap. 14.95 (*0-9645561-1-1*) Greathse Co.

Legal Assistance Foundation of Chicago. Authorization Agreements for Legal Services Clients. 52p. 1987. pap. 5.00 (*0-685-23156-9*, 42,246) NCLS Inc.

Legal Business Seminars Staff, jt. ed. see Law & Business Inc. Staff.

Legal Counsel for the Elderly Staff. Decisionmaking, Incapacity & the Elderly, 1987 (1990 Supplement) 186p. 1990. pap., suppl. ed. 30.00 (*0-933945-00-0*) Legal Coun Elderly.

— Medicare Practice Manual. 314p. 1990. pap. 25.00 (*0-933945-05-1*) Legal Coun Elderly.

— Organizing Your Future: A Guide to Decisionmaking in Your Later Years. 102p. 1993. pap. 50.00 (*0-933945-04-3*) Legal Coun Elderly.

— A Practical Guide to Nursing Home Advocacy. 245p. 1991. pap. 30.00 (*0-933945-02-7*) Legal Coun Elderly.

Legal Counsel for the Elderly Staff, jt. auth. see Brown, Robert N.

Legal Research Institute, Faculty of Law Staff, et al, trs. Turkish Code of Criminal Procedure. (American Series of Foreign Penal Codes: Vol. 5). x, 158p. 1962. 20.00 (*0-8377-0025-6*, Rothman) W S Hein.

Legal Research Network Staff, ed. Rules of the Road for the Information Superhighway: Electronic Communications & the Law. LC 95-61650. xxxv, 809p. (C). 1995. text 99.00 (*0-314-06663-2*) West Pub.

Legal Services Corporation Staff. Final Evaluation Report Demonstration: Computer Assisted Legal Research & Technological Improvements. (Illus.). 223p. (Orig.). 1981. pap. 5.00 (*0-941077-13-6*, 32,789) NCLS Inc.

Legal Star Communications Staff, jt. auth. see Nolo Staff Editors.

Legal Times Seminars Staff, jt. ed. see Law & Business Inc. Staff.

Legales, Patrick & Lequesne, Christian. Regions in Europe. LC 97-26562. 328p. (C). 1998. 90.00 (*0-415-16482-6*); pap. 27.99 (*0-415-16483-4*) Routledge.

LeGall, Jean, jt. ed. see Peck, Harry D., Jr.

LeGallienne, Eva. With a Quiet Heart: An Autobiography. LC 74-3745. (Illus.). 311p. 1974. reprint ed. lib. bdg. 65.00 (*0-8371-7470-8*, LEQH, Greenwood Pr) Greenwood.

LeGallienne, Richard. Robert Louis Stevenson & Other Poems, 1895. (Decadents, Symbolists, Anti-Decadents Ser.). 1996. 48.00 (*1-85477-151-5*) Continuum.

— Rudyard Kipling. LC 73-21739. (English Literature Ser.: No. 33). 1974. lib. bdg. 75.00 (*0-8383-1838-X*) M S G Haskell Hse.

Legany, Dezso. Liszt & His Country, 1874-1886. Smith-Csicsery-Ronay, Elizabeth, tr. from HUN. (Illus.). 331p. 1992. 39.50 (*0-911050-66-3*) Occidental.

Legard, Hilary & Launder, Elizabeth, eds. Understanding the Chambon. 88p. (C). 1990. 21.00 (*0-85131-439-2*, Pub. by J A Allen) St Mut.

***Legarda, Benito J., Jr.** After the Galleons: Foreign Trade, Economic Change & Entrepreneurship in the Nineteenth-Century Philippines. LC 98-61609. (Wisconsin Monographs in Southeast Asian Studies: Vol. M18). (Illus.). 416p. 1999. pap. write for info. (*1-881261-28-X*) U Wisc Ctr SE Asian.

LeGarde. Frommer's Amsterdam, 1995-1996. 1995. pap. 12.95 (*0-671-51760-0*) S&S Trade.

Legarde. Frommer's Belgium, Holland & Luxembourg, 1995-1996. 1994. pap. 16.95 (*0-671-51761-9*) S&S Trade.

LeGarde. Frommer's Boston, 1996. 1996. per. 13.00 (*0-671-52042-3*) S&S Trade.

— Frommer's Budget Travel Guide Paris on $50 a Day, 1996-1997. 1996. pap. 12.00 (*0-671-51889-5*) S&S Trade.

— Frommer's Comprehensive Travel Guide Santa Fe, Taos & Albuquerque 96. 1996. per. 12.95 (*0-671-52008-3*) S&S Trade.

— Frommer's New Mexico, 1995-1996. 1995. pap. 15.00 (*0-671-88495-6*) S&S Trade.

— Frommer's New Orleans, 1996. 1996. pap. 12.95 (*0-671-52043-1*) S&S Trade.

Legarde. Frommer's Santa Fe, Taos & Albuquerque, 1995-1996. 1995. pap. 13.00 (*0-671-88498-0*) S&S Trade.

LeGarde & Northrup. Frommer's New England, 1995. 1995. pap. 17.00 (*0-671-88816-1*) S&S Trade.

Legarde, Lisa. Frommer's New Mexico, 1997. 4th ed. (Illus.). 1997. 15.95 (*0-02-860907-7*) Macmillan.

— Frommer's New Orleans '97. 1996. 13.95 (*0-02-860906-9*) Macmillan.

— Frommer's Santa Fe, Taos & Albuquerque '96. 288p. 1995. 13.95 (*0-02-860874-7*) Macmillan.

— Frommer's Santa Fe, Taos & Albuquerque 98. 273p. 1997. 14.95 (*0-02-861782-7*) Macmillan.

— Frommer's Sante Fe, Taos & Alberquerque. 1996. 13.95 (*0-02-860908-5*) Macmillan.

— Frommer's Walking Tour: Boston. 176p. 1996. 11.95 (*0-02-860904-2*) Prntice Hall Bks.

— Paris. LC 93-6988. (Frommer's Walking Tours Ser.). 1993. pap. 12.00 (*0-671-79764-6*, P-H Travel) Prntice Hall Bks.

Legare, Jill. Enter Me: A Lesbian Memoir. 144p. 1998. pap. 9.95 (*0-87810-042-3*) Times Change.

Legare, Michel & Larson, Kermit D. Initiation A La Comptabilite Financiere, Vol. 2. 6th ed. 704p. (C). 1996. per. 34.95 (*0-256-20462-4*, Irwn McGrw-H) McGrw-H Hghr Educ.

Legare, Michel, et al. Initiation a la Comptabilite Financiere. 6th ed. (FRE.). 480p. (C). 1996. per. 36.95 (*0-256-17071-1*, Irwn McGrw-H) McGrw-H Hghr Educ.

— Initiation a la Comptabilite Financiere Recveil de Solutions Pour L'Etudiant. 6th ed. (FRE.). 112p. (C). 1996. text 15.62 (*0-256-21400-X*, Irwn McGrw-H) McGrw-H Hghr Educ.

— Initiation a la Comptabilite Financiere Recveil de Solutions pour L'Etudiant, Vol. 2. 6th ed. (FRE.). 112p. (C). 1996. text 18.12 (*0-256-21401-8*, Irwn McGrw-H) McGrw-H Hghr Educ.

Legare, Romain, jt. auth. see Dupuis, Hector.

Legarreta, Dorothy. The Guernica Generation: Basque Refugee Children of the Spanish Civil War. LC 84-13136. (Basque Ser.). (Illus.). 416p. 1985. 24.95 (*0-87417-088-5*) U of Nev Pr.

Legarsment, A. W. B. Yeats: Images of Ireland. 1996. 17.98 (*0-7628-0721-0*) Bk Sales Inc.

***Legaspi, Victor.** Abba's Touch. 1999. pap. write for info. (*1-58235-195-3*) Watermrk Pr.

Legasse, Paul. The Concise Columbia Encyclopedia. 3rd ed. LC 94-16721. (Illus.). 992p. 1994. 49.95 (*0-395-62439-8*) HM.

Legasse, Simon. Trial of Jesus. 1997. pap. 27.00 (*0-334-02679-2*) TPI PA.

LeGassick, T., tr. see Khalifeh, Sahar.

LeGassick, Trevor J., ed. Major Themes in Modern Arabic Thought: An Anthology. (ARA.). 225p. (C). 1997. reprint ed. pap. text 30.00 (*0-7881-3937-1*) DIANE Pub.

Legast, Anne. La Fauna en el Material Precolombino Calima. (SPA., Illus.). 116p. (Orig.). (C). 1993. pap. 9.50 (*1-877812-37-4*, BR033, Pub. by Banco de la Repub) UPLAAP.

Legasy, Karen L. Forest Plants of Northeastern Ontario. LC 96-171063. (Illus.). 448p. 1995. pap. 19.95 (*1-55105-064-1*) Lone Pine.

Legat, Michael. The Cast Iron Man. large type ed. 560p. 1988. 27.99 (*0-7089-1881-6*) Ulverscroft.

— Mario's Vineyard. large type ed. 752p. 1983. 27.99 (*0-7089-8099-6*, Charnwood) Ulverscroft.

— Putting on a Play. LC 84-13242. 208p. 1984. 12.95 (*0-685-08886-3*) St Martin.

***Legat, Michael.** Revision: An Author's Guide. 160p. 1999. pap. 14.95 (*0-7090-6079-3*, Pub. by R Hale Ltd) Seven Hills Bk.

Legat, Michael. The Shapiro Diamond. large type ed. 448p. 1984. 27.99 (*0-7089-8213-1*) Ulverscroft.

— The Silver Fountain. large type ed. 608p. 1984. 27.99 (*0-7089-8189-5*) Ulverscroft.

Legates. Genetics of Dairy Cattle. 1995. write for info. (*0-8493-8755-8*) CRC Pr.

Legates, J. E. & Warwick, E. J. Breeding & Improvement of Farm Animals. 8th ed. 342p. (C). 1990. 80.00 (*0-07-068376-X*) McGraw.

LeGates, John C. The Sound, the Fury, & the Significance. unabridged ed. LC 95-197745. 19p. (Orig.). 1995. pap. text. write for info. (*1-879716-22-4*, I-95-2) Ctr Info Policy.

LeGates, Marlene. Making Waves: A History of Feminism in Western Society. 397p. (C). 1996. text 25.95 (*0-7730-5483-9*) Addison-Wes.

Legates, Richard, jt. ed. see Stout, Frederic.

***LeGates, Richard T. & Stout, Frederic.** The City Reader. 2nd ed. LC 99-31896. 592p. 1999. pap. write for info. (*0-415-19071-1*) Routledge.

***LeGates, Richard T. & Stout, Frederic, eds.** City Reader. 2nd ed. LC 99-31896. 592p. (C). 1999. text. write for info. (*0-415-19070-3*) Routledge.

Legato, Marianne & Colman, Carol. What Women Need to Know: From Headaches to Heart Disease & Everything in Between. 239p. pap. write for info. (*1-58754-100-9*, Pub. by Olmstead Pr) LPC Group.

Legato, Marianne J. Female Heart: The Truth about Women & Coronary Artery Disease. 1991. pap. 19.95 (*0-13-321811-2*) P-H.

***Legato, Marianne J.** The Female Heart: The Truth about Women & Heart Disease. 272p. 2000. pap. 13.00 (*0-688-18065-5*, Quil) HarperTrade.

Legato, Marianne J. Gender-Specific Aspects of Human Biology for the Practicing Physician. LC 96-32122. 160p. 1996. 19.95 (*0-87993-648-7*) Futura Pub.

Legato, Marianne J., ed. The Developing Heart. 1984. text 141.00 (*0-89838-672-1*) Kluwer Academic.

— The Stressed Heart. (Developments in Cardiovascular Medicine Ser.). 1987. text 174.00 (*0-89838-849-X*) Kluwer Academic.

Legato, Marianne J. & Colman, Carol. The Female Heart: The Truth about Women & Coronary Artery Disease. (Illus.). 272p. 1992. pap. 21.00 (*0-671-76110-2*) S&S Trade.

Legator, Marvin S., et al, eds. The Health Detective's Handbook: A Guide to the Investigation of Environmental Health Hazards by Nonprofessionals. LC 84-20105. (Illus.). 272p. reprint ed. pap. 84.40 (*0-8357-6138-X*, 203414700089) Bks Demand.

Legator, Marvin S. & Strawn, Sabrina F., eds. Chemical Alert! A Community Action Handbook. rev. ed. LC 92-25304. Orig. Title: The Health Detective's Handbook. 254p. (C). 1993. text 35.00 (*0-292-74675-X*); pap. text 14.95 (*0-292-74676-8*) U of Tex Pr.

Legatos, Stephanie, ed. see Sweeney, Patricia M. & Gagnon, Donna.

***Legault, Alain.** Las Vegas. 2000. pap. 12.95 (*2-89464-269-5*, Pub. by Ulysses Travel) Globe Pequot.

Legault, Alain. Peru: Ulysses Travel Guide. Ulysses Travel Guide Staff, ed. (Ulysses Travel Guide Ser.). (Illus.). 1999. pap. 19.95 (*2-89464-122-2*) Ulysses Travel.

***Legault, Alain.** San Francisco. (Illus.). 2001. pap. 12.95 (*2-89464-391-8*) Ulysses Travel.

Legault, Alain. Ulysses Travel Guide: Miami. (Illus.). 336p. 1999. pap. 13.95 (*2-89464-211-3*, Pub. by Ulysses Travel) Globe Pequot.

Legault, Albert & Fortmann, Michel. A Diplomacy of Hope: Canada & Disarmament, 1945-1988. 696p. 1991. 75.00 (*0-7735-0920-8*, Pub. by McG-Queens Univ Pr) CUP Services.

— A Diplomacy of Hope: Canada & Disarmament, 1945-1988. 696p. 1992. pap. 29.95 (*0-7735-0955-0*, Pub. by McG-Queens Univ Pr) CUP Services.

Legault, Jim. Resume II: Artists, Galleries & Craftspersons of the Door Penisula. (Illus.). 64p. (Orig.). 1982. 12.75 (*0-933072-02-3*); pap. 6.50 (*0-933072-03-1*) Golden Glow.

Legault, R., jt. auth. see Biberman, L. M.

Legault, Rejean, jt. ed. see Goldhagen, Sarah Williams.

Legault, Robert, tr. see Emilio, Juan.

Legault, Robert, tr. see Noe & Barreiro.

Legault, Robert, tr. see Noe & Paya.

Legault, Robert, tr. see Paya & Revilla.

Legault, Robert, tr. see Prado, Miguelanxo.

Legault, Robert, tr. see Segrelles, Vicente.

Legault, Robert, tr. see Tobalina.

Legault, Roch, jt. ed. see McKercher, B. J. C.

Legay, Gilbert. Atlas of Indians of North America. LC 95-13019.Tr. of Atlas des Indiens d'Amerique du Nord. (Illus.). 96p. (YA). (gr. 8 up). 1995. 16.95 (*0-8120-6515-8*) Barron.

— Atlas of Indians of North America.Tr. of Atlas des Indiens d'Amerique du Nord. (Illus.). 96p. (YA). (gr. 6 up). 1997. lib. bdg. 25.95 (*1-56674-206-4*) Forest Hse.

LeGaye, Rocky. Authentic Civil War Battle Sites. 82p. 1991. pap. 15.95 (*0-941620-42-5*) Carson Ent.

— Gold! the ABC's of Panning. (Illus.). 96p. 1987. pap. 9.95 (*0-941620-04-2*) Carson Ent.

Lege, Cassie. What Does Heaven Look Like? A View of Heaven Through the Eyes of a Child. (Illus.). 58p. 1999. pap. 8.00 (*0-7392-0045-3*, PO2835) Morris Pubng.

Legeay, Yves, jt. auth. see Moraillon, Robert.

Legend. Shannara. 1995. pap. 33.00 (*1-880520-21-4*) Legend Enter.

Legend Enterprises Staff, ed. & photos by see American Horse Shows Association Staff.

Legend Staff. The Lost Adventures. 1996. 22.50 (*1-880520-28-1*) Legend Enter.

LeGendre. Mammals' Size & Climate. 1996. pap. text 19.95 (*0-226-47066-0*); lib. bdg. 54.50 (*0-226-47065-2*) U Ch Pr.

Legendre, A. F. Modern Chinese Civilization. Jones, Elsie M., tr. from FRE. LC 72-7076. (Select Bibliographies Reprint Ser.). 1977. reprint ed. 23.95 (*0-8369-6946-4*) Ayer.

Legendre, Geraldine. Topics in French Syntax. rev. ed. Hankamer, Jorge, ed. LC 93-46502. (Outstanding Dissertations in Linguistics Ser.). (Illus.). 346p. 1994. text 20.00 (*0-8153-1689-5*) Garland.

Legendre, L., jt. ed. see Legendre, P.

Legendre, Louis, jt. auth. see Legendre, Pierre.

Legendre, P. & Legendre, L., eds. Developments in Numerical Ecology. (NATO ASI Series G: Vol. 14). 600p. 1987. 245.00 (*0-387-16086-8*) Spr-Verlag.

Legendre, Philippe. Kids Can Draw African Animals. (Kids Can Draw Ser.). 24p. (J). (ps-2). 1997. pap. 3.95 (*1-56010-275-6*, KCD7) W Foster Pub.

— Kids Can Draw Animals of the World. (Kids Can Draw Ser.). 24p. (J). (ps-2). 1997. pap. 3.95 (*1-56010-276-4*, KCD8) W Foster Pub.

— Kids Can Draw Arctic Animals. (Kids Can Draw Ser.). 24p. (J). (ps-2). 1997. pap. 3.95 (*1-56010-269-1*, KCD1) W Foster Pub.

— Kids Can Draw Birds of the World. (Kids Can Draw Ser.). 24p. (J). (ps-2). 1997. pap. 3.95 (*1-56010-277-2*, KCD9) W Foster Pub.

— Kids Can Draw Dinosaurs. (Kids Can Draw Ser.). 24p. (J). (ps-2). 1997. pap. 3.95 (*1-56010-271-3*, KCD3) W Foster Pub.

— Kids Can Draw Fairy Tales. (Kids Can Draw Ser.). 24p. (J). (ps-2). 1997. pap. 3.95 (*1-56010-278-0*, KCD10) W Foster Pub.

— Kids Can Draw Farm Animals. (Kids Can Draw Ser.). 24p. (J). (ps-2). 1997. pap. 3.95 (*1-56010-280-2*, KCD12) W Foster Pub.

— Kids Can Draw Favorite Pets. (Kids Can Draw Ser.). 24p. (J). (ps-2). 1997. pap. 3.95 (*1-56010-272-1*, KCD4) W Foster Pub.

— Kids Can Draw Forest Animals. (Kids Can Draw Ser.). 24p. (J). (ps-2). 1997. pap. 3.95 (*1-56010-270-5*, KCD2) W Foster Pub.

— Kids Can Draw the Circus. (Kids Can Draw Ser.). 24p. (J). (ps-2). 1997. pap. 3.95 (*1-56010-279-9*, KCD11) W Foster Pub.

— Kids Can Draw the Mountains. (Kids Can Draw Ser.). 24p. (J). (ps-2). 1997. pap. 3.95 (*1-56010-274-8*, KCD6) W Foster Pub.

— Kids Can Draw the Ocean. (Kids Can Draw Ser.). 24p. (J). (ps-2). 1997. pap. 3.95 (*1-56010-273-X*, KCD5) W Foster Pub.

Legendre, Pierre. Ecrits Juridiques du Moyen Age Occidental. (Collected Studies: No. CS280). 280p. (C). 1988. reprint ed. text 113.95 (*0-86078-228-X*, Pub. by Variorum) Ashgate Pub Co.

***Legendre, Pierre.** Numerical Ecology. 2nd ed. (Developments in Environmental Modelling Ser.). 1998. 150.00 (*0-444-89249-4*) Elsevier.

Legendre, Pierre & Legendre, Louis. Numerical Ecology. 2nd ed. LC 98-45198. (Developments in Environmental Modelling Ser.: Vol. 20). 853p. 1998. pap. 73.50 (*0-444-89250-8*) Elsevier.

Legendre, Renald. Dictionnaire Actuel de l'Education. 2nd ed. (ENG & FRE.). 679p. 1993. 79.95 (*0-8288-1387-6*, M 520) Fr & Eur.

Legenfelder, Helga. Handbuch der Universitaten und Fachochschulen Bundesrepublik Deutschland, Osterreich, Schweiz. 9th ed. 1999. write for info. (*3-598-11388-9*) K G Saur Verlag.

Legenfelder, Helga, ed. World Guide to Libraries, 2 vols., Set. 14th ed. 1300p. 1999. 425.00 (*3-598-20725-5*) K G Saur Verlag.

Legenhausen, Gary, ed. & tr. see Taleqani, Mahmud & Mutahhari, Murtada.

Legenhausen, Gary, ed. & tr. see Talequani, Mahmud & Mutahhari, Murtada.

Legent, F., ed. Use of Ciprofloxacin in the Treatment of Chronic Otitis & Sinusitis & Malignant External Otitis. (Journal: Chemotherapy: Vol. 40, Suppl. 1, 1994). (Illus.). iv, 42p. 1994. pap. 14.00 (*3-8055-6071-0*) S Karger.

Leger, A., et al, eds. Polycyclic Aromatic Hydrocarbons & Astrophysics. 1986. text 184.00 (*90-277-2361-3*) Kluwer Academic.

Leger, Daniel W. & Dienstbier, Richard, eds. Nebraska Symposium on Motivation, 1987: Comparative Perspectives in Modern Psychology. LC 53-11655. (Nebraska Symposium on Motivation Ser.: Vol. 35). xvi, 327p. 1988. text 45.00 (*0-8032-2880-5*); pap. text 25.00 (*0-8032-7926-4*) U of Nebr Pr.

Leger, Dawn, jt. auth. see Bain, Beverly K.

Leger, Diane C. & Churcher, Dar. Maxine's Tree. (Illus.). 32p. (Orig.). (J). (gr. 1-4). 1990. pap. 5.95 (*0-920501-38-9*) Orca Bk Pubs.

Leger, E., et al. Second Career Vocations. O'Hara, F. & Lescoe, F., trs. from FRE. 20p. (C). 1986. pap. 1.50 (*0-910919-02-X*) Mariel Pubns.

Leger, Eugene. Complete Building Construction. 4th ed. 736p. 1994. pap. 39.95 (*0-02-517882-2*, Aude IN) IDG Bks.

Leger, Francois, jt. ed. see Pikulik, Ivan I.

Leger, Frederic J. Beyond the Therapeutic Relationship: Behavioral, Biological, & Cognitive Foundations of Psychotherapy. LC 97-16875. 330p. 1997. 49.95 (*0-7890-0291-4*); pap. 24.95 (*0-7890-0292-2*) Haworth Pr.

Leger, Jacques N. Haiti: Her History & Her Detractors. 1976. lib. bdg. 59.95 (*0-8490-1926-5*) Gordon Pr.

— Haiti, Her History & Her Detractors. LC 78-107482. 372p. 1970. reprint ed. lib. bdg. 35.00 (*0-8371-3784-5*, LEH&) Greenwood.

Leger, Jean-Claude. Le Genre Hymenochaete Leveille. (Bibliotheca Mycologica: Vol. 171). (FRE., Illus.). 320p. 1998. 83.00 (*3-443-59073-X*, Pub. by Gebruder Borntraeger) Balogh.

Leger Kelly, D. St., see St. Leger Kelly, D.

Leger, Marie, ed. Aboriginal Peoples: Toward Self-Government. 186p. 1995. 38.99 (*1-55164-011-2*, Pub. by Black Rose); pap. 19.99 (*1-55164-010-4*, Pub. by Black Rose) Consort Bk Sales.

Leger, Mary C. The Catholic Indian Missions in Maine (1611-1820) LC 73-3563. (Catholic University of America. Studies in Romance Languages & Literatures: No. 8). reprint ed. 39.50 (*0-404-57758-X*) AMS Pr.

Leger-Orine, Monique, jt. ed. see Schneider, Jean.

***Legere, James.** The Hare of the Hollow. (Illus.). 42p. (J). (ps-7). 1998. pap. 16.95 (*0-9677090-0-8*) We Believe Pubng.

Legere, Kersten. Dictionary German to Swahili. 3rd ed. (GER & SWA.). 267p. 1996. 95.00 (*0-320-00514-3*) Fr & Eur.

— Woerterbuch Deutsch-Swahili. (GER & SWA.). 267p. 1990. 65.00 (*0-7859-8311-2*, 3324005051) Fr & Eur.

Legere, Thomas E. Thoughts on the Run: Glimpses of Wholistic Spirituality. 144p. 1983. 7.95 (*0-86683-698-5*) Harper SF.

LeGeros, J P, jt. ed. see LeGeros, R Z.

LeGeros, R Z & LeGeros, J P, eds. Bioceramics 11: Proceedings of the 11th International Symposium on Ceramics in Medicine New York University, USA 5 - 8 November 1998. 800p. 148.00 (*981-02-3701-4*) World Scientific Pub.

LeGette, Bernard. LeGettes Calorie Encyclopedia. 448p. 1988. mass mkt. 5.99 (*0-446-35679-4*, Pub. by Warner Bks) Little.

— LeGette's Cholesterol Encyclopedia. 256p. (Orig.). 1989. mass mkt. 3.95 (*0-446-35092-3*, Pub. by Warner Bks) Little.

— LeGette's Guide to Fresh Food Shopping. 192p. 1985. mass mkt. 2.95 (*0-446-32421-3*, Pub. by Warner Bks) Little.

Legette, Helen. Parents, Kids & Character: 21 Strategies to Help Your Children Develop Good Character. 172p. 1998. pap. 15.95 (*1-892056-01-1*) Character Dev.

***Legewie, Jochen & Meyer-Ohle, Hendrick.** Corporate Strategies for Southeast Asia after the Crisis: A Comparison of Multinational Firms from Japan & Europe. LC 00-40447. 2000. write for info. (*0-312-23736-7*) St Martin.

Legey, Francoise. The Folklore of Morocco. Hotz, Lucy, tr. from FRE. LC 77-87639. reprint ed. 23.50 (*0-404-16428-5*) AMS Pr.

Legeza, Laszlo. Tao Magic: The Secret Language of Diagrams & Calligraphy. LC 86-51463. (Illus.). 167p. 1987. pap. 10.95 (*0-500-27062-7*, Pub. by Thames Hudson) Norton.

Legeza, Laszlo, jt. auth. see Rawson, Philip.

***LeGeza, Valentine.** Emigrants' Fairy Tales. Golikova, Arina, ed. LC 99-62684. (Illus.). 195p. 1999. pap. 9.99 (*0-9672614-0-6*) OKHO Pubg Co.

Legg, A. K. Haynes Audi 4000 Owners Workshop Manual, No. 165: '80-'87. 17.95 (*1-85010-242-2*) Haynes Manuals.

— Haynes Nissan Pulsar Owners Workshop Manual, No. 876: 1983 thru 1986. rev. ed. (Illus.). 301p. 1987. pap. 16.95 (*1-85010-322-4*) Haynes Manuals.

— Haynes Saab 99 Owners Workshop Manual, No. 247: 1969-1980. 1990. 16.95 (*0-85696-844-7*) Haynes Manuals.

Legg, A. K. & Haynes, J. H. Haynes BMW 528i Owners Workshop Manual: 1975-1980, No. 632. 16.95 (*0-85696-632-0*) Haynes Manuals.

Legg, A. K., jt. auth. see Haynes, J. H.

Legg, A. K., jt. auth. see Haynes, John Harold.

Legg, Adrian. Customising Your Electric Guitar. (Illus.). 64p. 1983. pap. 14.95 (*0-8256-2262-X*, AM40973) Music Sales.

***Legg, Adrian.** Pickin' 'n' Squintin' A Collection of 12 Fingerstyle Guitar Solos. 88p. 2000. otabind 19.95 (*1-57560-255-5*, Pub. by Cherry Lane) H Leonard.

Legg, Alicia & Smalley, Mary B., eds. Painting & Sculpture in the Museum of Modern Art: Catalog of the Collection, 1987. rev. ed. 136p. 1989. pap. 12.50 (*0-87070-572-5*) Mus of Modern Art.

Legg, C. R. Issues in Psychobiology. 256p. 1989. 47.50 (*0-415-01405-0*, 1091); pap. 17.95 (*0-415-01406-9*, A3367) Routledge.

Legg, Charles R. & Booth, David A., eds. Appetite: Neural & Behavioural Bases. LC 94-11806. (The European Brain & Behavior Ser.). (Illus.). 346p. 1995. text 65.00 (*0-19-854787-0*) OUP.

Legg, Gerald. Amazing Animals. LC 93-36703. (X-Ray Picture Bks.). (Illus.). 48p. (J). (gr. 5-8). 1994. lib. bdg. 24.00 (*0-531-14285-X*) Watts.

— From Caterpillar to Butterfly. (Life Cycles Ser.). (Illus.). 32p. (J). (gr. k-2). 1998. pap. 6.95 (*0-531-15332-0*) Watts.

— From Egg to Chicken. (Life Cycles Ser.). (Illus.). 32p. (J). (gr. k-2). 1998. pap. 6.95 (*0-531-15333-9*) Watts.

— From Seed to Sunflower. LC 97-16668. (Life Cycles Ser.). (Illus.). 32p. (J). 1998. 20.00 (*0-531-14492-5*) Watts.

— From Seed to Sunflower. (Life Cycles Ser.). (Illus.). 32p. (J). (gr. k-2). 1998. pap. 6.95 (*0-531-15334-7*) Watts.

— From Tadpole to Frog. (Life Cycles Ser.). 32p. 1998. 20.00 (*0-531-14491-7*) Watts.

— From Tadpole to Frog. (Life Cycles Ser.). (Illus.). 32p. (J). (gr. k-2). 1998. pap. 6.95 (*0-531-15335-5*) Watts.

— Incredible Creatures. LC 94-26901. (X-Ray Picture Bks.). (Illus.). 48p. (J). (gr. 5-8). 1995. lib. bdg. 24.00 (*0-531-14346-5*) Watts.

— Lifecyles, 4, Set. 1998. 80.00 (*0-531-19440-X*) Watts.

— Sharks. LC 97-5964. (Worldwise Ser.). 40p. (J). 1998. 23.00 (*0-531-14461-5*) Watts.

— Sharks. (Worldwise Ser.). (Illus.). 40p. (J). (gr. 2 up). 1998. pap. 7.00 (*0-531-15318-5*) Watts.

Legg, Gerald & Salariya, David. From Caterpillar to Butterfly. LC 97-14560. (Life Cycles Ser.). (Illus.). 32p. (J). 1998. 20.00 (*0-531-14493-3*) Watts.

— From Egg to Chicken. LC 97-14547. (Life Cycles Ser.). (Illus.). 32p. (J). 1998. 20.00 (*0-531-14490-9*) Watts.

Legg, J. Any Objections. 1995. pap. 4.99 (*0-85234-331-0*, Pub. by Evangelical Pr) P & R Pubng.

***Legg, J. Wickham.** The Westminster Missal. 1200p. 2000. 170.00 (*1-870252-12-8*, Henry Bradshaw Soc) Boydell & Brewer.

Legg, Jackie, ed. William & Mary Cookbook: A Treasury of Recipes & Memories of Good Eating at the College of William & Mary in Virginia Collected by Alumni & Friends. 276p. 1993. pap. 16.93 (*0-9615670-5-8*) Soc Alu Wm.

Legg, John. Apache Coffin. 1991. mass mkt. 3.50 (*0-8217-3476-8*, Zebra Kensgtn) Kensgtn Pub Corp.

— Blood in the Snow. 304p. 1993. mass mkt. 3.50 (*0-8217-4136-5*, Zebra Kensgtn) Kensgtn Pub Corp.

— Collecting Shane Stevens a.k.a. J. W. Rider. 88p. 1995. pap. 24.95 (*0-9644069-0-X*) Black Diamond.

— Shoshoni Vengeance. 304p. 1993. mass mkt. 3.50 (*0-8217-4334-1*, Zebra Kensgtn) Kensgtn Pub Corp.

— Vigilante Coffin. 304p. 1993. mass mkt. 3.50 (*0-8217-4228-0*, Zebra Kensgtn) Kensgtn Pub Corp.

— When We Don't Understand. 1992. pap. 6.99 (*0-85234-291-8*, Pub. by Evangelical Pr) P & R Pubng.

Legg, John D. Dear Tom: Letters to an Enquiring Christian. 1990. pap. 4.99 (*0-85234-275-6*, Pub. by Evangelical Pr) P & R Pubng.

Legg, John P. Guns of Arizona. 1992. mass mkt. 3.50 (*0-8217-3753-8*, Zebra Kensgtn) Kensgtn Pub Corp.

— Shinin' Trails: A Possibles Bag of Fur Trade Trivia. Smith, Monte, ed. (Illus.). 112p. 1988. per. 8.95 (*0-943604-20-6*, BOO/13) Eagles View.

— Showdown at Six-Gun Mine. (gr. k). 1989. mass mkt. 2.95 (*0-8217-2660-9*, Zebra Kensgtn) Kensgtn Pub Corp.

Legg, Keith R. Politics in Modern Greece. LC 69-18495. xii, 367p. 1969. 47.50 (*0-8047-0705-7*) Stanford U Pr.

Legg, Linda. Touring in Your Sea Kayak. (Nuts 'n Bolts Ser.). (Illus.). 32p. 1998. pap. 4.95 (*0-89732-263-0*) Menasha Ridge.

Legg, Marie L. Newspapers & Nationalism. LC 99-191735. 240p. 1999. boxed set 49.50 (*1-85182-341-7*, Pub. by Four Cts Pr) Intl Spec Bk.

***Legg, Marie-Louise.** Alfred Webb. 96p. 2000. pap. 12.95 (*1-85918-202-X*, Pub. by Cork Univ) Stylus Pub VA.

Legg, Mary L. The Synge Letters: Bishop Edward Synge to His Daughter Alicia. LC 96-133763. 576p. 1996. 70.00 (*1-874675-49-X*) Dufour.

L

An Asterisk (*) at the beginning of an entry indicates that the title is appearing for the first time.

Legg, Merle A. & Reid, Lynne M. Pulmonary Pathology: Proceedings of the 46th Annual Anatomic Pathology Slide Seminar. LC 86-7992. 156p. 1986. pap. text 35.00 (*0-89189-178-1*) Am Soc Clinical.

Legg, Michael, ed. Research Monograph, 1988, No. 17. 70p. 1988. pap. 7.50 (*1-879931-00-1*) Natl Assoc Interp.

Legg, Phillip R. Tales for Telling: Stories for Childrens Ministry, Vol. 2. (Illus.). 76p. (Orig.). (J). 1996. pap. text 13.50 (*0-8309-0749-1*) Herald Pub Hse.

Legg, Phyllida, jt. auth. see Harrold, Robert.

Legg, Sharon, jt. auth. see Griffin, Susan.

Legg, Stuart, jt. auth. see Klingender, F. D.

Legg, Sue M., et al, eds. Cognitive Assessment of Language & Math Outcomes. LC 90-36747. (Advances in Discourse Processes Ser.: Vol. 36). 304p. (C). 1990. text 78.50 (*0-89391-541-6*) Ablx Pub.

Legg, Sue M., jt. auth. see Wolcott, Willa.

Legg, W. Dorr, ed. Homophile Studies in Theory & Practice. 464p. (Orig.). 1994. 27.95 (*1-879194-16-3*); pap. 14.95 (*1-879194-17-1*) GLB Pubs.

***Leggat, Alexandra.** This Is Me since Yesterday. LC 99-488149. 64p. 1999. pap. 15.00 (*1-55245-036-8*, Pub. by Coach Hse Bks) SPD-Small Pr Dist.

Leggat, Bonnie-Alise. Punt, Pass & Point! Thatch, Nancy R., ed. LC 92-17598. (Books for Students by Students). (Illus.). 26p. (J). (gr. 3-5). 1992. lib. bdg. 15.95 (*0-933849-39-7*) Landmark Edns.

Leggatt, Alexander. English Drama 1590-1660. (Literature in English Ser.). 312p. (C). 1988. pap. text 28.50 (*0-582-49311-0*, 73571) Longman.

— English Stage Comedy, 1490-1990: The Persistence of a Genre. LC 98-12864. 224p. (C). 1998. 75.00 (*0-415-18936-5*); pap. 24.99 (*0-415-18937-3*) Routledge.

— Introduction To English Renaissance Comedy. LC 99-218153. 1999. 69.95 (*0-7190-4964-4*, Pub. by Manchester Univ Pr); pap. text 19.95 (*0-7190-4965-2*, Pub. by Manchester Univ Pr) St Martin.

— Shakespeare's Political Drama: The History Plays & the Roman Plays. 288p. (C). 1989. pap. 27.99 (*0-415-03888-X*) Routledge.

Leggatt, D. V., jt. auth. see Leggatt, P. O.

Leggatt, Jeremy, tr. see Bauby, Jean-Dominique.

Leggatt, Jeremy, tr. see Briant, Pierre.

Leggatt, Jeremy, tr. see Duchene, Herve.

Leggatt, Jeremy, tr. see Gerber, Alain.

Leggatt, Jeremy, tr. see Levy, Marc.

Leggatt, Jeremy, tr. see Raspail, Jean.

Leggatt, P. O. & Leggatt, D. V. The Healing Wells: Cornish Cults & Customs. (C). 1989. 45.00 (*1-85022-033-6*, Pub. by Dyllansow Truran) St Mut.

Leggatt, Stuart, ed. & tr. see Aristotle.

Legge, Allan H., jt. ed. see Krupa, Sagar V.

Legge, David. Bamboozled. LC 94-18647. (Illus.). 32p. (J). (ps-2). 1995. 14.95 (*0-590-47989-X*) Scholastic Inc.

Legge, David, jt. auth. see Barber, Paul J.

Legge, David R., jt. auth. see McCormack, John.

Legge, Debbie, jt. auth. see Brooman, Simon.

Legge, Elizabeth M. Max Ernst: The Psychoanalytic Sources. Foster, Stephen, ed. LC 89-31850. (Studies in the Fine Arts: The Avant-Garde: No. 67). 245p. reprint ed. 76.00 (*0-8357-1964-2*, 207073100004) Bks Demand.

Legge, Gordon. I Love Me. LC 95-215624. 216p. (Orig.). 1994. 15.95 (*0-7486-6184-0*, Pub. by Polygon) Subterranean Co.

— In Between Talking about the Football. 160p. 1997. reprint ed. pap. 15.95 (*0-7486-6112-3*, Pub. by Polygon) Subterranean Co.

Legge, J. D. Intellectuals & Nationalism in Indonesia No. 68: A Study of the Following Recruited by Sutan Sjahrir. (Modern Indonesia Project Ser.: Vol. 68). 159p. (Orig.). (C). 1988. pap. 8.00 (*0-87763-034-8*) Cornell SE Asia.

Legge, James. I Ching: Book of Changes. LC 95-49473. 448p. 1996. 9.99 (*0-517-14990-7*) Random.

— The Sacred Books of China, 6 vols. 1975. 1800.00 (*0-317-00108-6*) Krishna Pr.

— Works of Mencius. 587p. 1990. pap. 12.95 (*0-486-26375-4*) Dover.

Legge, James, tr. The Chinese Classics, 4 vols., Set. (CHI & ENG.). 1991. reprint ed. 135.00 (*957-638-038-3*, Pub. by SMC Pub) Antique Collect.

— The Ch'un Ts'ew with the Tso Chuen, Vol. IV. (CHI & ENG.). 1991. reprint ed. 35.00 (*957-638-042-1*, Pub. by SMC Pub) Antique Collect.

— Four Books of the Chinese Classics: Confucian Analects; Great Learning; Doctrine of the Mean, Works of Mencius, 4 vols., Vol. I. (CHI & ENG.). 1991. 35.00 (*957-638-039-1*, Pub. by SMC Pub) Antique Collect.

— The I Ching. 470p. 1992. 24.95 (*1-871948-60-6*) Heian Intl.

— I Ching. 2nd ed. 448p. 1963. pap. 7.95 (*0-486-21062-6*) Dover.

— A Record of Buddhistic Kingdoms. (C). 1991. 23.50 (*0-685-50018-7*, Pub. by M Manoharial) S Asia.

— The She King: or The Book of Poetry, Vol. III. (CHI & ENG.). 1991. reprint ed. 35.00 (*957-638-041-3*, Pub. by SMC Pub) Antique Collect.

— The Shoo King: or The Book of Historical Documents, Vol. II. (CHI & ENG.). 1991. reprint ed. 35.00 (*957-638-040-5*, Pub. by SMC Pub) Antique Collect.

— Tao Te Ching: An Illustrated Journey. LC 93-39655. (Illus.). 104p. 1994. 12.95 (*0-8212-2075-6*, Pub. by Bulfinch Pr) Little.

Legge, James, ed. see Confucius.

Legge, James, tr. see Confucius.

Legge, James, tr. see Lao Tze.

Legge, James, tr. see Muller, F. Max, ed.

Legge, James, tr. see Streep, Peg, ed.

Legge, James G. Rhyme & Revolution in Germany: A Study in German History, Life, Literature & Character. LC 72-126646. reprint ed. 33.45 (*0-404-03947-2*) AMS Pr.

Legge, Jerome S., Jr. Abortion Policy: An Evaluation of the Consequences for Maternal & Infant Health. LC 84-16356. 182p. (C). 1985. text 64.50 (*0-87395-958-2*); pap. text 21.95 (*0-87395-959-0*) State U NY Pr.

***Legge, John.** Product Management: Sharpening the Competitive Edge. 2000. pap. 52.95 (*0-7329-5408-8*, Pub. by Macmill Educ) Paul & Co Pubs.

Legge, John & Hindle, Kevin. Entrepreneurship: How Innovators Create the Future. (Illus.). 608p. 1998. 89.95 (*0-7329-3940-2*, Pub. by Macmill Educ); pap. 44.95 (*0-7329-3943-7*, Pub. by Macmill Educ) Paul & Co Pubs.

***Legge, John D.** Australian Outlook: A History of the Australian Institute of International Affairs. 250p. 2000. pap. 29.95 (*1-86508-095-0*, Pub. by Allen & Unwin Pty) Paul & Co Pubs.

Legge, Marilyn J. The Grace of Difference: A Canadian Feminist Theological Ethic. LC 92-16229. (American Academy of Religion Academy Ser.: Vol. 80). 312p. 1992. 29.95 (*1-55540-736-6*, 010180); pap. 19.95 (*1-55540-737-4*) OUP.

Legge, Mary D. Anglo-Norman Literature & Its Background. LC 78-17093. 389p. 1978. reprint ed. lib. bdg. 35.00 (*0-313-20588-4*, LEAL, Greenwood Pr) Greenwood.

Legge, Nancy J., jt. auth. see DiSanza, James R.

Legge, Ronald. Find Your Ancestors. 32p. 1987. pap. 25.00 (*0-85937-129-8*, Pub. by K Mason Pubns Ltd) St Mut.

Legge, Rupert. A Dangerous Age. 288p. 1996. mass mkt. 8.95 (*0-7472-4892-3*, Pub. by Headline Bk Pub) Trafalgar.

— A Dangerous Age. large type ed. (Black Satin Romance Ser.). 304p. 1996. 27.99 (*1-86110-011-6*) Ulverscroft.

Leggell, Chris & Teachout, Woden. Tracks & Trails: An Insider's Guide to the Best Cross-Country Skiing in the Northeast. LC 96-109294. (Illus.). 275p. 1995. pap. 14.95 (*0-933603-41-X*) Dawbert Pr.

Leggeri, Aldo, et al. Intraoperative Choledochoscopy. 116p. 1983. text 48.00 (*1-57235-041-5*) Piccin Nuova.

Legget, Robert F. The Ottawa River Canals & the Defence of British North America. (Illus.). 308p. 1988. text 35.00 (*0-8020-5794-2*) U of Toronto Pr.

— Ottawa Waterway: Gateway to a Continent. LC 75-6780. (Illus.). 303p. reprint ed. pap. 94.00 (*0-8357-8258-1*, 203405000088) Bks Demand.

— Rideau Waterway. LC 72-197084. 279p. reprint ed. pap. 86.50 (*0-608-15656-6*, 203191600077) Bks Demand.

— Rideau Waterway. rev. ed. LC 72-197084. 279p. reprint ed. pap. 86.50 (*0-608-12882-1*, 2023644) Bks Demand.

— Rideau Waterway. 2nd ed. (Illus.). 320p. 1986. pap. 17.95 (*0-8020-6591-0*); text 32.50 (*0-8020-2573-0*) U of Toronto Pr.

Legget, Robert F., ed. Geology under Cities. LC 82-20991. (Reviews in Engineering Geology Ser.: No. 5). (Illus.). 141p. reprint ed. pap. 43.80 (*0-7837-1848-9*, 204204800001) Bks Demand.

Legget, Robert F., ed. see Geological Society of America Staff.

Legget, Trevor. Fingers & Moons. 200p. 1995. pap. 10.95 (*0-946672-07-5*, Pub. by Buddhist Pub) Assoc Pubs Grp.

Leggett. A Guide to Effective Composition. 2nd ed. 1989. pap. 13.50 (*0-13-949785-4*) P-H.

Leggett, Abraham. Narrative of Major Abraham Leggett. LC 70-140871. (Eyewitness Accounts of the American Revolution Ser.). 1971. reprint ed. 16.95 (*0-405-01215-2*) Ayer.

Leggett, Anthony J., jt. ed. see Kagan, Yu A.

Leggett, Anthony J., tr. see Migdal, Arkadii B.

Leggett, B. J. Early Stevens: The Nietzschean Intertext. LC 91-34864. 285p. 1992. text 42.95 (*0-8223-1201-8*) Duke.

***Leggett, B. J.** Larkin's Blues: Jazz, Popular Music & Poetry. LC 98-43704. 208p. 1999. 45.00 (*0-8071-2342-0*) La State U Pr.

Leggett, Bobby J. Houseman's Land of Lost Content: A Critical Study of a Shropshire Lad. LC 71-100407. 172p. reprint ed. pap. 53.40 (*0-8357-8605-6*, 203500200091) Bks Demand.

— The Poetic Art of A. E. Housman: Theory & Practice. LC 77-15792. 173p. reprint ed. pap. 53.70 (*0-7837-6032-9*, 204584500008) Bks Demand.

— Wallace Stevens & Poetic Theory: Conceiving the Supreme Fiction. LC 86-16125. 236p. 1987. reprint ed. pap. 73.20 (*0-608-00292-5*, 205932000008) Bks Demand.

Leggett, Bobby J., jt. ed. see Serio, John N.

Leggett, Conway, & Co. Staff. The History of Marion County, Ohio. (Illus.). 915p. 1992. reprint ed. pap. 50.00 (*1-55613-549-1*) Heritage Bk.

— History of Wyandot Co., OH Vol. 2: A History of Its Townships. (Illus.). 627p. 1994. pap. 37.00 (*0-7884-0079-7*) Heritage Bk.

Leggett, Conway, & Co. Staff, ed. The History of Wyandot County, OH Vol. 1: A General History of the County. (Illus.). 297p. 1994. pap. text 22.00 (*0-7884-0061-4*) Heritage Bk.

Leggett, David, jt. auth. see Leggett, Kim.

Leggett, David J., ed. Computational Methods for the Determination of Formation Constants. LC 85-16991. (Modern Inorganic Chemistry Ser.). (Illus.). 494p. (C). 1985. text 167.00 (*0-306-41957-2*, Kluwer Plenum) Kluwer Academic.

Leggett, Glenn H., et al. Prentice Hall Handbook for Writers. 10th ed. LC 87-25927. Date not set. write for info. (*0-13-695728-5*) P-H.

Leggett, Grace P. Patchen: History & Genealogy of the Patchin-Patchen Family. Jillson, Myrtle M., ed. (Illus.). 1076p. 1995. reprint ed. pap. 145.00 (*0-8328-4816-6*); reprint ed. lib. bdg. 155.00 (*0-8328-4815-8*) Higginson Bk Co.

Leggett, Greene C. Bouvier des Flandres. (Illus.). 192p. 1995. 9.95 (*0-7938-0181-8*, KW168) TFH Pubns.

Leggett, J. K. Marine Clastic Sediment. 1987. text 265.00 (*0-86010-864-3*) Kluwer Academic.

Leggett, J. K., ed. Marine Clastic Sedimentology. (C). 1987. lib. bdg. 105.00 (*0-86010-897-X*, Pub. by Graham & Trotman) Kluwer Academic.

Leggett, Jeremy. El Calentamiento del Planeta (Global Warming) Informe de Greenpeace (The Greenpeace Report) (Ciencia para Todos Ser.). (SPA.). 523p. 1997. pap. text 39.99 (*968-16-5108-1*, Pub. by Fondo) Continental Bk.

Leggett, John. Race, Class & Political Consciousness. 243p. 1972. pap. 11.95 (*0-87073-257-9*) Schenkman Bks Inc.

— Race, Class, & Political Consciousness. 243p. 1972. boxed set 34.95 (*0-87073-256-0*) Transaction Pubs.

***Leggett, John.** Ross & Tom: Two American Tragedies. (Illus.). 464p. 2000. pap. 17.50 (*0-306-80992-3*, Pub. by Da Capo) HarpC.

Leggett, John C. Mining the Fields: Farmworkers Fight Back. (Illus.). 133p. (Orig.). (C). 1991. text 34.95 (*0-9625270-0-9*); pap. text 24.95 (*0-9625270-1-7*) Raritan Inst.

Leggett, John C. & Malm, Suzanne. The Eighteen Stages of Love: The Natural History, Fragrance, Celebration & Chase. Reynolds, Larry T., ed. LC 95-7515. (Reynolds Sociology Ser.). (Illus.). 270p. 1995. text 34.95 (*1-882289-34-X*); pap. text 24.95 (*1-882289-33-1*) Gen Hall.

***Leggett, Kim.** Leggetts' Antiques Atlas 2000: East. LC 98-34759. (Illus.). 418p. 1999. pap. 18.00 (*0-609-80490-1*, Three Riv Pr) Crown Pub Group.

— Leggetts' Antiques Atlas West 2000: The Guide to Antiquing in America. (Illus.). 512p. 1999. pap. 18.00 (*0-609-80492-8*, Three Riv Pr) Crown Pub Group.

Leggett, Kim & Leggett, David. The Antique Atlas. LC 96-93141. (Illus.). (Orig.). 1997. pap. 18.95 (*0-9656920-1-9*) Rainy Day TN.

Leggett, Kim & Leggett, David. The Antique Atlas - 1998. 2nd rev. ed. (Illus.). 640p. 1997. pap. 24.95 (*0-9656920-2-7*) Rainy Day TN.

Leggett, Kim & Leggett, David. Leggetts' Antiques Atlas West, 2000 Edition: The Guide to Antiquing in America. (Illus.). 512p. 1999. pap. 18.00 (*0-609-80498-7*, Three Riv Pr) Crown Pub Group.

Leggett, Linda R. & Andrews, Linda G. The Rose-Colored Glasses: Melanie Adjusts to Poor Vision. LC 79-12501. (Illus.). 32p. (J). (gr. 3 up). 1979. 16.95 (*0-87705-408-8*, Kluwer Acad Hman Sci) Kluwer Academic.

Leggett, M. D., ed. Subject-Matter Index of Patents for Inventions Issued by the United States Patent Office from 1790 to 1873, Inclusive, 3 vols., Set. LC 75-24110. (America in Two Centuries Ser.). 1976. reprint ed. 173.95 (*0-405-07737-8*) Ayer.

— Subject-Matter Index of Patents for Inventions Issued by the United States Patent Office from 1790 to 1873, Inclusive, 3 vols., Vol. 1. LC 75-24110. (America in Two Centuries Ser.). 1976. reprint ed. 58.95 (*0-405-07738-6*) Ayer.

— Subject-Matter Index of Patents for Inventions Issued by the United States Patent Office from 1790 to 1873, Inclusive, 3 vols., Vol. 2. LC 75-24110. (America in Two Centuries Ser.). 1976. reprint ed. 58.95 (*0-405-07739-4*) Ayer.

— Subject-Matter Index of Patents for Inventions Issued by the United States Patent Office from 1790 to 1873, Inclusive, 3 vols., Vol. 3. LC 75-24110. (America in Two Centuries Ser.). 1976. reprint ed. 58.95 (*0-405-07740-8*) Ayer.

Leggett, Susan, jt. ed. see Morgan, Michael.

Leggett, Trevor & Apastamba. Yoga & the Discovery of the Universal Self: A Practical Guide to Changing Individual Consciousness. LC 97-51365. 180p. 1998. 22.00 (*0-7103-0615-6*, Pub. by Kegan Paul Intl) Col U Pr.

Leggett, Trevor & Sankar, Acarya. A Training Manual for Spiritual Practice: A New Revelation of the Bhagavad Gita Yogas: Based on Sankara's Commentary. LC 97-51366. 180p. 1998. 25.50 (*0-7103-0616-4*, Pub. by Kegan Paul Intl) Col U Pr.

Leggett, Trevor, ed. & tr. see Pata, Njali & Sankar, Acarya.

Leggett, Trevor P. Encounters in Yoga & Zen: Meetings of Cloth & Stone. (Illus.). 112p. 1993. pap. 12.95 (*0-8048-1909-2*) Tuttle Pubng.

— First Zen Reader. LC 60-12739. (Illus.). 236p. 1960. pap. 12.95 (*0-8048-0180-0*) Tuttle Pubng.

— Realization of the Supreme Self: The Bhagavad Gita Yogas. (Illus.). 240p. 1995. 76.50 (*0-7103-0433-1*, Pub. by Kegan Paul Intl) Col U Pr.

— Sankara on the Yoga-Sutras: The Vivarana Sub-Commentary to Vyasa-Bhasya on the Yoga-Sultras of Pantanjali. 600p. 1981. text 30.00 (*0-7103-0277-0*) Routledge.

— Second Zen Reader: The Tiger's Cave & Translations of other Zen Writings. LC 87-50163. (Illus.). 196p. (Orig.). 1988. pap. 9.95 (*0-8048-1525-9*) Tuttle Pubng.

— Shogi: Japan's Game of Strategy. (Illus.). 100p. 1993. pap. 16.95 (*0-8048-1903-3*) Tuttle Pubng.

— The Spirit of Budo: Old Traditions for Present-Day Life. LC 96-14956. 128p. 1996. 42.50 (*0-7103-0562-1*, Pub. by Kegan Paul Intl) Col U Pr.

— Three Ages of Zen: Samurai, Feudal & Modern. 192p. 1993. pap. 12.95 (*0-8048-1898-3*) Tuttle Pubng.

— The Tiger's Cave: And Translations of Other Zen Writings. 192p. 1995. pap. 9.95 (*0-8048-2021-X*) Tuttle Pubng.

— Zen & the Ways. LC 87-50165. (Illus.). 258p. 1987. pap. 12.95 (*0-8048-1524-0*) Tuttle Pubng.

Leggett, Trevor P., tr. Sankara on the Yoga-Sutras: The Vivarana Sub-Commentary to Vyasa-Bhasya, 2 vols., 1. 220p. 1983. 30.00 (*0-7100-0826-0*, Routledge Thoemms) Routledge.

— Sankara on the Yoga-Sutras: The Vivarana Sub-Commentary to Vyasa-Bhasya, 2 vols., 2. 220p. 1983. 30.00 (*0-7100-9539-2*, Routledge Thoemms) Routledge.

Leggett, William. Collection of the Political Writings of William Leggett. LC 76-125702. (American Journalists Ser.). 1971. reprint ed. 30.95 (*0-405-01681-6*) Ayer.

— Democratick Editorials: Essays in Jacksonian Political Economy. White, Lawrence H., ed. LC 83-24893. 432p. (C). 1984. 12.00 (*0-86597-036-X*); pap. 6.00 (*0-86597-037-8*) Liberty Fund.

Leggewie, Robert. Anthologie de la Litterature Francaise: Des Origines a la fin du Dix-Huitieme Siecle, Tome I. 3rd ed. (Illus.). 464p. (C). 1990. pap. text 38.95 (*0-19-506276-0*) OUP.

— Anthologie de la Litterature Francaise: Dix-Neuvieme et Vinqtieme Siecles, Tome 2. 3rd ed. (Illus.). 480p. (C). 1990. pap. text 38.95 (*0-19-506277-9*) OUP.

***Legghorn, Tomhorn.** Hillbilly Dikshunery: The Tomhorn Legghorn Complete. LC 00-190678. (Illus.). 220p. 2000. pap. 11.99 (*0-9672121-0-3*) T C Legg.

Leggitt, W. E., ed. see Iron & Steel Society of AIME Staff.

Leggo, Carl. Growing up Perpendicular on the Side of a Hill. 96p. 1994. pap. 9.95 (*1-895387-36-1*) Creative Bk Pub.

***Leggo, Carleton D.** View from My Mother's House. (Illus.). 100p. 1999. pap. 9.95 (*1-894294-06-8*, Pub. by Creative Bk Pub) Genl Dist Srvs.

Leggott, Michele, ed. see Hyde, Robin.

Leggott, Michele, jt. ed. see Williams, Mark.

Leggott, Michele J. Reading Zukofsky's "80 Flowers" LC 88-6769. 464p. 1989. text 60.00 (*0-8018-3368-X*) Johns Hopkins.

Leghorn, Lindsay. Proud of Our Feelings. LC 95-1039. (Illus.). 32p. (J). (ps-3). 1995. 11.95 (*0-945354-68-1*) Am Psychol.

Legislative Administration Staff. Dictionary of Agri-Business: Dictionnaire Permanent Entreprise Agricole. (ENG & FRE.). 1722p. 1983. 195.00 (*0-8288-1173-3*, M15326) Fr & Eur.

Legislative Administrative Staff. Permanent Fiscal Dictionary: Dictionnaire Permanent Fiscal, 2 vols. (FRE.). 5000p. 1989. 495.00 (*0-7859-4928-3*) Fr & Eur.

Legislative Affairs Commission of the Standing Com, compiled by. The Laws of the People's Republic of China, 1987-1989, Vol. 3. 361p. 1996. 60.00 (*7-03-001951-2*, Pub. by Sci Pr) Lubrecht & Cramer.

— The Laws of the People's Republic of China, 1990-1992, Vol. 4. 533p. 1996. 90.00 (*7-03-003533-X*, Pub. by Sci Pr) Lubrecht & Cramer.

— The Laws of the People's Republic of China, 1993, Vol. 5. 385p. 1996. 75.00 (*7-03-004707-9*, Pub. by Sci Pr) Lubrecht & Cramer.

Legislative Drafting Research Fund, Columbia University Staff, contrib. by. Index Digest of State Constitutions. viii, 1546p. 1993. reprint ed. 125.00 (*0-8377-2177-6*, Rothman) W S Hein.

Legislative Management Staff. 1996 Election Results Directory. 1995. 35.00 (*1-55516-772-1*, 9371) Natl Conf State Legis.

Legislative Reference Bureau Staff. Laws of Pennsylvania, 1982, Vol. 2. 818p. 1983. text 7.70 (*0-8182-0015-4*) Commonweal PA.

— Pennsylvania Consolidated Statutes, Constitution: 1984 Permanent Edition. (Orig.). (C). 1984. pap. 4.00 (*0-8182-0046-4*) Commonweal PA.

— Pennsylvania Consolidated Statutes, Title 13: Commercial Code, 1992 Edition. 310p. (C). 1992. pap. 8.50 (*0-8182-0006-5*) Commonweal PA.

— Pennsylvania Consolidated Statutes, Title 18: Crime & Offence, 1995 Edition. rev. ed. 302p. (C). 1995. pap. text 8.74 (*0-8182-0007-3*) Commonweal PA.

— Pennsylvania Consolidated Statutes, Title 20 , Decedents, Estates & Fiduciaries: 1992 Edition. 278p. (C). 1992. pap. 7.50 (*0-8182-0008-1*) Commonweal PA.

— Pennsylvania Consolidated Statutes, Title 24, Education: 1994 Permanent Edition. (Orig.). (C). 1984. pap. 4.24 (*0-8182-0043-X*) Commonweal PA.

— Pennsylvania Consolidated Statutes, Title 30, Fish: 1989 Permanent Edition. (Orig.). (C). 1989. pap. 5.00 (*0-8182-0044-8*) Commonweal PA.

— Pennsylvania Consolidated Statutes, Title 42, Judiciary & Judicial Procedure: 1995 Edition. rev. ed. 554p. (C). 1995. pap. text 10.74 (*0-8182-0010-3*) Commonweal PA.

— Pennsylvania Consolidated Statutes, Title 71, State Government: 1994 Permanent Edition. (Orig.). (C). 1994. pap. 4.24 (*0-8182-0045-6*) Commonweal PA.

Legislative Reference Bureau Staff, intro. Pennsylvania Consolidated Statutes Title: 1992 Special Edition - Names. rev. ed. 29p. 1998. pap. text 3.74 (*0-8182-0011-1*) Commonweal PA.

Legislative Reference Bureau Staff, ed. see Commonwealth of Pennsylvania Staff.

Legisoft, Inc. Staff. Willmaker 6.O Macintosh. 6th ed. 464p. 1997. pap. 49.95 incl. mac hd (*0-87337-315-4*) Nolo com.

***Legler, Dixie.** Frank Lloyd Wright: The Western Work. LC 99-12150. (Illus.). 144p. 1999. 40.00 (*0-8118-1785-7*) Chronicle Bks.

Legler, Dixie. Prairie Style: Houses & Gardens by Frank Lloyd Wright & the Prairie School. LC 99-15471. (Illus.). 208p. 1999. text 45.00 (*1-55670-931-5*) Stewart Tabori & Chang.

Legler, Gretchen. All the Powerful Invisible Things: A Sportswoman's Notebook. LC 95-14254. 208p. 1995. pap. text 12.95 (*1-878067-69-9*) Seal Pr WA.

Legler, Henry E. Walt Whitman: Yesterday & Today. LC 76-2434. (Studies in Whitman: No. 28). 1976. lib. bdg. 49.00 (*0-8383-2118-6*) M S G Haskell Hse.

An Asterisk (*) at the beginning of an entry indicates that the title is appearing for the first time.

Legler, John B. Regional Distribution of Federal Receipts & Expenditures in the 19th Century: A Quantitative Study. Bruchey, Stuart, ed. LC 76-39833. (Nineteen Seventy-Seven Dissertations Ser.). (Illus.). 1977. lib. bdg. 23.95 (*0-405-09913-4*) Ayer.

Legman, G., ed. see Randolph, Vance.

Legman, Gershon. Love & Death: A Study in Censorship. 1963. pap. 1.75 (*0-87817-012-X*) Hacker.

Legman, Gershon, tr. & intro. see Afanasyev, Alexander.

Legmann, P., jt. auth. see Burstein, M.

Legner, E. F., jt. auth. see Moore, Ian.

Legner, G. E., et al, eds. Michie's Jurisprudence for Virginia & West Virginia, 1999 Replacement: A Complete Treatise of Virginia & West Virginia Law, Vol. 4A. 485p. 1999. write for info. (*0-327-01500-4*, 7472411) LEXIS Pub.

— Michie's Jurisprudence for Virginia & West Virginia, 1999 Replacement: A Complete Treatise of Virginia & West Virginia Law, Vol. 4B. 565p. 1999. write for info. (*0-327-01501-2*, 7473411) LEXIS Pub.

***Legner, G. E., et al, eds.** Michie's Jurisprudence of Virginia & West Virginia 2000 Replacement Vol. 11B: A Complete Treatise of Virginia-West Virginia, 51 vols. 576p. 2000. write for info. (*0-327-04943-X*, 7476811) LEXIS Pub.

— Michie's Jurisprudence of Virginia & West Virginia 2000 Replacement Vol. 16: A Complete Treatise of Virginia - West Virginia. 512p. 2000. write for info. (*0-327-04941-3*, 7479211) LEXIS Pub.

Legner, G. E., jt. ed. see Divine, M. J.

Legner, Gary, et al, eds. Michie on Banks & Banking: 1999 Cumulative Supplement. 1999. pap. write for info. (*0-327-01081-9*, 5011216) LEXIS Pub.

— Michie on Banks & Banking: 1999 Cumulative Supplement, Vol. 1A. 1999. suppl. ed. write for info. (*0-327-01071-1*, 5010016) LEXIS Pub.

— Michie on Banks & Banking: 1999 Cumulative Supplement, Vol. 1B. 1999. suppl. ed. write for info. (*0-327-01072-X*, 5010116) LEXIS Pub.

— Michie on Banks & Banking: 1999 Cumulative Supplement, Vol. 2. 1999. suppl. ed. write for info. (*0-327-01073-8*, 5010216) LEXIS Pub.

— Michie on Banks & Banking: 1999 Cumulative Supplement, Vol. 3. 1999. suppl. ed. write for info. (*0-327-01074-6*, 5010316) LEXIS Pub.

— Michie on Banks & Banking: 1999 Cumulative Supplement, Vol. 4. 1999. suppl. ed. write for info. (*0-327-01075-4*, 5010416) LEXIS Pub.

— Michie on Banks & Banking: 1999 Cumulative Supplement, Vol. 5A. 1999. suppl. ed. write for info. (*0-327-01076-2*, 5010516) LEXIS Pub.

— Michie on Banks & Banking: 1999 Cumulative Supplement, Vol. 5B. 1999. suppl. ed. write for info. (*0-327-01077-0*, 5010616) LEXIS Pub.

— Michie on Banks & Banking: 1999 Cumulative Supplement, Vol. 6A. 1999. suppl. ed. write for info. (*0-327-01078-9*, 5010716) LEXIS Pub.

— Michie on Banks & Banking: 1999 Cumulative Supplement, Vol. 6B. 1999. suppl. ed. write for info. (*0-327-01079-7*, 5010816) LEXIS Pub.

— Michie on Banks & Banking: 1999 Cumulative Supplement, Vol. 8. 1999. suppl. ed. write for info. (*0-327-01080-0*, 5011016) LEXIS Pub.

Legner, Gary, jt. ed. see Divine, M. J.

Lego. Gold Robber. LC 98-214240. 32p. (J). 1998. pap. 4.95 (*0-7894-3652-3*) DK Pub Inc.

— Jewel Thief. LC 98-214259. 32p. (J). 1998. pap. 4.95 (*0-7894-3653-1*) DK Pub Inc.

— Spy Catcher. LC 98-214250. 32p. (J). 1998. pap. 4.95 (*0-7894-3654-X*) DK Pub Inc.

— Treasure Smuggler. LC 98-214254. 32p. (J). (gr. 1-5). 1998. pap. 4.95 (*0-7894-3655-8*) DK Pub Inc.

Lego, Paul G., jt. auth. see Bragg, Steven M.

Lego Puzzle Books Staff. Castle Mystery. LC 99-177285. (Lego Puzzle Bks.). 32p. (J). 1998. pap. text 4.95 (*0-7894-3728-7*) DK Pub Inc.

— The Curse of the Mummy. LC 99-177286. (Lego Puzzle Bks.). 32p. (J). 1998. pap. text 4.95 (*0-7894-3729-5*) DK Pub Inc.

— Insectoid Invasion. LC 99-179206. (Lego Puzzle Bks.). 32p. (J). 1998. pap. text 4.95 (*0-7894-3730-9*) DK Pub Inc.

Lego, Suzanne, ed. Psychiatric Nursing: A Comprehensive Reference. 2nd ed. LC 95-26303. 655p. 1996. text 60.00 (*0-397-55266-1*) Lppncott W & W.

Legocki, A. B., et al, eds. Biological Fixation of Nitrogen for Ecology & Sustainable Agriculture. LC 96-39707. (NATO ASI Series G: Ecological Sciences: Vol. 39). (Illus.). 328p. 1997. 157.95 (*3-540-62056-7*) Spr-Verlag.

LeGoff, Jacques, ed. see Tilly, Charles.

LeGoff, Oliver. Ocean Liners, Vol. 1. 1999. 19.99 (*0-7858-1086-2*) Bk Sales Inc.

— World of Caviar, Vol. 1. 1999. 19.99 (*0-7858-1084-6*) Bk Sales Inc.

LeGoffe, Claude. French for Business. Le Francais des Affaires. Livret du Professeur. 2nd ed. (Hatier Ser.). (FRE.). 29p. 1989. pap. 12.95 (*2-218-02522-1*) Schoenhof.

Legomsky, Stephen H. Immigration & Refugee Law & Policy. 2nd ed. LC 97-25015. (University Casebook Ser.). 1107p. 1997. text 41.25 (*1-56662-466-5*) Foundation Pr.

— Immigration & Refugee Law & Policy, Teacher's Manual For. 2nd ed. (University Casebook Ser.). 423p. 1997. pap. text. write for info. (*1-56662-568-8*) Foundation Pr.

— Immigration Law & Policy. (University Casebook Ser.). 1111p. (C). 1991. text 45.25 (*0-88277-943-5*) Foundation Pr.

— Immigration Law & Policy: Teacher's Manual. (University Casebook Ser.). 416p. 1991. pap. text. write for info. (*0-88277-973-7*) Foundation Pr.

— Immigration Law & Policy: 1994 Supplement. (University Casebook Ser.). 100p. 1994. 7.95 (*1-56662-205-0*) Foundation Pr.

— Specialized Justice: Courts, Administrative Tribunals, & a Cross-National Theory of Specialization. (Illus.). 140p. 1990. text 55.00 (*0-19-825429-6*) OUP.

***Legon, Anne Marie.** My Soul's on a Journey. 50p. 1999. 6.95 (*1-885206-68-2*) Cader Pubng.

***Legoski, Robert J.** General George Crook's Campaign of 1876: Newspaper Accounts of the Day. (Illus.). 188p. 2000. per. 17.00 (*0-9701424-5-5*) R J Legoski.

LeGouis, Catherine. Positivism & Imagination: Scientism & Its Limits in Emile Hennequin, Wilhelm Scherer, & Dmitrii Pisarev. LC 96-15046. 272p. 1997. 39.50 (*0-8387-5323-X*) Bucknell U Pr.

Legouis, Emile H. The Early Life of William Wordsworth, 1770-1798. Mathews, J. W., tr. 494p. 1992. reprint ed. text 60.00 (*1-870352-30-0*, Pub. by Libris); reprint ed. pap. text 25.00 (*1-870352-01-7*, Pub. by Libris) Paul & Co Pubs.

— The Early Life of William Wordsworth, 1770-1798: A Study of the Prelude. Matthews, T. W., tr. from FRE. LC 74-145138. 1971. reprint ed. 49.00 (*0-403-01070-5*) Scholarly.

— Edmund Spenser. LC 71-172044. reprint ed. 27.50 (*0-404-03948-0*) AMS Pr.

— William Wordsworth & Annette Vallon. (BCL1-PR English Literature Ser.). 146p. 1992. reprint ed. lib. bdg. 69.00 (*0-7812-7680-2*) Rprt Serv.

Legowski, Margaret. Destination: Marshall Islands: Video Guide. (Illus.). 70p. 1998. reprint ed. pap. text 20.00 (*0-7881-4733-1*) DIANE Pub.

Legowski, Margaret, ed. see Kasubaite-Binder, Rima & Sheffield, Elise S.

Legowski, Margaret, jt. ed. see Koller, Mary.

Legoy, Marie-Dominique & Thomas, Daniel, eds. Enzyme Engineering XII Vol. 750: Proceedings of a Conference Sponsored by the Engineering Foundation & the American Institute of Chemical Engineers, September 19-24, 1993. 506p. 1995. 140.00 (*0-89766-927-4*) NY Acad Sci.

LeGrady, George. Stockfootage. (Illus.). 12p. 1984. pap. 10.00 (*0-939784-07-6*) CEPA Gall.

Legrain, L. Terra-cottas from Nippur. (Publications of the Babylonian Section: Vol. XVI). (Illus.). 52p. 1930. 60.00 (*0-686-11926-6*) U Museum Pubns.

Legrain, M. Nephrology. 400p. (gr. 13). 1987. 17.00 (*0-89352-230-9*) Mosby Inc.

— Le Petit Robert. (FRE.). 2551p. 1996. 70.00 (*2-85036-506-8*, Pub. by Robert) IBD Ltd.

Legrain, M., jt. auth. see Keen, Harry.

Legrand, et al. The Nature & Future of Episcopal Conferences. LC 88-28555. 410p. 1988. pap. 19.95 (*0-8132-0703-7*) Cath U Pr.

Legrand, A. P. & Flandrois, S., eds. Chemical Physics of Intercalation. LC 88-24688. (NATO ASI Series B, Physics: Vol. 172). 530p. 1988. 135.00 (*0-306-42831-8*, Plenum Trade) Perseus Pubng.

***Legrand, Andre P.** The Surface Properties of Silicas. LC 97-32242. 494p. 1998. 210.00 (*0-471-95332-6*) Wiley.

Legrand, B. APL, Management Problems with Answers & "Kit of Tools" Matthews, Julian G., tr. LC 83-25908. 167p. reprint ed. pap. 51.80 (*0-8357-5656-4*, 203266000080) Bks Demand.

— Learning & Applying APL. Matthews, Julian G., tr. LC 83-10620. 414p. reprint ed. pap. 128.40 (*0-608-17857-8*, 203265900080) Bks Demand.

Legrand, C., jt. ed. see De Cock, F.

Legrand, C., jt. ed. see Horellou, M. H.

LeGrand, Catherine. Frontier Expansion & Peasant Protest in Colombia, 1850-1936. LC 85-24244. 320p. reprint ed. pap. 99.20 (*0-7837-5870-7*, 204558900006) Bks Demand.

LeGrand, Donald G. & Bendler, John T. Handbook of Polycarbonate Science & Technology. LC 99-51829. (Plastics Engineering Ser.: Vol. 56). (Illus.). 357p. 1999. text 155.00 (*0-8247-9915-1*) Dekker.

Legrand, Emile. Bibliographie Hellenique, 4 vols. (FRE.). 1691p. 1997. reprint ed. 250.00 (*1-57898-049-6*) Martino Pubng.

— Bibliographie Ionienne, 2 vols. 862p. 1999. reprint ed. 95.00 (*1-57898-126-3*) Martino Pubng.

LeGrand, Harry. A Standardized System for Evaluating Waste Disposal Sites. 42p. 1983. 15.00 (*1-56034-043-6*, T005) Natl Grnd Water.

LeGrand, Jacques & Suk-Hbaatar, Tsegmidijn. Dictionnaire Mongol-Francais. (FRE & MON.). 288p. 1992. 49.95 (*0-7859-1018-2*, 2901795498) Fr & Eur.

Legrand, L. & Leroy, P. Prevention of Corrosion & Scaling in Water Supply Systems. (Ellis Horwood Series in Water & Waste Water Management). 1990. text 92.00 (*0-470-21647-6*) P-H.

***Legrand, Lucien.** The Bible on Culture: Belonging or Dissenting. (Faith & Cultures Ser.). 200p. 2000. pap. 20.00 (*1-57075-330-X*) Orbis Bks.

Legrand, M., ed. Cities & Subsurface Use: Proceedings of an International Conference, Bordeaux, 21-23 October 1987. 480p. (C). 1987. text 201.00 (*90-6191-715-8*, Pub. by A A Balkema) Ashgate Pub Co.

— Tunneling in Soft & Water-Bearing Grounds: Proceedings of an International Symposium, Lyon, 27-29 November 1984. 286p. (C). 1985. text 201.00 (*90-6191-590-2*, Pub. by A A Balkema) Ashgate Pub Co.

— Underground Crossing for Europe: Proceedings of an International Conference, Lille, 16 - 18 October 1990. (Illus.). 372p. (C). 1990. text 162.00 (*90-6191-157-5*, Pub. by A A Balkema) Ashgate Pub Co.

Legrand, Pierre. Dictionary of Lille Patois: Dictionnaire du Patois de Lille. (ENG & FRE.). 174p. 1990. pap. write for info. (*0-7859-4858-9*) Fr & Eur.

— Dictionnaire du Patois de Lille. fac. ed. (FRE.). 180p. 1987. pap. 79.95 (*0-7859-8229-9*, 2904951288) Fr & Eur.

Legrand, Ron. Fast Cash with Quick-Turn Real Estate: How Anyone Can Quickly Turn Single Family Houses into Cash. 2nd ed. 1997. pap. text 19.95 (*0-9654851-0-2*) Results Pub.

LeGrand, S. M. Web of Words: Selected Poetry & Prose from ShowEMall! Writers' Block http:// www.showemall.com/ x, 106p. 1997. pap. 15.00 (*0-9657917-1-8*) Show Em.

LeGrand, Y. & El Hage, S. G. Physiological Optics. (Optical Sciences Ser.: Vol. 13). (Illus.). 350p. 1980. 73.95 (*0-387-09919-0*) Spr-Verlag.

Legrendre, R. French-English Dictionary of Education with E-F Index. 2nd ed. (ENG & FRE.). 1500p. 1993. 150.00 (*2-86911-129-0*, Pub. by Eska Editions) IBD Ltd.

Legrenzi, Giovanni. Giovanni Legrenzi: Cantatas & Canzonets for Solo Voice I. Seay, Albert, ed. (Recent Researches in Music of the Baroque Era Ser.: Vol. RRB14). (Illus.). 107p. 1972. pap. 35.00 (*0-89579-045-9*) A-R Eds.

— Giovanni Legrenzi: Cantatas & Canzonets for Solo Voice II. Seay, Albert, ed. (Recent Researches in Music of the Baroque Era Ser.: Vol. RRB15). (Illus.). 109p. 1972. pap. 40.00 (*0-89579-046-7*) A-R Eds.

Legrez, Didier, jt. tr. see Horner, Robert C.

***Legriel, M. P.** Le Bresilien Sans Peine. (Methode Quotidienne Assimil Ser.). (SPA.). 1999. pap. 24.94 (*2-7005-0112-8*) Assimil.

Legris, Renee. Dictionnaire des Auteurs du Radio-Feuilleton Quebecois. (FRE.). 200p. 1981. pap. 29.95 (*0-7859-8026-1*, 2762110904) Fr & Eur.

Legris, Sylvia. Circuitry of Veins. LC 97-194759. 80p. pap. 7.95 (*0-88801-207-1*, Pub. by Turnstone Pr) Genl Dist Srvs.

Legro, Jeffrey W. Cooperation under Fire: Anglo-German Restraint During World War II. LC 94-35482. (Studies in Security Affairs). 272p. 1995. text 37.50 (*0-8014-2938-2*) Cornell U Pr.

LeGro, William E. Vietnam from Cease-Fire to Capitulation. 186p. 1996. per. 8.00 (*0-16-001929-X*) USGPO.

Legros. Materials Sciences, ser. vol. 6. (Advances in Space Research Ser.). 1988. pap. 56.00 (*0-08-036640-6*, Pergamon Pr) Elsevier.

Legros, Dominique. Tommy McGinty's Northern Tuchtone Story of Crow: A First Nation Elder Recounts the Creation of the World. (Mercury Ser.). 268p. 1999. pap. 27.95 (*0-660-17506-1*) CN Mus Civilization.

Legros, J. C., jt. auth. see Platten, J. K.

Legros, J. C., jt. ed. see Kaldis, E.

Legros, J. J., jt. ed. see Enjalbert, A.

LeGros, Lucy C. Activities & Games. 2nd rev. ed. (Illus.). 75p. (Orig.). (J). (gr. k-2). 1989. pap. 9.95 (*0-937306-02-9*) Creat Res NC.

— Instant Centers - Colors. (Illus.). 40p. (Orig.). (J). (gr. k-2). 1984. pap. 6.95 (*0-937306-03-7*) Creat Res NC.

— Instant Centers - Holidays. rev. ed. (Illus.). 51p. (Orig.). (J). (gr. k-2). 1988. teacher ed. 6.95 (*0-937306-06-1*) Creat Res NC.

— Instant Centers - Letters. (Illus.). 46p. (Orig.). (J). (gr. k-2). 1984. pap. 6.95 (*0-937306-04-5*) Creat Res NC.

— Instant Centers - Numbers. (Illus.). 48p. (Orig.). (J). (gr. k-2). 1984. pap. 6.95 (*0-937306-05-3*) Creat Res NC.

— Instant Centers - Numbers 10-20. (Illus.). 33p. (J). (gr. k-2). 1988. teacher ed. 6.95 (*0-937306-07-X*) Creat Res NC.

LeGros, Tom. Investigator's Guide to Ambulance Reports. 80p. (C). 1996. pap. text 35.00 (*0-918487-93-5*) Thomas Investigative.

LeGrys, Vicky, contrib. by. Sweat Testing: Sample Collection & Quantitative Analysis; Approved Guideline (1994) 1994. 75.00 (*1-56238-188-1*, C34-A) NCCLS.

LeGrys, Vicky A. The Laboratory Diagnosis of Selected Inborn Errors of Metabolism, 4. LC 83-22941. (Methods in Laboratory Medicine Ser.: Vol. 4). 154p. 1984. 45.00 (*0-275-91441-0*, C1441, Praeger Pubs) Greenwood.

Legters, Lyman H., ed. Eastern Europe - Transformation & Revolution, 1945-1991: Documents & Analyses. (Sources in Modern History Ser.). 665p. (C). 1992. pap. text 32.76 (*0-669-24994-7*) HM Trade Div.

Legters, Lyman H., et al, eds. Clinical Perspectives in Democracy. 188p. (C). 1994. pap. text 26.95 (*0-8476-7889-X*) Rowman.

— Clinical Perspectives on Democracy. 188p. (C). 1994. text 64.00 (*0-8476-7888-1*) Rowman.

Legters, Lyman H. & Lyden, Fremont J., eds. American Indian Policy: Self-Governance & Economic Development, 329. LC 93-9319. (Contributions in Political Science Ser.: No. 329). 240p. 1993. 59.95 (*0-313-28992-1*, G8892, Greenwood Pr) Greenwood.

Legters, Lyman H., jt. ed. see Lyden, Fremont J.

Legters, Lyman H., tr. see Litvan, Gyorgy.

LeGuin, Charles A., jt. auth. see Goucher, Candice L.

Leguineche, Manuel, jt. auth. see Torbado, Jesus.

***Leguineche, Miguel.** El Precio del Paraiso. (SPA.). 1998. pap. 9.95 (*84-8326-005-0*) E Martinez Roca.

Leguizamo, John. Freak: A Semi-Demi-Quasi-Pseudo Autobiography. 144p. 1998. pap. 11.00 (*1-57322-693-9*, Riverhd Trade) Berkley Pub.

Leguizamo, John & Katz, David B. Freak: A Semi-Demi-Quasi-Pseudo Autobiography. LC 97-26289. 144p. 1997. 19.95 (*1-57322-092-2*, Riverhead Books) Putnam Pub Group.

Leguizamon, Martha, tr. see Tobin, William J.

Legum, Colin. Africa Contemporary Record, Vol. XII: 1979-80. LC 70-7957. 1294p. 1981. 345.00 (*0-8419-0550-9*, Africana) Holmes & Meier.

— Africa Contemporary Record, Vol. 24. 1500p. 2000. 495.00 (*0-8419-0562-2*) Holmes & Meier.

— Africa Contemporary Record: Annual Survey & Documents 1986-1987, Vol. XIX. LC 70-7957. 1000p. 1988. lib. bdg. 345.00 (*0-8419-0557-6*, Africana) Holmes & Meier.

— Africa since Independence LC 99-29505. 1999. 9.95 (*0-253-21334-7*) Ind U Pr.

— The Battlefronts of Southern Africa. LC 87-25481. 1988. 49.50 (*0-8419-1135-5*) Holmes & Meier.

— The Battlefronts of Southern Africa. LC 87-25481. 1988. pap. 34.50 (*0-8419-1144-4*) Holmes & Meier.

— Pan-Africanism: A Short Political Guide. LC 75-25492. (Illus.). 296p. 1976. reprint ed. lib. bdg. 35.00 (*0-8371-8420-7*, LEPA, Greenwood Pr) Greenwood.

— Western Crisis Over Southern Africa. LC 79-9723. (Current Affairs Ser.). (Illus.). (C). 1979. pap. 17.95 (*0-8419-0496-0*, Africana) Holmes & Meier.

Legum, Colin, ed. Africa Contemporary Record, Vol. VIII: 1975-76. LC 70-7957. (Illus.). 1220p. 1976. 345.00 (*0-8419-0157-0*, Africana) Holmes & Meier.

— Africa Contemporary Record, Vol. X: 1977-78. LC 70-7957. 1472p. 1979. 345.00 (*0-8419-0159-7*, Africana) Holmes & Meier.

— Africa Contemporary Record, Vol. XI: 1978-79. LC 70-7957. 1354p. 1980. 345.00 (*0-8419-0160-0*, Africana) Holmes & Meier.

— Africa Contemporary Record, Vol. XIII: 1980-81. LC 70-7957. 1300p. 1982. 345.00 (*0-8419-0551-7*, Africana) Holmes & Meier.

— Africa Contemporary Record: Annual Survey & Documents, 1985-1986, Volume XVIII. 1392p. 1987. 345.00 (*0-8419-0556-8*, Africana) Holmes & Meier.

— Africa Contemporary Record Vol. VI: 1973-74. LC 70-7957. (Illus.). 1255p. 1974. 345.00 (*0-8419-0155-4*, Africana) Holmes & Meier.

— Africa Contemporary Record Vol. XIV: 1981-82. 1280p. 1983. 345.00 (*0-8419-0552-5*, Africana) Holmes & Meier.

— Africa Contemporary Record Vol. XV: 1982-83. 1216p. 1984. 345.00 (*0-8419-0553-3*, Africana) Holmes & Meier.

— Africa Contemporary Record Vol. XVI: 1983-84. (Illus.). 1344p. 1985. 345.00 (*0-8419-0554-1*, Africana) Holmes & Meier.

— Africa Contemporary Record Vol. 23: 1990-1992. (Illus.). 1500p. 1998. 495.00 (*0-8419-0561-4*, Africana) Holmes & Meier.

— Africa Contemporary Record Annual Survey & Documents 1968-69, Vol. I. 1972. 345.00 (*0-8419-0150-3*, Africana) Holmes & Meier.

— Africa Contemporary Record Annual Survey & Documents 1970-71, Vol. III. 1972. 345.00 (*0-8419-0152-X*, Africana) Holmes & Meier.

— Africa Contemporary Record Annual Survey & Documents 1971-72, Vol. IV. 1972. 345.00 (*0-8419-0153-8*, Africana) Holmes & Meier.

— Africa Contemporary Record Annual Survey & Documents 1972-73, Vol. V. 1973. 345.00 (*0-8419-0154-6*, Africana) Holmes & Meier.

— Africa Contemporary Record Annual Survey & Documents 1974-75, Vol. VII. LC 70-7957. (Illus.). 1185p. 1975. 345.00 (*0-8419-0156-2*, Africana) Holmes & Meier.

— Africa Contemporary Record Annual Survey & Documents 1976-77, Vol. IX. LC 70-7957. (Illus.). 1293p. 1978. 345.00 (*0-8419-0158-9*, Africana) Holmes & Meier.

— Africa Contemporary Record Annual Survey & Documents 1984-85, Vol. XVII. 1100p. 1986. 345.00 (*0-8419-0555-X*, Africana) Holmes & Meier.

— Middle East Contemporary Survey, 1976-1977, Vol. 1. (Illus.). 684p. 1978. 245.00 (*0-8419-0323-9*) Holmes & Meier.

Legum, Colin, et al, eds. Crisis & Conflict in the Middle East: The Changing Strategy, from Iran to Afghanistan. LC 81-84135. 160p. (C). 1982. pap. 14.50 (*0-8419-0784-6*) Holmes & Meier.

— Middle East Contemporary Survey, 1980-1981, Vol. 5. 896p. 1983. 245.00 (*0-8419-0825-7*) Holmes & Meier.

— Middle East Contemporary Survey, 1981-1982, Vol. 6. 957p. 1984. 245.00 (*0-8419-0878-8*) Holmes & Meier.

— Middle East Contemporary Survey, 1982-1983, Vol. 7. (Illus.). 950p. 1985. 245.00 (*0-8419-1014-6*) Holmes & Meier.

Legum, Colin & Doro, Marion, eds. Africa Contemporary Record Annual Survey & Documents 1987-88, Vol. XX. 1182p. 1990. 359.00 (*0-8419-0558-4*, Africana) Holmes & Meier.

Legum, Colin & Mmari, Geoffrey, eds. Mwalimu: The Influence of Nyerere. LC 95-3926. 1995. 49.95 (*0-86543-478-6*); pap. 16.95 (*0-86543-479-4*) Africa World.

Legum, Colin & Shaked, Haim, eds. Middle East Contemporary Survey, 1977-1978, Vol. 2. LC 78-648245. (Illus.). 824p. 1979. 245.00 (*0-8419-0398-0*) Holmes & Meier.

— Middle East Contemporary Survey, 1978-1979, Vol. 3. 1980. 245.00 (*0-8419-0514-2*) Holmes & Meier.

— Middle East Contemporary Survey, 1979-1980, Vol. 4. LC 78-648245. (Illus.). 890p. 1982. 245.00 (*0-8419-0609-2*) Holmes & Meier.

Legum, Colin, et al. Horn of Africa in Continuing Crisis. LC 79-873. (Current Affairs Ser.). (Illus.). 184p. (C). 1979. pap. 14.95 (*0-8419-0491-X*, Africana) Holmes & Meier.

Legum, Colin, jt. auth. see Cervenka, Zdenek.

Legum, Colin, jt. ed. see Doro, Marion E.

Legum, Colin, jt. ed. see Doro, Marion.

Legum, Stanley. High School Transcript Study Technical Report, 1994. 196p. 1997. pap. 17.00 (*0-16-049170-3*) USGPO.

L

An Asterisk (*) at the beginning of an entry indicates that the title is appearing for the first time.

L

Legum, Stanley, et al. High School Transcript Study Tabulations, 1994: Comparative Data on Credits Earned & Demographics for 1994, 1990, 1987 & 1982 High School Graduates. rev. ed. LC 98-203515. (Education Department Publication NCES 98 Ser.: Vol. 532). 636p. 1998. pap. 30.00 (*0-16-049723-X*) USGPO.

— The 1994 High School Transcript Study Tabulations: Comparative Data on Credits Earned & Demographics for 1994, 1990, 1987 & 1982 High School Graduates LC 97-188204. (E. D. Tabs Ser.). 1997. write for info. (*0-16-049176-2*) USGPO.

Leguori, Alphonsus. The Practice of the Love of Jesus Christ. rev. ed. Heinegg, Peter, tr. from ITA. LC 96-37868. 256p. 1997. pap. 13.00 (*0-7648-0031-0*) Liguori Pubns.

Legutke, Michael & Thomas, Howard. Process Experience Language Classroom. (Applied Linguistics & Language Ser.). 332p. (C). 1995. pap. text 34.74 (*0-582-01654-1*) Longman.

Legvold, Robert, jt. auth. see Garnett, Sherman W.

Legvold, Robert, jt. auth. see Task Force on Soviet New Thinking Staff.

Legvold, Robert H. Soviet Policy in West Africa. LC 79-115477. (Illus.). 386p. 1970. 40.50 (*0-674-82775-9*) HUP.

Legvold, Robert H., jt. ed. see Colton, Timothy J.

LeGwin, J. Hardy. Construction Inspection Checklist. 20p. 1994. pap. 19.00 (*1-55701-309-8*) BNI Pubns.

— Easyspec Construction Specifications. 300p. 1990. ring bd. 179.00 (*1-55701-303-9*) BNI Pubns.

— Easyspec Construction Specifications: PC Version for IBM. 300p. 1993. ring bd. 249.00 (*1-55701-302-0*) BNI Pubns.

— Easyspec Construction Specifications: PC Version for Mac. 300p. 1993. ring bd. 249.00 (*1-55701-301-2*) BNI Pubns.

— Minispec Residential Construction Specifications. 150p. 1991. ring bd. 79.00 (*1-55701-306-3*) BNI Pubns.

— Minispec Residential Construction Specifications: PC Version for IBM. 150p. 1991. ring bd. 99.00 (*1-55701-304-7*) BNI Pubns.

— Minispec Residential Construction Specifications: PC Version for MAC. 150p. 1991. 99.00 (*1-55701-305-5*) BNI Pubns.

— Project Checklist. 10p. 1991. pap. 15.00 (*1-55701-308-X*) BNI Pubns.

— Project Notebook: Basic Edition. 1990. ring bd. 29.95 (*1-55701-310-1*) BNI Pubns.

— Project Notebook: Professional Edition. Bicknell, Susan J., ed. 1991. ring bd. 59.95 (*1-55701-307-1*) BNI Pubns.

***Legwold, Gary.** The Last Toast to Lutefisk! 102 Toasts, Tidbits & Trifles for Your Next Lutefisk Dinner. LC 99-65890. (Illus.). 72p. 1999. pap. 8.95 (*0-9652027-1-2*) C Henry.

Legwold, Gary. The Last Word on Lute Lefse. 165p. 1991. pap. 9.95 (*0-934860-78-5*) Adventure Pubns.

— The Last Word on Lutefisk: Heartwarming Stories, Humor, History-Plus the Lutefisk Dinner Directory. LC 96-77791. (Illus.). viii, 168p. 1996. pap. 14.95 (*0-9652027-0-4*) C Henry.

***Leham, John & Ernest.** North by Northwest. (Illus.). 144p. 2000. pap. 14.00 (*0-571-20184-9*) Faber & Faber.

***Lehan, Claudia.** Get Lost! The Cool Guide to San Francisco. 2nd ed. 1999. pap. 13.00 (*90-802561-8-8*) SCB Distributors.

Lehan, Edward A. Simplified Governmental Budgeting. LC 81-82463. (Illus.). 86p. 1981. 30.00 (*0-686-84272-3*); student ed. 15.00 (*0-686-84273-1*) Municipal.

Lehan, Richard. City of Literature: An Intellectual & Cultural History. LC 97-3443. 307p. 1998. pap. text 17.95 (*0-520-21256-8*, Pub. by U CA Pr) Cal Prin Full Svc.

— The Great Gatsby: The Limits of Wonder. (Masterwork Studies). 128p. 1989. 29.00 (*0-8057-7960-4*, MWS-36) Macmillan.

— The Great Gatsby The Limits Of Wonder: The Limits of Wonder. (Masterwork Studies). 128p. 1989. pap. 18.00 (*0-8057-8013-0*) Macmillan.

Lehan, Richard, ed. see Dreiser, Theodore.

Lehan, Richard D. The City in Literature: An Intellectual & Cultural History from the Enlightenment to Postmodernism. LC 97-3443. 307p. 1998. 45.00 (*0-520-21042-5*, Pub. by U CA Pr) Cal Prin Full Svc.

Lehane, Brendan. The Quest of Three Abbots: The Golden Age of Celtic Christianity. 256p. 1994. reprint ed. pap. 16.95 (*0-940262-65-7*, Lindisfarne) Anthroposophic.

***Lehane, Brendan.** Wild Ireland: A Traveller's Guide. LC 99-87775. (Illus.). 2000. pap. 19.95 (*1-56656-363-1*) Interlink Pub.

Lehane, Dennis. Darkness, Take My Hand. LC 95-23609. 320p. 1996. 24.00 (*0-688-14380-6*, Wm Morrow) Morrow Avon.

— Darkness, Take My Hand. 1997. mass mkt. 5.99 (*0-614-27703-5*, Avon Bks) Morrow Avon.

— A Drink Before the War. LC 94-12274. 288p. 1994. 22.95 (*0-15-100093-X*) Harcourt.

— A Drink Before the War. LC 94-12274. 304p. 1996. mass mkt. 6.99 (*0-380-72623-8*, Avon Bks) Morrow Avon.

Lehane, Dennis. A Drink Before the War. 336p. write for info. (*0-7278-5537-9*) Severn Hse.

Lehane, Dennis. Gone, Baby, Gone. LC 98-14042. 448p. 1999. mass mkt. 6.99 (*0-380-73035-9*, Avon Bks) Morrow Avon.

— Gone, Baby, Gone: A Novel. LC 98-14042. 256p. 1998. 24.00 (*0-688-15332-1*, Wm Morrow) Morrow Avon.

***Lehane, Dennis.** Prayers for Rain. 416p. 2000. mass mkt. 6.99 (*0-380-73036-7*) Morrow Avon.

Lehane, Dennis. Prayers for Rain: A Novel. LC 99-22048. 352p. 1999. 25.00 (*0-688-15333-X*, Wm Morrow) Morrow Avon.

***Lehane, Dennis.** Prayers for Rain: A Novel. large type ed. LC 99-46176. (G. K. Hall Core Ser.). 570p. 1999. 28.95 (*0-7838-8786-8*, G K Hall Lrg Type) Mac Lib Ref.

Lehane, Dennis. Sacred: A Novel. LC 96-53115. 256p. 1997. 23.00 (*0-688-14381-4*, Wm Morrow) Morrow Avon.

— Sacred: A Novel. LC 96-53115. 384p. 1998. mass mkt. 6.99 (*0-380-72629-7*, Avon Bks) Morrow Avon.

***Lehane, Fleur Tully.** Heartbreak Corner. (Illus.). 1998. pap. 19.95 (*1-875998-61-6*, Pub. by Central Queensland) Accents Pubns.

Lehane, Michael J. & Billingsley, Peter B., eds. Biology of the Insect Midgut. (C). text 138.00 (*0-412-61670-X*) Chapman & Hall.

Lehane, Mike. Biology of Blood-Sucking Insects. 256p. (C). 1991. pap. 36.95 (*0-04-445410-4*, A8244); pap. 44.95 (*0-04-445409-0*, A8243) Thomson Learn.

Lehane, Stephen. Your Personally Tailored Diet. (Illus.). 1984. 15.95 (*0-13-980541-9*, Busn); pap. 5.95 (*0-13-980525-7*, Busn) P-H.

Lehaney, Brian, jt. auth. see Clarke, Steve.

Lehaney, Brian, jt. ed. see Clarke, Steve.

Lehar, Franz. The Merry Widow: Complete Score for Piano & Voice. (Music Ser.). 224p. 1983. reprint ed. pap. 10.95 (*0-486-24514-4*) Dover.

LeHardy, Judy N., jt. auth. see LeHardy, Ward M.

LeHardy, Ward M. & LeHardy, Judy N. Once Around. LC 96-92919. (Illus.). 292p. (Orig.). 1997. pap. 11.95 (*0-9656111-0-8*, A794-133) Once Around.

Lehbert, Margitt, jt. auth. see Kirsch, Sarah.

Lehbrink, H. Ferrari. (ENG, FRE, GER & SPA., Illus.). 382p. 1995. 39.95 (*3-89508-076-4*, 810023) Konemann.

— Ferrari Formula 1 Racing Cars. 1996. 49.98 (*0-7858-0717-9*) Bk Sales Inc.

— Grand Prix Fascination Formula 1. (SPA, GER, FRE & ENG., Illus.). 400p. 1994. 39.95 (*3-89508-006-3*, 810001) Konemann.

Lehbrink, Hartmut. Ferrari: Formula 1. (ENG, FRE & GER., Illus.). 320p. 1997. 39.95 (*3-89508-211-2*, 810067) Konemann.

— Mercedes, 2 Vols. 700p. 1998. boxed set 79.95 (*3-89508-899-4*, 520347) Konemann.

Lehenbauer, Ruth B. What's Happening in Utah Schools? Our Children in Crisis. (Illus.). 80p. (Orig.). 1996. pap. 5.98 (*0-9656244-0-4*) R B Lehenbauer.

Leheny, James, ed. see Addison, Joseph.

LeHeron, Richard, jt. ed. see Park, Sam O.

Lehey, Greg. The Complete FreeBSD, 2 disk 817p. (Orig.). 1996. pap. text 49.95 incl. cd-rom (*1-57176-159-4*) Walnut Creek.

— The Complete FreeBSD, 4 disc. 2nd ed. 1724p. (Orig.). 1999. pap. 69.95 incl. cd-rom (*1-57176-227-2*) Walnut Creek.

***Lehey, Greg.** Complete FreeBSD. 3rd ed. 1999. pap. text 69.95 (*1-57176-246-9*) Walnut Creek.

Lehey, Greg. Porting UNIX Software: From Download to Debug. 538p. 1995. pap. 29.95 (*1-56592-126-7*) Thomson Learn.

Lehfeldt, Martin C., jt. auth. see Hollowell, Louise.

Lehigh, David S. Restaurants - Conditions & Syndromes: Index of Actions & Reports. LC 90-56273. 160p. 1991. 47.50 (*1-55914-328-2*); pap. 44.50 (*1-55914-329-0*) ABBE Pubs Assn.

Lehigh University Staff. Study of the 'Clock' Reaction on Copper Surfaces. 87p. 1983. write for info. (*0-318-60086-2*, 333A) Intl Copper.

Lehiste, Ilse. Consonant Quantity & Phonological Units in Estonian. LC 66-63013. (Uralic & Altaic Ser.: Vol. 65). 73p. 1966. pap. text 8.00 (*0-87750-022-3*) Res Inst Inner Asian Studies.

Lehleiter, Robert. Die Familienstiftung als Instrument zur Sicherung der Unternehmenskontinuitat bei Familienunternehmen. (Europaische Hochschulschriften: Reibe 5: Bd. 1883). (GER., Illus.). 256p. 1996. pap. 51.95 (*3-631-30023-9*) P Lang Pubng.

Lehmacher, W. & Hoermann, A., eds. Statistik - Software Three: Konferenz Ueber die Wissenschaftliche Anwendung von Statistik-Software, 1985. (GER.). 393p. 1986. pap. 37.70 (*3-437-40170-X*) Lubrecht & Cramer.

Lehman. Applications for Business Communication. (PS - Communication/English Ser.). 1992. pap. 29.95 (*0-538-70524-8*) S-W Pub.

— Applications for Business Community Using Mac. (Communication-English Ser.). 1992. 3.95 (*0-538-70244-3*) S-W Pub.

— Thinking about Movies. (C). 1998. pap. text 46.50 (*0-15-500001-2*, Pub. by Harcourt Coll Pubs) Harcourt.

Lehman & Forde. Word Processing: Pearson & Associates. 2nd ed. (DF - Computer Applications Ser.). 1993. mass mkt. 19.95 (*0-538-61332-7*) S-W Pub.

Lehman & Lites, Emily. Visions. 1990. pap. text, teacher ed. 22.20 (*0-13-328824-2*) P-H.

***Lehman, et al.** Web Tutor on Webct to Accompany Business Communication. 12th ed. 1999. pap. 19.00 (*0-534-76476-2*) Wadsworth Pub.

Lehman, Ann W. & Zimmerman, Robert M. The Effective Nonprofit Board: Responsibilities & Recruitment. (Illus.). 29p. 1998. pap. 16.95 (*0-9665259-2-2*) Zmmrmn Lhmn.

Lehman, Anthony, jt. auth. see Bernheim, Kayla F.

Lehman, Anthony F. & Dixon, Lisa B., eds. Double Jeopardy: Chronic Mental Illness & Substance Use Disorders. (Chronic Mental Illness Ser.: Vol. 3). 304p. 1995. text 43.00 (*3-7186-0599-6*, Harwood Acad Pubs) Gordon & Breach.

Lehman, Benjamin H. Carlyle's Theory of the Hero. LC 76-181944. reprint ed. 24.50 (*0-404-03949-9*) AMS Pr.

— Carlyle's Theory of the Hero. (BCL1-PR English Literature Ser.). 212p. 1992. reprint ed. lib. bdg. 79.00 (*0-7812-7491-5*) Rprt Serv.

Lehman, Barbara, ed. see Casselberry, L. & Candy, F.

Lehman, Barbara, jt. ed. see Sorensen, Marilou.

Lehman, Barbara A., jt. auth. see Freeman, Evelyn B.

Lehman, Bruce A. The Conference on Fair Use: Final Report to the Commissioner on the Conclusion of the Conference on Fair Use. LC 98-49346. 1998. write for info. (*0-9668180-2-4*) Work Grp Intell Rghts.

***Lehman, Bruce A.** The Conference on Fair Use: Final Report to the Commissioner on the Conclusion of the Conference on Fair Use (1998) 189p. (C). 2000. reprint ed. pap. text 30.00 (*0-7881-8632-9*) DIANE Pub.

Lehman, Bruce A. How to Get a Patent. unabridged ed. Fife, Bruce, ed. LC 98-38653. 88p. 1998. pap. 10.00 (*0-941599-43-4*, Pub. by Piccadilly Bks) Empire Pub Srvs.

— Intellectual Property & the National Information Infrastructure: The Report of the Working Group on Intellectual Property Rights. 238p. (Orig.). (C). 1996. reprint ed. pap. text 35.00 (*0-7881-2415-3*, 310850) DIANE Pub.

Lehman, Carol M. & Himstreet, William C. Business Communications. 11th ed. (EC - HS Communication/English Ser.). (C). 1995. pap., student ed. 22.95 (*0-538-84779-4*) S-W Pub.

Lehman, Carol M., et al. Business Communication. 12th ed. LC 98-22969. (EC - HS Communication/English Ser.). 1998. pap. 85.95 (*0-538-87520-8*) S-W Pub.

— Business Communications. 11th ed. LC 95-12251. (C). 1995. pap. 67.95 (*0-538-84778-6*) S-W Pub.

Lehman, Celia, jt. auth. see Davis, Irma.

Lehman, Charles. Psalm Refrains: Reproducible Calligraphic Expressions of Sunday Responsorials. LC 97-132308. (Illus.). 128p. (Orig.). 1996. pap. 19.95 (*1-55612-855-X*, LL1855) Sheed & Ward WI.

— Signs of Christ: A Book of Clip Art. (Illus.). 128p. (Orig.). 1995. pap. 24.95 (*1-55612-822-3*) Sheed & Ward WI.

Lehman, Charles, jt. auth. see Gunderson, William.

Lehman, Charles A. Desert Survival Handbook: How to Prevent & Handle Emergency Situations. 2nd rev. ed. Fessler, Diane M., ed. (Illus.). 96p. 1998. pap. 7.95 (*0-935810-65-X*) R H Pub.

Lehman, Cheryl. Advances in Public Interest Accounting, Vol. 7. 1998. 78.50 (*1-55938-993-1*) Jai Pr.

Lehman, Cheryl, et al, eds. Advances in Public Interest Accounting, Vol. 1. 227p. 1986. 78.50 (*0-89232-516-X*) Jai Pr.

— Advances in Public Interest Accounting, Vol. 2. 197p. 1985. 78.50 (*0-89232-698-0*) Jai Pr.

— Advances in Public Interest Accounting, Vol. 3. 275p. 1990. 78.50 (*0-89232-784-7*) Jai Pr.

— Advances in Public Interest Accounting, Vol. 4. 261p. 1992. 78.50 (*1-55938-254-6*) Jai Pr.

— Advances in Public Interest Accounting, Vol. 5. 312p. 1993. 78.50 (*1-55938-496-4*) Jai Pr.

— Advances in Public Interest Accounting, Vol. 6. 376p. 1995. 78.50 (*1-55938-648-7*) Jai Pr.

***Lehman, Cheryl, et al, eds.** Advances in Public Interest Accounting, Vol. 8. 1999. 78.50 (*0-7623-0518-5*) Jai Pr.

Lehman, Cheryl R. Accounting's Changing Role in Social Conflict. LC 91-47864. (Critical Accounting Research Ser.). 196p. (C). 1995. 39.95 (*1-55876-030-X*); pap. text 24.95 (*1-55876-101-2*) Wiener Pubs Inc.

Lehman, Cheryl R. & Moore, Russell M., eds. Multinational Culture: Social Impacts of a Global Economy, 122. LC 91-27. (Contributions in Economics & Economic History Ser.: No. 122). 360p. 1992. 65.00 (*0-313-27822-9*, LMB, Greenwood Pr) Greenwood.

Lehman, Chester K. Biblical Theology No. 1: Old Testament. 1997. reprint ed. pap. 18.00 (*1-890133-12-4*) Biblical Viewpts.

— Biblical Theology No. 2: New Testament. 480p. 1997. reprint ed. pap. 18.00 (*1-890133-13-2*) Biblical Viewpts.

***Lehman, Chester K.** Fulfillment of Prophecy. (Mennonite Reprint Series: 1). 30p. (YA). 2000. pap. 2.95 (*1-883453-05-4*) Deutsche Buchhandlung.

— The Holy Spirit & the Holy Life. 3rd ed. 220p. 1999. reprint ed. pap. 8.00 (*1-890133-17-5*) Biblical Viewpts.

Lehman, Daniel W. Matters of Fact: Reading Nonfiction over the Edge. LC 97-26663. (Theory & Interpretation of Narrative Ser.). 234p. 1998. text 47.50 (*0-8142-0760-X*); pap. text 18.95 (*0-8142-0761-8*) Ohio St U Pr.

Lehman, David. The Best American Poetry. Rich, Adrienne, ed. 320p. 1996. 27.00 (*0-684-81455-2*) S&S Trade.

— The Best American Poetry. Hollander, John, ed. & intro. by. (Best American Poetry Ser.). 332p. 1998. pap. 14.00 (*0-684-81450-1*) Scribner.

— Best American Poetry, 1997. Tate, James, ed. 384p. 1997. per. 13.00 (*0-684-81452-8*) S&S Trade.

— Best American Poetry, 1997. 1997. 29.50 (*0-684-81454-4*) S&S Trade.

— The Best American Poetry, 1996. Rich, Adrienne, ed. 320p. 1996. per. 13.00 (*0-684-81451-X*) S&S Trade.

— The Big Question. LC 95-5493. (Poets on Poetry Ser.). 160p. 1995. pap. 13.95 (*0-472-06583-1*, 06583); text 39.50 (*0-472-09583-8*, 09583) U of Mich Pr.

— The Daily Mirror: A Journal in Poetry. LC 99-37041. 160p. 2000. 16.00 (*0-684-86493-2*) Scribner.

— The Last Avant-Garde: The Making of the New York School of Poets. LC 98-16249. 448p. 1998. 27.50 (*0-385-47542-X*) Doubleday.

***Lehman, David.** The Last Avant-Garde: The Making of the New York School of Poets. 464p. 1999. pap. 16.95 (*0-385-49533-1*, Anchor NY) Doubleday.

Lehman, David. The Line Forms Here. (Poets on Poetry Ser.). (Illus.). 264p. (C). 1992. pap. 13.95 (*0-472-06483-5*, 06483) U of Mich Pr.

— The Line Forms Here. (Poets on Poetry Ser.). (Illus.). 264p. (C). 1992. text 39.50 (*0-472-09483-1*, 09483) U of Mich Pr.

— The Perfect Murder: A Study in Detection. LC 99-42207. 288p. 2000. pap. 18.95 (*0-472-08585-9*, 08585) U of Mich Pr.

— Valentine Place: Poems. LC 95-38090. 96p. 1996. 24.50 (*0-684-81570-2*); per. 14.00 (*0-684-82279-2*) S&S Trade.

Lehman, David, ed. Beyond Amazement: New Essays on John Ashbery. LC 79-6850. 312p. 1980. 45.00 (*0-8014-1235-8*); pap. 18.95 (*0-8014-9183-5*) Cornell U Pr.

— Beyond Amazement: New Essays on John Ashbery. LC 79-6850. 295p. reprint ed. pap. 91.50 (*0-608-20092-1*, 207136400011) Bks Demand.

— Ecstatic Occasions, Expedient Forms: 85 Contemporary Poets Select & Comment on Their Poems. 2nd ed. LC 96-31099. 228p. 1996. pap. 17.95 (*0-472-06633-1*, 06633) U of Mich Pr.

— Ecstatic Occasions, Expedient Forms: 85 Contemporary Poets Select & Comment on Their Poems. 2nd ed. LC 96-31099. 228p. 1997. text 44.50 (*0-472-09633-8*, 09633) U of Mich Pr.

Lehman, David & Berger, Charles, eds. James Merrill: Essays in Criticism. 352p. 1982. text 47.50 (*0-8014-1404-0*) Cornell U Pr.

***Lehman, David & Black, Star.** The Kgb Bar Book of Poems. LC 00-26698. 288p. 2000. pap. 14.00 (*0-688-17109-5*, Quil) HarperTrade.

Lehman, David, jt. auth. see Bloom, Harold.

Lehman, David, jt. ed. see Bly, Robert W.

Lehman, David R. A Child's Gift of Lullabyes. (Illus.). 14p. (J). (ps). 1987. 12.95 incl. audio (*0-927945-01-0*) Someday Baby.

— A Child's Gift of Lullabyes. (Illus.). 14p. (J). (ps). 1991. 15.95 incl. audio compact disk (*0-927945-05-3*) Someday Baby.

Lehman, Dennis D., jt. auth. see Sackheim, George I.

Lehman, Donald R. & Winer, Russell S. Product Management. LC 93-10645. 464p. (C). 1993. text 68.95 (*0-256-11623-7*, Irwn McGrw-H) McGrw-H Hghr Educ.

Lehman, Donna. What on Earth Can You Do? Making Your Church a Creation Awareness Center. LC 93-600. 192p. (Orig.). 1993. pap. 10.99 (*0-8361-3632-2*) Herald Pr.

Lehman, Doris. Riviera off Season & On. LC 96-27796. (Illus.). 256p. 1996. pap. 15.95 (*0-312-14726-0*) St Martin.

***Lehman, Doris, et al.** London off Season & On. LC 99-36165. 272p. 1999. pap. 16.95 (*0-312-20447-7*) St Martin.

Lehman, Edward C., Jr. Gender & Work: The Case of the Clergy. LC 92-30543. (SUNY Series in Religion, Culture, & Society). 230p. (C). 1993. text 59.50 (*0-7914-1591-0*); pap. text 21.95 (*0-7914-1592-9*) State U NY Pr.

— Women Clergy in England: Sexism, Modern Consciousness, & Church Viability. LC 86-28547. (Studies in Religion & Society: Vol. 16). 232p. 1987. lib. bdg. 89.95 (*0-88946-858-3*) E Mellen.

Lehman, Edward R. Profits, Profitability, & the Oil Industry. Bruchey, Stuart, ed. LC 78-22694. (Energy in the American Economy Ser.). (Illus.). 1979. lib. bdg. 25.95 (*0-405-11997-6*) Ayer.

Lehman, Edward W. The Viable Polity. LC 92-9854. 296p. (C). 1992. 59.95 (*0-87722-994-5*) Temple U Pr.

***Lehman, Edward W., ed.** Autonomy & Order: A Communitarian Anthology. 320p. 2000. 70.00 (*0-8476-9702-9*); pap. 27.95 (*0-8476-9703-7*) Rowman.

Lehman, Elaine, et al. Big K: The Kundalini Story. LC 96-77148. 288p. 1996. pap. 15.95 (*1-883697-36-0*) Hara Pub.

Lehman, Eleanor R. & Grabowski, Barbara L. Constructivism: Its Foundations & Applications: A Selected Bibliography. LC 95-3903. 1995. pap. 24.95 (*0-87778-288-1*) Educ Tech Pubns.

Lehman, Elsie E. God Sends His Son Activity Book. (Story Bible Activity Ser.: Vol. 8). 80p. (Orig.). (J). (gr. 3-9). 1987. pap. 3.99 (*0-8361-3429-X*) Herald Pr.

— God's Wisdom & Power Activity Book. (Story Bible Activity Ser.). 80p. (J). (ps-1). 1985. pap. 3.99 (*0-8361-3391-9*) Herald Pr.

Lehman, Emil. Israel: Idea & Reality. (Illus.). (J). (gr. 8 up). 3.95 (*0-8381-0205-0*, 10-205) USCJE.

— The Tents of Michael: The Life & Times of Colonel Albert Williamson Goldsmid. LC 96-23696. 286p. 1996. lib. bdg. 39.50 (*0-7618-0426-9*) U Pr of Amer.

***Lehman, Eric G.** Summers House. LC 99-89930. 288p. 2000. text 23.95 (*0-312-24112-7*) St Martin.

Lehman, Ernest. North by Northwest: The Screenplay. 1976. 18.95 (*0-8488-0178-4*) Amereon Ltd.

— Sweet Smell of Success. 19.95 (*0-88411-447-3*) Amereon Ltd.

***Lehman, Ernest.** Sweet Smell of Success. 160p. 1998. pap. 14.95 (*0-571-19410-9*) Faber & Faber.

— Sweet Smell of Success: Short Fiction of Ernest Lehman. 240p. 2000. pap. 15.95 (*1-58567-047-2*, Pub. by Overlook Pr) Penguin Putnam.

Lehman, Fred, jt. auth. see Robinson, Keith.

Lehman, Gail, ed. see Shapiro, Michele.

Lehman, Gail, ed. see Shinpoch, Jan, et al.

Lehman, Gaylord L. Sunday Words for a Monday World. 75p. (Orig.). 1986. pap. 6.95 (*0-938828-03-7*) Falls Tar.

Lehman, George & Hunt, David. Carving 20 Realistic Game & Songbirds: Complete Patterns & Instructions. (Woodcarvers' Favorite Patterns Ser.: Bk. 1). 58p. 1991. spiral bd. 19.95 (*1-56523-004-3*) Fox Chapel Pub.

— Realism in Wood: Detailed Patterns & Instructions for Carving Twenty-Two Different Birds & Animals. (Woodcarvers' Favorite Patterns Ser.: Bk. 2). 64p. 1991. spiral bd. 19.95 (*1-56523-005-1*) Fox Chapel Pub.

Lehman, Glenn. Johnny Godshall: A Pilgrim's Process. LC 92-8226. 216p. (Orig.). 1992. pap. 8.99 (*0-8361-3597-0*) Herald Pr.

— You Can Lead Singing: A Song Leader's Manual. LC 95-6327. (Illus.). 94p. 1994. pap. 6.95 (*1-56148-117-3*) Good Bks PA.

An Asterisk (*) at the beginning of an entry indicates that the title is appearing for the first time.

***Lehman, Glenn M.** Johnny Godshell: A Pilgrim's Process. LC 00-32536. 2000. write for info. (*0-7862-2722-2*) Thorndike Pr.

Lehman, Glenn M., jt. auth. see Roth, Glen A.

Lehman, Godfrey D. The Ordeal of Edward Bushell. 276p. (Orig.). 1988. pap. 14.95 (*1-879563-04-5*) Lexicon CA.

— We the Jury: The Impact of Jurors on Our Basic Freedoms. LC 97-11435. 369p. 1997. 26.95 (*1-57392-144-0*) Prometheus Bks.

Lehman, Harvey C. Age & Achievement. LC 52-13159. (American Philosophical Society, Philadelphia. Memoirs Ser.: Vol. 33). 373p. reprint ed. pap. 115.70 (*0-8357-5249-6*, 200639600058) Bks Demand.

Lehman, Harvey C. & Witty, Paul A. Psychology of Play Activities. LC 75-35074. (Studies in Play & Games). (Illus.). 1976. reprint ed. 23.95 (*0-405-07924-9*) Ayer.

Lehman, Helmut T., jt. ed. see Bergendoff, Conrad.

Lehman, Howard P. Indebted Development: Strategic Bargaining & Economic Adjustment in the Third World. LC 92-47353. (International Political Economy Ser.). 240p. 1993. text 49.95 (*0-312-09635-6*) St Martin.

Lehman, Hugh. Rationality & Ethics in Agriculture. 239p. 1995. pap. text 24.95 (*0-89301-179-7*) U of Idaho Pr.

Lehman, J. Lee. The Book of Rulerships: Keywords from Classical Astrology. LC 92-60607. 352p. 1992. pap. 18.95 (*0-924608-13-7*, Whitford) Schiffer.

— Classical Astrology for Modern Living: From Ptolemy to Psychology & Back Again. LC 96-191936. 336p. 1996. pap. 19.95 (*0-924608-24-2*, Whitford) Schiffer.

— Essential Dignities. LC 89-51940. 256p. 1990. pap. 14.95 (*0-924608-03-X*, Whitford) Schiffer.

— The Ultimate Asteroid Book. LC 88-50479. (Illus.). 351p. 1988. pap. 18.95 (*0-914918-78-8*, Whitford) Schiffer.

Lehman, J. Lee, tr. see Papus, pseud.

Lehman, J. Lee, tr. see Partridge, John.

Lehman, James H. The Old Brethren. LC 76-20274. (Illus.). 384p. 1976. pap. 2.45 (*0-87178-650-8*, 8011) Brethren.

— The Owl & the Tuba. LC 91-73880. (Illus.). 32p. (J). 1991. 13.95 (*1-878925-02-4*) Brotherstone Pubs.

— The Saga of Shakespeare Pintlewood & the Great Silver Fountain Pen. LC 90-82303. (Illus.). 32p. (J). (gr. k-3). 1990. lib. bdg. 13.95 (*1-878925-00-8*) Brotherstone Pubs.

Lehman, Jane, jt. auth. see Kolzow, Lee V.

Lehman, Jean, jt. auth. see Lites, Emily.

***Lehman, Jeffrey.** Gale Encyclopedia of Multicultural America, 2 vols. LC 99-44219. 1999. write for info. (*0-7876-3992-3*) Gale.

Lehman, Jeffrey, ed. Gale Encyclopedia of Multicultural America: Primary Documents, 2 vols. LC 99-44219. 1100p. (J). 1999. 145.00 (*0-7876-3990-7*, GML00299-113793, Gale Res Intl) Gale.

Lehman, Jeffrey, jt. auth. see Dassanowsky, Robert.

Lehman, Jeffrey, jt. ed. see von Dassanowsky, Robert.

Lehman, Jeffrey S., jt. auth. see Kahn, Douglas A.

Lehman, Jerry D. Tracing Life's Footprints. LC 88-91214. 1989. 10.00 (*0-87212-218-2*) Libra.

Lehman, Jill F. Adaptive Parsing: Self-Extending Natural Language Interfaces. (C). 1991. text 104.00 (*0-7923-9183-7*) Kluwer Academic.

Lehman, Jill F., ed. see Cognitive Science Society Staff.

Lehman, Joanne. Traces of Treasure: Quest for God in the Commonplace. LC 93-36493. 160p. (Orig.). 1994. pap. 7.99 (*0-8361-3655-1*) Herald Pr.

Lehman, John. Facts & Circumstances. 219p. 1993. 19.95 (*0-8027-1230-4*) Walker & Co.

— Shrine of the Tooth Fairy. (Illus.). 80p. 1998. pap. 8.00 (*0-9660376-1-8*) Cambridge Bk Rev.

Lehman, John, jt. ed. see Day Lewis, Cecil.

Lehman, John A. Systems Design in the Fourth Generation Object-Based Development Using dBASE 3.0 & dBASE 4.0. LC 90-48154. 381p. 1991. text 70.95 (*0-471-52752-1*) Wiley.

Lehman, John F. Making War: The President & Congress from Barbary to Baghdad. 320p. 1992. text 24.00 (*0-684-19239-X*, Scribners Ref) Mac Lib Ref.

Lehman, John F. & Weiss, Seymour. Beyond the Salt II Failure. LC 81-2874. 195p. 1981. 49.95 (*0-275-90667-1*, C0667, Praeger Pubs) Greenwood.

***Lehman, John H.** Calibration Service for Spectral Responsivity of Laser & Optical-fiber Power Meters at Wavelengths Between 0.4 NM & 1.8 NM. 43p. 2000. pap. 4.25 (*0-16-059017-5*) USGPO.

Lehman, John H., ed. Standard History of Stark County: Authentic Narrative of the Past, with Particular Attention to the Modern Era; Chronicle of the People, with Family Lineag & Memoirs, 3 vols. (Illus.). 1114p. 1997. reprint ed. lib. bdg. 123.00 (*0-8328-6364-5*) Higginson Bk Co.

Lehman, John T. & International Decade for the East African Lakes St. Environmental Change & Response in East African Lakes: Contributions to Ideal, an International Decade for the East African Lakes. LC 98-23065. (Monographiae Biologicae). 236p. 1998. write for info. (*0-7923-5118-5*) Kluwer Academic.

Lehman, John W. General Chemistry. (C). 1992. 59.00 (*0-205-12850-5*, Macmillan Coll) P-H.

— Operational Organic Chemistry: A Problem-Solving Approach to the Laboratory Course. 3rd ed. LC 98-7010. 808p. 1998. 90.00 (*0-13-841917-5*) P-H.

***Lehman, Joyce Jordan.** Taking It to Extremes: A Christian's Journey to Self-Discovery. LC 99-65228. 192p. 2000. pap. 14.95 (*1-58501-055-3*, Pub. by CeShore Pubg) Natl Bk Netwk.

Lehman, Karl. Samothrace, a Guide to the Excavation & the Museum. 5th ed. LC 55-8563. pap. 12.00 (*0-685-73230-4*) J J Augustin.

Lehman, Karl, jt. auth. see Lehmann, Phyllis W.

Lehman, Katey & Lehman, Ross. Open House. (Illus.). 1989. 19.50 (*0-685-29451-X*) Bingham Bks.

Lehman, Kathleen, jt. auth. see Hatcher, Dale.

***Lehman, Kenneth D.** Bolivia & the United States: A Limited Partnership. LC 99-22737. (Illus.). 320p. 1999. 55.00 (*0-8203-2115-X*) U of Ga Pr.

— Bolivia & the United States: A Limited Partnership. LC 99-22737. (United States & the Americas Ser.). 320p. 1999. pap. text 20.00 (*0-8203-2116-8*) U of Ga Pr.

Lehman, Libby. Threadplay with Libby Lehman: Mastering Machine Embroidery Techniques. Reikes, Ursula, ed. LC 97-23692. (Illus.). 96p. (Orig.). 1997. pap. 24.95 (*1-56477-202-0*, B313) Martingale & Co.

Lehman, Lilli. My Path Through Life. Farkas, Andrew, ed. Seligman, Alice B., tr. LC 76-29947. (Opera Biographies Ser.). (Illus.). 1977. reprint ed. lib. bdg. 53.95 (*0-405-09689-5*) Ayer.

Lehman, M. M. & Belady, L. A. Program Evolution: Processes of Software Change. (APIC Studies in Data Processing). (C). 1989. pap. text 62.00 (*0-12-442441-4*) Acad Pr.

Lehman, Marcus. The Adopted Princess. Mindel, Nissan, tr. from GER. (Illus.). 74p. (YA). reprint ed. 11.00 (*0-8266-0334-3*, Merkos LInyonei Chinuch) Kehot Pubn Soc.

— Bustenai. (Illus.). 144p. (YA). 1982. reprint ed. 12.00 (*0-8266-0340-8*, Merkos LInyonei Chinuch) Kehot Pubn Soc.

— Meor Hagolah: Rabbenu Gershom. Hartheimer, Eva J., tr. from GER. (Illus.). 174p. (YA). reprint ed. 12.00 (*0-8266-0342-4*, Merkos LInyonei Chinuch) Kehot Pubn Soc.

— Out of the Depths. Mindel, Nissan, tr. from GER. (Illus.). 108p. (YA). reprint ed. 11.00 (*0-8266-0336-X*, Merkos LInyonei Chinuch) Kehot Pubn Soc.

— Unpaid Ransom. Mindel, Nissan, tr. from GER. (Illus.). 74p. (YA). reprint ed. 11.00 (*0-8266-0338-6*, Merkos LInyonei Chinuch) Kehot Pubn Soc.

Lehman, Mark W., et al. Marshall, Barrett & Co. A Word Processing Simulation. (C). 1989. pap. text 29.95 (*0-538-80124-7*, WS60AC) S-W Pub.

Lehman, Martin E. & Lehmann, Helmut T., eds. Luther's Works: Word & Sacrament IV, Vol. 38. LC 55-9893. 1971. 30.00 (*0-8006-0338-9*, 1-338, Fortress Pr) Augsburg Fortress.

Lehman, Maxwell, ed. Communication Technologies & Information Flow. (Policy Studies on Science & Technology). (Illus.). 175p. 1981. 48.00 (*0-08-027169-3*, Pergamon Pr); pap. 25.00 (*0-08-027528-1*, Pergamon Pr) Elsevier.

Lehman, Maxwell, jt. auth. see Costikyan, Edward N.

Lehman, Maxwell, jt. auth. see Costikyan, Edward N.

Lehman, Michael. The Newbie's Guide to the Microsoft Network. (Newbie's Guide Ser.). (Illus.). 240p. (Orig.). 1995. pap. 24.95 (*0-9637025-8-0*) Albion Bks.

Lehman, Michele K. Creating a Healthier Community: The Story of Ashtabula County Medical Center. 144p. 1997. 20.00 (*0-929690-32-X*) Herit Pubs AZ.

***Lehman, Patricia.** Cairn Terriers. LC 98-46011. (Complete Pet Owner's Manual Ser.). (Illus.). 104p. 1999. pap. 6.95 (*0-7641-0638-4*) Barron.

Lehman, Patricia. Life... A Soul's Journey Home. 2nd ed. (Illus.). Date not set. write for info. (*1-928587-04-6*) RoverMedia.

Lehman, Patricia F. Your Healthy Puppy. (Illus.). 64p. 1998. 12.95 (*0-7938-0326-8*, WW085) TFH Pubns.

Lehman, Paul, ed. Teaching Examples: Ideas for Music Educators. 142p. 1994. pap. 30.00 (*1-56545-041-8*, 1620) MENC.

Lehman, Paul E. Pistol Law. large type ed. (Linford Western Library). 280p. 1985. pap. 16.99 (*0-7089-6088-X*) Ulverscroft.

Lehman, Paul J. The Greatness Factor. 176p. 1989. pap. 13.95 (*0-9622035-0-5*) Universal Oregon.

Lehman, Paul J. & Ziegler, Rani. Reflections on Love. (Illus.). 80p. (Orig.). 1993. pap. 8.95 (*0-9622035-2-1*) Universal Oregon.

Lehman, Paul R. & Music Educators National Conference Staff. The National Standards: From Vision to Reality. 4p. 1994. pap. 6.75 (*1-56545-064-7*, 1606) MENC.

Lehman, Paula D. Journey with Justice. Hall, Eddy & Shelly, Maynard, eds. LC 90-81509. (Illus.). 100p. (YA). 1990. pap. 3.95 (*0-87303-139-3*) Faith & Life.

Lehman, Peter. Defining Cinema. LC 97-7710. (Depth of Field Ser.). 1997. pap. 18.00 (*0-8135-2302-8*) Rutgers U Pr.

***Lehman, Peter.** Masculinity: Bodies, Movies, Culture. 2000. 75.00 (*0-415-92323-9*) Routledge.

— Masculinity: Bodies, Movies, Culture. (AFI Film Readers Ser.). (Illus.). 2000. pap. 21.00 (*0-415-92324-7*) Routledge.

Lehman, Peter. Running Scared: Masculinity & the Representation of the Male Body. (Culture & the Moving Image Ser.). (C). 1994. pap. text 22.95 (*1-56639-222-5*) Temple U Pr.

Lehman, Peter, ed. Close Viewings: An Anthology of Film Criticism. 464p. 1990. 49.95 (*0-8130-0967-7*); pap. 24.95 (*0-8130-0991-X*) U Press Fla.

Lehman, Peter, ed. Defining Cinema. LC 97-7710. (Depth of Field Ser.). 216p. 1997. 48.00 (*0-8135-2301-X*) Rutgers U Pr.

Lehman, Peter & Luhr, William. Blake Edwards. LC 80-28440. (Illus.). 302p. 1981. 21.95 (*0-8214-0605-1*) Ohio U Pr.

Lehman, Peter, jt. auth. see Luhr, William.

Lehman, Phyllis W. & Frazer, Alfred, eds. Samothrace Vol. 10: The Propylon of Ptolemy II. (Bollingen Ser.: Vol. 60, No. 10). (Illus.). 224p. (C). 1990. text 145.00 (*0-691-09922-7*, Pub. by Princeton U Pr) Cal Prin Full Svc.

***Lehman, Richard A.** How to Prepare for the DAT: Dental Admissions Test. LC 98-33115. 496p. 1999. pap. 16.95 (*0-7641-0577-9*) Barron.

Lehman, Richard L., et al, eds. Handbook on Continuous Fiber-Reinforced Ceramic Matrix Composites. LC 95-48878. 1995. write for info. (*0-931682-43-6*) Purdue U Pubns.

Lehman, Richard S. Statistics & Research Design in the Behavioral Sciences: Answer Book. Date not set. write for info. (*0-534-13879-9*) Brooks-Cole.

Lehman, Richard S. Statistics in the Behavioral Sciences: A Conceptual Introduction. 1994. mass mkt., teacher ed. write for info. (*0-534-25321-0*) Brooks-Cole.

Lehman, Richard S. Statistics in the Behavioral Sciences: A Conceptual Introduction. LC 94-22175. 538p. 1994. pap. 92.95 (*0-534-25320-2*) Brooks-Cole.

Lehman, Richard S., ed. Programming for the Social Sciences: Algorithms & FORTRAN 77 Coding. 592p. (C). 1986. text 99.95 (*0-89859-588-6*) L Erlbaum Assocs.

Lehman, Ross, jt. auth. see Lehman, Katey.

Lehman, S. C. Nutrition & Food Preparation & Preventive Care & Maintenance. (Lifeworks Ser.). 1981. text 13.96 (*0-07-037094-X*) McGraw.

Lehman, Sandra D. Meditations for Moms-to-Be. LC 95-36210. 284p. 1995. pap. 7.95 (*1-56148-182-3*) Good Bks PA.

Lehman, Sarah, ed. see Lewitter, Sidney R.

***Lehman, Steve, photos by.** American Hollow. (Illus.). 128p. 1999. 35.00 (*0-8212-2631-2*, Pub. by Bulfinch Pr) Little.

Lehman, Steve, et al. Base Paths Vol. 1: The Best of the Minneapolis Review of Baseball, 1981-1987. 240p. 1991. text. write for info. (*0-697-13119-X*) Brown & Benchmark.

Lehman, Thomas A., jt. auth. see Busch, Kenneth L.

Lehman, Tim. Public Values, Private Lands: Farmland Preservation Policy. LC 94-19636. 240p. 1995. pap. text 19.95 (*0-8078-4491-8*); lib. bdg. 49.95 (*0-8078-2177-2*) U of NC Pr.

— Seeking the Wilderness: A Spiritual Journey. LC 93-71663. 240p. (Orig.). 1993. pap. 4.95 (*0-87303-205-5*) Faith & Life.

Lehman, Tom. A Winner Never Quits. 128p. 1999. 9.99 (*0-8499-5398-7*) Word Pub.

Lehman, Tom, frwd. The Golfer's Tee Time Devotional. 1997. 14.99 (*0-614-27171-1*) Honor Bks.

***Lehman, William.** Mr. Chairman: The Journal of a Congressional Appropriator. LC 99-49038. 728p. 2000. pap. 47.50 (*0-7618-1559-7*) U Pr of Amer.

Lehman-Wilzig, Sam. Wildfire: Grassroots Revolts in Israel in the Post-Socialist Era. LC 90-26930. (SUNY Series in Israeli Studies). 198p. (C). 1992. pap. text 18.95 (*0-7914-0872-8*) State U NY Pr.

Lehman-Wilzig, Sam N. Stiff-Necked People, Bottle-Necked System: The Evolution & Roots of Israeli Public Protest, 1949-1986. LC 89-45858. (Jewish Political & Social Studies). 224p. 1991. 27.50 (*0-253-33293-1*) Ind U Pr.

Lehman, Yvette K. Know & Tell: A Workbook for Parents & Children. Myles, Glenn, ed. 50p. (J). (ps-3). 1991. pap. write for info. (*0-318-68734-8*) Artmans Pr.

— Know & Tell: A Workbook for Parents & Children on How to Prevent Child Abuse. 2nd ed. Naeb, Yuli, tr. (CHI, ENG & SPA.). 46p. (J). (ps-4). 1992. student ed. 9.00 (*0-9638555-0-6*) Y K Lehman.

— Know & Tell: A Workbook for Parents & Children on How to Prevent Child Abuse. 2nd ed. Naeb, Yuli, tr. from CHI. (Illus.). 46p. (J). (ps-4). 1993. 9.00 (*0-9638555-2-2*) Y K Lehman.

— Saber y Decir: El Manual Para Padres e Hijos Sobre Como Prevenir el Abuso a los Ninos. 2nd ed. Chavez, Vivian & Costas, Gloria, trs. from ENG.Tr. of Know & Tell: A Workbook for Parents & Children on How to Prevent Child Abuse. (Illus.). 46p. (J). (ps-4). 1993. student ed. 9.00 (*0-9638555-1-4*) Y K Lehman.

Lehman, Yvonne. A Fighting Chance. LC 97-4709. (White Dove Romances Ser.: Bk. 5). 176p. (YA). (gr. 7-10). 1997. mass mkt. 4.99 (*1-55661-709-7*) Bethany Hse.

— Mirror of Dreams. (White Dove Romance Ser.: No. 3). 16p. (J). 1996. mass mkt. 4.99 (*1-55661-707-0*) Bethany Hse.

— More Than a Summer's Love, No. 23. (Serenade Serenata Ser.). 1985. pap. 2.50 (*0-310-47042-0*, 15557P) Zondervan.

— Picture Perfect. LC 96-45909. (White Dove Romance Ser.: No. 4). 176p. (YA). (gr. 7-10). 1997. mass mkt. 4.99 (*1-55661-708-9*) Bethany Hse.

— Secret Storm. (White Dove Romance Ser.: Vol. 2). 16p. (Orig.). (YA). (gr. 7 up). 1995. mass mkt. 4.99 (*1-55661-706-2*, Hampshire MN) Bethany Hse.

— Smoky Mountain Sunrise. (Serenade Serenata Ser.: No. 10). 192p. (Orig.). 1984. pap. 2.50 (*0-310-46562-1*, 15515P) Zondervan.

— Swept Away. LC 97-33883. 16p. (YA). 1998. mass mkt. 4.99 (*1-55661-710-0*) Bethany Hse.

— Tornado Alley. (White Dove Romance Ser.: Vol. 1). 176p. (Orig.). (YA). (gr. 7 up). 1995. mass mkt. 4.99 (*1-55661-705-4*, Hampshire MN) Bethany Hse.

Lehman, Yvonne, et al. Winter Wishes. 352p. 1999. pap. 4.97 (*1-57748-596-3*) Barbour Pub.

Lehmann. Carbohydrates. 98.00 (*0-86577-790-X*); pap. 49.00 (*0-86577-795-0*) Thieme Med Pubs.

— Introduction to Macroecon-Online. (C). 1999. pap. text, wbk. ed. 29.00 (*0-03-026001-9*) Harcourt Coll Pubs.

***Lehmann.** Nonparametrics. rev. ed. 480p. 1998. 65.20 (*0-13-997735-X*) P-H.

Lehmann. Real World Economic Applications. 5th ed. 1996. 35.74 (*0-256-14019-7*) McGraw.

— Statistical Reasoning: Lab Manual with Excel 5. LC 97-18069. (Statistics Ser.). 1997. pap., mass mkt., lab manual ed. 21.95 incl. disk (*0-534-51611-4*) Wadsworth Pub.

— Testing Statistical Hypotheses. 2nd ed. (Statistics). 624p. (C). 1991. pap. 66.95 (*0-534-15984-2*) Chapman & Hall.

— Theoretical Bases of Indo-European Languages. 336p. (C). 1996. pap. 29.99 (*0-415-13850-7*) Routledge.

Lehmann & Sandys, Cynthia. The Awakening Letters. 182p. 1986. pap. 11.95 (*0-85207-177-9*, Pub. by C W Daniel) Natl Bk Netwk.

Lehmann, jt. ed. see Krug.

Lehmann, Ann, jt. ed. see Sall, John.

Lehmann, Armin D. Travel & Tourism: An Introduction to Travel Agency Operations. LC 77-12589. 1978. pap. 18.95 (*0-672-97090-2*) Macmillan.

***Lehmann, Arthur C. & Myers, James E.** Magic, Witchcraft & Religion: An Anthropological Study of the Supernatural. 5th ed. LC 00-26306. 2000. write for info. (*0-7674-1692-9*) Mayfield Pub.

Lehmann, Arthur C. & Myers, James E., eds. Magic, Witchcraft, & Religion: An Anthropological Study of the Supernatural. 4th rev. ed. LC 96-19789. xii, 474p. (C). 1996. pap. text 46.95 (*1-55934-688-4*, 1688) Mayfield Pub.

Lehmann, Asher. Young Moses, Crown Prince of Egypt. Hirschler, Gertrude, tr. from GER. (Illus.). 150p. (YA). (gr. 9-12). 1987. 13.95 (*0-910818-74-6*); pap. 10.95 (*0-910818-64-9*) Judaica Pr.

Lehmann, Axel & Hahn, Winfried, eds. 9th European Simulation Symposium. 755p. 1997. 90.00 (*1-56555-125-7*) Soc Computer Sim.

Lehmann, Axel & Kaylan, Ali R., eds. 11th European Simulation Multiconference. 906p. 1997. 90.00 (*1-56555-115-X*) Soc Computer Sim.

Lehmann, B. Metallogeny of Tin. Bhattacharji, S. et al, eds. (Lecture Notes in Earth Sciences Ser.: Vol. 32). (Illus.). viii, 211p. 1990. 45.95 (*0-387-52806-7*) Spr-Verlag.

Lehmann, Brian, jt. auth. see Gennadi, Elfimov.

Lehmann, Christian. Ultimate Game. Rodarmor, William, tr. from FRE. LC 99-23133. 192p. (YA). (gr. 8 up). 1999. 15.95 (*1-56792-107-8*) Godine.

Lehmann, Claudia. Die Mittelmeerische Welt Als Geistige Landschaft und Geschichtsraum Im Fruhwerk von Albert Camus: Mit Ausblicken Auf Paul Valery, Giuseppe Tomasi di Lampedusa und Gottfried Benn. (Philosophie Ser.: Bd. 558). (GER.). 193p. 1998. 37.95 (*3-631-32626-2*) P Lang Pubng.

Lehmann, Conrad. Fischereiwirtschaft Band IV: Geschichte der Binnenfischerei, Teichwirtschaft und Kuenstliche Fischzucht. (Handbuch der Binnenfischerei Mitteleuropas Ser.: Lieferung 8). (GER., Illus.). xxi, 110p. 1945. 25.00 (*3-510-41023-8*, Pub. by E Schweizerbartsche) Balogh.

Lehmann, Craig A. Saunders Manual of Clinical Laboratory Science. Kaszczuk, Selma, ed. LC 97-27842. (Illus.). 1104p. 1998. text 69.95 (*0-7216-2185-6*, W B Saunders Co) Harcrt Hlth Sci Grp.

Lehmann, Danny. Before You Hit the Wall: Shaping up Spiritually to Win. 124p. 1991. pap. 7.99 (*0-927545-13-6*) YWAM Pub.

— Stoked: Firing up Your Passion for God. 165p. 1997. pap. 8.99 (*0-927545-93-4*) YWAM Pub.

Lehmann, David. Democracy & Development in Latin America: Economics, Politics & Religion in the Postwar Period. 1990. 59.95 (*0-87722-723-3*) Temple U Pr.

— Democracy & Development in Latin America: Economics, Politics & Religion in the Postwar Period. (C). 1992. pap. 24.95 (*1-56639-011-7*) Temple U Pr.

— Struggle for the Spirit: Religious Transformation & Popular Culture in Brazil & Latin America. LC 96-26914. 1996. 66.95 (*0-7456-1784-0*, Pub. by Polity Pr) Blackwell Pubs.

Lehmann, David, ed. Peasants, Landlords & Governments: Agrarian Reform in the Third World. LC 74-6091. 344p. (C). 1974. 37.00 (*0-8419-0162-7*); pap. 19.50 (*0-8419-0163-5*) Holmes & Meier.

Lehmann, Don. Marketing Research. (C). 1998. text. write for info. (*0-321-02879-1*) Addison-Wesley.

— Marketing Research. LC 97-34741. (Illus.). 950p. (C). 1997. 98.00 (*0-321-01416-2*, Prentice Hall) P-H.

Lehmann, Donald R. Analysis for Marketing Planning. 3rd ed. 1993. pap. text, teacher ed. 37.35 (*0-256-12291-1*) McGraw.

— Analysis for Marketing Planning. 4th ed. 208p. (C). 1996. text 37.35 (*0-256-21442-5*, Irwn McGrw-H) McGrw-H Hghr Educ.

— Product Management. 2nd ed. 512p. (C). 1996. text 68.95 (*0-256-21439-5*, Irwn McGrw-H) McGrw-H Hghr Educ.

Lehmann, Douglas K. The Postal History of Christmas Seals. (Illus.). 40p. (Orig.). 1990. pap. 9.95 (*1-878770-00-4*) Paragon OK.

Lehmann, E. Elements of Large Sample Theory. Casella, G. et al, eds. LC 98-34429. (Texts in Statistics Ser.). (Illus.). 624p. 1998. 79.95 (*0-387-98595-6*) Spr-Verlag.

Lehmann, E., jt. auth. see Hodges, J. L., Jr.

Lehmann, E. L. Nonparametrics: Statistical Methods Based on Ranks. LC 72-93538. 1975. text 49.95 (*0-8162-4994-6*) Holden-Day.

— Testing Statistical Hypotheses. 2nd ed. LC 96-48846. (Springer Texts in Statistics Ser.). 600p. 1997. 64.95 (*0-387-94919-4*) Spr-Verlag.

— Theory of Point Estimation. LC 97-10650. 1997. 64.95 (*0-387-98209-4*) Spr-Verlag.

Lehmann, E. L. & Casella, G. Theory of Point Estimation. 2nd rev. ed. LC 98-16687. (Texts in Statistics Ser.). 640p. 1998. 74.95 (*0-387-98502-6*) Spr-Verlag.

Lehmann, Elmar. Ordnung und Chaos: Das Englishce Restaurationsdrama, 1660-1685. (Beihefte zu Poetica Ser.: Vol. 19). (GER.). 194p. 1988. 56.00 (*90-6032-307-6*, Pub. by B R Gruner) Humanities.

Lehmann, Elmar & Lenz, Bernd, eds. Telling Stories: Studies in Honour of Ulrich Broich on the Occasion of His 60th Birthday. LC 92-12496. x, 335p. 1992. 76.00 (*90-6032-334-3*) J Benjamins Pubng Co.

L

An Asterisk (*) at the beginning of an entry indicates that the title is appearing for the first time.

Lehmann, F. Semantic Networks in Artificial Intelligence. (International Series in Modern Applied Mathematics: Vol. 24). 768p. 1992. 125.00 (0-08-042012-5, Pergamon Pr) Elsevier.

Lehmann, G. Danger on the Sunita. (J). (gr. 4-7). 1987. mass mkt. 4.95 (0-87508-438-9) Chr Lit.

— On the Trail of a Spy. (J). (gr. 3-6). 1987. mass mkt. 4.95 (0-87508-437-0) Chr Lit.

— The Red Gang. (J). (gr. 4-8). 1988. mass mkt. 4.95 (0-87508-439-7) Chr Lit.

Lehmann, G. & Coleman, C. Lehmann & Coleman: Taxation Law in Australia. 3rd ed. (Butterworths Australia Ser.). 1994. pap. write for info. (0-409-30524-3, MICHIE) LEXIS Pub.

Lehmann, G. D. The Curse of the Amulet. (Asha's Adventures Ser.). 164p. (J). (gr. 5-9). 1992. mass mkt. 4.95 (0-87508-443-5) Chr Lit.

— Saved by Fire. (Asha's Adventures Ser.). (Illus.). 125p. (J). (gr. 5-10). 1992. mass mkt. 4.95 (0-87508-441-9) Chr Lit.

Lehmann, Geoffrey & Coleman, Cynthia. Taxation Law in Australia. 4th ed. LC 96-161417. 1417p. 1996. pap. 96.00 (0-455-21407-7, Pub. by LawBk Co) Gaunt.

Lehmann, Gerhard. Beitraege zur Geschichte und Interpretation der Philosophie Kants. (GER.). (C). 1969. 107.70 (3-11-002561-2) De Gruyter.

Lehmann-Grube, F., ed. Lymphocytic Choriomeningitis. LC 70-167276. (Virology Monographs: Vol. 10). 1972. 47.00 (0-387-81017-X) Spr-Verlag.

Lehmann, Gunnar. Untersuchungen zur Spaten Eisenzeit in Syrien und Libanon: Stratigraphie und Keramikformen Zwischen ca. 720 bis 300 v. Chr. (Altertumskunde Des Vorderen Orients Ser.: No. 5). (Illus.). x, 548p. 1996. text 141.00 (3-927120-33-2, Pub. by UGARIT) Eisenbrauns.

Lehmann, H. E., ed. Non-Trycyclic & Non-Monamine Oxydase Inhibitors. (Modern Problems of Pharmacopsychiatry Ser.: Vol. 18). (Illus.). viii, 212p. 1982. 100.00 (3-8055-3428-0) S Karger.

Lehmann, H. E., jt. ed. see Ghadirian, A. M.

Lehmann, H. L., jt. ed. see Exwood, Maurice.

Lehmann, H. Peter, jt. ed. see Ban, T. A.

Lehmann, Hans & Lehmann, Thelma. Out of the Dustbin: Sentimental Musings on Art & Music in Seattle from 1936 to 1992. 112p. 1992. pap. 12.95 (0-9635567-0-3) H Lehmann.

*Lehmann, Hans-Ulrich, ed. Herman Krone 1827-1916: Werkverzeichnis (Catalogue Raisonnee) (GER., Illus.). 365p. 1998. text 72.00 (90-5705-086-2, Verlag Kunst) Gordon & Breach.

*Lehmann, Hartmut, et al, eds. In Search of Peace & Prosperity: New German Settlements in Eighteenth-Century Europe & America. LC 98-55335. 1999. write for info. (0-271-01928-X) Pa St U Pr.

Lehmann, Hartmut & Melton, James V., eds. Paths of Continuity: Central European Historiography from the 1930s Through the 1950s. (Publications of the German Historical Institute, Washington, D.C.). 416p. (C). 1994. text 80.00 (0-521-45199-X) Cambridge U Pr.

Lehmann, Hartmut & Roth, Guenther, eds. Weber's Protestant Ethic: Origins, Evidence, Contexts. (Publications of the German Historical Institute, Washington, D.C.). 411p. (C). 1993. text 69.95 (0-521-44062-9) Cambridge U Pr.

— Weber's Protestant Ethic: Origins, Evidence, Contexts. (Publications of the German Historical Institute, Washington, D.C.). 411p. (C). 1995. pap. text 21.95 (0-521-55829-8) Cambridge U Pr.

Lehmann, Hartmut & Sheehan, James J., eds. An Interrupted Past: German-Speaking Refugee Historians in the United States after 1933. (Publications of the German Historical Institute, Washington, D.C.). 272p. (C). 1991. text 54.95 (0-521-40326-X) Cambridge U Pr.

Lehmann, Hartmut & Wellenreuther, Hermann, eds. German & American Nationalism: A Comparative Perspective. (Germany & the U. S. A. Ser.). 512p. 1999. 65.00 (1-85973-271-2) Berg Pubs.

Lehmann, Hartmut, jt. auth. see Van Der Veer, Peter.

Lehmann, Hartmut, jt. ed. see Hutchison, William R.

Lehmann, Hartmut, jt. ed. see Po-Chia Hsia, R.

Lehmann-Haupt, Carl-Friedrich. Armenien Einst und Jetzt, 3 vols., Set. (GER.). xliv, 1714p. 1988. reprint ed. write for info. (3-487-09027-9) G Olms Pubs.

Lehmann-Haupt, Christopher. Crooked Man. 351p. 1995. 23.00 (0-671-73444-X) S&S Trade.

— A Crooked Man. 416p. 1996. mass mkt. 5.99 (1-57566-006-7) Kensgtn Pub Corp.

— Me & DiMaggio: A Baseball Fan Goes in Search of His Gods. LC 97-30433. 304p. 1998. reprint ed. pap. 14.95 (1-55821-623-5) Lyons Pr.

Lehmann-Haupt, Hellmut. An Introduction to the Woodcut of the Seventeenth Century. 1978. lib. bdg. 50.00 (0-913870-49-8) Abaris Bks.

— The Life of the Book. LC 75-17193. (Illus.). 240p. 1975. reprint ed. lib. bdg. 65.00 (0-8371-8293-X, LELB, Greenwood Pr) Greenwood.

— One Hundred Books about Bookmaking. LC 75-34148. 87p. 1976. reprint ed. lib. bdg. 55.00 (0-8371-8546-7, LEOB, Greenwood Pr) Greenwood.

Lehmann, Helm. Drivers Ed for Today's Managers: Six Leadership Strategies for the New Rules of the Road. (Illus.). 160p. (Orig.). 1997. pap. 15.95 (0-9659229-0-1) Org Perf & Plan.

Lehmann, Helmut T. & Atkinson, James, eds. Luther's Works: The Christian in Society I, Vol. 44. LC 55-9893. 1966. 30.00 (0-8006-0344-3, 1-344, Fortress Pr) Augsburg Fortress.

Lehmann, Helmut T. & Doberstein, John W., eds. Luther's Works: Sermons I, Vol. 51. LC 55-9893. 1959. 30.00 (0-8006-0351-6, 1-351, Fortress Pr) Augsburg Fortress.

Lehmann, Helmut T. & Gritsch, Eric W., eds. Luther's Works: Church & Ministry III, Vol. 41. LC 55-9893. 1966. 30.00 (0-8006-0341-9, 1-341, Fortress Pr) Augsburg Fortress.

Lehmann, Helmut T. & Kleiner, John W., trs. The Correspondence of Heinrich Melchior Muhlenberg Vol. 1: 1740-1748. LC 93-86108. 400p. 1993. 49.50 (0-89725-096-6, 1340) Picton Pr.

Lehmann, Helmut T., jt. auth. see Kleiner, John W.

Lehmann, Helmut T., jt. ed. see Bachmann, Theodore.

Lehmann, Helmut T., jt. ed. see Brandt, Walter I.

Lehmann, Helmut T., jt. ed. see Dietrich, Martin O.

Lehmann, Helmut T., jt. ed. see Fischer, Robert H.

Lehmann, Helmut T., jt. ed. see Forell, George W.

Lehmann, Helmut T., jt. ed. see Grimm, Harold J.

Lehmann, Helmut T., jt. ed. see Gritsch, Eric W.

Lehmann, Helmut T., jt. ed. see Hillerbrand, Hans J.

Lehmann, Helmut T., jt. ed. see Krodel, Gottfried G.

Lehmann, Helmut T., jt. ed. see Lehman, Martin E.

Lehmann, Helmut T., jt. ed. see Leupold, Ulrich S.

Lehmann, Helmut T., jt. ed. see Schultz, Robert C.

Lehmann, Helmut T., jt. ed. see Sherman, Franklin.

Lehmann, Helmut T., jt. ed. see Spitz, Lewis W.

Lehmann, Helmut T., jt. ed. see Tappert, Theodore G.

Lehmann, Helmut T., jt. ed. see Watson, Philip S.

Lehmann, Helmut T., jt. ed. see Wentz, Abdel R.

Lehmann, Helmut T., jt. ed. see Wiencke, Gustav K.

Lehmann, Helmut T., ed. & tr. see Muhlenburg, Heinrich M.

Lehmann, Henning & Weitenberg, J. J., eds. Armenian Texts, Tasks & Tools: How to Assess Variant Readings in Armenian Manuscripts. (Acta Jutlandica Ser.: No. 69:1). (Illus.). 128p. (Orig.). (C). 1993. pap. 27.00 (87-7288-111-9, Pub. by Aarhus Univ Pr) David Brown.

Lehmann, Hubert, jt. contrib. by see Hellwig, Peter.

Lehmann, Ingrid A. Peacekeeping & Public Information: Caught in the Crossfire. LC 98-47853. (Series on Peacekeeping: No. 5). (Illus.). 192p. 1999. 52.50 (0-7146-4930-9, Pub. by F Cass Pubs); pap. 24.50 (0-7146-4490-0, Pub. by F Cass Pubs) Intl Spec Bk.

Lehmann, Irvin J., jt. auth. see Mehrens, William A.

Lehmann, Jane, jt. auth. see Vogel, Lee.

*Lehmann, Jay. Intermediate Algebra. 4th ed. LC 99-87866. 584p. 2000. pap. text 79.00 (0-13-014498-3) P-H.

Lehmann, Jean-Pierre, jt. ed. see Henny, Sue.

Lehmann, Jennifer M. Deconstructing Durkheim. 288p. (C). 1995. pap. 24.99 (0-415-12374-7, C0393) Routledge.

— Durkheim & Women. LC 93-29360. x, 175p. 1994. text 45.00 (0-8032-2907-0) U of Nebr Pr.

Lehmann, Jennifer M., ed. Current Perspectives in Social Theory, Vol. 17. 1997. 73.25 (0-7623-0236-4) Jai Pr.

Lehmann, Jerry. We Walked to Moscow. Harvey, Arthur, ed. 100p. (Orig.). 1966. pap. 7.50 (0-934676-07-0) Greenlf Bks.

Lehmann, John. Christopher Isherwood: A Personal Memoir. LC 89-113990. viii, 150 p. 1987. write for info. (0-297-79179-6) Weidenfeld & Nicolson.

— The Craft of Letters in England. LC 74-2588. 248p. 1974. reprint ed. lib. bdg. 59.50 (0-8371-7410-4, LECL, Greenwood Pr) Greenwood.

— Open Night. LC 72-142654. (Essay Index Reprint Ser.). 1977. reprint ed. 18.95 (0-8369-2407-X) Ayer.

— Rupert Brooke: His Life & His Legend LC 80-502711. xiii, 178 p. 1980. write for info. (0-297-77757-2) Weidenfeld & Nicolson.

— Virginia Woolf. 2nd ed. LC 98-61521. (Literary Lives Ser.). (Illus.). 128p. 1999. reprint ed. pap. 12.95 (0-500-26026-5, Pub. by Thames Hudson) Norton.

— Virginia Woolf & Her World. LC 76-46232. (Illus.). 128p. 1977. pap. 4.95 (0-15-693581-3, Harvest Bks) Harcourt.

Lehmann, John, ed. New Writing: Spring, 1938. LC 72-178450. (Short Story Index Reprint Ser.). 1977. reprint ed. 19.95 (0-8369-4051-2) Ayer.

Lehmann, John, jt. ed. see Day Lewis, Cecil.

Lehmann, John, ed. see London Magazine Editors.

Lehmann, Justus F. Therapeutic Heat & Cold. 4th ed. (Rehabilitation Medicine Library). (Illus.). 752p. 1990. lib. bdg. 76.00 (0-683-04908-9) Lppncott W & W.

Lehmann, Justus F., jt. auth. see Kottke, Frederic J.

Lehmann, K. A. & Zech, D., eds. Transdermal Fentanyl. (Illus.). 192p. 1991. 69.95 (0-387-54440-2) Spr-Verlag.

Lehmann, Karl, et al, eds. Justification by Faith: Does the 16th-Century Condemnations Still Apply? LC 96-8821. 240p. 1996. pap. 39.95 (0-8264-0896-6) Continuum.

Lehmann, Karl & Lehmann, Phyllis W., eds. Samothrace - The Rotunda of Arisinoe Vol. 7: Excavations Conducted by the Institute of Fine Arts, New York University. (Bollingen Ser.: Vol. LX, Pt. 7). (Illus.). 416p. 1992. text 250.00 (0-691-09919-7, Pub. by Princeton U Pr) Cal Prin Full Svc.

Lehmann, Karl, ed. see Lehmann, Phyllis W. & Spittle, Denys.

Lehmann, Karl, ed. see McCredie, James R., et al.

Lehmann, Katharina. Franzosische Werbung Aus Semiotischer und Rhetorischer Sicht. (Franzosische Sprache und Literatur Ser.: Bd. 231). (GER., Illus.). 179p. 1998. 37.95 (3-631-33063-4) P Lang Pubng.

Lehmann, L. R. Blizzard. 240p. (Orig.). (YA). (gr. 9 up). 1997. pap. 4.95 (0-9659758-0-0) QuikReadPr.

Lehmann, Lilli. How to Sing. (Music Book Index Ser.). 303p. 1992. reprint ed. lib. bdg. 89.00 (0-7812-9508-4) Rprt Serv.

— How to Sing. rev. ed. Aldrich, Richard, tr. from GER. LC 92-43865. (Illus.). 128p. 1993. reprint ed. pap. 6.95 (0-486-27501-9) Dover.

— My Path Through Life. Seligman, Alice B., tr. LC 80-2286. (Illus.). reprint ed. 54.50 (0-404-18855-9) AMS Pr.

Lehmann, Linwood, tr. see Jefferson, Thomas.

Lehmann, Liza. The Life of Liza Lehmann. LC 79-25647. (Music Reprint Ser.). (Illus.). 1980. reprint ed. lib. bdg. 29.50 (0-306-76010-X) Da Capo.

Lehmann, Lotte. Midway in My Song: The Autobiography of Lotte Lehmann. (American Biography Ser.). 250p. 1991. reprint ed. lib. bdg. 69.00 (0-7812-8241-1) Rprt Serv.

— Midway in My Song, the Autobiography of Lotte Lehmann. LC 73-107813. (Select Bibliographies Reprint Ser.). 1977. 26.95 (0-8369-5186-7) Ayer.

— More Than Singing. Holden, Frances, tr. from GRE. LC 75-8688. 192p. 1975. reprint ed. lib. bdg. 55.00 (0-8371-8116-X, LEMT, Greenwood Pr) Greenwood.

— More Than Singing: The Interpretation of Songs. (Music Bks.). 192p. 1985. reprint ed. pap. 5.95 (0-486-24831-3) Dover.

— More Than Singing, the Interpretation of Songs: Music Book Index. 192p. 1993. reprint ed. lib. bdg. 69.00 (0-7812-9675-7) Rprt Serv.

— My Many Lives. Holden, Frances, tr. from GER. LC 74-3689. (Illus.). 262p. 1975. reprint ed. lib. bdg. 38.50 (0-8371-7361-2, LEML, Greenwood Pr) Greenwood.

— My Many Lives. (American Autobiography Ser.). 262p. 1995. reprint ed. lib. bdg. 79.00 (0-7812-8576-3) Rprt Serv.

— My Many Lives: Music Book Index. 262p. 1993. reprint ed. lib. bdg. 79.00 (0-7812-9633-1) Rprt Serv.

Lehmann, Manfred. On My Mind. LC 96-70932. (Illus.). 334p. 1997. 29.95 (0-88400-194-6, Shengold Bks) Schreiber Pub.

*Lehmann, Manfred, et al. Overload, Fatigue, Performance Incompetence & Regeneration. LC 99-15839. (Illus.). 1999. write for info. (0-306-46106-4, Kluwer Plenum) Kluwer Academic.

Lehmann, Marcus. The Lehmann Haggadah. 384p. 1983. 19.95 (0-87306-326-0) Feldheim.

Lehmann, Marcus & Prins, Eliezer. Lehmann-Prins Pirkei Avos. 1992. 24.95 (0-87306-589-1); pap. 20.95 (0-87306-593-X) Feldheim.

*Lehmann, Markus A. Negotiating Environmental Quality: Policy Implementation in Germany & the U. S. LC 00-37609. (New Horizons in Environmental Economics Ser.). 272p. 2000. text 95.00 (1-85898-976-0) E Elgar.

Lehmann, Martin E. A Biographical Study of Ingwer Ludwig Nommensen (1834-1918) Pioneer Missionary to the Bataks of Sumatra. LC 96-17515. (Studies in the History of Missions: Vol. 13). (Illus.). 384p. 1996. text 99.95 (0-7734-8963-0) E Mellen.

Lehmann, Michael B. The Business One Irwin Guide to Using the Wall Street Journal. 4th rev. ed. LC 92-39045. (Illus.). 416p. 1992. write for info. (1-55623-840-1, Irwn Prfssnl) McGraw-Hill Prof.

— The Business One Irwin Guide to Using the Wall Street Journal, College for Financial Planning Special Edition. 3rd ed. 400p. 1991. 12.00 (1-55623-519-4, Irwn Prfssnl) McGraw-Hill Prof.

— The Irwin Guide to Using the Wall Street Journal. 5th ed. (Illus.). 416p. 1997. pap. 19.95 (0-07-037119-9) McGraw.

— Irwin Guide to Using the Wall Street Journal. 6th ed. LC 99-16835. 366p. 2000. 29.95 (0-07-134649-X) McGraw.

— Real World Economic Applications: The Wall Street Journal. 2nd ed. 276p. (C). 1991. text 33.95 (0-256-09102-1, Irwn McGrw-H) McGrw-H Hghr Educ.

— Real World Economic Applications: The Wall Street Journal. 6th ed. 1997. pap., student ed. 45.63 (0-256-14024-3) McGraw.

Lehmann, Michael B., jt. ed. see Tapper, Colin.

Lehmann, O. J., et al, eds. Clinical Optics & Refraction. LC 97-51984. 160p. 1998. pap. text 36.50 (0-7506-2188-5) Buttrwrth-Heinemann.

Lehmann, Oscar M. Faith at the Brink: An Autobiography of the Formative Years Including the Holocaust Period & Historical Perspectives. Lehmann, Sara, ed. LC 96-94455. (Illus.). 360p. 1996. pap. 17.95 (0-9653098-1-9, Pub. by Lehmann Bks) Judaica Pr.

— Faith at the Brink: An Autobiography of the Formative Years Including the Holocaust Period & Historical Perspectives. unabridged ed. Lehmann, Sara, ed. LC 96-94455. (Illus.). 360p. 1996. 22.95 (0-9653098-0-0, Pub. by Lehmann Bks) Judaica Pr.

Lehmann, Oskar. Die Tachygraphischen Abkurzungen der Griechischen Handschriften. vi, 111p. 1965. reprint ed. write for info. (0-318-70957-0) G Olms Pubs.

Lehmann, Peggy & Pettus, Dania. Oh No . . . Not Another Summer. 224p. (Orig.). 1984. pap. 4.95 (0-9613376-0-5) P & L Res.

*Lehmann, Peter & Coady, Nick. Theoretical Perspectives for Direct Social Work: A Generalist-Eclectic Approach. LC 00-30744. 2001. pap. write for info. (0-8261-1369-9) Springer Pub.

Lehmann, Phyllis W. Cyriacus of Angona's Egyptian Visit & its Reflections in Gentili: Bellini & Hieronymus Bosch. LC 77-88599. (Flexner Lectures at Bryn Hawr College Ser.). 1978. 12.00 (0-686-92652-8) J J Augustin.

— The Pedimental Sculptures of the Hieron in Samothrace. LC 62-19124. (Illus.). 25.00 (0-685-71751-8) J J Augustin.

Lehmann, Phyllis W. & Lehman, Karl. Samothracian Reflections: Aspects of the Revival of the Antique. LC 71-163867. (Bollingen Ser.: No. 92). 216p. 1973. text 85.00 (0-691-09909-X, Pub. by Princeton U Pr) Cal Prin Full Svc.

Lehmann, Phyllis W. & Spittle, Denys. Samothrace: Excavations Conducted by the Institute of Fine Arts of New York University Vol. 5, Pt. 1: The Temenos. Lehmann, Karl, ed. LC 58-8985. (Bollingen Ser.: Vol. 60). 468p. 1958. reprint ed. pap. 145.10 (0-608-04570-5, 206534200005) Bks Demand.

— Samothrace: Excavations Conducted by the Institute of Fine Arts of New York University Vol. 5, Pt. 2: The Temenos. Lehmann, Karl, ed. LC 58-8985. (Bollingen Ser.: Vol. 60). 79p. 1958. reprint ed. pap. 30.00 (0-608-04571-3, 206534200006) Bks Demand.

Lehmann, Phyllis W., jt. ed. see Lehmann, Karl.

Lehmann, R., ed. see American Society of Mechanical Engineers Staff.

Lehmann, R., ed. see Dickens, Charles.

Lehmann, R., tr. see Michlin, S. G. & Prossdorf, S.

Lehmann, R. P. An Introduction to Old Irish. rev. ed. 1991. pap. 19.75 (0-87352-288-5, Z100P) Modern Lang.

Lehmann, Reinhard G. Friedrich Delitzsch und der Babel-Bibel-Streit. (Orbis Biblicus et Orientalis Ser.: Vol. 133). (GER.). 444p. 1994. text 91.00 (3-7278-0932-9, Pub. by Presses Univ Fribourg) Eisenbrauns.

Lehmann, Rosamond. Echoing Grove. LC 53-5646. 1953. 4.50 (0-15-127395-2) Harcourt.

— The Echoing Grove. LC 79-24170. 384p. 1980. pap. 5.95 (0-15-627487-6, Harvest Bks) Harcourt.

Lehmann, Rosamond, jt. auth. see Pole, Wellesley T.

Lehmann, Rosamond, ed. see Lady Sandys.

Lehmann, Rosamond, tr. see Cocteau, Jean.

Lehmann, Rudolf. The Leibstandarte, Vol. 1. Olcott, Nick, tr. from GER. (Illus.). 400p. 1987. 30.00 (0-921991-01-0) J J Fedorowicz.

Lehmann, Ruth P. Blessed Bastard: A Novel of Sir Galahad. (Illus.). 240p. 1997. pap. 20.00 (0-930324-35-8) Wings Pr.

Lehmann, Ruth P., tr. from ANG. Beowulf: An Imitative Translation. LC 88-10306. (Illus.). 127p. 1988. pap. 7.95 (0-292-70771-1) U of Tex Pr.

Lehmann, Sara, ed. see Lehmann, Oscar M.

Lehmann, Scott. Privatizing Public Lands. (Environmental Ethics & Science Policy Ser.). (Illus.). 264p. 1995. text 55.00 (0-19-508972-3) OUP.

Lehmann, Stephen, tr. see Nietzsche, Friedrich Wilhelm.

Lehmann, Thelma, jt. auth. see Lehmann, Hans.

Lehmann, Ulrich. Paleantologisches Woerterbuch. 3rd ed. (GER.). 739p. 1985. pap. 45.00 (0-8288-5506-4, M7577) Fr & Eur.

*Lehmann, Ulrich. Tigersprung: Fashion in Modernity. (Illus.). 520p. (C). 2000. 39.95 (0-262-12231-6) MIT Pr.

Lehmann, Ute. Your Kitten. LC 97-36139. 64p. 1998. pap. 6.95 (0-7641-0301-6) Barron.

Lehmann, W. P. & Hewitt, H. J., eds. Language Typology, 1988: Typological Models in the Service of Reconstruction. LC 91-12542. (Current Issues in Linguistic Theory Ser.: Vol. 81). vi, 182p. 1991. 50.00 (1-55619-136-7) J Benjamins Pubng Co.

Lehmann, W. P., jt. auth. see Heffner, Roe-Merrill S.

Lehmann, William. How to Be a Great First-Time Father. LC 94-23748. (How To Family Ser.). 144p. 1995. pap. 8.99 (0-570-04692-0, 12-3251) Concordia.

Lehmann, William C. John Millar of Glascow, 1735-1801. Mayer, J. P., ed. LC 78-67364. (European Political Thought Ser.). 1980. reprint ed. lib. bdg. 35.95 (0-405-11712-4) Ayer.

Lehmann, Winfred P. Development of Germanic Verse Form. LC 70-131252. 217p. 1971. reprint ed. 50.00 (0-87752-014-3) Gordian.

— A Gothic Etymological Dictionary Based on the Third Edition of Vergleichendes Worterbuch der Gotischen Sprache by Sigmund Feist. xx, 712p. 1986. 114.50 (90-04-08176-3) Brill Academic Pubs.

— Historical Linguistics. 3rd ed. LC 92-45655. 320p. (C). 1993. pap. 25.99 (0-415-07243-3, A9577) Routledge.

— Linguistische Theorien der Moderne. (Germanistische Lehrbuchsammlung Ser.: Vol. 19). (GER.). 173p. 1981. 9.00 (3-261-04889-1) P Lang Pubng.

Lehmann, Winfred P., contrib. by. Workbook for Historical Linguistics. 176p. 1992. pap. 13.60 (0-88312-272-3) S I L Intl.

Lehmann, Winfred P., ed. Language Typology, 1985: Papers from the Linguistic Typology Symposium, Moscow, 9-13 Dec. 1985. LC 86-26341. (Current Issues in Linguistic Theory Ser.: No. 47). viii, 200p. 1986. 52.00 (90-272-3541-4) J Benjamins Pubng Co.

— Language Typology 1987 - Systemic Balance in Language: Papers from the Linguistic Typology Symposium, Berkeley, 1-3, December 1987. LC 90-30. (Current Issues in Linguistic Theory Ser.: Vol. 67). x, 212p. 1990. 52.00 (90-272-3564-3) J Benjamins Pubng Co.

Lehmann, Winfred P. & Malkiel, Yakov, eds. Perspectives on Historical Linguistics: Papers From a Conference Held at the Meeting of the Language Theory Division, Modern Language Assn., San Francisco, 27-30 December 1979. (Current Issues in Linguistic Theory Ser.: No. 24). xii, 379p. 1982. 78.00 (90-272-3516-3) J Benjamins Pubng Co.

Lehmann, Winfred P., et al. Biblical Hebrew: An Analytical Introduction. LC 94-15418. (Berkeley Models of Grammar Ser.: Vol. 3). 1994. write for info. (0-8204-2283-5) P Lang Pubng.

— Biblical Hebrew: An Analytical Introduction. (ENG & HEB.). 400p. 1999. pap. 35.00 (0-930324-37-4) Wings Pr.

Lehmann, Winfred P., ed. see Bennett, William H.

Lehmberg, Janice, jt. auth. see Knapp, Ruthie.

Lehmberg, Stanford E. Cathedrals under Siege: Cathedrals in English Society, 1600-1700. LC 95-7502. 296p. 1996. 60.00 (0-271-01494-6) Pa St U Pr.

— The Reformation of Cathedrals: Cathedrals in English Society, 1485-1603. LC 88-9851. (Illus.). 335p. 1988. reprint ed. pap. 103.90 (0-608-07800-X, 205986700010) Bks Demand.

Lehmer. Keyboard Harmony. 1977. 25.00 (0-935058-00-1) Donato Music.

Lehmer, Emna, tr. see Delone, Boris N. & Faddeev, D. K.

An Asterisk (*) at the beginning of an entry indicates that the title is appearing for the first time.

Lehming, Rolf & Kane, Michael, eds. Improving Schools: Using What We Know. LC 81-8809. (Sage Focus Editions Ser.: No. 29). 312p. 1981. reprint ed. pap. 96.80 (*0-608-01540-7*, 205958400002) Bks Demand.

Lehmkuhl, Dennis, et al. Aquatic Insects. (Pictured Key Nature Ser.). 180p. (C). 1979. text. write for info. (*0-697-04767-9*, WCB McGr Hill) McGrw-H Hghr Educ.

Lehmkuhl, Don, ed. Brain Injury Glossary. 48p. 1993. reprint ed. pap. 9.50 (*1-882855-06-X*) HDI Pubs.

Lehmkuhl, Dorothy. Organizing for the Creative Person: How to Find the Organizing Style That Works for You. 1993. pap. 14.00 (*0-517-88164-0*, Crown) Crown Pub Group.

Lehmkuhl, John F., et al. Historical & Current Roles of Insects & Pathogens in Eastern Oregon & Washington Forested Landscapes: Vegetation Pattern & Insect & Disease Hazards. (Illus.). 100p. 1998. reprint ed. 17.00 (*0-89904-947-8*, Bear Meadows Resrch Grp); reprint ed. pap. 11.00 (*0-89904-948-6*, Bear Meadows Resrch Grp) Crumb Elbow Pub.

Lehmkuhl, Nonna. FORTRAN 77. 576p. (C). 1983. pap. 21.50 (*0-02-369390-8*, Macmillan Coll) P-H.

— An Introduction to VAX Assembly Language Programming. LC 86-24708. (Illus.). 486p. (C). 1987. pap. text, teacher ed. write for info. (*0-314-35222-8*) West Pub.

Lehmkuhl, Ursula, jt. ed. see Fiebig-von-Hase, Regnhild.

Lehmstedt, Mark. Ich Bin Nicht Gewohnt, Mit Kunstlern Zu Dingen. 46p. 1989. write for info. (*0-318-71837-5*) G Olms Pubs.

Lehn, Barbara. What Is a Scientist? LC 98-13984. 32p. (J). 1998. 19.90 (*0-7613-1272-2*) Millbrook Pr.

***Lehn, Barbara.** What Is a Scientist? (Illus.). 32p. (J). (gr. k-3). 1999. pap. 6.95 (*0-7613-1298-6*, Copper Beech Bks) Millbrook Pr.

— What Is a Teacher? LC 00-21495. 2000. write for info. (*0-7613-1713-9*) Millbrook Pr.

Lehn, Cornelia. I Heard Good News Today: Stories for Children. LC 83-80401. (Illus.). 148p. (J). (gr. 1-6). 1983. reprint ed. pap. 18.95 (*0-87303-073-7*) Faith & Life.

— Peace Be with You. LC 80-70190. (Illus.). 126p. (J). (gr. k-5). 1981. 6.95 (*0-87303-061-3*) Faith & Life.

Lehn, Howard M. Seventy Years of Commercial Aviation in the United States. 1998. pap. 19.95 (*0-87770-672-7*) Ye Galleon.

Lehn, J. M., ed. see Simon, J. & Andre, J. J.

Lehn, Jean-Marie. Supramolecular Chemistry: Concepts & Perspectives. LC 95-13502. 271p. 1995. pap. 74.95 (*3-527-29311-6*, Wiley-VCH) Wiley.

Lehn, Walter. The Development of Palestinian Resistance. (Information Papers: No. 14). 47p. (Orig.). (C). 1974. pap. 2.75 (*0-937694-30-4*) Assn Arab-Amer U Grads.

Lehn, Walter & Davies, Uri. The Jewish National Fund. 374p. 1987. 65.00 (*0-7103-0053-0*) Routledge.

Lehnartz, Klaus. New York in the Sixties. LC 78-53190. (Illus.). 144p. 1978. pap. 9.95 (*0-486-23674-9*) Dover.

Lehndorff, Peter G. & Tarcy, Brian. 60 Second Chronic Pain Relief: The Quickest Way to Soften the Throb, Cool the Burn, Ease the Ache. LC 96-68933. 160p. 1996. pap. 13.95 (*0-88282-151-2*) New Horizon NJ.

Lehndorff, Siegfried. Ein Leben mit Pferden: Ein Beitrag zur Geschichte der Pferdezucht. (GER., Illus.). 439p. 1956. write for info. (*3-487-08126-1*) G Olms Pubs.

Lehne. The Boy in the Candle Shop Window. (J). 1997. 15.00 (*0-689-81115-2*) S&S Childrens.

— If I Should Die Before I Wake. (J). 1999. 16.00 (*0-689-81116-0*) S&S Childrens.

Lehne, Inge & Johnson, Lonnie. Vienna: The Past in the Present. (Studies in Austrian Literature, Culture & Thought). (Illus.). 194p. 1995. pap. 15.95 (*1-57241-018-3*) Ariadne CA.

Lehne, Judith L. Coyote Girl. (J). 1995. 15.00 (*0-689-51156-6*) S&S Bks Yung.

— Kangaroos for Kids. LC 96-37145. (Wildlife for Kids Ser.). (Illus.). 48p. (Orig.). (J). (gr. 3-7). 1997. pap. 6.95 (*1-55971-595-2*, NorthWord Pr) Creat Pub Intl.

— The Never-Be-Bored Book: Quick Things to Make When There's Nothing to Do. LC 92-16529. (Illus.). 128p. (J). 1992. 17.95 (*0-8069-1254-5*) Sterling.

— When the Ragman Sings. LC 93-20346. 128p. (J). (gr. 3-7). 1993. 14.00 (*0-06-023316-8*); lib. bdg. 13.89 (*0-06-023317-6*) HarpC Child Bks.

Lehne, Judith Logan. Kangaroos for Kids. (Illus.). (J). 1997. 12.40 (*0-606-18079-6*) Turtleback.

Lehne, Richard. Casino Policy. 288p. 1986. lib. bdg. 40.00 (*0-8135-1153-4*) Rutgers U Pr.

***Lehne, Richard.** Government & Business: The United States in Comparative Perspective. 3rd ed. (Illus.). 300p. (C). 2000. pap. text 27.95 (*1-889119-38-5*, Chatham House Pub) Seven Bridges.

Lehne, Richard A. Pharmacology for Nursing Care. 2nd ed. (Illus.). 1994. teacher ed. write for info. (*0-7216-5167-4*, W B Saunders Co) Harcrt Hlth Sci Grp.

— Pharmacology for Nursing Care. 3rd ed. (Illus.). 1180p. 1998. teacher ed. write for info. (*0-7216-7151-9*, W B Saunders Co) Harcrt Hlth Sci Grp.

— Pharmacology for Nursing Care. 3rd ed. Connor, Maura, ed. LC 97-39758. (Illus.). 1184p. 1998. pap. text 55.95 (*0-7216-7150-0*, W B Saunders Co) Harcrt Hlth Sci Grp.

— Pharmacology for Nursing Care. 3rd ed. (C). 1998. pap. text, student ed. 17.95 (*0-7216-7069-5*, W B Saunders Co) Harcrt Hlth Sci Grp.

Lehne, Susanne. The New Covenant in Hebrews. (JSNT Supplement Ser.: Vol. 44). 184p. 1990. 57.50 (*1-85075-238-9*, Pub. by Sheffield Acad) CUP Services.

***Lehner, Christian P.** Die Heiler Von Samoa: O le Fofo Monographie Uber die Heiler Und die Naturheilmethoden in West-Samoa. 234p. 1999. 39.95 (*3-631-31127-3*) P Lang Pubng.

Lehner, Christine. Expecting. LC 82-8120. 192p. 1982. 12.95 (*0-8112-0848-6*, Pub. by New Directions) Norton.

— Expecting. LC 82-8120. 192p. 1984. pap. 6.95 (*0-8112-0898-2*, NDP573, Pub. by New Directions) Norton.

Lehner, David. Bright Day: A Novel. LC 99-30767. 112p. 2000. pap. 11.95 (*1-56474-315-2*) Fithian Pr.

Lehner, Ernst. Alphabets & Ornaments. (Pictorial Archive Ser.). (Illus.). 256p. 1968. pap. 12.95 (*0-486-21905-4*) Dover.

— Symbols, Signs & Signets. (Illus.). 221p. 1969. pap. 10.95 (*0-486-22241-1*) Dover.

— Symbols, Signs & Signets. (Illus.). 1990. 25.00 (*0-8446-0771-1*) Peter Smith.

Lehner, Ernst & Lehner, Johanna. Folklore & Symbolism of Flowers, Plants & Trees. (Illus.). 128p. 1990. reprint ed. lib. bdg. 55.00 (*1-55888-886-1*) Omnigraphics Inc.

— Picture Book of Devils, Demons, & Witchcraft. LC 72-137002. 174p. 1971. pap. 9.95 (*0-486-22751-0*) Dover.

***Lehner, F. K. & Urai, Janos Lajos, eds.** Aspects of Tectonic Faulting: In Honour of Georg Mandl. LC 00-38605. (Illus.). xviii, 226p. 2000. 99.00 (*3-540-65708-8*) Spr-Verlag.

Lehner, Johanna. Authentic Art Nouveau Lettering & Design in Full Color. 64p. 1989. pap. 11.95 (*0-486-25981-1*) Dover.

Lehner, Johanna, jt. auth. see Lehner, Ernst.

***Lehner, John.** OECD/CSNI Specialist Meeting on Advanced Instrumentation & Measurement Techniques: Held at Fess Parker's Red Lion Resort, Santa Barbara, California, March 17-20, 1997. 758p. 1998. per. 62.00 (*0-16-063028-2*) USGPO.

Lehner, Joseph. Discontinuous Groups & Automorphic Functions. LC 63-11987. (Mathematical Surveys & Monographs: Vol. 8). 425p. 1964. reprint ed. pap. 49.00 (*0-8218-1508-3*, SURV/8) Am Math.

Lehner, Lois. Lehner's Encyclopedia of U. S. Marks on Pottery, Porcelain & Clay. (Illus.). 636p. 1996. 24.95 (*0-89145-365-2*, 2379) Collector Bks.

Lehner, Mark. The Complete Pyramids. LC 97-60232. (Illus.). 256p. 1997. 39.95 (*0-500-05084-8*, Pub. by Thames Hudson) Norton.

***Lehner, Markus, et al, eds.** Applied Optical Measurements. LC 99-36705. (Heat & Mass Transfer Ser.). (Illus.). xix, 462p. 1999. 104.00 (*3-540-66173-5*) Spr-Verlag.

Lehner, Paul E. Artificial Intelligence & National Defense: Opportunity & Challenge. (Applications in Artificial Intelligence Ser.). (Illus.). xxxx, 240p. 1988. 34.95 (*0-89433-286-4*) Petrocelli.

***Lehner, Peter H., et al.** Stormwater Strategies: Community Responses to Runoff Pollution. (Illus.). 270p. 1999. pap. write for info. (*1-893340-20-1*) Natl Resources Defense Coun.

Lehner, Philip N. Handbook of Ethological Methods. 2nd ed. (Illus.). 692p. (C). 1998. reprint ed. pap. text 34.95 (*0-521-63750-3*) Cambridge U Pr.

Lehner, Susan & Sourek, Linda M. Presenting Harvard Graphics 3.0 for Windows. (DF - Computer Applications Ser.). 320p. 1995. mass mkt. 32.95 (*0-7895-0179-1*) Course Tech.

Lehner, T. & Mackey, P. J., eds. Co-Products & Minor Elements in Non-Ferrous Smelting: International Symposium Sponsored by the Extraction & Processing Division (1995: Las Vegas, Nevada) LC 95-75137. (Illus.). 370p. 1995. 20.00 (*0-87339-286-8*) Minerals Metals.

Lehner, T., jt. ed. see Ott, J.

Lehner, Theo, ed. see International Symposium on Injection in Process Me.

Lehner, Theo, jt. ed. see Nilmani, Madhu.

Lehner, Urban, ed. Let's Talk Turkey (about Japanese Turkey) And Other Tales from the Asian Wall Street Journal. LC 95-61323. (Illus.). 192p. (Orig.). 1996. pap. 9.95 (*0-8048-2051-1*) Tuttle Pubng.

Lehnerd, Alvin P., jt. auth. see Meyer, Mark H.

Lehnerdt, ed. Horatii Romani. (LAT.). 1973. reprint ed. pap. 24.95 (*3-519-01911-6*, T1911, Pub. by B G Teubner) U of Mich Pr.

***Lehnert.** A Beginner's Guide to the Internet & the World Wide Web. 1998. 50.00 (*0-201-39808-7*) P-H.

Lehnert, B. & Roy, S. Extended Electromagnetic Theory: Space Charge in Vacuo & the Rest Mass of the Photon. 330p. 1998. 54.00 (*981-02-3395-7*) World Scientific Pub.

Lehnert, Frederick, tr. see Schutz, Alfred.

***Lehnert, G.** Biological Exposure Values for Occupational Toxicants & Carcinogens Substances: (BAT Values & EKA), Critical Data Evaluation for BAT & EKA Values, Vol. 3. Henschler, D., ed. 284p. 1998. 155.00 (*3-527-27044-2*) Wiley.

Lehnert, G., jt. ed. see Henschler, Dietrich.

Lehnert, Gertrud. Fashion: An Illustrated Historical Overview. LC 98-70751. (Crash Course Ser.). (Illus.). 5p. 1998. pap. 13.95 (*0-7641-0437-3*) Barron.

Lehnert, Hendrik, et al, eds. Endocrine & Nutritional Control of Basic Biological Functions. LC 91-35313. (Neuronal Control of Bodily Function Ser.: Vol. 7). (Illus.). 580p. 1993. text 138.00 (*0-88937-076-1*) Hogrefe & Huber Pubs.

Lehnert, Herbert. Thomas Mann's "Doctor Faustus" A Novel at the Margin of Modernism. Pfeiffer, Peter, ed. (GERM Ser.: Vol. 49). (Illus.). xii, 226p. 1991. 65.00 (*0-938100-73-4*) Camden Hse.

Lehnert, Martin. Altenglisches Elementarbuch: Einfuehrung, Grammatik, Text mit Uebersetzung und Woerterbuch. 9th rev. ed. (Sammlung Goeschen Ser.: No. 2210). (GER.). (C). 1978. 9.85 (*3-11-007643-8*) De Gruyter.

— Altenglisches Elementarbuch: Einfuehrung, Grammatik, Woerterbuch. 10th ed. (ENG & GER.). 179p. 1990. 29.95 (*0-7859-8274-4*, 3110124718) Fr & Eur.

Lehnert, Tomek. Rogues in Robes: An Inside Chronicle of a Recent Chinese-Tibetan Intrique in the Karma-Kagyu Lineage of Diamond Way Buddhism. LC 98-28052. (Illus.). 336p. 1998. pap. 16.95 (*1-57733-026-9*) B Dolphin Pub.

Lehnert, Wendy G. Internet 101: Beginners Guide to the Internet & World Wide Web. 576p. (C). 1997. pap. text. write for info. (*0-201-35745-3*) Addison-Wesley.

— Light on the Internet. LC 97-34600. 513p. (C). 1997. pap. text 51.00 (*0-201-32553-5*) Addison-Wesley.

***Lehnert, Wendy G.** Light on the Internet. LC 98-52395. (Illus.). 249p. (C). 1999. pap. 25.00 (*0-201-61266-6*) Addison-Wesley.

— Web 101: Making the Net Work for You. LC 00-44798. (Illus.). 2001. write for info. (*0-201-70474-9*) Addison-Wesley.

Lehnert, Wendy G. & Ringle, Martin H., eds. Strategies for Natural Language Processing. (Illus.). 560p. 1982. pap. text 69.95 (*0-89859-266-6*) L Erlbaum Assocs.

Lehnhoff, Nora, ed. see Brooks, Robert E.

Lehnick, Dirk. Rate Ratios Und Odds Ratios In Zwei- Und Mehrdimensionalen Kontingenztafeln. (Illus.). 200p. 1998. 39.95 (*3-631-34096-6*) P Lang Pubng.

Lehnick, Ingo. Der Erzahler Heinrich Boll: Anderungen Seiner Narrativen Strategie und Ihre Hintergrunde. (GER.). 181p. 1997. 42.95 (*3-631-31437-X*) P Lang Pubng.

Lehnigk, S. H. The Generalized Feller Equation & Related Topics. 1993. lib. bdg. 100.00 (*0-582-08736-8*, Pub. by Addison-Wesley) Longman.

Lehning, James R. Peasant & French: Cultural Contact in Rural France During the Nineteenth Century. (Illus.). 251p. (C). 1995. text 64.95 (*0-521-46210-X*); pap. text 21.95 (*0-521-46770-5*) Cambridge U Pr.

— The Peasants of Marlhes: Economic Development & Family Organization in Nineteenth-Century France. LC 79-18707. 232p. reprint ed. pap. 72.00 (*0-7837-3760-2*, 204357700010) Bks Demand.

Lehning, Percy B. Civil Society & International Development. Bernard, Amanda et al, eds. LC 98-196422. 148p. 1998. pap. 22.00 (*92-64-16117-1*, 41 98 08 1 P, Pub. by European Conference Ministers Transp) OECD.

— Theories of Secession. LC 97-24742. 288p. (C). 1998. 85.00 (*0-415-17192-X*) Routledge.

Lehning, Percy B., jt. ed. see Weale, Albert.

***Lehninger.** Principles of Biochemistry. 3rd ed. 2000. pap. text, student ed. write for info. (*1-57259-167-6*) St Martin.

Lehninger. Principles of Biochemistry. 3rd ed. LC 99-49137. 2000. pap. text. write for info. (*1-57259-153-6*) W H Freeman.

Lehninger, Albert L. Biochemistry: The Molecular Basis of Cell Structure & Function. 2nd ed. LC 75-11082. 1975. text 69.95 (*0-87901-047-9*) Worth.

— Short Course in Biochemistry. 1973. 59.00 (*0-87901-024-X*) Worth.

Lehninger, Albert L., et al. Principles of Biochemistry. 2nd ed. (Illus.). 1013p. (C). 1984. teacher ed. 19.95 (*0-87901-178-5*) Worth.

— Principles of Biochemistry. 2nd ed. (Illus.). 1075p. (C). 1993. text 67.80 (*0-87901-711-2*) Worth.

Lehnus, Donald J. Angels to Zeppelins: A Guide to the Persons, Objects, Topics, & Themes on United States Postage Stamps, 1847-1980. LC 82-918. 279p. 1982. lib. bdg. 65.00 (*0-313-23475-2*, LPS, Greenwood Pr) Greenwood.

— Enchiridion of Form & Procedure for Typewritten Catalog Cards According to the International Standards of Bibliographic Description of Separately Published Monographs, Manual 2. (Serie Bibliotecologica). 28p. 1975. pap. 1.50 (*0-8477-0902-7*) U of PR Pr.

— Signaturas Librísticas: Normas para Su Aplicacion en Bibliotecas de Habla. (Serie Bibliotecologica). 35p. 1975. pap. text 1.50 (*0-8477-0903-5*) U of PR Pr.

Lehoczky, Sandor & Rusczyk, Richard. The Art of Problem Solving Vol. 1: The Basics. 361p. (YA). (gr. 7-12). Date not set. pap. 29.00 (*1-885875-01-0*) Mu Alpha Theta.

Lehoczky, Sandor, jt. auth. see Rusezyk, Richard.

Lehodey, Domitry V. The Ways of Mental Prayer. LC 82-50584. 408p. 1994. reprint ed. pap. 14.00 (*0-89555-178-0*) TAN Bks Pubs.

Leholzky, Sandor & Rusczyk, Richard. The Art of Problem Solving Vol. 2: And Beyond Solutions. 211p. (YA). (gr. 7-12). 1994. pap. text 8.00 (*1-885875-02-9*) Greater Testing.

— The Art of Problem Solving Vol. 2: And Beyond, Text. 389p. (YA). (gr. 7-12). 1994. pap. text 27.00 (*1-885875-03-7*) Mu Alpha Theta.

Lehotay, Denis C., ed. The Relationship of Man & Nature in the Modern Age: Dominion over the Earth. LC 93-10128. (Illus.). 284p. 1993. 89.95 (*0-7734-9273-9*) E Mellen.

Lehoucq, Richard, et al. Arpack Users' Guide: Solution of Large-Scale Eigenvalue Problems with Implicitly Restarted Arnoldi Methods. LC 98-60204. (Software, Environments & Tools Ser.: Vol. 6). (Illus.). xv, 142p. 1998. pap. 39.00 (*0-89871-407-9*, SE06) Soc Indus-Appl Math.

Lehr, jt. auth. see Ruben.

Lehr, Bill. 35 Places to Go & Things to Do: When Visiting Las Couccs, New Mexico or El Paso, Texas. LC 98-61625. 1998. pap. text 9.95 (*1-881325-34-2*) Yucca Tree Pr.

Lehr, Carol, jt. auth. see Levy, Susan L.

Lehr, Clair, jt. auth. see Spirson, Leslie L.

Lehr, Claire J., jt. auth. see Spirson, Leslie L.

Lehr, David. Austria Before & after the Anschluss: Personal Experiences, Observations & Comments. (Illus.). 416p. 2000. 20.00 (*0-8059-4778-7*) Dorrance.

***Lehr, Dick & O'Neill, Gerard.** Black Mass: The Irish Mob, the FBI & a Devil's Deal. 304p. 2000. 26.00 (*1-891620-40-1*, Pub. by PublicAffairs NY) HarpC.

Lehr, Donna H. & Brown, Fredda, eds. People with Disabilities Who Challenge the System. 1996. 34.00 (*1-55766-229-0*) P H Brookes.

Lehr, Edwin E. Colossus in Clay: Acme Brick Company: The Story of the Largest American Owned Brickmaker. LC 98-22161. 1998. write for info. (*1-57864-040-7*) Donning Co.

Lehr, Elizabeth D. King Lehr & the Gilded Age. (American Biography Ser.). 332p. 1991. reprint ed. lib. bdg. 79.00 (*0-7812-8242-X*) Rprt Serv.

— King Lehr & the Gilded Age: With Extracts from the Locked Diary of Harry Lehr. LC 75-1852. (Leisure Class in America Ser.). (Illus.). 1975. reprint ed. 29.95 (*0-405-06918-9*) Ayer.

Lehr, Fran. People of Gumption & Other Stories. 90p. 1987. pap. 7.95 (*0-935153-03-9*) Stormline Pr.

Lehr, Fran & Osborn, Jean, eds. Reading, Language, & Literacy: Reading Instruction for the Twenty-First Century. 312p. 1994. text 59.95 (*0-8058-1166-4*) L Erlbaum Assocs.

Lehr, Fran, jt. ed. see Osborn, Jean.

Lehr, Genevieve. Come & I Will Sing You: A Newfoundland Songbook. 234p. 1985. pap. 12.50 (*0-8020-6586-4*); text 27.50 (*0-8020-2567-6*) U of Toronto Pr.

Lehr, J. Harry. A Catalogue of the Flora of Arizona. 1978. 4.75 (*0-9605656-0-4*) Desert Botanical.

Lehr, Jane, jt. auth. see Collins, Tim.

Lehr, Jay & Swanson, Ken. Fit, Firm & Fifty: A Fitness Guide for Men-Women over 50. 328p. 1990. lib. bdg. 24.95 (*0-87371-399-0*, L399) Lewis Pubs.

***Lehr, Jay H.** Standard Handbook of Environmental Health, Science & Technology. 1600p. 2000. 150.00 (*0-07-038309-X*) McGraw-Hill Prof.

Lehr, Jay H., ed. Rational Readings on Environmental Concerns. 841p. 1992. 110.00 (*0-471-28485-8*, VNR) Wiley.

Lehr, Jay H., ed. Rational Readings on Environmental Concerns. (Environmental Engineering Ser.). (Illus.). 848p. 1992. text 81.95 (*0-442-01146-6*, VNR) Wiley.

Lehr, Jay H. & Rodriguez, Jose E. Orbital Management: Beyond the Hierarchy. LC 87-143. (Illus.). 120p. (Orig.). (C). 1987. pap. 9.95 (*0-8191-6265-5*); lib. bdg. 19.95 (*0-8191-6264-7*) U Pr of Amer.

Lehr, Judy, jt. auth. see Martin, Craig.

Lehr, Judy B. & Martin, Craig. Schools Without Fear: Group Activities for Building Community. LC 94-72561. (Illus.). 192p. (Orig.). (C). 1994. pap. text 19.95 (*0-932796-68-0*) Ed Media Corp.

Lehr, Marjorie. Getting Started with Elementary-Level Band. LC 99-160746. 47p. 1998. pap. 11.00 (*1-56545-110-4*, 1636) MENC.

Lehr, Middlebrooks & Proctor Staff, ed. see Sirote & Permutt Staff.

Lehr, Norma. Dance of the Crystal Skull. LC 98-49503. 115p. (J). (gr. 3-7). 1999. pap. 6.95 (*0-87358-725-1*, Rising Moon Bks); lib. bdg. 15.95 (*0-87358-724-3*, Rising Moon Bks) Northland AZ.

***Lehr, Norma.** Dance of the Crystal Skull. (Illus.). (J). 1999. 12.30 (*0-606-18310-8*) Turtleback.

— Haunting at Black Water Cove. LC 99-56358. 128p. (J). (gr. 3-7). 2000. pap. 6.95 (*0-87358-750-2*, Rising Moon Bks) Northland AZ.

— Haunting at Black Water Cove. (Illus.). (J). 2000. 12.30 (*0-606-18311-6*) Turtleback.

Lehr, Norma. The Secret of the Floating Phantom. LC 94-3004. 192p. (J). (gr. 3-6). 1994. lib. bdg. 19.95 (*0-8225-0736-6*, Lerner Publctns) Lerner Pub.

— The Shimmering Ghost of Riversend. (Lerner Mysteries Ser.). 168p. (J). (gr. 4-7). 1991. lib. bdg. 19.95 (*0-8225-0732-3*, Lerner Publctns) Lerner Pub.

— The Shimmering Ghost of Riversend. 168p. (J). (gr. 4-7). 1991. pap. 3.95 (*0-8225-9589-3*, First Ave Edns) Lerner Pub.

Lehr, Paul E. Weather, Air Masses, Clouds, Rainfall, Storms, Weather Maps, Climate. (Golden Guide Ser.). 1987. 11.05 (*0-606-12055-6*, Pub. by Turtleback) Demco.

Lehr, Rachel, jt. auth. see Perry, John R.

Lehr, Richard, et al. How to Avoid Charges of Age Discrimination. pap. 29.95 (*1-55840-211-X*) Exec Ent Pubns.

Lehr, Robert, jt. auth. see Katz, Marshall P.

Lehr, Stefan, jt. auth. see Riesenkampff, Alexander.

Lehr, Stephanie. Wir Leiden Fur Den Taufschein! Mission und Kolonialisierung Am Beispiel des Landkatechumenates in Nordostzaire. (Studien zur Interkulturellen Geschichte des Christentums, 0170-9240, Studies in the Intercultural History of Christianity: Bd. 87). (GER., Illus.). 445p. 1993. 62.80 (*3-631-45774-X*) P Lang Pubng.

***Lehr, Susan.** Images of Boys & Girls in Children's Literature. 2001. pap. text. write for info. (*0-325-00284-3*) Heinemann.

Lehr, Susan, ed. Battling Dragons: Issues & Controversy in Children's Literature. LC 94-31973. (Illus.). 287p. 1995. pap. text 27.50 (*0-435-08828-9*, 08828) Heinemann.

Lehr, Susan S. The Child's Developing Sense of Theme: A Response to Literature. (Language & Literacy Ser.: No. 3). 208p. (C). 1991. text 39.00 (*0-8077-3106-4*); pap. text 17.95 (*0-8077-3105-6*) Tchrs Coll.

***Lehr, Teresa K.** Let the Art of Medicine Flourish: The Centennial History of the Rochester Academy of Medicine. LC 00-27483. (Illus.). 2000. write for info. (*0-9665228-4-2*) Q Pubng VA.

Lehr, Teresa K. & Maples, Philip G. To Serve the Community: A Celebration of Rochester General Hospital, 1847-1997. LC 97-35662. 1997. write for info. (*1-57864-017-2*) Donning Co.

L

Lehr, Thomas A., ed. Industrial Energy Management: A Cost Cutting Approach. LC 82-62406. (Manufacturing Update Ser.). (Illus.). 270p. reprint ed. pap. 83.70 (*0-7837-6276-3*, 204599100010) Bks Demand.

***Lehr, Valerie.** Queer Family Values: Debunking the Myth of the Nuclear Family. LC 98-45411. (Queer Politics, Queer Theories Ser.). 224p. 1999. 59.50 (*1-56639-683-2*) Temple U Pr.

Lehr, Valerie. Queer Family Values: Debunking the Myth of the Nuclear Family. LC 98-45411. (Queer Politics, Queer Theories Ser.). 224p. 1999. pap. 19.95 (*1-56639-684-0*) Temple U Pr.

Lehr, William, ed. Quality & Reliability of Telecommunications Infrastructure. (Telecommunications Ser.). 256p. 1995. text 49.95 (*0-8058-1610-0*) L Erlbaum Assocs.

Lehrack, Otto J. No Shining Armor: The Marines at War in Vietnam. LC 91-39414. (Modern War Studies). (Illus.). 400p. 1992. 35.00 (*0-7006-0533-9*); pap. 15.95 (*0-7006-0534-7*) U Pr of KS.

Lehrberger, James, et al, eds. Saints, Sovereigns, & Scholars: Studies in Honor of Frederick D. Wilhelmsen. LC 92-34294. XXI, 409p. (C). 1993. text 63.00 (*0-8204-1929-X*) P Lang Pubng.

Lehrberger, John. Functor Analysis of Natural Language. LC 74-82387. (Janua Linguarum, Ser. Minor: No. 197). 155p. (C). 1974. pap. text 103.10 (*90-279-3342-1*) Mouton.

Lehrberger, John, jt. ed. see Kittredge, Richard.

Lehrer, Adrienne. Wine & Conversation. LC 82-48538. 256p. 1983. 35.00 (*0-253-36550-3*); pap. 18.95 (*0-253-20308-2*, MB-308) Ind U Pr.

Lehrer, Adrienne & Kittay, Eva F., eds. Frames, Fields & Contrasts: New Essays in Semantic & Lexical Organization. 480p. 1992. pap. 55.00 (*0-8058-1089-7*); text 99.95 (*0-8058-1088-9*) L Erlbaum Assocs.

Lehrer, Brian. The Korean Americans. rev. ed. LC 94-40428. (Immigrant Experience Ser.). 120p. (YA). (gr. 5 up). 1995. pap. text 9.95 (*0-7910-3374-0*); lib. bdg. 19.95 (*0-7910-3352-X*) Chelsea Hse.

Lehrer, G. I. Algebraic Groups & Lie Groups: A Volume of Papers in Honour of the late R. W. Richardson. (Australian Mathematical Society Lecture Ser.: Vol. 9). (Illus.). 380p. (C). 1997. pap. text 49.95 (*0-521-58532-5*) Cambridge U Pr.

Lehrer, Jim. Blue Hearts. large type ed. LC 93-39162. 344p. 1994. lib. bdg. 18.95 (*0-7862-0112-6*) Thorndike Pr.

***Lehrer, Jim.** A Bus of My Own. 2000. pap. 14.95 (*1-930709-12-9*) HAWK Pubng Grp.

Lehrer, Jim. Crown Oklahoma. 208p. 1991. pap. 3.95 (*0-345-36124-5*) Ballantine Pub Grp.

— Crown Oklahoma. LC 97-3437. (One-Eyed Mack Mystery Ser.). 223p. 1997. pap. 12.95 (*1-57178-040-8*) Coun Oak Bks.

— Crown Oklahoma. 224p. 1989. 18.95 (*0-399-13434-4*, G P Putnam) Peng Put Young Read.

— Fine Lines. large type ed. LC 94-13010. 249p. 1994. lib. bdg. 21.95 (*0-7862-0248-3*) Thorndike Pr.

— Kick the Can. LC 97-39748. 223p. (C). 1997. reprint ed. pap. 12.95 (*1-57178-059-9*) Coun Oak Bks.

***Lehrer, Jim.** The Last Debate. 2000. pap. 24.00 (*1-58648-004-9*) PublicAffairs NY.

Lehrer, Jim. The Last Debate. large type ed. (Niagara Large Print Ser.). 485p. 1996. 29.50 (*0-7089-5838-9*) Ulverscroft.

— Lost & Found. large type ed. LC 91-13716. 249p. 1991. reprint ed. lib. bdg. 21.95 (*1-56054-180-6*) Thorndike Pr.

— Purple Dots. large type ed. 1999. 27.95 (*0-7862-1809-6*) Mac Lib Ref.

— Purple Dots: A Novel. LC 98-12962. 262p. 1998. 23.95 (*0-679-45237-0*) McKay.

— Short List. large type ed. LC 92-6487. 303p. 1992. reprint ed. 20.95 (*1-56054-397-3*) Thorndike Pr.

— The Sooner Spy. LC 97-3972. (One-Eyed Mack Mystery Ser.). 222p. 1997. pap. 12.95 (*1-57178-041-6*) Coun Oak Bks.

— The Sooner Spy. large type ed. LC 90-45972. 290p. 1990. reprint ed. lib. bdg. 19.95 (*1-56054-067-2*) Thorndike Pr.

***Lehrer, Jim.** The Special Prisoner. 256p. 2000. 23.95 (*0-375-50371-4*) Random.

— White Widow. 224p. 2000. pap. 12.00 (*1-891620-41-X*) PublicAffairs NY.

Lehrer, Jim. White Widow. large type ed. LC 97-1178. (Basic Ser.). 312p. 1997. 24.95 (*0-7862-1088-5*) Thorndike Pr.

Lehrer, John. The World of Turtles & Tortoises. (Illus.). 160p. 1993. 26.95 (*1-56465-116-9*, 16089) Tetra Pr.

Lehrer, K., ed. Analysis & Metaphysics: Essays in Honour of R. M. Chisholm. (Philosophical Studies: 4). 327p. 1981. pap. text 59.00 (*90-277-1193-3*) Kluwer Academic.

Lehrer, Kate. Out of Eden. large type ed. (Niagara Large Print Ser.). 548p. 1997. 29.50 (*0-7089-5869-9*) Ulverscroft.

— When They Took Away the Man in the Moon. large type ed. LC 93-30904. 404p. 1993. lib. bdg. 17.95 (*0-7862-0042-1*) Thorndike Pr.

Lehrer, Keith. Metamind. 322p. 1990. text 45.00 (*0-19-824850-4*) OUP.

— Self-Trust: A Study of Reason, Knowledge, & Autonomy. LC 96-21872. (Illus.). 216p. 1997. pap. text 15.95 (*0-19-823694-8*) OUP.

— Theory of Knowledge. 224p. (C). 1990. pap. 25.00 (*0-8133-0571-3*, Pub. by Westview) HarpC.

— Theory of Knowledge. 2nd ed. (Dimensions of Philosophy Ser.). 224p. 2000. pap. 24.00 (*0-8133-9053-2*); text 60.00 (*0-8133-9052-4*) Westview.

— Thomas Reid. 400p. 1989. 49.95 (*0-415-03886-3*, A3536) Routledge.

Lehrer, Keith, ed. Analysis & Metaphysics: Essays in Honor of R. M. Chisholm. LC 75-5500. (Philosophical Studies: No. 4). 327p. 1975. lib. bdg. 146.00 (*90-277-0571-2*, D Reidel) Kluwer Academic.

— Austrian Philosophy Past & Present. LC 96-49725. (Boston Studies in Philosophy of Science: Vol. 190). 288p. (C). 1996. text 117.50 (*0-7923-4347-6*) Kluwer Academic.

— Knowledge, Teaching & Wisdom. (Philosophical Studies). 300p. (C). 1996. text 132.50 (*0-7923-3980-0*) Kluwer Academic.

Lehrer, Keith & Wagner, Carl. Rational Consensus in Science & Society: A Philosophical & Mathematical Study. 174p. 1981. lib. bdg. 70.50 (*90-277-1306-5*, D Reidel) Kluwer Academic.

Lehrer, Keith, ed. see Reid, Thomas.

Lehrer, Keith, ed. see Rosenberg, Alexander.

Lehrer, M. Orientation & Communication in Arthropods. LC 98-118531. (Experientia Supplementum Ser.: Vol. 84). (Illus.). 350p. 1997. text 160.00 (*3-7643-5693-6*) Birkhauser.

Lehrer, Marc, jt. auth. see Kopelman, Orion M.

Lehrer, Marc, jt. auth. see Van De Carr, F. Rene.

Lehrer, Mark. Intellektuelle Aporte und Literarische Originalitat: Wissenschaftgeschichtliche Studien zum Deutschen Realismus: Keller, Raabe und Fontane. LC 90-24409. (North American Studies in Nineteenth-Century German Literature: Vol. 8). XI, 169p. (C). 1991. text 36.95 (*0-8204-1476-X*) P Lang Pubng.

Lehrer, Matthew D., jt. auth. see Smith, Amy Sherman.

Lehrer, Melinda. Classical Myth & the "Polifemo" of Gongora. 130p. 1990. 39.50 (*0-916379-60-4*) Scripta.

Lehrer, Milton G. Transylvania: History & Reality. Martin, David, ed. & frwd. by. LC 86-25861. 320p. 1987. 18.95 (*0-910155-04-6*) Bartleby Pr.

Lehrer, Paul M. & Woolfolk, Robert L., eds. Principles & Practices of Stress Management. 2nd ed. LC 92-49253. 621p. 1993. pap. text 39.95 (*0-89862-162-3*) Guilford Pubns.

Lehrer, Paul M., jt. ed. see Woolfolk, Robert L.

Lehrer, Richard & Chazan, Daniel, eds. Designing Learning Environments for Developing Understanding of Geometry & Space. LC 97-48323. (Studies in Mathematical Thinking & Learning). 336p. 1998. write for info. (*0-8058-1948-7*); pap. write for info. (*0-8058-1949-5*) L Erlbaum Assocs.

Lehrer, Robert, et al. Immunologic Aspects of Infectious Diseases. Steigbigel, Roy, ed. (C). pap. text. write for info. (*1-878294-06-7*) Health Dimensions.

Lehrer, Ronald. Nietzsche's Presence in Freud's Life & Thought: On the Origins of a Psychology of Dynamic Unconscious Mental Functioning. LC 94-571. 370p. (C). 1994. text 69.50 (*0-7914-2145-7*); pap. text 23.95 (*0-7914-2146-5*) State U NY Pr.

Lehrer, Shlomo Zalman & Strassman, L. The Vanished City of Sanz. 402p. 1997. 23.95 (*1-56871-130-1*, Pub. by Targum Pr) Feldheim.

Lehrer, Stanley, jt. auth. see Ehrensperger, Harold A.

Lehrer, Stanley, jt. ed. see Brickman, William W.

Lehrer, Stephen M. Cooking with the Chicken Breast: Delicious Main Dishes Starring the Delectable Skinless & Boneless White Meat. LC 89-91671. (Illus.). 224p. (Orig.). 1990. pap. 11.95 (*0-9623104-8-4*) Madeira-Hudson Pub.

Lehrer, Steven. Understanding Lung Sounds. 2nd ed. (Illus.). 160p. 1993. pap. text 46.00 (*0-7216-4902-5*, W B Saunders Co) Harcrt Hlth Sci Grp.

Lehrer, Steven. Understanding Pediatric Heart Sounds. (Illus.). 248p. 1991. pap., pap. text 51.00 incl. digital audio (*0-7216-2387-5*, W B Saunders Co) Harcrt Hlth Sci Grp.

Lehrer, Steven, jt. auth. see Buck, Frank.

Lehrer, Susan. Origins of Protective Labor Legislation for Women, 1905-1925. LC 87-6485. (SUNY Series on Women & Work). 318p. (C). 1987. text 64.50 (*0-88706-506-6*); pap. text 21.95 (*0-88706-505-8*) State U NY Pr.

Lehrer, Tom. Tom Lehrer's Song Book. Date not set. reprint ed. lib. bdg. 16.95 (*0-89190-092-6*, Am Repr) Amereon Ltd.

— Too Many Songs by Tom Lehrer with Not Enough Pictures by Ronald Searle. (Illus.). 1981. pap. 17.00 (*0-394-74930-8*) Pantheon.

Lehrer, Warren. Brother Blue: A Narrative Portrait of Brother Blue, a. k. a. Dr. Hugh Morgan Hill. LC 95-5813. (Portrait Ser.). (Illus.). 272p. (Orig.). 1995. pap. 12.95 (*0-941920-36-4*) Bay Pr.

— Charlie: A Narrative Portrait of Charles Lang. LC 95-9933. (Portrait Ser.). (Illus.). 208p. (Orig.). 1995. pap. 12.95 (*0-941920-34-8*) Bay Pr.

— Claude: A Narrative Portrait of Claude Debs. LC 95-5812. (Portrait Ser.). (Illus.). 260p. (Orig.). 1995. pap. 12.95 (*0-941920-35-6*) Bay Pr.

— GRRRHHHH: A Study of Social Patterns. 462p. 1987. 100.00 (*0-9613871-1-4*) Ear Say.

— I Mean You Know. (Illus.). 156p. 1983. 25.00 (*0-89822-035-1*) Ear Say.

— Nicky D. A Narrative Portrait of Nicholas Detommaso. LC 95-5814. (Portrait Ser.). (Illus.). 268p. (Orig.). 1995. pap. 12.95 (*0-941920-37-2*) Bay Pr.

***Lehri, R. M.** Folk Designs & Motifs from India. LC 99-35142. (Design Library). 48p. 1999. pap. text 5.95 (*0-486-40706-3*) Dover.

Lehrke, Robert. Sex Linkage of Intelligence: The X-Factor. LC 96-53612. (Human Evolution, Behavior & Intelligence Ser.). 208p. 1997. 55.00 (*0-275-95903-1*, Praeger Pubs) Greenwood.

Lehrling, George. Machinist: Basic Skill Development. LC 77-73238. 256p. reprint ed. pap. 79.40 (*0-608-11689-0*, 201157500079) Bks Demand.

Lehrman, Edgar. A Handbook to the Russian Text of Crime & Punishment. 1977. 103.10 (*90-279-3327-8*) Mouton.

Lehrman, Edgar, tr. see Gorchakov, Nikolai A.

Lehrman, Frederica. Domestic Violence Practice & Procedure. 1996. ring bd. 150.00 (*0-8366-9007-9*) West Group.

Lehrman, Fredric. Loving the Earth. (Illus.). 48p. (YA). (gr. 6-12). 1990. 14.95 (*0-89087-603-7*) Celestial Arts.

— Prosperity Consciousness: How to Tap Your Unlimited Wealth. 1995. 16.00 incl. audio (*0-671-52975-7*) S&S Trade.

— The Sacred Landscape. LC 88-72301. (Illus.). 128p. 1995. pap. 29.95 (*0-89087-542-1*) Celestial Arts.

— The Sacred Landscape. deluxe ed. (Illus.). 128p. 1989. boxed set 100.00 (*0-89087-549-9*) Celestial Arts.

Lehrman, Jane A. Around Douglas & Beyond: A Collection of Columns about the People of Douglas County. Lehrman, Sally, ed. (Illus.). 123p. (Orig.). 1990. pap. text 24.50 (*0-922082-01-4*); lib. bdg. 27.50 (*0-685-46926-3*) Desk Top Pubs Inc.

Lehrman, Karen. The Lipstick Proviso: Women, Sex, & Power in the Real World. LC 96-49392. 240p. 1997. 23.95 (*0-385-47481-4*, Anchor NY) Doubleday.

Lehrman, Lewis. Dining Room Service. LC 70-142510. 1971. text. write for info. (*0-672-96065-6*) Macmillan.

Lehrman, Lewis B. Becoming a Successful Artist. (Illus.). 144p. 1996. pap. 24.99 (*0-89134-742-9*, North Lght Bks) F & W Pubns Inc.

— Energize Your Paintings with Color. (Elements of Painting Ser.). (Illus.). 144p. 1993. 27.95 (*0-89134-476-4*, 30522, North Lght Bks) F & W Pubns Inc.

— Freshen Your Paintings with New Ideas. (Illus.). 144p. 1995. 27.99 (*0-89134-566-3*, North Lght Bks) F & W Pubns Inc.

Lehrman, Lewis B., jt. auth. see Goerschner, Ted.

Lehrman, Lewis B., jt. auth. see Simandle, Marilyn.

Lehrman, Neil. Perdut. LC 78-20558. 1979. pap. 9.95 (*0-931848-23-7*) Dryad Pr.

— Perdut. deluxe limited ed. LC 78-20558. 1979. 15.00 (*0-931848-22-9*) Dryad Pr.

Lehrman, Paul. Getting into Digital Recording. 64p. 1996. pap. 9.95 (*0-7935-5947-2*) H Leonard.

Lehrman, Philip R., ed. see Freud, Anna & Burlingham, Dorothy T.

Lehrman, Robert. Juggling. LC 81-48654. 256p. (YA). (gr. 7 up). 1982. 11.50 (*0-06-023818-6*) HarpC Child Bks.

— The Store That Mama Built. LC 91-39983. 128p. (J). (gr. 3-7). 1992. lib. bdg. 13.95 (*0-02-754632-2*, Mac Bks Young Read) S&S Childrens.

Lehrman, Robert L. Physics the Easy Way. 3rd ed. LC 97-35217. 400p. 1998. pap. 12.95 (*0-7641-0236-2*) Barron.

Lehrman, S. M., tr. see Kahana, S. Z.

Lehrman, Sally, ed. see Lehrman, Jane A.

Lehrmann, Charles C. Jewish Influences on European Thought. Klin, George & Carpenter, Victor, trs. LC 72-3264. 323p. 1975. 27.50 (*0-8386-7908-0*) Fairleigh Dickinson.

Lehrmann, Paul & Tully, Tim. MIDI for the Professional. (Illus.). 240p. 1995. pap. 24.95 (*0-8256-1374-4*, AM91049) Music Sales.

Lehrs, Ernst. Man or Matter. pap. 24.00 (*0-85440-430-9*, 1027, Pub. by R Steiner Pr) Anthroposophic.

— Spiritual Science, Electricity & Michael Faraday. 30p. 1975. pap. 5.00 (*0-85440-296-9*, Pub. by R Steiner Pr) Anthroposophic.

Lehrs, Karl. De Aristarchi Studiis Homericis. x, 506p. 1964. reprint ed. write for info. incl. 3.5 hd (*0-318-70958-9*) G Olms Pubs.

— Kleine Schriften. viii, 582p. 1979. reprint ed. write for info. (*3-487-06756-0*) G Olms Pubs.

— Quaestiones Epicae. viii, 339p. 1977. reprint ed. write for info. (*3-487-06235-6*) G Olms Pubs.

Lehrs, Max. Geschichte & Kritscher Katalog des Deutschen, Niederlandischen & Franzosischen Kupferstichs im XV Jahrhundert, 9 Vols. (Illus.). 1969. 1320.00 (*0-8115-0044-6*) Periodicals Srv.

Lehrstuhl, Grundbau & Bodenmechanik, eds. 20 Jahre Grundbau und Bodenmechanik an der Ruhr-Universitat Bochum: Festschrift Anlasslich des 60.Geburtstages von Prof. Dr.-Ing, H. L. Jessberger, Devember 1992. 433p. 1992. 95.00 (*90-5410-301-9*, Pub. by A A Balkema) Ashgate Pub Co.

Lehtcmaa, Linda R., jt. auth. see McVey, Mary A.

***Lehti, Marko.** A Baltic League As a Construct of the New Europe: Envisioning a Baltic Region & Small State Sovereignty in the Aftermath of the First World War. (European University Studies: Vol. 817). 550p. 1999. 79.95 (*3-631-34045-1*) P Lang Pubng.

Lehti, Marko. A Baltic League As a Construct of the New Europe Vol. 817: Envisioning a Baltic Region & Small State Sovereignty in the Aftermath of the First World War. LC 99-36785. (European University Studies). 550p. 1998. pap. 79.95 (*0-8204-3635-6*) P Lang Pubng.

Lehtinen, Alice E., jt. auth. see Annett, Albert.

Lehtinen, Meri. Basic Course in Finnish. 3rd ed. Sebeok, Thomas A., ed. LC 63-64029. (Uralic & Altaic Ser.: Vol. 27). (FIN.). 700p. 1970. ring bd. write for info. (*0-87750-005-3*) Curzon Pr Ltd.

Lehtinen, Rick. Microsoft IIS 4 on Site: The Ultimate On-the-Job Solution Finder. 1998. pap. 39.99 (*1-57610-330-7*) Coriolis Grp.

Lehtinen, Ritva & Nurmi, Kari E. The Grandchildren of the Incas. (World's Children Ser.). (Illus.). 40p. (J). (gr. 3-6). 1991. lib. bdg. 21.27 (*0-87614-397-4*, Carolrhoda) Lerner Pub.

— The Grandchildren of the Incas. (Illus.). (J). (gr. 3-6). 1992. pap. 6.95 (*0-87614-566-7*, Carolrhoda) Lerner Pub.

***Lehtmets, Ann.** Sentence Siberia: A Story of Survival. 1998. 17.95 (*1-86254-313-5*) Wakefield Pr.

Lehto, J. Approaches to Alcohol Control Policy. LC 96-145877. (WHO Regional Publications, European Ser.: No. 60). 65p. Date not set. pap. text 20.00 (*92-890-1324-9*) World Health.

Lehto, J., jt. auth. see Anderson, P.

Lehto, Kerry. Official Microsoft Frontpage 98 Book. LC 97-33679. 416p. 1997. pap. text 24.99 (*1-57231-629-2*) Microsoft.

Lehto, Kerry A. & Polonsky, W. Brett. Introducing Microsoft FrontPage 97. LC 96-40955. 416p. 1996. 24.99 (*1-57231-571-7*) Microsoft.

Lehto, Manja I. Ingrian Finnish: Dialect Preservation & Change. (Studia Uralica Upsaliensia: Vol. 23). 194p. (Orig.). 1996. pap. 47.50 (*91-554-3688-9*) Coronet Bks.

Lehto, Mark R., ed. Hazard Communication: A Special Double Issue of the "International Journal of Cognitive Ergonomics" 175p. 1998. pap. write for info. (*0-8058-9822-0*) L Erlbaum Assocs.

Lehto, Mark R. & Miller, James M. Warnings Vol. 1: Fundamentals, Design & Evaluation Methodologies. LC 86-22866. (Illus.). 287p. 1986. 55.00 (*0-940537-00-1*) Fuller Tech.

Lehto, O. Univalent Functions & Teichmuller Spaces. (Graduate Texts in Mathematics Ser.: Vol. 109). (Illus.). 270p. 1986. 59.95 (*0-387-96310-3*) Spr-Verlag.

Lehto, O., ed. International Congress of Mathematicians: Proceedings, Helsinki, 1980, 2 vols., Set. 1022p. 1980. pap. 80.00 (*951-41-0352-1*, PICM/78) Am Math.

Lehto, Olli E. Mathematics Without Borders: A History of the International Mathematical Union. LC 97-37950. (Illus.). 368p. 1997. 35.00 (*0-387-98358-9*) Spr-Verlag.

Lehtonen, Risto. Story of a Storm: The Ecumenical Student Movement in the Turmoil of Revolution. LC 97-44688. 362p. 1998. pap. 20.00 (*0-8028-4429-4*) Eerdmans.

Lehtonen, Risto & Pahkinen, Erkki J. Practical Methods for Design & Analysis of Complex Surveys. LC 94-20917. (Statistics in Practice Ser.). 348p. 1995. 125.00 (*0-471-93934-X*) Wiley.

Lehtonen, Soila, jt. ed. see Hawkins, Hildi.

Lehu, Pierre, jt. auth. see Westheimer, Ruth K.

Lehu, Pierre A., jt. auth. see Westheimer, Ruth K.

***Lehuu, Isabelle.** Carnival on the Page: Popular Print Media in Antebellum America. LC 99-27582. 264p. 2000. pap. 17.95 (*0-8078-4832-8*) U of NC Pr.

— Carnival on the Page: Popular Print Media in Antebellum America. LC 99-27582. (Illus.). 264p. 2000. lib. bdg. 39.95 (*0-8078-2521-2*) U of NC Pr.

Lei, Chun, jt. ed. see Choquette, Kent D.

Lei, David, jt. auth. see Pitts, Robert A.

Lei, Donise. Ancient China: Its History & Culture from 2250 B.C. to A.D. 250 (A Learning Unit) LC 91-91297. (Illus.). 42p. (Orig.). (YA). (gr. 6 up). 1992. pap. text 7.95 (*1-879600-01-3*) Pac Asia Pr.

Lei, K. Y. Role of Copper in Lipid Metabolism. 296p. 1990. lib. bdg. 202.00 (*0-8493-5564-8*, QR186) CRC Pr.

Lei-Lanilau, Carolyn. Ono Ono Girl's Hula. LC 97-7216. 196p. 1997. 34.95 (*0-299-15630-3*); pap. 17.95 (*0-299-15634-6*) U of Wis Pr.

***Lei, Tan, ed.** The Mandelbrot Set, Theme & Variations. LC 99-54508. (London Mathematical Society Lecture Note Ser.: No. 274). (Illus.). 286p. 2000. pap. 44.95 (*0-521-77476-4*) Cambridge U Pr.

Leib, Frank B. Friendly Competitors: Fierce Companions: Men's Ways of Relating. LC 97-35247. 224p. (Orig.). 1998. pap. 16.95 (*0-8298-1211-3*) Pilgrim OH.

***Leib, Franklin A.** Behold a Pale Horse. LC 99-52421. 304p. 2000. 23.95 (*0-312-89064-8*, Pub. by Forge NYC) St Martin.

Leib, Franklin A. The House of Pain. LC 98-44609. 320p. 1999. 23.95 (*0-312-86616-X*, Pub. by Forge NYC) St Martin.

***Leib, Franklin Allen.** House of Pain. 368p. 2000. mass mkt. 6.99 (*0-8125-7781-7*) Tor Bks.

Leib, Garson, tr. see Margulis, Milia A., ed.

Leib, Kurt & Butterman, Steve. Ride Guide: Covered Bridges of Ohio. (Illus.). 128p. 1999. pap. 14.95 (*0-933855-16-8*) Anacus Pr.

Leib, Michael S. & Monroe, William E. Practical Small Animal Internal Medicine. Kersey, Ray, ed. 1008p. 1996. text 94.00 (*0-7216-4839-8*, W B Saunders Co) Harcrt Hlth Sci Grp.

Leibbrandt, G. Noncovariant Gauges: Quantization of Yang-Mills. 220p. 1994. text 48.00 (*981-02-1384-0*) World Scientific Pub.

Leibbrandt, Murray V., et al. The Contribution of Income Components to Income Inequality in South Africa: A Decomposable Gini Analysis. LC 96-16538. (LSMS Working Papers: No. 125). 40p. 1996. pap. 22.00 (*0-8213-3637-1*) World Bank.

***Leibe, Frankie.** Soft Toys. (Miller's Collectors' Guide Ser.). (Illus.). 64p. 2000. 9.95 (*1-84000-185-2*, Pub. by Millers Pubns) Antique Collect.

Leibe, Frankie, jt. auth. see Liebe, Frankie.

Leibel, Steven A. & Phillips, Theodore I. Textbook of Radiation Oncology: Principles. LC 96-4867. 1376p. (C). 1998. text 225.00 (*0-7216-5336-7*, W B Saunders Co) Harcrt Hlth Sci Grp.

Leibenluft, Ellen. Gender Differences in Mood & Anxiety Disorders: From Bench to Bedside. (Review of Psychiatry Ser.). 1999. 27.50 (*0-88048-958-8*) Am Psychiatric.

Leibenluft, Ellen, et al, eds. Less Time to Do More: Psychotherapy on the Short-Term Inpatient Unit. LC 93-20081. 321p. 1993. text 19.95 (*0-88048-512-4*, 8512) Am Psychiatric.

Leibenstein, Debby. Mab'Ei Hakittah: A Curriculum of Classroom Hebrew Expressions. 1997. pap. 3.75 (*1-878895-04-4*, C015) Torah Umesorah.

Leibenstein, Dov. Chumash & Rashi Curriculum. (Orig.). 1990. ring bd. 28.00 (*0-914131-94-X*, C030) Torah Umesorah.

An Asterisk (*) at the beginning of an entry indicates that the title is appearing for the first time.

Leibenstein, Harvey. Beyond Economic Man: A New Approach to Micro-Economic Theory. (Illus.). 302p. 1976. pap. 16.50 (*0-674-06892-0*) HUP.

— Inflation, Income Distribution & X-Efficiency Theory: A Study Prepared for the International Labour Office Within the Framework of the World Employment Programme. 122p. 1980. 45.00 (*0-06-494169-8*, 06556) B&N Imports.

— Inside the Firm: The Inefficiencies of Hierarchy. LC 87-8426. (Illus.). 304p. 1987. 43.00 (*0-674-45515-0*) HUP.

***Leibenstein, Margaret.** Cooking from the Garden: Original & Unusual Recipes to Enhance & Preserve Your Garden Harvest. LC 99-28991. (Taylor's Weekend Gardening Guides Ser.). (Illus.). 128p. 2000. pap. 14.00 (*0-395-88946-4*) HM.

Leiber. Frommer's Comprehensive Travel Guide Budapest. 2nd ed. 1996. per. 12.95 (*0-671-51941-7*) S&S Trade.

Leiber & Bailey. Swords against Shadowland. 1994. mass mkt. 4.50 (*0-8125-2388-1*) Tor Bks.

Leiber & Stoller. Jailhouse Rock, Kansas City, & Other Hits. (Piano-Vocal-Guitar Ser.). 80p. 1997. otabind 10.95 (*0-7935-7819-1*) H Leonard.

Leiber & Stoller. Jailhouse Rock, Kansas City, & Other Hits. 64p. 1997. pap. 8.95 (*0-7935-7820-5*) H Leonard.

— Jailhouse Rock, Kansas City, & Other Hits. (E-Z Play Today Ser.: Vol. #178). 64p. 1998. pap. 8.95 (*0-7935-8233-4*) H Leonard.

Leiber, Fritz. The Best of Fritz Leiber. Date not set. lib. bdg. 19.95 (*0-8488-2127-0*) Amereon Ltd.

— The Big Time. LC 99-86040. 128p. 2000. 21.95 (*0-312-89079-6*, Pub. by Tor Bks) St Martin.

— The Big Time. 1976. reprint ed. lib. bdg. 20.95 (*0-88411-931-9*) Amereon Ltd.

— The Big Time. 1990. reprint ed. lib. bdg. 25.95 (*0-89968-537-4*) Buccaneer Bks.

— Conjure Wife. 1993. reprint ed. lib. bdg. 18.95 (*0-89968-435-1*, Lghtyr Pr) Buccaneer Bks.

— Conjure Wife & Our Lady of Darkness. 352p. 1991. mass mkt. 4.99 (*0-8125-1296-0*, Pub. by Tor Bks) St Martin.

— Dark Ladies. LC 99-41092. 348p. 1999. pap. 17.95 (*0-312-86972-X*, Pub. by Tor Bks) St Martin.

— The Dealings of Daniel Kesserich. 128p. Date not set. pap. 9.95 (*0-312-86622-4*, Pub. by Tor Bks) St Martin.

— Farewell to Lankhmar. (Illus.). 1999. pap. 5.99 (*1-56504-897-0*, 12015, Borealis) White Wolf.

— Farewell to Lankhmar. (Lankhmar Ser.: Vol. 4). 1998. reprint ed. 21.99 (*1-56504-929-2*, 12003, Borealis) White Wolf.

— Green Millenium. 1976. 21.95 (*0-8488-1076-7*) Amereon Ltd.

— The Green Millenium. 1993. reprint ed. lib. bdg. 18.95 (*0-89968-348-7*, Lghtyr Pr) Buccaneer Bks.

— The Green Millennium. LC 80-22108. 256p. 1980. reprint ed. 25.00 (*0-8398-2641-9*) Ultramarine Pub.

— Gummitch & Friends. (Illus.). 224p. 1992. 30.00 (*1-880418-18-5*); 60.00 (*1-880418-17-7*) D M Grant.

— Heroes & Horrors. Schiff, Stuart D., ed. LC 78-64600. (Illus.). 1978. 15.00 (*0-918372-03-8*) Whispers.

— Ill Met in Lankhmar. (Illus.). 1996. pap. 5.99 (*1-56504-894-6*, 12011, Borealis) White Wolf.

— Lean Times in Lankhmar: Swords & Deviltry; Swords Against Death, 2 bks. in 1. (Lankhmar Ser.: Vol. 2). 1997. mass mkt. 5.99 (*1-56504-895-4*, WW 12013, Borealis) White Wolf.

— Night's Black Agent. 1976. reprint ed. lib. bdg. 21.95 (*0-88411-932-7*) Amereon Ltd.

— Night's Black Agent. 1990. reprint ed. 27.95 (*0-89968-538-2*) Buccaneer Bks.

— Night's Black Agents. LC 76-363952. x, 237p. (J). 1975. write for info. (*0-85978-013-9*) C W Daniel.

— Our Lady of Darkness. 1993. reprint ed. lib. bdg. 18.95 (*0-89968-436-X*, Lghtyr Pr) Buccaneer Bks.

— Pail of Air. 1976. reprint ed. lib. bdg. 20.95 (*0-88411-933-5*) Amereon Ltd.

— Return to Lankhmar. (Adventure of Fafhed & the Gray Mouser Ser.). 1998. pap. text 5.99 (*1-56504-896-2*, Borealis) White Wolf.

— Return to Lankhmar Vol. 3: The Adventures of Fafhrd & the Grey Mouser, 2 bks. in 1. rev. ed. (Illus.). 1997. 21.99 (*1-56504-928-4*, 12002, Borealis) White Wolf.

— The Secret Songs. 1999. lib. bdg. 21.95 (*1-56723-141-1*, 150) Yestermorrow.

— A Specter Is Haunting Texas. 256p. 1992. pap. 9.00 (*0-02-022347-1*) Macmillan.

— Swords of Lankhmar. 224p. Date not set. 21.95 (*0-8488-2352-4*) Amereon Ltd.

— Two Sought Adventure. 1993. reprint ed. lib. bdg. 18.95 (*0-89968-405-X*, Lghtyr Pr) Buccaneer Bks.

— The Wanderer. 1993. reprint ed. lib. bdg. 27.95 (*0-89968-349-5*, Lghtyr Pr) Buccaneer Bks.

Leiber, Joseph. Frommer's Budapest & Best of Hungary. 256p. 1995. 14.95 (*0-02-860703-1*) Macmillan.

Leiber, Joseph & Shea, Christina. Frommer's Budapest & Best of Hungary. 2nd ed. 240p. 1998. pap. 14.95 (*0-02-862082-8*) Macmillan.

Leiber, Justin. Can Animals & Machines Be Persons? A Dialogue. LC 85-21888. 88p. (C). 1985. pap. 5.95 (*0-87220-002-7*); lib. bdg. 24.95 (*0-87220-003-5*) Hackett Pub.

Leiber, Vivian. Always a Hero. (American Romance Ser.: No. 686). 1997. per. 3.75 (*0-373-16686-9*, 1-16686-7) Harlequin Bks.

***Leiber, Vivian.** Au Service de l'Amour. 1999. mass mkt. 3.99 (*0-373-39533-7*) Silhouette.

Leiber, Vivian. Baby Makes Nine. LC 95-6902. (American Romance Ser.). 251p. 1995. per. 3.50 (*0-373-16576-5*, 1-16576-0) Harlequin Bks.

— The Bewildered Wife. (Romance Ser.: No. 1237). 1997. per. 3.25 (*0-373-19237-1*, 1-19237-6) Silhouette.

— Blue-Jeaned Prince. (Harlequin American Romance Ser.: No. 640). 1996. per. 3.75 (*0-373-16640-0*, 1-16640-4) Harlequin Bks.

— Goody Two-Shoes. (Romance Ser.: No. 871). 1992. per. 2.69 (*0-373-08871-X*, 5-08871-1) Silhouette.

— Goody Two-Shoes. large type ed. 256p. 1992. reprint ed. lib. bdg. 13.95 (*1-56054-539-9*) Thorndike Pr.

— His Betrothed. (Intrigue Ser.). 1998. per. 3.99 (*0-373-22460-5*, 1-22460-9) Harlequin Bks.

— His Kind of Trouble. 1997. per. 3.75 (*0-373-22416-8*, 1-22416-1) Harlequin Bks.

— The Marriage Merger: Loving the Boss. (Romance Ser.: No. 1366). 1999. per. 3.50 (*0-373-19366-1*, 1-19366-3) Silhouette.

— Marrying Nicky. (American Romance Ser.: No. 655). 1996. per. 3.75 (*0-373-16655-9*, 1-16655-2) Harlequin Bks.

***Leiber, Vivian.** Men of Sugar Mountain: Two Hearts. (Zebra Bouquet Ser.: Vol. 49). 256p. 2000. pap. 3.99 (*0-8217-6623-6*, Zebra Kensgtn) Kensgtn Pub Corp.

Leiber, Vivian. A Million-Dollar Man: How to Marry. 1997. per. 3.75 (*0-373-16672-9*, 1-16672-7) Harlequin Bks.

— One Sexy Daddy. (American Romance Ser.). 1999. per. 3.99 (*0-373-16792-X*, 1-16792-3) Harlequin Bks.

***Leiber, Vivian.** One Touch, Vol. 41. (Zebra Bouquet Ser.). 2000. mass mkt. 3.99 (*0-8217-6577-9*, Zebra Kensgtn) Kensgtn Pub Corp.

Leiber, Vivian. An Ordinary Day. (American Romance Ser.: No. 712). 1998. per. 3.75 (*0-373-16712-1*, 1-16712-1) Harlequin Bks.

***Leiber, Vivian.** Safety of His Arms. 2000. mass mkt. 4.50 (*0-373-82211-1*, 1-82211-3) Harlequin Bks.

Leiber, Vivian. Safety of His Arms. (Romance Ser.). 1995. per. 2.99 (*0-373-19070-0*, 1-19070-1) Silhouette.

— The 6'2", 200 lb. Challenge. 1998. per. 3.50 (*0-373-19292-4*, 1-19292-1) Silhouette.

— Soldier & the Society Girl (He's My Hero!) (Silhouette Romance Ser.: No. 1358). 1999. per. 3.50 (*0-373-19358-0*, 1-19358-0) Harlequin Bks.

***Leiber, Vivian.** Three Wishes, Vol. 58. 2000. mass mkt. 3.99 (*0-8217-6668-6*) Kensgtn Pub Corp.

Leiber, Vivien. Secret Daddy: Gowns of White. 1999. per. 3.99 (*0-373-16761-X*, Harlequin) Harlequin Bks.

Leiberman, Jeffrey & Tasman, Allan. Psychiatric Drugs. LC 99-44546. (Illus.). 255p. 2000. pap. text. write for info. (*0-7216-5884-9*, W B Saunders Co) Harcrt Hlth Sci Grp.

Leiberman, Louis, jt. auth. see Westheimer, Ruth.

Leiberman, Marcia & Leiberman, Philip. Walking the Alpine Parks of France & Northwest Italy. (Illus.). 240p. 1994. pap. 14.95 (*0-89886-398-8*) Mountaineers.

Leiberman, Philip, jt. auth. see Leiberman, Marcia.

Leiberman, Sara. A Trip to Mezuza Land. Colish, Chanah, ed. (Illus.). 48p. (J). 1988. reprint ed. 12.00 (*0-8266-0364-5*, Merkos LInyonei Chinuch) Kehot Pubn Soc.

Leibfried, Kathleen H., jt. auth. see McNair, Carol J.

***Leibfried, Philip.** Rudyard Kipling & Sir Henry Rider Haggard on Screen, Stage, Radio & Television. LC 99-49415. (Illus.). 224p. 1999. boxed set 45.00 (*0-7864-0707-7*) McFarland & Co.

Leibfried, Stephan & Leisering, Lutz. Time & Poverty in Western Welfare States: United Germany in Perspective. LC 98-39070. (Illus.). 388p. 1999. 74.95 (*0-521-59013-2*) Cambridge U Pr.

Leibfried, Stephan, ed. see Pierson, Paul.

Leibholz-Bonhoeffer, Sabine. The Bonhoeffers: Portrait of a Family. (Orig.). 1994. pap. 12.95 (*0-910452-78-4*) Covenant.

Leibholz, Stephhen W., ed. see Hoeber, Francis P.

Leibig, Michael T. & Kahn, Wendy L. Public Employee Organizing & the Law. LC 87-18398. 258p. reprint ed. pap. 80.00 (*0-7837-4604-0*, 204432300002) Bks Demand.

Leibiger, Stuart Eric. Founding Friendship: George Washington, James Madison, & the Creation of the American Republic. LC 99-19854. 1999. 35.00 (*0-8139-1882-0*) U Pr of Va.

Leibing, Edward. NetWare User's Guide: Versions 3.11 & 3.12. LC 93-4987. 1995. pap. 34.95 (*1-55851-318-3*, M&T Bks) IDG Bks.

Leibling, Barbara, ed. see Imray Laurie Norie & Wilson, Ltd. Staff, et al.

Leiblum, Sandra R. Infertility: Psychological Issues & Counseling Strategies. LC 96-23253. (Wiley Series in Couples & Family Dynamics & Treatment). 278p. 1996. 64.50 (*0-471-12684-5*) Wiley.

***Leiblum, Sandra R.** Principles & Practice of Sex Therapy. 3rd ed. (Illus.). 518p. 2000. 50.00 (*1-57230-574-6*) Guilford Pubns.

Leiblum, Sandra R. & Rosen, Raymond C., eds. Principles & Practice of Sex Therapy: Update for the 1990s. 2nd ed. LC 89-7458. 413p. 1989. lib. bdg. 46.95 (*0-89862-389-8*) Guilford Pubns.

— Sexual Desire Disorders. LC 87-21192. 470p. 1992. reprint ed. pap. text 26.95 (*0-89862-153-4*) Guilford Pubns.

Leiblum, Sandra R., jt. auth. see Rosen, Raymond C.

Leiblum, Sandra R., jt. ed. see Rosen, Raymond C.

Leibman, Jack, jt. auth. see Wolfstone, Leon.

Leibman, Nina C. Living Room Lectures: The Fifties Family in Film & Television. LC 94-36606. (Texas Film Studies). (Illus.). 384p. 1995. pap. 18.95 (*0-292-74684-9*); text 45.00 (*0-292-74683-0*) U of Tex Pr.

Leibniz, Gottfried Wilhelm. Der Briefwechsel von Gottfried Wilhelm Leibniz Mit Mathematikern. xxviii, 760p. 1987. reprint ed. write for info. (*3-487-00343-0*) G Olms Pubs.

— Briefwechsel Zwischen Leibniz und Christian Wolff. 188p. 1971. reprint ed. write for info. (*0-318-71366-7*) G Olms Pubs.

— Catalogue Critique des Manuscrits de Leibniz Vol. Two: Mars 1672-Novembre 1676. xiv, 257p. 1986. reprint ed. write for info. (*3-487-07797-3*) G Olms Pubs.

— Correspondenz Von Leibniz Mit Caroline. (GER.). 1973. reprint ed. write for info. (*3-487-04542-7*) G Olms Pubs.

— Correspondenz Von Leibniz Mit der Prinzessin Sophie. (GER.). 1973. write for info. (*3-487-04857-4*) G Olms Pubs.

— De Summe-Rerum: Metaphysical Papers, 1675-1676. Parkinson, George H., tr. LC 91-30770. (Leibniz Ser.). 208p. (C). 1992. 47.50 (*0-300-05187-5*) Yale U Pr.

— Discourse on Metaphysics: Correspondence with Arnauld - Monadology. 2nd ed. LC 51-45405. 295p. 1973. reprint ed. pap. 9.00 (*0-87548-030-6*) Open Court.

— Discourse on Metaphysics & Other Essays. Garber, Daniel, ed. & tr. by. from FRE. Ariew, Roger, tr. from FRE. (HPC Classics Ser.). 96p. (C). 1991. pap. text 4.95 (*0-87220-132-5*); lib. bdg. 24.95 (*0-87220-133-3*) Hackett Pub.

— Discourse on Metaphysics & the Monadology. Montgomery, George R., tr. LC 93-33257. (Great Books in Philosophy). 88p. 1992. pap. 6.95 (*0-87975-775-2*) Prometheus Bks.

— General Investigations Concerning the Analysis of Concepts & Truths: A Translations & an Evaluation. O'Briant, Walter H., tr. LC 68-54890. (Georgia University Monographs: No. 17). 129p. reprint ed. pap. 40.00 (*0-608-10112-5*, 200285300015) Bks Demand.

— Leibniz: New Essays on Human Understanding. Remnant, Peter & Bennett, Jonathan, eds. LC 82-1334. (Cambridge Texts in the History of Philosophy Ser.). 648p. (C). 1996. text 59.95 (*0-521-57211-8*); pap. text 21.95 (*0-521-57660-1*) Cambridge U Pr.

— Leibniz & Ludolf on Things Linguistic: Excerpts from Their Correspondence, 1688-1703. Waterman, John T., ed. & tr. by. LC 77-83104. (University of California Publications in Social Welfare: No. 88). 101p. reprint ed. pap. 31.40 (*0-608-15272-2*, 202959300061) Bks Demand.

— Leibniz-Faksimiles, Bekanntes und Unbekanntes Aus Seinem Nachlass. (GER.). 1971. write for info. (*3-487-06525-8*) G Olms Pubs.

— Lettres de Leibniz a Arnauld D'Apres un Manuscrit Inedit. LC 84-48423. (Philosophy of Leibniz Ser.). 111p. 1985. text 15.00 (*0-8240-6536-0*) Garland.

— Lettres et Opuscules Inedits. cxii, 336p. 1975. reprint ed. write for info. (*3-487-05321-7*) G Olms Pubs.

— Mathematische Schriften, 7 vols., Set. xxviii, 3401p. 1971. reprint ed. write for info. (*0-318-71368-3*); reprint ed. pap. write for info. (*0-318-71369-1*) G Olms Pubs.

— Nachgelassene Schriften Physikalischen, Mechanischen und Technischen Inhalts. 1995. reprint ed. write for info. (*3-487-09855-5*) G Olms Pubs.

— Nouvelles Lettres et Opuscules Inedits de Leibniz. ccxix, 440p. 1971. reprint ed. write for info. (*3-487-04179-0*) G Olms Pubs.

— Oeuvres, 7 vols., Set. ccliv, 3472p. 1969. reprint ed. write for info. (*0-318-71370-5*) G Olms Pubs.

— Opera Omnia. (GER.). 1990. reprint ed. write for info. (*3-487-09233-6*) G Olms Pubs.

— Opuscules et Fragments Inedits. xiv, 682p. 1988. reprint ed. write for info. (*3-487-01197-2*); reprint ed. pap. write for info. (*3-487-00099-7*) G Olms Pubs.

— Philosophical Essays. Ariew, Roger & Garber, Daniel, eds. & trs. by. from FRE. LC 88-38259. (HPC Classics Ser.). 386p. (C). 1989. 37.95 (*0-87220-063-9*); pap. text 12.95 (*0-87220-062-0*) Hackett Pub.

— Philosophical Texts. Woolhouse, R. S. & Francks, Richard, trs. (Oxford Philosophical Texts Ser.). 320p. (C). 1998. pap. text 11.95 (*0-19-875153-2*) OUP.

— Philosophical Writings. rev. ed. Parkinson, George H., ed. 296p. 1995. pap. 7.50 (*0-460-87546-9*, Everyman's Classic Lib) Tuttle Pubng.

— Die Philosophischen Schriften, 7 vols., Set. 4040p. 1978. reprint ed. write for info. (*3-487-00064-4*); reprint ed. pap. write for info. (*3-487-00926-9*) G Olms Pubs.

— Political Writings. Riley, Patrick, ed. (Cambridge Texts in the History of Political Thought Ser.). 264p. 1988. text 64.95 (*0-521-35380-7*) Cambridge U Pr.

— Political Writings. Riley, Patrick, ed. (Cambridge Texts in the History of Political Thought Ser.). 264p. 1988. pap. text 21.95 (*0-521-35899-X*) Cambridge U Pr.

— The Preface to Leibniz' Novissima Sinice. Lach, Donald F., tr. LC 57-14876. 116p. reprint ed. pap. 36.00 (*0-608-30401-8*, 200116800065) Bks Demand.

— Reihe No. 2: Philosophischer Briefwechsel. (GER.). 1972. reprint ed. write for info. (*3-487-04102-2*) G Olms Pubs.

— Theodicy. LC 85-8833. 448p. (C). 1985. pap. 16.00 (*0-87548-437-9*) Open Court.

— Writings on China. Cook, Daniel J. & Rosemont, Henry, Jr., eds. 160p. 1994. 32.95 (*0-8126-9250-0*); pap. 17.95 (*0-8126-9251-9*) Open Court.

***Leibniz, Gottfried Wilhelm & Clarke, Samuel.** Correspondence. Ariew, Roger, ed. LC 99-52339. 112p. (C). 2000. pap. 8.95 (*0-87220-524-X*) Hackett Pub.

— G. W. Leibniz & Samuel Clarke: Correspondence. Ariew, Roger, ed. LC 99-52339. 112p. (C). 2000. lib. bdg. 24.95 (*0-87220-525-8*) Hackett Pub.

Leibniz, Gottfried Wilhelm & Lexicon. A Dual Concordance to Leibniz's Philosophische Schriften. Hunter, Graeme et al, eds. vii, 419p. 1988. write for info. (*3-487-09094-5*); fiche. write for info. (*3-487-09150-X*) G Olms Pubs.

***Leibniz, Gottfried Wilhelm, et al.** The Leibniz-Clarke Correspondence: With Extracts from Newton's Principia Opticks. LC 98-18298. 256p. 1998. pap. 24.95 (*0-7190-0669-4*, Pub. by Manchester Univ Pr) St Martin.

Leibniz, Gottfried Wilhelm, jt. auth. see Savile, Anthony.

Leibo, Steven A. East, Southeast Asia, & the Western Pacific, 1998. 31st ed. (World Today Ser.). 1998. pap. 11.50 (*1-887985-12-3*) Stryker-Post.

***Leibo, Steven A.** East Southeast Asia & Western Pacific: 1999 Edition. 32nd ed. 1999. pap. 11.50 (*1-887985-19-0*) Stryker-Post.

Leibo, Steven A. Transferring Technology to China: Prosper Giquel & the Self-Strengthening Movement. LC 85-60380. (China Research Monographs: No. 28). 175p. 1985. pap. 15.00 (*0-912966-76-9*) IEAS.

Leibo, Steven A., jt. auth. see Giquel, Prosper.

Leibold, Cheryl, jt. auth. see Danly, Susan.

Leibold, Cheryl, jt. ed. see Foster, Kathleen A.

Leibold, Jay. Ninja Avenger. (Choose Your Own Adventure Ser.: No. 179). (Illus.). 112p. (J). (gr. 4-8). 1997. mass mkt. 3.50 (*0-553-56750-0*) BDD Bks Young Read.

— Ninja Cyborg. (Choose Your Own Adventure Ser.: No. 155). (J). (gr. 4-8). 1995. 8.60 (*0-606-07952-1*, Pub. by Turtleback) Demco.

— Surf Monkeys. (Choose Your Own Adventure Ser.: No. 131). (J). (gr. 4-8). 1992. 8.35 (*0-606-02920-6*, Pub. by Turtleback) Demco.

— Treasure Hunt. (J). 1995. pap. 4.99 (*0-553-54210-9*) BDD Bks Young Read.

— You Are a Millionaire. (Choose Your Own Adventure Ser.: No. 98). (J). (gr. 4-8). 1990. 8.60 (*0-606-04430-2*, Pub. by Turtleback) Demco.

Leibold, Jay, ed. see Crozier-Hogle, Lois, et al.

Leibovic, K. N., ed. Science of Vision. (Illus.). 472p. 1990. 79.00 (*0-387-97270-6*) Spr-Verlag.

Leibovich, Anna F. The Russian Concept of Work: Suffering, Drama, & Tradition in Pre & Post Revolutionary Russia. LC 95-3869. 184p. 1995. 55.00 (*0-275-95135-9*, Praeger Pubs) Greenwood.

Leibovitch, K. A., tr. see Neuhaus, Heinrich.

Leibovitz, Annie. Olympians. LC 96-85445. (gr. 8). 1996. 29.95 (*0-8212-2366-6*) Little.

***Leibovitz, Annie.** Women. 256p. 2000. pap. 45.00 (*0-375-75646-9*) Random.

Leibovitz, Annie, photos by. Photo Ann Leibovitz. LC 90-56384. (Illus.). 232p. 1993. pap. 40.00 (*0-06-092346-6*, Perennial) HarperTrade.

Leibovitz, Brian. L-Carnitine. (Good Health Guides Ser.). 48p. 1999. pap. 3.95 (*0-87983-962-7*, 39627K, Keats Publng) NTC Contemp Pub Co.

Leibovitz, Clement & Finkel, Alvin. In Our Time: The Chamberlain-Hitler Collusion. LC 97-39461. 1998. 18.00 (*0-85345-998-3*, Pub. by Monthly Rev); pap. 48.00 (*0-85345-999-1*, Pub. by Monthly Rev) NYU Pr.

Leibovitz, Maury, ed. The Prints of LeRoy Neiman: A Catalogue Raisonne of Serigraphs, Lithographs & Etchings. (Illus.). 359p. 100.00 (*0-937608-00-9*) Knoedler.

Leibovitz, Maury & Lynch, Richard, eds. The Prints of LeRoy Neiman: A Catalogue Raisonne of Serigraphs & Etchings, 1980-1990. (Illus.). 212p. 1991. 150.00 (*0-685-40168-5*) Knoedler.

Leibovitz, Shirley. The Enduring Spirit: The Inspiring True Story of a Holocaust Survivor. 320p. 1993. pap. 14.95 (*0-9635993-0-5*) Gildith Pr.

Leibowitch, Michele, et al. An Atlas of Vulval Diseases: A Combined Dermatological, Gynecological & Venereological Approach. 1995. 65.00 (*1-85317-127-1*, M Dunitz) Scovill Paterson.

Leibowitt, S. David. Wit & Whimsy. (Illus.). 87p. (Orig.). 1989. pap. 5.95 (*0-9625362-0-2*) S D Leibowitt.

Leibowitz, A. H. Chochmas Hamussar. (Annual Fryer Memorial Lectures). 1982. 1.00 (*0-914131-11-7*, B150) Torah Umesorah.

Leibowitz, Alan. The Record Collector's Record Books. Adler, Roger & Adler, Andrew, eds. 1979. pap. 5.95 (*0-916844-07-2*) Turtle Pr.

Leibowitz, Amy. Law & Order in the 20th Century. 1997. pap. text 9.95 (*0-912517-30-1*) Bluewood Bks.

Leibowitz, Ann G., et al. Drafting Employment Documents in Massachusetts, 2 vols. LC 96-79510. 1146p. 1997. ring bd. 125.00 (*1-57589-046-1*, 97-15.05-BK) Mass CLE.

Leibowitz, Arnold. Defining Status: A Comprehensive Analysis of United States - Territorial Relations. (C). 1989. lib. bdg. 250.00 (*0-7923-0069-6*) Kluwer Academic.

Leibowitz, Arnold H. Embattled Island: Palau's Struggle for Independence. LC 95-30700. 256p. 1996. 59.95 (*0-275-95390-4*, Praeger Pubs) Greenwood.

Leibowitz, H. Majesty of Man. 1992. 19.99 (*0-89906-542-2*); pap. 16.99 (*0-89906-543-0*) Mesorah Pubns.

Leibowitz, Herbert. Fabricating Lives: Explorations in American Autobiography. LC 90-21152. (Illus.). 416p. 1991. reprint ed. pap. 14.95 (*0-8112-1168-1*, NDP715, Pub. by New Directions) Norton.

Leibowitz, Herbert, ed. Parnassus: Twenty Years of Poetry in Review. 432p. 1994. pap. 17.95 (*0-472-06577-7*, 06577) U of Mich Pr.

— Parnassus: Twenty Years of Poetry in Review. 432p. 1995. text 42.50 (*0-472-09577-3*, 09577) U of Mich Pr.

Leibowitz, Howard M. & Waring, George O. Corneal Disorders: Clinical Diagnosis & Management. 2nd ed. Lampert, Richard, ed. LC 97-44165. (Illus.). 1200p. (C). 1998. text 275.00 (*0-7216-5867-9*, W B Saunders Co) Harcrt Hlth Sci Grp.

Leibowitz, Jeff, jt. auth. see Park, Y. H.

Leibowitz, Joan. Yellow Ware. rev. ed. LC 85-61524. (Illus.). 119p. (Orig.). 1993. pap. 19.95 (*0-88740-508-8*) Schiffer.

Leibowitz, Judith. Narrative Purpose in the Novella. (De Proprietatibus Litterarum, Ser. Minor: No. 10). 139p. 1974. pap. text 32.35 (*90-279-3007-4*) Mouton.

Leibowitz, M. J., jt. auth. see Koltin, Y.

Leibowitz, Martin L. & Institute of Chartered Financial Analysts Staff. A New Perspective on Asset Allocation LC 99-207584. xiv, 75 p. 1987. write for info. (*0-943205-00-X*) RFICFA.

L

L

Leibowitz, Martin L., et al. Return Targets & Shortfall Risks: Studies in Strategic Asset Allocation. 448p. 1995. 70.00 (*1-55738-916-0*, Irwn Prfssnl) McGraw-Hill Prof.

Leibowitz, Marvin. Interpreting Projective Drawings: A Self Psychological Approach. LC 99-12635. 1999. 39.95 (*0-87630-933-3*) Brunner-Mazel.

Leibowitz, Rene. Schoenberg & His School: The Contemporary Stage of the Language of Music. Newlin, Dika, tr. from FRE. LC 75-115338. (Music Ser.). 1970. reprint ed. lib. bdg. 37.50 (*0-306-71930-4*) Da Capo.

— Thinking for Orchestra: Practical Exercises in Orchestration. 240p. reprint ed. lib. bdg. 39.00 (*0-685-14890-4*) Rprt Serv.

Leibowitz, Robert. The Defender: The Life & Career of Samuel Leibowitz. LC 81-5948. (Illus.). 255p. 1981. 15.00 (*0-685-03822-X*) P-H.

Leibowitz, Yeshayahu. The Faith of Maimonides. 228p. (Orig.). 1987. pap. 9.95 (*0-915361-93-0*) Lambda Pubs.

— Judaism, Human Values, & the Jewish State. Goldman, Eliezer, ed. & tr. by. Navon, Yoram et al, trs. 328p. (C). 1995. pap. text 18.50 (*0-674-48776-1*) HUP.

— Judaism, Human Values, & the Jewish State. Goldman, Eliezer, ed. & tr. by. Navon, Yoram et al, trs. 384p. (C). 1992. text 47.95 (*0-674-48775-3*) HUP.

Leibowitz, Zandy B., et al. Designing Career Development Systems. LC 86-45623. (Management Ser.). 341p. 1986. text 39.45 (*1-55542-024-9*) Jossey-Bass.

Leibrecht, Walter. Religion & Culture: Essays in Honor of Paul Tillich. LC 78-167376. (Essay Index Reprint Ser.). 1977. reprint ed. 26.95 (*0-8369-2558-0*) Ayer.

***Leibrich, Julie, ed.** The Gift of Stories: Realising How to Deal with Mental Illness. (Illus.). 160p. 1999. pap. 39.95 (*1-877133-83-3*, Pub. by Univ Otago Pr) Intl Spec Bk.

Leibrock, Cynthia A. Beautiful Barrier Free: A Visual Guide to Accessibility. (Illus.). 208p. 1993. text 64.95 (*0-442-00882-1*, VNR) Wiley.

— Beautiful Universal Design: A Visual Guide. 2nd ed. LC 98-36453. 224p. 1999. 64.95 (*0-471-29306-7*) Wiley.

— Design Details for Health: A Guide to Making the Most of Interior Design's Healing Potential. LC 99-29983. 288p. 1999. 75.00 (*0-471-24194-6*) Wiley.

Leibrockc. Beautiful Universal Design. 2nd ed. (Architecture Ser.). (C). 1998. text 64.95 (*0-442-02688-9*, VNR) Wiley.

Leibshaw, Robert. Rock Rabbit & the Rainbow: A Tribute to Laurens Van der Post. 214p. 1995. pap. 25.00 (*3-85630-540-8*) Continuum.

Leibsohn. Worktext Basic Counseling Responses. (Counseling Ser.). 1998. mass mkt. 14.95 (*0-534-35557-9*) Brooks-Cole.

Leibson, Art. Sam Dreben: The Fighting Jew. (Great West & Indian Ser.: No. 67). (Illus.). 208p. 1996. 26.95 (*0-87026-098-7*) Westernlore.

Leibson, David J. & Nowka, Richard H. Uniform Commercial Code of Kentucky, 1998 Cumulative Supplement. 210p. 1998. pap., suppl. ed. write for info. (*0-327-00701-X*, 6431611) LEXIS Pub.

Leibson, L. G. Vrach Russkogo Severa: Russian & Ukrainian Fairy Tales.Tr. of Doctor of Russian North. (RUS., Illus.). 126p. (Orig.). 1991. pap. text 20.00 (*0-914265-07-5*) New Eng Pub MA.

Leiby, Adrian C. Building on the Firm Foundation: The Buildings of South Church, Bergenfield, New Jersey. (Illus.). 72p. 1992. pap. 9.95 (*1-881576-10-8*) Providence Hse.

Leiby, Bruce R. Gordon MacRae: A Bio-Bibliography, 17. LC 90-29291. (Bio-Bibliographies in the Performing Arts Ser.: No. 17). 248p. 1991. lib. bdg. 49.95 (*0-313-26633-6*, LGM, Greenwood Pr) Greenwood.

— Howard Keel: A Bio-Bibliography, 67. LC 95-22407. (Bio-Bibliographies in the Performing Arts Ser.: Vol. 67). 344p. 1995. lib. bdg. 69.50 (*0-313-28456-3*, Greenwood Pr) Greenwood.

Leiby, G. Sterling. Verses & Re-Verses. LC 97-75516. 80p. 1998. pap. 10.95 (*1-57197-094-0*) Pentland Pr.

Leiby, James R. Carroll Wright & Labor Reform: The Origin of Labor Statistics. LC 60-15240. (Historical Monographs: No. 46). 251p. 1960. 15.00 (*0-674-09800-5*) HUP.

Leiby, Judy, ed. see Tepoot, Pabloo.

Leiby, Larry R. Florida Construction Law Manual. LC 81-5723. (Construction Law: Land Use-Environmental Publications). 500p. 1981. text 105.00 (*0-07-037076-1*) Shepards.

— Florida Construction Law Manual. 4th ed. LC 97-14461. (Construction Law Ser.). 1997. write for info. (*0-7620-0171-2*) West Group.

***Leiby, Richard A.** The Unification of Germany, 1989-1990. LC 98-22904. (Guides to Historic Events of the Twentieth Century Ser.). 240p. 1999. 39.95 (*0-313-29969-2*, Greenwood Pr) Greenwood.

Leicester. Disability Voice. 1. LC 99-164979. 1998. text 24.95 (*1-85302-355-8*) Jessica Kingsley.

Leicester, Charles. Bloodstock Breeding. 536p. 1990. 100.00 (*0-85131-349-3*, Pub. by J A Allen) Trafalgar.

Leicester, Colin. Britain 2001 Ad: An Analysis of Economic Activity, Work & Leisure Time At & Turn of the Century. LC 73-163070. vii, 46p. 1972. write for info. (*0-11-880282-8*) Statnry Office.

Leicester, H. Marshall, Jr. The Disenchanted Self: Representing the Subject in the Canterbury Tales. 1990. 65.00 (*0-520-06760-6*, Pub. by U CA Pr); pap. 19.95 (*0-520-06833-5*, Pub. by U CA Pr) Cal Prin Full Svc.

Leicester, Henry M. Historical Background of Chemistry. LC 79-166426. (Illus.). 260p. 1971. reprint ed. pap. text 8.95 (*0-486-61053-5*) Dover.

— Source Book in Chemistry, 1900-1950. (Source Books in the History of the Sciences). (Illus.). 432p. 1968. 35.95 (*0-674-82231-5*) HUP.

Leicester, Henry M., tr. see Lomonosov, Mikhail V.

Leicester, Mal. Race for a Change in Continuing & Higher Education. LC 93-1895. (Cutting Edge Ser.). 160p. 1993. 120.00 (*0-335-09768-5*); pap. 37.95 (*0-335-09767-7*) OpUniv Pr.

***Leicester, Mal, et al, eds.** Classroom Issues: Practice, Pedagogy & Curriculum. LC 99-39368. (Education, Culture & Values Ser.: Vol. III). 368p. 1999. 140.00 (*0-7507-1004-7*, Pub. by Falmer Pr UK) Taylor & Francis.

— Politics, Education & Citizenship. LC 99-36830. (Education, Culture & Values Ser.: Vol. VI). 368p. 1999. 140.00 (*0-7507-1007-1*, Pub. by Falmer Pr UK) Taylor & Francis.

— Spiritual & Religious Education. LC 99-36829. (Education, Culture & Values Ser.: Vol. V). 320p. 1999. 140.00 (*0-7507-1006-3*, Pub. by Falmer Pr UK) Taylor & Francis.

***Leicester, Mal, et al.** Institutional Issues. LC 99-36824. (Education, Culture & Values Ser.). 1999. write for info. (*0-7507-1003-9*, Falmer Pr) Taylor & Francis.

— Moral Education & Pluralism LC 99-36828. (Education, Culture & Values Ser.). 1999. write for info. (*0-7507-1005-5*) Taylor & Francis.

— Systems of Education. LC 99-36827. (Education, Culture & Values Ser.). 1999. write for info. (*0-7507-1002-0*, Falmer Pr) Taylor & Francis.

Leicester, Robert D. Correspondence of Robert Dudley, Earl of Leycester. Bruce, John, ed. LC 17-1209. (Camden Society, London. Publications, First Ser.: No. 27). reprint ed. 125.00 (*0-404-50127-3*) AMS Pr.

Leicester, Sandra, jt. auth. see Smith, David M.

Leichentritt, Hugo. Serge Koussevitsky, the Boston Symphony Orchestra & the New American Music: Music Book Index. 199p. 1993. reprint ed. lib. bdg. 69.00 (*0-7812-9636-6*) Rprt Serv.

Leicher, Eberhard. Woerterbuch der Arabischen Wirtschaftssprache und Rechtssprache: Arabisch-Deutsch. 609p. 1992. 225.00 (*0-7859-8473-9*, 3789027774) Fr & Eur.

Leichester Polytechnic University Library Staff, compiled by. Designers International Index, 3 vols., Set. 1700p. 1991. 730.00 (*0-86291-770-0*) U Pubns Amer.

Leichman, Larry, jt. auth. see Hochman, Joel.

Leichman, Laurence. 90Off! How & Where to Get the Lowest Possible Price on Absolutely Anything. 1995. pap. 14.95 (*0-9636867-5-5*) Leichman Assocs.

— The Real Estate Tycoon's Handbook! Secrets & Essentials of Today's Sharpest Property Magnates. 1995. pap. 14.95 (*0-9636867-1-2*) Leichman Assocs.

— Sell-Publish Your Own Best Seller! Complete Production & Marketing for Success & Profits. 1995. pap. 14.95 (*0-9636867-2-0*) Leichman Assocs.

— Steal These Homes! As Well As Vacation Houses, Retirement & Investment Real Estate & Commercial Property. 1995. pap. 14.95 (*0-9636867-4-7*) Leichman Assocs.

Leichman, Laurence, ed. see Investor Action Group Staff.

Leichman, Robert R., told to. Forces of the Zodiac. 448p. 2000. pap. text 19.99 (*0-89804-039-6*, Pub. by Ariel GA) Alliance Bk Co.

Leichner, Greg. Citizens for a Poodle-Free Montana. limited ed. Trusky, Tom, ed. (Hemingway Western Studies). (Illus.). 17p. (Orig.). 1995. 7.95 (*0-932129-22-6*) Heming W Studies.

— Man Alive! LC 97-91692. (Illus.). 220p. 1997. pap. 10.00 (*0-9661936-8-7*) Speed Light NM.

Leichner, Jeannine T. Called to His Supper. 119p. 1991. teacher ed., spiral bd. 13.95 (*0-87973-140-0*) Our Sunday Visitor.

Leichner, Jeannine T. Called to His Supper. (Illus.). 60p. (J). (gr. 1-3). 1991. pap. 5.95 (*0-87973-138-9*, 138) Our Sunday Visitor.

Leichner, Jeannine T. Joy Joy, the Mass: Our Family Celebration. (Illus.). 32p. (J). (gr. k-3). 1978. pap. 5.95 (*0-87973-350-0*); pap. 4.95 (*0-87973-348-9*, 348) Our Sunday Visitor.

— Making Things Right: The Sacrament of Reconciliation. (Illus.). 62p. (J). (gr. 2-4). 1980. pap. 5.95 (*0-87973-351-9*, 351) Our Sunday Visitor.

— Making Things Right: The Sacrament of Reconciliation. (SPA., Illus.). 62p. (J). (gr. 2-4). 1980. pap. 5.95 (*0-87973-349-7*, 349) Our Sunday Visitor.

Leichner, Nancy M., ed. see Murray, Coreen.

Leicht, Kevin. Research in Social Stratification & Mobility, Vol. 16. 1998. 73.25 (*0-7623-0279-8*) Jai Pr.

Leicht, Kevin, ed. Research in Social Stratification & Mobility, Vol. 13. 296p. 1994. 73.25 (*1-55938-711-4*) Jai Pr.

Leicht, S. & Karotemprel, Sebastian, eds. Early History of the Catholic Missions in North-East India. (C). 1989. 26.00 (*0-8364-2446-8*, Pub. by Firma KLM) S Asia.

Leicht, T., et al, eds. PCB Assembly Systems, 1989. (Illus.). 200p. 1989. 135.95 (*0-387-50938-0*) Spr-Verlag.

Leichtentritt, Hugo. Music, History, & Ideas. LC 38-17551. 320p. reprint ed. pap. 99.20 (*0-608-17492-0*, 202999200067) Bks Demand.

— Musical Form. LC 51-11139. 479p. reprint ed. pap. 148.50 (*0-7837-2292-3*, 205738000004) Bks Demand.

— Serge Koussevitsky, the Boston Symphony Orchestra & the New American Music. LC 75-41172. reprint ed. 32.50 (*0-404-14680-5*) AMS Pr.

Leichter, Hope J. & Mitchell, William E. Kinship & Casework. LC 66-24898. 344p. 1967. 39.95 (*0-87154-522-5*) Russell Sage.

Leichter, Howard M. Free to Be Foolish: Politics & Health Promotion in the United States & Great Britain. (Illus.). 294p. 1991. text 49.50 (*0-691-07867-X*, Pub. by Princeton U Pr) Cal Prin Full Svc.

Leichter, Howard M., ed. Health Policy Reform in America: Innovations from the States. LC 92-22293. 240p. (C). (gr. 13). 1992. 69.95 (*1-56324-053-X*) M E Sharpe.

— Health Policy Reform in America: Innovations from the States. 2nd ed. LC 96-43276. 280p. (C). (gr. 13). 1997. text 74.95 (*1-56324-899-9*) M E Sharpe.

Leichter, Howard M., ed. Health Policy Reform in America: Innovations from the States. LC 92-22293. 240p. (C). (gr. 13). 1992. pap. 34.95 (*1-56324-054-8*) M E Sharpe.

— Health Policy Reform in America: Innovations from the States. 2nd ed. LC 96-43276. 280p. (C). 1997. pap. text 30.95 (*1-56324-900-6*) M E Sharpe.

Leichter, Larry R. State Games. LC 89-62823. 1990. 20.00 (*0-87212-232-8*); pap. 15.00 (*0-87212-247-6*) Libra.

Leichtman, Caron, ed. see St. Laurent, Jonathan & Neave, Charles.

Leichtman, Ellen C., jt. auth. see Brandel, Rose.

Leichtman, Harry M. Helping Work Environments Work: Manual. 1996. pap. text, wbk. ed. 16.95 (*0-87868-549-9*) Child Welfare.

— Helping Work Environments Work Workbook. 1996. pap., wbk. ed. 9.95 (*0-87868-575-8*) Child Welfare.

Leichtman, Kerry, ed. see St. Laurent, Jonathan & Neave, Charles.

Leichtman, Martin. The Rorschach: A Developmental Perspective. 328p. 1996. text 45.00 (*0-88163-138-8*) Analytic Pr.

Leichtman, Robert. Recovering from Death: And Other Disasters. 128p. 2000. pap. 11.99 (*0-89804-077-9*, Pub. by Ariel GA) Alliance Bk Co.

Leichtman, Robert & Japikse, Carl. Completing the Masterpiece. (Art of Living Ser.: Vol. 5). 216p. 1999. pap. 13.99 (*0-89804-129-5*, Pub. by Ariel GA) Alliance Bk Co.

Leichtman, Robert R. Cheiro Returns. (From Heaven to Earth Ser.). (Illus.). 80p. (Orig.). 1979. pap. 3.50 (*0-89804-053-1*) Ariel GA.

— Churchill Returns. LC 81-66847. (From Heaven to Earth Ser.). (Illus.). 96p. (Orig.). 1981. pap. 3.50 (*0-89804-065-5*) Ariel GA.

— Destiny of America. (From Heaven to Earth Ser.). 1999. pap. 15.99 (*0-89804-086-8*, Pub. by Ariel GA) Alliance Bk Co.

— Dynamics of Creativity. (From Heaven to Earth Ser.). 256p. 1999. pap. 15.99 (*0-89804-085-X*, Pub. by Ariel GA) Alliance Bk Co.

— Edgar Cayce Returns: 20th Anniversary Edition. 20th anniversary ed. 96p. 1998. pap. 7.95 (*0-89804-839-7*) Ariel GA.

— Eileen Garrett Returns. (From Heaven to Earth Ser.). (Illus.). 96p. (Orig.). 1980. pap. 3.50 (*0-89804-061-2*) Ariel GA.

— Einstein Returns. LC 81-69184. (From Heaven to Earth Ser.). (Illus.). 112p. (Orig.). 1982. pap. 3.50 (*0-89804-068-X*) Ariel GA.

— Healing Emotional Wounds. 144p. 1999. pap. text 9.99 (*0-89804-832-X*) Alliance Bk Co.

— Healing Lines. 1989. pap. 7.95 (*0-7921-0557-5*) Paramount Video.

— The Hidden Side of Science. (From Heaven to Earth Ser.). 272p. 1992. pap. 11.95 (*0-89804-083-3*) Ariel GA.

— The Inner Side of Life. (From Heaven to Earth Ser.). 1991. pap. 11.95 (*0-89804-082-5*) Ariel GA.

— Jefferson Returns. (From Heaven to Earth Ser.). (Illus.). 64p. (Orig.). 1979. pap. 3.50 (*0-89804-057-4*) Ariel GA.

— Leadbeater Returns. (From Heaven to Earth Ser.). (Illus.). 96p. (Orig.). 1979. pap. 3.50 (*0-89804-055-8*) Ariel GA.

— Light of Learning. 188p. 1999. pap. text 13.95 (*0-89804-170-8*) Ariel Prods.

— Nikola Tesla Returns: 20th Anniversary Edition. 20th ed. 96p. 1998. pap. text 7.95 (*0-89804-840-0*) Ariel GA.

— Priests of God. (From Heaven to Earth Ser.). 1997. pap. 13.95 (*0-89804-084-1*) Ariel GA.

— The Psychic Perspective. (From Heaven to Earth Ser.). 1991. pap. 11.95 (*0-89804-081-7*) Ariel GA.

— Rembrandt Returns. (From Heaven to Earth Ser.). (Illus.). 96p. (Orig.). 1981. pap. 3.50 (*0-89804-064-7*) Ariel GA.

— Schweitzer Returns. (From Heaven to Earth Ser.). (Illus.). 104p. (Orig.). 1980. pap. 3.50 (*0-89804-063-9*) Ariel GA.

— Shakespeare Returns. (From Heaven to Earth Ser.). (Illus.). 70p. (Orig.). 1978. pap. 3.50 (*0-89804-051-5*) Ariel GA.

— Stewart White Returns. (From Heaven to Earth Ser.). (Illus.). 96p. (Orig.). 1980. pap. 3.50 (*0-89804-062-0*) Ariel GA.

— Yogananda Returns. (From Heaven to Earth Ser.). 104p. (Orig.). 1981. pap. 3.50 (*0-89804-066-3*) Ariel GA.

Leichtman, Robert R. & Japikse, Carl. The Act of Meditation. 96p. 1988. pap. 7.95 (*0-89804-830-3*, Pub. by Ariel GA) Alliance Bk Co.

— Active Meditation. 512p. 1982. pap. 19.95 (*0-89804-041-8*, Pub. by Ariel GA) Alliance Bk Co.

— The Art of Living, Vol. I. LC 70-76900. (Essay Index Reprint Ser.). 216p. 1979. pap. 9.95 (*0-89804-076-0*) Ariel GA.

— The Art of Living, Vol. II. (Illus.). 264p. 1980. pap. 7.95 (*0-89804-033-7*) Ariel GA.

— The Art of Living, Vol. III. LC 81-69186. (Illus.). 264p. 1982. pap. 7.95 (*0-89804-034-5*) Ariel GA.

— The Art of Living, Vol. IV. LC 83-703086. (Illus.). 280p. 1984. pap. 7.95 (*0-89804-035-3*) Ariel GA.

— Celebrating Life. 90p. 1994. pap. 7.95 (*0-89804-806-0*, Enthea Pr) Ariel GA.

— The Destiny of America. LC 83-70303. (From Heaven to Earth Ser.). 128p. 1984. 7.95 (*0-89804-075-2*); pap. 3.50 (*0-89804-074-4*) Ariel GA.

— Divine Workshop Vol V: Life of Spirit. Vol. 5. 234p. 1999. pap. text 14.95 (*0-89804-136-8*, Pub. by Ariel GA) Alliance Bk Co.

— Healing Emotional Wounds. 144p. 1998. pap. 9.95 (*0-89804-829-X*, Enthea Pr) Ariel GA.

— The Life of Spirit, Vol. I. (Illus.). 216p. (Orig.). 1986. pap. 8.95 (*0-89804-132-5*) Ariel GA.

— The Life of Spirit, Vol. II. (Illus.). 275p. (Orig.). 1987. pap. 8.95 (*0-89804-133-3*) Ariel GA.

— The Life of Spirit, Vol. III. (Illus.). 200p. (Orig.). 1988. pap. 8.95 (*0-89804-134-1*) Ariel GA.

— Making Prayer Work. 144p. 1996. pap. 9.95 (*0-89804-828-1*, Enthea Pr) Ariel GA.

— Mark Twain Returns. LC 81-69185. (From Heaven to Earth Ser.). 80p. (Orig.). 1982. pap. 3.50 (*0-89804-067-1*) Ariel GA.

— Our Spiritual Resources Vol. 4: The Life of Spirit. (Illus.). 216p. (Orig.). 1997. pap. 10.95 (*0-89804-135-X*) Ariel GA.

— The Way to Health. 128p. 1995. pap. 9.95 (*0-89804-805-2*, Enthea Pr) Ariel GA.

— Working with Angels. 90p. 1993. pap. 7.95 (*0-89804-824-9*, Enthea Pr) Ariel GA.

Leichtman, Robert R. & Japikse, Carl, eds. Books of Light. (Illus.). 160p. (Orig.). 1986. pap. 4.95 (*0-89804-155-4*) Ariel GA.

Leichtman, Robert R., jt. auth. see Japikse, Carl.

***Leichtweiss, Kurt.** Affine Geometry of Convex Bodies. 320p. 1998. 125.00 (*3-527-40261-6*) Wiley.

Leichty, E. V. The Series Summa Izbu. LC 66-25697. 38.00 (*0-685-71732-1*) J J Augustin.

Leichty, Erle, et al, eds. A Scientific Humanist: Studies in Memory of Abraham Sachs. (Occasional Publications of the Samuel Noah Kramer Fund: No. 9). xvi, 378p. 1988. 50.00 (*0-934718-90-3*) U Museum Pubns.

Leick, Alfred. GPS Satellite Surveying. 2nd ed. 584p. 1995. 99.00 (*0-471-30626-6*) Wiley.

Leick, Gwendolyn. A Dictionary of Ancient Near Eastern Mythology. (Illus.). 240p. 1998. pap. 27.99 (*0-415-19811-9*, D6639) Routledge.

— Sex & Eroticism in Mesopotamian Literature. LC 93-49776. (Illus.). 336p. (C). (gr. 13). 1994. 85.00 (*0-415-06534-8*, B4367) Routledge.

— Who's Who in the Ancient Near East. (Illus.). 320p. (C). 1998. 29.99 (*0-415-13230-4*) Routledge.

Leick, Nini & Davidsen-Nielsen, Marianne. Healing Pain: Attachment, Loss & Grief Therapy. LC 90-8509. 224p. (C). 1991. pap. 22.99 (*0-415-04795-1*, A5419) Routledge.

Leidecker, Kurt F. Scientific German by the Method of Discovery. 1947. 15.00 (*0-913298-67-0*) S F Vanni.

Leidecker, Kurt F., ed. The Record Book of the St. Louis Philosophical Society, Founded February, 1866. LC 89-37669. (Studies in the History of Philosophy: Vol. 14). (Illus.). 136p. 1990. lib. bdg. 69.95 (*0-88946-289-5*) E Mellen.

Leidelmeijer, Frans, et al. Dutch Decorative Arts, 1880-1940. (Illus.). 255p. 1997. 60.00 (*0-9627110-2-0*) Battledore Ltd.

***Leiden, Candace.** Linux Bible. (Bible Ser.). (Illus.). 1000p. 2000. pap. text 39.99 (*0-7645-4662-7*) IDG Bks.

— TCP/IP for Dummies. 4th ed. (For Dummies Ser.). (Illus.). 408p. 2000. pap. 24.99 incl. cd-rom (*0-7645-0726-5*) IDG Bks.

***Leiden, Candace & Wilensky, Marshall.** TCP/IP for Dummies. 3rd ed. LC TK5105.585.L45 1999. (For Dummies Ser.). 432p. 1999. pap. 24.99 (*0-7645-0473-8*) IDG Bks.

***Leider, Anna.** A's & B's of Academic Scholarships. 20th ed. 1998. pap. text 8.00 (*1-57509-033-3*) Octameron Assocs.

Leider, Anna. The A's & B's of Academic Scholarships. 21st ed. 1999. pap. 9.00 (*1-57509-055-4*, TN772820) Octameron Assocs.

— I Am Somebody: College Knowledge for the First-Generation Campus Bound. 8th ed. 1998. pap. 8.00 (*1-57509-040-6*, TN773008) Octameron Assocs.

***Leider, Anna & Leider, Robert.** Don't Miss Out: The Ambitiuos Student's Guide to Financial Aid. 23rd ed. 1998. pap. write for info. (*1-57509-032-5*) Octameron Assocs.

Leider, Anna & Leider, Robert. Don't Miss Out: The Ambitiuos Student's Guide to Financial Aid. 24th ed. 208p. 1999. pap. 9.00 (*1-57509-043-0*, TN772723) Octameron Assocs.

***Leider, Anna & Leider, Robert.** Leider's Lecture: A Complete Course in Understanding Financial Aid. 19th ed. 40p. 1999. pap. 15.00 (*1-57509-054-6*) Octameron Assocs.

***Leider, Anna J.** Loans & Grants from Uncle Sam. 7th ed. 1999. pap. 6.00 (*1-57509-044-9*) Octameron Assocs.

***Leider, Emily W.** Becoming Mae West. 472p. 2000. pap. text 18.00 (*0-306-80951-6*, Pub. by Da Capo) HarpC.

Leider, Emily W. Becoming Mae West. LC 96-43803. (Illus.). 448p. 1997. text 30.00 (*0-374-10959-1*) FS&G.

— California's Daughter: Gertrude Atherton & Her Times. LC 90-32410. 425p. 1991. 45.00 (*0-8047-1820-2*) Stanford U Pr.

— California's Daughter: Gertrude Atherton & Her Times. (Illus.). 425p. (C). 1993. pap. 14.95 (*0-8047-2219-6*) Stanford U Pr.

Leider, Frida. Playing My Part. Osborne, Charles, tr. LC 77-26171. (Music Reprint Ser.: 1978). (Illus.). 1978. reprint ed. lib. bdg. 32.50 (*0-306-77535-2*) Da Capo.

Leider, Richard & Shapiro, David. Repacking Your Bags: Lighten Your Load for the Rest of Your Life. LC 94-37974. 240p. 1996. pap. 15.95 (*1-881052-87-7*) Berrett-Koehler.

Leider, Richard, jt. auth. see Hagberg, Janet.

Leider, Richard J. Life Skills: Taking Charge of Your Personal & Professional Growth. 196p. 1996. pap. text 17.95 (*0-89384-230-3*, Pfffr & Co) Jossey-Bass.

— Life Skills: Taking Charge of Your Personal & Professional Growth. 196p. (C). 1996. pap. text 17.95 (*0-13-602616-8*) P-H.

Leider, Richard J. The Power of Purpose: Creating Meaning in Your Life & Work. LC 97-15571. 200p. 1997. 20.00 (*1-57675-021-3*) Berrett-Koehler.

An Asterisk (*) at the beginning of an entry indicates that the title is appearing for the first time.

***Leider, Richard J.** The Power of Purpose: Creating Meaning in Your Life & Work. 176p. 2000. 6.98 (*1-56731-406-6*, MJF Bks) Fine Comms.

***Leider, Richard J. & Shapiro, David A.** Repacking Your Bags. 240p. 2000. 6.98 (*1-56731-369-8*, MJF Bks) Fine Comms.

Leider, Richard J. & Shapiro, David A. Repacking Your Bags: Lighten Your Load for the Rest of Your Life. LC 94-37974. (Illus.). 250p. 1995. 21.95 (*1-881052-67-2*) Berrett-Koehler.

Leider, Robert, jt. auth. see Leider, Anna.

***Leiderman Davitz, Lois & Davitz, Joel R.** Fun? But We're Married! A Wise & Witty Guide to a Lasting Marriage. LC 99-61900. 157p. 1999. pap. 12.95 (*1-893732-02-9*) SORIN BKS.

Leiderman, Leonardo. Inflation & Disinflation: The Israeli Experiment. LC 92-37436. (Illus.). 344p. (C). 1993. 45.00 (*0-226-47110-1*) U Ch Pr.

Leiderman, Leonardo & Razin, Assaf, eds. Capital Mobility: The Impact on Consumption, Investment & Growth. (Illus.). 378p. (C). 1994. text 59.95 (*0-521-45438-7*) Cambridge U Pr.

Leiderman, Leonardo & Svensson, Lars E. Inflation Targets. 214p. (C). 1995. pap. 24.95 (*1-898128-21-9*) Brookings.

Leiderman, Marcos, et al, eds. Roots & New Frontiers in Social Group Work. LC 88-529. (Social Work with Groups Supplement Ser.: No. 3). 252p. 1989. text 49.95 (*0-86656-727-5*) Haworth Pr.

Leiderman, P. Herbert & Shapiro, David, eds. Psychobiological Approaches to Social Behavior. xv, 203p. 1964. 27.50 (*0-8047-0202-0*) Stanford U Pr.

— Psychobiological Approaches to Social Behavior. fac. ed. LC 64-170178. (Illus.). 221p. 1964. pap. 30.00 (*0-7837-7913-5*, 204766900008) Bks Demand.

Leidersdorf, Craig B., jt. ed. see Chen, Andrie T.

Leidheiser, H., Jr., ed. Corrosion Control by Organic Coatings. LC 81-84733. (Illus.). 300p. 1981. pap. 53.00 (*0-915567-93-8*) NACE Intl.

Leidheiser, Henry, Jr. The Corrosion of Copper, Tin, & Their Alloys. LC 78-12566. (Illus.). 426p. 1979. reprint ed. lib. bdg. 46.50 (*0-88275-752-0*) Krieger.

Leidholdt, Alexander S., jt. auth. see Chambers, Lenoir.

Leidholdt, Dorchen & Raymond, Janice G. The Sexual Liberals & the Attack on Feminism. (Athene Ser.). 256p. 1990. text 35.00 (*0-08-037458-1*, Pergamon Pr); pap. text 16.95 (*0-08-037457-3*, Pergamon Pr) Elsevier.

Leidholdt, Dorchen & Raymond, Janice G., eds. The Sexual Liberals & the Attack on Feminism. (Athene Ser.). 256p. (C). 1990. pap. text 17.95 (*0-8077-6238-5*) Tchrs Coll.

Leidig, jt. auth. see Pratt, James.

Leidig, Paul M., jt. auth. see Pratt, Philip J.

Leiding, Mel. How to Fight Your Traffic Ticket & Win: 206 Tips, Tricks & Techniques. LC 97-77718. (Illus.). 56p. 1998. pap. 15.95 (*1-891693-11-5*, 105) Avenir Intl.

Leidl, R., ed. Health Care & Its Financing in the Single European Market. LC 97-75040. (Biomedical & Health Research Ser.: Vol. 18). 330p. Date not set. 92.00 (*90-5199-359-5*, 359-5) IOS Press.

Leidner, Alan C. The Impatient Muse: Germany & the Sturm & Drang. LC 93-36492. (Germanic Languages & Literatures Ser.: No. 115). xii, 156p. (C). 1994. lib. bdg. 45.00 (*0-8078-8115-5*) U of NC Pr.

Leidner, Alan C. & Madland, Helga S., eds. Space to Act: The Theater of J. M. R. Lenz. LC 93-4998. (GERM Ser.). xvii, 194p. 1994. 60.00 (*1-879751-62-3*) Camden Hse.

Leidner, Alan C. & Wurst, Karin A. Unpopular Virtues: The Scholarly Reception of J. M. R. Lenz. LC 98-43007. (Literary Criticism in Perspective Ser.). 200p. 1999. 55.00 (*1-57113-093-4*) Camden Hse.

Leidner, Alan C., ed. see Schiller, Friedrich, et al.

***Leidner, Gordon.** Lincoln on God & Country. (Illus.). 241p. 2000. 19.95 (*1-57249-207-4*, WM Books) White Mane Pub.

***Leidner, Gordon & Lincoln, Abraham.** A Commitment to Honor: A Unique Portrait of Abraham Lincoln in His Own Words. LC 99-38776. 1999. 12.95 (*1-55853-786-4*) Rutledge Hill Pr.

Leidner, Jacob. Plastics Waste: Recovery of Economic Value. LC 81-2752. (Plastics Engineering Ser.: No. 1). 327p. reprint ed. pap. 101.40 (*0-7837-5885-5*, 204560500006) Bks Demand.

Leidner, Robin. Fast Food, Fast Talk: Service Work & the Routinization of Everyday Life. LC 92-38004. 1993. 55.00 (*0-520-08169-2*, Pub. by U CA Pr); pap. 18.95 (*0-520-08500-0*, Pub. by U CA Pr) Cal Prin Full Svc.

Leidy, Denise P. Treasures of Asian Art: The Asia Society's Mr. & Mrs. John D Rockefeller 3rd Collection. LC 94-9437. (Illus.). 320p. 1994. 65.00 (*1-55859-863-4*) Abbeville Pr.

Leidy, Denise P., jt. auth. see Desai, Vishakha N.

Leidy, Joseph. The Extinct Mammalian Fauna of Dakota & Nebraska, & a Account of Some Allied Forms from Other Localities: Synopsis of the Mammalian Remains of North America. 2nd ed. LC 73-17828. (Natural Sciences in America Ser.: Vol. 3). (Illus.). 536p. 1974. reprint ed. 41.95 (*0-405-05746-6*) Ayer.

***Leier, Mark.** Rebel Life: The Life & Times of Robert Gosden, Revolutionary, Mystic, Labour Spy. (Illus.). 244p. 1999. pap. 16.00 (*0-921586-69-8*, Pub. by New Star Bks) Genl Dist Srvs.

— Where the Fraser River Flows: A History of the Industrial Workers of the World in B. C. 138p. 1990. pap. 11.95 (*0-921586-01-9*, Pub. by New Star Bks) Genl Dist Srvs.

***Leier, Ray, et al.** Baskets: Tradition & Beyond. (Illus.). 128p. 2000. 27.99 (*1-893164-04-7*, Pub. by GUILDcom) F & W Pubns Inc.

— Contemporary Turned Wood: New Perspectives in a Rich Tradition. (Illus.). 128p. 1999. text. write for info. (*90-5703-652-5*, Pub. by Craftsman House) Gordon & Breach.

Leier, Ray, et al. Contemporary Turned Wood: New Perspectives in a Rich Tradition. 1999. 27.99 (*0-9658248-8-8*) GUILDcom.

Leies, John A., et al, eds. Handbook on Critical Life Issues. 6th rev. ed. LC 88-38958. 218p. 1988. pap. 9.95 (*0-935372-24-5*) NCBC.

Leies, John A., jt. ed. see McCarthy, Donald G.

Leif, Irving P. Children's Literature: A Historical & Contemporary Bibliography. xx, 338p. 1977. 35.00 (*0-87875-094-0*) Whitston Pub.

Leif, Irving P. Larry Eigner: A Bibliography of His Works. LC 88-27017. (Author Bibliographies Ser.: No. 84). (Illus.). 251p. 1989. 32.00 (*0-8108-2210-5*) Scarecrow.

Leif, Irving P. & Clark, Terry N. Community Power & Decision-Making. (Current Sociology - la Sociologie Contemporaine Ser.: Vol. 20, No. 2). 138p. 1973. pap. text 19.25 (*90-279-7941-3*) Mouton.

Leif, Norway. Sister City & Other Tales. (Illus.). 22p. (Orig.). 1971. pap. 2.50 (*0-932264-18-2*) Trask Hse Bks.

Leifchild, John R. Cornwall: Its Mines & Miners. 304p. 1968. reprint ed. 35.00 (*0-7146-1402-5*, Pub. by F Cass Pubs) Intl Spec Bk.

— Our Coal & Our Coal-Pits. (Illus.). 243p. 1968. reprint ed. 30.00 (*0-7146-1401-7*, Pub. by F Cass Pubs) Intl Spec Bk.

Leifer. Study Guide for Thompson's Introduction to Maternity & Pediatric Nursing. 3rd ed. Wood, Terri, ed. (Illus.). 275p. 1998. pap. text, student ed. write for info. (*0-7216-8018-6*, W B Saunders Co) Harcrt Hlth Sci Grp.

Leifer, Asa. The Kinetics of Environmental Aquatic Photochemistry: Theory & Practice. LC 88-16718. (Illus.). xxx, 304p. 1988. 64.95 (*0-8412-1464-6*, Pub. by Am Chemical) OUP.

— The Kinetics of Environmental Aquatic Photochemistry: Theory & Practice. LC 88-16718. (ACS Professional Reference Bk.). 336p. 1988. reprint ed. pap. 104.20 (*0-608-03840-7*, 206428700008) Bks Demand.

Leifer, Eric M. Actors as Observers: A Theory of Skill in Social Relationships. (Harvard Studies Sociology Ser.). 176p. 1991. text 20.00 (*0-8240-2524-5*) Garland.

Leifer, Eric M. Making the Majors: The Transformation of Team Sports in America. LC 95-13469. (Illus.). 400p. (C). 1996. 56.00 (*0-674-54322-X*) HUP.

— Making the Majors: The Transformation of Team Sports in America. (Illus.). 400p. 1998. pap. text 22.95 (*0-674-54331-9*) HUP.

***Leifer, Jack.** Introduction to Powerpoint. 175p. 2000. pap. 21.00 (*0-13-040214-1*) P-H.

Leifer, Jacqueline C. & Glomb, Michael B. Legal Obligations of Nonprofit Boards No. 39: A Guidebook for Board Members. 44p. 1997. reprint ed. pap. text 28.00 (*0-925299-79-0*) Natl Ctr Nonprofit.

Leifer, Michael. ASEAN & the Security of South-East Asia. 224p. (C). 1989. lib. bdg. 57.50 (*0-415-01008-X*, A2503) Routledge.

***Leifer, Michael.** Asian Nationalism. LC 99-86051. 2000. pap. write for info. (*0-415-23285-6*) Routledge.

Leifer, Michael. The ASKAN Regional Forum: Extending ASKAN's Regional Forum. (Adelphi Papers: No. 302). 66p. 1997. pap. text 28.00 (*0-19-829263-5*) OUP.

— Dictionary of the Modern Politics of South-East Asia. LC 96-11509. 304p. (C). 1996. pap. 29.99 (*0-415-13821-3*) Routledge.

— Indonesia's Foreign Policy. (Royal Institute of International Affairs Ser.). 224p. 1983. text 49.95 (*0-04-327069-7*) Routledge.

***Leifer, Michael.** Singapore's Foreign Policy: Coping with Vulnerability. LC 99-88864. (Politics in Asia Ser.). 2000. pap. write for info. (*0-415-23353-4*) Routledge.

Leifer, Michael, ed. Dictionary of the Modern Politics of South-East Asia. (Dictionaries of Contemporary Politics Ser.). (Illus.). 288p. (C). (gr. 13). 1994. 125.00 (*0-415-04219-4*, A9989) Routledge.

***Leifer, Michael & Australian National University Staff.** The Asian Regional Forum. LC 98-201940. (Working Paper/Dept. of International Relations Ser.). 16 p. 1998. write for info. (*0-7315-2869-7*, Pub. by Aust Nat Univ) UH Pr.

Leifer, Myra. Psychological Effects of Motherhood: A Study of First Pregnancy. LC 79-26179. 304p. 1980. 14.95 (*0-275-91691-X*, C1691, Praeger Pubs) Greenwood.

Leifer, Ron. The Happiness Project: Transforming the Three Poisons That Cause the Suffering We Inflict on Ourselves & Others. LC 97-11067. 260p. 1997. pap. 14.95 (*1-55939-079-4*) Snow Lion Pubns.

Leifert, Carlo. Nutrition, Physiology & Micro Biology of Plant Cell. 1999. 65.00 (*0-8493-8943-7*) CRC Pr.

Leiff, M. & Trechsel, Heinz R., eds. Moisture Migration in Buildings - STP 779. 291p. 1982. 39.00 (*0-8031-0605-X*, STP779) ASTM.

Leifman, Hakan. Perspectives on Alcohol Prevention. (Stockholm Studies in Sociology: NS 3). 195p. 1996. pap. 42.50 (*91-22-01732-1*) Coronet Bks.

Leifman, Lev J. Functional Analysis, Optimization, & Mathematical Economics: A Collection of Papers Dedicated to the Memory of Leonid Vital'evick Kantorovitch. (Illus.). 360p. 1990. text 110.00 (*0-19-505729-5*) OUP.

Leifman, Lev J., ed. Twelve Papers in Algebra. LC 82-24434. (Translations Ser.: Series 2, Vol. 119). 139p. 1983. 45.00 (*0-8218-3074-0*, TRANS2/119) Am Math.

Leigeber, Kaye M. German Colonization & Naturalization Cullman County, Alabama. fac. ed. 44p. 1982. pap. 10.00 (*0-944619-18-5*) Gregath Pub Co.

Leiggi, Patrick & May, Peter J., eds. Vertebrate Paleontological Techniques Vol. 1: Methods of Obtaining & Preparing Vertebrate Fossils. (Illus.). 366p. (C). 1995. text 74.95 (*0-521-44357-1*) Cambridge U Pr.

***Leigh.** The Plant Vacuole. (C). 1999. pap. text 59.95 (*0-12-441870-8*) Acad Pr.

Leigh. Satin Sheets. 1992. mass mkt. write for info. (*0-312-92793-2*) St Martin.

Leigh & Kalin, Martin. Tuning in the U. S. A. Listener Guide 2 FAUSA. 1991. pap. text 13.33 (*0-02-362975-4*, Macmillan Coll) P-H.

— Tuning in the U.S.A. Listener Guide 1 FAUSA. 1990. pap. text 13.33 (*0-02-345473-3*, Macmillan Coll) P-H.

***Leigh & Walters.** Effective Change: Twenty Ways to Make It Happen. 248p. 2000. pap. 38.95 (*0-8464-5035-6*) Beekman Pubs.

Leigh, et al. Using Microcomputers. pap. write for info. (*0-87835-221-X*) Thomson Learn.

***Leigh, Alison.** Mother in a Moment. 2001. mass mkt. 4.50 (*0-373-24367-7*, 1-24367-4) Silhouette.

***Leigh, Allison.** A Child for Christmas: Men of the Double-C Ranch, No. 129. 1999. mass mkt. 4.25 (*0-373-24290-5*) Silhouette.

— Married to a Stranger. (Special Edition Ser.: Bk. 1336). 2000. mass mkt. 4.50 (*0-373-24336-7*, 1-24336-9) Silhouette.

— Millionaire's Instant Baby. (Special Edition Ser.). 2000. per. 4.50 (*0-373-24312-X*) Silhouette.

Leigh, Allison. The Rancher & the Redhead: Men of the Double-C Ranch. Vol. 1212. 1998. per. 4.25 (*0-373-24212-3*, 1-24212-2) Silhouette.

— Stay . . . 1998. per. 4.25 (*0-373-24170-4*, 1-24170-2) Silhouette.

— A Wedding for Maggie: Men of the Double-C Ranch. 1999. per. 4.25 (*0-373-24241-7*, 1-24241-1) Silhouette.

Leigh, Ana. Forever, My Love. 384p. (Orig.). 1995. mass mkt. 4.99 (*0-380-77351-1*, Avon Bks) Morrow Avon.

— Luke. (Mackenzies Ser.: No. 1). 384p. (Orig.). 1996. mass mkt. 5.50 (*0-380-78098-4*, Avon Bks) Morrow Avon.

— The Mackenzies: David. 384p. 1998. mass mkt. 5.99 (*0-380-79337-7*, Avon Bks) Morrow Avon.

— The MacKenzies: Flint. 384p. (Orig.). 1996. mass mkt. 5.50 (*0-380-78096-8*, Avon Bks) Morrow Avon.

***Leigh, Ana.** The Mackenzies: Jake. 384p. 1999. mass mkt. 5.99 (*0-380-79339-3*, Avon Bks) Morrow Avon.

— The MacKenzies: Josh. 384p. 2000. mass mkt. 5.99 (*0-380-81102-2*, Avon Bks) Morrow Avon.

Leigh, Ana. The Mackenzies: Peter. LC 98-93176. (Mackenzies Trilogy Ser.: Vol. 2). 384p. 1998. mass mkt. 5.99 (*0-380-79338-5*, Avon Bks) Morrow Avon.

— Tender Is the Touch. 384p. (Orig.). 1994. mass mkt. 4.50 (*0-380-77350-3*, Avon Bks) Morrow Avon.

Leigh, Andrew. Decisions, Decisions! A Practical Guide to Problem Solving & Decision Making. 224p. (C). 1983. 63.00 (*0-85292-315-5*) St Mut.

— Effective Change: Twenty Ways to Make It Happen. 256p. (C). 1988. 54.00 (*0-85292-412-7*) St Mut.

***Leigh, Andrew.** Persuasive Reports & Proposals. 96p. 2000. pap. 17.95 (*0-8464-5131-X*) Beekman Pubs.

— 20 Ways to Manage Better. 224p. 2000. pap. 29.95 (*0-8464-4997-8*) Beekman Pubs.

Leigh, Andrew. 20 Ways to Manage Better. 2nd ed. 192p. 1995. pap. 35.00 (*0-85292-591-3*, Pub. by IPM Hse) St Mut.

— Understanding Management Software. 288p. (C). 1985. 69.00 (*0-333-40946-9*) St Mut.

Leigh, Andrew, ed. Twenty Ways to Manage Better. 192p. (C). 1984. 60.00 (*0-85292-334-1*) St Mut.

Leigh, Andrew & Maynard, Michael. ACE Teams: Creating Star Performance in Business. 280p. 1994. pap. text 28.95 (*0-7506-1883-3*) Buttrwrth-Heinemann.

— ACE Teams: Creating Star Performance in Business. LC 93-235010. (Illus.). reprint ed. pap. 70.70 (*0-608-07413-6*, 2067640) Bks Demand.

Leigh, Andrew & Maynard, Michael. Leading Your Team: How to Involve & Inspire Teams. (People Skills for Professionals Ser.). (Illus.). 232p. 1996. reprint ed. pap. 19.95 (*1-85788-101-X*) Nicholas Brealey.

Leigh, Anne. Referral & Termination Issues for Counsellors. LC 98-60212. (Professional Skills for Counsellors Ser.). ix, 150 p. 1998. write for info. (*0-8039-7475-2*) Sage.

Leigh, Barbara. For Love Alone. LC 95-6915. (Historical Ser.). 298p. 1995. per. 3.99 (*0-373-28854-9*, 1-28854-7) Harlequin Bks.

— For Love of Rory. LC 96-707. 299p. 1995. per. 4.50 (*0-373-28897-2*, 1-28897-6) Harlequin Bks.

— The Surrogate Wife. (Historical Ser.). 1999. per. 4.99 (*0-373-29078-0*, 1-29078-2) Harlequin Bks.

— Web of Loving Lies. (Historical Ser.). 1993. per. 3.99 (*0-373-28777-1*, 1-28777-0) Harlequin Bks.

Leigh-Bennett, Ernest. Handbook of the Early Church Fathers. 1980. lib. bdg. 75.00 (*0-8490-3107-9*) Gordon Pr.

Leigh, Bob, et al. Automatic, Manual Transmissions, Transaxles, & Drive Trains. rev. ed. Fennema, Roger L. & Lahue, Kalton C., eds. (Automobile Mechanics Refresher Course Ser.: Bk. 5). (Illus.). 84p. 1981. pap., student ed. 9.95 (*0-88098-066-4*, H M Gousha); audio 13.90 (*0-88098-072-9*, H M Gousha) Prntice Hall Bks.

— Brakes, Steering, Front Suspension, Wheels & Tires. rev. ed. Fennema, Roger L. & Shewan, Paul B., eds. (Automobile Mechanics Refresher Course Ser.: Bk. 4). (Illus.). 79p. 1981. pap., student ed. 9.95 (*0-88098-065-6*, H M Gousha); audio 13.90 (*0-88098-071-0*, H M Gousha) Prntice Hall Bks.

— Complete Automobile Mechanics Refresher Course. (Illus.). 441p. 1981. student ed. 79.95 (*0-88098-067-2*, H M Gousha) Prntice Hall Bks.

— Complete Automobile Mechanics Refresher Course, 5 cass., Set. rev. ed. (Illus.). 441p. 1981. audio 70.00 (*0-88098-073-7*, H M Gousha) Prntice Hall Bks.

— Electrical Systems, Heating, & Air Conditioning. rev. ed. Fenneman, Roger L. & Dark, Harris E., eds. (Automobile Mechanics Refresher Course Ser.: Bk. 3). (Illus.). 94p. 1981. pap., student ed. 9.95 (*0-88098-064-8*, H M Gousha); audio 13.90 (*0-88098-070-2*, H M Gousha) Prntice Hall Bks.

— Engines, Lubricating & Coding Systems. Fennema, Roger L. & Wiseman, Leslie A., eds. (Automobile Mechanics Refresher Course Ser.: Bk. 2). (Illus.). 80p. 1981. pap., student ed. 9.95 (*0-88098-063-X*, H M Gousha) Prntice Hall Bks.

— Engines, Lubricating & Coding Systems. rev. ed. Fennema, Roger L. & Wiseman, Leslie A., eds. (Automobile Mechanics Refresher Course Ser.: Bk. 2). (Illus.). 80p. 1981. audio 13.90 (*0-88098-069-9*, H M Gousha) Prntice Hall Bks.

— Tune-up Ignition & Fuel Induction Systems. Fennema, Roger L. et al, eds. (Automobile Mechanics Refresher Course Ser.: Bk. 1). (Illus.). 104p. 1981. pap., student ed. 9.95 (*0-88098-062-1*, H M Gousha) Prntice Hall Bks.

— Tune-up Ignition & Fuel Induction Systems. rev. ed. Fennema, Roger L. et al, eds. (Automobile Mechanics Refresher Course Ser.: Bk. 1). (Illus.). 104p. 1981. audio 13.90 (*0-88098-068-0*, H M Gousha) Prntice Hall Bks.

Leigh Brown, Alison. Fear, Truth, Writing: From Paper Village to Electronic Community. LC 94-32800. (SUNY Series in Postmodern Culture). 145p. (C). 1995. text 44.50 (*0-7914-2531-2*); pap. text 14.95 (*0-7914-2532-0*) State U NY Pr.

***Leigh, Carole.** Football Guide 1999: What You Always Wanted to Know about Football but Were Afraid to Ask. (Illus.). 85p. 1999. pap. 10.00 (*0-9638943-2-3*) Leigh Enter.

Leigh, Carole. What You Always Wanted to Know about Football but Were Afraid to Ask: The Beginner's Guide. Berg, Kristi K., ed. (Illus.). 65p. (Orig.). 1994. pap. 6.90 (*0-9638943-1-5*) Leigh Enter.

Leigh, Catherine. One Night Before Christmas. (Romance Ser.: No. 3533). 1998. per. 3.50 (*0-373-03533-0*, 1-03533-6) Harlequin Bks.

— One Night Before Christmas. large type ed. (Larger Print Ser.: No. 379). 1998. per. 3.50 (*0-373-15779-7*, 1-15779-1) Harlequin Bks.

— Rebel Without a Bride. 1997. per. 3.25 (*0-373-15715-0*, 1-15715-5); per. 3.25 (*0-373-03469-5*, 1-03469-3) Harlequin Bks.

— Something Old, Something New. (Romance Ser.). 1996. per. 3.25 (*0-373-03426-1*, 1-03426-3) Harlequin Bks.

Leigh, Colin H., jt. auth. see Aiken, S. Robert.

Leigh, D. Historical Development of British Psychiatry, Vol. 1: Eighteenth & Nineteenth Century. LC 61-14243. 1961. 129.00 (*0-08-009537-2*, Pub. by Pergamon Repr) Franklin.

Leigh, David. Designing & Delivering Training for Groups. rev. ed. (Practical Trainer Ser.). 192p. 1997. pap. 25.00 (*0-7494-2062-6*, Kogan Pg Educ) Stylus Pub VA.

— Fergie: The Very Private Life of the Duchess of York. LC 97-136230. 1996. mass mkt. 5.99 (*0-7860-0376-6*, Pinncle Kensgtn) Kensgtn Pub Corp.

— The Frontiers of Secrecy: Closed Government in Britain. LC 82-6757. 289p. 1980. lib. bdg. 55.00 (*0-313-27093-7*, U7093, Greenwood Pr) Greenwood.

— Interviewing TOPPICS. 200p. 1996. ring bd. 166.95 (*0-566-07660-8*, Pub. by Gower) Ashgate Pub Co.

Leigh, David J. Circuitous Journeys: Modern Spiritual Autobiography. (Studies in Religion & Literature: Vol. 2). 200p. 1999. 35.00 (*0-8232-1993-3*, Pub. by Fordham) BookMasters.

— Circuitous Journeys: Modern Spiritual Autobiography. (Studies in Religion & Literature: Vol. 2). 200p. 2000. pap. 17.00 (*0-8232-1994-1*, Pub. by Fordham) BookMasters.

Leigh, Duane E. Assisting Displaced Workers: Do the States Have a Better Idea? LC 89-5844. 172p. 1989. 22.00 (*0-88099-073-2*); pap. 12.00 (*0-88099-074-0*) W E Upjohn.

— Assisting Workers Displaced by Structural Change: An International Perspective. LC 95-21004. 220p. 1995. 35.00 (*0-88099-154-2*); pap. 17.00 (*0-88099-153-4*) W E Upjohn.

— Does Training Work for Displaced Workers? A Survey of Existing Evidence. LC 90-38433. 120p. 1990. 31.00 (*0-88099-093-7*); pap. 12.00 (*0-88099-094-5*) W E Upjohn.

Leigh, Edward. Critica Sacra. reprint ed. write for info. incl. 3.5 hd (*0-318-72037-X*) G Olms Pubs.

Leigh, Egbert G., Jr. Tropical Forest Ecology: A View from Barro Colorado Island. (Illus.). 264p. 1999. pap. 35.00 (*0-19-509603-7*); text 85.00 (*0-19-509602-9*) OUP.

Leigh, Egbert G., Jr., et al, eds. The Ecology of a Tropical Forest: Seasonal Rhythms & Long-Term Changes. 2nd ed. (Illus.). 480p. 1996. pap. text 32.95 (*1-56098-642-5*) Smithsonian.

Leigh, Elizabeth. Mountain Moonlight. 352p. 1997. mass mkt. 4.99 (*0-8217-5632-X*, Zebra Kensgtn) Kensgtn Pub Corp.

— Tennessee Waltz. 352p. 1998. mass mkt. 4.99 (*0-8217-5849-7*, Zebra Kensgtn) Kensgtn Pub Corp.

***Leigh, Elyssebeth.** Learning Through Fun & Games. (Illus.). 176p. (J). 1999. pap. 29.95 (*0-07-470768-X*) McGraw.

Leigh, Frances A., jt. auth. see Kemble, Frances A.

Leigh, Frances B. Ten Years on a Georgia Plantation since the War (1866-1876) 141p. 1992. 30.00 (*0-88322-010-5*) Beehive GA.

Leigh, Frederic A., jt. ed. see Godfrey, Donald G.

Leigh, G. J., et al. Principles of Chemical Nomenclature: A Guide to IUPAC Recommendations. LC 97-28587. (Illus.). 128p. 1998. pap. 28.95 (*0-86542-685-6*) Blackwell Sci.

Leigh, Gillian. All about Twins. 1985. pap. 8.95 (*0-7100-9888-X*, Routledge Thoemms) Routledge.

— All about Twins: A Handbook for Parents. (Illus.). 253p. (Orig.). 1984. pap. 14.95 (0-415-04287-9, 9888-X) Routledge.

Leigh, Glenn. Victims' Rights. LC 97-41945. (Contemporary World Issues Ser.). 231p. 1997. lib. bdg. 45.00 (0-87436-870-7) ABC-CLIO.

Leigh, H. Consultation-Liaison Psychiatry: 1990 & Beyond. (Illus.). 250p. (C). 1994. 75.00 (0-306-44725-8, Plenum Trade) Perseus Pubng.

Leigh, H., ed. Behavioral Medicine, Biofeedback, & Behavioral Approaches in Psychosomatic Medicine. (Journal: Psychotherapy & Psychosomatics: Vol. 36, No. 3-4, 1981). (Illus.). 122p. 1982. pap. 52.25 (3-8055-3521-X) S Karger.

Leigh, Heather. Comprende Usted? 1991. pap. text 10.00 (0-582-22344-X) Longman.

Leigh, Heather & Ortiz-Carboneres, Salvador. Conversaciones, Situaciones. 1984. pap. text 8.55 (0-582-22178-1, 70890); audio 22.61 (0-582-24270-3, 70971) Longman.

Leigh, Helena. The Grapes of Paradise. large type ed. 416p. 1986. 27.99 (0-7089-8326-X, Charnwood) Ulverscroft.

— Kingdoms of the Vine. large type ed. 352p. 1986. 27.99 (0-7089-8350-2) Ulverscroft.

— Wild Vines. large type ed. 448p. 1986. 27.99 (0-7089-8340-5) Ulverscroft.

Leigh, Hoyle, ed. Biopsychosocial Approaches in Primary Care: State of the Art & Challenges for the 21st Century. LC 97-3397. (Illus.). 252p. (C). 1997. text 89.50 (0-306-45582-X, Kluwer Plenum) Kluwer Academic.

Leigh, Hoyle & Reiser, Morton F. The Patient: Biological, Psychological & Social Dimensions of Medical Practice. 3rd ed. (Illus.). 528p. (C). 1992. text 45.00 (0-306-44142-X, Kluwer Plenum) Kluwer Academic.

***Leigh, Ian.** Law, Politics & Local Democracy. 300p. 2000. text 85.00 (0-19-825698-1) OUP.

Leigh, Ian, jt. auth. see Lustgarten, Laurence.

Leigh, Irene M., ed. Keratinocyte Methods. (Illus.). 223p. (C). 1995. spiral bd. 74.95 (0-521-45013-6) Cambridge U Pr.

Leigh, Irene M., et al, eds. The Keratinocyte Handbook. LC 93-21304. (Illus.). 584p. (C). 1995. text 220.00 (0-521-43416-5) Cambridge U Pr.

Leigh, Irene M. & Watt, Fiona M., eds. Keratinocyte: Methods. LC 93-42614. 310p. 1996. text 85.00 (0-521-45103-5) Cambridge U Pr.

Leigh, Irene M., jt. ed. see McKay, Ian.

Leigh, Irene W., ed. Psychotherapy with Deaf Clients from Diverse Groups. LC 99-40434. 290p. 1999. 65.00 (1-56368-083-1) Gallaudet Univ Pr.

Leigh, Ivan E., jt. ed. see Pesek, Joseph J.

Leigh, J. & Briggs, J. Rare or Threatened Australian Plants. 4th ed. (Illus.). 376p. (Orig.). 1996. pap. 44.95 (0-643-05798-6, Pub. by CSIRO) Accents Pubns.

Leigh, J. H. The Timber Trade: An Introduction to Commercial Aspects. LC 79-42776. 115p. 1980. 63.00 (0-08-024917-5, Pub. by Pergamon Repr) Franklin.

***Leigh, J. P., et al.** Costs of Occupational Injuries & Illnesses. LC 99-87029. (Illus.). 400p. (C). 2000. text 49.50 (0-472-11081-0, 11081) U of Mich Pr.

Leigh, J. Paul. Causes of Death in the Workplace. LC 94-36796. 328p. 1995. 67.95 (0-89930-951-8, Quorum Bks) Greenwood.

Leigh, J. R. Control Theory: A Guided Tour. (Control Engineering Ser.: No. 45). xii, 186p. 1992. 77.00 (0-86341-241-6, Pub. by Peregrinus); pap. 39.00 (0-86341-284-X, Pub. by Peregrinus) Dist Unknown.

— Functional Analysis & Linear Control Theory. (Mathematics in Science & Engineering Ser.). 1981. text 128.00 (0-12-441880-5) Acad Pr.

— Temperature Measurement & Control. (Control Engineering Ser.: No. 33). 208p. 1988. pap. 77.00 (0-86341-111-8, CE033) INSPEC Inc.

***Leigh, Jack.** Land I'm Bound To: Photographs. (Illus.). 2000. 75.00 (0-393-04931-0) Norton.

Leigh, Jack. Nets & Doors: Shrimping in Southern Waters. (Illus.). 96p. 1989. 45.00 (0-941711-12-9) Wyrick & Co.

— Seaport: A Waterfront at Work. LC 96-21783. (Illus.). 144p. 1996. 45.00 (0-941711-34-X) Wyrick & Co.

Leigh, Jackie D. Jinx. 182p. (Orig.). (J). 1997. pap. 12.00 (0-9659750-0-2) Dryden Press.

Leigh, James W. Communicating for Cultural Competence. LC 96-53189. 188p. 1997. pap. text 34.00 (0-205-18704-8) Allyn.

Leigh, Janet. House of Destiny. LC 95-19728. 512p. 1995. 19.95 (1-55166-125-X, Mira Bks) Harlequin Bks.

— House of Destiny. 1996. per. 5.99 (1-55166-159-4, 1-66159-4, Mira Bks) Harlequin Bks.

Leigh, Janet & Nickens, C. Psycho: Behind the Scenes of the Classic Thriller. 224p. 1995. 22.00 (0-517-70112-X) Harmony Bks.

Leigh, Jason. The Personality Factor. (Illus.). 120p. (Orig.). 1985. 5.95 (0-934145-01-6) Airborne Pr.

Leigh, Jo. Can't Resist a Cowboy. (American Romance Ser.: No. 768). 1999. per. 3.99 (0-373-16768-7, 1-16768-3) Harlequin Bks.

— Daddy 101. (American Romance Ser.: Vol. 736). 1998. per. 3.99 (0-373-16736-9, 1-16736-0) Harlequin Bks.

***Leigh, Jo.** Doctor, Darling. (American Romance Ser.: Bk. 832). 2000. per. 4.25 (0-373-16832-2, 1-16832-7) Harlequin Bks.

Leigh, Jo. Double Surprise pour une Ingenue. (Rouge Passion Ser.: Bk. 493). 1999. mass mkt. 3.50 (0-373-37493-3, 1-37493-3) Harlequin Bks.

— Everyday Hero. (Intimate Moments Ser.). 1996. per. 3.99 (0-373-07740-8, 1-07740-3) Silhouette.

— The $4.98 Daddy. 1999. mass mkt. 4.50 (0-373-82598-6, 1-82598-3) Harlequin Bks.

— Hot & Bothered: Blaze. (Temptation Ser.: No. 756). 1999. per. 3.75 (0-373-25856-9, 1-25856-5) Harlequin Bks.

— Hunted. (Intimate Moments Ser.). 1995. per. 3.75 (0-373-07659-2, 1-07659-5) Silhouette.

— Husband 101. (American Romance Ser.). 1998. per. 3.99 (0-373-16731-8, 1-16731-1) Harlequin Bks.

— If Wishes Were Daddies . . . Three Coins in a Fountain. (American Romance Ser.: Vol. 749). 1998. per. 3.99 (0-373-16749-0, 1-16749-3) Harlequin Bks.

***Leigh, Jo.** Ms. Taken. (Temptation Ser.). 2000. mass mkt. 3.99 (0-373-25909-3, 1259092) Harlequin Bks.

Leigh, Jo. One Wicked Night. (Temptation Ser.). 1998. per. 3.75 (0-373-25774-0, 1-25774-0) Harlequin Bks.

— Quick, Find a Ring! 1997. per. 3.75 (0-373-16695-8, 1-16695-8) Harlequin Bks.

— Seduction en Louisiane. (Rouge Passion Ser.: Vol. 503). (FRE.). 1999. mass mkt. 3.50 (0-373-37503-4, 1-37503-9) Harlequin Bks.

— Single Sheriff Seeks . . . Mail Order Men. (Temptation Ser.: Vol. 699). 1998. per. 3.75 (0-373-25799-6, 1-25799-7) Harlequin Bks.

— Suspect. 1994. per. 3.50 (0-373-07569-3) Silhouette.

***Leigh, Jo.** Tangled Sheets: The Wrong Bed. 1999. per. 3.75 (0-373-25827-5, 1-25826-6, Harlequin) Harlequin Bks.

***Leigh, John.** The Search for Enlightenment: An Introduction to Eighteenth-Century French Writing. 176p. 1999. pap. 24.00 (0-7425-0047-0) Rowman.

Leigh, John, jt. auth. see Wells, John.

Leigh-Jones, Nicholas, jt. auth. see MacGillivray, Evan James.

***Leigh, Julia.** The Hunter: A Novel. 176p. 2000. 20.00 (1-56858-169-6, Pub. by FWEW) Publishers Group.

Leigh, Julianne. My Beastiary. Mycue, Edward, ed. (Took Modern Poetry in English Ser.: No. 11). (Illus.). 28p. (Orig.). 1993. pap. 3.00 (1-879457-05-9) Norton Coker Pr.

Leigh, Juliette. Fifth Proposal, 1. (Zebra Regency Romance Ser.). 224p. 1999. mass mkt. 4.99 (0-8217-6265-6) Kensgtn Pub Corp.

— Sherry's Comet. (Zebra Romance Ser.). 224p. 1998. pap. 4.99 (0-8217-5891-8, Zebra Kensgtn) Kensgtn Pub Corp.

— Touch of Magic. 224p. 1998. mass mkt. 4.99 (0-8217-6065-3, Zebra Kensgtn) Kensgtn Pub Corp.

Leigh-Kendall, T. A., jt. auth. see Still, Tom.

Leigh, Keri. Stevie Ray: Soul to Soul. LC 93-24011. (Illus.). 200p. 1993. pap. 18.95 (0-87833-838-1) Taylor Pub.

Leigh-Kile, Donna. Lawyers: On the Spot. (Illus.). 180p. 1999. pap. 15.95 (1-883319-80-3) Frog Ltd CA.

— Sex Symbols. 1999. pap. 14.95 (1-883319-51-X) Frog Ltd CA.

Leigh, L. H. Leigh: Police Powers in England & Wales. 2nd ed. 1985. pap. 46.00 (0-406-84542-5, MICHIE) LEXIS Pub.

Leigh, L. H., et al. Introduction to Company Law. 4th ed. 1987. pap. 44.00 (0-406-63107-7, U.K., MICHIE) LEXIS Pub.

Leigh, Leonard & Beyani, Chaloka. Blackstone's Guide to the Asylum & Immigration Act, 1996. 149p. 1996. pap. 38.00 (1-85431-591-9, Pub. by Blackstone Pr) Gaunt.

Leigh, Linda. Book of Self Worth: Inspirations. Date not set. write for info. (1-891231-14-6) Word Assn.

Leigh, Margaret & MacLean, Katy. A Spade among the Rushes. LC 97-129019. (Illus.). 206p. pap. 13.95 (1-874744-64-5, Pub. by Birlinn Ltd) Dufour.

Leigh, Marion. Findhorn Flower Essences: Straight to the Heart of the Matter. (Illus.). 1997. pap. 16.95 (1-899171-96-7, Pub. by Findhorn Pr) Words Distrib.

Leigh, Mark & Lepine, Mike. The Book of Utterly Ridiculous Stupid Lists. 1998. mass mkt. 7.95 (0-7535-0262-3, Pub. by Virgin Bks) London Brdge.

Leigh, Matthew. Lucan: Spectacle & Engagement. (Oxford Classical Monographs). 376p. 1997. text 85.00 (0-19-815067-9) OUP.

Leigh, Maxwell. Touring Southern Africa. (Illus.). 1990. pap. 20.00 (0-87556-731-2) Saifer.

Leigh, Michael. Checklist of Holdings on Borneo in the Cornell University Libraries. LC 67-63728. (Cornell University, Southeast Asia Program, Data Paper Ser.: No. 62). 78p. reprint ed. pap. 30.00 (0-608-14386-3, 202184000023) Bks Demand.

— Mobilizing Consent: Public Opinion & American Foreign Policy, 1937-1947. LC 75-44656. 187p. 1976. 49.95 (0-8371-8772-9, LMC/, Greenwood Pr) Greenwood.

— The Velvet Underground. 192p. 1998. reprint ed. pap. 12.95 (1-871592-28-3, Velvet Pub) Creation Books.

Leigh, Michelle D. Inner Peace, Outer Beauty: Natural Japanese Health & Beauty Secrets Revealed. (Illus.). 224p. 1995. pap. 14.95 (0-8065-1628-3, Citadel Pr) Carol Pub Group.

— The Japanese Way of Beauty: Natural Beauty & Health Secrets. (Illus.). 208p. 1992. 22.50 (1-55972-065-4, Birch Ln Pr) Carol Pub Group.

— The Japanese Way of Beauty: Natural Beauty & Health Secrets. (Illus.). 224p. 1998. pap. 15.00 (0-7881-5296-3) DIANE Pub.

— The New Beauty. Calogeras, Meagan, ed. (Illus.). 240p. 1995. pap. 18.00 (4-7700-1869-X) Kodansha.

Leigh, Mike. Abigail's Party. 1979. pap. write for info. (0-573-11016-6) French.

— Career Girls. 128p. 1997. pap. text 13.95 (0-571-19404-4) Faber & Faber.

— Ecstacy. 128p. (Orig.). 1989. pap. 16.95 (1-85459-321-8, Pub. by N Hern Bks) Theatre Comm.

***Leigh, Mike.** The Gilbert & Sullivan Film. (Screenplays Ser.). (Illus.). 176p. 1999. pap. 14.00 (0-571-20206-3) Faber & Faber.

Leigh, Mike. Junior Judo. (Illus.). 132p. (Orig.). 1996. pap. 18.95 (0-572-01821-5, Pub. by W Foulsham) Trans-Atl Phila.

— Naked & Other Screenplays. LC 96-138277. 272p. (Orig.). 1995. pap. 21.95 (0-571-17386-1) Faber & Faber.

— Secrets & Lies. 128p. 1997. pap. 13.95 (0-571-19291-2) Faber & Faber.

— Smelling a Rat. 80p. (Orig.). 1996. pap. 14.95 (1-85459-316-1, Pub. by N Hern Bks) Theatre Comm.

Leigh, Mitch & Darion, Joe. Man of La Mancha: Complete Vocal Score. (Illus.). 150p. pap. 40.00 (0-89524-265-6, 3709) Cherry Lane.

— Man of La Mancha: Vocal Score. Flato, Ludwig, ed. (Illus.). 150p. (Orig.). 1990. pap. text 40.00 (0-89524-558-2, Pub. by Cherry Lane) H Leonard.

Leigh, Nancey G. Stemming Middle-Class Decline: The Challenges to Economic Development Planning. LC 94-18279. 236p. (C). 1994. pap. text 14.95 (0-88285-149-7) Ctr Urban Pol Res.

Leigh, Nila K. Learning to Swim in Swaziland: A Child's Eye-View of a Southern African Country. LC 92-13223. (Illus.). 48p. (J). (gr. k-3). 1993. 15.95 (0-590-45938-4) Scholastic Inc.

Leigh, P. N. & Swash, Michael, eds. Motor Neuron Disease. LC 94-14875. (Illus.). 486p. 1995. 135.00 (0-387-19685-4) Spr-Verlag.

Leigh-Phippard, Helen. Congress & U. S. Military Aid to Britain: Interdependence & Dependence, 1949-56. LC 94-35564. 199p. 1995. text 69.95 (0-312-12516-X) St Martin.

Leigh-Phippard, Helen, jt. auth. see Simpson, John.

Leigh-Pollitt, Piers, jt. auth. see Mullock, James.

***Leigh, R. A.** 3 Passports to Paradise. LC 99-91013. (Spectrutek Ser.). (Illus.). 176p. 1999. pap. 11.00 (0-9674557-0-7) Spectrutekcom.

Leigh, R. A. & Johnston, A. E., eds. Long-Term Experiments in Agricultural & Ecological Sciences. (Illus.). 448p. 1994. text 130.00 (0-85198-933-0) OUP.

Leigh, R. John. The Neurology of Eye Movements. 3rd ed. LC 98-37880. (Illus.). 656p. 1999. text 120.00 (0-19-512972-5) OUP.

Leigh, R. John & Zee, David S. The Neurology of Eye Movements. 3rd ed. (Contemporary Neurology Ser.). 1999. cd-rom 120.00 (0-19-512974-1) OUP.

— The Neurology of Eye Movements. 3rd ed. (Contemporary Neurology Ser.: No. 55). (Illus.). 656p. 1999. text 195.00 (0-19-512973-3) OUP.

Leigh, R. W. Dental Morphology & Pathology of Prehistoric Guam. (BMB Ser.). (Orig.). 1929. reprint ed. pap. 25.00 (0-527-01668-3) Periodicals Srv.

— Dental Pathology of Aboriginal California. fac. ed. (University of California Publications in American Archaeology & Ethnology: Vol. 23: 10). 53p. (C). 1928. reprint ed. pap. text 6.56 (1-55567-266-3) Coyote Press.

Leigh, Rhoda. Autumn Love. large type ed. (Linford Romance Library). 208p. 1993. pap. 16.99 (0-7089-7318-3, Linford) Ulverscroft.

***Leigh, Rhoda.** Faraway Love. large type ed. 256p. 1999. pap. 18.99 (0-7089-5522-3, Linford) Ulverscroft.

Leigh, Richard. The Copie of a Letter Sent out of England to Don B. Mendoza. LC 72-6010. (English Experience Ser.: No. 536). 1973. reprint ed. 20.00 (90-221-0536-9) Walter J Johnson.

Leigh, Richard, jt. auth. see Baigent, Michael.

Leigh, Robert. A Free & Responsible Press, a General Report on Mass Communication: Newspapers, Radio, Motion Pictures, Magazines & Books. Commission on Freedom of the Press, ed. LC 46-13. (Midway Reprint Ser.). 146p. 1974. reprint ed. pap. text 12.00 (0-226-47135-7) U Ch Pr.

— The Turner Journals. 288p. 1996. 22.95 (0-8027-3260-7) Walker & Co.

Leigh, Robert, compiled by. Index to Song Books. LC 72-8344. (Music Ser.). 242p. 1973. reprint ed. lib. bdg. 29.50 (0-306-70553-2) Da Capo.

Leigh, Robert D., jt. auth. see White, Llewellyn.

Leigh, Roberta. Bachelor at Heart. (Presents Ser.). 1993. mass mkt. 2.99 (0-373-11568-7, 1-11568-2) Harlequin Bks.

— Bachelor at Heart. large type ed. (Harlequin Ser.). 1993. lib. bdg. 19.95 (0-263-13355-9) Mac Lib Ref.

— Give a Man a Bad Name. 1994. per. 2.99 (0-373-11647-0) Harlequin Bks.

— Give a Man a Bad Name. large type ed. (Harlequin Ser.). 1994. lib. bdg. 19.95 (0-263-13660-4) Thorndike Pr.

— No Hay Olvido (The Wrong Kind of Wife) (SPA.). 1996. per. 3.50 (0-373-33382-X, 1-33382-2) Harlequin Bks.

— Not His Kind of Woman. large type ed. 1992. reprint ed. 18.95 (0-263-13097-5) Mac Lib Ref.

— Two-Faced Woman. (Presents Ser.). 1993. pap. 2.89 (0-373-11541-5, 1-11541-9) Harlequin Bks.

— Two-Timing Man. 1993. per. 2.99 (0-373-11609-8, 1-11609-4) Harlequin Bks.

— Two-Timing Man. large type ed. (Harlequin Ser.). 1993. lib. bdg. 18.95 (0-263-13423-7) Thorndike Pr.

— The Wrong Kind of Wife. large type ed. (Harlequin Romance Ser.). 283p. 1995. 19.95 (0-263-14213-2) Mac Lib Ref.

Leigh, Roberta & Wentworth, Sally. The Wrong Kind of Wife. LC 95-4588. (Presents Ser.). 189p. 1995. per. 3.25 (0-373-11725-6, 1-11725-8) Harlequin Bks.

Leigh, Robin. The Hawk & the Heather. 400p. (Orig.). 1992. mass mkt. 4.50 (0-380-76319-2, Avon Bks) Morrow Avon.

Leigh, Ronald W. Solid Modeling with AutoCAD, Release 12. 2nd ed. 271p. 1991. 29.95 (0-614-16834-1, V75) Am Soc Civil Eng.

Leigh, S. The Haunted Tower. (Puzzle Adventures Ser.). (Illus.). 48p. (J). (gr. 3-8). 1999. lib. bdg. 13.95 (0-88110-367-5, Usborne) EDC.

— Journey to the Lost Temple. (Puzzle Adventures Ser.). (Illus.). 48p. (J). (gr. 3-8). 1989. pap. 5.95 (0-7460-0308-0) EDC.

— Puzzle Castle. (Young Puzzles Ser.). (Illus.). 32p. (J). (ps up). 1993. text 5.95 (0-7460-1284-5); lib. bdg. 13.95 (0-88110-624-0) EDC.

— Puzzle Dungeon. (Young Puzzles Ser.). (Illus.). 32p. (J). (ps up). 1995. pap. 5.95 (0-7460-1679-4, Usborne); lib. bdg. 13.95 (0-88110-753-0, Usborne) EDC.

— Puzzle Farm. (Young Puzzles Ser.). (Illus.). 32p. (J). (ps up). 1992. pap. 5.95 (0-7460-0712-4, Usborne); lib. bdg. 13.95 (0-88110-555-4, Usborne) EDC.

— Puzzle Island. (Young Puzzles Ser.). (Illus.). 32p. (J). (ps up). 1991. lib. bdg. 13.95 (0-88110-558-9, Usborne) EDC.

— Puzzle Island. (Young Puzzles Ser.). (Illus.). 32p. (J). (ps up). 1991. pap. 5.95 (0-7460-0596-2, Usborne) EDC.

— Puzzle Town. (Young Puzzles Ser.). (Illus.). 32p. (J). (ps up). 1991. pap. 5.95 (0-7460-0681-0, Usborne); lib. bdg. 13.95 (0-88110-554-6, Usborne) EDC.

— Puzzle World (B - U) (Young Puzzles Ser.). (Illus.). 96p. (J). (ps up). 1992. pap. 9.95 (0-7460-0731-0) EDC.

— Uncle Pete the Pirate. (Young Puzzle Adventure Ser.). (Illus.). 32p. (J). (ps-2). 1994. pap. 5.95 (0-7460-1529-1, Usborne); lib. bdg. 13.95 (0-88110-713-1, Usborne) EDC.

Leigh, Scott H. Unemployed, Now What? A Handbook to Help Redirect Your Life When You Become Unemployed. 112p. 1998. pap. 14.95 (1-890622-34-6) Leathers Pub.

Leigh, Spencer, jt. auth. see Dawson, Jim.

Leigh, Stephen. Dark Water's Embrace. 352p. 1998. mass mkt. 3.99 (0-380-79478-0, Avon Bks) Morrow Avon.

— Ray Bradbury Presents: Dinosaur Conquest. 272p. (Orig.). 1995. mass mkt. 4.99 (0-380-76283-8, Avon Bks) Morrow Avon.

— Ray Bradbury Presents: Dinosaur Planet. 304p. (Orig.). 1993. mass mkt. 4.99 (0-380-76278-1, Avon Bks) Morrow Avon.

— Ray Bradbury Presents: Dinosaur Warriors. 327p. (Orig.). 1994. mass mkt. 4.99 (0-380-76280-3, Avon Bks) Morrow Avon.

— Ray Bradbury Presents Dinosaur World: Dinosaur World. 304p. (Orig.). 1992. mass mkt. 4.99 (0-380-76277-3, Avon Bks) Morrow Avon.

— Speaking Stones. 352p. 1999. mass mkt. 5.99 (0-380-79914-6, Eos) Morrow Avon.

Leigh, Stephen & Miller, John J. Ray Bradbury Presents: Dinosaur Empire. (Ray Bradbury Presents Ser.). 256p. (Orig.). 1995. mass mkt. 4.99 (0-380-76282-X, Avon Bks) Morrow Avon.

— Ray Bradbury Presents: Dinosaur Samurai. 256p. (Orig.). 1993. mass mkt. 4.99 (0-380-76279-X, Avon Bks) Morrow Avon.

Leigh, Sue, ed. see Burke, Peter.

Leigh, Sue, ed. see Egmond, Florike.

Leigh, Sue, ed. see Eyerman, Ron.

Leigh, Sue, ed. see Gilloch, Graeme.

Leigh, Sue, ed. see Hall, John.

Leigh, Sue, ed. see Horning, Karl H., et al.

Leigh, Sue, ed. see Moscovici, Serge.

Leigh, Sue, ed. see Nolan, Bryan.

Leigh, Susanna. Puzzle Train. (Young Puzzles Ser.). (Illus.). 32p. (J). (ps up). 1996. pap. 5.95 (0-7460-2331-6, Usborne); lib. bdg. 13.95 (0-88110-798-0, Usborne) EDC.

Leigh, Susannah. Ciudad Enigma: Lumen Puzzles Infantiles. (SPA., Illus.). (J). pap. 6.95 (950-724-182-5) Lumen ARG.

— Dream Pony. 112p. (gr. 4-8). 1997. pap. text 3.95 (0-7460-2490-8, Usborne) EDC.

Leigh, Susannah. Dream Pony. (Sandy Lane Stables Ser.). 112p. (J). (gr. 4-8). 1998. lib. bdg. 11.95 (0-88110-997-5) EDC.

Leigh, Susannah. Granja Enigma: Lumen Puzzles Infantiles. (SPA., Illus.). pap. 6.95 (950-724-226-0) Lumen ARG.

— Isla Enigma: Lumen Puzzles Infantiles. (SPA., Illus.). pap. 6.95 (950-724-183-3) Lumen ARG.

— L'Ile Fantastique: Fantastic Island. Gemmell, Kathy & Irving, Nicole, eds. (FRE., Illus.). 25p. (J). (gr. 2-3). reprint ed. 17.00 (0-7881-9300-7) DIANE Pub.

Leigh, Susannah. Moonwind. 512p. 1988. pap. 3.95 (0-317-66162-0, Sig) NAL.

— Puzzle Holiday. (Illus.). 32p. (J). (ps up). 1998. pap. 5.95 (0-7460-2680-3, Usborne); lib. bdg. 13.95 (0-88110-970-3, Usborne) EDC.

— Puzzle Jungle. (Young Puzzles Ser.). (Illus.). 32p. (J). (ps up). 1995. text 5.95 (0-7460-1707-3, Usborne); lib. bdg. 13.95 (0-88110-767-0, Usborne) EDC.

— Puzzle Ocean. (Young Puzzles Ser.). (Illus.). 32p. (J). (ps up). 1996. text 5.95 (0-7460-2333-2, Usborne); lib. bdg. 13.95 (0-88110-846-4, Usborne) EDC.

— Puzzle Planet. (Young Puzzles Ser.). (Illus.). 32p. (J). (ps up). 1993. pap. 5.95 (0-7460-1286-1, Usborne); lib. bdg. 13.95 (0-88110-646-1, Usborne) EDC.

— Puzzle School. Bates, Michelle, ed. (Young Puzzles Ser.). (Illus.). 32p. (Orig.). (J). (ps up). 1997. pap. 5.95 (0-7460-2678-1, Usborne); lib. bdg. 13.95 (0-88110-940-1, Usborne) EDC.

— Runaway Pony. (Sandy Lane Stables Ser.). (Illus.). 96p. (Orig.). (J). (gr. 4-8). 1997. pap. 3.95 (0-7460-2482-7, Usborne); lib. bdg. 11.95 (0-88110-942-8, Usborne) EDC.

— Uncle Pete's Pirate Adventure. (Young Puzzle Adventures Ser.). (Illus.). 32p. (J). (ps-2). 1997. pap. 5.95 (0-7460-2298-0, Usborne); lib. bdg. 13.95 (0-88110-918-5, Usborne) EDC.

Leigh, Susannah & Haw, Brenda. Complete Puzzle World. (Young Puzzles Ser.). (Illus.). 1192p. (J). (gr. 2 up). 1994. pap. 18.95 (0-7460-1859-2, Usborne) EDC.

— Puzzle Mountain. (Young Puzzles Ser.). (Illus.). 32p. (J). (ps up). 1994. pap. 5.95 (0-7460-1288-8, Usborne); lib. bdg. 13.95 (0-88110-665-8, Usborne) EDC.

Leigh, Susannah, jt. auth. see Bates, Michelle.

Leigh, Susannah, jt. auth. see Gammell, Kathy.

Leigh, Susannah, jt. auth. see Gemmell, Kathy.

An Asterisk (*) at the beginning of an entry indicates that the title is appearing for the first time.

Leigh, Ted. The Selected Letters of Fairfield Porter. (Illus.). (C). text. write for info. (*0-472-10976-6*) U of Mich Pr.

Leigh, Valentine. A Most Profitable Science of Surveying. LC 72-171772. (English Experience Ser.: No. 397). 128p. 1971. reprint ed. 45.00 (*90-221-0397-8*) Walter J Johnson.

Leigh, Vanora. Mental Illness. LC 98-8198. (Talking Points Ser.). 64p. (J). 1999. 27.12 (*0-8172-5311-4*) Raintree Steck-V.

Leigh, Victoria. Sizzling Southwest Cuisine. 48p. 1993. pap. 4.95 (*0-9642805-0-7*) Victoria Leigh.

Leigh, Wallace B. Devices for Optoelectronics. (Optical Engineering Ser.: Vol. 55). (Illus.). 336p. 1996. text 145.00 (*0-8247-9432-X*) Dekker.

Leigh, Wendy. Edward Windsor: Royal Enigma: The True Story of the Seventh in Line to the British Throne. 1999. 23.00 (*0-671-02825-1*) PB.

— Edward Windsor: Royal Enigma: The True Story of the Seventh in Line to the British Throne. 2000. pap. write for info. (*0-671-02826-X*) S&S Trade.

***Leigh, Wendy.** Prince Charming: The John F. Kennedy Jr. Story, Vol. 1. 1999. mass mkt. 6.99 (*0-451-40921-3*, Sig) NAL.

— Prince Charming: The John F. Kennedy, Jr. Story. 368p. 2000. pap. 9.95 (*0-451-20080-2*, Sig) NAL.

Leigh, Wilhelmina A. Shelter Affordability for Blacks: Crisis or Clamor? 90p. (Orig.). 1982. pap. 18.95 (*0-87855-901-9*) Transaction Pubs.

Leigh, Wilhelmina A. & Simms, Margaret C., eds. Job Creation Prospects & Strategies. LC 99-10620. (The/Black Worker in the 21st Century Ser.). 216p. 1999. 45.00 (*0-7618-1349-7*); pap. 23.50 (*0-7618-1350-0*) U Pr of Amer.

Leigh, Wilhelmina A. & Stewart, James B., eds. The Housing Status of Black Americans. 250p. (C). 1991. pap. text 24.95 (*1-56000-579-3*) Transaction Pubs.

Leigh, William, jt. auth. see Harrison, William.

Leigh, William E. Business Analysis & Decision Making with Spreadsheet Software. 1991. pap. 14.95 (*0-89600-017-6*) IE Pasadena.

— FORTRAN: The Engineers' & Science Language. 384p. (Orig.). (C). 1987. pap. text 28.95 (*0-938188-67-4*) Mitchell Pub.

***Leigh, William S.** Zentherapy: Bodywork from Rolf to Feldenkrais to Tanouye Rotaishi. (Illus.). 224p. 2000. pap. text 14.95 (*1-58063-098-7*) Renaissance.

Leighfield, M. LRTA (Leisure, Recreation, & Tourism Abstracts) A User Handbook. 125p. (Orig.). 1990. pap. text 35.00 (*0-85198-676-5*) OUP.

Leighland, James, jt. auth. see Hausker, Arthur J.

Leighninger, Leslie. Social Work: Search for Identity, 4. LC 86-12155. (Studies in Social Welfare Policies & Programs: No. 4). 262p. 1987. 59.95 (*0-313-24775-7*, LSW/, Greenwood Pr) Greenwood.

Leighninger, Leslie, jt. auth. see Popple, Philip R.

Leighow, Susan. Nurse's Questions/Women's Questions: The Impact of the Demographic Revolution & Feminism on United States Working Women, 1946-1986. (American University Studies Series XXVII: Vol. 5). VIII, 209p. (C). 1996. text 39.95 (*0-8204-2755-1*) P Lang Pubng.

Leight, Lynn. Raising Sexually Healthy Children. 304p. 1990. pap. 10.00 (*0-380-70857-4*, Avon Bks) Morrow Avon.

***Leight, Robert L. & Rinehart, Alice Duffy.** Country School Memories: An Oral History of One-Room Schooling, 74. LC 98-41417. (Contributions to the Study of Education: Vol. 74). 168p. 1999. 49.95 (*0-313-30919-1*, Greenwood Pr) Greenwood.

Leight, Samuel. The Futility of Reformism: A Case for Peaceful Democratic Social Revolution. (Illus.). 229p. 1984. pap. 12.95 (*0-9613654-0-4*) WWW Pubs.

— World Without Wages (Money, Poverty & War!) 229p. 1981. pap. text 12.95 (*0-9613654-1-2*) WWW Pubs.

Leight, Walter & Galowin, Lawrence, eds. Proceedings of the Open Forum on Laboratory Accreditation. 175p. (Orig.). (C). 1997. pap. text 40.00 (*0-7881-3899-5*) DIANE Pub.

Leight, Walter G., jt. auth. see Leuteritz, Krista J.

Leight, Warren. The Loop. Date not set. pap. 5.95 (*0-8222-1734-1*) Dramatists Play.

— Side Man. pap. 5.95 (*0-8222-1721-X*) Dramatists Play.

Leight, Warren. Side Man. LC 98-54092. 112p. 1999. pap. 12.00 (*0-8021-3622-2*, Grove) Grove-Atltic.

— Stray Cats. LC 99-231509. 1998. pap. 5.25 (*0-8222-1614-0*) Dramatists Play.

Leight, Wes. Indoor Soccer Tactics & Skills: The Player's, Coach's, & Fan's Guide to the Secrets of the Indoor Game. (Illus.). 139p. (Orig.). 1987. pap. 13.95 (*0-9619872-0-0*) Green Forest Prods.

***Leighten, Patricia.** Art Anarchism & Anarchy. 1998. pap. text 28.00 (*0-226-47140-3*) U Ch Pr.

— Art Anarchism & Audience. 1998. 45.00 (*0-226-47138-1*) U Ch Pr.

Leighton. First Course Ord Diff Equat 4th. 4th ed. (Math). 1976. 20.50 (*0-534-00435-0*) Brooks-Cole.

— Ordinary Differential Equa 3rd. 3rd ed. (Math). 1970. 13.50 (*0-534-01956-0*) Brooks-Cole.

Leighton, Albert C. Transport & Communication in Early Medieval Europe AD 500-1100. LC 72-182440. 257 p. 1972. write for info. (*0-7153-5439-6*) D & C Pub.

Leighton, Angela. Victorian Women Poets: Writing Against the Heart. (Victorian Literature & Culture Ser.). 336p. (C). 1992. pap. text 19.50 (*0-8139-1427-2*) U Pr of Va.

Leighton, Angela, ed. Victorian Women Poets: A Critical Reader. (Blackwell Critical Readers in Literature Ser.). 288p. (C). 1996. pap. 28.95 (*0-631-19757-5*) Blackwell Pubs.

Leighton, Angela & Reynolds, Margaret, eds. Victorian Women Poets: An Anthology. (Anthologies Ser.). 800p. 1995. 78.95 (*0-631-17608-X*, Pub. by Polity Pr); pap. 33.95 (*0-631-17609-8*, Pub. by Polity Pr) Blackwell Pubs.

Leighton, Ann. American Gardens in the Eighteenth Century: "For Use or for Delight" LC 86-6975. (Illus.). 544p. 1986. reprint ed. pap. 21.95 (*0-87023-531-1*) U of Mass Pr.

— American Gardens of the Nineteenth Century: "For Comfort & Affluence" LC 86-11330. (Illus.). 424p. 1987. 40.00 (*0-87023-532-X*); pap. 20.95 (*0-87023-533-8*) U of Mass Pr.

— Early American Gardens: "For Meate or Medicine" LC 86-6980. (Illus.). 464p. 1986. pap. 20.95 (*0-87023-530-3*) U of Mass Pr.

Leighton, Audrey O. Alaska Knock-Knock Jokes. pap. 4.95 (*0-9666647-2-8*, Pub. by Fly Frog) Todd Commns.

Leighton, Audrey O. A Window of Time. (Illus.). 32p. (J). 1995. 15.95 (*0-9636335-1-1*) Nadja Pub.

Leighton, B. C., jt. auth. see Bhatia, S. N.

Leighton, Beach. Mr. Dutch: The Arkansas Traveler. LC 91-60004. (Illus.). 263p. 1991. 19.95 (*0-915611-44-9*) Sports Pub.

Leighton, Bridget A. Malaina & the Magic Agate. LC 95-94588. (Illus.). 32p. (Orig.). (J). (gr. 1-6). 1995. pap. 8.95 (*0-9647549-9-1*) B A Leighton.

Leighton, C. D. Catholicism in a Protestant Kingdom: A Study of the Irish Ancient "Regime" LC 93-5866. (Studies in Modern History). 250p. 1994. text 69.95 (*0-312-10301-8*) St Martin.

Leighton, Caroline. Life at Puget Sound. (Illus.). 139p. 1980. 24.95 (*0-87770-209-8*) Ye Galleon.

Leighton, Caroline C. West Coast Journeys, 1865-1879: The Travelogue of a Remarkable Woman. LC 95-12198. 192p. 1995. pap. 14.95 (*1-57061-012-6*) Sasquatch Bks.

Leighton, Clare. Give Us This Day. LC 76-152187. (Essay Index Reprint Ser.). 1977. reprint ed. 19.95 (*0-8369-2513-0*) Ayer.

— Southern Harvest. LC 97-16773. (Illus.). 176p. 1997. reprint ed. 24.95 (*0-8203-1948-1*) U of Ga Pr.

— Tempestuous Petticoat: The Story of an Invincible Edwardian. 272p. 1984. reprint ed. pap. 10.00 (*0-89733-099-4*) Academy Chi Pubs.

— Where Land Meets Sea: The Enduring Cape Cod. LC 54-7922. (Illus.). 208p. 1973. reprint ed. pap. 14.95 (*0-85699-056-6*) Chatham Pr.

Leighton, Clare, jt. auth. see Hardy, Thomas.

Leighton, Clarence F. Leighton: Memorials of the Leightons of Ulishaven, Forfarshire, & Other Scottish Families of the Name, A. D. 1260-1518 (with Added Pedigrees Through 1920's) 126p. 1993. reprint ed. pap. 27.00 (*0-8328-3364-9*); reprint ed. lib. bdg. 37.00 (*0-8328-3363-0*) Higginson Bk Co.

Leighton, Daniel. Bodhisattva Archetype: Classic Buddhist Guides to Awakening & Their Modern Expression. LC 97-23841. (Illus.). 320p. 1998. pap. 14.95 (*0-14-019556-4*) Viking Penguin.

***Leighton, Daniel & Yi Wu.** Cultivating the Empty Field: The Silent Illumination of Zen Master Hongzhi. (Library of Enlightenment). 2001. pap. 16.95 (*0-8048-3240-4*, Periplus Eds) Tuttle Pubng.

Leighton, David, jt. auth. see Stevens, Anne.

Leighton, David L. The Biology & Culture of the California Abalone. (Illus.). 256p. 1999. 50.00 (*0-8059-4742-6*) Dorrance.

Leighton, Dorothea C. & Adair, John. People of the Middle Place: A Study of the Zuni Indians. LC 65-28463. (Monographs). 189p. 1966. pap. 10.00 (*0-87536-320-2*) HRAFP.

Leighton, Dorothea C., jt. auth. see Kluckhohn, Clyde.

Leighton, Douglas. Alberta Canadian West Edmonton Cover. 2nd ed. (Illus.). 96p. 1999. reprint ed. 29.95 (*1-55153-135-6*) Altitude Publ.

Leighton, F. Thomas. Introduction to Parallel Algorithms & Architectures: Arrays, Trees & Hypercubes. 831p. 1992. text 76.95 (*1-55860-117-1*) Morgan Kaufmann.

Leighton, Frances H. A Basis for Building a Course in Economics of the Home. LC 74-176983. (Columbia University. Teachers College. Contributions to Education Ser.: No. 459). reprint ed. 37.50 (*0-404-55459-8*) AMS Pr.

Leighton, Frances S., jt. auth. see Collier, Oscar.

Leighton, Frederick W., jt. auth. see Hardy, H. R.

Leighton, Frederick W., jt. auth. see Hardy, H. Reginald.

Leighton, George R. Five Cities: The Story of Their Youth & Old Age. 408p. 1974. reprint ed. 24.95 (*0-405-02802-4*) Ayer.

Leighton, George R., jt. auth. see Brenner, Anita.

Leighton, George R., jt. auth. see Brown, Earl L.

Leighton, Hal. How to Play the Harmonica for Fun & Profit. (Orig.). 1978. 6.50 (*0-87505-088-3*); pap. 3.00 (*0-87505-291-6*) Borden.

— Play Harmonica. 6.50 (*0-87505-262-2*) Borden.

Leighton-Hardman, A. C. Stallion Management. 1975. pap. 5.00 (*0-87980-297-9*) Wilshire.

Leighton, Hudson. City of Saint Paul, Minnesota: Enumeration Districts, 13th Federal Census, 1910. LC 97-2079. 1997. spiral bd. 21.95 (*0-915709-34-1*) Pk Geneal Bk.

— Gazetteer of Minnesota Railroad Towns, 1861-1997. LC 98-18734. (Illus.). 1998. pap. 12.00 (*0-915709-61-9*) Pk Geneal Bk.

Leighton, Isabel. Aspirin Age 1919-1941. Date not set. lib. bdg. 31.95 (*0-8488-1661-7*) Amereon Ltd.

Leighton, Janet. Lift High the Cross: The Story of Trinity Episcopal School for Ministry. 1995. 19.99 (*0-87788-474-9*, H Shaw Pubs) Waterbrook Pr.

Leighton, Jean. Simone de Beauvoir on Women. LC 74-3615. 230p. 1975. 35.00 (*0-8386-1504-X*) Fairleigh Dickinson.

Leighton, John. 1100 Designs & Motifs from Historic Sources. LC 95-40658. Orig. Title: Suggestions in Design. 144p. 1995. pap. 9.95 (*0-486-28730-0*) Dover.

— Van Gogh's House: A Pop-Up Carousel. (Illus.). 32p. 1998. 16.95 (*0-7893-0219-5*, Pub. by Universe) St Martin.

Leighton, John & Thomson, Richard. Seurat & the Bathers. LC 97-67662. 168 P. :p. 1997. write for info. (*1-85709-174-4*) Nat Gallery Pubns.

***Leighton, Judy.** A Path to Light: How to Not Not Make Healthy Choices. LC 00-190853. 327p. 2000. 25.00 (*0-7388-2029-6*); pap. 18.00 (*0-7388-2030-X*) Xlibris Corp.

Leighton, Kim. A Hard Chance: The Sydney-Hobart Race Disaster. LC 99-39554. (Illus.). 287p. 1999. 15.95 (*1-57223-282-X*, 282x) Willow Creek Pr.

— Seasons of the Yellowstone: An Angler's Year. LC 98-15959. (Great American Rivers Ser.). (Illus.). 160p. 1998. 29.50 (*1-57223-133-5*, 1335) Willow Creek Pr.

Leighton, Lauren G. A Bibliography of Alexander Pushkin in English. LC 98-53357. (Studies in Slavic Language & Literature Ser.: Vol. 12). 336p. 1999. text 99.95 (*0-7734-8170-2*) E Mellen.

— The Esoteric Tradition in Russian Romantic Literature: Decembrism & Freemasonry. LC 93-13983. 1994. 45.00 (*0-271-01024-X*) Pa St U Pr.

— Two Worlds, One Art: Literary Translation in Russia & America. LC 90-28531. 292p. 1991. lib. bdg. 35.00 (*0-87580-160-9*) N Ill U Pr.

Leighton, Lauren G., ed. Russian Romantic Criticism: An Anthology, 18. LC 86-29605. (Contributions to the Study of World Literature Ser.: No. 18). 227p. 1987. 55.00 (*0-313-25584-9*, LRU/, Greenwood Pr) Greenwood.

— Studies in Honor of Xenia Gasiorowska. (Illus.). 191p. (Orig.). 1983. pap. 19.95 (*0-89357-102-4*) Slavica.

Leighton, Lauren G., ed. & tr. see Chukovsky, Kornei.

Leighton, Lee. Beyond the Pass. 1997. 17.50 (*0-7451-4700-3*, Gunsmoke) Chivers N Amer.

***Leighton, Luke.** DCE/RPC over SMB. (Circle Ser.). 400p. 1999. 45.00 (*1-57870-150-3*) New Riders Pub.

Leighton, Marian. Soviet Propaganda As a Foreign Policy Tool. 198p. (C). 1991. 19.95 (*0-932088-51-1*) Freedom Hse.

— The Soviet Threat in NATO's Northern Flank. 95p. 1979. pap. 17.95 (*0-87855-803-9*) Transaction Pubs.

Leighton, Marie C. & Leighton, Robert. Michael Dred, Detective: The Unravelling of a Mystery of Twenty Years. LC 75-32761. (Literature of Mystery & Detection Ser.). (Illus.). 1976. reprint ed. 28.95 (*0-405-07882-X*) Ayer.

Leighton, Mary S. The Role of Leadership in Sustaining School Reform: Voices from the Field. (Illus.). 79p. (C). 1998. pap. text 20.00 (*0-7881-4861-3*) DIANE Pub.

Leighton, Mary S. Role of Leadership in Sustaining School Reform: Voices from the Field. 87p. 1996. pap. 7.00 (*0-16-048727-7*) USGPO.

Leighton, Maxinne R. An Ellis Island Christmas. (Illus.). 32p. (J). (ps-3). 1994. pap. 5.99 (*0-14-055344-4*, PuffinBks) Peng Put Young Read.

Leighton, Maxinne R., jt. auth. see Belle, John.

Leighton, Maxinne Rhea. Ellis Island Christmas. LC 91-47731. (Picture Puffin Ser.). (J). 1994. 10.19 (*0-606-06360-9*, Pub. by Turtleback) Demco.

Leighton, Patricia, et al. Today's Law Teachers: Lawyers or Academics?: A Research Report on Law Teachers in U. K. Higher Education, 1994. LC 96-195967. 81p. 1995. pap. 50.00 (*1-85941-009-X*, Pub. by Cavendish Pubng) Gaunt.

Leighton, Perly, compiled by. A Leighton Genealogy: Dscendants of Thomas Leighton of Dover New Hampshire, 2 vols. 1054p. 1989. 60.00 (*0-88082-023-3*, S3-33650) New Eng Hist.

Leighton, Peter. A Different Kind of Hero LC 99-189224. (Livewire Kaleidoscope Ser.). 44 p. 1998. write for info. (*0-89061-620-5*) NTC Contemp Pub Co.

— Variable Force Technique. LC 87-63607. (Illus.). 199p. 1988. ring bd. 39.95 (*0-945817-01-0*) Origin Bks.

Leighton, Philip. Planning Academic & Research Library Buildings. 3rd ed. LC 98-46757. 928p. 1999. 155.00 (*0-8389-0747-4*) ALA.

Leighton, Ralph. Deep in the Heart of Tuva, Vol. 1. (Musical Expeditions Ser.). (Illus.). 64p. 1996. 19.95 incl. audio compact disk (*1-55961-324-6*, CD4080); 16.95 incl. audio (*1-55961-325-4*, CT4080) Relaxtn Co.

***Leighton, Ralph.** Tuva or Bust! Richard Feyman's Last Journey. 256p. 2000. pap. text 13.95 (*0-393-32069-3*) Norton.

***Leighton, Ralph, et al.** Kazhyk! Sheepbone Dice Game Rules. Slone, J. Eric, ed. (Illus.). 20p. 2000. pap. 10.00 (*1-58490-030-X*) Scientific Consulting.

Leighton, Robert. Obedient & Patient Faith: An Exposition of 1st Peter. 1999. pap. text 16.95 (*1-879737-15-9*) Calvary Press.

— The Protohistoric Settlement on the Cittadella. (Morgantina Studies: No. 4). (Illus.). 265p. 1993. text 89.50 (*0-691-04015-X*, Pub. by Princeton U Pr) Cal Prin Full Svc.

— Sicily Before History: An Archaeological Survey from the Palaeolithic to the Iron Age. LC 98-30725. (Illus.). 224p. 1998. 49.95 (*0-8014-3620-6*); pap. 19.95 (*0-8014-8585-1*) Cornell U Pr.

Leighton, Robert & Thomas, Griffith. 1 & 2 Peter. abr. ed. LC 99-11104. (Crossway Classic Commentaries Ser.). 287p. 1999. pap. 14.99 (*1-58134-064-8*) Crossway Bks.

Leighton, Robert, jt. auth. see Leighton, Marie C.

***Leighton, Robert L.** Orthopedic Diseases of the Joints of the Dog. 230p. 2000. write for info. (*1-58692-029-4*) Copyright Mgmt.

Leighton, Robert L., ed. Some Techniques & Procedures in Small Animal Surgery. 3rd ed. 264p. 1982. text 15.00 (*0-935078-21-5*) Veterinary Med.

Leighton, Robert L. & Jones, Kathy. A Compendium of Small Animal Surgery. LC SF0911.L35. (Illus.). 282p. reprint ed. pap. 87.50 (*0-608-08710-6*, 206927800003) Bks Demand.

Leighton, Robert L., jt. auth. see Morgan, Joe P.

Leighton, Stephanie. It's Different for Guys. (Love Stories Super Edition Ser.). 224p. (YA). (gr. 7-12). 1997. mass mkt. 4.50 (*0-553-57048-X*) BDD Bks Young Read.

Leighton, Taigen D. & Okumura, Shohaku, trs. Dogen's Pure Standards for the Zen Community: A Translation of Eihei Shingi. LC 95-24658. (SUNY Series in Buddhist Studies). 272p. (C). 1995. text 59.50 (*0-7914-2709-9*); pap. text 19.95 (*0-7914-2710-2*) State U NY Pr.

Leighton, Taigen D., tr. see Hongzhi.

Leighton, Thomas. Modern Econometrics: An Introduction. LC 97-140273. (C). 1996. pap. text 98.00 (*0-201-87694-9*) Addison-Wesley.

Leighton, Thomson F. & Maggs, Bruce. Introduction to Parallel Algorithms & Architectures Vol. 2: Algorithms & VLSI. 1999. 59.95 (*1-55860-118-X*) Morgan Kaufmann.

Leighton, Timothy G., ed. The Acoustic Bubble. (Illus.). 638p. 1997. pap. text 56.00 (*0-12-441921-6*) Morgan Kaufmann.

Leighton, Tom, tr. see Manara, Milo.

***Leighton, Trevor.** The Jokers. (Illus.). 160p. 1999. 45.00 (*1-86205-252-2*, Pub. by Pavilion Bks Ltd) Trafalgar.

Leighton, Walter L. French Philosophers - New England Transcendentalism. LC 68-19289. 105p. 1970. reprint ed. lib. bdg. 45.00 (*0-8371-0143-3*, LEPT, Greenwood Pr) Greenwood.

Leighton, Willie E. Texas: The Way It Was. (Illus.). 272p. 1990. 19.95 (*0-9626069-0-1*) Insite Pub.

***Leighty, David.** Kentucky Employment & Labor Law: Forms & Practice Manual. LC 98-38053. 412p. 1998. ring bd. 169.95 (*1-57400-036-5*) Data Trace Pubng.

***Leighty, Paul.** Krewe of Infamy. 1. 337p. 1999. 22.95 (*0-9672791-0-0*) April Pr.

Leighwood, Kenneth, et al, eds. International Handbook of Educational Leadership & Administration. 1176p. 1996. lib. bdg. 395.00 (*0-7923-3530-9*) Kluwer Academic.

Leigland, James & Lamb, Robert B. WPPSS: Who Is to Blame for the WPPSS Disaster. LC 86-7924. 272p. 1986. text 34.95 (*0-88730-127-4*, HarpBusn) HarpInfo.

Leigland, Sam, ed. Radical Behaviorism: Willard Day on Psychology & Philosophy. 208p. (Orig.). (C). 1992. pap. text 29.95 (*1-878978-02-0*) Context Pr.

Leigou, et al. Youth Automation. LC 97-19070. (IFAC Postprint Ser.: 2). 680p. 1997. pap. 157.00 (*0-08-042369-8*, Pergamon Pr) Elsevier.

Leih, Janet. Publication Indexing, a Writer's Guide to Inventory. 12p. 1989. pap. 1.00 (*0-937953-14-8*) Tesseract SD.

— When Medicine Failed. 181p. 1998. pap. 15.00 (*1-877649-32-5*) Tesseract SD.

Leih, Janet, et al, eds. A Sixty Year Comprehensive Index of Pasque Petals (1926-1986) 328p. (Orig.). 1987. per. 5.00 (*0-945124-00-7*) Tesseract SD.

Leih, janet, ed. see Bakkum, Maria.

Leih, Janet, ed. see Bogue, Lois.

Leih, Janet, ed. see Christensen, Esther.

Leih, Janet, ed. see Dickerson, Stella M.

Leih, Janet, ed. see Edlosi, Mario.

Leih, Janet, ed. see Eikamp, Helen.

Leih, Janet, ed. see Farmer, Carol P.

Leih, Janet, ed. see Forelle, Helen.

Leih, Janet, ed. see Johnson, Gertrude.

Leih, Janet, ed. see Ovesen, Ellis.

Leih, Janet, ed. see Winklepleck-Stuefen, Fern E.

Leih, Janet, ed. & illus. see Todd, Wanda.

Leih, Janet, ed. & intro. see Leih, Ruth V.

Leih, Ruth V. Wahgancan Memories. Leih, Janet, ed. & intro. by. 32p. 1997. spiral bd. 5.00 (*1-877649-30-9*) Tesseract SD.

Leih, Virginia. Portrait of a Fulfilled Woman, Reflections from Proverbs 31. 132p. 1979. 4.95 (*0-8423-4860-3*) Tesseract SD.

***Leihner, Dietrich E. & Mitschein, Thomas A., eds.** A Third Millennium for Humanity? The Search for Paths of Sustainable Development. xiii, 423p. 1998. 67.95 (*3-631-34076-1*) P Lang Pubng.

Leihner, Dietrich E. & Mitschein, Thomas A., eds. A Third Millennium for Humanity? The Search for Paths of Sustainable Development. 423p. 1998. 67.95 (*0-8204-3637-2*) P Lang Pubng.

Leijenaar, Monique & European Commission. How to Create a Gender Balance in Political Decision-Making: A Guide to Implementing Policies for Increasing the Participation of Women in Political Decision-Making. LC 98-125521. (Employment & Social Affairs Ser.). 79 p. 1997. write for info. (*92-827-9833-X*) Comm Europ Commun.

Leijnse, Anton. Mathematical Tools - Changing Spatial Scales. 256p. 1993. boxed set 72.95 (*0-8493-8934-8*) CRC Pr.

***Leijonhufvud, Axel.** Macroeconomic Instability & Coordination: Selected Essays of Axel Leijonhufvud. LC 00-34121. (Economists of the Twentieth Century Ser.). 2000. write for info. (*1-85278-967-0*) E Elgar.

Leijonhufvud, Axel & Heymann, Daniel. High Inflation: The Arne Ryde Memorial Lectures. (Illus.). 246p. 1995. text 42.00 (*0-19-828844-1*) OUP.

Leijonhufvud, Goran. Going Against the Tide: A Study of Dissent in China. 286p. (C). 1996. pap. text 25.00 (*0-7007-0222-9*, Pub. by Curzon Pr Ltd) UH Pr.

Leijonhufvud, Jonas, tr. see Dahlstrom, Ake & Brost, Leif.

***Leik, Charles.** Barns. (Illus.). 72p. 2000. 6.98 (*1-58663-002-4*) M Friedman Pub Grp Inc.

L

L

Leik, Charles, intro. Barns. LC 98-46929. (Illus.). 72p. 1999. text 15.00 (*1-56799-802-X*) M Friedman Pub Grp Inc.

Leik, Robert K. Experimental Design & the Analysis of Variance. LC 96-47649. 1997. 19.95 (*0-8039-9006-5*) Pine Forge.

— Methods, Logic, & Research of Sociology. LC 72-85667. (Studies in Sociology). (C). 1972. pap. write for info. (*0-672-61242-9*, Bobbs) Macmillan.

Leiken, Robert S., ed. A New Moment in the Americas. LC 94-47503. 160p. (C). 1994. pap. 19.95 (*1-56000-811-3*, Pub. by U Miami N-S Ctr) L Rienner.

— Un Nuevo Momento en Nuestra America. (SPA.). 168p. (C). 1994. pap. 19.95 (*0-935501-89-4*, Pub. by U Miami N-S Ctr) L Rienner.

Leiken, Robert S., jt. auth. see Carnegie Endowment for International Peace Staff.

Leikin. Poisoning & Toxicology Compendium. 1997. 74.75 (*0-916589-61-7*) Lexi-Comp.

Leikin, Ezekiel. The Beilis Transcripts: The Anti-Semitic Trial That Shook the World. LC 92-39643. 280p. 1993. 40.00 (*0-87668-179-8*) Aronson.

Leikin, Molly-Ann. How to Make a Good Song a Hit Song: Rewriting & Marketing Your Lyrics & Music. 176p. 1995. per. 12.95 (*0-7935-5004-1*, 00330036) H Leonard.

— How to Write a Hit Song: The Complete Guide to Writing & Marketing Chart-Topping Lyrics & Music. 112p. 1989. reprint ed. per. 9.95 (*0-88188-881-8*, 00330006) H Leonard.

Leikola, J. & Contreras, M., eds. Blood Transfusion Services for the Developing World. (Journal Ser.: Vol. 67, Supplement 5, 1994). (Illus.). iv, 66p. 1994. pap. 30.50 (*3-8055-6094-X*) S Karger.

Leila El Khalidi. The Art of Palestinian Embroidery. LC 99-187426. 175p. 1999. write for info. (*0-86356-038-5*) Intl Spec Bk.

***Leila Simona Talani London School of Economics & Political Science Staff.** Betting for & Against EMU: Who Wins & Loses in Italy & in the UK from the Process of European Monetary Integration. 340p. 2000. text 70.95 (*0-7546-1054-3*, Pub. by Ashgate Pub) Ashgate Pub Co.

Leiman. Political Economy of Racism: A History. LC 92-8518. 421p. (C). 63.00 (*0-7453-0488-5*, Pub. by Pluto GBR); pap. 18.95 (*0-7453-0487-7*, Pub. by Pluto GBR) Stylus Pub VA.

Leiman, J., ed. see Freedman, Carleton H.

Leiman, Sid Z. The Canonization of Hebrew Scripture: The Talmudic & Midrashic Evidence. 2nd ed. LC 91-72569. (Transactions Ser.: Vol. 47). 242p. 1991. pap. 24.50 (*1-878508-04-0*) CT Acad Arts & Sciences.

Leiman, Sondra. America: The Jewish Experience. Sarna, Jonathan D., ed. LC 95-110776. (Illus.). (Orig.). (J). (gr. 4-6). 1994. pap., teacher ed. 15.00 (*0-8074-0501-9*, 208034); pap. text 12.00 (*0-8074-0500-0*, 123938) UAHC.

Leiman, Sondra, jt. auth. see Burstein, Chaya M.

***Leiman, Yehoshua, ed.** How to Teach Torah. 2nd rev. ed. (ENG & HEB.). 46p. 2000. pap. 3.00 (*1-878895-31-1*, M500) Torah Umesorah.

Leimann, Dan. The Achievers. Caton, Patrick, ed. 133p. 1996. 24.95 (*1-56245-251-7*) Great Quotations.

Leimbach, Parricia P. Harvest of Bittersweet. large type ed. LC 98-11914. 1998. 23.95 (*1-57490-134-6*, Beeler LP Bks) T T Beeler.

Leimberg, Stephan R. Stanley & Kilcullen's Federal Income Tax Law. 1994. pap. text 95.00 (*0-7913-1988-1*) Warren Gorham & Lamont.

Leimberg, Stephan R., et al. The New Book of Trusts. 2nd ed. LC 99-194028. 541p. 1997. pap. 49.95 (*0-9644565-2-4*) Leimberg.

— Stanley & Kilcullen's Federal Income Tax Law. LC 84-50708. 1991. pap. 95.00 (*0-7913-0971-1*, SK) Warren Gorham & Lamont.

— The Tools & Techniques of Financial Planning. 4th rev. ed. LC 88-62296. 545p. 1993. pap. 37.50 (*0-87218-114-6*) Natl Underwriter.

Leimberg, Stephan R., jt. auth. see Plotnick, Charles.

Leimberg, Stephen. Nonqualified Deferred Compensation. 95th ed. LC 95-142978. 1995. pap. text 35.00 (*0-15-602507-8*) Harcourt.

Leimberg, Stephen F. & Zaritsky, Howard M. Tax Planning with Life Insurance: Executive Edition. 832p. 1994. 79.95 (*0-7913-1311-5*) Warren Gorham & Lamont.

Leimberg, Stephen F., jt. auth. see Zaritsky, Howard M.

Leimberg, Stephen R. Federal Income Tax Law 1996. LC 87-50708. 1996. 98.00 (*0-7913-2741-8*, FXL) Warren Gorham & Lamont.

Leimberg, Stephen R., et al. The Book of Trusts: The Whole Truth about Trusts. 444p. 1996. 49.95 (*0-9644565-1-6*) Leimberg.

Leimbigler, Peter. Fast-Track Dutch, 6 cass., Set. unabridged ed. (DUT.). 344p. pap. 125.00 incl. audio (*0-88432-685-3*, FTDU20) Audio-Forum.

— Fast-Track German: Fast-Track Language Learning. unabridged ed. 340p. (C). 1985. pap., pap. text 125.00 incl. audio (*0-88432-123-1*, FTG100) Audio-Forum.

— Fast Track Mandarin: Fast-Track Language Learning. unabridged ed. 269p. (C). 1986. pap. text 155.00 incl. audio (*0-88432-122-3*, FTM520) Audio-Forum.

Leimbigler, Peter. Japanese, Fast-Track: Fast-Track Language Learning, 6 cass., Set unabridged ed. 367p. (C). 1985. pap. 155.00 incl. audio (*0-88432-121-5*, FTJ210) Audio-Forum.

Leimenstoll, Jo R. Turkey, Vol. IV. (Historic Preservation in Other Countries Ser.). (Illus.). 54p. (Orig.). (C). 1990. pap. text 15.00 (*0-911697-06-3*) US ICOMOS.

Leimer, Karl, jt. auth. see Gieseking, Walter.

Leimert, Karen M., jt. auth. see Mezek, Karen.

Leims, Thomas F. Die Entstehung des Kabuki: Transkulturation Europa-Japan im 16. und 17. Jahrhundert. (Japanese Studies Library: Vol. 2). (GER., Illus.). xv, 364p. 1990. 120.50 (*90-04-08988-8*) Brill Academic Pubs.

Lein, Alla Yu, jt. ed. see Brimblecombe, Peter.

Lein, Anatoly. In the World of Tactics, 1997, Vol. 1. 112p. 1998. pap. 14.95 (*1-886846-11-1*) Pickard & Son.

Lein, Anatoly & Archangelsky, Boris. Sharpen Your Tactics! 1125 Brilliant Sacrifices, Combinations, & Studies. Hays, Lou, ed. 270p. 1996. pap. 19.95 (*1-880673-13-4*) Hays Pub.

Lein, Clayton D., ed. British Prose Writers of the Early Seventeenth Century. LC 95-5786. (Dictionary of Literary Biography Ser.: Vol. 151). 400p. 1995. text 155.00 (*0-8103-5712-7*) Gale.

Lein, Eve L. Faith, Hope & Love & Other Wonderful Words. (Orig.). Date not set. pap. write for info. (*0-9655019-0-6*) E L Lein.

Lein, James K. Environmental Decision Making. LC 96-48895. (Illus.). 224p. 1997. boxed set 52.95 (*0-86542-466-7*) Blackwell Sci.

Lein, Laura & Richards, Robert C. Texas Probation Officers' Attitudes & Alternatives to Incarceration. (Policy Research Project Report Ser.: No. 95). 90p. 1992. pap. 9.50 (*0-89940-703-X*) LBJ Sch Pub Aff.

Lein, Laura & Rickards, Robert C. Policy Issues & Community Life in Texas: State Tax Issues, Child Care, Crime & Justice, & Hazardous Materials. (Special Project Reports). 80p. 1989. pap. 7.00 (*0-89940-868-0*) LBJ Sch Pub Aff.

— Property Crime Victims: An Analysis of Needs & Services in Texas. (Special Project Reports). 55p. 1992. pap. 9.50 (*0-89940-872-9*) LBJ Sch Pub Aff.

— Services for Crime Victims. (Policy Research Project Report: No. 92). 76p. 1991. pap. 9.50 (*0-89940-700-5*) LBJ Sch Pub Aff.

Lein, Laura & Sussman, Marvin B., eds. The Ties That Bind: Men's & Women's Social Networks. LC 82-23230. (Marriage & Family Review Ser.: Vol. 5, No. 4). 111p. 1983. text 39.95 (*0-86656-161-7*) Haworth Pr.

Lein, Laura, jt. auth. see Edin, Kathryn.

Lein, Laura, jt. auth. see Rickards, Robert C.

Lein, Linda F. Mother to Mother: A Companion Study Book. 70p. 1999. spiral bd., wbk. ed. 4.95 (*0-9670516-1-4*) Annika Pubns.

— Mother to Mother: Letters about Being a Mom. LC 99-94690. 60p. 1999. pap. 7.95 (*0-9670516-0-6*) Annika Pubns.

***Lein, Linda Frances.** Ephesians: A Study of Knowing & Living in God's Grace. 32p. 2000. spiral bd. 4.95 (*0-9670516-4-9*) Annika Pubns.

Leina, K., ed. Russian - German Dictionary. 10th rev. ed. (GER & RUS.). 736p. 1989. 25.95 (*0-8285-5386-6*) Firebird NY.

Leinbach, L. Carl, et al, eds. The Laboratory Approach to Teaching Calculus. rev. ed. LC 91-62171. (MAA Notes Ser.). 290p. 1991. pap. text 10.00 (*0-88385-074-5*, NTE-20R) Math Assn.

Leinbach, Philip E., ed. Personnel Administration in an Automated Environment. LC 90-39450. (Journal of Library Administration: Vol. 13, Nos. 1-2). 214p. 1990. text 49.95 (*1-56024-032-6*) Haworth Pr.

Leinbach, Richard B. Visualization Techniques. 2nd ed. 208p. 1990. pap. text 55.60 (*0-13-946518-9*) P-H.

Leinbach, T., jt. auth. see Brunn, S.

Leinbach, Thomas R. Southeast Asia: Diversity & Development. 594p. (C). 1999. 73.00 (*0-13-825126-6*, Macmillan Coll) P-H.

Leinbach, Thomas R. & Chai Lin Sien. South-East Asian Transport: Issues in Development. (South-East Asian Social Science Monographs). (Illus.). 284p. 1989. text 39.95 (*0-19-588895-2*) OUP.

Leinberger, Christopher B. Strategy for Real Estate Companies: Marketing, Finance, Organization. LC 93-61041. 136p. 1993. pap. text 41.95 (*0-87420-742-8*, S43) Urban Land.

Leindler, Laszlo. Strong Approximation by Fourier Series. 209p. (C). 1985. 80.00 (*963-05-4044-4*, Pub. by Akade Kiado) St Mut.

— Strong Approximation by Fourier Series. 210p. (C). 1985. 175.00 (*0-685-46648-5*, Pub. by Collets) St Mut.

***Leinecker, Richard.** COM+ Unleashed. 800p. 2000. 49.99 (*0-672-31887-3*) Sams.

Leinecker, Richard. Making Noise: Creating Sounds on Your PC. LC 94-26301. 1994. pap. 24.95 incl. disk (*1-55851-386-8*, M&T Bks) IDG Bks.

— Programming with Visual C++ 448p. (C). 1999. mass mkt., teacher ed. 49.95 (*0-7600-5019-8*) Course Tech.

— Programming with Visual C++ 10th ed. 656p. (C). 1998. pap. 51.95 (*0-7600-5018-X*) Course Tech.

Leinecker, Richard C. Windows 98 Programming Bible. (Bible Ser.). 1056p. 1998. pap. 49.99 (*0-7645-3185-9*) IDG Bks.

Leinecker, Richard C. & Smith, Kevin. Visual C++ 6 Bible. LC QA76.73.C153L4493. (Bible Ser.). (Illus.). 1278p. 1998. pap. 49.99 incl. cd-rom (*0-7645-3228-6*) IDG Bks.

Leinecker, Rick. Developing Dinosaurs & Ancient Worlds: All You Need to Create Your Own Dinosaur Park! (Illus.). 254p. (YA). 1998. reprint ed. pap. 20.00 incl. disk (*0-7881-5144-4*) DIANE Pub.

— Sams Teach Yourself Visual J++ 6 in 21 Days. LC 98-86423. 1998. pap. text 29.99 (*0-672-31351-0*) Sams.

Leinen, Margaret & Sarnthein, Michael, eds. Paleoclimatology & Paleometeorology: Modern & Past Patterns of Global Atmospheric Transport. (C). 1989. text 373.50 (*0-7923-0341-5*) Kluwer Academic.

Leinen, Patricia. Arthritis & Ulcer Disease: New Directions & Controversies. (Audioconference Workbook Ser.). (Illus.). 12p. 1994. write for info. (*0-944036-98-8*) Medicine Grp USA.

Leinen, Patricia, ed. Arthritis & Ulcer Disease: New Directions & Controversies NSAIDS in Arthritis. (Slide Resource Ser.: Pt. 1). (Illus.). (Orig.). 1994. write for info. (*1-57130-001-5*) Medicine Grp USA.

— Arthritis & Ulcer Disease New Directions & Controversies: Approaches for the Prevention of NSAID-Induced GI Damage & Complications. (Slide Resource Ser.: Pt. 4). (Illus.). (Orig.). 1994. write for info. (*1-57130-004-X*) Medicine Grp USA.

— Arthritis & Ulcer Disease New Directions & Controversies: Epidemiology of NSAID-Induced GI Damage. (Slide Resource Ser.: Pt. 3). (Illus.). (Orig.). 1994. write for info. (*1-57130-003-1*) Medicine Grp USA.

— Arthritis & Ulcer Disease New Directions & Controversies: Pathophysiology of GI Injury: NSAIDS & H. Pylori. (Slide Resource Ser.: Pt. 2). (Illus.). (Orig.). 1994. write for info. (*1-57130-002-3*) Medicine Grp USA.

Leinen, Patricia, et al, eds. Gene Therapy: Socioeconomic & Ethical Issues. 1996. write for info. (*1-57130-026-0*) Medicine Grp USA.

Leinen, Patty, ed. Dornase Alfa in Cystic Fibrosis: Clinical Use & Pharmaeconomic Issues. (Illus.). 1994. write for info. (*1-57130-010-4*) Medicine Grp USA.

Leinen, Ronald. Fear & Anxiety: Finding Peace in the Heart of Jesus. LC 98-61774. 55p. 1999. pap. 7.95 (*0-89622-971-8*) Twenty-Third.

— Quiet Times with Jesus LC 95-172280. 366 p. 1995. write for info. (*0-939025-03-5*) Cogan Productions.

Leinen, Stephen. Gay Cops. LC 93-9216. 320p. (C). 1993. 22.95 (*0-8135-2000-2*) Rutgers U Pr.

Leinen, Stephen H. Black Police, White Society. LC 83-23622. 250p. (C). 1985. pap. text 18.00 (*0-8147-5017-6*) NYU Pr.

***Leinenweber, John, ed. from LAT.** Pastoral Practice: Books 3 & 4 of the "Regula Pastoralis" by Saint Gregory the Great. LC 97-45169. 112p. 1998. pap. 12.00 (*1-56338-237-7*) TPI PA.

***Leiner, Frederick C.** Millions for Defense: The Subscription Warships of 1798. LC 99-15206. 1999. 36.95 (*1-55750-508-X*) Naval Inst Pr.

Leiner, Katherine. First Children. LC 95-2250. (Illus.). 1995. write for info. (*0-614-32221-9*, Wm Morrow) Morrow Avon.

— Halloween. LC 92-39343. (Illus.). 48p. (J). (gr. 2-6). 1993. 15.95 (*0-689-31769-7*) Atheneum Yung Read.

Leinert, Christoph, jt. ed. see Bowyer, Stuart.

Leinfelder, Karl F. & Taylor, Duane F. Laboratory & Clinical Dental Materials. 3rd ed. Moor, Douglas V., ed. (Dental Laboratory Technology Manuals Ser.). xiii, 202p. (C). 1982. pap. 34.95 (*0-8078-7906-1*) U of NC Pr.

Leinfelder, Karl F., et al. Dental Materials & Technical Application. 3rd ed. (Dental Assisting Manuals Ser.: No. 6). ix, 145p. (C). 1980. pap. 24.95 (*0-8078-1380-X*) U of NC Pr.

Leinfellner, Werner. Game Theory, Experience, Rationality: Foundations of Social Sciences, Economics & Ethics in Honor of John C. Harsanyi. (Vienna Circle Institute Yearbook Ser.). 472p. 1998. 159.00 (*0-7923-4943-1*) Kluwer Academic.

Leinfellner, Werner & Koehler, E. Developments in the Methodology of Social Science. LC 74-83003. (Theory & Decision Library: No. 6). 400p. 1974. pap. text 130.50 (*90-277-0539-9*); lib. bdg. 175.00 (*90-277-0493-7*) Kluwer Academic.

Leinfellner, Werner, jt. auth. see Gottinger, Hans W.

Leinhardt, Gaea & Beck, Isabel L., eds. Teaching & Learning in History. 280p. 1994. text 59.95 (*0-8058-1245-8*) L Erlbaum Assocs.

Leinhardt, Gaea, et al. Analysis of Arithmetic for Mathematics Teaching. 464p. 1992. text 89.95 (*0-8058-0929-5*) L Erlbaum Assocs.

Leinhardt, Samuel, ed. Sociological Methodology, 1982. LC 68-54940. (Jossey-Bass Social & Behavioral Science Ser.). (Illus.). 406p. reprint ed. pap. 125.90 (*0-8357-4901-0*, 203783100009) Bks Demand.

— Sociological Methodology, 1983-1984. LC 68-54940. (Jossey-Bass Social & Behavioral Science Ser.). 383p. reprint ed. pap. 118.80 (*0-8357-4902-9*, 203783200009) Bks Demand.

Leinhauser, Jean & Weiss, Rita. Seven-Day Afghans. LC 89-22038. (Illus.). 144p. 1990. pap. 14.95 (*0-8069-5709-3*) Sterling.

Leinieks, Valdis. The City of Dionysos: A Study of Euripedes' Bakchai. (Illus.). 407p. (C). 1996. text 100.00 (*3-519-07637-3*) B G Teubner.

Leinieks, Valdis, ed. The Structure of Latin: An Introductory Text Based on Caesar & Cicero. (LAT.). 423p. 1975. text 42.50 (*0-8422-5236-3*); pap. text 19.95 (*0-8290-0461-0*) Irvington.

Leining, Catherine R. Pollution Prevention: A Guide for Local Government. (Special Reports). (Illus.). 107p. 1994. pap. 28.00 (*0-87326-073-2*) Intl City-Cnty Mgt.

Leining, Michael. Dezentrale Losungsansatze in der Umweltpolitik: Eine Wirtschaftstheoretische Analyse Deutscher und Amerikanischer Umweltpolitischer Instrumente. (Europaische Hochschulschriften Ser.: Reihe 5, Vol. 2265). (Illus.). XII, 247p. 1998. pap. 48.95 (*3-631-32954-7*) P Lang Pubng.

***Leininger.** Transcultural Nursing 2000. 2000. 54.95 (*0-07-135397-6*) McGraw.

Leininger, Anita. Consulting & Independent Contracting. 55p. 1994. 30.00 (*0-914548-77-8*, 153-94) Soc Tech Comm.

Leininger, Gayle, et al. Making Wise Choices: Helping Children Understand Social & Moral Issues. Law, Jennifer, ed. 58p. (Orig.). (gr. 4). 1995. pap. text 6.95 (*1-56309-130-5*, N957102, New Hope) Womans Mission Union.

Leininger, James R. Daniel & the Lions' Den. (Beginners Bible Ser.). (Illus.). 1997. 2.99 (*0-310-97545-X*) Zondervan.

— David & Goliath. (Beginners Bible Ser.). 1997. 2.99 (*0-310-97537-9*) Zondervan.

— Jonah & the Big Fish. (Beginners Bible Ser.). (Illus.). 1997. 2.99 (*0-310-97541-7*) Zondervan.

— Noah & the Ark. (Beginners Bible Ser.). (Illus.). 1997. 2.99 (*0-310-97539-5*) Zondervan.

***Leininger, Joseph E. & Whalin, Terry.** Lessons from the Pit: A Successful Veteran of the Chicago Mercantile Exchange Shows Executives How to Thrive in a Competitive Environment. LC 98-49104. 224p. 1999. 14.99 (*0-8054-1699-4*) Broadman.

Leininger, Kevin E. AIX/6000 Developer's Tool Kit. LC 95-18964. (J. Ranade Workstation Ser.). 1995. 65.00 (*0-07-911992-1*) McGraw.

— HP-UX Development Tool Kit. 1996. text 60.00 incl. cd-rom (*0-07-912174-8*) McGraw.

— Java Developer's Toolkit. LC 97-1600. (Illus.). 201p. 1997. pap., pap. text 49.95 incl. cd-rom (*0-07-913106-9*) McGraw.

— Solaris Developer's Tool Kit. LC 94-34427. (J. Ranade Workstation Ser.). 1995. pap. 49.95 (*0-07-911852-6*) McGraw.

— UNIX Developer's Tool Kit. LC 93-44068. (J. Ranade Workstation Ser.). 1994. pap. text 49.95 (*0-685-70129-8*) McGraw.

Leininger, Laura & Rowan, Chris. Kid-Friendly Web Guide. (Illus.). 96p. (J). 1997. pap. 11.95 (*1-57612-023-6*, MM2049) Monday Morning Bks.

Leininger, M. Transcultural Nursing. 2nd ed. (C). 1995. pap. text 41.74 (*0-07-037660-3*) McGraw.

Leininger, Madeleine. Nursing & Anthropology: Two Worlds to Blend. 196p. (C). 1994. pap. text 17.95 (*1-57074-113-1*) Greyden Pr.

Leininger, Madeleine, ed. Culture Care Diversity & Universality: A Theory of Nursing. LC 15-2402. (Illus.). 448p. (Orig.). (C). 1991. pap. text 25.95 (*0-88737-519-7*) Natl League Nurse.

Leininger, Madeleine, jt. auth. see Reynolds, Cheryl L.

Leininger, Madeleine M., ed. Care: Discovery & Uses in Clinical & Community Nursing. LC 88-10804. (Human Care & Health Ser.). 202p. 1988. pap. 22.95 (*0-8143-1997-1*) Wayne St U Pr.

— Care: The Essence of Nursing & Health. LC 87-30043. (Human Care & Health Ser.). 278p. (C). 1988. reprint ed. pap. 22.95 (*0-8143-1995-5*) Wayne St U Pr.

— Caring - An Essential Human Need: Proceedings of the Three National Caring Conferences. LC 87-29577. (Human Care & Health Ser.). 178p. (C). 1988. reprint ed. pap. 22.95 (*0-8143-1993-9*) Wayne St U Pr.

— Ethical & Moral Dimensions of Care. LC 90-38404. (Human Care & Health Ser.). 116p. (C). 1986. pap. text 22.95 (*0-8143-2332-4*) Wayne St U Pr.

— Qualitative Research Methods in Nursing. 384p. 1985. text 64.00 (*0-8089-1676-9*, 792508, Grune & Strat) Harcrt Hlth Sci Grp.

Leininger, Madeleine M., jt. ed. see Gaut, Delores A.

Leininger, Madeline. Transcultural Nursing: Concepts, Theories & Practices. 547p. 1994. 25.95 (*1-57074-121-2*) Greyden Pr.

***Leininger-Miller, Theresa.** New Negro Artists in Paris: African American Painters & Sculptors in the City of Light, 1922-1934. LC 00-24449. (Illus.). 320p. (C). 2000. text 60.00 (*0-8135-2810-0*); pap. text 32.00 (*0-8135-2811-9*) Rutgers U Pr.

***Leininger-Miller, Theresa A.** New Negro Artists in Paris. LC 00-24449. 2000. pap. write for info. (*0-8135-2858-5*) Rutgers U Pr.

***Leininger, Nancy.** How to Prepare for the SAT9 2nd Grade. (Illus.). 115p. (J). (gr. 2-4). 1999. 19.95 (*1-930288-01-8*) Carney Ed Serv.

Leininger, Phillip, ed. see Hart, James D.

Leininger, Robert. Black Sun. 320p. (Orig.). 1991. mass mkt. 4.50 (*0-380-76012-6*, Avon Bks) Morrow Avon.

— Middlegame Strategy: With the Carlsbad Pawn Structure. 155p. 1997. pap. 17.50 (*1-886846-07-3*) Pickard & Son.

Leininger, Wayne E., jt. auth. see Hicks, James O., Jr.

Leininger, Wayne E., jt. auth. see Killough, Larry N.

***Leininter, James R.** Beginner's Bible, Vol. 1. 6p. 1999. boxed set 12.99 (*0-307-30340-3*, Goldn Books) Gldn Bks Pub Co.

Leino, Lily, tr. see Tuominen, Arvo.

***Leinonen, Eeva.** Children's Pragmatic Communication Difficulties. 2000. 42.95 (*1-86156-157-1*) Whurr Pub.

Leinonen, George, jt. auth. see Filer, Robert F.

Leinonen, Sandy. Gardens Are for Looking. 16p. (Orig.). (J). (ps-2). 1996. pap. text 7.50 (*0-9626823-7-3*) Perry ME.

Leins, Peter, et al, eds. Aspects of Floral Development: Proceedings of the Double Symposium "Floral Development - Evolutionary Aspects & Special Topics," Held at the 14. Internat. Botanical Congress Berlin, W-Germany, July 24-August 1, 1987. (Handbuch der Pflanzenanatomie Encyclopedia of Plant Anatomy - Traite d' Anatomie Vegetale Ser.). (Illus.). v, 239p. 1988. pap. 71.00 (*3-443-50011-0*, Pub. by Gebruder Borntraeger) Balogh.

Leinsdorf, Erich. Erich Leinsdorf on Music. LC 96-52635. (Illus.). 338p. 1997. 34.95 (*1-57467-028-X*, Amadeus Pr) Timber.

Leinster-Mackay, Donald & Sarfaty, Elizabeth. Education & the Times: An Index of Letters to 1910. 800p. 1995. text 190.00 (*0-7201-2101-9*) Continuum.

***Leinster, Murray.** First Contacts: The Essential Murray Leinster. Rico, Joe, ed. (NESFA's Choice Ser.). 464p. 1998. 25.00 (*0-915368-67-6*) New Eng SF Assoc.

Leinster, Murray. Forgotten Planet. 209p. 1990. pap. 3.95 (*0-88184-616-3*) Carroll & Graf.

— The Forgotten Planet. 1993. reprint ed. lib. bdg. 18.95 (*0-89968-350-9*, Lghtyr Pr) Buccaneer Bks.

An Asterisk (*) at the beginning of an entry indicates that the title is appearing for the first time.

— Quarantine World. 272p. 1992. mass mkt. 4.50 (*0-88184-844-1*) Carroll & Graf.

***Leinwand, Steven.** Sensible Sense-Making Mathematics: A Pracital Guide for Principals & Other School Leaders. 2000. pap. text 17.00 (*0-325-00277-0*) Heinemann.

Leinwand, Allan & Fang, Karen. Network Management: A Practical Perspective. 2nd ed. Stone, Tom, ed. LC 95-23029. 352p. (C). 1995. pap. text 39.95 (*0-201-60999-1*) Addison-Wesley.

Leinwand, Gerald. American Immigration: Should the Open Door Be Closed? (Impact Bks.). (Illus.). 128p. (YA). (gr. 9-12). 1995. lib. bdg. 24.00 (*0-531-13038-X*) Watts.

— Do We Need a New Constitution? LC 93-31847. (Democracy in Action Ser.). (Illus.). 128p. (YA). (gr. 9-12). 1994. lib. bdg. 24.00 (*0-531-11127-X*) Watts.

— The Environment. (American Issues Ser.). 128p. (YA). (gr. 7-12). 1990. 19.95 (*0-8160-2099-X*) Facts on File.

***Leinwand, Gerald.** 1927: High Tide of the 1920s. (Illus.). 368p. 2000. 32.00 (*1-56858-153-X*, Pub. by FWEW) Publishers Group.

Leinwand, Gerald. Public Education. (American Issues Ser.). 144p. (YA). (gr. 7-12). 1992. lib. bdg. 17.95 (*0-8160-2100-7*) Facts on File.

— Teaching of World History. LC 77-95099. (National Council for the Social Studies Bulletin: No. 54). 96p. reprint ed. pap. 30.00 (*0-608-17160-3*, 205219400056) Bks Demand.

Leinwand, Gerald, ed. see LeVert, Marianne.

Leinwand, Theodore B. The City Staged: Jacobean Comedy, 1603-1613. LC 86-1683. 240p. 1986. text 29.95 (*0-299-10670-5*) U of Wis Pr.

— Theatre, Finance & Society in Early Modern England. LC 99-211606. (Cambridge Studies in Renaissance Literature & Culture: No. 31). 216p. (C). 1999. text 54.95 (*0-521-64031-8*) Cambridge U Pr.

Leinward, Allen. Basic Router Configuration. 1997. 45.00 (*1-56205-814-2*) New Riders Pub.

Leinward, Allen & Pinsky, Bruce. Cisco Router Configuration. LC 97-81200. 400p. 1998. 40.00 (*1-57870-022-1*) Mac USA.

Leinwoll. Low Cholesterol Low Calorie Desserts. 1986. pap. 6.95 (*0-684-13380-6*, Scribners Ref) Mac Lib Ref.

Leipart, Charles. Deep Sleepers. 1989. pap. 5.25 (*0-8222-0297-2*) Dramatists Play.

— The Undefeated Rhumba Champ: One Act. 1982. pap. 3.25 (*0-8222-1193-9*) Dramatists Play.

Leiper, Brian. Gerbils & Jirds. (C). 1989. 40.00 (*0-946873-94-1*, Pub. by Basset Pubns) St Mut.

Leiper, Esther M. Flatlanders Guide to North Country Cooking. Moore, Eugenia, ed. (Illus.). 32p. 1988. pap. 3.95 (*0-9617284-5-0*) Sand & Silk.

— Home from the War. Dermen, Elizabeth & Moore, Eugenia, eds. (Illus.). 32p. (Orig.). 1989. pap. 3.95 (*0-9617284-6-9*) Sand & Silk.

— Tamar's Son & Other Christmas Sonnets. 28p. 1987. pap. 3.95 (*0-9617284-2-6*) Sand & Silk.

Leiper, Esther M., ed. see Lindow, Sandra.

Leiper, Esther M., ed. see Moore, Eugenia.

Leiper, Rob & Field, Vida, eds. Counting for Something: Effective User Feedback in Mental Health Services. 160p. 1993. 61.95 (*1-85628-477-8*, Pub. by Avebry) Ashgate Pub Co.

Leiper, Susan. Precious Cargo: The Scots Behind the China Trade. 112p. 1997. pap. 22.50 (*0-948636-90-4*, 904, Pub. by Natl Mus Scotland) A Schwartz & Co.

Leipert, Jack. Read the Fine Print Before You Say "I Do" LC 94-5156. 96p. (Orig.). 1994. pap. 5.95 (*0-8091-3464-0*) Paulist Pr.

***Leipertz, Harald.** Eliten: Ein Vergleich der Spezifischen Forschung Bei C. Wright Mills und Norbert Elias. XI, 115p. 1999. 28.95 (*3-631-34687-5*) P Lang Pubng.

***Leiphart, Suzanne.** Live the Evil: A Psychological Thriller about Overcoming Destructive Relationships. LC 99-91487. 218p. 2000. pap. 18.00 (*0-7388-0827-X*) Xlibris Corp.

— Love the Evil: A Psychological Thriller about Overcoming Destructive Relationships. LC 99-91487. 218p. 2000. 25.00 (*0-7388-0826-1*) Xlibris Corp.

Leiphart, Suzanne C. Love the Evil. 224p. 1999. pap. 14.95 (*0-7414-0013-8*) Buy Books.

Leipholz, Horst. Stability of Elastic Systems. (Mechanics of Elastic Stability Ser.: No. 7). 492p. 1980. text 241.50 (*90-286-0050-7*) Kluwer Academic.

Leipholz, Horst, ed. Structural Control. (C). 1987. text 405.50 (*90-247-3429-0*) Kluwer Academic.

Leipholz, Horst & Abdel-Rohman, M. Control of Structures. 1986. text 262.00 (*90-247-3321-9*) Kluwer Academic.

Leipman, Flora. The Long Journey Home: The Memoirs of Flora Leipman. large type ed. (Illus.). 464p. 1988. 15.95 (*0-7089-1801-8*) Ulverscroft.

Leipnitz, W. Dictionary of Coal Chemistry & Petrochemistry: English-German-French-Russian. (ENG, FRE, GER & RUS.). 340p. 1992. 158.00 (*0-7859-8833-5*) Fr & Eur.

Leipnitz, Walter. Woerterbuch Erdoelverarbeitung-Petrolchemie: Dictionary of Petroleum-Processing. (ENG, FRE, GER & RUS.). 1977. 125.00 (*0-8288-5568-4*, M6925) Fr & Eur.

Leipold, Alessandro, et al. International Capital Markets: Developments & Prospects. (World Economic & Financial Surveys Ser.). vii, 136p. 1991. pap. 20.00 (*1-55775-218-4*) Intl Monetary.

Leipold, Craig, jt. auth. see Oliver, Richard.

Leipold, Dieter. Beweismass und Beweislast im Zivilprozess. (Schriftenreihe der Juristischen Gesellschaft zu Berlin Ser.: Heft 93). (GER.). 26p. 1985. pap. 13.85 (*3-11-010580-2*) De Gruyter.

Leipold, L. Edmond. Dr. Christiaan N. Barnard, the Man with the Golden Hands. LC 78-118161. 179 p. 1971. write for info. (*0-513-01106-4*) Denison.

Leipoldt, Gabriele. Zur Biologie des Phytopathogenen Pilzes Gerlachia Nivalis (Erreger des Schneeschimmels) Molekularbiologische Untersuchungen an Verschiedenen Feldisolaten. (Bibliotheca Mycologica: Vol. 109). (GER., Illus.). 163p. (C). 1987. 53.00 (*3-443-59010-1*, Pub. by Gebruder Borntraeger) Balogh.

Leipp, Emile. The Violin: History, Aesthetics, Manufacture, & Acoustics. Parry, Hildegarde W., tr. LC 79-414278. (Illus.). 126p. reprint ed. pap. 39.10 (*0-608-10853-7*, 201429800094) Bks Demand.

Leippe, Michael R., jt. auth. see Zimbardo, Philip G.

Leipzig, Arthur. Sarah's Daughters: A Celebration of Jewish Women. Gould, Nathan & Vitiello, Jane K., eds. (Illus.). 94p. 1988. 25.00 (*0-685-26588-9*) Womens Am ORT.

Leipzig, Arthur, photos by. Growing up in New York: Photographs by Arthur Leipzig. (Imago Mundi Ser.). (Illus.). 132p. 1995. 40.00 (*1-56792-051-9*) Godine.

Leipzig, Bach-Archiv, ed. Leipziger Beitraege Zur Bachforschung Vol. 1: Bericht Uber die Wissenschaftliche Konferenz Anlablich des 69. Bach-Festes der Neuen Bachgesellschaft Leipzig, Marz 1994. (GER.). 280p. 1995. write for info. (*3-487-09974-8*) G Olms Pubs.

Leipzig, Marwayne. Beginner's Guide to Easy Horo Const. 1978. 9.00 (*0-86690-211-2*, L1273-014) Am Fed Astrologers.

Leipziger, Danny M. Korea: Transition to Maturity. (JWD Ser.: Vol. 16). 212p. 1988. 36.50 (*0-08-036812-3*, Pergamon Pr) Elsevier.

Leipziger, Danny M., ed. Lessons from East Asia. LC 96-35267. 608p. (C). 1997. text 90.00 (*0-472-10679-1*, 10679) U of Mich Pr.

***Leipziger, Danny M., ed.** Lessons from East Asia. (Studies in International Trade Policy). (Illus.). 608p. (C). 2000. pap. text 32.95 (*0-472-08722-3*, 08722) U of Mich Pr.

Leipziger, Danny M. & Petri, Peter A. Korean Industrial Policy: Legacies of the Past & Directions for the Future. LC 93-7329. (Discussion Paper, East Asia & Pacific Region Ser.: Vol. 197). 52p. 1993. pap. 22.00 (*0-8213-2414-4*, 12414) World Bank.

Leipziger, Danny M. & Thomas, Vinod. The Lessons of East Asia: An Overview of Country Experience - Experiencia de Asia Oriental. (SPA.). 52p. 1994. pap. 22.00 (*0-8213-2743-7*, 12743) World Bank.

Leipziger, Danny M. & Thomas, Vinrod. The Lessons of East Asia: An Overview of Country Experience - Experiencia de Asia Oriental. 48p. 1993. pap. 22.00 (*0-8213-2607-4*, 12607) World Bank.

Leipziger, Danny M., et al. The Distribution of Income & Wealth in Korea. LC 92-14468. (EDI Development Studies). 148p. 1993. pap. 22.00 (*0-8213-2124-2*, 12124) World Bank.

Leipziger, Danny M., jt. auth. see Kim, Kihwan.

Leipziger, Danny M., jt. ed. see Perry, Guillermo E.

Leir, Roger K. The Aliens & the Scalpel: Scientific Proof of Extraterrestrial Implants in Humans. Crissey, Brian, ed. LC 98-41509. (New Millennium Library: Vol. VI). (Illus.). 248p. 1999. pap. 18.95 (*1-893183-02-5*) Granite Pub.

***Leir, Roger K.** Casebook: Alien Implants. 256p. 2000. mass mkt. 6.99 (*0-440-23641-X*) Dell.

Leir, Roger K. The H/C Aliens & the Scalpel: Scientific Proof of Extraterrestrial Implants in Humans. LC 98-41509. (New Millenium Library). 248p. 1999. 24.95 (*1-893183-01-7*) Granite Pub.

Leira, Arnlaug, jt. auth. see Boje, Thomas P.

Leirado, Cayetano A. De La Barrera y, see De la Barrera Y Leirado, Cayetano A.

Leirbukt, Oddleif, jt. ed. see Debus, Friedhelm.

Leiren, Terje I. & Lovoll, Odd Sverre. Marcus Thrane: A Norwegian Radical in America. (Biographical Series: Special Publications). (Illus.). 167p. 1987. 15.00 (*0-87732-073-X*) Norwegian-Am Hist Assn.

Leiren, Terje I., jt. ed. see Adams, Ann-Charlotte Gavel.

Leiren, William. Shakespeare's Coloring Book. 50p. (YA). 1993. pap. 4.95 (*1-56850-032-7*) Chicago Plays.

Leiris, Joel De, see Hearse, David J., ed.

Leiris, Joel De, see Hearse, David J. & De Leiris, Joel, eds.

Leiris, Joel De, see Hearse, David J.

Leiris, Michel. L' Afrique Fantome. (FRE.). 1988. pap. 38.95 (*0-7859-2938-X*, 2070711889) Fr & Eur.

— Age d'Homme. (Folio Ser.: No. 435). (FRE.). pap. 8.95 (*2-07-036435-6*) Schoenhof.

— Aurora. (Imaginaire Ser.). (FRE.). 193p. 1977. pap. 11.95 (*2-07-029647-4*) Schoenhof.

— Aurora. Warby, Anna, tr. 160p. 1991. pap. 12.50 (*0-947757-25-2*) Serpents Tail.

— Biffures. (Imaginaire Ser.). (FRE.). 1975. pap. 13.95 (*2-07-072348-8*) Schoenhof.

— Brisees. (FRE.). 1992. pap. 19.95 (*0-7859-2826-X*, 2070326837) Fr & Eur.

— Fourbis. (Imaginaire Ser.). (FRE.). 1991. pap. 12.95 (*2-07-072347-X*) Schoenhof.

— Haut Mal. Autres Lancers. (Poesie Ser.). (FRE.). 256p. 1969. pap. 9.95 (*2-07-030166-4*) Schoenhof.

— Langage, Tangage Ou Ce Que les Mots Me Disent. (Gallimard Ser.). (FRE.). 188p. 1985. pap. 25.95 (*2-07-070442-4*) Schoenhof.

— Manhood: A Journey from Childhood into the Fierce Order of Virility. Howard, Richard, tr. LC 91-48195. 184p. (Orig.). 1992. pap. 13.95 (*0-226-47141-1*) U Ch Pr.

— Nights As Day, Days As Night. Sieburth, Richard, tr. from FRE. LC 87-83301.Tr. of Nuit sans Nuit. 198p. 1988. pap. 13.00 (*0-941419-07-X*, Eridanos Library) Marsilio Pubs.

— Operatics. Bennett, Guy, tr. from FRE. (Green Integer Bks.: No. 15). 100p. pap. 9.95 (*1-892295-03-2*, Pub. by Green Integer) Consort Bk Sales.

— La Regle du Jeu Vol. 1: Biffures. (FRE.). 1991. pap. 16.95 (*0-7859-2947-9*) Fr & Eur.

— La Regle du Jeu Vol. 2: Fourbis. (FRE.). 1991. pap. 15.95 (*0-7859-3395-6*) Fr & Eur.

— La Regle du Jeu Vol. 3: Fibrilles. (FRE.). 1991. pap. 16.95 (*0-7859-2953-3*) Fr & Eur.

— La Regle du Jeu Vol. 4: Frele Bruit. (FRE.). 1991. pap. 19.95 (*0-7859-2954-1*) Fr & Eur.

— Ruban au Cou D'Olympia. (Imaginaire Ser.). (FRE.). pap. 14.95 (*2-07-071702-X*) Schoenhof.

— Scraps. Davis, Lydia, tr. from FRE. LC 96-41035. (Rules of the Game Ser.). 256p. 1997. pap. 15.95 (*0-8018-5489-X*); text 35.00 (*0-8018-5488-1*) Johns Hopkins.

— Scratches. Davis, Lydia, tr. LC 96-23196. (Rules of the Game Ser.). 272p. 1997. pap. 15.95 (*0-8018-5486-5*); text 35.00 (*0-8018-5485-7*) Johns Hopkins.

— Zebrage. (FRE.). 1992. pap. 17.95 (*0-7859-2828-6*) Fr & Eur.

Leiris, Michel, pref. Picasso: Collected Writings. (Illus.). 456p. 1989. 70.00 (*1-55859-045-5*) Abbeville Pr.

Leiris, Michel, ed. see Miro, Joan.

Leirman, Walter & Kulich, Jindra, eds. Adult Education & the Challenges of the 1990's. 224p. 1987. lib. bdg. 47.50 (*0-7099-4169-2*, Pub. by C Helm) Routldge.

Leirner, Jac, text. Leirner, Jac. (Illus.). 1991. pap. 30.00 (*0-905836-74-X*, Pub. by Museum Modern Art) St Mut.

***Leis, A. Arturo & Trapani, Vicente C.** Atlas of Electromyography. LC 99-15580. 208p. 2000. write for info. (*0-19-511250-4*) OUP.

Leis, Brian N. Environmentally Assisted Cracking: Science & Engineering, STP 1049. Lisagore, W. Barry & Crooker, Thomas W., eds. LC 89-18581. (Special Technical Publication (STP) Ser.). (Illus.). 555p. 1990. text 112.00 (*0-8031-1276-9*, STP1049) ASTM.

Leis, Brian N., jt. ed. see Crooker, T. W.

Leis, Gina, ed. see Hockensmith, Sean.

Leis, Philip E. Enculturation & Socialization in an Ijaw Village. Spindler, Louise S. & Spindler, George D., eds. (Case Studies in Cultural Anthropology). 128p. 1983. reprint ed. pap. text 6.95 (*0-8290-0306-1*) Irvington.

Leis, R., jt. ed. see Hildebrandt, Stefan.

Leisch, Juanita. Introduction to Civil War Civilians. (Illus.). 86p. (C). 1994. pap. text 7.95 (*0-939631-70-9*) Thomas Publications.

— Who Wore What? Women's Wear, 1861-1865. (Illus.). 128p. (C). 1995. text 29.95 (*0-939631-81-4*) Thomas Publications.

Leisch, Juanita, ed. see Montez, Lola.

Leisching, Reihalter. Die Polnische Verfassung Vom 3. Mai 1791 Vor Dem Hintergrund der Europaischen Aufklarung. 99p. 1996. 29.95 (*3-631-30509-5*) P Lang Pubng.

Leisegang, Hans. Einfuehrung in die Philosophie. 8th ed. (Sammlung Goeschen Ser.: Vol. 4281). 148p. (C). 1973. pap. 12.95 (*3-11-004626-1*) De Gruyter.

— Pneuma Hagion. vi, 150p. 1970. reprint ed. write for info. (*0-318-70959-7*) G Olms Pubs.

Leisenring, A. C. Mathematical Logic & Hilbert's E-Symbol. x, 142p. 1969. text 249.00 (*0-677-61790-9*) Gordon & Breach.

Leiser, Andrew T., jt. auth. see Gray, Donald H.

Leiser, Burton M. Liberty, Justice & Morals: Contemporary Value Conflicts. 3rd ed. 579p. (C). 1985. pap. text 35.20 (*0-02-369530-7*, Macmillan Coll) P-H.

Leiser, Clara. Jean de Reszke & the Great Days of Opera. LC 77-107814. (Select Bibliographies Reprint Ser.). 1977. 30.95 (*0-8369-5187-5*) Ayer.

Leiser, D. & Gilleron, C. Cognitive Science & Genetic Epistemology: A Case Study of Understanding. LC 89-22970. (PATH in Psychology Ser.). (Illus.). 216p. (C). 1990. 55.00 (*0-306-43193-9*, Plenum Trade) Perseus Pubng.

Leiser, Eric. Book of Fly Patterns. LC 87-45102. 496p. 1987. 50.00 (*0-394-54394-7*) Knopf.

— The Complete Book of Fly Tying. LC 77-74975. 1977. 29.95 (*0-394-40047-X*) Knopf.

— The Dettes - A Catskill Legend: Their Story & Their Techniques. 264p. 1992. 35.00 (*0-9632705-0-8*) Willowkill Pr.

***Leiser, Eric.** Orvis Guide to Beginning Fly Tying. (Illus.). 2000. pap. 14.95 (*1-58574-096-9*) Lyons Pr.

Leiser, Gary. A History of Travis Air Force Base, 1943-1996. (Illus.). 122p. (Orig.). 1996. pap. 10.00 (*0-9655958-0-3*) Travis Air.

Leiser, Gary, ed. A History of the Seljuks: Ibrahim Kafesoglu's Interpretation & the Resulting Controversy. LC 87-26377. 219p. 1988. text 41.95 (*0-8093-1414-2*) S Ill U Pr.

Leiser, Gary, ed. & tr. see Koprulu, M. Fuad.

Leiser, Gary, ed. & tr. see Koprulu, Mehmed F.

Leiser, Gary, ed. & tr. see Olcen, Mehmet A.

Leiser, Joseph. American Judaism: The Religion & Religious Institutions of the Jewish People in the United States. LC 78-26230. 1979. reprint ed. lib. bdg. 75.00 (*0-313-20879-4*, LEAJ, Greenwood Pr) Greenwood.

Leisering, Lutz, jt. auth. see Leibfried, Stephan.

Leiserson, A., jt. auth. see Abel-Smith, B.

Leiserson, Avery. Administrative Regulation: A Study in Representation of Interests. rev. ed. LC 74-12761. 292p. 1975. reprint ed. lib. bdg. 22.50 (*0-8371-7744-8*, LEAR, Greenwood Pr) Greenwood.

Leiserson, Avery, et al. Political Research & Political Theory. Garceau, Oliver, ed. LC 68-28693. (Illus.). 268p. reprint ed. pap. 83.10 (*0-7837-4470-6*, 204417800001) Bks Demand.

Leiserson, Charles E. Area-Efficient VLSI Computation. (Association for Computing Machinery Doctoral Dissertation Award Ser.). (Illus.). 152p. 1983. 32.50 (*0-262-12102-6*) MIT Pr.

Leiserson, Charles E. & Cormen, Thomas H. Introduction to Algorithms. 1990. pap. text 43.50 (*0-262-53091-0*) MIT Pr.

Leiserson, Mark W. Wages & Economic Control in Norway, 1945-1957. LC 59-5565. (Wertheim Publications in Industrial Relations). (Illus.). 190p. 1959. 12.50 (*0-674-94470-4*) HUP.

Leiserson, William M. Adjusting Immigrant & Industry. LC 73-89747. (American Labor, from Conspiracy to Collective Bargaining Ser.: No. 1). 356p. 1974. reprint ed. 23.95 (*0-405-02135-6*) Ayer.

— American Trade Union Democracy. LC 75-40926. 354p. 1976. reprint ed. lib. bdg. 69.50 (*0-8371-8688-9*, LEAT, Greenwood Pr) Greenwood.

Leisey, Donald E., jt. auth. see Lavaroni, Charles.

***Leish, Kenneth W., ed.** Encyclopedia Puer Torriquena Siglo XXI, 6 vols. rev. ed. (SPA., Illus.). 1728p. 2000. lib. bdg. 460.00 (*0-7172-5164-0*) Grolier Educ.

Leisher, Gary, tr. & intro. see Koprulu, Mehmed F.

Leishman, Frank, et al, eds. Core Issues in Policing. LC 95-23758. vii, 273p. 1996. 64.00 (*0-582-24916-3*, 15737); pap. 25.00 (*0-582-24915-5*, 15737) Gaunt.

Leishman, J. B., tr. see Rilke, Rainer Maria.

***Leishman, J. Gordon.** Principles of Helicopter Aerodynamics. (Aerospace Ser.: Vol. 12). (Illus.). 560p. 2000. text 95.00 (*0-521-66060-2*) Cambridge U Pr.

Leishman, James. Voyaging under Power. 3rd ed. 1994. pap. 29.95 (*0-07-158019-0*) Intl Marine.

Leishman, Robert K., ed. see Marshburn, Tom.

Leisi, Ernst & Schlesinger, Eilhard. Der Zeuge im Attischen Recht & die Griechische Asylie, 2 vols. Vlastos, Gregory, ed. LC 78-14608. (Morals & Law in Ancient Greece Ser.). 1979. reprint ed. lib. bdg. 23.95 (*0-405-11584-9*) Ayer.

Leising, Marlene. Everyday & Gourmet Microwave Cookbook. 196p. 1980. pap. 8.95 (*0-9606096-0-1*) Micro Magic.

Leisinger, Andreas, tr. see Brinker, Helmut & Kanazawa, Hiroshi.

Leisinger, Klaus. All Our People: Population Policy with a Human Face. LC 93-50647. 350p. 1994. text 50.00 (*1-55963-292-5*, Pub. by IUCN) Island Pr.

— All Our People: Population Policy with a Human Face. LC 93-50647. 350p. 1994. pap. text 27.00 (*1-55963-293-3*) Island Pr.

Leisinger, Klaus M., jt. auth. see Hohn, Thomas.

Leisinger, Ulrich & Wollny, Peter. Die Bach-Quellen der Bibliotheken in Brussel - Katalog. (Leipziger Beitraege Zur Bachforschung Ser.: Vol. 2). 573p. 1997. write for info. (*3-487-10303-6*) G Olms Pubs.

***Leisink, Peter, ed.** Globalization & Labour Relations. LC 99-13584. 272p. 1999. 90.00 (*1-85898-669-9*) E Elgar.

Leisink, Peter, et al, eds. The Challenges to Trade Unions in Europe: Innovation or Adaptation. LC 95-23659. (Illus.). 320p. 1996. 95.00 (*1-85898-288-X*) E Elgar.

Leisink, Peter, jt. ed. see Coenen, Harry.

Leisner, Marcia. Literary Neighborhoods of New York. LC 88-34870. (Literary Cities Ser.). (Illus.). 72p. (Orig.). 1989. pap. 8.95 (*0-913515-40-X*, Starrhill Press) Black Belt Communs.

Leisner, Vera. Die Megalithgraber der Iberischen Halbinsel. 592p. 1997. text 281.00 (*3-11-014907-9*) De Gruyter.

Leisner, Walter, et al. Administrative Law: The Problem of Justice., Vol. 3. LC 97-228731. 1997. write for info. (*88-14-05114-3*) Giuffre.

Leiss, Bernd. Strukturbezogene Textur- und Korugefuegeuntersuchungen Plastisch Deformierter Dolomitgesteine Am Suedwestrand des Damara Orogens (Namibia) (Geotektonische Forschungen Ser.: Vol. 84). (GER.). ii, 130p. 1996. 70.00 (*3-510-50050-4*, Pub. by E Schweizerbartsche) Balogh.

Leiss, E. L. Language Equations. LC 98-31040. (Monographs in Computer Science). 304p. 1999. 64.95 (*0-387-98626-X*) Spr-Verlag.

— Software under Siege. vi, 136p. 1990. 105.00 (*0-946395-58-6*, Pub. by Elsvr Adv Tech) Elsevier.

Leiss, Elisabeth. Die Verbalkategorien des Deutschen: Ein Beitrag Zur Theorie der Sprachlichen Kategorisierung. (Studia Linguistica Germanica: No. 31). (GER.). vi, 334p. (C). 1992. lib. bdg. 107.70 (*3-11-012746-6*) De Gruyter.

Leiss, Ernst L. Principles of Data Security. LC 82-22272. (Foundations of Computer Science Ser.). (Illus.). 238p. (C). 1982. 71.00 (*0-306-41098-2*, Plenum Trade) Perseus Pubng.

Leiss, William. The Domination of Nature. LC 94-900223. 272p. (C). 1994. pap. text 19.95 (*0-7735-1198-9*, Pub. by McG-Queens Univ Pr) CUP Services.

— Ecology Versus Politics in Canada. 1979. pap. text 13.95 (*0-8020-6332-2*) U of Toronto Pr.

— The Limits to Satisfaction: An Essay on the Problem of Needs & Commodities. 184p. (C). 1988. reprint ed. pap. 19.95 (*0-7735-0688-8*, Pub. by McG-Queens Univ Pr) CUP Services.

— Under Technology's Thumb. 184p. (C). 1990. text 65.00 (*0-7735-0724-8*, Pub. by McG-Queens Univ Pr); pap. text 15.95 (*0-7735-0748-5*, Pub. by McG-Queens Univ Pr) CUP Services.

Leiss, William & Chociolko, Christina. Risk & Responsibility. LC 95-166763. 424p. 1994. 65.00 (*0-7735-1177-6*, Pub. by McG-Queens Univ Pr); pap. 19.95 (*0-7735-1194-6*, Pub. by McG-Queens Univ Pr) CUP Services.

Leiss, William, et al. Social Communication in Advertising: Persons, Products & Images of Well-Being. (Illus.). 327p. 1986. pap. 14.95 (*0-415-90084-0*, 9685) Routledge.

— Social Communication in Advertising: Persons, Products & Images of Well-Being. 2nd ed. (Illus.). 340p. (C). 1990. pap. 18.99 (*0-415-90354-8*, A4785) Routledge.

Leiss, William, jt. auth. see Powell, Douglas.

Leiss, William, jt. auth. see Salter, Liora.

Leissa, Arthur W. Vibration of Plates, Vol. 1. 353p. 1993. text 33.00 (1-56396-294-2) Acoustical Soc Am.

— Vibration of Shells. 428p. 1993. text 33.00 (1-56396-293-4) Acoustical Soc Am.

Leissring, J. C. The Life & Work of Michael Brenner, 1885-1969. (Illus.). 191p. 1991. 95.00 (0-9630085-0-1) J C Leissring.

— Songs My Father Never Sang. LC 96-94306. (Illus.). 476p. (Orig.). 1995. pap. 25.00 (0-9630085-1-X) J C Leissring.

Leist, Anja. Griechisch-Deutsche Zweisprachigkeit und Nonverbale Kommunikation: Eine Untersuchung Uber Gestik und Mimik Mit Vorschulkindern. (GER., Illus.). 145p. 1996. 35.95 (3-631-30371-8) P Lang Pubng.

Leist, Reiner. South Africa: Blue Portraits. (Illus.). 176p. 1996. pap. 35.00 (3-923922-42-6, Pub. by Nazraeli Pr) Dist Art Pubs.

— South Africa: Blue Portraits. (Illus.). 1996. 50.00 (3-923922-23-X, Pub. by Nazraeli Pr) Dist Art Pubs.

— Window. (Illus.). 146p. 85.00 (3-923922-61-2) Nazraeli Pr.

Leister, Elizabeth, tr. see Cera, Deanna F.

Leister, Jack, et al. California Politics & Government, 1970-1983: A Selected Bibliography. LC 84-23492. (Occasional Bibliographies Ser.: No. 3). 86p. reprint ed. pap. 30.00 (0-7837-2135-8, 204241700004) Bks Demand.

Leister, Mary. Wee Green Witch. LC 78-12380. (Illus.). 44p. (J). (ps up). 1978. 12.95 (0-916144-30-5) Stemmer Hse.

— Wildlings. LC 76-2063. (Illus.). 192p. 1976. 14.95 (0-916144-06-2) Stemmer Hse.

Leistico, Agnes. I Learn Better by Teaching Myself. 2nd ed. Hegener, Helen, ed. 152p. 1990. pap. 9.75 (0-945097-10-7) Home Educ Pr.

— I Learn Better by Teaching Myself & Still Teaching Ourselves. LC 97-178160. 304p. 1997. reprint ed. pap. 19.95 (0-913677-12-4) Holt Assocs.

— Still Teaching Ourselves. LC 95-10137. 214p. 1995. pap. 10.75 (0-945097-27-1) Home Educ Pr.

Leistico, Cathy R., ed. see LeBaron, Jeffery K.

Leistikow, Chad, jt. auth. see Finnie, Mike.

Leistner, Colette G., jt. auth. see Diabetes Care & Education Dietetic Practice Group.

Leistner, G. Abbreviations Guide to French Forms in Justice & Administration. 2nd ed. (ENG, FRE & GER.). 101p. 1975. 49.95 (0-8288-5785-7) Fr & Eur.

Leistritz, F. Larry & Hamm, Rita R., eds. Economic Development, 1975-1993: An Annotated Bibliography, Vol. 16. LC 94-6778. (Bibliographies & Indexes in Economics & Economic History Ser.: No. 16). 320p. 1994. lib. bdg. 79.50 (0-313-29159-4, Greenwood Pr) Greenwood.

Leistritz, F. Larry, jt. auth. see Murdock, Steve H.

Leistyna, Pepi. Presence of Mind: Education & the Politics of Deception. LC 98-34588. (Edge). 224p. (C). 1999. pap. 21.00 (0-8133-3476-4, Pub. by Westview); text 69.00 (0-8133-3475-6, Pub. by Westview) HarpC.

Leistyna, Pepi, et al, eds. Breaking Free: The Transformative Power of Critical Pedagogy. (Reprint Ser.: No. 27). 300p. (C). 1995. pap. 27.95 (0-916690-29-6) Harvard Educ Rev.

Leisure. Deer Hunter's Journal. 1995. pap. 5.95 (1-886558-05-1) Paladin Wrldwide.

— Film Fan's Movie Notebook. 1995. pap. 8.95 (1-886558-04-3) Paladin Wrldwide.

— Ice Fishing Journal. 1995. pap. 8.95 (1-886558-06-X) Paladin Wrldwide.

— Upland Game Hunter's Journal. 1995. pap. 5.95 (1-886558-07-8) Paladin Wrldwide.

***Leisure Arts Inc. Staff.** The Best of Teresa Wentzler Fantasy Collection. (Illus.). 96p. 2000. pap. 19.95 (1-57486-186-7) Leisure AR.

Leisure Arts Inc. Staff. Christmas Gifts of Good Taste, Vol. 4. LC 98-67372. (Illus.). 128p. 1999. 19.95 (1-57486-146-8) Oxmoor Hse.

***Leisure Arts Inc. Staff.** Crochet with Heart: Crochet with Heart: Best-Loved Afghans. (Illus.). 128p. 2000. 14.95 (1-57486-200-6) Leisure AR.

— Family Circle Big Book of Christmas. (Illus.). 160p. 2000. pap. 19.95 (1-57486-170-0) Leisure AR.

— 50 Fabulous Chairs. 1vol. (Illus.). 2000. pap. text 15.95 (1-57486-183-2) Leisure AR.

— Gooseberry Patch Christmas. LC 99-71586. (Illus.). 160p. 1999. 24.95 (1-57486-151-4) Oxmoor Hse.

— Gooseberry Patch Christmas, BK. 2. 160p. 2000. pap. 19.95 (1-57486-198-0) Leisure AR.

— Gooseberry Patch Christmas, BK. 2. (Illus.). 160p. 2000. 24.95 (1-57486-197-2) Leisure AR.

Leisure Arts Inc. Staff. Gooseberry Patch Christmas, BK.1. (Illus.). 160p. 1999. pap. 19.95 (1-57486-167-0) Oxmoor Hse.

***Leisure Arts Inc. Staff.** Gooseberry Patch Country Friends Go Quilting. (Illus.). 128p. 2000. pap. 19.95 (1-57486-201-4) Leisure AR.

— Great American Quilts, BK. 8. Vol. 8. (Illus.). 144p. 2000. pap. 19.95 (0-8487-1986-7) Leisure AR.

— 101 Christmas Ornaments. (Clever Crafter Series). (Illus.). 128p. 2000. 19.95 (1-57486-173-5) Leisure AR.

— The Perfect Party Planner. (Illus.). 128p. 2000. pap. 19.95 (1-57486-205-7) Leisure AR.

Leisure Arts Inc. Staff. Scrap - Happy Home Decor. (Clever Crafter Ser.). (Illus.). 128p. 1999. 19.95 (1-57486-140-9) Leisure AR.

***Leisure Arts Inc. Staff.** Southern Living Christmas Family Favorites Cookbook. (Illus.). 160p. 2000. 24.95 (0-8487-1947-6) Leisure AR.

Leisure Arts Inc. Staff. The Spirit of Christmas Cookbook, Vol. 4. 1999. 24.95 (1-57486-138-7) Oxmoor Hse.

***Leisure Arts Inc. Staff.** Trash to Treasure. 1999. 19.95 (1-57486-152-2) Oxmoor Hse.

— Year of Afghans, BK.5. (Illus.). 144p. 2000. pap. 14.95 (1-57486-175-1) Leisure AR.

Leisure Arts Inc. Staff & G+J USA Publishing Staff. Family Circle Big Book of Christmas. LC 98-66514. 160p. 1999. 19.95 (1-57486-098-4) Leisure AR.

Leisure Arts Staff. Aleene's Angels Made Easy A to Z. LC 96-72277. 144p. 1997. pap. 14.95 (0-8487-1610-8) Oxmoor Hse.

— Aleene's Iron-On Transfers. (Illus.). 160p. 1996. pap. 15.95 (1-57486-013-5, 1691) Leisure AR.

— Aleene's Something from Nothing: Treasures from Trash. (Illus.). 144p. 1998. pap. 19.95 (0-8487-1674-4) Oxmoor Hse.

— All about Memory Albums. (Illus.). 144p. 1998. pap. 19.95 (1-57486-093-3, 15840) Leisure AR.

— All Thru the House. LC 96-78949. (Illus.). 96p. 1997. 24.95 (0-8487-4158-7, 21494) Oxmoor Hse.

— American Country Christmas, Bk. 5. 160p. 1997. pap. 14.95 (0-8487-1520-9) Oxmoor Hse.

— Angels Remembered. LC 95-81459. 96p. 1996. 24.95 (0-942237-78-1); pap. 14.95 (1-57486-033-X, 33318) Leisure AR.

— The Best of Aleene's Creative Living. (Illus.). 144p. 1997. pap. 14.95 (0-8487-1614-0) Oxmoor Hse.

— Best of Christmas Is Coming. LC 97-65260. (Illus.). 144p. 1997. pap. 19.95 (0-8487-4137-4) Oxmoor Hse.

— The Best of Paula Vaughan, Bk. 1. 1994. 29.95 (0-942237-49-8) Leisure AR.

— The Best of Paula Vaughan, Bk. 1. 128p. 1997. pap. 24.95 (1-57486-084-4, 15833) Leisure AR.

— Best Selling Bazaar Patchwork. LC 92-80725. 160p. 1993. pap. 14.95 (0-8487-1172-6) Oxmoor Hse.

— Beyond the Garden Gate. LC 98-67371. 96p. 1999. text 24.95 (1-57486-066-6) Leisure AR.

— The Biggest & Best Iron-on Transfer Book. 165p. 1991. pap. 14.95 (0-942237-29-3) Leisure AR.

— Bubba Gump Shrimp Co. Cookbook: Recipes & Reflections from Forrest Gump. 1994. 179.40 (0-8487-4039-4) Oxmoor Hse.

— Christmas Cheer. LC 93-78285. 128p. 1993. 19.95 (0-942237-28-5) Leisure AR.

— Christmas from the Heart Iron-on Transfer Book. 1999. pap. text 15.95 (1-57486-147-6) Leisure AR.

— Christmas Gifts in Plastic Canvas. LC 98-75653. Vol. 13. 96p. 1999. pap. text 15.95 (1-57486-131-X) Leisure AR.

— Christmas Gifts of Good Taste. 128p. 1991. 19.95 (0-942237-13-7) Leisure AR.

— Christmas Gifts of Good Taste, Bk. 1. LC 96-78948. (Illus.). 128p. 1997. 19.95 (0-8487-4159-5, 33127) Oxmoor Hse.

— Christmas Gifts of Good Taste: 1998 Edition. 98th ed. LC 98-65190. 128p. 1998. 19.95 (1-57486-120-4) Oxmoor Hse.

— Christmas Gifts under $10. LC 96-78950. 128p. 1997. 19.95 (0-8487-4153-6, 33124) Oxmoor Hse.

— Christmas Handcrafts, Bk. 1. LC 92-60993. 144p. 1993. pap. 14.95 (0-8487-1170-X) Oxmoor Hse.

— Christmas Handcrafts, Bk. 2. LC 92-60993. 144p. 1994. pap. 14.95 (0-8487-1171-8) Oxmoor Hse.

— Christmas Handcrafts, Bk. 3. 144p. 1995. pap. 14.95 (0-8487-1415-6) Oxmoor Hse.

— Christmas Handcrafts, Bk. 4. 144p. 1996. pap. text 14.95 (0-8487-1470-9) Oxmoor Hse.

— Christmas Handcrafts, Vol. 5. (Illus.). 128p. 1997. pap. 14.95 (0-8487-4121-8) Oxmoor Hse.

— Christmas Is Coming, Vol. 3. LC 84-63030. 144p. 1993. pap. 9.99 (0-8487-1161-0) Oxmoor Hse.

— Christmas Is Coming!, Vol. 5. 144p. 1995. pap. 14.95 (0-8487-1441-5) Oxmoor Hse.

— Christmas Is Coming!, Vol. 6. 144p. 1996. pap. 14.95 (0-8487-1501-2) Oxmoor Hse.

***Leisure Arts Staff.** Christmas to Remember. 96p. 2000. 24.95 (1-57486-187-5) Leisure AR.

Leisure Arts Staff. Christmas with Southern Living, 1998. (Southern Living Ser.). (Illus.). 160p. 1998. 29.95 (0-8487-1800-3) Oxmoor Hse.

— The Cookie Jar. 128p. 1995. 19.95 (0-942237-50-1) Leisure AR.

— Cooking Light: Annual Recipes, 1998. (Illus.). 368p. 1997. 34.95 (0-8487-1598-5) Oxmoor Hse.

— Cooking Light: Light & Easy Cookbook. LC 97-68914. (Illus.). 240p. 1998. 29.95 (0-8487-1597-7) Oxmoor Hse.

— Cooking Light: Low-Fat Low-Calorie Quick & Easy Cookbook. LC 98-65944. (Illus.). 240p. 1998. 34.95 (0-8487-1591-8) Oxmoor Hse.

— Cooking Light Five-Star Recipes. LC 96-70980. 240p. 1996. 29.95 (0-8487-1540-3) Oxmoor Hse.

— The Creative Christmas Kitchen. 128p. 1992. 19.95 (0-942237-18-8) Leisure AR.

— Creative Touches. 1992. 19.95 (0-942237-16-1) Leisure AR.

— Creative Touches: How to Add Flair to Ready-to-Wear. 128p. 1996. pap. 14.95 (0-942237-86-2, 33312) Leisure AR.

— Cute As a Bug Iron-On Transfers. (Illus.). 165p. 1994. pap. 15.95 (0-942237-73-0, 1547) Leisure AR.

— Deck the Halls in Plastic Canvas: Over 75 All New Projects, Bk. 3. 96p. 1996. pap. text 15.95 (0-942237-42-0) Oxmoor Hse.

***Leisure Arts Staff.** Decorating Inside & Out. (Clever Crafter Series). (Illus.). 128p. 2000. 19.95 (1-57486-188-3) Leisure AR.

— Delicious Ways to Control Diabetes Cookbook, Bk. 2. (Illus.). 2000. 24.95 (0-8487-1968-9) Oxmoor Hse.

Leisure Arts Staff. Down Santa Claus Lane. LC 94-75391. 96p. 1994. 24.95 (0-942237-37-4) Leisure AR.

— Easy Does It. 1994. 19.95 (0-942237-39-0) Leisure AR.

— Easy Does It: Creative Decor & So Much More. 128p. 1995. pap. 14.95 (1-57486-004-6, 33303) Leisure AR.

— Fabulous Ideas for Flea Market Finds. 128p. 1995. 19.95 (0-942237-77-3) Leisure AR.

— Festive Christmas in Plastic Canvas. LC 98-65187. (Plastic Canvas Library Ser.). 1998. pap. text 15.95 (1-57486-067-4) Oxmoor Hse.

— Friendship Gifts. 144p. 1996. 19.95 (1-57486-056-9, 15826) Leisure AR.

— Friendship Gifts of Good Taste. 128p. 1991. 19.95 (0-942237-14-5) Leisure AR.

— Gifts Galore in Plastic Canvas, Bk. 4. LC 94-77912. 95p. 1996. pap. text 15.95 (0-942237-52-8) Oxmoor Hse.

— Gifts of Good Taste. 128p. 1989. 19.95 (0-942237-03-X) Leisure AR.

***Leisure Arts Staff.** Gifts of Good Taste, Vol. 3. 128p. 1999. 19.95 (1-57486-133-6) Leisure AR.

Leisure Arts Staff. God's Miracle Eye: Best-Loved Bible Stories in 3-D. LC 95-78900. (Illus.). 48p. 1995. 14.95 (1-57486-000-3) Leisure AR.

— Great American Quilts, Bk. 7. 144p. 1999. pap. 19.95 (0-8487-1893-3) Oxmoor Hse.

— Guideposts Christmas Celebration. LC 97-71975. 144p. 1997. 24.95 (0-8487-1645-0) Oxmoor Hse.

— Handmade by Design Presents Crafts in Minutes. (Illus.). 160p. 1997. pap. 14.95 (0-8487-1651-5) Oxmoor Hse.

— Healthy Heart One-Dish Meals. LC 95-73077. 240p. 1996. 29.95 (0-8487-1497-0, 102582) Oxmoor Hse.

— Heirloom Quilts. (Quick-Method Ser.). 160p. 1997. pap. 19.95 (1-57486-019-4) Oxmoor Hse.

— Holiday Crafts under $10. LC 97-73653. (Illus.). 128p. 1998. 19.95 (0-8487-1656-6) Oxmoor Hse.

— Holiday Fun in Plastic Canvas, 8. LC 96-76636. 96p. 1996. pap. text 15.95 (1-57486-052-6) Oxmoor Hse.

— Holiday Reverie. LC 97-75961. (Christmas Remembered Ser.). 1998. pap. text 24.95 (1-57486-104-2) Oxmoor Hse.

— Holidays in Plastic Canvas, 2. 96p. 1996. pap. text 15.95 (1-57486-050-X) Oxmoor Hse.

— Holidays Remembered. 96p. 1993. 24.95 (0-942237-20-X) Leisure AR.

— Holly Jolly Crafts under $10. Childs, Ann, ed. LC 99-71588. (Clever Crafter Series: Vol. 4). (Illus.). 128p. 1999. 19.95 (1-57486-125-5) Leisure AR.

— How to Arrange Dried Florals if You Think You Can't. LC 98-192719. 1998. pap. text 14.95 (1-57486-079-8) Oxmoor Hse.

— How to Arrange Seasonal Florals if You Think You Can't. LC 98-65608. 1998. pap. text 19.95 (1-57486-111-5) Leisure AR.

— How to Do Christmas Florals If You Think You Can't. (Illus.). 144p. 1997. pap. 19.95 (1-57486-073-9, 15828) Leisure AR.

— In the Nick of Time. LC 94-75390. 128p. 1994. 19.95 (0-942237-38-2) Leisure AR.

— Iron-On Transfers from the Heart. (Illus.). 165p. 1994. pap. 15.95 (0-942237-72-2, 1533) Leisure AR.

— It's in the Bag. LC 96-77627. 128p. 1997. 19.95 (1-57486-046-1) Oxmoor Hse.

— Leisure Arts Best 250 Christmas Quickies. 140p. 1995. pap. 19.95 (0-942237-76-5) Leisure AR.

— Let Us Pray. LC 96-77626. 96p. 1997. 24.95 (1-57486-047-X) Leisure AR.

— Looney Toon Big Book of Cross Stitch: 99 Designs. LC 98-65610. 1998. pap. 19.95 (1-57486-097-6) Leisure AR.

— Love, Life & Laughter. 1998. pap. text 19.95 (1-57486-113-1) Oxmoor Hse.

— Low-Fat Ways to Bake. (Illus.). 144p. 1998. 18.95 (0-8487-2216-7) Oxmoor Hse.

— Low-Fat Ways to Cook Family Favorites. LC 96-71086. (Illus.). 144p. 1997. 18.95 (0-8487-2215-9) Oxmoor Hse.

— Low-Fat Ways to Cook Soups & Stews. LC 96-71085. (Illus.). 144p. 1997. 18.95 (0-8487-2214-0) Oxmoor Hse.

— Low-Fat Ways to Cook Vegetarian. LC 96-67710. 144p. 1996. spiral bd. 18.95 (0-8487-2206-X, 104006) Oxmoor Hse.

— Low-Fat Ways to Lose Weight. LC 96-68032. 144p. 1996. spiral bd. 18.95 (0-8487-2208-6, 104007) Oxmoor Hse.

— Merry Christmas ABC. LC 93-78286. 96p. 1993. 24.95 (0-942237-27-7) Leisure AR.

— Mile-a-Minute Afghans. LC 96-76035. 128p. 1997. pap. 14.95 (1-57486-043-7) Oxmoor Hse.

— O Christmas Tree. 96p. 1992. 24.95 (0-942237-15-3) Leisure AR.

— Once upon a Christmas Time. (Christmas Remembered Ser.: No. 12). (Illus.). 96p. 1996. 24.95 (1-57486-010-0) Leisure AR.

— One-Hour Christmas Crafts. LC 98-65189. (Illus.). 128p. 1998. 19.95 (0-8487-6118-9) Oxmoor Hse.

— 150 Extra-Easy Ornaments in Plastic Canvas, Bk. 9. 96p. 1997. pap. 15.95 (1-57486-044-5) Oxmoor Hse.

— Our Best Thread Crochet. LC 96-77624. 128p. 1996. pap. 14.95 (1-57486-055-0, 2889) Leisure AR.

— Our Best 200+ Holiday Quickies. LC 97-70453. 144p. 1997. pap. 19.95 (1-57486-061-5) Oxmoor Hse.

— Precious Moments in Plastic Canvas, Bk. 10. (Illus.). 96p. 1997. pap. 16.95 (1-57486-051-8, 1763) Leisure AR.

— Precious Moments Iron-on Transfers. (Illus.). 170p. 1996. pap. 16.95 (1-57486-011-9, 1649) Leisure AR.

— Quick & Easy Christmas Crafts, Vol. 2. (Illus.). 144p. 1997. pap. 14.95 (0-8487-1622-1) Oxmoor Hse.

— Quick & Tasty Christmas Gifts. 128p. 1995. 19.95 (0-942237-67-6) Leisure AR.

— Quick As a Wink. 144p. 1996. pap. text 19.95 (1-57486-054-2) Oxmoor Hse.

— Quick Gifts of Good Taste. LC 93-80810. 128p. 1994. 19.95 (0-942237-35-8) Leisure AR.

— Quick Quilts. LC 91-61188. 160p. 1994. pap. 14.95 (0-8487-1427-X) Oxmoor Hse.

— The Romance of Paula Vaughan. 1992. 19.95 (0-942237-19-6) Leisure AR.

— The Romance of Paula Vaughan. 128p. 1996. pap. 14.95 (0-942237-91-9, 33306) Leisure AR.

— Santa Claus an American Treasure. Childs, Ann, ed. (Christmas Remembered Ser.). (Illus.). 96p. 1999. 24.95 (1-57486-132-8) Leisure AR.

— Santa Remembered. 96p. 1998. 24.95 (0-942237-05-6) Leisure AR.

— Seasons Remembered. 96p. 1995. 24.95 (0-942237-40-4) Leisure AR.

— Sew-No-More: Holiday Decor. LC 94-74353. 128p. 1995. 19.95 (0-942237-64-1, 33100) Leisure AR.

— Sew-No-More: Home Decor. 128p. 1995. pap. 14.95 (0-942237-93-5, 33300) Leisure AR.

— Southern Living: All-Time Favorite Pasta Recipes. LC 96-67712. (Illus.). 144p. 1996. pap. 14.95 (0-8487-2224-8) Oxmoor Hse.

— Southern Living: Our Best Easy Weeknight Favorites. LC 97-69946. (Southern Living Ser.). (Illus.). 240p. 1998. 29.95 (0-8487-1686-8) Oxmoor Hse.

— Southern Living All Time Favorite Low Fat Recipes. LC 95-74599. 144p. 1996. pap. 14.95 (0-8487-2223-X) Oxmoor Hse.

— Southern Living Best Recipes Made Lighter. LC 96-69579. 160p. 1997. 29.95 (0-8487-1548-9) Oxmoor Hse.

— The Southern Living Complete Do-Ahead Cookbook. LC 91-60996. 240p. 1993. pap. 14.99 (0-8487-1165-3) Oxmoor Hse.

— The Southern Living Cookbook: Updated for the Nineties. rev. ed. 520p. 1995. 29.95 (0-8487-1471-7) Oxmoor Hse.

— Southern Living Garden Guide Herbs. LC 96-67709. 128p. 1997. pap. 12.95 (0-8487-2247-7) Oxmoor Hse.

— Southern Living, 1995 Garden Annual. annuals 256p. 1995. pap. 14.95 (0-8487-1409-1) Oxmoor Hse.

— Southern Living Our Best Five-Star Recipes. LC 96-71641. 240p. 1997. 29.95 (0-8487-1567-5) Oxmoor Hse.

— Southern Living Our Best One-Dish Meals. 240p. 1995. 24.95 (0-8487-1438-5) Oxmoor Hse.

— Southern Living Quick Decorating. LC 93-87429. 160p. 1994. pap. 19.95 (0-8487-1416-4) Oxmoor Hse.

— Spirit of Christmas, 11. 1997. 24.95 (1-57486-064-X) Oxmoor Hse.

— Spirit of Christmas, Bk. 6. 6th ed. 160p. 1992. 24.95 (0-942237-17-X) Leisure AR.

— Spirit of Christmas, Bk. 7. 7th ed. LC 93-78118. 160p. 1993. 24.95 (0-942237-22-6) Leisure AR.

— Spirit of Christmas, Bk. 8. 8th ed. LC 93-80809. 160p. 1994. 24.95 (0-942237-36-6) Leisure AR.

— Spirit of Christmas, Bk. 9. 9th ed. 160p. 1995. 24.95 (0-942237-65-X) Leisure AR.

— The Spirit of Christmas, Bk. 11. LC 97-71976. (Illus.). 160p. 1997. 24.95 (0-8487-4150-1, 21558) Oxmoor Hse.

— The Spirit of Christmas, Bk. 13. Childs, Ann, ed. (Spirit of Christmas Ser.). (Illus.). 160p. 1999. 24.95 (1-57486-128-X) Leisure AR.

— The Spirit of Christmas, Vol. 10. 10th ed. (Illus.). 160p. 1996. 24.95 (1-57486-009-7) Leisure AR.

— Spirit of Christmas: Book 12. LC 98-65188. 1998. 24.95 (1-57486-119-0) Oxmoor Hse.

— The Spirit of Christmas Cookbook, Vol. 2. (Illus.). 176p. 1997. 24.95 (0-8487-4160-9, 15830) Oxmoor Hse.

— The Spirit of Christmas Cookbook, Vol. 3. Van Wagner-Child, Ann, ed. 1998. 24.95 (1-57486-124-7, 15836) Leisure AR.

***Leisure Arts Staff.** Spirit of Christmas Cookbook, Vol. 5. (Illus.). 2000. 24.95 (1-57486-180-8) Leisure AR.

Leisure Arts Staff. Stockings Were Hung. LC 98-65186. (Christmas Remembered Ser.). 1998. 24.95 (1-57486-122-0) Oxmoor Hse.

— Sweeter Than the Rose. 96p. 1996. pap. 14.95 (0-942237-85-4, 33309) Leisure AR.

— Sweeter That the Rose. LC 93-85969. 1994. 24.95 (0-942237-34-X) Leisure AR.

— Tasty Holiday Gifts. 128p. 1993. 19.95 (0-942237-21-8) Leisure AR.

— Teach Yourself Christmas Gifts under $10. 1997. 19.95 (1-57486-063-1) Oxmoor Hse.

— Teach Yourself Quick-Method Quilting. LC 96-77060. 96p. 1996. pap. 14.95 (1-57486-057-7, 1687) Leisure AR.

— Teddy Bear Treasury. LC 97-73652. (Illus.). 144p. 1997. pap. 19.95 (1-57486-077-1, 2994) Leisure AR.

— There's No Place Like Home, Bk. 12. Childs, Anne Van Wagner, ed. LC 98-65609. 1998. pap. 15.95 (1-57486-145-X, 1846) Leisure AR.

— 300+ Magnets in Plastic Canvas. (Illus.). 96p. (ps-3). 1998. pap. 15.95 (1-57486-096-8, 1807) Leisure AR.

— Timeless Ornaments. 96p. 1995. 24.95 (0-942237-66-8) Leisure AR.

***Leisure Arts Staff.** Tokens of Affection. (Christmas Remembered Ser.). (Illus.). 96p. 2000. 24.95 (1-57486-176-X) Leisure AR.

Leisure Arts Staff. Trash to Treasure, Bk. 1. LC 96-77625. 128p. 1996. 19.95 (1-57486-048-8) Leisure AR.

— Trash to Treasure Christmas, Bk. 3. (Trash to Treasure Ser.). 128p. 1999. 19.95 (1-57486-094-1) Leisure AR.

— The Ultimate Book of Memory Albums. (Illus.). 144p. 1997. pap. 19.95 (1-57486-075-5, 15829) Leisure AR.

— The Ultimate Christmas Iron-On Transfer Book. (Illus.). 170p. 1997. pap. 15.95 (1-57486-074-7, 1720) Leisure AR.

— Vanna's Afghans All Through the House. 144p. 1997. pap. 14.95 (0-8487-1602-7) Oxmoor Hse.

— Wonder-Under Book of Christmas Creations. LC 97-71086. 144p. 1997. pap. 14.95 (1-57486-062-3) Oxmoor Hse.

— Wonder-Under Book of Easy Applique. (Illus.). 160p. 1997. pap. 14.95 (0-8487-1572-1) Oxmoor Hse.
— Wonder-Under Sew No More Handmade Crafts. LC 98-65466. (Illus.). 160p. 1998. 14.95 (0-8487-1685-X, 108709) Oxmoor Hse.
— Year of Afghans. 144p. 1996. pap. text 14.95 (1-57486-049-6) Oxmoor Hse.
— Year of Afghans, Bk. 3. 1998. pap. text 14.95 (1-57486-117-4) Oxmoor Hse.
— Year of Gifts of Good Taste. LC 97-75960. 1998. 19.95 (1-57486-105-0) Oxmoor Hse.
Leisure Arts Staff, contrib. by. Christmas Keepsakes. 96p. 1990. 24.95 (0-942237-08-0) Leisure AR.
— Gifts That Taste Good. 128p. 1990. 19.95 (0-942237-09-9) Leisure AR.
— Great Works of Heart. 128p. 1991. 19.95 (0-942237-10-2) Leisure AR.
— Holiday Touches for the Country Home. 128p. 1990. 19.95 (0-942237-06-4) Leisure AR.
— Spirit of Christmas, Bk. 1. 160p. 1987. 24.95 (0-942237-00-5) Leisure AR.
— Spirit of Christmas, Bk. 2. 160p. 1988. 24.95 (0-942237-01-3) Leisure AR.
— Spirit of Christmas, Bk. 3. 160p. 1989. 24.95 (0-942237-04-8) Leisure AR.
— Spirit of Christmas, Bk. 4. 160p. 1990. 24.95 (0-942237-07-2) Leisure AR.
— Spirit of Christmas, Bk. 5. 160p. 1991. 24.95 (0-942237-11-0) Leisure AR.
***Leisure Arts Staff, ed.** Gifts of Good Taste Vol. 5: Yummy Recipes & Creative Crafts. Vol. 5. (Illus.). 160p. 2000. 24.95 (1-57486-166-2) Leisure AR.
— How to Decorate Your Home with Plastic Canvas. (Illus.). 2000. pap. text 15.95 (1-57486-165-4) Leisure AR.
— Spirit of Christmas, Bk 14. (Spirit of Christmas Ser.: Vol. 14). (Illus.). 2000. 24.95 (1-57486-178-6) Leisure AR.
— Trash to Treasure Vol. 5: The Year's Best Creative Crafts. (Illus.). 2000. 19.95 (1-57486-172-7) Leisure AR.
Leisure Arts Staff & Teske, Robert T. All-New Cookbook for Diabetics & Their Families. (Illus.). 234p. 1989. pap. 12.95 (0-8487-0750-8) Oxmoor Hse.
— Quick & Easy Cross-Stitch Gifts. 144p. 1991. 24.95 (0-8487-1069-X) Oxmoor Hse.
Leisure, Jerry, jt. auth. see Block, Jonathan.
Leisure Staff. Holiday in Cross Stitch, Vol. 2. (Illus.). 96p. 1997. pap. 14.95 (0-8487-4120-X) Oxmoor Hse.
***Leitao, Lino.** The Gift of the Holy Cross. 260p. 1999. pap. (0-948833-15-7, Pub. by Peepal Tree Pr) Paul & Co Pubs.
Leitch, A. R., et al. In Situ Hybridization. (Microscopy Handbooks Ser.: No. 27). (Illus.). 128p. 1994. pap. 39.50 (1-872748-48-1, Pub. by Bios Sci) Bks Intl VA.
Leitch, Alexander. A Princeton Companion. LC 78-51178. 576p. 1978. text 55.00 (0-691-04654-9, Pub. by Princeton U Pr) Cal Prin Full Svc.
Leitch, Barbara, et al. A Concise Dictionary of Indian Tribes of North American. 2nd rev. ed. Irvine, Keith, ed. write for info. (0-917256-48-4) Ref Pubns.
Leitch, E. C. & Scheibner, E., eds. Terrane Accretion & Orogenic Belts. (Geodynamics Ser.: Vol. 19). (Illus.). 343p. 1987. 38.00 (0-87590-516-1) Am Geophysical.
Leitch, Gordon, Jr. From Dollar to Counterfeit: The Path of American Government Dishonesty. LC 80-71064. (Illus.). 168p. (Orig.). (gr. 9-12). 1981. pap. 8.00 (0-9605734-1-0) Bicent Era.
— The Monetary Errors & Deceptions of the Supreme Court. LC 78-57901. 166p. (YA). (gr. 9-12). 1978. pap. 15.00 (0-9605734-0-2) Bicent Era.
— U. S. Government & IRS Tax Cheating. 7p. 1992. pap. 1.00 (0-9605734-2-9) Bicent Era.
Leitch, James W., tr. see Conzelmann, Hans.
Leitch, James W., tr. see Ebeling, Gerhard.
Leitch, James W., tr. see Moltmann, Jurgen.
***Leitch, Jay A.** Science & Policy: Interbasin Water Transfer of Aquatic Biota. 150p. 2000. pap. write for info. (0-911042-54-7) NDSU Inst Reg.
Leitch, Jay A. & Ekstrom, Brenda L. Wetland Economics & Assessment: An Annotated Bibliography. LC 88-30977. 203p. 1989. text 10.00 (0-8240-3648-4, SS508) Garland.
Leitch, Jay A. & Ludwig, Herbert R. Wetland Economics, 1989-1993: A Selected Annotated Bibliography, 17. LC 94-39564. (Bibliographies & Indexes in Economics & Economic History Ser.: Vol. 17). 152p. 1995. lib. bdg. 69.50 (0-313-29286-8, Greenwood Pr) Greenwood.
Leitch, Jeffrey, ed. see Condon, George.
Leitch, Margaret W., jt. auth. see Leitch, Mary.
Leitch, Mary. Seven Years in Ceylon: Stories of Mission Life. 1993. reprint ed. 24.00 (81-7013-105-7, Pub. by Navarang) S Asia.
Leitch, Mary & Leitch, Margaret W. Seven Years in Ceylon: Stories of Mission Life LC 99-932496. 1999. write for info. (81-206-1398-8, Pub. by Asian Educ Servs) S Asia.
Leitch, Mary, jt. auth. see Escalona, Sybelle K.
Leitch, Patricia. Cross Country Gallop. LC 96-4902. (Horseshoes Ser.). 1996. 9.05 (0-606-10214-0, Pub. by Turtleback) Demco.
— Perfect Horse. LC 95-26350. (Horseshoes Ser.). 1996. 9.15 (0-606-09431-8, Pub. by Turtleback) Demco.
Leitch, R. R., jt. auth. see Tokhi, M. O.
Leitch, Richard D., et al. Japan's Role in the Post Cold War World, 361. LC 95-9875. (Contributions in Political Science Ser.: Vol. 361). 240p. 1995. 62.95 (0-313-29731-2, Greenwood Pr) Greenwood.
Leitch, Robert A. & Davis, Roscoe K. Accounting Information Systems: Theory & Practice. 2nd ed. 768p. (C). 1992. text 66.80 (0-13-000032-1) P-H.
Leitch, Robert A., jt. auth. see McKeown, Patrick G.
Leitch, Roger D. Reliability Analysis for Engineers: An Introduction. (Illus.). 248p. 1995. text 80.00 (0-19-856372-8); pap. text 45.00 (0-19-856371-X) OUP.
Leitch, Thomas M. Lionel Trilling: An Annotated Bibliography. LC 92-23192. (Bibliographies of Modern Critics & Critical Schools Ser.: Vol. 19). 672p. 1992. text 40.00 (0-8240-7128-X, H1303) Garland.
— What Stories Are: Narrative Theory & Interpretation. LC 85-43559. 232p. 1986. 20.00 (0-271-00431-2) Pa St U Pr.
Leitch, Vincent. The Norton Anthology of Theory & Criticism. (C). pap. text. write for info. (0-393-97429-4) Norton.
— The Norton Anthology on Theory & Criticism. (C). pap. text. write for info. (0-393-97574-6) Norton.
Leitch, Vincent B. American Literary Criticism from the Thirties to the Eighties. 480p. 1989. pap. text 23.50 (0-231-06427-6) Col U Pr.
— Cultural Criticism, Literary Theory, Poststructuralism. 192p. 1992. 34.50 (0-231-07970-2) Col U Pr.
— Cultural Criticism, Literary Theory, Poststructuralism. 192p. 1994. pap. 18.50 (0-231-07971-0) Col U Pr.
— Deconstructive Criticism: An Advanced Introduction & Survey. LC 82-1120. 256p. 1982. text 66.00 (0-231-05472-6); pap. text 21.50 (0-231-05473-4) Col U Pr.
— Postmodernism - Local Effects, Global Flows. LC 95-38880. (SUNY Series in Postmodern Culture). 195p. (C). 1996. text 54.50 (0-7914-3009-X); pap. text 19.95 (0-7914-3010-3) State U NY Pr.
Leitch, William. South America's National Parks: A Visitor's Guide. LC 90-35389. (Illus.). 288p. (Orig.). 1990. 25.00 (0-89886-259-0); pap. 16.95 (0-89886-248-5) Mountaineers.
Leitch, William C. Argentine Trout Fishing: A Fly Fisherman's Guide to Patagonia. (Illus.). 192p. 1991. reprint ed. pap. 24.95 (1-878175-06-8) F Amato Pubns.
Leite, E. B., jt. ed. see Cunha-Vaz, J. G.
Leite, Eleni, tr. see Arthur, Kay & Domeij, Scoti.
Leite, Evelyn. Detachment: The Art of Letting Go While Living with an Alcoholic. 24p. 1981. pap. 3.00 (0-935908-02-1, 3218, HazeldenJohnson Inst) Hazelden.
— Mending Family Relationships. 44p. (Orig.). 1987. pap. 3.95 (0-9613416-7-X) Comm Intervention.
— Saving Face Through Surrender & Grace: A First Step Guide for Codependents. 24p. (Orig.). 1988. pap. 3.95 (0-945485-03-4) Comm Intervention.
Leite, Evelyn & Espeland, Pamela. Different Like Me: A Book for Teens Who Worry about Their Parents' Use of Alcohol - Drugs. (Illus.). 120p. (Orig.). 1987. pap. text 10.95 (0-935908-34-X, 3114, HazeldenJohnson Inst) Hazelden.
Leite, George & Porter, Bern, eds. Circle (Ten Issues), 2 vols., Set. (Avant-Garde Magazines Ser.). 890p. 1974. reprint ed. 60.95 (0-405-01756-1) Ayer.
— Circle (Ten Issues), 2 vols., Vol. 1. (Avant-Garde Magazines Ser.). 890p. 1974. reprint ed. 30.95 (0-405-01760-X) Ayer.
— Circle (Ten Issues), 2 vols., Vol. 2. (Avant-Garde Magazines Ser.). 890p. 1974. reprint ed. 30.95 (0-405-01761-8) Ayer.
Leite, J. R., et al, eds. Semiconductor Physics: Proceedings of the 5th Brazilian School. 450p. (C). 1992. text 127.00 (981-02-0613-5) World Scientific Pub.
Leiten, Georges K. Colonialism, Class & Nation: The Confrontation in Bombay 1930. 1985. 22.50 (0-8364-1274-5, Pub. by KP Bagchi) S Asia.
Leitenberg, H. Handbook of Social & Evaluation Anxiety. LC 90-6853. (Illus.). 570p. (C). 1990. 100.00 (0-306-43438-5, Kluwer Plenum) Kluwer Academic.
Leitenberg, Milton. Soviet Submarine Operations in Swedish Waters 1980-1986, 128. LC 87-13216. (Washington Papers: No. 128). 210p. 1987. 45.00 (0-275-92841-1, C2841, Praeger Pubs); pap. 15.95 (0-275-92842-X, B2842, Praeger Pubs) Greenwood.
***Leiter, Brian, ed.** Objectivity in Law & Morals. (Cambridge Studies in Philosophy & Law). 424p. 2000. write for info. (0-521-55430-6) Cambridge U Pr.
Leiter, Brian, ed. see Nietzsche, Friedrich Wilhelm.
Leiter, Edward & Atkinson, Mark. NOD Mice & Related Strains: Research Applications in Diabetes, AIDS, Cancer & Other Diseases. LC 97-31480. (Molecular Biology Intelligence Unit Ser.). 182p. 1999. 99.00 (1-57059-466-X) Landes Bioscience.
Leiter, Elliot, intro. The Second International Congress on Ethics in Medicine, 1987: Proceedings. 224p. 1988. 30.00 (0-685-22943-2) BIMC.
***Leiter, Gila & Kranz, Rachel.** Everything You Need to Know to Have a Healthy Twin Pregnancy. LC 00-31471. 2000. pap. 15.95 (0-440-50878-9) Dell.
Leiter, Irwin E. How to Buy a Condominium or Townhome. LC 97-14609. (Legal Survival Guides Ser.). 176p. (Orig.). 1997. pap. 16.95 (1-57071-164-X, Sphinx Pubng) Sourcebks.
Leiter, Jeffrey, et al, eds. Hanging by a Thread: Social Change in Southern Textiles. 256p. (Orig.). 1991. text 37.50 (0-87546-173-5, ILR Press); pap. text 14.95 (0-87546-174-3, ILR Press) Cornell U Pr.
Leiter, Kelly, et al. The Complete Reporter. 7th ed. LC 99-39519. 562p. (C). 1999. pap. text 50.00 (0-205-29586-X, Longwood Div) Allyn.
Leiter, Lawrence A., ed. The Endocrine Society Forty-Sixth Annual Postgraduate Assembly Syllabus, 1994. (Illus.). 350p. (C). 1994. pap. text 35.00 (1-879225-15-8) Endocrine Soc.
Leiter, Louis H., jt. auth. see Clerc, Charles.
Leiter, Michael P. & Webb, Mark. Developing Human Service Networks: Community & Organizatonal Relations. LC 83-4352. 279p. 1983. text 32.50 (0-8290-1262-1) Irvington.
Leiter, Michael P., jt. auth. see Maslach, Christina.
Leiter, Richard A. National Survey of State Laws, Vol. 1. 2nd ed. 605p. 1996. 75.00 (0-8103-9052-3) Gale.
— New Frontiers in Forensic & Demonstrative Evidence: A Bibliography. (Legal Bibliography Ser.: No. 29). 27p. (Orig.). 1985. pap. 15.00 (0-935630-12-0) U of Tex Tarlton Law Lib.
Leiter, Richard A. & White, Adrian Sherwood. Concordance of Federal Legislation. LC 98-35698. xii, 138p. 1998. pap. 22.50 (1-57588-429-1, 311710) W S Hein.
Leiter, Richard A., jt. compiled by see Mersky, Roy M.
Leiter, Robert D. Foreman in Industrial Relations. LC 68-58600. (Columbia University. Studies in the Social Sciences: No. 542). reprint ed. 20.00 (0-404-51542-8) AMS Pr.
Leiter, Robert D., jt. ed. see Galatin, Malcolm.
***Leiter, Samual L.** Great Stage Directors. 2000. mass mkt. 18.00 (0-306-80952-4, Pub. by Da Capo) HarpC.
Leiter, Samuel, et al. Zeami & the No Theatre in the World. 177p. 1998. pap. 15.00 (0-9666152-0-4) M E Segal.
Leiter, Samuel, ed. see Ortolani, Benito, et al.
Leiter, Samuel L. Art of Kabuki: Five Famous Plays. 2nd rev. ed. LC 99-46425. 2000. pap. text 18.95 (0-486-40872-8) Dover.
— The Encyclopedia of the New York Stage, 1930-1940. LC 88-5668. 1339p. 1989. lib. bdg. 215.00 (0-313-25509-1, LNY/, Greenwood Pr) Greenwood.
— The Encyclopedia of the New York Stage, 1940-1950. LC 92-7397. 1000p. 1992. lib. bdg. 215.00 (0-313-27510-6, LEY, Greenwood Pr) Greenwood.
— From Belasco to Brook. 1990. 18.95 (0-525-24594-4, 01840-550, Dutt) Dutton Plume.
— From Belasco to Brook: Representative Directors of the English-Speaking Stage, 33. LC 90-45350. (Contributions in Drama & Theatre Studies: No. 33). 320p. 1991. 65.00 (0-313-27662-5, LBB, Greenwood Pr) Greenwood.
— From Stanislavsky to Barrault, 34. LC 90-45612. (Contributions in Drama & Theatre Studies: No. 34). 264p. 1991. 49.95 (0-313-27661-7, LSE, Greenwood Pr) Greenwood.
— The Great Stage Directors: One Hundred Distinguished Careers of the Theater. LC 93-33380. (Illus.). 352p. 1994. 35.00 (0-8160-2602-5) Facts on File.
— New Kabuki Encyclopedia: A Revised Adaptation of Kabuki Jiten. rev. ed. LC 96-36530. 840p. 1997. lib. bdg. 115.00 (0-313-29288-4, Greenwood Pr) Greenwood.
— Ten Seasons: New York Theatre in the '70s, 21. LC 86-369. (Contributions in Drama & Theatre Studies). 257p. 1986. 59.95 (0-313-24994-6, LTS/, Greenwood Pr) Greenwood.
Leiter, Samuel L., ed. Shakespeare Around the Globe: A Guide to Notable Postwar Revivals. LC 85-27124. 987p. 1986. lib. bdg. 155.00 (0-313-23756-5, LES/, Greenwood Pr) Greenwood.
Leiter, Samuel L. & Hill, Holly, eds. The Encyclopedia of the New York Stage, 1920-1930, 2 vols., Set. LC 84-6558. 1331p. 1985. lib. bdg. 195.00 (0-313-23615-1, LEN/) Greenwood.
— The Encyclopedia of the New York Stage, 1920-1930, 2 vols., Vol. 1. LC 84-6558. xxxiii, 1331p. 1985. lib. bdg. 195.00 (0-313-25037-5, LEN/01) Greenwood.
— The Encyclopedia of the New York Stage, 1920-1930, 2 vols., Vol. 2. LC 84-6558. xxxiii, 1331p. 1985. lib. bdg. 195.00 (0-313-25038-3, LEN/02) Greenwood.
Leiter, Sharon. Prospects for Russian Military R&D. 95p. 1996. pap. text 15.00 (0-8330-2362-4, MR-709-A) Rand Corp.
Leiterer, Jurgen, jt. auth. see Henkin, Gennadi M.
Leiteritz, Christiane. Revolution Als Schauspiel: Beitrage zur Geschichte Einer Metapher Innerhalb der Europaeisch-Amerikanischen Literatur des 19. & 20. Jahrunderts. (Komparatistische Studien Ser.: Band 18). (GER.). xiv, 310p. (C). 1993. lib. bdg. 114.70 (3-11-013967-7) Mouton.
Leitermann, Bernhard. Wahl der Zusammenschlubform von Unternehmen Vol. XXIII: Eine Transaktionsokonomische Entscheidungskonzeption. (Schriften zue Unternehmensplanung Ser.: Bd. 41). (GER., Illus.). XXIII, 317p. 1996. pap. 57.95 (3-631-30834-5) P Lang Pubng.
Leites, D. A., tr. see Fomenko, A. T.
Leites, D. A., tr. see Leznov, A. N. & Saveliev, Mikhail V.
Leites, Edmund. The Puritan Conscience & Modern Sexuality. (C). 1995. pap. 13.00 (0-300-06549-3) Yale U Pr.
Leites, Edmund, ed. Conscience & Casuistry in Early Modern Europe. (Ideas in Context Ser.). 288p. 1988. text 59.95 (0-521-30113-0) Cambridge U Pr.
Leites, Nathan C. The Rules of the Game in Paris. Coltman, Derek, tr. LC 69-19276. 365p. reprint ed. pap. 113.20 (0-608-12563-6, 202405500035) Bks Demand.
Leitgeb, Grete, tr. see Saint-Exupery, Antoine de.
Leitgeb, H. Untersuchungen ueber die Lebermoose. 1970. 160.00 (3-7682-7187-0) Lubrecht & Cramer.
Leitgeb, Hanna. Der Ausgezeichnete Autor: Staeditsche Literaturpreise und Kulturpolitik in Deutschland 1926-1971. (European Cultures Ser.: No. 4). (GER.). 436p. (C). 1994. lib. bdg. 124.65 (3-11-014402-6) De Gruyter.
Leitgeb, Josef, tr. see Saint-Exupery, Antoine de.
Leitgeb, Norbert. Safety in Electromedical Technology. (Illus.). 184p. 1996. 119.00 (1-57491-014-0) Interpharm.
Leith. Japanese Hand Guns. LC 67-29814. 1968. 25.00 (0-87505-103-0) Borden.
Leith, Dick. A Social History of English. (Language & Society Ser.). 224p. 1983. pap. 14.95 (0-7100-9261-X, Routledge Thoemms) Routledge.
— A Social History of English. 2nd ed. 312p. (C). 1997. 75.00 (0-415-16456-7); pap. 21.99 (0-415-09797-5) Routledge.
Leith, J. Clark. Ghana. LC 74-77690. (Foreign Trade Regimes & Economic Development Ser.: No. 2). 238p. reprint ed. pap. 73.80 (0-8357-7575-5, 205689600096) Bks Demand.
— Ghana. (Special Conference Series on Foreign Trade Regimes & Economic Development: No. 2). 238p. 1974. reprint ed. 61.90 (0-87014-502-9) Natl Bur Econ Res.
Leith, James A. The Idea of Art As Propaganda in France, 1750-1799: A Study in the History of Ideas. LC 65-1875. (University of Toronto Romance Ser.: No. 8). 196p. reprint ed. pap. 60.80 (0-608-16235-3, 202646800049) Bks Demand.
— Space & Revolution: Projects for Monuments, Squares & Public Buildings in France, 1789-1799. (Illus.). 368p. 1991. 70.00 (0-7735-0757-4, Pub. by McG-Queens Univ Pr) CUP Services.
— Symbols in Life & Art. 166p. 1987. 65.00 (0-7735-0616-0, Pub. by McG-Queens Univ Pr) CUP Services.
Leith, James A., ed. Images of the Commune - Images De la Commune. (Illus.). 1978. 55.00 (0-7735-0297-1, Pub. by McG-Queens Univ Pr) CUP Services.
Leith, James A., ed. see Spencer, John H.
Leith, John H. Basic Christian Doctrine: A Summary of Christian Faith - Catholic, Protestant, & Reformed. 368p. (Orig.). 1993. pap. 26.95 (0-664-25192-7) Westminster John Knox.
— Crisis in the Church: The Plight of Theological Education. LC 97-12816. 128p. 1997. pap. 12.00 (0-664-25700-3) Westminster John Knox.
— Introduction to the Reformed Tradition. rev. ed. (Illus.). 253p. (C). 1981. pap. 19.95 (0-8042-0479-9) Westminster John Knox.
Leith, John H., ed. Creeds of the Churches: A Reader in Christian Doctrine from the Bible to the Present. 3rd ed. LC 82-48029. 1982. pap. 28.95 (0-8042-0526-4) Westminster John Knox.
Leith, John H., jt. ed. see Johnson, William S.
Leith, John T. & Dexter, Daniel L., eds. Mammalian Tumor Cell Heterogeneity. 160p. 1986. 94.00 (0-8493-6162-1, RC267, CRC Reprint) Franklin.
Leith, Larry M. Coaches Guide to Sport Administration. LC 89-39169. (ACEP Level Two Ser.). (Illus.). 96p. 1990. pap. text, teacher ed. 19.00 (0-88011-379-0, PLEI0379) Human Kinetics.
— Exercising Your Way to Better Mental Health. LC 97-61333. (Illus.). 120p. 1998. pap. 14.95 (1-885693-09-5) Fit Info Tech.
— Foundations of Exercise & Mental Health. LC 94-72237. 254p. (C). 1994. text 36.00 (0-9627926-6-7) Fit Info Tech.
— Sport Administration Study Guide. LC 89-39169. (ACEP Level Two Ser.). (Illus.). 96p. 1990. pap. text, student ed. 26.00 (0-88011-382-0, ACEP0206) Human Kinetics.
Leith, Linda. Introducing Hugh MacLennan's Two Solitudes. (Canadian Fiction Studies: No. 10). 92p. (C). 1990. text 18.95 (1-55022-018-7, Pub. by ECW) Genl Dist Srvs.
Leith, Linda, ed. see Diamond, Ann.
Leith, Linda, ed. see Ternar, Yeshim.
Leith, Mary J. Wadi Ed-Daliyeh I: The Wadi Ed-Daliyeh Seal Impressions. (Discoveries in the Judaean Desert Ser.: No. XXIV). (Illus.). 270p. 1997. text 120.00 (0-19-826935-8) OUP.
Leith, Philip. The Computerised Lawyer: A Guide to the Use of Computers in the Legal Profession. Morgan, G. G., ed. (Applications of Advanced Computing Techniques Ser.). (Illus.). 256p. 1991. 39.95 (0-387-19658-7) Spr-Verlag.
Leith, Philip & Hoey, Amanda. The Computerised Lawyer: A Guide to the Use of Computers in the Legal Profession. 2nd rev. ed. LC 97-33527. xii, 360p. (C). 1998. pap. 49.95 (3-540-76141-1) Spr-Verlag.
Leith, Philip, jt. auth. see Morison, John.
***Leith, Prue.** Leaving Patrick. large type ed. LC 99-87701. (General Ser.). 2000. pap. 23.95 (0-7862-2419-3) Thorndike Pr.
Leith, Ron. Torso Killer: Shocking True Crimes. 1991. mass mkt. 4.50 (1-55817-518-0, Pinncle Kensgtn) Kensgtn Pub Corp.
Leith-Ross, Prudence. The Florilegium of Alexander Marshall: In the Collection of Her Majesty the Queen at Windsor Castle. LC 99-70869. (Royal Collection Ser.). (Illus.). 368p. 2000. text 175.00 (0-500-97481-0, Pub. by Thames Hudson) Norton.
— The John Tradescants: Gardeners to the Rose & Lily Queen. 320p. 1984. 39.00 (0-317-61300-6, Pub. by P Owen Ltd) Dufour.
***Leith-Ross, Prudence.** The John Tradescants: The Gardners to the Rose & Lily Queen. 1999. pap. text 39.95 (0-7206-1073-7) P Owen Ltd.
Leith-Ross, Prudence, ed. The John Tradescants: Gardeners to the Rose & Lily Queen. 320p. 1984. 40.00 (0-7206-0612-8, Pub. by P Owen Ltd) Dufour.
Leith-Ross, Sylvia. African Women. LC 74-15062. (Illus.). reprint ed. 32.50 (0-404-12103-9) AMS Pr.
— Stepping Stones: Memoirs of Colonial Nigeria, 1907-1960. 191p. 1983. 30.00 (0-7206-0600-4, Pub. by P Owen Ltd) Dufour.
Leith, Royal W. A Quiet Devotion: The Life & Work of Henry Roderick Newman. LC 96-76318. (Illus.). 120p. (Orig.). 1996. pap. 50.00 (0-614-29361-8) V Jordan Fine Art.
Leith, Samuel. Man Under Authority. 9.99 (1-85792-016-3, Pub. by Christian Focus) Spring Arbor Dist.
— There Is an Answer. 1995. 6.99 (1-871676-06-1, Pub. by Christian Focus) Spring Arbor Dist.
— Time to Wake Up! 1992. pap. 8.99 (0-85234-296-9, Pub. by Evangelical Pr) P & R Pubng.

L

— Victorian Ornaments & Designs. LC 99-47030. 2000. pap. text 7.95 (0-486-40702-0) Dover.

***Leith, Valery.** Company of Glass Bk. One: Everien. LC 98-56460. 432p. 1999. pap. 13.95 (0-553-37938-0) Bantam.

— Company of Glass Bk. One: Everien. Vol. 1. 560p. 2000. mass mkt. 5.99 (0-553-57899-5) Bantam.

— The Riddled Night Bk. 2: Everien. 496p. 2000. pap. 13.95 (0-553-37939-9, Spectra) Bantam.

Leith, William R. Clinical Methods in Communication Disorders. 2nd ed. LC 92-17022. 288p. 1993. pap. text 31.00 (0-89079-568-1, 4047) PRO-ED.

Leithart, Peter. Wise Words: Family Stories that Bring the Proverbs to Life. (Illus.). 169p. 1996. pap. text 9.99 (1-880692-23-6) Holly Hall.

Leithart, Peter. Wise Words: Family Stories That Bring the Proverbs to Life. 167p. 1995. pap. 9.99 (1-888306-65-3) Holly Hall.

Leithart, Peter, jt. auth. see DeMar, Gary.

Leithart, Peter J. Brightest Heaven of Invention: A Christian Guide to Six Shakespeare Plays. 284p. (YA). (gr. 10-12). 1996. pap. 15.50 (1-885767-23-4) Canon Pr ID.

— Daddy, Why Was I Excommunicated? An Examination of Leonard J. Coppes, "Daddy, May I Take Communion?" 81p. 1992. pap. 7.00 (1-883690-00-5) Transfig Pr.

— Heroes of the City of Man: A Christian Guide to Select Ancient Literature. 400p. 1999. pap. 17.00 (1-885767-55-2) Canon Pr ID.

— The Kingdom & the Power: Rediscovering the Centrality of the Church. 270p. (Orig.). 1993. pap. 11.99 (0-87552-300-5) P & R Pubng.

Leithart, Peter J., jt. auth. see DeMar, Gary.

Leithauser, Brad. The Friends of Freeland. LC 96-19618. 1997. 26.00 (0-679-45083-1) Knopf.

— The Friends of Freeland. 528p. 1998. pap. 14.00 (0-679-77270-7) Vin Bks.

— The Odd Last Thing She Did: Poems. LC 98-14565. 96p. 1998. 22.00 (0-375-40141-5) Knopf.

***Leithauser, Brad.** The Odd Last Thing She Did: Poems. LC 98-14565. 96p. 2000. pap. 15.00 (0-375-70849-9) Knopf.

Leithauser, Brad. Penchants & Places: Essays & Criticism. LC 94-28629. 289p. 1995. 25.00 (0-679-42998-0) Knopf.

— Seaward. LC 92-31047. 1993. 25.00 (0-685-61666-5) Knopf.

— Seaward. LC 92-31047. (Borzoi Reader Ser). 1993. 23.00 (0-394-58587-9) Knopf.

Leithauser, Brad, ed. The Norton Book of Ghost Stories. LC 94-17383. 1994. 25.00 (0-393-03564-6) Norton.

Leithauser, Brad, jt. ed. see Jarrell, Randall.

Leithauser, David. Exploring Natural Language. 1991. 24.95 incl. disk (0-8306-6668-0); 24.95 incl. disk (0-8306-6669-9) McGraw-Hill Prof.

Leithe-Jasper, Manfred. Renaissance Master Bronzes from the Kunsthistorisches Museum, Vienna. (Illus.). 304p. 1986. lib. bdg. 35.00 (0-935748-69-5) Scala Books.

Leithe-Jasper, Manfred & Distelberger, Rudolf. The Kunsthistorisches Museum, Vienna: The Imperial & Ecclesiastical Treasury. (Illus.). 96p. 1998. 35.00 (1-85759-125-9) Scala Books.

Leitherer, C., et al, eds. From Stars to Galaxies. (ASP Conference Series Proceedings: Vol. 98). 624p. 1996. 34.00 (1-886733-19-8) Astron Soc Pacific.

Leitherer, Claus, et al, eds. Massive Stars in Starbursts: Proceedings of the Massive Stars in Starbursts Meeting, Baltimore, 1990 May 15-17. (Space Telescope Science Institute Symposium Ser.: No. 5). 349p. 1991. text 69.95 (0-521-40465-7) Cambridge U Pr.

Leithold & Gerber. Before Calculus. 3rd ed. 208p. (C). 1997. pap., student ed. 39.00 (0-673-46912-3) Addison-Wesley.

Leithold & Minnick. An Outline for the Study of Calculus, Vol. 2. 6th ed. 400p. (C). 1997. pap. 33.00 (0-06-044547-5) Addison-Wesley.

— Outline Student Calculus, Vol. 3. 6th ed. (C). 1997. pap. 31.00 (0-06-044548-3) Addison-Wesley.

Leithold, Esther M. Evans: Genealogy of the Evans Family, the Va. Biddles & Other Related Families. (Illus.). 78p. 1997. reprint ed. pap. 15.00 (0-8328-8508-8); reprint ed. lib. bdg. 25.00 (0-8328-8507-X) Higginson Bk Co.

Leithold, Louis. Before Calculus: Functions, Graphs, & Analytic Geometry. 3rd ed. LC 93-34084. 768p. (C). 1997. 99.00 (0-673-46911-5) Addson-Wesley Educ.

— Calculus Single Variable with Analytic Geometry. 6th ed. 880p. (C). 1997. pap. text, student ed. 104.00 (0-06-043930-0) Addson-Wesley Educ.

— Calculus with Analytic Geometry. 6th ed. 1280p. (C). 1997. pap. text 120.00 (0-06-044107-0) Addson-Wesley Educ.

— The Calculus 7 of a Single Variable. 7th ed. 1040p. (C). 1997. text 90.00 (0-673-46969-7) Addson-Wesley Educ.

— College Algebra. (Illus.). 482p. (C). 1989. text 50.00 (0-201-17051-5) Addison-Wesley.

— College Algebra & Trigonometry. (Illus.). 702p. (C). 1989. student ed. 18.25 (0-201-15732-2); text 50.50 (0-201-15730-6) Addison-Wesley.

— Computerized Testing. (Illus.). 702p. (C). 1989. teacher ed. 12.95 incl. disk (0-201-15700-4); student ed. 12.66 (0-201-17072-8) Addison-Wesley.

— Plane Trigonometry. (Illus.). (C). 1989. text 48.50 (0-201-17056-6); student ed. 18.25 (0-201-17058-2) Addison-Wesley.

— Print Tests of College Algebra Trigonometry. (Illus.). 702p. (C). 1989. pap. text, teacher ed. 12.95 (0-201-15733-0) Addison-Wesley.

— Printed Test Plane Trigo. (Illus.). (C). 1989. 12.95 (0-201-17059-0) Addison-Wesley.

***Leithwood, Kenneth.** Educational Accountability: The State of the Art International Network of Innovative School System. 1999. pap. 16.95 (3-89204-435-X) Bertelsmann Stiftung.

Leithwood, Kenneth, ed. Effective School District Leadership: Transforming Politics into Education. LC 94-3955. (SUNY Series, Educational Leadership). 360p. (C). 1995. text 64.50 (0-7914-2253-4); pap. text 21.95 (0-7914-2254-2) State U NY Pr.

Leithwood, Kenneth & Aitken, Robert. Making Schools Smarter: A System for Monitoring School & District Progress. (Illus.). 216p. 1995. pap. 34.95 (0-8039-6292-4) Corwin Pr.

Leithwood, Kenneth & Louis, Karen S. Organizational Learning in Schools. LC 98-52440. 394p. 1999. 83.00 (90-265-1539-1); pap. 29.00 (90-265-1540-5) Swets.

Leithwood, Kenneth & Steinbach, Rosanne. Expert Problem Solving: Evidence from School & District Leaders. LC 93-42686. (SUNY Series, Educational Leadership). 366p. (C). 1994. text 64.50 (0-7914-2107-4); pap. text 23.95 (0-7914-2108-2) State U NY Pr.

Leithwood, Kenneth, jt. ed. see Hallinger, Philip.

Leithwood, Kenneth A., et al, eds. Preparing School Leaders for Educational Improvement. (Educational Management Ser.). 224p. 1987. 45.00 (0-7099-4123-4, Pub. by C Helm) Routldge.

Leithwood, Kenneth A. & Musella, Donald F., eds. Understanding School System Administration: Studies of the Contemporary Chief Education Officer. 250p. 1991. 65.00 (1-85000-869-8, Falmer Pr) Taylor & Francis.

Leithwood, Kenneth A., et al. Changing Leadership for Changing Times. LC 98-36636. (Changing Education Ser.). 224p. 1999. pap. 29.95 (0-335-19522-9) OpUniv Pr.

***Leithwood, Kenneth A., et al.** Changing Leadership for Changing Times. LC 98-36636. (Changing Education Ser.). 1999. 95.00 (0-335-19523-7) OpUniv Pr.

— Making Schools Smarter: A System for Monitoring School & District Progress. 2nd ed. LC 00-29536. 2000. pap. write for info. (0-7619-7505-5) Corwin Pr.

Leithwood, Kenneth L. & Musella, Donald F., eds. Understanding School System Administration: Studies of the Contemporary Chief Education Officer. 250p. 1991. pap. 29.95 (1-85000-870-1, Falmer Pr) Taylor & Francis.

Leitinger, Ilse A., ed. from SPA. The Costa Rican Women's Movement: A Reader. LC 94-41579. (Latin American Ser.). (Illus.). 392p. (C). 1997. pap. 22.95 (0-8229-5543-1); text 49.95 (0-8229-3862-6) U of Pittsburgh Pr.

Leitman, Mark W. Manual for Eye Examination & Diagnosis. 4th ed. 1993. pap. 36.95 (0-86542-339-3) Blackwell Sci.

***Leitman, Mark W.** Manual for Eye Examination & Diagnosis. 5th ed. (Illus.). 98p. (C). 2000. pap. 39.95 (0-632-04542-6) Blackwell Sci.

Leitmann, G. The Calculus of Variations & Optimal Control. LC 81-4582. (Mathematical Concepts & Methods in Science & Engineering Ser.: Vol. 24). (Illus.). 328p. (C). 1981. text 75.00 (0-306-40707-8, Kluwer Plenum) Kluwer Academic.

Leitmann, G., et al, eds. Dynamics & Control. 272p. 1999. 120.00 (90-5699-172-8) Gordon & Breach.

Leitmann, Josef. Rapid Urban Environmental Assessment Vol. 1: Lessons from Cities in the Developing World, Methodology & Preliminary Findings. LC 94-10848. (Urban Management & the Environment Ser.: Vol. 14). 89p. 1994. pap. 22.00 (0-8213-2790-9, 12790) World Bank.

— Rapid Urban Environmental Assessment Vol. 2: Lessons from Cities in the Developing World, Tools & Outputs. LC 94-9395. (Urban Management Program Ser.: No. 15). 156p. 1994. pap. 22.00 (0-8213-2791-7, 12791) World Bank.

Leitmann, Joseph. Sustaining Cities: Environmental Planning & Management in Urban Design. LC 99-17193. (Professional Architelture Ser.). 416p. 1999. 69.95 (0-07-038316-2) McGraw.

***Leitner, Andreas & Burkhart, Dagmar.** Von Festen Un Feiren: Von Festen und Feiern In Den Slavischen Literaturen. (GER., Illus.). 304p. 1999. 57.00 (3-631-33293-9) P Lang Pubng.

Leitner, Bernhard. The Architecture of Ludwig Wittgenstein: A Second Look. 162p. 1997. 42.00 (3-211-82955-5) Spr-Verlag.

— Bernhard Leitner: Sound: Space. (Illus.). 340p. 1999. 65.00 (3-89322-444-0, 910302, Pub. by Dr Cantz sche Druckerei GmbH) Dist Art Pubs.

— Bernhard Leitner: Geometry of Sound. (Illus.). 80p. 1999. pap. 16.95 (3-89322-936-1) Dr Cantz sche Druckerei GmbH.

***Leitner, Bernhard.** The Wittgenstein House. (Illus.). 160p. 2000. 45.00 (1-56898-251-8) Princeton Arch.

***Leitner, David L.** Casemap: Case Knowledge Manager. LC 99-17009. 1999. write for info. (1-57073-683-9) Amer Bar Assn.

— The Law Firms's Quick Guide to Juris. LC 99-23755. 1999. write for info. (1-57073-669-3) Amer Bar Assn.

Leitner, David L., ed. Managed Care Liability: Examining Risks & Responsibilities in a Changing Health Care System. LC 96-80429. 488p. 1997. pap. 74.95 (1-57073-393-7) Amer Bar Assn.

Leitner, David L. & American Bar Association Staff. Emerging Issues in Employment Discrimination. LC 99-23198. 1999. write for info. (1-57073-715-0) Amer Bar Assn.

— Tobacco Litigation & Insurance. LC 97-4246. 1997. pap. 84.95 (1-57073-398-8) Amer Bar Assn.

Leitner, Erich, ed. Educational Research & Higher Education Reform in Eastern & Central Europe. LC 98-33927. (Studies in Comparative Education: Vol. 6). (Illus.). 231p. 1998. pap. text 39.95 (0-8204-3622-4) P Lang Pubng.

Leitner, Erich & Gellert, Claudius, eds. Educational Research & Higher Education Reform In Eastern & Central Europe. (Studies in Comparative Education: Vol. 6). (Illus.). 231p. 1998. pap. 39.95 (3-631-33751-5) P Lang Pubng.

Leitner, Gerhard. Gespraechsanalyse und Rundfunkkommmunikation. (GER.). iv, 224p. 1983. write for info. (3-487-07464-8) G Olms Pubs.

Leitner, Gerhard, ed. English Traditional Grammars: An International Perspective. LC 91-24951. (Studies in the History of the Language Sciences: Vol. 62). x, 392p. 1991. 89.00 (1-55619-357-2) J Benjamins Pubng Co.

— New Directions in English Language Corpora: Methdology, Results, Software Developments. LC 92-26798. (Topics in English Linguistics Ser.: Vol. 9). (Illus.). ix, 368p. 1992. lib. bdg. 136.95 (3-11-013201-X) Mouton.

***Leitner, Gerry.** Argentina Travel Companion. 2nd ed. (Illus.). 1050p. 2000. pap. 23.95 (0-9587498-1-7) Hunter NJ.

Leitner, Helga, jt. ed. see Nijkamp, Peter.

Leitner, Kerstin. Workers, Trade Unions & Peripheral Capitalism in Kenya after Independence. (European University Studies: Political Science: Ser. 31, Vol. 8). 184p. 1977. 32.00 (3-261-02962-5) P Lang Pubng.

Leitner, L. M. & Dunnett, N. G., eds. Critical Issues in Personal Construct Psychotherapy. 330p. (C). 1992. 37.50 (0-89464-519-6) Krieger.

— Critical Issues in Personal Construct Psychotherapy. 330p. (C). 1995. pap. 19.95 (0-89464-959-0) Krieger.

Leitner, L. M., jt. auth. see Faidley, A. J.

Leitner, Michael J. & Leitner, Sara F. Leisure in Later Life. 2nd ed. LC 95-45915. (Illus.). 466p. (C). 1996. pap. 24.95 (1-56024-966-8) Haworth Pr.

— Leisure in Later Life. 2nd ed. LC 95-45915. (Illus.). 466p. 1996. 49.95 (1-56024-965-X) Haworth Pr.

— Leisure in Later Life: A Sourcebook for the Provision of Recreation Services for Elders. LC 85-17635. (Activities, Adaptation & Aging Ser.: Vol. 7, Nos. 3-4). 341p. 1986. text 49.95 (0-86656-452-7); pap. text 24.95 (0-86656-476-4) Haworth Pr.

Leitner, Michael J., et al. Leisure Enhancement. 2nd ed. LC 95-36990. (Illus.). 447p. (C). 1996. 49.95 (1-56024-958-7); pap. 24.95 (1-56024-959-5) Haworth Pr.

Leitner, Patricia J., jt. auth. see Bach, Daniel J.

Leitner, Peter M. Decontrolling Strategic Technology, 1990-1992: Creating the Military Threats of the 21st Century. 242p. (C). Date not set. lib. bdg. 47.00 (0-7618-0034-4) U Pr of Amer.

— Reforming the Law of the Sea Treaty: Opportunities Missed, Precedents Set, & U. S. Sovereignty Threatened. 386p. 1996. pap. text 42.00 (0-7618-0394-7); lib. bdg. 62.00 (0-7618-0393-9) U Pr of Amer.

Leitner, Sara F., ed. Leisure Enhancement. LC 89-15549. (Illus.). 412p. 1989. pap. text 24.95 (0-86656-847-6) Haworth Pr.

— Leisure Enhancement. LC 89-15549. (Illus.). 412p. 1989. text 49.95 (0-86656-892-1) Haworth Pr.

Leitner, Sara F., jt. auth. see Leitner, Michael J.

Leitritz, Earl & Lewis, Robert C. Trout & Salmon Culture (Hatchery Methods) (Illus.). 197p. 1980. reprint ed. pap. 6.50 (0-931876-36-2, 4100) ANR Pubns CA.

Leitsch, Alexander. The Resolution Calculus. LC 96-39706. (Texts in Theoretical Computer Science Ser.). 312p. 1997. 45.95 (3-540-61882-1) Spr-Verlag.

***Leitsmann, H.** Tumornachsorge in der Gynakologie. xii, 276p. 1999. 71.50 (3-8055-6518-6) S Karger.

Leitz, Christian. Economic Relations Between Nazi Germany & Franco's Spain, 1936-1945. (Oxford Historical Monographs). (Illus.). 270p. 1996. text 75.00 (0-19-820645-3) OUP.

Leitz, Christian, ed. The Third Reich. LC 99-24872. (Essential Readings in History Ser.). 304p. 1999. 59.95 (0-631-20699-X); pap. 24.95 (0-631-20700-7) Blackwell Pubs.

***Leitz, Christian & Dunthorn, David J., eds.** Spain in International Context, 1936-1959. LC 99-31903. 334p. 1999. 69.95 (1-57181-956-8) Berghahn Bks.

Leitz, David. Casting in Dead Water. 1996. mass mkt. 5.50 (0-312-95779-3, Pub. by Tor Bks) St Martin.

— Fly Fishing Can Be Fatal. 1997. mass mkt. 5.99 (0-312-96162-6) St Martin.

— Fly-Fishing Can Be Fatal: A Max Adams Mystery. (Orig.). 1997. mass mkt. 5.99 (0-614-27785-X) St Martin.

Leitz, David E. The Fly Fishing Corpse. 160p. 1994. pap. 12.95 (1-882418-13-1) Centenn Pubns.

***Leitz, David E.** Hooked on Death: A Max Addams Fly Fishing Mystery. LC 00-190540. 2000. 25.00 (0-7388-1796-1); pap. 18.00 (0-7388-1797-X) Xlibris Corp.

Leitz, Pierr M., jt. auth. see Edge, Nellie.

Leitz, Robert C., III, jt. auth. see Price, Kenneth M.

Leitz, Robert C., III, ed. see London, Jack.

Leitzel, James R., ed. A Call for Change: Recommendations for the Mathematical Preparation of Teachers. (MAA Notes Ser.). 64p. 1991. pap. 6.00 (0-88385-072-9, CFC) Math Assn.

Leitzel, James R. & Tucker, Alan, eds. Assessing Calculus Reform Efforts: A Report to the Community. LC 94-72962. (MAA Notes Ser.). 100p. (C). 1994. pap. 9.60 (0-88385-093-1, ACRE) Math Assn.

Leitzel, Jim. Russian Economic Reform. LC 94-24768. 208p. (C). 1995. pap. 22.99 (0-415-12511-1, C0438) Routledge.

— Russian Economic Reform. LC 94-24768. 208p. (C). (gr. 13). 1995. 75.00 (0-415-12510-3, C0437) Routledge.

Leitzell, Terry L. Extinction, Evolution & Environmental Management. (Working Papers on the Preservation of Species). 1988. 2.50 (0-318-33311-2, PS2) IPPP.

Leitzmann, Albert, ed. see Luther, Martin.

Leitzmann, C. Worterbuch der Ernahrungswissenschaft. (ENG, FRE, GER, ITA & SPA.). 298p. 1988. lib. bdg. 115.00 (0-8288-3592-6, F113450) Fr & Eur.

Leitzmann, C., et al. Dictionary of Nutrition/Woerterbuch der Ernaehrung. 2nd ed. (FRE, GER & ITA.). 516p. 1996. 86.00 (3-8001-2148-4, Pub. by Eugen Ulmer) Balogh.

Leitzmann, Claus. Dictionary of Nutrition, English, French, German, Italian, Spanish. 2nd ed. (ENG, FRE, GER, ITA & SPA.). 516p. 1996. 195.00 (0-7859-9528-5) Fr & Eur.

Leitzmann, J. J., jt. auth. see Lipsius, J. G.

Leiva. Algebra Connections, Bk. 1. Date not set. text 91.96 (0-395-67136-1) HM.

— Algebra Connections, Bk. 2. 1996. text 91.96 (0-395-67138-8) HM.

— Algebra Connections Book. 1995. text 57.00 (0-395-67135-3) HM.

— Algebra Connections Book. 1996. text 59.80 (0-395-67137-X) HM.

— Algebra 2 Assessment Book. Date not set. pap. 122.00 (0-395-76958-2); pap., suppl. ed. write for info. (0-395-76960-4) HM.

— Algebra 1. Date not set. pap., suppl. ed. 46.76 (0-395-76989-2) HM.

— Algebra 1 Assessment Book. Date not set. pap. 118.48 (0-395-76957-4) HM.

— Algebra 1 Assessment Book Answer Key. Date not set. pap. write for info. (0-395-76959-0) HM.

— Algebra 1 Multi-Language Bookl. Date not set. pap. 48.88 (0-395-76987-6) HM.

— Algebra 1 Study Guide. Date not set. pap., student ed. 11.00 (0-395-76963-9) HM.

— Algebra 2. Date not set. pap., student ed. 13.28 (0-395-76964-7); pap., suppl. ed. 48.20 (0-395-76990-6) HM.

— Algebra 2 Multi-Language Book. Date not set. pap. 48.88 (0-395-76988-4) HM.

Leiva, Erasmo, tr. see Von Balthasar, Hans U.

Leiva, Manuel R. Relacion Hospedante-Parasito Mecanismo de Patogenicidad de los Microorganismos. (Serie de Biologia: No. 14). 91p. (C). 1981. pap. 3.50 (0-8270-1322-1) OAS.

Leiva-Merikakis, Erasmo. The Blossoming Thorn: Georg Trakl's Poetry of Atonement. LC 85-43246. 192p. 1987. 36.50 (0-8387-5102-4) Bucknell U Pr.

— Fire of Mercy, Heart of the Word: Meditations on the Gospel of St. Matthew. LC 95-75664. 730p. (Orig.). 1996. pap. 29.95 (0-89870-558-4) Ignatius Pr.

***Leiva-Merikakis, Erasmo.** Love's Sacred Order: The Four Loves Revisited. 165p. 2000. pap. 12.95 (0-89870-791-9, Pub. by Ignatius Pr) Midpt Trade.

Leiva-Merikakis, Erasmo, tr. see Auer, Johann.

Leiva-Merikakis, Erasmo, tr. see Von Balthasar, Hans U.

Leiva-Merikakis, Erasmo, tr. see Von Speyr, Adrienne.

Leiva, Miriam, ed. see Burton, Grace, et al.

Leiva, Miriam A., ed. see Burton, Grace, et al.

Leivadi, Stella, jt. ed. see Apostolopoulos, Yiorgis.

Leivant, Daniel, et al, eds. Logic & Computational Complexity: International Workshop, LCC '94, Bloomington, IN, October 13-16, 1994, Vol. VIII. LC 95-37560. (Lecture Notes in Computer Science Ser.: Vol. 960). 514p. 1995. 81.00 (3-540-60178-3) Spr-Verlag.

Leive, Loretta, ed. Bacterial Membranes & Walls. LC 73-82622. (Microbiology Ser.: No. 1). (Illus.). 515p. reprint ed. pap. 159.70 (0-7837-0905-6, 204121000019) Bks Demand.

Leivick, Joel. Carrara: The Marble Quarries of Tuscany. LC 98-45646. 1999. 60.00 (0-8047-3308-2) Stanford U Pr.

— The Enduring Illusion: Photographs from the Stanford University Museum of Art. (Illus.). 96p. (Orig.). 1996. pap. 24.95 (0-937031-06-2) Stanford Art.

Leivick, Joel, photos by. Carrara: The Marble Quarries of Tuscany. (Illus.). 1999. pap. 35.00 (0-8047-3637-5) Stanford U Pr.

Leiviska, K., ed. CIM in Process & Manufacturing Industries: IFAC Workshop, Espoo, Finland, 23-25 November 1992. LC 93-17913. (IFAC Pre-Print Ser.). 246p. 1993. pap. 94.00 (0-08-042182-2, Pergamon Pr) Elsevier.

***Leiviska, Karen.** The War with Grandpa: Literature Unit. (Illus.). 48p. 1999. pap., teacher ed. 7.95 (1-57690-334-6, TCM2334) Tchr Create Mat.

Leizman, Jon. Let's Kill 'Em: Understanding & Controlling Violence in Sports. LC 99-14399. 144p. 1999. pap. text 24.50 (0-7618-1378-0) U Pr of Amer.

***Leizman, Jon.** Let's Kill 'Em: Understanding & Controlling Violence in Sports. LC 99-14399. 144p. 1999. 42.00 (0-7618-1377-2) U Pr of Amer.

Leja, Jan. Surface Chemistry of Froth Flotation. 744p. 1981. 145.00 (0-306-40588-1, Plenum Trade) Perseus Pubng.

Leja, Laruen, et al. 5x5 Singles Club, Box. 84p. 1997. pap. 9.95 (0-941215-10-5) Primal Pub.

Leja, Michael. Reframing Abstract Expressionism: Subjectivity & Painting in the 1940s. LC 92-32992. (Illus.). 448p. (C). 1993. 63.00 (0-300-04461-5) Yale U Pr.

— Reframing Abstract Expressionism: Subjectivity & Painting in the 1940s. (Illus.). 400p. 1997. pap. 25.00 (0-300-07082-9) Yale U Pr.

Lejbowicz, Agnes. Omraam Mikhael Aivanhov: Master of the Great Universal White Brotherhood. (Testimonials Ser.). 115p. (Orig.). 1982. pap. 6.95 (2-85566-191-9, Pub. by Prosveta) Prosveta USA.

An Asterisk (*) at the beginning of an entry indicates that the title is appearing for the first time.

Lejcek, Pavel & Paidar, Vaclav, eds. Intergranular & Interphase Boundaries in Materials: IIB95. (Materials Science Forum Ser.: Vols. 294-296). (Illus.). 808p. (C). 1999. text 283.00 (*0-87849-823-0*, Pub. by Scitec Pubns) Enfield Pubs NH.

LeJeune, A., jt. auth. see Perdang, J. M.

Lejeune, Abbe P. An Introduction to the Mystical Life. 1977. lib. bdg. 59.95 (*0-8490-2070-0*) Gordon Pr.

Lejeune, Albert. L' Optique de Claude Ptolemee. 2nd ed. LC 89-9858. (Collection de Travaux de l'Academie Internationale d'Histoire des Sciences: Vol. 31). (FRE & LAT.). viii, 414p. 1989. reprint ed. 260.00 (*90-04-09126-2*) Brill Academic Pubs.

Lejeune, Anthony, ed. see Lejeune, C. A.

Lejeune, C. A. The C. A. Lejeune Film Reader. Lejeune, Anthony, ed. (Film Reader Ser.). 364p. 1995. 39.95 (*1-55783-207-2*) Applause Theatre Bk Pubs.

Lejeune-Dirichlet, P. G. Werke, 2 Vols. in 1. Kronecker, Leopold, ed. LC 68-54716. 1969. reprint ed. 75.00 (*0-8284-0225-6*) Chelsea Pub.

***Lejeune-Dirichlet, Peter G. & Dedekind, Richard.** Lectures on Number Theory. LC 99-35565. (History of Mathematics Source Ser.). 1999. write for info. (*0-8218-2017-6*) Am Math.

Lejeune, F. & Bunjes, Werner E. Dictionary for Physicians. 2nd ed. (ENG & GER.). 459p. 1968. 175.00 (*0-7859-0829-3*, M-7106) Fr & Eur.

— Woerterbuch fuer Aerzte: Dictionary for Physicians. 2nd ed. (GER.). 1968. pap. 55.00 (*0-685-01779-6*, M-6924) Fr & Eur.

Lejeune, F. & Stiennon. La Legende de Roland dans l'Art du Moyen Age. 125.00 (*0-685-34014-7*) Fr & Eur.

Lejeune, Jean-Francois, ed. Modern Cities. (New City Ser.: Vol. 3). (Illus.). 160p. (Orig.). 1996. pap. 25.00 (*1-56898-058-2*) Princeton Arch.

***Lejeune, Jean-Francois & Shulman, Allan T.** Making of Miami Beach, 1933-1941: The Architecture of Lawrence Murray Dixon. (Illus.). 240p. 2000. text 50.00 (*0-8478-2280-X*) Rizzoli Intl.

Lejeune, Jean-Francois, jt. ed. see Culot, Maurice.

Lejeune, John A. The Reminiscences of a Marine. Kohn, Richard H., ed. LC 78-22384. (American Military Experience Ser.). (Illus.). 1980. reprint ed. lib. bdg. 37.95 (*0-405-11860-0*) Ayer.

— The Reminiscences of a Marine. (Illus.). 488p. reprint ed. 8.95 (*0-686-30999-5*) Marine Corps.

Lejeune, P. Counsels of Perfection for Christian Mothers. 256p. 1998. reprint ed. 21.95 (*0-912141-58-1*) Roman Cath Bks.

Lejeune, Philippe. On Autobiography. Eakin, Paul J., ed. Leary, Katherine, tr. (Theory & History of Literature Ser.: Vol. 52). 1989. pap. 19.95 (*0-8166-1632-9*) U of Minn Pr.

LeJeune, Shonda. God Is... LC 97-140620. (Illus.). 28p. (J). 1996. 12.95 (*0-87516-689-X*) DeVorss.

— Love Is . . . LC 96-204003. (Illus.). 28p. (J). 1996. 12.95 (*0-87516-691-1*); pap. 9.95 (*0-87516-690-3*) DeVorss.

Lejins, Atis, jt. ed. see Huldt, Bo.

Lejk, Mark, jt. auth. see Deeks, David.

Lejnieks, Vincent Arturs, jt. auth. see Benson, Victoria Harnish.

Lejour, Madeleine. Vertical Mammaplasty & Liposuction. (Illus.). 1994. VHS 75.00 (*1-57626-042-9*) Quality Med Pub.

Lekachman. Capitalism for Beginners. (Documentary Comic Bks.). (Illus.). 1986. 6.95 (*0-317-03094-9*) Writers & Readers.

Lekai, Louis J. The Cistercians: Ideals & Reality. LC 77-3692. (Illus.). 534p. 1977. 35.00 (*0-87338-201-3*) Kent St U Pr.

— Nicolas Cotheret's Annals of Citeaux, Outlined from the Original French. (Cistercian Studies: 57). 1983. pap. 13.95 (*0-87907-857-X*) Cistercian Pubns.

Lekakis, J. N. Freer Trade, Sustainability & the Primary Production Sector: Unraveling the Evidence from Greece. LC 98-20770. (Economy & Environment Ser.). 30p. 1998. 99.00 (*0-7923-5151-7*) Kluwer Academic.

Lekas, Danny. Complete Works, Vol. 1. LC 84-90478. (Orig.). 1984. pap. 2.00 (*0-930759-00-1*) D Lekas.

— Complete Works, Vol. 2. LC 84-90478. (Orig.). 1985. pap. 2.00 (*0-930759-01-X*) D Lekas.

— PM. LC 84-91446. 1985. pap. 2.00 (*0-930759-05-2*) D Lekas.

Lekas, Steve, et al. Signal Conditioning & PC-Based Data Acquisition Handbook: A Reference on Analog & Digital Signal Conditioning for PC-Based Data Acquisition. LC 97-161602. (Illus.). 128p. 1997. pap. 25.95 (*0-9656789-0-3*) IOtech.

— Signal Conditioning & PC-Based Data Acquisition Handbook: A Reference on Analog & Digital Signal Conditioning for PC-Based Data Acquisition. (Illus.). 128p. 1998. pap. 25.95 (*0-9656789-1-1*) IOtech.

Lekatsas, Barbara. Persephone. Barkan, Stanley H., ed. Anghelaki-Rooke, Katerina, tr. (Review Woman Writers Chapbook Ser.: No. 1). (ENG & GRE.). 20p. 1986. 15.00 (*0-89304-400-8*, CCC160); pap. 5.00 (*0-89304-401-6*) Cross-Cultrl NY.

— Persephone: Mini Book. Barkan, Stanley H., ed. Anghelaki-Rooke, Katerina, tr. (Review Woman Writers Chapbook Ser.: No. 1). (ENG & GRE.). 20p. 1986. 15.00 (*0-89304-402-4*); pap. 5.00 (*0-89304-403-2*) Cross-Cultrl NY.

Lekatsas, Barbara, compiled by. The Howard L. & Muriel Weingrow Collection of Avant-Garde Art & Literature at Hofstra University: An Annotated Bibliography. LC 85-12659. (Illus.). 322p. 1985. lib. bdg. 195.00 (*0-313-25090-1*, LWC/, Greenwood Pr) Greenwood.

Lekatsos, Anthony, tr. see Makrakis, Apostolos.

LeKemp, pseud. A Boat Buyer's Guide: Answers to Questions You Have about Boating but Don't Know Who to Ask. rev. ed. Orig. Title: A Boat Buyer's Handbook. (Illus.). 1991. reprint ed. pap. 7.00 (*0-9627438-2-8*) L E Kemppainen.

Leker, Andrew, et al. Skyrealms of Jorune: The Role Playing Game. 3rd ed. (Illus.). 216p. 1992. pap. text 20.00 (*1-883240-00-X*) Chessex.

Leker, Andrew, jt. auth. see Coleman, Joseph S.

Lekeux, Martial. The Art of Prayer. Oligny, Paul J., tr. LC 59-14706. 314p. reprint ed. pap. 97.40 (*0-8357-5764-1*, 202257000028) Bks Demand.

Lekeux, Pierre. Pulmonary Function in Healthy, Exercising & Diseased Animals. (Illus.). 402p. 1993. 44.00 (*90-74070-02-7*) Vet Lrn Syst.

Lekhnitskii, S. G. Anisotropic Plates. 2nd ed. xvi, 534p. 1968. text 338.00 (*0-677-20670-4*) Gordon & Breach.

***Lekhnitskii, S. G. & Guegan, J. F., eds.** Artificial Neuronal Networks: Application to Ecology & Evolution. (Environmental Science Ser.). (Illus.). xviii, 244p. 2000. 92.00 (*3-540-66921-3*) Spr-Verlag.

Leki, Ilona. Academic Writing: Exploring Processes & Strategies. 2nd ed. 464p. (C). 1995. pap. text 24.95 (*0-521-65768-7*) Cambridge U Pr.

— Academic Writing: Exploring Processes & Strategies: Instructor's Manual. 30p. (C). 1995. pap., teacher ed. 6.00 (*0-521-65767-9*) Cambridge U Pr.

— Understanding ESL Writers: A Guide for Teachers. LC 91-35814. 151p. (C). 1992. pap. text 23.50 (*0-86709-303-X*, 0303, Pub. by Boynton Cook Pubs) Heinemann.

Lekic, Anita. The Poetry of Vasko Popa. LC 92-7285. (Balkan Studies: Vol. 2). XIV, 178p. (C). 1993. text 44.95 (*0-8204-1777-7*) P Lang Pubng.

Lekic, Maria. Articles from Obonyok: Everything You Need to Know to Meet New Challenges & Take Control of Your Career. 1994. 11.25 (*0-8442-4276-4*, VGM Career) NTC Contemp Pub Co.

Lekic, Maria D. Ogonyok. (RUS., Illus.). 128p. 1995. pap. 49.95 incl. audio (*0-8442-4273-X*) NTC Contemp Pub Co.

— Ogonyok: Advanced. (RUS.). 160p. (YA). 1994. teacher ed. 10.60 (*0-685-62844-2*, F4276-4, Natl Textbk Co) NTC Contemp Pub Co.

— Ogonyok: Advanced. (RUS.). 144p. (YA). 1994. pap. 26.75 (*0-8442-4275-6*, F4275-6, Natl Textbk Co) NTC Contemp Pub Co.

Lekic, Maria D., et al. Peers/Rovesniki: Russian Language Through Culture. Davidson, Dan, ed. (RUS., Illus.). 454p. (Orig.). 1995. pap. text, teacher ed. 20.00 (*0-9643332-2-8*); VHS 35.00 (*0-9643332-3-6*) ACIE.

— What Do You Think About That? (C). 1994. pap. text 29.90 (*0-9643332-0-1*) ACIE.

Lekieffre, Jean, jt. ed. see El-Sherif, Nabil.

Lekisch, Barbara. Tahoe Place Names. Browning, Peter, ed. LC 88-80574. (Illus.). 192p. (Orig.). (C). 1988. pap. 14.95 (*0-944220-01-0*) Great West Bks.

Lekkerkerker, C., jt. auth. see Gruber, P. M.

Lekner, John. Theory of Reflection of Electromagnetic & Particle Waves. 1987. text 193.50 (*90-247-3418-5*) Kluwer Academic.

Lekofka, Lenard. Secret of Bone Hill. 1981. 5.50 (*0-394-51425-4*) Random.

Lekorwe, M. H., jt. auth. see Edge, Wayne.

Lekshe Tsomo, Kama, ed. Buddhist Women Across Cultures: Realizations. LC 98-34325. (SUNY Series in Feminist Philosophy). 320p. (C). 1999. text 65.50 (*0-7914-4137-7*); pap. text 21.95 (*0-7914-4138-5*) State U NY Pr.

Lekson, Stephen H. The Chaco Meridian: Centers of Political Power in the Ancient Southwest. (Illus.). 234p. 1999. 62.00 (*0-7619-9180-8*); pap. 23.95 (*0-7619-9181-6*) AltaMira Pr.

— Mimbres Archaeology of the Upper Gila, New Mexico. LC 89-20538. (Anthropological Papers: No. 53). 116p. (Orig.). 1990. pap. 35.95 (*0-8165-1164-0*) U of Ariz Pr.

Lekson, Stephen H. & Swentzel, Rina. Ancient Land, Ancestral Places: Paul Logsdon in the Pueblo Southwest. (Illus.). 168p. 1994. pap. 29.95 (*0-89013-246-1*) Museum NM Pr.

***Leksukhum, Sankti.** Golden Temples of Thailand: Buddhist Paintings, 14th-19th Centuries. (Illus.). 2000. 75.00 (*0-8076-1476-9*) Braziller.

Lekven, Shelly D. When I Grow Up. (J). Date not set. 15.95 (*0-399-23124-2*) Putnam Pub Group.

LeLaCheur, Dan. Generational Legacy: Breaking a Curse - Starting a Blessing. LC 95-167518. 187p. 1994. pap. 8.99 (*0-9642286-0-2*) Family Survival.

Lelah, Michael D. & Cooper, Stuart L. Polyurethanes in Medicine. 256p. 1986. 136.00 (*0-8493-6307-1*, R857, CRC Reprint) Franklin.

Leland, Abby P. The Educational Theory & Practice of T. H. Green. LC 78-176984. (Columbia University. Teachers College. Contributions to Education Ser.: No. 46). reprint ed. 37.50 (*0-404-55046-0*) AMS Pr.

Leland, Abigail T. Way Back Yonder. Perkins, Priscilla L., ed. (Illus.). 64p. (Orig.). 1993. pap. 10.00 (*1-881459-11-X*) Eagle Pr SC.

Leland, Arthur & Leland, Lorna. Playground Technique & Playcraft. 1982. 23.95 (*0-8434-0432-9*, Pub. by McGrath NH) Ayer.

Leland, Bruce. Connections: Reading & Writing. 364p. (C). 1995. pap. text 28.95 (*0-8403-7769-X*) Kendall-Hunt.

— Discovery: Writing to Learn. 304p. (C). 1995. per. 28.95 (*0-8403-8230-8*) Kendall-Hunt.

Leland, C. G. Kuloskap the Master & Other Algonquin Poems. 1977. lib. bdg. 59.95 (*0-8490-2120-0*) Gordon Pr.

Leland, Candance. Feelings of Love. 1997. pap. write for info. (*1-57553-537-8*) Watermrk Pr.

Leland, Carole A., jt. auth. see Astin, Helen S.

Leland, Caryn. Licensing Art & Design. rev. ed. LC 95-75288. (Illus.). 128p. 1995. pap. 16.95 (*1-880559-27-7*) Allworth Pr.

Leland, Charles G. The Algonquin Legends of New England. (Illus.). 416p. 1991. reprint ed. pap. 8.95 (*0-486-26944-2*) Dover.

— Aradia: The Gospel of the Witches. 1995. reprint ed. pap. 8.95 (*1-872189-15-6*, Pub. by Mandrake Pr) Holmes Pub.

— Aradia Basic Edition: Gospel of the Witches. 148p. 1989. pap. 7.95 (*0-919345-10-7*) Phoenix WA.

— Aradia or the Gospel of the Witches. White, Nelson & White, Anne, eds. LC 85-52307. 100p. (Orig.). 1986. pap. 18.00 (*0-939856-54-9*) Tech Group.

— Etruscan Roman Remains in Popular Tradition. (Illus.). 392p. 1999. pap. 18.50 (*0-919345-29-8*) Phoenix WA.

— The Gypsies. LC 75-3460. reprint ed. 37.50 (*0-404-16891-4*) AMS Pr.

— Gypsy Sorcery. (Illus.). 288p. 1993. reprint ed. text 45.00 (*1-872736-10-6*, Pub. by Mandrake Pr) Holmes Pub.

— Gypsy Sorcery & Fortune Telling. 304p. 1995. 7.98 (*0-7858-0440-4*) Bk Sales Inc.

— Gypsy Sorcery & Fortune Telling. 1990. pap. 12.95 (*0-8065-1198-2*, Citadel Pr) Carol Pub Group.

— Hans Breitmann's Ballads. 260p. 1965. pap. 2.95 (*0-486-21444-3*) Dover.

— Meister Karl's Sketch-Book. LC 75-104510. reprint ed. lib. bdg. 22.50 (*0-8398-1154-3*) Irvington.

— Memoirs. (American Biography Ser.). 439p. 1991. reprint ed. lib. bdg. 89.00 (*0-7812-8243-8*) Rprt Serv.

— The Mystic Will. 1976. reprint ed. 11.00 (*0-911662-58-8*) Yoga.

— Pidgin-English Sing-Song. LC 74-166796. 1971. reprint ed. 25.00 (*0-403-01418-2*) Scholarly.

Leland, Charles G. & Pazzaglini, Mario. Aradia - Expanded Edition: Gospel of the Witches. expanded ed. (Illus.). 450p. 1998. pap. 21.50 (*0-919345-34-4*) Phoenix WA.

Leland, Charles G., et al. English-Gypsy Songs: In Romany, with Metrical English Translations. LC 75-3459. reprint ed. 32.50 (*0-404-16890-6*) AMS Pr.

Leland, Charles G., tr. see Heine, Heinrich.

Leland, Christopher. The Last Happy Men: The Generation of 1922, Fiction, & the Argentine Reality. (Illus.). 232p. 1986. text 39.95 (*0-8156-2376-3*) Syracuse U Pr.

Leland, Christopher T. Art of Compelling Fiction. LC 97-45986. 224p. 1998. 17.99 (*1-884910-30-0*, Story Press) F & W Pubns Inc.

— Letting Loose. LC 96-16396. 384p. 1996. 23.95 (*0-944072-69-0*) Zoland Bks.

— The Professor of Aesthetics. LC 93-38225. 160p. 1994. 18.95 (*0-944072-37-2*) Zoland Bks.

Leland, Debbie. Aggie Goose Rhymes. (Illus.). 24p. (J). (ps-3). 1998. 17.95 (*0-9667086-0-1*) Wildflower Run.

Leland, Diane S. Clinical Virology. Ozmat, Selma, ed. LC 95-30881. 224p. 1996. pap. text 31.50 (*0-7216-4958-0*, W B Saunders Co) Harcrt Hlth Sci Grp.

Leland, Dorothy K. Sallie Fox: The Story of a Pioneer Girl. LC 95-61289. (Illus.). 128p. (Orig.). (J). (gr. 4-6). 1995. pap. 8.95 (*0-9617357-6-7*) Tomato Enter.

Leland, Dorothy Kupcha. Sallie Fox: The Story of a Pioneer Girl. 1995. 14.05 (*0-606-08862-8*, Pub. by Turtleback) Demco.

Leland, Elizabeth. A Place for Joe. (Illus.). 166p. 1997. 19.95 (*1-878086-60-X*, Pub. by Down Home NC) Blair.

— The Vanishing Coast. (Illus.). 142p. (Orig.). 1996. pap. 10.95 (*0-89587-149-1*) Blair.

Leland, F. G. Advancement of Gear Technology. (Technical Papers: Vol. P229.12). (Illus.). 15p. 1968. pap. text 30.00 (*1-55589-279-5*) AGMA.

Leland, G. Waldo & Mereness, Newton D. Introduction to the American Official Sources for the Economic & Social History of the World War. LC 74-75248. (United States in World War I Ser.). xlvii, 532p. 1974. reprint ed. lib. bdg. 64.95 (*0-89198-109-8*) Ozer.

Leland, Gregory. Presidential Indiscretions: The Unofficial, Unexpurgated Guide to Naughty Behavior Kept Under Wraps (or Under the Covers) by the White House! LC 98-53045. 256p. 1999. pap. 9.95 (*0-440-50792-8*, Dell Trade Pbks) Dell.

Leland, Irene. Amazein' St. Louis. (Illus.). 60p. 1999. pap. write for info. (*0-9646386-2-2*) Uplifting Pr.

— The Maze Comes to Life. LC 95-90293. (Illus.). 199p. 1995. 19.95 (*0-9646386-1-4*) Uplifting Pr.

— On the Right Course. (Illus.). 26p. (J). 1993. pap. text 11.95 (*0-9646386-0-6*) Uplifting Pr.

Leland, Isabella G. Charleston, S. C. Crossroads of History. 1980. 17.95 (*0-89781-008-2*, 3286) Am Historical Pr.

Leland, Jane V., ed. see American Chemical Society Staff.

Leland, John. The Labouryouse Journey & Serche of Johan Leylande for Englandes Antiquitees. LC 74-28871. (English Experience Ser.: No. 750). 1975. reprint ed. 25.00 (*90-221-0750-7*) Walter J Johnson.

— A Voice from South Carolina. LC 72-37310. (Black Heritage Library Collection). 1977. reprint ed. 20.95 (*0-8369-8947-3*) Ayer.

— Writings of the Late Elder John Leland, Including Some Events of His Life. Greene, L. F., ed. LC 73-83420. (Religion in America, Ser. 1). 1977. reprint ed. 60.95 (*0-405-00245-9*) Ayer.

Leland, Joy H. Firewater Myths: North American Indian Drinking & Alcohol Addiction. LC 75-620113. (Monographs: No. 11). 1976. 6.00 (*0-911290-43-5*) Rutgers Ctr Alcohol.

***Leland, Karen.** Customer Service for Dummies. 2nd ed. (For Dummies Ser.). 384p. 1999. pap. 19.99 (*0-7645-5209-0*) IDG Bks.

Leland, L. S., Jr., jt. auth. see Wood, G. A.

Leland, Lorna, jt. auth. see Leland, Arthur.

Leland, Lorrin, ed. The Kansas Experience in Poetry. rev. ed. LC 80-621211. (Kansas Studies). 150p. (Orig.). 1986. reprint ed. pap. text 7.00 (*0-936352-01-9*, B929) U of KS Cont Ed.

Leland, Louis S., jt. ed. see Harris, William.

***Leland, Mary.** The Lie of the Land: Journeys Through Literary Cork. (Illus.). 170p. 2000. pap. 15.95 (*1-85918-231-3*, Pub. by Cork Univ) Stylus Pub VA.

Leland, Nita. Creative Artist. (Illus.). 160p. 1993. pap. 24.99 (*0-89134-465-9*, 30479, North Lght Bks) F & W Pubns Inc.

— Exploring Color. rev. ed. LC 98-16932. (Illus.). 144p. 1998. pap. 24.99 (*0-89134-846-8*, North Lght Bks) F & W Pubns Inc.

***Leland, Nita.** Exploring Color Coloring Book. (Illus.). 50p. 2000. pap., wbk. ed. 29.99 (*0-9677804-3-8*, CB2000) Moonflower.

Leland, Nita & Williams, Virginia L. Creative Collage Techniques. (Illus.). 144p. 1994. 28.99 (*0-89134-563-9*, North Lght Bks) F & W Pubns Inc.

Leland, Ottilie M. & Dubbs Millbrook, Minnie. Master of Precision: Henry M. Leland. LC 66-10501. (Great Lakes Bks.). (Illus.). 300p. 1996. pap. 17.95 (*0-8143-2665-X*) Wayne St U Pr.

Leland, R. P. Stochastic Models for Laser Propagation in Atmospheric Turbulence. (Lecture Notes in Control & Information Sciences: Vol. 133). (Illus.). xii, 145p. 1989. pap. 35.00 (*0-387-51538-0*) Spr-Verlag.

Leland, Thomas. Longsword, Earl of Salisbury: An Historical Romance, 2 vols., Set. LC 73-22765. 420p. 1975. reprint ed. 87.95 (*0-405-06016-5*) Ayer.

Leland, Thomas, tr. see Demosthenes.

Leland, Toni M. Show Your Mini! A Complete How-to Workbook for the First Time Exhibitor. rev. ed. LC 95-74741. (Illus.). 86p. 1998. ring bd. 13.95 (*1-887932-06-2*, SYM, Small Horse Pr) Equine Graph Pubng.

Leland, Toni M., ed. Look It Up! A Comprehensive Equine Glossary. LC 95-74741. (Illus.). 64p. (Orig.). 1996. pap. 6.95 (*1-887932-09-7*, GLS) Equine Graph Pubng.

— The Miniature Horse in Review: A Collection of Articles on Miniature Horses, 1. rev. ed. LC 95-74741. (Illus.). 136p. (Orig.). 1999. pap. text 21.95 (*1-887932-04-6*) Equine Graph Pubng.

— The Miniature Horse in Review Vol. 2: A Collection of Articles on Miniature Horses. rev. ed. (Illus.). 144p. 1998. pap. 23.95 (*1-887932-08-9*, Small Horse Pr) Equine Graph Pubng.

***Leland, Toni M., ed.** So You're Expecting a Foal! A Basic Foaling Handbook. (Illus.). 32p. 1999. pap. 10.00 (*1-887932-07-0*, Small Horse Pr) Equine Graph Pubng.

***Leland, Toni M.** Mini Manual for New Owners: A Guided Tour for the First-Time Miniature Horse Owner. 66p. 1999. pap. 21.95 (*1-887932-05-4*, Small Horse Pr) Equine Graph Pubng.

Leland, Toni M., ed. see Porter, Lorle.

Leland, Toni M., ed. see Tunstall, Cynthia.

Leland, W. G. Guide to Materials for American History in the Libraries & Archives of Paris, 2 Vols. Set. (Carnegie Institute Ser.: Vol. 12). 1969. reprint ed. 120.00 (*0-527-00692-0*) Periodicals Srv.

Leland, W. G., jt. auth. see Van Tyne, C. H.

***Leland Wilder, Effie.** Older but Wilder: More Notes from the Pasture. LC 99-89392. (Paperback Ser.). 2000. 23.95 (*0-7838-8959-3*, G K Hall Lrg Type) Mac Lib Ref.

Leland Wilder, Effie. Older but Wilder: More Notes from the Pasture. LC 98-19371. (Illus.). 179p. (J). 1998. 14.95 (*1-56145-182-7*, Peachtree) Peachtree Pubs.

***Leland Wilder, Effie.** One More Time: (Just for the Fun of It) LC 99-46811. (Illus.). 192p. 1999. 14.95 (*1-56145-213-0*) Peachtree Pubs.

— One More Time: Just for the Fun of It! Notes from Fairacres. large type ed. LC 99-462092. (Paperback Ser.). 160p. 2000. pap. 23.95 (*0-7838-8960-7*, G K Hall Lrg Type) Mac Lib Ref.

Leland Wilder, Effie. Out to Pasture: But Not over the Hill. LC 94-48008. (Illus.). 177p. 1995. 14.95 (*1-56145-101-0*) Peachtree Pubs.

— Over What Hill? Notes from the Pasture. large type ed. LC 96-16513. (Illus.). 180p. 1996. 14.95 (*1-56145-131-2*) Peachtree Pubs.

Lelande, A. Technical & Critical Vocabulary of Philosophy: Vocabulaire Technique et Critique de la Philosophie. 13th ed. (FRE.). 1323p. 1980. 150.00 (*0-8288-2274-3*, F18440) Fr & Eur.

***Lelas, Srdan.** Science & Modernity - Toward an Integral Theory of Science. 304p. 2000. 129.00 (*0-7923-6303-5*) Kluwer Academic.

Lelash, Marjorie, jt. tr. see Pack, Robert.

Lelchuk, Alan. Brooklyn Boy. 298p. 1996. pap. 11.00 (*1-880909-43-X*, Basset Bks) Baskerville.

— On Home Ground. LC 87-8496. (Illus.). 80p. (YA). (gr. 5 up). 1987. 9.95 (*0-15-200560-9*, Gulliver Bks) Harcourt.

— Playing the Game. 361p. 1995. 23.00 (*1-880909-32-4*) Baskerville.

Lelchuk, Janna. I Want to Speak Russian. (Illus.). 204p. 1997. 14.95 (*0-9661269-0-4*) J L Lelchuk

Lele, J. K. & Singh, R. Language & Society: Steps Towards an Integrated Theory. LC 88-24107. (Monographs & Theoretical Studies in Sociology & Anthropology in Honour of Nels Anderson: No. 27). xix, 146p. (Orig.). 1989. pap. 49.00 (*90-04-08789-3*) Brill Academic Pubs.

Lele, Jayant. Elite Pluralism & Class Rule: Political Development in Maharashtra, India. LC 78-21167. 301p. reprint ed. pap. 93.40 (*0-608-16221-3*, 202646700050) Bks Demand.

Lele, Jayant & Tettey, Wisdom, eds. Asia - Who Pays for Growth? Women, Environment, & Popular Movements. LC 95-39635. (Illus.). 296p. 1996. text 79.95 (*1-85521-751-1*, Pub. by Dartmth Pub) Ashgate Pub Co.

L

Lele, Jayant & Vora, Rajendra, eds. Boeings & Bullock Carts Vol. 5: State & Society in India. 1990. 54.00 (*81-7001-067-5*, Pub. by Chanakya) S Asia.

Lele, Jayant, ed. see Navaratna-Bandara, Abeysinghe M.

Lele, Milind M. Creating Strategic Leverage: Matching Company Strengths with Market Opportunities. 352p. 1991. 45.00 (*0-471-63142-6*) Wiley.

Lele, R. D. The Clinical Approach: A Companion for the Practising Doctor. LC 97-164935. (Illus.). 372p. 1997. 49.50 (*0-19-563729-1*) OUP.

Lele, Uma. Agricultural Growth & Assistance to Africa: Lessons of a Quarter Century. LC 89-48873. 106p. 1990. pap. 14.95 (*1-55815-063-3*) ICS Pr.

— The Design of Rural Development: Lessons from Africa. LC 75-10896. 290p. 1984. reprint ed. pap. 89.90 (*0-608-03734-6*, 206455900009) Bks Demand.

***Lele, Uma, et al, eds.** Intellectual Property Rights in Agriculture: The World Bank's Role in Assisting Borrower & Member Countries. LC 99-15437. (Environmentally & Socially Sustainable Development-Rural Development Ser.). 100p. 1999. pap. 22.00 (*0-8213-4496-X*, 14496) World Bank.

Lele, Uma & Nabi, Ijaz, eds. Transitions in Development: The Role of Aid & Commercial Flows. LC 89-26922. 535p. 1990. 34.95 (*1-55815-078-1*); pap. 19.95 (*1-55815-093-5*) ICS Pr.

Leledakis, Kanakis. Society & Psyche: Social Theory & the Unconscious Dimension of the Social. 240p. 1995. 50.00 (*1-85973-062-0*, Pub. by Berg Pubs); pap. 19.50 (*1-85973-067-1*, Pub. by Berg Pubs) NYU Pr.

LeLeers, Stephen V. The Laborer Is Worthy of His Hire, Vol. VII, No. 5. 5th rev. ed. (Illus.). 74p. 1996. pap. 12.00 (*0-9653675-0-9*) NFPC.

Leleu, Joseph Mary. Pray the Rosary. (Illus.). 1980. pap. 0.85 (*0-89942-040-0*, 40/05) Catholic Bk Pub.

— Recemos el Santo Rosario. (SPA., Illus.). 1978. pap. 0.95 (*0-89942-048-6*, 48/S) Catholic Bk Pub.

Leleu, Joseph Mary, tr. see Augustine, Saint.

Leleux, Benoit, jt. auth. see Molian, David.

***LeLeux, Ron.** Louisiana Stories: Growing Up in the Bayou State. 80p. 2000. 29.95 (*0-9700746-0-3*) Sat Morn Pubng.

— West Elizabeth Street: Portraits & Letters. 56p. 1999. pap. 12.00 (*0-9700746-1-1*) Sat Morn Pubng.

Lelevkin, V. M., et al. Physics of Non-Equilibrium Plasmas. LC 92-44398. xviii, 418p. 1992. 166.75 (*0-444-89533-7*, North Holland) Elsevier.

Lelewer, Nancy. Something's Not Right: One Family's Struggle with Learning Disabilities. LC 94-60521. 184p. 1994. 21.95 (*0-9641089-0-9*); pap. 14.95 (*0-9641089-1-7*) VanderWyk & Burnham.

Leliard, J. D. Judicial Terminology. 4th rev. ed. (DUT & FRE.). 413p. 1992. 95.00 (*0-8288-9436-1*) Fr & Eur.

Lelic, Muhidin, jt. auth. see Gajic, Zoran.

Lelie, Herman, jt. auth. see Bateson, Margaret.

Leliepvre, Eugene, jt. auth. see Chartrand, Rene.

Lelievre, Eva, jt. auth. see Courgeau, Daniel.

Lelievre, Jacques-Felix. Jacques-Felix Lelievre's New Louisiana Gardener. Reeves, Sally K., tr. from FRE.Tr. of Jardinier de la Louisiane. (Illus.). 216p. 2000. 29.95 (*0-8071-2479-6*) La State U Pr.

LeLievre, Roger. Know Your Ships 1998: Guide to Boats & Boatwatching on the Great Lakes & St. Lawrence Seaway. 39th ed. (Illus.). 128p. 1998. pap. 12.95 (*1-891849-00-X*) Marine Pub MI.

— Know Your Ships, 1997: Guide to Boatwatching on the Great Lakes & St. Lawrence Seaway. 38th rev. ed. (Illus.). 124p. 1997. pap. 12.95 (*0-9626930-8-1*) Marine Pub MI.

LeLievre, Roger A. & Clayton, Philip A., eds. Know Your Ships, 1999: Guide to Boats & Boatwatching on the Great Lakes & St. Lawrence Seaway. annuals 40th rev. ed. (Illus.). 144p. 1999. pap. 14.95 (*1-891849-01-8*, Pub. by Marine Pub MI) Partners Pubs Grp.

Lelke & Rosenheck, K. Stimulus/Sec Coup/Chrom Cells. 200p. 1987. 115.00 (*0-8493-6536-8*, CRC Reprint) Franklin.

Lelkes, P. I., jt. auth. see Rosenheck, K.

***Lelkes, Peter, ed.** Mechanical Forces & the Endothelium. (Endothelial Cell Research Ser.). 392p. 1999. text 115.00 (*90-5702-447-0*, Harwood Acad Pubs) Gordon & Breach.

Lella, Alexander A. di, see Hartman, Louis F.

Lella, Alexander A. di, see Hartman, Louis F. & Di Lella, Alexander A.

Lella, Alexander A. di, see Sehan, Patrick W.

Lella, Alexander A. di, see Sehan, Patrick W. & Di Lella, Alexander A.

Lella, Alexander Di, see Di Lella, Alexander.

Lellag. Looking Ahead, Level 2. LC 98-128134. (Global Esl/Elt Ser.). 288p. (J). 1998. pap. 29.95 (*0-8384-7911-1*) Heinle & Heinle.

Lellenberg, Jon L. Nova 57 Minor: The Waxing & Waning of the Sixty-First Adventure of Sherlock Holmes. LC 89-80834. (Illus.). 109p. 1990. 19.00 (*0-934468-26-5*, Pub. by Gaslight) Empire Pub Srvs.

Lellenberg, Jon L., ed. Irregular Proceedings of the Mid 'Forties: Archival History of the Baker Street Irregulars. limited ed. (B.S.I. History Ser.: Vol. 4). (Illus.). 400p. (Orig.). 1995. pap. 24.95 (*0-9648788-0-1*) Baker St Irregulars.

Lellepvre, Eugene, jt. auth. see Chartrand, Rene.

Lellie, Herman & Bateson, Margaret. A Victorian Doll House. (Illus.). 4p. (J). 1991. text 19.95 (*0-312-06228-1*) St Martin.

Lellinger, David B. The Ferns & Fern-Allies of Costa Rica, Panama & the Choco Pt. 1: Psilotaceae Through Dicksoniaceae. LC 89-6461. (Pteridolgia Ser.: No. 2A). (Illus.). 364p. 1989. pap. 32.00 (*0-933500-01-7*) Am Fern Soc.

— A Field Manual of the Ferns & Fern-Allies of the United States & Canada. LC 84-22216. (Illus.). 446p. 1985. pap. 34.95 (*0-87474-603-5*, LEFNP) Smithsonian.

Lellis, George P. Bertolt Brecht, "Cahiers du Cinema", & Contemporary Film Theory. Kirkpatrick, Diane, ed. LC 82-2051. (Studies in Cinema: No. 13). 207p. 1982. reprint ed. pap. 64.20 (*0-8357-1300-8*, 207033200078) Bks Demand.

Lello, John. Accountability in Practice. Sayer, John, ed. (Education Ser.). 128p. 1994. 90.00 (*0-304-32748-4*); pap. 33.95 (*0-304-32740-9*) Continuum.

Lello, Richard Di, see Di Lello, Richard.

Lello, Ronald, jt. auth. see Robson, Eric.

Lelmar, Bernard, jt. auth. see Wilson, Samuel.

Leloir, Michel. Dictionnaire du Costume. (FRE.). 400p. 1992. 295.00 (*0-8288-9477-9*) Fr & Eur.

Lelong-Mainaud, Ariane, jt. auth. see Dupin, Jacques.

Lelong, P. Plurisubharmonic Functions & Positive Differential Forms. (Notes on Mathematics & Its Applications Ser.). x, 78p. 1969. text 142.00 (*0-677-30220-7*) Gordon & Breach.

Lelong, P., et al, eds. Seminaire d'Analyse. (Lecture Notes in Mathematics Ser.: Vol. 1198). x, 260p. 1986. 38.95 (*0-387-16762-5*) Spr-Verlag.

Lelong, P. & Gruman, L. Entire Functions of Several Complex Variables. (Grundlehren der Mathematischen Wissenschaften Ser.: Vol. 282). 285p. 1986. 155.95 (*0-387-15296-2*) Spr-Verlag.

***Lelong, Pierre & Dolbeault, P.** Complex Analysis & Geometry: International Conference in Honor of Pierre Lelong. LC 00-37854. (Progress in Mathematics Ser.). 2000. write for info. (*0-8176-6352-5*) Birkhauser.

Lelooska. The Traditional Art of the Mask: Carving a Transformation Mask. (Illus.). 80p. 1996. pap. 19.95 (*0-7643-0028-8*) Schiffer.

Lelooska, Chief. Echoes of the Elders: The Stories & Paintings of Chief Lelooska. Normandin, Christine & Danese, Andrea, eds. LC 97-34242. (Illus.). 38p. (J). (gr. 4-7). 1997. 24.95 incl. audio compact disk (*0-7894-2455-X*) DK Pub Inc.

Leloudis, James L. Schooling the New South: Pedagogy, Self, & Society in North Carolina, 1880-1920. LC 95-26137. (Fred W. Morrison Series in Southern Studies). (Illus.). 352p. (C). 1996. text 45.00 (*0-8078-2265-5*) U of NC Pr.

— Schooling the New South: Pedagogy, Self & Society in North Carolina, 1880-1920. LC 95-26137. (Fred W. Morrison Series in Southern Studies). (Illus.). 358p. (C). 1999. pap. 18.95 (*0-8078-4808-5*) U of NC Pr.

Leloup. American Politics: Institutions & Policies. (C). 1999. pap. text 44.50 (*0-15-507368-0*) Harcourt Coll Pubs.

— American Politics: Policymaking I. (C). 1999. pap. text 36.00 (*0-15-502217-2*, Pub. by Harcourt Coll Pubs) Harcourt.

Leloup, Jean-Yves, compiled by. The Wisdom of Jesus. LC 96-8010. (Illus.). 56p. 1996. 8.95 (*0-7892-0239-5*) Abbeville Pr.

LeLoup, Lance T. The Fiscal Congress: Legislative Control of the Budget, 47. LC 79-6823. (Contributions in Political Science Ser.: No. 47). (Illus.). 227p. 1980. 59.95 (*0-313-22009-3*, LFC/, Greenwood Pr) Greenwood.

Leloup, Lance T. & Shull, Steven A. The President & Congress: Collaboration & Combat in National Policymaking. LC 98-13341. 278p. 1998. pap. text 39.06 (*0-205-26534-0*) Allyn.

Lelvy, Richard N. On Wings of Freedom: The Hillel Haggadah. 15.00 (*0-88125-319-7*) Ktav.

Lelwical, Michelle Mary. Starving for Salvation: The Spiritual Dimensions of Eating Problems among American Girls & Women. LC 98-50120. 224p. 1999. 25.00 (*0-19-512743-9*) OUP.

Lely, Gilbert. Vie du Marquis de Sade. 24.40 (*0-685-34061-9*) Fr & Eur.

Lely, Gilbert, ed. see DeSade, Marquis.

Lelyveld, Arthur. The Steadfast Stream: An Introduction to Jewish Social Values. LC 94-39947. 120p. 1995. pap. 10.95 (*0-8298-1023-4*) Pilgrim OH.

Lelyveld, David. Aligarh's First Generation: Muslim Solidarity in British India. LC 77-71990. 406p. reprint ed. pap. 125.90 (*0-8357-3299-1*, 203952200013) Bks Demand.

Lelyveld, I., jt. auth. see Hutzinger, O.

Lem, Carol. The Hermit's Journey: Tarot Poems for Meditation. 53p. 1992. pap. 9.95 (*1-882868-00-5*) Peddler Pr.

— Moe, Remembrance: (March 17, 1983-February 20, 1996) LC 97-204922. 36p. 1996. pap. 10.00 (*1-882868-05-6*) Peddler Pr.

Lem, Carol, ed. see Lem, Dean P.

Lem, Dean P. Graphics Master No. 6: A Workbook of Planning Aids, Reference Guides, & Graphic Tools for the Design, Planning, Estimating, Preparation & Production of Typography, Electronic Prepress Imaging, Printing, Print Advertising & Desktop Publishing. LC 96-94580. (Illus.). 162p. 1996. 74.50 (*0-914218-10-7*) D Lem Assocs.

— Graphics Master No. 6: A Workbook of Planning Aids, Reference Guides, & Graphic Tools for the Design, Planning, Estimating, Preparation & Production of Typography, Electronic Prepress Imaging, Printing, Print Advertising & Desktop Publishing. LC 96-94580. (Illus.). 162p. (C). 1996. pap. text 54.50 (*0-914218-11-5*) D Lem Assocs.

***Lem, Dean P.** Graphics Master Seven: The One-Volume Workbook of Planning AIDS, Reference Guides & Graphic Tools for Prepress Imaging, Print Production & Internet Publishing. 7th rev ed. Lem, Carol, ed. LC 99-96129. (Illus.). 158p. 2000. 79.50 (*0-914218-12-3*) D Lem Assocs.

Lem, Stanislaw. The Cyberiad: Fables for the Cybernetic Age. Kandel, Michael, tr. LC 84-22589. (Illus.). 304p. (C). 1985. pap. 11.00 (*0-15-623550-1*, Harvest Bks) Harcourt.

— Eden. Heine, Marc E., tr. 1989. 19.95 (*0-15-127580-7*) Harcourt.

— Fiasco. Kandel, Michael, tr. (Helen & Kurt Wolff Bk.). 1987. 17.95 (*0-15-130640-0*) Harcourt.

— Futurological Congress. 1999. lib. bdg. 18.95 (*1-56723-145-4*, 154) Yestermorrow.

— The Futurological Congress. Kandel, Michael, tr. from POL. LC 85-5500. 156p. 1985. reprint ed. pap. 10.00 (*0-15-634040-2*, Harvest Bks) Harcourt.

— Highcastle: A Remembrance. Kandel, Michael, tr. from POL. LC 95-7882.Tr. of Wysoki Zamek. 144p. 1995. 22.00 (*0-15-140218-3*) Harcourt.

— Highcastle: A Remembrance.Tr. of Wysoki Zamek. 160p. 1997. pap. 11.00 (*0-15-600472-0*) Harcourt.

***Lem, Stanislaw.** His Master's Voice. Kandel, Michael, tr. from POL. LC 99-41917. 208p. 1999. pap. 14.95 (*0-8101-1731-2*) Northwestern U Pr.

Lem, Stanislaw. Hospital of the Transfiguration. 228p. 1991. pap. 9.95 (*0-15-642176-3*, Harvest Bks) Harcourt.

— Microworlds: Writings on Science Fiction & Fantasy. Rottensteiner, Franz, ed. 288p. 1986. pap. 11.00 (*0-15-659443-9*, Harvest Bks) Harcourt.

— Mortal Engines. 256p. 1992. pap. 8.95 (*0-15-662161-4*, Harvest Bks) Harcourt.

— One Human Minute. Leach, Catherine S., tr. 112p. 1986. pap. 5.00 (*0-15-668795-X*, Harvest Bks) Harcourt.

— Peace on Earth. Ford, Elinor & Kandel, Michael, trs. from POL. 240p. 1996. pap. 12.00 (*0-15-600242-6*, Harvest Bks) Harcourt.

***Lem, Stanislaw.** A Perfect Vacuum. Kandel, Michael, tr. from POL. LC 99-42422. 240p. 1999. pap. 14.95 (*0-8101-1733-9*) Northwestern U Pr.

Lem, Stanislaw. Return from the Stars. 256p. 1989. pap. 7.95 (*0-15-676593-4*) Harcourt.

— Solaris. 212p. (C). 1987. pap. 11.00 (*0-15-683750-1*, Harvest Bks) Harcourt.

— Solaris. 1999. lib. bdg. 22.95 (*1-56723-146-2*, 155) Yestermorrow.

— Solaris. 1993. reprint ed. lib. bdg. 18.95 (*0-89968-351-7*, Lghtyr Pr) Buccaneer Bks.

— The Star Diaries. Kandel, Michael, tr. LC 83-26385. (Illus.). 286p. 1985. pap. 8.95 (*0-15-684905-4*, Harvest Bks) Harcourt.

— Tales of Pirx the Pilot. Iribarne, Louis, tr. 216p. 1990. pap. 7.95 (*0-15-688150-0*, Harvest Bks) Harcourt.

Lem, Stanislaw & Swirski, Peter. The Lem Reader. LC 97-23102. (Rethinking Theory Ser.). 1997. 49.95 (*0-8101-1494-1*); pap. 14.95 (*0-8101-1495-X*) Northwestern U Pr.

Lem, Winnie. Cultivating Dissent: Work, Identity & Praxis in Rural Languedoc. LC 98-54770. (SUNY Series in National Identities). 268p. (C). 1999. pap. text 19.95 (*0-7914-4188-1*) State U NY Pr.

***Lem, Winnie.** Cultivating Dissent: Work, Identity & Praxis in Rural Languedoc. LC 98-54770. (SUNY Series in National Identities). 2p. (C). 1999. text 59.50 (*0-7914-4187-3*) State U NY Pr.

Lema, Jose & Trevino, Esthela, eds. Theoretical Analysis of Romance Languages: Selected Papers from the 26th Linguistic Symposium on Romance Languages LSRL XXVI, Mexico City, 28-30, 1996. LC 98-13797. (Current Issues in Linguistic Theory Ser.: Vol. 157). viii, 380p. 1998. 89.00 (*1-55619-873-6*) J Benjamins Pubng Co.

Lema, Jose, jt. ed. see Trevino, Esthela.

***Lema Publications Staff.** Aircraft Carriers, Submarines & Cruisers. 1999. pap. text 16.95 (*84-95323-12-5*) LEMA.

— Destroyers, Frigates & Corvettes. 1999. pap. text 16.95 (*84-95323-13-3*) LEMA.

— Diverse Subjects Step by Step. 1999. pap. text 16.95 (*84-95323-08-7*) LEMA.

— Fighter & Stealth Aircraft. 1999. pap. text 16.95 (*84-95323-15-X*) LEMA.

— Minehunters, Patrol Boats & Logistics. 1999. pap. text 16.95 (*84-95323-14-1*) LEMA.

— Techniques & Color. 1999. pap. text 16.95 (*84-95323-10-9*) LEMA.

— Transport, Aircraft & Specialized Carriers. 1999. pap. text 16.95 (*84-95323-17-6*) LEMA.

— Watercolor Painting Flowers. 1999. pap. text 18.95 (*84-89730-97-0*) LEMA.

Lemagny, Jean-Claude, intro. Visionary Architects: Boullee, Ledoux, Lequeu. (Illus.). 240p. 1968. pap. 27.95 (*0-914412-21-3*, Inst Arts Catalogues) Menil Found.

***Lemahan, Rod.** Confrontation Zone: 1989 US Intervention into Panama Operation Just Cause. LC 99-70127. (Illus.). 356p. 1999. 29.95 (*1-886391-40-8*) Narwhal Pr.

LeMahieu, D. L. A Culture for Democracy: Mass Communication & the Cultivated Mind in Britain Between the Wars. (Illus.). 408p. 1988. text 85.00 (*0-19-820137-0*) OUP.

— The Mind of William Paley: A Philosopher & His Age. LC 75-22547. 229p. reprint ed. pap. 71.00 (*0-7837-6172-4*, 204589400009) Bks Demand.

Lemaine, Gerard. Perspectives on the Emergence of Scientific Disciplines. 1977. text 38.50 (*90-279-7743-7*) Mouton.

Lemaine, Gerard & Lemaine, Jean-Marie. Psychologie Sociale et Experimentation. (Textes de Sciences Sociales Ser.: No. 2). 1969. pap. 26.95 (*90-279-6308-8*) Mouton.

Lemaine, Gerard, et al, eds. Strategies et Choix dans la Recherche. (Maison des Sciences de l'Homme, Paris, Publications: No. 5). 1977. pap. 33.85 (*90-279-7674-0*) Mouton.

***Lemaine, Jean G.** La Pareja Humana: Su Vida, Muerte y Estructura. rev. ed. 358p. 1999. pap. 8.99 (*968-16-2140-9*) Fondo CA.

Lemaine, Jean-Marie, jt. auth. see Lemaine, Gerard.

Lemaire. Applications of Statistics & Probability, Vol. 1. 707p. 1995. 110.00 (*90-5410-564-X*) Ashgate Pub Co.

Lemaire & Favre. Applications of Statistics & Probability, Vol. 2. 700p. 1995. 110.00 (*90-5410-565-8*) Ashgate Pub Co.

Lemaire, Anika. Jacques Lacan. 292p. (C). 1979. pap. 27.99 (*0-415-07844-X*) Routledge.

— Jacques Lacan. Macey, David, tr. from FRE. 1979. reprint ed. pap. 14.95 (*0-7100-0350-1*, Routledge Thoemms) Routledge.

***Lemaire, Barbara, ed.** ElectriGuide 2000: A Comprehensive Directory of the Electrical Industry. 502p. 2000. pap. 39.95 (*0-915955-16-4*) Trade Srv Corp.

Lemaire, Donald, jt. ed. see Boyle, Richard.

Lemaire, F., ed. Mechanical Ventilation. xii, 198p. 1991. pap. 63.00 (*0-387-53322-2*) Spr-Verlag.

LeMaire, Francois, jt. ed. see Zapol, Warren M.

***Lemaire, G., et al, eds.** Grassland Ecophysiology & Grazing Ecology. (Cabi Publishing Ser.). (Illus.). 352p. 2000. text 100.00 (*0-85199-452-0*) OUP.

Lemaire, Gerard-Georges, ed. Calder. Hawkes, Sophie, tr. from FRE. (Great Modern Masters Ser.). (Illus.). 64p. 1998. 11.98 (*0-8109-4668-8*, Pub. by Abrams) Time Warner.

Lemaire, Gilles. Diagnosis of the Nitrogen Status in Crops. LC 96-52379. (Applied Agriculture Ser.). 1997. write for info. (*3-540-62223-3*) Spr-Verlag.

LeMaire, H. Paul. Personal Decisions. LC 81-43668. 220p. (Orig.). 1982. pap. text 21.50 (*0-8191-2330-7*) U Pr of Amer.

Lemaire, J., et al. Radiation Belts: Models & Standards. LC 96-48740. (Geophysical Monographs: Vol. 97). 1996. 55.00 (*0-87590-079-8*) Am Geophysical.

Lemaire, J. F. & Gringauz, K. I. The Earth's Plasmasphere. LC 96-38481. (Cambridge Atmospheric & Space Science Ser.). (Illus.). 372p. (C). 1998. text 90.00 (*0-521-43091-7*) Cambridge U Pr.

Lemaire, Jean. Automobile Insurance: Actuarial Models. (S. S. Huebner International Ser.). 1985. lib. bdg. 72.50 (*0-89838-166-5*) Huebner Foun Insur.

— Automobile Insurance: Actuarial Models. (C). 1985. 340.00 (*0-7855-4318-X*, Pub. by Witherby & Co) St Mut.

— Bonus-Malus Systems in Automobile Insurance. LC 94-41825. (Huebner International Series on Risk, Insurance, & Economic Security: Vol. 19). 312p. (C). 1995. lib. bdg. 85.00 (*0-7923-9545-X*) Huebner Foun Insur.

Lemaire, Jean & Subramanian, Krupa. Insurance Regulation in Europe & the United States. LC 97-66208. (S. S. Huebner International Ser.). 152p. 1997. pap. 22.95 (*0-918930-16-2*) Huebner Foun Insur.

Lemaire, Jeanie. The Body Talks & I Can Hear It. Codye, Corinn, ed. LC 95-80304. 272p. 1995. pap. 14.95 (*0-9648540-0-7*) Balancing Arts.

Lemaire, Jeanie & Codye, Corinn. Magical Essence of Being: Human & Divine Imagenetics & Humanology in Motion. LC 98-71299. (Illus.). 224p. 1998. pap. 17.95 (*0-9648540-1-5*) Balancing Arts.

Lemaire, Luc, jt. auth. see Eells, James.

Lemaire, M., et al, eds. Applications of Statistics & Probability-Civil Engineering Reliability & Risk Analysis: Proceedings of the 7th International Conference, Paris, 10-13 July 1995, 3 vols. (Illus.). 1800p. (C). 1995. 291.00 (*90-5410-563-1*, Pub. by A A Balkema) Ashgate Pub Co.

Lemaire, Maurice, et al, eds. Applications of Statistics & Probability: Civil Engineering Reliability & Risk Analysis: Proceedings, ICASP 7 Conference on Applications of Statistics & Probability, 1995, Paris, France. 1540p. 1996. 110.00 (*90-5410-566-6*, Pub. by A A Balkema) Ashgate Pub Co.

Lemaire, P. G. Les Ondelettes en, 1989: Seminaire d'Analyse Harmonique Universite de Paris-Sud, Orsay. Dold, A. et al, eds. (Lecture Notes in Mathematics Ser.: Vol. 1438). v, 212p. 1990. 41.95 (*0-387-52932-2*) Spr-Verlag.

LeMaistre, JoAnn. After the Diagnosis. LC 95-61134. 228p. (Orig.). 1996. pap. 12.95 (*1-56975-046-7*) Ulysses Pr.

— Beyond Rage: Mastering Unavoidable Health Changes. rev. ed. LC 93-36467. 208p. 1993. 24.95 (*0-931712-11-4*) Alpine Guild.

Lemaitre, ed. see Enerval, Gerard.

LeMaitre, Corene. April Rising. 288p. 2000. 23.95 (*0-7867-0654-6*) Carroll & Graf.

Lemaitre, Georges E. From Cubism to Surrealism in French Literature. LC 77-18121. (Illus.). 256p. 1978. reprint ed. lib. bdg. 65.00 (*0-313-20112-9*, LEFC, Greenwood Pr) Greenwood.

Lemaitre, Henri. Dictionnaire Bordas de Litterature Francaise, 4 vols. (FRE.). 1994. 780.00 (*0-7859-8614-6*, 204019682X) Fr & Eur.

— Le Litterature Francaise, 5 tomes. Incl. Tome I. Du Moyen Age a L'age Baroque. 29.95 Tome II. Des Classiques aux Philosophes. 29.95 Tome III. Evolutions du Dix-Neuvieme Siecle. 29.95 Tome IV. Metamorphoses du Vingtieme Siecle. 29.95 Tome V. Litterature Aujourd'hui. 17.50 write for info. (*0-318-52038-9*) Fr & Eur.

— Poesie Depuis Baudelaire. 368p. 1965. 39.95 (*0-8288-7422-0*) Fr & Eur.

Lemaitre, Henri, ed. Litterature Francaise, 5 tomes, Vol. 1. write for info. (*0-8288-7876-6*, FA104) Fr & Eur.

Lemaitre, Henri, ed. see Baudelaire, Charles.

Lemaitre, Jean P. A Course on Damage Mechanics. (Illus.). 250p. 1992. 103.95 (*0-387-53609-4*) Spr-Verlag.

An Asterisk (*) at the beginning of an entry indicates that the title is appearing for the first time.

— A Course on Damage Mechanics. 2nd enl. ed. LC 96-15592. 210p. 1996. pap. 59.95 (*3-540-60980-6*) Spr-Verlag.

Lemaitre, Jean P. & Chaboche, Jean-Louis. Mechanics of Solid Materials. (Illus.). 582p. (C). 1994. pap. text 39.95 (*0-521-47758-1*) Cambridge U Pr.

Lemaitre, Jean P. & Krajcinovic, Dusan, eds. Continuum Damage Mechanics: Theory & Applications. (CISM Ser.: Vol. 295). (Illus.). v, 294p. 1988. 59.95 (*0-387-82011-6*) Spr-Verlag.

Lemaitre, Joseph. French: How to Speak & Write It. (Illus.). 403p. 1962. pap. 8.95 (*0-486-20268-2*) Dover.

Lemaitre, Jules. On the Margins of Old Books. Stratton, Clarence, tr. LC 70-163041. (Short Story Index Reprint Ser.). 1977. reprint ed. 23.95 (*0-8369-3955-7*) Ayer.

Lemaitre, Jules & Cavaignac, Godegroy. En Marge des Vieux Livres: Contes, 2 vols. LC 75-41173. (FRE.). reprint ed. 72.50 (*0-404-15020-9*) AMS Pr.

Lemaitre, Nicole, et al. Dictionnaire Culturel du Christianisme. (FRE.). 332p. 1994. write for info. (*0-7859-7723-6*, 2091800813) Fr & Eur.

Lemaitre, Pascal. Zelda's Secret. LC 93-28448. (Illus.). (J). (ps-3). 1997. pap. 3.95 (*0-8167-3310-4*, Troll Medallion) Troll Communs.

Lemaitre, Rafael. A Review of the Hermit Crabs of the Genus Xylopagurus A. Milne Edwards, 1880 (Crustacea: Decapoda: Paguridae), Including Descriptions of Two New Species. LC 94-37724. (Smithsonian Contributions to Zoology Ser.: Vol. 570). 31p. 1995. reprint ed. pap. 30.00 (*0-608-00511-8*, 206133100008) Bks Demand.

Lemaitre, Solange. Ramakrishna & the Vitality of Hinduism. Markmann, Charles L., tr. from FRE. LC 68-54059. (Spiritual Masters Ser.). (Illus.). 224p. 1984. 18.95 (*0-87951-194-X*, Pub. by Overlook Pr) Penguin Putnam.

— Ramakrishna & the Vitality of Hinduism. Markmann, Charles L., tr. from FRE. LC 68-54059. (Spiritual Masters Ser.). (Illus.). 224p. 1986. pap. 9.95 (*0-87951-241-5*, Pub. by Overlook Pr) Penguin Putnam.

Lemak, N. A., jt. auth. see Gehan, E. A.

Lemak, Noreen A., jt. auth. see Fields, William S.

Lemak, Noreen A., jt. auth. see Freireich, Emil J.

Leman, jt. auth. see Byram, Michael.

Leman, Arthur. Boats, Planes & Murphy's Law. (Illus.). 173p. 1999. write for info. (*0-9649988-0-7*) Attleborough.

Leman, Bonnie & Martin, Judy. Log Cabin Quilts. 36p. 1980. pap. 5.95 (*0-9602970-1-4*) Leman Pubns.

— Taking the Math Out of Making Patchwork Quilts. (Illus.). (Orig.). 1981. pap. 4.95 (*0-9602970-3-0*) Leman Pubns.

Leman, Bonnie & Townsend, Louise O. How to Make a Quilt: Twenty-Five Easy Lessons for Beginners. 2nd rev. ed. (Illus.). 44p. 1986. reprint ed. pap. 7.95 (*0-9602970-4-9*) Leman Pubns.

Leman, Bonnie, jt. auth. see Quilter's Newsletter Magazine Editors.

Leman Chall, Sally. Making God Real to Your Children. 192p. (Orig.). (gr. 11). 1995. mass mkt. 5.99 (*0-8007-8630-0*, Spire) Revell.

Leman, Chris, jt. auth. see Leman, Laurie.

***Leman, Derek.** Proverbial Wisdom & Common Sense: A Messianic Jewish Approach to Today's Issues from the Proverbs. LC 99-32303. 248p. 1999. pap. 12.99 (*1-880226-78-2*, Pub. by M J Pubs) Spring Arbor Dist.

Leman, Derek. The Y'shua Challenge Pt. II: A Basic Study Guide. 28p. 1998. pap. 3.00 (*1-881022-38-2*, BT042) Purple Pomegranate.

***Leman, Elena M.** Cheyenne Major Constituent Order. 106p. 1999. pap. 15.00 (*1-55671-015-1*) S I L Intl.

Leman, J. From Challenging Culture to Challenged Culture: The Sicilian Cultural Code & the Socio-Cultural Praxis of Sicilian Immigrants in Belgium. (Studia Anthropologica Ser.: No. 1). 197p. (Orig.). 1987. pap. 44.00 (*90-6186-235-3*, Pub. by Leuven Univ) Coronet Bks.

Leman, Johan, ed. The Dynamics of Emerging Ethnicities: Immigrant & Indigenous Ethnogenesis in Confrontation. LC 98-205665. 179p. 1998. pap. 19.95 (*3-631-33107-X*) P Lang Pubng.

Leman, Kevin. El Amor Comienza en la Cocina. Farias, Monica R., tr. from ENG.Tr. of Sex Begins in the Kitchen. (SPA.). 144p. 1986. pap. 7.99 (*0-88113-013-3*) Caribe Betania.

— Becoming a Couple of Promise. (Illus.). 174p. 1999. pap. 12.00 (*1-57683-129-9*) NavPress.

— Becoming the Parent God Wants You to Be. LC 98-230256. 1998. pap. 12.00 (*1-57683-100-0*) NavPress.

— The Birth Order Book: Why You Are The Way You Are. 256p. 1992. pap. 10.95 (*0-440-50471-6*, Dell Trade Pbks) Dell.

— Bonkers: Why Women Get Stressed Out & What They Can Do about It. 302p. (gr. 11). 1994. mass mkt. 5.99 (*0-8007-8612-2*, Spire) Revell.

— Bringing up Kids Without Tearing Them Down. 1995. 16.99 (*1-56179-276-4*) Focus Family.

— Bringing up Kids Without Tearing Them Down. 384p. 1995. pap. 12.99 (*0-7852-7806-0*, J Thoma Bks) Nelson.

— Chicas Inteligentes No lo Hacen. 1997. pap. text 14.98 (*968-13-1791-2*) Edit Diana.

— Keeping Your Family Together When the World Is Falling Apart. LC 93-5068. 1993. reprint ed. 14.99 (*1-56179-180-6*) Focus Family.

— Living in a Stepfamily Without Getting Stepped On. LC 94-3565. 1994. 19.99 (*0-8407-3492-1*) Nelson.

— Making Children Mind Without Losing Yours. 192p. 1987. pap. 10.95 (*0-440-55184-6*) Dell.

— Making Children Mind Without Losing Yours. 192p. (gr. 10). 1994. pap. 10.99 (*0-8007-5256-2*) Revell.

***Leman, Kevin.** Making Children Mind Without Losing Yours. 2nd ed. 272p. 2000. pap., student ed. 12.99 (*0-8007-5731-9*) Chosen Bks.

Leman, Kevin. The New Birth Order Book: Why You Are the Way You Are. 2nd rev. ed. LC 98-28465. 368p. 1998. pap. 11.99 (*0-8007-5679-7*) Revell.

— Obtenga Lo Mejor de Sus Hijos, Antes Que Acaben Con Usted.Tr. of Getting the Best out of Your Kids, Before They Get the Best of You. (SPA.). 192p. 1996. 8.99 (*0-88113-141-5*, B023-1415) Caribe Betania.

— Sex Begins in the Kitchen: Because Love Is an All-Day Affair. 2nd ed. LC 99-22767. 269p. 1999. pap. 11.99 (*0-8007-5709-2*) Revell.

— Sexo y Comunicacion en el Matrimonio. (Serie Enfoque a la Familia - Focus on the Family Ser.).Tr. of Sex & Communication in Marriage. (SPA.). 30p. 1992. pap. 1.99 (*1-56063-260-7*, 497416) Editorial Unilit.

— The Six Stress Points in a Woman's Life. LC 98-31891. Orig. Title: Bonkers. 192p. 1999. pap. 9.99 (*0-8007-5691-6*, Bonkers) Revell.

— What a Difference a Daddy Makes: The Indelible Imprint a Dad Leaves on His Daughter's Life. LC 99-22184. 256p. 2000. 19.99 (*0-8407-3449-2*) Nelson.

— When Your Best Is Not Good Enough: The Secret of Measuring Up. LC 97-25997. 256p. 1997. pap. 9.99 (*0-8007-5636-3*, Measuring Up) Revell.

— Winning the Rat Race Without Becoming a Rat: The Psychology of Winning in Business. LC 96-14886. 256p. 1996. 19.99 (*0-8407-3491-3*, J Thoma Bks) Nelson.

— Women Who Try Too Hard: Breaking the Pleaser Habits. LC 97-53306. 320p. 1998. pap. 10.99 (*0-8007-5652-5*, The Pleasers) Revell.

Leman, Kevin & Carlson, Randy. Unlocking the Secrets of Your Childhood Memories. 288p. 1990. mass mkt. 5.99 (*0-671-70317-X*) PB.

Leman, Laurie & Leman, Chris. Mountain Bike! Oregon. LC 98-30987. (Mountain Bike! Ser.). (Illus.). 400p. 1998. pap. 15.95 (*0-89732-281-9*) Menasha Ridge.

Leman, Marc. Music & Schema Theory: Cognitive Foundations of Systematic Musicology, Vol. 31. LC 95-4478. (Springer Series in Information Sciences). 1995. 84.95 (*3-540-60021-3*) Spr-Verlag.

Leman, Marc, ed. Music, Gestalt, & Computing: Studies in Cognitive & Systematic Musicology, Vol. 131. LC 97-39887. (Lecture Notes in Artificial Intelligence: Vol. 1317). ix, 524p. 1997. pap. 69.00 (*3-540-63526-2*) Spr-Verlag.

Leman-Stefanovic, I. The Event of Death: A Phenomenological Enquiry. 362p. (C). 1986. text 161.50 (*90-247-3414-2*) Kluwer Academic.

Leman, Walter M. Memoirs of an Old Actor. LC 78-91905. 1972. 26.95 (*0-405-08741-1*) Ayer.

— Memories of an Old Actor. (American Biography Ser.). 406p. 1991. reprint ed. lib. bdg. 89.00 (*0-7812-8244-6*) Rprt Serv.

— Memories of an Old Actor. LC 70-106905. 1970. reprint ed. 16.00 (*0-403-00199-4*) Scholarly.

Leman, Wayne, jt. auth. see Risingsun, Ted.

Lemann, Arthur A., III. Hail to the Dragon Slayer. Neil, Winter C., III, ed. (Illus.). 256p. 1998. 24.95 (*0-9653145-6-1*, VCCI) Pontalba Pr.

Lemann, Bernard, et al, eds. Talk about Architecture: A Century of Architectural Education at Tulane. LC 93-60383. (Illus.). 247p. 1993. 40.00 (*0-9637302-0-7*) Tulane U Archit.

Lemann, Nancy. The Fiery Pantheon: A Novel. LC 97-28222. 256p. 1998. 21.50 (*0-684-84114-2*) S&S Trade.

— The Fiery Pantheon: A Novel. 256p. 1999. per. 11.00 (*0-684-85205-5*) S&S Trade.

— Lives of the Saints. (Voices of the South Ser.). 160p. 1997. pap. 13.95 (*0-8071-2162-2*) La State U Pr.

— Sportsman's Paradise. LC 99-15678. (Voices of the South Ser.). 240p. 1999. pap. 15.95 (*0-8071-2417-6*) La State U Pr.

Lemann, Nicholas. The Big Test: The Secret History of the American Meritocracy. LC 99-32036. 368p. 1999. 27.00 (*0-374-29984-6*) FS&G.

***Lemann, Nicholas.** The Big Test: The Secret History of the American Meritocracy. 416p. 2000. pap. 15.00 (*0-374-52751-2*) FS&G.

Lemann, Nicholas. On Meritocracy. 1999. write for info. (*0-679-42176-9*) Knopf.

— Out of the Forties. 152p. 1998. pap. 24.95 (*1-56098-772-3*) Smithsonian.

— The Promised Land. 320p. 1992. pap. 16.00 (*0-679-73347-7*) McKay.

— The Promised Land: The Great Black Migration & How It Changed America. 1992. pap. 13.00 (*0-685-57357-5*) Vin Bks.

Lemanski, A. J. Advanced Measuring Technique for In-Process Control of Spiral Bevel Gearing. (1985 Fall Technical Meeting Ser.: Vol. 85FTM10). (Illus.). 15p. 1985. pap. text 30.00 (*1-55589-103-9*) AGMA.

Lemanski, A. J., jt. auth. see Kelley, B. W.

Lemanski, Pietrek. Performance Acrobatics. unabridged ed. Fife, Bruce, ed. LC 98-38270. (Illus.). 80p. 1998. pap. 10.00 (*0-941599-38-8*, Pub. by Piccadilly Bks) Empire Pub Srvs.

Lemar, Natalie. Why the Mirrors Speak So Loud: The Journey to Inner Peace. 92p. 1999. pap. 9.95 (*0-9668953-0-4*) Lipstick Publ.

Lemar, J. & Mast, Lois A. A Journey Through Europe. 20p. 1992. pap. 4.00 (*1-883294-06-1*) Masthof Pr.

Lemarchand-Beraud, T. & Fossati, P., eds. Androgens: Pathophysiological & Behavioural Aspects. (Journal: Hormone Research Ser.: Vol. 18, No. 1-3). (Illus.). 152p. 1983. pap. 71.50 (*3-8055-3728-X*) S Karger.

Lemarchand-Beraud, T. & Vanhaelst, L., eds. Actual Trends in Thyroid Physiopathology. (Journal: Hormone Research Ser.: Vol. 26, No. 1-4, 1987). ii, 230p. 1987. 168.75 (*3-8055-4582-7*) S Karger.

Lemarchand, Elizabeth. The Affacombe Affair. large type ed. 1979. 12.00 (*0-7089-0280-4*) Ulverscroft.

— Buried in the Past. large type ed. 1976. 12.00 (*0-85456-431-4*) Ulverscroft.

— Death on Doomsday. large type ed. 1973. 12.00 (*0-85456-173-0*) Ulverscroft.

— The Glade Manor Murder. large type ed. (Mystery Ser.). 304p. 1992. 11.50 (*0-7089-2647-9*) Ulverscroft.

— Light Through Glass. large type ed. 288p. 1986. 15.95 (*0-7089-1505-1*) Ulverscroft.

— Who Goes Home? 192p. 1987. 15.95 (*0-8027-5675-1*) Walker & Co.

— Who Goes Home? large type ed. 304p. 1987. 27.99 (*0-7089-1599-X*) Ulverscroft.

Lemarchand, Guillermo A., ed. Scientists, Peace & Disarmament. 396p. (C). 1988. text 89.00 (*9971-5-0761-7*) World Scientific Pub.

Lemarchand, Rene. Burundi: Ethnic Conflict & Genocide. LC 96-233050. (Woodrow Wilson Center Press Ser.). 232p. 1996. pap. text 18.95 (*0-521-56623-1*) Cambridge U Pr.

— Burundi: Ethnocide As Discourse & Practice. (Woodrow Wilson Center Press Ser.). 232p. (C). 1994. text 64.95 (*0-521-45176-0*) Cambridge U Pr.

Lemarchand, Rene, ed. African Kingships in Perspective: Political Change & Modernization in Monarchical Settings. 325p. 1977. 55.00 (*0-7146-3027-6*, Pub. by F Cass Pubs) Intl Spec Bk.

— American Policy in Southern Africa: The Stakes & the Stance. 2nd ed. LC 80-6222. 513p. (C). 1981. lib. bdg. 57.00 (*0-8191-1436-7*) U Pr of Amer.

— The Green & the Black: Qadhafi's Policies in Africa. LC 87-46088. (Indiana Series in Arab & Islamic). (Illus.). 198p. 1988. 32.50 (*0-253-32678-8*) Ind U Pr.

Lemarchand, Rene, et al. Political Awakening in the Belgian Congo. LC 82-2986. (Illus.). 357p. 1982. reprint ed. lib. bdg. 75.00 (*0-313-23415-9*, LEP0L, Greenwood Pr) Greenwood.

Lemarchand, Rene, ed. see Eisenstadt, Samuel N.

Lemarchand, Yannick & Parker, R. H., eds. Accounting in France/La Comptabilite en France: Historical Essays/Etudes Historiques. LC 95-51118. (New Works in Accounting History). (FRE & ENG.). 456p. 1996. reprint ed. text 108.00 (*0-8153-2270-4*) Garland.

Lemard, Joseph A. History of Olmsted County, Minnesota. (Illus.). 674p. 1994. reprint ed. lib. bdg. 67.50 (*0-8328-3617-6*) Higginson Bk Co.

Lemare, Edwin H. Organs I Have Met. (Illus.). 137p. 1992. 25.00 (*0-913746-32-0*) Organ Lit.

Lemarechal, Claude, jt. auth. see Hiriart-Urruty, Jean-Baptiste.

Lemarechal, Claude, jt. auth. see Hiriart-Urruty, Jean-Baptiste.

LeMarr, John. America's Best Hoax: How Doctors Get Fat on Fitness. LC 93-77223. (Illus.). 160p. (Orig.). 1993. pap. 12.95 (*0-9632923-7-4*) HealthMasters.

***Lemartine, M.** Maverick Gun. large type ed. 264p. 1999. pap. 18.99 (*0-7089-5620-3*, Linford) Ulverscroft.

— Valley of the Lawless. large type ed. 264p. 2000. pap. 18.99 (*0-7089-5624-6*, Linford) Ulverscroft.

LeMassena, Robert. America's Workhorse Locomotive: The 2-8-2. 1993. pap. 14.95 (*0-915276-54-2*) Quadrant Pr.

LeMassena, Robert A. American Steam Vol. 2: Locomotives of the Northeast. (Illus.). 256p. 1989. 32.00 (*0-913582-05-0*) Sundance.

— Colorado's Mountain Railroads. rev. ed. LC 63-23230. (Illus.). 384p. 1994. 55.00 (*0-913582-35-2*, 0003) Sundance.

— Denver & Rio Grande Western: Superpower Railroad of the Rockies. (Illus.). 112p. 1999. 28.95 (*1-883089-48-4*, Pub. by TLC VA) Motorbooks Intl.

***Lemaster & Baer.** Superwrite Alphabetic Writing System, for Post Secondary. 1998. pap., wbk. ed. 12.75 (*0-538-72161-8*) Sth-Wstrn College.

Lemaster & Hankin. Superwrite: An Alphabetic Writing System. (C). 1989. text 9.50 (*0-538-60786-6*) Thomson Learn.

Lemaster & Hankin. Superwrite Alpha Writing System Dictionary. 1989. 229.25 (*0-538-60764-5*) S-W Pub.

Lemaster, A. James. Dictionary, Superwrite, Alphabetic Writing System. 2nd ed. (KB - Notemaking Ser.). 1995. 9.25 (*0-538-63078-7*) S-W Pub.

— Notemaking & Study Skills, Superwrite. 2nd ed. (KB - Notemaking Ser.). 1995. text 37.95 (*0-538-63276-3*) S-W Pub.

— Notemaking & Study Skills, Superwrite. 2nd ed. (KB - Notemaking Ser.). 1996. wbk. ed. 12.00 (*0-538-63277-1*) S-W Pub.

— Notemaking Superwrite: Alphabetic Writing System. (KB - Notemaking Ser.). 1989. mass mkt. 15.00 (*0-538-60763-7*) S-W Pub.

— Notemaking, Superwrite Alpha Writing System. 2nd ed. (KB - Notemaking Ser.). 1995. 240.25 (*0-538-63080-9*) S-W Pub.

— Notemaking, Superwrite Alpha Writing System. 2nd ed. (KB - Notemaking Ser.). 1995. text 15.00 (*0-538-63079-5*) S-W Pub.

— Superwrite. (KB - Notemaking Ser.). 1989. mass mkt. 15.00 (*0-538-60525-1*) S-W Pub.

— Superwrite: Alphabetic Writing System. (KB - Notemaking Ser.). 1990. pap., wbk. ed. 11.75 (*0-538-60801-3*) S-W Pub.

LeMaster, A. James. Superwrite: Alphabetic Writing System: Comprehensive Course, 2 vols., Set. 1991. 33.50 (*0-538-61798-5*) S-W Pub.

Lemaster, A. James. SuperWrite: Notemaking & Study Skills. (KB - Notemaking Ser.). 1991. mass mkt. 22.50 (*0-538-61817-5*) S-W Pub.

— Superwrite: Notemaking & Study Skills. (KB - Notemaking Ser.). (C). 1991. mass mkt., suppl. ed. 11.75 (*0-538-70513-2*) S-W Pub.

— Superwrite: Notemaking & Study Skills. (KB - Notemaking Ser.). 1991. pap. 12.00 (*0-538-61818-3*) S-W Pub.

— Superwrite Vol. 1: Alphabetic Writing System, Vol. 1. (KB - Notemaking Ser.). 1990. mass mkt. 20.25 (*0-538-60800-5*) S-W Pub.

— Superwrite Vol. 2: An Alphabetic Writing System. (KB - Notemaking Ser.). 1991. mass mkt., wbk. ed. 12.50 (*0-538-60804-8*) S-W Pub.

— SuperWrite Vol. 2: An Alphabetic Writing System, Vol. 2. (KB - Notemaking Ser.). 1990. text 20.25 (*0-538-70512-4*) S-W Pub.

— Superwrite, Brief Course: Alphabetic Writing System. 2nd ed. (KB - Notemaking Ser.). 1995. 15.00 (*0-538-62845-6*); suppl. ed. 240.25 (*0-538-62847-2*) S-W Pub.

— Superwrite Dictionary. (KB - Notemaking Ser.). 1989. mass mkt. 9.25 (*0-538-60526-X*) S-W Pub.

— Superwrite, Post Sec: Alphabetic Writing System. (KB - Notemaking Ser.). (C). 1990. mass mkt. 18.75 (*0-538-70510-8*) S-W Pub.

Lemaster, A. James & Baer, John. Superwrite: Alphabetic Writing System: Office Professional. 2nd ed. LC 98-34130. (C). 1998. 26.95 (*0-538-72163-4*) Thomson Learn.

LeMaster, Carolyn G. A Corner of the Tapestry: A History of the Jewish Experience in Arkansas, 1820s - 1990s. LC 93-48940. 632p. 1994. text 52.00 (*1-55728-304-4*) U of Ark Pr.

LeMaster, Dennis C., ed. Community Stability in Forest-Based Economies. LC 88-24831. 198p. 1989. text 34.95 (*0-88192-129-7*) Timber.

LeMaster, J. R. Journey to Beijing: Poems. LC 92-6726. 100p. 1992. pap. 14.95 (*0-7734-0030-3*) E Mellen.

LeMaster, J. R., ed. Jesse Stuart on Education. LC 91-24688. 176p. 1992. text 21.50 (*0-8131-1765-8*) U Pr of Ky.

— The World of Jesse Stuart: Selected Poems. 303p. 1975. 40.00 (*0-07-062212-4*) McGraw.

LeMaster, J. R. & Clarke, Mary W., eds. Jesse Stuart, Essays on His Work. fac. ed. LC 76-46032. 173p. 1994. pap. 53.70 (*0-7837-7594-6*, 204734700007) Bks Demand.

LeMaster, J. R. & Kummings, Donald D., eds. The Walt Whitman Encyclopedia. LC 98-14072. (Illus.). 847p. 1998. 125.00 (*0-8153-1876-6*, H1877) Garland.

LeMaster, J. R. & Wilson, James D., eds. The Mark Twain Encyclopedia. LC 92-45662. 888p. 1993. text 100.00 (*0-8240-7212-X*, H1249) Garland.

Lemaster, Melanie M. Starting College on the Right Foot. 96p. (C). 1992. per. 21.95 (*0-8403-7903-X*) Kendall-Hunt.

LeMaster, Richard. The Great Gallery of Ducks & Other Waterfowl. LC 94-28557. 1995. 59.95 (*0-8117-0706-7*) Stackpole.

— Waterfowl Identification: The LeMaster Method. LC 96-20744. (Illus.). 76p. 1996. pap., spiral bd. 7.95 (*0-8117-2982-6*) Stackpole.

LeMaster, Ron. The Skier's Edge. LC 98-30822. (Illus.). 160p. 1998. pap. 19.95 (*0-88011-982-9*, PLEM0982) Human Kinetics.

LeMasters, E. E. Blue Collar Aristocrats: Life Styles at a Working-Class Tavern. LC 74-27309. 228p. 1976. pap. 14.95 (*0-299-06554-5*) U of Wis Pr.

LeMasters, E. E. & Defrain, John D. Parents in Contemporary America: A Sympathetic View. 4th ed. 304p. (C). 1983. pap. write for info. (*0-534-10669-2*) Wadsworth Pub.

Lemasters, J. J., et al, eds. Integration of Mitochondrial Function. LC 88-22444. (Illus.). 678p. 1988. 135.00 (*0-306-42999-3*, Plenum Trade) Perseus Pubng.

LeMasters, J. R. Jesse Stuart: Selected Criticism. LC 76-584. 140p. 1978. 10.00 (*0-912760-21-4*) Valkyrie Pub Hse.

Lemasters, John J., jt. ed. see Herman, Brian.

LeMasters, Philip. Discipleship Between Creation & Redemption: Toward a Believers' Church Social Ethic. LC 97-27214. 108p. (C). 1997. 42.50 (*0-7618-0858-2*); pap. 22.50 (*0-7618-0859-0*) U Pr of Amer.

— Discipleship for All Believers: Christian Ethics & the Kingdom of God. LC 91-36402. 160p. (Orig.). 1992. pap. 15.99 (*0-8361-3579-2*) Herald Pr.

— The Import of Eschatology in John Howard Yoder's Critique of Constantinianism. LC 91-44635. 264p. 1992. lib. bdg. 89.95 (*0-7734-9808-7*) E Mellen.

LeMasurier, W. E. & Thomson, J. W., eds. Volcanoes of the Antarctic Plate & Southern Oceans. (Antarctic Research Ser.: Vol. 48). 512p. 1990. 55.00 (*0-87590-172-7*) Am Geophysical.

Lemay. DOS & Windows Protected Mode. (C). 1995. pap. text 10.25 (*0-8053-6372-6*) Benjamin-Cummings.

Lemay & Perkins. Teach Yourself Java 1.1 in 21 Days. 2nd ed. Date not set. 39.99 (*1-57521-374-5*) Sams.

Lemay, Shawna. All the God-Sized Fruit. pap. 12.95 (*0-7735-1902-5*) McG-Queens Univ Pr.

***Lemay, A. & Maheux, R., eds.** Understanding & Managing Endometriosis: Advances in Research & Practice: The Proceedings of the 6th World Congress of Endometriosis. LC 99-30330. (Illus.). 288p. 1999. 98.00 (*1-85070-070-2*) Prthnon Pub.

LeMay, Alan. The Searchers. 1998. reprint ed. 35.95 (*1-56849-704-0*) Buccaneer Bks.

— The Smoky Years. large type ed. LC 96-36880. (Sagebrush Large Print Westerns Ser.). 1996. lib. bdg. 17.95 (*1-57490-052-8*) T T Beeler.

— The Smoky Years. 304p. 1997. reprint ed. mass mkt. 4.99 (*0-8439-4333-5*, Leisure Bks) Dorchester Pub Co.

— Spanish Crossing: Western Stories. LC 98-22723. 1998. 18.95 (*0-7862-1158-X*) Thorndike Pr.

— Spanish Crossing: Western Stories, Vol. 1. LC 99-21864. 1999. 22.95 (*0-7862-1170-9*) Thorndike Pr.

L

Lemay, Allan. The Searchers. reprint ed. lib. bdg. 23.95 (*0-88411-179-2*) Amereon Ltd.

Lemay, Anne. Dog Days & Winter Ways: Skits to Promote Reading All Year Long. LC 94-7904. 56p. 1994. pap. 6.50 (*0-917846-40-0*, 33899, Alleyside) Highsmith Pr.

LeMay, Brian W., ed. Science, Ethics, & Food: Papers & Proceedings of a Colloquium Organized by the Smithsonian Institution. LC 88-18399. (Illus.). 144p. (Orig.). 1988. pap. text 14.95 (*0-87474-605-1*) Smithsonian.

Lemay, Edna H. Dictionnaire des Constituants, 1789-1991, 2 vols. (FRE.). 1991. 395.00 (*0-7859-8019-9*, 2740000030) Fr & Eur.

Lemay, Eric C. Heidegger for Beginners. LC 94-60330. (Illus.). 160p. 1994. pap. 9.95 (*0-86316-172-3*) Writers & Readers.

Lemay, Gerald. MS-DOS & Windows Essentials. 80p. 1995. pap. text 21.33 (*0-8053-6373-4*) Benjamin-Cummings.

— MS-DOS & Windows Essentials. 1995. teacher ed. 11.67 (*0-8053-6548-6*) Benjamin-Cummings.

Lemay, Gerald J. C for Pascal & FORTRAN Programmers. 114p. (C). 1993. student ed. 15.00 (*1-883496-02-0*); pap. text 25.00 (*1-883496-01-2*) P S Melvil Pr.

Lemay, Helen R. Women's Secrets: A Translation of Pseudo-Albertus Magnus' De Secretis Mulierum with Commentaries. LC 91-30690. (SUNY Series in Medieval Studies). 200p. (C). 1992. pap. text 21.95 (*0-7914-1144-3*) State U NY Pr.

LeMay, Iain & Schetky, McDonald, eds. Copper in Iron & Steel. LC 82-17615. 446p. 1986. 59.50 (*0-471-05913-7*) Krieger.

Lemay, J. A. The Canon of Benjamin Franklin, 1722-1776: New Attributions & Reconsiderations. LC 85-40530. 160p. 1986. 28.50 (*0-87413-290-8*) U Delaware Pr.

— New England's Annoyances: America's First Folk Song. LC 84-40414. (Illus.). 160p. 1985. 29.50 (*0-87413-278-9*) U Delaware Pr.

Lemay, J. A., ed. Deism, Masonry, & the Enlightenment: Essays Honoring Alfred Owen Aldrige. LC 86-40585. (Illus.). 216p. 1987. 32.50 (*0-87413-317-3*) U Delaware Pr.

— Reappraising Benjamin Franklin: A Bicentennial Perspective. LC 91-50237. (Illus.). 504p. (C). 1993. 39.50 (*0-87413-448-X*) U Delaware Pr.

Lemay, J. A., ed. see Franklin, Benjamin.

Lemay, J. A. Leo. Did Pocahontas Save Captain John Smith? LC 92-791. (Illus.). 144p. 1993. 25.00 (*0-8203-1461-7*) U of Ga Pr.

Lemay, J. A. Leo, ed. see Franklin, Benjamin, et al.

Lemay, J. Leo. The Frontiersman from Lout to Hero: Notes on the Significance of the Comparative Method & the Stage Theory in Early American Literature & Culture. 1979. pap. 3.50 (*0-912296-39-9*) Am Antiquarian.

— The Oldest Revolutionary: Essays on Benjamin Franklin. LC 75-41618. x, 165p. 1976. write for info. (*0-8122-7707-4*) U of Pa Pr.

Lemay, J. Leo, ed. The Oldest Revolutionary: Essays on Benjamin Franklin. 165p. (C). 1999. reprint ed. 25.00 (*0-7881-6093-1*) DIANE Pub.

Lemay, Joseph A. The American Dream of Captain John Smith. LC 91-2285. (Illus.). 299p. reprint ed. pap. 92.70 (*0-608-10489-2*, 207111800009) Bks Demand.

***Lemay, K.** Seattle. (Illus.). 260p. 1999. pap. 12.95 (*2-89464-206-7*, Pub. by Ulysses Travel) Globe Pequot.

LeMay, Konnie, ed. see Marshall, James R.

Lemay, Laura. Official Marimba Guide to Castanet. LC 96-71499. 354p. 1997. 39.99 (*1-57521-255-2*) Sams.

— Public Administration. (Political Science). 2001. pap. text 37.00 (*0-534-57663-X*) Wadsworth Pub.

***Lemay, Laura.** Sams Teach Yourself Java 2 Platform in 21 Days. (Illus.). 680p. 1999. pap. 29.99 (*0-672-31638-2*) Sams.

— Sams Teach Yourself Java 2 in 21 Days. 2nd ed. (Teach Yourself... in 21 Days Ser.). (Illus.). 800p. 2000. pap. 29.99 (*0-672-31958-6*) Sams.

— Sams Teach Yourself Perl in 21 Days. LC 98-84939. (Teach Yourself Ser.). (Illus.). 680p. 1999. pap. 29.99 (*0-672-31305-7*) Sams.

Lemay, Laura. Sams Teach Yourself Web Publishing with HTML 3.2 in 14 Days. 2nd ed. LC 97-65453. 1176p. 1997. 59.99 incl. cd-rom (*1-57521-305-2*) Sams.

— Sams Teach Yourself Web Publishing with HTML 4 in 14 Days: Professional Reference Edition. 3rd ed. (Teach Yourself Ser.). 1999. 49.99 (*0-672-31408-8*) Sams.

***Lemay, Laura.** Sams Teach Yourself Web Publishing with HTML 4 in 21 Days. 2nd ed. (Teach Yourself... in 21 Days Ser.). (Illus.). 1200p. 2000. 74.95 (*0-672-31838-5*) Sams.

Lemay, Laura. Teach Yourself Java for Macintosh in 21 Days. 1996. 40.00 (*1-56830-292-4*) Hayden.

***Lemay, Laura.** Teach Yourself Java 1.2 in 21 Days, 1. (Teach Yourself Ser.). 1998. pap. text 49.99 (*0-672-31534-3*) Sams.

Lemay, Laura. Sams' Teach Yourself More Java 1.1 in 21 Days. LC 97-68011. 479p. 1997. 29.99 (*1-57521-347-8*) Sams.

— Teach Yourself More Web Publishing with HTML in a Week. (Illus.). 480p. 1995. pap. 29.99 (*1-57521-005-3*) Sams.

— Teach Yourself Sunsoft Java Workshop in 21 Days. LC 96-68937. 656p. 1996. pap. text 39.99 incl. cd-rom (*1-57521-159-9*) Sams.

— Teach Yourself Web Publishing with HTML 3.0 in 14 Days: Premier. 2nd ed. LC 96-67214. 1104p. 1996. 59.99 incl. cd-rom (*1-57521-096-7*) Sams.

— Teach Yourself Web Publishing with HTML 3.2 in a Week. 3rd ed. LC 96-70053. (Illus.). 600p. 1997. pap. 29.99 (*1-57521-192-0*) Sams.

Lemay, Laura & Cadenhead, Rogers. Sams Teach Yourself Java 1.2 in 21 Days: Professional Reference Edition. LC 98-86994. 1999. 49.99 incl. cd-rom (*0-672-31438-X*) Sams.

— Teach Yourself Java 2 Platform in 21 Days With CDROM. (Teach Yourself Ser.). 700p. 1999. pap. 49.99 (*0-672-31647-1*) Sams.

Lemay, Laura & Holzschlag, Molly. Laura Lemay's Guide to Sizzling Web Site Design. LC 96-70712. 256p. 1997. 45.00 (*1-57521-221-8*) Sams.

Lemay, Laura & Morrison, Michael. Teach Yourself Java 1.1 in 21 Days: Professional Reference Edition. 1296p. 1997. pap. 59.99 (*1-57521-382-6*) Sams.

Lemay, Laura & Perkins, Charles L. Teach Yourself Java 1.1 in 21 Days. 2nd ed. LC 96-68602. 816p. 1997. 39.99 (*1-57521-142-4*) Sams.

Lemay, Laura & Samsnet Publishing Staff. Teach Yourself Web Publishing with HTML in 14 Days: Premier Edition. 2nd ed. LC 95-70177. (Illus.). 840p. (Orig.). 1995. pap. 39.99 (*1-57521-014-2*) Sams.

Lemay, Laura & Tyler, Denise. Laura Lemay's Web Workshop: Microsoft FrontPage 97. 2nd ed. 832p. 1997. 39.99 (*1-57521-223-4*) Sams.

Lemay, Laura & Winters, Patrick. Teach Yourself Visual J++ in 21 Days. 2nd ed. 600p. 1999. 39.99 (*1-57521-244-7*) Sams.

Lemay, Laura, jt. auth. see Holzschlag, Molly.

Lemay, Laura, jt. auth. see Tyler, Denise.

Lemay, Marc-Henry & Cocks, C. Bordeaux & Its Wines. 15th ed. LC 99-183805. 2016p. 1998. 250.00 (*0-470-25012-7*) Halsted Pr.

LeMay, Michael C. Anatomy of a Public Policy: The Reform of Contemporary American Immigration Law. LC 94-6376. 224p. 1994. 59.95 (*0-275-94902-8*, Praeger Pubs) Greenwood.

— From Open Door to Dutch Door: An Analysis of U. S. Immigration Policy since 1820. LC 87-2368. 200p. 1987. pap. 19.95 (*0-275-92628-1*, B2628) Greenwood.

— From Open Door to Dutch Door: An Analysis of U. S. Immigration Policy since 1820. LC 87-2368. 200p. 1987. 55.00 (*0-275-92492-0*, C2492, Praeger Pubs) Greenwood.

***LeMay, Michael C.** The Perennial Struggle: Race, Ethnicity Minority Groups in the United States. LC 99-58622. 350p. 2000. pap. text 42.00 (*0-13-020547-8*) P-H.

Lemay, Michael C., ed. The Gatekeepers: Comparative Immigration Policy. LC 88-17993. 228p. 1989. 55.00 (*0-275-93079-3*, C3079, Praeger Pubs) Greenwood.

Lemay, Michele H. & Hale, Lynne Z. Coastal Resources Management: A Guide to Public Education Programs & Materials. LC 89-27274. 58p. 1989. pap. 11.95 (*0-931816-80-7*) Kumarian Pr.

— Coastal Resources Management: A Guide to Public Education Programs & Materials. fac. ed. LC 89-27274. (Kumarian Press Library of Management for Development). 62p. 1994. pap. 30.00 (*0-7837-7571-7*, 204732400007) Bks Demand.

Lemay, R. Coinage of Siam. (Illus.). 1989. pap. 15.00 (*0-932106-29-3*) S J Durst.

Lembark, Connie W. The Prints of Sam Francis: A Catalogue Raisonne, 1960-1990, 2 vols., Set. LC 91-58633. (Illus.). 612p. 1992. boxed set 125.00 (*1-55595-062-0*) Hudson Hills.

Lembcke, B., et al, eds. Systemic Manifestations of IBD: The Pending Challenge for Subtle Diagnosis & Treatment. LC 98-133583. (Falk Symposium Ser.). 416p. 1998. 175.00 (*0-7923-8734-1*) Kluwer Academic.

Lembcke, Jerry. Capitalist Development & Class Capacities: Marxist Theory & Union Organization, 25. LC 87-37546. (Contributions in Labor Studies: No. 25). 213p. 1988. 57.95 (*0-313-26209-8*, LCD/, Greenwood Pr) Greenwood.

***Lembcke, Jerry.** Spitting Image. (Illus.). 280p. 2000. pap. 18.95 (*0-8147-5147-4*) NYU Pr.

Lembcke, Jerry. The Spitting Image: Myth, Memory, & the Legacy of Vietnam. LC 98-9048. 230p. 1998. 24.95 (*0-8147-5146-6*) NYU Pr.

Lembcke, Jerry & Tattam, William. One Union in Wood. LC 84-15808. 210p. 1984. pap. 7.95 (*0-7178-0619-7*) Intl Pubs Co.

Lembeck, Fred. Science Alternative Animal Experiments. 1990. boxed set. write for info. (*0-318-68271-0*) P-H.

Lembeck, Fred, ed. Scientific Alternatives to Animal Experiments. Welch, Jacqui, tr. from GER. (Ellis Horwood Series in Biochemistry & Biotechnology). 300p. 1990. mass mkt. 90.95 (*0-412-02771-2*, A4476, Chap & Hall NY) Chapman & Hall.

Lembeck, Frederick. Beat the House: Sixteen Ways to Win at Blackjack, Craps, Roulette, Baccarat & Other Table Games. LC 98-102756. 224p. 1995. pap. 12.95 (*0-8065-1607-0*, Citadel Pr) Carol Pub Group.

Lembeck, Karl-Heinz. Gegenstand Geschichte. 272p. 1988. lib. bdg. 177.50 (*90-247-3635-8*, Pub. by Kluwer Academic) Kluwer Academic.

Lembeck, Michael, ed. see Lazar, Edward.

Lembede, Anton M. Freedom in Our Lifetime: The Collected Writings of Anton Muziwakhe. Edgar, Robert R. & Msumza, Luyanda K., eds. (Illus.). 224p. (C). 1996. text 29.95 (*0-8214-1149-7*) Ohio U Pr.

Lembeke, Jerry, jt. ed. see Levine, Rhonda F.

Lember, Barbara H. The Shell Book. LC 96-22172. (Illus.). 32p. (J). 1997. 14.95 (*0-395-72030-3*) HM.

Lember, Barbara H., photos by. Book of Fruit. LC 94-4067. (Illus.). 32p. (J). (ps-2). 1994. 14.95 (*0-395-66989-8*) Ticknor & Flds Bks Yng Read.

Lemberg, Alexis, jt. auth. see Lemberg, Ray.

Lemberg, H. L., jt. ed. see Ferrard, J. M.

Lemberg, Lauri. St. Croix Avenue. Eldridge, Miriam, tr. 424p. 1992. pap. 14.95 (*0-9633780-0-7*) Tyomies Soc.

Lemberg, R., jt. auth. see Falk, J.

Lemberg, Ray & Lemberg, Alexis. Daddy, Me & the Adventures of Growing Up. (Illus.). 32p. (Orig.). (J). (gr. k-4). 1988. pap. 6.45 (*0-9619208-5-8*) Small Hands Pr.

Lemberg, Raymond & Cohn, Leigh. Eating Disorders: A Reference Sourcebook. 2nd rev. ed. LC 98-48506. 272p. 1998. pap. 49.95 (*1-57356-156-8*) Oryx Pr.

Lemberg, Sally, jt. auth. see Griffith, Ernest R.

Lemberg, Stephen H. Singin' Steve's Learning Land & Rainbow Village. (Singin' Steve's SmartSongs Ser.). (Illus.). (J). (ps-1). 1999. 14.95 incl. audio (*1-882500-17-2*) SmartSong.

Lemberger, LeAnn. The Cooke Family in England & America. 79p. 1998. pap. 9.95 (*0-9641275-6-3*) PBL Ltd.

— Dear Leigh Michaels... A Novelist Answers the Most-Asked Questions about Getting Published. LC 95-106996. 84p. (Orig.). 1994. pap. 9.95 (*0-9641275-0-4*) PBL Ltd.

Lemberger, Mark. Crime of Magnitude: The Murder of Little Annie. LC 93-6866. (Illus.). 320p. 1993. 23.95 (*1-879483-12-2*); pap. 14.95 (*1-879483-13-0*) Prairie Oak Pr.

Lemberger, Nancy. Bilingual Education: Teachers' Narratives. LC 97-6296. 1997. pap. write for info. (*0-8058-2258-5*) L Erlbaum Assocs.

***Lembersky, Mark.** The Spirit of Mount Saint Helens. (Illus.). 2000. 24.95 (*0-936085-49-5*, Cloudbank); pap. 19.95 (*0-936085-48-7*, Cloudbank) Blue Heron OR.

Lembersky, Mark R., photos by. Nisqually Watershed: Glacier to Delta, a River's Legacy. deluxe ed. LC 95-11067. (Illus.). 128p. 1995. pap. 19.95 (*0-89886-453-4*) Mountaineers.

***Lembey, Stephen H. & Bavid, Maria Elean.** Singin' Steve's Smart Class: An Early Childhood Supplementary Curriculum Kit, 3 vols. 300p. (J). (ps-3). 1999. pap. text 139.95 (*1-882500-20-2*) SmartSong.

Lembi, Carole A. & Waaland, J. Robert, eds. Algae & Human Affairs. (Illus.). 606p. 1989. text 95.00 (*0-521-32115-8*) Cambridge U Pr.

Lembi, Carole A., et al. Green Algae, II: Cytology. LC 73-10108. 216p. (C). 1973. 29.00 (*0-8422-7161-9*) Irvington.

Lembke, Bud. Ups & Downs in a Flying Fortress: "Were Those Trips Necessary" (Illus.). 200p. (Orig.). 1997. pap. 24.95 (*0-9657814-0-2*) Pulse Pr.

Lembke, Janet. Dangerous Birds. 192p. 1996. pap. text 16.95 (*1-55821-514-X*) Lyons Pr.

— Dangerous Birds: A Naturalist's Aviary. 192p. 1992. 21.95 (*1-55821-190-X*) Lyons Pr.

***Lembke, Janet.** Despicable Species. LC 99-15220. 216p. 1999. 22.95 (*1-55821-635-9*) Lyons Pr.

Lembke, Janet. Hecuba. Reckford, Kenneth J., ed. (Greek Tragedy in New Translations Ser.). 112p. 1991. pap. 8.95 (*0-19-506874-2*) OUP.

— River Time: Life on an American Frontier. 176p. 1997. pap. 14.95 (*1-55821-657-X*) Lyons Pr.

— Shake Them 'Simmons down & Other Adventures in the Lives of Trees. LC 96-14375. (Illus.). 224p. 1996. 22.95 (*1-55821-350-3*) Lyons Pr.

— Skinny Dipping: And Other Immersions in Water, Myth & Being Human. LC 94-15378. 192p. 1994. 21.95 (*1-55821-274-4*) Lyons Pr.

Lembke, Janet & Herington, C. John, trs. Persians. (Greek Tragedy in New Translations Ser.). 144p. 1991. reprint ed. pap. 8.95 (*0-19-507008-9*) OUP.

Lembke, Janet, tr. see Euripides.

Lembke, Melody B., compiled by. Legal L. C. Subject Headings Weekly Lists: Cumulation. LC 86-529. (AALL Publications Ser.: No. 26). viii, 38p. 1986. ring bd. 57.50 (*0-8377-0125-2*, Rothman) W S Hein.

Lembke, Melody B. & Lawrence, Rhonda K. Cataloging Legal Literature: A Manual on AACR2R & Library of Congress Subject Headings for Legal Materials. 3rd ed. LC 96-32561. (AALL Publications: No. 22). (Illus.). xx, 646p. 1997. ring bd. 125.00 (*0-8377-9313-0*, Rothman) W S Hein.

Lembke, Ruth C. Calico's Country Cats. LC 82-80861. (Illus.). 64p. 1982. 5.95 (*0-686-39811-4*) R C Lembke.

Lembke, Valdean C., jt. auth. see Baker, Richard E.

Lembo, Ann & Surkiewicz, Joe. Short Bike Rides Philadelphia: Rides for the Casual Cyclist. 3rd ed. LC 99-45047. (Short Bike Rides Ser.). (Illus.). 160p. 2000. pap. text 11.95 (*0-7627-0408-X*) Globe Pequot.

Lembo, J. Lawrence, ed. see Whitman, Walt.

Lembo, John M. The Counseling Process: A Cognitive-Behavioral Approach. LC 76-4232. 1976. 10.95 (*0-87212-060-0*) Libra.

— How to Cope with Your Fears & Frustrations. LC 76-52139. 1977. 10.95 (*0-87212-091-0*) Libra.

***Lembo, Ron.** Thinking Through Television. LC 99-56422. (Cambridge Cultural Social Studies). 264p. 2000. write for info. (*0-521-58465-5*); pap. write for info. (*0-521-58577-5*) Cambridge U Pr.

Lemche, Niels P. The Canaanites & Their Land: The Tradition of the Canaanites. (Journal for the Study of the Old Testament Supplement Ser.: Vol. 110). 192p. 1991. 57.50 (*1-85075-310-5*, Pub. by Sheffield Acad) CUP Services.

— Early Israel: Anthropological & Historical Studies on the Israelite Society before the Monarchy. (Supplements to Vetus Testamentum Ser.: No. 37). (Illus.). xv, 496p. 1986. 127.50 (*90-04-07853-3*) Brill Academic Pubs.

— Prelude to Israel's Past: Background & Beginnings of Israelite History & Identity. Maniscalco, E. F., tr. from GER. Orig. Title: Die Vorgeschichte Israels. 248p. 1998. 24.95 (*1-56563-343-1*) Hendrickson MA.

Lemche, Niels Peter. Ancient Israel: A New History of Israelite Society. (Biblical Seminar Ser.: Vol. 5). 276p. 1988. pap. 24.95 (*1-85075-017-3*, Pub. by Sheffield Acad) CUP Services.

— Israelites in History & Tradition: Library of Ancient Israel. LC 98-22300. (Library of Ancient Israel Ser.). 224p. 1998. 25.00 (*0-664-22075-4*) Westminster John Knox.

Lemcio, Eugene E. The Past of Jesus in the Gospels. (Society for New Testament Studies Monographs: No. 68). 204p. (C). 1991. text 59.95 (*0-521-40113-5*) Cambridge U Pr.

Lemcio, Eugene E., jt. auth. see Wall, Robert W.

Lemcke, Dawn P. Primary Care of Women. (Illus.). 624p. (C). 1996. pap. text 39.95 (*0-8385-9813-7*, A9813-5, Apple Lange Med) McGraw.

Lemcke, Kur. Das Bayerische Alpenvorland vor der Eiszeit: Erdgeschichte---Bau---Bodenschaetze. (Geologie Von Bayern Ser.: Band 1). vii, 175p. 1988. 32.00 (*3-510-65135-9*, Pub. by E Schweizerbartsche) Balogh.

Lemco, Gary. Nietzsche As Educator. LC 92-4107. 160p. 1992. lib. bdg. 69.95 (*0-7734-9962-8*) E Mellen.

Lemco, Jonathan. Canada & the Crisis in Central America. LC 90-43134. 208p. 1991. 55.00 (*0-275-93718-6*, C3718, Praeger Pubs) Greenwood.

— Political Stability in Federal Governments. LC 91-6777. 224p. 1991. 57.95 (*0-275-93854-9*, C3854, Praeger Pubs) Greenwood.

— Turmoil in the Peacable Kingdom: The Quebec Sovereignty Movement & Its Implications for Canada & the U. S. (Illus.). 266p. 1994. pap. 17.95 (*0-8020-6970-3*); text 50.00 (*0-8020-0532-2*) U of Toronto Pr.

Lemco, Jonathan, ed. The Canada - United States Relationship: The Politics of Energy & Environmental Coordination. LC 91-34774. 240p. 1992. 52.95 (*0-275-94239-2*, C4239, Praeger Pubs) Greenwood.

— National Health Care: Lessons for the United States & Canada. 304p. 1994. text 54.50 (*0-472-10440-3*, 10440) U of Mich Pr.

— Tensions at the Border: Energy & Environmental Concerns in Canada & the United States. LC 91-34775. 216p. 1992. 55.00 (*0-275-94001-2*, C4001, Praeger Pubs) Greenwood.

Lemco, Jonathan & Robson, William B., eds. Ties Beyond Trade: Labor & Environmental Issues under the NAFTA. 162p. (Orig.). 1993. pap. text 14.95 (*0-89068-120-1*, CAC 61(NPA 265)) Natl Planning.

Lemco, Jonathan, jt. ed. see Belous, Richard S.

Leme, J. Garcia, ed. Hormones & Inflammation. 248p. 1988. 143.00 (*0-8493-5928-7*, RB131, CRC Reprint) Franklin.

Leme, R. A. Dictionary of Geotechnical Engineering. (ENG & POR.). 159p. 1980. pap. 39.95 (*0-8288-0958-5*, M6073) Fr & Eur.

LeMehaute, Alain, et al, eds. Curves & Surfaces in Geometric Design. LC 94-11335. (Illus.). 490p. (C). 1994. text 82.00 (*1-56881-039-3*) AK Peters.

LeMehaute, Alain, ed. see Laurent, Pierre-Jean.

Lemehaute, Bernard & Hanes, Daniel M. The Sea: Ocean Engineering Science, Vol. 9. 640p. 1990. write for info. (*0-471-52855-2*); write for info. (*0-471-52856-0*) Wiley.

— The Sea: Ocean Engineering Science Set, 2 vols., Vol. 9, 2 Vol. Set, Ocean Engineering Science. 1344p. 1990. 400.00 (*0-471-63393-3*) Wiley.

***Lemel, Harold, ed.** Rural Property & Economy in Post-Communist Albania. 184p. 2000. 45.00 (*1-57181-150-8*) Berghahn Bks.

Lemelin, Evelina E., jt. compiled by see Benamati, Dennis C.

Lemelin, Maurice. The Public Service Alliance of Canada: A Look at a Union in the Public Sector. (Monograph & Research Ser.: No. 21). 1978. 6.50 (*0-89215-085-8*) U Cal LA Indus Rel.

Lemelle. Readings in the Sociology of AIDS. LC 99-27564. 322p. 1999. pap. text 29.40 (*0-13-639261-X*) P-H.

Lemelle, Anthony J. Black Male Deviance. LC 94-25040. 208p. 1994. 59.95 (*0-275-95004-2*, Praeger Pubs) Greenwood.

Lemelle, Anthony J., Jr. Black Male Deviance. LC 94-25040. 208p. 1997. pap. 20.95 (*0-275-95913-9*, Praeger Pubs) Greenwood.

Lemelle, Sid. Pan-Africanism for Beginners. LC 91-50561. (Writers & Readers Documentary Comic Bks.). 176p. (Orig.). (C). 1992. pap. 9.95 (*0-86316-148-0*) Writers & Readers.

Lemelle, Sidney. Imagining Home: Class, Culture & Nationalism in the African Diaspora. LC 94-41699. 320p. (C). 1994. pap. 20.00 (*0-86091-585-9*, Pub. by Verso) Norton.

Lemelman, Martin. Chanukah Is... (Illus.). 10p. (J). (ps). 1988. bds. 4.95 (*0-8074-0424-1*, 102003) UAHC.

— My Jewish Home. (Illus.). 10p. (J). (ps). 1988. bds. 3.95 (*0-8074-0415-2*, 102002) UAHC.

***Lemelman, Martin.** Circus Opposites: With Disappearing Animals. (Wacky Flaps Book Ser.). 10p. (J). (ps-k). 2000. 7.99 (*1-58476-016-8*) Innovative Kids.

Lemelman, Martin. The Jewish Holiday Book. 10p. (J). 1989. bds. 4.95 (*0-8074-0431-4*, 102004) UAHC.

— My Jewish Home: Bath Book. 10p. (J). (ps). 1987. vinyl bd. 3.95 (*0-8074-0327-X*, 102001) UAHC.

LeMenager, Charles R. Flying after 50: You're Not Too Old to Start. LC 95-25137. (Illus.). 206p. reprint ed. pap. 63.90 (*0-608-09065-4*, 206969900005) Bks Demand.

— Julian City & Cuyamaca Country: A History & Guide to the Past & Present. (Illus.). 256p. 1992. 19.95 (*0-9611102-5-2*); pap. 12.95 (*0-9611102-4-4*) Eagle Peak Pub.

— Lemenager Family History: America's Wastines Legacy. (Illus.). 150p. 1998. pap. text 19.95 (*0-9611102-6-0*) Eagle Peak Pub.

— Off the Main Road: San Vicente & Barona. 2nd ed. (Illus.). 206p. (Orig.). 1997. reprint ed. pap., per. 10.95 (*0-9611102-3-6*) Eagle Peak Pub.

An Asterisk (*) at the beginning of an entry indicates that the title is appearing for the first time.

— Ramona & Round About: A History of San Diego County's Little Known Back Country. (Illus.). 252p. 1995. reprint ed. pap. 12.95 (*0-9611102-2-8*) Eagle Peak Pub.

Lemer, Andrew C., jt. auth. see Bernstein, Harvey M.

Lemer, Andrew C., ed. see National Research Council Staff.

Lemer, Paule. Astrological Key to Mahabharata. (C). 1989. 21.00 (*81-208-0453-8*, Pub. by Motilal Bnarsidass) S Asia.

Lemerand, Pamela. SAFE, Student Assistance & Family Education Program: A Dynamic Program for Elementary Schools. LC 92-40065. 208p. 1993. pap. 44.00 (*1-56246-053-6*, 3204, HazeldenJohnson Inst) Hazelden.

Lemercier. Pinto. Perry, ed. (Exeter French Texts Ser.: Vol. 21). (FRE.). 187p. Date not set. pap. text 19.95 (*0-85989-011-2*, Pub. by Univ Exeter Pr) Northwestern U Pr.

Lemercier-Quelquejay, Chantal, jt. auth. see Bennigsen, Alexandre.

Lemers, Andrew C., ed. see National Research Council Staff.

Lemert, Charles. Postmodernism Is Not What You Think. (Twentieth-Century Social Theory Ser.). 240p. 1997. pap. 21.95 (*1-55786-286-9*) Blackwell Pubs.

— Social Things: An Introduction to the Sociological Life. LC 97-7372. 222p. 1997. 17.95 (*0-8476-8538-1*); pap. 13.95 (*0-8476-8539-X*) Rowman.

Lemert, Charles, ed. Social Theory: The Multicultural & Classic Readings. 2nd ed. LC 98-11803. 688p. 1998. pap. 35.00 (*0-8133-3472-1*, Pub. by Westview) HarpC.

Lemert, Charles & Bhan, Esme, eds. The Voice of Anna Julia Cooper: Including "A Voice from the South" LC 97-37767. 382p. (Orig.). 1997. pap. 15.95 (*0-8476-8408-3*) Rowman.

— The Voice of Anna Julia Cooper: Including "A Voice from the South" LC 97-37767. 382p. (Orig.). 1997. text 58.00 (*0-8476-8407-5*) Rowman.

Lemert, Charles & Branaman, Ann, eds. The Goffman Reader. LC 96-26921. 474p. (C). 1997. text 66.95 (*1-55786-893-X*); pap. text 28.95 (*1-55786-894-8*) Blackwell Pubs.

Lemert, Charles, ed. see Denzin, Norman K.

Lemert, Charles C. Sociology & the Twilight of Man: Homocentrism & Discourse in Sociological Theory. LC 78-17146. 276p. 1980. pap. 9.95 (*0-8093-0975-0*) S Ill U Pr.

Lemert, Charles C., ed. French Sociology: Rupture & Renewal Since 1968. LC 80-25714. 528p. 1981. text 81.00 (*0-231-04698-7*) Col U Pr.

— Intellectuals & Politics: Social Theory Beyond the Academy. (Key Issues in Sociological Theory Ser.: Vol. 5). (Illus.). 224p. (C). 1990. text 56.00 (*0-8039-3731-8*); pap. text 26.00 (*0-8039-3732-6*) Sage.

— Intellectuals & Politics: Social Theory in a Changing World. LC 90-21368. (Key Issues in Sociological Theory Ser.: Vol. 5). 198p. reprint ed. pap. 61.40 (*0-608-09786-1*, 206996000007) Bks Demand.

Lemert, Charles C. & Gillan, Garth. Michel Foucault: Social Theory & Transgression. LC 82-4276. 187p. reprint ed. pap. 58.00 (*0-8357-7782-0*, 203614200002) Bks Demand.

Lemert, Charles C., ed. see Lemert, Edwin M.

Lemert, E. M., jt. auth. see Heizer, R. F.

***Lemert, Edwin M.** Crime & Deviance: Essays & Innovations of Edwin M. Lemert. Lemert, Charles C. & Winter, Michael, eds. 272p. 2000. 75.00 (*0-8476-9816-5*); pap. 29.95 (*0-8476-9817-3*) Rowman.

Lemert, Edwin M. The Trouble with Evil: Social Control at the Edge of Morality. LC 96-30388. (SUNY Series in Deviance & Social Control). 185p. (C). 1997. text 49.50 (*0-7914-3243-2*) State U NY Pr.

— The Trouble with Evil: Social Control at the Edge of Morality. LC 96-30388. (SUNY Series in Deviance & Social Control). 185p. (C). 1997. pap. text 16.95 (*0-7914-3244-0*) State U NY Pr.

Lemert, James B. Criticizing the Media: Empirical Approaches. (CommText Ser.: Vol. 21). 160p. (C). 1989. text 42.00 (*0-8039-2636-7*); pap. text 18.95 (*0-8039-2637-5*) Sage.

Lemert, James B., et al. News Verdicts, the Debates, & Presidential Campaigns. LC 91-8749. 312p. 1991. 62.95 (*0-275-93758-5*, C3758, Praeger Pubs) Greenwood.

— The Politics of Disenchantment: Bush, Clinton, Perot, & the Press. LC 95-51055. 384p. 1996. text 75.00 (*1-57273-058-7*); pap. text 28.50 (*1-57273-059-5*) Hampton Pr NJ.

***Lemery, D. & Santolaya-Forgas, Joaquin.** Interventional Ultrasound in Obstetrics, Gynecology & the Breast. LC 98-12984. (Illus.). 384p. 1998. 145.00 (*0-632-03874-8*) Blackwell Sci.

***Lemeseurier, Peter.** Nostradamus & Beyond: 128 New Prophecies Based on His Techniques. LC 99-39414. (Illus.). 128p. 1999. pap. 16.95 (*0-8069-9911-X*) Sterling.

Lemeshow, S., jt. auth. see Lwanga, Stephen K.

Lemeshow, Stanley, jt. auth. see Hosmer, David W., Jr.

Lemeshow, Stanley, jt. auth. see Hosmer, David W.

Lemeshow, Stanley, jt. auth. see Hosmer, David W., Jr.

Lemeshow, Stanley, jt. auth. see Levy, Paul S.

Lemesis, G. Victor, jt. auth. see Meehan, Robert H.

LeMesuier, Charles & Arnold, Marc. Storage & Preservation of Defence Equipment. 2nd ed. (Market Intelligence - Related Special Reports). 1999. 695.00 (*0-7106-1833-6*) Janes Info Group.

LeMesurier, Charles & Arnold, Marc. Advanced Composite Markets. 2nd ed. (Market Intelligence - Related Special Reports). 1998. 695.00 (*0-7106-1832-8*) Janes Info Group.

— Armed Forces of the European Union. (Geopolitical-Emerging Threats - Related Special Reports). 1997. 695.00 (*0-7106-1655-4*) Janes Info Group.

— Armoured & Logistic Vehicle Markets. 2nd ed. (Land Forces - Related Special Reports). 1998. 695.00 (*0-7106-1666-X*) Janes Info Group.

— China's Aerospace Industry. (Market Intelligence - Related Special Reports). 1997. 695.00 (*0-7106-1624-4*) Janes Info Group.

— Defence & the Environment. 2nd ed. (Market Intelligence - Related Special Reports). 1997. 695.00 (*0-7106-1665-1*) Janes Info Group.

— Defence Modernisation Markets - Western Europe. (Market Intelligence - Related Special Reports). 1997. 695.00 (*0-7106-1497-7*) Janes Info Group.

— Electronic Warfare - The Development of an Air EW Capability. (Air-Space - Related Special Reports). 1996. 695.00 (*0-7106-1501-9*) Janes Info Group.

— The Future Land Battlefield. (Land Forces - Related Special Reports). 1999. 695.00 (*0-7106-1831-X*) Janes Info Group.

— International Defence Markets. (Market Intelligence - Related Special Reports). 1996. 695.00 (*0-7106-1414-4*) Janes Info Group.

— Japan's Defence Industry - Capabilities & Future Trends. (Market Intelligence - Related Special Reports). 1998. 695.00 (*0-7106-1822-0*) Janes Info Group.

— Maritime Communications - Electronic Warfare Systems. (Special Reports). 1996. 695.00 (*0-7106-1394-6*) Janes Info Group.

— Naval Mine Warfare Markets. (Special Reports). 1997. 695.00 (*0-7106-1503-5*) Janes Info Group.

— Non-Nuclear Submarines - The World Market. (Special Reports). 1996. 695.00 (*0-7106-1502-7*) Janes Info Group.

— Police Markets of North America & The European Union. (Law Enforcement - Related Special Report Ser.). 1997. 695.00 (*0-7106-1511-6*) Janes Info Group.

— Security & Stability in South Asia. (Geopolitical-Emerging Threats - Related Special Reports). 1996. 695.00 (*0-7106-1425-X*) Janes Info Group.

— Terrorism. (Geopolitical-Emerging Threats - Related Special Reports). 1997. 695.00 (*0-7106-1662-7*) Janes Info Group.

— Trends in Maritime Violence. (Geopolitical-Emerging Threats - Related Special Reports). 1997. 695.00 (*0-7106-1403-9*) Janes Info Group.

— 24 Hour Battle. (Military Systems - Related Special Reports). 1996. 695.00 (*0-7106-1415-2*) Janes Info Group.

— Unstable Russia - A Regional Commercial Risk Assessment. (Geopolitical-Emerging Threats - Related Special Reports). 1996. 695.00 (*0-7106-1426-8*) Janes Info Group.

— Virtual Reality - Trends & Technologies. (Military Systems - Related Special Reports). 1988. 695.00 (*0-7106-1664-3*) Janes Info Group.

— World Military Aircraft Market Forecast. (Air-Space - Related Special Reports). 1997. 695.00 (*0-7106-1399-7*) Janes Info Group.

LeMesurier, Charles & Arnold, Marc, eds. European Defence Procurement. (Market Intelligence - Related Special Reports). 1998. 695.00 (*0-7106-1215-X*) Janes Info Group.

Lemesurier, Peter. The Armageddon Script: Prophecy in Action. (Illus.). 270p. 1993. pap. 15.95 (*0-906540-37-2*, Pub. by Element MA) Penguin Putnam.

***Lemesurier, Peter.** Decoding the Great Pyramid. 256p. 1999. pap. 29.95 (*1-86204-588-7*, Pub. by Element MA) Penguin Putnam.

Lemesurier, Peter. Essential Nostradamus. (Piatkus Guides Ser.). 1999. pap. 6.95 (*0-7499-1868-3*, Pub. by Piatkus Bks) London Brdge.

— Gods of the Dawn: The Message of the Pyramids & the True Stargate Mystery. (Illus.). 1999. pap. 13.00 (*0-7225-3699-2*) Thorsons PA.

— Gospel of the Stars: The Mystery of the Cycle of the Ages. (Illus.). 144p. 1993. pap. 12.95 (*1-85230-148-1*, Pub. by Element MA) Penguin Putnam.

— The Great Pyramid Decoded. rev. ed. 432p. 1996. pap. 16.95 (*1-85230-793-5*, Pub. by Element MA) Penguin Putnam.

— Great Pyramid Your Personal Guide. 1993. pap. 17.95 (*1-85230-016-7*, Pub. by Element MA) Penguin Putnam.

— The Healing of the Gods: The Magic of Symbols & the Practice of Theotherapy. 208p. 1993. pap. 12.95 (*1-85230-033-7*, Pub. by Element MA) Penguin Putnam.

— Nostradamus: Final Reckoning. LC 97-110464. 208p. 1997. reprint ed. pap. 12.95 (*0-425-15610-9*) Berkley Pub.

— Nostradamus: The Next Fifty Years. 304p. 1994. pap. 12.95 (*0-425-14433-X*) Berkley Pub.

— Nostradamus Encyclopedia. LC 98-223000. (Illus.). 288p. 1997. text 29.95 (*0-312-17093-9*) St Martin.

— Nostradamus Encyclopedia. 2nd ed. 1999. pap. 21.95 (*0-312-19994-5*) St Martin.

Lemeunier. Dictionnaire Juridique. (FRE.). 1988. pap. 75.00 (*0-7859-3914-8*) Fr & Eur.

Lemic, Jesse. Quitting in Time: How to Stop Smoking on Your Own. (Illus.). 39p. (Orig.). 1987. write for info. (*0-944566-00-6*) Start Today.

Lemiech, Johanna K. Classroom Management: Methods & Techniques for Elementary & Secondary Teachers. 3rd rev. ed. LC 99-193706. (Illus.). 383p. (C). 1998. pap. text 24.95 (*1-57766-033-1*) Waveland Pr.

Lemieux. A Light Place. (Fairy Lair Ser.: No. 3). (J). 1998. pap. 16.00 (*0-689-81874-2*) S&S Childrens.

— Love Speed. 2001. per. 4.50 (*0-689-81799-1*) S&S Childrens.

— A Magic Place. LC 98-29378. (Fairy Lair Ser.: 3). 160p. (J). (gr. 4-6). 1998. mass mkt. 3.99 (*0-689-81727-4*) S&S Childrens.

Lemieux, A. C. Do Angels Sing the Blues? LC 94-26411. 1996. 9.60 (*0-606-09197-1*, Pub. by Turtleback) Demco.

LeMieux, A. C. Do Angels Sing the Blues. LC 94-26411. 224p. (YA). (gr. 7-12). 1996. mass mkt. 4.50 (*0-380-72399-9*, Avon Bks) Morrow Avon.

Lemieux, A. C. Fruit Flies, Fish & Fortune Cookies. (J). 1995. 9.09 (*0-606-07553-4*) Turtleback.

LeMieux, A. C. The TV Guidance Counselor. 192p. (YA). 1994. mass mkt. 3.99 (*0-380-72050-7*, Avon Bks) Morrow Avon.

Lemieux, A.C. TV Guidance Counselor. 1994. 9.09 (*0-606-07126-1*, Pub. by Turtleback) Demco.

Lemieux, Andre. Canadian Mines: Perspective: Production, Reserves, Development, Exploration-1991. (Mineral Bulletin Ser.: No. 233). (FRE., Illus.). 42p. (Orig.). 1993. pap. 24.65 (*0-660-58966-4*, Pub. by Canadian Govt Pub) Accents Pubns.

LeMieux, Anne. The Fairy Lair: A Special Place. LC 97-29540. 144p. (J). (gr. 3-7). 1997. 16.00 (*0-689-81854-8*) S&S Childrens.

— The Fairy Lair: A Special Place. LC 97-29540. (Fairy Lair Ser.: Bk. 1). 158p. (J). (gr. 3-7). 1997. per. 3.99 (*0-689-81725-8*) S&S Childrens.

— A Safe Place. LC 98-13730. (Fairy Lair Ser.: 2). 144p. (J). 1998. mass mkt. 3.99 (*0-689-81726-6*) S&S Childrens.

— Super Snoop Sam Snout & the Case of the Missing Marble. 64p. (Orig.). (J). (ps-3). 1994. pap. 3.50 (*0-380-77460-7*, Avon Bks) Morrow Avon.

— Super Snoop Sam Snout & the Case of the Stolen Snowman. 64p. (Orig.). (J). (ps-3). 1994. pap. 3.50 (*0-380-77459-3*, Avon Bks) Morrow Avon.

— Super Snoop Sam Snout & the Case of the Yogurt-Poker. 64p. (Orig.). (J). (ps-3). 1994. pap. 3.50 (*0-380-77462-3*, Avon Bks) Morrow Avon.

LeMieux, Anne C. All The Answers. pap. 4.95 (*0-380-72890-7*) Morrow Avon.

— All the Answers. LC 99-27179. 160p. (J). (gr. 4-7). 2000. 15.00 (*0-380-97771-0*, Avon Bks) Morrow Avon.

LeMieux, Anne C. Dare to Be, M. E.! LC 96-36034. 224p. (J). 1997. mass mkt. 14.00 (*0-380-97496-7*, Avon Bks) Morrow Avon.

— Dare to Be, M. E.! 240p. (J). (gr. 3-7). 1998. pap. 3.99 (*0-380-72889-3*, Avon Bks) Morrow Avon.

Lemieux, Christina M. Coping with the Loss of a Pet: A Gentle Guide for All Who Love a Pet. LC 91-73129. (Illus.). 60p. (Orig.). 1992. reprint ed. pap. 11.95 (*0-9622158-1-3*) W R Clark Co.

— Coping with the Loss of a Pet: A Gentle Guide for All Who Love a Pet. rev. ed. LC 91-73129. (Illus.). 60p. (Orig.). 1989. 14.95 (*0-9622158-0-5*) W R Clark Co.

LeMieux, David. The Ancient Tarot & Its Symbolism: A Guide to the Secret Keys of the Tarot Cards. LC 84-4318. (Illus.). 208p. 1985. 25.00 (*0-8453-4714-4*, Cornwall Bks) Assoc Univ Prs.

***LeMieux, Dennis H. & Snell, John R., eds.** Thermosense XXI. 534p. 1999. pap. text 120.00 (*0-8194-3174-5*) SPIE.

LeMieux, Dotty. Let Us Not Blame Foolish Women. (Desert Island Chapbook Ser.). 32p. 1983. pap. text 3.50 (*0-939180-26-X*) Tombouctou.

Lemieux, G., ed. see Symposium, Montreal Staff.

Lemieux, Luc, ed. The Real World of Engineering: Case History, No. 60. 3.50 (*0-614-05229-7*, CHN06005923.5M) ASFE.

Lemieux, Margo. The Fiddle Ribbon. LC 95-19536. (Illus.). 32p. (J). (gr. 1-3). 1996. 13.95 (*0-382-39097-0*, Dillon Silver Burdett); pap. 5.95 (*0-382-39098-9*, Dillon Silver Burdett) Silver Burdett Pr.

— The Fiddle Ribbon. LC 95-19536. (Illus.). 32p. (J). (gr. 1-3). 1999. lib. bdg. 22.00 (*0-382-39096-2*, Dillon Silver Burdett) Silver Burdett Pr.

— Paul & the Wolf. LC 95-9686. (Illus.). 32p. (J). (gr. k-2). 1995. 13.95 (*0-382-39100-4*) Silver Burdett Pr.

— Paul & the Wolf. (Illus.). 32p. (J). (gr. 1-3). 1995. pap. 5.95 (*0-382-39101-2*); lib. bdg. 15.95 (*0-382-39099-7*, Silver Pr NJ) Silver Burdett Pr.

Lemieux, Mario & McMillan, Tom. Mario Lemieux: The Final Period. (Illus.). 128p. 1997. 50.00 (*1-57243-253-5*) Triumph Bks.

Lemieux, Michele. Peter & the Wolf. (J). (ps-3). 1996. mass mkt. 4.95 (*0-688-14728-3*, Wm Morrow) Morrow Avon.

— Stormy Night. (Illus.). 240p. (J). (gr. 3-7). 1999. 18.95 (*1-55074-692-8*) Kids Can Pr.

— What's That Noise. unabridged ed. (Illus.). 32p. (J). (ps-2). 1998. pap. 4.95 (*0-921103-69-7*, Pub. by Kids Can Pr) Genl Dist Srvs.

Lemieux, Michele. Peter & the Wolf. 32p. (J). 1991. pap. 4.95 (*1-55074-174-8*) Kids Can Pr.

Lemieux, Michele. Peter & the Wolf. LC 90-6486. 32p. 1991. 13.95 (*0-688-09846-0*, Wm Morrow) Morrow Avon.

Lemieux, P. Chaos & Society. LC 94-74250. (gr. 12). 1995. 75.00 (*90-5199-214-9*) IOS Press.

Lemieux, Raymond U. Raymond U. Lemieux: Explorations with Sugar: How Sweet It Was. LC 90-38333. (Illus.). 185p. 1990. text 36.00 (*0-8412-1777-7*, Pub. by Am Chemical) OUP.

Lemieux, Wayne K. Public Agency Officials' Complete Source Book. abr. ed. 851p. 1998. lib. bdg. write for info. (*0-327-00883-0*, 8097411) LEXIS Pub.

— Public Agency Officials' Complete Source Book. 4th ed. 1998. disk. write for info. (*0-327-00903-9*) LEXIS Pub.

Leming. Understanding Death, Dying & Bereavement. 3rd ed. (C). 1994. pap. text, teacher ed. 8.50 (*0-15-501311-4*) Harcourt Coll Pubs.

— Understanding Dying & Death. 4th ed. LC 97-74390. (C). 1997. text 69.50 (*0-15-505174-1*) Harcourt.

Leming, J. C. Basic Gearing. (1985 Gear Manufacturing Symposium Ser.: 85GMS1). 88p. 1985. pap. text 30.00 (*1-55589-014-8*) AGMA.

Leming, James S., compiled by. Foundations of Moral Education: An Annotated Bibliography. LC 83-12834. 325p. 1983. lib. bdg. 69.50 (*0-313-24165-1*, LME/, Greenwood Pr) Greenwood.

Leming, John C. High Contact Ratio (2+) Spur Gears. (Technical Papers: Vol. P209.11). (Illus.). 14p. 1977. pap. text 30.00 (*1-55589-137-3*) AGMA.

Leming, Michael & Dickinson, George. Understanding Dying, Death, & Bereavement. 3rd ed. LC 93-77913. 552p. (C). 1994. text 65.00 (*0-15-500632-0*, Pub. by Harcourt Coll Pubs) Harcourt.

Leming, Michael, et al. Mechanical Behavior of High Performance Concretes Vol. 4: High Early Strength Concrete. 179p. (C). 1993. pap. text 15.00 (*0-309-05756-6*, SHRP-C-364) SHRP.

Leming, Ron, jt. auth. see Anthony, Piers.

Leming, Shirley, ed. see Arnzen, Michael.

Leming, Shirley, ed. see Pa. Public Utility Commission Staff.

Leming, Shirley, ed. see Pennsylvania Public Utility Commission.

Lemire, Beverly. Fashion's Favourite: The Cotton Trade & the Consumer in Britain, 1660-1800. (Illus.). 272p. 1992. text 79.00 (*0-19-921062-4*) OUP.

Lemire, Maurice. Dictionnaire des Oeuvres Litteraires du Quebec des Origines a 1900, 6 vols. (FRE.). 1994. 995.00 (*0-7859-9477-7*) Fr & Eur.

— Dictionnaires des Oeuvres Litteraires du Quebec Vol. 1: Origines a 1900. rev. ed. (FRE.). 998p. 1980. 250.00 (*0-7859-5221-7*) Fr & Eur.

Lemire, Ronald J., et al. Anencephaly. LC 77-83688. (Illus.). 281p. reprint ed. pap. 87.20 (*0-7837-7116-9*, 204694500004) Bks Demand.

***Lemire, Sandra.** Yorkies Head to Tail: The Essential Care Guide. 304p. 1999. pap. 15.95 (*1-879706-83-0*) Paper Chase.

LeMire, Vic. Drive to the Net: Becoming a Two-Way Power Forward. Frizzell, Colleen, ed. (Illus.). 161p. 1998. pap. 19.95 (*1-892640-02-3*) Vics Hockey Schls.

— Goaltenders Are Not Targets: How to Coach & Play Hockey Goaltending. rev. ed. Frizzell, Colleen, ed. (Illus.). 1998. pap. 19.95 (*1-892640-00-7*) Vics Hockey Schls.

— Off the Post: Advanced Goaltending Techniques & Strategies. Frizzell, Colleen, ed. (Illus.). 158p. 1998. pap. 19.95 (*1-892640-01-5*) Vics Hockey Schls.

— Solid on Defense: How to Dominate on Defense. Frizzell, Colleen, ed. (Illus.). 153p. 1998. pap. 19.95 (*1-892640-03-1*) Vics Hockey Schls.

Lemisch, Jesse. Jack Tar in the Streets: Merchant Seamen in the Politics of Revolutionary America. (Irvington Reprint Series in American History). (C). 1991. reprint ed. pap. text 2.90 (*0-8290-2613-4*, H-431) Irvington.

— Jack Tar vs. John Bull: The Role of New York's Seamen in Precipitating the Revolution. LC 97-10449. (Studies in African American History & Culture). 200p. 1997. text 45.00 (*0-8153-2788-9*) Garland.

Lemish, Michael. War Dogs: Canines in Combat. (Illus.). 304p. 1996. 24.95 (*1-57488-017-9*) Brasseys.

— War Dogs: Canines in Combat. (Illus.). 224p. 1998. pap. 17.95 (*0-02-881135-6*); pap. 17.95 (*1-57488-195-7*) Brasseys.

***Lemish, Michael G.** War Dogs: A History of Loyalty & Heroism. 1999. pap. text 15.95 (*1-57488-216-3*) Brasseys.

Lemius, J. B. Catechism of Modernism. LC 81-52536. 160p. 1992. reprint ed. pap. 5.00 (*0-89555-167-5*) TAN Bks Pubs.

Lemke, A. B., tr. see Schweitzer, Albert.

Lemke, Bob. Sports Collector's Digest Baseball Card Pocket Price Guide. 576p. (Orig.). 1990. mass mkt. 5.95 (*0-446-36048-1*, Pub. by Warner Bks) Little.

***Lemke, Bob.** Standard Catalog of Baseball Cards 2001. 10th rev. ed. LC 88-80850. (Illus.). 1,664p. 2000. pap. 39.95 (*0-87341-936-7*, SB10) Krause Pubns.

***Lemke, Bob, ed.** Standard Catalog of Minor League Baseball Cards: The Most Comprehensive Price Guide Ever Published. LC 99-68108. (Illus.). 480p. 2000. pap. 24.95 (*0-87341-876-X*) Krause Pubns.

— 2000 Standard Catalog of Baseball Cards. 9th ed. LC 88-80850. (Illus.). 1664p. 1999. pap. 39.95 (*0-87341-767-4*) Krause Pubns.

Lemke, Bob & Grace, Sally. Sportscard Counterfeit Detector. 3rd ed. LC 91-77563. (Illus.). 272p. 1994. pap. 17.95 (*0-87341-284-2*, BD03) Krause Pubns.

— Sportscard Counterfeit Detector (1993) 2nd ed. (Illus.). 239p. 1998. reprint ed. pap. text 14.00 (*0-7881-5113-4*) DIANE Pub.

Lemke, Bradley N. & Della Rocca, Robert C. Surgery of the Eyelids & Orbit: An Anatomical Approach. (Illus.). 322p. (C). 1992. pap. text 195.00 (*0-8385-7500-5*, A7500-0, Apple Lange Med) McGraw.

Lemke, C. E., jt. ed. see Cottle, Richard W.

Lemke, Christiane, ed. German Democratic Republic in Eastern Europe. (Eastern Europe after Communism). (C). 1996. pap. text 42.50 (*0-8133-7901-6*) Westview.

Lemke, Christiane & Marks, Gary, eds. The Crisis of Socialism in Europe. LC 91-14680. 264p. 1991. pap. text 19.95 (*0-8223-1197-6*) Duke.

— The Crisis of Socialism in Europe. LC 91-14680. 264p. 1992. text 49.95 (*0-8223-1180-1*) Duke.

Lemke, Christiane, jt. ed. see Rueschemeyer, Marilyn.

***Lemke, D., et al.** ISO Surveys of a Dusty Universe: Proceedings of a Ringberg Workshop Held at Ringberg Castle, Tegernsee, Germany, 8-12 November, 1999. LC 00-41289. (Lecture Notes in Physics Ser.). 2000. write for info. (*3-540-67479-9*) Spr-Verlag.

Lemke, Douglas, jt. ed. see Kugler, Jacek.

L

***Lemke, Elisabeth & David, Thomas.** Marc Chagall: What Colour Is Paradise? (Illus.). 30p. 2000. 14.95 (*3-7913-2393-8*) Prestel.

Lemke, Gayle. The Art of the Fillmore: The Poster Series, 1966-1971. Kastor, Jacaeber, ed. (Illus.). 240p. 1997. 40.00 (*1-888358-09-2*) Acid Test Prodns.

***Lemke, Gayle, et al.** The Art of the Fillmore: The Poster Series 1966-1971. (Illus.). 240p. 1999. pap. 29.95 (*1-56025-242-1*, Thunders Mouth) Avalon NY.

***Lemke, H. U.** Cars 2000: Computer Assisted Radiology & Surgery: Proceedings of the 14th International Congress & Exhibition, San Francisco, June 28-July 1, 2000. LC 00-34105. (International Congress Ser.). 2000. write for info. (*0-444-50536-9*) Elsevier.

Lemke, H. U. Computer Assisted Radiology: Proceedings of the International Symposium on Computer & Communication Systems for Image Guided Diagnosis & Therapy, Paris, June 1996, No. 1124. 1148p. 1996. 336.50 (*0-444-82497-9*) Elsevier.

Lemke, H. U., et al, eds. CAR'97 Computer Assisted Radiology & Surgery: Proceedings of the 11th International Symposium & Exhibition, Berlin, Germany, 25-28 June 1997. (International Congress Ser.: No. 1134). 1108p. 1997. 340.75 (*0-444-82756-0*) Elsevier.

— Computer Assisted Radiology - Computergestutze Radiologie: Proceedings of the International Symposium. (Illus.). xxxv, 836p. 1993. 180.00 (*0-387-56595-7*) Spr-Verlag.

— Computer Assisted Radiology Computergestutzte Radiologie: Proceedings of the International Symposium Vortrage des Internationalen Symposiums, CAR '91 Computer Assisted Radiology. (Illus.). 944p. 1991. 207.95 (*0-387-54143-8*) Spr-Verlag.

— Computer Assisted Radiology-Computergestutzte Radiologie CAR '87. (Illus.). 900p. 1987. 118.95 (*0-387-17812-0*) Spr-Verlag.

— Computer Assisted Radiology-Computergestutzte Radiologie CAR' 89. (Illus.). xxxiii, 860p. 1989. 150.95 (*0-387-50890-2*, 2903) Spr-Verlag.

Lemke, H. U., jt. auth. see CARS '99 Staff.

Lemke, H. U., ed. see International Symposium CAR '95 Staff.

Lemke, Heinz. Car '98 Vol. 12: International Symposium & Exhibition. 998p. 1998. 310.50 (*0-444-82973-3*) Elsevier.

Lemke, Horst. Places & Faces. LC 78-160446. 32p. (J). (ps). 14.95 (*0-87592-041-1*) Scroll Pr.

Lemke, Ian. Changeling: The Dreaming. 2nd ed. (Changeling: The Dreaming Ser.). (Illus.). (Orig.). 1997. 30.00 (*1-56504-716-8*, 7300) White Wolf.

— Changeling: The Dreaming Dice. 2nd ed. (Changeling: The Dreaming Ser.). 1997. pap. 6.99 (*1-56504-798-2*) White Wolf.

— Changeling Player's Guide: For Changeling: The Dreaming. (Changeling: The Dreaming Ser.). (Illus.). 192p. (Orig.). 1996. pap. 22.00 (*1-56504-701-X*, 7100) White Wolf.

— Immortal Eyes: Court of All Kings, Vol. 3. (Changeling: The Dreaming Ser.). (Illus.). 136p. (Orig.). 1996. pap. 15.00 (*1-56504-713-3*, 7202) White Wolf.

— Kithbook: Troll. (Changeling: The Dreaming Ser.). (Illus.). 1996. pap. 12.00 (*1-56504-725-7*, 7050) White Wolf.

Lemke, Ian & Dansky, Richard. Kithbook: Slaugh. (Changeling: The Dreaming Ser.). (Illus.). 72p. (Orig.). 1997. pap. 12.00 (*1-56504-726-5*, 7051) White Wolf.

Lemke, Ian & Fisci, Beth. Isle of the Mighty. (Changeling: The Dreaming Ser.). (Illus.). 192p. (Orig.). 1997. pap. 22.00 (*1-56504-712-5*, 7007) White Wolf.

Lemke, Ian, et al. Immortal Eyes: Shadows on the Hill, Vol. 2. (Changeling: The Dreaming Ser.). (Illus.). 128p. (Orig.). 1996. pap. 15.00 (*1-56504-705-2*, 7201) White Wolf.

Lemke, J. Textual Politics: Discourse & Social Dynamics. (Critical Perspectives on Literacy & Education Ser.). 240p. 1995. 89.95 (*0-7484-0215-2*); pap. 24.95 (*0-7484-0216-0*) Taylor & Francis.

Lemke, Jay, jt. auth. see Hetteen, Edgar.

Lemke, Jay L. Talking Science: Language, Learning & Values. Green, Judith, ed. (Language & Educational Processes Ser.: Vol. 1). 288p. (C). 1990. pap. 39.50 (*0-89391-566-1*); text 73.25 (*0-89391-565-3*) Ablx Pub.

— Using Language in the Classroom. (C). 1985. pap. 38.00 (*0-7300-0308-6*, ECS805, Pub. by Deakin Univ) St Mut.

— Using Language in the Classroom. (Language Education Ser.). 60p. 1989. pap. text 7.95 (*0-19-437157-3*) OUP.

Lemke, Jeffrey J., jt. auth. see Thompson, J. Mark.

Lemke, Jurgen. Gay Voices from East Germany. Borneman, John, ed. LC 90-43690. 208p. 1991. pap. 14.95 (*0-253-20630-8*, MB-630) Ind U Pr.

Lemke, Karen. Return of the Downeast Detective. (Illus.). 192p. (Orig.). 1998. pap. 9.95 (*0-924771-94-1*, Covered Brdge Pr) Douglas Charles Ltd.

Lemke, Kenneth W., jt. ed. see Sterling, Robert R.

Lemke, Nancy. Cabrillo: First European Explorer of California Coast. (Illus.). 128p. 1991. pap. 8.95 (*0-945092-19-9*) EZ Nature.

— Missions of Southern Coast. (J). (gr. 4-7). pap. 5.95 (*0-8225-9837-X*) Lerner Pub.

— Missions of the Southern Coast. LC 95-16619. (California Missions Ser.). 80p. (J). (gr. 4-7). 1996. lib. bdg. 23.93 (*0-8225-1925-9*, Lerner Publctns) Lerner Pub.

Lemke, P. A., ed. Systematics & Cell Structure, No. 7. (Mycota: Vol. VII). Date not set. write for info. (*3-540-58008-5*) Spr-Verlag.

Lemke, P. A., jt. ed. see Esser, Karl.

Lemke, P. A., ed. see Melton, A. C.

Lemke, Raymond L. Yes You Can! An Innovative Approach to Happiness. Wilcox, Lucie, ed. LC 88-61002. (Illus.). 192p. (Orig.). 1988. pap. 6.95 (*0-929099-00-1*) Omaha Pr Pub.

Lemke, Robert F., jt. auth. see Krause, Chester L.

Lemke, Robert J. & Diedrich, Karen K. Misconceptions about Radiation, Facts Are Stranger Than Fiction in Hiroshima, Nagasaki, Marshall Islands, No. 1. (Illus.). 1994. pap. 35.00 (*0-9645418-3-1*) F T Cua.

— 101 Ways to Enrich Your Life: Clear Mindsets & Simple Tools That Help You See Everyday Experiences in a Different Way, & Handle them with Confidence. LC 98-89943. 232p. 1998. pap. 12.95 (*0-9669686-0-3*) Living Rich.

Lemke-Santangelo, Gretchen. Abiding Courage: African American Migrant Women & the East Bay Community. LC 95-23508. (Illus.). 232p. (C). 1996. pap. 17.95 (*0-8078-4563-9*); lib. bdg. 39.95 (*0-8078-2256-6*) U of NC Pr.

Lemke, Sieglinde. Primitivist-Modernism: Black Culture & the Origins of Transatlantic Modernism. LC 97-1352. (W. E. B. Dubois Institute Ser.). (Illus.). 192p. 1998. text 45.00 (*0-19-510403-X*) OUP.

Lemke, Sonne, jt. auth. see Moos, Rudolf H.

Lemke, Stefan. Gran Atlas del Mundo Para Ninos. 14p. 1991. pap. 24.95 (*0-8477-0079-8*) U of PR Pr.

Lemke, Steve, et al, eds. Biblical Hermeneutics: A Comprehensive Introduction to Interpreting Scripture. LC 95-46615. 432p. 1996. 34.99 (*0-8054-1147-X*, 4211-47) Broadman.

Lemke, Thomas & Lins, Gerald T. Regulation of Investment Advisers, 1995. (Securities Law Ser.). 1991. pap. 137.50 (*0-614-07306-5*) West Group.

Lemke, Thomas L. Review of Organic Functional Groups: Introduction to Medicinal Organic Chemistry. 3rd ed. LC 91-4855. (Illus.). 142p. 1991. pap. 25.95 (*0-8121-1428-0*) Lppncott W & W.

— Science of Drug Action: Course Outline. 4th ed. 208p. 1994. spiral bd. 13.95 (*0-8403-8318-5*) Kendall-Hunt.

Lemke, Thomas P. & Lins, Gerald T. How to Read a Mutual Fund Prospectus: A Practical Guide to Getting the Most Out of a Mutual Fund Prospectus. 300p. 1999. pap. 19.95 (*0-9655374-1-2*) Mercer Point.

Lemke, William. A Pride of Lions: Joshua Chamberlain & Other Maine Civil War Heroes. (Illus.). 256p. (Orig.). 1997. pap. 16.95 (*0-924771-95-X*, Covered Brdge Pr) Douglas Charles Ltd.

— The Wild, Wild East: Unusual Tales of Maine History. (Illus.). 188p. (Orig.). 1994. reprint ed. pap. 10.95 (*1-56626-116-3*, Cntry Rds Pr) NTC Contemp Pub Co.

Lemkey, F. D., et al, eds. High-Temperature/High-Performance Composites. (Symposium Proceedings Ser.: Vol. 120). 1988. text 17.50 (*0-931837-90-1*) Materials Res.

Lemkhin, Mikhail. Joseph Brodsky: Leningrad. LC 97-44215. (Illus.). 240p. 1998. text 35.00 (*0-374-15831-2*) FS&G.

Lemkhin, Mikhail, photos by. Missing Frames. LC 95-1321. (Illus.). 72p. (Orig.). 1995. pap. 24.00 (*1-55779-083-3*) Hermitage Pubs.

— Russkie Razgovory: Antologiia Sovremennoi Prozy. LC 92-17803. (RUS., Illus.). 200p. (Orig.). (C). 1992. pap. 10.00 (*1-55779-049-3*) Hermitage Pubs.

Lemkow, Anna F. The Wholeness Principle: Dynamics of Unity Within Science, Religion & Society. 2nd ed. LC 94-34924. 355p. 1995. pap. 14.00 (*0-8356-0715-1*, Quest) Theos Pub Hse.

Lemkow, Jytte, jt. auth. see Kyrklund, Kyra.

Lemkow, Louis. Public Attitudes to Genetic Engineering: Some European Perspectives. (Illus.). 44p. (Orig.). (C). 1995. pap. text 25.00 (*0-7881-1883-8*) DIANE Pub.

Lemkowitz, Florence. Mexico, 1985. Fisher, Robert C., ed. (Fisher Annotated Travel Guides Ser.). 448p. 1984. 13.95 (*0-8116-0068-8*) NAL.

Lemkowitz, S. M., jt. auth. see De Zeeuw, M. A.

Lemlech, Johanna K. Curriculum & Instructional Methods for the Elementary & Middle School. 4th ed. LC 97-21783. 413p. (C). 1997. 73.00 (*0-13-262130-4*) P-H.

Lemlech, Johanna K., ed. Becoming a Professional Leader. LC 94-29653. (Leadership Policy Research Ser.). (Illus.). 240p. (C). 1995. 24.95 (*0-590-49334-5*) Scholastic Inc.

Lemler, Kathleen. Transformation Through Flowers: Spiritual & Physical Healing. (Illus.). 128p. (Orig.). 1993. pap. 5.95 (*0-9635987-0-8*) Express of Nature.

Lemley, Amy, jt. auth. see Berent, Jonathan.

Lemley, Amy, jt. auth. see Koch-Sheras, Phyllis.

Lemley, Jo, jt. auth. see Lemley, Virg.

***Lemley, Mark A.** Software & Internet Law. LC 00-22064. 2000. boxed set 56.00 (*0-7355-1312-0*) Panel Pubs.

***Lemley, Mark A., et al.** Software & Internet Law: With Teacher's Manual. large type ed. (Casebook Ser.). 800p. 2000. write for info. (*0-7355-1313-9*) Panel Pubs.

***Lemley, Victor.** History of Cities: 500 BC to Present, 10 vols. Incl. History of Cities: Jerusalem. 2000. 55.00 (*0-9675028-5-3*); History of Cities: Paris. 2000. 55.00 (*0-9675028-6-1*); 2000. 550.00 (*0-9675028-4-5*) Beacon Light Bks.

Lemley, Virg & Lemley, Jo. Children's Cookery, Naturally, Vol. 1. (Illus.). 57p. (J). (gr. 1-10). 1980. pap. 5.99 (*0-931798-05-1*) Wilderness Hse.

— Soybean Cookery. 1975. pap. 5.99 (*0-931798-04-3*) Wilderness Hse.

— Zucchini Cookery, Vol. 1. 56p. 1976. pap. 5.99 (*0-931798-02-7*) Wilderness Hse.

Lemlich, Jeffrey M. Savage Lost: Florida Garage Bands - The '60s & Beyond. LC 91-15241. (Illus.). 424p. 1992. pap. 19.95 (*0-942963-12-1*) Distinctive Pub.

Lemlin, Jeanne. Main-Course Vegetarian Pleasures. LC 94-23966. 272p. 1998. pap. 17.00 (*0-06-095022-6*) HarpC.

— Quick Vegetarian Pleasures: Fast, Delicious, & Healthy Meatless Recipes. LC 91-50515. (Illus.). 288p. 1998. pap. 17.00 (*0-06-096911-3*, Perennial) HarperTrade.

— Simple Vegetarian Pleasures. LC 97-43360. 336p. 1998. 24.00 (*0-06-019135-X*) HarpC.

***Lemlin, Jeanne.** Simple Vegetarian Pleasures. (Illus.). 336p. 2000. pap. 15.00 (*0-06-093246-5*, Quil) HarperTrade.

— Vegetarian Classics. 2001. write for info. (*0-06-019482-0*) HarpC.

— Vegetarian Classics. 2002. pap. write for info. (*0-06-093273-2*, Perennial) HarperTrade.

Lemm, W. Langenscheidt German/Japanese/German Dictionary. 9th ed. (GER & JPN.). 379p. 1995. 29.95 (*0-320-00540-2*) Fr & Eur.

Lemm, W., ed. The Reference Materials of the European Communities: Results of Hemocompatibility Tests. LC 92-30458. 272p. (C). 1992. text 148.50 (*0-7923-2002-6*) Kluwer Academic.

Lemm, W., jt. ed. see Missirlis, Y. F.

Lemma, Aklilu, et al. Phytolacca Dodecandra (Endod) 332p. 1984. pap. 40.00 (*0-907567-85-1*, Tycooly Pub); text 60.00 (*0-907567-84-3*, Tycooly Pub) Weidner & Sons.

Lemma, Alessandra. Introduction to Psychopathology. LC 96-68912. 240p. 1996. 42.50 (*0-8039-7470-1*); pap. 13.99 (*0-8039-7471-X*) Sage.

Lemma-Wright, Alessandra. Invitation to Psychodynamic Psychology. 150p. 1995. pap. 24.95 (*1-56593-500-4*, 1158) Singular Publishing.

Lemme. Development in Adulthood. 2nd ed. LC 98-17281. 544p. 1998. 77.33 (*0-205-27366-1*) Allyn.

Lemme, Margaret L., ed. Clinical Aphasiology, Vol. 21. LC 86-647891. 364p. (C). 1992. text 49.00 (*0-89079-564-9*, 1808) PRO-ED.

— Clinical Aphasiology, Vol. 22. 363p. (C). 1994. text 49.00 (*0-89079-595-9*, 1809) PRO-ED.

— Clinical Aphasiology, Vol. 24. 277p. 1996. text 49.00 (*0-89079-695-5*, 6901) PRO-ED.

Lemmen, Jan. Integrating Financial Markets in the European Union. LC 98-23715. 240p. 1998. 85.00 (*1-85898-730-X*) E Elgar.

Lemmens, Maarten. Lexical Perspectives on Transitivity & Ergativity: Causatives Constructions in English. LC 98-36270. (Current Issues in Linguistic Theory Ser.: Vol. 166). xii, 268p. 1998. 69.00 (*1-55619-882-5*) J Benjamins Pubng Co.

Lemmens, P. & Raes, S., eds. Civil Procedure. 1991. ring bd. write for info. (*0-318-68488-8*) Kluwer Law Intl.

Lemmens, R. H., et al, eds. Timber Trees: Minor Commercial Timbers. (PROSEA Ser.: No. 5.2). (Illus.). 655p. 1995. 150.00 (*90-73348-44-7*, Pub. by Backhuys Pubs) Balogh.

Lemmens, R. H. & Wulijarni-Soetjipto, N., eds. Dye & Tannin-Producing Plants. (PROSEA Ser.: No. 3). (Illus.). 196p. 1991. 100.00 (*90-220-0987-4*, Pub. by Backhuys Pubs); pap. 36.00 (*979-8316-03-7*, Pub. by Backhuys Pubs) Balogh.

Lemmens, R. H., jt. ed. see Soerianegara, I.

Lemmer, B. & Huller, H., eds. Clinical Chronopharmacology. (Clinical Pharmacology Ser.: Vol. 6). (Illus.). 208p. 1990. text 48.00 (*3-88603-374-0*, Pub. by W Zuckschwerdt) Scholium Intl.

Lemmer, Bill & Smits, Martin. Facilitating Change in Mental Health. 236p. 1990. pap. 25.50 (*0-412-33010-5*, A4458) Chapman & Hall.

Lemmer, E. M. & Badenhorst, D. C. Foundations of Education: An Orientation to Teaching Practice in South Africa. LC 97-226029. 440p. 1997. pap. 69.95 (*0-7021-3819-3*, Pub. by Juta & Co) Intl Spec Bk.

Lemmer, Eleanor. Winning at Work. 1998. pap. text 14.00 (*0-627-02084-4*, Pub. by J L Van Schaik) BHB Intl.

Lemmer, George F. The Lao Crisis of 1959. 61p. 1961. reprint ed. pap. text 9.50 (*0-923135-38-3*) Dalley Bk Service.

Lemmer, Gerhard, et al. Nelles Guide to Norway. (Illus.). 256p. 1999. pap. 15.95 (*3-88618-048-4*) Hunter NJ.

Lemmer, R. H. Multistep Direct Reactions. 236p. 1992. text 81.00 (*981-02-1171-6*) World Scientific Pub.

***Lemmermeyer, F.** Reciprocity Laws: From Euler to Eisenstein. (Monographs in Mathematics). xix, 487p. 2000. (*3-540-66957-4*) Spr-Verlag.

Lemmerz, A. H. Basiswissen-Ekg-Registrierung: 2., Erweiterte Auflage. (Illus.). viii, 96p. 1975. 16.75 (*3-8055-2298-3*) S Karger.

— Examples Illustrating the Use of Frank Leads. (Illus.). 48p. 1972. pap. 10.50 (*3-8055-1294-5*) S Karger.

Lemmerz, A. H. & Schmidt, R. R. Auswertung und Deutung des EKG. 12th ed. (Illus.). xii, 260p. 1981. pap. 41.75 (*3-8055-1932-X*) S Karger.

Lemmi, Charles W. The Classic Deities in Bacon: A Study in Mythological Symbolism. 234p. 1997. reprint ed. pap. 24.95 (*0-7661-0096-0*) Kessinger Pub.

***Lemmings, David.** Professors of the Law: Barristers & English Legal Culture in the Eighteenth Century. (Illus.). 408p. 2000. text 88.00 (*0-19-820721-2*) OUP.

Lemmink, Jos, jt. ed. see Kunst, Paul.

Lemmo, Edward A. Silica. (Good Health Guides Ser.). pap. 3.95 (*0-87983-905-8*, 39058K, Keats Publng) NTC Contemp Pub Co.

Lemmo, Peter S., jt. auth. see Greenblatt, Miriam.

Lemmo, Peter S., ed. see Schoendorf, Robert.

Lemmo, Steven & Grehan, Rick. The Client/Server Toolkit for C & C++ Programmers. (Illus.). 410p. (Orig.). 1996. pap. write for info. (*0-9657512-0-1*) NobleNet.

Lemmon, Alfred E. La Musica de Guatemala en el Siglo XVIII: Music from Eighteenth Century Guatemala. LC 85-63627. (ENG & SPA., Illus.). 174p. (Orig.). 1986. pap. 14.00 (*0-910443-03-3*) Plumsock Meso Studies.

Lemmon, David. The Benson & Hedges British Theatre Yearbook, 1992. (Illus.). 376p. 1993. pap. 34.95 (*0-233-98780-0*, Pub. by Andre Deutsch) Trafalgar.

Lemmon, E. J. Beginning Logic. LC 98-49119. 240p. 1971. per. 41.95 (*0-412-38090-0*) CRC Pr.

— Beginning Logic. LC 78-51926. 235p. (C). 1978. pap. text 15.95 (*0-915144-50-6*) Hackett Pub.

Lemmon, Ed. Boss Cowman: The Recollections of Ed Lemmon, 1857-1946. LC 69-10313. (Pioneer Heritage Ser.: No. 6). 341p. reprint ed. pap. 105.80 (*0-7837-6464-2*, 204646800001) Bks Demand.

Lemmon, James T., ed. Liberal Dreams & Nature'S Limits: Great Cities Of North America Since 1600. LC 97-141393. (Illus.). 342p. 1997. pap. text 42.00 (*0-19-540793-8*) OUP.

Lemmon, Jennifer. The Gift. (Animal Tales Ser.). (Illus.). 12p. (J). (ps-2). 1995. pap. 4.95 (*0-909991-86-3*) Bahai.

— Story of Calvin Caterpillar. (Illus.). 12p. (J). (ps-2). 1994. pap. 4.95 (*0-909991-82-0*) Bahai.

— The Story of Rosie Redbird. (Illus.). 12p. (J). (ps-2). 1995. pap. 4.95 (*0-909991-74-X*) Bahai.

Lemmon, Jim. The Log of Rowing at the University of California Berkeley, 1870-1987. LC 88-33945. (Western Heritage Bks.). (Illus.). 160p. 1989. 35.00 (*0-9621956-0-X*) Wstrn Heritage.

Lemmon, John A. Family Mediation Practice. 244p. 1985. 29.95 (*0-02-918550-5*) Free Pr.

Lemmon, John A., jt. auth. see Brieland, Donald.

Lemmon, M., jt. ed. see Goin, J.

Lemmon, Michael. Competitively Inhibited Neural Networks for Adaptive Parameter Estimation. (C). 1990. text 91.50 (*0-7923-9086-5*) Kluwer Academic.

Lemmon, Nadine, jt. ed. see Druckrey, Timothy.

Lemmon, Nicolette. Almost Famous: How to Market Yourself for Success. (Illus.). 108p. (Orig.). 1996. pap., wbk. ed. 18.95 (*0-9650880-0-6*) Lemmon Pubng Grp.

— Successful Product Development: From Research to Results. 108p. (Orig.). 1995. pap. 89.00 (*1-889394-20-3*) Credit Union Execs.

***Lemmon, Nicolette, et al.** Member Acceptance of Electronic Access Systems: Innovators vs. Laggards. 74p. 1999. pap. 100.00 (*1-880572-36-2*, 1752-43) Filene Res.

Lemmon, Randy. A Golfer's Guide to Gardening. Billac, Pete, ed. LC 97-65259. (Illus.). 104p. (Orig.). 1997. pap. 9.95 (*0-943629-28-4*) Swan Pub.

Lemmon, Sarah M. North Carolina & the War of 1812. (Illus.). ix, 54p. 1984. pap. 5.00 (*0-86526-087-7*) NC Archives.

— North Carolina's Role in the First World War. (Illus.). viii, 91p. 1975. pap. 5.00 (*0-86526-094-X*) NC Archives.

— North Carolina's Role in World War II. (Illus.). viii, 69p. 1995. reprint ed. pap. 5.00 (*0-86526-095-8*) NC Archives.

Lemmon, Sarah M., ed. The Pettigrew Papers, 1819-1843, Vol. 2. (Pettigrew Papers). (Illus.). xlv, 631p. 1988. 45.00 (*0-86526-069-9*) NC Archives.

Lemmons, Robert & Stancil, Mary H. Through the Eyes of a Recovering Addict. (Illus.). 120p. 1998. pap. 7.95 (*1-892212-02-1*) Love Pubg Co.

Lemmons, Russel G. Goebbels & der Angriff. LC 93-33405. 184p. (C). 1994. 24.95 (*0-8131-1848-4*) U Pr of Ky.

Lemmons, Thom. Daughter of Jerusalem. LC 98-50035. (Daughters of Faith Ser.: Vol. 1). 325p. 1999. pap. 12.99 (*1-57673-477-3*) Multnomah Pubs.

***Lemmons, Thom.** Woman of Means: Lydia, Merchant of Philippi. LC 99-88654. (Daughters of Faith Ser.: Vol. 2). 320p. 2000. pap. 10.99 (*1-57673-612-1*, Pub. by Multnomah Pubs) GL Services.

Lemmons, Thom, jt. auth. see Mirza, William.

Lemoalle, Jacques, jt. auth. see Talling, Jack F.

***Lemoff, Theodore C.** National Fire Gas Code Handbook, 4, 1. 3rd ed. LC 99-75206. (Illus.). 422p. 2000. 18.00 (*0-87765-446-8*, 54HB99) Natl Fire Prot.

Lemoff, Theodore C., et al. National Fuel Gas Code Handbook. 3rd ed. LC 97-81708. xiii, 547p. 1997. 78.00 (*0-87765-409-3*) Natl Fire Prot.

Lemoine, A., et al. Esvitaf Vitamin Status in Three Groups of French Adults: Control, Obese Subjects, Alcohol Drinkers. (Journal: Annals of Nutrition & Metabolism: Vol. 30, Suppl. 1, 1986). (ENG & FRE., Illus.). 96p. 1986. pap. 25.25 (*3-8055-4244-5*) S Karger.

Lemoine, Bertrand. Architecture in France, 1800 to 1900. Bonfante-Warren, Alexandra, tr. LC 97-45861. (Illus.). 200p. 1998. 45.00 (*0-8109-4090-6*, Pub. by Abrams) Time Warner.

***Lemoine, Bertrand.** Birkhauser Architectural Guide France. (Illus.). 352p. 2000. 40.00 (*3-7643-6222-7*, Pub. by Birkhauser) Princeton Arch.

LeMoine, Fannie & Kleinhenz, Christopher, eds. Saint Augustine the Bishop: A Book of Essays. LC 94-7258. (Medieval Casebooks Ser.: Vol. 9). (Illus.). 232p. 1994. text 43.00 (*0-8153-1639-9*, H1830) Garland.

LeMoine, Fannie, jt. auth. see Kleinhenz, Christopher.

LeMoine, Fannie, jt. ed. see Kleinhenz, Christopher.

Lemoine, Francoise, jt. auth. see Sokoloff, Georges.

Lemoine, Georges. Pied. (Gallimard - Mes Premieres Decouvertes Ser.: No. 9). (FRE.). (J). (ps-1). 1989. 12.95 (*2-07-035701-5*) Schoenhof.

Lemoine, Georges, ed. see Fallis, James C., et al.

Lemoine, H. Dictionnaire des Communes Vol. 1: Departement de la Meuse. fac. ed. (FRE.). 1991. pap. 185.00 (*0-7859-8250-7*, 2909112047) Fr & Eur.

— Etudes Enfantines for Piano, Op. 37. (Carl Fischer Music Library: No. 323). 52p. (J). 1904. pap. 8.95 (*0-8258-0106-0*, L 323) Fischer Inc NY.

LeMoine, J. M. The Scot in New France: An Ethnological Study. 85p. 1998. reprint ed. pap. 10.00 (*1-58211-057-3*, 097651) Quintin Pub RI.

Lemoine, Jacques. The International Civil Servant: An Endangered Species. LC 95-11895. 1995. lib. bdg. 142.00 (*0-7923-3444-2*) Kluwer Academic.

Lemoine, Laura F., jt. auth. see Rasberry, Robert W.

Lemoine, Michel, ed. see ESEC/FSE '99 Staff, et al.

Lemoine, N. & Cooper, D. N. Gene Therapy. (Human Molecular Genetics Ser.). 320p. 1996. text 130.00 (*1-85996-205-X*, Pub. by Bios Sci) Bks Intl VA.

An Asterisk (*) at the beginning of an entry indicates that the title is appearing for the first time.

***Lemoine, Nicholas.** Gene Therapy. 343p. 1999. 105.00 (*0-12-220435-2*) Acad Pr.

Lemoine, Nicholas R. The Molecular Pathology of Cancer. LC 93-246938. (Cancer Surveys Ser.: No. 16). (Illus.). 252p. 1993. pap. 78.20 (*0-608-04957-3*, 206553600004) Bks Demand.

Lemoine, Nicholas R. & Epenetos, Agamemnon A., eds. Mutant Oncogenes: Targets for Therapy. LC 92-48907. 224p. (gr. 13). 1993. text 132.95 (*0-412-48110-3*) Chapman & Hall.

Lemoine, Roy E. The Anagogic Theory of Wittgenstein's Tractatus. LC 74-80541. (Janua Linguarum, Series Minor: No. 214). 215p. (Orig.). 1975. pap. text 44.65 (*90-279-3393-6*) Mouton.

Lemoine, Stewart. Cocktails at Pam's & Evelyn Strange: A Mystery, 2 bks. in 1. (Playwrights Canada Ser.). 120p. 1998. pap. 15.95 (*0-88754-539-4*) Theatre Comm.

***Lemole, Gerald M.** The River of Life. 2001. write for info. (*0-688-17073-0*, Wm Morrow) Morrow Avon.

Lemon. Collected Practical Problems. (C). 1959. 110.00 (*0-685-36030-X*, Pub. by British Textile Tech) St Mut.

— Geography Change South Africa. 274p. 1994. pap. text 59.95 (*0-471-95619-8*) Wiley.

— Physical Geology. 608p. 1995. 37.95 (*0-8016-2571-8*) Mosby Inc.

— Physical Geology Study Guide. 192p. 1994. pap. 16.95 (*0-8016-2556-4*) Mosby Inc.

— The Third Planet: An Introduction to Earth Science. 608p. 1994. 39.95 (*0-8016-7470-0*) Mosby Inc.

— Vanishing World. 1992. teacher ed. 25.62 (*0-697-11250-0*) McGraw.

Lemon, Anthony, ed. Homes Apart: South Africa's Segregated Cities. LC 91-72181. (Illus.). 252p. 1991. 21.00 (*0-253-33321-0*) Ind U Pr.

Lemon, Anthony & Pollock, Norman C. Studies in Overseas Settlement & Population. LC 79-42738. 133p. reprint ed. pap. 41.30 (*0-608-14478-9*, 202527400043) Bks Demand.

***Lemon, Bill.** Professional Secrets of Nude & Beauty Photography: Techniques & Images in Black & White. (Illus.). 128p. 2000. pap. 29.95 (*1-58428-044-1*, Pub. by Amherst Media) IPG Chicago.

LeMon, Cal. Unreported Miracles: What . . . Do Not Know about Your Child's School Bus. 3rd ed. LC 99-165256. 72p. 1998. per. 10.00 (*0-7872-4893-2*, 41489301) Kendall-Hunt.

Lemon, Charles, ed. Bronte's Family History, 6 vols. 2000p. (C). 1998. 700.00 (*0-415-16873-2*) Routledge.

Lemon, Harvey B. From Galileo to the Nuclear Age: An Introduction to Physics. LC QC0023.L4. (Phoenix Science Ser.). 480p. reprint ed. pap. 148.80 (*0-608-10007-2*, 202010400016) Bks Demand.

Lemon, Jack E., jt. auth. see Ratner, Buddy D.

Lemon, Jennifer. The Secret. (Illus.). 11p. (J). (ps-2). 1994. pap. 4.95 (*0-909991-80-4*) Bahai.

— Story of Riaz Redfin. (Illus.). 12p. (J). (ps-2). 1995. pap. 4.95 (*0-909991-84-7*) Bahai.

Lemon, Lee T. Portraits of the Artist in Contemporary Fiction. LC 84-22005. 281p. 1985. reprint ed. pap. 87.20 (*0-608-02382-5*, 206302400004) Bks Demand.

Lemon, Lee T. & Reis, Marion J., trs. Russian Formalist Criticism: Four Essays. LC 65-21899. (Regents Critics Ser.). xvii, 143p. 1965. pap. text 14.00 (*0-8032-5460-1*) U of Nebr Pr.

***Lemon, Mark, ed.** Exploring Environmental Change Using an Integrative Method. (Illus.). 260p. 1999. 90.00 (*90-5699-193-0*, Harwood Acad Pubs) Gordon & Breach.

Lemon, Nancy K., ed. Domestic Violence Law: A Comprehensive Overview of Cases & Sources. 822p. (C). 1996. text 69.95 (*1-57292 023 8*); pap. text 49.95 (*1-57292-022-X*) Austin & Winfield.

***Lemon, Nancy K. D.** Domestic Violence Cases in Criminal Law. LC 96-85790. (California Judges Benchbook Ser.). 198p. 2000. 65.00 (*0-7626-0458-1*, CR-33270) Cont Ed Bar-CA.

Lemon, Peter C. Beyond the Medal: A Journey from Their Hearts to Yours. LC 96-47641. (Illus.). 192p. 1997. 24.95 (*1-55591-358-X*) Fulcrum Pub.

Lemon, R., ed. Collected Practical Problems. 1959. 80.00 (*0-7855-1014-1*) St Mut.

***Lemon, Ralph.** Geography: Art - Race - Exile. 2000. 29.95 (*0-8195-6443-5*, Wesleyan Univ Pr) U Pr of New Eng.

Lemon, Roger, jt. auth. see Porter, Robert.

Lemon, Roy R. Vanished Worlds: An Introduction to Historical Geology. 496p. (C). 1992. text. write for info. (*0-697-11249-7*, WCB McGr Hill) McGrw-H Hghr Educ.

Lemon, Sandra, tr. see Isaac, Mia.

Lemon, Sandra E. From Captivity to Comeback. LC 90-85375. 328p. (Orig.). 1991. pap. 17.95 (*0-935132-20-1*) C H Fairfax.

Lemon-Swindle, Liz & Easton-Black, Susan. Joseph Smith: Impressions of a Prophet. LC 97-46357. 1998. write for info. (*1-57345-316-1*) Deseret Bk.

Lemon, Tess. Chimpanzees. (Illus.). 112p. text 19.95 (*1-873580-04-5*, Pub. by Whittet Bks) Diamond Farm Bk.

LeMoncheck, Linda. Dehumanizing Women: Treating Persons As Sex Objects. (New Feminist Perspectives Ser.). 180p. 1985. 55.00 (*0-8476-7331-6*) Rowman.

— Dehumanizing Women: Treating Persons As Sex Objects. (New Feminist Perspectives Ser.). 184p. 1985. pap. 21.00 (*0-8476-7386-3*) Rowman.

LeMoncheck, Linda & Hajdin, Mane. Sexual Harassment: A Debate. LC 96-43497. (Point/Counterpoint Ser.: No. 94). 252p. 1997. 55.50 (*0-8476-8424-5*); pap. 17.95 (*0-8476-8425-3*) Rowman.

***LeMoncheck, Linda & Sterba, James P.** Sexual Harassment: Issues & Answers. 384p. (C). 2000. pap. 25.00 (*0-19-513481-8*); text 45.00 (*0-19-514299-3*) OUP.

LeMoncheck, Linda J. Loose Women, Lecherous Men: A Feminist Philosophy of Sex. LC 96-34477. 320p. 1997. pap. 22.00 (*0-19-510556-7*) OUP.

LeMond, Greg & Gordis, Kent. Greg LeMond's Complete Book of Bicycling. 2nd ed. (Illus.). 352p. 1990. pap. 14.95 (*0-399-51594-1*, Perigee Bks) Berkley Pub.

***LeMonds, James.** Deadfall: Generations of Logging in the Pacific Northwest. (Illus.). 272p. 2000. pap. 14.00 (*0-87842-421-0*) Mountain Pr.

LeMonds, James. South of Seattle: Notes on Life in the Northwest Woods. LC 97-28352. 122p. 1997. pap. 10.00 (*0-87842-363-X*) Mountain Pr.

LeMone, jt. auth. see Lillis.

LeMone, Charles S. A Dance in the Street. 256p. (Orig.). 1993. mass mkt. 3.99 (*0-380-76713-9*, Avon Bks) Morrow Avon.

Lemone, Karen A. Assembly Language & Systems for the IBM PC. 1985. 19.95 (*0-316-52069-1*) Little.

— Design of Compilers: Techniques of Programming Language Translation. 336p. 1992. lib. bdg. 69.95 (*0-8493-7342-5*, QA76) CRC Pr.

— Fundamentals of Compilers: An Introduction to Computer Language Translation. (Illus.). 600p. 1991. lib. bdg. 58.00 (*0-8493-7341-7*, TP308) CRC Pr.

LeMone, Priscilla. Clinical Handbook Medical Surgical Nuring: Critical Thinking in Client Care. 2nd ed. LC 99-34472. (C). 1999. pap. text 22.00 (*0-8053-8126-0*) Benjamin-Cummings.

— Fluid & Electrolytes. 2nd ed. 55p. (C). 1999. pap. 9.95 (*0-8053-8128-7*) Benjamin-Cummings.

***Lemone, Priscilla.** Medical & Surgical Nursing: Study Guide. 2nd ed. 448p. (C). 1999. pap. text, student ed. 19.93 (*0-8053-8127-9*) Benjamin-Cummings.

LeMone, Priscilla & Burke, Karen M., eds. Medical Surgical Nursing: Critical Thinking in Client Care. 2nd ed. LC 99-32955. 2170p. (C). 1999. student ed. 80.00 (*0-8053-8121-X*) Benjamin-Cummings.

LeMone, Priscilla, ed. see North American Nursing Diagnosis Association Staff.

Lemonick, Michael. Other Worlds: The Search for Life in the Universe. (Illus.). 272p. 1999. pap. 14.00 (*0-684-85313-2*, Touchstone) S&S Trade Pap.

— Science Alive, No. 1. (J). 1998. write for info. (*0-7868-0133-6*) Hyperion.

— Science Alive, No. 1. (J). Date not set. lib. bdg. write for info. (*0-7868-2106-X*) Hyprn Child.

— Science Alive, Vol. 2. (J). Date not set. write for info. (*0-7868-0134-4*) Hyperion.

Lemonick, Michael D. The Light at the Edge of the Universe: Dispatches from the Front Lines of Cosmology. LC 94-39324. 336p. 1995. pap. text 14.95 (*0-691-00158-8*, Pub. by Princeton U Pr) Cal Prin Full Svc.

— Other Worlds: The Search for Life in the Universe. LC 97-49006. 272p. 1998. 24.50 (*0-684-83294-1*) S&S Trade.

Lemonnier, Augustin-Michel, ed. see Fesch, Jacques.

Lemonnier, D., et al, eds. Advanced Concepts & Techniques in Thermal Modelling. (Proceedings of the Eurotherm Seminar Ser.: No. 36). 380p. 109.00 (*2-906077-77-1*) Elsevier.

Lemonnier, Pierre. Elements for an Anthropology of Technology. LC 92-19485. (Anthropological Papers Ser.: No. 88). 1992. pap. 15.00 (*0-915703-30-0*) U Mich Mus Anthro.

Lemons, C. Dale. Education & Training for a Technological World. 42p. 1984. 4.25 (*0-318-22084-9*, IN267) Ctr Educ Trng Employ.

Lemons, Don S. Perfect Form: Variational Principles, Methods, & Applications in Elementary Physics. LC 96-9639. 144p. 1997. text 39.50 (*0-691-02664-5*, Pub. by Princeton U Pr) Cal Prin Full Svc.

Lemons, J. Stanley. The Woman Citizen: Social Feminism in the 1920s. 288p. 1990. reprint ed. pap. text 16.50 (*0-8139-1302-0*) U Pr of Va.

Lemons, Jack E., ed. Quantitative Characterization & Performance of Porous Implants for Hard Tissue Applications. LC 87-33430. (Special Technical Publication Ser.: No. 953). 420p. 1988. text 75.00 (*0-8031-0965-2*, STP953) ASTM.

Lemons, Jack E., jt. ed. see Brown, Stanley A.

Lemons, John. National Environmental Policy ACT: Readings from the Environmental Professional. LC 96-125265. 1995. write for info. (*0-86542-462-4*) Blackwell Sci.

Lemons, John, ed. Scientific Uncertainty & Its Implications for Environmental Problem Solving. LC 95-36595. (Environmental Sciences Library). (Illus.). 512p. 1996. boxed set 91.95 (*0-86542-476-4*) Blackwell Sci.

Lemons, John, et al, eds. Ecological Sustainability & Integrity: Concepts & Approaches. LC 97-49832. (Environmental Science & Technology Library). 315p. 1998. 145.00 (*0-7923-4909-1*) Kluwer Academic.

Lemons, John & Brown, Donald A., eds. Sustainable Development: Science, Ethics, & Public Policy. LC 95-10769. (Environmental Science & Technology Library). 304p. (C). 1995. text 154.50 (*0-7923-3500-7*) Kluwer Academic.

Lemons, John, jt. ed. see Westra, Laura.

Lemons, John, jt. ed. see Wright, R. Gerald.

Lemons Pollack, Ann, jt. auth. see Pollack, Joe.

Lemons, Rhonda K., ed. see Woytowich, Andy.

Lemons, Ted, jt. auth. see Droms, Ralph E.

***Lemons, Terry.** Where There's Love There's Miracles. Page, Deanna, ed. 2000. pap. write for info. (*0-9679539-0-1*) Lemons Pub.

Lemont, Harvey, jt. auth. see Witkowski, Joseph A.

Lemont, Levi P. Historical Dates of the Town & City of Bath, ME, & Town of Georgetown, from 1604 to 1874. 104p. 1995. reprint ed. pap. 15.00 (*0-8328-4462-4*) Higginson Bk Co.

Lemos, Anna. Archaic Pottery of Chios, 2 vols. (Illus.). 300p. 1992. 135.00 (*0-947816-30-5*, Pub. by Oxford Univ Comm Arch) David Brown.

Lemos, Charles. Everybody's San Francisco Cookbook: Recipes Celebrating the City's Best Ethnic Cooking. (Illus.). 288p. 1998. pap. text 16.95 (*1-886776-01-6*) Good Life.

Lemos, Claudia De, see Camaioni, Luigia & De Lemos, Claudia, eds.

Lemos, Gerard, jt. auth. see Young, Michael Dunlop.

Lemos, M. C., et al, eds. Wave Breaking: A Numerical Study. (Lecture Notes in Engineering Ser.: Vol. 71). (Illus.). viii, 196p. 1992. 68.95 (*0-387-54942-0*) Spr-Verlag.

Lemos, Noah M. Intrinsic Value: Concept & Warrant. LC 93-48142. (Cambridge Studies in Philosophy). 233p. (C). 1994. text 69.95 (*0-521-46207-X*) Cambridge U Pr.

Lemos, Ramon M. Metaphysical Investigations. LC 86-46324. 288p. 1988. 38.50 (*0-8386-3307-2*) Fairleigh Dickinson.

— The Nature of Value: Axiological Investigations. LC 95-1079. 240p. 1995. 39.95 (*0-8130-1366-6*) U Press Fla.

— Rights, Goods & Democracy. LC 85-47801. 208p. 1986. 38.50 (*0-87413-312-2*) U Delaware Pr.

Lemos, William. LorcaLines: Combinations Inspired by Federico Garcia Lorca. LC 94-72532. (Illus.). 60p. (Orig.). 1994. pap. 12.95 (*0-9642125-1-X*) Daylight Ducks.

Lemp, Helena B. Manual for the Organization of Scientific Congresses. 1978. pap. 28.75 (*3-8055-2962-7*) S Karger.

Lemp, M. A. & Marquardt, R., eds. The Dry Eye: A Comprehensive Guide. (Illus.). 256p. 1992. 145.00 (*0-387-53308-7*) Spr-Verlag.

Lemp, Michael A., jt. auth. see Snell, Richard S.

Lempereur, Agnes, jt. auth. see Thines, Georges.

Lemperle, G. & Nievergelt, J. Plastic & Reconstructive Breast Surgery. (Illus.). x, 192p. 1991. 262.00 (*0-387-52868-7*) Spr-Verlag.

Lempert, David H. Daily Life in a Crumbling Empire: The Absorption of Russia into the World Economy, 2 vols. 1200p. 1996. 168.00 (*0-88033-341-3*, 444, Pub. by East Eur Monographs) Col U Pr.

— Escape from the Ivory Tower: Student Adventures in Democratic Experiential Education. LC 95-22192. (Higher & Adult Education Ser.). 400p. 1995. text 32.95 (*0-7879-0136-9*) Jossey-Bass.

Lempert, David H. & McCarty, Kim. A Model Development Plan: New Strategies & Perspectives. LC 95-2225. 320p. 1998. pap. 24.95 (*0-275-96360-8*, Praeger Pubs) Greenwood.

Lempert, David H., et al. A Model Development Plan: New Strategies & Perspectives. LC 95-2225. 320p. 1995. 65.00 (*0-275-95068-9*) Greenwood.

Lempert, Leo. Industrialisation of Developing Countries. 363p. 1973. pap. 24.00 (*0-8464-1471-6*) Beekman Pubs.

— Millionaires & Managers: Structure of U. S. Financial Oligarchy. (Illus.). 1969. pap. 22.00 (*0-8464-0632-2*) Beekman Pubs.

Lempert, Michael & Sangpo, Tenzing. Tibetan Newspaper Reader. Hackett, Paul, ed. LC 96-83390. 1996. 44.00 (*1-881265-40-4*) Dunwoody Pr.

Lempert, Richard & Sanders, Joseph A. An Invitation to Law & Social Science. LC 85-12899. (Law in Social Context Ser.). 541p. 1989. pap. text 21.95 (*0-8122-1329-7*) U of Pa Pr.

Lempert, Richard O. & Saltzburg, Stephen A. A Modern Approach to Evidence: Teacher's Manual. 2nd ed. (American Casebook Ser.). 553p. (C). 1983. pap. text, teacher ed. write for info. (*0-314-76113-6*) West Pub.

— A Modern Approach to Evidence: Text, Problems, Transcripts & Cases. 2nd ed. LC 82-13578. (American Casebook Ser.). 1232p. (C). 1982. reprint ed. 62.50 (*0-314-67594-9*) West Pub.

Lempert, Robert J. & Bonomo, James L. New Methods for Robust Science & Technology Planning. (Illus.). 50p. 1998. pap. 6.00 (*0-8330-2585-6*, DB-238-DARPA) Rand Corp.

Lempert, Robert J. & Schwabe, William L. Transition to Sustainable Waste Management: A Simulation Gaming Approach. LC 93-14765. 1993. pap. 13.00 (*0-8330-1339-4*, MR-183-EAC) Rand Corp.

Lempert, Todd E., jt. auth. see Truwit, Charles L.

Lempfrit, Honore-Timothee. His Oregon Trail Journal of Father Lempfrit, OMI. Meyer, Patricia & Levesque, Catou, eds. (Illus.). 260p. 1985. 18.95 (*0-87770-347-7*) Ye Galleon.

Lempicka-Foxhall, Kizette De, see De Lempicka-Foxhall, Kizette.

Lempinen, M., ed. see European Society for Surgical Research Staff.

Lempp, Otto. Das Problem der Theodicee in der Philosophie und Literatur des 18. Jahr-Hunderts bis auf Kant und Schiller. (GER.). vi, 432p. 1976. write for info. (*3-487-05879-0*) G Olms Pubs.

Lempp, Steffen, jt. ed. see Arslanov, Marat.

***Lemprecht, Barbara.** Richard Neutra: Complete Works. (Illus.). 2000. 149.99 (*3-8228-6622-9*) Taschen Amer.

Lemprecht, Sandra J. California: A Bibliography of Theses & Dissertations in Geography, No. 753. 1975. 5.50 (*0-686-20344-5*, Sage Prdcls Pr) Sage.

Lempriere, John A. A Classical Dictionary, 2 vols, Set. 1973. lib. bdg. 600.00 (*0-87968-878-5*) Gordon Pr.

Lems-Dworkin, Carol. Africa in Scott Joplin's Music. LC 96-94101. (Illus.). 29p. (Orig.). 1991. pap. 12.00 (*0-9637048-0-X*) C Lems-Dworkin Pubs.

— African Music: A Pan African Annotated Bibliography. (Illus.). 400p. 1991. 50.00 (*0-905450-91-4*) C Lems-Dworkin Pubs.

— Videos of African & African-Related Performance: An Annotated Bibliography. annot. ed. (Illus.). 35300p. 1996. pap. 57.00 (*0-9637048-1-8*) C Lems-Dworkin Pubs.

Lems-Tardif, Gina. Pilgrim Children Had Many Chores, Vol. 3902. Williams, Rozanne L., ed. (Social Studies Learn to Read Ser.). (Illus.). 8p. (J). (ps-2). 1996. pap. 1.75 (*1-57471-121-0*, 3902) Creat Teach Pr.

— Pilgrim Children Had Many Chores, Vol. 3959. Williams, Rozanne L., ed. (Social Studies Big Bks.). (Illus.). 8p. (J). (ps-2). 1997. pap. 8.98 (*1-57471-167-9*, 3959) Creat Teach Pr.

Lemsine, Aicha. Beneath a Sky of Porphyry. Blair, Dorothy, tr. from FRE. 224p. 1990. pap. 11.95 (*0-7043-0161-X*, Pub. by Quartet) Interlink Pub.

— The Chrysalis. Blair, Dorothy S., tr. 189p. 1993. 19.95 (*0-7043-7034-4*, Pub. by Quartet) Interlink Pub.

Lemstra, P. J., jt. auth. see Kleintjens, L. A.

Lemstra, Tjitske & Doornenbal, Baukje. Home Making: Nurturing Your Family in Today's World. LC 98-126756. 80p. 1997. pap. 5.00 (*1-57683-017-9*) NavPress.

Lemstra, Tjitske, jt. auth. see Doornenbal, Baukje.

Lemu, Ahmed. A Book of Fasting. 2nd ed. Lemu, Bridget, ed. LC 96-35052. 86p. (Orig.). (C). 1996. reprint ed. pap. text 4.00 (*1-881963-01-2*) Al-Saadawi Pubns.

Lemu, Aisha & Heeren, Fatima. Women in Islam. 51p. (Orig.). 1978. pap. 3.50 (*0-86037-004-6*, Pub. by Islamic Fnd) New Era Publns MI.

Lemu, B. A. Islamic Aqidah & Fiqh: A Textbook of Islamic Belief & Jurisprudence. adapted ed. Quraishi-Ahmed, Huda & Akhtar, Hina, eds. LC 96-79297. 218p. (J). (gr. 6-8). 1997. pap. text 8.00 (*1-56316-061-7*) Iqra Intl Ed Fdtn.

Lemu, B. Aisha. The Ideal Muslim Husband. 22p. 1996. pap. 2.00 (*0-614-21459-9*, 485) Kazi Pubns.

— Islam & Alcohol. 2nd ed. LC 96-35049. 18p. (Orig.). 1996. pap. text 2.00 (*1-881963-02-0*) Al-Saadawi Pubns.

— Islamic Tahdhib & Akhlaq: Theory & Practice. rev. ed. Akhtar, Hina N. & Ahmed, Huda Q., eds. LC 97-71699. 219p. 1997. pap. text 8.00 (*1-56316-320-9*) Iqra Intl Ed Fdtn.

— Women in Islam. 51p. 1996. pap. 3.95 (*0-614-21401-7*, 1327) Kazi Pubns.

Lemu, Bridget, ed. see Lemu, Ahmed.

Lemu, Sheikh A. A Book of Fasting. 90p. 1996. pap. 3.00 (*0-614-21454-8*, 111) Kazi Pubns.

Lemuel. Introduction to Solid State Devices. (Electrical Engineering Ser.). 192p. 1997. pap. text 19.95 (*0-340-66275-1*) Wadsworth Pub.

Lemus, Vera. Pushkin, Palaces & Parks. (Illus.). 170p. (C). 1984. 250.00 (*0-7855-6499-3*, Pub. by Collets) St Mut.

Lemut, Enrica, et al, eds. Cognitive Models & Intelligent Environments for Learning Programming. LC 93-25348. (NATO ASI Series F: Computer & Systems Sciences, Special Programme AET: Vol. 111). 315p. 1993. 78.95 (*0-387-56580-9*) Spr-Verlag.

Len Sen, George A., tr. see Bolkhovitinov, Nikolai.

Lena, Dan & Lena, Marie. I Am Special & You Are Special Too! (Illus.). 35p. (Orig.). (J). (gr. k-4). 1995. pap. write for info. (*0-9645027-1-2*) S-Team Unltd.

— My Power Book. (Self Help Motivation Ser.). (Illus.). 60p. (YA). 1991. student ed. 10.00 (*0-9617032-0-2*) D & M Lena.

Lena, Hugh. Primis Reader in Sociology. 1992. pap. text. write for info. (*0-07-037581-X*) McGraw.

Lena, Marie, jt. auth. see Lena, Dan.

Lena, P. Observational Astrophysics. (Astronomy & Astrophysics Library). (Illus.). 340p. 1988. 79.95 (*0-387-18433-5*) Spr-Verlag.

Lena, Pierre & Lebrun, Francoise. Observational Astrophysics. 2nd enl. rev. ed. LC 97-47092. (Astronomy & Astrophysics Library). (Illus.). xiii, 518p. 1998. 62.00 (*3-540-63482-7*) Spr-Verlag.

Lena, Willie, jt. auth. see Howard, James H.

Lenaerts, Vincent M. & Gurny, Robert, eds. Bioadhesive Drug Delivery Systems. LC 96-21434. (Illus.). 272p. 1989. lib. bdg. 210.00 (*0-8493-5367-X*, RS201) CRC Pr.

Lenagan, Thomas H., jt. auth. see Krause, G. R.

Lenaghan, Jo, ed. Hard Choices in Health Care. LC 97-151067. 204p. 1996. pap. text 26.00 (*0-7279-1081-7*, 345300260, Pub. by BMJ Pub) Login Brothers Bk Co.

Lenaghan, John, tr. see Baily, Samuel L. & Ramella, Franco, eds.

Lenaghan, Kim. A Little Book of Irish Superstitions. (Little Irish Bookshelf Ser.). (Illus.). 60p. 1995. 9.95 (*0-86281-545-2*, Pub. by Appletree Pr) Irish Bks Media.

Lenaghan, Michael J. Reader to Social Environment: Anthology. (C). 1996. pap. 20.00 (*0-536-59828-2*) Pearson Custom.

Lenaghan, Patrick. From Goya to Picasso: A Century of Spanish Printmaking. (Illus.). 64p. 1998. pap. 15.00 (*0-87535-151-4*) Hispanic Soc.

Lenahan, Philip. The Family Financial Organizer. 1996. ring bd. 14.95 (*0-9652869-1-6*) Finan Fnds.

Lenahan, Philip. Finances for Today's Catholic Family. (Illus.). 96p. 1996. pap. 12.95 (*0-9652869-0-8*) Finan Fnds.

Lenahan, Rod. Crippled Eagle: A Historical Perspective of U. S. Special Operations, 1976-1996. LC 98-65032. 1998. pap. 19.95 (*1-886391-23-8*, Shipwreck Pr) Narwhal Pr.

Lenahan, Thomas & Blanchfield, Thomas. New York Security Officer Training Manual. 120p. pap. 12.95 (*0-87526-425-5*) Gould.

***Lenahan, Tom.** Turnaround Management. LC 99-34593. 183p. 1999. pap. text 85.00 (*0-7506-4283-1*) Buttrwrth-Heinemann.

L

L

Lenain, Patrick, jt. ed. see Cornelius, Peter K.

Lenain, Thierry. Monkey Painting. (Illus.). 208p. 1997. 24.95 (*1-86189-003-6*, Pub. by Reaktion Bks) Consort Bk Sales.

Lenamon, C. E. Potholes & Pigsties, a Prodigal's Journey Home. Weber, Kathy D., ed. LC 97-92182. (Illus.). 208p. (Orig.). 1997. pap. 14.95 (*0-9658964-0-4*) Pippin Publ.

Lenanton, John. The Home Gardener. 2nd ed. (Illus.). 291p. (C). 1980. pap. 35.95 (*0-943281-00-8*) Matrix Grp.

Lenarcic, J., et al. Advances in Robot Kinematics: Analysis & Control. LC 98-24598. 1998. 254.00 (*0-7923-5169-X*) Kluwer Academic.

Lenarcic, J., jt. ed. see Stifter, S.

Lenarcic, Jadran & Ravani, Bahram, eds. Advances in Robot Kinematics & Computational Geometry. LC 94-21074. (Diversity & Direction in Children's Literature Ser.). 520p. (C). 1994. text 306.50 (*0-7923-2983-X*) Kluwer Academic.

Lenarcic, Jadran, ed. see Parenti-Castelli, Vincenzo.

***Lenard.** Invitation to Languages. 1998. teacher ed. 28.25 (*0-02-640869-4*) Glencoe.

Lenard. Parole & Pensee. 5th ed. (College French Ser.). (C). 1991. mass mkt., teacher ed. 7.95 (*0-8384-3692-7*) Heinle & Heinle.

Lenard, Alexander, tr. see Milne, A. A., pseud.

Lenard, Catherine. All I Ever Wanted Was a Lot of Money & a Husband: Instead I Got Enlightenment. LC 97-90275. (Illus.). 129p. 1997. pap. 11.95 (*0-9657692-3-2*) Your Hands.

Lenard, J. G., ed. Modelling Hot Deformation of Steels. (Illus.). viii, 145p. 1989. 76.95 (*0-387-50754-X*) Spr-Verlag.

***Lenard, J. G., et al.** Mathematical & Physical Simulation of the Properties of Hot Rolled Products. 376p. 1999. 140.00 (*0-08-042701-4*) Elsevier.

Lenard, J. G., jt. auth. see Pietrzyk, M.

***Lenard, Lane.** The Smart Guide to Andro: The Safe & Natural Testosterone Precursor for Sex & Athletic Enhancement. LC 98-88353. (Illus.). 80p. 1999. pap. 6.95 (*0-9627418-5-X*) Smart Pubns CA.

Lenard, Lane, jt. auth. see Morgenthaler, John.

Lenard, Lane, jt. auth. see Wright, Jonathan.

***Lenard, Larry.** Sturgeon Fishing. 2nd rev. ed. (Illus.). 64p. 2000. pap. 12.95 (*1-57188-198-0*) F Amato Pubns.

Lenard, Lisa, jt. auth. see Gerwick-Brodeur, Madeline.

Lenard, Lisa, jt. auth. see Lagerquist, Kay.

Lenard, Lisa, jt. auth. see Tognetti, Arlene.

Lenard, Madelyn & Johnson, Greg. Complete Guide to Word Perfect 6.X for DOS: Your Law Office Power Tool. LC 96-37713. 600p. (C). 1997. pap. text. write for info. (*0-314-20464-4*) West Pub.

***Lenard, Mary.** Preaching Pity: Dickens, Gaskell & Sentimentalism in Victorian Culture. LC 97-32896. (Studies in Nineteenth-Century British Literature: Vol. 11). viii, 157p. (C). 1999. text 43.95 (*0-8204-3903-7*) P Lang Pubng.

Lenard, Philipp E. Great Men of Science. Hatfield, H. Stafford, tr. LC 74-105026. (Essay Index Reprint Ser.). 1977. 27.95 (*0-8369-1614-X*) Ayer.

Lenard, Thomas M., jt. auth. see Block, Michael K.

***Lenard, Yvonne.** The Magic of Provence: Pleasures of Southern France. LC 99-51797. 324p. 2000. 22.00 (*0-87127-212-1*) Princeton Bk Co.

Lenardon, Robert J. Classical Myth Companion. 5th ed. 1997. pap. 28.95 (*0-471-36907-1*) Wiley.

Lenardon, Robert J., jt. auth. see Morford, Mark P.

Lenardon, Robert J., jt. ed. see Morford, Mark P.

***Lenaricibc, J. & Staniisic, M. M.** Advances in Robot Kinematics. LC 00-42658. 2000. write for info. (*0-7923-6426-0*) Kluwer Academic.

***Lenart, Curt.** How to Shop for a Cell Phone: Herbie's Guide Through the Cellular Maze. Pearson, Keith & Knox, Dahk, eds. (Illus.). 41p. 1999. pap. 9.95 (*1-58275-008-4*, Pub. by Black Forest Pr) Epic Bk Promo.

Lenart, Istvan. Non-Euclidean Adventures on the Lenart Sphere. (Illus.). 244p. (YA). (gr. 6 up). 1995. pap. text 15.95 (*1-55953-103-7*) Key Curr Pr.

***Lenart, Marie.** Child of Divorce. 1999. pap. 11.95 (*1-881545-73-3*) Angelas Bkshelf.

Lenart, Silvo. Shaping Political Attitudes: The Impact of Interpersonal Communication & Mass Media. LC 94-15533. 192p. 1994. 42.00 (*0-8039-5708-4*); pap. 19.50 (*0-8039-5709-2*) Sage.

Lenau, H., jt. ed. see Volkmar, Tilsner.

Lenaz, Giorgio & Milazzo, Giulio. Bioelectrochemistry of Biomacromolecules. LC 96-47676. (Bioelectrochemistry Ser.). 1997. 198.00 (*0-8176-5296-5*) Birkhauser.

***Lenberg, Carrie, ed.** Checklists for Skills Demonstration & Guidelines for Their Administration. 2nd ed. 26p. 1999. pap. write for info. (*1-930304-06-4*) Home Care Univ.

***Lenberg, Kinda, ed.** 101 Winning Drills from the AVCA. (Illus.). 160p. 1999. pap. 16.95 (*1-58382-039-6*) Coaches Choice.

Lenburg, Jeff. The Encyclopedia of Animated Cartoons. 2nd rev. ed. LC 98-46100. (Illus.). 512p. 1999. pap. 24.95 (*0-8160-3832-5*) Facts on File.

— The Encyclopedia of Animated Cartoons. 2nd rev. ed. LC 98-46100. (Illus.). 608p. 1999. 50.00 (*0-8160-3831-7*) Facts on File.

— The Great Cartoon Directors. LC 82-23923. (Illus.). 190p. 1983. lib. bdg. 28.50 (*0-89950-036-6*) McFarland & Co.

— The Great Cartoon Directors. rev. ed. LC 93-2928. (Illus.). 272p. 1993. reprint ed. pap. 15.95 (*0-306-80521-9*) Da Capo.

Lenburg, Jeff, jt. auth. see Gatlin, Larry.

Lencastre, Armando. Handbook of Hydraulic Engineering. (Civil & Mechanical Engineering Ser.). 520p. 1987. text 179.00 (*0-470-20828-7*) P-H.

Lence, Ross M., ed. see Calhoun, John C.

Lencek, Lena & Bosker, Gideon. Beach: The History of Paradise on Earth. 1999. pap. 13.95 (*0-14-027802-8*, PuffinBks) Peng Put Young Read.

Lencek, Lena, jt. auth. see Bosker, Gideon.

Lencek, Rado L., et al, eds. SSS Newsletter, 11 vols. 238p. 1978. write for info. (*0-318-60013-7*) Soc Slovene Studies.

Lencek, Rado L. & Cooper, Henry R., Jr., eds. Papers in Slavic Philology No. 2: To Honor Jernej Kopitar. 1982. pap. 10.00 (*0-930042-46-8*) Mich Slavic Pubns.

Lencer, Lena, jt. ed. see Bosker, Gideon.

Lences, Z., jt. ed. see Sajgalik, P.

Lenchek, Allen M. Physics of Pulsars. (Topics in Astrophysics & Space Physics Ser.). x, 174p. (C). 1972. text 252.00 (*0-677-14290-0*) Gordon & Breach.

***Lenchitz, Ken.** Autism & Post-Traumatic Stress Disorder: Ending Autistic Fixation. LC 00-32543. 2000. pap. write for info. (*0-398-07097-0*) C C Thomas.

Lenchner, George. Creative Problem sloving in School Mathematics. (Illus.). 296p. (YA). (gr. 4-10). 1983. reprint ed. pap. 25.75 (*0-9626662-2-X*) Glenwood Pubns.

Lenchner, George. Math Olympiad Contest Problems for Elementary & Middle Schools. 2nd expanded rev. ed. Kessler, Gilbert W. & Zimmerman, Lawrence J., eds. LC 96-77380. Orig. Title: Mathematical Olympiad Contest Problems for Children. (Illus.). 280p. (Orig.). (J). (gr. 4-8). 1997. pap. 24.95 (*0-9626662-1-1*) Glenwood Pubns.

Lenchner, Orna & Podhajski, Blanche. Sound Start: Teaching Phonological Awareness in the Classroom. (Illus.). 111p. 1997. teacher ed., spiral bd. 95.00 (*0-9657567-0-X*) Stern Ctr.

Lenci, Francesco, et al, eds. Biophysics of Photoreceptors & Photomovements in Microorganisms. (NATO ASI Ser.: Vol. 211). (Illus.). 366p. (C). 1991. text 150.00 (*0-306-44022-9*, Kluwer Plenum) Kluwer Academic.

Lenci, Francesco, jt. ed. see Colombetti, Giuliano.

Lencioni, Patrick. The Five Temptations of a CEO: A Leadership Fable. LC 98-9097. (Business & Management Ser.). 134p. 1998. 20.00 (*0-7879-4433-5*) Jossey-Bass.

***Lencioni, Patrick M.** Obsessions of an Extraordinary Executive: The Four Disciplines at the Heart of Making Any Organi. 180p. 2000. 22.00 (*0-7879-5403-9*) Jossey-Bass.

Lencioni, R., jt. ed. see Bartolozzi, C.

Lencsis, Peter M. Insurance Regulation in the United States: An Overview for Business & Government. LC 96-32507. 160p. 1997. 55.00 (*1-56720-085-0*, Quorum Bks) Greenwood.

— Workers Compensation: A Reference & Guide. LC 97-46649. 192p. 1998. 59.95 (*1-56720-174-1*, Quorum Bks) Greenwood.

Lenczewski, Romuald, jt. ed. see Gruber, Bruno.

Lenczowski, George. American Presidents & the Middle East. LC 89-17056. 368p. (C). 1989. text 45.95 (*0-8223-0963-7*) Duke.

— Oil & State in the Middle East. LC 60-476. 399p. reprint ed. pap. 123.70 (*0-608-08538-3*, 206906100002) Bks Demand.

Lenczowski, George. Russia & the West in Iran, 1918-1948: A Study in Big Power Rivalry. LC 68-23307. (Illus.). 383p. 1968. reprint ed. lib. bdg. 75.00 (*0-8371-0144-1*, LERW, Greenwood Pr) Greenwood.

Lenczowski, George, ed. Iran under the Pahlavis. LC 76-26773. (Publication Ser.: No. 164). (Illus.). xxii, 550p. 1978. text 45.00 (*0-8179-6641-2*) Bibliotheca Persica.

— Political Elites in the Middle East. LC 75-10898. (Foreign Affairs Study Ser.: No. 19). 235p. reprint ed. pap. 72.90 (*0-8357-4522-8*, 203738300008) Bks Demand.

Lenczowski, John. The Sources of Soviet Perestroika. (Essay Ser.: No. 2). 60p. (Orig.). (C). 1990. pap. text 3.00 (*1-878802-01-1*) J M Ashbrook Ctr Pub Affairs.

— Soviet Perceptions of U. S. Foreign Policy: A Study of Ideology, Power & Consensus. LC 81-70713. 319p. reprint ed. pap. 98.90 (*0-608-08539-1*, 206906200002) Bks Demand.

Lenczycki, Donna M., jt. auth. see Zeilenga, Donald G.

***Lend'el, V. I., et al.** Electron Scattering on Complex Atoms (Ions) Vol. 234: In Horizons in World Physics. LC 00-25270. (Horizons in World Physics Ser.). 213p. 2000. lib. bdg. 89.00 (*1-56072-804-3*) Nova Sci Pubs.

Lendenmann, Rolf & International Business Machines Corporation Staff. An Introduction to Tivoli's TME 10. LC 97-18175. 416p. (C). 1997. pap. 66.00 (*0-13-899717-9*) P-H.

Lender, Mark E. Dictionary of American Temperance Biography: From Temperance Reform to Alcohol Research, the 1600s to the 1980s. LC 83-12589. 572p. 1984. lib. bdg. 105.00 (*0-313-22335-1*, LAT/, Greenwood Pr) Greenwood.

— The Middlesex Water Company: A Business History. 235p. 1994. 20.00 (*0-9642916-0-6*) Upland Press.

Lender, Mark E. & Martin, James K. Drinking in America. rev. ed. 222p. 1987. pap. 16.95 (*0-02-918570-X*) Free Pr.

Lender, Mark E., jt. auth. see Martin, James K.

Lender, Theodore. Dictionary of Biology: Diccionario de Biologia. 2nd ed. (ENG & SPA.). 208p. 1985. 30.95 (*0-7859-4915-1*) Fr & Eur.

— Dictionnaire de Biologie. 2nd ed. (FRE.). 448p. 1992. 275.00 (*0-7859-7747-3*, 2130447031) Fr & Eur.

Lender, W. G. & Leader, L. Lecturing at Your Best. 92p. (C). 1990. pap. 125.00 (*0-85297-214-8*, Pub. by Chartered Bank) St Mut.

Lenderink, R. S. & Siebrand, Jan C. A Disequilibrium Analysis of the Labour Market. 126p. 1975. text 59.95 (*90-237-2277-9*, Pub. by Avebry) Ashgate Pub Co.

Lenderman, Teddy. The Complete Idiot's Guide to the Perfect Wedding. 350p. 1995. 16.99 (*1-56761-532-5*, Alpha Ref) Macmillan Gen Ref.

— Complete Idiot's Guide to the Perfect Wedding. 2nd ed. LC 97-73181. (Illus.). 332p. 1997. 17.95 (*0-02-861963-3*) Macmillan Gen Ref.

***Lenderman, Teddy.** Complete Idiot's Guide to the Perfect Wedding. 3rd ed. (Complete Idiot's Guides (Lifestyle) Ser.). (Illus.). 352p. 2000. pap. text 18.95 (*0-02-863894-8*, Alpha Ref) Macmillan Gen Ref.

***Lenders, Jac.** Excess of Love. 256p. 2000. mass mkt. 7.95 (*1-56201-168-5*) Blue Moon Bks.

Lenderyou, Gill & Ray, Caroline, eds. Let's Hear It for the Boys! Supporting Sex & Relationships Education for Boys & Young Men. LC 98-180602. 64p. 1998. pap. 22.00 (*1-900990-15-6*, Pub. by Natl Childrens Bur) Paul & Co Pubs.

Lenderyou, Gill, jt. auth. see Patel-Kanwal, Hansa.

Lendhoff, Janet. The Noontime Walker's Guide to Downtown Los Angeles. (Illus.). 16p. 1994. 5.95 (*1-883897-04-1*) River Rock CA.

Lendi, K., jt. auth. see Alicki, R.

***Lendinara, Patrizia.** Anglo-Saxon Glosses & Glossaries. LC 98-50875. (Variorum Collected Studies Ser.). 1999. 110.95 (*0-86078-672-2*) Ashgate Pub Co.

Lendler, Marc. Crisis & Political Beliefs: The Case of the Colt Firearms Strike. LC 96-9747. 200p. 1997. 35.00 (*0-300-06746-1*) Yale U Pr.

— Just the Working Life: Opposition & Accommodation in Daily Industrial Life. LC 89-70267. 224p. (gr. 13). 1990. text 70.95 (*0-87332-608-3*) M E Sharpe.

Lendon, J. E. Empire of Honour: The Art of Government in the Roman World. 332p. 1997. text 75.00 (*0-19-815079-2*) OUP.

Lendon, Nigel, jt. ed. see Caruana, Wally.

Lendrum, Susan & Syme, Gabrielle. Gift of Tears: A Practical Approach to Loss & Bereavement Counselling. LC 91-43922. 240p. (C). 1992. pap. 16.95 (*0-415-07349-9*, A7649, Pub. by Tavistock) Routldge.

Lendrum, Susan, jt. auth. see Tolan, Janet.

Lendt, C. K. Kiss & Sell: The Making of a Supergroup. LC 96-52637. (Illus.). 352p. 1997. 18.95 (*0-8230-7551-6*, Billboard Bks); 24.95 (*0-8230-7604-0*) Watsn-Guptill.

Lendvai, Erno. Bela Bartok: An Analysis of His Music. 1991. 16.95 (*0-912483-33-4*) Pro-Am Music.

— Verdi & Wagner. Palos, Monika & Pokoly, Judit, trs. 504p. 36.50 (*0-685-30700-X*, Pub. by Intl Hse) Pro-Am Music.

Lendvai, J. Structure Development in Condensed Matter. (Solid State Phenomena Ser.: Vol. 56). (Illus.). 260p. (C). 1998. text 94.00 (*3-908450-26-8*, Pub. by Scitec Pubns) Enfield Pubs NH.

Lendvai, J., ed. Nonequilibrium Materials. (Key Engineering Materials Ser.: Vol. 103). 260p. 1995. 100.00 (*0-87849-694-7*, Pub. by Trans T Pub) Enfield Pubs NH.

Lendvai, J., jt. ed. see Kovacs, I.

Lendvai, Paul. Blacklisted: A Journalist's Life in Central Europe. 256p. 1998. text 39.50 (*1-86064-268-3*, Pub. by I B T) St Martin.

— Hungary: The Art of Survival. 160p. 1990. text 59.50 (*1-85043-118-3*, Pub. by I B T) St Martin.

Lendvay, E., ed. Epitaxial Crystal Growth. 1000p. 1991. text 316.00 (*0-87849-616-5*, Pub. by Trans T Pub) Enfield Pubs NH.

— Gallium Arsenide. 374p. 1987. text 133.00 (*0-87849-555-X*, Pub. by Trans T Pub) Enfield Pubs NH.

Leneaux, Grant F., tr. see Duhem, Pierre M.

Leneghan, Kim. A Little History of Golf. (Illus.). 60p. 1996. 7.95 (*0-8118-1266-9*) Chronicle Bks.

Lenehan, Arthur F., ed. The Best of Bits & Pieces. 300p. 29.95 (*0-910187-08-8*) Economics Pr.

Lenehan, Gail P., jt. auth. see Sheehy, Susan B.

***Lenehan, Jim.** A Rotten Borough: Politics & Society in Athlone, 1830-85. LC 99-31100. (Maynooth Studies in Local History). 64p. 1999. 10.95 (*0-7165-2676-X*, Pub. by Irish Acad Pr) Intl Spec Bk.

Lenehan, William, ed. see Irving, Washington.

Lenel, Fritz V. Powder Metallurgy: Principles & Applications. LC 80-81890. (Illus.). 602p. reprint ed. pap. 186.70 (*0-7837-1562-5*, 204185400024) Bks Demand.

***LeNell, Wayne Martin.** Tax Considerations for the Newly Ordained Priest. 20p. 1999. pap. text. write for info. (*1-893060-01-2*) NFPC.

Leneman, Helen. Bar/Bat Mitzvah Basics: A Practical Family Guide to Coming of Age Together. LC 96-1613. 240p. 1996. pap. 16.95 (*1-879045-54-0*) Jewish Lights.

Leneman, Helen, ed. Bar - Bat Mitzvah Education: A Sourcebook. LC 93-70473. 370p. 1993. pap. text 25.00 (*0-86705-031-4*) A R E Pub.

***Leneman, Leah.** Alienated Affections: Divorce & Separation in Scotland, 1684-1830. 256p. 1998. 30.00 (*0-7486-1031-6*, Pub. by Edinburgh U Pr); lib. bdg. 60.00 (*0-7486-1030-8*, Pub. by Edinburgh U Pr) Col U Pr.

Leneman, Leah. Elsie Inglis. LC 99-189637. (Illus.). 96p. 1998. pap. 7.95 (*1-901663-09-4*) A Schwartz & Co.

— Fit for Heroes? Land Settlement in Scotland after World War I. (Illus.). 1989. text 35.00 (*0-08-037720-3*, Pergamon Pr) Elsevier.

— A Guid Cause: The Women's Suffrage Movement in Scotland. rev. ed. 320p. 1996. pap. 60.00 (*1-873644-48-5*, Pub. by Mercat Pr Bks) St Mut.

— In the Service of Life. 300p. 1996. pap. 60.00 (*1-873644-26-4*, Pub. by Mercat Pr Bks) St Mut.

— International Tofu Cookery Book. 1986. pap. 8.50 (*0-7102-0702-6*, Routledge Thoemms) Routledge.

— Living in Atholl, 1685-1785. 200p. 1986. 30.00 (*0-85224-507-6*, Pub. by Edinburgh U Pr) Col U Pr.

— Perspectives in Scottish Social History: Essays in Honour of Rosalind Mitchison. 200p. 1988. pap. text 29.95 (*0-08-036574-4*, Pub. by Aberdeen U Pr) Macmillan.

— The Tofu Cookbook. (Illus.). 1992. pap. 14.00 (*0-7225-2587-7*) Thorsons PA.

— Tofu Cookbook: Over 150 Quick & Easy Recipes. 192p. 1998. pap. 11.00 (*0-7225-3667-4*) Thorsons PA.

***Leneman, Leah.** Vegan Cooking for One: Over 150 Simple & Appetizing Meals. (Illus.). 2000. pap. 14.95 (*0-7225-3923-1*) Thorsons.

Leneman, Leah. Women's Suffrage Movement in Scotland: A Guid Cause. (SWSS Ser.). (Illus.). 192p. 1991. pap. text 23.90 (*0-08-041201-7*, Pub. by Aberdeen U Pr) Macmillan.

Leneman, Leah & Kidd, Dorothy I. Into the Foreground: A Century of Scottish Women in Photography. (Photography Ser.). (Illus.). 132p. 1995. 32.50 (*0-7509-0444-5*, 444-5, Pub. by Natl Mus Scotland) A Schwartz & Co.

— Into the Foreground: A Century of Scottish Women in Photography. (Photography Ser.). (Illus.). 132p. 1996. pap. 19.95 (*0-7509-5395-0*, 539-5, Pub. by Natl Mus Scotland) A Schwartz & Co.

Leneman, Leah & Mitchison, Rosalind, eds. Sin in the City: Sexuality & Social Control in Urban Scotland, 1660-1780. 128p. 1997. pap. 27.00 (*1-898218-90-0*) St Mut.

Leneman, Leah, jt. auth. see Mitchison, Rosalind.

Lener, Dewayne J. Paper Preservation-Conservation Techniques & Methodology. (Illus.). 123p. 1988. pap. 19.95 (*0-945433-04-2*) Herit Quest.

Lenero, Carmen. Lucas Afuera, Lucas Adentro (Lucas Outside, Lucas Inside) (SPA., Illus.). (J). (gr. 5-6). 1997. pap. 5.99 (*968-16-5434-X*, Pub. by Fondo) Continental Bk.

Lenero, Vicente. Contemporary Mexican Drama in Translation: No One Knows Anything, Vol. II. Gann, Myra S., tr. from SPA. & intro. by. 125p. (C). 1995. pap. text 15.00 (*0-9643288-1-X*) Danzon Pr.

— The Gospel of Lucas Gavilan. Mowry, Robert G., tr. 272p. (Orig.). (C). 1991. pap. text 33.00 (*0-8191-7959-0*); lib. bdg. 54.00 (*0-8191-7958-2*) U Pr of Amer.

***Lenes, Jill R.** Meant to Be. LC 99-96803. 2000. pap. 7.95 (*0-533-13349-1*) Vantage.

Lenett, Robin, et al. Sometimes It's O.K. to Tell Secrets! 128p. (Orig.). (J). 1986. pap. 3.95 (*0-8125-9454-1*, Pub. by Tor Bks) St Martin.

Leney, Terttu. Teach Yourself Finnish. (ENG & FIN.). 1993. pap. 29.95 incl. audio (*0-7859-1053-0*, 0-340-561734) Fr & Eur.

Lenfant, C. L., et al, eds. Growth Factors of the Vascular & Nervous Systems: Functional Characterization & Biotechnology. (Illus.). viii, 132p. 1992. 108.00 (*3-8055-5475-3*) S Karger.

Lenfant, C. L., jt. auth. see Wood, Lenfant.

Lenfant, Claude, et al, eds. Biotechnology of Dyslipoproteinemias: Applications in Diagnosis & Control. LC 89-70044. (Atherosclerosis Reviews Ser.: Vol. 20). 352p. 1990. reprint ed. pap. 109.20 (*0-608-04745-7*, 206556500004) Bks Demand.

Lenfant, Claude, et al. Asthma in the Elderly: Considerations for Diagnosing & Managing Asthma in the Elderly. (Illus.). 50p. (C). 1997. reprint ed. pap. text 25.00 (*0-7881-4229-1*) DIANE Pub.

L'Enfant, Julie. William Rossetti's Art Criticism: The Search for Truth in Victorian Art. 392p. 1998. 46.00 (*0-7618-1290-3*) U Pr of Amer.

***Lenfestey, James P.** Urban Coyote: Howlings on Family, Community & the Search for Peace & Quiet. LC 99-68388. 264p. 1999. pap. 16.00 (*0-931714-86-9*, Pub. by Nodin Pr) Bookmen Inc.

Lenfestey, Thompson. Facts on File Dictionary of Nautical Terms. (Dictionaries Ser.). (Illus.). 560p. 1993. lib. bdg. 40.00 (*0-8160-2087-6*) Facts on File.

Leng, Felicity, tr. see Guitton, Jean.

***Leng, Flavia.** Daphne du Maurier. 1999. pap. text 13.95 (*1-84018-190-7*, Pub. by Mainstream Pubng) Trafalgar.

Leng, Flavia. Daphne du Maurier: A Daughter's Memoir. large type ed. 208p. 1997. text 22.95 (*1-85695-128-6*, Pub. by ISIS Lrg Prnt) Transaction Pubs.

Leng, Gareth, ed. Pulsatility in Neuroendocrine Systems. 272p. 1988. 155.00 (*0-8493-4944-3*, QP356, CRC Reprint) Franklin.

Leng, Marguerite L., et al. Agrochemical Environmental Fate Studies: State of the Art. 432p. 1995. lib. bdg. 95.00 (*1-56670-034-5*, L1034) Lewis Pubs.

Leng, Nicholas R. Psychological Care in Old Age. 140p. 1990. 59.95 (*1-56032-049-4*) Taylor & Francis.

Leng, P. & Charlton, C. Principles of Computer Organisation: A First Course Using the 68000 Processor. 288p. (C). 1990. 47.81 (*0-07-707217-0*) McGraw.

Leng-Peschlow, Elke, ed. Senna & Its Rational Use. (Journal: Pharmacology: Vol. 44, Suppl. 1, 1992). (Illus.). iv, 52p. 1992. pap. 17.50 (*3-8055-5574-1*) S Karger.

Leng, Roger. Right to Silence in Police Interrogation: Study of Some Issues Underlying Debate. (Research Studies: No. 10). 86p. 1993. pap. 20.00 (*0-11-341063-8*, HM10638, Pub. by Statnry Office) Bernan Associates.

Leng, Roger & Manchester, Colin. A Guide to the Criminal Justice Act 1991. 424p. 1991. 90.00 (*1-85190-152-3*, Pub. by Tolley Pubng) St Mut.

Leng, Roger & Taylor, Richard. Blackstone's Guide to the Criminal Procedure & Investigations Act, 1996. 219p. 1996. pap. 38.00 (*1-85431-588-9*, Pub. by Blackstone Pr) Gaunt.

Leng, Russell J. Bargaining & Learning in Recurring Crises: The Soviet-American, Egyptian-Israeli & Indo-Pakistani Rivalries. (Illus.). 336p. (C). text 64.50 (*0-472-09703-2*, 09703); pap. text 24.95 (*0-472-06703-6*, 06703) U of Mich Pr.

Leng, Russell J. Interstate Crisis Behavior, 1816-1980: Realism vs. Reciprocity. LC 92-32370. (Studies in International Relations: No. 28). (Illus.). 278p. (C). 1993. text 59.95 (*0-521-39141-5*) Cambridge U Pr.

An Asterisk (*) at the beginning of an entry indicates that the title is appearing for the first time.

Leng, Shao-Chuan. Japan & Communist China. LC 75-11893. 166p. 1975. reprint ed. lib. bdg. 35.00 (*0-8371-8134-8*, LEJC, Greenwood Pr) Greenwood.

Leng, Shao-Chuan, ed. Chiang Ching-Kuo's Leadership in the Development of the Republic of China on Taiwan, Vol. III. LC 92-31103. (Miller Center Series on Asian Political Leadership). 230p. (Orig.). (C). 1993. pap. text 24.50 (*0-8191-8904-9*, Pub. by White Miller Center); lib. bdg. 54.00 (*0-8191-8903-0*, Pub. by White Miller Center) U Pr of Amer.

— Coping with Crises: How Governments Deal with Emergencies, Vol. II. LC 89-16734. (Miller Center Series on Asian Political Leadership). 242p. (Orig.). (C). 1990. pap. text 24.00 (*0-8191-7585-4*, Pub. by White Miller Center); lib. bdg. 47.00 (*0-8191-7584-6*, Pub. by White Miller Center) U Pr of Amer.

— Post-Mao China & U. S.-China Trade. LC 77-20811. 168p. reprint ed. pap. 52.10 (*0-8357-2713-0*, 203982700013) Bks Demand.

— Reform & Development in Deng's China. LC 94-4725. (Miller Center Series on Asian Political Leadership: Vol. 4). 214p. (C). 1994. pap. text 26.00 (*0-8191-9504-9*); lib. bdg. 54.50 (*0-8191-9503-0*) U Pr of Amer.

Leng, Shao-Chuan & Chiu, Hungdah, eds. Criminal Justice in Post-Mao China: Analysis & Documents. LC 84-16362. 330p. (C). 1985. pap. text 24.95 (*0-87395-950-7*) State U NY Pr.

Leng, Shao-Chuan, jt. ed. see Chiu, Hungdah.

***Leng, Simon.** Soul Sacrifice: The Story of Santana. (Illus.). 256p. 2000. pap. 18.95 (*0-946719-29-2*) SAF Pub.

Leng, Tse-Kang. The Taiwan-China Connection: Democracy & Development across the Taiwan Straits. LC 96-8991. (Transitions: Asia & Asian America Ser.). (C). 1996. pap. 23.00 (*0-8133-9006-0*, Pub. by Westview) HarpC.

Leng, Vikki. The Vibrant Vegetarian. (Illus.). 192p. 1998. pap. 15.95 (*0-7322-5831-6*) HarpC.

Leng, Virginia. Training the Event Horse. (Illus.). 224p. 1991. 24.95 (*0-943955-38-6*, Trafalgar Sq Pub) Trafalgar.

Lengauer, Christian, et al, eds. Euro-Par '97 Parallel Processing: Third International Euro-Par Conference, Passau, Germany, August 26-29, 1997, Proceedings, Vol. 130. LC 97-30390. (Lecture Notes in Computer Science Ser.: Vol. 1300). xxx, 1380p. 1997. pap. 149.00 (*3-540-63440-1*) Spr-Verlag.

Lengauer, Thomas, ed. Algorithms - ESA '93: First Annual European Symposium, Bad Honnef, Germany, September 30-October 2, 1993 Proceedings, Vol. 726. LC 93-34004. 1993. 61.95 (*0-387-57273-2*) Spr-Verlag.

***Lengauer, Thomas, et al, eds.** Proceedings of the Seventh International Conference on Intelligent Systems for Molecular Biology. (Illus.). 324p. 1999. pap. text 45.00 (*1-57735-083-9*) AAAI Pr.

Lengauer, Thomas, jt. ed. see Choffrut, C.

Lengefeld, Uelaine. Study Skills Strategies: Your Guide to Critical Thinking. rev. ed. Crisp, Michael, ed. LC 93-74051. (Fifty-Minute Ser.). (Illus.). 89p. (Orig.). 1994. pap. 10.95 (*1-56052-260-7*) Crisp Pubns.

Lengel, Darlene. Effective Conversations. (Illus.). 120p. (J). (gr. 1-8). 1994. 18.95 (*0-937857-52-1*, 1483) Speech Bin.

— Effective Listening. (Illus.). 144p. 1998. 24.95 (*0-937857-79-3*, 1355) Speech Bin.

***Lengel, Laura B.** Culture & Technology in the New Europe: Civic Discourse in Transformation in Post-Socialist Nations. LC 99-34301. (Civic Discourse for the Third Millennium Ser.). 1999. write for info. (*1-56750-467-1*) Ablx Pub.

Lengel, Robert H., jt. auth. see Daft, Richard L.

Lengeler. Biology of the Procaryotes. LC 98-36569. (Illus.). 1000p. 1998. 89.00 (*0-86577-760-8*) Thieme Med Pubs.

Lengeler, B., et al. Formation of Semiconductor Interfaces: Proceedings of the 4th International Conference. 816p. 1994. text 178.00 (*981-02-1559-2*) World Scientific Pub.

Lengeler, Joseph W., et al. Biology of the Prokaryotes. LC 98-36569. (Illus.). xxvii, 955p. 1999. 89.95 (*0-632-05357-7*) Blackwell Sci.

— Biology of the Prokaryotes. LC 98-36569. 1998. write for info. (*3-13-108411-1*) Thieme Med Pubs.

Lengelt, J. & Kendall, D. Kids, Computers & Homework. 1996. pap. 16.00 (*0-8129-6382-2*) Random.

Lengenfelder, Jack W. A Picture Postcard History of U. S. Aviation. LC 88-36433. (Illus.). 100p. (Orig.). 1989. pap. 12.95 (*0-930256-19-0*, Vestal Pr) Madison Bks UPA.

Lengermann. Women Founders, 1830-1930. LC 97-41765. 336p. 1997. pap. 32.19 (*0-07-037169-5*) McGraw.

Lengerova, Alena, ed. see Symposium, Liblice Prague Staff.

Lenges, J., jt. ed. see Morton, I. D.

Lenghardtova. Spanielska Konverzacia. (SLO.). 280p. 1996. write for info. (*80-08-01245-5*, Pub. by Slov Pegagog Naklad) IBD Ltd.

Lengjak, Laura S., ed. United States Export Policy on Technology Transfer. (Wisconsin International Law Journal, 1982 Ser.: Vol. 1983). 228p. (Orig.). 1984. pap. 8.00 (*0-933431-01-5*) U Wisc Law Madison.

Lengle, James I. Representation & Presidential Primaries: The Democratic Party in the Post-Reform Era, 57. LC 80-1791. (Contributions in Political Science Ser.: No. 57). (Illus.). 131p. 1981. 52.95 (*0-313-22482-X*, LEP/, Greenwood Pr) Greenwood.

L'Engle, Madeleine. An Acceptable Time. 352p. (YA). (gr. 7 up). 1989. 18.00 (*0-374-30027-5*) FS&G.

— Acceptable Time. (J). 1990. 10.09 (*0-606-04598-8*, Pub. by Turtleback) Demco.

— An Acceptable Time. LC 89-84882. 368p. (J). (gr. 7-12). 1990. reprint ed. mass mkt. 5.99 (*0-440-20814-9*, LLL BDD) BDD Bks Young Read.

— And Both Were Young. (Young Love Romance Ser.). 256p. (YA). (gr. 7 up). 1983. mass mkt. 4.99 (*0-440-90229-0*, LLL BDD) BDD Bks Young Read.

— And Both Were Young. 1983. 9.60 (*0-606-01439-X*, Pub. by Turtleback) Demco.

— And It Was Good: Reflections on Beginnings. LC 83-8518. (Wheaton Literary Ser.). 216p. 1983. 14.99 (*0-87788-046-8*, H Shaw Pubs) Waterbrook Pr.

— Anytime Prayers. 1997. pap. text 15.99 (*0-87788-017-4*, H Shaw Pubs) Waterbrook Pr.

— The Arm of the Starfish. 240p. (YA). (gr. 7 up). 1979. mass mkt. 4.99 (*0-440-90183-9*, LLL BDD) BDD Bks Young Read.

— The Arm of the Starfish. LC 65-10919. 256p. (J). (gr. 7 up). 1965. 18.00 (*0-374-30396-7*) FS&G.

— Arm of the Starfish. (Laurel-Leaf Suspense Ser.). 1965. 10.09 (*0-606-00290-1*, Pub. by Turtleback) Demco.

— Una Arruga en el Tiempo.Tr. of Wrinkle in Time. (SPA.). (J). (gr. 1-6). 15.95 (*84-204-4074-4*) Santillana.

— Una Arruga en el Tiempo.Tr. of Wrinkle in Time. 1996. 21.05 (*0-606-10526-3*, Pub. by Turtleback) Demco.

— Austin Family Christmas. LC 99-36819. 48p. (J). 1999. 12.99 (*0-87788-020-4*, H Shaw Pubs) Waterbrook Pr.

— Camila. Barbadillo, Pedro, tr. (SPA.). 197p. (YA). (gr. 9-12). 1992. pap. write for info. (*84-204-4555-X*) Santillana.

— Camilla. (Young Love Romance Ser.). 288p. (YA). (gr. 7 up). 1982. mass mkt. 4.50 (*0-440-91171-0*, LLL BDD) BDD Bks Young Read.

L'Engle, Madeleine. Camilla. 278p. (YA). (gr. 7 up). pap. 4.95 (*0-8072-1359-4*) Listening Lib.

L'Engle, Madeleine. Camilla. 1995. 18.75 (*0-8446-6833-8*) Peter Smith.

— Camilla. (J). 1965. 9.60 (*0-606-01947-2*, Pub. by Turtleback) Demco.

— Certain Women. LC 91-34048. 351p. 1992. text 21.00 (*0-374-12025-0*) FS&G.

— Certain Women: A Novel. LC 92-56136. 368p. 1993. pap. 15.00 (*0-06-065207-1*, Pub. by Harper SF) HarpC.

— A Circle of Quiet. 256p. 1984. pap. 14.00 (*0-06-254503-5*, Perennial) HarperTrade.

— A Circle of Quiet, 3 vols., Set. (Crosswicks Journal Trilogy Ser.). 246p. 1977. 13.00 (*0-685-06341-0*) Harper SF.

— Crosswicks Journal. 1983. 23.85 (*0-8164-2617-1*) Harper SF.

— A Cry Like a Bell. LC 87-26940. (Wheaton Literary Ser.). 120p. (Orig.). 1987. pap. 8.99 (*0-87788-148-0*, H Shaw Pubs) Waterbrook Pr.

— Dance in the Desert. LC 68-29465. (Illus.). 64p. (J). (ps up). 1969. 14.95 (*0-374-31684-8*) FS&G.

— Dance in the Desert. LC 68-29465. (Sunburst Ser.). (Illus.). 56p. (J). (gr. 2 up). 1988. pap. 6.95 (*0-374-41684-2*) FS&G.

— Dragons in the Waters. 336p. (YA). (gr. 7 up). 1982. mass mkt. 4.99 (*0-440-91719-0*, LLL BDD) BDD Bks Young Read.

— Dragons in the Waters. (J). 1976. 10.09 (*0-606-00428-9*, Pub. by Turtleback) Demco.

— The Glorious Impossible. (Illus.). 64p. (J). (gr. 3 up). 1990. per. 22.00 (*0-671-68690-9*) Litle Simon.

— A House Like a Lotus. 320p. (YA). (gr. 6-12). 1985. mass mkt. 4.99 (*0-440-93685-3*, LLL BDD) BDD Bks Young Read.

— A House Like a Lotus. LC 84-48471. 307p. (YA). (gr. 7 up). 1984. 17.00 (*0-374-33385-8*) FS&G.

— The Irrational Season. (Crosswicks Journal Trilogy Ser.). 224p. 1983. 12.95 (*0-8164-0324-4*) Harper SF.

— The Irrational Season. (Crosswicks Journal Trilogy Ser.). 224p. 1984. pap. 13.00 (*0-86683-946-1*, Pub. by Harper SF) HarpC.

— The Irrational Season. large type ed. 430p. 1985. reprint ed. pap. 13.95 (*0-8027-2476-0*) Walker & Co.

— The Journey with Jonah. 72p. (J). (ps up). 1991. pap. 5.95 (*0-374-43858-7*) FS&G.

— A Live Coal in the Sea. 352p. 1996. 24.00 (*0-374-18989-7*) FS&G.

— A Live Coal In The Sea. LC 96-4909. 336p. 1997. pap. 14.00 (*0-06-065286-1*, Pub. by Harper SF) HarpC.

— Love Letters. 303p. 1996. 19.99 (*0-87788-528-1*, H Shaw Pubs) Waterbrook Pr.

— Many Waters. 310p. (YA). (gr. 5-9). 1987. pap. 5.50 (*0-440-40548-3*) Dell.

— Many Waters. (J). 1991. mass mkt. 4.99 (*0-440-80265-2*) Dell.

— Many Waters. LC 86-14911. 310p. (J). (gr. 4 up). 1986. 17.00 (*0-374-34796-4*) FS&G.

L'Engle, Madeleine. Many Waters. 1986. 9.60 (*0-606-05091-4*, Pub. by Turtleback) Demco.

— Many Waters. 1998. 10.60 (*0-606-13596-0*, Pub. by Turtleback) Demco.

L'Engle, Madeleine. Many Waters. anniversary rev. ed. (Illus.). 336p. (J). (gr. 8-12). 1998. mass mkt. 5.99 (*0-440-22770-4*) BDD Bks Young Read.

— Meet the Austins. 192p. (YA). (gr. 5-9). 1981. mass mkt. 4.99 (*0-440-95777-X*, LE) Dell.

— Meet the Austins. LC 96-27655. (Illus.). 224p. (J). (gr. 5-9). 1997. 16.00 (*0-374-34929-0*) FS&G.

L'Engle, Madeleine. Meet the Austins. (J). 1960. 9.60 (*0-606-02172-8*, Pub. by Turtleback) Demco.

L'Engle, Madeleine. Miracle on 10th Street: And Other Christmas Writings. LC 98-24322. 144p. 1998. 16.99 (*0-87788-531-1*, H Shaw Pubs) Waterbrook Pr.

— The Moon by Night. 256p. (YA). (gr. 6 up). 1981. mass mkt. 4.99 (*0-440-95776-1*, LE) Dell.

— The Moon by Night. LC 63-9072. 224p. (J). (gr. 5-9). 1963. 16.00 (*0-374-35049-3*) FS&G.

L'Engle, Madeleine. The Moon by Night. (Austin Family Ser.). (J). 1963. 9.60 (*0-606-02181-7*, Pub. by Turtleback) Demco.

L'Engle, Madeleine. Moses, Prince of Egypt: Storyteller's Edition. 48p. 1998. 15.99 (*0-525-46051-9*, PuffinBks) Peng Put Young Read.

L'Engle, Madeleine. Mothers & Daughters. LC 96-50117. 112p. 1997. 17.99 (*0-87788-561-3*, H Shaw Pubs) Waterbrook Pr.

L'Engle, Madeleine. Mothers & Sons. LC 98-55387. (Illus.). 105p. 1999. 17.99 (*0-87788-567-2*, H Shaw Pubs) Waterbrook Pr.

***L'Engle, Madeleine.** My Own Small Place: Developing the Writing Life. LC 98-23519. 1998. write for info. (*0-87788-571-0*, H Shaw Pubs) Waterbrook Pr.

L'Engle, Madeleine. The Other Side of the Sun. large type ed. LC 93-35731. 1993. lib. bdg. 20.95 (*0-7862-0089-8*) Thorndike Pr.

— The Other Side of the Sun: A Novel. (Wheaton Literary Ser.). 384p. 1996. 19.99 (*0-87788-615-6*, H Shaw Pubs) Waterbrook Pr.

— Penguins & Golden Calves: Icons & Idols. (Wheaton Literary Ser.). 192p. 1996. 17.99 (*0-87788-631-8*, H Shaw Pubs) Waterbrook Pr.

L'Engle, Madeleine. Un Raccourci Sans Le Temps. 4th ed. 1997. pap. 12.95 (*2-266-08159-4*) Distribks Inc.

L'Engle, Madeleine. A Ring of Endless Light. (Austin Family Ser.: Vol. 3). 332p. (J). (gr. 4-7). 1981. mass mkt. 5.50 (*0-440-97232-9*, LLL BDD) BDD Bks Young Read.

— A Ring of Endless Light. (J). 1995. mass mkt. 5.99 (*0-440-91081-1*) BDD Bks Young Read.

— A Ring of Endless Light. (Austin Family Ser.). (J). 1980. 10.09 (*0-606-02243-0*, Pub. by Turtleback) Demco.

— The Rock That Is Higher: Story As Truth. (Wheaton Literary Ser.). 296p. 1998. pap. 14.99 (*0-87788-808-6*, H Shaw Pubs) Waterbrook Pr.

— A Severed Wasp. 388p. 1983. pap. 13.00 (*0-374-51783-5*) FS&G.

— The Small Rain: A Novel. LC 84-47839. 371p. (J). (gr. 7 up). 1984. 14.95 (*0-374-26637-9*) FS&G.

— The Small Rain: A Novel. LC 84-47839. 371p. (J). (gr. 7 up). 1985. pap. 13.00 (*0-374-51912-9*) FS&G.

— Sold into Egypt: Joseph's Journey into Human Being. LC 89-32030. (Wheaton Literary Ser.). 240p. 1989. 14.99 (*0-87788-766-7*, H Shaw Pubs) Waterbrook Pr.

— The Sphinx at Dawn: Two Stories. (Illus.). 48p. (J). 1984. 8.20 (*0-8164-0527-1*) Harper SF.

— A Stone for a Pillow: Journeys with Jacob. LC 86-6487. (Wheaton Literary Ser.). 240p. 1986. 14.99 (*0-87788-789-6*, H Shaw Pubs) Waterbrook Pr.

— The Summer of the Great-Grandmother. (Crosswicks Journal Trilogy Ser.). 256p. 1984. pap. 14.00 (*0-06-254506-X*, Pub. by Harper SF) HarpC.

— A Swiftly Tilting Planet. 272p. (YA). (gr. 7 up). 1979. mass mkt. 5.50 (*0-440-90158-8*, LLL BDD) BDD Bks Young Read.

— A Swiftly Tilting Planet. 304p. (J). (gr. 4-7). 1980. pap. 5.99 (*0-440-40158-5*) Dell.

— A Swiftly Tilting Planet. LC 78-9648. 288p. (J). (gr. 5 up). 1978. 17.00 (*0-374-37362-0*) FS&G.

L'Engle, Madeleine. A Swiftly Tilting Planet. 228p. (YA). (gr. 5 up). pap. 5.50 (*0-8072-1495-7*) Listening Lib.

L'Engle, Madeleine. A Swiftly Tilting Planet. 1978. 10.09 (*0-606-01841-7*, Pub. by Turtleback) Demco.

— A Swiftly Tilting Planet. large type ed. LC 93-21812. (J). 1993. 15.95 (*1-56054-710-3*) Thorndike Pr.

— A Swiftly Tilting Planet: Digest Edition. 1998. 10.60 (*0-606-13831-5*, Pub. by Turtleback) Demco.

— The Time Trilogy: A Wrinkle in Time; A Wind in the Door; A Swiftly Tilting Planet, 3 vols., Set. 710p. (J). (gr. 5-7). 1979. boxed set 51.00 (*0-374-37592-5*) FS&G.

— Troubling a Star. (J). 1995. mass mkt. 5.99 (*0-440-91058-7*) BDD Bks Young Read.

— Troubling a Star. 304p. (YA). (gr. 5 up). 1995. mass mkt. 5.50 (*0-440-21950-7*, LLL BDD) BDD Bks Young Read.

— Troubling a Star. LC 93-50956. 304p. (J). (gr. 4-7). 1994. 17.00 (*0-374-37783-9*) FS&G.

— Troubling a Star. (J). 1995. 10.09 (*0-606-08318-9*, Pub. by Turtleback) Demco.

— The Twenty-Four Days Before Christmas. 80p. (J). (gr. k-6). 1987. pap. 3.99 (*0-440-40105-4*, YB BDD) BDD Bks Young Read.

L'Engle, Madeleine. Twenty-Four Days Before Christmas. (Dell Young Yearling Ser.). (J). 1984. 9.19 (*0-606-04059-5*, Pub. by Turtleback) Demco.

L'Engle, Madeleine. Two-Part Invention: The Story of a Marriage. LC 89-15652. 240p. 1989. pap. 14.00 (*0-06-250501-7*, Pub. by Harper SF) HarpC.

— Walking on Water: Reflections on Faith & Art. LC 94-47655. 198p. (Orig.). 1995. pap. 11.00 (*0-86547-487-7*) N Point Pr.

— Walking on Water: Reflections on Faith & Art. (Wheaton Literary Ser.). 198p. (Orig.). 1998. pap. 9.99 (*0-87788-896-5*, H Shaw Pubs) Waterbrook Pr.

— The Weather of the Heart. LC 78-62202. (Wheaton Literary Ser.). 96p. 1978. pap. 9.99 (*0-87788-931-7*, H Shaw Pubs) Waterbrook Pr.

— A Wind in the Door. 224p. (YA). (gr. 5-9). 1976. mass mkt. 5.50 (*0-440-98761-X*, LLL BDD) BDD Bks Young Read.

— A Wind in the Door. (Yearling Book Ser.). 240p. (J). (gr. 4-7). 1974. pap. 5.99 (*0-440-48761-7*) Dell.

— A Wind in the Door. LC 73-75176. 224p. (J). (gr. 7 up). 1973. 17.00 (*0-374-38443-6*) FS&G.

L'Engle, Madeleine. A Wind in the Door. 211p. (YA). (gr. 5 up). pap. 5.50 (*0-8072-1466-3*) Listening Lib.

L'Engle, Madeleine. A Wind in the Door. 1973. 10.09 (*0-606-05084-1*, Pub. by Turtleback) Demco.

— A Wind in the Door. (J). 1979. 10.60 (*0-606-13920-6*, Pub. by Turtleback) Demco.

— A Wind in the Door. large type ed. 270p. (J). 1993. reprint ed. lib. bdg. 15.95 (*1-56054-615-8*) Thorndike Pr.

— A Winter's Love. 1984. mass mkt. 4.95 (*0-345-30644-9*) Ballantine Pub Grp.

— A Wrinkle in Time. 224p. (YA). (gr. 5-9). 1976. mass mkt. 5.99 (*0-440-99805-0*, LLL BDD) BDD Bks Young Read.

— A Wrinkle in Time. 240p. (J). (gr. 5-9). 1998. pap. 5.99 (*0-440-49805-8*, YB BDD) BDD Bks Young Read.

— A Wrinkle in Time. LC 62-7203. 224p. (J). (gr. 7 up). 1962. 17.00 (*0-374-38613-7*) FS&G.

L'Engle, Madeleine. A Wrinkle in Time. 211p. (YA). (gr. 5 up). pap. 5.99 (*0-8072-1460-4*) Listening Lib.

L'Engle, Madeleine. A Wrinkle in Time, 2 vols. 20.00 (*0-89064-014-9*) NAVH.

— A Wrinkle in Time. (Scholastic Literature Guide Ser.). 16p. (J). 1997. pap. text 3.95 (*0-590-37360-9*) Scholastic Inc.

— A Wrinkle in Time. 1962. 10.60 (*0-606-05085-X*, Pub. by Turtleback) Demco.

— A Wrinkle in Time. (J). 1976. 10.60 (*0-606-13931-1*, Pub. by Turtleback) Demco.

— The Young Unicorns. 288p. (YA). (gr. 8 up). 1989. mass mkt. 4.99 (*0-440-99919-7*, LLL BDD) BDD Bks Young Read.

— The Young Unicorns. LC 68-13682. 256p. (YA). (gr. 7 up). 1968. 16.00 (*0-374-38778-8*) FS&G.

— The Young Unicorns. (J). 1968. 9.60 (*0-606-01893-X*, Pub. by Turtleback) Demco.

L'Engle, Madeleine & Chase, Carole F. Glimpses of Grace: Daily Thoughts & Reflections. LC 95-50088. 384p. 1998. pap. 14.00 (*0-06-065281-0*, Pub. by Harper SF) HarpC.

L'Engle, Madeleine & Shaw, Luci. Friends for the Journey: Two Extraordinary Women Celebrate Friendships Made & Sustained Through the Seasons of Life. LC 98-29264. 271 p. 1998. write for info. (*0-7540-3561-1*, Galaxy Child Lrg Print) Chivers N Amer.

— Friends for the Journey: Two Extraordinary Women Celebrate Friendships Made & Sustained Through the Seasons of Life. large type ed. LC 98-29264. 272p. 1998. 23.95 (*0-7862-1612-3*, G K Hall Lrg Type) Mac Lib Ref.

***L'Engle, Madeleine & Shaw, Luci.** A Prayerbook for Spiritual Friends: Partners in Prayer. LC 99-25817. (Illus.). 96p. 1999. pap. 10.99 (*0-8066-3892-3*) Augsburg Fortress.

L'Engle, Madeleine, et al. The Swiftly Tilting Worlds of Madeleine L'Engle: Essays in Her Honor. Shaw, Luci, ed. LC 97-49159. 220p. 1998. pap. 14.99 (*0-87788-483-8*, H Shaw Pubs) Waterbrook Pr.

— Things in Heaven & Earth: Exploring the Supernatural. Fickett, Harold, ed. LC 98-18983. 200p. 1998. 20.00 (*1-55725-188-6*, 930-005, Pub. by Paraclete MA) BookWorld.

L'Engle, Madeleine, jt. auth. see Shaw, Lucy.

Lengnick, H. Experiencing Quality. (C). 1994. pap. text 34.00 (*0-03-009254-X*) Harcourt Coll Pubs.

Lengnick-Hall, Cynthia A. & Lengnick-Hall, Mark L. Interactive Human Resource Management & Strategic Planning. LC 90-8959. 200p. 1990. 55.00 (*0-89930-502-4*, LHA/, Quorum Bks) Greenwood.

Lengnick-Hall, Mark L., jt. auth. see Lengnick-Hall, Cynthia A.

Lenguage, Inc., Translation Services Staff, tr. see Walls, James, III, ed.

Lengwin, Ron. Praying the Rosary: The Companion Volume to the Catholic Prayer Book. large type ed. LC 92-410. 96p. 1995. pap. 6.95 (*0-8027-2671-2*) Walker & Co.

Lengy, J. I., tr. see Nikol'skii, G. V.

Lengyel. Atom Clock. pap. 1.00 (*0-686-00466-3*) Fantasy Pub Co.

Lengyel, A. & Radan, G. T., eds. The Archaeology of Roman Pannonia. LC 81-51021. (Illus.). 674p. 1981. 75.00 (*0-8131-1370-9*) U Pr of Ky.

Lengyel, Alfonz. Archaeology for Museologists. (Museum Study Ser.: No. 2). (Illus.). 158p. (Orig.). 1993. pap. 20.00 (*0-9626500-1-3*) Fudan Mus Fndtn.

— Chinese Chronological History: From Prehistory Through 1950. (Museum Study Ser.: No. 4). 108p. (Orig.). 1993. pap. 20.00 (*0-9626500-3-X*) Fudan Mus Fndtn.

— Public Relations in Museums. 1990. pap. 15.00 (*0-9626500-0-5*) Fudan Mus Fndtn.

Lengyel, Alfonz & Liu-Lengyel, Hongying. Ray Leight & Shanghai Cartoonists' Views of Columbus. (Museum Study Ser.: No. 3). (Illus.). 17p. (Orig.). (C). 1992. pap. 8.00 (*0-9626500-2-1*) Fudan Mus Fndtn.

Lengyel, Cornel. The Case of Benedict Arnold. LC 79-56427. (New Poetic Drama Ser.: No. 2). 1982. pap. 3.50 (*0-934218-20-X*) Dragons Teeth.

— Four Dozen Songs. LC 72-96887. (Living Poets' Library). pap. 2.50 (*0-686-02577-6*) Dragons Teeth.

— Late News from Adam's Acres. (Living Poets' Library). 1983. pap. 3.50 (*0-934218-25-0*) Dragons Teeth.

— The Lookout's Letter. LC 75-148857. (Living Poets' Library). pap. 2.50 (*0-686-05006-1*) Dragons Teeth.

— The Master Plan. (Living Playwrights' Library). 1978. pap. 2.50 (*0-686-00548-1*) Dragons Teeth.

Lengyel, Cornel, ed. History of Music in San Francisco, 7 vols., Set. reprint ed. 364.50 (*0-404-07240-2*) AMS Pr.

Lengyel, Emil. Americans from Hungary. (History - United States Ser.). 319p. 1993. reprint ed. lib. bdg. 89.00 (*0-7812-4868-X*) Rprt Serv.

— The Land & People of Hungary. rev. ed. LC 72-37763. (Portraits of the Nations Ser.). (Illus.). (J). (gr. 5-9). 1972. lib. bdg. 12.89 (*0-397-31545-7*) HarpC Child Bks.

Lengyel, Eva, tr. see Agoston, Vilmos, ed.

Lengyel, Gyhorgy, jt. auth. see Higley, John.

Lengyel, Gyorgy, ed. Hungarian Economy & Society During World War II. (Atlantic Studies on Society & Change: No. 74). 240p. (C). 1993. text 37.50 (*0-88033-259-X*, 362, Pub. by East Eur Monographs) Col U Pr.

Lengyel, Gyorgy, jt. ed. see Higley, John.

L

Lengyel, I. A. Palaeoserology: Blood Typing with Fluorescent Antibody Method. 240p. (C). 1975. 60.00 (*963-05-0355-7*, Pub. by Akade Kiado) St Mut.

Lengyel, Joszef. Acta Sanctorum. 1970. 20.00 (*0-8464-0109-6*) Beekman Pubs.

Lengyel, Jozsef. Prenn Drifting. 293p. 1966. 19.95 (*0-8464-0747-7*) Beekman Pubs.

***Lengyel, Kathy.** Celebration of Summer: Machine Applique Quilt Projects for the Home. (Illus.). 36p. 1999. pap. 19.95 (*0-9675275-0-3*) Artistic.

Lengyel, Olga. Five Chimneys: A Woman's True Story of Auschwitz. 221p. 1995. pap. 12.00 (*0-89733-376-4*) Academy Chi Pubs.

— Five Chimneys: A Woman's True Story of Auschwitz. LC 81-20260. 213p. 1983. reprint ed. 25.00 (*0-86527-343-X*) Fertig.

Lengyel, Olga. Hornos de Hitler. (SPA.). 1997. pap. 19.98 (*968-13-1010-1*) Edit Diana.

Lengyel, Peter. Cobblestone: A Detective Novel. Batki, John, tr. from HUN. 450p. (Orig.). (C). 1993. pap. 14.95 (*0-930523-86-5*) Readers Intl.

— International Social Science: The UNESCO Experience. 145p. 1986. 39.95 (*0-88738-085-9*); pap. 24.95 (*0-88738-629-6*) Transaction Pubs.

Lengyel, Peter, jt. ed. see Bornschier, Volker.

Lengyel, V. I., et al. Resonance Phenomena in Electron-Atom Collisions. (Atoms & Plasmas Ser.: Vol. 11). (Illus.). 200p. 1992. 92.95 (*0-387-54093-8*) Spr-Verlag.

Lengyel, Zsolt, jt. ed. see Singleton, David.

Lenhard, Elizabeth. Bettypalooza. 4th ed. (Clueless Ser.: No. 20). 160p. (YA). (gr. 6-12). 1999. pap. 4.99 (*0-671-03438-3*) PB.

***Lenhard, Elizabeth.** Charlie's Angels. 192p. 2000. 5.99 (*0-7434-1023-8*) PB.

Lenhard, Peter, jt. auth. see Dutton, Harry J.

***Lenhard, Raymond E., Jr., et al, eds.** Clinical Oncology. (Illus.). 800p. 2000. 49.95 incl. cd-rom (*0-944235-15-8*, Pub. by Am Cancer NY) Blackwell Sci.

Lenhardt. Critical Care. (Pearls of Wisdom Ser.). 1998. pap. 88.00 (*1-890369-16-0*) Boston Medical.

Lenhardt, Christian, tr. see Habermas, Jurgen.

Lenhardt, Richard. Pulmonary Pearls of Wisdom. (Pearls of Wisdom Ser.). 1998. pap. 88.00 (*1-890369-17-9*) Boston Medical.

Lenhart, Gary. Father & Son Night. 1999. 21.00 (*1-882413-65-2*); pap. 13.00 (*1-882413-64-4*) Hanging Loose.

— Light Heart. 1991. 15.00 (*0-914610-92-9*); pap. 9.00 (*0-914610-91-0*) Hanging Loose.

— One at a Time. 1983. pap. 4.00 (*0-935992-06-5*) United Art Bks.

Lenhart, Gary, ed. The Teachers & Writers Guide to William Carlos Williams. LC 98-7381. (Illus.). 200p. 1998. pap. 14.95 (*0-915924-57-9*) Tchrs & Writers Coll.

Lenhart, Harry A., Jr. Pacific Northwest Gateway: A Historical & Contemporary Portrait of Portland International Airport. LC 97-66363. (Illus.). 120p. 1997. 34.95 (*1-882933-15-X*) Cherbo Pub Grp.

Lenhart, John N. Gershom Carmichael on Samuel Pufendor's de Officio Hominis et Civis Juxta Legem Naturalem Libro Duo. Reeves, Charles H., tr. LC 85-80343. (Illus.). 64p. (Orig.). 1985. pap. 4.00 (*0-9615380-0-7*) Lenhart.

***Lenhart, John P.** Seven Secrets of Anti-Aging. Marcou, Diane, ed. 2000. pap. 24.95 (*1-930822-00-6*) Medfo.

Lenhart, Maria. Hidden Oregon. 3rd rev. ed. (Hidden Travel Ser.). (Illus.). 270p. 1999. pap. 14.95 (*1-56975-177-3*) Ulysses Pr.

Lenhart, Steven W. Histoplasmosis: Protecting Workers at Risk. 32p. 1997. pap. 3.50 (*0-16-061561-5*) USGPO.

Lenhart, Volker, jt. auth. see Boehm, Ullrich.

Lenhart, Volker, jt. auth. see O'hrs, Herman R.

Lenhart, Volker, jt. ed. see Rohrs, Hermann.

Lenhoff, Arthur. Comments, Cases & Other Materials on Legislation. xxxvii,1046p. 1954. reprint ed. lib. bdg. 40.00 (*0-89941-603-9*, 501960) W S Hein.

Lenhoff, Gail. The Martyred Princes Boris & Gleb: A Social-Cultural Study of the Cult & the Texts. (UCLA Slavic Studies: Vol. 19). 168p. 1989. 18.95 (*0-89357-204-7*) Slavica.

Lenhoff, H. M., jt. auth. see Ngo, T. T.

Lenhoff, Howard M. Conception to Birth: Human Reproduction, Genetics & Development. rev. ed. 400p. (C). 1994. per. 29.95 (*0-8403-9213-3*) Kendall-Hunt.

Lenhoff, Howard M., ed. Experimental Coelenterate Biology. LC 73-127331. 291p. reprint ed. pap. 90.30 (*0-608-17227-8*, 202702800053) Bks Demand.

— Hydra: Research Methods. LC 82-24648. 496p. 1983. 110.00 (*0-306-41086-9*, Plenum Trade) Perseus Pubng.

Lenhoff, Howard M., tr. see Trembley, Abraham.

Lenhoff, Sylvia, tr. see Trembley, Abraham.

Leniashin, O. Soviet Art, 1920s-1930s. (C). 1990. 170.00 (*0-7855-4446-1*, Pub. by Collets) St Mut.

Leniashin, Vladimir A., compiled by. The Russian Museum, Leningrad. (C). 1987. 195.00 (*0-7855-3317-6*, Pub. by Collets) St Mut.

Lenic, Zdenko, ed. see Samokovlija, Isak, et al.

Lenica, Jan, jt. auth. see Kamyszew, Christopher D.

Lenier, Minnette & Maker, Janet. College Reading, Bk. 1. 2nd ed. 351p. (C). 1987. pap. write for info. (*0-534-08964-X*) Wadsworth Pub.

— College Reading, Bk. 1. 3rd ed. 375p. (C). 1991. mass mkt. 25.50 (*0-534-15390-9*) Wadsworth Pub.

— Keys to a Powerful Vocabulary, Level II. 3rd ed. LC 93-10923. 304p. (C). 1993. pap. text 41.00 (*0-13-668955-8*) Prntice Hall Bks.

— Keys to College Success: Reading & Study Improvement. 4th ed. LC 97-7828. 364p. 1997. pap. text 37.00 (*0-13-270935-X*) P-H.

Lenier, Minnette, jt. auth. see Maker, Janet.

Lenier, Susan J. Rain Following: Poems. (Modern Poets Ser.: Vol. 13). 64p. 1984. 15.00 (*0-906672-19-8*); pap. 8.95 (*0-906672-20-1*) Oleander Pr.

— Swansongs: Poems. (Modern Poets Ser.: Vol. 12). (Illus.). (Orig.). 1982. 15.00 (*0-906672-04-X*); pap. 8.95 (*0-906672-03-1*) Oleander Pr.

Lenihan, Dan, jt. auth. see Hackman, Gene.

Lenihan, Daniel F. Shipwrecks of Isle Royale National Park: The Archeological Survey. LC 94-77712. (Illus.). 212p. 1994. pap. 34.95 (*0-942235-18-5*) LSPC Inc.

— Underwater Wonders of the National Parks. LC 97-36765. (Compass American Guides Ser.). 272p. 1997. pap. 19.95 (*0-679-03386-6*, Compass Amrcn) Fodors Travel.

Lenihan, Daniel F., jt. auth. see Hackman, Gene.

Lenihan, Donald G., et al. Reclaiming the Middle Ground. 162p. 1995. pap. 16.95 (*0-88645-167-1*, Pub. by Inst Res Pub) Ashgate Pub Co.

Lenihan, Eddie. Defiant Irish Women. 142p. 1997. pap. 9.95 (*1-85635-188-2*, Pub. by Mercier Pr) Irish Amer Bk.

— Gruesome Irish Tales for Children. 96p. (J). (gr. 4-7). 1998. pap. 7.95 (*1-85635-197-1*, Pub. by Mercier Pr) Irish Amer Bk.

— Humorous Irish Tales for Children. 1998. pap. text (*1-85635-238-2*) Irish Amer Bk.

— A Spooky Irish Tale for Children. (Illus.). 96p. (J). 1997. pap. 7.95 (*1-85635-150-5*, Pub. by Mercier Pr) Irish Amer Bk.

— Stories of Old Ireland for Children. (Illus.). 98p. 1986. pap. 7.95 (*0-85342-927-8*, Pub. by Mercier Pr) Music Sales.

Lenihan, Edmund. Ferocious Irish Women. 144p. 1991. pap. 12.95 (*0-85342-977-4*) Dufour.

— Long Ago by Shannon Side. 1982. pap. 7.95 (*0-85342-671-6*) Dufour.

— Stories of Old Ireland for Children. (J). 1990. pap. 9.95 (*0-85342-777-1*) Dufour.

Lenihan, John. How the Body Works. LC 94-42774. 200p. 1995. pap. 17.95 (*0-944838-48-0*, Cogito Bks) Med Physics Pub.

— Human Engineering: The Body Re-Examined. LC 74-25318. 212p. 1975. 7.95 (*0-8076-0782-7*) Braziller.

— Well It's Not My Fault! About the San Andreas Fault & Other Things. LC 87-28103. (Illus.). 223p. (gr. 12 up). 1988. pap. 7.95 (*0-944838-00-6*) Med Physics Pub.

Lenihan, John H. Showdown: Confronting Modern America in the Western Film. LC 79-25271. (Illus.). 224p. 1985. pap. text 14.95 (*0-252-01254-2*) U of Ill Pr.

Lenihan, John M. A. The Crumbs of Creation: Trace Elements in History, Medicine, Industry, Crime & Folklore. (Illus.). 176p. 1988. 34.00 (*0-85274-390-4*) IOP Pub.

Lenihan, John M. A. & Fletcher, William Whigham. The Chemical Environment. LC 78-106912. (Environment & Man Ser.). 163 p. 1977. write for info. (*0-12-443506-8*) Acad Pr.

Lenihan, Mary, ed. see Brown, Kendall, et al.

***Lenihan, Padraig.** Catholic Confederates at War, 1641-1648. 320p. 2000. 65.00 (*1-85918-244-5*, Pub. by Cork Univ) Stylus Pub VA.

***Lenik, Edward J.** Indians in the Ramapos: Survival, Persistence & Presence. (Illus.). 107p. 1999. pap. 13.00 (*0-9675706-0-3*) N J Highlands.

Lenik, Edward J. Iron Mine Trails. LC 96-30423. 1996. 8.95 (*1-880775-07-7*) NY-NJ Trail Confer.

Lenin, Vladimir Il'ich. British Labour & British Imperialism. 316p. 1969. 25.00 (*0-8464-0214-9*) Beekman Pubs.

— Collected Works. 1977. 24.95 (*0-8464-4441-0*); 24.95 (*0-8464-4442-9*); 24.95 (*0-8464-4443-7*); 24.95 (*0-8464-4444-5*); 24.95 (*0-8464-4445-3*) Beekman Pubs.

— Development of Capitalism in Russia. Date not set. pap. 29.95 (*0-8464-4446-1*) Beekman Pubs.

— Essential Works of Lenin: "What Is to Be Done?" & Other Writings. Christman, Henry M., ed. 372p. 1987. reprint ed. pap. 10.95 (*0-486-25333-3*) Dover.

— Imperialism: The Highest Stage of Capitalism. 128p. 1969. pap. text 2.95 (*0-7178-0098-9*) Intl Pubs Co.

— Imperialism: The Highest Stage of Capitalism. 144p. 1996. 35.00 (*0-7453-1036-2*, Pub. by Pluto GBR) Stylus Pub VA.

Lenin, Vladimir Il'ich. Imperialism: The Highest Stage of Capitalism. 144p. 1996. pap. 12.95 (*0-7453-1035-4*, Pub. by Pluto GBR) Stylus Pub VA.

Lenin, Vladimir Il'ich. Imperialism, the Highest Stage of Capitalism. 1975. reprint ed. pap. 3.95 (*0-8351-0113-4*) China Bks.

— Introduction to Marx, Engels & Marxism. Smith, Betty, ed. LC 86-21012. 108p. 1987. pap. text 4.95 (*0-7178-0647-2*) Intl Pubs Co.

— Left-Wing Communism, an Infantile Disorder. 95p. 1988. reprint ed. pap. 2.50 (*0-7178-0107-1*) Intl Pubs Co.

— Lenin: Against Imperialist War. 1978. pap. 24.95 (*0-8464-0554-7*) Beekman Pubs.

— Lenin: Against Liquidationism. 1978. 29.95 (*0-8464-0553-9*) Beekman Pubs.

— Lenin: On Utopian & Scientific Socialism. 1978. pap. 24.95 (*0-8464-0558-X*) Beekman Pubs.

— Lenin on War & Peace: Three Articles. 107p. 1966. pap. 1.95 (*0-8351-0130-4*) China Bks.

— Lenin's Final Fight: Speeches & Writings, 1922-1923. Fyson, George, ed. LC 95-68455. 320p. 1995. pap. 19.95 (*0-87348-807-5*); lib. bdg. 50.00 (*0-87348-808-3*) Pathfinder NY.

— Lenin's Struggle for a Revolutionary International: Documents: 1907-1916, the Preparatory Years. 2nd ed. Riddell, John, ed. LC 84-61519. 604p. 1986. pap. 32.95 (*0-913460-95-8*); lib. bdg. 75.00 (*0-913460-94-X*) Pathfinder NY.

— Letter to American Workers. 1970. pap. 0.45 (*0-87898-047-4*) New Outlook.

— New Data for Lenin's "Imperialism, the Highest Stage of Capitalism." Varga, E. & Mendelsohn, L., eds. LC 71-121288. reprint ed. 22.75 (*0-404-03965-0*) AMS Pr.

— The Right of Nations to Self Determination: Selected Writings. LC 77-23314. 128p. 1977. reprint ed. lib. bdg. 38.50 (*0-8371-9731-7*, LERN, Greenwood Pr) Greenwood.

— State & Revolution. 1965. pap. 3.95 (*0-8351-0372-2*) China Bks.

— State & Revolution. 103p. (C). 1932. pap. text 4.95 (*0-7178-0196-9*) Intl Pubs Co.

— The State & Revolution. Service, Robert W., tr. & intro. by. 192p. 1993. pap. 11.95 (*0-14-018435-X*, Penguin Classics) Viking Penguin.

— State & Revolution: Marxist Teachings about the Theory of the State & the Tasks of the Proletariat in the Revolution. LC 78-2228. 104p. 1978. reprint ed. lib. bdg. 35.00 (*0-313-20351-2*, LESTR, Greenwood Pr) Greenwood.

— Two Tactics of Social Democracy in the Democratic Revolution. Trachtenberg, Alexander, tr. from RUS. xxx, 128p. 1989. reprint ed. pap. 3.25 (*0-7178-0206-X*) Intl Pubs Co.

— La Ultima Lucha de Lenin: Discursos Y Escritos. Madrid, Luis, ed.Tr. of Lenin's Final Fight. (SPA.). 325p. 1997. pap. 21.95 (*0-87348-843-1*) Pathfinder NY.

— The Unknown Lenin: From the Secret Archive. Pipes, Richard et al, eds. Fitzpatrick, Catherine A., tr. LC 96-8415. (Annals of Communism Ser.). (Illus.). 256p. 1996. 27.50 (*0-300-06919-7*) Yale U Pr.

— What Is to Be Done? Burning Questions of Our Movement. Allen, James S., ed. LC 69-18884. 200p. (C). 1969. pap. 6.95 (*0-7178-0218-3*) Intl Pubs Co.

— Will the Bolsheviks Maintain Power? 128p. 1997. pap. 6.95 (*0-7509-1677-X*, Pub. by Sutton Pub Ltd) Intl Pubs Mktg.

Lenin, Vladimir Il'ich & Trotsky, Leon. Kronstadt. Mutnick, Barbara, ed. Wright, John G. et al, trs. LC 78-65893. 159p. 1979. pap. 15.95 (*0-913460-74-5*); lib. bdg. 45.00 (*0-913460-73-7*) Pathfinder NY.

Lenin, Vladimir Il'ich, et al. Bolshevism & the Russian Revolution. 68p. pap. 8.00 (*0-87348-671-4*) Pathfinder NY.

Lening, Paul F., ed. see Kellogg, Dale C., et al.

Lenington, Robert L. Managing Higher Education As a Business. LC 96-7617. (American Council on Education). 184p. 1996. boxed set 29.95 (*1-57356-023-5*) Oryx Pr.

Leniston. Decorative Bird Prints. 1998. pap. text 3.95 (*0-486-26510-2*) Dover.

Leniston, Florence. Easy-to-Cut Mother Goose Silhouettes. (Illus.). 1990. pap. 2.95 (*0-486-26450-5*) Dover.

— Popular Irish Songs. 160p. 1992. pap. 9.95 (*0-486-26755-5*) Dover.

Leniston, Florence, ed. La Mode Illustree Fashion Plates in Full Color. Olian, JoAnne, tr. LC 97-22623. (Illus.). 64p. 1997. pap. 12.95 (*0-486-29819-1*) Dover.

Lenius, Oscar. A Well-Dressed Gentleman's Pocket Guide. (Illus.). 226p. 1998. 21.95 (*1-85375-276-2*) Prion.

Lenk. Practical Design Power Supplies. 1998. 69.95 (*0-07-134324-5*) McGraw.

Lenk, Hans. Social Philosophy of Athletics. 1979. pap. text 9.60 (*0-87563-165-7*) Stipes.

Lenk, Hans & Paul, Gregor, eds. Epistemological Issues in Classical Chinese Philosophy. LC 92-17185. (SUNY Series in Chinese Philosophy & Culture). 194p. (C). 1993. text 59.50 (*0-7914-1449-3*); pap. text 19.95 (*0-7914-1450-7*) State U NY Pr.

Lenk, John D. Circuit Troubleshooting Handbook. LC 98-39250. 390p. 1998. 59.50 (*0-07-038185-2*); pap. 39.95 (*0-07-038186-0*) McGraw.

— Complete Guide to Stereo Television (MIS-MCS) Troubleshooting & Repair. (Illus.). 160p. (C). 1988. text 44.00 (*0-13-160839-8*) P-H.

— Handbook of Basic Electronic Troubleshooting. (Illus.). 1979. 15.50 (*0-13-372474-3*) P-H.

— Handbook of Digital Electronics. (Illus.). 384p. 1981. pap. text 39.00 (*0-13-377184-9*) P-H.

— Handbook of Modern Solid State Amplifiers. (Illus.). 400p. 1974. pap. text 39.00 (*0-13-380394-5*) P-H.

— Handbook of Oscilloscopes: Theory & Application. enl. rev. ed. (Illus.). 320p. (C). 1982. text 44.00 (*0-13-380576-X*) P-H.

— Handbook of Practical CB Service. (Illus.). 1978. 15.50 (*0-13-380550-6*) P-H.

— Handbook of Practical Electronic Circuits. (Illus.). 352p. 1982. pap. text 39.00 (*0-13-380741-X*) P-H.

— Handbook of Simplified Electrical Wiring Design. (Illus.). 416p. 1978. 19.50 (*0-13-381681-8*) P-H.

— A Hobbyist's Guide to Computer Experimentation. (Illus.). 288p. (C). 1985. pap. text 39.00 (*0-13-392473-4*) P-H.

— Lenk's Audio Handbook: Operation & Troubleshooting. 350p. 1991. 39.50 (*0-07-037503-8*) McGraw.

— Lenk's Audio Handbook: Operation & Troubleshooting. 1992. pap. text 22.95 (*0-07-004276-4*) McGraw.

— Lenk's Audio Handbook: Operation & Troubleshooting. 304p. 1992. pap. 22.95 (*0-8306-4276-5*, 4309) McGraw-Hill Prof.

— Lenk's Laser Handbook: Featuring CD, CDV, & CD-Rom Technology. 1993. pap. 22.95 (*0-8306-4429-6*) McGraw-Hill Prof.

— Lenk's Laser Handbook: Featuring CD, CDV & CD-Rom Technology. 352p. 1992. 39.50 (*0-07-037505-4*) McGraw.

— Lenk's Video Handbook. 2nd ed. LC 96-34523. 1996. pap. text 29.95 (*0-07-037617-4*) McGraw.

— Lenk's Video Handbook: Operation & Troubleshooting. 384p. 1992. pap. 22.95 (*0-8306-4072-X*) McGraw.

— Lenk's Video Handbook: Operation & Troubleshooting. 2nd ed. LC 96-34523. (Illus.). 512p. 1996. 49.50 (*0-07-037616-6*) McGraw.

— McGraw-Hill Circuit Encyclopedia & Troubleshooting Guide, Vol. 2. (Illus.). 707p. 1996. pap. 39.95 (*0-07-037611-5*) McGraw.

— McGraw-Hill Circuit Encyclopedia & Troubleshooting Guide, Vol. 3. (Illus.). 706p. 1996. 59.50 (*0-07-037716-2*); pap. 36.95 (*0-07-037717-0*) McGraw.

— McGraw-Hill Circuit Encyclopedia & Troubleshooting Guide, Vol. No. 1. (Illus.). 647p. 1996. pap. 39.95 (*0-07-038076-7*) McGraw.

— Optimizing Wireless /RF Circuits. (Electronics Workbench Circuit Solution Ser.). 300p. 1999. 60.00 (*0-07-134376-8*) McGraw-Hill Prof.

— Simplified Design of Data Converters. LC 96-48397. (Lenk Ser.). 242p. 1997. text 19.95 (*0-7506-9509-9*) Buttrwrth-Heinemann.

— Simplified Design of IC Amplifiers. (Lenk Ser.). (Illus.). 239p. 1996. text 19.95 (*0-7506-9508-0*) Buttrwrth-Heinemann.

— Simplified Design of Linear Power Supplies. LC 94-16077. (EDN Ser.). 240p. 1994. 39.95 (*0-7506-9506-4*) Buttrwrth-Heinemann.

— Simplified Design of Linear Power Supplies. (Lenk Ser.). (Illus.). 246p. 1996. pap. text 19.95 (*0-7506-9820-9*) Buttrwrth-Heinemann.

— Simplified Design of Micropower & Battery Circuits. LC 95-4867. (Lenk Ser.). (Illus.). 255p. 1995. text 19.95 (*0-7506-9510-2*, Focal) Buttrwrth-Heinemann.

— Simplified Design of Microprocessor Supervisory Circuits. LC 97-52061. 256p. 1998. text 19.95 (*0-7506-9652-4*, Newnes) Buttrwrth-Heinemann.

— Simplified Design of Switching Power Supplies. (Lenk Ser.). (Illus.). 240p. 1996. pap. text 19.95 (*0-7506-9821-7*) Buttrwrth-Heinemann.

— Simplified Design of Voltage-Frequency Converters. LC 97-15943. (Lenk Ser.). 224p. 1997. pap. text 19.95 (*0-7506-9654-0*) Buttrwrth-Heinemann.

Lenk, John D., jt. auth. see Marcus, Abraham.

Lenk, Krzysztof, jt. auth. see Kahn, Paul.

Lenk, Robert P. Breast Cancer: The Fight of Your Life. (Illus.). 193p. (Orig.). 1999. pap. 19.95 (*1-56072-322-X*, Nova Kroshka Bks) Nova Sci Pubs.

— Breast Cancer Treatment Options. (Illus.). 279p. 1998. lib. bdg. 37.00 (*1-56072-396-3*) Nova Sci Pubs.

Lenk, Ron. Practical Design of Power Supplies. 288p. 1998. 69.95 (*0-7803-3458-2*, PC5715-QOE) Inst Electrical.

Lenke, Leif. Alcohol & Criminal Violence: Time Series Analyses in a Comparative Perspective. 187p. (Orig.). 1990. pap. 47.50 (*91-22-01415-2*) Coronet Bks.

Lenker, Lagretta T., jt. ed. see Deats, Sara M.

Lenker, Lagretta T., jt. ed. see Moxley, Joseph M.

Lenker, Lagretta Tallent, jt. ed. see Deats, Sara Munson.

Lenker, Susan, ed. Exemplary Programs in Introductory College Mathematics: Innovative Programs Using Technology. LC 98-88602. (MAA Notes: No. 27). 140p. 1998. pap. text 28.95 (*0-88385-159-8*) Math Assn.

Lenkert, Erica. Frommer's San Francisco. 1996. 13.95 (*0-02-861105-5*) Macmillan.

***Lenkert, Erika.** Frommer's San Francisco 2001. (Illus.). 352p. 2000. pap. 14.99 (*0-7645-6128-6*) IDG Bks.

Lenkert, Erika, ed. Southern California Best Places: Restaurants, Lodgings, Touring. (Illus.). 492p. 1999. pap. 19.95 (*1-57061-181-5*) Sasquatch Bks.

Lenkert, Erika & Poole, Mathew R. Frommer's San Francisco from $60 a Day. 298p. 1997. pap. 14.95 (*0-02-862087-9*, Pub. by Macmillan) S&S Trade.

Lenkert, Erika, et al. Frommer's California from $60 a Day with Coupons. 2nd ed. (Frommer's California from $60 a Day Ser.). (Illus.). 664p. 1999. pap. 19.95 (*0-02-862577-3*, Pub. by Macmillan) S&S Trade.

— Frommer's California 1998. 688p. 1997. 18.95 (*0-02-861778-9*) Macmillan.

Lenkert, Erika, jt. auth. see Juliano.

Len'kov, V. D., et al. The Komandorskii Camp of the Bering Expedition: An Experiment in Complex Study. Arndt, Katherine L., tr. from RUS. (Illus.). 176p. (Orig.). 1992. pap. 12.00 (*0-940521-00-8*) AK Hist Soc.

Lenman, Bruce. Integration, Enlightenment, & Industrialization: Scotland, 1746-1832. LC 81-193623. (New History of Scotland Ser.: No. 6). 192p. reprint ed. pap. 59.60 (*0-608-16633-2*, 202636900049) Bks Demand.

— Jacobite Clans of the Great Glen, 1650-1784. 248p. 1990. pap. 39.00 (*1-898218-19-6*) St Mut.

— Jacobite Risings in Britain, 1689-1746. 320p. 1990. pap. 45.00 (*1-898218-20-X*) St Mut.

***Lenman, Bruce, ed.** Chambers Dictionary of World History. (Illus.). 960p. 2000. 47.95 (*0-550-13000-4*, Chambers LKC) LKC.

Lenman, Bruce, ed. Larousse Dictionary of North American History. 320p. 1995. pap. 8.95 (*0-7523-0005-9*, Larousse LKC) LKC.

— Larousse Dictionary of World History. 1024p. 1995. pap. 18.95 (*0-7523-5008-0*, Chambers LKC) LKC.

Lenman, Bruce P. Integration & Enlightenment: Scotland, 1746-1832. (New History of Scotland Ser.). 200p. 1993. pap. 20.00 (*0-7486-0385-9*, Pub. by Edinburgh U Pr) Col U Pr.

Lenman, J. A., jt. auth. see Davidson, D. L.

Lenman, Karin, ed. see Forsee, David.

Lenman, Karin, ed. see Radha, Sivananda.

Lenn, Dorothy, tr. see Steiner, Rudolf.

Lenn, Marjorie P. & Campos, Lenora. Globalization of the Professions & the Quality Imperative: Professional Accreditation, Certification, Licensure. LC 97-1213. 162p. 1997. pap. 55.00 (*0-912150-46-7*) Atwood Pub LLC.

Lenn, Marjorie P. & Campos, Lenora, eds. Globalization of the Professions & the Quality Imperative: Professional Accreditation, Certification & Licensure. 162p. 1997. pap. text 55.00 (*1-891859-13-7*) Atwood Pub LLC.

An Asterisk (*) at the beginning of an entry indicates that the title is appearing for the first time.

Lenna, Harry R., jt. auth. see Woodman, Natalie J.

Lennan, Richard. The Ecclesiology of Karl Rahner. 300p. 1998. reprint ed. pap. text 19.95 (*0-19-826955-2*) OUP.

— An Introduction to Catholic Theology. LC 98-20642. 208p. 1998. pap. 15.95 (*0-8091-3808-5*) Paulist Pr.

Lennan, Richard, ed. Redefining the Church: Vision & Practice. 176p. 1996. pap. 9.95 (*0-85574-230-5*, Pub. by E J Dwyer) Morehouse Pub.

Lennander, Jean. Crafty Recycling: Wallpaper Craft from Throw-Aways. LC 93-86374. (Illus.). 192p. (Orig.). 1994. pap. 12.95 (*0-9639009-1-9*) Tassel Pr.

Lennard, Erica. Classic Gardens. LC 83-80908. (Illus.). 128p. 1982. 27.95 (*0-912810-38-6*) Lustrum Pr.

Lennard, Henry L. & Gralnick, Alexander, eds. The Psychiatric Hospital: Context, Values & Therapeutic Process. 221p. 1986. 35.95 (*0-89885-297-8*, Kluwer Acad Hman Sci) Kluwer Academic.

Lennard, Henry L. & Lennard, Suzanne H., eds. Ethics of Health Care: Dilemmas of Technology & Techniques in Health Care & Psychotherapy. LC 79-57022. 174p. (Orig.). 1979. pap. 16.00 (*0-935824-01-4*) Gondolier.

Lennard, Henry L., jt. auth. see Crowhurst-Lennard, Suzanne H.

Lennard, Henry L., jt. auth. see Lennard, Suzanne H.

Lennard, John. But I Digress: The Exploitation of Parentheses in English Printed Verse. (Illus.). 340p. (C). 1992. text 80.00 (*0-19-811247-5*) OUP.

— The Poetry Handbook: A Guide to Reading Poetry in English for Pleasure & Practical Criticism. 238p. 1996. pap. text 14.95 (*0-19-871149-2*) OUP.

— The Poetry Handbook: A Guide to Reading Poetry in English for Pleasure & Practical Criticism. 238p. 1997. text 60.00 (*0-19-871154-9*) OUP.

Lennard-Jones, John E., jt. ed. see Kamm, Michael A.

Lennard, Reginald V. Rural England, 1086 to 1135: A Study of Social & Agrarian Conditions. LC 80-2222. reprint ed. 49.50 (*0-404-18767-6*) AMS Pr.

Lennard, Suzanne H., et al, eds. Making Cities Livable: Wege Zur Menschlichen Stadt. (ENG & GER., Illus.). 460p. 1997. 49.00 (*0-935824-07-3*); pap. 38.00 (*0-935824-08-1*) Gondolier.

Lennard, Suzanne H. & Lennard, Henry L. Livable Cities Observed: A Source Book of Images & Ideas. (Illus.). 272p. (Orig.). 1995. 38.00 (*0-935824-05-7*); pap. 33.00 (*0-935824-06-5*) Gondolier.

Lennard, Suzanne H., jt. ed. see Lennard, Henry L.

***Lennard, Ted A., ed.** Pain Procedure in Clinical Practice. 2nd rev. ed. LC 99-42857. (Illus.). 350p. (C). 2000. text 75.00 (*1-56053-367-6*, Pub. by Harcourt Coll Pubs) Harcourt.

Lennard, Ted A., ed. Physiatric Procedures in Clinical Practice. (Illus.). 400p. 1995. text 76.00 (*1-56053-069-3*) Hanley & Belfus.

Lennard, Vic. Midi Survival Guide. (Illus.). 96p. 1996. pap. 13.95 (*1-870775-28-7*, Pub. by PC Pubg) Cimino Pub Grp.

Lennard, Vic, jt. auth. see Buick, Peter.

Lennbe, Jillian M., jt. ed. see Wood, D.

Lenne, J. M. Diseases & Pests of Sweet Potato. 116p. 1991. pap. 45.00 (*0-85954-294-7*, Pub. by Nat Res Inst) St Mut.

Lenne, J. M. & Trutmann, P., eds. Diseases of Tropical Pasture Plants. LC 97-179022. (Illus.). 480p. 1994. text 140.00 (*0-85198-917-9*) OUP.

Lenne, J. M., jt. auth. see Boa, E.

Lenne, J. M., jt. ed. see Allen, D. J.

Lenn'e, J. M., jt. ed. see Waller, J. M.

Lenneberg, Hans. Witness & Scholars: Studies in Musical Biography. (Monographs on Musicology: Vol. 5). 1988. text 44.00 (*2-88124-210-3*, ML3797.L46) Gordon & Breach.

Lenneberg, Hans, ed. The Dissemination of Music: Studies in the History of Music Publishing. (Musicology: A Book Ser.). 192p. 1994. text 29.00 (*2-88449-117-1*) Gordon & Breach.

Lenneberg, Hans, tr. Breitkoph & Hartel in Paris (1833-1844) The Letters of Heinrich Probst. LC 90-7036. (Musical Life in Nineteenth-Century France Ser.: No. 5). (GER., Illus.). 200p. 1990. lib. bdg. 47.00 (*0-918728-64-9*) Pendragon NY.

Lennerstrand, G., et al, eds. Strabismus & Amblyopia: Experimental Basis for Advances in Clinical Management. (Wenner-Gren International Symposia Ser.: Vol. 49). (Illus.). 452p. 1988. 110.00 (*0-306-42943-8*, Plenum Trade) Perseus Pubng.

Lennerstrand, Gunnar & American Association for Pediatric Ophthalmology &, eds. Update on Strabismus & Pediatric Ophthalmology: Proceedings of the June, 1994 Joint ISA & AAPO&S Meeting, Vancouver, Canada. LC 94-46587. 752p. 1995. boxed set 244.95 (*0-8493-8961-5*, 8961) CRC Pr.

Lennerstrand, Gunnar & Ygge, J. Eye Movements in Reading. LC 94-19379. (Wenner-Gren International Ser.: Vol. 64). 390p. 1994. 179.25 (*0-08-042509-7*, Pergamon Pr) Elsevier.

Lennert, K. & Feller, A. C. Histopathology of Non-Hodgkin's Lymphomas: Based on the Updated Kiel Classification. 2nd rev. ed. (Illus.). xiv, 312p. 1994. 176.00 (*0-387-51270-5*) Spr-Verlag.

Lennert, K. & Hubner, K., eds. Pathology of the Bone Marrow. (Illus.). 426p. 1984. lib. bdg. 115.00 (*0-89574-195-4*, Pub. by Gustav Fischer) Balogh.

Lennert, Kristen, jt. auth. see Clark, Sheree.

Lennette, Edwin H., ed. Laboratory Diagnosis of Viral Infections. 2nd expanded rev. ed. (Illus.). 800p. 1991. text 215.00 (*0-8247-8585-1*) Dekker.

Lennette, Edwin H., et al, eds. Diagnostic Procedures for Viral, Rickettsial & Chlamydial Infections. 7th ed. LC 96-147851. 633p. (C). 1995. pap., lab manual ed. 96.00 (*0-87553-220-9*) Am Pub Health.

— Laboratory Diagnosis of Infectious Diseases: Principles & Practice, Vol. 2. (Illus.). 825p. 1988. 350.00 (*0-387-96756-7*) Spr-Verlag.

***Lennette, Edwin H. & Smith, Thomas F.** Laboratory Diagnosis of Viral Infections 3rd rev. expanded ed. LC 99-22924. (Illus.). 880p. 1999. text 195.00 (*0-8247-1952-2*) Dekker.

Lennette, Edwin H., ed. see American Society for Microbiology Staff, et al.

Lennick, Douglas. The Simple Genius (You) Johnson, Marietta, ed. (Illus.). 93p. 1984. pap. 8.00 (*0-9673838-0-3*) DL Wright Pubng.

Lennick, Douglas & Geer, Roy. How to Get What You Want & Remain True to Yourself. (Illus.). 103p. 1989. pap. 10.00 (*0-9673838-1-1*) DL Wright Pubng.

Lennie. Seeing. 350p. 1998. 79.95 (*0-12-443760-5*) Acad Pr.

Lennig, Arthur. Stroheim. LC 99-27365. (Illus.). 550p. 2000. 30.00 (*0-8131-2138-8*) U Pr of Ky.

Lennihan, Begabati, ed. see De Schepper, Luc.

Lenning, Janet, ed. see Clark, Jim, et al.

Lenning, Janet, ed. see Hoffman, Mark, et al.

Lenning, Michael L. Inside the Crosshairs: Snipers in Vietnam. LC 98-92560. 1998. mass mkt. 6.99 (*0-8041-1620-2*) Ivy Books.

***Lenning, Oscar T. & Ebbers, Larry H.** The Powerful Potential of Learning Communities: Improving Education for the Future. LC 98-88007. (ASHE-ERIC Higher Education Report: Vol. 26, No. 6). 100p. 1999. pap. 24.00 (*1-878380-86-9*) GWU Grad Schl E&HD.

Lennon, ed. Social Psychology. (C). 1998. text. write for info. (*0-321-01152-X*) Addson-Wesley Educ.

Lennon & McCartney. Beatles Greatest Hits: Notes with Tablature. 64p. 1991. pap. 9.95 (*0-7935-0878-9*, 00702072) H Leonard.

— The John Lennon Collection, Vol. 158. Vol. 158. 56p. 1985. pap. 6.95 (*0-7935-2559-4*, 00101769) H Leonard.

Lennon & McCartney. Lennon & McCartney 60 Greatest Hits: Violin. 64p. 1986. pap. 9.95 (*0-7935-3300-7*, 00844286) H Leonard.

Lennon & McCartney. Lennon & McCartney 60 Greatest Hits: Clarinet. 64p. 1986. pap. 6.95 (*0-7935-3294-9*, 00844282) H Leonard.

— Lennon & McCartney 60 Greatest Hits: Flute. 64p. 1986. pap. 6.95 (*0-7935-3299-X*, 00844281) H Leonard.

Lennon, Alex. History of the Cocker Spaniel. (Illus.). 350p. 1988. 39.95 (*0-911949-00-3*); pap. 19.95 (*0-911949-01-1*) Big Sand Pub.

Lennon, Alexander T., jt. ed. see Mazarr, Michael J.

Lennon, Andy. The Basics of Model Aircraft Design. (Illus.). 120p. 1996. pap. text 19.95 (*0-911295-40-2*) Air Age.

Lennon, Biddy W. Eating at Home Cookbook. 180p. (Orig.). 1990. pap. 10.95 (*1-85371-096-2*, Pub. by Poolbeg Pr) Dufour.

— The Poolbeg Book of Traditional Irish Cooking. 186p. 1990. pap. 9.95 (*1-85371-092-X*, Pub. by Poolbeg Pr) Dufour.

Lennon, Bill. Black & White Model Photography. LC 98-70349. (Illus.). 128p. 1998. pap. 29.95 (*0-936262-68-0*) Amherst Media.

Lennon, Brian. After the Ceasefires: Catholics & the Future of Northern Ireland. 172p. 1997. 59.95 (*1-57309-297-5*, Cath Scholar Pr) Intl Scholars.

— After the Ceasefires: Catholics & the Future of Northern Ireland. LC 95-122543. 172p. 1997. pap. 49.95 (*1-85607-122-7*, Cath Scholar Pr) Intl Scholars.

Lennon, Cheryl, ed. see Frederickson, Jeanette A. & Holton, Court C.

***Lennon, Colm.** An Irish Prisoner of Conscience in the Tudor Era: Archbishop Richard Creagh. 176p. 1999. 45.00 (*1-85182-473-1*, Pub. by Four Cts Pr) Intl Spec Bk.

Lennon, Colm. The Lords of Dublin in the Age of Reformation. 320p. 1989. 45.00 (*0-7165-2419-8*, Pub. by Irish Acad Pr) Intl Spec Bk.

— Sixteenth Century Ireland: The Incomplete Conquest. LC 94-32460. 1995. text 45.00 (*0-312-12462-7*) St Martin.

***Lennon, Colm & Murray, James, eds.** The Dublin City Franchise Roll, 1468-1512. LC 99-190934. (Illus.). 164p. 1999. 55.00 (*0-9505301-6-6*, Pub. by Four Cts Pr) Intl Spec Bk.

Lennon, Colm, jt. ed. see Hill, Jacqueline.

Lennon, Donald R., jt. auth. see Bennett, Charles E.

Lennon, Edith, ed. The CQ Amateur Radio Equipment Buyer's Guide. LC 97-76812. (Illus.). 136p. 1997. mass mkt. 15.95 (*0-943016-19-3*) CQ Commns Inc.

Lennon, Florence B. Victoria Through the Looking Glass: The Life of Lewis Carroll. 27.95 (*0-89190-991-5*) Amereon Ltd.

***Lennon, Frank.** Nirvana. (Poetry New York Pamphlet Ser.: No. 28). 30p. 1999. pap. 5.00 (*0-923389-42-3*) Meet Eyes Bind.

Lennon, Gerard P., ed. Symposium on Ground Water. LC 91-21956. 344p. 1991. pap. text 38.00 (*0-87262-817-5*) Am Soc Civil Eng.

Lennon, Gered, et al. Living with the South Carolina Coast. LC 96-17857. (Living with the Shore Ser.). (Illus.). 264p. 1996. pap. 18.95 (*0-8223-1815-6*); text 49.95 (*0-8223-1809-1*) Duke.

Lennon, J. Hypermedia Systems & Applications: World Wide Web & Beyond. LC 97-13552. 250p. 1997. pap. 31.95 (*3-540-62697-2*) Spr-Verlag.

***Lennon, J. John & Foley, Malcolm.** Dark Tourism. 256p. 2000. pap. 24.95 (*0-8264-5064-4*) Continuum.

— Dark Tourism. 256p. 2000. 82.95 (*1-85567-520-X*, Pub. by P P Pubs) Continuum.

Lennon, J. Michael, ed. Conversations with Norman Mailer. LC 87-34316. (Literary Conversations Ser.). 396p. 1988. pap. 15.95 (*0-87805-352-2*); text 39.50 (*0-87805-351-4*) U Pr of Miss.

***Lennon, J. Robert.** The Funnies. 2000. pap. 13.00 (*1-57322-781-1*, Riverhd Trade) Berkley Pub.

Lennon, J. Robert. The Funnies. LC 98-42363. 320p. 1999. 23.95 (*1-57322-126-0*, Riverhead Books) Putnam Pub Group.

— The Light of Falling Stars. LC 97-10972. 307p. 1998. reprint ed. pap. 13.00 (*1-57322-682-3*, Riverhd Trade) Berkley Pub.

Lennon, James M. & Taylor, Susan, eds. The Natural Hygiene Diet. 128p. 1999. pap. 10.95 (*0-914532-44-8*, ANHS 254) Amer Natural Hygiene.

— The Natural Hygiene Handbook. LC 96-86830. 128p. (Orig.). 1996. pap. 10.95 (*0-914532-40-5*, ANHS 0238) Amer Natural Hygiene.

Lennon, Jane. Happier in the Country. LC 87-61162. (Illus.). (Orig.). 1987. 12.95 (*0-941526-04-6*) Prospect Hill.

***Lennon, Joan.** There's a Kangaroo in My Soup! (Illus.). (J). 2000. 15.95 (*0-8126-2898-5*) Front St-Cricket Bks.

Lennon, John. Grow Old With Me: Vocal-High Voice. 6p. 1997. pap. 3.95 (*0-7935-8513-9*) H Leonard.

— Grow Old With Me: Vocal-Low Voices. 6p. 1997. pap. 3.95 (*0-7935-8514-7*) H Leonard.

— Imagine. 1990. 13.95 (*1-55972-038-7*, Birch Ln Pr) Carol Pub Group.

— In His Own Write. 1995. reprint ed. lib. bdg. 27.95 (*1-56849-147-6*) Buccaneer Bks.

— In His Own Write: John Lennon. 1987. pap. text 4.95 (*0-06-097123-1*, Harp PBks) HarpC.

— Misadventures of Sherlock Holmes. 1991. 16.95 (*0-8065-1245-8*) Carol Pub Group.

— Real Love: The Drawings for Sean. LC 98-50003. (Illus.). 48p. (J). (gr. 4-7). 1999. 12.99 (*0-375-80174-X*, Pub. by Random Bks Yng Read) Random.

— Real Love_drawings for Sean. LC 98-50003. (Illus.). 48p. (J). (gr. 4-7). 1999. lib. bdg. 14.99 (*0-375-90174-4*) Random.

— Skywriting by Word of Mouth: And Other Writings, Including the Ballad of John & Yoko. LC 86-54312. (Illus.). 208p. 1987. pap. 13.00 (*0-06-091444-0*, PL/1444, Perennial) HarperTrade.

— A Spaniard in the Works. 1995. reprint ed. 27.95 (*1-56849-299-5*) Buccaneer Bks.

— A Spaniard in the Works: John Lennon. 1987. pap. text 4.95 (*0-06-097122-3*) HarpC.

Lennon, John & McCartney, Paul. Easy Beatle Hits. (Easy Piano Ser.). 48p. 1988. pap. 6.95 (*0-7935-2788-0*, 00364116) H Leonard.

— Yellow Submarine. (Piano-Vocal-Guitar Ser.). 6p. 1987. pap. 3.95 (*0-88188-959-8*, 00355727) H Leonard.

— Yellow Submarine. (Sing-a-Song Storybooks Ser.). (Illus.). 24p. (J). 1993. 9.95 (*0-7935-1859-8*, 00183013) H Leonard.

Lennon, John, et al. Misadventures of Sherlock Holmes. Wolfe, Sebastian, ed. 1991. pap. 10.95 (*0-8065-1235-0*) Carol Pub Group.

Lennon, Kathleen, jt. ed. see Whitford, Margaret.

Lennon, Kathleen H., jt. auth. see Dacey, John S.

Lennon, Kethleen, jt. ed. see Charles, David.

Lennon, Mary I. Mind Your P's & Q's: Your B's, D's & S's Too! LC 97-92243. (Illus.). 32p. (Orig.). (J). (gr. k-3). 1998. mass mkt., per. 6.25 (*0-9658531-0-1*) Acrospire Bk.

Lennon, Michael J. Patent License Agreements: Information Technology, Computers, Electronics. LC 98-40535. 1998. ring bd. 160.00 (*0-7355-0237-4*) Panel Pubs.

***Lennon, Michael J.** Technology Transfer Guide. LC 00-35587. 2000. write for info. (*0-7355-1352-X*) Panel Pubs.

Lennon, Michael J., jt. auth. see Mailer, Norman.

Lennon, Nigey. Alfred Jarry: The Man with the Axe. (Illus.). 128p. 1991. pap. 9.95 (*0-86719-382-4*) Last Gasp.

— Alfred Jarry: The Man with the Axe. (Illus.). 120p. 1984. 15.95 (*0-915572-74-5*); pap. 6.95 (*0-915572-73-7*) Panjandrum.

— Being Frank: My Time with Frank Zappa. (Illus.). 160p. (Orig.). 1995. pap. 14.95 (*1-879395-55-X*) CA Classics Bks.

— The Sagebrush Bohemian: Mark Twain in California. (Illus.). 203p. 1994. pap. 10.95 (*1-56924-946-6*) Marlowe & Co.

Lennon, Nigey, jt. auth. see Rolfe, Lionel.

Lennon, Patricia & Moore, Douglas. Te Toca a Ti. (Aiming for Proficiency Ser.). (SPA., Illus.). 160p. (Orig.). 1990. student ed. 14.95 (*1-879279-04-5*, TX 3-018-188) Proficiency Pr.

Lennon, Patricia, et al. The Foreign Language Teacher's Handbook: Aiming for Proficiency in Spanish. (SPA., Illus.). 208p. (Orig.). 1989. teacher ed. 28.95 (*1-879279-01-0*, TX 2-670-457) Proficiency Pr.

Lennon, Rebecca D. Keyboard Capers: Music Theory for Children. 143p. (J). 1993. pap. text 18.95 (*1-884098-01-0*) Elijah Co.

Lennon, Robin. Home Design from the Inside Out: Feng Shui, Color Therapy & Self Awareness. LC 96-43800. (Illus.). 288p. 1997. pap. 14.95 (*0-14-019539-4*, Arkana) Viking Penguin.

Lennon, Robin. Home for Your Heart. 1999. pap. 14.95 (*0-14-026055-2*) Viking Penguin.

Lennon, Rosemarie. David Letterman: On Stage & 320p. 1994. mass mkt. 4.99 (*0-7860-0084-8*, Pinncle Kensgtn) Kensgtn Pub Corp.

Lennon, Sharron J., et al. Social Science Aspects of Dress: New Directions. (ITAA Special Publications: No. 5). 211p. (C). 1993. pap. text 35.00 (*1-885715-01-3*) Intl Textile.

Lennon, Sharron J., jt. ed. see Johnson, Kim K.

Lennon, Thomas M. The Battle of the Gods & Giants: The Legacies of Descartes & Gassendi, 1655-1715. LC 92-26088. (Studies in Intellectual History & the History of Philosophy). 456p. 1993. text 57.50 (*0-691-07400-3*, Pub. by Princeton U Pr) Cal Prin Full Svc.

— Reading Bayle. 240p. 1999. text 60.00 (*0-8020-4488-3*); pap. text 19.95 (*0-8020-8266-1*) U of Toronto Pr.

Lennon, Thomas M., et al, eds. Problems of Cartesianism. (Studies in the History of Ideas). 272p. 1982. 65.00 (*0-7735-1000-1*, Pub. by McG-Queens Univ Pr) CUP Services.

Lennon, Thomas M. & Olscamp, Paul J., eds. The Search after Truth: With "Elucidations of the Search after Truth" (Cambridge Texts in the History of Philosophy Ser.). 821p. (C). 1997. text 80.00 (*0-521-58004-8*); pap. text 29.95 (*0-521-58995-9*) Cambridge U Pr.

Lennon, Thomas M., tr. see Malebranche, Nicolas.

Lennon, Todd M., ed. Statistics on Social Work Education in the United States, 1997. 128p. 1998. pap. 16.00 (*0-87293-066-1*) Coun Soc Wk Ed.

Lennon, Tom. When Love Comes to Town. 176p. 1997. pap. 9.95 (*0-86278-361-5*, Pub. by OBrien Pr) Irish Amer Bk.

Lennor, Linda A., jt. auth. see Miller, Ruth M.

Lennox. Gray's Anatomy Colouring Book. 1997. pap. text 21.95 (*0-443-05727-3*, W B Saunders Co) Harcrt Hlth Sci Grp.

Lennox-Boyd, et al. Traditional English Gardens. 1998. pap. 16.95 (*0-7538-0264-3*) Phoenix Hse.

Lennox-Boyd, Christopher, et al. George Stubbs. (Illus.). 432p. 1990. 290.00 (*0-85667-375-7*, Pub. by P Wilson) Hoovers TX.

Lennox-Boyd, Edward, ed. Masterpieces of English Furniture: The Gerstenfeld Collection. (Illus.). 272p. 1999. 125.00 (*0-903432-56-0*, Pub. by CMW Ltd) Antique Collect.

Lennox, C. Shakespeare Illustrated, 3 vols. LC 72-172047. reprint ed. 135.00 (*0-404-03970-7*) AMS Pr.

Lennox, C. M., jt. ed. see McLatchie, G.

Lennox, Carolyn E., ed. Redecision Therapy: A Brief, Action-Oriented Approach. LC 96-41624. 336p. 1997. 40.00 (*0-7657-0043-3*) Aronson.

Lennox, Charlotte. Euphemia. LC 88-38442. 256p. 1989. 50.00 (*0-8201-1435-9*) Schol Facsimiles.

— The Female Quixote: Or the Adventures of Arabella. (Illus.). 461p. 1998. pap. 11.95 (*0-19-283572-6*) OUP.

— The Female Quixote, or the Adventures of Arabella, 2 vols. in one. LC 79-104511. 603p. reprint ed. lib. bdg. 77.50 (*0-8398-1155-1*) Irvington.

— The Life of Harriot Stuart, Written by Herself. Kubica, Susan, ed. & intro. by. LC 94-29387. 328p. 1995. 45.00 (*0-8386-3579-2*) Fairleigh Dickinson.

Lennox, Daphne. See Me after School: Identifying & Helping Children with Emotional & Behavioral Problems. 144p. (Orig.). 1991. pap. 29.95 (*1-85346-163-6*, Pub. by David Fulton) Taylor & Francis.

Lennox, Duncan, ed. Jane's Air-Launched Weapons. (Illus.). 260p. 595.00 (*0-7106-0866-7*) Janes Info Group.

— Jane's Strategic Weapon Systems. (Illus.). 250p. 1996. ring bd. 595.00 (*0-7106-0880-2*) Janes Info Group.

Lennox, E. S., jt. ed. see Birch, J. R.

Lennox, Elsie, jt. auth. see Cohen, Daniel.

Lennox, Gladys R. Mists & Megaliths of Michael in the Mount. 1986. 39.00 (*0-7223-2036-1*, Pub. by A H S Ltd); pap. 35.00 (*0-7223-2091-4*, Pub. by A H S Ltd) St Mut.

***Lennox, James G.** Aristotle's Philosophy of Biology: Studies in the Origins of Life Science. (Cambridge Studies in Philosophy & Biology). (Illus.). 312p. (C). 2000. 64.95 (*0-521-65027-5*); pap. text 22.95 (*0-521-65976-0*) Cambridge U Pr.

Lennox, James G., jt. ed. see Gill, Mary L.

Lennox, John. Ralph Connor & His Works. (Canadian Author Studies). 60p. (C). 1988. pap. text 9.95 (*0-920763-78-2*, Pub. by ECW) Genl Dist Srvs.

Lennox, John & Lacombe, Michele, eds. Dear Bill: The Correspondence of William Arthur Deacon. 400p. 1988. text 40.00 (*0-8020-2624-9*) U of Toronto Pr.

Lennox, John & Paterson, Janet M., eds. Challenges, Projects, Texts: Canadian Editing: Papers Given at the Conference on Editorial Problems, University of Toronto, 17-18, November, 1989. LC 91-12400. (Conference on Editorial Problems Ser.: No. 25). Orig. Title: Defis, Projets et Textes dans l'Edition Critique au Canada. 120p. 1993. 42.50 (*0-404-63675-6*) AMS Pr.

Lennox, John, jt. auth. see Gooding, David.

Lennox, John, jt. auth. see Thomas, Clara.

Lennox, John, ed. see Laurence, Margaret.

Lennox, John C., tr. see Adian, S. I.

***Lennox, Judith.** Footprints on the Sand. 2000. pap. 14.00 (*0-688-17243-1*) Morrow Avon.

— The Secret Years. 2000. pap. 8.95 (*0-552-14331-6*, Pub. by Transworld Publishers Ltd) Trafalgar.

— Some Old Lover's Ghost. 2000. 29.95 (*0-385-40675-4*, Pub. by Transworld Publishers Ltd); pap. 10.95 (*0-552-14333-2*, Pub. by Transworld Publishers Ltd) Trafalgar.

Lennox, Judith. Some Old Lover's Ghost. 480p. 1999. reprint ed. pap. 14.00 (*0-688-17219-9*, Wm Morrow) Morrow Avon.

— Winter House. 1998. mass mkt. 8.99 (*0-552-14332-4*) Bantam.

***Lennox, Kara.** Twin Expectations. (American Romance Ser.). 2000. mass mkt. 4.25 (*0-373-16856-X*, 1168566) Harlequin Bks.

— Virgin Promise. (American Romance Ser.). 2000. mass mkt. 4.25 (*0-373-16840-3*, 1-16840-0) Harlequin Bks.

***Lennox, Marion.** The Baby Affair. large type ed. 288p. 1999. 25.99 (*0-263-16032-7*, Pub. by Mills & Boon) Ulverscroft.

— Bachelor Cure. (Readers Choice Ser.). 2000. mass mkt. 4.50 (*0-373-51124-8*, 1511245) Harlequin Bks.

Lennox, Marion. Cruel Country. large type ed. (Magna Large Print Ser.). 272p. 1996. 27.99 (*0-7505-0964-3*, Pub. by Mgna Lrg Print) Ulverscroft.

— Dr. McIver's Baby. (Promo Ser.). 1999. per. 3.75 (*0-373-83383-0*, 1-83383-9) Harlequin Bks.

An Asterisk (*) at the beginning of an entry indicates that the title is appearing for the first time.

— Legacy of Shadows. large type ed. 259p. 1996. 27.99 (*0-7505-0818-3*, Pub. by Mgna Lrg Print) Ulverscroft.

— A Loving Legacy. large type ed. 301p. 1995. 11.50 (*0-7505-0817-5*, Pub. by Mgna Lrg Print) Ulverscroft.

***Lennox, Muriel A.** Northern Dancer: The Legend & His Legacy. (Illus.). 222p. 1999. pap. 13.95 (*0-9699025-1-4*) King3gfisher Communs.

— Northern Dancer: The Legend & His Legacy. 2nd ed. (Illus.). 222p. 1998. write for info. (*0-9699025-0-6*) BEA1.

***Lennox, Rowena.** Fighting Spirit of East Timor: The Life of Martinho Da Costa Lopes. LC 00-24637. 2000. boxed set. write for info. (*1-85649-833-6*, Pub. by Zed Books) St Martin.

Lennox, Shelley S., jt. auth. see Bedell, Jeffrey R.

***Lennox, Stephen J.** Proverbs: A Bible Commentary in the Wesleyan Tradition. LC 99-174410. 326 p. 1998. write for info. (*0-89827-197-5*) Wesleyan Pub Hse.

— Psalms: A Bible Commentary in the Wesleyan Tradition. 1999. 24.95 (*0-89827-204-1*) Wesleyan Pub Hse.

Lennox, Thompson. How to Develop an Import/Export Business. unabridged ed. 84p. 1995. pap. 24.95 (*1-890283-00-2*, 9403) L Thompson NY.

— How to Interview for a Job. unabridged ed. 30p. (Orig.). 1995. pap. 21.95 (*1-890283-01-0*, 9401) L Thompson NY.

— How to Turn the Newspapers & Magazines You Read into Mega Cash. unabridged ed. 50p. (Orig.). 1995. pap. 17.95 (*1-890283-02-9*, 9402) L Thompson NY.

— I Sleep in Doorways. unabridged ed. 71p. (Orig.). 1996. pap. 12.00 (*1-890283-05-3*, 9602) L Thompson NY.

— Poems from the Heart. unabridged ed. 66p. (Orig.). 1996. pap. 12.00 (*1-890283-06-1*, 9601) L Thompson NY.

— Sonnets for Lovers. unabridged ed. 74p. (Orig.). 1997. pap. 12.00 (*1-890283-03-7*, 9702) L Thompson NY.

— Where No Wind Blows. unabridged ed. 74p. (Orig.). 1997. pap. 12.00 (*1-890283-04-5*, 9701) L Thompson NY.

Leno, Garth. Hebrews: The Superiority of Christ. LC 96-85150. (Deeper Life Pulpit Commentary Ser.). 370p. 1996. pap. 12.99 (*0-87509-626-3*) Chr Pubns.

Leno, Jay. Jay Leno's Police Blotter: Real-Life Crime Headlines from "The Tonight Show with Jay Leno" LC 94-207296. 160p. 1994. pap. 6.95 (*0-8362-1751-9*) Andrews & McMeel.

— Leading with My Chin. 304p. 1997. mass mkt. 6.50 (*0-06-109492-7*, Harp PBks) HarpC.

— Leading with My Chin. large type ed. LC 98-52520. (Paperback Ser.). 1999. 22.95 (*0-7838-8524-5*) Thorndike Pr.

— More Headlines. 1990. mass mkt. 6.95 (*0-446-39236-7*, Pub. by Warner Bks) Little.

Leno, Jay, compiled by. Headlines IV: The Next Generation. (Illus.). 192p. (Orig.). 1992. mass mkt. 6.99 (*0-446-39417-3*, Pub. by Warner Bks) Little.

— Headlines III: Not the Movie, Still the Book. 1991. mass mkt. 6.99 (*0-446-39374-6*, Pub. by Warner Bks) Little.

Lenoble, Jacqueline. Atmospheric Radiative Transfer. LC 93-12711. (Illus.). 500p. 1993. 94.00 (*0-937194-21-2*) A Deepak Pub.

Lenoble, Jacqueline, ed. Radiative Transfer in Scattering & Absorbing Atmospheres: Standard Computational Procedures. LC 85-31116. 300p. 1985. 71.00 (*0-937194-05-0*) A Deepak Pub.

Lenoble, Jacqueline & Geleyn, J. F., eds. IRS '88 - Current Problems in Atmospheric Radiation: Proceedings of the International Radiation Symposium, Lille, France, 18-24 August 1988. LC 89-33588. (Illus.). 653p. 1989. 82.00 (*0-937194-16-6*) A Deepak Pub.

Lenoir, Anna. Napoleon Daze, 2 vols. Roberts, Sherry, ed. Incl. Vol. 1. Napoleon Daze. 2nd ed. Bilyeu, Jesse. LC 96-75801. 150p. (J). (gr. 4-6). 1997. reprint ed. lib. bdg. 14.95 (*1-889567-16-7*); Vol. 2. The Adventure Continues. Bilyeu, Sherry. LC 96-75795. 150p. (J). (gr. 6-9). 1997. lib. bdg. 9.99 (*1-889567-17-5*); 24.99 (*1-889567-18-3*) Chldrens Mus Coll.

LeNoir, Anna & Carlson, Melanie. Napoleon Days: Historical Reenactment Script with Insights for Beginning & Intermediate Creative Writing Student. Glass, I., ed. (Illus.). 150p. (Orig.). (J). (gr. 1-6). 1996. write for info. (*0-614-13274-6*) Chldrens Mus Coll.

LeNoir, Cathie. Born to Be One, No. 29. (Serenade Serenata Ser.). 1985. pap. 2.50 (*0-310-47062-5*, 15559P) Zondervan.

Lenoir, Jane, jt. auth. see Sargent, Dave.

Lenoir, Jane, jt. illus. see Sargent, Dave.

Lenoir, Jane, jt. illus. see Sargent.

Lenoir, Michel, jt. ed. see Dibble, Harold L.

Lenoir, Robert. The Language of Business: Dictionnaire Commercial et Economique Bilingue: French-English, English-French. (ENG & FRE.). 920p. 1989. pap. 105.00 (*0-7859-7954-9*, 2717817182) Fr & Eur.

Lenoir, Timothy. Instituting Science: The Cultural Production of Scientific Disciplines. 1997. pap. text 22.50 (*0-8047-2925-5*) Stanford U Pr.

— Instituting Science: The Cultural Production of Scientific Disciplines. LC 97-29112. (Writing Science Ser.). 1998. write for info. (*0-8047-2776-7*); pap. write for info. (*0-8047-2777-5*) Stanford U Pr.

— The Strategy of Life. 326p. 1982. lib. bdg. 191.50 (*90-277-1363-4*, D Reidel) Kluwer Academic.

— The Strategy of Life: Teleology & Mechanics in Nineteenth Century German Biology. (Illus.). 328p. 1989. pap. text 18.00 (*0-226-47183-7*) U Ch Pr.

Lenoir, W. B. History of Sweetwater Valley (Tennessee) 438p. 1998. reprint ed. pap. 32.00 (*0-7884-0904-2*, L158) Heritage Bk.

Lenora. A Black Entrepreneur's Prayer & Other Motivational Poems. 36p. 1994. pap. 5.00 (*0-9642175-0-3*) N Williams Commun.

Lenore, Linda. The Gift of the Red Envelope: A Guide to Designing Balance, Order & Beauty in Your New Home. LC 99-175851. 159 p. 1998. write for info. (*0-9664428-0-6*) Beautiful Ctr.

Lenormand, Rene & Carner, Mosco. A Study of Twentieth-Century Harmony: Harmony in France to 1914 & Contemporary Harmony, 2 vols. in 1. LC 76-40058. (Music Reprint Ser.). 1975. reprint ed. lib. bdg. 32.50 (*0-306-70717-9*) Da Capo.

Lenormant, Francois. Chaldean Magic: Its Origin & Development. LC 98-49347. (Weiser Classic Ser.). Orig. Title: La Magie Chez les Chaldeensis. 448p. 1999. reprint ed. 40.00 (*0-87728-924-7*) Weiser.

— Chaldean Magic Its Origin & Development. 449p. 1994. reprint ed. pap. 27.00 (*1-56459-468-8*) Kessinger Pub.

— Essai sur l'Organisation Politique et Economique de la Monnaie dans L'antiquite. (FRE.). 192p. (Orig.). (C). 1970. reprint ed. pap. 37.00 (*90-70265-22-2*, Pub. by Gieben) J Benjamins Pubng Co.

Lenoski, Daniel E. & Weber, Wolf-Dietrich. Scalable Shared Memory Multiprocessing. 341p. 1995. text 63.95 (*1-55860-315-8*) Morgan Kaufmann.

Lenowitz, Harris. The Jewish Messiahs: From the Galilee to Crown Heights. (Illus.). 312p. 1998. text 45.00 (*0-19-511492-2*) OUP.

— Origins: Creation Texts from the Ancient Mediterranean. Doria, Charles, ed. LC 74-18844. 1976. lib. bdg. 32.50 (*0-404-14849-2*) AMS Pr.

Lenowitz, Harris, ed. Exiled in the Word: Poems & Other Visions of the Jews from Tribal Times to Present. rev. ed. LC 89-61458. (Illus.). 288p. (Orig.). 1989. reprint ed. pap. 12.00 (*1-55659-026-1*) Copper Canyon.

Lenowitz, Harris, jt. auth. see Rothenberg, Jerome.

Lenox-Conyngham, Melosina. Diaries of Ireland: An Anthology, 1590-1987. LC 98-147644. 276p. 1998. 55.00 (*1-874675-88-0*) Dufour.

Lenox, Edward H. Overland to Oregon. LC 93-13113. Orig. Title: Overland to Oregon in the Tracks of Lewis & Clarke. 1993. 15.95 (*0-87770-520-8*) Ye Galleon.

***Lenox Hill Hospital Staff.** Symptoms & Solutions: The Ultimate Home Health Guide-What to Watch For, What to Do. (Illus.). 176p. 2000. pap. text 14.95 (*1-57954-259-X*) Rodale Pr Inc.

Lenrott, Katherine F., jt. auth. see Lundberg, Emma O.

***Lens, Al.** Optics, Retinoscopy & Refractometry. LC 98-50141. (Basic Bookshelf for Eyecare Professionals Ser.). (Illus.). 144p. 1999. pap. 30.00 (*1-55642-397-7*, 63977) SLACK Inc.

Lens, Ken, ed. Washington's Backcountry Access Guide: National Parks, National Forests, Wilderness Areas. annuals rev. ed. LC 98-161212. (Illus.). 96p. 1998. pap. 5.95 (*0-89886-571-9*) Mountaineers.

Lens, P. & Vander Wal, G., eds. Problem Doctors: A Conspiracy of Silence. LC 96-77816. 300p. (gr. 12). 1997. 76.00 (*90-5199-287-4*, 287-4) IOS Press.

Lens, W. & Nuttin, J. M. Future Time Perspective & Motivation: Theory & Research Method. 235p. (Orig.). 1984. pap. 46.50 (*90-6186-172-1*, Pub. by Leuven Univ) Coronet Bks.

Lens, W., jt. ed. see D'Ydewalle, G.

Lens, Willy, jt. ed. see D'Ydewalle, Gery.

Lensberg, Terje, jt. auth. see Thomson, William.

***Lensch, Carol R.** Making Sense of Attention Deficit/Hyperactivity Disorder LC 99-36508. 168p. 2000. 55.00 (*0-89789-700-5*, Bergin & Garvey) Greenwood.

***Lensch, Rodney.** Be All Thy Graces Outpoured. LC 98-88658. 212p. (Orig.). 1998. pap. write for info. (*1-890676-31-4*, Pub. by Beavers Pond) Bookman Bks.

Lenschen, Walter, ed. Literatur Ebersetzen in der DDR La Traduction Litteraire en RDA: La Traduction Litteraire en RDA. (GER., Illus.). 178p. 1998. 27.95 (*3-906760-19-7*) P Lang Pubng.

Lenschou, Donald H., ed. Probing the Atmospheric Boundary Layer. (Illus.). 269p. 1986. 45.00 (*0-933876-63-7*) Am Meteorological.

Lenschow, Sabine. Die Funktion und Verwendung der Propria in der Mittelhochdeutschen Dietrich-Epik, Vol. 1. x, 313p. 1997. write for info. (*3-487-10200-5*) G Olms Pubs.

Lense, Esther. Easter Is Forever: A Children's Program. 16p. (Orig.). 1978. reprint ed. pap. 2.25 (*0-89536-302-X*) CSS OH.

— Light Triumphant. 1977. pap. 3.50 (*0-89536-301-1*, 1253) CSS OH.

Lense, Esther, jt. ed. see Kingery, W. E.

Lenselaer, A. Swahili-French Dictionary (Dictionnaire Swahili-Francais) (FRE & SWA.). 646p. 1983. 175.00 (*0-8288-1100-8*, F60950) Fr & Eur.

Lensen, George A. The Damned Inheritance: The Soviet Union & the Manchurian Crises, 1924-1935. LC 74-186318. (Illus.). 533p. 1974. 19.80 (*0-910512-17-5*) Diplomatic IN.

— Japanese Recognition of the U. S. S. R. Soviet-Japanese Relations, 1921-1930. LC 77-186316. 419p. 1970. 15.00 (*0-910512-09-4*) Diplomatic IN.

— Report from Hokkaido: The Remains of Russian Culture in Northern Japan. LC 73-2878. (Illus.). 216p. 1974. reprint ed. lib. bdg. 55.00 (*0-8371-6818-X*, LERH, Greenwood Pr) Greenwood.

— Russia's Japan Expedition of 1885. LC 82-9156. (Illus.). 208p. 1982. reprint ed. lib. bdg. 59.50 (*0-313-23621-6*, LERJ, Greenwood Pr) Greenwood.

— The Strange Neutrality: Soviet - Japanese Relations During the Second World War, 1941-1945. LC 72-178091. (Illus.). 332p. 1972. 15.00 (*0-910512-14-0*) Diplomatic IN.

Lensen, George A., compiled by. Japanese Diplomatic & Consular Officials in Russia: A Handbook of Japanese Representatives in Russia from 1874 to 1968. LC 68-26392. 230p. 1968. 15.00 (*0-910512-05-1*) Diplomatic IN.

Lensen, George A., ed. Russian Diplomatic & Consular Officials in East Asia. LC 68-26393. (Monuments Nipponica Monograph). 294p. 1968. 15.00 (*0-910512-06-X*) Diplomatic IN.

Lensen, George A., ed. & tr. see Poutiatine, Olga.

Lensing, George S. Wallace Stevens: A Poet's Growth. LC 86-7280. xii, 313p. 1986. pap. text 19.95 (*0-8071-1671-8*) La State U Pr.

Lensing, George S. & Moran, Ronald. Four Poets & the Emotive Imagination - Robert Bly, James Wright, Louis Simpson & William Stafford. fac. ed. LC 75-5348. 240p. 1976. reprint ed. pap. 74.40 (*0-7837-7803-1*, 204755900007) Bks Demand.

Lensing, Leo A., ed. see Fassbinder, Rainer Werner.

Lensink, Judy N. A Secret to Be Burried: The Diary & Life of Emily Hawley Gillespie, 1858-1888. LC 88-38514. (Bur Oak Original Ser.). (Illus.). 472p. 1989. pap. 17.95 (*0-87745-237-7*); text 42.95 (*0-87745-229-6*) U of Iowa Pr.

Lensink, R. Structural Adjustment in Africa. LC 95-21944. 160p. (C). 1996. pap. text 23.25 (*0-582-24886-8*) Addison-Wesley.

Lensink, Robert, jt. auth. see Gupta, Kanhaya L.

Lensink, Robert, jt. ed. see Hermes, Niels.

Lenska, R. Mammoth Hunt: In Search of the Giant Elephants of Nepal. 1996. pap. 219.00 (*0-7855-7434-4*, Pub. by Ratna Pustak Bhandar) St Mut.

Lenski. Human Societies. 8th ed. 200p. 1998. pap., student ed. 14.69 (*0-07-292820-4*) McGraw.

Lenski, et al. Reading - Learning Strategies. 352p. 1999. per. 32.95 (*0-7872-5607-2*, 41560701) Kendall-Hunt.

Lenski, Al. Magic 100. 112p. Date not set. 24.95 (*1-56311-222-1*) Turner Pub KY.

Lenski, Gerhard E. Power & Privilege: A Theory of Social Stratification. LC 83-26049. 512p. 1984. reprint ed. pap. 22.50 (*0-8078-4119-6*) U of NC Pr.

— The Religious Factor: A Sociological Study of Religion's Impact on Politics, Economics, & Family Life. LC 77-1275. 381p. 1977. reprint ed. lib. bdg. 38.50 (*0-8371-9506-3*, LERF, Greenwood Pr) Greenwood.

— Status Crystallization: A Non-Vertical Dimension of Social Status. (Reprint Series in Social Sciences). (C). 1993. reprint ed. pap. text 5.00 (*0-8290-3968-6*, S-168) Irvington.

Lenski, Gerhard E., et al. Human Societies: An Introduction to Macrosociology. 7th ed. LC 94-15796. 560p. (C). 1994. 68.13 (*0-07-037631-X*) McGraw.

— Human Societies: An Introduction to Macrosociology. 7th ed. 560p. (C). 1995. student ed. 14.69 (*0-07-037698-0*) McGraw.

Lenski, Gerhard E., jt. auth. see Nolan, Patrick.

Lenski, J. W., jt. auth. see Drago, Raymond J.

Lenski, Jean. Genesis. 176p. (Orig.). 1993. pap. 9.95 (*1-879934-25-6*) St Andrews NC.

— Genesis: The Poetry of Jean Lenski. 168p. Date not set. reprint ed. pap. 9.95 (*1-879934-21-3*) St Andrews NC.

Lenski, Lois. Adventures in Understanding. 1968. 4.95 (*0-9607778-1-4*) Friends Fla St.

— Adventures in Understanding. deluxe ed. 1968. 12.50 (*0-9607778-2-2*) Friends Fla St.

— Bayou Suzette. 1976. 20.95 (*0-8488-4049-6*) Amereon Ltd.

— Bound Girl of Cobble Hill. 23.95 (*0-89190-632-0*) Amereon Ltd.

***Lenski, Lois.** I Like Winter. (Illus.). (J). 2000. 9.95 (*0-375-81068-4*, Pub. by Random Bks Yng Read); 11.99 (*0-375-91068-9*) Random Bks Yng Read.

Lenski, Lois. Indian Captive: The Story of Mary Jemison. LC 41-51956. (Illus.). 272p. (J). (gr. 5 up). 1994. lib. bdg. 16.89 (*0-397-30076-X*) HarpC Child Bks.

— Indian Captive: The Story of Mary Jemison. 1995. 10.05 (*0-606-07706-5*, Pub. by Turtleback) Demco.

— Judy's Journey. LC 47-4504. (Regional Stories Ser.). (Illus.). (J). (gr. 4-6). 1947. lib. bdg. 13.89 (*0-397-30131-6*) HarpC Child Bks.

***Lenski, Lois.** Little Auto. (J). 2001. mass mkt. 13.99 (*0-375-91073-5*, Pub. by Random Bks Yng Read); mass mkt. 11.95 (*0-375-81073-0*, Pub. by Random Bks Yng Read) Random.

— Little Fire Engine. (Illus.). (J). 2000. 13.95 (*0-375-81070-6*) Random.

— Little Fire Engine. (Illus.). (J). 2000. 15.99 (*0-375-91070-0*) Random Bks Yng Read.

— Little Train. (Illus.). (J). 2000. 13.95 (*0-375-81071-4*) Random.

— Little Train. (Illus.). (J). 2000. 15.99 (*0-375-91071-9*) Random Bks Yng Read.

Lenski, Lois. Lois Lenski's Christmas Stories. LC 68-24417. (Illus.). 160p. (J). (gr. 4-6). 1968. 12.95 (*0-397-31031-5*) HarpC Child Bks.

***Lenski, Lois.** Now It's Fall. (Illus.). (J). 2000. 9.95 (*0-375-81069-2*) Random.

— Now It's Fall. (Illus.). (J). 2000. 11.99 (*0-375-91069-7*) Random Bks Yng Read.

— Policeman Small. (J). 2001. mass mkt. 11.95 (*0-375-81072-2*) Random.

— Policeman Small. (J). 2001. mass mkt. 13.99 (*0-375-91072-7*, Pub. by Random Bks Yng Read) Random.

Lenski, Lois. Prairie School. LC 51-11169. (Illus.). 208p. (J). (gr. 4-7). 1951. lib. bdg. 15.89 (*0-397-30194-4*) HarpC Child Bks.

— Sing a Song of People. (Illus.). 32p. (J). (gr. k-3). 1996. pap. 5.95 (*0-316-52070-5*) Little.

— Sing a Song of People. 1987. 10.15 (*0-606-09858-5*, Pub. by Turtleback) Demco.

***Lenski, Lois.** Slump. (Illus.). (J). 2000. pap. 4.50 (*0-440-41514-4*, YB BDD) BDD Bks Young Read.

Lenski, Lois. Strawberry Girl. 1976. 20.95 (*0-8488-1410-X*) Amereon Ltd.

— Strawberry Girl. LC 45-7609. (Illus.). 192p. (J). (gr. 4-6). 1945. lib. bdg. 16.89 (*0-397-30110-3*) HarpC Child Bks.

— Strawberry Girl. LC 45-7609. (Illus.). 208p. (J). (gr. 4-7). 1945. 17.95 (*0-397-30109-X*) HarpC Child Bks.

— Strawberry Girl. LC 45-7609. (Illus.). 208p. (J). (gr. 5-9). 1995. pap. 5.95 (*0-06-440585-0*, HarpTrophy) HarpC Child Bks.

— Strawberry Girl. (J). 1995. 11.30 (*0-606-08209-3*) Turtleback.

Lenski, Lois. Indian Captive: The Story of Mary Jemison. LC 41-51956. (Trophy Nonfiction Bk.). 320p. (J). (gr. 5-9). 1995. pap. 5.95 (*0-06-446162-9*, HarpTrophy) HarpC Child Bks.

Lenski, Lois & Cushman, Karen. Newbery Library III: Walk Two Moons, Catherine, Called Birdy, Indian Captive, 4 vols., Set. (J). 1996. pap., boxed set 14.85 (*0-06-449627-9*, HarpTrophy) HarpC Child Bks.

Lenski, Richard C. Commentary on the New Testament, 12 vols., Set. 11894p. 1998. reprint ed. 495.00 (*1-56563-408-X*) Hendrickson MA.

Lensky, Yaacov, jt. ed. see Mizrahi, Avshalom.

Lenskyj, Helen. Out of Bounds: Women, Sport & Sexuality. 180p. reprint ed. pap. 10.95 (*0-88961-105-X*, Pub. by Womens Pr) LPC InBook.

***Lenskyj, Helen Jefferson.** Inside the Olympic Industry: Power, Politics, & Activism. LC 00-20164. 2000. pap. 19.95 (*0-7914-4756-1*) State U NY Pr.

***Lensmire, Timothy J.** Powerful Writing/Responsible Teaching. LC 00-21070. (Critical Issues in Educational Leadership Ser.). 2000. write for info. (*0-8077-3957-X*) Tchrs Coll.

Lensmire, Timothy J. When Children Write: Critical Re-Visions of the Writing Workshop. LC 93-44983. 192p. (C). 1994. text 38.00 (*0-8077-3329-6*); pap. text 17.95 (*0-8077-3328-8*) Tchrs Coll.

Lensmith, Lawrence E. Persuasive Resume! A Guide to Writing, Formatting & Finishing. 1991. pap. text 7.95 (*1-880381-00-1*) Desktop Impress.

Lenson, Barry, jt. auth. see Caliandro, Arthur.

Lenson, Barry, jt. auth. see Schreiber, Alfred L.

Lenson, Barry, jt. auth. see Shoup, Richard C.

Lenson, David. The Birth of Tragedy: A Commentary. (Twayne's Masterwork Studies). 152p. 1987. 23.95 (*0-8057-7968-X*, Twayne); pap. 13.95 (*0-8057-8008-4*, Twayne) Mac Lib Ref.

— The Gambler. LC 76-55929. 57p. 1978. pap. 7.00 (*0-89924-013-5*) Lynx Hse.

— On Drugs. 256p. 1995. 29.95 (*0-8166-2710-X*) U of Minn Pr.

— Ride the Shadow. LC 78-78115. 53p. 1979. pap. 3.75 (*0-934332-13-4*) LEpervier Pr.

Lenson, Eileen S. Succeeding in Private Practice: A Business Guide for Psychotherapists. (Illus.). 296p. (C). 1993. text 55.00 (*0-8039-4957-X*); pap. text 25.50 (*0-8039-4958-8*) Sage.

Lenssen, Nicholas. Empowering Development: The New Energy Equation. 70p. (Orig.). 1992. pap. 5.00 (*1-878071-12-2*) Worldwatch Inst.

— Nuclear Waste: The Problem That Won't Go Away. 70p. (Orig.). 1991. pap. 5.00 (*1-878071-07-6*) Worldwatch Inst.

Lenssen, Nicholas & Roodman, David. A Building Revolution: How Ecology & Health Concerns Are Transforming Construction. 70p. (Orig.). 1995. pap. 5.00 (*1-878071-25-4*) Worldwatch Inst.

Lenssen, Nicholas, jt. auth. see Flavin, Christopher.

Lenssen, Polly, jt. auth. see Aker, Saundra N.

Lenstra, A. K. & Lenstra, H. W., Jr. The Development of the Number Field Sieve. LC 93-5229. (Lecture Notes in Mathematics Ser.: Vol. 1554). 1994. 29.95 (*0-387-57013-6*) Spr-Verlag.

Lenstra, Daan, jt. ed. see Van Haeringen, Willem.

Lenstra, H. W., Jr., ed. The Number Field Sieve. (Lecture Notes in Mathematics Ser.: Vol. 1554). (Illus.). vii, 132p. 1993. pap. write for info. (*3-540-57013-6*) Spr-Verlag.

Lenstra, H. W., Jr., jt. auth. see Lenstra, A. K.

Lenstra, Jan K., jt. ed. see Aarts, Emile L.

Lensveld, Jim. Harley-Davidson: Factory & Custom Dream Machines. unabridged ed. LC 96-13204. (Illus.). 160p. 24.98 (*1-57145-030-0*, Thunder Bay) Advantage Pubs.

***Lent, Adam.** Ruby & Fred. LC 99-48328. (Illus.). 32p. (ps-1). 2000. text 16.00 (*0-8050-6117-7*) St Martin.

Lent, Adam, ed. Political Thought Today: An Introduction. LC 98-199743. 224p. 1998. pap. 20.00 (*0-85315-859-2*, Pub. by Lawrence & Wishart) NYU Pr.

Lent, Adam, jt. ed. see Jordan, Tim.

***Lent, Anne & Wolhandler, Harry.** Computers, Home Electronics & Office Supplies: Building Consumer Loyalty Online, 2 vols. unabridged ed. Gurney, Margaret, ed. (Illus.). 300p. 2000. ring bd. 1295.00 (*1-58637-040-5*) ActivMedia.

— Consumable Products: Building Consumer Loyalty Online, 2 vols. unabridged ed. Gurney, Margaret, ed. (Illus.). 300p. 2000. ring bd. 1295.00 (*1-58637-034-0*) ActivMedia.

***Lent, Anne Fischer & Wolhandler, Harry.** Real Numbers Behind the Online Retail Industry. unabridged ed. Gurney, Margaret, ed. (Illus.). 116p. 1999. 1495.00 (*1-58637-010-3*) ActivMedia.

Lent, Blair. Tikki Tikki Tembo. LC 68-11839. (Owlet Book Ser.). 46p. (J). (ps-3). 1989. pap. 5.95 (*0-8050-1166-8*, Bks Young Read) H Holt & Co.

Lent, Deane. Analysis & Design of Mechanisms. 2nd ed. (Technology Ser.). (C). 1970. text 51.00 (*0-13-032797-2*) P-H.

Lent, George E. Impact of the Undistributed Profits Tax, 1936-37. LC 68-58601. (Columbia University. Studies in the Social Sciences: No. 539). reprint ed. 20.00 (*0-404-51539-8*) AMS Pr.

An Asterisk (*) at the beginning of an entry indicates that the title is appearing for the first time.

— The Ownership of Tax-Exempt Securities, 1913-1953. (Occasional Papers: No. 47). 150p. 1955. reprint ed. 39.00 (0-87014-361-1) Natl Bur Econ Res.

Lent, Jeffrey. In the Fall. LC 99-30862. 560p. 2000. 25.00 (0-87113-765-8, Pub. by Grove-Atltic) Publishers Group.

***Lent, Jeffrey.** In the Fall. LC 00-42580. 2000. write for info. (0-7862-2783-4) Thorndike Pr.

Lent, John, ed. Animation, Caricature & Gag & Political Cartoons in the United States: An International Bibliography, 3. LC 94-14433. (Bibliographies & Indexes in Popular Culture Ser.: No. 3). 440p. 1994. lib. bdg. 85.00 (0-313-28681-7, Greenwood Pr) Greenwood.

Lent, John A. The Asian Film Industry. (Film Studies). (Illus.). 320p. 1990. text 32.50 (0-292-70421-6) U of Tex Pr.

— Assorted Themes & Issues in Asian Cartooning. LC 98-36403. 212 p. 1998. pap. 21.95 (0-87972-780-2) Bowling Green Univ Popular Press.

— Assorted Themes & Issues in Asian Cartooning: Cute, Cheap, Mad, & Sexy. LC 98-36403. 212p. 1998. 49.95 (0-87972-779-9) Bowling Green Univ Popular Press.

— Bibliographic Guide to Caribbean Mass Communication, 5. LC 92-19373. (Bibliographies & Indexes in Mass Media & Communications Ser.: No. 5). 320p. 1992. lib. bdg. 69.50 (0-313-28210-2, LBM, Greenwood Pr) Greenwood.

— Bibliography of Cuban Mass Communications, 6. LC 92-24462. (Bibliographies & Indexes in Mass Media & Communications Ser.: No. 6). 384p. 1992. lib. bdg. 75.00 (0-313-28455-5, LBN, Greenwood Pr) Greenwood.

— Caribbean Popular Culture. LC 90-83084. (Illus.). 156p. (C). 1990. 26.95 (0-87972-499-4) Bowling Green Univ Popular Press.

— Global Guide to Media & Communications. 160p. 1986. 49.50 (0-914746-49-9); write for info. (0-317-39334-0) G Kurian.

— Mass Communications in the Caribbean. LC 90-33583. (Illus.). 412p. 1990. reprint ed. pap. 127.80 (0-608-06886-1, 206709400009) Bks Demand.

— Pulp Demons: International Dimensions of the Postwar Anti-Comics Campaign. LC 98-30640. 1999. 49.50 (0-8386-3784-1) Fairleigh Dickinson.

— Third World Mass Media & Their Search for Modernity: The Case of Commonwealth Caribbean, 1717-1976. LC 75-39110. 405p. 1978. 45.00 (0-8387-1896-5) Bucknell U Pr.

Lent, John A., compiled by. Comic Art in Africa, Asia, Australia & Latin America: A Comprehensive, International Bibliography, 7. LC 95-31367. (Bibliographies & Indexes in Popular Culture Ser.: No. 7). (Illus.). 560p. 1996. lib. bdg. 99.50 (0-313-29343-0, Greenwood Pr) Greenwood.

Lent, John A., compiled by. Women & Mass Communications: An International Annotated Bibliography, 11. LC 90-23780. (Bibliographies & Indexes in Women's Studies: No. 11). 504p. 1991. lib. bdg. 89.50 (0-313-26579-8, LWM/, Greenwood Pr) Greenwood.

***Lent, John A., compiled by.** Women & Mass Communications in the 1990s: An International, Annotated Bibliography, Vol. 29. LC 99-21787. (Bibliographies & Indexes in Women's Studies: No. 29). 528p. 1999. lib. bdg. 79.50 (0-313-30209-X, GR0209, Greenwood Pr) Greenwood.

Lent, John A., ed. Comic Art of Europe: An International, Comprehensive Bibliography, 5. LC 94-14432. (Bibliographies & Indexes in Popular Culture Ser.: No. 5). 688p. 1994. lib. bdg. 105.00 (0-313-28212-9, Greenwood Pr) Greenwood.

— Comic Books & Comic Strips in the United States: An International Bibliography, 4. LC 94-10852. (Bibliographies & Indexes in Popular Culture Ser.: No. 4). 624p. 1994. lib. bdg. 99.50 (0-313-28211-0, Greenwood Pr) Greenwood.

Lent, John A., ed. see Splichal, Slavko.

Lent, John A., jt. ed. see Sussman, Gerald.

Lent, Joy. Houston's Heritage: Using Antique Postcards. (Illus.). pap., per. 12.95 (0-9643284-0-2) Clem Interests.

Lent, Penny. Young Writer's Contest Manual: Competitions for Students Work. 2nd rev. ed. LC 94-79466. (Young Writers Ser.). 68p. (J). (gr. k up). 1994. pap., per. 7.95 (1-885371-05-5) Kldoscope Pr.

— Young Writer's Manuscript Manual: A Guide on How to Send Writing for Publication. rev. ed. LC 94-76618. (Young Writers Ser.). (Illus.). 84p. 1994. pap. 7.95 (1-885371-01-2) Kldoscope Pr.

— Young Writer's Market Manual: Publications Seeking Student Work. 2nd rev. ed. LC 94-76617. (Young Writers Ser.). 80p. 1994. pap. 7.95 (1-885371-02-0) Kldoscope Pr.

Lent, Penny, ed. Meeker Mansion Mysteries: A Fiction Anthology. LC 94-76615. (Illus.). 84p. (Orig.). 1994. pap. 5.95 (1-885371-03-9) Kldoscope Pr.

Lent, Penny, ed. see Amos, Chuck & Amos, Sheila.

Lent, Penny, ed. see Bird, Tia.

Lent, Penny, ed. see Bond, Jan.

Lent, Penny, ed. see Etchison, Birdie.

Lent, Penny, ed. see Rabe, Sheila & Schneider, Eric S.

Lent, Penny, ed. see Reece, Colleen L.

***Lent, Peter C.** Muskoxen & Their Hunters: A History. LC 99-15298. (Animal Natural History Ser.). 352p. 1999. 57.50 (0-8061-3170-5) U of Okla Pr.

Lent, Robert W., jt. auth. see Brown, Steven D.

Lent, Robert W., jt. ed. see Brown, Steve D.

Lent, Robert W., jt. ed. see Savickas, Mark L.

Lent, Roberto, ed. The Visual System from Genesis to Maturity. LC 92-21738. xii, 285p. 1992. 108.00 (0-8176-3598-X) Birkhauser.

Lent, Tami, ed. see Gordon, Jeff.

Lentchner, Harvey, ed. see Homer, Lawrence.

Lenters, William R. & Avila A., Mariano. Alcoholismo, Alcohol y Otras Drogas: Una Guia de Estudio y Accion. (SPA.). 115p. 5.95 (1-55883-091-X, 6765-0220C) Libros Desafio.

Lentfoehr, Therese. Words & Silence: On the Poetry of Thomas Merton. LC 78-21475. 1979. 12.50 (0-8112-0712-9, Pub. by New Directions) Norton.

Lenth. Design, Data & Deduction. (Statistics-Probability Ser.). 2001. pap. 12.95 (0-534-92380-1) Wadsworth Pub.

Lenth, Charles L. The Tuition Dilemma: State Policies & Practices for Pricing Public Higher Education. 1993. 15.00 (1-881543-02-1) SHEEO.

Lenth, Charles S., ed. Using National Data Bases. LC 85-645339. (New Directions for Institutional Research Ser.: No. IR 69). 1991. 22.00 (1-55542-791-X) Jossey-Bass.

Lenthall, Lisa-Theresa, jt. ed. see Elliott, Lynn.

Lenti, Paul, tr. see De La Colina, Jose & Turrent, Tomas P.

Lenti, Paul, tr. see De la Colina, Jose & Turrent, Tomas P.

Lentin, A., ed. Voltaire & Catherine the Great: Selected Correspondence. (Illus.). 196p. 1974. 16.00 (0-89250-099-9) Orient Res Partners.

Lentin, Ponit, ed. Gender & Catastrophe. LC 98-170587. 256p. (C). 1998. text 22.50 (1-85649-446-2, Pub. by Zed Books) St Martin.

***Lentin, Ronit.** Israel & the Daughters of the Shoah: Reoccupying the Territories of Silence. 288p. 2000. 59.95 (1-57181-774-3); pap. 19.95 (1-57181-775-1) Berghahn Bks.

Lentin, Ronit. Songs on the Death of Children. 220p. 1997. pap. 13.95 (1-85371-625-1, Pub. by Poolbeg Pr) Dufour.

Lentin, Ronit, ed. Gender & Catastrophe. LC 98-170587. 256p. (C). 1998. text 62.50 (1-85649-445-4, Pub. by Zed Books) St Martin.

Lentinello, Richard. Corvette. LC 99-18997. (Autofocus Ser.). (Illus.). 96p. 1999. text 18.50 (1-56799-847-X) M Friedman Pub Grp Inc.

***Lentinello, Richard A.** Porsche 911. LC 00-33568. (Illus.). 2000. write for info. (1-58663-028-8, Friedman-Fairfax) M Friedman Pub Grp Inc.

Lentle. Radiation & Medicine. (Radiation Physics & Chemistry Ser.). 1985. pap. 61.00 (0-08-032402-9, Pergamon Pr) Elsevier.

Lentner, Howard H. International Politics: Theory & Practice. LC 96-9253. 400p. 1996. 56.95 (0-314-20203-X) West Pub.

— State Formation in Central America: The Struggle for Autonomy, Development, & Democracy, 2. LC 93-12603. (Contributions in Latin American Studies: No. 2). 264p. 1993. 65.00 (0-313-28921-2, GM8921) Greenwood.

Lentner, Marvin & Bishop, Thomas. Experimental Design & Analysis. (Illus.). xi, 565p. (C). 1986. text 32.75 (0-9616255-0-3) Valley Bk.

Lentner, Timothy H., jt. ed. see Cooper, Saul.

Lento, Robert. Handbook of Practical Woodworking Techniques. LC 99-12493. (Illus.). 224p. 2000. 17.95 (0-8069-1351-7) Sterling.

— Woodworking: Tools, Fabrication, Design, & Manufacturing. (Illus.). 1979. student ed. 24.95 (0-685-03911-0) P-H.

Lento, Takako, tr. see Makoto, Ooka.

Lento, Thomas, tr. see Makoto, Ooka.

***Lenton, Anthony.** Murder City. large type ed. 248p. 1999. pap. 18.99 (0-7089-5595-9, Linford) Ulverscroft.

Lenton, H. T. British & Empire Warships of the Second World War. LC 97-76482. 1998. 125.00 (1-55750-048-7) Naval Inst Pr.

Lenton, Sarah. Backstage at the Opera. (Illus.). 212p. 1998. 28.95 (1-86105-155-7, Pub. by Robson Bks) Parkwest Pubns.

Lentricchia, Frank. After the New Criticism. LC 79-23715. 398p. 1981. pap. text 18.95 (0-226-47198-5) U Ch Pr.

— Ariel & the Police: Michel Foucault, William James, Wallace Stevens. LC 87-18885. 208p. 1989. pap. text 15.95 (0-299-11544-5) U of Wis Pr.

— Criticism & Social Change. LC 83-9299. viii, 184p. 1985. pap. text 12.95 (0-226-47200-0) U Ch Pr.

— Criticism & Social Change. LC 83-9299. 182p. 1996. 19.95 (0-226-47199-3) U Ch Pr.

— Modernist Quartet. 319p. (C). 1994. pap. text 18.95 (0-521-46975-9) Cambridge U Pr.

— The Music of the Inferno. LC 99-14974. (SUNY Series in Italian/American Culture). 220p. (C). 1999. 24.50 (0-7914-4347-7) State U NY Pr.

— The Music of the Inferno. LC 99-14974. 220p. (C). 2000. pap. 19.95 (0-7914-4348-5) State U NY Pr.

Lentricchia, Frank, ed. Introducing Don DeLillo. LC 90-15567. 221p. 1991. pap. text 16.95 (0-8223-1144-5) Duke.

— New Essays on "White Noise" (American Novel Ser.). 127p. (C). 1991. text 32.95 (0-521-39291-8) Cambridge U Pr.

Lentricchia, Frank & McLaughlin, Thomas, eds. Critical Terms for Literary Study. LC 89-4910. 388p. 1990. lib. bdg. 45.00 (0-226-47201-9) U Ch Pr.

— Critical Terms for Literary Study. LC 89-4910. 378p. 1997. pap. text 16.95 (0-226-47202-7) U Ch Pr.

— Critical Terms for Literary Study. 2nd ed. LC 94-43640. 496p. 1995. pap. text 17.95 (0-226-47203-5) U Ch Pr.

— Critical Terms for Literary Study. 2nd ed. (Literary Studies). 496p. 1996. lib. bdg. 47.50 (0-226-47204-3) U Ch Pr.

Lentricchia, Frank, jt. auth. see McLaughlin, Thomas.

Lents, Don G., jt. auth. see Hansen, Charles.

Lentz, Alice B. Mountain Magic. LC 98-11050. (Illus.). (J). 1998. 12.99 (0-8499-5841-5) Tommy Nelson.

— Tweetsie Adventure. (Illus.). 32p. (J). (ps-3). 1995. 9.95 (1-57072-025-8) Overmountain Pr.

Lentz, Andrea D. A Guide to the Manuscripts at the Ohio Historical Society. 281p. 1972. pap. 5.00 (0-318-00848-3) Ohio Hist Soc.

— The Warren G. Harding Papers: An Inventory to the Microfilm Edition. 283p. 1970. 4.00 (0-318-03212-0) Ohio Hist Soc.

Lentz, Bernard F. & Laband, David N. Sex Discrimination in the Legal Profession. LC 95-3777. 256p. 1995. 57.95 (0-89930-928-3, Quorum Bks) Greenwood.

Lentz, Bernard F., jt. auth. see Laband, David N.

Lentz, Carola, ed. Changing Food Habits: Case Studies from Africa, South America, & Europe. (Food in History & Culture Ser.: Vol. 2). 296p. 1999. text 54.00 (90-5702-564-7, ECU45, Harwood Acad Pubs) Gordon & Breach.

Lentz, David B. The Silver King. 193p. 1999. pap. 13.95 (0-7414-0031-6) Buy Books.

***Lentz, David B., ed.** Imperfect Balance: Landscape Transformations in the Pre-Columbian Americas. 788p. 2000. text 65.00 (0-231-11156-8) Col U Pr.

***Lentz, David Lewis.** An Imperfect Balance: Landscape Transformations in the PreColumbian Americas. LC 00-22681. (Historical Ecology Ser.). (Illus.). 2000. 30.00 (0-231-11157-6) Col U Pr.

Lentz, Donald A. The Gamelan Music of Java & Bali: An Artistic Anomaly Complementary to Primary Tonal Theoretical Systems. LC 65-10545. 78p. reprint ed. pap. 30.00 (0-608-12627-6, 202542800043) Bks Demand.

Lentz, Ed. As It Were: Stories of Old Columbus. (Illus.). 208p. 1998. pap. 12.00 (0-9667950-0-8) Red Mntn Pr.

Lentz, Florence K. Centennial Snapshots: Historic Places Around King County from the First Twenty-Five Years of Statehood. (Illus.). 119p. (Orig.). 1991. pap. text 8.95 (0-914019-28-7) NW Interpretive.

***Lentz, Gretchen M., ed.** Urogynecology. LC 99-40831. (An Arnold Publication). (Illus.). 368p. 2000. text 89.50 (0-340-74230-5, Pub. by E A) OUP.

Lentz, Harold B. The Pop-Up Goldilocks & the Three Bears. LC 95-77080. (Illus.). 24p. (J). (ps-5). 1995. 14.95 (1-55709-239-7) Applewood.

— The Pop-Up Mother Goose. LC 94-71382. (Illus.). 24p. (J). (ps-3). 1994. 14.95 (1-55709-237-0) Applewood.

— The Pop-Up Puss-in-Boots. (Illus.). 24p. (J). (ps-3). 1995. 14.95 (1-55709-238-9) Applewood.

***Lentz, Harold H.** Preaching the Miracles: Series III, Cycle B. LC 99-36619. 132p. 1999. pap. 12.00 (0-7880-1358-0) CSS OH.

Lentz, Harris M., III. Assassinations & Executions: An Encyclopedia of Political Violence, 1865-1986. LC 87-46383. 296p. 1988. lib. bdg. 45.00 (0-89950-312-8) McFarland & Co.

— Biographical Dictionary of Professional Wrestling. LC 96-46346. (Illus.). 383p. 1997. boxed set 55.00 (0-7864-0303-9) McFarland & Co.

Lentz, Harris M., 3rd. Encyclopedia of Heads of States & Governments, 1900-1945. LC 98-53751. 520p. 1999. lib. bdg. 75.00 (0-7864-0500-7) McFarland & Co.

Lentz, Harris M., III. Heads of States & Governments: A Worldwide Encyclopedia of over 2,300 Leaders, 1945-1992. LC 94-13310. 924p. 1994. lib. bdg. 95.00 (0-89950-926-6) McFarland & Co.

— Obituaries in the Performing Arts, 1995: Film, Television, Radio, Theatre, Dance, Music, Cartoons & Pop Culture. (Illus.). 218p. 1996. pap. 30.00 (0-7864-0253-9) McFarland & Co.

— Obituaries in the Performing Arts, 1994: Film, Television, Radio, Theatre, Dance, Music, Cartoons & Pop Culture. (Illus.). 207p. 1996. pap. 30.00 (0-7864-0254-7) McFarland & Co.

— Obituaries in the Performing Arts, 1996: Film, Television, Radio, Theatre, Dance, Music, Cartoons & Pop Culture. (Illus.). 221p. 1997. pap. 30.00 (0-7864-0302-0) McFarland & Co.

***Lentz, Harris M., III.** Obituaries in the Performing Arts 1998: Film, Television, Radio, Theatre, Dance, Music, Cartoons & Pop Culture. (Illus.). 255p. 1999. pap. 30.00 (0-7864-0748-4) McFarland & Co.

— Obituaries in the Performing Arts, 1999: Film, Television, Radio, Theatre, Dance, Music, Cartoons & Pop Culture. 254p. 2000. 30.00 (0-7864-0919-3) McFarland & Co.

Lentz, Harris M., III. Obituaries in the Performing Arts, 1997: Film, Television, Radio, Theatre, Dance, Music, Cartoons & Pop Culture. (Illus.). 206p. 1998. pap. 30.00 (0-7864-0460-4) McFarland & Co.

***Lentz, Harris M., III.** Science Fiction, Horror & Fantasy Film & Television Credits, Vol. 1. 2nd ed. 920p. 2000. 115.00 (0-7864-0950-9) McFarland & Co.

— Science Fiction, Horror & Fantasy Film & Television Credits, Vol. 2. 2nd ed. 936p. 2000. 115.00 (0-7864-0951-7) McFarland & Co.

— Science Fiction, Horror & Fantasy Film & Television Credits, Vol. 3. 2nd ed. 480p. 2000. lib. bdg. 75.00 (0-7864-0952-5) McFarland & Co.

Lentz, Harris M., III. Science Fiction, Horror & Fantasy Film & Television Credits Through 1993 Suppl. 2. LC 93-33878. 864p. 1994. lib. bdg. 85.00 (0-89950-927-4) McFarland & Co.

— Television Westerns Episode Guide: All United States Series, 1949-1996. LC 97-10085. 576p. 1997. lib. bdg. 95.00 (0-7864-0377-2) McFarland & Co.

***Lentz, Harris M., III.** The Volcano Registry: Names, Locations, Descriptions & Histories for over 1500 Sites. LC 99-19961. 200p. 1999. lib. bdg. 29.95 (0-7864-0732-8) McFarland & Co.

Lentz, Harris M., III. Western & Frontier Film & Television Credits: 1903-1995, 2 vols., Set. LC 95-43360. 1796p. 1996. lib. bdg. 175.00 (0-7864-0158-3) McFarland & Co.

— Western & Frontier Film & Television Credits: 1903-1995, Vol. 1. 1015p. 1996. lib. bdg. 115.00 (0-7864-0217-2) McFarland & Co.

— Western & Frontier Film & Television Credits: 1903-1995, Vol. 2. 781p. 1996. lib. bdg. 95.00 (0-7864-0218-0) McFarland & Co.

Lentz, Harris M., ed. Heads of States & Governments since 1945. 925p. 1996. lib. bdg. 125.00 (1-884964-44-3) Fitzroy Dearborn.

Lentz, John D. Effective Handling of Manipulative Persons. (Illus.). 112p. 1989. pap. 25.95 (0-398-06227-7) C C Thomas.

— Effective Handling of Manipulative Persons. (Illus.). 112p. (C). 1989. text 35.95 (0-398-05555-6) C C Thomas.

Lentz, Jon. Deconstructing Web Graphics 2. 1998. 39.99 (1-56205-859-2, New Riders Sftwre) MCP SW Interactive.

Lentz, Lloyd C., III. Guthrie: A History of the Capital City, 1889-1910. LC 90-62164. (Illus.). 165p. 1990. pap. 25.00 (0-9603564-2-8) Thirty Seconds.

Lentz, Nugent. Ethnicity in Ghana LC 99-23357. 1999. text 65.00 (0-312-22405-2) St Martin.

Lentz, Perry. The Falling Hills: A Novel of the Civil War. LC 93-24496. 470p. (C). 1994. reprint ed. pap. 14.95 (0-87249-988-X) U of SC Pr.

Lentz, Robert J. Lee Marvin: His Films & Career. LC 99-43492. (Illus.). 238p. 1999. boxed set 45.00 (0-7864-0723-9) McFarland & Co.

Lentz, Robert J., jt. auth. see Paul, Gordon L.

Lentz, Steve, ed. see Shakespeare, William.

Lentz, Steve, ed. see Thoreau, Henry David.

Lentz, Theodore F. An Experimental Method for the Discovery & Development of Tests of Character. LC 71-176985. (Columbia University. Teachers College. Contributions to Education Ser.: No. 180). reprint ed. 37.50 (0-404-55180-7) AMS Pr.

— Towards a Science of Peace. 1955. 4.00 (0-318-03980-X) Lentz Peace Res.

— Towards a Technology of Peace. 1972. pap. 3.00 (0-933061-11-0) Lentz Peace Res.

Lentz, Theodore F., ed. Humatriotism. 1976. 6.00 (0-933061-07-2) Lentz Peace Res.

Lentz, Theodore F., jt. auth. see Eckhardt, William.

Lentz, Thomas L. Primitive Nervous Systems. LC 68-27760. 160p. reprint ed. pap. 49.60 (0-8357-8283-2, 203379900087) Bks Demand.

Lentz, Thomas W., jt. auth. see De Angelis, Michele A.

Lentz, Thomas W., jt. auth. see Lawton, Thomas.

Lentz, Tony M. Orality & Literacy in Hellenic Greece. LC 88-14152. 232p. (C). 1989. text 26.95 (0-8093-1359-6) S Ill U Pr.

Lentze, M., ed. see Falk Symposium Staff.

Lentzner, Harold R., jt. ed. see Kramarow, Ellen A.

Lenway, Stefanie A., et al. Remembering U. S. Memories: The Fate of the U. S. Semiconductor Production Consortium. (Pew Case Studies in International Affairs). 50p. (C). 1996. pap. text 3.50 (1-56927-722-2, GU Schl Foreign) Geo U Inst Dplmcy.

Lenway, Stephanie A. The Politics of U. S. International Trade. LC 84-25395. (Business & Public Policy Ser.). 288p. 1986. text 28.00 (0-273-02250-4, HarpBusn) HarpInfo.

Lenyashin, Vladimir, jt. auth. see Kruglov, Vladimir.

Lenz. Das Feuerschiff. text 8.95 (0-88436-276-0) EMC-Paradigm.

— Lehmanns Erzahlungen: C level. text 8.95 (0-8219-0852-9) EMC-Paradigm.

— So Zartlich War Suleyken: C Level. text 8.95 (0-8219-1055-8) EMC-Paradigm.

***Lenz & Sampson.** Career Dev & Planning: A Cognitive Approach. (Counseling Ser.). 1999. pap. text, student ed. 21.50 (0-534-36684-8) Brooks-Cole.

Lenz, jt. auth. see Reardon.

Lenz, A. C. Bulletins of American Paleontology Vol. 104: Upper Wenlock & Ludlow (Silurian) Plectograptinae (Retiolitid Graptolites), Cape Phillips Formation, Arctic Canada, Vol. 342. 1993. 45.00 (0-87710-427-1) Paleo Res.

Lenz, A. N. Bonsai from the Wild. (Illus.). 124p. 1997. pap. 24.95 (0-9658313-0-2) Am Bonsai.

Lenz, Allen J. Beyond Blue Economic Horizons: U. S. Trade Performance & International Competitiveness in the 1990s. LC 90-7625. 288p. 1990. 49.95 (0-275-93624-4, C3624, Praeger Pubs) Greenwood.

— Narrowing the U. S. Current Account Deficit: A Sectoral Assessment. LC 92-8778. 627p. 1992. reprint ed. pap. 194.40 (0-7837-9049-X, 204980000003) Bks Demand.

Lenz, B. Keith, et al. Teaching Learning Strategies to Adolescents & Adults with Learning Disabilities. LC 94-41597. 234p. 1996. pap. 29.00 (0-89079-650-5, 6960) PRO-ED.

Lenz, B. Keith, jt. auth. see Schumaker, Jean B.

Lenz, Bernd, jt. ed. see Lehmann, Elmar.

Lenz, Brenda S., jt. auth. see Finley, James R.

Lenz, Christian. The Neue Pinakothek, Munich. (Illus.). 132p. 1989. 30.00 (1-870248-19-8) Scala Books.

Lenz, Diane, ed. see Henderson, Carol.

Lenz, E. E. Lenz Family: History of the American Branch Established at Stone Arabia, N.Y., in 1854, by Friedrich Konrad Lenz of Werdorf, Germany. (Illus.). 187p. 1993. reprint ed. pap. 31.00 (0-8328-3700-8); reprint ed. lib. bdg. 41.00 (0-8328-3699-0) Higginson Bk Co.

Lenz, Elinor. Rights of Passage: How Women Can Find a New Freedom in Their Midyears. 224p. 1993. pap. 14.95 (1-56565-076-X, Woman-Woman) Lowell Hse.

— Rights of Passage: How Women Can Find a New Freedom in Their Midyears. 209p. 1998. reprint ed. pap. 15.00 (0-7881-5216-5) DIANE Pub.

Lenz, Elinor, jt. auth. see Adams, Linda.

Lenz, F., et al, eds. Lectures on QCD: Applications. LC 97-37132. (Lecture Notes in Physics Ser.: Vol. 496). vii, 483p. 1997. text 110.00 (3-540-63442-8) Spr-Verlag.

L

Lenz, F., et al. Lectures on QCD. Vol. 481. LC 97-11040. (Lecture Notes in Physics Ser.). 1997. write for info. (*3-540-62543-7*) Spr-Verlag.

Lenz, F. W. Ovid's Metamorphoses: Prolegomena to a Revision of Hugo Magnus' Edit. iv, 104p. 1967. write for info. (*3-296-14180-4*) G Olms Pubs.

Lenz, Frederick. Snowboarding to Nirvana. (Illus.). 240p. 1998. pap. 10.95 (*0-312-18179-5*) St Martin.

— Snowboarding to Nirvana: A Novel. LC 96-45535. (Illus.). 256p. 1997. text 16.95 (*0-312-15293-0*) St Martin.

— Surfing the Himalayas. LC 96-44195. 240p. 1996. pap. 10.95 (*0-312-15217-5*) St Martin.

— Surfing the Himalayas: Conversations & Travels with Master Fwap. 256p. 1995. text 14.95 (*0-312-14147-5*) St Martin.

Lenz, G. & Pakesch, G., eds. The Polydiagnostic Approach in Psychiatry. (Journal: Psychopathology: Vol. 19, No. 5, 1986). (Illus.). 76p. 1987. pap. 38.50 (*3-8055-4540-1*) S Karger.

Lenz, H. J., et al, eds. Frontiers in Statistical Quality Control 3. x, 265p. 1987. 89.00 (*0-387-91315-7*) Spr-Verlag.

— Frontiers in Statistical Quality Control 4. (Illus.). x, 266p. 1996. 88.00 (*0-387-91434-X*) Spr-Verlag.

Lenz, H. J., jt. ed. see Fisher, Doug.

Lenz, H. P. Mixture Formation for Spark Ignition Engines. 416p. 1992. 19.00 (*1-56091-188-3*, R-113) Soc Auto Engineers.

Lenz, Hans-Joachim & Wilrich, P. T., eds. Frontiers in Statistical Quality Control 5, Vol. X. LC 97-7880. (Illus.). 297p. 1997. pap. 68.00 (*3-7908-0984-5*) Spr-Verlag.

***Lenz, Hans Peter & Cozzarini, Christian.** Emissions & Air Quality. LC 99-14564. 140p. 1999. 25.00 (*0-7680-0248-6*, R-237) Soc Auto Engineers.

Lenz, Harry. Seeds of Knowledge: The Core of Success. 1999. 7.95 (*1-56245-378-5*) Great Quotations.

Lenz, Heinz W. & Murray, John L. Fit for Life: An Annapolis Way. LC 82-84099. (Illus.). 352p. 1985. reprint ed. pap. 109.20 (*0-608-07099-8*, 206732600009) Bks Demand.

Lenz, J. E., ed. Simulation in Manufacturing. 260p. 1986. 158.95 (*0-387-16329-8*) Spr-Verlag.

Lenz, J. M. Prince Tandi of Cumba: or The New Menoza. Hill, David & Butler, Michael, eds. & trs. by. from GER. (Contemporary Theatre Studies: Vol. 9). 127p. 1996. text 36.00 (*3-7186-5595-0*, ECU43, Harwood Acad Pubs); pap. text 18.00 (*3-7186-5603-5*, ECU14, Harwood Acad Pubs) Gordon & Breach.

— The Tutor & the Soldiers. Northcott, Kenneth J., ed. Yuill, William E., tr. from GER. LC 72-80812. (German Literary Classics in Translation Ser.). 1993. pap. text 1.95 (*0-226-47211-6*, P469) U Ch Pr.

Lenz, Janet G., jt. auth. see Reardon, Robert C.

Lenz, Jerry, ed. Power Tool Kit. 84p. 1995. teacher ed., ring bd. 59.95 incl. audio, trans. (*1-57405-002-8*) CharismaLife Pub.

Lenz, John W., ed. see Hume, David.

Lenz, K. & Laggner, A. N., eds. Patient Data Management in Intensive Care, No. 6. (Illus.). 157p. 1995. 39.00 (*0-387-82513-4*) Spr-Verlag.

Lenz, Lee W. An Annotated Catalogue of the Plants of Baja California Sur, Mexico. 128p. 1993. pap. 16.50 (*0-9634595-0-3*) Cape Pr.

— Marcus Jones: Western Geologist, Mining Engineer & Botanist. LC 85-61956. (Illus.). xv, 486p. 1986. 28.00 (*0-9605808-2-4*) Rancho Santa Ana.

Lenz, Lee W. & Dourley, John. California Native Trees & Shrubs for Garden & Environmental Use in Southern California & Adjacent Areas. LC 81-50257. (Illus.). xiii, 232p. (C). 1981. kivar 23.50 (*0-9605808-1-6*) Rancho Santa Ana.

Lenz, Leslie, ed. see Shelton, Connie.

Lenz, Mario, et al, eds. Case-Based Reasoning Technology: From Foundations to Applications, Vol. 140. LC 98-22158. (Lecture Notes in Computer Science Ser.: Vol. 1400). xviii, 405p. 1998. pap. 49.00 (*3-540-64572-1*) Spr-Verlag.

Lenz, Mario & Ashley, Kevin, eds. Textual Case-Based Reasoning: Papers from the AAAI Workshop. (Technical Reports: Vol. WS-98-12). (Illus.). 61p. 1998. spiral bd. 25.00 (*1-57735-065-0*) AAAI Pr.

Lenz, Mark J. God's Providence. LC 96-71377. (People's Bible Teachings Ser.). 146p. 1997. pap. 8.99 (*0-8100-0673-1*, 15N0604) Northwest Pub.

— Leviticus. LC 88-61920. (People's Bible Ser.). 246p. 1988. pap. 10.99 (*0-8100-0298-1*, 15N0459) Northwest Pub.

— Leviticus. (The People's Bible Ser.). 62p. 1989. pap. text, student ed. 5.00 (*0-938272-68-3*, 22-2214) WELS Board.

— Sing along with Saints & Angels. 38p. (Orig.). 1985. pap., teacher ed. 7.50 (*0-8100-0207-8*, 22N0796); pap., student ed. 5.00 (*0-8100-0206-X*, 22N0795) Northwest Pub.

Lenz, Martin. Computed Tomography & Magnetic Resonance Imaging of Head & Neck Tumors: Methods, Guidelines, Differential Diagnoses, & Clinical Results. Bergman, Clifford, tr. LC 93-28314.Tr. of Computertomographie und Kernspintomographie Bei Kopf-Hals-Tumoren. 206p. 1993. 115.00 (*0-86577-504-4*) Thieme Med Pubs.

Lenz, Mary. The Complete Help Desk Guide. 300p. 1996. per. 24.95 (*0-936648-96-1*, P60015) Telecom Bks.

Lenz, Millicent & Meachem, Mary. Young Adult Literature & Nonprint Materials: Resources for Selection. LC 94-13774. 1994. 39.50 (*0-8108-2906-1*) Scarecrow.

Lenz, P. H., et al, eds. Zooplankton: Sensory Ecology & Physiology. 570p. 1997. text 98.00 (*90-5699-022-5*) Gordon & Breach.

Lenz, Paul & Sikka, Anju, eds. Reengineering Health Care: A Practical Guide. LC 97-77266. 264p. 1998. pap. 50.00 (*0-924674-58-X*) Am Coll Phys Execs.

Lenz, R. W. & Ciardelli, I., eds. Advances in the Preparation & Properties of Stereo-Regular Polymers. (NATO Advanced Study Institutes Series C, Mathematical & Physical Sciences: No. 51). 1979. text 141.50 (*90-277-1055-4*) Kluwer Academic.

Lenz, Ralph C. & Vanston, Lawrence K. Personal Communications: Perspectives, Forecasts, & Impacts. 99p. 1993. pap. 45.00 (*1-884154-02-6*) Tech Futures.

Lenz, Richard, jt. auth. see McDonald, Marge.

Lenz, Richard J. The Civil War in Georgia: An Illustrated Travelers Guide: Historic Homes, Battlefields, Museums, Cemeteries, Memorials, Parks, Attractions, Maps. LC 95-81860. (Illus.). 116p. (Orig.). 1995. pap. 19.95 (*0-9650305-0-4*) Infinity Pr GA.

— Longstreet Highroad Guide to the Georgia Coast & Okefenokee. LC 98-89179. (Illus.). 320p. 1999. pap. 18.95 (*1-56352-542-9*) Longstreet.

Lenz, Robert R. Explosives & Bomb Disposal Guide. (Illus.). 320p. 1976. pap. 39.95 (*0-398-06228-5*) C C Thomas.

— Explosives & Bomb Disposal Guide. fac. ed. (Illus.). 320p. 1976. 57.95 (*0-398-01097-8*) C C Thomas.

Lenz, Robert W. Biodegradable Polymers & Plastics in Japan: Research, Development, & Applications. unabridged ed. LC 96-224103. (JTEL Monographs Ser.). 33p. (Orig.). 1995. pap. write for info. (*1-883712-38-6*) Intl Tech Res.

Lenz, Siegfried. The German Lesson. Kaiser, Ernst & Wilkins, Eithne, trs. from GER. LC 77-163567. (New Directions Classics Ser.). 480p. 1986. reprint ed. pap. 15.95 (*0-8112-0982-2*, NDP618, Pub. by New Directions) Norton.

— The Selected Stories. Mitchell, Breon, ed. & tr. by. LC 89-13120. 1989. 19.95 (*0-8112-1105-3*, Pub. by New Directions) Norton.

— The Selected Stories of Siegfried Lenz. Mitchell, Breon, ed. LC 95-36430. 232p. (C). 1995. pap. 15.95 (*0-8101-1314-7*) Northwestern U Pr.

Lenz, Vicki. Don't Forget Your Customers! A Marketing Guide for Small Businesses. LC 96-96150. (Illus.). xiii, 90p. (Orig.). 1996. pap. 10.95 (*0-9651641-0-1*) Emphasis Custom.

— Employees Serving Customers: Your Starring Role in the Big Picture! LC 97-93035. (Illus.). 64p. (Orig.). 1997. pap. 9.95 (*0-9651641-1-X*) Emphasis Custom.

— The Saturn Difference: Creating Customer Loyalty in Your Company. LC 98-38406. 274p. 1999. 24.95 (*0-471-31449-8*) Wiley.

Lenz, Wilhelm Von, see Von Lenz, Wilhelm.

Lenz, William E. Fast Talk & Flush Times: The Confidence Man as a Literary Convention. LC 84-2200. (Illus.). 248p. 1985. text 29.95 (*0-8262-0450-3*) U of Mo Pr.

— The Poetics of the Antarctic: A Study in Nineteenth-Century American Cultural Perceptions. LC 94-27300. (Studies in Nineteenth-Century American Literature: Vol. 5). (Illus.). 248p. 1995. text 46.00 (*0-8153-1473-6*, H1785) Garland.

Lenze, David. Florida Long-Term Economic Forecast, 1997, Vol. 1. West, Carol T., ed. Date not set. pap. write for info. (*0-930885-24-4*) Bur Econ & Bus Res.

— Florida Long-Term Economic Forecast, 1997, Vol. 1 & 2. West, Carol T., ed. Date not set. pap. write for info. (*0-930885-23-6*) Bur Econ & Bus Res.

— Florida Long-Term Economic Forecast, 1997, Vol. 2. West, Carol T., ed. Date not set. pap. write for info. (*0-930885-27-9*) Bur Econ & Bus Res.

Lenze, David, jt. auth. see West, Carol T.

Lenzen, Charlotte. Reading Step-by-Step: A Winning Formula. rev. ed. (Illus.). 286p. 1997. ring bd. 99.95 (*0-9623658-3-1*) Chalen Edu Systs.

Lenzen, Dieter, jt. ed. see Benner, Dietrich.

Lenzen, Donald L. Ancient Metrology. (Illus.). 108p. 1989. 14.95 (*0-9625309-0-5*) D L Lenzen.

Lenzen, V. F. Benjamin Peirce & the U. S. Coast Survey. (Illus.). 1968. 20.00 (*0-911302-06-9*) San Francisco Pr.

Lenzen, Victor F. Procedures of Empirical Science. LC 71-131570. (Foundations of the Unity of Science Ser.: Vol. 1, No. 5). 1993. pap. text 1.95 (*0-226-57580-2*, P404) U Ch Pr.

Lenzen, Wolfgang. Das System der Leibnizschen Logik. (Foundations of Communication & Cognition Ser.). xvi, 235p. (C). 1990. lib. bdg. 83.10 (*3-11-012353-3*) De Gruyter.

Lenzen, Wolfgang, ed. Das Weite Spektrum der Analytischen Philosophie: Festschrift Fuer Franz von Kutschera. (Perspektiven der Analytischen Philosophie - Perspectives in Analytical Philosophy Ser.: Vol. 14). (GER.). vii, 463p. (C). 1997. lib. bdg. 203.45 (*3-11-015386-6*) De Gruyter.

***Lenzendorf, Dennis.** Effigy Mounds National Monument Handbook. (Illus.). 124p. 2000. pap. 14.95 (*1-888213-52-3*) Eastern National.

Lenzenweger, Mark F. & Dworkin, Robert H., eds. Origins & Development of Schizophrenia: Advances in Experimental Psychopathology. LC 97-52362. 557p. 1998. 49.95 (*1-55798-497-2*, 431-8730) Am Psychol.

Lenzenweger, Mark F., jt. ed. see Clarkin, John F.

Lenzenweger, Mark F., jt. ed. see Haugaard, Jeffery J.

Lenzenweger, R. Bibliotheca Phycologica, Vol. 104. (Desmidiaceenflora von Oesterreich Ser.: Teil 3). (Illus.). 218p. 1997. 55.00 (*3-443-60031-X*, Pub. by Gebruder Borntraeger) Balogh.

Lenzenweger, Rupert. Desmidiaceenflora Von Osterreich, Teil 1, Pt. VIII. (Bibliotheca Phycologica Ser.: Vol. 101). (Illus.). 162p. 1996. pap. 53.00 (*3-443-60028-X*, Pub. by Gebruder Borntraeger) Balogh.

— Desmidiaceenflora Von Osterreich, Teil 2. (Bibliotheca Phycologica Ser.: Vol. 102). (Illus.). 216p. 1997. pap. 57.00 (*3-443-60029-8*, Pub. by Gebruder Borntraeger) Balogh.

Lenzer, Gertrud, ed. Auguste Comte & Positivism: The Essential Writings. LC 97-30353. 555p. 1997. pap. 29.95 (*0-7658-0412-3*) Transaction Pubs.

Lenzer, Gertrud, ed. see Comte, Auguste.

Lenzerini, Maurizio. AI*IA 97 - Advances in Artificial Intelligence: 5th Congress of the Italian Association for Artificial Intelligence, Rome, Italy, September 17-19, 1997 : Proceedings. Carbonell, J. G. & Siekmann, J., eds. LC 97-37170. (Lecture Notes in Computer Science Ser.: Vol. 1321). xii, 459p. 1997. pap. 69.00 (*3-540-63576-9*) Spr-Verlag.

Lenzi, Diana E. Dike Eddleman: Illinois' Greatest Athlete. (Illus.). 192p. 1998. 19.95 (*1-57167-199-4*) Sports Pub.

Lenzi, G. L., jt. ed. see Orgogozo, J. M.

Lenzi, Gian L., jt. ed. see Fieschi, C.

Lenzi, J. Arthur. Food for Thoughts & Thoughts for Food: 80 Recipes & 400 Opinions of a 1950's Thinker. viii, 160p. 1999. pap. 14.95 (*0-9667914-0-1*) Nova Grp.

Lenzi, John D. Epistemo Philiac's Delight. 50p. (YA). (gr. 9 up). 1998. 9.95 (*0-9663744-0-1*, TXU 766-059) Epistemo MN.

Lenzi, S. & Descovich, G. C., eds. Atherosclerosis & Cardiovascular Disease. 1984. text 225.00 (*0-85200-793-0*) Kluwer Academic.

— Atherosclerosis & Cardiovascular Disease. (C). 1987. text 288.00 (*0-85200-836-8*) Kluwer Academic.

Lenzi, S., jt. ed. see Descovich, G.

Lenzing, H., jt. auth. see Jensen, C. U.

Lenzing, Helmut, jt. ed. see Dlab, Vlastimil.

***Lenzke, James T.** Standard Catalog of American Light-Duty Trucks, 1896-2000. 3rd rev. ed. LC 86-83144. (Illus.). 1,008p. 2000. pap. 34.95 (*0-87341-933-2*, PT03) Krause Pubns.

— Standard Catalog of Cadillac, 1903-2000. 2nd rev. ed. LC 91-61301. (Illus.). 304p. 2000. pap. 21.95 (*0-87341-925-1*, AL02) Krause Pubns.

Lenzke, James T. 2000 Standard Guide to Cars & Prices. 12th ed. Buttolph, Ken, ed. LC 89-80091. (Illus.). 696p. 1999. pap. 16.95 (*0-87341-766-6*) Krause Pubns.

Lenzke, James T., jt. ed. see Gunnell, John.

Lenzke, James T., ed. see Kowalke, Ron.

Lenzkes, Susan. Crossing the Bridge Between You & Me: Friendship-Building Devotions for Women. 128p. 1993. pap. 8.99 (*0-929239-83-0*) Discovery Hse Pubs.

— Everybody's Breaking Pieces off of Me: Stress Relieving Devotions for Women. 128p. 1992. pap. 8.99 (*0-929239-58-X*) Discovery Hse Pubs.

— No Rain, No Gain: Growing Through Life's Storms. 128p. (Orig.). 1995. pap. 10.99 (*0-929239-93-8*) Discovery Hse Pubs.

— A Silver Pen for Cloudy Days. 144p. 1987. pap. 7.95 (*0-310-43671-0*, 6893P) Zondervan.

— When Life Takes What Matters: Devotions to Comfort You Through Crisis & Change. LC 92-31268. 128p. 1993. pap. 8.99 (*0-929239-70-9*) Discovery Hse Pubs.

— When the Handwriting on the Wall Is in Brown Crayon. 1986. pap. 6.99 (*0-310-43631-1*, 6891P) Zondervan.

Lenzkes, Susan L. When Life Takes What Matter: Devotions to Comfort You Through Crisis & Change; No Rain, No Gain: Growing Through Life's Storms. LC 99-26172. 240p. 1999. pap. 11.99 (*1-57293-057-8*) Discovery Hse Pubs.

***Lenzkes, Susan L.** When the Handwriting on the Wall Is in Brown Crayon. LC 00-31543. 2000. write for info. (*1-57293-014-4*) Discovery Hse Pubs.

Lenzo, Fran. Angel John's Little Book of Angelic Wisdom: Affirmations of Love, Healing, Hope & Faith for Renewal of Heart, Spirit & Soul. (Illus.). (Orig.). 1996. pap. 7.00 (*0-9644821-1-8*) Angel Guidance.

— Angel Messages from Above: Stories, Poems, Essays & Loving Words from John, My Guardian Angel. Lenzo, Jerry, ed. (Illus.). 224p. (Orig.). 1995. pap. 14.95 (*0-9644821-0-X*) Angel Guidance.

Lenzo, Fran, jt. auth. see Payne, Donna.

Lenzo, Jerry, ed. see Lenzo, Fran.

Lenzo, Lisa. Within the Lighted City. LC 97-15908. (John Simmons Short Fiction Award Ser.). 112p. 1997. 19.95 (*0-87745-611-9*) U of Iowa Pr.

Leo, A. Practical Astrology. 228p. 1988. 10.95 (*0-318-36378-X*) Asia Bk Corp.

Leo A. Orleans for the Committee on Scholarly Comm, jt. auth. see National Academy of Sciences Staff.

Leo, Alan. Astrology for All. 336p. 1996. reprint ed. spiral bd. 19.00 (*0-7873-0553-7*) Hlth Research.

— Esoteric Astrology. (Astrologer's Library). 320p. 1989. pap. 16.95 (*0-89281-181-1*, Destiny Bks) Inner Tradit.

— Jupiter the Preserver. 102p. 1998. reprint ed. pap. 14.95 (*0-7661-0444-3*) Kessinger Pub.

— Mars: The War Lord. 99p. 1993. reprint ed. spiral bd. 9.00 (*0-7873-0550-2*) Hlth Research.

— Practical Astrology. 224p. 1996. reprint ed. spiral bd. 16.00 (*0-7873-1059-X*) Hlth Research.

— Progressed Horoscope (1923) 378p. 1998. reprint ed. pap. 15.95 (*0-7661-0552-0*) Kessinger Pub.

— Thousand & One Notable Nativities: Astrologer's "Who's Who" 4th ed. 130p. 1996. reprint ed. spiral bd. 11.00 (*0-7873-0551-0*) Hlth Research.

Leo, Alan & Robson, Vivian E. Alan Leo's Dictionary of Astrology. 224p. 1981. pap. 12.00 (*0-89540-101-0*, SB-101, Sun Bks) Sun Pub.

Leo, Albert, jt. auth. see Hansch, Corwin.

***Leo Baeck Institute Staff.** Year Book, 1999. 2000. 59.95 (*1-57181-184-2*) Berghahn Bks.

Leo, Bessie. The Romance of the Stars. (Being a Series of Astrological Stories). 201p. 1997. pap. 18.00 (*0-89540-344-7*, SB-344, Sun Bks) Sun Pub.

Leo, Carl & Zavin, Benjamin. The Family Man. 1956. pap. 5.25 (*0-8222-0383-9*) Dramatists Play.

Leo, Christopher. Land & Class in Kenya. (Political Economy of World Poverty Ser.: No. 3). 256p. 1984. pap. 13.95 (*0-8020-6547-3*); text 30.00 (*0-8020-2532-3*) U of Toronto Pr.

Leo, D. De, see De Leo, D.

Leo, Eleanor. Powerful Reading, Efficient Learning. LC 93-886. 462p. (C). 1993. pap. text 38.00 (*0-02-369762-8*, Macmillan Coll) P-H.

Leo, Evan T. Regulation of Telecommunications Carriers: Telecommunications Management & Law. LC 98-41882. 735p. 1998. 99.00 (*0-89006-714-7*) Artech Hse.

***Leo, Frank.** Shanghai Remebrance. LC 00-101991. 240p. 2000. 19.95 (*1-56167-596-2*) Am Literary Pr.

Leo, Friedrich. Geschichte der Romischen Literatur, Band I: Die Archaische Literatur. (GER.). iv, 496p. 1967. write for info. (*3-296-14200-2*) G Olms Pubs.

— Die Griechisch-Romische Biographie Nach Ihrer Literarischen Form. (GER.). x, 330p. 1991. reprint ed. write for info. (*3-487-00986-2*) G Olms Pubs.

— Plutinische Forschungen Zur Kritik und Geschichte der Komodie. (GER.). vii, 375p. 1973. write for info. (*3-296-14210-X*) G Olms Pubs.

Leo, Friedrich & Kiessling, Adolf. Philologische Untersuchungen Heft 2: Zu Augusteischen Dichtern. 122p. write for info. (*0-318-70816-7*) G Olms Pubs.

Leo, Friedrich, ed. see Plautus.

Leo, Friedrich, ed. see Seneca, Lucius Annaeus.

***Leo, Hildegund.** Musik Im Fernsehwerbespot. (GER., Illus.). 164p. 1999. 32.00 (*3-631-34527-5*) P Lang Pubng.

Leo, Jana, jt. auth. see Potter, Keith R.

Leo, Jennifer, jt. auth. see Gher, Nancy.

Leo, Johannes. A Geographical Historie of Africa. Pory, John, tr. LC 72-213. (English Experience Ser.: No. 133). 420p. 1969. reprint ed. 125.00 (*90-221-0133-9*) Walter J Johnson.

***Leo, John.** Incorrect Thoughts: Notes on Our Wayward Culture. 327p. 2000. 29.95 (*0-7658-0038-1*) Transaction Pubs.

Leo, John. Two Steps Ahead of the Thought Police. 320p. 1994. 22.00 (*0-671-88698-3*) S&S Trade.

— Two Steps Ahead of the Thought Police. 2nd ed. LC 98-10023. 345p. 1998. pap. text 19.95 (*0-7658-0400-X*) Transaction Pubs.

Leo, John R. Guide to Poetry Explication: American Poetry, Vol. 2. (Poetry Explication Ser.). 450p. 1989. 55.00 (*0-8161-8918-8*, Hall Reference) Macmillan.

Leo, K. J. Company Accounting in Australia PPR. 1985. pap. text 33.25 (*0-471-33393-X*) Wiley.

Leo, Kathleen R. The Circle Is Assembled. 14p. 1994. pap. 7.00 (*0-941543-08-0*) Sun Dog Pr.

— Inner Timbres. LC 81-90254. (Illus.). 60p. (Orig.). 1981. pap. 4.95 (*0-9606678-0-6*) Sylvan Pubns.

— The Old Ways. Berlinski, Allen, ed. 12p. (Orig.). 1990. pap. 4.95 (*0-941543-01-3*) Sun Dog Pr.

Leo, Kathleen R., et al, eds. Waiting for the Apples. LC 82-62746. (Illus.). 100p. (Orig.). (J). (gr. k up). 1983. pap. 6.50 (*0-9606678-2-2*) Sylvan Pubns.

Leo, Kathleen R., ed. see Blain, Alexander.

Leo, Mabel R. America - The Italian Dream: Living the Italian Way in the U. S. A. LC 99-188623. 206p. 1998. pap. 14.95 (*0-9650787-2-8*) MIBS Publishing.

— The Saga of Jack Durant. unabridged ed. (Illus.). 208p. (Orig.). 1996. pap., per. 14.95 (*0-9650787-0-1*) MIBS Publishing.

Leo, Punana. Pai Ka Leo. (Illus.). 40p. (J). (ps-6). 1989. pap. 14.95 (*0-935848-63-0*) Bess Pr.

Leo, Ray. Little C++ (Made Easy) (Illus.). 200p. (Orig.). 1996. pap. 14.95 (*0-9654634-1-9*) Leo Pr.

Leo-Rhynie, Elsa, et al, eds. Gender: A Caribbean Multidisciplinary Approach. 358p. 1996. pap. 22.95 (*976-8100-68-0*) Women Ink.

Leo, Richard. Way Out Here: Modern Life in Ice-Age Alaska. 208p. (Orig.). 1996. pap. 14.95 (*1-57061-061-4*) Sasquatch Bks.

Leo, Richard A. & Thomas, George C., III, eds. The Miranda Debate: Law, Justice, & Policing. LC 98-9496. (Illus.). 352p. 1998. text 55.00 (*1-55553-338-8*) NE U Pr.

***Leo, Richard A. & Thomas, George C., III, eds.** The Miranda Debate: Law, Justice, & Policing. LC 98-9496. 352p. 2000. pap. text 24.95 (*1-55553-422-8*) NE U Pr.

Leo, Sweeney S. Divine Infinity in Greek & Medieval Thought. 2nd ed. XX, 569p. (C). 1998. reprint ed. pap. text 39.95 (*0-8204-4043-4*) P Lang Pubng.

Leo the Great. Letters. Hunt, Edmund, tr. LC 63-18826. (Fathers of the Church Ser.: Vol. 34). 312p. 1957. 17.95 (*0-8132-0034-2*) Cath U Pr.

Leo, Titus, jt. auth. see Kumar, Vinodh.

Leo, Veronica & Daknewa, Tashi. The Three Silver Coins: A Folk Story from Tibet. Aberg, Nina, tr. LC 94-39648. (Illus.). 32p. (J). (gr. 5-8). 1995. pap. 12.95 (*1-55939-040-9*) Snow Lion Pubns.

Leo, Vince, ed. Heads up - Hands On: A Guide to Youth Arts Activities in the Twin Cities. (Illus.). 140p. (Orig.). 1995. pap. 7.95 (*0-9645862-0-7*) United Arts.

— Heads up/Hands On: A Guide to Youth Arts Activities in the Twin Cities. 2nd ed. (Illus.). 150p. 1996. pap. text 7.95 (*0-9645862-1-5*) United Arts.

***Leo, Vince, et al.** Angel of Histories: Dorit Cypis. (Illus.). 16p. 2000. 15.00 (*0-932173-18-7*) Sweeney Art Gallery.

Leo, Vincent Z. De, see Buckner, Allen Z. & De Leo, Vincent Z.

Leo, William R. Techniques for Nuclear & Particle Physics Experiments: A How-To Approach. LC 92-7633. 1992. write for info. (*3-540-17386-2*) Spr-Verlag.

— Techniques for Nuclear & Particle Physics Experiments: A How-To Approach. (Illus.). xvi, 368p. 1992. reprint ed. pap. 49.50 (*0-387-17386-2*) Spr-Verlag.

An Asterisk (*) at the beginning of an entry indicates that the title is appearing for the first time.

— Techniques for Nuclear & Particle Physics Experiments: A How-To Approach. 2nd rev. ed. LC 93-38494. (Illus.). 378p. 1996. 64.95 (*0-387-57280-5*) Spr-Verlag.

***Leo XIII, pseud.** Custodi di Quella Fede: Guardians of That Faith. Desmarais, Norman, tr. from ITA. 14p. 1998. reprint ed. pap. 2.45 (*0-935952-62-4*) Angelus Pr.

Leo XIII, pseud. The Great Encyclical Letters of Pope Leo XIII (1878-1903): or A Light in the Heavens. LC 95-60850. 580p. 1995. reprint ed. pap. 21.00 (*0-89555-529-8*, 1276) TAN Bks Pubs.

***Leo XIII, pseud.** Humanum Genus: On Freemasonry. 28p. 1998. pap. 3.45 (*0-935952-64-0*) Angelus Pr.

— "Libertas Praestantissimum" On Human Liberty. 34p. 1998. pap. 3.95 (*0-935952-48-9*) Angelus Pr.

Leo XIII, pseud. On Freemasonry - Humanum Genus. 32p. 1992. reprint ed. pap. 1.50 (*0-89555-171-3*) TAN Bks Pubs.

— On the Condition of the Working Classes: Rerum Novarum. 56p. pap. 3.50 (*0-8198-1492-X*) Pauline Bks.

***Leo XIII, pseud.** Quo Graviora: Condemnation of Freemasonry. 33p. 1998. pap. 3.45 (*0-935952-60-8*) Angelus Pr.

Leocha, Charles. Myths, Legends & Tales of Europe for Travellers. 360p. (Orig.). Date not set. pap. 14.95 (*0-915009-15-3*) World Leis Corp.

***Leocha, Charles.** Ski America & Canada: Top Winter Resorts in the U. S. A. & Canada. 13th ed. 512p. 2000. pap. 24.95 (*0-915009-72-2*, Pub. by World Leis Corp) Midpt Trade.

Leocha, Charles. Ski Europe 2000: Guide to Europe's Top Resorts. 12th ed. 364p. 1999. pap. 21.95 (*0-915009-66-8*, Pub. by World Leis Corp) BookWorld.

— Skiing America 2000: Top Winter Resorts in U. S. A. & Canada. 12th ed. Scholfield, Diane & Nangle, Hilary, eds. 496p. 1999. pap. 24.95 (*0-915009-67-6*, Pub. by World Leis Corp) BookWorld.

— Travel Rights. 2nd ed. 191p. 1998. pap. 9.95 (*0-915009-57-9*) World Leis Corp.

Leocha, Charles, jt. auth. see McSweeney, Jeanne.

***Leochko, Dave.** 25 Quick Mini-Lessons to Teach Narrative Writing: Classroom Tested Lessons with Reproducibles. (Illus.). 80p. 2000. pap. text 11.95 (*0-439-06396-5*) Scholastic Inc.

Leodhas, Sorche N. Always Room for One More. LC 65-12881. (Illus.). 32p. (J). (ps-2). 1995. pap. 5.95 (*0-8050-0330-4*, Bks Young Read) H Holt & Co.

Leoff, Eve. Monarch Notes on Shakespeare's A Midsummer Night's Dream. (Orig.). (C). 3.95 (*0-671-00638-X*, Arco) Macmillan Gen Ref.

Leogrande, Dennis. Cello Extensions for the Student. 37p. 1993. pap. write for info. (*0-615-11753-8*) Rubato Mus.

— Ten Duets for the Beginning Cellist. (Illus.). 17p. 1993. pap. write for info. (*0-615-11752-X*) Rubato Mus.

LeoGrande, William M. Our Own Backyard: The United States in Central America, 1977-1992. LC 97-18198. 790p. 1998. 45.00 (*0-8078-2395-3*) U of NC Pr.

***LeoGrande, William M.** Our Own Backyard: The United States in Central America, 1977-1992. LC 97-18198. 790p. 2000. pap. 24.95 (*0-8078-4857-3*) U of NC Pr.

LeoGrande, William M. The United States & Cuba after the Cold War: The 1994 Refugee Crisis. (Pew Case Studies in International Affairs). 50p. (C). 1995. pap. text 3.50 (*1-56927-367-7*, GU Schl Foreign) Geo U Inst Dplmcy.

Leohr, T. M., ed. Iron Carriers & Iron Proteins. 5. 533p. 1989. 265.00 (*0-471-18703-8*) Wiley.

Leoin, Larry. Telecommunications for Information Specialties. (Library, Information, & Computer Science Ser.: No. 11). (Illus.). 180p. (Orig.). 1989. pap. 15.00 (*1-55653-075-7*) OCLC Online Comp.

Leok & Associates Staff, et al. The Nursing Procedures Manual for Skin Diseases. 1995. pap. text. write for info. (*0-07-113835-8*) McGraw.

Leokum, Arkady. Neighbors. 1972. pap. 3.25 (*0-8222-0809-1*) Dramatists Play.

***Leominster Historical Society Staff.** Leominster. (Images of America Ser.). 1999. pap. 18.99 (*0-7524-0996-4*) Arcadia Publng.

Leon. Lo Que el Varon Debe Ser y Como Debe Amar.Tr. of What a Man Should Be & How He Should Love. (SPA.). 44p. 1995. 2.29 (*1-56063-687-4*, 496222) Editorial Unilit.

— Poesia. unabridged ed. (SPA.). pap. 5.95 (*84-410-0049-2*, Pub. by Bookking Intl) Distribks Inc.

— Railroad Terminology Dictionary: German, French, English, Catalan, Basque, Galician. 693p. 1997. 140.00 (*84-7978-291-9*, Pub. by Ediciones Diaz) IBD Ltd.

***Leon.** Uppity Women of Shakespearean Times. 320p. 2000. 7.98 (*1-56731-373-6*, MJF Bks) Fine Comms.

Leon, A. K. Haynes Mazda 626 Owners Workshop Manual, No. 648: 1979-1982. 16.95 (*0-85696-996-6*) Haynes Manuals.

Leon, Abraham. Die Judische Frage: Ein Marxistische Darstellung. Orig. Title: La Conception Materialiste de la Question Juive. (GER.). 205p. (Orig.). 1995. pap. 19.95 (*3-88634-064-3*) Mehring Bks.

Leon, Abram. The Jewish Question: A Marxist Interpretation. LC 76-108721. 270p. 1970. reprint ed. lib. bdg. 50.00 (*0-87348-133-X*) Pathfinder NY.

— The Jewish Question: A Marxist Interpretation. LC 76-108721. 270p. 1971. reprint ed. pap. 17.95 (*0-87348-134-8*) Pathfinder NY.

Leon, Adolfo, jt. auth. see Christophersen, Merrill G.

Leon, Adriano G. Viejo. 304p. 1995. pap. 14.95 (*0-679-76337-6*) Vin Bks.

***Leon, Alexis.** Guide to Software Configuration Management. LC 00-21719. (Illus.). (Regional Handbooks of Economic Development Ser.). (Illus.). 384p. 2000. 79.00 (*1-58053-072-9*) Artech Hse.

Leon, Arnold De, see Calvert, Robert A. & De Leon, Arnold.

Leon, Arnoldo De. The Mexican Image in Nineteenth Century Texas. (Texas History Ser.). (Illus.). 45p. 1983. pap. text 9.95 (*0-89641-106-0*) American Pr.

Leon, Arnoldo De, see De Leon, Arnoldo.

Leon, Arnoldo De, see Griswold del Castillo, Richard & De Leon, Arnoldo.

Leon, Arnoldo De, see De Leon, Arnoldo.

Leon, Arthur S., ed. Physical Activity & Cardiovascular Health: A National Consensus. LC 96-50955. (Illus.). 288p. (Orig.). (C). 1997. pap. text 22.00 (*0-88011-610-2*, BLEO0610) Human Kinetics.

***Leon, Bonnie.** Harvest of Truth. LC 99-45733. (Sowers Trilogy Ser.: Vol. 3). 320p. 2000. pap. 12.99 (*0-8054-1274-3*) Broadman.

Leon, Bonnie. In Fields of Freedom. LC 98-48985. (Sowers Triology Ser.: No. 2). 320p. 1999. pap. 12.99 (*0-8054-1273-5*) Broadman.

— Return to the Misty Shore: A Novel, Vol. 3. LC 96-42385. (Northern Lights Ser.). 1997. pap. text 10.99 (*0-7852-7413-8*) Nelson.

***Leon, Bonnie.** A Sacred Place: A Novel. 320p. 2000. pap. 12.99 (*0-8054-2152-1*) Broadman.

Leon, Bonnie. Where Freedom Grows. LC 98-15558. (Sowers Triology Ser.: Vol. 1). 300p. 1998. pap. 12.99 (*0-8054-1272-7*) Broadman.

***Leon, Burke.** Insider's Guide to Buying a New or Used Car. 3rd ed. (Illus.). 256p. 2000. pap. 14.99 (*1-55870-566-X*, Betrwy Bks) F & W Pubns Inc.

Leon, Burke & Leon, Stephanie. The Insider's Guide to Buying a New or Used Car. 2nd ed. LC 96-41140. 224p. 1997. pap. 12.99 (*1-55870-453-1*, Betrwy Bks) F & W Pubns Inc.

Leon-Carribon, Jose, jt. auth. see Pontbon, Marcel O.

Leon-Carrion, Jose, ed. Neuropsychological Rehabilitation: Fundamentals, Innovations & Directions. (Illus.). 500p. 1997. lib. bdg. 89.95 (*1-57444-039-X*) St Lucie Pr.

Leon, Celine & Walsh, Sylvia. Feminist Interpretations of Soren Kierkegaard. LC 96-49105. (Re-Reading the Canon Ser.). 1997. 55.00 (*0-271-01698-1*); pap. 18.95 (*0-271-01699-X*) Pa St U Pr.

Leon, Coralee, jt. auth. see Songdahl, Harold.

Leon, D. La Institucion Divina del Matrimonio.Tr. of Divine Institution of Marriage. (SPA.). 46p. 1995. 2.29 (*1-56063-685-8*, 496220) Editorial Unilit.

Leon, Dan, tr. see Rubinstein, Danny.

Leon, Daniel, jt. auth. see Santano, Daniel.

Leon, Daniel de, see De Leon, Daniel.

***Leon, David & Walt, Gill, eds.** Poverty, Inequality & Health: An International Perspective. (Illus.). 336p. 2001. pap. text 55.00 (*0-19-263196-9*) OUP.

Leon, David De, see De Leon, David.

Leon, De, see De Leon.

Leon, Donna. Acqua Alta: A Venetian Mystery. 22.50 (*0-614-23187-6*) HarpC.

— The Anonymous Venetian. large type ed. 512p. 1996. 27.99 (*0-7089-3616-4*) Ulverscroft.

— Death at La Fenice. 288p. 1995. mass mkt. 5.99 (*0-06-104337-0*, Harp PBks) HarpC.

— A Venetian Reckoning. large type ed. (Large Print Ser.). 480p. 1997. 27.99 (*0-7089-3668-7*) Ulverscroft.

Leon-Dufour, Xavier. Diccionario del Nuevo Testamento.Tr. of Dictionary of the New Testament. (SPA.). 480p. 1977. 29.95 (*0-8288-5329-0*, S50103) Fr & Eur.

— Woerterbuch Zum Neuen Testament. (GER.). 469p. 1977. 39.95 (*0-7859-8384-8*, 3466202191) Fr & Eur.

— Woerterbuch Zur Biblischen Botschaft. 2nd ed. (GER.). 826p. 1981. 95.00 (*0-7859-8373-2*, 3451141779) Fr & Eur.

Leon-Dufour, Xavier & Viola, G. Dictionary of Biblical Theology: Dizionario di Teologia Biblica. (ITA.). 1424p. 1980. 110.00 (*0-8288-2314-6*, M7691) Fr & Eur.

Leon, Edel, ed. see James, Henry.

Leon, Fray L. de. De Los Nombres de Cristo. Sanchez Zamarreno, Antonio, ed. (Nueva Austral Ser.: Vol. 190). (SPA.). 1991. pap. text 32.95 (*84-239-1990-0*) Elliots Bks.

Leon Freyre, Ponce De, see De Leon Freyre, Ponce.

Leon-Garcia. Communication Networks. 768p. 1999. 27.50 (*0-07-022839-6*) McGraw-Hill Prof.

Leon-Garcia, Albert. Probability & Random Processes for Electrical Engineering: Instructor's Solutions Manual. 2nd ed. 1994. teacher ed. 18.00 (*0-201-55739-8*) Addison-Wesley.

Leon-Garcia, Alberto. Pasupathy Communications. (C). 2000. 95.00 (*0-201-52528-3*) Addison-Wesley.

— Probability & Random Processes. 2nd ed. 128p. (C). 1993. pap. text 18.00 (*0-201-55738-X*) Addison-Wesley.

— Probability & Random Processes for Electrical Engineering. (Electrical & Computer Engineering Ser.). (Illus.). 488p. (C). 1989. text 62.50 (*0-201-12906-X*) Addison-Wesley.

— Probability & Random Processes for Electrical Engineering. 2nd ed. (Illus.). 606p. (C). 1993. 99.00 (*0-201-50037-X*) Addison-Wesley.

Leon, Gary. The Way it Was: A Jew's Struggle Through Two World Wars. (Illus.). 108p. 1997. 38.50 (*1-85776-250-9*, Pub. by Book Guild Ltd) Trans-Atl Phila.

Leon, George B. The Greek Socialist Movement & the First World War. (East European Monographs: No. 18). 204p. 1976. text 52.50 (*0-914710-11-7*, Pub. by East Eur Monographs) Col U Pr.

Leon, George D. How to Make Simple, Sturdy, Attractive, Inexpensive Furniture from Cardboard. (Illus.). 96p. 1994. pap. 12.95 (*0-8117-2548-0*) Stackpole.

— The Story of Electricity: With Twenty Easy-to-Perform Experiments. (Illus.). 112p. 1988. reprint ed. pap. 4.95 (*0-486-25581-6*) Dover.

Leon, George de, see De Leon, George.

Leon, Georgina L. El Flamboyan Amarillo. 50p. (J). (gr. 1-3). 1997. 10.50 (*0-929157-33-8*) Ediciones Huracan.

Leon, Gloria R. Case Histories of Psychopathology. 4th ed. 368p. 1989. pap. text 43.00 (*0-205-12085-7*, H20852) Allyn.

Leon, H. & Alain, Hermano. Flora de Cuba, 3 vols. (Contribuc. Ocasionales del Museo de Historia Natural de la Salle Ser.: Nos. 8, 10, 13, 16, Pt. 5). (LAT & SPA., Illus.). 2317p. 1974. reprint ed. 486.20 (*3-87429-077-8*, 006877, Pub. by Koeltz Sci Bks) Lubrecht & Cramer.

Leon, Harry J. The Jews of Ancient Rome. rev. ed. (Illus.). 394p. 1995. 24.95 (*1-56563-076-9*) Hendrickson MA.

Leon, Irving G. When a Baby Dies: Psychotherapy for Pregnancy & Newborn Loss. 248p. (C). 1992. reprint ed. pap. 16.00 (*0-300-05230-8*) Yale U Pr.

Leon, J. Becoming Best Friend. 1993. pap. 4.99 (*0-425-13959-X*) Berkley Pub.

Leon, J. K. How to Test & Buy a Used Car. (Illus.). 29p. (Orig.). 1984. pap. 4.95 (*0-932675-00-X*) Used Car Pubns.

Leon, J. Mustrede. Nonlinear Evolutions. 808p. (C). 1988. text 143.00 (*9971-5-0458-8*) World Scientific Pub.

Leon, J. Mustrede, et al, eds. Susy & Grand Unification from Strings to Collider Phenomenology: Proceedings of the 3rd CSIC Workshop; Madrid, Spain Jan-Feb 1985. 530p. 1986. text 117.00 (*9971-978-62-8*) World Scientific Pub.

Leon, J. Mustrede, jt. ed. see Barthes, M.

Leon, Jane E. Becoming Best Friends. 1993. mass mkt. 4.99 (*0-425-13956-5*) Berkley Pub.

Leon, Jeffrey C. Science & Philosophy in the West. LC 98-2872. 330p. (C). 1998. pap. text 48.00 (*0-13-647439-X*) P-H.

Leon, Joel, jt. auth. see Hayslip, Bert, Jr.

Leon, Jorge A. Hacia una Sicologia Pastoral Para los Anos 2000.Tr. of Pastoral Psychology. (SPA.). 240p. 1996. 10.99 (*0-89922-576-4*, C042-5764) Caribe Betania.

***Leon, Jorge A.** Psicologia Pastoral Para Toda la Familia. 1998. pap. text 9.99 (*0-89922-426-1*) Caribe Betania.

Leon, Joseph J., et al. Survey Techniques for Homeowners Associations & Property Managers: Mail-Out & Hand-Out Questionnaires. unabridged ed. 71p. 1997. pap. 39.95 (*0-9668165-0-1*, SS-1) Streamline Surv.

Leon, Joseph J., jt. ed. see Cretser, Gary A.

Leon, Judene. Bible Games for Teams & Groups. (Illus.). 64p. 1984. 6.95 (*0-86683-832-5*) Harper SF.

***Leon, Luis & Laderman, Gary.** Encyclopedia of Religion & American Cultures, 4 Vols. 2002. lib. bdg. 375.00 (*1-57607-238-X*) ABC-CLIO.

Leon, Luis de, see Luis de Leon, Fray.

Leon, Luis De, see De Leon, Luis.

Leon, M. Ponz De, see De Leon, M. Ponz.

Leon, Margaret. Barnaby Bear. (Illus.). 32p. (J). (ps-8). 1983. 7.95 (*0-920806-42-2*, Pub. by Penumbra Pr) U of Toronto Pr.

Leon, Mariette, tr. see Grousset, Rene.

Leon, Mario. Polytechnical Railroad Dictionary, Basque, Catalan, English, French, German, Spanish. (BAQ, CAT, ENG, FRE & GER.). 717p. 1997. 295.00 (*0-7859-9577-3*) Fr & Eur.

Leon, Marjorie, jt. auth. see Jackson, Lewis.

Leon, Mark. The Gaia War. 320p. (Orig.). 1995. mass mkt. 4.99 (*0-380-77873-4*, Avon Bks) Morrow Avon.

— Mind-Surfer. 272p. (Orig.). 1995. mass mkt. 4.99 (*0-380-77582-4*, Avon Bks) Morrow Avon.

— The Unified Field. 288p. (Orig.). 1996. mass mkt. 5.99 (*0-380-78651-6*, Avon Bks) Morrow Avon.

Leon, Martin B., et al. Interventional Cardiology Self-Assessment & Review. 380p. (C). Date not set. pap. text 45.00 (*1-890114-04-9*) Physicians Pr.

Leon, Marynel, jt. auth. see Noel, Leon.

Leon, Monique. Exercises Systematique. (FRE.). 183p. 1991. 24.95 (*0-8288-7483-2*) Fr & Eur.

— Exercises Systematiques de Prononciation Francaise. (FRE.). 55p. 1969. pap. write for info. (*0-7859-4634-9*) Fr & Eur.

— Prononciation du Francais Standard. (Coll. Linguistique Appliquee). 16.50 (*0-685-36699-5*); 39.95 (*0-8288-7873-0*, F139430); audio 59.95 (*0-685-36700-2*) Fr & Eur.

Leon, N. H. Chemical Reactivity & Modification of Keratin Fibres. 81p. 1975. 120.00 (*0-7855-7186-8*) St Mut.

Leon, Napoleon B. De, see De Leon, Napoleon B.

Leon Nunez, Victor. Diccionario de Argot Espanol. 9th ed. (SPA.). 160p. 1991. pap. 8.95 (*0-7859-5720-0*, 8420617660) Fr & Eur.

Leon, Pablo M. Mendes De, see Masson-Zwaan, Tanja L., ed.

Leon, Pablo M. Mendes De, see Masson-Zwaan, Tanja L. & Mendes de Leon, Pablo M., eds.

***Leon, Philip W.** Bullies & Cowards 1898-1901: The West Point Hazing Scandal, 186. LC 99-32002. Vol. 186. 208p. 1999. 55.00 (*0-313-31222-2*) Greenwood.

Leon, Philip W. Mark Twain & West Point: America's Favorite Storyteller at the U. S. Military Academy. LC 97-200367. (Illus.). 276p. 1996. pap. 15.95 (*1-55022-277-5*, Pub. by ECW) LPC InBook.

— Walt Whitman & Sir William Osler: A Poet & His Physician. LC 95-232905. (Illus.). 212p. 1995. 32.00 (*1-55022-251-1*, Pub. by ECW) LPC InBook.

— Walt Whitman & Sir William Osler, a Poet & His Physician: A Poet & His Physician. LC 95-232905. (Illus.). 212p. 1995. pap. 29.95 (*1-55022-252-X*, Pub. by ECW) Genl Dist Srvs.

Leon Pinelo, Antonio De, see De Leon Pinelo, Antonio.

Leon, Ponce De, see De Leon, Ponce.

Leon-Portilla, Miguel. Los Antiguos Mexicanos (The Ancient Mexicans) (SPA., Illus.). 203p. 1990. reprint ed. pap. 7.99 (*968-16-1506-9*, Pub. by Fondo) Continental Bk.

— The Aztec Image of Self & Society: An Introduction to Nahua Culture. LC 90-53559. (Illus.). 264p. (C). 1992. 27.50 (*0-87480-360-8*) U of Utah Pr.

— Aztec Thought & Culture: A Study of the Ancient Nahuatl Mind. Davis, Jack E., tr. from SPA. LC 63-11019. (Civilization of the American Indian Ser.: Vol. 67). (Illus.). 264p. 1990. reprint ed. pap. 17.95 (*0-8061-2295-1*) U of Okla Pr.

— Endangered Cultures. Goodson-Lawes, Julie, tr. from SPA. LC 90-52658. (Illus.). 276p. 1990. pap. text 14.95 (*0-87074-311-2*) SMU Press.

***Leon-Portilla, Miguel.** Fifteen Poets of the Aztec World. (Illus.). 328p. 2000. pap. 12.95 (*0-8061-3291-4*) U of Okla Pr.

Leon-Portilla, Miguel. Fifteen Poets of the Aztec World. LC 92-7108. (Illus.). 328p. 1992. 29.95 (*0-8061-2441-5*) U of Okla Pr.

— Pre-Columbian Literatures of Mexico. Lobanov, Grace, tr. LC 79-32551. (Civilization of the American Indian Ser.: Vol. 92). (Illus.). 256p. (Orig.). 1986. pap. 15.95 (*0-8061-1974-8*) U of Okla Pr.

— Time & Reality in the Thought of the Maya. Boiles, Charles L. & Horcasitas, Fernando, trs. from SPA. LC 88-40207. (Civilization of the American Indian Ser.: Vol. 190). (Illus.). 256p. 1990. pap. 14.95 (*0-8061-2308-7*) U of Okla Pr.

Leon-Portilla, Miguel, ed. The Broken Spears: The Aztec Account of the Conquest of Mexico. rev. ed. LC 91-35657. (Illus.). 224p. 1992. pap. 15.50 (*0-8070-5501-8*) Beacon Pr.

— Native Meso-American Spirituality. Anderson, Arthur J. et al, trs. LC 80-80821. (Classics of Western Spirituality Ser.). 320p. 1980. pap. 17.95 (*0-8091-2231-6*) Paulist Pr.

Leon-Portilla, Miguel, jt. ed. see Gossen, Gary H.

Leon, Roberto T., et al, eds. Effects on Soils & Structures: Proceedings of the U. S. - Costa Rica Workshop on the Costa Rica Earthquakes of 1990-1991. 171p. 1993. pap. 15.00 (*0-943198-35-6*, 93-A) Earthquake Eng.

Leon, Ruth. Applause: New York's Guide to the Performing Arts. (Companion Ser.). (Illus.). 516p. 1992. pap. 15.95 (*1-55783-096-7*) Applause Theatre Bk Pubs.

Leon, Ruth, jt. auth. see Morley, Sheridan.

Leon, Silvia. Songs for Little Ones (Canciones Para Pequenos) Teacher's Guide (Guia de Maestros) (Illus.). 61p. (Orig.). 1995. pap. text 8.95 (*0-9643490-0-0*) Smarty Kat.

Leon, Stephanie, jt. auth. see Leon, Burke.

Leon, Steven J. Linear Algebra with Applications. 5th ed. LC 97-31804. 491p. 1997. 93.33 (*0-13-849308-1*) P-H.

Leon, Steven J., et al. At Last Computer Exercises Linear. LC 97-110086. 232p. (C). 1996. pap. text 17.33 (*0-13-270273-8*) P-H.

Leon, Sula, jt. auth. see Rose, Evelyn.

Leon, Sy. None of the Above: Why Non-Voters Are America's Political Majority. 191p. 1996. reprint ed. pap. 12.95 (*0-930073-17-7*) Fox & Wilkes.

Leon-Talley, Andre. X-Ray. LC 99-32081. (Illus.). 256p. 1999. 110.00 (*1-57687-035-9*, pwerHse Bks) pwerHse Cultrl.

***Leon-Talley, Andre.** X-Ray. 1999. 110.00 (*1-57687-063-4*) pwerHse Cultrl.

***Leon, Tania F.** Finally Home. 70p. 1999. pap. 7.00 (*1-882695-11-9*) Patagonia Pr.

Leon, Teadoro Bonzales De, see Bonzales De Leon, Teadoro, pref.

Leon, Thomas C. De, see De Leon, Thomas C.

Leon, V. Slang Dictionary of Spanish: Diccionario del Argot Espanol. (SPA.). 157p. 1983. pap. 9.95 (*0-8288-2050-3*, S33020) Fr & Eur.

Leon, Vicki. Hearst Castle Photo Tour Guide. 2nd ed. (Illus.). 32p. 1983. pap. 6.95 (*0-918303-04-4*) Blake Pub.

— Monterey Peninsula. (Illus.). 56p. (Orig.). 1985. pap. 7.95 (*0-918303-03-6*) Blake Pub.

— Outrageous Women of Ancient Times. LC 97-10836. (Outrageous Women Ser.). 128p. (YA). (gr. 5-9). 1997. pap. 12.95 (*0-471-17006-2*) Wiley.

— Outrageous Women of Ancient Times. LC 97-30307. (Outrageous Women Ser.). 128p. (J). (gr. 4-7). 1998. pap. 12.95 (*0-471-17004-6*) Wiley.

***Leon, Vicki.** Outrageous Women of the Renaissance. LC 98-30357. (Outrageous Women Ser.). (Illus.). 128p. (YA). (gr. 5-12). 1999. pap. text 12.95 (*0-471-29684-8*) Wiley.

Leon, Vicki. Parrots, Macaws & Cockatoos. LC 94-30908. (Close up: A Focus on Nature Ser.). (Illus.). 40p. (YA). (gr. 5 up). 1994. pap. 7.95 (*0-382-24899-6*); lib. bdg. 14.95 (*0-382-24898-8*) Silver Burdett Pr.

— A Pod of Killer Whales: The Mysterious & Beautiful Life of the Orca. LC 94-30906. (Close Up Ser.). (Illus.). 40p. (YA). (gr. 5 up). 1994. pap. 7.95 (*0-382-24901-1*); lib. bdg. 14.95 (*0-382-24900-3*) Silver Burdett Pr.

***Leon, Vicki.** A Raft of Sea Otters: An Affectionate Portrait. (Illus.). 40p. 1999. reprint ed. pap. 7.95 (*0-945092-43-1*, Pub. by EZ Nature) Cntrl Coast Pr.

Leon, Vicki. San Luis Obispo County Coast & Castle. (Illus.). 72p. (Orig.). 1986. pap. 9.95 (*0-918303-11-7*) Blake Pub.

— Scenic Highway One: Monterey to Morro Bay. rev. ed. (Illus.). 64p. (Orig.). 1984. pap. 8.95 (*0-918303-02-8*) Blake Pub.

— Seals & Sea Lions: An Affectionate Portrait. LC 94-31827. (Close Up Ser.). (Illus.). 40p. (YA). (gr. 5 up). 1994. pap. 7.95 (*0-382-24890-2*); lib. bdg. 14.95 (*0-382-24889-9*) Silver Burdett Pr.

***Leon, Vicki.** Seals & Sea Lions: An Affectionate Portrait. (Illus.). 40p. 1999. reprint ed. pap. 7.95 (*0-945092-44-X*, Pub. by EZ Nature) Cntrl Coast Pr.

Leon, Vicki. A Tangle of Octopuses: Plus Cuttlefish, Nautilus & a Giant Squid or Two. LC 97-10935. (Close Up Ser.). (J). 1998. 23.00 (*0-382-39726-6*); pap. write for info. (*0-382-39727-4*) Silver Burdett Pr.

— Uppity Women of Ancient Times. (Illus.). 256p. 1995. pap. 14.95 (*1-57324-010-9*) Conari Press.

L

— Uppity Women of Ancient Times. LC 97-75623. (Illus.). 256p. 1998. reprint ed. 8.98 (1-56731-249-7, MJF Bks) Fine Comms.

— Uppity Women of Medieval Times. LC 97-4483. (Illus.). 256p. 1997. pap. 14.95 (1-57324-039-7) Conari Press.

— Uppity Women of Medieval Times. LC 97-75624. (Illus.). 256p. 1998. reprint ed. 8.98 (1-56731-250-0, MJF Bks) Fine Comms.

— Uppity Women of the Renaissance. LC 98-43618. 1999. pap. text 14.95 (1-57324-127-X) Conari Press.

— Wetlands: All about Bogs, Bayous, Swamps, Sloughs & a Salt Marsh or Two. LC 97-10936. (Close Up Ser.). (J). 1998. pap. write for info. (0-382-39724-X); pap. write for info. (0-382-39725-8) Silver Burdett Pr.

***Leon, Vicki, ed.** A Pod of Killer Whales: The Mysterious & Beautiful Life of the Orca. (Illus.). 40p. 2000. reprint ed. pap. 7.95 (0-945092-46-6, Pub. by EZ Nature) Cntrl Coast Pr.

Leon, Vicki, ed. A Raft of Sea Otters: An Affectionate Portrait. rev. ed. LC 94-31826. (Close Up Ser.). (Illus.). 48p. (YA). (gr. 5 up). 1994. pap. 7.95 (0-382-24886-4); lib. bdg. 14.95 (0-382-24885-6) Silver Burdett Pr.

Leon, Vicki, jt. auth. see Barnhart, Diana.

Leon, Vicki, ed. see Berger, Bruce.

Leon, Vicki, ed. see Brody, Jean.

Leon, Vicki, ed. see Fourie, Denise K.

Leon, Vicki, ed. see Gohier, Francois.

Leon, Vicki, ed. see Hall, Howard.

Leon, Vicki, ed. see Hamilton, Jean.

Leon, Vicki, ed. see Holing, Dwight, et al.

Leon, Vicki, ed. see Hunt, Joni P.

Leon, Vicki, ed. see Wilson, Barbara.

Leon, Warren & Rosenzweig, Roy, eds. History Museums in the United States: A Critical Assessment. LC 88-27883. (Illus.). 360p. 1989. pap. text 17.95 (0-252-06064-4) U of Ill Pr.

Leon-Yanez, Susana, jt. ed. see Jorgensen, Peter M.

Leonaites, Joseph. New Genesis & the Technoid Movement. (Illus.). 1977. pap. write for info. (0-9601272-1-6) Leonaitis.

Leonard. Biocom. (UK - Science Ser.). 1997. mass mkt., student ed. 43.95 (0-538-65208-X) S-W Pub.

— Biocom. (UK - Science Ser.). 1997. teacher ed. 127.95 (0-538-65210-1) S-W Pub.

— Biocom. annot. ed. (UK - Science Ser.). 1998. pap., teacher ed. 71.95 (0-538-65209-8) S-W Pub.

— Biology: A Community Context. (UK - Science Ser.). 1996. mass mkt., student ed. 3.95 (0-538-66751-6) S-W Pub.

Leonard. Cake Decorating Special Occasion. 1992. text 34.50 (0-8050-1550-7) St Martin.

Leonard. Database Design Theory. 1997. text 25.95 (0-333-53813-7, Pub. by Macmillan) St Martin.

— Elections in Britain Today. 3rd ed. LC 96-24401. 240p. 1996. text 59.95 (0-312-16349-5) St Martin.

***Leonard.** Human Nutritional Ecology. 2000. pap. 22.00 (0-8133-3772-0, Pub. by Westview) HarpC.

— Human Nutritional Ecology & Evolution. 2000. 60.00 (0-8133-3771-2, Pub. by Westview) HarpC.

Leonard. Kitten for Christmas. 1988. pap. 2.95 (0-8167-1489-4) Troll Communs.

— Medicine & Public Health. 1995. pap. text. write for info. (0-582-22670-8, Pub. by Addison-Wesley) Longman.

— Neuroscience of Human Movement: A Primer. LC 98-221239. (Illus.). 272p. (gr. 13). 1997. pap. text 25.00 (0-8151-5371-6, 26560) Mosby Inc.

***Leonard.** A Sociological Perspective of Sport. 5th ed. LC 97-47213. 450p. (C). 1998. pap. text 52.00 (0-205-27506-0) Allyn.

Leonard. Trajectories of Mystic Theory. LC 99-39494. 220p. 1999. text 55.00 (0-312-22492-3) St Martin.

— Wish on a Star. 1988. pap. 2.95 (0-8167-1491-6) Troll Communs.

***Leonard, et al.** Student Resource,Biology: A Community Context. 1998. pap. 19.75 (0-538-68573-5) Thomson Learn.

Leonard, jt. auth. see Imwinkelried, Edward A.

Leonard, jt. auth. see Lawrence.

Leonard, A. Britain's Economy: The Roots of Stagnation. LC 73-536665. 27 p. 1970. write for info. (0-7223-0030-1) A H Stockwell.

Leonard, A. B., jt. auth. see Murray, Harold D.

Leonard, Alan, jt. auth. see Baker, Rodney.

Leonard, Albert, Jr. The Excavations at Kom Ge'lf. Lapp, Nancy, ed. LC 97-28045. (Annual of the American Schools of Oriental Research Ser.: Vol. 54). (Illus.). 415p. (C). 1999. 75.00 (0-7885-0392-8, Pub. by Am Sch Orient Res) David Brown.

— An Index to the Late Bronze Age Aegean Pottery from Syria-Palestine. (Studies in Mediterranean Archaeology: Vol. CXIV). (Illus.). 270p. 1994. 78.00 (91-7081-067-2, Pub. by P Astroms) Coronet Bks.

— The Jordan Valley Survey, 1953: Some Unpublished Soundings Conducted by James Mellaart. (Annual of the American Schools of Oriental Research Ser.: No. 50). (Illus.). vii, 199p. 1992. text 55.00 (0-931464-72-2) Eisenbrauns.

Leonard, Albert, Jr. & Williams, Bruce B., eds. Essays in Ancient Civilization Presented to Helen J. Kantor. LC 89-60852. (Studies in Ancient Oriental Civilization: No. 47). (Illus.). xxxix, 393p. 1989. pap. 55.00 (0-918986-57-5) Orient Inst.

Leonard, Alfred. Prescription for Life. 124p. (Orig.). 1997. pap. write for info. (0-9653271-0-8) J Witty.

Leonard, Alice M. Judging Inequality: The Effectiveness of the Tribunal System in Sex. (C). 1988. 49.00 (0-900137-28-2, Pub. by NCCL) St Mut.

Leonard, Alice M., jt. auth. see Gaylord, Catherine L.

Leonard, Alison. Telling Our Stories: Wrestling with a Fresh Language for the Spiritual Journey. pap. write for info. (0-232-52097-6) S Asia.

Leonard, Allenna, jt. ed. see Harnden, Roger.

Leonard, Andrea. A Crocker Genealogy. 311p. (Orig.). 1995. pap. text 23.00 (0-7884-0197-1) Heritage Bk.

— A Crocker Genealogy, Vol. 2. vi, 244p. (Orig.). 1997. pap. 16.50 (0-7884-0776-7, L157) Heritage Bk.

— Records of the Proprietors of the Common Lands in the Town of Barnstable, Massachusetts 1703-1795. iv, 234p. (Orig.). 1996. pap. 21.00 (0-7884-0572-1, L156) Heritage Bk.

Leonard, Andrea, jt. auth. see Halverstadt, Amy.

Leonard, Andrew. Bots: The Origin of New Species. 224p. 1998. pap. 13.95 (0-14-027566-5) Viking Penguin.

— Bots: The Origin of New Species. LC 97-9274. 218p. 1997. 21.95 (1-888869-05-4) Wired Bks.

Leonard, Angela M., ed. Antislavery Materials at Bowdoin College: A Finding Aid. LC 92-70213. (Illus.). 100p. (Orig.). 1992. pap. 7.95 (0-916606-22-8) Bowdoin Coll.

Leonard, Ann, ed. Proceedings of the Fifteenth Annual Conference. LC 76-643241. iii, 79p. (Orig.). 1983. pap. 10.00 (0-933438-07-9) APLIC Intl.

— Seeds 2: Supporting Women's Work Around the World. 207p. 1995. pap. 12.95 (1-55861-106-1); lib. bdg. 35.00 (1-55861-107-X) Feminist Pr.

Leonard, Ann M. I Spy Something: A Practical Guide for Using Observation Tools in the Preschool Classroom. unabridged ed. (Illus.). 120p. 1997. pap. 12.00 (0-942388-24-0) So Early Chldhood Assn.

Leonard, Anne. Homes of Their Own: A Community Care Initiative for Children with Learning Difficulties. (Studies in Cash & Care). 161p. 1991. text 66.95 (1-85628-156-6, Pub. by Avebry) Ashgate Pub Co.

Leonard, Anne & Terrell, John. Patterns of Paradise: The Styles & Significance of Bark Cloth Around the World. Bushman, Tanisse, ed. LC 80-65125. 1980. pap. 10.95 (0-914868-05-5) Field Mus.

Leonard, Arthur G. Lower Niger & Its Tribes. 564p. 1968. reprint ed. 57.50 (0-7146-1687-7, Pub. by F Cass Pubs) Intl Spec Bk.

Leonard, Arthur S. Gay & Lesbian Rights & the Law, Vol. 2. Finkelman, Paul, ed. (Controversies in Constitutional Law Ser.). 350p. 1998. text 75.00 (0-8153-2637-8) Garland.

— Gay & Lesbian Rights & the Law, Vol. 3. Finkelman, Paul, ed. (Controversies in Constitutional Law Ser.). 350p. 1998. text 75.00 (0-8153-2638-6) Garland.

— Gay & Lesbian Rights & the Law, Vol. 4. Finkelman, Paul, ed. (Controversies in Constitutional Law Ser.). 350p. 1998. text 75.00 (0-8153-2639-4) Garland.

Leonard, Arthur S., compiled by. AIDS Legal Bibliography. (Legal Bibliography Ser.: No. 33). 25p. 1989. 40.00 (0-935630-28-7) U of Tex Tarlton Law Lib.

— AIDS Legal Bibliography. 2nd ed. (Tarlton Law Library Legal Bibliography Ser.: No. 37). 97p. 1993. 40.00 (0-935630-39-2) U of Tex Tarlton Law Lib.

Leonard, Arthur S., ed. Sexuality & the Law: An Encyclopedia of Major Legal Cases, Vol. 3. LC 92-45133. 736p. 1993. text 105.00 (0-8240-3421-X, H1272) Garland.

Leonard, Arthur S. & Finkelman, Paul, eds. Homosexuality & the Constitution: Cases & Readings, 4 vols., Vol. 4. LC 97-33515. (Controversies in Constitutional Law Ser.). 1560p. 1997. reprint ed. text 330.00 (0-8153-2636-X) Garland.

***Leonard, Barry.** Electric Current Abroad: 1998 Edition. 3rd rev. ed. 30p. (C). 2000. pap. text 15.00 (0-7881-8800-3) DIANE Pub.

Leonard, Barry. Niosh Pocket Guide to Chemical Hazards. (Illus.). 440p. 1998. pap. text 35.00 (0-7881-4923-7) DIANE Pub.

— United States Court Directory (1996) 604p. (C). 1998. pap. text 60.00 (0-7881-4931-8) DIANE Pub.

***Leonard, Barry, ed.** Achieving the National Education Goals Goal 1: All Children in America Will Start School Ready to Learn. 78p. 1999. pap. text 30.00 (0-7881-7572-6) DIANE Pub.

Leonard, Barry, ed. African Merc Combat Manual. (Illus.). 203p. 1998. pap. text 25.00 (0-7881-5492-3) DIANE Pub.

***Leonard, Barry, ed.** Air Force Manufacturing Technology Year 2000 Project Book: A Digest of the Air Force[0012]s Mantech Activities. 124p. 2000. pap. text 35.00 (0-7881-8786-4) DIANE Pub.

Leonard, Barry, ed. Air Force Research Laboratory: Manufacturing Technology: 1999 Project Book Update. 82p. (C). 1999. pap. text 25.00 (0-7881-7898-9) DIANE Pub.

— Air Force Research Laboratory Manufacturing Technology: 1998 Project Book. 187p. (C). 1998. pap. text 35.00 (0-7881-7310-3) DIANE Pub.

— Airport Services Manual Pt. 7: Airport Emergency Planning. (Illus.). 75p. (C). 1999. pap. text 20.00 (0-7881-8006-1) DIANE Pub.

— America Goes Back to School: A Place for Families & the Community: Partner's Activity Guide. 66p. (C). 1998. pap. text 20.00 (0-7881-7124-0) DIANE Pub.

***Leonard, Barry, ed.** Americans with Disabilities Act: Accessibility Guidelines for Buildings & Facilities CADAAG. rev. ed. (Illus.). 125p. (C). 2000. reprint ed. pap. text 30.00 (0-7881-8524-1) DIANE Pub.

Leonard, Barry, ed. The Annual Report on Transport Economy: In Quest of Transport Resistible to Disaster (FY 1995) (Illus.). 124p. (Orig.). 1996. pap. text 30.00 (0-7881-3261-X) DIANE Pub.

— Answers to Questions about the National Flood Insurance Program. rev. ed. 63p. (C). 1999. pap. text 15.00 (0-7881-7608-0) DIANE Pub.

— Approved Drug Products with Therapeutic Equivalence Evaluations. 18th ed. 770p. (C). 1999. pap. text 95.00 (0-7881-7324-3) DIANE Pub.

***Leonard, Barry, ed.** Approved Drug Products with Therapeutic Equivalence Evaluations, 1999. 19th ed. 800p. (C). 2000. pap. text 95.00 (0-7881-8679-5) DIANE Pub.

Leonard, Barry, ed. ATP Focused Program Competition: Digital Video in Information Networks, Selective-Membrane Platforms, Premium Power, Catalysis & Biocatalysis Technologies, & Tools for DNA Diagnostics. (Illus.). 144p. (C). 1998. pap. text 50.00 (0-7881-7450-9) DIANE Pub.

— Automated Local Flood Warning Systems Handbook. (Illus.). 138p. (C). 1998. pap. text 35.00 (0-7881-7029-5) DIANE Pub.

— The Bank Office of Contemporary Japan. (JPN., Illus.). 115p. 1998. pap. text 25.00 (0-7881-5891-0) DIANE Pub.

***Leonard, Barry, ed.** Basic Facts about the United Nations. rev. ed. 341p. 1999. reprint ed. pap. text 20.00 (0-7881-7002-3) DIANE Pub.

Leonard, Barry, ed. Basic Guide to the National Labor Relations Act: General Principles of Law under the Statute & Procedures of the National Labor Relations Boards. rev. ed. (Illus.). 53p. (C). 1999. pap. text 20.00 (0-7881-8110-6) DIANE Pub.

***Leonard, Barry, ed.** Bibliography on Smoking & Health (to 1990) 343p. (C). 2000. reprint ed. pap. text 30.00 (0-7881-8966-2) DIANE Pub.

— Bibliography on Treatment of Gunshot & Blast Injuries, 1984-1990. 54p. (C). 1999. reprint ed. pap. text 20.00 (0-7881-8379-6) DIANE Pub.

Leonard, Barry, ed. Biomedical Technology Resources: A Research Resources Directory. 92p. 1998. reprint ed. pap. text 25.00 (0-7881-4187-2) DIANE Pub.

— BMDO Technologies, 1998. (Illus.). 53p. (C). 1999. pap. text 20.00 (0-7881-7753-2) DIANE Pub.

***Leonard, Barry, ed.** Building on Beijing: United States NGOs Shape a Women's National Action Agenda. 77p. 1999. reprint ed. pap. text 20.00 (0-7881-8172-6) DIANE Pub.

— California Consumer Beverage Recycling Survey. (Illus.). 106p. (C). 1999. pap. text 25.00 (0-7881-8360-5) DIANE Pub.

Leonard, Barry, ed. The Capitol: A Pictoral History of the Capitol & of the Congress. 9th ed. (Illus.). 192p. 1998. pap. text 30.00 (0-7881-7051-1) DIANE Pub.

***Leonard, Barry, ed.** Catalog of Federal Domestic Assistance, 1999. 34th ed. 1580p. (C). 1999. pap. text 125.00 (0-7881-8308-7) DIANE Pub.

— Catalog of School Reform Models. 233p. 2000. reprint ed. pap. text 40.00 (0-7881-8867-4) DIANE Pub.

— CERCLA Priority List of Hazardous Substances That Will be the Subject of Toxicological Profiles & Support Document, 1997. 160p. (C). 2000. reprint ed. pap. text 30.00 (0-7881-8880-1) DIANE Pub.

Leonard, Barry, ed. Chemotherapy & You: A Guide to Self-Help During Treatment. (Illus.). 56p. (C). 2000. pap. text 15.00 (0-7881-7518-1) DIANE Pub.

***Leonard, Barry, ed.** Child Labor Reserach Needs: Recommendations from the NIOSH Child Labor Working Team. 62p. 1999. pap. text 20.00 (0-7881-8127-0) DIANE Pub.

— Child Maltreatment Report (Minnesota), 1982-1991. (Illus.). 66p. (C). 1999. reprint ed. pap. text 15.00 (0-7881-8215-3) DIANE Pub.

Leonard, Barry, ed. China in the 21st Century: Long-Term Global Implications. 110p. (C). 1998. pap. text 35.00 (0-7881-3873-1) DIANE Pub.

***Leonard, Barry, ed.** Christmas Songs & Stories for All the Family: Arranged for Piano-Vocal with Full Lyrics, Chords & Illustrations. 192p. 1999. reprint ed. pap. text 18.00 (0-7881-6840-1) DIANE Pub.

Leonard, Barry, ed. Chronic Fatiques Syndrome: Information for Physicians. 60p. (C). 1998. pap. text 20.00 (0-7881-4378-6) DIANE Pub.

— A Citizen's Guide to the Federal Budget. (Illus.). 42p. 1999. reprint ed. pap. text 15.00 (0-7881-7010-4) DIANE Pub.

***Leonard, Barry, ed.** A Citizen's Guide to the Federal Budget: Fiscal Year 2000. 5th ed. (Illus.). 57p. 2000. pap. text 20.00 (0-7881-8830-5) DIANE Pub.

— Clean Air Act - Confidential Business Information: Security Manual. rev. ed. (Illus.). 102p. 2000. reprint ed. pap. text 25.00 (0-7881-8974-3) DIANE Pub.

Leonard, Barry, ed. Clean Coal Technology Demonstration Program: Program Update 1996-97. (Illus.). 259p. (C). 1998. pap. text 40.00 (0-7881-7034-1) DIANE Pub.

***Leonard, Barry, ed.** Clearing the Air: An Updated Report on Emission Trends in Selected Cities. (Illus.). 65p. (C). 2000. pap. text 25.00 (0-7881-8661-2) DIANE Pub.

— Colorectal Cancer Screening: Technical Review. 154p. 2000. reprint ed. pap. text 30.00 (0-7567-0052-3) DIANE Pub.

— Concept for Future Joint Operations: Expanding Joint Vision 2010. (Illus.). 88p. (C). 2000. reprint ed. pap. text 25.00 (0-7881-8633-7) DIANE Pub.

Leonard, Barry, ed. Convention on International Civil Aviation (1968) 6th ed. 42p. (C). 1998. pap. text 20.00 (0-7881-3901-0) DIANE Pub.

— Convention on the Marking of Plastic Explosives for the Purpose of Detection. 44p. (C). 1999. reprint ed. pap. text 20.00 (0-7881-7991-8) DIANE Pub.

— Correctional Populations in the United States, 1995. (Illus.). 215p. 1998. pap. text 40.00 (0-7881-7018-X) DIANE Pub.

***Leonard, Barry, ed.** The Cost of Tuberculosis Control in Minnesota: A Report to the Legislature. 48p. (C). 1999. reprint ed. pap. text 20.00 (0-7881-8195-5) DIANE Pub.

— Creating Safe & Drug-Free-Schools: An Action Guide. 140p. (C). 1999. reprint ed. pap. text 25.00 (0-7881-8622-1) DIANE Pub.

— Crime in the United States: 1997 Uniform Crime Reports. (Illus.). 420p. 1999. pap. text 50.00 (0-7881-8070-3) DIANE Pub.

Leonard, Barry, ed. Cumulative Impact of Environmental Regulations on the U. S. Petroleum Refining, Transportation & Marketing Industries. 200p. (C). 1998. pap. text 30.00 (0-7881-7299-9) DIANE Pub.

— Cyber Risk '97: Conference Proceedings. (Illus.). 195p. (C). 1998. pap. text 40.00 (0-7881-7452-5) DIANE Pub.

— Defense Communications: Agreement Signed Between the United States of America & Australia, Signed at Canberra November 6, 1989 with Annexes. 51p. (C). 1999. reprint ed. pap. text 20.00 (0-7881-7609-9) DIANE Pub.

***Leonard, Barry, ed.** Description & Analysis of Tax Proposals Relating to Individual Saving & IRAs: Senate Committee on Finance. (Illus.). 71p. 2000. pap. text 20.00 (0-7881-8512-8) DIANE Pub.

Leonard, Barry, ed. Developing Objectives for Healthy People 2010. (Illus.). 180p. (C). 1999. pap. text 30.00 (0-7881-7577-7) DIANE Pub.

— Diccionario de la Diabetes. (SPA., Illus.). 65p. (C). 1998. pap. text 20.00 (0-7881-7136-4) DIANE Pub.

***Leonard, Barry, ed.** Dictionary of Phrase & Fable. 252p. 1999. reprint ed. pap. text 15.00 (0-7881-6738-3) DIANE Pub.

— Dictionary of Rail & Steam. 187p. 2000. reprint ed. 17.00 (0-7881-9318-X) DIANE Pub.

Leonard, Barry, ed. Digest of State Alcohol-Highway Related Legislation Current As of January 1, 1998. 16th ed. 568p. (C). 1999. pap. text 50.00 (0-7881-7678-1) DIANE Pub.

***Leonard, Barry, ed.** Diplomatic List: Foreign Diplomatic Staffs in the U. S. 78p. (C). 2000. pap. text 20.00 (0-7881-8997-2) DIANE Pub.

Leonard, Barry, ed. Diplomatic List: Foreign Diplomatic Staffs in the U. S., 1998. 76p. (C). 1999. pap. text 25.00 (0-7881-4105-8) DIANE Pub.

***Leonard, Barry, ed.** Diplomatic List: Foreign Diplomatic Staffs in the U. S. (1999) 80p. 1999. pap. text 25.00 (0-7881-8230-7) DIANE Pub.

Leonard, Barry, ed. Disability Evaluation under Social Security. rev. ed. (Illus.). 205p. (C). 1999. text 30.00 (0-7881-7883-0) DIANE Pub.

— Eating Habits for Cancer Patients: Before, During & after Treatment. rev. ed. (Illus.). 60p. 1999. pap. text 15.00 (0-7881-8047-9) DIANE Pub.

***Leonard, Barry, ed.** The Effects of Great Lakes Contaminants on Human Health: Report to Congress, 1995. (Illus.). 95p. (C). 2000. reprint ed. pap. text 20.00 (0-7881-8722-8) DIANE Pub.

— Eighth Annual Report on Carcinogens: 1998 Summary. (Illus.). 252p. (C). 1999. pap. text 50.00 (0-7881-8396-6) DIANE Pub.

Leonard, Barry, ed. Electric Power Annual, 1995. (Illus.). 144p. (C). 1998. pap. text 30.00 (0-7881-7266-2) DIANE Pub.

***Leonard, Barry, ed.** Emergency Response Guidebook (2000) A Guidebook for First Responders During the Initial Phase of a Dangerous Goods/ Hazardous Materials Incident. 384p. 2000. pap. 30.00 (0-7881-8399-0) DIANE Pub.

Leonard, Barry, ed. Energy Education Resources: Kindergarten Through 12th Grade. 123p. 1998. pap. text 20.00 (0-7881-7056-2) DIANE Pub.

— Environmental Restoration Acceleration Report: Expediting the Cleanup. (Illus.), 43p. 1999. reprint ed. pap. text 25.00 (0-7881-8057-6) DIANE Pub.

— EPA's 33/50 Program Company Profile Reduction Highlights, & Company Profiles Vol. II: Eastman Kodak Company, Emerson, & Chrysler Corporation. (Illus.). 87p. (C). 1998. reprint ed. pap. text 25.00 (0-7881-3399-3) DIANE Pub.

— Evaluation of Financing Options for Biomass Facilities in Minnesota. 53p. (C). 1999. text 20.00 (0-7881-7926-8) DIANE Pub.

— Examining the Relationship Between Housing, Education, & Persistent Segregation: Final Report. (Illus.). 139p. (C). 1999. pap. text 30.00 (0-7881-4106-6) DIANE Pub.

— Excellence & Accountability in Teaching: A Guide to U. S. Department of Education Programs & Resources. 74p. 1998. pap. text 20.00 (0-7881-7320-0) DIANE Pub.

***Leonard, Barry, ed.** FDA's Cosmetics Handbook. 60p. (C). 2000. reprint ed. pap. text 20.00 (0-7881-8898-4) DIANE Pub.

— Federal Benefits for Veterans & Dependents. 88p. 1999. pap. text 20.00 (0-7881-8068-1) DIANE Pub.

Leonard, Barry, ed. Finding Resources for Healthy Heart Programs at Work. (Illus.). 92p. 1998. pap. text 20.00 (0-7881-7290-5) DIANE Pub.

***Leonard, Barry, ed.** Fire in the United States 1986-1995. 10th ed. (Illus.). 201p. (C). 1999. reprint ed. pap. text 35.00 (0-7881-8337-0) DIANE Pub.

Leonard, Barry, ed. Fire Management Preparedness & Planning Handbook: U. S. Fish & Wildlife Service. 184p. 1999. reprint ed. text 35.00 (0-7881-7909-8) DIANE Pub.

— Fire Safety Education Resource Directory. (Illus.). 654p. 1998. pap. text 75.00 (0-7881-7308-1) DIANE Pub.

***Leonard, Barry, ed.** Flood Proofing Performance: Successes & Failures. (Illus.). 116p. 2000. reprint ed. pap. text 30.00 (0-7881-8988-3) DIANE Pub.

— Florida Citrus Production Trends 1997-98 Through 2006-07. (Illus.). 43p. (C). 2000. pap. text 25.00 (0-7881-4452-9) DIANE Pub.

Leonard, Barry, ed. Food Safety from Farm to Table: A National Food-Safety Initiative. 56p. (C). 1998. pap. text 20.00 (0-7881-7421-5) DIANE Pub.

— Foreign Labor Trends: Mexico (1995-1996) 39p. (C). 1998. reprint ed. pap. text 20.00 (0-7881-7218-2) DIANE Pub.

An Asterisk (*) at the beginning of an entry indicates that the title is appearing for the first time.

*Leonard, Barry, ed.** Full Cost Accounting for Municipal Solid Waste Management: A Handbook. 70p. (C). 2000. pap. text 20.00 (*0-7881-8212-9*) DIANE Pub.

Leonard, Barry, ed. General Industry Digest: Safety & Health Standards. 86p. 1998. reprint ed. pap. text 25.00 (*0-7881-7214-X*) DIANE Pub.

— General Information Concerning Patents. rev. ed. 87p. (C). 1999. pap. text 20.00 (*0-7881-7585-8*) DIANE Pub.

— General/Flag Officer Worldwide Roster, 1998. 48p. (C). 1999. pap. text 25.00 (*0-7881-7612-9*) DIANE Pub.

***Leonard, Barry, ed.** Getting HIV-Positive Youth into Care: Issues & Opportunities: A Study of the Special Projects of National Significance Program Adolescent Care Projects, 1997. 90p. (C). 2000. reprint ed. pap. text 20.00 (*0-7881-8482-2*) DIANE Pub.

Leonard, Barry, ed. Glossary of HIV/AIDS - Related Terms. 110p. 1999. reprint ed. pap. text 25.00 (*0-7881-7014-7*) DIANE Pub.

— Green Paper on Vertical Restraints in EC Competition Policy. (Illus.). 82p. (C). 1999. reprint ed. pap. text 20.00 (*0-7881-7520-3*) DIANE Pub.

***Leonard, Barry, ed.** Growth, Employment & Convergence on the Road to Emu: 1997 Annual Economic Report. (Illus.). 102p. 1999. reprint ed. pap. text 30.00 (*0-7881-7981-0*) DIANE Pub.

Leonard, Barry, ed. A Guide to Aviation Education Resources. 72p. 1998. pap. text 25.00 (*0-7881-7036-8*) DIANE Pub.

— Guide to E-2 Trial Procedures: OSHA Review Commission Trial. 51p. 1998. pap. text 20.00 (*0-7881-7121-6*) DIANE Pub.

— A Guide to Home Ownership: Annotatd Bibliography. 114p. 1998. reprint ed. pap. text 30.00 (*0-7881-3946-0*) DIANE Pub.

***Leonard, Barry, ed.** Guide to Investigating Child Abuse. (Illus.). 56p. (C). 1999. reprint ed. pap. text 20.00 (*0-7881-7521-1*) DIANE Pub.

Leonard, Barry, ed. A Guide to the Preservation of Federal Judges' Papers. 83p. (C). 1998. pap. text 25.00 (*0-7881-7020-1*) DIANE Pub.

***Leonard, Barry, ed.** Guidelines for Developmental Risk Toxicity: Risk Assessment Forum. 118p. 2000. reprint ed. pap. text 30.00 (*0-7881-8417-2*) DIANE Pub.

— Handbook on Child Support Enforcement. 51p. (C). 1999. reprint ed. pap. text 15.00 (*0-7881-8218-8*) DIANE Pub.

Leonard, Barry, ed. High School/High Tech: Establishing a Program to Promote Science, Engineering, & Technology Careers for Students with Disabilities. 67p. (C). 1998. reprint ed. pap. text 20.00 (*0-7881-7441-X*) DIANE Pub.

***Leonard, Barry, ed.** Highway Special Investigation Report: Selective Motorcoach Issues. (Illus.). 57p. 2000. pap. text 20.00 (*0-7567-0045-0*) DIANE Pub.

Leonard, Barry, ed. Hints to Exporters Visiting Brazil. (Illus.). 120p. 1999. pap. text 30.00 (*0-7881-8035-5*) DIANE Pub.

— Hints to Exporters Visiting Mexico. (Illus.). 96p. 1999. pap. text 25.00 (*0-7881-8036-3*) DIANE Pub.

***Leonard, Barry, ed.** HIV Disease in Correctional Facilities: Report of the National Commission on AIDS, 1991. 43p. (C). 1999. reprint ed. pap. text 20.00 (*0-7881-8323-0*) DIANE Pub.

Leonard, Barry, ed. Hungary: Country Commercial Guide, Fiscal Year 1998. 74p. (C). 1999. pap. text 25.00 (*0-7881-3978-9*) DIANE Pub.

— I Have Diabetes - How Much Should I Eat? What Should I Eat? When Should I Eat? (Illus.). 68p. 1998. pap. text 20.00 (*0-7881-8055-X*) DIANE Pub.

***Leonard, Barry, ed.** Importing into the United States: A Guide for Commercial Importers. rev. ed. 110p. 1999. pap. text 25.00 (*0-7881-8069-X*) DIANE Pub.

— Improving America's Schools Act of 1994. 544p. 1999. reprint ed. pap. text 50.00 (*0-7881-7003-1*) DIANE Pub.

— Info War Con: Electronic Civil Defense for the 21st Century-Proceedings. (Illus.). 200p. (C). 1999. reprint ed. pap. text 50.00 (*0-7881-8228-5*) DIANE Pub.

— Infrastructure of Home & Community Based Services for the Functionally Impaired Elderly: State Source Book. (Illus.). 140p. 2000. reprint ed. pap. text 25.00 (*0-7881-8711-2*) DIANE Pub.

— Intergovernmental Conference 1996: Commission Report for the Reflection Group. (Illus.). 100p. 2000. reprint ed. pap. text 25.00 (*0-7881-4289-5*) DIANE Pub.

— Investigation of Human Factors in Accidents & Incidents (Involving Aviation) (Illus.). 57p. 2000. reprint ed. pap. text 20.00 (*0-7881-8702-3*) DIANE Pub.

Leonard, Barry, ed. An Investigation of the Safety Implications of Wireless Communications in Vehicles. (Illus.). 274p. (C). 1999. reprint ed. pap. text 35.00 (*0-7881-7749-4*) DIANE Pub.

***Leonard, Barry, ed.** Investing in Partnerships for Student Success: A Basic Tool for Community Stakeholders to GuideEducational Partnership Development & Management. (Illus.). 70p. 2000. pap. text 25.00 (*0-7881-8469-5*) DIANE Pub.

— Irish Fairy Tales: Fairy Legends & Traditions. (Illus.). 311p. 1999. reprint ed. pap. text 20.00 (*0-7881-6802-9*) DIANE Pub.

Leonard, Barry, ed. Jazz Fake Book: The Official Red Book: More Than 200 Favorite Traditional Jazz Songs. (Illus.). 230p. 1998. pap. text 35.00 (*0-7881-7460-6*) DIANE Pub.

— Kennedy Assassination: Surveillance of Civil Rights Activists. 321p. 1998. pap. text 50.00 (*0-7881-7359-6*) DIANE Pub.

***Leonard, Barry, ed.** Key Officers of Foreign Service Posts: Guide for Business Representatives (1998) 151p. 1999. pap. text 25.00 (*0-7881-8229-3*) DIANE Pub.

— Land Application of Sewage Sludge: A Guide for Land Appliers on the Requirements of the Federal Standards for the Use or Disposal of Sewage Sludge, 40 CFR, Part 503. (Illus.). 107p. (C). 2000. pap. text 30.00 (*0-7881-8710-4*) DIANE Pub.

Leonard, Barry, ed. Land Areas of the National Forest System. (Illus.). 126p. 1998. pap. text 25.00 (*0-7881-1677-0*) DIANE Pub.

— Leukemia: A Research Report. 2nd ed. 63p. (C). 1998. pap. text 15.00 (*0-7881-7189-5*) DIANE Pub.

— Library Resources for the Blind & Physically Handicapped: A Directory with FY 1996 Statistics on Readership, Circulation, Budget, Staff, & Collections. (Illus.). 96p. (C). 1998. pap. text 20.00 (*0-7881-7437-1*) DIANE Pub.

— Local Government Network Regional Workshop Meeting Summary. (Illus.). 71p. 1998. pap. text 20.00 (*0-7881-7022-8*) DIANE Pub.

***Leonard, Barry, ed.** The Madonna: An Anthology of Verse & Prose. (Illus.). 64p. 1999. text 20.00 (*0-7881-6567-4*) DIANE Pub.

— Mandatory Purchase of Flood Insurance Guidelines. (Illus.). 150p. (C). 1999. reprint ed. pap. text 25.00 (*0-7881-7866-0*) DIANE Pub.

— MANTECH Project Book (1995) (Illus.). 120p. (C). 1999. reprint ed. pap. text 50.00 (*0-7881-2667-9*) DIANE Pub.

Leonard, Barry, ed. Manual for Courts-Martial United States. 800p. (C). 1999. pap. text 95.00 (*0-7881-7756-7*) DIANE Pub.

— Memorandum on ICAO: The Story of the International Civil Aviation Organization. (Illus.). 61p. 1998. reprint ed. pap. text 20.00 (*0-7881-2780-2*) DIANE Pub.

***Leonard, Barry, ed.** Metropolitan Area Exports: An Export Performance Report on over 250 U.S. Cities, 1993-1998. (Illus.). 96p. (C). 2000. pap. text 25.00 (*0-7567-0010-8*) DIANE Pub.

— Military Operations in Low Intensity Conflict. 150p. 1999. reprint ed. pap. text 35.00 (*0-7881-7894-6*) DIANE Pub.

Leonard, Barry, ed. Minnesota Public Health Goals, 1995. (Illus.). 185p. 1998. pap. text 35.00 (*0-7881-7186-0*) DIANE Pub.

— The National Dam Safety Program Act: Implementation Plan. (Illus.). 46p. (C). 1999. text 20.00 (*0-7881-7924-1*) DIANE Pub.

— National Laboratories & Public Research Organizations in Japan. (Illus.). 264p. (C). 1998. pap. text 50.00 (*0-7881-7369-3*) DIANE Pub.

— National Listing of Medicare Providers Furnishing Kidney Dialysis & Transplant Services. 234p. 1999. pap. text 30.00 (*0-7881-7566-1*) DIANE Pub.

— Navy Song Book. (Illus.). 216p. 1998. reprint ed. pap. text 25.00 (*0-7881-7468-1*) DIANE Pub.

***Leonard, Barry, ed.** Nicotine in Cigarettes & Smokeless Tobacco Products Is a Drug & These Products Are Nicotine Delivery Devices & under the Federal Food, Drug & Cosmetic Act - Appendices. 313p. (C). 1999. reprint ed. pap. text 60.00 (*0-7881-8222-6*) DIANE Pub.

Leonard, Barry, ed. Opportunities to Improve Air Quality Through Transportation Pricing Programs. (Illus.). 130p. (C). 1998. pap. text 25.00 (*0-7881-3943-6*) DIANE Pub.

***Leonard, Barry, ed.** Oscar Wilde: Trial & Punishment, 1895-1897. (Illus.). 52p. 1999. pap. text 25.00 (*0-7881-8126-2*) DIANE Pub.

— Overseas Employment Opportunities for Educators: Department of Defense Dependents Schools. (Illus.). 44p. 1999. pap. text 20.00 (*0-7881-8075-4*) DIANE Pub.

— Passing on Failure: District Promotion Practices & Policies. 58p. (C). 1999. reprint ed. pap. text 20.00 (*0-7881-7998-5*) DIANE Pub.

— Personal Watercraft Safety. (Illus.). 98p. 2000. reprint ed. pap. text 25.00 (*0-7881-8870-4*) DIANE Pub.

— Plan Letters: Managing Correspondence: A Records Management Handbook. (Illus.). 51p. 2000. reprint ed. pap. 20.00 (*0-7881-8934-4*) DIANE Pub.

Leonard, Barry, ed. Poland: Country Commercial Guide, 1998. (Illus.). 88p. (C). 1999. pap. text 25.00 (*0-7881-7564-5*) DIANE Pub.

— Precursors & Chemicals Frequently Used in the Illicit Manufacture of Narcotic Drugs & Psychotropic Substances. (Illus.). 89p. (C). 1998. pap. text 25.00 (*0-7881-7394-4*) DIANE Pub.

***Leonard, Barry, ed.** Privitization Potential of Mississippi's State Programs & Services. 79p. 2000. reprint ed. pap. text 20.00 (*0-7881-4486-3*) DIANE Pub.

— Public/Private Partnerships: Implications for Innovation in Transportation. 52p. (C). 2000. reprint ed. pap. text 20.00 (*0-7881-8692-2*) DIANE Pub.

Leonard, Barry, ed. Recent Changes in Health Care Law: Questions & Answers. 66p. 1999. reprint ed. pap. text 20.00 (*0-7881-8004-5*) DIANE Pub.

***Leonard, Barry, ed.** Recommended National Procedures & Out-of-Service Criteria for the Enhanced Safety Inspection of Commercial Highway Vehicles Transporting Transuranics, Spent Nuclear Fuel & High-Level Radioactive Waste. 110p. (C). 1999. reprint ed. pap. text 40.00 (*0-7881-4552-5*) DIANE Pub.

— Report on United States Barriers to Trade & Investment 1997. 50p. 1999. reprint ed. pap. text 20.00 (*0-7881-8131-9*) DIANE Pub.

— Report on United States Barriers to Trade & Investment, 1999. (Illus.), 63p. (C). 2000. pap. text 20.00 (*0-7881-8856-9*) DIANE Pub.

Leonard, Barry, ed. Research & Development in Industry, 1997: Funds, 1997; Scientists & Engineers, January 1998. (Illus.). 200p. (C). 1999. pap. text 35.00 (*0-7881-7752-4*) DIANE Pub.

***Leonard, Barry, ed.** Review of Gender Equity in Interscholastic Athletic Opportunities in Minnesota's Secondary Schools. (Illus.). 100p. (C). 1999. pap. text 20.00 (*0-7881-8225-0*) DIANE Pub.

Leonard, Barry, ed. Risk Management of Financial Derivatives: Comptroller's Handbook. 190p. 1999. reprint ed. pap. text 40.00 (*0-7881-8020-7*) DIANE Pub.

— The River Law in Japan. 69p. (C). 1999. pap. text 20.00 (*0-7881-7676-5*) DIANE Pub.

***Leonard, Barry, ed.** The Rural Fire Problem in the United States. (Illus.). 55p. (C). 1999. pap. text 20.00 (*0-7881-8335-4*) DIANE Pub.

Leonard, Barry, ed. Seals & Other Devices in Use at the Government Printing Office. (Illus.). 70p. (C). 1999. reprint ed. pap. text 20.00 (*0-7881-7710-9*) DIANE Pub.

— Seismicity Catalog: Data for Four Million Earthquakes, 2100 B. C. to 1996 A. D., 2 vols. (C). 1998. pap. 225.00 incl. cd-rom (*0-7881-3874-X*) DIANE Pub.

***Leonard, Barry, ed.** Sexual Harassment in the Workplace (Law Enforcement) Guidelines & Curriculum 1994. 85p. (C). 1999. reprint ed. pap. text 20.00 (*0-7881-8197-1*) DIANE Pub.

Leonard, Barry, ed. Social Security Handbook, 1997. 13th ed. 570p. (C). 1999. pap. text 50.00 (*0-7881-7675-7*) DIANE Pub.

***Leonard, Barry, ed.** Soil Survey Manual. rev. ed. (Illus.). 437p. 2000. text 60.00 (*0-7881-8799-6*) DIANE Pub.

Leonard, Barry, ed. Space Cooperation: Memorandum of Understanding Between the United States of America & the European Space Agency, Signed at Washington November 30, 1989. 73p. (C). 1999. reprint ed. pap. text 20.00 (*0-7881-7610-2*) DIANE Pub.

— Special Early Childhood Report, 1997: National Education Goals Report - Goal 1. (Illus.). 39p. 1998. pap. text 20.00 (*0-7881-7024-4*) DIANE Pub.

— Standards for the Use & Disposal of Sewage Sludge. 69p. (C). 1999. reprint ed. pap. text 20.00 (*0-7881-7910-1*) DIANE Pub.

— State of Idaho Guidelines for Coordinating Action on Child Abuse Problems. (Illus.). 113p. 1998. pap. text 30.00 (*0-7881-7017-1*) DIANE Pub.

***Leonard, Barry, ed.** Strengthening the Circle: Child Support for Native American Children. (Illus.). 57p. (C). 2000. reprint ed. pap. text 20.00 (*0-7881-8990-5*) DIANE Pub.

Leonard, Barry, ed. Study on Emergency Stockpiles. 2nd ed. 51p. (C). 1996. pap. 20.00 (*0-7881-7413-4*) DIANE Pub.

— Subsistence Management Regulations for the Harvest of Fish & Wildlife on Federal Public Lands in Alaska. (Illus.). 178p. (C). 1999. pap. text 30.00 (*0-7881-7681-1*) DIANE Pub.

— Sustainable Agriculture in Print: Current Books, 1997. 126p. (C). 1998. pap. text 25.00 (*0-7881-7495-9*) DIANE Pub.

***Leonard, Barry, ed.** Teaching Human Rights: Practical Activities for Primary & Secondary Schools. 56p. 2000. reprint ed. pap. text 20.00 (*0-7881-8575-6*) DIANE Pub.

Leonard, Barry, ed. Telematics for Flexible & Distance Learning: 1994 Delta Catalogue. (Illus.). 62p. (C). 1998. reprint ed. pap. text 20.00 (*0-7881-7445-2*) DIANE Pub.

— U. S. Army Field Manual 100-5: Fighting Future Wars. (Illus.). 280p. 1999. reprint ed. pap. text 22.00 (*0-7881-6092-3*) DIANE Pub.

***Leonard, Barry, ed.** The Unfolding World of Mysterious Places. (Illus.). 49p. 1999. reprint ed. pap. text 6.00 (*0-7881-6410-4*) DIANE Pub.

— Using Data to Assess HIV/AIDS Service Needs: A Guide for Ryan White/Care Act Planning Groups. (Illus.). 106p. (C). 2000. pap. text 25.00 (*0-7881-8784-8*) DIANE Pub.

— Voices from the Landscape: "Living in the Landscape," a Flathead Community Celebration. (Illus.). 95p. 2000. pap. text 20.00 (*0-7881-8676-0*) DIANE Pub.

— Webster's Concise Biographical Dictionary. 372p. 1999. reprint ed. 20.00 (*0-7881-6335-3*) DIANE Pub.

— Webster's Dictionary of American Women. rev. ed. (Illus.). 696p. 1999. text 25.00 (*0-7881-6333-7*) DIANE Pub.

— Webster's New Business Writers Guide. 440p. 1999. reprint ed. text 20.00 (*0-7881-6334-5*) DIANE Pub.

Leonard, Barry, ed. Welcome to Washington: A Guide to the Capital. (Illus.). 46p. 1998. pap. text 15.00 (*0-7881-7462-2*) DIANE Pub.

***Leonard, Barry, ed.** What You Should Know about Your Pension Rights. 48p. 2000. reprint ed. pap. text 15.00 (*0-7881-8780-5*) DIANE Pub.

Leonard, Barry, ed. Youth Violence in America: Recommendations from the IACP Summit. (Illus.). 46p. (C). 1998. pap. text 15.00 (*0-7881-7427-4*) DIANE Pub.

Leonard, Barry, ed. see Diane Publishing Staff.

Leonard, Barry, ed. see Gaskill, Stephen.

Leonard-Barton. Wellspring of Knowlege. 288p. 1995. 29.95 (*0-07-103640-7*) McGraw.

Leonard-Barton, Dorothy. Wellsprings of Knowledge: Building & Sustaining the Sources of Innovation. LC 95-14582. 352p. 1995. 29.95 (*0-87584-612-2*) Harvard Busn.

Leonard, Bernardo & Golenbock, Peter. The Superstar Hitter's Bible. LC 97-40103. (Illus.). 128p. 1997. pap. 12.95 (*0-8092-3000-3*, 300030, Contemporary Bks) NTC Contemp Pub Co.

Leonard, Beth A. Following Seas: Sailing the Globe, Sounding a Life. LC 98-61719. (Illus.). 272p. 1999. 29.95 (*1-55949-369-0*); pap. 19.95 (*1-55949-370-4*) Tide-Mark.

— Voyager's Handbook: The Essential Guide To Blue Water Cruising. LC 97-23130. (Illus.). 448p. 1998. 34.95 (*0-07-038143-7*) McGraw.

***Leonard, Bill J.** Dictionary of Baptists in America. 320p. 1998. pap. 18.00 (*1-57312-255-6*) Smyth & Helwys.

— La Naturaleza de la Iglesia. Clark, Stanley, Jr., tr. from ENG.Tr. of Nature of the Church. (SPA.). 156p. 1989. pap. 6.75 (*0-311-09122-9*) Casa Bautista.

Leonard, Bill J. Risk the Journey: Answering God's Call to Proclaim His Word. Edwards, Judith, ed. 130p. 1995. pap. text 4.95 (*1-56309-122-4*, W953102) Womans Mission Union.

— Word of God Across the Ages: Using Christian History in Preaching. enl. ed. 110p. 1993. reprint ed. pap. text 10.00 (*0-9628455-5-8*) Smyth & Helwys.

Leonard, Bill J., ed. Christianity in Appalachia: Profiles in Regional Pluralism. LC 98-40115. (Illus.). 360p. 1999. pap. text 17.50 (*1-57233-040-6*) U of Tenn Pr.

— Christianity in Appalachia: Profiles in Regional Plurlism. LC 98-40115. (Illus.). 360p. 1999. text 35.00 (*1-57233-039-2*) U of Tenn Pr.

Leonard, Bill J., jt. ed. see Shriver, George H.

Leonard, Brian. Fundamentals of Psychopharmacology. LC 96-49182. 408p. 1997. pap. 59.95 (*0-471-96115-9*) Wiley.

Leonard, Brian E. & Miller, Klara, eds. Stress, the Immune System & Psychiatry. LC 94-30641. 252p. 1995. 175.00 (*0-471-95258-3*) Wiley.

Leonard, Buck. Buck Leonard: In His Own Words. 1976. 30.95 (*0-8488-1544-0*) Amereon Ltd.

Leonard, Buck, jt. auth. see Riley, James A.

Leonard, Calista V. Guess Who. 36p. (J). (ps-6). 1992. lib. bdg. write for info. (*0-9634165-0-2*) Vistoso Bks.

Leonard, Carol S. Reform & Regicide: The Reign of Peter III of Russia. LC 92-5176. (Indiana-Michigan Series in Russian & East European Studies). 244p. 1993. 35.00 (*0-253-33322-9*) Ind U Pr.

Leonard, Carolyn, ed. see Waugh, Meredith.

Leonard, Charles, jt. auth. see Warner, David.

Leonard, Charles R., jt. auth. see Bruce, Roy W.

Leonard, Charlotte. Tied Together: Topics & Thoughts for Introducing Children's Books. LC 80-11135. 261p. 1980. lib. bdg. 31.00 (*0-8108-1293-2*) Scarecrow.

***Leonard, Christine J.** Charter Schools: Professional Guide. (Illus.). 1999. pap. 9.95 (*1-57690-479-2*) Tchr Create Mat.

***Leonard, Christopher.** MCSE Database Design on SQL Server 7 Exam Prep. LC 99-42704. (Exam Prep Ser.). 1999. pap. 44.99 (*1-57610-519-9*) Coriolis Grp.

Leonard Clayton Gallery Staff, jt. auth. see Royal Cortissoz.

Leonard, Curtis & Kappele, William. Contemporary Wire Wrapped Jewelry. LC 95-75187. (Illus.). 144p. (Orig.). 1995. pap. text 15.95 (*0-935182-71-3*) Gem Guides Bk.

Leonard, Cynthia M., compiled by. The General Assembly of Virginia, July 30, 1619-January 11, 1978: A Bicentennial Register of Members. xxxi, 884p. 1978. 29.95 (*0-88490-008-8*) Library of VA.

Leonard, Daniel. Massachusettensis. LC 72-10246. (American Revolutionary Ser.). 1979. reprint ed. lib. bdg. 22.50 (*0-8398-1180-2*) Irvington.

Leonard, Daniel & Long, Ngo V. Optimal Control Theory & Static Optimization in Economics. (Illus.). 365p. (C). 1992. text 85.00 (*0-521-33158-7*); pap. text 39.95 (*0-521-33746-1*) Cambridge U Pr.

Leonard, David C. & Dillon, Patrick M. Multimedia & the Web from A to Z. 2nd enl. rev. ed. LC 98-34083. 384p. 1998. pap. 39.95 (*1-57356-132-0*) Oryx Pr.

Leonard, David K. African Successes: Four Public Managers of Kenyan Rural Development. LC 90-11089. (Illus.). 390p. 1991. 60.00 (*0-520-07075-5*, Pub. by U CA Pr); pap. 22.50 (*0-520-07076-3*, Pub. by U CA Pr) Cal Prin Full Svc.

***Leonard, David K.** Africa's Changing Markets for Health & Veterinary Services. LC 99-88269. 2000. pap. 25.00 (*0-312-23267-5*); text 79.95 (*0-312-23266-7*) St Martin.

Leonard, David K. Reaching the Peasant Farmer: Organization Theory & Practice in Kenya. LC 77-1823. xxii, 298p. 1994. pap. text 17.00 (*0-226-47261-2*) U Ch Pr.

Leonard, David P. New Wigmore. 5th ed. LC 95-77279. 986p. 1995. 155.00 (*0-316-26232-3*) Little.

Leonard, David W. Delayed Frontier: The Peace River Country to 1909. LC 96-134985. (Illus.). 256p. 1995. pap. write for info. (*1-55059-111-8*) Detselig Ents.

Leonard, Deni. Contemporary Indigenous Issues: Economic Sovereignty. LC 96-96571. (C). 1996. text. write for info. (*0-9653383-2-0*); pap. text. write for info. (*0-9653383-3-9*) DLA Finan.

— Contemporary Indigenous Issues: Public Policy. LC 96-96571. (C). 1996. text. write for info. (*0-9653383-0-4*); pap. text. write for info. (*0-9653383-1-2*) DLA Finan.

Leonard, Dennis. Overcoming Depression. 1991. pap. 4.95 (*1-880809-01-X*) D Leonard Pubns.

— You Can Forgive Yourself: If God Can Forgive You...You Can Forgive Yourself. 1991. pap. 4.95 (*1-880809-00-1*) D Leonard Pubns.

Leonard, Diana & Allen, Sheila. Dependence & Exploitation in Work & Marriage. LC 75-43517. 265 p. 1976. 16.00 (*0-582-48673-4*) Addison-Wesley.

Leonard, Diana, jt. auth. see Delphy, Christine.

Leonard, Diana, jt. ed. see Adkins, Lisa.

Leonard, Don, jt. auth. see Waters, Max L.

Leonard, Donald, et al. Readings & Materials for Managerial Communication. 315p. (C). 1991. pap. text 52.00 (*0-536-57984-9*) Pearson Custom.

Leonard, Donald E. A Pragmatic Guide to Advertising. 336p. (C). 1992. pap. text, per. 37.95 (*0-8403-7429-1*) Kendall-Hunt.

— A Pragmatic Guide to Consumer Behavior. 308p. 1993. per. 34.95 (*0-8403-8256-1*) Kendall-Hunt.

— A Pragmatic Guide to Marketing. 272p. (C). 1990. per. 32.95 (*0-8403-6371-0*) Kendall-Hunt.

Leonard, Donald J., jt. auth. see Smeltzer, Larry R.

Leonard, Donald J., jt. ed. see Holland, G. Pepper.

Leonard, Dorothy. Wellsprings of Knowledge. 352p. 1998. pap. 16.95 (*0-87584-859-1*) Harvard Busn.

Leonard, Dorothy & Swap, Walter C. When Sparks Fly: Igniting Creativity in Groups. LC 99-20608. 224p. 1999. 24.95 (*0-87584-865-6*) Harvard Busn.

Leonard, E. WordPerfect 6.0 for Windows. 156p. 1994. pap. 59.95 (*1-85805-097-9*, Pub. by DP Publns) St Mut.

L

An Asterisk (*) at the beginning of an entry indicates that the title is appearing for the first time.

Leonard, E. Bruce & Besant, Christopher W., eds. Current Issues in Cross-Border Insolvency & Reorganizations. LC 94-7617. (International Bar Association Ser.). 432p. (C). 1994. lib. bdg. 123.00 (*1-85333-958-X*, Pub. by Graham & Trotman) Kluwer Academic.

Leonard, E. G. Histoire Universelle: De la Reforme a nos Jours, Vol. 3. 2340p. write for info. (*0-318-52027-3*) Fr & Eur.

— Histoire Universelle, Vol. 3: De la Reforme a Nos Jours. (FRE.). 1340p. 1958. 135.00 (*0-7859-4547-4*) Fr & Eur.

Leonard, E. G., jt. auth. see Grousset, R.

Leonard, Edmund A. Packaging: Specifications, Purchasing, & Quality Control. 4th ed. (Packaging & Converting Technology Ser.: Vol. 7). (Illus.). 304p. 1996. text 95.00 (*0-8247-9755-8*) Dekker.

Leonard, Edson. Feather in the Breeze. (Illus.). 1974. 7.95 (*0-88395-026-X*) Freshet Pr.

Leonard, Edwin, jt. auth. see Hilgert, Raymond.

Leonard, Edwin C., jt. auth. see Hilgert, Raymond L.

Leonard, Eileen B., et al, eds. In Search of Community: Essays in Memory of Werner Stark, 1905-1985. LC 91-30219. vi, 256p. 1993. 40.00 (*0-8232-1352-8*) Fordham.

Leonard, Eliot. Operating a Bookstore: Practical Details for Improving Profit. 120p. (Orig.). 1992. pap. 12.95 (*1-879923-04-1*) Booksellers Pub.

Leonard, Elisabeth A., ed. Into Darkness Peering: Race & Color in the Fantastic, 74. LC 97-5596. (Contributions to the Study of Science Fiction & Fantasy: Vol. 74). 208p. 1997. 57.95 (*0-313-30042-9*, Greenwood Pr) Greenwood.

Leonard, Elizabeth. Painting Flowers. (Illus.). 144p. 1991. pap. 18.95 (*0-8230-3630-8*) Watsn-Guptill.

Leonard, Elizabeth D. All the Daring of the Soldier: Women of the Civil War Armies. LC 98-52304. (Illus.). 320p. 1999. text 27.95 (*0-393-04712-1*) Norton.

— Yankee Women: Gender Battles in the Civil War. (Illus.). 336p. 1995. pap. 13.95 (*0-393-31372-7*, Norton Paperbks) Norton.

Leonard, Elizabeth L. Friendly Rebel: A Personal & Social History of Eduard C. Lindeman. LC 91-31364. 1991. 25.00 (*0-912362-11-1*) Adamant Pr.

Leonard, Ellen. Unresting Transformation: The Theology & Spirituality of Maude Petre. 256p. (Orig.). (C). 1991. pap. text 29.00 (*0-8191-8221-4*); lib. bdg. 51.00 (*0-8191-8220-6*) U Pr of Amer.

Leonard, Ellen M. Creative Tension: The Spiritual Legacy of Friedrich Von Hugel. LC 97-17784. 1997. 24.95 (*0-940866-66-8*); pap. 18.95 (*0-940866-67-6*) U Scranton Pr.

Leonard, Elmore. Bandits. LC 99-206318. 352p. 1999. pap. 12.00 (*0-688-16639-3*, Quil) HarperTrade.

— Bandits. 384p. 1988. mass mkt. 5.99 (*0-446-30130-2*, Mysterious Paperbk) Warner Bks.

— Be Cool. LC 98-36601. 304p. 1999. 24.95 (*0-385-33391-9*) Delacorte.

***Leonard, Elmore.** Be Cool. 1999. mass mkt. 7.99 (*0-440-29577-7*) Dell.

— Be Cool. 368p. 2000. mass mkt. 7.50 (*0-440-23505-7*) Dell.

Leonard, Elmore. Be Cool. large type ed. LC 99-10429. 1999. lib. bdg. 30.00 (*0-7862-1838-X*) Thorndike Pr.

— Be Cool. large type ed. LC 99-10429. (Paperback Bestsellers Ser.). 383p. 2000. pap. 27.95 (*0-7862-1839-8*) Thorndike Pr.

— The Big Bounce. 256p. 2000. mass mkt. 6.99 (*0-440-23611-8*) Dell.

— La Brava. 256p. 1984. mass mkt. 4.99 (*0-380-69237-6*, Avon Bks) Morrow Avon.

— Cat Chaser. LC 98-41166. 288p. 1998. pap. 12.00 (*0-688-16341-6*, Quil) HarperTrade.

— Cat Chaser. 288p. 1983. mass mkt. 6.50 (*0-380-64642-0*, Avon Bks) Morrow Avon.

— City Primeval: High Noon in Detroit. 224p. 1982. mass mkt. 6.50 (*0-380-56952-3*, Avon Bks) Morrow Avon.

***Leonard, Elmore.** City Primeval: High Noon in Detroit. LC 99-26538. 288p. 1999. reprint ed. pap. 12.00 (*0-688-16970-8*, Wm Morrow) Morrow Avon.

— Cuba Libre. 352p. 2000. reprint ed. pap. 9.95 (*0-385-32384-0*, Delta Trade) Dell.

— Cuba Libre: A Novel. LC 97-24541. 352p. (YA). 1998. 23.95 (*0-385-32383-2*) Delacorte.

Leonard, Elmore. Cuba Libre: A Novel. 416p. 1999. mass mkt. 7.50 (*0-440-22559-0*) Dell.

— Cuba Libre: A Novel. large type ed. LC 98-26431. (Wheeler Large Print Book Ser.). 1998. 27.95 (*1-56895-600-2*) Wheeler Pub.

— Elmore Leonard: Three Complete Novels. 688p. 1992. 10.99 (*0-517-06492-8*) Random Hse Value.

— Elmore Leonard's Western Roundup #1: Valdez in Coming & Hombre, Vol. 1. LC 98-23509. 512p. 1998. pap. 12.95 (*0-385-33322-6*) Dell.

— Elmore Leonard's Western Roundup #2: Valdez in Coming & Hombre. LC 98-26094. 496p. 1998. pap. 12.95 (*0-385-33323-4*) Dell.

— Elmore Leonard's Western Roundup #3: Valdez in Coming & Hombre. LC 98-27963. 304p. 1998. pap. 12.95 (*0-385-33324-2*) Dell.

— Freaky Deaky. LC 98-13560. 352p. 1998. pap. 12.00 (*0-688-16096-4*, Quil) HarperTrade.

— Freaky Deaky. 1989. mass mkt. 5.95 (*0-446-35039-7*, Pub. by Warner Bks) Little.

— Get Shorty. 384p. 1991. mass mkt. 6.99 (*0-440-20980-3*) Dell.

— Get Shorty. 304p. 1998. pap. 9.95 (*0-385-32398-0*) Dell.

***Leonard, Elmore.** Get Shorty. 368p. 2000. mass mkt. 4.99 (*0-440-23614-2*) Dell.

Leonard, Elmore. Get Shorty. large type ed. LC 93-1992. 1993. pap. 18.95 (*0-8161-5809-6*, G K Hall Lrg Type) Mac Lib Ref.

— Glitz. 1986. mass mkt. 3.95 (*0-446-32920-7*, Pub. by Warner Bks) Little.

— Glitz. 368p. 1987. mass mkt. 6.99 (*0-446-34343-9*) Warner Bks.

— Glitz: A Novel. LC 98-14730. 256p. 1998. pap. 9.95 (*0-688-16095-6*, Quil) HarperTrade.

— Gold Coast. 224p. 1990. mass mkt. 6.99 (*0-440-20832-7*) Dell.

Leonard, Elmore. Hombre. 1980. mass mkt. 1.75 (*0-345-28850-5*) Ballantine Pub Grp.

— Hombre. 1984. mass mkt. 2.25 (*0-345-31606-1*) Ballantine Pub Grp.

Leonard, Elmore. Killshot. LC 99-201114. 288p. 1999. pap. 12.00 (*0-688-16638-5*, Quil) HarperTrade.

— Killshot. 352p. 1990. reprint ed. mass mkt. 5.95 (*0-446-35041-9*) Warner Bks.

— Labrava. LC 98-13559. 288p. 1998. pap. 9.95 (*0-688-16097-2*, Wm Morrow) Morrow Avon.

— Last Stand at Saber River. 1994. reprint ed. lib. bdg. 29.95 (*1-56849-301-0*) Buccaneer Bks.

— Maximum Bob. 352p. 1992. mass mkt. 6.99 (*0-440-21218-9*) Dell.

— Maximum Bob. 304p. 1998. pap. 9.95 (*0-385-32396-4*, Delta Trade) Dell.

— Mr. Majestyk. 224p. 2000. mass mkt. 6.99 (*0-440-23610-X*) Dell.

— Mr. Majestyk. 192p. 1986. mass mkt. 5.99 (*0-445-40228-8*, Mysterious Paperbk) Warner Bks.

— The Moonshine War. 224p. 1985. mass mkt. 6.99 (*0-440-15807-9*) Dell.

— Notebooks. limited ed. 60p. 1990. 50.00 (*0-935716-52-1*) Lord John.

— Out of Sight. 352p. 1997. mass mkt. 6.99 (*0-440-21442-4*) Dell.

— Out of Sight. 304p. 1998. pap. 9.95 (*0-385-33291-2*, 892924Q, Delta Trade) Dell.

— Out of Sight. large type ed. LC 96-44356. 1996. 26.95 (*1-56895-385-2*) Wheeler Pub.

— Out of Sight: International Edition. 1997. mass mkt. 6.50 (*0-440-29553-X*) Dell.

***Leonard, Elmore.** Pagan Babies. 224p. 2000. 24.95 (*0-385-33392-7*) Delacorte.

— Pagan Babies. large type ed. 2000. 24.95 (*0-375-43086-5*) Random Hse Lrg Prnt.

Leonard, Elmore. Pronto. 272p. 1998. pap. 9.95 (*0-385-33290-4*) Doubleday.

— Riding the Rap. 336p. 1995. mass mkt. 6.50 (*0-440-29539-4*) Dell.

— Riding the Rap. 304p. 1998. pap. 9.95 (*0-385-32417-0*, Delta Trade) Dell.

— Riding the Rap. large type ed. LC 95-10890. (Large Print Bks.). 1995. 26.95 (*1-56895-224-4*) Wheeler Pub.

— Rum Punch. 304p. 1998. pap. 9.95 (*0-385-33280-7*) Doubleday.

— Rum Punch. large type ed. LC 93-35521. (General Ser.). 376p. 1994. pap. 18.95 (*0-8161-5807-X*, G K Hall Lrg Type) Mac Lib Ref.

— Split Images. 288p. 1983. mass mkt. 6.50 (*0-380-63107-5*, Avon Bks) Morrow Avon.

***Leonard, Elmore.** Split Images: A Novel. LC 99-23233. 288p. 1999. reprint ed. pap. 12.00 (*0-688-16971-6*, Wm Morrow) Morrow Avon.

Leonard, Elmore. Stick. 304p. 1984. mass mkt. 6.50 (*0-380-67652-4*, Avon Bks) Morrow Avon.

— Stick. LC 98-41165. 304p. 1998. pap. 12.00 (*0-688-16340-8*, Wm Morrow) Morrow Avon.

— Swag. 240p. 1978. mass mkt. 6.99 (*0-440-18424-X*) Dell.

***Leonard, Elmore.** Swag. large type ed. LC 00-38335. 308p. 2000. lib. bdg. 28.95 (*1-58547-041-4*) Ctr Point Pubg.

Leonard, Elmore. The Switch. 224p. 1990. mass mkt. 6.99 (*0-440-20831-9*) Dell.

— The Switch. large type ed. LC 93-24852. 258p. 1993. pap. 17.95 (*0-8161-5653-0*, G K Hall Lrg Type) Mac Lib Ref.

— The Tonto Woman & Other Western Stories. LC 98-21566. 352p. 1998. 23.95 (*0-385-32386-7*); pap. 12.95 (*0-385-32387-5*) Dell.

***Leonard, Elmore.** Touch. LC 99-53349. 256p. 2000. pap. 12.00 (*0-688-17572-4*, Quil) HarperTrade.

Leonard, Elmore. Touch. 240p. 1988. mass mkt. 6.50 (*0-380-70386-6*, Avon Bks) Morrow Avon.

— Unknown Man, No. 89. 272p. 1984. mass mkt. 6.50 (*0-380-67041-0*, Avon Bks) Morrow Avon.

— Unknown Man: No. 89, No. 89. large type ed. LC 92-35897. (General Ser.). 379p. 1993. pap. 17.95 (*0-8161-5696-4*, G K Hall Lrg Type) Mac Lib Ref.

— Valdez Is Coming. 1993. reprint ed. lib. bdg. 21.95 (*1-56849-176-X*) Buccaneer Bks.

Leonard, Elmore, et al. Western Movies. 256p. 25.00 (*0-7278-5207-8*) Severn Hse.

Leonard, Elmore, jt. auth. see Tarantino, Quentin.

Leonard, Eugenie. Concerning Our Girls & What They Tell Us: A Study of Some Phases of the Confidential Relationship of Mothers & Adolescent Daughters. LC 75-176986. (Columbia University. Teachers College. Contributions to Education Ser.: No. 430). reprint ed. 37.50 (*0-404-55430-X*) AMS Pr.

Leonard, F. Quotationary. LC 98-30433. (Random House Business Division Ser.). 800p. 1998. 45.00 (*0-679-44850-0*) Random Ref & Info.

Leonard, Fannie A., jt. auth. see Leonard, Justin W.

Leonard, Frances. Money & the Mature Woman: How to Hold on to Your Income, Keep Your Home, Plan Your Estate. LC 92-34822. 1993. 19.95 (*0-201-60897-9*) Addison-Wesley.

— Time Is Money: A Million-Dollar Investment Plan for Today's Twenty & Thirty-Somethings. LC 95-17911. 1995. pap. 12.00 (*0-201-40962-3*) Addison-Wesley.

Leonard, Frances M. Laughter in the Courts of Love: Comedy in Allegory, from Chaucer to Spencer. LC 81-10676. 184p. 1981. 18.95 (*0-937664-54-5*) Pilgrim Bks OK.

Leonard, Francis. Money & the Mature Woman: How to Hold on to Your Income, Keep Your Home, Plan Your Estate. (Illus.). 288p. 1994. pap. 11.95 (*0-201-62700-0*) Addison-Wesley.

Leonard, Frank. A Thousand Blunders: The Grand Pacific Railway & Northern British Columbia. (Illus.). 355p. 1995. pap. 25.95 (*0-7748-0552-8*) U of Wash Pr.

— A Thousand Blunders: The Grand Trunk Pacific Railway & Northern British Columbia. LC 96-132748. (Illus.). 355p. 1995. 49.95 (*0-7748-0532-3*) U of Wash Pr.

Leonard, Garry. Advertising & Commodity Culture in Joyce. LC 98-30330. (Florida James Joyce Ser.). 224p. 1998. 49.95 (*0-8130-1632-0*) U Press Fla.

Leonard, Garry M. Reading Dubliners Again: A Lacanian Perspective. LC 92-33860. (Irish Studies). 384p. (C). 1993. pap. text 18.95 (*0-8156-2600-2*) Syracuse U Pr.

Leonard, Gary. Eucalypts: A Bushwalker's Guide from Newcastle to Wollongong. LC 95-109284. (Bush Bks.). 88p. 1993. 11.95 (*0-86840-348-2*) NSW U Pr.

— Eucalypts of the Sydney Region: A Bushwalker's Guide. (Illus.). 88p. 1998. reprint ed. pap. 19.95 (*0-86840-340-7*, Pub. by New South Wales Univ Pr) Intl Spec Bk.

— Take My Picture Gary Leonard. LC 98-88688. (Illus.). 192p. 1999. pap. 17.95 (*1-893329-00-3*) Really Great Bks.

Leonard, George. Education & Ecstasy: With the Great School Reform Hoax. rev. ed. 288p. 1987. pap. 12.95 (*1-55643-005-1*); text 25.00 (*1-55643-007-8*) North Atlantic.

— Mastery: The Keys to Long-Term Success & Fulfillment. LC 91-38072. 192p. 1992. reprint ed. pap. 12.95 (*0-452-26756-0*, Plume) Dutton Plume.

***Leonard, George.** The Ultimate Athlete. 2nd rev. ed. (Illus.). 300p. (C). 2000. pap. 16.95 (*1-55643-349-2*) North Atlantic.

— User's Guide to the Universe: Finding Love, Power & Joy Through the Philosophy of Aikido. 224p. 2000. pap. 12.95 (*0-452-27972-0*, Plume) Dutton Plume.

Leonard, George. The Way of Aikido: Life Lessons from an American Sensei. LC 98-54339. 206p. 1999. 22.95 (*0-525-94413-3*) NAL.

Leonard, George & Murphy, Michael. The Life We Are Given: A Daily Program for Realizing the Potential of Body, Mind, Heart, & Soul. LC 95-8623. (Inner Work Bks.). (Illus.). 288p. 1995. pap. 15.95 (*0-87477-792-5*, Tarcher Putnam) Putnam Pub Group.

Leonard, George J. Break Your Writer's Block. 39p. 1997. pap. text 11.95 (*0-87411-948-0*, Copley Custom Pub Grp) Copley Pub.

Leonard, George J. Into the Light of Things: The Art of the Commonplace from Wordsworth to John Cage. (Literary Studies Art Philosophy). 268p. 1995. pap. text 15.95 (*0-226-47253-1*) U Ch Pr.

— Into the Light of Things: The Art of the Commonplace from Wordsworth to John Cage. LC 93-24555. 268p. (C). 1997. 24.95 (*0-226-47252-3*) U Ch Pr.

— The Italian American Heritage: A Companion to Literature & Arts. D'Acierno, Pellegrino, ed. LC 98-7963. (Illus.). 790p. 1998. 100.00 (*0-8153-0380-7*, H1473) Garland.

Leonard, George J., ed. The Asian Pacific American Heritage: A Companion to Literature & Arts. LC 98-33468. (Illus.). 690p. 1999. 100.00 (*0-8153-2980-6*, H2109) Garland.

Leonard, Glen M., et al. A History of Davis County. LC 98-61323. (Illus.). write for info. (*0-913738-43-3*) Utah St Hist Soc.

Leonard, Glen M., jt. auth. see Allen, James B.

Leonard, Grant. Harley Davidson. 1993. 6.98 (*1-55521-862-8*) Bk Sales Inc.

Leonard, H. Jeffrey. Pollution & the Struggle for the World Product: Multinational Corporations, Environment, & International Comparative Advantage. (Illus.). 272p. 1988. text 85.00 (*0-521-34042-X*) Cambridge U Pr.

Leonard, H. Jeffrey, ed. Divesting Nature's Capital: The Political Economy of Environmental Abuse in the Third World. LC 83-18534. 350p. 1985. 59.50 (*0-8419-0897-4*) Holmes & Meier.

Leonard, H. Jeffrey, et al. Environment & the Poor: Development Strategies for a Common Agenda. Feinberg, Richard E. & Kallab, Valeriana, eds. (U. S. Third World Policy Perspectives Ser.: No. 11). 192p. 1989. text 39.95 (*0-88738-282-7*); pap. text 21.95 (*0-88738-786-1*) Transaction Pubs.

***Leonard, Hal.** Christmas Hits, Level 1. (Alfred's Basic Adult Piano Course Ser.). 32p. 1999. pap. 7.50 (*0-7390-0404-2*, 17108) Alfred Pub.

— Christmas Hits, Level 2. (Alfred's Basic Adult Piano Course Ser.). 32p. 1999. pap. 7.50 (*0-7390-0405-0*, 17109) Alfred Pub.

— Great Movie Music of the 20th Century, 1927-1999. (Illus.). 320p. 1999. otabind 19.95 (*0-634-00987-7*) H Leonard.

— Greatest Hits Level 1. (Alfred's Basic Adult Piano Course Ser.). 48p. 1999. pap. 7.95 (*0-7390-0281-3*, 16505) Alfred Pub.

— Greatest Hits Level Two. (Alfred's Basic Adult Piano Course Ser.). 48p. 1999. pap. 7.95 (*0-7390-0282-1*, 16506) Alfred Pub.

— Top Hits! Duet Book, Level 2. (Alfred's Basic Piano Library). 1999. pap. 6.95 (*0-7390-0835-8*, 17166) Alfred Pub.

— Top Hits! Level 4. (Alfred's Basic Piano Library). 32p. 1999. pap. 6.95 (*0-7390-0299-6*, 16499) Alfred Pub.

— Top Hits! Christmas Book, Level 1B. (Alfred's Basic Piano Library). 24p. 1999. pap. 6.50 (*0-7390-0400-X*, 16936) Alfred Pub.

— Top Hits Christmas Book, Level 4. (Alfred's Basic Piano Library). 24p. 1999. pap. 6.50 (*0-7390-0403-4*, 16939) Alfred Pub.

— Top Hits! Christmas Book Level 3. (Alfred's Basic Piano Library). 24p. 1999. pap. 6.50 (*0-7390-0402-6*, 16938) Alfred Pub.

— Top Hits! Christmas Book Level 2. (Alfred's Basic Piano Library). 24p. 1999. pap. 6.50 (*0-7390-0401-8*, 16937) Alfred Pub.

— Top Hits! Duet Book, Level 4. (Alfred's Basic Piano Library). 1999. pap. 7.95 (*0-7390-0837-4*, 17168) Alfred Pub.

— Top Hits! Duet Book, Level 1B. (Alfred's Basic Piano Library). 1999. pap. 6.95 (*0-7390-0834-X*, 17165) Alfred Pub.

— Top Hits! Duet Book, Level 3. (Alfred's Basic Piano Library). 1999. pap. 7.50 (*0-7390-0836-6*, 17167) Alfred Pub.

— Top Hits! Solo Book, Level 1B. (Alfred's Basic Piano Library). 23p. 1999. pap. 5.95 (*0-7390-0296-1*, 16496) Alfred Pub.

— Top Hits! Solo Book, Level 3. (Alfred's Basic Piano Library). 32p. 1999. pap. 6.95 (*0-7390-0298-8*, 16498) Alfred Pub.

— Top Hits! Solo Book, Level 2. (Alfred's Basic Piano Library). 32p. 1999. pap. 6.95 (*0-7390-0297-X*, 16497) Alfred Pub.

Leonard, Hal, Corporation Staff. Aladdin: Illustrated Songbook. 1994. 14.95 (*0-7935-3412-7*) H Leonard.

Leonard, Hal, Corporation Staff. Andrew Lloyd Webber Collection for Five Finger Piano. 48p. 1996. pap. 7.95 (*0-7935-5725-9*) H Leonard.

— Another Op'nin', Another Show. 176p. (YA). (gr. 7-13). 1998. otabind 12.95 (*0-7935-8953-3*) H Leonard.

— Artie Traum Teaches 101 Essential Riffs for Acoustic Guitar. (Listen & Learn Ser.). 56p. 1998. pap. 14.95 incl. audio compact disk (*0-7935-8859-6*) H Leonard.

— The Award-Winning Songs of the Country Music Association, 1984-1996. 3rd rev. ed. (Illus.). 216p. 1997. per. 17.95 (*0-7935-8483-3*, HL00313081) H Leonard.

Leonard, Hal, Corporation Staff. Best Broadway Songs Ever. (Best Ever Ser.). 256p. 1985. otabind 19.95 (*0-7935-0628-X*) H Leonard.

Leonard, Hal, Corporation Staff. Best Children's Song Ever. 304p. 1998. otabind 19.95 (*0-7935-8966-5*) H Leonard.

— Best Chord Changes for the Most Popular Songs. 208p. 1998. otabind 24.95 (*0-7935-7339-4*) H Leonard.

Leonard, Hal, Corporation Staff. Best Easy Listening Songs Ever. (Best Ever Ser.). 296p. 1986. otabind 18.95 (*0-7935-0867-3*) H Leonard.

— Best Fake Book Ever. (Fake Book Ser.). 864p. 1990. spiral bd. 45.00 (*0-7935-0021-4*) H Leonard.

Leonard, Hal, Corporation Staff. Best Latin Songs Ever. 248p. 1998. otabind 17.95 (*0-7935-8934-7*) H Leonard.

Leonard, Hal, Corporation Staff. Best Movie Songs Ever. (Best Ever Ser.). 296p. 1995. otabind 19.95 (*0-7935-4765-2*) H Leonard.

Leonard, Hal, Corporation Staff. The Best of Lerner & Loewe. 96p. 1981. per. 10.95 (*0-7935-8245-8*, HL00312240) H Leonard.

— Best of Sepultura for Bass. 1996. pap. 18.95 (*1-57560-004-8*, Pub. by Cherry Lane) H Leonard.

Leonard, Hal, Corporation Staff. Best of Yanni: New Age Piano Solos. 80p. 1993. otabind 14.95 (*0-7935-1709-5*) H Leonard.

— Best Rock Songs Ever. (Best Ever Ser.). 248p. 1990. otabind 17.95 (*0-7935-0071-0*) H Leonard.

— Best Songs Ever: 4th Revised Ed. 4th ed. (Best Ever Ser.). 280p. 1983. otabind 19.95 (*0-7935-0445-7*) H Leonard.

Leonard, Hal, Corporation Staff. Big Book of Ballads. 288p. 1999. otabind 19.95 (*0-634-00468-9*) H Leonard.

Leonard, Hal, Corporation Staff. Big Book of Christmas Songs. 272p. 1991. otabind 19.95 (*0-7935-0783-9*) H Leonard.

Leonard, Hal, Corporation Staff. Big Book of Early Rock 'n' Roll. 336p. 1998. otabind 19.95 (*0-7935-9495-2*) H Leonard.

Leonard, Hal, Corporation Staff. Big Book of Latin American Songs. (Big Books of Music Ser.). 320p. 1992. otabind 19.95 (*0-7935-1383-9*) H Leonard.

Leonard, Hal, Corporation Staff. The Big Book of Swing. (Illus.). 320p. 1998. otabind 19.95 (*0-7935-8963-0*, HL00310359) H Leonard.

— Birth of Rock n' Roll: From Rhythm & Blues to Rockabilly, from the Roots of Rock to Elvis. (Piano-Vocal-Guitar History of Rock Ser.). 136p. (Orig.). 1991. per. 12.95 (*0-88188-995-4*, HL00490216) H Leonard.

Leonard, Hal, Corporation Staff. Blues. (Paperback Songs Ser.). 256p. 1995. per. 6.95 (*0-7935-5259-1*) H Leonard.

Leonard, Hal, Corporation Staff. Blues Fake Book 400 Songs. 408p. 1999. spiral bd. 35.00 (*0-7935-5855-7*) H Leonard.

Leonard, Hal, Corporation Staff. Bob Marley: Songs of Freedom. 216p. 1992. otabind 24.95 (*0-7935-1684-6*) H Leonard.

Leonard, Hal, Corporation Staff. The Bonnie Raitt Collection. 1997. pap. 22.95 (*0-89524-991-X*, Pub. by Cherry Lane) H Leonard.

— The Book of Greatest Movie Music. (Illus.). 200p. 1998. otabind 14.95 (*0-7935-8806-5*, HL00310346) H Leonard.

— The British Invasion. 176p. 1997. otabind 14.95 (*0-7935-7904-X*) H Leonard.

***Leonard, Hal, Corporation Staff.** Broadway in the '90s. 192p. 1998. otabind 16.95 (*0-7935-9526-6*) H Leonard.

— Broadway Love Songs. (Broadway's Best Ser.). 192p. 1992. otabind 14.95 (*0-7935-1249-2*) H Leonard.

— Canciones De Amor; Latin Love Songs. 144p. 1998. otabind 14.95 (*0-7935-9306-9*) H Leonard.

Leonard, Hal, Corporation Staff. Chicago: The Ballads. 104p. 1997. otabind 16.95 (*0-7935-7080-8*) H Leonard.

Leonard, Hal, Corporation Staff. Christmas Songs. (Xylotone Fun! Ser.). 272p. 1992. pap. text 14.95 (*0-7935-1781-8*) H Leonard.

— Classic Rock. (Paperback Songs Ser.). 256p. 1995. per. 6.95 (*0-7935-4653-2*) H Leonard.

— Classical Fake Book: The Encyclopedia of over 650 Classical Themes & Melodies. (Fake Book Ser.). 416p. 1992. spiral bd. 24.95 (*0-7935-1329-4*) H Leonard.

Leonard, Hal, Corporation Staff. Cole Porter Love Songs. 168p. 1998. otabind 12.95 (*0-7935-8956-8*) H Leonard.

— Complete Cabaret Collection. 176p. 1999. otabind 16.95 (*0-7935-9411-1*) H Leonard.

— The Concise Beatles Complete. 382p. 1996. per. 24.95 (*0-7935-7048-4*, HL00306120) H Leonard.

— Contemporary Latin Songs. (Piano-Vocal-Guitar Ser.). 120p. (Orig.). 1993. per. 14.95 (*0-7935-1576-9*, 00311581) H Leonard.

Leonard, Hal, Corporation Staff. Country Hits. (Paperback Songs Ser.). 256p. 1995. per. 6.95 (*0-7935-5258-3*) H Leonard.

Leonard, Hal, Corporation Staff. The Country Music Hall of Fame, Vol. 1. 120p. 1998. per. 12.95 (*0-7935-6765-3*, HL00313058) H Leonard.

— The Country Music Hall of Fame, Vol. 3. 112p. 1998. otabind 12.95 (*0-7935-6767-X*, HL00313060) H Leonard.

— The Country Music Hall of Fame, Vol. 4. 112p. 1998. per. 12.95 (*0-7935-6768-8*, HL00313061) H Leonard.

— The Country Music Hall of Fame, Vol. 5. 120p. 1998. per. 12.95 (*0-7935-6769-6*, HL00313062) H Leonard.

— Danzas Cubanas: Suite for Piano Solo. 24p. 1984. pap. 5.95 (*0-7935-1642-0*) H Leonard.

Leonard, Hal, Corporation Staff. Disney Afternoon Songbook: Easy Piano. 104p. 1991. per. 12.95 (*0-7935-0346-9*) H Leonard.

— Disney Collection: Best-loved Songs from Disney Movie Television Shows & Theme Parks, Revise. 160p. 1992. otabind 17.95 (*0-7935-0832-0*) H Leonard.

Leonard, Hal, Corporation Staff. Disney's Mulan. (Illus.). 56p. 1998. per. 14.95 (*0-7935-9308-5*) H Leonard.

— Disney's Sebastian Party Gras! 64p. 1992. pap. 7.95 (*0-7935-1491-6*) H Leonard.

— Disney's Tarzan. 448p. 1999. pap. 19.95 (*0-634-00334-8*) H Leonard.

— Disney's Tarzan. 274p. (ps up). 1999. pap. text 14.95 (*0-634-00335-6*) H Leonard.

***Leonard, Hal, Corporation Staff.** Dixieland. 88p. 1998. otabind 10.95 (*0-7935-9545-2*) H Leonard.

— 80's to 90's Rock. 256p. 1999. per. 6.95 (*0-7935-9824-9*) H Leonard.

Leonard, Hal, Corporation Staff. Elvis Fake Book. 152p. 1998. spiral bd. 19.95 (*0-7935-8976-2*) H Leonard.

— Elvis Presley Sings Leiber & Stoller. 64p. 1997. per. 14.95 (*0-7935-8075-7*, HL00306167) H Leonard.

— Evita. 80p. 1997. otabind 12.95 (*0-7935-7845-0*, HL00120077) H Leonard.

— Favorite Classical Themes. (World's Great Classical Music Ser.). 224p. 1999. per. 14.95 (*0-634-00212-0*) H Leonard.

Leonard, Hal, Corporation Staff. Fifty Nifty Novelty Songs. 216p. 1996. per. 17.95 (*0-7935-6535-9*) H Leonard.

— Forty Songs for a Better World. 176p. 1996. otabind 15.95 (*0-7935-5696-1*) H Leonard.

Leonard, Hal, Corporation Staff. Great American Songwriters. 248p. 1998. otabind 17.95 (*0-7935-8948-7*) H Leonard.

Leonard, Hal, Corporation Staff. Great Ballads for Singers. 176p. 1993. per. 14.95 (*0-7935-2223-4*) H Leonard.

— Great Big Book Of Children's Songs. 224p. 1995. otabind 14.95 (*0-7935-3918-8*) H Leonard.

— Great Film Scores: 39 Themes by 17 Composers. 144p. 1996. otabind 16.95 (*0-7935-5250-8*) H Leonard.

Leonard, Hal, Corporation Staff. Great Masterworks. (World's Great Classical Music Ser.). 240p. 1999. per. 14.95 (*0-634-00211-2*) H Leonard.

Leonard, Hal, Corporation Staff. Great Movie Musical Songbook. 256p. (Orig.). 1994. per. 19.95 (*0-7935-3364-3*) H Leonard.

Leonard, Hal, Corporation Staff. Guitar of Jorma Kaukonen: Detailed Analysis of 8 Classic Songs & Instrumentals. (Listen & Learn Ser.). 64p. 1998. pap. 19.95 incl. audio compact disk (*0-7935-8176-1*) H Leonard.

— Guitar World Presents Kiss. (Guitar World Presents Ser.). 144p. 1997. per. 14.95 (*0-7935-8078-1*, HL00330291) H Leonard.

— Guitar World Presents Metallica. (Guitar World Presents Ser.). 144p. 1997. per. 14.95 (*0-7935-8079-X*, HL00330292) H Leonard.

— Guitar World Presents Stevie Ray Vaughan. (Guitar World Presents Ser.). 144p. 1997. per. 14.95 (*0-7935-8080-3*, HL00330293) H Leonard.

— Guitar World Presents Van Halen. (Guitar World Presents Ser.). 208p. 1997. per. 14.95 (*0-7935-8081-1*, HL00330294) H Leonard.

— The Guitarist's Almanac. LC 97-51796. 80p. 1998. per. 12.95 (*0-7935-6851-X*) H Leonard.

— Hal Leonard Electric Bass Method. 144p. 1996. per. 14.95 (*0-7935-6382-8*) H Leonard.

Leonard, Hal, Corporation Staff. Hal Leonard Electric Bass Method. 144p. 1996. pap. 24.95 (*0-7935-6383-6*) H Leonard.

Leonard, Hal, Corporation Staff. Hal Leonard Electric Bass Method, Bk. 1. 48p. 1996. pap. 5.95 (*0-7935-6376-3*) H Leonard.

— Hal Leonard Electric Bass Method, Bk. 2. 48p. 1996. pap. 5.95 (*0-7935-6378-X*) H Leonard.

— Hal Leonard Electric Bass Method, Bk. 3. 48p. 1996. pap. 5.95 (*0-7935-6380-1*); pap. 9.95 (*0-7935-6381-X*) H Leonard.

— The Hal Leonard Guitar Superbook. (Guitar Method Ser.). 176p. 1996. otabind 29.95 incl. audio compact disk (*0-7935-6253-8*) H Leonard.

— The Hal Leonard Mandolin Method Book. 64p. 1986. pap. 6.95 (*0-7935-8586-4*) H Leonard.

— The Hal Leonard Pocket Music Dictionary. 240p. 1993. per. 4.95 (*0-7935-1654-4*, 00183006) H Leonard.

— Harmonica Fun! 50p. 1999. pap. text 9.95 (*0-634-00332-1*) H Leonard.

— Hercules Harmonica Fun! (Music Fun Ser.). 48p. (J). (gr. 3). 1997. pap. 9.95 (*0-7935-7771-3*) H Leonard.

— Hercules Piano Fun! (Music Fun Ser.). 272p. (J). (gr. 3). 1997. pap. 19.95 (*0-7935-7769-1*) H Leonard.

— Hercules Recorder Fun! (Music Fun Ser.). 840p. (J). (ps-3). 1997. pap. 9.95 (*0-7935-7768-3*) H Leonard.

— Hercules Xylotone Fun! (Music Fun Ser.). 272p. (J). (ps-3). 1997. pap. 14.95 (*0-7935-7770-5*) H Leonard.

— History of Rock: Late 50s. 176p. 1991. per. 14.95 (*0-7935-0019-2*, HL00490321) H Leonard.

Leonard, Hal, Corporation Staff. Hollywood Love Songs. (Illus.). 256p. 1997. otabind 16.95 (*0-7935-8345-4*, HL00310318) H Leonard.

Leonard, Hal, Corporation Staff. How to Play Rock Guitar. 112p. 1997. per. 14.95 (*0-7935-6829-3*) H Leonard.

Leonard, Hal, Corporation Staff. I'll Be Seeing You: Fifty Songs of World War II. 192p. 1995. otabind 19.95 (*0-7935-3761-4*) H Leonard.

— Irving Berlin Fake Book. (Fake Book Ser.). 184p. 1992. spiral bd. 19.95 (*0-7935-1294-8*) H Leonard.

Leonard, Hal, Corporation Staff. Jump, Jive, Wail & Swing. 176p. 1999. otabind 16.95 (*0-634-00023-3*) H Leonard.

— Learning Unlimited Basic Bass Guitar. 40p. 1970. pap. 10.95 incl. audio (*0-7935-1900-4*) H Leonard.

— Leiber & Stoller Songbook. 160p. 1997. pap. 22.95 (*0-7935-8073-0*, HL00313079) H Leonard.

***Leonard, Hal, Corporation Staff.** Lilith Fair: A Celebration of Women in Music. 144p. 1998. otabind 19.95 (*0-7935-9772-2*) H Leonard.

— Love Songs of the 80's. (Decades of Love Songs Ser.). 160p. 1995. per. 14.95 (*0-7935-4592-7*) H Leonard.

— Love Songs of the 50's. (Decades of Love Songs Ser.). 160p. 1995. per. 14.95 (*0-7935-4457-2*) H Leonard.

— Love Songs of the 40's. (Decades of Love Songs Ser.). 160p. 1995. per. 14.95 (*0-7935-4445-9*) H Leonard.

— Love Songs of the 90's. 160p. 1995. otabind 14.95 (*0-7935-4593-5*) H Leonard.

— Love Songs of the 70's. (Decades of Love Songs Ser.). 160p. 1995. otabind 14.95 (*0-7935-4591-9*) H Leonard.

— Love Songs of the 60's. 160p. 1995. per. 14.95 (*0-7935-4456-4*) H Leonard.

— Love Songs of the 30's. (Decades of Love Songs Ser.). 160p. 1995. per. 14.95 (*0-7935-4441-6*) H Leonard.

— Love Songs of the 20's. (Decades of Love Songs Ser.). 160p. 1995. per. 14.95 (*0-7935-4442-4*) H Leonard.

— Marlene Dietrich: The Songbook. 1999. pap. text 14.95 (*0-7119-7022-X*) H Leonard.

Leonard, Hal, Corporation Staff. Motown Anthology. 312p. 1998. otabind 19.95 (*0-7935-9201-1*) H Leonard.

— Motown Hits. 256p. 1999. per. 6.95 (*0-7935-9823-0*) H Leonard.

— The Movie Fake Book. 2nd ed. 352p. 1995. spiral bd. 29.95 (*0-7935-8244-X*, HL00240033) H Leonard.

— Movie Music. 256p. 1998. per. 6.95 (*0-7935-8870-7*) H Leonard.

***Leonard, Hal, Corporation Staff.** New Standards. 176p. 1998. otabind 12.95 (*0-7935-9284-4*) H Leonard.

Leonard, Hal, Corporation Staff. #1 Country Songs of the 80's. 168p. 1997. otabind 12.95 (*0-7935-8552-X*) H Leonard.

— Piano Lessons. (Student Piano Library). 1p. 1996. pap. text 10.95 incl. audio compact disk (*0-7935-6263-5*) H Leonard.

— Piano Lessons. (Student Piano Library). 1p. 1996. pap. text 10.95 incl. audio compact disk (*0-7935-6268-6*) H Leonard.

— Piano Lessons. (Student Piano Library: Bk. 1). 64p. 1996. pap. 5.95 (*0-7935-6260-0*) H Leonard.

— Piano Lessons, Bk. 2. (Student Piano Library). 48p. 1996. pap. 5.95 (*0-7935-6265-1*) H Leonard.

— Piano Lessons, Bk. 3. (Student Piano Library). 48p. 1996. pap. 5.95 (*0-7935-6270-8*) H Leonard.

— Piano Lessons: General MIDI. (Student Piano Library). 1p. 1996. pap. text 14.95 incl. disk (*0-7935-6269-4*) H Leonard.

— Piano Lessons: General MIDI, Bk. 3. (Student Piano Library). 1p. 1996. pap. text 14.95 (*0-7935-6274-0*) H Leonard.

— Piano Practice Games, Bk. 1. (Student Piano Library). 48p. 1996. pap. 5.50 (*0-7935-6261-9*) H Leonard.

— Piano Practice Games, Bk. 2. (Student Piano Library). 40p. 1996. pap. 5.50 (*0-7935-6266-X*) H Leonard.

— Piano Solos, Bk. 1. (Student Piano Library). 32p. 1996. pap. 4.95 (*0-7935-6262-7*) H Leonard.

— Piano Solos, Bk. 2. (Student Piano Library). 32p. 1996. pap. 4.95 (*0-7935-6267-8*) H Leonard.

— Piano Solos, Bk. 3. (Student Piano Library). 32p. 1996. pap. 4.95 (*0-7935-6272-4*) H Leonard.

— Pooh's Grand Adventure. 56p. 1998. pap. 9.95 (*0-7935-8968-1*) H Leonard.

— Professional Singer's Pop/Rock Fake Book. 168p. 1998. per. 19.95 (*0-7935-5989-8*); per. 19.95 (*0-7935-5990-1*) H Leonard.

— The Ray Lynch Songbook. (Orig.). 1995. pap. text 14.95 (*0-7935-2160-2*) H Leonard.

— Really Big Book of Children's Songs. 256p. 1998. otabind 15.95 (*0-7935-9265-8*) H Leonard.

— Recorder Fun! 841p. 1999. pap. text 9.95 (*0-634-00331-3*) H Leonard.

— Recorder Fun! Teach Yourself the Easy Way! 48p. 1996. pap. text 7.95 incl. audio compact disk (*0-7935-6650-9*) H Leonard.

— Richard Rodgers Love Songs. 1999. otabind 14.95 (*0-7935-8955-X*) H Leonard.

Leonard, Hal, Corporation Staff. Rock & Roll Collection. (Paperback Songs Ser.). 256p. 1995. per. 6.95 (*0-7935-5984-7*) H Leonard.

— Romance; Boleros Favoritos. 192p. 1998. otabind 16.95 (*0-7935-9304-2*) H Leonard.

Leonard, Hal, Corporation Staff. Selections from the Beatles Anthology, Vol. 3. 112p. 1997. per. 17.95 (*0-7935-7536-2*, HL00306144) H Leonard.

— Side Show Vocal Selections. 104p. 1998. otabind 17.95 (*0-7935-9162-7*) H Leonard.

— Sing the Songs of Rodgers & Hammerstein: High Voice. 40p. 1998. pap. 17.95 incl. audio compact disk (*0-7935-8352-7*, 00740092) H Leonard.

— Sing the Songs of Rodgers & Hammerstein: Low Voice. 40p. 1998. pap. 17.95 incl. audio compact disk (*0-7935-8374-8*, 00740093) H Leonard.

— Singer's Christian Wedding Collection-High Voice. 152p. 1999. otabind 14.95 (*0-7935-9367-0*) H Leonard.

— Singer's Christian Wedding Collection-Low Voice. 152p. 1999. otabind 14.95 (*0-7935-9368-9*) H Leonard.

— Smokey Joe's Cafe: The Songs of Leiber & Stoller. 68p. 1997. otabind 16.95 (*0-7935-8074-9*, HL00313080) H Leonard.

Leonard, Hal, Corporation Staff. Songs for Kids. (Xylotone Fun! Ser.). 272p. 1992. pap. text 14.95 (*0-7935-1770-2*) H Leonard.

Leonard, Hal, Corporation Staff. Songs of Bacharach & David. 96p. 1999. otabind 14.95 (*0-7935-9839-7*) H Leonard.

— Songs of Stephen Foster. 96p. 1999. otabind 10.95 (*0-7935-9122-8*) H Leonard.

Leonard, Hal, Corporation Staff. Songs of the 1890's. 200p. 1994. per. 12.95 (*0-7935-3125-X*) H Leonard.

— Songs of the 1900's: 1900-1909. (Decade Ser.). 208p. 1994. per. 12.95 (*0-7935-3126-8*) H Leonard.

— Sound of Music; Broadway Souvenir, Broadway Souvenir Folio ed. 136p. 1998. otabind 15.95 (*0-7935-9876-1*) H Leonard.

— Souvenir Disney Songbook: Favorite Songs from Disneyland & Walt Disney World. 96p. 1994. per. 19.95 (*0-7935-0835-5*) H Leonard.

Leonard, Hal, Corporation Staff. Standard Ballads: Cabaret Arrangements for Singer & Trio (Piano, Bass, Drums), Men's ed. (Singer's Ser.). 72p. 1998. pap. 19.95 (*0-7935-8349-7*) H Leonard.

— Standard Ballads: Cabaret Arrangements for Singer & Trio (Piano, Bass, Drums), Womens ed. (Singer's Ser.). 72p. 1998. pap. 19.95 (*0-7935-8348-9*) H Leonard.

Leonard, Hal, Corporation Staff. Steely Dan Complete. 256p. 1995. otabind 24.95 (*0-7935-4874-8*) H Leonard.

— Stevie Ray Vaughan: Signature Guitar Licks. 80p. 1991. student ed. 19.95 incl. audio compact disk (*0-7935-0824-X*) H Leonard.

— Swinging Love. 176p. 1998. per. 14.95 (*0-7935-9294-1*) H Leonard.

Leonard, Hal, Corporation Staff. Titanic - Easy Piano. (Illus.). 72p. 1998. per. 16.95 (*0-7935-9485-5*, HL00316030) H Leonard.

***Leonard, Hal, Corporation Staff.** Tonight at the Lounge. 184p. 1998. otabind 14.95 (*0-7935-9538-X*) H Leonard.

— Torch Songs. 224p. 1991. otabind 16.95 (*0-7935-0289-6*) H Leonard.

Leonard, Hal, Corporation Staff. Torch Songs: Men's ed. (Singer's Ser.). 1999. pap. text 19.95 (*0-7935-8347-0*) H Leonard.

— Torch Songs: Women's ed. (Singer's Ser.). 64p. 1999. pap. text 19.95 (*0-7935-8346-2*) H Leonard.

— TV Themes: Past & Present. 112p. 1998. otabind 12.95 (*0-7935-8098-6*) H Leonard.

— Twila Paris--Perennial. 64p. 1998. otabind 14.95 (*0-7935-9381-6*) H Leonard.

— Ultimate Elton John Collection. 522p. 1998. pap. 49.90 (*0-7935-9416-2*) H Leonard.

***Leonard, Hal, Corporation Staff.** Ultimate Guitar Songbook: The Complete Resource for Every Guitar Player ! 240p. 1998. otabind 17.95 (*0-7935-8554-6*) H Leonard.

— Vaudeville Songbook. 200p. 1995. otabind 18.95 (*0-7935-3703-7*) H Leonard.

Leonard, Hal, Corporation Staff. Very Best of Sting & the Police. 72p. 1998. per. 16.95 (*0-7935-9424-3*) H Leonard.

Leonard, Hal, Corporation Staff. Windham Hill Guitar Sampler: 18 Transcriptions from the Modern Masters of the Acoustic Guitar. 112p. 1994. otabind 18.95 (*0-7935-2488-1*) H Leonard.

Leonard, Hal, Corporation Staff. Winnie the Pooh. 40p. 1998. pap. 10.95 (*0-7935-8754-9*) H Leonard.

***Leonard, Hal, Corporation Staff.** WWF: The Music Guitar Tab Edition: Original Arena Entrance Theme Songs of the World Wrestling Federation, Vol. 3. 64p. 1999. per. 19.95 (*1-57560-250-4*, Pub. by Cherry Lane) H Leonard.

Leonard, Hal, Corporation Staff, abr. Disney Songs From Animated Film Classics With Zylotone. 256p. 1992. 14.95 (*0-7935-1393-6*) H Leonard.

Leonard, Hal, Corporation Staff, ed. Piano Theory Workbook. (Hal Leonard Student Piano Library). 40p. 1997. pap. 5.50 (*0-7935-7689-X*) H Leonard.

— Titanic Piano Selections. 56p. 1998. per. 16.95 (*0-7935-9224-0*) H Leonard.

Leonard, Harry, ed. J. N. Andrews: The Man & the Mission. LC 85-71649. 368p. (Orig.). 1985. pap. 16.99 (*0-943872-91-X*) Andrews Univ Pr.

Leonard, Helen, jt. auth. see Cox, Eve.

Leonard, Helen M. Conger Family in America: Descendants of John Belconger, 1640 & His Six Sons. 844p. 1998. reprint ed. pap. 99.50 (*0-8328-9647-0*); reprint ed. lib. bdg. 109.50 (*0-8328-9646-2*) Higginson Bk Co.

— The Janesvillians, 1849-1974. (Illus.). 250p. 1998. reprint ed. lib. bdg. 35.00 (*0-8328-9703-5*) Higginson Bk Co.

Leonard, Henrietta L., jt. auth. see Swedo, Susan Anderson.

Leonard, Henry B. The Open Gates: The Protest Against the Movement to Restrict European Immigration, 1896-1924. Cordasco, Francesco, ed. LC 80-875. (American Ethnic Groups Ser.). 1981. lib. bdg. 35.95 (*0-405-13437-1*) Ayer.

Leonard, Herman. History of the Oregon Territory from its First Discovery up to the Present Time. 88p. 1980. 14.95 (*0-87770-230-6*) Ye Galleon.

Leonard, Herman B. By Choice or By Chance? Tracking the Values in Massachusetts' Public Spending. (Pioneer Paper Ser.: No. 6). 168p. (Orig.). 1992. pap. 10.00 (*0-929930-08-8*) Pioneer Inst.

Leonard, Holli, ed. see Belle, Laval W.

Leonard, Hugh. Out after Dark. 192p. 1991. 24.95 (*0-233-98474-7*, Pub. by Andre Deutsch) Trafalgar.

— Selected Plays of Hugh Leonard. LC 91-25924. (Irish Drama Selections Ser.). 464p. 1992. pap. 16.95 (*0-8132-0760-6*); text 49.95 (*0-8132-0759-2*) Cath U Pr.

Leonard, I. R., compiled by. Historical Sketch of Gowanda, in Commemoration of the 50th Anniversary of Its Incorporation, August 8, 1898. (Illus.). 147p. 1997. reprint ed. lib. bdg. 25.00 (*0-8328-6152-9*) Higginson Bk Co.

Leonard, Irving. La Epoca Barroca en el Mexico Colonial (The Baroque Epoch in Colonial Mexico) (SPA.). 335p. 1974. pap. 8.99 (*968-16-2377-0*, Pub. by Fondo) Continental Bk.

Leonard, Irving A. Baroque Times in Old Mexico: Seventeenth-Century Persons, Places, & Practices. (Illus.). 288p. 1959. pap. text 18.95 (*0-472-06110-0*, 06110, Ann Arbor Bks) U of Mich Pr.

— Baroque Times in Old Mexico: Seventeenth-Century Persons, Places, & Practices. LC 80-29256. (Illus.). 260p. 1981. reprint ed. lib. bdg. 65.00 (*0-313-22826-4*, LEBT, Greenwood Pr) Greenwood.

— Books of the Brave: Being an Account of Books & of Men in the Spanish Conquest & Settlement of the Sixteenth-Century New World. (C). 1992. 50.00 (*0-520-07990-6*, Pub. by U CA Pr); pap. 18.95 (*0-520-07816-0*, Pub. by U CA Pr) Cal Prin Full Svc.

— Colonial Travelers in Latin America. Bryant, William C., ed. (Estudios de Literatura Latinoamericana Ser.: Vol. 1). 235p. 1972. 15.50 (*0-936388-30-7*); pap. 10.50 (*0-936388-29-3*) Juan de la Cuesta.

— Mercurio Volante of Don Carlos de Siguenza y Gongora. LC 67-24715. (Quivira Society Publications, Vol. 3). 1967. reprint ed. 19.95 (*0-405-00073-1*) Ayer.

Leonard, Irving A., ed. Spanish Approach to Pensacola, 1689-1693. LC 67-24720. (Quivira Society Publications: Vol. 9). 1967. reprint ed. 19.95 (*0-405-00083-9*) Ayer.

Leonard, Irving A., tr. see Picon-Salas, Mariano.

Leonard, J. Contribution a l'Etude de la Flore et de la Vegetation des Deserts d'Iran, Fasc. 1-10. (Illus.). 1992. 235.00 (*1-878762-87-7*) Balogh.

— Una Gran Fe.Tr. of Great Faith. (SPA.). 134p. pap. 5.99 (*1-56063-616-5*, 495014) Editorial Unilit.

Leonard, J. E. Come Out of Her, My People: A Study of the Revelation to John. 208p. 1991. pap. 9.75 (*1-884454-00-3*) Laudemont Pr.

— Heritage from the Lord: The Place of Children in Worship. 56p. 1993. pap. 6.95 (*1-884454-02-X*) Laudemont Pr.

— I Will Be Their God: Understanding the Covenant. 160p. 1992. pap. 7.95 (*1-884454-01-1*) Laudemont Pr.

— Processions of God: The Significance of Ceremony. 60p. 1995. pap. 5.95 (*1-884454-03-8*) Laudemont Pr.

Leonard, J. E., jt. auth. see Leonard, R. C.

Leonard, J. Michael. French Pieces for Saxophone. 88p. 1997. pap. 11.95 (*0-7866-0861-7*, 95524) Mel Bay.

— Solo Pieces for the Advanced Saxophonist. 80p. 1997. pap. 10.95 (*0-7866-0862-5*, 95523) Mel Bay.

— Solo Pieces for the Beginning Saxophonist. 96p. 1997. pap. 10.95 (*0-7866-0864-1*, 95521) Mel Bay.

— Solo Pieces for the Intermediate Saxophonist. 112p. 1997. pap. 12.95 (*0-7866-0863-3*, 95522) Mel Bay.

Leonard, J. W., III, ed. Coal Preparation. 5th ed. LC 91-61678. (Illus.). 1154p. (C). 1991. 89.00 (*0-87335-104-5*) SMM&E Inc.

Leonard, Jack & Shapira, Sid. The Time of My Life. (Illus.). 189p. 1993. 14.95 (*0-9639900-0-4*) Drumalee.

Leonard, Jacob C. Centennial History of Davidson County. (Illus.). 523p. 1995. reprint ed. lib. bdg. 55.00 (*0-8328-5089-6*) Higginson Bk Co.

***Leonard, James.** The Pool Birds. (Illus.). 24p. 2000. pap. 8.00 (*0-8059-4761-2*) Dorrance.

Leonard, James F. The New Philosophy for K-12 Education: A Deming Framework for Transforming America's Schools. 330p. 1996. 35.00 (*0-87389-363-8*, H0924) ASQ Qual Pr.

Leonard, James S. Making Mark Twain Work in the Classroom. LC 98-42358. 1999. write for info. (*0-8223-2278-1*); pap. 17.95 (*0-8223-2297-8*) Duke.

Leonard, James S., ed. Author-ity & Textuality: Current Views of Collaborative Writing. LC 94-15111. (Locust Hill Literary Studies: No. 14). (Illus.). 254p. (C). 1994. lib. bdg. 30.00 (*0-933951-57-4*) Locust Hill Pr.

Leonard, James S., et al, eds. Satire or Evasion? Black Perspectives on Huckleberry Finn. LC 91-14315. 288p. 1991. lib. bdg. 45.00 (*0-8223-1163-1*) Duke.

— Satire or Evasion? Black Perspectives on Huckleberry Finn. LC 91-14315. 288p. 1992. pap. text 19.95 (*0-8223-1174-7*) Duke.

Leonard, James V., jt. auth. see Zobrist, George W.

Leonard, Jane F., et al. Keys to Parenting a Child with Cerebral Palsy. LC 97-12492. (Parenting Keys Ser.). 208p. 1997. pap. text 6.95 (0-7641-0091-2) Barron.

Leonard, Jane K. Controlling from Afar: The Daoguang Emperor's Management of the Grand Canal Crisis, 1824-1826. LC 95-50275. (Michigan Monographs in Chinese Studies: No. 69). 334p. 1996. text 50.00 (0-89264-114-2) Ctr Chinese Studies.

— Controlling from Afar: The Daoguang Emperor's Management of the Grand Canal Crisis, 1824-1826. (Michigan Monographs in Chinese Studies: No. 69). (Illus.). 334p. 1996. pap. 25.00 (0-89264-119-3) Ctr Chinese Studies.

— Wei Yuan & China's Rediscovery of the Maritime World. (East Asian Monographs: No. 111). (Illus.). 300p. 1984. 30.00 (0-674-94855-6) Harvard E Asian.

Leonard, Jane K. & Watt, John R., eds. To Achieve Security & Wealth: The Qing Imperial State & the Economy, 1644-1911. (Cornell East Asia Ser.: No. 56). (Illus.). 206p. (Orig.). (C). 1993. pap. 11.90 (0-939657-56-2) Cornell East Asia Pgm.

Leonard, Janice E. Therese of Lisieux. (Illus.). 104p. (Orig.). 1997. pap. 8.95 (1-884454-50-X) Lampstand Pub.

Leonard, Jean-Francois & Leveillee, Jacques. Montreal after Drapeau. Roussopoulos, Dimitrios I., tr. & intro. by. (FRE.). 134p. 1986. write for info. (0-920057-89-6); pap. write for info. (0-920057-88-8) Black Rose.

Leonard, Jerry D., ed. Legal Studies As Cultural Studies: A Reader in (Post)Modern Critical Theory. LC 94-9240. 392p. (C). 1995. text 59.50 (0-7914-2295-X); pap. text 19.95 (0-7914-2296-8) State U NY Pr.

Leonard, Jim, Jr. And They Dance Real Slow in Jackson. 91p. 1986. pap. 5.25 (0-8222-0045-7) Dramatists Play.

Leonard, Jim. The Skill of Happiness: Creative Daily Ecstacy with Vivation. 187p. (Orig.). 1996. pap. 12.95 (1-881952-09-6) Three Blue Herons.

***Leonard, Joan.** Twice Blessed: Everything You Need to Know About Having a Second Child Preparing Yourself, Your Marriage, & Your Firstborn for a New Family of Four. 224p. 2000. pap. 12.95 (0-312-25430-X) St Martin.

Leonard, Joann. All the World's a Stage. 114p. 1997. pap. 5.00 (0-87440-039-2) Bakers Plays.

— All the World's a Stage Vol. II. 101p. 1998. pap. 5.00 (0-87440-077-5) Bakers Plays.

***Leonard, Joann.** Cooking with Herbs & Spices: A Reference Manual. 167p. 2000. pap. write for info. (1-56072-518-4, Nova Kroshka Bks) Nova Sci Pubs.

— The Soup Has Many Eyes: From Shtetl to Chicago - A Memoir of One Family's Journey Through History. LC 99-39229. 192p. 2000. 18.95 (0-553-80159-7) Bantam.

Leonard, JoAnn K. A Wedding Planner for Brides: Questions You Need to Ask When Planning the Perfect Wedding. rev. ed. 190p. 1994. reprint ed. pap. 24.95 (0-9629412-5-5) Garnet Rose.

Leonard, Joe & Nelson-Pallmeyer, Jack. Study Guide to "Families Valued" Parenting & Politics for the Good of All Children. 32p. 1997. pap., student ed. 4.95 (0-377-00310-7) Friendship Pr.

Leonard, Joe H., ed. Church Family Gatherings: Programs & Plans. LC 78-9548. (Illus.). 94p. 1978. reprint ed. pap. 30.00 (0-608-00217-8, 206101100006) Bks Demand.

Leonard, Joe H., Jr., jt. auth. see Olson, Richard P.

Leonard, John. Crybaby of the Western World: A Novel of Petit Guignol in Long Beach, California. LC 71-380796. 308p. (J). 1968. write for info. (0-356-02457-1) Little Brown.

— The Last Innocent White Man in America: And Other Writings. 320p. 1997. pap. 13.00 (1-56584-348-7, Pub. by New Press NY) Norton.

— The Last Innocent White Man in America & Other Writings. LC 92-50838. 320p. 1993. 21.95 (1-56584-072-0, Pub. by New Press NY) Norton.

— Naming in Paradise: Milton & the Language of Adam & Eve. 318p. (C). 1990. 75.00 (0-19-812958-0) OUP.

Leonard, John. 100 Elegies for Modernity. LC 97-152974. (Illus.). 1997. write for info. (0-86806-617-6) Hale & Iremnger.

Leonard, John. Smoke & Mirrors: Violence, Television & Other American Cultures. 1998. pap. 13.00 (1-56584-443-2, Pub. by New Press NY) Norton.

— What to Do about Your Child's Manners. LC 98-5416. (Parenting Guides Ser.). (Illus.). 96p. 1998. 12.95 (0-7621-0101-6, Pub. by RD Assn) Penguin Putnam.

***Leonard, John.** When the Kissing Had to Stop: Cult Studs, Khmer Newts, Langley Spooks, Techno-Geeks, Video Drones. (Illus.). 2000. reprint ed. pap. 15.95 (1-56584-643-5, Pub. by New Press NY) Norton.

Leonard, John. When the Kissing Had to Stop: Cult Studs, Khmer Newts, Langley Spooks, Techno-Geeks, Video Drones, Author Gods, Serial Killers. LC 98-44584. 362p. 1999. 25.00 (1-56584-533-1, Pub. by New Press NY) Norton.

Leonard, John, ed. Australian Verse: An Oxford Anthology. LC 99-165081. 456p. 1999. pap. 35.00 (0-19-550699-5) OUP.

Leonard, John, et al, eds. Smoke & Mirrors: Violence, Television & Other American Cultures. LC 94-41459. 494p. 1997. 23.00 (1-56584-226-X, Pub. by New Press NY) Norton.

Leonard, John, jt. auth. see American Sport Education Program Staff.

Leonard, John, jt. auth. see Frumkin, Lyn.

Leonard, John, jt. auth. see Mitchell, Nathan D.

Leonard, John, ed. & pref. see Milton, John.

Leonard, John J. Directed Sonar Sensing for Mobile Robot Navigation. (International Series in Engineering & Computer Science, VLSI, Computer Architecture, & Digital Screen Processing). 208p. (C). 1992. text 113.50 (0-7923-9242-6) Kluwer Academic.

Leonard, John L. Yum! Irresistible, Fun-to-Create, Reliable Recipes. LC 95-94321. (Illus.). 394p. 1995. text 17.95 (0-9646465-5-2) Heron Hill Pr.

Leonard, Jonathan G. & Bell, Ross Taylor. Northeastern Tiger Beetles: Field Guide to Tiger Beetles of New England & Eastern Canada. LC 98-41599. 192p. 1998. otabind 49.95 (0-8493-1915-3, 1915) CRC Pr.

Leonard, Jonathan N. Crusaders of Chemistry. LC 72-8533. (Essay Index Reprint Ser.). 1977. reprint ed. 26.95 (0-8369-7320-8) Ayer.

Leonard, Joseph M. Pocket Power No. 1: Medical. 48p. (Orig.). 1988. pap. 2.95 (0-945893-00-0) Pocket Power.

Leonard, Joseph M., jt. auth. see Augustine, John L.

Leonard, Joseph M., jt. auth. see Brannon, Wayne A.

Leonard, Joseph M., ed. see Burnette, Allyson C.

Leonard, Joseph M., ed. see Leonard, Lois L.

Leonard, Joseph M., ed. see Stoodt, Douglas A.

Leonard, Joseph W., jt. ed. see Humphreys, Kenneth K.

Leonard, Justin W. & Leonard, Fannie A. Mayflies of Michigan Trout Streams. LC 62-9726. (Bulletin Ser.: No. 43). 139p. 1962. pap. 8.50 (0-87737-020-6) Cranbrook.

Leonard, Karen I. Making Ethnic Choices: California's Punjabi Mexican Americans. (Asian American History & Culture Ser.). 368p. (C). 1992. 59.95 (0-87722-890-6) Temple U Pr.

— Making Ethnic Choices: California's Punjabi Mexican Americans. (Asian American History & Culture Ser.). 368p. (C). 1994. pap. 22.95 (1-56639-202-0) Temple U Pr.

— Social History of an Indian Caste: The Kayasths of Hyderabad. (C). 1995. 16.00 (81-250-0032-1, Pub. by UBS Pubs Dist) S Asia.

— Social History of an Indian Caste: The Kayasths of Hyderabad. LC 76-52031. (Illus.). 371p. reprint ed. pap. 115.10 (0-7837-4846-9, 204449300003) Bks Demand.

— The South Asian Americans. LC 97-2219. (New Americans Ser.). 208p. 1997. 39.95 (0-313-29788-6, Greenwood Pr) Greenwood.

Leonard, Kathy & Shua, Ana M., eds. Cruel Fictions, Cruel Realities: Short Stories by Latin American Women Writers. LC 97-13681. (Discoveries Ser.). 160p. 1997. pap. 15.95 (0-935480-87-0) Lat Am Lit Rev Pr.

Leonard, Kathy S., compiled by. Index to Translated Short Fiction by Latin American Women in English Language Anthologies, 25. LC 97-33141. (Bibliographies & Indexes in Women's Studies: Vol. 25). 136p. 1997. lib. bdg. 65.00 (0-313-30046-1, Greenwood Pr) Greenwood.

Leonard, Kathy S., jt. ed. see Benner, Susan E.

Leonard, Kay. How to Read a Painting: Lessons in Proportion, Balance & Symmetry. (Illus.). 102p. 1988. student ed. 9.95 (0-9623455-1-2) Eye Cue.

— Paper Kaleidoscopes. (Illus.). 40p. (J). (gr. k-12). 1989. pap. 6.95 (0-9623455-0-4) Eye Cue.

Leonard, Keith. The Phoebe Chronicles, Vol. 1. LC 97-199837. (Illus.). 64p. 1997. pap. 9.95 (1-56163-182-5, Amerotica) NBM.

— The Phoebe Chronicles Vol. 2: Angels of Death. (Illus.). 64p. 1998. pap. 9.95 (1-56163-221-X, Amerotica) NBM.

***Leonard, Kenneth E. & Blane, Howard T., eds.** Psychological Theories of Drinking & Alcoholism. 2nd ed. LC 99-29558. (Substance Abuse Ser.). 467p. 1999. lib. bdg. 49.00 (1-57230-410-3) Guilford Pubns.

Leonard, Kimberly K., et al, eds. Minorities in Juvenile Justice. LC 95-15769. 242p. (C). 1995. 48.00 (0-8039-7264-4) Sage.

— Minorities in Juvenile Justice. 232p. (C). 1995. pap. 22.95 (0-8039-7265-2) Sage.

***Leonard, L. Larry, et al.** International Regulation of Fisheries. LC 99-48874. (Carnegie Endowment for International Peace Monograph Ser.: No. 7). x, 201p. 2000. reprint ed. 42.00 (1-57588-564-6, 323960) W S Hein.

Leonard, Lana S. Victim or Hero? Writing Your Own Life Story: A Passage Guide for Life's Transitions. (Orig.). 1996. pap. write for info. (0-9656370-0-X) Teaching Peace.

Leonard, Larry. Far Walker. LC 88-12290. (Illus.). 120p. (J). (gr. 1 up). 1988. 12.95 (0-932576-60-5) Breitenbush Bks.

— Fishing the Lower Columbia: The Greatest Salmon Hole in the World. (Illus.). 64p. 1993. pap. 8.95 (1-878175-53-X) F Amato Pubns.

Leonard, Laura L. Energy-Generating Resources: Index of New Information. 150p. 1994. 47.50 (0-7883-0026-1); pap. 44.50 (0-7883-0027-X) ABBE Pubs Assn.

Leonard, Laurence. Children with Specific Language Impairment. LC 96-37594. (Language, Speech & Communication Ser.). 347p. 1997. 60.00 (0-262-12206-5, Bradford Bks) MIT Pr.

Leonard, Laurence, jt. ed. see Taylor, Orlando L.

Leonard, Laurence B. Children with Specific Language Impairment. (Language, Speech & Communication Ser.). (Illus.). 352p. 1997. pap. 27.50 (0-262-62136-3) MIT Pr.

***Leonard, Lawrence.** 1812 & All That: A Concise History of Music from 30,000 BC to the Millennium. (Illus.). 128p. 2000. pap. 14.95 (0-920151-33-7, Pub. by Sound & Vision) Firefly Bks Ltd.

Leonard, Leah W. Jewish Cookery. (International Cookbook Ser.). 1994. 15.00 (0-517-09758-3, Crown) Crown Pub Group.

Leonard, Linda S. On Way to Wedding. 1986. 15.95 (0-394-55250-4) Random.

Leonard, Linda S. The Wounded Woman: Healing the Father-Daughter Relationship. LC 83-42801. 179p. 1983. pap. 12.00 (0-394-72183-7, Pub. by Shambhala Pubns) Random.

— The Wounded Woman: Healing the Father-Daughter Relationship. 1998. pap. 12.00 (1-57062-411-9, Pub. by Shambhala Pubns) Random.

— The Wounded Woman: Healing the Father-Daughter Relationship. LC 82-6289. xx, 186p. 1982. 24.95 (0-8040-0397-1) Swallow.

Leonard, Linda Schierse. The Call to Create: Liberating Everyday Genius. LC 99-41778. 304p. 2000. 25.00 (0-609-60093-1) Harmony Bks.

***Leonard, Linda Schierse.** Creation's Heartbeat: Following the Reindeer. 240p. 1999. reprint ed. text 22.00 (0-7881-6713-8) DIANE Pub.

Leonard, Lois L. Pocket Power No. 2: Taxes. Leonard, Joseph M., ed. 48p. (Orig.). 1988. pap. text 2.95 (0-945893-01-9) Pocket Power.

***Leonard, Lorenzo D.** Abstract Freedom: Creating Emotional Integrity in Relationships. McCoy, Lisa, ed. LC 98-68578. 211p. 1999. pap. 17.95 (0-9660092-2-3) Puget Sound.

Leonard, Lorenzo D. Relationships...Shattering the Lies We Live By: Solutions for Conflict & Prejudice. LC 97-92512. 166p. 1998. pap. 14.95 (0-9660092-0-7) Puget Sound.

***Leonard, Lorenzo D.** Who We Are vs. What We Are. deluxe ed. McCoy, Lisa, ed. LC 99-67412. (Illus.). 200p. 2000. pap. 15.95 (0-9660092-6-6) Puget Sound.

Leonard Lowdermilk, Deitra, et al. Maternity Nursing. 5th ed. LC 98-33732. 1998. 54.00 (0-323-00215-3) Mosby Inc.

Leonard, Lynn, ed. Get a Jump on College & Careers in Ohio: Career Exploration & College Planning Made Easy. rev. ed. (Illus.). 148p. 1997. pap. text 8.95 (0-9657427-1-7) Thomson Ctrl OH.

Leonard, M. Leonard Memorial: Genealogy, History, & Biography of Solomon Leonard; 1637, of Duxbury & Bridgewater, Mass., & Some of His Descendants. (Illus.). 454p. 1989. reprint ed. pap. 68.00 (0-8328-0766-4); reprint ed. lib. bdg. 76.00 (0-8328-0765-6) Higginson Bk Co.

Leonard, M. C., ed. The Illustrated Guide to the Florida West Coast. (Illus.). 64p. (Orig.). 1992. pap. text 3.95 (0-9634223-0-8) Purple Islands.

Leonard, Madeleine. Informal Economic Activity in Belfast. 224p. 1994. 66.95 (1-85628-478-6, Pub. by Avebry) Ashgate Pub Co.

Leonard, Madeleine & Byrne, Anne, eds. Irish Women: Sociological Profiles. 640p. 1997. pap. 51.00 (1-85594-153-8, Pub. by Attic Press) Intl Spec Bk.

Leonard, Madeleine, jt. ed. see Byrne, Anne.

Leonard, Maggie. Elizabeth Cat. (Illus.). iv, 92p. 1998. 17.95 (0-9659853-0-X); pap. 17.95 (0-9659853-1-8) M Leonard.

Leonard, Marcellus J. Cardboard Ears: The Early Poems. 1999. pap. 10.00 (1-928795-01-3) M Leonard IL.

— Nubian Cousins: Adventures in Verse. (Illus.). 35p. 1999. pap. 5.00 (1-928795-00-5, Glass Cage) M Leonard IL.

Leonard, Marcia. Alphabets Bandits: An ABC Book. 1990. pap. text 16.95 (0-8167-2652-3) Troll Communs.

— Animal Talk. LC 99-63970. (Illus.). 24p. (J). (ps-k). 2000. 7.95 (0-694-01363-3) HarpC Child Bks.

***Leonard, Marcia.** Babies Help Out. LC 99-69952. 24p. (J). 2001. pap. 7.95 (0-694-01369-2, HarpFestival) HarpC Child Bks.

Leonard, Marcia. The Bad News Bully. (The Kids on Bus 5 Ser.: No. 1). (Illus.). 80p. (J). (gr. 2-4). 1996. per. 3.50 (0-671-54188-9) PB.

— Bear's Busy Year: A Book about Seasons. LC 89-4946. (Illus.). 24p. (J). (gr. k-2). 1990. pap. 2.50 (0-8167-1721-4); lib. bdg. 14.50 (0-8167-1720-6) Troll Communs.

***Leonard, Marcia.** Best Friends. LC 99-11179. (Real Kids Readers Ser.). (Illus.). 30p. (J). (ps-k). 1999. lib. bdg. 16.90 (0-7613-2064-4, Copper Beech Bks) Millbrook Pr.

— Best Friends. LC 99-11179. (Real Kids Readers Ser.). (Illus.). 30p. (J). (gr. k-1). 1999. pap. 3.99 (0-7613-2089-X, Copper Beech Bks) Millbrook Pr.

Leonard, Marcia. Best Snowman Ever. (Illus.). 10p. (J). (ps). 1996. pap. 2.95 (0-8167-1488-6) Troll Communs.

— Big Ben. LC 98-10041. (Real Kids Readers Ser.). (Illus.). 32p. (J). (ps-1). 1998. pap. 3.99 (0-7613-2038-5); lib. bdg. 16.90 (0-7613-2013-X) Millbrook Pr.

— Busy Babies. LC 99-63971. (Illus.). 24p. (J). (ps-k). 2000. 7.95 (0-694-01364-1) HarpC Child Bks.

— Counting Kangaroos, a Book about Numbers. LC 89-4960. (Illus.). 24p. (J). (gr. k-2). 1990. lib. bdg. 14.50 (0-8167-1722-2) Troll Communs.

— Counting Kangaroos, a Book about Numbers. LC 89-4960. (Illus.). 24p. (J). (gr. k-2). 1997. pap. 2.50 (0-8167-1723-0) Troll Communs.

— Crickets Jokes Riddles. (J). 1984. pap. 5.95 (0-87548-416-6) Open Court.

— Dan & Dan. LC 97-31375. (Real Kids Readers Ser.). (Illus.). 32p. (J). (ps). 1998. pap. 3.99 (0-7613-2028-8) Millbrook Pr.

***Leonard, Marcia.** Dan & Dan. LC 97-31375. (Real Kids Readers Ser.). (Illus.). 32p. (J). (ps). 1998. lib. bdg. 16.90 (0-7613-2003-2) Millbrook Pr.

Leonard, Marcia. Dress-Up. LC 98-38105. (Real Kids Readers Ser.). (Illus.). 32p. (J). 1999. pap. 3.99 (0-7613-2078-4, Copper Beech Bks); lib. bdg. 16.90 (0-7613-2053-9, Copper Beech Bks) Millbrook Pr.

***Leonard, Marcia.** Favorite Colors. 24p. (J). (ps up). 2001. pap. 7.95 (0-694-01370-6, HarpFestival) HarpC Child Bks.

Leonard, Marcia. Finders Keepers. (The Kids on Bus 5 Ser.: No. 3). (J). (gr. 2-4). 1997. per. 3.50 (0-671-54211-7) PB.

— Food Is Fun! LC 99-63972. (Illus.). 24p. (J). (ps-k). 2000. 7.95 (0-694-01366-8) HarpC Child Bks.

— Get the Ball, Slim. LC 97-31376. (Real Kids Readers Ser.). (Illus.). 32p. (J). (ps-1). 1998. pap. 3.99 (0-7613-2025-3) Millbrook Pr.

***Leonard, Marcia.** Get the Ball, Slim. LC 97-31376. (Real Kids Readers Ser.). (Illus.). 32p. (J). (ps-1). 1998. lib. bdg. 16.90 (0-7613-2000-8) Millbrook Pr.

Leonard, Marcia. The Giant Baby & Other Giant Tales. LC 93-6225. (Hello Reader! Ser.: Level 4). (Illus.). 48p. (J). (ps-3). 1994. pap. 3.50 (0-590-46892-8) Scholastic Inc.

***Leonard, Marcia.** Guess Who. LC 99-6182. (Illus.). 20p. (J). (ps up). 2000. 7.95 (0-694-01374-9, HarpFestival) HarpC Child Bks.

Leonard, Marcia. Haunted House. (J). 1996. pap. 2.95 (0-8167-1889-X) Troll Communs.

— Hop, Skip, Run. LC 98-10252. (Real Kids Readers Ser.). (Illus.). 32p. (J). (ps-1). 1998. pap. 3.99 (0-7613-2040-7, Copper Beech Bks); lib. bdg. 16.90 (0-7613-2015-6, Copper Beech Bks) Millbrook Pr.

— How I Feel - Angry. (How I Feel Ser.). (Illus.). 24p. (J). 2000. pap. text 3.95 (1-891100-00-9) Smart Kids Publ.

— How I Feel - Happy. (How I Feel Ser.). (Illus.). 24p. (J). 2000. pap. text 3.95 (1-891100-01-7) Smart Kids Publ.

— How I Feel - Scared. (How I Feel Ser.). (Illus.). 24p. (J). 2000. pap. text 3.95 (1-891100-02-5) Smart Kids Publ.

— How I Feel - Silly. (How I Feel Ser.). (Illus.). 24p. (J). 2000. pap. text 3.95 (1-891100-03-3) Smart Kids Publ.

***Leonard, Marcia.** I Like Mess. LC 97-31368. (Real Kids Readers Ser.). (Illus.). 32p. (J). (ps-1). 1998. pap. 3.99 (0-7613-2027-X); lib. bdg. 16.90 (0-7613-2002-4) Millbrook Pr.

Leonard, Marcia. Is That Really You, Amy? (Here Comes the Brownies Ser.: No. 8). (Illus.). 64p. (J). (gr. 1-4). 1994. pap. 3.95 (0-448-40839-2, G & D) Peng Put Young Read.

— Jo Ann & the Surprise Party: A Brownie Girl Scout Book. (Here Comes the Brownies Ser.: No. 11). (Illus.). 64p. (J). (gr. 1-4). 1996. pap. 4.95 (0-448-40884-8, G & D) Peng Put Young Read.

— King Lionheart's Castle. (What Belongs? Ser.). (Illus.). 24p. (J). (ps-1). 1992. 5.95 (0-382-72974-9); lib. bdg. 9.98 (0-382-72973-0) Silver.

— The Kitten Twins: A Book about Opposites. LC 89-4945. (Illus.). 24p. (J). (gr. k-2). 1990. pap. 2.50 (0-8167-1725-7); lib. bdg. 14.50 (0-8167-1724-9) Troll Communs.

— Krissy & the Big Snow: A Brownie Girl Scout Book. LC 95-36195. (Here Comes the Brownies Ser.: No. 12). (Illus.). 64p. (Orig.). (J). (gr. 1-4). 1996. pap. 4.95 (0-448-40886-4, G & D) Peng Put Young Read.

***Leonard, Marcia.** Let's Go Baby-o! LC 99-66434. (Hanna Bks.). 24p. (J). 2000. 7.95 (0-694-01367-6, HarpFestival) HarpC Child Bks.

Leonard, Marcia. Mouse's Christmas. (Illus.). 16p. 1997. pap. 2.95 (0-8167-1494-0) Troll Communs.

— My Camp-Out. (Real Kids Readers Ser.). (Illus.). 32p. (J). (gr. k-1). 1999. lib. bdg. 16.90 (0-7613-2052-0, Copper Beech Bks) Millbrook Pr.

***Leonard, Marcia.** My Camp-Out. LC 98-38106. (Real Kids Readers Ser.). (Illus.). 32p. (J). (gr. k-1). 1999. pap. 3.99 (0-7613-2077-6, Copper Beech Bks) Millbrook Pr.

Leonard, Marcia. My Pal Al. LC 97-40289. (Real Kids Readers Ser.). (Illus.). 32p. (J). (ps-1). 1998. pap. 3.99 (0-7613-2026-1, Copper Beech Bks); lib. bdg. 16.90 (0-7613-2001-6, Copper Beech Bks) Millbrook Pr.

***Leonard, Marcia.** No New Pants! LC 98-52514. (Illus.). 32p. (J). 1999. 16.90 (0-7613-2063-6, Copper Beech Bks) Millbrook Pr.

Leonard, Marcia. No New Pants! LC 98-52514. (Real Kids Readers Ser.). (Illus.). 32p. (J). (gr. k-1). 1999. pap. 3.99 (0-7613-2088-1, Copper Beech Bks) Millbrook Pr.

— Noisy Neighbors: A Book about Animal Sounds. LC 89-4959. (Illus.). 24p. (J). (gr. k-2). 1990. pap. 2.50 (0-8167-1727-3); lib. bdg. 14.50 (0-8167-1726-5) Troll Communs.

***Leonard, Marcia.** The Opposite of Stop Is Go. LC 99-64436. (Hanna Bks.). 24p. (J). (ps up). 2000. 7.95 (0-694-01368-4, HarpFestival) HarpC Child Bks.

Leonard, Marcia. Paintbox Penguins, A Book about Colors. LC 89-4979. (Illus.). 24p. (J). (gr. k-2). 1990. lib. bdg. 14.50 (0-8167-1716-8) Troll Communs.

— Paintbox Penguins, A Book about Colors. LC 89-4979. (Illus.). 24p. (J). (gr. k-2). 1997. pap. 2.50 (0-8167-1717-6) Troll Communs.

— Paintbox Penguins, A Book about Colors. 1999. pap. text 16.95 (0-8167-2657-4) Troll Communs.

***Leonard, Marcia.** Peekaboo, Baby! LC 99-66183. (Illus.). 20p. (J). (ps-k). 2000. 7.95 (0-694-01373-0, HarpFestival) HarpC Child Bks.

Leonard, Marcia. The Pet Vet. LC 98-34285. (Real Kids Readers Ser.). (Illus.). 32p. (J). (ps-1). 1999. pap. 3.99 (0-7613-2075-X, Copper Beech Bks); lib. bdg. 16.90 (0-7613-2050-4, Copper Beech Bks) Millbrook Pr.

— Pine Cones & Holly. 1996. pap. 2.95 (0-8167-1493-2) Troll Communs.

— Pumpkin Magic. (J). 1996. pap. 2.95 (0-8167-1888-1) Troll Communs.

— Santa Bear. (Illus.). 16p. 1996. pap. 2.95 (0-8167-1495-9) Troll Communs.

— Splish, Splash! LC 99-63969. (Illus.). 24p. (J). (ps up). 2000. 7.95 (0-694-01365-X) HarpC Child Bks.

— Spots. LC 98-13970. (Real Kids Readers Ser.). (Illus.). 32p. (J). (ps-1). 1998. pap. 3.99 (0-7613-2041-5, Copper Beech Bks); lib. bdg. 16.90 (0-7613-2016-4, Copper Beech Bks) Millbrook Pr.

— The Tin Can Man. LC 98-10042. (Real Kids Readers Ser.). (Illus.). 32p. (J). (ps-1). 1998. pap. 3.99 (0-7613-2037-7); lib. bdg. 16.90 (0-7613-2012-1) Millbrook Pr.

— Waiting for Christmas. (Illus.). 16p. 1988. pap. 2.95 (0-8167-1490-8) Troll Communs.

— What Next?, 4 bks., Set. (Illus.). 24 pgs ea.p. (J). (ps-1). 1990. 19.80 (0-671-94102-X, Julian Messner); lib. bdg. 27.80 (0-671-94101-1, Julian Messner) Silver Burdett Pr.

An Asterisk (*) at the beginning of an entry indicates that the title is appearing for the first time.

— When the Giants Came to Town. (Hello, Reader! Ser.). (J). 1994. 8.70 (0-606-07137-7, Pub. by Turtleback) Demco.

— Wild Man at the Wheel. (The Kids on Bus 5 Ser.: No. 2). (J). (gr. 2-4). 1996. per. 3.50 (0-671-54191-9) PB.

Leonard, Marcia, jt. auth. see Brookes, Diane.

Leonard, Margaret. Headgear for the Future. 1987. pap. 3.50 (0-942396-43-X) Blackberry ME.

Leonard, Marica. I Survived on Bus 5. (The Kids on Bus 5 Ser.: No. 4). 80p. (J). (gr. 2-4). 1997. per. 3.50 (0-671-54215-X) PB.

Leonard, Mark, jt. auth. see Carr, Dawson.

Leonard, Mary A. Anderson - Denny, - Denny. William Anderson & Rebecca Denny & Their Descendants, 1706-1914. (Illus.). 287p. 1997. reprint ed. pap. 44.00 (0-8328-7265-2); reprint ed. lib. bdg. 54.00 (0-8328-7264-4) Higginson Bk Co.

Leonard, Maurice. Mae West: Empress of Sex. (Illus.). 424p. 1992. 22.50 (1-55972-151-0, Birch Ln Pr) Carol Pub Group.

***Leonard, Michael.** Lettergrams Find-a-Bible Word. Fittro, Pat, ed. 48p. 1999. pap. 1.49 (0-7847-1072-4, 02803) Standard Pub.

Leonard, Naomi E. Using MATLAB to Analyze & Design Control Systems. 2nd ed. 164p. (C). 1995. pap. text 34.80 (0-8053-2193-4) Benjamin-Cummings.

— Using MatLab to Analyze & Design Control Systems. 3rd ed. (C). 2000. pap. text. write for info. (0-201-35090-4) Addison-Wesley.

Leonard, Neil. Jazz & the White Americans: The Acceptance of a New Art Form. LC 62-19626. 225p. reprint ed. pap. 69.80 (0-608-16599-9, 202678000052) Bks Demand.

— Wellington's Army: Recreated in Colour Photographs. (Europa Militaria Ser.: No. 15). (Illus.). 96p. 1994. pap. 19.95 (1-872004-79-2, Pub. by Windrow & Green) Motorbooks Intl.

Leonard, Pamela & Hoffmann, Walter. Effective Global Environmental Protection: World Federalist Proposals to Strengthen the Role of the U. N. 42p. 1990. pap. 5.00 (1-880533-00-6) Wrld Federal.

Leonard, Pat. Damned If You Do. LC 93-90854. 260p. 1994. lib. bdg. 10.00 (0-9632933-2-X) Leonard Pubns.

— Proceed with Caution. LC 92-93411. 254p. 1992. pap. 19.95 (0-9632933-1-1); lib. bdg. 10.00 (0-9632933-0-3) Leonard Pubns.

Leonard, Paul. Genocide. (Doctor Who Ser.). 1998. pap. 5.95 (0-563-40572-4) BBC.

— Revolution Man. 1999. mass mkt. 5.95 (0-563-55570-X) BBC Worldwide.

Leonard, Paul & Mortimore, Jim. Decolog 5: Wonders. (Orig.). 1997. mass mkt. 6.95 (0-426-20515-4, Pub. by Virgin Bks) London Brdge.

Leonard, Paul & Walters, Nick. New Advanced Dry Pilgrimage. (New Adventures Ser.). mass mkt. 5.95 (0-426-20525-1, Pub. by Virgin Bks) London Brdge.

Leonard, Paul A. Commercial Bank Underwriting of Municipal Revenue Bonds. Dufey, Gunter, ed. LC 82-4753. (Research for Business Decisions Ser.: No. 48). 107p. 1982. reprint ed. pap. 33.20 (0-8357-1332-6, 207008000063) Bks Demand.

Leonard, Paul H., jt. auth. see Boone, J. Allen.

Leonard, Pauline, jt. auth. see Halford, Susan.

Leonard, Pauline, jt. ed. see Begley, Paul.

Leonard, Peggy C. Building a Medical Vocabulary. 3rd ed. (Illus.). 1993. pap., teacher ed. write for info. (0-7216-4739-1, W B Saunders Co) Harcrt Hlth Sci Grp.

— Building a Medical Vocabulary. 4th ed. LC 96-15373. (Illus.). 555p. 1997. pap. text 38.00 (0-7216-9642-2, W B Saunders Co) Harcrt Hlth Sci Grp.

— Building a Medical Vocabulary. 4th ed. (Illus.). 555p. 1997. pap., teacher ed. write for info. (0-7216-9643-0, W B Saunders Co) Harcrt Hlth Sci Grp.

Leonard, Peggy C. Instructor's Manual to Accompany Quick & Easy Medical Terminology. 3rd ed. (Illus.). 175p. Date not set. pap. text, teacher ed. write for info. (0-7216-8272-3, W B Saunders Co) Harcrt Hlth Sci Grp.

Leonard, Peggy C. Quick & Easy Medical Terminology. 2nd ed. (Illus.). 369p. 1995. pap., teacher ed., spiral bd. write for info. (0-7216-5687-0, W B Saunders Co) Harcrt Hlth Sci Grp.

— Quick & Easy Medical Terminology. 2nd ed. 352p. 1995. pap. text 30.00 (0-7216-5686-2, W B Saunders Co) Harcrt Hlth Sci Grp.

Leonard, Peter. Personality & Ideology. (Critical Texts in Social Work & the Welfare State). 225p. (C). 1997. text 21.95 (0-333-34726-9, Pub. by Macmillan) Humanities.

— Postmodern Welfare: Reconstructing & Empancipatory Project. LC 97-65514. 224p. 1997. text 69.95 (0-8039-7609-7); pap. text 23.95 (0-8039-7610-0) Sage.

— Records of a Voyage to the Western Coast of Africa in His Majesty's Ship Dryad & of Service on That Station for the Suppression of the Slave Trade in the Years 1830, 1831 & 1832. (B. E. Ser.: No. 154). 1833. 30.00 (0-8115-3072-8) Periodicals Srv.

— Saigon Guidebook. (Illus.). 96p. (Orig.). 1995. pap. 9.95 (0-9645457-9-9) VietnAm Trading.

Leonard, Peter, jt. ed. see McLaren, Peter.

Leonard, Peter, jt. ed. see Nichols, Barbara.

Leonard, Phyllis B. & Montgomery, Paula K. Cues: Choose, Use, Enjoy, Share: A Model for Educational Enrichment Through the School Library Media Center. 2nd ed. LC 98-8405. (Library & Information Problem-Solving Skills Ser.). 209p. 1998. 26.00 (1-56308-550-X) Teacher Ideas Pr.

Leonard, Pola, et al, eds. Not the Last Word: New Work from the Institute of American Indian Arts. 154p. (Orig.). (C). 1997. pap. text 8.00 (1-881396-13-4) IOA Indian Arts.

Leonard, R. C. & Leonard, J. E. The Promise of His Coming: Interpreting New Testament Statements Concerning the Time of Christ's Appearance. 223 p. (Orig.). 1996. pap. 12.95 (1-884454-05-4) Laudemont Pr.

Leonard, R. C., jt. auth. see Roulston, J. E.

***Leonard, R. L. & Mortimore, Roger.** Elections in Britain: A Voter's Guide. LC 00-41489. 2000. write for info. (0-333-91799-5, Pub. by Macmillan) St Martin.

Leonard, R. Leon. Air Quality Permitting. LC 96-20443. 224p. 1996. lib. bdg. 59.95 (0-87371-790-2, L790) Lewis Pubs.

Leonard, R. M., ed. A Book of Light Verse. LC 71-168784. (Granger Index Reprint Ser.). 1977. reprint ed. 24.95 (0-8369-6304-0) Ayer.

Leonard, R. V., ed. see Gotliffe, Harvey L.

Leonard, Raymond S. Construction Robotics: A Primer on Construction Automation. (Civil Engineering - Advisors Ser.). 1999. 55.00 (0-8493-7482-0) CRC Pr.

***Leonard, Raymond W.** Secret Soldiers of The Revolution 1918-1933: Soviet Military Intelligence, 183. LC 99-32003. Vol. 183. 240p. 1999. 59.95 (0-313-30990-6) Greenwood.

Leonard, Rebecca & Kendall, Katherine. Dysphagia Assessment & Treatment Planning: A Team Approach. LC 97-23885. (Illus.). 328p. (Orig.). 1997. pap. 65.00 (1-56593-749-X, 1458) Thomson Learn.

Leonard, Richard. With Unveiled Face: Charismatic Christians & Fulfilled Eschatology. 44p. 1993. pap. 4.95 (1-884454-04-6) Laudemont Pr.

Leonard, Richard A. A History of Russian Music. LC 77-6760. 395p. 1977. reprint ed. lib. bdg. 75.00 (0-8371-9658-2, LERM, Greenwood Pr) Greenwood.

— The Stream of Music: Music Book Index. 454p. 1993. reprint ed. lib. bdg. 99.00 (0-7812-9581-5) Rprt Serv.

Leonard, Richard G. Nothing Diplomatic: Five Decades of True & Witty Tales from a Globetrotting Diplomat. LC 96-86103. (Illus.). 128p. (Orig.). 1997. pap. 14.00 (1-885884-84-2) Cormorant Pr.

Leonard, Rita, jt. auth. see Our Lady of Perpetual Help Church Women's Guild St.

Leonard, Robert E., jt. auth. see Mundis, Jerrold J.

Leonard, Robert J. Human Gross Anatomy: An Outline Text. 456p. 1995. pap. text 27.95 (0-19-509003-9) OUP.

— Stupid Stories: Nonstop Nonsense for Children of All Ages. (Illus.). 108p. (Orig.). (J). (gr. 5-10). 1989. pap. 5.95 (0-930753-05-4) Spect Ln Pr.

Leonard, Robert J. & De Beer, Peter H. A Survival Kit for Teachers of Composition: Skill-by-Skill Writing Improvement Program. 256p. 1982. pap. text 26.95 (0-87628-777-1) Ctr Appl Res.

Leonard, Robert S., et al. The Arsenal Ship Acquisition Process Experience: Contrasting & Common Impressions from the Contractor Teams & Joint Program Office. LC 98-52862. (Illus.). 157p. 1999. pap. text 15.00 (0-8330-2690-9, MR-1030-DARPA) Rand Corp.

Leonard, Robert T. & Hepler, Peter K., eds. Calcium in Plant Growth: Thirteenth Annual Symposium in Plant Physiology. LC 89-82676. (Current Topics in Plant Physiology: an American Society of Plant Physiologists Ser.: Vol. IV). (Illus.). 275p. (Orig.). 1990. pap. 25.00 (0-943088-18-6) Am Soc of Plan.

Leonard, Robin. Bankruptcy: Is It the Right Solution to Your Debt Problems? LC 98-27090. (Quick & Legal Ser.). (Illus.). 300p. 1998. pap. 15.95 (0-87337-449-5) Nolo com.

— Chapter 13 Bankruptcy: Repay Your Debts. 3rd rev. ed. (Illus.). 368p. 1997. pap. 29.95 (0-87337-340-5) Nolo com.

— Chapter 13 Bankruptcy: Repay Your Debts. 4th ed. LC 98-39118. 368p. 1999. 29.95 (0-87337-501-7) Nolo com.

***Leonard, Robin.** Credit Repair. 4th ed. (Quick & Legal Ser.). 2000. pap. 18.95 (0-87337-565-3) Nolo com.

— Credit Repair: Quick & Legal. 3rd ed. Irving, Shae, ed. LC 98-51170. (Quick & Legal Ser.). (Illus.). 232p. 1999. pap. 15.95 (0-87337-516-5) Nolo com.

Leonard, Robin. Money Troubles: Legal Strategies to Cope with Your Debts. 4th ed. LC 96-7907. 360p. 1996. 19.95 (0-87337-341-3) Nolo com.

— Take Control of Your Student Loans. 2nd ed. LC 99-20334. 1999. pap. text 19.95 (0-87337-514-9) Nolo com.

Leonard, Robin & Elias, Stephen R. Nolo's Pocket Guide to Family Law. 4th ed. LC 95-26806. (Illus.). 208p. 1996. pap. text 14.95 (0-87337-322-7) Nolo com.

Leonard, Robin & Stewart, Marcia. 101 Law Forms for Personal Use. LC 98-5035. (Quick & Legal Ser.). (Illus.). 272p. (Orig.). 1997. pap. 24.95 (0-87337-412-6) Nolo com.

Leonard, Robin, ed. see Daily, Frederick W.

Leonard, Robin, ed. see Devine, George.

Leonard, Robin, ed. see Duncan, Roderic.

Leonard, Robin, ed. see Lyster, Mimi E.

Leonard, Robin, ed. see Starnes, Tanya.

Leonard, Robin, ed. see Warner, Ralph E. & Devine, George.

Leonard, Roger K. Triptychos by Thrice by Thrice. 76p. 1993. write for info. (0-9637851-0-9) R K Leonard.

Leonard, Ron. The Transcendental Philosophy of Franklin Merrell-Wolff. LC 98-53600. (SUNY series in Western Esoteric Traditions). 352p. (C). 1999. text 65.50 (0-7914-4215-2); pap. text 21.95 (0-7914-4216-0) State U NY Pr.

Leonard, Rosa M., ed. see Deans, Mary L.

Leonard, Sam. Mediation: The Book: A Step-by-Step Guide for Dispute Resolvers. LC 94-199240. (Illus.). 208p. (Orig.). 1994. pap. 19.95 (1-879260-25-5) Evanston Pub.

***Leonard, Schalk & Lin, Marjorie.** Dictionary of 1,000 Chinese Idioms. 160p. 2000. pap. 14.95 (0-7818-0820-0) Hippocrene Bks.

Leonard, Schalk & Lin, Marjorie, eds. Dictionary of 1,000 Chinese Proverbs. LC 98-7813. (Chinese Proverbs Ser.). 131p. 1998. pap. 11.95 (0-7818-0682-8) Hippocrene Bks.

Leonard, Scott, jt. ed. see Knowles, Sebastian.

Leonard, Scott A. Biotechnology: Gene Gun/Biolistic Technology: Bibliography: Jan. '92-Mar. '96. 58p. 1998. reprint ed. pap. text 25.00 (0-7881-3860-X) DIANE Pub.

Leonard, Scott A., ed. Biotechnology: Public Perception: Bibliography January 1992-March 1996. 39p. (C). 1997. pap. text 20.00 (0-7881-4886-9) DIANE Pub.

Leonard, Scott A. & Dobert, Raymond. Biotechnology: Legislation & Regulation: Bibliography: January 1991-March 1996. 52p. (Orig.). 1997. pap. text 30.00 (0-7881-3869-3) DIANE Pub.

— Herbicide Tolerance/Resistance in Plants: Bibliography: January 1991-June 1996. 68p. (Orig.). 1997. pap. text 35.00 (0-7881-3866-9) DIANE Pub.

***Leonard, Sean.** The Dragon Awakens: China's Long March to Geneva. 1999. 171.00 (1-874698-82-1, Pub. by Cameron May) Gaunt.

Leonard, Sheldon. And the Show Goes On: Broadway & Hollywood Adventures. LC 94-40934. (Illus.). 256p. 1995. 25.00 (0-87910-184-9) Limelight Edns.

Leonard, Siobhan, jt. ed. see Hegarty, Angela.

Leonard, Stephen J. & Noel, Thomas J. Denver: Mining Camp to Metropolis. (Illus.). 560p. 1991. pap. 34.95 (0-87081-240-8) Univ Pr Colo.

***Leonard, T.** A Course in Categorical Data Analysis. LC 99-47135. 224p. 1999. 49.95 (0-8493-0323-0) CRC Pr.

Leonard, Ted H. Alaskan Mail-Order Bride: An Alaskan Romance. LC 95-81186. (Illus.). 184p. (Orig.). 1996. pap. 9.50 (0-9641553-2-X) Alaska Wrd Wrks.

— Alaskan Wildlife: Humorous Perspectives on Life in the Bush. (Illus.). 160p. (Orig.). 1997. pap. 10.00 (0-9641553-3-8) Alaska Wrd Wrks.

— Are We Having Fun Yet? For Better or Verse. (Illus.). 64p. (Orig.). 1997. pap. 7.00 (0-9641553-4-6) Alaska Wrd Wrks.

— Neath the Midnight Sun: Alaskan Adventure. abr. ed. 196p. 1995. pap. 7.95 (1-56901-407-8) Alaska Wrd Wrks.

— Now! We're Having Fun: Humorous Anecdotes of Life on the Last Frontier. (Illus.). 160p. 1994. pap. 9.50 (0-9641553-0-3) Alaska Wrd Wrks.

— Now! We're Having Fun: Humorous Anecdotes of Life on the Last Frontier. rev. ed. (Illus.). 160p. 1997. pap. 10.00 (0-9641553-1-1) Alaska Wrd Wrks.

***Leonard, Terri.** In the Women's Clubhouse: The Greatest Women Golfers in Their Own Words. LC 99-40484. 256p. 2000. 22.95 (0-8092-2425-9, 242590, Contemporary Bks) NTC Contemp Pub Co.

Leonard, Thomas & Hsu, John S.J. Bayesian Methods: An Analysis for Statisticians & Interdisciplinary Researchers. LC 98-54415. (Cambridge Series in Statistical & Probabilistic Mathematics: Vol. 5). (Illus.). 350p. (C). 1999. text 64.95 (0-521-59417-0) Cambridge U Pr.

Leonard, Thomas, et al. Day by Day: The Seventies, 2 vols., Set. (Day by Day Ser.). (Illus.). 1328p. 1988. 195.00 (0-8160-1020-X) Facts on File.

Leonard, Thomas, jt. illus. see Daly, Catherine.

Leonard, Thomas C. News at the Hearth: A Drama of Reading in Nineteenth-Century America. 1993. pap. 7.00 (0-944026-42-7) Am Antiquarian.

— News for All: America's Coming-of-Age with the Press. (Illus.). 304p. 1995. text 30.00 (0-19-506454-2) OUP.

Leonard, Thomas J. The Portable Coach: 28 Surefire Strategies for Business & Personal Success. abr. ed. 1998. 17.00 incl. audio (0-671-58216-X, Audioworks) S&S Trade.

— Working Wisdom: Top 10 Lists for Improving Your Business. LC 97-28851. 218p. 1997. pap. 14.95 (1-885167-26-1) Bard Press.

***Leonard, Thomas J. & Laursen, Byron.** The Portable Coach: 28 Sure-Fire Strategies for Business & Personal Success. LC 98-26631. 336p. 1998. 23.00 (0-684-85041-9) Scribner.

Leonard, Thomas M. Castro & the Cuban Revolution. LC 98-41685. (Guides to Historic Events of the Twentieth Century Ser.). 224p. 1999. 39.95 (0-313-29979-X, Greenwood Pr) Greenwood.

— Central America & the United States: The Search for Stability. LC 90-24818. (United States & the Americas Ser.). 256p. 1991. pap. 20.00 (0-8203-1321-1) U of Ga Pr.

— Central America & the United States: The Search for Stability. LC 90-24818. (United States & the Americas Ser.). 256p. 1991. 40.00 (0-8203-1320-3) U of Ga Pr.

— A Guide to Central American Collections in the United States, 3. LC 94-10359. (Reference Guides to Archival & Manuscript Sources in World History Ser.: No. 3). 200p. 1994. lib. bdg. 75.00 (0-313-28689-2, Greenwood Pr) Greenwood.

***Leonard, Thomas M.** James K. Polk: A Clear & Unquestionable Destiny. LC 00-32961. (Biographies in American Foreign Policy Ser.). 2000. 17.95 (0-8420-2647-9) Scholarly Res Inc.

— James K. Polk: A Clear & Unquestionable Destiny. (Illus.). 2000. 50.00 (0-8420-2646-0) Scholarly Res Inc.

Leonard, Thomas M. Panama, the Canal, & the United States: A Guide to Issues & References. LC 93-26255. (Guides to Contemporary Issues Ser.: No. 9). 1993. 21.95 (0-941690-55-5); pap. 11.95 (0-941690-56-3) Regina Bks.

— The United States & Central America, 1944-1949: Perceptions of Political Dynamics. LC 83-5032. 230p. 1984. pap. 71.30 (0-608-05134-9, 206569500005) Bks Demand.

Leonard, Thomas M., ed. United States - Latin American Relations, 1850-1903: Establishing a Relationship. LC 98-58026. 392p. 1999. 44.95 (0-8173-0937-3) U of Ala Pr.

Leonard, Timothy. Geno: A Biography of Eugene Walsh, SS. 1988. pap. 12.95 (0-912405-42-2, Pastoral Press) OR Catholic.

***Leonard, Tina.** Cowboy Be Mine. (American Romance Ser.: No. 811). 2000. per. 4.25 (0-373-16811-X, 1-16811-1, Harlequin) Harlequin Bks.

Leonard, Tina. Cowboy Cootchie-Coo: (Accidental Dads) (American Romance Ser.: Vol. 748). 1998. per. 3.99 (0-373-16748-2, 1-16748-5) Harlequin Bks.

— Daddy's Little Darlings: Gowns of White. 1998. per. 3.99 (0-373-16758-X, 1-16758-4, Mira Bks) Harlequin Bks.

— Desperado. (Scarlet Ser.). 1998. mass mkt. 3.99 (1-85487-881-6, Pub. by Scarlet Bks) London Brdge.

— It Takes Two: Battle of the Sexes. 400p. (Orig.). 1996. mass mkt. 3.99 (1-85487-482-9, Pub. by Scarlet Bks) London Brdge.

***Leonard, Tina.** A Man of Honor: A Crookseye Canyon Story, Vol. 576. (Intrigue Ser.). 2000. mass mkt. 4.25 (0-373-22576-8, 1-22576-2) Harlequin Bks.

Leonard, Tina. A Match Made in Texas. (American Romance Ser.: No. 796). 1999. per. 3.99 (0-373-16796-2, 1-16796-4) Harlequin Bks.

***Leonard, Tina.** The Most Eligible . . . Daddy: Sexy Single Dads. 1999. per. 3.99 (0-373-16771-7, 1-16771-7, Harlequin) Harlequin Bks.

Leonard, Tina. Never Say Never. 400p. (Orig.). 1997. mass mkt. 3.99 (1-85487-715-1, Pub. by Scarlet Bks) London Brdge.

— Secret Sins. (Scarlet Ser.). (Orig.). 1997. mass mkt. 3.99 (1-85487-955-3, Pub. by Scarlet Bks) London Brdge.

***Leonard, Tina.** Special Order Groom. (American Romance Ser.: Bk. 846). 2000. mass mkt. 4.25 (0-373-16846-2, 1-16846-7) Harlequin Bks.

— Surprise! Surprise! Maitland Maternity: Double Deliveries. (American Romance Ser.: Bk. 829). 2000. per. 4.25 (0-373-16829-2, 1-6829-3) Harlequin Bks.

***Leonard, Tom.** A Course in Categorical Data Analysis. (Texts in Statistical Science Ser.). 208p. 1999. per. 49.95 (1-58488-180-1, Chap & Hall CRC) CRC Pr.

Leonard, Tom. On the Mass Bombing of Kuwait, Commonly Known As the "Gulf War" 24p. (Orig.). 1992. pap. 4.00 (1-873176-25-2, AK Pr San Fran) AK Pr Dist.

Leonard, Tom, ed. Radical Renfrew. 1990. 24.00 (0-7486-6028-3, Pub. by Polygon) Subterranean Co.

Leonard, V. A. & More, Harry W. Police Organization & Management. 8th ed. (Police Science Ser.). 650p. (C). 1993. text 34.95 (1-56662-049-X) Foundation Pr.

Leonard, Venelda H. Sourwood. 430p. 1995. 24.95 (0-9647919-0-0) Leonard Publ.

Leonard, Vincent F., Jr. Analog Circuit Design. Fry, Jim, ed. LC 84-21727. (Circuit Design Ser.). (Illus.). 750p. 1984. ring bd. 69.95 (0-87119-102-4, EE-1003) Heathkit-Zenith Ed.

— Passive Circuit Design. (Engineering Design Ser.). (Illus.). 583p. (C). 1983. pap. text 17.95 (0-87119-020-6); student ed., ring bd. 10.95 (0-87119-021-4); ring bd. 49.95 (0-87119-019-2, EE-1001); 9.95 (0-87119-022-2) Heathkit-Zenith Ed.

— Transistor Circuit Design. (Engineering Design Ser.). (Illus.). 583p. (C). 1983. teacher ed. 9.95 (0-87119-018-4); student ed. 10.95 (0-87119-017-6); pap. text 19.95 (0-87119-016-8); ring bd. 59.95 (0-87119-015-X, EE-1002) Heathkit-Zenith Ed.

Leonard, Virginia. Politicians, Pupils, & Priests: Argentino Education since 1743. (American University Studies: Ser. XXII, Vol. 2). XIV, 456p. (C). 1989. text 59.95 (0-8204-0748-8) P Lang Pubng.

Leonard, W. A. Stephen Banks Leonard of Owego, Tioga Co., N. Y. (Illus.). 342p. 1990. reprint ed. pap. 52.00 (0-8328-1491-1); reprint ed. lib. bdg. 60.00 (0-8328-1490-3) Higginson Bk Co.

Leonard, Wilbert M., 2nd. Basic Social Statistics. 458p. (C). 1996. pap. text 31.95 (0-87563-580-6) Stipes.

Leonard, Willard. Horse Sense. (Illus.). 144p. 1984. 15.95 (0-87595-115-5); pap. 9.95 (0-87595-116-3) Oregon Hist.

Leonard, William, jt. auth. see Barba, James.

Leonard, William E. Byron & Byronism in America. LC 64-23597. 126p. (C). 1964. lib. bdg. 75.00 (0-8383-0582-2) M S G Haskell Hse.

— Byron & Byronism in America. LC 65-24997. 126p. 1965. reprint ed. 50.00 (0-87752-062-3) Gordian.

Leonard, William E., ed. see Lucretius.

Leonard, William F. & Martin, Thomas L. Electronic Structure & Transport Properties of Crystals. LC 79-13471. 720p. (Orig.). 1980. lib. bdg. 79.50 (0-88275-986-8) Krieger.

Leonard, William J. The Letter Carrier: Autobiography of William J. Leonard, S.J. LC 93-18887. 384p. (Orig.). 1993. 29.95 (1-55612-651-4); pap. 15.95 (1-55612-671-9) Sheed & Ward WI.

— Where Thousands Fell. 256p. (Orig.). 1995. pap. 15.95 (1-55612-755-3); pap. 29.95 (1-55612-756-1) Sheed & Ward WI.

Leonard, William L. Radiography Assess Test. 2nd ed. 1995. 19.95 (0-9644624-1-9) JLW Pub.

— Radiography Examination Review. 8th ed. (Illus.). 174p. (C). 29.95 (0-9644624-0-0) JLW Pub.

— Radiography Examination Review. 9th rev. ed. (Illus.). 174p. (C). 1997. pap. text 29.95 (0-9644624-2-7) JLW Pub.

— Self-Study Exercises in Radiography. 2nd ed. (Illus.). 260p. (C). 1998. pap. text 29.95 (0-9644624-3-5) JLW Pub.

L

L

Leonard, William N. Railroad Consolidation under the Transportation Act of 1920. LC 68-58602. (Columbia University. Studies in the Social Sciences: No. 522). reprint ed. 29.50 (*0-404-51522-3*) AMS Pr.

Leonard, William P., et al. Amphibians of Washington & Oregon. (Trailside Ser.). (Illus.). 168p. 1996. reprint ed. pap. 14.95 (*0-914516-10-8*) Seattle Audubon Soc.

Leonard, William P., jt. auth. see West, Larry.

Leonard, William P., jt. ed. see Storm, Robert M.

Leonard, William R., et al. U. N. Development Aid: Criteria & Methods of Evaluation. LC 75-140126. (UNITAR Studies). 1971. 23.95 (*0-405-02235-2*) Ayer.

Leonard, William T. Masquerade in Black. LC 86-6597. (Illus.). 443p. 1986. 50.00 (*0-8108-1895-7*) Scarecrow.

— Theatre: Stage to Screen to Television, 2 vols. LC 80-22987. 1812p. 1981. 99.50 (*0-8108-1374-2*) Scarecrow.

Leonard, Zenas. Adventures of a Mountain Man: The Narrative of Zenas Leonard. Quaife, Milo M., ed. LC 78-17427. (Illus.). xx, 274p. 1978. reprint ed. text 25.00 (*0-8032-2853-8*) U of Nebr Pr.

— Adventures of a Mountain Man: The Narrative of Zenas Leonard. Quaife, Milo M., ed. LC 78-17427. (Illus.). xx, 274p. 1978. reprint ed. pap. 12.95 (*0-8032-7903-5*, Bison Books) U of Nebr Pr.

Leonard, Zoe, photos by. The Fae Richards Photo Archive. (Illus.). 34p. 15.00 (*0-9631095-8-8*) Artspace Bks.

Leonarda, Isabella. Isabella Leonarda: Selected Compositions. Carter, Stewart, ed. (Recent Researches in Music of the Baroque Era Ser.: Vol. RRB59). (Illus.). xxii, 104p. 1988. pap. 40.00 (*0-89579-227-3*) A-R Eds.

Leonardelli, Carol A. The Milwaukee Evaluation of Daily Living Skills: Evaluation in Long-Term Psychiatric Care (MEDLS) LC 88-42542. 136p. 1988. pap. 25.00 (*1-55642-039-0*) SLACK Inc.

Leonardi, Dell. The Reincarnation of John Wilkes Booth: A Study in Hypnotic Regression. LC 74-27952. 180p. reprint ed. pap. 55.80 (*0-608-30772-6*, 202271000029) Bks Demand.

Leonardi, E. & Madhusudana, C. V. Heat & Mass Transfer Australasia, 1996: Proceedings of the Sixth Australasian Heat & Mass Transfer Conference, December 9-12, 1996, Sydney, Australia. LC 97-52398. 596p. 1998. write for info. (*1-56700-099-1*) Begell Hse.

Leonardi, Leonardo & Ribolini, Gabriele. Pocket Watches: L'Orologio da Tasca. LC 93-48527. (Bella Cosa Ser.). (ITA & ENG., Illus.). 144p. 1994. pap. 12.95 (*0-8118-0753-3*) Chronicle Bks.

Leonardi Leone, Norma. A Mother's Guide to Computers. Koenemann, Jean, ed. LC 85-46037. (Illus.). 102p. (Orig.). 1986. pap. 5.95 (*0-936635-03-7*) Lion Pr & Vid.

***Leonardi, Louis.** The Ultimate Experience of Fire & Ice. 173p. 1998. 22.95 (*0-9664677-1-X*, Pub. by Da Vinci Pr); pap. 14.95 (*0-9664677-0-1*, Pub. by Da Vinci Pr) New Leaf Dist.

Leonardi, Paolo & Santambrogio, Marco, eds. On Quine: New Essays. (Illus.). 371p. (C). 1995. text 80.00 (*0-521-47091-9*) Cambridge U Pr.

Leonardi, Robert. Italian Politics, Vol. 1. 204p. 1987. text 40.00 (*0-86187-691-1*, Pub. by P P Pubs) Cassell & Continuum.

Leonardi, Robert, ed. The Regions & the European Community: The Regional Response to the Single Market in the Underdeveloped Areas. LC 92-28756. 1992. 37.50 (*0-7146-3460-3*, Pub. by F Cass Pubs) Intl Spec Bk.

Leonardi, Robert & Anderlini, Fausto, eds. Italian Politics Vol. 6: A Review. 250p. 1992. text 59.00 (*1-85567-047-X*, Pub. by P P Pubs) Cassell & Continuum.

Leonardi, Robert & Corbetta, Piergiorgio, eds. Italian Politics Vol. 4: A Review. 250p. 1990. text 47.50 (*0-86187-852-3*, Pub. by P P Pubs) Cassell & Continuum.

Leonardi, Robert & Nanetti, Rafaella Y., eds. Regional Development in a Modern European Economy: The Case of Tuscany. 256p. 1994. 49.00 (*1-85567-155-7*, Pub. by P P Pubs) Cassell & Continuum.

— The Regions & European Integration. 1992. text 39.00 (*0-86187-149-9*) St Martin.

Leonardi, Robert & Nanetti, Raffaella. Regional Development in a Modern European Economy: The Case of Tuscany. 2nd ed. LC 97-38231. 1998. 69.95 (*1-85567-515-3*) Bks Intl VA.

Leonardi, Robert & Nanetti, Raffaella Y. Italy: Politics & Policy. (European Political Economy Ser.). (Illus.). 265p. 1996. text 77.95 (*1-85521-764-3*, Pub. by Dartmth Pub) Ashgate Pub Co.

Leonardi, Robert, jt. ed. see Nanetti, Rafaella Y.

Leonardi, Rosarius R. Fire on the Beach. LC 96-11183. 60p. 1996. pap. 14.95 (*0-7734-2686-8*, Mellen Poetry Pr) E Mellen.

Leonardi, Susan J. Dangerous by Degrees: Women at Oxford & the Somerville College Novelists. (Illus.). 260p. 1989. text 45.00 (*0-8135-1365-0*); pap. text 12.95 (*0-8135-1366-9*) Rutgers U Pr.

Leonardi, Susan J. & Pope, Rebbecca A. The Diva's Mouth: Body, Voice, Prima Donna Politics. (Illus.). 325p. (C). 1996. text 50.00 (*0-8135-2303-6*); pap. text 17.95 (*0-8135-2304-4*) Rutgers U Pr.

Leonardi, Tom. The Secrets of Sensual Love. 1999. pap. 9.95 (*0-452-27457-5*, Plume) Dutton Plume.

Leonardi, Tommy. Secrets of Sensual Lovemaking: The Ultimate in Female Ecstasy. 1998. mass mkt. 5.99 (*0-451-18477-7*, Sig) NAL.

Leonardis, David J. de, see De Leonardis, David J.

Leonardis, Rocco. Systematic Guide to Perspective: A Step-by-Step Handbook for the Classroom & the Professional. LC 97-75490. (Illus.). 120p. 1998. pap. text 15.00 (*1-890053-01-5*) NY Schl Interior Des.

Leonardo, Bianca & Rugg, Winnifred K. Anne Hutchinson: Unsung Heroine of History 1591-1643. 2nd rev. unabridged ed. LC 95-3439. Orig. Title: Unafraid: A Life of Anne Hutchinson. (Illus.). 350p. (Orig.). 1995. pap. 19.95 (*0-930852-30-3*) Tree Life Pubns.

Leonardo, Bianca, jt. auth. see Gregory, Scott J.

Leonardo, Bianca, jt. auth. see Welsh, Philip J.

Leonardo, Bianca, ed. see Brandt, Johanna.

Leonardo, Bianca, ed. see Conwell, Russell H.

Leonardo, Bianca, ed. see Gregory, Scott J.

Leonardo, Bianca, ed. see Notovitch, Nicolas.

Leonardo, Bianca, ed. & intro. see Conwell, Russell H.

Leonardo da Vinci. Drawings of Da Vinci. Belt, Elmer, ed. (Master Draughtsman Ser.). (Illus.). (Orig.). 1962. pap. 4.95 (*0-87505-157-X*) Borden.

— Leonardo da Vinci: Artist - Scientist - Inventor. (Illus.). 224p. 1996. pap. 35.00 (*3-7757-0625-9*, 620162, Pub. by Gerd Hatje) Dist Art Pubs.

— Leonardo da Vinci Drawings. (Illus.). 64p. 1980. pap. 4.95 (*0-486-23951-9*) Dover.

— Leonardo on the Human Body. (Fine Art Ser.). (Illus.). 506p. 1983. reprint ed. pap. 21.95 (*0-486-24483-0*) Dover.

— Notebooks of Leonardo Da Vinci, 1. (Illus.). 860p. 1970. reprint ed. pap. 18.95 (*0-486-22572-0*) Dover.

— Notebooks of Leonardo Da Vinci, 2. (Illus.). 860p. 1970. reprint ed. pap. 19.95 (*0-486-22573-9*) Dover.

Leonardo, J., jt. auth. see Carroll, S.

Leonardo, Joe, ed. see International SAMPE Technical Conference Staff.

Leonardo, Zeus, jt. ed. see Tejeda, Carlos.

***Leonardy, Ernst & Roland, Hubert.** Deutsch-Belgische Beziehungen Im Kulturellen Und Literarischen Bereich 1890-1940 les Relations Culturelles et Litteraires Belgo-Allemandes 1890-1940. (Illus.). 289p. 1999. 48.95 (*3-631-34294-2*) P Lang Pubng.

Leonberger, F. J., et al, eds. Picosecond Electronics & Optoelectronics II. (Electronics & Photonics Ser.: Vol. 24). (Illus.). 280p. 1987. 75.95 (*0-387-18329-9*) Spr-Verlag.

Leonbruno, Frank. Lake George Reflections: Island History & Lore. Henry, Ginger, ed. LC 98-7370. (Illus.). 236p. 1998. pap. 18.00 (*0-935796-97-5*) Purple Mnt Pr.

Leoncavallo, Ruggiero. I Pagliacci: Vocal Score. (ENG & ITA.). 212p. 1986. pap. 20.95 (*0-7935-2548-9*, 50338260) H Leonard.

— Pagliacci in Full Score. 304p. 1993. text 16.95 (*0-486-27363-6*) Dover.

— Pagliacci Libretto. (ENG & ITA.). 32p. 1986. pap. 4.95 (*0-7935-2616-7*, 50340300) H Leonard.

***Leoncini, Luca.** Living in History. 1999. pap. 55.00 (*88-422-0841-8*) Dist Art Pubs.

Leoncini, Mauro, jt. auth. see Codenotti, B.

Leoncker, Tracy, ed. Computing in Civil Engineering. LC 86-25911. (Proceedings of the Fourth Conference Ser.). 1018p. 1986. pap. 11.00 (*0-87262-569-9*) Am Soc Civil Eng.

Leondar, Barbara, jt. ed. see Perkins, David.

Leondes. Fuzzy Theory Systems: Techniques & Applications, Vol. 1. 1999. text 150.00 (*0-12-443871-7*) Acad Pr.

— Neural Network Systems Techniques & Applications, 7 vols. 1997. write for info. (*0-12-443860-1*) Acad Pr.

Leondes, Cornelius T. Fuzzy Theory Systems, 4 vols. 1856p. 1999. 550.00 (*0-12-443870-9*) Acad Pr.

— Fuzzy Theory Systems, Vol. 3. 1999. text 150.00 (*0-12-443873-3*) Acad Pr.

— Fuzzy Theory Systems: Techniques & Applications, Vol. 2. 1999. text 150.00 (*0-12-443872-5*) Acad Pr.

— Fuzzy Theory Systems: Techniques & Applications, Vol. 4. 1999. text 150.00 (*0-12-443874-1*) Acad Pr.

***Leondes, Cornelius T.** Knowledge-Based Systems: Techniques & Applications, 4 vols. 1700p. 2000. 895.00 (*0-12-443875-X*) Acad Pr.

Leondes, Cornelius T. Structural Dynamic Systems Computational Techniques & Optimization: Finite Element Analysis Techniques. (Engineering, Technology, & Applied Science Ser.: Vol. 8). 336p. 1998. text 120.00 (*90-5699-643-6*, ECU81, Harwood Acad Pubs) Gordon & Breach.

Leondes, Cornelius T., ed. Control & Dynamic Systems Vol. 68: Digital Signal Processing Systems Implementation Techniques. (Illus.). 400p. 1995. text 104.00 (*0-12-012768-7*) Acad Pr.

— Control & Dynamic Systems Vol. 69: Multidimentional Systems: Advances in Theory & Applications. (Multidimensional Systems: Vol. 69). (Illus.). 441p. 1995. text 104.00 (*0-12-012769-5*) Acad Pr.

— Control & Dynamic Systems Vol. 70: Digital Control Systems Implementation Techniques. (Illus.). 383p. 1995. text 104.00 (*0-12-012770-9*) Acad Pr.

— Control & Dynamic Systems Vol. 71: Discrete-Time Control System Analysis & Design. (Illus.). 349p. 1995. text 104.00 (*0-12-012771-7*) Acad Pr.

— Control & Dynamic Systems Vol. 72: Discrete-Time Control System Implementation Techniques. (Illus.). 351p. 1995. text 104.00 (*0-12-012772-5*) Acad Pr.

— Control & Dynamic Systems Vol. 73: Techniques in Discrete-Time Stochastic Control Systems. (Illus.). 319p. 1995. text 104.00 (*0-12-012773-3*) Acad Pr.

— Control & Dynamic Systems Vol. 74: Techniques in Discrete & Continuous Robust Systems, Vol. 74. (Illus.). 313p. 1996. text 99.00 (*0-12-012774-1*) Acad Pr.

— Control & Dynamic Systems Vol. 75: Computer Techniques & Algorithms in Digital Signal Processing, Vol. 75. (Illus.). 411p. 1996. text 99.00 (*0-12-012775-X*) Acad Pr.

— Control & Dynamic Systems Vol. 76: Stochastic Digital Control System Techniques. (Illus.). 427p. 1996. text 99.00 (*0-12-012776-8*) Acad Pr.

— Control & Dynamic Systems Vol. 77: Multidimensional Systems Signal Processing Algorithms & Application Techniques. (Illus.). 401p. 1996. text 99.00 (*0-12-012777-6*) Acad Pr.

— Control & Dynamic Systems Vol. 78: Digital Control & Signal Processing Systems & Techniques. (Illus.). 388p. 1996. text 99.00 (*0-12-012778-4*) Acad Pr.

— Control & Dynamic Systems Vol. 79: Digital Control Systems Implementation & Computational Techniques. (Illus.). 393p. 1996. text 99.00 (*0-12-012779-2*) Acad Pr.

— Medical Imaging Systems Techniques & Applications: Brain & Skeletal Systems. (International Series in Engineering, Technology & Applied Science: Vol. 2). 258p. 1997. text 52.00 (*90-5699-541-3*) Gordon & Breach.

— Medical Imaging Systems Techniques & Applications: Cardiovascular Systems. (Gordon & Breach International Ser. I). 226p. 1997. text 49.00 (*90-5699-509-X*) Gordon & Breach.

— Medical Imaging Systems Techniques & Applications: Computational Techniques. (International Series in Engineering, Technology & Applied Science: Vol. 6). 264p. 1998. text 89.00 (*90-5699-620-7*) Gordon & Breach.

— Medical Imaging Systems Techniques & Applications: Diagnosis Optimization Techniques. (International Series in Engineering, Technology & Applied Science: Vol. 3). 336p. 1997. text 52.00 (*90-5699-595-2*) Gordon & Breach.

— Medical Imaging Systems Techniques & Applications: General Anatomy, Vol. 4. (International Series in Engineering, Technology & Applied Science). 334p. 1997. text 58.00 (*90-5699-597-9*) Gordon & Breach.

— Medical Imaging Systems Techniques & Applications: Modalities. (Gordon & Breach International Ser. I). 340p. 1997. text 58.00 (*90-5699-610-X*) Gordon & Breach.

— Neural Network Systems Techniques & Applications Vol. 1: Algorithms & Architecture. LC 97-80441. (Illus.). 480p. 1997. text 69.95 (*0-12-443861-X*) Morgan Kaufmann.

— Neural Network Systems Techniques & Applications Vol. 2: Neural Network Systems, Vol. 2. (Neural Network Systems Techniques & Applications Ser.). (Illus.). 398p. 1997. text 69.95 (*0-12-443862-8*) Morgan Kaufmann.

— Neural Network Systems Techniques & Applications Vol. 3: Implementation Techniques, Vol. 3. (Neural Network Systems Techniques & Applications Ser.). (Illus.). 432p. 1997. text 69.95 (*0-12-443863-6*) Morgan Kaufmann.

— Neural Network Systems Techniques & Applications Vol. 4: Industrial & Manufacturing Systems, Vol. 4. (Neural Network Systems Techniques & Applications Ser.). (Illus.). 384p. 1997. text 69.95 (*0-12-443864-4*) Morgan Kaufmann.

— Neural Network Systems Techniques & Applications Vol. 5: Image Processing & Pattern Recognition, Vol. 5. (Neural Network Systems Techniques & Applications Ser.). (Illus.). 416p. 1997. text 69.95 (*0-12-443865-2*) Morgan Kaufmann.

— Neural Network Systems Techniques & Applications Vol. 6: Fuzzy Logic & Expert Systems Applications, Vol. 6. (Neural Network Systems Techniques & Applications Ser.). (Illus.). 384p. 1997. text 69.95 (*0-12-443866-0*) Morgan Kaufmann.

— Neural Network Systems Techniques & Applications Vol. 7: Control & Dynamic Systems, Vol. 7. (Neural Network Systems Techniques & Applications Ser.). (Illus.). 438p. 1997. text 69.95 (*0-12-443867-9*) Morgan Kaufmann.

***Leondes, Cornelius T., ed.** Optimization Techniques. 284p. 1998. text 120.00 (*90-5699-644-4*, Harwood Acad Pubs) Gordon & Breach.

— Reliability & Damage Tolerance. 304p. 1998. text 120.00 (*90-5699-652-5*, Harwood Acad Pubs) Gordon & Breach.

— Seismic Techniques. 252p. 1999. 120.00 (*90-5699-656-8*, Harwood Acad Pubs) Gordon & Breach.

Leondes, Cornelius T., ed. Structural Dynamic Systems Computational Techniques & Optimization: Computer-Aided Design & Engineering. (Engineering, Technology, & Applied Science Ser.: Vol. 7). 268p. 1998. text 120.00 (*90-5699-642-8*, ECU81, Harwood Acad Pubs) Gordon & Breach.

***Leondes, Cornelius T., ed.** Structural Dynamic Systems Computational Techniques & Optimization: Dynamic Analysis & Control Techniques. 324p. 1999. text 120.00 (*90-5699-658-4*, G & B Science) Gordon & Breach.

— Structural Dynamic Systems Computational Techniques & Optimization: Nonlinear Techniques. 344p. 1999. 120.00 (*90-5699-659-2*) Gordon & Breach.

— Structural Dynamic Systems Computational Techniques & Optimization: Parameters. 295p. 1999. text 120.00 (*90-5699-657-6*, Harwood Acad Pubs) Gordon & Breach.

— Techniques in Buildings & Bridges. 300p. 1998. text 120.00 (*90-5699-655-X*, Harwood Acad Pubs) Gordon & Breach.

Leondopoulos, Jordan. Still the Moving World: Intolerance, Modernism, & Heart of Darkness. LC 90-35558. (Literature & the Visual Arts: Ser.: Vol. 7). XII, 210p. (C). 1991. text 40.95 (*0-8204-1388-7*) P Lang Pubng.

Leone. Atlas of Orbital Surgery. 1992. text 95.00 (*0-7216-3215-7*, W B Saunders Co) Harcrt Hlth Sci Grp.

Leone, A. & Mercer, J. F. B., eds. Copper Transport & Its Disorders: Molecular & Cellular Aspects. LC 98-46056. (Advances in Experimental Medicine & Biology Ser.: 448). (Illus.). 269p. (C). 1999. text 149.50 (*0-306-46045-9*, Kluwer Plenum) Kluwer Academic.

Leone, A., jt. ed. see Grillo, S.

Leone, Annalisa, et al. Fundamentals of Engineering Afternoon Exam for Chemical Engineering. (Illus.). 454p. (C). Date not set. pap. text 60.00 (*1-882767-23-3*) ETS.

Leone, Anthony, jt. auth. see Turner Publishing Company Staff.

Leone, Bill, jt. auth. see Corbett, Lynn.

Leone, Bruno, ed. Communism: Opposing Viewpoints. 2nd rev. ed. LC 86-338. (Isms Ser.). (Illus.). 210p. (Orig.). 1986. lib. bdg. 26.20 (*0-89908-385-4*) Greenhaven.

— Free Speech. LC 93-19855. (Current Controversies Ser.). 240p. (YA). 1994. pap. 16.20 (*1-56510-077-8*); lib. bdg. 26.20 (*1-56510-078-6*) Greenhaven.

— Nationalism. 2nd rev. ed. LC 86-324. (Isms Ser.). (Illus.). 150p. (YA). (gr. 9-12). 1986. lib. bdg. 26.20 (*0-89908-387-0*) Greenhaven.

Leone, Bruno & De Koster, Katie, eds. Rape on Campus. LC 94-42400. (At Issue Ser.). 1995. lib. bdg. 18.70 (*1-56510-296-7*) Greenhaven.

Leone, Bruno, jt. ed. see DeKoster, Katie.

Leone, Carmen J. Rose Street: A Family History. 2nd ed. LC 99-191293. 267p. 1998. write for info. (*0-917530-52-7*) Pig Iron Pr.

***Leone, Carmen J.** Rose Street Revisited, 2 vols. 2000. pap. 10.95 (*0-936369-48-5*) Son-Rise Pubns.

Leone, Dan. Eat This, San Francisco: A Narrated Roadmap to Dives, Joints, All-Night Cafes, Noodle Houses, Buffets & Other Cheap Places to Eat in the Bay Area. LC 99-15348. (Illus.). 348p. 1999. pap. 16.95 (*1-57061-184-X*) Sasquatch Bks.

***Leone, Dan.** The Meaning of Lunch. LC 99-65036. 257p. (YA). 2000. pap. 14.95 (*0-9666028-7-0*, Pub. by Mammoth Press) SPD-Small Pr Dist.

Leone, Dan. Meaning of Lunch: The Collected Restaurant Ramblings of San Francisco's Cheapest Eater. 1998. pap. text 13.95 (*0-9653524-9-8*) Russn Hill Pr.

Leone, Daniel, ed. Physician-Assisted Suicide. LC 97-27792. (At Issue Ser.). 107p. (YA). (gr. 5-12). 1997. 18.70 (*1-55610-019-0*); pap. 11.20 (*1-56510-018-2*) Greenhaven.

— The Spread of AIDS. LC 96-42912. (At Issue Ser.). 96p. (J). (gr. 5-12). 1997. pap. 11.20 (*1-56510-537-0*) Greenhaven.

Leone, Daniel, ed. The Spread of AIDS. LC 96-42912. (At Issue Ser.). (J). (gr. 5-12). 1997. lib. bdg. 18.70 (*1-56510-538-9*) Greenhaven.

Leone, Daniel A., ed. The Ethics of Euthanasia. LC 98-36587. (At Issue Ser.). 96p. (YA). (gr. 9-12). 1998. lib. bdg. 21.20 (*0-7377-0005-X*) Greenhaven.

***Leone, Daniel A., ed.** The Ethics of Euthanasia. LC 98-36587. (At Issue Ser.). 96p. (YA). (gr. 9-12). 1998. pap. 12.45 (*0-7377-0004-1*) Greenhaven.

Leone, Dee. The Stories of Noah & Joseph. (Bible-Time Puzzle Ser.). (Illus.). 48p. (J). (ps-1). 1992. 7.95 (*0-86653-645-0*, SS2811, Shining Star Pubns) Good Apple.

***Leone, Diana.** Attic Windows: A New View. 2nd rev. ed. LC 99-66145. (Illus.). 96p. 2000. pap. 19.95 (*0-87341-834-4*, ATWI) Krause Pubns.

Leone, Diana. Crazy with Cotton. Aneloski, Elizabeth, ed. (Illus.). 96p. (Orig.). 1996. pap. 21.95 (*1-57120-017-7*, 10141) C & T Pub.

— Diana's Watercolor Jacket. (Illus.). 32p. 1995. pap. text 14.95 (*0-942786-37-8*) Eddies Q Bee.

— The New Sampler Quilt. McAndrew, Maura, ed. LC 95-83398. (Illus.). 144p. 1993. reprint ed. 24.95 (*1-57120-011-8*, 10135) C & T Pub.

***Leone, Diana & Walter, Cindy.** Fine Hand Quilting. 2nd ed. LC 99-66142. (Illus.). 112p. 2000. pap. 19.95 (*0-87341-835-2*, FHQU) Krause Pubns.

Leone, Edward. Seasons of Love. LC 92-7373. 80p. 1992. 9.95 (*0-87319-035-1*) Hallberg Pub Corp.

Leone, Francis. The Atom: Heart & Science & Technology. LC 86-81737. (Illus.). 177p. 1986. 24.95 (*0-914587-03-X*) Helix Pr.

— Genetics: The Mystery & the Promise. 240p. 1991. 24.95 (*0-8306-3068-6*) McGraw-Hill Prof.

— Genetics: The Mystery & the Promise. (Illus.). 240p. 1991. pap. 14.95 (*0-8306-3067-8*) McGraw-Hill Prof.

Leone, Gene. Leone's Italian Cookbook. 1994. lib. bdg. 37.95 (*1-56849-509-9*) Buccaneer Bks.

Leone, Jacqueline, ed. see Ambrosino, Salvatore V.

Leone, Laura. The Black Sheep. (Desire Ser.: No. 696). 1992. per. 2.79 (*0-373-05696-6*, 5-05696-5) Harlequin Bks.

— Fever Dreams. 352p. 1997. mass mkt. 4.99 (*0-7860-0354-5*, Pinncle Kensgtn) Kensgtn Pub Corp.

— Under the Voodoo Moon. (Desire Ser.). 1994. per. 2.99 (*0-373-05834-9*, 5-05834-2) Silhouette.

Leone, Mark P. Roots of Modern Mormonism. LC 78-25965. 259p. 1979. 23.95 (*0-674-77970-3*) HUP.

Leone, Mark P., ed. Contemporary Archaeology: A Guide to Theory & Contributions. LC 79-156779. (Illus.). 476p. 1972. pap. 21.95 (*0-8093-0534-8*) S Ill U Pr.

Leone, Mark P. & Potter, Parker B. A Historical Archaeology of Capitalism. LC 98-45788. (Contributions to Global Historical Archaeology Ser.). 1998. pap. 37.50 (*0-306-46068-8*) Plenum.

***Leone, Mark P. & Potter, Parker B.** A Historical Archaeology of Capitalism. LC 98-45788. (Contributions to Global Historical Archaeology Ser.). 248p. 1998. 85.00 (*0-306-46067-X*) Plenum.

Leone, Mark P. & Silberman, Neil A. Invisible America: Unearthing Our Hidden History. (Illus.). 88p. 1995. 35.00 (*0-8050-3525-7*) H Holt & Co.

Leone, Mark P., jt. ed. see Zaretsky, Irving I.

Leone, Michele. L' Industria Nella Letteratura Italiana Contemporanea. (Stanford French & Italian Studies: No. 2). (ITA.). 156p. 1976. pap. 56.50 (*0-915838-30-3*) Anma Libri.

Leone, Norma L. Computers Made Really Easy for Beginners. LC 95-2941. 120p. (Orig.). 1995. pap. 8.95 (*0-936635-08-8*) Lion Pr & Vid.

Leone, Norma L., jt. auth. see O'Connell, Avice M.

Leone, Norma L., jt. auth. see Parkman, Elmerina L.

An Asterisk (*) at the beginning of an entry indicates that the title is appearing for the first time.

Leone, Norma Leonardi, see Leonardi Leone, Norma.
Leone, Paul, jt. auth. see Poshka, Mary.
Leone, Paul, ed. see Pettit, Eber M.
Leone, Peter E., ed. Understanding Troubled & Troubling Youth. LC 90-8228. (Sage Focus Editions Ser.: Vol. 116). (Illus.). 317p. reprint ed. pap. 98.30 (*0-608-08565-0*, 206908800002) Bks Demand.
— Understanding Troubled & Troubling Youth: Multiple Perspectives. (Focus Editions Ser.: Vol. 116). (Illus.). 320p. (C). 1990. 59.95 (*0-8039-3442-4*); pap. 26.00 (*0-8039-3443-2*) Sage.
Leone, Ray. Success Secrets of the Sales Funnel. 1992. 24.95 (*1-881196-25-9*) SSS Pub.
Leone, Roland, contrib. by. Joe Pass Live!! 72p. 1990. spiral bd. 14.95 (*0-87166-972-2*, 94380) Mel Bay.
— Joe Pass Live!! 72p. 1996. 29.95 incl. audio compact disk (*0-7866-1861-2*, 94380CDP) Mel Bay.
— Joe Pass Plays the Blues. 48p. 1987. 9.95 (*0-87166-885-8*, 94109) Mel Bay.
— Joe Pass Plays the Blues. 1993. 19.95 incl. audio (*0-7866-0972-9*, 94109P); audio 10.98 (*1-56222-625-8*, 94109C) Mel Bay.
Leone, Roland, tr. Joe Pass - Off the Record. 56p. 1993. pap. 9.95 (*1-56222-687-8*, 94890) Mel Bay.
— Joe Pass - Off the Record. 1995. 24.95 incl. audio compact disk (*0-7866-1744-6*, 94890CDP) Mel Bay.
— Joe Pass Note by Note. 1993. 19.95 incl. audio (*1-56222-849-8*, 95019P); pap. 9.95 (*1-56222-847-1*, 95019) Mel Bay.
Leone, Sierra. Conditions of Trust. 256p. (Orig.). 1995. pap. 3.95 (*1-877606-00-6*) R Romance.
— Love Express. 256p. (Orig.). 1995. pap. 3.95 (*1-877606-01-4*) R Romance.
— Southern Enchantment. 256p. (Orig.). 1995. pap. text 3.95 (*1-877606-02-2*) R Romance.
Leone, Ugo, ed. The Death Penalty: A Bibliographic Research. 119p. (Orig.). (C). 1995. pap. text 40.00 (*0-7881-1573-1*) DIANE Pub.
Leone, William C. Production Automation & Numerical Control. LC 67-21679. (Illus.). 245p. reprint ed. pap. 76.00 (*0-608-11695-5*, 201241900081) Bks Demand.
Leonelli, Joseph & Althouse, Mark L., eds. Air Monitoring & Detection of Chemical & Biological Agents, Vol. 3533. 270p. 1999. 69.00 (*0-8194-2994-5*) SPIE.
Leonenko, N. N. Limit Theorems for Random Fields with Singular Spectrum LC 99-18120. 1999. write for info. (*0-7923-5635-7*) Kluwer Academic.
Leonenko, N. N., jt. auth. see Ivanov, Alexander V.
***Leonessa, A., et al.** Hierarchical Nonlinear Switching Control Design with Applications to Propulsion Systems. LC 00-41936. (Lecture Notes in Control & Information Sciences). 2000. write for info. (*1-85233-335-9*) Spr-Verlag.
Leonessa, Anna. Journal Entries Acapulco 93. limited ed. (Codex Edition Ser.). (Illus.). 12p. 1993. 20.00 (*1-884185-01-0*) O Zone.
— The Last Poem. limited ed. (Illus.). 1995. pap. 5.00 (*1-884185-09-6*) O Zone.
Leonetti, Gastone & Cuspidi, Cesare, eds. Hypertension in the Elderly, No. 157. LC 94-12005. (Developments in Cardiovascular Medicine Ser.: Vol. 157). 152p. 1994. text 98.00 (*0-7923-2852-3*) Kluwer Academic.
Leonetti, Mike. The Game We Knew: Hockey in the Fifties. (Illus.). 128p. 1997. write for info. (*1-55192-111-1*) Raincoast Bk.
— Hockey in the Seventies: The Game We Knew. (Illus.). 128p. 1999. 26.95 (*1-55192-260-6*, Pub. by Raincoast Bk) Orca Bk Pubs.
***Leonetti, Mike.** Hockey Now! (Illus.). 168p. (J). 1999. pap. 19.95 (*1-55209-397-2*) Firefly Bks Ltd.
Leonetti, Mike. Hockey's Golden Era. (Illus.). 160p. 1993. 29.95 (*1-895629-20-9*) Warwick Publ.
— Hockey's Golden Era: Stars of the Original Six. (Illus.). 160p. 1998. pap. 19.95 (*1-55209-318-2*) Firefly Bks Ltd.
Leonetti, Mike, jt. auth. see Henderson, Paul.
Leong. Career Development & Vocational Behavior of Racial & Ethnic Minorities. 1996. pap. 36.00 (*0-8058-2692-0*) L Erlbaum Assocs.
— Family Law in Singapore. 431p. 1990. boxed set 185.00 (*0-409-99583-5*, MICHIE) LEXIS Pub.
— Handbook of Surgical Pathology. 1996. text 56.00 (*0-443-05121-6*, W B Saunders Co) Harcrt Hlth Sci Grp.
Leong, A. S., ed. Principles & Practice of Medical Laboratory Science Vol. 1: Basic Histotechnology. (Illus.). 172p. 1996. pap. write for info. (*0-443-05369-3*) Church.
— Principles & Practice of Medical Laboratory Science Vol. 2: Medical Microbiology, Virology & Molecular Technology. (Illus.). 252p. 1997. pap. write for info. (*0-443-05982-9*) Church.
Leong, A. S., jt. auth. see Forbes, I. J.
Leong, Albert, ed. The Millenium: Christianity & Russia (AD 988-1988) LC 90-46791. 224p. 1990. pap. 13.95 (*0-88141-080-2*) St Vladimirs.
— Oregon Studies in Chinese & Russian Culture. LC 90-5520. (American University Studies: Slavic Languages & Literature: Ser. XII, Vol. 13). (Illus.). XVIII, 376p. (C). 1990. text 72.95 (*0-8204-1309-7*) P Lang Pubng.
— Proceedings of the Summer 1986 Intensive Workshop in Chinese & Russian. 1987. 15.00 (*0-87114-177-9*) U Oreg Russian Dept.
Leong, Albert, ed. see Niezvestny, Ernst.
Leong, Andrew P. & Kheong, Chin Yoong. Cheshire, Fifoot & Furmston's Law of Contract: Singapore & Malaysian Edition. 1006p. 1994. pap. 186.00 (*0-409-99682-3*, SI, MICHIE) LEXIS Pub.
Leong, Anthony S., ed. Applied Immunohistochemistry for the Surgical Pathologist. 448p. 1993. text 150.00 (*0-340-55148-8*, Pub. by E A) OUP.
Leong, Anthony S., et al. Hepatocellular Carcinoma: Diagnosis Investigation & Management. LC 99-24540. (An Arnold Publication). (Illus.). 304p. 1999. text 110.00 (*0-340-74096-5*, Pub. by E A) OUP.
— Immunohistology & Electron Microscopy of Anaplastic & Pleomorphic Tumors. LC 96-47099. (Illus.). 300p. (C). 1997. text 125.00 (*0-521-44092-0*) Cambridge U Pr.
Leong, Carol. Serials Cataloging Handbook: An Illustrative Guide to the Use of AACR2 & L C Rule Interpretations. 320p. 1989. text 55.00 (*0-8389-0501-3*) ALA.
Leong, Che K. Children with Specific Reading Disabilities. xvi, 360p. 1987. 93.25 (*90-265-0291-5*) Swets.
Leong, Che K., ed. Developmental & Acquired Dyslexia: Neuropsychological & Neurolinguistic Perspectives. (Neuropsychology & Cognition Ser.). 300p. (C). 1995. text 148.50 (*0-7923-3166-4*) Kluwer Academic.
Leong, Che K. & Joshi, R. Malatesha, eds. Cross-Language Studies of Learning to Read & Spell: Phonologic & Orthographic Processing. LC 97-5686. 1997. lib. bdg. 207.50 (*0-7923-4457-X*) Kluwer Academic.
Leong, Che K. & Randhawa, Bikkar S., eds. Understanding Literacy & Cognition: Theory, Research & Application. LC 89-77899. (Illus.). 330p. (C). 1989. 126.00 (*0-306-43489-X*, Plenum Trade) Perseus Pubng.
Leong, Che K., jt. ed. see Joshi, R. Malatesha.
Leong, Che Kan & Tamaoka, Katsuo. Cognitive Processing of the Chinese & the Japanese Languages. LC 98-51872. (Neuropsychology & Cognition Ser.). 11p. 1999. write for info. (*0-7923-5479-6*) Kluwer Academic.
***Leong, Cheong Cheng & Wiley, Mark.** The Secrets of Phoenix-Eye Fist Kung-Fu. 2000. pap. 16.95 (*0-8048-3178-5*) Tuttle Pubng.
Leong, Deborah J. & Bodrova, Elena. Tools of the Mind: The Vygotskian Approach to Early Childhood. 192p. 1995. pap. 30.00 (*0-02-369874-8*, Macmillan Coll) P-H.
Leong, Deborah J., jt. auth. see McAfee, Oralie.
Leong, Eric, ed. see Truscott, Alan.
Leong, Frederick, ed. Career Development & Vocational Behavior of Racial & Ethnic Minorities. (Vocational Psychology Ser.). 312p. 1995. text 59.95 (*0-8058-1303-9*) L Erlbaum Assocs.
Leong, Frederick T. & Austin, James T., eds. The Psychology Research Handbook: A Primer for Graduate Students & Research Assistants. LC 96-10017. 408p. 1996. 36.00 (*0-8039-7048-X*); pap. 16.99 (*0-8039-7049-8*) Sage.
Leong, Frederick T., ed. see Sekaran, Uma.
Leong, Frederick T. L. & Whitfield, James R., eds. Asians in the United States: Abstracts of the Psychological & Behaviorial Literature, 1967-1991. LC 92-17379. (Bibliographies in Psychology Ser.: No. 11). 216p. 1992. pap. 19.95 (*1-55798-178-7*) Am Psychol.
Leong, H. W., et al, eds. Algorithms & Computation: 8th International Symposium, ISAAC'97, Singapore, December 17-19, 1997, Proceedings. (Lecture Notes in Computer Science Ser.: Vol. 1350). xv, 426p. 1997. pap. text 67.00 (*3-540-63890-3*) Spr-Verlag.
Leong, Hong Va, ed. see International Conference on Mobile Data Access Staff.
Leong, Kenneth S. The Zen Teachings of Jesus. 202p. (Orig.). 1995. pap. 14.95 (*0-8245-1481-5*) Crossroad NY.
***Leong, Kenneth S.** The Zen Teachings of Jesus. rev. ed. (Orig.). 2001. pap. 19.95 (*0-8245-1883-7*) Crossroad NY.
Leong, Laurence W., jt. ed. see Sullivan, Gerard.
Leong, Peng C. Nutrition Bibliography of Malaya. LC 52-40995. 32p. reprint ed. pap. 30.00 (*0-608-11254-2*, 200135900076) Bks Demand.
Leong, Po Shun, jt. auth. see Lydgate, Tony.
***Leong, Roger.** From Russia with Love: Costumes for the Ballets Russes, 1909-1933. (Illus.). 96p. 2000. pap. text 27.95 (*0-642-54116-7*, AusInfo) Aust Gov Pub.
Leong, Russell. The Country of Dreams & Dust. 71p. 1993. pap. 8.95 (*0-931122-76-7*) West End.
Leong, Russell, ed. Asian American Sexualities: Dimensions of the Gay & Lesbian Experience. LC 95-538. 256p. (C). 1995. pap. 18.99 (*0-415-91437-X*) Routledge.
— Asian American Sexualities: Dimensions of the Gay & Lesbian Experience. LC 95-538. 256p. (C). (gr. 13). 1995. 70.00 (*0-415-91436-1*) Routledge.
Leong, Russell, intro. Moving the Image: Independent Asian Pacific American Media Arts 1970-1990. LC 90-71789. (Illus.). 312p. 1992. pap. 25.00 (*0-934052-13-1*) UCLA Asian Am Studies Ctr.
Leong, Russell, jt. ed. see Chang, Edward T.
Leong, Russell, ed. see Him Mark Lai.
Leong, Russell, ed. see Robles, Al.
***Leong, Russell Charles.** Phoenix Eyes & Other Stories. 208p. 2000. 30.00 (*0-295-97944-5*); pap. 16.95 (*0-295-97945-3*) U of Wash Pr.
Leong, Sally A. & Berka, Randy, eds. Molecular Industrial Mycology: Systems & Applications for Filamentous Fungi. (Mycology Ser.: Vol. 8). (Illus.). 304p. 1990. text 145.00 (*0-8247-8392-1*) Dekker.
Leong, Sow-Theng & Wright, Tim. Migration & Ethnicity in Chinese History: Hakkas, Pengmin & Their Neighbors. LC 97-413. (Illus.). 274p. 1997. 42.50 (*0-8047-2857-7*) Stanford U Pr.
Leong, Toong Pen. The Business of Banking in Malaysia. LC 98-944380. 172p. 1998. write for info. (*967-978-624-2*) Pelanduk.
Leong, Y. S. Silver: An Analysis of Factors Affecting Its Price. 2nd ed. (Brookings Institution Reprint Ser.). reprint ed. lib. bdg. 42.50 (*0-697-00162-8*) Irvington.
Leong, Yu K., jt. ed. see Cheng, Kai N.
Leonhard, K. Classification of Endogenous Psychoses & Their Differentiated Etiology. 2nd enl. rev. ed. Beckmann, H., ed. Cahn, Charles H., tr. from GER. LC 99-35446. 450p. 1999. 62.00 (*3-211-83259-9*) Spr-Verlag.
Leonhard, Alan T. & Mercuro, Nicholas, eds. Neutrality: Changing Concepts & Practices. LC 88-21755. 164p. (Orig.). (C). 1988. pap. text 18.00 (*0-8191-7141-7*) U Pr of Amer.
Leonhard, Charles. The Status of Arts Education in American Public Schools. 1992. 15.00 (*0-317-05162-8*) U IL Sch Music.
— The Status of Arts Education in American Public Schools: Summary & Conclusions. 1992. 5.00 (*0-317-05163-6*) U IL Sch Music.
Leonhard, Charles M., jt. auth. see Johnston, Albert M., Jr.
Leonhard, Gwen & Mast, Jennie. Feathering Your Nest: An Interactive Workbook & Guide to a Loving Lesbian Relationship. unabridged ed. Boojamra, Lee, ed. LC 96-67601. 256p. (Orig.). 1996. pap. 14.99 (*1-883061-13-X*) Rising AZ.
Leonhard, Robert R. The Art of Maneuver: Maneuver-Warfare Theory & AirLand Battle. LC 91-12820. 336p. 1995. pap. 21.95 (*0-89141-532-7*) Presidio Pr.
— Fighting by Minutes: Time & the Art of War. LC 93-50685. 216p. 1994. 59.95 (*0-275-94736-X*, Praeger Pubs) Greenwood.
Leonhard, Robert R. The Principles of War for the Information Age. LC 98-8287. 288p. 1998. 29.95 (*0-89141-647-1*, Pub. by Presidio Pr) Natl Bk Netwk.
***Leonhard, Robert R.** The Principles of War for the Information Age. (Illus.). 304p. 2000. pap. 19.95 (*0-89141-713-3*) Presidio Pr.
Leonhard, W. Control of Electrical Drives. (Electric Energy Systems & Engineering Ser.). 315p. 1991. 79.00 (*0-387-13650-9*) Spr-Verlag.
— Control of Electrical Drives. 2nd ed. LC 98-162081. 440p. 1996. 79.00 (*3-540-59380-2*) Spr-Verlag.
Leonhard, Woody. CD Mania. (C). 1995. pap. text. write for info. (*0-201-48915-5*) Addison-Wesley.
Leonhard, Woody. The Mother of All Windows Books, Set. 1072p. 1993. 39.95 incl. disk (*0-201-62475-3*) Addison-Wesley.
Leonhard, Woody. Mother of All Windows CD Rom Swap for 62475. (C). 1994. cd-rom 10.00 (*0-201-40693-4*) Addison-Wesley.
— The Underground Guide to Telecommuting: Slightly Askew Advice on Leaving the Rat Race Behind. LC 95-9089. (Underground Guide Ser.). 336p. 1995. pap. 24.95 (*0-201-48343-2*) Addison-Wesley.
— Underground Guide to Word for Windows: Slightly Askew Advice from a Winword Wizard. 336p. 1994. pap. 19.95 (*0-201-40650-0*) Addison-Wesley.
Leonhard, Woody. Windows Programming for Mere Mortals. 560p. (Orig.). (C). 1992. pap. 36.95 incl. disk (*0-201-60832-4*) Addison-Wesley.
Leonhard, Woody. Woody Leonhard Teaches Microsoft Office. LC 98-85051. 716p. 1998. 19.99 (*0-7897-1705-0*) Que.
— Woody Leonhard Teaches Microsoft Office 2000. (Illus.). 650p. 1999. pap. 19.99 (*0-7897-1871-5*) Que.
Leonhard, Woody & Chen, Vincent. Hacker's Guide to Word for Windows, Set. 2nd ed. 928p. (C). 1994. pap. 39.95 incl. disk (*0-201-40763-9*) Addison-Wesley.
Leonhard, Woody & Deegan, Peter. Word in a Nutshell. Mott, Troy, ed. (Illus.). 500p. 1999. pap. 24.95 (*1-56592-489-4*) OReilly & Assocs.
Leonhard, Woody & Simon, Barry. Mom 95. 960p. 1995. pap. 39.95 incl. cd-rom (*0-201-40971-2*) Addison-Wesley.
Leonhard, Woody & Simon, Barry. The Mother of All Windows 98 Books. LC 98-39309. 864p. (C). 1998. pap. 39.95 (*0-201-43312-5*) Addison-Wesley.
Leonhard, Woody & Simon, Barry. PC-mom: The Mother of All PC Books. 784p. 1994. pap. 49.95 (*0-201-40681-0*) Addison-Wesley.
Leonhard, Woody, et al. Excel '97 Annoyances. LC 97-208356. (Illus.). 336p. (Orig.). 1997. pap. 21.95 (*1-56592-309-X*) OReilly & Assocs.
— Office '97 Annoyances. (Illus.). 396p. (Orig.). 1997. pap. 21.95 (*1-56592-310-3*) OReilly & Assocs.
— Outlook Annoyances. Petrusha, Ron, ed. (Illus.). 400p. 1998. pap. 24.95 (*1-56592-384-7*) OReilly & Assocs.
— Word 97 Annoyances. LC 97-208729. (Illus.). 356p. (Orig.). 1997. pap. 24.95 (*1-56592-308-1*) OReilly & Assocs.
Leonhard, Woody, jt. auth. see Bott, Ed.
Leonhardt, Albrecht, tr. see Voss, Knud.
Leonhardt, Alice. Hostage! LC 99-53506. 2001. pap. 4.99 (*0-679-89366-0*) Random.
— Ocean Life: Tide Pool Creatures. 40p. (J). (gr. 2-4). 1999. pap. 5.95 (*0-7398-1481-8*) Raintree Steck-V.
— Pursuit! 2001. pap. 4.99 (*0-679-89367-9*) Random.
Leonhardt, Barbara, tr. see Voss, Knud.
Leonhardt, Barbara A. & Beroza, Morton. Insect Pheromone Technology: Chemistry & Applications. LC 82-8714. (ACS Symposium Ser.: Vol. 190). 271p. 1982. reprint ed. pap. 84.10 (*0-608-03115-1*, 206356800007) Bks Demand.
Leonhardt, Barbara A. & Berzoa, Morton, eds. Insect Pheromone Technology: Chemistry & Applications. LC 82-8714. (ACS Symposium Ser.: No. 190). 1982. 43.95 (*0-8412-0724-0*) Am Chemical.
Leonhardt, Cheryl. Breaking the Grass Ceiling: A Woman's Guide to Golf for Business. LC 98-4466. (Illus.). 288p. 1998. pap. 15.95 (*1-57243-276-4*) Triumph Bks.
Leonhardt, Cheryl A. Breaking the Glass Ceiling: A Woman's Guide to Golf As a Business Tool. (Illus.). 144p. 1995. pap. 16.95 (*0-9649725-3-0*) Grist Mill Pr.
Leonhardt, Fritz, jt. auth. see Heinle, Erwin.
Leonhardt, H. Fundamentals of Electroacupuncture According to Voll. Sarkisyanz, Helga, tr. from GER. (Illus.). 284p. 1980. text 98.00 (*3-88136-081-6*, Pub. by ML-Verlag) Medicina Bio.
Leonhardt, Helmut. Human Histology, Cytology & Microanatomy. 4th ed. (Illus.). 1977. pap. 20.95 (*0-8151-5375-9*) Mosby Inc.
***Leonhardt, Kenneth & Sewake, Kelvin.** Growing Dendrobium Orchids in Hawaii: Production & Pest Management Guide. (Illus.). iv, 92p. 1999. pap. 13.00 (*1-929325-03-7*) UOH Agric & Trop Res.
Leonhardt-Lupa, Merete. A Mother Is Born: Preparing for Motherhood During Pregnancy. LC 94-29716. 176p. 1995. 16.95 (*0-89789-353-0*, Bergin & Garvey) Greenwood.
Leonhardt, Mary. Keeping Kids Reading: How to Raise Avid Readers in the Video Age. 272p. 1998. pap. 12.00 (*0-517-88849-1*, Crown) Crown Pub Group.
— 99 Ways to Get Kids to Love Reading. LC 96-51711. 1997. pap. 10.00 (*0-609-80113-9*) Crown Pub Group.
— 99 Ways to Get Kids to Love Writing: And 10 Easy Tips for Teaching Them Grammar. LC 98-21340. 128p. 1998. pap. 8.00 (*0-609-80320-4*) Crown Pub Group.
***Leonhardt, Mary.** 99 Ways to get Your Kids to Do Their Homework: And Not Hate It. LC 00-28660. (Illus.). 124p. 2000. pap. 10.00 (*0-609-80638-6*, EDU022000, Three Riv Pr) Crown Pub Group.
Leonhardt, Mary. Parents Who Love Reading, Kids Who Don't. 1995. pap. 12.00 (*0-517-88222-1*, Crown) Crown Pub Group.
Leonhardt, Thomas W., ed. Advances in Collection Development & Resource Management, Vol. 1. 185p. 1995. 78.50 (*1-55938-213-9*) Jai Pr.
— Advances in Collection Development & Resource Management, Vol. 2. 1996. 78.50 (*0-7623-0097-3*) Jai Pr.
— Advances in Collection Development & Resource Management, Vol. 3. 258p. Date not set. 78.50 (*0-7623-0407-3*) Jai Pr.
— Foundations in Library & Information Science: Look of the West: Teaching & Learning in a Climate of Change, Vol. 34. (Monographs). 264p. 1996. 78.50 (*0-7623-0099-X*) Jai Pr.
— Information Technology: It's for Everyone! 206p. 1992. pap. 11.00 (*0-8389-7634-4*, Z678) ALA.
— Technical Services in Libraries: Systems & Applications. LC 91-43729. (Foundations in Library & Information Science: Vol. 25). 279p. 1992. 78.50 (*1-55938-214-7*) Jai Pr.
Leonhardt, Ulf. Measuring the Quantum State of Light. LC 96-44409. (Studies in Modern Optics: Vol. 22). (Illus.). 202p. (C). 1997. text 59.95 (*0-521-49730-2*) Cambridge U Pr.
Leonhardy, Frank C. Domebo: A Paleo-Indian Mammoth Kill in the Prairie-Plains. LC 65-26284. (Contributions of the Museum of the Great Plains Ser.: No. 1). 1966. 6.95 (*0-685-85506-6*) Mus Great Plains.
— Test Excavations in the Mangum Reservoir Area of Southwestern Oklahoma. (Contributions of the Museum of the Great Plains Ser.: No. 2). (Illus.). 1966. 4.00 (*0-685-85507-4*) Mus Great Plains.
Leonhart, Rochus. Gluck als Vollendung des Menschseins. 336p. 1997. text 99.00 (*3-11-015691-1*) De Gruyter.
Leonhart, Rodney W. Calibration Service for Laser Power & Energy At 248 Nm. 38p. 1998. pap. 3.50 (*0-16-056700-9*) USGPO.
Leoni, Bruno. Freedom & the Law. LC 91-3283. 274p. (C). 1991. pap. 7.50 (*0-86597-097-1*); text 17.50 (*0-86597-096-3*) Liberty Fund.
***Leoni, Edgar.** Nostradamus & His Prophecies. LC 00-29513. 2000. pap. 18.95 (*0-486-41468-X*) Dover.
Leoni, Edgar. Nostradamus & His Prophecies. LC 82-9479. (Illus.). 832p. 1988. 12.99 (*0-517-38809-X*) Random Hse Value.
Leonida, G. Handbook of Printed Circuit Design, Manufacture, Components & Assembly. 559p. 1997. pap. 308.00 (*0-901150-09-6*) St Mut.
Leonidov, Pavel. U Nikh V Michigane. LC 85-61782. 120p. (Orig.). 1987. pap. 12.50 (*0-89830-100-9*) Russica Pubs.
***Leonidov, Vladimir & O'Hare, P. A. G.** Fluorine Calorimetry: A Translation & Complete Update of Ftornaya Kalorimetriya. LC 00-25781. 1999. write for info. (*1-56700-146-7*) Begell Hse.
Leonidova. Russian-Bulgarian Dictionary. (BUL & RUS.). 463p. 1978. 14.95 (*0-8288-5269-3*, M9101) Fr & Eur.
***Leonik, Tom.** Home Automation Basics: Practical Applications Using Visual Basic 6. (Illus.). 2000. pap. 34.95 (*0-7906-1214-3*) Prompt Publns.
Leonin, Mia A. Braid. LC 98-73409. 65p. 1999. pap. 11.00 (*0-938078-57-7*, Pub. by Anhinga Pr) SPD-Small Pr Dist.
Leonis, James. Filmed on Location: A Guide to Leasing Your Property As a Film Location. 1994. pap. 28.00 (*0-9639781-0-1*) Premiere Pub.
Leonoff, Cyril E. Bridges of Light: Otto Landauer of Leonard Frank Photographs, 1945-1980. LC 98-110462. (Illus.). 208p. 1997. 36.95 (*0-88922-376-9*, Pub. by Talonbks) Genl Dist Srvs.
Leonor, M. D. & Richards, P. J., eds. Target Setting for Basic Needs: The Operation of Selected Government Services. vii, 130p. 1982. 22.50 (*92-2-102946-8*) Intl Labour Office.
Leonov, A. I., jt. auth. see Tikhonov.
Leonov, G. A., et al. Frequency-Domain Methods for Nonlinear Analysis: Theory & Application. (Series on Nonlinear Science). 450p. 1996. text 78.00 (*981-02-2146-0*) World Scientific Pub.
— Frequency Methods in Oscillation Theory. LC 95-11150. (Mathematics & Its Applications Ser.: Vol. 357). 416p. (C). 1996. text 206.00 (*0-7923-3896-0*) Kluwer Academic.

L

An Asterisk (*) at the beginning of an entry indicates that the title is appearing for the first time.

L

Leonov, Leonid. Skutarevsky. Brown, Alec, tr. LC 76-135250. 444p. 1971. reprint ed. lib. bdg. 85.00 (*0-8371-5170-8*, LESK, Greenwood Pr) Greenwood.

Leonov, M. V., jt. auth. see Pimenov, M. G.

Leonov, Sergey A. & Barton, William F. Russian-English & English-Russion Dictionary of Radar & Electronics. LC 93-30104. (ENG & RUS.). 1993. 45.00 (*0-89006-705-8*) Artech Hse.

Leonov, Yu G. & Khain, Victor E., eds. Global Correlation of Tectonics Movements. fac. ed. LC 86-13361. (Illus.). 318p. 1994. pap. 98.60 (*0-7837-7656-X*, 204740900007) Bks Demand.

***Leonowens, Anna.** The English Governess at the Siamese Court. 304p. 1999. pap. 4.50 (*0-8125-7062-6*) Tor Bks.

***Leonowens, Anna H.** Siamese Harem Life. 228p. 2000. text 110.00 (*0-7103-0692-X*) Col U Pr.

Leonowens, Anna Harriette. The English Governess at the Siamese Court: Being Recollections of Six Years in the Royal Palace at Bangkok. (Illus.). 338p. 1989. pap. 9.95 (*0-19-588897-9*) OUP.

Leons, Madeline B. & Rothstein, Frances A., eds. New Directions in Political Economy: An Approach from Anthropology, 22. LC 78-4290. (Contributions in Economics & Economic History Ser.: No. 22). 350p. 1979. 69.50 (*0-313-20414-4*, LND/) Greenwood.

Leons, Madeline B. & Sanabria, Harry, eds. Coca, Cocaine, & the Bolivian Reality. LC 96-45353. (Illus.). 310p. (C). 1997. text 59.50 (*0-7914-3481-8*); pap. text 19.95 (*0-7914-3482-6*) State U NY Pr.

Leonsis, Ted, jt. auth. see Chposky, James.

Leontaritis, George B. Greece & the First World War: From Neutrality to Intervention, 1917-1918. (East European Monographs). 640p. 1990. text 115.00 (*0-88033-181-X*, Pub. by East Eur Monographs) Col U Pr.

Leont'eva, G. K. Karl Briullov. (RUS.). 336p. 1983. 65.00 (*0-7855-1561-5*) St Mut.

Leontiades, James. Multinational Corporate Strategy. 228p. 1987. pap. 25.95 (*0-669-16038-5*) Lxngtn Bks.

Leontidou, Lila. The Mediterranean City in Transition: Social Change & Urban Development. (Cambridge Human Geography Ser.). (Illus.). 314p. (C). 1990. text 80.00 (*0-521-34467-0*) Cambridge U Pr.

Leontief, Estelle. Sellie & Dee: A Friendship. LC 93-29920. (Crimson Edge Chapbook Ser.). 1993. pap. 7.95 (*0-9619111-6-6*) Chicory Blue.

Leontief, Wassily. Essays in Economics: Theories, Theorizing, Facts, & Policies. 423p. (C). 1985. pap. 24.95 (*0-87855-993-0*) Transaction Pubs.

— Essays in Economics Vol. 1: Theories & Theorizing, Vol. I. LC 76-21999. 252p. (C). (gr. 13). 1976. reprint ed. text 93.95 (*0-87332-091-3*) M E Sharpe.

— Essays in Economics Vol. II: Theories, Facts & Politics, Vol. II, Vol. II. LC 77-79062. 168p. (C). (gr. 13). 1978. text 93.95 (*0-87332-092-1*) M E Sharpe.

— Input-Output Economics. 2nd ed. (Illus.). 436p. 1986. pap. text 41.95 (*0-19-503527-5*) OUP.

— The Structure of the American Economy 1919-1939: An Empirical Application of Equilibrium Analysis. 2nd enl. ed. LC 76-17415. 264p. (C). (gr. 13). 1977. reprint ed. text 91.95 (*0-87332-087-5*) M E Sharpe.

— Studies in the Structure of the American Economy: Theoretical & Empirical Explorations in Input-Output Analysis. LC 76-16433. 562p. (C). (gr. 13). 1977. reprint ed. text 91.95 (*0-87332-086-7*) M E Sharpe.

Leontief, Wassily, jt. auth. see Georgescu-Roegen, Nicholas.

Leontis, Artemis. Topographies of Hellenism: Mapping the Homeland. (Myth & Poetics Ser.). 240p. 1995. text 32.50 (*0-8014-3057-7*) Cornell U Pr.

Leontis, Artemis, ed. Greece: A Traveler's Literary Companion. LC 97-13267. (Travelers' Literary Companions Ser.: Vol. 5). (Illus.). 256p. 1997. pap. 13.95 (*1-883513-04-9*) Whereabouts.

Leontis, Neocles B., ed. see American Chemical Society Staff.

***Leontos, Carolyn.** What to Eat When You Get Diabetes: Easy & Appetizing Ways to Make Healthful Changes in Your Diet. 256p. 2000. pap. 14.95 (*0-471-38139-X*) Wiley.

Leontos, Carolyn. What to Eat When Your Doctor Says It's Diabetes. 224p. 1998. pap. 14.95 (*0-945448-98-8*) Am Diabetes.

Leontos, Carolyn & Palmer, Jeanne. Chefs Creating Lean: A Nutrition Course for Food Professionals. LC 94-38126. 1994. ring bd. 95.00 (*0-88091-136-0*) Am Dietetic Assn.

Leontovich, M. A. English Russian Dictionary of Quantum Electronics & Holography. (ENG & RUS.). 1977. 49.95 (*0-8288-3960-3*, M8921) Fr & Eur.

Leontovich, M. A., ed. Reviews of Plasma Physics, Vol. 4, 1966. Lashinsky, Herbert, tr. from RUS. LC 64-23244. (Illus.). 249p. reprint ed. pap. 77.20 (*0-8357-4388-8*, 203724300004) Bks Demand.

— Reviews of Plasma Physics, Vol. 10. Glebov, Oleg H., tr. from RUS. LC 64-23244. 526p. 1986. 125.00 (*0-306-11000-8*, Kluwer Plenum) Kluwer Academic.

— Reviews of Plasma Physics, Vol. 11. Hugill, J., tr. from RUS. LC 64-23244. 316p. 1986. 89.50 (*0-306-11001-6*, Kluwer Plenum) Kluwer Academic.

Leontovich, M. A., et al, eds. Reviews of Plasma Physics, Vol. 12. LC 64-23244. (Illus.). 364p. 1987. 95.00 (*0-306-11002-4*, Kluwer Plenum) Kluwer Academic.

Leontovich, Mary. Close Encounters: Systems & Interactions. (Explore! Science Ser.). (Illus.). 48p. (J). (gr. 3-6). 1995. 12.95 (*0-673-36220-5*, GoodYrBooks); pap. 4.95 (*0-673-36215-9*, GoodYrBooks) Addson-Wesley Educ.

— Force, of Course! Force & Motion. (Explore! Science Ser.). (Illus.). 48p. (J). (gr. 3-6). 1995. pap. 4.95 (*0-673-36213-2*, GoodYrBooks) Addson-Wesley Educ.

Leontsinis, Pat. Automatically . . . Light! Easy Low-Fat Recipes Using Time-Saving Appliances & the Heatproof Oven Bag. LC 97-93565. (Illus.). 280p. (Orig.). 1997. pap. 19.95 (*0-9658382-7-7*) Autocook.

Leontyev, L. Political Economy: A Condensed Course. (Rus. Ser.). (Illus.). 248p. 1974. pap. 19.95 (*0-8464-1268-3*) Beekman Pubs.

Leontyeva, Galina. Bruillov. (Illus.). 176p. 1997. 40.00 (*1-85995-298-4*) Parkstone Pr.

Lenozio, Claudio, ed. see Fossi, M. Cristina.

Leopard, J. C., et al. History of Daviess & Gentry Counties. (Illus.). 1035p. 1997. reprint ed. lib. bdg. 99.50 (*0-8328-6832-9*) Higginson Bk Co.

Leopard Productions Inc. Staff, ed. see Troy, Gene.

Leopardi, Giacomo. The Canti with a Selection of His Prose: The Centenary Edition. Nichols, J. G., tr. 192p. 1998. pap. 19.95 (*1-85754-359-9*, Pub. by Carcanet Pr) Paul & Co Pubs.

— Concordanze Diacroniche Delle 'Operette Morali' Di Giacomo Leopardi. (Alpha-Omega, Series F, Italienische Autoren). xiii, 775p. 1988. write for info. incl. 3.5 hd (*3-487-07757-4*) G Olms Pubs.

— Leopardi: Poems & Prose. Flores, Angel, ed. LC 86-29460. 256p. 1987. reprint ed. lib. bdg. 77.50 (*0-313-25769-8*, FLLE, Greenwood Pr) Greenwood.

— Leopardi: Poems: Bilingual. 2nd ed. Vivante, Arturo, tr. from ITA. & intro. by. 85p. 1994. pap. 12.00 (*0-9620305-0-3*) Delphinium Pr.

— Leopardi: Selected Poems. Grennan, Eamon, tr. from ITA. LC 96-47721. (Lockert Library of Poetry in Translation). 104p. 1997. pap. 9.95 (*0-691-01644-5*, Pub. by Princeton U Pr); text 27.50 (*0-691-01643-7*, Pub. by Princeton U Pr) Cal Prin Full Svc.

— A Leopardi Reader. fac. ed. Casale, Ottavio M., ed. & tr. by. LC 80-29068. 288p. 1994. pap. 89.30 (*0-7837-7611-X*, 204736300007) Bks Demand.

— The Moral Essays. Creagh, Patrick, tr. from ITA. LC 82-23473. Orig. Title: Operette Morali. 265p. 1985. pap. text 21.00 (*0-231-05707-5*) Col U Pr.

— The Moral Essays. Operette Morali. Creagh, Patrick, tr. from ITA. LC 82-23473. 265p. 1985. text 49.00 (*0-231-05706-7*) Col U Pr.

— The Moral Essays: Operette Morali. Creagh, Patrick, tr. from ITA. LC 82-23473. (Works of Giacomo Leopardi: Vol. 1). 265p. reprint ed. pap. 82.20 (*0-7837-0429-1*, 204075200018) Bks Demand.

— Operette Morali: Essays & Dialogues. Del Cecchetti, Giovanni, tr. from ITA. LC 82-2627. (Biblioteca Italiana Ser.: No. 3). 672p. 1982. pap. 15.95 (*0-520-04928-4*, Pub. by U CA Pr) Cal Prin Full Svc.

— Pensieri. Di Piero, W. S., tr. LC 81-11745. 180p. reprint ed. pap. 55.80 (*0-7837-8809-6*, 204945500011) Bks Demand.

— Quarterly Review of Literature: The 1950s, Special Issue, Vol. VIII, No. 1. 1950. pap. 10.00 (*1-888545-22-4*) Quarterly Rev.

— Zibaldone: A Selection by Giacomo Leopardi. King, Martha, ed. & intro. by. Bini, Daniela, intro. LC 91-43276. (Studies in Italian Culture: Literature in History: Vol. 8). XXII, 209p. (C). 1993. text 46.95 (*0-8204-1723-8*) P Lang Pubng.

Leopardi, Linda. Policy for School Boards. (School Board Library Ser.). 68p. (Orig.). 1983. pap. 9.95 (*0-912337-03-6*) NJ Schl Bds.

Leopold, A. Carl, ed. Membranes, Metabolism & Dry Organisms. LC 86-47646. (Comstock Bk.). (Illus.). 352p. 1986. 55.00 (*0-8014-1979-4*) Cornell U Pr.

Leopold, A. Starker. The California Quail. LC 76-48003. (Illus.). 1978. pap. 16.95 (*0-520-05456-3*, Pub. by U CA Pr) Cal Prin Full Svc.

Leopold, A. Starker, et al. Wild California: Vanishing Lands, Vanishing Wildlife. Dasmann, Raymond F., ed. (Illus.). 150p. 1985. pap. 29.95 (*0-520-06024-5*, Pub. by U CA Pr) Cal Prin Full Svc.

***Leopold, Aldo.** The Essential Aldo Leopold: Quotations & Commentaries. Meine, Curt D. & Knight, Richard L., eds. LC 99-6424. (Illus.). 384p. 1999. text 27.95 (*0-299-16550-7*) U of Wis Pr.

— For the Health of the Land: Previously Unpublished Essays & Other Writings. Callicott, J. Baird & Freyfogle, Eric T., eds. LC 99-16797. (Illus.). 240p. 1999. 22.95 (*1-55963-763-3*, Shearwater Bks) Island Pr.

Leopold, Aldo. Game Management. LC 86-40055. 512p. 1986. reprint ed. pap. 24.95 (*0-299-10774-4*) U of Wis Pr.

— The River of the Mother of God: And Other Essays by Aldo Leopold. Flader, Susan L. & Callicott, J. Baird, eds. LC 90-45491. (Illus.). 400p. 1993. reprint ed. pap. 19.95 (*0-299-12764-8*) U of Wis Pr.

— A Sand County Almanac: And Sketches Here & There. (Illus.). 256p. 1989. pap. 10.95 (*0-19-505928-X*) OUP.

— A Sand County Almanac: And Sketches Here & There. 2nd ed. (Illus.). 269p. 1968. pap. 10.95 (*0-19-500777-8*) OUP.

— A Sand County Almanac: And Sketches Here & There: Commemorative Edition. (Illus.). 256p. 1987. text 25.00 (*0-19-505305-2*) OUP.

— A Sand County Almanac: With Essays on Conservation from Round River. (Ecological Main Event Ser.). (Illus.). 295p. 1991. mass mkt. 6.99 (*0-345-34505-3*) Ballantine Pub Grp.

***Leopold, Astara.** The Cosmic Woman. 128p. 2001. pap. 12.95 (*1-885226-29-2*) StarLineage.

— Mosaic of the Ineffable. 144p. 2001. pap. 13.95 (*1-885226-27-6*) StarLineage.

Leopold, Astara L. Celestial Liaisons. LC 96-92178. 96p. 1996. pap. 11.95 (*1-885226-25-X*) StarLineage.

— Jewels! LC 96-92716. 144p. (Orig.). 1998. pap. 13.95 (*1-885226-28-4*) StarLineage.

— Muses for the Ammi Shaddai. 144p. Date not set. pap. 13.95 (*1-885226-26-8*) StarLineage.

— Quintessential Apotheoses. 128p. Date not set. pap. 12.95 (*1-885226-22-5*) StarLineage.

— Refulgent Peregrinations. LC 96-92180. 112p. 1996. pap. 11.95 (*1-885226-21-7*) StarLineage.

Leopold, Astara Ladyvienna. The Stardream Chronicles, No. 1. large type ed. LC 96-92179. 96p. (J). (gr. 1-8). 1996. pap. 11.95 (*1-885226-46-2*) StarLineage.

— Stardream Chronicles, Vol. 2. 128p. (J). (gr. 1-8). Date not set. pap. 12.95 (*1-885226-45-4*) StarLineage.

Leopold, Dennette C., jt. auth. see Michaels, Carolyn.

Leopold, Donald J., et al. Trees of the Central Hardwood Forests of North America: An Identification & Cultivation Guide. LC 97-6200. (Illus.). 509p. 1998. 49.95 (*0-88192-406-7*) Timber.

Leopold, Donald J., jt. auth. see Raynal, Dudley J.

***Leopold, Ellen.** A Darker Ribbon: A Twentieth-Century Story of Breast Cancer, Women & Their Doctors. LC 99-27201. 224p. 1999. 27.50 (*0-8070-6512-9*) Beacon Pr.

— A Darker Ribbon: Breast Cancer, Women & Their Doctors in the Twentieth Century. 2000. pap. 18.00 (*0-8070-6513-7*) Beacon Pr.

Leopold, Ellen, jt. auth. see Fine, Ben.

Leopold, George, ed. Clinical Ultrasound, Vol. 11. 1983. text 57.00 (*0-471-88978-4*) Wiley.

Leopold, George R. Ultrasound in Breast & Endocrine Disease. fac. ed. LC 83-21054. (Clinics in Diagnostic Ultrasound Ser.: No. 12). (Illus.). 210p. 1984. reprint ed. pap. 65.10 (*0-7837-7878-3*, 204763500007) Bks Demand.

***Leopold, H., et al, eds.** Multimedia Applications, Services & Techniques - ECMAST'99: Proceedings of the 4th European Conference, Madrid, Spain, May 26-28, 1999. LC 99-34565. (Lecture Notes in Computer Science Ser.: Vol. 1629). xv, 574p. 1999. pap. 85.00 (*3-540-66082-8*) Spr-Verlag.

Leopold, J., et al, eds. Beyond Reason: The National Health Service & the Limits of Management. (Stirling School of Management Ser.). 288p. 1996. 77.95 (*1-85972-031-5*, Pub. by Avebry) Ashgate Pub Co.

Leopold, Joan. Contributions to Comparative Indo-European, African, & Chinese Linguistics. LC 94-27056. (Prix Volney Essay Ser.: Vol. 3). 1994. lib. bdg. write for info. (*0-7923-2507-9*) Kluwer Academic.

— The Letter Liveth: The Life, Work & Library of August Friedrich Pott (1802-1887) (Library & Information Sources in Linguistics: 9). clii, 438p. 1983. 130.00 (*90-272-3733-6*) J Benjamins Pubng Co.

Leopold, Joan, ed. The Prix Volney: Its History & Significance for the Development of Linguistic Research, 1. LC 94-27057. (Prix Volney Essay Ser.). 1994. lib. bdg. write for info. (*0-7923-2505-2*, Pub. by Kluwer Academic) Kluwer Academic.

Leopold, Joan, ed. see Swiggers, Pierre & Boewe, Charles.

***Leopold, John, et al.** Strategic Human Resourcing: Principles, Perspectives & Practices. 544p. (Orig.). 1999. pap. 59.50 (*0-273-63164-0*, Pub. by F T P-H) Trans-Atl Phila.

Leopold, John A. Alfred Hugenberg: The Radical Nationalist Campaign Against the Weimar Republic. LC 77-4026. (Illus.). 314p. reprint ed. pap. 97.40 (*0-8357-5303-4*, 203213500078) Bks Demand.

Leopold, Kathleen & Orians, Thomas, eds. Theological Pastoral Resources: A Collection of Articles on Homosexuality from a Pastoral Perspective. rev. ed. LC 81-69476. 81p. 1985. pap. 4.00 (*0-940680-01-7*) Dignity Inc.

Leopold, L., jt. auth. see Rubin, R.

Leopold, Luna B. A View of the River. LC 93-34698. (Illus.). 320p. 1994. 45.95 (*0-674-93732-5*) HUP.

— Water, Rivers & Creeks. LC 97-9507. 1997. 30.00 (*0-935702-98-9*) Univ Sci Bks.

Leopold, Luna B., ed. Round River: From the Journals of Aldo Leopold. (Illus.). 286p. (C). 1972. reprint ed. pap. 11.95 (*0-19-501563-0*) OUP.

Leopold, Luna B., et al. Fluvial Processes in Geomorphology. (Illus.). 535p. 1999. pap. text 17.95 (*0-486-68588-8*) Dover.

— Reference Reach Field Book. (C). 1998. text 19.95 (*0-9653289-2-9*) Wildlnd Hydrology.

Leopold, Luna B., jt. auth. see Dunne, Thomas.

Leopold, Marlene, jt. auth. see Thomas, Frank.

Leopold, Nathan F., Jr. Life Plus Ninety-Nine Years. LC 73-16644. 381p. 1974. reprint ed. lib. bdg. 69.50 (*0-8371-7207-1*, LELP, Greenwood Pr) Greenwood.

Leopold, Niki. Once I Was.... LC 98-15461. (Illus.). 32p. (J). (gr. k up). 1999. 15.99 (*0-399-23105-6*, G P Putnam) Peng Put Young Read.

Leopold, Nikia C. Sandcastle Seahorses. LC 87-35978. 45p. (Orig.). (J). 1988. pap. 5.95 (*0-913123-17-X*) Galileo.

Leopold-Rieks, Monika. Ein Viertel in Bewegung: Hausbesitz, Mobilitaet und Wohnverhalten in der Suedlichen Vorstadt Bremens Zwischen 1875 und 1914. (Europaeische Hochschulschriften Ser.: Reihe 3, Band 785). (GER., Illus.). 552p. 1998. pap. 79.95 (*3-631-33104-5*) P Lang Pubng.

Leopold, Robert L., jt. ed. see Duhl, Leonard J.

Leopold, Simon R. Spiritual Aspects of Indian Music. 1985. 22.50 (*0-8364-1258-3*, Pub. by Sundeep Prak) S Asia.

Leopold, Vincent. The Alliance & Labor Songster. LC 74-30660. (American Farmers & the Rise of Agribusiness Ser.). 1975. reprint ed. 16.95 (*0-405-06837-9*) Ayer.

Leopold, Werner F. Bibliography of Child Language. LC 71-128944. (Northwestern Humanities Ser.: No. 28). reprint ed. 27.50 (*0-404-50728-X*) AMS Pr.

— Speech Development of a Bilingual Child, 4 vols. Incl. Vol. 6. Vocabulary Growth in the First Two Years. reprint ed. 38.75 (*0-404-50706-9*); Vol. 11. Sound-Learning in the First Two Years. reprint ed. 38.75 (*0-404-50711-5*); Vol. 18. Grammar & General Problems in the First Two Years. reprint ed. 38.75 (*0-404-50718-2*); Vol. 19. Diary from Age Two. reprint ed. 38.75 (*0-404-50719-0*); (Northwestern University. Humanities Ser.). 155.00 (*0-404-50749-2*) AMS Pr.

Leopold-Wildburger, U., et al, eds. Modelling & Decisions in Economics: Essays in Honor of Franz Ferschl. LC 99-30479. (Illus.). viii, 298p. 1999. 79.95 (*3-7908-1219-6*) Spr-Verlag.

Leopold-Wildburger, U., jt. auth. see Heuer, Gerald A.

Leopoldo, Solis M., jt. ed. see Norton, Roger D.

Leopoldseder, H. Prix Ars Electronica '96: International Compendium of the Computer Arts. (Illus.). 240p. 1996. pap. text 38.00 (*3-211-82863-X*) Spr-Verlag.

Leopoldseder, H., ed. Cyberarts 98: International Compendium Prix Ars Electronica. LC 99-170923. 300p. 1998. pap. 39.95 (*3-211-83135-5*) Spr-Verlag.

***Leopoldseder, H. & Schopf, C., eds.** Cyberarts 99: International Compendium Prix Ars Electronica. (Illus.). 240p. 1999. 35.00 (*3-211-83367-6*) Spr-Verlag.

Leopoldseder, Hannes & Schspf, C., eds. Cyberarts: Internationales Kompendium Prix Ars Electronica/International Compendium Prix Ars Electronica. 270p. 1997. 30.00 (*3-211-82998-9*) Spr-Verlag.

Leopoldt, Heinrich W., ed. see Hasse, Helmut.

Leopole, David, ed. see Stirner, Max.

Leos, Frances, tr. see Bridwell, Norman.

Leos, Ruben. Twenty-Five Romantic Lines to Say to Your Lover in Spanish. 28p. (Orig.). 1987. pap. 1.50 (*0-945228-00-7*) Chico Bks.

— Twenty-Five Ways to Tell Someone off in Spanish. 28p. (Orig.). 1987. pap. 1.50 (*0-945228-01-5*) Chico Bks.

Leotta, G. G., jt. ed. see Brunelli, B.

Leoung & Mills. Opportunistic Infections in Patients with the Acquired Immunodeficiency Syndrome. (Infectious Disease & Therapy Ser.: Vol. 3). (Illus.). 476p. 1989. text 155.00 (*0-8247-8080-9*) Dekker.

***Leoussi, Athena S.** Encyclopaedia of Nationalism. 2000. 125.00 (*0-7658-0002-0*) Transaction Pubs.

Leoussi, Eleni. Rehearsal: Photographs of Dance. (Illus.). 140p. 1999. 55.00 (*1-899235-02-7*, Pub. by Dewi Lewis) Dist Art Pubs.

Lep, Annette. Crocheting Fashion Sweaters for Women: Directions for 12 Cardigans, Pullovers & Vests. 48p. 1986. pap. 2.95 (*0-486-24957-3*) Dover.

— Crocheting Patchwork Patterns. (Illus.). 50p. (Orig.). 1981. pap. 3.95 (*0-486-23967-5*) Dover.

Lepa, E., tr. see Goldman, I. I. & Krivchenkov, V. D.

Lepa, Eugene, tr. see Maurin, Krzysztof.

Lepa, Maria O., tr. see Nowak, Stefan.

LePage, Andy. Transforming Education: The New Three R's. LC 87-18534. 218p. (Orig.). 1987. pap. 14.95 (*0-941079-03-1*) Oakmore Hse.

LePage, Elaine B. Brain Surgery: What to Know & Ask. Hollingsworth, Anna, ed. LC 93-23725. (Illus.). 36p. (Orig.). 1994. pap. text 7.75 (*0-939838-36-2*) Pritchett & Hull.

LePage, Jane W. Women Composers, Conductors & Musicians of the Twentieth Century: Selected Biographies, Vol. I. LC 80-12162. 388p. 1980. 41.50 (*0-8108-1298-3*) Scarecrow.

— Women Composers, Conductors & Musicians of the Twentieth Century: Selected Biographies, Vol. III. LC 80-12162. (Illus.). 333p. 1988. 37.00 (*0-8108-2082-X*) Scarecrow.

LePage-Lees, Pamela. From Disadvantaged Girls to Successful Women: Education & Women's Resiliency. LC 97-11080. 184p. 1997. 55.00 (*0-275-95752-7*, Praeger Pubs) Greenwood.

LePage, Raoul & Billard, Lynne. Exploring the Limits of Bootstrap. LC 91-31546. (Probability & Mathematical Statistics: Applied Probability & Statistics Section Ser.). 448p. 1992. 124.95 (*0-471-53631-8*) Wiley.

Lepage, Robert. Robert Lepage: Connecting Flights: In Conversation with Remy Charest. Charest, Remy & Romer Taylor, Wanda, trs. from FRE. LC 99-18990. (Illus.). 208p. 1999. reprint ed. pap. 15.95 (*1-55936-165-4*, Pub. by Theatre Comm) Consort Bk Sales.

LePage, Wilbur R. Complex Variables & the Laplace Transform for Engineers. (Illus.). 483p. 1980. reprint ed. pap. text 12.95 (*0-486-63926-6*) Dover.

***LePage, Yves.** UNIX Bible. 2nd ed. (Bible Ser.). (Illus.). 900p. 2000. pap. text 39.99 (*0-7645-4687-2*) IDG Bks.

LePage, Yves & Iarrera, Paul. UNIX System Administrator's Bible. (Bible Ser.). 672p. 1998. pap. 49.99 incl. cd-rom (*0-7645-3162-X*) IDG Bks.

LePain, Marc A., tr. see Kriegel, Blandine.

Lepak. Politics, an Initial Inquiry. (C). 2001. pap. 33.33 (*0-205-28901-0*, Longwood Div) Allyn.

Lepak, Anne F. The Frary Family in America: A Continuation. enl. ed. Frary, Robert Barnes, ed. (Illus.). 296p. 1985. 16.00 (*0-9616030-1-1*) Frary Family.

Lepak, Anne F., jt. auth. see Frary, Marty M.

Lepak, Keith J. Prelude to Solidarity: Poland & the Politics of the Gierek Regime. 320p. 1988. text 61.50 (*0-231-06608-2*) Col U Pr.

***LePan, Don.** The Book of Common Errors in English: A Guide to Righting Wrongs. 4th ed. 304p. (Orig.). 1999. pap. 9.95 (*1-55111-318-X*) Broadview Pr.

LePan, Don. The Broadview Book of Common Errors in English. 2nd ed. Broadview Press Staff, ed. 240p. (C). 1993. pap. text 12.95 (*0-921149-96-4*) Broadview Pr.

— The Cognitive Revolution in Western Culture. 388p. 1989. pap. 19.95 (*1-55111-081-4*, Pub. by Macmillan) Scholium Intl.

LePan, Don, jt. auth. see Babington, Doug.

LePan, Don, jt. auth. see Boyne, Martin.

LePan, Douglas. Macalister: or Dying in the Dark. LC 95-157703. 144p. 1995. pap. 14.95 (*1-55082-139-3*, Pub. by Quarry Pr) LPC InBook.

An Asterisk (*) at the beginning of an entry indicates that the title is appearing for the first time.

LePar, William A. Spiritual Harvest: Discourses on the Path to Fulfillment. LC 97-61832. 240p. 1998. pap. 14.95 (*1-885728-01-8*) Solar Press.

LePar, William A., et al. Life after Death: A New Revelation. LC 94-66952. (Illus.). 256p. (Orig.). 1994. pap. 14.95 (*1-885728-00-X*) Solar Press.

Lepard, Brian D. & Gerhart, Frederick J. Unrelated Business Income Tax Issues in Health Care. (BNA's Health Law & Business Ser.: No. 2000). 1996. 125.00 (*1-55871-342-5*) BNA.

LePard, Don. When the Saints Come Marching In. LC 98-89384. 112p. 1999. pap. 12.95 (*1-56167-511-3*) Am Literary Pr.

Leparski, E., jt. auth. see Puska, P.

Leparsky, E. & Nussel, F. E., eds. Protocol & Guidelines for Monotoring & Evaluation Procedures. xiii, 60p. 1987. pap. 32.70 (*0-387-18458-9*) Spr-Verlag.

Lepawsky, Albert, jt. auth. see Lepawsky, Rosalind.

Lepawsky, Rosalind & Lepawsky, Albert. Coalition & Coalescence: Berkeley Links Ecology & Ethnicity. (Environmental Studies: No. 1). 8p. 1972. 1.00 (*0-912102-46-2*) Cal Inst Public.

LePeau, Andrew T. & LePeau, Phyllis J. Ephesians. (LifeGuide Bible Studies). 60p. (Orig.). 1985. pap., wbk. ed. 4.99 (*0-8308-1012-9*, 1012) InterVarsity.

— James: Faith That Works. (LifeGuide Bible Studies). 64p. 1987. pap., wbk. ed. 4.99 (*0-8308-1018-8*, 1018) InterVarsity.

— James: Faith That Works. rev. ed. (Life Guide Bible Studies Ser.). 63p. 1999. pap. 4.99 (*0-8308-3018-9*, 3018) InterVarsity.

LePeau, Phyllis J. Gentleness. (Fruit of the Spirit Bible Studies). 48p. 1991. mass mkt. 5.99 (*0-310-53691-X*) Zondervan.

— Joy. (Fruit of the Spirit Bible Studies). 48p. 1991. pap. 5.99 (*0-310-53711-8*) Zondervan.

— Kindness. (Fruit of the Spirit Bible Studies). 48p. 1991. mass mkt. 5.99 (*0-310-53701-0*) Zondervan.

LePeau, Phyllis J., jt. auth. see LePeau, Andrew T.

Lepell, Rachel. Time Dance. LC 97-28679. 1997. pap. 6.00 (*0-88734-483-6*) Players Pr.

Lepelletier, Edmond A. Paul Verlaine: His Life, His Work. Lang, E. M., tr. LC 71-128944. (Illus.). reprint ed. 55.00 (*0-404-03968-5*) AMS Pr.

Lepelley, Rene. Dictionnaire du Francais Regional de Normandie. (FRE.). 157p. 1993. 39.95 (*0-7859-8121-7*, 2862531502) Fr & Eur.

— Dictionnaire Etymologique des Noms de Communes de Normandie. (FRE.). 1993. write for info. (*0-7859-8096-2*, 2-85480-455-4) Fr & Eur.

Lepenies, Wolf. Between Literature & Science: The Rise of Sociology. Hollingdale, R. J., tr. (Cambridge Ideas in Context Ser.). 400p. 1988. pap. text 24.95 (*0-521-33810-7*) Cambridge U Pr.

— Melancholy & Society. Gaines, Jeremy & Jones, Doris L., trs. from GER. 272p. (C). 1992. 51.95 (*0-674-56468-5*) HUP.

Leperlier, Francois. Claude Cahun: Masks & Metamor Phases. 2000. pap. 30.00 (*1-85984-199-6*, Pub. by Verso) Norton.

— Claude Cahun: Masks & Metamorphoses. (C). 2000. 75.00 (*1-85984-828-1*, Pub. by Verso) Norton.

Leperlier, Francois, jt. auth. see Bate, David.

Lepesant, Gilles, jt. ed. see Lewis, David W. P.

Lepeschkin, E., ed. see Body Surface Mapping of Cardiac Fields Symposium S.

Lepetit, Bernard. The Pre-Industrial Urban System: France, 1740-1840. Rogers, Godfrey, tr. LC 93-26676. (Themes in International Urban History Ser.: No. 2). (Illus.). 503p. (C). 1994. text 80.00 (*0-521-41734-1*) Cambridge U Pr.

Lepetit, Bernard, jt. ed. see Clark, Peter.

Lepeudry, Jean-Michel. Hunting Dogs from Around the World. LC 97-12172. (Illus.). 224p. 1997. 24.95 (*0-8120-6632-4*) Barron.

Lepgold. Introduction to International Relations. 2000. pap. text. write for info. (*0-312-15334-1*) St Martin.

Lepgold, Joseph. The Declining Hegemon: The United States & European Defense, 1960-1990. LC 90-7116. (Contributions in Military Studies Ser.: No. 103). 232p. 1990. pap. 21.95 (*0-275-93657-0*, LDH, Praeger Pubs) Greenwood.

— The Declining Hegemon: The United States & European Defense, 1960-1990, 103. LC 90-3132. (Contributions in Military Studies Ser.: No. 103). 232p. 1990. 57.95 (*0-313-26373-6*, B3657, Greenwood Pr) Greenwood.

Lepgold, Joseph & Weiss, Thomas G., eds. Collective Conflict Management & Changing World Politics. LC 97-35892. (SUNY Series in Global Politics). (Illus.). 245p. (C). 1998. pap. text 19.95 (*0-7914-3844-9*) State U NY Pr.

— Collective Conflict Management & Changing World Politics. LC 97-35892. (SUNY Series in Global Politics). (Illus.). 245p. (C). 1998. text 59.50 (*0-7914-3843-0*) State U NY Pr.

Lepgold, Joseph, jt. ed. see Nincic, Miroslav.

***Lephart, Scott M. & Fu, Freddie H., eds.** Proprioception & Neuromuscular Control in Joint Stability. (Illus.). 464p. 1999. 59.00 (*0-88011-864-4*) Human Kinetics.

Lepi, Steven M. Practical Guide to Finite Elements: A Solid Mechanics Approach. LC 97-52825. (Mechanical Engineering Ser.: Vol. 115). (Illus.). 544p. 1998. text 165.00 (*0-8247-0075-9*) Dekker.

***Lepiane, Mark.** Music for the Recorder - Folk Songs of the U. S. Beginning-Intermediate Level. 64p. 1999. pap. 9.95 (*0-7866-3080-9*, 96738) Mel Bay.

Lepidis, Clement. Un Itineraire Espagnol. (FRE., Illus.). 160p. 1995. pap. 49.95 (*2-86808-005-7*) Intl Scholars.

Lepidus, Henry. The History of Mexican Journalism. 1976. 59.95 (*0-8490-1978-8*) Gordon Pr.

Lepik, E. E. Floral Evolution in Relation to Pollination Ecology. 164p. 1977. 35.00 (*0-685-59956-6*) Scholarly Pubns.

Lepine, Bob. The Christian Husband: God's Vision of Loving & Caring for Your Wife. LC 98-52015. 1999. pap. 11.99 (*1-56955-130-8*) Servant.

Lepine, Christopher. God Without the Garbage: A Reasonable Approach to God. 64p. (Orig.). 1993. pap. 2.25 (*0-9634081-0-0*) Revelation DE.

— The Universal Religion: Essentials for a Joyful Life. LC 99-90736. xvi, 240p. 1999. pap. 14.00 (*0-9634081-1-9*) Revelation DE.

Lepine, David. A Brotherhood of Canons Serving God: English Secular Cathedrals in the Later Middle Ages. (Studies in the History of Medieval Religion: No. 8). 256p. (C). 1995. 75.00 (*0-85115-620-7*) Boydell & Brewer.

Lepine, Mike, jt. auth. see Leigh, Mark.

Lepine, Pierre. Dictionnaire Francais-Anglais et Anglais-Francais des Termes Medicaux et Biologiques. 2nd ed. (ENG & FRE.). 896p. 1974. 175.00 (*0-8288-6027-0*, M4665) Fr & Eur.

— French-English - English-French Dictionary of Medical & Biological Terms. 2nd ed. (ENG & FRE.). 1991. 162.50 (*0-7859-8938-2*) Fr & Eur.

— French-English - English-French Dictionary of Medical & Biological Terms. 2nd ed. (ENG & FRE.). 876p. 1991. reprint ed. 132.00 (*2-257-10598-2*) IBD Ltd.

Leping, A. A. Russisch-Deutsches Woerterbuch. 34th ed. (GER & RUS.). 514p. 1992. 29.95 (*0-7859-8573-5*, 5200021472) Fr & Eur.

Lepingle, Dominique, jt. auth. see Bouleau, Nicolas.

***Lepinoux, Johel.** Multiscale Phenomena in Plasticity: From Experiments to Phenomenology, Modelling 7 Materials Engineering. LC 00-26055. (NATO Science Ser.). 2000. write for info. (*0-7923-6251-9*) Kluwer Academic.

***Lepist, Enn.** Cultural IQ Factor: Test Your Education & Awareness of the World Around You. (Illus.). 104p. 1999. pap. 16.95 (*1-930105-07-X*) MUR.

Lepisto, Lawrence. Consumer Relationships with Financial Institutions. 57p. 1993. pap. 100.00 (*1-880572-08-7*) Filene Res.

— Psychological & Demographic Factors Affecting Relationships with Financial Institutions. 47p. 1994. pap. 100.00 (*1-880572-12-5*) Filene Res.

Lepke, Helen S., ed. Shaping the Future: Challenges & Opportunities. (Reports of the Northeast Conference on the Teaching of Foreign Languages). 164p. 1989. pap. 10.95 (*0-915432-89-7*) NE Conf Teach Foreign.

Lepkowski, Ronald J., jt. auth. see Williams, David.

LePla, F. Joseph, jt. auth. see Parker, Lynn M.

Lepley, Lynne. Scrumptious Scriptures. (Illus.). 96p. (J). (ps-k). 1998. pap. 11.95 (*1-885358-46-6*, RB36821) Rainbow CA.

Lepley, Marvin, jt. auth. see Esch, Dortha.

Lepley, Mary M., jt. auth. see LaBaw, Jeanine L.

Lepley, William M. Serial Reactions Considered As Conditioned Reactions. (Psychology Monographs General & Applied: Vol. 46). 1974. reprint ed. 55.00 (*0-8115-1445-5*) Periodicals Srv.

Leplin, Jarrett. A Novel Defense of Scientific Realism. LC 96-29086. (Illus.). 224p. 1997. text 39.95 (*0-19-511363-2*) OUP.

Leplin, Jarrett, ed. The Creation of Ideas in Physics: Studies for Methodology of Theory Construction. LC 95-13782. (University of Western Ontario Series in Philosophy of Science WONS: Vol. 55). 260p. (C). 1995. lib. bdg. 125.00 (*0-7923-3461-2*, Pub. by Kluwer Academic) Kluwer Academic.

Leplin, Jarrett, jt. ed. see Fine, Arthur.

LePlongeon, Augustus. Sacred Mysteries among the Mayas & Quiches. 163p. 1996. reprint ed. spiral bd. 15.50 (*0-7873-0554-5*) Hlth Research.

LePlongeon, Augustus & Allen, Paul M. Maya-Atlantis: Queen Moo & the Egyptian Sphinx. LC 73-186768. (Illus.). 424p. 1991. reprint ed. pap. 16.95 (*0-89345-238-6*, Steinerbks) Garber Comm.

LePoer, Barbara L., ed. Thailand: A Country Study. 6th ed. LC 88-600485. (Area Handbook Ser.). (Illus.). 396p. 1989. text 23.00 (*0-16-001732-7*, S/N 008-020-01184-3) USGPO.

LePoff, Arlene, jt. auth. see Prager, Janice.

Lepoittevin, J. P. & Karlberg, A. T., eds. Allergic Contact Dermatitis: The Molecular Basis. LC 97-28047. x, 186p. 1997. 59.00 (*3-540-61833-3*) Spr-Verlag.

Lepoma, Ed, et al. A Passion for People: The Story of Mary Mahoney & Her Old French House Restaurant. LC 98-28077. 168p. 1998. pap. 9.95 (*0-937552-94-1*) Quail Ridge.

Lepon, Elimelech, tr. see Zalman, Avraham B.

Lepon, S. Torah Rhymes & Riddles. 1992. 13.99 (*0-89906-995-9*); pap. 10.99 (*0-89906-996-7*) Mesorah Pubns.

Lepon, Shoshana. Hanukkah Carousel. (Illus.). (J). (ps-1). 1993. 12.95 (*0-943706-11-4*) Pitspopany.

— Hillel Builds a House. LC 92-39383. (Illus.). (J). (ps-2). 1993. pap. 5.95 (*0-929371-42-9*) Kar-Ben.

— Hillel Builds a House. (J). 1993. 11.15 (*0-606-08772-9*, Pub. by Turtleback) Demco.

— Holiday Rhymes & Riddles. (Illus.). (J). 1994. 13.99 (*0-89906-820-0*, HR1H); pap. 10.99 (*0-89906-821-9*) Mesorah Pubns.

— No Greater Treasure: Stories of Extraordinary Women Drawn from the Talmud & Misdrash. 190p. 1990. 16.95 (*0-944070-62-0*) Targum Pr.

— Noah & the Rainbow. LC 92-26431. (Illus.). (J). (gr. k-4). 1993. 12.95 (*1-880582-04-X*); pap. 9.95 (*1-880582-05-8*) Judaica Pr.

— The Ten Plagues of Egypt. Goldstein-Alpern, Neva, ed. (Illus.). 32p. (J). (gr. k-4). 1988. 12.95 (*0-910818-77-0*); pap. 9.95 (*0-910818-76-2*) Judaica Pr.

— The Ten Tests of Abraham. (Judaica Bible Series for Young Children). (Illus.). 32p. (J). (gr. k-4). 1986. pap. 7.95 (*0-910818-67-3*) Judaica Pr.

***Lepon, Shoshana.** The Ten Tests of Avraham. LC 00-35231. (Illus.). 2000. pap. write for info. (*1-880582-61-9*) Judaica Pr.

Lepon, Shoshona. Joseph the Dreamer. (Bible Series for Young Children). (Illus.). 32p. (J). (gr. k-4). 1991. 12.95 (*0-910818-92-4*); pap. 9.95 (*0-910818-93-2*) Judaica Pr.

Lepor, Herbert. Prostatic Disease. LC 99-48130. 1999. text. write for info. (*0-7216-7416-X*, W B Saunders Co) Harcrt Hlth Sci Grp.

Lepor, Herbert & Lawson, Russell K., eds. Prostate Diseases. LC 92-49620. (Illus.). 512p. 1993. text 115.00 (*0-7216-4545-3*, W B Saunders Co) Harcrt Hlth Sci Grp.

— Therapy for Genitourinary Cancer. (Cancer Treatment & Research Ser.). 176p. (C). 1992. text 148.50 (*0-7923-1412-3*) Kluwer Academic.

Lepor, Herbert & McGuire, William L., eds. Urologic Oncology. (Cancer Treatment & Research Ser.). (C). 1989. text 174.00 (*0-7923-0161-7*) Kluwer Academic.

Lepor, Keith P., ed. After the Cold War: Essays on the Emerging World Order. LC 96-23670. 344p. 1997. 34.95 (*0-292-74693-8*) U of Tex Pr.

Leporati, Ezio. The Assessment of Structural Safety: A Comparative Statistical Study of the Evolution & Use of Levels 1, 2, & 3. Grimoldi, Nicoletta, tr. LC 79-50708. (Series in Cement & Concrete Research: No. 1). (Illus.). 143p. reprint ed. pap. 44.40 (*0-8357-8808-3*, 203334400085) Bks Demand.

Lepore, Bruce A. & Lepore, Chris N. The Employer's Back Injury Prevention Handbook. (Illus.). 164p. (C). 1984. pap. 24.95 (*0-9613365-0-1*) Bridgeview.

— Not Tonite Dear, My Back Is Killing Me! (Illus.). 52p. 1986. pap. 5.95 (*0-9613365-5-2*) Bridgeview.

Lepore, Chris N., jt. auth. see Lepore, Bruce A.

Lepore, Domenico & Cohen, Oded. Deming & Goldratt: The Theory of Constraints & the System of Profound Knowledge. 1999. pap. 19.95 (*0-88427-163-3*) North River.

Lepore, Donald. The Ultimate Healing System. 402p. 1987. pap. 19.95 (*0-913923-63-X*) Woodland UT.

— Ultimate Healing System. 1996. 19.95 (*1-885670-08-7*) Woodland UT.

***Lepore, Ernest.** Meaning & Argument: An Introduction to Logic. 300p. 1999. 62.95 (*0-631-20581-0*); pap. 29.95 (*0-631-20582-9*) Blackwell Pubs.

LePore, Ernest. New Directions in Semantics. (Cognitive Science Ser.: No. 2). 512p. 1987. text 139.00 (*0-12-444040-1*) Acad Pr.

Lepore, Ernest & Pylyshyn, Zenon, eds. What Is Cognitive Science? LC 98-47772. 496p. 1999. pap. 29.95 (*0-631-20494-6*) Blackwell Pubs.

***Lepore, Ernest & Pylyshyn, Zenon, eds.** What Is Cognitive Science? LC 98-47772. 496p. 1999. 59.95 (*0-631-20493-8*) Blackwell Pubs.

Lepore, Ernest, jt. auth. see Fodor, Jerry.

Lepore, Jill. Early American Encounters: A History in Documents. LC 99-45335. (Pages from History Ser.). (Illus.). 176p. (YA). 2000. text 32.95 (*0-19-510513-3*) OUP.

— The Name of War: King Philiip's War & the Origins of American Identity. (Illus.). 337p. 1999. pap. 15.00 (*0-375-70262-8*) Vin Bks.

— The Name of War: King Philip's War & the Origins of American Identity. LC 97-2820. (Illus.). 337p. 1998. 30.00 (*0-679-44686-9*) Random.

Lepore, Monica, et al. Adapted Aquatics Programming: A Professional Guide. LC 98-22953. (Illus.). 328p. 1998. text 37.00 (*0-88011-695-1*, BLEP0695) Human Kinetics.

Leporin, Dorothea C. Grundliche Untersuchung der Ursachen, die das Weibliche Geschlecht vom Studiren Abhalten. (GER.). 250p. 1987. reprint ed. write for info. (*3-487-05875-8*) G Olms Pubs.

Lepow, Lauren. Enacting the Sacrament: Counter-Lollardy in the Towneley Cycle. LC 90-55003. 168p. 1991. 28.50 (*0-8386-3368-4*) Fairleigh Dickinson.

Lepowsky, James & Primc, M. Structure of the Standard Modules for the Affine Lie Algebra A - Sub 1. LC 85-15639. (Contemporary Mathematics Ser.: Vol. 46). 84p. 1985. pap. 21.00 (*0-8218-5048-2*, CONM/46) Am Math.

Lepowsky, James, jt. auth. see Dong, Chong-Ying.

Lepowsky, Maria A. Fruit of the Motherland: Gender in an Egalitarian Society. LC 93-8314. 383p. 1994. 61.50 (*0-231-08120-0*); pap. 22.00 (*0-231-08121-9*) Col U Pr.

Lepp, Bil, jt. auth. see Lepp, Paul.

Lepp, George & Dickerson, Joe. Canon Lenses. (Magic Lantern Guides Ser.). (Illus.). 176p. (Orig.). (C). 1998. pap. 19.95 (*1-883403-16-2*, H 112, Silver Pixel Pr) Saunders Photo.

Lepp, George D. Beyond the Basics: Innovative Techniques for Nature Photography. LC 93-91588. 156p. 1993. pap. 32.95 (*0-9637313-0-0*) Lepp & Assocs.

— Beyond the Basics II: More Innovative Techniques for Nature Photography. LC 96-95518. (Illus.). 180p. 1997. pap. 32.95 (*0-9637313-1-9*) Lepp & Assocs.

***Lepp, Matt.** When Worst Comes to Verse. 1999. pap. write for info. (*1-58235-324-7*) Watermrk Pr.

Lepp, Paul & Lepp, Bil. The Monster Stick & Other Appalachian Tall Tales. LC PS3562.E6132M66 1999. 160p. (YA). (gr. 10 up). 1999. pap. 9.95 (*0-87483-577-1*) August Hse.

Leppa, S., jt. auth. see Albrecht, H.

Leppakoski, Markku. The Transcendental How: Kant's Transcendental Deduction of Objective Cognition. (Stockholm Studies in Philosophy: No. 13). 280p. (Orig.). 1993. pap. 53.00 (*91-22-01560-4*) Coronet Bks.

Leppaluoto, Jean R., ed. Women on the Move: A Feminist Perspective. 306p. 1972. pap. 6.00 (*0-317-34800-0*, X050) Know Inc.

Leppanen, Pentti A., jt. auth. see Glisic, Savo G.

Leppanen, Pentti A., jt. ed. see Glisic, Savo G.

Leppard, Barbara & Ashton, Richard. Treatment in Dermatology. rev. ed. Wieder, Joshua & Lowe, Nicholas J., eds. LC 94-40427. 1995. 39.95 (*1-85775-135-3*, Radcliffe Med Pr); text 115.00 (*1-85775-130-2*, Radcliffe Med Pr) Scovill Paterson.

— Treatment in Dermatology. 2nd ed. 1995. pap. 39.95 (*1-870905-52-0*, Radcliffe Med Pr) Scovill Paterson.

Leppard, Barbara, jt. auth. see Ashton, Richard.

Leppard, J. W., jt. auth. see McDonald, M. H.

Leppard, John & Molyneux, Liz. Auditing Your Customer Service: The Foundation for Success. LC 93-41814. (Marketing for Managers Ser.). 176p. (C). 1994. pap. 16.95 (*0-415-09732-0*, B3937) Thomson Learn.

Leppard, John W., jt. auth. see McDonald, Malcolm.

Leppard, John W., jt. auth. see Vyakarnam, Shailendra.

Leppard, Lois G. Mandie: My Diary. 256p. (J). 1997. text 9.99 (*0-7642-2022-5*, 232022) Bethany Hse.

— Mandie & Her Missing Kin. (Mandie Bks.: No. 25). 16p. (J). (gr. 4-7). 1995. mass mkt. 4.99 (*1-55661-511-6*) Bethany Hse.

— Mandie & Her Missing Kin. (Mandie Bks.: No. 25). (J). (gr. 4-7). 1995. 10.09 (*0-606-10868-8*, Pub. by Turtleback) Demco.

— Mandie & Joe's Christmas Suprise. 128p. (J). (gr. 3-8). 1995. text 9.99 (*1-55661-552-3*) Bethany Hse.

***Leppard, Lois G.** Mandie & Joe's Christmas Surprise. 128p. (J). (gr. 3-9). 2000. mass mkt. 4.99 (*0-7642-2414-X*) Bethany Hse.

Leppard, Lois G. Mandie & Jonathan's Predicament. LC 97-21027. (Mandie Bks.: No. 28). 176p. (J). (gr. 4-7). 1997. mass mkt. 4.99 (*1-55661-555-8*) Bethany Hse.

— Mandie & Mollie: The Angel's Visit. LC 97-45479. 128p. (J). 1998. text 9.99 (*0-7642-2063-2*) Bethany Hse.

— Mandie & the Abandoned Mine. LC 87-70883. (Mandie Bks.: No. 8). 16p. (J). (gr. 4-9). 1987. mass mkt. 4.99 (*0-87123-932-9*) Bethany Hse.

Leppard, Lois G. Mandie & the Abandoned Mine. (Mandie Bks.: No. 8). (J). (gr. 4-9). 1987. 10.09 (*0-606-06123-1*, Pub. by Turtleback) Demco.

Leppard, Lois G. Mandie & the Angel's Secret. (Mandie Bks.: No. 22). 16p. (J). (gr. 4-7). 1993. mass mkt. 4.99 (*1-55661-370-9*) Bethany Hse.

— Mandie & the Angel's Secret. (Mandie Bks.: No. 22). (J). (gr. 4-7). 1993. 10.09 (*0-606-06124-X*, Pub. by Turtleback) Demco.

***Leppard, Lois G.** Mandie & the Buried Stranger. LC 99-6446. (Mandie Bks.: No. 31). 176p. (J). (gr. 4-7). 1999. pap. text 4.99 (*1-55661-384-9*) Bethany Hse.

Leppard, Lois G. Mandie & the Charleston Phantom. LC 86-7098. (Mandie Bks.: No. 7). 144p. (J). (gr. 4-7). 1986. mass mkt. 4.99 (*0-87123-650-8*) Bethany Hse.

Leppard, Lois G. Mandie & the Charleston Phantom. (Mandie Bks.: No. 7). (J). (gr. 4-7). 1986. 10.09 (*0-606-06125-8*, Pub. by Turtleback) Demco.

Leppard, Lois G. Mandie & the Cherokee Legend. LC 83-70894. (Mandie Bks.: No. 2). 144p. (J). (gr. 4-8). 1983. mass mkt. 4.99 (*0-87123-321-5*) Bethany Hse.

Leppard, Lois G. Mandie & the Cherokee Legend. (Mandie Bks.: No. 2). (J). (gr. 4-7). 1983. 10.09 (*0-606-06126-6*, Pub. by Turtleback) Demco.

Leppard, Lois G. Mandie & the Courtroom Battle. LC 96-51197. (Mandy Ser.: No. 27). 176p. (J). (gr. 4-7). 1996. mass mkt. 4.99 (*1-55661-554-X*) Bethany Hse.

— Mandie & the Courtroom Battle. (Mandie Bks.: No. 27). (J). (gr. 4-7). 1996. 10.09 (*0-606-10869-6*, Pub. by Turtleback) Demco.

— Mandie & the Dangerous Imposter. LC 93-74539. (Mandie Bks.: No. 23). 176p. (J). (gr. 4-7). 1994. mass mkt. 4.99 (*1-55661-459-4*) Bethany Hse.

Leppard, Lois G. Mandie & the Dark Alley. (Mandie Bks.: No. 33). (J). (gr. 4-7). mass mkt. 4.99 (*0-7642-1674-0*) Bethany Hse.

— Mandie & the Dark Alley. (Mandie Bks.: No. 33). (Illus.). 176p. (J). (gr. 4-7). 2000. mass mkt. 4.99 (*1-55661-674-0*) Bethany Hse.

Leppard, Lois G. Mandie & the Fiery Rescue. (Mandie Bks.: No. 21). 16p. (J). (gr. 4-7). 1993. mass mkt. 4.99 (*1-55661-289-3*) Bethany Hse.

Leppard, Lois G. Mandie & the Fiery Rescue. (Mandie Bks.: No. 21). (J). (gr. 4-7). 1993. 10.09 (*0-606-06127-4*, Pub. by Turtleback) Demco.

Leppard, Lois G. Mandie & the Forbidden Attic. LC 84-72710. (Mandie Bks.: No. 4). 128p. (J). (gr. 4-7). 1985. mass mkt. 4.99 (*0-87123-822-5*) Bethany Hse.

Leppard, Lois G. Mandie & the Forbidden Attic. (Mandie Bks.: No. 4). (J). (gr. 4-7). 1985. 10.09 (*0-606-06128-2*, Pub. by Turtleback) Demco.

Leppard, Lois G. Mandie & the Foreign Spies. (Mandie Bks.: No. 15). 16p. (J). (gr. 4-7). 1990. mass mkt. 4.99 (*1-55661-147-1*) Bethany Hse.

Leppard, Lois G. Mandie & the Foreign Spies. (Mandie Bks.: No. 15). (J). (gr. 4-7). 1990. 10.09 (*0-606-06129-0*, Pub. by Turtleback) Demco.

Leppard, Lois G. Mandie & the Ghost Bandits. LC 84 71151. (Mandie Bks.: No. 3). 128p. (J). (gr. 4-7). 1984. mass mkt. 4.99 (*0-87123-442-4*) Bethany Hse.

Leppard, Lois G. Mandie & the Ghost Bandits. (Mandie Bks.: No. 3). (J). (gr. 4-7). 1984. 10.09 (*0-606-06130-4*, Pub. by Turtleback) Demco.

Leppard, Lois G. Mandie & the Hidden Treasure. LC 87-71606. (Mandie Bks.: No. 9). 16p. (J). (gr. 4-7). 1987. mass mkt. 4.99 (*0-87123-977-9*) Bethany Hse.

Leppard, Lois G. Mandie & the Hidden Treasure. (Mandie Bks.: No. 9). (J). (gr. 4-7). 1987. 10.09 (*0-606-06131-2*, Pub. by Turtleback) Demco.

Leppard, Lois G. Mandie & the Holiday Surprise. LC 88-71502. (Mandie Bks.: No. 11). 16p. (J). (gr. 4-7). 1988. mass mkt. 4.99 (*1-55661-036-X*) Bethany Hse.

L

L

Leppard, Lois G. Mandie & the Holiday Surprise. (Mandie Bks.: No. 11). (J). (gr. 4-7). 1988. 10.09 (*0-606-06132-0*, Pub. by Turtleback) Demco.

Leppard, Lois G. Mandie & the Invisible Troublemaker. LC 94-25134. (Mandie Bks.: No. 24). 176p. (J). (gr. 4-7). 1994. mass mkt. 4.99 (*1-55661-510-8*) Bethany Hse.

— Mandie & the Jumping Juniper. (Mandie Bks.: No. 18). 16p. (J). (gr. 4-7). 1991. mass mkt. 4.99 (*1-55661-200-1*) Bethany Hse.

Leppard, Lois G. Mandie & the Jumping Juniper. (Mandie Bks.: No. 18). (J). (gr. 4-7). 1991. 10.09 (*0-606-06133-9*, Pub. by Turtleback) Demco.

Leppard, Lois G. Mandie & the Long Goodbye. (Mandie Bks.: No. 30). 16p. (J). (gr. 4-7). 1998. mass mkt. 4.99 (*1-55661-557-4*) Bethany Hse.

— Mandie & the Medicine Man. LC 85-73426. (Mandie Bks.: No. 6). 128p. (J). (gr. 4-7). 1986. mass mkt. 4.99 (*0-87123-891-8*) Bethany Hse.

Leppard, Lois G. Mandie & the Medicine Man. (Mandie Bks.: No. 6). (J). (gr. 4-7). 1986. 10.09 (*0-606-06134-7*, Pub. by Turtleback) Demco.

Leppard, Lois G. Mandie & the Midnight Journey. (Mandie Bks.: No. 13). 16p. (J). (gr. 4-7). 1989. mass mkt. 4.99 (*1-55661-084-X*) Bethany Hse.

— Mandie & the Midnight Journey. (Mandie Bks.: No. 13). (J). (gr. 4-7). 1989. 10.09 (*0-606-06135-5*, Pub. by Turtleback) Demco.

— Mandie & the Mysterious Bells. LC 87-72792. (Mandie Bks.: No. 10). 16p. (J). (gr. 4-7). 1988. mass mkt. 4.99 (*1-55661-000-9*) Bethany Hse.

— Mandie & the Mysterious Bells. (Mandie Bks.: No. 10). (J). (gr. 4-7). 1988. 10.09 (*0-606-06136-3*, Pub. by Turtleback) Demco.

— Mandie & the Mysterious Fisherman. (Mandie Bks.: No. 19). 176p. (J). (gr. 4-7). 1992. mass mkt. 4.99 (*1-55661-235-4*) Bethany Hse.

— Mandie & the Mysterious Fisherman. (Mandie Bks.: No. 19). (J). (gr. 4-7). 1992. 10.09 (*0-606-06137-1*, Pub. by Turtleback) Demco.

— Mandie & the Schoolhouse's Secret. (Mandie Bks.: No. 26). 176p. (J). (gr. 4-7). 1996. mass mkt. 4.99 (*1-55661-553-1*) Bethany Hse.

— Mandie & the Schoolhouse's Secret. (Mandie Bks.: No. 26). (J). (gr. 4-7). 1996. 10.09 (*0-606-10870-X*, Pub. by Turtleback) Demco.

— Mandie & the Seaside Rendezvous. (Mandie Bks.: No. 32). 176p. (J). (gr. 4-7). 1999. pap. text 4.99 (*1-55661-673-2*) Bethany Hse.

— Mandie & the Secret Tunnel. LC 82-74053. (Mandie Bks.: No. 1). 144p. (J). (gr. 4-7). 1983. mass mkt. 4.99 (*0-87123-320-7*) Bethany Hse.

— Mandie & the Secret Tunnel. (Mandie Bks.: No. 1). (J). (gr. 4-7). 1983. 10.09 (*0-606-06138-X*, Pub. by Turtleback) Demco.

— Mandie & the Shipboard Mystery. (Mandie Bks.: No. 14). 16p. (J). (gr. 4-7). 1990. mass mkt. 4.99 (*1-55661-120-X*) Bethany Hse.

— Mandie & the Shipboard Mystery. (Mandie Bks.: No. 14). (J). (gr. 4-7). 1990. 10.09 (*0-606-06139-8*, Pub. by Turtleback) Demco.

— Mandie & the Silent Catacombs. (Mandie Bks.: No. 16). 16p. (J). (gr. 4-7). 1990. mass mkt. 4.99 (*1-55661-148-X*) Bethany Hse.

— Mandie & the Silent Catacombs. (Mandie Bks.: No. 16). (J). (gr. 4-7). 1990. 10.09 (*0-606-06140-1*, Pub. by Turtleback) Demco.

— Mandie & the Singing Chalet. (Mandie Bks.: No. 17). 176p. (J). (gr. 4-7). 1991. mass mkt. 4.99 (*1-55661-198-6*) Bethany Hse.

— Mandie & the Singing Chalet. (Mandie Bks.: No. 17). (J). (gr. 4-7). 1991. 10.09 (*0-606-06141-X*, Pub. by Turtleback) Demco.

Leppard, Lois G. Mandie & the Trunk's Secret. (Mandie Bks.: No. 5). (J). (gr. 4-7). 1985. 10.09 (*0-606-06142-8*, Pub. by Turtleback) Demco.

Leppard, Lois G. Mandie & the Trunk's Secret, Bk. 5. LC 85-71474. (Mandie Bks.: No. 5). 128p. (J). (gr. 4-7). 1985. mass mkt. 4.99 (*0-87123-839-X*) Bethany Hse.

— Mandie & the Unwanted Gift, 29. LC 97-33827. (Mandie Bks.: No. 29). 176p. (J). (gr. 4-7). 1997. mass mkt. 4.99 (*1-55661-556-6*) Bethany Hse.

Leppard, Lois G. Mandie & the Washington Nightmare. (Mandie Bks.: No. 12). (J). (gr. 4-7). 1989. 10.09 (*0-606-06143-6*, Pub. by Turtleback) Demco.

Leppard, Lois G. Mandie & the Washington Nightmare, Bk. 12. LC 88-63464. (Mandie Bks.: No. 12). 176p. (J). (gr. 4-7). 1989. mass mkt. 4.99 (*1-55661-065-3*) Bethany Hse.

— Mandie & the Windmill's Message. LC 92-73061. (Mandie Bks.: No. 20). 16p. (J). (gr. 4-7). 1992. mass mkt. 4.99 (*1-55661-288-5*) Bethany Hse.

Leppard, Lois G. Mandie & the Windmill's Message. (Mandie Bks.: No. 20). (J). (gr. 4-7). 1992. 10.09 (*0-606-06144-4*, Pub. by Turtleback) Demco.

Leppard, Lois G. Mandie Books. 1998. pap., boxed set 24.99 (*0-7642-8390-1*) Bethany Hse.

— Mandie Books Boxed Set: Mandie & the Holiday Surprise; Mandie & the Washington Nightmare; Mandie & the Midnight Journey; Mandie & the Shipboard Mystery; Mandie & the Foreign Spies. (Mandie Bks.: Nos. 11-15). (J). (gr. 4-7). 1990. boxed set 24.99 (*1-55661-758-5*) Bethany Hse.

— Mandie Books Boxed Set: Mandie & the Medicine Man; Mandie & the Charleston Phantom; Mandie & the Abandoned Mine; Mandie & the Hidden Treasure; Mandie & the Mysterious Bells. (Mandie Bks.: Nos. 6-10). (J). (gr. 4-7). 1988. pap., boxed set 24.99 (*1-55661-752-6*, 252752) Bethany Hse.

— Mandie Books Boxed Set: Mandie & the Secret Tunnel; Mandie & the Cherokee Legend; Mandie & the Ghost Bandits; Mandie & the Forbidden Attic; Mandie & the Trunk's Secret. (Mandie Bks.: Nos. 1-5). (J). (gr. 4-7). 1987. boxed set 24.99 (*1-55661-750-X*) Bethany Hse.

— Mandie Books Boxed Set: Mandie & the Silent Catacombs; Mandie & the Singing Chalet; Mandie & the Jumping Juniper; Mandie & the Mysterious Fisherman; Mandie & the Windmill's Message. (Mandie Bks.: Nos. 16-20). (J). (gr. 4-7). 1992. boxed set 24.99 (*1-55661-769-0*) Bethany Hse.

— Mandie's Cookbook. 112p. (Orig.). (J). (gr. 3-8). 1991. pap. 9.99 (*1-55661-224-9*) Bethany Hse.

***Leppard, Lois G.** Merry Christmas from Mandie. (Young Mandie Christmas Special Mysteries Ser.). (Illus.). (J). 2000. pap. 4.50 (*0-553-48720-5*, Skylark BDD) BDD Bks Young Read.

Leppard, Lois G. My Datebook: A Keepsake Book of Special Days. 112p. (J). 1997. text 7.99 (*0-7642-2021-7*) Bethany Hse.

— Mystery at Miss Abigail's. 128p. 1999. pap. 4.50 (*0-553-48661-6*) Bantam.

— The New Girl. (Mantlemass Ser.: No. 2). 118p. (J). (gr. 2-5). 1999. pap. 4.50 (*0-553-48660-8*) BDD Bks Young Read.

***Leppard, Lois G.** The Secret in the Woods. (J). 2001. pap. 4.50 (*0-553-48717-5*, Pub. by BDD Bks Young Read) Random House.

— The Talking Snowman. (Young Mandie Mysteries Ser.). (J). 2001. pap. 4.50 (*0-553-48662-4*, Skylark BDD) BDD Bks Young Read.

Leppard, Louis Gladys, jt. auth. see Bryant, Bonnie.

Leppard, Raymond. Authenticity in Music. 88p. (Orig.). 1989. pap. 8.50 (*0-931340-20-9*, Amadeus Pr) Timber.

— Raymond Leppard on Music: An Anthology of Critical & Personal Writings. Lewis, Thomas P., ed. (Illus.). 760p. 1993. 45.00 (*0-912483-96-2*) Pro-Am Music.

Leppard, Shannon M. The Ballet Class Mystery. LC 96-45834. (Adventures of Callie Ann Ser.). 8p. (J). (gr. 1-5). 1997. pap. 3.99 (*1-55661-814-X*) Bethany Hse.

— The Hospital Caper. LC 97-21040. (Adventures of Callie Ann Ser.: No. 3). 8p. (J). 1997. pap. 3.99 (*1-55661-815-8*) Bethany Hse.

— Miss Kitty Mystery. LC 97-21041. (Adventures of Callie Ann Ser.: No. 4). 8p. (J). 1997. pap. 3.99 (*1-55661-816-6*) Bethany Hse.

— Summer Surprise. LC 96-45833. (Adventures of Callie Ann Ser.). 8p. (J). (gr. 2-5). 1997. pap. 3.99 (*1-55661-813-1*) Bethany Hse.

Leppart, Jerry. Headwaters. LC 98-6593. 256p. 1998. pap. 14.95 (*1-880090-66-X*) Galde Pr.

— Pest Control. LC 99-47726. 224p. 2000. pap. 14.95 (*1-880090-95-3*) Galde Pr.

Leppek, Chris. Surrogate Assassin. 418p. 1998. 24.95 (*1-885173-54-7*) Write Way.

Leppelman, John. Blood on the Risers: An Airborne Soldier's Thirty-Five Months in Vietnam. (Orig.). 1991. mass mkt. 6.99 (*0-8041-0562-6*) Ivy Books.

***Lepper, Bradley T.** People of the Mounds: Ohio's Hopewell Culture. rev. ed. (Illus.). 22p. 1999. reprint ed. pap. 1.95 (*1-888213-48-5*) Eastern National.

Lepper, F. A. Trajan's Parthian War. rev. ed. (ENG & GRE.). xv, 262p. (C). 1994. text 30.00 (*0-89005-530-0*) Ares.

***Lepper, Frank & Frere, Sheppard.** Trajan's Column. (Illus.). 456p. 2000. pap. 29.95 (*0-7509-2466-7*) Sutton Publng.

Lepper, J. D. Mediterranean Orchids. 86p. (C). 1990. pap. 35.00 (*0-7223-2450-2*, Pub. by A H S Ltd) St Mut.

— Orchids of Greece. 60p. 1982. 35.00 (*0-7223-1450-7*, Pub. by A H S Ltd) St Mut.

Lepper, Marion J. De, see De Lepper, Marion J., ed.

Leppert, Clara. Simple Times. (Folk Literature Ser.). 48p. 1993. pap. 5.95 (*1-878781-07-3*) Free River Pr.

Leppert, G., jt. auth. see Farrell, R. E.

Leppert, Mary & Leppert, Michael. Homeschooling Annual. LC 99-27553. 624p. 1999. per. 24.95 (*0-7615-2014-7*) Prima Pub.

Leppert, Michael, jt. auth. see Leppert, Mary.

Leppert, Paul. Doing Business with China. LC 94-9350. (Global Business Ser.). 166p. (Orig.). 1994. pap. 12.95 (*0-87573-045-0*) Jain Pub Co.

— Doing Business with Korea. 2nd ed. LC 95-14750. (Global Business Ser.). Orig. Title: Doing Business with the Koreans. 144p. (Orig.). 1997. pap. 12.95 (*0-87573-043-4*) Jain Pub Co.

— Doing Business with Mexico. LC 95-20285. (Global Business Ser.). 144p. (Orig.). 1996. pap. 12.95 (*0-87573-046-9*) Jain Pub Co.

— Doing Business with Singapore. 2nd ed. LC 95-14751. (Global Business Ser.). Orig. Title: Doing Business in Singapore. 144p. (Orig.). 1997. pap. 12.95 (*0-87573-042-6*) Jain Pub Co.

— Doing Business with Taiwan. 2nd ed. LC 95-14753. (Global Business Ser.). Orig. Title: Doing Business with the Chinese. 144p. (Orig.). 1997. pap. 12.95 (*0-87573-041-8*) Jain Pub Co.

— Doing Business with Thailand. 2nd ed. LC 95-14752. (Global Business Ser.). Orig. Title: Doing Business with the Thais. 166p. (Orig.). 1997. pap. 12.95 (*0-87573-044-2*) Jain Pub Co.

Leppert, Phyllis. Primary Care for Women. LC 96-30176. 1,048p. 1996. text 79.00 (*0-397-51523-5*) Lppncott W & W.

Leppert, Phyllis C. & Woessner, J. Frederick, eds. The Extracellular Matrix of the Uterus, Cervix & Fetal Membranes: Synthesis, Degradation & Hormonal Regulation. (Research in Perinatal Medicine Ser.: No. X). (Illus.). 296p. 1991. 110.00 (*0-916859-43-6*) Perinatology.

Leppert, Richard. Art & the Committed Eye: The Cultural Functions of Imagery. LC 95-19092. (Cultural Studies). (Illus.). 368p. (C). 1996. pap. 30.00 (*0-8133-1540-9*, Pub. by Westview) HarpC.

— The Sight of Sound: Music, Representation, & the History of the Body. LC 92-39075. 345p. 1995. pap. 19.95 (*0-520-20342-9*, Pub. by U CA Pr) Cal Prin Full Svc.

***Leppert, Richard.** The Sight of Sound: Music, Representation & the History of the Body. (Illus.). 316p. 2000. reprint ed. pap. text 25.00 (*0-7881-9132-2*) DIANE Pub.

Leppert, Richard D. Arcadia at Versailles: Noble Amateur Musicians & Their Musettes & Hurdy-Gurdies at the French Court (C. 1660-1789), a Visual Study. x, 138p. 1978. pap. text 26.00 (*90-265-0246-X*) Swets.

— Music & Image: Domesticity, Ideology & Socio-Cultural Formation in 18th Century England. (Illus.). 264p. (C). 1993. pap. text 25.95 (*0-521-44854-9*) Cambridge U Pr.

— The Sight of Sound: Music, Representation, & the History of the Body. LC 92-39075. 1993. 55.00 (*0-520-08174-9*, Pub. by U CA Pr) Cal Prin Full Svc.

Leppert, Richard D. & McClary, Susan, eds. Music & Society: The Politics of Composition, Performance, & Reception. LC 86-31672. (Illus.). 224p. 1989. pap. text 21.95 (*0-521-37977-6*) Cambridge U Pr.

Leppien, Patsy A. & Smith, J. Kincaid. What's Going on among the Lutherans? A Comparison of Beliefs. LC 92-80393. 400p. (Orig.). 1992. pap. 13.99 (*0-8100-0427-5*, 15N0544) Northwest Pub.

Leppihalme, Ritva. Culture Bumps: An Empirical Approach to the Translation of Allusions. LC 97-7446. (Topics in Translation Ser.). 240p. 1997. 95.00 (*1-85359-374-5*, Pub. by Multilingual Matters); pap. 39.95 (*1-85359-373-7*, Pub. by Multilingual Matters) Taylor & Francis.

***Leppik, Ilo E.** Managing Your Epilepsy. (Illus.). 130p. 2000. pap. 29.95 (*1-884065-81-3*, Hndbks Hlth Care) Assocs in Med.

Leppik, Ilo E., ed. Rational Plypharmacy. LC 96-43598. (Epilepsy Research Supplements Ser.: No. 11). 274p. 1997. text 172.00 (*0-444-82455-3*) Elsevier.

Leppin, Paul. The Road to Darkness. 1997. pap. text 11.95 (*1-57241-052-3*) Ariadne CA.

Lepple-Wienhues, A., jt. ed. see Cahalan, M. D.

Leppmann, P., tr. see Hoermann, H.

Leppmann, Wolfgang. Rilke: A Life. Stockman, Russell M., tr. from GER. LC 84-6062.Tr. of Rilke-Sein Leben, Seine Welt, Sein Werk. (Illus.). 421p. 1995. pap. 14.95 (*1-88064-015-4*) Fromm Intl Pub.

LePre, C. Gerard. God's Money-Back Guarantee: The Seven Steps to Financial Success. LC 93-40623. (Illus.). 248p. 1994. 21.95 (*1-56554-027-1*) Pelican.

Lepre, George. Himmler's Bosnian Division: The Waffen-SS Handschar Division, 1943-1945. LC 96-69809. (Illus.). 400p. 1997. 39.95 (*0-7643-0134-9*) Schiffer.

Lepre, J. P. The Egyptian Pyramids: A Comprehensive, Illustrated Reference. LC 89-43623. (Illus.). 359p. 1990. lib. bdg. 62.50 (*0-89950-461-2*) McFarland & Co.

LePrestre, Philippe G., ed. French Security Policy in a Disarming World: Domestic Challenges & International Constraints. LC 88-21703. 152p. 1988. lib. bdg. 30.00 (*1-55587-132-1*) L Rienner.

Leprince de Beaumont, De, see De Leprince de Beaumont.

Leprince de Beaumont, Marie & Perrault, Charles. Beauty & the Beast & Other Fairy Tales. (Illus.). 96p. (Orig.). (J). (ps-3). 1994. pap. 1.00 (*0-486-28032-2*) Dover.

Leprince-Ringuet, Louis. Atoms & Men. Halperin, Elaine P., tr. LC 61-11292. 128p. reprint ed. pap. 39.70 (*0-8357-5859-1*, 202020000016) Bks Demand.

Leps, Marie-Christine. Apprehending the Criminal: The Production of Deviance in Nineteenth-Century Discourse. LC 92-7451. (Post-Contemporary Interventions Ser.). (Illus.). 277p. 1992. text 54.95 (*0-8223-1255-7*); pap. text 18.95 (*0-8223-1271-9*) Duke.

Lepsch-Cunha, Nadja, jt. auth. see Mori, Scott A.

Lepschy. History of Linguistics, Vol. 2. 1994. text. write for info. (*0-582-09490-9*, Pub. by Addison-Wesley) Longman.

— History of Lingus , Vol. 3. 1998. 61.44 (*0-582-09492-5*) Addison-Wesley.

***Lepschy.** History of Lingus , Vol. 4. 1998. text 69.12 (*0-582-29477-0*) Addison-Wesley.

Lepschy, Anna Laura & Lepschy, Giulio C. The Italian Language Today. 2nd ed. LC 88-5320. 260p. (C). 1988. pap. text 16.95 (*0-941533-22-0*, NAB) I R Dee.

Lepschy, Anna Laura & Lepschy, Guilio. The Italian Language Today. 2nd ed. LC 92-6700. 272p. (C). 1989. pap. 25.99 (*0-415-07862-8*, A8529) Routledge.

Lepschy, Giulio, ed. History of Linguistics. LC 93-31169. text. write for info. (*0-582-09488-7*, Pub. by Addison-Wesley) Longman.

Lepschy, Giulio C., jt. auth. see Lepschy, Anna Laura.

Lepschy, Guilio, jt. auth. see Lepschy, Anna Laura.

Lepscky. Amadeus Mozart. (Illus.). 28p. (J). (gr. 5-9). 1982. 9.95 (*0-8120-5465-2*) Barron.

— Leonardo da Vinci. (Famous People Ser.). (Illus.). 28p. (gr. k-3). 1984. 9.95 (*0-8120-5512-8*) Barron.

Lepscky, Ibi. Albert Einstein. (Famous People Ser.). (Illus.). 28p. (J). (gr. k-3). 1992. pap. 5.95 (*0-8120-1452-9*) Barron.

— Amadeus Mozart. (Famous People Ser.). (Illus.). 28p. (J). (gr. k-3). 1992. pap. 5.95 (*0-8120-1493-6*) Barron.

— Leonardo da Vinci. (Famous People Ser.). (Illus.). 28p. (J). (gr. k-3). 1992. pap. 4.95 (*0-8120-1451-0*) Barron.

— Leonardo da Vinci. (Children of Genius Ser.). (J). 1992. 10.15 (*0-606-05423-5*, Pub. by Turtleback) Demco.

— Marie Curie. (Famous People Ser.). (Illus.). 28p. (J). (gr. k-3). 1993. pap. 5.95 (*0-8120-1558-4*) Barron.

— Marie Curie. LC 92-38955. (Famous People Ser.). (Illus.). 28p. (J). (ps-3). 1993. 9.95 (*0-8120-6340-6*) Barron.

— Pablo Picasso. LC 83-347. (Famous People Ser.). (Illus.). 24p. (J). (gr. k-3). 1984. 9.95 (*0-8120-5511-X*) Barron.

— Pablo Picasso. (Famous People Ser.). (Illus.). 28p. (J). (gr. k-3). 1992. pap. 5.95 (*0-8120-1450-2*) Barron.

— William Shakespeare. (Famous People Ser.). (Illus.). 28p. (J). (gr. k-3). 1989. 7.95 (*0-8120-6106-3*) Barron.

Lepsinger, Richard & Lucia, Antoinette D. The Art & Science of 360 Degree Feedback. LC 96-39195. 288p. 1997. 44.95 (*0-7879-0855-X*) Jossey-Bass.

Lepsius, Richard. Standard Alphabet for Reducing Unwritten Languages & Foreign Graphic Systems to a Uniform Orthography in European Letters. 2nd rev. ed. Kemp, J. Alan, ed. & intro. by. (Amsterdam Classics in Linguistics Ser.: Vol. 5). xvii, 336p. 1981. 87.00 (*90-272-0876-X*) J Benjamins Pubng Co.

Lepsky, Michele. Pathway to Promise. LC 93-19926. 250p. (Orig.). 1993. pap. 4.99 (*1-56722-008-8*) Word Aflame.

Lepson, Ruth. Dreaming in Color. LC 79-54882. (Illus.). 72p. 1980. pap. 3.95 (*0-914086-27-8*) Alice James Bks.

Lepthien, Emilie U. Beavers. LC 92-14909. (New True Books Ser.). (Illus.). 48p. (J). (gr. k-4). 1992. lib. bdg. 21.00 (*0-516-01131-6*) Childrens.

— The Cherokee. rev. ed. LC 84-27476. (New True Books Ser.). (Illus.). 48p. (J). (gr. k-4). 1992. pap. 5.50 (*0-516-41938-2*) Childrens.

— The Cherokee. rev. ed. LC 84-27476. (New True Books Ser.). (Illus.). 48p. (J). (ps-3). 1992. lib. bdg. 21.00 (*0-516-01938-4*) Childrens.

— The Choctaw. rev. ed. LC 87-14583. (New True Books Ser.). (Illus.). 48p. (J). (ps-3). 1992. lib. bdg. 21.00 (*0-516-01240-1*) Childrens.

— The Choctaw. rev. ed. LC 87-14583. (New True Books Ser.). (Illus.). 48p. (J). (gr. k-4). 1994. pap. 5.50 (*0-516-41240-X*) Childrens.

— Coyotes. LC 92-35050. (New True Books Ser.). (Illus.). 48p. (J). (gr. k-4). 1993. pap. 5.50 (*0-516-41331-7*); lib. bdg. 21.00 (*0-516-01331-9*) Childrens.

— Elk. LC 94-10469. (New True Books Ser.). (Illus.). 48p. (J). (gr. k-4). 1994. lib. bdg. 21.00 (*0-516-01063-8*) Childrens.

— Giraffes. (True Bk.). 48p. (J). (gr. 3-5). 1996. lib. bdg. 21.00 (*0-516-20158-1*) Childrens.

— Giraffes. (True Bks.). 48p. (J). (gr. 3-5). 1997. pap. 6.95 (*0-516-26098-7*) Childrens.

— Grizzlies. (True Bk.). 48p. (J). (gr. 3-5). 1996. lib. bdg. 21.00 (*0-516-20159-X*) Childrens.

— Grizzlies. (True Bks.). 48p. (J). (gr. 3-4). 1997. pap. 6.95 (*0-516-26100-2*) Childrens.

— Kangaroos. LC 94-36351. (New True Books Ser.). (Illus.). 48p. (J). (gr. k-4). 1995. lib. bdg. 21.00 (*0-516-01075-1*) Childrens.

— Koalas. LC 90-2219. (New True Books Ser.). (Illus.). 48p. (J). (gr. k-4). 1990. lib. bdg. 21.00 (*0-516-01108-1*) Childrens.

— Llamas. (True Bk.). 48p. 1996. lib. bdg. 21.00 (*0-516-20160-3*) Childrens.

— Llamas. (True Bks.). 48p. (J). (gr. 3-4). 1997. pap. 6.95 (*0-516-26108-8*) Childrens.

— Manatees. LC 90-21138. (New True Books Ser.). (Illus.). 48p. (J). (gr. k-4). 1991. lib. bdg. 21.00 (*0-516-01114-6*) Childrens.

— Manatees. LC 90-21138. (New True Books Ser.). (Illus.). 48p. (J). (ps-3). 1991. pap. 5.50 (*0-516-41114-4*) Childrens.

— The Mandans. rev. ed. LC 89-22235. (New True Books Ser.). (Illus.). 48p. (J). (ps-3). 1992. lib. bdg. 21.00 (*0-516-01180-4*) Childrens.

— Monarch Butterflies. LC 89-456. (New True Books Ser.). (Illus.). 48p. (J). (gr. k-4). 1989. lib. bdg. 21.00 (*0-516-01165-0*) Childrens.

— Ostriches. LC 93-3407. (New True Books Ser.). (Illus.). 48p. (J). (gr. k-4). 1993. pap. 5.50 (*0-516-41193-4*) Childrens.

— Otters. LC 93-33515. (New True Books Ser.). (Illus.). 48p. (J). (gr. 2-4). 1994. pap. 5.50 (*0-516-41056-3*) Childrens.

— Penguins. LC 82-17911. (New True Books Ser.). (Illus.). 48p. (J). (gr. k-4). 1983. pap. 5.50 (*0-516-41683-9*) Childrens.

— Polar Bears. LC 91-8892. (New True Books Ser.). (Illus.). 48p. (J). (ps-3). 1991. pap. 5.50 (*0-516-41127-6*); lib. bdg. 21.00 (*0-516-01127-8*) Childrens.

— Sea Turtles. (True Bk.). 48p. (J). 1996. lib. bdg. 21.00 (*0-516-20161-1*) Childrens.

— Sea Turtles. (True Bks.). 48p. (J). (gr. 3-4). 1997. pap. 6.95 (*0-516-26113-4*) Childrens.

— The Seminole. rev. ed. LC 84-23141. (New True Books Ser.). (Illus.). 48p. (J). (gr. k-4). 1992. pap. 5.50 (*0-516-41941-2*) Childrens.

— Skunks. LC 93-3410. (New True Books Ser.). (Illus.). 48p. (J). (gr. k-4). 1993. pap. 5.50 (*0-516-41197-7*); lib. bdg. 21.00 (*0-516-01197-9*) Childrens.

— South Dakota. rev. ed. LC 90-21137. (America the Beautiful Ser.). (Illus.). 144p. (J). (gr. 5-8). 1991. lib. bdg. 28.00 (*0-516-00487-5*) Childrens.

— Squirrels. LC 92-9207. (New True Books Ser.). (Illus.). 48p. (J). (ps-3). 1992. lib. bdg. 21.00 (*0-516-01947-3*) Childrens.

— Squirrels. LC 92-9207. (New True Books Ser.). (Illus.). 48p. (J). (gr. k-4). 1993. pap. 5.50 (*0-516-41947-1*) Childrens.

— Walruses. LC 96-13921. (True Bks.). 48p. (J). (gr. 2-4). 1996. lib. bdg. 21.00 (*0-516-20162-X*) Childrens.

— Walruses. (True Bks.). 48p. (J). (gr. 2-4). 1997. pap. 6.95 (*0-516-26117-7*) Childrens.

— Wolves. LC 91-3035. (New True Books Ser.). (Illus.). 48p. (J). (gr. k-4). 1991. pap. 5.50 (*0-516-41129-2*) Childrens.

— Wolves. LC 91-3035. (New True Books Ser.). (Illus.). 48p. (J). (ps-3). 1991. lib. bdg. 21.00 (*0-516-01129-4*) Childrens.

— Zebras. LC 94-10945. (New True Books Ser.). (Illus.). 48p. (J). (gr. 2-4). 1994. lib. bdg. 21.00 (*0-516-01072-7*) Childrens.

Lepthien, Emilie U. & Kalbacken, Joan. Foxes. LC 93-3409. (New True Books Ser.). (Illus.). 48p. (J). (gr. 3-5). 1993. lib. bdg. 21.00 (*0-516-01191-X*) Childrens.

An Asterisk (*) at the beginning of an entry indicates that the title is appearing for the first time.

— Recycling. LC 90-21275. (New True Books Ser.). (Illus.). 48p. (J). (gr. k-4). 1991. lib. bdg. 21.00 (*0-516-01118-9*) Childrens.

— Wetlands. LC 92-35051. (New True Books Ser.). (Illus.). 48p. (J). (gr. 2-4). 1993. pap. 5.50 (*0-516-41334-1*) Childrens.

Leptich, Anne & Evans, Jacque. Calligraphy for Fun & Profit. 1982. pap. 7.00 (*0-87980-385-1*) Wilshire.

Leptin, Horst & Ludwig, Jean. Unitary Representation Theory of Exponential Lie Groups. LC 94-27983. (Expositions in Mathematics Ser.: Vol. 18). 210p. (C). 1994. lib. bdg. 109.95 (*3-11-013938-3*) De Gruyter.

Lepuil, Roger, jt. auth. see Guegan, Yannick.

LeQuesne, Caroline. Reforming World Trade: The Social & Environmental Priorities. (Oxfam Insight Ser.). 80p. 1996. pap. 7.95 (*0-85598-346-9*, Pub. by Oxfam Pub) Stylus Pub VA.

LeQuesne, Caroline, jt. auth. see Coote, Belinda.

Lequesne, Christian, jt. auth. see Legales, Patrick.

Lequeux, James. Structure & Evolution of Galaxies. (Documents on Modern Physics Ser.). xii, 220p. 1969. text 274.00 (*0-677-30110-3*) Gordon & Breach.

***Lequeux, Pierre.** Financial Markets Tick by Tick: In-Depth Analysis of Share Price Movement. LC 98-35143. 426p. 1999. 79.95 (*0-471-98160-5*) Wiley.

LeQueux, William. Spies of the Kaiser. 255p. Date not set. 22.95 (*0-8488-2353-2*) Amereon Ltd.

Lequin, Frank, ed. The Private Correspondence of Isaac Titsingh, 1785-1811, Vol. 1. (Japonica Neerlandica Ser.: Vol. 4). (DUT.). xlix, 534p. 1990. 94.00 (*90-5063-052-9*, Pub. by Gieben) J Benjamins Pubng Co.

LeQuire, Stan L., ed. The Best Preaching on Earth: Sermons on Caring for Creation. 248p. (Orig.). 1996. pap. 16.00 (*0-8170-1239-7*) Judson.

***Lequyer, Jules.** Jules Lequyer's Abel & Abel Followed by "Incidents in the Life & Death of Jules Lequyer" A Philosophical Biography. West, Mark, tr. from FRE. LC 99-32856. (Studies in the History of Philosophy: Vol. 51). 208p. 1999. text 89.95 (*0-7734-7934-1*) E Mellen.

Lequyer, Jules. Translation of Works of Jules Lequyer: The Hornbeam Leaf, The Dialogue of the Predestinate & the Reprobate, Eugene & Theophilus. Viney, Donald W., ed. LC 98-23584. (Studies in the History of Philosophy: Vol. 48). 184p. 1998. text 79.95 (*0-7734-8366-7*) E Mellen.

Lera, Thomas M. Bats in Philately. (Illus.). 64p. 1995. pap. 10.00 (*0-935991-24-7*) Am Topical Assn.

Lerai, Brandon. How to Get a Woman No Matter How You Look: How to Please a Woman Mentally & Physically - Mind, Body & Soul. rev. ed. LC 87-90520. xvii, 218p. 1998. pap. 10.95 (*0-9618677-1-X*) Lerai Enterprises.

Leranbaum, Miriam. Alexander Pope's Opus Magnum, 1729-1744. (Illus.). 204p. 1977. text 24.95 (*0-19-812051-6*) OUP.

Leranger, Jim. In the Shadow of the Cloud: Photographs & Histories of America's Atomic Veterans. LC 87-33682. (Illus.). 128p. 1988. 23.95 (*1-55591-030-0*) Fulcrum Pub.

Lerangis, Peter. Attack of the Killer Potatoes. (J). 1997. pap. text 3.99 (*0-590-93971-8*, Little Apple) Scholastic Inc.

— Attack of the Killer Potatoes. 1997. 9.09 (*0-606-12880-8*, Pub. by Turtleback) Demco.

— Driver's Dead. 192p. (YA). (gr. 7-9). 1994. pap. 3.50 (*0-590-46677-1*) Scholastic Inc.

***Lerangis, Peter.** Escape from Disaster. (Antarctica Ser. : Vol. 2). (Illus.). 160p. (J). (gr. 4-7). 2000. pap. 4.50 (*0-439-16388-9*) Scholastic Inc.

— Escape from Disaster. (Illus.). (J). 2000. 9.85 (*0-606-18865-7*) Turtleback.

Lerangis, Peter. I.D., 3. (Watchers Ser.: No. 3). (J). (gr. 4-7). 1999. pap. text 3.99 (*0-590-10998-7*) Scholastic Inc.

— Island, Vol. 5. (Watchers Ser.: No. 5). (J). (gr. 4-7). 1999. pap. 4.50 (*0-590-11500-6*) Scholastic Inc.

— It Came from the Cafeteria. (J). (gr. 3-7). 1996. pap. 3.50 (*0-590-93970-X*) Scholastic Inc.

***Lerangis, Peter.** Journey to the North Pole. (Antarctica Ser. : Vol. 1). (Illus.). 160p. (J). (gr. 4-7). 2000. pap. 4.50 (*0-439-16387-0*) Scholastic Inc.

— Journey to the North Pole. (Illus.). (J). 2000. 9.85 (*0-606-18864-9*) Turtleback.

— Lab 6. (Watchers Ser.: No. 6). (J). (gr. 4-7). 1999. pap. 4.50 (*0-590-11501-4*, Apple Classics) Scholastic Inc.

Lerangis, Peter. Last Stop. (Watchers Ser.: No. 1). 176p. (J). (gr. 4-7). 1998. pap. text 3.99 (*0-590-10996-0*) Scholastic Inc.

— Puzzles & Games. Sovndal, Jane, ed. (Thinking Skills Library). (Illus.). 106p. (Orig.). (J). (gr. 2-5). 1997. pap., teacher ed. 9.95 (*1-56784-712-9*) Newbridge Educ.

— Rewind. (Watchers Ser.: No. 2). 176p. (J). (gr. 4-7). 1998. pap. text 3.99 (*0-590-10997-9*) Scholastic Inc.

***Lerangis, Peter.** Road to El Dorado: Junior Novelization. (Gold & Glory Ser.). 115p. (J). 2000. mass mkt. 4.99 (*0-14-130712-9*) Viking Penguin.

Lerangis, Peter. Special Class Projects. Buckingham, Anne, ed. (Thinking Skills Library). (Illus.). 108p. (Orig.). (J). (gr. 2-5). 1997. pap., teacher ed. 9.95 (*1-56784-710-2*) Newbridge Educ.

— Spring Break. (J). 1997. mass mkt. 3.99 (*0-590-69771-4*) Scholastic Inc.

— War. (Watchers Ser.: 4). (J). (gr. 4-7). 1999. pap. text 4.50 (*0-590-10999-5*) Scholastic Inc.

— Yearbook. 176p. (YA). (gr. 7 up). 1994. pap. 3.50 (*0-590-46678-X*) Scholastic Inc.

L'Erario, Joe, jt. auth. see Feldman, Ed.

Lerat, Pierre. Dictionnaire Juridique: Terminologie du Contrat - Anglais, Francais, Allemand. (ENG, FRE & GER.). 239p. 1994. 95.00 (*0-7859-9176-X*) Fr & Eur.

Lerat, Pierre & Sourioux, Jean-Louis. French Dictionary of Contract Law with Equivalent Terms in German & English. 1994. 62.00 (*2-85319-257-1*) IBD Ltd.

— French Law Dictionary of Contract Terminology with Equivalents in English & German. (ENG, FRE & GER.). 239p. 1994. 95.00 (*0-7859-8892-0*) Fr & Eur.

Leray, Jean. Jean Leray Selected Papers - Oeuvres Scientifiques. Malliavin, P., ed. xxiv, 1693p. 1998. 325.00 (*3-540-60949-0*) Spr-Verlag.

Lerberghe, K. Van, see Van Lerberghe, K.

Lerbinger, Otto. The Crisis Manager: Facing Risk & Responsibility. (Communication Ser.). 384p. (C). 1996. text 79.95 (*0-8058-2386-7*); pap. text 37.50 (*0-8058-2387-5*) L Erlbaum Assocs.

Lerbinger, Otto, ed. Who's Who in Public Relations. 6th ed. 762p. 1992. 50.00 (*0-9632901-0-X*) P R Pub Co.

Lerch, Jennifer M. 500 Ways to Beat the Hollywood Script Reader: Writing the Screenplay the Reader Will Recommend. LC 99-25212. 176p. 1999. per. 12.00 (*0-684-85640-9*) S&S Trade Pap.

Lerch, Louise. Teens Musical Theatre Collection: Young Womens Edition. 160p. 1997. otabind 14.95 (*0-7935-8225-3*) H Leonard.

Lerch, Marilyn, jt. auth. see Siddiqui, Ashoaf.

Lerche, Charles, ed. Emergence: Dimensions of a New World. 180p. 1991. pap. 15.50 (*1-870989-22-8*) Bahai.

Lerche, Charles O., Jr. America in World Affairs. LC 79-26759. (Foundations of American Government & Political Science Ser.). (Illus.). 118p. 1980. reprint ed. lib. bdg. 55.00 (*0-313-22315-7*, LEAMW, Greenwood Pr) Greenwood.

Lerche, Charles O., Jr., et al. Concepts of International Politics. 4th ed. LC 94-24776. 336p. 1994. pap. text 49.00 (*0-13-174640-5*) P-H.

Lerche, H. R. Boundary Crossing of Brownian Motion. (Lecture Notes in Statistics Ser.: Vol. 40). 142p. 1986. 43.95 (*0-387-96433-9*) Spr-Verlag.

Lerche, I. & Petersen, K. Salt & Sediment Dynamics. LC 95-2515. 336p. 1995. boxed set 224.95 (*0-8493-7684-X*) CRC Pr.

Lerche, I. & Thomsen, Rene O. Hydrodynamics of Oil & Gas. LC 94-48514. (Illus.). 318p. (C). 1995. 85.00 (*0-306-44872-6*, Plenum Trade) Perseus Pubng.

Lerche, I., jt. ed. see Bachmann, G. H.

Lerche, Ian. Economic Risk in Hydrocarbon Exploration. LC 98-86364. 1998. 129.00 (*0-12-444165-3*) Acad Pr.

— Geological Risk & Uncertainty in Oil Exploration. LC 97-9787. (Illus.). 658p. 1997. text 140.00 (*0-12-444174-2*) Morgan Kaufmann.

— Oil Exploration: Basin Analysis & Economics. (Illus.). 178p. 1992. text 77.00 (*0-12-444175-0*) Acad Pr.

Lerche, Mario R. Deutsch-Spanisches Glossarium Finanz und Wirtschaft: German - Spanish Glossary of Finance & Economics. (GER & SPA.). 460p. 1967. 75.00 (*0-8288-6671-6*, M8176) Fr & Eur.

Lerchner, Gotthard, et al. Chronologische, Areale und Situative Varietaten des Deutschen in der Sprachhistoriographie: Festschrift fur Rudolf Grobe. (Leipziger Arbeiten zur Sprach- und Kommunikationsgeschichte Ser.: Bd. 2). (GER., Illus.). XII, 501p. 1995. 108.95 (*3-631-47613-2*) P Lang Pubng.

Lerchner, Gotthard, jt. auth. see Fix, Ulla.

Lerchner, Gotthard, jt. auth. see Helbig, Gerhard.

Lerda, Alberto. Anyons: Quantum Mechanics of Particles with Fractional Statistics. LC 92-33779. (Lecture Notes in Physics, New Series, Monographs; Vol. 14). 1992. 50.95 (*0-387-56105-6*) Spr-Verlag.

Lerdahl, Fred & Jackendoff, Ray S. A Generative Theory of Tonal Music. (Illus.). 384p. 1996. pap. text 29.00 (*0-262-62107-X*) MIT Pr.

Lerdau, Enrique, tr. see Escarpenter, Claudio & Fargas.

Lerdau, Federico, tr. see Escarpenter, Claudio & Fargas.

***Lerdorf, Rasmus.** PHP Pocket Reference. Ferguson, Paula, ed. LC 99-86930. (Illus.). 120p. 2000. pap. 9.95 (*1-56592-769-9*) OReilly & Assocs.

Lereah, David. The Rules for Growing Rich: 201 Ways to Make Money in Any Market. LC 99-56474. 2000. 25.00 (*0-8129-3056-8*, Times Bks) Crown Pub Group.

Lereah, David A. Insurance Markets: Information Problems & Regulation. LC 84-26403. 192p. 1985. 57.95 (*0-275-90135-1*, C0135, Praeger Pubs) Greenwood.

— Insurance Markets: Information Problems & Regulations. (C). 1985. 330.00 (*0-7855-4128-4*, Pub. by Witherby & Co) St Mut.

Lerebours, N. P. A Treatise on Photography. LC 72-9215. (Literature of Photography Ser.). 1973. reprint ed. 19.95 (*0-405-04923-4*) Ayer.

Lerer, Bernard, et al, eds. Ect: Basic Mechanisms. LC 86-3507. 189p. 1984. reprint ed. pap. 58.60 (*0-608-06664-8*, 206686100009) Bks Demand.

Lerer, Bernard & Gershon, Samuel, eds. New Directions in Affective Disorders. (Illus.). 625p. 1989. 244.00 (*0-387-96769-9*) Spr-Verlag.

Lerer, Seth. Boethius & Dialogue: Literary Method in the Consolation of Philosophy. LC 85-42937. 277p. 1985. reprint ed. pap. 85.90 (*0-7837-9372-3*, 206011600004) Bks Demand.

— Chaucer & His Readers: Imagining the Author in Late Medieval England. LC 92-33454. (Illus.). 320p. (C). 1993. text 45.00 (*0-691-06811-9*, Pub. by Princeton U Pr) Cal Prin Full Svc.

— Chaucer & His Readers: Imagining the Author in Late-Medieval England. 328p. 1993. pap. text 16.95 (*0-691-02923-7*, Pub. by Princeton U Pr) Cal Prin Full Svc.

— Courtly Letters in the Age of Henry VIII: Literary Culture & the Arts of Deceit. (Cambridge Studies in Renaissance Literature & Culture: Vol. 18). (Illus.). 268p. (C). 1997. text 59.95 (*0-521-59001-9*) Cambridge U Pr.

— Literacy & Power in Anglo-Saxon Literature. LC 90-40463. (Regents Studies in Medieval Culture). xii, 269p. 1991. text 45.00 (*0-8032-2895-3*) U of Nebr Pr.

— Reading from the Margins: Textual Studies, Chaucer & Medieval Literature. LC 96-31096. 1996. pap. 12.00 (*0-87328-163-2*) Huntington Lib.

Lerer, Seth, ed. Literary History & the Challenge of Philology: The Legacy of Erich Auerbach. LC 95-10992. 308p. 1996. 45.00 (*0-8047-2545-4*) Stanford U Pr.

— Reading from the Margins: Textual Studies, Chaucer & Medieval Literature. LC 96-31096. (Huntington Library Quarterly: Vol. 58, No. 1). 168p. 1996. reprint ed. pap. 52.10 (*0-608-03465-7*, 206417200008) Bks Demand.

Lerer, Susan. African Metalwork & Ivory. (Illus.). 48p. (Orig.). (C). 1993. pap. 22.00 (*0-9635857-0-3*) Images of Cult.

Leresche, G. & Bovet, J., eds. Relations Between Psychopathological & Socio-Professional Factors in Out-Patient Department Psychiatry. (Journal: Psychopathology: Vol. 19, Suppl. 1, 1986). (Illus.). 260p. 1986. pap. 68.00 (*3-8055-4332-8*) S Karger.

Lergessner, J. White Specks on Dark Shores. 80p. (C). 1990. pap. 30.00 (*0-86439-147-1*, Pub. by Boolarong Pubns) St Mut.

Lerho, Perry. The Greatest Show on Turf: A History of the Breeders' Cup. LC 96-86136. (Illus.). 224p. 1996. 24.95 (*0-9648493-3-X*) Daily Racing.

Leridon, Henri. Human Fertility: The Basic Components. Helzner, Judith F., tr. from FRE. LC 77-1913. 208p. 1977. lib. bdg. 25.50 (*0-226-47297-3*) U Ch Pr.

Leridon, Henri, jt. ed. see Bozon, Michel.

Leridon, Henri, jt. ed. see Gray, Ronald.

Lerin, Alfredo, compiled by. Quinientas Ilustraciones: 500 Illustrations. (SPA.). 324p. 1966. reprint ed. pap. 12.99 (*0-311-42037-0*) Casa Bautista.

Leritz, Len. No-Fault Negotiating: A Practical Guide to the New Dealmaking Strategy That Lets Both Sides Win. 1990. pap. 12.95 (*0-446-39104-2*) Warner Bks.

Lerma, Olivia, tr. see Harmon, Ed & Jarmin, Marge.

Lermack, Paul. How to Get into the Right Law School. LC 92-14744. 160p. 1994. pap. 14.95 (*0-8442-4165-2*, VGM Career) NTC Contemp Pub Co.

— How to Get into the Right Law School. 2nd ed. LC 96-26638. (Illus.). 192p. 1996. pap. 14.95 (*0-8442-4127-X*, 4127X) NTC Contemp Pub Co.

Lerman, A. & Meybeck, M., eds. Physical & Chemical Weathering in Geochemical Cycles. (C). 1988. text 201.00 (*90-277-2821-6*) Kluwer Academic.

Lerman, Abraham, et al, eds. Physics & Chemistry of Lakes. 2nd ed. (Illus.). 351p. 1995. 97.95 (*0-387-57891-9*) Spr-Verlag.

Lerman, Abraham, ed. see Chou, L. M.

Lerman, Alice. Birth Environments: Emerging Trends & Implications for Design. (Publications in Architecture & Urban Planning: No. R91-3). (Illus.). 110p. (C). 1991. 15.00 (*0-938744-76-3*) U of Wis Ctr Arch-Urban.

Lerman, Andrea B. The Macrobiotic Community Cookbook: Favorite Recipes from America's Macrobiotic Leaders. LC 88-32260. (Illus.). 224p. (Orig.). pap. 12.95 (*0-89529-396-X*, Avery) Penguin Putnam.

Lerman, Antony, ed. The Jewish Communities of the World: A Contemporary Guide. 4th ed. LC 88-30991. 216p. 1989. reprint ed. pap. 67.00 (*0-7837-9911-X*, 206063700006) Bks Demand.

Lerman, Dan & Linne, Eric B., eds. Hospital Home Care: Strategic Management for Integrated Care Delivery. LC 93-16411. 328p. 1993. pap. 60.00 (*1-55648-096-2*, 079200) AHPI.

Lerman, Dan & Tehan, Claire, eds. Hospital-Hospice Mangement Models: Integration & Collaboration. LC 95-14333. 1995. pap. 32.00 (*1-55648-137-3*) AHPI.

Lerman, Eleanor. Armed Love. LC 73-6013. (Wesleyan Poetry Ser.). 64p. 1973. pap. 12.95 (*0-8195-1068-8*, Wesleyan Univ Pr) U Pr of New Eng.

— Come the Sweet By & By. LC 75-8449. 80p. 1975. 15.00 (*0-87023-194-4*); pap. 9.95 (*0-87023-195-2*) U of Mass Pr.

***Lerman, Eleanor.** The Mystery of Meteors: Poems. LC 00-41309. 2001. write for info. (*1-889330-55-8*) Sarabande Bks.

***Lerman, Evelyn.** Safer Sex: The New Morality. 224p. 2000. 21.95 (*1-885356-65-X*, Pub. by Morning Glory); pap. 14.95 (*1-885356-66-8*, Pub. by Morning Glory) IPG Chicago.

Lerman, Evelyn. Teen Moms: The Pain & the Promise. LC 97-20134. (Illus.). 224p. 1997. 21.95 (*1-885356-24-2*); pap. 14.95 (*1-885356-25-0*) Morning Glory.

— Teen Moms: The Pain & the Promise Student Workbook. 24p. 1998. pap., student ed., wbk. ed. 2.50 (*1-885356-46-3*) Morning Glory.

— Teen Moms: The Pain & the Promise Teacher Guide. 16p. 1998. pap., teacher ed. 2.50 (*1-885356-45-5*) Morning Glory.

Lerman, G. & Rudolph, L. Parallel Evolution of Parallel Processors. (Frontiers of Computer Science Ser.). (Illus.). 284p. (C). 1994. 75.00 (*0-306-44537-9*, Plenum Trade) Perseus Pubng.

Lerman-Golomb, Barbara. AIDS. LC 94-30055. (Teen Hotline Ser.). 80p. (YA). 1995. lib. bdg. 25.68 (*0-8114-3814-7*) Raintree Steck-V.

***Lerman-Golomb, Barbara.** Teen Hot Line. 1999. 215.78 (*0-8114-3819-8*) Raintree Steck-V.

Lerman, Hallie. Crying for Imma: Battling for the Soul on Golon Heights. (Illus.). 300p. 1999. 25.00 (*0-9665722-0-3*) Night Vision.

Lerman, Hannah & Porter, Natalie, eds. Feminist Ethics in Psychotherapy. LC 90-9625. 288p. 1990. 39.95 (*0-8261-6290-8*) Springer Pub.

Lerman, J. M., tr. see Kahana, S. Z.

Lerman, Jona, jt. auth. see Kurtis, Arlene.

***Lerman, L. M., et al, eds.** Methods of Qualitative Theory of Differential Equations & Related Topics. (TRANS2 Ser.: Vol. 200). 196p. 2000. 89.00 (*0-8218-2663-8*) Am Math.

Lerman, L. M. & Umanskiy, Y. L. Four-Dimensional Integrable Hamilton Systems with Simple Singular Point (Topological Aspects) LC 98-15030. (Translations of Mathematical Monographs: Vol. 176). (Illus.). 177p. 1998. 79.00 (*0-8218-0375-1*, MMONO-LERMAN) Am Math.

Lerman, Laura. Supermax. LC 97-6767. (Illus.). (J). 1998. 11.99 (*0-679-88659-1*); lib. bdg. 13.99 (*0-679-98659-6*) Random.

Lerman, Leonard S., ed. DNA Probes: Applications in Genetic & Infectious Disease & Cancer. LC 86-212410. (Current Communications in Molecular Biology Ser.). 198p. reprint ed. pap. 61.40 (*0-8357-2755-6*, 203987100013) Bks Demand.

Lerman, Lisa G. Legal Help for Battered Women. 3rd rev. ed. 12p. 1989. pap. 4.00 (*1-877966-02-9*) Ctr Women Policy.

Lerman, Liz. Teaching Dance to Senior Adults. (Illus.). 190p. 1984. pap. text 22.95 (*0-398-06641-8*) C C Thomas.

— Teaching Dance to Senior Adults. (Illus.). 190p. (C). 1984. text 36.95 (*0-398-04903-3*) C C Thomas.

Lerman, M. Degrees of Unsolvability: Local & Global Theory. (Perspectives in Mathematical Logic Ser.). (Illus.). 307p. 1983. 146.95 (*0-387-12155-2*) Spr-Verlag.

Lerman, M., ed. see Ebbinghaus, Heinz-Dieter & Flum, Jorg.

Lerman, Matthew. Marine Biology. (Illus.). 510p. (C). 1986. pap. text 57.00 (*0-8053-6402-1*) Benjamin-Cummings.

Lerman, Ora, et al. Inside the Ark. 32p. 1995. pap. 10.00 (*0-9645942-7-7*) Lerman Studios.

Lerman, Paul. The Parents' Perspective: Delinquency, Aggression & Mental Health. (Applied Social Problems & Intervention Ser.: Vol. 1). 248p. 1995. pap. text 20.00 (*3-7186-0582-1*, Harwood Acad Pubs) Gordon & Breach.

Lerman, Paul & Pottick, Kathleen J. The Parents' Perspective: Delinquency, Aggression & Mental Health. (Applied Social Problems & Intervention Ser.: Vol. 1). 248p. 1995. text 50.00 (*3-7186-0581-3*, Harwood Acad Pubs) Gordon & Breach.

Lerman, Philip, jt. auth. see Walsh, John.

Lerman, Rhoda. Animal Acts. 272p. 1995. write for info. (*0-8050-1418-7*) H Holt & Co.

— Call Me Ishtar. LC 98-3287. 1998. pap. 18.95 (*0-8156-0533-1*) Syracuse U Pr.

— God's Ear: A Novel. LC 96-29026. (Library of Modern Jewish Literature). 309p. 1996. reprint ed. pap. 17.95 (*0-8156-0427-0*, LEGEP) Syracuse U Pr.

Lerman, Robert A., jt. auth. see Kolk, W. Richard.

Lerman, Robert I. Young Unwed Fathers: Changing Roles & Emerging Policies. (C). 1994. pap. text 22.95 (*1-56639-318-3*) Temple U Pr.

Lerman, Robert I. & Ooms, Theodora J., eds. Young Unwed Fathers: Changing Roles & Emerging Policies. LC 92-39617. 384p. 1993. 69.95 (*1-56639-048-6*) Temple U Pr.

Lerman, Rory S. Charlie's Checklist. LC 96-28383. (Illus.). 32p. (J). (ps-3). 1997. pap. 14.95 (*0-531-30001-3*) Orchard Bks Watts.

***Lerman, Rory S.** Charlie's Checklist. 32p. 2000. pap. 6.95 (*0-531-07173-1*) Orchard Bks Watts.

Lerman, Sidney & Tripathi, Ramesh C. Ocular Toxicology. LC 91-5822. (Illus.). 410p. 1989. text 160.00 (*0-8247-8309-3*) Dekker.

Lerman, Stephen, ed. Cultural Perspectives on the Mathematics Classroom. (Mathematics Education Library: Vol. 14). 218p. (C). 1994. lib. bdg. 102.00 (*0-7923-2931-7*, Pub. by Kluwer Academic) Kluwer Academic.

Lerman, Steven, jt. auth. see Ben-Akiva, Moshe.

Lerman, Steven R. Problem Solving & Computation for Scientists: An Introduction Using C. LC 92-24326. 544p. 1992. pap. 67.00 (*0-13-482126-2*, Pub. by P-H) S&S Trade.

Lerman, Z., ed. see Gorbatskii, Vitalii G.

Lerman, Zafra, jt. auth. see Spiro, Thomas G.

Lerman, Zvi, et al. Land Reform & Farm Restructuring in Moldova: Progress & Prospects. LC 98-27897. (Discussion Paper Ser.: No. 398). 121p. 1998. pap. 22.00 (*0-8213-4317-3*, 14317) World Bank.

— Land Reform & Farm Restructuring in Ukraine. LC 94-43327. (Discussion Paper Ser.: Vol. 270). 125p. 1995. pap. 22.00 (*0-8213-3149-3*, 13149) World Bank.

— Land Reform & Farm Restructuring in Ukraine. (RUS.). 148p. 1995. pap. 22.00 (*0-8213-3242-2*, 13242) World Bank.

Lerman, Zvi, jt. auth. see Csaki, Csaba.

Lermond, Lucia. The Form of Man: Human Essence in Spinoza's Ethic. LC 88-5039. (Brill's Studies in Intellectual History). ix, 87p. 1988. 38.50 (*90-04-08829-6*) Brill Academic Pubs.

Lermontov. Taman Lermontov: A Level. text 7.95 (*0-88436-270-1*) EMC-Paradigm.

Lermontov, Mikhail. A Hero of Our Time. Nabokov, Vladimir & Nabokov, Dmitri, trs. (World's Classics Ser.). 200p. 1984. pap. write for info. (*0-19-281401-X*) OUP.

— A Hero of Our Time. Cornwell, Neil, ed. 208p. 1995. pap. 8.50 (*0-460-87566-3*, Everyman's Classic Lib) Tuttle Pubng.

— A Hero of Our Time. Foote, Paul, tr. (Classics Ser.). 192p. 1966. pap. 15.99 (*0-14-044176-X*, Penguin Classics) Viking Penguin.

— Hero of Our Time. 1992. 15.00 (*0-679-41327-8*, Evrmns Lib) Knopf.

— A Hero of Our Time. Nabokov, Vladimir & Nabokov, Dmitri, trs. from RUS. 210p. 1988. reprint ed. pap. 12.95 (*0-87501-049-0*) Ardis Pubs.

An Asterisk (*) at the beginning of an entry indicates that the title is appearing for the first time.

— Hero of Our Time. unabridged ed. (World Classic Literature Ser.). (RUS.). pap. 6.95 (*2-87714-259-0*, Pub. by Bookking Intl) Distribks Inc.

— Un Heroes de Montre Temps, La Princess Ligovskoi. (FRE.). 1976. pap. 11.95 (*0-7859-4031-6*) Fr & Eur.

Lermontov, Mikhail, et al. Eros Russe: Russkii Erot ne Dlia Dam. 3rd ed. (RUS., Illus.). 94p. 1995. reprint ed. pap. 7.95 (*1-57201-004-5*) Berkeley Slavic.

LERN Staff. Front-Line Staff Training Manual. 47p. 24.95 (*0-914951-68-8*) LERN.

— Ratios for Success. 42p. 39.95 (*0-914951-69-6*) LERN.

Lerner. Catalytic Antibodies. Date not set. 1.20 (*0-7167-9276-1*) W H Freeman.

— Learning Disabilities, 6 vols. (C). 1992. pap., teacher ed. 3.16 (*0-395-64010-5*) HM.

— Learning Disabled, 7 vols. 7th ed. (C). 1996. pap. text, student ed. 21.16 (*0-395-79486-2*) HM.

— Learning Disabled: Testbank, 7 vols. (C). Date not set. pap., teacher ed. 11.96 (*0-395-79487-0*) HM.

***Lerner.** Western Civilization, Their History & Their Culture, Vol. 1. 1998. pap. text 47.00 (*0-393-97296-8*) Norton.

— Western Civilization, Their History & Their Culture, Vol. 1. 1999. pap. text 22.00 (*0-393-97449-9*) Norton.

— Western Civilization With Perspectives From the Past, 2 vols., Set. 13th ed. 1998. text 91.00 (*0-393-97324-7*) Norton.

— Western Civilization with Study Guide, Vol. 2. 13th ed. 1998. pap. text 47.00 (*0-393-97302-6*) Norton.

Lerner & Lee. Physics, Science & Engineering, Vol. 2. (Physics Ser.). 312p. 1996. pap., teacher ed. 50.00 (*0-7637-0206-4*) Jones & Bartlett.

Lerner & Loewe. Camelot: Easy Piano Vocal Selections. 16p. 1981. pap. 6.95 (*0-7935-3609-X*, 00300285) H Leonard.

— My Fair Lady, Vol. 77. (EZ Play Today Ser.: Series B). 24p. 1981. pap. 5.95 (*0-7935-2651-5*, 00100489) H Leonard.

Lerner, A. W. The Manipulators: Personality & Politics in Multiple Perspectives. 168p. (C). 1989. text 39.95 (*0-8058-0335-1*) L Erlbaum Assocs.

Lerner, Abba P. The Economics of Control: Principles of Welfare Economics. LC 75-107922. (Reprints of Economic Classics Ser.). (Illus.). xxii, 428p. 1970. reprint ed. 45.00 (*0-678-00618-0*) Kelley.

— Economics of Employment. LC 77-18756. (Economics Handbook Ser.). 397p. 1978. reprint ed. lib. bdg. 38.50 (*0-313-20181-1*, LEEE, Greenwood Pr) Greenwood.

Lerner, Abe, ed. see Rathe, John F.

Lerner, Abe, ed. see Schmoller, Hans.

Lerner, Abram. An Introduction to the Hirshhorn Museum & Sculpture Garden, Smithsonian Institution LC 74-11204. 70p. 1974. write for info. (*0-8109-2051-4*) Abrams.

Lerner, Adam. Fantasy Football: Playing to Win. (Illus.). 124p. (J). 1998. pap. text 5.95 (*0-8225-9968-6*) Lerner Pub.

Lerner, Adam & Charpentier, Cliff. Fantasy Football: Playing to Win. LC 97-52253. (J). 1998. 19.93 (*0-8225-7778-X*) Lerner Pub.

Lerner, Adam, jt. auth. see Contemporary Museum Staff.

Lerner, Adam, jt. ed. see Ringrose, Marjorie.

Lerner, Alan J. The Musical Theatre: A Celebration. (Quality Paperbacks Ser.). (Illus.). 256p. 1989. pap. 16.95 (*0-306-80364-X*) Da Capo.

— The Street Where I Live. (Illus.). 333p. 1994. reprint ed. pap. 13.95 (*0-306-80602-9*) Da Capo.

Lerner, Alan J., ed. The Little Black Book of Neurology: A Manual for Neurological House Officers. 3rd ed. LC 94-22738. (Illus.). 456p. (C). (gr. 13). 1994. pap. text 37.95 (*0-8151-5440-2*, 24022) Mosby Inc.

Lerner, Alan J. & Lane. On a Clear Day You Can See Forever. 120p. 1994. per. 35.00 (*0-7935-3408-9*, 00312501) H Leonard.

Lerner, Alexander. Change of Heart. (Illus.). 1992. lib. bdg. write for info. (*0-86689-030-0*) Balaban Intl Sci Serv.

Lerner, Allan W. & King, B. Kay. Continuing Higher Education: The Coming Wave. 176p. (C). 1992. text 31.00 (*0-8077-3197-8*) Tchrs Coll.

Lerner, Allan W. & Wanat, John. Public Administration: Scenarios in Public Management. LC 92-16366. 192p. (C). 1993. pap. text 23.60 (*0-13-739046-7*) P-H.

Lerner, Andrea, ed. Dancing on the Rim of the World: An Anthology of Contemporary Northwest Native American Writing. LC 90-11006. (Sun Tracks Ser.: Vol. 19). (Illus.). 266p. (Orig.). 1990. pap. 19.95 (*0-8165-1215-9*) U of Ariz Pr.

Lerner, Andy, jt. auth. see Herzog, Brad.

Lerner, Arthur. Poetry in the Therapeutic Experience. (Illus.). 144p. (Orig.). (C). 1994. pap. 14.95 (*0-918812-79-8*) MMB Music.

— Words for All Seasons. (Illus.). 104p. (Orig.). 1983. pap. 6.95 (*0-938292-06-4*) Being Bks.

Lerner, Arthur & Mahlendorf, Ursula R. Life Guidance Through Literature. LC 91-27499. 236p. (C). 1992. text 25.00 (*0-8389-0580-3*) ALA.

Lerner, Arthur, ed. see Weyand, Clinton.

Lerner, B. Rosie & Netzhammer, Beverly S. Possum in the Pawpaw Tree: A Seasonal Guide to Midwestern Gardening. LC 94-12066. (Illus.). 300p. 1994. 27.95 (*1-55753-053-X*); pap. 24.95 (*1-55753-054-8*) Purdue U Pr.

Lerner, Barbara. Minimum Competence, Maximum Choice: Educational Vouchers for Children Who Need Them Most. (C). 1982. text 22.50 (*0-8290-0414-9*) Irvington.

— Therapy in the Ghetto: Political Impotence & Personal Disintegration. LC 74-186606. 240p. reprint ed. pap. 74.40 (*0-608-06077-1*, 206640900008) Bks Demand.

Lerner, Barbara & Vining, Daniel R. Intelligence & National Achievement. Cattell, Raymond B., Jr., ed. (C). 1984. lib. bdg. 40.00 (*0-941694-14-3*); lib. bdg. 28.00 (*0-941694-48-8*) Inst Study Man.

Lerner, Barron H. Contagion & Confinement: Controlling Tuberculosis along the Skid Road. LC 98-5700. (Illus.). 264p. 1998. 42.50 (*0-8018-5898-4*) Johns Hopkins.

***Lerner, Betsy.** The Forest for the Trees: An Editor's Advice to Writers. LC 99-53355. 304p. 2000. 21.95 (*1-57322-152-X*, Riverhead Books) Putnam Pub Group.

Lerner, Beverly, jt. auth. see Bell, Lisa.

Lerner, Carol. Backyard Birds of Summer. (Illus.). (J). 1996. 16.00 (*0-688-13600-1*, Wm Morrow); lib. bdg. 15.93 (*0-688-13601-X*, Wm Morrow) Morrow Avon.

— Backyard Birds of Winter. LC 94-3036. (Illus.). 48p. (J). 1994. 16.00 (*0-688-12819-X*, Wm Morrow); lib. bdg. 15.93 (*0-688-12820-3*, Wm Morrow) Morrow Avon.

Lerner, Carol. Butterflies in the Garden. 1924. lib. bdg. write for info. (*0-688-17479-5*, Wm Morrow) Morrow Avon.

— Cactus. LC 91-35678. (Illus.). 32p. (J). (ps-3). 1992. lib. bdg. 14.93 (*0-688-09637-9*, Wm Morrow) Morrow Avon.

Lerner, Carol. My Backyard Garden. LC 97-6460. (Illus.). 48p. (J). (gr. 4-6). 1998. lib. bdg. 15.93 (*0-688-14756-9*, Wm Morrow) Morrow Avon.

— My Backyard Garden. LC 97-6460. (Illus.). 48p. (J). (ps-3). 1998. 16.00 (*0-688-14755-0*, Wm Morrow) Morrow Avon.

— My Backyard Garden. 1998. 16.00 (*0-676-57322-3*) Random.

***Lerner, Carol.** My Indoor Garden. LC 98-18929. (Illus.). 48p. (J). 1999. 15.89 (*0-688-14754-2*, Wm Morrow) Morrow Avon.

Lerner, Carol. My Indoor Garden. LC 98-18929. (Illus.). 48p. (J). (ps-3). 1999. 16.00 (*0-688-14753-4*, Wm Morrow) Morrow Avon.

— On the Wing. (J). 1924. 15.95 (*0-688-16649-0*, Wm Morrow); lib. bdg. 15.89 (*0-688-16650-4*, Wm Morrow) Morrow Avon.

***Lerner, Claire & Dombro, Amy.** Learning & Growing Together: Understanding Your Child's Development. Levine, Karen, ed. 56p. 2000. pap. 15.00 (*0-943657-05-9*) ZERO TO THREE.

Lerner, Daniel. Single Malt & Scotch Whiskey: Select & Savor over 200 Brands & Varieties. (Essential Connoisseur Ser.: No. 5). (Illus.). 192p. 1996. 10.98 (*1-884822-76-2*) Blck Dog & Leventhal.

Lerner, Daniel, ed. Human Meaning of the Social Sciences. 1990. 16.50 (*0-8446-2281-8*) Peter Smith.

— Propaganda in War & Crisis. LC 72-4669. (International Propaganda & Communications Ser.). 516p. 1978. reprint ed. 30.95 (*0-405-04754-1*) Ayer.

Lerner, Daniel & Nelson, Lyle M., eds. Communication Research: A Half-Century Appraisal. LC 77-89616. 359p. reprint ed. pap. 111.30 (*0-7837-3976-1*, 204380600011) Bks Demand.

Lerner, Daniel, jt. ed. see Lasswell, Harold D.

Lerner, Daniel, jt. ed. see Schramm, Wilbur L.

Lerner, David. Pray Like the Hunted. 91p. (Orig.). 1992. pap. 6.00 (*0-929730-38-0*) Zeitgeist Pr.

Lerner, David & Walton, Nick, eds. Contaminated Land & Groundwater: Future Directions. (Geological Society Engineering Geology Special Publication Ser.: No. 14). 256p. 1998. 107.00 (*1-86239-001-0*, Pub. by Geol Soc Pub Hse) AAPG.

Lerner, Deborah, jt. auth. see Pardini, Alan.

Lerner, Devon A. Celebrating Interfaith Marriages: Creating Your Jewish/Christian Ceremony. LC 98-38274. 256p. 1999. pap. 13.95 (*0-8050-6083-9*, Pub. by H Holt & Co) VHPS.

Lerner, E., ed. Methods for the Study of Personality in Young Children. (SRCD M Ser.: Vol. 6, No. 4). 1941. 25.00 (*0-527-01520-2*) Periodicals Srv.

Lerner, Edward M. Probe. 1991. mass mkt. 4.99 (*0-446-36081-3*) Warner Bks.

Lerner, Elaine & Abbott, C. B. The Way to Go: A Woman's Guide to Careers in Travel. 208p. 1982. mass mkt. 6.95 (*0-446-37022-3*, Pub. by Warner Bks) Little.

Lerner, Eric. The Big Bang Never Happened. 1992. pap. 17.00 (*0-679-74049-X*) Vin Bks.

— The Big Bang Never Happened: A Startling Refutation of the Dominant Theory of the Origin of the Universe. 480p. 1991. 21.95 (*0-8129-1853-3*, Times Bks) Crown Pub Group.

Lerner, Eric K. & Hombs, Mary E. AIDS Crisis in America: A Reference Handbook. 2nd ed. LC 98-25764. (Contemporary World Issues Ser.). 344p. 1998. lib. bdg. 45.00 (*1-57607-070-0*) ABC-CLIO.

Lerner, Fred. A Bookman's Fantasy: How Science Fiction Became Respectable & Other Essays. LC 94-73980. iv, 97p. (Orig.). 1995. pap. 11.95 (*0-915368-65-X*) New Eng SF Assoc.

— Libraries Through the Ages. LC 99-33321. (Illus.). 1999. 17.95 (*0-8264-1201-7*) Continuum.

Lerner, Fred. Pilots Database User's Guide. 254p. 1995. per. 22.00 (*0-16-062478-9*, Veterans Affairs) USGPO.

Lerner, Fred, ed. A Silverlock Companion: The Life & Works of John Myers Myers. (Illus.). 52p. (Orig.). 1988. pap. 7.95 (*0-910619-02-6*) Niekas Pubns.

Lerner, Frederick A. Modern Science Fiction & the American Literary Community. LC 85-1874. 343p. 1985. 31.00 (*0-8108-1794-2*) Scarecrow.

— The Story of Libraries: From the Invention of Writing to the Computer Age. LC 98-22748. (Illus.). 264p. 1998. 24.95 (*0-8264-1114-2*) Continuum.

Lerner Geography Department Staff. Dazzling! Jewelry of the Ancient World. LC 94-21445. (Buried Worlds Ser.). (YA). (gr. 6 up). 1994. lib. bdg. 23.93 (*0-8225-3203-4*, Runestone Pr) Lerner Pub.

— United States in Pictures. LC 94-44841. (Visual Geography Ser.). (J). 1995. lib. bdg. 19.93 (*0-8225-1896-1*) Lerner Pub.

— Uruguay in Pictures. (Visual Geography Ser.). (Illus.). 64p. (YA). (gr. 5 up). 1987. lib. bdg. 19.95 (*0-8225-1823-6*, Lerner Publctns) Lerner Pub.

Lerner Geography Department Staff, ed. Albania in Pictures. LC 94-10616. (Visual Geography Ser.). (Illus.). 64p. (YA). (gr. 5 up). 1995. lib. bdg. 19.93 (*0-8225-1902-X*, Lerner Publctns) Lerner Pub.

— Algeria in Pictures. (Visual Geography Ser.). (Illus.). 64p. (YA). (gr. 5 up). 1992. lib. bdg. 19.93 (*0-8225-1901-1*, Lerner Publctns) Lerner Pub.

— Armenia. (Then & Now Ser.). (Illus.). 64p. (YA). (gr. 5 up). 1993. lib. bdg. 23.93 (*0-8225-2806-1*, Lerner Publctns) Lerner Pub.

Lerner Geography Department Staff, ed. Azerbaijan. (Then & Now Ser.). (Illus.). 64p. (YA). (gr. 5 up). 1993. lib. bdg. 23.93 (*0-8225-2810-X*, Lerner Publctns) Lerner Pub.

Lerner Geography Department Staff, ed. Belarus. (Then & Now Ser.). (Illus.). 64p. (YA). (gr. 5 up). 1993. lib. bdg. 23.93 (*0-8225-2811-8*, Lerner Publctns) Lerner Pub.

— Belgium in Pictures. (Visual Geography Ser.). (Illus.). 64p. (YA). (gr. 5 up). 1991. lib. bdg. 19.93 (*0-8225-1889-9*, Lerner Publctns) Lerner Pub.

— Brazil in Pictures. rev. ed. (Visual Geography Ser.). (Illus.). 64p. (YA). (gr. 5 up). 1987. lib. bdg. 19.93 (*0-8225-1802-3*, Lerner Publctns) Lerner Pub.

— Cyprus in Pictures. (Visual Geography Ser.). (Illus.). 64p. (YA). (gr. 5 up). 1992. lib. bdg. 19.93 (*0-8225-1910-0*, Lerner Publctns) Lerner Pub.

— Denmark in Pictures. (Visual Geography Ser.). (Illus.). 64p. (YA). (gr. 5 up). 1991. reprint ed. lib. bdg. 19.93 (*0-8225-1880-5*, Lerner Publctns) Lerner Pub.

— Dig This! How Archaeologists Uncover Our Past. LC 92-28305. (Buried Worlds Ser.). (YA). (gr. 6 up). 1993. lib. bdg. 23.93 (*0-8225-3200-X*, Lerner Publctns) Lerner Pub.

— The Dominican Republic in Pictures. rev. ed. (Visual Geography Ser.). (Illus.). 64p. (YA). (gr. 5 up). 1997. lib. bdg. 19.93 (*0-8225-1812-0*, Lerner Publctns) Lerner Pub.

— Estonia. (Then & Now Ser.). (Illus.). 64p. (YA). (gr. 5 up). 1992. lib. bdg. 23.93 (*0-8225-2803-7*, Lerner Publctns) Lerner Pub.

— Georgia. (Then & Now Ser.). (Illus.). 64p. (YA). (gr. 5 up). 1993. lib. bdg. 23.93 (*0-8225-2807-X*, Lerner Publctns) Lerner Pub.

— Greece in Pictures. rev. ed. (Visual Geography Ser.). (Illus.). 64p. (YA). (gr. 5 up). 1996. lib. bdg 19.93 (*0-8225-1882-1*, Lerner Publctns) Lerner Pub.

— Iceland in Pictures. rev. ed. (Visual Geography Ser.). (Illus.). 64p. (YA). (gr. 5 up). 1996. lib. bdg. 19.93 (*0-8225-1892-9*, Lerner Publctns) Lerner Pub.

— Kazakhstan. (Then & Now Ser.). (Illus.). 64p. (YA). (gr. 5 up). 1993. lib. bdg. 23.93 (*0-8225-2815-0*, Lerner Publctns) Lerner Pub.

— Latvia. LC 92-7260. (Then & Now Ser.). (Illus.). 64p. (YA). (gr. 5 up). 1992. lib. bdg. 23.93 (*0-8225-2802-9*, Lerner Publctns) Lerner Pub.

— Lithuania. LC 92-9698. (Then & Now Ser.). (Illus.). 64p. (YA). (gr. 6-9). 1992. lib. bdg. 23.93 (*0-8225-2804-5*, Lerner Publctns) Lerner Pub.

— Moldova. (Then & Now Ser.). (Illus.). 64p. (YA). (gr. 6-9). 1992. lib. bdg. 23.93 (*0-8225-2809-6*, Lerner Publctns) Lerner Pub.

— Northern Ireland in Pictures. (Visual Geography Ser.). (Illus.). 64p. (YA). (gr. 5 up). 1991. reprint ed. lib. bdg. 19.95 (*0-8225-1898-8*, Lerner Publctns) Lerner Pub.

— Portugal in Pictures. (Visual Geography Ser.). (Illus.). 64p. (J). 1995. reprint ed. lib. bdg. 19.95 (*0-8225-1886-4*, Lerner Publctns) Lerner Pub.

— Russia. (Then & Now Ser.). (Illus.). 64p. (YA). (gr. 5 up). 1992. lib. bdg. 23.93 (*0-8225-2805-3*, Lerner Publctns) Lerner Pub.

— Sold! The Origins of Money & Trade. LC 93-37782. (Buried Worlds Ser.). (Illus.). (YA). (gr. 6 up). 1994. lib. bdg. 23.93 (*0-8225-3206-9*, Runestone Pr) Lerner Pub.

Lerner Geography Department Staff, ed. Spain in Pictures. (Illus.). 64p. (YA). (gr. 5 up). 1995. lib. bdg. 19.95 (*0-8225-1887-2*, Lerner Publctns) Lerner Pub.

Lerner Geography Department Staff, ed. Tajikistan. (Then & Now Ser.). (Illus.). 64p. (YA). (gr. 5 up). 1993. lib. bdg. 23.93 (*0-8225-2816-9*, Lerner Publctns) Lerner Pub.

— Turkmenistan. (Then & Now Ser.). (Illus.). 64p. (YA). (gr. 5 up). 1993. lib. bdg. 23.93 (*0-8225-2813-4*, Lerner Publctns) Lerner Pub.

— Uzbekistan. (Then & Now Ser.). (Illus.). 64p. (YA). (gr. 5 up). 1993. lib. bdg. 23.93 (*0-8225-2812-6*, Lerner Publctns) Lerner Pub.

Lerner Geography Department Staff, ed. see Brown, Dottie.

Lerner Geography Department Staff, ed. see Fredeen, Charles.

Lerner Geography Department Staff, ed. see Gelman, Amy.

Lerner Geography Department Staff, ed. see LaDoux, Rita C.

Lerner Geography Department Staff, ed. see Porter, A. P.

Lerner Geography Department Staff, ed. see Sitvaitis, Karen.

Lerner Geography Department Staff, ed. see Swain, Gwenyth.

Lerner Geography Department Staff, ed. see Verba, Joan M.

Lerner Geography Departmment Staff, ed. Finland in Pictures. rev. ed. (Visual Geography Ser.). (Illus.). 64p. (YA). (gr. 5 up). 1995. lib. bdg. 19.93 (*0-8225-1881-3*, Lerner Publctns) Lerner Pub.

Lerner, Gerda. Black Women in White America: A Documentary History. 630p. 1992. pap. 16.00 (*0-679-74314-6*) Vin Bks.

— The Creation of Feminist Consciousness: From the Middle Ages to Eighteen-Seventy. 416p. 1994. reprint ed. pap. 16.95 (*0-19-509060-8*) OUP.

— The Creation of Patriarchy. LC 85-21578. (Women & History Ser.). (Illus.). 368p. 1986. reprint ed. text 35.00 (*0-19-503996-3*) OUP.

— The Creation of Patriarchy. LC 85-21578. (Women & History Ser.). (Illus.). 344p. 1987. reprint ed. pap. 15.95 (*0-19-505185-8*) OUP.

— The Feminist Thought of Sarah Grimke. LC 97-42197. 208p. 1998. pap. 16.95 (*0-19-510605-9*) OUP.

— The Grimke Sisters of South Carolina. LC 97-42210. 382p. 1998. reprint ed. pap. 17.95 (*0-19-510603-2*) OUP.

— The Majority Finds Its Past: Placing Women in History. 250p. 1981. pap. 9.95 (*0-19-502899-6*) OUP.

— Why History Matters: Life & Thought. LC 96-41288. 272p. (C). 1997. 30.00 (*0-19-504644-7*) OUP.

— Why History Matters: Life & Thought. 272p. 1998. reprint ed. pap. 14.95 (*0-19-512289-5*) OUP.

Lerner Group Staff. Create-a-Story Book. (Illus.). 28p. 1995. pap. text 3.95 (*0-8225-9998-8*) Lerner Pub.

Lerner, H. R. Plant Responses to Environmental Stresses: From Phytohormones to Genome Reorganization. LC 99-30941. (Books in Soils, Plants & the Environment). (Illus.). 752p. 1999. text 195.00 (*0-8247-0044-9*) Dekker.

***Lerner, Harriet.** Franny B. Kranny, There's a Bird in Your Hair! 40p. (J). (ps-1). 2001. 15.95 (*0-06-024683-9*) HarpC Child Bks.

Lerner, Harriet G. The Dance of Anger: A Woman's Guide to Changing the Patterns of Intimate Relationships. LC 85-42576. (Illus.). 256p. 1997. pap. 14.00 (*0-06-091565-X*, Perennial) HarperTrade.

Lerner, Harriet G. The Dance of Anger: Lerner,&Harriet, Set. abr. ed. 1997. audio 18.00 (*0-89845-796-3*, CPN 2112, Pub. by HarperAudio) Lndmrk Audiobks.

Lerner, Harriet G. The Dance of Deception: Pretending & Truth-Telling in Women's Lives. 272p. 1997. pap. 13.50 (*0-06-092463-2*, Perennial) HarperTrade.

— The Dance of Intimacy: A Woman's Guide to Courageous Acts of Change in Key Relationships. LC 88-45519. (Illus.). 272p. 1997. reprint ed. pap. 14.00 (*0-06-091646-X*, Perennial) HarperTrade.

Lerner, Harriet G. Dance of Intimacy: Lerner,&Harriet Gold. abr. ed. 1997. audio 18.00 (*1-55994-147-2*, CPN 2144) HarperAudio.

Lerner, Harriet G. Life Preservers: Staying Afloat in Love & Life. 335p. 1998. pap. text 13.00 (*0-7881-5906-2*) DIANE Pub.

— Life Preservers: Staying Afloat in Love & Life. 368p. 1997. pap. 13.50 (*0-06-092835-2*, Perennial) HarperTrade.

— The Mother Dance: How Children Change Your Life. LC 97-51852. 336p. 1998. 25.00 (*0-06-018768-9*) HarpC.

— The Mother Dance: How Children Change Your Life. LC 97-51852. 336p. 1999. pap. 14.00 (*0-06-093025-X*) HarpC.

***Lerner, Harriet G.** The Mother Dance: How Children Change Your Life, Set. abr. ed. 1998. audio 18.00 (*0-694-51974-X*, AF07R) HarperAudio.

Lerner, Harriet G. Women in Therapy. LC 87-19326. 320p. 1992. reprint ed. 60.00 (*0-87668-978-0*) Aronson.

— Women in Therapy. LC 88-45938. 320p. 1994. reprint ed. pap. 13.50 (*0-06-097228-9*, PL 7228, Perennial) HarperTrade.

Lerner, Harriet G. & Goldhor, Susan H. What's So Terrible About Swallowing an Apple Seed. LC 94-2769. (Illus.). 40p. (J). (ps-3). 1996. 15.95 (*0-06-024523-9*) HarpC Child Bks.

Lerner, Herbert J. & Antes, Richard S. Federal Income Taxation of Corporations Filing Consolidated Returns, 4 vols. 2nd ed. LC 97-22504. (C). 1997. ring bd. 650.00 (*0-8205-1227-3*) Bender.

Lerner, Howard D. & Lerner, Paul M., eds. Primitive Mental States & the Rorschach Test. 1988. 80.00 (*0-8236-4295-X*) Intl Univs Pr.

Lerner, I. Michael, tr. see Medvedev, Zhores A.

Lerner, I. V., et al, eds. Supersymmetry & Trace Formulae: Chaos & Disorder. LC 98-42555. (NATO ASI Series B: Vol. 370). (Illus.). 404p. (C). 1998. text. write for info. (*0-306-45933-7*) Plenum.

Lerner, Isha & Lerner, Mark. Inner Child Cards: A Journey into Fairy Tales, Myth & Natūre. (Illus.). 336p. (Orig.). 1992. text 34.95 (*0-939680-95-5*) Bear & Co.

Lerner, Jacqueline V. Working Mothers & Their Families. (Family Studies Text Ser.: Vol. 13). (Illus.). 128p. (C). 1993. text 42.00 (*0-8039-4209-5*); pap. text 18.95 (*0-8039-4210-9*) Sage.

Lerner, Jacqueline V. & Galambos, Nancy L., eds. Employed Mothers & Their Children. LC 90-25897. (Reference Books on Family Issues: Vol. 17). 320p. 1991. text 42.00 (*0-8240-6344-9*, 475) Garland.

Lerner, Jacqueline V., jt. auth. see Lerner, Richard.

Lerner, Janet, et al. Cases in Learning & Behavior Problems: A Guide to Individualized Education Programs. 354p. (C). 1992. reprint ed. pap. text, student ed. 28.95 (*1-879215-06-3*) Sheffield WI.

— Preschool Children with Special Disabilities. LC 97-33961. 400p. 1998. 57.00 (*0-205-26735-1*) P-H.

— Preschoolers with Special Needs: Children-at-Risk or Who Have Disabilities: Instructor's Manual with Tests. (C). 1998. text, teacher ed. write for info. (*0-205-26736-X*, T6736-7) Allyn.

Lerner, Janet M. Restoring Families Facilitator's Guide: Overcoming Abusive Relationships Through Christ. pap. 12.00 (*1-58119-031-X*) T P Min.

An Asterisk (*) at the beginning of an entry indicates that the title is appearing for the first time.

— Restoring Families Members Guide: Overcoming Abusive Relationships Through Christ. pap. 10.00 (*1-58119-032-8*) T P Min.

Lerner, Janet W. Learning Disabilities: Theories, Diagnosis, & Teaching Strategies. 4th ed. LC 84-82413. 640p. (C). 1984. student ed. 14.76 (*0-685-10561-X*) HM.

— Learning Disabilities: Theories, Diagnosis, & Teaching Strategies. 5th ed. 1988. teacher ed. write for info. (*0-318-63320-5*); student ed. 13.96 (*0-318-36897-8*) HM.

— Learning Disabled, 7 vols. 7th ed. LC 96-76924. (C). 1996. text 69.16 (*0-395-79685-7*) HM.

— Learning Disablities, 6 vols. (C). 1992. pap., student ed. 20.36 (*0-395-64011-3*) HM.

Lerner, Janet W., et al. Attention Deficit Disorders: Assessment & Teaching. LC 94-20274. (Special Education Ser.). 258p. 1994. 36.95 (*0-534-25044-0*) Brooks-Cole.

Lerner, Janet W., et al. Special Education for the Early Childhood Years. 416p. 1981. text 24.95 (*0-13-826461-9*) P-H.

Lerner, Janet W., jt. ed. see Cruickshank, William M.

Lerner, Jeff R. The Complete Manual of Ice Dance Patterns. (Illus.). 402p. 1992. student ed. 40.00 (*0-9696538-0-8*) Platoro Pr.

Lerner, Jesse, jt. auth. see Gonzales, Rita.

Lerner, Joel. Complete Home Landscape Designer. rev. ed. 1995. 22.95 (*0-312-13672-2*) St Martin.

— Financial Planning for the Utterly Confused. 5th ed. LC 97-43777. 400p. 1998. pap. 12.95 (*0-07-038164-X*) McGraw.

— Our Thought for the Day: The Best of Professor Joel Lerner's Lifetime Collection of Quotes. 366p. 1995. pap., spiral bd. 6.50 (*1-56245-182-0*) Great Quotations.

— Schaum's Outline of Basic Business Mathematics. 2nd ed. LC 99-29346. (Schaum's Outlines Ser.). 249p. 1999. pap. 15.95 (*0-07-038182-8*) McGraw.

Lerner, Joel J. Financial Planning for the Utterly Confused. 4th ed. 264p. 1993. pap. 9.95 (*0-07-037647-6*) McGraw.

— Schaum's Outline of Principles of Accounting I. 5th ed. LC 98-35909. (Schaum's Outline Ser.). (Illus.). 388p. 1998. pap. 15.95 (*0-07-038149-6*) McGraw.

— Schaum's Outline of Theory & Problems of Bookkeeping & Accounting. 3rd ed. LC 93-41304. 384p. (C). 1994. pap. 15.95 (*0-07-037593-3*) McGraw.

Lerner, Joel J. & Cashin, James A. Schaum's Outline of Principles of Accounting II. 4th ed. LC 92-4387. (Schaum's Outline Ser.). 306p. (C). 1994. pap. 12.95 (*0-07-037589-5*) McGraw.

Lerner, Joel J. & Zima, P. Schaum's Outline of Theory & Problems of Business Mathematics. 304p. (C). 1984. pap. 15.95 (*0-07-037212-8*) McGraw.

Lerner, Joel J., tr. see Herczl, Moshe Y.

Lerner, Joel M. The Complete Home Landscape Designer. LC 95-25817. (Illus.). 144p. (Orig.). 1991. pap. 22.95 (*0-312-06937-5*) St Martin.

Lerner, Jonathan. Caught in a Still Place. 128p. (Orig.). 1990. pap. 9.95 (*1-85242-146-0*) Serpents Tail.

Lerner, Joseph. A Review of Amino Acid Transport Processes in Animal Cells & Tissues. LC 78-55683. 1977. text 20.00 (*0-89101-036-X*) U Maine Pr.

Lerner, Josh. Venture Capital & Private Equity: A Casebook. LC 99-33115. 560p. 1999. text 66.75 (*0-471-32286-5*) Wiley.

Lerner, Josh, jt. auth. see Gompers, Paul A.

Lerner, Julie & Lerner, Paul. Lerner Survey of Health Care in New York: Your Consumer Guide to HMOs, Health Insurance Plans, Hospitals, Free & Low-Cost Services & Your Legal Rights. LC 99-94087. 320p. 1999. pap. 17.95 (*0-9669999-1-6*) Lerner.

Lerner, Julie, jt. auth. see Lerner, Paul.

Lerner, L. Scott, ed. L' Affaire Dreyfus: Et l'Emergence de la France Moderne.Tr. of Dreyfus Affair: The Making of Modern France. (FRE.). 80p. 1997. text 95.00 (*1-57803-048-X*) Primary Srce Media.

Lerner, Laurence. Angels & Absences: Child Deaths in the Nineteenth Century. LC 97-4572. (Illus.). 268p. 1997. 29.95 (*0-8265-1287-9*) Vanderbilt U Pr.

— A.R.T.H.U.R. The Life & Opinions of a Digital Computer. LC 74-21241. 66p. 1975. reprint ed. pap. 9.95 (*0-87023-181-2*) U of Mass Pr.

— Baudelaire. 128p. 1999. pap. 3.50 (*0-460-87993-6*) Tuttle Pubng.

— Philip Larkin. (Writers & Their Work Ser.). 80p. (Orig.). 1997. pap. 17.00 (*0-7463-0838-8*, Pub. by Northcote House) U Pr of Miss.

Lerner, Laurence, ed. The Victorians. LC 78-15642. (Context of English Literature Ser.). 228p. 1978. 35.95 (*0-8419-0419-7*); pap. 19.95 (*0-8419-0420-0*) Holmes & Meier.

Lerner, Lawrence. Modern Physics Scientists & Engineers, Vol. II. (Physics Ser.). 240p. (C). 1996. pap. 33.75 (*0-86720-487-7*) Jones & Bartlett.

— Physics, Vol. 2. 656p. Date not set. pap. 43.75 (*0-86720-492-3*) Jones & Bartlett.

— Physics, Vol. 2, Chapters 23-39. 536p. 1997. pap. 46.25 (*0-7637-0460-1*) Jones & Bartlett.

— Physics for Scientists & Engineers. (Physics Ser.). 1168p. (C). 1996. text 83.75 (*0-86720-479-6*) Jones & Bartlett.

Lerner, Lawrence & French. Physics. Student Study Guide. 136p. 1996. pap. 22.50 (*0-7637-0204-8*) Jones & Bartlett.

— Physics Vol. 2: Student Study Guide. 144p. 1996. pap. 22.50 (*0-7637-0340-0*) Jones & Bartlett.

Lerner, Lawrence, jt. auth. see Lee, Dean.

Lerner, Lawrence, jt. auth. see Strawbridge, Steven J.

Lerner, Lawrence S. Physics, Vol. 1. LC 96-9427. 1996. pap. 48.75 (*0-86720-491-5*) Jones & Bartlett.

— Physics for Scientists & Engineers. LC 96-9427. Date not set. 80.00 (*0-7637-0253-6*) Jones & Bartlett.

Lerner, Lawrence S., ed. & tr. see Bruno, Giordano.

Lerner, Leon L. Babel: A Play of Ideas. 84p. 1996. write for info. (*0-9607964-4-4*) Galaxy Pr MD.

— Being Human. 86p. 1982. pap. 5.95 (*0-9607964-0-1*) Galaxy Pr MD.

— Biography of a Century & Other Poems. 80p. 1976. pap. 8.95 (*0-9607964-1-X*) Galaxy Pr MD.

— In These Strange Times: Poetry As News. 189p. 1993. 21.99 (*0-9607964-2-8*); pap. 14.99 (*0-9607964-3-6*) Galaxy Pr MD.

— Words & Thoughts. 60p. (Orig.). 1996. pap. 11.95 (*0-9607964-5-2*) Galaxy Pr MD.

Lerner, Linda. Anytime Blues. (Illus.). 70p. 1999. pap. 10.00 (*1-889289-36-1*) Ye Olde Font Shoppe.

— City Girl. 32p. (Orig.). 1990. pap. text 4.00 (*0-935839-09-7*) Virgin Press.

— New & Selected Poems. (Illus.). 90p. 1999. pap. 12.00 (*1-889289-24-8*) Ye Olde Font Shoppe.

Lerner, Loren R. Canadian Film & Video/Film et Video Canadiens: A Bibliography & Guide to the Literature/Bibliographie Analytique Sur le Cinema & la Video Au Canada, 2 vols., Set. (Illus.). 1256p. 1996. text 275.00 (*0-8020-2988-4*) U of Toronto Pr.

Lerner, Loren R., jt. auth. see Sacca, Elizabeth J.

Lerner, M. J. The Belief in a Just World: A Fundamental Delusion. LC 80-16359. (Perspectives in Social Psychology Ser.). (Illus.). 224p. (C). 1980. 55.00 (*0-306-40495-8*, Plenum Trade) Perseus Pubng.

Lerner, M. J. & Lerner, S. C. The Justice Motive in Social Behavior: Adapting to Times of Scarcity & Change. LC 81-10605. (Critical Issues in Social Justice Ser.). (Illus.). 516p. (C). 1981. 80.00 (*0-306-40675-6*, Plenum Trade) Perseus Pubng.

Lerner, M. J. & Mikula, G. Entitlement & the Affectional Bond: Justice in Close Relationships. (Illus.). 374p. (C). 1994. 54.50 (*0-306-44699-5*, Kluwer Plenum) Kluwer Academic.

Lerner, M. J., jt. auth. see Montada, L.

Lerner, Marcia. Cracking the MAT 1998. 2nd ed. 1997. pap. 20.00 (*0-679-77866-7*) Random.

Lerner, Marcia. Math Smart II. LC 98-132835. (Princeton Review Ser.). 288p. 1997. pap. 12.00 (*0-679-78383-0*) Random.

— Writing Smart: Your Guide to Great Writing. (Princeton Review Ser.). 1994. pap. 12.00 (*0-679-75360-5*) Villard Books.

Lerner, Marcia & Princeton Review Publishing Staff. Math Smart: Essential Math for These Numeric Times. LC 93-18543. (Princeton Review Ser.). 304p. 1993. pap. 12.00 (*0-679-74616-1*) Villard Books.

Lerner, Marcia, jt. auth. see Princeton Review Publishing Staff.

Lerner, Mark. Mysteries of Venus. (Illus.). 208p. (Orig.). 1986. pap. 10.95 (*0-938559-00-1*) Great Bear Pr.

Lerner, Mark & Philips, Laura. Baseball Tarot. LC 98-49626. (Illus.). 324p. 1999. pap. 20.00 (*0-7611-0347-3*) Workman Pub.

Lerner, Mark, jt. auth. see Lerner, Isha.

Lerner, Mark, ed. see Richie, Jason.

Lerner, Mark, tr. see Mitgutsch, Ali, et al.

Lerner, Martin, jt. auth. see Felten, Wolfgang.

Lerner, Max. Articulation Between For-Profit Private Occupational Schools & Secondary Vocational Programs: Colleges & Universities. 39p. 1987. 5.25 (*0-318-23410-6*, IN315) Ctr Educ Trng Employ.

— Ideas Are Weapons: The History & Uses of Ideas. 585p. (C). 1990. 29.95 (*0-88738-364-5*) Transaction Pubs.

— Ideas for the Ice Age: Studies in a Revolutionary Era. 450p. (C). 1992. pap. 29.95 (*1-56000-595-5*) Transaction Pubs.

— It Is Later Than You Think. 278p. 1989. 39.95 (*0-88738-782-9*) Transaction Pubs.

— Magisterial Imagination: Six Masters of the Human Sciences. LC 93-39856. 212p. (C). 1994. 34.95 (*1-56000-168-2*) Transaction Pubs.

— Nine Scorpions in a Bottle: Great Judges & Cases of the Supreme Court. Cummings, Richard, Jr., ed. LC 93-24463. 352p. 1995. pap. 13.45 (*1-55970-291-5*, Pub. by Arcade Pub Inc) Time Warner.

— Nine Scorpions in a Bottle: Great Judges, & Cases of the Supreme Court. LC 93-24463. 544p. 1994. 27.45 (*1-55970-168-4*, Pub. by Arcade Pub Inc) Time Warner.

— Thomas Jefferson: America's Philosopher-King. 155p. 1997. text 29.95 (*1-56000-262-X*) Transaction Pubs.

— Tocqueville & American Civilization. LC 93-5992. 136p. (C). 1993. reprint ed. pap. text 21.95 (*1-56000-703-6*) Transaction Pubs.

— Wounded Titans: American Presidents & the Perils of Power. 464p. 1996. 29.45 (*1-55970-339-3*, Pub. by Arcade Pub Inc) Time Warner.

Lerner, Max, intro. The Mind & Faith of Justice Holmes: His Speeches, Essays, Letters, & Judicial Opinions. 500p. 1989. pap. 24.95 (*0-88738-765-9*) Transaction Pubs.

Lerner, Melvin J., jt. ed. see Montada, Leo.

Lerner, Michael. Choice in Healing: Integrating the Best of Conventional & Alternative Approaches to Cancer. LC 93-39913. (Illus.). 693p. 1994. 38.50 (*0-262-12180-8*) MIT Pr.

— Choices in Healing: Integrating the Best of Conventional & Alternative Approaches to Cancer. 696p. 1996. reprint ed. pap. text 20.00 (*0-262-62104-5*) MIT Pr.

— Jewish Renewal: A Path to Healing & Transformation. 464p. 1995. pap. 15.00 (*0-06-097675-6*, Perennial) HarperTrade.

***Lerner, Michael.** Middleware Networks: Concept, Design & Deployment of Internet Infrastructure. LC 00-35404. (International Series on Advances in Database Systems). 2000. write for info. (*0-7923-7840-7*) Kluwer Academic.

Lerner, Michael. The Politics of Meaning: Restoring Hope & Possibility in an Age of Cynicism. LC 97-194468. 355p. 1996. pap. 13.00 (*0-201-15489-7*) Addison-Wesley.

Lerner, Michael. The Socialism of Fools: Anti-Semitism on the Left. (C). 1992. pap. 10.00 (*0-03-593305-4*) Harcourt Coll Pubs.

Lerner, Michael. The Socialism of Fools: Anti-Semitism on the Left. 1992. pap. 10.00 (*0-935933-05-0*) Inst Labor & Mental.

***Lerner, Michael.** Spirit Matters. 256p. 2000. 22.95 (*1-57174-195-X*) Hampton Roads Pub Co.

Lerner, Michael. Surplus Powerlessness. LC 85-62314. 320p. 1986. 14.95 (*0-935933-01-8*); pap. 9.95 (*0-935933-02-6*) Inst Labor & Mental.

— Surplus Powerlessness: The Psychodynamics of Everyday Life & the Psychology of Individual & Social Transformation. LC 91-7279. 424p. (C). 1991. pap. 18.50 (*0-391-03706-4*) Humanities.

***Lerner, Michael.** Surplus Powerlessness: The Psychodynamics of Everyday Life & the Psychology of Individual & Social Transformation. LC 98-54286. 1998. write for info. (*1-57392-299-4*, Humanity Bks) Prometheus Bks.

Lerner, Michael. Tikkun: To Heal, Repair & Transform the World. 1992. 39.95 (*0-935933-03-4*); pap. 16.95 (*0-935933-04-2*) Inst Labor & Mental.

Lerner, Michael & West, Cornel. Jews & Blacks: A Dialogue on Race, Religion, & Culture in America. 288p. 1996. pap. 12.95 (*0-452-27591-1*, Plume) Dutton Plume.

Lerner, Michael, jt. auth. see O'Manique, John.

Lerner, Michael G. Pierre Loti. LC 73-2368. (Twayne's World Authors Ser.). 172p. (C). 1974. lib. bdg. 17.95 (*0-8057-2546-6*) Irvington.

— Pierre Loti's Dramatic Works. LC 98-45070. (Studies in French Literature). 103 p. 1998. write for info. (*0-88946-572-X*) E Mellen.

— Pierre Loti's Dramatic Works. LC 98-45070. (Studies in French Literature: Vol. 30). 103p. 1998. text 79.95 (*0-7734-8247-4*) E Mellen.

Lerner, Morris W. The Analysis of Elemental Boron. LC 74-607964. (AEC Critical Review Ser.). 137p. 1970. pap. 11.25 (*0-87079-134-6*, TID-25190); fiche 9.00 (*0-87079-135-4*, TID-25190) DOE.

Lerner, Natan. Group Rights & Discrimination in International Law. (International Studies in Human Rights). (C). 1990. lib. bdg. 100.50 (*0-7923-0853-0*) Kluwer Academic.

***Lerner, Natan.** Religion, Beliefs, & International Human Rights. LC 99-86309. (Religion & Human Rights Ser.). 160p. 2000. pap. 25.00 (*1-57075-301-6*) Orbis Bks.

Lerner, Natan. United Nations Convention on the Elimination of All Forms of Racial Dicrimination. LC 80-51738. 278p. 1980. lib. bdg. 87.00 (*90-286-0160-0*) Kluwer Academic.

Lerner, Neal, jt. auth. see Gillespie, Paula.

Lerner, Nicolas, jt. ed. see Colombini, F.

Lerner, Norbert & Sobel, Max A. College Algebra. 4th ed. LC 94-11437. 590p. (C). 1995. 86.00 (*0-13-311614-X*) P-H.

— Precalculus Mathematics. 5th ed. LC 94-11433. 778p. (C). 1995. 90.00 (*0-13-112095-6*) P-H.

Lerner, Norbert, jt. auth. see Sobel, Max A.

***Lerner, Paul & Lerner, Julie.** Lerner's Consumer Guide to Health Care: How to Get the Best Health Care for Less. 224p. 2000. pap. 13.95 (*0-9669999-2-4*, Pub. by Lerner) IPG Chicago.

Lerner, Paul, jt. auth. see Lerner, Julie.

Lerner, Paul M. Psychoanalytic Perspectives on the Rorschach. LC 97-51640. 512p. 1998. 59.95 (*0-88163-231-1*) Analytic Pr.

— Psychoanalytic Theory & the Rorschach. 1996. pap. 29.95 (*0-88163-255-4*) Analytic Pr.

— Psychoanalytic Theory & the Rorschach. 2nd ed. 312p. 1990. text 39.95 (*0-88163-122-1*) Analytic Pr.

Lerner, Paul M., ed. Handbook of Rorschach Research Scales. LC 73-7022. 523p. 1974. 77.50 (*0-8236-2305-X*) Intl Univs Pr.

Lerner, Paul M., jt. ed. see Lerner, Howard D.

Lerner, Preston. Fools on the Hill. 352p. (Orig.). 1995. mass mkt. 5.50 (*0-671-51048-7*) PB.

Lerner Publications, Department of Geography Staff. Botswana in Pictures. (Visual Geography Ser.). (Illus.). 64p. (YA). (gr. 5 up). 1990. lib. bdg. 19.93 (*0-8225-1856-2*, Lerner Publctns) Lerner Pub.

— Cambodia in Pictures. LC 95-37200. (Visual Geography Ser.). (Illus.). (J). 1996. lib. bdg. 19.93 (*0-8225-1905-4*, Lerner Publctns) Lerner Pub.

— Canada in Pictures. (Visual Geography Ser.). (Illus.). 64p. (YA). (gr. 5 up). 1989. lib. bdg. 19.93 (*0-8225-1870-8*, Lerner Publctns) Lerner Pub.

***Lerner Publications, Department of Geography Staff.** Congo (Formerly Zaire)-- In Pictures. LC 98-44336. (Visual Geography Ser.). (Illus.). 1998. lib. bdg. 21.27 (*0-8225-1900-3*) Lerner Pub.

Lerner Publications, Department of Geography Staff. Costa Rica in Pictures. (Visual Geography Ser.). (Illus.). 64p. (YA). (gr. 5 up). 1993. lib. bdg. 19.93 (*0-8225-1805-8*, Lerner Publctns) Lerner Pub.

— Czech Republic in Pictures. LC 94-37432. (Visual Geography Ser.). 1995. lib. bdg. 19.93 (*0-8225-1879-1*) Lerner Pub.

— Ecuador in Pictures. rev. ed. LC 98-217556. (Visual Geography Ser.). (Illus.). 64p. (YA). (gr. 5 up). 1987. lib. bdg. 19.93 (*0-8225-1813-9*, Lerner Publctns) Lerner Pub.

— Germany - in Pictures. LC 93-40971. (Visual Geography Ser.). (Illus.). 64p. (YA). (gr. 5 up). 1994. lib. bdg. 19.93 (*0-8225-1873-2*, Lerner Publctns) Lerner Pub.

— Ghana in Pictures. rev. ed. (Visual Geography Ser.). (Illus.). 64p. (YA). (gr. 5 up). 1988. lib. bdg. 19.93 (*0-8225-1829-5*, Lerner Publctns) Lerner Pub.

— Guatemala in Pictures. rev. ed. (Visual Geography Ser.). (Illus.). 64p. (YA). (gr. 5 up). 1987. lib. bdg. 19.93 (*0-8225-1803-1*, Lerner Publctns) Lerner Pub.

— Guyana in Pictures. rev. ed. (Visual Geography Ser.). (Illus.). 64p. (YA). (gr. 5 up). 1997. lib. bdg. 19.93 (*0-8225-1815-5*, Lerner Publctns) Lerner Pub.

— Haiti in Pictures. (Visual Geography Ser.). (Illus.). 64p. (YA). (gr. 5 up). 1995. lib. bdg. 19.93 (*0-8225-1816-3*, Lerner Publctns) Lerner Pub.

— Honduras in Pictures. rev. ed. (Visual Geography Ser.). (Illus.). 64p. (YA). (gr. 5 up). 1987. lib. bdg. 19.93 (*0-8225-1804-X*, Lerner Publctns) Lerner Pub.

— Iraq in Pictures. rev. ed. (Visual Geography Ser.). (Illus.). 64p. (YA). (gr. 5 up). 1992. lib. bdg. 19.93 (*0-8225-1847-3*, Lerner Publctns) Lerner Pub.

— Italy - In Pictures. LC 95-45609. (Visual Geography Ser.). (J). 1997. lib. bdg. 19.93 (*0-8225-1884-8*, Lerner Publctns) Lerner Pub.

— Jamaica in Pictures. rev. ed. (Visual Geography Ser.). (Illus.). 64p. (YA). (gr. 5 up). 1987. lib. bdg. 19.93 (*0-8225-1814-7*, Lerner Publctns) Lerner Pub.

— Japan in Pictures. rev. ed. (Visual Geography Ser.). (Illus.). 64p. (YA). (gr. 5 up). 1994. lib. bdg. 19.93 (*0-8225-1861-9*, Lerner Publctns) Lerner Pub.

— Kenya in Pictures. rev. ed. (Visual Geography Ser.). (Illus.). 64p. (YA). (gr. 5 up). 1997. lib. bdg. 19.93 (*0-8225-1830-9*, Lerner Publctns) Lerner Pub.

— Laos in Pictures. LC 95-37182. (Visual Geography Ser.). (Illus.). (J). 1996. lib. bdg. 19.93 (*0-8225-1906-2*, Lerner Publctns) Lerner Pub.

— New Zealand in Pictures. (Visual Geography Ser.). (Illus.). 64p. (YA). (gr. 5 up). 1990. lib. bdg. 19.95 (*0-8225-1862-7*, Lerner Publctns) Lerner Pub.

— Panama in Pictures. (Visual Geography Ser.). (Illus.). 64p. (YA). (gr. 5 up). 1987. lib. bdg. 19.95 (*0-8225-1818-X*, Lerner Publctns) Lerner Pub.

— Peru in Pictures. (Visual Geography Ser.). (Illus.). 64p. (YA). (gr. 5 up). 1987. lib. bdg. 19.95 (*0-8225-1820-1*, Lerner Publctns) Lerner Pub.

— Puerto Rico in Pictures. (Visual Geography Ser.). (Illus.). 64p. (YA). (gr. 5 up). 1989. lib. bdg. 19.95 (*0-8225-1821-X*, Lerner Publctns) Lerner Pub.

— Romania: In Pictures. LC 92-32861. (Visual Geography Ser.). (J). 1993. lib. bdg. 19.95 (*0-8225-1894-5*, Lerner Publctns) Lerner Pub.

— Slovakia in Pictures. LC 94-45803. (Visual Geography Ser.). (Illus.). 64p. (YA). (gr. 5 up). 1995. lib. bdg. 19.95 (*0-8225-1912-7*) Lerner Pub.

— Switzerland-In Pictures. LC 95-2807. (Visual Georgraphy Ser.: Vol. 27, No. 16). (Illus.). (J). 1996. lib. bdg. 19.95 (*0-8225-1895-3*, Lerner Publctns) Lerner Pub.

— Syria in Pictures. (Visual Geography Ser.). (Illus.). 64p. (YA). (gr. 5 up). 1990. lib. bdg. 19.95 (*0-8225-1867-8*, Lerner Publctns) Lerner Pub.

— Venezuela in Pictures. (Visual Geography Ser.). (Illus.). 64p. (YA). (gr. 5 up). 1987. lib. bdg. 19.95 (*0-8225-1824-4*, Lerner Publctns) Lerner Pub.

Lerner Publications, Department of Geography Staff, compiled by. Libya - In Pictures. LC 95-39567. (Visual Geography Ser.). (Illus.). (J). 1996. lib. bdg. 19.93 (*0-8225-1907-0*, Lerner Publctns) Lerner Pub.

Lerner Publications, Department of Geography Staff, compiled by. Ukraine. LC 92-10284. (Then & Now Ser.). (Illus.). 64p. (YA). (gr. 5 up). 1993. lib. bdg. 22.95 (*0-8225-2808-8*, Lerner Publctns) Lerner Pub.

Lerner Publications, Department of Geography Staff, ed. Afghanistan in Pictures. (Visual Geography Ser.). (Illus.). 64p. (YA). (gr. 5 up). 1989. lib. bdg. 19.93 (*0-8225-1849-X*, Lerner Publctns) Lerner Pub.

— Argentina in Pictures. (Visual Geography Ser.). (Illus.). 64p. (YA). (gr. 5 up). 1988. lib. bdg. 19.93 (*0-8225-1807-4*, Lerner Publctns) Lerner Pub.

— Australia in Pictures. (Visual Geography Ser.). (Illus.). 64p. (J). (gr. 5 up). 1990. lib. bdg. 19.93 (*0-8225-1855-4*, Lerner Publctns) Lerner Pub.

— Austria in Pictures. (Visual Geography Ser.). (Illus.). 64p. (YA). (gr. 5 up). 1991. lib. bdg. 19.93 (*0-8225-1888-0*, Lerner Publctns) Lerner Pub.

— Bolivia in Pictures. (Visual Geography Ser.). (Illus.). 64p. (YA). (gr. 5 up). 1987. lib. bdg. 19.93 (*0-8225-1808-2*, Lerner Publctns) Lerner Pub.

— Cameroon in Pictures. (Visual Geography Ser.). (Illus.). 64p. (YA). (gr. 5 up). 1989. lib. bdg. 19.93 (*0-8225-1857-0*, Lerner Publctns) Lerner Pub.

— Central African Republic in Pictures. (Visual Geography Ser.). (Illus.). 64p. (YA). (gr. 5 up). 1989. lib. bdg. 19.93 (*0-8225-1858-9*, Lerner Publctns) Lerner Pub.

— Chile in Pictures. (Visual Geography Ser.). (Illus.). 64p. (YA). (gr. 5 up). 1988. lib. bdg. 19.93 (*0-8225-1809-0*, Lerner Publctns) Lerner Pub.

— China in Pictures. (Visual Geography Ser.). (Illus.). 64p. (YA). (gr. 5 up). 1989. lib. bdg. 19.93 (*0-8225-1859-7*, Lerner Publctns) Lerner Pub.

— Colombia in Pictures. (Visual Geography Ser.). (Illus.). 64p. (YA). (gr. 5 up). 1987. lib. bdg. 19.93 (*0-8225-1810-4*, Lerner Publctns) Lerner Pub.

— England in Pictures. rev. ed. (Visual Geography Ser.). (Illus.). 64p. (YA). (gr. 5 up). 1990. lib. bdg. 19.93 (*0-8225-1874-0*, Lerner Publctns) Lerner Pub.

— India in Pictures. rev. ed. (Visual Geography Ser.). (Illus.). 64p. (YA). (gr. 5 up). 1995. lib. bdg. 19.93 (*0-8225-1852-X*, Lerner Publctns) Lerner Pub.

— Indonesia in Pictures. rev. ed. (Visual Geography Ser.). (Illus.). 64p. (YA). (gr. 5 up). 1995. lib. bdg. 19.93 (*0-8225-1860-0*, Lerner Publctns) Lerner Pub.

— Iran in Pictures. rev. ed. (Visual Geography Ser.). (Illus.). 64p. (YA). (gr. 5 up). 1992. lib. bdg. 19.93 (*0-8225-1848-1*, Lerner Publctns) Lerner Pub.

L

An Asterisk (*) at the beginning of an entry indicates that the title is appearing for the first time.

L

— Ireland in Pictures. rev. ed. (Visual Geography Ser.). (Illus.). 64p. (YA). (gr. 5 up). 1997. lib. bdg. 19.93 (0-8225-1878-3, Lerner Publctns) Lerner Pub.
— Kuwait in Pictures. rev. ed. (Visual Geography Ser.). (Illus.). 64p. (YA). (gr. 5 up). 1995. lib. bdg. 19.93 (0-8225-1846-5, Lerner Publctns) Lerner Pub.
— Lebanon in Pictures. rev. ed. (Visual Geography Ser.). (Illus.). 64p. (YA). (gr. 5 up). 1992. lib. bdg. 19.93 (0-8225-1832-5, Lerner Publctns) Lerner Pub.
— Malaysia in Pictures. rev. ed. (Visual Geography Ser.). (Illus.). 64p. (YA). (gr. 6-9). 1997. lib. bdg. 19.93 (0-8225-1854-6, Lerner Publctns) Lerner Pub.
— Mali in Pictures. rev. ed. (Visual Geography Ser.). (Illus.). 64p. (YA). (gr. 6-9). 1996. lib. bdg. 19.93 (0-8225-1869-4, Lerner Publctns) Lerner Pub.
— Morocco in Pictures. rev. ed. (Visual Geography Ser.). (Illus.). 64p. (YA). (gr. 6-9). 1996. lib. bdg. 19.93 (0-8225-1843-0, Lerner Publctns) Lerner Pub.
— Nepal in Pictures. (Visual Geography Ser.). (Illus.). 64p. (YA). (gr. 5 up). 1993. lib. bdg. 19.95 (0-8225-1851-1, Lerner Publctns) Lerner Pub.
— Norway in Pictures. (Visual Geography Ser.). (Illus.). 64p. (YA). (gr. 5 up). 1990. lib. bdg. 19.95 (0-8225-1871-6, Lerner Publctns) Lerner Pub.
— Pakistan in Pictures. (Visual Geography Ser.). (Illus.). 64p. (YA). (gr. 5 up). 1989. lib. bdg. 19.95 (0-8225-1850-3, Lerner Publctns) Lerner Pub.
— Philippines in Pictures. (Visual Geography Ser.). (Illus.). 64p. (YA). (gr. 5 up). 1995. lib. bdg. 19.95 (0-8225-1863-5, Lerner Publctns) Lerner Pub.
— Scotland in Pictures. (Visual Geography Ser.). (Illus.). 64p. (YA). (gr. 5 up). 1991. lib. bdg. 19.95 (0-8225-1875-9, Lerner Publctns) Lerner Pub.
— South Korea in Pictures. (Visual Geography Ser.). (Illus.). 64p. (YA). (gr. 5 up). 1989. lib. bdg. 19.95 (0-8225-1868-6, Lerner Publctns) Lerner Pub.
— Soviet Union in Pictures. (Visual Geography Ser.). (Illus.). 64p. (YA). (gr. 5 up). 1989. lib. bdg. 19.95 (0-8225-1864-3, Lerner Publctns) Lerner Pub.
— Sri Lanka in Pictures. (Visual Geography Ser.). (Illus.). 64p. (YA). (gr. 5 up). 1988. lib. bdg. 19.95 (0-8225-1853-8, Lerner Publctns) Lerner Pub.
— Sweden in Pictures. LC 98-217405. (Visual Geography Ser.). (Illus.). 64p. (YA). (gr. 5 up). 1993. lib. bdg. 19.95 (0-8225-1872-4, Lerner Publctns) Lerner Pub.
— Taiwan in Pictures. (Visual Geography Ser.). (Illus.). 64p. (YA). (gr. 5 up). 1989. lib. bdg. 19.95 (0-8225-1865-1, Lerner Publctns) Lerner Pub.
— Thailand in Pictures. (Visual Geography Ser.). (Illus.). 64p. (YA). (gr. 5 up). 1994. lib. bdg. 19.95 (0-8225-1866-X, Lerner Publctns) Lerner Pub.
— Tunisia in Pictures. (Visual Geography Ser.). (Illus.). 64p. (YA). (gr. 5 up). 1989. lib. bdg. 19.95 (0-8225-1844-9, Lerner Publctns) Lerner Pub.
— Wales in Pictures. (Visual Geography Ser.). (Illus.). 64p. (YA). (gr. 5 up). 1990. lib. bdg. 19.95 (0-8225-1877-5, Lerner Publctns) Lerner Pub.

Lerner, R. G. & Trigg, George L. Encyclopedia of Physics. 2nd ed. 1408p. 1990. 159.00 (0-471-18719-4) Wiley.

Lerner, Ralph. Revolutions Revisited: Two Faces of the Politics of Enlightenment. LC 93-36438. xvi, 136p. (C). 1994. 27.50 (0-8078-2136-5) U of NC Pr.
— The Thinking Revolutionary: Principle & Practice in the New Republic. LC 87-5287. 256p. (C). 1987. text 39.95 (0-8014-2007-5) Cornell U Pr.

Lerner, Ralph & Mahdi, Muhsin, eds. Medieval Political Philosophy: A Sourcebook. (Agora Paperback Editions Ser.). 544p. 1972. pap. text 18.95 (0-8014-9139-8) Cornell U Pr.

***Lerner, Ralph & Maimonides.** Maimonides' Empire of Light: Popular Enlightenment in an Age of Belief. LC 00-21360. 1999. 35.00 (0-226-47313-9) U Ch Pr.

Lerner, Ralph, jt. auth. see Kurland, Philip B.

Lerner, Ralph, jt. ed. see Kurland, Philip B.

Lerner, Ralph E. & Bresler, Judith. Art Law: The Guide for Collectors, Investors, Dealers, & Artists. LC 89-63038. 1244p. 1989. text, suppl. ed. 125.00 (0-87224-000-2, G6-2005) PLI.
— Art Law: The Guide for Collectors, Investors, Dealers, & Artists - 1992. 2nd ed. 478p. 1992. pap. 50.00 (0-685-69381-3) PLI.

Lerner, Reuven. CGI Programming Interactive Course. LC 97-15948. 1997. write for info. (1-57169-101-4) Sams.

Lerner, Richard. Hiking with Your Dog. (Nuts-n-Bolts Guides Ser.). (Illus.). 32p. (Orig.). 1995. pap. 4.95 (0-89732-164-2) Menasha Ridge.

***Lerner, Richard & Lerner, Jacqueline V.** Adolescence in America: An Encyclopedia, 2 Vols. 2000. lib. bdg. 150.00 (1-57607-205-3) ABC-CLIO.

Lerner, Richard A. Concepts & Theories of Human Development. 2nd ed. 512p. 1985. text 34.50 (0-89859-886-9) L Erlbaum Assocs.

Lerner, Richard A., et al, eds. Vaccines, '85: Molecular & Chemical Basis of Resistance to Parasitic, Bacterial & Viral Diseases. LC 84-29372. 407p. (Orig.). 1985. pap. 75.00 (0-87969-181-6) Cold Spring Harbor.
— Vaccines, '89: Modern Approaches to New Vaccines Including the Prevention of AIDS. (Illus.). 1989. pap. 100.00 (0-87969-323-1) Cold Spring Harbor.

Lerner, Richard A., jt. ed. see Chanock, Robert M.

Lerner, Richard M. America's Children & Youth in Crisis: Challenges & Options for Programs & Policies. 160p. 1994. 45.00 (0-8039-7068-4); pap. 21.00 (0-8039-7069-2) Sage.
— Concepts & Theories of Human Development. 2nd ed. 1996. 49.95 (0-8058-2682-3) L Erlbaum Assocs.
— Concepts & Theories of Human Development. 2nd ed. 512p. (C). 1986. text. write for info. (0-07-554899-2) McGraw.
— Final Solutions: Biology, Prejudice, & Genocide. (Illus.). 224p. 1992. text 35.00 (0-271-00793-1) Pa St U Pr.

***Lerner, Richard M., ed.** Adolescence: Development, Diversity, & Context, Vols. 1-6. (Illus.). 1999. reprint ed. 475.00 (0-8153-3289-0) Garland.
— Adolescents & Their Families: Structure, Function, & Parent-Youth Relationships. LC 99-33729. (Adolescence Ser.: Vol. 4). (Illus.). 392p. 1999. reprint ed. 80.00 (0-8153-3293-9) Garland.
— Cognitive & Moral Development & Academic Achievement in Adolescence. LC 99-33731. (Adolescence Ser.: Vol. 2). (Illus.). 376p. 1999. reprint ed. 80.00 (0-8153-3291-2) Garland.
— The Development of Personality, Self, & Ego in Adolescence. LC 99-33730. (Adolescence Ser.: Vol. 3). (Illus.). 376p. 1999. reprint ed. 80.00 (0-8153-3292-0) Garland.

Lerner, Richard M., ed. Developmental Psychology: Historical & Philosophical Perspectives. 288p. (C). 1983. text 49.95 (0-89859-247-X) L Erlbaum Assocs.
— Early Adolescence: Perspectives on Research, Policy, & Intervention. (Penn State Series on Child & Adolescent Development). 528p. 1993. text 99.95 (0-8058-1164-8) L Erlbaum Assocs.

***Lerner, Richard M., ed.** Risks & Problem Behaviors in Adolescence. LC 99-33727. (Adolescence Ser.: Vol. 5). (Illus.). 368p. 1999. reprint ed. 80.00 (0-8153-3294-7) Garland.
— Social Interactions in Adolescence & Promoting Positive Social Contributions of Youth. LC 99-33728. (Adolescence Ser.: Vol. 6). (Illus.). 336p. 1999. reprint ed. 80.00 (0-8153-3295-5) Garland.
— Theoretical Foundations & Biological Bases of Development in Adolescence. LC 99-33732. (Adolescence Ser.: Vol. 1). (Illus.). 360p. 1999. reprint ed. 80.00 (0-8153-3290-4) Garland.

Lerner, Richard M., et al, eds. University-Community Collaborations for the Twenty-First Century: Outreach Scholarship for Youth & Families. LC 97-30385. (Michigan State University Series on Children, Youth, & Families: Vol. 4). (Illus.). 544p. 1997. text 94.00 (0-8153-2445-6, SS1119) Garland.

Lerner, Richard M. & Foch, Terryl, eds. Biological-Psychosocial Interactions in Early Adolescence: A Life-Span Perspective. (Child Psychology Ser.). 408p. 1987. text 69.95 (0-89859-787-0) L Erlbaum Assocs.

Lerner, Richard M. & Galambos, Nancy L., eds. Experiencing Adolescents: A Sourcebook for Parents, Teachers & Teens. LC 87-10129. 432p. reprint ed. pap. 134.00 (0-7837-3886-2, 204373400010) Bks Demand.

***Lerner, Richard M., et al.** Family Diversity & Family Policy: Strengthening Families for America's Children. LC 99-40718. (Outreach Scholarship Ser.). 192p. 1999. 99.00 (0-7923-8612-4) Kluwer Academic.

Lerner, Richard M., jt. auth. see Chiucos, Thomas R.

Lerner, Richard M., jt. auth. see Ford, Donald H.

Lerner, Richard M., jt. ed. see Brandtstadter, Jochen.

Lerner, Richard M., jt. ed. see Fisher, Celia B.

Lerner, Richard M., jt. ed. see Kreppner, Kurt.

Lerner, Richard M., jt. ed. see Villaruel, Francisco A.

Lerner, Rita G. & Trigg, George L., eds. Concise Encyclopedia of Solid State Physics. 300p. (C). 1983. 55.95 (0-201-14204-X); pap. 40.95 (0-201-14205-8) Addison-Wesley.
— Encyclopedia of Physics. 2nd ed. xiv, 1,408p. (C). 1991. 95.00 (0-89573-752-3) Wiley.

Lerner-Robbins, Helene. Our Power As Women: Wisdom & Strategies of Highly Successful Women. 200p. (Orig.). 1996. pap. 11.95 (0-943233-91-7) Conari Press.

Lerner, Robert, et al. American Elites. LC 96-16343. (Illus.). 192p. 1996. 30.00 (0-300-06534-5) Yale U Pr.
— Molding the Good Citizen: The Politics of High School History Texts. LC 94-32922. 200p. 1995. 59.95 (0-275-94919-2, Praeger Pubs); pap. 20.95 (0-275-95100-6) Greenwood.

Lerner, Robert E. The Heresy of the Free Spirit in the Later Middle Ages. LC 78-45790. (C). 1991. reprint ed. pap. text 18.50 (0-268-01094-3) U of Notre Dame Pr.

***Lerner, Robert E.** Western Civilization With Perspectives From the Past, Vol. 1. 13th ed. 1998. text 69.00 (0-393-97317-4); pap. text 57.50 (0-393-97310-7) Norton.
— Western Civilization With Perspectives From the Past, Vol. 2. 13th ed. 1998. text 68.50 (0-393-97306-9); pap. text 57.50 (0-393-97313-1) Norton.

Lerner, Robert E. Western Civilizations, 2 vols., Vol. 2. 2nd ed. 1999. pap. text. write for info. (0-393-99015-X) Norton.

***Lerner, Robert E., et al, contrib. by.** Western Civilizations, Their History & Their Culture, Vol. 1. 13th ed. LC 97-32338. (Illus.). 1998. 42.00 (0-393-97200-3) Norton.
— Western Civilizations, Their History & Their Culture, Vol. 2. 13th ed. LC 97-32338. (Illus.). 1998. pap. text 42.00 (0-393-97220-8) Norton.

Lerner, Robert E., et al. Western Civilizations, Their History & Their Culture. 13th ed. LC 97-32338. 1998. text 78.00 (0-393-97192-9) Norton.

Lerner, Rokelle. Affirmations for the Inner Child. 380p. 1990. pap. 6.95 (1-55874-054-6) Health Comm.
— Boundaries for Codependents. pap. 2.00 (0-89486-560-9, 5217 B) Hazelden.
— Daily Affirmations for Adult Children of Alcoholics. 372p. 1986. pap. 7.95 (0-932194-27-3, 4273) Health Comm.
— Living in the Comfort Zone: The Gift of Boundaries in Relationships. 200p. 1995. pap. 9.95 (1-55874-370-7, 3707) Health Comm.

Lerner, S. A. & Kaatz, G. W. Bacterial Resistance to Antimicrobial Agents. (Infectious Disease & Therapy Ser.). Date not set. write for info. (0-8247-9404-4) Dekker.

Lerner, S. C., jt. auth. see Lerner, M. J.

Lerner, Shalom, jt. ed. see Ziegel, Jacob.

Lerner, Sharon. Big Bird Says...A Game to Read & Play. LC 85-1959. (Step into Reading Ser.: A Step 1 Book). (Illus.). 31p. (J). (ps-3). 1985. pap. 3.99 (0-394-87499-4, Pub. by Random Bks Yng Read) Random.
— Big Bird's Copycat Day. LC 84-6869. (Step into Reading Ser.: A Step 1 Book). (Illus.). 32p. (J). (ps-1). 1984. pap. 3.99 (0-394-86912-5, Pub. by Random Bks Yng Read) Random.
— Big Bird's Copycat Day. LC 98-87191. (Step into Reading Ser.: A Step 1 Book). (Illus.). 12p. (J). (ps-1). 1999. 4.99 (0-375-80129-4, Pub. by Random Bks Yng Read) Random.

Lerner, Sharon. Big Bird's Copycat Day. (Step into Reading Ser.: A Step 1 Book). (J). (ps-1). 1984. 9.19 (0-606-12190-0, Pub. by Turtleback) Demco.
— Follow the Monsters! (Step into Reading Ser.: A Step 1 Book). (J). (ps-1). 1985. 9.19 (0-606-12292-3, Pub. by Turtleback) Demco.
— Follow the Monsters. (Illus.). (J). 1999. pap. 11.10 (0-8085-3580-3) Econo-Clad Bks.

Lerner, Sharon. Follow the Monsters! large type ed. LC 98-87127. (Step into Reading Ser.: A Step 1 Book). (Illus.). 12p. (J). (ps-1). 1999. 4.99 (0-375-80130-8) Random.
— Follow the Monsters! large type ed. LC 84-18031. (Step into Reading Ser.: A Step 1 Book). (Illus.). 32p. (J). (ps-3). 1985. pap. 3.99 (0-394-87126-X, Pub. by Random Bks Yng Read) Random.

Lerner, Sharon, ed. Noah's Ark. LC 77-92377. (Pictureback Ser.). (Illus.). (J). (ps-2). 1978. pap. 3.25 (0-394-83861-0, Pub. by Random Bks Yng Read) Random.

Lerner, Sharon, ed. see Berenstain, Stan & Berenstain, Jan.

Lerner, Steve. Beyond the Earth Summit: Conversations with Advocates of Sustainable Development. 294p. 1992. pap. 12.50 (0-943004-07-1) Common Knowledge.
— Bodily Harm: The Pattern of Fear & Violence at the California Youth Authority. 72p. 1986. pap. 4.95 (0-943004-03-9) Common Knowledge.
— The CYA Report: Conditions of Life at the California Youth Authority. LC 82-4973. 164p. (Orig.). 1982. pap. 5.95 (0-943004-00-4) Common Knowledge.
— Earth Summit: Conversations with Architects of an Ecologically Sustainable Future. 263p. 1991. pap. 9.95 (0-943004-06-3) Common Knowledge.
— Eco-Pioneers: Practical Visionaries Solving Today's Environmental Problems. LC 97-8333. (Illus.). 440p. 1997. 29.95 (0-262-12207-3) MIT Pr.
— Eco-Pioneers: Practical Visionaries Solving Today's Environmental Problems. (Illus.). 480p. 1998. pap. text 15.00 (0-262-62124-X) MIT Pr.
— The Good News about Juvenile Justice: The Movement Away from Large Institutions & Toward Community-Based Services. 128p. 1990. pap. 5.95 (0-943004-05-5) Common Knowledge.

Lerner, Stewart M., jt. auth. see Paterson, Lee T.

***Lerner, Vladimir S.** Information Systems Analysis & Modeling. LC 99-48108. (International Series In Engineering & Computer Science). 1999. write for info. (0-7923-8683-3) Kluwer Academic.

Lerner, Wayne M., ed. Anatomy of a Merger: BJC Health System. LC 96-37336. 1997. pap. 44.00 (1-56793-052-2) Health Admin Pr.

Lerner, William D. & Barr, Marjorie A. Handbook of Hospital Based Substance Abuse Treatment. (Illus.). 256p. 1990. 50.00 (0-08-036077-7, Pub. by PPI); pap. 25.00 (0-08-036076-9, Pub. by PPI) McGraw.

Lerner, William J. The Irwin Directory of Emerging Market Brokers. LC 96-3989. (Illus.). 341p. 1996. 65.00 (0-7863-0719-6, Irwn Prfssnl) McGraw-Hill Prof.

Lernet-Holenia, Alexander. Baron Bagge & Count Luna. Winston, Richard et al, trs. from GER. LC 88-80805. 256p. 1988. pap. 14.00 (0-941419-21-5, Eridanos Library) Marsilio Pubs.
— The Resurrection of Maltravers. Neugroschel, Joachim, tr. from GER. LC 88-80806. 246p. 1989. pap. 14.00 (0-941419-23-1, Eridanos Library) Marsilio Pubs.

Lernhilfen, Mentor. Bausteine U Spielregeln Unserer Sprache. (GER.). 21.00 (3-580-64150-6) Langenscheidt.
— Den Haufigsten Fehlern Auf der Spur. (GER.). 19.25 (3-580-64180-8) Langenscheidt.
— Horen., Verstehen, Richtig Schreiben. (GER.). 17.50 (3-580-64130-1) Langenscheidt.
— In 33 Tagen Durch das Land Fehlerlos. (GER.). 21.00 (3-580-64100-X) Langenscheidt.
— In 33 Tagen Wort-und Satzbaumeister. (GER.). 21.00 (3-580-64110-7) Langenscheidt.
— Richtig Schreiben Leicht Gelemt. (GER.). 21.00 (3-580-64120-4) Langenscheidt.
— Satze, Geschichten, Aufsatze. (GER.). 17.50 (3-580-64090-9) Langenscheidt.
— Vorsicht Fehler! Deutsch. (GER.). 1993. 21.95 (3-580-64070-4) Langenscheidt.

Lernout, Geert. The French Joyce. 308p. (C). 1992. pap. text 19.95 (0-472-08180-2, 08180) U of Mich Pr.
— The Poet As Thinker: Holderlin in France. (COMLIT Ser.). xii, 138p. 1994. 60.00 (1-879751-98-4) Camden Hse.

Lernoux, Penny. Hearts on Fire, 1993: The Story of the Maryknoll Sisters. LC 93-36831. 328p. 1995. pap. 23.00 (1-57075-019-X) Orbis Bks.

Leroe, E. W. Nasty the Snowman. LC 96-7434. (Friendly Corners Ser.: Vol. 4). (Illus.). 128p. (J). (gr. 3-7). 1996. pap. 3.95 (0-7868-1098-X, Pub. by Hyprn Ppbks) Little.
— Pizza Zombies. LC 95-45998. (Friendly Corners Ser.: No. 2). (Illus.). 128p. (J). (gr. 4-7). 1996. pap. 3.95 (0-7868-1096-3, Pub. by Hyprn Ppbks) Little.
— Revenge of the Hairy Horror. LC 96-4318. (Friendly Corners Ser.: No. 3). (Illus.). 128p. (J). (gr. 3-7). 1996. pap. 3.95 (0-7868-1097-1, Pub. by Hyprn Ppbks) Little.

***Leroe, Ellen.** Disaster! 144p. (J). (gr. 3-7). 2000. 15.99 (0-7868-0544-7, Pub. by Hyprn Child) Time Warner.
— Disaster! Three Real - Life Stories of Survival. 2000. 16.49 (0-7868-2474-3) Hyperion.

Leroe, Ellen. Ghost Dog. LC 92-72020. (Illus.). 64p. (J). (gr. 2-5). 1993. 12.95 (1-56282-268-3, Pub. by Hyprn Child) Time Warner.
— Ghost Dog. LC 92-72020. 1994. 8.15 (0-606-06407-9, Pub. by Turtleback) Demco.
— Have a Heart, Cupid. (J). 1987. mass mkt. 3.95 (0-553-16800-2) BDD Bks Young Read.
— Have a Heart, Cupid Delaney. 160p. (J). (gr. 5 up). 1988. mass mkt. 2.95 (0-553-27002-8, Starfire BDD) BDD Bks Young Read.
— Heebie Jeebies at H.O.W.L. High. MacDonald, Patricia, ed. 144p. (J). (gr. 3-6). 1992. per. 2.99 (0-671-75415-7, Minstrel Bks) PB.
— H.O.W.L. High, No. 1. MacDonald, Patricia, ed. 144p. (J). (gr. 4-7). 1991. pap. 2.95 (0-671-68568-6, Minstrel Bks) PB.
— H.O.W.L. High Goes Bats. MacDonald, Patricia, ed. 144p. (Orig.). (YA). 1993. per. 2.99 (0-671-79838-3, Minstrel Bks) PB.
— Racetrack Robbery. LC 95-8912. (Illus.). 64p. (J). (gr. 2-4). 1996. 13.95 (0-7868-0093-3, Pub. by Hyprn Child) Little.
— Racetrack Robbery. LC 95-8912. (Illus.). 64p. (J). (gr. 2-4). 1996. pap. 3.95 (0-7868-1092-0, Pub. by Hyprn Ppbks) Little.
— Robot Raiders. LC 86-45782. 192p. (J). (gr. 6-9). 1987. 11.95 (0-06-023835-6) HarpC Child Bks.
— Single Bed Blues. Fitzgerald, Elisa B., ed. LC 81-23307. 72p. 1981. pap. 5.95 (0-913024-12-0) Tandem Pr.

Leroe, Ellen W. Monster Vision. LC 95-45994. (F(r)iendly Corners Ser.: Vol. 1). (Illus.). 128p. (J). (gr. 4-7). 1996. pap. 3.95 (0-7868-1095-5, Pub. by Hyprn Ppbks) Little.

Leroi & Gibrat. Pinocchia. (Illus.). 50p. 1996. pap. 11.95 (1-56163-169-8, Eurotica) NBM.

Leroi, A. The Cell, the Human Organism & Cancer. 1973. lib. bdg. 79.95 (0-87968-538-7) Krishna Pr.

Leroi-Gourham, Andre. Gesture & Speech. Berger, Anna B., tr. (October Bks.). (Illus.). 360p. 1993. 49.50 (0-262-12173-5) MIT Pr.

Leroi-Gourhan, Andre. Dictionnaire de la Prehistoire. (FRE.). 1288p. 1994. 295.00 (0-7859-9267-7) Fr & Eur.

Leroi, Rita. An Anthroposophical Approach to Cancer. 45p. (Orig.). 1982. pap. 5.50 (0-936132-21-3) Merc Pr NY.

LeRoith, D. & Raizada, M. K. Current Directions in Insulin-Like Growth Factor Research. LC 93-46649. (Advances in Experimental Medicine & Biology Ser.: Vol. 343). (Illus.). 430p. (C). 1994. text 130.00 (0-306-44622-7, Kluwer Plenum) Kluwer Academic.

LeRoith, D., jt. ed. see Raizada, Mohan K.

LeRoith, Derek. Insulin-Like Growth Factors: Molecular & Cellular Aspects. (Illus.). 305p. 1991. lib. bdg. 219.00 (0-8493-5712-8, QP552) CRC Pr.

LeRoith, Derek, ed. Advances in Molecular & Cellular Endocrinology, Vol. 1. 286p. 1997. 128.50 (0-7623-0158-9) Jai Pr.
— Advances in Molecular & Cellular Endocrinology, Vol. 2. 216p. 1998. 128.50 (0-7623-0292-5) Jai Pr.

LeRoith, Derek, et al, eds. Diabetes Mellitus. LC 96-10271. 896p. 1996. text 209.00 (0-397-51456-5) Lppncott W & W.
— Purification of Fermentation Products: Applications to Large-Scale Processes. LC 84-24316. (ACS Symposium Ser.: No. 271). 198p. 1985. lib. bdg. 49.95 (0-8412-0890-5) Am Chemical.
— Purification of Fermentation Products: Applications to Large-Scale Processes - Based on a Symposium Sponsored by the Division of Microbial & Biochemical Technology. LC 84-24316. (ACS Symposium Ser.: No. 271). 208p. reprint ed. pap. 64.50 (0-7837-1966-3, 205244400001) Bks Demand.

LeRoith, Derek & Bondy, Carolyn, eds. Growth Factors & Cytokines in Health & Disease Vols. 2A & 2B: Cytokines. 864p. 1997. 257.00 (0-7623-0117-1) Jai Pr.
— Growth Factors & Cytokines in Health & Disease Vols. 3A & 3B: Systems. 568p. 1997. 257.00 (0-7623-0118-X) Jai Pr.

LeRoith, Derek, et al. Diabetes Mellitus: A Fundamental & Clinical Text. 2nd ed. 1072p. text 225.00 (0-7817-2058-3) Lppncott W & W.

LeRoith, Derek, jt. ed. see Draznin, Boris.

Leron, Uri, jt. auth. see Dubinsky, E.

Leron, Uri, jt. auth. see Dubinsky, Ed.

Lerond, A. Dictionnaire de la Prononciation.Tr. of Pronounciation Dictionary. (FRE.). 589p. 1980. 45.00 (0-8288-1943-2, M9124) Fr & Eur.

LeRoque, Ellen E. A Tale of a Teddy Bear. (Illus.). 28p. (Orig.). (J). (ps-2). 1985. pap. 3.95 (0-932967-03-5) Pacific Shoreline.

Leroque, Noel C. Martin Luther's Friends. 1997. pap. text 18.95 (1-57736-022-2) Providence Hse.

***Leroque, Noel C.** Paul Confronts the World Again: The Apostle's Voice in Augustine, Luther, Wesley & Barth. LC 99-65172. 192p. 1999. pap. 18.95 (1-57736-153-9) Providence Hse.

LeRose, Joanne, ed. see Gerdeman, Jim.

LeRossignol, James E. The Habitant-Merchant. LC 70-167461. (Short Story Index Reprint Ser.). (Illus.). 1977. reprint ed. 23.95 (0-8369-3987-5) Ayer.

Lerot, Jacques. Analyse Grammaticale. (FRE.). 130p. lib. bdg. 24.95 (0-8288-3324-9, 2801106100) Fr & Eur.

LeRougetel, Hazel. The Chelsea Gardener: Philip Miller, 1691-1771. 2nd ed. (Illus.). 228p. 1990. 29.95 (0-88192-176-9) Timber.

Leroux, Gaston. The Bride of the Sun. Reginald, R. & Melville, Douglas, eds. LC 78-84248. (Lost Race & Adult Fantasy Ser.). 1978. reprint ed. lib. bdg. 26.95 (0-405-10994-6) Ayer.

An Asterisk (*) at the beginning of an entry indicates that the title is appearing for the first time.

— Le Fantome De l'Opera.Tr. of Phantom of the Opera. (FRE., Illus.). 152p. 1994. pap. 9.95 (*0-8442-1233-4*, 12334, Natl Textbk Co) NTC Contemp Pub Co.

***Leroux, Gaston.** The Mystery of the Yellow Room, Set. unabridged ed. 1999. 35.95 incl. audio (*1-55685-594-X*) Audio Bk Con.

Leroux, Gaston. The Mystery of the Yellow Room: Extraordinary Adventures of Joseph Rouletabille, Reporter. 1992. lib. bdg. 27.95 (*0-89966-141-6*) Buccaneer Bks.

— The Mystery of the Yellow Room: Extraordinary Adventures of Joseph Rouletabille, Reporter. Hale, Terry, ed. (European Classics). 256p. 1997. pap. 11.99 (*1-873982-38-0*, Pub. by Dedalus) Subterranean Co.

— The Mystery of the Yellow Room: Extraordinary Adventures of Joseph Rouletabille, Reporter. LC 75-32762. (Literature of Mystery & Detection Ser.). 1976. reprint ed. 33.95 (*0-405-07883-8*) Ayer.

— The Perfume of the Lady in Black. 1975. lib. bdg. 16.70 (*0-89966-138-6*) Buccaneer Bks.

— The Perfume of the Lady in Black. Hale, Terry, ed. Anon, tr. from FRE. (Dedalus European Classics Ser.). 326p. 1998. pap. 13.99 (*1-873982-98-4*, Pub. by Dedalus) Subterranean Co.

***Leroux, Gaston.** The Perfume of the Lady in Black, Set. unabridged ed. 1998. 47.95 incl. audio (*1-55685-589-3*) Audio Bk Con.

Leroux, Gaston. The Phantom of the Opera. Date not set. lib. bdg. 26.95 (*0-8488-1652-8*) Amereon Ltd.

— The Phantom of the Opera. 288p. 1990. mass mkt. 4.95 (*0-553-21376-8*) Bantam.

— The Phantom of the Opera. 1975. lib. bdg. 28.95 (*0-89966-136-X*) Buccaneer Bks.

— The Phantom of the Opera. (Signet Classics Ser.). 1989. mass mkt. 4.95 (*0-451-52482-9*, Sig Classics) NAL.

— The Phantom of the Opera. (Classics for Young Readers Ser.). (Illus.). 352p. (YA). (gr. 5 up). 1994. pap. 3.99 (*0-14-036813-2*, PuffinBks) Peng Put Young Read.

— The Phantom of the Opera. LC 88-34079. (Bullseye Chillers Ser.). (Illus.). 96p. (J). (gr. 3-7). 1989. pap. 3.99 (*0-394-83847-5*, Pub. by Random Bks Yng Read) Random.

— The Phantom of the Opera. 1938. 10.60 (*0-606-03258-4*, Pub. by Turtleback) Demco.

— The Phantom of the Opera. 1995. mass mkt. 5.95 (*0-352-31716-7*, Pub. by Virgin Bks) London Brdge.

— The Phantom of the Opera. 272p. 1986. mass mkt. 5.99 (*0-446-30120-5*) Warner Bks.

— The Phantom of the Opera. (Classics Library). 224p. 1998. pap. 3.95 (*1-85326-273-0*, 2730WW, Pub. by Wrdsworth Edits) NTC Contemp Pub Co.

— The Phantom of the Opera. abr. ed. Bair, Lowell, tr. LC 98-8845. 336p. (YA). 1998. mass mkt. 3.99 (*0-440-22774-7*) BDD Bks Young Read.

— The Phantom of the Opera. large type ed. (Large Print Heritage Ser.). 420p. (J). (gr. 7-12). 1999. lib. bdg. 35.95 (*1-58118-043-8*, 22512) LRS.

***Leroux, Gaston.** The Phantom of the Opera: Abraham,&F. Murray, Set. abr. ed. 1998. audio 18.00 (*0-89845-776-9*, CPN 2108) HarperAudio.

Leroux, Gaston. The Phantom of the Opera: The Original Novel. LC 87-45635. 368p. 1988. reprint ed. mass mkt. 7.00 (*0-06-080924-8*, PL-7140, Perennial) HarperTrade.

— The Phantom of the Opera, the Play. 1979. pap. 5.50 (*0-87129-363-3*, P45) Dramatic Pub.

— The Secret of the Night. 1975. lib. bdg. 16.70 (*0-89966-139-4*) Buccaneer Bks.

Leroux, Jean-Francois. Cistercian Abbeys: History & Architecture. (Illus.). 400p. 1998. 39.95 (*3-89508-894-3*, 520586) Konemann.

Leroux, Marcel. Dynamic Analysis of Weather & Climate: Atmospheric Circulation, Perturbations, Climatic Evolution. LC 98-3120. (Atmospheric Physics & Climatology Ser.). 376p. 1998. 165.00 (*0-471-98291-1*) Wiley.

Leroux, Marine, jt. auth. see Dell, Thomas R.

Leroux, Marine, jt. auth. see Dell, Tom.

Leroux, Michele. Instant Visual Basic Animation. LC 96-60774. 1996. pap. 34.95 incl. cd-rom (*1-874416-78-8*) Wrox Pr Inc.

Leroux, Odette, ed. Inuit Women Artists. (Illus.). 256p. 1995. text 32.00 (*976-641-012-7*) Gordon & Breach.

Leroux, Pierre. Encyclopedie Nouvelle ou Dictionnaire Philosophique, Scientifique, Litteraire et Industriel, Offrant le Tableaux des Connaissances Humaines au XIXe Siecle, 6 vols. (FRE.). 5060p. 1991. pap. 3850.00 (*0-7859-7713-9*, 2051011664) Fr & Eur.

Leroux, Pierre, jt. ed. see Labelle, G.

Leroy, Andre L. David Hume. Mayer, J. P., ed. LC 78-67413. (European Political Thought Ser.). (FRE.). 1980. reprint ed. lib. bdg. 28.95 (*0-405-11713-2*) Ayer.

Leroy, Annick M., jt. auth. see Rousseeuw, Peter J.

Leroy, Beatrice. Le Royaume de Navarre a la Fin du Moyen Age: Gouvernement et Societe. (Collected Studies: No. CS 335). (FRE.). 320p. 1991. text 109.95 (*0-86078-284-0*, Pub. by Variorum) Ashgate Pub Co.

Leroy-Beaulieu, Anatole. Empire of the Tsars & the Russians, 3 vols., Set. Ragozin, Zenaide A., tr. LC 70-86377. reprint ed. 265.00 (*0-404-03990-1*) AMS Pr.

— Israel among the Nations: A Study of the Jews & Antisemitism. Hellman, Frances, tr. from FRE. LC 74-27996. (Modern Jewish Experience Ser.). (ENG.). 1975. reprint ed. 35.95 (*0-405-06723-2*) Ayer.

LeRoy, Bernard. Dictionnaire Encyclopedique des Sports, des Sportifs et des Performances. (FRE.). 864p. 1973. 135.00 (*0-8288-6266-4*, M-6353) Fr & Eur.

LeRoy, Bridget & Clavin, Tom. We're Not Normal! (Illus.). 176p. 1997. pap. 10.00 (*0-9659103-0-X*) IndyBooks.

Leroy, Catherine, jt. auth. see Clifton, Tony.

LeRoy, Clarice, ed. see Schumacher, Claire W.

Leroy, Claude E., et al. Portugues Para Principiantes. (POR., Illus.). xii, 422p. (C). 1993. text 18.00 (*0-9636612-0-5*) U WI Dept Span.

LeRoy, D. O., jt. auth. see LeRoy, L. W.

LeRoy, D. O., jt. ed. see LeRoy, L. W.

LeRoy, Douglas. Basic Bible Study. LC 78-65822. 72p. (Orig.). 1983. pap. text 1.29 (*0-87148-699-7*) Pathway Pr.

Leroy, F., ed. Blastocyst-Endometrium Relationships. (Progress in Reproductive Biology & Medicine Ser.: Vol. 7). (Illus.). 338p. 1980. 172.25 (*3-8055-0988-X*) S Karger.

Leroy, Fabrice, jt. auth. see Berg, R. J.

LeRoy, Gaylord C. & Beitz, Ursula. Preserve & Create: Essays in Marxist Literary Criticism. LC 72-75793. (AIMS Monogram Ser.: No. 4). iv, 276p. 1973. write for info. (*0-391-00233-3*) Humanities.

LeRoy, Gen. Not Waving . . . LC 98-228482. 1998. pap. 5.25 (*0-8222-1612-4*) Dramatists Play.

LeRoy, Gene, ed. see Schumacher, Claire W.

LeRoy, Greg. Between the Beholders: A Two Wheeled Tramp Around the World. (Illus.). 184p. 1998. pap. text 10.00 (*0-945210-15-9*) Public Search.

— Pantex Plant: Practices, Policy, & the Environmental Impact of the Final Assembly Point. rev. ed. (Illus.). 35p. 1996. pap. text 4.00 (*0-945210-00-0*) Public Search.

— Research Centers: The Pentagon Moves the High-Tech Battlefield on Campus. rev. ed. (Illus.). 22p. (Orig.). 1996. pap. text 3.00 (*0-945210-01-9*) Public Search.

***Leroy, J. T.** Sarah. 160p. 2000. pap. 19.95 (*1-58234-076-5*) Bloomsbury Pubg.

Leroy, Jackson, see Thomas, J. L., pseud.

Leroy, Jacques D., ed. see Sainte-Beuve, Charles-Augustin.

Leroy, Jacques L., jt. ed. see Pagel, Maurice.

***Leroy, Jean-Louis.** La Polarisation de la Lumiere et L'observation Astronomique. 212p. 1998. text 70.00 (*90-5699-110-8*, Harwood Acad Pubs); pap. text 30.00 (*90-5699-111-6*, Harwood Acad Pubs) Gordon & Breach.

Leroy, Jeremy. Angel Tears. 1999. 22.00 (*0-609-60157-1*) C Potter.

Leroy, Jules, tr. see Cartan, Elie.

LeRoy, L. David. Biography of Gerald R. Ford. 1974. 4.75 (*0-87948-036-X*) Beatty.

LeRoy, L. W. & Finney, J. J. Fading Shadows. LC 73-620142. 182p. 1999. pap. 5.00 (*0-87108-900-9*) Colo Sch Mines.

LeRoy, L. W. & LeRoy, D. O. Red Rocks Park: Geology & Flowers. LC 78-15784. 29p. 1978. pap. 3.00 (*0-918062-02-0*) Colo Sch Mines.

LeRoy, L. W. & LeRoy, D. O., eds. Subsurface Geology: Petroleum, Mining, Construction. 4th ed. LC 76-51265. 941p. 1977. 21.00 (*0-918062-00-4*) Colo Sch Mines.

Leroy, L. W. & Weimer, Robert J. Professional Contributions, No. 7. 1984. pap. 2.00 (*0-685-09169-4*) Colo Sch Mines.

Leroy, Michael. Comparative Politics: An Introduction Using ExplorIt. 5th ed. (C). 1999. pap. text 18.00 (*0-922914-36-2*) Thomson Learn.

Leroy, O. & Breazeale, M. A., eds. Physical Acoustics: Fundamentals & Applications. (Illus.). 724p. (C). 1991. text 198.00 (*0-306-43883-6*, Kluwer Plenum) Kluwer Academic.

Leroy, P., jt. auth. see Legrand, L.

***Leroy, Peter & Nelissen, Nico.** Social & Political Sciences of the Environment: Three Decades of Research in the Netherlands. 112p. 2000. pap. 12.00 (*90-5727-031-5*, Pub. by Intl Bks) Paul & Co Pubs.

Leroy, R. Supernatural Spine. 1993. pap. text 5.95 (*1-878209-09-4*) Hunter Bks.

***LeRoy, Stephen F. & Werner, Jan.** Principles of Financial Economics. (Illus.). 300p. 2001. write for info. (*0-521-58434-5*); pap. write for info. (*0-521-58605-4*) Cambridge U Pr.

LeRoy, Thomas, jt. auth. see Adams, William D.

Leroy, X., et al, eds. Types in Compilation: Second International Workshop, TIC'98, Kyoto, Japan, March 25-27, 1998, Proceedings, Vol. 147. LC 98-30696. (Lecture Notes in Computer Science Ser.: Vol. 1473). viii, 299p. 1998. pap. 55.00 (*3-540-64925-5*) Spr-Verlag.

Lerrick, Alison, jt. auth. see Mian, Q. Javed.

Lerrigo, Marion O. Health Problem Sources. LC 76-176989. (Columbia University. Teachers College. Contributions to Education Ser.: No. 224). reprint ed. 37.50 (*0-404-55224-2*) AMS Pr.

***Lerron, Bruce.** From Earth Spirits to Sky Gods: The Socioecological Origins of Monotheism, Individualism & Hyper-Abstract Reasoning, from the Stone Age to the Axial Iron Age. LC 99-57664. 352p. 2000. 68.00 (*0-7391-0098-X*) Lxngtn Bks.

Lersch, Laurenz. Die Griechischs-Romische Biographie Nach Ihrer Literarischen Form, 3 vols. in 1. (GER.). xxii, 701p. 1971. reprint ed. write for info. (*0-318-70778-0*) G Olms Pubs.

Lerski & Morley. Ultrasound Eighty-Two. (Ultrasound in Medicine & Biology). 1983. pap. 8.65 (*0-08-030769-8*, Pergamon Pr) Elsevier.

Lerskl, George J. Historical Dictionary of Poland, 966-1945. LC 94-46940. 784p. 1996. lib. bdg. 135.00 (*0-313-26007-9*, Greenwood Pr) Greenwood.

Lerski, George J., ed. Herbert Hoover & Poland: A Documentary History of a Friendship. LC 77-72051. (Publication Ser.: No. 174). (Illus.). 124p. 1977. 4.38 (*0-8179-6741-9*) Hoover Inst Pr.

Lerski, George J. & Lerski, Halina T., compiled by. Jewish-Polish Co-Existence, 1772 to 1939: A Topical Bibliography, 5. LC 86-12119. (Bibliographies & Indexes in World History Ser.: No. 5). 244p. 1986. lib. bdg. 55.00 (*0-313-24758-7*, LJP/) Greenwood.

Lerski, Halina T., jt. compiled by see Lerski, George J.

Lerstrom, Kirsten, jt. auth. see Bernsen, Jens.

Lertz, Laurie, ed. see De'Medici, Lorenza.

Lerud, Joan V., ed. see Geoscience Information Society Meeting Staff.

Lerude, Warren, jt. auth. see Merriman, Marion.

***Lerup, Lars.** After the City. LC 99-56867. (Illus.). 216p. 2000. 24.95 (*0-262-12224-3*) MIT Pr.

Lerup, Lars. Building the Unfinished: Architecture & Human Action. LC 77-12370. (Sage Library of Social Research: No. 53). (Illus.). 171p. reprint ed. pap. 53.10 (*0-8357-8447-9*, 203471100091) Bks Demand.

— Planned Assaults: The No Family House, Love-House, Texas Zero. (Illus.). 112p. (Orig.). 1987. 35.00 (*0-262-12123-9*) MIT Pr.

Lerup, Lars & Farokhi, Sohela. Room. LC 99-61006. (Illus.). 64p. (C). 1999. pap. 15.00 (*0-939594-48-X*, Pub. by Menil Found) RAM Publications.

Lerup, Lars, et al. Martin Wagner: Urban Projects in Rural Contexts 1988-1993.Tr. of Urbane Provekte Im Landlichen Umfeld 1988-1993. (Illus.). 120p. 1996. 50.00 (*0-9651144-0-6*) W K Stout.

Leruste, C., jt. auth. see Karoubi, M.

Lervik, Leif Magne, jt. ed. see Moen, Ole O.

Lerwick, Alan. The Kilted Fiddler: A Collection of 167 Scottish Fiddle Tunes. (Illus.). 208p. (Orig.). 1996. pap. 19.95 (*1-57424-029-3*) Centerstream Pub.

Lerwick, R. W. The Pipemajor's Handbook: How to Tune, Maintain, & Set up a Band for Competition. 2nd rev. ed. Croft, Joseph & Croft, Ceilidh, eds. LC 98-60286. (Illus.). 144p. 1998. pap. text 19.95 (*0-9663321-2-1*) Shetland Piper.

— The Zerland Tunebook, Vol. 1. Croft, Ceilidh & Croft, Joseph, eds. 77p. 1998. pap. 14.95 (*0-9663321-1-3*) Shetland Piper.

Lerzundi, Patricio C., ed. see Lihn, Enrique.

Les Benedict, Michael. The Blessings of Liberty: A Concise History of the Constitution of the United States. 389p. (C). 1996. pap. text 24.76 (*0-669-35290-X*) HM Trade Div.

***Les Benedict, Michael.** The Impeachment & Trial of Andrew Johnson. 224p. 1999. pap. 12.95 (*0-393-31982-2*) Norton.

Les Benedict, Michael, ed. Sources in American Constitutional History. 330p. (C). 1996. pap. text 24.76 (*0-669-39471-8*) HM Trade Div.

Les, M., jt. auth. see Hudgeons.

Les Strang, Jacques. Cargo Carriers of the Great Lakes. 3rd ed. (Illus.). 193p. 1985. reprint ed. pap. 15.00 (*0-937360-06-6*) Harbor Hse MI.

Lesaffre, Gulhelm. Collins Watch Guide: Wildlife of the Town. (Illus.). 1997. pap. 11.95 (*0-00-220091-0*, Pub. by HarpC) Trafalgar.

Lesage, Alain-Rene. Histoire de Gil Blas de Santillane, 2 tomes, Set. Bardon, ed. (Coll. Prestige). 99.95 (*0-685-34040-6*) Fr & Eur.

— Turcaret. pap. 4.95 (*0-685-11607-7*) Fr & Eur.

LeSage, Joan & Barhyte, Diana Y. Nursing Quality Assurance in Long-Term Care. 288p. 1989. 58.00 (*0-8342-0066-X*, 20066) Aspen Pub.

Lesage, Julia, jt. auth. see Kintz, Linda.

LeSage, L. G., ed. see Sarkisov, A. A.

Lesage, Suzanne & Jackson, Richard E., eds. Groundwater Contamination & Analysis at Hazardous Waste Sites. LC 92-20758. (Environmental Science & Pollution Control Ser.: Vol. 4). (Illus.). 552p. 1992. text 230.00 (*0-8247-8720-X*) Dekker.

Lesak, Anne E., jt. auth. see Donnersberger, Anne B.

Lesak, David M. Hazardous Materials: Strategies & Tactics. LC 98-18780. 496p. 1998. 74.00 (*0-8359-5209-6*) P-H.

LeSaux, Francoise, ed. The Text & Tradition of Layamon's Brut. LC 94-10443. (Arthurian Studies: No. XXXIII). (Illus.). 284p. (C). 1994. 75.00 (*0-85991-417-7*, DS Brewer) Boydell & Brewer.

LeSaux, Francoise H., ed. Cultural Intermediaries in Medieval Britain: Collected Essays. LC 94-37245. 212p. 1995. text 89.95 (*0-7734-9119-8*) E Mellen.

Lesavoy, Malcolm A., jt. auth. see Meals, Roy A.

Lesbaupin, Ivo. Blessed Are the Persecuted: Christian Life in the Roman Empire, A.D. 64-313. Barr, Robert R., tr. from POR. LC 87-5746.Tr. of A Bem-Aventuranca da Persecucion & La Bienaventuranza de la Persecucion. 112p. (Orig.). reprint ed. pap. 34.80 (*0-8357-2682-7*, 204021800015) Bks Demand.

Lesbia de Varona, Ana R., jt. ed. see Martin, Rita.

Lesbian & Gay Community Services, National Museum & Program of the Lesbian & Gay Community Community S. The Lesbian Almanac: The Most Comprehensive Reference Source Available. 534p. 1996. pap. 16.95 (*0-425-15301-0*) Berkley Pub.

Lesbian Writing & Publishing Collective Staff, ed. Dykeversions: Lesbian Short Fiction. 186p. reprint ed. pap. 9.95 (*0-88961-110-6*, Pub. by Womens Pr) LPC InBook.

— Dykewords: An Anthology of Lesbian Writing. 268p. pap. 9.95 (*0-88961-149-1*, Pub. by Womens Pr) LPC InBook.

Lesbirel, S. Hayden. Nimby Politics in Japan: Energy Sitting & the Management of Environmental Conflict. LC 98-38148. (Illus.). 187p. 1999. 33.95 (*0-8014-3537-4*) Cornell U Pr.

Lescanne, P., ed. Rewriting Techniques & Applications. (Lecture Notes in Computer Science Ser.: Vol. 256). vi, 285p. 1987. 36.00 (*0-387-17220-3*) Spr-Verlag.

Lescarbot, Marc. History of New France, 3 vols., Vol. 1. LC 68-28596. 331p. 1969. reprint ed. lib. bdg. 65.00 (*0-8371-5039-6*, LHFA) Greenwood.

— History of New France, 3 vols., Vol. 7. LC 68-28596. 584p. 1969. reprint ed. lib. bdg. 75.00 (*0-8371-5040-X*, LHFB) Greenwood.

— History of New France, 3 vols., Vol. 11. LC 68-28596. 555p. 1969. reprint ed. lib. bdg. 75.00 (*0-8371-5041-8*, LHFC) Greenwood.

— Nova Francia, or the Description of That Part of New France, Which Is One Continent with Virginia. Erondelle, Pierre E., tr. LC 77-7415. (English Experience Ser.: No. 877). 1977. reprint ed. lib. bdg. 31.00 (*90-221-0877-5*) Walter J Johnson.

Lescarboura, Austin C. Behind the Motion-Picture Screen. LC 75-174878. (Illus.). 1972. reprint ed. 30.95 (*0-405-08742-X*, Pub. by Blom Pubns) Ayer.

Lescault, Anthoni M., ed. Problemas Sexuales del Hombre. deluxe ed. (SPA., Illus.). 192p. 1999. pap. 5.95 (*0-939193-29-9*) Edit Concepts.

Lescault, Anthonii M., ed. Conflictos Conyugales. deluxe ed. (SPA., Illus.). 1998. pap. 5.95 (*0-939193-38-8*) Edit Concepts.

Lesce, Tony. Secrets of Successful Job Hunting: Surefire Tactics for Finding Hidden Jobs, Writing Effective Resumes, Handling Tough Interviews, & Beating Chemical & Psychological Tests. (Illus.). 104p. 1994. pap. 14.00 (*0-87364-776-9*) Paladin Pr.

— The Shotgun in Combat. (Illus.). 152p. 1984. pap. 14.00 (*0-87364-314-3*) Paladin Pr.

— They're Watching You: The Age of Surveillance. 1998. pap. text 12.95 (*0-9666932-2-1*) Breakout Prods Inc.

Lesce, Tony, jt. auth. see Cheek, John C.

Lesce, Tony, jt. auth. see Turner, Donald M.

Lescelius, Robert H. Lordship Salvation: Some Crucial Questions & Answers. 1992. pap. 6.99 (*1-56632-001-1*) Revival Lit.

Lescelius, Robert H. The Spirit Directed Life: The Spirit's Leadership into Christ's Life, Service & Warfare. 114p. 1981. pap. 4.99 (*1-56632-095-X*) Revival Lit.

Lescelius, Robert H. What Is God Like? The Biblical God for Contemporary Man. (Roadbuilding for Revival Ser.). 26p. (Orig.). 1996. pap. 1.99 (*1-56632-100-X*) Revival Lit.

Lesch, Ann, jt. auth. see Wondu, Steven.

Lesch, Ann M. Israel, Egypt, & the Palestinians: From Camp David to Intifada. LC 88-45448. (Indiana Series in Arab & Islamic Studies). (Illus.). 314p. 1989. reprint ed. pap. 97.40 (*0-7837-9657-9*, 205929000005) Bks Demand.

— Transition to Palestinian Self-Government: Practical Steps Toward Israeli-Palestinian Peace. (Illus.). 160p. (C). 1992. 29.95 (*0-253-33326-1*, MB-794); pap. 11.95 (*0-253-20794-0*) Ind U Pr.

Lesch, Ann M. & Tschirgi, Dan. Origins & Development of the Arab-Israeli Conflict. LC 97-49481. 240p. 1998. 39.95 (*0-313-29970-6*) Greenwood.

Lesch, Barry M. & Pettibone, James P. Meeting Statutory Deadlines: Workers' Compensation - Action Guide - Summer 1996. Tindel, Kay E., ed. 96p. 1996. pap. 58.00 (*0-7626-0024-1*, WC-11403) Cont Ed Bar-CA.

Lesch, Christiane. A Farmyard Morning. Lawson, Polly, tr. from GER. (Illus.). 24p. (J). (ps). 1990. reprint ed. lib. bdg. 12.95 (*0-86315-117-5*, Pub. by Floris Bks) Gryphon Hse.

Lesch, David W., ed. The Middle East & the United States: A Historical & Political Reassessment. 460p. (C). 1996. pap. 32.00 (*0-8133-2405-X*, Pub. by Westview) HarpC.

— The Middle East & the United States: A Historical & Political Reassessment. 2nd ed. LC 98-40724. 496p. (C). 1999. pap. 32.00 (*0-8133-3559-0*, Pub. by Westview) HarpC.

Lesch, Harald, et al, eds. The Physics of Galactic Halos. 324p. 1997. 175.00 (*3-527-40111-3*) Wiley.

Lesch, Harald & Dettmar, Ralf J., eds. The Physics of Galactic Halos: Proceedings of the 156th WE-Heraeus Seminar, Bad Honnef, Germany, February 1996. LC 97-175783. 324p. 1997. 125.00 (*3-05-501752-8*, Wiley-VCH) Wiley.

Lesch, William C. & Rupert, David. New Product Screening: A Step-Wise Approach. LC 93-15579. (Illus.). 116p. 1994. lib. bdg. 39.95 (*1-56024-404-6*) Haworth Pr.

LeSchack, Leonard A., jt. auth. see Leary, William M.

Leschak, Peter M. The Bear Guardian. LC 90-47257. (Illus.). 184p. 1990. pap. 9.95 (*0-87839-061-8*) North Star.

— Bumming with the Furies: Out on the Trail of Experience. LC 93-7993. (Illus.). 1993. pap. 12.95 (*0-87839-078-2*) North Star.

— Hellroaring: The Life & Time of a Fire Bum. (Illus.). 240p. 1994. pap. 14.95 (*0-87839-087-1*) North Star.

— Letters from Side Lake: A Chronicle of Life in the North Woods. LC 92-8713. 208p. 1992. pap. 14.95 (*0-8166-2243-4*) U of Minn Pr.

***Leschak, Peter M.** Rogues & Toads: A Poetry Collection. (Illus.). 64p. 1999. pap. 9.95 (*0-87839-117-7*) North Star.

Leschak, Peter M. Seeing the Raven. 208p. 1999. pap. 14.95 (*0-8166-2430-5*, Pub. by U of Minn Pr) Chicago Distribution Ctr.

— Seeing the Raven: A Narrative of Renewal. LC 93-27943. 1994. 18.95 (*0-8166-2429-1*) U of Minn Pr.

— The Snow Lotus: Exploring the Eternal Moment. LC 95-52674. (C). 1996. 18.95 (*0-8166-2820-3*) U of Minn Pr.

***Leschak, Peter M.** Trials by Wildfire: In Search of the New Warrior Spirit. LC 99-6690. 192p. 1999. pap. 14.95 (*1-57025-198-3*) Pfeifer-Hamilton.

Leschen, Ann. Comp. Skills - Reading. Tindale, Judy, ed. 1982. 4.95 (*1-55708-198-0*, MCR861) McDonald Pub Co.

— Poetry. 1981. 4.95 (*1-55708-233-2*, MCR243) McDonald Pub Co.

Leschen, Ann & Tisdale, Judy. Comp. Skills - Math. 1982. 4.95 (*1-55708-231-6*, MCR863) McDonald Pub Co.

Leschen, Ann & Witcher, Marie. Comp. & Speed-Book B. Allen, Yvonne, ed. 1979. 4.95 (*1-55708-170-0*, MCR253) McDonald Pub Co.

— Study Skills-Book A. Allen, Yvonne, ed. 1977. 4.95 (*1-55708-171-9*, R255) McDonald Pub Co.

An Asterisk (*) at the beginning of an entry indicates that the title is appearing for the first time.

Leschen, Ann, et al. Comp. & Speed-Book A. Allen, Yvonne, ed. 1979. 4.95 (*1-55708-169-7*, MCR251) McDonald Pub Co.

Leschen, Ann, jt. ed. see Green, Irvin.

Leschen, Anne. Test Taking: Language & Reading. 1980. 4.95 (*1-55708-249-9*, R831) McDonald Pub Co.

Lescher, John F. Online Market Research: Cost-Effective Searching of the Internet & Online Databases. LC 95-4739. 288p. (C). 1995. pap. text 19.95 (*0-201-48929-5*) Addison-Wesley.

Lescher, Marianne L. Portfolios: Assessing Learning in the Primary Grades. LC 95-4295. (What Research Says to the Teacher Ser.). 1995. pap. 5.95 (*0-8106-1094-9*) NEA.

Leschert, Dale F., jt. auth. see National Association of Baptist Professors of Reli.

Leschied, Alan W., et al, eds. Young Offenders Act Revolution: Changing the Face of Canadian Juvenile Justice. 256p. 1991. pap. 24.95 (*0-8020-6714-X*); text 60.00 (*0-8020-2623-0*) U of Toronto Pr.

***Leschinsky, Achim & Mayer, Karl U., eds.** The Comprehensive School Experiment Revisited: Evidence from Western Europe. 2nd enl. ed. LC 99-45996. (Comparative Studies Ser.: Vol. 2). 216p. (C). 1999. pap. text 37.95 (*0-8204-3594-5*) P Lang Pubng.

***Leschinsky, Achim & Mayer, Karl Ulrich, eds.** The Comprehensive School Experiment Revisited: Evidence from Western Europe. 2nd enl. ed. 216p. 1999. pap. 37.95 (*3-631-33297-1*) P Lang Pubng.

Leschmelle, Pierre. Montaigne: or The Anguished Soul. Beck, William J., tr. from FRE. LC 93-46833. (Currents in Comparative Romance Languages & Literatures Ser.: Vol. 29). XVII, 222p. (C). 1994. text 51.95 (*0-8204-2476-5*) P Lang Pubng.

Leschnitzer, Adolf. The Magic Background of Modern Anti-Semitism: An Analysis of the German-Jewish Relationship. LC 55-6501. 246p. reprint ed. pap. 76.30 (*0-608-11737-4*, 201043700070) Bks Demand.

Leschot, Nico J. & Vejerslev, Lars O., eds. Prenatal Diagnosis in Europe Proceedings of an EUCROMC Workshop, Paris, May 1996. (European Journal of Human Genetics Ser.: Vol. 5, Suppl. 1, 1997). (Illus.). iv, 90p. 1997. pap. text 36.50 (*3-8055-6506-2*) S Karger.

Leschziner, M. A., jt. ed. see Ervine, A.

Lescoe, F., ed. see Dennehy, R. & Grisez, G.

Lescoe, F., ed. see Krapiec, Mieczyslaw A.

Lescoe, F., ed. see Lawler, R. & May, W.

Lescoe, F., tr. see Leger, E., et al.

Lescoe, M., tr. see Krapiec, Mieczyslaw A.

Lescohier, Don D. Knights of St. Crispin, 1867 to 1874. LC 77-89748. (American Labor, from Conspiracy to Collective Bargaining Ser., No. 1). 101p. 1974. reprint ed. 17.95 (*0-405-02136-4*) Ayer.

Lescop, Christine. Global Surgery Formula for the Casson-Walker Invariant. (Annals of Mathematics Studies: Vol. 140). 150p. 1996. text 49.50 (*0-691-02133-3*, Pub. by Princeton U Pr); pap. text 19.95 (*0-691-02132-5*, Pub. by Princeton U Pr) Cal Prin Full Svc.

Lescourret, Marie-Anne. Rubens: A Double Life. Powell, Elfreda, tr. from FRE. (Illus.). 304p. 1993. text 27.50 (*1-56663-015-0*) I R Dee.

Lescow, Theodor. Das Stufenschema: Unterschungen zur Struktur Alttestamentlicher Texte. (Beiheft zur Zeitschrift fuer die Alttestamentliche Wissenschaft Ser.: Bd. 211). (GER.). x, 282p. (C). 1992. lib. bdg. 98.50 (*3-11-013768-2*) De Gruyter.

***Lescroart, John.** Nothing But the Truth. 2000. mass mkt. 7.99 (*0-440-22664-3*) Dell.

Lescroart, John T. A Certain Justice. 1996. pap. 6.99 (*0-440-29547-5*) Bantam.

— A Certain Justice. 544p. 1996. mass mkt. 7.50 (*0-440-22104-8*, Island Bks) Dell.

— A Certain Justice. large type ed. 756p. 1996. 25.95 (*0-7838-1565-4*, G K Hall Lrg Type) Mac Lib Ref.

— Dead Irish. 416p. 1990. mass mkt. 7.50 (*0-440-20783-5*) Dell.

— Guilt. 656p. 1998. mass mkt. 6.99 (*0-440-22281-8*) Doubleday.

— Guilt. large type ed. LC 97-29619. (Large Print Book Ser.). 1997. 25.95 (*1-56895-477-8*) Wheeler Pub.

— Hard Evidence. (Northern California Mysteries Ser.). 1994. mass mkt. 5.99 (*0-8041-1275-4*) Ivy Books.

***Lescroart, John T.** The Hearing. LC 00-34119. (Illus.). (YA). 2001. write for info. (*0-525-94575-X*, Dutton Child) Peng Put Young Read.

Lescroart, John T. The Mercy Rule. 640p. 1999. mass mkt. 7.99 (*0-440-22282-6*) Bantam Dell.

— The Mercy Rule. large type ed. 684p. 1999. pap. 26.95 (*0-7838-0394-X*, G K Hall Lrg Type) Mac Lib Ref.

— The Mercy Rule: A Novel. LC 98-16726. 480p. 1998. 24.95 (*0-385-31658-5*) Doubleday.

***Lescroart, John T.** Nothing but the Truth. 1999. mass mkt. 7.50 (*0-440-29574-2*) Bantam Dell.

— Nothing but the Truth. large type ed. LC 99-59449. 2000. 26.95 (*1-56895-813-7*) Wheeler Pub.

— Nothing but the Truth: A Novel. LC 99-32584. 435p. 2000. 24.95 (*0-385-33353-6*) Delacorte.

Lescroart, John T. Son of Holmes & Rasputin's Revenge: The Early Works of John T. Lescroart. 544p. 1995. pap. 16.95 (*1-55611-437-0*, Pub. by D I Fine) Penguin Putnam.

— The 13th Juror: A Novel. 544p. 1995. mass mkt. 7.50 (*0-440-22079-3*, Island Bks) Dell.

— The Vig. 384p. 1991. mass mkt. 7.50 (*0-440-20986-2*) Dell.

Lescroart, Yves, jt. auth. see Faucaon, Regis.

Lescure, Karine & Trintignac, Florence. International Justice for Former Yugoslavia: The Workings of the International Criminal Tribunal of the Hague. LC 96-4889. (Nijhoff Law Specials Ser.: Vol. 20). 1996. pap. 84.00 (*90-411-0201-9*) Kluwer Law Intl.

Lescure, Marc, jt. ed. see Bosch, Thierry.

Lesdain, De, see De Lesdain.

Leseho, Johanna & Howard-Rose, Dawn. Anger in the Classroom: A Practical Guide for Teachers. (Illus.). 96p. (C). 1994. pap. text 14.95 (*1-55059-080-4*) Temeron Bks.

Lesell, Colin. Textbook of Dental Homoeopathy. pap. 29.95 (*0-8464-4494-1*) Beekman Pubs.

— World Traveller's Manual of Homoeopathy. pap. 33.95 (*0-8464-4497-6*) Beekman Pubs.

Lesem, Jeanne. Preserving Today. LC 96-29834. 288p. 1997. pap. 15.95 (*0-8050-4881-2*) H Holt & Co.

Leseman, Paul, jt. ed. see Eldering, Lotty.

Lesemann, D. E., jt. ed. see Mendgen, K.

Lesemann, Frederic. Services & Circuses: Community & the Welfare State. Huston, Lorne & Heap, Margaret, trs. from FRE. Orig. Title: Du Pain et des Services. 277p. 1984. 41.99 (*0-920057-06-3*, Pub. by Black Rose); pap. 12.99 (*0-920057-05-5*, Pub. by Black Rose) Consort Bk Sales.

Leser. Diercke Woerterbuch Allgemeinisches Geographie: A-M, Vol. 1. (GER.). 29.95 (*0-614-00365-2*) Fr & Eur.

— Diercke Woerterbuch Allgemeinisches Geographie: N-Z, Vol. 1. (GER.). 29.95 (*0-614-00366-0*, 3423034181) Fr & Eur.

— Diercke Woerterbuch Umwel Oekologie, Vol. 2. (GER.). 29.95 (*0-614-00367-9*, 3423034203) Fr & Eur.

Leser, C. E. Econometric Techniques & Problems. 2nd ed. 1974. 25.00 (*0-85264-218-0*) Lubrecht & Cramer.

***Leser, David.** The Whites of Their Eyes. 296p. 2000. 19.95 (*1-86508-114-0*, Pub. by Allen & Unwin Pty) Paul & Co Pubs.

Leser, Esther H. Thomas Mann's Short Fiction: An Intellectual Biography. LC 87-45369. 352p. 1989. 47.50 (*0-8386-3319-6*) Fairleigh Dickinson.

Leserman, Lee, jt. auth. see Machy, Patrick.

Lesesne, Tamara S. & Harrill, Helen S. I'm Special: A Program for Third & Fourth Graders. 2nd ed. (Illus.). 142p. (C). 1992. teacher ed. 25.00 (*0-934337-04-7*) Drug Ed Ctr.

Leseur, Elisabeth. Light in the Darkness: How to Bring Christ to the Souls You Meet Each Day. rev. ed. LC 98-12657. Orig. Title: La Vie Spirituelle. 157p. 1998. pap. 12.95 (*0-918477-72-7*) Sophia Inst Pr.

— My Spirit Rejoices: The Diary of a Christian Soul in an Age of Unbelief. LC 96-6442. 265p. 1996. pap. 16.50 (*0-918477-40-9*) Sophia Inst Pr.

LeSeur, Geta. Ten Is the Age of Darkness: The Black Bildungsroman. 248p. 1995. text 34.95 (*0-8262-1011-2*) U of Mo Pr.

Lesgold, Alan, ed. see Boy, Guy A.

Lesgold, Alan, ed. see National Research Council Staff.

Lesgold, Alan M., et al, eds. Cognitive Psychology & Instruction. LC 77-27133. (NATO Conference Series III, Human Factors: Vol. 5). 540p. 1978. 75.00 (*0-306-32886-0*, Plenum Trade) Perseus Pubng.

Lesgold, Alan M. & Glaser, Robert, eds. Foundations for a Psychology of Education. 328p. 1988. 69.95 (*0-8058-0296-7*) L Erlbaum Assocs.

Lesgold, Alan M. & Perfetti, Charles A., eds. Interactive Processes in Reading. LC 80-21048. 448p. 1981. text 89.95 (*0-89859-079-5*) L Erlbaum Assocs.

Lesgold, Alan M., jt. ed. see Mandl, Heinz.

Lesh, Donald. Treatise on Thoroughbred Selection. 80p. 1990. pap. 21.00 (*0-85131-296-9*, Pub. by J A Allen) St Mut.

Lesh, Janet R., tr. see Kourganoff, Vladimir.

Lesh, Kay, jt. auth. see Ealy, C. Diane.

Lesh, Kay, jt. auth. see Golden, Bonnie J.

***Lesh, Michael D. & Roithinger, Franz X.** Atrial Tachycardia. LC 99-40659. (Clinical Approaches to Tachyarrhythmias Ser.: Vol. 11). (Illus.). 80p. 1999. pap. 19.00 (*0-87993-442-5*) Futura Pub.

Lesh, O. E., jt. ed. see Tyndall, John W.

Lesh, Richard & Lamon, Susan J., eds. Assessment of Authentic Performance in School Mathematics. 456p. 1994. pap. 39.95 (*0-8058-1877-4*) L Erlbaum Assocs.

Lesh, Richard & Landau, Marsha, eds. Acquisitions of Mathematics Concepts & Processes. LC 83-2845. 1983. text 95.00 (*0-12-444220-X*) Acad Pr.

Lesh, Richard, jt. ed. see Kelly, Anthony.

Lesh, Steven G. Clinical Orthopedics for the Physical Therapist Assistant. (Illus.). 560p. (C). 2000. pap. text 39.95 (*0-8036-0449-1*) Davis Co.

LeShan, Eda. Grandparenting in a Changing World. LC 93-24988. 208p. 1993. 19.95 (*1-55704-175-X*, Pub. by Newmarket) Norton.

— Grandparenting in a Changing World. LC 93-24988. 208p. 1997. reprint ed. pap. 11.95 (*1-55704-307-8*, Pub. by Newmarket) Norton.

— I Want More of Everything. LC 94-22544. 256p. 1994. 20.00 (*1-55704-211-X*, Pub. by Newmarket) Norton.

— I Want More of Everything. LC 94-22544. 256p. 1997. pap. 11.95 (*1-55704-247-0*, Pub. by Newmarket) Norton.

— It's Better to Be over the Hill Than under It. LC 90-41274. 240p. 1997. pap. 11.95 (*1-55704-251-9*, Pub. by Newmarket) Norton.

***LeShan, Eda.** It's Better to Be over the Hill Than under It: Thoughts on Life over Sixty. large type ed. LC 00-24250. (Senior Lifestyles Ser.). 272p. 2000. 24.95 (*0-7862-2527-0*) Thorndike Pr.

LeShan, Eda. Learning to Say Good-Bye: When a Child's Parent Dies. 128p. 1978. pap. 8.00 (*0-380-40105-3*, Avon Bks) Morrow Avon.

— When Grownups Drive You Crazy. LC 87-22005. 128p. (J). (gr. 3-7). 1988. mass mkt. 14.00 (*0-02-756340-5*, Mac Bks Young Read) S&S Childrens.

Leshan, Eda. When Your Child Drives You Crazy. 1992. mass mkt. 5.99 (*0-312-92930-7*) St Martin.

LeShan, Lawrence. Beyond Technique: Psychotherapy for the 21st Century. LC 95-10750. 216p. 1996. 40.00 (*1-56821-550-9*) Aronson.

— Cancer As a Turning Point: A Handbook for People with Cancer, Their Families & Health Professionals. rev. ed. 240p. 1994. pap. 12.95 (*0-452-27137-1*) NAL.

— An Ethic for the Age of Space. 160p. (Orig.). 1996. pap. 12.95 (*0-87728-854-2*) Weiser.

— How to Meditate: A Guide to Self-Discovery. 176p. 1984. mass mkt. 6.50 (*0-553-24453-1*) Bantam.

— How to Meditate: A Guide to Self-Discovery. 240p. 1999. pap. 10.00 (*0-316-88062-0*, Back Bay) Little.

— The Psychology of War: Comprehending Its Mystique & Its Madness. LC 92-50438. 163p. 1992. 16.95 (*1-879360-20-9*) Noble Pr.

— Toward a General Theory of the Paranormal. 3rd ed. LC 73-80027. (Parapsychological Monographs: No. 9). 1969. pap. 7.00 (*0-912328-13-4*) Parapsych Foun.

— You Can Fight for Your Life: Emotional Factors in the Treatment of Cancer. LC 76-30464. 216p. 1980. pap. 9.95 (*0-87131-494-0*) M Evans.

Leshane, Patricia. Vegetarian Cooking for People with Diabetes. LC 94-16298. 144p. 1994. pap. 12.95 (*0-913990-22-1*) Book Pub Co.

Leshay, Jeff. How to Launch Your Career in TV News. (Illus.). 144p. 1994. pap. 14.95 (*0-8442-4138-5*, 41385, VGM Career) NTC Contemp Pub Co.

Leshchisky, D., jt. auth. see Tatsuoka, F.

Leshe, Leta, ed. I Remember: Childhood Memories of the Leshe Family. (Illus.). 48p. (Orig.). 1995. pap. 5.00 (*0-9645451-5-2*) F Swann Pubns.

Leshe, Leta, ed. see Peckel, Floyd A.

Leshe, Leta, ed. & illus. see Peckel, Floyd A.

Leshem, Elazar & Shuval, Judith T., eds. Immigration to Israel: Sociological Perspectives Studies of Israeli Society. LC 98-213200. 370p. 1998. text 49.95 (*1-56000-346-4*); pap. text 24.95 (*1-56000-997-7*) Transaction Pubs.

Leshem, O. Alice & Varholak, Dorothy M., eds. Long Term Care Nursing Standards Manual, Policies, & Procedures, Suppl. 6. 1998. ring bd. 69.00 (*0-8342-0331-6*, S5406) Aspen Pub.

Leshem, Ya'acov Y. Plant Membranes: A Biophysical Approach. 280p. (C). 1992. text 218.00 (*0-7923-1353-4*) Kluwer Academic.

Lesher, A. Jean. O Holy Night: Timeless Meditations on Christmas. Koch, Carl, ed. LC 99-179987. (Illus.). 168p. 1998. pap. 16.95 (*0-88489-534-3*) St Marys.

Lesher, A. Jean, ed. Prayers for the Common Good. LC 97-47076. 208p. 1998. 18.95 (*0-8298-1248-2*) Pilgrim OH.

Lesher, Emerson L. The Muppie Manual. LC 85-80988. (Illus.). 96p. 1985. pap. 4.95 (*0-934672-31-8*) Good Bks PA.

***Lesher, J. H.** The Greek Philosophers. (GRE.). 160p. (C). 1999. pap. text 20.95 (*1-85399-562-2*, Pub. by Brist Class Pr) Focus Pub-R Pullins.

Lesher, J. H., ed. Xenophanes of Colophon: Fragments - A Text & Translation with a Commentary. (Phoenix Supplementary Volumes Ser.: No. XXX: Pre-Socratics). 380p. 1992. text 45.00 (*0-8020-5990-2*) U of Toronto Pr.

Lesher, J. L., ed. An Atlas of Microbiology of the Skin. LC 98-50050. (Encyclopedia of Visual Medicine Ser.). (Illus.). 132p. 1999. 89.00 (*1-85070-904-1*) Prthnon Pub.

Lesher, James, jt. ed. see Marolda, Edward J.

***Lesher, Linda P.** The Best Novels of the Nineties: A Reader's Guide. LC 99-44233. 488p. 2000. pap. 39.95 (*0-7864-0742-5*) McFarland & Co.

Lesher, Stephan. George Wallace: American Populist. LC 93-40384. 608p. 1993. 29.95 (*0-201-62210-6*) Addison-Wesley.

— George Wallace: American Populist. 608p. 1994. pap. 15.00 (*0-201-40798-1*) Addison-Wesley.

Lesher, Tina. Suburban Mothers: The Funny Life. (Illus.). 40p. 1998. pap. 6.95 (*1-892657-05-8*) Town Bk Pr.

Leshikar, Chuck, ed. Delta Raiders: D Company, 2/501 Infantry 101st Airborne (AMBL) 328p. 1998. 29.95 (*0-941072-34-7*) Southern Herit.

***Leshin.** Internet for Educators: Integrating the Internet into the Curriculum. (C). 1998. VHS 57.00 (*0-205-28503-1*, Macmillan Coll) P-H.

***Leshin, Cynthia.** Focus in Curriculum Integrated Through Internet Adventures. LC 98-209685. 96p. (C). 1998. pap. text 7.00 (*0-205-28414-0*) P-H.

Leshin, Cynthia. Internet Adventures: Step-By-Step Guide to Finding & Using Educational Resources. (Internet Adventures Ser.). (Illus.). 320p. (Orig.). 1995. pap. text 24.95 (*0-9645588-0-7*) XPlora.

— Internet Adventures: Step-by-Step Guide to Netscape Navigator & the World Wide Web. (Internet Adventures Ser.). (Illus.). 120p. (Orig.). 1995. pap. text 22.95 (*0-9645588-1-5*) XPlora.

— Student Resource Guide to the Internet: Student Success On-Line. LC 97-22922. (Illus.). 241p. (C). 1997. pap. text 14.80 (*0-13-621079-1*) P-H.

Leshin, Cynthia B. Dictionary of the World Wide Web. LC 97-17899. 207p. (C). 1997. pap. text 33.00 (*0-13-758319-2*) P-H.

Leshin, Cynthia B. Internet Adventures: Integrating the Internet into the Curriculum. 2nd ed. LC 98-125207. 314p. (C). 1997. pap. text 30.00 (*0-205-27883-3*) Allyn.

— Internet Investigations in Electronic Technology. LC 97-115568. (Illus.). 144p. (C). 1996. pap. text 21.00 (*0-13-496076-9*) P-H.

— Internet Investigations in Hospitality/Travel/Tourism. LC 97-105130. 192p. (C). 1996. pap. text 21.00 (*0-13-495946-9*) P-H.

— Management on Worldwide Web. LC 96-47385. (Illus.). 266p. (C). 1996. pap. text 13.20 (*0-13-268871-9*) P-H.

Leshin, Cynthia B. Netscape Adventures: Step-by-Step Guide to Netscape Navigator & the World Wide Web. LC 96-18106. 316p. (C). 1996. pap. text 62.00 (*0-13-255092-X*) P-H.

Leshin, Cynthia B., et al. Instructional Design Strategies & Tactics. LC 91-32884. (Illus.). 360p. (Orig.). 1992. pap. 39.95 (*0-87778-240-7*) Educ Tech Pubns.

Leshin, George, et al. Speech for the Hearing-Impaired Child. LC 75-327202. (Illus.). 159p. 1975. pap. 49.30 (*0-608-05646-4*, 206610000006) Bks Demand.

Leshin, Geraldine & Schwartz, Rosalind M., eds. EEO for Practitioners, 1988. (Current Issues Ser.: No. 8). 52p. 1993. reprint ed. pap. 7.50 (*0-89215-146-3*) U Cal LA Indus Rel.

— EEO Update: California Threshold Issues. (Current Issues Ser.: No. 7). 21p. 1993. reprint ed. pap. 5.00 (*0-89215-144-7*) U Cal LA Indus Rel.

— Issues in Public Sector Employment. (Current Issues Ser.: No. 11). 48p. 1993. reprint ed. pap. 7.50 (*0-89215-156-0*) U Cal LA Indus Rel.

Leshin, Michael L. Massachusetts Family Law Sourcebook, 1997 Edition. rev. ed. LC 97-70501. Orig. Title: Compendium of Massachusetts Family Law. 450p. 1997. pap. text 50.00 (*1-57589-057-7*, 97-10.23-BK) Mass CLE.

Leshinskie, Matthew, jt. auth. see Gustafson, Bruce.

Leshko, Jaroslaw, jt. auth. see Davis, John.

***Leshner, Alan I., pref.** Principles of Drug Addiction Treatment: A Research--Based Guide. 54p. 2000. pap. text 20.00 (*0-7567-0065-5*) DIANE Pub.

Leshy, John D. Arizona State Constitution: A Reference Guide, 15. LC 92-35922. (Reference Guides to the State Constitutions of the United States Ser.: No. 15). 456p. 1993. lib. bdg. 99.50 (*0-313-27266-2*, LAH/, Greenwood Pr) Greenwood.

— The Mining Law: A Study in Perpetual Motion. LC 86-42610. 521p. 1987. 50.00 (*0-915707-26-8*) Resources Future.

Leshy, John D., ed. see Coggins, George C. & Wilkinson, Charles F.

***Lesi, Frank A., et al.** Ophthalmic & Facial Plastic Surgery: A Compendium of Reconstructive & Aesthetic Techniques. 400p. (C). 2000. text 130.00 (*1-55642-451-5*) SLACK Inc.

Lesiak, Judi L., jt. auth. see Bradley-Johnson, Sharon.

Lesiak, Judi L., jt. auth. see Lesiak, Walter J.

***Lesiak, Liz.** Mother's Blood. LC 99-67406. 112p. 1999. pap. 16.00 (*1-892323-18-4*) Vivisphere.

Lesiak, Walter J. & Lesiak, Judi L. Developmental Tasks for Kindergarten Readiness II (DTKR II) Assessment of Prekindergarten Children to Determine Kindergarten Readiness. LC 93-41855. 72p. 1994. pap. 19.95 (*0-88422-095-8*) Clinical Psych.

Lesic, Zdenko, ed. Children of Atlantis: Voices from the Former Yugoslavia. (Central European University Press Bk.). 184p. 1995. pap. 16.95 (*1-85866-041-6*) Ctrl Europ Univ.

Lesick, Lawrence T. The Lane Rebels: Evangelicalism & Antislavery in Antebellum America. LC 80-24123. (Studies in Evangelicalism: No. 2). 287p. 1980. 29.00 (*0-8108-1372-6*) Scarecrow.

LeSieg, Theo, pseud. Come over to My House. (J). 1999. lib. bdg. 11.99 (*0-679-98255-8*, Pub. by Random Bks Yng Read) Random.

— Come over to My House. (J). (ps-3). 1999. 7.99 (*0-679-88255-3*, Pub. by Random Bks Yng Read) Random.

— The Eye Book. LC 98-25120. (Illus.). 48p. (ps-3). 1999. 7.99 (*0-375-80033-6*) Random.

— The Eye Book. LC 98-25120. (Illus.). 48p. (J). (ps-3). 1999. lib. bdg. 11.99 (*0-375-90033-0*) Random.

— The Eye Book. (Bright & Early Bks.). (Illus.). (J). (ps-1). 1968. lib. bdg. 11.99 (*0-394-91094-X*, BE2, Pub. by Random Bks Yng Read) Random.

— I Can Write! A Book by Me, Myself. (Bright & Early Bks.). (Illus.). 32p. (J). (ps-1). 1993. pap. 2.99 (*0-679-84700-6*, Pub. by Random Bks Yng Read) Random.

— I Wish That I Had Duck Feet. LC 65-21211. (Beginner Bks.). (Illus.). 64p. (J). (ps-2). 1965. 7.99 (*0-394-80040-0*, Pub. by Random Bks Yng Read) Random.

— I Wish That I Had Duck Feet. LC 65-21211. (Beginner Bks.). (Illus.). 64p. (J). (ps-3). 1965. lib. bdg. 11.99 (*0-394-90040-5*, Pub. by Random Bks Yng Read) Random.

— I Wish That I Had Duck Feet. (J). 1991. 7.99 (*0-606-04941-X*, Pub. by Turtleback) Demco.

— In a People House. (Bright & Early Bks.: No. 12). (Illus.). (J). (ps-1). 1972. lib. bdg. 9.99 (*0-394-92395-2*, Pub. by Random Bks Yng Read) Random.

— Please Try to Remember the 1st of October. LC 77-4504. (Illus.). 48p. (J). (gr. k-3). 1977. lib. bdg. 11.99 (*0-394-93563-2*) Beginner.

— The Pop-Up Mice of Mr. Brice. LC 89-60507. (Illus.). 20p. (J). (ps-3). 1989. 16.00 (*0-679-80132-4*, Pub. by Random Bks Yng Read) Random.

— Ten Apples up on Top. LC 61-7068. (Illus.). 72p. (J). (gr. 1-2). 1961. lib. bdg. 11.99 (*0-394-90019-7*) Beginner.

— Ten Apples up on Top. LC 97-76121. (J). 1998. 4.99 (*0-679-89247-8*, Pub. by Random Bks Yng Read) Random.

— Ten Apples Up on Top! LC 61-7068. (Illus.). 72p. (J). (ps-3). 1961. 7.99 (*0-394-80019-2*) Random House.

An Asterisk (*) at the beginning of an entry indicates that the title is appearing for the first time.

— The Tooth Book. LC 80-28320. (Bright & Early Bks.: No. 25). (Illus.). 48p. (J). (ps-1). 1981. lib. bdg. 11.99 (*0-394-94825-4*, Pub. by Random Bks Yng Read) Random.

— The Tooth Book. LC 80-28320. (Bright & Early Bks.: No. 25). (Illus.). 48p. (J). (ps-3). 1981. 7.99 (*0-394-84825-X*, XBYR, Pub. by Random Bks Yng Read) Random.

***LeSieg, Theo, pseud.** Tooth Book. LC 00-20436. (Bright & Early Bks.). (Illus.). 48p. (J). (ps-3). 2000. 7.99 (*0-375-81039-0*) Random.

LeSieg, Theo, pseud. Wacky Wednesday. LC 74-5520. (Illus.). 48p. (J). (gr. k-4). 1974. 7.99 (*0-394-82912-3*); lib. bdg. 11.99 (*0-394-92912-8*) Beginner.

***LeSieg, Theo, pseud & Mathieu, Joseph.** The Tooth Book. LC 00-20436. (Illus.). 48p. (J). (ps-3). 2000. lib. bdg. 11.99 (*0-375-91039-5*) Random.

Lesieur. Turbulence in Fluids. 1997. pap. text 73.50 (*0-7923-4416-2*) Kluwer Academic.

Lesieur, Guillaume, jt. auth. see Guild, Elspeth.

Lesieur, Henry. The Chase: The Compulsive Gambler. LC 84-10533. 352p. 1984. 29.95 (*0-87073-642-6*); pap. 18.95 (*0-87073-643-4*) Schenkman Bks Inc.

— Understanding Compulsive Gambling. 32p. 1994. pap. 2.50 (*0-89486-388-6*, 5497) Hazelden.

Lesieur, Marcel. Turbulence in Fluids. 2nd rev. ed. (C). 1990. lib. bdg. 137.50 (*0-7923-0645-7*) Kluwer Academic.

— Turbulence in Fluids. 3rd ed. LC 96-51041. 515p. 1997. lib. bdg. 225.00 (*0-7923-4415-4*) Kluwer Academic.

— Turbulence in Fluids: Stochastic & Numerical Modelling. 1987. text 172.00 (*90-247-3470-3*) Kluwer Academic.

Lesieur, Marcel, jt. ed. see Metais, O.

Lesikar. Fundamentals of Management Communications. 2nd ed. 1998. 21.00 (*0-07-229360-8*) McGraw.

Lesikar, et al. Business Communication: Theory & Application. 7th ed. 1993. 67.95 (*0-87393-216-1*) Dame Pubns.

Lesikar, Raymond V., Sr. Basic Business Communication. 5th ed. (Business Communication Ser.). (C). 1990. student ed. 17.95 (*0-256-08614-1*, Irwn McGrw-H) McGrw-H Hghr Educ.

Lesikar, Raymond Vincent. CPS - Report Writing for Business Select Chapters. 9th ed. 204p. (C). 1995. text 20.95 (*0-256-20304-0*, Irwn McGrw-H) McGrw-H Hghr Educ.

Lesikar, Raymond Vincent & Flatley, Marie E. Lesikar's Basic Business Communication. 8th ed. LC 98-21173. 1998. 77.00 (*0-07-292990-1*) McGraw.

Lesikar, Raymond Vincent & Petit, John D., Jr. Report Writing for Business. 9th ed. 1995. pap. write for info. (*0-256-18021-0*, Irwn McGrw-H) McGrw-H Hghr Educ.

Lesikar, Raymond Vincent & Pettit, John D. Lesikar's Basic Business Communication. 8th ed. 640p. 1998. pap., student ed. 71.88 (*0-07-561942-3*) McGraw.

— Report Writing for Business. 9th ed. LC 94-12499. 480p. (C). 1994. text 61.50 (*0-256-11565-6*, Irwn McGrw-H) McGrw-H Hghr Educ.

— Report Writing for Business. 10th ed. LC 97-41363. (Illus.). 448p. (C). 1998. text 64.38 (*0-256-23691-7*) McGraw-Hill Prof.

Lesikar, Raymond Vincent, et al. Basic Business Communication. 7th ed. LC 95-12695. 688p. (C). 1995. text 64.50 (*0-256-14078-2*, Irwn Prfssnl) McGraw-Hill Prof.

— Basic Business Communication, Canadian. 688p. (C). 1993. text 43.75 (*0-256-11690-3*, Irwn McGrw-H) McGrw-H Hghr Educ.

— Lesikar's Basic Business Communication. 7th ed. 128p. (C). 1995. text, student ed. 23.43 (*0-256-14079-0*, Irwn McGrw-H) McGrw-H Hghr Educ.

Lesina, D. Roberto. Software & Hardware Dictionary: Italian - English, English - Italian. (ENG & ITA.). 1991. 89.95 (*0-7859 3709 9*, 8808114880) Fr & Eur.

— Software & Hardware Dictionary: Italian-English - English-Italian. 416p. 1991. 85.00 (*88-08-11488-0*, Pub. by Zanichelli) IBD Ltd.

Lesina, R. Italian Style Manual.Tr. of Nuovo Manuale Di Stile. 383p. 1994. 55.00 (*88-08-09602-5*, Pub. by Zanichelli) IBD Ltd.

Lesins. Genus. 1979. 212.00 (*90-6193-598-9*, Pub. by Kluwer Academic) Kluwer Academic.

***Lesinski, Jeanne M.** Bill Gates. LC 99-34009. (A&E Biography Ser.). (Illus.). 128p. (YA). (gr. 6-9). 2000. 25.26 (*0-8225-4949-2*, Lerner Publctns); pap. 7.95 (*0-8225-9689-X*, First Ave Edns) Lerner Pub.

— Bill Gates. (Illus.). (J). 2000. 13.30 (*0-606-18814-2*) Turtleback.

Lesinski, Jeanne M. Exotic Invaders: Killer Bees, Fire Ants & Other Alien Species Are Infesting America! LC 95-20908. (Illus.). 48p. (J). (gr. 4-6). 1996. 16.95 (*0-8027-8390-2*); lib. bdg. 17.85 (*0-8027-8391-0*) Walker & Co.

— MIAs: A Reference Handbook. LC 98-42275. (Contemporary World Issues Ser.). 256p. 1998. lib. bdg. 45.00 (*0-87436-954-1*) ABC-CLIO.

Lesk, Arthur M., ed. Computational Molecular Biology: Sources & Methods for Sequence Analysis. (Illus.). 272p. 1989. 55.00 (*0-19-854218-6*) OUP.

— Protein Architecture: A Practical Approach. (Practical Approach Ser.). (Illus.). 312p. 1991. pap. 45.00 (*0-19-963055-0*) OUP.

Lesk, Michael. Practical Digital Libraries: Books, Bytes, & Bucks. LC 97-22069. (Illus.). 300p. 1997. text 49.95 (*1-55860-459-6*) Morgan Kaufmann.

— Preservation of New Technology: A Report of the Technology Assessment Advisory Committee. 19p. 1992. pap. 5.00 (*1-887334-19-X*) Coun Lib & Info.

Lesk, Sara M., ed. see Time-Life Books Editors.

Leske, Steven. Sir Richard & the Dragon. 14p. (J). (gr. k-6). 1992. pap. text 5.99 (*1-881617-01-7*) Teapot Tales.

— A Two Headed Tale. 16p. (J). (gr. k-6). 1992. pap. text 5.99 (*1-881617-02-5*) Teapot Tales.

Lesker, G. A., ed. Three Late Medieval Morality Plays: Mankind, Everyman & Mundis et Infans. (New Mermaids Ser.). (C). 1984. pap. text 11.25 (*0-393-90054-1*) Norton.

Leskes, Andrea, tr. see Bebel-Gisler, Dany.

Leskes, Andrea, tr. see Lopes, Henri.

Leski, J., jt. auth. see Czogala, E.

Leskiewicz, H. J., ed. see IFAC Symposium Staff.

Leskiw, Donald M., jt. auth. see Miller, Kenneth S.

***Lesko.** Free Stuff for Everyone Made E-Z. 224p. 2000. pap. 17.95 (*1-56382-459-0*) E-Z Legal.

Lesko. Readings in Social Psychology. 4th ed. LC 99-20563. 413p. (C). 1999. pap. text 37.00 (*0-205-28720-4*, Macmillan Coll) P-H.

***Lesko & Goldstein.** Free Legal Help Made E-Z. 224p. 2000. pap. 17.95 (*1-56382-458-2*) E-Z Legal.

***Lesko, Barbara S.** The Great Goddesses of Egypt. LC 99-11850. 336p. 1999. pap. 19.95 (*0-8061-3202-7*) U of Okla Pr.

Lesko, Barbara S. The Remarkable Women of Ancient Egypt. 3rd rev. ed. (Illus.). 68p. 1996. pap. 16.95 (*0-930548-13-2*) B C Scribe.

Lesko, Barbara S. & Larkin, Diana W. Joseph Lindon Smith: Paintings from Egypt - An Exhibition, Brown University, October 8-November 21, 1998. Lesko, Leonard H., ed. (Illus.). 64p. 1998. pap. 20.00 (*0-9662685-1-2*) Brown U Egyptology.

Lesko, Diane. James Ensor: The Creative Years. LC 84-26452. (Illus.). 191p. reprint ed. pap. 59.30 (*0-8357-6552-0*, 203591600097) Bks Demand.

Lesko, Diane, et al, eds. Catalogue of the Collection Museum of Fine Arts, St. Petersburg, Florida. LC 93-78274. (Illus.). 367p. (Orig.). (C). 1993. pap. 35.00 (*1-878390-02-3*) Mus St Pete.

Lesko, Jim. Industrial Design: Materials & Manufacturing Guide. LC 97-33670. (Illus.). 256p. 1997. pap. 49.95 (*0-442-02409-6*, VNR) Wiley.

— Industrial Design: Materials & Manufacturing Guide. (Illus.). 224p. 1998. pap. 49.95 (*0-471-29769-0*) Wiley.

Lesko, John, et al, eds. Technology Exchange in the Information Age: A Guide to Successful Cooperative R&D Partnerships. 2nd ed. LC 97-30038. 202p. 1998. pap. text 29.95 (*1-57477-037-3*) Battelle.

Lesko, Kathleen M. Black Georgetown Remembered: A History of Its Black Community from the Founding of "the Town of George" in 1751 to the Present Day. LC 91-29357. (Illus.). 200p. reprint ed. pap. 62.00 (*0-608-09708-X*, 2069874) Bks Demand.

Lesko, Kathleen M., et al. Black Georgetown Remembered: A History of Its Black Community from the Founding of "The Town of George" in 1751 to the Present Day. LC 91-29357. (Illus.). 210p. 1999. reprint ed. pap. 19.95 (*0-87840-526-7*) Georgetown U Pr.

Lesko, Leonard H. King Tut's Wine Cellar. LC 77-85654. (Illus.). 1977. pap. 3.95 (*0-930548-00-0*) B C Scribe.

Lesko, Leonard H., ed. Ancient Egyptian & Mediterranean Studies in Memory of William A. Ward. (Illus.). xx, 271p. (C). 1998. 89.95 (*0-9662685-0-4*) Brown U Egyptology.

— Dictionary of Late Egyptian, Vol. 1 of 4 Vols. (EGY.). 1982. pap. text 20.00 (*0-930548-04-3*); lib. bdg. 35.00 (*0-930548-03-5*) B C Scribe.

— Pharaoh's Workers: The Villagers of Deir el Medina. (Illus.). 212p. 1994. text 37.50 (*0-8014-2915-3*); pap. text 15.95 (*0-8014-8143-0*) Cornell U Pr.

Lesko, Leonard H., ed. see Brown University Staff & Malamat, Abraham.

Lesko, Leonard H., ed. see Lesko, Barbara S. & Larkin, Diana W.

Lesko, Marian, ed. see Arnold, Marti.

Lesko, Matthew. Everything You Need to Run a Business at Home. Martello, Mary A., ed. (Illus.). 765p. (Orig.). 1996. pap. 29.95 (*1-878346-36-9*) Info USA.

***Lesko, Matthew.** Free College Money & Training for Women. 2000. pap. text 24.95 (*1-878346-52-0*) Info USA.

Lesko, Matthew. Free Health Care. 603p. 1995. pap. 19.95 (*1-878346-34-2*) Info USA.

— Free Legal Help. 367p. (Orig.). 1996. pap. 14.95 (*1-878346-35-0*) Info USA.

***Lesko, Matthew.** Free Money & Help for Women Entrepreneurs. 2000. pap. text 24.95 (*1-878346-51-2*) Info USA.

Lesko, Matthew. Free Money to Change Your Life. 1148p. (Orig.). 1997. pap. text 37.95 (*1-878346-40-7*) Info USA.

***Lesko, Matthew.** Free Stuff for Busy Moms. (Illus.). 1999. pap. 24.95 (*1-878346-49-0*) Info USA.

— Free Stuff for Pet Lovers. (Illus.). 2000. pap. 19.95 (*1-878346-48-2*) Info USA.

Lesko, Matthew. Free Stuff for Seniors. Naprawa, Andrew, ed. 693p. (Orig.). 1995. pap. 19.95 (*1-878346-30-X*) Info USA.

***Lesko, Matthew.** Free Stuff for Women's Health, Fitness & Nutrition. 2000. pap. text 24.95 (*1-878346-50-4*) Info USA.

— Get to Know Perot. (Illus.). pap. 23.75 (*1-878346-15-6*) Info USA.

Lesko, Matthew. Getting Yours: The Complete Guide to Government Money. 3rd ed. LC 86-22688. 336p. 1987. pap. 14.95 (*0-14-046760-2*, Penguin Bks) Viking Penguin.

— Gobs & Gobs of Free Stuff. (Illus.). 494p. (Orig.). 1996. pap. 19.95 (*1-878346-33-4*) Info USA.

— Government Giveaways for Entrepreneurs III. 5th exp. ed. Murray, Toni & Naprawa, Andrew, eds. (Government Giveaways for Entrepreneurs Ser.). 785p. 1996. pap. 37.95 (*1-878346-39-3*) Info USA.

— Info-Fobia: How to Survive in an Information Society. (Illus.). 423p. (Orig.). 1996. pap. 17.95 (*1-878346-38-5*) Info USA.

— Information U. S. A. (Handbooks Ser.). 1288p. 1986. pap. 29.95 (*0-14-046745-9*, Penguin Bks) Viking Penguin.

— Lesko's Info-Power, Vol. 2. 1600p. 1993. pap. 29.95 (*0-8103-9485-5*) Visible Ink Pr.

Lesko, Matthew. Lesko's Info-Power III. 3rd ed. Naprawa, Andrew, ed. 1519p. 1996. pap. text 39.95 (*1-878346-37-7*) Info USA.

Lesko, Matthew. Lesko's Info Power III, Vol. III. 3rd ed. 1600p. 1996. 29.95 (*0-7876-0880-7*) Visible Ink Pr.

Lesko, Matthew & Martello, Mary A. Free College Money, Term Papers, Sex (Ed) Hess, Martha, ed. LC 96-141016. 1053p. (Orig.). 1994. pap. 36.95 (*1-878346-24-5*) Info USA.

***Lesko, Nancy, ed.** Masculinities at School. LC 99-6785. (Research on Men & Masculinities Ser.: No. 11). 360p. 2000. 74.95 (*0-7619-1493-5*) Sage.

Lesko, Wendy S. No Kidding Around! America's Young Activists Are Changing Our World & You Can Too. (Illus.). 250p. (Orig.). 1992. pap. 18.95 (*1-878346-10-5*) Info USA.

Leskov. Short Stories. unabridged ed. (World Classic Literature Ser.). (RUS.). pap. 8.95 (*2-87714-273-6*, Pub. by Bookking Intl) Distribks Inc.

Leskov, Chtchedri, jt. auth. see Leskov, Saltykov-Chtchedrine.

Leskov, Nicolas. Lady Macbeth au Village, l'Ange Scelle, la Vagabond Enchante. (FRE.). 1982. pap. 17.95 (*0-7859-4174-6*) Fr & Eur.

Leskov, Nikolai. On the Edge of the World. Prokurat, Michael, tr. from RUS. LC 92-31940.Tr. of Na Kraiu Sveta. 136p. 1993. pap. 8.95 (*0-88141-118-3*) St Vladimirs.

— Schism in High Society: Granville Waldergrave Lord Radstock & His Followers. Muckle, James, tr. LC 96-110236. 1995. 30.00 (*0-9517853-5-4*, Pub. by Bramcote Pr); pap. 19.95 (*0-9517853-4-6*, Pub. by Bramcote Pr) Intl Spec Bk.

— Vale of Tears & on Quakeresses. 1991. pap. 16.95 (*0-9517853-0-3*, Pub. by Bramcote Pr) Intl Spec Bk.

Leskov, Nikolai S. Five Tales. Shotton, Michael, tr. from RUS. 192p. 1984. pap. 13.95 (*0-946162-13-1*) Dufour.

— The Sealed Angel & Other Stories. Lantz, K. A., ed. LC 83-14547. 267p. reprint ed. pap. 82.80 (*0-7837-7080-4*, 204689200004) Bks Demand.

Leskov, Nikolay. Five Tales. Shotton, Michael, tr. from RUS. & intro. by. 192p. 1984. 25.00 (*0-946162-12-3*) Dufour.

Leskov, Saltykov-Chtchedrine. Oeuvres. 1676p. 42.95 (*0-686-56534-7*) Fr & Eur.

Leskov, Saltykov-Chtchedrine & Leskov, Chtchedri. Oeuvres. Luneau, Andre, ed. (FRE.). 1676p. 1967. lib. bdg. 110.00 (*0-7859-3764-1*, 2070103102) Fr & Eur.

Leskova, T. & Plisek, V. Czech-English Technical Textile Dictionary. (CZE & ENG.). 468p. 1980. 60.00 (*0-7855-7261-9*) St Mut.

Leskovsek, Valentin. Slovenia: A Bibliography in Foreign Languages, Vol. 1. 105p. 1990. 12.00 (*0-685-34712-5*) Studia Slovenica.

— Slovenia: A Bibliography in Foreign Languages, Vol. 2. 115p. 1991. 12.00 (*0-685-41046-3*) Studia Slovenica.

— Yugoslavia Vol. 1: A Bibliography. LC 77-374918. 192p. 1974. 10.00 (*0-686-28383-X*) Studia Slovenica.

— Yugoslavia Vol. 2: A Bibliography. LC 77-374918. 168p. 1978. 10.00 (*0-686-28386-4*) Studia Slovenica.

— Yugoslavia Vol. 3: A Bibliography. LC 77-374918. 120p. 1980. pap. 10.00 (*0-686-26712-5*) Studia Slovenica.

— Yugoslavia Vol. 4: A Bibliography. LC 77-374918. 153p. 1982. 10.00 (*0-938616-15-3*) Studia Slovenica.

***Leskowitz, Eric D.** Transpersonal Hypnosis. LC 97-32274. 208p. 1999. boxed set 39.95 (*0-8493-2237-5*) CRC Pr.

Lesky, Albin. Historia de la Literatura Griega. (SPA.). 1004p. 1993. 200.00 (*84-249-3132-7*) Elliots Bks.

— A History of Greek Literature. Willis, James & De Heer, Cornelis, trs. LC 96-78783. 944p. (C). 1996. reprint ed. pap. text 29.95 (*0-87220-350-6*); reprint ed. lib. bdg. 59.95 (*0-87220-351-4*) Hackett Pub.

— Thalatta: Der Weg der Griechen Zum Meer. LC 72-7899. (Greek History Ser.). (GER.). 1980. reprint ed. 31.95 (*0-405-04798-3*) Ayer.

Lesky, Erna. The Vienna Medical School of the 19th Century. LC 76-24938. 677p. 1976. reprint ed. pap. 200.00 (*0-608-03715-X*, 206454000009) Bks Demand.

Lesky, Erna, ed. see Frank, Johann P.

Leslau. Falasha Anthology Translated from Ethiopic Sources. 1987. pap. 17.00 (*0-300-03927-1*) Yale U Pr.

Leslau, Charlotte & Leslau, Wolf, eds. African Love Poems & Proverbs. (Petites Ser.). (Illus.). 80p. 1995. 4.95 (*0-88088-791-5*) Peter Pauper.

Leslau, Wolf. Concise Amharic Dictionary. (AMH & ENG.). 95.00 (*0-8288-1153-9*, F 55180) Fr & Eur.

— Concise Amharic Dictionary. 538p. (C). 1996. pap. 27.50 (*0-520-20501-4*, Pub. by U CA Pr) Cal Prin Full Svc.

— Ethiopians Speak: Studies in Cultural Background, Vol. 2: Chana. LC 66-64912. (University of California Publications, Near Eastern Studies: Vol. 7). 225p. reprint ed. pap. 64.20 (*0-608-10875-8*, 2014803) Bks Demand.

— Ethiopians Speak: Studies in Cultural Background, Vol. 3: Soddo. LC 66-64912. (University of California Publications, Near Eastern Studies: Vol. 11). 246p. reprint ed. pap. 76.30 (*0-608-11087-6*, 202137800021) Bks Demand.

— Etymological Dictionary of Gurage (Ethiopic), 3 vols., Set. 2950p. 1980. 495.00 (*0-8288-1775-8*, M15182) Fr & Eur.

— Gafat Documents: Records of a South-Ethiopic Language. (American Oriental Ser.: Vol. 28). 1945. pap. 5.00 (*0-940490-28-5*) Am Orient Soc.

Leslau, Wolf, jt. auth. see Courlander, Harold.

Leslau, Wolf, jt. ed. see Leslau, Charlotte.

Leslee, Ray & Welsh, Kenneth. Standup Shakespeare. 1998. pap. 6.00 (*0-8222-1526-8*) Dramatists Play.

LeSleg, Theo & Cumings, Art. Please Try to Remember the 1st of October. LC 77-4504. (Illus.). 48p. (J). (gr. k-3). 1977. 7.99 (*0-394-83563-8*, 565683) Beginner.

Lesley, Alexander. McD. (Illus.). 1989. pap. 9.95 (*0-317-93841-X*) Palm Tree Words.

***Lesley, Craig.** River Song. LC 99-39794. 320p. 1999. pap. 14.00 (*0-312-24491-6*, Picador USA) St Martin.

Lesley, Craig. Sky Fisherman. LC 96-16227. 304p. 1996. pap. 13.00 (*0-312-14738-4*) St Martin.

***Lesley, Craig.** Storm Riders: Novel. LC 99-55046. 352p. 2000. text 24.00 (*0-312-24554-8*, Picador USA) St Martin.

Lesley, Craig. Talking Leaves: Contemporary Native American Short Stories. 1991. 18.05 (*0-606-00793-8*, Pub. by Turtleback) Demco.

— Winterkill. 336p. 1990. pap. 11.95 (*0-385-31180-X*, Delta Trade) Dell.

— Winterkill. LC 96-48912. 336p. 1996. pap. 14.00 (*0-312-15244-2*) St Martin.

Lesley, Craig, ed. Talking Leaves. 416p. 1991. reprint ed. pap. 13.95 (*0-385-31272-5*, Delta Trade) Dell.

Lesley, Dawn, ed. see Klopping, Paul H., et al.

Lesley, Jason, jt. auth. see Wineka, Mark.

Lesley, Millard. Adult Learners: Study Skills & Teaching Methods. (C). 1981. 35.00 (*0-7855-6562-0*, Pub. by Univ Nottingham) St Mut.

Lesley, Philip. Lesly's Handbook of Public Relations & Communications. 35th ed. LC 96-40864. (Illus.). 224p. 1997. 100.00 (*0-8442-3257-2*, 35272) NTC Contemp Pub Co.

Lesley, Robert W., et al. History of the Portland Cement Industry in the United States. LC 72-5061. (Technology & Society Ser.). (Illus.). 346p. 1972. reprint ed. 23.95 (*0-405-04712-6*) Ayer.

Lesley, Susan I., jt. ed. see Tiffany, Nina M.

Lesley, Ted. Paramiracles. Minch, Stephen, ed. Palmer, Bill & Erens, Oliver, trs. (Illus.). 213p. 1994. 35.00 (*0-945296-12-6*) Hermetic Pr.

Leslie. Blue Moon. 1999. mass mkt. 6.50 (*0-671-53515-3*) S&S Trade.

— Core Mathematics (Custom Publication) 1991. pap. write for info. (*0-07-037220-9*) McGraw.

— Diabetes. 1989. text 99.00 (*0-443-04069-9*, W B Saunders Co) Harcrt Hlth Sci Grp.

— Labor Law. 3rd ed. 1248p. 1992. 56.00 (*0-316-52165-5*, Aspen Law & Bus) Aspen Pub.

— Mass Communications. (C). 1999. pap. text 37.16 (*0-395-90490-0*) HM.

— Statutory Supplement to Cases & Materials on Labor Law. 284p. 1992. 17.95 (*0-316-52167-1*, Aspen Law & Bus) Aspen Pub.

Leslie, ed. Three Old English Elegies. 108p. 1988. pap. text 12.95 (*0-85989-184-4*, Pub. by Univ Exeter Pr) Northwestern U Pr.

— The Wanderer. 116p. 1985. pap. text 12.95 (*0-85989-261-1*, Pub. by Univ Exeter Pr) Northwestern U Pr.

Leslie, et al. Land Use Regulation: A Handbook for the Eighties. 171p. 1984. 12.00 (*0-318-04412-9*) Stanford Enviro.

Leslie, jt. auth. see Scott.

Leslie, A., et al, eds. A Tribute to Hermann Weigand. 144p. 1982. pap. 9.95 (*0-911173-00-5*) Dimension Pr.

***Leslie, Alfred, ed.** The Hasty Papers: Millennium Edition of the Legendary 1960 One-Shot-Review. Arrowsmith, William, tr. LC 96-75157. (Illus.). 256p. 1999. 35.00 (*0-924047-12-7*) Host Pubns.

***Leslie, Alison.** Rounders. (Skills of the Game Ser.). 1999. pap. 19.95 (*1-86126-234-5*, Pub. by Crolwood) Trafalgar.

***Leslie, Amanda.** Are Chickens Stripy? (Illus.). 12p. (J). 2000. 5.99 (*1-58048-088-8*) Sandvik Pub.

— Are Chickens Stripy? Two Lift-the-Flap Books. (Illus.). 24p. (J). 2000. 4.95 (*1-929766-09-2*) Handprint.

— Do Crocodiles Moo? (Illus.). 12p. (J). 2000. 5.99 (*1-58048-087-X*) Sandvik Pub.

— Do Crocodiles Moo? Two Lift-the-Flap Books. (Illus.). 24p. (J). 2000. 4.95 (*1-929766-08-4*) Handprint.

— Flappy, Waggly, Wiggly. (Illus.). (J). 1999. 9.99 (*1-58048-089-6*) Sandvik Pub.

— Flappy Waggy Wiggly: A Peckaboo Riddle Book. (Illus.). 34p. (J). (ps-k). 1999. 12.99 (*0-525-46182-5*, Dutton Child) Peng Put Young Read.

Leslie, Amanda. Let's Look Inside the Red Car. LC 96-84555. (Illus.). 10p. (J). (ps up). 1997. 9.99 (*0-7636-0089-X*) Candlewick Pr.

— Let's Look Inside the Yellow Truck. LC 96-84560. (Illus.). 10p. (J). (ps up). 1997. 8.99 (*0-7636-0104-7*) Candlewick Pr.

Leslie, Andrew, ed. Passport's Guide to the Best of Scotland. (Illus.). 522p. 1996. pap. 17.95 (*0-8442-4874-6*, 48746, Passprt Bks) NTC Contemp Pub Co.

Leslie, Ann R. Integrated Pest Management for Environmentally Compatible Agricultural. 224p. 1992. lib. bdg. 99.95 (*0-87371-502-0*, L502) Lewis Pubs.

Leslie, Anne R. Integrated Pest Management. 672p. 1994. lib. bdg. 95.00 (*0-87371-350-8*, L350) Lewis Pubs.

Leslie, Anne R., jt. ed. see Nash, Ralph G.

Leslie, Anne R., jt. ed. see Racke, Kenneth D.

Leslie, Benjamin C. Trinitaria Hermeneutics: The Hermeneutical Significance of Karl Barth's Doctrine of the Trinity. LC 91-17450. (American University Studies: Theology & Religion: Ser. VII, Vol. 66). XII, 286p. (C). 1991. text 47.95 (*0-8204-1461-1*) P Lang Pubng.

Leslie, Bennett, jt. auth. see Daley, Dennis.

Leslie, Bruce R. Ronsard's Successful Epic Venture: The Epyllion. LC 78-52838. (French Forum Monographs: No. 11). 137p. (Orig.). 1979. pap. 9.95 (*0-917058-10-0*) French Forum.

L

L

Leslie, C. R. Memoirs of the Life of John Constable. rev. ed. Mayne, Jonathan, ed. LC 96-138171. (Arts & Letters Ser.). (Illus.). 464p. (C). 1995. pap. 14.95 (*0-7148-3360-6*, Pub. by Phaidon Press) Phaidon Pr.

Leslie, Candace. From Forge & Anvil: Erich Riesel, Hill Country Iron Worker. LC 98-71227. (Illus.). 96p. 1992. 29.95 (*0-9626069-7-9*) Insite Pub.

— Hidden Florida Keys & Everglades. 6th rev. ed. (Hidden Travel Ser.). (Illus.). 192p. 1999. pap. 12.95 (*1-56975-193-5*, Pub. by Ulysses Pr) Publishers Group.

Leslie, Charles & Young, Allan, eds. Paths to Asian Medical Knowledge. 306p. 1993. 39.50 (*81-215-0608-5*, Pub. by M Manoharial) Coronet Bks.

***Leslie, Charles M.** Asian Medical Systems: A Comparative Study. LC 98-904382. (Indian Medical Tradition Ser.). xvii, 419 p. 1998. write for info. (*81-208-1537-8*, Pub. by Motilal Bnarsidass) S Asia.

Leslie, Charles M. Now We Are Civilized: A Study of the World View of the Zapotec Indians of Mitla, Oaxaca. LC 60-7651. 133p. reprint ed. pap. 38.00 (*0-7837-3686-X*, 2043560) Bks Demand.

— Now We Are Civilized: A Study of the World View of the Zapotec Indians of Mitla, Oaxaca. LC 81-14. (Illus.). 108p. 1981. reprint ed. lib. bdg. 55.00 (*0-313-22847-7*, LENW, Greenwood Pr) Greenwood.

Leslie, Charles M. & Young, Allan H., eds. Paths to Asian Medical Knowledge. LC 91-796. (Comparative Studies of Health Systems & Medical Care: Vol. 32). 296p. (C). 1992. 50.00 (*0-520-07317-7*, Pub. by U CA Pr); pap. 17.95 (*0-520-07318-5*, Pub. by U CA Pr) Cal Prin Full Svc.

Leslie, Charles M., ed. see Kunitz, Stephen J.

Leslie, Clare W. The Art of Field Sketching. 208p. (C). 1995. pap. text, per. 20.95 (*0-7872-0579-6*) Kendall-Hunt.

— Nature All Year Long. LC 90-47866. (Illus.). 56p. (J). (ps up). 1991. 18.00 (*0-688-09183-0*, Grenwillow Bks) HarpC Child Bks.

— Nature Drawing: A Tool for Learning. 208p. (C). 1995. pap. text, per. 20.95 (*0-7872-0580-X*) Kendall-Hunt.

***Leslie, Clare Walker & Gerace, Frank E.** The Ancient Celtic Festivals: And How We Celebrate Them Today. (Illus.). 64p. (gr. 3-7). 2000. 18.00 (*0-89281-822-0*) Inner Tradit.

***Leslie, Clare Walker & Roth, Charles E.** Keeping a Nature Journal: Discover a Whole New Way of Seeing the World Around You. (Illus.). 192p. 2000. pap. 16.95 (*1-58017-306-3*, 67306) Storey Bks.

***Leslie, Clare Walker, et al.** Into the Field: A Guide to Locally Focused Teaching. (Nature Literacy Ser.: No. 3). 83p. 1999. pap. 8.00 (*0-913098-52-3*) Orion Society.

Leslie, Clare Walker, see Walker Leslie, Clare.

Leslie, Darla G., jt. ed. see Summers, Joseph B.

Leslie, David. The Mountain Bike Book. (Illus.). 144p. 1996. 21.95 (*0-7063-7373-1*, Pub. by WrLock) Sterling.

— The Mountain Bike Book. (Illus.). 144p. 1997. pap. 16.95 (*0-7063-7526-6*, Pub. by WrLock) Sterling.

Leslie, David W. & Fretwell, E. K., Jr. Wise Moves in Hard Times: Creating & Managing Resilient Colleges & Universities. LC 95-40653. (Higher & Adult Education Ser.). 320p. 1996. 34.45 (*0-7879-0196-2*) Jossey-Bass.

Leslie, David W., et al. Part-Time Faculty in American Higher Education. LC 81-13773. 151p. 1982. 45.00 (*0-275-90846-1*, C0846, Praeger Pubs) Greenwood.

Leslie, David W., jt. auth. see Gappa, Judith M.

Leslie, Derek. Advanced Macroeconomics: Beyond IS-LM. LC 92-38140. 1993. 17.95 (*0-07-707724-5*) McGraw.

Leslie, Derek, ed. An Investigation of Racial Disadvantage. LC 98-222090. 256p. 1998. text 79.95 (*0-7190-5036-7*, Pub. by Manchester Univ Pr) St Martin.

***Leslie, Diane.** Fleur de Leigh's Life of Crime: A Novel. LC 98-53353. 301p. 1999. 22.50 (*0-684-85695-6*) S&S Trade.

— Fleur de Leigh's Life of Crime: A Novel. 304p. 2000. pap. 12.00 (*0-684-86741-9*, Fireside) S&S Trade Pap.

Leslie, D.M. & Seru, V.B. Fiji Soil Taxonomic Unit Description Handbook, 2 vols. (Illus.). 800p. 1998. reprint ed. pap. 50.00 (*0-478-09318-7*) Balogh.

Leslie, Donald, tr. see Hallyn, Fernand.

Leslie, Doris. The Great Corinthian. large type ed. (Shadows of the Crown Ser.). 1974. 27.99 (*0-85456-597-3*) Ulverscroft.

— The Sceptre & the Rose. large type ed. (Shadows of the Crown Ser.). 1974. 27.99 (*0-85456-618-X*) Ulverscroft.

— That Enchantress. large type ed. (Shadows of the Crown Ser.). 1974. 27.99 (*0-85456-593-0*) Ulverscroft.

Leslie, Douglas L. Cases & Materials on Labor Law: Process & Policy. 2nd ed. 1247p. 1985. 42.00 (*0-316-52161-2*, Aspen Law & Bus) Aspen Pub.

— Labor Law in a Nutshell. 2nd ed. (Nutshell Ser.). 388p. (C). 1991. reprint ed. pap. 21.00 (*0-314-92205-9*) West Pub.

***Leslie, Douglas L.** Labor Law in a Nutshell. 4th ed. 2000. pap. text 23.50 (*0-314-23151-X*) West Pub.

Leslie, Edmund N. Skaneateles: History of Its Earliest Settlement & Reminiscences of Later Times. (Illus.). 477p. 1997. reprint ed. lib. bdg. 49.00 (*0-8328-6241-X*) Higginson Bk Co.

Leslie, Edward E. Desperate Journeys, Abandoned Souls: True Stories of Castaways & Other Survivors. 608p. 1998. pap. 14.00 (*0-395-91150-8*, Mariner Bks) HM.

— The Devil Knows How to Ride: The True Story of William Clarke Quantrill & His Confederate Raiders. LC 98-7156. (Illus.). 516p. 1998. reprint ed. pap. 17.95 (*0-306-80865-X*) Da Capo.

Leslie, Eliza. Directions for Cookery, in Its Various Branches. with Improvements, Supplementary Receipts, & a New Appendix. LC 72-9797. (Cookery Americana Ser.). 1973. reprint ed. 17.95 (*0-405-05050-X*) Ayer.

— Miss Leslie's Behaviour Book: A Guide & Manual for Ladies. LC 72-2611. (American Women Ser.: Images & Realities). 340p. 1974. reprint ed. 24.95 (*0-405-04465-8*) Ayer.

***Leslie, Eliza.** Miss Leslie's Directions for Cookery. unabridged ed. LC 98-55116. 1999. reprint ed. pap. 14.95 (*0-486-40614-8*) Dover.

Leslie, Eliza. Miss Leslie's Secrets: What Every Bride Should Know. Franks, James A. & McKenzie, Elizabeth, eds. (Cookbook Ser.). 528p. 1999. 18.95 (*0-9657173-2-1*) Wld Goose Pr.

— Seventy-Five Receipts for Pastry, Cakes & Sweetmeats. LC 93-12983. 88p. 1988. reprint ed. pap. 7.95 (*1-55709-116-1*) Applewood.

***Leslie, Esther.** Walter Benjamin: Overpowering Conformism. LC 00-20282. (Modern European Thinkers Ser.). 2000. 59.95 (*0-7453-1573-9*) Pluto GBR.

— Walter Benjamin: Overpowering Conformism. 2000. pap. 17.95 (*0-7453-1568-2*, Pub. by Pluto GBR) Stylus Pub VA.

Leslie, Esther, tr. see Lukacs, Georg.

Leslie, F. & Helmers, C. H. Project Planning & Income Distribution. (Studies in Development & Planning: Vol. 9). 1979. lib. bdg. 71.50 (*0-89838-010-3*) Kluwer Academic.

Leslie, G. B. & Lunau, F. W., eds. Indoor Air Pollution: Problems & Priorities. (Illus.). 341p. (C). 1994. pap. text 31.95 (*0-521-47794-8*) Cambridge U Pr.

Leslie, Gay, ed. see Udell, Jon G.

Leslie, George D. The Inner Life of the Royal Academy, with an Account of Its Schools & Exhibitions, Principally in the Reign of Queen Victoria. 1972. 21.95 (*0-405-18181-7*, 1730) Ayer.

Leslie, Gerald R. & Korman, Sheila K. The Family in Social Context. 7th ed. (Illus.). 624p. (C). 1989. text 47.95 (*0-19-504974-8*) OUP.

Leslie-Hynan, Lauren, jt. auth. see Hynan, Michael T.

Leslie, J. D., ed. see Solar Energy Conversion Course, 5th, University of.

Leslie, Jacques. The Mark: A War Correspondent's Memoir of Vietnam & Cambodia. LC 94-38062. (Illus.). 305p. 1995. 22.00 (*1-56858-024-X*) FWEW.

Leslie, James W. Land of Cypress & Pine: More Southeast Arkansas History. (Illus.). 216p. 1976. 19.95 (*0-914546-09-0*) J W Bell.

— Saracen's Country: Some Southeast Arkansas History. (Illus.). 216p. 1974. 19.95 (*0-914546-03-1*) J W Bell.

Leslie, Jan. Routt County Rural Schools, 1883-1960: Windows to Yesterday. LC 98-66349. 90p. 1998. write for info. (*0-9666054-0-3*) Legacy Bks & Res.

Leslie, Jean. Glimpses of Calgary Past. (Illus.). 128p. (Orig.). 1994. pap. write for info. (*1-55059-099-5*) Detselig Ents.

Leslie, Jean B. & Fleenor, John W. Feedback to Managers: A Review & Comparison of Multi-Rater Instruments for Management Development. 3rd expanded rev. ed. LC 98-5006. 348p. 1998. pap. text 60.00 (*1-882197-35-6*) Ctr Creat Leader.

Leslie, Jean B. & Van Velsor, Ellen. A Cross-National Comparison of Effective Leadership & Teamwork Toward a Global Workforce: Toward a Global Work Force. LC 97-40879. 55p. 1998. pap. text 15.00 (*1-882197-34-8*) Ctr Creat Leader.

— A Look at Derailment Today: North America & Europe. LC 95-52011. 69p. 1996. pap. text 20.00 (*1-882197-15-1*) Ctr Creat Leader.

***Leslie, Jeremy & Blackwell, Lewis.** Issues: New Magazine Design. (Illus.). 172p. 2000. pap. 45.00 (*1-58423-025-8*) Gingko Press.

Leslie, Jeremy, jt. auth. see Burgoyne, Patrick.

Leslie, John. Blue Moon. LC 99-166546. Vol. 4. 256p. 1998. 23.00 (*0-671-53514-5*, Pocket Books) PB.

— Damaged Goods. Grad, Doug, ed. 320p. (Orig.). 1993. mass mkt. 5.50 (*0-671-72479-7*) PB.

— The End of the World: The Science & Ethics of Human Extinction. LC 95-38891. 320p. (C). 1996. 32.99 (*0-415-14043-9*) Routledge.

— The End of the World: The Science & Ethics of Human Extinction. (Illus.). 336p. 1998. pap. 17.99 (*0-415-18447-9*) Routledge.

— Havana Hustle. 1994. mass mkt. 5.50 (*0-671-78166-9*) PB.

— History of Scotland, from the Death of King James First in the Year 1436, to the Year 1561. LC 78-172315. (Bannatyne Club, Edinburgh. Publications: No. 38). reprint ed. 42.50 (*0-404-52744-2*) AMS Pr.

— Killing Me Softly. Grose, Bill, ed. 256p. (Orig.). 1995. mass mkt. 5.50 (*0-671-86421-1*) PB.

— Love for Sale. (Gideon Lowry Mystery Ser.). 272p. 1997. per. 6.50 (*0-671-51126-2*) PB.

— Love for Sale: A Gideon Lowry Mystery. LC 96-8554. 1997. 22.00 (*0-671-51127-0*) PB.

— Night & Day. 1996. pap. 5.99 (*0-671-86423-8*) PB.

— Universes. 256p. (C). 1990. text 25.00 (*0-415-04144-9*, A4027) Routledge.

— Universes. 240p. (C). 1996. pap. 20.99 (*0-415-13955-4*) Routledge.

Leslie, John, ed. Modern Cosmology & Philosophy. 330p. 1998. reprint ed. pap. 19.95 (*1-57392-250-1*) Prometheus Bks.

Leslie, John K. Spanish for Conversation. 4th ed. LC 75-3774. 170p. (C). 1976. pap. text 7.00 (*0-471-01417-6*) Wiley.

Leslie, Julia, ed. Myth & Mythmaking: Continuous Evolution in Indian Tradition. LC 96-153476. (SOAS Collected Papers on South Asia: No. 12). 260p. (C). 1996. text 45.00 (*0-7007-0303-9*, Pub. by Curzon Pr Ltd) UH Pr.

— Roles & Rituals for Hindu Women. LC 91-18883. 256p. 1991. 42.50 (*0-8386-3475-3*) Fairleigh Dickinson.

***Leslie, Julia & McGee, Mary, eds.** Gender Constructs, Indian Religion & Society. (School of Oriental & African Studies). 328p. 2000. text 24.95 (*0-19-565293-2*) OUP.

Leslie, Julian. Principles of Behavioural Analysis. 3rd ed. 340p. 1996. text 38.00 (*3-7186-5901-8*, Harwood Acad Pubs); pap. text 15.00 (*3-7186-5902-6*, Harwood Acad Pubs) Gordon & Breach.

***Leslie, Julian & O'Reilly, Mark F.** Behavior Analysis: Foundations & Applications to Psychology. 384p. 2000. text 45.00 (*90-5702-485-3*, Harwood Acad Pubs); pap. text 22.00 (*90-5702-486-1*, Harwood Acad Pubs) Gordon & Breach.

***Leslie, Julian C. & Blackman, Derek E.** Experimental & Applied Analysis of Human Behavior. LC 99-52328. 1999. write for info. (*1-878978-37-3*) Context Pr.

Leslie, K. H. Leslie: Historical Records of the Family of Leslie, 3 vols. 1991. reprint ed. pap. 134.50 (*0-8328-2159-4*); reprint ed. lib. bdg. 144.50 (*0-8328-2158-6*) Higginson Bk Co.

Leslie, Karen. Faith & Little Children: A Guide for Parents & Teachers. LC 89-51903. 128p. (Orig.). 1990. pap. 7.95 (*0-89622-404-X*) Twenty-Third.

Leslie, Kathleen. Cities Around the World. LC 97-215111. (Pair-it Bks.). 25p. 1998. write for info. (*0-8172-7281-X*) Raintree Steck-V.

Leslie, Kent A. Woman of Color, Daughter of Privilege: Amanda America Dickson, 1849-1893. LC 94-17033. (Illus.). 240p. 1995. 29.95 (*0-8203-1688-1*) U of Ga Pr.

— Woman of Color, Daughter of Privilege: Amanda America Dickson, 1849-1893. 1996. pap. text 15.95 (*0-8203-1871-X*) U of Ga Pr.

Leslie, Kevin, jt. auth. see Stein, Elissa.

Leslie, Kim C., ed. Roots of America: A Anthology of Documents Relating to American History in the West Sussex Record Office. 114p. 1976. 75.00 (*0-7855-7276-7*) St Mut.

Leslie, Larry L., jt. auth. see Anderson, Richard E.

Leslie, Larry L., jt. auth. see Slaughter, Sheila.

Leslie, Laura, ed. see Kemp, Jerrold E.

Leslie, Lauren & Caldwell, JoAnne. Qualitative Reading Inventory. 278p. (C). 1997. pap. text 41.40 (*0-673-18791-8*) Addson-Wesley Educ.

***Leslie, Lauren & Caldwell, JoAnne.** Qualitative Reading Inventory, 3. LC 00-30498. 2001. write for info. (*0-321-03786-3*) Longman.

Leslie, Lauren & Caldwell, JoAnne. Qualitative Reading Inventory, II. 2nd rev. ed. LC 94-18636. 277p. (C). 1997. pap. text 40.75 (*0-673-99086-9*) Addson-Wesley Educ.

Leslie, Lauren, et al. Authentic Literacy Assessment: An Ecological Approach. LC 96-51525. 320p. (C). 1997. pap. 41.40 (*0-321-01235-6*) Addson-Wesley Educ.

Leslie, Leigh A., jt. ed. see Sollie, Donna L.

Leslie, Louis A. Twenty Thousand Words. 7th large type ed. 300p. (YA). (gr. 7 up). 1981. reprint ed. 75.50 (*0-317-01950-3*, J-26190-00) Am Printing Hse.

Leslie, Louis A. & Zoubek, Charles E. Gregg Shorthand for the Electronic Office, Pt. I. (Short Course Ser.: No. 90). 320p. 1984. text 29.96 (*0-07-037914-9*) McGraw.

— Gregg Shorthand for the Electronic Office: Short Course, Pt. II. (Series 90). 320p. 1984. text 29.96 (*0-07-037917-3*) McGraw.

— Gregg Shorthand Functional Method. 2nd ed. (Diamond Jubilee Ser.). 1971. text 25.00 (*0-07-037255-1*) McGraw.

— Gregg Transcription. 2nd ed. (Diamond Jubilee Ser.). 1971. text 25.00 (*0-07-037262-4*) McGraw.

Leslie, Louis A., et al. Gregg Dictation: Diamond Jubilee Series. 2nd ed. 1970. pap. text 24.12 (*0-07-037257-8*) McGraw.

— Gregg Notehand. 2nd ed. 1968. text 20.24 (*0-07-037331-0*) McGraw.

— Gregg Shorthand for Colleges, Vol. 1. (Series 90). 1998. text 96.20 (*0-07-037749-9*) McGraw.

— Gregg Shorthand for Colleges, Vol. 2. (Series 90). 1980. text 101.40 (*0-07-037754-5*) McGraw.

— Gregg Shorthand One Series Ninety: A Gregg Text-Kit in Continuing Education. (Microcomputer Software Program Ser.). 1983. 62.92 (*0-07-037769-3*) McGraw.

— Gregg Shorthand 2: A Gregg Text-Kit in Continuing Education. (Series 90). 1983. 69.92 (*0-07-037770-7*) McGraw.

— Gregg Transcription. (Series 90). 1979. text 24.56 (*0-07-037740-5*) McGraw.

Leslie, Louise. Tazewell County. (Illus.). 794p. 1995. reprint ed. 34.95 (*1-57072-031-2*) Overmountain Pr.

Leslie, Lynn. Courage, My Love: Women Who Dare. (Superromance Ser.). 1993. mass mkt. 3.50 (*0-373-70566-2*, 1-70566-4) Harlequin Bks.

— Night of the Nile. (Intrigue Ser.). 1994. per. 2.99 (*0-373-22287-4*, 1-22287-6) Harlequin Bks.

— The Other Amanda. (Loving Dangerously Ser.). 1997. per. 3.99 (*0-373-70735-5*, 1-70735-5) Harlequin Bks.

— Passion Sans Escale. (Amours d'Aujourd'Hui Ser.). 1999. mass mkt. 4.99 (*0-373-38327-4*, 1-38327-2) Harlequin Bks.

— Singapore Fling. (Superromance Ser.). 1994. per. 3.50 (*0-373-70604-9*, 1-70604-3) Harlequin Bks.

Leslie, Marina. Renaissance Utopias & the Problem of History. LC 98-17865. (Illus.). 176p. 1998. text 35.00 (*0-8014-3400-9*) Cornell U Pr.

Leslie, Marina, jt. auth. see Kelly, Kathleen C.

Leslie, Marsha R., ed. The Single Mother's Companion: Essays & Stories by Women. LC 94-10613. 288p. (Orig.). 1994. pap. 12.95 (*1-878067-56-7*) Seal Pr WA.

Leslie, Mary E., et al, eds. American Women in Sport, 1887 - 1987: A 100-Year Chronology. LC 89-6150. (Illus.). 173p. 1989. 31.00 (*0-8108-2205-9*) Scarecrow.

Leslie, Mei, ed. see Gray, Margie.

Leslie-Melville, Betty. Walter Warthog. large type ed. 1993. 13.50 (*0-614-09859-9*, L-34123-00) Am Printing Hse.

Leslie, Michael & Raylor, Timothy, eds. Culture & Cultivation in Early Modern England. 256p. 1994. pap. 19.95 (*0-7185-2148-X*) St Martin.

— Culture & Cultivation in Early Modern England: Writing & the Land. LC 92-8560. 1992. 59.00 (*0-7185-1399-1*) St Martin.

Leslie, Naton. Their Shadows Are Dark Daughters. (Chapbook Ser.: No. 1). (Illus.). 40p. 1998. pap. 5.00 (*1-886350-50-7*) Pavement Saw.

Leslie, Noel. Three Plays. LC 79-50026. (One-Act Plays in Reprint Ser.). 1980. reprint ed. 20.00 (*0-8486-2050-X*) Roth Pub Inc.

Leslie, Patty, jt. auth. see Cox, Paul W.

Leslie, Paul, ed. The Gulf War As Popular Entertainment: An Analysis of the Military-Industrial Media Complex. LC 97-2065. (Symposium Ser.: Vol. 42). 72p. 1997. text 49.95 (*0-7734-8666-6*) E Mellen.

Leslie, Paul, jt. auth. see Little, Michael.

Leslie, Paula & Fox, John. Anger in the Workplace, a Catalyst for Change: A Handbook for Women. (Illus.). 96p. (Orig.). 1998. pap. 17.95 (*0-9662691-0-1*) Essent Life Strat.

Leslie, Peter. Baltic Commando. 224p. 25.00 (*0-7278-5208-6*) Severn Hse.

***Leslie, Peter.** Blitz Harvest. 1999. 26.00 (*0-7278-5440-2*, Pub. by Severn Hse) Chivers N Amer.

Leslie, Peter. Flames over Provence. 224p. 1998. 24.00 (*0-7278-5340-6*) Severn Hse.

— No Deal in Diamonds. 224p. 1992. 19.00 (*0-7278-4371-0*) Severn Hse.

Leslie, Peter M. Federal State, National Economy. 213p. 1987. pap. 19.95 (*0-8020-6611-9*) U of Toronto Pr.

Leslie, R. D., ed. Causes of Diabetes: Genetic & Environmental Factors. LC 93-11222. 376p. 1993. 314.00 (*0-471-94040-2*) Wiley.

Leslie, R. D. & Robbins, David C., eds. Diabetes: Clinical Science in Practice. (Illus.). 508p. (C). 1995. text 165.00 (*0-521-45029-2*) Cambridge U Pr.

Leslie, R. F. Reform & Insurrection in Russian Poland, 1856-1865, 13--13. LC 72-91767. 272p. 1970. reprint ed. lib. bdg. 35.00 (*0-8371-2415-8*, LERI, Greenwood Pr) Greenwood.

Leslie, R. F., jt. ed. see Brook, G. L.

***Leslie, Richard.** Pablo Picasso: A Modern Master. (Illus.). 1998. 16.98 (*1-880908-73-5*) Todtri Prods.

Leslie, Richard, ed. see Chalifoux, Paul R.

Leslie, Richard D., ed. Molecular Pathogenesis of Diabetes Mellitus. LC 96-24159. (Frontiers of Hormone Research Ser.: Vol. 22, 1997). (Illus.). viii, 228p. 1997. 198.25 (*3-8055-6373-6*) S Karger.

Leslie, Robert, ed. see Parra, Mario & Canterbury, Gloria.

Leslie, Robert F. In the Shadow of a Rainbow. 192p. 1996. pap. 11.00 (*0-393-31452-9*, Norton Paperbks) Norton.

— In the Shadow of a Rainbow: The True Story of a Friendship Between Man & Wolf. 192p. 1986. reprint ed. pap. 9.95 (*0-393-30392-6*) Norton.

Leslie, Roderick, jt. auth. see Avery, Mark.

***Leslie, Ron A., et al.** Antisense Technology in the Central Nervous System. LC 99-16187. 1999. write for info. (*0-19-850316-4*) OUP.

***Leslie, Ron A. & Robertson, Harry A., eds.** Differential Display: A Practical Approach. (The Practical Approach Ser.: No. 224). (Illus.). 288p. 2000. pap. text 55.00 (*0-19-963758-X*) OUP.

— Differential Display: A Practical Approach. LC 99-57575. 288p. 2000. write for info. (*0-19-963759-8*) OUP.

Leslie, Ronald A., et al, eds. Antisense Technology in the Central Nervous System. LC 99-16187. (Illus.). 272p. 2000. pap. text 39.95 (*0-19-850538-8*) OUP.

Leslie, Russell P. & Conway, Kathryn M. The Lighting Pattern Book for Homes. LC 93-80008. (Illus.). 232p. 1993. 40.00 (*1-883297-00-1*) RPI Lght Res.

Leslie, Shane. Men Were Different: Five Studies in Late Victorian Biography. LC 67-26754. (Essay Index Reprint Ser.). 1977. 20.95 (*0-8369-0615-2*) Ayer.

— Salutation to Five: Mrs. Fitzherbert, Edmund Warre, Sir William Butler, Leo Tolstoy, Sir Mark Sykes. LC 75-126231. (Biography Index Reprint Ser.). 1977. 19.95 (*0-8369-8027-1*) Ayer.

— The Skull of Swift. LC 79-169767. (Select Bibliographies Reprint Ser.). 1977. reprint ed. 26.95 (*0-8369-5987-6*) Ayer.

— Studies in Sublime Failure. LC 70-117817. (Essay Index Reprint Ser.). 1977. 23.95 (*0-8369-1670-0*) Ayer.

Leslie-Smith, L. H., ed. The Universal Flame. 263p. 1975. 9.95 (*0-8356-7506-8*) Theos Pub Hse.

Leslie-Spinks, Tim & Andres, Alice. Treasures of Trinkamalee. (Illus.). 32p. (J). (gr. 4-7). 1993. pap. 5.95 (*1-55037-323-4*, Pub. by Annick); lib. bdg. 15.95 (*1-55037-320-X*, Pub. by Annick) Firefly Bks Ltd.

Leslie, Stephen W., jt. auth. see Savitz, Gail.

Leslie, Stuart W. The Cold War & American Science. 320p. 1993. text 57.50 (*0-231-07958-3*) Col U Pr.

— Cold War & American Science. 1994. pap. 20.50 (*0-231-07959-1*) Col U Pr.

Leslie, Susan. The Happiness of God. (C). 1988. 39.00 (*0-85439-272-6*, Pub. by St Paul Pubns) St Mut.

— The Happiness of God: Holiness in Therese of Lisieux. LC 88-21658. 81p. 1988. pap. 4.95 (*0-8189-0540-9*) Alba.

Leslie, Tanya, tr. see Ernaux, Annie.

Leslie, Thomas E. Essays in Political Economy. 2nd ed. LC 69-20305. (Reprints of Economic Classics Ser.). xii, 437p. 1969. reprint ed. 49.50 (*0-678-00480-3*) Kelley.

— Land Systems & Industrial Economy of Ireland, England, & Continental Countries. LC 67-18570. (Reprints of Economic Classics Ser.). vi, 379p. 1968. reprint ed. 49.50 (*0-678-00346-7*) Kelley.

***Leslie, Tim, ed.** Electronic Banking & Trading of Securities: Public Hearing. 97p. 2000. pap. text 25.00 (0-7881-8907-7) DIANE Pub.

Leslie, W. Bruce. Gentlemen & Scholars: College & Community in the "Age of the University" (Illus.). 320p. 1993. 49.50 (0-271-00829-6) Pa St U Pr.

Leslie, Warren, et al. Dallas Public & Private: Aspects of an American City. LC 98-14808. 276p. 1998. reprint ed. pap. 14.95 (0-87074-428-3) SMU Press.

Leslie, Wendy, ed. see Zablocki, Craig.

Leslie, William C. The Physical Metallurgy of Steels. (Illus.). 408p. (C). 1991. reprint ed. 88.00 (1-878907-25-5) TechBooks.

Lesly, Elizabeth. The Network: Inside the Tight-Knit World of Black America's Power Brokers. 1996. 22.00 (0-614-15441-3) McGraw.

— The Network: Inside the Tight-Knit World of Black America's Power Brokers. (Illus.). 304p. 1996. text 22.00 (0-07-037800-2) McGraw.

Lesly, Philip. Bonanzas & Fool's Gold: Treasures & Dross from the Nuggetizing of Our Lives. 180p. 1987. pap. 9.95 (0-9602866-2-4) Lesly Co.

— Selections from Managing the Human Climate. 178p. (Orig.). 1979. pap. 9.00 (0-9602866-0-8) Lesly Co.

Lesman, Ann S., et al. Espanol para Hoy: En el Mundo y la Comunidad. (SPA.). 388p. (Orig.). (C). 1992. pap. text 42.50 (0-8191-8858-1) U Pr of Amer.

Lesman, Helen. Friend to Friend. rev. ed. 366p. 1995. spiral bd. 6.50 (1-879127-63-6) Lighten Up Enter.

— Heart Delights. rev. ed. 366p. 1995. spiral bd. 6.50 (1-879127-57-1) Lighten Up Enter.

Lesman, Helen. Heart-to-Heart. pap. 8.95 (1-879127-02-4) Lighten Up Enter.

Lesman, Helen. Heart to Heart. rev. ed. 366p. 1995. spiral bd. 6.50 (1-879127-56-3) Lighten Up Enter.

— Hugs for the Heart. rev. ed. 366p. 1995. spiral bd. 6.50 (1-879127-55-5) Lighten Up Enter.

Lesman, Helen. Running Starts: Teens. pap. 8.95 (1-879127-04-0) Lighten Up Enter.

Lesman, Helen & Cleaveland, Teta. Heart Delights for Mothers & Daughters. rev. ed. 366p. 1995. spiral bd. 6.50 (1-879127-58-X) Lighten Up Enter.

Lesman, Helen, et al. The Best of Hearts. 10th anniversary ed. (Illus.). 368p. 1994. spiral bd. 6.50 (1-879127-30-X) Lighten Up Enter.

Lesman, Helen, jt. auth. see Estrem, Victoria L.

Lesmes, George R. & Hearst, Margo R. Intervention Information Systems: Smoking Cessation. (Illus.). 13p. (C). 1993. write for info. (1-882953-04-5); student ed. write for info. (1-882953-03-7); write for info. (1-882953-06-1); audio. write for info. (1-882953-05-3) Intervent Info.

— Intervention Information Systems: Smoking Cessation, Pt. I. (Illus.). 150p. (C). 1993. teacher ed. write for info. (1-882953-01-0) Intervent Info.

— Intervention Information Systems: Smoking Cessation, Pt. II. (Illus.). 150p. (C). 1993. write for info. (1-882953-02-9) Intervent Info.

— Intervention Information Systems: Smoking Cessation, Set. (Illus.). (C). 1993. write for info. (1-882953-00-2) Intervent Info.

Lesmian, Boleslaw. Mythematics & Extropy II: Selected Literary Criticism of Boleslaw Lesmian. Chciuk-Celt, Alexandra, ed. & tr. by. from POL. LC 91-20519. (American University Studies: Slavic Languages & Literature: Ser. XII, Vol. 3). 158p. (C). 1992. text 29.95 (0-8204-1636-3) P Lang Pubng.

Lesmueller, A. Thurn, ed. Iosephi Genesii Regum Libri Quattuor. (Corpus Fontium Historiae Byzantinae Ser.: Vol. XIV). (C). 1978. 119.25 (3-11-006599-1) De Gruyter.

Lesne, Annick. Renormalization Methods: Critical Phenomena, Chaos, Fractal Structures. LC 97-43772. 374p. 1998. 165.00 (0-471-96689-4) Wiley.

Lesner, Patricia A. Pediatric Nursing. (LPN/LVN Nursing Ser.). 1983. pap., teacher ed. 10.00 (0-8273-1933-9) Delmar.

— Pediatric Nursing. LC 81-82910. (Illus.). 544p. 1983. text 35.95 (0-8273-1932-0) Delmar.

Lesner, Sharon A., jt. auth. see Kricos, Patricia B.

Lesniak, James. Contemporary Authors New Revision, Vol. 44. Draper, James P. & Trosky, Susan M., eds. (Contemporary Authors Revised Ser.). 500p. 1994. text 150.00 (0-8103-1929-2, 000084) Gale.

— Contemporary Authors New Revision Series, Vol. 42. (Contemporary Authors Revised Ser.). 500p. 1993. text 150.00 (0-8103-1973-X, 000082) Gale.

— Contemporary Authors New Revision Series & Contemporary Authors Index, Vol. 43. 500p. 1994. text 150.00 (0-8103-1974-8, 000083) Gale.

Lesniak, James, ed. Contemporary Authors, Vol. 31. (New Revision Ser.). 500p. 1990. text 150.00 (0-8103-1985-3) Gale.

— Contemporary Authors New Revision Series, Vol. 30. 500p. 1990. text 150.00 (0-8103-1984-5) Gale.

Lesniak, James, jt. auth. see May, Hal.

Lesniak, James, jt. auth. see Trosky, Susan M.

Lesniak, James, ed. see Gale Research Staff.

Lesniak, James, jt. ed. see May, Hal.

Lesniak, Linda, jt. auth. see Chartrand, Gary.

Lesniak, Louis A. Human Psychology of the Single Person: Index of New Information with Authors, Subjects & Bibliography. rev. ed. 135p. 1997. 47.50 (0-7883-1480-7); pap. 44.50 (0-7883-1481-5) ABBE Pubs Assn.

***Lesniak, Slawomir.** Der Begriff der Einbildungskraft Bei Rudolf Kassner. (Europaische Hochschulschriften Ser.). 137p. 1999. 26.95 (3-631-35542-4) P Lang Pubng.

Lesnick. Excerpts. (American Casebook Ser.). (C). 1995. write for info. (0-314-06787-6) West Pub.

Lesnick, Howard. Becoming a Lawyer: Individual Choice & Responsibility in the Practice of Law, Teacher's Manual to Accompany. (American Casebook Ser.). 100p. (C). 1992. pap. text. write for info. (0-314-01332-6) West Pub.

— Being a Lawyer: Individual Choice & Responsibility in the Practice of Law. LC 92-16679. (American Casebook Ser.). 422p. (C). 1992. pap. 36.50 (0-314-00916-7) West Pub.

— Listening for God: Religion & Moral Discernment. LC 98-18062. xiii, 249p. 1998. 29.95 (0-8232-1860-0); pap. 18.95 (0-8232-1861-9) Fordham.

Lesnick, Howard, et al. Becoming a Lawyer: A Humanistic Perspective on Legal Education & Professionalism. LC 80-26225. 211p. (C). 1980. reprint ed. pap. 22.50 (0-8299-2126-5) West Pub.

Lesnick, Irving, jt. auth. see Harnett, Bertram.

Lesnick, Leslie & Dahl, Andrew. Lotus Notes: Administration Survival Guide. 672p. 1996. 55.00 incl. cd-rom (0-672-30844-4, Bobbs) Macmillan.

Lesnick, Leslie, jt. auth. see Dahl, Andrew.

Lesnick, Michael E. Skilled Nursing Facility Management: Cost Reporting. LC 97-13983. 250p. 1995. 175.00 (1-55738-637-4, Irwn Prfssnl) McGraw-Hill Prof.

— Skilled Nursing Facility Management: Coverage Issues. 200p. 1995. 175.00 (1-55738-638-2, Irwn Prfssnl) McGraw-Hill Prof.

— Skilled Nursing Facility Management: New Directions in Long Term Care. 250p. 1995. 50.00 (1-55738-639-0, Irwn Prfssnl) McGraw-Hill Prof.

— Skilled Nursing Facility Management: Optimizing Reimbursement. 300p. 1995. 175.00 (1-55738-636-6, Irwn Prfssnl) McGraw-Hill Prof.

Lesnick, Michael T. & Crowfoot, James E. A Bibliography for the Study of Natural Resource & Environmental Conflict. (CPL Bibliographies Ser.: No. 64). 55p. 1981. 10.00 (0-86602-064-0, Sage Prdcls Pr) Sage.

Lesniewicz, Paul. Bonsai: Complete Guide to Art & Techniques. (Illus.). 192p. 1998. pap. 21.95 (0-304-34943-7, Pub. by Cassell) Sterling.

— Bonsai in Your Home: An Indoor Grower's Guide. (Illus.). 208p. 1997. pap. 19.95 (0-8069-0781-9) Sterling.

— Indoor Bonsai. (Illus.). 208p. (Orig.). 1986. pap. 16.95 (0-7137-1700-9, Pub. by Blandford Pr) Sterling.

Lesniewski. Collected Works. (Nips Ser.). Date not set. lib. bdg. write for info. (90-277-0996-3) Kluwer Academic.

Lesniewski, John, jt. auth. see Lesniewski, Karen.

Lesniewski, Karen & Lesniewski, John. Kiss Collectibles: Identification & Price Guide. 200p. (Orig.). 1993. pap. 10.00 (0-380-77166-7, Avon Bks) Morrow Avon.

Lesniewski, Stanislaw. Collected Works, 2 vols., Set, Vols. I & II. Surma, S. J. et al, eds. (Nijhoff International Philosophy Ser.: No. 44). 810p. 1991. lib. bdg. 468.00 (0-7923-1512-X, Pub. by Kluwer Academic) Kluwer Academic.

Lesnik, Bogdan. Countering Discrimination in Social Work. (International Perspectives in Social Work Ser.). 208p. 1998. text 59.95 (1-85742-436-0, Pub. by Ashgate Pub) Ashgate Pub Co.

— International Perspectives in Social Work: Change in Social Work. LC 97-39720. 1997. 46.95 (1-85742-407-7, Pub. by Arena) Ashgate Pub Co.

Lesnik, Milton & Anderson, Bernice E. Nursing Practice & the Law. 2nd ed. LC 75-45453. 400p. 1976. reprint ed. lib. bdg. 75.00 (0-8371-8729-X, LENP, Greenwood Pr) Greenwood.

Lesnik-Oberstein, Karin. Children's Literature: Criticism & the Fictional Child. LC 93-35484. 258p. 1994. text 45.00 (0-19-811998-4) OUP.

Lesnoff-Caravaglia, Gari. Handbook of Applied Gerontology. LC 86-20811. 460p. 1987. 54.95 (0-89885-314-1, Kluwer Acad Hman Sci) Kluwer Academic.

— Health Aspects of Aging: The Experience of Growing Old. LC 99-44461. 206p. 1999. text 39.95 (0-398-07011-3); pap. text 27.95 (0-398-07012-1) C C Thomas.

Lesnoff-Caravaglia, Gari, ed. Aging & the Human Condition, Vol. II. LC 81-6630. (Frontiers in Aging Ser.). 160p. 1982. 32.95 (0-89885-029-0, Kluwer Acad Hman Sci) Kluwer Academic.

— Aging in a Technological Society, Vol. VI. (Frontiers in Aging Ser.). 264p. 1988. 43.95 (0-89885-382-6, Kluwer Acad Hman Sci) Kluwer Academic.

— Health Care of the Elderly: Strategies for Prevention & Intervention. LC 79-19192. (Frontiers in Aging Ser.: Vol. I). 232p. 1980. 42.95 (0-87705-417-7, Kluwer Acad Hman Sci) Kluwer Academic.

— Values, Ethics & Aging, Vol. IV. (Frontiers in Aging Ser.). (Illus.). 196p. 1985. 35.95 (0-89885-162-9, Kluwer Acad Hman Sci) Kluwer Academic.

Lesnoff-Caravaglia, Gari, tr. see Pitskhelauri, G. Z.

Lesobre, Jacques, et al. Risk Insurance Reinsurance Lexicon: Francais - English - American. 3rd ed. (ENG & FRE.). 375p. 1993. pap. 150.00 (0-7859-1079-4, 290218945X) Fr & Eur.

Lesoil, M. French-Norwegian Dictionary: Fransk-Norsk-Ordbok. (FRE & NOR.). 435p. 1986. 49.95 (0-8288-1032-X, M9457) Fr & Eur.

— Norsk-Fransk Ordbok: Norwegian-French Dictionary. (FRE.). 445p. 1978. 39.95 (0-8288-5258-8, M9463) Fr & Eur.

Lesoing, Jan. Forever Yesterday. 1988. pap. 3.95 (0-517-00623-5) Random Hse Value.

Leson, Nancy, ed. Northwest Budget Traveler: Cheap Eats, Cheap Sleeps, Affordable Adventure. 3rd rev. ed. (Best Places Ser.). Orig. Title: Northwest Cheap Sleeps. (Illus.). 320p. 1998. pap. 16.95 (1-57061-126-2) Sasquatch Bks.

Leson, Nancy & Irving, Stephanie, eds. Seattle Best Places: The Most Discriminating Guide to Seattle's Restaurants, Shops, Hotels, Nightlife, Arts, Sights, & Outings. 7th rev. ed. LC 95-22919. (Best Places Guidebooks Ser.). 448p. 1996. pap. 16.95 (1-57061-055-X) Sasquatch Bks.

Lesonsky, Rieva. Get Smart: 365 Tips to Boost Your Entrepreneurial IQ. LC 99-39749. 400p. 1999. pap. 12.95 (1-891984-09-8, Pub. by Entrepreneur) Natl Bk Netwk.

Lesonsky, Rieva & Anderson, Leann. 303 Marketing Tips: Guaranteed to Boost Your Business. LC 98-41359. 350p. 1999. pap. 17.95 (1-891984-02-0, Pub. by Entrepreneur) Natl Bk Netwk.

***Lesonsky, Rieva & Sato Stodder, Gayle.** Young Millionaires: Inspiring Stories to Ignite Your Entrepreneurial Dreams. LC 98-27541. 200p. 1998. pap. 14.95 (1-891984-01-2, Pub. by Entrepreneur) Natl Bk Netwk.

Lesonsky, Rieva, jt. ed. see Entrepreneur Media Staff.

Lesort, Jean-Baptiste, ed. Transportation & Traffic Theory: Proceedings of the 13th International Symposium on Transportation & Traffic Theory, Lyon, France, 24-26 July 1996. 772p. 1996. text 173.00 (0-08-042586-0, Pergamon Pr) Elsevier.

LeSota, Stan, ed. Coatings Encyclopedic Dictionary. 1995. 135.00 (0-934010-04-8); pap. 105.00 (0-934010-05-6) Fed Soc Coat Tech.

Lesoult, G. & Lacaze, J., eds. Physical Metallurgy of Cast Iron V. LC 99-515148. (Advanced Materials Research Ser.: Vols. 4-5). (Illus.). 600p. (C). 1998. text 215.00 (3-908450-28-4, Pub. by Scitec Pubns) Enfield Pubs NH.

Lesourd, Jean-Baptiste, et al, eds. Models for Energy Policy. LC 95-813. (New International Studies in Economic Modelling Ser.). 288p. (C). (gr. 13). 1995. 115.00 (0-415-12975-3) Routledge.

Lesourd, Leonard. The Rookie. 1996. 18.99 (0-345-40504-8) Ballantine Pub Grp.

LeSourd, Leonard, jt. auth. see Marshall, Catherine.

LeSourd, Leonard E., ed. The Best of Catherine Marshall. large type ed. LC 94-42713. 384p. 1995. pap. 14.95 (0-8027-2687-9) Walker & Co.

— The Best of Catherine Marshall: Her Intimate Life. 352p. 1995. reprint ed. pap. 9.00 (0-380-72383-2, Avon Bks) Morrow Avon.

LeSourd, Leonard E., ed. see Marshall, Catherine.

LeSourd, Philip S. Accent & Syllable Structure in Passamaquoddy. LC 92-36574. (Outstanding Dissertations in Linguistics Ser.). 496p. 1992. text 20.00 (0-8153-0213-4) Garland.

Lesourd, Sandra Simpson. Woman's Journey to Freedom. 1998. 11.99 (0-88486-198-8, Inspirational Pr) Arrowood Pr.

LeSourd, Sandra Simpson, see Simpson LeSourd, Sandra.

Lesourne, Jacques. After Communism: From the Atlantic to the Urals. 271, viip. 1991. pap. text 36.00 (3-7186-5212-9, Harwood Acad Pubs) Gordon & Breach.

— The Economics of Order & Disorder. (Illus.). 224p. 1992. text 49.95 (0-19-828739-9) OUP.

— World Perspectives: A European Assessment. Romeo, Sharon L., tr. (FRE.). viii, 352p. 1986. text 80.00 (2-88124-179-4) Gordon & Breach.

Lesourne, Jacques & Lecomte, Bernard. After Communism: From the Atlantic to the Urals. vii, 271p. 1991. text 94.00 (3-7186-5211-0, HX) Gordon & Breach.

Lesourne, Jacques, ed. see Anas, Alex.

Lesourne, Jacques, ed. see Hahn, R. W.

Lesourne, Jacques, ed. see Hartwick, John M.

Lesourne, Jacques, ed. see Mokyr, J.

Lesourne, Jacques, ed. see Pollard, S.

Lesourne, Jacques, ed. see Vogelsang, Ingo.

Lesourne, Jacques, ed. see Weiss, A.

Lesowitz, Nina & Starr, Laura Morris. The Party Girl Cookbook: Your Complete Guide to Throwing a Smashing Bash, with Ideas for Themes, Invitations, Costumes, & More Than 150 Recipes. LC 99-16035. 272p. 1999. pap. 14.95 (1-57324-167-9) Conari Press.

Lesowske, Charles J., ed. see Edske, James A.

L'Esperance, Carrie. The Ancient Cookfire: How to Rejuvenate Body & Spirit Through Seasonal Foods & Fasting. LC 97-52212. (Illus.). 288p. 1998. pap. 18.00 (1-879181-51-7) Bear & Co.

L'Esperance, Francis A., jt. auth. see Friedman, Eli A.

Lesperance, Gary L. & Purvins, John J. Computers Simplified & Illustrated Bk. 1: Learn the Easy Way. (Illus.). 80p. (Orig.). (C). 1985. pap. 5.95 (0-932285-00-7) Rockway Hse.

Lesperance, Yves, jt. auth. see Jennings, Nick.

Lespes, Anthony. Les Semences de la Colere. (B. E. Ser.: No. 49). (FRE.). 1949. 35.00 (0-8115-3000-0) Periodicals Srv.

LesPes, Claudine & Oluer-Zimmerman, Joelle. Dinou et Dina: Introductory French. 1993. write for info. (0-8013-0811-9) Longman.

Lespy, V. Dictionary Barnais Ancien, Moderne. (FRE.). 1998. 175.00 (0-320-00262-4) Fr & Eur.

Less, Menahem, et al. Evaluating Driving Potential of Persons With Physical Disabilities. LC 78-62052. (Illus.). 36p. 1978. 4.25 (0-686-38803-8) Human Res Ctr.

— Hand Controls & Assistive Devices for the Physically Disabled Driver. (Illus.). 60p. 1977. 5.00 (0-686-38804-6) Human Res Ctr.

Lessa, Christina. Gymnastics: Balancing Acts. (Illus.). 160p. 1997. 45.00 (0-7893-0113-X, Pub. by Universe) St Martin.

— Gymnastics: Balancing Acts. (Illus.). 160p. 1997. pap. 27.50 (0-7893-0105-9) St Martin.

***Lessa, Christina.** Women to Women: A New Plan for Success & Well-Being from Today's Most Celebrated Women. 2000. 29.95 (0-7893-0356-6) Universe.

Lessa, Christina. Women Who Win: Stories of Triumph in Sports & Life. (Illus.). 160p. 2000. pap. 27.50 (0-7893-0233-0, Pub. by Universe) St Martin.

— Women Who Win: Stories of Triumph in Sports & Life. 512th ed. (Illus.). 160p. 2000. 45.00 (0-7893-0208-X, Pub. by Universe) St Martin.

Lessa, William A. Spearhead Governatore: Remembrances of the Campaign in Italy. (Illus.). 257p. 1998. reprint ed. text 20.00 (0-7881-5147-9) DIANE Pub.

— Ulithi: A Micronesian Design for Living. (Illus.). 118p. (C). 1986. reprint ed. pap. text 10.50 (0-88133-212-7) Waveland Pr.

Lessa, William A. & Vogt, Evon Z. Reader in Comparative Religion: An Anthropological Approach. 4th ed. 488p. (C). 1997. pap. text 78.00 (0-06-043991-2) Addson-Wesley Educ.

Lessac, Arthur. The Use & Training of the Human Voice: A Bio-Dynamic Approach to Vocal Life. 3rd rev. ed. LC 96-18629. (Illus.). 291p. 1996. pap. text 40.00 (1-55934-696-5, 1696) Mayfield Pub.

Lessac, Frane. Caribbean Canvas. LC 88-36555. (Illus.). 24p. (J). (ps up). 1989. 14.95 (0-397-32367-0); lib. bdg. 14.89 (0-397-32368-9) HarpC Child Bks.

— My Little Island. LC 84-48355. (Illus.). 48p. (J). (gr. 1-4). 1985. 14.00 (0-397-32114-7); lib. bdg. 15.89 (0-397-32115-5) HarpC Child Bks.

— My Little Island. LC 84-48355. (Trophy Picture Bk.). (Illus.). 48p. (J). (gr. 1-4). 1987. reprint ed. pap. 5.95 (0-06-443146-0, HarpTrophy) HarpC Child Bks.

Lessard, Betty. Picturing Manchester Vol. 1: A Selection of Images from the Manchester Historic Association. Babin, Holly, ed. (Illus.). 92p. 1997. mass mkt. 19.95 (0-9660881-0-7) Manchest Hist.

***Lessard, Bill.** NetSlaves: True Tales of Working the Web. 256p. 2000. pap. 12.95 (0-07-136480-3) McGraw.

Lessard, Bill & Baldwin, Steve. Net Slaves: True Tales of Working the Web. LC 00-687334. 240p. 1999. 19.95 (0-07-135243-0) McGraw.

Lessard, Donald R., ed. International Financial Management: Theory & Application. 2nd ed. LC 84-15378. 606p. reprint ed. pap. 187.90 (0-7837-2378-4, 204006400006) Bks Demand.

Lessard, Donald R. & Williamson, John. Capital Flight: The Problem & Policy Responses. LC 87-17279. (Policy Analyses in International Economics Ser.: No. 23). 77p. reprint ed. pap. 30.00 (0-7837-6407-3, 204638700012) Bks Demand.

— Capital Flight & Third World Debt. LC 87-17279. 271p. reprint ed. pap. 84.10 (0-7837-4222-3, 204391100012) Bks Demand.

— Financial Intermediation Beyond the Debt Crisis. LC 85-18092. (Policy Analyses in International Economics Ser.: No. 12). 132p. (Orig.). 1985. pap. 41.00 (0-7837-8494-5, 204930100010) Bks Demand.

Lessard, Donald R., jt. auth. see Miller, Roger.

Lessard, Gregory, jt. ed. see Hamm, Jean-Jaques.

Lessard, Gregory, ed. see Stendhal, pseud.

Lessard, Marc. Colombia: Ulysses Travel Guide. Ulysses Travel Guide Staff, ed. (Ulysses Travel Guide Ser.). 1999. pap. 21.95 (2-89464-089-7) Ulysses Travel.

Lessard, P., jt. ed. see Beck, M. B.

Lessard, Paul N. Fun & Easy Easter Pageant: CD Soundtrack Inside: Life Savers. LC 96-2944. 1997. 24.99 incl. audio compact disk (1-55945-499-7) Group Pub.

— Sermons Alive! 52 Short Dramatic Sketches for Sunday Worship. Wray, Rhonda, ed. LC 92-44911. 208p. (Orig.). 1993. pap. 12.95 (0-916260-95-X, B132) Meriwether Pub.

Lessard, Paul N., jt. ed. see Nappa, Mike.

Lessard, R. A., jt. auth. see Lampropoulos, G. A.

Lessard, Roger A., ed. Photopolymer Device Physics, Chemistry & Applications III, Vol. 2851. 168p. 1996. 56.00 (0-8194-2239-8) SPIE.

***Lessard, Roger A., ed.** Photopolymer Device Physics, Chemistry & Applications IV, No. 3417. LC 99-170361. 1998. 69.00 (0-8194-2871-X) SPIE.

Lessard, Roger A. & Manivannan, Gurusamy, eds. Selected Papers on Photopolymers: Physics, Chemistry, & Applications, Vol. MS 114. LC 95-23392. (SPIE Milestone Ser.). 1995. text 110.00 (0-8194-2000-X) SPIE.

Lessard, Roger A., et al. Materials Characterization & Optical Probes Techniques: Proceedings of a Conference Held 27-30 July 1997, San Diego, California. LC 97-23156. (Critical Reviews of Optical Science Technology Ser.). 1997. pap. write for info. (0-8194-2600-8) SPIE.

— Polymers in Optics: Physics, Chemistry, & Applications. LC 96-22980. (Critical Reviews of Optical Science & Technology Ser.). 1996. pap. 70.00 (0-8194-2255-X) SPIE.

Lessard, Sabin, ed. Mathematical & Statistical Developments of Evolutionary Theory: Proceedings of the NATO Advanced Study Institute Dordrecht, The Netherlands & Seminaire de Mathematiques Superleures Held in Montreal, Canada, August 3-21, 1987. (C). 1990. text 207.50 (0-7923-0595-7) Kluwer Academic.

Lessard, Sabin, jt. auth. see Karlin, Samuel.

Lessard, Suzannah. The Architect of Desire: Beauty & Danger in the Stanford White Family. (Illus.). 334p. 1996. 24.95 (0-385-31445-0, Dial Pr) Dell.

Lessard, Suzannah. The Architect of Desire: Beauty & Danger in the Stanford White Family. 352p. 1997. pap. 14.95 (0-385-31942-8) Doubleday.

Lessard, Victoria C., jt. auth. see Hall, Jack.

L

Lessard, W. O. The Complete Book of Bananas. Wilbur, Joan, ed. (Illus.). 120p. 1992. text 35.00 (*0-9633161-0-9*) W O Lessard.

Lesschaeve, Jacqueline, jt. auth. see Cunningham, Merce.

Lesse, Nicholas, tr. see Erasmus, Desiderius.

Lesse, Stanley. Masked Depression. 1996. pap. text 60.00 (*1-56821-871-0*) Aronson.

Lesse, Stanley, ed. Masked Depression. LC 73-17744. 394p. 1983. 60.00 (*0-87668-688-9*) Aronson.

Lessel, William M. Creating Graphics That Communicate: Illustrated Manual for Graphic Artists. rev. ed. LC 87-182991. (Illus.). 133 p. 1987. write for info. (*0-8024-3046-5*) Moody.

Lessel, Colin B. Infinitesimal Dose. 1994. pap. 19.95 (*0-8464-4392-9*) Beekman Pubs.

Lessel, Uta, jt. auth. see Schomburg, Dietmar.

Lessell, Colin. Infinitesimal Dose. 107p. 1995. pap. 19.95 (*0-85207-276-7*, Pub. by C W Daniel) Natl Bk Netwk.

— A Textbook of Dental Homeopathy: For Dental Surgeons, Homeopathists & General Medicine Practitioners. 111p. 1995. pap. 25.95 (*0-85207-281-3*, Pub. by C W Daniel) Natl Bk Netwk.

— The World Travellers' Manual of Homoeopathy. 373p. pap. 25.95 (*0-85207-242-2*, Pub. by C W Daniel) Natl Bk Netwk.

***Lessell, Colin B.** The World Travellers' Manual of Homoeopathy. 2000. pap. 25.95 (*0-85207-330-5*) C W Daniel.

Lessels, Bruce. Classic Northeastern Whitewater Guide. 3rd ed. LC 98-13403. 1998. pap. text 19.95 (*1-878239-63-5*) AMC Books.

— Whitewater Handbook. 3rd ed. LC 93-21066. (Illus.). 288p. 1994. pap. 14.95 (*1-878239-01-5*) AMC Books.

Lessels, John, intro. Australia's Greenhouse Policy Seminar. (Illus.). 137p. (Orig.). 1992. pap. text 36.00 (*0-85825-569-3*, Pub. by Inst Engrs Aust-EA Bks) Accents Pubns.

— Wheels '92. (Illus.). 259p. (Orig.). 1992. pap. 57.75 (*0-85825-584-7*, Pub. by Inst Engrs Aust-EA Bks) Accents Pubns.

***Lessem.** All Dirt on Dinosaurs. 1999. mass mkt. 4.99 (*0-8125-6798-6*) Tor Bks.

Lessem. Raptors! (J). 1996. pap. write for info. (*0-316-87929-0*) Little.

Lessem, Don. All the Dirt on Dinosaurs. (J). 1997. write for info. (*0-614-29308-1*) Tor Bks.

— Bigger Than T-Rex. (Illus.). 32p. (J). (gr. 4-6). 1997. 18.00 (*0-517-70930-9*) Random Hse Value.

— Dinosaur Worlds: New Dinosaurs - New Discoveries. LC 95-83194. (Illus.). 192p. (J). (gr. 5-9). 1996. 19.95 (*1-56397-597-1*) Boyds Mills Pr.

— Dinosaurs Rediscovered: New Discoveries That Are Revolutionizing Our Understanding of Dinosaurs. (Illus.). 320p. 1992. 25.00 (*0-671-73491-1*) S&S Trade.

— Dinosaurs to Dodos: An Encyclopedia of Extinct Animals. LC 98-25863. (Illus.). 112p. (J). (gr. 3-7). 1999. 16.95 (*0-590-31684-2*, Pub. by Scholastic Inc) Penguin Putnam.

— Ornithomimids, the Fastest Dinosaur. LC 93-10264. (Special Dinosaurs Ser.). (Illus.). (J). (gr. 2-5). 1993. lib. bdg. 19.95 (*0-87614-813-5*, Carolrhoda) Lerner Pub.

— Raptors! The Nastiest Dinosaurs. LC 95-7110. (Illus.). 32p. (J). (gr. 1-5). 1996. 14.95 (*0-316-52119-1*) Little.

— Raptors: The Nastiest Dinosaurs. 32p. (J). (gr. k-3). 1998. pap. 5.95 (*0-316-56428-1*) Little.

— Seismosaurus: The Longest Dinosaur. LC 95-36473. (Illus.). (J). (gr. 2-5). 1996. lib. bdg. 14.95 (*0-87614-987-5*, Carolrhoda) Lerner Pub.

— Skeleton Detective. (J). 1997. 16.00 (*0-517-70932-5*) Random Hse Value.

— Supergiants! The Biggest Dinosaurs. LC 96-15418. (Illus.). 32p. (J). (gr. 1-5). 1997. 14.95 (*0-316-52118-3*) Little.

— Troodon, the Smartest Dinosaur. LC 92-44689. (Illus.). (J). (gr. 2-5). 1995. lib. bdg. 14.96 (*0-87614-798-8*, Carolrhoda) Lerner Pub.

Lessem, Ronnie. Business as a Learning Community. LC 92-44981. 1993. 19.95 (*0-07-707787-3*) McGraw.

— Enterprise Development. 200p. 1986. text 65.95 (*0-566-02601-5*, Pub. by Gower) Ashgate Pub Co.

— Entrepreneurship: Developing the Individual in Business. 220p. 1987. pap. text 25.95 (*0-7045-0577-0*, Pub. by Gower) Ashgate Pub Co.

— From Management Education to Civic Reconstruction: The Emerging Ecology of Organisation. LC 98-35446. (Managing Across Cultures Ser.). 1999. write for info. (*0-415-18232-8*); pap. write for info. (*0-415-18233-6*) Routledge.

— Management Development Through Cultural Diversity. LC 97-45920. 432p. (C). 1998. 100.00 (*0-415-17875-4*); pap. 34.99 (*0-415-17876-2*) Routledge.

— Managing Corporate Culture. (Illus.). 240p. 1990. text 78.95 (*0-566-02774-7*, Pub. by Gower) Ashgate Pub Co.

— Total Quality Learning. 1994. pap. 26.95 (*0-631-19306-5*) Blackwell Pubs.

Lessem, Ronnie & Neubauer, Fred. European Management Systems: Towards Unity Out of Cultural Diversity. LC 93-29857. 1993. write for info. (*0-07-707908-6*) McGraw.

Lessem, Ronnie, ed. see Jaques, Elliott & Clement, Stephen D.

Lessen. Exceptional Persons Society. 2nd ed. LC 95-102861. 464p. 1994. pap. text 56.00 (*0-536-58666-7*) Pearson Custom.

Lessen, Don, jt. auth. see Horner, John R.

Lessen, Elliott. Exceptional Persons in Society. 346p. (C). 1994. text 28.00 (*0-536-58685-3*) Pearson Custom.

Lessen, Knots. The Adventures of Roundup & the Sacred Cow Cattle Drive. 145p. (Orig.). 1992. pap. 8.50 (*0-9632144-0-3*) Unidox Print.

Lessen, Laurie S. The Dance of the Carbon-Atom. LC 95-3921. 68p. 1996. pap. 14.95 (*0-7734-2723-6*, Mellen Poetry Pr) E Mellen.

Lesseps, Ferdinand M. De, see De Lesseps, Ferdinand M.

Lesseps, Jean De, see De Lesseps, Jean.

***Lesser.** Business,Society & Public Policy. 1999. text 41.75 (*0-03-010218-9*, Pub. by Harcourt Coll Pubs) Harcourt.

Lesser. Linguistic Investigations of Aphasia. 2nd ed. 1989. 64.50 (*1-56593-541-1*, 0045) Singular Publishing.

Lesser, ed. Introduction to Environmental Economics. (C). 1999. text. write for info. (*0-321-01441-3*) Addson-Wesley Educ.

Lesser, jt. auth. see Mayes.

Lesser, A. Harry, ed. Ageing, Autonomy & Resources. LC 99-72599. (Avebury Series in Philosophy). 256p. 1999. text 65.95 (*1-84014-971-X*, Pub. by Ashgate Pub) Ashgate Pub Co.

Lesser, Adrienne E., ed. Stock Photo Deskbook. 6th rev. ed. LC 98-70953. 536p. 1998. pap. 48.95 (*0-9662915-0-6*) Exeter Co.

Lesser, Alayne, jt. auth. see Battle, Dee.

Lesser, Alexander. Pawnee Ghost Dance Hand Game. LC 79-82340. (Columbia Univ. Contributions to Anthropology Ser.: Vol. 16). 1969. reprint ed. 37.00 (*0-404-50566-X*) AMS Pr.

— The Pawnee Ghost Dance Hand Game: Ghost Dance Revival & Ethnic Identity. LC 96-28279. (Illus.). xx, 342p. 1996. pap. 17.50 (*0-8032-7965-5*, Bison Books) U of Nebr Pr.

— The Pawnee Ghost Dance Hand Game: Ghost Dance Revival & Ethnic Identity. LC 77-91056. (Illus.). 368p. reprint ed. pap. 114.10 (*0-608-07016-5*, 206722300009) Bks Demand.

Lesser, Allen. Israel's Impact, 1950-1951: A Personal Record. LC 84-12013. (Orig.). 1984. pap. text 29.00 (*0-8191-4126-7*); lib. bdg. 52.50 (*0-8191-4125-9*) U Pr of Amer.

Lesser, Andrew J. Drive with Less Stress: A Motorist's Survival Guide for the 90's. Brown, Jane W., ed. LC 90-91498. (Illus.). 176p. (Orig.). 1990. pap. 5.95 (*0-945375-01-8*) Less Stress Pr.

Lesser, Barbara. Welcome to America: Memories of a Bintel Brief. LC 96-37911. 128p. Date not set. pap. 7.95 (*1-55783-259-5*) Applause Theatre Bk Pubs.

Lesser, Barry, jt. auth. see Tillet, Anthony.

Lesser, Carolyn. Flamingo Knees. 3rd ed. 52p. (J). (gr. 5 up). 1991. pap. 10.00 (*0-9630604-0-6*) Oakwood MO.

— Flamingo Knees. 4th ed. (Illus.). 52p. (J). (gr. k up). 1993. 10.00 (*0-9630604-2-2*) Oakwood MO.

— The Goodnight Circle. LC 84-4501. (Illus.). 32p. (J). (ps-3). 1984. 14.95 (*0-15-232158-6*, Harcourt Child Bks) Harcourt.

— The Goodnight Circle. LC 84-4501. (Illus.). 32p. (J). (ps-3). 1991. pap. 7.00 (*0-15-232159-4*, Harcourt Child Bks) Harcourt.

— Great Crystal Bear. LC 95-12383. (Illus.). 32p. (J). (gr. k-4). 1996. 15.00 (*0-15-200667-2*) Harcourt.

— The Knees Knock Again. 2nd ed. 56p. (J). 1991. pap. 10.00 (*0-9630604-1-4*) Oakwood MO.

— The Knees Knock Again. 3rd ed. (Illus.). 56p. (J). (gr. k up). 1993. pap. 10.00 (*0-9630604-3-0*) Oakwood MO.

— Spots: Counting Creatures from Sky to Sea. LC 97-37571. (Illus.). 32p. (J). 1999. 16.00 (*0-15-200666-4*) Harcourt.

— Storm on the Desert. LC 95-44923. (Illus.). 40p. (J). 1997. 16.00 (*0-15-272198-3*) Harcourt.

Lesser, Carolyn. What a Wonderful Day to Be a Cow. (Illus.). 32p. (J). (ps-2). 1999. pap. 6.99 (*0-375-80212-6*, Pub. by Knopf Bks Yng Read) Random.

***Lesser, Carolyn.** What a Wonderful Day to Be a Cow. (Illus.). (J). 1999. 13.35 (*0-606-16958-X*, Pub. by Turtleback) Demco.

Lesser, Charles H. Relic of the Lost Cause: The Story of South Carolina's Ordinance of Secession. rev. ed. Andrews, Judith M., ed. 32p. 1996. pap. 9.00 (*1-880067-36-6*) SC Dept of Arch & Hist.

— South Carolina Begins: The Records of a Proprietary Colony, 1663-1721. LC 95-622449. 540p. 1995. pap. 40.00 (*1-880067-31-5*) SC Dept of Arch & Hist.

Lesser, Charles H., jt. ed. see White, J. Todd.

***Lesser, Elizabeth.** The New American Spirituality: A Seeker's Guide. LC 98-50310. 352p. 1999. 25.95 (*0-375-50010-3*) Random House.

— Seeker's Guide: Making Your Life a Spiritual Adventure. 2000. pap. 14.95 (*0-679-78359-8*) Villard Books.

***Lesser, Eric.** Knowledge & Social Capital, Foundations & Applications. LC 99-48591. 208p. 2000. pap. text 21.95 (*0-7506-7222-6*) Buttrwrth-Heinemann.

***Lesser, Eric, et al.** Knowledge & Communities. LC 00-39808. (Resources for the Knowledge-Based Economy Ser.). 2000. pap. write for info. (*0-7506-7293-5*) Buttrwrth-Heinemann.

Lesser, Eugene. Drug Abuse in Marin County. 136p. (Orig.). 1985. pap. 8.95 (*0-912449-09-8*) Floating Island.

— A Palindrome Is a Pal Indeed. 16p. (Orig.). 1991. pap. 5.00 (*0-912449-38-1*) Floating Island.

Lesser, Gary S. 457 Answer Book. annuals 832p. boxed set 118.00 (*1-56706-389-6*, 63896) Panel Pubs.

— 457 Answer Book. LC 97-136419. 832p. 1997. boxed set 118.00 (*1-56706-365-9*, 63659) Panel Pubs.

***Lesser, Gary S.** Roth IRA Answer Book, 1. LC 99-201100. 468p. 1999. boxed set 125.00 (*0-7355-0408-3*) Panel Pubs.

Lesser, Gary S. SEP & SARSEP Answer Book. annuals 472p. 1995. 126.00 incl. disk (*1-56706-176-1*) Panel Pubs.

— SEP & SARSEP Answer Book. 2nd ed. LC 97-122182. 928p. 1996. 126.00 (*1-56706-359-4*) Aspen Pub.

— Simple, SEP & SARSEP 4th ed. LC 98-215843. (Answer Book Ser.). 1998. write for info. (*0-7355-0000-2*) Panel Pubs.

— Simple, Sep, & Sarsep Answer Book. 3rd ed. LC 98-107095. (Panel Answer Bks). 1998. write for info. (*1-56706-435-3*) Panel Pubs.

Lesser, Gary S. & Starr, Lawrence C. Life Insurance Answer Book: For Qualified Plans & Estate Planning. 2nd ed. LC 98-44299. (Panel Answer Book Ser.). 1997. boxed set 118.00 (*1-56706-886-3*) Aspen Law.

Lesser, Gary S. & Starr, Lawrence C., eds. Life Insurance Answer Book: For Qualified Plans & Estate Planning. annuals LC 97-202983. 1152p. 1999. boxed set 118.00 (*1-56706-424-8*, 64248) Panel Pubs.

Lesser, Gerald S., jt. auth. see Kandel, Denise B.

Lesser, Gerald S., ed. see Conference on Contemporary Issues in Thematic Appe.

Lesser, Harry, jt. auth. see Loizou, Andros.

***Lesser, Ian, et al.** The Future of NATO's Mediterranean Initiative: Evolution & Next Steps. xv, 47p. 2000. pap. 10.00 (*0-8330-2812-X*, MR-1164-SMD) Rand Corp.

Lesser, Ian O. Bridge or Barrier? Turkey & the West after the Cold War. LC 92-17308. 1992. pap. text 4.00 (*0-8330-1256-8*, R-4204-AF/A) Rand Corp.

***Lesser, Ian O.** NATO Looks South: New Challenges & New Strategies in the Mediterranean. LC 99-87790. xv, 66p. 2000. pap. 12.00 (*0-8330-2810-3*, MR-1126-AF) Rand Corp.

Lesser, Ian O. Security in North Africa: Internal & External Challenges. 90p. 1993. pap. 15.00 (*0-8330-1380-7*, MR-203) Rand Corp.

Lesser, Ian O. & Tellis, Ashley J. Strategic Exposure: Proliferation Around the Mediterranean. LC 96-3054. 125p. 1996. pap. 15.00 (*0-8330-2373-X*, MR-742-A) Rand Corp.

Lesser, Ian O., et al. Countering the New Terrorism. LC 98-51685. (Illus.). 160p. 1999. pap. 15.00 (*0-8330-2667-4*, MR-989-AF) Rand Corp.

Lesser, Ian O., jt. auth. see Fuller, Graham E.

Lesser, Ian O., jt. ed. see Khalilzad, Zalmay.

Lesser, Isaac. The Pentateuch-Haftaroth & Sabbath Prayers: Hebrew with English. (ENG & HEB.). 32.50 (*0-87559-197-3*) Shalom.

Lesser, Jeff. Negotiating National Identity: Immigrants, Minorities, & the Struggle for Ethnicity in Brazil. LC 98-38238. 1999. 49.95 (*0-8223-2260-9*); pap. 17.95 (*0-8223-2292-7*) Duke.

Lesser, Jeffrey. Welcoming the Undesirables: Brazil & the Jewish Question. LC 93-21199. 1994. 48.00 (*0-520-08412-8*, Pub. by U CA Pr); pap. 18.95 (*0-520-08413-6*, Pub. by U CA Pr) Cal Prin Full Svc.

Lesser, Jeffrey, jt. ed. see Klich, Ignacio.

Lesser, Joe & Youngblood, Pete. Realistic Railroading with Toy Trains: Building the O Gauge Hi-Rail JL/ATSF Railway. (Illus.). 96p. (Orig.). 1995. pap. 17.95 (*0-89778-399-9*, 10-7975, Greenberg Books) Kalmbach.

Lesser, Jonathan A., et al. Environmental Economics. LC 96-44798. 751p. (C). 1997. 98.00 (*0-673-98210-6*) Addison-Wesley.

Lesser, Lawrence M., jt. auth. see Mayes, Robert L.

Lesser, M. X. Jonathan Edwards. (United States Authors Ser.: No. 537). 152p. 1988. 26.95 (*0-8057-7519-6*, TUSAS 537) Macmillan.

— Jonathan Edwards: An Annotated Bibliography, 1979-1993, 30. LC 94-31540. (Bibliographies & Indexes in Religious Studies). 232p. 1994. lib. bdg. 69.50 (*0-313-29237-X*) Greenwood.

Lesser, Martin. Analysis of Complex Nonlinear Mechanical Systems: A Computer Algebra Assisted Approach. 340p. 1995. text 62.00 (*981-02-2209-2*) World Scientific Pub.

Lesser, Maximus. The Historical Development of the Jury System. 1976. lib. bdg. 34.95 (*0-8490-1957-5*) Gordon Pr.

Lesser, Maximus A. The Historical Development of the Jury System. LC 92-28982. 284p. 1992. reprint ed. 62.00 (*0-89941-816-3*, 307690) W S Hein.

Lesser, Rika. All We Need of Hell. LC 94-40015. 87p. 1995. pap. 10.95 (*0-929398-92-0*) UNTX Pr.

— Growing Back: Poems, 1972-1992. LC 97-21149. 90p. 1997. 15.95 (*1-57003-232-7*); pap. 9.95 (*1-57003-233-5*) U of SC Pr.

— Hansel & Gretel. LC 99-10198. 1999. 16.99 (*0-525-46152-3*, Dutton Child) Peng Put Young Read.

Lesser, Rika. Hansel & Gretel. (J). 1996. 12.15 (*0-606-04241-5*, Pub. by Turtleback) Demco.

Lesser, Rika, ed. & tr. see Sonnevi, Goran.

Lesser, Rika, tr. see Andersson, Claes.

Lesser, Rika, tr. see Dahlback, Helena.

Lesser, Rika, tr. see Gripe, Maria.

Lesser, Rika, tr. see Hesse, Hermann.

Lesser, Rika, tr. see Jersild, P. C.

Lesser, Rika, tr. see Schami, Rafik.

Lesser, Ronnie & Schoenberg, Erica, eds. Naming the Unnamed: Interdisciplinary Discussion of Freud's Female Homosexual. LC 98-41836. 288p. (C). (gr. 13). 1999. 65.00 (*0-415-91670-4*) Routledge.

Lesser, Ronnie C. & Schoenberg, Erica. That Obscure Subject of Desire: Freud's Female Homosexual Revisited. LC 98-41836. 1999. pap. 18.99 (*0-415-91671-2*) Routledge.

Lesser, Ronnie C., jt. ed. see Domenici, Thomas.

Lesser, Rosemary. Yoga Manual, 1. 1998. 16.98 (*1-57717-093-8*) Todtri Prods.

Lesser, Simon O. Fiction & the Unconscious. (Midway Reprint Ser.). xiv, 322p. 1975. pap. text 16.00 (*0-226-47331-7*) U Ch Pr.

— The Whispered Meanings: Selected Essays of Simon O. Lesser. Sprich, Robert W. & Noland, Richard W., eds. LC 77-73480. 248p. 1977. pap. 17.95 (*0-87023-244-4*) U of Mass Pr.

Lesser, Stephen, jt. ed. see Morsberger, Robert.

Lesser, Victor & Gasser, Les, eds. Proceedings of the First International Conference on Multiagent Systems: June 12-14, 1995, San Francisco. (AAAI Press Ser.). (Illus.). 490p. (C). 1995. pap. text 77.00 (*0-262-62102-9*) MIT Pr.

Lesser, W. The Role of Intellectual Property Rights in Biotechnology Transfer under the Convention on Biological Diversity. (ISAAA Briefs Ser.: Vol. 3). (Illus.). vi, 22p. 1997. pap. 10.00 (*1-892456-03-6*) Agri-Biotech.

— Sustainable Use of Genetic Resources under the Convention on Biological Diverstiy: Exploring Access & Benefit Sharing Issues. LC 97-23972. (A CAB International Publication). 232p. 1998. text 65.00 (*0-85199-197-1*) OUP.

Lesser, Wendy. The Amateur: An Independent Life of Letters. LC 98-26157. 274p. 1999. 24.00 (*0-375-40402-3*) Pantheon.

***Lesser, Wendy.** The Amateur: An Independent Life of Letters. 2000. pap. 13.00 (*0-375-70381-0*) Vin Bks.

Lesser, Wendy. A Director Calls. LC 97-20476. 250p. 1997. pap. 15.95 (*0-520-21262-2*, Pub. by U CA Pr) Cal Prin Full Svc.

— His Other Half: Men Looking at Women Through Art. LC 90-37165. (Illus.). 304p. 1991. text 36.00 (*0-674-39210-8*, LESHIS) HUP.

— His Other Half: Men Looking at Women Through Art. (Illus.). 304p. 1992. pap. text 12.95 (*0-674-39211-6*) HUP.

— Pictures at an Execution. LC 93-7336. 288p. 1993. 25.95 (*0-674-66735-2*) HUP.

— Pictures at an Execution: An Inquiry into the Subject of Murder. (Illus.). 288p. (Orig.). (C). 1995. pap. 14.95 (*0-674-66736-0*) HUP.

Lesser, Wendy, intro. Hiding in Plain Sight: Essays in Criticism & Autobiography. LC 92-42345. 344p. 1993. 21.95 (*1-56279-037-4*) Mercury Hse Inc.

Lesser, William. Marketing Livestock & Meat. 471p. 1993. pap. 59.95 (*1-56022-017-1*) Haworth Jrnl Co-Edits.

— Marketing Livestock & Meat. LC 91-32989. (Illus.). 484p. 1993. lib. bdg. 69.95 (*1-56022-016-3*) Haworth Pr.

Lesses, Rebecca M. Ritual Practices to Gain Power: Angels, Incantations & Revelation in Early Jewish Mysticism. LC 97-45492. (Harvard Theological Studies: Vol. 44). 320p. 1997. pap. 24.00 (*1-56338-219-9*) TPI PA.

***Lessie, Par.** How to Spell Homophones. Kelly, Walter, ed. (Illus.). 48p. (J). (gr. 3-6). 1999. pap., teacher ed. 7.95 (*1-57690-499-7*, TCM2499) Tchr Create Mat.

***Lessie, Pat.** Fablesauce. LC 99-45092. (Illus.). 80p. 1999. 16.95 (*1-884540-48-1*); pap. 9.95 (*1-884540-46-5*) Haleys.

***Lessig, Robert J.** Poetry with Some Flowers, Birds & Teddy Bears: Inspirational, Romance & Life. LC 00-104494. (Illus.). 104p. 2000. pap. 17.95 (*0-9667763-0-5*) Biblical Rsrch.

Lessin, Alexander. Great Relations: Do-It-Yourself Counseling for Couples. (Lessin's Lessons Ser.). (Illus.). (Orig.). 1988. pap. 12.00 (*0-945596-00-6*) Schl Counsel Psy.

Lessin, Barton M., ed. Off-Campus Library Services: Selected Readings from Central Michigan University's Conferences. LC 91-38119. 256p. 1991. 31.50 (*0-8108-2512-0*) Scarecrow.

Lessin, Roy. Como Criar Hijos Felices y Obedientes. 160p. 1981. 6.99 (*0-88113-037-0*) Caribe Betania.

— Como Disciplinar a Tus Hijos.Tr. of Spanking: Why, When, How. 96p. 1982. 6.99 (*0-88113-032-X*) Caribe Betania.

***Lessin, Roy.** Continue On. 2000. 12.99 (*0-7814-3346-0*) Chariot Victor.

Lessin, Roy. Forgiven. (Illus.). 64p. 1996. 24.99 (*1-884009-07-7*) DaySpring.

***Lessin, Roy.** From God's Heart to Yours: Words of Hope & Comfort. 2000. 9.99 (*1-56292-642-X*) Honor Bks OK.

Lessin, Roy. God Sent Us a Savior. LC 98-17288. 1998. 24.99 (*1-56476-735-3*, Victor Bks) Chariot Victor.

— How to Be the Parents of Happy & Obedient Children. 156p. (C). 1978. pap. text 9.99 (*0-86694-130-4*) Omega Pubns OR.

— Knowing His Best . . . Walking in Rest. 96p. 1993. pap. 5.95 (*1-884009-03-4*) DaySpring.

— Never Forgotten, Always Loved. 96p. 1992. pap. 5.95 (*1-884009-00-X*) DaySpring.

— Receiving His Blessing, Giving His Love. 96p. 1993. pap. 5.95 (*1-884009-02-6*) DaySpring.

— Spanking: Why? When? How? LC 79-54028. 96p. 1979. mass mkt. 4.99 (*0-87123-494-7*) Bethany Hse.

— Within His Hands, Without a Fear. 96p. 1993. pap. 5.95 (*1-884009-01-8*) DaySpring.

***Lessin, Roy & Solum, Heather.** Patterns of Grace Gift Book: The Wonderful Ways God Touches Our Lives. 1999. 12.99 (*1-58375-464-4*) Garborgs.

Lessin, Roy A. A Father's Heritage. (Illus.). 84p. 1998. 24.99 (*1-884009-75-1*) DaySpring.

Lessing. Nathan der Weise. (GER.). (C). 1989. 19.95 (*0-8442-2776-5*, X2776-5) NTC Contemp Pub Co.

— Nathan der Weise - Minna Von Barnhelm. unabridged ed. (World Classic Literature Ser.). (GER.). pap. 5.95 (*3-89507-015-7*, Pub. by Bookking Intl) Distribks Inc.

— Proper Marriage. 1969. pap. text 3.95 (*0-586-02116-7*) HarpC.

Lessing, Carl. Scriptorum Historiae Augustae Lexicon. iii, 747p. 1964. reprint ed. write for info. (*0-318-71160-5*); reprint ed. write for info. (*0-318-72038-8*) G Olms Pubs.

Lessing, Doris. African Laughter: Four Visits to Zimbabwe. LC 92-52590. 464p. 1993. reprint ed. pap. 15.00 (*0-06-092433-0*, Perennial) HarperTrade.

***Lessing, Doris.** Ben, In the World: The Sequel to The Fifth Child. LC 99-89804. 160p. 2000. 23.00 (*0-06-019628-9*, HarpCollins) HarperTrade.

An Asterisk (*) at the beginning of an entry indicates that the title is appearing for the first time.

Lessing, Doris. Briefing for a Descent into Hell. LC 80-6142. 308p. 1981. pap. 3.95 (*0-685-04268-5*, V-662) Vin Bks.

— The Fifth Child. 1991. pap. text. write for info. (*0-582-06021-4*, Pub. by Addison-Wesley) Longman.

— The Fifth Child. (International Ser.). 133p. 1989. pap. 10.00 (*0-679-72182-7*) Vin Bks.

— The Four-Gated City: A Novel. LC 95-31487. 672p. 1995. pap. 16.00 (*0-06-097667-5*, Perennial) HarperTrade.

— Going Home. LC 96-4329. 320p. 1996. pap. 15.00 (*0-06-097630-6*) HarpC.

— The Golden Notebook: Perennial Classics edition. LC 98-47608. 672p. 1999. pap. 15.00 (*0-06-093140-X*) HarpC.

— The Good Terrorist. LC 86-40142. 400p. 1986. pap. 12.00 (*0-394-74629-5*) Vin Bks.

Lessing, Doris. The Grass Is Singing. LC 72-550467. (New Windmill Ser.). 256p. (J). 1969. write for info. (*0-435-12129-4*) Heinemann.

— The Grass Is Singing: A Novel. LC 99-35316. 256p. 2000. pap. 13.00 (*0-06-095346-2*) HarpC.

Lessing, Doris. In Pursuit of the English: A Documentary. 240p. 1996. pap. 14.00 (*0-06-097629-2*) HarpC.

— Landlocked: A Novel. LC 95-31489. 352p. 1995. pap. 13.00 (*0-06-097665-9*, Perennial) HarperTrade.

— Love, Again. large type ed. LC 96-8526. (Large Print Bks). 1996. 25.95 (*1-56895-341-0*, Compass) Wheeler Pub.

— Love Again: Novel, A. LC 95-53317. 368p. 1997. pap. 13.00 (*0-06-092796-8*, Perennial) HarperTrade.

— Mara & Dann: An Adventure. LC 98-30782. 416p. 1999. 25.00 (*0-06-018294-6*, HarperFlamingo) HarpC.

— Mara & Dann: An Adventure. 416p. 2000. pap. 14.00 (*0-06-093056-X*) HarpC.

— Martha Quest. LC 95-33106. (Children of Violence Ser.: Vol. 1). 336p. 1995. pap. 14.00 (*0-06-097666-7*, Perennial) HarperTrade.

— The Memoirs of a Survivor. Freedgood, Anne, ed. LC 87-45951. 224p. 1988. reprint ed. pap. 12.00 (*0-394-75759-9*) Vin Bks.

*__Lessing, Doris.__ Particularly Cats. LC 99-89340. (Illus.). 160p. 2000. reprint ed. pap. 14.95 (*1-58080-036-X*) Burford Bks.

Lessing, Doris. Prisons We Choose To. LC 87-45064. 96p. 1987. 10.00 (*0-06-039077-8*) HarperTrade.

— A Proper Marriage: A Novel. LC 95-33114. (Children of Violence Ser.). 448p. 1995. pap. 15.00 (*0-06-097663-2*, Perennial) HarperTrade.

— The Real Thing: Stories & Sketches. LC 91-59932. 224p. 1993. pap. 12.00 (*0-06-092417-9*, Perennial) HarperTrade.

— A Ripple From the Storm: A Novel. LC 95-31488. (Children of Violence Ser.). 336p. 1995. pap. 14.00 (*0-06-097664-0*, Perennial) HarperTrade.

— The Summer Before Dark. LC 82-40421. 256p. 1983. pap. 10.00 (*0-394-71095-9*) Vin Bks.

— Under My Skin: My Autobiography, to 1949, Vol. 1. 448p. 1995. pap. 15.00 (*0-06-092664-3*, Perennial) HarperTrade.

— Walking in the Shade: Volume Two of My Autobiography--1949-1962. LC 97-9959. (Illus.). 432p. 1998. pap. 15.00 (*0-06-092956-1*, Perennial) HarperTrade.

Lessing, Erich, jt. auth. see Huguenin, Daniel.

Lessing, Eva M. The Road to Financial Success: A Money Management Tool. 2nd ed. Lessing, J. W., ed. LC 98-50344. (Illus.). 90p. 1998. reprint ed. pap. 9.95 (*0-9666338-1-4*) W L Pubns.

Lessing, Eva M., ed. see Lessing, J. W.

Lessing, Ferdinand D. & Wayman, Alex. Introduction to the Buddhist Tantric System. 1978. 14.50 (*0-89684-037-9*, Pub. by Motilal Bnarsidass) S Asia.

Lessing, Gotthold Ephraim. Emilia Galotti: A Tragedy in Five Acts. Dvoretzky, Edward, tr. from GER. & pref. by. 82p. (C). 1999. pap. text 6.95 (*0-917324-17-X*) German Bk Ctr.

— Lacoon. McCormick, Edward A., tr. 1962. pap. 5.50 (*0-672-60260-1*, Bobbs) Macmillan.

— Laocoon: An Essay on the Limits of Painting & Poetry. McCormick, Edward A., tr. LC 83-23880. 259p. 1984. pap. 15.95 (*0-8018-3139-3*) Johns Hopkins.

— Lessings Saemtliche Schriften, 23 vols., Set. 3rd ed. Lachmann, Karl, ed. (C). 1968. reprint ed. 1523.10 (*3-11-005161-3*) De Gruyter.

— Lessing's Theological Writings: Selections in Translation. Chadwick, Henry, tr. 110p. 1957. reprint ed. pap. 10.95 (*0-8047-0335-3*) Stanford U Pr.

— Minna Von Barnhelm. Northcott, Kenneth J., ed. LC 70-189867. (German Literary Classics in Translation Ser.). 1973. pap. text 1.95 (*0-226-47342-2*, P488) U Ch Pr.

— Minna Von Barnhelm. Northcott, Kenneth J., tr. from GER. & intro. by. LC 70-189867. (German Literary Classics in Translation Ser.). 116p. (C). 1992. lib. bdg. 10.00 (*0-226-47341-4*) U Ch Pr.

— Minna von Barnhelm or the Soldier's Fortune. Grunwald, Arnold P., tr. LC 98-90813. 1999. pap. 8.95 (*0-533-12925-7*) Vantage.

— Nathan der Weise. Schweitzer, Christoph, ed. LC 83-18169. (Suhrkamp/Insel Ser.). (ENG & GER.). 165p. 1984. pap. 9.00 (*3-518-02974-6*, Pub. by Suhr Verlag) Intl Bk Import.

*__Lessing, Hans-Erhard & Ritchie, Andrew, eds.__ Cycle History 10: Proceedings of the 10th International Cycling History Conference. LC 00-131378. (Illus.). 160p. 2000. 45.00 (*1-892495-05-8*, 5058, Pub. by Van der Plas) Seven Hills Bk.

Lessing, J. W. Become a Successful Truck Owner Operator: Business Guide & Information Package. 2nd ed. Lessing, Eva M., ed. LC 92-50344. (Illus.). 90p. 1992. reprint ed. pap. 9.95 (*0-9666338-0-6*) W L Pubns.

Lessing, J. W., ed. see Lessing, Eva M.

Lessing, John & Corkery, Jim, eds. Corporate Insolvency Law. 350p. 1995. 60.00 (*0-7331-0006-6*, Pub. by Bond Univ) Gaunt.

*__Lessing, Lawrence.__ Code. 2000. pap. 14.00 (*0-465-03913-8*, Pub. by Basic) HarpC.

Lessing, Lawrence. Code: And Other Laws of Cyberspace. (Illus.). 240p. 1999. 30.00 (*0-465-03912-X*, Pub. by Basic) HarpC.

Lessing, Mary Alice, tr. see Araujo, Luis.

Lessing, Otto E. Masters in Modern German Literature. LC 67-23239. (Essay Index Reprint Ser.). 1977. 19.95 (*0-8369-0616-0*) Ayer.

*__Lessing, Pamela.__ First Week with My New Computer: A Very Basic Guide for Grandparents Who Want to "Get Connected" (Illus.). 2000. pap. 12.95 (*1-892123-22-3*) Capital VA.

Lessinge, Leon M., jt. auth. see Salowe, Allen E.

Lessinger, Jack. The Crash of Suburbia: The Coming Boom of Small Towns. rev. ed. (Illus.). 1990. write for info. (*0-318-66598-0*) Socioeconomics.

— Penturbia: Where Real Estate Will Boom After the Crash of Suburbia. (Illus.). 1991. 22.95 (*0-9625182-5-5*) Socioeconomics.

Lessinger, Johanna. From the Ganges to the Hudson: Indian Immigrants in New York City. Foner, Nancy, ed. LC 96-170388. (New Immigrants Ser.). 100p. (C). 1996. pap. 20.00 (*0-205-16701-2*) Allyn.

Lessinger, Leon & Salowe, Allen. Game Time: The Educator's Playbook for the New Global Economy. LC 97-60629. 220p. 1997. pap. text 29.95 (*1-56676-542-0*) Scarecrow.

Lessinger, Leon, jt. auth. see Burt, Samuel M.

Lessiter, Frank. Centennial Farm: How Six Generations Farmed the Land. 368p. 1997. mass mkt. 29.95 (*0-944079-05-9*) Lessiter Pubns.

Lessiter, Frank D. Horsepower. LC 76-45044. 256p. 1977. pap. 11.95 (*0-89821-018-6*, 0186) Reiman Pubns.

Lessiter, Frank D., ed. see Herrick, John B.

Lessiter, Kelly, ed. see Herrick, John B.

Lessiter, Mike, ed. Country Chuckles, Cracks & Knee-Slappers. rev. ed. 256p. 1997. pap. 11.95 (*0-944079-27-X*) Lessiter Pubns.

Lessius, Leonard & Cornaro, Luigi. A Treatise of Health & Long Life with the Future Means of Attaining It. Kastenbaum, Robert J., ed. Smith, Timothy, tr. LC 78-22206. (Aging & Old Age Ser.). 1979. reprint ed. lib. bdg. 17.95 (*0-405-11821-X*) Ayer.

Lessius, Leonardus & Matthew, Tobie. A Consultation What Faith & Religion Is Best to Be Imbraced. LC 76-362276. (English Recusant Literature, 1558-1640 Ser.). 430 p. 1975. write for info. (*0-85967-226-3*) Scolar Pr.

Lessler, F. H., jt. auth. see Korepin, V. E.

Lessler, Judith T. & Kalsbeek, William D. Nonsampling Error in Surveys. LC 91-31950. (Probability & Mathematical Statistics: Applied Probability & Statistics Section Ser.). 432p. 1992. 145.00 (*0-471-86908-2*) Wiley.

Lessler, Richard S., jt. auth. see Wedding, C. Nugent.

Lessman, F., jt. auth. see Levy, H.

Lessmann, Andreas. Datenbanken-Zugang Zu Urheberrechtlich Geschutztem Material In der Informationsgesellschaft. XVI, 169p. 1998. 39.95 (*3-631-34154-7*) P Lang Pubng.

Lessmann, Heinrich. Aufgaben und Ziele der Vergleichenden Mythenforschung: Tasks & Goals of Comparative Mythology. Bolle, Kees W., ed. LC 77-79138. (Mythology Ser.). (GER.). 1978. reprint ed. lib. bdg. 19.95 (*0-405-10548-7*) Ayer.

Lessmann, Judith. Be a Natural Woman: Fitness for Teens. Kaste, Harry, ed. LC 81-80111. (Illus.). 184p. (Orig.). (gr. 7-12). 1981. pap. 5.95 (*0-939390-00-0*) Pizzazz Pr.

Lessmann, Sabine. The Future of Party Government, Vol. 4 - Budgetary Politics & Elections: An Investigation of Public Expenditures. Wildenmann, Rudolf, ed. (European University Institute, Series C (Political & Social Science): No. 5-4). xii, 212p. 1987. lib. bdg. 68.60 (*3-11-010943-3*) De Gruyter.

Lessmeier, Friedhelm. The British Shorthair Cat. LC 96-54580. (Complete Pet Owner's Manual Ser.). (Illus.). 120p. 1997. pap. 6.95 (*0-7641-0056-4*) Barron.

Lessner, Grace, ed. see Fitch, David A.

Lessner, Richard, ed. see Benson, Steve & Keane, Bill.

Lessnoff, M. Social Contract Theory. 330p. (C). 1990. pap. text 18.50 (*0-8147-5055-9*) NYU Pr.

Lessnoff, Michael. Political Philosophers of the Twentieth Century. LC 98-22987. 300p. 1998. 59.95 (*0-631-20260-9*); pap. 29.95 (*0-631-20261-7*) Blackwell Pubs.

Lessnoff, Michael H. The Spirit of Capitalism & the Protestant Ethic: An Enquiry into the Weber Thesis. 160p. 1994. 85.00 (*1-85278-875-5*) E Elgar.

Lessof, M. H. Food Allergy & Other Adverse Reactions to Food. (Illus.). 22p. 1994. pap. text 12.50 (*0-944398-19-7*) ILSI.

Lessof, M. H., et al. Allergy: Immunological & Clinical Aspects. 2nd ed. 670p. 1987. 142.50 (*0-471-90927-0*) Wiley.

Lessof, Maurice H., ed. Immunology of Cardiovascular Disease. LC 81-15208. (Basic & Clinical Cardiology Ser.: No. 1). 447p. reprint ed. pap. 138.60 (*0-7837-3355-0*, 204331300008) Bks Demand.

Lessoff, Alan. The Nation & Its City: Politics, Corruption, & Progress in Washington, D.C., 1861-1902. LC 93-17513. 337p. 1994. 48.00 (*0-8018-4464-9*) Johns Hopkins.

Lessom, Don. Utahraptor: The Deadliest Dinosaur. (J). (gr. 2-5). 1996. lib. bdg. 14.95 (*0-87614-988-3*, Carolrhoda) Lerner Pub.

Lesson, Pierre A. Les Polynesiens: Leur Origine, Leurs Migrations, Leur Langage, 4 vols., Set. LC 75-35201. reprint ed. 162.50 (*0-404-14270-2*) AMS Pr.

Lesson, Rene P. Voyage Autour du Monde... Sur la Corvette LaCoquille, Tome 1. (Discovery of the Pacific & Australia Ser.). (FRE., Illus.). 518p. 1998. reprint ed. pap. 240.00 (*1-85297-006-5*, Pub. by Archival Facs) St Mut.

*__Lessop, Mike, et al.__ Differential Diagnosis: Tortoises, Reptiles, Amphibians. (Illus.). 256p. 2000. pap. 59.00 (*0-7506-4189-4*) Buttrwrth-Heinemann.

*__Lessow-Hurley, Judith.__ The Foundations of Dual Language Instruction. 3rd ed. 186p. (Orig.). (C). 1999. pap. text 35.66 (*0-8013-3071-8*) Longman.

*__Lester.__ Cupid. 2001. write for info. (*0-15-202056-X*) Harcourt.

Lester. The Essential Guide to Writing Research Papers. 321st ed. LC 98-7342. 208p. (C). (gr. 3). 1998. spiral bd. 15.73 (*0-321-02406-0*) Addson-Wesley Educ.

— From Colonization to Democracy: A History Geography of South Africa. 1998. pap. 22.50 (*1-86064-176-8*, Pub. by I B T) St Martin.

— Look to the East. 15.95 (*0-685-22017-6*) Wehman.

*__Lester.__ Public Policy: An Evolutionary Approach. 2nd ed. LC 99-462500. (Political Science Ser.). 1999. pap. 57.95 (*0-534-55008-8*) Wadsworth Pub.

— Revision Chart: Writer's Handbook. rev. ed. (C). 1991. pap. text 6.00 (*0-15-597653-2*, Pub. by Harcourt Coll Pubs) Harcourt.

— Text & Thought: An Integrated Approach to College Reading & Writing. LC 99-43140. 512p. (C). 2000. pap. text 41.40 (*0-321-04576-9*) Addison-Wesley.

Lester. Visual Communication. 2nd ed. LC 99-19632. (Mass Communication Ser.). 1999. pap. 56.95 (*0-534-56142-X*) Wadsworth Pub.

— A Writer's Handbook: Test Bank. (C). 1991. pap. text, teacher ed., suppl. ed. 15.00 (*0-15-597658-3*, Pub. by Harcourt Coll Pubs) Harcourt.

— Writing Research Papers. 9th ed. 400p. (C). 1998. spiral bd. 26.00 (*0-321-04978-0*) Addison-Wesley.

Lester, jt. auth. see Schneider.

Lester, ed. see Clark.

*__Lester, Albert.__ Project Planning & Control. 3rd ed. 448p. 2000. 66.95 (*0-7506-4261-0*) Buttrwrth-Heinemann.

Lester, Albert. Project Planning & Control. 3rd ed. (Illus.). 256p. 2000. 91.95 (*0-7506-1100-6*) Buttrwrth-Heinemann.

Lester, Alison. Alice & Aldo. 32p. (J). (ps-2). 1998. 15.00 (*0-395-87092-5*) HM.

— Bibs & Boots. (Illus.). 7p. (J). (ps). 1997. bds. 3.95 (*1-86448-178-1*, Pub. by Allen & Unwin Pty) IPG Chicago.

— La Cama de Isabella (Isabella's Bed) (Illus.). 32p. (J). (gr. 1 up). 1998. 15.95 (*980-257-118-0*, Pub. by Ediciones Ekare) Kane-Miller Bk.

*__Lester, Alison.__ Celeste Sails to Spain. LC 98-42747. (Illus.). 32p. (J). (ps-3). 1999. 15.00 (*0-395-97395-3*, W Lorraine) HM.

Lester, Alison. Crashing & Splashing. (Illus.). 7p. (J). (ps). 1997. 3.95 (*1-86448-175-7*, Pub. by Allen & Unwin Pty) IPG Chicago.

— I'm Green & I'm Grumpy. (Open-the-Door Bks.). 16p. (J). (ps-1). 1993. pap. 4.99 (*0-14-054478-X*, PuffinBks) Peng Put Young Read.

— Imagine. 40p. (J). (ps-3). 1993. pap. 6.95 (*0-395-66953-7*) HM.

— Isabella's Bed. LC 92-22935. (Illus.). 32p. (J). (gr. k-3). 1993. reprint ed. 14.95 (*0-395-65565-X*) HM.

— Journey Home. 1991. 10.15 (*0-606-07751-0*, Pub. by Turtleback) Demco.

— My Farm. LC 93-30894. (Illus.). 32p. (J). 1994. 14.95 (*0-395-68193-6*) HM.

— My Farm. (Illus.). 32p. (J). (ps-3). 1999. pap. 5.95 (*0-395-97721-5*, W Lorraine) HM.

— The Quicksand Pony. LC 98-6930. 162p. (J). (gr. 4-7). 1998. 15.00 (*0-395-93749-3*) HM.

— Tessa Snaps Snakes. LC 91-2665. (Illus.). 32p. (J). (ps). 1991. pap. 13.95 (*0-685-52551-1*, Sandpiper) HM.

— When Frank Was Four. LC 95-38276. (Illus.). 32p. (J). (gr. k-3). 1996. 15.00 (*0-395-74275-7*) HM.

Lester, Alsion. Happy & Sad. (Illus.). 7p. (J). (ps). 1997. bds. 3.95 (*1-86448-176-5*, Pub. by Allen & Unwin Pty) IPG Chicago.

Lester, Andrew D. Coping with Your Anger: A Christian Guide. LC 82-24730. 114p. 1983. pap. 12.95 (*0-664-24471-8*) Westminster John Knox.

— Hope in Pastoral Care & Counseling. LC 94-36895. 176p. 1995. pap. 19.00 (*0-664-25588-4*) Westminster John Knox.

— Pastoral Care with Children in Crisis. LC 84-21901. 7p. (Orig.). (C). 1985. pap. 15.95 (*0-664-24598-6*) Westminster John Knox.

Lester, Andrew D. & Lester, Judith L. It Takes Two: The Joy of Intimate Marriage. LC 97-50587. 232p. 1998. pap. 20.00 (*0-664-25594-9*) Westminster John Knox.

— Understanding Aging Parents. LC 80-17832. (Christian Care Bks.: No. 8). 120p. reprint ed. pap. 37.20 (*0-7837-2636-8*, 204298700006) Bks Demand.

Lester, Barry M. & Boukydis, C. F., eds. Infant Crying: Theoretical & Research Perspectives. LC 84-26414. (Illus.). 400p. (C). 1985. 108.00 (*0-306-41775-8*, Plenum Trade) Perseus Pubng.

Lester, Barry M., jt. auth. see Fitzgerald, Hiram E.

Lester, Benisse. The Acute Hand. LC 97-11816. 600p. 1998. text 85.00 (*0-8385-0258-X*, A-0258-2, Apple Lange Med) McGraw.

Lester, C. B. Hydraulics for Pipeliners, Vol. 1. 2nd ed. 300p. 1994. 85.00 (*0-88415-400-9*, 5400) Gulf Pub.

Lester, C. R. Stoke to Market Drayton Line & Associated Canals & Mineral Branches. 52p. (C). 1985. 39.00 (*0-85361-293-5*) St Mut.

Lester, Charles E. The Life of Sam Houston: The Only Authentic Memoir of Him Ever Published. LC 70-38360. (Select Bibliographies Reprint Ser.). 1977. reprint ed. 25.95 (*0-8369-6777-1*) Ayer.

Lester, Cheryl, tr. see Lacoue-Labarthe, Philippe & Nancy, Jean-Luc.

Lester, David. Can We Prevent Suicide? LC 87-47813. (Studies in Modern Society: Political & Social Issues: No. 20). 1987. 34.50 (*0-404-61627-5*) AMS Pr.

*__Lester, David.__ Crime & the Native American. LC 99-31537. 200p. 1999. pap. 26.95 (*0-398-06984-0*); pap. 39.95 (*0-398-06983-2*) C C Thomas.

Lester, David. The Cruelest Death: The Enigma of Adolescent Suicide. LC 92-34448. 160p. (Orig.). (C). 1992. pap. text 20.95 (*0-914783-64-5*) Charles.

— The Death Penalty: Issues & Answers. 2nd ed. LC 97-34267. 174p. 1998. text 41.95 (*0-398-06822-4*); pap. text 27.95 (*0-398-06823-2*) C C Thomas.

— Encyclopedia of Famous Suicides. 175p. 1997. lib. bdg. 85.00 (*1-56072-413-7*) Nova Sci Pubs.

— Gun Control: Issues & Answers. 146p. 1983. pap. 26.95 (*0-398-04880-0*) C C Thomas.

— The Murderer & His Murder: A Review of Research. LC 85-48007. (Studies in Modern Society: Political & Social Issues: No. 19). 1986. 32.50 (*0-404-61626-7*) AMS Pr.

— Patterns of Suicide & Homicide in the World. LC 97-130538. (Illus.). (C). 1996. lib. bdg. 95.00 (*1-56072-392-0*) Nova Sci Pubs.

— Patterns of Suicide & Homocide in America. 143p. (C). 1994. lib. bdg. 115.00 (*1-56072-148-0*) Nova Sci Pubs.

— Questions & Answers about Murder. LC 91-23439. 192p. (Orig.). 1991. pap. text 16.95 (*0-914783-46-7*) Charles.

— Questions & Answers about Suicide. LC 89-60683. 184p. (Orig.). (C). 1989. pap. text 17.95 (*0-914783-31-9*) Charles.

— Serial Killers: The Insatiable Passion. LC 95-19309. 208p. (Orig.). 1995. pap. 18.95 (*0-914783-77-7*) Charles.

— Suicide from a Psychological Perspective. 142p. 1988. pap. 26.95 (*0-398-06233-1*) C C Thomas.

— Suicide from a Psychological Perspective. 142p. (C). 1988. text 39.95 (*0-398-05489-4*) C C Thomas.

— Suicide in African-Americans. LC 98-7496. 1998. 75.00 (*1-56072-562-1*) Nova Sci Pubs.

— Suicide in American Indians. LC 97-12613. 237p. (C). 1997. lib. bdg. 65.00 (*1-56072-429-3*) Nova Sci Pubs.

— Suicide in Creative Women. 189p. (C). 1997. lib. bdg. 115.00 (*1-56072-150-2*) Nova Sci Pubs.

— Suicide in Creative Women. (Illus.). 161p. 1998. pap. 16.95 (*1-56072-345-9*) Nova Sci Pubs.

*__Lester, David.__ Suicide Prevention: Resources for the Millenium. LC 00-40341. (Series in Death, Dying & Bereavement). 2000. write for info. (*0-87630-987-2*) Brunner-Mazel.

Lester, David. Theories of Personality. 200p. 1995. 69.95 (*1-56032-350-7*); pap. 34.95 (*1-56032-351-5*) Taylor & Francis.

— Understanding & Preventing Suicide: New Perspectives. (Illus.). 134p. 1990. pap. 21.95 (*0-398-06235-8*) C C Thomas.

— Understanding & Preventing Suicide: New Perspectives. (Illus.). 134p. (C). 1990. text 35.95 (*0-398-05709-5*) C C Thomas.

— Understanding Suicide: A Case Study Approach. 221p. (C). 1994. lib. bdg. 115.00 (*1-56072-149-9*) Nova Sci Pubs.

— Why People Kill Themselves: A 1990s Summary of Research Findings on Suicidal Behavior. 3rd ed. 464p. 1992. pap. 56.95 (*0-398-06236-6*) C C Thomas.

— Why People Kill Themselves: A 1990s Summary of Research Findings on Suicidal Behavior. 3rd ed. 464p. (C). 1992. text 71.95 (*0-398-05767-2*) C C Thomas.

Lester, David, ed. Emile Durkheim: Le Suicide One Hundred Years Later. LC 94-1056. 348p. 1994. lib. bdg. 42.95 (*0-914783-73-4*) Charles.

— Making Sense of Suicide: An In-Depth Look at Why People Kill Themselves. LC 97-10780. 208p. (Orig.). 1997. pap. text 22.95 (*0-914783-82-3*) Charles.

— Mechanical Rights. 183p. 1992. pap. 102.00 (*90-6215-313-5*, Pub. by Maklu Uitgev) Gaunt.

Lester, David, ed. Current Concepts of Suicide. LC 90-1600. 256p. (Orig.). 1990. pap. text 20.95 (*0-914783-45-9*) Charles.

Lester, David & Brockopp, Gene W. Crisis Intervention & Counseling by Telephone. (Illus.). 336p. 1976. pap. 41.95 (*0-398-06230-7*); text 54.95 (*0-398-02641-6*) C C Thomas.

Lester, David & Danto, Bruce L. Suicide Behind Bars: Prediction & Prevention. LC 92-27480. 176p. 1993. pap. 21.50 (*0-914783-62-9*) Charles.

Lester, David & Tallmer, Margot, eds. Now I Lay Me Down: Suicide & the Elderly. LC 93-25814. 252p. (Orig.). 1994. pap. 22.95 (*0-914783-65-3*) Charles.

Lester, David & Yang, Bijou. The Economy & Suicide: Economic Perspectives on Suicide. 237p. (C). 1997. lib. bdg. 75.00 (*1-56072-423-4*) Nova Sci Pubs.

Lester, David, jt. ed. see Canetto, Silvia S.

Lester, David, jt. ed. see Leenaars, Antoon A.

Lester, David S., et al. Imaging Brain Structure & Function: Emerging Technologies in the Neurosciences. LC 97-13820. (Annals of the New York Academy of Sciences Ser.). 1997. pap. 130.00 (*1-57331-069-7*) NY Acad Sci.

— Imaging Brain Structure & Function: Emerging Technologies in the Neurosciences. (Annals of the New York Academy of Sciences Ser.: Vol. 820). 185p. 1997. 130.00 (*1-57331-068-9*) NY Acad Sci.

Lester, Dee G. & Thomson, Kenneth, Jr. Around Gallatin & Sumner County, Tennessee. (Images of America Ser.). (Illus.). 128p. 1999. pap. 18.99 (*0-7524-1220-5*) Arcadia Publng.

L

Lester, Dee Gee, et al. Around Gallatin & Sumner County, Tennessee. (Images of America Ser.). (Illus.). 128p. 1998. pap. 16.99 (0-7524-0929-8) Arcadia Publng.

Lester, DeeGee. Roosevelt Research: Collections for the Study of Theodore, Franklin & Eleanor, 23. LC 92-10072. (Bibliographies & Indexes in American History Ser.: No. 23). 224p. 1992. lib. bdg. 65.00 (0-313-27204-2, LRC/, Greenwood Pr) Greenwood.

Lester, DeeGee, compiled by. Irish Research: A Guide to Collections in North America, Ireland, & Great Britain, 9. LC 87-25150. 376p. 1987. lib. bdg. 79.50 (0-313-24664-5, LIR/, Greenwood Pr) Greenwood.

Lester, DeeGee, jt. compiled by see Weaver, Jack W.

Lester, Donna. Macon County, Missouri Pictorial History. (Illus.). 110p. 1993. 35.00 (0-88107-214-1) Curtis Media.

Lester, E. W., jt. auth. see Hickman, James.

Lester, Ed. Writing Research Papers: A Complete Guide. 7th ed. (C). 1997. pap. text 26.40 (0-673-46644-2) Addson-Wesley Educ.

Lester, Elizabeth. Legendary King of San Miguel. 1979. pap. 6.50 (0-87461-027-3) McNally & Loftin.

Lester, Ellen C., ed. see Hendricks, Douglas L., et al.

Lester, Ellen C., ed. see Holderness, Richard A.

Lester, Ellen C., ed. see Rehon, Peter M.

Lester, Ellen C., ed. see Reinbolt, Jacob C.

Lester, Ellen C., ed. see Tussman, Davida S. & Hansen, Charles A.

***Lester, Esther.** One Woman's Reflections. 80p. 1999. pap. 7.95 (1-56167-547-4) Am Literary Pr.

Lester, Eva P., jt. auth. see Gabbard, Glen O.

Lester, G. A. The Index of Middle English Prose Handlist II: Manuscripts in the John Rylands Chetham's Libraries, Manchester. LC 85-2105. 128p. 1985. 55.00 (0-85991-189-6) Boydell & Brewer.

— Sir John Paston's Grete Boke: A Descriptive Catalogue with an Introduction, of British Library Ms. Lansdowne 285. 197p. 1984. 75.00 (0-85991-161-6) Boydell & Brewer.

Lester, Gary & Lester, Tina. Feyetteville, Arkansas, National Cemetery. 90p. 1996. reprint ed. pap. 20.00 (1-56546-075-8) Arkansas Res.

— Ft. Smith, Arkansas, National Cemetery. 163p. 1996. reprint ed. pap. 25.00 (1-56546-076-6) Arkansas Res.

Lester, Gary Robert. Mosquitoes to Wolves: The Evolution of the Airborne Forward Air Controller. LC 97-18377. (Illus.). 294p. 1987. pap. 18.00 (1-58566-033-7) Air Univ.

Lester, Gene & Laufer, Peter. When Hollywood Was Fun: Snapshots of an Era. (Illus.). 224p. 1993. 24.95 (1-55972-197-9, Birch Ln Pr) Carol Pub Group.

Lester, Genie, ed. see O'Donnell, John.

Lester, Geoff A., ed. Chaucer in Perspective: Middle English Essays in Honour of Norman Blake. (SAP Individual Title Ser.). 400p. 1999. 95.00 (1-85075-988-X, Pub. by Sheffield Acad) CUP Services.

Lester, Gillian, jt. auth. see Kelman, Mark.

Lester, Gordon H., jt. auth. see Scoon-Rogers, Lydia.

Lester, Helen. A la Cima. Palacios, Argentina, tr. (Spanish Whole Language Big Bks.).Tr. of Hop to the Top. (SPA., Illus.). 16p. (Orig.). (J). (ps-2). 1994. pap. 14.95 (1-56784-097-3) Newbridge Educ.

— Author: A True Story. LC 96-9645. (Illus.). 32p. (J). 1997. 11.00 (0-395-82744-2) HM.

— La Bolsa de Kathy. Palacios, Argentina, tr. (Spanish Whole Language Big Bks.).Tr. of Kathy's Pocket. (SPA., Illus.). 16p. (Orig.). (J). (ps-2). 1994. pap. 16.95 (1-56784-098-1) Newbridge Educ.

— Hooway for Wodney Wat. LC 98-46149. (Illus.). 32p. (J). (ps-3). 1999. 15.00 (0-395-92392-1) HM.

— Hop to the Top. (Whole-Language Big Bks.). (Illus.). 16p. (Orig.). (J). (ps-2). 1994. pap. 16.95 (1-56784-070-1) Newbridge Educ.

— It Wasn't My Fault, 001. LC 84-19212. (Illus.). 32p. (J). (gr. k-3). 1985. 16.00 (0-395-35629-6) HM.

— It Wasn't My Fault. LC 84-19212. (Illus.). 32p. (J). (ps-3). 1989. pap. 6.95 (0-395-51007-4, Sandpiper) HM.

— Kathy's Pocket. (Whole-Language Big Bks.). (Illus.). 16p. (Orig.). (J). (ps-2). 1994. pap. 16.95 (1-56784-071-X) Newbridge Educ.

— Listen, Buddy. LC 94-33634. (Illus.). 32p. (J). (gr. k-3). 1995. 15.00 (0-395-72361-2) HM.

— Listen, Buddy. 32p. 1997. pap. 5.95 (0-395-85402-4) HM.

— Listen, Buddy. (J). 1997. pap. text 4.95 (0-395-72631-X) HM.

— Listen, Buddy. (J). 1997. 10.15 (0-606-11567-6, Pub. by Turtleback) Demco.

— Me First. LC 91-45808. (Illus.). 32p. (J). (ps up). 1992. 15.00 (0-395-58706-9) HM.

— Me First. LC 91-45808. (Illus.). 32p. (J). (gr. k-3). 1995. pap. 5.95 (0-395-72022-2, Sandpiper) HM.

— Me First. (J). 1992. 11.15 (0-606-07855-X) Turtleback.

— La Mochila de Lin. 3rd ed. Ada, Alma F., tr. (Dejame Leer).Tr. of Lin's Backpack. (SPA., Illus.). 8p. (J). (ps-1). 1995. bds. 2.95 (0-673-36291-4, GoodYrBooks) Addson-Wesley Educ.

— Pookins Gets Her Way. (Illus.). 32p. (J). (ps-3). 1990. pap. 7.95 (0-395-53965-X) HM.

— A Porcupine Named Fluffy, 001. LC 85-24820. (Illus.). 32p. (J). (ps-3). 1986. 16.00 (0-395-36895-2) HM.

— A Porcupine Named Fluffy. LC 85-24820. (Illus.). 32p. (J). (ps-3). 1989. pap. 6.95 (0-395-52018-5) HM.

Lester, Helen. A Porcupine Named Fluffy. (J). 1986. 11.15 (0-606-02251-1, Pub. by Turtleback) Demco.

Lester, Helen. Princess Penelope's Parrot. LC 95-53266. (Illus.). 32p. (J). (ps-3). 1996. 14.95 (0-395-78320-8) HM.

— Tacky in Trouble. LC 97-442. (Illus.). 32p. 1998. 15.00 (0-395-86113-6) HM.

— Tacky the Penguin. LC 87-30684. (Illus.). 32p. (J). (ps-3). 1988. 15.00 (0-395-45536-7) HM.

— Tacky the Penguin. LC 87-30684. (Illus.). 32p. (J). (ps-3). 1990. pap. 5.95 (0-395-56233-3) HM.

— Tacky the Penguin. (J). 1988. 11.15 (0-606-04552-X, Pub. by Turtleback) Demco.

— Three Cheers for Tacky. LC 93-14342. (Illus.). 32p. (J). 1994. 14.95 (0-395-66841-7) HM.

— Three Cheers for Tacky. LC 93-14342. (Illus.). 32p. (J). (ps-3). 1996. pap. 5.95 (0-395-82740-X) HM.

Lester, Helen. Three Cheers for Tacky. LC 93-14342. (J). 1994. 11.15 (0-606-10344-9, Pub. by Turtleback) Demco.

Lester, Helen. The Wizard, the Fairy, & the Magic Chicken, 001. (Illus.). 32p. (J). (ps-3). 1983. 16.00 (0-395-33885-9) HM.

— The Wizard, the Fairy, & the Magic Chicken. LC 82-21302. (Illus.). 32p. (J). (gr. k-3). 1988. pap. 6.95 (0-395-47945-2) HM.

Lester, Helen & Lester, Robin. Muttsy's Mystery. LC 94-24224. (Gund Children's Library). (Illus.). (J). 1995. write for info. (1-56402-499-7) Candlewick Pr.

***Lester, Helen & Munsinger, Lynn.** Tacky & the Emperor's New Clothes. LC 99-89159. (J). 2000. 15.00 (0-395-98120-4) HM.

Lester, Helen, jt. auth. see Lester, Robin.

***Lester, J. C.** Escape from Leviathan: Liberty, Welfare & Anarchy Reconciled. LC 00-25475. 2000. write for info. (0-312-23416-3) St Martin.

Lester, J. C. Liberty, Utility & Anarchy: A Philosophical & Economic Reconciliation. (Studies in Social, Political, & Legal Philosophy: No. 70). 256p. 1998. 62.50 (0-8476-8451-2); pap. 23.95 (0-8476-8452-0) Rowman.

Lester, J. C. & Wilson, D. L. Ku Klux Klan, Its Origin, Growth & Disbandment. LC 70-144650. reprint ed. 29.50 (0-404-00195-5) AMS Pr.

— Ku Klux Klan, Its Origin, Growth & Disbandment. LC 72-131766. 1973. reprint ed. 25.00 (0-403-00653-8) Scholarly.

Lester, J. N. Heavy Metals in Wastewater & Sludge Treatment Processes Vo. 1: Sources Analysis & Legislation. LC 87-10329. 1987. 113.00 (0-8493-4668-1, CRC Reprint) Franklin.

— Heavy Metals in Wastewater & Sludge Treatment Processes Vol. 2: Treatment & Disposal. LC 87-10329. 1987. 99.00 (0-8493-4669-X, TD758, CRC Reprint) Franklin.

— Microbiology & Chemistry for Environmental Scientists & Engineers. LC 98-49280. 1999. pap. write for info. (0-419-22680-X) Routledge.

Lester, J. N., ed. Heavy Metals in Wastewater & Sludge Treatment Processes, 2 vols., Set. LC 87-10329. 176p. 1987. 211.00 (0-8493-4667-3, TD758, CRC Reprint) Franklin.

Lester, J. N. & Sterritt, R. M. Microbiology for Public Health & Environmental Engineers. 284p. 1988. text 65.00 (0-419-12760-7, E & FN Spon); pap. text 29.50 (0-419-12770-4, E & FN Spon) Routledge.

Lester, James D. Argument & Research. (C). 1999. pap. text 8.44 (0-321-02759-0) Addison-Wesley Educ.

— Daughters of the Revolution: Classic Essays by Women. LC 95-11910. (Library of Classic Essays). 224p. 1995. pap. text, student ed. 14.95 (0-8442-5880-6) NTC Contemp Pub Co.

— Daughters of the Revolution: Classic Essays by Women. (Library of Classic Essays). 1998. pap., teacher ed. 16.95 (0-8442-5881-4) NTC Contemp Pub Co.

— Diverse Identities: Classic Multicultural Essays. (Library of Classic Essays). 1998. pap., teacher ed. 23.99 (0-8442-5885-7) NTC Contemp Pub Co.

— Diverse Identities: Classical Multicultural Essays. LC 95-11019. (Library of Classic Essays). 272p. 1995. pap. text, student ed. 14.95 (0-8442-5884-9) NTC Contemp Pub Co.

— Literature & Research. (C). 1999. pap. text 7.50 (0-321-02764-7) Addison-Wesley Educ.

— Of Bunsen Burners, Bones, & Belles Lettres: Classic Essays Across the Curriculum. LC 95-11060. (Library of Classic Essays). 240p. 1995. pap. text, student ed. 14.95 (0-8442-5882-2) NTC Contemp Pub Co.

— Of Bunsen Burners, Bones, & Belles Lettres: Classic Essays Across the Curriculum. (Library of Classic Essays). 1998. pap., teacher ed. 23.99 (0-8442-5883-0) NTC Contemp Pub Co.

— Plato's Heirs: Classic Essays. (Library of Classic Essays). 1998. pap., teacher ed. 23.99 (0-8442-5879-2) NTC Contemp Pub Co.

— WRI RSRCH PPR REP99& PKG. 9th ed. (C). 1998. pap. text 22.00 (0-321-02766-3) Addison-Wesley.

— A Writer's Handbook: Style & Grammar. 512p. (C). 1990. pap. text 35.50 (0-15-597648-6) Harcourt Coll Pubs.

— Writing Across the Curriculum. 96p. (C). 1998. pap. text 10.00 (0-321-02761-2) Addison-Wesley Educ.

— Writing Research Paper: Reporting & Writing. 9th ed. (C). 1998. pap. text 22.00 (0-321-02768-X) Addison-Wesley.

— Writing Research Papers. 6th ed. (C). 1997. pap. 12.33 (0-673-38798-4) Addson-Wesley Educ.

— Writing Research Papers. 8th ed. (C). 1996. spiral bd. 18.95 (0-321-02644-6) Addson-Wesley Educ.

— Writing Research Papers. 9th ed. 386p. (C). 1998. reprint ed. pap. 22.00 (0-321-04980-2) Addison-Wesley.

— Writing Research Papers: A Complete Guide. 7th ed. 1993. write for info. (0-318-69537-5) HarperTrade.

— Writing Research Papers: A Complete Guide. 7th ed. (Illus.). 382p. 1999. reprint ed. pap. text 15.00 (0-7881-6226-8) DIANE Pub.

— Writing Research Papers: A Complete Guide. 9th ed. (C). 1998. pap. text 22.00 (0-321-02767-1) Addison-Wesley.

Lester, James D., compiled by. Plato's Heirs: Classic Essays. LC 95-8290. (Library of Classic Essays). 304p. 1995. pap. text, student ed. 14.95 (0-8442-5878-4) NTC Contemp Pub Co.

Lester, James D., Sr. & Lester, James D., Jr. The Research Paper Handbook. (Illus.). 232p. (Orig.). 1991. pap. 7.95 (0-673-36016-4, GoodYrBooks) Addson-Wesley Educ.

— Writing: Style & Grammar. 400p. (J). (gr. 6-10). 1994. pap. 9.95 (0-673-36093-8, GoodYrBooks); spiral bd. 14.95 (0-673-36128-4, GoodYrBooks) Addson-Wesley Educ.

Lester, James D., Jr., jt. auth. see Lester, James D., Sr.

Lester, James P., ed. Environmental Politics & Policy: Theories & Evidence. 2nd ed. LC 94-38244. (Illus.). 384p. 1995. text 59.95 (0-8223-1558-0); pap. text 24.95 (0-8223-1569-6) Duke.

Lester, James P. & Bowman, Ann, eds. The Politics of Hazardous Waste Management. LC 83-16595. (Duke Press Policy Studies). x, 317p. (Orig.). 1983. pap. text 20.95 (0-8223-0523-2) Duke.

Lester, James P. & Stewart, Joseph, Jr. Public Policy: An Evolutionary Approach. 350p. (C). 1996. 36.75 (0-314-06750-7) West Pub.

***Lester, James P., et al.** Environmental Injustice in the United States: Myth & Realities. 192p. 2000. pap. 19.00 (0-8133-3819-0) Westview.

Lester, James P., jt. ed. see Davis, Charles E.

Lester, James P., jt. ed. see Davis, Charles.

***Lester, Jane.** An American College Girl in Hitler's Germany: A Memoir. LC 99-52236. 1999. write for info. (0-7734-7852-3) E Mellen.

Lester, Jane. The House at Cheltonwood. large type ed. (Linford Romance Library). 1991. pap. 16.99 (0-7089-7100-8) Ulverscroft.

— Love's Golden Touch. large type ed. (Linford Romance Library). 272p. 1985. pap. 16.99 (0-7089-6055-3, Linford) Ulverscroft.

— Nurse at High Hedges. large type ed. 288p. 1988. 27.99 (0-7089-1882-4) Ulverscroft.

— Nurse in the East. large type ed. (Linford Romance Library). 336p. 1985. pap. 16.99 (0-7089-6098-7, Linford) Ulverscroft.

— Nurse Rita's Request. large type ed. 281p. 1989. 27.99 (0-7089-1933-2) Ulverscroft.

— The Reluctant Heart. large type ed. 416p. 1988. 27.99 (0-7089-1802-6) Ulverscroft.

— Sister March's Secret. large type ed. (Linford Romance Library). 296p. 1984. pap. 16.99 (0-7089-6047-2) Ulverscroft.

— You Are Very Lucky, My Father Said... & Other Poems. LC 98-48979. 60p. 1998. pap. 14.95 (0-7734-3110-1) E Mellen.

***Lester, Jeremy.** The Dialogue of Negation: Debates on Hegemony in Russia & the West. 240p. 2000. pap. 27.50 (0-7453-1629-8, Pub. by Pluto GBR); text 79.95 (0-7453-1630-1, Pub. by Pluto GBR) Stylus Pub VA.

Lester, Jeremy. Modern Tsars & Princes: The Struggle for Hegemony in Russia. LC 95-23359. 224p. (C). 1995. pap. 20.00 (1-85984-039-6, Pub. by Verso) Norton.

— Modern Tsars & Princes: The Struggle for Hegemony in Russia. LC 95-23359. 224p. (C). (gr. 13 up). 1995. 65.00 (1-85984-914-8, Pub. by Verso) Norton.

Lester, Jim. Fallout. 224p. (J). 1997. mass mkt. 3.99 (0-440-22683-X) Dell.

— Fallout. 1997. 9.09 (0-606-11312-6, Pub. by Turtleback) Demco.

— Man for Arkansas: Sid McMath & the Southern Reform Tradition. (Illus.). 303p. 1976. 19.95 (0-914546-11-2) J W Bell.

Lester, Joan S. Taking Charge: Every Woman's Action Guide to Personal, Political & Professional Success. 250p. (Orig.). 1996. pap. 14.95 (1-57324-052-4) Conari Press.

Lester, Joanne, et al. Statement on the Scope & Standards of Advanced Practice in Oncology Nursing. rev. ed. LC 98-204655. 28p. 1997. pap. text 9.50 (1-890504-05-X) Oncology Nursing.

***Lester, Joe N.** I Am Not Afraid to Dream, 1. 193p. 1999. 19.99 (0-9671344-0-4) Joewolf Pubs.

Lester, Joel. Analytical Approaches to Twentieth-Century Music. (C). 1989. text 50.75 (0-393-95762-4); pap. text. write for info. (0-393-95816-7) Norton.

— Bach's Works for Solo Violin: Style, Structure, Performance. LC 98-27735. (Illus.). 200p. 1999. 29.95 (0-19-512097-3) OUP.

— Between Modes & Keys: German Theory 1592-1802. LC 87-14864. (Harmonologia Ser.: No. 3). (Illus.). 250p. 1990. lib. bdg. 54.00 (0-918728-77-0) Pendragon NY.

— Compositional Theory in the Eighteenth Century. (Illus.). 368p. 1993. text 49.95 (0-674-15522-X) HUP.

— Compositional Theory in the Eighteenth Century. (Illus.). 368p. 1994. pap. 31.00 (0-674-15523-8) HUP.

— Harmony in Tonal Music, 2 vols. LC 81-12350. (C). 1982. student ed. 8.00 (0-685-07494-3, KnopfC) Knopf.

— Harmony in Tonal Music, 2 vols., Vol. 2: Chromatic Practices. LC 81-12350. (C). 1982. student ed. 7.95 (0-685-07493-5, KnopfC) Knopf.

Lester, John & Spoerri, Pierre. Rediscovering Freedom. (Illus.). 149p. (Orig.). 1992. pap. 12.95 (1-85239-016-6) Grosvenor USA.

Lester, John A. Journey Through Despair, 1880-1914: Transformations in British Literary Culture. LC 68-15767. 235p. reprint ed. pap. 72.90 (0-608-16115-2, 201602100006) Bks Demand.

Lester, John C. Ku Klux Klan, Its Origin, Growth, & Disbandment. (History - United States Ser.). 198p. 1992. reprint ed. lib. bdg. 69.00 (0-7812-6204-6) Rprt Serv.

Lester, John R. Frontline Airline: Troop Carrier Pilot in World War II. (Illus.). 194p. 1994. pap. text 17.95 (0-89745-179-1) Sunflower U Pr.

Lester, Judith L., jt. auth. see Lester, Andrew D.

Lester, Juliette N., jt. auth. see Hoyt, Kenneth B.

***Lester, Julius.** Ackamarackus. LC 00-37185. (Illus.). (J). 2001. write for info. (0-590-48913-5) Scholastic Inc.

— Albidaro & the Mischievous Dream. (Illus.). 40p. (J). (ps-3). 2000. 16.99 (0-8037-1987-6, Dial Yng Read) Peng Put Young Read.

Lester, Julius. And All Our Wounds Forgiven. LC 93-50049. 256p. 1994. 19.45 (1-55970-258-3, Pub. by Arcade Pub Inc) Time Warner.

— And All Our Wounds Forgiven. 240p. 1996. pap. 12.00 (0-15-600330-9, Harvest Bks) Harcourt.

— The Autobiography of God. 2000. write for info. (1-55970-112-9) Arcade Pub Inc.

— Black Folktales. LC 91-7619. 128p. 1991. pap. 11.00 (0-8021-3242-1, Grove) Grove-Atltic.

— From Slave Ship to Freedom Road. LC 96-44422. (Illus.). 40p. (YA). (gr. 5-9). 1998. 17.99 (0-8037-1893-4, Dial Yng Read) Peng Put Young Read.

***Lester, Julius.** From Slave Ship to Freedom Road. (Illus.). (YA). (gr. 3 up). 1999. pap. 6.99 (0-14-056669-4, PuffinBks) Peng Put Young Read.

Lester, Julius. How Many Spots Does a Leopard Have? And Other Tales. 80p. (J). (gr. 4-7). 1994. pap. 5.95 (0-590-41972-2) Scholastic Inc.

— Jazz 48p. (J). 2001. 14.99 (0-7868-0463-7) Little.

— John Henry. LC 93-34583. (Illus.). 40p. (J). (ps-3). 1994. 17.99 (0-8037-1606-0, Dial Yng Read) Peng Put Young Read.

***Lester, Julius.** John Henry. (Illus.). 40p. (J). (ps-3). 1999. pap. 6.99 (0-14-056622-8, PuffinBks) Peng Put Young Read.

— Let's Talk about Race. 32p. (J). 15.95 (0-06-028596-6); 15.89 (0-06-028598-2); 5.95 (0-06-446226-9) HarpC.

Lester, Julius. The Long Journey Home: Stories from Black History. LC 98-115427. 160p. (YA). (gr. 6 up). 1998. pap. 4.99 (0-14-038981-4, PuffinBks) Peng Put Young Read.

— The Long Journey Home: Stories from Black History. (J). 1998. 10.09 (0-606-12987-1, Pub. by Turtleback) Demco.

***Lester, Julius.** Long Journey Home: Stories from Black History. (YA). (gr. 6 up). 2000. 19.25 (0-8446-7148-7) Peter Smith.

Lester, Julius. Lovesong: Becoming a Jew. (Illus.). 256p. 1995. reprint ed. pap. 12.45 (1-55970-316-4, Pub. by Arcade Pub Inc) Time Warner.

— The Man Who Was Horse. LC 97-25210. (Illus.). 40p. (J). (gr. k-3). 1998. 16.99 (0-8037-1787-3, Dial Yng Read) Peng Put Young Read.

***Lester, Julius.** Pharaoh's Daughter: A Novel of Ancient Egypt. LC 99-6403. (Illus.). 192p. (YA). (gr. 7 up). 2000. 17.00 (0-15-201826-3) Harcourt.

Lester, Julius. Sam & the Tigers. (Illus.). 1996. pap. 15.99 (0-8037-2216-8, Dial Yng Read) Peng Put Young Read.

— Sam & the Tigers: A Retelling of Little Black Sambo. LC 95-43080. (Illus.). 40p. (J). (ps-3). 1996. 15.99 (0-8037-2028-9, Dial Yng Read) Peng Put Young Read.

— Shining. LC 95-48904. (Illus.). (J). 1999. 17.00 (0-15-200773-3) Harcourt.

— Tales of Uncle Remus: The Adventures of Brer Rabbit. (Illus.). 160p. (J). (gr. 3 up). 1999. pap. 6.99 (0-14-130347-6, PuffinBks) Peng Put Young Read.

— This Strange New Feeling. LC 81-68782. 172p. (YA). (gr. 7 up). 1985. pap. 2.75 (0-590-44047-0) Scholastic Inc.

***Lester, Julius.** To Be a Slave. (Illus.). 176p. (J). (gr. 5-9). 2000. pap. 5.99 (0-14-131001-4, PuffinBks) Peng Put Young Read.

Lester, Julius. To Be a Slave. LC 77-587047. (Illus.). 160p. (YA). (gr. 7-12). 1986. pap. 3.99 (0-590-42460-2) Scholastic Inc.

— To Be a Slave. (YA). 1968. 9.09 (0-606-00989-2, Pub. by Turtleback) Demco.

— To Be a Slave. 30th ed. LC 98-5213. (YA). (gr. 7 up). 1998. 20.00 (0-8037-2347-4, Dial Yng Read) Peng Put Young Read.

Lester, Julius. To Be a Slave, Set. unabridged ed. (YA). (gr. 8). 1997. pap. 39.75 incl. audio (0-7887-0961-5, 40269) Recorded Bks.

Lester, Julius. What a Truly Cool World! LC 96-31438. (Illus.). 40p. (J). (ps-2). 1997. 15.95 (0-590-86468-8) Scholastic Inc.

— When the Beginning Began: Stories about God, the Creatures & Us. LC 97-37352. (Illus.). 112p. (J). 1999. 17.00 (0-15-201238-9) Harcourt.

***Lester, Julius & Isadora, Rachel.** Sam & the Tigers. (Picture Puffin Ser.). (Illus.). 40p. (J). (ps-3). 2000. 6.99 (0-14-056288-5, PuffinBks) Peng Put Young Read.

Lester, Julius & Seeger, Pete. Folksinger's Guide to the Twelve-String Guitar As Played by Leadbelly. (Illus.). 80p. 1965. pap. 14.95 (0-8256-0023-5, OK61440, Oak) Music Sales.

Lester, June, ed. Libraries & Information Services Today: The Yearly Chronicle, 1991. LC Z 0731.L53. (Illus.). 318p. 1991. reprint ed. pap. 98.60 (0-7837-9681-1, 206041000005) Bks Demand.

Lester, K. AS/400 Security, Audit & Control. 140p. 1993. 272.25 (1-85617-182-5, Pergamon Pr) Elsevier.

***Lester, Katherine Morris.** Historic Costume: A Resume of the Characteristic Types of Costume from the Most Remote Time to the Present Dau. LC 99-28698. 244p. 1999. reprint ed. 45.00 (0-7808-0310-8) Omnigraphics Inc.

***Lester, Katherine Morris & McAfee, Ila.** Historic Costume. LC 99-28698. 1999. lib. bdg. write for info. (1-55888-291-X) Omnigraphics Inc.

Lester, Kent, jt. auth. see McGuerty, David.

Lester, Kit. A Practical Approach to Data Structures: Related Algorithms in Pascal with Applications. 1990. text 49.95 (0-470-21504-6) P-H.

An Asterisk (*) at the beginning of an entry indicates that the title is appearing for the first time.

Lester, L. & Benning, B. Procurement in the Process Industry. 258p. 1989. 400.00 (*0-7855-5755-5*, Pub. by Inst Pur & Supply) St Mut.

Lester, L. J., jt. auth. see Fast, A. W.

Lester, Lane P. & Bohlin, Raymond G. The Natural Limits to Biological Change. 160p. 1984. pap. 10.95 (*0-310-44511-6*, 12211P) Zondervan.

— The Natural Limits to Biological Change. 2nd ed. LC 89-70041. (Illus.). 207p. 1989. reprint ed. pap. 12.99 (*0-945241-06-2*) Probe Bks.

Lester, Lane P. & Hefley, James C. Human Cloning: Playing God or Scientific Progress? LC 98-23847. 176p. 1998. pap. 9.99 (*0-8007-5668-1*) Revell.

***Lester, Larry, et al.** Black Baseball in Chicago. LC 00-101510. (Black America Ser.). (Illus.). 128p. 2000. pap. 18.99 (*0-7385-0704-0*) Arcadia Publng.

— Black Baseball in Detroit. (Black America Ser.). (Illus.). 128p. 2000. pap. 18.99 (*0-7385-0707-5*) Arcadia Publng.

Lester, Lilly. A Woman's Heart. 37p. 1998. pap. 8.95 (*0-533-12341-0*) Vantage.

Lester, Margot. So You Want to be Rich & Happy: 110 Simple Ways to Bring Wealth & Satisfaction to Your Life. 1998. pap. 9.95 (*1-890586-40-4*) Pipeline Pr.

Lester, Margot C. Real Life Guide to Starting Your Career: How to Get the Right Job Right Now! Foster, Kerry & Poole, Laura, eds. (Real Life Guide Ser.). 224p. (Orig.). 1998. pap. 16.95 (*1-890586-02-1*) Pipeline Pr.

Lester, Marion, jt. auth. see Hughes, Elizabeth.

Lester, Mark. Grammar in the Classroom. LC 89-33800. 352p. 1989. 62.00 (*0-02-370060-2*, Macmillan Coll) P-H.

Lester, Mark, jt. auth. see Elder, Dana C.

Lester, Mark, jt. ed. see Germidis, Dimitri.

Lester, Mark, tr. see Deleuze, Gilles.

Lester, Mary. Hand Me That Corkscrew, Bacchus. LC 73-82326. 160p. 1973. 15.00 (*0-87832-007-5*) Piper.

Lester, Mike. A Is for Salad. LC 99-20900. (Illus.). 40p. (ps-3). 1999. 9.99 (*0-399-23388-1*, Putnam & Grosset) Putnam Pub Group.

Lester, Mike, jt. auth. see Hall, Katy.

Lester, Mike, jt. auth. see Winter, Rick.

Lester, Nancy B. & Onore, Cynthia S. Learning Change: One School District Meets Language Across the Curriculum. LC 89-36956. 220p. (C). 1990. pap. text 22.00 (*0-86709-254-8*, 0254, Pub. by Boynton Cook Pubs) Heinemann.

Lester, Neal A. Understanding Zora Neale Hurston's Their Eyes Were Watching God: A Student Casebook to Issues, Sources & Historical Documents. LC 98-55342. (Literature in Context Ser.). 200p. 1999. 39.95 (*0-313-30210-3*) Greenwood.

Lester, Neal A. & Shange, Ntozake. Ntozake Shange: A Critical Study of the Plays. LC 94-36113. (Critical Studies in Black Life & Culture: Vol. 21). 336p. 1995. text 58.00 (*0-8153-0314-9*, H1441) Garland.

Lester, Patricia, ed. see Oklahoma Department of Libraries Staff.

Lester, Patrick D. The Biographical Directory of Native American Painters. limited ed. LC 95-69012. (Illus.). 744p. 1995. 245.00 (*0-9640706-3-4*) Cock-a-Hoop.

Lester, Patrick D., ed. The Biographical Directory of Native American Painters. LC 95-69012. 720p. 1995. 49.95 (*0-8061-9936-9*) U of Okla Pr.

Lester, Paul. Blur: The Illustrated Story. (Illus.). 80p. 1995. pap. 14.95 (*0-7935-4730-X*, 00330025) H Leonard.

***Lester, Paul.** Great Galveston Disaster. (Illus.). 576p. 2000. pap. 17.95 (*1-56554-784-5*) Pelican.

Lester, Paul. Oasis: The Illustrated Story. (Illus.). 80p. pap. 14.95 (*0-600-58761-4*, HL00330020) H Leonard.

— Oasis: The Illustrated Story. 80p. 1995. pap. 14.95 (*0-7935-4729-6*, 00330020) H Leonard.

***Lester, Paul.** The Prodigy. (Illustrated Story Ser.). (Illus.). 80p. 2000. pap. 9.95 (*0-600-59511-0*, Pub. by P HM) Trafalgar.

Lester, Paul. Pulp: The Illustrated Story. (Illus.). 80p. 1996. pap. text 14.95 (*0-7935-6439-5*, 00330227) H Leonard.

***Lester, Paul.** The Verve. (Illustrated Story Ser.). (Illus.). 80p. 2000. pap. 9.95 (*0-600-59592-7*, Pub. by P HM) Trafalgar.

Lester, Paul M. Desktop Computing Workbook: A Guide for Using 15 Programs in Macintosh & Windows Formats. (Mass Communication Ser.). (C). 1995. 50.95 (*0-534-50566-X*) Wadsworth Pub.

— Images That Injure: Pictorial Stereotypes in the Media. LC 95-34418. 296p. 1996. 65.00 (*0-275-94928-1*, Praeger Pubs) Greenwood.

— Images That Injure: Pictorial Stereotypes in the Media. LC 95-34418. 296p. 1996. pap. 22.95 (*0-275-95357-2*, Praeger Pubs) Greenwood.

— Visual Communication: Images with Messages. (Mass Communication Ser.). 1999. pap. 12.00 (*0-534-76771-0*) Thomson Learn.

Lester, Paul M. Visual Communication: Images with Messages. LC 94-19173. 450p. 1994. pap. 36.25 (*0-534-19530-X*) Wadsworth Pub.

Lester, Paula. Teacher Job Satisfaction: An Annotated Bibliography & Guide to Research. McCarthy, Joseph M., ed. LC 88-9768. (Bibliographies in Contemporary Education Ser.: Vol. 7). 362p. 1988. text 65.00 (*0-8240-8922-7*) Garland.

Lester, Paula & Bishop, Lloyd. Handbook of Tests & Measurement in Education & the Social Sciences. LC 96-60521. 240p. 1997. pap. text 39.95 (*1-56676-434-3*) Scarecrow.

Lester, Paula, jt. auth. see Bishop, Lloyd.

***Lester, Paula E. & Bishop, Lloyd K.** Handbook of Tests & Measurement in Education & the Social Sciences. 2nd ed. LC 00-41964. 2000. pap. write for info. (*0-8108-3863-X*) Scarecrow.

Lester, Paula E. & Norton, Marcia M. K-12 Case Studies for School Administrators: Problems, Issues, & Resources. LC 98-16204. (Source Books on Education: Vol. 52). 216p. 1998. 50.00 (*0-8153-2570-3*, SS1139) Garland.

Lester, Peter F. Aviation Weather. LC 95-7862. 1995. write for info. (*0-88487-178-9*) Jeppesen Sanderson.

— Turbulence: A New Perspective for Pilots. LC 93-13133. (Illus.). 280p. 1994. 24.95 (*0-88487-176-2*) Jeppesen Sanderson.

Lester, R. G., ed. Information Sources in Finance & Banking. 818p. 1995. 125.00 (*1-85739-037-7*) Bowker-Saur.

Lester, Ralph P. Look to the East. 15.00 (*0-911164-18-9*) Powner.

— Look to the East! A Ritual of the First Three Degrees of Freemasonry. 220p. 1998. reprint ed. pap. 19.95 (*0-7661-0465-6*) Kessinger Pub.

Lester, Richard, jt. auth. see Soderbergh, Steven.

Lester, Richard A. As Unions Mature: An Analysis of the Evolution of American Unionism. LC 58-10048. 183p. 1958. reprint ed. pap. 56.80 (*0-7837-9373-1*, 206011700004) Bks Demand.

— Labor Arbitration in State & Local Government: An Examination of Experience in Eight States & New York City. 1984p. pap. 10.00 (*0-318-20241-7*) PU Indust Rel.

— Manpower Planning in a Free Society. LC 66-14890. 241p. reprint ed. pap. 74.80 (*0-8357-8945-4*, 203339800085) Bks Demand.

— Monetary Experiments: Early American & Recent Scandinavian. LC 70-75796. (Reprints of Economic Classics Ser.). (Illus.). xvii, 316p. 1970. reprint ed. 45.00 (*0-678-05547-5*) Kelley.

***Lester, Richard K.** Productive Edge: A New Strategy for Economic Growth. 368p. 2000. pap. 16.95 (*0-393-32038-3*) Norton.

Lester, Richard K. The Productive Edge: How U. S. Industries Are Pointing the Way to a New Era of Economic Growth. LC 97-35029. 350p. 1998. 29.95 (*0-393-04574-9*) Norton.

Lester, Richard K., jt. ed. see Berger, Suzanne.

Lester, Robert & Dente-Cassidy, Marie. Intravenous Medications for Critical Care. 2nd ed. LC 95-3557. (Illus.). 387p. 1995. pap. text 26.00 (*0-7216-4887-8*, W B Saunders Co) Harcrt Hlth Sci Grp.

Lester, Robert & Dwight D. Eisenhower Library. The Papers of the President's Science Advisory Committee, 1957-1961: Microfilmed from the Holdings of the Dwight D. Eisenhower Library. LC 91-486. (Science & Technology : Research Collections in U.S. Public Policy). 3 p. 1991. write for info. (*0-89093-979-9*) U Pubns Amer.

— President Eisenhower's Meetings with Legislative Leaders, 1953-1961: Microfilmed from the Holdings of the Dwight D. Eisenhower Library. LC 90-28587. (Research Collections in American Politics Ser.). 2p. 1986. write for info. (*0-89093-980-2*) U Pubns Amer.

Lester, Robert & Hydrick, Blair D. Civil War Battles & Campaigns. LC 96-48360. 1996. 16920.00 (*1-55655-589-X*) U Pubns Amer.

***Lester, Robert & Hydrick, Blair D.** Confidential U. S. State Department Central Files: Foreign Affairs, Decimal Numbers 693 & 693A, 693B, 693C, 611.93, 611.93A, 611.93B & 611.93C. LC 00-38159. 1998. write for info. (*1-55655-705-1*) U Pubns Amer.

Lester, Robert & John F. Kennedy Library Staff. The John F. Kennedy National Security Files: National Security Files, 1961-1963. LC 93-629992. 10p. 1987. write for info. (*1-55655-006-5*) U Pubns Amer.

Lester, Robert & University Publications of America (Firm). Native Americans & the New Deal: The Office Files of John Collier, 1933-1945 LC 94-9017. 18 p. 1993. write for info. (*1-55655-491-5*) U Pubns Amer.

— Records of the Bureau of Indian Affairs: Central Classified Files, 1907-1939. LC 95-18006. 1995. write for info. (*1-55655-599-7*) U Pubns Amer.

Lester, Robert & US Army Military History Institute. Records of the Military Assistance Command, Vietnam. LC 90-12374. 1988. write for info. (*1-55655-106-1*) U Pubns Amer.

***Lester, Robert, et al.** Confidential U. S. State Department Central Files. LC 00-29020. 2000. pap. write for info. (*1-55655-703-5*) U Pubns Amer.

— Confidential U. S. State Department Central Files. LC 00-36333. 2000. write for info. (*1-55655-704-3*) University Pub.

Lester, Robert, et al. Confidential U. S. State Department Central Files: Internal & Foreign Affairs. LC 98-15144. 1998. write for info. (*1-55655-701-9*) U Pubns Amer.

— The Indian Wars of the West & Frontier Army Life, 1862-1898: Official Histories & Personal Narratives. LC 98-12605. 1998. write for info. (*1-55655-598-9*) U Pubns Amer.

— The John F. Kennedy National Security Files: National Security Files, 1961-1963. LC 91-31371. 10p. 1987. write for info. (*1-55655-010-3*); write for info. (*1-55655-013-8*) U Pubns Amer.

— The John F. Kennedy National Security Files: National Security Files, 1961-1963. LC 88-121. 3 p. 1988. write for info. (*1-55655-002-2*) U Pubns Amer.

— The John F. Kennedy Presidential Oral History Collection. LC 89-5736. (The Presidential Oral History Ser.). 24p. 1989. write for info. (*1-55655-078-2*) U Pubns Amer.

— The Johnson Administration & Pacification in Vietnam: The Robert Komer-william Leonhart Files, 1966-1968 LC 93-28321. (Vietnam War Research Collections). 15p. 1993. write for info. (*1-55655-474-5*) U Pubns Amer.

— The Lyndon B. Johnson National Security Files: National Security Files, 1963-1969 LC 93-629993. 15p. 1987. write for info. (*0-89093-996-9*); write for info. (*1-55655-018-9*) U Pubns Amer.

— The Lyndon B. Johnson National Security Files: National Security Files, 1963-1969 LC 98-159133. (National Security Files Ser.). 12 p. 1996. write for info. (*1-55655-642-X*) U Pubns Amer.

— The Lyndon B. Johnson National Security Files: National Security Files, 1963-1969. LC 87-27901. 1 p. 1987. write for info. (*0-89093-966-7*); write for info. (*1-55655-004-9*) U Pubns Amer.

— The Lyndon B. Johnson National Security Files: National Security Files, 1963-1969. LC 93-47284. (National Security Files Ser.). 34p. 1993. write for info. (*1-55655-470-2*) U Pubns Amer.

— President Dwight D. Eisenhower's Office Files, 1953-1961. LC 91-43074. (Research Collections in American Politics Ser.). 64p. 1990. write for info. (*1-55655-166-5*) U Pubns Amer.

— President Franklin D. Roosevelt's Office Files, 1933-1945. LC 92-25443. (Research Collections in American Politics Ser.). 1990. write for info. (*1-55655-265-3*) U Pubns Amer.

— U.S. Army Build-Up & Activities in South Vietnam, 1965-1972: Microfilmed from the Holdings of the Library of the U.S. Army Military History Institute, Carlisle Barracks, Pennsylvania LC 91-24540. (Vietnam War Research Collections). 29p. 1989. write for info. (*1-55655-156-8*) U Pubns Amer.

— Vietnam, the Media, & Public Support for the War: Selections from the Holdings of the Lyndon B. Johnson Library. LC 87-6248. (The Presidential Documents Ser.). 11p. 1986. write for info. (*0-89093-496-7*) U Pubns Amer.

Lester, Robert C. Buddhism: The Path to Nirvana. (Illus.). 160p. (C). 1998. reprint ed. pap. text 11.50 (*1-57766-013-7*) Waveland Pr.

Lester, Robert E. Records of the Bureau of Indian Affairs Central Classified Files, 1907-1939 Series A, Pt. 3: Indian Delegations to Washington. LC 95-18006. 1995. 3450.00 (*1-55655-550-4*) U Pubns Amer.

Lester, Robert E., jt. auth. see Hydrick, Blair D.

Lester, Robin. Stagg's University: The Rise, Decline & Fall of Big-Time Football at The University of Chicago. LC 94-34018. (Sport & Society Ser.). (Illus.). 344p. 1995. 32.95 (*0-252-02128-2*) U of Ill Pr.

— Stagg's University: The Rise, Decline & Fall of Big-Timw Football at Chicago. (Sport & Society Ser.). 344p. 1999. pap. text 18.95 (*0-252-06791-6*) U of Ill Pr.

Lester, Robin & Lester, Helen. Wuzzy Takes Off. LC 95-10694. (Gund Children's Library). (Illus.). 32p. (J). (ps up). 1995. 9.99 (*1-56402-498-9*) Candlewick Pr.

— Wuzzy Takes Off. LC 95-10694. (Gund Children's Library). (Illus.). 32p. (J). (ps up). 1997. reprint ed. pap. 3.99 (*0-7636-0097-0*) Candlewick Pr.

Lester, Robin, jt. auth. see Lester, Helen.

Lester, Ronald H., et al, eds. Quality Control for Profit. 3rd expanded rev. ed. (Illus.). 592p. 1992. text 115.00 (*0-8247-8658-0*) Dekker.

Lester, Susan C. Handbook of Surgical Pathology. 380p. 1998. text 86.00 (*0-443-07918-8*) Church.

Lester, Teri. Dawn of Love. 1977. mass mkt. 1.75 (*0-451-07804-7*, E7804, Sig) NAL.

Lester, Teri, jt. auth. see Nichols, Pamela.

Lester, Thomas, jt. auth. see Gehrmann, James.

Lester, Tina, jt. auth. see Lester, Gary.

***Lester, Tyler.** Welcome to Dyslexic Park. large type ed. (Illus.). 25p. 1999. 15.00 (*0-938911-16-3*) Indiv Ed - Poppy Ln.

Lester, V. Markham. Victorian Insolvency: Bankruptcy, Imprisonment for Debt, & Company Winding-up in Nineteenth-Century England. (Oxford Historical Monographs). (Illus.). 368p. 1995. text 69.00 (*0-19-820518-X*) OUP.

Lester, Valerie. Fasten Your Seat Belts! History & Heroism in the Pan Am Cabin. (Illus.). 304p. 1995. 30.00 (*0-9626483-8-8*) Paladwr Pr.

Lester, Vivian. Wee-Dolph, the Tiniest Reindeer. (Illus.). 22p. (J). (ps-3). pap. 4.00 (*1-929785-01-1*) Connexions KY.

Lester, Vivian & Luhrs, Jeannece Jackson. Alphabet Alive Lesson Plans Books. 78p. (J). pap. text 9.95 (*1-929785-03-8*) Connexions KY.

Lester, W. A., Jr., et al. Lecture Notes on Theoretical Chemistry. 436p. (C). 1994. text 74.00 (*981-02-0321-7*); pap. text 36.00 (*981-02-0322-5*) World Scientific Pub.

Lester, W. Hunter. Battle at Corricks Ford. 1993. pap. 5.00 (*0-87012-504-4*) McClain.

The BATTLE AT CORRICKS FORD & subsequent death of Confederate General Robert S. Garnett near Parsons, West Virginia have long been footnotes to the 1861 (West) Virginia campaign of Major General George B. McClellan. McClellan's victories of Rich Mountain & Corricks Ford were instrumental in the creation of the state of West Virginia in 1863. They also precipitated McClellan's meteoric rise to general-in-chief of the United States armies less than four months later. *Publisher Paid Annotation.*

Lester, William, tr. see Scupoli, Dom L.

Lester, William K. Gemini Fraud. 208p. 1997. 17.95 (*1-887750-52-5*) Rutledge Bks.

Lesthaeghe, Ron J. The Decline of Belgian Fertility, 1800-1970. LC 77-71991. 280p. 1977. reprint ed. pap. 86.80 (*0-7837-9374-X*, 206011800004) Bks Demand.

Lesthaeghe, Ron J., ed. Reproduction & Social Organization in Sub-Saharan Africa. 1989. 80.00 (*0-520-06363-5*, Pub. by U CA Pr) Cal Prin Full Svc.

Lesti, Paul, et al. Structured Settlements. 2nd ed. LC 86-80969. 1993. 135.00 (*0-685-59909-4*) West Group.

Lestienne, Patrick, ed. Mitochondrial Diseases: Models & Methods. LC 99-25405. (Illus.). 350p. 1999. 156.00 (*3-540-64177-7*) Spr-Verlag.

Lestienne, Remy. The Children of Time: Causality, Entropy, Becoming. Neher, E. C., tr. from FRE. LC 94-20269.Tr. of Fils du Temps. 240p. 1995. 17.95 (*0-252-06427-5*); text 45.95 (*0-252-01959-8*) U of Ill Pr.

Lestina, Peggy, ed. see Pompelli, Jean.

Lestourgeon, Diana E. Rosamond Lehmann. LC 64-8331. (Twayne's English Authors Ser.). 157p. (C). 1965. lib. bdg. 20.95 (*0-8290-1723-2*) Irvington.

L'Estrange, Francis L. Random Talks with the Living Christ. 107p. 1988. 30.00 (*0-7223-2038-8*, Pub. by A H S Ltd) St Mut.

LeStrange, G. & Nicholson, R. A., eds. The Farsnama: By Ibnu 'I-Balkt. 2nd ed. (E. J. W. Gibb Memorial Series: Vol. 1). (PER.). 200p. 1998. reprint ed. 40.00 (*0-906094-34-8*) David Brown.

LeStrange, Guy. Baghdad During the Abbasid Caliphate: From Contemporary Arabic & Persian Sources. LC 82-15143. 381p. 1983. reprint ed. lib. bdg. 99.75 (*0-313-23198-2*, LEBC, Greenwood Pr) Greenwood.

LeStrange, H. LeStrange Records: A Chronicle of the Early LeStranges of Norfolk, England, & the March of Wales, 1100-1310. (Illus.). 407p. 1993. reprint ed. pap. 61.00 (*0-8328-3702-4*); reprint ed. lib. bdg. 71.00 (*0-8328-3701-6*) Higginson Bk Co.

L'Estrange, Hamon. Alliance of Divine Offices. LC 71-172316. (Library of Anglo-Catholic Theology: No. 12). reprint ed. 40.00 (*0-404-52104-5*) AMS Pr.

***L'Estrange, Hamon.** Americans No Jewes: or Improbabilities That the Americans Are of That Race. (LC History-America-E). 80p. 1999. reprint ed. lib. bdg. 69.00 (*0-7812-4347-5*) Rprt Serv.

L'Estrange, Roger. Citt & Bumpkin: In a Dialogue over a Pot of Ale, Governing Matters of Religion & Government. LC 92-24280. (Augustan Reprints Ser.: No. 117). 1965. reprint ed. 14.50 (*0-404-70117-5*, PR3541) AMS Pr.

— Selections from the Observator. LC 92-24819. (Augustan Reprints Ser.: No. 141). 1970. reprint ed. 14.50 (*0-404-70141-8*, DA452) AMS Pr.

L'Estrange, Roger, tr. see Aesop.

Lestrel, Pete E. Morphometrics for the Life Sciences. (Recent Advances in Human Biology Ser.). 1999. 38.00 (*981-02-3610-7*) World Scientific Pub.

Lestrel, Pete E., ed. Fourier Descriptors & Their Applications in Biology. (Illus.). 478p. (C). 1997. text 95.00 (*0-521-45201-5*) Cambridge U Pr.

Lestrieux, Elisabeth De, see Hageman, Kees.

Lestrieux, Elisabeth De, see De Lestrieux, Elisabeth.

Lestrieux, Elisabeth De, see Hageman, Kees.

Lestringant, Frank. Cannibals: The Discovery & Representation of the Cannibal from Columbus to Jules Verne. Morris, Rosemary, tr. from FRE. LC 96-39830. (New Historicis Ser.: Vol. 37). 1997. 38.00 (*0-520-20240-6*, Pub. by U CA Pr) Cal Prin Full Svc.

— Mapping the Renaissance World: The Geographical Imagination in the Age of Discovery. LC 93-40812. (New Historicism: Studies in Cultural Poetics). 1994. 45.00 (*0-520-08871-9*, Pub. by U CA Pr) Cal Prin Full Svc.

Lestz, Gerald S. To Lancaster with Love. (Illus.). 68p. 1992. 26.95 (*1-880976-02-1*); pap. 18.95 (*1-880976-01-3*) Brookshire Pubns.

***Lesuer, D., et al, eds.** Mechanical Performance of Laminated Composites. (Illus.). 267p. 1999. 110.00 (*0-87339-414-3*, 4143) Minerals Metals.

Lesuer, D. R., et al, eds. Thermomechanical Processing & Mechanical Properties of Hypereutectoid Steels & Cast Irons. LC 97-73311. (Illus.). 267p. 1997. 74.00 (*0-87339-383-X*, 383X) Minerals Metals.

LeSueur, Annette. Timeless Treasure: The Art of Stephen Gjertson. LC 93-70682. (Illus.). 64p. (Orig.). 1993. pap. 29.95 (*0-9636180-0-8*) AS Class Realism.

LeSueur, Charlie. The Legends Live On: Interviews with the Cowboy Stars of the Silver Screen. 136p. 1999. pap. 11.95 (*1-885162-25-1*, CL-25-1) Norseman.

LeSueur, Gavin. Multihull Seamanship: An A-Z of Skills for Catamarans & Trim. (Illus.). 143p. 1998. pap. 21.95 (*1-898660-31-X*) Motorbooks Intl.

***Lesueur, James W.** Indian Legends. (LC History-America-E). 339p. 1999. reprint ed. lib. bdg. 99.00 (*0-7812-4298-3*) Rprt Serv.

LeSueur, Joe, ed. Homage to Frank O'Hara. 3rd rev. ed. (Illus.). 224p. 1988. pap. 12.00 (*0-929844-12-2*) Big Sky Bolinas.

LeSueur, Meridel, jt. intro. see Darrow, Clarence.

LeSueur, Stephen C. The Eighteen Thirty-Eight Mormon War in Missouri. LC 86-16090. (Illus.). 296p. 1990. pap. 16.95 (*0-8262-0729-4*) U of Mo Pr.

Lesure, Francois, ed. see Debussy, Claude.

Lesurf, J. C. Information & Measurement. (Illus.). 260p. 1998. pap. 30.00 (*0-7503-0519-3*) IOP Pub.

Lesurf, James C. Millimetre-Wave Optics, Devices & Systems. (Illus.). 268p. 1990. 130.00 (*0-85274-129-4*) IOP Pub.

Lesurf, James C., ed. Selected Papers on Gaussian Beam Mode Optics for Millimeter Wave & Terahertz Systems. LC 92-31312. (Milestone Ser.: Vol. 68). 1992. pap. 45.00 (*0-8194-1060-8*) SPIE.

— Selected Papers on Gaussian Beam Mode Optics for Millimeter Wave & Terahertz Systems. LC 92-31312. (Milestone Ser.: Vol. 68/HC). 1992. 55.00 (*0-8194-1061-6*) SPIE.

Lesy, Michael. Dreamland: America at the Dawn of the Twentieth Century. 240p. 1997. 40.00 (*1-56584-382-7*, Pub. by New Press NY) Norton.

— Dreamland: America at the Dawn of the Twentieth Century. (Illus.). 224p. 1998. pap. 22.50 (*1-56584-485-8*, Pub. by New Press NY) Norton.

L

Lesyk, Jack J. Developing Sport Psychology Within Your Clinical Practice. LC 97-45764. 224p. 1998. 34.95 (*0-7879-4046-1*) Jossey-Bass.

Lesynski, Loris. Boy Soup: Or When Giant Caught Cold. (Illus.). 32p. (J). (ps-2). 1996. pap. 16.95 (*1-55037-417-6*, Pub. by Annick) Firefly Bks Ltd.

— Boy Soup: Or When Giant Caught Cold. (Illus.). 32p. (J). (ps-3). 1996. pap. 5.95 (*1-55037-416-8*, Pub. by Annick) Firefly Bks Ltd.

— Catmagic. (Illus.). 32p. (J). (ps-3). 1998. pap. 5.95 (*1-55037-532-6*, Pub. by Annick Pr); text 15.95 (*1-55037-533-4*, Pub. by Annick Pr) Firefly Bks Ltd.

***Lesynski, Loris.** Dirty Dog Boogie. (Illus.). 32p. (J). (gr. k-2). 1999. pap. 6.95 (*1-55037-572-5*, Pub. by Annick Pr); lib. bdg. 16.95 (*1-55037-573-3*, Pub. by Annick Pr) Firefly Bks Ltd.

— Night School. (Illus.). 32p. 2000. 15.95 (*1-55037-585-7*, Pub. by Annick Pr); pap. 5.95 (*1-55037-584-9*, Pub. by Annick Pr) Firefly Bks Ltd.

Lesynski, Loris. Ogre Fun. (Illus.). 32p. (J). (ps-2). 1997. pap. 5.95 (*1-55037-446-X*, Pub. by Annick); lib. bdg. 15.95 (*1-55037-447-8*, Pub. by Annick) Firefly Bks Ltd.

— Ogre Fun. 1997. 11.15 (*0-606-12784-4*, Pub. by Turtleback) Demco.

Leszcz, Molyn. Treating the Elderly with Psychotherapy. Sadavoy, Joel, ed. LC 86-10487. 390p. 1987. 57.50 (*0-8236-6647-6*, BN-06647) Intl Univs Pr.

Leszczynski, Jerzy. Computational Chemistry: Reviews of Current Trends. Vol. 3. 350p. 74.00 (*981-02-3752-9*) World Scientific Pub.

Leszczynski, Jerzy. Computational Chemistry Reviews of Current Trends. 1999. 82.00 (*981-02-4000-7*) World Scientific Pub.

***Leszczynski, Jerzy.** Computational Molecular Biology. LC 99-31225. (Theoretical & Computational Chemistry Ser.). 662p. 1999. 327.50 (*0-444-50030-8*) Elsevier.

Leszczynski, Jerzy, ed. Computational Chemistry: Reviews of Current Trends. LC 95-49000. 284p. 1996. write for info. (*981-02-2572-5*) World Scientific Pub.

Leszczynski, Nancy A. Planting the Landscape: A Professional Approach to Garden Design. LC 97-17966. (Illus.). 224p. 1998. 42.95 (*0-442-02429-0*, VNR) Wiley.

— Planting the Landscape: A Professional Approach to Garden Design. (Illus.). 224p. 1998. 59.95 (*0-471-29215-X*) Wiley.

Leszkiewicz, Ted. To the Top Without a Glass. LC 86-50264. 180p. (Orig.). 1986. pap. 7.95 (*0-938287-00-1*) Warren Bk Pub.

Leszynski, Stan. Access 97 Expert Solutions: Expert Solutions. LC 95-72581. (Illus.). 1000p. (Orig.). 1997. 59.99 (*0-7897-0367-X*) Que.

Letablier, Marie-Therese, jt. auth. see Hantrais, Linda.

Letac, Gerald. Exercises & Solutions Manual for Integration & Probability. 152p. 1996. 29.95 (*0-387-94421-4*) Spr-Verlag.

L'Etang, Jacquie. Critical Perspectives in Public Relations. LC 96-38881. (Illus.). 350p. 1996. pap. 19.99 (*0-415-12300-3*) Thomson Learn.

L'Etang, Jacquie & Pieczka, Magda. Critical Perspectives in Public Relations. 350p. 1996. pap. 69.95 (*0-415-12299-6*) Thomson Learn.

Letarouilly, Paul. Letarouilly on Renaissance Rome: An American Student Edition. abr. ed. Bayley, John B., ed. (Classical America Series in Art & Architecture). (Illus.). xiv, 160p. 1984. pap. text 14.95 (*0-8038-9250-0*) Archit CT.

Letarouilly, Paul M. Edifices de Rome Moderne. (Illus.). 368p. (C). 1983. reprint ed. 65.00 (*0-910413-00-2*) Princeton Arch.

***Letbetter, Dennis.** Jane: 30 April 1985, Masonic Avenue. (Illus.). 64p. 2000. 100.00 (*0-9676251-0-6*) Greenwood Pr CA.

Letch, Rachael. Special People. (Who Cares Ser.). (ITA.). (J). 1990. pap. 3.99 (*0-85953-580-0*) Childs Play.

— Special People. LC 90-48944. (Who Cares Ser.). 32p. (J). (gr. 4 up). 1990. 5.99 (*0-85953-360-3*); pap. 3.99 (*0-85953-350-6*) Childs Play.

Letch, Ralph A. Myths of the Atonement. 1985. 30.00 (*0-7223-1657-7*, Pub. by A H S Ltd) St Mut.

Letcher, Gary. Canoeing the Delaware River. rev. ed. LC 97-5684. (Illus.). 228p. 1997. pap. 16.95 (*0-8135-2451-2*) Rutgers U Pr.

Letcher, John S. Good-Bye to Old Peking: The Wartime Letters of U. S. Marine Captain John Seymour Letcher, 1937-1939. Jeans, Roger B. & Lyle, Katie L., eds. LC 97-49200. xx, 242p. 1998. text 34.95 (*0-8214-1228-0*) Ohio U Pr.

Letcher, Owen. The Gold Mines of Southern Africa: The History Technology & Statistics of the Gold Industry, Vol. 18. LC 74-353. (Illus.). 580p. 1974. reprint ed. 47.95 (*0-405-05915-9*) Ayer.

***Letcher, T. M.** Chemical Thermodynamics. LC 98-30308. (IUPAC Chemical Data Ser.). (Illus.). xiv, 348 p. 1999. 115.00 (*0-632-05127-2*) Blackwell Sci.

Letchikov, A. V. Localization of One-Dimensional Random Walks in Random Environment, Vol. 8. (SSR SEC Mathematical Physics Review Ser.: Vol. 8, No. 3). ii, 52p. 1989. pap. text 106.00 (*3-7186-4866-0*) Gordon & Breach.

Letchworth, Celesta & Letchworth, Tom. Meet Me at Luigi's: An Interactive Dinner Theatre Event in Six Scenes. 1998. pap. 8.99 (*0-8341-9105-9*) Lillenas.

Letchworth, Celesta, jt. auth. see Letchworth, Tom.

Letchworth, L. Tom. Superlove Says. LC 77-71488. 168p. 1977. pap. 4.00 (*0-9602334-0-7*) Superlove.

Letchworth, Tom & Letchworth, Celesta. Mysteries with a Message. 1995. pap. 8.99 (*0-8341-9351-5*, MP-762) Nazarene.

Letchworth, Tom, jt. auth. see Letchworth, Celesta.

Letchworth, William P. Homes of Homeless Children: Report on Orphan Asylums & Institutions for Care of Children, Vol. 4. LC 74-1693. (Children & Youth Ser.). 632p. 1974. reprint ed. 50.95 (*0-405-05969-8*) Ayer.

Lete, Gregorio Del Olmo, see Del Olmo Lete, Gregorio.

***Letelier, Hernan Rivera.** La Reina Isabel Cantaba Rancheras. 1998. 22.95 (*84-08-02300-4*) Planeta Edit.

Letelier, P. S., Jr., jt. auth. see Rodrigues, W. A.

Letellier, Bernadette, jt. auth. see Berman, Lawrence M.

Letellier, Esther M. The Man Who Works . . . 154p. 1984. per. 10.00 (*0-614-24794-2*) Tesseract SD.

Letellier, Joel, et al. Word & Spirit No. 16: The Monastery & the City. (Word & Spirit Ser.). 160p. (Orig.). 1994. pap. 8.00 (*1-879007-10-X*) St Bedes Pubns.

Letellier, Patrick, jt. auth. see Island, David.

Letellier, Phyllis M. A Stock Tank of Petunias on Poverty Flat. LC 98-12894. 1998. 10.50 (*0-914565-48-6*) Capstan Pubns.

Letellier, Robert. Sir Walter Scott & the Gothic Novel. LC 94-38897. (Salzburg University Studies). 236p. 1994. text 89.95 (*0-7734-1276-X*) E Mellen.

Letellier, Robert I. Day in Mamre, Night in Sodom: Abraham & Lot in Genesis 18 & 19. LC 94-47520. (Biblical Interpretation Ser.: Vol. 10). xv, 296p. 1995. 101.50 (*90-04-10250-7*) Brill Academic Pubs.

Letellier, Robert I. The English Novel, 1660-1700: An Annotated Bibliography, Vol. 53. LC 97-22560. (Bibliographies & Indexes in World Literature: Vol. 53). 488p. 1997. lib. bdg. 85.00 (*0-313-30368-1*, Greenwood Pr) Greenwood.

***LeTendre, Brenda Guenther.** Getting Answers to Your Questions: A Middle-level Educator's Guide to Program Evaluation. LC 99-72585. 1999. write for info. (*0-926842-94-3*) CG Pubs Inc.

***LeTendre, Gerald K.** Appropriate Behavior: Defining Adolescence in U. S. & Japanese Middle Schools. LC 00-36641. (Illus.). 256p. 2000. 30.00 (*0-300-08438-2*) Yale U Pr.

LeTendre, Gerald K., ed. Competitor or Ally? Japan's Role in American Educational Debates. (Reference Books in International Education: No. 45). 200p. 1999. reprint ed. 50.00 (*0-8153-3273-4*) Garland.

LeTendre, Gerald K., jt. ed. see Rohlen, Thomas P.

Letendre, Joseph L. Preparing for Confession. 1987. pap. 2.95 (*0-937032-52-2*) Light&Life Pub Co MN.

LeTendre, Walter G., ed. see VMSB-343 Reunion Association Staff.

Letessier, Fernand, jt. auth. see De Chateaubriand, Rene.

Letessier, Fernand, ed. see Chateaubriand, Francois-Rene de.

Letessier, Fernand, ed. see De Lamartine, Alphonse.

Letessier, J., et al. Hot Hadronic Matter: Theory & Experiment. LC 95-17273. (NATO ASI Series B: Vol. 346). (Illus.). 574p. (C). 1995. text 155.00 (*0-306-45008-9*) Plenum.

Leth, Carl M. A Holy Encounter: Meeting God in His Word. LC 97-45876. 112p. (Orig.). 1998. pap. 9.99 (*0-8341-1633-2*) Beacon Hill.

***Lethaby, Jo, ed.** Indian Food & Folklore: A Guide to the Cooking, Myths & History of India. (Illus.). 144p. 2000. 19.95 (*1-57145-624-4*, Laurel Glen Pub) Advantage Pubs.

Lethaby, Nick. Bird Finding Guide to Alaska. (ENG.). 151p. 1994. pap. text 14.00 (*1-57833-065-3*) Todd Commns.

Lethaby, W. R. Medieval Art. 20.00 (*0-8196-2015-7*) Biblo.

Lethaby, William R. Londinium: Architecture & the Crafts. LC 72-83273. (Illus.). 1972. reprint ed. 18.95 (*0-405-08743-8*) Ayer.

— Mediaeval Art: From the Peace of the Church to the Eve of the Renaissance, 312-1350. LC 70-157345. (Select Bibliographies Reprint Ser.). 1977. reprint ed. 30.95 (*0-8369-5806-3*) Ayer.

— Silverwork & Jewelry Handbook of 1903. (Illus.). 343p. 1988. reprint ed. pap. 25.00 (*0-87556-362-7*) Saifer.

— Westminster Abbey & the King's Craftsmen. LC 69-13243. (Illus.). 398p. 1972. reprint ed. 27.95 (*0-405-08745-4*, Pub. by Blom Pubns) Ayer.

— Westminster Abbey Re-Examined. LC 69-13244. (Illus.). 306p. 1972. reprint ed. 27.95 (*0-405-08744-6*, Pub. by Blom Pubns) Ayer.

Letham, D. S., jt. ed. see Stewart, P. R.

Letham, Lawrence. Best Hikes with Children in Arizona. LC 97-44974. (Best Hikes with Children Ser.). (Illus.). 230p. 1998. pap. 14.95 (*0-89886-515-8*) Mountaineers.

— GPS Made Easy: Using Global Positioning Systems in the Outdoors. 2nd ed. LC 98-38724. (Illus.). 224p. 1998. pap. 14.95 (*0-89886-592-1*) Mountaineers.

Lethbride, T. Prominent Indians of Victorian Age: A Biographical Dictionary. 600p. 1986. 120.00 (*0-7855-1827-4*, Pub. by Archives Pubs) St Mut.

***Lethbridge, David, et al.** The Business Environment in Hong Kong. 4th ed. LC 99-52330. 304p. 2000. pap. 24.95 (*0-19-590566-0*) OUP.

Lethbridge, David. Mind in the World: The Marxist Psychology of Self-Actualization. LC 91-37124. (Studies in Marxism: Vol. 26). 186p. 1992. 39.95 (*0-930656-61-X*); pap. 19.95 (*0-930656-62-8*) MEP Pubns.

Lethbridge, David G., ed. Government & Industry Relationships: The Lubbock Memorial Lectures, 1975. LC 75-38968. 200p. 1976. pap. 97.00 (*0-08-019732-9*, Pub. by Pergamon Repr) Franklin.

Lethbridge, David G. & Ng Sek Hong. The Business Environment in Hong Kong. (Illus.). 244p. 1995. 65.00 (*0-19-585163-3*) OUP.

— The Business Environment in Hong Kong. 3rd ed. (Illus.). 242p. 1995. pap. text 26.00 (*0-19-586533-2*) OUP.

Lethbridge, Dona J. & Hanna, Kathleen M. Promoting Effective Contraceptive Use. LC 96-46782. (Illus.). 264p. 1997. 38.95 (*0-8261-7840-5*) Springer Pub.

Lethbridge, Henry J. Hong Kong: Stability & Change: A Collection of Essays. (C). 1979. 39.95 (*0-19-580402-3*) OUP.

Lethbridge, John. The Yachtsman's Guide to Jamaica. 1996. pap. 125.00 (*976-610-030-6*, Pub. by Laurie Norie & Wilson Ltd) St Mut.

Lethbridge, Melvin W., compiled by. Montgomery County, New York Marriage Records, Performed by Reverend Elijah Herrick, 1795-1844; Also Record of Reverend Calvin Herricl, 1834-1876; Reverend John Calvin Toll, 1803-1844. (Illus.). 38p. 1997. reprint ed. pap. 8.00 (*0-8328-7145-1*) Higginson Bk Co.

Lethbridge, Robert & Keefe, Terry, eds. Zola & the Craft of Fiction. 240p. 1990. text 49.00 (*0-7185-1312-6*, Pub. by Leicester U Pr) Cassell & Continuum.

— Zola & the Craft of FIction. 188p. 1993. pap. 14.95 (*1-85567-166-2*, Pub. by P P Pubs) Cassell & Continuum.

Lethbridge, Robert, jt. ed. see Collier, Peter.

Lethbridge, Robert, ed. see Zola, Emile.

Lethbridge, Thomas C. Herdsmen & Hermits: Celtic Seafarers in the Northern Seas. 1950. 49.50 (*0-317-07648-5*) Elliots Bks.

— Herdsmen & Hermits: Celtic Seafarers in the Northern Seas. 1977. lib. bdg. 59.95 (*0-8490-1941-9*) Gordon Pr.

— Witches. LC 68-28449. (Illus.). 1969. reprint ed. 5.95 (*0-8065-0221-5*, Citadel Pr); reprint ed. pap. 2.45 (*0-685-08138-9*, Citadel Pr) Carol Pub Group.

Lethco, Amanda Vick, et al. Alfred's Basic Adult All-in-One-Course: Italian Edition, Bk. 5. Subrizi, Paolo, tr. (ITA.). 1998. pap. 5.95 (*0-88284-867-4*, 14569) Alfred Pub.

— Alfred's Basic Piano All-in-One-Course: Italian Edition, Bk. 4. Subrizi, Paolo, tr. (ITA.). 1998. pap. 5.95 (*0-88284-866-6*, 14568) Alfred Pub.

— Basic Book of Scales, Chords, Arpeggios, & Cadences. 1994. pap. 6.95 (*0-88284-859-3*, 5754) Alfred Pub.

— Merry Christmas: Level 1A. (Alfred's Basic Piano Library). 16p. 1982. pap. 5.50 (*0-7390-0309-7*) Alfred Pub.

Lethcoe, Athena. Valiant Lancer of Prince William. 12p. (J). 1987. 7.95 incl. audio (*0-9613146-7-2*) Prince W Sound.

Lethcoe, Jim. An Observer's Guide to the Geology of Prince William Sound. (Illus.). 190p. (Orig.). 1989. pap. 19.95 (*1-877900-00-1*) Prince W Sound.

Lethcoe, Jim & Lethcoe, Nancy. A Cruising Guide to Prince William Sound. rev. ed. (Illus.). 184p. 1998. pap. 39.95 (*1-877900-10-9*) Prince W Sound.

— Valdez Gold Rush Trails, 1898-99. (Illus.). 144p. (Orig.). 1996. pap. 14.95 (*1-877900-05-2*) Prince W Sound.

***Lethcoe, Nancy.** Habitats of Change. (Illus.). 1999. 7.95 (*1-877900-11-7*) Prince W Sound.

Lethcoe, Nancy & Nurnberger, Lisa, eds. Prince William Sound Environmental Reader. (Illus.). 118p. (J). 1989. pap. 12.00 incl. audio (*0-9613146-9-9*) Prince W Sound.

Lethcoe, Nancy, jt. auth. see Lethcoe, Jim.

Letheby. A Bird Finding Guide to Alaska. (Illus.). 152p. (Orig.). 1994. pap. 14.95 (*0-9637765-9-2*) Cinclus Pubns.

Lethem, Christopher J. Police Detention: A Practical Guide to Advising the Suspect. (Waterlow Procedure Notes Ser.). (Illus.). 208p. 1991. pap. 33.90 (*0-685-48858-6*) Macmillan.

— A Practical Guide to Arrest & Detention. (Waterlow Procedure Notes Ser.). 128p. 1991. pap. 33.90 (*0-08-036919-7*) Macmillan.

Lethem, Jonathan. Amnesia Moon. 256p. 1996. pap. 12.95 (*0-312-86220-2*) St Martin.

— As She Climbed Across the Table. LC 97-36287. 1998. pap. 12.00 (*0-375-70012-9*) Vin Bks.

— Girl in the Landscape. LC 98-41173. 288p. 1999. pap. 12.00 (*0-375-70391-8*) Vin Bks.

— Gun, with Occasional Music. LC 93-4864. 1994. 19.95 (*0-15-136458-3*) Harcourt.

— Gun, with Occasional Music. 272p. 1995. pap. 12.95 (*0-312-85878-7*, Pub. by Tor Bks) St Martin.

— Motherless Brooklyn. LC 99-18194. 320p. 1999. 23.95 (*0-385-49183-2*) Doubleday.

***Lethem, Jonathan.** Motherless Brooklyn. 2000. pap. 13.00 (*0-375-72483-4*) Knopf.

— Motherless Brooklyn. LC 00-33759. 2000. write for info. (*0-7862-2695-1*) Thorndike Pr.

Lethem, Jonathan. Wall of Sky, Wall of Eye. LC 97-5835. 304p. 1997. pap. 13.95 (*0-312-86353-5*) St Martin.

— The Wall of the Sky, the Wall of the Eye. 1997. pap. write for info. (*0-614-27321-8*) Tor Bks.

***Lethem, Jonathan, ed.** The Vintage Book of Amnesia. (Crime - Black Lizard Ser.). 352p. 2000. pap. 14.00 (*0-375-70661-5*) Vin Bks.

Lethem, M. I., jt. auth. see Rogers, D. F.

Letheren, Carole A. & Mathieu, Richard. Marketing Health Care. (Illus.). 127p. (C). 1991. text 29.95 (*1-878487-32-9*, ME043) Practice Mgmt Info.

Lethert, Michael J., jt. auth. see Faletti, Gerald M.

***Lethiers, F.** Evolution de la Biosphere et Evenements Geologiques. 336p. 1998. text 65.00 (*90-5699-123-X*, Harwood Acad Pubs); pap. text 30.00 (*90-5699-124-8*, Harwood Acad Pubs) Gordon & Breach.

Letiche, H. K., et al, eds. The Practitioner's Power of Choice in Staff-Development & Inservice Training. 184p. 1991. pap. 23.50 (*90-265-1124-8*) Swets.

Letiche, Hugo Kuyper. Learning & Hatred for Meaning. 263p. 1984. pap. 33.00 (*90-272-2016-6*) J Benjamins Pubng Co.

Letiche, John M. Balance of Payments & Economic Growth. LC 66-21681. (Reprints of Economic Classics Ser.). (Illus.). xiii, 378p. 1967. reprint ed. 45.00 (*0-678-00267-3*) Kelley.

Letinsky, Laura. MFA, 1996. Smith, Courtenay, ed. & pref. by. Mapp, Tom, pref. (Illus.). 13p. (Orig.). 1996. pap. text 2.95 (*0-935573-16-X*) D & A Smart Museum.

***Letinsky, Laura & Berlant, Lauren Gail.** Venus Inferred. LC 99-86912. 1998. 45.00 (*0-226-47345-7*) U Ch Pr.

Letinsky, Laura & Bloom, Elizabeth. Space/Sight/Self. Smith, Courtenay, ed. LC 98-73407. (Illus.). 76p. 1998. 15.00 (*0-935573-22-4*) D & A Smart Museum.

Letis, Theodore P. The Ecclesiastical Text: Text Criticism, Biblical Authority, & the Popular Mind. LC 97-74091. 232p. 1997. pap. 19.95 (*0-9658607-0-1*) Inst Ren Ref Bib Studies.

Letis, Theodore P., intro. Majority Text: Essays & Reviews in the Continuing Debate. 210p. (Orig.). (C). 1987. pap. 10.95 (*0-944355-00-5*) IBTS.

Letko, Ken. The Kerf: May, 1998. 1998. pap. 5.00 (*0-9646865-3-8*) Col of Redwoods.

***Letko, Ken.** The Kerf: May 2000. 54p. 2000. pap. write for info. (*0-9646865-6-2*) Col of Redwoods.

Letko, Ken, ed. see College of the Redwoods, Del Norte Staff.

Letley, Emma, ed. see Stevenson, Robert Louis.

Letley, Emma, ed. & intro. see Stevenson, Robert Louis.

Letman, Sloan T. Urban Alcoholism. 104p. (C). 1993. pap. text 25.00 (*1-884028-00-4*) Justice Research.

Letman, Sloan T., ed. Criminal Justice at the Crossroads. 195p. (Orig.). (C). 1994. pap. text 20.00 (*1-884028-09-8*) Justice Research.

— International Issues in Criminal Justice. 100p. (Orig.). (C). 1994. pap. text 20.00 (*1-884028-07-1*) Justice Research.

Letman, Sloan T., jt. auth. see Edwards, Dan W.

***Letnanova, Elena.** Beginner's Slovak. (Beginners Ser.). 180p. 2000. pap. 14.95 (*0-7818-0815-4*) Hippocrene Bks.

Letnanova, Elena. Piano Interpretations of the Seventeenth, Eighteenth & Nineteenth Centuries: A Study of Theory & Practice Using Original Documents. LC 91-52596. (Illus.). 196p. 1991. lib. bdg. 39.95 (*0-89950-616-X*) McFarland & Co.

Letner, Kenneth L., jt. auth. see Percy, Walker.

Letner, Ruth, ed. see Flores, Bettina R.

Leto, Julie E. Private Lessons (Blaze) (Temptation Ser.: No. 724). 1999. per. 3.75 (*0-373-25824-0*, 1-25824-3) Harlequin Bks.

— Seducing Sullivan. (Temptation Ser.). 1998. per. 3.75 (*0-373-25786-4*, 1-25786-4) Harlequin Bks.

***Leto, Julie Elizabeth.** Good Girls Do! 216p. 2000. mass mkt. 3.99 (*0-373-25883-6*) Harlequin Bks.

Leto, M. J. The Larder Chef. 3rd ed. 1989. pap. 39.95 (*0-7506-0943-5*) Buttrwrth-Heinemann.

Leto, Steve. What Dreams Remember. 24p. 1995. pap. 5.00 (*1-889806-09-9*) Devils Millhopper.

Letokhov, V. S. IR Multiple Photon, Vol. 8, Nos. 2-4. Joussot-Dubien, J. et al, eds. (Laser Chemistry Ser.: Vol. 8 Nos. 2-4). 182p. 1988. text 370.00 (*3-7186-4847-4*) Gordon & Breach.

Letokhov, V. S. Lasers in Atomic, Molecular & Nuclear Physics: Proceedings of the 3rd International School on Laser Applications in Atomic, Molecular & Nuclear Physics, August 27-September 4, 1984, Vilnius, U. S. S. R. xii, 610p. 1986. text 403.00 (*3-7186-0348-9*) Gordon & Breach.

— Nonlinear Laser Chemistry: Multiple-Photon Excitation. (Chemical Physics Ser.: Vol. 22). (Illus.). 417p. 1983. 69.95 (*0-387-11705-9*) Spr-Verlag.

Letokhov, V. S., ed. Laser Spectroscopy of Highly Vibrationally Excited Molecules. (Illus.). 396p. 1989. 212.00 (*0-85274-217-7*) IOP Pub.

— Lasers in Atomic, Molecular & Nuclear Physics. 432p. (C). 1989. text 125.00 (*9971-5-0623-8*) World Scientific Pub.

Letokhov, V. S. & Chebotayev, V. P. Nonlinear Laser Spectroscopy. (Optical Sciences Ser.: Vol. 4). (Illus.). 1977. 46.00 (*0-387-08044-9*) Spr-Verlag.

***Letokhov, V. S. & Meystre, P., eds.** Advances in Laser Physics, Vol. 21. 108p. 2000. text 58.00 (*90-5823-010-4*, Harwood Acad Pubs) Gordon & Breach.

Letokhov, V. S. & Ustinov, N. D., eds. Power Lasers & Their Applications. viii, 128p. 1983. text 172.00 (*3-7186-0166-4*) Gordon & Breach.

Letokhov, V. S. & Zharov, V. P. Laser Optoacoustic Spectroscopy. (Optical Sciences Ser.: Vol. 37). (Illus.). 345p. 1986. 118.95 (*0-387-11795-4*) Spr-Verlag.

Letokhov, V. S., jt. auth. see Balykin, V. I.

Letokhov, V. S., jt. auth. see Minogin, V. G.

Letokhov, V. S., ed. see Borshch, A. A., et al.

Letokhov, V. S., jt. ed. see Feld, M. S.

Letokhov, V. S., ed. see Khmanov, S. A., et al.

Letokhov, V. S., ed. see Otten, E. W.

Letokhov, V. S., ed. see Phillips, D. & Grice, R.

Letokhov, V. S., ed. see Rudolph, W. & Wilhelmi, B.

Letokhov, V. S., ed. see Weitz, E.

***Letona, Maria E.** State Government Provision of HIV/AIDS Prevention Programs: Towards a Partnership Model of the Contractual Relationship Between State Governments & Community Agencies. LC 99-34308. (Health Care Policy in the United States Ser.). 280p. 1999. 64.00 (*0-8153-3454-0*) Garland.

Letona, Rene, jt. contrib. by see Sierra, Carmen.

Letonturier, P. Mini Medical Encyclopedia: Mini-Encyclopedie Medicale. 8th ed. (FRE.). 416p. 1984. 25.00 (*0-8288-1816-9*, M8935) Fr & Eur.

LeTord, Bijou. Sing a New Song: A Book of Psalms. LC 96-33231. (Illus.). 32p. (J). (ps-2). 1997. 15.00 (*0-8028-5139-8*, Eerdmans Bks) Eerdmans.

Letoublon, F., ed. La Langue et les Textes en Grec Ancien: Actes du Colloque Pierre Chantraine (Grenoble, 5-8 Septembre 1989) 377p. 1992. pap. 97.00 (*90-5063-066-9*, Pub. by Gieben) J Benjamins Pubng Co.

Letoublon, Francoise. Les Lieux Communs du Roman: Stereotypes Grecs d'Aventure & d'Amour. (Mnemosyne Ser.: Supplement 123). (FRE., Illus.). 248p. 1993. 86.00 (*90-04-09724-4*) Brill Academic Pubs.

An Asterisk (*) at the beginning of an entry indicates that the title is appearing for the first time.

Letourneau, Barbara & Curry, Wesley. In Search of Physician Leadership. LC 98-13927. 180p. 1998. 45.00 (*1-56793-082-4*) Health Admin Pr.

Letourneau, David, et al. Bent but Not Broken: Today's Canadian Church. 176p. pap. (*0-9695180-1-3*) Sh1oreline.

— Bent but Not Broken: Today's Canadian Church. 1994. pap., student ed. (*0-9695180-2-1*) Sh1oreline.

Letourneau, Deborah K., jt. ed. see Barbosa, Pedro.

Letourneau, Kim, ed. see Letourneau, Tom.

Letourneau, Kim, ed. see LeTourneau, Tom.

Letourneau, P. A. Caterpillar Photo Gallery. LC 97-70622. (Photo Gallery Ser.). (Illus.). 288p. (Orig.). 1997. pap. 24.95 (*1-882256-70-0*) Iconografix.

— Farmall Cub Photo Archive: Photographs from the McCormick-International Harvester Company Collection. LC 97-70639. (Photo Archive Ser.). (Illus.). 128p. (Orig.). 1997. pap. 29.95 (*1-882256-71-9*) Iconografix.

— Fordson 1917-1928 Photo Archive. LC 94-74208. (Photo Archive Ser.). (Illus.). 144p. 1995. pap. text 29.95 (*1-882256-33-6*) Iconografix.

Letourneau, P. A., ed. Case Tractors 1912-1959 Photo Archive. LC 94-74207. (Photo Archive Ser.). 144p. 1995. pap. 29.95 (*1-882256-32-8*, CS-001) Iconografix.

— Caterpillar Military Tractors Vol. 1: The Vital Edge of Victory, Photo Archive. LC 94-76266. (Photo Archive Ser.: Vol. 1). (Illus.). 144p. 1994. pap. 29.95 (*1-882256-16-6*) Iconografix.

— Caterpillar Military Tractors Vol. 2: Workpower on the Side of Victory, Photo Archive. LC 94-76266. (Photo Archive Ser.: Vol. 2). (Illus.). 144p. 1994. pap. 29.95 (*1-882256-17-4*) Iconografix.

— Caterpillar Sixty Photo Archive. LC 93-78195. (Photo Archive Ser.). (Illus.). 144p. 1993. pap. 29.95 (*1-882256-05-0*) Iconografix.

— Chicago, St. Paul, Minneapolis & Omaha Railway, 1880-1940 Photo Archive: Photographs from the State Historical Society of Wisconsin. LC 96-78344. (Photo Archive Ser.). (Illus.). 128p. 1997. pap. 29.95 (*1-882256-67-0*) Iconografix.

— Cletrac & Oliver Crawlers Photo Archive. LC 95-82097. (Photo Archive Ser.). (Illus.). 128p. 1996. pap. 29.95 (*1-882256-43-3*) Iconografix.

— Dodge Trucks 1948-1960 Photo Archive. LC 95-77489. (Photo Archive Ser.). (Illus.). 128p. 1995. pap. 29.95 (*1-882256-37-9*) Iconografix.

— Farmall F Series Photo Archive: The Models F-12, F-14, F-20 & F-30. LC 93-77113. (Photo Archive Ser.). (Illus.). 144p. 1993. pap. 29.95 (*1-882256-02-6*) Iconografix.

— Farmall Model H Photo Archive. LC 93-77114. (Photo Archive Ser.). (Illus.). 144p. 1993. pap. 29.95 (*1-882256-03-4*) Iconografix.

— Farmall Model M Photo Archive. LC 94-75855. (Photo Archive Ser.). (Illus.). 144p. 1994. pap. 29.95 (*1-882256-15-8*) Iconografix.

— Farmall Regular Photo Archive. LC 94-75854. (Photo Archive Ser.). (Illus.). 144p. 1994. pap. 29.95 (*1-882256-14-X*) Iconografix.

— Farmall Super Series Photo Archive. LC 96-76057. (Photo Archive Ser.). (Illus.). 128p. 1996. pap. 29.95 (*1-882256-49-2*) Iconografix.

— Hart-Parr Photo Archive. LC 93-61075. (Illus.). 144p. 1993. pap. 29.95 (*1-882256-08-5*) Iconografix.

— Holt Tractors Photo Archive: An Album of Steam & Early Gas Tractors. LC 93-80439. (Photo Archive Ser.). (Illus.). 144p. 1993. pap. text 29.95 (*1-882256-10-7*) Iconografix.

— Imperial 1955-1963 Photo Archive. LC 94-78694. (Photo Archive Ser.). (Illus.). 144p. 1994. pap. 29.95 (*1-882256-22-0*) Iconografix.

— Imperial 1964-1968 Photo Archive. LC 94-78695. (Photo Archive Ser.). (Illus.). 144p. 1994. pap. 29.95 (*1-882256-23-9*) Iconografix.

— International TD Crawlers 1933-1962 Photo Archive: Photographs from the McCormick-International Harvester Company Collection. LC 97-70640. (Photo Archive Ser.). (Illus.). 128p. 1997. pap. 29.95 (*1-882256-72-7*) Iconografix.

— International TracTracTor Photo Archive: Photographs from the McCormick-International Harvester Company Collection. LC 96-76056. (Photo Archive Ser.). (Illus.). 128p. 1996. pap. 29.95 (*1-882256-48-4*) Iconografix.

— John Deere Model A Photo Archive. LC 94-75631. (Photo Archive Ser.). (Illus.). 144p. 1994. pap. 29.95 (*1-882256-12-3*) Iconografix.

— John Deere Model B Photo Archive: The "Unstyled" & "Styled" Model "B" LC 92-74595. (Photo Archive Ser.). (Illus.). 144p. 1993. pap. 29.95 (*1-882256-01-8*) Iconografix.

— John Deere Model D Photo Archive: The "Unstyled" Model "D", 1923-1938. LC 92-74596. (Photo Archive Ser.). (Illus.). 144p. 1993. pap. 29.95 (*1-882256-00-X*) Iconografix.

— John Deere 30 Series Photo Archive. LC 94-75639. (Photo Archive Ser.). (Illus.). 144p. 1994. pap. 29.95 (*1-882256-13-1*) Iconografix.

— Milwaukee Road 1850-1960 Photo Archive. LC 96-76223. (Photo Archive Ser.). (Illus.). 128p. 1996. pap. 29.95 (*1-882256-61-1*) Iconografix.

— Minneapolis-Moline U Series Photo Archive. LC 93-79371. (Photo Archive Ser.). (Illus.). 141p. 1993. pap. text 29.95 (*1-882256-07-7*) Iconografix.

— Oliver Tractors Photo Archive. LC 93-61074. (Photo Archive Ser.). (Illus.). 144p. 1993. pap. 29.95 (*1-882256-09-3*) Iconografix.

— Russell Graders Photo Archive. LC 93-80438. (Photo Archive Ser.). (Illus.). 144p. 1993. pap. text 29.95 (*1-882256-11-5*) Iconografix.

— Twin City Tractor Photo Archive. LC 93-79372. (Photo Archive Ser.). (Illus.). 144p. 1993. pap. 29.95 (*1-882256-06-9*) Iconografix.

— Wisconsin Central Railway 1871-1909 Photo Archive: Photographs from the Wisconsin Historical Society. LC 97-75275. (Illus.). 128p. 1998. pap. 29.95 (*1-882256-78-6*) Iconografix.

Letourneau, Paul C., ed. The Nerve Growth Cone. 558p. 1991. text 104.00 (*0-88167-816-3*) Lppncott W & W.

Letourneau, Paul C., et al, eds. The Nerve Growth Cone. LC 91-19165. (Illus.). 557p. reprint ed. pap. 172.70 (*0-608-09746-2*, 206991500007) Bks Demand.

Letourneau, Paul R. The Secrets to Saving Big Bucks at the Grocery Store: How to Save 50& More Every Time You Buy Groceries! (Illus.). 50p. 1995. pap. 7.00 (*0-9662014-1-8*) P Letourneau.

Letourneau, Peter. John Deere Limited Production & Experimental Tractors. (Illus.). 144p. 1994. pap. 14.98 (*0-87938-951-6*) MBI Pubg.

— Vintage Case Tractors. LC 96-35225. (American Legends Ser.). (Illus.). 112p. 1997. 24.95 (*0-89658-335-X*) Voyageur Pr.

LeTourneau, R. G. Mover of Men & Mountains. mass mkt. 6.99 (*0-8024-3818-0*, 222) Moody.

LeTourneau, Richard H. Democracy in Trouble: There's Only One Way Back to Greatness. LC 85-91035. (LeTourneau One-Way Ser.: Vol. 5). (Illus.). 138p. (Orig.). 1985. pap. 12.95 (*0-935899-01-4*) LeTourneau Pr.

***LeTourneau, Richard H.** The Earthensteel Report: An Angel's Report on the Life of R. G. LeTourneau. 128p. (Orig.). 1999. pap. 19.95 (*0-935899-10-3*) LeTourneau Pr.

LeTourneau, Richard H. Finding Your Niche in Life: There's Only One Way to Live Especially When Your Father Is R. G. LeTourneau. LC 85-91033. (LeTourneau One-Way Ser.: Vol. 8). 317p. (Orig.). 1985. pap. 15.95 (*0-935899-04-9*) LeTourneau Pr.

LeTourneau, Richard H., jt. ed. see Dick, Louise L.

LeTourneau, Tom. 50 More Strategies to Increase Your Sales. Letourneau, Kim, ed. 64p. (Orig.). 1994. pap. 15.00 (*1-885074-08-5*) Kito Enter.

— 50 Strategies for Great Customer Service. Letourneau, Kim, ed. 64p. (Orig.). 1994. pap. 15.00 (*1-885074-01-8*) Kito Enter.

— 50 Strategies to Increase Your Sales. Letourneau, Kim, ed. 64p. (Orig.). 1994. pap. 15.00 (*1-885074-00-X*) Kito Enter.

— Lighting Techniques for Video Production: The Art of Casting Shadows. 172p. 1996. reprint ed. pap. 34.95 (*0-240-80248-9*, Focal) Buttrwrth-Heinemann.

Letourneau, Tom. 101 Favorite Quotations. 101p. 1998. pap. 15.00 (*1-885074-20-4*) Kito Enter.

LeTourneau, Tom. Placing Shadows: The Art of Video Lighting. 2nd ed. 224p. 1998. pap. 39.95 (*0-240-80313-2*, Focal) Buttrwrth-Heinemann.

Letourneau, Tom. Sales Managers Meeting Guide. Letourneau, Kim, ed. 175p. 1998. ring bd. 149.00 (*1-885074-21-2*) Kito Enter.

LeTourneau, Tom, jt. auth. see Gloman, Chuck.

Letournel, E. & Judet, R. Fracture to the Acetabulum. (Illus.). 420p. 1981. 175.00 (*0-387-09875-5*) Spr-Verlag.

— Fractures of the Acetabulum. 2nd enl. rev. ed. Elson, Reginald A., ed. & tr. by. LC 92-48836. 1994. 215.00 (*0-387-52189-5*) Spr-Verlag.

Letourneux, A., jt. auth. see Hanoteau, A.

Letouzey & Ane. Dictionnaire d'Archeologie Chretienne et de Liturgie, 28 vols. (FRE.). 1903. 4500.00 (*0-7859-0497-2*, 2706301562) Fr & Eur.

Letouzey, J., ed. Petroleum & Tectonics in Mobile Belts: 4th IFP Exploration & Production Research Conference, Bordeaux, 1988. (Illus.). 224p. (C). 1990. 370.00 (*2-7108-0579-0*, Pub. by Edits Technip) Enfield Pubs NH.

Letov, Aleksandr M. Stability in Nonlinear Control Systems. Adashko, J. George, tr. LC 59-5599. 332p. 1961. reprint ed. pap. 103.00 (*0-608-02933-5*, 206399900008) Bks Demand.

Letovsky, Robert & Dwyer, Brian. Protecting Endangered Species: U. S. Trade Policy & the Cases of China & Taiwan. (Pew Case Studies in International Affairs). 50p. (C). 1997. pap. text 3.50 (*1-56927-218-2*) Geo U Inst Dplmcy.

***Letovsky, Stanley.** Bioinformatics: Databases & Systems. LC 99-28476. 304p. 1999. write for info. (*0-7923-8573-X*, Kluwer Plenum) Kluwer Academic.

LeTraunik, Kenneth F., jt. auth. see Hanapel, James A.

LeTraunik, Kenneth R., jt. auth. see Hanapel, James A.

Letringer, Sylvere, ed. see Virilio, Paul.

Letrouneux, J. & Vinet, Luc. Quantum Groups, Integrable Models & Statistical Systems. 300p. 1993. text 95.00 (*981-02-1555-X*) World Scientific Pub.

Let's Go, Inc. Editorial Staff. The Unoffical Guide to Life at Harvard. 327p. 1995. pap. 7.95 (*0-9634820-0-9*) Harvard Student Agencies Inc.

***Lets Go Inc. Staff.** Let's Go Map Guide: San Francisco. 3rd ed. 20p. 2000. pap. 8.95 (*0-312-24642-0*) St Martin.

— Let's Go Map Guide: Washington DC. 3rd ed. 2000. pap. 8.95 (*0-312-24643-9*) St Martin.

— Lets Go Map Guide Hong Kong. 2000. pap. 8.95 (*0-312-24638-2*) St Martin.

***Let's Go Staff.** Alaska & the Pacific Northwest. (Let's Go 2001 Ser.). (Illus.). 560p. 2000. pap. 19.99 (*0-312-24344-8*, St Martin Griffin) St Martin.

— Australia. (Let's Go 2001 Ser.). (Illus.). 704p. 2000. pap. 22.99 (*0-312-24345-6*, St Martin Griffin) St Martin.

— Austria & Switzerland. rev. ed. (Let's Go 2001 Ser.). (Illus.). 544p. 2000. pap. 19.99 (*0-312-24346-4*, St Martin Griffin) St Martin.

— Boston. rev. ed. (Let's Go 2001 Ser.). (Illus.). 336p. 2000. pap. 16.99 (*0-312-24692-7*, St Martin Griffin) St Martin.

— Britain & Ireland. (Let's Go 2001 Ser.). (Illus.). 784p. 2000. pap. 21.99 (*0-312-24569-6*, St Martin Griffin) St Martin.

— California. (Let's Go 2001 Ser.). (Illus.). 544p. 2000. pap. 19.99 (*0-312-24668-4*, St Martin Griffin) St Martin.

— Central America. rev. ed. (Let's Go 2001 Ser.). (Illus.). 624p. 2000. pap. 19.99 (*0-312-24669-2*, St Martin Griffin) St Martin.

— China. rev. ed. (Let's Go 2001 Ser.). (Illus.). 800p. 2000. pap. 24.99 (*0-312-24670-6*, St Martin Griffin) St Martin.

— Eastern Europe. rev. ed. (Let's Go 2001 Ser.). (Illus.). 864p. 2000. pap. 22.99 (*0-312-24671-4*, St Martin Griffin) St Martin.

— Europe. rev. ed. (Let's Go 2001 Ser.). (Illus.). 992p. 2000. pap. 22.99 (*0-312-24673-0*, St Martin Griffin) St Martin.

Let's Go Staff. Europe, 2000. (Let's Go Ser.). 992p. 1999. pap. 22.99 (*0-312-24466-5*) St Martin.

***Let's Go Staff.** France. rev. ed. (Let's Go 2001 Ser.). (Illus.). 768p. 2000. pap. 21.99 (*0-312-24674-9*, St Martin Griffin) St Martin.

— Germany. rev. ed. (Let's Go 2001 Ser.). (Illus.). 624p. 2000. pap. 21.99 (*0-312-24676-5*, St Martin Griffin) St Martin.

— Greece. rev. ed. (Let's Go 2001 Ser.). (Illus.). 592p. 2000. pap. 19.99 (*0-312-24677-3*, St Martin Griffin) St Martin.

— India & Nepal. rev. ed. (Let's Go 2001 Ser.). (Illus.). 864p. 2000. pap. 22.99 (*0-312-24678-1*, St Martin Griffin) St Martin.

— Ireland. rev. ed. (Let's Go 2001 Ser.). (Illus.). 528p. 2000. pap. 19.99 (*0-312-24679-X*, St Martin Griffin) St Martin.

— Israel. rev. ed. (Let's Go 2001 Ser.). (Illus.). 400p. 2000. pap. 17.99 (*0-312-24680-3*, St Martin Griffin) St Martin.

— Italy. rev. ed. (Let's Go 2001 Ser.). (Illus.). 720p. 2000. pap. 21.99 (*0-312-24681-1*, St Martin Griffin) St Martin.

— Let's Go Map Guide: Boston. 3rd ed. 2000. pap. 8.95 (*0-312-24632-3*) St Martin.

— Lets Go Map Guide Florence. 32p. 2000. pap., student ed. 8.95 (*0-312-24633-1*) St Martin.

— Lets Go Map Guide London. 32p. 2000. pap., student ed. 8.95 (*0-312-24635-8*) St Martin.

— Lets Go Map Guide New York City. 32p. 2000. pap., student ed. 8.95 (*0-312-24636-6*) St Martin.

— Let's Go Map Guides: Amsterdam. 2nd ed. 16p. 2000. pap. 8.95 (*0-312-24631-5*) St Martin.

— London. rev. ed. (Let's Go 2001 Ser.). (Illus.). 336p. 2000. pap. 16.99 (*0-312-24682-X*, St Martin Griffin) St Martin.

— Mexico. rev. ed. (Let's Go 2001 Ser.). (Illus.). 688p. 2000. pap. 21.99 (*0-312-24683-8*, St Martin Griffin) St Martin.

— Middle East. rev. ed. (Let's Go 2001 Ser.). (Illus.). 736p. 2000. pap. 22.99 (*0-312-24693-5*, St Martin Griffin) St Martin.

— New York City. rev. ed. (Let's Go 2001 Ser.). (Illus.). 368p. 2000. pap. 16.99 (*0-312-24684-6*, St Martin Griffin) St Martin.

— New Zealand. rev. ed. (Let's Go 2001 Ser.). (Illus.). 416p. 2000. pap. 18.99 (*0-312-24685-4*, St Martin Griffin) St Martin.

— Paris. rev. ed. (Let's Go 2001 Ser.). (Illus.). 368p. 2000. pap. 16.99 (*0-312-24686-2*, St Martin Griffin) St Martin.

— Peru, Bolivia & Ecuador Including the Galapagos. rev. ed. (Let's Go 2001 Ser.). (Illus.). 640p. 2000. pap. 22.99 (*0-312-24672-2*, St Martin Griffin) St Martin.

— Rome. rev. ed. (Let's Go 2001 Ser.). (Illus.). 336p. 2000. pap. 16.99 (*0-312-24687-0*, St Martin Griffin) St Martin.

— San Francisco. rev. ed. (Let's Go 2001 Ser.). (Illus.). 336p. 2000. pap. 16.99 (*0-312-24691-9*, St Martin Griffin) St Martin.

— South Africa. rev. ed. (Let's Go 2001 Ser.). (Illus.). 608p. 2000. pap. 21.99 (*0-312-24688-9*, St Martin Griffin) St Martin.

— Southeast Asia. rev. ed. (Let's Go 2001 Ser.). (Illus.). 944p. 2000. pap. 23.99 (*0-312-24689-7*, St Martin Griffin) St Martin.

— Spain & Portugal, Including Morocco. rev. ed. (Let's Go 2001 Ser.). (Illus.). 768p. 2000. pap. 21.99 (*0-312-24690-0*, St Martin Griffin) St Martin.

— Turkey. rev. ed. (Let's Go 2001 Ser.). (Illus.). 512p. 2000. pap. 19.99 (*0-312-24694-3*, St Martin Griffin) St Martin.

— U. S. A. rev. ed. (Let's Go 2001 Ser.). (Illus.). 992p. 2000. pap. 22.99 (*0-312-24695-1*, St Martin Griffin) St Martin.

— Washington, D. C. rev. ed. (Let's Go 2001 Ser.). (Illus.). 336p. 2000. pap. 16.99 (*0-312-24696-X*, St Martin Griffin) St Martin.

— Western Europe. rev. ed. (Let's Go 2001 Ser.). (Illus.). 960p. 2000. pap. 22.99 (*0-312-26961-7*, St Martin Griffin) St Martin.

Letsch-Brunner, Silvia. Marcella - Discipula et Magistra: Auf den Spuren einer römischen Christin des 4. Jahrhunderts. 304p. 1998. 105.00 (*3-11-015808-6*) De Gruyter.

Letschert, Ulrike. Zum Mineralstoffhaushalt Einiger Chenopo Diaceae Bei Hohen Bor- und Salzangeboten: Freilandstudiens in den Suedwestlichen U. S. A. und Kulturversuche mit Atriplex Halimus L. und Hortensis L. (Dissertationes Botanicae Ser.: Band 96). (GER., Illus.). 244p. 1986. pap. 53.00 (*3-443-64008-7*, Pub. by Gebruder Borntraeger) Balogh.

Letshama. Old People Say! The Wisdom of the Forefathers in Setswana Proverbs. (Illus.). 87p. 1999. pap. 9.00 (*0-627-02247-2*, Pub. by J L Van Schaik) BHB Intl.

Letsinger-Miller, Lyn. The Artists of Brown County. LC 93-48931. 264p. 1994. 49.95 (*0-253-33354-7*) Ind U Pr.

Letson, Ben H. Davidson's Theory of Truth & Its Implications for Rorty's Pragmatism. LC 96-28077. (American University Studies Series 5: Vol. 178). 136p. (C). 1997. 33.95 (*0-8204-3138-9*) P Lang Pubng.

Letson, Chaddie, ed. see Schweinhart, Belinda.

Letson, Douglas & Higgins, Michael. The Jesuit Mystique. LC 95-20288. (Illus.). 276p. (C). 1995. 24.95 (*0-8294-0865-7*, Jesuit Way) Loyola Pr.

***Letson, Tom.** 4 Downs to Anger Control: Control Anger & Strengthen Character with Football Concepts & Principles. Corey, Ron & Corey, Lillian, eds. LC 98-94943. (Illus.). 144p. 1999. pap. 10.95 (*0-9669618-0-3*) Finish Line Pr.

Letson, Vivian I. The Heart is Highland: A True Story of Scots in Early Wyoming. (Illus.). 144p. (Orig.). 1991. pap. 9.95 (*0-9630487-3-2*) V I Letson.

Lett, jt. auth. see Austin.

Lett, Amelia Moreland, jt. auth. see Web, Wilma.

***Lett, Ann.** Reflex Zone Therapy for Health Professionals. 2nd ed. 2000. pap. 35.00 (*0-443-06015-0*) C Lvngstone UK.

Lett, Denise P. In Pursuit of Status: The Making of South Korea's "New" Urban Middle Class, Vol. 170. LC 97-37532. (Harvard East Asian Monographs). 260p. 1998. 40.00 (*0-674-44595-3*) HUP.

Lett, Didier, jt. auth. see Alexandre-Bidon, Daniele.

Lett, James. Science, Reason, & Anthropology: A Guide to Critical Thinking. 160p. 1997. 58.00 (*0-8476-8592-6*); pap. 17.95 (*0-8476-8593-4*) Rowman.

Lett, John, et al, compiled by. Old Settlers' History of York County & Individual Biographies. (Illus.). 175p. 1997. reprint ed. lib. bdg. 25.00 (*0-8328-6872-8*) Higginson Bk Co.

Lett, John T., et al, eds. Advances in Radiation Biology Vol. 18: Relative Radiation Sensitivities of Human Organ Systems, Vol. 18. (Illus.). 232p. 1994. boxed set 110.00 (*0-12-034518-8*) Acad Pr.

Lett, Monica. Rent Control: Concepts, Realities, & Mechanisms. 294p. 1976. boxed set 17.95 (*0-87855-152-2*) Transaction Pubs.

Letta, Corrado G. M. Listen to the Emerging Markets of Southeast Asia: Long Term Strategies for Effective Partnerships. LC 96-22604. 240p. 1999. 189.95 (*0-471-96448-4*) Wiley.

Letta, Elisabetta M. Pontormo-Rosso Fiorentino. Brierly, Anthony, tr. from ITA. (Library of Great Masters). (Illus.). 80p. (Orig.). 1995. pap. 12.99 (*1-878351-48-6*) Riverside NY.

Letta, G. & Pratelli, M., eds. Probability & Analysis. (Lecture Notes in Mathematics Ser.: Vol. 1206). viii, 283p. 1986. 48.95 (*0-387-16787-0*) Spr-Verlag.

***Lette, Kathy.** Altar Ego. LC 99-34255. 368p. 1999. 23.00 (*0-688-17145-1*, Wm Morrow) Morrow Avon.

— Altar Ego: A Novel. 368p. 2000. pap. 13.00 (*0-688-17781-6*, Quil) HarperTrade.

Lettenmaier, Dennis P., jt. ed. see Cassidy, John J.

Letterheads. Atkinson Reproduced in Color. (Illus.). 112p. 1994. pap. 25.00 (*0-944094-04-X*) ST Pubns.

Letteri, J. M., ed. Schreiner Festschrift, George E. Journal: Mineral & Electrolyte Metabolism, Vol. 13, No. 6, 1987. (Illus.). vi, 118p. 1987. pap. 69.75 (*3-8055-4651-3*) S Karger.

Letteri, Richard. A Handbook of Public Speaking. 2nd rev. ed. LC 97-206204. 212p. (Orig.). (C). 1996. pap. text 18.95 (*0-943025-90-7*) Cummngs & Hath.

Letteris, Meir H. Dibre Shir(Poems) Literaria Judaica No. 41. reprint ed. 49.50 (*0-404-13862-4*) AMS Pr.

Letteris, Meir H., ed. Megillat Esther: The Story of Esther. 1979. pap. 1.95 (*0-88482-583-3*) Hebrew Pub.

Letterman, David. Late Night Top Ten Lists. 1994. mass mkt. 5.99 (*0-671-51143-2*) PB.

— New Late Night Top 10 Lists. 1994. per. 5.99 (*0-671-51144-0*) PB.

Letterman, David, et al, creators. David Letterman's Book of Top Ten Lists. 176p. 1995. 16.00 (*0-553-10222-2*) Bantam.

Letterman, David & Late Show with David Letterman Writers Staff. David Letterman's Book of Top Ten Lists, Vol. 2. 176p. 1996. 16.00 (*0-553-10243-5*) Bantam.

Letterman, David, jt. auth. see Late Night with David Letterman Writers Staff.

Letterman, Dorothy. Home Cookin' with Dave's Mom. 1996. write for info. (*0-614-96846-1*) PB.

***Letterman, Dorothy & Cagle, Jess.** Home Cookin' with Dave's Mom: By Dave's Mom, Dorothy. (Illus.). 176p. 1999. reprint ed. text 20.00 (*0-7881-6720-0*) DIANE Pub.

Letterman, Dorothy, jt. auth. see Cagle, Jess.

Letterman, G. Gregory. Letterman's Guide to International Business, 4 vols. LC 96-18160. (International Business & Law Ser.). 1996. ring bd. write for info. (*0-8366-1045-8*) West Group.

— Letterman's Law of Private International Business, 3 vols., Set. annuals rev. ed. LC 89-64180. (International Business & Law Ser.). 1990. suppl. ed. 375.00 (*0-685-59810-1*) West Group.

Letterman, Jonathan & Clements, Bennett A. Medical Recollections of the Army of Potomac with Memoir of Jonathan Letterman. rev. ed. Archer, Edgar G., ed. (Illus.). 250p. 1991. reprint ed. write for info. (*1-877791-01-6*) Bohemian Brigade.

Letterman, Raymond D. Filtration Strategies to Meet the Surface Water Treatment Rule. 184p. 1991. pap. 45.00 (*0-89867-554-5*, 20268) Am Water Wks Assn.

Letterman, T., jt. auth. see Buning, Hans K.

Lettieri. Adesso. 2nd ed. (College Italian Ser.). (C). 1997. pap., wbk. ed., lab manual ed. 31.95 (*0-8384-6710-5*) Heinle & Heinle.

Lettieri, Carol, tr. see Dib, Mohammed.

Lettieri, Carol, tr. see Spaziani, Maria L.

Lettieri, Dan J., ed. Drugs & Suicide: When Other Coping Strategies Fail. LC 78-50826. (Sage Annual Reviews of Drug & Alcohol Abuse Ser.: No. 2). (Illus.). 303p. reprint ed. pap. 94.00 (*0-8357-8448-7*, 203471200091) Bks Demand.

L

An Asterisk (*) at the beginning of an entry indicates that the title is appearing for the first time.

L

Lettieri, Dan J., pref. Research Strategies in Alcoholism Treatment Assessment. LC 88-7212. (Drugs & Society Ser.: Vol. 2, No. 2). (Illus.). 123p. 1989. text 39.95 (0-86656-782-8) Haworth Pr.

Lettieri, Dan J., jt. auth. see Neuringer, Charles.

Lettieri, Michael, jt. auth. see Bancheri, Salvatore.

Lettieri, Michael, ed. see Trissino, Giovanni G., et al.

Lettieri, Robert, jt. auth. see Stern, Judith.

Lettieri, Robert A., jt. auth. see Stern, Judith.

Lettin, A. W., jt. auth. see Donell, S. T.

***Lettinck, Paul.** Aristotle's Meteorology & its Reception in the Arab World: With an Edition & Translation of Ibn Suwar's <i>Treatise on Meteorological Phenomena</i> & Ibn Bajja's <i>Commentary on the Meteorology</i> Vol. 10. (ARA., Illus.). x, 506p. 1999. text 147.00 (90-04-10933-1) Brill Academic Pubs.

Lettinck, Paul, tr. see Philoponus & Simplicius.

Lettinga, Gatze, jt. auth. see Van Haandel, Adrianus C.

***Lettinga, J.P.** Grammaire de 'hebreu Biblique et Volume Complementaire. xiv, 202p. 1999. pap. 41.00 (90-04-11473-4) Brill Academic Pubs.

Lettis, Richard. The Dickens Aesthetic. LC 87-45808. (Studies in the Nineteenth Century: No. 6). 1989. 37.50 (0-404-61486-8) AMS Pr.

— Dickens on Literature: A Continuing Study of His Aesthetic. LC 89-45850. (Studies in the Nineteenth Century: No. 8). 1990. 42.50 (0-404-61488-4) AMS Pr.

Lettmann, Vicky Hodges, see Hodges Lettmann, Vicky.

Lettner, Margot, jt. auth. see Ames, Janet.

Lettnin, Heinz K. International Textbook of Mixed Gas Diving. LC 95-80957. (Illus.). 350p. 1998. pap. text 14.95 (0-941332-50-0, D809) Best Pub Co.

Letto-Gilles, jt. auth. see John.

Letton, Frances, jt. auth. see Letton, Jennette F.

Letton, Francis, jt. auth. see Letton, Jennette.

Letton, Francis, jt. auth. see Letton, Jennette F.

Letton, Jennette & Letton, Francis. The Young Elizabeth. 1955. pap. 5.25 (0-8222-1290-0) Dramatists Play.

Letton, Jennette F. The Robsart Affair. 268p. 1976. reprint ed. lib. bdg. 22.95 (0-89244-015-5, Queens House) Amereon Ltd.

Letton, Jennette F. & Letton, Frances. The Young Elizabeth. reprint ed. lib. bdg. 23.95 (0-89244-014-7, Queens House) Amereon Ltd.

Letton, Jennette F. & Letton, Francis. The Robsart Affair. reprint ed. lib. bdg. 22.95 (0-89190-237-6, Rivercity Pr) Amereon Ltd.

Letton, Donna. Highlander: Barricades. 224p. (Orig.). 1999. mass mkt. 6.50 (0-446-60573-5, Aspect) Warner Bks.

— Highlander: Zealot. 256p. (Orig.). 1997. reprint ed. mass mkt. 5.99 (0-446-60457-7, Pub. by Warner Bks) Little.

Lettow, Lucille, jt. auth. see Harms, Jeanne M.

Lettow Vorbeck, Paul Von, see Von Lettow Vorbeck, Paul.

Letts, Billie. The Honk & Holler Opening Soon. LC 97-51230. 290p. (YA). 1998. 22.00 (0-446-52158-2, Pub. by Warner Bks) Little.

— The Honk & Holler Opening Soon. 305p. 1999. mass mkt. 13.99 (0-446-67505-9, Pub. by Warner Bks) Little.

***Letts, Billie.** The Honk & Holler Opening Soon. large type ed. LC 00-41402. 2000. write for info. (1-57490-283-0, Beeler LP Bks) T T Beeler.

Letts, Billie. Where the Heart Is. LC 94-43079. 368p. 1995. 17.95 (0-446-51972-3, Pub. by Warner Bks) Little.

— Where the Heart Is. 336p. 1996. mass mkt. 5.99 (0-446-60365-1, Pub. by Warner Bks) Little.

— Where the Heart Is. 1998. 17.95 (0-446-78928-3); pap. 12.00 (0-446-78929-1) Warner Bks.

***Letts, Billie.** Where the Heart Is. 2000. pap. 12.00 (0-446-78770-1) Warner Bks.

Letts, Billie. Where the Heart Is. large type ed. LC 95-30936. 427p. 1995. 23.95 (0-7838-1478-X, G K Hall Lrg Type) Mac Lib Ref.

— Where the Heart Is. LC 94-43079. 376p. 1998. reprint ed. mass mkt. 12.00 (0-446-67221-1, Pub. by Warner Bks) Little.

***Letts, G. L., ed.** Inflammatory Processes: Molecular Mechanisms & Therapeutic Opportunities. (Progress in Inflammation Research Ser.). (Illus.). 200p. 2000. 119.00 (3-7643-6025-9) Birkhauser.

Letts, Janet. Legendary Lives in 'La Princesse de Cleves' LC 97-31021. (EMF Monographs). 286p. 1998. lib. bdg. 49.95 (1-886365-08-3) Rookwood Pr.

Letts, Malcolm. Sir John Mandeville: The Man & His Book. LC 70-161957. 192p. 1949. reprint ed. 25.00 (0-403-01318-6) Scholarly.

Letts, Malcolm, ed. from SPA. Travels & Adventures of Pero Tafur (1435-149) (Curzon Travellers Ser.). (C). 1996. text 65.00 (0-7007-0348-9, Pub. by Curzon Pr Ltd) Paul & Co Pubs.

Letts, Marceil F. & Quinlan, Beverly A. An Heirloom Book of the Nativity. Golden, Marcia & Spengler, Kenneth J., eds. (Heirloom Book). (Illus.). 80p. 1989. 24.95 (0-685-26593-5) Heirloom NJ.

Letts, Nancy. Creating a Caring Classroom: Hundreds of Practical Ways to Make It Happen. 96p. 1997. pap. 12.95 (0-590-70131-2) Scholastic Inc.

Letts, Penny. Managing Other People's Money. (C). 1989. 35.00 (0-86242-090-3, Pub. by Age Concern Eng) St Mut.

Letts, R. Mervyn. Principles of Seating the Disabled. (Illus.). 384p. 1991. lib. bdg. 139.00 (0-8493-6021-8, RD757) CRC Pr.

Letts, Richard. Successful Promotion by Musicians: The Art of Self-Promotion. 224p. 1997. pap. 19.95 (1-86448-272-9, Pub. by Allen & Unwin Pty) Paul & Co Pubs.

Letts, Robert M., ed. Management of Pediatric Fractures. (Illus.). 1296p. 1993. text 294.00 (0-443-08860-8) Church.

Letts, Vanessa. New York: Manhattan. 2nd ed. (Cadogan Guide Ser.). (Illus.). 224p. 1997. pap. text 14.95 (1-86011-072-X, Pub. by Cadgn Bks) Globe Pequot.

***Letts, William J., IV & Sears, James T., eds.** Queering Elementary Education: Advancing the Dialogue about Sexualities & Schooling. LC 99-23762. 320p. 1999. pap. 19.95 (0-8476-9369-4); text 65.00 (0-8476-9368-6) Rowman.

Lettunich, Janice, jt. auth. see Klug, Gary.

Lettunich, Mateo. Martha Polo. 272p. 1998. 24.00 (1-887750-92-4) Rutledge Bks.

Leturgie, Jean & Fauche, Xavier. The Tomb of Ice: Percevan.Tr. of Le Tombeau des Glaces. (ENG & FRE., Illus.). 48p. (YA). (gr. 6 up). 1996. pap. 8.95 (1-887911-57-X) Fantsy Flight.

Leturgie, Jean & Luguy, Phillipe. The Three Stars of Ingaar. Decker, Dwight R., tr. from FRE. (Percevan Ser.). (Illus.). 48p. (Orig.). (YA). (gr. 5 up). 1996. pap. 8.95 (1-887911-53-7) Fantsy Flight.

Letvin, Alice. Sacrifice in Surrealist Novel: The Impact of Early Theories of Primitive Religion on the Depiction of Violence in Modern Fiction. LC 90-23039. (Studies in Comparative Literature). 350p. 1991. reprint ed. 20.00 (0-8240-5473-3) Garland.

Letvin, N. L. & Desrosiers, R. C., eds. Simian Immuno-Deficiency Virus. (Currents Topics in Microbiology & Immunology Ser.: Vol. 188). (Illus.). 250p. 1994. 158.95 (0-387-57274-0) Spr-Verlag.

Letwenk. Bible Book Worm. (Jeremy the Bible Bookworm Ser.). (J). 1996. pap. 3.95 (0-88271-309-4) Regina Pr.

Letwenko, Edward. Jeremy & Creation. (Jeremy the Bible Bookworm Ser.). 1996. pap. 3.95 (0-88271-310-8) Regina Pr.

— Jeremy & Noah's Ark. (Jeremy the Bible Bookworm Ser.). (J). 1996. pap. 3.95 (0-88271-311-6) Regina Pr.

— Jeremy & the Easter Story. (Jeremy the Bible Bookworm Ser.). (J). 1996. pap. 3.95 (0-88271-314-0) Regina Pr.

— Jeremy & the Life of Jesus. (Jeremy the Bible Bookworm Ser.). (J). 1996. pap. 3.95 (0-88271-313-2) Regina Pr.

— Jeremy & the Lord's Prayer. (Jeremy the Bible Bookworm Ser.). (J). 1996. pap. 3.95 (0-88271-466-X) Regina Pr.

— Jeremy & the Nativity. (Jeremy the Bible Bookworm Ser.). (J). 1996. pap. 3.95 (0-88271-312-4) Regina Pr.

— Jeremy & the Parables. (Jeremy the Bible Bookworm Ser.). (J). 1996. pap. 3.95 (0-88271-465-1) Regina Pr.

— Jeremy's Book of Prayers. (Jeremy the Bible Bookworm Ser.). (J). 1996. pap. 3.95 (0-88271-467-8) Regina Pr.

Letwenko, Edward, jt. auth. see Letwenko, Roberta.

Letwenko, Roberta & Letwenko, Edward. Book of Prayers. (Jeremy the Bible Bookworm Ser.). (Illus.). 32p. 3.95 (0-614-22057-2) Regina Pr.

— Creation. (Jeremy the Bible Bookworm Ser.). (Illus.). 32p. (J). 3.95 (0-614-22059-9); mass mkt. 3.95 (0-614-24937-6); mass mkt. 3.95 (0-614-24964-3) Regina Pr.

— The Easter Story. (Jeremy the Bible Bookworm Ser.). (Illus.). 32p. (J). 3.95 (0-614-22063-7) Regina Pr.

— Jeremy the Bible Bookworm. (Illus.). 32p. (J). 3.95 (0-614-22058-0) Regina Pr.

— The Life of Jesus. (Jeremy the Bible Bookworm Ser.). (Illus.). 32p. (J). 3.95 (0-614-22062-9) Regina Pr.

— The Lord's Prayer. (Jeremy the Bible Bookworm Ser.). (Illus.). 32p. (J). 3.95 (0-614-22066-1) Regina Pr.

— The Nativity. (Jeremy the Bible Bookworm Ser.). (Illus.). 32p. (J). 3.95 (0-614-22061-0) Regina Pr.

— Noah's Ark. (Jeremy the Bible Bookworm Ser.). (Illus.). 32p. (J). 3.95 (0-614-22060-2) Regina Pr.

— The Parables. (Jeremy the Bible Bookworm Ser.). (Illus.). 32p. (J). 3.95 (0-614-22065-3) Regina Pr.

— 10 Commandments. (Jeremy the Bible Bookworm Ser.). (Illus.). 32p. (J). 3.95 (0-614-22064-5) Regina Pr.

Letwin. Evidence Law: Commentary, Problems & Cases. 1986. teacher ed. write for info. (0-8205-0142-5) Bender.

— Evidence Law: Commentary, Problems & Cases. 1988. suppl. ed. write for info. (0-8205-0143-3) Bender.

Letwin, Daniel. The Challenge of Interracial Unionism: Alabama Coal Miners, 1878-1921. LC 97-9365. 368p. (gr. 13). 1998. pap. 19.95 (0-8078-4678-3); lib. bdg. 49.95 (0-8078-2377-5) U of NC Pr.

Letwin, Shirley R. The Anatomy of Thatcherism. 377p. (C). 1993. text 34.95 (1-56000-106-2) Transaction Pubs.

— The Gentlemen in Trollope: Individuality & Moral Conduct. LC 81-6252. 315p. 1982. 34.50 (0-674-34755-2) HUP.

— The Pursuit of Certainty: David Hume, Jeremy Bentham, John Stuart Mill, Beatrice Webb. LC 97-47485. 1998. 18.50 (0-86597-194-3); pap. 9.50 (0-86597-195-1) Liberty Fund.

Letwin, Shirley R., ed. see Oakeshott, Michael.

Letwin, William. Law & Economic Policy in America: The Evolution of the Sherman Antitrust Act. LC 81-7551. xii, 316p. 1981. pap. text 12.00 (0-226-47353-8) U Ch Pr.

— Law & Economic Policy in America: The Evolution of the Sherman Antitrust Act. LC 80-21868. 304p. 1980. reprint ed. lib. bdg. 35.00 (0-313-22651-2, LELE, Greenwood Pr) Greenwood.

— The Origins of Scientific Economics. LC 75-8721. 316p. 1975. reprint ed. lib. bdg. 65.00 (0-8371-8038-4, LEOS, Greenwood Pr) Greenwood.

Letwinch, Joanne C. Soaring Through the Universe: Astronomy Through Children's Literature. LC 98-53234. (Illus.). xvi, 191 p. 1999. pap., teacher ed. 23.00 (1-56308-560-7) Libs Unl.

Letyagin, V. P., et al. Modern Approaches to the Treatment of Initial Stages of Breast Cancer. (Soviet Medical Reviews Ser.: Vol. 3). iv, 84p. 1989. pap. text 87.00 (3-7186-4912-8) Gordon & Breach.

Letz, Hans. Music for Violin & Viola. 107p. 1993. reprint ed. lib. bdg. 69.00 (0-7812-9690-0) Rprt Serv.

Letzgus, Oliver. Die Oekonomie Internationalen Umweltschutzes. (Illus.). 366p. 1998. 67.95 (3-631-34265-9) P Lang Pubng.

Letzter, E. S., jt. auth. see Goodearl, K. R.

***Leu.** Handbook of Rapid Prototyping & Layered Manufacturing. 1999. 99.00 (0-12-444610-8) Morgan Kaufmann.

Leu, Deborah D., jt. auth. see Leu, Donald J.

Leu, Donald J. & Kinzer, Charles K. Effective Literacy Instruction, K-8. 4th ed. LC 98-19877. 384p. 1998. 72.00 (0-13-907544-5, Merrill Coll) P-H.

Leu, Donald J. & Leu, Deborah D. Teaching with the Internet: Lessons from the Classroom, 1999 Edition. 2nd rev. ed. (Illus.). 348p. 1999. pap. text 36.95 (0-926842-85-4) CG Pubs Inc.

Leu, H. J., ed. Ruettner, J. R. Festschrift. (Journal: Experimental Cell Biology: Vol. 56, No. 4, 1988). (Illus.). 60p. 1988. pap. 35.00 (3-8055-4923-7) S Karger.

Leuba, James H. Psychological Study of Religion: Its Origin, Function, & Future. LC 75-98628. reprint ed. 49.50 (0-404-03969-3) AMS Pr.

Leubben, Craig. Knots for Climbers. LC 96-162922. (How to Rock Climb Ser.). (Illus.). 40p. (Orig.). 1995. pap. 4.95 (0-934641-58-7) Falcon Pub Inc.

Leube, Kurt R., ed. The Essence of Friedman. 566p. 1987. 44.95 (0-8179-8661-8, P-366) Hoover Inst Pr.

Leube, Kurt R. & Moore, Thomas G., eds. The Essence of Stigler. (Publication Ser.: No. 346). 377p. (C). 1986. text 34.95 (0-8179-8461-5); pap. text 20.95 (0-8179-8462-3) Hoover Inst Pr.

Leube, Kurt R., ed. see Bartley, W. W., III, et al.

Leube, Kurt R., jt. ed. see Nishiyama, Chiaki.

Leucht, Dagmar, jt. auth. see Leucht, Wolfgang.

Leucht, Wolfgang & Leucht, Dagmar. Teaching Atlas of Breast Ultrasound. 2nd ed. LC 95-39577. (Illus.). 250p. 1996. text 99.00 (0-86577-572-9) Thieme Med Pubs.

Leuchtag, Richard H., jt. auth. see Smith, C. U.

***Leuchtenburg, William, ed.** American Places: Encounters with History. (Illus.). 400p. 2000. 30.00 (0-19-513026-X) OUP.

Leuchtenburg, William E. The FDR Years: On Roosevelt & His Legacy. LC 95-13282. 350p. 1995. 47.50 (0-231-08298-3) Col U Pr.

— FDR Years: On Roosevelt & His Legacy. 377p. 1997. pap. 19.50 (0-231-08299-1) Col U Pr.

— Franklin D Roosevelt. LC 63-12053. (New American Nation Ser.). 432p. 1963. pap. 16.00 (0-06-133025-6, TB3025, Torch) HarpC.

— In the Shadow of FDR: From Harry Truman to Bill Clinton. rev. ed. LC 92-54825. 408p. 1993. pap. text 17.95 (0-8014-8123-6) Cornell U Pr.

— 1984 Election in Historical Perspective. LC 86-72071. (Charles Edmondson Historical Lectures). 43p. (Orig.). 1986. pap. 5.95 (0-918954-45-2) Baylor Univ Pr.

— Perils of Prosperity: Nineteen Fourteen to Nineteen Thirty-Two. LC 58-5680. (Chicago History of American Civilization Ser.). 1995. pap. text 9.95 (0-226-47369-4, CHAC12) U Ch Pr.

— The Perils of Prosperity, 1914-1932. 2nd ed. LC 92-44912. (Chicago History of American Civilization Ser.). 325p. (C). 1993. pap. text 13.00 (0-226-47371-6) U Ch Pr.

— The Perils of Prosperity, 1914-1932. 2nd ed. LC 92-44912. (Chicago History of American Civilization Ser.). 320p. (C). 1997. lib. bdg. 33.00 (0-226-47370-8) U Ch Pr.

Leuchtenburg, William E., ed. Political Parties. LC 76-54572. (Great Contemporary Issues Ser.). 1977. lib. bdg. 27.95 (0-405-09866-9) Ayer.

Leuchtenburg, William E., ed. see Anderson, David L.

Leuchtenburg, William E., ed. see Billings-Yun, Melanie.

Leuchtenburg, William E., ed. see Tucker, Nancy B.

Leuchter, Fred. Leuchter Report. 67p. 1989. pap. 20.00 (1-872197-00-0, Pub. by Focal Pt) Legion Survival.

Leuchtmann, Horst. Dictionary of Terms in Music, English-German/German-English. 5th ed. (ENG & GER.). 347p. 1998. 150.00 (0-7859-9622-2) Fr & Eur.

— Multilingual Dictionary of Musical Terms in Seven Languages. (ENG, FRE, GER, HUN & ITA.). 798p. Date not set. 95.00 (0-7859-9628-1) Fr & Eur.

— Polygot Dictionary of Musical Terms. 2nd ed. (ENG, FRE, GER, ITA & POL.). 805p. 1980. 195.00 (0-8288-2186-0, M9436) Fr & Eur.

— Woeterbuch Musik: Dictionary of Terms in Music. 3rd ed. (ENG, FRE & GER.). 560p. 1981. 125.00 (0-8288-2174-7, M6911) Fr & Eur.

Leuci, Bob. Captain Butterfly. 240p. 1987. 16.95 (0-317-58348-4) Freundlich.

— Doyle's Disciples. 272p. 1984. 14.95 (0-88191-006-6) Freundlich.

***Leuci, Robert.** Blaze. LC 99-16670. 400p. 1999. 24.00 (0-380-97625-0, Avon Bks) Morrow Avon.

Leuci, Robert. Captain Butterfly. LC 97-41893. 254p. (Orig.). 1998. pap. 10.95 (1-55921-253-5) Moyer Bell.

— Fence Jumpers: A Novel. 1996. mass mkt. 5.99 (0-312-95937-0) St Martin.

— Odessa Beach. LC 85-20716. 240p. 1985. 15.95 (0-88191-029-5) Freundlich.

***Leuci, Robert.** Odessa Beach. LC 99-48429. 288p. 2000. pap. 10.95 (1-55921-242-X, Pub. by Moyer Bell) Publishers Group.

Leuci, Robert. Snitch. LC 96-34917. 384p. 1997. text 24.95 (0-312-14739-2) St Martin.

— Snitch, Vol. 1. 1998. 6.99 (0-312-96510-9, Pub. by Tor Bks) St Martin.

Leuck, Laura. Goodnight Baby Monster. 32p. (ps-1). 14.95 (0-06-029151-6); pap. 4.95 (0-06-443723-X); lib. bdg. 14.89 (0-06-029152-4) HarpC.

Leuck, Laura. My Baby Brother Has Ten Tiny Toes. LC 96-32815. (Illus.). 24p. (J). (ps). 1997. lib. bdg. 14.95 (0-8075-5310-7) A Whitman.

— My Baby Brother Has Ten Tiny Toes. (Prairie Paperback Bks.). (Illus.). 24p. (J). 1999. pap. 5.95 (0-8075-5311-5) A Whitman.

***Leuck, Laura.** My Monster Mama Loves Me So. LC 98-48141. (Illus.). (J). (ps). 1999. lib. bdg. 15.93 (0-688-16867-1) Lothrop.

— My Monster Mama Loves Me So. LC 98-48141. (Illus.). 24p. (J). (ps-k). 1999. 16.00 (0-688-16866-3) Lothrop.

Leuck, Laura. Sun is Falling, Night Is Calling. LC 93-22837. (Illus.). 32p. (J). (ps-k). 1994. mass mkt. 15.00 (0-671-86940-X) S&S Bks Yung.

— Teeny, Tiny Mouse: A Book about Colors. (Illus.). 32p. (J). (ps-1). 1998. pap. 5.95 (0-8167-4898-5) Troll Communs.

— The Teeny Tiny Mouse: A Book about Colors. LC 97-30887. (Illus.). 32p. (J). 1998. 15.95 (0-8167-4547-1) BrdgeWater.

Leucocyte Culture Conference Staff. Leucocyte Culture Conference: Proceedings, 4th, 1969, Hanover. McIntyre, O. Ross, ed. LC 69-19545. 607p. reprint ed. pap. 188.20 (0-608-16616-2, 202630200049) Bks Demand.

Leuder, Andreas. Historie und Dogmatik: Ein Beitrag zur Genese und Entfaltung von Johann Salomo Semlers Verstaendnis des Alten Testaments. (Beiheft zur Zeitschrift fuer die Alttestamentliche Wissenschaft Ser.: No. 233). (GER.). x, 259p. (C). 1995. lib. bdg. 121.55 (3-11-014627-4) De Gruyter.

Leue, A. E., jt. auth. see Brandt, P. A.

Leue, Holger & Lay, Graeme. Auckland & Beyond. (Panoramic Ser.). (Illus.). 128p. 1999. 24.95 (1-86436-470-X, Pub. by New Holland) BHB Intl.

***Leue, Holger & Lay, Graeme.** The Magic of New Zealand. (Panoramic Ser.). (Illus.). 128p. 1999. 24.95 (1-86436-471-8, Pub. by New Holland) BHB Intl.

Leue, Mary M. The Flying Bird Brings the Message: Lessons from My Life As Metaphor. (Orig.). 1993. pap. 12.95 (1-878115-06-5) Dwn-To-Erth Bks.

— India Journal - Pilgrimage Toward the Self. (Illus.). 190p. (Orig.). 1993. pap. 12.95 (1-878115-08-1) Dwn-To-Erth Bks.

— Jessica Dragonette's Fiery Breath: A Fable for Little Girls Who Love Their Daddies. 2nd ed. (Illus.). 46p. (J). (gr. k-6). 1993. reprint ed. pap. 9.95 (1-878115-00-6) Dwn-To-Erth Bks.

— Looking for One's Shadow at Noon Vol. I: Looking for the Self in Family & Society. 1993. pap. 7.95 (1-878115-03-0) Dwn-To-Erth Bks.

— Looking for One's Shadow at Noon Vol. II: Finding the Self in School & Community. 116p. (Orig.). 1993. pap. 7.95 (1-878115-02-2) Dwn-To-Erth Bks.

— Rushing to Eva: A Pilgrimage in Search of the Great Mother. 3rd ed. (Illus.). 337p. 1992. reprint ed. pap. 12.95 (1-878115-04-9) Dwn-To-Erth Bks.

Leue, Mary M., ed. Challenging the Giant: The Best of SKOLE, the Journal of Alternative Education, Vol. I. (Illus.). 488p. (Orig.). 1992. pap. 14.95 (1-878115-05-7, Pub. by Dwn-To-Erth Bks) Baker & Taylor.

Leue, Mary M., ed. see Free School Community Members.

Leue, Mary M., ed. see Gatto, John T. & Mercogliano, Chris.

Leue, Mary M., ed. & intro. see Miller, Ron, et al.

Leuenberger, Hans G., et al, eds. A Multilingual Glossary of Biotechnological Terms. (Verlag Helvetica Chimica Acta Publication Ser.). (ENG, FRE, GER, JPN & POR.). 252p. 1995. 69.95 (3-906390-13-6, Wiley-VCH) Wiley.

Leuenberger, Theodor, et al, eds. From Technology Transfer to Technology Management in China. (Europe-Asia-Pacific Studies in Economy & Technology). (Illus.). viii, 283p. 1990. 82.95 (0-387-52478-9) Spr-Verlag.

Leuenberger, Theodor & Weinstein, Martin E., eds. Europe, Japan, & America in the 1990s: Cooperation & Competition. LC 92-36244. (Europe-Asia-Pacific Studies in Economy & Technology). vi, 289p. 1992. 109.00 (0-387-55856-X) Spr-Verlag.

Leuf, Bo, jt. auth. see Syroid, Tom.

Leuilliot, B., ed. Anthologie de la Poesie Francaise du XIX Siecle, de Chateaubriand a Baudelaire. (Poesie Ser.). (FRE.). pap. 18.95 (2-07-032258-0) Schoenhof.

Leukart, Hank. Hank Leudart's Hacker's Guide to DOOM. 256p. 1995. pap. 21.95 incl. cd-rom (1-55828-428-1, MIS Pr) IDG Bks.

Leukefeld, C. G., et al. AIDS & Intravenous Drug Use: Community Intervention & Prevention. 300p. 1990. 42.95 (1-56032-141-5) Hemisp Pub.

Leukefeld, Carl, jt. auth. see Daugherty, Raymond P.

Leukefeld, Carl G., et al, eds. Prevention Practice in Substance Abuse. LC 95-13748. (Drugs & Society Ser.: Vol. 8, No. 3 & 4). 141p. 1995. 39.95 (1-56024-734-7) Haworth Pr.

Leukefeld, Carl G. & Fimbres, Manuel F., eds. Responding to AIDS: Psychosocial Initiatives. LC 87-15211. 95p. 1987. 12.95 (0-87101-148-4) Natl Assn Soc Wkrs.

***Leukefeld, Carl G., et al.** Behavioral Therapy for Rural Substance Abusers. LC 99-47768. 224p. (C). 2000. pap. 18.00 (0-8131-0984-1) U Pr of Ky.

Leukefeld, Carl G., jt. auth. see Ries, Joanne B.

Leukefeld, Karl G., jt. auth. see Ries, Joanne B.

Leukroth, K. Glossary for International Conferences. 3rd ed. (DAN, DUT, ENG, FRE & GER.). 174p. 1984. pap. 24.95 (0-8288-1508-9, F137200) Fr & Eur.

Leumann, Christian, jt. ed. see Ernst, Beat.

***Leumann, E. & Capeller, C., eds.** Sanskrit-English Dictionary. 2nd ed. 1369p. 1999. 67.50 (81-215-0200-4, Pub. by M Manoharlal) Coronet Bks.

Leun, Gerard Van Der, see Doyle, Arthur Conan & Van Der Leun, Gerard.

Leun, Gerard Van Der, see Mandel, Thomas.

Leun, Gerard Van Der, see Mandel, Thomas & Van Der Leun, Gerard.

An Asterisk (*) at the beginning of an entry indicates that the title is appearing for the first time.

Leuner, Hanscarl, et al. Guided Affective Imagery with Children & Adolescents. LC 83-8050. (Emotions, Personality, & Psychotherapy Ser.). 208p. 1983. 55.00 (*0-306-41232-2*, Plenum Trade) Perseus Pubng.

Leuner, Jean D., et al. Mastering the Nursing Process: A Case Method Approach. LC 89-71523. (Illus.). 494p. (Orig.). (C). 1990. pap. text 26.95 (*0-8036-5588-6*) Davis Co.

LeUnes, Arnold & Nation, Jack R. Sport Psychology: An Introduction. 2nd ed. LC 95-41298. (Nelson-Hall Series in Psychology). 592p. 1996. text 60.95 (*0-8304-1306-5*) Thomson Learn.

Leung. Development Land & Development Charge in Singapore. 1987. 74.00 (*0-409-99537-1*, MICHIE) LEXIS Pub.

Leung, Priscilla Mei-Fun & Chu, Kuo-Pin. The Basic Law of the HKSAR: From Theory to Practice. LC 98-214602. xxxvii, 419 p. 1998. write for info. (*0-409-99964-4*) Buttrwrth-Heinemann.

Leung, A. Y. Dynamic Stiffness & Substructures. LC 93-15461. 1993. 227.95 (*0-387-19807-5*) Spr-Verlag.

Leung, A. Y., jt. auth. see Chen, Y.

Leung, A. Y., jt. auth. see Cheung, Y. K.

Leung, Albert, jt. auth. see Kim, Haksu.

Leung, Albert Y. Better Health with (Mostly) Chinese Herbs & Foods. (Illus.). 128p. 1984. pap. 9.95 (*0-9634979-1-X*) AYSL.

— Chinese Healing Foods & Herbs. Orig. Title: Chinese Herbal Remedies. (Illus.). 192p. reprint ed. pap. 10.95 (*0-9634979-0-1*) AYSL.

Leung, Albert Y. & Foster, Steven. Encyclopedia of Common Natural Ingredients Used in Food, Drugs & Cosmetics. 2nd ed. LC 94-49668. 688p. 1995. 175.00 (*0-471-50826-8*) Wiley.

Leung, Anskar Y. The Epididymis as a Chloride-Secreting Organ. 173p. (Orig.). (C). 1995. pap. 49.50 (*962-201-673-1*, Pub. by Chinese Univ) Coronet Bks.

Leung, Anthony W. Systems of Nonlinear Partial Differential Equations: Applications to Biology & Engineering. (C). 1989. text 202.50 (*0-7923-0138-2*) Kluwer Academic.

Leung, Beatrice. Sino-Vatican Relations: Problems in Conflicting Authority, 1976-1986. (London School of Economics Monographs in International Studies). (Illus.). 432p. (C). 1992. text 85.00 (*0-521-38173-8*) Cambridge U Pr.

Leung, Beatrice & Cheng, Joseph, eds. Hong Kong SAR: In Pursuit of Domestic & International Order. LC 97-218956. 334p. 1998. pap. 27.50 (*962-201-785-1*, Pub. by Chinese Univ) U of Mich Pr.

Leung, Benjamin K. Perspectives on Hong Kong Society. LC 96-232403. (Illus.). 210p. 1996. pap. text 28.00 (*0-19-586535-9*) OUP.

Leung, Benjamin K., ed. Social Issues in Hong Kong. 250p. (C). 1990. 29.95 (*0-19-584008-9*) OUP.

Leung, Benjamin K., jt. ed. see Pearson, Veronica.

Leung, C. F., et al, eds. Centrifuge 94: Proceedings of the International Conference Singapore, 31 August - 2 September 1994. (Illus.). 854p. (C). 1994. text 149.00 (*90-5410-352-3*, Pub. by A A Balkema) Ashgate Pub Co.

***Leung, C. F., et al, eds.** Field Measurements in Geomechanics: Proceedings of the 5th International Symposium, FMGM99, Singapore, 1-3 December 1999. 610p. (C). 1999. text 95.00 (*90-5809-066-3*, Pub. by A A Balkema) Ashgate Pub Co.

Leung, C. K. & Ginsburg, Norton, eds. China: Urbanization & National Development. LC 80-29142. (University of Chicago, Department of Geography, Research Paper Ser.: No. 196). 296p. 1980. reprint ed. pap. 91.80 (*0-608-02289-6*, 206293000004) Bks Demand.

Leung, Chi-Keung. China: Railway Patterns & National Goals. LC 80-17030. (University of Chicago, Department of Geography, Research Paper Ser.: No. 195). (Illus.). 263p. reprint ed. pap. 81.60 (*0-8357-3723-3*, 203644500003) Bks Demand.

Leung, Clement H. Quantitative Analysis of Computer Systems. LC 87-2046. 184p. 1988. reprint ed. pap. 57.10 (*0-608-04601-9*, 206537100003) Bks Demand.

Leung, Clement H., ed. Visual Information Systems, Vol. 130. LC 97-35097. (Lecture Notes in Computer Science Ser.: Vol. 1306). x, 274p. 1997. pap. 49.00 (*3-540-63636-6*) Spr-Verlag.

Leung, Conita S., jt. ed. see Tay, Alice Erh-Soon.

Leung, Debbie. Self Defense: The Womanly Art of Self-Care, Intuition & Choice. LC 91-61404. (Illus.). 176p. 1991. pap. 12.95 (*0-929838-08-4*) Blue Zoo.

Leung, Donald. New Directions in the Clinical Use of Intravenous Immunoglobulin, Vol. I. (Illus.). 60p. 1989. write for info. (*0-318-65779-1*) Health Dimensions.

Leung, Donald V. M., et al, eds. Superantigens: Molecular Biology, Immunology & Relevance to Human Disease. LC 96-40407. (Illus.). 624p. 1997. text 195.00 (*0-8247-9813-9*) Dekker.

Leung, Donald V. M. & Szefler, S. J., eds. Severe Asthma, No. 86. (Lung Biology in Health & Disease Ser.: Vol. 86). (Illus.). 640p. 1995. text 215.00 (*0-8247-9511-3*) Dekker.

***Leung, Donald Y. M. & Greaves, Malcolm W., eds.** Allergic Skin Disease: A Multidisciplinary Approach. 532p. 2000. 165.00 (*0-8247-0287-5*) Dekker.

Leung, Ed, et al, contrib. by. Errant Bodies: Toys. (Illus.). 80p. 1998. pap. 6.00 (*0-9655570-1-4*, 810683) Errant Bodies.

Leung, Edwin P., ed. Historical Dictionary of Revolutionary China, 1839-1976. LC 91-15990. 584p. 1992. lib. bdg. 99.50 (*0-313-26457-0*, LHD, Greenwood Pr) Greenwood.

Leung, Edwin P., jt. ed. see Leung, Philip Y.

Leung, H. & Leung, Thomas. The Art of H. Leung & Thomas Leung. deluxe ed. (Illus.). 212p. 1996. 50.00 (*0-9649629-0-X*) Galleria Fine Art.

Leung, H. F. Distributed Constraint Logic Programming. 350p. 1993. text 74.00 (*981-02-1456-1*) World Scientific Pub.

Leung, H. M., jt. auth. see Thoburn, John T.

***Leung, Helen & Marshall, Mark.** Problems & Solutions to Accompany Changes Physical Chemistry for the Chemical & Biological Sciences. (Illus.). 496p. 2000. pap. text 52.00 (*1-891389-11-4*) Univ Sci Bks.

Leung, Jimmy, jt. auth. see Coel, Marc.

Leung, Joe C. & Nann, Richard C. Authority & Benevolence: Social Welfare in China. LC 95-10896. 1995. pap. 39.95 (*0-312-12747-2*) St Martin.

Leung, John, tr. see Dawson, David.

Leung, John K., jt. ed. see Kau, Michael Y.

Leung, K. C. Critical Observations Versus Physical Models for Close Binary Systems: Proceedings of the Colloquium in Beijing, China, Nov, 1985. xvi, 472p. 1988. text 264.00 (*0-677-22070-7*) Gordon & Breach.

Leung, K. C. & Nha, I. S., eds. New Frontiers in Binary Research. (ASP Conference Series Proceedings: Vol. 38). 471p. 1993. 34.00 (*0-937707-57-0*) Astron Soc Pacific.

Leung, K. S., et al. Biodegradable Implants in Fracture Fixation: Proceedings of the ISFR Symposium. 308p. 1994. text 86.00 (*981-02-1796-X*) World Scientific Pub.

Leung, K. S., jt. auth. see Yam, Y.

Leung, K. T. & Cheung, P. H. Fundamental Concepts of Mathematics. 260p. (C). 1991. pap. text 17.95 (*962-209-181-4*, Pub. by HK Univ Pr) Coronet Bks.

Leung, K. T. & Suen, S. N. Vectors, Matrices & Geometry: Introducing Finite-Dimensional Vector Spaces. 356p. 1994. pap. 29.50 (*962-209-360-4*, Pub. by HK Univ Pr) Coronet Bks.

Leung, K. T., et al. Polynomials & Equations. 240p. (C). 1992. pap. text 20.00 (*962-209-271-3*, Pub. by HK Univ Pr) Coronet Bks.

Leung, Kam-Ching. The 3rd Pacific Rim Conference on Recent Developments on Binary Star Research: Proceedings of a Conference Held in Chiang Mai, Thailand, October 26-November 1, 1995. (ASP Conference Series Proceedings: Vol. 130). 341p. 1997. 34.00 (*1-886733-50-3*) Astron Soc Pacific.

***Leung, Kim K. & Vojcic, Branimir.** Multiaccess, Mobility & Teletraffic for Wireless Communications. LC 99-189927. 1999. write for info. (*0-7923-8353-2*) Kluwer Academic.

***Leung, Kwok.** Conflict Management in the Asia Pacific: Perspectives in International Business. LC 98-40355. 350p. 1999. 60.50 (*0-471-24858-4*) Wiley.

***Leung, Kwok, et al.** Progress in Asian Social Psychology, Vol. 1. Kashima, Yoshihisa, tr. 1998. 55.00 (*0-471-24865-7*) Wiley.

Leung, Kwok, jt. auth. see Van De Vijver, Fons.

Leung, Kwong Sak, jt. auth. see Wong, Man Leung.

Leung, Lai-Ching. Lone Mothers, Social Security & the Family in Hong Kong. LC 97-77889. (Illus.). 239p. 1998. text 59.95 (*1-84014-320-7*, Pub. by Ashgate Pub) Ashgate Pub Co.

Leung, Laifong. Morning Sun: Interviews with Chinese Writers of the Lost Generation. LC 92-33902. (Studies on Contemporary China). 440p. (C). (gr. 13). 1994. text 85.95 (*1-56324-093-9*, East Gate Bk) M E Sharpe.

Leung, Laifong. Morning Sun: Interviews with Chinese Writers of the Lost Generation. LC 92-33902. (Studies on Contemporary China). 440p. (C). (gr. 13). 1994. pap. text 39.95 (*1-56324-130-7*, East Gate Bk) M E Sharpe.

Leung, Mai. The Classic Chinese Cook Book. LC 75-9354. (Illus.). 1976. 16.95 (*0-685-02047-9*, Perennial) HarperTrade.

Leung, Martha C., jt. auth. see Lin, Sharon C.

Leung, P. C. Info-Med Orthopaedics, Vol. 2. (Illus.). 690p. 1996. write for info. (*962-356-008-7*) Lppncott W & W.

Leung, P. C. Jotting Writing by Surgery. 260p. 1994. pap. text 11.00 (*1-879771-13-6*) Global Pub NJ.

Leung, P. C. & Gu, Y. D. Microsurgery in Orthopaedic Practice. LC 94-43237. 360p. 1995. text 61.00 (*9971-5-0860-5*) World Scientific Pub.

Leung, P. C. & Kraicer, P. F., eds. Hormone Receptors & Signaling in Reproduction. (Journal Ser.: Vol. 5, No. 2, 1996). (Illus.). 64p. 1996. pap. 28.00 (*3-8055-6341-8*) S Karger.

Leung, Patrick, jt. auth. see Kantambu, Latting J.

Leung, Peter C. Current Trends in Bone Grafting. (Illus.). 130p. 1988. 85.95 (*0-387-50139-8*) Spr-Verlag.

Leung, Peter C., et al, eds. Burns: Treatment & Research. 324p. (C). 1991. text 104.00 (*9971-5-0674-2*) World Scientific Pub.

— Endocrinology & Physiology of Reproduction. LC 87-11280. (Illus.). 372p. 1987. 95.00 (*0-306-42583-1*, Plenum Trade) Perseus Pubng.

— Molecular Basis of Reproductive Endocrinology. LC 92-2304. (Serono Symposia Ser.). (Illus.). 312p. 1992. 130.00 (*0-387-97861-5*); write for info. (*3-540-97861-5*) Spr-Verlag.

Leung, Peter C., jt. ed. see Adashi, Eli Y.

Leung, Peter C., jt. ed. see Chang, T. S.

Leung, Philip Y. & Leung, Edwin P., eds. Modern China in Transition: Studies in Honor of Immanuel C. Y. Hsu. LC 95-30491. 1995. 36.95 (*0-941690-63-6*); pap. 17.95 (*0-941690-68-7*) Regina Bks.

Leung, Ping-Chung, ed. Current Practice of Fracture Treatment: New Concepts & Common Problems. 1994. 199.00 (*0-387-57367-4*) Spr-Verlag.

Leung, PingSun, jt. ed. see Roecklein, John C.

***Leung, S. K.** Nature of the Self: A Philosophy on Human Nature. 416p. 2000. 32.00 (*1-902835-07-7*, Pub. by Empiricus Bks); pap. 19.95 (*1-902835-03-4*, Pub. by Empiricus Bks) Paul & Co Pubs.

— Politics & Human Nature: Ideological Rooting of the Left. 195p. 2000. 29.95 (*1-902835-08-5*, Pub. by Empiricus Bks); pap. 16.95 (*1-902835-02-6*, Pub. by Empiricus Bks) Paul & Co Pubs.

Leung, Sai-Wing. The Making of an Alienated Generation: The Political Socialization of Secondary School Students in Transitional Hong Kong. LC 97-73878. (Illus.). 344p. 1997. text 83.95 (*1-84014-159-X*, Pub. by Ashgate Pub) Ashgate Pub Co.

Leung, Stephen J. NSW Sniper Log Book. (Model 9600 - Waterproof Ser.). 268p. 1996. 85.00 (*1-885633-05-X*) Iron Brigade.

Leung, Steven S. & Shanblatt, Michael A. ASIC System Design with VHDL: A Paradigm. (C). 1989. text 114.50 (*0-7923-9032-6*) Kluwer Academic.

Leung, Suiwah, ed. Vietnam & the East Asian Crisis. LC 99-21830. 256p. 1999. 90.00 (*1-84064-089-8*) E Elgar.

— Vietnam Assessment: Creating a Sound Investment Climate. (Illus.). 123p. (Orig.). (C). 1997. pap. text 45.00 (*0-7881-3706-9*) DIANE Pub.

***Leung, Tao.** First Aid for the USMLE Step 1: A Student-to-Student Guide 2000. 10th ed. (Illus.). 425p. 2000. pap. 27.95 (*0-07-135849-8*) McGraw.

Leung, Tao & Anderson, Shelli. Communications 101: Easy Beginner's Guide to Computer Communications... Churchman, Michael, ed. (Illus.). 154p. (Orig.). 1996. pap. 19.95 (*0-9655291-0-X*) Pacific Image Communs Inc.

Leung, Thomas, jt. auth. see Leung, H.

Leung, Vincent W., jt. auth. see Roberts, Gordon W.

Leung, Wai-Ching. Clinical Examination for Medical Students. LC 97-171541. 208p. pap. text 17.95 (*0-340-66192-5*, Pub. by E A) Routldge.

— Clinical Medicine: Key Questions Answered. LC 98-15855. (Key Questions Answered Ser.). 300p. (Orig.). 1998. pap. text 32.50 (*0-19-262891-7*) OUP.

***Leung, Wai-Ching.** Law & Medicine: Common Legal Problems in Everyday Practice. 224p. 2000. pap. 44.00 (*0-7506-4190-8*) Buttrwrth-Heinemann.

— Law for Doctors. LC 00-20659. 224p. 2000. pap. 45.00 (*0-632-05243-0*) Blackwell Sci.

Leung, Wai-Ching. MCQs in Integrated Sciences. LC 99-11697. 1999. write for info. (*0-443-06239-0*) Church.

— Revision in Optics & Refraction. LC 97-164764. (An Arnold Publication). 144p. 1997. pap. text 24.50 (*0-340-64613-6*, Pub. by E A) OUP.

Leung, Wai-Ching & Mindford, Adrian. Self Assessment for the Diploma in Child Health. LC 97-20459. (An Arnold Publication). (Illus.). 208p. 1997. pap. text 24.95 (*0-340-67720-1*, Pub. by E A) OUP.

Leung, Wallace W. Industrial Centrifugation Technology. LC 97-49814. (Illus.). 304p. 1998. 70.00 (*0-07-037191-1*) McGraw-Hill Prof.

Leung, Y. C. Physics of Dense Matter. 280p. 1985. text 61.00 (*9971-978-10-5*) World Scientific Pub.

Leung, Yee. Intelligent Spatial Decision Support Systems. LC 97-13123. (Advances in Spatial Science Ser.). 1997. write for info. (*3-540-62518-6*) Spr-Verlag.

Leung, Yiu-Nam, ed. see Aldridge, Alfred O.

Leuning, Kevin. Archie Givens Sr. Collection Curriculum Guide. x, 30p. (J). (ps-12). 1988. pap. text. write for info. (*0-9632976-0-0*) A Givens Sr Collect.

Leunissen, Jan L., jt. ed. see Verkleij, A. J.

Leunissen, K. L., jt. ed. see Widere, T. E.

Leunissen, K. M., ed. International Society of Blood Purification 12th Annual Meeting, Maastricht, September 1994 Abstracts: Journal: Blood Purification, Vol. 12, No. 3. (Journal: Blood Purification). (Illus.). 62p. 1994. pap. 47.00 (*3-8055-6052-4*) S Karger.

Leunissen, Paul M. M. Konsulin und Konsulare in der Zeit von Commodus bis Severus Alexander (180-235 n. Chr.) (GER.). 505p. 1989. 110.00 (*90-5063-028-6*, Pub. by Gieben) J Benjamins Pubng Co.

Leunk, Thea. Which Way to God? A Christian Look at World Religions. 100p. 1998. pap. 13.75 (*1-56212-347-5*, 1180-0110) CRC Pubns.

Leupelt, M., jt. ed. see Muller, F.

Leupen, Bernard, et al. Design & Analysis. LC 97-3505. (Architecture Ser.). 224p. 1997. text 34.95 (*0-442-02580-7*, VNR) Wiley.

Leupen, Bernard, et al. Design & Analysis. 224p. 1997. 49.95 (*0-471-28841-1*, VNR) Wiley.

Leupen, P., ed. Philip of Leyden - A Fourteenth Century Jurist: A Study of His Life & Treatise de Cura Republicae et Sorte Principantis. (Rechtshistorische Studies: No. 7). xviii, 300p. 1992. pap. 68.00 (*90-271-1678-4*, Pub. by Egbert Forsten) Hodlder & Stoughton.

Leupers, Rainer. Retargetable Code Generation for Digital Signal Processors. LC 97-17690. 1997. text 126.50 (*0-7923-9958-7*) Kluwer Academic.

Leupin, Alexandre. Barbarolexis: Medieval Writing & Sexuality. Cooper, Kate M., tr. from FRE. LC 89-1999. 272p. 1989. 49.95 (*0-674-06170-5*) HUP.

Leupin, Alexandre, ed. Lacan & the Human Sciences. LC 90-39325. viii, 191p. 1991. text 45.00 (*0-8032-2894-5*) U of Nebr Pr.

Leupold, Bernd. Weder Anglophil Noch Anglophob. 367p. 1997. 63.95 (*3-631-49784-9*) P Lang Pubng.

Leupold, Ulrich S. & Lehmann, Helmut T., eds. Luther's Works: Liturgy & Hymns, Vol. 53. LC 55-9893. 1965. 30.00 (*0-8006-0353-2*, 1-353, Fortress Pr) Augsburg Fortress.

Leupp, Francis E. Indian & His Problem. LC 72-137175. (Poverty U. S. A. Historical Record Ser.). 1975. reprint ed. 26.95 (*0-405-03114-9*) Ayer.

Leupp, Gary P. Male Colors: The Construction of Homosexuality in Tokugawa Japan. LC 94-40395. (Illus.). 317p. 1996. 45.00 (*0-520-08627-9*, Pub. by U CA Pr) Cal Prin Full Svc.

— Male Colors: The Construction of Homosexuality in Tokugawa Japan. LC 94-40395. (Illus.). 1997. pap. 19.95 (*0-520-20900-1*, Pub. by U CA Pr) Cal Prin Full Svc.

— Servants, Shophands, & Laborers. 250p. 1992. pap. text 17.95 (*0-691-02961-X*, Pub. by Princeton U Pr) Cal Prin Full Svc.

— Servants, Shophands, & Laborers in the Cities of Tokugawa Japan. (Illus.). 252p. 1992. text 37.50 (*0-691-03139-8*) Princeton U Pr.

L

Leupp, Roderick T. Knowing the Name of God: A Trinitarian Tapestry of Grace, Faith & Community. 216p. 1996. pap. 14.99 (*0-8308-1874-X*, 1874) InterVarsity.

Leurquin, Regine. Theodore Meliteniote: Tribiblos Astronomique, Livre I. (Corpus des Astronomes Byzantins Ser.: Vol. 4). (FRE.). 436p. 1990. pap. 94.00 (*90-5063-045-6*, Pub. by Gieben) J Benjamins Pubng Co.

Leurs, Robert. A Resource Guide for Trainers & Facilitators of PLA. 120p. 1996. pap. 20.00 (*1-888753-00-5*) PACT Pubns.

Leurs, Robert & Timmerman, Henk. The Histamine H3 Receptor: A Target for New Drugs. LC 98-48712. xi, 291 p. 1998. write for info. (*0-444-82936-9*) Elsevier.

Leuschner, Eckhard. Persona, Larva, Maske: Ikonologische Studien zum 16. bis Fruhen 18. Jahrhundert. (Europaische Hochschulschriften, Reihe 28: Bd. 292). (GER., Illus.). 566p. 1997. 95.95 (*3-631-31340-3*) P Lang Pubng.

Leuschner, R. & Boehm, G., eds. Advances in Aerobiology. (BioSeries-EXS: No. 51). 300p. 1987. 99.00 (*0-8176-1803-1*) Birkhauser.

Leuschner, U., jt. ed. see Berg, P. A.

Leuschner, U., jt. ed. see Fromm, H.

Leuschner, William A. Introduction to Forest Resource Management. LC 91-21718. 304p. (C). 1992. reprint ed. lib. bdg. 52.50 (*0-89464-641-9*) Krieger.

Leusen, Isadore, ed. see International Congress of Physiological Sciences,.

Leuser, Claudia. Theologie und Anthropologie: Die Erziehung des Menschengeschlechts Bei Johann Gottfried Herder. (Wurzburger Studien Zur Fundamentaltheologie Ser.: Bd. 19). (GER.). 472p. 1996. 76.95 (*3-631-30388-2*) P Lang Pubng.

Leuser, David V. How to Send Healing Energy: Diccionari Enciclopedic D'abast Universal, 8 vols., Set. (CAT.). 3500p. 1974. 375.00 (*0-8288-6053-X*, S50517) Fr & Eur.

Leushina, A. M. The Development of Elementary Mathematical Concepts in Preschool Children. Steffe, Leslie P., ed. Teller, Joan W., tr. from RUS. LC 91-3865. (Soviet Studies in Mathematics Education). (Illus.). 481p. 1991. pap. 17.50 (*0-87353-299-6*) NCTM.

Leutenberg, Estelle A., jt. auth. see Korb-Khalsa, Kathy L.

***Leuteritz, Krista J. & Leight, Walter G.** Toward a National Standards Strategy: Conference Report. (Illus.). 115p. (C). 1999. pap. text 30.00 (*0-7881-8184-X*) DIANE Pub.

Leuthauser, Gabriele & Feierabend, Peter. Potsdam. (ENG, FRE & GER., Illus.). 300p. 1997. 39.95 (*3-89508-238-4*, 810499) Konemann.

Leuthauser, Karl. Character Counts! 40 Youth Ministry Devotions from Extraordinary Christians. LC 99-18665. 1999. 14.99 (*0-7644-2075-5*) Group Pub.

Leuthauser, Karl, ed. Student Led Discussions: How Can I Know God Exists? LC 98-5947. (Illus.). 96p. (YA). 1998. per. 6.99 (*0-7644-2071-2*, Vital Ministry) Group Pub.

Leuthausser, Werner. Die Entwicklung Staatlich Organisierter Herrschaft in Fruehen Hochkulturen Am Beispiel des Vorderen Orients. (Europaische Hochschulschriften Ser.: Reihe 22, Band 317). (GER.). 336p. 1998. pap. 51.95 (*3-631-33426-5*) P Lang Pubng.

Leuthold, David. Campaign Missouri Nineteen Ninety-Two. (Illus.). 288p. 1994. pap. 22.95 (*0-8262-0977-7*) U of Mo Pr.

Leuthold, Raymond M., et al. The Theory & Practice of Futures Markets. LC 87-45248. 432p. 1989. 46.95 (*0-669-16260-4*) Free Pr.

***Leuthold, Raymond M., et al.** The Theory & Practice of Futures Markets. 408p. 1999. pap. text 32.80 (*0-87563-944-5*) Stipes.

Leuthold, Scott. Dale Earnhardt. (Stats & Standings Ser.). 12p. 1999. pap. 5.95 (*1-58224-014-0*) Futech Interactive.

— Dale Jarrett: NASCAR. (Stats & Standings Ser.). 12p. 1999. pap. text 5.95 (*1-58224-017-5*) Futech Interactive.

— Jeff Gordon. (Stats & Standings Ser.). 12p. (ps-3). 1999. pap. text 5.95 (*1-58224-015-9*) Futech Interactive.

— Rusty Wallace: NASCAR. (Stats & Standings Ser.). 12p. 1999. pap. text 5.95 (*1-58224-016-7*) Futech Interactive.

Leuthold, Steven. Indigenous Aesthetics: Native Art, Media, & Identity. LC 97-37343. (Illus.). 240p. (C). 1998. 30.00 (*0-292-74702-0*, LEUIND); pap. 16.95 (*0-292-74703-9*, LEUINP) U of Tex Pr.

Leutholtz, Brian C. Exercise & Disease Management. LC 99-26886. 240p. 1999. boxed set 149.95 (*0-8493-8713-2*) CRC Pr.

Leutholtz, Brian C., jt. auth. see Swain, David P.

Leutinen, Mary T. Blossoms in the Wind: And Other Poems. 90p. (Orig.). 1994. pap. text 7.95 (*1-886698-01-5*) Sampo Pub.

Leutloff, D. & Srivastava, R. C., eds. Computational Fluid Dynamics: Selected Topics. LC 94-48557. 1995. 98.95 (*3-540-58757-8*) Spr-Verlag.

Leutner, Robert W. Shikitei Sanba & the Comic Tradition in Edo Fiction. (Harvard-Yenching Institute Monographs: No. 25). 300p. 1986. 30.00 (*0-674-80646-8*) HUP.

Leutsch, E. & Schneidewin, F. G., eds. Corpus Paroemiographorum Graecorum. 3.5 hd. write for info. (*0-318-70795-0*) G Olms Pubs.

L

Leutsch, E. L. & Schneidewin, F. Corpus Paroemiographorum Graecorum, 2 vols., Set. (GER.). 1468p. 1958. reprint ed. pap. write for info. (*0-318-70499-4*) G Olms Pubs.

Leutwiler, Heinz, jt. auth. see Arsove, Maynard.

Leutz, H., jt. auth. see Barletta, W.

Leutz, Walter N., et al. Care for Frail Elders: Developing Community Solutions. LC 92-11506. 315p. 1992. 59.95 (*0-86569-029-4*, T029, Auburn Hse) Greenwood.

Leutzbach, W. Introduction to the Theory of Traffic Flow. (Illus.). 180p. 1987. 86.95 (*0-387-17113-4*) Spr-Verlag.

Leutzbach, William. Traffic & Transport Systems: English-German, German-English. (ENG & GER.). 143p. 1991. 125.00 (*0-7859-9999-X*) Fr & Eur.

Leutzeler, H. Bildwoerterbuch der Kunst. 2nd ed. (GER.). 404p. 1962. 45.00 (*3-427-85012-9*, M-7310) Fr & Eur.

Leutzinger, John F. The Handstamps of Wells, Fargo & Co. 1852 to 1895. 2nd ed. Spelman, Henry M., III, ed. LC 93-77466. (Illus.). 384p. 1993. 45.00 (*0-917528-11-5*) L H Hartmann.

Leutzinger, Larry, ed. Mathematics in the Middle. LC 98-52986. (Illus.). 218p. 1998. pap. 28.50 (*0-87353-460-3*) NCTM.

Leutzinger, Richard. Lefty O'Doul - The Legend That Baseball Nearly Forgot: The Story of the Hall of Fame's Missing Star. (Illus.). 170p. (Orig.). 1997. pap. 19.95 (*1-883532-03-5*) Carmel Bay.

Leuven, Edwin P. Van, see Van Leuven, Edwin P.

Leuven, Hendrik Van, see Breitstein, Ron & Van Leuven, Hendrik.

Leuven, J. V. Prehistoric Religion in Greece. (Illus.). 280p. 1987. lib. bdg. 84.00 (*0-317-54494-2*, Pub. by AM Hakkert) Coronet Bks.

Leuven, Nancy Van, see Van Leuven, Nancy.

Leuven, R. S., ed. see Nienhuis, P. H.

Leuver, Peter. Fur & Feather: Fly-Tying for Trout. (Illus.). 224p. 1999. 25.50 (*0-684-86844-X*) S&S Trade.

Leuverink, Margaret, ed. The Mind: Our Greatest Gift. (Mananam Ser.). (Illus.). 111p. 1995. 7.00 (*1-880687-09-7*) Chinmaya Pubns.

— The Sages Speak about Immortality. LC 95-68108. (Mananam Ser.). (Illus.). 106p. 1995. 7.00 (*1-880687-08-9*) Chinmaya Pubns.

— The Sages Speak about Life & Death. LC 94-21223. (Mananam Ser.). (Illus.). 107p. pap. 7.00 (*1-880687-07-0*) Chinmaya Pubns.

Leuverunk, Margaret, ed. The Path of Love. (Manaham Ser.). (Illus.). 121p. (Orig.). 1996. pap. text 10.00 (*1-880687-10-0*) Chinmaya Pubns.

Leuw, Ed & Marshall, I. Haen, eds. Between Prohibition/Legalization: The Dutch Experiment in Drug Policy. LC 94-1664. (Studies on Crime & Justice Ser.). (Illus.). 335p. 1994. pap. 47.50 (*90-6299-103-3*, Criminal Justice) Willow Tree NY.

Leuz, Christian. Rechnungslegung und Kreditfinanzierung: Zum Zusammenhang von Ausschuttungsbegrenzung, Bilanzieller Gewinnermittlung und Vorsichtiger Rechnungslegung. (Betriebswirtschaftliche Studien: Bd. 32). (GER., Illus.). XLV, 250p. 1996. pap. 54.95 (*3-631-30150-2*) P Lang Pubng.

Leuzinger-Bohleber, M., et al, eds. Two Butterflies on My Head: Psychoanalysis in the Interdisciplinary Scientific Dialogue. (Illus.). 280p. 1992. pap. 40.00 (*0-387-53899-2*) Spr-Verlag.

Leuzinger, Elsy. Arte del Africa Negra. (ENG, FRE, GER & SPA., Illus.). 388p. 1993. 100.00 (*84-343-0176-8*) Elliots Bks.

Leuzzi, Linda. A Creative Life: The Young Person's Guide. LC 98-42890. 144p. (YA). (gr. 5-8). 1999. 24.00 (*0-531-11527-5*) Watts.

— Education. LC 97-27664. (Life in America 100 Years Ago Ser.). (Illus.). 100p. (YA). (gr. 5 up). 1997. lib. bdg. 19.95 (*0-7910-2849-6*) Chelsea Hse.

— Industry & Business. LC 96-45199. (Life in America 100 Years Ago Ser.). (Illus.). 100p. (YA). (gr. 5 up). 1996. lib. bdg. 19.95 (*0-7910-2846-1*) Chelsea Hse.

***Leuzzi, Linda.** Life Connections: Pioneers in Ecology LC 99-33075. (Lives in Science Ser.). 2000. 25.00 (*0-531-11566-6*) Watts.

Leuzzi, Linda. A Matter of Style: Women in the Fashion Industry. LC 96-33960. (Women Then - Women Now Ser.). 160p. (YA). (gr. 8-12). 1996. lib. bdg. 24.00 (*0-531-11303-5*) Watts.

— A Matter of Style: Women in the Fashion Industry. (Women Then - Women Now Ser.). 160p. (J). 1997. pap. 9.95 (*0-531-15831-4*) Watts.

— To the Young Environmentalist: Lives Dedicated to Preserving the Natural World. LC 97-1042. (J). 1997. lib. bdg. 24.00 (*0-531-11359-0*) Watts.

— To the Young Environmentalist: Lives Dedicated to Preserving the Natural World. (To the Young Ser.). 1998. pap. 6.95 (*0-531-15895-0*) Watts.

— Transportation. LC 94-17183. (Life in America 100 Years Ago Ser.). (Illus.). 100p. (YA). (gr. 5 up). 1995. lib. bdg. 19.95 (*0-7910-2840-2*) Chelsea Hse.

— Urban Life. LC 94-24617. (Life in America 100 Years Ago Ser.). (Illus.). 100p. (YA). (gr. 5 up). 1995. lib. bdg. 19.95 (*0-7910-2841-0*) Chelsea Hse.

Lev, jt. auth. see Balkin, Jack.

Lev, Baruch. Accounting & Information Theory, Vol. 2. (Studies in Accounting Research). 84p. 1969. 12.00 (*0-86539-014-2*) Am Accounting.

Lev, Baruch & Weiss, H. J. Introduction to Mathematical Programming: Quantitative Tools for Decision Making. 290p. 1981. 46.00 (*0-444-00591-9*, North Holland) Elsevier.

Lev, Daniel S. & McVey, Ruth T., eds. Making Indonesia. (Studies on Southeast Asia: SOSEA 20). 201p. (Orig.). 1996. pap. 18.00 (*0-87727-719-2*, SOSEA 20) Cornell SE Asia.

***Lev, Donald.** Enemies of Time. 2000. pap. 12.00 (*0-942292-16-2*) Warthog Pr.

Lev, Donald. Footnotes. Barkan, Stanley H., ed. (Cross-Cultural Review Chapbook Ser.: No. 11). 16p. 1981. 15.00 (*0-89304-850-X*, CCC138); pap. 5.00 (*0-89304-810-0*); audio 10.00 (*0-89304-835-6*) Cross-Cultrl NY.

— Intercourse with the Dead. 63p. 1980. pap. 7.50 (*0-685-49041-6*) Cross-Cultrl NY.

— Intercourse with the Dead. 60p. 1980. per. 2.50 (*0-917402-11-1*) Downtown Poets.

Lev, Loseff. Tainyi Sovetnik. LC 87-35388. (RUS.). 128p. (Orig.). 1988. pap. 8.00 (*0-938920-97-9*) Hermitage Pubs.

Lev, M. C., jt. ed. see Martinez, M. R.

Lev, Maurice, jt. auth. see Bharati, Saroja.

Lev, Omri B. Jokes for Your John: The Full Bathroom Reader. LC 95-51072. (Illus.). 96p. 1996. reprint ed. 10.00 (*1-56980-063-4*) Barricade Bks.

Lev, Ovadia E., ed. Structural Optimization: Recent Developments & Applications. LC 81-69232. 220p. 1981. pap. 5.00 (*0-87262-281-9*) Am Soc Civil Eng.

***Lev, Peter.** American Films of the 70's: Conflicting Visions. LC 99-53348. (Illus.). 248p. 2000. 40.00 (*0-292-74715-2*); pap. 19.95 (*0-292-74716-0*) U of Tex Pr.

Lev, Peter. Claude Lelouch, Film Director. LC 81-72036. (Illus.). 184p. 1983. 29.50 (*0-8386-3114-2*) Fairleigh Dickinson.

— The Euro-American Cinema. LC 92-42794. (Film Studies). (Illus.). 188p. (C). 1993. text 27.50 (*0-292-74677-6*) U of Tex Pr.

Lev, R. Adenomatous Polyps of the Colon. (Illus.). 160p. 1989. 87.00 (*0-387-96985-3*, 2730) Spr-Verlag.

***Lev, Yaacov.** Saladin in Egypt. Vol. 21. (Illus.). Xvi, 216p. 1998. text (*90-04-11221-9*) Brill Academic Pubs.

Lev, Yaacov. State & Society in Fatimid Egypt. LC 90-24522. (AHC Ser.: No. 1). xi, 217p. 1991. 82.00 (*90-04-09344-3*) Brill Academic Pubs.

Lev, Yaacov, ed. War & Society in the Eastern Mediterranean, 7th-15th Centuries. LC 96-16295. (Medieval Mediterranean Ser.: Vol. 9). (Illus.). xii, 412p. 1996. 160.00 (*90-04-10032-6*, NLG252) Brill Academic Pubs.

Leva, Patricia. Traveling the Interstate of Consciousness: A Driver's Instruction Manual: Using Hemi-Sync to Access States of Non-Ordinary Reality. LC 97-92502. (Illus.). xiii, 394p. 1997. pap. 18.00 (*0-9658963-8-2*) Q Central.

Leva-Skrovanova, Vera. Contemporary Bohemian Lace. 1987. 6.00 (*0-85219-735-7*) Robin & Russ.

Levaar, Liz, jt. auth. see Lee, Annabel.

Levacic, Rosalind. Financial Management in Education. (Management in Education Ser.). 192p. 1989. pap. 34.95 (*0-335-09246-2*) OpUniv Pr.

— Local Management of Schools: Analysis & Practice. LC 95-5855. 240p. 1995. pap. 37.95 (*0-335-19375-7*) OpUniv Pr.

Levack, Brain P. Witch Hunt. (C). 1995. pap. text 28.95 (*0-582-02357-2*) Addison-Wesley.

Levack, Brian P. The Witch-Hunt in Early Modern Europe. 267p. (C). 1987. text 23.75 (*0-582-49122-3*, 73488); pap. text 24.95 (*0-582-49123-1*, 73488) Longman.

— Witch Hunt in Early Modern Europe. 2nd ed. 320p. (C). 1995. pap. text 29.06 (*0-582-08069-X*, 76887) Longman.

Levack, Brian P., ed. Anthropological Studies of Witchcraft, Magic, & Religion. LC 92-21028. (Articles on Witchcraft, Magic, & Demonology Ser.: Vol. 1). 416p. 1992. text 77.00 (*0-8153-1023-4*) Garland.

— The Literature of Witchcraft. LC 92-21029. (Articles on Witchcraft, Magic, & Demonology Ser.: Vol. 4). 352p. 1992. text 68.00 (*0-8153-1026-9*) Garland.

— Possession & Exorcism. LC 92-22857. (Witchcraft, Magic, & Demonology Ser.: Vol. 9). 352p. 1992. text 68.00 (*0-8153-1031-5*) Garland.

— Renaissance Magic. LC 92-22912. (Articles on Witchcraft, Magic, & Demonology Ser.: Vol. 11). 336p. 1992. text 68.00 (*0-8153-1034-X*) Garland.

— Witch-Hunting in Continental Europe: Regional & Local Studies. LC 92-22856. (Witchcraft Magic, Demonology Ser.: Vol. 5). 304p. 1992. text 66.00 (*0-8153-1027-7*) Garland.

— Witch-Hunting in Early Modern Europe: General Studies. LC 92-21027. (Articles on Witchcraft, Magic, & Demonology Ser.: Vol. 3). 392p. 1992. text 77.00 (*0-8153-1025-0*) Garland.

— Witchcraft & Demonology in Art & Literature. LC 92-22872. (Articles on Witchcraft, Magic, & Demonology Ser.: Vol. 12). (Illus.). 360p. 1992. text 77.00 (*0-8153-1035-8*) Garland.

— Witchcraft in Colonial America. LC 92-22874. (Articles on Witchcraft, Magic, & Demonology Ser.: Vol. 8). 416p. 1992. text 79.00 (*0-8153-1030-7*) Garland.

— Witchcraft in England. LC 92-21032. (Articles on Witchcraft, Magic, & Demonology Ser.: Vol. 6). 344p. 1992. text 68.00 (*0-8153-1028-5*) Garland.

— Witchcraft in Scotland. LC 92-21033. (Articles on Witchcraft, Magic, & Demonology Ser.: Vol. 7). 408p. 1992. text 77.00 (*0-8153-1029-3*) Garland.

— Witchcraft in the Ancient World & the Middle Ages. LC 92-20731. (Articles on Witchcraft, Magic, & Demonology Ser.: Vol. 2). 344p. 1992. text 68.00 (*0-8153-1024-2*) Garland.

Levack, Brian P., intro. Witchcraft, Magic & Demonology: An Anthology of Scholarly Articles, 12 vols., Set. 1992. 710.00 (*0-8153-1022-6*) Garland.

Levack, Daniel J. Amber Dreams: A Roger Zelazny Bibliography. 151p. 1983. lib. bdg. 49.95 (*0-313-27678-1*) Greenwood.

— The Dune Master: A Frank Herbert Bibliography, 2. 300p. 1988. lib. bdg. 59.95 (*0-313-27679-X*) Greenwood.

— PKD: A Philip K. Dick Bibliography, 1. (Bibliographies on Science Fiction, Fantasy & Horror Ser.: No. 1). 160p. 1988. lib. bdg. 69.50 (*0-313-27680-3*) Greenwood.

Levack, Daniel J. & Willard, Mark. The Dune Master: A Frank Herbert Bibliography. LC 87-25034. (Meckler's Bibliographies on Science Fiction, Fantasy, & Horror Ser.). xx, 176 p. 1988. write for info. (*0-88736-099-8*) Mecklermedia.

Levack, Daniel J., jt. auth. see Laughlin, Charlotte.

Levack, Mary I., ed. see Quick, William K.

Levack, Nancy. Low Vision: A Resource Guide with Adaptations for Students with Visual Impairments. 2nd ed. LC 94-6108. 1994. pap. 25.00 (*1-880366-12-6*) TSBVI.

Levack, Nancy, jt. auth. see Loumiet, Robin.

Levack, Nancy, jt. auth. see Miller, Cyral.

Levack, Nancy, jt. auth. see Smith, Millie.

***Levack, Rusty.** The Westerner. 144p. 1999. pap. 13.00 (*0-8059-4787-6*) Dorrance.

Levacy, William R. Beneath a Vedic Sky: A Beginner's Guide to the Astrology of Ancient India. LC 98-41294. (Illus.). 432p. 1999. pap. 19.95 (*1-56170-524-1*, 570) Hay House.

Levadie, Benjamin, ed. see American Society for Testing & Materials Staff.

Levaditis, Alexandra M., ed. see Lasham, Charles & Scallan, Andrew.

Levaggi, Rosella. Fiscal Federalism & Grants-in-Aid: The Problem of Asymmetrical Information. 208p. 1991. text 82.95 (*1-85628-242-2*, Pub. by Avebry) Ashgate Pub Co.

Levai, Imre, jt. ed. see Sharma, R. R.

Levaillant, Maurice. Les Aventures du Scepticisme: Essai sur l'Evolution Intellectuelle d'Anatole France. (FRE.). 38.95 (*0-8288-9969-X*, F59035) Fr & Eur.

— Passionate Exiles: Madame de Stael & Madame Recamier. Barnes, Malcolm, tr. from FRE. LC 73-160923. (Biography Index Reprint Ser.). 1977. reprint ed. 23.95 (*0-8369-8086-7*) Ayer.

Levaillant, Maurice, jt. auth. see Merimee, Prosper.

Levaillant, Maurice, jt. auth. see Sainte-Beuve, Charles-Augustin.

Levaillant, Maurice, ed. see De Chateaubriand, Francois-Rene.

Leval, Georges de, see De Leval, Georges, ed.

Leval, Susana T. Artists Talk Back - Los Artistas Responden: Visual Conversations with el Museo, Pt. 1: Reclaiming History - Conversando en Imagenes Con el Museo, El Rescate de la Historia. (ENG & SPA.). 52p. (Orig.). (C). 1994. pap. 20.00 (*1-882454-01-4*) El Museo Barrio.

Leval, Susana T., et al. Antonio Martorell: A House for Us All. (ENG & SPA., Illus.). 56p. (Orig.). 1992. pap. 20.00 (*1-882454-00-6*) El Museo Barrio.

Leval, Susana Torruella, see Ponce de Leon, Carolina & Torruella Leval, Susana.

Leval, Susana Torruella, jt. text see Sullivan, Edward J.

LeValley, Norma. A Tree for Me. LC 87-70974. (Illus.). 50p. (J). (ps-2). 1987. pap. 5.95 (*0-9618740-0-7*) Caring Tree.

LeValliant, Ted & Theroux, Marcel. What's the Verdict? Real Life Court Cases to Test Your Legal IQ. LC 90-28616. (Illus.). 128p. 1991. pap. 5.95 (*0-8069-7466-4*) Sterling.

Levan, Christopher. Living in the Maybe: A Steward Confronts the Spirit of Fundamentalism. LC 97-48603. (Faith's Horizons Ser.: Vol. 4). 160p. 1998. pap. 18.00 (*0-8028-4347-6*) Eerdmans.

Levan, Gerald. The Survival Guide for Business Families. LC 98-7429. 256p. 1998. 30.00 (*0-415-92086-8*) Routledge.

***LeVan, Lisa.** The Psoriasis Cure: A Drug-Free Guide to Stopping & Reversing the Symptoms of Psoriasis. LC 99-28980. 154p. 1999. pap. 13.95 (*0-89529-917-8*, Avery) Penguin Putnam.

LeVan, M. Douglas, ed. Fundamentals of Adsorption: Proceedings of the Fifth International Conference on Fundamentals of Adsorption. LC 96-14812. (Kluwer International Series in Engineering & Computer Science: Vol. 356). 1096p. (C). 1996. text 333.00 (*0-7923-9713-4*) Kluwer Academic.

Levan, N. Systems & Signals. (University Series in Modern Engineering). 173p. 1983. pap. 33.00 (*0-387-90900-1*) Spr-Verlag.

— Systems & Signals. 2nd rev. ed. LC 86-31158. (University Series in Modern Engineering). 176p. (C). 1987. text 29.50 (*0-911575-40-5*) Optimization Soft.

— Systems & Signals. 3rd enl. rev. ed. LC 92-28882. (University Series in Modern Engineering). 240p. 1992. pap. text 43.00 (*0-911575-63-4*) Optimization Soft.

LeVan, Russell. The Great War of Destruction. LC 98-65635. (Illus.). 960p. 1998. 49.95 (*1-57197-114-9*) Pentland Pr.

Levan, Susie. God Has Your Best Interest at This Time. 400p. 1996. 24.95 (*0-87418-279-4*) Sanctuary FL.

LeVan, Timothy. Masters of the French Art Song: Translations of the Complete Songs of Chausson, Debussy, Duparc, Favre & Ravel. LC 91-41123. 457p. 1991. 50.00 (*0-8108-2522-8*) Scarecrow.

— Masters of the Italian Art Song: Word-by-Word & Poetic Translations of the Complete Songs for Voice & Piano. LC 90-8955. 333p. 1990. 45.00 (*0-8108-2363-2*) Scarecrow.

Levander, Caroline F. Voices of the Nation: Women & Public Speech in 19th-Century American Literature & Culture. LC 97-24281. (Studies in American Literature & Culture: Vol. 114). 200p. (C). 1998. text 54.95 (*0-521-59374-3*) Cambridge U Pr.

Levander, Orville A., ed. AIN Symposium Proceedings, Nutrition '87. (Illus.). 157p. (Orig.). 1987. pap. 15.00 (*0-943029-01-5*) Am Soc Nutr Sci.

Levandoski, Rob. Going to Chicago. LC 96-44831. 208p. 1997. 22.00 (*1-877946-98-2*) Permanent Pr.

***Levandoski, Rob.** Serendipity Green. LC 99-39277. 270p. 2000. 25.00 (*1-57962-063-9*) Permanent Pr.

Levang, Curtis. Looking Good Outside, Feeling Bad Inside: Freedom from the Shame That Hides the Real You. 142p. (Orig.). 1995. pap. 9.99 (*1-883002-11-7*) Emerald WA.

Levang, Elizabeth. Remembering with Love: Messages of Love for the First Year of Grieving & Beyond. 1995. pap. 11.95 (*0-925190-86-1*) Fairview Press.

— When Men Grieve: Why Men Grieve Differently & How You Can Help. LC 98-28694. 224p. 1998. 19.95 (*1-57749-078-9*, Pub. by Fairview Press) Natl Bk Netwk.

Levang, J. H. Living Lutheran Christianity. 129p. (Orig.). 1991. pap. 8.95 (*0-943167-14-0*) Faith & Fellowship Pr.

Levangie, Pamela K., jt. auth. see Norkin, Cynthia C.

***Levangle, Pamela K. & Norkin, Cynthia C.** Joint Structure & Function: A Comprehensive Analysis. 3rd rev. ed. (Illus.). 512p. 2000. pap. text 43.95 (*0-8036-0710-5*) Davis Co.

Levaniouk, Olga, jt. ed. see Carlisle, Miriam.

Levanon, Haim, jt. auth. see Gamliel, Dan.

Levanon, Nadav. Radar Principles. LC 87-29832. 320p. 1988. 105.00 (*0-471-85881-1*) Wiley.

Levanoni, Amalia. A Turning Point in Mamluk History: The Third Reign of Al-Nasir Muhammad ibn Qalawun (1310-1341) (Islamic History & Civilization, Studies & Texts Ser.). ix, 221p. 1995. 81.00 (*90-04-10182-9*) Brill Academic Pubs.

Levant, Glenn A. Keeping Kids Drug Free: D. A. R. E. Official Parent's Guide. LC 97-37097. (Illus.). 276p. 1998. pap. 13.95 (*1-57145-625-2*, Laurel Glen Pub) Advantage Pubs.

Levant, J. Selecting the Right People. 1996. pap. 129.00 (*1-85953-010-9*, Pub. by Tech Comm) St Mut.

Levant, Jessica. HRD Survival Skills. LC 98-15721. (Improving Human Performance Ser.). 150p. 1998. 36.00 (*0-88415-270-7*, 5270) Gulf Pub.

Levant, Jonathan. Five Days Shy of February. 30p. 1997. pap. 5.00 (*1-57141-040-6*) Runaway Spoon.

— Oedipus the Anti-Sociopath: or Autumn Angst. 24p. (Orig.). 1992. pap. 5.00 (*0-926935-62-3*) Runaway Spoon.

Levant, Leonid, tr. see Meerson, Felix Z.

Levant, Nancy. Generations of Sara. 20p. 1995. pap. 5.00 (*1-57141-012-0*) Runaway Spoon.

Levant, Oscar. The Memoirs of an Amnesiac. LC 89-36545. 320p. 1989. pap. 12.95 (*0-573-60698-6*) S French Trade.

— A Smattering of Ignorance. Date not set. lib. bdg. 22.95 (*0-8488-2152-1*) Amereon Ltd.

Levant, Ronald & Pollack, William, eds. The New Psychology of Men. LC 94-41028. 352p. 1995. pap. 42.00 (*0-465-08656-X*, Pub. by Basic) HarpC.

Levant, Ronald F. & Brooks, Gary R. Men & Sex: New Psychological Perspectives. LC 97-12813. 283p. 1997. 75.00 (*0-471-16903-X*) Wiley.

Levant, Ronald F. & Shlien, John M., eds. Client-Centered Therapy & the Person-Centered Approach: New Directions in Theory, Research & Practice. LC 84-6832. 480p. 1984. 69.50 (*0-275-91215-9*, C1215, Praeger Pubs) Greenwood.

— Client-Centered Therapy & the Person-Centered Approach: New Directions in Theory, Research, & Practice. LC 84-6832. 480p. 1987. pap. 19.95 (*0-275-92821-7*, B2821, Praeger Pubs) Greenwood.

Levant, Ronald F., jt. auth. see Pollack, William S.

Leventhal, Sallye, ed. see Anthony, Robert.

Leventhal, Sallye, ed. see Hernacki, Mike.

Levantrosser, William F., ed. Harry S. Truman, the Man from Independence, 145. LC 85-21962. (Contributions in Political Science Ser.: No. 145). 437p. 1986. 69.50 (*0-313-25178-9*, LTR/, Greenwood Pr) Greenwood.

Levantrosser, William F., jt. ed. see Friedman, Leon.

Levanyuk, A. P. & Sigov, A. S. Defects & Structural Phase Transitions. 244p. 1988. text 312.00 (*2-88124-067-4*) Gordon & Breach.

Levanyuk, A. P., jt. auth. see Strukov, Boris A.

***Levaren.** Blue Ribbon Science Fair. 2nd ed. LC 99-48586. 100p. 1999. 12.95 (*0-07-134668-6*) McGraw.

Levarie, Norma. The Art & History of Books. LC 82-8984. (Illus.). 328p. 1995. 45.00 (*1-884718-02-7*); pap. 29.95 (*1-884718-03-5*) Oak Knoll.

Levarie, Siegmund. Fundamentals of Harmony. (Wissenschaftliche Abhandlungen-Musicological Studies: Vol. 5). 150p. 1965. pap. 5.20 (*0-912024-75-5*) Inst Mediaeval Mus.

— Mozart's Le Nozze Di Figaro. LC 77-5150. (Music Reprint Ser.). 1977. reprint ed. lib. bdg. 32.50 (*0-306-70897-3*) Da Capo.

Levarie, Siegmund & Levy, Ernest. Musical Morphology: A Discourse & a Dictionary. LC 82-21274. 355p. reprint ed. pap. 110.10 (*0-7837-5124-9*, 204485200004) Bks Demand.

Levarie, Siegmund & Levy, Ernst. A Dictionary of Musical Morphology. (Wissenschaftliche Abhandlungen-Musicological Studies: Vol. 29). viii, 400p. 1980. lib. bdg. 34.00 (*0-912024-32-1*) Inst Mediaeval Mus.

— Tone: A Study in Musical Acoustics. 2nd ed. LC 80-29383. (Illus.). 256p. 1981. reprint ed. lib. bdg. 65.00 (*0-313-22499-4*, LETO, Greenwood Pr) Greenwood.

Levarie, Siegmund, tr. see Dahlhaus, Carl.

Levarie, Siegmund, tr. see Mertin, Josef.

LeVarn, Caspar L. The Early History of Wilmot. (Illus.). 214p. 1995. reprint ed. lib. bdg. 32.50 (*0-8328-5063-2*) Higginson Bk Co.

Levasics, E. & Suranyi, M. Serbo-Croatian-Hungarian Concise Dictionary. 848p. 1988. 36.00 (*963-205-216-1*, Pub. by Akade Kiado) St Mut.

— Serbocroatian-Hungarian Concise Dictionary. 3rd ed. (HUN & SER.). 848p. 1982. 39.95 (*0-8288-1668-9*, M 8578) Fr & Eur.

Levasseur, Alain A. Louisiana Law of Obligations in General: A Precis. 350p. (C). 1988. pap. 39.50 (*0-409-25390-1*, MICHIE) LEXIS Pub.

— Louisiana Law of Quasi-Contracts or Unjust Enrichment: A Precis. LC 92-28451. 1992. pap. 35.00 (*0-409-25521-1*, MICHIE) LEXIS Pub.

— Louisiana Law of Unjust Enrichment in Quasi-Contracts. 490p. 1991. ring bd. 110.00 (*0-409-25600-5*, MICHIE) LEXIS Pub.

Levasseur, Alain A. & Baker, John S., eds. An Introduction to the Law of the United States. 492p. (C). 1991. lib. bdg. 68.00 (*0-8191-8462-4*) U Pr of Amer.

Levasseur, Alain A. & Dahl, Enrique, eds. Multinational Corporations: Investments, Technology, Tax, Labor & Securities: European, North & Latin American Perspectives with Summaries in French & Spanish. LC 86-13192. 404p. (C). 1986. lib. bdg. 58.00 (*0-8191-5496-2*) U Pr of Amer.

Levasseur, Alain A., tr. see Alter, Michel.

Levasseur, Alain A., tr. see Atias, Christian.

Levasseur, Emile. The American Workman. Stein, Leon & Marburg, Theodore, eds. Adams, Thomas S., tr. LC 77-70510. 1977. lib. bdg. 47.95 (*0-405-10180-5*) Ayer.

— Histoire des Classes Ouvrieres et de L'industrie en France de 1789-1870, 2 vols. 2nd ed. LC 78-92175. (FRE.). reprint ed. 225.00 (*0-404-03977-4*) AMS Pr.

LeVasseur, Michal. Finding a Way: Encouraging Underrepresented Groups in Geography: An Annotated Bibliography. (Pathways in Geography Ser.: No. 5). 63p. (Orig.). 1993. pap. text 5.00 (*0-9627379-6-8*) NCFGE.

Levasseur, Raymond L., jt. auth. see Blunk, Tim.

Levasseur-Regourd, A. C. & Hasegawa, H., eds. Origin & Evolution of Interplanetary Dust. 450p. (C). 1992. text 226.50 (*0-7923-1365-8*) Kluwer Academic.

Levasseur-Regourd, A. C. & Raulin, F., eds. Prebiotic Chemistry in Space: Proceedings of Symposium B1.4 of COSPAR Scientific Commission B & Symposium F3.3 of COSPAR Scientific Commission F Which Were Held During the 30th COSPAR Scientific Assembly, Hamburg, Germany, 11-21 July, 1994. (Advances in Space Research Ser.: Vol. 16). 120p. 1995. pap. 97.75 (*0-08-042622-0*, Pergamon Pr) Elsevier.

Levasseur, Robert E. Breakthrough Golf for High Handicappers. LC 96-83808. 62p. (Orig.). 1996. pap. 9.95 (*0-9651154-0-2*) Develop Pr.

Levasseur, T. & Stafford, J. Rings of Differential Operators on Classical Rings of Invariants. LC 89-15147. (Memoirs Ser.: Vol. 81/412). 117p. 1989. pap. 21.00 (*0-8218-2475-9*, MEMO/81/412) Am Math.

Levathes, Louise. When China Ruled the Seas: The Treasure Fleet of the Dragon Throne 1403-1433. LC 93-42773. (Illus.). 256p. 1994. 23.00 (*0-671-70158-4*) S&S Trade.

— When China Ruled the Seas: The Treasure Fleet of the Dragon Throne, 1405-1433. (Illus.). 256p. 1997. pap. 15.95 (*0-19-511207-5*) OUP.

Levatino, Madeline. Past Masters: The History & Hauntings of Destrehan Plantation. (Illus.). 100p. (Orig.). 1991. pap. 9.50 (*0-9630144-6-3*) M Levatino.

Levaux, Hugh P., jt. auth. see Lorell, Mark A.

Levay, Bela, jt. ed. see Vertes, Attila.

LeVay, D., tr. see Bricout, N.

LeVay, David. Scenes from Surgical Life. 200p. 1976. 22.95 (*0-8464-0813-9*) Beekman Pubs.

LeVay, David, tr. see Roth, Joseph.

LeVay, Simon. Queer Science: The Use & Abuse of Research into Homosexuality. (Illus.). 374p. (C). 1996. 32.00 (*0-262-12199-9*) MIT Pr.

Levay, Simon. Queer Science: The Use & Abuse of Research into Homosexuality. (Illus.). 374p. 1997. reprint ed. pap. text 16.95 (*0-262-62119-3*) MIT Pr.

LeVay, Simon. The Sexual Brain. (Illus.). 184p. 1994. pap. text 13.00 (*0-262-62093-6*, Bradford Bks) MIT Pr.

LeVay, Simon & Nonas, Elisabeth. City of Friends: A Portrait of the Gay & Lesbian Community in America. (Illus.). 464p. (C). 1995. 32.00 (*0-262-12194-8*, Bradford Bks) MIT Pr.

Levay, Simon & Nonas, Elisabeth. City of Friends: A Portrait of the Gay & Lesbian Community in America. (Illus.). 468p. 1997. reprint ed. pap. text 18.95 (*0-262-62113-4*) MIT Pr.

LeVay, Simon, jt. auth. see Koerner, David W.

LeVay, Simon, jt. auth. see Sieh, Kerry.

Levceque, Francois, jt. auth. see Carraro, Carlo.

Levchev, Lyubomir. Sky Break: Nebesen Sriv - Poems. Halatcheva-Roussesv, Chtiliana, tr. from BUL. LC 97-7225. (BUL & ENG., Illus.). 112p. (Orig.). (C). 1997. pap. 12.00 (*1-57889-034-9*) Passeggiata.

— Sky Break: Poems by Lyubomir Levchev. limited ed. 60p. 1995. 95.00 (*0-9646958-1-2*) Griffis Art Ctr.

— Stolen Fire: Selected Poems. Osers, Ewald, tr. LC 85-82112. (Illus.). 105p. 1986. pap. 13.95 (*0-948259-04-3*, Pub. by Forest Bks) Dufour.

Levchev, Vladimir. Black Book of the Endangered Species. Taylor, Henry, tr. LC 98-61424. (BUL & ENG.). 88p. (Orig.). 1999. pap. text 10.00 (*0-915380-42-0*) Word Works.

***Levchuck, Caroline M.** Learning about Charity from the Life of Princess Diana. LC 98-22111. (Character Building Book 1). (Illus.). 24p. (J). 1999. 17.26 (*0-8239-5344-0*, PowerKids) Rosen Group.

***Levchuck, Caroline M. & Drohan, Michele I.** Healthy Living, 3 vols. LC 99-53258. 600p. (J). 1999. text 95.00 (*0-7876-3918-4*) Gale.

***Levchuck, Caroline M. & Drohan, Michele Ingber.** Healthy Living, 3 vols. LC 99-53258. 2000. write for info. (*0-7876-3921-4*) Gale.

Levchuk. Ukrainian-English Phrasebook. 2nd ed. (ENG & UKR.). 190p. 1980. 7.95 (*0-8288-1730-8*, F65560) Fr & Eur.

Levchuk, Helen. The Dingles. LC 85-240770. (Illus.). 24p. (J). (ps-1). 1991. pap. 4.95 (*0-88899-044-8*) Publishers Group.

— Doris Dingle's Crafty Cat Activity Book: Games, Toys & Hobbies to Keep Your Cat's Mind Active. LC 91-2701. (Illus.). 96p. (Orig.). 1991. pap. 12.95 (*0-88240-415-6*, Alaska NW Bks) Gr Arts Ctr Pub.

Leve, Robert M. Child & Adolescent Psychotherapy: Process & Integration. 368p. 1994. pap. text 51.40 (*0-205-14907-3*, Longwood Div) Allyn.

LeVeau, Barney F. Williams & Lissner's Biomechanics of Human Motion. 3rd ed. (Illus.). 340p. 1991. pap. text 47.00 (*0-7216-5743-5*, W B Saunders Co) Harcrt Hlth Sci Grp.

***Leveau, P., et al, eds.** Environmental Reconstruction in Mediterranean Landscape Archaeology. (Archaeology of the Mediterranean Landscape, Populus Monograph: Vol. 2). (Illus.). 224p. 2000. 72.95 (*1-900188-63-5*, Pub. by Oxbow Bks) David Brown.

LeVeen, E. Phillip. British Slave Trade Suppression Policies 1821-1865: Impact & Implications. Bruchey, Stuart, ed. LC 77-77179. (Dissertations in European Economic History Ser.). (Illus.). 1978. lib. bdg. 26.95 (*0-405-10792-7*) Ayer.

Leveen, J. The Hebrew Bible in Art. (British Academy, London, Schweich Lectures on Biblical Archaeology Series, 1930). 1969. reprint ed. pap. 30.00 (*0-8115-1281-9*) Periodicals Srv.

Leveen, Louis & Priver, David. Intimacy: Our Quest for Completeness. 144p. (Orig.). 1994. pap. 9.95 (*1-885637-17-9*) Bluefish Pr.

LeVeen, Phillip, jt. auth. see Runsten, David.

Leveille, Gary T. Around Great Barrington & Stockbridge. (Images of America Ser.). 1997. pap. 16.99 (*0-7524-0557-8*) Arcadia Publng.

Leveille, Paul. Drawing Expressive Portraits. (Illus.). 128p. 1996. 24.99 (*0-89134-614-7*, North Lght Bks) F & W Pubns Inc.

— Painting Expressive Pastel Portraits. LC 98-6131. (Illus.). 128p. 1998. 27.99 (*0-89134-815-8*, North Lght Bks) F & W Pubns Inc.

— Painting Expressive Portraits in Oil. LC 96-37071. (Illus.). 128p. 1997. 27.99 (*0-89134-726-7*, North Lght Bks) F & W Pubns Inc.

Leveille, Thomas M., ed. Tennessee Legal & Business Forms. LC 94-40878. 1994. 330.00 (*0-614-32171-9*) West Group.

Leveille, Thomas M. & Fleishman, Lori F. Tennessee Litigation Forms & Analysis. LC 95-82074. (Practitioner's Ser.). 1800p. 1995. text. write for info. (*0-7620-0031-7*) West Group.

Leveillee, Jacques, jt. auth. see Leonard, Jean-Francois.

Level, Jeff, et al. The Precision Type Font Reference Guide Version 5.0: Complete Front Software Resource for Electronic Publishing. 653p. 2000. pap. 39.95 (*0-88179-182-2*, Pub. by Hartley & Marks) Andrews & McMeel.

— Precision Type Font Reference Guide 5.0: The Complete Font Software Resource for Electronic Publishing. (Illus.). 704p. (Orig.). 1996. pap. 39.95 (*0-9646252-0-2*) Precision Type.

Level, M. S., jt. ed. see Cardew, P. T.

Levell, Dorsey, jt. auth. see Groner, Wayne.

Levell, John P. Field Guide to Reptiles & the Law. 2nd rev. ed. (Illus.). 270p. (Orig.). 1997. pap. 29.95 (*1-885209-06-1*); text 49.95 (*1-885209-07-X*) Serpents Tale.

Levelt, A. M., jt. auth. see Van den Essen, A. P.

Levelt, Willem J. Crossing the Boundaries in Linguistics. Klein, Wolfgang, ed. 302p. 1981. text 164.50 (*90-277-1259-X*, D Reidel) Kluwer Academic.

— Formal Grammars in Linguistics & Psycholinguistics: An Introduction to the Theory of Formal Languages & Automata, Vol. 1. Barnas, Andrew, tr. from DUT. (Janua Linguarum, Ser. Minor: No. 192). (Illus.). 143p. 1974. pap. text 20.80 (*90-279-2666-2*) Mouton.

— Formal Grammars in Linguistics & Psycholinguistics: Applications in Linguistic Theory, Vol. 2. (Janua Linguarum, Ser. Minor: No. 192-2). (Illus.). viii, 194p. (Orig.). 1974. pap. text 26.15 (*90-279-2708-1*) Mouton.

— Formal Grammars in Linguistics & Psycholinguistics: Psycholinguistics Applications, Vol. 3. (Janua Linguarum, Ser. Minor: No. 192-3). 206p. 1974. pap. text 32.35 (*90-279-3352-9*) Mouton.

Levelt, Willem J. & Flores d'Arcais, G. B., eds. Studies in the Perception of Language. LC 78-2548. 353p. reprint ed. pap. 100.70 (*0-608-20462-6*, 2029858) Bks Demand.

Levelt, William J. M. Speaking: From Intention to Articulation. (ACL-MIT Series in Natural Language Processing). (Illus.). 584p. 1993. pap. text 27.50 (*0-262-62089-8*, Bradford Bks) MIT Pr.

Leven, E. Ja., et al, eds. Permian Stratigraphy & Fusulinida of Afghanistan. Shalashilina, Tatyana Y., tr. LC 96-51130. (Special Papers: No. 316). 1997. pap. 45.00 (*0-8137-2316-7*) Geol Soc.

Leven, Maurice. Income in the Various States: Its Sources & Distribution, 1919, 1920, & 1921. (General Ser.: No. 7). 306p. 1925. reprint ed. 79.60 (*0-87014-006-X*) Natl Bur Econ Res.

Leven, Samuel J., jt. ed. see Levine, Daniel S.

Leven, Stephen T. & Elwell, David M. Manhattan Apartment Finder. 97p. (Orig.). 1996. pap. 19.95 (*0-9651014-0-1*, 1001) Greener Pastures.

Levenard, J. M., et al, eds. Anthology of the Paradoxist Literary Movement: Multicultural Essays. LC 65-900. (ENG & FRE., Illus.). 176p. reprint ed. pap. 54.60 (*0-608-10448-5*, 207108300008) Bks Demand.

Levenard, Jim, et al. Anthology of the Paradoxist Literary Movement: Essays. Dinca, C., ed. (Illus.). 174p. 1993. pap. text 9.99 (*1-879585-34-0*) Erhus Univ Pr.

Levenbach, Hans, et al. Modern Forecasting. 400p. boxed set. write for info. (*0-534-26268-6*, Pub. by Brooks-Cole) Thomson Learn.

Levenback, Charles, jt. auth. see Eifel, Patricia J.

Levenback, Karen L. Virginia Woolf & the Great War. LC 98-27678. 1998. 34.95 (*0-8156-0546-3*) Syracuse U Pr.

Levenberg, Haim. Military Preparations of the Arab Community in Palestine, 1945-1948. LC 92-18785. 281p. 1993. text 52.50 (*0-7146-3439-5*, Pub. by F Cass Pubs) Intl Spec Bk.

Levenberg, Juri. Russian Wristwatches: Pocket Watches, Stop Watches, Onboard Clock & Chronometers. Hechl, Gertraud, tr. LC 95-34594. (Illus.). 96p. 1995. pap. 19.95 (*0-88740-873-7*) Schiffer.

Levenberg, N., et al. The Metric Induced by the Robin Function. LC 91-13768. (Memoirs Ser.: No. 448). 156p. 1991. pap. 25.00 (*0-8218-2520-8*, MEMO/92/448) Am Math.

Levenberg, Patricia B., et al. Guidelines for Adolescent Preventive Services (gaps) Clinical Evaluation & Management Handbook. LC 98-147764. 152 p. 1995. write for info. (*0-89970-745-9*) AMA.

Levenberg, S. The Enigma of Soviet Jewry, Historical Background By. 687p. (C). 1995. 75.00 (*1-870360-15-X*) St Mut.

Levenburg, Nancy M. Production-Operations Management Curricula: Thoughts from Practitioners & Professors. (E & R Foundation Research Papers). 38p. (Orig.). 1996. pap. 25.00 (*1-55822-156-5*) Am Prod & Inventory.

Levenda, Peter. Unholy Alliance: A History of Nazi Involvement with the Occult. LC 95-94487. 393p. (Orig.). 1995. mass mkt. 6.99 (*0-380-77722-3*, Avon Bks) Morrow Avon.

Levendel, Isaac. Not the Germans Alone: A Son's Search for the Truth of Vichy. LC 99-19628. 280p. 1999. 25.95 (*0-8101-1663-4*) Northwestern U Pr.

***Levendel, Isaac.** Not the Germans Alone: A Son's Search for the Truth of Vichy. 2000. pap. 15.95 (*0-8101-1843-2*) Northwestern U Pr.

Levendorskii, Serge. Asymptotic Distribution of Eigenvalues of Differential Operators. (C). 1990. text 226.50 (*0-7923-0539-6*) Kluwer Academic.

— Degenerate Elliptic Equations. LC 93-13188. (Mathematics & Its Applications Ser.: Vol. 258). 460p. (C). 1993. text 285.50 (*0-7923-2305-X*) Kluwer Academic.

Levendosky, Charles. Circle of Light. 74p. (Orig.). 1995. pap. 9.95 (*0-931271-32-0*) Hi Plains Pr.

Levendusk, Christine, ed. see Rowson, Susanna Haswell.

Levenduski, Cristine. Peculiar Power: A Quaker Woman Preacher in 18th-Century America. LC 95-48862. 208p. 1996. text 36.95 (*1-56098-670-0*) Smithsonian.

Levene. Color Atlas of Hair & Nail Diagnosis. (Illus.). 1991. write for info. (*0-8151-5437-2*) Mosby Inc.

Levene, Rebecca & Winstone, Simon. Where Angels Fear. mass mkt. 6.95 (*0-426-20530-8*) London Brdge.

Levene, Bruce. 1995 Market Scope: The Desktop Guide to Supermarket Share & Category Sales. Toth, Adrienne et al, eds. (Illus.). 940p. 1995. pap. 299.00 (*0-911790-28-4*) Trade Dimensns.

Levene, Bruce, ed. James Dean in Mendocino: The Making of the Movie East of Eden. (Illus.). 64p. (Orig.). 1994. pap. 12.95 (*0-933391-13-7*) Pac Transcript.

— Mendocino & the Movies: Hollywood & Television Motion Pictures Filmed on the Mendocino Coast. (Illus.). 144p. 1998. pap. 18.95 (*0-933391-14-5*) Pac Transcript.

Levene, Clara M., jt. auth. see Schuchardt, Charles.

Levene, D. S. Religion in Livy. LC 93-11077. (Mnemosyne Ser.: Supplement 127). xii, 260p. 1993. 99.00 (*90-04-09617-5*) Brill Academic Pubs.

Levene, Donald L., ed. Chest Pain: An Integrated Diagnostic Approach. LC 77-8297. 222p. reprint ed. pap. 68.90 (*0-608-17765-2*, 205651700069) Bks Demand.

Levene, Donna B. Music Through Children's Literature: Theme & Variations. (Illus.). viii, 117p. (Orig.). 1993. pap. text 22.50 (*1-56308-021-4*) Teacher Ideas Pr.

Levene, G. M. & Goolamali, S. K. Diagnostic Picture Tests in Dermatology. (Illus.). 128p. (C). 1986. text. write for info. (*0-8151-5407-0*, 09893) Mosby Inc.

Levene, John R., ed. see International Symposium on Visual Science Staff.

Levene, M. The Nested Universal Relation Database Model. Goos, G. & Hartmanis, J., eds. LC 92-10727. (Lecture Notes in Computer Science Ser.: Vol. 595). x, 177p. 1992. pap. 31.00 (*0-685-59405-X*) Spr-Verlag.

Levene, Malcolm I., et al, eds. Fetal & Neonatal Neurology & Neurosurgery. (Illus.). 640p. 1988. text 180.00 (*0-443-03713-2*) Church.

— Fetal & Neonatal Neurology & Neurosurgery. 2nd ed. LC 94-24322. 1995. text 199.00 (*0-443-04910-6*) Church.

***Levene, Malcolm I. & Rudolf, Mary C. J.** Paediatrics & Child Health. LC 98-24257. (Illus.). 10p. 1999. pap. 54.95 (*0-86542-957-X*) Blackwell Sci.

Levene, Malcolm I. & Tudehope, David. Essential of Neonatal Medicine. 2nd ed. LC 92-49090. (Essentials Ser.). 448p. 1993. pap. 49.95 (*0-632-03558-7*) Blackwell Sci.

***Levene, Malcolm I., et al.** Essentials of Neonatal Medicine. 3rd ed. LC 99-38947. (Illus.). 352p. 2000. pap. 49.95 (*0-632-05163-9*) Blackwell Sci.

Levene, Malcolm I., et al. Ultrasound of the Infant Brain. (Clinics in Developmental Medicine Ser.: No. 92). (Illus.). 148p. (C). 1991. text 39.95 (*0-521-41212-9*, Pub. by Mc Keith Pr) Cambridge U Pr.

Levene, Mark. A Guided Tour of Relational Databases & Beyond. LC 98-46727. xiv, 634p. 1999. pap. 59.95 (*1-85233-008-2*) Spr-Verlag.

— War, Jews, & the New Europe: The Diplomacy of Lucien Wolf, 1914-1919. (Littman Library of Jewish Civilization). (Illus.). 346p. 1992. 45.00 (*0-19-710072-4*) Intl Spec Bk.

Levene, Mark & Roberts, Penny, eds. The Massacre in History. LC 97-38276. (Illus.). 320p. 1998. pap. 25.00 (*1-57181-935-5*) Berghahn Bks.

— The Massacre in History. LC 97-38276. (Illus.). 320p. 1999. 65.00 (*1-57181-934-7*) Berghahn Bks.

Levene, Nancy. Cherry Cola Champions. LC 88-12294. (Alex Ser.). (Illus.). 120p. (J). (gr. 3-7). 1988. pap. 4.99 (*1-55513-519-6*, Chariot Bks) Chariot Victor.

— French Fry Forgiveness. LC 87-5268. 120p. (J). (gr. 3-6). 1987. pap. 4.99 (*1-55513-302-9*, Chariot Bks) Chariot Victor.

— Peach Pit Popularity. LC 89-33900. (Illus.). 128p. (J). (gr. 2-5). 1994. pap. 4.99 (*1-55513-529-3*, Chariot Bks) Chariot Victor.

— Peanut Butter & Jelly Secrets. LC 87-5247. 128p. (J). (gr. 3-6). 1987. pap. 4.99 (*1-55513-303-7*, Chariot Bks) Chariot Victor.

— Salty Scarecrow Solution. LC 89-31274. 128p. (J). (gr. 3-6). 1989. pap. 4.99 (*1-55513-523-4*, Chariot Bks) Chariot Victor.

— Shoelaces & Brussel Sprouts. LC 87-5267. 120p. (J). (gr. 3-6). 1994. pap. 4.99 (*1-55513-301-0*, Chariot Bks) Chariot Victor.

— T-Bone Trouble. LC 90-32906. 128p. (J). (gr. 3-6). 1990. pap. 4.99 (*1-55513-765-2*, Chariot Bks) Chariot Victor.

Levene, Nancy Simpson. Cherry Cola Champions, 6. LC 88-12294. (The Alex Ser.). (Illus.). 128p. (J). (gr. 2-5). 1999. pap. text 4.99 (*0-7814-3372-X*) Chariot Victor.

Levene, Nancy S. Alex's Triple Treat. 384p. (J). (gr. 3-7). 1996. pap. 7.99 (*0-7814-0303-0*) Chariot Victor.

— Chocolate Chips & Trumpet Tricks. Reck, Sue, ed. LC 93-36195. 192p. (J). (gr. 3-6). 1994. pap. 5.99 (*0-7814-0103-8*) Chariot Victor.

— Crocodile Meatloaf. LC 92-32615. 128p. (J). (ps-6). 1994. pap. 4.99 (*0-7814-0000-7*, Chariot Bks) Chariot Victor.

— The Fastest Car in the County. LC 91-33539. Vol. 2. 96p. (J). (gr. 4-7). 1992. pap. 4.99 (*1-55513-395-9*, Chariot Bks) Chariot Victor.

— Grapefruit Basket Upset. Reck, Sue, ed. LC 91-9359. 128p. (J). (gr. 3-6). 1991. pap. 4.99 (*1-55513-768-7*, Chariot Bks) Chariot Victor.

— Hero for a Season. Reck, Sue, ed. LC 93-21126. (T. J. Ser.: Vol. 4). (Illus.). 96p. (J). (gr. 2-5). 1994. pap. 4.99 (*0-7814-0702-8*) Chariot Victor.

— Mint Cookie Miracles. LC 88-11902. (Alex Ser.). 120p. (J). (gr. 3-7). 1988. pap. 4.99 (*1-55513-514-5*, Chariot Bks) Chariot Victor.

— The Pet That Never Was. LC 91-33518. Vol. 1. 96p. (J). (gr. 5-7). 1992. pap. 4.99 (*1-55513-394-0*, Chariot Bks) Chariot Victor.

— Trouble in the Deep End. LC 93-16602. (T. J. Ser.). 96p. (J). 1993. pap. 4.99 (*0-7814-0701-X*, Chariot Bks) Chariot Victor.

Levene, Peter. How to Start & Run Your Own Shop. 2nd ed. 192p. (C). 1988. pap. text 17.50 (*1-85333-033-7*, Pub. by Graham & Trotman); lib. bdg. 36.00 (*1-85333-107-4*, Pub. by Graham & Trotman) G & T Inc.

— The Shopkeeper's Handbook. (C). 1989. pap. text 18.50 (*1-85333-171-6*, Pub. by Graham & Trotman); lib. bdg. 39.00 (*1-85333-170-8*, Pub. by Graham & Trotman) Kluwer Academic.

Levene, Philip & Sergel, Sherman L. The Christmas Miser. 69p. 1965. pap. 3.50 (*0-87129-988-7*, C49) Dramatic Pub.

Levene, Simon. Causes of Action. 296p. 1997. pap. 61.50 (*1-85811-070-X*, Pub. by CLT Prof) Gaunt.

— Heads of Damage. 180p. 1996. pap. 53.00 (*1-85811-069-6*, Pub. by CLT Prof) Gaunt.

— Heads of Damage. 2nd ed. 256p. 1998. pap. 61.50 (*1-85811-178-1*, Pub. by CLT Prof) Gaunt.

Levene, Simon, jt. auth. see Rodway, Susan.

Levenfish, Gregory. Moscow International Chess Tournament, 1936. Adams, Jimmy, tr. from RUS. (Tournament Bk.). (Illus.). 245p. 1988. 34.00 (*0-939433-08-7*) Caissa Edit.

Levenhagen, John I. HVAC Control System Diagrams. LC 98-34733. (Illus.). 438p. 1998. 79.00 (*0-07-038129-1*) McGraw.

— HVAC Controls & Systems. 334p. 1993. 49.00 (*0-07-037509-7*) McGraw.

***Levenkron.** Cutting: Understanding & Overcoming Self-Mutilation. LC 98-10274. 269p. 1999. pap. 14.00 (*0-393-31938-5*) Norton.

Levenkron, Steven. Anatomy of Anorexia. LC 99-39958. 288p. 2000. text 24.95 (*0-393-04835-7*) Norton.

Levenkron, Steven. The Anatomy of Anorexia. pap. 14.95 (*0-393-32101-0*) Norton.

Levenkron, Steven. The Best Little Girl in the World. 1979. 10.09 (*0-606-01011-4*, Pub. by Turtleback) Demco.

— The Best Little Girl in the World. 256p. 1989. mass mkt. 6.99 (*0-446-35865-7*, Pub. by Warner Bks) Little.

— Cutting: Understanding & Overcoming Self-Mutilation. LC 98-10274. 256p. 1998. 25.00 (*0-393-02741-4*) Norton.

— The Luckiest Girl in the World. LC 96-44353. 192p. 1998. pap. 9.95 (*0-14-026625-9*) Viking Penguin.

— Obsessive-Compulsive Disorders: Treating & Understanding Crippling Habits. 1992. mass mkt. 14.99 (*0-446-39348-7*, Pub. by Warner Bks) Little.

— Treating & Overcoming Anorexia Nervosa. 240p. 1988. mass mkt. 5.99 (*0-446-34416-8*, Pub. by Warner Bks) Little.

Levenok, O. Fetal Monitoring. (C). Date not set. 45.00 (*0-8385-2571-7*) Appleton & Lange.

Levens. Problems in Mechanical Drawing. 6th ed. 1985. 45.66 (*0-07-037471-6*) McGraw.

Levens, A. S. & Cooper, S. J. Problems in Mechanical Drawing. 6th ed. (Illus.). 224p. (C). 1985. write for info. (*0-07-022334-3*) McGraw.

An Asterisk (*) at the beginning of an entry indicates that the title is appearing for the first time.

Levens, A. S. & Edstrom, A. E. Problems in Mechanical Drawing. 4th ed. 1974. text 23.16 (*0-07-037349-3*) McGraw.

Levens, Ann, jt. auth. see Renshaw, Polly.

Levens, Mary. Magical Control of the Body: The Treatment of Eating Disorders Through Art Therapy. LC 94-23957. (Illus.). 160p. (C). 1995. 65.00 (*0-415-12216-3*, C0393) Routledge.

— Magical Control of the Body: The Treatment of Eating Disorders Through Art Therapy. LC 94-23957. (Illus.). 160p. (C). (gr. 13). 1995. pap. 24.99 (*0-415-12217-1*, RC552) Routledge.

Levens, Peter. Manipulus Vocabulorum. (Camden Society, London. Publications, First Ser.: No. 95). reprint ed. 90.00 (*0-404-50195-8*) AMS Pr.

— Manipulus Vocabulorum: Rhyming Dictionary of the English Language. (EETS, OS Ser.: No. 27). 1969. reprint ed. 63.00 (*0-527-00027-2*) Periodicals Srv.

Levens, R. G., ed. A Book of Latin Letters. (Classical Texts Ser.). 196p. 1989. pap. 13.95 (*0-631-13867-6*) Blackwell Pubs.

— Cicero: Verrine V. (Bristol Latin Texts Ser.). (LAT.). 256p. 1980. reprint ed. 22.95 (*0-906515-74-2*, Pub. by Brist Class Pr) Focus Pub-R Pullins.

Levensohn, Lotta, tr. see Herzl, Theodor.

***Levenson, Alan.** Modern Jewish Thinkers: An Introduction. LC 99-41430. 300p. 2000. 25.00 (*0-7657-6121-1*) Aronson.

Levenson, Alvin J. & Hall, Richard C., eds. Neuropsychiatric Manifestations of Physical Disease in the Elderly. LC 79-5420. (Aging Ser.: Vol. 14). 168p. 1981. reprint ed. pap. 52.10 (*0-608-00417-0*, 206113200007) Bks Demand.

Levenson, Ana & Eggly, Susan. Gramatica Espanola para Estudiantes de Ingles. Morton, Jacqueline, ed. (SPA.). 208p. 1993. pap. text 12.95 (*0-934034-17-6*) Olivia & Hill.

Levenson, Barry. Exciting Concepts for Blues Guitar Soloing. Gordon, Andrew D., ed. (Illus.). 1994. 22.95 incl. cd-rom (*1-882146-32-8*) A D G Prods.

Levenson, Carl. Socrates among the Corybantes: Dionysian Spirituality & the Philosophy of Plato. LC 99-41161. 174p. 2000. pap. 17.50 (*0-88214-226-7*, Pub. by Spring Pubns) Continuum.

Levenson, Carl, jt. ed. see Westphal, Jonathan.

Levenson, Christopher. Arriving at Night. 80p. 1995. pap. 8.95 (*0-88962-341-4*) Mosaic.

Levenson, Christopher, tr. see Bauer, Wolfgang.

Levenson, Claire B. Temple Israel of Tallahassee, Florida, 1937-1987. (Illus.). 96p. 1987. text 6.95 (*0-9616000-1-2*) Peninsular Pub Co.

Levenson, Claude B. The Dalai Lama: A Biography. 320p. 2000. text 29.95 (*0-19-565017-4*) OUP.

— Symbols of Tibetan Buddhism. 1997. 40.00 (*2-908228-86-6*, Pub. by Assouline) Rizzoli Intl.

Levenson, David. Julian & Jerusalem: The Sources & the Tradition. (Series in Jewish Studies: No. 15). 250p. 1998. 87.50 (*90-04-10167-5*) Brill Academic Pubs.

Levenson, Dorothy. Mind & Body: A History of the American Psychosomatic Society. LC 94-5786. 1994. write for info. (*0-683-05840-1*) Lppncott W & W.

Levenson, Edgar A. The Purloined Self: Interpersonal Perspective in Psychoanalysis. 266p. 1991. 30.95 (*0-9629993-0-X*); pap. 24.95 (*0-9629993-1-8*) Contemp Psycho.

Levenson, Edie & Rosenkranz, John. Golf Obsession Register. (Illus.). 128p. (Orig.). 1995. pap. 12.95 (*1-887765-95-6*) That Reminds Me.

Levenson, Edie, jt. auth. see Rosenkranz, John.

Levenson, Elaine. Teaching Children about Life & Earth Science: Ideas & Activities Every Teacher & Parent Can Use. LC 93-40784. (Illus.). 256p. (J). (gr. k-3). 1994. pap. 19.95 (*0-07-037655-7*) McGraw.

— Teaching Children about Science: Ideas & Activities Every Teacher & Parent Can Use. LC 93-34326. (Illus.). 256p. (J). (gr. k-3). 1994. pap. 19.95 (*0-07-037619-0*) McGraw-Hill Prof.

— Teaching Children about Science Ideas & Activities Teachers & Parents Can Use. 2nd ed. 1993. pap. text 19.95 (*0-8306-4598-5*) TAB Bks.

Levenson, Eleanore, jt. auth. see Goldberg, Louis P.

Levenson-Estrada, Deborah. Trade Unionists Against Terror: Guatemala City, 1954-1985. LC 93-32054. (Illus.). 310p. (C). 1994. text 59.95 (*0-8078-2131-4*); pap. text 19.95 (*0-8078-4440-3*) U of NC Pr.

Levenson, George. Pumpkin Circle: The Story of a Garden. LC 99-20081. (Illus.). 40p. (J). (gr. k-3). 1999. 14.95 (*1-58246-004-3*) Tricycle Pr.

Levenson, Hanna. Time-Limited Dynamic Psychotherapy: A Guide to Clinical Practice. LC 95-13934. 256p. 1995. 37.00 (*0-465-08651-9*, Pub. by Basic) HarpC.

Levenson, Hanna, et al. Concise Guide to Brief Dynamic Psychotherapy. (Concise Guides/American Psychiatric Press Ser.). 224p. 1997. pap. text 22.95 (*0-88048-346-6*, 8346) Am Psychiatric.

Levenson, Harvey R. Complete Dictionary of Graphic Arts & Desktop Publishing Terminology: With Overview of Industry Growth & Technology. (Illus.). 276p. (Orig.). 1994. pap. 19.95 (*0-932423-09-4*) Summa Bks.

Levenson, Harvey R. & Kinsey, Thomas D. Graphic Arts & Desktop Publishing Pocket Dictionary. (Illus.). 256p. (Orig.). 1995. 9.95 (*0-932423-10-8*) Summa Bks.

***Levenson, Harvey Robert.** Understanding Graphic Communication: Selected Reading. LC 99-64459. 264p. (C). 2000. 75.00 (*0-88362-227-0*) GATFPress.

Levenson, Howard. The Price of Justice, No. AJ3. 87p. (C). 1981. pap. 30.00 (*0-900137-17-7*, Pub. by NCCL) St Mut.

Levenson, J. C., ed. see Adams, Henry (Brooks).

Levenson, J. C., ed. see Crane, Stephen.

***Levenson, James B.** Depression. (Key Diseases Series). 340p. 2000. pap. text 35.00 (*0-943126-85-1*, 330300790) Amer Coll Phys.

Levenson, Jay. Circa, 1492: Art in the Age of Exploration. LC 91-50590. (Illus.). 512p. (C). 1991. 30.00 (*0-300-05167-0*) Yale U Pr.

Levenson, Jay, ed. The Age of the Baroque in Portugal. (Illus.). 256p. 1993. 65.00 (*0-300-05841-1*) Yale U Pr.

Levenson, Jay A., ed. The Age of Baroque in Portugal. LC 93-5424. 303p. 1994. pap. 25.00 (*0-89468-198-2*) Natl Gallery Art.

***Levenson, Jill, et al, eds.** Romeo & Juliet 1597. (Malone Society Reprints Ser.: Vol. 163). 94p. 2000. text 45.00 (*0-19-729039-6*) OUP.

Levenson, Jill L., ed. see Shakespeare, William.

***Levenson, Jill S. & Morin, John W.** Treating Non-Offending Parents in Child Sexual Abuse Cases: Connections for Family Safety. LC 00-9511. 2000. write for info. (*0-7619-2192-3*) Sage Pub.

Levenson, Jill S., jt. auth. see Morin, John W.

Levenson, John R. & Pope-Levenson, Priscilla, eds. Return to Babel: Global Perspectives on the Bible. LC 98-49512. 216p. 1999. pap. 19.00 (*0-664-25823-9*) Westminster John Knox.

Levenson, Jon D. Creation & the Persistence of Evil: The Jewish Prama of Divine Omnipotence. LC 94-31950. 200p. 1994. pap. text 15.95 (*0-691-02950-4*, Pub. by Princeton U Pr) Cal Prin Full Svc.

— Death & Resurrection of the Beloved Son: The Transformation of Child Sacrifice in Judaism. 1995. pap. 16.00 (*0-300-06511-6*) Yale U Pr.

— Esther: A Commentary. LC 96-43247. (Old Testament Library). 152p. 1997. 22.00 (*0-664-22093-2*) Westminster John Knox.

— Sinai & Zion: An Entry into the Jewish Bible. 240p. (Orig.). 1987. pap. 15.00 (*0-06-254828-X*, Pub. by Harper SF) HarpC.

— Theology of the Program of Restoration of Ezekiel 40-48. LC 76-3769. (Harvard Semitic Monographs: No. 10). 186p. reprint ed. pap. 57.70 (*0-7837-5416-7*, 204518000005) Bks Demand.

Levenson, Jon D., jt. ed. see Halpern, Baruch.

Levenson, Jordan. How to Buy & Understand Refracting Telescopes. 3rd ed. LC 90-26742. (Illus.). 192p. (Orig.). 1991. 43.50 (*0-914442-13-9*) Levenson Pr.

— University Degree, Fellow, & Honours Abbreviations Listed Alphabetically, & Their Meanings, As Used by Authors, Writers, & Other Persons after Their Names, in England, Scotland, Wales, Northern Ireland, & the Republic of Ireland: Plus Five Articles by the Author on Other Subjects, LC 98-21333. (Illus.). 44p. 1998. 44.95 (*0-914442-14-7*) Levenson Pr.

— Your First Trip to Europe: Where, What & How, Vol. 1. LC 84-82461. 110p. 1985. pap. 18.50 (*0-914442-11-2*) Levenson Pr.

Levenson, Joseph R. Revolution & Cosmopolitanism: The Western Stage & the Chinese Stages. LC 73-121188. 196p. reprint ed. pap. 60.80 (*0-7837-4833-7*, 204448000003) Bks Demand.

Levenson, Laurie L. Criminal Law. LC 97-16998. 464p. 1997. pap. text 21.95 (*1-56706-459-0*) Aspen Law.

— West's California Criminal Procedure. LC 95-24212. (West's Criminal Law Ser.). 1400p. (C). 1995. text. write for info. (*0-314-07049-4*) West Pub.

Levenson, Leah & Natterstad, Jerry. Granville Hicks: The Intellectual in Mass Society. LC 93-16145. (Critical Perspectives on the Past Ser.). (Illus.). 336p. 1993. 49.95 (*1-56639-104-0*) Temple U Pr.

Levenson, Leah & Natterstad, Jerry H. Hanna Sheehy-Skeffington, Irish Feminist. LC 85-26223. (Irish Studies). (Illus.). 240p. 1986. reprint ed. pap. 74.40 (*0-608-06988-4*, 206719600009) Bks Demand.

Levenson, Lester. Keys to the Ultimate Freedom: Thoughts & Talks on Personal Transformation. 395p. (Orig.). 1993. pap. 17.97 (*0-915721-03-1*) Sedona Inst.

Levenson, M. D., et al, eds. Resonances: A Volume in Honor of Professor N. Bloembergen on His 70th Birthday. 512p. (C). 1990. text 99.00 (*981-02-0377-2*); pap. text 48.00 (*981-02-0378-0*) World Scientific Pub.

Levenson, Marc D., jt. ed. see Yen, W. M.

Levenson, Marcia, tr. see Krupnik, Igor I.

Levenson, Michael. A Genealogy of Modernism: A Study of English Literary Doctrine 1908-1922. 264p. 1986. pap. text 22.95 (*0-521-33800-X*) Cambridge U Pr.

Levenson, Michael, ed. The Cambridge Companion to Modernism. (Cambridge Companions to Literature Ser.). (Illus.). 272p. (C). 1999. text 54.95 (*0-521-49516-4*); pap. text 19.95 (*0-521-49866-X*) Cambridge U Pr.

Levenson, Michael H., jt. auth. see Chase, Karen.

Levenson, Milton, jt. auth. see National Research Council Staff.

Levenson, Rosaline. Contractural Services in Government: Selected Bibliography on Practice in Federal, State & Local Agencies, Education in Foreign Countries, No. 980. 1976. 6.00 (*0-686-20386-0*, Sage Prdcls Pr) Sage.

— The Short-Lived Exploration of Isadore Meyerowitz. LC 94-77679. (Illus.). 80p. (Orig.). 1994. pap. 9.95 (*0-936029-35-8*) Western Bk Journ.

Levenson, Rustin S., jt. auth. see Kirsh, Andrea.

Levenson, Steven A., ed. Medical Direction in Long-Term Care: A Guidebook for the Future. 2nd ed. LC 93-72380. 694p. 1993. 65.00 (*0-89089-547-3*) Carolina Acad Pr.

Levenson, Thomas. Measure for Measure: A Musical History of Science. LC 97-19859. 1997. write for info. (*0-19-288049-7*) OUP.

Levenson, William B. & Stasheff, Edward. Teaching Through Radio & Television. rev. ed. LC 72-92303. 560p. 1969. reprint ed. lib. bdg. 38.50 (*0-8371-2414-X*, LERT, Greenwood Pr) Greenwood.

Levenspiel, O. Engineering Flow & Heat Exchange. rev. ed. LC 97-17294. (Chemical Engineering Ser.). (Illus.). 380p. (C). 1998. text 89.50 (*0-306-45682-6*, Kluwer Plenum) Kluwer Academic.

Levenspiel, Octave. Chemical Reaction Engineering. 3rd ed. LC 97-46872. 688p. 1998. text 106.95 (*0-471-25424-X*) Wiley.

— Chemical Reactor Omnibook. pap. 30.00 (*0-88246-170-2*) Oreg St U Bkstrs.

Levenspiel, Octave & Kunii, Daizo. Fluidization Engineering. 2nd ed. (Chemical Engineering Ser.). 491p. 1991. text 199.00 (*0-409-90233-0*) Buttrwrth-Heinemann.

Levenstein, Aaron. Escape to Freedom: The Story of the International Rescue Committee, 2. LC 82-21078. (Studies in Freedom: No. 2). (Illus.). 339p. 1983. 55.00 (*0-313-23815-4*, LSC/, Greenwood Pr) Greenwood.

Levenstein, Adolf. Die Arbeiterfrage: The Labor Question: with Particular Consideration of the Social Psychological Side of Modern Large-Scale Industry & Its Psycho-Physical Effect on Workers. LC 74-25767. (European Sociology Ser.). 410p. 1975. reprint ed. 34.95 (*0-405-06521-3*) Ayer.

Levenstein, Charles & Wooding, John. Work, Health & Environment: Old Problems, New Solutions. LC 97-17255. (Democracy & Ecology Ser.). 536p. 1997. pap. text 26.95 (*1-57230-234-8*) Guilford Pubns.

Levenstein, Charles & Wooding, John. Work, Health & Environment: Old Problems, New Solutions. LC 97-17255. (Democracy & Ecology Ser.). 536p. 1997. lib. bdg. 44.95 (*1-57230-233-X*, -0233) Guilford Pubns.

Levenstein, Charles, jt. auth. see Wooding, John.

Levenstein, Harvey A. Communism, Anticommunism, & the CIO, 91. LC 80-787. (Contributions in American History Ser.: No. 91). 364p. 1981. 59.95 (*0-313-22072-7*, LEC/, Greenwood Pr) Greenwood.

— Labor Organization in the United States & Mexico: A History of Their Relations, 13. LC 79-133498. 258p. 1971. 59.95 (*0-8371-5151-1*, LLO/, Greenwood Pr) Greenwood.

— Paradox of Plenty: A Social History of Eating in Modern America. (Illus.). 368p. 1994. reprint ed. pap. 12.95 (*0-19-508918-9*) OUP.

— Revolution at the Table: The Transformation of the American Diet. (Illus.). 292p. 1988. text 30.00 (*0-19-504365-0*) OUP.

***Levenstein, Harvey A.** Seductive Journey, Vol. 2. 1998. 25.00 (*0-226-47378-3*) U Ch Pr.

— Seductive Journey: American Tourists in France from Jefferson to the Jazz Age. LC 97-49389. (Illus.). 432p. 1998. 30.00 (*0-226-47376-7*) U Ch Pr.

***Levenstein, Harvey A.** Seductive Journey: American Tourists in France from Jefferson to the Jazz Age. (Illus.). 2000. pap. 17.00 (*0-226-47377-5*) U Ch Pr.

Levenstein, Margaret. Accounting for Growth: Information Systems & the Creation of the Large Corporation. LC 97-39376. 1998. 49.50 (*0-8047-3003-2*) Stanford U Pr.

Levenston, Eddie, tr. see Hoffmann, Yoel.

Levenston, Edward A. & Sivan, Reuven. The New Bantam-Megiddo Hebrew Dictionary. (HEB.). 736p. 1984. mass mkt. 6.99 (*0-553-26387-0*) Bantam.

Leventhal, Debra. What Is Your Language? (Picture Puffin Ser.). (J). 1998. 11.19 (*0-606-13901-X*, Pub. by Turtleback) Demco.

— What Is Your Language? 32p. (J). (ps-1). 1998. pap. 5.99 (*0-14-056315-6*) Viking Penguin.

Leventhal, F. M., ed. Twentieth-Century Britain: An Encyclopedia. LC 95-30749. (Illus.). 944p. 1995. text 95.00 (*0-8240-7205-7*, H1378) Garland.

***Leventhal, F. M. & Quinault, Roland E.** Anglo-American Attitudes: From Revolution to Partnership. LC 00-38982. 2000. pap. write for info. (*0-7546-0030-0*) Ashgate Pub Co.

Leventhal, F. M., jt. auth. see Behlmer, George K.

Leventhal, Jean H. Echoes in the Text: Musical Citation in German Narratives from Theodor Fontane to Martin Walser. (Studies in Modern German Literature: Vol. 64). 260p. (C). 1995. text 51.95 (*0-8204-2372-6*) P Lang Pubng.

***Leventhal, Josh.** The Beer Lover's Companion: A Guide to Producing, Brewing, Tasting, Rating & Drinking Around the World. LC 98-50119. (Essential Connoisseur Ser.: Vol. 7). (Illus.). 192p. 1999. pap. 10.98 (*1-57912-062-8*) Blck Dog & Leventhal.

— Take Me Out to the Ballpark: An Illustrated Guide to Baseball Parks Past & Present. (Illus.). 128p. 2000. 29.98 (*1-57912-112-8*) Blck Dog & Leventhal.

— Tugs: The World's Hardest Working Boats. LC 99-40545. (Illus.). 112p. 1999. 24.98 (*1-57912-085-7*) Blck Dog & Leventhal.

Leventhal, Judith, jt. auth. see Halberstam, Yitta.

Leventhal, Judith, jt. auth. see Halbertstam, Yitta H.

Leventhal, Lance A. Assembly Language Subroutines for the 6809. 1989. text 26.95 (*0-07-707152-2*) McGraw.

— Assembly Language Subroutines for the 8086. 1989. text 26.95 (*0-07-707151-4*) McGraw.

— Microcomputer Experimentation with the IBM PC. (Oxford Series in Electrical & Computer Engineering). (Illus.). 464p. (C). 1995. pap. text 44.00 (*0-03-009542-5*) OUP.

— Microcomputer Experimentation with the MOS Technology KIM-1. (Illus.). 480p. (C). 1982. pap. text 41.00 (*0-13-580779-4*) P-H.

— Microcomputer Experimentation with the Motorola MC6800ECB. 368p. (C). 1988. write for info. (*0-03-211783-3*) SCP.

— Microcomputer Experimentation with the Synertek SYM-1. (Illus.). 512p. (C). 1983. text 37.00 (*0-13-580910-X*) P-H.

— Turbo C. Quickstart. LC 91-53069. (Lance A. Leventhal Microtrend Ser.). 375p. (Orig.). 1992. pap. 29.95 (*0-915391-67-8*) Slawson Comm.

Leventhal, Lance A., ed. UNIX User's Handbook. LC 91-53067. (Lance A. Leventhal Microtrend Ser.). 600p. (Orig.). 1992. pap. 29.95 (*0-915391-47-3*) Slawson Comm.

Leventhal, Lance A., ed. see Antonovich, Michael P.

Leventhal, Lance A., ed. see Antonvich, Michael.

Leventhal, Lance A., ed. see Chambers, Bill.

Leventhal, Lance A., ed. see Del Rossi, Robert.

Leventhal, Lance A., ed. see Heiser, Paul W.

Leventhal, Lance A., ed. see Moss, Julian V.

Leventhal, Lance A., ed. see Occhiogrosso, James J.

Leventhal, Lance A., ed. see Powe, James E.

Leventhal, Lance A., ed. see Powell, James E.

Leventhal, Lance A., ed. see Powell, Jim.

Leventhal, Lance A., ed. see Schmieder, Valerie.

Leventhal, Lance A., ed. see Spence, Rick.

Leventhal, Lance A., ed. see Taylor, Allan G.

Leventhal, Lance A., ed. see Taylor, Billy P.

Leventhal, Lance A., ed. see Teja, Ed & Johnson, Laura.

Leventhal, Lance A., ed. see Thro, Ellen.

Leventhal, Lance A., ed. see Vang, Soren.

Leventhal, Robert S. The Disciplines of Interpretation: Lessing, Herder, Schlegel, & Hermeneutics in Germany 1750-1800. LC 94-19772. No. 5. 362p. (C). 1994. lib. bdg. 98.00 (*3-11-014424-7*) De Gruyter.

Leventhal, Robert S., ed. Reading after Foucault: Institutions, Disciplines, & Technologies of the Self in Germany, 1750-1830. LC 94-16730. (Kritik: German Literary Theory & Cultural Studies). (Illus.). 278p. 1995. text 39.95 (*0-8143-2510-6*) Wayne St U Pr.

Leventhal, Ruth & Cheadle, Russell F. Medical Parasitology: A Self-Instructional Text. 4th ed. LC 95-4649. (Illus.). 178p. (C). 1995. pap. 37.95 (*0-8036-0041-0*) Davis Co.

Leventhal, Ruth & Shoop, Diane. Closing the Male-Female Earnings Gap in Pennsylvania. 16p. (Orig.). 1994. pap. text 15.00 (*0-939667-29-0*, SDC1P2-94) Penn State Data Ctr.

Leventhal, Stan. Barbie in Bondage. (Orig.). 1996. mass mkt. 6.95 (*1-56333-415-1*, Hard Candy) Masquerade.

— Skydiving on Christopher Street. (Orig.). 1995. mass mkt. 6.95 (*1-56333-287-6*, Hard Candy) Masquerade.

Leventhal, Steven. Saving Your Qualified Plans: IRS Employee Plans Administrative Enforcement. 300p. 1998. text 89.00 (*0-8080-0276-7*) CCH INC.

— Working with Tax-Sheltered Annuities: 403(b) Plans Explained. LC 98-123535. 368p. 1997. 69.00 (*0-8080-0194-9*, 5490) CCH INC.

Leventhal, Willy S., ed. The Children Coming On... A Retrospective of the Montgomery Bus Boycott. 4th ed. LC 97-6989. 256p. 1999. pap. text 21.95 (*1-881320-83-9*, Black Belt) Black Belt Communs.

Leventman, Seymour, jt. ed. see Figley, Charles R.

Leveque, Ch., et al. Biologie et Ecologie des Poissons d'Eau Douce Africains (Biology & Ecology of African Freshwater Fishes) (ENG & FRE.). 512p. 1988. pap. 40.00 (*2-7099-0929-4*, Pub. by LInstitut Francais) Balogh.

Leveque, Ch., jt. auth. see Durand, J. R.

Leveque, Christian. Biodiversity Dynamics & Conservation: The Freshwater Fish of Tropical Africa. (Illus.). 451p. (C). 1997. text 85.00 (*0-521-57033-6*) Cambridge U Pr.

Leveque, Francois, ed. Environmental Policy in Europe: Industry, Competition, & the Policy Process. LC 96-600. (Illus.). 232p. 1996. 90.00 (*1-85898-466-1*) E Elgar.

***Leveque, Georges & Valery, Marie-Francoise.** French Garden Style. 240p. 1999. 35.00 (*0-7112-1061-6*, Pub. by F Lincoln) Antique Collect.

Leveque, H. Dictionnaire Thematique Francais-Argot. (FRE.). 1991. 49.95 (*0-685-48813-6*, F83770) Fr & Eur.

— Thematic French-Argot Dictionary: Dictionnaire Thematique Francais-Argot. (FRE.). 1991. 49.95 (*0-8288-3914-X*, F83770) Fr & Eur.

Leveque, Jean-Luc, ed. Cutaneous Investigation in Health & Disease: Noninvasive Methods & Instrumentation. (Basic & Clinical Dermatology Ser.: Vol. 1). (Illus.). 464p. 1988. text 210.00 (*0-8247-7967-3*) Dekker.

Leveque, Jean-Luc & Agache, Pierre G. Aging Skin: Properties & Functional Changes. (Basic & Clinical Dermatology Ser.: Vol. 4). (Illus.). 320p. 1992. text 189.00 (*0-8247-8791-9*) Dekker.

Leveque, Joseph D. Manual of Personnel Policies, Procedures & Operations. 2nd ed. LC 93-9305. 512p. (C). 1993. ring bd. 79.95 (*0-13-020231-2*) P-H.

Leveque, Mimi, ed. see Friedman, Florence Dunn, et al.

Leveque, Pierre. The Birth of Greece. (Discoveries Ser.). (Illus.). 176p. 1994. pap. 12.95 (*0-8109-2843-4*, Pub. by Abrams) Time Warner.

Leveque, Pierre, jt. auth. see Vidal-Naquet, Pierre.

LeVeque, Randall J. Numerical Methods for Conservation Laws. (Lectures in Mathematics ETH Zurich: Vol. 1). 232p. 1990. 24.50 (*0-8176-2464-3*) Birkhauser.

LeVeque, Randall J., et al. Computational Methods for Astrophysical Fluid Flow: Saas-Fee Advances Course 27. Lecture Notes, 1997 Swiss Society for, Vol. 199. LC 98-27205. (Saas-Fee Advances Course Ser.: No. 27). (Illus.). xiv, 520p. 1998. 72.00 (*3-540-64448-2*) Spr-Verlag.

Leveque, William J. Elementary Theory of Numbers. 144p. 1990. pap. 6.95 (*0-486-66348-5*) Dover.

LeVeque, William J. Fundamentals of Number Theory. unabridged ed. (Illus.). 288p. 1996. reprint ed. pap. 8.95 (*0-486-68906-9*) Dover.

LeVeque, William J., ed. Reviews in Number Theory: 1940-72, 6 vols., Set. LC 74-11335. 2931p. 1974. pap. 534.00 (*0-8218-0226-7*, REVNUM) Am Math.

L

— Reviews in Number Theory: 1940-72, 6 vols., Vol. 1. LC 74-11335. 420p. 1974. pap. 123.00 (*0-8218-0203-8*, REVNUM/1) Am Math.

— Reviews in Number Theory: 1940-72, 6 vols., Vol. 2. LC 74-11335. 672p. 1974. pap. 123.00 (*0-8218-0204-6*, REVNUM/2) Am Math.

— Reviews in Number Theory: 1940-72, 6 vols., Vol. 3. LC 74-11335. 377p. 1974. pap. 123.00 (*0-8218-0205-4*, REVNUM/3) Am Math.

— Reviews in Number Theory: 1940-72, 6 vols., Vol. 4. LC 74-11335. 582p. 1974. pap. 123.00 (*0-8218-0206-2*, REVNUM/4) Am Math.

— Reviews in Number Theory: 1940-72, 6 vols., Vol. 5. LC 74-11335. 470p. 1974. pap. 123.00 (*0-8218-0207-0*, REVNUM/5) Am Math.

— Reviews in Number Theory: 1940-72, 6 vols., Vol. 6. LC 74-11335. 410p. 1974. pap. 123.00 (*0-8218-0208-9*, REVNUM/6) Am Math.

LeVeque, William J. & Straus, E. G., eds. Number Theory. LC 70-78057. (Proceedings of Symposia in Pure Mathematics Ser.). 98p. 1970. reprint ed. pap. 34.00 (*0-8218-1412-5*, PSPUM/12) Am Math.

Lever. Gene Therapy, Vol. 51/1. 1995. text 115.00 (*0-443-05333-2*, W B Saunders Co) Harcrt Hlth Sci Grp.

— Industrial Change in U. K. 1987. pap. text. write for info. (*0-582-30141-6*, Pub. by Addison-Wesley) Longman.

— Naturlized Birds of World. 1987. pap. text. write for info. (*0-582-46055-7*, Pub. by Addison-Wesley) Longman.

Lever, A. P., jt. ed. see Solomon, Edward I.

***Lever, Evelyne.** Marie Antoinette: A Biography. Temerson, Catherine, tr. from FRE. (Illus.). 352p. 2000. 30.00 (*0-374-19938-8*) FS&G.

Lever, A. B. Inorganic Electronic Spectroscopy. (Studies in Physical & Theoretical Chemistry: Vol. 33). xvi, 864p. 1984. reprint ed. 279.50 (*0-444-42389-3*, I-314-84) Elsevier.

Lever, A. B., ed. Excited States & Reactive Intermediates: Photochemistry, Photophysics, & Electrochemistry. LC 86-7908. (ACS Symposium Ser.: Vol. 307). 288p. 1986. reprint ed. pap. 89.30 (*0-608-03513-0*, 206423200008) Bks Demand.

— Excited States & Reactive Intermediates Photochemistry, Photophysics, & Eletrochemistry. LC 86-7908. (ACS Symposium Ser.: No. 307). (Illus.). xii, 276p. 1986. 62.95 (*0-8412-0971-5*) Am Chemical.

Lever, A. B. & Gray, H. B., eds. Iron Porphyrins, Vol. 4. 322p. 1989. 105.00 (*0-471-18715-1*) Wiley.

Lever, A. B. & Gray, Harry B., eds. Iron Porphyrins, Pt. 1. (Physical Bioinorganic Chemistry Ser.). 256p. (C). 1982. write for info. (*0-201-05816-2*) Addison-Wesley.

— Iron Porphyrins, Pt. 2. (Physical Bioinorganic Chemistry Ser.). 256p. (C). 1982. write for info. (*0-201-05817-0*) Addison-Wesley.

Lever, A. B. & Leznoff, Clifford C., eds. Phthalocyanines: Properties & Applications, Vol. 1. 448p. 1989. 195.00 (*0-471-18720-8*) Wiley.

— Phthalocyanines: Properties & Applications, Vol. 2. 305p. 1992. 195.00 (*0-471-18828-X*) Wiley.

Lever, A. B. & Leznoff, Clifford C., eds. Phthalocyanines: Properties & Applications, Vol. 3. (Illus.). xi, 303p. 1993. 150.00 (*1-56081-638-4*, Wiley-VCH) Wiley.

Lever, A. B. & Leznoff, Clifford C., eds. Phthalocyanines: Properties & Applications, Vol. 3. 303p. 1993. 195.00 (*0-471-18863-8*) Wiley.

Lever, A. B. & Leznoff, Clifford C., eds. Phthalocyanines: Properties & Applications, Vol. 4. (Illus.). 550p. 1996. 150.00 (*1-56081-916-2*, Wiley-VCH) Wiley.

Lever, A. B. & Leznoff, Clifford C., eds. Phthalocyanines: Properties & Applications, Vol. 4. 524p. 1996. 195.00 (*0-471-18629-5*) Wiley.

Lever, A. B., jt. ed. see Leznoff, Clifford C.

Lever, A. B., jt. ed. see Solomon, Edward I.

Lever, A. M., ed. The Molecular Biology of HIV & AIDS. LC 95-19768. (Molecular Medical Science Ser.). 232p. 1996. 137.95 (*0-471-96094-2*) Wiley.

Lever, A. Phillip, jt. ed. see Leznoff, Clifford C.

Lever, B., ed. see Parker, John L.

***Lever, Charles.** Charles O'Malley, the Irish Dragoon. 252p. 2000. pap. 9.95 (*0-594-00792-5*) Eightn Hundrd.

— If You Can't Climb the Wall, Build a Door! Vol. 1: Principles to Live by When Quitting Is Not an Option. Price, Steve, ed. 168p. 1997. pap. 11.95 (*0-9632667-7-2*) INTI.

— Jack Hinton. 252p. 2000. pap. 9.95 (*0-594-00795-X*) Eightn Hundrd.

— The Knight of Gwynne, Vol. I. 252p. 2000. pap. 9.95 (*0-594-03096-X*) Eightn Hundrd.

— The Knight of Gwynne, Vol. II. 252p. 2000. pap. 9.95 (*0-594-03171-0*) Eightn Hundrd.

— Maurice Tierney. 252p. 2000. pap. 9.95 (*0-594-03101-X*) Eightn Hundrd.

— The O'Donoghue. 252p. 2000. pap. 9.95 (*0-594-00621-X*) Eightn Hundrd.

— Tom Burke of "Ours" 252p. 2000. pap. 9.95 (*0-594-00726-7*) Eightn Hundrd.

Lever, Christopher. The Mandarin Duck. (Natural History Ser.: No. 24). (Illus.). 24p. 1989. pap. 5.25 (*0-7478-0055-3*, Pub. by Shire Pubns) Parkwest Pubns.

— The Naturalized Fishes of the World. (Illus.). 432p. 1996. text 49.95 (*0-12-444745-7*) Acad Pr.

Lever, Darcy. The Young Sea Officer's Sheet Anchor, or a Key to the Leading of Rigging & to Practical Seamanship. 2nd unabridged ed. LC 98-7018. 126p. 1998. pap. 12.95 (*0-486-40220-7*) Dover.

— The Young Sea Officer's Sheet Anchor, or, a Key to the Leading of Rigging, or to Practical Seamanship - With Appendix. 2nd ed. (Illus.). 124p. 1997. reprint ed. lib. bdg. 35.00 (*0-8328-4490-X*) Higginson Bk Co.

***Lever, E. & Lovett, K.** Animals Are Fun!, 4 bks. Incl. Dolphins. Slater, P. LC 99-54138. (Illus.). 16p. (J). (ps up). 1999. lib. bdg. 17.27 (*0-8368-2612-4*); Frogs. Slater, P. LC 99-54135. (Illus.). 16p. (J). (ps up). 1999. lib. bdg. 17.27 (*0-8368-2613-2*); Kangaroos. Slater, P. LC 99-54136. (Illus.). 16p. (J). (ps up). 1999. lib. bdg. 17.27 (*0-8368-2614-0*); Koalas. Slater, S. LC 99-53400. (Illus.). 16p. (J). (ps up). 1999. lib. bdg. 17.27 (*0-8368-2615-9*); (Illus.). 16p. (J). (ps up). 1999. Set lib. bdg. 69.08 (*0-8368-2611-6*) Gareth Stevens Inc.

Lever, J. L. & Boer, H. H., eds. Molluscan Neuro-Endocrinology. (Illus.). 268p. 1983. 32.00 (*0-444-85572-6*, North Holland) Elsevier.

Lever, J. L., jt. auth. see Cosh, J. A.

Lever, J. W., ed. As You Like It. (New Swan Shakespeare Ser.). 1989. pap. 2.95 (*0-582-52725-2*) Longman.

— Sonnets of the English Renaissance. LC 75-305102. (Renaissance Library). 186p. (C). 1974. pap. 22.00 (*0-485-12604-4*, Pub. by Athlone Pr) Humanities.

Lever, J. W., ed. see Shakespeare, William.

Lever, Janet. Soccer Madness. LC 82-13416. 200p. 1993. lib. bdg. 17.50 (*0-226-47382-1*) U Ch Pr.

— Soccer Madness. LC 82-13416. 200p. 1994. pap. text 12.95 (*0-226-47384-8*) U Ch Pr.

— Soccer Madness: Brazil's Passion for the World's Most Popular Sport. rev. ed. (Illus.). 200p. (C). 1995. pap. text 12.50 (*0-88133-843-5*) Waveland Pr.

Lever, Janet, jt. auth. see Schwartz, Pepper.

Lever, Nik. Animation Magic: The Fun Way to Learn Structured Programming Using Visual Basic. LC 97-11046. 480p. (C). 1997. pap. text 44.95 (*0-13-842296-6*) P-H.

Lever, O. W., ed. New Horizons in Carbonyl Chemistry: Reagents for Nucleophilic Acylation. 29p. 1976. pap. 12.75 (*0-08-021334-0*, Pergamon Pr) Elsevier.

Lever, Phillip & Gray, H. B., eds. Iron Porphyrins, Vol. 4, Pt. 3. LC 82-6786. (Physical Bioinorganic Chemistry Ser.). 309p. 1989. 70.00 (*0-89573-718-3*, Wiley-VCH) Wiley.

Lever, Phillip, jt. ed. see Leznoff, Clifford C.

Lever, Richard, et al. Post-Colonial Literatures in English: Australia, 1970-1992. LC 95-44820. (Reference Publication in Literature Ser.). 361p. 1996. 60.00 (*0-8161-7375-3*, G K Hall & Co) Mac Lib Ref.

Lever, Susan. The Oxford Book of Australian Women's Verse. 282p. (C). 1996. pap. text 29.95 (*0-19-553505-7*) OUP.

Lever, Susan & Pratt, Catherine, eds. Henry Handel Richardson: The Getting of Wisdom, Stories, Selected Prose & Correspondence. LC 97-169585. 300p. 1997. pap. 26.95 (*0-7022-2918-0*, Pub. by Univ Queensland Pr) Intl Spec Bk.

Lever, Thomas. Sermons, 1550. Arber, Edward, ed. 143p. 1990. pap. 15.00 (*0-87556-200-0*) Saifer.

Lever, Thomas. Sermons of 1550. pap. 15.00 (*0-87556-649-9*) Saifer.

Lever, W. F., jt. auth. see Daniels, P. W.

Lever, Walter F. & Elder, David E. Lever's Histopathology of the Skin. 8th ed. LC 96-30912. 1104p. 1997. text 173.00 (*0-397-51500-6*) Lppncott W & W.

Lever, William & Bailly, Antione, eds. The Spatial Impact of Economic Changes in Europe. LC 96-83276. (ESF Ser.). 384p. (C). 1996. 87.95 (*1-85628-611-8*, Pub. by Avebry) Ashgate Pub Co.

Lever, William & Moore, Chris. The City in Transition: Policies & Agencies for the Economic Regeneration of Clydeside. (ESRC Research Programme: Inner City in Context Ser.). (Illus.). 144p. 1986. pap. 16.95 (*0-19-823267-5*) OUP.

***Levere, Debra.** Starstruck. 160p. (J). 2001. pap. 12.99 (*0-7868-1511-6*, Pub. by Disney Pr) Time Warner.

Levere, Trevor H. Affinity & Matter: Elements of Chemical Philosophy, 1800-1865. LC 92-45001. (Classics in the History & Philosophy of Science Ser.: Vol. 12). 264p. 1993. pap. text 49.00 (*2-88124-583-8*) Gordon & Breach.

— Chemists & Chemistry in Nature & Society, 1770-1878. (Collected Studies: No. CS 439). 314p. 1994. 98.95 (*0-86078-412-6*, Pub. by Variorum) Ashgate Pub Co.

— Poetry Realized in Nature: Samuel Taylor Coleridge & Early Nineteenth-Century Science. LC 81-1930. 296p. 1981. text 69.95 (*0-521-23920-6*) Cambridge U Pr.

— Science & the Canadian Arctic: A Century of Exploration, 1918-1920. (Illus.). 454p. (C). 1993. text 69.95 (*0-521-41933-6*) Cambridge U Pr.

Levere, Trevor H., ed. Editing Texts in the History of Science & Medicine: Papers Given at the Seventeenth Annual Conference on Editorial Problems. LC 82-15800. (Conference on Editorial Problems Ser.: No. 17). 1987. 42.50 (*0-404-63667-5*) AMS Pr.

Levere, Trevor H. & Shea, William R., eds. Nature, Experiment, & the Sciences. 360p. (C). 1990. lib. bdg. 186.00 (*0-7923-0420-9*, Pub. by Kluwer Academic) Kluwer Academic.

Levere, Trevor H., jt. auth. see Holmes, Frederic L.

Leverence, John. And the Winner Is: Using Awards to Promote Your Company & Encourage Your Employees. 328p. (Orig.). 1997. pap. 19.95 (*1-56343-147-5*) Silver Lake.

— Irving Wallace, a Writer's Profile. LC 73-93855. 454p. 1974. 7.95 (*0-87972-063-8*) Bowling Green Univ Popular Press.

Leverenz, David. The Language of Puritan Feeling: An Exploration in Literature, Psychology, & Social History. LC 79-18579. 357p. reprint ed. pap. 110.70 (*0-8357-7948-3*, 205702300002) Bks Demand.

— Manhood & the American Renaissance. LC 88-47914. 384p. 1989. text 47.50 (*0-8014-2281-7*) Cornell U Pr.

— Manhood & the American Renaissance. LC 88-47914. 384p. 1990. reprint ed. pap. text 18.95 (*0-8014-9743-4*) Cornell U Pr.

Leverenz, Jon, ed. see Nebenzahl, Kenneth.

Leveretle, Rebekah, jt. auth. see McRae, Barbara.

Leverett, Brian. The Complete Book of Gardening. (Illus.). 320p. (Orig.). 1994. pap. 17.95 (*0-572-01986-6*, Pub. by W Foulsham) Trans-Atl Phila.

— Complete Guide to Home Winemaking. 192p. (Orig.). 1996. pap. 7.95 (*1-85327-099-7*, Pub. by Prism Pr) Assoc Pubs Grp.

— Water Gardens: Step by Step to Success. (Crowood Gardening Guides Ser.). (Illus.). 128p. 1996. pap. 17.95 (*1-85223-977-8*, Pub. by Cro1wood) Trafalgar.

— Winemaking Month by Month. 3rd rev. ed. (Illus.). 144p. 1979. pap. text 10.95 (*1-85327-096-2*, Pub. by Prism Pr) Assoc Pubs Grp.

Leverett, Bruce W. Register Allocation in Optimizing Compilers. Stone, Harold, ed. LC 83-18297. (Computer Science: Systems Programming Ser.: No. 19). 234p. 1983. reprint ed. pap. 72.60 (*0-8357-1530-2*, 207031300066) Bks Demand.

Leverett, James, et al, eds. New Plays U. S. A. Four. 254p. (C). 1988. 24.95 (*0-930452-80-1*); pap. 12.95 (*0-930452-81-X*) Theatre Comm.

Leverett, James & Osborn, M. Elizabeth, eds. New Plays U. S. A. Three. 300p. (Orig.). (C). 1986. pap. 11.95 (*0-930452-54-2*) Theatre Comm.

Leverett, Les. Blue Moon of Kentucky: A Journey into the World of Bluegrass & Country Music As Seen Through the Camera Lens of Photo-Journalist Les Leverett. large type ed. LC 96-86528. (Illus.). 136p. (Orig.). 1996. pap. 15.00 (*0-944019-23-4*) Empire NC.

— The Long Journey Home: The Bluegrass Chronicles of Les Leverett. 96p. 1998. pap. text 12.95 (*1-880756-15-3*) Riverwood Pr.

Leverett, Rudy H. Legend of the Free State of Jones. LC 84-7513. (Illus.). 151p. (Orig.). reprint ed. pap. 46.90 (*0-7837-1070-4*, 204159300021) Bks Demand.

Leverett, Simon, jt. auth. see Carcach, Carlos.

Leverett, Trish. Birdies in the Oven: Aces in the Kitchen. (Illus.). 228p. (Orig.). 1986. pap. 10.00 (*0-317-58354-9*) Miss Annies Pubns.

Leverett, Willard M. How to Buy a Good Used Piano. rev. ed. Roehl, Harvey N., ed. LC 88-91309. (Illus.). 76p. 1988. pap. 8.95 (*0-9621063-0-5*) W Leverett.

Leverich, Kathleen. Best Enemies. LC 88-19150. (Illus.). (J). (gr. 1 up). 1989. 15.00 (*0-688-08316-1*, Grenwillow Bks) HarpC Child Bks.

***Leverich, Kathleen.** Best Enemies. 80p. (J). (gr. 2 up). 1998. mass mkt. 4.95 (*0-688-15853-6*, Wm Morrow) Morrow Avon.

Leverich, Kathleen. Best Enemies. 1998. 10.05 (*0-606-13195-7*, Pub. by Turtleback) Demco.

— Best Enemies Again. 96p. (J). 1999. mass mkt. 4.95 (*0-688-16197-9*, Wm Morrow) Morrow Avon.

— Best Enemies Forever. LC 94-26790. (Illus.). 136p. (J). (gr. 2 up). 1995. 14.00 (*0-688-13963-9*, Grenwillow Bks) HarpC Child Bks.

— Best Enemies Forever. 144p. (J). (gr. 2 up). 1998. pap. 4.95 (*0-688-15854-4*, Wm Morrow) Morrow Avon.

— Brigid Beware! 1995. 9.19 (*0-606-07321-3*, Pub. by Turtleback) Demco.

— Brigid Beware, No. 2. LC 94-28614. (Illus.). 1995. pap. 3.99 (*0-679-85429-0*) Random.

— Brigid, Bewitched. LC 93-43221. (First Stepping Stone Bks.). (Illus.). 80p. (J). (gr. 1-4). 1994. lib. bdg. 11.99 (*0-679-95433-3*, Pub. by Random Bks Yng Read) Random.

Leverich, Kathleen. Brigid, Bewitched. LC 93-43221. 1994. 8.19 (*0-606-06252-1*, Pub. by Turtleback) Demco.

Leverich, Kathleen. Brigid the Bad. LC 95-5305. (Illus.). 72p. (J). (ps-3). 1995. pap. 3.99 (*0-679-87340-6*) Random.

— Cricket's Expeditions. (Illus.). (J). 1984. pap. text 5.95 (*0-87548-414-X*) Open Court.

— Daisy. LC 96-8469. (Flower Girls Ser.: Vol. 2). (Illus.). 96p. (J). (gr. 1-4). 1997. pap. 4.25 (*0-06-442019-1*, HarpTrophy) HarpC Child Bks.

— Heather. LC 96-49267. (Flower Girls Ser.: Vol. 3). (Illus.). 96p. (J). (gr. 1-4). 1997. pap. 3.95 (*0-06-442021-3*, HarpTrophy) HarpC Child Bks.

— Hilary & the Troublemakers. (Illus.). 144p. (gr. 1-4). 1999. mass mkt. 4.95 (*0-688-16453-6*, Wm Morrow) Morrow Avon.

— The New You. LC 97-32322. 128p. (YA). (gr. 5-9). 1998. 15.00 (*0-688-16076-X*, Grenwillow Bks) HarpC Child Bks.

***Leverich, Kathleen.** The New You. (Illus.). 112p. (J). (gr. 4-7). 2000. pap. 4.50 (*0-439-10801-2*) Scholastic Inc.

Leverich, Kathleen. Rose. LC 96-38907. (Flower Girls Ser.: Vol. 4). (Illus.). 96p. (J). (gr. 1-4). 1997. pap. 3.95 (*0-06-442020-5*, HarpTrophy) HarpC Child Bks.

— Violet. LC 96-111. (Flower Girls Ser.: Vol. 1). (Illus.). 96p. (J). (gr. 1-4). 1997. pap. 3.95 (*0-06-442018-3*, HarpTrophy) HarpC Child Bks.

Leverich, Lyle. Tom. 1995. 30.00 (*0-614-15414-6*, Crown) Crown Pub Group.

— Tom: The Unknown Tennessee Williams. (Illus.). 644p. (C). 1997. pap. 18.00 (*0-393-31663-7*) Norton.

Leveridge, ed. Therapy for the Burn Patient. 182p. 1991. pap. 43.25 (*1-56593-013-4*, 0255) Thomson Learn.

***Leveridge, Brett.** Men My Mother Dated: And Other Mostly True Tales. LC 99-55381. 192p. 2000. 19.95 (*0-375-50400-1*) Villard Books.

Levering, Bas, jt. auth. see Van Manen, Max.

***Levering, Donald.** Horsetail. Sheldon, Bill, ed. 84p. 2000. pap. 7.00 (*0-939391-28-7*) B Woodley Pr.

Levering, Donald. Mister Ubiquity. 30p. 1997. pap. 7.95 (*0-944754-50-3*) Pudding Hse Pubns.

— Outcroppings from Navajoland: Poems. LC 83-73475. 72p. 1985. 5.00 (*0-912586-52-4*) Dine College Pr.

Levering, Frank. Blue Light: Poems from a Life. unabridged ed. 140p. (Orig.). 1997. pap. write for info. (*0-9656330-0-4*) Orchard Gap Pr.

Levering, Frank & Urbanska, Wanda. Simple Living: One Couple's Search for a Better Life. 288p. 1993. pap. 12.95 (*0-14-012339-3*, Penguin Bks) Viking Penguin.

Levering, Joseph M. History of Bethlehem, Pennsylvania 1741-1892. LC 74-134432. reprint ed. 95.00 (*0-404-07218-6*) AMS Pr.

— History of Bethlehem, 1741-1892, with Some Account of Its Founders & Their Early Activity in America. (Illus.). 809p. 1997. reprint ed. lib. bdg. 79.50 (*0-8328-6392-0*) Higginson Bk Co.

Levering, Marcy, ed. see Brunson, Dorothy & Bolton, Barbara.

Levering, Marcy, ed. see Brunson, Dorothy & DaHarb, Peggy.

Levering, Miriam, ed. Rethinking Scripture: Essays from a Comparative Perspective. LC 87-9919. 276p. 1988. text 21.50 (*0-88706-613-5*) State U NY Pr.

***Levering, Miriam, ed.** Zen: Images, Text, & Teachings. LC 00-24651. (Illus.). 160p. 2000. 25.00 (*1-57965-166-6*) Artisan.

Levering, Miriam L., et al. Love, Mom: Stories from the Life of a Global Activist, Teacher & Mother of Six. unabridged ed. (Illus.). 196p. 1996. pap. 14.95 (*0-9656330-1-2*) Orchard Gap Pr.

Levering, Miriam L., jt. auth. see Levering, Ralph B.

Levering, Ralph B. The Cold War, 1945-1987. 2nd ed. Eisenstadt, A. S. & Franklin, John H., eds. LC 87-25459. (American History Ser.). (Illus.). 240p. (C). 1988. pap. text 11.95 (*0-88295-858-5*) Harlan Davidson.

— The Cold War, 1945-1991: A Post-Cold War History. Eisenstadt, A. S. & Franklin, John H., eds. (American History Ser.). (Illus.). 200p. (C). 1994. pap. text 12.95 (*0-88295-912-3*) Harlan Davidson.

***Levering, Ralph B. & Levering, Miriam L.** Citizen Action for Global Change: The Neptune Group & Law of the Sea. LC 98-45026. (Syracuse Studies on Peace & Conflict Resolution). (Illus.). 373p. 1999. 45.00 (*0-8156-2794-7*) Syracuse U Pr.

Levering, Ralph B. & Levering, Miriam L. Citizen Action for Global Change: The Neptune Group & Law of the Sea. LC 98-45026. (Studies on Peace & Conflict Resolution). 373p. 1999. pap. text 19.95 (*0-8156-2795-5*) Syracuse U Pr.

Levering, Robert. Friends & Alcohol: Recovering a Forgotten Testimony. LC 94-65301. 1994. pap. 4.00 (*0-87574-313-7*) Pendle Hill.

— A Great Place to Work. 336p. 1990. reprint ed. pap. 9.95 (*0-380-71103-6*, Avon Bks) Morrow Avon.

Levering, Robert & Moskowitz, Milton. The One Hundred Best Companies to Work for in America. LC 93-6406. 528p. 1994. pap. 15.95 (*0-452-27123-1*, Plume) Dutton Plume.

Levering, Samauel R. Quaker Peacemakers: A Saga of Fruitgrowing & Christian Service. unabridged ed. (Illus.). 81p. 1993. pap. 7.50 (*0-9656330-3-9*) Orchard Gap Pr.

Levering, Ted. The Other Side of the Bridge. LC 91-91144. (Illus.). 400p. (Orig.). 1990. pap. 14.95 (*0-9640957-7-7*) Willowmead.

Leverington, David. A History of Astronomy: From 1890 to the Present. LC 95-12034. (Practical Astronomy Ser.). (Illus.). 365p. 1995. 32.00 (*3-540-19915-2*) Spr-Verlag.

***Leveritt, Mara.** The Boys on the Tracks: Death, Denial & a Mother's Crusade to Bring Her Son's Killer to Justice. LC 99-21877. 384p. 1999. text 25.95 (*0-312-19841-8*) St Martin.

Leveriza, Jose P. Rage in the Hearts: A Historical Novel. 167p. (Orig.). (C). 1989. pap. 12.50 (*971-10-0382-1*, Pub. by New Day Pub) Cellar.

***Levermore, G. J.** Building Energy Management Systems: Application to Heating Natural Ventilation Lighting & Occupant Satisfaction. 2nd ed. LC 99-39663. 2000. pap. write for info. (*0-419-22590-0*, E & FN Spon) Routledge.

Levermore, G. J. Building Energy Management Systems: The Basics. (C). 1988. pap. 320.00 (*0-86022-205-5*, Pub. by Build Servs Info Assn) St Mut.

— Building Energy Management Systems for the Operator. 1989. pap. 320.00 (*0-86022-216-0*, Pub. by Build Servs Info Assn) St Mut.

— Control with a Building Energy Management System. (C). 1988. pap. 320.00 (*0-86022-204-7*, Pub. by Build Servs Info Assn) St Mut.

— Monitoring & Targeting with a Building & Energy Management System. 1989. pap. 320.00 (*0-86022-239-X*, Pub. by Build Servs Info Assn) St Mut.

— Presenting a Case for a Building & Energy Management System. 1989. pap. 320.00 (*0-86022-241-1*, Pub. by Build Servs Info Assn) St Mut.

Levermore, J. G. Staff Reaction to Building Energy Management Systems. 1999. pap. 320.00 (*0-86022-233-0*, Pub. by Build Servs Info Assn) St Mut.

Leverne. Black Girl. LC 99-93950. (YA). (gr. 7-9). 1997. pap. 8.95 (*0-533-12256-2*) Vantage.

Levernier. Phillis Wheatley. 1998. 22.95 (*0-8057-4019-8*) Macmillan.

Levernier, James A. & Cohen, Hennig, compiled by. The Indians & Their Captives, 31. LC 76-57831. (Contributions in American Studies: No. 31). 291p. 1977. 65.00 (*0-8371-9535-7*, CIC/, Greenwood Pr) Greenwood.

Levernier, James A. & Wilmes, Douglas R., eds. American Writers Before Eighteen Hundred: A Biographical & Critical Reference Guide, 3 vols., Set. LC 82-933. 1764p. 1984. lib. bdg. 295.00 (*0-313-22229-0*, LWB/) Greenwood.

— American Writers Before Eighteen Hundred: A Biographical & Critical Reference Guide, 3 vols., Vol. 1. LC 82-933. 1984. lib. bdg. 125.00 (*0-313-23476-0*, LWB/01) Greenwood.

— American Writers Before Eighteen Hundred: A Biographical & Critical Reference Guide, 3 vols., Vol. 2. LC 82-933. 1984. lib. bdg. 125.00 (*0-313-23477-9*, LWB/02) Greenwood.

— American Writers Before Eighteen Hundred: A Biographical & Critical Reference Guide, 3 vols., Vol. 3. LC 82-933. 1984. lib. bdg. 125.00 (*0-313-24096-5*, LWB/03) Greenwood.

***Levero, Diane.** What So Proudly We Hail'd. Kemnitz, Myrna, ed. 302p. (YA). 1999. pap. 7.99 (*0-88092-054-8*, 0548) Royal Fireworks.

Levers-Carter, M., jt. auth. see Newdick, Jane.

Levers, Phyllis, ed. see Druhot, George S.

***Leversedge, Terry.** CF-105 Arrow MK1: Pilot Operating Instructions & RCAF Testing/Basing Plans. (Illus.). 160p. 1999. pap. text 27.95 (*1-55046-310-1*) Bomporto.

***LeversedgeE, T F J.** Cf-105 Arrow Mk1: Pilot's Operating Instructions & RCAF Testing/Basing Plans. 160p. 1999. pap. text 39.95 (*1-55046-293-8*, Pub. by Boston Mills) Genl Dist Srvs.

LeVert, Marianne. AIDS: A Handbook for the Future. LC 96-3186. (Illus.). 144p. (YA). (gr. 7 up). 1996. lib. bdg. 23.90 (*1-56294-660-9*) Millbrook Pr.

— Crime. Leinwand, Gerald, ed. (American Issues Ser.). 160p. (YA). (gr. 9-12). 1991. 19.95 (*0-8160-2102-3*) Facts on File.

— The Welfare System: Help or Hindrance to the Poor? LC 94-21815. (Issue & Debate Ser.). (Illus.). 112p. (YA). (gr. 7 up). 1995. lib. bdg. 23.90 (*1-56294-455-X*) Millbrook Pr.

Levert, Mireille. Charlotte Dejeune. (Collection Charlotte Nounours: No. 1).Tr. of Molly's Breakfast. (FRE., Illus.). 12p. (J). (ps). 1997. bds. 4.95 (*1-55037-423-0*, Pub. by Annick) Firefly Bks Ltd.

— Charlotte Joue. (Collection Charlotte Nounours: No. 3).Tr. of Molly's Toys. (FRE., Illus.). 12p. (J). (ps). 1997. bds. 4.95 (*1-55037-427-3*, Pub. by Annick) Firefly Bks Ltd.

— Charlotte Se Lave. (Collection Charlotte Nounours: No. 4).Tr. of Molly's Bath. (FRE., Illus.). 12p. (J). (ps). 1997. bds. 4.95 (*1-55037-429-X*, Pub. by Annick) Firefly Bks Ltd.

— Charlotte S'Habille. (Collection Charlotte Nounours: No. 2).Tr. of Molly's Clothes. (FRE., Illus.). 12p. (J). (ps). 1997. bds. 4.95 (*1-55037-425-7*, Pub. by Annick) Firefly Bks Ltd.

Levert, Mireille. Molly Counts. (Molly Bear Bks.: No. 5). (Illus.). 16p. (J). (ps). 1998. bds. 4.95 (*1-55037-547-4*, Pub. by Annick Pr) Firefly Bks Ltd.

— Molly Draws. (Molly Bear Bks.: No. 6). (Illus.). 16p. (J). (ps). 1998. bds. 4.95 (*1-55037-546-6*, Pub. by Annick Pr) Firefly Bks Ltd.

— Molly's Bath. LC 96-931194. (Molly Bear Bks.: No. 4). (Illus.). 12p. (J). (ps). 1997. bds. 4.95 (*1-55037-428-1*, Pub. by Annick) Firefly Bks Ltd.

— Molly's Breakfast. LC 96-931195. (Molly Bear Bks.: No. 1). (Illus.). 12p. (J). (ps). 1997. bds. 4.95 (*1-55037-422-2*, Pub. by Annick) Firefly Bks Ltd.

— Molly's Clothes. (Molly Bear Bks.: No. 2). (Illus.). 12p. (J). (ps). 1997. bds. 4.95 (*1-55037-424-9*, Pub. by Annick) Firefly Bks Ltd.

— Molly's Toys. (Molly Bear Bks.: No. 2). (Illus.). 12p. (J). (ps). 1997. bds. 4.95 (*1-55037-426-5*, Pub. by Annick) Firefly Bks Ltd.

— Rose by Night. (Illus.). 32p. (J). (gr. 3-5). 1998. bds. write for info. (*0-88899-313-7*, Pub. by Gro1undwood-Douglas) Publishers Group.

LeVert, Mireille, jt. illus. see Cuyler, Margery.

LeVert, Suanne, jt. auth. see Rothfeld, Glenn S.

LeVert, Susan, jt. auth. see San, Rosa Lo.

LeVert, Suzanne. Hillary Rodham Clinton: First Lady. LC 93-13836. (Gateway Biographies Ser.). (Illus.). 48p. (J). (gr. 2-4). 1994. lib. bdg. 20.90 (*1-56294-432-0*) Millbrook Pr.

— Hillary Rodham Clinton: First Lady. 1994. 12.15 (*0-606-12334-2*, Pub. by Turtleback) Demco.

Levert, Suzanne. Hillary Rodham Clinton: First Lady. LC 93-13836. (Gateway Biographies Ser.). 48p. (J). (gr. 2-4). 1994. pap. 7.95 (*1-56294-726-5*) Millbrook Pr.

— Human Growth Hormone: The Promise of Eternal Youth. LC 97-93167. 256p. 1997. mass mkt. 5.99 (*0-380-78885-3*, Avon Bks) Morrow Avon.

LeVert, Suzanne. Let's Discover Canada, 14 vols. (Illus.). (J). (gr. 3 up). 1991. lib. bdg. 237.30 (*0-7910-1021-X*) Chelsea Hse.

***LeVert, Suzanne.** Massachusetts, 5 vols. , Set. LC 98-52549. (Celebrate the States Ser.). 144p. (J). (gr. 4-7). 2000. 35.64 (*0-7614-0666-2*, Benchmark NY) Marshall Cavendish.

— Melatonin: The Anti-Aging Hormone. 272p. (Orig.). 1998. mass mkt. 5.99 (*0-380-78304-5*, Avon Bks) Morrow Avon.

LeVert, Suzanne. Quebec. (Let's Discover Canada Ser.). (Illus.). 64p. (YA). (gr. 3 up). 1991. lib. bdg. 16.95 (*0-7910-1030-9*) Chelsea Hse.

— Saskatchewan. (Let's Discover Canada Ser.). (Illus.). 64p. (J). (gr. 3 up). 1991. lib. bdg. 16.95 (*0-7910-1024-4*) Chelsea Hse.

— Teens Face to Face with Chronic Illness. LC 92-45819. (YA). 1993. pap. 7.95 (*0-671-74541-7*, Julian Messner) Silver Burdett Pr.

Levert, Suzanne. Teens Face to Face with Chronic Illness. 1993. 13.05 (*0-606-06048-0*, Pub. by Turtleback) Demco.

LeVert, Suzanne & McClain, Gary. Complete Idiot's Guide to Breaking Bad Habits. LC 97-80969. (Illus.). 336p. 1997. 16.95 (*0-02-862110-7*) Macmillan Gen Ref.

LeVert, Suzanne, jt. auth. see Ferber, Jane S.

LeVert, Suzanne, jt. auth. see Greenspan, Peter R.

LeVert, Suzanne, jt. auth. see Moore-Ede, Martin C.

LeVert, Suzanne, jt. auth. see Murphy, Kevin.

LeVert, Suzanne, jt. auth. see Rothfeld, Glenn.

LeVert, Suzanne, jt. auth. see Rothfeld, Glenn S.

LeVert, Suzanne, ed. see Keene, Carolyn.

Leverton, William H. Through the Box-Office Window. LC 79-8069. (Illus.). reprint ed. 26.50 (*0-404-18379-4*) AMS Pr.

Levertov, Denise. Breathing the Water. LC 86-23658. 96p. 1987. pap. 10.95 (*0-8112-1027-8*, NDP640, Pub. by New Directions) Norton.

— Candles in Babylon. LC 81-22289. 144p. (C). 1982. pap. 7.95 (*0-8112-0831-1*, NDP533, Pub. by New Directions) Norton.

— Collected Earlier Poems, 1940-1960. LC 78-26199. 133p. 1979. pap. 9.95 (*0-8112-0718-8*, NDP475, Pub. by New Directions) Norton.

— A Door in the Hive. LC 89-8304. 96p. 1989. pap. 9.95 (*0-8112-1119-3*, NDP685, Pub. by New Directions) Norton.

— The Double Image. limited ed. 56p. 1991. 125.00 (*0-918116-65-1*) Brooding Heron Pr.

— Evening Train. LC 96-23850. 128p. 1993. reprint ed. pap. 9.95 (*0-8112-1220-3*, NDP750, Pub. by New Directions) Norton.

— The Freeing of the Dust. LC 75-8568. 128p. 1975. pap. 7.95 (*0-8112-0582-7*, NDP401, Pub. by New Directions) Norton.

— The Great Unknowing: Last Poems. LC 98-51469. 68p. 1999. 19.95 (*0-8112-1403-6*, Pub. by New Directions) Norton.

— The Life Around Us: Selected Poems on Nature. LC 96-52901. 80p. 1997. 19.95 (*0-8112-1351-X*, Pub. by New Directions); pap. 8.95 (*0-8112-1352-8*, NDP843, Pub. by New Directions) Norton.

— Life in the Forest. LC 78-9356. 1978. pap. 7.95 (*0-8112-0693-9*, NDP461, Pub. by New Directions) Norton.

— Light up the Cave. LC 81-11295. 224p. 1982. 8.95 (*0-8112-0813-3*, Pub. by New Directions) Norton.

— New & Selected Essays. LC 92-17887. 256p. 1992. pap. 12.95 (*0-8112-1218-1*, NDP749, Pub. by New Directions) Norton.

— Oblique Prayers: New Poems with Fourteen Translations from Jean Joubert. LC 84-1103. 96p. 1984. 9.95 (*0-8112-0909-1*, NDP578, Pub. by New Directions) Norton.

— Poems, 1968-1972: Including Relearning the Alphabet, To Stay Alive & Footprints. LC 86-5389. 288p. 1987. pap. 12.95 (*0-8112-1005-7*, NDP629, Pub. by New Directions) Norton.

— Poems, 1960-1967: Including The Jacob's Ladder, O Taste & See, & The Sorrow Dance. LC 82-2263. 256p. 1983. pap. 11.95 (*0-8112-0859-1*, NDP549, Pub. by New Directions) Norton.

— Sands of the Well. 1998. pap. 19.95 (*1-85224-433-X*, Pub. by Bloodaxe Bks) Dufour.

— Sands of the Well. LC 96-4324. 144p. 1996. 10.95 (*0-8112-1316-1*, Pub. by New Directions) Norton.

— The Stream & the Sapphire: Selected Poems on Religious Themes. LC 96-30012. 80p. 1997. pap. 8.95 (*0-8112-1354-4*, NDP844, Pub. by New Directions) Norton.

— Tesserae. LC 95-2954. 160p. 1995. 18.95 (*0-8112-1292-0*, Pub. by New Directions) Norton.

— Tesserae: Memories & Suppositions. LC 95-2954. 160p. 1996. pap. 9.95 (*0-8112-1337-4*, NDP832, Pub. by New Directions) Norton.

***Levertov, Denise.** This Great Unknowing. 2000. pap. 9.95 (*0-8112-1458-3*, Pub. by New Directions) Norton.

Levertov, Denise & Williams, William Carlos. The Letters of Denise Levertov & William Carlos Williams. MacGowan, Christopher, ed. LC 98-34194. 192p. 1998. 24.95 (*0-8112-1392-7*, Pub. by New Directions) Norton.

***Levertov, Denise, et al.** Food Poems. Garrison, David L. & Hermsen, Terry, eds. (Pocket Poems Ser.). 42p. 1998. pap. 2.50 (*0-933087-48-9*) Bottom Dog Pr.

Levertov, Denise, ed. & tr. see Guillevic.

Levertov, Denise, jt. tr. see Dimock, Edward C., Jr.

Levertov, Denise, tr. see Guillevic, Eugene.

Levertov, Denise, tr. see Joubert, Jean.

Levertov, Denise, tr. see Meredith, William, ed.

Leveson, Irving, ed. Quantitative Explorations in Drug Abuse Policy. LC 79-21399. 183p. 1980. 45.00 (*0-88331-192-5*) R B Luce.

Leveson, Irving, jt. auth. see Fuchs, Victor R.

Leveson, Irving F. American Challenges: Business & Government in the World of the 1990s. LC 90-39104. 216p. 1991. 55.00 (*0-275-93644-9*, C3644, Praeger Pubs) Greenwood.

Leveson, Nancy G. Safeware: System Safety & Computers. LC 94-19779. (Computer Science & Electrical Engineering Ser.). 704p. (C). 1995. 49.95 (*0-201-11972-2*) Addison-Wesley.

Levesque, Allen H., jt. auth. see Michelson, Arnold M.

Levesque, Allen H., jt. auth. see Pahlavan, Kaveh.

Levesque, Catherine. Journey Through Landscape in Seventeenth-Century Holland: The Harlem Print Series & Dutch Identity. LC 94-8293. 1995. 75.00 (*0-271-01049-5*) Pa St U Pr.

Levesque, Catherine, ed. The Illustrated Bartsch Vol. 6, Commentary: Netherlandish Artists. 1986. lib. bdg. 149.00 (*0-89835-105-7*) Abaris Bks.

Levesque, Catou, ed. see Lempfrit, Honore-Timothee.

Levesque, Claude, jt. ed. see De Koninck, Jean-Marie.

Levesque, D., jt. auth. see Nadeau, M.

***Levesque, Daniel.** The Weider Weight Training Log: The IFBB Worldwide Official Training Log. 416p. 1999. spiral bd. 18.95 (*0-9684004-0-X*) Cole Pubg.

Levesque, George A. Black Boston: African American Life in Urban America, 1750-1860. LC 94-899. (Studies in African American History & Culture). 1994. write for info. (*0-8153-1003-X*) Garland.

Levesque, George H. Social Credit & Catholicism. 1979. lib. bdg. 39.95 (*0-8490-3006-4*) Gordon Pr.

***Levesque, H. J., et al, eds.** Logical Foundations for Cognitive Agents: Contributions in Honor of Ray Reiter. LC 99-23785. (Artificial Intelligence Ser.). 400p. 1999. 56.00 (*3-540-66012-7*) Spr-Verlag.

***Levesque, Hector J & Lakemeyer, Gerhard.** The Logic of Knowledge Bases. LC 00-25413. (Illus.). 583p. 2000. 45.00 (*0-262-12232-4*) MIT Pr.

Levesque, Hector J., jt. ed. see Brachman, Ronald J.

Levesque, Jacques. Enigma of 1989: The U. S. S. R. & the Liberation of Eastern Europe. Martin, Keith, tr. LC 96-52426. 275p. 1997. 35.00 (*0-520-20631-2*, Pub. by U CA Pr) Cal Prin Full Svc.

Levesque, Jacques, jt. auth. see Lewis, Zack.

Levesque, Jacques, jt. ed. see David, Charles-Philippe.

Levesque, Jerome, et al. A Clinical Guide to Primary Bone Tumors. LC 97-34657. 301p. 1998. 99.00 (*0-683-30255-8*) Lppncott W & W.

Levesque, John. Geneva Farewell: A Novel. 1998. pap. 22.95 (*0-88962-669-3*) Mosaic.

— Stranded on the Information Highway. 200p. (Orig.). 1996. pap. 16.95 (*0-88962-608-1*) Mosaic.

— Waiting for Aquarius. 200p. 1993. pap. 14.95 (*0-88962-537-9*) Mosaic.

Levesque, Joseph D. The Complete Hiring Manual: Policies, Practices & Procedures. 700p. 1991. 80.00 (*0-685-52664-X*) P-H.

***Levesque, Karen.** Vocational Education in the United States Toward the Year 2000. 424p. 2000. per. 38.00 (*0-16-050279-9*) USGPO.

Levesque, Karen, et al. At Your Fingertips: Using Everyday Data to Improve Schools. LC 98-233036. (Illus.). ix, 208p. 1998. pap. 39.95 (*0-9662883-0-0*) MPR Assocs.

Levesque, Paul. Symbols of Transcendence: Religious Expression in the Thought of Louis Dupre. (Louvain Theological & Pastoral Monographs). 1997. pap. text 30.00 (*0-8028-4488-X*) Eerdmans.

— The WOW Factory: Creating a Customer Focus Revolution in Your Business. LC 94-31410. 192p. 1994. text 22.95 (*0-7863-0386-7*, Irwn Prfssnl) McGraw-Hill Prof.

Levesque, Paul, et al. Breakaway Planning: 8 Big Questions to Guide Organizational Change. LC 98-27143. 272p. 1998. 40.95 (*0-8144-0426-X*) AMACOM.

Levesque, Roger J. Sexual Abuse of Children: A Human Rights Perspective. LC 98-48401. 574p. 1999. text 39.95 (*0-253-33471-3*) Ind U Pr.

***Levesque, Roger J. R.** Adolescents, Sex & the Law: Preparing Adolescents for Responsible Citizenship. LC 99-38670. (Law & Public Policy Ser.: Vol. 4). 398p. 1999. 39.95 (*1-55798-609-6*, 431-626A) Am Psychol.

— Culture & Family Violence: Fostering Change Through Human Rights Law. LC 00-33195. (Law & Public Policy Ser.). 2000. write for info. (*1-55798-682-7*) Am Psychol.

Levesque, Suzanne, tr. see Zeman, Ludmila.

Levetan, Resa. Day by Day Diabetes: 1998 Calendar. 370p. 1997. pap. 9.95 (*1-883205-41-7*) Intl Med Pub.

— Day-by-Day Diabetes 2000 Calendar. (Day-by-Day Year 2000 Calendars Ser.). 320p. 1999. pap. 15.95 (*1-883205-74-3*) Intl Med Pub.

— Day-by-Day Obesity 2000 Calendar. (Day-by-Day Year 2000 Calendars Ser.). 120p. 1999. pap. 12.95 (*1-883205-67-0*) Intl Med Pub.

Levetan, Resa, et al. Day-by-Day Diabetes, 1999 Calendar. (Day-by-Day Calendars Ser.). 320p. 1999. pap. 15.95 (*1-883205-36-0*) Intl Med Pub.

Levete, Gina. Letting Go of Loneliness: A Positive Approach. 1993. pap. 12.95 (*1-85230-398-0*, Pub. by Element MA) Penguin Putnam.

***Levete, Sarah.** Being Jealous. LC 98-44972. (How Do I Feel About... Ser.). (Illus.). 24p. (J). (gr. 1-3). 1999. lib. bdg. 19.90 (*0-7613-0911-X*, Copper Beech Bks) Millbrook Pr.

Levete, Sarah. Looking after Myself. LC 97-41644. (How Do I Feel About... Ser.). (Illus.). 24p. (J). (gr. k-4). 1998. lib. bdg. 19.90 (*0-7613-0809-1*, Copper Beech Bks) Millbrook Pr.

— Making Friends. LC 97-41646. (How Do I Feel About... Ser.). (Illus.). 24p. (J). (gr. k-4). 1998. lib. bdg. 19.90 (*0-7613-0808-3*, Copper Beech Bks) Millbrook Pr.

***Levete, Sarah.** Rivers & Lakes. LC 99-29594. (Illus.). 32p. (J). 1999. 20.90 (*0-7613-0904-7*, Copper Beech Bks) Millbrook Pr.

Levete, Sarah. When People Die. LC 98-16959. (How Do I Feel About... Ser.). (Illus.). 24p. (J). (gr. 1-3). 1998. lib. bdg. 19.90 (*0-7613-0870-9*, Copper Beech Bks) Millbrook Pr.

Levetin. Plants & Society. 2nd ed. LC 98-18213. 496p. 1998. pap. 57.50 (*0-697-34552-1*) McGraw.

Levetin, Estelle. Plants & Society. 3rd ed. 2002. 53.25 (*0-07-290949-8*) McGraw.

Levetin, Estelle & McMahon, Karen. Plants & Society. 416p. (C). 1995. text. write for info. (*0-697-14064-4*, WCB McGr Hill) McGrw-H Hghr Educ.

Leveton, Deborah. Iowa Artists, 1990. LC 90-82944. (Illus.). 50p. 1990. pap. 10.00 (*1-879003-01-5*) Edmundson.

— Iowa Artists, 1993. (Illus.). 48p. 1993. pap., spiral bd. 10.00 (*1-879003-09-0*) Edmundson.

— Selections from the Print Collection of John Huseby. (Illus.). 26p. 1995. pap. 7.00 (*0-614-31047-4*) Edmundson.

Leveton, Deborah & Danoff, I. Michael. Will Mentor: Food & Ornament. (Illus.). 55p. 1996. pap. 12.00 (*1-879003-14-7*) Edmundson.

Leveton, Deborah & Heartney, Eleanor. Parts: Work by Rita McBride. LC 92-73382. (Illus.). 42p. 1992. pap. 16.00 (*1-879003-06-6*) Edmundson.

Leveton, Deborah, jt. auth. see Danoff, I. Michael.

Leveton, Deborah, jt. auth. see Rowe, M. Jessica.

Leveton, Deborah, ed. see Moore, Henry & Scott, Deborah E.

Leveton, Eva. A Clinician's Guide to Psychodrama. 2nd ed. LC 91-4823. Orig. Title: Psychodrama for the Timid Clinician. (Illus.). 192p. 1991. pap. 29.95 (*0-8261-2262-0*) Springer Pub.

Leveton, Lauren B., ed. see Institute of Medicine Staff.

Levett, Ann, et al, eds. Culture, Power & Difference: Discourse Analysis in South Africa. LC 96-28127. 224p. 1997. pap. 22.50 (*1-85649-472-1*, Pub. by Zed Books); text 62.50 (*1-85649-471-3*, Pub. by Zed Books) St Martin.

Levett, Gordon. Flying under Two Flags. 1994. pap. 19.50 (*0-7146-4102-2*, Pub. by F Cass Pubs) Intl Spec Bk.

Levett, John. The Ordering of Bees. LC 70-171773. (English Experience Ser.: No. 398). 96p. 1971. reprint ed. 35.00 (*90-221-0398-6*) Walter J Johnson.

Levett, M. J., tr. see Burnyeat, Myles F.

Levett, M. J., tr. see Plato.

Levett, Paul N., ed. Anaerobic Microbiology: A Practical Approach. (Practical Approach Ser.). (Illus.). 328p. 1992. pap. text 49.95 (*0-19-963262-6*) OUP.

Levetto, Guido C. The Mist of Yesterday. 2nd rev. ed. Todd, William E., ed. 157p. 1997. reprint ed. pap. 10.50 (*0-9667870-1-3*) G C Levetto.

— A Return to Yesterday. 3rd rev. ed. (Illus.). 181p. 1997. reprint ed. pap. 10.50 (*0-9667870-0-5*) G C Levetto.

Levey, jt. auth. see Hammel.

Levey, Ann. Limits of Property Rights Libertarianism. 1998. text 34.95 (*0-8133-2020-8*) Westview.

— Limits of Property Rights Libertarianism. (C). 1999. pap. text 14.95 (*0-8133-2021-6*) Westview.

Levey, Barry. Fishing the Oceans, Lakes - Rivers. (Illus.). 1992. 17.95 (*1-885422-06-7*) Fishermans Tales.

— Florida: Fishing & Diving the Wrecks & Artificial Reefs. (Illus.). 1994. 10.95 (*1-885422-10-5*) Fishermans Tales.

— Wonders of the Oceans: Sharks - Marine Mammals. (Illus.). 1995. spiral bd. 10.95 (*1-885422-13-X*) Fishermans Tales.

Levey, Bob & Siemer, Nan. Washington: City on a Hill. LC 97-12602. (Urban Tapestry Ser.). (Illus.). 256p. 1997. 44.95 (*1-881096-41-6*) Towery Pub.

Levey, Bob, jt. auth. see Levey, Jane Freundel.

Levey, Brian C., ed. Massachusetts Zoning & Land Use Law: 1996 Edition. 417p. 1996. 95.00 (*1-55834-407-1*, 64525, MICHIE) LEXIS Pub.

— Massachusetts Zoning & Land Use Law: 1998 Supplement. 50p. 1998. 29.50 (*0-327-00790-7*, 6452611) LEXIS Pub.

Levey, Gerald S., ed. Hormone-Receptor Interaction: Molecular Aspects. LC 76-583. (Modern Pharmacology-Toxicology Ser.: No. 9). (Illus.). 488p. reprint ed. pap. 151.30 (*0-7837-0834-3*, 204114800019) Bks Demand.

Levey, Idelle, jt. auth. see Topalanski, Julie.

Levey, Jane & Morrison, Bob. Background Music. (Illus.). 40p. Date not set. 30.00 (*0-918196-20-5*) American Music.

***Levey, Jane Freundel & Levey, Bob.** The Washington Album: A Pictorial History of the Nation's Capital. (Illus.). 250p. 2000. pap. 24.95 (*1-930691-00-9*, Pub. by Washington Post) Wash Bk Distrib.

Levey, Joel & Levey, Michelle. The Fine Arts of Relaxation, Concentration & Meditation: Ancient Skills for Modern Minds. rev. ed. LC 94-1269. (Illus.). 232p. 1994. pap., wbk. ed. 14.95 (*0-86171-040-1*) Wisdom MA.

— Living in Balance: A Dynamic Approach for Creating Harmony & Wholeness in a Chaotic World. LC 97-31200. (Illus.). 333p. (Orig.). 1998. pap. 17.95 (*1-57324-032-X*) Conari Press.

— Simple Meditation & Relaxation. LC 99-24221. (Simple Wisdom Ser.). 320p. 1999. 13.95 (*1-57324-151-2*) Conari Press.

***Levey, Joel & Levey, Michelle.** Wisdom at Work: Simple Meditation & Relaxation. LC 99-24223. 1999. 14.95 (*1-57324-180-6*) Conari Press.

Levey, Joseph. The Jazz Experience: A Guide to Appreciation. 168p. (C). 1987. reprint ed. pap. text 18.00 (*0-8191-6068-7*) U Pr of Amer.

Levey, Judith. The World Almanac Book for Kids. (J). (gr. 3-7). pap. 8.95 (*0-614-19263-3*, World Almanac) Newspaper Ent.

— The World Almanac Book for Kids, 1997. (J). (gr. 3-7). 16.95 (*0-614-19262-5*, World Almanac) Newspaper Ent.

Levey, Judith, ed. The Macmillan First Dictionary. rev. ed. LC 90-6062. (Dictionaries Ser.). (Illus.). 416p. (J). (gr. k-4). 1990. lib. bdg. 14.00 (*0-02-761731-9*, Mac Bks Young Read) S&S Childrens.

— The Macmillan Picture Wordbook. rev. ed. LC 90-8274. (Dictionaries Ser.). (Illus.). 64p. (J). (ps-1). 1990. lib. bdg. 8.95 (*0-02-754641-1*, Mac Bks Young Read) S&S Childrens.

Levey, Judith S. The Concise Columbia Encyclopedia. large type ed. 1985. text 468.00 (*0-231-06026-2*) Col U Pr.

— The World Almanac for Kids, 1998. LC 96-658610. 1995. 14.05 (*0-606-10719-3*, Pub. by Turtleback) Demco.

Levey, Judith S., ed. see Scholastic, Inc. Staff.

Levey, Marc, et al. How to Succeed on a Majority Campus: A Guide for Minority Students. LC 97-26358. (Freshman Orientation Ser.). (C). 1997. 13.95 (*0-534-50671-2*); 11.95 (*0-534-50672-0*) Wadsworth Pub.

Levey, Mare M. U. S. Taxation of Foreign Controlled Businesses. Davis, D, ed. 1200p. 1995. 195.00 (*0-7913-2293-9*) Warren Gorham & Lamont.

Levey, Michael. Florence: A Portrait. LC 95-31215. (Illus.). 560p. 1996. 35.00 (*0-674-30657-0*) HUP.

— Florence: A Portrait. (Illus.). 560p. 1998. pap. 22.95 (*0-674-30658-9*) HUP.

An Asterisk (*) at the beginning of an entry indicates that the title is appearing for the first time.

— From Giotto to Cezanne: A Concise History of Painting. LC 84-50479. (World of Art Ser.). (Illus.). 324p. 1985. pap. 16.95 (*0-500-20024-6*, Pub. by Thames Hudson) Norton.

— Giambattista Tiepolo: His Life & Art. (Illus.). 302p. 1994. pap. 35.00 (*0-300-06046-7*) Yale U Pr.

— The Later Italian Pictures in the Collection of Her Majesty the Queen. 2nd ed. (Pictures in the Royal Collections). (Illus.). 490p. (C). 1991. text 159.95 (*0-521-26328-X*) Cambridge U Pr.

— The Painter Depicted: Painters As a Subject in Painting. (Illus.). 1982. 10.95 (*0-500-55013-1*, Pub. by Thames Hudson) Norton.

— Painting & Sculpture in France, 1700-1789. LC 92-32503. (Pelican History of Art Ser.). (Illus.). 304p. (C). 1993. 60.00 (*0-300-05344-4*) Yale U Pr.

— Painting & Sculpture in France, 1700-1789. 1995. pap. 30.00 (*0-300-06494-2*) Yale U Pr.

— Painting in Eighteenth-Century Venice. 3rd ed. LC 94-17558. 267p. 1994. pap. 22.50 (*0-300-06057-2*) Yale U Pr.

— Rococo to Revolution. (World of Art Ser.). (Illus.). 252p. 1985. pap. 14.95 (*0-500-20050-5*, Pub. by Thames Hudson) Norton.

— The Seventeenth & Eighteenth Century Italian Schools. (National Gallery Publications). (Illus.). 1989. pap. 25.00 (*0-300-06142-0*) Yale U Pr.

Levey, Michelle, jt. auth. see Levey, Joel.

Levey, R. A., et al, compiled by. CD-ROM: Targeted Technology Applications for Infield Reserve Growth. 1994. 20.00 (*0-614-01873-0*) Bur Econ Geology.

— 3-D Seismic & Well Log Data Set: Fluvial Reservoir Systems-Stratton Field, South Texas. 30p. 1994. pap. text 40.00 incl. audio, 3.5 hd (*0-614-01872-2*) Bur Econ Geology.

Levey, R. A., ed. Core & Log Analyses of Depositional Systems & Reservoir Properties of Gulf Coast Natural Gas Reservoirs No. GC92-1: An Integrated Approach to Infield Reserve Growth in Frio, Vicksburg, & Wilcox Sandstones. (Illus.). 56p. 1992. pap. 3.50 (*0-317-05170-9*, GC92-1) Bur Econ Geology.

Levey, R. A., et al. Quantifying Secondary Gas Resources in Fluvial-Deltaic Reservoirs: A Case History from Stratton Field, South Texas. (Reports of Investigations: No. RI 221). (Illus.). 38p. 1994. pap. 4.00 (*0-614-01870-6*) Bur Econ Geology.

Levey, Robert. Reengineering COBOL with Objects: Step by Step Tp Sustainable Legacy Systems. 272p. 1995. 40.00 (*0-07-037774-X*) McGraw.

Levey, S. M., jt. auth. see King, D.

Levey, Samson H. The Messiah: An Aramoic Interpretation. 1974. 25.00 (*0-87820-402-4*) Ktav.

Levey, Samuel. The Rise of a University Teaching Hospital: A Leadership Perspective: The University of Iowa Hospitals & Clinics. LC 96-36389. 618p. 1996. 24.00 (*1-56793-048-4*) Health Admin Pr.

Levey, Santina M. Elizabethan Treasures: The Hardwick Hall Textiles. (Illus.). 112p. 1998. 35.00 (*0-8109-6353-1*, Pub. by Abrams) Time Warner.

Levey, Zach. Israel & the Western Powers, 1952-1960. LC 97-12363. 218p. (gr. 13). 1997. 45.00 (*0-8078-2368-6*) U of NC Pr.

Levez, Belinda. How to Win at Card Games. (Illus.). 72p. 1997. pap. 5.95 (*0-8442-3721-3*, Teach Yrslf) NTC Contemp Pub Co.

— Teach Yourself How to Win at Casino Games. (Illus.). 96p. 1997. pap. 5.95 (*0-8442-3078-2*, Teach Yrslf) NTC Contemp Pub Co.

— Teach Yourself How to Win at Poker. (Illus.). 72p. 1997. pap. 5.95 (*0-8442-3079-0*, Teach Yrslf) NTC Contemp Pub Co.

Levgers, Karen & Stangler, Kathy. LIFE: Learning Independence Through Functional Experiences. (Illus.). 204p. 1995. spiral bd. 24.00 (*1-884135-13-7*) Mayer-Johnson.

Levi. Group Dynamics in Teams. (SWC-Business Communication Ser.). 2000. pap. 29.00 (*0-324-01410-4*) Thomson Learn.

— International Finance. 1998. 32.00 (*0-07-228668-7*) McGraw.

— Supply Chain Management. 1999. 67.50 (*0-256-26168-7*) McGraw.

Levi & Pellegrin-Resci. Social as Metaphor & Cooperatives as Reaction. 68.95 (*1-84014-489-0*) Ashgate Pub Co.

Levi & Scharff. Intrapsychic & Interpersonal Dimensions: An Unresolved Dilemma. (Psychoanalytic Inquiry Ser.: Vol. 8, No. 4). 1988. 20.00 (*0-88163-960-5*) Analytic Pr.

Levi, A. H., ed. Guide to French Literature Vol. 2: Beginnings to 1789, Vol. 2. 1111p. 1993. 140.00 (*1-55862-159-8*) St James Pr.

Levi, A. H., ed. & tr. see Erasmus, Desiderius.

Levi, Adoff Jaime. Please Don't Hit It to Me. 1924. write for info. (*0-688-17532-5*); lib. bdg. write for info. (*0-688-17533-3*) Lothrop.

— Rock-n-Roll Dad. 1924. write for info. (*0-688-17550-3*); lib. bdg. write for info. (*0-688-17551-1*) Lothrop.

Levi, Albert W. Philosophy As Social Expression. LC 73-84191. xii, 328p. 1992. pap. text 4.25 (*0-226-47390-2*, P668) U Ch Pr.

— Varieties of Experience: An Introduction to Philosophy. LC 57-6807. 537p. reprint ed. pap. 166.50 (*0-608-10037-4*, 201255500081) Bks Demand.

Levi, Albert W. & Smith, Ralph A. Art Education: A Critical Necessity. (Disciplines in Art Education, Contexts of Understanding Ser.). (Illus.). 280p. 1991. pap. text 16.95 (*0-252-06185-3*) U of Ill Pr.

Levi, Alberto, jt. ed. see Concaro, Edoardo.

***Levi, Anthony.** Cardinal Richelieu: And the Making of France. (Illus.). 256p. 2000. 26.00 (*0-7867-0778-X*, Pub. by Carroll & Graf) Publishers Group.

Levi, Anthony, ed. Guide to French Literature: 1789 to the Present, 2 vols., Set. 93rd ed. 1994. 100.00 (*1-55862-320-5*, 200234-M99109) St James Pr.

— Guide to French Literature Vol. 1: 1789 to the Present. LC 92-165633. (Reference Guide to French Literature Ser.: Vol. 1). 884p. 1992. 140.00 (*1-55862-086-9*, 200116) St James Pr.

Levi, Anthony, tr. see Pascal, Blaise.

Levi, Anthony H., ed. Guide to French Literature: 1789 to the Present, 2 vols., Set. 900p. 1992. 210.00 (*1-55862-161-X*, 200158-M99019) St James Pr.

Levi, Antonia. Samurai from Outer Space: Understanding Japanaese Animation. (Illus.). 180p. (Orig.). 1996. pap. 18.95 (*0-8126-9332-9*) Open Court.

Levi, Avraham & Levi, Ruth. Bazak Guide to Israel/Jordan 1996-1997: Jordan 1996-97. 34th ed. (Illus.). 624p. 1996. pap. 21.95 (*0-8069-8199-7*) Sterling.

Levi, Barbara, et al, eds. The Future of Land-Based Strategic Missiles. (Illus.). 290p. 1989. 59.95 (*0-88318-619-5*) Spr-Verlag.

Levi, Benjamin H. Respecting Patient Autonomy. LC 98-25360. 296p. 1999. pap. 19.95 (*0-252-06749-5*) U of Ill Pr.

— Respecting Patient Autonomy. LC 98-25360. 296p. 1999. 45.95 (*0-252-02441-9*) U of Ill Pr.

Levi, C., ed. Sponges of the New Caledonian Lagoon. 3rd ed. (Illus.). xxxiii, 216p. 1998. 59.00 (*2-7099-1354-2*, Pub. by LInstitut Francais) Balogh.

Levi, Carlo. Le Christ S'Est Arrete a Eboli. (FRE.). 1977. pap. 11.95 (*0-7859-4085-5*) Fr & Eur.

— Christ Stopped at Eboli. Frenaye, Frances, tr. from ITA. 272p. 1947. pap. 10.00 (*0-374-50316-8*) FS&G.

— The Watch: A Novel. LC 99-15665. (Steerforth Italia Ser.). 440p. 1999. reprint ed. pap. 16.00 (*1-883642-81-7*) Steerforth Pr.

Levi-Civita, Tullio. The Absolute Differential Calculus: Calculus of Tensors. Persico, Enrico, ed. Long, Marjorie, tr. from ITA. LC 76-27497. (Illus.). 452p. 1977. reprint ed. pap. text 11.95 (*0-486-63401-9*) Dover.

— N-Body Problem in General Relativity. Knodel, Arthur J., tr. from FRE. 120p. 1965. text 113.00 (*90-277-0106-7*) Kluwer Academic.

Levi, Constance A., jt. auth. see Levi, James H.

***Levi, D. & Ragnisco, O., eds.** Symmetries & Integrability of Difference Equations. 444p. 2000. 99.00 (*0-8218-2128-8*) Am Math.

Levi, D. & Winternitz, P., eds. Painleve Transcendents: Their Asymptotics & Physical Applications. LC 96-5775. (NATO ASI Ser.: Vol. 278). (Illus.). 472p. (C). 1992. text 162.00 (*0-306-44050-4*, Kluwer Plenum) Kluwer Academic.

Levi, D. & Winternitz, Pavel, eds. Symmetries & Nonlinear Phenomena: Paipa, Columbia, Feb. 22-26, 1988. 472p. 1988. text 102.00 (*9971-5-0663-7*) World Scientific Pub.

Levi, D., et al. Symmetries & Integrability of Difference Equations. LC 96-26796. (CRM Proceedings & Lecture Notes Ser.: Vol. 9). 388p. 1996. pap. 98.00 (*0-8218-0601-7*, CRMP/9) Am Math.

Levi, Darrell E. Michael Manley: The Making of a Leader. LC 86-30826. (Illus.). 364p. 1990. 35.00 (*0-8203-1221-5*) U of Ga Pr.

Levi, Don S. Critical Thinking & Logic. 449p. (C). 1991. pap. text 32.95 (*1-879215-01-2*) Sheffield WI.

Levi, Donald R. How to Teach Adults: A Handbook for Real Estate Instructors. 2nd ed. 1996. pap. 9.95 (*0-9621154-1-X*) Real Est Educ.

— How to Teach Real Estate to Adults: A Handbook for Instructors. 134p. (Orig.). 1989. pap. text 9.95 (*0-9621154-0-1*) Real Est Educ.

Levi, Dorothy H. A Very Special Sister. (Awareness & Caring Ser.). (Illus.). 32p. (J). (gr. k-3). 1992. lib. bdg. 13.95 (*1-56674-033-9*) Forest Hse.

***Levi, Dror Shai.** The Sacred Redwood Forest. (Illus.). 40p. (J). (gr. k-5). 1999. 15.95 (*1-56167-558-X*) Am Literary Pr.

Levi, Edward H. Introduction to Legal Reasoning. rev. ed. LC 49-11213. 112p. 1962. pap. text 7.00 (*0-226-47408-9*, P84) U Ch Pr.

Levi, Eliphas. The Book of Splendours. LC 84-214089. 192p. 1973. pap. 12.95 (*0-87728-614-0*) Weiser.

— The Conjuration of the Four. Doubleday, Abner, tr. from FRE. 1991. pap. 3.95 (*1-55818-140-7*, Sure Fire) Holmes Pub.

— The Elements of the Kabbalah. Kuntz, Darcy, ed. Hamilton-Jones, J. W., tr. 1998. pap. 6.95 (*1-55818-366-3*) Holmes Pub.

***Levi, Eliphas.** The Great Secret. 192p. 2000. pap. (*1-57863-938-7*) Weiser.

— The Great Secret: or Occultism Unveiled. 192p. 2000. pap. 16.95 (*0-87728-938-7*) Weiser.

Levi, Eliphas. History of Magic. 1973. 250.00 (*0-8490-0332-6*) Gordon Pr.

— The History of Magic. Waite, Arthur E., tr. from FRE. LC 98-48102. (Weiser Classic Ser.). (Illus.). 384p. 1999. reprint ed. pap. 16.95 (*0-87728-929-8*) Weiser.

— The History of Magic: Including a Clear & Precise Exposition of Its Procedures, Its Rites & Its Mysteries. Waite, Arthur E., tr. (Illus.). 560p. 1993. reprint ed. pap. 29.95 (*1-56459-404-1*) Kessinger Pub.

— The Kabbalistic Prayer. Westcott, W. W., tr. 1989. reprint ed. pap. 3.95 (*1-55818-119-9*, Sure Fire) Holmes Pub.

— The Magical Ritual of the Sanctum Regnum. Bouleur, Joseph & Westcott, W. Wynn, eds. 1992. reprint ed. pap. 8.95 (*1-55818-184-9*, Sure Fire) Holmes Pub.

— The Magical Ritual of the Sanctum Regnum. Westcott, W. Wynn, ed. 108p. 1992. reprint ed. pap. 7.95 (*0-922802-95-5*) Kessinger Pub.

***Levi, Eliphas.** Mysteries of the Qabalah. (Illus.). 288p. 2000. (*1-57863-940-9*) Weiser.

— The Mysteries of The Qabalah: or Occult Agreement of the Two Testaments. (Illus.). 288p. 2000. pap. 18.95 (*0-87728-940-9*) Weiser.

Levi, Eliphas. The Paradoxes of the Highest Science. 172p. 1992. reprint ed. pap. 14.95 (*1-56459-020-8*) Kessinger Pub.

— The Paradoxes of the Highest Science. 2nd ed. 172p. 1996. reprint ed. spiral bd. 16.50 (*0-7873-0555-3*) Hlth Research.

— The Paradoxes of the Highest Science: A New Translation. Bouleur, Joseph, ed. & tr. by. from FRE. 1996. pap. 8.95 (*1-55818-341-8*) Holmes Pub.

— Science of Hermes. Waite, Arthur E., tr. from FRE. 1993. pap. 4.95 (*1-55818-207-1*) Holmes Pub.

— Transcendental Magic. Waite, A. E., tr. from FRE. LC 72-16629. (Illus.). 438p. 1968. reprint ed. pap. 14.95 (*0-87728-079-7*) Weiser.

— Transcendental Magic: Its Doctrine & Ritual (1910) 450p. 1998. reprint ed. pap. 27.50 (*0-7661-0297-1*) Kessinger Pub.

— Transcendental Magic, Its Doctrine & Ritual. 420p. 1996. reprint ed. pap. 30.00 (*0-7873-0556-1*) Hlth Research.

Levi, Enrique J. The Shadow. Zimmerman, Samuel A., tr. from SPA. LC 96-17103. (Discoveries Ser.). 119p. (C). 1996. pap. 13.95 (*0-935480-78-1*) Lat Am Lit Rev Pr.

Levi, Enrique J., ed. When New Flowers Bloomed: Short Stories by Women Writers from Costa Rica & Panama. LC 91-26038. (Discoveries Ser.). 208p. 1988. pap. 14.95 (*0-935480-47-1*) Lat Am Lit Rev Pr.

Levi, Enrique J. & Chambers, Leland H., eds. Contemporary Short Stories from Central America. (Institute of Latin American Studies). 320p. (Orig.). (C). 1994. pap. 17.95 (*0-292-74034-4*); text 37.50 (*0-292-74030-1*) U of Tex Pr.

Levi, Enzo. The Science of Water: The Foundation of Modern Hydraulics. Edina, Daniel E., tr. from SPA. LC 94-44189.Tr. of Agua Segun la Ciencia. 649p. 1995. 109.00 (*0-7844-0005-9*) Am Soc Civil Eng.

***Levi-Faur, David, et al, eds.** Israel: The Dynamics of Change & Continuity. LC 99-25984. (History, Politics & Society Ser.). 312p. 1999. 57.50 (*0-7146-5012-9*); pap. 24.50 (*0-7146-8062-1*) F Cass Pubs.

Levi, G. & Rodriguez-Artalejo, M., eds. Algebraic & Logic Programming: 4th International Conference, ALP '94, Madrid, Spain, September 14 16, 1994. Proceedings. (Lecture Notes in Computer Science Ser.: Vol. 850). 304p. 1994. 50.95 (*3-540-58431-5*) Spr-Verlag.

Levi, G., tr. see Segal, B., ed.

Levi, G. Ional. Static Analysis: 5th International Symposium, SAS'98, Pisa, Italy, September 14-16, 1998, Proceedings, Vol. 150. Goos, G. et al, eds. LC 98-40040. (Lecture Notes in Computer Science Ser.: Vol. 1503). ix, 383p. 1998. pap. 59.00 (*3-540-65014-8*) Spr-Verlag.

Levi, Gershon, ed. & tr. see Alon, Gedaliah.

Levi, Gerson B., ed. see Hirsch, Emil G.

Levi, Giorgio, ed. Advances in Logic Programming Theory. (International Schools for Computer Scientists Ser.). (Illus.). 268p. 1995. text 76.00 (*0-19-853853-7*) OUP.

Levi, Giorgio & Artalejo, Mario R. Algebraic & Logic Programming: Proceedings of the 4th International Conference, ALP '94, Madrid, Spain, September 1994. LC 94-33286. (Series Lecture Notes in Computer Science Ser.: 850). 1994. write for info. (*0-387-58431-5*) Spr-Verlag.

Levi, Giorgio, jt. ed. see Kirchner, H.

Levi, Giovanni. Inheriting Power: The Story of an Exorcist. Cochrane, Lydia G., tr. (Illus.). xviii, 210p. 1994. pap. text 12.95 (*0-226-47418-6*) U Ch Pr.

— Inheriting Power: The Story of an Exorcist. Cochrane, Lydia G., tr. (Illus.). xviii, 228p. 1998. lib. bdg. 36.00 (*0-226-47417-8*) U Ch Pr.

— Stormy Evolution to Modern Times, Vol. 2. (History of Young People Ser.). 1999. pap. 19.95 (*0-674-40408-4*) HUP.

Levi, Giovanni & Schmitt, Jean C., eds. A History of Young People in the West Vol. 1: Ancient & Medieval Rites of Passage. Naish, Camille, tr. from ITA. LC 96-34751. (Illus.). 396p. 1997. 35.00 (*0-674-40405-X*) Belknap Pr.

— A History of Young People in the West Vol. 2: Stormy Evolution to Modern Times. Volk, Carol, tr. from ITA. LC 96-34751. (Illus.). 409p. 1997. 35.00 (*0-674-40406-8*) Belknap Pr.

***Levi, Giovanni & Schmitt, Jean-Claude, eds.** Ancient & Medieval Rites of Passage. Naish, Camille, tr. (History of Young People Ser.: Vol. 1). 1999. pap. 19.95 (*0-674-40407-6*) HUP.

Levi, H. Dowling. The Aquarian Gospel of Jesus Christ. 1972. 20.95 (*0-87516-041-7*) DeVorss.

Levi, Herbert Walter. Spiders & Their Kin. (Golden Guide Ser.). 1990. 11.05 (*0-606-11873-X*, Pub. by Turtleback) Demco.

Levi, Honor, tr. see Pascal, Blaise.

Levi, Howard. Elements of Algebra. 4th ed. 189p. (C). 1990. text 12.95 (*0-8284-0103-9*, 103) Chelsea Pub.

— Topics in Geometry. LC 75-19477. 112p. 1976. reprint ed. 13.50 (*0-88275-280-4*) Krieger.

Levi, Isaac. The Covenant of Reason: Rationality & the Commitments of Thought. LC 97-2958. 272p. (C). 1997. text 59.95 (*0-521-57288-6*); pap. text 19.95 (*0-521-57601-6*) Cambridge U Pr.

— The Enterprise of Knowledge: An Essay on Knowledge, Credal Probability & Chance. 480p. 1983. pap. text 16.00 (*0-262-62043-X*) MIT Pr.

— The Fixation of Belief & Its Undoing: Changing Beliefs Through Inquiry. 204p. (C). 1991. text 59.95 (*0-521-41266-8*) Cambridge U Pr.

— For the Sake of the Argument: Ramsey Test Conditionals, Inductive Inference & Nonmonotonic Reasoning. 361p. (C). 1996. text 69.95 (*0-521-49713-2*) Cambridge U Pr.

— Hard Choices: Decision Making under Unresolved Conflict. 262p. (C). 1990. pap. text 24.95 (*0-521-38630-6*) Cambridge U Pr.

Levi, J. N. & Walker, A. G. Language in the Judicial Process. (Law, Society, & Policy Ser.: Vol. 5). (Illus.). 402p. (C). 1990. 65.00 (*0-306-43551-9*, Plenum Trade) Perseus Pubng.

Levi, James H. & Levi, Constance A. Larchmont, New York, the Way It Was: Picture Postcards of Old Larchmont. (Illus.). 52p. 1990. pap. 14.95 (*0-9628437-0-9*) J H Levi.

Levi, Jan H. A Muriel Rukeyser Reader. Rukeyser, Muriel, ed. 320p. 1995. pap. 15.00 (*0-393-31323-9*) Norton.

— Once I Gazed at You in Wonder. LC 98-50182. 96p. 1999. 19.95 (*0-8071-2364-1*); pap. 12.95 (*0-8071-2365-X*) La State U Pr.

Levi, Jan H., ed. see Morin, France, et al.

Levi, Jean. The Chinese Emperor. Bray, Barbara, tr. 1987. 18.95 (*0-15-117649-3*) Harcourt.

Levi, John. Rabbi Jacob Danglow: The Uncrowned Monarch of Australian Jews. LC 95-202213. 340p. 1995. 49.95 (*0-522-84645-9*, Pub. by Melbourne Univ Pr) Paul & Co Pubs.

Levi, John & Havinden, Michael. Economics of African Agriculture. LC 82-165400. (Illus.). 183p. reprint ed. pap. 56.80 (*0-8357-6102-9*, 203443600090) Bks Demand.

Levi, Jonathan. Treen for the Table. LC 99-494960. (Illus.). 224p. 1998. 69.50 (*1-85149-284-4*) Antique Collect.

Levi, Joseph A., ed. Alfonso X, el Sabio, Estoria de Alexandre el Grand, General Estoria (Quarta Parte) - The Life of Alexander the Great As Narrated by King Alfonso X the Wise, of Castile, in the General Estoria: Manuscript U. Vatican Urb. Lat. 539. LC 95-14847. (Hispanic Literature Ser.: Vol. 26). (Illus.). 224p. 1996. text 89.95 (*0-7734-8900-2*) E Mellen.

— Hernando del Pulgar: Los Claros Varones de Espana (ca. 1483), a Semi-paleographic Edition. (American University Studies II: Vol. 220). (SPA.). XXIII, 118p. (C). 1996. text 32.95 (*0-8204-3030-7*) P Lang Pubng.

Levi, Joseph Abraham, jt. ed. see Coblin, W. South.

Levi, Ken, ed. Violence & Religious Commitment: Implications of Jim Jones's People's Temple Movement. LC 81-83147. (Illus.). 224p. (C). 1982. 28.50 (*0-271-00296-4*) Pa St U Pr.

Levi, L. Stress in Industry: Cause, Effects, & Prevention. (Occupational Safety & Health Ser.: No. 51). vi, 70p. (Orig.). 1984. pap. 11.25 (*92-2-103539-5*) Intl Labour Office.

Levi, Leo, ed. Handbook of Tables of Functions for Applied Optics, CRC. (Handbook Ser.). 640p. 1974. 347.00 (*0-87819-371-5*, QC, CRC Reprint) Franklin.

Levi, Louise L. Sweet on My Lips: The Love Poems of Mirabai. LC 96-83816. (Illus.). 112p. pap. 12.95 (*1-887276-04-1*, Coolgrve Pr) Cool Grove Pub.

— Sweet on My Lips: The Love Poems of Mirabai. LC 96-83816. 112p. 1997. 18.00 (*1-887276-07-6*, Coolgrve Pr) Cool Grove Pub.

Levi, Louise L., tr. see Daumal, Rene.

Levi, Louise Landes. Guru Punk. deluxe ed. (Illus.). 125p. 2000. pap. 10.95 (*1-887276-15-7*) Cool Grove Pub.

Levi, M. Franz Kafka & Anarchism. 1972. 250.00 (*0-87700-189-8*) Revisionist Pr.

Levi, Makeda, ed. see Lewis, Yohanan.

Levi, Makedah, ed. see Lewis, Johanan.

Levi, Malkeyan, ed. see Lewis, Johanan.

Levi-Malvano, E. Montesquieu & Machiavelli. Pansini, Anthony J., ed. & comment by. 90p. (Orig.). (C). 1991. pap. 15.00 (*0-911876-05-7*) Greenvale.

Levi, Margaret. Consent, Dissent, & Patriotism. (Political Economy of Institutions & Decisions Ser.). (Illus.). 272p. (C). 1997. text 59.95 (*0-521-59055-8*); pap. text 19.95 (*0-521-59961-X*) Cambridge U Pr.

— Of Rule & Revenue. (California Series on Social Choice & Political Economy: Vol. 13). 1988. pap. 16.95 (*0-520-06750-9*, Pub. by U CA Pr) Cal Prin Full Svc.

Levi, Margaret, ed. Marxism, 2 vols. (Schools of Thought in Politics Ser.: No. 1). 1188p. 1991. text 385.00 (*1-85278-355-9*) E Elgar.

Levi, Margaret, jt. ed. see Braithwaite, Valerie A.

Levi, Margaret, jt. ed. see Cook, Karen S.

Levi, Mark. Qualitative Analysis of the Periodically Forced Relaxation Oscillations. LC 81-3642. (Memoirs of the American Mathematical Society Ser.: No. 32/224). 147p. 1981. pap. 17.00 (*0-8218-2244-6*, MEMO/32/244) Am Math.

Levi, Mark L. & Salam, Fathi M., eds. Dynamical Systems Approaches to Nonlinear Problems in Systems & Circuits. LC 87-63139. (Proceedings in Applied Mathematics Ser.: No. 31). (Illus.). xvi, 413p. 1988. text 49.75 (*0-89871-218-1*) Soc Indus-Appl Math.

Levi, Maurice. Economics & the Modern World. (C). 1994. text, teacher ed. 2.66 (*0-669-21669-0*); text, student ed. 24.36 (*0-669-21670-4*) HM.

— Economics & the Modern World. LC 93-70462. 637p. (C). 1994. pap. 58.36 (*0-669-21668-2*) HM Trade Div.

— International Finance: The Markets & Financial Management of Multinational Business. 3rd ed. LC 95-19667. (Finance Ser.). (Illus.). 520p. (C). 1995. 81.56 (*0-07-037687-5*) McGraw.

Levi, Maurice D., jt. auth. see Kupferman, Martin.

***Levi, Michael.** Fraud: Organization, Motivation & Control. LC 98-34351. (International Library of Criminology, Criminal Justice & Penology). 1999. 323.95 (*1-85521-716-3*) Ashgate Pub Co.

Levi, Michael. Regulating Fraud: White-Collar Crime & the Criminal Process. 416p. 1990. 55.00 (*0-422-61160-3*, A0718) Routledge.

L

An Asterisk (*) at the beginning of an entry indicates that the title is appearing for the first time.

L

***Levi, Michael & Pithouse, Andrew.** White Collar Crime & It's Victims: The Social & Media Construction of Business Fraud. (Clarendon Studies in Criminology). 300p. 2000. text 75.00 (*0-19-826254-X*, Clarendon Pr) OUP.

Levi, Mike, ed. Relections on Organized Crime: Patterns & Control. 112p. 1999. pap. 29.95 (*0-631-21436-4*) Blackwell Pubs.

Levi, Mike, jt. ed. see Nelken, David.

Levi, Miriam. Effective Jewish Parenting. 1986. pap. 17.95 (*0-87306-405-4*) Feldheim.

Levi-Montalcini, Rita. Saga of the Nerve Growth Factor. LC 97-180647. 1997. 84.00 (*981-02-2604-7*) World Scientific Pub.

Levi, Patricia E., jt. ed. see Chambers, Janice E.

Levi, Peta. New British Design, 1998. (Illus.). 272p. 1998. 85.00 (*1-84000-099-6*, Pub. by Conran Octopus) Antique Collect.

Levi, Peter. Atlas of the Greek World. (Cultural Atlas Ser.). (Illus.). 240p. 1981. 45.00 (*0-87196-448-1*) Facts on File.

— Collected Poems, 1955-1975. 2nd ed. 256p. 1984. 34.95 (*0-85646-134-2*, Pub. by Anvil Press); pap. 21.95 (*0-85646-135-0*, Pub. by Anvil Press) Dufour.

— Edward Lear: A Biography. 362p. 1995. 30.00 (*0-684-19688-3*) S&S Trade.

— Five Ages. Date not set. 18.95 (*0-85646-036-2*, Pub. by Anvil Press) Dufour.

— Goodbye to the Art of Poetry. 40p. 1989. pap. 9.95 (*0-85646-212-8*, Pub. by Anvil Press) Dufour.

— Horace: A Life. LC 97-35012. 270p. 1998. 40.00 (*0-415-92008-6*) Routledge.

— Knit One, Drop One. 1987. 15.95 (*0-8027-5688-3*) Walker & Co.

***Levi, Peter.** Light Garden of the Angel King: Travels in Afghanistan. (Illus.). 2000. pap. 18.95 (*1-873429-35-5*) Pallas Athene.

Levi, Peter. The Noise Made by Poems. 2nd ed. 108p. 1984. 24.95 (*0-85646-132-6*, Pub. by Anvil Press); pap. 17.95 (*0-85646-133-4*, Pub. by Anvil Press) Dufour.

— The Rags of Time. 90p. 1994. pap. 17.95 (*0-85646-258-6*, Pub. by Anvil Press) Dufour.

— Reed Music. LC 97-149362. 80p. 1997. pap. 18.95 (*0-85646-279-9*, Pub. by Anvil Press) Dufour.

— Shadow & Bone. 118p. 1989. pap. 17.95 (*0-85646-211-X*, Pub. by Anvil Press) Dufour.

— Shakespeare's Birthday. 38p. 1985. pap. 11.95 (*0-85646-142-3*, Pub. by Anvil Press) Dufour.

— Virgil: His Life & Times. LC 98-47718. 256p. 1999. text 27.95 (*0-312-19352-1*) St Martin.

Levi, Peter, et al. The Lamentation of the Dead: With the Lament for Arthur O'Leary. 40p. 1984. pap. 11.95 (*0-85646-140-7*, Pub. by Anvil Press) Dufour.

Levi, Peter, jt. auth. see Brewster, Harry.

Levi, Peter, ed. & intro. see Johnson, Samuel, et al.

Levi, Peter, ed. & intro. see Kipling, Rudyard.

Levi, Peter, tr. see Papadiamantis, Alexandros.

Levi, Peter, tr. & intro. see Pausanias.

Levi, Peter S. Water, Rock & Sand: Poems. LC 63-2158. 1962. 15.95 (*0-8023-1071-0*) Dufour.

Levi, Primo. The Drowned & the Saved. Rosenthal, Raymond, tr. (International Ser.). 1989. pap. 12.00 (*0-679-72186-X*) Vin Bks.

— If Not Now, When? Weaver, William, tr. (Twentieth-Century Classics Ser.). 356p. 1995. pap. 13.95 (*0-14-018893-2*, Penguin Classics) Viking Penguin.

— Moments of Reprieve. (Twentieth-Century Classics Ser.). 176p. 1995. pap. 11.95 (*0-14-018895-9*, Penguin Classics) Viking Penguin.

— The Monkey's Wrench. Feldman, Ruth, tr. (Twentieth-Century Classics Ser.). 176p. 1995. pap. 12.95 (*0-14-018892-4*, Penguin Classics) Viking Penguin.

— The Periodic Table. Rosenthal, Raymond, tr. 1996. 17.00 (*0-679-44463-7*) Fodors Travel.

— The Periodic Table. 240p. 1995. pap. 11.00 (*0-8052-1041-5*) Schocken.

— The Reawakening. 240p. 1995. per. 11.00 (*0-684-82635-6*) S&S Trade.

— Survival in Auschwitz. (U Ser.). 192p. 1995. per. 11.00 (*0-684-82680-1*) S&S Trade.

— Survival in Auschwitz & The Reawakening: Two Memoirs. Woolf, Stuart, tr. from ITA. 384p. 1986. 19.45 (*0-671-60541-0*) Summit Bks.

***Levi, Primo.** The Voice of Memory. Belpoliti, Marco, ed. Gordon, Robert, tr. from ITA. 2001. 24.95 (*1-56584-645-1*, Pub. by New Press NY) Norton.

Levi-Provencal, E., ed. see Menendez Pidal, Ramon.

Levi, Ran. On Finite Groups & Homotopy Theory. LC 95-34452. (Memoirs of the American Mathematical Society Ser.: No. 567). 100p. 1995. pap. 35.00 (*0-8218-0401-4*, MEMO/118/567) Am Math.

Levi, Robert B. Fifth Discipline Study. 1910. mass mkt. 10.95 (*0-385-49085-2*) Doubleday.

Levi, Ruth, jt. auth. see Levi, Avraham.

Levi, S. M., jt. auth. see Zelikman, Vitalii L.

Levi, Salvator & Chervenak, Frank A., eds. Ultrasound Screening for Fetal Anomalies: Is It Worth It? LC 98-17556. (Annals of the New York Academy of Sciences Ser.). 350p. 1998. 140.00 (*1-57331-123-5*); pap. 140.00 (*1-57331-124-3*) NY Acad Sci.

Levi, Samuel. Iginia d'Asti. (Italian Opera 1810-1840 Ser.). 250p. 1985. text 30.00 (*0-8240-6558-1*) Garland.

— Ildegonda. (Italian Opera Ser., 1810-1840). 255p. 1986. text 30.00 (*0-8240-6559-X*) Garland.

Levi-Setti, Riccardo. Elementary Particles. LC 63-22713. (Chicago Lectures in Physics Ser.). 172p. 1996. pap. text 10.95 (*0-226-47446-1*) U Ch Pr.

— Elementary Particles. LC 63-22713. (Chicago Lectures in Physics: Vol. 8, No. 3). 180p. reprint ed. pap. 55.80 (*0-608-09462-5*, 205426200005) Bks Demand.

— Trilobites. 2nd ed. LC 92-38716. (Illus.). 352p. (C). 1993. 45.00 (*0-226-47451-8*) U Ch Pr.

— Trilobites. 2nd ed. (Illus.). x, 342p. 1995. pap. 27.95 (*0-226-47452-6*) U Ch Pr.

— Trilobites: A Photographic Atlas. LC 74-7555. (Illus.). 222p. reprint ed. pap. 68.90 (*0-608-18212-5*, 205661600078) Bks Demand.

Levi-Setti, Riccardo & Lasinski, Thomas. Strongly Interacting Particles. LC 73-83750. (Chicago Lectures in Physics). 328p. reprint ed. pap. 101.70 (*0-608-18242-7*, 205665600078) Bks Demand.

Levi, Stephen. Daphne in Cottage D. 1968. pap. 5.25 (*0-8222-0270-0*) Dramatists Play.

Levi, Steven. A Destiny Going Sour. 1991. 5.00 (*0-932593-19-4*) Black Bear.

Levi, Steven C. Cowboys of the Sky: The Story of Alaska's Bush Pilots. (Illus.). 128p. (YA). (gr. 5 up). 1996. 17.95 (*0-8027-8331-7*); lib. bdg. 18.85 (*0-8027-8332-5*) Walker & Co.

— Deadwood Dick: The Black Cowboy. 224p. 1996. reprint ed. mass mkt. 5.99 (*0-87067-872-8*, BH872-8) Holloway.

— Our National Tapestry. 1986. 2.00 (*0-932593-06-2*) Black Bear.

Levi-Strauss, Claude. De Pres et de Loin: Entretiens: Deux Ans Apres. (FRE.). 1991. pap. 16.95 (*0-7859-3935-0*) Fr & Eur.

— Elementary Structures of Kinship. Bell, James H. et al, trs. LC 68-12840. (Illus.). 1971. reprint ed. pap. 24.00 (*0-8070-4669-8*) Beacon Pr.

— Entretiens avec Claude Live-Strauss. (FRE.). 188p. 1989. pap. 13.95 (*0-7859-4446-X*, 2266032631) Fr & Eur.

— From Honey to Ashes: Introduction to a Science of Mythology, Vol. 2. Weightman, John & Weightman, Doreen, trs. LC 82-15965. 512p. 1993. pap. text 13.00 (*0-226-47489-5*) U Ch Pr.

— L' Identite. (FRE.). 1987. pap. 20.95 (*0-7859-3008-6*) Fr & Eur.

— Introduction to the Work of Marcel Mauss. Baker, Felicity, tr. (ASA Monographs Ser.). 88p. (C). 1987. pap. 20.99 (*0-7100-9066-8*, Routledge Thoemms) Routledge.

— The Jealous Potter. Chorier, Benedicte, tr. (Illus.). 264p. 1988. 23.95 (*0-226-47480-1*) U Ch Pr.

— The Jealous Potter. Chorier, Benedicte, tr. (Illus.). viii, 252p. 1996. pap. 15.95 (*0-226-47482-8*) U Ch Pr.

— Look, Listen, Read. Singer, Brian C., tr. from ENG. LC 96-51629. (Illus.). 224p. 1997. 24.00 (*0-465-06880-4*, Pub. by Basic) HarpC.

— Look, Listen, Read. 224p. 2000. pap. 10.00 (*0-465-06881-2*, Pub. by Basic) HarpC.

— Myth & Meaning. LC 78-25833. 80p. 1995. pap. 10.00 (*0-8052-1038-5*) Schocken.

— Myth & Meaning: Five Talks for Radio. LC 78-5212. (Massey Lectures: 1977). 64p. reprint ed. pap. 30.00 (*0-8357-8240-9*, 203403000088) Bks Demand.

— The Naked Man Vol. 4: Mythologiques. Weightman, John & Weightman, Doreen, trs. LC 79-3399. (Illus.). 746p. 1990. pap. text 25.95 (*0-226-47496-8*) U Ch Pr.

— The Origin of Table Manners Vol. 3: Mythologiques. Weightman, John & Weightman, Doreen, trs. (Illus.). 590p. 1990. pap. text 23.95 (*0-226-47493-3*) U Ch Pr.

— El Pensamiento Salvaje. (Breviarios Ser.). (SPA.). pap. 9.99 (*968-16-0933-6*, Pub. by Fondo) Continental Bk.

— Pensee Sauvage. rev. ed. (FRE.). 1985. 15.95 (*2-266-03816-8*) Adlers Foreign Bks.

— Race et Histoire. (FRE.). 1987. pap. 12.95 (*0-7859-3970-9*) Fr & Eur.

— Race et Histoire. (Folio Essais Ser.: No. 58). (FRE.). 127p. 1987. pap. 9.95 (*2-07-032413-3*) Schoenhof.

— The Raw & the Cooked: Introduction to a Science of Mythology, Vol. 1. Weightman, John & Weightman, Doreen, trs. LC 82-15895. (Illus.). 406p. 1983. pap. text 24.95 (*0-226-47487-9*) U Ch Pr.

— Saudades do Brasil: A Photographic Memoir. Modelski, Sylvia, tr. LC 95-21579. (Illus.). 224p. (C). 1995. 50.00 (*0-295-97472-9*) U of Wash Pr.

— Saudades do Brasil: A Photographic Memoir. Modelski, Sylvia, tr. LC 95-21579. (Illus.). 224p. 1996. pap. 29.95 (*0-295-97566-0*) U of Wash Pr.

— Savage Mind. LC 66-28197. (Nature of Human Society Ser.). 1968. pap. 16.95 (*0-226-47484-4*, P325) U Ch Pr.

— The Story of Lynx. Tihanyi, Catherine, tr. from FRE. LC 94-34811.Tr. of Histoire de Lynx. (Illus.). 294p. 1995. 24.95 (*0-226-47471-2*) U Ch Pr.

— The Story of Lynx. Tihanyi, Catherine, tr.Tr. of Histoire de Lynx. (Illus.). xviii, 276p. 1996. pap. 17.95 (*0-226-47472-0*) U Ch Pr.

— Structural Anthropology, Vol. 1. LC 63-17344. 432p. 2000. pap. 22.00 (*0-465-09516-X*, Pub. by Basic) HarpC.

— Structural Anthropology, Vol. 2. Layton, Monique, tr. LC 82-16115. xvi, 400p. 1983. pap. text 21.00 (*0-226-47491-7*) U Ch Pr.

— Totemism. Needham, Rodney, tr. 1963. pap. 15.00 (*0-8070-4671-X*) Beacon Pr.

— Tristes Tropiques. LC 97-11778. 1997. 22.00 (*0-679-60246-1*) Modern Lib NY.

— Tristes Tropiques. Weightman, John & Weightman, Doreen, trs. (Illus.). 432p. 1992. pap. 16.95 (*0-14-016562-2*, Penguin Bks) Viking Penguin.

— Tristes Tropiques. rev. ed. (FRE., Illus.). 1984. 17.95 (*2-266-02612-7*) Adlers Foreign Bks.

— The View from Afar. Neugroschel, Joachim & Hoss, Phoebe, trs. 328p. 1992. pap. 16.50 (*0-226-47474-7*) U Ch Pr.

— The Way of the Masks. Modelski, Sylvia, tr. from FRE. LC 82-2723. (Illus.). 276p. 1988. pap. 22.50 (*0-295-96636-X*) U of Wash Pr.

Levi-Strauss, Claude & Eribon, Didier. Conversations with Claude Levi-Strauss. Wissing, Paula, tr. LC 90-11052. 192p. 1991. 19.95 (*0-226-47475-5*) U Ch Pr.

Levi-Strauss, David, et al. Francesca Woodman. (Illus.). 160p. 1998. 39.95 (*3-931141-96-9*, Pub. by Scalo Pubs) Dist Art Pubs.

Levi, Trude. A Cat Called Adolf. LC 94-18872. (Library of Holocaust Testimonies). 180p. 1995. pap. 19.50 (*0-85303-289-0*, Pub. by M Vallentine & Co) Intl Spec Bk.

Levi-Valensi. Les Critiques de Notre Temps et Camus. (FRE.). 13.95 (*0-7859-0036-5*, F91100) Fr & Eur.

Levi, Vicki G. & Eisenberg, Lee. Atlantic City: One Hundred Twenty-Five Years of Ocean Madness. LC 93-46513. (Illus.). 224p. 1994. pap. 22.95 (*0-89815-613-0*) Ten Speed Pr.

Levi, Vicki Gold, jt. auth. see Shepard, Richard F.

Levi, Virgil. John Paul Ii: A Tribute in Words & Pictures. LC 99-23941. (Illus.). 160p. 1999. 25.00 (*0-688-16621-0*, Wm Morrow) Morrow Avon.

Levi, Wendell M. Encyclopedia of Pigeon Breeds. 1965. 56.50 (*0-910876-02-9*) Levi Pub.

— Making Pigeons Pay. rev. ed. 1984. reprint ed. 20.00 (*0-910876-03-7*) Levi Pub.

— The Pigeon. 1986. reprint ed. 52.00 (*0-910876-01-0*) Levi Pub.

Levi, Werner. The Coming End of War. LC 80-39568. (Sage Library of Social Research: No. 117). 183p. reprint ed. pap. 56.80 (*0-8357-4819-7*, 203775600009) Bks Demand.

— From Alms to Liberation: The Catholic Church, the Theologians, Poverty, & Politics. LC 88-29009. 183p. 1989. 49.95 (*0-275-93171-4*, C3171, Praeger Pubs) Greenwood.

— International Politics: Foundations of the System. LC 73-84786. 285p. reprint ed. pap. 88.40 (*0-7837-2938-3*, 205751600006) Bks Demand.

Levi, Yaakov, jt. auth. see Radday, Yehuda T.

Levi, Yehuda. Facing Current Challenges: Essays on Judaism. 502p. 38.00 (*0-87559-226-0*) Shalom.

Levi, Yehuda. Torah Study: A Survey of Classic Sources on Timely Issues. 22.95 (*0-87306-555-7*) Feldheim.

Levia, Oz, ed. see Bergee, Jean-Michel.

Levialdi, Stefano & Bernardelli, C. Representation: Relationship Betwen Language & Image. 236p. 1994. text 71.00 (*981-02-1690-4*) World Scientific Pub.

***Leviant, Curt.** Diary of an Adulterous Woman: A Novel. 440p. 2000. 29.95 (*0-8156-0670-2*) Syracuse U Pr.

Leviant, Curt. The Man Who Thought He Was Messiah. 226p. 1990. 9.95 (*0-8276-0371-1*) JPS Phila.

— Masterpieces of Hebrew Literature: A Treasury of 2000 Years of Jewish Creativity. 1969. pap. 24.95 (*0-87068-079-X*) Ktav.

***Leviant, Curt.** Partita in Venice: A Novel. unabridged ed. LC 99-64440. 208p. 1999. 24.00 (*0-942979-64-8*) Livingston AL.

— Partita in Venice: A Novel. unabridged ed. 192p. 2000. pap. 12.00 (*0-942979-63-X*) Livingston U Pr.

— The Yemenite Girl: A Novel. LC 99-34414. 192p. 1999. pap. text 17.95 (*0-8156-0619-2*) Syracuse U Pr.

Leviant, Curt, jt. auth. see Aleichem, Sholem.

Leviant, Curt, tr. see Kipnis, Itzik.

Leviant, Curt, tr. see Singer, Isaac Bashevis.

Leviatan, D., jt. ed. see Baron, S.

Leviatan, Uriel, ed. see Quarter, Jack.

Leviatin. How the Other Half Lives. 274p. 1996. pap. text 11.95 (*0-312-11700-0*) St Martin.

Leviatin, David. Prague Sprung: Notes & Voices from the New World. LC 93-2869. 160p. 1993. 57.95 (*0-275-94536-7*, C4536, Praeger Pubs) Greenwood.

Levibiel, Timothy. The Deer Family. (Zoobooks Ser.). 24p. (J). (gr. 1-7). 1993. 13.95 (*0-937934-97-6*) Wildlife Educ.

Levibiel, Timothy, jt. auth. see Wildlife Education, Ltd. Staff.

Levich, A. P. On the Way to Understanding the Time Phenomenon: The Constructions of Time in Natural Science. (Series on Advances in Mathematics for Applied Sciences). 216p. 1995. text 48.00 (*981-02-1360-3*) World Scientific Pub.

— On the Way to Understanding the Time Phenomenon: The Constructions of Time in Natural Science, Pt. 2. (Series on Advances in Mathematics for Applied Sciences). 500p. 1996. text 109.00 (*981-02-1606-8*) World Scientific Pub.

Levich, Eugene W. The Kwangsi Way in Kuomintang China, 1931-1939. LC 92-37094. (Studies on Modern China). 336p. (C). (gr. 13). 1993. text 81.95 (*1-56324-200-1*, East Gate Bk) M E Sharpe.

Levich, M., jt. auth. see Crandall, R.

Levich, Marvin, jt. auth. see Crandall, Richard.

Levich, Richard, ed. Emerging Market Capital Flows: Proceedings of a Conference Held at the Stern School of Business, New York University on May 23-24, 1996. LC 97-23943. (New York University Salomon Center Series on Financial Markets & Institutions). 474p. 1998. lib. bdg. 129.95 (*0-7923-9976-5*) Kluwer Academic.

Levich, Richard M. International Financial Markets. 2nd ed. 2000. 63.50 (*0-07-233865-2*) McGraw.

— International Financial Markets: Prices & Policies. LC 97-11583. 736p. (C). 1997. text 54.95 (*0-256-13011-6*, Irwn McGrw-H) McGrw-H Hghr Educ.

— The International Money Market: An Assessment of Forecasting Techniques & Market Efficiency. Altman, Edward I. & Walter, Ingo I., eds. LC 78-13841. (Contemporary Studies in Economic & Financial Analysis: Vol. 22). 178p. 1979. 78.50 (*0-89232-109-1*) Jai Pr.

— Overshooting in the Foreign Exchange Market. (Occasional Paper Ser.: Vol. 5). 38p. 1981. pap. 7.00 (*1-56708-004-9*) Grp of Thirty.

Levick, Barbara. Claudius: The Corruption of Power. LC 89-51800. 272p. (C). 1993. pap. 19.00 (*0-300-05831-4*) Yale U Pr.

***Levick, Barbara.** The Government of the Roman Empire: A Sourcebook. LC 00-25440. 2000. pap. write for info. (*0-415-23237-6*) Routledge.

Levick, Barbara. Tiberius the Politician. (Classical Lives Ser.). (Illus.). 256p. 1986. reprint ed. pap. 16.95 (*0-7099-4132-3*, Pub. by C Helm) Routldge.

***Levick, Barbara.** Tiberius the Politician. 2nd ed. 1999. pap. 24.99 (*0-415-21753-9*) Routledge.

Levick, Barbara. Vespasian. LC 98-52448. 376p. 1999. 40.00 (*0-415-16618-7*) Routledge.

Levick, Barbara, jt. ed. see Hawley, Richard.

Levick, Dwight E. Risk Management & Insurance Audit Techniques. rev. ed. 952p. 1996. ring bd. 169.00 (*0-923240-17-9*) Stndrd Publishing.

Levick, Dwight E. & Grzincic, Barbara. Workers Compensation: Exposures, Coverage, Claims. Standard Publishing Corporation Staff, ed. 608p. 1994. 155.00 (*0-923240-12-8*) Stndrd Publishing.

Levick, Edwin, jt. auth. see Jobson, Gary A.

Levick, Hugh, tr. see Camus, Albert.

Levick, J. R. An Introduction to Cardiovascular Physiology. 2nd ed. LC 94-45631. (Illus.). 320p. 1995. pap. text 45.00 (*0-7506-2167-2*, Focal) Buttrwrth-Heinemann.

***Levick, J. R.** An Introduction to Cardiovascular Physiology. 3rd ed. 384p. 2000. pap. 37.50 (*0-7506-4593-8*) Buttrwrth-Heinemann.

Levick, Melba. Japanese-style Gardens of the Pacific West Coast. LC 98-48810. 1999. 45.00 (*0-8478-2109-9*, Pub. by Rizzoli Intl) St Martin.

Levick, Melba, photos by. Antonio Gaudi: Master Architect. LC 99-59876. (Tiny Folio Ser.). (Illus.). 144p. (J). 2000. 35.00 (*0-7892-0220-4*, Abbeville Kids) Abbeville Pr.

— Barcelona. LC 92-30383. (Illus.). 332p. 1993. 85.00 (*0-8109-3125-7*, Pub. by Abrams) Time Warner.

— Paradise Found: The Beautiful Retreats & Sanctuaries of California & the Southwest. (Illus.). 132p. 1995. pap. 18.95 (*0-8118-0687-1*) Chronicle Bks.

Levick, Melba & Young, Stanley. Missions of California. (Illus.). 138p. 1988. pap. 16.95 (*0-87701-540-6*) Chronicle Bks.

Levick, Melba, et al. Reflections on the Pool: California Designs for Swimming. LC 96-44236. (Illus.). 160p. 1997. 45.00 (*0-8478-2014-9*, Pub. by Rizzoli Intl) St Martin.

Levick, Melba, jt. auth. see Permanyer, Lluis.

Levick, Myra. See What I'm Saying: What Children Tell Us Through Their Art. LC 97-72127. (Illus.). xi, 138p. 1997. pap. 19.95 (*1-888461-04-7*) Islewest Pub.

Levick, Myra F. They Could Not Talk & So They Drew: Children's Styles of Coping & Thinking. (Illus.). 240p. 1983. pap. 40.95 (*0-398-06518-7*); text 56.95 (*0-398-04800-2*) C C Thomas.

Levicki, Cyril. The Leadership Gene: Character, Management & Leadership. 1998. 52.50 (*0-273-63557-3*, Pub. by Pitman Pub) Trans-Atl Phila.

— The Stratgey Workout: Build & Implement a Robust Strategic Plan. (Illus.). 250p. (Orig.). 1997. pap. 25.00 (*0-273-62442-3*) F T P-H.

Levicki, Nancy. College Cookbook for Students by Students. 1994. pap. text 12.95 (*0-9631318-2-6*) NJL Interests.

— The College Cookbook, No. Two: By Students, for Students. 2nd rev. ed. (Illus.). 170p. 1993. pap. 11.95 (*0-9631318-1-8*) NJL Interests.

Levicki, Nancy, jt. auth. see Silkwood, Chris.

Levicki, Nancy S. Your Housekeeper's Cookbook: Bilingual Recipes, Menus & More. fac. ed. LC 85-5179. (ENG.). 151p. pap. 46.90 (*0-7837-7415-X*, 204721000006) Bks Demand.

Levicoff, Judith, et al. The Butterfly Garden. (Illus.). 48p. (Orig.). (J). (gr. 1-4). 1994. pap. 10.95 (*1-880812-17-7*) S Ink WA.

Levidow, Les, jt. ed. see Gill, Dawn.

Levie, Alison, ed. French Fashions of Good Taste, 1920-1922: From Pochoir Illustrations. (Illus.). 144p. 1998. 39.95 (*0-7643-0604-9*) Schiffer.

Levie, Alison, photos by. Useful Beauty: Turning Practical Items on a Wood Lathe. LC 95-22738. (Illus.). 64p. (Orig.). 1995. pap. 12.95 (*0-88740-851-6*) Schiffer.

Levie, Alison, jt. auth. see Sing, Dick.

Levie, Alvin. Nicaragua: The People Speak. LC 85-13485. (Illus.). 221p. 1985. pap. 12.95 (*0-89789-084-1*, Bergin & Garvey) Greenwood.

Levie, Alvin. Nicaragua: The People Speak. (Illus.). 221p. 1985. 34.94 (*0-89789-083-3*, Bergin & Garvey) Greenwood.

Levie, Arlette. Half a World Away. (FRE.). 32p. (J). 1990. pap. 3.99 (*0-85953-458-8*); pap. 3.99 (*0-85953-555-X*) Childs Play.

Levie, Betty B. Christmas Magic. (J). 1995. pap. 19.00 (*0-9638776-4-X*) Pea Pod Tree.

Levie, Eleanor. Creations in Miniature: 101 Tiny Treasures to Stitch & Craft. LC 98-84107. (Illus.). 128p. 1998. pap. 19.95 (*0-87341-574-4*, TINYT) Krause Pubns.

— The Halloween Costume Book. 160p. (Orig.). 1994. pap. text 4.99 (*0-425-15831-4*) Berkley Pub.

— Halloween Fun. pap. 4.99 (*0-425-13958-1*) Berkley Pub.

— Halloween Fun. LC 97-48511. 1998. 5.99 (*0-517-18816-3*) Random Hse Value.

— Halloween Fun: One-Hundred-One Ways to Have a Safe & Scary Halloween. 192p. 1993. mass mkt. 4.99 (*0-425-13955-7*) Berkley Pub.

Levie, Howard S. The Law of Non-International Armed Conflicts: Protocol II to the 1949 Geneva Conventions. LC 87-1706. 1987. lib. bdg. 217.50 (*90-247-3491-6*) Kluwer Academic.

— Mine Warfare at Sea. 236p. (C). 1992. lib. bdg. 111.00 (*0-7923-1526-X*) Kluwer Academic.

An Asterisk (*) at the beginning of an entry indicates that the title is appearing for the first time.

L

— Terrorism in War: The Law of War Crimes. LC 93-25148. (Terrorism). 721p. 1993. text 105.00 (*0-379-20148-8*) Oceana.

Levie, Hugo, et al, eds. Fighting Closures: De-industrialization & the Trade Unions 1979-1983. 233p. 1984. 42.50 (*0-85124-361-4*, Pub. by Spkesman) Coronet Bks.

Levie, Hugo, jt. ed. see Hastings, Sue.

Levie, W. Howard, jt. ed. see Fleming, Malcolm.

Levien, Alisa & Barad, Leona G. The Soap Opera Companion: Your Complete Guide to Shows, Resources, Collectibles, & More. (Illus.). xii, 436p. 1998. pap. 23.95 (*0-9662310-0-7*) Stonyridge Pr.

Levien, D. J. Wormwood. LC 98-43840. 256p. 1999. 22.95 (*0-7868-6506-7*, Pub. by Hyperion) Time Warner.

— Wormwood: A Novel. 256p. 2000. pap. 14.00 (*0-7868-8436-3*, Pub. by Hyperion) Little.

Levien, David. Rounders: A Screenplay. 208p. 1998. pap. 10.95 (*0-7868-8422-3*, Pub. by Hyperion) Time Warner.

Levien, David H. Introduction to Surgery. 2nd ed. LC 92-48894. (Illus.). 304p. 1993. pap. text 31.95 (*0-7216-6647-7*, W B Saunders Co) Harcrt Hlth Sci Grp.

— Introduction to Surgery. 3rd ed. Bralow, Lisette, ed. LC 98-36803. (Illus.). 335p. 1999. pap. text. write for info. (*0-7216-7652-9*, W B Saunders Co) Harcrt Hlth Sci Grp.

***Levien, Frederic H.** Overview of Information Warfare: Principles & Practice. (Overview Summary Ser.). (Illus.). 32p. 1999. pap. 8.00 (*1-885897-11-1*) Lynx Pubng.

***Levien, Helen.** Change That Garden: Transforming Furniture, Ornaments & Pots. (Illus.). 96p. 2000. pap. 17.95 (*0-85532-890-8*) Srch Pr.

— Change That Garden: Transforming Furniture, Ornaments & Pots. 96p. 2000. 29.99 (*0-85532-940-8*, Pub. by Srch Pr) Midpt Trade.

Levien, J. R., compiled by. Anatomy of a Crash: Nineteen Twenty-Nine. LC 89-84135. (Illus.). 1989. reprint ed. pap. 12.00 (*0-87034-037-9*) Fraser Pub Co.

Levien, Julia. Duncan Dance: A Guide for Young People Ages Six to Sixteen. (Illus.). 112p. (Orig.). (J). (gr. 1-11). 1994. pap. 12.95 (*0-87127-198-2*) Princeton Bk Co.

Levien, Michael, ed. see Maurois, Andre.

Levien, Michael, ed. see Sadleir, Michael.

Levien, Roger E. Taking Technology to Market. 1997. pap. text 12.95 (*1-56052-439-1*) Crisp Pubns.

Levier, Francis A., jt. auth. see Edmunds, David R.

Levieux, Eleanor & Levieux, Michel. Insiders' French: Beyond the Dictionary. 1999. 30.00 (*0-226-47502-6*) U Ch Pr.

— Insiders' French: Beyond the Dictionary. LC 98-49005. (Illus.). 288p. 1999. pap. 12.00 (*0-226-47503-4*) U Ch Pr.

Levieux, Eleanor, tr. see Duby, Georges.

Levieux, Eleanor, tr. see Gauguin, Paul.

Levieux, Eleanor, tr. see Memmi, Albert.

Levieux, Eleanor, tr. see Zola, Emile.

Levieux, Michel, jt. auth. see Levieux, Eleanor.

Leviev, G. I. Nonlinear Effects in Metals in the Microwave Band, Vol. 11. (Soviet Scientific Reviews Ser.: Vol. 11, Pt. 2). ii, 94p. 1989. pap. text 106.00 (*3-7186-4903-9*) Gordon & Breach.

Levignac, Jacque & Wolfe, S. Anthony, eds. The Chin. (Illus.). 174p. 1990. text. write for info. (*0-443-04221-7*) Church.

Levigne, Heather, jt. auth. see Kalman, Bobbie.

Levill. Concrete Defects. LC 98-107946. (Illus.). 136p. (C). 1997. 60.00 (*0-419-21690-1*, E & FN Spon) Routledge.

Levillain, Philippe. Dictionnaire Historique de la Papaute. (FRE.). 1776p. 375.00 (*0-7859-8720-7*) Fr & Eur.

Levillot, B., ed. see Hugo, Victor.

Levin. Balm in Gilead. 1997. pap. write for info. (*0-8052-1085-7*) Schocken.

— Condition England Question: Carlyle, Mill, Engels. LC 98-10759. 208p. 1998. text 65.00 (*0-312-21411-1*) St Martin.

— Contemporary Physical Geology. 3rd ed. (C). 1990. pap. text, student ed. 19.00 (*0-03-033187-0*, Pub. by Harcourt Coll Pubs) Harcourt.

— Continuing Physical Geology. 3rd ed. (C). 1990. pap. text, teacher ed. 34.00 (*0-03-031138-1*) Harcourt Coll Pubs.

— The Earth Through Time. 5th ed. (C). 1995. 246.00 (*0-03-015647-5*) Harcourt Coll Pubs.

— The Earth Through Time. 6th ed. 192p. (C). 1998. pap. text, student ed. 28.00 (*0-03-021783-0*, Pub. by Harcourt Coll Pubs) Harcourt.

— The Earth Through Time: Test Bank. 5th ed. (C). 1995. pap. text, teacher ed. 42.00 (*0-03-015637-8*) Harcourt.

***Levin.** Elementary Statistics in Social Research. 8th ed. LC 99-22898. (Illus.). 432p. (C). 1999. 78.00 (*0-321-04460-6*) Allyn.

Levin. Principles of Experimental Psychology: Instructor's Course Planner. 1994. 14.68 (*0-697-12795-8*) McGraw.

— Prose Models. 10th ed. (C). 1995. pap. text 35.50 (*0-15-502167-2*, Pub. by Harcourt Coll Pubs); pap. text, teacher ed. 30.00 (*0-15-502168-0*) Harcourt Coll Pubs.

Levin. Quick & Fun Learning Activities for Babies. 1996. pap. text, wbk. ed. 8.95 (*1-55734-553-8*) Tchr Create Mat.

Levin. Returns Only - Sg Earth Through Time 4e. 4th ed. (C). 1993. pap. text 11.50 (*0-03-097764-9*) Harcourt.

***Levin.** Setting the Agenda. 2000. 65.00 (*0-8133-6640-2*, Pub. by Westview) HarpC.

Levin. Sociological Ideas. (Sociology - Introductory Level Ser.). 1984. pap., teacher ed. write for info. (*0-534-03206-0*) Wadsworth Pub.

— Sociological Ideas. 3rd ed. (Sociology - Intro Level Ser.). 1990. mass mkt., teacher ed. write for info. (*0-534-14647-3*) Wadsworth Pub.

— Testbank/Continuing Physical Geology. 3rd ed. (C). 1990. pap. text, student ed., suppl. ed. 40.50 (*0-03-032659-1*, Pub. by Harcourt Coll Pubs) Harcourt.

— Venture Capital. 1995. 125.00 (*0-316-52276-7*) Little.

Levin, ed. United States School Laws & Rules, 1998. 1392p. 1998. text 45.00 (*0-314-23071-8*) West Pub.

Levin & Emblad. Pediatric Medical Student Pearls of Wisdom. (Pearls of Wisdom Ser.). 1999. pap. 32.00 (*1-890369-24-1*) Boston Medical.

Levin & Rubin. Stats for Management. 7th ed. 1997. pap. text, student ed. 22.20 (*0-13-619636-5*) P-H.

Levin, et al. Civil Procedure: 1998 Supplement. 1998. write for info. (*1-56662-645-5*) Foundation Pr.

— Pediatrics Pearls of Wisdom. (Pearls of Wisdom Ser.). 1998. pap. 88.00 (*1-890369-07-1*) Boston Medical.

Levin, jt. auth. see Fox.

Levin, Herbert & Levin, Gail. Learning Through Music. LC 99-163021. (Illus.). 150p. 1998. pap. text 28.00 (*1-891278-00-2*) Barcelona Pubs.

— Learning Through Songs. 80p. 1997. pap. text 16.00 (*1-891278-01-0*) Barcelona Pubs.

Levin, A., tr. see Gedalge, Andre.

Levin, A. E., jt. auth. see Brush, Stephen G.

Levin, A. L. & Lubinsky, D. S. Christoffel Functions & Orthogonal Polynomials for Exponential Weights. LC 94-17089. (Memoirs of the American Mathematical Society Ser.: Vol. 535). 146p. 1994. pap. 35.00 (*0-8218-2599-2*, MEMO/111/535) Am Math.

Levin, A. Leo, et al. Cases & Materials on Civil Procedure: Successor Edition. (University Casebook Ser.). 815p. (C). 1991. text 41.95 (*0-88277-942-7*) Foundation Pr.

— Civil Procedure: Cases & Materials, Successor Edition, 1994 Supplement. (University Casebook Ser.). 80p. 1994. 6.50 (*1-56662-206-9*) Foundation Pr.

— Civil Procedure: 1997 Supplement to Cases & Materials. (University Casebook Ser.). 368p. (C). 1997. pap. text. write for info. (*1-56662-490-8*) Foundation Pr.

— Civil Procedure, Teacher's Manual for Cases & Materials on Civil Procedure Successor Edition. (University Casebook Ser.). 106p. (C). 1992. pap. text. write for info. (*1-56662-032-5*) Foundation Pr.

Levin, A. Leo, ed. see Wheeler, Russell R.

Levin, Aaron. Testament: At the Creation of the State of Israel. LC 97-46031. (Illus.). 192p. 1998. 35.00 (*1-885183-94-1*, 85094) Artisan.

Levin, Adeline L. The Caboose Tenants. LC 96-94711. (Illus.). 54p. (Orig.). (J). (gr. 6-9). 1997. pap., per. write for info. (*0-9654486-0-6*) Kitonia Pub.

Levin, Alan M. & Page, Wayne E. Everything You Need to Do to Get Hired (& How to Do It) Projects & Guides. LC 93-90356. 358p. 1993. student ed., ring bd. write for info. (*1-883552-02-8*) Career Adv MD.

— Getting Yourself Hired: The Self-Directed Job Search. LC 93-90357. 380p. 1993. student ed., ring bd. write for info. (*1-883552-01-X*) Career Adv MD.

— Gopp, Inc. The Company That Always Gets You Hired. LC 93-90358. 166p. (Orig.). 1993. write for info. (*1-883552-00-1*) Career Adv MD.

— My Job-Search Record: Records Project. LC 93-71441. 142p. 1993. student ed., ring bd. write for info. (*1-883552-03-6*) Career Adv MD.

Levin, Alex V. & Sheridan, Mary S. Munchausen Syndrome by Proxy: Issues in Diagnosis & Treatment. LC 95-3324. 479p. 1996. 49.95 (*0-02-918606-4*) Jossey-Bass.

Levin, Alexandra L., ed. Henrietta Srold & the Youth Aliyah: Family Letters, 1934-1944. (Illus.). 100p. (Orig.). 1986. write for info. (*0-318-61349-2*) Herzl Pr.

Levin, Alice B. Eleanor Powell: First Lady of Dance. LC 97-76809. (Illus.). 160p. 1997. 24.95 (*0-944019-24-2*) Empire NC.

Levin, Amy K. The Suppressed Sister: A Relationship in Novels by Nineteenth- & Twentieth-Century British Women. LC 91-55127. 160p. 1992. 29.50 (*0-8387-5211-X*) Bucknell U Pr.

Levin, Arthur & Rapoport, Mitchell, eds. Focus on Health: Issues & Events of 1978 from the New York Times Information Bank. LC 78-31464. (News in Print Ser.). 1980. lib. bdg. 30.95 (*0-405-12874-6*) Ayer.

***Levin, Arthur H.** Hillside Building: Design & Construction. 2nd ed. (Illus.). 163p. 1999. pap. 29.95 (*1-889892-19-X*) Builders Bk Inc.

Levin, Arthur H. Hillside Building Design & Construction. LC 90-81793. (Illus.). 192p. (Orig.). 1990. pap. 19.95 (*0-931228-19-0*) Arts & Arch.

Levin, Aryeh. Envoy to Moscow: Memoirs of an Israeli Ambassador, 1988-1992. LC 96-223590. (Cummings Center Ser.). 456p. 1996. 49.50 (*0-7146-4597-4*, Pub. by F Cass Pubs) Intl Spec Bk.

— Envoy to Moscow: Memoirs of an Israeli Ambassador, 1988-92. (Cummings Center Ser.). 456p. 1996. pap. 25.00 (*0-7146-4248-7*, Pub. by F Cass Pubs) Intl Spec Bk.

Levin Associates Staff. Bar Mitzvah Book. 1987. 19.95 (*0-88363-482-1*) H L Levin.

— Irish Book of Days. (Illus.). 128p. 1994. 10.95 (*0-88363-294-2*) H L Levin.

Levin, B., jt. auth. see Finkelstein, Michael O.

Levin, B. Y., ed. Entire & Subharmonic Functions. LC 91-640741. (Advances in Soviet Mathematics Ser.: Vol. 11). 275p. 1992. text 147.00 (*0-8218-4110-6*, ADVSOV/11) Am Math.

Levin, B. Y., et al. Lectures on Entire Functions. LC 96-318. (Translations of Mathematical Monographs: Vol. 150). 265p. 1996. text 99.00 (*0-8218-0282-8*, MMONO/150) Am Math.

Levin, Barry & Ferrier, David O. Defending the Vietnam Combat Veteran. Caney-Peterson, Susan, ed. LC 89-193635. 345p. 1989. pap. text 29.95 (*0-9626742-0-6*) VVLAP.

Levin, Barry B. Benji Lopez: A Picaresque Tale of Puerto Rican Emigration & Return. 202p. 1932. boxed set 95.00 (*0-465-00653-1*) Transaction Pubs.

Levin, Beatrice. John Hawk: Seminole Saga. 2nd ed. LC 94-66098. (Council for Indian Education Ser.). (Illus.). 182p. 1994. pap. 9.95 (*1-57098-000-4*) Roberts Rinehart.

Levin, Beatrice & Vanderveld, Marjorie. Me Run Fast Good: Biographies of Tewanima (Hopi), Carlos Montezuma (Apache) & John Horse (Seminole) 32p. (J). (gr. 5-9). 1983. pap. 3.95 (*0-89992-087-X*) Coun India Ed.

Levin, Benjamin & Riffel, Anthony. Schools & the Changing World: Struggling Towards the Future. (Education Policy Perspectives Ser.). 224p. 1997. 79.95 (*0-7507-0662-7*, Falmer Pr); pap. 29.95 (*0-7507-0617-1*, Falmer Pr) Taylor & Francis.

Levin, Berard. The Way We Live Now. large type ed. (Illus.). 200p. 1991. 22.95 (*1-85290-019-9*, Pub. by ISIS Lrg Prnt) Transaction Pubs.

Levin, Bernard. American Cancer Society - Colorectal Cancer: Cancer: A Thorough & Compassionate Resource for Patients & Their Families. LC 98-35323. (Illus.). 336p. 1999. pap. 14.95 (*0-679-77813-6*) Random.

Levin, Bernard, jt. ed. see DeMeester, Tom R.

Levin, Bernard M. Human Behavior in Fire: What We Know Now. 1984. 4.65 (*0-318-03820-X*, TR84-3) Society Fire Protect.

Levin, Beth. English Verb Classes & Alternations: A Preliminary Investigation. 368p. (C). 1993. pap. text 18.95 (*0-226-47533-6*); lib. bdg. 45.00 (*0-226-47532-8*) U Ch Pr.

Levin, Beth & Hovav, Malka R. Unaccusativity: At the Syntax-Lexical Semantics Interface. LC 94-17439. (Linguistic Inquiry Monographs: Vol. 26). 350p. 1994. 42.00 (*0-262-12185-9*); pap. text 21.00 (*0-262-62094-4*) MIT Pr.

Levin, Betsy, ed. see Hawley, Willis D.

Levin, Betty. Away to Me, Moss. LC 93-48136. 176p. (J). (gr. 5 up). 1994. 15.00 (*0-688-13439-4*, Grenwillow Bks) HarpC Child Bks.

***Levin, Betty.** The Banished. LC 98-39889. (Illus.). 160p. (YA). (gr. 5-9). 1999. 16.00 (*0-688-16602-4*, Grenwillow Bks) HarpC Child Bks.

Levin, Betty. Creature Crossing. LC 98-5435. (Illus.). 96p. (J). (gr. 3-7). 1999. 15.00 (*0-688-16220-7*, Grenwillow Bks) HarpC Child Bks.

— Fire in the Wind. LC 94-48801. 176p. (J). (gr. 7 up). 1995. 15.00 (*0-688-14299-0*, Grenwillow Bks) HarpC Child Bks.

— Fire in the Wind. LC 94-48801. 144p. (J). (gr. 3-7). 1997. mass mkt. 4.95 (*0-688-15495-6*, Wm Morrow) Morrow Avon.

— Fire in the Wind. 1997. 10.05 (*0-606-11327-4*, Pub. by Turtleback) Demco.

— Gift Horse. LC 95-41840. (Illus.). 176p. (YA). (gr. 4-7). 1996. 15.00 (*0-688-14698-8*, Grenwillow Bks) HarpC Child Bks.

— Island Bound. LC 96-45411. 224p. (YA). (gr. 5-9). 1997. 15.00 (*0-688-15217-1*, Grenwillow Bks) HarpC Child Bks.

***Levin, Betty.** Island Bound. LC 96-45411. 272p. (J). (gr. 3-7). 2000. mass mkt. 4.95 (*0-380-73174-6*, Grenwillow Bks) HarpC Child Bks.

Levin, Betty. Look Back, Moss. LC 97-34510. (Illus.). 152p. (J). (gr. 3-7). 1998. 15.00 (*0-688-15696-7*, Grenwillow Bks) HarpC Child Bks.

***Levin, Betty.** Shadow-Catcher. LC 99-45087. 160p. (YA). (gr. 5 up). 2000. 15.95 (*0-688-17862-6*, Grenwillow Bks) HarpC Child Bks.

Levin, Betty. Starshine & Sunglow. LC 93-26672. (J). (gr. 4-7). 1994. 14.00 (*0-688-22806-2*, Grenwillow Bks) HarpC Child Bks.

— Starshine & Sunglow. LC 93-26672. (Illus.). 96p. (J). (gr. 4-7). 1994. 14.00 (*0-688-12806-8*, Grenwillow Bks) HarpC Child Bks.

Levin, Betty B., jt. auth. see Christensen, Janet.

Levin, Bob. Fully Armed: The Story of Jimmy Don Polk. 245p. 1995. 21.00 (*1-880909-38-3*) Baskerville.

Levin, Boris J. Distribution of Zeros of Entire Functions. rev. ed. Boas, Ralph P. et al, trs. LC 80-36891. (Translations of Mathematical Monographs: Vol. 5). 524p. 1980. pap. 70.00 (*0-8218-4505-5*, MMONO/5) Am Math.

Levin, Boris M. Crryetbl: N35Pahhoe. (Illus.). 317p. (Orig.). 1994. 12.00 (*0-9643641-0-7*) B Levin.

Levin, Brian, jt. auth. see Halpern, Thomas.

Levin, Bruce A. & Coyne, Robert, eds. Tort Reform & Related Proposals: Annotated Bibliographies on Product Liability & Medical Malpractice. LC 79-54074. xiii, 249p. 1979. 36.00 (*0-910058-94-6*, 305050) W S Hein.

Levin, Bruce L. & Petrila, John, eds. Mental Health Services: A Public Health Perspective. (Illus.). 448p. 1996. text 49.95 (*0-19-508800-X*) OUP.

Levin, Bruce L., et al. Women's Mental Health Services: A Public Health Perspective. LC 97-45341. 496p. 1998. 39.00 (*0-7619-0508-1*); pap. 17.99 (*0-7619-0509-X*) Sage.

Levin, Buck. Environmental Nutrition: Understanding the Link between Environment, Food Quality & Nutrition. (Illus.). 304p. (C). 1999. pap. 39.95 (*0-9671283-0-7*) HingePin Pub.

***Levin, Carl, ed.** Oversight of U. S. Trade Policy with Japan: Hearing Before the Committee on Governmental Affairs, U. S. Senate, 1991. 283p. (C). 2000. reprint ed. pap. text 40.00 (*0-7881-7270-0*) DIANE Pub.

Levin, Carole. The Heart & Stomach of a King: Elizabeth I & the Politics of Sex & Power. LC 94-7315. (New Cultural Studies). (Illus.). 256p. (Orig.). (C). 1994. pap. text 14.95 (*0-8122-1533-8*) U of Pa Pr.

— Propaganda in the English Reformation: Heroic & Villainous Images of King John. LC 87-31949. (Studies in British History: Vol. 11). 306p. 1988. lib. bdg. 99.95 (*0-88946-463-4*) E Mellen.

Levin, Carole & Robertson, Karen, eds. Sexuality & Politics in Renaissance Drama. LC 91-25367. (Studies in Renaissance Literature: Vol. 10). 289p. 1991. lib. bdg. 89.95 (*0-88946-078-7*) E Mellen.

Levin, Carole & Sullivan, Patricia A., eds. Political Rhetoric, Power, & Renaissance Women. LC 94-32811. (SUNY Series in Speech Communication). 293p. (C). 1995. text 57.50 (*0-7914-2545-2*); pap. text 19.95 (*0-7914-2546-0*) State U NY Pr.

Levin, Carole & Watson, Jeanie, eds. Ambiguous Realities: Women in the Middle Ages & Renaissance. LC 87-21671. 264p. 1987. pap. 18.95 (*0-8143-1873-8*) Wayne St U Pr.

— Ambiguous Realties: Women in the Middle Ages & Renaissance. LC 87-21671. (Illus.). 264p. reprint ed. pap. 81.90 (*0-608-10532-5*, 2071152) Bks Demand.

***Levin, Carole, et al.** Extraordinary Women of the Medieval & Renaissance World: A Biographical Dictionary. LC 99-55218. 352p. 2000. 65.00 (*0-313-30659-1*, GR0659, Greenwood Pr) Greenwood.

Levin, Caroline D. Blind Dog Stories: Tales of Triumph, Humor & Heroism. unabridged ed. (Illus.). 107p. 1999. pap. 12.95 (*0-9672253-1-0*) Lantern Pubns.

— Living with Blind Dogs: A Resource Book & Training Guide for the Owners of Blind & Low-Vision Dogs. unabridged ed. (Illus.). 181p. 1998. pap. 29.95 (*0-9672253-0-2*) Lantern Pubns.

Levin, Charles. Jean Baudrillard: A Study in Cultural Metaphysics. LC 95-22659. (Modern Cultural Theorists Ser.). 192p. (C). 1996. pap. text 25.00 (*0-13-433368-3*) P-H.

Levin, Charles, tr. see Baudrillard, Jean.

Levin, Craig, jt. auth. see Erlank, Steve.

***Levin, D. L. & Morris, F. C., eds.** Essentials of Pediatric Intensive Care - A Pocket Companion. 2nd ed. 1998. pap. write for info. (*0-443-07613-8*) Church.

Levin, Dan. From the Battlefield: Dispatches of a World War II Marine. LC 94-19370. (Illus.). 133p. 1995. 23.95 (*1-55750-515-2*) Naval Inst Pr.

Levin, Dana. In the Surgical Theatre. 96p. 1999. 23.00 (*0-9663395-2-5*, Pub. by Amer Poet); pap. 14.00 (*0-9663395-3-3*, Pub. by Amer Poet) Copper Canyon.

Levin, Daniel L. Representing Popular Sovereignty: The Constitution in American Political Culture. LC 98-27368. (SUNY Series, American Constitutionalism). 224p. (C). 1999. text 59.50 (*0-7914-4105-9*); pap. text 19.95 (*0-7914-4106-7*) State U NY Pr.

Levin, Daniel L. & Morris, Frances C. Essentials of Pediatric Intensive Care. 2nd ed. LC 96-53381. 1997. text 65.00 (*0-443-05932-2*) Church.

Levin, Daniel L. & Morriss, Frances C. Essentials of Pediatric Intensive Care. 2nd ed. LC 96-53381. 1997. text 65.00 (*0-443-05931-4*) Church.

Levin, Daniel L. & Morriss, Francis C. Essentials of Pediatric Intensive Care, 2 vols. 2nd ed. Fletcher, Judy, ed. LC 96-53381. (Illus.). 1890p. 1999. pap. text 120.00 (*0-443-05930-6*) Church.

Levin, David. Cotton Mather: The Young Life of the Lord's Remembrancer, 1663-1703. LC 78-2355. (Illus.). 382p. 1978. 43.50 (*0-674-17507-7*) HUP.

— Forms of Uncertainty: Essays in Historical Criticism. LC 91-32563. 329p. reprint ed. pap. 102.00 (*0-608-08546-4*, 206906900002) Bks Demand.

— Riddler's Riddle Book. (Illus.). 128p. 1991. pap. 3.50 (*0-8125-1353-3*, Pub. by Tor Bks) St Martin.

Levin, David, jt. ed. see Levin, Richard.

Levin, David, ed. see Mather, Cotton.

Levin, David, ed. see Orwell, George.

Levin, David, ed. see Parkman, Francis.

Levin, David, ed. & intro. see Parkman, Francis.

Levin, David H. Chess Puzzles for Children. (Illus.). 124p. (Orig.). (J). (gr. 2-6). 1994. pap. 11.95 (*0-9638001-1-6*) Syllogism Pr.

— Position & Pawn Tension in Chess. (Illus.). 118p. (Orig.). 1993. pap. 13.95 (*0-9638001-0-8*) Syllogism Pr.

Levin, David J. Opera Through Other Eyes. (Illus.). 288p. (C). 1994. 39.50 (*0-8047-2239-0*); pap. 15.95 (*0-8047-2240-4*) Stanford U Pr.

***Levin, David J.** Richard Wagner, Fritz Lang & the Nibelungen: The Dramaturgy of Disavowal. LC 97-27022. (Princeton Series in Opera). 224p. 1998. text 29.95 (*0-691-02621-1*, Pub. by Princeton U Pr) Cal Prin Full Svc.

— Richard Wagner, Fritz Lang & the Nibelungen: The Dramaturgy of Disavowal. (Studies in Opera). 2000. pap. text 14.95 (*0-691-04971-8*) Princeton U Pr.

Levin, David M. The Listening Self: Personal Growth, Social Change & the Closure of Metaphysics. 352p. (C). 1989. pap. 26.99 (*0-415-02583-4*, A3269) Routledge.

— The Listening Self: Personal Growth, Social Change & the Closure of Metaphysics. 320p. 1989. 47.00 (*0-415-02582-6*, A1581) Routledge.

— The Opening of Vision: Nihilism & the Postmodern Situation. 480p. 1988. text 59.95 (*0-415-00412-8*) Routledge.

— The Opening of Vision: Nihilism & the Postmodern Situation. 480p. (C). 1988. pap. 25.99 (*0-415-00173-0*) Routledge.

***Levin, David M.** The Philosopher's Gaze: Modernity in the Shadows of Enlightenment LC 98-43812. 412p. 1999. 50.00 (*0-520-21780-2*, Pub. by U CA Pr) Cal Prin Full Svc.

Levin, David M., ed. Modernity & the Hegemony of Vision. LC 93-1523. 1993. 55.00 (*0-520-07972-8*, Pub. by U CA Pr); pap. 24.95 (*0-520-07973-6*, Pub. by U CA Pr) Cal Prin Full Svc.

L

— Sites of Vision: The Discursive Construction of Sight in the History of Philosophy. LC 96-41860. 506p. 1997. 50.00 (*0-262-12203-0*) MIT Pr.

Levin, David M., jt. auth. see Gendlin, Eugene T.

Levin, David R. & Ferrera, Tess J. ERISA Fiduciary Answer Book. annuals 3rd ed. LC 98-137842. 792p. 1994. boxed set 118.00 (*1-56706-419-1*, 64191) Panel Pubs.

Levin, David S. Developmental Experiences: Treatment of Developmental Disorders in Children. LC 84-24318. 352p. 1985. 60.00 (*0-87668-760-5*) Aronson.

— How to Use UNIX & Xenix. Jonas, Jacqueline & Menges, Patricia A., eds. (Illus.). 95p. (C). 1991. pap. text 245.00 incl. audio (*0-917792-49-1*, 122) OneOnOne Comp Trng.

Levin, Diane. Teaching Young Children in Violent Times: Building a Peaceable Classroom. 194p. 1996. pap. text, per. 16.95 (*0-7872-2220-8*) Kendall-Hunt.

Levin, Diane, jt. auth. see Carlsson-Paige, Nancy.

Levin, Diane E. Remote Control Childhood? Combating the Hazards of Media Culture. LC 97-80647. (Illus.). 184p. 1998. pap. 8.00 (*0-935989-84-6*) Natl Assn Child Ed.

— Teaching Young Children in Violent Times: Building a Peaceable Classroom. (Illus.). 176p. 1994. pap. 21.95 (*0-86571-316-2*) New Soc Pubs.

Levin, Diane E., jt. auth. see Carlsson-Paige, Nancy.

Levin, Donald. The House of Grins. 330p. (Orig.). 1992. pap. 13.95 (*0-9628647-0-6*) Sewickley Pr.

***Levin, Donald A.** The Origin, Expansion & Demise of Plant Species. LC 99-34861. (Oxford Series in Ecology & Evolution). (Illus.). 240p. 2000. text 70.00 (*0-19-512728-5*); pap. text 35.00 (*0-19-512729-3*) OUP.

Levin, Donna. Get That Novel Started! (And Keep Going 'Til You Finish) 176p. 1992. 17.99 (*0-89879-517-6*, Wrtrs Digest Bks) F & W Pubns Inc.

— Get That Novel Written! LC 96-11139. 208p. 1996. 18.99 (*0-89879-696-2*, Wrtrs Digest Bks) F & W Pubns Inc.

Levin, Doron. Behind the Wheel at Chrysler: The Iacocca Legacy. (Illus.). 354p. 1996. pap. 15.00 (*0-15-600474-7*, Harvest Bks) Harcourt.

Levin, Doron P. Behind the Wheel at Chrysler: The Iacocca Legacy. 339p. 1995. 25.00 (*0-15-111703-9*) Harcourt.

— Irreconcilable Differences: Ross Perot Versus General Motors. (Illus.). 320p. 1989. 18.95 (*0-316-52211-2*, Aspen Law & Bus) Aspen Pub.

Levin, Dov. Fighting Back: Lithuanian Jewry's Armed Resistance to the Nazis. LC 83-12605. 325p. 1985. 49.50 (*0-8419-0831-1*) Holmes & Meier.

— Fighting Back: Lithuanian Jewry's Armed Resistance to the Nazis, 1941-1945. 300p. (C). 1997. reprint ed. pap. 17.50 (*0-8419-1389-7*) Holmes & Meier.

— The Lesser of 2 Evils: Eastern European Jewry under Soviet Rule. 1995. 29.95 (*0-8276-0518-8*) JPS Phila.

***Levin, Dov.** The Litvaks: A Short History of the Jews in Lithuania. 300p. 2000. 39.95 (*965-308-084-9*, Pub. by Yad Vashem Pubns) Berghahn Bks.

— The Litvaks: A Short History of the Jews of Lithuania. LC 00-37841. 2001. write for info. (*1-57181-264-4*) Berghahn Bks.

Levin, Edward. I Will Be Sanctified: Religious Responses to the Holocaust. Fogel, Yehezkel, ed. LC 96-31143. 213p. 1998. 35.00 (*1-56821-943-1*) Aronson.

Levin, Edward & Grody, Donald. Witnesses in Arbitration: Selection, Preparation, & Presentation. LC 86-32727. (BNA Books Arbitration Ser.). 258p. 1987. reprint ed. pap. 80.00 (*0-608-00713-7*, 206148600009) Bks Demand.

Levin, Edward, tr. see Kotler, Yair.

Levin, Edward, tr. see Raz, Simcha.

Levin, Edward D., et al, eds. Neurotransmitter Interactions & Cognitive Function. LC 92-17848. xiv, 362p. 1992. 120.00 (*0-8176-3617-X*) Birkhauser.

Levin, Edward J., jt. auth. see Albert, Charles T.

Levin, Edward S., jt. auth. see Morris, Ellen K.

Levin, Elaine. The History of American Ceramics: 1607 to the Present from Pikkpkins & Bean Pots to Contemporary Forms. (Illus.). 352p. 1998. 65.00 (*0-8109-1172-8*, Pub. by Abrams) Time Warner.

Levin, Elaine, et al. Paul Soldner: A Retrospective. LC 91-53090. (Illus.). 128p. 1992. pap. 24.95 (*0-295-97159-2*) U of Wash Pr.

Levin, Elliott. Does It Swing? (Open Mouth Poetry Ser.). 95p. (Orig.). 1996. pap. 9.95 (*1-884773-03-6*) Heat Press.

Levin, Ellis, jt. ed. see Samson, Willis K.

Levin, Ellis R. Endocrinology of Cardiovascular Function. LC 98-12410. (Endocrine Updates Ser.). 1998. 189.95 (*0-7923-8217-X*) Kluwer Academic.

Levin, Enid, et al. Families, Services & Confusion in Old Age. 338p. 1989. text 82.95 (*0-566-05714-X*, Pub. by Avebry) Ashgate Pub Co.

***Levin-Epstein, Michael.** Wage & Hour Compliance Handbook: Practical Guide to Law & Administration. LC 98-230213. 1998. write for info. (*0-87622-781-7*) Aspen Pub.

Levin, Ernest M., et al, eds. Phase Diagrams for Ceramists Vol. 1: Oxides & Salts, Vol. 1. (Illus.). 602p. 1964. 150.00 (*0-916094-04-9*, PH01) Am Ceramic.

— Phase Diagrams for Ceramists Vol. II: Oxides & Salts. 626p. 1969. 150.00 (*0-916094-05-7*, PH02) Am Ceramic.

Levin, Ernest M. & McMurdie, Howard F., eds. Phase Diagrams for Ceramists Vol. III: Oxides & Salts. 514p. 1975. 150.00 (*0-916094-06-5*, PH03) Am Ceramic.

Levin, Eve. Sex & Society in the World of the Orthodox Slavs, 900-1700. LC 89-30075. (Illus.). 344p. 1989. text 47.50 (*0-8014-2260-4*) Cornell U Pr.

— Sex & Society in the World of the Orthodox Slavs, 900-1700. (Illus.). 344p. 1995. pap. text 17.95 (*0-8014-8304-2*) Cornell U Pr.

Levin, Eve, ed. & tr. see Pushkareva, Natalia.

Levin, Evgenii M., jt. auth. see Beletsky, Vladimir V.

Levin, F. S. & Micha, D. A. Coulomb Interactions in Nuclear & Atomic Few-Body Collisions. LC 95-51224. (Finite Systems & Multiparticle Dynamics Ser.). (Illus.). 335p. (C). 1996. text 95.00 (*0-306-45149-2*, Kluwer Plenum) Kluwer Academic.

— Long-Range Casimir Forces: Theory & Recent Experiments on Atomic Systems. (Finite Systems & Multiparticle Dynamics Ser.: Vol. 1). (Illus.). 374p. (C). 1993. text 85.00 (*0-306-44385-6*, Kluwer Plenum) Kluwer Academic.

Levin, F. S., jt. auth. see Feshbach, Herman.

Levin, Flora, tr. see Nicomachus the Pythagorean.

***Levin, Floyd.** Classic Jazz: A Personal View of the Music & the Musicians. LC 00-22554. (Illus.). 384p. 2000. 37.50 (*0-520-21360-2*, Pub. by U CA Pr) Cal Prin Full Svc.

Levin, Frank. Complete Traditional Holiday Season Folk Book. 144p. 1997. spiral bd. write for info. (*0-7866-3255-0*, 96870) Mel Bay.

***Levin, Fred.** Mapping the Mind: The Intersection of Psychoanalysis & Neuroscience. 1999. pap. 39.95 (*0-88163-320-8*) Analytic Pr.

***Levin, Freddie.** 1 - 2 - 3 Draw Dinosaurs & Other Prehistoric Animals. (Illus.). 64p. (J). (gr. 1-7). 2000. pap. 8.95 (*0-939217-41-4*) Peel Prod.

— 1 - 2 - 3 Draw Pets & Farm Animals. (Illus.). 64p. (J). (gr. 1-7). 2000. pap. 8.95 (*0-939217-40-6*) Peel Prod.

Levin, Fredric G. Effective Opening Statements: The Attorney's Master Key to Courtroom Victory. LC 83-14034. 1983. text 59.95 (*0-13-244418-6*) Exec Reports.

***Levin, Gabriel.** Ostraca. 70p. 2000. pap. 18.95 (*0-85646-317-5*, Pub. by Anvil Press) Dufour.

Levin, Gail. The Early Drawings of Edward Hopper. (Illus.). 16p. 1995. pap. 10.00 (*0-87920-052-9*) Kennedy Gall.

Levin, Gail. Edward Hopper. 1996. pap. write for info. (*0-679-77286-3*) McKay.

— Edward Hopper: A Catalogue Raisonne, 3 vols., Set. (Illus.). 1056p. 1995. boxed set 750.00 incl. cd-rom (*0-393-03786-X*) Norton.

— Edward Hopper: An Intimate Biography. LC 95-2114. 704p. 1995. 45.00 (*0-394-54664-4*) Knopf.

— Edward Hopper: An Intimate Biography. LC 97-53182. 695p. 1998. pap. text 19.95 (*0-520-21475-7*, Pub. by U CA Pr) Cal Prin Full Svc.

— Edward Hopper: The Art & the Artist. 320p. 1999. pap. 39.95 (*0-393-31577-0*) Norton.

— Edward Hopper: The Art & the Artist. (Illus.). 1981. reprint ed. 50.00 (*0-393-01374-X*) Norton.

— Edward Hopper: The Complete Prints. (Illus.). 1979. 15.95 (*0-393-01275-1*) Norton.

— Hopper's Places. LC 98-16450. 145p. 1998. 35.00 (*0-520-21737-3*, Pub. by U CA Pr); pap. 19.95 (*0-520-21676-8*, Pub. by U CA Pr) Cal Prin Full Svc.

Levin, Gail. The Paintings of Edward Hopper. 125.00 (*0-393-04996-5*) Norton.

Levin, Gail. Poetry of Solitude: A Tribute to Edward Hopper. (Illus.). 80p. 1995. 19.95 (*0-7893-0017-6*, Pub. by Universe) St Martin.

***Levin, Gail.** Silent Places: A Tribute to Edward Hopper. (Illus.). 80p. 2000. text 19.95 (*0-7893-0398-1*) Universe.

Levin, Gail. Twentieth-Century American Painting: The Thyssen-Bornemisza Collection. LC 87-61728. (Illus.). 408p. 1988. 95.00 (*0-85667-332-3*, Pub. by P Wilson) Hoovers TX.

Levin, Gail. Watercolors of Edward Hopper. 125.00 (*0-393-04995-7*) Norton.

Levin, Gail, text. Marsden Hartley: Six Berlin Paintings. (Illus.). 1992. pap. 15.00 (*1-58821-038-3*) Salander OReilly.

***Levin, Gail & Tick, Judith.** Aaron Copland's America: A Cultural Perspective. (Illus.). 176p. 2000. 29.95 (*0-8230-0110-5*) Watsn-Guptill.

Levin, Gail & Van Sickle, John B., texts. Elie Nadelman: New Classicism. (Illus.). 30p. 1997. pap. 25.00 (*1-58821-049-9*) Salander OReilly.

Levin, Gail, jt. auth. see Levin, Herbert.

Levin, George. Laser Isotope Separation Research & Development in the U. S. S. R. Johnson, Anne H., ed. xi, 120p. (Orig.). 1989. pap. text 75.00 (*1-55831-093-2*) Delphic Associates.

Levin, Gerald. The Educated Reader. 641p. (C). 1988. pap. text, teacher ed. 4.50 (*0-15-520718-0*) Harcourt Coll Pubs.

— The Macmillan College Handbook. 2nd ed. (C). 1990. teacher ed. write for info. (*0-02-370232-X*, U4240-0) Allyn.

— The Macmillan College Handbook. 2nd ed. LC 90-36315. 834p. (C). 1990. 46.00 (*0-02-370231-1*, Macmillan Coll) P-H.

— Prose Models. 9th ed. 576p. (C). 1992. pap. text, teacher ed. 5.00 (*0-15-500297-X*) Harcourt Coll Pubs.

— Short Essays. 5th ed. 512p. (C). 1989. pap. text 18.75 (*0-15-580920-2*, Pub. by Harcourt Coll Pubs) Harcourt.

— Short Essays. 7th ed. LC 94-76300. (C). 1994. pap. text 32.50 (*0-15-501188-X*, Pub. by Harcourt Coll Pubs) Harcourt.

— Short Essays. 7th ed. (C). 1994. pap. text, teacher ed. 33.75 (*0-15-502145-1*) Harcourt Coll Pubs.

— Short Essays. 8th ed. (C). 1997. pap. text. write for info. (*0-15-503969-5*) Harcourt.

— Writing & Logic. 276p. (C). 1982. pap. text, teacher ed. 3.75 (*0-15-597789-X*) Harcourt Coll Pubs.

Levin-Gervasi, Stephanie. The Back Pain Sourcebook. 2nd rev. ed. (Illus.). 256p. 1998. pap. 17.00 (*0-7373-0015-9*, 00159W) NTC Contemp Pub Co.

— Yoga. LC 99-31068. (Smart Guides Ser.). 220p. 1999. pap. 12.95 (*0-471-35648-4*) Wiley.

Levin, Gina, ed. see Dolinjak, Igor.

Levin, Ginger, jt. auth. see Ward, J. Leroy.

Levin, Ginger, jt. auth. see Ward, J. LeRoy.

Levin, Ginny, jt. auth. see Levin, Ted.

Levin, H. Toward Stendhal. LC 75-22213. (Studies in French Literature: No. 45). 1975. lib. bdg. 75.00 (*0-8383-2083-X*) M S G Haskell Hse.

Levin, H., ed. Lawyers & Lawmakers of Kentucky. (Illus.). 777p. 1982. reprint ed. 40.00 (*0-89308-319-4*) Southern Hist Pr.

Levin, H. A. Quotations for Successful Living: How to Live Life. 2nd rev. ed. 128p. (Orig.). 1997. reprint ed. mass mkt. 7.95 (*0-9636211-6-5*) A Lincoln Pr.

Levin, Harold L. Ancient Invertebrates & Their Living. LC 98-2690. 358p. 1998. 68.00 (*0-13-748955-2*) P-H.

— Ancient Invertebrates & Their Living Relatives. (Illus.). 350p. (C). 1995. write for info. (*0-521-33450-0*); pap. write for info. (*0-521-33671-6*) Cambridge U Pr.

— The Earth Through Time. 5th ed. (C). 1995. pap. text, student ed. 15.75 (*0-03-015638-6*) Harcourt Coll Pubs.

— The Earth through Time. 5th ed. (C). 1996. text 52.50 (*0-03-005167-3*) Harcourt Coll Pubs.

— The Earth Through Time. 6th ed. LC 98-84385. 656p. (C). 1998. text 50.00 (*0-03-023751-3*, Pub. by SCP) Harcourt.

Levin, Harold L., et al. Laboratory Studies in Earth History. 6th ed. 256p. (C). 1996. text. write for info. (*0-697-25256-6*, WCB McGr Hill) McGrw-H Hghr Educ.

Levin, Harriet. The Christmas Show. LC 96-35462. 79p. 1997. pap. 12.00 (*0-8070-6837-3*) Beacon Pr.

Levin, Harry. Genetic Engineering. LC 99-28264. (Contemporary World Issues Ser.). 264p. 1999. lib. bdg. 45.00 (*0-87436-962-2*) ABC-CLIO.

— Grounds for Comparison. LC 72-75402. (Harvard Studies in Comparative Literature: No. 32). 437p. reprint ed. pap. 135.50 (*0-7837-6094-9*, 205914000007) Bks Demand.

— James Joyce: A Critical Introduction. LC 60-9222. (C). 1960. pap. 9.95 (*0-8112-0089-2*, NDP87, Pub. by New Directions) Norton.

— Memories of the Moderns. LC 80-36827. 256p. 1980. 15.95 (*0-8112-0733-1*, Pub. by New Directions) Norton.

— Memories of the Moderns. LC 80-36827. 256p. 1982. pap. 7.95 (*0-8112-0842-7*, NDP539, Pub. by New Directions) Norton.

— The Power of Blackness: Hawthorne, Poe, Melville. LC 80-83221. 286p. 1980. reprint ed. pap. 14.95 (*0-8214-0581-0*) Ohio U Pr.

***Levin, Harry.** Scene a Faire. 280p. 2000. 65.00 (*0-8153-3636-5*) Garland.

Levin, Harry, ed. see Shakespeare, William.

Levin, Harry, ed. & intro. see James, Henry.

Levin, Harry T. Why Literary Criticism Is Not an Exact Science. abr. ed. LC 68-7221. 27p. 1967. pap. 5.00 (*0-674-95235-9*) HUP.

Levin, Harry T., jt. auth. see Gibson, Eleanor J.

Levin, Harry T., ed. see Hawthorne, Nathaniel.

Levin, Harvey J. Fact & Fancy in Television Regulation: An Economic Study of Policy Alternatives. LC 79-90148. 544p. 1980. 49.95 (*0-87154-531-4*) Russell Sage.

— The Invisible Resource: Use & Regulation of the Radio Spectrum. LC 71-148951. (Resources for the Future Ser.). (Illus.). 432p. 1971. 30.00 (*0-8018-1316-6*) Johns Hopkins.

— The Invisible Resource: Use & Regulation of the Radio Spectrum. LC 71-148951. (Illus.). 466p. reprint ed. pap. 144.50 (*0-608-18093-9*, 203215900078) Bks Demand.

Levin, Harvey S., et al, eds. Catastrophic Brain Injury. (Illus.). 282p. 1996. text 42.50 (*0-19-508533-7*) OUP.

— Frontal Lobe Function & Dysfunction. (Illus.). 448p. (C). 1991. text 58.00 (*0-19-506284-1*) OUP.

— Mild Head Injury. (Illus.). 304p. 1989. text 49.50 (*0-19-505301-X*) OUP.

— Neurobehavioral Recovery from Head Injury. (Illus.). 446p. 1987. text 49.95 (*0-19-504287-5*) OUP.

***Levin, Harvey S. & Grafman, Jordan, eds.** Cerebral Reorganization of Function after Brain Damage. (Illus.). 416p. 2000. text 55.00 (*0-19-512026-4*) OUP.

Levin, Harvey S., et al. Neurobehavioral Consequences of Closed Head Injury. (Illus.). 280p. (C). 1982. text 47.50 (*0-19-503008-7*) OUP.

Levin, Henry M. Cost-Effectiveness: A Primer, No. 4. (New Perspectives in Evaluation Ser.: Vol. 4). 168p. 1983. 42.00 (*0-8039-2152-7*); pap. 18.95 (*0-8039-2153-5*) Sage.

— Education & Jobs in a Technological World. 28p. 1984. 3.25 (*0-318-22083-0*, IN265) Ctr Educ Trng Employ.

Levin, Henry M. & Lockheed, Marlaine E., eds. Effective Schools in Developing Countries. LC 92-42862. 188p. 1993. 75.00 (*0-7507-0173-0*, Falmer Pr) Taylor & Francis.

***Levin, Henry M. & McEwan, Patrick J.** Cost-Effectiveness Analysis: Methods & Applications. 2nd ed. LC 00-9499. 2000. pap. write for info. (*0-7619-1934-1*) Sage.

Levin, Henry M. & Schutze, Hans G., eds. Financing Recurrent Education: Strategies for Increasing Employment, Job Opportunities, & Productivity. LC 83-11214. 320p. reprint ed. pap. 99.20 (*0-8357-8488-6*, 203476100091) Bks Demand.

Levin, Henry M., jt. auth. see Carnoy, Martin.

Levin, Henry M., jt. auth. see Rumberger, Russell W.

Levin, Henry M., jt. ed. see James, Thomas.

Levin, Herbert J. Reflections of a Family Doctor: Writings of Herbert J. Levin, M.D. 185p. (Orig.). (C). 1994. pap. text 19.95 (*0-9642777-0-0*) Levin Family.

Levin, Ina & Levin, Michael. Read to Me! Read to Me! LC 97-62340. (Creative Kids Ser.). 144p. (J). (gr. 1-3). 1997. pap. 14.95 (*1-57690-365-5*) Tchr Create Mat.

Levin, Ina M., ed. see Denny, Philip.

Levin, Ina M., ed. see Kane, Susan, et al.

Levin, Ina M., ed. see Larsen, Linda J.

Levin, Ina M., ed. see Schaff, Barbara & Roth, Sue.

Levin, Ina M., ed. see Thomas, Jennifer.

Levin, Ina M., ed. see Wallace, Annette H.

***Levin, Ina Massler & Levin, Michael H.** Party Time: Creative Kids. (Illus.). 160p. 1999. pap., teacher ed. 14.95 (*1-57690-510-1*, TCM2510) Tchr Create Mat.

Levin, Ira. Critic's Choice. 1962. pap. 5.25 (*0-8222-0252-2*) Dramatists Play.

— Deathtrap. 1979. pap. 5.25 (*0-8222-0294-8*) Dramatists Play.

— Dr. Cook's Garden. 1968. pap. 5.25 (*0-8222-0328-6*) Dramatists Play.

— General Seeger. 1962. pap. 5.25 (*0-8222-0437-1*) Dramatists Play.

***Levin, Ira.** A Kiss Before Dying. 304p. 2000. mass mkt. 5.95 (*0-7867-0728-3*, Pub. by Carroll & Graf) Publishers Group.

Levin, Ira. A Kiss Before Dying. Peters, Sally, ed. 304p. 1991. reprint ed. mass mkt. 5.50 (*0-671-68388-8*) PB.

— Rosemary's Baby. 1991. lib. bdg. 25.95 (*1-56849-065-8*) Buccaneer Bks.

— Rosemary's Baby. 320p. 1997. mass mkt. 6.99 (*0-451-19400-4*, Sig) NAL.

— Silver. 1992. 5.99 (*0-685-53447-2*) Bantam.

— Sliver. large type ed. LC 93-40533. 248p. 1994. pap. 18.95 (*0-8161-5939-4*, G K Hall Lrg Type) Mac Lib Ref.

— Son of Rosemary. 1998. mass mkt. 6.99 (*0-451-19472-1*, Onyx) NAL.

— Son of Rosemary: The Sequel to Rosemary's Baby. large type ed. LC 97-41718. 1997. 26.95 (*0-7862-1272-1*) Mac Lib Ref.

***Levin, Ira, contrib. by.** A Kiss Before Dying. LC 99-31440. 1999. write for info. (*0-7621-0251-9*) RD Assn.

Levin, Ira, jt. auth. see Hyman, Mac.

Levin, Irene & Sussman, Marvin B., eds. Stepfamilies: History, Research, & Policy. LC 97-39585. 328p. 1997. pap. 24.95 (*0-7890-0337-6*); pap. 24.95 (*0-7890-0338-4*) Haworth Pr.

Levin, Iris & Strauss, Sidney, eds. Stage & Structure: Reopening the Debate. LC 85-15624. (Human Development Ser.: Vol. 1). 336p. 1986. text 73.25 (*0-89391-224-7*) Ablx Pub.

Levin, Irwin P. Relating Statistics & Research Design: An Introduction. LC 98-40176. (Quantitative Applications in the Social Sciences Ser.). 1999. write for info. (*0-7619-1472-2*) Sage.

Levin, Irwin P., et al. Experimental Psychology: Contemporary Methods & Applications. 432p. (C). 1994. text. write for info. (*0-697-12794-X*) Brown & Benchmark.

***Levin, Itamar.** The Last Deposit: Swiss Banks & Holocaust Victims' Accounts. Dornberg, Natasha, tr. from HEB. LC 98-53398. 280p. 1999. 29.95 (*0-275-96520-1*, Praeger Pubs) Greenwood.

Levin, Itamar, tr. see Yalon-Fortus, Judith.

Levin, Iurii D. Shakespeare & Literature in Nineteenth Century Russia. 368p. 69.50 (*0-85496-891-1*) Berg Pubs.

Levin, J. & Fox, J. A. Mass Murder: America's Growing Menace. LC 84-26585. (Illus.). 270p. (C). 1985. 19.95 (*0-306-41943-2*, Plenum Trade) Perseus Pubng.

Levin, J. & McDevitt, J. Hate Crimes: The Rising Tide of Bigotry & Bloodshed. (Illus.). 306p. (C). 1993. 23.95 (*0-306-44471-2*, Plenum Trade) Perseus Pubng.

Levin, J. R., jt. ed. see Presley, M.

Levin, Jack. Sociological Snapshots: Seeing Social Structure & Change in Everyday Life. 3rd ed. LC 98-9081. (Illus.). 232p. (C). 1998. pap. text 13.95 (*0-7619-8592-1*) Pine Forge.

Levin, Jack, et al, eds. Bacterial Endotoxins: Lipopolysaccharides from Genes to Therapy, No. 392. LC 95-22164. (Progress in Clinical & Biological Research Ser.: Vol. 392). 608p. 1995. 184.50 (*0-471-12133-9*, Wiley-Liss) Wiley.

***Levin, Jack, et al, eds.** Endotoxin & Sepsis: Molecular Mechanisms of Pathogenesis, Host Resistance & Therapy. LC 97-50215. 398p. 1998. 154.00 (*0-471-19432-8*, Wiley-Liss) Wiley.

Levin, Jack & Arluke, Arnold. Sociology: Snapshots & Portraits of Society. LC 95-37238. 1996. pap. 19.95 (*0-8039-9084-7*) Pine Forge.

Levin, Jack & Levin, William C. The Functions of Discrimination & Prejudice. 2nd ed. LC 81-6794. 270p. reprint ed. pap. 83.70 (*0-7837-4509-5*, 204428600001) Bks Demand.

Levin, Jack, et al. Social Problems: Causes, Consequences, Interventions. 2nd rev. ed. LC 97-40027. (Illus.). 425p. (C). 1999. pap. text. write for info. (*0-935732-96-9*) Roxbury Pub Co.

Levin, Jack, jt. auth. see Bourne, Richard.

Levin, Jack, jt. auth. see Ferman, Gerald S.

Levin, Jack, jt. auth. see Fox, James.

Levin, Jack, jt. auth. see Fox, James A.

Levin, Jack, ed. see Fourth International Conference on Endotoxins Staf.

Levin, Jack S. Structuring Venture Capital, Private Equity, & Entrepreneurial Transactions. annuals 912p. 1997. pap. 125.00 (*0-316-52282-1*, 22821) Aspen Law.

— Structuring Venture Capital, Private Equity, & Entrepreneurial Transactions. annuals 912p. pap. 125.00 (*1-56706-468-X*, 6468X) Panel Pubs.

***Levin, Jack S.** Structuring Venture Capital, Private Equity & Entrepreneurial Transactions, 1. 1040p. 1999. pap. text 165.00 (*0-7355-0505-5*) Panel Pubs.

***Levin, Jack S. & Ginsburg, Martin D.** Mergers, Acquisitions & Buyouts: Combo, October 1999, 3. 2450p. 2000. pap. text 450.00 (*0-7355-1255-8*) Panel Pubs.

An Asterisk (*) at the beginning of an entry indicates that the title is appearing for the first time.

— Mergers, Acquisitions & Buyouts April 1999, 3. 3160p. 1999. pap. 295.00 (*0-7355-0422-9*) Panel Pubs.

— Mergers, Acquisitions & Buyouts, October 1999: A Transactional Analysis of the Governing Tax, Legal & Accounting Considerations, 3 vols. 3160p. 2000. pap. 325.00 incl. disk (*0-7355-1104-7*, 11047) Panel Pubs.

Levin, Jack S., jt. auth. see Ginsburg, Martin D.

Levin, Jackie. Expressions of the Human Spirit. 1998. 9.95 (*0-9666667-0-4*) AbleNet Inc.

Levin, Jackie, jt. auth. see Locke, Peggy.

Levin, Jacqueline B. Wise Women Said These Things. LC 99-203183. (Pocket Gift Editions Ser.). 64p. 1998. 4.95 (*0-88088-089-9*) Peter Pauper.

Levin, James, photos by. All in a Day's Play. LC 98-173977. (Tonka Photo Board Bks.). (Illus.). 16p. (J). 1998. bds. 4.99 (*0-590-76344-X*) Scholastic Inc.

— What Do Trucks Do? (Tonka Photo Board Bks.). (Illus.). 16p. (J). (ps). 1998. bds. 4.99 (*0-590-76343-1*) Scholastic Inc.

Levin, James & Cederquist, Natalie. A Celebration of Wellness. (Illus.). 308p. 1990. pap. 16.95 (*0-9628698-1-3*) GLO Inc.

— A Celebration of Wellness: An Easy to Use Vegetarian Cookbook... with Over 300 Lowfat & Nonfat Heart Healthy, No Dairy, No Cholesterol Recipes. (Illus.). 334p. Date not set. pap. 17.95 (*0-89529-684-5*, Avery) Penguin Putnam.

— A Vegetarian's Ecstasy. (Illus.). 321p. 1992. pap. 16.95 (*0-9628698-7-2*) GLO Inc.

— Vibrant Living. (Illus.). 261p. 1993. pap. 14.95 (*0-9628698-2-1*) GLO Inc.

***Levin, James & Nolan, James F.** Principles of Classroom Management. 3rd ed. LC 99-12693. 246p. (C). 1999. pap. text 36.00 (*0-205-28862-6*, Longwood Div) Allyn.

Levin, James & Shanken-Kaye, John. The Self-Control Classroom: Understanding & Managing the Disruptive Behavior of All Students Including Students with ADHD. 182p. 1996. pap. text 27.00 (*0-7872-1299-7*) Kendall-Hunt.

Levin, James, jt. auth. see Danielson, Eric W.

***Levin, Jay.** The Inn at Little Washington. LC 99-59967. (Illus.). 160p. 2000. 27.95 (*0-86730-804-4*) Lebhar Friedman.

Levin, Jeffrey. Picture L. A. Landmarks of a New Generation. LC 94-31176. (Illus.). 120p. (Orig.). 1994. pap. 19.95 (*0-89236-305-3*, Pub. by J P Getty Trust) OUP.

Levin, Jeffrey S., ed. Religion in Aging & Health: Theoretical Foundations in Methodological Frontiers. (Focus Editions Ser.: Vol. 166). (Illus.). 320p. (C). 1993. text 59.95 (*0-8039-5438-7*); pap. text 26.00 (*0-8039-5439-5*) Sage.

Levin, Jeffrey S., jt. auth. see Jonas, Wayne B.

Levin, Jenifer. Love & Death, & Other Disasters: Stories, 1977-1995. LC 96-41687. 144p. (Orig.). 1996. pap. 10.95 (*1-56341-078-8*) Firebrand Bks.

Levin, Jenifer. Love & Death, & Other Disasters: Stories, 1977-1995. LC 96-41687. 144p. (Orig.). 1996. lib. bdg. 22.95 (*1-56341-079-6*) Firebrand Bks.

Levin, Jenifer. Power & Surrender. 1999. pap. 20.95 (*0-525-93907-5*) Viking Penguin.

— The Sea of Light. LC 93-45971. 400p. 1994. pap. 12.95 (*0-452-27059-6*, Plume) Dutton Plume.

— Shimoni's Lover. 1987. 18.95 (*0-15-181990-4*) Harcourt.

Levin, Jennifer, jt. auth. see Boon, Andrew.

Levin, Jeremy. Energy-Saving Devices & Equipment: Residential & Commercial. LC 98-120550. (Report Ser.: No. E-070R). 132p. 1997. 3150.00 (*1-56965-166-3*) BCC.

***Levin, Jerome.** From Slavery to Freedom: Therapeutic Strategies in the treatment of Addiction. 2001. 50.00 (*0-7657-0287-8*) Aronson.

— Introduction to Chemical Dependency Counseling (A1) 2001. 50.00 (*0-7657-0289-4*) Aronson.

Levin, Jerome D. The Clinton Syndrome: The President & the Self-Destructive Nature of Sexual Addiction. LC 98-18359. 250p. 1998. 24.95 (*0-7615-1628-X*) Prima Pub.

— Couple & Family Therapy of Addiction. LC 97-29588. (Illus.). 368p. 1998. 60.00 (*1-56821-641-6*) Aronson.

— Introduction to Alcoholism Counselling: A Bio-Psycho-Social Approach. 2nd ed. 225p. 1995. 79.95 (*1-56032-355-8*); pap. 29.95 (*1-56032-358-2*) Taylor & Francis.

— Primer for Treating Substance Abusers. LC 98-6397. 1998. 30.00 (*0-7657-0078-6*) Aronson.

— Recovery from Alcoholism. LC 93-74242. 296p. 1994. reprint ed. pap. 30.00 (*1-56821-186-4*) Aronson.

— Recovery from Alcoholism: Beyond Your Wildest Dreams. LC 90-1232. 296p. 1991. 50.00 (*0-87668-625-0*) Aronson.

— Slings & Arrows: Narcissistic Injury & Its Treatment. LC 93-13285. 336p. 1993. 50.00 (*0-87668-550-5*) Aronson.

— Theories of the Self. LC 92-12864. 1992. 29.95 (*1-56032-260-8*); pap. 29.95 (*1-56032-261-6*) Hemisp Pub.

— Treatment of Alcoholism & Other Addictions: A Self-Psychology Approach. LC 87-19563. 433p. 1987. 60.00 (*0-87668-947-0*) Aronson.

— Treatment of Alcoholism & Other Addictions: A Self-Psychology Approach. LC 87-19563. 448p. 1994. pap. 65.00 (*0-87668-521-1*) Aronson.

Levin, Jerome D., ed. see Weiss, Ronna H.

Levin, Joel. Getting Published: The Educators' Resource Book. LC 83-10042. 288p. 1983. lib. bdg. 16.95 (*0-685-06781-5*, Arco) Macmillan Gen Ref.

— How Judges Reason. LC 91-37405. 267p. (C). 1992. text 39.95 (*0-8204-1549-9*) P Lang Pubng.

Levin, Joel & Kevelson, Roberta, eds. Revolutions, Institutions, Law: Eleventh Round Table on Law & Semiotics. LC 98-5646. (Semiotics & the Human Sciences). 275p. 1998. 50.95 (*0-8204-3482-5*) P Lang Pubng.

Levin, Joel, jt. ed. see Kratochwill, Thomas R.

Levin, Joel M. Ascent of the Primal Eye. (Illus.). 30p. (Orig.). 1982. pap. text 3.00 (*1-879594-04-8*) Androgyne Bks.

— Tigerskin. 14p. (Orig.). 1981. pap. text 0.75 (*1-879594-05-6*) Androgyne Bks.

Levin, Johathan. The Banking Law Reference Guide for National Banks. 2nd ed. 250p. 1991. pap. 29.95 (*0-13-093972-2*, 130401) P-H.

***Levin, Jonathan.** The Poetics of Transition: Emerson, Pragmatism, & American Literary Modernism. LC 98-8840. (New Americanists Ser.). 1999. write for info. (*0-8223-2277-3*) Duke.

Levin, Jonathan. The Poetics of Transition: Emerson, Pragmatism & American Literary Modernism. LC 98-8840. (New Americanists Ser.). 1999. pap. 17.95 (*0-8223-2296-X*) Duke.

Levin, Jonathan, ed. see Whitman, Walt.

Levin, Jonathan L. The Guide to National Banking Law. LC 96-13012. 229p. 1996. pap. 37.50 (*0-7863-1057-X*, Irwn Prfssnl) McGraw-Hill Prof.

Levin, Jules F. The Slavic Element in the Old Prussian Elbing Vocabulary. LC 72-619636. (U. C. Publ. in Linguistics Ser.: Vol. 77). 124p. reprint ed. 38.50 (*0-8357-9639-6*, 201511600092) Bks Demand.

Levin, Jules F., et al. Reading Modern Russian. (Illus.). vi, 321p. 1979. pap. text 18.95 (*0-89357-059-1*) Slavica.

Levin, Karen A. Meatless Dishes in Twenty Minutes. 144p. 1993. pap. 9.95 (*0-8092-3810-1*, 381010, Contemporary Bks) NTC Contemp Pub Co.

— Twenty-Minute Chicken Dishes. 128p. 1991. pap. 12.95 (*0-8092-4033-5*, 403350, Contemporary Bks) NTC Contemp Pub Co.

Levin, Kenneth. Solace & Romance. LC 95-70438. 341p. 1996. 24.95 (*0-9647566-0-9*) Sorenson Bks.

— Unconscious Fantasy in Psychotherapy: Its Meaning & Mastery in Psychotherapy. LC 92-49153. 320p. 1994. 50.00 (*0-87668-260-3*) Aronson.

***Levin, Kim.** Bark & Smile. 2000. 10.95 (*0-7407-0566-0*) Andrews & McMeel.

— Dogs Are Funny. (Illus.). (J). 2000. pap. 4.95 (*0-7407-1048-6*) Andrews & McMeel.

— Dogs Love... (Illus.). (J). 2000. pap. 4.95 (*0-7407-1049-4*) Andrews & McMeel.

— John Salvest: Time on His Hands. LC 99-48795. 1999. pap. 5.00 (*0-910407-37-1*) Phoenix Art.

Levin, Kim. Why We Love Dogs: A Bark & Smile Book. LC 98-85159. (Bark & Smile Book Ser.). (Illus.). 160p. 1998. 12.95 (*0-8362-6971-3*) Andrews & McMeel.

***Levin, Kim.** Why We Really Love Dogs: A Bark & Smile Book. 2000. 12.95 (*0-7407-0670-5*) Andrews & McMeel.

Levin, Kim, ed. Beyond Walls & Wars: Art, Politics, & Multiculturalism. LC 91-68502. 1993. pap. text 15.50 (*1-877675-11-3*) Midmarch Arts.

Levin, Kim, jt. auth. see Crary, Jonathan.

Levin, L., jt. auth. see Gantmakher, F.

Levin, L. I. Electrochemistry of Non-Ferrous Metals. Murty, Ram, tr. from RUS. (Illus.). 282p. (C). 1989. 40.00 (*81-204-0458-0*) S Asia.

Levin, L. I., et al. Energy Reviews: Scientific & Technical Progress in District Heating & Cogeneration, Vol. 4. Rudenko, Y. N., ed. (Soviet Technology Reviews Ser.: Vol. 4, Pt. 3). iv, 146p. 1990. pap. text 142.00 (*3-7186-4899-7*) Gordon & Breach.

Levin, L. S., et al, eds. Economic Change, Social Welfare, & Health in Europe. (WHO Regional Publications: No. 54). xii, 131p. 1995. pap. text 26.10 (*92-890-1318-4*, 1310054) World Health.

***Levin, Laura Victoria & O'Hara, John.** Elvis & You: Your Guide to the Pleasures of Being an Elvis Fan. LC 99-39295. 1999. pap. 18.95 (*0-399-52565-3*, Perigee Bks) Berkley Pub.

Levin, Laurie & Bellotti, Laura G. Creative Weddings: An Up-to-Date Guide to Making Your Wedding As Unique As You Are. LC 93-31490. 192p. (Orig.). 1994. pap. 12.95 (*0-452-27203-3*, Plume) Dutton Plume.

Levin, Lawrence M., ed. see Galdos, Benito Perez.

Levin, Leonard, jt. auth. see Holzman, Red.

Levin, Leslie. Metaphors of Conversion in Seventeenth-Century Spanish Drama, Vol. 174. LC 98-29030. (Spanish, Portuguese, Latin American Studies). (SPA.). 160p. 1998. 60.00 (*1-85566-057-1*) Boydell & Brewer.

Levin, Lester. An Investigative Approach to Industrial Hygiene. (Illus.). 288p. 1996. text 41.95 (*0-442-01925-4*, VNR) Wiley.

Levin, Lester. An Investigative Approach to Industrial Hygiene Sleuth. (Industrial Health & Safety Ser.). 274p. 1996. 54.95 (*0-471-28662-1*, VNR) Wiley.

Levin, Lewis M. Medical Staff Privileges. Karaffa, Melanie C., ed. 220p. (C). 1992. text 49.95 (*1-878487-36-1*, ME046) Practice Mgmt Info.

Levin, Linda & Bropson, Eileen. My Baby Manual: An Easy Reference Guide to Your Baby's First Year. LC 98-60125. (ENG & SPA., Illus.). 192p. 1998. spiral bd. 19.95 (*0-9655703-2-0*) Square Peg Pr.

Levin, Linda L. Mass Communication Law in Rhode Island. (State Law Ser.). 114p. (Orig.). 1993. pap. text 12.95 (*0-913507-45-8*) New Forums.

Levin, Lois, ed. see Levin, Sidney.

Levin, Lori, jt. auth. see Weber, Shirley.

Levin, Louis. Phantastica: A Classic Survey on the Use & Abuse of Mind-Altering Plants. Wirth, P. H., tr. LC 98-9484. 320p. 1998. pap. 16.95 (*0-89281-783-6*, Inner Trad) Inner Tradit.

Levin, Louis & Levin, Samuel. Practical Benchwork for Horologists. 8th rev. ed. (Illus.). 382p. 1988. reprint ed. pap. 19.95 (*0-930163-12-5*) Arlington Bk.

Levin, Lowell S., et al. Self-Care: Lay Initiatives in Health. LC 76-29361. 1976. pap. 7.95 (*0-88202-111-7*) Watson Pub Intl.

Levin, Lubov, ed. Drugie: Anthology of Modern Poetry. LC 93-70690.Tr. of Others. (RUS.). 150p. 1993. pap. text 19.95 (*0-914265-24-5*) New Eng Pub MA.

— I Vsjakie: Anthology of Modern Poetry. LC 93-77711.Tr. of Any Anyone. (RUS.). 134p. 1993. pap. text 19.95 (*0-914265-50-4*) New Eng Pub MA.

Levin, Lubov, ed. see Perelishin, Valeriy.

Levin, Lubov, ed. see Sonynn, Roman.

Levin, Lubov, ed. see Tkachev, Marian.

Levin, Lubov, ed. & illus. see Sonynn, Roman.

Levin, Maksim G. Ethnic Origins of the Peoples of Northeastern Asia. Michael, Henry N., ed. LC 63-4343. (Arctic Institute of North America-Anthropology of the North; Translation from Russian Sources Ser.: No. 3). 367p. reprint ed. pap. 113.80 (*0-608-10905-3*, 202049900018) Bks Demand.

Levin, Marcia O. The Baby's Book. (Illus.). 64p. 1984. 19.95 (*0-88363-084-2*) H L Levin.

— Baby's First Year. 1998. 9.99 (*1-57866-033-5*) Galahad Bks.

— The Bride's Book. (Illus.). 64p. 1985. 19.95 (*0-88363-085-0*) H L Levin.

— Bride's Book. 1999. 9.99 (*1-57866-051-3*) Galahad Bks.

— The Cat Lovers' Book of Days. (Illus.). 128p. 1992. 10.95 (*0-88363-092-3*) H L Levin.

— Grandmother's Book. (Illus.). 64p. 1998. pap. 9.99 (*1-57866-035-1*) Galahad Bks.

— Grandmother's Book. (Illus.). 64p. 1987. 19.95 (*0-88363-588-7*) H L Levin.

— Jewish Book of Days. (Illus.). 128p. 1987. 10.95 (*0-88363-388-4*) H L Levin.

— Physicians' Book of Days. (Illus.). 128p. 1992. 10.95 (*0-88363-392-2*) H L Levin.

— Women Artist Book of Days. 1989. 10.95 (*0-88363-481-3*) S&S Trade.

Levin, Marian S. Grandparents' Little Dividends: How to Stay in Touch with Your Grandkids. (Illus.). 64p. (Orig.). 1991. pap. text 7.95 (*0-9623521-0-1*) Grandparents Little Div.

Levin, Marjorie, et al. The Jews of Wilkes-Barre: 150 Years (1845-1995) in the Wyoming Valley of Pennsylvania. LC 87-66460. (Illus.). ix, 375p. 1998. 39.95 (*0-9664784-0-1*) Jewish Com Ctr.

***Levin, Mark.** EXP3-- Journalism: A Handbook for Journalists. LC 99-33230. 1999. write for info. (*0-8442-2392-1*) NTC Contemp Pub Co.

Levin, Mark. The Gift of Leadership: How to Relight the Volunteer Spirit in the 21st Century. (Illus.). 180p. 1997. pap. 21.95 (*0-9660080-1-4*) BAI Inc.

— Membership Development: 101 Ways to Get & Keep Your Members. 5th ed. 176p. 1995. reprint ed. pap. 29.95 (*0-9660080-0-6*) BAI Inc.

***Levin, Mark.** Millenium Membership: How to Attract & Keep Members in the New Marketplace. LC 99-50222. (Illus.). xvi, 151p. 1999. pap. 35.00 (*0-88034-163-7*) Am Soc Assn Execs.

— The Reporter's Notebook: Writing Tools for Student Journalists. 100p. (J). (gr. 3-8). 2000. pap. 10.00 (*0-9676409-0-3*) Mind Stretch.

Levin, Mark S. Combinatorial Engineering of Decomposable Systems. LC 97-50332. 392p. 1998. text. write for info. (*0-7923-4950-4*) Kluwer Academic.

Levin, Marlin. The Birth of Israel: Celebrating Fifty Years of Life, 1948-1998. (Illus.). 64p. 1998. pap. 14.95 (*965-229-186-2*, Pub. by Gefen Pub Hse) Gefen Bks.

— It Takes a Dream: The Story of Hadassah. LC 97-19184. 1997. 19.95 (*965-229-179-X*, Pub. by Gefen Pub Hse) Gefen Bks.

Levin, Marshall N. & Hake, Theodore L. Buttons in Sets. (Illus.). 88p. 1984. pap. 12.00 (*0-918708-04-4*) Hake.

Levin, Martha, ed. see Spring Hill Center Staff.

***Levin, Martin A.** After the Cure: Managing AIDS & Other Public Health Crises. 256p. 2000. text 35.00 (*0-7006-1022-7*); pap. text 16.95 (*0-7006-1023-5*) U Pr of KS.

Levin, Martin A. Urban Politics & the Criminal Courts. LC 76-8084. 1992. lib. bdg. 22.50 (*0-226-47529-8*, P822) U Ch Pr.

— Urban Politics & the Criminal Courts. LC 76-8084. 1994. pap. text 6.95 (*0-226-47530-1*, P822) U Ch Pr.

Levin, Martin A. & Ferman, Barbara. The Political Hand: Policy Implementation & Youth Employment Programs. (Government & Politics Ser.). 160p. 1985. text 37.50 (*0-08-031604-2*, Pergamon Pr); pap. text 18.95 (*0-08-031603-4*, Pergamon Pr) Elsevier.

Levin, Martin A., jt. ed. see Landy, Marc K.

Levin, Marvin E., ed. see Pfeiffer, Michael A.

***Levin, Mary Gjetson & Forde, Catherine Turmo.** Dear John: Love Letters & Lessons Learned from the Wife of an Alcoholic. LC 99-50381. 172p. 1999. pap. 21.95 (*0-8281-1349-1*) Forb Custom Pub.

Levin, Maurice I. Russian Declension & Conjugation: A Structural Description with Exercises. x, 159p. 1978. pap. 15.95 (*0-89357-048-6*) Slavica.

Levin, Meir. Novarodok: A Movement That Lived in Struggle & Its Unique Approach to the Problem of Man. LC 96-11264. 216p. 1997. pap. 30.00 (*1-56821-603-3*) Aronson.

Levin, Melvin R. American Experience & China's Urban Choices. (Working Papers: No. 8). 54p. 1987. 5.00 (*0-913749-18-4*) U MD Urban Stud.

— Ending Unemployment: Alternatives for Public Policy. LC 82-84540. (Urban Studies: No. 1). 393p. 1982. 12.00 (*0-913749-06-0*) U MD Urban Stud.

— Planning in Government: Shaping Programs that Succeed. (Illus.). 257p. (Orig.). (C). 1987. pap. 24.95 (*0-918286-44-1*, Planners Press) Am Plan Assn.

— Teleworking & Urban Development Patterns: Goodbye Uglyville - Hello Paradise. LC 98-16374. (Illus.). 256p. 1998. 52.00 (*0-7618-1117-6*); pap. 36.00 (*0-7618-1118-4*) U Pr of Amer.

Levin, Melvin R., intro. The Best of Planning. LC 88-83721. (Illus.). 614p. (Orig.). 1989. pap. text 34.95 (*0-918286-60-3*, Planners Press) Am Plan Assn.

L

Levin, Meyer. Beginnings in Jewish Philosophy. LC 76-116677. (Jewish Heritage Ser.). (Illus.). 192p. (YA). (gr. 9-11). 1971. pap. text 7.95 (*0-87441-063-0*) Behrman.

— Citizens: A Novel. LC 74-22793. reprint ed. 39.00 (*0-404-58447-0*) AMS Pr.

— Classic Chassidic Tales. LC 96-4370. (Illus.). 378p. 1996. pap. 30.00 (*1-56821-911-3*) Aronson.

— Compulsion. 416p. 1996. pap. 11.95 (*0-7867-0319-9*) Carroll & Graf.

— The Old Bunch. 976p. 1985. reprint ed. 19.95 (*0-8065-0974-0*, Citadel Pr); reprint ed. pap. 14.95 (*0-8065-0967-8*, Citadel Pr) Carol Pub Group.

Levin, Meyer, tr. see Asch, Sholem.

Levin, Michael. The Adventures of Huckleberry Finn: Literature Unit. (Literature Unit Ser.). (Illus.). 48p. 1996. pap. text, wbk. ed. 7.95 (*1-55734-564-3*) Tchr Create Mat.

Levin, Michael. Brain Teasers. (Illus.). 32p. (YA). (gr. 6 up). 1997. pap., teacher ed. 2.95 (*1-57690-260-9*, TCM2260) Tchr Create Mat.

— Brain Teasers 5. (Brain Teasers Ser.). 16p. 1997. pap., wbk. ed. 2.95 (*1-57690-259-5*) Tchr Create Mat.

— Brain Teasers 4. (Brain Teasers Ser.). 16p. 1997. pap., wbk. ed. 2.95 (*1-57690-258-7*) Tchr Create Mat.

— Brain Teasers 1. (Brain Teasers Ser.). 16p. 1997. pap., wbk. ed. 2.95 (*1-57690-255-2*) Tchr Create Mat.

— Brain Teasers 3. (Brain Teasers Ser.). 16p. 1997. pap., wbk. ed. 2.95 (*1-57690-257-9*) Tchr Create Mat.

— Brain Teasers 2. (Brain Teasers Ser.). 16p. pap., wbk. ed. 2.95 (*1-57690-256-0*) Tchr Create Mat.

— By the Great Horn Spoon! (Literature Unit Ser.). (Illus.). 48p. 1996. pap., teacher ed. 7.95 (*1-55734-528-7*) Tchr Create Mat.

— Feminism & Freedom. 490p. 1994. 44.95 (*0-88738-125-1*) Transaction Pubs.

— Feminism & Freedom. 490p. 1994. pap. 24.95 (*0-88738-670-9*) Transaction Pubs.

— The Guide to the Jewish Internet. (Illus.). 344p. 1996. pap. text 27.95 incl. disk (*1-886411-16-6*) No Starch Pr.

— Janine & Alex, Alex & Janine. 256p. (J). (gr. 5-11). 1997. mass mkt. 4.50 (*0-425-16042-4*) Berkley Pub.

— Maniac Magee. (Literature Unit Ser.). (Illus.). 48p. 1995. pap., teacher ed. 7.95 (*1-55734-537-6*) Tchr Create Mat.

— A Man's Guide to Being a Woman's Best Friend. 96p. (Orig.). 1996. pap. 4.95 (*0-8362-2581-3*) Andrews & McMeel.

***Levin, Michael.** Modern Architecture in Israel. (Illus.). 404p. 2000. 55.00 (*88-8118-523-7*, Pub. by Skira IT) Abbeville Pr.

Levin, Michael. Old Yeller: A Literature Unit. (Literature Units Ser.). (Illus.). 48p. (Orig.). 1993. pap., student ed. 7.95 (*1-55734-427-2*) Tchr Create Mat.

— Pennsylvania School Laws & Rules Annotated: 1997-98 Edition. annuals (Practice Ser.). 1407p. 1997. pap. text, suppl. ed. write for info. (*0-314-22780-6*) West Pub.

— Sam & Derek, Derek & Sam. 256p. (J). (gr. 5-11). 1997. mass mkt. 4.50 (*0-425-16041-6*) Berkley Pub.

— The Spectre of Democracy: The Rise of Modern Democracy As Seen by Its Opponents. 272p. (C). 1992. text 50.00 (*0-8147-5060-5*) NYU Pr.

— What Every Jew Needs to Know about God. LC 96-16444. 1997. 23.00 (*0-88125-537-8*) Ktav.

***Levin, Michael.** Where There's Smoke, There's Salmon: The Book of Jewish Proverbs. LC 99-27704. 160p. 1999. pap. text 10.95 (*0-8065-2146-5*, Citadel Pr) Carol Pub Group.

Levin, Michael. A Woman's Guide to Being a Man's Best Friend. LC 96-85618. 96p. (Orig.). 1996. pap. 4.95 (*0-8362-2582-1*) Andrews & McMeel.

— Writer's Internet Sourcebook. LC 97-8055. 283p. 1997. pap. text 18.95 (*1-886411-11-5*) No Starch Pr.

Levin, Michael, ed. Ethnicity & Aboriginality: Case Studies in Ethnonationalism. 1993. pap. text 20.95 (*0-8020-7423-5*) U of Toronto Pr.

— Ethnicity & Aboriginality: Case Studies in Ethnonationalism. 1993. text 50.00 (*0-8020-2918-3*) U of Toronto Pr.

— Pennsylvania School Laws & Rules Annotated, 1995-1996. 1050p. 1995. pap. write for info. (*0-314-07660-3*) West Pub.

Levin, Michael, jt. auth. see Brod, Harry.

Levin, Michael, jt. auth. see Grant, Susan H.

Levin, Michael, jt. auth. see Levin, Ina.

Levin, Michael, jt. auth. see McMullan, Jim.

Levin, Michael E. Why Race Matters: Race Differences & What They Mean. LC 96-36361. (Human Evolution, Behavior, & Intelligence Ser.). 432p. 1997. 65.00 (*0-275-95789-6*, Praeger Pubs) Greenwood.

Levin, Michael H. Roll of Thunder, Hear My Cry: A Literature Unit. (Literature Units Ser.). (Illus.). 48p. 1994. student ed. 7.95 (*1-55734-439-6*) Tchr Create Mat.

Levin, Michael H., jt. auth. see Levin, Ina Massler.

Levin, Michael I. Pennsylvania School Personnel Actions. 3rd ed. 428p. 1991. pap. 59.00 (*0-8322-0511-7*) Banks-Baldwin.

Levin, Michael I., ed. Pennsylvania School Laws & Rules, 1994-95. 905p. 1992. pap. 81.00 (*0-8322-0512-5*) Banks-Baldwin.

An Asterisk (*) at the beginning of an entry indicates that the title is appearing for the first time.

Levin, Michael L. Leo Tolstoy, a Signature on a Portrait, Highlights of Tolstoy's Thought. 2nd ed. (Illus.). 136p. (Orig.). 1995. per. 9.95 (*0-9628473-2-1*) Levin Pr.

***Levin, Michal.** The Pool of Memory: The Autobiography of an Unwilling Intuitive LC 99-194274. x, 269 p. 1998. write for info. (*0-7171-2757-5*, Pub. by Gill & MacMill) St Mut.

Levin, Mikael. In Search: War Story Aftermath. 1997. 29.95 (*3-929078-44-9*) Dist Art Pubs.

— War Story. (Illus.). 272p. 1998. pap. 35.00 (*3-929078-52-X*, Kehayoff) te Neues.

Levin, Milton. Noel Coward. (English Authors Ser.: No. 73). 130p. 1989. 22.95 (*0-8057-6978-1*, TEAS 73, Twyne) Mac Lib Ref.

Levin, Miriam. In the Beginning. LC 96-4172. (Illus.). 24p. (J). (ps-1). 1996. 14.95 (*0-929371-94-1*); pap. 5.95 (*0-929371-95-X*) Kar-Ben.

***Levin, Miriam, ed.** Cultures of Control. (Studies in the History of Science, Technology & Medicine: Vol. 9). 288p. 2000. 54.00 (*90-5823-012-0*, Harwood Acad Pubs); pap. 24.00 (*90-5823-013-9*, Harwood Acad Pubs) Gordon & Breach.

Levin, Miriam R. Republican Art & Ideology in Late Nineteenth-Century France. LC 85-21021. (Studies in the Fine Arts - Art Theory: No. 11). (Illus.). 355p. reprint ed. pap. 110.10 (*0-8357-1670-8*, 207060800005) Bks Demand.

— When the Eiffel Tower Was New: French Visions of Progress at the Centennial of the Revolution. LC 88-63428. (Illus.). 128p. 1989. pap. 18.95 (*0-87023-673-3*) U of Mass Pr.

Levin, Monroe. Clues to American Music. LC 91-42562. (Clues to American Arts Ser.). (Illus.). 72p. (Orig.). 1992. pap. 7.95 (*0-913515-62-0*, Starrhill Press) Black Belt Communs.

Levin, Morris, jt. ed. see Vinik, Ave.

Levin, Morris A. Biotreatment of Industrial & Hazardous Waste. 331p. 1993. 60.00 (*0-07-037554-2*) McGraw.

Levin, Morris A. & Israeli, Eitan. Engineered Organisms in Environmental Settings: Biotechnical & Agricultural Applications. 224p. 1996. boxed set 94.95 (*0-8493-4465-4*) CRC Pr.

Levin, Morten, jt. auth. see Greenwood, Davydd J.

Levin, Morton L., jt. ed. see Kessler, Irving I.

Levin, Moshe C., ed. see Schneersohn, Yosef Y.

Levin, Murray B. & Blackwood, George. The Compleat Politician: Political Strategy in Massachusetts. LC 62-18204. 1962. 32.50 (*0-672-51133-9*) Irvington.

Levin, Murray Barton. Teach Me. LC 98-13444. 174p. 1998. 23.00 (*0-85345-932-0*, Pub. by Monthly Rev) NYU Pr.

Levin, Murray Burton. Teach Me. LC 98-13444. 1998. pap. write for info. (*0-85345-931-2*) Monthly Rev.

Levin, N. D., et al. The Wary Warriors: Future Directions in Japanese Security Policies. 146p. 1993. pap. 15.00 (*0-8330-1406-4*, MR-101) Rand Corp.

Levin, N. Gordon, Jr. Woodrow Wilson & World Politics: America's Response to War & Revolution. LC 68-15893. 352p. 1970. pap. text 23.95 (*0-19-500803-0*) OUP.

Levin, Nancy E. Free Willy: Talking to Animals. LC 95-224949. (Illus.). 32p. (J). (ps-3). 1995. pap. 2.50 (*0-590-25352-2*) Scholastic Inc.

Levin, Nicky. Kanal Griboedova. Levin, Roman, ed. (RUS.). 208p. (Orig.). 1986. 20.00 (*0-914265-05-9*); pap. 12.00 (*0-914265-04-0*) New Eng Pub MA.

Levin, Nora. The Holocaust: The Nazi Destruction of European Jewelry, 1933-1945. LC 89-2315. (Anvil Ser.). 384p. (C). 1990. pap. text 22.50 (*0-89464-223-5*) Krieger.

— How to Care for Your Parents: A Practical Guide. LC 96-20955. 192p. 1997. 23.00 (*0-393-03987-0*) Norton.

— The Jews in the Soviet Union since 1917, 2 vols., 1. 1017p. (C). 1990. pap. text 25.00 (*0-8147-5051-6*) NYU Pr.

— The Jews in the Soviet Union since 1917, 2 vols., 2. 1017p. (C). 1990. pap. text 25.00 (*0-8147-5052-4*) NYU Pr.

— The Jews in the Soviet Union since 1917, 2 vols., Set. 1017p. (C). 1990. pap. text 50.00 (*0-8147-5050-8*) NYU Pr.

Levin, Nora Jean. How to Care for Your Parents: A Practical Guide. LC 96-20955. 192p. 1997. pap. 12.00 (*0-393-31526-6*) Norton.

***Levin, Norman D.** The Shape of South Korea's Future: Korean Attitudes Toward Unification & Long-Term Security. (Illus.). xix, 48p. 1999. pap. 7.50 (*0-8330-2759-X*, MR-1092-CAPP) Rand Corp.

Levin, P., et al. Studies in Honor of Jaan Puhvel, Pt. 1. Disterheft, Dorothy & Greppin, John, eds. LC 97-204933. (Journal of Indo-European Monograph Ser.: No. 20). 266p. (C). 1997. pap. 48.00 (*0-941694-54-2*) Inst Study Man.

Levin, P., ed. see European Congress on Sleep Research Staff.

Levin, Pam. Tyra Banks. (Black Americans of Achievement Ser.). (Illus.). (YA). (gr. 4 up). 1999. pap. 9.95 (*0-7910-4962-0*) Chelsea Hse.

Levin, Pamela. Becoming the Way We Are. rev. ed. Stern, Nora G., ed. LC 84-70759. (Illus.). 120p. 1985. pap. text 6.95 (*0-939688-12-3*) Directed Media.

***Levin, Pamela.** Perfect Bones: A Six Point Plan to Keep or Regain Healthy Bones. LC 99-96171. 304p. 2000. pap. 39.95 (*0-9672718-0-0*) Nourishing Co.

Levin, Pamela. Tyra Banks: Model. LC 99-16764. (Illus.). 144p. (YA). (gr. 5 up). 1999. 19.95 (*0-7910-5195-1*); pap. 9.95 (*0-7910-5196-X*) Chelsea Hse.

Levin, Pamela W., ed. Catastrophe Losses. LC 96-18019. 1996. pap. write for info. (*1-57073-335-X*) Amer Bar Assn.

Levin, Paul. Claims & Changes: Handbook for Construction Contract Management. Jones, Bruce & Jones, Angier, eds. (Illus.). 222p. 23.50 (*0-686-36279-9*) Constr Ind Pr.

— Construction Contract, Claims, Changes & Dispute Resolution. LC 97-28354. 272p. 1997. 49.00 (*0-7844-0276-0*) Am Soc Civil Eng.

— Time Management for Engineers & Constructors. 2nd rev. ed. LC 97-47451. 160p. 1998. pap. 35.00 (*0-7844-0303-1*) Am Soc Civil Eng.

Levin, Paul, jt. auth. see Jervis, Bruce M.

Levin, Peter. Making Social Policy: The Mechanisms of Government & Politics, & How to Investigate Them. LC 95-50905. 256p. (C). 1996. pap. 28.95 (*0-335-19084-7*) OpUniv Pr.

Levin, Peter J. Making Social Policy: The Mechanisms of Government & Politics, & How to Investigate Them. LC 95-50905. 256p. (C). 1996. 94.00 (*0-335-19085-5*) OpUniv Pr.

Levin, Phillis. The Afterimage. LC 94-19640. 63p. (Orig.). 1995. pap. 9.95 (*0-914278-67-3*) Copper Beech.

Levin, R. The Long Journey Home: The Story of a Jew's Modern-Day Pilgrimage to Christ. LC 94-76014. xvii, 171 p. 1995. pap. 10.00 (*0-9640720-0-9*) My Fathrs Busn SC.

Levin, Rhoda F. Heartmates: A Guide for the Spouse & Family of the Heart Patient. rev. ed. LC 87-11392. 368p. 1995. pap. 18.95 (*0-9637795-1-6*) MinervaPress.

— Heartmates: A Guide for the Spouse & Family of the Heart Patient. rev. unabridged ed. LC 87-11392. 1998. audio 24.95 (*0-9637795-4-0*) MinervaPress.

— The Heartmates Meditation Journal: A Companion for Partners of People with Heart Disease. 256p. (Orig.). 1995. otabind 15.00 (*0-9637795-2-4*) MinervaPress.

Levin, Rhonda F. HeartMates: A Guide for the Spouse & Family of the Heart Patient. rev. ed. 340p. 1994. mass mkt. 5.99 (*0-671-51095-9*) PB.

***Levin, Rich.** Microsoft Windows. 2000. pap. 18.95 (*0-7894-5982-5*) DK Pub Inc.

Levin, Richard. Computer Virus Handbook. 1990. text 24.95 (*0-07-881647-5*) Osborne-McGraw.

— Love & Society in Shakespearean Comedy: A Study of Dramatic Form & Content. LC 84-40060. 208p. 1985. 32.50 (*0-87413-266-5*) U Delaware Pr.

— Multiple Plot in English Renaissance Drama. LC 75-130306. 1994. lib. bdg. 22.00 (*0-226-47526-3*) U Ch Pr.

— New Readings vs. Old Plays. LC 78-10695. xiv, 278p. (C). 1994. pap. text 8.95 (*0-226-47521-2*) U Ch Pr.

— New Readings vs. Old Plays: Recent Trends in the Reinterpretation of English Renaissance Drama. LC 78-10695. 1994. lib. bdg. 24.00 (*0-226-47520-4*) U Ch Pr.

Levin, Richard. When the Sleeping Grass Awakens: Land & Power in Swaziland. 300p. 1997. pap. 49.95 (*1-86814-301-5*, U Pr W Africa) Intl Scholars.

Levin, Richard & Levin, David, eds. Tragedy: Plays, Theory & Criticism. (Harbrace Sourcebooks Ser.). 217p. (Orig.). (C). 1960. pap. text 31.00 (*0-15-592346-3*, Pub. by Harcourt Coll Pubs) Harcourt.

Levin, Richard & Weiner, Daniel, eds. No More Tears... Struggles for Land in Mpumalanga, South Africa. LC 96-45355. 300p. 1996. 69.95 (*0-86543-508-1*); pap. 18.95 (*0-86543-509-X*) Africa World.

Levin, Richard, ed. see Middleton, Thomas.

Levin, Richard I. & Rubin, David S. Statistics for Management, 7th ed. LC 96-17344. 1026p. 1997. 99.00 (*0-13-476292-4*) P-H.

Levin, Richard I., et al. Quantitative Approaches to Management. 8th ed. (C). 1992. pap., student ed. 26.88 (*0-07-037579-8*) McGraw.

Levin, Richard J., jt. auth. see Mackavey, Maria G.

Levin, Richard L. New Reading vs. Old Plays: Recent Trends in the Reinterpretation of English Renaissance Drama. LC 78-10695. 292p. reprint ed. pap. 90.60 (*0-608-09463-3*, 205426300005) Bks Demand.

Levin, Rob, ed. Quiet Contentment: The Art of Henrietta Milan. Milan, Henrietta C., tr. 160p. 1998. write for info. (*0-9669657-0-1*) Milan Pubg.

Levin, Rob & Eanes, Jennifer, eds. Seven Days in Winston-Salem. 240p. 1994. 32.95 (*1-883987-02-4*) Riverbend Bks.

Levin, Robert. The Lizard & the Fly. 320p. 1998. pap. 13.95 (*0-9665127-0-7*) Voyage Bks.

— Talks on the Origins of Public Education. 1996. pap. text. write for info. (*0-07-037711-1*) McGraw.

Levin, Robert, jt. auth. see Rosse, Joseph G.

Levin, Robert, jt. ed. see Rivelli, Pauline.

Levin, Robert A. Educating Elementary School Teachers: The Struggle for Coherent Vision, 1909-1978. LC 93-29001. 200p. (Orig.). (C). 1994. text 49.50 (*0-8191-9276-7*); pap. text 17.95 (*0-8191-9277-5*) U Pr of Amer.

Levin, Robert D. Who Wrote the Mozart Four-Wind Concertante? Authenticity, Origin & Reconstruction. LC 84-26365. 1989. 62.00 (*0-918728-31-2*) Pendragon NY.

Levin, Roman, ed. see Levin, Nicky.

Levin, Roman, ed. see Pereleshin, Valeriy.

Levin, Ron. Devil's Gut: A Novel of Good & Evil. 240p. (Orig.). 1996. pap. 9.95 (*0-9640720-1-7*) My Fathrs Busn SC.

Levin, Ronald M., jt. auth. see Gellhorn, Ernest.

***Levin, Ronit & McVeigh, Robbie, eds.** Racism & Anti-Racism in Irish Society. 224p. 2000. 57.50 (*0-7165-2648-4*, Pub. by Irish Acad Pr); pap. 26.50 (*0-7165-2652-2*, Pub. by Irish Acad Pr) Intl Spec Bk.

Levin, Ross. The Wealth Management Index: The Financial Advisor's System for Assessing & Managing Your Client's Plans & Goals. LC 96-3466. 168p. 1996. 50.00 (*0-7863-1020-0*, Irwn Prfssnl) McGraw-Hill Prof.

Levin, S. A., ed. Frontiers in Mathematical Biology. LC 94-33688. (Lecture Notes in Biomathematics Ser.: Vol. 100). 1994. write for info. (*0-387-58466-8*) Spr-Verlag.

— Frontiers in Mathematical Biology. LC 94-33688. (Lecture Notes in Biomathematics Ser.: Vol. 100). 1995. 74.95 (*3-540-58466-8*) Spr-Verlag.

Levin, S. A., et al, eds. Applied Mathematical Ecology. (Biomathematics Ser.: Vol. 18). (Illus.). 505p. 1989. 97.95 (*0-387-19465-7*, 2440) Spr-Verlag.

— Ecotoxicology: Problems & Approaches. (Advanced Texts in Life Sciences Ser.). (Illus.). 530p. 1988. 102.00 (*0-387-96762-1*) Spr-Verlag.

— Patch Dynamics. (Lecture Notes in Biomathematics Ser.: Vol. 96). xiii, 307p. 1995. 75.95 (*0-387-56525-6*) Spr-Verlag.

Levin, S. A. & Hallam, T. G., eds. Mathematical Ecology: Proceedings of the Autumn Research Seminar, Held at the International Centre for Theoretical Physics, Miramare-Trieste, Italy, November 29-December 10, 1982. (Lecture Notes in Biomathematics Ser.: Vol. 54). xii, 513p. 1984. 59.95 (*0-387-12919-7*) Spr-Verlag.

Levin, S. A., ed. see Busenberg, Stavros N., et al.

Levin, S. A., ed. see Cohen, J. E., et al.

Levin, S. A., ed. see Cressman, R.

Levin, S. A., ed. see Lyubich, Y. I.

Levin, S. A., ed. see Murray, J. D.

Levin, S. A., ed. see Nagylaki, T.

Levin, S. A., ed. see Taib, Ziad.

Levin, S. A., ed. see Tyson, J. J.

Levin, S. A., ed. see Wiegel, F. W.

***Levin, Sally & Mass, Rochelle.** Taproot Literary Review Willow Tree: Poetry & Short Stories: An International Collection. 12th ed. Feinstein, Tikvah, ed. (Tree Ser.: Vol 2). (Illus.). 94p. 1999. pap. 6.95 (*1-890269-09-3*, 16) Taproot Press.

Levin, Samuel. Shades of Meaning: Reflections on the Use, Misuse & Abuse of English. LC 97-48286. 224p. (C). 1998. pap. 16.00 (*0-8133-9028-1*, Pub. by Westview) HarpC.

Levin, Samuel, jt. auth. see Levin, Louis.

Levin, Samuel R. Linguistic Structures in Poetry. (Janua Linguarum, Ser. Minor: No. 23). 1973. pap. text 20.00 (*90-279-0678-5*) Mouton.

— The Semantics of Metaphor. LC 77-4550. 176p. reprint ed. pap. 54.60 (*0-608-14809-1*, 202562600045) Bks Demand.

Levin, Samuil. Dvadtsat' Pjat' Pljus Desjat' LC 91-68153.Tr. of Twenty-Five Plus Ten. (RUS.). 176p. 1992. pap. 12.50 (*0-914265-22-9*) New Eng Pub MA.

Levin, Saul. Semitic & Indo-European: The Principal Etymologies: With Observations on Afro-Asiatic. LC 95-19984. (Current Issues in Linguistic Theory Ser.: No. 129). xxii, 514p. 1995. lib. bdg., student ed. 97.00 (*1-55619-583-4*) J Benjamins Pubng Co.

Levin, Saul, jt. ed. see Bernardo, Aldo S.

Levin, Shalom D. Zichron Livnei Yisroel: Memoirs of Rabbi Israel Jacobson 1907-39. (HEB., Illus.). 302p. 1996. 25.00 (*0-8266-5338-3*) Kehot Pubn Soc.

Levin, Shalom D., ed. Igrois Kodesh: Admur Hazoken, Emzoee, Tzemech Tzedek, Maharasu. LC 80-81177. (HEB.). 64p. 1990. pap. 3.00 (*0-8266-5542-4*) Kehot Pubn Soc.

— Ma'asar U'geulat Admor Ha'emtzai. (HEB.). 214p. 1997. pap. 5.00 (*0-8266-5339-1*) Kehot Pubn Soc.

Levin, Shalom D., ed. see Schneersohn, Yosef Y.

Levin, Shirley. Summer on Campus. LC 96-101943. 321p. (C). 1995. pap. 15.00 (*0-87447-526-0*) College Bd.

Levin, Shmarya. The Arena. Samuel, Maurice, tr. LC 74-27999. (Modern Jewish Experience Ser.). (ENG.). 1975. reprint ed. 28.95 (*0-405-06726-7*) Ayer.

— Childhood in Exile. Samuel, Maurice, tr. LC 74-27997. (Modern Jewish Experience Ser.). 1975. reprint ed. 25.95 (*0-405-06724-0*) Ayer.

— Youth in Revolt. Samuel, Maurice, tr. LC 74-27998. (Modern Jewish Experience Ser.). 1975. reprint ed. 26.95 (*0-405-06725-9*) Ayer.

Levin, Sholom Douber, see Douber Levin, Sholom.

Levin, Sidney. Facilitating Psychotherapy. Levin, Lois, ed. 221p. 1987. text 32.95 (*0-8290-2137-X*) Irvington.

Levin, Sidney & Kahana, Ralph J., eds. Psychodynamic Studies on Aging: Creativity, Reminiscing & Dying. LC 67-27427. 345p. 1967. 50.00 (*0-8236-5640-3*) Intl Univs Pr.

Levin, Sidney L., jt. auth. see Stillman, Deborah L.

Levin, Simon. The Emergence of Diversity. 1999. write for info. (*0-201-15694-6*) Addison-Wesley.

— Fragile Dominion: Complexity & the Commons. 256p. 1999. 27.00 (*0-7382-0111-1*, Pub. by Perseus Pubng) HarpC.

***Levin, Simon, ed.** Encyclopedia of Biodiversity, 10 vols. Set. 3100p. 2000. 795.00 (*0-12-226865-2*) Acad Pr.

***Levin, Simon A.** Fragile Dominion: Complexity & the Commons. 272p. 2000. pap. text 16.00 (*0-7382-0319-X*) Perseus Pubng.

Levin, Simon A., ed. Population Biology. LC 83-21389. (Proceedings of Symposia in Applied Mathematics Ser.: Vol. 30). 101p. 1984. pap. 31.00 (*0-8218-0083-3*, PSAPM/30) Am Math.

— Some Mathematical Questions in Biology. LC 77-25086. (Lectures on Mathematics in the Life Sciences: Vol. 12). 218p. 1979. reprint ed. pap. 34.00 (*0-8218-1162-2*, LLSCI/12) Am Math.

— Some Mathematical Questions in Biology, Pt. VI. (Lectures on Mathematics in the Life Sciences: Vol. 7). 232p. 1975. pap. 47.00 (*0-8218-9902-3*, LLSCI/7) Am Math.

— Some Mathematical Questions in Biology, Pt. VIII. (Lectures on Mathematics in the Life Sciences: Vol. 9). 186p. 1977. pap. 35.00 (*0-8218-1159-2*, LLSCI/9) Am Math.

— Some Mathematical Questions in Biology, Pt. IX. (Lectures on Mathematics in the Life Sciences: Vol. 10). 244p. 1978. pap. 36.00 (*0-8218-1160-6*, LLSCI/0) Am Math.

— Some Mathematical Questions in Biology, Pt. X. (Lectures on Mathematics in the Life Sciences: Vol. 11). 179p. 1979. pap. 27.00 (*0-8218-1161-4*, LLSCI/11) Am Math.

— Some Mathematical Questions in Biology Pt. VII. (Lectures on Mathematics in the Life Sciences: Vol. 8). 182p. 1976. pap. 37.00 (*0-8218-1158-4*, LLSCI/8) Am Math.

Levin, Simon A., ed. see Symposium on Mathematical Biology Staff.

Levin-Stankevich, Brian, jt. auth. see Popovych, Erika.

Levin, Stefan L. & Knight, Connie H., eds. Genetic & Environmental Hearing Loss: Syndromic & Nonsyndromic. (Alan R. Liss Ser.: Vol. 16, No. 7). 1980. 16.00 (*0-685-03288-4*) March of Dimes.

Levin, Steffanie, ed. ABC Slide. (Illus.). (J). 1998. pap. 12.99 (*0-525-46076-4*, Dutton Child) Peng Put Young Read.

Levin, Steve. Seven Days in Tucson. 192p. 1994. 32.95 (*1-883987-01-6*) Riverbend Bks.

Levin, Sue. In the Pink: The Making of Successful Gay- & Lesbian-Owned Businesses. LC 98-39346. 172p. (C). 1998. lib. bdg. 24.95 (*0-7890-0579-4*, Harrington Park) Haworth Pr.

— In the Pink: The Making of Successful Gay- & Lesbian-Owned Businesses. LC 98-39346. (Illus.). 171p. (C). 1999. pap. 17.95 (*1-56023-941-7*) Haworth Pr.

Levin, Sunie. Mingled Roots: A Guide for Jewish Grandparents of Interfaith Grandchildren. (Illus.). 84p. (Orig.). 1992. pap. 13.95 (*0-9632259-0-1*) Bnai Brith Wom.

— You & Your Grandchildren: Special Ways to Keep in Touch. (Illus.). 56p. 1991. pap. 7.95 (*0-8431-2873-9*) Grandparents Little Div.

Levin, Susan, jt. auth. see Tracy, Gloria.

***Levin, Susan B.** The Ancient Quarrel Between Philosophy & Poetry Revisited: Plato & the Greek Literary Tradition. LC 99-54667. 208p. 2000. 39.95 (*0-19-513606-3*) OUP.

Levin, Susan M. Harry the Hairy Monster. (Illus.). 16p. (Orig.). (J). (ps-2). 1994. pap. write for info. (*0-9642777-1-9*) Levin Family.

— The Romantic Art of Confession: De Quincey, Musset, Sand, Lamb, Hogg, Fremy, Soulie, Janin. LC 97-41773. (Studies in Comparative Literature). 220p. 1998. 55.00 (*1-57113-189-2*) Camden Hse.

Levin, Susanna, jt. auth. see Smith, Kathy.

Levin, Sydney S., jt. ed. see Touchstone, Joseph C.

Levin, Ted. Backtracking: The Way of a Naturalis. LC 86-32717. (Illus.). 231p. reprint ed. pap. 71.70 (*0-608-08579-0*, 206910200002) Bks Demand.

— Blood Brook: A Naturalist's Home Ground. LC 92-16626. 224p. reprint ed. pap. 69.50 (*0-608-08578-2*, 206910100002) Bks Demand.

Levin, Ted & Levin, Ginny. Creepy Crawly Creatures: A National Geographic Pop-Up Book. LC 95-17399. (Pop-Up Bks.). (Illus.). 10p. (YA). (ps up). 1996. 16.00 (*0-7922-2975-4*, Pub. by Natl Geog) Publishers Group.

Levin, Ted, jt. auth. see National Parks & Conservation Association Staff.

Levin, Theodore. The Hundred Thousand Fools of God: Musical Travels in Central Asia (& Queens, New York) LC 96-7607. (Illus.). 346p. 1997. text 39.95 incl. audio compact disk (*0-253-33206-0*) Ind U Pr.

***Levin, Theodore.** The Hundred Thousand Fools of God: Musical Travels in Central Asia (And Queens, New York) LC 96-7607. (Illus.). 346p. 1999. pap. 24.95 incl. audio compact disk (*0-253-21310-X*) Ind U Pr.

Levin, Thomas Y., ed. & tr. see Kracauer, Siegfried.

Levin, Tony. Beyond the Bass Clef: The Life & Art of Bass Playing. (Illus.). 203p. 1998. pap. 14.99 (*0-9668137-0-7*) Papa Bear Records.

Levin, Victor. Death in Scarsdale. 32p. 1983. pap. 3.50 (*0-87129-158-4*, D40) Dramatic Pub.

Levin, Victor A., ed. Cancer in the Nervous System. LC 95-35116. 474p. 1995. text 120.00 (*0-443-08880-2*) Church.

Levin, Vladimir & Meltser, David. Chernaya Kniga S Kraenymi Stranitsami: Tragedy & Heroism of Bellorussian Jewry. LC 96-60904.Tr. of Black Book with Red Pages. (Illus.). 590p. 1996. pap. 15.00 (*1-885563-05-1*) VIA Press MD.

Levin-Waldman, Oren M. Automatic Adjustment of the Minimum Wage. (Public Policy Brief Highlights Ser.: Vol. 42A). 4p. 1998. pap. write for info. (*0-941276-50-3*) J Levy.

— Automatic Adjustment of the Minimum Wage: Linking the Minimum Wage to Productivity. (Public Policy Brief Ser.: Vol. 42). 39p. 1998. pap. write for info. (*0-941276-49-X*) J Levy.

***Levin-Waldman, Oren M.** The Case of the Minimum Wage: Competing Policy Models. LC 00-38770. (C). 2001. pap. text 20.95 (*0-7914-4856-8*) State U NY Pr.

— The Case of the Minimum Wage: Competing Policy Models. LC 00-38770. (C). 2001. text 62.50 (*0-7914-4855-X*) State U NY Pr.

Levin-Waldman, Oren M. The Consolidated Assistance Program: Reforming Welfare by Synchronizing Public Assistance Benefits. (Public Policy Briefs Ser.: No. 21). 54p. (Orig.). 1995. pap. write for info. (*0-941276-66-X*) J Levy.

***Levin-Waldman, Oren M.** Institutions Affect the Wage Structure? (Public Policy Brief Highlights Ser.: No. 57A). 6p. 1999. pap. write for info. (*0-941276-87-2*) J Levy.

— Institutions Affect the Wage Structure? Right-to-Work

An Asterisk (*) at the beginning of an entry indicates that the title is appearing for the first time.

Laws, Unionization, & the Minimum Wage. (Public Policy Brief Ser.: No. 57). 32p. 1999. pap. write for info. (*0-941276-86-4*) J Levy.

Levin-Waldman, Oren M. Making Unemployment Insurance Work: Reforming Unemployment Insurance: Toward Greater Employment. (Public Policy Brief Ser.: Vol. 26). 54p. (Orig.). 1996. pap. text 3.00 (*0-941276-17-1*) J Levy.

— A New Path from Welfare to Work. (Public Policy Brief Highlights Ser.: Vol. 31A). 4p. 1997. pap. write for info. (*0-941276-26-0*) J Levy.

— A New Path from Welfare to Work: The New Welfare & the Potential for Workforce Development. (Public Policy Briefs Ser.: Vol. 31). (Illus.). 36p. 1997. pap. text 3.00 (*0-941276-24-4*) J Levy.

— Plant Closure, Regulation, & Liberalism: The Limits to Liberal Public Philosophy. LC 92-16876. 200p. (C). 1992. lib. bdg. 49.50 (*0-8191-8760-7*) U Pr of Amer.

— Plant Closure, Regulation, & Liberalism: The Limits to Liberal Public Philosophy. LC 92-16876. 200p. (C). 1992. pap. text 26.00 (*0-8191-8761-5*) U Pr of Amer.

— Reconceiving Liberalism: Dilemmas of Contemporary Liberal Public Policy. LC 96-25190. (Pitt Series in Political Science). 256p. 1997. pap. 19.95 (*0-8229-5594-6*); text 44.95 (*0-8229-3937-1*) U of Pittsburgh Pr.

— Small Business & Welfare Reform. (Public Policy Briefs Highlights Ser.: 51A). 6p. (Orig.). 1999. pap. write for info. (*0-941276-69-4*) J Levy.

***Levin-Waldman, Oren M.** Small Business & Welfare Reform: Levy Institute Survey of Hiring & Employment Practices. (Public Policy Briefs Ser.: 51). 36p. (Orig.). 1999. pap. write for info. (*0-941276-68-6*) J Levy.

Levin-Waldman, Oren M., intro. Homosexuality & the Military: A Sourcebook of Official, Uncensored U. S. Government Documents. (Illus.). 256p. (Orig.). (C). 1993. pap. text 35.00 (*1-56806-282-6*) DIANE Pub.

Levin, Wayne, et al, photos by. Kaho'olawe: Na Leo O Kanaloa. (Illus.). 136p. 1995. 55.00 (*1-883528-01-1*) Ai Pohaku Pr.

Levin, Wayne, photos by. Kalaupapa: A Portrait. (Illus.). 1989. 19.95 (*0-930897-45-5*, SP91) Bishop Mus.

Levin, William C. Sociological Ideas: Concepts & Applications. 342p. (C). 1984. pap. write for info. (*0-534-03205-2*) Wadsworth Pub.

— Sociological Ideas: Concepts & Applications. 2nd ed. 342p. (C). 1987. pap. write for info. (*0-534-08892-9*) Wadsworth Pub.

— Sociological Ideas: Concepts & Applications. 3rd ed. 416p. (C). 1990. pap. 24.95 (*0-534-14646-5*) Wadsworth Pub.

— Sociological Ideas: Concepts & Applications. 4th ed. LC 93-3256. 473p. 1993. 28.00 (*0-534-20856-8*) Wadsworth Pub.

Levin, William C., jt. auth. see Levin, Jack.

Levin, William E. Trade Dress Protection. LC 96-15608. 1996. ring bd. write for info. (*0-8366-1031-8*) West Group.

Levina, Anna. Brak Po Emigrantski - Marriage Emigre Style. LC 96-24318. (RUS., Illus.). 176p. 1996. pap. 10.00 (*1-55779-093-0*) Hermitage Pubs.

***Levina, Anna.** Ekh, Iablochko... Tstoriia V Dollarakh, Rubliakh I Kopeikakh. (Illus.). 364p. 1999. pap. 12.00 (*1-55779-117-1*) Hermitage Pubs.

***Levina-Rozengolts, Eva, et al.** Eva Levina-Rozengolts: Her Life & Work. LC 99-15942. 1999. write for info. (*0-940979-40-3*) Natl Museum Women.

Levina, Valentina M., tr. see Gorelik, Gennady E. & Frenkel, Victor Y.

Levinas, Emmanuel. Alterity & Transcendence. LC 98-47784. 144p. 1999. 29.50 (*0-231-11650-0*) Col U Pr.

***Levinas, Emmanuel.** Alterity & Transcendence. Smith, Michael B., tr. 2000. reprint ed. pap. 18.50 (*0-231-11651-9*) Col U Pr.

Levinas, Emmanuel. Autrement Qu'etre Ou Au-dela de l'Essence. (Phaenomenologica Ser.: Vol. 54). 243p. 1978. lib. bdg. 106.00 (*90-247-2030-3*, Pub. by M Nijhoff) Kluwer Academic.

— Beyond the Verse: Talmudic Readings & Lectures. Mole, Gary D., tr. LC 94-8618. 240p. 1994. 35.00 (*0-253-33288-5*) Ind U Pr.

— Collected Philosophical Papers. Lingis, Alphonso, tr. from FRE. LC 98-29198. 218p. 1998. pap. 24.95 (*0-8207-0306-0*) Duquesne.

— Collected Philosophical Papers. Lingis, Alphonso, ed. 318p. 1987. lib. bdg. 118.50 (*90-247-3272-7*, Pub. by M Nijhoff) Kluwer Academic.

— Difficult Freedom: Essays on Judaism. Hand, Sean, tr. from FRE. LC 90-31771. (Jewish Studies). 368p. 1991. text 45.00 (*0-8018-4074-0*) Johns Hopkins.

— Difficult Freedom: Essays on Judaism. Hand, Sean, tr. LC 90-31771. (Jewish Studies). 320p. 1997. pap. text 15.95 (*0-8018-5783-X*) Johns Hopkins.

— Discovering Existence with Husserl. Cohen, Richard A. & Smith, Michael B., trs. LC 98-3984. (Studies in Phenomenology & Existential Philosophy). 232p. 1997. 69.95 (*0-8101-1360-0*); pap. 18.95 (*0-8101-1361-9*) Northwestern U Pr.

— Entre Nous: Essays on Thinking-of-the-Other. Smith, Michael B. & Harshav, Barbara, trs. from FRE. LC 97-51471. (European Perspectives Ser.). 256p. 1998. 35.00 (*0-231-07910-9*) Col U Pr.

— Ethics & Infinity. Cohen, Richard, tr. from FRE. LC 85-1542.Tr. of Ethique et Infini. 136p. 1985. pap. text 14.95 (*0-8207-0178-5*) Duquesne.

— Existence & Existents. Lingis, Alphonso, tr. from FRE. 101p. 1978. pap. text 43.00 (*90-247-2048-6*, Pub. by M Nijhoff) Kluwer Academic.

— In the Time of the Nations. Smith, Michael B., tr. LC 94-8617. 224p. 1994. 32.50 (*0-253-33295-8*) Ind U Pr.

— New Talmudic Readings. LC 99-6128. 136p. 1999. 24.00 (*0-8207-0297-8*) Duquesne.

— Nine Talmudic Readings by Emmanuel Levinas. Aronwicz, Annette, tr. LC 89-46329. 240p. 1990. 31.95 (*0-253-33379-2*) Ind U Pr.

— Nine Talmudic Readings by Emmanuel Levinas. Aronwicz, Annette, tr. LC 89-46329. 240p. 1994. pap. 14.95 (*0-253-20876-9*) Ind U Pr.

— Of God Who Comes to Mind. Bergo, Bettina, tr. from FRE. LC 97-49446. (Meridian Crossing Aesthetics Ser.). 274p. 1998. 45.00 (*0-8047-3093-8*); pap. 17.95 (*0-8047-3094-6*) Stanford U Pr.

— Otherwise Than Being or Beyond Essence. Lingis, Alphonso, tr. from FRE. LC 98-19597. 205p. 1998. pap. text 22.50 (*0-8207-0299-4*) Duquesne.

— Otherwise Than Being or Beyond Essence. Lingis, Alphonso, tr. (Martinus Nijhoff Philosophy: No. 3). 273p. 1981. lib. bdg. 85.50 (*90-247-2374-4*, Pub. by M Nijhoff) Kluwer Academic.

— Outside the Subject. LC 92-83918. 128p. (C). 1993. 35.00 (*0-8047-2197-1*); pap. 12.95 (*0-8047-2199-8*) Stanford U Pr.

— Proper Names. Smith, Michael B., tr. (Meridian: Crossing Aesthetics Ser.). 208p. 1997. 35.00 (*0-8047-2351-6*); pap. 15.95 (*0-8047-2352-4*) Stanford U Pr.

— The Theory of Intuition in Husserl's Phenomenology. 2nd ed. Orianne, Andre, tr. LC 95-14655. (Studies in Phenomenology & Existential Philosophy). 163p. 1995. pap. text 19.95 (*0-8101-1281-7*) Northwestern U Pr.

— Time & the Other. Cohen, Richard A., tr. from FRE. & intro. by. LC 87-6900.Tr. of Le/Temps et L'Autre. 149p. (C). 1987. reprint ed. pap. text 19.95 (*0-8207-0233-1*) Duquesne.

— Totalite et Infini. (Phaenomenologica Ser.: No. 8). 302p. 1981. lib. bdg. 112.00 (*90-247-5105-5*, Pub. by M Nijhoff) Kluwer Academic.

— Totalite et Infini: Essai sur l'Exteriorite. 4th ed. (Phaenomenologica Ser.: Vol. 8). (FRE.). 302p. 1984. pap. text 49.50 (*90-247-2971-8*, Pub. by M Nijhoff) Kluwer Academic.

— Totality & Infinity. Lingis, Alphonso, tr. LC 69-14431. 307p. 1969. pap. text 23.50 (*0-8207-0245-5*) Duquesne.

— Totality & Infinity. Lingis, Alphonso, tr. (Martinus Nijhoff Philosophy: Vol. 1). 307p. 1980. lib. bdg. 85.50 (*90-247-2288-8*, Pub. by M Nijhoff) Kluwer Academic.

Levine. Advances in Metabolism, Vol. 12. 1997. write for info. (*0-12-027312-8*) Acad Pr.

— Advances in Metabolism, Vol. 13. 1997. write for info. (*0-12-027313-6*) Acad Pr.

***Levine.** Applied Statistics for Engineers & Scientists. 750p. 2000. 86.67 (*0-13-488801-4*) P-H.

Levine. Cinderella & the Glass Hill. LC 99-21161. 112p. (J). (gr. 2-7). pap. 4.95 (*0-06-442104-X*) HarpC Child Bks.

— Discovering Calculus. 1993. 21.00 (*0-07-037555-0*) McGraw.

— Fine Motor Dysfunction. (C). 1998. text 78.00 (*0-12-785029-5*) Acad Pr.

— Frommer's California, 1995. 1994. pap. 17.00 (*0-671-88367-4*) S&S Trade.

— Frommer's Comprehensive Travel Guide California, 1996. 1996. per. 16.00 (*0-671-52058-X*) S&S Trade.

— Frommer's Comprehensive Travel Guide Los Angeles 96. 1996. per. 12.95 (*0-671-52013-X*) S&S Trade.

— Frommer's Comprehensive Travel Guide Prague. 2nd ed. 1996. per. 12.95 (*0-671-51947-6*) S&S Trade.

— Frommer's Los Angeles, 1995-1996. 1995. pap. 13.00 (*0-671-88491-3*) S&S Trade.

— Great Beginnings - Nouns 1. 1988. 37.00 (*0-7616-2221-7*) Commun Skill.

— Great Beginnings - Nouns 2. 1988. 37.00 (*0-7616-2222-5*) Commun Skill.

— Great Beginnings-Associations. 1988. 57.00 (*0-7616-2225-X*) Commun Skill.

— Great Beginnings-Concepts. 1988. 110.50 (*0-7616-2223-3*) Commun Skill.

— Great Beginnings-Prepositions. 1988. 37.00 (*0-7616-2227-6*) Commun Skill.

— Great Beginnings-Verbs. 1988. 44.00 (*0-7616-2226-8*) Commun Skill.

Levine. Industrial Retardation in Britain. 216p. 1993. 61.95 (*0-7512-0171-5*) Ashgate Pub Co.

Levine. Internet E-Mail for Dummies. LC 96-75409. 408p. 1996. pap. 24.99 (*1-56884-235-X*) IDG Bks.

***Levine.** Introduction to Biology Survival Skills. 2000. pap. text. write for info. (*0-7167-3970-4*) W H Freeman.

— Introduction to Biology Survival Skills. 2001. pap. text. write for info. (*0-7167-3971-2*) W H Freeman.

Levine. Introductory Biology. 2000. pap. text. write for info. (*0-7167-3184-3*) W H Freeman.

***Levine.** Issues in Biology. 2000. pap. text. write for info. (*0-7167-3973-9*); pap. text. write for info. (*0-7167-3974-7*) W H Freeman.

Levine. The Magnet Book. (Illus.). 80p. (J). (gr. 3-7). 1998. pap. 10.95 (*0-8069-9944-6*) Sterling.

— Physical Chemistry. 5th ed. 2000. 65.25 (*0-07-231808-2*) McGraw.

— Point Counterpoint. 5th ed. 1994. pap. text, teacher ed. 5.00 (*0-312-11143-6*) St Martin.

— Point Counterpoint. 6th ed. LC 97-65190. 400p. 1997. pap. text 24.95 (*0-312-14987-5*) St Martin.

— Radiology of the Esophagus. 1989. text 155.00 (*0-7216-2906-7*, W B Saunders Co) Harcrt Hlth Sci Grp.

***Levine.** Science in the News Booklet. 2000. pap. text. write for info. (*0-7167-3972-0*) W H Freeman.

Levine. Seeking Alternatives: American Women in Progressive Era, 1900. 2000. 26.95 (*0-8057-1633-5*) Mac Lib Ref.

— Taking Sides:bioethical. 8th ed. 384p. 1999. pap., student ed. 18.44 (*0-07-303190-9*) McGraw.

— Tracheostomy. 2nd ed. pap. 13.00 (*0-86577-294-0*) Thieme Med Pubs.

— The World of Abnormal Psychology: A New Way of Teaching About Behavior. 10th ed. (C). 1996. pap. text, student ed. 23.44 (*0-673-98162-2*) Addson-Wesley Educ.

Levine, ed. Sexual Abuse. (Psychoanalytic Inquiry Ser.: Vol. 17, No. 3). 1997. pap. 20.00 (*0-88163-934-6*) Analytic Pr.

***Levine & Miller.** Introductory Biology. 2001. pap. text. write for info. (*0-7167-3515-6*) W H Freeman.

***Levine & Reed, eds.** Clinical Aspects of Compliance. (Psychoanalytic Inquiry Ser.: Vol. 19, No. 1). 1999. pap. 20.00 (*0-88163-926-5*) Analytic Pr.

Levine & Shefner. Fundamentals of Sensation & Perception. (Adaptable Courseware Ser.). 1996. reprint ed. 50.00 (*0-534-49779-9*) Brooks-Cole.

Levine, et al. Frommer's Comprehensive Travel Guide Florida, 1996. 1995. pap. 18.00 (*0-671-51878-X*) S&S Trade.

Levine, jt. auth. see Berenson.

Levine, jt. auth. see Chatelaine.

Levine, jt. ed. see Reed.

Levine, A. Fugitives of the Forest. LC 98-232437. (Original Six Ser.). 400p. 1999. 24.95 (*0-7737-3127-X*, Pub. by Stoddart Publ) Genl Dist Srvs.

Levine, A., jt. auth. see Neft, N.

Levine, A. J., jt. ed. see Knippers, R.

***Levine, Aaron.** Case Studies in Jewish Business Ethics. 419p. 2000. 49.50 (*0-88125-673-0*); pap. 29.50 (*0-88125-664-1*) Ktav.

Levine, Aaron. Economic Public Policy & Jewish Law. LC 93-16847. (Library of Jewish Law & Ethics: Vol. 19). 1993. 29.50 (*0-88125-437-1*) Ktav.

— Free Enterprise & Jewish Law: Aspects of Jewish Business Ethics. 1979. 22.95 (*0-87068-702-6*) Ktav.

— To Comfort the Bereaved: A Guide for Mourners & Those Who Visit Them. LC 93-39381. 288p. 1994. 30.00 (*1-56821-109-0*) Aronson.

— To Comfort the Bereaved: A Guide for Mourners & Those Who Visit Them. LC 93-39381. 288p. 1996. pap. 40.00 (*1-56821-966-0*) Aronson.

Levine, Aaron, jt. auth. see Jung, Leo.

Levine, Aaron, jt. auth. see Pava, Moses L.

Levine, Aaron, ed. see Pelletier, James L.

Levine, Abby. Abby Levine: A Man of Action. Winters, Kate, ed. (Illus.). 200p. 1998. 35.00 (*1-888069-11-2*) Biography For Everyone.

— Gretchen Groundhog, It's Your Day! LC 98-11465. (Illus.). 32p. (J). (gr. k-3). 1998. lib. bdg. 15.95 (*0-8075-3058-1*) A Whitman.

— Ollie Knows Everything. LC 93-29600. (J). 1994. 12.15 (*0-606-09706-6*, Pub. by Turtleback) Demco.

— Ollie Knows Everything. (Illus.). 32p. (J). (ps-2). 1996. reprint ed. pap. 6.95 (*0-8075-6021-9*) A Whitman.

— This Is the Pumpkin. LC 97-6156. (Illus.). 24p. (J). (ps-1). 1997. lib. bdg. 13.95 (*0-8075-7886-X*) A Whitman.

— This Is the Pumpkin. (Illus.). 24p. (J). (ps-1). 1998. pap. 6.95 (*0-8075-7887-8*) A Whitman.

***Levine, Abby.** This Is the Turkey. LC 00-8175. (Illus.). 32p. (J). (ps-1). 2000. lib. bdg. 14.95 (*0-8075-7888-6*) A Whitman.

Levine, Abby, ed. see Adorjan, Carol.

Levine, Abby, ed. see Bernstein, Sharon C.

Levine, Abby, ed. see Brown, Drollene p.

Levine, Abby, ed. see Corey, Dorothy.

Levine, Abby, ed. see Emmert, Michelle.

Levine, Abby, ed. see Girard, Linda W.

Levine, Abby, ed. see Hickman, Martha W.

Levine, Abby, ed. see James, Synthia S.

Levine, Abby, ed. see Jordan, MaryKate.

Levine, Abby, ed. see Kehret, Peg.

Levine, Abby, ed. see Kite, Patricia.

Levine, Abby, ed. see Krisher, Trudy.

Levine, Abby, ed. see Lawlor, Laurie.

Levine, Abby, ed. see Limmer, Milly J.

Levine, Abby, ed. see London, Jonathan.

Levine, Abby, ed. see Monsell, Mary E.

Levine, Abby, ed. see Mueller, Virginia.

Levine, Abby, ed. see Nerlove, Miriam.

Levine, Abby, ed. see Nikola-Lisa, W.

Levine, Abby, ed. see Ostrow, William & Ostrow, Vivian.

Levine, Abby, ed. see Sills, Leslie.

Levine, Abby, ed. see St. James, Synthia.

Levine, Abby, ed. see Tucker, Kathy.

Levine, Abby, ed. see Vigna, Judith.

Levine, Abby, ed. see Whitelaw, Nancy.

Levine, Abby, ed. see Wolf, Sallie.

***Levine, Alan.** Discovering Higher Mathematics. 336p. 1999. 59.95 (*0-12-445460-7*) Acad Pr.

Levine, Alan, ed. Early Modern Skepticism & the Origins of Toleration. LC 98-47858. (Applications of Political Theory Ser.). 266p. 1999. pap. 22.95 (*0-7391-0024-6*) Lxngtn Bks.

***Levine, Alan J.** Captivity, Flight, & Survival in World War II. LC 99-86095. 2000. write for info. (*0-275-96955-X*, Praeger Pubs) Greenwood.

— From the Normandy Beaches to the Baltic Sea: The Northwest Europe Campaign, 1944-1945. LC 99-59562. 240p. 2000. 67.50 (*0-275-96920-7*, C6920, Praeger Pubs) Greenwood.

Levine, Alan J. The Missile & Space Race. LC 93-23673. 256p. 1994. 59.95 (*0-275-94451-4*, Praeger Pubs) Greenwood.

— The Pacific War: Japan vs. the Allies, 130. LC 94-39948. 216p. 1995. 55.00 (*0-275-95102-2*, Praeger Pubs) Greenwood.

— Race Relations Within Western Expansion. LC 95-43772. 184p. 1996. 55.00 (*0-275-95037-9*, Praeger Pubs) Greenwood.

— The Soviet Union, the Communist Movement, & the World Prelude to the Cold War. LC 89-16335. 189p. 1990. 49.95 (*0-275-93443-8*, C3443, Greenwood Pr) Greenwood.

— The Strategic Bombing of Germany, 1940-1945. LC 91-45610. 248p. 1992. 59.95 (*0-275-94319-4*, C4319, Praeger Pubs) Greenwood.

— The United States & the Struggle for Southeast Asia, 1945-1975. LC 95-6928. 200p. 1995. 52.95 (*0-275-95124-3*, Praeger Pubs) Greenwood.

***Levine, Alan J.** The War Against Rommel's Supply Lines, 1942-1943. LC 98-50242. 232p. 1999. 59.95 (*0-275-96521-X*, Praeger Pubs) Greenwood.

Levine, Alan M. Orthopaedic Knowledge Update: Trauma. 350p. 1996. pap. 115.00 (*0-89203-126-3*) Amer Acad Ortho Surg.

— Spine Trauma. Lampert, Richard, ed. LC 97-39760. (Illus.). 720p. 1998. text 140.00 (*0-7216-2957-1*, W B Saunders Co) Harcrt Hlth Sci Grp.

Levine, Albert K., ed. Lasers, Vol. 1. LC 66-11288. (Illus.). 3771p. reprint ed. pap. 107.50 (*0-608-31014-X*) Bks Demand.

Levine, Albert K. & DeMaria, Anthony J., eds. Lasers, Vol. 1. LC 66-11288. (Illus.). 377p. reprint ed. pap. 116.90 (*0-608-10669-0*, 205507100001) Bks Demand.

— Lasers, Vol. 3. LC 66-11288. 383p. reprint ed. pap. 109.20 (*0-608-16654-5*, 2027814) Bks Demand.

— Lasers, Vol. 3. LC 66-11288. (Illus.). 383p. reprint ed. pap. 118.80 (*0-608-10670-4*, 202781400003) Bks Demand.

— Lasers, Vol. 4. LC 66-11288. 343p. reprint ed. pap. 106.40 (*0-7837-0022-9*, 202781400004) Bks Demand.

Levine, Alexander J., tr. see Hoyningen-Huene, Paul.

Levine, Alice, ed. see Byron, George Gordon.

Levine, Amy J. The Social & Ethnic Dimensions of Matthean Salvation History: "Go Nowhere among the Gentiles..." (Matt. 10.5b) LC 88-12701. (Studies in the Bible & Early Christianity: Vol. 14). 319p. 1989. lib. bdg. 99.95 (*0-88946-614-9*) E Mellen.

Levine, Andrew. The End of the State: A Marxist Reflection on an Idea of Rousseau's. 208p. (C). 1987. pap. 19.00 (*0-86091-881-5*, Pub. by Verso) Norton.

— The General Will: Rousseau, Marx, Communism. LC 93-2768. 238p. (C). 1993. text 69.95 (*0-521-44322-9*) Cambridge U Pr.

— Liberal Democracy: A Critique of Its Theory. LC 81-1204. 224p. reprint ed. pap. 69.50 (*0-608-15783-X*, 203101500073) Bks Demand.

— Rethinking Liberal Equality: From a "Utopian" Point of View. LC 98-6790. 1998. write for info. (*0-8014-3543-9*); pap. 30.00 (*0-8014-8523-1*) Cornell U Pr.

Levine, Andrew, ed. The State & Its Critics, 2 vols., Set. (Schools of Thought in Politics Ser.: Vol. 3). 832p. 1992. text 300.00 (*1-85278-413-X*) E Elgar.

Levine, Andrew S. & Levine, Valerie J. The Bodywork & Massage Sourcebook. LC 99-14297. (Illus.). 336p. 1999. pap. 16.95 (*0-7373-0098-1*, 00981W) NTC Contemp Pub Co.

Levine, Ann, jt. auth. see Gelles, Richard J.

Levine, Ann, jt. auth. see Steinberg, Laurence.

***Levine, Annalee.** Running on Eggs. LC 99-31984. 128p. (YA). (gr. 5-9). 1999. 15.95 (*0-8126-2875-6*, Pub. by Front St-Cricket Bks) Publishers Group.

Levine, Annalee, et al. The Teen Quiz Book. LC 97-47056. ix, 230 p. (YA). 1998. pap. 9.95 (*0-8362-5415-5*) Andrews & McMeel.

Levine, Anne-Marie. Euphorbia, Vol. III. Busa, Christopher, ed. LC 94-65401. (Provincetown Poets Ser.: III). (Illus.). 76p. 1994. 28.00 (*0-944854-12-5*); pap. 10.00 (*0-944854-11-7*) Provincetown Arts.

Levine, Arlene G. 39 Ways to Open Your Heart. (Illus.). 96p. 1996. 12.95 (*0-943233-90-9*) Conari Press.

Levine, Arnold, jt. auth. see Brockett, Patrick.

Levine, Arnold J., et al, eds. The Transformed Phenotype. LC 83-26318. (Cancer Cells Ser.: No. 1). 320p. reprint ed. pap. 99.20 (*0-7837-2003-3*, 204227700002) Bks Demand.

Levine, Arnold J., et al. The Harvey Lecture Series 90. Losick, Richard et al, eds. (Harvey Lectures). 168p. 1996. 89.95 (*0-471-14622-6*) Wiley.

Levine, Arnold S. & Luck, Jeff. The New Management Paradigm: A Review of Principles & Practices. LC 94-28874. 1994. pap. 13.00 (*0-8330-1571-0*, MR-458-AF) Rand Corp.

Levine, Arthur. All the Lights in the Night. LC 90-47496. (Illus.). 32p. (J). 1997. pap. 4.95 (*0-688-15592-8*, Wm Morrow) Morrow Avon.

— When Hope & Fear Collide: A Portrait of Today's College Student. LC 97-42414. 1998. 30.95 (*0-7879-3877-7*) Jossey-Bass.

Levine, Arthur, ed. Higher Learning in America, 1980-2000. LC 92-19746. 392p. 1993. text 40.00 (*0-8018-4457-6*) Johns Hopkins.

— Higher Learning in America, 1980-2000. 392p. (C). 1994. reprint ed. pap. text 17.95 (*0-8018-4861-X*) Johns Hopkins.

Levine, Arthur & Nidiffer, Jana. Beating the Odds: How the Poor Get to College. LC 95-9137. (Higher & Adult Education Ser.). 224p. 1995. text 29.95 (*0-7879-0132-6*) Jossey-Bass.

Levine, Arthur & Weingart, John R. Reform of Undergraduate Education. LC 73-7154. (Jossey-Bass Higher Education Ser.). 176p. reprint ed. 54.60 (*0-8357-9343-5*, 201396000087) Bks Demand.

Levine, Arthur, jt. auth. see Boyer, Ernest L.

Levine, Arthur A. All the Lights in the Night. LC 90-47496. (Illus.). 32p. (J). (ps-3). 1991. 16.00 (*0-688-10107-0*, Wm Morrow) Morrow Avon.

L

L

— The Boy Who Drew Cats: A Japanese Folktale. LC 91-46232. (J). (ps-3). 1994. 16.99 (0-8037-1172-7, Dial Yng Read) Peng Put Young Read.

Levine, Arthur S., ed. Etiology of Cancer in Man. (Cancer Growth & Progression Ser.). (C). 1989. text 207.50 (0-89838-995-X) Kluwer Academic.

Levine, B. E. The Luck of Charlie Spinoza. 265p. (Orig.). 1995. pap. 12.00 (0-9646002-1-8) Off the Grid.

Levine, Barbara, compiled by. Sidney Hook: A Checklist of Writings. LC 88-15043. 120p. 1989. 21.95 (0-8093-1510-6) S Ill U Pr.

— Works about John Dewey, 1886-1995. 536p. (C). 1996. 49.95 (0-8093-2056-8); pap. 24.95 (0-8093-2058-4) S Ill U Pr.

— Works about John Dewey, 1886-1995. 536p. 1996. 79.95 incl. cd-rom (0-8093-2063-0); pap. 59.95 incl. cd-rom (0-8093-2064-9) S Ill U Pr.

Levine, Barbara G., jt. auth. see Mogil, H. Michael.

Levine, Barbara H. Your Body Believes Every Word You Say: The Language of the Body & Mind Connection. LC 90-1169. 224p. (Orig.). 1990. pap. 13.95 (0-944031-07-2) Aslan Pub.

Levine, Barbara Hoberman. Your Body Believes Every Word You Say: The Language of the Bodymind Connection. 2nd ed. LC 99-22896. 2000. write for info. (0-944031-84-6) Aslan Pub.

Levine, Barry. The Kiss Years. expanded ed. Conte, Robert V., ed. (Illus.). 160p. (Orig.). 1998. pap. 29.95 (1-890313-02-5, RCTP9701.1) Studio Chikara.

— The Kiss Years. limited ed. (Illus.). 144p. (Orig.). 1997. pap. 24.95 (1-890313-00-9, Silver Skull) Studio Chikara.

— Principles of Forensic Toxicology. 363p. 1998. pap. 49.00 (1-890883-07-7, 202024) Am Assn Clinical Chem.

Levine, Barry, ed. The Caribbean Exodus. LC 86-21217. 300p. 1986. pap. 24.95 (0-275-92183-2, B2183, Praeger Pubs) Greenwood.

— The Caribbean Exodus. LC 86-21217. 300p. 1987. 55.00 (0-275-92182-4, C2182, Praeger Pubs) Greenwood.

Levine, Barry, jt. auth. see Okrand, Mark.

Levine, Barry A. Current Practice of Cardiothoracic Surgery. LC 93-49075. 1994. pap. text 39.00 (0-443-08976-0) Church.

— Current Practice of Gastrointestinal & Abdominal Surgery. LC 93-50705. 1994. pap. text 58.00 (0-443-08975-2) Church.

— Current Practice of Pediatric Surgery. LC 93-49044. 1994. pap. text 34.00 (0-443-08978-7) Church.

Levine, Barry A., ed. Current Practice of Breast, Skin & Soft Tissue Surgery. LC 93-50590. 1994. pap. text 34.00 (0-443-08974-4) Church.

— Current Practice of Vascular Surgery. LC 93-50706. 1994. pap. text 39.00 (0-443-08977-9) Church.

Levine, Barry A., et al, eds. Current Practice of Surgery, 3 vols., Set. (Illus.). 2848p. 1993. text 315.00 (0-443-08767-9) Church.

— Current Practice of Surgery Essentials. LC 93-48804. 1994. pap. text 48.00 (0-443-08972-8) Church.

Levine, Barry A., et al. Current Practice of Trauma Surgery. LC 93-48362. 1994. pap. text 34.00 (0-443-08973-6) Church.

Levine, Barry K. Pattern Recognition Analysis via Genetic Algorithms & Multivariate Statistical Methods. (Fundamental & Applied Aspects of Chemometrics Ser.). 1999. 69.95 (0-8493-7324-7, 7324) CRC Pr.

Levine, Baruch. Group Psychotherapy: Practice & Development. (Illus.). 352p. (C). 1991. reprint ed. text 34.95 (0-88133-598-3) Waveland Pr.

— Group Work with the Emotionally Disabled. LC 90-4281. (Social Work with Groups Ser.: Vol. 13, No. 1). 133p. 1990. text 39.95 (0-86656-994-4) Haworth Pr.

— Numbers 1 to 20: A New Translation with Introduction & Commentary. LC 92-12262. (Anchor Bible Ser.: Vol. 4). 544p. 1993. 42.50 (0-385-15651-0) Doubleday.

Levine, Baruch & Gallogly, Virginia. Group Therapy with Alcoholics: Outpatient & Inpatient Approaches. (Human Services Guides Ser.: Vol. 40). 136p. (Orig.). (C). 1985. pap. text 18.95 (0-8039-2504-2) Sage.

Levine, Baruch, jt. auth. see Hudson, Michael.

Levine, Baruch, jt. ed. see Ahituv, Shmuel.

Levine, Baruch, jt. ed. see Hudson, Michael.

Levine, Baruch A. The JPS Torah Commentary: Leviticus. 330p. 60.00 (0-8276-0328-2) JPS Phila.

***Levine, Baruch A.** Numbers 21-36. LC 99-28025. (Anchor Bible Ser.: Vol. 4). 496p. 2000. 45.00 (0-385-41256-8) Doubleday.

Levine, Becky, ed. see Bakhtiar-van Dillen, Lailee.

Levine, Bernard. Levine's Guide to Knives & Their Values: The Complete Handbook of Knife Collecting. 4th ed. LC 85-71895. (Illus.). 512p. 1997. pap. 27.95 (0-87349-189-0, LGK4(DBI9746)) Krause Pubns.

***Levine, Bernard.** Levine's Guide to Knives & Their Values: The Complete Handbook of Knife Collecting. 5th rev. ed. LC 85-71895. (Illus.). 544p. 2000. pap. 29.95 (0-87341-945-6, LGK5) Krause Pubns.

Levine, Bernard R. Knifemakers of Old San Francisco. 2nd ed. LC 98-143737. 160p. 1998. 39.95 (0-87364-974-5) Paladin Pr.

Levine, Bertram J., jt. auth. see Wolpe, Bruce C.

Levine, Beth. Divorce: Young People Caught in the Middle. LC 94-33430. (Issues in Focus Ser.). 112p. (YA). (gr. 6 up). 1995. lib. bdg. 20.95 (0-89490-633-X) Enslow Pubs.

Levine, Bev, jt. auth. see Pastor, Iris.

Levine, Bobbie & Lichter, Carolyn. A Child's Walk Through Africa. (Illus.). 38p. (J). (gr. 3-6). 1987. spiral bd. 1.50 (0-912303-38-7) Michigan Mus.

— A Child's Walk Through Asia. (Illus.). 25p. (J). (gr. 2-6). 1984. spiral bd. 1.50 (0-912303-31-X) Michigan Mus.

Levine, Bobbie, et al. A Child's Walk Through Twentieth Century American Painting & Sculpture. (Illus.). 29p. (J). (gr. 2-6). 1986. spiral bd. 1.50 (0-912303-37-9) Michigan Mus.

Levine, Brian. Cripple Creek: City of Influence. (Illus.). 150p. (Orig.). 1994. pap. 5.95 (0-9655012-0-5) City of Cripple.

Levine, Bruce. Half Slave & Half Free. Foner, Eric, ed. (American Century Ser.). 292p. 1992. pap. 12.00 (0-374-52309-6) FS&G.

— Manhattan Living. Weisberg, Michael, ed. (Illus.). 304p. (Orig.). 1985. pap. 14.95 (0-9614421-0-7) M K L Ltd.

Levine, Bruce S. The Spirit of 1848: German Immigrants, Labor Conflict, & the Coming of the Civil War. (Working Class in American History Ser.). 400p. 1992. text 34.95 (0-252-01873-7) U of Ill Pr.

Levine, C. & Berg, N. It's about Time. (Tamar Bks.). 1992. 16.99 (0-89906-111-7); pap. 13.99 (0-89906-112-5) Mesorah Pubns.

Levine, Carol. Guide to Wildflowers in Winter. LC 94-46215. (Illus.). 329p. 1995. pap. 20.00 (0-300-06560-4) Yale U Pr.

— Guide to Wildflowers in Winter: Herbaceous Plants of Northeastern North America. LC 94-46215. 329p. (C). 1995. 45.00 (0-300-06207-9) Yale U Pr.

— Rough Crossings: Family Caregivers' Odysseys Through the Health Care System. LC 98-38769. (A Special Report). 1998. write for info. (1-881277-43-7) United Hosp Fund.

— Taking Sides: Clashing Views on Controversial Bioethical Issues. 7th ed. (C). 1997. text 14.88 (0-697-37535-8) Brown & Benchmark.

Levine, Carol, ed. A Death in the Family: Orphans of the HIV Epidemic. LC 93-21517. 1993. 10.00 (1-881277-13-5) United Hosp Fund.

Levine, Carol, ed. Taking Sides: Clashing Views on Controversial Bioethical Issues. 6th ed. LC 94-45959. 400p. (C). 1995. text 13.95 (1-56134-328-5, Dshkn McGraw-Hill) McGrw-H Hghr Educ.

Levine, Carol, jt. auth. see Dane, Barbara O.

Levine, Carol, jt. ed. see Dane, Barbara O.

Levine, Caroline, jt. auth. see Levine, Sumner N.

Levine, Caroline, tr. see Loraux, Nicole.

Levine, Charles H., ed. Managing Fiscal Stress: The Crisis in the Public Sector. LC 79-27266. (Chatham House Series on Change in American Politics). (Illus.). 352p. reprint ed. pap. 109.20 (0-8357-4830-8, 203776700009) Bks Demand.

— Managing Human Resources: A Challenge to Urban Governments. LC 77-79869. (Urban Affairs Annual Reviews Ser.: No. 13). 319p. reprint ed. pap. 98.90 (0-8357-8491-6, 203476500091) Bks Demand.

— The Unfinished Agenda for Civil Servivce Reform: Implications of the Grace Commission Report. LC 85-71183. (Dialogues on Public Policy Ser.). 142p. 1985. pap. 10.95 (0-8157-5251-2) Brookings.

Levine, Charles H. & Rubin, Irene, eds. Fiscal Stress & Public Policy. LC 80-24515. (Sage Yearbooks in Politics & Public Policy Ser.: No. 9). 314p. reprint ed. pap. 97.40 (0-8357-8419-3, 203468400091) Bks Demand.

Levine, Charles H., et al. The Politics of Retrenchment: How Local Governments Manage Fiscal Stress. LC 81-9241. (Sage Library of Social Research: No. 130). 224p. reprint ed. pap. 69.50 (0-8357-8490-8, 203476400091) Bks Demand.

Levine, Claire. The Bud That Stays, Poetry, Prose & Drawings of Laurence Levine, CD Included. 220p. (Orig.). 1998. pap. 20.00 incl. audio compact disk (1-56439-070-5) Ridgeway.

Levine, D. S. Introduction to Cognitive & Neural Modeling. 456p. (C). 1991. pap. 27.50 (0-8058-0268-1) L Erlbaum Assocs.

Levine, Dan. Avant-Guide London: Insider's Guide for Cosmopolitan Travelers. 1999. pap. text 19.95 (1-891603-02-7) Empire Pr.

— Avant-Guide New York City: Insiders' Guide for Cosmopolitan Travelers. (Illus.). 284p. 1998. pap. 19.95 (1-891603-01-9, Pub. by Empire Pr) Publishers Group.

***Levine, Dan.** Avant-Guide Paris: Insiders' Guide for Cosmopolitan Travelers. (Avant-Guide Bks.). (Illus.). 288p. 2000. pap. 19.95 (1-891603-06-X) Empire Pr.

— Avant-Guide San Francisco: Insider's Guide for Cosmopolitan Travelers. 264p. 1999. pap. text 19.95 (1-891603-03-5) Empire Pr.

Levine, Dan. Avant Guide to Prague. 1998. pap. text 19.95 (1-891603-00-0) Empire Pr.

***Levine, Dan.** Las Vegas: Insiders' Guide for Cosmopolitan Travelers. (Avant-Guide Bks.). (Illus.). 2000. pap. 19.95 (1-891603-11-6) Empire Pr.

Levine, Dan. London. (Frommer's Walking Tours Ser.). (Illus.). 176p. 1993. pap. 12.00 (0-671-79836-7, P-H Travel) Prntice Hall Bks.

***Levine, Dan.** New Orleans: Insiders' Guide for Cosmopolitan Travelers. (Avant-Guide Bks.). (Illus.). 2000. pap. 19.95 (1-891603-10-8) Empire Pr.

— New York City: Insiders' Guide for Cosmopolitan Travelers. 2nd ed. (Avant-Guide Bks.). (Illus.). 2000. pap. 19.95 (1-891603-08-6) Empire Pr.

— Prague: Insiders' Guide for Cosmopolitan Travelers. 2nd ed. (Avant-Guide Bks.). (Illus.). 2000. pap. 19.95 (1-891603-09-4) Empire Pr.

Levine, Dan & Crosby, Alan. Frommer's Prague & Best of Czech. 288p. 1996. 14.95 (0-02-860903-4) Macmillan.

Levine, Daniel. Bayard Rustin & the Civil Rights Movement. LC 99-34245. (Illus.). 352p. 1999. text 35.00 (0-8135-2718-X) Rutgers U Pr.

— Jane Addams & the Liberal Tradition. LC 80-18807. (Illus.). 277p. 1980. reprint ed. lib. bdg. 38.50 (0-313-22691-1, LEJA, Greenwood Pr) Greenwood.

— Poverty & Society: The Growth of the American Welfare State in International Comparison. 368p. (C). 1988. pap. text 19.00 (0-8135-1353-7) Rutgers U Pr.

— Varieties of Reform Thought. LC 79-28658. 149p. 1980. reprint ed. lib. bdg. 49.75 (0-313-22345-9, LEVR, Greenwood Pr) Greenwood.

Levine, Daniel A., tr. see Vorobyov, N. N.

Levine, Daniel B., ed. see National Research Council (U. S.), Panel on Immigration Statistics Staff.

Levine, Daniel H. Conflict & Political Change in Venezuela. LC 75-39790. 299p. reprint ed. pap. 92.70 (0-8357-3401-3, 203965800013) Bks Demand.

— Popular Voices in Latin American Catholicism. (Studies in Church & State). (Illus.). 424p. 1992. pap. text 22.95 (0-691-02459-6, Pub. by Princeton U Pr) Cal Prin Full Svc.

Levine, Daniel H., ed. Churches & Politics in Latin America. LC 79-23827. (Sage Focus Editions Ser.: No. 14). 288p. reprint ed. pap. 89.30 (0-8357-8489-4, 203476200091) Bks Demand.

— Constructing Culture & Power in Latin America. (Comparative Studies in Society & History). 488p. 1993. text 65.00 (0-472-09456-4, 09456); pap. text 24.95 (0-472-06456-8, 06456) U of Mich Pr.

— Religion & Political Conflict in Latin America. LC 85-24525. xiii, 266p. (C). 1986. 34.95 (0-8078-1689-2); pap. 17.95 (0-8078-4150-1) U of NC Pr.

Levine, Daniel S. Disgruntled: The Darker Side of the World of Work. LC 99-218597. 304p. 1998. pap. 12.00 (0-425-16507-8) Blvd Books.

***Levine, Daniel S.** Introduction to Neural & Cognitive Modeling. 2nd ed. 325p. 1999. teacher ed. write for info. (0-8058-2007-8); text. write for info. (0-8058-2005-1); pap. text. write for info. (0-8058-2006-X) L Erlbaum Assocs.

Levine, Daniel S., et al, eds. Osillations in Neural Systems. LC 99-39666. 448p. 1999. 99.95 (0-8058-2066-3) L Erlbaum Assocs.

Levine, Daniel S. & Aparicio, Manuel, IV, eds. Neural Networks for Knowledge Representation & Inference. 512p. 1994. pap. 45.00 (0-8058-1159-1); text 99.95 (0-8058-1158-3) L Erlbaum Assocs.

Levine, Daniel S. & Elsberry, Wesley R., eds. Optimality in Biological & Artificial Networks. (INNS Series of Texts, Monographs, & Proceedings). 400p. (C). 1996. 89.95 (0-8058-1561-9) L Erlbaum Assocs.

Levine, Daniel S. & Leven, Samuel J., eds. Motivation, Emotion, & Goal Direction in Neural Networks. 472p. (C). 1992. text 99.95 (0-8058-0447-1) L Erlbaum Assocs.

Levine, Danny. The Birth of the Irgun Zvai Leumi: The Jewish Resistance Movement. 202p. 1992. pap. 9.95 (965-229-071-8, Pub. by Gefen Pub Hse) Gefen Bks.

***Levine, David.** At the Dawn of Modernity: Biology, Culture & Material Life in Europe after the Year 1000. LC 00-34384. 2001. write for info. (0-520-22058-7) U CA Pr.

— Dance of a Child's Dreams. 32p. 1998. pap. 23.95 incl. audio compact disk (0-7866-3088-4, 96790CDP) Mel Bay.

— Dance of a Child's Dreams - Songs for Home & School: Beginning-Intermediate Level. 32p. 1998. pap. 8.95 (0-7866-3048-5, 96790) Mel Bay.

Levine, David. In That Day: How Jesus Is Revealing Himself to the Jewish People in the Last Days. LC 98-3981. 1998. pap. 12.99 (0-88419-545-7) Creation House.

Levine, David, et al, eds. Rethinking Schools: A Collection from the Leading Journal of School Reform. LC 94-34347. 304p. 1995. 25.00 (1-56584-214-6, Pub. by New Press NY) Norton.

Levine, David, intro. Defending the Earth: Debate Between Murray Bookchin & Dave Foreman. 120p. 1991. write for info. (0-921689-89-6); pap. write for info. (0-921689-88-8) Black Rose.

Levine, David & Bailer, Darice. Head-to-Head Football: Troy Aikman & Steve Young. Sieck, Margaret, ed. LC 96-206371. (Illus.). 144p. (Orig.). (J). (gr. 5). 1996. pap. 4.95 (1-886749-14-0) SI For Kids.

Levine, David & Minton, Gabriel. Wireless Data Solutions. 448p. 1999. pap. 39.99 (0-471-32335-7) Wiley.

Levine, David & Negreiros, Almada. The Man Who Never Was. LC 81-83226. 195p. (Orig.). 1982. pap. 7.50 (0-943722-08-X); text 17.50 (0-943722-07-1) Gavea-Brown.

Levine, David, jt. auth. see Wrightson, Keith.

Levine, David, ed. see Nebraska Symposium on Motivation Staff.

Levine, David, tr. see Ibn Al-Fayyumi, Nathanael.

Levine, David A. Internal Combustion: The Races in Detroit 1915-1926, 24. LC 75-35347. 222p. 1976. 69.50 (0-8371-8588-2, LIC/, Greenwood Pr) Greenwood.

Levine, David A. & Wrightson, Keith. The Making of an Industrial Society: Whickham, 1560-1765. (Oxford Studies in Social History). (Illus.). 478p. 1991. text 120.00 (0-19-820066-8) OUP.

Levine, David I. Working in the 21st Century: Policies for Economic Growth Through Training, Opportunity & Education. LC 98-13865. (Issues in Work & Human Resources Ser.). 304p. (C). (gr. 13). 1998. pap. text 27.95 (0-7656-0304-7) M E Sharpe.

— Working in the Twenty-First Century: Policies for Economic Growth Through Training, Opportunity & Education. LC 98-13865. (Issues in Work & Human Resources Ser.). 304p. (C). (gr. 13). 1998. text 65.95 (0-7656-0303-9) M E Sharpe.

Levine, David I., ed. Reinventing the Workplace: How Business & Employees Can Both Win. LC 94-24066. 222p. (C). 1995. 38.95 (0-8157-5232-6); pap. 16.95 (0-8157-5231-8) Brookings.

Levine, David I., et al, eds. Civil Procedure Anthology. 600p. 1998. pap. 29.95 (0-87084-140-8) Anderson Pub Co.

Levine, David I., et al. California Civil Procedures: Teacher's Manual, Cases & Materials On. (American Casebook Ser.). 95p. 1991. pap. text. write for info. (0-314-00482-3) West Pub.

— Cases & Materials on California Civil Procedure. (American Casebook Ser.). 546p. (C). 1991. 50.50 (0-314-84826-6) West Pub.

— Cases & Materials on Remedies: Public & Private. 2nd ed. LC 96-372. (American Casebook Ser.). 850p. (C). 1996. 57.50 (0-314-06778-7) West Pub.

Levine, David I., jt. auth. see Kane, Mary K.

Levine, David K. & Lippman, Steven A., eds. The Economics of Information, 2 Vols. (International Library of Critical Writings in Economics: Vol. 53). 944p. 1995. 365.00 (1-85278-511-X) E Elgar.

Levine, David K., jt. auth. see Fudenberg, Drew.

***Levine, David M., et al.** Business Statistics: A First Course. 2nd ed. LC 99-56620. (Illus.). 654p. 1999. pap. text 75.00 (0-13-086754-3) P-H.

Levine, David M., jt. auth. see Berenson, Mark.

Levine, David M., jt. auth. see Berenson, Mark L.

Levine, David P. Needs, Rights & the Market. LC 88-4543. 158p. 1988. lib. bdg. 35.00 (1-55587-115-1) L Rienner.

***Levine, David P.** Normative Political Economy: Subjective Freedom, the Market & the State. LC 00-34482. 2000. write for info. (0-415-23529-4) Routledge.

Levine, David P. Self-Seeking & the Pursuit of Justice. LC 97-73205. (Avebury Series in Philosophy). 144p. 1997. text 59.95 (1-84014-113-1, Pub. by Ashgate Pub) Ashgate Pub Co.

— Wanting & Choosing: Essays on Subjectivity in Political Economy. LC 97-23783. 176p. (C). 1989. 70.00 (0-415-16661-6) Routledge.

— Wealth & Freedom: An Introduction to Political Economy. (Illus.). 203p. (C). 1995. pap. text 18.95 (0-521-44791-7) Cambridge U Pr.

Levine, David P., et al, eds. Rethinking Schools: A Collection from the Leading Journal of School Reform. LC 94-34347. 304p. 1995. pap. 16.00 (1-56584-215-4, Pub. by New Press NY) Norton.

Levine, David P., jt. auth. see Caporaso, James A.

Levine, David U. & Levine, Rayna F. Society & Education. 9th ed. 624p. 1995. 77.00 (0-205-18935-0) Allyn.

Levine, David Z. Care of the Renal Patient: A Family Medicine Guide. 3rd ed. Kersey, Ray, ed. LC 96-26583. 315p. 1997. text 52.00 (0-7216-6243-9, W B Saunders Co) Harcrt Hlth Sci Grp.

Levine, Deb. The Joy of Cybersex: A Guide for Creative Lovers. LC 98-21013. 256p. 1998. pap. 12.00 (0-345-42580-4) Ballantine Pub Grp.

Levine, Deborah J. Religious Diversity in Public Schools: A Suburban Case Study. 64p. (Orig.). 1996. spiral bd. write for info. (0-9640706-9-3) Cock-a-Hoop.

— Teaching Christian Children about Judaism. LC 94-48369. 64p. (Orig.). 1995. pap. 18.00 incl. audio (1-56854-076-0, TCCAJ) Liturgy Tr Pubns.

Levine, Deborah R., jt. auth. see Christy, Dennis T.

Levine, Deena R. & Adelman, Mara B. Beyond Language: Cross Cultural Communication. 2nd ed. LC 92-28675. 288p. (C). 1992. pap. 31.93 (0-13-094855-1) P-H.

Levine, Deena R., et al. The Culture Puzzle: Cross-Cultural Communication for English As a Second Language. (Illus.). 256p. (C). 1987. pap. text 31.80 (0-13-195520-9) P-H.

Levine, Don & Michlig, John. G. I. Joe: Masterpiece Edition. deluxe ed. (Illus.). 96p. 1996. 60.00 (0-8118-1388-6); 60.00 (0-8118-1464-5) Chronicle Bks.

Levine, Donald N. The Flight from Ambiguity: Essays in Social & Cultural Theory. LC 85-8762. x, 258p. 1988. pap. text 23.00 (0-226-47556-5) U Ch Pr.

— The Flight from Ambiguity: Essays in Social & Cultural Theory. LC 85-8762. x, 266p. 1996. lib. bdg. 33.00 (0-226-47555-7) U Ch Pr.

— Greater Ethiopia: The Evolution of a Multiethnic Society. LC 73-91233. (Illus.). 246p. 2000. pap. text 17.95 (0-226-47560-3, P721) U Ch Pr.

— Greater Ethiopia: The Evolution of a Multiethnic Society. 2nd ed. 2000. pap. text 16.00 (0-226-47561-1) U Ch Pr.

— Simmel & Parsons: Two Approaches to the Study of Society. Zuckerman, Harriet & Merton, Robert K., eds. LC 79-9011. (Dissertations on Sociology Ser.). 1980. lib. bdg. 30.95 (0-405-12979-3) Ayer.

— Visions of the Sociological Tradition. LC 95-3389. 381p. 1995. pap. text 15.95 (0-226-47547-6) U Ch Pr.

— Visions of the Sociological Tradition. LC 95-3389. 380p. 1995. lib. bdg. 47.50 (0-226-47546-8) U Ch Pr.

— Wax & Gold: Tradition & Innovation in Ethiopian Culture. LC 65-18340. xvi, 316p. 1994. reprint ed. pap. text 18.00 (0-226-47566-2) U Ch Pr.

Levine, Donald N., ed. Performance Contracting in Education - An Appraisal: Toward a Balanced Perspective. LC 72-12681. 192p. 1973. pap. 24.95 (0-87778-046-3) Educ Tech Pubns.

Levine, Donald N., ed. see Simmel, Georg.

Levine, Donald P. & Sobel, Jack D., eds. Infections in Intravenous Drug Abusers. (Illus.). 416p. 1990. text 75.00 (0-19-506223-X) OUP.

Levine, Doug. You. 1997. pap. 16.00 (0-679-76715-0) McKay.

Levine, Dov, tr. The Torah Discourses of the Holy Tzaddik Reb Menachem Mendel of Rimanov, 1745-1815. LC 96-248. (ENG, HEB & YID.). 1996. 35.00 (0-88125-540-8) Ktav.

LeVine, Duane G. The City As a Human Environment. LC 94-1146. (Only One Earth Ser.). 216p. 1994. 59.95 (0-275-94659-2, Praeger Pubs) Greenwood.

An Asterisk (*) at the beginning of an entry indicates that the title is appearing for the first time.

LeVine, Duane G. & Upton, Arthur C., eds. Management of Hazardous Agents Vol. 1: Industrial & Regulatory Approaches, Vol. 1. LC 92-167. (Only One Earth Ser.). 208p. 1992. 59.95 (*0-275-94322-4*, C4322, Praeger Pubs) Greenwood.

— Management of Hazardous Agents Vol. 2: Social, Political, & Policy Aspects, Vol. 2. LC 92-167. (Only One Earth Ser.). 200p. 1992. 59.95 (*0-275-94323-2*, C4323, Praeger Pubs) Greenwood.

Levine, E. Legal Justice & Social Change, a Philosophy of Law. 256p. 1990. 67.00 (*965-09-0125-6*, 73865, Pub. by R Mass Ltd) Lambda Pubs.

Levine, Ed. New York Eats (More) The Food Shopper's Guide to the Freshest Ingredients, the Best Take-out & Baked Goods, & the Most Unusual Marketplaces in All of New York. LC 97-11456. 1997. pap. 18.95 (*0-312-15605-7*) St Martin.

Levine, Edna S. Lisa & Her Soundless World. (Illus.). (J). (gr. 1-5). 1984. 18.95 (*0-87705-104-6*, Kluwer Acad Hman Sci); pap. 10.95 (*0-89885-204-8*, Kluwer Acad Hman Sci) Kluwer Academic.

Levine, Edward M. The Irish & Irish Politicians: A Study of Cultural & Social Alienation. LC 66-24921. 253p. reprint ed. pap. 78.50 (*0-608-15653-1*, 203191100077) Bks Demand.

Levine, Eileen, ed. Directory of Pathology Training Programs, 1999-2000 in the U. S. & Canada: Anatomic, Clinical, Specialized & Information about Pathology As a Career in Medicine. 31st ed. 649p. 1998. pap. 25.00 (*0-937888-15-X*) Intersoc Comm Path Info.

***Levine, Elaine & Sallee, Alvin L.** Child Welfare: Clinical Theory & Practice. LC 99-195307. 1999. pap. 34.95 (*0-945483-91-0*) E Bowers Pub.

Levine, Elaine S., ed. Successful Vines for the Peninsula: A Selection by the Members of the Western Horticultural Society. LC 96-60292. (Illus.). 104p. (Orig.). 1996. pap. 15.00 (*0-9622226-1-5*) West Hort Soc.

Levine, Eli. Golden Key. (Illus.). 1981. lib. bdg. 25.00 (*0-915262-52-5*) S J Durst.

Levine, Elise. Driving Men Mad. 128p. 1995. pap. write for info. (*0-88984-155-1*) Porcup Quill.

Levine, Elizabeth R. A Ceremonies Sampler. LC 90-70834. 127p. (Orig.). 1991. pap. 9.95 (*0-9608054-9-4*) Womans Inst-Cont Jewish Ed.

Levine, Ellen. Anna Pavlova: Genius of the Dance. LC 94-7310. (Illus.). 160p. (J). (gr. 3-7). 1995. 14.95 (*0-590-44304-6*) Scholastic Inc.

— Darkness over Denmark: The Danish Resistance & the Rescue of the Jews. LC 99-25607. (Illus.). 128p. 1999. 18.95 (*0-8234-1447-7*) Holiday.

— A Fence Away from Freedom: Japanese Americans & World War II. LC 95-13357. (Illus.). 224p. (YA). (gr. 6 up). 1995. 18.95 (*0-399-22638-9*, G P Putnam) Peng Put Young Read.

***Levine, Ellen.** Freedom's Children. (Illus.). 192p. (J). (gr. 4-7). 2000. pap. 6.99 (*0-698-11870-7*, PuffinBks) Peng Put Young Read.

— Freedom's Children: Young Civil Rights Activists Tell Their Own Stories. (J). 1993. 9.60 (*0-606-05835-4*, Pub. by Turtleback) Demco.

Levine, Ellen. Freedom's Children: Young Civil Rights Activists Tell Their Own Stories. large type ed. (Illus.). 1995. 46.50 (*0-614-08366-4*, L-81893-00) Am Printing Hse.

— Freedom's Children: Young Civil Rights Activists Tell Their Own Stories. large type ed. LC 93-10388. (Illus.). 242p. (J). 1993. pap. 16.95 (*1-56054-744-8*) Thorndike Pr.

Levine, Ellen. I Hate English! 1989. 10.19 (*0-606-07684-0*, Pub. by Turtleback) Demco.

Levine, Ellen. If You Lived At the Time of Martin Luther King. (Illus.). 80p. (J). (gr. 2-5). 1990. pap. 5.99 (*0-590-42582-X*) Scholastic Inc.

Levine, Ellen. If You Lived at the Time of Martin Luther King. (If You Lived at the Time of . . . Ser.). (J). 1994. 11.19 (*0-606-05884-2*, Pub. by Turtleback) Demco.

Levine, Ellen. If You Lived at the Time of the Great San Francisco Earthquake. (Illus.). 64p. (J). (gr. 4-7). 1992. pap. 5.99 (*0-590-45157-X*) Scholastic Inc.

Levine, Ellen. If You Lived at the Time of the Great San Francisco Earthquake. (J). 1992. 11.19 (*0-606-01854-9*, Pub. by Turtleback) Demco.

Levine, Ellen. If You Lived with the Iroquois. LC 99-186732. (Illus.). 80p. (gr. 2-5). 1999. pap. text 5.99 (*0-590-67445-5*) Scholastic Inc.

***Levine, Ellen.** If You Lived with the Iroquois. (Illus.). (J). 1998. 11.44 (*0-606-18564-X*) Turtleback.

Levine, Ellen. If You Traveled on the Underground Railroad. (Illus.). 64p. (J). (gr. 4-7). 1993. pap. 5.99 (*0-590-45156-1*) Scholastic Inc.

Levine, Ellen. If You Traveled on the Underground Railroad. (J). 1988. 11.19 (*0-606-03591-5*, Pub. by Turtleback) Demco.

Levine, Ellen. If You Traveled West in a Covered Wagon. (Illus.). 80p. (J). (gr. 2-5). 1992. pap. 4.95 (*0-590-45158-8*) Scholastic Inc.

Levine, Ellen. If You Traveled West in a Covered Wagon. (J). 1992. 11.19 (*0-606-01855-7*, Pub. by Turtleback) Demco.

Levine, Ellen. If Your Name Was Changed at Ellis Island. LC 92-27940. (Illus.). 80p. (J). (gr. 2-5). 1993. 15.95 (*0-590-46134-6*) Scholastic Inc.

— If Your Name Was Changed at Ellis Island. LC 92-27940. (Illus.). 80p. (J). (gr. 4-7). 1994. pap. 5.95 (*0-590-43829-8*) Scholastic Inc.

— If Your Name Was Changed at Ellis Island. LC 92-27940. 1993. 11.15 (*0-606-06494-X*, Pub. by Turtleback) Demco.

— If Your Name Was Changed at Ellis Island. large type ed. (Illus.). 1994. 22.50 (*0-614-09556-5*, L-77896-00) Am Printing Hse.

— Notes on the Pumpkin. 16p. (Orig.). 1979. pap. 3.00 (*0-89924-020-8*) Lynx Hse.

— The Tree That Would Not Die. LC 94-8394. (Illus.). 32p. (J). (gr. 2-4). 1995. 14.95 (*0-590-43724-0*, Scholastic Hardcover) Scholastic Inc.

Levine, Ellen, ed. Freedom's Children: Young Civil Rights Activists Tell Their Own Stories. 224p. 1994. mass mkt. 4.99 (*0-380-72114-7*, Avon Bks) Morrow Avon.

Levine, Ellen, intro. Periodical Guide for Computerists, 1982: Annual since 1975-76. 70p. (Orig.). 1982. pap. 15.95 (*0-686-40864-0*) Applegate Comp Ent.

Levine, Ellen & Bjorkman, Steven. I Hate English. 32p. (J). 1995. pap. 3.95 (*0-590-42304-5*) Scholastic Inc.

Levine, Erwin L. Theodore Francis Green: The Rhode Island Years, 1906-1936. LC 63-18096. (Brown University Bicentennial Publications). 234p. 1963. reprint ed. pap. 72.60 (*0-608-08471-9*, 202751100055) Bks Demand.

— Theodore Francis Green: The Washington Years, 1937-1960. LC 73-127366. 191p. 1971. reprint ed. pap. 59.30 (*0-608-08472-7*, 202751200055) Bks Demand.

Levine, Esther, jt. auth. see Montross, Constance M.

Levine, Esther, ed. see Levine, Sy.

Levine, Esther, ed. see Levine, Sy, et al.

Levine, Etan. The Aramaic Version of the Bible: Contents & Context. xiv, 258p. (C). 1988. lib. bdg. 55.40 (*3-11-011474-7*) De Gruyter.

Levine, Etan, ed. Voices from Israel: Understanding the Israeli Mind. LC 85-47911. 288p. 1986. 19.95 (*0-8453-4825-6*, Cornwall Bks) Assoc Univ Prs.

Levine, Eugene, et al. Nursing Practice in the U. K. & North America. LC 92-12312. 1993. 49.50 (*1-56593-024-X*, 0267) Thomson Learn.

Levine, Eugene, jt. auth. see Abdellah, Faye G.

Levine, Evan. Kids Pick the Best Videos for Kids. LC 93-43784. (J). 1994. pap. 9.95 (*0-8065-1498-1*, Citadel Pr) Carol Pub Group.

— Not the Piano, Mrs. Medley! (Illus.). (J). (ps-3). 1996. pap. 15.95 incl. audio (*0-87499-373-3*) Live Oak Media.

— Not the Piano, Mrs. Medley! LC 90-29085. (Illus.). 32p. (J). (ps-2). 1991. 15.95 (*0-531-05956-1*); lib. bdg. 16.99 (*0-531-08556-2*) Orchard Bks Watts.

— Not the Piano, Mrs. Medley! LC 90-29085. (Illus.). 32p. (J). (ps-2). 1995. pap. text 5.95 (*0-531-07062-X*) Orchard Bks Watts.

— Not the Piano, Mrs. Medley! 1995. 11.15 (*0-606-08835-0*, Pub. by Turtleback) Demco.

— Not the Piano, Mrs. Medley! unabridged ed. (Illus.). (J). (ps-3). 1996. 24.95 incl. audio (*0-87499-374-1*) Live Oak Media.

— Not the Piano, Mrs. Medley!, 4 bks., Set. (Illus.). (J). (ps-3). 1996. pap., teacher ed. 33.95 incl. audio (*0-87499-375-X*) Live Oak Media.

Levine, Evelyn, jt. auth. see Grubbs, Arlene.

Levine, Felice J. & Rosich, Katherine J. Social Causes of Violence: Crafting a Science Agenda. LC 96-83435. x, 114p. (Orig.). 1996. pap. 15.00 (*0-912764-26-0*) Am Sociological.

Levine, Frances. Our Prayers Are in This Place: Centuries of Pecos Pueblo Identity. LC 98-58039. 1999. 39.95 (*0-8263-2044-9*) U of NM Pr.

— Salads from A to Z, Vol. 3. 60p. 1996. spiral bd. 14.95 (*0-938911-10-4*) Indiv Ed - Poppy Ln.

— Soups from A - Z. 1994. LC 94-132755. 59p. 1994. spiral bd. 14.95 (*0-938911-08-2*) Indiv Ed - Poppy Ln.

Levine, Francis, et al. Santa Fe: History of an Ancient City. Noble, David G., ed. LC 89-4214. (Illus.). 168p. 1989. pap. 19.95 (*0-933452-27-6*) Schol Am Res.

Levine, Fred. Road Construction Ahead. LC 94-35519. (J). 1995. 12.95 (*0-06-025427-0*) HarpC Child Bks.

Levine, Frederic M. & Sandeen, Evelyn. Conceptualization in Psychotherapy: The Models Approach. 232p. (C). 1985. text 49.95 (*0-89859-549-5*) L Erlbaum Assocs.

Levine, Frederick G. The Psychic Sourcebook: How to Choose & Use a Psychic. 368p. (Orig.). 1988. mass mkt. 9.95 (*0-446-38729-0*, Pub. by Warner Bks) Little.

Levine, Frederick G. & Israel, Peter. The New Age Dictionary of Mysticism & the Occult. LC 90-6744. 1990. write for info. (*0-8022-2575-6*) Philosophical Bk Service.

Levine, G., ed. A Guide to SPSS-X for Analysis of Variance. 176p. (C). 1991. pap. 22.50 (*0-8058-0941-4*); text 39.95 (*0-8058-0939-2*) L Erlbaum Assocs.

***Levine, Gail Carson.** Cinderellis & the Glass Hill. LC 99-21161. (Illus.). 112p. (J). (gr. 2-7). 2000. 8.95 (*0-06-028336-X*) HarpC Child Bks.

— Cinderellis & the Glass Hill. LC 99-21161. (Illus.). 112p. (J). (gr. 4-7). 2000. lib. bdg. 8.89 (*0-06-028337-8*) HarpC Child Bks.

Levine, Gail Carson. Dave at Night. LC 98-50069. 288p. (J). (gr. 3-7). 1999. 15.95 (*0-06-028153-7*) HarpC Child Bks.

— Dave at Night. LC 98-50069. (Illus.). 288p. (J). (gr. 3-7). 1999. lib. bdg. 15.89 (*0-06-028154-5*) HarpC Child Bks.

— Dave at Night. LC 98-50069. (J). 2001. pap. 4.95 (*0-06-440747-0*, HarpTrophy) HarpC Child Bks.

— Ella Enchanted. LC 96-30734. 240p. (J). (gr. 3-7). 1997. 15.95 (*0-06-027510-3*); lib. bdg. 15.89 (*0-06-027511-1*) HarpC Child Bks.

— Ella Enchanted. LC 96-30734. 240p. (J). (gr. 3-7). 1998. pap. 5.95 (*0-06-440705-5*) HarpC Child Bks.

— Ella Enchanted. (J). 1998. 10.05 (*0-606-13099-3*, Pub. by Turtleback) Demco.

— The Fairy's Mistake. LC 98-27871. (Princess Tales Bks.). (Illus.). 96p. (J). (gr. 2-7). 1999. 9.95 (*0-06-028060-3*); lib. bdg. 8.89 (*0-06-028061-1*) HarpC Child Bks.

— Princess Sonora & the Long Sleep. LC 98-53740. (Princess Tales Ser.). (Illus.). 107p. (J). (gr. 2-7). 1999. 8.95 (*0-06-028064-6*) HarpC Child Bks.

— Princess Sonora & the Long Sleep. LC 98-53470. (Princess Tales Ser.). (Illus.). 112p. (J). (gr. 2-7). 1999. lib. bdg. 8.89 (*0-06-028065-4*) HarpC Child Bks.

— The Princess Test. LC 98-27960. (Princess Tales Ser.). (Illus.). 96p. (J). (gr. 2-7). 1999. 9.95 (*0-06-028062-X*) HarpC Child Bks.

— The Princess Test. LC 98-27960. (Princess Tales Ser.). (Illus.). 96p. (J). (gr. 2-7). 1999. lib. bdg. 8.89 (*0-06-028063-8*) HarpC Child Bks.

— The Wish. LC 98-19087. (Illus.). 208p. (J). (gr. 3-7). 2000. pap. 15.95 (*0-06-027900-1*); lib. bdg. 15.89 (*0-06-027901-X*) HarpC Child Bks.

Levine, Gail Carson. Wolf Picture Book. (Illus.). 32p. (J). (ps-3). 15.95 (*0-06-028763-2*) HarpC.

— Wolf Picture Book. (Illus.). 32p. (J). (ps-3). 15.89 (*0-06-028764-0*); 5.95 (*0-06-443640-3*) HarpC Child Bks.

Levine, Gary. Jack "Legs" Diamond: Anatomy of a Gangster. 2nd ed. LC 95-13601. (Illus.). 159p. 1995. pap. 15.00 (*0-935796-55-X*) Purple Mnt Pr.

Levine, Gene N., ed. see Drury, Ruth.

Levine, George. Lifebirds. LC 94-41058. (Illus.). 180p. (C). 1995. 24.95 (*0-8135-2202-1*) Rutgers U Pr.

— Lifebirds. (Illus.). 180p. 1997. pap. 17.00 (*0-8135-2495-4*) Rutgers U Pr.

Levine, George, ed. Aesthetics & Ideology. LC 93-31173. 325p. (C). 1994. text 48.00 (*0-8135-2058-4*); pap. text 20.00 (*0-8135-2059-2*) Rutgers U Pr.

— Constructions of the Self. LC 91-27274. (Illus.). 325p. 1992. pap. text 20.00 (*0-8135-1773-7*) Rutgers U Pr.

— One Culture: Essays in Science & Literature. LC 87-40143. (Science & Literature Ser.). 368p. 1987. pap. text 14.95 (*0-299-11304-3*) U of Wis Pr.

— Realism & Representation: Essays on the Problem of Realism in Relation to Science, Literature & Culture. LC 92-26774. (Science & Literature Ser.). 348p. (Orig.). (C). 1993. 50.00 (*0-299-13630-2*) U of Wis Pr.

Levine, George, jt. ed. see Kaplan, E. Ann.

Levine, George L. Darwin & the Novelists: Patterns of Science in Victorian Fiction. LC 87-36201. 336p. 1988. 43.50 (*0-674-19285-0*) HUP.

— Darwin & the Novelists: Patterns of Science in Victorian Fiction. LC 87-36201. 334p. 1991. pap. text 19.50 (*0-226-47574-3*) U Ch Pr.

— The Realistic Imagination: English Fiction from Frankenstein to Lady Chatterley. LC 80-17444. 358p. 1993. pap. text 10.95 (*0-226-47551-4*) U Ch Pr.

— The Realistic Imagination: English Fiction from Frankenstein to Lady Chatterley. LC 80-17444. 367p. reprint ed. pap. 113.80 (*0-608-09017-4*, 206965200005) Bks Demand.

Levine, George L., ed. One Culture: Essays in Science & Literature. LC 87-40143. (Science & Literature Ser.). 368p. (C). 1988. text 45.00 (*0-299-11300-0*) U of Wis Pr.

Levine, George L. & Knoepflmacher, U. C., eds. The Endurance of Frankenstein: Essays on Mary Shelley's Novel. LC 77-20325. 1979. pap. 16.95 (*0-520-04640-4*, Pub. by U CA Pr) Cal Prin Full Svc.

— The Endurance of Frankenstein: Essays on Mary Shelley's Novel. LC 77-20325. (Illus.). 361p. reprint ed. pap. 112.00 (*0-608-17933-7*, 202905000058) Bks Demand.

***Levine, Gilbert.** Music from the Silence. 2001. 24.00 (*0-609-60457-0*, Pub. by Crown Pub Group) Random House.

Levine, Gilbert & Vookles, Laura L. The Jeweler's Eye: Nineteenth-Century Jewelry in the Collection of Nancy & Gilbert Levine. LC 86-21490. (Illus.). 112p. (Orig.). 1986. pap. 9.50 (*0-943651-02-6*) Hudson Riv.

Levine, Gilbert, jt. ed. see Kahnert, Friedrich.

Levine, Glenn N. Diagnosing & Treating Arrhythmias Made Easy. LC 98-3821. 85p. 1998. 10.00 (*1-57626-106-9*) Quality Med Pub.

— Pocket Guide to Commonly Prescribed Drugs. 2nd ed. (C). 1996. pap. text 18.95 (*0-8385-8099-8*, A8099-2) Appleton & Lange.

— Pocket Guide to Commonly Prescribed Drugs. 3rd ed. 480p. 1999. pap. 19.95 (*0-8385-8146-3*, Apple Lange Med) McGraw.

— Primary Care Cardiology. LC 99-42866. 205p. 2000. 19.95 (*0-683-30688-X*) Lppncott W & W.

***Levine, Gloria.** Across Five Aprils. 44p. (YA). 1999. 11.95 (*1-56137-491-1*) Novel Units.

— The Adventures of Huckleberry Finn. 40p. 1999. 9.95 (*1-56137-182-3*) Novel Units.

— All Quiet on the Western Front. 44p. (YA). 1999. 11.95 (*1-56137-620-5*) Novel Units.

— All Quiet on the Western Front. 28p. 1999. 9.95 (*1-56137-619-1*) Novel Units.

Levine, Gloria. Anne of Green Gables: A Study Guide. (Novel-Ties Ser.). (J). (gr. 6-8). 1989. pap. text, teacher ed., student ed. 15.95 (*0-88122-056-6*) Lrn Links.

***Levine, Gloria.** Billy Budd. 44p. (YA). 1999. 11.95 (*1-56137-916-6*) Novel Units.

— Bless the Beasts & Children. 36p. 1999. 9.95 (*1-56137-148-3*) Novel Units.

— Bridge to Terabithia. 36p. (J). 1998. 11.95 (*1-56137-488-1*) Novel Units.

— The Call of the Wild. 44p. (YA). 1999. student ed., wbk. ed. 11.95 (*1-56137-529-2*) Novel Units.

— The Call of the Wild. 28p. 1999. 9.95 (*1-56137-138-6*) Novel Units.

— The Cat Ate My Gymsuit. 40p. 1999. 9.95 (*1-56137-287-0*) Novel Units.

— The Catcher in the Rye. 36p. 1999. 9.95 (*1-56137-449-0*) Novel Units.

— Charlie & the Chocolate Factory. 36p. 1999. 9.95 (*1-56137-190-4*) Novel Units.

— The Chocolate War. 32p. 1999. 9.95 (*1-56137-206-4*) Novel Units.

— The Chocolate War. 44p. (YA). 1999. 11.95 (*1-56137-629-9*) Novel Units.

— The Contender. 32p. 1999. 9.95 (*1-56137-121-1*) Novel Units.

Levine, Gloria. The Cricket in Times Square: A Study Guide. (Novel-Ties Ser.). (J). (gr. 3-5). 1987. pap. text, teacher ed., student ed. 15.95 (*0-88122-073-6*) Lrn Links.

***Levine, Gloria.** Cry the Beloved Country. 44p. 1999. 9.95 (*1-56137-354-0*) Novel Units.

— Death of a Salesman. 40p. 1999. 9.95 (*1-56137-185-8*) Novel Units.

— A Doll's House/Hedda Gabler. 36p. 1999. 9.95 (*1-56137-892-5*) Novel Units.

— The Door in the Wall. 32p. 1999. 9.95 (*1-56137-288-9*) Novel Units.

— Ethan Frome. (YA). 1999. 11.95 (*1-56137-513-6*) Novel Units.

Levine, Gloria. Fantastic Mr. Fox: A Study Guide. (Novel-Ties Ser.). (J). (gr. 3-5). 1985. pap. text, teacher ed. 15.95 (*0-88122-076-0*) Lrn Links.

***Levine, Gloria.** A Farewell to Arms. 40p. 1999. 9.95 (*1-56137-454-7*) Novel Units.

— A Farewell to Arms. 40p. (YA). 1999. 11.95 (*1-56137-455-5*) Novel Units.

— The Fighting Ground. 40p. 1999. 9.95 (*1-56137-189-0*) Novel Units.

— Flowers for Algernon. 36p. (YA). 1999. 11.95 (*1-56137-409-1*) Novel Units.

— Frankenstein. 44p. (YA). 1999. 11.95 (*1-56137-751-1*) Novel Units.

— Frankenstein. 40p. 1999. 9.95 (*1-56137-750-3*) Novel Units.

— Hamlet. 44p. (YA). 1998. 11.95 (*1-56137-419-9*) Novel Units.

— Hatchet. 40p. (YA). 1998. 11.95 (*1-56137-493-8*) Novel Units.

— Johnny Tremain. 44p. (YA). 1999. student ed., wbk. ed. 11.95 (*1-56137-530-6*) Novel Units.

— Joy Luck Club. 44p. 1999. 9.95 (*1-56137-894-1*) Novel Units.

— The Light in the Forest. 40p. (YA). 1999. 11.95 (*1-56137-467-9*) Novel Units.

Levine, Gloria. Mr. Popper's Penguins: A Study Guide. (Novel-Ties Ser.). (J). (gr. 3-5). 1989. pap. text, teacher ed., student ed. 15.95 (*0-88122-049-3*) Lrn Links.

***Levine, Gloria.** Mythology. 44p. (YA). 1999. 11.95 (*1-56137-817-8*) Novel Units.

— Native Son. 44p. (YA). 1999. 11.95 (*1-56137-624-8*) Novel Units.

— Of Mice & Men. 32p. 1998. 9.95 (*1-56137-187-4*) Novel Units.

— Othello. 32p. 1999. 9.95 (*1-56137-520-9*) Novel Units.

— Othello. 40p. (YA). 1999. wbk. ed. 11.95 (*1-56137-521-7*) Novel Units.

— Our Town. 44p. (YA). 1999. 11.95 (*1-56137-626-4*) Novel Units.

— The Phantom Tollbooth. 32p. 1999. 9.95 (*1-56137-290-0*) Novel Units.

— The Pigman. 40p. 1999. 9.95 (*1-56137-389-3*) Novel Units.

Levine, Gloria. Pippi Longstocking: A Study Guide. (Novel-Ties Ser.). (J). (gr. 3-5). 1989. pap. text, teacher ed., student ed. 15.95 (*0-88122-050-7*) Lrn Links.

— Roll of Thunder, Hear My Cry: Study Guide. Friedland, Joyce & Kessler, Rikki, eds. (Novel-Ties Ser.). (J). (gr. 6-8). 1993. pap. text 15.95 (*0-88122-126-0*) Lrn Links.

— Trouble River: A Study Guide. (Novel-Ties Ser.). (J). (gr. 3-5). 1988. pap. text, teacher ed., student ed. 15.95 (*0-88122-065-5*) Lrn Links.

— The White Mountains: A Study Guide. (Novel-Ties Ser.). (J). (gr. 5-7). 1987. pap. text, teacher ed., wbk. ed. 15.95 (*0-88122-097-3*) Lrn Links.

— The Wind in the Willows: A Study Guide. (Novel-Ties Ser.). (J). (gr. 5-7). 1989. pap. text, teacher ed., wbk. ed. 15.95 (*0-88122-058-2*) Lrn Links.

Levine, Gloria & Fischer, Kathleen. The Wave - Study Guide. Friedland, Joyce & Kessler, Rikki, eds. (Novel-Ties Ser.). (YA). (gr. 9-12). 1993. pap. text 15.95 (*0-88122-132-5*) Lrn Links.

Levine, Gloria, et al. The High King: A Study Guide. (Novel-Ties Ser.). (J). (gr. 5-7). 1988. pap. text, teacher ed. 15.95 (*0-88122-093-0*) Lrn Links.

Levine, Gustav & Parkinson, Stanley. Experimental Methods in Psychology. 496p. 1994. text 39.95 (*0-8058-1438-8*) L Erlbaum Assocs.

Levine, H. Classifying Immersions into IR4 over Stable Maps of 3-Manifolds into IR2. (Lecture Notes in Mathematics Ser.: Vol. 1157). 163p. 1985. 34.95 (*0-387-15995-9*) Spr-Verlag.

Levine, H. & Slade, L. Water Relationships in Foods: Advances in the 1980s & Trends for the 1990s. (Advances in Experimental Medicine & Biology Ser.: Vol. 302). (Illus.). 852p. (C). 1991. text 195.00 (*0-306-43936-0*, Kluwer Plenum) Kluwer Academic.

Levine, H. B. & Levine, Marlene W. Urbanization in Papua New Guinea: A Study of Ambivalent Townsmen. LC 78-58795. 169p. reprint ed. pap. 48.20 (*0-608-15747-3*, 2031682) Bks Demand.

Levine, Hal & Ploeg, Anton, eds. Work in Progress: Essays in New Guinea Highlands Ethnography in Honour of Paula Brown Glick. (Illus.). 362p. 1996. pap. 61.95 (*0-8204-2991-0*, GN671) P Lang Pubng.

Levine, Hal B. Constructing Collective Identity: A Comparative Analysis of New Zealand Jews, Maori, & Urban Papua New Guineans. LC 97-35706. (Illus.). 179p. 1997. pap. 44.95 (*0-8204-3291-1*) P Lang Pubng.

— Constructing Collective Identity: A Comparative Analysis of New Zealand Jews, Maori & Urban Papua New Guineans. LC 97-35706. (Illus.). 179p. 1997. pap. 44.95 (*3-631-31944-4*) P Lang Pubng.

Levine, Harold. The Joy of Vocabulary. 416p. 1997. mass mkt. 6.99 (*0-451-19396-2*, Sig) NAL.

— Partial Differential Equations. LC 97-27385. (AMS/IP Studies in Advanced Mathematics: Vol. 6). 706p. 1997. text 69.00 (*0-8218-0775-7*) Am Math.

Levine, Harold, jt. ed. see Langness, Lewis L.

Levine, Harry G., jt. auth. see Reinarman, Craig.

Levine, Hedi. Good Health Low-Fat Low Sodium Clay Pot Cookbook. (Illus.). 120p. 1996. 14.95 (*1-882606-58-2*) Peoples Med Soc.

— Natural Recipes for the Good Life: Using Wholesome Ingredients for Better Health. LC 96-50005. (Illus.). 256p. 1997. pap. 16.95 (*1-882606-74-4*) Peoples Med Soc.

Levine, Henry D. & Anderson, David R. Negotiating Telecommunications Contracts: Business & Legal Aspects. (Illus.). vi, 457p. write for info. (*0-318-60200-8*) Harcourt.

Levine, Henry D. & Witten, Roger M. Negotiating Telecommunications Contracts. annuals 2nd ed. v, 301p. write for info. (*0-318-61625-4*) Harcourt.

Levine, Herb. Animal Rights. LC 97-1223. (American Issues Debated Ser.). 128p. (J). 1999. lib. bdg. 19.98 (*0-8172-4350-X*) Raintree Steck-V.

Levine, Herbert A., jt. auth. see Kerrison, Irvine L.

Levine, Herbert J. Sing unto God a New Song: A Contemporary Reading of the Psalms. LC 94-21826. 308p. 1995. 39.95 (*0-253-33341-5*) Ind U Pr.

— Yeats's Daimonic Renewal. LC 83-6989. (Studies in Modern Literature: No. 16). 179p. reprint ed. pap. 55.50 (*0-8357-1427-6*, 207050300097) Bks Demand.

Levine, Herbert J. & Gaasch, William H., eds. The Ventricle: Basic & Clinical Aspects. LC 85-4976. 1985. text 247.50 (*0-89838-721-3*) Kluwer Academic.

Levine, Herbert J., jt. ed. see Gaasch, William H.

***Levine, Herbert M.** Chemical & Biological Weapons in Our Times. LC 99-49982. 2000. 25.00 (*0-531-11852-5*) Watts.

Levine, Herbert M. The Drug Problem. LC 97-17074. (American Issues Debated Ser.). 128p. (J). (gr. 7-8). 1997. 28.55 (*0-8172-4354-2*) Raintree Steck-V.

— Gun Control. LC 97-12423. (American Issues Debated Ser.). 128p. (J). 1998. lib. bdg. 27.83 (*0-8172-4351-8*) Raintree Steck-V.

— Immigration. LC 97-13238. (American Issues Debated Ser.). 128p. (J). 1998. lib. bdg. 28.55 (*0-8172-4353-4*) Raintree Steck-V.

— Political Issues Debated: An Introduction to Politics. (Illus.). 352p. (C). 1982. pap. 15.95 (*0-13-685032-4*) P-H.

— Political Issues Debated: An Introduction to Politics. 4th ed. 322p. 1992. pap. text 34.60 (*0-13-681644-4*) P-H.

— The Politics of American Government: Instructor's Manual. 2nd ed. 1997. teacher ed. 13.33 (*0-312-15315-5*) St Martin.

— The Politics of American Government: Study Guide. 2nd ed. 1997. pap. text, student ed. 23.95 (*0-312-11148-7*) St Martin.

— World Politics Debated. 4th ed. (C). 1991. text 26.50 (*0-07-037512-7*) McGraw.

Levine, Herbert M., ed. What If the American Political System Were Different? LC 91-26730. 304p. (gr. 13). 1992. text 75.95 (*1-56324-009-2*) M E Sharpe.

Levine, Herbert M., ed. What If the American Political System Were Different? LC 91-26730. 304p. (gr. 13). 1992. pap. text 35.95 (*1-56324-010-6*) M E Sharpe.

Levine, Herbert M., jt. auth. see Collins, Winifred Q.

Levine, Herbert S., jt. ed. see Bergson, Abram.

Levine, Hillel. Economic Origins of Antisemitism. (Illus.). 288p. (C). 1991. 45.00 (*0-300-04987-0*) Yale U Pr.

— Economic Origins of Antisemitism: Poland & Its Jews in the Early Modern Period. LC 90-26565. 284p. (C). 1993. reprint ed. pap. 22.50 (*0-300-05248-0*) Yale U Pr.

— In Search of Sugihara. LC 96-42108. 256p. 1996. 24.50 (*0-684-83251-8*) S&S Trade.

Levine, Hillel & Harmon, Lawrence. The Death of an American Jewish Community: A Tragedy of Good Intentions. 370p. 1993. per. 13.95 (*0-02-913866-3*) Free Pr.

Levine, Howard. Steps on the Ladder. LC 99-61096. 256p. 2000. pap. 14.95 (*0-88739-261-X*) Creat Arts Bk.

Levine, Howard, ed. Structures under Extreme Loading Conditions, 1998: Proceedings, ASME/JSME Joint Pressure Vessels & Piping Conference (1998, San Diego, CA) LC 98-207928. (PVP Ser.: 361). 339p. 1998. pap. 120.00 (*0-7918-1857-8*) ASME.

***Levine, Howard & McCullum, Richard E.** Developing Teaching Professionals Vol. II: The California Eisenhower State Program Experience, 1997 & 1998. 80 +p. 1999. pap. write for info. (*0-9673336-0-1*) CA Post Educ.

Levine, Howard, jt. auth. see Kraus, Dennis H.

Levine, Howard, ed. see Mathog, Robert H., et al.

Levine, Howard B., ed. Adult Analysis & Childhood Sexual Abuse. 248p. 1990. text 34.50 (*0-88163-083-7*) Analytic Pr.

— Adult Analysis & Childhood Sexual Abuse. 248p. 1998. reprint ed. pap. 29.95 (*0-88163-306-2*) Analytic Pr.

Levine, Howard B., et al, eds. Psychoanalysis & the Nuclear Threat: Clinical & Theoretical Studies. 304p. 1988. text 34.50 (*0-88163-062-4*) Analytic Pr.

Levine, Howard L. & May, Mark. Endoscopic Sinus Surgery. LC 92-49512. (Rhinology & Sinusology Ser.). (Illus.). 256p. 1993. 145.00 (*0-86577-474-9*) Thieme Med Pubs.

Levine, Ira A. Left-Wing Dramatic Theory in the American Theatre. LC 84-28018. (Theater & Dramatic Studies: No. 24). (Illus.). 249p. reprint ed. pap. 77.20 (*0-8357-1599-X*, 207055700001) Bks Demand.

Levine, Ira N. Molecular Spectroscopy. 512p. 1975. 125.00 (*0-471-53128-6*) Wiley.

— Physical Chemistry. 3rd rev. ed. 920p. (C). 1988. text 73.50 (*0-07-037474-0*) McGraw.

— Physical Chemistry. 4th ed. LC 93-48561. 920p. (C). 1994. 95.94 (*0-07-037528-3*) McGraw.

— Physical Chemistryon. 4th ed. (C). 1994. pap. text, student ed. 35.00 (*0-07-037686-7*) McGraw.

***Levine, Ira N.** Quantum Chemistry. 5th ed. LC 99-28558. 1999. write for info. (*0-13-685511-3*) P-H.

— Quantum Chemistry. 5th ed. LC 99-28558. 739p. (C). 1999. 96.00 (*0-13-685512-1*) P-H.

Levine, Isaac D. Mitchell, Pioneer of Air Power. LC 71-169426. (Literature & History of Aviation Ser.). 1972. reprint ed. 33.95 (*0-405-03777-5*) Ayer.

Levine, J. R. & Eggleston, J. R. The Anthracite Basins of Eastern Pennsylvania: Field Trip Guide Book. (Illus.). 54p. (Orig.). (C). 1994. pap. text 40.00 (*1-56806-478-0*) DIANE Pub.

Levine, Jack. The Complete Graphic Work of Jack Levine. (Fine Art Ser.). (Illus.). 112p. (Orig.). 1984. pap. 11.95 (*0-486-24481-4*) Dover.

— United States Cryptographic Patents, 1861-1989. LC Z 0103.L49. (Illus.). 125p. 1991. reprint ed. pap. 38.80 (*0-608-03153-4*, 206360600007) Bks Demand.

Levine, Jacques. Hitler's Secret Diaries. 160p. (Orig.). 1988. pap. 14.95 (*0-934579-00-8*) Aiglon Pr.

Levine, James. Getting Men Involved: Strategies for Early Childhood Programs. 1993. pap. 12.95 (*0-590-49605-0*) Scholastic Inc.

Levine, James A. New Expectations: Community Strategies for Responsible Fatherhood. 230p. 1995. pap. 22.00 (*1-888324-00-7*) Families & Work.

Levine, James A. & Pittinsky, Todd L. Working Fathers. LC 97-2067. 1997. 23.00 (*0-201-14938-9*) Addison-Wesley.

— Working Fathers: New Strategies for Balancing Work & Family. LC 98-16196. 288p. (C). 1998. pap. 13.00 (*0-15-600603-0*, Harvest Bks) Harcourt.

***Levine, James A., et al.** Getting Men Involved: Strategies for Early Childhood Programs. 96p. 1998. pap. 13.00 (*1-888324-28-7*) Families & Work.

Levine, James P. Juries & Politics. LC 91-11960. 202p. (C). 1991. 19.50 (*0-534-14754-2*) Wadsworth Pub.

Levine, James P., et al. Criminal Justice in America: The Law in Action. LC 85-9303. 198p. 1986. pap. text 18.50 (*0-471-84943-X*) P-H.

— Criminal Justice in America: The Law in Action. 2nd ed. LC 85-9303. 684p. 1986. text 37.95 (*0-471-88626-2*) P-H.

Levine, James P., jt. auth. see Abbott, David W.

Levine, James S. Schaum's Outline of Russian Grammar. LC 99-30512. (ENG & RUS., Illus.). 335p. 1999. pap. 14.95 (*0-07-038238-7*) McGraw.

Levine, Jan M. & Sampson, Kathryn A. Analytical Assignments for Integrating Legal Research & Writing (1996-97 Edition) 306p. (Orig.). (C). 1996. wbk. ed. write for info. (*0-916951-06-5*) Adams & Ambrose.

Levine, Janet. The Enneagram Intelligences: Understanding Personality for Effective Teaching & Learning. LC 98-20129. 320p. 1999. 59.95 (*0-89789-561-4*, Bergin & Garvey); pap. 24.95 (*0-89789-562-2*, Bergin & Garvey) Greenwood.

Levine, Jason & Bhalla, Sarab. Bugcards: The Complete Microbiology Review for Class, the Boards & the Wards. (Illus.). 154p. (C). 1998. 26.50 (*0-9671655-0-4*) B L Publishing.

Levine, Jeffrey. Pittsburgh Business Directory. 2nd rev. ed. 1041p. 1997. 49.95 (*0-9650280-1-1*) Pittsbrgh Busn.

Levine, Jeffrey P. Doing Business in Boston. 2nd ed. 974p. (Orig.). 1996. pap. 55.00 (*0-9640989-1-1*) Boston Business.

Levine, Jeffrey S. Repair, Replacement & Maintenance of Historic Slate Roofs. 16p. 1993. pap. 1.25 (*0-16-061656-5*) USGPO.

Levine, Jennifer. Forever in My Heart: A Story to Help Children Participate in Life As a Parent Dies. LC 92-50678. (Illus.). 32p. (Orig.). (J). (gr. 1-6). 1992. pap. 6.95 (*1-878321-08-0*) Compassion Bks.

— My Foster Family: A Story for Children Entering Foster Care. (Illus.). (J). (gr. k-6). 1994. pap. 6.95 (*0-87868-537-5*) Child Welfare.

Levine, Jeremiah, jt. auth. see Pettei, Michael.

Levine, Jessica, tr. see Le Dantec, Denise & Le Dantec, Jean-Pierre.

Levine, Jessica, tr. see Tafuri, Manfredo.

Levine, Jessie, ed. see Winters, Manque.

Levine, Joan, ed. see Mestre, Kenneth.

Levine, Joanne, jt. auth. see Karger, Howard J.

Levine, Jodi, jt. auth. see Shapiro, Nancy S.

***Levine, Jodi H., ed.** Learning Communities: New Structures, New Partnerships for Learning. (Freshman Year Experience Monograph Ser.: No. 26). 120p. 1999. pap. 30.00 (*1-889271-27-6*) Nat Res Ctr.

Levine, Joel M., jt. auth. see Borman, Suzanne.

Levine, Joel S., ed. Biomass Burning & Global Change Vol. 1: Remote Sensing & Modeling of Biomass Burning, & Biomass Burning in the Boreal Forest. LC 96-35030. (Illus.). 622p. (C). 1996. 85.00 (*0-262-12201-4*) MIT Pr.

— Biomass Burning & Global Change Vol. 2: Biomass Burning in the Tropical & Temperate Ecosystems. LC 96-35030. (Illus.). 454p. (C). 1996. 75.00 (*0-262-12202-2*) MIT Pr.

— Global Biomass Burning: Atmospheric, Climatic & Biospheric Implications. (Illus.). 600p. 1991. 85.00 (*0-262-12159-X*) MIT Pr.

Levine, Joel S., jt. auth. see Jacobson, Eugene D.

Levine, Joel Seth. Decision Making in Gastroenterology, No. 2. 512p. (C). (gr. 13). 1992. text 79.95 (*1-55664-323-3*) Mosby Inc.

Levine, John. Business Statistics for Quality & Productivity. 771p. 1994. 68.00 (*0-13-352311-X*) P-H.

— The Internet for Dummies. (Illus.). 350p. 1993. pap. 19.95 (*1-56884-024-1*) IDG Bks.

— The Internet for Dummies. 1997. pap. 47.22 (*84-283-2380-1*, Pub. by Paraninfo) IBD Ltd.

Levine, John. Internet for Dummies Quick Reference. 2nd ed. 224p. 1995. spiral bd. 12.99 (*1-56884-977-X*) IDG Bks.

— Linkers & Loaders. LC 99-47127. (Operating Systems Ser.). 400p. 1999. pap. 36.95 (*1-55860-496-0*, Pub. by Morgan Kaufmann) Harcourt.

— Linux. 1999. pap. write for info. (*0-201-35456-X*) Peachpit Pr.

Levine, John. QR/Internet for Dummies. LC 94-75909. 176p. 1994. spiral bd. 8.95 (*1-56884-168-X*) IDG Bks.

***Levine, John, ed.** Internet Secrets. 2nd ed. LC 99-58439. (Secrets Ser.). 1128p. 2000. 39.99 incl. cd-rom (*0-7645-0508-4*) IDG Bks.

Levine, John & Baroudi, Carol. The Internet for Dummies. 2nd ed. 384p. 1994. pap. 19.99 (*1-56884-222-8*) IDG Bks.

— The Internet for Dummies. 3rd ed. 432p. 1995. pap. 19.99 (*1-56884-620-7*) IDG Bks.

***Levine, John & IDG Books Staff.** Internet for Dummies Quick Reference. 4th ed. LC 98-70126. (For Dummies). (Illus.). 224p. 1998. spiral bd. 12.99 (*0-7645-0355-3*) IDG Bks.

— The Internet for Dummies Starter Kit. 2nd ed. LC TK5105.875.I57L395. (For Dummies Ser.). 432p. (Orig.). 1998. pap. 24.99 incl. cd-rom (*0-7645-0356-1*) IDG Bks.

Levine, John & Young, Margaret L. The Internet for Windows for Dummies Starter Kit. 456p. 1995. pap. 34.99 (*1-56884-237-6*) IDG Bks.

— Internet Windows for Dummies Starter Kit. 448p. 1995. pap. 39.99 (*1-56884-246-5*) IDG Bks.

***Levine, John, et al.** The Internet for Dummies. 5th ed. LC 99-60534. (For Dummies). 224p. 1999. spiral bd. 12.99 (*0-7645-0508-4*) IDG Bks.

Levine, John, et al. Lex & Yacc. 2nd ed. (Computer Science). 366p. 1992. pap. 29.95 (*1-56592-000-7*) Thomson Learn.

Levine, John, jt. auth. see Young, Margaret L.

Levine, John, jt. auth. see Young, Margaret Levine.

Levine, John R. Comp-Compilers 1990 Annual. 700p. (Orig.). (C). 1991. pap. text 50.00 (*0-944954-02-2*) Ctr Bk Pubs.

— Internet E-Mail for Dummies. 2nd ed. LC 97-72416. 384p. 1997. pap. 24.99 incl. cd-rom (*0-7645-0131-3*) IDG Bks.

***Levine, John R.** The Internet for Dummies. 7th ed. (For Dummies Ser.). 384p. 2000. pap. 19.99 (*0-7645-0674-9*) IDG Bks.

— Internet for Dummies. 7th ed. 408p. 2000. pap. 24.99 incl. cd-rom (*0-7645-0700-1*) IDG Bks.

— Internet for Dummies Quick Reference. 6th ed. (For Dummies Ser.). (Illus.). 224p. 2000. pap. 12.99 (*0-7645-0675-7*) IDG Bks.

Levine, John R. Internet Secrets. 1032p. 1995. pap. 39.99 (*1-56884-452-2*) IDG Bks.

— More Internet for Dummies. 4th ed. LC TK5105.875.I57L483. 420p. 1998. pap. 22.99 (*0-7645-0369-3*) IDG Bks.

— Programming for Graphics Files: In C & C Plus Plus. 512p. 1994. pap. 49.95 incl. disk (*0-471-59856-9*); disk 20.00 (*0-471-59857-7*) Wiley.

— Programming for Graphics Files: In C & C Plus Plus. 512p. 1994. pap. 29.95 (*0-471-59854-2*) Wiley.

Levine, John R., ed. Computer Compilers Annual, 1991. 900p. (Orig.). 1992. pap. text 70.00 (*0-944954-03-0*) Ctr Bk Pubs.

Levine, John R. & Levine, Margaret. Windows 98: The Complete Reference. LC 98-174547. 1001p. 1998. pap. text 39.99 incl. cd-rom (*0-07-882343-9*) Osborne-McGraw.

Levine, John R. & Nelson, Russell. Qmail. O'Reilly, Tim, ed. (Illus.). 400p. 1999. pap. 29.95 (*1-56592-628-5*) OReilly & Assocs.

***Levine, John R. & Young, Margaret Levine.** The Internet for Microsoft Windows Millenium for Dummies. (For Dummies Ser.). 384p. 2000. pap. 19.99 (*0-7645-0739-7*) IDG Bks.

— UNIX for Dummies. (Illus.). 408p. 1993. pap. 19.95 (*1-878058-58-4*) IDG Bks.

Levine, John R. & Young, Margaret Levine. UNIX for Dummies. 4th ed. (For Dummies Ser.). 408p. 1998. pap. 19.99 (*0-7645-0419-3*) IDG Bks.

Levine, John R., et al. Internet for Dummies. abr. ed. (For Dummies Ser.). 1996. audio 12.00 (*0-694-51667-8*, CPN 10070) HarperAudio.

— The Internet for Dummies. 6th ed. LC 99-60184. (For Dummies Ser.). (Illus.). 416p. 1999. pap. 24.99 incl. cd-rom (*0-7645-0507-6*); pap. 19.99 (*0-7645-0506-8*) IDG Bks.

Levine, John R., jt. auth. see Kay, David C.

Levine, John R., jt. auth. see Young, Margaret Levine.

Levine, Jon E. & Conn, P. Michael, eds. Methods in Neurosciences Vol. 20: Pulsatility in Neuroendocrine Systems. (Illus.). 510p. 1994. text 104.00 (*0-12-185289-X*) Acad Pr.

Levine, Jonathan D., ed. A Minyan of Comfort: Evening Services for the House of Mourning. 1990. 10.95 (*0-87677-078-2*) Prayer Bk.

Levine, Jonathan D., jt. auth. see Greenberg, Sidney.

Levine, Jonathan D., jt. auth. see Preeg, Ernest H.

Levine, Jonathan D., jt. ed. see Greenberg, Sidney.

Levine, Joseph. The Battle of the Books: History & Literature in the Augustan Age. (Illus.). 448p. 1994. pap. text 18.95 (*0-8014-8199-6*) Cornell U Pr.

***Levine, Joseph.** Purple Haze: The Puzzle of Consciousness. LC 99-87912. (Philosophy of Mind Ser.). 224p. 2000. 29.95 (*0-19-513235-1*) OUP.

— Rise & Be Seated: The Ups & Downs of Jewish Worship. LC 99-59863. 2001. 40.00 (*0-7657-6137-8*) Aronson.

Levine, Joseph & Miller, Kenneth R. Biology: Discovering Life. 2nd ed. 988p. (C). 1994. text 72.76 (*0-669-33494-4*) HM Trade Div.

Levine, Joseph & Suzuki, David. The Secret of Life: Redesigning the Living World. 280p. 1998. pap. text 14.95 (*0-7167-3311-0*) W H Freeman.

Levine, Joseph A. Synagogue Song in America. Date not set. pap. write for info. (*0-7657-6139-4*) Aronson.

Levine, Joseph M. Autonomy of History: Truth & Method from Erasmus to Gibbon. LC 99-30861. (Illus.). 192p. 2000. 27.50 (*0-226-47541-7*) U Ch Pr.

— The Battle of the Books: History & Literature in the Augustan Age. LC 90-55735. (Illus.). 448p. 1991. text 49.95 (*0-8014-2537-9*) Cornell U Pr.

***Levine, Joseph M.** Between the Ancients & the Moderns: Baroque Culture in Restoration England. LC 99-26545. (Illus.). 352p. 1999. 40.00 (*0-300-07914-1*) Yale U Pr.

Levine, Joseph M. Dr. Woodward's Shield: History, Science & Satire in Augustan England. LC 75-27927. (Illus.). 376p. 1991. reprint ed. pap. text 17.95 (*0-8014-9935-6*) Cornell U Pr.

— Humanism & History: Origins of Modern English Historiography. LC 86-16776. (Illus.). 304p. (C). 1987. text 42.50 (*0-8014-1885-2*) Cornell U Pr.

Levine, Joseph S. & Miller, Kenneth R. Biology: Discovering Life. 2nd ed. (C). 1994. text, teacher ed. 73.96 (*0-669-34075-8*); text, teacher ed. 2.66 (*0-669-34076-6*); pap. text, student ed. 27.96 (*0-669-34081-2*) HM Trade Div.

— Biology: Discovering Life, 4 vols., Vol. III: Plant Systems. LC 90-82264. 71p. (C). 1990. pap. text 11.16 (*0-669-28842-X*) HM Trade Div.

— Biology Pt. 5: Discovering Life: Diversity of Life. 2nd ed. 115p. (C). 1994. pap. text 13.56 (*0-669-34078-2*) HM Trade Div.

— Biology Pts. 1-4: Discovering Life: Molecules of Life. 2nd ed. 478p. (C). 1994. pap. text 48.36 (*0-669-34077-4*) HM Trade Div.

— Biology: Discovering Life: Core Concepts. 2nd ed. (C). 1994. text, teacher ed. 49.56 (*0-669-34080-4*) HM Trade Div.

***Levine, Josh.** David E. Kelley: The Man Behind "Ally McBeal" (Illus.). 200p. 1999. pap. 16.95 (*1-55022-372-0*) ECW.

Levine, Josh. Jerry Seinfeld: Much Ado about Nothing. (Illus.). 140p. 1993. pap. 14.95 (*1-55022-201-5*, Pub. by ECW) Genl Dist Srvs.

Levine, Joshua. The Rise & Fall of the House of Barneys: A Family Tale of Chutzpah, Glory & Greed. LC 98-51429. (Illus.). 272p. 1999. 25.00 (*0-688-15502-2*, Wm Morrow) Morrow Avon.

Levine, Josie. Bilingual Learners & Mainstream Curriculum: Integrated Approaches to Learning & the Teaching & Learning of English As a Second Language. 225p. 1990. pap. 39.95 (*1-85000-495-1*, Falmer Pr) Taylor & Francis.

Levine, Joya. A Beginner's Guide to Astrological Interpretation. 144p. (Orig.). 1995. pap. 11.95 (*1-885856-09-1*) Vizualizations.

Levine, Judi. Helping Your Child Lose Weight: A Healthy Approach to Weight Control. (Illus.). 320p. 1998. pap. text 14.95 (*0-8065-1979-7*, Citadel Pr) Carol Pub Group.

Levine, Judith & Bine, Linda. Helping Your Child Lose Weight the Healthy Way: A Family Approach to Weight Control. 256p. 1996. 18.95 (*1-55972-345-9*, Birch Ln Pr) Carol Pub Group.

Levine, Judy & Jackson, Nancy. How to Speak New Yorkese: A Hand Guide to the World's Most Improbable Language. (Illus.). 96p. (Orig.). 1989. pap. 6.95 (*0-930753-07-0*) Spect Ln Pr.

Levine, Julia B. Practicing for Heaven. (Anhinga Prize for Poetry Ser.). 96p. 1999. pap. 12.00 (*0-938078-62-3*) Anhinga Pr.

Levine, June P. Creation & Criticism: A Passage to India. LC 78-134772. 218p. reprint ed. pap. 67.60 (*0-608-13198-9*, 205594500040) Bks Demand.

Levine, Karen. Keeping Life Simple: Guiding Principles, 500 Tips & Ideas. LC 96-7623. 160p. (Orig.). 1996. pap. 9.95 (*0-88266-943-5*) Storey Bks.

— What to Do When Your Child Has Trouble in School. LC 97-2469. (What to Do Parenting Guides Ser.). (Illus.). 96p. 1997. 12.95 (*0-89577-985-4*, Pub. by RD Assn) Penguin Putnam.

Levine, Karen, ed. see Lerner, Claire & Dombro, Amy.

Levine, Katherine G. When Good Kids Do Bad Things. Rubenstein, Julie, ed. 272p. 1993. reprint ed. pap. 10.00 (*0-671-79296-2*) PB.

Levine, Kathy. We Should Be So Lucky. LC 97-30614. 1997. 24.00 (*0-671-00848-X*, PB Hardcover) PB.

Levine, Kathy & Scovell, Jane. It's Better to Laugh . . . Life, Good Luck, Bad Hair Day, & QVC. 1996. per. 6.99 (*0-671-51108-4*) PB.

Levine, Kenneth. Social Context of Literacy. (Language, Education & Society Ser.). 247p. (C). 1986. text 42.50 (*0-7100-9745-X*, Routledge Thoemms); pap. text 19.95 (*0-685-12291-3*, Routledge Thoemms) Routledge.

— The Social Context of Literacy. 272p. (C). 1986. pap. 19.95 (*0-7102-1391-3*, Routledge Thoemms) Routledge.

***Levine, Ketzel.** Plant This! Best Bets for Year - Round Gorgeous Gardens. (Illus.). 224p. 2000. pap. 19.95 (*1-57061-245-5*) Sasquatch Bks.

Levine, Kristin J. Development of Pre-Writing & Scissor Skills: A Visual Analysis. 38p. 1995. pap. text 87.00 incl. vdisk (*0-7616-4363-X*) Commun Skill.

— Fine Motor Dysfunction: Therapeutic Strategies in the Classroom. (Illus.). 593p. 1991. pap. text 79.00 (*0-7616-4704-X*) Commun Skill.

Levine, L. Construction Machinery. 215p. 1998. 1995.00 (*0-318-03907-9*) Lead Edge Reports.

— Industrial Furnaces, Kilns & Ovens. 190p. 1999. 1995.00 (*0-945235-15-1*) Lead Edge Reports.

An Asterisk (*) at the beginning of an entry indicates that the title is appearing for the first time.

— The Market for Leather Accessories & Travelware: A Product-by-Product Marketing Analysis & Competitor Profile. 300p. 1999. 1295.00 (*0-317-55201-5*) Busn Trend.

— The Market for Poultry & Small Game. (Illus.). 270p. 1999. pap. 1995.00 (*0-318-04171-5*) Lead Edge Reports.

— The Markets for Salt-Free & Sugar-Free Foods: A Product-by-Product Marketing Analysis & Competitor Profile. 300p. 2000. 1995.00 (*0-317-55191-4*) Lead Edge Reports.

— Outlook for Mining Equipment. 308p. 1997. 1995.00 (*0-945235-55-0*) Lead Edge Reports.

— Security Industry Markets: Products & Services. 200p. 2000. 1995.00 (*0-945235-69-0*) Lead Edge Reports.

— Trends in Construction Machinery. 220p. 1998. 1995.00 (*0-945235-54-2*) Lead Edge Reports.

*__Levine, L.__ The U. S. Farm Machinery & Equipment Market. 480p. 2000. 1995.00 (*0-318-03906-0*) Lead Edge Reports.

Levine, L. The U. S. Outlook for Mining Machinery & Equipment Industry. 190p. 1997. 1995.00 (*0-318-00500-X*) Lead Edge Reports.

— Wire Harness Markets. 160p. 2000. 1995.00 (*0-945235-70-4*) Lead Edge Reports.

— World Markets for Tire & Rubber. 340p. 1998. 1995.00 (*0-945235-39-9*) Lead Edge Reports.

Levine, L., ed. Arachidonate Metabolism in Immunologic Systems. (Progress in Allergy Ser.: Vol. 44). (Illus.). viii, 216p. 1988. 128.75 (*3-8055-4773-0*) S Karger.

Levine, L., et al. The American Urological Association Erectile Dysfunction Clinical Guidelines Panel Report on the Treatment of Organic Erectile Dysfunction. 80p. 1996. pap. 67.00 (*0-9649702-1-X*) Am Urological.

Levine, L. S., jt. auth. see News, M. I.

Levine, Larry. PCMCIA Primer. LC 95-24177. 89p. 1995. pap. 24.95 (*1-55828-437-0*, MIS Pr) IDG Bks.

*__Levine, Larry.__ Torts. 3rd ed. (Quick Sum & Substance Review Ser.). 1999. pap. 18.95 (*0-314-24286-4*) West Pub.

Levine, Laura. Wig! The B-52's. LC 94-33486. 32p. (J). (ps-3). 1995. 14.95 (*0-7868-0079-8*, Pub. by Hyprn Child); lib. bdg. 14.89 (*0-7868-2064-0*, Pub. by Hyprn Child) Little.

Levine, Laurence W. U. S. - China Relations. 1972. 7.95 (*0-8315-0136-7*) Speller.

*__Levine, Laurie B.__ Spiritual Medicine. 148p. 2000. pap. 12.00 (*0-684-87210-2*) S&S Trade.

Levine, Laurie B., jt. auth. see Atwood, Joan D.

*__Levine, Laurie Leah.__ Spiritual Medicine: Transform Your Health, Life & Relationships. (Illus.). 200p. (C). 2000. pap. 14.95 (*1-58394-021-9*) Frog Ltd CA.

Levine, Lawrence C., et al, eds. A Torts Anthology. 2nd ed. 596p. (C). 1999. pap. 29.95 (*0-87084-843-7*) Anderson Pub Co.

Levine, Lawrence O., jt. ed. see Montgomery, Joseph C.

Levine, Lawrence W. Black Culture & Black Consciousness: Afro-American Folk Thought from Slavery to Freedom. LC 76-9223. 542p. 1978. reprint ed. pap. text 16.95 (*0-19-502374-9*) OUP.

— Defender of the Faith: William Jennings: The Last Decade 1915-1925. LC 86-25679. 400p. 1987. pap. 18.00 (*0-674-19542-6*) HUP.

— Highbrow-Lowbrow: The Emergence of Cultural Hierarchy in America. (William E. Massey Sr. Lectures in the History of American Civilization). (Illus.). 320p. 1990. pap. text 17.95 (*0-674-39077-6*) HUP.

— The Opening of the American Mind: Canons, Culture, & History. LC 96-33866. 240p. 1997. pap. 14.00 (*0-8070-3119-4*) Beacon Pr.

— The Unpredictable Past: Explorations in American Cultural History. (Illus.). 384p. 1993. pap. 18.95 (*0-19-508297-4*) OUP.

Levine, Lee, ed. Jerusalem: Its Sanctity & Centrality to Judaism, Christianity, & Islam. LC 98-15267. (Illus.). 540p. 1998. 75.00 (*0-8264-1024-3*) Continuum.

Levine, Lee I. Ancient Synagogue: The/First Thousand Years. LC 98-52667. (Illus.). 608p. 1999. 70.00 (*0-300-07475-1*) Yale U Pr.

— Judaism & Hellenism in Antiquity: Conflict or Confluence? LC 97-46205. (Samuel & Althea Stroum Lectures in Jewish Studies). (Illus.). 242p. 1999. pap. 20.00 (*0-295-97682-9*) U of Wash Pr.

*__Levine, Lee I.__ Judaism & Hellenism in Antiquity: Conflict or Confluence. (Illus.). 240p. 1999. pap. 19.95 (*1-56563-488-8*) Hendrickson MA.

Levine, Lee I. The Synagogue in Late Antiquity. (JTS & the American Schools of Oriental Research Ser.). 1987. pap. 19.95 (*0-685-19157-5*); bds. 26.95 (*0-317-64344-4*) Jewish Sem.

Levine, Lee I., ed. The Galilee in Late Antiquity. (Jewish Theological Seminary Ser.). (Illus.). 410p. 1994. pap. 17.95 (*0-674-34114-7*, LEVGAX) HUP.

— The Galilee in Late Antiquity. LC 92-12475. 1992. 35.00 (*0-674-34113-9*) Jewish Sem.

Levine, Leonard P., jt. auth. see Besag, Frank P.

Levine, Leonore S., jt. ed. see New, Maria I.

Levine, Les. Art Can See, Media Sculpture. LC 98-116057. 1998. pap. 39.95 (*3-89322-913-2*) Dist Art Pubs.

Levine, Leslie B. Clinical Management of the Disabled Dental Patient: A Working Manual for Dental Professionals, Vol. 1. Mason, Leslie C., ed. (Illus.). 65p. (Orig.). (C). 1989. pap. text 10.95 (*0-9622139-0-X*) Denta Pr.

Levine, Leslie G. Will This Place Ever Feel Like Home? Simple Advice for Settling in after Your Move. LC 98-38605. 256p. 1998. pap. 17.95 (*0-7931-2870-6*, 19135301, Real Estate Ed) Dearborn.

Levine, Lewis & Hughey, Lucinda S. Changing Times: Toward an Integrated Approach to Reading. (Illus.). 300p. (C). 1985. pap. text 34.40 (*0-13-128182-8*) P-H.

Levine, Linda, ed. Diffusion, Transfer, & Implementation of Information Technology: Proceedings of the IFIP TC8 Working Conference on Diffusion, Transfer, & Implementation of Information Technology, Pittsburgh, PA, U.S.A., 11-13 October 1993. LC 94-4643. (IFIP Transactions A: Computer Science & Technology Ser.: Vol. A-45). 444p. 1994. 152.50 (*0-444-81856-1*, North Holland) Elsevier.

Levine, Linda G., et al, eds. Spanish Women Writers: A Bio-Bibliographical Source Book. LC 92-42432. 632p. 1993. lib. bdg. 105.00 (*0-313-26823-1*, LSB, Greenwood Pr) Greenwood.

Levine, Lois, jt. auth. see Burros, Marian.

*__Levine, Lori D., et al.__ Building Leadership for Community Development: A Training Curriculum to Support Free to Grow Program Implementation. 2000. ring bd. write for info. (*1-930951-00-0*) Free Grow Natl.

Levine, Louis, pseud. The Women's Garment Workers. LC 72-89752. (American Labor, from Conspiracy to Collective Bargaining Ser., No. 1). 608p. 1976. reprint ed. 23.95 (*0-405-02139-9*) Ayer.

Levine, Louis, pseud, ed. Genetics of Natural Populations: The Continuing Importance of Theodosius Dobzhansky. LC 94-29691. 1995. 99.00 (*0-231-08116-2*) Col U Pr.

*__Levine, Lynn.__ A Few Questions about Paradise. (Illus.). 64p. 2000. pap. 10.95 (*0-926147-11-0*) Loonfeather.

Levine, M. D., jt. auth. see Noble, P. B.

Levine, M. J. Worker Rights & Labor Standards in Asia's Four New Tigers: A Comparative Perspective. LC 97-8964. (Illus.). 492p. (C). 1997. 69.50 (*0-306-45477-7*, Plenum Trade) Perseus Pubng.

Levine, M. Walter. The Golfer's Dream. (Illus.). 16p. (Orig.). 1995. pap. 6.95 (*0-9651109-0-7*) Amtax.

Levine, Madeline. See No Evil: A Guide to Protecting Our Children from Media Violence. LC 98-15191. (Health & Psychology Ser.). 304p. 1998. pap. 16.95 (*0-7879-4347-9*) Jossey-Bass.

Levine, Madeline, tr. see Fink, Ida.

Levine, Madeline, tr. see Milosz, Czeslaw.

Levine, Madeline, tr. & intro. see Bialoszewski, Miron.

Levine, Madeline G., tr. see Milosz, Czeslaw.

Levine, Madeline G., tr. see Tuszynska, Agata.

Levine, Madeline G., tr. see Wojdowski, Bogdan.

Levine, Marc. Mixed Motives. LC 98-4734. (Mathematical Surveys & Monographs). 515p. 1998. 125.00 (*0-8218-0785-4*, SURV-LEVINE) Am Math.

Levine, Marc S., et al. Drug Therapy Decision Making Guide. (Illus.). 574p. 1995. pap. text 49.95 (*0-7216-4215-2*, W B Saunders Co) Harcrt Hlth Sci Grp.

Levine, Marc S., jt. auth. see Gore, Richard M.

Levine, Marc S., jt. ed. see Laufer, Igor.

Levine, Marc V. The Reconquest of Montreal: Language Policy & Social Change in a Bilingual City. (Conflicts in Urban & Regional Development Ser.). (Illus.). 320p. 1990. 49.95 (*0-87722-703-9*) Temple U Pr.

— The Reconquest of Montreal: Language Policy & Social Change in a Bilingual City. (Conflicts in Urban & Regional Development Ser.). (Illus.). 320p. 1991. pap. 22.95 (*0-87722-899-X*) Temple U Pr.

Levine, Margaret, jt. auth. see Levine, John R.

Levine, Marian, ed. Cookies!, Vol. 26. 64p. 1989. pap., per. 3.95 (*0-942320-33-6*) Am Cooking.

Levine, Marian, ed. see Bloom, Leslie.

Levine, Marian, ed. see Clingerman, Polly.

Levine, Marian, ed. see Rosenberg, Lawrence M.

Levine, Marian, ed. see Torine, Len.

Levine, Marie. Great White Sharks. LC 97-11463. (Untamed World Ser.). (Illus.). 64p. (J). (gr. 5-9). 1998. lib. bdg. 27.12 (*0-8172-4569-3*) Raintree Steck-V.

— Great White Sharks. (Untamed World Ser.). 1998. pap. 8.95 (*0-8172-8012-X*) Raintree Steck-V.

Levine, Marilyn A. The Found Generation: Chinese Communists in Europe During the Twenties. LC 92-46157. (Jackson School Publications in International Studies). 296p. 1993. 35.00 (*0-295-97240-8*) U of Wash Pr.

*__Levine, Marilyn A. & Chen, San-Ching.__ The Guomindang in Europe: A Sourcebook of Documents. LC 99-86515. (China Research Monographs). 2000. write for info. (*1-55729-068-7*) IEAS.

*__Levine, Mark.__ Enola Gay. LC 99-16316. 100p. 2000. 30.00 (*0-520-22259-8*, Pub. by U CA Pr) Cal Prin Full Svc.

— Enola Gay. LC 99-16316. (New California Poetry Ser.: Vol. 2). 86p. 2000. 13.95 (*0-520-22260-1*, Pub. by U CA Pr) Cal Prin Full Svc.

Levine, Mark. The Jazz Piano Book. (Illus.). 307p. (Orig.). (C). 1990. pap. text 28.00 (*0-9614701-5-1*) Sher Music.

— The Jazz Theory Book. 522p. 1996. pap. text 38.00 (*1-883217-04-0*) Sher Music.

*__Levine, Mark.__ Lifescripts For the Self Employed. LC 98-52419. (Lifescripts Ser.). (Illus.). 161p. 1999. pap. 14.95 (*0-02-862621-4*, Pub. by Macmillan) S&S Trade.

Levine, Mark. Manual of Oculoplastic Surgery. 2nd ed. (Illus.). 336p. 1996. text 70.00 (*0-7506-9634-6*, Focal) Buttrwrth-Heinemann.

Levine, Mark, jt. auth. see Caplan, Michael.

Levine, Mark, jt. auth. see Kelly, Pat.

Levine, Mark, jt. auth. see Pollan, Stephen.

Levine, Mark, jt. auth. see Pollan, Stephen M.

Levine, Mark, ed. see Pollan, Stephen M. & Tower, Roni Beth.

Levine, Mark L. Builders' Liability. 1980. write for info. (*0-318-02240-0*) Prof Pubns & Educ.

— Exchanging Real Estate, 2 vols. 1997. 115.00 (*0-317-01847-7*) Prof Pubns & Educ.

— Landlords'-Owners' Liability (1981) 1989. write for info. (*0-317-00909-5*) Prof Pubns & Educ.

— Levine's Real Estate Transactions. 1991. pap. write for info. (*0-314-86700-7*) West Pub.

— Negotiating a Book Contract: A Guide for Authors, Agents & Lawyers. 96p. (Orig.). 1988. pap. 12.95 (*0-918825-69-5*) Moyer Bell.

— Real Estate Appraiser's Liabiity. 1997. write for info. (*0-317-01846-9*) Prof Pubns & Educ.

— Real Estate Appraisers' Liability. annuals rev. ed. LC 91-60906. (Real Property-Zoning Ser.). 1991. suppl. ed. 135.00 (*0-685-59814-4*) West Group.

— Real Estate Fundamentals. LC 76-3508. 440p. reprint ed. pap. 136.40 (*0-608-12019-7*, 202284300030) Bks Demand.

— Real Estate Tax Update Outline (1987) 1997. write for info. (*0-318-58317-8*) Prof Pubns & Educ.

— Real Estate Transactions, Tax Planning. 1998. write for info. (*0-317-01848-5*) Prof Pubns & Educ.

— Real Estate Transactions, Tax Planning & Consequences. 1390p. (C). 1993. pap. text. write for info. (*0-314-02383-6*) West Pub.

— Real Estate Transactions, Tax Planning & Consequences. 1375p. (C). 1997. pap. text. write for info. (*0-314-21623-5*) West Pub.

— Real Estate Transactions, Tax Planning & Consequences: 1995 Edition. 1450p. (C). 1995. pap. text. write for info. (*0-314-06362-5*) West Pub.

— Realtors' Liability. 1979. write for info. (*0-317-00910-9*) Prof Pubns & Educ.

Levine, Mark L. & Rachlis, Eugene, eds. The Complete Book of Bible Quotes from the New Testament. LC 95-42294. 288p. 1996. pap. 16.00 (*0-671-53797-0*, PB Trade Paper) PB.

Levine, Mark R., ed. Manual of Oculoplastic Surgery. LC 88-18903. (Illus.). 284p. reprint ed. pap. 88.10 (*0-7837-6254-2*, 204596600010) Bks Demand.

Levine, Mark S. Canonical Analysis & Factor Comparison. LC 77-75941. (Quantitative Applications in the Social Sciences Ser.: Vol. 6). 62p. 1977. 10.95 (*0-8039-0655-2*) Sage.

Levine, Marlene W., jt. auth. see Levine, H. B.

Levine, Marsha, ed. Professional Practice Schools: Integrating School Reform & Teacher Education. 192p. (C). 1992. text 38.00 (*0-8077-3176-5*); pap. text 17.95 (*0-8077-3175-7*) Tchrs Coll.

*__Levine, Marsha, et al, eds.__ Late Prehistoric Exploitation of the Eurasian Steppe. (Monographs Ser.). (Illus.). 224p. 1999. lib. bdg. 70.00 (*1-902937-03-1*, Pub. by McDonald Inst) David Brown.

Levine, Marsha & Trachman, Roberta, eds. Making Professional Development Schools Work: Politics, Policy & Practice. LC 97-1604. (School Reform Ser.). 272p. (C). 1997. text 50.00 (*0-8077-3634-1*); pap. text 22.95 (*0-8077-3633-3*) Tchrs Coll.

Levine, Marshall & Wood, Jeremy. Construction Insurance & U. K. Construction Contracts. 336p. 1991. 140.00 (*1-85044-375-0*) LLP.

Levine, Martin. Age Discrimination & the Mandatory Retirement Controversy. LC 88-9280. 253p. reprint ed. pap. 78.50 (*0-608-06078-X*, 206641000008) Bks Demand.

*__Levine, Martin.__ Compassion Reconsidered. LC 99-96698. 2000. 12.95 (*0-533-13293-2*) Vantage.

Levine, Martin. Legal Education. LC 93-27764. (International Library of Essays in Law & Legal Theory: Vol. 5). (C). 1993. lib. bdg. 150.00 (*0-8147-5065-6*) NYU Pr.

Levine, Martin L., ed. Law & Psychology. LC 95-7995. (International Library of Essays in Law & Legal Theory: No. 16). 500p. (C). 1995. lib. bdg. 150.00 (*0-8147-5064-8*) NYU Pr.

Levine, Martin N. Mental Retardation Handbook. 147p. 1989. pap. text 39.50 (*0-87424-230-4*, W-230) Western Psych.

Levine, Martin P. Gay Macho. LC 97-21215. 260p. 1998. text 50.00 (*0-8147-4694-2*); pap. text 18.00 (*0-8147-4695-0*) NYU Pr.

Levine, Martin P., ed. In Changing Times: Gay Men & Lesbians Encounter HIV-AIDS. LC 97-3414. 248p. 1997. lib. bdg. 55.00 (*0-226-27856-5*) U Ch Pr.

— In Changing Times: Gay Men & Lesbians Encounter HIV-AIDS. LC 97-3414. (Illus.). 248p. 1997. pap. text 17.95 (*0-226-27857-3*) U Ch Pr.

Levine, Martin P., jt. auth. see Markisz, John A.

Levine, Marvin. Look down from Clouds: New Poems. Axelrod, David B., ed. & pref. by. 52p. 1997. pap. 12.00 (*0-925062-09-X*) Writers Ink Pr.

*__Levine, Marvin.__ The Positive Psychology of Buddhism & Yoga: Paths to Mature Happiness. LC 00-22894. 2000. write for info. (*0-8058-3349-8*) L Erlbaum Assocs.

Levine, Marvin J. Effective Problem Solving. 2nd ed. LC 93-31281. 146p. (C). 1993. pap. text 32.40 (*0-13-245481-5*) P-H.

— Public Personnel Management: Structure, Process & Practice. 1983. 22.95 (*0-913878-27-8*) T Horton & Dghts.

Levine, Mary Ann E., ed. see Nassaney, Michael.

Levine, Mel. Illusion. LC 98-68266. 272p. 1999. pap. 16.95 (*1-57197-147-5*) Pentland Pr.

— Life in the Trash Lane: Cash, Cars & Corruption, a Sports Agent's True Story. LC 93-44457. 192p. 1993. pap. 9.95 (*0-942963-48-2*) Distinctive Pub.

— Pediatric Early Elementary Examination (PEEX 2) 2nd rev. ed. Winkleby, Diane, ed. 80p. 1996. pap. 15.40 (*0-8388-2806-X*, 82806) Ed Pub Serv.

— Peeramid II Pediatric Examination of Educational Readiness at Middle School. rev. ed. Winkleby, Diane, ed. (Illus.). 80p. 1996. pap. 15.40 (*0-8388-1994-X*, 81998) Ed Pub Serv.

Levine, Mel, et al. The Mind That's Mine. Brown, Ruth, ed. (Illus.). 74p. 1997. pap. text, student ed. write for info. (*1-891000-01-2*); teacher ed., ring bd. 65.00 (*1-891000-02-0*) All Kinds Minds.

— The Mind That's Mine: A Program to Help Young Learners Learn about Learning. Brown, Ruth, ed. 1997. 370.00 (*1-891000-00-4*) All Kinds Minds.

Levine, Melinda. Colors for Living: Living Rooms. 128p. 1996. 24.99 (*1-56496-104-4*) Rockport Pubs.

— Colors for Living: Living Rooms. (Colors for Living Ser.). (Illus.). 128p. 1998. pap. 19.99 (*1-56496-553-8*) Rockport Pubs.

Levine, Melvin D. All Kinds of Minds: A Young Student's Book about Learning Abilities & Learning Disorders. 296p. (J). 1993. pap. 24.75 (*0-8388-2090-5*, 2090) Ed Pub Serv.

— Concentration Cockpit: Explaining Attention Deficits to Children. 2nd rev. ed. 1995. 15.00 (*0-8388-1991-5*) Ed Pub Serv.

— Developmental Variation & Learning Disorders. rev. ed. 672p. 1998. 69.00 (*0-8388-1992-3*, 1992) Ed Pub Serv.

— Educational Care: A System for Understanding & Helping Children with Learning Problems at Home & in School. 327p. 1994. 31.50 (*0-8388-1987-7*, 1987) Ed Pub Serv.

— Guidelines for All Kinds of Minds: A Manual for Adults to Use in Their Work with Children. 56p. 1993. pap. 11.00 (*0-8388-2098-0*, 2098) Ed Pub Serv.

— Keeping a Head in School: A Student's Book about Learning Abilities & Learning Disorders. rev. ed. (Illus.). 299p. (J). (gr. 4-10). 1991. reprint ed. pap. 24.75 (*0-8388-2069-7*, 2069) Ed Pub Serv.

Levine, Melvin D. Keeping a Head in School: A Student's Book about Learning Abilities & Learning Disorders, Set. unabridged ed. (J). (gr. 4-10). audio 44.00 (*0-8388-2070-0*, 2070) Ed Pub Serv.

Levine, Melvin D. Language Parts Catalog. Noon, Jennifer, ed. (Illus.). (YA). (gr. 7-10). 1999. pap., wbk. ed. 9.00 (*0-8388-1980-X*) Ed Pub Serv.

— Memory Factory: Guidelines for Use with Students. Arnold, Tim, ed. (Illus.). (YA). (gr. 6-12). 1999. pap., wbk. ed. 9.00 (*0-8388-1982-6*) Ed Pub Serv.

— PEET: Pediatric Examination at Three. (Pediatric Assessment Systems Ser.). 64p. 1986. pap. 13.75 (*0-8388-1795-5*) Ed Pub Serv.

Levine, Melvin D., et al, eds. Developmental-Behavioral Pediatrics. 2nd ed. (Illus.). 809p. 1992. text 155.00 (*0-7216-3189-4*, W B Saunders Co) Harcrt Hlth Sci Grp.

Levine, Michael. The Address Book. 8th rev. ed. 288p. 1997. pap. 12.00 (*0-399-52274-3*, Perigee Bks) Berkley Pub.

— The Address Book. 9th ed. 304p. 1999. pap. 12.00 (*0-399-52487-8*, Perigee Bks) Berkley Pub.

— The Address Book No. 7: How to Reach Anyone Who Is Anyone. 7th ed. LC 94-33188. 288p. (Orig.). 1995. pap. 11.00 (*0-399-52149-6*, Perigee Bks) Berkley Pub.

— Guerrilla PR: How to Wage an Effective Publicity Campaign - Without Going Broke. LC 92-53331. 256p. 1993. 20.00 (*0-88730-608-X*, HarpBusn) HarpInfo.

— Guerrilla PR: How You Can Wage an Effective Publicity Campaign . . . Without Going Broke. LC 92-53331. 256p. 1994. pap. 13.00 (*0-88730-664-0*, HarpBusn) HarpInfo.

— The Health Address Book: How to Locate the Best Healthcare Information in America. LC 98-19911. 240p. 1998. pap. 14.95 (*1-58063-024-3*, Pub. by Renaissance) St Martin.

— Julia: Nothing Lasts Forever. (Party of Five Ser.: No. 4). (J). (gr. 3-6). 1998. pap. 4.50 (*0-671-01773-X*, Archway) PB.

*__Levine, Michael.__ The Kid's Address Book. 1999. pap. 11.95 (*0-399-52516-5*, Perigee Bks) Berkley Pub.

Levine, Michael. The Kid's Address Book. rev. ed. 240p. (J). 1994. pap. 9.95 (*0-399-51875-4*, Perigee Bks) Berkley Pub.

— The Kid's Address Book: Over 3,000 Addresses of Celebrities, Athletes, Entertainers, & More...Just for Kids! 3rd rev. ed. 304p. 1997. pap. 10.95 (*0-399-52304-9*, Perigee Bks) Berkley Pub.

— Lessons at the Halfway Point: Wisdom for Midlife. 150p. 1995. bds. 12.95 (*0-89087-744-0*) Celestial Arts.

Levine, Michael. Music Address Book. 2nd ed. LC 93-21463. 240p. 1994. pap. 16.00 (*0-06-273257-9*, Harper Ref) HarpC.

Levine, Michael. The Princess & the Package. LC 98-26672. 304p. 1998. 24.95 (*1-58063-028-6*) Renaissance.

*__Levine, Michael.__ The Princess & the Package, abr. ed. 1998. pap. 16.95 incl. audio (*1-55927-511-1*) Audio Renaissance.

Levine, Michael. Raise Your Social I.Q. How to Do the Right Thing in Any Situation. LC 98-29053. (Illus.). 224p. 1998. pap. 12.95 (*0-8065-2047-7*, Citadel Pr) Carol Pub Group.

— Selling Goodness: The Guerrilla P. R. Guide to Promoting Your Charity, Nonprofit Organization, or Fund-Raising Event. LC 97-52572. 288p. 1998. 22.95 (*1-58063-009-X*, Pub. by Renaissance) St Martin.

— Take It from Me: Practical & Inspiring Career Advice from the Celebrated & the Successful. 208p. (Orig.). 1996. pap. 12.00 (*0-399-52217-4*, Perigee Bks) Berkley Pub.

— Triangle of Death: Deep Cover II. 1997. mass mkt. 6.99 (*0-440-22111-0*) Dell.

Levine, Michael, tr. see Semyonova Tian-Shanskaia.

Levine, Michael G. Writing Through Repression: Literature, Censorship, Psychoanalysis. 232p. (C). 1994. text 35.00 (*0-8018-4835-0*) Johns Hopkins.

Levine, Michael K. Inside International Trade Policy Formulation: A History of the 1982 US-EC Steel Arrangements. LC 85-3724. 176p. 1985. 47.95 (*0-275-90136-X*, C0136, Praeger Pubs) Greenwood.

Levine, Michael L. African Americans & Civil Rights: From 1619 to the Present. LC 96-8923. (Social Issues in American History Ser.). (Illus.). 344p. 1996. boxed set 35.95 (*0-89774-859-X*) Oryx Pr.

L

L

Levine, Michael P. Analytic Freud: Philosophy & Psychoanalysis. LC 99-24182. 1999. pap. 27.99 (*0-415-18040-6*) Routledge.
— Hume & the Problem of Miracles: A Solution. 200p. (C). 1988. lib. bdg. 130.50 (*0-7923-0043-2*, Pub. by Kluwer Academic) Kluwer Academic.
***Levine, Michael P., ed.** Analytic Freud: Philosophy & Psychoanalysis. LC 99-24182. 400p. (C). 1999. text. write for info. (*0-415-18039-2*) Routledge.
Levine, Michael S., ed. Glutamate & Dopamine in the Developing & Adult Neostriatum. (Developmental Neuroscience Ser.: Vol. 20, Nos. 2 & 3, 1998). (Illus.). 172p. 1998. pap. 86.25 (*3-8055-6684-0*) S Karger.
Levine, Michael S., jt. ed. see Franks, Jacqueline.
Levine, Michelle J. I Wish I Were Thin - I Wish I Were Fat: The Real Reasons We Overeat & What We Can Do about It. LC 97-60106. 240p. 1997. 23.95 (*0-9656686-4-9*) Vanderbilt Press.
Levine, Michelle Joy. I Wish I Were Thin, I Wish I Were Fat: The Real Reasons We Overeat & What We Can Do about It. LC 98-54812. 240p. 1999. per. 12.00 (*0-684-85738-3*, Fireside) S&S Trade Pap.
***Levine, Mike.** Fundamentals of Sensation & Perception. 3rd ed. LC 99-89741. 576p. 2000. text 75.00 (*0-19-852467-6*) OUP.
Levine, Mike. How to Be a Working Musician: A Practical Guide to Earning Money in the Music Business. LC 97-19904. (Illus.). 224p. 1997. 16.95 (*0-8230-8329-2*, Billboard Bks) Watsn-Guptill.
Levine, Mindy N., ed. see Dance Theater Workshop Staff.
Levine, Mindy N., ed. see De Natale, Douglas & Ito, Karen L.
Levine, Mira, jt. ed. see Kaufman, Menahem.
Levine, Miriam. A Guide to Writers' Homes in New England. rev. ed. (Illus.). 186p. 1997. pap. 14.95 (*0-918222-51-6*) Applewood.
Levine, Mortimer. The Early Elizabethan Succession Question, 1558-1568. viii, 245p. 1966. 32.50 (*0-8047-0299-3*) Stanford U Pr.
— The Early Elizabethan Succession Question, 1558-1568. fac. ed. LC 66-17563. 255p. 1966. reprint ed. pap. 30.00 (*0-7837-7911-9*, 204766700008) Bks Demand.
— Tudor England, 1485-1603. LC 68-12060. (Conference on British Studies, Bibliographical Handbooks). 127p. reprint ed. pap. 36.20 (*0-608-16808-4*, 2027230) Bks Demand.
***Levine, Murray.** Hegemony. 2000. pap. 18.00 (*0-7388-2221-3*) Xlibris Corp.
Levine, Murray. The History & Politics of Mental Health. 232p. 1981. pap. text 19.95 (*0-19-502956-9*) OUP.
Levine, Murray & Doueck, Howard J. Psychotherapy & Mandated Reporting of Child Maltreatment. LC 95-18434. (Practice Ser.). 169p. (C). 1995. 45.00 (*0-8039-5472-7*); pap. 18.95 (*0-8039-5473-5*) Sage.
Levine, Murray & Perkins, David V. Principles of Community Psychology: Perspectives & Trends. 2nd ed. (Illus.). 512p. (C). 1996. text 54.95 (*0-19-509844-7*) OUP.
Levine, Myron A., jt. auth. see Ross, Bernard H.
Levine, Myron M. New Generation Vaccines. 2nd ed. LC 97-12541. (Illus.). 1240p. 1997. text 195.00 (*0-8247-0061-9*) Dekker.
Levine, Nancy D., ed. The Older Volunteer: An Annotated Bibliography, 21. LC 92-41898. (Bibliographies & Indexes in Gerontology Ser.: No. 21). 136p. 1993. lib. bdg. 49.95 (*0-313-28125-4*, BOV, Greenwood Pr) Greenwood.
Levine, Nancy E. The Dynamics of Polyandry: Kinship, Domesticity, & Population on the Tibetan Border. (Illus.). 344p. 1996. lib. bdg. 57.00 (*0-226-47568-9*) U Ch Pr.
— The Dynamics of Polyandry: Kinship, Domesticity, & Population on the Tibetan Border. (Illus.). 344p. 1998. pap. text 21.95 (*0-226-47569-7*) U Ch Pr.
Levine, Nancy Goldberg, see Goldberg Levine, Nancy.
Levine, Naomi & Hochbaum, Martin, eds. Poor Jews: An American Awakening. LC 73-85097. 206p. 1974. 32.95 (*0-87855-073-9*); pap. 18.95 (*0-87855-570-6*) Transaction Pubs.
Levine, Naomi B. Politics, Religion, & Love: The Story of H. H. Asquith, Venetia Stanley & Edwin Samuel Montagu, Based on the Life & Letters of Edwin Samuel Montagu. (Illus.). 843p. (C). 1991. text 45.00 (*0-8147-5057-5*) NYU Pr.
Levine, Nathan. Typing & Keyboarding for Everyone. 10th ed. 160p. 1996. 14.95 (*0-02-860597-7*) Macmillan.
— Typing & Keyboarding for Everyone. 11th ed. LC 97-81013. 144p. 1998. pap. 14.95 (*0-02-862194-8*, Arc) IDG Bks.
— Typing & Keyboarding for Everyone, with Typing Tutor 6. 11th ed. 1998. pap. text 19.95 (*0-02-862476-9*, Arc) IDG Bks.
Levine, Ned, jt. auth. see Glickfeld, Madelyn J.
Levine, Neil. The Architecture of Frank Lloyd Wright. 544p. 1996. pap. text 49.50 (*0-691-02745-5*, Pub. by Princeton U Pr) Cal Prin Full Svc.
— The Architecture of Frank Lloyd Wright. LC 95-32307. (Illus.). 524p. (C). 1996. text 90.00 (*0-691-03371-4*, Pub. by Princeton U Pr) Cal Prin Full Svc.
Levine, Neil & Lipman, Jonathan. The Wright State: Frank Lloyd Wright in Wisconsin. LC 92-30063. (Illus.). 96p. 1992. pap. 19.95 (*0-944110-27-4*) Milwauk Art Mus.
Levine, Newton, ed. see Mestre, Kenneth.
Levine, Nina S. Women's Matters: Politics, Gender, & Nation in Shakespeare's Early History Plays. LC 97-41515. 192p. 1998. 36.00 (*0-87413-654-7*) U Delaware Pr.
Levine, Norma. The Blessing Power of the Buddhas: Sacred Objects, Secret Lands. 1993. pap. 15.95 (*1-85230-305-0*, Pub. by Element MA) Penguin Putnam.
— A Yearbook of Buddhist Wisdom. (Illus.). 128p. 1996. 24.00 (*0-8356-0743-7*, Quest) Theos Pub Hse.
Levine, Norman. Canada Made Me. 304p. 1993. pap. write for info. (*0-88984-168-3*) Porcup Quill.
— The Discourses of Love: Paganism. LC 97-13341. 330p. (C). 1998. 64.00 (*0-7618-0826-4*); pap. 42.50 (*0-7618-0827-2*) U Pr of Amer.
— From a Seaside Town. 160p. 1993. pap. write for info. (*0-88984-170-5*) Porcup Quill.
***Levine, Norman.** Howard Frye & Me: Reminiscenses of a Mandolin Great. (Illus.). 117p. 1999. 24.00 (*0-9614120-8-9*, PSE 006) Plucked.
Levine, Norman. I Don't Want to Know Anyone Too Well & Other Stories. LC 72-191174. 160 p. (J). 1971. write for info. (*0-333-12959-8*) Motilal Bnarsidass.
— Pigmentation & Pigmentary Disorders. 576p. 1993. lib. bdg. 199.00 (*0-8493-7353-0*, RL790) CRC Pr.
— Selected Stories LC 75-1983. 116 p. 1975. write for info. (*0-88750-151-6*) Oberon Pr.
— She'll Only Drag You Down: A Novel LC 77-376865. 220p. 1975. write for info. (*0-7737-7091-7*) Stoddart Publ.
— Skin Healthy: Everyone's Guide to Great Skin. LC 95-9070. 184p. 1995. pap. 12.95 (*0-87833-900-0*) Taylor Pub.
Levine, Norman, ed. The US & the EU: Economic Relations in a World of Transition. LC 96-21502. 358p. 1996. pap. text 39.50 (*0-7618-0398-X*) U Pr of Amer.
— The U.S. & the E.U. Economic Relations in a World of Transition. LC 96-21502. 358p. 1996. lib. bdg. 64.50 (*0-7618-0397-1*) U Pr of Amer.
Levine, Norman, ed. see Bauer, Walter K.
Levine, Norman, tr. see Lukacs, Georg.
Levine, Norman D. Veterinary Protozoology. LC 84-27867. (Illus.). 414p. 1985. text 64.95 (*0-8138-1861-3*) Iowa St U Pr.
Levine, Norman D., ed. Natural Nidality of Diseases & Questions of Parasitology. Plous, Frederick K., Jr., tr. LC 68-11027. (Illus.). 495p. reprint ed. 153.50 (*0-8357-9691-4*, 201903100010) Bks Demand.
— The Protozoan Phylum Apicomplexa, 2 vols., Vol. I. 240p. 1988. 124.00 (*0-8493-4653-3*, SF780, CRC Reprint) Franklin.
— The Protozoan Phylum Apicomplexa, 2 vols., Vol. II. 176p. 1988. 98.00 (*0-8493-4654-1*, CRC Reprint) Franklin.
Levine, Norman D. & Ivens, Virginia R., eds. Coccidian Parasites of Rodents. 150p. 1989. lib. bdg. 139.00 (*0-8493-4898-6*, QL368) CRC Pr.
Levine, Norman D., ed. see Drake, Daniel.
Levine, Norman D., ed. see Naumov, N. P.
Levine, Norman D., ed. see Pavlovsky, Evgeny N.
Levine, Norman G. A Norman Levine Reader: Insights on Achieving Success & Fulfillment. Ragaglia, Brad, ed. 280p. 1998. pap. 24.99 (*1-891042-01-7*) Million Dollar.
***Levine, Norman G.** Passion for Compassion: The Formula for Successful Financial Advisors. 286p. 2000. pap. 24.95 (*1-891042-10-6*, 59934) Million Dollar.
Levine, Norman S. Current Treatment in Dental Practice. (Illus.). 533p. 1986. text 89.00 (*0-7216-1198-2*, W B Saunders Co) Harcrt Hlth Sci Grp.
Levine, Ondrea & Levine, Stephen. The Heart of Relationship. unabridged ed. 1992. audio 11.00 (*0-87773-678-2*, Pub. by Shambhala Pubns) Random.
Levine, Ondrea, jt. auth. see Levine, Stephen.
Levine, Paul. False Dawn. 368p. 1994. mass mkt. 5.99 (*0-553-56504-4*) Bantam.
— Flesh & Bones. (Jake Lassiter Mystery Ser.). 352p. 1998. mass mkt. 5.99 (*0-380-72591-6*, Avon Bks) Morrow Avon.
— Flesh & Bones: A Jake Lassiter Novel. large type ed. LC 96-37988. 468p. 1997. write for info. (*0-7838-8065-0*, G K Hall Lrg Type) Mac Lib Ref.
— Flesh & Bones: A Jake Lassiter Novel. large type ed. LC 96-35364. 336p. 1997. 23.00 (*0-688-14305-9*, Wm Morrow) Morrow Avon.
— Fool Me Twice. 352p. 1996. mass mkt. 5.99 (*0-380-72590-8*, Avon Bks) Morrow Avon.
— Making Kitchen Cabinets: A Foolproof System for the Home Workshop. LC 87-51674. (Illus.). 192p. 1988. pap. 19.95 (*0-918804-94-9*, 070067) Taunton.
Levine, Paul. Making Kitchen Cabinets with Paul Levine: A Foolproof System for the Home Workshop. LC 87-51674. (Illus.). 192p. 1988. 19.95 incl. VHS (*0-918804-95-7*) Taunton.
Levine, Paul. Mortal Sin. 352p. 1995. mass mkt. 5.50 (*0-380-72161-9*, Avon Bks) Morrow Avon.
— Night Vision. 448p. 1992. mass mkt. 5.99 (*0-553-29762-7*) Bantam.
— 9 Scorpions. LC 98-15064. 448p. 1999. 23.00 (*0-671-01939-2*, Pocket Books) PB.
— 9 Scorpions. 1999. reprint ed. per. 7.50 (*0-671-01940-6*, Pocket Books) PB.
— To Speak for the Dead. 400p. 1991. mass mkt. 5.99 (*0-553-29172-6*) Bantam.
Levine, Paul, et al. Building Backyard Structures: Sheds, Barns, Bins, Gazebos & Other Outdoor Construction. LC 96-53254. (Illus.). 192p. 1997. pap. 19.95 (*0-8069-4216-9*) Sterling.
Levine, Paul, jt. auth. see Currie, David.
Levine, Paul A. From Indifference to Activism: Swedish Diplomacy & the Holocaust, 1938-44. 2nd ed. (Acta Universitatis Upsaliensis Studia Historica Upsaliensia). 309p. 1998. pap. 65.00 (*91-554-4249-8*) Coronet Bks.
Levine, Paul A., et al. Electrocardiography of Rate-Modulated Pacemaker Rhythms. (Illus.). 90p. (Orig.). (C). 1990. pap. 40.00 (*0-9626364-0-1*); pap. 40.00 (*0-9626364-1-X*) Siemens Pacesetter.
Levine, Paul H. & Patarca, Roberto. Clinical Management of Chronic Fatigue Syndrome: Clinical Conference, American Association of Chronic Fatigue Syndrome. Klimas, Nancy G. et al, eds. LC 95-47749. (Journal of Chronic Fatigue Syndrome: Vol. 1, Nos. 3/4). 244p. (C). 1996. 39.95 (*1-56024-792-4*, Hawrth Medical) Haworth Pr.
LeVine, Peg, ed. see Morita, Shoma.
Levine, Peter. A. G. Spalding & the Rise of Baseball: The Promise of American Sport. (Illus.). 184p. 1998. pap. text 10.00 (*0-7881-5239-4*) DIANE Pub.
— The Behavior of State Legislative Parties in the Jacksonian Era New Jersey: 1829-1844. LC 75-18248. 285p. 1977. 25.00 (*0-8386-1800-6*) Fairleigh Dickinson.
— Ellis Island to Ebbets Field: Sport & the American Jewish Experience. 1992. 24.95 (*0-685-61042-X*) OUP.
— Living Without Philosophy: On Narrative, Rhetoric, & Morality. LC 98-7524. 352p. (C). 1998. text 68.50 (*0-7914-3897-X*); pap. text 22.95 (*0-7914-3898-8*) State U NY Pr.
***Levine, Peter.** New Progressive Era: Toward a Fair & Deliberative Democracy. LC 99-45647. 304p. 2000. pap. 19.95 (*0-8476-9574-3*); text 65.00 (*0-8476-9573-5*) Rowman.
Levine, Peter. Nietzsche & the Modern Crisis of the Humanities. LC 94-11021. 279p. (C). 1995. pap. text 18.95 (*0-7914-2328-X*) State U NY Pr.
— Nietzsche & the Modern Crisis of the Humanities. LC 94-11021. 279p. (C). 1995. text 57.50 (*0-7914-2327-1*) State U NY Pr.
— The Rabbi of Swat. LC 99-6026. 266p. 1999. 19.95 (*0-87013-517-1*) Mich St U Pr.
— Something to Hide: A Novel. 288p. 1996. 22.95 (*0-312-14047-9*) St Martin.
Levine, Peter, ed. Baseball History. (Illus.). 160p. 1990. reprint ed. pap. 14.95 (*0-9625132-1-0*) Cyberbooks.
Levine, Peter A. & Frederick, Ann. Waking the Tiger - Healing Trauma: The Innate Capacity to Transform Overwhelming Experiences. LC 97-3918. (Illus.). 256p. (Orig.). 1997. pap. 16.95 (*1-55643-233-X*) North Atlantic.
Levine, Philip. Don't Ask. LC 80-24992. (Poets on Poetry Ser.). 192p. 1981. pap. 13.95 (*0-472-06327-8*, 06327) U of Mich Pr.
— The Look of Things. 1996. pap. 13.00 (*0-614-20812-2*) Knopf.
— Mercy. LC 98-43353. 80p. 1999. 22.00 (*0-375-40138-5*) Knopf.
— The Mercy: Poems. LC 98-43353. 80p. 2000. pap. 15.00 (*0-375-70135-4*) Knopf.
— New Selected Poems. 1992. pap. 20.00 (*0-679-74056-2*) McKay.
— Not This Pig: Poems. LC 68-16006. (Wesleyan Poetry Program Ser.: Vol. 38). 80p. 1968. pap. 12.95 (*0-8195-1038-6*, Wesleyan Univ Pr) U Pr of New Eng.
— One for the Rose. LC 98-74552. (Classic Contemporaries Ser.). 80p. 1999. reprint ed. pap. 12.95 (*0-88748-307-0*, Pub. by Carnegie-Mellon) Cornell U Pr.
— The Simple Truth: Poems. 1996. pap. 15.00 (*0-679-76584-0*) Knopf.
— Unselected Poems. (Orig.). 1997. pap. 13.95 (*0-9655239-0-X*) Greenhouse Review Pr.
— What Work Is. 1992. pap. 15.00 (*0-679-74058-9*) McKay.
Levine, Philip, tr. City of God Against the Pagans, 7 vols, IV. (Loeb Classical Library: No. 411-417). 592p. 1966. 18.95 (*0-674-99456-6*) HUP.
***Levine, Philip & Miller, Richard Copeland.** Passage Europe. (Illus.). 156p. 2000. 50.00 (*1-888899-05-0*) Lodima.
Levine, Philip, et al. Earth, Stars, & Writers. LC 92-36089. (National Book Week Lectures). 1992. write for info. (*0-8444-0771-2*) Lib Congress.
Levine, Philip, jt. auth. see Miller, Richard Copeland.
Levine, Philip, ed. see Levis, Larry.
Levine, Philippa. The Bread of Time: Toward a Autobiography. (Illus.). (C). pap. text. write for info. (*0-472-08625-1*) U of Mich Pr.
Levine, Philippa. Victorian Feminism, 1850-1900. LC 94-11565. 176p. 1989. pap. 17.95 (*0-8130-1321-6*) U Press Fla.
Levine, Phillip. Sweet Will. 1985. pap. 5.95 (*0-689-11586-5*) Atheneum Yung Read.
— They Feed the Lion & The Names. LC 99-10987. 1999. pap. 17.00 (*0-375-70629-1*) Knopf.
Levine, Phillip J. Chemical Use among Older Adults: Risks, Reactions, & Concerns. 40p. 1993. pap. 4.95 (*1-56246-071-4*, 3261, HazeldenJohnson Inst) Hazelden.
Levine-Provost, Gail, jt. auth. see Provost, Gary.
Levine, R. D., jt. auth. see Iachello, F.
Levine, R. J., jt. ed. see Bankowski, Z.
Levine, R. L. & Fitzgerald, H. E. Analysis of Dynamic Psychological Systems Vol. 1: Basic Approaches to General Systems, Dynamic Systems, & Cybernetics. (Illus.). 352p. (C). 1992. 60.00 (*0-306-43745-7*, Plenum Trade) Perseus Pubng.
Levine, R. L. & Fitzgerald, H. E. Analysis of Dynamic Psychological Systems Vol. 2: Methods & Applications. (Illus.). 422p. (C). 1992. 70.00 (*0-306-43746-5*, Plenum Trade) Perseus Pubng.
Levine, Raphael D. Quantum Mechanics of Molecular Rate Processes. unabridged ed. LC 99-21051. 335p. 1999. pap. text 12.95 (*0-486-40692-X*) Dover.
Levine, Rayna F., jt. auth. see Levine, David U.
Levine, Rhonda F. Class Struggle & the New Deal: Industrial Labor, Industrial Capital, & the State. LC 88-17183. (Studies in Historical Social Change). 232p. 1988. 29.95 (*0-7006-0373-5*); pap. 14.95 (*0-7006-0496-0*) U Pr of KS.
Levine, Rhonda F., ed. Social Class & Stratification: Classic Statements & Theoretical Debates. LC 98-14690. 288p. 1998. 62.50 (*0-8476-8542-X*); pap. 17.95 (*0-8476-8543-8*) Rowman.
Levine, Rhonda F. & Lembeke, Jerry, eds. Recapturing Marxism: An Appraisal of Recent Trends in Sociological Theory. LC 87-11589. 263p. 1987. 59.95 (*0-275-92576-5*, C2576, Praeger Pubs); pap. 17.95 (*0-275-92638-9*, B2638, Praeger Pubs) Greenwood.
Levine, Richard & Harte, Lawrence. GSM Superphones: Technologies & Services. (Telecommunications Ser.). (Illus.). 348p. 1998. 60.00 (*0-07-038177-1*) McGraw.
***Levine, Rick, et al.** The Cluetrain Manifesto: The End of Business as Usual. 224p. 1999. text 23.00 (*0-7382-0244-4*, Pub. by Perseus Pubng) HarpC.
Levine, Robert. Conspiracy & Romance: Studies in Brockden Brown, Cooper, Hawthorne & Melville. (Cambridge Studies in American Literature & Culture: No. 33). 312p. (C). 1989. text 69.95 (*0-521-36654-2*) Cambridge U Pr.
Levine, Robert. Neural Networks The Second Generation. pap. text 24.95 (*0-07-037486-4*) Gregg-McGraw.
LeVine, Robert. The Uniform Commercial Code: An Operational Translation. LC 80-68569. 1980. pap. 16.50 (*0-933718-00-4*) Browning Pubns.
Levine, Robert, ed. Formal Grammar: Theory & Implementation. (Vancouver Studies in Cognitive Science: Vol. 2). (Illus.). 448p. 1992. text 85.00 (*0-19-507314-2*); pap. text 45.00 (*0-19-507310-X*) OUP.
Levine, Robert, ed. A Thirteenth-Century Life of Charlemagne. LC 91-13581. (Library of Medieval Literature: Vol. 80A). 170p. 1991. text 15.00 (*0-8153-0397-1*) Garland.
Levine, Robert, tr. The Deeds of God Through the Franks: A Translation of Guibert de Nogent's 'Gesta Dei Per Francos' LC 96-46270. 172p. 1997. 75.00 (*0-85115-693-2*) Boydell & Brewer.
— France Before Charlemagne: A Translation from the Grandes Chroniques. LC 89-13819. (Studies in French Civilization: Vol. 3). 296p. 1990. lib. bdg. 89.95 (*0-88946-640-8*) E Mellen.
Levine, Robert & Lutyens, Elizabeth. Opera Small Talk: Pocket Plots, Crucial Characters, & Amusing Asides. LC 93-80148. (Illus.). 100p. 1993. pap. 9.95 (*0-9638743-0-6*) Cherubino Pr.
Levine, Robert, jt. ed. see Rodrigues, Aroldo.
Levine, Robert, tr. see Minstrel of Reims.
Levine, Robert A. The Arms Debate. LC 63-17204. 364p. reprint ed. pap. 112.90 (*0-7837-4478-1*, 204418600001) Bks Demand.
— Not with a Bang but a Whimper: Western Europe Approaches the Third Millenium. LC 96-17907. 95p. 1996. pap. 15.00 (*0-8330-2401-9*, MR-765-AF/A/OSD) Rand Corp.
— The SDI Debate As a Continuation of History. (CISA Working Papers: No. 55). 57p. (Orig.). 1986. pap. 15.00 (*0-86682-070-1*) Ctr Intl Relations.
— Still the Arms Debate. 420p. 1990. text 77.95 (*1-85521-071-1*, Pub. by Dartmth Pub) Ashgate Pub Co.
— Uniform Deterrence of Nuclear First Use. LC 93-25248. 1993. pap. 15.00 (*0-8330-1401-3*, MR-231) Rand Corp.
— Western Europe, 1979-2009: A View from the United States. LC 98-34304. (Illus.). 61p. 1998. pap. 15.00 (*0-8330-2648-8*) Rand Corp.
LeVine, Robert A., ed. Culture & Personality: Contemporary Readings. LC 79-16915. 466p. 1974. pap. text 31.95 (*0-202-01122-4*) Aldine de Gruyter.
Levine, Robert A. & Estan, Peter J. Macroeconomic Strategy for the 1990's: Getting the Long Run Right. LC 93-6415. 1993. pap. 15.00 (*0-8330-1449-8*, MR-325-RC) Rand Corp.
LeVine, Robert A., et al. Child Care & Culture: Lessons from Africa. LC 93-33584. (Illus.). 368p. (C). 1994. text 59.95 (*0-521-33171-4*) Cambridge U Pr.
— Child Care & Culture: Lessons from Africa. 366p. 1996. pap. text 21.95 (*0-521-57546-X*) Cambridge U Pr.
Levine, Robert A., jt. auth. see Hosek, James R.
Levine, Robert A., jt. ed. see Shweder, Richard A.
Levine, Robert B. When You Are the Partner of a Rape or Incest Survivor: A Workbook for You. LC 96-161017. 104p. 1996. pap. 14.95 (*0-89390-329-9*) Resource Pubns.
Levine, Robert D. & Green, Georgia M., eds. Studies in Contemporary Phrase Structure Grammar. LC 98-36961. (Illus.). 342p. 2000. 64.95 (*0-521-65107-7*) Cambridge U Pr.
Levine, Robert J. Ethics & Regulation of Clinical Research. 2nd ed. LC 87-28955. 1988. pap. 23.00 (*0-300-04288-4*) Yale U Pr.
Levine, Robert J., jt. auth. see Young, Brugruet L.
Levine, Robert M. Brazilian Legacies. LC 96-38568. (Perspectives on Latin America & the Caribbean Ser.). 224p. (C). (gr. 13). 1997. pap. 28.95 (*0-7656-0009-9*) M E Sharpe.
Levine, Robert M. Brazilian Legacies. LC 96-38568. (Perspectives on Latin America & the Caribbean Ser.). (Illus.). (C). (gr. 13). 1997. 74.95 (*0-7656-0008-0*) M E Sharpe.
— Cuba in the 1850's: Through the Lens of Charles DeForest Fredricks. 86p. 1990. 24.95 (*0-8130-1010-1*) U Press Fla.
— Father of the Poor? Vargas & His Era. LC 97-11309. (New Approaches to the Americas Ser.). (Illus.). 204p. (C). 1998. text 54.95 (*0-521-58515-5*); pap. text 15.95 (*0-521-58528-7*) Cambridge U Pr.
— Historical Dictionary of Brazil. LC 78-10178. (Latin American Historical Dictionaries Ser.: No. 19). 309p. 1979. lib. bdg. 35.00 (*0-8108-1178-2*) Scarecrow.
— The History of Brazil. LC 99-21711. (Histories of the Modern Nations Ser.). 232p. 1999. 35.00 (*0-313-30390-8*) Greenwood.
— Images of History: Nineteenth- & Early Twentieth-Century Latin American Photographs As Documents. LC 88-26741. (Illus.). 228p. (C). 1990. reprint ed. pap. text 39.95 (*0-8223-0999-8*) Duke.

An Asterisk (*) at the beginning of an entry indicates that the title is appearing for the first time.

— Life & Death of C. M. De Jesus. (Dialogos Ser.). (Illus.). 162p. 1996. pap. 15.95 (*0-8263-1648-4*) U of NM Pr.
— Race & Ethnic Relations in Latin America & the Caribbean: An Historical Dictionary & Bibliography. LC 80-15179. 260p. 1980. 24.00 (*0-8108-1324-6*) Scarecrow.
— Tropical Diaspora: The Jewish Experience in Cuba. LC 93-12542. (Illus.). 400p. (C). 1993. 39.95 (*0-8130-1218-X*) U Press Fla.
— Vale of Tears: Revisiting the Canudos Massacre in Northeastern Brazil, 1893-1897. LC 91-36011. (C). 1992. 45.00 (*0-520-07524-2*, Pub. by U CA Pr) Cal Prin Full Svc.
— Vale of Tears: Revisiting the Canudos Massacre in Northeastern Brazil, 1893-1897. LC 91-36011. 365p. 1995. pap. 17.95 (*0-520-20343-7*, Pub. by U CA Pr) Cal Prin Full Svc.
— The Vargas Regime. LC 78-115222. (Institute of Latin American Studies). 270p. (C). 1970. text 57.50 (*0-231-03370-2*) Col U Pr.
Levine, Robert M., ed. Windows on Latin America: Understanding Society Through Photographs. (Illus.). 154p. 1987. pap. 21.95 (*0-935501-06-1*, WL001, Pub. by U Miami N-S Ctr) L Rienner.
***Levine, Robert M. & Asis, Moises.** Cuban Miami. LC 99-45919. (Illus.). 176p. (C). 2000. 32.00 (*0-8135-2780-5*) Rutgers U Pr.
Levine, Robert M. & Crocitti, John J., eds. The Brazil Reader: History, Culture, Politics. (Illus.). 576p. 1999. 64.95 (*0-8223-2258-7*); pap. 21.95 (*0-8223-2290-0*) Duke.
Levine, Robert M. & Naylor, Genevieve. The Brazilian Photographs of Genevieve Naylor, 1940-1943. LC 97-41666. 1998. write for info. (*0-8223-2160-2*); pap. write for info. (*0-8223-2189-0*) Duke.
Levine, Robert M., ed. see De Jesus, Carolina M.
Levine, Robert M., tr. see De Jesus, Carolina M.
Levine, Robert N. Geography of Time: On Tempo, Culture & the Pace of Life. 288p. 1998. pap. 14.00 (*0-465-02642-7*, Pub. by Basic) HarpC.
— Where Are You When I Need You? Befriending God When Life Hurts. LC 95-25507. 1996. pap. 10.00 (*0-06-251352-4*) Harper SF.
Levine, Robert S. Martin Delany, Frederick Douglass, & the Politics of Representative Identity. LC 96-9614. 352p. (C). (gr. 13). 1997. 49.95 (*0-8078-2323-6*); pap. 19.95 (*0-8078-4633-3*) U of NC Pr.
Levine, Robert S., ed. The Cambridge Companion to Herman Melville. LC 97-33339. (Cambridge Companions to Literature Ser.). 326p. (C). 1998. text 59.95 (*0-521-55477-2*); pap. text 17.95 (*0-521-55571-X*) Cambridge U Pr.
Levine, Robert S. & Pagni, Patrick J. Fire Science for Fire Safety. (Combustion Science & Technology Ser.). iv, 506p. 1984. pap. text 274.00 (*2-88124-115-8*) Gordon & Breach.
***Levine, Robert T.** Story of the Orchestra: A Child's Introduction to the Instruments, the Music, the Musicians & the Composers. 96p. 2000. 19.98 (*1-57912-148-9*) Blck Dog & Leventhal.
Levine, Roger E., et al. Public School Districts in the United States: A Statistical Profile, 1987-88 to 1993-94. LC 98-176202. (Statistical Analysis Report National Center for Education Statistics Reports). 1998. write for info. (*0-16-049420-6*) USGPO.
Levine, Ronald L., jt. ed. see Sanfilippo, Joseph S.
Levine, Roz. Palmistry: How to Chart the Lines of Your Life. (Illus.). 128p. (Orig.). 1993. pap. 15.00 (*0-671-78501-X*, Fireside) S&S Trade Pap.
— Seasonings. 366p. (Orig.). 1993. pap. 8.95 (*1-56245-075-1*) Great Quotations.
Levine, Ruth R. Pharmacology: Drug Actions & Reactions. 3rd ed. (Illus.). 1983. 24.50 (*0-316-52222-8*, Little Brwn Med Div) Lppncott W & W.
***Levine, Ruth R. & Walsh, Carol T.** Pharmacology: Drug Actions & Reactions. 6th ed. (Illus.). 590p. 2000. pap. 51.45 (*1-85070-497-X*) Prthnon Pub.
Levine, Ruth R., et al. Pharmacology: Drug Actions & Reactions. 5th ed. LC 96-29172. (Illus.). 586p. 1996. pap. text 44.95 (*1-85070-780-4*) Prthnon Pub.
Levine, S., ed. Flight Vehicle Materials, Structures, & Dynamics Vol. 3: Ceramics & Ceramic Matrix Composites. 1992. 105.00 (*0-685-70654-0*, 100322) ASME.
Levine, S. B. Sexual Life: A Clinician's Guide. (Critical Issues in Psychiatry Ser.). (Illus.). 250p. (C). 1992. 54.00 (*0-306-44287-6*, Plenum Trade) Perseus Pubng.
Levine, S. J., tr. see Infante, G. Cabrera.
Levine, S. N. Selected Papers on Desalination & Ocean Technology. (Illus.). 1990. 15.50 (*0-8446-2459-4*) Peter Smith.
Levine, Sally S. Oh Yes, I Still Will Write My Poem. Edelman, Ann B., ed. 57p. (Orig.). 1993. pap. 10.00 (*0-9637922-2-9*) Cherry Stne Bks.
Levine, Samuel. You Take Jesus, I'll Take God. LC 80-82731. 134p. (Orig.). 1980. pap. 6.95 (*0-9604754-1-9*) Hamoroh Pr.
Levine, Samuel P. Ham, Kosher Style! LC 79-89747. 1979. 9.95 (*0-9602906-1-3*); pap. 5.95 (*0-9602906-0-5*) S P Levine.
Levine, Sanford. 247 Best Movie Scenes in Film History: A Filmgoer's Guide to Cigar Scenes, Car Chase Scenes, Haircut Scenes, Whistling Scenes, Dentist Scenes, Fluttering Drapes, Funny Walks, Mirrors, Name Mispronunciations, Parking Meters, Sagging Shoulders, Steambaths, & Numerous Other Scenes Long Noted . . LC 91-50953. (Illus.). 192p. 1992. lib. bdg. 29.95 (*0-89950-671-2*) McFarland & Co.
Levine, Sarah. Mothers & Wives: Gusii Women of East Africa. LC 78-21573. 391p. reprint ed. pap. 121.30 (*0-608-09464-1*, 205426400005) Bks Demand.
Levine, Sarah & Correa, Clara S. Dolor y Alegria: Women & Social Change in Urban Mexico. LC 92-39037. (Life Course Studies). (Illus.). 254p. (Orig.). 1993. 39.95 (*0-299-13790-2*); pap. 19.95 (*0-299-13794-5*) U of Wis Pr.
LeVine, Sarah, et al. Mothers & Wives: Gusii Women of East Africa. LC 78-21573. 1994. lib. bdg. 26.00 (*0-226-47548-4*) U Ch Pr.
Levine, Sarah L. Promoting Adult Growth in Schools: The Promise of Professional Development. 342p. (Orig.). (C). 1995. pap. 19.50 (*0-9636513-2-3*) Assn Ind Sch.
Levine, Sarah L., ed. A Passion for Teaching. LC 99-6340. (Illus.). 209p. 1999. pap. 23.95 (*0-87120-354-5*, 199224) ASCD.
Levine, Saul V. Radical Departures: Desperate Detours to Growing Up. LC 83-26491. 216p. 1986. pap. 4.95 (*0-15-675799-0*, Harvest Bks) Harcourt.
Levine, Seymour & Ursin, Holger, eds. Coping & Health. LC 79-28833. (NATO Conference Series III, Human Factors: Vol. 12). 372p. 1980. 85.00 (*0-306-40422-2*, Plenum Trade) Perseus Pubng.
Levine, Shar. Fun with Your Microscope. 1999. pap. text 10.95 (*0-8069-9946-2*) Sterling.
— Marbles. LC 98-26083. (Illus.). 96p. 1998. 17.95 (*0-8069-4262-2*) Sterling.
***Levine, Shar.** Marbles: A Player's Guide. (J). 1999. pap. text 9.95 (*0-8069-6257-7*) Sterling.
— The Optics Book: Fun Experiments with Light, Vision & Color. (J). 1999. pap. text 9.95 (*0-8069-9942-X*) Sterling.
Levine, Shar. The Paper Book & Paper Maker. LC 92-72021. (Illus.). 32p. (J). (gr. k-5). 1993. pap. 12.95 (*1-56282-235-7*, Pub. by Hyprn Child) Time Warner.
— Shocking Science: Fun & Fascinating Electrical Experiments. LC 99-43501. 1999. 19.95 (*0-8069-3946-X*) Sterling.
— Wormworld Book & Tank. (Illus.). 64p. (J). (gr. 1-7). 1998. pap. 14.95 (*1-895897-84-X*) Somerville Hse.
***Levine, Shar & Bowden, Robert.** Awesome Yo-Yo Tricks. LC 99-51642. (Illus.). (J). 2000. 9.95 (*0-8069-4468-4*) Sterling.
Levine, Shar & Grafton, Allison. Einstein's Party Book: Simple Instructions for Spy Parties, Bubble Parties, & Much, Much More. 112p. 1994. pap. 12.95 (*0-471-59646-9*) Wiley.
— Projects for a Healthy Planet: Simple Environmental Experiments for Kids. LC 91-42406. (Illus.). 96p. (J). 1992. pap. 10.95 (*0-471-55484-7*) Wiley.
Levine, Shar & Johnstone, Leslie. Everyday Science: Fun & Easy Projects for Making Practical Things. LC 94-24700. 101p. (J). 1995. pap. 9.95 (*0-471-11014-0*) Wiley.
— The Magnet Book. LC 97-13987. (Illus.). 80p. (J). 1997. 19.95 (*0-8069-9943-8*) Sterling.
— The Microscope Book. LC 95-43239. (Illus.). 80p. (J). (gr. 5). 1996. 19.95 (*0-8069-4898-1*) Sterling.
— The Microscope Book. (Illus.). 80p. 1997. pap. 9.95 (*0-8069-4899-X*) Sterling.
— Science Around the World: Travel Through Time & Space with Fun Experiments & Projects. LC 95-44029. (Illus.). 96p. (J). (gr. 3-6). 1996. pap. 10.95 (*0-471-11916-4*) Wiley.
— Silly Science: Strange & Startling Projects to Amaze Your Family & Friends. LC 94-24698. 95p. (J). 1995. pap. 9.95 (*0-471-11013-2*) Wiley.
Levine, Shar & Scudamore, Vicki. Chocolate Lover's Cookbook. LC 96-46686. (Illus.). 96p. 1997. 10.95 (*0-8069-4825-6*) Sterling.
***Levine, Shar, et al.** The Paper Book & Paper Maker: With Plastic Paper Maker. (Illus.). 56p. (J). (gr. 1-5). 1998. pap. 12.95 (*0-921051-75-1*) Somerville Hse.
— Quick-but-Great Science Fair Projects. LC 99-87162. (Illus.). (J). 2000. 19.95 (*0-8069-5939-8*) Sterling Pub.
— 3-D Bees & Micro Fleas. (Micro-Stereo Ser.: No. 2). (Illus.). 48p. (J). (gr. 3 up). 1998. pap. 10.95 (*1-894042-18-2*) Somerville Hse.
— 3-D Bees & Micro Fleas. (Eye to Eye Series). (Illus.). 48p. (J). (gr. 3-7). 1999. pap. 9.99 (*1-58184-061-6*) Somerville Hse.
Levine, Shar, et al. 3-D Lungs & Micro Tongues. (Micro-Stereo Ser.: No. 1). (Illus.). 48p. (J). (gr. 3 up). 1998. pap. 10.95 (*1-894042-16-6*) Somerville Hse.
***Levine, Shar, et al.** 3-D Lungs & Micro Tongues. (Eye to Eye Series). (Illus.). 48p. (J). (gr. 3-7). 1999. pap. 9.99 (*1-58184-060-8*) Somerville Hse.
Levine, Sharon. Microscope II. LC 97-27609. (Illus.). 80p. (J). 1998. 19.95 (*0-8069-9945-4*) Sterling.
Levine, Sharon, et al. The Optics Book: Fun Experiments with Light, Vision & Color. LC 98-26732. (Illus.). 80p. (J). (gr. 4-7). 1998. 19.95 (*0-8069-9947-0*) Sterling.
***Levine, Sheldon.** Hello, Baby Good-bye, Baby Fat. (Illus.). 288p. 2000. reprint ed. pap. 13.00 (*0-688-17578-3*, Wm Morrow) Morrow Avon.
Levine, Sheldon. Hello, Baby! Good-Bye, Baby Fat! LC 98-47154. (Illus.). 288p. 1999. 23.00 (*0-688-15750-5*, Wm Morrow) Morrow Avon.
— The Redux Revolution: Everything You Need to Know about the Most Important Weight Loss Discovery of the Century. LC 96-26000. 192p. 1996. 20.00 (*0-688-15153-1*, Wm Morrow) Morrow Avon.
Levine, Shirley S. The Reading Workout. (Illus.). (Orig.). 1995. pap. 10.00 (*0-9648436-0-9*) Readsmart.
Levine, Shlomo D. The Singular Problems of the Single Jewish Parent. 39p. (Orig.). 1981. pap. text 1.25 (*0-8381-2115-2*) United Synagogue.
Levine, Sidney R. Math Verses with Twists, Vol. I. 30p. 1989. pap. write for info. (*0-88092-008-4*, Kav Bks) Royal Fireworks.
Levine, Sol & Lilienfeld, Abraham M. Epidemiology & Health Policy. (Contemporary Issues in Health, Medicine & Social Policy Ser.). 290p. 1987. text 37.50 (*0-422-78000-6*, Pub. by Tavistock) Routldge.
Levine, Sol, jt. auth. see Croog, Sydney.
Levine, Stacey. Dra. (New American Fiction Ser.: No. 39). 170p. 1997. pap. 11.95 (*1-55713-288-7*) Sun & Moon CA.
— My Horse & Other Stories. (New American Fiction Ser.: No. 28). 150p. (Orig.). 1990. pap. 11.95 (*1-55713-124-4*) Sun & Moon CA.
***Levine, Steffanie, told to.** Mrs. Potato Head Goes Shopping. 1999. 6.99 (*0-525-46234-1*, Playskool) Peng Put Young Read.
Levine, Stephen. A Gradual Awakening. 2nd ed. 192p. 1989. pap. 10.95 (*0-385-26218-3*, Anchor NY) Doubleday.
— Guided Meditations, Explorations & Healing. 352p. 1991. pap. 12.95 (*0-385-41737-3*, Anchor NY) Doubleday.
— Healing into Life & Death. 264p. Date not set. 9.95 (*0-614-97097-0*, Anchor NY) Doubleday.
— Healing into Life & Death. 312p. 1989. pap. 12.95 (*0-385-26219-1*, Anchor NY) Doubleday.
— Meetings at the Edge: Dialogues with the Grieving & the Dying, the Healing & the Healed. 264p. 1989. pap. 11.95 (*0-385-26220-5*, Anchor NY) Doubleday.
— The New Zealand Jewish Community. LC 98-52719. 384p. 1999. 65.00 (*0-7391-0003-3*) Lxngtn Bks.
— Who Dies? An Ivestigation of Conscious Living & Conscious Dying. 336p. 1989. pap. 12.95 (*0-385-26221-3*, Anchor NY) Doubleday.
— A Year to Live: How to Live This Year As If It Were Your Last. 192p. 1998. pap. 10.00 (*0-609-80194-5*) Bell T.
— A Year to Live: How to Live This Year As If It Were Your Last. large type ed. LC 97-41489. 240p. 1997. 24.95 (*0-7838-8326-9*, G K Hall Lrg Type) Mac Lib Ref.
Levine, Stephen, ed. Israeli Elections of 1988. (WVSS on the Middle East Ser.). (C). 1996. pap. text 22.50 (*0-8133-7377-8*) Westview.
Levine, Stephen & Levine, Ondrea. Embracing the Beloved: Relationship as a Path of Awakening. 320p. 1996. pap. 12.95 (*0-385-42527-9*, Anchor NY) Doubleday.
Levine, Stephen & Newcombe, Barbara. Paper Trails: A Guide to Public Records in California. 2nd ed. 244p. (C). 1996. pap. 18.95 (*0-9621793-2-9*) CA News Pubs Assn.
Levine, Stephen, jt. auth. see Dass, Ram.
Levine, Stephen, jt. auth. see Levine, Ondrea.
***Levine, Stephen B.** Sexuality in Mid-Life. LC 98-10284. (Illus.). 172p. (C). 1998. text 35.00 (*0-306-45742-3*, Kluwer Plenum) Kluwer Academic.
Levine, Stephen B. Solving Common Sexual Problems: Toward a Problem-Free Sexual Life. LC 97-28092. 296p. 1997. pap. 30.00 (*0-7657-0121-9*) Aronson.
Levine, Stephen B., jt. ed. see Pariser, Stephen F.
Levine, Stephen K. Poiesis: The Language of Psychology & the Speech of the Soul. LC 97-200969. 141p. 1997. pap. 24.95 (*1-85302-488-0*, Pub. by Jessica Kingsley) Taylor & Francis.
Levine, Stephen R. Planning for Strikes: Obtaining Maximum Performance with Minimum Personnel. 54p. 1975. pap. 25.00 (*0-941496-00-7*) Model Cities.
Levine, Steve. The Cycles of Heaven. (Morning Coffee Chapbook Ser.). (Illus.). 11p. (Orig.). 1988. pap. 15.00 (*0-918273-38-2*) Coffee Hse.
— To & For. LC 92-3245. 72p. 1992. pap. 10.95 (*0-918273-71-4*) Coffee Hse.
Levine, Steve, ed. see Scholnick, Michael.
Levine, Steven I., jt. ed. see Hsiung, James C.
Levine, Steven I., tr. see Vishnyakova-Akimova, Vera V.
Levine, Steven P., jt. ed. see Martin, William F.
***Levine, Steven R. & Brey, Robin L.** Clinical Approach to Antiphospholipid Antibodies. (Illus.). 168p. 2000. text 59.95 (*0-7506-7177-7*) Buttrwrth-Heinemann.
Levine, Steven Z. Monet, Narcissus, & Self-Reflection: The Modernist Myth of the Self. LC 94-1105. 388p. 1994. pap. text 29.95 (*0-226-47544-1*); lib. bdg. 70.00 (*0-226-47543-3*) U Ch Pr.
Levine, Stewart. Getting to Resolution: Turning Conflict into Collaboration. LC 97-47473. 200p. 1998. 19.95 (*1-57675-005-1*) Berrett-Koehler.
***Levine, Stewart.** Getting to Resolution: Turning Conflict into Collaboration. 200p. 2000. reprint ed. pap. 16.95 (*1-57675-115-5*, Pub. by Berrett-Koehler) Publishers Group.
Levine, Stuart. The Monday-Wednesday-Friday Girl & Other Stories. 238p. 1994. pap. 10.00 (*0-939391-20-1*) B Woodley Pr.
Levine, Stuart, ed. see Poe, Edgar Allan.
***Levine, Stuart P.** Dr. Seuss. LC 00-9242. (Importance of Ser.). 2001. write for info. (*1-56006-748-9*) Lucent Bks.
Levine, Stuart P. The Elephant. LC 97-28532. (Overview Ser.). (Illus.). (YA). (gr. 4-12). 1997. lib. bdg. 22.45 (*1-56006-522-2*) Lucent Bks.
***Levine, Stuart P.** The Orangutan. LC 99-37697. (Overview Ser.). (Illus.). 128p. (YA). (gr. 6-9). 2000. lib. bdg. 23.70 (*1-56006-560-5*) Lucent Bks.
— The Tiger. LC 98-27237. (Overview Ser.). (Illus.). 128p. (YA). (gr. 4-12). 1998. lib. bdg. 23.70 (*1-56006-465-X*) Lucent Bks.
Levine, Sumner N. Global Investing: A Handbook for Sophisticated Investors. LC 91-58499. 512p. 1992. 50.00 (*0-88730-498-2*, HarpBusn) HarpInfo.
— Investing in Bankruptcies & Turnarounds: Spotting Investment Values in Distressed Businesses. 1008p. 1991. 69.95 (*0-88730-459-1*, HarpBusn) HarpInfo.
Levine, Sumner N., ed. The Acquisitions Manual: A Guide to Negotiating & Evaluating Business Acquisitions. 1989. 64.95 (*0-317-03936-9*) NY Inst Finance.
Levine, Sumner N. & Levine, Caroline. The Irwin Business & Investment Almanac, 1994: Dow Jones & Company Edition. 18th ed. 864p. 1994. per. 75.00 (*1-55623-927-0*, Irwn Prfssnl) McGraw-Hill Prof.
Levine, Sura & Landes, Joan. Representing Revolution: French & British Images, 1789-1804. (Illus.). 56p. 1989. pap. 12.00 (*0-914337-13-0*) Mead Art Mus.
Levine, Susan. Degrees of Equality: The American Association of University Women & The Challenge of Twentieth Century Feminism. LC 94-44693. (Critical Perspectives on the Past Ser.). 1995. 44.95 (*1-56639-326-4*) Temple U Pr.
— Useful Servants: Psychodynamic Theories from a Clinical Perspective. 320p. 1996. 40.00 (*1-56821-844-3*) Aronson.
Levine, Susan, ed. see Poe, Edgar Allan.
Levine, Susan P., et al. Recreation Experiences for the Severely Impaired or Nonambulatory Child. (Illus.). 96p. 1983. spiral bd. 20.95 (*0-398-04783-9*) C C Thomas.
***Levine, Suzanne.** Your Feet Dont Have to Hurt. LC 00-24609. (Illus.). 304p. 2000. text 24.95 (*0-312-26276-0*) St Martin.
Levine, Suzanne, ed. Return to Life/Volver a Vivir. LC 96-83386. (Illus.). 56p. (Orig.). 1996. pap. 16.00 (*0-9620222-6-8*) Chardon Pr.
Levine, Suzanne Braun. Father Courage: What Happens When Men Put Family First. 288p. 2000. 24.00 (*0-15-100382-3*) Harcourt.
***Levine, Suzanne J.** Manuel Puig & the Spider Woman. LC 99-39130. (Illus.). 426p. 2000. text 27.50 (*0-374-28190-4*) FS&G.
Levine, Suzanne J. Subversive Scribe: Translating Latin American Fiction. 224p. 1991. pap. 12.00 (*1-55597-146-6*) Graywolf.
Levine, Suzanne J., tr. see Bioy Casares, Adolfo.
Levine, Suzanne J., tr. see Puig, Manuel.
Levine, Suzanne J., tr. see Rios, Julian.
Levine, Suzanne J., tr. see Sarduy, Severo.
Levine, Suzanne Jill, tr. see Donoso, Jose.
Levine, Suzanne S. The Child Development Program: Preventing & Remediating Learning Problems. LC 96-28755. (Education Ser.). (Illus.). 582p. 1996. pap. 95.00 (*0-89503-146-9*) Baywood Pub.
Levine, Suzanne Sosna. Developing Learning Readiness: A Visual-motor-tactile Skills Program : Teacher's Manual. LC 97-141212. (Illus.). 1997. write for info. (*0-89503-145-0*) Baywood Pub.
Levine, Sy. Discrete Semiconductors & Opto-Electronics. 2nd ed. Levine, Esther & Worthing, Jerry, eds. (A Library on Basic Electronics: Vol. 2). (Illus.). 356p. Date not set. text 35.00 (*0-939527-06-5*) Electro Horiz.
— Integrated Circuits & Computer Concepts. Levine, Esther & Worthing, Jerry, eds. (Library on Basic Electronics: Vol. 3). (Illus.). 320p. 1989. text 35.00 (*0-939527-02-2*) Electro Horiz.
Levine, Sy, et al. Basic Concepts & Passive Components. 3rd ed. Levine, Esther & Worthing, Jerry, eds. LC 85-71203. (Library on Basic Electronics: Vol. 1). (Illus.). 305p. Date not set. text 35.00 (*0-939527-05-7*) Electro Horiz.
Levine, Theodore A. & Pitt, Harvey L. Securities & Litigation. (Illus.). iv, 714p. write for info. (*0-318-57842-5*) Harcourt.
Levine, Theodore A., jt. auth. see Fedders, John M.
Levine, Toby K., et al. The Africans: Study Guide. LC 85-28166. 1986. pap. 13.95 (*0-275-92074-7*, B2074, Praeger Pubs) Greenwood.
***Levine, Toby Kleban.** The Healthy Steps Interactive Multimedia Training & Resource Kit User Manual. McDonald, Kelley & Welsh, Joan Seidman, eds. (Illus.). 48p. 2000. pap. write for info. (*1-930783-11-6*) Independ Prod.
— The Healthy Steps Multimedia Training & Resource Kit, 9 cass. McDonald, Kelley et al, eds. (Illus.). 48p. 2000. pap., student ed., boxed set 350.00 incl. VHS (*1-930783-00-0*) Independ Prod.
Levine, Tom. Tom Levine: Paintings & Drawings. (Illus.). 80p. 1999. pap. 35.00 (*3-89322-339-8*) Dr Cantz sche Druckerei GmbH.
Levine, Valerie J., jt. auth. see Levine, Andrew S.
Levine, Victor, jt. auth. see Allen, David N.
Levine, Victor T. & Luke, Timothy W. The Arab-African Connection: Political & Economic Realities. (Special Studies on Africa & the Middle East). 1979. text 35.50 (*0-89158-398-X*) Westview.
Levine, Victoria L. Music in the Ruben Cobos Collection of Spanish New Mexican Folklore: A Descriptive Catalogue. Chace, Amanda, ed. (ENG & SPA.). 200p. 1998. pap. 25.00 (*0-935052-30-5*) Colorado College.
Levine, Victoria L., jt. auth. see Howard, James H.
***Levine, W. S.** Control System Applications. LC 99-48035. 360p. 1999. boxed set 69.95 (*0-8493-0054-1*) CRC Pr.
— Control System Fundamentals. LC 99-48036. 466p. 1999. boxed set 89.95 (*0-8493-0053-3*) CRC Pr.
Levine, W. S., et al, eds. Issues in Control of Urban Traffic Systems. LC 81-71830. 268p. 1982. pap. 50.00 (*0-939204-07-X*) Eng Found.
Levine, William S., ed. Control Engineering. Date not set. write for info. (*0-614-30186-6*) Spr-Verlag.
— The Control Handbook. LC 95-25551. (Electrical Engineering Handbook Ser.). 1568p. 1996. boxed set 159.95 (*0-8493-8570-9*, 8570) CRC Pr.
***Levine-Young.** Wordperfect for Linux for Dummies. (For Dummies Ser.). 408p. 1999. pap. 24.99 incl. cd-rom (*0-7645-0657-9*) IDG Bks.
Levine-Young, Margaret. Dummies 101: The Internet for Windows 98. 2nd ed. 288p. 1998. pap. 24.99 incl. cd-rom (*0-7645-0207-7*) IDG Bks.
— Internet FAQs. 448p. 1995. pap. 19.99 (*1-56884-476-X*) IDG Bks.

L

L

— WordPerfect 8 for Windows for Dummies. LC 97-72404. (For Dummies Ser.). (Illus.). 432p. 1997. pap. 19.99 (*0-7645-0186-0*) IDG Bks.

Leviner, Betty C., jt. auth. see Gilliam, Jan K.

Leving, Jeffery M. & Dachman, Kenneth A. Father's Rights. 224p. 1998. pap. 14.00 (*0-465-02362-2*, Pub. by Basic) HarpC.

Levinger, Beryl. Achieving Education for All: Nutrition, Health & School Performance. 72p. 1993. pap. text. write for info. (*0-9637044-3-5*) PACT Pubns.

— Critical Transitions: Human Capacity Development Across the Lifespan. 155p. (Orig.). (C). 1996. pap. text. write for info. (*0-89292-282-6*) Educ Dev Ctr.

— La Nutricion, la Salud y la Educacion para Todos. Vanderschoot, Fauvette, tr. (C). 1993. pap. write for info. (*0-9637044-4-3*) PACT Pubns.

Levinger, Beryl & National Council for International Health (U.S.) S. Capacity, Capital, & Calories. LC 96-45936. (Martin J. Forman Memorial Lectures). 1996. write for info. (*0-915173-04-2*) Helen Keller Intl.

Levinger, Carl & Schefres, Itzchack. Everything You Need to Get a Psychology Internship. 2nd rev. ed. LC 96-90348. 153p. 1996. pap. 24.95 (*0-9648043-1-X*) Windmill Lane Pr.

Levinger, George & Raush, Harold L., eds. Close Relationships: Perspectives on the Meaning of Intimacy. LC 77-900. (Illus.). 208p. 1977. 30.00 (*0-87023-238-X*) U of Mass Pr.

Levinger, Jasna, tr. see Selimovic, Mesa.

***Levinger, Matthew.** Enlightened Nationalism: The Transformation of Prussian Political Culture, 1806-1848. LC 99-32583. (Illus.). 304p. 2000. text 49.95 (*0-19-513185-1*) OUP.

Levinger, Michael. How to Select, Implement, & Use Support Technologies. Bultema, Patrick et al, eds. (Illus.). 178p. (Orig.). pap. write for info. (*1-57125-014-X*) Help Desk Inst.

Levings, Charles S., III & Vasil, Indra K., eds. The Molecular Biology of Plant Mitochondria. (Advances in Cellular & Molecular Biology of Plants: Vol. 3). 676p. (C). 1995. text 368.00 (*0-7923-3224-5*) Kluwer Academic.

Levingston, Steven, jt. auth. see Seto, Matt.

Levinkind, Susan, jt. auth. see Elias, Stephen.

Levinon, Sanford, ed. Responding to Imperfection: The Theory & Practice of Constitutional Amendment. LC 94-27766. 352p. 1995. text 59.50 (*0-691-08657-5*, Pub. by Princeton U Pr); pap. text 20.95 (*0-691-02570-3*, Pub. by Princeton U Pr) Cal Prin Full Svc.

Levins. Quick & Fun Learning Activities for 2 Years Old. (Illus.). 80p. 1996. pap. 8.95 (*1-55734-555-4*) Tchr Create Mat.

Levins, Hoag. American Sex Machines: The Hidden History of Sex at the U. S. Patent Office. (Illus.). 256p. (Orig.). 1996. pap. text 9.95 (*1-55850-534-2*) Adams Media.

Levins, Richard. Evolution in Changing Environments: Some Theoretical Explorations. LC 68-20871. (Monographs in Population Biology: No. 2). (Illus.). 130p. reprint ed. pap. 40.30 (*0-7837-0558-1*, 204090200019) Bks Demand.

— Willard Cochrane & the American Family Farm. (Our Sustainable Future Ser.). (Illus.). 128p. 2000. text 30.00 (*0-8032-2935-6*) U of Nebr Pr.

Levins, Richard & Lewontin, Richard C. The Dialectical Biologist. LC 84-22451. (Illus.). 336p. 1985. pap. 22.95 (*0-674-20283-X*) HUP.

Levins, Richard, jt. auth. see Haila, Yrjo.

Levins, Richard, jt. auth. see Puccia, Charles J.

Levinshtein, M. A Best of Soviet Semiconductor Physics & Technology (1989-1990) 900p. 1995. text 109.00 (*981-02-1579-7*) World Scientific Pub.

Levinshtein, M., et al. Getting to Know Semiconductors. 200p. (C). 1992. text 36.00 (*981-02-0760-3*) World Scientific Pub.

— Handbook Series on Semiconductor Parameters, Vol. 1. 300p. 1997. text 99.00 (*981-02-1420-0*) World Scientific Pub.

***Levinshtein, Mikhail.** Properties of Advanced Semiconductor Materials: G An, Aln, Inn, Bn, Sic, Sige. 165p. 2001. 74.95 (*0-471-35827-4*) Wiley.

Levinshtein, Mikhail, ed. Best of Soviet Semiconductor Physics & Technology, 1987-1988. 360p. 1991. 119.95 (*0-88318-782-5*); pap. 59.95 (*0-88318-783-3*) Spr-Verlag.

Levinshtein, Mikhail & Schur, Michael. Semiconductor Technology: Processing & Novel Fabrication Techniques. LC 97-1734. 264p. 1997. 89.95 (*0-471-12792-2*) Wiley.

Levinskaja. Russian-Polish Dictionary. (POL & RUS.). 320p. 1981. 14.95 (*0-8288-0488-5*, F 47670) Fr & Eur.

Levinskaya, Irina. The Book of Acts in Its Diaspora Setting, Vol. 5. LC 96-46659. 1996. 38.00 (*0-8028-2437-4*) Eerdmans.

Levinskaya, Victoria, jt. auth. see Shermukhamedov, Said.

Levinsky, Norman, jt. auth. see Wilkins, Richard.

Levinsky, Norman G., ed. see Institute of Medicine, Committee for the Study of.

Levinsky, Ruth. Nathalie Sarraute & Fedor Dostoevsky: Their Philosophy, Psychology, & Literary Techniques. (Graduate Studies: No. 3). 44p. (Orig.). 1973. pap. 2.00 (*0-89672-010-1*) Tex Tech Univ Pr.

Levinsky, Sara A. & Steindl-Rast, David. A Bridge of Dreams: The Story of Paramananda, a Modern Mystic. LC 83-82698. (Illus.). 632p. (Orig.). 1984. pap. 12.95 (*0-940262-12-6*, Lindisfarne) Anthroposophic.

Levinsohn, Allan G., jt. auth. see Huxhold, William E.

Levinsohn, Florence H. Belgrade: Among the Serbs. 351p. 1994. text 27.50 (*1-56663-061-4*) I R Dee.

— Looking for Farrakhan. LC 97-11335. 320p. 1997. 25.00 (*1-56663-157-2*, Pub. by I R Dee) Natl Bk Netwk.

Levinsohn, Florence H. & Wright, Benjamin D. School Desegregation: Shadow & Substance. 1976. pap. 3.95 (*0-226-47577-8*) U Ch Pr.

Levinsohn, Florence H. & Wright, Benjamin D., eds. School Desegregation: Shadow & Substance. LC 76-17291. 224p. reprint ed. pap. 69.50 (*0-608-16603-0*, 202678100052) Bks Demand.

Levinsohn, Mark E., jt. auth. see Martire, Joseph R.

Levinsohn, Stephen, ed. Discourse Features of Ten Languages of West- Central Africa. LC 94-67160. (Publications in Linguistics). 256p. (Orig.). 1995. pap. 30.00 (*0-88312-619-2*) S I L Intl.

***Levinsohn, Stephen H.** Discourse Features of New Testament Greek: A Coursebook on the Information Structure of New Testament Greek. 2nd ed. 316p. 2000. pap. 32.00 (*1-55671-093-3*) S I L Intl.

Levinsohn, Stephen H. The Inga Language. (Janua Linguarum, Series Practica: No. 188). (Illus.). (Orig.). 1976. pap. text 44.65 (*90-279-3381-2*) Mouton.

Levinsohn, Sylvia. Jewish Puzzle Book. 1995. pap. 12.95 (*0-8246-0379-6*) Jonathan David.

Levinson. Designing & Managing Your Career. 391p. 1989. 39.95 (*0-07-103249-5*) McGraw.

— Encyclopedia of Marriage & the Family, 2 vols. Incl. Vol. 1. Encyclopedia of Marriage & the Family. 2nd ed. 1995. 110.00 (*0-02-897236-8*); Vol. 2. Encyclopedia of Marriage & the Family. 2nd ed. 1995. 110.00 (*0-02-897237-6*); 1995. 210.00 (*0-02-897235-X*) Macmillan.

— Mastering Hebrew. (Foreign Service Institute Language Ser.). (HEB & ENG.). 1988. pap. 16.95 (*0-8120-3990-4*) Barron.

***Levinson.** Say Cheese. (Illus.). 32p. (J). 2000. write for info. (*0-307-46110-6*) Gldn Bks Pub Co.

Levinson, contrib. by. Mastering Hebrew. (Foreign Service Institute Language Ser.). (HEB & ENG.). 1988. pap. 79.95 incl. audio (*0-8120-7478-5*) Barron.

Levinson & Droga, eds. Somatization: Bodily Experience & Mental States. (Psychoanalytic Inquiry Ser.: Vol. 17, No.2). 1997. pap. 20.00 (*0-88163-935-4*) Analytic Pr.

Levinson, A. A., ed. Apollo Eleven Lunar Science Conference, Jan., 1970: Proceedings, 3 vols. Incl. Vol. 1. Mineralogy & Petrology. LC 72-119485. 1970. Vol. 2. Chemical & Isotope Analysis. LC 72-119485. 1970. Vol. 3. Physical Properties. LC 72-119485. 1970. LC 72-119485. 1970. 1110.00 (*0-08-016392-0*, Pub. by Pergamon Repr) Franklin.

***Levinson, A. A. & Dyachkov, P. N.** Heteroligand Molecular Systems: Bonding, Shapes & Isomer Stabilities. 280p. 2000. text 90.00 (*90-5699-045-4*, G & B Science) Gordon & Breach.

Levinson, A. A., et al. Practical Problems in Exploration Geochemistry. LC 86-72694. (Illus.). 269p. 1987. 80.00 (*0-915834-05-7*) Applied Pub.

Levinson, A. A., jt. auth. see Lunar & Planetary Institute Staff.

Levinson, A. A., ed. see Beus, Alexei A. & Grigorian, S. V.

Levinson, Abraham. The Mentally Retarded Child. enl. rev. ed. LC 77-25884. (Illus.). 187p. 1978. reprint ed. lib. bdg. 48.50 (*0-313-20123-4*, LEMR, Greenwood Pr) Greenwood.

Levinson, Andre. Bakst: The Story of the Artist's Life. LC 68-57182. (Illus.). 1978. reprint ed. 36.95 (*0-405-08233-9*) Ayer.

Levinson, Arnold I. New Directions in the Clinical Use of Intravenous Immunoglobulin, Vol. II. (Illus.). 60p. 1990. write for info. (*0-318-65780-5*) Health Dimensions.

Levinson, Arnold I. & Paterson, Yvonne, eds. Molecular & Cellular Biology of the Allergic Response. LC 94-4449. (Clinical Allergy & Immunology Ser.: Vol. 3). (Illus.). 473p. 1994. text 185.00 (*0-8247-8876-1*) Dekker.

Levinson, Arthur T. The Web of Their Lives: Macbeth & Human Greatness. 120p. 1984. pap. 7.95 (*0-9613268-0-8*) Byrnam Pr.

Levinson, Barbara, tr. see Shapiro, Eugene.

Levinson, Barry. Avalon, Tin Men, & Diner: Three Screenplays. LC 90-41929. 400p. 1990. pap. 12.95 (*0-87113-435-7*, Atlntc Mnthly) Grove-Atltic.

Levinson, Bernard M. Deuteronomy & the Hermeneutics of Legal Innovation. LC 96-47389. 224p. 1997. text 39.95 (*0-19-511280-6*) OUP.

— Theory & Method in Biblical & Cuneiform Law: Revision, Interpolation & Development. LC 94-234263. (Journal for the Study of the Old Testament Supplement Ser.: Vol. 181). 200p. 1996. 57.50 (*1-85075-498-5*, Pub. by Sheffield Acad) CUP Services.

Levinson, Betty, contrib. by. Handling the Domestic Violence Case. LC 99-159951. (Tax Law & Estate Plannig Ser.). 416p. 1998. 129.00 (*0-87224-526-8*) PLI.

Levinson Bks Staff. Stack-A-Boat. 1999. 12.95 (*1-899607-56-0*) Levinson Bks.

— Stack-A-Car. 1999. 12.95 (*1-899607-92-7*) Levinson Bks.

— Stack-A-Plane. 1999. 12.95 (*1-899607-91-9*) Levinson Bks.

Levinson, Boris M. & Mallon, Gerald P. Pet-Oriented Child Psychotherapy. 2nd ed. LC 96-8968. 242p. 1996. text 48.95 (*0-398-06673-6*); pap. text 33.95 (*0-398-06674-4*) C C Thomas.

Levinson, Bradley, jt. ed. see Sutton, Margaret A.

Levinson, Bradley A., et al, eds. The Cultural Production of the Educated Person: Critical Ethnographies of Schooling & Local Practice. LC 95-8931. (SUNY Series, Power, Social Identity, & Education). 338p. (C). 1996. pap. text 24.95 (*0-7914-2860-5*) State U NY Pr.

***Levinson, Bradley A.U., et al, eds.** Schooling the Symbolic Animal: Social & Cultural Dimensions of Education. 416p. 2000. 71.00 (*0-7425-0119-1*); pap. 25.95 (*0-7425-0120-5*) Rowman.

Levinson, Brett. Secondary Moderns: Mimesis, History, & Revolution in Lezama Lima's "American Expression" LC 95-50475. 208p. (C). 1996. 33.50 (*0-8387-5300-0*) Bucknell U Pr.

Levinson, Bruce S., jt. auth. see Modesitt, L. E., Jr.

Levinson, Charles. Food & Beverage Operations: Cost Control Systems Management. 2nd ed. LC 88-9683. 336p. 1988. 115.00 (*0-13-322819-3*) P-H.

— Industry's Democratic Revolution. 350p. 1974. pap. 25.00 (*0-8464-1322-1*) Beekman Pubs.

Levinson, Christopher, ed. see Shields, Carol.

Levinson, Daniel. Seasons of Womans Life. 464p. 1997. pap. 15.00 (*0-345-31174-4*, Ballantine) Ballantine Pub Grp.

Levinson, Daniel J. The Seasons of a Woman's Life. 448p. 1996. 27.50 (*0-394-53235-X*) Random.

Levinson, Daniel J. & Levinson, Judy D. The Seasons of a Woman's Life. LC 95-20893. 438p. 1996. 27.50 (*0-614-09477-1*) Knopf.

Levinson, Daniel J., et al. The Seasons of a Man's Life. 1986. pap. 14.00 (*0-345-33901-0*) Ballantine Pub Grp.

Levinson, David. Aggression & Conflict: A Cross-Cultural Encyclopedia. (Human Experience Ser.). 234p. 1994. lib. bdg. 49.50 (*0-87436-728-X*) ABC-CLIO.

— The Encyclopedia of World Cultures Vol. 10: Cumulated Indexes, Bibliographies & Maps. 1995. 110.00 (*0-8161-1817-5*, G K Hall & Co) Mac Lib Ref.

***Levinson, David.** Encyclopedia of World Sport: From Ancient Times to the Present. 512p. 1999. 45.00 (*0-19-513195-9*) OUP.

Levinson, David. Ethnic Relations: A Cross-Cultural Encyclopedia. LC 94-40253. (Human Experience Ser.). 293p. 1995. lib. bdg. 55.00 (*0-87436-735-2*) ABC-CLIO.

— Family Violence in Cross-Cultural Perspectives. (Frontiers of Anthropology Ser.: Vol. 1). 200p. (C). 1989. text 52.00 (*0-8039-3075-5*); pap. text 25.00 (*0-8039-3076-3*) Sage.

— Human Environments: A Cross-Cultural Encyclopedia. LC 95-39798. (Human Experience Ser.). 284p. (YA). (gr. 10 up). 1995. lib. bdg. 65.00 (*0-87436-784-0*) ABC-CLIO.

— Religion: A Cross-Cultural Dictionary. (Oxford Paperback Reference Ser.). (Illus.). 312p. 1998. reprint ed. pap. 17.95 (*0-19-512311-5*) OUP.

— Religion: A Cross-Cultural Encyclopedia. LC 96-45172. (Encyclopedia of Human Experiences Ser.). 352p. 1996. lib. bdg. 49.50 (*0-87436-865-0*) ABC-CLIO.

Levinson, David, ed. The Encyclopedia of World Cultures: Sponsored by the Human Relations Area Files at Yale University, 10 vols. (Illus.). 6500p. 1994. 800.00 (*0-685-40448-X*, Hall Reference) Macmillan.

— The Encyclopedia of World Cultures: Sponsored by the Human Relations Area Files at Yale University, 10 vols., Set. (Illus.). 6500p. 1996. 1200.00 (*0-8161-1840-X*, Hall Reference) Macmillan.

— A Guide to Alcoholism Treatment Research. Incl. Vol. I Behavioral Medicine - Behavior Modification. 525p. (Orig.). 1981. pap. 45.00 (*0-87536-736-4*); Vol. III. Alcoholics Anonymous & Counseling. 553p. (Orig.). 1984. pap. 45.00 (*0-87536-740-2*); (Theoretical Information Control Guides Ser.). write for info. (*0-318-57544-2*) HRAFP.

— A Guide to Alcoholism Treatment Research, Vol. 2. LC 82-105273. (HRAF Theoretical Information Control System Ser.: No. 4). 494p. reprint ed. pap. 153.20 (*0-608-16290-6*, 202717200002) Bks Demand.

— A Guide to Social Theory: Worldwide Cross-Cultural Tests, 5 vols. 1700p. 1978. 495.00 (*0-317-34231-2*) HRAFP.

***Levinson, David, ed. The Wilson Chronology of the World's Religions. LC 99-52362. (Wilson Chronologies Series). 500p. 1999. 80.00 (0-8242-0978-8) Wilson.**

The Wilson Chronology Of the World's Religions. This volume provides a fascinating timeline & narrative for a broad range of religions, including information about leaders, beliefs, influence over time & more. In addition to thousands of insightful entries, the chronology includes nearly 200 sidebars that shed light on the histories of the various religious movements & events. To order: H.W. Wilson - 1-800-367-6770 (1-718-588-8400 outside U.S. & Canada); custserv@hwwilson.com , or visit www.hwwilson.com. *Publisher Paid Annotation.*

Levinson, David, et al, eds. Encyclopedia of Human Emotions, 2 vols. LC 99-31198. 768p. 1999. 200.00 (*0-02-864766-1*) S&S Trade.

Levinson, David & Christensen, Karen. The Global Village Companion: An A-to-Z Guide to Current World Affairs. LC 96-38457. 438p. 1996. lib. bdg. 65.00 (*0-87436-829-4*) ABC-CLIO.

Levinson, David & Christensen, Karen, eds. Dictionary of World Sport: From Ancient Times to the Present. LC 98-27052. 512p. 1999. pap. 19.95 (*0-19-512778-1*) OUP.

— Encyclopedia of World Sport: From Ancient Times to the Present. write for info. (*0-614-26612-2*) ABC-CLIO.

— Encyclopedia of World Sport: From Ancient Times to the Present, 3 vols. LC 96-45437. 1317p. 1997. lib. bdg. 275.00 (*0-87436-819-7*) ABC-CLIO.

***Levinson, David & Christensen, Karen, eds.** Famous First Facts about Human Rights. 900p. 2000. 85.00 (*0-8242-0972-9*) Wilson.

Levinson, David & Ember, Melvin, eds. Encyclopedia of Cultural Anthropology: Sponsored by the Human Relations Area Files, 4 vols., Set. LC 95-37237. (Illus.). 1700p. 1995. lib. bdg. 395.00 (*0-8050-2877-3*) H Holt & Co.

Levinson, David & Gaccione, Laura. Health & Illness: A Cross-Cultural Encyclopedia. LC 97-29638. (Human Experience Ser.). 253p. 1997. lib. bdg. 65.00 (*0-87436-876-6*) ABC-CLIO.

Levinson, David & Human Relations Area Files at Yale University & St, eds. The Encyclopedia of World Cultures Vol. 2: Oceania, Vol. 2. large type ed. 650p. 1991. 125.00 (*0-8161-1809-4*, Hall Reference) Macmillan.

Levinson, David & Malone, Martin J. Toward Explaining Human Culture: A Critical Review of the Findings of Worldwide Cross-Cultural Research. LC 80-83324. (Comparative Studies). 412p. 1980. 20.00 (*0-87536-339-3*) HRAFP.

Levinson, David & O'Leary, Timothy J., eds. The Encyclopedia of World Cultures Vol. 1: North America, Vol. 1. 2nd large type ed. 600p. 1991. 125.00 (*0-8161-1808-6*, Hall Reference) Macmillan.

Levinson, David & Ponzetti, James J., Jr. Encyclopedia of Human Emotions, Vol. 2. 1999. 130.00 (*0-02-864767-X*); 195.00 (*0-02-864768-8*) S&S Trade.

Levinson, David, ed. see Yale University Staff.

Levinson, David H. Ethnic Groups Worldwide: A Ready Reference Handbook. LC 98-13274. (Illus.). 448p. (YA). (gr. 5 up). 1998. boxed set 65.00 (*1-57356-019-7*) Oryx Pr.

Levinson, Debra. The Truth about Chiropractic. (Illus.). 1993. 39.95 (*0-9633577-0-0*) Max Pubns.

Levinson, Edward. I Break Strikes: The Technique of Pearl L. Bergoff. LC 75-89750. (American Labor, from Conspiracy to Collective Bargaining Series, No. 1). 314p. 1974. reprint ed. 21.95 (*0-405-02137-2*) Ayer.

— Labor on the March. (Literature of American Labor Ser.). 344p. 1995. pap. text 17.95 (*0-87546-340-1*, ILR Press) Cornell U Pr.

— Labor on the March. 329p. 1993. reprint ed. lib. bdg. 89.00 (*0-7812-5249-0*) Rprt Serv.

Levinson, Edward M. Transdisciplinary Vocational Assessment: Issues in School-based Programs. LC 92-53226. 1993. pap. 42.50 (*0-88422-118-0*) Clinical Psych.

— Transition: Facilitating the Post-School Adjustment of Individuals with Disabilities. 1998. pap. 17.95 (*0-8133-2516-1*, 846573Q) Westview.

— Transition: Planning for the Postschool Adjustment of Students with Disabilities. LC 97-47025. 200p. (C). 1998. text 69.00 (*0-8133-2515-3*, Pub. by Westview) HarpC.

Levinson, Ellis. Hiring Contractors Without Going Through Hell: How to Find, Hire, Supervise, & Pay Professional Help. 174p. (Orig.). 1992. 23.95 (*0-8027-1194-4*); pap. 14.95 (*0-8027-7381-8*) Walker & Co.

Levinson, Gerald B., jt. auth. see Laurenzi, Elise.

Levinson, Gershon, jt. auth. see Shnider, Sol M.

Levinson, Hanna, jt. auth. see Reif, Joseph A.

Levinson, Harold, jt. auth. see England, Arthur.

Levinson, Harold M. Collective Bargaining by British Local Authority Employees. LC 74-634398. (Comparative Studies in Public Employment Labor Relations Ser.). 1971. 10.00 (*0-87736-013-8*); pap. 5.00 (*0-87736-014-6*) U of Mich Inst Labor.

— Collective Bargaining by Public Employees in Sweden. LC 72-619516. (Comparative Studies in Public Employment Labor Relations Ser.). 120p. 1972. 10.00 (*0-87736-023-5*); pap. 5.00 (*0-87736-024-3*) U of Mich Inst Labor.

Levinson, Harold N. A Scientific Watergate - Dyslexia: How & Why Countless Millions Are Deprived of Breakthrough Medical Treatment. LC 93-87064. (Illus.). 455p. 1994. 24.95 (*0-9639303-0-3*) Stonebrdge Pubng.

— Smart but Feeling Dumb. LC 84-40090. 256p. 1988. mass mkt. 10.95 (*0-446-38841-6*, Pub. by Warner Bks) Little.

— Smart but Feeling Dumb. rev. ed. 320p. 1994. mass mkt. 14.95 (*0-446-39545-5*, Pub. by Warner Bks) Little.

— Total Concentration: How to Understand Attention Deficit Disorder, Maximize Your Mental Energy, & Reach Your Full Potential. LC 90-48943. 1992. pap. 15.95 (*0-87131-708-7*) M Evans.

***Levinson, Harold N. & Carter, Steven.** Phobia Free. 304p. 1999. 7.98 (*1-56731-318-3*, MJF Bks) Fine Comms.

Levinson, Harold N. & Carter, Steven. Phobia Free: A Medical Breakthrough Linking Ninety Percent of all Phobias & Panic Attacks to a Hidden Physical Problem. LC 86-6303. 300p. 1988. pap. 15.95 (*0-87131-539-4*) M Evans.

Levinson, Harold N. & Sanders, Addie. Turning Around the Upside-Down Kids: Helping Dyslexic Kids Overcome Their Disorder. LC 92-13440. 180p. 1992. 17.95 (*0-87131-700-1*) M Evans.

— The Upside-Down Kids: Helping Dyslexic Children Understand Themselves & Overcome Their Disorder. LC 91-4420. 168p. 1991. 17.95 (*0-87131-625-0*) M Evans.

Levinson, Harry. Career Mastery: Keys to Taking Charge of Your Career Throughout Your Work Life. LC 92-20192. 250p. (Orig.). 1992. pap. 15.95 (*1-881052-05-2*) Berrett-Koehler.

— The Exceptional Executive: A Psychological Conception. LC 68-25615. 311p. 1968. reprint ed. pap. 96.50 (*0-7837-1713-X*, 205724200024) Bks Demand.

— Executive. rev. ed. LC 80-26107. 382p. 1981. pap. 20.50 (*0-674-27396-6*) HUP.

— Paint & Paper: Pleasures of Home. (Illus.). 128p. 1998. pap. 14.95 (*0-304-35090-7*) Continuum.

— Paint & Repair. (Pleasures of Home Ser.). (Illus.). 128p. 1997. 21.95 (*0-304-34628-4*, Pub. by Cassell) Sterling.

Levinson, Harry, et al. Organizational Diagnosis. LC 71-168429. (Illus.). 575p. 1976. pap. 21.00 (*0-674-64346-1*) HUP.

Levinson, Harry J. Lithography Process Control. LC 98-44433. (Tutorial Texts in Optical Engineering Ser.). 190p. 1999. pap. text 42.00 (*0-8194-3052-8*) SPIE.

Levinson, Henry S. The Religious Investigations of William James. LC 80-26109. 323p. reprint ed. pap. 100.20 (*0-7837-3767-X*, 204358400010) Bks Demand.

An Asterisk (*) at the beginning of an entry indicates that the title is appearing for the first time.

— Santayana, Pragmatism, & the Spiritual Life. LC 91-50785. (Illus.). xvi, 348p. (C). 1992. 59.95 (*0-8078-2031-8*) U of NC Pr.
— Science, Metaphysics, & the Chance of Salvation: An Interpretation of the Thought of William James. LC 78-7383. (American Academy of Religion. Dissertation Ser.: No. 24). 266p. reprint ed. pap. 82.50 (*0-7837-5467-1*, 204523200005) Bks Demand.
Levinson, Irving J. Introduction to Mechanics. 2nd ed. (C). 1968. 63.80 (*0-13-487660-1*) P-H.
Levinson, Irving J. Preparing for the Engineer-in-Training Examination. 3rd ed. LC 82-18251. 242p. 1992. 29.50 (*0-910554-85-4*) Engineering.
— Statics & Strength of Materials. (C). 1970. text 69.80 (*0-13-844506-0*) P-H.
Levinson, Isabel S. Gibbons vs. Ogden: Controlling Trade Between States. LC 98-34011. (Landmark Supreme Court Cases Ser.). 112p. (YA). (gr. 6 up). 1999. lib. bdg. 20.95 (*0-7660-1086-4*) Enslow Pubs.
Levinson, James H. Another Line. 145p. 1990. pap. 8.50 (*0-922820-03-1*) Watermark Pr.
***Levinson, James Heller.** Because You Wanted a Wedding Ring. iv, 20p. 1999. pap. 5.00 (*0-9674900-2-2*, Implodal Pr) Wordrunner.
***Levinson, Jay.** Questioned Documents: A Lawyer's Handbook. 260p. 2000. 69.95 (*0-12-445490-9*) Acad Pr.
Levinson, Jay & Godin, Seth. Get What You Deserve! How to Guerrilla Market Yourself. LC 97-3149. 256p. 1997. mass mkt. 23.00 (*0-380-97410-X*, Avon Bks) Morrow Avon.
Levinson, Jay A., et al. Early Italian Engravings from the National Gallery of Art. (Illus.). 616p. 1973. pap. 150.00 (*1-55660-188-3*) A Wofsy Fine Arts.
Levinson, Jay C. Earning Money Without a Job. rev. ed. 1995. pap. 9.95 (*0-8050-1458-6*, Owl) H Holt & Co.
— Five Hundred Fifty-Five Ways to Earn Extra Money. rev. ed. LC 81-47471. 432p. (Orig.). 1995. pap. 14.95 (*0-8050-1459-4*, Owl) H Holt & Co.
— Guerrilla Marketing. 1985. pap. 7.95 (*0-685-10137-1*) HM.
— Guerrilla Marketing Attack. 1989. 17.95 (*0-318-41374-4*); pap. 7.95 (*0-318-41375-2*) HM.
— Guerrilla Marketing Attack: New Strategies, Tactics, & Weapons for Winning Big Profits. 224p. 1989. pap. 13.00 (*0-395-50220-9*) HM.
— Guerrilla Marketing Excellence: The 50 Golden Rules for Small Business Success. LC 92-20533. 288p. 1993. pap. 14.00 (*0-395-60844-9*) HM.
— Guerrilla Marketing Weapons: 100 Affordable Marketing Methods for Maximizing Profits from Your Small Business. 240p. 1990. pap. 13.95 (*0-452-26519-3*, Plume) Dutton Plume.
— The Ninety Minute Hour: Combining Time-Saving Technology with New Age Psychology to Take You Beyond Time Management. 1990. 17.95 (*0-317-02816-2*, Dutt) Dutton Plume.
Levinson, Jay C. & Godin, Seth. Guerrilla Marketing for the Home-Based Business. (Guerrilla Marketing Ser.). 240p. 1995. pap. 13.00 (*0-395-74283-8*) HM.
Levinson, Jay C. & Rubin, Charles. Guerrilla Advertising: Cost-Effective Tactics for Small Business Success. 304p. 1994. pap. 13.00 (*0-395-68718-7*) HM.
— Guerrilla Marketing Handbook. (Illus.). 304p. 1994. pap. 18.00 (*0-395-70013-2*) HM.
— Guerrilla Marketing Online Weapons. 1996. 11.95 (*0-614-14432-9*) HM Soft-Ref Div.
— Guerrilla Marketing Online Weapons: 100 Low-Cost, High-Impact Weapons for Online Profits & Prosperity. 224p. 1996. pap. 14.00 (*0-395-77019-X*) HM.
— Guerrilla Selling: Unconventional Tactics for Increasing Your Sales. 224p. 1992. pap. 13.00 (*0-395-57820-5*) HM.
Levinson, Jay C., et al. Guerilla Negotiating: Unconventional Weapons & Tactics to Get What You Want. LC 98-48158. 272p. (C). 1999. pap. 19.95 (*0-471-33021-3*) Wiley.
— Guerilla Trade Show Selling. LC 96-25074. (More People, Get More Leads, & Close More Sales Ser.). 320p. 1997. pap. 19.95 (*0-471-16568-9*) Wiley.
***Levinson, Jay C., et al.** Guerrilla Teleselling: New Unconventional Weapons & Tacticis to Sell. LC 98-21027. (When You Can't Be There in Person Ser.). 304p. 1998. pap. 17.95 (*0-471-24279-9*) Wiley.
Levinson, Jay C., jt. auth. see Blechman, Bruce J.
Levinson, Jay Conrad. Guerilla Marketing Through Technology. LC 97-26619. 240p. 1997. pap. 15.00 (*0-201-32804-6*) Addison-Wesley.
— Guerrilla Marketing Online. 2nd rev. ed. LC 97-25296. 314p. 1997. pap. 14.00 (*0-395-86061-X*) HM.
***Levinson, Jay Conrad.** Marketing de Guerrilla: Los Secretos Para Obtener Grandes Ganancias de Sus Pequenas y Medianas Empresas. Savage, Steve, ed. Zambrano, Helena, tr.Tr. of Guerrilla Marketing. (SPA.). 432p. 2000. pap. 19.95 (*0-9627848-1-8*) Savage Mktg.
Levinson, Jay Conrad. Mastering Guerrilla Marketing: 100 Profit-Producing Insights That You Can Take to the Bank. LC 99-33627. 256p. 1999. pap. 14.00 (*0-395-90875-2*) HM.
— Secrets for Making Big Profits from Your Small Business. 3rd ed. LC 98-24984. (Guerrilla Marketing Ser.). 388p. 1998. pap. 13.00 (*0-395-90625-3*) HM.
— The Way of the Guerrilla: Achieving Success & Balance As an Entrepreneur in the Twenty-First Century. 256p. 1998. pap. 13.00 (*0-395-92478-2*) HM.
***Levinson, Jay Conrad & Tyler, Kathryn.** Guerrilla Saving: Secrets for Keeping Profits in Your Home-Based Business. LC 99-43408. 288p. 2000. pap. 19.95 (*0-471-34542-3*) Wiley.
***Levinson, Jay Conrad, et al.** Guerrilla Marketing for Writers: 100 No-Cost Low-Cost Weapons to Help You Sell Your Work. 224p. 2000. pap. 14.99 (*0-89879-983-X*, Wrtrs Digest Bks) F & W Pubns Inc.
Levinson, Jeffrey L. & Edwards, Randy L. Missile Inbound: The Attack on the "Stark" in the Persian Gulf. LC 97-2087. (Illus.). 176p. 1997. 28.95 (*1-55750-517-9*) Naval Inst Pr.
Levinson, Jerome I. Unrequited Toil: Denial of Labor Rights in Mexico & Implications for NAFTA. Reding, Andrew A., ed. (North America Project Special Reports). 28p. 1993. pap. 5.00 (*0-911646-53-1*) World Policy.
— World's Bankers: The Multilateral Financial Institutions in the 1900's. LC 94-8560. 1993. pap. 9.95 (*0-87078-181-2*) Century Foundation.
Levinson, Jerrold. Music, Art, & Metaphysics: Essays in Philosophical Aesthetics. LC 90-55138. (Illus.). 432p. 1991. text 57.50 (*0-8014-2342-2*); pap. text 19.95 (*0-8014-9591-1*) Cornell U Pr.
— Music in the Moment. LC 97-19847. 176p. 1997. 25.00 (*0-8014-3129-8*) Cornell U Pr.
— The Pleasures of Aesthetics: Philosophical Essays. (Illus.). 320p. 1996. text 52.50 (*0-8014-3059-3*); pap. text 18.95 (*0-8014-8226-7*) Cornell U Pr.
Levinson, Jerrold, ed. Aesthetics & Ethics: Essays at the Intersection. LC 97-21284. (Studies in Philosophy & the Arts). (Illus.). 336p. (C). 1998. text 59.95 (*0-521-58513-9*) Cambridge U Pr.
***Levinson, Jerrold, ed.** Aesthetics & Ethics: Essays at the Intersection. (Cambridge Studies in Philosophy & the Arts Ser.). (Illus.). 336p. (C). 2000. pap. 19.95 (*0-521-78805-6*) Cambridge U Pr.
Levinson, Joel B. & Nega, Susan L., photos by. Pittsburgh: Views into the 21st Century. (Illus.). 96p. (Orig.). 1996. pap. 16.50 (*0-914355-23-6*) J B Jeffers.
Levinson, John M. & Ger, Errol, eds. Safe Passage Questioned: Medical Care & Safety for the Polar Tourist. LC 97-41984. 192p. 1998. pap. 24.95 (*0-87033-504-9*) Cornell Maritime.
Levinson, John M. & Headley, Somers G. Shorebirds: The Birds, the Hunters, the Decoys. LC 91-50581. (Illus.). 158p. 1991. 49.95 (*0-87033-424-7*, Tidewtr Pubs) Cornell Maritime.
Levinson, John M., ed. see Eastman, Peter F.
Levinson, John R. Portraits of Adam in Early Judaism: From Sirach to 2 Baruch. (Journal for the Study of the Pseudepigrapha Supplement Ser.: No. 1). 254p. 1988. 75.00 (*1-85075-062-9*, Pub. by Sheffield Acad) CUP Services.
Levinson, Judy D., jt. auth. see Levinson, Daniel J.
Levinson, Kathy. First Aid for Tantrums. Orloff, Erica, ed. LC 93-93066. (Illus.). 176p. (Orig.). 1997. pap. 12.95 (*1-885843-04-6*) Saturn Press.
Levinson, L. Harold. State Administrative Law. write for info. (*0-318-59313-0*, Aspen Law & Bus) Aspen Pub.
Levinson, L. Harold, jt. auth. see England, Arthur J., Jr.
Levinson, Lee A. East Side, West Side: A Guide to New York City Parks in All Five Boroughs. (Illus.). 228p. (Orig.). 1997. pap. 18.95 (*1-881907-14-7*) Two Bytes Pub.
Levinson, Lionel M. Electronic Ceramics: Properties, Devices & Applications. (Electrical Engineering & Electronics Ser.: Vol. 44). (Illus.). 552p. 1987. text 195.00 (*0-8247-7761-1*) Dekker.
Levinson, Lionel M. & Hirano, Shin-ichi, eds. Grain Boundaries & Interfacial Phenomena in Electronic Ceramics. LC 94-4933. (Ceramic Transactions Ser.: Vol. 41). 390p. 1994. 88.00 (*0-944904-73-4*, CT041) Am Ceramic.
Levinson, Lisa, jt. auth. see Chernoff-Rosen, Diane.
Levinson, Luisa M. The Two Siblings & Other Stories. Miller, Yvette E., ed. Lipp, Sylvia E., tr. from SPA. LC 96-17097. (Discoveries Ser.). 157p. 1996. pap. 14.95 (*0 935480-74-9*) Lat Am Lit Rev Pr.
Levinson, Luna. Tried & True: Tested Ideas for Teaching & Learning from the Regional Educational Laboratories. 96p. 1997. pap. 9.00 (*0-16-049309-9*) USGPO.
Levinson, Luna, ed. Mathematics, Science & Technology Education Programs That Work: A Collection of Exemplary Educational Programs & Practices in the National Diffusion Network. 145p. (Orig.). (C). 1994. pap. text 30.00 (*0-7881-1525-1*) DIANE Pub.
Levinson, Marilyn. The Fourth-Grade Four. LC 89-31109. (Illus.). 64p. (J). (gr. 2-4). 1995. pap. 4.95 (*0-8050-1640-6*, Owlet BYR) H Holt & Co.
— No Boys Allowed. LC 93-22335. (Illus.). 128p. (J). (gr. 5-8). 1996. pap. 13.95 (*0-8167-3135-7*) BrdgeWater.
— No Boys Allowed. LC 93-22335. (Illus.). 128p. (J). (gr. 5-8). 1994. pap. 2.95 (*0-8167-3136-5*, Rainbow NJ) Troll Communs.
Levinson, Marilyn. No Boys Allowed. 1993. 8.05 (*0-606-07059-1*, Pub. by Turtleback) Demco.
Levinson, Marjorie. The Romantic Fragment Poem: A Critique of a Form. LC 85-28927. x, 268p. 1986. 45.00 (*0-8078-1684-1*) U of NC Pr.
Levinson, Meira. The Demands of Liberal Education. LC 99-24528. 250p. 1999. 35.00 (*0-19-829544-8*) OUP.
Levinson, Nadine, jt. auth. see Schuker, Eleanor.
Levinson, Nancy S. Clara & the Bookwagon. (I Can Read Bks.). (Illus.). 64p. (J). (gr. 2-4). 1988. lib. bdg. 15.89 (*0-06-023838-0*) HarpC Child Bks.
— Clara & the Bookwagon. LC 86-45773. (I Can Read Bks.). (Illus.). 64p. (J). (ps-3). 1991. pap. 3.95 (*0-06-444134-2*, HarpTrophy) HarpC Child Bks.
— Clara & the Bookwagon. (I Can Read Bks.). (J). (gr. 2-4). 1991. 8.95 (*0-606-04636-4*, Pub. by Turtleback) Demco.
— If You Lived in the Alaska Territory. (Illus.). 80p. (J). (gr. 2-5). 1998. pap. text 5.99 (*0-590-74449-6*) Scholastic Inc.
— She's Been Working on the Railroad. LC 97-1058. (Illus.). 96p. (YA). (gr. 5). 1997. 16.99 (*0-525-67545-0*, Dutton Child) Peng Put Young Read.
— Snowshoe Thompson. (I Can Read Bks.). (Illus.). 64p. (J). (gr. 2-4). 1992. lib. bdg. 15.89 (*0-06-023802-X*) HarpC Child Bks.
— Snowshoe Thompson. LC 90-37401. (I Can Read Bks.). (Illus.). 64p. (J). (ps-3). 1996. pap. 3.95 (*0-06-444206-3*, HarpTrophy) HarpC Child Bks.
— Snowshoe Thompson. (I Can Read Bks.). (J). (gr. 2-4). 1996. 8.95 (*0-606-09868-2*, Pub. by Turtleback) Demco.
— Thomas Alva Edison, Great Inventor. LC 97-135053. (J). (gr. 3-7). 1996. mass mkt. 3.50 (*0-590-52767-3*) Scholastic Inc.
Levinson, Nancy S. & Burman, Shirley. Women & the Railroads. (J). 1997. write for info. (*0-614-29259-X*, Dutton Child) Peng Put Young Read.
***Levinson, Nancy S. & Petrone, Valeria.** Say Cheese! Road to Reading. LC 99-24461. (Road to Reading Ser.). 32p. (J). 2000. pap. text 3.99 (*0-307-26110-7*, Whitman Coin) St Martin.
***Levinson, Nancy Smiler.** If You Lived in the Alaska Territory. 1998. 11.09 (*0-606-13515-4*, Pub. by Turtleback) Demco.
— Levinson I Can Read: Chapter Book. 48p. (J). (gr. 2-4). 14.89 (*0-06-028002-6*) HarpC Child Bks.
— Thomas Alva Edison, Great Inventor. (Scholastic Biography Ser.). (J). 1996. 8.70 (*0-606-11981-7*, Pub. by Turtleback) Demco.
***Levinson, Nancy Smiler & Hearn, Diane Dawson.** Death Valley Desert. LC 00-23305. (Illus.). 2001. write for info. (*0-8234-1566-X*) Holiday.
Levinson, Norma. Paper Children. large type ed. 560p. 1988. 27.99 (*0-7089-1852-2*) Ulverscroft.
Levinson, Norman. Gap & Density Theorems. LC 41-6147. (Colloquium Publications: Vol. 26). 246p. 1940. pap. 34.00 (*0-8218-1026-X*, COLL/26) Am Math.
Levinson, Norman, et al. Selected Papers of Norman Levinson. LC 97-38621. (Contemporary Mathematicians Ser.). 1997. write for info. (*3-7643-3862-8*); write for info. (*3-7643-3979-9*) Birkhauser.
Levinson, Norman, jt. auth. see Coddington, Earl A.
Levinson, Orde. The African Dream: Themes & Images of John Muafangejo. LC 92-70865. (Illus.). 120p. 1993. pap. 14.95 (*0-500-27682-X*, Pub. by Thames Hudson) Norton.
— Quality & Experiment: The Prints of John Piper (1903-92) (Illus.). 192p. 1996. 99.00 (*0-85331-690-2*, Pub. by Lund Humphries) Antique Collect.
Levinson, Paul. Digital McLuhan: Guide to the Information Millennium. LC 98-40359. 211p. 1999. 27.50 (*0-415-19251-X*) Routledge.
— Electronic Chronicles: Columns of the Changes in Our Time. LC 92-18689. 224p. (Orig.). 1992. pap. 14.95 (*0-9631203-3-6*) Anamnesis Pr.
— Mind at Large: Knowing in the Technological Age. Ferre, Frederick et al, eds. 271p. 1998. pap. 25.75 (*0-7623-0018-3*) Jai Pr.
***Levinson, Paul.** The Silk Code. LC 99-33992. 319p. 1999. 23.95 (*0-312-86823-5*, Pub. by Tor Bks) St Martin.
Levinson, Paul. The Soft Edge: A Natural History & Future of the Information Revolution. LC 97-7248. 280p. (C). 1997. 29.99 (*0-415-15785-4*) Routledge.
— The Soft Edge: A Natural History & Future of the Information Revolution. 264p. 1998. reprint ed. pap. 16.99 (*0-415-19772-4*) Routledge.
Levinson, Peter J. Trumpet Blues: The Life of Harry James. LC 99-11507. (Illus.). 368p. 1999. 30.00 (*0-19-511030-7*) OUP.
***Levinson, Phil.** Essentials of Subfile Programming & Advanced Topics in RPG IV. LC 99-6493. 260p. 1999. pap. text 45.00 (*1-58304-051-X*) News Four-Hund.
Levinson, Phil. Essentials of Subfile Programming & Advanced Topics in RPG/400. LC 98-8863. 300p. 1998. pap. text 45.00 (*1-882419-64-2*) News Four-Hund.
Levinson, Ralph & Thomas, Jeffrey N. Science Today: Problem or Crisis? LC 96-43790. 248p. (C). 1997. pap. 22.99 (*0-415-13531-1*) Routledge.
Levinson, Richard & Link, William. Rehearsal for Murder. 1983. pap. 5.50 (*0-87129-279-3*, R36) Dramatic Pub.
Levinson, Richard, et al. Murder by Natural Causes. 64p. (YA). (gr. 10 up). 1985. pap. 5.50 (*0-87129-850-3*, M61) Dramatic Pub.
Levinson, Riki. Watch the Stars Come Out. (Illus.). 32p. (J). (ps up). 1995. pap. 5.99 (*0-14-055506-4*, PuffinBks) Peng Put Young Read.
Levinson, Riki. Watch the Stars Come Out. 1995. 11.19 (*0-606-08352-9*, Pub. by Turtleback) Demco.
Levinson, Risha. Information & Referral Networks: Doorways to Human Services. (Social Work Ser.). 256p. (C). 1987. 31.95 (*0-8261-4820-4*) Springer Pub.
Levinson, Risha W. & Haynes, Karen S., eds. Accessing Human Services: International Perspectives. LC 84-16012. (Social Science Delivery Systems Ser.: No. 7). 320p. reprint ed. pap. 99.20 (*0-8357-4820-0*, 203775700009) Bks Demand.
Levinson, Robert. The Jews in the California Gold Rush. 2nd ed. (Illus.). 1994. pap. 19.95 (*0-943376-62-9*) Magnes Mus.
Levinson, Robert, jt. ed. see Epstein, Susan.
Levinson, Robert B. Unit Management in Prisons & Jails. LC 98-20708. 281p. 1999. pap. 29.95 (*1-56991-079-0*, 198) Am Correctional.
Levinson, Robert E. Super Savvy: How to Get It, How to Use It, How to Make A Fortune with It! Lauer, Mark T., ed. LC 94-14016. 256p. 1994. pap. 14.95 (*1-880539-29-2*) Garrett FL.
***Levinson, Robert S.** The Elvis & Marilyn Affair. LC 99-22197. 304p. 1999. 24.95 (*0-312-86968-1*, Pub. by Forge NYC) St Martin.
— Elvis & Marilyn Affair: A Neil Gulliver & Stevie Marriner Novel. 416p. 2000. mass mkt. 6.99 (*0-8125-8432-5*) Forge NYC.
— The James Dean Affair. 320p. 2000. 24.95 (*0-312-87268-2*) Forge NYC.
Levinson, Robin, jt. auth. see Acheson, David.
Levinson, Robin, jt. auth. see Granet, Roger.
Levinson, Robin, ed. see Bruchi, Phil.
Levinson, Robin K., jt. auth. see Hanson, Harry.
Levinson, Ronald B., ed. see Plato.
***Levinson, Ronnen.** Much Ado about Ballroom Dancing: Pointers on Learning to Dance, Choosing Shoes, Finding Dance Music, & More! (Illus.). iv, 68p. 2000. pap. 14.95 (*0-9679909-0-4*) R Levinson.
Levinson, Rosalie & Bodensteiner, Ivan E. Civil Rights Legislation & Litigation. 738p. 1998. ring bd. 71.00 (*1-879581-57-4*) Lupus Pubns.
Levinson, Rosalie B., jt. auth. see Bodensteiner, Ivan E.
Levinson, Samuel A. & MacFate, Robert P. Clinical Laboratory Diagnosis. 7th ed. LC 68-18867. 1343p. reprint ed. pap. 200.00 (*0-608-13666-2*, 205543600022) Bks Demand.
Levinson, Sanford. Written in Stone: Public Monuments in Changing Societies. LC 97-49361. (Public Planet Bks.). 143p. 1998. pap. 13.95 (*0-8223-2220-X*) Duke.
— Written in Stone: Public Monuments in Changing Societies. LC 97-49361. (Public Planet Bks.). 143p. 1998. 39.95 (*0-8223-2204-8*) Duke.
Levinson, Sanford, jt. auth. see Brest, Paul.
Levinson, Sanford, jt. auth. see McCloskey, Robert G.
Levinson, Sanford, jt. ed. see Mailloux, Steven.
Levinson, Sanford, ed. see McCloskey, Robert G.
Levinson, Sanford V., jt. ed. see Eskridge, William N., Jr.
***Levinson, Sidney B.** Application of Paints & Coatings. (Illus.). 49p. 1998. pap. 30.00 (*0-934010-09-9*) Fed Soc Coat Tech.
Levinson, Stephen C. Pragmatics. LC 82-14701. (Cambridge Textbooks in Linguistics Ser.). 434p. 1983. pap. text 29.95 (*0-521-29414-2*) Cambridge U Pr.
***Levinson, Stephen C.** Presumptive Meanings: The Theory of Generalized Conversational Implicature. LC 99-46140. (Language, Speech & Communication Ser.). 1999. text 85.00 (*0-262-12218-9*) MIT Pr.
Levinson, Stephen C. Presumptive Meanings: The Theory of Generalized Conversational Implicature. LC 99-46140. (Illus.). 450p. 1999. pap. 35.00 (*0-262-62130-4*) MIT Pr.
Levinson, Stephen C., jt. auth. see Brown, Penelope.
Levinson, Stephen C., jt. ed. see Bowerman, Melissa.
Levinson, Stephen C., jt. ed. see Gumperz, John J.
Levinson, Stephen E. & Shepp, Lawrence A. Image Models (And Their Speech Model Cousins) LC 96-18353. (IMA Volumes in Mathematics & Its Applications Ser.). 216p. 1996. 65.95 (*0-387-94806-6*) Spr-Verlag.
Levinson, Steve & Greider, Pete C. Following Through: A Revolutionary New Model for Finishing Whatever You Start. LC 99-217327. 223p. 1998. pap. 13.00 (*1-57566-348-1*) Kensgtn Pub Corp.
***Levinson, Steven W. & Nowakowski, Richard S., eds.** Neuroepithelial Stem Cells & Progenitors. (Developmental Neuroscience Ser.: Vol. 22, Nos. 1-2). (Illus.). 178p. 2000. pap. 45.25 (*3-8055-6976-9*) S Karger.
***Levinson, Warren & Jawetz, Ernest.** Medical Microbiology & Immunology: Examination & Board Review. 6th ed. (Illus.). 600p. 2000. write for info. (*0-8385-6410-0*) McGraw.
Levinson, Warren E. Medical Microbiology & Immunology: Examination & Board Review. 4th ed. (C). 1996. pap. text 31.95 (*0-8385-6225-6*, A6225-5) Appleton & Lange.
Levinson, Warren E. & Jawetz, Ernest. Medical Microbiology & Immunology: Examination & Board Review. 5th ed. (Illus.). 547p. (C). 1998. pap. 34.95 (*0-8385-6287-6*, Apple Lange Med) McGraw.
***Levinson, William A.** ISO 9000 at the Front Line. LC 00-36216. 2000. write for info. (*0-87389-397-2*) ASQ Qual Pr.
Levinson, William A. Study Guide for Engineering & the Physical Sciences. (Illus.). 101p. (Orig.). 1988. pap. text 7.00 (*0-913811-04-1*) Northeast A S.
— The Way of Strategy. 246p. 1995. text 30.00 (*0-87389-228-3*, H0778) ASQ Qual Pr.
Levinson, William A., ed. Leading the Way to Competitive Excellence: The Harris Mountaintop Case Study. LC 97-17504. 346p. 1997. 38.00 (*0-87389-376-X*, H0954) ASQ Qual Pr.
Levinson, William A. & Tumbelty, Frank. SPC Essentials & Productivity Improvement: A Manufacturing Approach. 266p. (Orig.). 1997. pap. 35.00 (*0-87389-372-7*, H0937) ASQ Qual Pr.
Levinson, William A., jt. auth. see Tumbelty, Frank.
Levinson, Yaakov. The Jewish Guide to Natural Nutrition. 1995. 18.95 (*0-87306-706-1*) Feldheim.
Levinstein, Edward. Morbid Craving for Morphia: Die Morphiumsucht. Grob, Gerald N., ed. Harrer, Charles, tr. LC 80-1259. (Addiction in America Ser.). 1981. reprint ed. lib. bdg. 15.95 (*0-405-13602-1*) Ayer.
Levinstein, Jerry. The Complete Carpet Manual. (Illus.). 376p. 1992. 59.95 (*0-912526-60-2*) Lib Res.
Levinstein, Mark S., jt. auth. see Cozzillio, Michael J.
Levinthal, Charles F. Drugs, Behavior, & Modern Society. 2nd ed. LC 98-15221. 390p. 1998. pap. text 57.00 (*0-205-27703-9*) Allyn.
Levinthal, David. David Levinthal 1975-1996. (Illus.). 1997. 45.00 (*0-614-28258-6*) DAP Assocs.
— Desire. 1993. pap. 15.00 (*1-881616-11-8*) Dist Art Pubs.
***Levinthal, David.** Modern Romance. 2000. 65.00 (*0-9671744-1-4*) St Anns Pr.
Levinthal, David. Small Wonder: Worlds in a Box. LC 95-25368. (Illus.). 112p. 1995. pap. 35.00 (*1-881616-39-8*) Dist Art Pubs.
Levinthal, David, photos by. Barbie Millicent Roberts. LC 98-6828. (Illus.). 1998. 30.00 (*0-375-40425-2*) Pantheon.

L

— David Levinthal: Blackface. (Illus.). 156p. 1999. 65.00 (*1-892041-06-5*, Pub. by Arena Editions) Dist Art Pubs.

Levinton, Jeffrey. Genetics, Paleontology & Macroevolution. (Illus.). 656p. 1988. text 69.95 (*0-521-24933-3*) Cambridge U Pr.

Levinton, Jeffrey S. Marine Biology: Function, Biodiversity, Ecology. (Illus.). 448p. (C). 1995. text 62.95 (*0-19-508573-6*) OUP.

Leviq, Enrique J. Duplications: And Other Stories. Miller, Yvette E., ed. Chambers, Leland H., tr. from SPA. LC 94-19375. (Discoveries Ser.). 192p. 1994. pap. 15.95 (*0-935480-65-X*) Lat Am Lit Rev Pr.

L

Levis, A. H. & Stephanou, H. E. Distributed Intelligence Systems. (IFAC Symposia Ser.: Vol. 9204). 266p. 1992. 105.75 (*0-08-041272-6*, Pergamon Pr) Elsevier.

Levis, Albert J. Conflict Analysis-The Formal Theory of Behavior: A Theory & Its Experimental Validation. LC 88-90914. (Illus.). 500p. (C). 1989. 60.00 (*0-929642-00-7*) Normative Pubns.

— Conflict Analysis Training: A Program of Emotional Education. LC 88-90913. (Illus.). 160p. (Orig.). (C). 1989. pap. 35.00 (*0-929642-01-5*) Normative Pubns.

Levis, Alexander H. & Levis, Ilze S., eds. Science of Command & Control Pt. 3: Coping with Change. LC 94-34428. (AIP Information Systems: Vol. III). 200p. (Orig.). (C). 1994. pap. 18.95 (*0-916159-25-6*) AFCEA Intl Pr.

Levis, Alexander H., jt. ed. see Johnson, Stuart E.

Levis, Allen. General Merchandise - HBA Mgt & OPS. 1989. pap. 32.95 (*0-86730-313-1*) Lebhar Friedman.

Levis, Bob, ed. see Malmuth, Mason.

Levis, G. Liz & Beth Bk. 1: A Good Licking. Verre, Tom, ed. Jordan, Gil, tr. (Eros Graphic Novel Ser.: No. 8). (Illus.). 88p. 1993. pap. 13.95 (*1-56097-205-X*) Fantagraph Bks.

— Liz & Beth Bk. 2: Coffee, Tea, or Me? (Eros Graphic Novel Ser.: No. 12). 112p. 1994. pap. 12.95 (*1-56097-210-6*) Fantagraph Bks.

— Liz & Beth Bk. 3: Tit for Twat. (Eros Graphic Novel Ser.: No. 20). 104p. 1995. pap. 12.95 (*1-56097-218-1*) Fantagraph Bks.

Levis, Howard C. A Descriptive Bibliography of the Most Important Books in the English Language Relating to the Art & History of Engraving & the Collecting of Prints. 714p. 1999. reprint ed. 80.00 (*1-57898-128-X*) Martino Pubng.

Levis, Ilze S., jt. ed. see Levis, Alexander H.

Levis, Larry. The Afterlife. LC 97-76758. (Classic Contemporaries Ser.). 64p. 1997. pap. 12.95 (*0-88748-279-1*) Carnegie-Mellon.

— The Afterlife: Poems. LC 77-8598. 61p. reprint ed. pap. 30.00 (*0-8357-3840-X*, 203657200004) Bks Demand.

— The Dollmaker's Ghost. 1997. pap. text 12.95 (*0-88748-094-2*) Carnegie-Mellon.

— The Dollmaker's Ghost. LC 91-70995. (Classic Contemporaries Ser.). 72p. 1997. pap. 12.95 (*0-88748-282-1*) Carnegie-Mellon.

— The Dollmaker's Ghost. 2nd ed. LC 91-70995. 72p. 1992. reprint ed. pap. 12.95 (*0-88748-125-6*) Carnegie-Mellon.

— Elegy. Levine, Philip, ed. LC 97-21097. (Pitt Poetry Ser.). 85p. 1997. pap. 12.95 (*0-8229-5648-9*); text 25.00 (*0-8229-4043-4*) U of Pittsburgh Pr.

***Levis, Larry.** The Gazer Within. (Illus.). 160p. (C). 2000. pap. 14.95 (*0-472-06718-4*, 06718); text 42.50 (*0-472-09718-0*, 09718) U of Mich Pr.

— The Selected Levis. St. John, David, ed. (Pitt Poetry Ser). 110p. 2000. 22.50 (*0-8229-4141-4*) U of Pittsburgh Pr.

Levis, Larry. The Widening Spell of the Leaves. LC 90-21308. (Poetry Ser.). 77p. (C). 1991. pap. 10.95 (*0-8229-5454-0*); text 19.95 (*0-8229-3675-5*) U of Pittsburgh Pr.

— Winter Stars. LC 84-21957. (Poetry Ser.). 104p. 1985. pap. 10.95 (*0-8229-5368-4*); text 19.95 (*0-8229-3511-2*) U of Pittsburgh Pr.

— Wrecking Crew: Poems. LC 78-181398. (Pitt Poetry Ser.). 72p. 1972. reprint ed. pap. 30.00 (*0-608-02057-5*, 206271000003) Bks Demand.

Levis, M. Empirical Issues in Raising Equity Capital. LC 96-47154. (Advances in Finance, Investment & Banking Ser.: Vol. 2). 412p. 1996. 129.50 (*0-444-82469-3*) Elsevier.

Levis, Nicholas, ed. & tr. see Billstein, Reinhold, et al.

Levis, Nicholas, tr. see Giesen, Bernhard.

Levison, Ann, ed. see Van Dinh, Tran.

Levison, Arnold B. Knowledge & Society: An Introduction to the Philosophy of the Social Sciences. LC 72-88122. 1974. 29.50 (*0-672-53661-7*) Irvington.

Levison, Catherine. A Charlotte Mason Education: A How to Manual. O'Brien, Deborah, ed. (Illus.). 96p. 1996. pap. 7.95 (*0-9655044-0-9*) C Mason Commns.

Levison, Catherine. A Charlotte Mason Education: A How to Manual. 1996. pap. text 8.95 (*1-891400-16-9*) Champion Pr.

— More Charlotte Mason Education: A Homeschooling How to Manual. 2000. pap. 13.95 (*1-891400-17-7*) Champion Pr.

Levison, H. Textbook for Dental Nurses. 8th ed. LC 97-1020. 1997. pap. 34.95 (*0-632-04031-9*) Blackwell Sci.

Levison, John R. The Spirit in First Century Judaism. (Arbeiten zur Geschichte des Antiken Judentums und des Urchristentums Ser.: No. 29). 296p. 1997. 93.00 (*90-04-10739-8*) Brill Academic Pubs.

***Levison, John R.** The Spirit in Second Temple. LC 99-50560. 1998. pap. 8.95 (*0-941037-74-6*) D & F Scott.

Levison, John R., jt. ed. see Feldman, Louis H.

Levison, Julie H., jt. ed. see Agosin, Marjorie.

Levison, Lee M. Community Service Programs in Independent Schools: The Processes of Implementation & Institutionalization of Peripheral Educational Innovations. rev. ed. LC 93-49428. (Non-profit Institutions in America Ser.). 208p. 1994. text 10.00 (*0-8153-0907-4*) Garland.

Levison, Lorie & St. Onge, Isabelle. Disability Awareness in the Classroom: A Resource Tool for Teachers & Students. LC 99-17943. (Illus.). 230p. 1999. spiral bd. 38.95 (*0-398-06953-0*) C C Thomas.

***Levison, Louise.** Filmmakers & Financing: Business Plans for Independents. 224p. 2001. pap. 24.95 (*0-240-80432-5*, Focal) Buttrwrth-Heinemann.

Levison, Louise. Filmmakers & Financing: Business Plans for Independents. 2nd ed. LC 97-13434. 192p. 1998. pap. 24.95 (*0-240-80300-0*, Focal) Buttrwrth-Heinemann.

Levison, Mary, ed. Wrestling with the Church. (C). 1992. pap. 24.00 (*0-85305-307-3*, Pub. by Arthur James) St Mut.

Levison, Matthew E., ed. The Pneumonias: Clinical Approaches to Infectious Diseases of the Lower Respiratory Tract. LC 83-10473. 592p. reprint ed. pap. 183.60 (*0-8357-7864-9*, 203628100002) Bks Demand.

Levison, Michael, et al. The Settlement of Polynesia: A Computer Simulation. LC 72-92337. 145p. reprint ed. pap. 45.00 (*0-608-14636-6*, 205588800039) Bks Demand.

Levison, N. The Jewish Background of Christianity: 586 B.C. to A.D. 1. 1977. lib. bdg. 59.95 (*0-8490-2100-6*) Gordon Pr.

Levison, Teddi, jt. auth. see Faber, Stuart J.

Levison, William H. Black Diamonds; or Humor, Satire & Sentiment... LC 75-91083. (American Humorists Ser.). reprint ed. lib. bdg. 32.50 (*0-8398-1156-X*) Irvington.

Levit, Fred. A Dickens Glossary for American Readers. 458p. (Orig.). 1996. pap. 10.00 (*0-924312-00-9*) Hall Des.

Levit, Herschel, jt. auth. see Piranesi, Giovanni B.

Levit, Kathryn, jt. auth. see Ryerson, Susan.

Levit, Nancy. Gender Line. pap. text 19.50 (*0-8147-5122-9*) NYU Pr.

Levit, Nancy. The Gender Line: Men, Women, & the Law. LC 97-45398. 312p. 1998. text 35.00 (*0-8147-5121-0*) NYU Pr.

Levit, Nancy, jt. auth. see Hayman, Robert L.

Levit, Robert A. & Gikakis, Christina, eds. Shared Wisdom: Development & Succession Planning. (Best Practices Ser.: No. 2). 300p. 1994. pap. text 25.00 (*1-881115-05-4*) Human Res Plan.

Levit, Sarah. Fashion in Photographs, 1880-1900. (Illus.). 144p. (C). 1992. text 85.00 (*0-7134-6120-9*) B&N Imports.

***Levit, Saul D.** Pennsylvania Domestic Relations, Issue 9. 100p. 1999. ring bd. write for info. (*0-327-01383-4*, 8231515) LEXIS Pub.

Levit, Saul D. Pennsylvania Domestic Relations Forms. 540p. 1989. spiral bd. 169.00 (*0-8342-0075-9*, MICHIE) LEXIS Pub.

— Pennsylvania Domestic Relations Forms. 1994. ring bd., suppl. ed. 80.00 (*0-685-74634-8*, MICHIE) LEXIS Pub.

— Pennsylvania Domestic Relations Forms, Issue 9. LC 89-6074. 200p. 1998. ring bd. write for info. (*0-327-00229-8*, 82315-14) LEXIS Pub.

— Pennsylvania Domestic Relations Forms, Set. 1994. disk 50.00 (*0-614-03766-2*, MICHIE) LEXIS Pub.

Levitan, Alexis, tr. see De Andrade, Eugenio.

Levitan, B. M. & Sargsjan, I. S. Introduction to Spectral Theory: Selfadjoint Ordinary Differential Operators. Feinstein, A., tr. LC 75-15565. (Translations of Mathematical Monographs: Vol. 39). 525p. 1975. text 129.00 (*0-8218-1589-X*, MMONO/39) Am Math.

— Strum-Liouville & Dirac Operators. (C). 1990. text 248.50 (*0-7923-0992-8*) Kluwer Academic.

Levitan, B. M., et al. Six Papers in Analysis. LC 73-15614. (Translations Ser.: Series 2, Vol. 101). 250p. 1973. text 59.00 (*0-8218-3051-1*, TRANS2/101) Am Math.

Levitan, Ben. Too Easy Gourmet: The World's First Non-Fiction Cookbook. LC 94-90329. (Orig.). 1995. pap. 6.95 (*0-9640023-0-2*) Too Easy Gourmet.

Levitan, Cayli H. Minister to Minister Vol. I: Alternative Services for All Occasions. 100p. (Orig.). 1992. pap. 13.95 (*0-9632747-0-8*) C H Levitan.

***Levitan, Diane & Wildman, Jeanne.** Manual of Procedures. rev. ed. Burfield, Lori, ed. (Illus.). 164p. 2000. 33.00 (*1-930866-02-X*) IES.

Levitan, Donald. Guide to Grants: Governmental & Nongovernmental. 2nd ed. 230p. (C). 1985. pap. 25.00 (*0-931684-09-9*) Gov Res Pubns.

Levitan, Donald & Mariner, Elwyn. Your Massachusetts Government. 10th ed. LC 84-13554. (Illus.). 272p. (Orig.). 1984. pap. text 25.00 (*0-931684-07-2*) Gov Res Pubns.

Levitan, Donald, jt. auth. see Seagrave, Jane.

Levitan, Irwin B. & Kaczmarek, Leonard K. The Neuron: Cell & Molecular Biology. 2nd ed. (Illus.). 560p. 1996. pap. text 49.95 (*0-19-510021-2*) OUP.

Levitan, Irwin B., jt. auth. see Kaczmarek, Leonard K.

Levitan, Jean E., jt. auth. see Blonna, Richard.

Levitan, Kalman L. In Search of Miniature Books. 68p. 1985. text 19.95 (*0-9614884-4-1*) Kaycee Pr.

Levitan, Karen B., ed. Government Infostructures: A Guide to the Networks of Information Resources & Technologies at Federal, State, & Local Levels. LC 86-27119. 342p. 1987. lib. bdg. 75.00 (*0-313-24864-8*, LGI/, Greenwood Pr) Greenwood.

Levitan, Linda, jt. auth. see Moore, Matthew S.

Levitan, Mark. New York City's Labor Market, 1994-1997: Profiles & Perspectives. 124p. 1998. 15.00 (*0-88156-253-X*) Comm Serv Soc NY.

— Opportunity at Work: The New York City Garment Industry. 80p. 1998. 12.00 (*0-88156-216-5*) Comm Serv Soc NY.

Levitan, Max. Human Genetics. 3rd ed. (Illus.). 456p. 1988. text 59.95 (*0-19-504935-7*) OUP.

Levitan, Richard, jt. auth. see Shubik, Martin.

Levitan, Sar A. Antipoverty Work & Training Efforts: Goals & Reality. 2nd ed. (Policy Papers in Human Resources & Industrial Relations Ser.: No. 3). (Orig.). 1970. pap. 5.00 (*0-87736-103-7*) U of Mich Inst Labor.

— Design of Federal Antipoverty Strategy. (Policy Papers in Human Resources & Industrial Relations Ser.: No. 1). (Orig.). (C). 1967. pap. 5.00 (*0-87736-101-0*) U of Mich Inst Labor.

— Employment & Earnings Inadequacy: A New Social Indicator. LC 74-6831. (Policy Studies in Employment & Welfare: No. 19). 128p. reprint ed. pap. 39.70 (*0-608-15039-8*, 202312100031) Bks Demand.

— Federal Aid to Depressed Areas: An Evaluation of the Area Redevelopment Administration. LC 64-16310. 288p. reprint ed. pap. 89.30 (*0-608-13718-9*, 202047000018) Bks Demand.

— The Great Society's Poor Law: A New Approach to Poverty. LC 74-82450. 362p. reprint ed. pap. 112.30 (*0-608-13765-0*, 202047400018) Bks Demand.

— Programs in Aid of the Poor. rev. ed. LC 84-28890. 176p. 1990. pap. text 12.95 (*0-8018-4040-6*) Johns Hopkins.

— Programs in Aid of the Poor. 5th ed. LC 84-28890. 165p. reprint ed. pap. 51.20 (*0-8357-6904-6*, 203796200009) Bks Demand.

— Programs in Aid of the Poor. 6th rev. ed. LC 84-28890. 176p. 1990. text 29.50 (*0-8018-4039-2*) Johns Hopkins.

— Programs in Aid of the Poor. 7th ed. Mangum, Garth L. & Mangum, Stephen L., eds. LC 97-15768. 264p. 1998. pap. text 13.95 (*0-8018-5713-9*) Johns Hopkins.

— Programs in Aid of the Poor. 7th ed. Mangum, Garth L. & Mangum, Stephen L., eds. LC 97-15768. 264p. 1999. text 35.00 (*0-8018-5688-4*) Johns Hopkins.

— Programs in Aid of the Poor for the 1980's. 4th ed. LC 80-8093. (Policy Studies in Employment & Welfare: No. 1). 169p. reprint ed. pap. 52.40 (*0-608-15001-0*, 202588500046) Bks Demand.

Levitan, Sar A. & Alderman, Karen C. Child Care & ABC's Too. LC 75-11355. 144p. 1975. reprint ed. pap. 44.70 (*0-608-03719-2*, 206454400009) Bks Demand.

Levitan, Sar A. & Belous, Richard. Shorter Hours, Shorter Weeks: Spreading the Work to Reduce Unemployment. LC 77-4787. (Johns Hopkins University Policy Studies in Employment & Welfare: No. 30). (Illus.). 107p. reprint ed. pap. 33.20 (*0-8357-9286-2*, 201657300004) Bks Demand.

Levitan, Sar A. & Belous, Richard S. More Than Subsistence: Minimum Wages for the Working Poor. LC 79-11688. (Policy Studies in Employment & Welfare: Vol. 34). 193p. 1979. reprint ed. pap. 59.90 (*0-608-03720-6*, 206454500009) Bks Demand.

Levitan, Sar A. & Cooper, Martha R. Business Lobbies: The Public Good & the Bottom Line. LC 83-48071. 167p. 1984. reprint ed. pap. 51.80 (*0-608-03716-8*, 206454100009) Bks Demand.

Levitan, Sar A. & Gallo, Frank. A Second Chance: Training for Jobs. LC 87-37266. 220p. 1988. text 26.00 (*0-88099-057-0*); pap. text 16.00 (*0-88099-056-2*) W E Upjohn.

Levitan, Sar A. & Johnson, Clifford M. Second Thoughts on Work. LC 82-13532. 241p. 1982. text 24.00 (*0-88099-000-7*); pap. text 14.00 (*0-88099-001-5*) W E Upjohn.

Levitan, Sar A. & Johnston, William B. Indian Giving: Federal Programs for Native Americans. LC 75-11354. (Policy Studies in Employment & Welfare: No. 20). 94p. reprint ed. pap. 30.00 (*0-8357-8179-8*, 203415000088) Bks Demand.

Levitan, Sar A. & Mangum, Garth L. Federal Training & Work Programs in the Sixties. LC 78-626163. (Orig.). 1969. 13.00 (*0-87736-305-6*); pap. 6.50 (*0-87736-306-4*) U of Mich Inst Labor.

— Making Sense of Federal Manpower Policy. 2nd ed. (Policy Papers in Human Resources & Industrial Relations Ser.: No. 2). (Orig.). (C). 1973. pap. 5.00 (*0-87736-102-9*) U of Mich Inst Labor.

Levitan, Sar A. & Mangum, Garth L., eds. The T in CETA: Local & National Perspectives. LC 81-19791. 433p. 1981. text 14.00 (*0-911558-94-2*); pap. text 10.00 (*0-911558-93-4*) W E Upjohn.

Levitan, Sar A. & Noden, Alexandra B. Working for the Sovereign: Employee Relations in the Federal Government. LC 82-49064. (Policy Studies in Employment & Welfare: No. 39). 165p. 1983. reprint ed. pap. 51.20 (*0-608-03721-4*, 206454600009) Bks Demand.

Levitan, Sar A. & Taggart, Robert. Jobs for the Disabled. LC 76-49910. (Policy Studies in Employment & Welfare: No. 28). 143p. reprint ed. pap. 44.40 (*0-608-30471-9*, 201756800007) Bks Demand.

— The Promise of Greatness. 325p. 1977. pap. 17.00 (*0-674-71456-3*) HUP.

Levitan, Sar A. & Taggart, Robert, 3rd. Social Experimentation & Manpower Policy: The Rhetoric & the Reality. LC 78-153557. (Policy Studies in Employment & Welfare: Vol. 9). 124p. 1971. reprint ed. pap. 38.50 (*0-608-03718-4*, 206454300009) Bks Demand.

Levitan, Sar A. & Werneke, Diane. Productivity: Problems, Prospects, & Policies. LC 83-22184. (Policy Studies in Employment & Welfare: Vol. 40). 143p. 1984. reprint ed. pap. 44.40 (*0-608-03717-6*, 206454200009) Bks Demand.

Levitan, Sar A. & Wurzburg, Gregory K. Evaluating Federal Social Programs: An Uncertain Art. LC 79-17946. 148p. 1979. pap. 8.00 (*0-911558-64-0*); text 18.00 (*0-911558-65-9*) W E Upjohn.

Levitan, Sar A. & Zickler, Joyce K. The Quest for a Federal Manpower Partnership. LC 74-16541. 141p. reprint ed. pap. 43.80 (*0-7837-4140-5*, 205796300011) Bks Demand.

Levitan, Sar A., et al. Economic Opportunity in the Ghetto: The Partnership of Government & Business. LC 70-108580. (Policy Studies in Employment & Welfare: No. 3). 94p. reprint ed. pap. 30.00 (*0-608-15064-9*, 202312000032) Bks Demand.

— Protecting American Workers: An Assessment of Government Programs. LC 86-13681. 294p. 1986. reprint ed. pap. 91.20 (*0-608-00703-X*, 206147500009) Bks Demand.

— Still a Dream: The Changing Status of Blacks Since 1960. LC 74-16539. 398p. 1976. pap. 16.50 (*0-674-83856-4*) HUP.

— What's Happening to the American Family? Tensions, Hopes, Realities. rev. ed. LC 87-46304. (Illus.). 240p. 1988. reprint ed. pap. 74.40 (*0-8357-8374-X*, 203413200088) Bks Demand.

— Working but Poor: America's Contradiction. rev. ed. LC 92-34719. (Illus.). 160p. 1993. pap. text 12.95 (*0-8018-4575-0*) Johns Hopkins.

Levitan, Sar A., jt. auth. see Davidson, Roger H.

Levitan, Stephan J. & Berkowitz, Howard L., eds. New Developments in Pain Research & Treatment. LC 84-28254. (Clinical Insights Ser.). 87p. reprint ed. pap. 30.00 (*0-8357-7817-7*, 203618900002) Bks Demand.

Levitan, Tina. First Facts in American Jewish History: From 1492 to the Present. LC 96-1791. 432p. 1996. 40.00 (*1-56821-895-8*) Aronson.

***Levitan, Valerie F.** Thank You for Asking: A Response-Resource Coping Book. 100p. 1998. pap. 15.00 (*0-9659941-4-7*) Natl Spasmodic Dysphonia.

Levitan, Valerie F., ed. see Ross, Karen K.

Levitas, Ruth. The Concept of Utopia. 224p. (C). 1991. text 45.00 (*0-8156-2513-8*); pap. text 19.95 (*0-8156-2514-6*) Syracuse U Pr.

Levitas, Ruth & Guy, Will, eds. Intrepreting Offical Statistics. 224p. (C). 1996. 80.00 (*0-415-10835-7*); pap. 24.99 (*0-415-10836-5*) Routledge.

Levitas, Susan, ed. Railroad Ties: Industry & Culture in Hagerstown, Maryland. LC 94-33071. (Illus.). 64p. 1994. pap. 14.00 (*1-878399-64-0*, MD Hist Trust) Div Hist Cult Progs.

Levitas, V. I. Large Deformation of Materials with Complex Rheological Properties at Normal & High Pressure. 323p. 1996. 175.00 (*1-56072-085-9*) Nova Sci Pubs.

Levitch, Edward J. From Beginning to Beginning. Rowe, Fran, ed. LC 98-146028. (Illus.). 130p. (Orig.). 1997. pap. 14.95 (*0-9655974-0-7*) Mad Dog Pub.

Levitch, Timothy. Speed's New York: A Guide to Life. 240p. 2000. pap. 16.95 (*1-55970-496-9*, Pub. by Arcade Pub Inc) Time Warner.

Levite, Allan. Guilt, Blame & Politics. LC 98-96566. 259p. 1998. pap. 16.95 (*0-9666943-0-9*) Stanyan Pr.

Levite, Ariel E. Intelligence & Strategic Surprises. LC 86-17401. 300p. 1987. text 46.00 (*0-231-06374-1*) Col U Pr.

Levite, Ariel E., et al, eds. Foreign Military Intervention: The Dynamics of Protracted Conflict. (Illus.). 312p. 1992. text 46.00 (*0-231-07294-5*) Col U Pr.

Levite, Bernard L. Structured COBOL Programming: Interactive & Batch Processing. 1994. write for info. (*0-614-32025-9*) Course Tech.

***Levite, Bob.** Dave Thomas: A Decade of Dave in Advertising. (Illus.). 128p. 1999. write for info. (*0-9659352-8-0*) DaScribe Lit.

Levite, George. By George for Lilly - Love Letters to a Potbellied Stove. Griffis, Molly L., ed. LC 87-90704. (Illus.). 160p. 1992. pap. 11.95 (*0-927562-13-8*) Levite Apache.

Levithan, David. In the Eye of the Tornado. (Disaster Zone Ser.: Vol. 1). (J). 1998. pap. 3.99 (*0-590-12915-5*) Scholastic Inc.

— In the Eye of the Tornado. (Disaster Zone Ser.). 1998. 9.09 (*0-606-13334-8*, Pub. by Turtleback) Demco.

— In the Heart of the Quake. (Disaster Zone Ser.: Vol. 2). (J). 1998. mass mkt. 3.99 (*0-590-12916-3*, Apple Paperbacks) Scholastic Inc.

***Levithan, David.** In the Heart of the Quake, 2. (Disaster Zone Ser.). 1998. 9.09 (*0-606-13335-6*, Pub. by Turtleback) Demco.

— Journey Through the Lost Canyon. (Pokemon Challenge Ser.). (Illus.). 128p. (J). (gr. 4-7). 2000. pap. 4.50 (*0-439-15407-3*) Scholastic Inc.

— Sixth Sense. (Illus.). (YA). 2000. pap. text 59.85 (*0-439-21195-6*) Scholastic Inc.

— Sixth Sense. Vol. 1. (Illus.). 160p. (gr. 4-7). 2000. pap. text 4.99 (*0-439-20270-1*) Scholastic Inc.

Leviticus. Sefer Ha'hinnuch Vol. 5. Pt. 2: Bemidbar & Devarim. 1985. 22.95 (*0-87306-297-3*) Feldheim.

Levitin & McMahon. Plants & Society. 1995. teacher ed. 15.31 (*0-697-24323-0*, WCB McGr Hill) McGrw-H Hghr Educ.

Levitin, Alexis, ed. see De Andrade, Eugenio.

Levitin, Alexis, tr. see De Andrade, Eugenio.

Levitin, Alexis, tr. see Lispector, Clarice.

Levitin, Anany. Data Quality Foundations. 2nd rev. ed. Snow, Kimberly, ed. (AT&T Quality Library). (Illus.). 50p. (Orig.). 1992. pap. 22.45 (*0-932764-26-6*, 500-490) AT&T Customer Info.

Levitin, Dan. From Demo Tape to Record Deal. (Alfred Handy Guide Ser.). 48p. 1992. pap. 4.50 (*0-88284-494-6*, 4422) Alfred Pub.

Levitin, Howard. Pre-Med Handbook. 336p. (Orig.). 1986. mass mkt. 12.95 (*0-446-38291-4*, Pub. by Warner Bks) Little.

Levitin, Isabella, tr. see Yanovsky, Vassily.

Levitin, Michael, jt. auth. see Sverdlin, Alexey.

Levitin, Michael J., jt. auth. see Wiegley, Roger D.

An Asterisk (*) at the beginning of an entry indicates that the title is appearing for the first time.

Levitin, Moshe S., ed. see American Institute of Certified Public Accountants.

Levitin, Nancy. America's Health Care Crisis - Who's Responsible? Who's Responsible? LC 94-15523. (Impact Bks.). (Illus.). 128p. (YA). (gr. 7-12). 1994. lib. bdg. 24.00 (*0-531-11187-3*) Watts.

— Health Care Rights. LC 95-49196. 256p. (Orig.). 1996. pap. 14.00 (*0-380-78025-9*, Avon Bks) Morrow Avon.

Levitin, Sonia. Annie's Promise. 192p. (YA). (gr. 5 up). 1993. text, lib. bdg. 15.00 (*0-689-31752-2*) Aladdin.

— Annie's Promise. (Illus.). 192p. (YA). (gr. 7). 1996. per. 3.99 (*0-689-80440-7*) Aladdin.

— Annie's Promise. LC 92-16819. 1996. 9.09 (*0-606-09007-X*, Pub. by Turtleback) Demco.

— Boom Town. LC 96-53302. (Illus.). 32p. (J). (gr. k-4). 1997. 16.95 (*0-531-30043-9*); lib. bdg. 17.99 (*0-531-33043-5*) Orchard Bks Watts.

— The Cure. LC 98-33907. 180p. (YA). (gr. 5 up). 1999. 16.00 (*0-15-201827-1*) Harcourt.

***Levitin, Sonia.** The Cure. LC 98-33907. 256p. (J). (gr. 7 up). 2000. mass mkt. 4.95 (*0-380-73298-X*) Morrow Avon.

— Dream Freedom. 288p. (YA). (gr. 4-7). 2000. 17.00 (*0-15-202404-2*, Harcourt Child Bks) Harcourt.

Levitin, Sonia. Escape from Egypt. 272p. (YA). (gr. 7 up). 1996. pap. 4.99 (*0-14-037537-6*, PuffinBks) Peng Put Young Read.

Levitin, Sonia. Escape from Egypt: A Novel. 1996. 10.09 (*0-606-08678-1*, Pub. by Turtleback) Demco.

Levitin, Sonia. Evil Encounter. (J). 1997. mass mkt. 4.50 (*0-689-80601-9*) Aladdin.

— Evil Encounter. 1997. 9.60 (*0-606-12694-5*, Pub. by Turtleback) Demco.

— Evil Encounter: A Compelling Timely Novel about a Charismatic Leader's Hypnotic Power. 256p. (YA). (gr. 7 up). 1996. mass mkt. 17.00 (*0-689-80216-1*) S&S Bks Yung.

— Incident at Loring Groves. 160p. (gr. 7 up). 1990. mass mkt. 4.50 (*0-449-70347-9*, Juniper) Fawcett.

— Journey to America. 2nd ed. LC 70-98616. (Illus.). 160p. (J). (gr. 3-7). 1993. text 16.00 (*0-689-31829-4*) Atheneum Yung Read.

Levitin, Sonia. Journey to America. 2nd ed. 1987. 9.05 (*0-606-00503-X*, Pub. by Turtleback) Demco.

Levitin, Sonia. Journey to America. 2nd ed. LC 86-22234. (Illus.). 160p. (J). (gr. 4-7). 1987. reprint ed. mass mkt. 3.95 (*0-689-71130-1*) Aladdin.

— The Man Who Kept His Heart in a Bucket. (Baby-Sitters Club Ser.). (J). 1995. 11.19 (*0-606-07837-1*) Turtleback.

— Nine for California. LC 96-1958. (Illus.). 32p. (J). (gr. k-4). 1996. 15.95 (*0-531-09527-4*) Orchard Bks Watts.

***Levitin, Sonia.** Nine for California. 40p. 2000. pap. 6.95 (*0-531-07176-6*) Orchard Bks Watts.

Levitin, Sonia. The Return. LC 86-25891. 224p. (YA). (gr. 5 up). 1987. 16.00 (*0-689-31309-8*) Atheneum Yung Read.

— The Return. 192p. (gr. 7 up). 1988. mass mkt. 4.50 (*0-449-70280-4*, Juniper) Fawcett.

— Rita, the Weekend Rat. (Illus.). 144p. (Orig.). (J). (gr. 3-7). 1980. pap. 1.95 (*0-590-30378-3*) Scholastic Inc.

— Silver Days. 1992. 9.05 (*0-606-01597-3*, Pub. by Turtleback) Demco.

— Silver Days. LC 91-22581. 192p. (J). (gr. 5 up). 1992. reprint ed. mass mkt. 3.95 (*0-689-71570-6*) Aladdin.

***Levitin, Sonia.** The Singing Mountain. 304p. (YA). (gr. 7-12). 2000. pap. 4.99 (*0-689-83523-X*) Aladdin.

Levitin, Sonia. The Singing Mountain. LC 97-33365. 272p. (YA). (gr. 7-12). 1998. 17.00 (*0-689-80809-7*) S&S Childrens.

— A Single Speckled Egg. LC 75-4189. (Illus.). 40p. (J). (ps-3). 1976. 6.95 (*0-87466-074-2*) HM.

— Taking Charge. LC 98-36623. (Illus.). 32p. (J). (gr. k-4). 1999. 16.95 (*0-531-30149-4*); lib. bdg. 17.99 (*0-531-33149-0*) Orchard Bks Watts.

— Yesterday's Child. LC 96-31649. 256p. (J). (gr. 7 up). 1997. 17.00 (*0-689-80810-0*) S&S Childrens.

— Yesterday's Child. LC 96-31649. 272p. (J). (gr. 7). 1998. per. 4.99 (*0-689-82073-9*) S&S Childrens.

Levitin, Teresa E., jt. auth. see Miller, Warren E.

Levitin, Victor. TraX: Simulation & Analysis of Dynamical Systems. Millstein, Jeffrey A., ed. 73p. 1990. 345.00 (*1-884977-10-3*); teacher ed. 695.00 (*1-884977-11-1*) Applied Biomath.

Levitine, George. Culture & Revolution: Cultural Ramifications of the French Revolution. Libby, Susan & Hall, Pam, eds. (Illus.). 336p. (C). 1989. write for info. (*0-9625932-0-6*) Univ MD Dept Art Hist.

Leviton. Elements of Mediation. 2nd ed. (Counseling Ser.). 2002. pap. 13.50 (*0-534-36758-5*) Brooks-Cole.

— Handbook to Middle East Amphibians & Reptiles. LC 90-63909. 1992. write for info. (*0-916984-23-0*) SSAR.

Leviton, Alan E., et al, eds. Frontiers of Geological Exploration of Western North America. LC 82-71290. 248p. (Orig.). 1982. 16.95 (*0-934394-03-2*) AAASPD.

Leviton, Alan E. & Aldrich, Michele L., eds. Theodore Henry Hittell's the California Academy of Sciences, a Narrative History, 1853-1906. unabridged ed. (Memoirs of the California Academy of Sciences Ser.: Vol. 22). (Illus.). 640p. 1997. lib. bdg. 42.00 (*0-940228-39-4*) Calif Acad Sci.

Leviton, Alan E., jt. ed. see Kockelman, W. J.

Leviton, Alan E., jt. ed. see Taylor, Ronald J.

Leviton, Charles. There Is No Bad Truth. 288p. 1995. pap. text, per. 26.25 (*0-7872-1093-5*) Kendall-Hunt.

Leviton, Daniel. Horrendous Deaths, Health & Well-Being. 1990. 82.95 (*1-56032-033-8*) Hemisp Pub.

Leviton, Daniel, ed. Horrendous Death & Health: Towards Action. (Death Education, Aging & Health Care Ser.). 408p. 1991. 99.95 (*1-56032-186-5*) Hemisp Pub.

Leviton, Laura C., et al. Confronting Public Health Risks: A Decision Maker's Guide. LC 97-33795. 1997. write for info. (*0-8039-5356-9*); pap. write for info. (*0-8039-5357-7*) Sage.

Leviton, Richard. Anthroposophic Medicine Today. 40p. 1988. pap. 5.95 (*0-88010-265-9*) Anthroposophic.

— Brain Builders: A Lifelong Guide to Sharper Thinking, Better Memory, & an Age-Proof Mind. LC 95-32233. 432p. (C). 1995. pap. text 14.95 (*0-13-303603-0*) P-H.

— Brain Builders: A Lifelong Guide to Sharper Thinking, Better Memory, & an Age-Proof Mind. 432p. (C). 1995. text 29.95 (*0-13-303611-1*) P-H.

— The Imagination of Pentecost: Rudolf Steiner & Contemporary Spirituality. 464p. 1994. pap. 24.95 (*0-88010-379-5*) Anthroposophic.

— Looking for Arthur: A Once & Future Travelogue. LC 96-48775. 600p. 1995. pap. text 16.95 (*1-886449-13-9*) Barrytown Ltd.

***Leviton, Richard.** Physician: Medicine & the Unsuspected Battle for Human Freedom. 480p. 2000. pap. 16.95 (*1-57174-168-2*) Hampton Roads Pub Co.

Leviton, Richard. Weddings by Design: A Guide to Non-Traditional Ceremonies. LC 92-53058. 208p. 1994. pap. 15.00 (*0-06-251007-X*, Pub. by Harper SF) HarpC.

Leviton, Richard, jt. auth. see Lewis, Judith.

Leviton, Sharon C. & Greenstone, James L. The Elements of Mediation. LC 96-31849. (Counseling Ser.). 200p. (C). 1996. pap. 18.95 (*0-534-23982-X*) Brooks-Cole.

Leviton, Sharon C., jt. auth. see Greenstone, James L.

Levitov, Leo. Solution of the Voynich Manuscript. 182p. (Orig.). 1987. pap. 34.80 (*0-89412-148-0*) Aegean Park Pr.

Levitskiy, Semyon P. & Shulman, Zinoviy P. Bubbles in Polymeric Liquids. LC 94-61880. 307p. 1995. pap. text 99.95 (*1-56676-247-2*) Technomic.

Levitsky, David, jt. auth. see Garrison, Terry N.

Levitsky, David A. Malnutrition, Environment, & Behavior: New Perspectives. LC 78-58016. (Illus.). 299p. reprint ed. pap. 92.70 (*0-608-08540-5*, 206906300002) Bks Demand.

***Levitsky, Jacob.** Business Development Services. 224p. 2000. 25.00 (*1-85339-506-4*, Pub. by Intermed Tech) Stylus Pub VA.

Levitsky, Jacob, ed. Small Business in Transition Economies: Promoting Enterprise in Central & Eastern Europe & the Former Soviet Union. 160p. (Orig.). 1996. pap. 19.95 (*1-85339-343-6*) Women Ink.

Levitsky, Michael G. Pulmonary Physiology. 5th ed. (Illus.). 320p. 1999. pap. text 29.95 (*0-07-134543-4*) McGraw-Hill HPD.

Levitsky, Rachel. 2 (1+1) Portraits. 20p. 1998. pap. 5.00 (*1-887997-10-5*) Baksun Bks.

Levitsky, Ronald. The Innocence That Kills. LC 93-42385. 254p. 1994. text 20.00 (*0-684-19707-3*, Scribners Ref) Mac Lib Ref.

— The Wisdom of Serpents: A Nate Rosen Mystery. 256p. 1992. text 19.00 (*0-684-19411-2*) S&S Trade.

Levitsky, Serge L. Copyright, Defamation & Privacy in Soviet Civil Law, No. 22. (Law in Eastern Europe Ser.). 517p. 1979. lib. bdg. 98.50 (*90-286-0139-2*) Kluwer Academic.

Levitsky, Serge L., ed. see Boguslavsky, M. M. & Smirnov, P. S.

Levitsky, Sidney & Fitzgerald, Jeanne T., eds. Using CPT for Cardiothoracic Reimbursement: A Manual for Surgeons & Insurance Billing Specialists. 105p. (Orig.). 1990. 25.00 (*0-9626174-0-7*) Soc Thor Surgeons.

Levitt. Genres & Genders of Surrealism. LC 99-33344. 2000. text 45.00 (*0-312-12050-8*) St Martin.

— Raquets Unlimited. (KM - Office Procedures Ser.). 1982. pap., wbk. ed. 13.95 (*0-538-23501-2*) S-W Pub.

— The Reorganized National Health Service. 4th ed. 146p. 1991. pap. 52.50 (*1-56593-016-9*, 0259) Thomson Learn.

Levitt. Spin Dynamics. text. write for info. (*0-471-48921-2*); pap. text. write for info. (*0-471-48922-0*) Wiley.

Levitt. State & Local Government & Politics. 4th ed. 138p. (C). 1997. spiral bd. 34.95 (*0-7872-4307-8*, 41430701) Kendall-Hunt.

— Your Career: How to Make It Happen. 4th ed. (Career Development Ser.). (C). 1999. pap. 28.95 (*0-538-72191-X*) Thomson Learn.

Levitt & Mertelsmann, R. Hematopoietic Stem Cells: Biology & Therapeutic Applications. (Illus.). 681p. 1995. text 195.00 (*0-8247-9305-6*) Dekker.

Levitt, A. R., jt. auth. see MacLeod, J. S.

Levitt, Alan M. Disaster Planning & Recovery: A Guide for Facility Professionals. LC 96-35914. 432p. 1997. 69.95 (*0-471-14205-0*) Wiley.

Levitt, Annette S. The Intertextuality of Joyce Cary's "The Horse's Mouth" LC 93-32507. 186p. 1993. text 79.95 (*0-7734-9353-0*) E Mellen.

Levitt, Annette S., jt. ed. see Bertholf, Robert J.

Levitt, Anthony J., jt. ed. see Joffe, Russell T.

Levitt, Atma J. The Kripalu Cookbook: Gourmet Vegetarian Recipes. LC 94-38742. 416p. 1995. pap. 16.95 (*0-936399-65-1*) Berkshire Hse.

Levitt, B. Blake, jt. auth. see Sussman, John R.

Levitt, Blake B. Electromagnetic Fields. (Illus.). 400p. 1995. pap. 15.00 (*0-15-628100-7*) Harcourt.

Levitt, Cyril. Children of Privilege: Student Revolt in the Sixties. 288p. 1984. text 40.00 (*0-8020-5636-9*) U of Toronto Pr.

— Children of Privilege: Student Revolt in the Sixties: a Study of Student Movements in Canada, the United States & West Germany. LC 84-211030. (Illus.). 280p. reprint ed. pap. 86.80 (*0-7837-0526-3*, 204085200019) Bks Demand.

***Levitt, Cyril, et al, eds.** Mistaken Identities: The Second Wave of Controversy over "Political Correctness" LC 99-22413. 339p. 1999. pap. text 29.95 (*0-8204-4137-6*) P Lang Pubng.

Levitt, Cyril, ed. see DeGre, Gerard.

Levitt, Cyril, jt. ed. see Greenspan, Louis.

Levitt, David, jt. auth. see Schwanauer, Stephan.

Levitt, Diane. Private Sins. 1993. mass mkt. 4.99 (*1-55817-738-8*, Pinncle Kensgtn) Kensgtn Pub Corp.

— Teen Families & Welfare Dependency in California: Background Briefing Report with Seminar Presentations. 137p. 1994. pap. 15.00 (*0-929722-83-3*) CA State Library Fndtn.

Levitt, Eleanor. Natural Food Cookery. Orig. Title: The Wonderful World of Natural-Food Cookery. (Illus.). 320p. 1979. reprint ed. pap. 6.95 (*0-486-23851-2*) Dover.

Levitt, Eugene E. The Clinical Application of MMPI Special Scales. 136p. 1989. 29.95 (*0-8058-0047-6*) L Erlbaum Assocs.

— The Psychology of Anxiety. 2nd ed. LC 80-107. 188p. 1980. text 29.95 (*0-89859-040-X*) L Erlbaum Assocs.

Levitt, Eugene E. & Gotts, Edward E. The Clinical Application of MMPI Special Scales. 2nd ed. 200p. 1995. text 39.95 (*0-8058-1770-0*) L Erlbaum Assocs.

Levitt, Eugene E., et al. Depression: Concepts, Controversies & Some New Facts. 2nd ed. 264p. 1983. text 39.95 (*0-89859-278-X*) L Erlbaum Assocs.

Levitt, Geoffrey M. The Western Response to State-Supported Terrorism, 134. LC 88-9859. (Washington Papers: No. 134). (Illus.). 156p. 1988. 39.95 (*0-275-93021-1*, C3021, Praeger Pubs); pap. 9.95 (*0-275-93022-X*, B3022, Praeger Pubs) Greenwood.

***Levitt, Gerald M.** The Turk, Chess Automation. (Illus.). 256p. 2000. lib. bdg. 50.00 (*0-7864-0778-6*) McFarland & Co.

Levitt, H. N. Achilles' Memoirs. LC 98-36307. 64p. 1998. pap. 14.95 (*0-7734-3084-9*, Mellen Poetry Pr) E Mellen.

Levitt, Helen. Helen Levitt: Mexico City. LC 97-2724. 128p. 1997. 35.00 (*0-393-04549-8*) Norton.

— In the Street: Chalk Drawings & Messages, New York City, 1938-1948. LC 86-29367. (Illus.). 112p. 1987. pap. 26.95 (*0-8223-0771-5*) Duke.

— Photographers on Photographers: Aperture 151. (Illus.). 80p. 1998. pap. 27.95 (*0-89381-773-2*) Aperture.

— A Way of Seeing. rev. ed. LC 81-82838. (Illus.). 100p. 1989. reprint ed. pap. 26.95 (*0-8223-1005-8*) Duke.

— A Way of Seeing. 3rd rev. ed. LC 81-82838. (Illus.). 100p. 1989. reprint ed. text 49.95 (*0-8223-1004-X*) Duke.

Levitt, I. M. & Marshall, Roy K. Star Maps for Beginners: Fiftieth Anniversary Edition. 50th anniversary ed. (Illus.). 64p. 1992. per. 10.00 (*0-671-79187-7*) S&S Trade Pap.

Levitt, Ian. Poverty & Welfare in Scotland, 1890-1948. 200p. 1989. 68.00 (*0-85224-558-0*, Pub. by Edinburgh U Pr) Col U Pr.

— Poverty & Welfare in Scotland, 1890-1948. 256p. 1990. pap. text 28.00 (*0-85224-583-1*, Pub. by Edinburgh U Pr) Col U Pr.

Levitt, Irene. Brainwriting - for Sales. (Illus.). 48p. 1997. pap. 9.95 (*0-9656723-0-1*) Serena Pub.

Levitt, J. Stanley. A Beginner's Guide to Investing in No-Load Mutual Funds. 127p. (Orig.). 1998. pap. 15.95 (*0-9631039-0-3*) J S Levitt.

Levitt, Jason, jt. auth. see Husain, Kamran.

Levitt, Jesse, et al, eds. Geolinguistic Perpectives: Proceedings of the International Conference Celebrating the Twentieth Anniversary of the American Society of Geolinguistics, 1985. 398p. (Orig.). 1987. pap. text 33.00 (*0-8191-6046-6*) U Pr of Amer.

Levitt, Jesse, jt. ed. see Thomas, T. M.

Levitt, JoAnn & Norian, Todd, eds. Sounds of the Sacred: Chants of Love & Prayer. LC 90-62313. (Illus.). 158p. (Orig.). pap. 14.95 (*0-940258-23-4*) Kripalu Pubns.

Levitt, Joanna J. Sex & Psychology of Sexual Offenses: Index of New Information with Authors, Subjects & Bibliography. 180p. 1993. 47.50 (*1-55914-768-7*); pap. 44.50 (*1-55914-769-5*) ABBE Pubs Assn.

— Sex & Psychology of Sexual Offenses: Index of New Information with Authors, Subjects & Bibliography. rev. ed. 151p. 1998. 47.50 (*0-7883-1850-0*); pap. 44.50 (*0-7883-1851-9*) ABBE Pubs Assn.

Levitt, Joel. Complete Guide to Fleet Management. 220p. 1989. boxed set 39.00 (*0-13-159328-5*) P-H.

— Handbook of Maintenance Management. 476p. 1997. 59.95 (*0-8311-3075-X*) Indus Pr.

— Internet Guide for Maintenance Managers. LC 98-42765. (Illus.). 160p. 1998. pap. 24.95 (*0-8311-3081-4*) Indus Pr.

— Managing Factory Maintenance. (Illus.). 290p. 1996. 39.95 (*0-8311-3063-6*) Indus Pr.

Levitt, Joel H. Small Signal Analysis: By Computer, by Inspection. LC 82-83970. (Illus.). 184p. (C). 1983. pap. text 11.25 (*0-9609892-0-X*) Haywood Pr.

Levitt, Johathan. Secrets of Spectacular Chess. 1995. pap. 23.00 (*0-8050-3901-5*) H Holt & Co.

Levitt, Jonathan. Genius in Chess!! LC 97-71878. (New American Batsford Chess Library). 144p. (Orig.). 1997. pap. 19.50 (*1-879479-57-5*) ICE WA.

Levitt, Joseph. Pearson & Canada's Role in Nuclear Disarmament & Arms Control Negotiations, 1945-1957. (Illus.). 344p. 1993. 60.00 (*0-7735-0905-4*, Pub. by McG-Queens Univ Pr) CUP Services.

***Levitt, Joy & Strassfeld, Michael, eds.** A Night of Questions: A Passover Haggadah. (Illus.). 160p. 2000. pap. 12.95 (*0-935457-49-6*, Pub. by Reconstructionist Pr) Fordham.

Levitt, Julie G. Your Career: How to Make It Happen. 3rd ed. (CA - Career Development Ser.). (C). 1995. mass mkt. 23.25 (*0-538-71259-7*) S-W Pub.

Levitt, Laura. Jews & Feminism: Ambivalent Search for Home. LC 97-2757. 240p. (C). 1997. pap. 19.99 (*0-415-91445-0*) Routledge.

— Jews & Feminism: Ambivalent Search for Home. LC 97-2757. 240p. (C). 1997. 70.00 (*0-415-91444-2*) Routledge.

Levitt, Laura, jt. ed. see Peskowitz, Miriam.

Levitt, Lawrence P., jt. auth. see Weiner, Howard L.

Levitt, M. & Belforte, David A., eds. Industrial Laser Handbook. (Illus.). 400p. 1992. 238.95 (*0-387-97751-1*) Spr-Verlag.

Levitt, Mairi. Nice When They Are Young: Contemporary Christianity in Families & Schools. 181p. 1996. text 63.95 (*1-85972-388-8*, Pub. by Avebry) Ashgate Pub Co.

***Levitt, Malcolm & Lord, Christopher.** The Political Economy of Monetary Union. LC 99-88066. 2000. write for info. (*0-312-23189-X*) St Martin.

Levitt, Marc J. Johnny Appleseed: Gentle Hero. unabridged ed. (J). (gr. k-6). 1991. 12.00 incl. audio (*0-87483-176-8*) August Hse.

Levitt, Marcus C. Russian Literary Politics & the Pushkin Celebration of 1880. LC 88-43237. (Studies of the Harriman Institute). (Illus.). 240p. 1989. text 39.95 (*0-8014-2250-7*) Cornell U Pr.

Levitt, Marcus C., ed. Early Modern Russian Writers: Late Seventeenth & Eighteenth Centuries. LC 95-1711. (Dictionary of Literary Biography Ser.: Vol. 150). 465p. 1995. text 155.00 (*0-8103-5711-9*) Gale.

Levitt, Martin J. Confessions of a Union Buster. LC 93-14736. 1993. 25.00 (*0-517-58330-5*, Crown) Crown Pub Group.

Levitt, Michael, jt. auth. see Conner, Dennis.

Levitt, Mimi, tr. see Durrenmatt, Friedrich & Selz, Peter H.

Levitt, Morris J. State & Local Government & Politics: A Simulation. 3rd ed. 136p. 1993. spiral bd. 20.95 (*0-8403-8741-5*) Kendall-Hunt.

Levitt, Mortimer. The Executive Look & How to Get It: Professional Guidelines for Putting Together Executive Wardrobes for Men & Women. LC 79-18848. (AMA Management Briefing Ser.). 76p. reprint ed. pap. 30.00 (*0-608-13398-1*, 205574100034) Bks Demand.

Levitt, Morton. The Cretan Glance: The World & Art of Nikos Kazantzakis. LC 79-23990. 203p. reprint ed. pap. 63.00 (*0-608-09851-5*, 206981600006) Bks Demand.

***Levitt, Morton.** James Joyce & Modernism: Beyond Dublin. LC 99-47959. (Studies in Irish Literature Ser.: Vol. 2). 296p. 2000. 89.95 (*0-7734-7869-8*) E Mellen.

Levitt, Morton & Rubenstein, Ben, eds. The Mental Health Field: A Critical Appraisal. LC 70-135397. 387p. reprint ed. pap. 120.00 (*0-608-16629-4*, 202768100055) Bks Demand.

— Youth & Social Change. LC 73-157414. 420p. reprint ed. pap. 130.20 (*0-608-15233-1*, 202749900055) Bks Demand.

Levitt, N. J. Grassmannians & Gauss Maps in Piecewise-Linear & Piecewise-Differential Topology. (Lecture Notes in Mathematics Ser.: Vol. 1366). 203p. 1989. 37.95 (*0-387-50756-6*) Spr-Verlag.

Levitt, Norman. Prometheus Bedeviled: Science & the Contradictions of Contemporary Culture. LC 98-37628. 420p. (C). 1999. 32.00 (*0-8135-2652-3*) Rutgers U Pr.

Levitt, Norman, jt. auth. see Gross, Paul R.

Levitt, Paul M. A Structural Approach to the Analysis of Drama. LC 79-159466. (De Proprietatibus Litterarum, Ser. Major: No. 15). 119p. 1971. text 25.40 (*90-279-1841-4*) Mouton.

Levitt, Paul M. & Gurainick, Elissa S. You Can Make It Back: Coping with Serious Illness. LC 84-26049. 226p. reprint ed. pap. 70.10 (*0-7837-1362-2*, 204151000021) Bks Demand.

***Levitt, Paul M. & Guralnick, Elissa S.** How Raven Found the Daylight: And Other American Indian Stories. 120p. 2000. 29.95 (*0-87081-601-2*); pap. 14.95 (*0-87081-586-5*) U of Okla Pr.

Levitt, Paul M. & Guralnick, Elissa S. The Weighty Word Book. 2nd ed. LC 99-29881. (Illus.). 96p. (J). (gr. 4-7). 1999. 17.95 (*1-57098-313-5*, Pub. by Roberts Rinehart) Publishers Group.

Levitt, Paul M., et al. The Cancer Reference Book: Direct & Clear Answers to Everyone's Questions. LC 78-26046. 299p. reprint ed. pap. 92.70 (*0-7837-1571-4*, 204186300024) Bks Demand.

— The Weighty Word Book. LC PZ7.L5824 W4. (Illus.). 99p. (J). (gr. 4-9). 1990. reprint ed. 17.95 (*0-9627979-0-1*) Manuscripts.

Levitt, Paul M., ed. see Lowry, Ed, et al.

Levitt, Peter, ed. see Dunitz, Jay.

Levitt, Peter, ed. & intro. see Hanh, Thich Nhat.

Levitt, R., et al. The Reorganized National Health Service. 320p. 1995. 38.25 (*0-614-10678-8*, 1220) Singular Publishing.

Levitt, Rachelle, ed. Cities Reborn. LC 87-50398. 203p. 1987. pap. 53.95 (*0-87420-667-7*, C32) Urban Land.

Levitt, Rachelle L., jt. ed. see Waite, Margaret M.

Levitt, Ray E., jt. auth. see Dym, Clive L.

Levitt, Raymond E. & Samelson, Nancy M. Construction Safety Management. 2nd ed. LC 93-4539. 304p. 1993. 90.00 (*0-471-59933-6*) Wiley.

Levitt, Richard, ed. see Jarrell, David G.

***Levitt, Ruth & Wall, Andrew.** The Reorganized National Health Service. 6th ed. (Illus.). 352p. 1999. pap. 37.50 (*0-7487-3894-0*) Standard Pub.

Levitt, Ruth, tr. see Claus, Hugo.

Levitt, Ruth, tr. see De Loo, Tessa.

Levitt, Ruth, tr. see Minco, Marga, et al.

Levitt, S. H., et al. Levitt & Tapley's Technological Basis of Radiation Therapy. 2nd ed. (Illus.). 414p. 1992. text 82.00 (*0-8121-1466-3*) Lppncott W & W.

L

Levitt, Sarah. Victorians Unbuttoned: Registered Designs for Clothing, Their Makers & Wearers, 1839-1900. (Illus.). 246p. 1986. 34.95 (*0-04-391013-0*) Routledge.

Levitt, Saul. The Andersonville Trial. 1961. pap. 5.25 (*0-8222-0042-2*) Dramatists Play.

— Jim Thorpe, All American: Playscript. (J). (gr. 4 up). 1980. 6.50 (*0-87602-237-9*) Anchorage.

Levitt, Seymour H., et al, eds. Levitt & Tapley's Technological Basis of Radiation Therapy: Clinical Applications. 3rd ed. LC 98-3836. 560p. 1998. 89.00 (*0-683-30123-3*) Lppncott W & W.

Levitt, Sophie. Treatment of Cerebral Palsy & Motor Delay. 3rd ed. LC 94-16798. (Illus.). 312p. 1995. pap. 44.95 (*0-632-03873-X*, Pub. by Blckwll Scitfc UK) Blackwell Sci.

Levitt, Susan. Taoist Feng Shui: The Ancient Roots of the Chinese Art of Placement. (Illus.). 176p. 2000. pap. 14.95 (*0-89281-723-2*) Inner Tradit.

Levitt, Susan & Tang, Jean. Taoist Astrology: A Handbook of the Authentic Chinese Tradition. LC 97-10330. (Illus.). 224p. 1997. pap. 14.95 (*0-89281-606-6*) Inner Tradit.

Levitt, Theodore. The Marketing Imagination. LC 83-47989. 256p. (C). 1983. 9.95 (*0-02-918840-7*) Free Pr.

— The Marketing Imagination. enl. ed. 218p. 1986. pap. 16.95 (*0-02-919090-8*) Free Pr.

— Thinking about Management. 160p. 1990. 22.95 (*0-02-918605-6*) Free Pr.

Levitte, Elaine. Step-by-Step Table Decorating. (Step-by-Step Ser.). (Illus.). 96p. 1998. pap. text 10.95 (*1-58062-022-1*) Adams Media.

***LeVitus, Bob.** Apple Works 5.0 for Dummies. LC 99-61338. (For Dummies Ser.). 408p. 1999. pap. 19.99 (*0-7645-0557-2*) IDG Bks.

— AppleWorks X for Dummies. 408p. 2000. pap. 19.99 (*0-7645-0636-6*) IDG Bks.

LeVitus, Bob. Clarisworks Office for Dummies. 2nd ed. LC 97-80750. (For Dummies Ser.). 384p. 1997. pap. 19.99 (*0-7645-0113-5*) IDG Bks.

— Dr. Macintosh: Tips, Techniques & Advice for Mastering Your Macintosh. 350p. 1989. pap. text 19.95 (*0-201-51733-7*) Addison-Wesley.

— Dr. Macintosh's Guide to the On-Line Universe. 384p. (C). 1992. pap. 24.95 (*0-201-58125-6*) Addison-Wesley.

***LeVitus, Bob.** Imac! I Didn't Know You Could Do That... 4th ed. 400p. 1999. pap. text 19.99 (*0-7821-2589-1*) Sybex.

LeVitus, Bob. Mac OS 8 for Dummies. LC 97-80123. 432p. 1997. pap. 19.99 (*0-7645-0271-9*) IDG Bks.

— Mac OS 8.5 for Dummies. LC QA76.76.O63L48684. (For Dummies Ser.). 432p. 1998. pap. 19.99 (*0-7645-0397-9*) IDG Bks.

***LeVitus, Bob.** Mac OS 9 for Dummies. LC 99-66422. (For Dummies Ser.). (Illus.). 432p. 1999. pap. 19.99 (*0-7645-0652-8*) IDG Bks.

LeVitus, Bob. Macintosh System 7.5 for Dummies. LC 94-77742. 432p. 1994. pap. 19.95 (*1-56884-197-3*) IDG Bks.

***LeVitus, Bob.** MacWorld Microsoft Office "X" Bible. (Bible Ser.). (Illus.). 900p. 2000. pap. text 39.99 (*0-7645-3462-9*) IDG Bks.

LeVitus, Bob. MW Office 98 Bible. 880p. 1998. pap. 39.99 (*0-7645-4041-6*) IDG Bks.

— Stupid Beyond Belief PC. 128p. 1992. pap. 19.95 incl. disk (*0-201-63235-7*) Addison-Wesley.

LeVitus, Bob & Brisbin, Shelly. Mac Answers! Certified Tech Support. LC 99-176038. 458p. 1998. pap. 24.99 (*0-07-211919-5*) McGraw.

LeVitus, Bob & Evans, Jeff. Webmaster Macintosh. 2nd ed. LC 97-122070. (Illus.). 525p. 1997. pap., pap. text 34.95 incl. cd-rom (*0-12-445602-2*) Morgan Kaufmann.

— Webmaster Windows. 2nd ed. (Illus.). 490p. 1997. pap., pap. text 34.95 incl. cd-rom (*0-12-445600-6*) Morgan Kaufmann.

LeVitus, Bob & Pitts, Natanya. The Official BBEdit Book. 350p. 1997. 39.99 (*1-56276-505-1*, Ziff-Davis Pr) Que.

***LeVitus, Bob, et al.** Tango 2000 for Dummies. (For Dummies Ser.). (Illus.). 384p. 2000. pap. 24.99 incl. cd-rom (*0-7645-0645-5*) IDG Bks.

Levitus, Geoff, ed. Lying about the Landscape. 1997. text 30.00 (*90-5704-031-X*, Pub. by Craftsman House) Gordon & Breach.

Levitus, Sydney & Boyer, Timothy P. World Ocean Atlas, 1994 Vol. 4: Temperature. (Illus.). 117p. (Orig.). (C). 1996. pap. text 50.00 (*0-7881-3077-3*) DIANE Pub.

Levitus, Sydney, et al. World Ocean Atlas, 1994 Vol. 5: Interannual Variability of Upper Ocean Thermal Structure. (Illus.). 176p. (Orig.). (C). 1996. pap. text 50.00 (*0-7881-3078-1*) DIANE Pub.

Levitz, Linda C. The Dark Face of Planting: Poems. LC 96-27674. (Illus.). 80p. (Orig.). 1997. pap. 9.95 (*1-56474-205-9*) Fithian Pr.

Levitz, Mitchell. Count Us In: Growing up with Down Syndrome. 208p. 1994. pap. 9.95 (*0-15-622660-X*, Harvest Bks) Harcourt.

Levitz, Mitchell & Kingsley. Count Us In: Growing up with Down Syndrome. 1994. 19.95 (*0-15-150447-4*) Harcourt.

Levitz, Nancy, ed. see Weidemann, Sela.

Levitz, Paul. Legion of Superheroes, Vol. 1. 1989. pap. 10.00 (*0-912771-52-6*) Mayfair Games.

Levitz, Paul, ed. see O'Neil, Dennis.

Levitzki, Alexander, jt. ed. see Schulster, Dennis.

Levitzky, et al. Introduction to Respiratory Care. (Illus.). 608p. 1990. text 67.00 (*0-7216-1090-0*, W B Saunders Co) Harcrt Hlth Sci Grp.

Levitzky, Michael G., et al. Cardiopulmonary Physiology in Anesthesiology. LC 94-2822. (Illus.). 384p. 1996. text 49.00 (*0-07-037534-8*) McGraw-Hill HPD.

Levkoff, Alice F., jt. auth. see Whitelaw, Robert N.

***Levkoff, Mary L.** Rodin in His Time. (Illus.). 232p. 2000. 65.00 (*0-8478-2299-0*) Rizzoli Intl.

***Levkoff, Sue.** Recruitment & Retention in Minority Populations: Lessons Learned in Conducting Research on Health Promotion & Minority Aging. LC 00-30138. 2000. write for info. (*0-8261-1375-3*) Springer Pub.

***Levkoff, Sue & Chee, Yeon Kyung.** Aging in Good Health: Multidiscinplinary Perspectives. LC 00-30091. 2000. write for info. (*0-8261-1366-4*) Springer Pub.

Levkoff, Sue, jt. auth. see Wei, Jeanne.

Levkowitz, H., jt. ed. see Grinstein, George G.

Levkowitz, Haim. Color Theory & Modeling for Computer Graphics, Visualization & Multimedia. LC 97-12567. (Kluwer International Series in Engineering & Computer Science: Vol. 402). 1997. text 165.00 (*0-7923-9928-5*) Kluwer Academic.

Levmore, jt. auth. see Scott.

Levmore, Saul. Foundations of Tort Law. LC 92-45580. (Interdisciplinary Readers in Law Ser.). (Illus.). 368p. 1993. text 62.95 (*0-19-508391-1*) OUP.

Levmore, Saul, et al. Foundations of Tort Law, Vol. 1. LC 92-45580. (Interdisciplinary Readers in Law Ser.). (Illus.). 368p. 1993. pap. text 27.95 (*0-19-508392-X*) OUP.

Levno, Arley W. Rencontres Culturelles: Cross-Cultural Mini-Dramas. Snyder, Barbara, ed. (FRE.). 120p. (C). 1984. pap. 12.65 (*0-8442-1247-4*, VF1247-4) NTC Contemp Pub Co.

LeVoir, John M., jt. auth. see Hogan, Richard M.

Levokove, Michael. The Selling Edge: Winning over Today's Business Customers. LC 92-75676. 200p. 1993. 18.95 (*0-944435-21-1*) Glenbridge Pub.

Levonen, Jarmo J. & Tukiainen, Markku, eds. Complex Learning in Computer Environments: A Special Issue of Machine-Mediated Learning, Vol. 5, No. 2. 115p. 1996. pap. 20.00 (*0-8058-9921-9*) L Erlbaum Assocs.

Levorsen, Arville L., ed. see American Association of Petroleum Geologists Staff.

Levorsen, Bella, ed. see Sierra Nevada Dog Drivers, Inc. Staff.

LeVot, Andre. F. Scott Fitzgerald. LC 80-2420. 1984. mass mkt. 9.95 (*0-446-38065-2*, Pub. by Warner Bks) Little.

Levow, David E. Banking & Financial Services: Glossary of Terms. 5th ed. 108p. 1998. reprint ed. spiral bd. 9.95 (*0-9661656-0-8*) Levow Info Systs.

— Banking & Financial Services: Glossary of Terms. 6th rev. ed. 120p. Date not set. spiral bd. 11.95 (*0-9661656-1-6*) Levow Info Systs.

Levoy, Bob. 101 Secrets of a High-Performance Veterinary Practice. LC 96-60137. (Illus.). 101p. 1996. pap. 29.95 (*0-935078-60-6*) Veterinary Med.

***Levoy, Gregg.** Callings: Finding & Following an Authentic Life. 339p. 1998. pap. 14.00 (*0-609-80370-0*, Three Riv Pr) Crown Pub Group.

Levoy, Gregg. Callings: Finding & Following an Authentic Life. LC 97-6116. 352p. 1997. 23.00 (*0-517-70569-9*) Random.

Levoy, Myron. Alan & Naomi. LC 76-41522. (Trophy Bk.). 192p. (J). (gr. 4-7). 1987. pap. 4.95 (*0-06-440209-6*, HarpTrophy) HarpC Child Bks.

— Alan & Naomi. LC 76-41522. 1987. 10.05 (*0-606-03543-5*, Pub. by Turtleback) Demco.

— Kelly 'n' Me. LC 91-35807. (Charlotte Zolotow Bk.). 208p. (YA). (gr. 7 up). 1992. 15.00 (*0-06-020838-4*) HarpC Child Bks.

***Levoy, Myron.** Kelly 'n' Me. 202p. (gr. 7-12). 2000. pap. 13.95 (*0-595-09356-6*) iUniversecom.

Levoy, Myron. The Magic Hat of Mortimer Wintergreen. LC 87-45292. (Charlotte Zolotow Bk.). (Illus.). 224p. (J). (gr. 3-7). 1988. 11.95 (*0-06-023841-0*) HarpC Child Bks.

Levoy, Myron. Witch of 4th Street. LC 74-183174. (Illus.). 128p. (J). (gr. 3-7). 1974. pap. 4.95 (*0-06-440059-X*, HarpTrophy) HarpC Child Bks.

Levoy, Myron. The Witch of Fourth Street & Other Stories. (J). (gr. 3-6). 1991. 19.00 (*0-8446-6450-2*) Peter Smith.

Levoy, Myron. Witch of Fourth Street, & Other Stories. (J). 1972. 9.60 (*0-606-02370-4*, Pub. by Turtleback) Demco.

Levoy, Robert P. 101 Secrets of a High-Performance Dental Practice: From the Success Files of Bob Levoy. LC 96-51693. 1996. 44.95 (*0-87814-593-1*) PennWell Bks.

— Successful Professional Practice. LC 74-97581. (Illus.). 192p. 1970. 39.95 (*0-13-868307-7*, Busn) P-H.

Levra, John & Peterson, James A. Coaching Defensive Lineman. LC 98-87855. (Art & Science of Coaching Ser.). (Illus.). 240p. 1998. pap. 17.95 (*1-57167-207-9*) Coaches Choice.

Levran, Aharon. Israel after the Storm: Strategic Lessons from the Second Gulf War. LC 97-10552. 169p. (Orig.). 1997. 52.50 (*0-7146-4755-1*, Pub. by Irish Acad Pr); pap. 24.50 (*0-7146-4316-5*, Pub. by Irish Acad Pr) Intl Spec Bk.

Levring, Tore, ed. Tenth International Seaweed Symposium. (Illus.). 780p. 1981. 150.00 (*3-11-008389-2*) De Gruyter.

Levshin, A. L., jt. auth. see Kaufman, Alexander A.

***Levstik, Linda S. & Barton, Keith C.** Doing History: Investigating with Children in Elementary & Middle Schools. 2nd ed. LC 00-24495. 256p. 2000. pap. write for info. (*0-8058-3562-8*) L Erlbaum Assocs.

Levstik, Linda S. & Barton, Keith C. Doing History in the K-8 Classroom: Investigating with Children in Elementary & Middle Schools. 208p. 1996. pap. text 25.00 (*0-8058-8040-2*) L Erlbaum Assocs.

Levtzion, Nehemia. Islam in West Africa: Religion, Society & Politics to 1800. (Collected Studies: CS 462). 336p. 1994. 115.95 (*0-86078-444-4*, Pub. by Variorum) Ashgate Pub Co.

Levtzion, Nehemia, ed. Conversion to Islam. LC 77-26771. 265p. 1979. 45.00 (*0-8419-0343-3*) Holmes & Meier.

Levtzion, Nehemia, ed. from ARA. Medieval West Africa Before 1400: Ghana, Takrur, Gao (Songhay) & Mali as Described by Arab Scholars & Merchants. rev. ed. Hopkins, J. F., tr. from ARA. Orig. Title: Corpus of Early Arab Sources for West African History. (Illus.). 320p. (C). Date not set. text 44.95 (*1-55876-164-0*); pap. text 22.95 (*1-55876-165-9*) Wiener Pubs Inc.

***Levtzion, Nehemia & Pouwels, Randall L., eds.** The History of Islam in Africa. LC 99-27729. 640p. 1999. 75.00 (*0-8214-1296-5*) Ohio U Pr.

— The History of Islam in Africa. LC 99-27729. (Illus.). 640p. 1999. pap. 26.95 (*0-8214-1297-3*) Ohio U Pr.

***Levtzion, Nehemiah.** Corpus of Early Arab Sources for West African History. Hopkins, J. F. P., ed. 516p. 2000. reprint ed. pap. text 28.95 (*1-55876-241-8*) Wiener Pubs Inc.

Levush, Ruth, ed. Campaign Financing of National Elections in Foreign Countries. 199p. (Orig.). (C). 1992. pap. text 40.00 (*1-56806-108-0*) DIANE Pub.

Levvasseur, K., jt. auth. see Hibbard, Allen C.

Levy. AIDS: Pathogenesis & Treatment. (Immunology Ser.: Vol. 44). (Illus.). 720p. 1988. text 165.00 (*0-8247-7684-4*) Dekker.

— Bankruptcy Handbook. 2nd ed. 1993. 125.00 (*0-316-52253-8*, Aspen Law & Bus) Aspen Pub.

— Connectionist Models Mem & Language. 288p. 1995. 59.95 (*1-85728-368-6*, Pub. by UCL Pr Ltd) Taylor & Francis.

Levy. Dans le Metro. pap. text 3.95 (*0-88436-907-2*) EMC-Paradigm.

Levy. Essential Life & Health. 4th ed. 1988. wbk. ed. 18.50 (*0-07-556984-1*) McGraw.

— Essentials of Investments. 2000. 61.00 (*0-324-00217-3*) S-W Pub.

— Fronteras, Vol. 3. (SPA.). 1989. pap. text, teacher ed. 81.00 (*0-03-021413-0*) Holt R&W.

— Fronteras: Gramatica. 3rd ed. (C). 1996. student ed. 37.00 (*0-03-016978-X*) Harcourt Coll Pubs.

— Hebrew for All. Date not set. 16.50 (*0-85303-191-6*, Pub. by M Vallentine & Co) Intl Spec Bk.

— Imagenes: Guia Al Mundo Hispan. (C). 1998. pap. text 25.00 (*0-03-026387-5*) Harcourt Coll Pubs.

— The Infant. (C). Date not set. 46.00 (*0-205-28086-2*, Macmillan Coll) P-H.

— Introduction to Investments. 2nd ed. LC 98-29096. (FD - Investments Ser.). 1998. mass mkt. 97.95 (*0-538-87737-5*) S-W Pub.

— Introduction to Investments. 2nd ed. (FD - Investments Ser.). (C). 1999. pap., student ed. 19.00 (*0-538-88552-1*) S-W Pub.

***Levy.** Introduction to Investments. 3rd ed. 2000. pap. 54.00 (*0-324-07082-9*) Sth-Wstrn College.

Levy. Inventing & Patenting Sourcebook. 2nd ed. 1992. 95.00 (*0-8103-7616-4*) Gale.

***Levy.** Law & Ethics. 440p. 1999. pap. text 24.00 (*0-536-02757-9*) Pearson Custom.

Levy. Life & Health: Target Wellness. 1992. pap. text, teacher ed. 13.43 (*0-07-037497-X*) McGraw.

***Levy.** Maine Family Law: 1999 Edition. 700p. 1999. write for info. (*0-327-04993-6*, 8164013) LEXIS Pub.

Levy. Massachusetts Zoning & Land Use Law. 1994. write for info. (*1-56257-217-2*, MICHIE) LEXIS Pub.

— Modern City & Metro Area. LC 99-32735. 302p. 1999. pap. 35.00 (*0-13-287111-4*) P-H.

— Modern Drama: Selected Plays from 1879 to the Present. LC 98-4292. 985p. 1998. pap. text 55.00 (*0-13-226721-7*) P-H.

***Levy.** On Wings of Light: A Shabat Siddur. 2000. write for info. (*0-88125-638-2*) Ktav.

— Packaging, Policy & the Environment. LC 99-51890. 448p. 1999. 135.00 (*0-8342-1718-X*, 1718X) Aspen Pub.

Levy. Principles of Corporate Finance. (FN - Financial Management Ser.). 1998. pap. 19.95 (*0-538-85438-3*) S-W Pub.

— Principles of Corporate Finance. 2nd ed. (SWC-Finance Ser.). 2001. pap. text 57.00 (*0-324-02394-4*) Sth-Wstrn College.

— Project Management in Construction. 3rd ed. LC 99-36049. 352p. 1999. 64.95 (*0-07-134230-3*) McGraw.

***Levy.** Remember Every Name, Every Time. 2001. write for info. (*0-684-87393-1*) S&S Trade.

Levy. Retailing Management. 4th ed. 2000. 65.50 (*0-07-231577-6*) McGraw.

— Role of Procoagulant Activity in Health & Disease. 1993. 165.00 (*0-317-05735-9*, QR186, CRC Reprint) Franklin.

— Subcontractors' Operation Manual. LC 99-14448. 360p. 1999. 69.95 (*0-07-134858-1*) McGraw.

— Targeting Wellness. 1992. teacher ed. 26.87 (*0-07-037576-3*) McGraw.

— Telecommunications & the Internet. (DF - Computer Applications Ser.). 1997. pap., teacher ed. 14.95 (*0-538-67251-X*) S-W Pub.

— Tools of Critical Thinking: Metathoughts for Psychology. (C). 2001. pap. 21.00 (*0-205-28063-3*, Macmillan Coll) P-H.

— A Traveler from Altruria. 184p. 1996. pap. text 12.95 (*0-312-11799-X*) St Martin.

— Ultimate Universe. 1998. 29.95 (*0-671-01204-5*) S&S Trade.

— Videomundo. 3rd ed. (C). 1996. pap. text, teacher ed. 42.00 incl. trans. (*0-03-017014-1*) Harcourt Coll Pubs.

— Viewer's Manual: Videomundo. 3rd ed. (C). 1996. pap. text, lab manual ed. 20.50 (*0-03-017017-6*) Harcourt Coll Pubs.

Levy & Karst. Encyclopedia of the American Constitution. 2000. 110.00 (*0-02-864880-3*) S&S Trade.

Levy & Kindler, eds. Psychoanalytic Supervision. (Psychoanalytic Inquiry Ser.: Vol. 15, No. 2). 1995. 20.00 (*0-88163-995-8*) Analytic Pr.

Levy & Perry. Principles of Corporate Finance. LC 97-36159. (AB - Accounting Principles Ser.). (C). 1997. mass mkt. 98.95 (*0-538-84741-7*) S-W Pub.

Levy & Sabnat. Modern Portfolio & Investment Selection. 2nd ed. (FN - Financial Mangement Ser.). 2002. mass mkt. 74.95 (*0-538-86601-2*) S-W Pub.

Levy, jt. auth. see Berne, Robert M.

Levy, jt. auth. see McCarthy.

Levy, jt. auth. see Orlando.

Levy, Habib. Comprehensive History of the Jews of Iran (Tarikh-e Yahud-e Iran) The Outset of Diaspora. Ebrami, Hooshang, ed. LC 99-20731. (Illus.). 540p. 1999. lib. bdg. 49.95 (*1-56859-086-5*) Mazda Pubs.

Levy, A. Deep Inelastic Scattering & Related Subjects: Proceedings of the International Workshop. 552p. 1995. text 124.00 (*981-02-2053-7*) World Scientific Pub.

Levy, A., et al, eds. Endogenous Peptides & Centrally Acting Drugs. (Progress in Biochemical Pharmacology Ser.: Vol. 16). (Illus.). xvi, 160p. 1980. 71.50 (*3-8055-0831-X*) S Karger.

Levy, A. E., jt. auth. see Butler-Sloss, Elizabeth.

Levy, A. V., ed. Proceedings: Corrosion-Erosion-Wear of Materials at Elevated Temperatures. (Illus.). 700p. 1991. 10.00 (*1-877914-18-5*) NACE Intl.

***Levy, Aaron Uri, ed.** Math Practice Grades 5-6. (Kelley Wingate Ser.). (Illus.). vii, 128p. (J). (gr. 5-6). 1999. pap. 10.95 (*0-88724-529-3*, CD-3748) Carson-Dellos.

— Math Practice Grades 4-5. (Kelley Wingate Ser.). (Illus.). vii, 128p. (J). (gr. 4-5). 1999. pap. 10.95 (*0-88724-528-5*, CD-3747) Carson-Dellos.

— Math Practice Grades K-1. (Kelley Wingate Ser.). (Illus.). iii, 128p. (J). (gr. k-1). 1999. pap. 10.95 (*0-88724-527-7*, CD-3746) Carson-Dellos.

— Math Practice Grades 7-8. (Kelley Wingate Ser.). (Illus.). vi, 128p. (YA). (gr. 7-8). 1999. pap. 10.95 (*0-88724-531-5*, CD-3750) Carson-Dellos.

— Math Practice Grades 6-7. (Kelley Wingate). (Illus.). vii, 128p. (YA). (gr. 6-7). 1999. pap. 10.95 (*0-88724-530-7*, CD-3749) Carson-Dellos.

Levy, Abraham, jt. auth. see Gubbay, Lucien.

Levy, Adam. Jazz Guitar Sightreading. 1996. pap. 7.95 (*0-88284-807-0*) Alfred Pub.

— Jazz Guitar Sightreading. 1997. pap. 17.90 incl. audio compact disk (*0-88284-834-8*) Alfred Pub.

Levy, Adam, jt. auth. see Davidson, Martin.

Levy, Adolph. Solving Statute of Limitations Problems: 1988 Supplement. 1989. pap. write for info. (*0-87473-464-9*, 64336-10, MICHIE) LEXIS Pub.

— Solving Statute of Limitations Problems: 1992 Cumulative Supplement. 193p. 1992. 40.00 (*0-87473-829-6*, 64337-10, MICHIE) LEXIS Pub.

Levy, Adolph J. Solving Statute of Limitations Problems. 800p. 1987. suppl. ed. 85.00 (*0-930273-65-6*, 64335-10, MICHIE) LEXIS Pub.

Levy, Aharon, et al, eds. New Frontiers in Stress Research: Modulation of Brain Function. (Illus.). 320p. 1998. text 80.00 (*90-5702-266-4*, Harwood Acad Pubs) Gordon & Breach.

Levy, Alan. Ezra Pound: The Voice of Silence. LC 82-83126. 160p. (C). 1982. pap. 16.00 (*0-932966-25-X*) Permanent Pr.

— Ezra Pound: Voice of Silence. 160p. 18.95 (*0-8488-2638-8*) Amereon Ltd.

— So Many Heroes. rev. ed. LC 80-65002. Orig. Title: Rowboat to Prague. 384p. 1980. reprint ed. pap. 16.00 (*0-933256-16-7*) Second Chance.

— So Many Heroes. 2nd rev. ed. LC 80-65002. Orig. Title: Rowboat to Prague. 384p. 1980. reprint ed. 22.00 (*0-933256-12-4*) Second Chance.

— Vladimir Nabokov: The Velvet Butterfly. LC 83-63247. (Illus.). 164p. (C). 1984. pap. 16.00 (*0-932966-41-1*) Permanent Pr.

— W. H. Auden: In the Autumn of the Age of Anxiety. LC 82-84008. (Illus.). 160p. (C). 1983. pap. 16.00 (*0-932966-31-4*) Permanent Pr.

Levy, Alan H. Edward MacDowell: An American Master. LC 98-7958. (Illus.). 352p. 1998. 65.00 (*0-8108-3463-4*) Scarecrow.

— Elite Education & the Private School: Excellence & Arrogance at Phillips Exeter Academy. LC 90-38906. (Studies in Education: Vol. 11). 104p. 1990. lib. bdg. 59.95 (*0-88946-947-4*) E Mellen.

— Government & the Arts: Debates over Federal Support of the Arts in America from George Washington to Jesse Helms. LC 96-52505. 160p. 1997. text 57.50 (*0-7618-0674-1*) U Pr of Amer.

— Musical Nationalism: American Composers' Search for Identity, 66. LC 82-12168. (Contributions in American Studies: No. 66). 168p. 1983. 47.95 (*0-313-23709-3*, LMN/, Greenwood Pr) Greenwood.

— Radical Aesthetics & Music Criticism in America, 1930-1950. LC 91-35626. 80p. 1991. lib. bdg. 49.95 (*0-7734-9621-1*) E Mellen.

***Levy, Alan H.** Rube Waddell: The Zany, Brilliant Life of a Strikeout Artist. (Illus.). 327p. 2000. 29.95 (*0-7864-0786-7*) McFarland & Co.

Levy, Alan S., et al. A Study of Nutrition Label Formats: Performance & Preference. 55p. (Orig.). (C). 1992. pap. text 20.00 (*1-56806-050-5*) DIANE Pub.

Levy, Alan V. Solid Particle Erosion & Erosion-Corrosion of Materials. (Illus.). 225p. 1995. 122.00 (*0-87170-519-2*, 6469) ASM.

Levy, Alexander. Loss of a Parent: Understanding & Coping with Grief & Change after the Death of Our Parents. LC 99-64773. 208p. 1999. text 24.00 (*0-7382-0099-9*, Pub. by Perseus Pubng) HarpC.

***Levy, Alexander.** The Orphaned Adult: Understanding & Coping with Grief & Change After the Death of Our Parents. 208p. 2000. reprint ed. pap. text 14.00 (*0-7382-0361-0*, Pub. by Perseus Pubng) HarpC.

***Levy, Allan M. & Fuerst, Mark L.** Golf Injury Handbook: Professional Advice for Amature Athletes. LC 98-24885. 171p. 1999. pap. 14.95 (*0-471-24853-3*) Wiley.

An Asterisk (*) at the beginning of an entry indicates that the title is appearing for the first time.

Levy, Allan M. & Fuerst, Mark L. The Sports Injury Handbook: Professional Advice for Amateur Athletes. LC 92-29435. 304p. 1993. pap. 19.95 (*0-471-54737-9*) Wiley.

***Levy, Allan M. & Fuerst, Mark L.** Tennis Injury Handbook: Professional Advice for Amateur Athletes. LC 98-33165. 192p. 1999. pap. 14.95 (*0-471-24854-1*) Wiley.

Levy, Allen, ed. 1898 Bing Toy Catalogue. (Illus.). 160p. 1992. 45.00 (*1-872727-70-0*) Pincushion Pr.

— Great Toys of Georges Carette. (Illus.). 300p. 1996. 49.95 (*0-904568-02-4*, Pub. by New Cavendish) Pincushion Pr.

— The Meccano Magazine: Anthology. (Hornby Companion Ser.: Vol. 7A). 1072p. 1992. 75.00 (*1-872727-80-8*) Pincushion Pr.

— The 1906 Bing Toy Catalogue: Including 1907 Supplement. (Illus.). 500p. 1992. 55.00 (*0-904568-52-0*) Pincushion Pr.

Levy, Allen, ed. see Ottenheimer, Peter.

Levy, Alon, jt. ed. see Knoblock, Craig.

Levy, Amihay, ed. see Carmi, Amnon.

Levy, Amir & Merry, Uri. Organizational Transformation: Approaches, Strategies, & Theories. LC 86-9389. 347p. 1986. 65.00 (*0-275-92147-6*, C2147, Praeger Pubs) Greenwood.

Levy, Amnon. Economic Dynamics: Applications of Difference Equations, Differential Equations & Optimal Control. 213p. 1992. 87.95 (*1-85628-404-2*, Pub. by Avebry) Ashgate Pub Co.

Levy, Amy. Reuben Sachs: A Sketch. LC 78-37699. reprint ed. 39.50 (*0-404-56758-4*) AMS Pr.

***Levy, Andre.** Chinese Literature, Ancient & Classical. Nienhauser, William H., Jr., tr. from FRE. LC 99-34024. 152p. 2000. 22.95 (*0-253-33656-2*) Ind U Pr.

Levy, Andre. Jin Ping Mei, Vol. 1. deluxe ed. (FRE.). 1424p. 1985. 125.00 (*0-7859-5017-6*) Fr & Eur.

— Jin Ping Mei, Vol. 2. (FRE.). 1985. pap. 125.00 (*0-7859-5018-4*) Fr & Eur.

Levy, Andre & Duffour, Jacqueline. Dictionnaire Pratique de l'Alimentation. (FRE.). 1987. 69.95 (*0-7859-7914-X*, 2-7021-1649-3) Fr & Eur.

Levy, Andre, ed. see Wu Ch'eng-en.

Levy, Andre, ed. see Wu Cheng'en.

Levy, Andrea T. Odyssey of a Public Intellectual: Andri Gorz in Perspective. 320p. 2000. 53.99 (*1-55164-155-0*, Pub. by Black Rose) Consort Bk Sales.

— Odyssey of a Public Intellectual: Andri Gorz in Perspective. 320p. 2000. pap. 24.99 (*1-55164-154-2*) Consort Bk Sales.

Levy, Andrew. Continuous Discontinuous: Curve 2. LC 98-104318. 136p. (C). 1997. pap. 13.50 (*0-937013-68-4*) Potes Poets.

— Curve. LC 94-65732. 80p. 1994. 10.00 (*1-882022-20-3*) O Bks.

— Democracy Assemblages. 32p. 1990. 7.50 (*0-911623-08-6*) I Klang.

***Levy, Andrew.** The Man Who Got Lost in Duty Free & Other Video-Illustrated Case Studies for Examinations. LC 99-24400. (Video Casebook Ser.: Vol. II). (Illus.). 1999. pap. 29.95 incl. cd-rom (*0-632-05382-8*) Blackwell Sci.

— Paper Head Last Lyrics. 112p. 2000. pap. 11.95 (*0-937804-83-5*, Pub. by Segue NYC) SPD-Small Pr Dist.

Levy, Andrew. The Toy Boy & the Burgundy Car. LC 99-21518. (Video Casebook Ser.: Vol. I). (Illus.). 1999. pap. 29.95 incl. cd-rom (*0-632-05122-1*) Blackwell Sci.

— Values Chauffeur You. LC 90-60632. 88p. 1991. 9.00 (*1-882022-06-8*) O Bks.

Levy, Andrew & Lightman, Stafford L. Endocrinology. LC 97-7853. (Oxford Core Texts Ser.). (Illus.). 398p. 1997. pap. text 37.50 (*0-19-262766-X*) OUP.

Levy, Anita. Other Women: The Writing of Class, Race & Gender, 1832-1898. (Illus.). 250p. 1991. pap. text 11.95 (*0-691-01493-0*, Pub. by Princeton U Pr) Cal Prin Full Svc.

— Other Women: The Writing of Class, Race, & Gender, 1832-1898. LC 90-42210. 184p. 1991. reprint ed. pap. 57.10 (*0-608-04593-4*, 206536300004) Bks Demand.

***Levy, Anita.** Reproductive Urges Popular Novel-Reading, Sexuality, & the English Nation. LC 99-20435. 1999. 37.50 (*0-8122-3497-9*) U of Pa Pr.

***Levy, Ann S.** Acts of Living: A Cookbook - Journal for Those Who Don't Cook... Yet. (Illus.). 91p. 1999. pap. 24.00 (*0-9675856-1-9*) Little App Pr.

Levy, Anne. Workplace Sexual Harassment. LC 96-22254. 168p. (C). 1996. pap. text 41.00 (*0-13-450560-3*, Pub. by P-H) S&S Trade.

Levy, April L. Writing College English: A Composition Handbook for Speakers of English As a Second Language. 340p. 1998. pap. text 20.00 (*0-7881-5634-9*) DIANE Pub.

Levy, Arnold Bruce. Hit & Run. 2000. pap. 14.95 (*1-56980-140-1*) Barricade Bks.

***Levy, Audrey.** Exotic Gift Ideas. 48p. 2000. pap. 7.95 (*1-56167-515-6*, Five Star Spec Ed) Am Literary Pr.

Levy, Avigdor, ed. The Jews of the Ottoman Empire. LC 92-2991. (Illus.). 783p. (C). 1994. text 49.95 (*0-87850-090-1*) Darwin Pr.

Levy, Azriel. A Hierarchy of Formulas in Set Theory. LC 52-42839. (Memoirs Ser.: No. 1/57). 76p. 1983. reprint ed. pap. 21.00 (*0-8218-1257-2*, MEMO/1/57) Am Math.

— A Hierarchy of Formulas in Set Theory. LC 52-42839. (American Mathematical Society Ser.: No. 57). 78p. reprint ed. pap. 30.00 (*0-608-09211-8*, 205271500005) Bks Demand.

***Levy, B.** How to Draw Dogs. (J). 2000. pap. 2.50 (*0-486-41058-7*) Dover.

Levy, B. A. Sea Life Follow the Dots. (J). (ps-3). 1997. mass mkt. 1.00 (*0-486-29446-3*) Dover.

Levy, B. Barry. Planets, Potions & Parchments: Scientifica Hebraica from the Dead Sea Scrolls to the Eighteenth Century. (Illus.). 152p. 1990. pap. 32.95 (*0-7735-0791-4*, Pub. by McG-Queens Univ Pr) CUP Services.

— Planets, Potions & Parchments: Scientifica Hebraica from the Dead Sea Scrolls to the Eighteenth Century. (Illus.). 152p. 1990. 65.00 (*0-7735-0793-0*, Pub. by McG-Queens Univ Pr) CUP Services.

— Targum Neophyti One: A Textual Study: Leviticus, Numbers, Deuteronomy, Vol. 2. LC 86-11117. (Brown Classics in Judaica Ser.). 396p. (Orig.). (C). 1987. pap. text 32.00 (*0-8191-6314-7*); lib. bdg. 56.50 (*0-8191-6313-9*) U Pr of Amer.

— Targun Neophyti One: A Textual Study: Introduction, Genesis, Exodus. LC 86-11117. (Studies in Judaism). 470p. (Orig.). (C). 1986. pap. text 35.50 (*0-8191-5465-2*) U Pr of Amer.

Levy, B. H. La Barbarie a Visage Humaine. (FRE.). 1985. pap. 12.95 (*0-7859-3127-9*) Fr & Eur.

— Eloge des Intellectuels. (FRE.). 1988. pap. 9.95 (*0-7859-3146-5*, 2253047759) Fr & Eur.

— Mordecai Sheftall: Jewish Revolutionary Patriot. LC 99-73260. (Illus.). 150p. 1999. 15.00 (*1-881682-07-2*) GA Hist Soc.

— Questions de Principe, Vol. 2. 1986. pap. 18.95 (*0-7859-3133-3*) Fr & Eur.

— Questions de Principe Vol. 3: La Suite dans les Idees. (FRE.). 1990. pap. 18.95 (*0-7859-3156-2*, 2253054321) Fr & Eur.

— Questions de Principe Vol. 4: Idees Fixes. (FRE.). 1992. pap. 22.95 (*0-7859-3172-4*, 2253061743) Fr & Eur.

Levy, Barbar Soloff. How to Draw Wild Animals. LC 99-32164. 32p. 1999. pap. text 2.50 (*0-486-40821-3*) Dover.

Levy, Barbara. How to Draw Clowns. LC 91-17171. (Illus.). 32p. (J). (gr. 2-6). 1991. pap. 2.95 (*0-8167-2478-4*); lib. bdg. 17.25 (*0-8167-2477-6*) Troll Communs.

***Levy, Barbara.** Ht Draw Clowns. (Illus.). 1999. pap. text 9.90 (*0-7857-6349-X*) Econo-Clad Bks.

Levy, Barbara. Ladies Laughing: Wit As Control in Contemporary American Women Writers. (Studies in Humor & Gender: Vol. 3). 200p. 1997. text 26.00 (*90-5699-542-1*); pap. text 17.00 (*90-5699-543-X*) Gordon & Breach.

Levy, Barbara R. & Marion, Barbara. Successful Special Events: Planning, Hosting & Evaluating. LC 97-11358. 200p. 1997. pap. 59.00 (*0-8342-0935-7*, 09357) Aspen Pub.

Levy, Barbara R., ed. see National Society of Fund Raising Executives Staff.

Levy, Barbara S. How to Draw Cats. LC 96-47816. 1999. pap. 2.50 (*0-486-29621-0*) Dover.

***Levy, Barbara S.** Invisible Jewish Magic Picture Book. (Little Activity Bks.). (Illus.). (J). 1999. pap. 1.00 (*0-486-40764-0*) Dover.

***Levy, Barbara W.** Barbara's View Vol. XXVI 302-100: Milan, Italy. 2000. pap. 12.00 (*1-882340-56-6*) Barbaras View.

— Barbara's View Vol. XXVI 303-100: Florence, Italy. 2000. pap. 12.00 (*1-882340-57-4*) Barbaras View.

Levy, Barbara W. Barbara's View Vols. XXV, 290-199: Miami & South Florida. (Illus.). 1999. pap. 12.00 (*1-882340-44-2*) Barbaras View.

***Levy, Barbara W. & Hughes, Lauren.** Barbara's View Vol. XXVI 301-100: London, England. 2000. pap. 12.00 (*1-882340-55-8*) Barbaras View.

— Barbara's View Vol. XXVI 304-100: Rome, Italy. 2000. pap. 12.00 (*1-882340-58-2*) Barbaras View.

— Barbara's View Vol. XXVI 305-100: New York, New York. 2000. pap. 12.00 (*1-882340-59-0*) Barbaras View.

— Barbara's View Vol. XXVI 305-100: Paris, France. 2000. pap. 12.00 (*1-882340-54-X*) Barbaras View.

— Barbara's View Vol. XXVI 306-100: Miami & South Florida. 2000. pap. 12.00 (*1-882340-60-4*) Barbaras View.

— Barbara's View Vol. XXVI 307-100: Los Angeles, CA. 2000. pap. 12.00 (*1-882340-61-2*) Barbaras View.

— Barbara's View Vol. XXVI 308-100: Atlanta, Georgia. 2000. pap. 12.00 (*1-882340-62-0*) Barbaras View.

Levy, Barnet M. & Dreizen, S. Handbook of Experimental Stomatology. LC 81-7734. (Experimental Oral Biology Ser.). 224p. 1982. 131.00 (*0-8493-3161-7*, RC815, CRC Reprint) Franklin.

Levy, Barnet M., et al. The Marmoset Periodontium in Health & Disease. Myers, H. M., ed. (Monographs in Oral Science: Vol. 1). 1972. 34.00 (*3-8055-1366-6*) S Karger.

Levy, Barrie. In Love & in Danger: A Teen's Guide to Breaking Free of Abusive Relationships. 2nd rev. ed. LC 92-41914. (New Leaf Ser.). 126p. (Orig.). (YA). (gr. 8-12). 1998. pap. 10.95 (*1-58005-002-6*) Seal Pr WA.

Levy, Barrie, ed. Dating Violence: Young Women in Danger. 2nd rev. ed. LC 90-24538. (New Leaf Ser.). 324p. (Orig.). 1998. pap. 18.95 (*1-58005-001-8*) Seal Pr WA.

Levy, Barrie & Griggans, Patricia. What Parents Need to Know about Dating Violence. LC 94-42614. 196p. (Orig.). 1995. pap. 10.95 (*1-878067-47-8*) Seal Pr WA.

Levy, Barrie & Los Angeles Commission on Assaults Against Women S. Jovenes, Enamorados y en Peligro: Una Guia para Jovenes: Como Librarse de Relaciones Abusivas. LC 99-45631. (SPA., Illus.). 126p. 1999. pap. 10.95 (*1-58005-027-1*, Pub. by Seal Pr WA) Publishers Group.

Levy, Barrie, jt. auth. see Giggans, Patricia O.

Levy, Barry. Quakers & the American Family: British Quakers in the Delaware Valley, 1650-1765. (Illus.). 368p. 1992. reprint ed. pap. text 19.95 (*0-19-504976-4*) OUP.

Levy, Barry & Wegman, David H., eds. Occupational Health: Recognizing & Preventing Work-Related Disease. 3rd ed. LC 94-13146. 800p. 1995. pap. text 50.00 (*0-316-52271-6*, Little Brwn Med Div) Lppncott W & W.

Levy, Barry S. & Sidel, Victor W., eds. War & Public Health. (Illus.). 432p. 1996. text 55.00 (*0-19-510814-0*) OUP.

***Levy, Barry S. & Wegman, David H.** Occupational Health: Recognizing & Preventing Work-Related Disease & Injury. LC 99-35194. 842p. 1999. pap. write for info. (*0-7817-1954-2*) Lppncott W & W.

Levy, Benny, jt. auth. see Sartre, Jean-Paul.

Levy, Bernard. Multidimensional Filter Banks & Wavelets: Basic Theory & Cosine Modulated Filter Banks. Basu, Sankar, ed. LC 96-23407. 160p. (C). 1996. text 111.00 (*0-7923-9757-6*) Kluwer Academic.

Levy, Bernard, et al. Multidimensional Filter Banks & Wavelets: Research Developments & Applications. Basu, Sankar, ed. LC 96-45465. 244p. (C). 1997. text 125.00 (*0-7923-9848-3*) Kluwer Academic.

Levy, Bernard I. & Tedguin, Alain. Biology of the Arterial Wall. LC 98-55059. (Basic Science for the Cardiologist Ser.). 278p. 1999. 155.00 (*0-7923-8458-X*) Kluwer Academic.

Levy, Bernard S., ed. The Bible in the Middle Ages: Its Influence on Literature & Art. (Medieval & Renaissance Texts & Studies: Vol. 89). 224p. 1992. 25.00 (*0-86698-101-2*, MR89) MRTS.

Levy, Bernard S. & Szarmach, Paul E., eds. The Alliterative Tradition in the Fourteenth Century. LC 80-28821. 227p. reprint ed. pap. 70.40 (*0-7837-0293-0*, 204061400018) Bks Demand.

Levy, Bertram L. & White, Benjamin T. Georgia Estate Planning, Will Drafting & Estate Administration Forms, 2 vols. 1994. ring bd., suppl. ed. 89.00 (*0-685-70883-7*, MICHIE) LEXIS Pub.

— Georgia Estate Planning, Will Drafting & Estate Administration Forms, 2 vols., Set. 980p. 1994. spiral bd. 239.00 (*0-87189-062-3*, 80946-10, MICHIE) LEXIS Pub.

Levy, Bertram L., jt. auth. see White, Benjamin T.

Levy, Beryl H. Anglo-American Philosophy of Law: An Introduction to Its Development & Outcome. 456p. (C). 1990. text 49.95 (*0-88738-344-0*) Transaction Pubs.

***Levy, Beth & Solomon, Brian.** Chemical & Biological Warfare LC 99-33264. (Reference Shelf Ser.). 1999. write for info. (*0-8242-0964-8*) Wilson.

Levy, Beth, jt. auth. see Bonilla, Denise M.

Levy, Bill. John Ford: A Bio-Bibliography, 78. LC 98-36558. (Bio-Bibliographies in the Performing Arts Ser.: Vol. 78). 384p. 1998. lib. bdg. 75.00 (*0-313-27514-9*, Greenwood Pr) Greenwood.

— Shazaam! The Fractured Phrases of Basketball. (Illus.). 96p. 1996. pap. 6.95 (*1-885590-18-0*) Golden West Pub.

***Levy, Bob.** Broken Hearts: A Novel of Suspense. 288p. 2000. 24.95 (*0-86534-312-8*) Sunstone Pr.

Levy, Brian & Spiller, Pablo T., eds. Regulations, Institutions, & Commitment: Comparative Studies of Telecommunications. (Political Economy of Institutions & Decisions Ser.). (Illus.). 308p. (C). 1996. text 59.95 (*0-521-55013-0*); pap. text 19.95 (*0-521-55996-0*) Cambridge U Pr.

***Levy, Brian & Wackers, Paul, eds.** Reinardus Vol. 12: Yearbook of the International Reynard Society. vi, 248p. 1999. pap. 83.00 (*1-55619-769-1*) J Benjamins Pubng Co.

Levy, Brian, et al. Fulfilling the Export Potential of Small & Medium Firms. LC 98-51684. 1999. write for info. (*0-7923-8430-X*) Kluwer Academic.

Levy, Brooks E. & Bastien, Pierre C. Roman Coins in the Princeton Library, I. Republic to Commodus. (Editions NR, 1985 Ser.). 191p. 1994. 100.00 (*0-685-72019-5*) Am Numismatic.

Levy-Bruhl, Lucien. How Natives Think. Coser, Lewis A. & Powell, Walter W., eds. Clare, Lilian A., tr. LC 79-7006. (Perennial Works in Sociology). 1980. reprint ed. lib. bdg. 31.95 (*0-405-12104-0*) Ayer.

— La Mythologie Primitive. 2nd ed. LC 75-35138. 1976. reprint ed. 57.50 (*0-404-14154-4*) AMS Pr.

— The Philosophy of Auguste Comte. 1976. lib. bdg. 59.95 (*0-8490-2430-7*) Gordon Pr.

— Primitive Mentality. Clare, Lilian A., tr. LC 75-41174. 1976. reprint ed. 69.50 (*0-404-14568-X*) AMS Pr.

— Primitives & the Supernatural. LC 73-4358. (Studies in Comparative Literature: No. 35). 1972. reprint ed. lib. bdg. 75.00 (*0-8383-1589-5*) M S G Haskell Hse.

***Levy, Burt.** The Last Open Road. rev. ed. LC 98-12324. 354p. 1998. 25.00 (*0-9642107-2-X*) Think Fast Ink.

— Montezuma's Ferrari: And Other Adventures. LC 99-93834. (Last Open Road Ser.). 416p. 1999. 30.00 (*0-9642107-1-1*) Think Fast Ink.

Levy, C. Michael & Ransdell, Sarah, eds. The Science of Writing. LC 96-84604. 456p. 1996. text 89.95 (*0-8058-2108-2*); pap. text 45.00 (*0-8058-2109-0*) L Erlbaum Assocs.

***Levy, Carl, ed.** Gramsci & the Anarchists. 320p. 1999. 65.00 (*1-85973-984-9*, Pub. by Berg Pubs) NYU Pr.

Levy, Carl, ed. Italian Regionalism: History, Identity & Politics. LC 97-151075. 224p. 1996. 55.00 (*1-85973-131-7*, Pub. by Berg Pubs); pap. 16.50 (*1-85973-156-2*, Pub. by Berg Pubs) NYU Pr.

— Socialism & the Intelligentsia: 1880-1914. (History Workshop Ser.). 224p. (C). 1988. pap. text 22.00 (*0-7102-1257-7*, Routledge Thoemms); lib. bdg. 59.95 (*0-7102-0722-0*, Routledge Thoemms) Routledge.

Levy, Carl, jt. auth. see Bloch, Alice.

Levy, Carol. Reading Readiness Book: For the New Hebrew & Heritage Siddur Program. (Illus.). (J). 1995. pap. 4.95 (*0-87441-518-7*) Behrman.

Levy, Celia, ed. Stuttering Therapies: Practical Approaches. 224p. 1987. pap. text 25.95 (*0-7099-4145-5*, Pub. by C Helm) Routldge.

Levy, Charles. Crocodiles & Alligators. 1991. 9.98 (*1-55521-714-1*) Bk Sales Inc.

— Human Biology: Text & Laboratory Manual. 340p. (C). 1996. 52.95 (*0-8403-9618-X*) Kendall-Hunt.

Levy, Charles K. Biology: Study Guide & Workbook. 3rd ed. LC 81-17556. (Biology Ser.). (Illus.). 620p. 1983. pap. text, student ed. 11.25 (*0-201-04566-4*) Addison-Wesley.

— Elements of Biology. 3rd ed. LC 81-17556. (Biology Ser.). (Illus.). 620p. 1983. text 25.00 (*0-201-04564-8*) Addison-Wesley.

— Evolutionary Wars. LC 99-39982. (Illus.). 278p. 1999. pap. text 29.95 (*0-7167-3483-4*) W H Freeman.

— Evolutionary Wars: The Battle of Species on Land, Sea & Air. 278p. 1999. pap. text 16.95 (*0-7167-3775-2*) W H Freeman.

Levy, Charles S. Guide to Ethical Decisions & Actions for Social Service Administrators: A Handbook for Managerial Personnel. LC 81-13511. (Supplement to Administration in Social Work Ser.: No. 1). 160p. 1982. text 32.95 (*0-86656-106-4*) Haworth Pr.

— Social Work Ethics. LC 75-11007. 266p. 1976. 42.95 (*0-87705-254-9*, Kluwer Acad Hman Sci); pap. 20.95 (*0-87705-493-2*, Kluwer Acad Hman Sci) Kluwer Academic.

— Social Work Ethics on the Line. LC 92-3349. 130p. 1993. lib. bdg. 39.95 (*1-56024-282-5*) Haworth Pr.

Levy, Charlotte L. Computer-Assisted Litigation Support: An Annotated Bibliography. LC 84-1756. (CompuBibs Ser.: No. 4). 31p. 1984. pap. 10.00 (*0-914791-02-8*) Vantage Info.

Levy, Charlotte L. & Robbins, Sara. Library Automation: A Systems & Software Sampler. (CompuBibs Ser.: No. 11). 87p. 1985. pap. 15.50 (*0-914791-10-9*) Vantage Info.

Levy, Claire M. The Civilian Airline Industry's Role in Military Pilot Retention: Beggarman or Thief? 54p. 1995. pap. text 6.00 (*0-8330-2300-4*, DB-118-OSD) Rand Corp.

Levy, Claude. Emancipation, Sugar, & Federalism: Barbados & the West Indies, 1833-1876. LC 79-18084. (University of Florida Latin American Monographs: No. 25). (Illus.). viii, 206p. 1980. 29.95 (*0-8130-0655-4*) U Press Fla.

Levy, Constance. A Crack in the Clouds & Other Poems. LC 98-10652. (Illus.). 48p. (J). (gr. 3-7). 1998. per. 15.00 (*0-689-82204-9*) McElderry Bks.

— I'm Going to Pet a Worm Today: And Other Poems. LC 91-7485. (Illus.). 48p. (J). (ps-3). 1991. 14.00 (*0-689-50535-3*) McElderry Bks.

— A Tree Place: And Other Poems. LC 93-20586. (Illus.). 48p. (J). (gr. k-5). 1994. mass mkt. 15.00 (*0-689-50599-X*) McElderry Bks.

— When Whales Exhale & Other Poems. LC 95-52560. 48p. (J). (ps-3). 1996. 15.00 (*0-689-80946-8*) S&S Bks Yung.

Levy, Cynthia J. & Schultz, Jeffrey D., eds. Global Links: A Guide to People & Institutions Worldwide. LC 98-26643. 192p. 1998. pap. 59.95 (*1-57356-224-6*) Oryx Pr.

Levy, D. A. The Buddhist Third Class Junk Mail Chronicle: The Art & Poetry of D. A. Levy. Golden, Mike, ed. & frwd. by. LC 98-35490. (Illus.). 336p. 1999. pap. 21.95 (*1-888363-88-6*) Seven Stories.

— The Madison Poems & Collages. 1980. 12.00 (*0-685-04199-9*) Quixote.

Levy, D. A., et al. Zen Concrete & Etc. Swanberg, Ingrid, ed. LC 91-70949. (Illus.). 274p. 1991. pap. 27.50 (*0-941160-04-1*) Ghost Pony Pr.

Levy, D. E. & Tang, C. The Chemistry of C-Glycosides. LC 95-38444. (Tetrahedron Organic Chemistry Ser.). 290p. 1995. text 115.50 (*0-08-042080-X*, Pergamon Pr); pap. text 50.00 (*0-08-042081-8*, Pergamon Pr) Elsevier.

Levy, Dana, jt. ed. see O'Connor, Letitia Burns.

Levy, Daniel, tr. from HEB. The Ben Ish Hai Anthology Vol. 1: Between Heaven & Earth. LC 99-201674. 1998. 22.95 (*965-222-676-9*) Feldheim.

Levy, Daniel, tr. Ben Ish Hai Anthology Vol. 2: The Challenge of Wealth & Poverty. 22.95 (*1-58330-167-4*) Feldheim.

— Ben Ish Hai Anthology Vol. 3: In the Service of the King. 1997. 22.95 (*1-58330-166-6*) Feldheim.

— Ben Ish Hai Anthology Vol. 4: Dawn of a Nation. 1998. 22.95 (*1-58330-165-8*) Feldheim.

— Ben Ish Hai Anthology Vol. 5: If I Forget Thee. 1998. 22.95 (*0-87306-905-6*) Feldheim.

— Ben Ish Hai Anthology Vol. 6: Israel & the Nations. 22.95 (*0-87306-904-8*) Feldheim.

Levy, Daniel C. Building the Third Sector: Latin America's Private Research Centers & Nonprofit Development. (Latin American Ser.). 348p. (C). 1996. pap. 19.95 (*0-8229-5603-9*); text 45.00 (*0-8229-3944-4*) U of Pittsburgh Pr.

— Higher Education & the State in Latin America: Private Challenges to Public Dominance. LC 85-21023. xviii, 464p. (C). 1986. 33.00 (*0-226-47608-1*) U Ch Pr.

— University & Government in Mexico: Autonomy in a Authoritarian System. LC 79-21134. 173p. 1980. 49.95 (*0-275-90512-8*, C0512, Praeger Pubs) Greenwood.

Levy, Daniel C., ed. Private Education & Public Policy: Studies in Choice & Public Policy. LC 85-15568. 288p. 1986. text 55.00 (*0-19-503710-3*) OUP.

Levy, Daniel C., jt. auth. see De Moura Castro, Claudio.

Levy, Daniel S., et al. Conceptual & Statistical Issues in Contingent Valuation: Estimating the Value of Altered Visibility in the Grand Canyon. LC 93-48695. 54p. 1995. pap. text 13.00 (*0-8330-1500-1*, MR-344-RC) Rand Corp.

L

Levy, Darline G. The Ideas & Careers of Simon-Nicolas-Henri Linguet: A Study in Eighteenth-Century French Politics. LC 79-24109. (Illus.). 394p. 1980. 39.95 (*0-252-00311-X*) U of Ill Pr.

Levy, Darline G., et al, eds. Women in Revolutionary Paris, 1789-1795. 326p. 1980. pap. text 15.95 (*0-252-00855-3*) U of Ill Pr.

Levy, Darline G., jt. ed. see Applewhite, Harriet B.

Levy, David. Comets: Creators & Destroyers. LC 98-3113. (Illus.). 256p. 1998. pap. 12.00 (*0-684-85255-1*, Touchstone) S&S Trade Pap.

— Executive Jungle: A Novel. LC 98-37788. 300p. 1998. 25.95 (*1-57392-245-5*) Prometheus Bks.

— Joel: The Day of the Lord. LC 86-82328. 1986. pap. text 8.95 (*0-915540-37-1*) Frnds Israel.

***Levy, David.** Scientific American Book of the Cosmos. (Illus.). 416p. 2000. text 29.95 (*0-312-25453-9*) St Martin.

— What Every Jewish Person Should Ask. 32p. 2000. pap. 4.99 (*0-7369-0163-9*) Harvest Hse.

Levy, David, contrib. by. Administering Stock Options Plans: A Guide to Implementing a Recordkeeping & Reporting System. LC 98-180372. (Building Blocks Ser.: Vol. 45). (Illus.). 1998. pap. 24.95 (*1-57963-057-X*) Am Compensation.

Levy, David, jt. auth. see Bishop, Deborah.

Levy, David, jt. auth. see Keene, Raymond.

Levy, David, jt. auth. see Levy, S. Jay.

Levy, David, jt. ed. see National Industrial Council Staff.

Levy, David A. Europe's Digital Revolution: Broadcasting Regulation, the Eu, & the Nation State LC 99-17496. (Routledge Research in European Public Policy Ser.). 1999. write for info. (*0-415-17196-2*) Routledge.

— Tools of Critical Thinking. LC 96-27649. 224p. 1996. pap. text 29.00 (*0-205-26083-7*) Allyn.

Levy, David B. Beethoven: The Ninth Symphony. (Monuments of Western Music Ser.). (Illus.). 226p. 1995. 37.00 (*0-02-871363-X*, Schirmer Books) Mac Lib Ref.

Levy, David Benjamin. Beethoven: The Ninth Symphony. 1998. pap. 15.00 (*0-02-864861-7*) S&S Trade.

***Levy, David H.** Eclipse: A Journey to Darkness & Light. 2000. 18.00 (*0-7434-0727-X*, Pub. by ibooks) S&S Trade.

Levy, David H. Impact Jupiter: The Crash of Comet Shoemaker-Levy 9. LC 95-33339. (Illus.). 304p. (C). 1995. 25.95 (*0-306-45088-7*, Plenum Trade) Perseus Pubng.

— The Man Who Sold the Milky Way: A Biography of Bart Bok. LC 93-4039. (Illus.). 246p. 1993. 38.00 (*0-8165-1149-7*) U of Ariz Pr.

— The Man Who Sold the Milky Way: A Biography of Bart Bok. LC 93-4039. (Illus.). 246p. 1995. pap. 15.95 (*0-8165-1524-7*) U of Ariz Pr.

— Observing Variable Stars: A Guide for the Beginner. 2nd ed. (Illus.). 224p. (C). 1998. reprint ed. pap. 16.95 (*0-521-62755-9*) Cambridge U Pr.

— The Quest for Comets: An Explosive Trail of Beauty & Danger. 304p. 1995. reprint ed. pap. 12.50 (*0-380-72526-6*, Avon Bks) Morrow Avon.

***Levy, David H.** Shoemaker by Levy: The Man Who Made an Impact. LC 00-38523. (Illus.). 256p. 2000. 24.95 (*0-691-00225-8*, Pub. by Princeton U Pr) Cal Prin Full Svc.

Levy, David H. The Sky: A User's Guide. (Illus.). 315p. (C). 1993. pap. 18.95 (*0-521-45958-3*) Cambridge U Pr.

***Levy, David H.** Skywatching. (Nature Company Guides Ser.). (Illus.). 288p. 2000. pap. write for info. (*0-7370-0079-1*) Time-Life Educ.

Levy, David H. Stars & Planets. LC 95-32799. (Nature Company Discoveries Library). (Illus.). 64p. (J). (gr. 3-8). 1997. 16.00 (*0-8094-9246-6*) Time-Life.

— Variable Star Observing. 224p. 1989. text 49.95 (*0-521-32113-1*) Cambridge U Pr.

Levy, David H., ed. The Sky: A User's Guide. (Illus.). 315p. (C). 1991. text 49.95 (*0-521-39112-1*) Cambridge U Pr.

Levy, David H., et al. Sharing the Sky: A Parent's & Teacher's Guide to Astronomy. LC 97-35720. (Illus.). 324p. (C). 1997. pap. 18.95 (*0-306-45639-7*, Kluwer Plenum) Kluwer Academic.

— Sharing the Sky: A Parent's & Teacher's Guide to Astronomy. LC 97-35720. (Illus.). 324p. (C). 1997. 29.95 (*0-306-45638-9*, Plenum Trade) Perseus Pubng.

Levy, David H., jt. auth. see Edberg, Stephen J.

Levy, David J. The Measure of Man: Incursions in Philosophical & Political Anthropology. 248p. (C). 1993. text 34.95 (*0-8262-0899-1*) U of Mo Pr.

Levy, David M. The Economic Ideas of Ordinary People: From Preferences to Trade. 304p. (C). (gr. 13). 1991. text 79.95 (*0-415-06770-7*, A6163) Routledge.

— Guarding the Gospel of Grace: Contending for the Faith in the Face of Comprise. 1997. pap. 10.95 (*0-915540-26-6*) Frnds Israel.

— Malachi: Messenger of Rebuke & Renewal. 1992. pap. 8.95 (*0-915540-20-7*) Frnds Israel.

— Maternal Overprotection. (C). 1966. pap. 3.50 (*0-393-00349-3*) Norton.

***Levy, David M.** Revelation: Hearing the Last Word. LC 98-74877. (Illus.). 250p. 1999. pap. 11.95 (*0-915540-60-6*) Frnds Israel.

— Scrolling Forward: Making Sense of Documents in the Digital Age. (Illus.). 2000. 24.95 (*1-55970-553-1*, Pub. by Arcade Pub Inc) Time Warner.

Levy, David M. The Tabernacle: Shadows of the Messiah. 1993. pap. 9.95 (*0-915540-17-7*) Frnds Israel.

Levy, David M., contrib. by. When Prophets Speak of Judgement: Habakkuk, Zephaniah, Haggai. LC 98-72175. 1998. pap. 10.95 (*0-915540-35-5*) Frnds Israel.

Levy, David N. Chess & Computers. LC 77-473857. (Chess Bks). vi, 145p. 1976. write for info. (*0-7134-3178-4*) B T B.

Levy, David N., ed. Computer Chess Compendium. 450p. 1989. 73.54 (*0-387-91331-9*) Spr-Verlag.

— Learn Chess from the World Champions. 214p. 1979. pap. text 17.95 (*0-08-021388-X*, Pergamon Pr) Elsevier.

Levy, David N. & Beal, Don, eds. Heuristic Programming in Artificial Intelligence: The First Computer Olympiad. (Artificial Intelligence Ser.). 1990. text 59.95 (*0-470-21659-X*) P-H.

Levy, David N. & O'Connell, Kevin J. How to Play the Sicilian Defense: Primary Level. (Chess Library). (Illus.). 160p. 1988. pap. 14.95 (*0-02-029191-4*) Macmillan.

— Instant Chess. (Chess Ser.). (Illus.). 83p. 1984. 17.90 (*0-08-024122-0*, Pergamon Pr); pap. 11.90 (*0-08-024121-2*, Pergamon Pr) Elsevier.

Levy, David N., jt. auth. see Hayes, Jean E.

Levy, David W., ed. see Brandeis, Louis D.

Levy, David W., jt. ed. see Buhite, Russell D.

Levy, David W., jt. ed. see Urofsky, Melvin I.

***Levy, Debbie.** Civil Liberties. LC 99-33792. (Overview Ser.). (Illus.). 112p. (YA). (gr. 6-9). 2000. lib. bdg. 23.70 (*1-56006-611-3*) Lucent Bks.

— Kidding Around Washington, D. C. A Fun-Filled, Fact-Packed Travel & Activity Book. 2nd ed. (Kidding Around Ser.). (Illus.). 144p. (J). (gr. 1-5). 2000. pap. 8.95 (*1-56261-588-2*) Avalon Travel.

Levy, Deborah. Billy & Girl. 185p. 1996. text. write for info. (*0-7475-2835-7*, Pub. by Blmsbury Pub) AMACOM.

— Billy & Girl. LC 98-49257. 192p. 1998. pap. 13.95 (*1-56478-202-6*) Dalkey Arch.

— Heresies & Evan & Moses. (Methuen New Theatrescripts Ser.). 34p. (C). 1988. pap. write for info. (*0-413-17170-1*, A0123, Methuen Drama) Methn.

— Ophelia's Great Idea. 1999. pap. 6.95 (*0-14-011786-5*, Viking) Viking Penguin.

Levy, Deborah, ed. Walks on Water. 160p. (C). 1992. pap. write for info. (*0-413-67120-8*, A0655, Methuen Drama) Methn.

Levy, Delores G. Branching Out: Emmy's Story. (Illus.). 136p. (Orig.). (YA). (gr. 7-12). 1995. pap. 7.95 (*0-9642639-0-4*) Portraits West.

— Branching Out: Emmy's Story. (Illus.). (Orig.). (YA). (gr. 8-12). 1995. pap. 13.95 (*0-9642639-1-2*) Portraits West.

Levy, Dominique, jt. auth. see Dumenil, Gerard.

Levy, Donald. Freud among the Philosophers: The Psychoanalytic Unconscious & Its Philosophical Critics. LC 96-2169. 200p. 1996. 27.00 (*0-300-06632-5*) Yale U Pr.

Levy, Donald, jt. auth. see Goldsmith, Donald.

Levy, Donald, jt. auth. see Seymon-Hersch, Barbara.

Levy, Donald R. Answer Book 403 (b) Forms & Worksheets. 2nd ed. LC 96-232946. 560p. 1996. 96.00 (*1-56706-350-0*) Aspen Pub.

***Levy, Donald R.** Estate & Retirement Planning Answer Book: Forms & Checklists. 2nd ed. LC 99-199407. (Answer Book Ser.). 1999. write for info. (*1-56706-869-3*) Panel Pubs.

Levy, Donald R. 403(b) Answer Book. 2nd ed. 704p. 1996. 130.00 (*1-56706-119-2*) Aspen Pub.

— 403(b) Answer Book: Forms & Worksheets. annuals 3rd ed. LC 98-106675. 560p. 1999. pap. 96.00 incl. disk (*1-56706-744-1*, 67441) Panel Pubs.

— 403(b) Answer Book: Forms & Checklists. annuals 432p. 1995. pap. 96.00 incl. disk (*1-56706-099-4*) Panel Pubs.

— Individual Retirement Account Answer Book. annuals 2nd ed. 848p. 1995. 118.00 (*1-56706-105-2*, S117) Panel Pubs.

— Individual Retirement Account Answer Book. 3rd ed. LC 96-224888. 1048p. 1996. 118.00 (*1-56706-351-9*) Panel Pubs.

— Individual Retirement Account Answer Book: Forms & Worksheets. 3rd ed. 740p. pap. 89.00 (*1-56706-310-1*, 63101) Panel Pubs.

*** Levy JD MBA, Donald R.** State by State Guide to Managed Care Law. 368p. 1999. pap. text 165.00 (*0-7355-0490-3*) Panel Pubs.

Levy, Donald R., ed. Estate & Retirement Planning Answer Book: Forms & Checklists. LC 98-127526. 500p. 1999. pap. 96.00 incl. disk (*1-56706-413-2*, 64132) Panel Pubs.

Levy, Donald R., et al. 403(b) Answer Book. annuals 3rd ed. LC 97-195565. 768p. 1997. boxed set 136.00 (*1-56706-388-8*) Panel Pubs.

— 403(b) Answer Book. 4th ed. LC 98-184407. (Panel Answer Book Ser.). 1998. boxed set 136.00 (*0-7355-0074-6*) Panel Pubs.

— Individual Retirement Account Answer Book. annuals 4th ed. LC 98-107122. 1224p. 1999. boxed set 118.00 (*1-56706-396-9*, 63969) Panel Pubs.

***Levy, Donald R., et al.** Individual Retirement Account Answer Book 5th ed. LC 99-188130. (Answer Book Ser.). 1999. write for info. (*1-56706-875-8*) Panel Pubs.

Levy, Donald R., et al. Managed Care Answer Book: Forms & Checklists, 1. 2nd ed. LC 99-171120. (Panel Answer Book Ser.). 560p. 1998. pap. 96.00 (*1-56706-968-1*) Panel Pubs.

Levy, Doran J., jt. auth. see Morgan, Carol M.

Levy, Dore J. Chinese Narrative Poetry: The Tradition in Shih from the Late Han Through T'ang Dynasties. LC 88-14712. 224p. (C). 1988. text 42.95 (*0-8223-0863-0*) Duke.

— Ideal & Actual in the Story of the Stone. LC 98-44246. 35p. 1999. 42.50 (*0-231-11406-0*) Col U Pr.

— Ideal & Actual in the Story of the Stone. LC 98-44246. 1999. pap. text 16.50 (*0-231-11407-9*) Col U Pr.

***Levy, E.** Just One More Dance. 1999. 35.00 (*1-84018-134-6*, Pub. by Mainstream Pubng) Trafalgar.

Levy, E. Provencal-Francais. 5th ed. 387p. 1973. pap. 70.00 (*3-533-01393-6*) IBD Ltd.

Levy, E., ed. Le Systeme Palatial en Orient, en Grece et a Rome: Acts du Collogie de Strasbourg, 19-22 Juin 1985. (Travaux du Centre de Recherche sur le Proche Orient et la Grece Antiques Ser.: Vol. 9). (Illus.). 502p. 1987. pap. 110.50 (*90-04-08520-3*) Brill Academic Pubs.

Levy, E. & Herrington, C. S., eds. Non-Isotopic Methods in Molecular Biology: A Practical Approach. (Practical Approach Ser.: Vol. 153). (Illus.). 244p. 1995. text 110.00 (*0-19-963456-4*) OUP.

— Non-Isotopic Methods in Molecular Biology: A Practical Approach, No. 153. (Practical Approach Ser.: Vol. 153). (Illus.). 244p. 1995. pap. text 55.00 (*0-19-963455-6*) OUP.

Levy, E., jt. auth. see World Association of Societies of Pathology Staff.

Levy, E. J., jt. auth. see Liebman, S. A.

Levy, Edmond. Making a Winning Short. 1995. pap. 14.95 (*0-8050-2680-0*) H Holt & Co.

Levy, Elie. Dictionnaire de Physique. (FRE.). 890p. 1988. 250.00 (*0-7859-8622-7*, 213039311x) Fr & Eur.

Levy, Elinor & Monte, Tom. The 10 Best Tools to Boost Your Immune System. 256p. 1997. pap. 14.00 (*0-395-69460-4*) HM.

Levy, Elizabeth. Big Trouble in Little Twinsville. 96p. mass mkt. 4.25 (*0-06-442116-3*) HarpC.

— Big Trouble in Little Twinsville. (J). 2001. write for info. (*0-06-028590-7*); lib. bdg. write for info. (*0-06-028591-5*) HarpC Child Bks.

Levy, Elizabeth. Cheater, Cheater. 176p. (J). (gr. 4-7). 1994. pap. 3.50 (*0-590-45866-3*) Scholastic Inc.

— Cold As Ice. 176p. 1989. pap. 2.95 (*0-380-70315-7*, Avon Bks) Morrow Avon.

— The Creepy Computer Mystery. LC 95-30914. (Invisible Inc. Ser.: Vol. 4). (Illus.). 32-48p. (J). (gr. 2-4). 1996. pap. 3.99 (*0-590-60322-1*, Cartwheel) Scholastic Inc.

— Creepy Computer Mystery. (Hello, Reader! Ser.). 1996. 9.19 (*0-606-09473-3*, Pub. by Turtleback) Demco.

— Double Standard. 160p. (YA). (gr. 7 up). 1984. pap. 2.25 (*0-380-87379-6*, 87379-6, Avon Bks) Morrow Avon.

— Dracula Is a Pain in the Neck. LC 82-47707. (Trophy Bk.). (Illus.). 96p. (J). (gr. 2-6). 1984. pap. 4.25 (*0-06-440146-4*, HarpTrophy) HarpC Child Bks.

Levy, Elizabeth. Dracula is a Pain in the Neck. LC 82-47707. (Trophy Chapter Bks.). 1984. 9.15 (*0-606-06335-8*, Pub. by Turtleback) Demco.

Levy, Elizabeth. The Drowned. (Illus.). 192p. (YA). (gr. 7 up). 1995. 16.95 (*0-7868-0135-2*, Pub. by Hyprn Child) Little.

— First Date. (Gymnasts Ser.: No. 13). 112p. (J). (gr. 3-7). 1990. pap. 2.75 (*0-590-42825-X*) Scholastic Inc.

— Frankenstein Moved in on the Fourth Floor. (J). 1979. 9.15 (*0-606-02115-9*, Pub. by Turtleback) Demco.

— Frankenstein Moved In on the Fourth Floor. (J). 1990. mass mkt. 3.50 (*0-06-107013-0*, Harp PBks) HarpC.

— Frankenstein Moved In on the Fourth Floor. LC 78-19830. (Trophy Bk.). (Illus.). 80p. (J). (gr. 1-5). 1981. pap. 4.95 (*0-06-440122-7*, HarpTrophy) HarpC Child Bks.

— The Great Laugh Off. LC 97-3842. 192p. (J). (gr. 3-7). 1997. lib. bdg. 14.89 (*0-06-026603-1*) HarpC Child Bks.

— If You Were There When They Signed the Constitution. 80p. (J). (gr. 4-7). 1992. pap. 5.99 (*0-590-45159-6*) Scholastic Inc.

— If You Were There When They Signed the Constitution. (J). 1992. 11.19 (*0-606-01856-5*, Pub. by Turtleback) Demco.

— Invisible Inc. #2: The Mystery of the Missing Dog. (Hello, Reader! Ser.). (J). 1995. 9.19 (*0-606-07712-X*, Pub. by Turtleback) Demco.

— Karate Class Mystery. (Hello, Reader! Ser.). 1996. 9.19 (*0-606-09474-1*, Pub. by Turtleback) Demco.

— The Karate Class Mystery: Invisable Ink. LC 95-50527. (Hello Reader! Ser.: No. 5). (Illus.). (J). (ps-3). 1996. 3.99 (*0-590-60323-X*, Cartwheel) Scholastic Inc.

— Keep Ms. Sugarman in the Fourth Grade. LC 91-22576. (Illus.). 96p. (J). (gr. 3-6). 1992. 13.95 (*0-06-020426-5*) HarpC Child Bks.

— Keep Ms. Sugarman in the Fourth Grade. LC 91-22576. (Illus.). 96p. (J). (gr. 4-7). 1992. lib. bdg. 14.89 (*0-06-020427-3*) HarpC Child Bks.

— Keep Ms. Sugarman in the Fourth Grade. LC 91-22576. (Trophy Bk.). (Illus.). 96p. (J). (gr. 3-6). 1993. pap. 4.95 (*0-06-440487-0*, HarpTrophy) HarpC Child Bks.

— Keep Ms. Sugarman in the Fourth Grade. (J). 1993. 9.15 (*0-606-05390-5*, Pub. by Turtleback) Demco.

Levy, Elizabeth. Levy Chapter Book. 96p. (J). (gr. 2-5). 14.89 (*0-06-028593-1*) HarpC Child Bks.

Levy, Elizabeth. A Mammoth Mix-Up. LC 94-47960. (Brian & Pea Brain Mystery Ser.). (Illus.). 96p. (J). (gr. 2-5). 1995. lib. bdg. 12.89 (*0-06-024815-7*) HarpC Child Bks.

— A Mammoth Mix-Up. LC 94-47960. (Brian & Pea Brain Mystery Ser.). (Illus.). 96p. (J). (gr. 2-5). 1996. pap. 3.95 (*0-06-442043-4*, HarpTrophy) HarpC Child Bks.

— Mammoth Mix-Up: Starring Brian & Pea Brain. 1996. 9.15 (*0-606-09590-X*, Pub. by Turtleback) Demco.

— My Life as a Fifth-Grade Comedian. LC 97-3842. 192p. (J). (gr. 3-7). 1998. pap. 4.95 (*0-06-440723-3*) HarpC.

— My Life as a Fifth-Grade Comedian. LC 97-3842. 192p. (J). (gr. 3-7). 1997. 15.95 (*0-06-026602-3*) HarpC Child Bks.

— The Mystery of the Missing Dog. LC 94-38765. (Invisible Inc. Ser.: Vol. 2). (Illus.). 48p. (J). (ps-3). 1995. pap. 3.50 (*0-590-47484-7*, Cartwheel) Scholastic Inc.

Levy, Elizabeth. The Night of the Living Gerbil. 96p. 14.95 (*0-06-028588-5*) HarpC.

— The Night of the Living Gerbil. 96p. (J). (gr. 2-5). 14.89 (*0-06-028589-3*) HarpC.

Levy, Elizabeth. Out of Control. (Gymnasts Ser.: No. 12). 112p. (J). (gr. 4-7). 1990. pap. 2.75 (*0-590-42824-1*) Scholastic Inc.

— Parents' Night Fright. LC 97-14294. (Hello Reader! Ser.). (Illus.). (J). (gr. 2-4). 1998. 3.99 (*0-590-60324-8*) Scholastic Inc.

— Parents' Night Fright, 6. (Invisible Inc. Ser.). 1998. 9.09 (*0-606-13526-X*, Pub. by Turtleback) Demco.

— Return of the Jedi. (Illus.). 1995. pap. 3.99 (*0-679-87205-1*) Random.

— Rude Rowdy Rumors: Starring Brian & Pea Brain. LC 93-46792. (Trophy Chapter Bk.). (Illus.). 96p. (J). (gr. 2-5). 1995. pap. 3.95 (*0-06-442002-7*, HarpTrophy) HarpC Child Bks.

— Rude Rowdy Rumors Starring Brian & Pea Brain. (J). 1995. 9.15 (*0-606-08441-X*, Pub. by Turtleback) Demco.

— School Spirit Sabotage: Starring Brian & Pea Brain. LC 93-23029. (Trophy Chapter Bk.). (Illus.). 96p. (J). (gr. 4-7). 1995. pap. 4.25 (*0-06-442013-2*, HarpTrophy) HarpC Child Bks.

— School Spirit Sabotage Starring Brian & Pea Brain. (J). 1995. 9.15 (*0-606-08440-1*, Pub. by Turtleback) Demco.

— The Schoolyard Mystery. (Hello Reader!, Invisible Inc. Ser.: Level 4, Bk. 1). (Illus.). 48p. (J). (gr. 2-3). 1994. pap. 3.99 (*0-590-47483-9*, Cartwheel) Scholastic Inc.

— The Schoolyard Mystery. (Invisible Inc. Ser.). 1994. 9.19 (*0-606-06499-0*, Pub. by Turtleback) Demco.

***Levy, Elizabeth.** Seventh Grade Tango. LC 99-53124. 160p. (J). (gr. 3-7). 2000. 16.00 (*0-7868-0498-X*, Pub. by Disney Pr) Time Warner.

— Seventh Grade Tango. LC 99-53124. 144p. (YA). (gr. 3-7). 2000. 16.49 (*0-7868-2427-1*, Pub. by Hyprn Child) Time Warner.

Levy, Elizabeth. The Snack Attack Mystery. LC 95-11036. (Invisible Inc. Ser.: Vol. 3). (Illus.). 32-48p. (J). (gr. 2-4). 1996. pap. 3.99 (*0-590-60289-6*, Cartwheel) Scholastic Inc.

— Snack Attack Mystery. (Hello, Reader! Ser.). 1995. 9.19 (*0-606-09472-5*, Pub. by Turtleback) Demco.

— Something Queer at the Haunted School. LC 81-1940. 1982. 8.89 (*0-440-08355-9*) Dell.

— Something Queer at the Haunted School. (J). 1983. 8.70 (*0-606-02814-5*, Pub. by Turtleback) Demco.

— Something Queer at the Library. (Something Queer Ser.). (Illus.). 48p. (J). (gr. 1-4). 1989. pap. 3.50 (*0-440-48120-1*, YB BDD) BDD Bks Young Read.

— Something Queer at the Library: A Mystery. (Dell Young Yearling Ser.). (J). 1977. 8.70 (*0-606-02263-5*, Pub. by Turtleback) Demco.

— Something Queer at the Scary Movie. LC 94-45618. (Something Queer Ser.). (Illus.). 48p. (J). (gr. 2-5). 1995. 14.95 (*0-7868-0150-6*, Pub. by Hyprn Child) Time Warner.

— Something Queer at the Scary Movie. 1995. 10.15 (*0-606-08875-X*, Pub. by Turtleback) Demco.

— Something Queer in Outer Space. 1993. 10.15 (*0-606-08876-8*, Pub. by Turtleback) Demco.

— Something Queer in the Cafeteria. 1994. 10.15 (*0-606-06749-3*, Pub. by Turtleback) Demco.

— Something Queer in the Cafeteria. 11th ed. LC 93-31343. (Something Queer Ser.: Bk. 2). (Illus.). 48p. (J). (gr. 2-5). 1994. 13.95 (*0-7868-0001-1*, Pub. by Hyprn Child) Time Warner.

— Something Queer in the Wild West. LC 96-2554. (Illus.). 48p. (J). 1997. 14.95 (*0-7868-0258-8*, Pub. by Hyprn Child) Time Warner.

— Something Queer in the Wild West. LC 96-2554. (Illus.). 48p. (J). (gr. 2-5). 1997. pap. 4.95 (*0-7868-1117-X*, Pub. by Hyprn Ppbks) Little.

— Something Queer in the Wild West. 1997. 10.40 (*0-606-11859-4*) Turtleback.

— Something Queer Is Going On. unabridged ed. (Follow the Reader Ser.). (J). (gr. 1-3). 1983. pap. 15.98 incl. audio (*0-8072-0046-8*, FTR 78 SP) Listening Lib.

Levy, Elizabeth. Something Queer Is Going On: A Mystery. (Dell Young Yearling Ser.). (J). 1973. 8.70 (*0-606-02264-3*, Pub. by Turtleback) Demco.

Levy, Elizabeth. Third Grade Bullies. LC 96-49018. (Hyperion Chapters Ser.). (Illus.). 64p. (J). (ps-4). 1997. lib. bdg. 14.49 (*0-7868-2264-3*, Pub. by Hyprn Ppbks) Little.

— Third Grade Bullies. LC 96-49018. (Hyperion Chapters Ser.). (Illus.). 64p. (J). (gr. 3-6). 1998. pap. 3.95 (*0-7868-1214-1*, Pub. by Hyprn Ppbks) Little.

— 3rd Grade Bullies. (Hyperion Chapters Ser.). 1998. 9.05 (*0-606-13844-7*, Pub. by Turtleback) Demco.

— Wolfman Sam. LC 96-2542. (Trophy Chapter Bk.). (Illus.). 128p. (J). (gr. 2-5). 1996. pap. 3.95 (*0-06-442048-5*, HarpTrophy) HarpC Child Bks.

— Wolfman Sam. LC 96-2542. (J). 1996. 9.15 (*0-606-10081-4*, Pub. by Turtleback) Demco.

Levy, Elizabeth, ed. Greenberg Van Doren Gallery Selected Works. (Illus.). 88p. 1998. 20.00 (*0-942779-08-8*) Greenberg Van Doren.

Levy, Elizabeth & Brunkus, Denise. Invisible Inc. 2: The Mystery of the Missing Dog. (Hello Reader! (Je Peux Lire!) Ser.).Tr. of Invisible et Cie: Le Mystere du Chien Disparu. (FRE., Illus.). (J). pap. 5.99 (*0-590-16010-9*) Scholastic Inc.

***Levy, Emanuel.** Cinema of Outsiders: The Rise of American Independent Film. LC 99-6746. 600p. 1999. 34.95 (*0-8147-5123-7*) NYU Pr.

Levy, Emanuel. John Wayne: Prophet of the American Way of Life. LC 87-28410. (Illus.). 399p. 1988. 41.50 (*0-8108-2054-4*) Scarecrow.

— John Wayne: Prophet of the American Way of Life. (Illus.). 410p. 1998. pap. 19.95 (*0-8108-3531-2*) Scarecrow.

***Levy, Emanuel.** Oscar Fever: The History & Politics of the Academy Awards. 384p. 2000. 19.95 (*0-8264-1284-X*) Continuum.

Levy, Emil. Petit Dictionnaire Provencal-Francais. (FRE & PRO.). 387p. 1990. pap. 59.95 (*0-7859-8169-1*, 2869712790) Fr & Eur.

An Asterisk (*) at the beginning of an entry indicates that the title is appearing for the first time.

Levy, Emilie De Vidas, see De Vidas Levy, Emilie.

Levy, Eric, ed. 1999 Comparative Performance Data Sourcebook. 496p. 1998. pap. 265.00 (*1-57987-082-1*) Faulkner & Gray.

— 1999 Patient Resources on the Internet. 512p. 1998. pap. 195.00 (*1-57987-044-9*) Faulkner & Gray.

— 1999 Wellness & Prevention Sourcebook. 496p. 1998. pap. 235.00 (*1-57987-081-3*) Faulkner & Gray.

Levy, Eric & Coughlin, Kenneth, eds. 1999 Telemedicine Sourcebook. 512p. 1998. pap. 275.00 (*1-57987-046-5*) Faulkner & Gray.

Levy, Eric P. Beckett & the Voice of Species: A Study of the Prose Fiction. 145p. 1980. 44.00 (*0-389-20004-2*, 06781) B&N Imports.

Levy, Ernest, jt. auth. see Levarie, Siegmund.

Levy, Ernst. Pauli Sententiae: A Palingenesia of the Opening Titles as a Specimen of Research in West Roman Vulgar Law. xii, 130p. 1970. reprint ed. 35.00 (*0-8377-2400-7*, Rothman) W S Hein.

— A Theory of Harmony. LC 85-12604. (SUNY Series in Cultural Perspectives). (Illus.). 99p. (C). 1985. pap. text 19.95 (*0-87395-992-2*) State U NY Pr.

Levy, Ernst, jt. auth. see Levarie, Siegmund.

Levy, Esther. Jewish Cookery Book. 200p. 1988. reprint ed. 11.95 (*1-55709-109-9*) Applewood.

— Jewish Cookery Book on Principles of Economy Adapted for Jewish Housekeepers. LC 74-28000. (Modern Jewish Experience Ser.). 1975. reprint ed. 23.95 (*0-405-06727-5*) Ayer.

Levy, Eugene. James Weldon Johnson: Black Leader, Black Voice. LC 72-95134. (Negro American Biographies & Autobiographies Ser.). 393p. pap. 121.90 (*0-8357-8927-6*, 205678600085) Bks Demand.

— James Weldon Johnson: Black Leader, Black Voice. Franklin, John H., ed. LC 72-95134. (Negro American Biographies & Autobiographies Ser.). (Illus.). 1976. pap. text 5.95 (*0-226-47604-9*, P700) U Ch Pr.

Levy, Faye. Classic Techniques for Fine Cooking. LC 94-28039. (Kitchen Arts Ser.). (Illus.). 128p. 1995. pap. 11.95 (*1-56426-071-2*) Cole Group.

Levy, Faye. Faye Levy's International Chicken Cookbook. 422p. 1992. 29.95 (*0-446-51569-8*, Pub. by Warner Bks) Little.

Levy, Faye. Faye Levy's International Jewish Cookbook. LC 91-50083. (Illus.). 364p. 1991. 29.95 (*0-446-51568-X*, Pub. by Warner Bks) Little.

— Faye Levy's International Jewish Cookbook. 384p. 1995. mass mkt. 14.99 (*0-446-67126-6*, Pub. by Warner Bks) Little.

— Faye Levy's International Vegetable Cookbook: Over 300 Sensational Recipes from Argentina to Zaire & Artichokes to Zucchini. LC 92-51034. (Illus.). 453p. 1993. 29.95 (*0-446-51719-4*, Pub. by Warner Bks) Little.

— Low Fat Kosher Cookbook. LC 96-29192. 1997. 24.95 (*0-517-70364-5*) Random Hse Value.

— The New Casserole. LC 97-6059. (Illus.). 192p. 1997. 15.00 (*0-02-860993-X*) Macmillan.

— 1,000 Jewish Recipes. LC 99-55743. 640p. 2000. 32.50 (*0-02-862337-1*) Macmillan.

— Sensational Chocolate. (Illus.). 192p. 1992. pap. 14.95 (*1-55788-049-2*, HP Books) Berkley Pub.

— 30 Low-Fat Meals in 30 Minutes. 208p. (Orig.). 1995. mass mkt. 9.99 (*0-446-67059-6*, Pub. by Warner Bks) Little.

— 30 Low-Fat Vegetarian Meals in 30 Minutes. 176p. (Orig.). 1997. mass mkt. 11.99 (*0-446-67211-4*, Pub. by Warner Bks) Little.

Levy, Fran J., ed. Dance & Other Expressive Art Therapies: When Words Are Not Enough. LC 95-16839. (Illus.). 273p. (C). 1995. 70.00 (*0-415-91228-8*); pap. 25.99 (*0-415-91229-6*) Routledge.

Levy, Fran S. Dance Movement Therapy: A Healing Art. rev. ed. (Illus.). 377p. (C). 1992. pap. text 34.00 (*0-88314-531-6*) AAHPERD.

Levy, Francis A., ed. Crystallography & Crystal Chemistry of Materials with a Layered Structure. (Physics & Chemistry of Materials with Layered Structures Ser.: No. 2). 380p. 1976. text 199.50 (*90-277-0586-0*) Kluwer Academic.

— Fritz Hulliger: Structural Chemistry of Layer-Type Phases. LC 76-26635. (Physics & Chemistry of Materials with Layered Structures Ser.: No. 5). 1977. text 199.50 (*90-277-0714-6*) Kluwer Academic.

— Intercalated Layered Materials. (Physics & Chemistry of Materials with Layered Structures Ser.: No. 6). 1979. text 239.50 (*90-277-0967-X*) Kluwer Academic.

Levy, Frank. Dollars & Dreams: The Changing American Income Distribution. LC 86-42952. (Population of the United States in the 1980s: A Census Monograph Ser.). 256p. (Orig.). 1987. 34.95 (*0-87154-523-3*) Russell Sage.

— The New Dollars & Dreams: American Incomes & Economic Change. rev. ed. LC 98-20635. (Illus.). 256p. (C). 1998. 39.95 (*0-87154-514-4*); pap. 16.95 (*0-87154-515-2*) Russell Sage.

Levy, Frank, et al. Running in Place: Recent Trends in U. S. Living Standards. (Illus.). 88p. (C). 1998. reprint ed. pap. text 25.00 (*0-7881-4573-8*) DIANE Pub.

Levy, Frank, jt. auth. see Murnane, Richard J.

Levy, Frank S. & Michel, Richard C. The Economic Future of American Families: Income & Wealth Trends. LC 90-20278. (Illus.). 148p. (C). 1991. pap. text 18.50 (*0-87766-487-0*); lib. bdg. 33.50 (*0-87766-486-2*) Urban Inst.

***Levy, Frederick.** Hollywood 101: The Film Industry. 336p. 2000. pap. text 19.95 (*1-58063-123-1*) Renaissance.

— The Ultimate Boy Band Book. (Illus.). 160p. 2000. mass mkt. 4.99 (*0-7434-0669-9*, Archway) PB.

Levy, Fritz J., ed. see Bacon, Francis.

Levy, G. & De Vachon, M. La Douleur. 162p. 1993. pap. text 33.00 (*2-88124-893-4*) Gordon & Breach.

Levy, Gail, ed. see Stodden, Norma J.

Levy, Gail, ed. see Stodden, Norma J. & McCormick, Linda.

Levy, Gary & White, Graham, eds. Provincial & Territorial Legislatures in Canada. 369p. 1989. pap. 18.95 (*0-8020-6734-4*) U of Toronto Pr.

Levy, Gary A. Role of Procoagulant Activity in Health & Disease. 240p. 1993. lib. bdg. 179.00 (*0-8493-5566-4*, QP93) CRC Pr.

Levy, Gary A., jt. ed. see Talbot, Pierre J.

Levy, Gayle A. Refiguring the Muse. (Currents in Comparative Romance Languages & Literatures Ser.: Vol. 59). 186p. (C). 1999. text 44.95 (*0-8204-3782-4*) P Lang Pubng.

Levy, Genevieve. The Puzzle of Pain. (Illus.). 176p. 1994. text 43.00 (*976-8097-89-2*) Gordon & Breach.

***Levy, Geoffrey M.** Packaging in the Environment. 273p. 1998. 140.00 (*0-8342-1347-8*) Aspen Pub.

Levy, George. To Die in Chicago: Confederate Prisoners at Camp Douglas, 1862-65. 2nd ed. LC 98-21807. (Illus.). 448p. 1998. 29.95 (*1-56554-331-9*) Pelican.

— To Die in Chicago: Confederate Prisons at Camp Douglas, 1862-1865. (Illus.). 325p. 1994. boxed set 25.00 (*1-879260-20-4*) Evanston Pub.

Levy, George C., ed. NMR Spectroscopy: New Methods & Applications. LC 82-11458. (ACS Symposium Ser.: Vol. 191). 398p. 1982. reprint ed. pap. 123.40 (*0-608-03116-X*, 206356900007) Bks Demand.

— Topics in Carbon-13 NMR Spectroscopy, Vol. 4. (Topics in Carbon-13 NMR Spectroscopy Ser.: 1-683). 282p. 1984. 199.00 (*0-471-09857-4*) Wiley.

Levy, George C., et al. Carbon-13 Nuclear Magnetic Resonance Spectroscopy. 2nd ed. 352p. (C). 1992. reprint ed. lib. bdg. 59.95 (*0-89464-796-2*) Krieger.

Levy, Gerald M., ed. Arbitration of Real Estate Valuation Disputes. LC 87-71510. 1987. pap. 19.95 (*0-943001-21-8*) Am Arbitration.

Levy, Gerard. Behind the Walls. (Illus.). 96p. 1999. 45.00 (*3-929078-90-2*, Pub. by G Kehayoff) te Neues.

— Skin. (Illus.). 120p. 1998. 45.00 (*3-929078-73-2*, Kehayoff) te Neues.

Levy, Gerhard, ed. see Benet, Leslie Z., et al.

Levy, Gerold H., jt. auth. see Kofke, W. Andrew.

Levy, H. The Universe of Science. LC 74-26272. (History, Philosophy & Sociology of Science Ser.). 1975. reprint ed. 23.95 (*0-405-06600-7*) Ayer.

Levy, H. & Lessman, F. Finite Difference Equations. unabridged ed. LC 92-20438. (Illus.). vii, 278p. 1992. reprint ed. pap. text 8.95 (*0-486-67260-3*) Dover.

Levy, H. M., Jr., ed. see Partee, Phillip E.

Levy, Haim. Introduction to Investments. 960p. (C). 1996. text. write for info. (*0-201-51372-2*) Addison-Wesley.

— Introduction to Investments. LC 95-32312. 1995. 59.50 (*0-538-85998-9*) S-W Pub.

***Levy, Haim.** Microscopic Simulation of Financial Markets: From Investor Behavior to Market Phenomena. 2000. 69.95 (*0-12-445890-4*) Acad Pr.

Levy, Haim. Stochastic Dominance: Investment Decision Making under Uncertainty. LC 98-34577. (Studies in Risk & Uncertainty). 1998. 159.95 (*0-7923-8260-9*) Kluwer Academic.

Levy, Haim, jt. auth. see Brooks.

Levy, Harlan. And the Blood Cried Out. 272p. 1997. mass mkt. 5.99 (*0-380-73061-8*, Avon Bks) Morrow Avon.

Levy, Harold B. Square Pegs, Round Holes: The Learning-Disabled Child in the Classroom & at Home. LC 73-3422. (Illus.). 288p. 1974. 8.95 (*0-316-52232-5*, Little Brwn Med Div) Lppncott W & W.

Levy, Harold L., ed. The Language Teacher. 84p. 1958. pap. 10.95 (*0-915432-58-7*) NE Conf Teach Foreign.

Levy, Harold P. There Were Days Like That. DeWitt, Beverley J., ed. (Illus.). 164p. (Orig.). 1985. pap. 9.95 (*0-9615303-0-8*) Blue Whale Pr.

Levy, Harriet L. 920 O'Farrell Street: A Jewish Girlhood in Old San Francisco. 216p. 1996. pap. 12.95 (*0-930588-91-6*) Heyday Bks.

— Nine-Twenty O'Farrell Street. LC 74-29501. (Modern Jewish Experience Ser.). (Illus.). 1975. reprint ed. 25.95 (*0-405-06728-3*) Ayer.

Levy, Harry. Chain of Custody. 1999. mass mkt. 6.99 (*0-449-00449-X*) Fawcett.

— The Dark Side of the Sky: The Story of a Young Jewish Airman in Nazi Germany. (Illus.). 189p. 1996. 29.95 (*0-85052-498-9*, Pub. by Leo Cooper) Trans-Atl Phila.

Levy, Harry L. A Latin Reader for Colleges. LC 62-18119. 1962. pap. text 9.00 (*0-226-47602-2*) U Ch Pr.

— A Latin Reader for Colleges. LC 62-18119. (Midway Reprint Ser.). xii, 276p. 1989. reprint ed. pap. text 17.95 (*0-226-47601-4*) U Ch Pr.

Levy, Helen F. Fiction of the Home Place: Jewett, Cather, Glasgow, Porter, Welty, & Naylor. LC 91-35996. 272p. 1993. reprint ed. pap. text 17.95 (*0-87805-663-7*) U Pr of Miss.

Levy, Henry L. Finding Your Self & Helping Others: The Holistic Way. Widosh, Kathleen & Widosh, Bud, eds. (Illus.). 210p. (Orig.). 1995. pap. 14.00 (*0-9645413-9-4*) Ctr Psychol.

Levy, Henry M. & Eckhouse, Richard H., Jr. Computer Programming & Architecture: The VAX. 2nd ed. LC 88-22887. 464p. reprint ed. pap. 143.90 (*0-608-08849-8*, 206948800004) Bks Demand.

Levy, Herbert. Voices from the Past: From German Jew to British Patriot. 122p. 1995. 19.95 (*1-85776-087-5*, Pub. by Book Guild Ltd) Trans-Atl Phila.

Levy, Hermann. Monopoly & Competition: A Study in English Industrial Organisation. Wilkins, Mira, ed. LC 76-29993. (European Business Ser.). 1977. reprint ed. lib. bdg. 31.95 (*0-405-09771-4*) Ayer.

Levy, Hilton B., ed. The Biochemistry of Viruses. LC 75-90149. (Illus.). 671p. reprint ed. pap. 200.00 (*0-7837-0951-X*, 204125600019) Bks Demand.

Levy, Howard. Child Maltreatment - Illustrated Dictionary: Physical, Psychological & Legal Terminology of Child Abuse & Neglect. (Illus.). 600p. (C). 1999. text 69.95 (*1-878060-30-9*) GW Medical.

***Levy, Howard S.** A Day This Lit. LC 00-35846. 2000. pap. write for info. (*0-9678856-1-2*) Cavankerry.

Levy, Howard S. One Hundred Haiku. (East Asian Poetry in Translation Ser.: No. 5). 1976. pap. 8.00 (*0-89986-300-0*) Oriental Bk Store.

Levy, Howard S., tr. Korean Love Poems, Vol. 2. 1976. pap. 8.00 (*0-89986-258-6*) Oriental Bk Store.

Levy, Howard S. & Ishihara, Akira. The Tao of Sex. 2nd ed. (Illus.). 241p. 1989. pap. 14.95 (*0-941255-44-1*) Integral Pub.

Levy, Ian H. Hitomaro & the Birth of Japanese Lyricism. LC 83-42564. 185p. reprint ed. pap. 57.40 (*0-608-06342-8*, 206670400008) Bks Demand.

***Levy, Ian Hideo.** Love Songs from the Man'yoshu: Selections from a Japanese Classic. 2000. pap. 25.00 (*4-7700-2642-0*) Kodansha.

Levy, Isaac, tr. from GER. The Pentateuch: Hebrew Text, English Translation & Commentary Digest, 7 vols. (ENG & HEB.). 4257p. 1962. 149.95 (*0-910818-12-6*) Judaica Pr.

***Levy, Isaac J.** And the World Stood Silent: Sephardic Poetry of the Holocaust. 2000. pap. 16.95 (*0-252-06861-0*) U of Ill Pr.

Levy, Isaac J. Jewish Rhodes: A Lost Culture. (Illus.). 96p. 1989. 9.95 (*0-943376-44-0*) Magnes Mus.

Levy, J., jt. auth. see Hoffmann, G.

Levy, J. A., ed. The Retroviridae, Vol. 1. (Viruses Ser.). (Illus.). 504p. (C). 1992. text 110.00 (*0-306-44074-1*, Kluwer Plenum) Kluwer Academic.

— The Retroviridae, Vol. 2. (Viruses Ser.). (Illus.). 458p. (C). 1993. text 110.00 (*0-306-44369-4*, Kluwer Plenum) Kluwer Academic.

— The Retroviridae, Vol. 3. (Viruses Ser.). (Illus.). 564p. (C). 1994. text 120.00 (*0-306-44693-6*, Kluwer Plenum) Kluwer Academic.

Levy, Jack, jt. ed. see Wubbels, Theo.

***Levy, Jacob T.** The Multiculturalism of Fear. 220p. 2000. 29.95 (*0-19-829712-2*) OUP.

Levy, Jacques. Where the River Meets the Sea: Coastal Landscapes, 1980-1998. unabridged ed. LC 98-96139. (Illus.). 56p. 1998. pap. 24.95 (*0-9663863-0-2*, 101) RiverSea Pr.

Levy, Jade, jt. ed. see Levy, Lynnie.

Levy, Jane & Helzel, Florence B. The Jewish Illustrated Book: Catalog of the collections - Selected. LC 86-80427. (Illus.). 150p. (Orig.). 1986. pap. 16.95 (*0-943376-33-5*) Magnes Mus.

Levy, Janet & Levy, Nathan. There Are Those. rev. ed. (Illus.). 40p. (J). (gr. 1-12). 1994. pap. 9.95 (*1-878347-41-1*) NL Assocs.

Levy, Janice. Abuelito Eats with His Fingers. LC 97-51134. (Illus.). 32p. (J). 1998. 14.95 (*1-57168-177-9*, Eakin Pr) Sunbelt Media.

— The Spirit of Tio Fernando. Mlawer, Teresa, tr. LC 95-1318.Tr. of El Espiritu de Tio Fernando: Una Historia del Dia de los Muertos. (ENG & SPA., Illus.). 32p. (J). (gr. k-3). 1995. 14.95 (*0-8075-7585-2*) A Whitman.

— The Spirit of Tio Fernando. Fuenmayor, Morella, tr. LC 95-1318.Tr. of El Espiritu de Tio Fernando: Una Historia del Dia de los Muertos. (Illus.). 32p. (J). (gr. k-3). 1995. pap. 6.95 (*0-8075-7586-0*) A Whitman.

Levy, Jay A. HIV & the Pathogenesis of AIDS. 2nd rev. ed. LC 97-42731. (Illus.). 600p. (C). 1997. pap. 65.95 (*1-55581-122-1*) ASM Pr.

Levy, Jay A., ed. The Retroviridae, Vol. 4. (Viruses Ser.). (Illus.). 684p. (C). 1995. text 139.50 (*0-306-45033-X*, Kluwer Plenum) Kluwer Academic.

Levy, Jay A., et al, eds. Cancer, AIDS & Quality of Life: Proceedings of the Second International Conference of the International Council for Global Health Progress (ICGHP) Held in Paris, France, January 15-17, 1996. LC 97-5782. (Illus.). 211p. 1997. 85.00 (*0-306-45517-X*, Kluwer Plenum) Kluwer Academic.

Levy, Jean-Jacques, jt. ed. see Kanchanasut, Kanchana.

Levy, Jean-Pierre & Schram, Gunnar G. United Nations Conference on Straddling Fish Stocks & Highly Migratory Fish Stocks: Selected Documents. LC 96-28964. 1996. lib. bdg. 283.50 (*90-411-0270-1*, Pub. by M Nijhoff) Kluwer Academic.

***Levy, Jennifer, et al.** Kids' Rooms: Ideas & Projects for Children's Spaces. LC 00-24044. (Illus.). 2001. pap. write for info. (*0-8118-2841-7*) Chronicle Bks.

Levy, Jerome S. & Prather, Robert C. Texas Alternative Dispute Resolution Practice Guide. Thomas, Susan & Esping, Edward K., eds. LC 95-80676. 600p. 1995. text. write for info. (*0-7620-0013-9*) West Group.

Levy, Jerrold, et al. Hand Trembling, Frenzy Witchcraft, & Moth Madness: A Study of Navajo Seizure Disorders. LC 87-19445. 196p. 1995. pap. 18.95 (*0-8165-1572-7*) U of Ariz Pr.

Levy, Jerrold E. In the Beginning: The Navajo Genesis. 325p. 1998. 45.00 (*0-520-21128-6*, Pub. by U CA Pr); pap. 16.95 (*0-520-21277-0*, Pub. by U CA Pr) Cal Prin Full Svc.

Levy, Jerrold E. & Kunitz, Stephen J. Indian Drinking: Navajo Practices & Anglo-American Theories. LC 73-17173. 271p. reprint ed. pap. 84.10 (*0-8357-9910-7*, 205512200008) Bks Demand.

Levy, Jerrold E. & Pepper, Barbara. Orayvi Revisited: Social Stratification in an "Egalitarian" Society. (Resident Scholar Ser.). (Illus.). 216p. 1992. 35.00 (*0-933452-33-0*) Schol Am Res.

Levy, Jerrold E., jt. auth. see Kunitz, Stephen J.

Levy, Jerrold H. Anaphylactic Reactions in Anesthesia & Intensive Care. 2nd ed. 266p. 1992. text 65.00 (*0-7506-9064-X*) Buttrwrth-Heinemann.

— Anaphylactic Reactions in Anesthesia & Intensive Care. 3rd ed. 272p. 1998. text 65.00 (*0-7506-9827-6*) Buttrwrth-Heinemann.

Levy, Jill. Take Command of Your Writing. LC 98-92668. (Illus.). 670p. 1998. pap. 49.95 (*0-9651516-1-1*) Firebelle.

Levy, Jill M. The First Responder's Pocket Guide to Hazardous Materials Emergency Response. LC 96-96169. (Illus.). 224p. (Orig.). 1996. pap. 19.95 (*0-9651516-0-3*) Firebelle.

Levy, Jo, tr. see Adamov, Arthur.

Levy, Jo, tr. see Aragon, Louis.

Levy, Joan U. ACT: American College Testing Program 1999 Edition. 608p. 1998. pap. text 13.95 (*0-02-862466-1*, Arco) Macmillan Gen Ref.

— Act with Study-Planning Software: 1999 Edition. 616p. 1998. pap. 29.95 incl. cd-rom (*0-02-862478-5*, Arco) Macmillan Gen Ref.

— Advance Placement Exam in U.S. Government & Politics. 192p. 1994. pap. 15.00 (*0-671-84780-5*, Arco) Macmillan Gen Ref.

— Arco Mechanical Aptitude & Spatial Relations Tests. 3rd ed. LC 96-106713. 288p. 1995. pap. 15.95 (*0-02-860600-0*, Arco) Macmillan Gen Ref.

— Praxis II, NTE, MSAT. 12th ed. 416p. 1995. 14.95 (*0-02-860601-9*) Macmillan.

Levy, Joan U. & Levy, Norman. ACT: American College Testing Program. 15th ed. LC 93-48848. 576p. 1994. 12.00 (*0-671-88822-6*, Arco) Macmillan Gen Ref.

— AP European History: Advanced Placement Examination. 3rd ed. LC 97-70063. (Illus.). 224p. 1997. pap. 14.95 (*0-02-861716-9*, Arc) IDG Bks.

— AP U. S. Government & Politics: Advanced Placement Examination. 2nd ed. (Illus.). 192p. 1997. pap. 15.95 (*0-02-861714-2*, Arc) IDG Bks.

— Arco ACT: With Study-Planning Software. (Illus.). 616p. 1997. pap. 29.95 incl. disk (*0-02-861920-X*, Arco) Macmillan Gen Ref.

— Essential Math for College-Bound Students: A Self-Study Program for Aptitude, Achievement, & Placement Tests. 2nd ed. 416p. 1996. pap., student ed. 14.95 (*0-02-861313-9*, Arc) IDG Bks.

— Praxis II. 13th ed. 325p. 1997. 15.95 (*0-02-862198-0*, Arc) IDG Bks.

— Praxis II Preparation Kit. 13th ed. 336p. 1998. pap. 19.95 incl. audio (*0-02-862197-2*, Arc) IDG Bks.

Levy, Joan U., et al. Advanced Placement Examination in European History. 2nd ed. LC 92-34477. 240p. 1993. pap. 14.00 (*0-671-84777-5*, Arco) Macmillan Gen Ref.

Levy, Joan U., jt. auth. see Levy, Norman.

Levy, JoAnn. Daughter of Joy. LC 97-35924. 320p. 1997. 23.95 (*0-312-86502-3*, Pub. by Forge NYC) St Martin.

— Daughter of Joy. (Women of the West Ser.). 1999. mass mkt. 6.99 (*0-8125-4029-8*, Pub. by Forge NYC) St Martin.

***Levy, JoAnn.** For California's Gold. LC 99-89207. 280p. 2000. 24.95 (*0-87081-566-0*, Pub. by Univ Pr Colo) U of Okla Pr.

Levy, JoAnn. They Saw the Elephant: Women in the California Gold Rush. LC 89-78223. (Illus.). xxii, 265p. (C). 1990. lib. bdg. 32.50 (*0-208-02273-2*, Archon Bks) Shoe String.

— They Saw the Elephant: Women in the California Gold Rush. LC 92-54146. (Illus.). 288p. 1992. reprint ed. pap. 13.95 (*0-8061-2473-3*) U of Okla Pr.

Levy, Jodi. The Healing Handbook: A Beginner's Guide to Meditation. 128p. (Orig.). 1999. per. 10.00 (*0-671-02759-X*, PB Trade Paper) PB.

Levy, Joe & Skintik, Catherine. Telecommunications & the Internet. (DF - Computer Applications Ser.). 1996. mass mkt., teacher ed. 24.95 (*0-538-67250-1*) S-W Pub.

***Levy, Joel & The Cryptozoological Society of London Staff.** A Natural History of the Unnatural World: Discover What Gryptozoology Can Teach Us about Over One Hundred Fabulous & Legendary Creatures That Inhabit Earth, Sea & Sky. (Illus.). 224p. 2000. text 25.95 (*0-312-20703-4*, Thomas Dunne) St Martin.

Levy, John. We Don't Kill Snakes Where We Come From: Two Years in a Greek Village. LC 92-81744. 128p. 1994. pap. 8.00 (*1-882168-02-X*) Querencia Bks.

Levy, John M. Contemporary Urban Planning. 5th ed. LC 98-55576. 354p. 1999. pap. text 54.00 (*0-13-083574-9*) P-H.

— Economic Development Programs for Cities, Counties & Towns. 2nd ed. LC 90-32301. 192p. 1990. 49.95 (*0-275-93366-0*, C3366, Praeger Pubs); pap. 21.95 (*0-275-93760-7*, B3760, Praeger Pubs) Greenwood.

— Essential Microeconomics for Public Policy Analysis. LC 95-7990. 248p. 1995. 69.50 (*0-275-94362-3*, Praeger Pubs); pap. 27.95 (*0-275-94363-1*, Praeger Pubs) Greenwood.

Levy, John M., jt. auth. see Moliterno, James E.

Levy, John M., ed. see Moliterno, James E.

Levy, Jon. Maine Family Law, 1998 Supplement. 150p. 1998. pap., suppl. ed. write for info. (*0-327-00716-8*, 8164310) LEXIS Pub.

Levy, Jon D. Maine Family Law: Divorce, Separation & Annulment, 2000 Edition. 808p. 1998. pap. 105.00 (*0-327-12448-2*) LEXIS Pub.

Levy, Jon D. Maine Family Law, 1988-1991: Divorce, Separation & Annulment. 380p. 1994. spiral bd. 85.00 (*0-89442-076-3*, MICHIE) LEXIS Pub.

Levy, Jon D., jt. auth. see Murray, Peter L.

Levy, Jonah D. Tocqueville's Revenge: State, Society & Economy in Contemporary France. LC 98-45015. 1999. 55.00 (*0-674-89432-4*) HUP.

Levy, Jonathan. Charlie the Chicken & Other Plays. 86p. (Orig.). 1990. 10.00 (*0-685-32638-1*) Playsmith.

— The Gymnasium of the Imagination: A Collection of

L

L

Children's Plays in English, 1780-1860, 40. LC 91-16448. (Contributions in Drama & Theatre Studies: No. 40). 296p. 1992. 59.95 (*0-313-26697-2*, LGN, Greenwood Pr) Greenwood.

— Marco Polo. 1977. pap. 5.25 (*0-8222-0732-X*) Dramatists Play.

— A Theatre of the Imagination. 56p. pap. 7.95 (*0-932720-75-7*) New Plays Inc.

Levy, Joseph. Welcome to . . . Networks: A Guide to LAN'S. 1995. pap. 19.95 (*1-55828-259-9*, MIS Pr) IDG Bks.

Levy, Joseph, pref. Play Behavior. LC 83-6102. 250p. (C). 1983. reprint ed. text 29.50 (*0-89874-627-2*) Krieger.

Levy, Joseph R. Building LANtastic Networks. LC 94-36561. 600p. 1994. pap. 34.95 incl. disk (*1-55851-394-9*, M&T Bks) IDG Bks.

— Create Your Own Virtual Reality System. 1994. 44.95 (*0-07-037651-4*) McGraw.

Levy, Joseph V. & Bach-Y-Rita, Paul. Vitamins: Their Use & Abuse. 155p. 1976. 8.95 (*0-87140-616-0*, Pub. by Liveright) Norton.

Levy, Judith. Grandfather Remembers: Memories for my Grandchild. LC 85-45645. (Illus.). 64p. 1993. 18.95 (*0-06-015561-2*) HarperTrade.

— My Baby & Me: A Journal for the Single Parent. (Illus.). 64p. 1999. text 17.95 (*1-55670-890-4*) Stewart Tabori & Chang.

Levy, Judith & Pelikan, Judy. Grandmother Remembers Songbook. LC 92-50287. (Illus.). 96p. 1992. 15.95 (*1-56305-316-0*, 3316) Workman Pub.

Levy, Judith, jt. auth. see Rascon, Bonnie.

Levy, Judith A., jt. ed. see Albrecht, Gary L.

Levy, Judith A., ed. see Austin, David M.

Levy, Judith A., ed. see Ingersoll, Virginia H. & Adams, Guy B.

Levy, Judith A., ed. see Niv, Amittai & Bar-On, Dan.

Levy, Judith A., ed. see Perry, Ronald W. & Hirose, Hirotada.

Levy, Judith A., jt. ed. see Perry, Ronald W.

Levy, Julien. Surrealism. LC 68-9469. 1968. reprint ed. 18.95 (*0-405-00299-8*) Ayer.

— Surrealism. (Illus.). 202p. 1995. reprint ed. pap. 17.95 (*0-306-80663-0*) Da Capo.

Levy, Julien, ed. see Berman, Eugene.

Levy, Juliette D. The Complete Herbal Handbook for Farm & Stable. 384p. (Orig.). 1991. pap. 21.95 (*0-571-16116-2*) Faber & Faber.

Levy, Juliette D. The Complete Herbal Handbook for the Dog & Cat. rev. ed. (Orig.). 1991. pap. 16.00 (*0-571-16115-4*) Faber & Faber.

Levy, Juliette de Bairacli, see De Bairacli Levy, Juliette.

Levy, Justine. The Rendezvous. Davis, Lydia, tr. LC 97-3150. 142p. 1997. 21.50 (*0-684-82579-1*) S&S Trade.

— The Rendezvous: A Novel. Davis, Lydia, tr. 144p. 1999. pap. 11.00 (*0-684-84632-2*) S&S Trade.

Levy, Karen B. The Politics of Women's Health Care: Medicalization As a Form of Social Control. LC 92-39492. (Woman in History Ser.: Vol. 60). (Illus.). 133p. 1992. pap. 10.00 (*0-86663-201-8*) Ide Hse.

Levy, Kelley & Associates Staff. Demystifying Sap. 1998. 49.99 (*0-7897-1563-5*, Que New Media) MCP SW Interactive.

Levy, Kenneth. Gregorian Chant & the Carolingians. LC 97-21957. 296p. 1998. text 49.50 (*0-691-01733-6*, Pub. by Princeton U Pr) Cal Prin Full Svc.

— Music: A Listener's Introduction. 526p. (C). 1997. pap. 68.00 (*0-06-043933-5*) Addson-Wesley Educ.

***Levy, Kenneth A., et al, eds.** Guide to Telephone Regulation: FCC Rules. annot. ed. 816p. 1999. 495.00 (*0-9673156-0-3*) Indep NECA.

Levy-Ko. Asi Es. 2nd ed. (C). 1996. student ed. 103.00 (*0-15-505164-4*) Harcourt.

— Asi Es. 2nd ed. (C). 1995. text 76.00 (*0-15-501284-3*, Pub. by Harcourt Coll Pubs) Harcourt.

— Asi Es With Liscass & Workbook. (C). 1995. 99.50 (*0-15-503335-2*) Harcourt.

— Asi Es with List Cassettes. 2nd ed. (C). 1996. student ed. 77.50 (*0-15-502002-1*) Harcourt.

— Nuevas Fronteras. 3rd ed. (SPA.). (C). 1996. 35.50 incl. audio (*0-03-017233-0*) Harcourt.

— Nuevas Frontieras. 3rd ed. (C). 1996. 51.00 (*0-03-013403-X*) Harcourt.

— Nuevas Fronteras. 5th ed. 1995. 246.00 (*0-03-015708-0*) Harcourt Coll Pubs.

Levy-Konesky, Nancy & Daggett, Karen. Asi Es. (ENG & SPA.). (C). 1991. text. write for info. incl. VHS (*0-318-69165-5*) Harcourt Coll Pubs.

— Asi Es. (SPA., Illus.). 560p. (C). 1992. teacher ed. write for info. (*0-03-049482-6*) Harcourt Coll Pubs.

***Levy-Konesky, Nancy & Daggett, Karen.** Asi Es. 3rd ed. LC 99-42033. 1999. write for info. (*0-03-025928-2*) H Holt & Co.

Levy-Konesky, Nancy & Daggett, Karen. Revista. Perez-Abreu, Marilyn et al, eds. 250p. (C). 1988. pap. text 42.50 (*0-03-014214-8*) Harcourt Coll Pubs.

Levy-Konesky, Nancy, et al. Fronteras: Gramatica y Conversacion. 2nd ed. (ENG & SPA.). 352p. (C). 1992. student ed. write for info. (*0-318-69166-3*) Harcourt Coll Pubs.

— FRONTERAS GRAMMAR, 3/E. 3rd ed. (SPA.). (C). 1996. pap. text 49.00 (*0-03-013399-8*) Holt R&W.

Levy-Konesky, Nancy, et al. FRONTERAS LITERATURE, 3/E. 3rd ed. (SPA.). 366p. (C). 1996. pap. text 34.00 (*0-03-013404-8*) Holt R&W.

Levy-Konesky, Nancy, et al. Viewer's Manual: Camara. 2nd ed. (ENG & SPA.). 352p. (C). 1990. pap. text, student ed. 24.50 (*0-03-049033-2*) Harcourt Coll Pubs.

Levy, L., jt. auth. see Bilgram, Hugo.

***Levy, L. A. & Hetherington, V. J.** Principles & Practice of Podiatric Medicine. 2nd ed. (Illus.). 854p. 1998. text. write for info. (*0-443-07940-4*) Church.

***Levy, Lance.** Understanding Obesity: The Five Medical Causes. (Your Personal Health Ser.). (Illus.). 200p. 2000. pap. 14.95 (*1-55209-479-0*) Firefly Bks Ltd.

Levy, Larry. I Would Stay Forever If I Could. 36p. 1999. pap. (*0-932412-14-9*) Mayapple Pr.

***Levy, Laurent-Patrick.** Magnetism & Superconductivity. LC 99-56699. (Texts & Monographs in Physics). (Illus.). xi, 461p. (C). 2000. 58.95 (*3-540-66688-5*) Spr-Verlag.

Levy, Laurie, ed. see Morton Press Staff.

Levy, Lawrence & Morgan, Brian D. Golf: Tours & Detours. (Illus.). 160p. 1988. 24.95 (*0-88162-362-8*, Pergamon Pr) Elsevier.

Levy, Lawrence & White, Gordon S., Jr. A Victory for Jamie: The Story of Greg Norman & Jamie Hutton. (Illus.). 64p. 1989. 20.00 (*0-9615344-4-3*) Intl Merc OH.

Levy, Leah. Kathryn Gustafson: Sculpting the Land. Landecker, Heidi, ed. (Landmarks Ser.: Vol. 5). (Illus.). 66p. 1998. pap. 24.95 (*1-888931-06-X*) Spacemkr Pr.

— Peter Walker: Minimalist Gardens. (Illus.). 210p. 1997. pap. 45.00 (*1-888931-00-0*) Spacemkr Pr.

Levy, Leah, ed. see Hood, Walter.

Levy-Leblond, J. M., jt. auth. see Beltrametti, E. G.

Levy-Leblond, Jean-Marc & Balibar, F. Quantics: Rudiments. Ali, S. T., tr. xx, 540p. 1990. 177.25 (*0-444-87424-0*) Elsevier.

— Quantics: Rudiments. Ali, S. T., tr. xx, 540p. 1990. pap. 72.25 (*0-444-88120-4*) Elsevier.

Levy-Leblond, Jean-Marc, jt. ed. see Cini, M.

Levy-Leboyer, Claude. Le Psychologue et L'Entreprise. LC HF5548.8.P76. (Collection De Psychologie Appliquee). (FRE.). 175p. reprint ed. pap. 54.30 (*0-7837-6951-2*, 204678000003) Bks Demand.

— Psychology & Environment. Canter, David & Griffiths, Ian, trs. LC 81-21382. 197p. reprint ed. pap. 61.10 (*0-8357-4821-9*, 203775800009) Bks Demand.

Levy, Leo B., jt. ed. see McNeir, Waldo F.

Levy, Leon S. Fundamental Concepts of Computer Science: Mathematical Foundations of Programming. LC 88-392. (Illus.). 320p. (C). 1988. reprint ed. pap. 23.95 (*0-932633-06-4*) Dorset Hse Pub Co.

Levy, Leon S., jt. auth. see Kowalski, Thaddeus J.

Levy, Leonard. The Fifth Amendment. Date not set. pap. write for info. (*0-679-43435-6*) Fodors Travel.

Levy, Leonard, et al, eds. Encyclopedia of The American Constitution, 2 vols. 2196p. 1990. 175.00 (*0-685-47371-6*) Macmillan.

Levy, Leonard A. & Thompson, Anne K., eds. Podiatric Medical Assisting. 2nd ed. (Illus.). 295p. 1992. pap. text 56.00 (*0-443-08760-1*) Church.

Levy, Leonard W. Blasphemy: Verbal Offense Against the Sacred, from Moses to Salman Rushdie. LC 94-31365. 688p. 1995. pap. 22.50 (*0-8078-4515-9*) U of NC Pr.

Levy, Leonard W. Blasphemy in Massachusetts: Freedom of Conscience & the Abner Kneeland Case. LC 70-16634. 592p. 1973. lib. bdg. 65.00 (*0-306-70221-5*) Da Capo.

— Encyclopedia of American Presidency, Vol. 4. 1995. 100.00 (*0-13-275975-6*) P-H.

— Encyclopedia of the American Presidency, Vol. 1. 1995. 100.00 (*0-13-276197-1*) P-H.

— Encyclopedia of the American Presidency, Vol. 3. 1995. 100.00 (*0-13-275967-5*) P-H.

— Essays on the Making of the Constitution. 2nd ed. LC 86-16255. 350p. (Orig.). 1987. pap. text 20.95 (*0-19-504902-0*) OUP.

— The Establishment Clause: Religion & the First Amendment. 2nd ed. LC 94-1046. 300p. 1994. 45.00 (*0-8078-2156-X*); pap. 18.95 (*0-8078-4466-7*) U of NC Pr.

— Freedom of the Press from Zenger to Jefferson. LC 95-69528. 496p. (C). 1996. reprint ed. pap. 22.50 (*0-89089-837-5*) Carolina Acad Pr.

— Jefferson & Civil Liberties: The Darker Side. 264p. 1989. reprint ed. pap. text 10.95 (*0-929587-11-1*, Elephant Paperbacks) I R Dee.

— Law of the Commonwealth & Chief Justice Shaw. 400p. 1987. text 57.00 (*0-19-504865-2*) OUP.

Levy, Leonard W. Law of the Commonwealth & Chief Justice Shaw. 400p. 1987. pap. text 24.95 (*0-19-504866-0*) OUP.

Levy, Leonard W. A License to Steal: The Forfeiture of Property. LC 95-14497. (Illus.). 288p. (C). 1995. 39.95 (*0-8078-2242-6*) U of NC Pr.

— Original Intent & the Framer's Constitution. 288p. 1988. text 19.95 (*0-02-918791-5*) Free Pr.

***Levy, Leonard W.** Original Intent & the Framers' Constitution. 544p. 2000. reprint ed. pap. 19.95 (*1-56663-312-5*, Pub. by I R Dee) Natl Bk Netwk.

Levy, Leonard W. Origins of the Bill of Rights. LC 98-44965. (Contemporary Law Ser.). (Illus.). 304p. 1999. 30.00 (*0-300-07802-1*) Yale U Pr.

— Origins of the Fifth Amendment: The Right Against Self-Incrimination. LC 99-34149. 561p. 1999. pap. 18.95 (*1-56663-270-6*, Pub. by I R Dee) Natl Bk Netwk.

— Origins of the Fifth Amendment: The Right Against Self-Incrimination. 576p. 1986. reprint ed. pap. 14.95 (*0-02-919580-2*); reprint ed. text 23.99 (*0-02-919570-5*) Free Pr.

— The Palladium of Justice: Origins of Trial by Jury. 108p. 1999. 18.95 (*1-56663-259-5*, Pub. by I R Dee) Natl Bk Netwk.

***Levy, Leonard W.** The Palladium of Justice: Origins of Trial by Jury. 128p. 2000. reprint ed. pap. 12.95 (*1-56663-313-3*, Pub. by I R Dee) Natl Bk Netwk.

— Ranters Run Amok: And Other Adventures in the History of the Law. LC 99-52807. 256p. 2000. text 26.50 (*1-56663-277-3*, Pub. by I R Dee) Natl Bk Netwk.

Levy, Leonard W. Seasoned Judgments: Constitutional Rights & American History. 410p. (C). 1994. 44.95 (*1-56000-170-4*) Transaction Pubs.

Levy, Leonard W., ed. Encyclopedia of the American Constitution, Vol. 2. 1986. 100.00 (*0-02-918630-7*) Mac Lib Ref.

— Encyclopedia of the American Constitution, Vol. 3. 1986. 100.00 (*0-02-918640-4*) Mac Lib Ref.

— Encyclopedia of the American Constitution, Vols. 1 & 2. 1991. 133.00 (*0-02-918680-3*) Mac Lib Ref.

— Encyclopedia of the American Constitution, Vols. 3 & 4. 1991. 133.00 (*0-02-918690-0*) Mac Lib Ref.

Levy, Leonard W., et al, eds. American Constitutional History. (Readings from the Encyclopedia of the American Constitution Ser.). 352p. (C). 1989. 15.95 (*0-02-897231-7*) Macmillan.

— Encyclopedia of the American Constitution, Vol. 1. 1986. 100.00 (*0-02-918620-X*) Mac Lib Ref.

Levy, Leonard W. & Fisher. Encyclopedia of the American Presidency, Vol. 2. 1995. 100.00 (*0-13-276148-3*) Mac Lib Ref.

Levy, Leonard W. & Mahoney, Dennis J. The Framing & Ratification of the Constitution. 1987. write for info. (*0-317-62103-3*) Macmillan.

Levy, Leonard W. & Mahoney, Dennis J., eds. The Constitution: A History of Its Framing & Ratification. 352p. 1987. 23.99 (*0-02-918790-7*) Free Pr.

Levy, Lester, ed. Take Me Out to the Ball Game & Other Favorite Song Hits, 1906-1908. 128p. 1984. pap. 9.95 (*0-486-24662-0*) Dover.

Levy, Lillian, ed. Space: Its Impact on Man & Society. LC 72-13181. (Essay Index Reprint Ser.). 1977. reprint ed. 19.95 (*0-8369-8164-2*) Ayer.

***Levy, Linda & Bernier, Julie.** Therapeutic Exercise for Athletic Training Lab Manual. 100p. (C). 2000. pap., lab manual ed. write for info. (*0-7360-3382-3*) Human Kinetics.

Levy, Linda & Grabowski, Francine. Low-Fat Living for Real People: The Fat-Free Chocolate-Covered Creme-Filled Mini-Cakes Diet & Other Confusions of Low-Fat Eating Explained. 2nd rev. ed. LC 97-75607. 1998. pap. text 14.95 (*0-9627403-9-X*) Lake Isle Pr.

Levy-Livermore, Amnon. Economic Analyses of Financial Crises. 320p. 1995. 87.95 (*1-85972-244-X*, Pub. by Avebry) Ashgate Pub Co.

Levy-Livermore, Amnon, ed. Handbook on the Globalization of the World Economy. LC 97-44513. 776p. 1998. 215.00 (*1-85898-467-X*) E Elgar.

Levy, Lois. Undress Your Stress: 30 Curiously Fun Ways to Take off Tension. LC 99-36917. 128p. 1999. pap. 9.95 (*1-57071-482-7*) Sourcebks.

Levy, Lorraine. Picasso. (Illus.). 160p. 1998. reprint ed. 19.95 (*1-56852-172-3*, Konecky & Konecky) W S Konecky Assocs.

Levy, Lou, ed. Day Walks in the Santa Monica Mountains. rev. ed. 125p. (Orig.). 1986. pap. 3.95 (*0-9619564-0-2*) SMMTF.

Levy, Louis E. The Jewish Year. 1979. lib. bdg. 59.95 (*0-685-96463-9*) Revisionist Pr.

Levy, Louise, jt. auth. see Kohan, Darius.

Levy, Lynn. Echoes on RimRock: In Pursuit of the Chukar Partridge. LC 98-41458. (Illus.). 158p. 1998. 21.95 (*0-87108-882-7*) Pruett.

Levy, Lynnie & Levy, Jade, eds. Of Like Mind Source Book II: For Spiritually-Minded Women. 2nd ed. 122p. 1995. pap. 14.95 (*0-9626751-0-5*) Triple Crescent.

Levy, M., et al, eds. Z Degree Physics: Cargese, 1990. (NATO ASI Ser.: Vol. 261). (Illus.). 568p. (C). 1991. text 174.00 (*0-306-43934-4*, Kluwer Plenum) Kluwer Academic.

Levy, M., et al. Frontiers in Particle Physics: Cargese 1994. (NATO ASI Ser.: Vol. 350). (Illus.). 468p. (C). 1996. text 135.00 (*0-306-45129-8*, Kluwer Plenum) Kluwer Academic.

— Quantitative Particle Physics: Cargese 1992. (NATO ASI Ser.: Vol. 311). (Illus.). 444p. (C). 1993. text 129.50 (*0-306-44560-3*, Kluwer Plenum) Kluwer Academic.

Levy, M. J. The Mistresses of King George IV. LC 96-144880. (Illus.). 224p. 1996. 34.95 (*0-7206-0956-9*, Pub. by P Owen Ltd) Dufour.

Levy, M. J., ed. Perdita: The Memoirs of Mary Robinson, 1758-1800. 1995. 35.00 (*0-614-07439-8*, Pub. by P Owen Ltd) Dufour.

***Levy, Marc.** If Only It Were True. Leggatt, Jeremy, tr. 218p. 2000. 22.95 (*0-7434-0617-6*, PB Hardcover) PB.

Levy, Marc. Rhodesia Becomes Zimbabwe: The United States & the Internal Settlement & The Lancaster House Conference. (Pew Case Studies in International Affairs). 50p. (C). 1989. pap. text 3.50 (*1-56927-442-8*) Geo U Inst Dplmcy.

— When Liberty & Justice Were Won. LC 97-8188. 112p. 1997. 12.95 (*0-944957-92-7*) Rivercross Pub.

Levy, Marc A., jt. ed. see Keohane, Robert O.

Levy, Margot, ed. Annual Obituary, 1984. 84th ed. 1986. 100.00 (*0-912289-53-8*) St James Pr.

Levy, Marguerite F., ed. Research & Theory in Developmental Psychology: Awards Papers of the New York State Psychological Association. 1983. 30.50 (*0-8290-1067-X*) Irvington.

Levy, Marilyn. Is That Really Me in the Mirror? 176p. (Orig.). 1991. mass mkt. 3.95 (*0-449-70343-6*, Juniper) Fawcett.

— Run for Your Life. LC 95-24379. 224p. (J). (gr. 5-9). 1996. 15.00 (*0-395-74520-9*) HM.

— Run for Your Life. LC 95-24379. 224p. (J). (gr. 5-9). 1997. pap. 5.99 (*0-698-11608-9*, PapStar) Peng Put Young Read.

— Run for Your Life. 1997. 11.05 (*0-606-12802-6*, Pub. by Turtleback) Demco.

Levy, Marion. Modernization & the Structure of Societies, 2 Vols., Set. 920p. 1996. pap. text 49.95 (*1-56000-897-0*) Transaction Pubs.

— Modernization & the Structure of Societies: Aspects of Social Structure in Modernized & Non-Modernized Societies, 2 Vols., Vol. 1. 432p. 1996. pap. text 29.95 (*1-56000-893-8*) Transaction Pubs.

— Modernization & the Sturcture of Societies: The Organization Contexts of Societies, 2 Vols., Vol. 2. 488p. 1996. pap. text 29.95 (*1-56000-896-2*) Transaction Pubs.

— Seasoned Judgments: The American Constitution, Rights, & History. 468p. 1996. pap. text 25.95 (*1-56000-925-X*) Transaction Pubs.

Levy, Marion F. Each in Her Own Way: Five Women Leaders of the Developing World. LC 87-26844. 182p. 1988. pap. text 17.95 (*1-55587-094-5*) L Rienner.

Levy, Marion J., Jr. Maternal Influence: The Search for Social Universals. 263p. (C). 1992. pap. 24.95 (*1-56000-614-5*) Transaction Pubs.

— Our Mother-Tempers. 1989. 48.00 (*0-520-06422-4*, Pub. by U CA Pr) Cal Prin Full Svc.

***Levy, Mark.** Accidental Genius: Revolutionize Your Thinking Through Private Writing. 180p. 2000. pap. 16.95 (*1-57675-083-3*, Pub. by Berrett-Koehler) Publishers Group.

Levy, Mark. Joan Brown: The Golden Age. LC 86-50213. (Illus.). 40p. (Orig.). 1986. pap. 12.00 (*0-937097-00-4*) SDSU Univ Art.

— Technicians of Ecstasy: Shamanism & the Modern Artist. LC 93-14704. (Illus.). 360p. (Orig.). 1993. pap. 14.95 (*0-9626184-4-6*) Bramble Co.

Levy, Mark R., ed. The VCR Age. (Focus Editions Ser.: Vol. 105). 280p. (C). 1989. text 59.95 (*0-8039-3299-5*); pap. text 26.00 (*0-8039-3300-2*) Sage.

— The VCR Age: Home Video & Mass Communication. LC 89-5852. (Sage Focus Editions Ser.: No. 105). (Illus.). 274p. 1989. reprint ed. pap. 85.00 (*0-608-04317-6*, 206509600012) Bks Demand.

Levy, Mark R. & Gurevitch, Michael. Defining Media Studies: Reflections on the Future of the Field. 448p. (C). 1994. pap. text 27.95 (*0-19-508788-7*) OUP.

— Defining Media Studies: Reflections on the Future of the Field. (Illus.). 448p. (C). 1994. text 57.95 (*0-19-508787-9*) OUP.

Levy, Mark R., jt. auth. see Robinson, John P.

Levy, Mark R., jt. ed. see Biocca, Frank.

Levy, Markus, jt. auth. see Dipert, Brian.

Levy, Marlon F., jt. auth. see Klintmalm, Goran B.

Levy-Marschal, Claire & Czernichow, P., eds. Epidemiology & Etiology of Insulin-Dependent Diabetes in the Young. (Pediatric & Adolescent Endocrinology Ser.: Vol. 21). (Illus.). xii, 242p. 1992. 208.75 (*3-8055-5521-0*) S Karger.

Levy, Martin, tr. see Al-Kindi.

Levy, Martin J., ed. Perdita: The Memoirs of Mary Robinson. LC 95-112570. 168p. 1995. 35.00 (*0-7206-0930-5*) Dufour.

Levy, Marvin, et al. Essentials of Life & Health. 5th ed. 486p. (C). 1987. text 24.95 (*0-685-18212-6*) McGraw.

Levy, Matthew N., jt. auth. see Berne, Robert M.

Levy, Matthew N., jt. ed. see Berne, Robert M.

Levy, Matthew N., jt. ed. see Schwartz, Peter J.

Levy, Matthys. Why Buildings Fall Down. 1994. pap. 13.00 (*0-393-31152-X*) Norton.

— Why the Earth Quakes: The Story of Earthquakes & Volcanoes. 224p. 1997. pap. 13.00 (*0-393-31527-4*) Norton.

***Levy, Matthys & Panchyk, Richard.** Engineering the City: How Infrastructure Works. 160p. 2000. pap. 14.95 (*1-55652-419-6*, Pub. by Chicago Review) IPG Chicago.

Levy, Matthys & Salvadori, Mario G. Why the Earth Quakes: The Story of Earthquakes & Volcanoes. (Illus.). 256p. 1995. 25.00 (*0-393-03774-6*) Norton.

Levy, Matthys, jt. auth. see Salvadori, Mario G.

Levy, Maurice. Lovecraft: A Study in the Fantastic. Joshi, S. T., tr. from FRE. LC 87-36470. 148p. 1988. 31.95 (*0-8143-1955-6*); pap. 16.95 (*0-8143-1956-4*) Wayne St U Pr.

Levy, Maurice, et al, eds. Particle Physics: Cargese, 1985. Weyers, Jacques & Castamans, Raymond, trs. (NATO ASI Series B, Physical Sciences: Vol. 150). 447p. 1987. 110.00 (*0-306-42562-9*, Plenum Trade) Perseus Pubng.

— Particle Physics: Cargese, 1987. LC 88-4180. (NATO ASI Series B, Physics: Vol. 173). (Illus.). 684p. 1988. 155.00 (*0-306-42835-0*, Plenum Trade) Perseus Pubng.

— Particle Physics: Cargese, 1989. (NATO ASI Series B, Physics: Vol. 223). (Illus.). 368p. 1990. 110.00 (*0-306-43601-9*, Plenum Trade) Perseus Pubng.

Levy, Maurice & Jean, M., eds. Cargese Lectures in Physics, 1966-1968, Vol. 2. 432p. (Orig.). 1968. 175.00 (*0-677-12720-0*) Gordon & Breach.

Levy, Maurice & Robinson, John L., eds. Energy & Agriculture: Their Interacting Futures Policy & Implications & Global Models. (Golbal Modelling & Applications Ser.: Vol. I). xii, 372p. 1984. text 317.00 (*3-7186-0187-7*) Gordon & Breach.

Levy, Maurice, ed. see North Atlantic Treaty Organization Staff.

Levy, Maya. Acting Scenes & Monologues for Young Women. LC 98-49593. 192p. 1999. pap. 14.95 (*1-56608-049-5*) Meriwether Pub.

Levy, Michael. Computer-Assisted Language Learning: Context & Conceptualization. LC 96-35169. (Illus.). 298p. 1997. pap. 28.00 (*0-19-823631-X*); text 65.00 (*0-19-823632-8*) OUP.

— Enjoy Yourself, Its Later Than You Think. (What Is the Point Ser.: No. 3). 128p. 1999. pap. 9.95 (*0-9668069-2-1*) Point of Life Inc.

— Minds of Blue Souls of Gold: What's the Point II. 128p. 1999. pap. 9.95 (*0-9668069-1-3*) Point of Life Inc.

An Asterisk (*) at the beginning of an entry indicates that the title is appearing for the first time.

— Natalie Babbit. (Twayne's United States Authors Ser.: No. 573). 136p. (C). 1991. 21.95 (*0-8057-7612-5*, Twyne) Mac Lib Ref.

— Political Thought in America: An Anthology. 2nd ed. 596p. (C). 1992. reprint ed. pap. text 30.95 (*0-88133-688-2*) Waveland Pr.

— Retailing Management. 3rd ed. LC 97-25683. (Series in Marketing). 1997. write for info. (*0-07-115387-X*) McGraw.

— Retailing Management. 3rd ed. LC 97-25683. (Series in Marketing). (C). 1997. text 77.51 (*0-256-22346-7*, Irwn Prfssnl) McGraw-Hill Prof.

— What Is the Point: The Essence of Life. vi, 111p. 1998. pap. 9.95 (*0-9668069-0-5*) Point of Life Inc.

***Levy, Michael & Gray, Sherylann.** From God with Love. (Illus.). 128p. 2000. pap. 9.95 (*0-9668069-3-X*) Point of Life Inc.

Levy, Michael & Weitz, Barton A. Essentials of Retailing. 496p. (C). 1995. text 54.95 (*0-256-16348-0*, Irwn Prfssnl) McGraw-Hill Prof.

— Retailing Management. 2nd ed. LC 94-26274. (Marketing Ser.). 736p. (C). 1994. text 69.95 (*0-256-13661-0*, Irwn McGrw-H) McGrw-H Hghr Educ.

Levy, Michael, et al. Statmaster for Business & Economics. (C). 1987. pap. text 19.00 (*0-673-39523-5*) Addson-Wesley Educ.

Levy, Michael, ed. see Academy of Marketing Science Staff.

Levy, Michael, ed. see Hewson, brendan.

Levy, Michael B., jt. ed. see Abbot, Philip.

Levy, Michael B., jt. ed. see Portis, Edward B.

Levy, Michael H., jt. auth. see Green, Helen I.

***Levy, Michael M.** Portrayal of Southeast Asian Refugees in Recent American Children's Books. LC 00-31041. (Studies in American Literature: Vol. 35). (Illus.). 116p. 2000. 59.95 (*0-7734-7753-5*) E Mellen.

Levy, Michele F., et al, eds. Borders of Culture, Margins of Identity: Seventh Annual Colloquium of the Interdisciplinary Nineteenth Century Studies Association, New Orleans, 1992. (Occasional Publications: No. 3). (Illus.). 95p. (Orig.). 1994. pap. 8.95 (*1-883275-01-6*) Xavier Rev.

Levy, Mike & Thomas, Gill. Managing the Millennium Bug: And Its Implications for Your Organization LC 99-18668. 1999. 78.95 (*0-566-08177-6*, Pub. by Gower) Ashgate Pub Co.

Levy, Mike, jt. ed. see Debski, Robert.

***Levy, Mireille F.** Parabolic Equation Methods for Electromagnetic Wave Propagation. (IEE Electromagnetic Waves Ser.: No. 45). 350p. 2000. boxed set 85.00 (*0-85296-764-0*, Pub. by INSPEC Inc) Whitehurst & Clark.

Levy, Miriam J. Governance & Grievance: Habsburg Policy & Italian Tyrol in the Eighteenth Century. LC 87-15189. 272p. (Orig.). 1988. pap. 21.95 (*0-911198-86-5*) Purdue U Pr.

Levy, Morten. The World of the Gorrlaus Slatts: A Morphological Investigation of a Branch of Norwegian Fiddle Music Tradition, 3 vols. (Illus.). 960p. (Orig.). 1989. pap. 142.50 (*87-89160-02-9*) Coronet Bks.

Levy, Moses E. A Plan for the Abolition of Slavery: Consistently with the Interests of All Parties Concerned. 2nd annot. ed. Monaco, Chris, ed. (Illus.). 64p. 1999. reprint ed. 14.95 (*0-9653864-0-6*) Wacahoota Pr.

Levy, Myrna N. The Summer Kid. 80p. (J). (gr. 1-5). 1991. pap. 5.95 (*0-929005-20-1*, Pub. by Sec Story Pr) LPC InBook.

***Levy, Naomi.** To Begin Again: The Journey Toward Comfort, Strength & Faith in Difficult Times. 1999. pap. 12.95 (*0-345-41383-0*, Ballantine) Ballantine Pub Grp.

***Levy, Nathan.** American History. Kristensen, Renee & Sculthorp, Jeffrey A., eds. LC 99-68389. (Whose Clues? Ser.). 32p. (YA). (gr. 3-12). 2000. pap., teacher ed. 5.99 (*1-889319-39-2*, MindMotion) Trend Enterprises.

— Characters in Literature. Kristensen, Renee & Sculthorp, Jeffrey A., eds. LC 99-69315. (Whose Clues? Ser.). 32p. (YA). (gr. 3-12). 2000. pap., teacher ed. 5.99 (*1-889319-42-2*, MindMotion) Trend Enterprises.

Levy, Nathan. Each Life Is Once. (J). (gr. k up). 1993. pap. 9.95 (*1-878347-15-2*) NL Assocs.

***Levy, Nathan.** Famous Authors. Kristensen, Renee & Sculthorp, Jeffrey A., eds. LC 99-69316. (Whose Clues? Ser.). 32p. (YA). (gr. 3-12). 2000. pap., teacher ed. 5.99 (*1-889319-43-0*, MindMotion) Trend Enterprises.

— Inventors & Scientists. Kristensen, Renee & Sculthorp, Jeffrey A., eds. LC 99-69265. (Whose Clues? Ser.). 32p. (YA). (gr. 3-12). 2000. pap., teacher ed. 5.99 (*1-889319-40-6*, MindMotion) Trend Enterprises.

— Musicians & Composers. Kristensen, Renee & Sculthorp, Jeffrey A., eds. LC 99-69276. (Whose Clues? Ser.). 32p. (YA). (gr. 3-12). 2000. pap., teacher ed. 5.99 (*1-889319-41-4*, MindMotion) Trend Enterprises.

Levy, Nathan. Nathan Levy's 100 Hundred Intriguing Questions, Bk. 1. (J). (gr. 3 up). 1993. 7.50 (*1-878347-35-7*) NL Assocs.

— Nathan Levy's 100 Hundred Intriguing Questions, Bk. 2. (J). (gr. 3 up). 1994. 7.50 (*1-878347-36-5*) NL Assocs.

— Nathan Levy's 100 Hundred Intriguing Questions, Bk. 3. (J). (gr. 3 up). 1994. 7.50 (*1-878347-37-3*) NL Assocs.

— Nathan Levy's 100 Intriguing Questions, Bk. 4. 52p. 1994. pap. 7.50 (*1-878347-38-1*) NL Assocs.

— Nathan Levy's 100 Intriguing Questions, Bk. 5. 52p. 1994. pap. 7.50 (*1-878347-40-3*) NL Assocs.

— Nathan Levy's 100 Intriguing Questions, Bk. 6. 52p. 1994. pap. 7.50 (*1-878347-42-X*) NL Assocs.

— Personality Probe. (J). (gr. k up). 1990. pap. 21.95 (*1-878347-07-1*) NL Assocs.

***Levy, Nathan.** Sports Heroes. Kristensen, Renee & Sculthorp, Jeffrey A., eds. LC 99-69317. (Whose Clues? Ser.). 32p. (YA). (gr. 3-12). 2000. pap., teacher ed. 5.99 (*1-889319-44-9*, MindMotion) Trend Enterprises.

— Stories with Holes, Vol. 1. Gordon, Juli A., ed. (Illus.). 32p. (YA). (gr. 2-12). 2000. pap., teacher ed. 5.99 (*1-889319-49-X*, MindMotion) Trend Enterprises.

Levy, Nathan. Stories with Holes, Vol. II. (J). (gr. 3 up). 1996. pap. 7.50 (*1-878347-00-4*) NL Assocs.

***Levy, Nathan.** Stories with Holes, Vol. 2. Gordon, Juli A., ed. LC 99-69753. (Illus.). 32p. (YA). (gr. 2-12). 2000. pap., teacher ed. 5.99 (*1-889319-50-3*, MindMotion) Trend Enterprises.

Levy, Nathan. Stories with Holes, Vol. III. (J). (gr. 3 up). 1996. pap. 7.50 (*1-878347-01-2*) NL Assocs.

***Levy, Nathan.** Stories with Holes, Vol. 3. Gordon, Juli A., ed. LC 99-69753. (Illus.). (YA). (gr. 2-12). 2000. pap., teacher ed. 5.99 (*1-889319-51-1*, MindMotion) Trend Enterprises.

Levy, Nathan. Stories with Holes, Vol. IV. (J). (gr. 3 up). 1996. pap. 7.50 (*1-878347-02-0*) NL Assocs.

***Levy, Nathan.** Stories with Holes, Vol. 4. Gordon, Juli A., ed. LC 99-69753. (Illus.). (YA). (gr. 2-12). 2000. pap., teacher ed. 5.99 (*1-889319-52-X*, MindMotion) Trend Enterprises.

Levy, Nathan. Stories with Holes, Vol. V. (J). (gr. 3 up). 1996. pap. 7.50 (*1-878347-03-9*) NL Assocs.

***Levy, Nathan.** Stories with Holes, Vol. 5. Gordon, Juli A., ed. LC 99-69753. (Illus.). (YA). (gr. 2-12). 2000. pap., teacher ed. 5.99 (*1-889319-53-8*, MindMotion) Trend Enterprises.

Levy, Nathan. Stories with Holes, Vol. VI. (J). (gr. 3 up). 1996. pap. 7.50 (*1-878347-09-8*) NL Assocs.

***Levy, Nathan.** Stories with Holes, Vol. 6. Gordon, Juli A., ed. LC 99-69753. (Illus.). (YA). (gr. 2-12). 2000. pap., teacher ed. 5.99 (*1-889319-54-6*, MindMotion) Trend Enterprises.

Levy, Nathan. Stories with Holes, Vol. VII. (J). (gr. 3 up). 1996. pap. 7.50 (*1-878347-10-1*) NL Assocs.

***Levy, Nathan.** Stories with Holes, Vol. 7. Gordon, Juli A., ed. LC 99-69753. (Illus.). (YA). (gr. 2-12). 2000. pap., teacher ed. 5.99 (*1-889319-55-4*, MindMotion) Trend Enterprises.

Levy, Nathan. Stories with Holes, Vol. VIII. 20p. (J). (gr. 3 up). 1996. pap. 7.50 (*1-878347-11-X*) NL Assocs.

***Levy, Nathan.** Stories with Holes, Vol. 8. Gordon, Juli A., ed. LC 99-69753. (Illus.). (YA). (gr. 2-12). 2000. pap., teacher ed. 5.99 (*1-889319-56-2*, MindMotion) Trend Enterprises.

Levy, Nathan. Stories with Holes, Vol. IX. (J). (gr. 3 up). 1996. pap. 7.50 (*1-878347-17-9*) NL Assocs.

***Levy, Nathan.** Stories with Holes, Vol. 9. Gordon, Juli A., ed. LC 99-69753. (Illus.). (YA). (gr. 2-12). 2000. pap., teacher ed. 5.99 (*1-889319-57-0*, MindMotion) Trend Enterprises.

Levy, Nathan. Stories with Holes, Vol. X. (J). (gr. 3 up). 1996. pap. 7.50 (*1-878347-21-7*) NL Assocs.

***Levy, Nathan.** Stories with Holes, Vol. 10. Gordon, Juli A., ed. LC 99-69753. (Illus.). (YA). (gr. 2-12). 2000. pap., teacher ed. 5.99 (*1-889319-58-9*, MindMotion) Trend Enterprises.

Levy, Nathan. Stories with Holes, Vol. XI. (J). (gr. 3 up). 1996. pap. 10.00 (*1-878347-22-5*) NL Assocs.

***Levy, Nathan.** Stories with Holes, Vol. 11. Gordon, Juli A., ed. LC 99-69753. (Illus.). (YA). (gr. 2-12). 2000. pap., teacher ed. 5.99 (*1-889319-59-7*, MindMotion) Trend Enterprises.

Levy, Nathan. Stories with Holes, Vol. XII. (J). (gr. 3 up). 1996. pap. 10.00 (*1-878347-26-8*) NL Assocs.

***Levy, Nathan.** Stories with Holes, Vol. 12. Gordon, Juli A., ed. LC 99-69753. (Illus.). (YA). (gr. 2-12). 2000. pap., teacher ed. 5.99 (*1-889319-60-0*, MindMotion) Trend Enterprises.

Levy, Nathan. Stories with Holes, Vol. XIII. (J). (gr. 3 up). 1996. pap. 10.00 (*1-878347-27-6*) NL Assocs.

— Stories with Holes, Vol. XIV. (J). (gr. 3 up). 1996. pap. 10.00 (*1-878347-28-4*) NL Assocs.

— Stories with Holes, Vol. XV. (J). (gr. 3 up). 1996. pap. 10.00 (*1-878347-29-2*) NL Assocs.

— Stories with Holes, Vol. XVI. (J). (gr. 3 up). 1996. pap. 10.00 (*1-878347-30-6*) NL Assocs.

— Stories with Holes, Vol. XVII. (J). (gr. 3 up). 1996. pap. 7.50 (*1-878347-31-4*) NL Assocs.

— Stories with Holes, Vol. XVIII. (J). (gr. 3 up). 1996. pap. 7.50 (*1-878347-32-2*) NL Assocs.

— Stories with Holes, Vol. XIX. 40p. 1996. pap. 7.50 (*1-878347-44-6*) NL Assocs.

— Stories with Holes, Vol. XX. (Illus.). 40p. 1997. pap. 7.50 (*1-878347-46-2*) NL Assocs.

Levy, Nathan & Burke, Amy M. Tools of the Trade. (J). (gr. 4-12). 1992. pap. 7.95 (*1-878347-18-7*) NL Assocs.

Levy, Nathan & Pastis, Steven. Who Am I? Vol. 5: Inventors. (J). (gr. 4-8). 1992. pap. 7.50 (*1-878347-19-5*) NL Assocs.

Levy, Nathan, et al. Who Am I? Vol. 1: History. (J). (gr. 4-8). 1990. pap. 7.50 (*1-878347-04-7*) NL Assocs.

— Who Am I? Vol. 2: Literature Authors. (J). (gr. 4-8). 1991. pap. 7.50 (*1-878347-12-8*) NL Assocs.

— Who Am I? Vol. 3: Music. (J). (gr. 4-8). 1991. pap. 7.50 (*1-878347-13-6*) NL Assocs.

— Who Am I? Vol. 4: Literature Characters. (J). (gr. 2-8). 1991. pap. 7.50 (*1-878347-14-4*) NL Assocs.

Levy, Nathan, jt. auth. see Levy, Janet.

***Levy, Neil M.** Moon Handbooks: Micronesia. 5th rev. ed. Vol. 5. (Illus.). 340p. 2000. pap. 16.95 (*1-56691-162-1*, Moon Handbks) Avalon Travel.

Levy, Neil M., et al. California Torts, 6 vols. LC 85-61608. 1985. ring bd. 1080.00 (*0-8205-1116-1*, 116) Bender.

Levy, Nino S. Managing High Technology & Innovation. LC 97-37465. 274p. 1998. pap. text 36.20 (*0-02-370462-4*) Macmillan.

Levy, Norman. Essential Math For the College Bound Student: College Entrance & Placement Tests. 3rd ed. 416p. 1988. pap. 14.00 (*0-671-79971-1*) Macmillan.

Levy, Norman & Levy, Joan U. Mechanical Aptitude & Spatial Relations Tests. 2nd ed. 256p. 1991. pap. 12.00 (*0-13-568692-X*, Arco) Macmillan Gen Ref.

***Levy, Norman & Levy, Joan U.** New York State Teacher Certification Exam. (Illus.). 256p. 1999. pap. text 19.95 (*0-02-863534-5*) S&S Trade.

Levy, Norman & Levy, Joan U. S. A. T. Math Preparatory Set. 600p. 1989. pap. text 10.95 (*1-55637-085-7*) Visual Educ.

Levy, Norman, jt. auth. see Levy, Joan U.

Levy, Norman B., ed. Psychonephrology Vol. 1: Psychological Factors in Hemodialysis & Transplantation. LC 80-20681. 306p. 1981. 75.00 (*0-306-40586-5*, Plenum Trade) Perseus Pubng.

— Psychonephrology Vol. 2: Psychological Problems in Kidney Failure & Their Treatment. LC 83-8015. 312p. 1983. 85.00 (*0-306-41154-7*, Plenum Trade) Perseus Pubng.

Levy, Norman B., jt. ed. see Solomon, Kenneth.

Levy, Oscar. The Revival of Aristocracy. 1972. 59.95 (*0-8490-0952-9*) Gordon Pr.

Levy, Oscar, ed. see Nietzsche, Friedrich Wilhelm.

Levy, Oscar, tr. see Nietzsche, Friedrich Wilhelm.

Levy, Owen, ed. Party Planner. (Party Planner Ser.). (Illus.). 96p. 1991. 18.95 (*0-9629770-0-4*) Langston Pr.

***Levy, P.** Ghana, 6 vols., Set. LC 98-49004. (Cultures of the World Ser.). (Illus.). 128p. (YA). (gr. 5 up). 1999. lib. bdg. 35.64 (*0-7614-0952-1*) Marshall Cavendish.

Levy, Pamela R. Otto's Rainy Day. LC 99-19695. (Illus.). (J). 2000. write for info. (*1-57091-400-1*) Charlesbridge Pub.

***Levy, Patricia.** Essential Malta & Gozo. (AAA Essential Guides Ser.). 128p. 2000. pap. 8.95 (*0-658-00628-2*, 006282) NTC Contemp Pub Co.

— In Ancient Rome. (People Who Made History in Ser.). (Illus.). (J). 2000. 27.11 (*0-7398-2749-9*) Raintree Steck-V.

— Scotland. (Cultures of the World Ser.). (Illus.). (J). 2000. 35.64 (*0-7614-1159-3*, Benchmark NY) Marshall Cavendish.

Levy, Patricia M. Culture Shock! Ireland. LC 95-79455. 240p. 1995. pap. text 12.95 (*1-55868-247-3*) Gr Arts Ctr Pub.

Levy, Patricia M., jt. auth. see Sheehan, Sean.

Levy, Paul. Random Functions: A Laplacian Random Function Depending on a Point of Hilbert Space. LC 56-8639. (University of California Publications in Social Welfare: Vol. 2, No. 10). 14p. reprint ed. pap. 30.00 (*0-608-11618-1*, 2021182000022) Bks Demand.

— Turtle Who Lost His Shell. Larsen, Margie, ed. LC 95-75420. (Barney Ser.). (Illus.). 24p. (J). (ps-3). 1996. pap. 6.95 incl. audio (*1-57064-096-3*) Lyrick Pub.

Levy, Paul S. & Lemeshow, Stanley. Sampling of Populations: Methods & Applications. 3rd ed. LC 98-20498. (Series in Probability & Statistics). 568p. 1999. 89.95 (*0-471-15575-6*, Wiley-Interscience) Wiley.

Levy, Paula, jt. ed. see Lorena, Jeanne Marie.

Levy, Peter. The Complete Car Cost Guide, 1991. 368p. 1991. pap., per. 39.00 (*0-941443-11-6*) IntelliChoice.

— The Complete Car Cost Guide, 1992. 353p. 1992. pap., per. 39.00 (*0-941443-13-2*) IntelliChoice.

— The Complete Car Cost Guide, 1993. 379p. 1993. pap., per. 45.00 (*0-941443-15-9*) IntelliChoice.

— The Complete Small Truck Cost Guide, 1991. 281p. 1991. pap., per. 39.00 (*0-941443-12-4*) IntelliChoice.

— The Complete Small Truck Cost Guide, 1992. 250p. 1992. pap., per. 39.00 (*0-941443-14-0*) IntelliChoice.

— The Complete Small Truck Cost Guide, 1993. 312p. 1993. pap., per. 45.00 (*0-941443-16-7*) IntelliChoice.

***Levy, Peter.** Getting Started with the Internet: An Easy & Practical Guide for Teachers. (Illus.). 2000. pap. 10.95 (*0-439-14114-1*) Scholastic Inc.

Levy, Peter B. The Civil Rights Movement. LC 97-22553. (Greenwood Press Guides to Historic Events of the Twentieth Century Ser.). 264p. 1998. 39.95 (*0-313-29854-8*, Greenwood Pr) Greenwood.

— Encyclopedia of the Reagan-Bush Years. LC 95-37336. 456p. 1996. 49.95 (*0-313-29018-0*, Greenwood Pr) Greenwood.

— The New Left & Labor in the 1960s. LC 93-30844. (Illus.). 328p. 1994. text 49.95 (*0-252-02074-X*); pap. text 16.95 (*0-252-06367-8*) U of Ill Pr.

Levy, Peter B., ed. America in the Sixties. LC 98-22911. 344p. 1998. lib. bdg. 79.50 (*0-313-29936-6*, Greenwood Pr) Greenwood.

— America in the Sixties--Right, Left & Center: A Documentary History. LC 98-22911. 344p. 1998. pap. 22.95 (*0-275-95516-8*) Greenwood.

— Documentary History of the Modern Civil Rights Movements. LC 91-27240. 296p. 1992. lib. bdg. 59.95 (*0-313-27233-6*, LMR/, Greenwood Pr) Greenwood.

Levy, Peter B., ed. Let Freedom Ring: A Documentary History of the Modern Civil Rights Movement. LC 91-27717. 296p. 1992. pap. 19.95 (*0-275-93434-9*, B3434, Praeger Pubs) Greenwood.

Levy, Peter B., ed. 100 Key Documents in American Democracy. LC 93-1137. 536p. 1993. 59.95 (*0-313-28424-5*, LVK/, Greenwood Pr) Greenwood.

— 100 Key Documents in American Democracy. LC 93-1137. 528p. 1999. pap. 27.50 (*0-275-96525-2*, Praeger Pubs) Greenwood.

Levy, Peter E., tr. see Corti, Eugenio.

Levy, Philippa. Interpersonal Skills. LC 94-11002. (Library Training Guides Ser.). (Illus.). 70p. Date not set. reprint ed. pap. 30.00 (*0-608-20727-6*, 2071825000002) Bks Demand.

Levy, Phyllis J. Peace Within My Borders: A Bible Study. 63p. 1998. pap. 5.00 (*0-9660929-1-0*) Glory Communs.

***Levy, Pierre.** Becoming Virtual: Reality in the Digital Age. LC 98-5698. (Illus.). 120p. (C). 1998. 26.95 (*0-306-45788-1*, Plenum Trade) Perseus Pubng.

Levy, Pierre. Collective Intelligence: Mankind's Emerging World in Cyberspace. Bononno, Robert, tr. LC 97-26272. (Illus.). 308p. (C). 1997. 27.95 (*0-306-45635-4*, Plenum Trade) Perseus Pubng.

***Levy, Pierre.** Collective Intelligence: Mankind's Emerging World in Cyberspace. 312p. 1999. pap. text 17.00 (*0-7382-0261-4*, Pub. by Perseus Pubng) HarpC.

Levy-Provencal, E. Historia de Espana No. 4: Espana Musulmana (711-1031): La Conquista, el Emirato, el Califato. 568p. 1992. 189.50 (*84-239-4806-4*) Elliots Bks.

— Historia de Espana No. 5: Espana Musulmana (711-1031): Instituciones y Vida Social e Intelectual. 862p. 1992. 189.50 (*84-239-4807-2*) Elliots Bks.

Levy, R. A., ed. Microelectronic Materials & Processes. (C). 1989. pap. text 196.50 (*0-7923-0154-4*); lib. bdg. 348.50 (*0-7923-0147-1*) Kluwer Academic.

— Novel Silicon Based Technologies. (C). 1991. text 146.50 (*0-7923-1112-4*) Kluwer Academic.

— Reduced Thermal Processing for ULSI. LC 89-23011. (NATO ASI Ser.: Vol. 207). (Illus.). 450p. (C). 1989. text 162.00 (*0-306-43382-6*, Kluwer Plenum) Kluwer Academic.

Levy, R. I. Mesocosm: Hinduism & the Organization of a Traditional Newar City in Nepal. (C). 1992. 108.00 (*0-7855-0192-4*, Pub. by Ratna Pustak Bhandar) St Mut.

Levy, R. I., ed. A New Era of Lipid-Lowering Drug Alternative: Journal: Cardiology, Vol. 76, Suppl. 1, 1989. (Illus.). iv, 102p. 1989. pap. 23.25 (*3-8055-5023-5*) S Karger.

Levy, Ralph D. The Symbolism of the Azazel Goat. LC 98-20477. 140p. 1998. 74.95 (*1-57309-323-8*, Christ Univ Pr) Intl Scholars.

Levy, Ran. Wild Flowers of Japan: A Field Guide. Lancet, Barry, ed. 224p. 1995. pap. 25.00 (*4-7700-1809-6*) Kodansha.

Levy, Raphael. Contribution a la Lexicographie Francaise Selon D'anciens Textes D'origies Juive. (FRE.). 1960. 75.00 (*0-89366-103-1*) Ultramarine Pub.

***Levy, Ray, et al.** Try & Make Me! 2001. 19.95 (*1-57954-335-9*, Daybrk) Rodale Pr Inc.

Levy, Raymond. Making Mechanical Marvels in Wood. LC 91-9634. (Illus.). 200p. 1991. pap. 14.95 (*0-8069-7358-7*) Sterling.

Levy, Raymond, et al, eds. Treatment & Care in Old Age Psychiatry. LC 93-3405. 256p. 1993. pap. 85.00 (*1-871816-17-3*, Pub. by Wrightson Biomed) Taylor & Francis.

Levy, Raymond & Howard, Robert, eds. Developments in Dementia & Functional Disorders in the Elderly. LC 94-47442. 232p. 1995. 75.00 (*1-871816-27-0*, Pub. by Wrightson Biomed) Taylor & Francis.

***Levy-Reiner, Sherry.** Adaptable Brain, Papers Presented at a Symposium Series Cosponsored by the National Institute of Mental Health of the National Institutes of Health & the Library of Congress. 100p. 1999. per. 12.00 (*0-16-061814-2*, Library of Cong) USGPO.

Levy-Reiner, Sherry, ed. see National Institutes of Mental Health (U.S.) & Library of Congress.

Levy, Ren H., et al. Metabolic Drug Interactions. 750p. text 159.00 (*0-7817-1441-9*) Lppncott W & W.

Levy, Rene H., et al, eds. Antiepileptic Drugs. LC 88-42524. 1053p. 1989. reprint ed. pap. 200.00 (*0-608-03427-4*, 206412600008) Bks Demand.

— Antiepileptic Drugs. 4th ed. 1056p. 1995. text 194.00 (*0-7817-0246-1*) Lppncott W & W.

— Metabolism of Antiepileptic Drugs. LC 84-3436. (Illus.). 263p. 1984. reprint ed. pap. 81.60 (*0-608-00624-6*, 206121100007) Bks Demand.

Levy, Rene H. & Penry, J. Kiffin, eds. Idiosyncratic Reactions to Valproate: Clinical Risk Patterns & Mechanisms of Toxicity. LC 91-27480. (Illus.). 179p. 1991. reprint ed. pap. 55.50 (*0-608-05864-5*, 205983100007) Bks Demand.

***Levy, Reuben.** The Social Structure of Islam. LC 99-53541. (Orientalism Ser.). 2000. write for info. (*0-415-20910-2*) Routledge.

Levy, Reuben, tr. from PER. The Epic of the Kings: Shah-nama - the National Epic of Persia. 2nd rev. ed. (Persian Heritage Ser.: Vol. 2). xlvi, 423p. 1996. reprint ed. pap. text 15.00 (*1-56859-035-0*) Bibliotheca Persica.

Levy, Reynold. Give & Take: A Candid Account of Corporate Philanthropy. LC 98-52016. 336p. 1999. 24.95 (*0-87584-893-1*) Harvard Busn.

Levy, Richard C. Inventor's Desktop Companion: A Guide to Successfully Marketing & Protecting Your Ideas. 1990. 24.95 (*0-8103-7943-0*) Visible Ink Pr.

— The Inventor's Desktop Companion: A Guide to Successfully Marketing & Protecting Your Ideas. 2nd ed. (Illus.). 440p. 1998. pap. 24.95 (*0-7876-0490-9*) Visible Ink Pr.

— Secret of Selling Inventions. 2nd ed. Levy, Sheryl, ed. 200p. (Orig.). 1986. 49.50 (*0-931347-00-9*) Riesher Pub Ltd.

Levy, Richard N., ed. On the Wings of Awe: A Machzor for Rosh Hashanah & Yom Kippur. 1985. 13.95 (*0-685-31415-4*) Bnai Brith-Hillel.

Levy, Richard S. The Downfall of the Anti-Semitic Political Parties in Imperial Germany. LC 74-20083. (Yale Historical Publications: Miscellany: No. 106). 345p. reprint ed. pap. 107.00 (*0-8357-8101-1*, 203380000087) Bks Demand.

Levy, Richard S., ed. Antisemitism in the Modern World: An Anthology of Texts. LC 90-81852. (Sources in Modern History Ser.). 270p. (C). 1990. pap. text 28.76 (*0-669-24340-X*) HM Trade Div.

Levy, Richard S., ed. & tr. see Segel, Binjamin W.

***Levy, Robert.** Ana Pauker. LC 99-87890. 2000. write for info. (*0-520-22395-0*) U CA Pr.

Levy, Robert. Escape from Exile. LC 92-20443. 176p. (J). (gr. 5-9). 1993. 16.00 (*0-395-64379-1*) HM.

— Prisons & the Law. 1995. boxed set. write for info. (*0-406-02514-2*, UK, MICHIE) LEXIS Pub.

Levy, Robert, jt. ed. see Berger, Joseph R.

Levy, Robert I. Mesocosm: Hinduism & the Organization of a Traditional Newar City in Nepal. 1992. 180.00 (*0-7855-0260-2*, Pub. by Ratna Pustak Bhandar) St Mut.

— Mesocosm: Hinduism & the Organization of a Traditional Newar City in Nepal. (Illus.). 800p. 1990. 85.00 (*0-520-06911-0*, Pub. by U CA Pr) Cal Prin Full Svc.

— Tahitians: Mind & Experience in the Society Islands. (Illus.). 576p. 1997. pap. text 19.95 (*0-226-47611-1*, Midway Reprint) U Ch Pr.

— Tahitians: Mind & Experience in the Society Islands. LC 73-77136. (Illus.). xxviii, 576p. 1975. reprint ed. pap. text 30.00 (*0-226-47607-3*, P649) U Ch Pr.

Levy, Robert I., et al, eds. Nutrition, Lipids & Coronary Heart Disease: A Global View. fac. ed. LC 78-67020. (Nutrition in Health & Disease Ser.: No. 1). (Illus.). 578p. pap. 179.20 (*0-7837-7529-6*, 204697500005) Bks Demand.

Levy, Robert J. Chefs at Twilight. 28p. (Orig.). 1996. pap. 5.00 (*0-9637849-8-6*) Bacchae Pr.

— Introductory Logic. 110p. (Orig.). 1984. pap. text 15.00 (*0-8191-4179-8*) U Pr of Amer.

Levy, Robert J., jt. auth. see Foote, Caleb.

Levy, Robert M. & North, Richard B., eds. Neurosurgical Management of Pain. LC 95-23662. 376p. 1996. 160.00 (*0-387-94256-4*) Spr-Verlag.

Levy, Robert M. & Rubenstein, Leonard S. The Rights of People with Mental Disabilities: The Authoritative ACLU Guide to the Rights of People with Mental Illness & Mental Retardation. LC 95-36408. (American Civil Liberties Union Handbook Ser.). 424p. 1996. 34.95 (*0-8093-1989-6*) S Ill U Pr.

— The Rights of People with Mental Disabilities: The Basic ACLU Guide to the Rights of People with Mental Illness & Mental Retardation. LC 95-36408. (American Civil Liberties Union Handbook Ser.). 424p. (C). 1996. pap. 13.95 (*0-8093-1990-X*) S Ill U Pr.

Levy, Rodd. Takeovers Law & Strategy. LC 96-150603. 265p. 1996. pap. 85.00 (*0-455-21398-4*, Pub. by Cavendish Pubng) Gaunt.

Levy, Roger. French Interests & Policies in the Far East. LC 75-30110. (Institute of Pacific Relations Ser.). 1976. reprint ed. 45.00 (*0-404-59540-5*) AMS Pr.

*__Levy, Roger.__ Implementing European Union Public Policy. LC 00-34829. (New Horizons in Public Policy Ser.). 2000. write for info. (*1-85898-880-2*) E Elgar.

Levy, Rona, jt. auth. see Jayaratne, Srinika.

Levy, Roy. Structural Engineering of Microwave Antennas: For Electrical, Mechanical, & Civil Engineers. LC 95-45351. 376p. 1996. 149.95 (*0-7803-1020-9*, PC3681) Inst Electrical.

Levy, Ruth, jt. auth. see Mahrer, Debi.

Levy, Ruth, jt. auth. see Thomson, Ruth.

Levy, S. A Scout Is Born. 1999. pap. 4.99 (*1-892213-11-7*) Mixx Enter Inc.

— Starting from Scratch: One Classroom Builds an Authentic Curriculum. LC 96-4126. 205p. 1996. pap. text 22.00 (*0-435-07205-6*) Heinemann.

Levy, S. & Seroul, R. A Beginner's Book of TEX. 284p. 1995. reprint ed. 36.95 (*0-387-97562-4*) Spr-Verlag.

Levy, S., tr. see Berger, M.

Levy, S., tr. see Hirsch, Francis & Lacombe, G.

Levy, S., tr. see Janich, K.

Levy, S. B. The Antibiotic Paradox: How Miracle Drugs Are Destorying the Miracle. (Illus.). 294p. (C). 1992. 24.95 (*0-306-44331-7*, Plenum Trade) Perseus Pubng.

Levy, S. C. & Bro, P. Battery Hazards & Accident Prevention. (Illus.). 366p. (C). 1994. text 59.50 (*0-306-44758-4*, Kluwer Plenum) Kluwer Academic.

Levy, S. C., jt. auth. see Bro, P.

Levy, S. Jay. The Economics of Aging: Can We Afford Grandma & Grandpa? (Public Policy Brief Ser.: Vol. 18). 32p. (Orig.). 1995. pap. 3.00 (*0-941276-06-6*) J Levy.

Levy, S. Jay & Caclette, Walter M. Overcoming America's Infrastructure Deficit. (Public Policy Brief Highlights Ser.: No. 40A). (Illus.). 6p. 1998. pap. write for info. (*0-941276-48-1*) J Levy.

Levy, S. Jay & Cadette, Walter M. Overcoming America's Infrastructure Deficit: A Fiscally Responsible Plan for Public Capitol Investment. (Public Policy Brief Ser.: No. 40). (Illus.). 28p. 1998. pap. write for info. (*0-941276-47-3*) J Levy.

Levy, S. Jay & Levy, David. Surviving the Contained Depression of the 1990's. LC 92-56827. 96p. 1994. 16.00 (*0-679-42401-6*) Random.

Levy, S. Leon. Nassau W. Senior, 1790-1864: Critical Essayist, Classical Economist & Adviser of Governments. rev. ed. LC 67-30861. 336p. 1970. 45.00 (*0-678-05676-5*) Kelley.

Levy, S. Leon, ed. see Senior, Nassau W.

Levy-Salomone, Rosemary. An Analysis of the Effects of Language Acquisitions Context upon the Dual Language Development of Non-English Dominant Students. Cordasco, Francesco, ed. LC 77-90557. (Bilingual-Bicultural Education in the U. S. Ser.). 1978. lib. bdg. 36.95 (*0-405-11095-2*) Ayer.

Levy, Samuel J. Applied Geometric Tolerancing II: (AGT II) 720p. 1993. pap. 59.00 (*1-883467-00-4*) Intl Geometric.

— Computer Aided Tolerancing Analysis (CATA) Manual. 175p. 1986. ring bd. 34.00 (*1-883467-02-0*) Intl Geometric.

— Summary Fact Data Sheets. 20p. 1990. ring bd. 24.00 (*1-883467-01-2*) Intl Geometric.

Levy, Samuel L. Nassau W. Senior: The Prophet of Modern Capitalism. 1943. 30.00 (*0-686-17409-7*) R S Barnes.

Levy, Sandra & Siegel, Barbara. Electronic Keyboard for Kids. (Illus.). 80p. 1988. pap. 11.95 (*0-8256-1185-7*, AM70483) Music Sales.

Levy, Sandra M. Behavior & Cancer: Life-Style & Psychosocial Factors in the Initiation & Progression of Cancer. LC 85-45061. (Joint Publication in the Jossey-Bass Social & Behavioral Science Series & the Jossey-Bass Health Ser.). 279p. reprint ed. pap. 86.50 (*0-7837-2521-3*, 204268000006) Bks Demand.

Levy, Sara. Stiletto Talk: Poems by Sara Levy. Baker, R. D., ed. (Poetry Chapbook Ser.). (Illus.). 28p. (Orig.). 1995. pap. 4.00 (*1-887641-06-8*) Argonne Hotel Pr.

Levy, Sara G. Mother Goose Rhymes for Jewish Children. (Illus.). (J). (ps-2). 1979. reprint ed. pap. 8.95 (*0-8197-0254-4*) Bloch.

Levy, Saul. Account's Legal Reponsibility. Brief, Richard P., ed. LC 80-1509. (Dimensions of Accounting Theory & Practice Ser.). 1980. reprint ed. lib. bdg. 31.95 (*0-405-13534-3*) Ayer.

Levy, Seymour. A Guide to Counseling: Developing Employees through Performance Reviews. LC 76-16912. 1976. pap. 9.75 (*0-935198-01-6*) M M Bruce.

Levy, Shawn. King of Comedy. (Illus.). 528p. 1997. pap. 15.95 (*0-312-16878-0*) St Martin.

— Rat Pack Confidential. (Illus.). 368p. 1999. pap. 14.00 (*0-385-49576-5*, Main St Bks) Doubleday.

— Rat Pack Confidential: Frank, Dean, Sammy, Peter, Joey, & the Last Great Showbiz Party. LC 97-36760. (Illus.). 352p. 1998. 23.95 (*0-385-48751-7*) Doubleday.

Levy, Shem, jt. auth. see Adler, Irit.

Levy, Sheryl, ed. see Levy, Richard C.

Levy, Shimon. Here, There & Everywhere: Notions of Comparative Space in Canadian & Israeli Drama. LC 95-210176. 220p. 1995. pap. 24.95 (*1-898723-16-8*, Pub. by Sussex Acad Pr) Intl Spec Bk.

Levy, Shimon, ed. Bible As Theatre. LC 99-48949. (Illus.). 246p. 1997. 59.50 (*1-898723-50-8*, Pub. by Sussex Acad Pr) Intl Spec Bk.

— Bible as Theatre. LC 99-48949. 246p. 2000. pap. 24.95 (*1-898723-51-6*, Pub. by Sussex Acad Pr) Intl Spec Bk.

— Theatre & Holy Script. LC 98-41068. 272p. 1997. 59.50 (*1-898723-53-2*, Pub. by Sussex Acad Pr) Intl Spec Bk.

Levy, Shlomit, ed. Louis Guttman on Theory & Methodology: Selected Writings. (Benchmark Ser.). 448p. 1994. 91.95 (*1-85521-389-3*, Pub. by Dartmth Pub) Ashgate Pub Co.

Levy, Sidney, et al. Dartnell's Marketing Manager's Handbook. 3rd ed. 1432p. 1994. 69.95 (*0-85013-203-7*) Dartnell Corp.

— Plastics Extrusion Technology Handbook. 2nd ed. (Illus.). 398p. 1989. 44.95 (*0-8311-1185-2*) Indus Pr.

*__Levy, Sidney J.__ Brands, Consumers, Symbols & Research. Rook, Dennis W., ed. LC 99-6225. 590p. 1999. 84.00 (*0-7619-1696-2*) Sage.

Levy, Sidney J., ed. Creating Winning Marketing Plans. (Illus.). 273p. 1996. 39.95 (*0-85013-254-1*) Dartnell Corp.

Levy, Sidney J. & Robles, Albert G. The Image of Archivists: Resource Allocators' Perceptions. 61p. (Orig.). 1984. pap. text 7.00 (*0-931828-35-X*) Soc Am Archivists.

Levy, Sidney M. Build, Operate, Transfer: Paving the Way for Tomorrow's Infrastructure. LC 96-10268. 411p. 1996. 80.00 (*0-471-11992-X*) Wiley.

— Construction Building Envelope & Interior Finishes Databook. write for info. (*0-07-135167-1*) McGraw.

*__Levy, Sidney M.__ Construction Building Envelope & Interior Finishes Databook. (Construction Databook Ser.). (Illus.). 600p. 2000. 79.95 (*0-07-136022-0*) McGraw-Hill Prof.

Levy, Sidney M. Construction Daily Log. (Illus.). 448p. 1996. 54.95 (*0-07-038078-3*) McGraw.

— Construction Databook. LC 98-40478. (Illus.). 700p. 1998. 79.95 (*0-07-038365-0*) McGraw-Hill Prof.

— Construction Portable Field Handbook. (Illus.). 356p. 1998. 54.95 (*0-07-038122-4*) McGraw-Hill Prof.

*__Levy, Sidney M.__ Construction Site Work, Sub-Utilities & Substructures Databook. (Construction Databook Ser.). (Illus.). 600p. 2000. 79.95 (*0-07-136021-2*) McGraw-Hill Prof.

Levy, Sidney M. Japanese Construction: An American Perspective. (Illus.). 250p. (gr. 13). 1990. text 60.95 (*0-442-31865-0*) Chapman & Hall.

*__Levy, Sidney M.__ MEP Databook. (Construction Databook Ser.). 600p. 2000. 79.95 (*0-07-136020-4*) McGraw-Hill Prof.

Levy, Sidney M. Project Management in Construction. 2nd ed. LC 93-21585. 310p. 1992. 59.95 (*0-07-037590-9*) McGraw.

*__Levy, Sidney M.__ Subcontractor's Operations Manual. LC 99-14448. 1999. write for info. (*0-07-038239-5*) McGraw.

Levy, Silvano. Desmond Morris: 50 Years of Surrealism. (Illus.). 224p. 1997. 65.00 (*0-7126-7298-2*, Pub. by Barrie & Jenkins) Trafalgar.

— Surrealism: Surrealist Visuality. LC 96-36461. 1997. text 50.00 (*0-8147-5128-8*); pap. text 20.00 (*0-8147-5127-X*) NYU Pr.

— Understanding French Accounts: Language & Terminology. 128p. (Orig.). 1995. pap. 42.50 (*0-273-60307-8*, Pub. by Pitman Pub) Trans-Atl Phila.

Levy, Silvano, ed. see Donaghy, Peter & Laidler, John.

Levy, Silvano, ed. see Hofften, Adelheid & Edelsbacher, Johanna.

Levy, Silvio, ed. The Eightfold Way: The Beauty of the Klein Quartic. LC 98-51730. (Mathematical Sciences Research Institute Publications: No. 35). 240p. (C). 1999. 49.95 (*0-521-66066-1*) Cambridge U Pr.

— Flavors of Geometry. LC 97-213171. (Mathematical Sciences Research Institute Publications: Vol. 31). 204p. (C). 1997. text 59.95 (*0-521-62048-1*); pap. text 19.95 (*0-521-62962-4*) Cambridge U Pr.

Levy, Silvio, jt. auth. see Knuth, Donald E.

Levy, Silvio, jt. auth. see Thurston, William P.

Levy, Silvio, tr. see Schwarz, Albert S.

Levy, Solly, tr. see Kelly, Tim.

Levy, Stanley R. & Kozoll, Charles E. A Guide to Decision Making in Student Affairs: A Case Study Approach. LC 98-16397. 194p. 1998. text 43.95 (*0-398-06871-2*); pap. text 29.95 (*0-398-06872-0*) C C Thomas.

Levy, Stephen. California County Projections: 1999 Edition. LC 90-660111. 180p. 1999. pap. 225.00 (*1-878316-38-9*) CCSCE.

— California Economic Growth: 1999 Edition. 300p. 1999. pap. 225.00 (*1-878316-37-0*) CCSCE.

*__Levy, Stephen.__ California Economic Growth: 2000 Edition. 300p. 2000. pap. 225.00 (*1-878316-40-0*) CCSCE.

Levy, Stephen. California Population Characteristics: 1995 Edition. LC 90-660112. (California Economic Reports 1995-96 Projection). 160p. 1995. 225.00 (*1-878316-20-6*) CCSCE.

*__Levy, Stephen.__ Outlook for the California Economy: Summer, 1999. 60p. 1999. 75.00 (*1-878316-39-7*) CCSCE.

Levy, Steven. Artificial Life: A Report from the Frontier Where Computers Meet Biology. LC 92-50600. 400p. 1993. pap. 17.00 (*0-679-74389-8*) Vin Bks.

— Crypto. 2001. 24.95 (*0-670-85950-8*) Viking Penguin.

— Insanely Great: The Life & Times of Macintosh, the Computer That Changed Everything. 320p. 1995. pap. 13.95 (*0-14-023237-0*, Penguin Bks) Viking Penguin.

*__Levy, Steven.__ Insanely Great: The Life & Times of Macintosh, the Computer That Changed Everything. 336p. 2000. pap. 13.95 (*0-14-029177-6*) Viking Penguin.

Levy, Steven. The Unicorn's Secret: A Murder in the Age of Aquarius. LC 99-215412. (Illus.). 1990. mass mkt. 6.99 (*0-451-40166-2*, Onyx) NAL.

Levy, Steven T., ed. The Therapeutic Alliance. LC 99-22442. (Workshop Series of the American Psychoanalytic Association). 155p. 1999. 27.50 (*0-8236-6471-6*, No. 06471) Intl Univs Pr.

*__Levy, Stu.__ Sushi Girl, Vol. 2. 96p. 2000. pap. 11.95 (*1-892213-40-0*) Mixx Enter Inc.

Levy, Stuart B. & Novick, Richard, eds. Antibiotic Resistance Genes: Ecology, Transfer, & Expression. LC 86-24361. (Banbury Reports: No. 24). 436p. 1986. text 68.00 (*0-87969-224-3*) Cold Spring Harbor.

*__Levy, Stuart J.__ Power of Love. 1999. pap. 4.99 (*1-892213-13-3*, SMILE Bks) Mixx Enter Inc.

Levy, Susan L. & Lehr, Carol. Your Body Can Talk: Learning to Listen to What Your Boby Knows & Needs Through Simple Muscle Testing. LC 96-14124. (Illus.). 390p. (Orig.). 1996. pap. 19.95 (*0-934252-68-8*) Hohm Pr.

Levy, Susan P., jt. auth. see Persky, Robert S.

Levy, Susan P., ed. see Cisek, Eugene & Persky, Robert S.

Levy, Susan P., ed. see Davis, Harold.

Levy, Sydney. The Play of the Text: Max Jacob's "Le Cornet a Des" Schneider, Judith M., tr. LC 80-52298. 173p. 1981. reprint ed. pap. 53.70 (*0-608-01969-0*, 206262400003) Bks Demand.

Levy, Sydney, ed. Asylum Based on Sexual Orientation: A Resource Guide. 550p. 1996. pap. 50.00 (*1-884955-00-2*) Intl Gay & Lesbian.

*__Levy, Terry M., ed.__ Handbook of Attachment Interventions. 384p. 1999. 59.95 (*0-12-445860-2*) Acad Pr.

Levy, Terry M. & Orlans, Michael. Attachment, Trauma & Healing: Understanding & Treating Attachment Disorder in Children & Families. LC 98-25993. (Illus.). 313p. 1998. pap. 34.95 (*0-87868-709-2*, 7092, CWLA Pr) Child Welfare.

Levy, Thomas. Archaeology of Society in the Holy Land. 624p. 1998. pap. text 35.00 (*0-7185-0165-9*) Bks Intl VA.

Levy, Thomas, ed. The Archaeology of Society in the Holy Land. (Illus.). 640p. 1994. 85.00 (*0-8160-2855-9*) Facts on File.

Levy, Thomas E., jt. auth. see Huggins, Hal A.

Levy, Thomas E., jt. ed. see Holl, Augustin.

Levy, Tina. Vital Signs: Mathematics in Everyday Life. 326p. (C). 1991. pap. text 27.95 (*0-89863-144-0*) Star Pub CA.

Levy-Toledano, S., et al, eds. International Congress on Thrombosis - 14th Congress, Montpellier, October 1996: Abstracts. (Haemostasis Ser.: Vol. 26, Supplement 3, 1996). (Illus.). 344p. 1996. pap. 104.50 (*3-8055-6399-X*) S Karger.

*__Levy-Toledano, S. & Hemker, H. C., eds.__ Fundamental Mechanisms Implicated in Thrombosis: New Aspects Selected Plenary Lectures - 15th International Congress on Thrombosis, Antalya, October, 1998. (Haemostasis Ser.: Vol. 29, No. 1). (Illus.). 72p. 1999. pap. 25.25 (*3-8055-6951-3*) S Karger.

— Venous & Arterial Thrombosis: Pathophysiological & Clinical Aspects, Selected Plenary Lectures: 15th International Congress on Thrombosis, Antalya, October 1998. (Haemostasis Ser.: Vol. 29, Nos. 2 & 3). (Illus.). 116p. 1999. pap. 34.00 (*3-8055-6958-0*) S Karger.

*__Levy, Udi.__ Lost Civilization of Petra. 2000. 45.00 (*0-86315-298-8*) Floris Bks.

Levy, V. M. Financial Management of Hospitals. 3rd ed. xxii, 510p. 1985. pap. 74.50 (*0-455-20296-6*, Pub. by LawBk Co) Gaunt.

— Financial Management of Hospitals. 4th ed. 486p. 1992. pap. 75.00 (*0-455-21060-8*, Pub. by LawBk Co) Gaunt.

Levy, Viv. Beginner's Guide to Figure Drawing. 1993. 12.98 (*1-55521-854-7*) Bk Sales Inc.

Levy, W. J., et al. Magnetic Motor Stimulation. (Supplements to Electroencephalography & Clinical Neurophysiology Ser.: Vol. 43). 394p. 1991. 218.00 (*0-444-81351-9*) Elsevier.

Levy, Walter & Hallowell, Christopher. Green Perspectives: Thinking & Writing about Nature. 650p. (C). 1997. pap. text 48.00 (*0-06-501500-2*) Addson-Wesley Educ.

Levy, Walter, jt. auth. see Keating, Helene L.

Levy, Walter A., jt. ed. see Summer, Claire.

Levy, Walter J., jt. ed. see Keating, Helene L.

*__Levy-Warren, Marsha.__ The Adolescent Journey. 2000. pap. 40.00 (*0-7657-0285-1*) Aronson.

Levy, William, et al, eds. Synaptic Modification, Neuron Selectivity & Nervous System Organization. 280p. (C). 1985. text 59.95 (*0-89859-344-1*) L Erlbaum Assocs.

Levy, William S. Skin Problems of the Amputee. LC 78-50196. (Illus.). 324p. 1983. 49.95 (*0-87527-181-2*) Green.

Levy, William T. & Russett, Cynthia E. The Extraordinary Mrs. R. A Friend Remembers: Eleanor Roosevelt. LC 99-20989. 257p. 1999. 22.95 (*0-471-33177-5*) Wiley.

Levy, William T., jt. auth. see Scherle, Victor.

Levy, Yagil. Trial & Error: Israel's Route from War to De-Escalation. LC 96-42064. (SUNY Series in Israeli Studies). 282p. (C). 1997. text 57.50 (*0-7914-3429-X*); pap. text 18.95 (*0-7914-3430-3*) State U NY Pr.

Levy, Yamin. Confronting the Loss of a Baby: A Personal & Jewish Perspective. LC 97-29989. xxi, 156p. 1998. 23.00 (*0-88125-609-9*) Ktav.

Levy, Yonata, ed. Other Children, Other Languages: Issues in the Theory of Language Acquisition. 424p. 1994. text 79.95 (*0-8058-1330-6*) L Erlbaum Assocs.

Levy, Ze'ev. Baruch or Benedict: On Some Jewish Aspects of Spinoza's Philosophy. LC 89-8257. (American University Studies: Philosophy: Ser. V, Vol. 81). XI, 224p. (C). 1989. text 39.50 (*0-8204-0986-3*) P Lang Pubng.

— David Baumgardt & Ethical Hedonism. 1989. 39.50 (*0-88125-304-9*) Ktav.

Levy, Zvi, intro. Negotiating Positive Identity in a Group Care Community: Reclaiming Uprooted Youth. LC 93-34917. (Child & Youth Services Ser.: Vol. 16, No. 2). (Illus.). 141p. 1993. lib. bdg. 39.95 (*1-56024-514-X*) Haworth Pr.

Lew, Alan. Eight Monologs. 64p. (Orig.). 1980. pap. 3.50 (*0-931416-01-9*) Open Books.

Lew, Alan & Jaffe, Sherril. One God Clapping: The Spiritual Path of a Zen Rabbi. LC 99-29401. 1999. 24.00 (*1-56836-287-0*) Kodansha.

Lew, Alan A. & Van Otten, George A., eds. Tourism & Gaming on American Indian Lands. LC 98-6261. (Tourism Dynamics Ser.). 275p. (C). 1998. pap. text 30.00 (*1-882345-21-5*) Cognizant Comm.

Lew, Amy & Bettner, Betty L. A Parent's Guide to Understanding & Motivating Children. 459p. 1996. pap. 5.00 (*0-9624841-8-0*) Connex Pr.

— Responsibility in the Classroom: A Teacher's Guide to Understanding & Motivating Students. rev. ed. (Raising Kids Who Can Ser.). 72p. 1998. pap. 6.00 (*0-9624841-0-5*) Connex Pr.

Lew, Amy & Bettner, Betty Lou. Cinderella, the Sequal: When the Fairytale Ends & Real Life Begins. (Illus.). 49p. (Orig.). 1997. pap. 12.00 (*0-9624841-9-9*) Connex Pr.

— A Parent's Guide to Understanding & Motivating Children. 78p. 2000. pap. 7.00 (*0-9624841-3-X*) Connex Pr.

Lew, Amy, jt. auth. see Bettner, Betty L.

Lew, Art. Computer Science, A Mathematical Introduction: Applied Mathematics--modeling, Analysis, & Optimization Techniques with Applications to Software Systems. LC 84-8374. (Prentice-hall International Computer Science Ser.). xxvi, 421 p. 1985. write for info. (*0-13-164062-3*) Prntice Hall Bks.

Lew, Christina, jt. auth. see Womack, Randy L.

Lew, Dayan. Humanity of Jewish Law. 220p. 1986. 13.95 (*0-900689-87-0*) Soncino Pr.

Lew, Edward A. & Gajewski, Jerzy, eds. Medical Risks: Trends in Mortality by Age & Time Elapsed, 2 vols., Set. LC 90-7707. 1512p. 1990. 195.00 (*0-275-93786-0*, C37860, Praeger Pubs) Greenwood.

— Medical Risks: Trends in Mortality by Age & Time Elapsed, 2 vols., Vol. 1. LC 90-7707. 368p. 1990. 195.00 (*0-275-93787-9*, C37861, Praeger Pubs) Greenwood.

— Medical Risks: Trends in Mortality by Age & Time Elapsed, 2 vols., Vol. 2. LC 90-7707. 368p. 1990. 195.00 (*0-275-93788-7*, C37862, Praeger Pubs) Greenwood.

Lew, Ellen F. Ellen Lew's Far East Favorites Cookbook. 200p. 1992. pap. 7.98 (*0-9623626-0-3*) E F Lew.

— Ellen Lew's Pacific Rim Light & Low Recipes. (Illus.). 200p. 1992. 10.00 (*0-9623626-1-1*) E F Lew.

Lew, Ellen F. & Akins, Harold D. Rice: A Food for All Seasons Cookbook. (Illus.). 1989. 10.00 (*0-317-93880-0*) H D Akins.

Lew, Ellen F., jt. auth. see Akins, H. D.

Lew, Gena A., ed. Perspectives on Affirmative Action . . . & Its Impact on Asian Pacific Americans. 39p. (Orig.). (C). 1996. pap. text 25.00 (*0-7881-2330-0*) DIANE Pub.

Lew, H. Kim & Cisco Systems Staff. The Internetwork Troubleshooting Handbook. 500p. 1996. 65.00 (*1-56205-653-0*) New Riders Pub.

Lew, Helen. Medical ADP Systems: Defense's Tools & Methodology for Managing CHCs Performance Needs Strengthening. (Illus.). 44p. 1998. pap. text 30.00 (*0-7881-4507-X*) DIANE Pub.

*__Lew, Helen.__ Year 2000 Computing Crisis: Biomedical Equipment Items. 117p. 1999. pap. text 30.00 (*0-7881-7640-4*) DIANE Pub.

Lew, Irvina. Romantic Weekends: New York. (Romantic Weekends Ser.). (Illus.). 224p. (Orig.). 1997. pap. 14.95 (*1-55650-771-2*) Hunter NJ.

Lew, James. The Art of Stretching & Kicking. LC 80-106144. (Illus.). 104p. 1977. pap. 7.95 (*0-86568-007-8*, 206) Unique Pubns.

Lew, Jennifer F., jt. auth. see Proctor, Richard M.

Lew, Jonathan, jt. auth. see Wong, Mary.

An Asterisk (*) at the beginning of an entry indicates that the title is appearing for the first time.

Lew, Judy, jt. auth. see Poladitmontri, Panurat.
Lew, Kim & Chang, Wei. Remote Access Networking. 1997. 50.00 (*1-56205-815-0*) New Riders Pub.
Lew, Kim & Cheng, Wei. Remote Access Networking. 550p. 1998. pap. 50.00 (*1-57870-029-9*) Mac USA.
Lew, Meyer S., ed. see Marmorstein, Arthur.
***Lew, Mike.** Leaping upon the Mountains: Men Proclaiming Victory over Sexual Child Abuse. 320p. 2000. pap. 19.95 (*1-55643-345-X*, Pub. by North Atlantic) Publishers Group.
Lew, Mike. Victims No Longer: Men Recovering from Incest & Other Childhood Sexual Abuse. LC 89-45839. 352p. 1990. reprint ed. pap. 20.00 (*0-06-097300-5*, Perennial) HarperTrade.
Lew, Peter & Lamb, John P. Lotus Notes Network Design Release 5. LC 97-30082. (Illus.). 575p. 1997. pap., text 44.95 incl. cd-rom (*0-07-913241-3*) McGraw.
Lew, Walter K. Excerpts from, IKJH Dikte for Dictee 1982. (Critical Collage Ser.: No. 1). (Illus.). (Orig.). (C). pap. 17.95 (*89-7427-000-5*, Pub. by Yeul Eum SA Pubng) SPD-Small Pr Dist.
Lew, Walter K., ed. Muae: A Journal of Transcultural Production, Vol. 1. (Illus.). 272p. (Orig.). 1995. pap. 19.95 (*1-885030-15-0*) Kaya Prod.
— Premonitions: The Kaya Anthology of New Asian American Poetry. LC 94-75916. (Illus.). 616p. 1995. 44.95 (*1-885030-13-4*); pap. 22.95 (*1-885030-14-2*) Kaya Prod.
Lew, William J. Understanding the Chinese Personality: Parenting, Schooling, Values, Morality, Relations & Personality. LC 98-26729. (Chinese Studies: Vol. 6). 412p. 1998. text 109.95 (*0-7734-8298-9*) E Mellen.
Lewald, Ann & Jenkins, William. Developing College Skills in Writing Literature. 2nd ed. 436p. (C). 1995. text 37.20 (*0-536-58823-6*) Pearson Custom.
Lewald, Fanny. The Education of Fanny Lewald: An Autobiography. Lewis, Hanna B., ed. & tr. by. from GER. LC 91-35930. (SUNY Series, Women Writers in Translation). 341p. (C). 1992. text 64.50 (*0-7914-1147-8*); pap. text 21.95 (*0-7914-1148-6*) State U NY Pr.
— Prinz Louis Ferdinand. Rogols-Siegel, Linda, tr. from GER. LC 88-13957. (Studies in German Thought & History: Vol. 6). 507p. 1989. lib. bdg. 119.95 (*0-88946-357-3*) E Mellen.
Lewald, Herald E., ed. The Cry of Home: Cultural Nationalism & the Modern Writer. LC 76-173656. 1972. 20.00 (*0-87049-135-0*) Lib Soc Sci.
— The Cry of Home: Cultural Nationalism & the Modern Writer. LC 76-173656. 412p. reprint ed. 127.80 (*0-608-16824-6*, 202755900055) Bks Demand.
Lewallen, Arrie. Prayers, Praises & Professing. 1988. pap. write for info. (*0-938645-03-X*) In His Steps.
Lewallen, Constance. Gigi Janchang: 1998 Adaline Kent Award. LC 98-60571. (Illus.). 28p. 1998. pap. 5.00 (*0-930495-33-0*) San Fran Art Inst.
Lewallen, Constance, et al. Jay DeFeo: Selected Works 1952-1989. Longhauser, Elsa, ed. LC 96-77338. (Illus.). 40p. 1996. pap. 25.00 (*1-58442-009-X*) Galleries at Moore.
Lewallen, Constance, jt. auth. see Ross, David A.
Lewallen, Dale. Help! Excel for Windows. 1993. 27.95 (*1-56276-165-X*, Ziff-Davis Pr) Que.
— PC - Computing Guide to Excel 4.0 for Windows. (Guide to...Ser.). (Illus.). 643p. (Orig.). 1992. pap. 27.95 (*1-56276-048-3*, Ziff-Davis Pr) Que.
— PC - Computing Guide to Excel 3.0. (Guide to...Ser.). (Illus.). 434p. (Orig.). 1991. pap. 24.95 (*1-56276-019-X*, Ziff-Davis Pr) Que.
— This Old PC. 640p. 1993. pap. 29.95 incl. disk (*1-56276-108-0*, Ziff-Davis Pr) Que.
— Upgrade Your PC Now. 500p. 1997. pap. text 30.00 (*1-56276-545-0*, Ziff-Davis Pr) Que.
Lewallen, Eleanor & Lewallen, John. Sea Vegetable Gourmet Cookbook & Wildcrafter's Guide. 128p. 1996. pap. 19.95 (*0-9647643-7-7*) Mendocino Sea.
Lewallen, James E. The Camp: A Story of Homelessness -- Life, Death & Reunion. Murphy, Gael, ed. 140p. 1998. pap. 11.95 (*0-9669843-0-7*) Natl Coal Home.
Lewallen, John, jt. auth. see Lewallen, Eleanor.
Lewallen, Susan, jt. auth. see Courtright, Paul.
***Lewalski, Barbara.** The Life of John Milton. 2001. 39.95 (*0-631-17665-9*) Blackwell Pubs.
Lewalski, Barbara K. Donne's Anniversaries & the Poetry of Praise: The Creation of a Symbolic Mode. LC 72-14027. 399p. reprint ed. pap. 123.70 (*0-8357-3689-X*, 203641300003) Bks Demand.
— Milton's Brief Epic: The Genre, Meaning, & Art of "Paradise Regained" LC 66-10282. (Brown University Bicentennial Publications). 448p. reprint ed. pap. 127.70 (*0-7837-2620-1*, 2042956) Bks Demand.
— Protestant Poetics & the Seventeenth-Century Religious Lyric. LC 78-70305. (Illus.). 563p. reprint ed. pap. 174.60 (*0-8357-4284-9*, 203708300007) Bks Demand.
— Writing Women in Jacobean England. (Illus.). 431p. (C). 1993. text 47.50 (*0-674-96242-7*) HUP.
— Writing Women in Jacobean England. (Illus.). 448p. 1994. pap. text 19.95 (*0-674-96243-5*, LEWWRX) HUP.
Lewalski, Barbara K., ed. Renaissance Genres: Essay on Theory, History & Interpretation. (English Studies: No. 14). 448p. 1986. pap. 11.95 (*0-674-76041-7*) HUP.
— Renaissance Genres: Essays on THeory, History & Interpretation. (English Studies: No. 14). 512p. 1986. 27.95 (*0-674-76040-9*) HUP.
Lewalski, Barbara K., ed. see Speght, Rachel.
***Lewalski, Barbara Kiefer.** Form & Reform in Renaissance England: Essays in Honor of Barbara Kiefer Lewalski. Boesky, Amy & Crane, Mary Thomas, eds. LC 99-39234. (Illus.). 376p. 2000. 49.50 (*0-87413-691-1*) U Delaware Pr.
Lewalski, Zdzislaw M. Product Esthetics: An Interpretation for Designers. (Illus.). 240p. (Orig.). 1988. pap. 17.95 (*0-944327-04-4*) Design & Dev Engineering Pr.
Lewan, Lloyd S. & Billingsley, Ronald G. Women in the Workplace: A Man's Perspective. LC 88-90731. (Illus.). 125p. (Orig.). 1988. pap. 6.95 (*0-9620360-0-5*) Remington Pr.
Lewan, M. D., jt. ed. see Pittman, E. D.
***Lewan, Todd.** Storm Gods & Heroes. 2001. write for info. (*0-06-019648-3*) HarpC.
— Storm Gods & Heroes. 2002. pap. write for info. (*0-06-095623-2*, Perennial) HarperTrade.
Lewandoski, Theodor. Linguistics Dictionary: Linguistisches Woerterbuch. 3 vols., Set. 5th ed. (GER.). 1287p. 1985. 150.00 (*0-8288-1977-7*, M15160) Fr & Eur.
Lewandowsi, Joseph J. Alaskan Environmental Impact Statements: A Bibliography. LC 81-623250. (Occasional Papers Ser.: No. 7). 235p. 1980. pap. text 7.50 (*0-937592-05-6*) U Alaska Rasmuson Lib.
Lewandowska, Marysia, jt. auth. see Cummings, Neil.
***Lewandowska-Tomaszczyk, Barbara.** Cognitive Perspectives on Language. LC 99-50177. (Polish Studies in English Language & Literature: Vol. 1). 235p. (C). 1999. pap. text 37.95 (*0-8204-4370-0*) P Lang Pubng.
***Lewandowska-Tomaszczyk, Barbara, ed.** Cognitive Perspectives on Language. (Polish Studies in English Language & Literature). 235p. 1999. 37.95 (*3-631-35314-6*) P Lang Pubng.
Lewandowska-Tomaszczyk, Barbara, jt. ed. see Tomaszczyk, Jerzy.
Lewandowski, A., et al, eds. Methodology, Implementation & Applications of Decision Support Systems. (CISM International Centre for Mechanical Sciences Ser.: Vol. 320). (Illus.). vi, 322p. 1991. 52.95 (*0-387-82297-6*) Spr-Verlag.
— Multiple Criteria Decision Support: Proceedings of the International Workshop Held in Helsinki, Finland, August 7-11, 1989. (Illus.). xii, 392p. 1991. 65.00 (*0-387-53895-X*) Spr-Verlag.
Lewandowski, A. & Stanchev, I., eds. Methodology & Software for Interactive Decision Support. (Lecture Notes in Economics & Mathematical Systems Ser.: Vol. 337). viii, 308p. 1989. 44.95 (*0-387-51572-0*) Spr-Verlag.
Lewandowski, A. & Volkovich, V., eds. Multiobjective Problems of Mathematical Programming: Proceedings of the International Conference on Multiobjective Problems of Mathematical Programming Held in Yalta, U. S. S. R., October 26-November 2, 1988. (Lecture Notes in Economics & Mathematical Systems Ser.: Vol. 351). (Illus.). vii, 314p. 1990. 46.00 (*0-387-53432-6*) Spr-Verlag.
Lewandowski, A. & Wierzbicki, A. P., eds. Aspiration Based Decision Support Systems. (Lecture Notes in Economics & Mathematical Systems Ser.: Vol. 331). x, 399p. 1989. 55.95 (*0-387-51213-6*) Spr-Verlag.
***Lewandowski, David A.** Design of Thermal Oxidation Systems for Volatile Organic Compounds. LC 99-35424. 348p. 1999. 79.95 (*1-56670-410-3*) Lewis Pubs.
Lewandowski, Frrich. Babci's Angel. LC 96-96834. (Illus.). 20p. (J). (gr. 2-3). 1998. 9.50 (*0-9646439-5-2*) Ambasdr Bks.
— The First Easter Bunny. LC 98-74525. (Illus.). 24p. (J). (gr. 2-3). 1999. 9.50 (*0-9646439-2-8*) Ambasdr Bks.
— Shooting Stardust. LC 98-9253. (Illus.). 20p. (J). (gr. 2-3). 1998. 9.50 (*0-9646439-4-4*) Ambasdr Bks.
Lewandowski, Gordon A. & DeFilippi, Louis J. Biological Treatment of Hazardous Wastes. LC 97-10384. 416p. 1997. 87.95 (*0-471-04861-5*) Wiley.
Lewandowski, J. J., et al, eds. Layered Materials for Structural Applications. (MRS Symposium Proceedings Ser.: Vol. 434). 314p. 1996. 68.00 (*1-55899-337-1*, 434) Materials Res.
Lewandowski, J. J. & Hunt, W. H., eds. Intrinsic & Extrinsic Fracture Mechanisms in Inorganic Composite Systems: Proceedings: Symposium Sponsored by the Structural Materials Division of TMS (1995: Las Vegas, Nevada) Proceedings. LC 94-74271. (Illus.). 246p. 1995. 20.00 (*0-87339-284-1*, 2841) Minerals Metals.
***Lewandowski, Jeff.** Assessment of Non-Orthopedic Sports Injuries: A Sideline Reference Manual. (Illus.). 176p. 2000. pap. 28.00 (*1-55642-444-2*) SLACK Inc.
***Lewandowski, Jergen, et al.** Audi TT. (Illus.). 140p. 2000. 34.95 (*3-7688-1167-0*, 130086AP, Pub. by Klasing & Co) Motorbooks Intl.
Lewandowski, Joe, jt. auth. see Holdeman, Paul H.
Lewandowski, Lawrence J. & Leavell, Carol A. The Clinical Neuropsychology of Children & Adults. (C). 1995. 43.95 (*0-205-16759-4*, Macmillan Coll) P-H.
Lewandowski, Marcia. Folk Mittens: Techniques & Patterns for Handknitted Mittens. LC 97-9475. (Illus.). 120p. 1997. write for info. (*1-883010-34-9*) Interweave.
Lewandowski, Rainer. Die Filme von Alexander Kluge. (Weitere Monographien Zur Filmgeschichte Ser.). (GER.). 359p. 1980. write for info. (*3-487-08209-8*) G Olms Pubs.
— Die Filme von Volker Schlondorff. (Weitere Monographien Zur Filmgeschichte Ser.). (GER.). 293p. 1981. write for info. (*3-487-08232-2*) G Olms Pubs.
Lewandowski, Ronald J., et al, eds. Helmet- & Head-Mounted Displays III. LC 99-182524. (Proceedings of SPIE Ser.: Vol. 3362). 396p. 1998. 80.00 (*0-8194-2811-6*) SPIE.
Lewandowski, Ronald J., ed. see Girolamo, Henry J.
Lewandowski, Susan. Migration & Ethnicity in Urban India. 1982. 18.00 (*0-8364-0833-0*, Pub. by Manohar) S Asia.
Lewandowski, Theodor. Dictionary of Linguistics: Diccionario de Linguistica. 2nd ed. (ENG & SPA.). 464p. 1986. pap. 59.95 (*0-7859-4953-4*) Fr & Eur.
Lewandowsky, Stephen, et al, eds. Implicit Memory: Theoretical Issues. 352p. (C). 1989. text 79.95 (*0-8058-0358-0*) L Erlbaum Assocs.
Lewandowsky, Stephen, jt. ed. see Hockley, William.
Lewanski, Bob, ed. see Gleason, Ronne R.
Lewanski, Richard C., ed. Guide to Polish Libraries & Archives. (East European Monographs: No. 6). 209p. 1974. text 60.00 (*0-231-03896-8*) East Eur Monographs.
Lewanski, Robert T. & Zuraw, Robert A. Health Force. 2nd rev. ed. (Illus.). 252p. 1982. 14.95 (*0-9608030-0-9*) Taoist Pubs.
Lewanski, Robert T., jt. auth. see Zuraw, Robert A.
Lewarch, Dennis E., jt. ed. see O'Brien, Michael J.
Lewarne, Charles P. Utopias on Puget Sound, 1885-1915. (Illus.). 346p. 1995. pap. 18.95 (*0-295-97444-3*) U of Wash Pr.
LeWarne, Charles P. Washington State. rev. ed. LC 85-20977. (Illus.). 438p. 1993. text 50.00 (*0-295-97301-3*) U of Wash Pr.
LeWarne, Charles P., jt. auth. see Ficken, Robert E.
Lewart, Cass R. Modem Handbook for the Communications Professional. 320p. 1987. 40.25 (*0-444-01279-6*) P-H.
— Science & Engineering Sourcebook. LC 82-80269. (Illus.). 96p. (Orig.). 1982. pap. 9.95 (*0-942412-02-8*); audio 8.95 (*0-686-98227-4*) Micro Text Pubns.
— Scientific & Engineering Sourcebook: Professional Programs for the Timex Sinclair 1000. LC 82-62818. (Illus.). 120p. (Orig.). 1983. pap. text 15.95 (*0-07-037444-9*, BYTE Bks) McGraw.
— The Ultimate Modem Handbook. 426p. (C). 1997. pap. text 39.95 (*0-13-849415-0*) P-H.
Lewbart, Greg. Ivory Hunters. LC 96-32808. 224p. 1996. reprint ed. 17.50 (*1-57524-009-2*) Krieger.
— Ivory Hunters: A Novel of Extinction. LC 95-71272. 211p. 1996. pap. 9.95 (*1-884570-40-2*) Research Triangle.
— Pavilion Key: Isle of Buried Treasure. LC 99-35645. 212p. 2000. 18.50 (*1-57524-079-3*) Krieger.
Lewbart, Gregory, ed. Self-Assessment Color Review of Ornamental Fish. LC 99-160214. (Illus.). 192p. 1998. pap. text 34.95 (*0-8138-2619-5*) Iowa St U Pr.
Lewbel, George S. Lonely Planet Diving & Snorkeling Guide to Curacao. 2nd ed. LC 96-39573. (Pisces Diving & Snorkeling Guides Ser.). 96p. 1997. 14.95 (*1-55992-095-5*, 2095, Pisces Books) Lonely Planet.
Lewbel, George S. & Martin, Larry R. Diving Bonaire. rev. ed. LC 91-71777. (Illus.). 132p. (Orig.). 1998. pap. 18.95 (*0-9623389-4-X*) Aqua Quest.
— Lonely Planet Diving & Snorkeling Guide to Cozumel. 2nd ed. (Pisces Diving & Snorkeling Guides Ser.). 96p. 1991. pap. 14.95 (*1-55992-034-3*, Pisces Books) Lonely Planet.
— Lonely Planet Diving & Snorkeling Guide to Cozumel. 3rd ed. (Illus.). 96p. 1998. pap. 14.95 (*0-86442-574-0*) Lonely Planet.
***Lewchanin, Shari & Zimmerman, Ellen.** Clinical Assessment of Juvenile Animal Cruelty. 65p. 2000. 39.95 (*1-879418-31-2*) Biddle Pub.
Lewchanin, Shari, jt. auth. see Zimmerman, Ellen.
Lewcock, Ronald. Non- Western Architecture. write for info. (*0-393-73044-1*) Norton.
***Lewellen & Halloran.** Practical Financial Management. 2nd ed. 2001. pap. 51.00 (*0-324-07173-6*) Sth-Wstrn College.
***Lewellen, et al.** Financial Management. (SWC-Finance Ser.). (C). 2000. pap. 19.00 (*0-324-05599-4*) Sth-Wstrn College.
— Financial Management: An Introduction to Principles & Practices. (SWC-Finance Ser.). 1999. pap. 19.75 (*0-324-00435-4*) Sth-Wstrn College.
Lewellen, James B. A Parent's Guide to Quality Schools: Taking Charge of Your Child's Education. 1994. 12.95 (*0-533-10794-6*) Vantage.
Lewellen, Judie. The Teen Body Book: A Guide to Your Changing Body. LC 99-73107. (Illus.). 144p. (YA). (gr. 3-7). 1999. pap. 11.95 (*0-7373-0165-1*, 01651W) NTC Contemp Pub Co.
Lewellen, Ted C. Dependency & Development: An Introduction to the Third World. LC 94-39193. 288p. 1995. 69.50 (*0-89789-399-9*, Bergin & Garvey); pap. 24.95 (*0-89789-400-6*, Bergin & Garvey) Greenwood.
— Political Anthropology: An Introduction. 2nd ed. LC 91-44660. 248p. 1992. 57.95 (*0-89789-289-5*, H289, Bergin & Garvey); pap. 24.95 (*0-89789-290-9*, G290, Bergin & Garvey) Greenwood.
Lewellen, Wilbur G. Executive Compensation in Large Industrial Corporations. (Fiscal Studies Ser.: No. 11). 396p. 1968. 103.30 (*0-87014-481-2*) Natl Bur Econ Res.
— Executive Compensation in Large Industrial Corporations. LC 67-29643. (National Bureau of Economic Research, Fiscal Studies: No. 11). (Illus.). 397p. reprint ed. pap. 123.10 (*0-8357-7573-9*, 205689400096) Bks Demand.
— The Ownership Income of Management. (Fiscal Studies Ser.: No. 14). 220p. 1971. reprint ed. 57.20 (*0-87014-222-4*) Natl Bur Econ Res.
Lewellen, Wilbur G. & Halloran, John A. Financial Management: An Introduction to Principles & Practice. 2nd ed. (C). Date not set. text 56.00 (*0-324-04350-3*) Thomson Learn.
Lewellen, Wilbur G., et al. Financial Management: An Introduction to Principles & Practice. LC 99-10753. (SWC-Finance). 1999. text 96.95 (*0-538-87589-5*) S-W Pub.
Lewellyn, Angie, et al. Oral Histories & the 1960s. 2nd ed. Cole, Vicki, ed. (Series of Lesson Plans: Ser. 2, No. 23). (Illus.). 16p. (J). (gr. k-12). 1997. write for info. (*1-889030-05-8*) FL Div Hist Res.
Lewellyn, Harry. Glovebox Guide to Unpaved Southern California. 2nd ed. 348p. (Orig.). 1993. spiral bd. 14.95 (*0-944781-01-2*) Glovebox Pubns.
Lewellyn, Les. The Burnt Hills. large type ed. (Linford Western Library Ser.). 272p. 1997. pap. 16.99 (*0-7089-5090-6*, Linford) Ulverscroft.
— Cimarron. large type ed. (Linford Western Large Print Ser.). 256p. 1997. pap. 16.99 (*0-7089-5054-X*) Ulverscroft.
Lewellyn, Marion. Poems of Inspiration & Guidance. 1998. pap. write for info. (*1-57553-972-1*) Watermrk Pr.
Lewels, Joe. The God Hypothesis: Extraterrestrial Life & Its Implications for Science & Religion. (Illus.). 300p. 1997. pap. 18.95 (*1-893183-12-2*, Pub. by Granite Pub) ACCESS Pubs Network.
— The God Hypothesis: The Hidden Truth Behind UFOs, Aliens, Angels & Gods. LC 96-40867. 300p. 1997. pap. 18.95 (*0-926524-40-2*) Granite WI.
Lewen, Si. A Journey. LC 80-67120. 86p. 1980. 30.00 (*0-87982-032-2*) Art Alliance.
Lewenhak, Sheila. The Revaluation of Women's Work. 288p. 1988. lib. bdg. 57.50 (*0-415-01863-3*) Routledge.
Lewens, George. My Lives Between Hitler & Stalin. (Illus.). 160p. (Orig.). 1992. pap. 12.95 (*0-9631336-0-8*) Lewens Pub.
Lewenson, Sandra B. Taking Charge: Nursing, Suffrage, & Feminism in America, 1873-1920. LC 93-11137. (Development of American Feminism Ser.: Vol. 1). 368p. 1993. text 20.00 (*0-8240-6897-1*) Garland.
Lewenson, Sandra B., jt. auth. see Feldman, Harriet R.
Lewenson, Sandra B., jt. ed. see Birnbach, Nettie.
Lewenstam. Applications of Ion-Selective Electrodes in Clinical Chem. 1995. 75.00 (*0-8493-4209-0*) CRC Pr.
Lewenstein, Barbara, jt. auth. see Mikolajewska, Barbara.
Lewenstein, Essie. The Case of the Lost Identity. Felder, Ilana, ed. (Bina Gold Mystery Ser.). (Illus.). (YA). 1998. pap. 9.95 (*0-911643-22-2*) Aura Bklyn.
Lewenstein, M., jt. ed. see Kujawski, A.
Lewenstein, Oscar. Kicking Against the Pricks: A Producer in the Theatre of Dissent. 256p. 1994. 39.95 (*1-85459-171-1*, Pub. by N Hern Bks) Theatre Comm.
Lewenstein, Suzanne H., jt. auth. see Rovner, Irwin.
Lewenstein, Suzanne M. Stone Tool Use at Cerros: The Ethnoarchaeological & Use-Wear Evidence. LC 86-24910. (Illus.). 238p. 1987. text 42.50 (*0-292-77590-3*) U of Tex Pr.
Lewenz, Marie A., tr. see Bulow, Bernhard H.
Lewer, Nicholas & Schofield, Steven. Non-Lethal Weapons: A Fatal Attraction? Military Strategies & Technologies for 21st Century Conflict. LC 96-34465. 192p. 1997. pap. 19.95 (*1-85649-486-1*, Pub. by Zed Books) St Martin.
Lewer, Nick. Physicians & the Peace Movement. 140p. 1992. text 29.50 (*0-7146-3438-7*, Pub. by F Cass Pubs) Intl Spec Bk.
Lewerentz, Claus & Lindner, Thomas, eds. Formal Development of Reactive Systems: Case Study Production Cell. LC 94-44675. (Lecture Notes in Computer Science Ser.: No. 891). 394p. 1995. pap. 62.00 (*0-387-58867-1*) Spr-Verlag.
Lewerentz, Sigurd. Sigurd Lewerentz: Two Churches. (Illus.). 90p. 1998. 34.95 (*91-86050-40-0*) Gingko Press.
Lewerenz, Alfred S. Antique Auto Body Brass Work for the Restorer. (Vintage Craft Ser.: No. 5). (Illus.). 1970. pap. 6.95 (*0-911160-05-1*) Post Group.
Lewerenz, Alfred S., ed. Antique Auto Body Accessories for the Restorer. (Vintage Craft Ser.: No. 7). (Illus.). 1970. pap. 6.95 (*0-911160-07-8*) Post Group.
Lewerenz, H. J., jt. auth. see Campbell, S. A.
Lewerth, Margaret. Stuyvesant Square. 464p. 1989. mass mkt. 4.50 (*0-380-70596-6*, Avon Bks) Morrow Avon.
Lewery, Tony. Flowers Afloat: Folk Artists of the Canals. (Illus.). 128p. 1996. 27.95 (*0-7153-0145-4*, Pub. by D & C Pub) Sterling.
Lewes, Darby. Dream Revisionaries: Gender & Genre in Women's Utopian Fiction, 1870-1920. LC 94-40947. 216p. 1995. text 36.95 (*0-8173-0795-8*) U of Ala Pr.
***Lewes, Darby.** Nudes from Nowhere: Utopian Sexual Landscapes. 240p. 2000. 67.00 (*0-8476-9814-9*); pap. 26.95 (*0-8476-9815-7*) Rowman.
Lewes, George Henry. Literary Criticism of George Henry Lewes. Kaminsky, Alice R., ed. LC 64-17230. (Regents Critics Ser.). 183p. reprint ed. pap. 56.80 (*0-7837-6014-0*, 204582500008) Bks Demand.
— On Actors & the Art of Acting. LC 68-56038. (Illus.). 237p. 1970. reprint ed. lib. bdg. 59.50 (*0-8371-0533-1*, LEAA, Greenwood Pr) Greenwood.
Lewes, George Henry. The Physical Basis of Mind. 511p. 120.00 (*1-85506-666-1*) Thoemmes Pr.
Lewes, George Henry. Rose, Blanche & Violet, 3 vols., 2 bks., Set. LC 79-8153. reprint ed. 84.50 (*0-404-61975-4*) AMS Pr.
— The Spanish Drama: Lope De Vaga & Calderon. 1980. lib. bdg. 59.95 (*0-8490-3201-6*) Gordon Pr.
Lewes, George Henry, et al. Problems of Life & Mind, 5 vols., Set. Incl. Foundations of a Creed., 2 vols. LC 78-72805. 75.00 (*0-404-60871-X*); Physical Basis of Mind. LC 78-72805. 42.50 (*0-404-60874-4*); Study of Psychology & Mind As a Function of the Organism., 2 vols. LC 78-72805. 62.50 (*0-404-60875-2*); LC 78-72805. (Illus.). 180.00 (*0-404-60870-1*) AMS Pr.
Lewes, Henry. Working in Photography: How to Obtain the Right Qualifications, Training & Employment. (Jobs & Careers Ser.). (Illus.). 128p. 1996. pap. 19.95 (*1-85703-220-9*, Pub. by How To Bks) Trans-Atl Phila.
***Lewes, John.** Jock Lewes: Co-Founder of the SAS. 2000. 34.95 (*0-85052-743-0*, Pub. by Pen & Sword Bks Ltd) Combined Pub.
Lewes, Kenneth. Psychoanalysis & Male Homosexuality. LC 94-49189. 328p. 1995. pap. 50.00 (*1-56821-484-7*) Aronson.
Lewfishman. Golf Magazine Shortcuts to Better Golf. 1993. 6.98 (*0-88365-820-8*) Galahad Bks.
Lewi, Grant. Astrology for the Millions. 6th rev. ed. LC 90-31242. (Classics of Astrology Library). (Illus.). 464p. 1990. pap. 14.95 (*0-87542-438-4*) Llewellyn Pubns.

L

An Asterisk (*) at the beginning of an entry indicates that the title is appearing for the first time.

— Astrology Kit. 1997. pap. text 29.95 (*0-88079-500-X*, ASK50) US Games Syst.

— Heaven Knows What. 9th rev. ed. LC 84-48086. (Popular Astrology Ser.). (Illus.). 468p. 1999. pap. 14.95 (*0-87542-444-9*) Llewellyn Pubns.

— Que Te Dicen las Estrellas? Tu Horoscopo en Minutos. (SPA.). 400p. Date not set. 14.95 (*1-56718-426-X*) Llewellyn Pubns.

Lewi, Grant & Greene, Liz. Astrology Kit. 1987. text 27.95 (*0-312-01350-7*) St Martin.

Lewi, P. J., jt. auth. see Massart, D. L.

Lewi, Paul J. Multivariate Data Analysis in Industrial Practice. LC 82-6906. (Chemometrics Research Studies: No. 3). (Illus.). 258p. reprint ed. pap. 80.00 (*0-8357-6228-9*, 203422900089) Bks Demand.

Lewi, Paul J., jt. auth. see Van Horebeek, I.

Lewicki. The Essentials of Negotiation. 2nd ed. 288p. 2000. pap. 37.50 (*0-07-231285-8*) McGraw.

— Negotiation: Readings, Exercises & Cases. 3rd ed. LC 97-44924. 1998. text 29.80 (*0-256-21591-X*, Irwn McGrw-H) McGrw-H Hghr Educ.

Lewicki, G., jt. auth. see Odyniec, W.

Lewicki, Krys V. Fetons l'Action de Graces. Warnant-Cote, Marie-Andree, tr. (FRE., Illus.). 40p. 1993. 14.95 (*0-929141-17-2*) Napoleon Publ.

— Thanksgiving Day in Canada. (Illus.). 40p. (J). (gr. 2-3). 1993. 12.95 (*0-929141-18-0*) Napoleon Publ.

— Thanksgiving Day in Canada. (Illus.). 40p. (J). (gr. 2-3). 1995. pap. 9.95 (*0-929141-36-9*) Napoleon Publ.

Lewicki, R. Hand-Dictionary KFZ. 2nd ed. (GER & POL.). 220p. 1995. 59.95 (*0-320-02701-5*) Fr & Eur.

***Lewicki, Roy & Hiam, Alexander.** The Fast Forward MBA in Negotiating & Deal Making. LC 98-24242. (Fast Forward MBA Ser.). 288p. 1998. pap. 14.95 (*0-471-25698-6*) Wiley.

Lewicki, Roy J. Essentials of Negotiation. 224p. (C). 1996. text 29.95 (*0-256-24168-6*, Irwn McGrw-H) McGrw-H Hghr Educ.

— Negotiation: Readings, Cases & Exercises. 3rd ed. LC 99-10103. (Illus.). 528p. (C). 1999. text 59.25 (*0-256-20832-8*, Irwn McGrw-H) McGrw-H Hghr Educ.

— Think Before You Speak: A Complete Guide to Strategic Negotiations. LC 95-45411. (Portable MBA Ser.). 304p. 1996. 29.95 (*0-471-01321-8*) Wiley.

Lewicki, Roy J., et al, eds. Research on Negotiation in Organizations, Vol. 1. 344p. 1986. 78.50 (*0-89232-638-7*) Jai Pr.

— Research on Negotiation in Organizations, Vol. 2. 269p. 1990. 78.50 (*0-89232-639-5*) Jai Pr.

— Research on Negotiation in Organizations, Vol. 3: Handbook of Negotiation Research. 332p. 1991. 78.50 (*1-55938-249-X*) Jai Pr.

— Research on Negotiation in Organizations, Vol. 4. 240p. 1994. 78.50 (*1-55938-555-3*) Jai Pr.

— Research on Negotiation in Organizations, Vol. 5. 276p. 1995. 78.50 (*1-55938-928-1*) Jai Pr.

— Research on Negotiation in Organizations, Vol. 6. 1997. 78.50 (*0-7623-0022-1*) Jai Pr.

— Research on Negotiation in Organizations, Vol. 7. Date not set. 78.50 (*0-7623-0314-X*) Jai Pr.

Lewicki, Roy J. & Litterer, Joseph A. Negotiation. 368p. (C). 1985. text 49.95 (*0-256-02633-5*, Irwn McGrw-H) McGrw-H Hghr Educ.

— Negotiation: Readings, Exercises & Cases. (C). 1985. pap. text 29.95 (*0-256-02634-3*, Irwn McGrw-H) McGrw-H Hghr Educ.

Lewicki, Roy J., et al. Experiences in Management & Organizational Behavior. 3rd ed. LC 87-25353. (Management Ser.). 384p. 1988. pap. 43.95 (*0-471-83796-2*) Wiley.

— Negotiation. 2nd ed. LC 93-40307. 496p. (C). 1994. text 51.95 (*0-256-10163-9*, Irwn McGrw-H) McGrw-H Hghr Educ.

— Negotiation: Readings, Exercises & Cases. 2nd ed. LC 92-11882. 784p. (C). 1992. text 37.25 (*0-256-10164-7*, Irwn McGrw-H) McGrw-H Hghr Educ.

Lewicki, Roy J., jt. auth. see Bowditch, James L.

Lewicki, Roy J., jt. ed. see Bazerman, Max H.

Lewicki, Zbigniew. The Bang & the Whimper: Apocalypse & Entropy in American Literature, 71. LC 83-12678. (Contributions in American Studies: No. 71). 135p. 1984. 45.00 (*0-313-23674-7*, LBW/, Greenwood Pr) Greenwood.

Lewiecki-Wilson, Cynthia. Writing Against the Family: Gender in Lawrence & Joyce. LC 93-7829. (Illus.). 288p. 1994. 36.95 (*0-8093-1881-4*) S Ill U Pr.

Lewin. Stalinism & Seeds Soviet: The Debates of the 1960's. (C). pap. 22.95 (*0-7453-0427-3*, Pub. by Pluto GBR) Stylus Pub VA.

— Van Day Truex: A Biography. 1998. 40.00 (*0-8050-5468-5*) H Holt & Co.

Lewin & Appelman. Tumors of the Esophagus & Stomach. (AFIP Atlas of Tumor Pathology Ser.: Vol. 18). (Illus.). 467p. 1996. pap. text 69.00 (*1-881041-27-1*) Am Registry Path.

Lewin & Pearce, eds. Handbook of Fiber Chemistry. 2nd ed. LC 97-44119. (Illus.). 1112p. 1998. text 275.00 (*0-8247-9471-0*) Dekker.

Lewin & Sello, S. Handbook of Fiber Science & Technology, Vol. 1, Pt. B Vol. 1, Pt. B: Chemical Processing of Fibers & Fabrics: Fundamentals & Preparation. (International Fiber Science & Technology Ser.). (Illus.). 368p. 1984. text 225.00 (*0-8247-7117-6*) Dekker.

Lewin & Lewin Staff. Thesaurus of Slang. (Reference Library). 1998. pap. 6.95 (*1-85326-360-5*, 3605WW, Pub. by Wrdsworth Edits) NTC Contemp Pub Co.

Lewin, Albert E., jt. auth. see Lewin, Esther.

Lewin, Arthur. Africa Is Not a Country: It's a Continent. (Illus.). 77p. 1991. pap. 9.95 (*0-9628911-1-8*) Clarendon NJ.

— The Law, Procedure & Conduct of Meetings. 5th ed. 280p. 1985. pap. 30.00 (*0-7021-1528-2*, Pub. by Juta & Co) Gaunt.

Lewin, B. Sex & Family Planning - How We Teach the Young: Report on a Study. (Public Health in Europe Ser.: No. 23). 170p. 1984. pap. text 19.00 (*92-890-1159-9*) World Health.

Lewin, B. & Bruno. Small Dictionary of Japanology: Kleines Woerterbuch der Japanologie. 2nd ed. (GER & JPN.). 596p. 1981. 85.00 (*0-8288-1019-2*, M7512) Fr & Eur.

Lewin, Benjamin. Gene Expression, Vol. 1. LC 73-14382. (Illus.). 660p. 1974. reprint ed. pap. 200.00 (*0-608-08276-7*, 202789000001) Bks Demand.

— Gene Expression Vol. 2: Eucaryotic Chromosomes. 2nd ed. LC 80-10849. 1178p. 1980. reprint ed. pap. 200.00 (*0-608-08277-5*, 205630000056) Bks Demand.

— Genes V. (Illus.). 180p. (C). 1995. trans. 200.00 (*0-19-510532-X*) OUP.

***Lewin, Benjamin.** Genes VII. LC 99-54243. 1999. write for info. (*0-19-879277-8*) OUP.

— Genes VII. LC 99-54243. (Illus.). 992p. (C). 1999. text 79.95 (*0-19-879276-X*) OUP.

Lewin, Bertram D. The Image & the Past. LC 68-59121. 128p. 1969. 27.50 (*0-8236-2505-2*) Intl Univs Pr.

Lewin, Betsy. Booby Hatch. LC 94-19309. (Illus.). 32p. (J). (ps-3). 1995. 14.95 (*0-395-68703-9*, Clarion Bks) HM.

— Booby Hatch. (Illus.). 32p. (J). (ps-3). 1997. pap. 4.95 (*0-395-84516-5*, Clarion Bks) HM.

— Booby Hatch. 1997. 10.15 (*0-606-11155-7*, Pub. by Turtleback) Demco.

— Chubbo's Pool. LC 95-20467. (Illus.). 32p. (J). (ps-3). 1996. 14.95 (*0-395-72807-X*, Clarion Bks) HM.

— Chubbo's Pool. LC 95-20467. (Illus.). 32p. (J). (ps-3). 1998. pap. 5.95 (*0-395-92863-X*, Clarion Bks) HM.

— Groundhog Day. LC 99-24784. (Hello Reader! Ser.). (Illus.). (J). 2000. pap. 10.01 (*0-439-10802-0*) Scholastic Inc.

— Walk a Green Path. LC 94-14824. (Illus.). 32p. (J). (gr. k up). 1995. 15.00 (*0-688-13425-4*) Lothrop.

— Wiley Learns to Spell. LC 97-41142. (Hello Reader! Ser.). (Illus.). 32p. (J). (ps-1). 1998. pap. 3.50 (*0-590-10835-2*, Pub. by Scholastic Inc) Penguin Putnam.

***Lewin, Betsy.** Wiley Learns to Spell. (Hello, Reader! Ser.). (J). 1998. 8.70 (*0-606-13916-8*, Pub. by Turtleback) Demco.

***Lewin, Betsy.** Promises. LC 99-27186. 32p. (J). (gr. k-3). 2000. 16.00 (*0-395-82272-6*, Clarion Bks) HM.

Lewin, Betsy, jt. auth. see Lewin, Ted.

Lewin, Betsy, jt. auth. see Maccarone, Grace.

Lewin, Bruno. Kleines Woerterbuch der Japanologie. (GER.). 593p. 1968. 125.00 (*0-7859-8365-1*, 3447005300) Fr & Eur.

Lewin, Cheryl. Great Package Design: Creating the Competitive Edge. Holland, D. K., ed. (Illus.). 192p. 1992. pap. 44.95 (*1-56496-128-1*, 30639) Rockport Pubs.

Lewin, Cheryl, jt. auth. see Holland, D. K.

Lewin, David, et al, eds. Advances in Industrial & Labor Relations, Vol. 4. 251p. 1987. 78.50 (*0-89232-909-2*) Jai Pr.

— Advances in Industrial & Labor Relations, Vol. 6. 236p. 1994. 78.50 (*1-55938-488-3*) Jai Pr.

— Advances in Industrial & Labor Relations, Vol. 7. 1996. 78.50 (*1-55938-925-7*) Jai Pr.

— Advances in Industrial & Labor Relations, Vol. 8. 1998. 78.50 (*0-7623-0245-3*) Jai Pr.

— The Human Resource Management Handbook. LC 96-38022. (Monographs in Organizational Behavior & Industrial Relations: Vol. 19). 1997. 78.50 (*1-55938-921-4*) Jai Pr.

— Research Frontiers in Industrial Relations & Human Resources. 1992. 22.50 (*0-913447-53-6*) Indus Relations Res.

Lewin, David & Mitchell, Daniel J. Human Resource Management: An Economic Approach. 2nd ed. LC 94-34201. (C). 1994. pap. 94.95 (*0-538-84487-6*) S-W Pub.

Lewin, David & Peterson, Richard B. The Modern Grievance Procedure in the United States. LC 87-32612. (Illus.). 301p. 1988. 69.50 (*0-89930-149-5*, LMG/, Quorum Bks) Greenwood.

Lewin, David, et al. The Human Resource Management Handbook, 3 pts. Incl. Pt. 1. LC 96-38022. 1997. pap. text 86.25 (*0-7623-0247-X*); Pt. 2. LC 96-38022. 1997. pap. text 86.25 (*0-7623-0248-8*); Pt. 3. LC 96-38022. 1997. pap. text 86.25 (*0-7623-0249-6*); 1997. Set pap. text 250.00 (*0-7623-0246-1*) Jai Pr.

— Public Sector Labor Relations. 3rd ed. LC 82-64038. 648p. (C). 1988. pap. 29.95 (*0-669-12893-7*) Lxngtn Bks.

Lewin, Debra H., jt. auth. see Haan, Ellen De.

Lewin, Douglas, jt. ed. see Boulaye, G.

Lewin, Elizabeth. J. K. Lasser's Women on Their Own Again: Financial Planning for Women on Their Own Again. 256p. 1998. 15.95 (*0-02-862530-7*) Macmillan.

— Kiss the Rat Race Good-Bye: Achieve Financial Independence Within 15 Years: A Step-by-Step Program. LC 94-31504. 272p. 1994. pap. 12.95 (*0-8027-7438-5*) Walker & Co.

Lewin, Elizabeth & Ryan, Bernard, Jr. Simple Ways to Help Your Kids Become Dollar-Smart. LC 93-36832. 128p. (Orig.). 1994. pap. 8.95 (*0-8027-7429-6*) Walker & Co.

Lewin, Elizabeth S. Financial Fitness for Living Together. LC 96-5792. (Illus.). 176p. 1996. pap. 14.95 (*0-8160-3281-5*) Facts on File.

— Financial Fitness for New Families. 176p. 1989. pap. 12.95 (*0-8160-1980-0*) Facts on File.

— Financial Fitness for New Families. LC 89-17110. 170p. 1989. reprint ed. pap. 52.70 (*0-608-02818-5*, 206388500007) Bks Demand.

— Financial Fitness for Newlyweds. fac. ed. LC 83-14139. 188p. 1984. reprint ed. pap. 58.30 (*0-7837-8141-5*, 204794900008) Bks Demand.

— Financial Fitness Through Divorce: A Guide to the Financial Realities of Divorce. LC 86-24383. 156p. reprint ed. pap. 48.40 (*0-8357-3497-8*, 203975700013) Bks Demand.

— Your Personal Financial Fitness Program, 1995-96. (Illus.). 156p. 1995. pap. 13.95 (*0-8160-3146-0*) Facts on File.

— Your Personal Financial Fitness Program, 1997-98. rev. ed. (Illus.). 160p. 1997. pap. 14.95 (*0-8160-3575-X*) Facts on File.

Lewin, Ellen. Lesbian Mothers: Accounts of Gender in American Culture. LC 92-54977. (Anthropology of Contemporary Issues Ser.). 256p. 1993. text 39.95 (*0-8014-2857-2*); pap. text 15.95 (*0-8014-8099-X*) Cornell U Pr.

— Mothers & Children. Cortes, Carlos E., ed. LC 79-6215. (Hispanics in the United States Ser.). (Illus.). 1981. lib. bdg. 23.95 (*0-405-13163-1*) Ayer.

— Recognizing Ourselves: Ceremonies of Lesbian & Gay Commitment. LC 97-45672. (Between Men - Between Women Ser.). (Illus.). 278p. 1998. 31.50 (*0-231-10392-1*) Col U Pr.

— Recognizing Ourselves: Ceremonies of Lesbian & Gay Commitment. 288p. 1999. pap. 16.95 (*0-231-10393-X*) Col U Pr.

Lewin, Ellen, ed. Inventing Lesbian Cultures in America. LC 96-12406. 224p. 1996. pap. 17.00 (*0-8070-7943-X*) Beacon Pr.

Lewin, Ellen & Leap, William L., eds. Out in the Field: Reflections of Lesbian & Gay Anthropolgists. LC 95-32456. 312p. 1996. 16.95 (*0-252-06518-2*); text 39.95 (*0-252-02219-X*) U of Ill Pr.

Lewin, Elsa. I, Anna. 312p. 1987. reprint ed. mass mkt. 3.50 (*0-445-40300-4*, Mysterious Paperbk) Warner Bks.

Lewin-Epstein, Noah, jt. auth. see Semyonov, Moshe.

Lewin, Esther & Lewin, Albert E. The Thesaurus of Slang. rev. ed. LC 98-113686. 464p. 1997. pap. 24.95 (*0-8160-3661-6*) Facts on File.

— The Thesaurus of Slang: Over 165,000 Uncensored Contemporary Slang Terms, Common Idioms, & Colloquialisms, Updated for the 1990's & Arranged for Quick & Easy Reference. rev. ed. LC 93-42890. 464p. 1994. 50.00 (*0-8160-2898-2*) Facts on File.

Lewin, Evans. The Germans & Africa. 1977. lib. bdg. 59.95 (*0-8490-1886-2*) Gordon Pr.

— Subject Catalogue of the Library of the Royal Empire Society, 1930-1937, 4 vols. Incl. Vol. 1. British Empire. 850p. 1967. reprint ed. 40.00 Vol. 2. Australia, New Zealand, South Pacific, Antarctic. 770p. 1967. reprint ed. 40.00 Vol. 3. Canada, Newfoundland, West Indies, Colonial America. 830p. 1967. reprint ed. 40.00 Vol. 4. Mediterranean Colonies, Middle East, Indian Empire, Far East. 820p. 1967. reprint ed. 40.00 1967. write for info. (*0-318-51038-3*); Set pap. 160.00 (*0-8464-0894-5*) Beekman Pubs.

Lewin, Frank & Auld, Louis E. Burning Bright: The Genesis of an Opera. (Monograph: No. 1). (Illus.). 100p. (Orig.). 1985. pap. 15.00 (*0-937129-00-3*) Lyrica.

Lewin, Hugh. Bandiet-Seven Years in a South African Prison. (African Writers Ser.). 230p. (Orig.). (C). 1981. pap. 8.95 (*0-435-90251-2*) Heinemann.

— Jafta. (Jafta Collection). (Illus.). 24p. (J). (ps-3). 1983. reprint ed. pap. 4.95 (*0-87614-494-6*, Carolrhoda) Lerner Pub.

— Jafta: The Journey. LC 84-4326. (The Jafta Bks.). (Illus.). 24p. (J). (ps-3). 1994. pap. 4.95 (*0-87614-644-2*, Carolrhoda); lib. bdg. 18.60 (*0-87614-265-X*, Carolrhoda) Lerner Pub.

— Jafta: The Town. LC 84-4950. (The Jafta Bks.). (Illus.). 24p. (J). (ps-3). 1994. pap. 4.95 (*0-87614-645-0*, Carolrhoda) Lerner Pub.

— Jafta - The Town. LC 84-4950. (Illus.). 24p. (J). (ps-3). 1994. lib. bdg. 18.60 (*0-87614-266-8*, Carolrhoda) Lerner Pub.

— Jafta & the Wedding. LC 82-12836. (Jafta Collection). (Illus.). 24p. (J). (ps-3). 1983. pap. 4.95 (*0-87614-497-0*, Carolrhoda) Lerner Pub.

— Jafta's Father. (Jafta Collection). (Illus.). 24p. (J). (ps-3). 1983. lib. bdg. 18.60 (*0-87614-209-9*, Carolrhoda) Lerner Pub.

— Jafta's Father. (Jafta Collection). (Illus.). 24p. (J). (ps-3). 1989. reprint ed. pap. 4.95 (*0-87614-496-2*, Carolrhoda) Lerner Pub.

— Jafta's Mother. LC 82-12863. (J). (ps-3). 1983. lib. bdg. 18.60 (*0-87614-208-0*, Carolrhoda) Lerner Pub.

— Jafta's Mother. (Jafta Collection). (Illus.). 24p. (J). (ps-3). 1989. reprint ed. pap. 4.95 (*0-87614-495-4*, Carolrhoda) Lerner Pub.

— The Picture That Came Alive. (Junior African Writers Ser.). (Illus.). 80p. (J). (gr. 3 up). 1992. pap. 4.95 (*0-7910-2912-3*) Chelsea Hse.

Lewin, Isaac, jt. auth. see Kranzler, David.

Lewin, Jack. Hydraulic Gates & Valves in Free Surface Flow & Submerged Outlets. LC 95-209399. 238p. 1995. 105.00 (*0-7277-2020-1*) Am Soc Civil Eng.

***Lewin, Jackie.** Death Flies on Final. LC 98-96849. 192p. 1999. lib. bdg. 18.95 (*0-8034-9338-X*, Avalon Bks) Bouregy.

— Murder Flies Left Seat. LC 97-97218. 192p. 1998. 18.95 (*0-8034-9288-X*, Avalon Bks) Bouregy.

***Lewin, Jackie.** Murder Flies Left Seat. 2000. mass mkt. 5.99 (*0-373-26357-0*, Wrldwide Lib) Harlequin Bks.

Lewin, Jacqueline A. & Taylor, Marilyn S. The St. Joe Road: Emigration Mid Eighteen Hundreds. 64p. 1992. pap. 12.00 (*1-884483-00-3*) St Joseph Mus.

Lewin, James. Die Lehre Von den Ideen Bei Malebranche. (Abhandlungen Zur Philosophie und Ihrer Geschichte Ser.: No. 35). viii, 165p. 1981. reprint ed. write for info. (*3-487-06787-0*) G Olms Pubs.

Lewin, Jane E., tr. see Genette, Gerard.

Lewin, Jeanne E. & Reed, Colleen A., eds. Creative Problem Solving in Occupational Therapy. LC 97-48862. (Illus.). 304p. 1998. pap. text 43.95 (*0-397-55233-5*) Lppncott W & W.

Lewin, Jeffrey L., jt. ed. see Kaufman, Howard H.

Lewin, John, et al, eds. Mediterranean Quaternary River Environments: Refereed Proceedings of an International Conference, University of Cambridge, UK, 28-29 September 1992. (Illus.). 300p. (C). 1995. text 97.00 (*90-5410-191-1*, Pub. by A A Balkema) Ashgate Pub Co.

Lewin, Jonathan. Precalculus... Notebook. 2nd ed. 314p. (C). 1999. per. 51.95 (*0-7872-5798-2*, 41579802) Kendall-Hunt.

— Precalculus with Scientific Notebook. 310p. (C). 1997. per. 41.95 (*0-7872-3935-6*) Kendall-Hunt.

Lewin, Jonathan, jt. auth. see Yang, Wei-Chi.

Lewin, Joseph. Differential Games: Theory & Methods for Solving Game Problems with Singular Surfaces. LC 93-33448. (Illus.). 262p. 1993. 59.95 (*0-387-19841-5*) Spr-Verlag.

Lewin, Julius. Politics & Law in South Africa: Essays on Race Relations. LC DT0763. 116p. reprint ed. pap. 36.00 (*0-608-11630-0*, 200169500014) Bks Demand.

— Studies in African Native Law. 173p. 1998. reprint ed. pap. 35.95 (*1-58073-008-6*) BCP Bks.

— Studies in African Native Law. 173p. 1998. reprint ed. pap. 35.95 (*0-933121-90-3*) Black Classic.

Lewin, Karl K. Brief Encounters (Brief Psychotherapy) LC 78-96987. 288p. 1970. 15.00 (*0-87527-048-4*) Green.

— Heritage of Illusions. LC 76-528. 192p. 1977. 12.50 (*0-87527-157-X*) Green.

— Sexual Self-Destruct: Conscience of the West. LC 79-54918. 166p. 1980. 15.00 (*0-87527-197-9*) Green.

Lewin, Keith M., jt. auth. see Colclough, Christopher.

Lewin, Klaus J., et al. Gastrointestinal Pathology & Its Clinical Implications, 2 vols., Set. LC 88-28473. (Illus.). 1488p. 1992. text 345.00 (*0-89640-153-7*) Igaku-Shoin.

Lewin, Kurt. The Complete Social Scientist: A Kurt Lewin Reader. Gold, Martin, ed. LC 98-48619. 363p. 1999. pap. 29.95 (*1-55798-532-4*) Am Psychol.

— Resolving Social Conflicts & Field Theory in Social Science. LC 96-40386. 422p. 1997. pap. 19.95 (*1-55798-415-8*) Am Psychol.

Lewin, Kurt I. A Journey Through Illusions. (Illus.). 464p. 1997. pap. 14.95 (*1-56474-211-3*) Fithian Pr.

Lewin, L. Structural Properties of Polylogarithms. LC 91-18172. (Mathematical Surveys & Monographs: No. 37). 412p. 1991. text 133.00 (*0-8218-1634-9*, SURV/37) Am Math.

***Lewin, Larry.** Enhancing Language Arts/Social Studies Curriculum with the Net: Grades 7-12. 165p. 1999. 19.95 (*1-893243-06-0*) Forefront.

— Teaching with Technology-Language Arts & Social Studies: Grades 5-12. 160p. 1999. 19.95 (*1-893243-07-9*) Forefront.

Lewin, Larry & Shoemaker, Betty J. Great Performances: Creating Classroom-Based Assessment Tasks. LC 98-40133. 167p. 1998. pap. 17.95 (*0-87120-339-1*, 198184) ASCD.

Lewin, Larry, jt. auth. see Knight, Tanis.

Lewin, Leif. Governing Trade Unions in Sweden. LC 79-26724. (Illus.). 180p. 1980. 36.50 (*0-674-35875-9*) HUP.

— Ideology & Strategy: A Century of Swedish Politics. (Political Economy of Institutions & Decisions Ser.: No. 3). (Illus.). 360p. 1989. text 80.00 (*0-521-34330-5*) Cambridge U Pr.

— Self Interest & Public Interest in Western Politics. Lavery, Donald S., tr. (Comparative Politics Ser.). (Illus.). 152p. 1991. text 55.00 (*0-19-827726-1*, 11906); pap. text 18.95 (*0-19-827725-3*) OUP.

Lewin, Leif & Vedung, Evert, eds. Politics As Rational Action: Essays in Public Choice & Policy Analysis. (Theory & Decision Library: No. 23). 276p. 1980. lib. bdg. 96.00 (*90-277-1040-6*) Kluwer Academic.

Lewin, Leif, jt. ed. see Gustavsson, Sverker.

Lewin, Leonard. On the Possibility & Desirability of Peace. abr. ed. LC 67-27553. 43p. 1987. reprint ed. pap. 5.00 (*0-942153-18-9*) Entropy Conserv.

— Science & the Paranormal. 16p. 1979. pap. 6.00 (*0-904674-07-X*, Pub. by Octagon Pr) ISHK.

Lewin, Leonard, ed. Telecommunications: An Interdisciplinary Survey. LC 78-26665. (Illus.). 722p. reprint ed. pap. 200.00 (*0-8357-7923-8*, 203634900002) Bks Demand.

— Telecommunications: An Interdisciplinary Text. LC 84-70225. (Illus.). 709p. reprint ed. pap. 200.00 (*0-7837-1188-3*, 204171800023) Bks Demand.

— Telecommunications in the U. S. Trends & Policies. LC 81-67809. (Illus.). 487p. reprint ed. pap. 151.00 (*0-8357-4190-7*, 203696800006) Bks Demand.

Lewin, Leonard B. Shopping for Furniture: A Consumer's Guide. LC 98-35042. (Illus.). 128p. 1998. pap. 14.95 (*0-941936-39-2*) Linden Pub Fresno.

***Lewin, Leonard Bruce.** Shopping for Fine Furniture on the Internet: What You Must Know Before You Buy. 128p. 2000. pap. 12.95 (*0-941936-58-9*, Pub. by Linden Pub Fresno) IPG Chicago.

Lewin, Leonard C. Report from Iron Mountain: On the Possibility & Desirability of Peace. 110p. 1993. reprint ed. lib. bdg. 25.95 (*0-89968-322-3*) Buccaneer Bks.

Lewin, Lewis M., jt. auth. see Lundervold, Duane A.

***Lewin, Linda.** Pioneer Women of California. (California Biography Ser.). (Illus.). 48p. (J). (gr. 4-8). 1999. pap. text 14.95 (*1-884925-81-2*) Toucan Valley.

An Asterisk (*) at the beginning of an entry indicates that the title is appearing for the first time.

Lewin, Linda. Politics & Parentela in Paraiba: A Case Study of Family-Based Oligarchy in Brazil. LC 86-42850. 524p. 1987. reprint ed. pap. 162.50 (*0-7837-9375-8*, 20601190004) Bks Demand.

Lewin, M. & Preston, J. Handbook of Fiber Science & Technology: High Technology Fibers, Pt. B. (International Fiber Science & Technology Ser.: Vol. 9). (Illus.). 360p. 1989. text 225.00 (*0-8247-8066-3*) Dekker.

Lewin, M. & Preston, Jack. HB of Fiber Science & Technology Vol. 3, Pt. A: High Technology Fibers. (International Fiber Science & Technology Ser.: Vol. 5). (Illus.). 424p. 1985. text 225.00 (*0-8247-7279-2*) Dekker.

Lewin, M. & Sello, S. Handbook of Fiber Science & Technology: Chemical Processing of Fibers & Fabrics, Pt. B: Functional Finishes. (International Fiber Science & Technology Ser.: Vol. 2). (Illus.). 544p. 1984. text 225.00 (*0-8247-7118-4*) Dekker.

Lewin, M. H. Elements of C. LC 86-4910. (Foundations of Computer Science Ser.). (Illus.). 260p. (C). 1986. 65.00 (*0-306-42182-8*, Plenum Trade) Perseus Pubng.

Lewin, Marion E., ed. see Institute of Medicine, Committee to Increase Minor.

Lewin, Marion E., ed. see Institute of Medicine Staff.

Lewin, Marsha D. The Consultant's Survival Guide. LC 96-36659. 231p. 1997. 24.95 (*0-471-16079-2*) Wiley.

— The Overnight Consultant. LC 95-17526. 234p. 1995. 55.00 (*0-471-11944-X*); pap. 19.95 (*0-471-11945-8*) Wiley.

Lewin, Marsha D. & Rosenau, Milton D., Jr. Software Project Management: Step by Step. 313p. 1988. text 35.00 (*0-9627022-0-X*) M D Lewin Assocs.

Lewin, Menachem. Polymers for Advanced Technologies: IUPAC International Symposium. LC 88-177. 953p. 1988. 150.00 (*0-89573-293-9*, Wiley-VCH) Wiley.

Lewin, Menachem & Goldstein, Irving S., eds. Wood Structure & Composition. (International Fiber Science & Technology Ser.: Vol. 11). (Illus.). 512p. 1991. text 225.00 (*0-8247-8233-X*) Dekker.

Lewin, Menachem & Preston, Jack, eds. Handbook of Fiber Science & Technology Vol. III: High Technology Fibers Part D. (International Fiber Science & Technology Ser.: Vol. 14). (Illus.). 312p. 1996. text 165.00 (*0-8247-9470-2*) Dekker.

Lewin, Menachem, et al. Flame-Retardant Polymeric Materials, Vol. 3. LC 75-26781. 248p. 1982. 75.00 (*0-306-40868-6*, Plenum Trade) Perseus Pubng.

Lewin, Menachem, ed. see Preston, Jack.

Lewin, Michael Z., ed. see Codey, Liza.

Lewin, Michael Z. And Baby Will Fall. 1990. mass mkt. 3.50 (*0-373-26042-3*) Harlequin Bks.

Lewin, Michael Z. And Baby Will Fall. large type ed. LC 88-28361. 304 p. 1989. pap. write for info. (*1-55504-755-6*) Chivers N Amer.

Lewin, Michael Z. Called by a Panther. 272p. 1992. mass mkt. 4.99 (*0-446-40159-5*, Pub. by Warner Bks) Little.

— Cutting Loose. LC 99-10997. 528p. (YA). (gr. 8 up). 1999. 23.95 (*0-8050-6225-4*) H Holt & Co.

— Family Business: A Novel of Detection. (Lunghi Family Mystery Ser.). 176p. 1995. reprint ed. 20.00 (*0-88150-348-7*, Foul Play) Norton.

***Lewin, Michael Z.** Family Planning. LC 99-33280. 272p. 1999. text 23.95 (*0-312-24391-X*) St Martin.

Lewin, Michael Z. Hard Line. (Lt. Leroy Powder Novel Ser.). 256p. 1996. reprint ed. pap. 10.00 (*0-88150-346-0*, Foul Play) Norton.

— Late Payments. (Lt. Leroy Powder Novel Ser.). 216p. 1996. reprint ed. pap. 10.00 (*0-88150-347-9*, Foul Play) Norton.

— Missing Woman. 1991. mass mkt. 4.99 (*0-446-40026-2*, Mysterious Paperbk) Warner Bks.

— Rover's Tales. LC 97-41881. 1998. text 21.95 (*0-312-18169-8*) St Martin.

— Underdog. 272p. 1993. 18.95 (*0-89296-440-5*) Mysterious Pr.

— Underdog. 256p. 1995. mass mkt. 5.50 (*0-446-40436-5*, Pub. by Warner Bks) Little.

Lewin, Michael Z., ed. see Cody, Liza.

Lewin, Miriam. Understanding Psychological Research. LC 87-3507. 464p. (C). 1987. reprint ed. lib. bdg. 49.50 (*0-89464-230-8*) Krieger.

Lewin, Miriam, ed. In the Shadow of the Past: Psychology Portrays the Sexes. LC 83-10072. 338p. 1986. pap. 22.00 (*0-231-05303-7*) Col U Pr.

Lewin, Morton H. Logic Design & Computer Organization. LC 81-20636. 478p. 1983. text 38.36 (*0-201-04144-8*) Addison-Wesley.

Lewin, Moshe. The Gorbachev Phenomenon: A Historical Interpretation. enl. rev. ed. LC 90-46995. 208p. 1991. pap. 14.95 (*0-520-07429-7*, Pub. by U CA Pr) Cal Prin Full Svc.

— The Making of the Soviet System: Essays in the Social History of Interwar Russia. 368p. 1994. pap. 16.95 (*1-56584-125-5*, Pub. by New Press NY) Norton.

— Russia - U. S. S. R. - Russia: The Drive & Drift of a Superstate. (Illus.). 384p. 1995. 30.00 (*1-56584-123-9*, Pub. by New Press NY) Norton.

— Russian Peasants & Soviet Power: A Study of Collectivization. 544p. (C). 1975. reprint ed. pap. 21.75 (*0-393-00752-9*) Norton.

Lewin, Moshe. Stalinism & the Seeds of Soviet Reform: The Debates of the 1960s. LC 91-8701. (Socialism & Social Movements Ser.). 414p. (C). (gr. 13). 1991. pap. text 43.95 (*0-87332-858-2*) M E Sharpe.

Lewin, Moshe, jt. ed. see Kershaw, Ian.

Lewin, Paulina, intro. Seventeenth-Century Writings on the Kievan Caves Monastery. LC 87-83705. (Harvard Library of Early Ukrainian Literature: Vol. 4). 468p. (C). 1989. text 15.00 (*0-916458-24-5*) Harvard Ukrainian.

***Lewin, Peter A.** The Role Of Capital In A Changing World / LC 98-54231. (Foundations of the Market Economy Ser.). 6p. 1998. write for info. (*0-415-14706-9*) Routledge.

Lewin, Peter A., jt. ed. see Ziskin, Marvin C.

Lewin, Rachel. Holistic Healing. (Healing Ser.). (Illus.). 160p. 1998. pap. 8.95 (*965-494-042-6*, Pub. by Astrolog Pub) Assoc Pubs Grp.

***Lewin, Ralph A.** Abacus & Swallows: Poems about Animals & Plants. LC 00-32439. 76p. 2000. pap. text 14.95 (*0-7734-1260-3*) E Mellen.

Lewin, Ralph A. The Biology of Algae & Diverse Other Verses. 1987. pap. 9.95 (*0-940168-11-1*) Boxwood.

— Merde: Excursions in Scientific Cultural & Sociological Historical Coprology. LC 98-27259. 187p. 1999. 19.95 (*0-375-50198-3*) Random.

Lewin, Ralph A., tr. see Thurber, James.

Lewin, Rhoda G., ed. Witnesses to the Holocaust: An Oral History. (Oral History Ser.: No. 2). (Illus.). 240p. 1989. 20.95 (*0-8057-9100-0*) Macmillan.

— Witnesses to the Holocaust: An Oral History. (Twayne's Oral History Ser.: No. 2). 240p. 1991. pap. 20.00 (*0-8057-9126-4*) Macmillan.

Lewin, Rod. Steel Spine, Iron Will. LC 91-78105. 320p. (Orig.). 1992. pap. 18.95 (*0-9632031-0-X*) Boomerang Bks.

Lewin, Roger. Bones of Contention: Controversies in the Search for Human Origins. 2nd ed. LC 97-972. 1997. pap. text 18.95 (*0-226-47651-0*) U Ch Pr.

— Complexity: Life at the Edge of Chaos. 2nd ed. LC 99-38597. 2000. pap. 15.00 (*0-226-47655-3*); lib. bdg. 28.00 (*0-226-47654-5*) U Ch Pr.

— Human Evolution. 3rd ed. LC 92-48913. (Illus.). 208p. 1993. pap. 26.95 (*0-86542-262-1*) Blackwell Sci.

— Human Evolution: An Illustrated Introduction. 4th ed. LC 98-35384. (Illus.). 1998. pap. 31.95 (*0-632-04309-1*) Blackwell Sci.

— New Wrinkles. LC 96-85400. (Illus.). 64p. (Orig.). 1996. pap. 9.95 (*1-886094-42-X*) Chicago Spectrum.

— The Origin of Modern Humans. 1998. pap. 19.95 (*0-7167-6023-1*) W H Freeman.

— Patterns of Evolution: The New Molecular View. 1999. pap. text 19.95 (*0-7167-6036-3*, Sci Amer Lib Paperbacks) W H Freeman.

— Principles of Human Evolution. LC 97-21774. (Illus.). 224p. (C). 1997. pap. text 51.95 (*0-86542-542-6*) Blackwell Sci.

— Thread of Life: The Smithsonian Looks at Evolution. LC 82-16834. (Illus.). 256p. (C). 1989. text 35.00 (*0-89599-010-5*) Smithsonian.

***Lewin, Roger & Regine, Birute.** The Soul at Work: Listen... Respond... Let Go. LC 99-16253. 304p. 2000. 26.00 (*0-684-84384-6*) S&S Trade.

***Lewin, Roger & Swisher, Carl C., 3rd.** Java Man: How Two Geologists Changed the History of Human Evolution. 256p. 2000. 27.00 (*0-684-80000-4*) Scribner.

Lewin, Roger, jt. auth. see Leakey, Richard.

Lewin, Roger, jt. auth. see Leakey, Richard E.

Lewin, Roger, jt. auth. see Savage-Rumbaugh, E. Sue.

Lewin, Roger A. Compassion: The Core Value That Animates Psychotherapy. LC 95-23012. 1996. 50.00 (*1-56821-678-5*) Aronson.

— Creative Collaboration in Psychotherapy: Making Room for Life. LC 97-5353. 208p. 1997. text 35.00 (*0-7657-0075-1*) Aronson.

Lewin, Roger A. & Schulz, Clarence. Losing & Fusing: Borderline Transitional Object & Self Relations. LC 92-6219. 368p. 1992. 55.00 (*0-87668-490-8*) Aronson.

Lewin, Ronald. Churchill As Warlord. LC 72-96544. (Illus.). 308p. (C). 1982. 10.95 (*0-8128-6099-3*, Scrbrough Hse) Madison Bks UPA.

— Montgomery. (Military Commanders Ser.). 1998. pap. 18.95 (*0-938289-17-9*, 289179) Combined Pub.

***Lewin, Ronald.** Slim. 1999. pap. 12.99 (*1-84022-214-X*) Wrdsworth Edits.

Lewin, Sam. How to Win at the Races. 1979. pap. 5.00 (*0-87980-244-8*) Wilshire.

Lewin, Samuel. Between Two Abysses, Pt. 1. Leftwich, Joseph, tr. LC 85-22377. (Trilogy Ser.). 224p. 1988. 12.95 (*0-8453-4795-0*, Cornwall Bks) Assoc Univ Prs.

— Between Two Abysses: A Trilogy, 3 pts. Leftwich, Joseph, tr. boxed set 29.50 (*0-318-36511-1*, Cornwall Bks) Assoc Univ Prs.

— Between Two Abysses: A Trilogy, 3 vols. Leftwich, Joseph, tr. 1988. boxed set 29.50 (*0-8453-4818-3*, Cornwall Bks) Assoc Univ Prs.

— Between Two Abysses: A Trilogy, 3 pts., Pt. 1: Between Two Abysses. Leftwich, Joseph, tr. 12.95 (*0-318-36512-X*, Cornwall Bks) Assoc Univ Prs.

— Between Two Abysses: A Trilogy, Pt. 3. Leftwich, Joseph, tr. write for info. (*0-318-63293-4*, Cornwall Bks) Assoc Univ Prs.

— Dark Mountains & Blue Valleys, Pt. 2. Leftwich, Joseph, tr. LC 85-22377. (Trilogy Ser.). 160p. 1988. 12.95 (*0-8453-4803-4*, Cornwall Bks) Assoc Univ Prs.

— Singing Through the Clouds, Pt. 3. Leftwich, Joseph, tr. LC 85-22377. (Trilogy Ser.). 160p. 1988. 12.95 (*0-8453-4805-1*, Cornwall Bks) Assoc Univ Prs.

— The Turning of the Tide. Leftwich, Joseph, tr. 8.95 (*0-8453-2087-4*, Cornwall Bks) Assoc Univ Prs.

Lewin-Spstein, Noah, et al, eds. Russian Jews on Three Continents: Emigration & Resettlement. LC 97-9891. (The Cummings Center Ser.: Vol. 6). 568p. (C). 1997. text 64.50 (*0-7146-4726-8*, Pub. by F Cass Pubs); pap. text 29.50 (*0-7146-4276-2*, Pub. by F Cass Pubs) Intl Spec Bk.

Lewin, Susan G. Contemporary American Art Jewelry. LC 94-1413. (Illus.). 224p. 1994. 49.50 (*0-8109-3198-2*) Abrams.

Lewin, Ted. Elephant Quest. LC 99-55369. 48p. (J). (gr. 1 up). 2000. lib. bdg. 15.89 (*0-688-14112-9*, Wm Morrow) Morrow Avon.

— Elephant Quest. LC 99-55369. (Illus.). 48p. (J). (gr. 1-4). 2000. 15.95 (*0-688-14111-0*, Wm Morrow) Morrow Avon.

— Fair! LC 96-51146. (Illus.). 40p. (J). 1997. lib. bdg., lab manual ed. 15.93 (*0-688-12851-3*) Lothrop.

— Fair! LC 96-51146. (Illus.). 40p. (J). (gr. k-3). 1997. 16.00 (*0-688-12850-5*) Lothrop.

— I Was a Teenage Professional Wrestler. LC 94-2132. 128p. (J). (gr. 5-9). 1994. pap. 6.70 (*0-7868-1009-2*, Pub. by Hyprn Ppbks) Little.

— I Was a Teenage Professional Wrestler. LC 92-31523. (Illus.). 128p. (YA). (gr. 6 up). 1993. 18.95 (*0-531-05477-2*) Orchard Bks Watts.

Lewin, Ted. I Was a Teenage Professional Wrestler. LC 94-2132. 1994. 12.05 (*0-606-06488-5*, Pub. by Turtleback) Demco.

Lewin, Ted. Market! LC 95-7439. (Illus.). 48p. (J). (gr. k up). 1996. lib. bdg. 15.93 (*0-688-12162-4*) Lothrop.

— Market! LC 95-7439. (Illus.). 32p. (J). (ps up). 1996. 16.00 (*0-688-12161-6*) Lothrop.

***Lewin, Ted.** Market! LC 95-7439. (Illus.). 48p. (YA). (gr. k-3). 2000. mass mkt. 5.95 (*0-688-17520-1*, Wm Morrow) Morrow Avon.

Lewin, Ted. Nilo & the Tortoise. LC 98-27489. (J). 1999. write for info. (*0-590-73912-3*) Scholastic Inc.

— Nilo & the Tortoise. LC 98-27489. 40p. (J). (gr. k-3). 1999. 16.95 (*0-590-96004-0*) Scholastic Inc.

— The Reindeer People. LC 93-19252. (Illus.). 40p. (J). (gr. 1-4). 1994. mass mkt. 14.95 (*0-02-757390-7*, Mac Bks Young Read) S&S Childrens.

— Sacred River. LC 94-18370. (Illus.). 32p. (J). (gr. 1-5). 1995. 14.95 (*0-395-69846-4*, Clarion Bks) HM.

— Something Special. LC 98-40548. (J). 1999. 15.00 (*0-688-14109-9*) Lothrop.

— Storyteller. LC 97-15744. (Illus.). 40p. 1998. lib. bdg. 15.93 (*0-688-15179-5*) Lothrop.

— Storyteller. LC 97-15744. (Illus.). 40p. (J). (gr. k-4). 1998. 16.00 (*0-688-15178-7*) Lothrop.

***Lewin, Ted & Lewin, Betsy.** Gorilla Walk. LC 98-44727. (Illus.). 48p. (YA). (gr. 4 up). 1999. lib. bdg. 15.93 (*0-688-16510-9*) Lothrop.

— Gorilla Walk. LC 98-44727. 48p. (J). 1999. 16.00 (*0-688-16509-5*) Lothrop.

Lewin, Thomas H. A Manual of Tibetan Being: A Guide to the Colloquial Speech of Tibet in a Series of Progressive Exercises. (C). 1985. reprint ed. 18.50 (*0-8364-2411-5*, Pub. by Asian Educ Servs) S Asia.

Lewin, Vozar. Yo, Hungry Wolf! (J). 1992. 12.95 (*0-385-44580-6*) Doubleday.

Lewin, Walter H., et al, eds. High Energy Astrophysics: American & Soviet Perspectives/Proceedings from the U. S.-U. S. S. R. Workshop. 424p. 1991. pap. text 30.00 (*0-309-04334-4*) Natl Acad Pr.

— X-Ray Binaries. (Cambridge Astrophysics Ser.: No. 26). (Illus.). 674p. (C). 1995. text 100.00 (*0-521-41684-1*) Cambridge U Pr.

— X-Ray Binaries. (Illus.). 674p. 1997. pap. text 42.95 (*0-521-59934-2*) Cambridge U Pr.

Lewine, Carol F. The Sistine Chapel Walls & the Roman Liturgy. (Illus.). 192p. (C). 1993. 45.00 (*0-271-00792-3*) Pa St U Pr.

Lewine, D. A., ed. see Eighty-Eight Open Consortium Staff.

Lewine, Donald. POSIX Programmer's Guide. Dougherty, Dale, ed. LC 92-225989. (Computer Science Ser.). (Illus.). 640p. 1991. reprint ed. pap. 37.95 (*0-937175-73-0*) OReilly & Assocs.

Lewine, Harris, jt. auth. see Driggs, Frank.

Lewine, Harris, jt. auth. see Humphrey, Mark.

Lewine, Harris, jt. ed. see Okrent, Daniel.

***Lewine, J.** Bibliography of XVIII Century Art & Illustrated Books. 615p. 1998. reprint ed. 70.00 (*1-57898-103-4*) Martino Pubng.

Lewine, Richard & Simon, Alfred. Songs of the Theater: A Definitive Index to the Songs of the Musical Stage. LC 84-13068. 916p. 1984. 82.00 (*0-8242-0706-8*) Wilson.

Lewine, Richard R., jt. auth. see Bernheim, Kayla F.

***Lewing, Harold.** When God Changes His Mind. 60p. 1999. pap. text 9.95 (*1-893693-08-2*) Sweet Dreams.

Lewington, Anna. Antonio's Rain Forest. (Photo Bks.). (Illus.). 48p. (J). (ps-5). 1993. lib. bdg. 22.60 (*0-87614-749-X*, Carolrhoda) Lerner Pub.

— Antonio's Rainforest. (Illus.). 48p. (J). (ps-5). 1996. pap. 7.95 (*0-87614-992-1*) Lerner Pub.

— Mexico: A Study of an Economically Developing Country. (Illus.). 48p. (J). (gr. 3-5). 1996. lib. bdg. 24.26 (*0-8172-4528-6*) Raintree Steck-V.

— What Do We Know about Amazonian Indians? LC 93-1736. (What Do We Know about...? Ser.). (Illus.). 44p. (J). (gr. 3 up). 1993. pap. 8.95 (*0-87226-262-6*, 62626B, P Bedrick Books) NTC Contemp Pub Co.

— What Do We Know about Amazonian Indians? LC 93-1736. (What Do We Know about...? Ser.). (Illus.). 40p. (YA). (gr. 3 up). 1993. lib. bdg. 18.95 (*0-87226-367-3*, 63673B, P Bedrick Books) NTC Contemp Pub Co.

Lewington, Anna & Parker, Edward. People of the Rain Forests. LC 97-38626. (Wide World Ser.). 48p. (J). (gr. 4-7). 1998. 25.69 (*0-8172-5061-1*) Raintree Steck-V.

***Lewington, John Henry.** Ferret Husbandry Medicine & Surgery. (Illus.). 256p. 2000. pap. text 63.75 (*0-7506-4251-3*) Buttrwrth-Heinemann.

Lewington, Peter. No Right-of-Way: How Democracy Came to the Oil Patch. LC 90-20444. (Illus.). 290p. 1991. reprint ed. pap. 89.90 (*0-608-06875-6*, 206708300009) Bks Demand.

Lewington, R., jt. auth. see Tolman, T.

***Lewington, Richard.** How to Identify Butterflies: Britain & Europe. (Illus.). 150p. 2000. 22.95 (*0-00-220123-2*, Pub. by HarpC) Trafalgar.

Lewins, Frank. Bioethics for Health Professionals: An Introduction & Critical Approach. 160p. 1997. 59.95 (*0-7329-3045-6*, Pub. by Macmill Educ); pap. 24.95 (*0-7329-3046-4*, Pub. by Macmill Educ) Paul & Co Pubs.

— Social Science Methodology. 16.95 (*0-7329-1331-4*, Pub. by Macmill Educ) Paul & Co Pubs.

— Transsexualism in Society: A Sociology of Male-to-Female Transsexuals. 184p. 1995. 49.95 (*0-7329-3043-X*); pap. 24.95 (*0-7329-3044-8*) Paul & Co Pubs.

Lewins, Frank & Ly, Judith. The First Wave: The Settlement of Australia's First Vietnam Refugees. 124p. 1985. text 21.95 (*0-86861-461-0*) Routledge.

Lewins, J. & Becker, M. Advances in Nuclear Science & Technology, Vol. 20. (Illus.). 242p. (C). 1988. text 95.00 (*0-306-43082-7*, Kluwer Plenum) Kluwer Academic.

Lewins, J. & Becker, M. Advances in Nuclear Science & Technology, Vol. 21. LC 62-13039. (Illus.). 308p. (C). 1990. text 95.00 (*0-306-43614-0*, Kluwer Plenum) Kluwer Academic.

Lewins, J. & Becker, M. Advances in Nuclear Science & Technology, Vol. 22. (Illus.). 246p. (C). 1992. text 95.00 (*0-306-44094-6*, Kluwer Plenum) Kluwer Academic.

Lewins, J. & Becker, M. Advances in Nuclear Science & Technology, Vol. 23. (Illus.). 212p. (C). 1996. text 102.00 (*0-306-45184-0*, Kluwer Plenum) Kluwer Academic.

— Advances in Nuclear Science & Technology, Vol. 24. (Illus.). 332p. (C). 1997. 110.00 (*0-306-45515-3*, Kluwer Plenum) Kluwer Academic.

Lewins, J. & Becker, M. Advances in Nuclear Science & Technology, Vol. 25. 302p. (C). 1997. 110.00 (*0-306-45604-4*, Plenum Trade) Perseus Pubng.

— Advances in Nuclear Science & Technology, Vol. 26. 172p. 1999. write for info. (*0-306-46110-2*, Kluwer Plenum) Kluwer Academic.

Lewins, Jeffery D. Importance of the Adjoint Function: Physical Basis of Variational & Perturbation Theory in Transport & Diffusion Problems. LC 65-142230. 1965. 91.00 (*0-08-013836-5*, Pub. by Pergamon Repr) Franklin.

— Nuclear Reactor Kinetics & Control. LC 77-8107. 1978. 129.00 (*0-08-021682-X*, Pub. by Pergamon Repr) Franklin.

Lewins, Jeffery D., ed. Teaching Thermodynamics. 538p. 1986. 125.00 (*0-306-42207-7*, Plenum Trade) Perseus Pubng.

Lewins, Jeffery D. & Becker, Martin, eds. Advances in Nuclear Science & Technology, Vol. 14: Sensitivity & Uncertainty Analysis of Reactor Performance Paramaters. LC 82-3654. 388p. 1982. 105.00 (*0-306-40994-1*, Plenum Trade) Perseus Pubng.

— Advances in Nuclear Science & Technology, Vol. 15. LC 62-13039. 418p. 1983. 105.00 (*0-306-41392-2*, Plenum Trade) Perseus Pubng.

— Advances in Nuclear Science & Technology, Vol. 16. LC 62-13039. 596p. 1983. 135.00 (*0-306-41486-4*, Plenum Trade) Perseus Pubng.

— Advances in Nuclear Science & Technology, Vol. 17: Simulators for Nuclear Power. LC 85-31170. 244p. 1986. 75.00 (*0-306-42234-4*, Plenum Trade) Perseus Pubng.

— Advances in Nuclear Science & Technology, Vol. 18. LC 62-13059. 434p. 1987. 105.00 (*0-306-42289-1*, Plenum Trade) Perseus Pubng.

— Advances in Nuclear Science & Technology, Vol. 19: Festschrift in Honor of Eugene Wigner. LC 62-13039. 508p. 1987. 120.00 (*0-306-42543-2*, Plenum Trade) Perseus Pubng.

Lewinska, Pelagia. Twenty Months in Auschwitz. Teichner, Albert, tr. 1968. 4.95 (*0-8184-0090-0*) Carol Pub Group.

Lewinski, John S. Developer's Guide to Computer Game Design. LC 99-36673. 1999. pap. 49.95 (*1-55622-667-5*) Wordware Pub.

***Lewinski, John Scott.** The Screenwriter's Guide to Agents & Managers. 256p. 2000. pap. 18.95 (*1-58115-079-2*, Pub. by Allworth Pr) Watsn-Guptill.

Lewinski, Marcel. Great Decisions 1997. Hoepli-Phalon, Nancy, ed. (Illus.). 48p. 1997. pap. text, teacher ed. 11.95 (*0-87124-174-9*) Foreign Policy.

— Great Decisions Teacher's Guide, 1999. Rohan, Karen M., ed. (Illus.). 44p. 1999. pap. text, teacher ed. 19.00 (*0-87124-188-9*) Foreign Policy.

— Great Decisions Teacher's Guide 1996. Hoepli-Phalon, Nancy L. & Foreign Policy Association Staff, eds. LC 58-59828. (Illus.). 60p. 1996. pap., teacher ed. 11.95 (*0-87124-167-6*) Foreign Policy.

Lewinski, Marcel, jt. auth. see Foreign Policy Association Staff.

Lewinski, Ron. Worship: A Parish Planning Workbook. (Follow Me! Ser.). 1998. pap. 9.95 (*1-881307-13-1*, B7131) Natl Pastoral LC.

Lewinski, Ronald J. Guide for Sponsors. 3rd ed. Tufano, Victoria M., ed. LC 93-30922. 54p. 1993. pap. 5.00 (*1-56854-007-8*, GSPON3) Liturgy Tr Pubns.

— Making Parish Policy: A Workbook on Sacramental Policies. 264p. 1996. pap. 19.00 (*1-56854-116-3*, PARPOL) Liturgy Tr Pubns.

— El Privilegio de Ser Padrino o Madrina: Guia para los Patrocinadores del Catecumenado. Rodriguez, Pedro, tr. from ENG. (SPA.). 68p. 1990. pap. 4.50 (*0-929650-25-5*, SGSPON) Liturgy Tr Pubns.

— Welcoming the New Catholic. 3rd rev. ed. LC 93-50845. (Font & Table Ser.). 98p. 1994. pap. 10.00 (*1-56854-013-2*, WNEW/3) Liturgy Tr Pubns.

L

Lewinski, T. & Telega, J. J. Plates, Laminates & Shells Asymptotic Analysis & Homogenization. LC 99-40193. 450p. 1999. text 58.00 (981-02-3206-3) World Scientific Pub.

Lewinsky, Monica S., et al. Open City Vol. 6: The Only Woman He's Ever Left. Beller, Thomas & Pinchdeck, Daniel, eds. 220p. 1998. pap. 8.00 (1-890447-17-X, 700002) Open City Bks.

Lewinsohn, Peter M., et al. Control Your Depression. 1978. 12.95 (0-13-171702-2, Spectrum IN) Macmillan Gen Ref.

— Control Your Depression. 256p. 1992. pap. 11.00 (0-671-76242-7, Fireside) S&S Trade Pap.

Lewinstein, Bruce, ed. When Science Meets the Public. 164p. 1992. 14.00 (0-87168-440-3, 92-06S) AAAS.

Lewinter, Martin M., et al, eds. Cardiac Energetics: From Emax to Pressure-Volume Area. (Developments in Cardiovascular Medicine Ser.: Vol. 177). 256p. (C). 1995. text 141.50 (0-7923-3721-2) Kluwer Academic.

Lewinter, Martin M., jt. auth. see Gaasch, William.

Lewinter, Renee. Digital Photography. 1997. pap. 45.00 (1-56830-330-0) Hayden.

LeWinter, Renee & Nolan, Michael J. Fine Art Photoshop: Lessons in Digital Drawing & Painting. LC 97-81026. 220p. 1997. pap. 39.99 (1-56205-829-0) New Riders Pub.

LeWinter, Renee, jt. auth. see Schulman, Ted.

Lewinter-Suskind, Leslie, jt. auth. see Suskind, Robert M.

Lewinter-Suskind, Leslie, jt. ed. see Suskind, Robert M.

Lewis. After Atheism. LC 99-15906. 1999. text 59.95 (0-312-22692-6) St Martin.

— Australia, Vol. 1. Date not set. 17.95 (0-914629-63-8) St Martin.

***Lewis.** Automotive Engine Machining. (C). 2001. pap. 38.25 (0-7668-1576-5) Delmar.

— Automotive Machining & Engine Repair. (C). 2000. pap. 36.00 (0-7668-1578-1) Delmar.

Lewis. Basic Ekg Rhythm Ident/Analysis. (Allied Health Ser.). (C). 2000. pap. text 25.95 (0-7668-0522-0) Delmar.

— Basis Lotus 123 4.0 Windows. (C). 1995. pap. text. write for info. (0-201-83712-9) Addison-Wesley.

— Basis Wordperfect 6.0 Windows. (C). 1995. pap. text. write for info. (0-201-83709-9) Addison-Wesley.

— Beginnings of Life. 2nd ed. 1994. teacher ed. 20.62 (0-697-13662-0) McGraw.

— Beginnings of Life. 2nd ed. 1994. 388.75 (0-697-13664-7, WCB McGr Hill) McGrw-H Hghr Educ.

— Bid for the Moon. 1996. pap. write for info. (0-08-018301-8, Pergamon Pr) Elsevier.

— Biology: Concepts & Implications. Date not set. pap. text 34.00 (0-697-12943-8) McGraw.

— Brand New Moon. 1996. pap. write for info. (0-08-019753-1, Pergamon Pr) Elsevier.

— Carpentry. 2nd ed. 48p. 1995. pap. text, teacher ed. 16.95 (0-8273-7029-6) Delmar.

— Carpentry. 2nd ed. (Construction & Building Trades Ser.). 1995. text, teacher ed. 39.95 (0-8273-7116-0) Delmar.

***Lewis.** Carpentry Level 2: Textnotes. (C). 2000. text 20.25 (0-7668-1782-2) Delmar.

— Cases Hospitality Strategy Tm. 1998. pap. text. write for info. (0-471-24802-9) Wiley.

— Cisco Switched Internetworks. 500p. 1999. pap. 55.00 (0-07-134646-5) McGraw.

— Clinical Anatomy & Physiology of the Swallow Mechanism. 2000. pap. 49.95 (1-56593-967-0) Singular Publishing.

Lewis. Close Ups of the Past, Vol. 7. (C). 2000. pap. text 23.50 (0-15-505398-1) Harcourt Coll Pubs.

— Comprehensive Chemical Contaminants. 1996. 650.00 (0-442-02290-5, VNR) Wiley.

— Data Structures & Their Algorithms. 2nd ed. (C). 1998. text. write for info. (0-673-99751-0) Addison-Wesley.

— The Economics of Marketing. (General Business & Business Education Ser.). 1996. pap. 16.00 (0-8273-6607-8) Delmar.

— Encyclopedia of Religious Fundamentalism & Modernism in America. 1996. 80.00 (0-13-061383-5) P-H.

— English Thru Computers Bk 2. 1998. 16.50 (84-7615-677-4) McGraw.

— Ethnomedicine & Chemistry of South American Plants, Vol. 1. (Illus.). 640p. 1997. text. write for info. (0-412-71310-1, Chap & Hall NY) Chapman & Hall.

— Ethnomedicine & Chemistry of South American Plants, Vol. 2. (Illus.). 640p. 1997. text. write for info. (0-412-71320-9, Chap & Hall NY) Chapman & Hall.

— Ethnomedicine & Chemistry of South American Plants, Vol. 3. (Illus.). 640p. 1997. text. write for info. (0-412-71330-6, Chap & Hall NY) Chapman & Hall.

— Exercise Tiger. 1991. per. 12.95 (0-13-292897-3) P-H.

— Facility Manager's Portable Handbook. LC 99-33971. 441p. 1999. 54.95 (0-07-135121-3) McGraw.

***Lewis.** Hackh's Chemical Dictionary. 6th ed. 2001. 99.95 (0-07-135889-7) McGraw.

Lewis. Human Genetics. 1994. pap. text, teacher ed. 8.12 (0-697-16199-4) McGraw.

— Human Genetics. 1993. 3.43 (0-697-23710-9, WCB McGr Hill) McGrw-H Hghr Educ.

— Human Genetics. 3rd ed. 1998. boxed set 58.50 (0-07-229261-X) McGraw.

— Human Genetics. 3rd ed. LC 98-18209. 1998. 47.50 (0-697-42296-8, WCB McGr Hill) McGrw-H Hghr Educ.

— Human Genetics. 4th ed. 480p. 2000. 74.69 (0-07-231898-8) McGraw.

— Human Genetics. 4th ed. 2000. 56.00 (0-07-231897-X) McGraw.

Lewis. IM OLP Mentor Guide. 96p. 1997. pap. text 44.95 (0-7506-3677-7) Buttrwrth-Heinemann.

— IM OLP User Guide. 100p. 1997. pap. text 44.95 (0-7506-3676-9) Buttrwrth-Heinemann.

Lewis. Index of Reviews in Organic Chemistry, 1972. 1989. suppl. ed. 11.00 (0-85186-519-4) CRC Pr.

— Index of Reviews in Organic Chemistry, 1973. 1989. suppl. ed. 11.00 (0-85186-529-1) CRC Pr.

— Introduction to Sociology. LC 95-131916. 1995. pap. 10.50 (0-314-04906-1) West Pub.

— Language Therapy. 300p. 1990. 64.50 (1-56593-542-X, 0215) Singular Publishing.

— Life. 3rd ed. 1999. text 50.00 (0-07-235234-5) McGraw.

— Life. 4th ed. 2001. pap. 62.25 (0-07-027134-8) McGraw.

***Lewis.** Life: Ready Notes. 3rd ed. 1999. 9.06 (0-07-234545-4) McGraw.

Lewis. Life & Study Guide. 3rd ed. 1998. text 62.25 (0-07-561735-8) McGraw.

Lewis. Marketing Leadership Hospitali. 2nd ed. 1997. pap. text. write for info. (0-471-28647-8) Wiley.

Lewis. Mental Arithmetic & Problem Solving 5. Date not set. pap. text. write for info. (0-582-87525-0, Pub. by Addison-Wesley) Longman.

— Mental Arithmetic & Problem Solving 6. Date not set. pap. text. write for info. (0-582-87526-9, Pub. by Addison-Wesley) Longman.

— Microsoft Works 3.0 for DOS+ (C). 1994. pap. text 27.00 (0-03-004804-4) Harcourt Coll Pubs.

— Novel Idea. 1986. 13.12 (0-07-040717-7) McGraw.

— On Call: Pediatrics. (C). 1998. text. write for info. (0-8089-2096-0, Grune & Strat) Harcrt Hlth Sci Grp.

— Organic Chemistry. 2nd ed. 2000. 17.74 (0-697-14370-8) McGraw.

— Photojournalism. 2nd ed. 1994. teacher ed. 11.87 (0-697-14630-8, WCB McGr Hill) McGrw-H Hghr Educ.

— The Power of Art. (C). 1994. pap. text, teacher ed., suppl. ed. 33.75 (0-15-501214-2) Harcourt Coll Pubs.

— Primarily Speaking Vol. 3: Reverence/Articles of One Faith. 1989. pap. 7.95 (0-88494-718-1) Bookcraft Inc.

— The Project Manager's Desk Reference: A Comprehensive Guide to Project Planning, Evaluation & Control. 2nd ed. LC 99-32834. 546p. 1999. 70.00 (0-07-134750-X) McGraw.

— The Reckoning. large type ed. LC 98-42039. 1999. 24.95 (0-7862-1691-3) Thorndike Pr.

— Rhythm Analysis Using 12-Lead ECG. LC 99-44880. (Allied Health Ser.). 275p. (C). 2000. pap. text 31.95 (0-7668-0524-7) Delmar.

Lewis. Roger Hilton. 61.95 (1-84014-673-7) Ashgate Pub Co.

— School Nursing. 2nd ed. 2001. pap. text. write for info. (0-7216-8521-8, W B Saunders Co) Harcrt Hlth Sci Grp.

Lewis. Sensible ECG Analysis. LC 99-29634. (Allied Health Ser.). (C). 1999. pap. text 41.95 (0-7668-0520-4) Delmar.

***Lewis.** Special Education Technology: Practical Applications. 2nd ed. (Education Ser.). 2001. 48.00 (0-534-52157-6) Wadsworth Pub.

Lewis. Tips for Teaching Sociology. 2nd ed. (Sociology - Intro Level Ser.). 1997. pap. 10.50 (0-534-54513-0) Wadsworth Pub.

— Trial of Mary Queen of Scots. LC 98-86159. (Bedford Series in History & Culture). 138p. 1998. pap. text 11.95 (0-312-15439-9) St Martin.

— The Trial of Mary Queen of Scots: Sixteenth Century Crisis of Female Sovereignty. LC 98-86159. 192p. 1998. text 39.95 (0-312-21815-X) St Martin.

Lewis & Barton. A&I Review General Patholgy. 4th ed. 1999. pap. text 34.95 (0-8385-0396-9) Appleton & Lange.

Lewis & Brod. Making Benefit-Cost Analysis Work. 59.95 (1-85972-247-4) Ashgate Pub Co.

Lewis & Charnock. Index of Reviews in Organic Chemistry, 1979. 1989. suppl. ed. 18.00 (0-85186-820-7) CRC Pr.

Lewis & Dana. Substance Abuse Counseling. 3rd ed. (Counseling Ser.). 2001. 27.00 (0-534-36428-4) Brooks-Cole.

Lewis & Denenberg, Larry. Data Structure & Algorithm. (C). 1991. pap. text, teacher ed. 9.38 (0-673-49381-4) Addison-Wesley Educ.

Lewis & Emory. The United States Conquest of California: An Original Anthology. Cortes, Carlos E., ed. LC 76-7303. (Chicano Heritage Ser.). (Illus.). 1977. 57.95 (0-405-09542-2) Ayer.

Lewis & Gaspar. Carpentry. 3rd ed. LC 99-57913. (Construction/Building Trades Ser.). (C). 2000. pap. 64.95 (0-7668-1081-X); pap., wbk. ed. 18.00 (0-7668-1082-8) Delmar.

Lewis & Goodman. Management: Challenges in the 21st Century. 3rd ed. (SWC-Management Ser.). 2000. pap. 46.75 (0-324-00993-3); pap., student ed. 16.00 (0-324-01200-4) Thomson Learn.

— Management: Challenges in 21st Century. 2nd ed. LC 97-20809. (SWC-Management Ser.). 1997. pap. 76.95 (0-538-87899-1) S-W Pub.

Lewis & Goodman. Management, Challenges in the 21st Century: Insights : Readings in Small Business Management. 2nd ed. (SWC-Management Ser.). 1997. pap. 14.50 (0-538-88036-8) Sth-Wstrn College.

— Student Notetaking Guide for Management: Challenges in the 21st Century. 2nd ed. (SWC-Management Ser.). 1997. pap. 14.50 (0-538-88035-X) Sth-Wstrn College.

Lewis & Mitchell. Children's Early Understanding of Mind: Origins & Development. 1997. pap. 24.95 (0-86377-352-4) L Erlbaum Assocs.

Lewis & Ray, Mary F. Exploring Professional Cooking. 3rd rev. ed. (YA). (gr. 9-12). 1988. teacher ed. 37.01 (0-02-667980-9); student ed. 7.27 (0-02-667960-4) Glencoe.

***Lewis & Sargeant.** Essentials of Employment Law 2000. 464p. 2000. pap. 59.95 (0-8464-5171-9) Beekman Pubs.

Lewis & Sines, eds. Fracture Mechanics Vol. 1: Fourteenth Symposium: Theory & Analysis - STP 791. 610p. 1983. 75.00 (0-8031-0728-5, \) ASTM.

— Fracture Mechanics: Fourteenth Symposium - STP 791, 2 vols., Set. 1983. 135.00 (0-8031-0730-7, STP791) ASTM.

Lewis & Walla. Policies into Practice. 1984. text 72.95 (0-435-83488-6); text 35.95 (0-435-83489-4) Ashgate Pub Co.

Lewis & Winningham. Medical-Surgical Nursing: Critical Thinking in Medical-Surgical Settings. 1995. text 93.00 (0-8151-9672-5, 29185) Mosby Inc.

— Medical-Surgical Nursing: Critical Thinking in Medical-Surgical Settings, 2 vols. 1996. text 99.00 (0-8151-4496-2, 30630) Mosby Inc.

Lewis, et al. Management of Human Services Programs. 2nd ed. LC 90-46530. 321p. (C). 1990. mass mkt. 41.00 (0-534-13074-7) Brooks-Cole.

— Management of Human Services Programs. 3rd ed. 2000. pap. text 48.00 (0-534-36886-7) Thomson Learn.

— Manual of Psychosocial Nursing Interventions: Promoting Mental Health in Medical-Surgical Settings. 288p. 1989. text 44.00 (0-7216-5763-X, W B Saunders Co) Harcrt Hlth Sci Grp.

— Revised Sg:mgt:challenges 21stcentury. 2nd rev. ed. (SWC-Management). 1998. mass mkt. 15.00 (0-324-00157-6) S-W Pub.

***Lewis, et al.** Web Tutor on Webct to Accompany Management: Challenges in 21st Century. 3rd ed. 2000. pap. 19.00 (0-324-06452-7) Sth-Wstrn College.

Lewis, jt. auth. see Fifield.

Lewis, jt. auth. see Meidan.

Lewis, jt. auth. see Morrison.

Lewis, jt. auth. see Peterson.

Lewis, jt. auth. see Sanders.

Lewis, jt. auth. see Saunders.

Lewis, Agnes Smith, jt. auth. see Gibson, Margaret Dunlop.

Lewis, Jeremy. Cyril Connoly: A Life. LC 97-179762. 675p. 1998. 50.00 (0-224-03710-2, Pub. by Jonathan Cape) Trafalgar.

Lewis, Jewel. Just Imagine: A Past Life with John Lennon? LC 96-28822. 129p. 1995. pap. 12.95 (1-55056-354-8) Toad Hall PA.

***Lewis, Joan Germann.** A Nature Journal. (Illus.). 208p. (C). 2000. 30.00 (0-9677024-0-2) J G Lewis.

Lewis, Omar. The Wonderful World of Myat, Vol. 1. large type ed. (Illus.). 36p. (J). (gr. 1-3). 1998. pap. 5.95 (0-9667858-0-0) Brkthrough Images.

Lewis (Jones), Jel D. The Perfect Lady. LC 95-148997. 200p. 1994. pap. 12.95 (0-9639917-0-1) Writers Unltd.

Lewis, A., jt. ed. see Dauben, Joseph W.

Lewis, A. C. Nahanni Remembered, Vol. 2. (Northwest Passage Ser.). (Illus.). 312p. (Orig.). 1997. pap. 19.95 (1-896300-18-9) NeWest Pubs.

Lewis, A. D. & Ibbetson, D. J., eds. The Roman Law Tradition. 248p. (C). 1994. text 59.95 (0-521-44199-4) Cambridge U Pr.

Lewis, A. D., jt. ed. see Chen, Wai-Fah.

Lewis, A. D., jt. ed. see Foxhall, L.

Lewis, A. D., jt. ed. see Freeman, Michael D.

Lewis, A. F. Graphic Arts Blue Book: 1998-1999 Texas-Central Edition. Vanstock, Marguerite, ed. 800p. 1998. pap. text 85.00 (0-910880-88-3) Lewis.

— Graphic Arts Blue Book, 1998-99 Northeastern: 1998 Northeast Edition. 700p. 1998. pap. text 85.00 (0-910880-89-1) Lewis.

Lewis, A. F., & Company Staff. Graphic Arts Blue Book: 1997-98 Delaware Valley-Ohio Edition. 600p. 1998. pap. text 85.00 (0-910880-81-6) Lewis.

— Graphic Arts Blue Book Texas-Central Edition: 1997-98 Southeastern Edition. 800p. 1998. pap. text 85.00 (0-910880-82-4) Lewis.

Lewis, A. H. Critical History of Sunday Legislation from 321 to 1888 A.D. LC 97-73087. 1997. reprint ed. 75.00 (1-57588-385-6, 311410) W S Hein.

Lewis, A. H., jt. auth. see MacEwen, William A.

Lewis, A. J. Zinzendorf the Ecumenical Pioneer. LC 63-7179. 208p. 1998. reprint ed. pap. 10.00 (1-878422-39-1) Moravian Ch in Amer.

Lewis, A. J., jt. auth. see Henderson, F. M.

Lewis, A. J., tr. see Romen, A. S.

Lewis, A. Rodger. Battle for Bali: The Story of Rodger & Lelia Lewis. (Jaffray Collection). 213p. pap. 9.99 (0-87509-827-4) Chr Pubns.

***Lewis, A. S. & Footitt, R. J.** Canning of Fish & Meat. 310p. 1998. 145.00 (0-8342-1291-9) Aspen Pub.

Lewis, A. S., jt. auth. see Borwein, J. J.

Lewis, Adam. Salmon of the Pacific. LC 94-16591. (Illus.). 96p. (Orig.). 1994. pap. 14.95 (1-57061-016-9) Sasquatch Bks.

Lewis, Adele, jt. auth. see Grappo, Gary J.

Lewis, Adele, jt. auth. see Wilson, Robert F.

Lewis, Adele B. & Corwin, Gene. Better Resumes for Sales & Marketing Personnel. 2nd ed. LC 95-37704. 180p. 1996. pap. 12.95 (0-8120-9597-9) Barron.

Lewis, Adele B. & Saltman, David A. Better Resumes for Attorneys & Paralegals. 1986. pap. 10.95 (0-8120-3649-2) Barron.

Lewis, Adele B., jt. auth. see Schuman, Nancy.

Lewis, Adrian & Pomeroy, Derek. A Bird Atlas of Kenya. 650p. 1988. 141.00 (90-6191-716-6, Pub. by A A Balkema) Ashgate Pub Co.

Lewis Advertising, Inc. Staff. The American Dream. LC 98-174515. (Illus.). 80p. 1997. per. 29.00 (0-9659039-0-7) Orig Log Cabin.

Lewis, A.F. & Co. Staff (X). Graphic Arts Blue Book: 1999 Midwestern Edition. 900p. 1999. pap. text 85.00 (0-910880-93-X) Lewis.

Lewis, Alan, et al, eds. New Perspectives in Anti-Inflammatory Therapies. LC 86-43103. (Advances in Inflammation Research Ser.: Vol. 12). 352p. 1988. reprint ed. pap. 109.20 (0-608-00434-0, 206114900007) Bks Demand.

Lewis, Alan, et al. The New Economic Mind: The Social Psychology of Economic Behavior. LC 94-31583. 332p. 1995. pap. 42.00 (0-7450-1325-2, Pub. by Wheatsheaf Bks) P-H.

Lewis, Alan E. Apocalypse Soon? Christian Responsibility & the Book of Revelation. 1987. 50.00 (0-7855-2137-2, Pub. by Wild Goose Pubns) St Mut.

Lewis, Alan E., ed. Motherhood of God, Report of the Woman's Guild/Panel on Doctrine Study Group. 80p. 1984. pap. 2.95 (0-7152-0577-3) Outlook.

Lewis, Alan E., jt. auth. see Clouatre, Dallas.

Lewis, Alan J. & Furst, Daniel E., eds. Nonsteroidal Anti-Inflammatory Drugs: Mechanisms & Clinical Uses. 2nd ed. LC 93-34984. (Illus.). 480p. 1993. text 240.00 (0-8247-8856-7) Dekker.

***Lewis, Alan L.** Option Valuation under Stochastic Volatility: With Mathematica Code. LC 99-91935. (Illus.). 360p. (C). 2000. pap. 97.50 (0-9676372-0-1) Finance Pr.

Lewis, Alaric. Prayerstarters in Times of Pain or Illness. LC 99-72387. (Prayerstarters Ser.). 72p. 1999. pap. 4.95 (0-87029-327-3, 20110) Abbey.

Lewis, Albert B. Danger Insurance Fraud in Progress: How to Avoid Becoming A Victim. LC 87-71527. 381p. (Orig.). 1987. pap. text, spiral bd. 80.00 (0-939713-02-0) Carriage House.

— Gotcha! Swindles, Scams, Cons & Rip-Offs. (Illus.). 177p. 1998. pap. 12.00 (0-9665965-0-1) Papillon Pubg.

— A Guide to Understanding & Using the Property & Casualty Statutory Statements for Banks, Investors & Brokers. LC 86-72094. (Orig.). 1987. pap. 15.00 (0-939713-00-4) Carriage House.

Lewis, Albert C. Albert Einstein, 1879-1955: A Centenary Exhibit. (Illus.). 40p. 1979. pap. 7.50 (0-87959-090-4) U of Tex H Ransom Ctr.

Lewis, Albert C., intro. Albert Einstein: Four Commemorative Lectures. 1979. 10.00 (0-87959-093-9) U of Tex H Ransom Ctr.

Lewis, Albert C., jt. auth. see Griffin, Nicholas.

Lewis, Albert C., ed. see Russell, Bertrand.

Lewis, Albert D., Jr. The Great Spiritual War, 7 vols. Incl. Vol. 7. Great Spiritual War: My Personal Testimony.Tr. of 7. (Illus.). 106p. (Orig.). 1997. pap. 8.99 (0-9633356-7-7); Vol. 1. What Is It? (Illus.). 64p. (Orig.). 1997. pap. 4.99 (0-9633356-1-8); Vol. 2. Our Real Foe(s) - Who Are They? (Illus.). 30p. (Orig.). 1997. pap. 2.99 (0-9633356-2-6); Vol. 3. Idol Worship. (Illus.). 26p. (Orig.). 1997. pap. 2.99 (0-9633356-3-4); Vol. 4. AIDS & Abortion. (Illus.). 60p. (Orig.). 1997. pap. 6.99 (0-9633356-4-2); Vol. 5. The Great Tribulation. (Illus.). 30p. (Orig.). 1997. pap. 2.99 (0-9633356-5-0); Vol. 6. Suicide; Forgiveness; Repentance: The Weapons of Our Warfare & a Letter to the President. (Illus.). 38p. (Orig.). 1997. pap. 4.99 (0-9633356-6-9); 33.99 (0-9633356-9-3) Harvest Time.

Lewis, Alcinda C., jt. ed. see Brooklyn Botanic Garden Botanists.

Lewis, Alfred. Pak: Using American Law Books. 4th ed. 304p. (C). 1995. pap. text 39.95 (0-7872-0734-9, 41073401) Kendall-Hunt.

Lewis, Alfred & Pescetto, Gioia, eds. Europe & U. S. Banking in the 1990s. (Illus.). 224p. 1996. text 49.95 (0-12-446640-0) Acad Pr.

Lewis, Alfred, jt. ed. see Ullmann, Arieh A.

***Lewis, Alfred A.** Ladies & Not So Gentle Women: Elisabeth Marbury, Anne Morgan, Elsie de Wolfe, Anne Vanderbilt & Their Times. LC 99-55217. 688p. 2000. 39.95 (0-670-85810-2, Viking) Viking Penguin.

Lewis, Alfred H. Apaches of New York. LC 73-37277. (Short Story Index Reprint Ser.). 1977. reprint ed. 23.95 (0-8369-4088-1) Ayer.

— The Boss. LC 67-29272. (Americans in Fiction Ser.). reprint ed. pap. text 6.95 (0-89197-684-1); reprint ed. lib. bdg. 22.00 (0-8398-1157-8) Irvington.

— Faro Nell & Her Friends: Wolfville Stories. LC 73-163042. (Short Story Index Reprint Ser.). (Illus.). 1977. reprint ed. 24.95 (0-8369-3956-5) Ayer.

— Sandburrs. LC 72-90585. (Short Story Index Reprint Ser.). (Illus.). 1977. 21.95 (0-8369-3068-1) Ayer.

— Sandburrs. LC 72-104512. (Illus.). 318p. reprint ed. lib. bdg. 21.00 (0-8398-1158-6) Irvington.

— Sandburrs. 318p. (C). 1986. reprint ed. pap. text 7.95 (0-8290-2029-2) Irvington.

— Wolfville. 1998. mass mkt. 4.99 (0-8125-8045-1, Pub. by Tor Bks) St Martin.

— Wolfville. 1972. reprint ed. lib. bdg. 32.00 (0-8422-8090-1) Irvington.

— Wolfville. 1986. reprint ed. pap. text 11.95 (0-8290-1957-X) Irvington.

Lewis, Alfred H., ed. Old Wolfville: Chapters from the Fiction of Alfred Henry Lewis. LC 68-13363. (Illus.). 274p. reprint ed. pap. 85.00 (0-608-14200-X, 202171500023) Bks Demand.

Lewis, Alfred J. Using American Law Books: Including Online & CD-ROM Services. 4th ed. LC 95-77139. 224p. 1995. pap. 26.88 (0-7872-0735-7) Kendall-Hunt.

— Using California Law Books. 100p. (C). 1994. pap. text, per. 17.95 (0-8403-2982-2) Kendall-Hunt.

Lewis, Alison. Subverting Patriarchy. 300p. 1995. 59.50 (0-85496-322-7) Berg Pubs.

***Lewis, Allen & Westcott, Rich.** No-Hitters: The 223 Games, 1893-1998. LC 99-59282. (Illus.). 424p. 2000. lib. bdg. 45.00 (0-7864-0722-0) McFarland & Co.

Lewis, Allison, et al. La Ensenanza de la Sexualidad Humana en las Escuelas: Un Manual para el Educador. Jaimes, Rene, ed.Tr. of Teaching Human Sexuality in Caribbean Schools-a Teacher's Handbook. (SPA., Illus.). 236p. (Orig.). 1985. write for info. (*0-916683-11-7*) Intl Plan Parent.

— Teaching Human Sexuality in Caribbean Schools: A Teachers Handbook. Jaimes, Rene, ed. (Illus.). 306p. (Orig.). pap. 15.00 (*0-916683-07-9*) Intl Plan Parent.

***Lewis, Allyson.** The Million Dollar Car & $250,000 Pizza: How Every Dollar You Save Builds Your Financial Future. LC 99-54458. (Illus.). 322p. 2000. pap. 18.95 (*0-7931-3593-1*) Dearborn.

Lewis, Alonzo & Newhall, James R. History of Lynn, Including Lynnfield, Saugus, Swampscott & Nahant. rev. ed. (Illus.). 620p. 1989. reprint ed. lib. bdg. 65.00 (*0-8328-0840-7*, MA0072) Higginson Bk Co.

***Lewis, Alvin D.** Cultural Diversity in Sexual Abuser Treatment: Issues & Approaches. Bear, Euan, ed. LC 98-35773. 256p. 1999. 22.00 (*1-884444-49-0*, WP066) Safer Soc.

Lewis, Amanda. Lettering: Make Your Own Cards, Signs, Gifts & More. (Kids Can Crafts Ser.). (Illus.). 48p. (J). 1996. 16.99 (*1-55074-312-0*) Kids Can Pr.

Lewis, Amanda. Lettering: Make Your Own Cards, Signs, Gifts & More. unabridged ed. (Kids Can Crafts Ser.). (Illus.). 48p. (J). (gr. 3 up). 1997. pap. 5.95 (*1-55074-232-9*, Pub. by Kids Can Pr) Genl Dist Srvs.

— Writing: A Fact & Fun Book. unabridged ed. (Illus.). 96p. (J). (gr. 3-8). 1992. pap. 9.95 (*1-55074-052-0*, Pub. by Kids Can Pr) Genl Dist Srvs.

Lewis, Amanda & Melo, Esperanca. Making Memory Books. LC 99-63007. (Kids Can Do It Ser.). 40p. (J). (gr. 3-7). 1999. 5.95 (*1-55074-567-0*) Kids Can Pr.

Lewis, Amanda & Wynne-Jones, Tim. Rosie Backstage. unabridged ed. (Illus.). 96p. (J). (gr. 3-7). 1994. 21.95 (*1-55074-209-4*, Pub. by Kids Can Pr) Genl Dist Srvs.

— Rosie Backstage. unabridged ed. (Illus.). 96p. (J). (gr. 3-7). 1997. pap. 10.95 (*1-55074-148-9*, Pub. by Kids Can Pr) Genl Dist Srvs.

Lewis, Amy, jt. ed. see Sader, Marion.

Lewis, Andrew. The Stone Dragon. (Illus.). 17p. (J). (ps-5). 1996. spiral bd. write for info. (*0-9659217-0-0*) High Popples.

Lewis, Andrew, ed. Current Legal Problems Vol. 48, Pt. 1: Annual Review. 242p. 1995. pap. text 38.00 (*0-19-826041-5*) OUP.

Lewis, Andrew, ed. Current Legal Problems, 1996 Vol. 49, Pt. 1: Annual Review. 232p. 1996. pap. text 60.00 (*0-19-826279-5*) OUP.

Lewis, Andrew, jt. ed. see Freeman, Michael.

Lewis, Andrew B., jt. ed. see Lassiter, Matthew D.

Lewis, Andrew D. E., jt. ed. see Freeman, Michael.

Lewis, Andrew M., jt. ed. see Brown, Fred.

Lewis, Andrew W. Royal Succession in Capetian France: Studies on Familial Order & the State. LC 81-6360. (Historical Studies: No. 100). (Illus.). 374p. 1982. 37.00 (*0-674-77985-1*) HUP.

Lewis, Ann. Chairing Child Protection Conferences: An Exploration of Role & Attitude. 144p. 1994. 61.95 (*1-85628-691-6*, Pub. by Avebry) Ashgate Pub Co.

— Children's Understanding of Disability. LC 94-34162. 224p. (C). 1995. pap. 24.99 (*0-415-10132-8*, B4018) Routledge.

— Confederate Jasmine & the Fat Tuesday Tree: A Poetic Herbarium. LC 96-44576. 1997. 22.95 (*0-8118-1308-8*) Chronicle Bks.

Lewis, Ann E. Reuniting Refugee Families: An Attorney's Guide to Law & Procedure. Marks, Stephanie & Black, George, eds. 200p. (Orig.). 1994. pap. text 25.00 (*0-934143-70-6*) Lawyers Comm Human.

Lewis, Ann E., ed. Fifty Georgia Stories. LC 87-26193. (Illus.). 320p. 1987. pap. 14.95 (*0-87797-270-2*) Cherokee.

***Lewis, Ann G.** The Minnesota Guide. LC 99-31529. (Illus.). 320p. 1999. pap. 21.95 (*1-55591-362-8*) Fulcrum Pub.

Lewis, Anna M. The Adventures of Beulah & Lora: Life on the Farm in the Early 1900's. Lewis, Michael R., ed. & intro. by. (Illus.). 165p. (J). 1990. 14.95 (*0-9628358-0-3*) M R Lewis.

Lewis, Anne. Leadership Styles. 63p. 1993. pap. 9.95 (*0-87652-178-2*) Am Assn Sch Admin.

Lewis, Anne, ed. Teaching Basis Riding. 93p. (C). 1990. pap. 21.00 (*0-85131-460-0*, Pub. by J A Allen) Trafalgar.

Lewis, Anne & Lindsay, Geoffrey A. Researching Children's Perspectives. LC 99-13289. 234p. 1999. 29.95 (*0-335-20279-9*) OpUniv Pr.

Lewis, Anne, ed. see Rambon, Sheppard.

Lewis, Anthony. Concordance to Cordwainer Smith. 2nd ed. 1994. pap. 10.00 (*0-915368-57-9*) New Eng SF Assoc.

— Gideon's Trumpet. 1980. 6.95 (*0-394-74410-1*) Vin Bks.

— Gideon's Trumpet. 233p. 1989. pap. 11.00 (*0-679-72312-9*) Vin Bks.

— Make No Law: The Sullivan Case & the First Amendment. LC 92-50104. 368p. 1992. pap. 14.00 (*0-679-73939-4*) Vin Bks.

Lewis, Anthony. A Treasury of Pony Stories. LC 96-1906. 160p. (J). (gr. k-4). 1996. 6.95 (*0-7534-5029-1*) LKC.

Lewis, Anthony & Saucedo, Aracely. Scriptures Said It, Jesus Accomplished It. unabridged ed. 26p. 1998. pap. 6.95 (*1-892651-07-6*) Columbia Pubns.

Lewis, Anthony, jt. auth. see Llewellyn, Claire.

Lewis, Anthony, jt. auth. see McAfee, Annalena.

Lewis, Anthony, jt. auth. see McCormick, Rosie.

Lewis, Anthony, jt. auth. see Mccormick, Rosie.

Lewis, Anthony, jt. auth. see McCormick, Rosie.

Lewis, Anthony, ed. see Budrys, Algis.

Lewis, Anthony, jt. ed. see Fortune, Nigel.

Lewis, Anthony J. The Love Story in Shakespearean Comedy. LC 91-45643. 248p. 1992. 29.95 (*0-8131-1786-0*) U Pr of Ky.

Lewis, Anthony J., jt. ed. see Henderson, Floyd M.

Lewis, Anthony R. An Annotated Bibliography of Recursive Science Fiction. iv, 56p. 1990. pap. 6.00 (*0-915368-47-1*) New Eng SF Assoc.

Lewis, Anthony R., jt. auth. see Bova, Ben.

Lewis, Anthony R., ed. see Clement, Hal.

Lewis, Anthony R., ed. see Malzberg, Barry N.

Lewis, Anthony R., jt. ed. see Olson, Mark L.

Lewis, Archibald Ross. Medieval Society in Southern France & Catalonia. (Collected Studies: No. CS197). 280p. (C). 1984. reprint ed. lib. bdg. 89.95 (*0-86078-145-3*, Pub. by Variorum) Ashgate Pub Co.

— Nomads & Crusaders, A.D. 1000-1368. LC 87-45588. (Illus.). 224p. 1988. 26.95 (*0-253-34787-4*) Ind U Pr.

— The Sea & Medieval Civilizations. LC 79-314124. 320 p. 1978. 16.00 (*0-86078-027-9*) Variorum.

Lewis, Arne. A Book of Rules. LC 83-80760. (Illus.). 48p. 1983. 22.95 (*0-912810-41-6*) Lustrum Pr.

Lewis, Arnold. American Country Houses of the Gilded Age: Sheldon's "Artistic Country-Seats" (Illus.). 128p. (C). 1982. pap. 10.95 (*0-486-24301-X*) Dover.

— An Early Encounter with Tomorrow: Europeans, Chicago's Loop & the World's Columbian Exposition. LC 96-25325. 376p. 1997. 34.95 (*0-252-02305-6*) U of Ill Pr.

Lewis, Arnold & Morgan, Keith, eds. American Victorian Architecture. LC 73-92261. Orig. Title: L' Architecture American. (Illus.). 152p. 1975. reprint ed. pap. 12.95 (*0-486-23177-1*) Dover.

Lewis, Arnold, et al. The Opulent Interiors of the Gilded Age: All 203 Photographs from Artistic Houses, with New Text. (Illus.). 192p. 1987. pap. 15.95 (*0-486-25250-7*) Dover.

Lewis, Arthur. European Community Law. (International Business Ser.). 1997. pap. 25.00 (*1-872807-47-X*) Kogan Page Ltd.

— Judges & Ruth. (Everyman's Bible Commentary Ser.). 1979. pap. 9.99 (*0-8024-2007-9*) Moody.

Lewis, Arthur H. The Day They Shook the Plum Tree. 251p. Date not set. 22.95 (*0-8488-2354-0*) Amereon Ltd.

— The Day They Shook the Plum Tree. 250p. 1985. reprint ed. lib. bdg. 35.95 (*0-89966-600-0*) Buccaneer Bks.

— Jueces y Rut (Comentario Biblico Portavoz) Orig. Title: Judges & Ruth (Everyman's Bible Commentary). (SPA.). 128p. 1982. pap. 6.99 (*0-8254-1434-2*, Edit Portavoz) Kregel.

— Lament for the Molly Maguires. 308p. 1990. reprint ed. lib. bdg. 26.95 (*0-89966-722-8*) Buccaneer Bks.

Lewis, Arthur M. Evolution-Social & Organic: Linnaeus, Darwin, Kropotkin, Marx. (Science for the Workers Ser.). 186p. 1984. 17.95 (*0-88286-088-7*) C H Kerr.

— Vital Problems in Social Evolution: An Introduction to the Materialist Conception of History. (Science for the Workers Ser.). 192p. 1984. 17.95 (*0-88286-089-5*) C H Kerr.

Lewis, Arthur M., jt. auth. see Darrow, Clarence.

Lewis, Arthur M., jt. auth. see Darrow, Clarence S.

Lewis, Arthur O., ed. American Utopias: Selected Short Fiction. LC 77-154448. (Utopian Literature Ser.). 1973. reprint ed. 23.95 (*0-405-03530-6*) Ayer.

— Utopian Literature, 41 bks. 1971. 932.50 (*0-405-03510-1*) Ayer.

Lewis, Arthur O., et al, eds. Anglo-German & American-German Crosscurrents, Vol. 4. (Illus.). 204p. (C). 1990. lib. bdg. 42.00 (*0-8191-7474-2*) U Pr of Amer.

Lewis, Arthur W. Basic Bookbinding. (Illus.). 144p. 1957. pap. 4.95 (*0-486-20169-4*) Dover.

Lewis, Aubrey. The Later Papers of Sir Aubrey Lewis. 1979. text 37.50 (*0-19-712150-0*) OUP.

Lewis, Audie G. Career Progression Guide for Soldiers. LC 97-34504. 160p. 1998. pap. 12.95 (*0-8117-2712-2*) Stackpole.

— Year 2000 Health Care Survival Guide: Strategies & Solutions for Executives. LC 98-36700. 90p. 1998. pap. 35.00 (*1-55648-254-X*) AHPI.

Lewis, Audrey. Madame Audrey's Guide to Mostly Cheap but Good Reference Books for Small & Rural Libraries. LC 98-30767. 352p. 1998. 45.00 (*0-8389-0733-4*) ALA.

— Through the Eyes of a Child. 88p. 1993. pap. 12.95 (*0-938645-89-7*) In His Steps.

Lewis, Audrey, jt. auth. see Falk, Peter Hastings.

Lewis, Audrey King. Big Momma & Celeste: Innocence - Seduction - Revenge. 200p. 1999. pap. 13.95 (*1-881524-50-7*, Prof Busn) Milligan Bks.

Lewis, Audrey N. Dreamseeker Wish Keeper. LC 98-94830. (Illus.). 32p. (J). 1998. pap. 7.95 (*0-9668406-0-7*) Dreamseekers.

Lewis, B., ed. Bioacoustics: A Comparative Approach. (Illus.). 1983. text 136.00 (*0-12-446550-1*) Acad Pr.

Lewis, B., jt. ed. see Bosworth, C. E.

Lewis, B. A. & Cribb, P. J. Orchids of the Solomon Islands & Bougainville. (Illus.). ix, 335p. 1991. pap. 40.00 (*0-947643-27-3*, Pub. by Royal Botnic Grdns) Balogh. Orchids of Vanuatu. (Illus.). 171p. 1989. pap. 24.00 (*0-947643-16-8*, Pub. by Royal Botnic Grdns) Balogh.

Lewis, B. J. Ready-to-Use Cowboy & Western Illustrations: 110 Different Copyright-Free Designs Printed One Side. (Clip Art Ser.). (Illus.). 64p. 1996. pap. text 5.95 (*0-486-29066-2*) Dover.

Lewis, B. P., jt. ed. see Brown, F.

Lewis, B. S. & Kimchi, A., eds. Heart-Failure Mechanisms & Management. (Illus.). 480p. 1991. 125.00 (*0-387-53145-9*) Spr-Verlag.

Lewis, B. Victor & Magos, Adam L., eds. Endometrial Ablation. LC 92-21014. 232p. 1993. text 105.00 (*0-443-04587-9*) Church.

Lewis, Barbara. The Young Lions: Ordinary Kids with Extraordinary Courage. (Illus.). 243p. (Orig.). 1993. pap. 9.95 (*0-87579-771-7*) Deseret Bk.

Lewis, Barbara & Littler, Dale, eds. The Blackwell Encyclopedic Dictionary of Marketing. (Blackwell Encyclopedia of Management Ser.). 320p. 1999. reprint ed. pap. 29.95 (*0-631-21485-2*) Blackwell Pubs.

Lewis, Barbara, tr. see Glissant, Edouard.

Lewis, Barbara A. Basic Music Theory. (TEE Ser.). 128p. 1980. 5.95 (*1-879892-21-9*) Editorial Bautista.

***Lewis, Barbara A.** Being Your Best: Character Building for Kids 7-10. LC 99-41180. (Illus.). 172p. (J). (gr. 2-5). 1999. pap. 14.95 (*1-57542-063-5*) Free Spirit Pub.

Lewis, Barbara A. The Kid's Guide to Service Projects: Over 500 Service Ideas for Young People Who Want to Make a Difference. LC 94-47933. 184p. (Orig.). (YA). (gr. 5 up). 1995. pap. 12.95 (*0-915793-82-2*) Free Spirit Pub.

— Kid's Guide to Social Action: How to Solve the Social Problems You Choose - And Turn Creative Thinking into Positive Action. expanded rev. ed. LC 98-11036. (Illus.). 224p. (YA). (gr. 5 up). 1998. pap. 18.95 (*1-57542-038-4*) Free Spirit Pub.

— Kids with Courage: True Stories about Young People Making a Difference. LC 91-46726. 184p. (J). (gr. 5 up). 1992. pap. 10.95 (*0-915793-39-3*) Free Spirit Pub.

Lewis, Barbara A. Kids with Courage: True Stories about Young People Making a Difference. (Illus.). (J). 1992. 16.30 (*0-606-18164-4*) Turtleback.

Lewis, Barbara A. A Leader's Guide to Being Your Best: Character Building for Kids 7-10. LC 99-46768. 128p. (J). (gr. 2-5). 1999. pap., teacher ed. 18.95 (*1-57542-064-3*) Free Spirit Pub.

— Teoria de la Musica. (TEE Ser.). (SPA.). 137p. 1983. 5.95 (*1-879892-20-0*) Editorial Bautista.

— What Do You Stand For? A Kid's Guide to Building Character. LC 97-13952. (Illus.). 284p. (YA). (gr. 6 up). 1997. 19.95 (*1-57542-029-5*) Free Spirit Pub.

Lewis, Barbara B., tr. see Glissant, Edouard.

Lewis, Barbara R., jt. auth. see Varey, Richard J.

Lewis, Barbara R., jt. ed. see Littler, Dale.

Lewis, Barrie, jt. ed. see Marsh, Graham.

Lewis, Barry. Inside Endurance. (Illus.). 192p. 1996. pap. 14.95 (*0-8117-2551-0*) Stackpole.

— Kew Gardens: Urban Village in the Big City an Architectural History of Kew Gardens. Berger, Murray H. & Hack, Martin, eds. (Illus.). 69p. 1999. pap. 10.95 (*0-9670954-0-9*) Kew Gardens Coun.

— Running the Trans America Footrace: Trials & Triumphs of Life on the Road. (Illus.). 160p. 1994. pap. 14.95 (*0-8117-2582-0*) Stackpole.

Lewis, Barry, jt. auth. see Davis, Peter.

Lewis, Bea. Quick & Easy Low-Fat, Low-Cholesterol Recipes Kids Will Love. 128p. (Orig.). 1990. pap. 3.95 (*0-380-76079-7*, Avon Bks) Morrow Avon.

***Lewis, Beca.** Power Shift to Gracious Abundance: Spirituality Made Practical for All Aspects of Life. 250p. 2000. pap. 14.95 (*0-915009-71-4*, Pub. by World Leis Corp) Midpt Trade.

Lewis-Beck. Economics & Democracy. (C). 2001. pap. 21.00 (*0-205-28259-8*, Macmillan Coll) P-H.

Lewis-Beck, Michael S. Applied Regression: An Introduction, No. 22. (Quantitative Applications in the Social Sciences Ser.: Vol. 22). (Illus.). 79p. 1980. pap. 10.95 (*0-8039-1494-6*) Sage.

— Data Analysis: An Introduction, No. 103. (Quantitative Applications in the Social Science Ser.). 96p. 1995. pap. text 10.95 (*0-8039-5772-6*) Sage.

— Economics & Elections: The Major Western Democracies. (Illus.). 204p. (C). 1990. pap. text 18.95 (*0-472-08133-0*, 08133) U of Mich Pr.

— Forecasting Elections. 163p. 1992. 22.95 (*0-87187-600-0*) Congr Quarterly.

Lewis-Beck, Michael S., et al, eds. How France Votes. LC 98-58099. (Illus.). 304p. (C). 1999. pap. text 24.95 (*1-56643-069-0*, Chatham House Pub) Seven Bridges.

Lewis-Beck, Michael S., jt. ed. see Berry, William D.

Lewis-Beck, Michael S., jt. ed. see Eulau, Heinz.

Lewis, Benjamin & Paranhos Velloso, Rodrigo. Eat Dangerously: Blow Health Out Your Ass!!! Cookbook. unabridged ed. 122p. 1999. pap. 14.95 (*0-9670029-0-7*) Holl & Hech.

Lewis, Bernard. The Arabs in History. 6th ed. LC 92-43000. 256p. (C). 1993. 14.95 (*0-19-285258-2*) OUP.

— The Assassins: A Radical Sect in Islam. (Illus.). 183p. 1987. pap. text 11.95 (*0-19-520550-2*) OUP.

— Cultures in Conflict: Christians, Muslims & Jews in the Age of Discovery. (Illus.). 126p. 1996. reprint ed. pap. 10.95 (*0-19-510283-5*) OUP.

— Emergence of Modern Turkey. 2nd ed. (Royal Institute of International Affairs Ser.). (Illus.). 542p. (C). 1969. pap. text 24.95 (*0-19-500344-6*) OUP.

***Lewis, Bernard.** The Future of the Middle East. (Predictions Ser.). 58p. 1999. pap. 3.95 (*0-297-81980-1*, Pub. by Weidenfeld & Nicolson) Trafalgar.

Lewis, Bernard. Islam & the West. 240p. 1994. reprint ed. pap. 14.95 (*0-19-509061-6*) OUP.

— Islam in History: Ideas, People, & Events in the Middle East. 2nd rev. ed. LC 92-46218. 492p. 1993. 59.95 (*0-8126-9216-0*) Open Court.

— Istanbul & the Civilization of the Ottoman Empire. LC 63-17161. (Centers of Civilization Ser.: Vol. 9). (Illus.). 1972. reprint ed. pap. 11.95 (*0-8061-1060-0*) U of Okla Pr.

— The Jews of Islam. LC 84-42575. (Illus.). 259p. 1984. pap. text 15.95 (*0-691-00807-8*, Pub. by Princeton U Pr) Cal Prin Full Svc.

***Lewis, Bernard.** Land of the Enchanters: Egyptian Short Stories from the Earliest Times to the Present. rev. ed. Burstein, Stanley M., ed. 200p. 2000. 38.95 (*1-55876-249-3*); pap. 18.95 (*1-55876-250-7*) Wiener Pubs Inc.

Lewis, Bernard. Middle East. 448p. 1997. per. 15.00 (*0-684-83280-1*, Touchstone) S&S Trade Pap.

— The Middle East: A Brief History of the Last 2,000 Years. (Illus.). 433p. 1996. 29.50 (*0-684-80712-2*) S&S Trade.

— Multiple Identities of the Middle East. LC 99-20735. 176p. 1999. pap. text 21.00 (*0-8052-4172-8*) Schocken.

— The Muslim Discovery of Europe. (Illus.). 352p. 1985. pap. 13.95 (*0-393-30233-4*) Norton.

— The Origins of Isma'ilism: A Study of the Historical Background of the Fatimid Caliphate. LC 74-180357. reprint ed. 29.50 (*0-404-56289-2*) AMS Pr.

— The Political Language of Islam. LC 87-19222. (Exxon Lectures). viii, 184p. 1991. pap. 12.00 (*0-226-47693-6*) U Ch Pr.

— The Political Language of Islam. (Illus.). x, 168p. 1992. 19.95 (*0-226-47692-8*) U Ch Pr.

— Race & Slavery in the Middle East: An Historical Enquiry. (Illus.). 224p. 1992. pap. 14.95 (*0-19-505326-5*) OUP.

— Semites & Anti-Semites: An Inquiry into Conflict & Prejudice. 288p. 1999. pap. 14.00 (*0-393-31839-7*, Norton Paperbks) Norton.

— The Shaping of the Modern Middle East. rev. ed. (Illus.). 200p. (C). 1994. pap. text 21.95 (*0-19-507282-0*) OUP.

***Lewis, Bernard, ed.** Middle East Mosaic: Fragments of Life, Letters & History. LC 99-10150. (Illus.). 512p. 2000. 35.00 (*0-679-45191-9*) Random.

Lewis, Bernard, ed. World of Islam. LC 91-65146. (Illus.). 360p. 1992. reprint ed. pap. 29.95 (*0-500-27624-2*, Pub. by Thames Hudson) Norton.

Lewis, Bernard, ed. Islam - From the Prophet Muhammad to the Capture of Constantinople Vol. 1: Politics & War, Vol. 1. (Illus.). 303p. 1987. pap. text 21.95 (*0-19-505087-8*) OUP.

— Islam - From the Prophet Muhammad to the Capture of Constantinople Vol. 3: Religion & Society, Vol. 2. (Illus.). 352p. 1987. pap. text 22.95 (*0-19-505088-6*) OUP.

***Lewis, Bernard & Kramer, Martin S.** The Jewish Discovery of Islam: Studies in Honor of Bernard Lewis. LC 99-461273. 311p. 1999. 24.95 (*965-224-040-0*, Pub. by Moshe Dayan Ctr) Syracuse U Pr.

Lewis, Bernard & Schnapper, Dominique, eds. Muslims in Europe. LC 94-13756. (Social Change in Western Europe Ser.). 1994. 39.00 (*1-85567-250-2*); pap. 15.00 (*1-85567-214-6*) St Martin.

Lewis, Bernard & Von Elbe, Guenther, eds. Combustion, Flames, & Explosions of Gases. 3rd ed. 739p. 1987. text 116.00 (*0-12-446751-2*) Acad Pr.

Lewis, Bernard, jt. auth. see Cohen, Amnon.

Lewis, Bernard, jt. ed. see Braude, Benjamin.

Lewis, Bernard, ed. see Frye, Richard N.

Lewis, Bernard, ed. see Goldziher, Ignaz.

Lewis, Bernard, ed. see Halm, Heinz.

Lewis, Bernard, ed. see Nagel, Tilman.

Lewis, Bernard T. Building Maintenance Engineering Price Book 1985-86. 300p. 1986. 39.95 (*0-412-01071-2*, 9666, Chap & Hall NY) Chapman & Hall.

Lewis, Bernnard T. Facility Manager's Operation & Maintenance Handbook. LC 98-34425. 1999. 99.95 (*0-07-040048-2*) McGraw.

Lewis, Beth I. George Grosz: Art & Politics in the Weimar Republic. rev. ed. LC 91-4300. (Illus.). 362p. 1991. reprint ed. pap. 112.30 (*0-608-07792-5*, 205985900010) Bks Demand.

Lewis, Betty. Holy City: Riker's Religious Roadside Attraction. (Topics in Monterey Bay Area History Ser.). (Illus.). 100p. 1992. pap. 8.95 (*0-9617681-5-0*) Otter B Bks.

— Monterey Bay Yesterday: A Nostalgic Era in Postcards. (Illus.). 124p. (Orig.). 1987. reprint ed. pap. 4.98 (*0-9617681-1-8*) Otter B Bks.

— Watsonville: Memories That Linger, Vol. 1. LC 76-41500. 220p. 1986. 13.95 (*0-9617681-0-X*) Otter B Bks.

— Watsonville: Memories That Linger, Vol. 2. LC 76-41500. (Illus.). 154p. 1980. 13.95 (*0-934136-08-4*) Otter B Bks.

Lewis, Betty J. & Edwards, Judith. Hand in Hand: Partners Working Together with God. 88p. 1996. pap. text 7.95 (*1-56309-163-1*, W963103) Womans Mission Union.

Lewis, Beverly. Annika's Secret Wish. text 14.99 (*0-7642-2181-7*) Bethany Hse.

Lewis, Beverly. Backyard Bandit Mystery. LC 97-21033. (Cul-de-Sac Kids Ser.: Vol. 15). 80p. (J). (gr. 2-5). 1997. pap. 3.99 (*1-55661-986-3*) Bethany Hse.

***Lewis, Beverly.** Better Than Best. (Girls Only Go Ser.: Vol. 6). (Illus.). 128p. (J). (gr. 3-8). 2000. pap. 5.99 (*1-55661-641-4*) Bethany Hse.

— Big Bad Beans. LC 99-6753. (Cul-de-Sac Kids Ser.: Vol. 22). (Illus.). 80p. (J). (gr. 2-5). 2000. pap. 3.99 (*0-7642-2127-2*) Bethany Hse.

Lewis, Beverly. California Christmas. (Holly's Heart Ser.: Vol. 5). 144p. (J). (gr. 6-9). 1994. pap. 6.99 (*0-310-43321-5*) Zondervan.

— Catch a Falling Star. (SummerHill Secrets Ser.: Bk. 3). 144p. (J). (gr. 6-9). 1995. pap. 5.99 (*1-55661-478-0*) Bethany Hse.

— The Chicken Pox Panic. LC 94-49117. (Cul-de-Sac Kids Ser.: Vol. 2). 80p. (J). (gr. 2-5). 1995. pap. 3.99 (*1-55661-626-0*) Bethany Hse.

— The Confession. LC 97-21118. (Heritage of Lancaster County Ser.: No. 2). 288p. (J). 1997. pap. 10.99 (*1-55661-867-0*) Bethany Hse.

— The Confession. large type ed. LC 98-23163. 1998. 23.95 (*0-7862-1522-4*) Mac Lib Ref.

An Asterisk (*) at the beginning of an entry indicates that the title is appearing for the first time.

L

— The Crabby Cat Caper. LC 96-45851. (Cul-de-Sac Kids Ser.: Vol. 12). 80p. (J). (gr. 2-5). 1997. pap. 3.99 (*1-55661-912-X*) Bethany Hse.

— The Crazy Christmas Angel. (Cul-de-Sac Kids Ser.). 80p. (J). (gr. 2-5). 1995. pap. 3.99 (*1-55661-627-9*) Bethany Hse.

— Creepy Sleep-Over. LC 97-33925. (Cul-de-Sac Kids Ser.: Vol. 17). (Illus.). 80p. (J). (gr. 2-5). 1998. pap. 3.99 (*1-55661-988-X*) Bethany Hse.

***Lewis, Beverly.** The Crossroad. LC 99-6719. 368p. 1999. 15.99 (*0-7642-2239-2*); 15.99 (*0-7642-2240-6*); pap. text 10.99 (*0-7642-2212-0*) Bethany Hse.

Lewis, Beverly. A Cry in the Dark. (Summerhill Secrets Ser.: Vol. 5). 144p. (J). (gr. 4-7). 1996. pap. 5.99 (*1-55661-480-2*) Bethany Hse.

— The Cul-de-Sac Kids Series Books 1-6. (Cul-de-Sac Kids Ser.). (J). (gr. 2-5). 1995. pap., boxed set 23.99 (*1-55661-804-2*, 252804) Bethany Hse.

— The Cul-de-Sac Kids Series Books 7-12. (Cul-de-Sac Kids Ser.). (J). (gr. 2-5). 1997. boxed set 23.99 (*0-7642-8155-0*) Bethany Hse.

— The Cul-de-Sac Kids Series Books 13-18. (Cul-de-Sac Kids Ser.). (J). (gr. 2-5). 1998. pap., boxed set 23.99 (*0-7642-8258-1*, 258258) Bethany Hse.

— The Double Dabble Surprise. LC 94-49116. (Cul-de-Sac Kids Ser.: Vol. 1). 80p. (J). (gr. 2-5). 1995. pap. 3.99 (*1-55661-625-2*) Bethany Hse.

— Dreams on Ice. LC 98-220297. (Girls Only Go Ser.). 128p. (J). 1998. pap. 5.99 (*0-7642-2058-6*) Bethany Hse.

— Echoes in the Wind. LC 97-4707. (Summerhill Secrets Ser.: No. 7). 144p. (J). (gr. 6-9). 1997. pap. 5.99 (*1-55661-873-5*) Bethany Hse.

— Eight Is Enough, Bk. 13. LC 96-43887. (Holly's Heart Ser.: Vol. 13). 144p. (Orig.). (J). (gr. 6-9). 1997. pap. 6.99 (*0-310-20844-0*) Zondervan.

— Fiddlesticks. LC 96-45852. (Cul-de-Sac Kids Ser.: Vol. 11). 80p. (J). (gr. 2-5). 1997. pap. 3.99 (*1-55661-911-1*) Bethany Hse.

***Lewis, Beverly.** Follow the Dream. LC 00-8102. (Girls Only Go Ser.: Vol. 5). 128p. (J). (gr. 3-8). 2000. pap. 5.99 (*1-55661-640-6*) Bethany Hse.

Lewis, Beverly. Frog Power. LC 95-22385. (Cul-de-Sac Kids Ser.: Vol. 5). 80p. (J). (gr. 2-5). 1995. pap. 3.99 (*1-55661-645-7*) Bethany Hse.

— Good-Bye Dressel Hills. (Holly's Heart Series: Vol. 7). 160p. (J). 1994. pap. 6.99 (*0-310-44410-1*) Zondervan.

— Granny Game. (Cul-de-Sac Kids Ser.). 80p. (J). (gr. 2-5). 1999. pap. 3.99 (*0-7642-2125-6*) Bethany Hse.

— Great TV Turn-Off. LC 97-33924. (Cul-de-Sac Kids Ser.: Vol. 18). 80p. (J). (gr. 2-5). 1998. pap. 3.99 (*1-55661-989-8*) Bethany Hse.

— Green Gravy. LC 97-21032. (Cul-de-Sac Kids Ser.: Vol. 14). 80p. (J). (gr. 2-5). 1997. pap. 3.99 (*1-55661-985-5*) Bethany Hse.

— The Heritage of Lancaster County: The Shunning, The Confession & The Reckoning. 1998. pap., boxed set 32.99 (*0-7642-8382-0*) Bethany Hse.

— Hide Behind the Moon. LC 97-45421. (Summerhill Secrets Ser.). 144p. (YA). 1998. pap. 5.99 (*1-55661-874-3*) Bethany Hse.

— Holly's First Love. LC 92-47055. (Holly's Heart Series: Vol. 1). 160p. (J). 1993. pap. 6.99 (*0-310-38051-0*) Zondervan.

— House of Secrets. (Summerhill Secrets Ser.: No. 6). 144p. (J). (gr. 6-9). 1996. pap. 5.99 (*1-55661-872-7*) Bethany Hse.

— It's a Girl Thing, Bk. 14. LC 97-2142. (Holly's Heart Ser.: Vol. 14). 144p. (Orig.). (J). (gr. 6-9). 1997. pap. 6.99 (*0-310-20845-9*) Zondervan.

— Little White Lies, Bk. 10. LC 95-30920. (Holly's Heart Ser.: Vol. 10). 160p. (J). (gr. 5-9). 1995. pap. 6.99 (*0-310-20194-2*) Zondervan.

— Mailbox Mania. (Cul-de-Sac Kids Ser.). 80p. (J). (gr. 2-5). 1996. pap. 3.99 (*1-55661-729-1*) Bethany Hse.

— The Mudhole Mystery. LC 96-45853. (Cul-de-Sac Kids Ser.). (Illus.). 80p. (J). (gr. 2-5). 1997. pap. 3.99 (*1-55661-910-3*) Bethany Hse.

***Lewis, Beverly.** Mystery Mutt. LC 99-6754. (Cul-de-Sac Kids Ser.: Vol. 21). (Illus.). 80p. (J). (gr. 2-5). 2000. pap. 3.99 (*0-7642-2126-4*) Bethany Hse.

Lewis, Beverly. The Mystery of Case D. Luc. (Cul-de-Sac Kids Ser.). (Illus.). 80p. (J). (gr. 2-5). 1995. pap. 3.99 (*1-55661-646-5*) Bethany Hse.

— Night of the Fireflies. LC 95-43838. (Summerhill Secrets Ser.: Vol. 4). 144p. (Orig.). (J). (gr. 6-9). 1995. pap. 5.99 (*1-55661-479-9*) Bethany Hse.

— No Grown-Ups Allowed. LC 95-23931. (Cul-de-Sac Kids Ser.: Vol. 4). (Illus.). 80p. (J). (gr. 2-5). 1995. pap. 3.99 (*1-55661-644-9*) Bethany Hse.

— Only the Best. LC 98-220293. 128p. 1998. pap. 5.99 (*0-7642-2059-4*) Bethany Hse.

— A Perfect Match, Vol. 3. LC 99-6718. (Girls Only Go Ser.). 128p. (J). (gr. 3-8). 1999. pap. text 5.99 (*0-7642-2060-8*) Bethany Hse.

— Pickle Pizza. (Cul-de-Sac Kids Ser.). 80p. (J). (gr. 2-5). 1996. pap. 3.99 (*1-55661-728-3*) Bethany Hse.

— Piggy Party. (Cul-de-Sac Kids Ser.). 80p. (J). (gr. 2-5). 1999. pap. 3.99 (*0-7642-2124-8*) Bethany Hse.

— Postcard. LC 99-6378. 1999. pap. 15.99 (*0-7642-2225-2*); text 15.99 (*0-7642-2224-4*) Bethany Hse.

— The Postcard. LC 99-6378. 288p. 1999. pap. text 10.99 (*0-7642-2211-2*) Bethany Hse.

***Lewis, Beverly.** Reach for the Stars, 4. LC 99-6717. (Girls Only Go Ser.). (J). (gr. 3-8). 1999. pap. text 5.99 (*0-7642-2061-6*) Bethany Hse.

Lewis, Beverly. The Reckoning. LC 98-220299. 288p. 1998. pap. 10.99 (*1-55661-868-9*) Bethany Hse.

***Lewis, Beverly.** Redemption of Sarah Cain. (Heritage of Lancaster County Ser.). 320p. 2000. pap. 10.99 (*0-7642-2329-1*) Bethany Hse.

— The Redemption of Sarah Cain. 320p. 2000. 15.99 (*0-7642-2388-7*) Bethany Hse.

— The Redemption of Sarah Cain. large type ed. 384p. 2000. pap. 15.99 (*0-7642-2390-9*) Bethany Hse.

Lewis, Beverly. Second-Best Friend. (Holly's Heart Ser.: Vol. 6). 160p. (J). (gr. 6-9). 1994. pap. 6.99 (*0-310-43331-2*) Zondervan.

— Secret in the Willows. (Summerhill Secrets Ser.: Bk. 2). 144p. (J). (gr. 6-9). 1995. pap. 5.99 (*1-55661-477-2*) Bethany Hse.

***Lewis, Beverly.** Shadows Beyond the Gate. LC 99-50589. (Summerhill Secrets Ser.: 10). 144p. (YA). 1999. pap. 5.99 (*1-55661-876-X*) Bethany Hse.

Lewis, Beverly. The Shunning. LC 97-45444. 1998. 11.99 (*0-7642-2076-4*) Bethany Hse.

— The Shunning, Vol. 1. LC 97-4648. (The Heritage of Lancaster County Ser.). 288p. 1997. pap. 10.99 (*1-55661-866-2*) Bethany Hse.

— The Stinky Sneakers Mystery. LC 96-4439. (Cul-de-Sac Kids Ser.: Vol. 7). 80p. (J). (ps-3). 1996. pap. 3.99 (*1-55661-727-5*) Bethany Hse.

— Straight - A Teacher. (Holly's Heart Ser.: Vol. 8). 160p. (J). 1994. pap. 6.99 (*0-310-46111-1*) Zondervan.

— SummerHill Secrets, Vols. 1-5. (J). 1996. boxed set 29.99 (*0-7642-8029-5*) Bethany Hse.

— The Sunroom. large type ed. LC 98-22314. 204p. 1998. 23.95 (*0-7838-0281-1*, G K Hall Lrg Type) Mac Lib Ref.

— Tarantula Toes. LC 97-21031. (Cul-de-Sac Kids Ser.: Vol. 13). 80p. (J). (gr. 2-5). 1997. pap. 3.99 (*1-55661-984-7*) Bethany Hse.

— Tree House Trouble. LC 97-33884. (Cul-de-Sac Kids Ser.: Vol. 16). 80p. (J). (gr. 2-5). 1998. pap. 3.99 (*1-55661-987-1*) Bethany Hse.

— The Trouble with Weddings. (Holly's Heart Ser.: Vol. 4). 160p. (J). (gr. 6-9). 1993. 6.99 (*0-310-38081-2*) Zondervan.

— Whispers down the Lane. (Summerhill Secrets Ser.: Bk. 1). 144p. (J). (gr. 6-9). 1995. pap. 5.99 (*1-55661-476-4*) Bethany Hse.

— Windows on the Hill. (Summerhill Secrets Ser.). 144p. 1999. pap. 5.99 (*1-55661-875-1*) Bethany Hse.

***Lewis, Beverly R.** The Postcard. LC 00-42579. 2000. write for info. (*0-7862-2713-3*) Thorndike Pr.

Lewis, Bil. Threads Primer: A Guide to Multithreaded Programming. 352p. 1995. pap. 46.00 (*0-13-443698-9*) P-H.

***Lewis, Bil & Berg, Daniel.** Multithreaded JAVA Programming. LC 99-51538. (Java Ser.). (Illus.). 461p. 1999. pap. text 39.99 (*0-13-017007-0*) P-H.

Lewis, Bil & Berg, Daniel J. Multithreaded Programming with Pthreads. LC 97-31758. 432p. (C). 1997. pap. text 34.95 (*0-13-680729-1*) P-H.

***Lewis, Bil, et al.** The GNU Emacs Lisp Reference Manual: Emacs Version 21. 900p. 1999. per. 60.00 (*1-882114-73-6*) Free Software.

Lewis, Bill. Grafting & Budding Fruit & Nut Trees: A Practical Guide. (Illus.). 48p. (Orig.). pap. 19.95 (*0-643-06387-0*, Pub. by CSIRO) Accents Pubns.

Lewis, Bill. West Texas Adventure. 180p. 1993. pap. 9.95 (*1-57087-007-1*) Prof Pr NC.

Lewis, Blair S., jt. auth. see Rex, Douglas K.

Lewis, Blake, jt. auth. see Williams, Basil.

Lewis-Blue, Tabitha. A Walk Back in Time. Wade, C. Hsanni, ed. (Illus.). 84p. (Orig.). 1996. pap. 8.75 (*0-9655369-0-4*) Ts Enterprises.

***Lewis, Bob.** IS Survival Guide. LC 98-86977. 332p. 1999. pap. 24.99 (*0-672-31437-1*) Sams.

Lewis, Bob. The Lost Plates of Laman. LC 97-33412. (Illus.). 76p. 1997. pap. 12.95 (*1-56085-097-3*) Signature Bks.

— Romantic Places on the Westside. 3rd rev. ed. (Illus.). 80p. 1996. pap. 4.95 (*0-9650931-3-1*) B Lewis.

Lewis, Bob, et al. WordPerfect Version 6.0 for DOS. (C). 1995. pap. text. write for info. (*0-201-83710-2*) Addison-Wesley.

***Lewis, Bonnie B. & Kaahanui, MaryAnn.** Creating Fabulous Footwear for Fantastic Dolls. 2nd rev. ed. Orig. Title: Creating Fabulous Footwear for Cloth Dolls. (Illus.). 118p. 1998. spiral bd. 22.95 (*0-9674219-0-X*) Dollmakers.

— Creating Heavenly Hats for Discriminating Dolls. (Illus.). 181p. 1999. spiral bd. 28.95 (*0-9674219-1-8*) Dollmakers.

Lewis, Bonnie Sue, jt. intro. see Drury, Clifford M.

Lewis, Brad & Goldstein, Gabriella. Olympic Results, Barcelona 1992: A Complete Compilation of Results from the Games of the XXV Olympiad. LC 93-15813. 648p. 1993. text 30.00 (*0-8153-0333-5*, H1752) Garland.

Lewis, Brad, jt. auth. see Berle, William.

Lewis, Brad, jt. auth. see Maxwell, John.

Lewis, Brad A. Assault on Lake Casitas. 177p. 1990. pap. 11.95 (*1-888478-00-4*) Shark Pr.

— The Idiot Years. 189p. 1993. pap. 9.95 (*1-888478-01-2*) Shark Pr.

— Wanted: Rowing Coach. 213p. (Orig.). 1995. pap. 11.95 (*1-888478-02-0*) Shark Pr.

Lewis, Brenda J. Little Foster & His Friends: A Program to Develop Self Concept & Tolerance. (Illus.). 21p. (Orig.). (J). (ps-2). 1993. pap. 6.95 (*1-884063-58-6*) Mar Co Prods.

— Little Foster & Maria: A Program about Abuse. LC 93-79189. 32p. (J). (ps-2). 1993. 6.95 (*1-884063-04-7*) Mar Co Prods.

— Little Foster & Miss Mable: A Program about Death & Grief. LC 95-78484. (Illus.). 31p. (J). (ps-2). 1995. 6.95 (*1-884063-67-5*) Mar Co Prods.

— Little Foster & Sam: A Program about Drugs. LC 93-81084. 24p. (J). (ps-2). 1994. 6.95 (*1-884063-18-7*) Mar Co Prods.

***Lewis, Brenda R.** Focus on Coins & Currency. (Illus.). 76p. (gr. 6-10). 1999. reprint ed. text 15.00 (*0-7881-6578-X*) DIANE Pub.

Lewis, Brenda Ralph. Aztecs. 1999. pap. text 9.95 (*0-7509-2222-2*) Sutton Pub Ltd.

Lewis, Brian. Jean Mitry & the Aesthetics of the Cinema. Kirkpatrick, Diane, ed. LC 84-138. (Studies in Cinema: No. 25). 150p. reprint ed. 46.50 (*0-8357-1553-1*, 207045700093) Bks Demand.

Lewis, Brian, jt. auth. see Horabin, Ivan.

Lewis, Brian, ed. see IPM Committee on International Affairs Staff.

Lewis, Brian L. The Novice Nomad. (Illus.). 84p. pap. 9.95 (*1-928693-00-8*) Novice Nomad.

***Lewis, Brian Leslie.** The Alaskan Nomad's Journal (14 Page Version) A Journey Through the Wilds of Alaska. 16p. 1999. pap. 6.95 (*1-928693-02-4*) Novice Nomad.

— A Musher's Journal. 16p. 1999. pap. 6.95 (*1-928693-04-0*) Novice Nomad.

— My Holiday Journal. 16p. (J). 1999. pap. 6.95 (*1-928693-05-9*) Novice Nomad.

— My Journal (14 Page Version) 16p. (J). (gr. k). 1999. pap. 6.95 (*1-928693-01-6*) Novice Nomad.

— The Nomad's Journal: International - 30 Day. 32p. 1999. pap. 9.95 (*1-928693-03-2*) Novice Nomad.

— A Nomad's Journal - 72 Page: (Magehan's Version) 72p. 1999. pap. 7.95 (*1-928693-06-7*) Novice Nomad.

Lewis, Bruce, jt. auth. see Eldred, Tim.

Lewis, Byron A. & Pucelik, Frank. Magic of NLP Demystified: A Pragmatic Guide to Communication & Change. rev. ed. LC 90-5742. (Positive Change Guide Ser.). (Illus.). 176p. 1990. pap. 9.95 (*1-55552-017-0*) Metamorphous Pr.

Lewis, C. Data Structures & Their Algorithms. 2nd ed. (C). 1998. pap. text, teacher ed. write for info. (*0-673-97131-7*) Addison-Wesley.

— A Wish to Be. 1994. pap. 11.95 (*1-85230-534-7*, Pub. by Element MA) Penguin Putnam.

Lewis, C., et al. Marketing Peanut Butter: A Microcomputer Simulation. 1984. 271.72 (*0-07-079588-6*) McGraw.

Lewis, C., jt. auth. see Lewis, P. C.

Lewis, C., jt. auth. see Trotta, V.

Lewis, C., jt. ed. see Bennett, D.

Lewis, C. A. An Encounter with a Prophet, Vol. 1. LC 97-92241. 173p. (Orig.). 1997. pap. 14.95 (*0-9658574-0-9*) Amadon Publ.

Lewis, C. F., jt. ed. see Kohel, R. J.

Lewis, C. J. & Lewis, J. Norman. Natality & Fecundity: A Contribution to National Demography. LC 75-38135. (Demography Ser.). 1976. reprint ed. 19.95 (*0-405-07988-5*) Ayer.

***Lewis, C. Jonathan.** The Telephone Troubleshooting Desk Reference. McCay, William et al, eds. (Illus.). viii, 40p. 1999. pap. 4.50 (*0-9675451-0-2*) C J Lewis Assocs.

Lewis, C. P. The Haskins Society Journal No. 8, 1996: Studies in Medieval History. Cownie, Emma, ed. 192p. 1999. 60.00 (*0-85115-724-6*, Boydell Pr) Boydell & Brewer.

Lewis, C. P. & Cownie, Emma, eds. The Haskins Society Journal No. 7, 1995: Studies in Medieval History. (Illus.). 208p. 1997. 75.00 (*0-85115-696-7*) Boydell & Brewer.

Lewis, C. P., jt. ed. see Currie, C. R.

Lewis, C. Patrick. Building a Shared Vision: A Leader's Guide to Aligning the Organization. LC 96-43390. (Illus.). 150p. 1997. 45.00 (*1-56327-163-X*) Productivity Inc.

Lewis, C. Roy, jt. auth. see Carter, Harold.

***Lewis, C. S.** The Abolition of Man. 1999. pap. 6.00 (*0-8054-2047-9*) Broadman.

Lewis, C. S. The Abolition of Man. 112p. 1996. per. 6.00 (*0-684-82371-3*, Touchstone) S&S Trade Pap.

— All My Road Before Me: The Diary of C. S. Lewis, 1922-1927. Hooper, Walter, ed. 1991. 24.95 (*0-15-104609-3*) Harcourt.

— All My Road Before Me: The Diary of C. S. Lewis, 1922-1927. (Illus.). 536p. 1992. pap. 16.00 (*0-15-604643-1*, Harvest Bks) Harcourt.

— The Allegory of Love: A Study of Medieval Tradition. 390p. 1985. pap. 21.95 (*0-19-281220-3*) OUP.

***Lewis, C. S.** L' Armoire Magique. 6th ed. Orig. Title: The Lion, the Witch & the Wardrobe. (FRE.). (J). (gr. 4-7). 1999. pap. 12.95 (*2-08-164414-2*) Distribks Inc.

Lewis, C. S. Aslan. LC 97-2046. (World of Narnia Ser.: Bk. 3). (Illus.). 40p. (J). (gr. k-4). 1998. 15.95 (*0-06-027636-3*) HarpC.

— Aslan's Triumph. LC 97-28642. (Illus.). 40p. (J). (gr. k-4). 1998. 14.95 (*0-06-027638-X*) HarpC.

— Aslan's Triumph. LC 97-28642. (Narnia Ser.). (Illus.). 40p. (J). (gr. k-4). 1999. pap. 5.95 (*0-06-443575-X*) HarpC.

***Lewis, C. S.** Aslan's Triumph. (Illus.). (J). 1999. 11.40 (*0-606-18675-1*) Turtleback.

Lewis, C. S. A Book of Narnians: The Lion, the Witch & the Others. LC 94-29069. (Illus.). 96p. (J). (gr. 4-7). 1995. 16.95 (*0-06-025009-7*) HarpC Child Bks.

— A Book of Narnians: The Lion, the Witch & the Others. LC 94-29069. (Narnia Ser.). (Illus.). 96p. (J). (gr. 3-7). 1997. reprint ed. pap. 9.95 (*0-06-446203-X*, HarpTrophy) HarpC Child Bks.

— Boxen: The Imaginary World of the Young C. S. Lewis. (Illus.). 216p. 1986. pap. 4.95 (*0-15-614000-4*, Harvest Bks) Harcourt.

— The Business of Heaven: Daily Readings from C. S. Lewis. Hooper, Walter, ed. 384p. (C). 1984. pap. 9.95 (*0-15-614863-3*, Harvest Bks) Harcourt.

— C. S. Lewis at the Breakfast Table & Other Reminiscences. Como, James T., ed. 1985. 10.95 (*0-02-570620-9*) Macmillan.

***Lewis, C. S.** The Case for Christianity. 1999. pap. 6.00 (*0-8054-2044-4*) Broadman.

Lewis, C. S. The Case for Christianity. 64p. 1996. per. 6.00 (*0-684-82373-X*) S&S Trade Pap.

— A Christian for All Christians: Essays in Honor of C. S. Lewis. Walker, Andrew & Patrick, James, eds. LC 91-46764. 258p. 1992. pap. 10.95 (*0-89526-735-7*) Regnery Pub.

— Christian Mythmakers: Lewis, L'Engle, Tolkien & Others. LC 98-20706. 300p. 1998. pap. 13.95 (*0-940895-31-5*) Cornerstone IL.

— Christian Reflections. 1976. 20.95 (*0-8488-1077-5*) Amereon Ltd.

— Christian Reflections. 190p. 1967. pap. 12.00 (*0-8028-0869-7*) Eerdmans.

Lewis, C. S. The Chronicles of Narnia, 7 vols. (Chronicles of Narnia Ser.: Bks. 1-7). (Illus.). (J). (gr. 4-7). 1994. pap., boxed set 34.65 (*0-06-447119-5*, HarpTrophy) HarpC Child Bks.

Lewis, C. S. The Chronicles of Narnia, 7 bks., Set. (Chronicles of Narnia Ser.: Bks. 1-7). (Illus.). (J). (gr. 4-8). 1994. boxed set 111.65 (*0-06-024488-7*); pap., boxed set 48.65 (*0-06-440537-0*, HarpTrophy) HarpC Child Bks.

Lewis, C. S. The Chronicles of Narnia Audio Collection, Set. unabridged ed. (YA). (gr. 3 up). 1991. audio 25.00 (*1-55994-501-X*, SBN 123, Pub. by HarperAudio) Lndmrk Audiobks.

— The Chronicles of Narnia Box Set: Full-Color Collector's Edition. (Chronicles of Narnia Ser.: Bks. 1-7). (Illus.). (J). (gr. 4-7). 2000. pap., boxed set 55.65 (*0-06-440939-2*, HarpTrophy) HarpC Child Bks.

Lewis, C. S. Collected Works of C. S. Lewis. 544p. 1996. 14.99 (*0-88486-151-1*) Arrowood Pr.

— The Complete Chronicles of Narnia. deluxe ed. (Chronicles of Narnia Ser.). (Illus.). 528p. (YA). (gr. 3 up). 1998. 50.00 (*0-06-028137-5*) HarpC.

— C.S. Lewis: Readings for Meditation & Reflection. Hooper, Walter, ed. LC 95-21947. 176p. 1996. pap. 13.00 (*0-06-065285-3*, Pub. by Harper SF) HarpC.

— The Dark Tower & Other Stories. Hooper, Walter, ed. LC 76-52387. 160p. (C). 1977. pap. 10.00 (*0-15-623930-2*, Harvest Bks) Harcourt.

— The Discarded Image: An Introduction to Medieval & Renaissance Literature. (Canto Book Ser.). 242p. (C). 1994. pap. 10.95 (*0-521-47735-2*) Cambridge U Pr.

— Edmund & the White Witch. LC 96-23202. (World of Narnia Ser.: Bk. 2). (Illus.). 40p. (J). (gr. k-4). 1997. 12.95 (*0-06-027516-2*); lib. bdg. 12.89 (*0-06-027517-0*) HarpC.

— Edmund & the White Witch. LC 96-23202. (World of Narnia Ser.). (Illus.). 40p. (J). (gr. k-4). 1998. pap. 5.95 (*0-06-443506-7*) HarpC.

— The Essential C. S. Lewis. 560p. 1996. per. 14.00 (*0-684-82374-8*) S&S Trade Pap.

***Lewis, C. S.** Essential C. S. Lewis. 1999. pap. 15.00 (*0-8054-2050-9*) Broadman.

Lewis, C. S. An Experiment in Criticism. 152p. (C). 1961. text 59.95 (*0-521-05553-9*) Cambridge U Pr.

— An Experiment in Criticism. (Canto Book Ser.). 151p. (C). 1992. pap. 10.95 (*0-521-42281-7*) Cambridge U Pr.

— The Four Loves. (Modern Classic Ser.). 1991. 18.00 (*0-15-132916-8*) Harcourt.

— The Four Loves. LC 60-10920. 141p. 1971. reprint ed. pap. 10.00 (*0-15-632930-1*, Harvest Bks) Harcourt.

— God in the Dock: Essays on Theology & Ethics. Hooper, Walter, ed. 346p. 1972. pap. 16.00 (*0-8028-0868-9*) Eerdmans.

— The Grand Miracle. (Epiphany Bks.). 176p. 1986. mass mkt. 5.99 (*0-345-33658-5*) Ballantine Pub Grp.

***Lewis, C. S.** The Great Divorce. 1999. pap. 7.00 (*0-8054-2048-7*) Broadman.

Lewis, C. S. The Great Divorce. 128p. 1996. per. 6.00 (*0-684-82376-4*, Touchstone) S&S Trade Pap.

— A Grief Observed. 160p. 1983. mass mkt. 6.50 (*0-553-27486-4*) Bantam.

— A Grief Observed. 1984. 7.20 (*0-8164-0137-3*) Harper SF.

— A Grief Observed. 96p. 1994. pap. 11.00 (*0-06-065284-5*, Pub. by Harper SF) HarpC.

— A Grief Observed. gif. ed. LC 88-45674. 96p. 1989. reprint ed. 13.00 (*0-06-065273-X*, Pub. by Harper SF) HarpC.

— A Grief Observed. large type ed. 96p. 1985. reprint ed. pap. 7.95 (*0-8027-2470-1*) Walker & Co.

— The Horse & His Boy. LC 93-14300. (Chronicles of Narnia Ser.: Bk. 5). (Illus.). 240p. (J). (gr. 3-7). 1994. pap. 6.95 (*0-06-440501-X*, HarpTrophy) HarpC Child Bks.

— The Horse & His Boy. LC 93-14300. (Chronicles of Narnia Ser.: Bk. 5). (Illus.). 240p. (J). (gr. 4-7). 1994. 16.95 (*0-06-023488-1*); pap. 4.95 (*0-06-447106-3*, Harper Keypoint); lib. bdg. 16.89 (*0-06-023489-X*, HarpTrophy) HarpC Child Bks.

Lewis, C. S. The Horse & His Boy. LC 93-14300. (Chronicles of Narnia Ser.: Bk. 5). (J). (gr. 4-8). 1994. 12.05 (*0-606-06470-2*, Pub. by Turtleback); 10.05 (*0-606-06471-0*, Pub. by Turtleback) Demco.

— The Horse & His Boy. large type ed. LC 99-57459. (Chronicles of Narnia Ser.: Bk. 5). 246p. (J). (gr. 8-12). 1950. 30.00 (*0-7862-2233-6*) Mac Lib Ref.

— The Horse & His Boy: Full-Color Collector's Edition. LC 93-14300. (Chronicles of Narnia Ser.: Bk. 5). (Illus.). 240p. (J). (gr. 4-7). 2000. mass mkt. 7.95 (*0-06-440940-6*, HarpTrophy) HarpC Child Bks.

Lewis, C. S. Inspirational Writing. 544p. 1994. 14.98 (*0-88486-108-2*) Arrowood Pr.

— Inspirational Writings of C. S. Lewis. 1987. 12.98 (*0-88486-016-7*, Inspirational Pr) Arrowood Pr.

— Inspirational Writings of C. S. Lewis. 1991. 12.98 (*0-88486-047-7*, Inspirational Pr) Arrowood Pr.

***Lewis, C. S.** The Joyful Christian. 1999. pap. 10.00 (*0-8054-2041-X*) Broadman.

An Asterisk (*) at the beginning of an entry indicates that the title is appearing for the first time.

Lewis, C. S. The Joyful Christian. 256p. 1996. per. 9.00 (*0-684-82377-2*) S&S Trade Pap.

— The Last Battle. LC 93-14302. (Chronicles of Narnia Ser.: Bk. 7). (Illus.). 224p. (J). (gr. 4-7). 1994. 16.95 (*0-06-023493-8*); pap. 6.95 (*0-06-440503-6*); pap. 4.95 (*0-06-447108-X*, HarpTrophy); lib. bdg. 16.89 (*0-06-023494-6*) HarpC Child Bks.

Lewis, C. S. The Last Battle. (Chronicles of Narnia Ser.: Bk. 7). (J). (gr. 4-8). 1950. 30.00 (*0-7862-2237-9*) Mac Lib Ref.

Lewis, C. S. The Last Battle. (Chronicles of Narnia Ser.: Bk. 7). 192p. (J). (gr. 4-8). 1970. pap. 3.95 (*0-02-044210-6*) Macmillan.

Lewis, C. S. The Last Battle. LC 93-14302. (Chronicles of Narnia Ser.: Bk. 7). (J). (gr. 4-8). 1994. 12.05 (*0-606-06517-2*, Pub. by Turtleback); 10.05 (*0-606-06518-0*, Pub. by Turtleback) Demco.

— The Last Battle: Full-Color Collector's Edition. LC 93-14302. (Chronicles of Narnia Ser.: Bk. 7). (Illus.). 224p. (J). (gr. 4-7). 2000. mass mkt. 7.95 (*0-06-440941-4*, HarpTrophy) HarpC Child Bks.

— El Leon, La Bruja y El Armario. (Chronicles of Narnia Ser.). 1996. 17.05 (*0-606-10412-7*, Pub. by Turtleback) Demco.

Lewis, C. S. The Letters of C. S. Lewis. Hooper, Walter & Lewis, W. H., eds. 528p. 1994. pap. 14.95 (*0-15-650871-0*) Harcourt.

— Letters to an American Lady. Kilby, Clyde S., ed. 128p. 1967. pap. 8.00 (*0-8028-1428-X*) Eerdmans.

***Lewis, C. S.** Letters to Children. (J). 1999. pap. 8.00 (*0-8054-2043-6*) Broadman.

Lewis, C. S. Letters to Malcolm: Chiefly on Prayer. LC 64-11536. 136p. 1973. reprint ed. pap. 9.00 (*0-15-650880-X*, Harvest Bks) Harcourt.

— The Lion, the Witch & the Wardrobe. (Chronicles of Narnia Ser.: Bk. 1). (J). (gr. 4-8). 1976. 20.95 (*0-8488-0823-1*) Amereon Ltd.

— The Lion, the Witch & the Wardrobe. (Chronicles of Narnia Ser.: Bk. 1). (J). (gr. 4-8). 1989. pap. 5.95 (*0-87129-265-3*, L62) Dramatic Pub.

— The Lion, the Witch & the Wardrobe. LC 93-8889. (Chronicles of Narnia Ser.: Bk. 1). (Illus.). 208p. (J). (gr. 4-7). 1994. 16.95 (*0-06-023481-4*); pap. 4.95 (*0-06-447104-7*, HarpTrophy); lib. bdg. 16.89 (*0-06-023482-2*) HarpC Child Bks.

***Lewis, C. S.** The Lion, the Witch & the Wardrobe. (Chronicles of Narnia Ser.: Bk. 1). 40p. (J). (gr. 4-8). 1999. 9.95 (*1-56137-243-9*) Novel Units.

— The Lion, the Witch & the Wardrobe. (Chronicles of Narnia Ser.: Bk. 1). (J). (gr. 4-8). 1999. 11.95 (*1-56137-704-X*) Novel Units.

Lewis, C. S. The Lion, the Witch & the Wardrobe. LC 83-61572. (Chronicles of Narnia Ser.: Bk. 1). (Illus.). 160p. (J). (gr. 4-8). 1988. lib. bdg. 22.95 (*0-02-758200-0*, Mac Bks Young Read) S&S Childrens.

***Lewis, C. S.** The Lion, the Witch & the Wardrobe. 112p. 1999. pap. 10.95 (*1-84002-049-0*, Pub. by Theatre Comm) Consort Bk Sales.

— The Lion, the Witch & the Wardrobe. LC 99-57460. (Chronicles of Narnia Ser.: Bk. 1). (Illus.). (J). (gr. 4-8). 1950. 21.95 (*0-7862-2232-8*) Thorndike Pr.

— The Lion, the Witch & the Wardrobe. LC 93-8889. (Chronicles of Narnia Ser.: Bk. 1). (J). (gr. 4-8). 1994. 12.05 (*0-606-06532-6*, Pub. by Turtleback); 10.05 (*0-606-06533-4*, Pub. by Turtleback) Demco.

Lewis, C. S. The Lion, the Witch & the Wardrobe. (Chronicles of Narnia Ser.: Bk. 1). (J). (gr. 4-8). 1995. 16.15 (*0-606-07791-X*) Turtleback.

— The Lion, the Witch & the Wardrobe. abr. ed. LC 93-8889. (Chronicles of Narnia Ser.: Bk. 1). (Illus.). 208p. (J). (gr. 4-7). 1994. pap. 6.95 (*0-06-440499-4*) HarpC Child Bks.

— The Lion, the Witch & the Wardrobe. abr. ed. LC 94 13165. (Trophy Picture Bk.). (Illus.). 64p. (J). (gr. 4-7). 1995. pap. 11.95 (*0-06-443399-4*, HarpTrophy) HarpC Child Bks.

— The Lion, the Witch & the Wardrobe. (Chronicles of Narnia Ser.: Bk. 1). (J). (gr. 4-8). 1986. reprint ed. pap. 7.95 (*0-02-044490-7*) Macmillan.

***Lewis, C. S.** The Lion, the Witch & the Wardrobe: Bound Complete Narnia Teacher's Guide. (Chronicles of Narnia Ser.). (J). 2000. pap. write for info. (*0-06-449255-9*, HarpTrophy) HarpC Child Bks.

— The Lion, the Witch & the Wardrobe: (C. Birmingham Edition) abr. ed. LC 99-51480. (Illus.). 48p. (J). (gr. 1-5). 2000. 15.95 (*0-06-029011-0*) HarpC Child Bks.

Lewis, C. S. The Lion, the Witch & the Wardrobe: (El Lion, la Bruja y el Armario) LC 49-124440. (SPA.). (J). (gr. 4-7). 1995. 11.95 (*84-204-4564-9*) Santillana.

***Lewis, C. S.** The Lion, the Witch & the Wardrobe: Full-Color Collector's Edition. LC 93-8889. (Chronicles of Narnia Ser.: Bk. 1). (Illus.). 208p. (J). (gr. 4-7). 2000. mass mkt. 7.95 (*0-06-440942-2*, HarpTrophy) HarpC Child Bks.

— The Lion, the Witch & the Wardrobe: Teacher's Guide. (J). 2000. pap., teacher ed. write for info. (*0-06-447260-4*, HarpTrophy) HarpC Child Bks.

Lewis, C. S. The Lion, the Witch & the Wardrobe - One Act - Two Character. 30p. 1989. pap. 5.50 (*0-87129-668-3*, L54) Dramatic Pub.

Lewis, C. S. The Lion, the Witch & the Wardrobe Deluxe Edition: Deluxe Edition. deluxe ed. LC 96-49854. (Chronicles of Narnia Ser.: Bk. 1). (Illus.). 176p. (J). (gr. 3-7). 1994. 24.95 (*0-06-027724-6*) HarpC.

Lewis, C. S. Lucy Steps Through the Wardrobe. LC 96-23200. (World of Narnia Ser.: Bk. 1). (Illus.). 40p. (J). (gr. k-4). 1997. 12.95 (*0-06-027450-6*) HarpC.

— Lucy Steps Through the Wardrobe. LC 96-23200. (World of Narnia Ser.). (Illus.). 40p. (J). (gr. k-4). 1998. pap. 5.95 (*0-06-443505-9*) HarpC.

Lewis, C. S. The Magician's Nephew. 1984. 5.95 (*0-87129-541-5*, M57) Dramatic Pub.

Lewis, C. S. The Magician's Nephew. LC 93-14301. (Chronicles of Narnia Ser.: Bk. 6). (Illus.). 208p. (J). (gr. 3 up). 1994. 16.95 (*0-06-023497-0*) HarpC Child Bks.

— The Magician's Nephew. LC 93-14301. (Chronicles of Narnia Ser.: Bk. 6). (Illus.). 208p. (J). (gr. 4-7). 1994. pap. 6.95 (*0-06-440505-2*, HarpTrophy); pap. 4.95 (*0-06-447110-1*, HarpTrophy) HarpC Child Bks.

Lewis, C. S. The Magician's Nephew. LC 93-14301. (Chronicles of Narnia Ser.: Bk. 6). (J). (gr. 4-8). 1994. 12.05 (*0-606-06553-9*, Pub. by Turtleback); 10.05 (*0-606-06554-7*, Pub. by Turtleback) Demco.

Lewis, C. S. The Magician's Nephew. abr. ed. (Chronicles of Narnia Ser.). (J). (gr. 4-7). 1997. audio 18.00 (*0-553-47768-4*) BDD Aud Pub.

***Lewis, C. S.** The Magician's Nephew. large type ed. LC 99-49183. (Chronicles of Narnia Ser.: Bk. 6). 210p. (J). (gr. 4-7). 2000. 21.95 (*0-7862-2231-X*) Silhouette.

— The Magician's Nephew: Full-Color Collector's Edition. LC 93-14301. (Chronicles of Narnia Ser.: Bk. 6). (Illus.). 208p. (J). (gr. 4-7). 2000. mass mkt. 7.95 (*0-06-440943-0*, HarpTrophy) HarpC Child Bks.

Lewis, C. S. The Magician's Nephew: One-Act. 1985. pap. 5.95 (*0-87129-368-4*, M86) Dramatic Pub.

— Mere Christianity. 190p. 1986. pap. 3.95 (*0-02-086940-1*) Macmillan.

— Mere Christianity. 1997. 18.00 (*0-684-84638-1*) S&S Trade.

— Mere Christianity. rev. ed. LC 84-20027. 192p. 1996. per. 6.00 (*0-684-82378-0*, Touchstone) S&S Trade Pap.

— Mere Christianity: A Revised & Enlarged Edition, with a new introduction, of the three books, The case for Christianity, Christian behaviour, & Beyond Personality. large type enl. rev. ed. LC 86-30451. (Large Print Inspirational Ser.). 384p. 1987. pap. 16.95 (*0-8027-2575-9*) Walker & Co.

***Lewis, C. S.** Miracles. 1999. pap. 7.00 (*0-8054-2045-2*) Broadman.

Lewis, C. S. Miracles. 240p. 1996. per. 7.00 (*0-684-82379-9*, Touchstone) S&S Trade Pap.

— The Narnia Trivia Book: Inspired by The Chronicles of Narnia by C.S. Lewis. LC 98-56502. (Narnia Ser.). (Illus.). 128p. (J). (gr. 3-7). 1999. pap. 4.95 (*0-06-446212-9*, HarpTrophy) HarpC Child Bks.

— Narrative Poems. Hooper, Walter, ed. LC 78-15062. 192p. (C). 1978. pap. 4.95 (*0-15-665327-3*, Harvest Bks) Harcourt.

— Of Other Worlds: Essays & Stories. Hooper, Walter, ed. LC 75-6785. 168p. (C). 1975. pap. 10.00 (*0-15-667897-7*, Harvest Bks) Harcourt.

— On Stories: And Other Essays on Literature. Hooper, Walter, ed. LC 81-48014. 180p. 1982. pap. 8.00 (*0-15-668788-7*, Harvest Bks) Harcourt.

— Out of the Silent Planet. 1980. 14.95 (*0-02-570790-6*) Macmillan.

— Out of the Silent Planet. LC 96-10402. 160p. 1996. per. 6.95 (*0-684-82380-2*) S&S Trade.

— Out of the Silent Planet. LC 96-30110. 160p. 1996. 21.50 (*0-684-83364-6*) S&S Trade.

— Out of the Silent Planet. 1965. 12.05 (*0-606-01214-1*, Pub. by Turtleback) Demco.

— Out of the Silent Planet. 1998. lib. bdg. 20.95 (*1-56723-071-7*) Yestermorrow.

— Out of the Silent Planet. large type ed. 234p. 1998. 23.95 (*0-7838-0411-3*) Mac Lib Ref.

— Out of the Silent Planet. 1991. reprint ed. lib. bdg. 21.95 (*1-56849-039-9*) Buccaneer Bks.

— Out of the Silent Planet. 174p. 1990. reprint ed. 45.00 (*0-02-570795-7*, Hudson Rvr Edtn) S&S Trade.

— Perelandra. (J). 1976. 21.95 (*0-8488-0564-X*) Amereon Ltd.

— Perelandra. 1965. 12.05 (*0-606-00445-9*, Pub. by Turtleback) Demco.

— Perelandra: A Novel. LC 96-10403. (Space Trilogy Ser.: No. 2). 224p. 1996. per. 6.95 (*0-684-82382-9*) S&S Trade.

— Perelandra: A Novel. LC 96-20724. 192p. 1996. 21.50 (*0-684-83365-4*) S&S Trade.

— Perelandra: A Novel. (Space Trilogy Ser.: No. 2). 222p. 1990. reprint ed. 40.00 (*0-02-570845-7*, Hudson Rvr Edtn) S&S Trade.

— The Pilgrims Regress: An Allegorical Apology for Christianity, Reason, & Romanticism. 219p. 1992. pap. 14.00 (*0-8028-0641-4*) Eerdmans.

— Poems. Hooper, Walter, ed. LC 77-4733. 168p. 1977. pap. 10.00 (*0-15-672248-8*, Harvest Bks) Harcourt.

— Poetry & Prose in the Sixteenth Century. (Oxford History of English Literature Ser.: Vol. IV). 704p. (C). 1990. text 75.00 (*0-19-812231-4*) OUP.

— A Preface to Paradise Lost. 154p. 1961. text 14.95 (*0-19-500345-4*) OUP.

— Present Concerns. Hooper, Walter, ed. 112p. 1987. pap. 10.00 (*0-15-673840-6*, Harvest Bks) Harcourt.

Lewis, C. S. Prince Caspian. LC 99-57458. (Chronicles of Narnia Ser.: Bk. 2). (J). (gr. 4-8). 1950. 30.00 (*0-7862-2234-4*) Mac Lib Ref.

Lewis, C. S. Prince Caspian. (Chronicles of Narnia Ser.: Bk. 2). 224p. (J). (gr. 4-8). 1970. pap. 3.95 (*0-02-044240-8*) Macmillan.

Lewis, C. S. Prince Caspian. (Chronicles of Narnia Ser.: Bk. 2). (J). (gr. 4-8). 1994. 12.05 (*0-606-06680-2*, Pub. by Turtleback); 10.05 (*0-606-06681-0*, Pub. by Turtleback) Demco.

— Prince Caspian. (Chronicles of Narnia Ser.: Bk. 2). (J). (gr. 4-8). 1998. lib. bdg. 18.95 (*1-56723-072-5*) Yestermorrow.

Lewis, C. S. Prince Caspian. LC 85-18999. (Chronicles of Narnia Ser.: Bk. 2). (Illus.). 192p. (J). (gr. 4-8). 1986. reprint ed. pap. 7.95 (*0-02-044430-3*) Macmillan.

***Lewis, C. S.** Prince Caspian: Full-Color Collector's Edition. LC 93-11514. (Chronicles of Narnia Ser.: Bk. 2). (Illus.). 240p. (J). (gr. 4-7). 2000. mass mkt. 7.95 (*0-06-440944-9*, HarpTrophy) HarpC Child Bks.

Lewis, C. S. Prince Caspian: The Return to Narnia. LC 93-11514. (Chronicles of Narnia Ser.: Bk. 2). (Illus.). 240p. (J). (gr. 4-7). 1994. 16.95 (*0-06-023483-0*); pap. 6.95 (*0-06-440500-1*, HarpTrophy); pap. 4.95 (*0-06-447105-5*, Harper Keypoint); lib. bdg. 16.89 (*0-06-023484-9*) HarpC Child Bks.

Lewis, C. S. Prince Caspian Audio. abr. ed. (Chronicles of Narnia Ser.). (J). (gr. 4-7). 1989. audio 11.95 (*0-89845-090-X*, CPN 1603) HarperAudio.

Lewis, C. S. The Problem of Pain. 144p. 1996. per. 6.00 (*0-684-82383-7*, Touchstone) S&S Trade Pap.

***Lewis, C. S.** Problem of Pain. 1999. pap. 7.00 (*0-8054-2049-5*) Broadman.

Lewis, C. S. The Problem with Pain - A Grief Observed. LC 99-37904. (Shepherd's Notes Ser.). 1999. pap. 5.95 (*0-8054-9353-0*) Broadman.

— The Quotable Lewis. Martindale, Wayne & Root, Jerry, eds. (Illus.). 651p. 1990. 19.99 (*0-8423-5115-9*) Tyndale Hse.

— Readings for Meditation & Reflection. Hooper, Walter, ed. LC 98-35482. 1998. pap. text 15.95 (*0-8027-2735-2*) Walker & Co.

— Reflections on the Psalms. LC 58-10910. 160p. 1964. pap. 9.00 (*0-15-676248-X*, Harvest Bks) Harcourt.

— Rehabilitations & Other Essays. LC 71-167377. (Essay Index Reprint Ser.). 1977. reprint ed. 18.95 (*0-8369-2559-9*) Ayer.

— Rehabilitations & Other Essays. reprint ed. 14.00 (*0-403-04233-X*) Somerset Pub.

— The Screwtape Letters. 20.95 (*0-89190-989-3*) Amereon Ltd.

— The Screwtape Letters. 112p. 1995. mass mkt. 4.50 (*0-553-21443-8*, Bantam Classics) Bantam.

***Lewis, C. S.** The Screwtape Letters. 1999. pap. 7.00 (*0-8054-2040-1*) Broadman.

Lewis, C. S. The Screwtape Letters. 128p. 1996. per. 6.00 (*0-684-83117-1*, Touchstone) S&S Trade Pap.

— The Screwtape Letters. 1988. 11.09 (*0-606-12505-1*, Pub. by Turtleback) Demco.

— The Seeing Eye & Other Selected Essays from Christian Reflections. 256p. 1986. mass mkt. 6.99 (*0-345-32866-3*) Ballantine Pub Grp.

— The Shadow Lands of C. S. Lewis: The Man Behind the Movie. Kreeft, Peter, ed. LC 94-75772. 221p. 1994. pap. 12.95 (*0-89870-493-6*) Ignatius Pr.

— The Silver Chair. LC 93-14299. (Chronicles of Narnia Ser.: Bk. 4). (Illus.). 256p. (J). (gr. 4-7). 1994. 16.95 (*0-06-023495-4*); pap. 4.95 (*0-06-447109-8*); pap. 6.95 (*0-06-440504-4*, HarpTrophy) HarpC Child Bks.

Lewis, C. S. The Silver Chair. LC 99-57456. (Chronicles of Narnia Ser.: Bk. 4). (J). (gr. 4-8). 1950. 30.00 (*0-7862-2236-0*) Mac Lib Ref.

— The Silver Chair. (Chronicles of Narnia Ser.: Bk. 4). (J). (gr. 4-8). 1994. 12.05 (*0-606-06737-X*, Pub. by Turtleback); 10.05 (*0-606-06738-8*, Pub. by Turtleback) Demco.

— The Silver Chair: Full-Color Collector's Edition. LC 93-14299. (Chronicles of Narnia Ser.: Bk. 4). (Illus.). 256p. (J). (gr. 4-7). 2000. mass mkt. 7.95 (*0-06-440945-7*, HarpTrophy) HarpC Child Bks.

Lewis, C. S. Six by Lewis, 6 vols. 1978. boxed set 27.95 (*0-02-086770-0*) Macmillan.

— Six by Lewis. 1996. per. 34.95 (*0-684-83119-8*) Simon & Schuster.

— Space Trilogy. 1996. pap., per., boxed set 20.85 (*0-684-83118-X*) Simon & Schuster.

— Space Trilogy, 3 vols. 2nd ed. 1986. pap. 16.95 (*0-02-022360-9*) Macmillan.

— Spirits in Bondage: A Cycle of Lyrics. Hooper, Walter, ed. 132p. 1984. pap. 10.00 (*0-15-684748-5*, Harvest Bks) Harcourt.

— Studies in Medieval & Renaissance Literature. Hooper, Walter, ed. LC 99-174745. (Canto Book Ser.). 196p. 1998. pap. 12.95 (*0-521-64584-0*) Cambridge U Pr.

— Studies in Words. (Canto Book Ser.). 349p. (C). 1990. pap. 12.95 (*0-521-39831-2*) Cambridge U Pr.

— Surprised by Joy. 22.95 (*0-8488-1078-3*) Amereon Ltd.

— Surprised by Joy: The Shape of My Early Life. LC 56-5329. 238p. (C). 1975. pap. 11.00 (*0-15-687011-8*, Harvest Bks) Harcourt.

— Surprised by Joy: The Shape of My Early Life. LC 96-112306. 240p. (C). 1995. 17.00 (*0-15-100185-5*) Harcourt.

— Surprised by Joy: The Shape of My Early Life. large type ed. (Large Print Inspirational Ser.). 368p. 1986. pap. 15.95 (*0-8027-2536-8*) Walker & Co.

— That Hideous Strength: A Modern Fairy-Tale for Grownups. LC 68-7663. 384p. 1996. per. 6.95 (*0-684-82385-3*) S&S Trade.

— That Hideous Strength: A Modern Fairy-Tale for Grownups. LC 96-20722. 384p. 1996. 22.50 (*0-684-83367-0*) S&S Trade.

Lewis, C. S. That Hideous Strength; A Modern Fairy-Tale for Grownups. 1965. 11.05 (*0-606-05067-1*, Pub. by Turtleback) Demco.

Lewis, C. S. That Hideous Strength: A Modern Fairy-Tale for Grownups. 382p. 1990. reprint ed. 60.00 (*0-02-571255-1*, Hudson Rvr Edtn) S&S Trade.

— Till We Have Faces: A Myth Retold. LC 79-24272. (Illus.). 313p. (C). 1980. pap. 13.00 (*0-15-690436-5*, Harvest Bks) Harcourt.

— Till We Have Faces: A Myth Retold. large type ed. LC 98-21638. 325 p. 1998. pap. 24.95 (*0-7838-0275-7*, G K Hall Lrg Type) Mac Lib Ref.

— The Visionary Christian. 288p. 1996. per. 11.00 (*0-684-82386-1*, Touchstone) S&S Trade Pap.

***Lewis, C. S.** Visionary Christian. 1999. pap. 12.00 (*0-8054-2042-8*) Broadman.

Lewis, C. S. The Voyage of the Dawn Treader. LC 93-11515. (Chronicles of Narnia Ser.: Bk. 2). (Illus.). 288p. (J). (gr. 4-7). 1994. pap. 4.95 (*0-06-447107-1*) HarpC Child Bks.

— The Voyage of the Dawn Treader. LC 93-11515. (Chronicles of Narnia Ser.: Bk. 3). (Illus.). 256p. (J). (gr. 4-7). 1994. 16.95 (*0-06-023486-5*); pap. 6.95 (*0-06-440502-8*, HarpTrophy) HarpC Child Bks.

Lewis, C. S. The Voyage of the Dawn Treader. LC 99-57457. (Chronicles of Narnia Ser.: Bk. 3). (J). (gr. 4-8). 1950. 30.00 (*0-7862-2235-2*) Mac Lib Ref.

— The Voyage of the Dawn Treader. (Chronicles of Narnia Ser.: Bk. 3). (J). (gr. 4-8). 1994. 11.05 (*0-606-06851-1*, Pub. by Turtleback); 10.05 (*0-606-06852-X*, Pub. by Turtleback) Demco.

— The Voyage of the Dawn Treader: Full-Color Collector's Edition. LC 93-11515. (Chronicles of Narnia Ser.: Bk. 3). (Illus.). 256p. (J). (gr. 4-7). 2000. mass mkt. 7.95 (*0-06-440946-5*, HarpTrophy) HarpC Child Bks.

Lewis, C. S. The Weight of Glory & Other Addresses. Hooper, Walter, ed. 144p. 1996. per. 10.00 (*0-684-82384-5*, Touchstone) S&S Trade Pap.

— The Wood Between the Worlds. LC 98-17130. (Illus.). 40p. (J). (gr. k-4). 1999. 14.95 (*0-06-027640-1*) HarpC Child Bks.

***Lewis, C. S.** The Wood Between the Worlds. LC 98-17130. (Illus.). 40p. (J). (gr. k-4). 2000. pap. 5.95 (*0-06-443641-1*, HarpTrophy) HarpC Child Bks.

Lewis, C. S. The World's Last Night & Other Essays. LC 73-4887. 128p. 1973. reprint ed. pap. 9.00 (*0-15-698360-5*, Harvest Bks) Harcourt.

***Lewis, C. S. & Calabria, Don G.** The Latin Letters of C. S. Lewis. Moynihan, Martin, ed. & tr. by. LC 98-18477. Orig. Title: Letters: A Study in Friendship. (LAT.). 126p. 1998. 18.00 (*1-890318-34-5*) St Augustines Pr.

Lewis, C. S. & Dorsett, Lyle W. C. S. Lewis' Letters to Children. 128p. 1996. per. 8.00 (*0-684-82372-1*, Touchstone) S&S Trade Pap.

Lewis, C. S. & Lawrie, Robin. The Magician's Nephew. abr. ed. LC 98-24263. (Chronicles of Narnia Ser.: Bk. 6). (Illus.). 64p. (J). (gr. 3-7). 1999. pap. 10.95 (*0-06-443515-6*, HarpTrophy) HarpC Child Bks.

Lewis, C. S. & Maze, Deborah. Aslan. LC 97-2046. (Narnia Ser.). (Illus.). 40p. (J). (gr. k-4). 1999. pap. 5.95 (*0-06-443527-X*) HarpC.

***Lewis, C. S. & Parry, Jay A.** Favorite Quotations from C. S. Lewis for Latter-Day Saints. LC 00-31524. 2000. write for info. (*1-57345-799-X*) Deseret Bk.

Lewis, C. S. & Scholastic, Inc. Staff. The Lion, the Witch & the Wardrobe. anniversary ed. (Chronicles of Narnia Ser.: Bk. 1). 16p. (J). (gr. 4-8). 1997. pap. text 3.95 (*0-590-36647-5*) Scholastic Inc.

***Lewis, C. S., et al.** The Lion, the Witch & the Wardrobe. LC 99-51480. (Illus.). (J). 2000. lib. bdg. 14.89 (*0-06-029013-7*) HarpC.

Lewis, C. S., et al. Narnia: The Short Musical Version. 1995. 5.95 (*0-87129-565-2*, N02) Dramatic Pub.

Lewis, C. S., jt. auth. see Forsyth, James.

Lewis, C. S., jt. auth. see Gresham, Douglas H.

Lewis, C. S., jt. auth. see Lindskoog, Kathryn.

Lewis, C. S., jt. auth. see Shepherd, Michael.

Lewis, C. S., jt. auth. see Sibley, Brian.

Lewis, C. S., ed. see MacDonald, George.

Lewis, Candace, jt. auth. see Mann, Peter.

Lewis, Carenza, jt. ed. see Aston, Michael.

Lewis, Carla & Bertolino, Angela. "Extra" Work for Brain Surgeons, No. 13. rev. ed. Bontrager, Jennifer, ed. 265p. 1999. spiral bd. 20.00 (*1-893899-00-4*) Holly Op Sys.

***Lewis, Carla & Bertolino, Angela.** Extra Work for Brain Surgeons, Vol. 14. Bontrager, Jennifer, ed. 282p. 1999. 20.00 (*1-893899-01-2*) Holly Op Sys.

— "Extra" Work for Brain Surgeons, Vol. 15. Bontrager, Jennifer, ed. 282p. 1999. (*1-893899-02-0*) Holly Op Sys.

Lewis, Carla, jt. auth. see Bertolino, Angela.

Lewis, Carol & Sternheimer, Stephen. Soviet Urban Management: With Comparisons to the United States. LC 78-19748. (Praeger Special Studies). 216p. 1979. 59.95 (*0-275-90381-8*, C0381, Praeger Pubs) Greenwood.

***Lewis, Carol Ann.** San Diego Coloring Book. (Illus.). 32p. (J). (ps-6). 2000. pap. 5.95 (*0-9678482-0-2*) Here & There Pubns.

Lewis, Carol M., jt. ed. see Beck, Araidne P.

Lewis, Carol R. Listening to Children. LC 84-11154. 208p. 1992. pap. 35.00 (*0-87668-285-9*) Aronson.

Lewis, Carol W. The Ethics Challenge in Public Service: A Problem-Solving Guide. LC 91-3401. (Public Administration Ser.). 252p. 1991. 33.95 (*1-55542-383-3*) Jossey-Bass.

Lewis, Carol W. & Walker, A. Grayson, III. Casebook in Public Budgeting & Financial Management. (Illus.). 384p. (C). 1984. pap. text 30.80 (*0-13-115402-8*) P-H.

Lewis, Carola R. Ramblings. LC 73-91452. 104p. 1974. 10.00 (*0-87012-161-8*) McClain.

Lewis, Carole & McNerney, Therese. Functional Toolbox, Vol. II. 300p. 1997. write for info. (*0-9643582-3-9*) Learn Pubns.

Lewis, Carole & Whalin, W. T. First Place. LC 97-45914. 272p. 1998. pap. 12.99 (*0-8054-0179-2*) Broadman.

Lewis, Carole, et al. Orthopedic Flash. 725p. 1997. text 249.00 (*0-9643582-4-7*) Learn Pubns.

Lewis, Carole B. Aging: The Health Care Challenge. 3rd ed. (Illus.). 494p. (C). 1995. pap. text 43.95 (*0-8036-0042-9*) Davis Co.

— Clinical Measures of Functional Outcomes: The Functional Tool Box. McNerney, Therese, ed. 240p. 1994. student ed. 149.00 (*0-9643582-0-4*) Learn Pubns.

L

— Improving Mobility in Older Persons: A Manual for Geriatric Specialists. LC 88-24244. 172p. (C). 1989. 56.00 (0-8342-0020-1) Aspen Pub.

Lewis, Carole B. & Knortz, Karen A. Orthopaedic Assessment & Treatment of the Geriatric Patient. (Illus.). 424p. (C). (gr. 13). 1993. text 69.00 (0-8016-6512-4, 06512) Mosby Inc.

Lewis, Carole B. & McNerney, Therese. Exercise Handouts for Rehabilitation. (Aspen Series on Physical Therapy). 536p. 1993. ring bd. 89.00 (0-8342-0372-3, 20372) Aspen Pub.

Lewis, Caroline, jt. ed. see Jay, Peter.

Lewis, Caroline T. Prenatal Care in the United States, 1980-94. 23p. 1996. pap. 3.00 (0-16-061446-5) USGPO.

Lewis, Carolyn D. Reporting for Television. LC 83-7568. (Illus.). 192p. 1984. text 41.00 (0-231-05538-2) Col U Pr.

***Lewis, Carroll.** Alice's Adventures in Wonderland. (Aladdin Classics Ser.). 160p. (J). 2000. per. 3.99 (0-689-83375-X) Aladdin.

Lewis, Carroll. Treasures of Galveston Bay. (Illus.). 1966. 13.95 (0-87244-052-4) Texian.

Lewis, Carson M., et al. Superficial Liposculpture: Manual of Technique. LC 92-49210. 137p. 1996. text 180.00 (0-387-97917-4) Spr-Verlag.

***Lewis, Catherine.** Considerable Passions: Golf, the Masters & the Legacy of Bobby Jones. (Illus.). 208p. 2000. 39.95 (1-57243-354-X) Triumph Bks.

Lewis, Catherine. Dry Fire: A Novel. 288p. 1996. 21.00 (0-393-03835-1) Norton.

***Lewis, Catherine.** Postcards to Father Abraham. LC 99-27005. (Illus.). 304p. (J). 2000. 17.00 (0-689-82852-7) Atheneum Yung Read.

Lewis, Catherine, jt. auth. see Mannis, Barbara.

Lewis, Catherine C. Educating Hearts & Minds: Reflections on Japanese Preschool & Elementary Education. (Illus.). 261p. (C). 1995. pap. text 16.95 (0-521-45832-3) Cambridge U Pr.

Lewis, Catherine F., jt. auth. see Haywood, Kathleen M.

Lewis, Catherine H. Horry County, South Carolina, 1730-1993. LC 97-21012. (Illus.). 224p. 1998. lib. bdg. 24.95 (1-57003-207-6) U of SC Pr.

Lewis, Cathy, ed. see Bianchi, Susan & Butler, Jan.

Lewis, Catriona J., jt. auth. see Kirkwood, Evelyne M.

Lewis, Cecil. All My Yesterdays: An Autobiography. LC 93-14870. 1993. pap. 24.95 (1-85230-405-7, Pub. by Element MA) Penguin Putnam.

— Farewell to Wings. Gibert, James, ed. LC 79-7279. (Flight: Its First Seventy-Five Years Ser.). (Illus.). 1980. reprint ed. lib. bdg. 15.95 (0-405-12188-1) Ayer.

Lewis, Cecil Day, see Day Lewis, Cecil, ed.

Lewis, Celeste, jt. auth. see Johnson, Paul B.

Lewis, Chad T., et al. Managerial Skills in Organizations. 350p. 1990. teacher ed. write for info. incl. disk (0-318-66374-0, H23377) P-H.

Lewis, Charles. America's Frontline Trade Officials. 204p. (Orig.). 1994. pap. text 20.00 (0-8191-9921-4) U Pr of Amer.

***Lewis, Charles.** Outlaw Class. 2001. write for info. (0-380-97682-X, Wm Morrow) Morrow Avon.

Lewis, Charles. State & Diplomatic Immunity. 3rd rev. ed. 224p. 1990. 120.00 (1-85044-254-1) LLP.

***Lewis, Charles & Center for Public Integrity Staff.** The Buying of the President 2000. LC 99-55251. 384p. 2000. pap. 14.00 (0-380-79519-1, Avon Bks) Morrow Avon.

Lewis, Charles & Lewis, Karoki. Delhi's Historic Villages: A Photographic Evocation. LC 97-905060. (C). 1997. 58.00 (81-7530-011-6, Pub. by Ravi Dayal) S Asia.

Lewis, Charles & O'Brien, Margaret, eds. Reassessing Fatherhood. LC 87-60199. 288p. (C). 1987. text 45.00 (0-8039-8019-1); pap. text 24.00 (0-8039-8020-5) Sage.

Lewis, Charles, jt. ed. see Keren, Gideon.

Lewis, Charles A. Green Nature - Human Nature: The Meaning of Plants in Our Lives. LC 95-17506. (Environment & the Human Condition Ser.). (Illus.). 160p. 1996. 14.95 (0-252-06510-7); text 32.95 (0-252-02213-0) U of Ill Pr.

Lewis, Charles B. Bessie Bane: or The Mormon's Victim. (Notable American Authors Ser.). 1999. reprint ed. lib. bdg. 125.00 (0-7812-3791-2) Rprt Serv.

— Brother Gardner's Lime-Kiln Club. LC 76-104513. (Illus.). reprint ed. lib. bdg. 22.00 (0-8398-1159-4) Irvington.

— Brother Gardner's Lime-Kiln Club. (Notable American Authors Ser.). 1999. reprint ed. lib. bdg. 125.00 (0-7812-3793-9) Rprt Serv.

— The Comic Biography of James A. Garfield. (Notable American Authors Ser.). 1999. reprint ed. lib. bdg. 125.00 (0-7812-3792-0) Rprt Serv.

— Goaks & Tears. (Notable American Authors Ser.). 1999. reprint ed. lib. bdg. 125.00 (0-7812-3790-4) Rprt Serv.

— Quad's Odds. (Notable American Authors Ser.). 1999. reprint ed. lib. bdg. 125.00 (0-7812-3789-0) Rprt Serv.

— Sawed-Off Sketches. (Notable American Authors Ser.). 1999. reprint ed. lib. bdg. 125.00 (0-7812-3794-7) Rprt Serv.

— Sparks of Wit & Humor. (Notable American Authors Ser.). 1999. reprint ed. lib. bdg. 125.00 (0-7812-3795-5) Rprt Serv.

— Trials & Troubles of the Bowser Family. (Notable American Authors Ser.). 1999. reprint ed. lib. bdg. 125.00 (0-7812-3796-3) Rprt Serv.

***Lewis, Charles B.** Workers' Compensation Guide for Employers: Regulations - Checklists - Forms. 4th ed. 600p. 2000. ring bd. 119.50 (1-56759-062-4) Summers Pr.

Lewis, Charles B., ed. see Kirk, H. Ray.

Lewis, Charles C., jt. auth. see Lord, Richard A.

Lewis, Charles E., Jr. Getting What You Want & Being Liked for It! How to Resolve Conflicts, Problems, & Situations with Anyone about Anything. (Illus.). 320p. 1998. pap. 19.95 (0-9661001-0-7) Littlejohn Pub.

Lewis, Charles F., jt. ed. see Christiansen, M. N.

Lewis, Charles J. Medical Negligence: A Practical Guide. 567p. 1992. 165.00 (0-85459-643-7, Pub. by Tolley Pubng) St Mut.

— Medical Negligence: A Practical Guide. 600p. 1995. 310.00 (1-86012-073-3, Pub. by Tolley Pubng) St Mut.

Lewis, Charles L. Admiral De Grasse & American Independence. LC 79-6113. (Navies & Men Ser.). (Illus.). 1980. reprint ed. lib. bdg. 44.95 (0-405-13042-2) Ayer.

— David Glasgow Farragut. LC 79-6115. (Navies & Men Ser.). (Illus.). 1980. lib. bdg. 38.95 (0-405-13043-0); lib. bdg. 44.95 (0-405-13044-9) Ayer.

— Famous American Naval Officers. rev. ed. LC 76-142655. (Essay Index Reprint Ser.). 1977. 31.95 (0-8369-2170-4) Ayer.

— Famous Old-World Sea Fighters. LC 70-99708. (Essay Index Reprint Ser.). 1977. 31.95 (0-8369-1419-8) Ayer.

— Famous Sea Fighters: Outstanding Naval Engagements Over 23 Centuries of Sea History with a Bibliography of 102 Works. 1977. lib. bdg. 75.00 (0-8490-1804-8) Gordon Pr.

— Matthew Fontaine Maury. LC 79-6116. (Navies & Men Ser.). (Illus.). 1980. reprint ed. lib. bdg. 31.95 (0-405-13045-7) Ayer.

— Matthew Fontaine Maury, the Pathfinder of the Seas. LC 72-98638. reprint ed. 34.50 (0-404-03984-7) AMS Pr.

— The Romantic Decatur. LC 79-164614. (Select Bibliographies Reprint Ser.). 1977. reprint ed. 23.95 (0-8369-5898-5) Ayer.

Lewis, Charles M., ed. Relativism & Religion. LC 94-43978. 256p. 1995. text 55.00 (0-312-12392-2) St Martin.

***Lewis, Charles R.** A Coincidence of Wants: The Novel & Neoclassical Economics. rev. ed. LC 99-52038. (Literary Criticism & Cultural Theory Ser.). 160p. 2000. 60.00 (0-8153-3648-9) Garland.

Lewis, Charlton M. Prologue to the Chinese Revolution: The Transformation of Ideas & Institutions in Hunan Province, 1891-1907. (East Asian Monographs: No. 70). 216p. 1976. 21.00 (0-674-71441-5) HUP.

Lewis, Charlton T. Elementary Latin Dictionary. (ENG & LAT.). 964p. 1969. text 35.00 (0-19-910205-8) OUP.

Lewis, Charlton T. & Short, Charles. Latin Dictionary: Founded on Andrews Edition of Freund's Latin Dictionary. (LAT.). 2,024p. 1956. text 175.00 (0-19-864201-6) OUP.

***Lewis, Cherry.** The Dating Game: One Man's Search for the Age of the Earth. (Illus.). 216p. (C). 2000. 24.95 (0-521-79051-4) Cambridge U Pr.

Lewis, Cherry, ed. see Jekyll, Gertrude.

***Lewis, Chris.** Cisco TCP/IP: Professional Reference. 3rd ed. 2000. pap. text 55.00 (0-07-212557-8) McGraw.

Lewis, Chris. Cisco TCP/IP Routing Professional Reference. 2nd ed. LC 98-26959. 1998. pap. 55.00 (0-07-041130-1) McGraw.

— Cisco TCP/IP Routing Toolkit. LC 97-23553. (Computer Communications Ser.). (Illus.). 416p. 1997. pap. 50.00 (0-07-041088-7) McGraw.

***Lewis, Chris.** The Day Trader's Guide to Technical Analysis: How to Use Level II & Time of Sales to Profit in Electronic Markets. LC 00-29202. (Illus.). 300p. 2000. 49.95 (0-07-135979-6) McGraw.

Lewis, Christine L., et al. Gemini: Gifted Education Manual for Individualizing Networks of Instruction. 50p. 1980. pap., teacher ed. 15.00 (0-89824-015-8) Trillium Pr.

— Pegasus: Providing Enrichment for the Gifted by Adapting Selected Units of Study. Cantor, Marjorie A., ed. 119p. 1980. pap., teacher ed. 15.00 (0-89824-017-4) Trillium Pr.

Lewis, Christine L., ed. see Barzun, Jacques, et al.

Lewis, Christine L., ed. see Wheelwright, Steven C., et al.

Lewis, Christopher. Antiques Roadshow: Experts on Objects. LC 89-174855. 192 p. 1987. write for info. (0-563-20602-0, BBC Bks) BBC Worldwide.

Lewis, Christopher. Employee Selection. 2nd ed. 190p. 1999. pap. 67.50 (0-7487-1371-9, Pub. by S Thornes Pubs) Trans-Atl Phila.

Lewis, Christopher, jt. ed. see Cohn-Sherbok, Dan.

Lewis, Christopher O. Tonal Coherence in Mahler's Ninth Symphony. LC 84-2754. (Studies in Musicology: No. 79). 148p. reprint ed. pap. 45.90 (0-8357-1585-X, 207055800001) Bks Demand.

Lewis, Christopher P., jt. ed. see Thacker, Alan T.

Lewis, Chuck. All the Riches of Job, a True Story of Success, & What Came After. LC 93-83590. (Illus.). 128p. (Orig.). (C). 1993. pap. text 8.95 (0-9635854-0-1) Serendpty Pr.

Lewis, Claire E., et al, eds. Cell Proliferation in Cancer: Regulatory Mechanisms of Neoplastic Cell Growth. (Illus.). 418p. 1996. text 145.00 (0-19-854791-9) OUP.

Lewis, Clara M., jt. auth. see Bailey, Carolyn S.

Lewis, Clarence Irving. Mind & the World Order: Outline of a Theory of Knowledge. 446p. 1991. pap. 9.95 (0-486-26564-1) Dover.

***Lewis, Clarence M.** Law of Leases. xliii, 674p. 2000. reprint ed. 180.00 (1-56169-578-5) Gaunt.

Lewis, Clarence O. The Seven Sutherland Sisters. rev. ed. 56p. 1991. reprint ed. 4.00 (0-614-13513-3) Niagara Cnty Hist Soc.

Lewis, Clarissa. The Problem with Cameron. LC 95-70502. (Illus.). 24p. (J). (gr. 4-8). 1995. 12.95 (0-9647148-0-9) Pocket Change.

— Vay Kamo, Vay! Andonian, Aramais, tr. from ENG. (ARM., Illus.). 28p. (J). (ps-2). 1995. boxed set 14.00 (1-886434-00-X) Blue Crane Bks.

Lewis, Claudia L. Indian Families of the Northwest Coast: The Impact of Change. LC 70-108776. 236p. reprint ed. pap. 73.20 (0-608-16493-3, 202673600051) Bks Demand.

— Long Ago in Oregon. LC 86-45781. (Charlotte Zolotow Bk.). (Illus.). 64p. (J). (gr. 3-7). 1987. 11.95 (0-06-023839-9) HarpC Child Bks.

Lewis, Clay. Battlegrounds of Memory. LC 98-4906. 248p. 1998. 24.95 (0-8203-2009-9) U of Ga Pr.

Lewis, Clement E. When It's Twilight Time: Thirty Worship Services for Health Care Centers, Retirement Homes, & Other Special Life Settings. LC 93-42515. 133p. 1994. pap. 12.50 (1-55673-837-4) CSS OH.

Lewis, Cleona. International Accounts. (Brookings Institution Reprint Ser.). reprint ed. lib. bdg. 32.50 (0-697-00163-6) Irvington.

Lewis, Cleona & Schlotterbeck, Karl T. America's Stake in International Investments. Bruchey, Stuart & Bruchey, Eleanor, eds. LC 76-5015. (Essay Index Reprint Ser.). 1976. reprint ed. 62.95 (0-405-09283-0) Ayer.

Lewis, Cliff & Britch, Carroll, eds. Rediscovering Steinbeck - Revisionist Views of His Art, Politics, & Intellect. (Studies in American Literature: Vol. 3). 277p. 1989. 89.95 (0-88946-169-4) E Mellen.

Lewis, Colin. Bonsai: A Care Manual, 6 vols. LC 97-15154. (Care Manual Ser.). (Illus.). 128p. 1997. 19.95 (1-57145-609-0, Laurel Glen Pub) Advantage Pubs.

— Bonsai Survival Manual: Tree-By-Tree Guide to Buying, Maintaining, & Problem Solving. LC 96-1719. (Illus.). 160p. 1996. pap. 21.95 (0-88266-853-6, Garden Way Pub) Storey Bks.

— Demand Forecasting & Inventory Control. 157p. 1998. 65.00 incl. disk (0-471-25338-3) Wiley.

— Practical Bonsai. (Illus.). 64p. 1992. pap. 8.95 (1-85223-661-2, Pub. by Crolwood) Trafalgar.

Lewis, Colin A. Horse Breeding in Ireland. 232p. 1990. pap. 50.00 (0-85131-315-9, Pub. by J A Allen) St Mut.

Lewis, Colin D. Demand Forcasting & Inventory Control: A Computer Aided Learning Approach. LC 98-227907. 176p. 1997. boxed set 105.00 (1-85573-241-6) Buttrwrth-Heinemann.

Lewis, Colin M. British Railways in Argentina, 1857-1914: A Case Study of Foreign Investment. (Institute of Latin American Studies Monographs: No. 12). (Illus.). 259p. (C). 1983. text 42.50 (0-485-17712-9, Pub. by Athlone Pr) Humanities.

Lewis, Colleen, jt. ed. see Bryett, Keith.

Lewis, Colleen, jt. ed. see Goldsmith, Andrew.

Lewis, Copeland C. Mother's First Year. 1992. pap. 5.50 (0-425-13488-1) Berkley Pub.

Lewis, Crystal. Gold. LC 98-15699. 176p. 1998. 12.99 (0-7852-7470-7) Nelson.

— Oro Puro.Tr. of Gold. 1998. pap. text 6.99 (0-88113-521-6) Caribe Betania.

Lewis, Curtis L. & Underwood, Dennis D. The Great American Horse Race of 1976: A Photographic Documentary. (Illus.). 224p. (Orig.). 1993. pap. 16.95 (0-9638302-0-1) Buckboard Pub.

Lewis, Cynthia. Particular Saints: Shakespeare's Four Antonios, Their Contexts, & Their Plays. LC 96-38090. (Illus.). 256p. 1997. 39.50 (0-87413-630-X) U Delaware Pr.

Lewis, Cynthia A., jt. auth. see Thunder, James M.

***Lewis, Cynthia C.** Diet Fads & Facts: A Hot Issue. LC 99-41409. (Hot Issues Ser.). (Illus.). 64p. (J). (gr. 6 up). 2000. lib. bdg. 19.95 (0-7660-1194-1) Enslow Pubs.

Lewis, Cynthia C. Dilly's Big Sister Diary. LC 97-47431. (Illus.). 32p. (J). (gr. k-4). 1998. 9.95 (0-7613-0441-X, Copper Beech Bks) Millbrook Pr.

— Hello, Alexander Graham Bell Speaking. (Taking Part Ser.). (Illus.). 64p. (J). (gr. 3 up). 1991. lib. bdg. 13.95 (0-87518-461-8, Dillon Silver Burdett) Silver Burdett Pr.

— Mother's First Year: A Realistic Guide to the Changes & Challenges of Motherhood. 384p. 1997. reprint ed. pap. 12.00 (0-425-15677-X) Berkley Pub.

— Really Important Stuff My Kids Have Taught Me. Kovalchick, Sally, ed. LC 94-31588. (Illus.). 416p. (Orig.). 1994. pap. 6.95 (1-56305-700-X, 3700) Workman Pub.

Lewis, Cynthia C. & Lewis, Thomas. Best Hikes with Children in Vermont, New Hampshire & Maine. LC 91-26465. (Best Hikes with Children Ser.). (Illus.). 224p. 1991. pap. 14.95 (0-89886-281-7) Mountaineers.

Lewis, Cynthia C. & Lewis, Thomas J. Best Hikes with Children in Connecticut, Massachusetts, & Rhode Island. 2nd ed. LC 97-47609. (Best Hikes with Children Ser.). (Illus.). 230p. 1998. pap. 14.95 (0-89886-543-3) Mountaineers.

***Lewis, Cynthia C. & Lewis, Thomas J.** Best Hikes with Children in Vermont, New Hampshire & Maine. 2nd ed. LC 00-8219. (Best Hikes with Children Ser.). (Illus.). 256p. 2000. pap. 16.95 (0-89886-611-1) Mountaineers.

Lewis, Cynthia C. & Lewis, Tom. Best Hikes with Children in the Catskills & Hudson River Valley. LC 92-5135. (Best Hikes with Children Ser.). (Illus.). 230p. (Orig.). 1992. pap. 14.95 (0-89886-322-8) Mountaineers.

Lewis, Cynthia C., et al. In-Line Skate New England: The Complete Guide to the Best 101 Tours. LC 96-39388. (Illus.). 240p. (Orig.). 1997. pap. 17.00 (0-88150-393-2, Pub. by Countryman) Norton.

Lewis, Cynthia Copeland. Dilly's Summer Camp Diary. LC 98-36182. 32p. (J). (gr. 2-4). 1999. 18.90 (0-7613-1416-4, Copper Beech Bks) Millbrook Pr.

— Dilly's Summer Camp Diary. LC 98-36182. (Illus.). 32p. (J). (gr. k-3). 1999. 6.95 (0-7613-0990-X, Copper Beech Bks) Millbrook Pr.

Lewis, D. Matrix Theory. 300p. (C). 1991. text 44.00 (981-02-0689-5) World Scientific Pub.

Lewis, D., jt. auth. see Bartenieff, Irmgard.

Lewis, D. A. Anti-Inflammatory Drugs from Plant & Marine Sources. (Agents & Actions Supplements Ser.: No. 27). 371p. 1989. 97.00 (0-8176-2265-9) Birkhauser.

Lewis, D. A., jt. auth. see Hawkey, P. M.

Lewis, D. Geraint, ed. Termau Llwydraeth Leol: A Glossary of Local Government Terms. (ENG & WEL.). 1996. pap. 18.00 (0-8464-4618-9) Beekman Pubs.

Lewis, D. Gregory. Photojournalism: Content & Technique. 2nd ed. 352p. (C). 1994. text. write for info. (0-697-14629-4) Brown & Benchmark.

Lewis, D. H., ed. Induced Skeletal Muscle Ischemia in Man. (Illus.). iv, 180p. 1982. pap. 100.00 (3-8055-3427-2) S Karger.

Lewis, D. H., ed. see Conference of the European Society for Microcircul.

Lewis, D. H., ed. see Conference on Microcirculation, 6th, Aalborg, 1970.

Lewis, D. H., ed. see Conference on Microcirculation, 6th European, Aalb.

Lewis, D. H., ed. see Easter School in Agricultural Science (8th 1961, U.

Lewis, D. H., ed. see European Conference on Microcirculation Staff.

Lewis, D. M., et al, eds. The Fifth Century B. C. 2nd ed. (Cambridge Ancient History Ser.: Vol. 5, Pt. 2). 617p. 1992. text 120.00 (0-521-23347-X) Cambridge U Pr.

— The Fourth Century B. C. 2nd ed. (Cambridge Ancient History Ser.: Vol. 6). (Illus.). 1097p. 1994. text 170.00 (0-521-23348-8) Cambridge U Pr.

Lewis, D. M., jt. auth. see Perkins, Alan C.

Lewis, D. V. P., jt. ed. see Ionnides, C.

Lewis, Dale. Roy Houck Buffalo Man. 148p. text 20.00 (0-614-07280-8) Buffalo Pr.

Lewis, Dale & Carter, Nick. Voices from Africa: Local Perspectives on Conservation. LC 93-4758. 216p. (Orig.). 1993. pap. 19.95 (0-89164-124-6) World Wildlife Fund.

Lewis, Dallas & Lewis, Lisa. The Planet Yes. (Illus.). 32p. (Orig.). (J). (gr. 3). 1994. 13.95 (0-9634087-1-2); pap. 6.95 (0-9634087-2-0) Silly Billys Bks.

Lewis, Dallas & Lewis, Lisa M. The Last Book. (Illus.). 32p. (J). (gr. 1-2). 1992. 16.00 (0-9634087-0-4) Silly Billys Bks.

Lewis, Dallas, jt. auth. see Lewis, Lisa.

Lewis, Dan. Eight Thousand Miles of Dirt. 2nd rev. ed. (Illus.). 188p. 1992. pap. 16.95 (0-941875-16-4) Wolverine Distrib.

— Floater's Guide to Wyoming Rivers: Paddle & Portage. (Illus.). 186p. 1991. pap. 12.95 (0-941875-15-6) Wolverine Distrib.

Lewis, Dan A. & Lurigio, Arthur J. The State Mental Patient & Urban Life: Moving in & Out of the Institution. 146p. 1994. pap. 26.95 (0-398-06238-2) C C Thomas.

— The State Mental Patient & Urban Life: Moving in & Out of the Institution. 146p. (C). 1994. text 39.95 (0-398-05901-2) C C Thomas.

Lewis, Dan A. & Nakagawa, Kathryn. Race & Educational Reform in the American Metropolis: A Study of School Decentralization. LC 94-9565. (SUNY Series, Frontiers in Education). 176p. (C). 1994. pap. text 18.95 (0-7914-2134-1) State U NY Pr.

Lewis, Dan A. & Salem, Greta W. Fear of Crime: Incivility & the Production of a Social Problem. (New Observations Ser.). 145p. (Orig.). 1986. 39.95 (0-88738-086-7) Transaction Pubs.

Lewis, Dan A., et al. The Social Construction of Reform: Crime Prevention & Community Organization. 192p. 1988. 34.95 (0-88738-138-3) Transaction Pubs.

— Worlds of the Mentally Ill: How Deinstitutionalization Works in the City. LC 89-18058. 208p. (C). 1990. text 31.95 (0-8093-1477-0) S Ill U Pr.

Lewis, Dana, tr. see Kobayashi, Makoto.

Lewis, Dana, tr. see Otomo, Kat S.

Lewis, Dana, tr. see Samura, Hiroaki.

Lewis, Dana K. Working with Children: Effective Communication Through Self-Awareness. LC 81-2668. (Sage Human Services Guides Ser.: No. 22). 160p. reprint ed. pap. 49.60 (0-8357-4755-7, 203767700009) Bks Demand.

Lewis, Daniel. Victorian Houses Coloring Book. (Illus.). (J). (gr. k-3). 1980. pap. 2.95 (0-486-23908-X) Dover.

Lewis, Daniel, ed. Dance in Hispanic Cultures: Papers of the Conference of Dance History Scholars, Miami, 1991, Vol. 3, Part 4. (Choreography & Dance Studies: Vol. 3, Pt. 4). 136p. 1994. pap. text 16.00 (3-7186-5534-9, ECU21, Harwood Acad Pubs) Gordon & Breach.

Lewis, Daniel, et al, eds. Self-Assessment Color Review of Small Animal Orthopedics. LC 99-174419. (Illus.). 192p. 1998. pap. text 34.95 (0-8138-2947-X) Iowa St U Pr.

Lewis, Daniel D. Illustrated Dance Technique of Jose Limon. (Illus.). 208p. 1999. pap. text 24.95 (0-87127-209-1) Princeton Bk Co.

Lewis, Daniel I. & Lee, Winnie. Bank President. (Chief Executive Ser.). 64p. (Orig.). 1984. 74.95 incl. disk (0-915847-00-0); pap. 9.95 (0-915847-02-7) Lewis Lee Corp.

Lewis, Daniel J. 3 Crucial Questions about the Last Days. LC 98-23845. (Three Crucial Questions Ser.). 168p. (C). 1998. pap. 11.99 (0-8010-5820-1) Baker Bks.

Lewis, Daniel M., jt. auth. see Burrell, Robert.

Lewis, Danny, jt. auth. see Lewis, JoLinda.

Lewis, Danny, tr. see Heider, Ulrike.

Lewis, Daphne. Illuminations: An Interweave of Thought, Identity, & Love. Ferguson, Wynne L., ed. LC 92-24817. (Illus.). 108p. 1992. 19.95 (1-880292-21-1) LangMarc.

Lewis, Daphne B. Hardy Bamboos for Shoots & Poles: Thirty Varieties of Bamboo for Farms in USDA Zones 7, 8, 9. Cooper, Gib et al, eds. 28p. 1998. pap. 10.00 (0-9668142-0-7) Daphne Works.

Lewis, Darrell, jt. auth. see Schultz, Charlie.

An Asterisk (*) at the beginning of an entry indicates that the title is appearing for the first time.

Lewis, Darrell L. & Stoeppelwerth, Walter W. Kitchen & Bath Installation, Vol. 1. (Illus.). 270p. (Orig.). 1995. pap. text 50.00 (*1-887127-08-9*) Natl Kit Bath.
— Kitchen & Bath Installation: Installation Business Management, Vol. 2. (Illus.). 140p. (Orig.). 1995. pap. text 50.00 (*1-887127-09-7*) Natl Kit Bath.
Lewis, Darrell R., jt. auth. see Boyer, Carol M.
Lewis, Darrell R., jt. ed. see Clark, Shirley M.
Lewis, Dartrey B., jt. ed. see Dove, Allan B.
Lewis, Daryl W. When You Are at a Loss for Words: Love Is Wonderful, the Second Time Around. (Illus.). 166p. 1998. 17.95 (*0-89896-429-6*, Am Intl Bk) Larksdale.
Lewis, Dave. Cod Fishing: The Complete Guide. (Illus.). 160p. 1997. 35.00 (*1-86126-017-2*, Pub. by Crolwood) Trafalgar.
— Led Zeppelin. (Complete Guides to the Music Of...Ser.). (Illus.). 104p. (Orig.). pap. 8.95 (*0-7119-3528-9*, OP 47350, Pub. by Omnibus Press) Omnibus NY.
— Led Zeppelin: A Celebration. (Illus.). 128p. pap. 24.95 (*0-7119-2416-3*, OP 46135) Omnibus NY.
Lewis, Dave & Pallett, Simon. Led Zeppelin: The Concert File. (Illus.). 176p. 1997. pap. 24.95 (*0-7119-5307-4*, OP47805) Omnibus NY.
Lewis, David. The Body Language of Children: How Children Talk Before they Can Speak. (Illus.). 288p. 1996. pap. text 12.95 (*0-285-63336-8*, Pub. by Souvenir Pr Ltd) IPG Chicago.
— Chevrolet Small Block V-8 Interchange Manual. (Illus.). 144p. 1989. pap. 19.95 (*0-87938-357-7*) MBI Pubg.
— Counterfactuals. LC 72-78430. 1973. 10.00 (*0-674-17540-9*) HUP.
— Counterfactuals. LC 72-78430. 156p. 1987. pap. 12.95 (*0-674-17541-7*) HUP.
— The Creative Producer: A Memoir of the Studio System. Curtis, James, ed. (Filmmakers Ser.: No. 36). (Illus.). 272p. 1993. 39.50 (*0-8108-2720-4*) Scarecrow.
— Dying to Tell. LC 92-70085. 179p. 1992. pap. 11.95 (*0-89112-152-8*) Abilene Christ U.
— Essentials of Employment Law. 288p. (C). 1986. 120.00 (*0-85292-357-0*, Pub. by IPM Hse) St Mut.
— Essentials of Employment Law. 352p. 1993. pap. 125.00 (*0-85292-536-0*, Pub. by IPM Hse) St Mut.
*__Lewis, David.__ Essentials of Employment Law 1997. 352p. 2000. pap. 56.95 (*0-8464-5048-8*) Beekman Pubs.
Lewis, David. Finite Counterforce. (Working Papers on Nuclear Deterrence). 1988. 2.50 (*0-318-33326-0*, SB1) IPPP.
— How to Get Your Message Across: A Practical Guide to Power Communication. (Illus.). 282p. 1997. 24.95 (*0-285-63348-1*, Pub. by Souvenir Pr Ltd) IPG Chicago.
— Index of Childhood Immunization. Date not set. 19.95 (*1-873413-02-5*, 8290) Merit Pub Intl.
— Papers in Ethics & Social Philosophy. (Studies in Philosophy). (Illus.). 304p. (C). 1999. 54.95 (*0-521-58249-0*); pap. 19.95 (*0-521-58786-7*) Cambridge U Pr.
— Papers in Metaphysics & Epistemology. LC 98-25689. (Studies in Philosophy). 288p. (C). 1999. text 64.95 (*0-521-58248-2*); pap. text 19.95 (*0-521-58787-5*) Cambridge U Pr.
— Papers in Philosophical Logic, Vol. 1. LC 97-6656. (Studies in Philosophy). 272p. (C). 1997. text 54.95 (*0-521-58247-4*); pap. text 17.95 (*0-521-58788-3*) Cambridge U Pr.
— The Public Image of Henry Ford: An American Folk Hero & His Company. LC 76-807. (Great Lakes Bks.). (Illus.). 600p. 1987. pap. 24.95 (*0-8143-1892-4*) Wayne St U Pr.
— Secret Languages of Success. 1995. 7.98 (*0-88365-894-1*) Galahad Bks.
— Sloss Furnaces & the Rise of the Birmingham District: An Industrial Epic. LC 93-48178. (History of American Science & Technology Ser.). 672p. 1994. text 39.95 (*0-8173-0708-7*) U of Ala Pr.
— Stress for Success. pap. 10.95 (*0-7867-0872-7*) Carroll & Graf.
Lewis, David. Stress for Success. 208p. 10.95 (*0-88184-872-7*) Carroll & Graf.
Lewis, David. Terry Frost. Knowles, Elizabeth, ed. (Illus.). 252p. 1994. 87.95 (*1-85928-041-2*, Pub. by Scolar Pr) Ashgate Pub Co.
— Thaddeus Mosley: African-American Sculptor. (Illus.). 128p. 1997. pap. 24.95 (*0-8229-5634-9*) U of Pittsburgh Pr.
— Warren MacKenzie, Potter: A Retrospective. Brown, Susan Taylor, ed. LC 89-51231. (Illus.). 128p. (Orig.). 1989. pap. text 30.00 (*0-938713-05-1*) Univ MN Art Mus.
— We, the Navigators: The Ancient Art of Landfinding in the Pacific. 2nd ed. Oulton, Derek, ed. LC 93-44019. (Illus.). 384p. (C). 1994. pap. 24.95 (*0-8248-1582-3*) UH Pr.
Lewis, David, contrib. by. Guinea Pigs. LC 97-33123. (Junior Pet Care Ser.). (Illus.). 48p. (J). (gr. 2 up). 1999. 16.95 (*0-7910-4908-6*) Chelsea Hse.
— Hamsters. LC 97-28351. (Junior Pet Care Ser.). (Illus.). 48p. (J). (gr. 2 up). 1999. 16.95 (*0-7910-4907-8*) Chelsea Hse.
— Kittens. LC 97-28350. (Junior Pet Care Ser.). (Illus.). 48p. (J). (gr. 2 up). 1999. lib. bdg. 15.95 (*0-7910-4906-X*) Chelsea Hse.
— Parakeets (Budgerigars) (Junior Pet Care Ser.). (Illus.). 48p. (J). (gr. 2 up). 1999. lib. bdg. 14.95 (*0-7910-4909-4*) Chelsea Hse.
— Puppies. LC 97-29293. (Junior Pet Care Ser.). (Illus.). 48p. (J). (gr. 2 up). 1999. 16.95 (*0-7910-4905-1*) Chelsea Hse.
— Rabbits. LC 97-27744. (Junior Pet Care Ser.). (Illus.). 48p. (J). (gr. 2 up). 1999. 15.95 (*0-7910-4904-3*) Chelsea Hse.
— Snakes. LC 97-28374. (Junior Pet Care Ser.). (Illus.). 48p. (J). (gr. 2 up). 1999. 16.95 (*0-7910-4910-8*) Chelsea Hse.
— Turtles. (Junior Pet Care Ser.). (Illus.). 48p. (J). (gr. 2 up). 1999. 14.95 (*0-7910-4911-6*) Chelsea Hse.
Lewis, David, ed. Byzantine Butterflies: The Folk Painting of Peter Contis & Helen Contis. (Illus.). 160p. 1999. reprint ed. pap. 25.00 (*0-8229-5701-9*) U of Pittsburgh Pr.
— Byzantine Butterflies: The Folk Painting of Peter Contis & Helen Contis. (Illus.). 160p. 1999. reprint ed. text 45.00 (*0-8229-4100-7*) U of Pittsburgh Pr.
— Oil Painting Techniques: Learn How to Master Oil Painting Working Techniques to Create Your Own Successful Paintings. (Illus.). 144p. 1983. pap. 16.95 (*0-8230-3261-2*) Watsn-Guptill.
— Pencil Drawing Techniques. (Illus.). 144p. 1984. pap. 16.95 (*0-8230-3991-9*) Watsn-Guptill.
— Watercolor Painting Techniques. (Illus.). 144p. 1983. pap. 16.95 (*0-8230-5669-4*) Watsn-Guptill.
Lewis, David, et al, eds. Inscriptiones Graecae. 176p. 1998. 143.00 (*3-11-016183-4*) De Gruyter.
— Inscriptiones Graecae, Vol. 1, Fasc. 2: Consilio et Auctoritate Academiae Scientiarum Berolinensis et Brandenburgensis Editae. (LAT.). xiv, 998p. 1993. lib. bdg. 715.40 (*3-11-010362-1*) De Gruyter.
*__Lewis, David & Bridger, Darren.__ The Soul of New Consumer: Authenticity: What We Buy & Why in the New Economy. (Illus.). 256p. 2000. 25.00 (*1-85788-246-6*, Pub. by Nicholas Brealey) Natl Bk Netwk.
Lewis, David & Greene, James. Thinking Better. LC 83-8389. 324p. 1995. pap. 9.95 (*0-8050-0022-4*, Owl) H Holt & Co.
Lewis, David & James, Philip. Discipline. 128p. (C). 1992. 85.00 (*0-85292-485-2*, Pub. by IPM Hse) St Mut.
Lewis, David & Norton, James J. On Call Pediatrics. Schmitt, Bill, ed. LC 96-49867. (Illus.). 336p. 1997. pap. text 21.95 (*0-7216-6757-0*, W B Saunders Co) Harcrt Hlth Sci Grp.
Lewis, David & Shreckhise, Robert. UFO: End-Time Delusion. LC 91-61713. 256p. (Orig.). 1991. pap. 10.95 (*0-89221-213-6*) New Leaf.
*__Lewis, David & Williams, Fred.__ Policy & Planning As Public Choice. LC 99-72332. 304p. 1999. 78.95 (*0-7546-1067-5*) Ashgate Pub Co.
Lewis, David, et al. The Gospel According to Generation X--The Culture of Adolescent Faith. 1995. pap. 14.95 (*0-89112-015-7*) Abilene Christ U.
Lewis, David, jt. auth. see Bolanos, Harry.
Lewis, David, jt. auth. see Gardner, Katy.
Lewis, David, jt. auth. see Moore, Karl.
Lewis, David, ed. see Coleman, Kenneth.
Lewis, David, ed. see Jeffrey, Grant, et al.
Lewis, David, tr. see Miyazaki, Hayao.
Lewis, David, tr. see Sander, Nicolas.
Lewis, David, tr. see St. John of the Cross.
Lewis, David, tr. see St. Teresa of Avila & Zimmerman, Benedict.
Lewis, David A. Can Israel Survive in a Hostile World? LC 93-87251. 352p. 1994. pap. 11.95 (*0-89221-260-8*) New Leaf.
— Magog, 1982 Cancelled: Did Israel Prevent the Third World War? LC 82-62079. 144p. 1982. pap. 4.95 (*0-89221-103-2*) New Leaf.
— Prophecy, 2000. LC 90-60310. (Illus.). 432p. 1990. pap. 11.95 (*0-89221-179-2*) New Leaf.
— Signs of His Coming: Startling Proof That the Coming of Jesus Is Near at Hand. LC 97-65169. 400p. 1997. pap. 12.95 (*0-89221-347-7*) New Leaf.
— Smashing the Gates of Hell: In the Last Days. LC 86-65887. 226p. 1987. 10.95 (*0-89221-143-1*) New Leaf.
Lewis, David Allen. Dreamland: An Inside View of the Race for Peace in the Middle East. Date not set. pap. text 12.99 (*0-89221-424-4*) New Leaf.
*__Lewis, David C.__ After Atheism: Religion & Ethnicity in Russia & Central Asia. 288p. 1999. (*0-7007-1164-3*, Pub. by Curzon Pr Ltd) Paul & Co Pubs.
Lewis, David E. Organic Chemistry: A Modern Perspective. 1152p. (C). 1996. text. write for info. (*0-697-35091-6*, WCB McGr Hill) McGrw-H Hghr Educ.
Lewis, David F. Cytochromes P450: Structure, Function & Mechanism. 330p. 1996. 165.00 (*0-7484-0443-0*) Taylor & Francis.
Lewis, David H. Roller Skating for Gold. LC 96-21274. (American Sports History Ser.: No. 5). 232p. 1996. 42.50 (*0-8108-3048-5*) Scarecrow.
Lewis, David J., et al. Trading the Silver Seed: Local Knowledge & Market Moralities in Aquaculture Development. (Orig.). 1996. pap. 30.00 (*1-85339-342-8*, Pub. by Intermed Tech) Stylus Pub VA.
Lewis, David J., jt. ed. see Farrington, John W.
Lewis, David K. Convention: A Philosophical Study. LC 69-12727. (Illus.). 1969. 15.00 (*0-674-17025-3*) HUP.
— Convention: A Philosophical Study. LC 69-12727. 224p. 1987. pap. 14.50 (*0-674-17026-1*) HUP.
— Konventionen: Eine Sprachphilosophische Abhandlung. Posher, Roland & Wenzel, Detlef, trs. (Grundlagen der Kommunikation Ser.). (GER.). xiv, 224p. (C). 1975. pap. 29.25 (*3-11-004608-3*) De Gruyter.
Lewis, David L. The Civil Rights Movement in America: Essays. Eagles, Charles W., ed. LC 86-5665. (Chancellor's Symposium Ser.). 202p. reprint ed. pap. 62.70 (*0-608-08715-7*, 206928300003) Bks Demand.
— District of Columbia: A Bicentennial History. (States & the Nation Ser.). (Illus.). 1976. 14.95 (*0-393-05601-5*) Norton.
*__Lewis, David L.__ Ford Country. LC 99-462669. (Illus.). 228p. 1999. pap. 24.95 (*1-880524-33-3*, 128440AP) Cars & Parts.
Lewis, David L. Ford Country II. (Illus.). 296p. 1999. 24.95 (*1-880524-34-1*, 128445AP) Cars & Parts.
— King: A Biography. 2nd ed. (Blacks in the New World Ser.). 481p. 1978. pap. text 15.95 (*0-252-00680-1*) U of Ill Pr.
— Neither Wolf Nor Dog: American Indians, Environment & Agrarian Change. (Illus.). 256p. 1994. text 45.00 (*0-19-506297-3*) OUP.
— Prisoners of Honor: The Dreyfus Affair. LC 94-31878. 1995. pap. 12.00 (*0-8050-3766-7*) H Holt & Co.
— The Race to Fashoda: Colonialism & African Resistance. LC 94-36013. 1995. pap. 13.95 (*0-8050-3556-7*, Owl) H Holt & Co.
— When Harlem Was in Vogue. LC 97-201415. (Illus.). 432p. 1997. pap. 14.95 (*0-14-026334-9*) Viking Penguin.
Lewis, David L., ed. The Portable Harlem Renaissance Reader. 816p. 1995. pap. 15.95 (*0-14-017036-7*) Viking Penguin.
Lewis, David L. & Goldstein, Laurence, eds. The Automobile & American Culture. 440p. 1983. pap. text 22.95 (*0-472-08044-X*, 08044) U of Mich Pr.
Lewis, David L., jt. auth. see Flammang, James M.
Lewis, David L., jt. auth. see Rauhauser, Bill.
Lewis, David L., ed. see Du Bois, W. E. B.
Lewis, David Levering. W. E. B. Du Bois: Biography of a Race, 1868-1919. 1995. pap. 17.95 (*0-8050-3568-0*) H Holt & Co.
— W. E. B. Du Bois: Biography of a Race, 1868-1919. LC 93-16617. (Illus.). 700p. 1995. 35.00 (*0-8050-2621-5*) H Holt & Co.
— W. E. B. Du Bois: Biography of a Race, 1868-1919. 1997. pap. 4.99 (*0-681-06937-6*) Waldenbooks Co Inc.
— W. E. B. Du Bois: The Fight for Equality & the American Century, 1919-1963. Vol. II. (Illus.). 608p. 2000. 35.00 (*0-8050-2534-0*) H Holt & Co.
Lewis, David M. Selected Papers in Greek & Near Eastern History. Rhodes, P. J., ed. LC 96-399750. (Illus.). 430p. (C). 1997. text 90.00 (*0-521-46564-8*) Cambridge U Pr.
Lewis, David M. & Pickard-Cambridge, Arthur W. The Dramatic Festivals of Athens. 2nd ed. (Illus.). 392p. 1989. text 95.00 (*0-19-814258-7*) OUP.
Lewis, David M., jt. ed. see Meiggs, Russell.
Lewis, David R. Chillin Out: In the Language of Today's Inner-City Youth. (Illus.). 40p. (J). (gr. 1-11). 1990. pap. 5.95 (*1-56411-185-7*) Untd Bros & Sis.
— Neither Wolf nor Dog: American Indians, Environment & Agrarian Change. (Illus.). 256p. 1997. pap. 17.95 (*0-19-511794-8*) OUP.
Lewis, David V. Power Negotiating Tactics & Techniques. LC 81-5164. 243p. 1984. 19.95 (*0-13-686808-8*, Busn); pap. 5.95 (*0-13-687740-0*, Busn) P-H.
Lewis, David W. French for Business & International Careers: Vocabulary, Stylistics, Culture; A College Reader. (American University Studies: Foreign Language Instruction: Ser. VI, Vol. 4). 650p. 1989. text 58.00 (*0-8204-0513-2*) P Lang Pubng.
— The Road to Europe: History, Institutions & Prospects of European Integration 1945-1993. XIX, 488p. 1994. pap. 29.95 (*0-8204-2113-8*) P Lang Pubng.
— The Road to Europe: The Past & Future of European Integration, 1945-1993. LC 91-16050. XIX, 488p. (C). 1993. text 69.95 (*0-8204-1640-1*) P Lang Pubng.
Lewis, David W., Jr., ed. see Fine, Norman M.
*__Lewis, David W. P. & Lepesant, Gilles, eds.__ What Security for Which Europe? Case Studies from the Baltic to the Black Sea. LC 99-16298. 208p. (C). 1999. text 50.95 (*0-8204-4268-2*) P Lang Pubng.
Lewis, Day C. Otterbury Incident. 1961. pap. 12.95 (*0-14-030163-1*, Pub. by Pnguin Bks Ltd) Trafalgar.
Lewis Deans, Mary. Like the Moon. 179p. (Orig.). 1989. pap. 7.95 (*0-9624388-0-4*) Flatrock Bks.
Lewis, Deborah. Kirkwood Fires. (Orig.). 1978. mass mkt. 1.95 (*0-89083-405-9*, Zebra Kensgtn) Kensgtn Pub Corp.
— The Wind at Winter's End. (Orig.). 1979. mass mkt. 1.95 (*0-89083-540-3*, Zebra Kensgtn) Kensgtn Pub Corp.
Lewis, Deborah S. & Lewis, Gregg A., photos by. When You Were a Baby. LC 94-44691. (Illus.). 48p. (J). (ps-1). 1995. 13.95 (*1-56145-102-9*) Peachtree Pubs.
Lewis, Deborrah. The Sculpture of Pol Bury: Shapes in Space & Time. 1978. pap. 4.95 (*0-614-02731-4*) J S Blanton Mus.
Lewis, Delano E. & McCracken, Edward R. Kickstart Initiative: Connecting America's Communities to the Information Superhighway. (Illus.). 176p. (Orig.). 1997. pap. text 40.00 (*0-7881-3859-6*) DIANE Pub.
Lewis, Dennis. Martini-Henry .450 Rifles & Carbines. LC 96-204563. (British Firearms Ser.: Vol. 6). (Illus.). 72p. (Orig.). 1996. pap. 11.95 (*1-880677-12-1*) Excalibur AZ.
— The Tao of Natural Breathing: For Health, Well-Being & Inner Growth. LC 96-75684. (Illus.). 208p. (Orig.). 1996. pap. 17.95 (*0-9651611-0-2*) Mtn Wind.
Lewis, Dennis & Washburn, Robert. British Point Twenty-Two RF Training Rifles. (British Firearms Ser.: Vol. 3). (Illus.). 64p. 1993. pap. 10.95 (*1-880677-03-2*) Excalibur AZ.
Lewis, Dennis M., ed. Proceedings of the Second Champlain Valley Symposium, 1982. 38p. 1982. pap. 5.00 (*1-890402-05-2*) Clinton Cnty Hist.
Lewis, Denslow. Gynecologic Consideration of the Sexual Act. Hollender, Marc H., ed. 1970. 20.00 (*0-87730-002-X*) M & S Pr.
Lewis, Derek & McKenzie, John R., eds. The New Germany: Social, Political, & Cultural Challenges of Unification. 352p. (C). 1995. text 59.95 (*0-85989-494-0*, Pub. by Univ Exeter Pr) Northwestern U Pr.
Lewis, Derek & McKenzie, John R. P., eds. The New Germany: Social, Political, & Cultural Challenges in Unification. 352p. 1995. pap. text 29.95 (*0-85989-442-8*) Northwestern U Pr.
Lewis, Derrick. Great Knots & How to Tie Them. LC 97-33673. (Illus.). 128p. 1998. 19.95 (*0-8069-4860-4*) Sterling.
— Great Knots & How to Tie Them. 1999. pap. text 13.95 (*0-8069-4889-2*) Sterling.
Lewis, Diana. Magical Chango: An Enchanting Book on Manners & Friendship. Widmer, Jeri D., ed. (Illus.). 24p. (J). (ps-4). 1997. pap. 9.95 (*0-9659901-3-3*) DiLee Publ.
Lewis, Diana, jt. auth. see Lewis, G. W.
Lewis, Diane. Fifty Ways to Recycle Fruit Cake. 106p. 1992. pap. 5.95 (*0-934860-94-7*) Adventure Pubns.
Lewis, Dianne. Jan Compagnie in the Straits of Malacca, 1641-1795. LC 95-15868. (Monographs in International Studies, Southeast Asia Ser.: No. 96). (Illus.). 176p. (Orig.). (C). 1995. pap. text 18.00 (*0-89680-187-X*) Ohio U Pr.
Lewis, Dio. Chastity: Our Secret Sins. LC 73-20634. (Sex, Marriage & Society Ser.). 324p. 1974. reprint ed. 26.95 (*0-405-05809-8*) Ayer.
— Our Girls. LC 74-3958. (Women in America Ser.). 388p. 1974. reprint ed. 34.95 (*0-405-06106-4*) Ayer.
Lewis, Dominic B. Doctor Rabelais. LC 69-10117. 274p. 1969. reprint ed. lib. bdg. 65.00 (*0-8371-0145-X*, LEDR, Greenwood Pr) Greenwood.
— James Boswell, a Short Life. 2nd ed. LC 79-25846. (Illus.). 285p. 1980. reprint ed. lib. bdg. 65.00 (*0-313-22232-0*, LEJB, Greenwood Pr) Greenwood.
Lewis, Dominic B. & Lee, Charles, eds. The Stuffed Owl: An Anthology of Bad Verse. LC 76-42707. (Illus.). reprint ed. 20.00 (*0-404-15371-2*) AMS Pr.
Lewis, Don. Don Lewis Pagan/Magical PCX Clip Art. 12p. 1995. 25.00 incl. disk (*1-57353-901-5*) Eschaton Prods.
Lewis, Don, jt. auth. see Lewis, Kathy.
Lewis, Donald. Alexander & the United Snakes of America: A Play about Tolerance. 1999. pap. 3.00 (*1-57514-341-0*, 3040) Encore Perform Pub.
— Uptown Country: Food with Style. 1991. 12.95 (*5-550-37028-X*) Precision Foods.
Lewis, Donald, jt. ed. see McGrath, Alister E.
Lewis, Donald J., ed. Number Theory Institute, 1969: Proceedings of Symposia in Pure Mathematics, 20th, Stony Brook, N. Y., 1969. LC 76-125938. (Proceedings of Symposia in Pure Mathematics Ser.: Vol. 20). 451p. 1971. text 60.00 (*0-8218-1420-6*, PSPUM/20) Am Math.
Lewis, Donald M. Lighten Their Darkness: The Evangelical Mission to Working-Class London, 1828-1860, 19. LC 86-12104. (Contributions to the Study of Religion Ser.: No. 19). (Illus.). 386p. 1986. 69.50 (*0-313-25577-6*, LLD/, Greenwood Pr) Greenwood.
Lewis, Donald M., intro. The Blackwell Dictionary of Evangelical Biography, 1730-1860. 1201p. 1995. 232.95 (*0-631-17384-6*) Blackwell Pubs.
*__Lewis, Donald P., Jr.__ Employee Embezzlement & Fraud in the Dental Office: Scams, Schemes & Broken Dreams. (Illus.). 272p. 1999. pap. write for info. (*0-9673901-4-1*) J D S G Intl.
Lewis, Donna & Slanker, Craig A. Hurry Home Elvis Vol. I: Donna Lewis Diaries, 1962-1966. LC 96-79197. (Illus.). 226p. 1996. pap. 12.95 (*0-9655086-3-3*) Busted Burd Prods.
— Hurry Home Elvis Vol. II: Donna Lewis Diaries, 1967-1968. (Illus.). 308p. 1997. pap. 14.95 (*0-9655086-2-5*) Busted Burd Prods.
Lewis, Donna, jt. auth. see Milady Inc. Staff.
Lewis, Dorothy. I Close My Eyes & See: Vision for the Inner Journey. (Guidebooks for Growth Together). 176p. (Orig.). 1996. pap. 10.95 (*1-899171-11-8*, Pub. by Findhorn Pr) Words Distrib.
— The Way Home. 140p. (Orig.). 1996. pap. 10.95 (*1-899171-60-6*, Pub. by Findhorn Pr) Words Distrib.
Lewis, Dorothy O. Guilty by Reason of Insanity: A Psychiatrist Explores the Minds of Killers. LC 97-46400. 301p. 1998. 25.00 (*0-449-00277-2*) Fawcett.
— Guilty by Reason of Insanity: A Psychiatrist Explores the Minds of Killers. 1999. mass mkt. 7.99 (*0-8041-1887-6*) Ivy Books.
Lewis, Dottie L., ed. Baseball in Cincinnati: From Wooden Fences to Astroturf. (Illus.). 64p. (Orig.). 1988. pap. text 7.50 (*0-911497-10-2*) Cin Mus Ctr.
— The Taft Museum: A Cincinnati Legacy. (Illus.). 63p. (Orig.). 1988. pap. text 7.50 (*0-911497-09-9*) Cin Mus Ctr.
Lewis, E. A., jt. auth. see Parrish, W. R.
Lewis, E. E. Introduction to Reliability Engineering. 2nd ed. LC 95-13533. 435p. 1995. text 102.95 (*0-471-01833-3*) Wiley.
Lewis, E. E. & Miller, W. F., Jr. Computational Methods of Neutron Transport. 2nd ed. LC 93-36902. 401p. 1993. 50.00 (*0-89448-452-4*) Am Nuclear Soc.
Lewis, E. Glyn. Linguistics & Second Language Pedagogy: A Theoretical Study. LC 73-79891. (Janua Linguarum, Ser. Didactica: No. 10). 137p. (Orig.). 1974. pap. text 32.35 (*90-279-2707-3*) Mouton.
— Multilingualism in the Soviet Union: Aspects of Language Policy & Its Implementation. (Contributions to the Sociology of Language Ser.: No. 3). (Illus.). 332p. (Orig.). 1972. pap. text 70.80 (*90-279-2352-3*) Mouton.
*__Lewis, E. R.__ Introduction to Bioengineering. Berger, S. A. & Goldsmith, W., eds. 2000. pap. 49.95 (*0-19-856515-1*) OUP.
Lewis, E. R. Network Models in Population Biology. LC 77-5873. (Biomathematics Ser.: Vol 7). 1977. 52.95 (*0-387-08214-X*) Spr-Verlag.
Lewis, E. Ridley. Acts of the Apostles & the Letters of St. Paul. (London Divinity Ser.). 160p. 1964. reprint ed. 6.50 (*0-227-67519-3*) Attic Pr.
— Johannine Writings & Other Epistles. (London Divinity Ser.). 144p. 1961. 6.50 (*0-227-67663-7*) Attic Pr.

Lewis, Earl. In Their Own Interests: Race, Class & Power in Twentieth-Century Norfolk, Virginia. (Illus.). 288p. 1990. 45.00 (*0-520-06644-8*, Pub. by U CA Pr); pap. 15.95 (*0-520-08444-6*, Pub. by U CA Pr) Cal Prin Full Svc.

***Lewis, Earl.** Love on Trial: An American Scandal in Black & White. (Illus.). 320p. 2000. 26.95 (*0-393-05013-0*) Norton.

Lewis, Earl, jt. ed. see Kelley, Robin D. G.

Lewis, Earl, jt. ed. see Trotter, Joe W., Jr.

Lewis, Earl B. New King. 1999. pap. 4.99 (*0-14-055729-6*) Viking Penguin.

Lewis, Earl B., jt. auth. see Steptoe, John L.

Lewis, Earl B., jt. illus. see Clifton, Lucille.

Lewis, Eddie. The Wedding's Over: What Now? 1989. 10.95 (*0-89137-583-X*) Quality Pubns.

***Lewis, Edith.** Willa Cather Living: A Personal Record. 215p. 2000. pap. 15.00 (*0-8032-7996-5*, Bison Books) U of Nebr Pr.

Lewis, Edith M. Haiku Is . . . A Feeling. LC 89-64144. (Illus.). 63p. (J). (ps-3). 1990. 5.95 (*0-9624993-0-7*) Pippin Bks.

Lewis, Edmund J., et al, eds. Lupus Nephritis. LC 98-39265. (Oxford Clinical Nephrology Ser.). (Illus.). 336p. 1999. text 125.00 (*0-19-262755-4*) OUP.

Lewis, Edna. Southern Cooking. 1998. write for info. (*0-375-40035-4*) Knopf.

— The Taste of Country Cooking. 1976. pap. 22.50 (*0-394-73215-4*) Knopf.

***Lewis, Edna & Goodbody, Mary.** In Pursuit of Flavor. LC 99-88305. (Illus.). 323p. 2000. pap. 15.95 (*0-8139-1989-4*) U Pr of Va.

Lewis, Edna & Peterson, Evangeline. The Edna Lewis Cookbook. (Cookbook Ser.). 200p. 1989. reprint ed. pap. 9.95 (*0-88001-193-9*) HarpC.

Lewis, Edward. Bracketing: A Constructive Way to Learn Basic English Grammar. 3rd ed. 254p. (C). 1992. pap. text 41.00 (*0-536-58238-6*) Pearson Custom.

— From a Different Angle: Observations on Being Human. (Illus.). 64p. 1993. pap. 12.95 (*1-880823-01-2*) N Star Pubns.

***Lewis, Edward.** Hostile Ground: Defusing & Restraining Violent Behavior & Physical Assaults. (Illus.). 152p. 2000. pap. 15.00 (*1-58160-054-2*) Paladin Pr.

Lewis, Edward, tr. see Heil, A. & Wesch.

Lewis, Edward A. American Shortline Railway Guide. 5th ed. Drury, George H., ed. LC 96-215170. (Railroad Reference Ser.: No. 17). (Illus.). 368p. 1994. pap. 24.95 (*0-89024-290-9*, 01073, Kalmbach Books) Kalmbach.

Lewis, Edward E. The Mobility of the Negro. LC 68-58603. (Columbia University. Studies in the Social Sciences: No. 342). reprint ed. 20.00 (*0-404-51342-5*) AMS Pr.

***Lewis, Edward Lyn & Jones, E. Peter.** The Freshwater Budget of the Arctic Ocean. LC 00-42087. (NATO Science Ser.). (Illus.). 2000. write for info. (*0-7923-6439-2*) Kluwer Academic.

Lewis, Edward S. A Biography of Distinguished Scientist Gilbert Newton Lewis. LC 98-25084. (Illus.). 152p. 1998. text 69.95 (*0-7734-8284-9*) E Mellen.

Lewis, Edward V., ed. Principles of Naval Architecture, 3 vols., Set. LC 88-60829. 1988. 180.00 (*0-685-56498-3*) Soc Naval Arch.

— Principles of Naval Architecture, 3 vols., Set. rev. ed. 1988. 192.00 (*0-614-06723-5*) Soc Naval Arch.

— Principles of Naval Architecture Vol. I: Stability & Strength, 3 vols. LC 88-60829. 320p. 1988. 90.00 (*0-939773-00-7*) Soc Naval Arch.

Lewis, Edwin. Teach Yourself Welsh Dictionary. (Teach Yourself Ser.). 1992. 15.95 (*0-8288-8412-9*) Fr & Eur.

— Teach Yourself Welsh Dictionary. (Teach Yourself Ser.). (WEL., Illus.). 256p. 1994. pap. 14.95 (*0-8442-3842-2*, Teach Yrslf) NTC Contemp Pub Co.

Lewis, Edwin H. The History of the English Paragraph. 1976. lib. bdg. 59.95 (*0-8490-1996-6*) Gordon Pr.

Lewis, Edwin R., et al, eds. The Vertebrate Inner Ear. 256p. 1985. 148.00 (*0-8493-6465-5*, QP461, CRC Reprint) Franklin.

Lewis, Elaine, jt. auth. see Lewis, Paul.

Lewis, Eleanor, ed. Darkroom. LC 76-57201. (Illus.). 184p. (Orig.). 1979. pap. 17.50 (*0-912810-19-X*) Lustrum Pr.

Lewis, Eleanor P. Nelly Custis Lewis's Housekeeping Book. Schmit, Patricia B., ed. LC 82-81038. (Illus.). x, 134p. 1982. 14.95 (*0-917860-09-8*) Historic New Orleans.

Lewis, Eleanore G., jt. auth. see Holmes, Roger.

Lewis, Elizabeth B. Christmas Songs from the Plains & Songs from Small-Town Dakota. 29p. 1990. pap. 3.50 (*0-614-24772-1*) Tesseract SD.

— First Songs from the Plains. 25p. 1990. pap. 3.50 (*0-614-24768-3*) Tesseract SD.

— More Songs from the Plains. 26p. 1990. pap. 3.50 (*0-614-24769-1*) Tesseract SD.

— Songs from Seasons on the Plains. 37p. 1990. pap. 3.50 (*0-614-24770-5*) Tesseract SD.

— Two Epics from the Plains. 14p. 1990. pap. 3.50 (*0-614-24771-3*) Tesseract SD.

Lewis, Elizabeth F. Young Fu of the Upper Yangtze. 288p. (J). (gr. k-6). 1990. pap. 5.50 (*0-440-49043-X*, YB BDD) BDD Bks Young Read.

— Young Fu of the Upper Yangtze. (J). 1996. pap. 5.99 (*0-440-91160-5*) BDD Bks Young Read.

— Young Fu of the Upper Yangtze. LC 72-91654. (Illus.). 268p. (J). (gr. 4-6). 1995. 18.95 (*0-8050-0549-8*, Bks Young Read) H Holt & Co.

Lewis, Elizabeth H. Young Fu of the Upper Yangtze. (J). 1960. 10.09 (*0-606-04431-0*, Pub. by Turtleback) Demco.

Lewis, Elizabeth N. Manual of Patient Classification: Systems & Techniques for Practical Application. 432p. 1988. 167.00 (*0-87189-898-5*, 510) Aspen Pub.

Lewis, Emmanuel R. Seacoast Fortifications of the United States: An Introductory History. (Illus.). 145p. 1993. pap. 18.95 (*1-55750-502-0*) Naval Inst Pr.

Lewis, Eric, tr. see Alexander of Aphrodisias.

Lewis, Eric C. & Caveney, Mike. The Genius of Robert Harbin: A Personal Biography. LC 97-76603. (Illus.). 1997. write for info. (*0-915181-30-4*) Magic Words.

Lewis, Eric C., jt. auth. see Brislin, Ralph F.

Lewis, Ernest A. The Fremont Cannon, High Up & Far Back. 2nd rev. ed. LC 92-60710. (Illus.). 96p. (C). 1992. reprint ed. pap. 14.95 (*0-9633604-1-8*) Western Trails.

— The Great Lost Fremont Cannon Expedition: The Fremont Cannon High Up & Far Back. 3rd rev. ed. LC 92-60780. (Illus.). 96p. 1992. reprint ed. pap. 12.95 (*0-9633604-2-6*) Western Trails.

Lewis, Ethan. Gospels of Wealth: How the Rich Portray Their Lives. LC 94-33272. 304p. 1994. 69.50 (*0-275-94643-6*, Praeger Pubs) Greenwood.

Lewis, Ethan, jt. auth. see McGregor, Robert Kuhn.

Lewis, Eugene. American Politics in a Bureaucratic Age: Citizens, Constituents, Clients & Victims. 192p. (C). 1988. reprint ed. pap. text 19.50 (*0-8191-7049-6*) U Pr of Amer.

— Public Entrepreneurship: Toward a Theory of Bureaucratic Political Power. LC 79-2451. 286p. reprint ed. pap. 88.70 (*0-8357-3953-8*, 205704900004) Bks Demand.

Lewis, Evelyn Jones & Ray, Mary F. Exploring Professional Cooking. 3rd rev. ed. (YA). (gr. 9-12). 1988. text 36.99 (*0-02-667950-7*) Glencoe.

Lewis, Evelyn L. & Turner, Carolyn S. Housing Decisions. LC 99-19060. (Illus.). 543p. (YA). (gr. 9-12). 2000. text 45.00 (*1-56637-651-3*) Goodheart.

Lewis, Evelyn Stryker. Neptune & Shark River Hills. LC 98-87778. (Images of America Ser.). (Illus.). 128p. 1998. pap. 16.99 (*0-7524-0997-2*) Arcadia Publng.

Lewis, F. A. & Aladjem, A., eds. Hydrogen Metal Systems I. (Solid State Phenomena Ser.: Vols. 49-50). (Illus.). 460p. (C). 1995. text 200.00 (*3-908450-12-8*, Pub. by Scitec Pubns) Enfield Pubs NH.

Lewis, F. L., jt. auth. see Kim, Young H.

Lewis, F. L., jt. ed. see Sadegh, N.

Lewis, F. R. & Pfeiffer, U. J., eds. Practical Applications of Fiberoptics in Critical Care Monitoring. 204p. 1990. 55.95 (*0-387-51718-9*) Spr-Verlag.

Lewis, F. W. Neural Network Control of Robot Manipulators & Non-Linear Systems. LC 99-178266. 1998. 99.00 (*0-7484-0596-8*) Taylor & Francis.

Lewis-Ferguson, Julinda. Alvin Ailey, Jr. A Life in Dance. LC 93-17906. 64p. (J). (gr. 3-8). 1994. 14.95 (*0-8027-8239-6*); lib. bdg. 15.85 (*0-8027-8241-8*) Walker & Co.

Lewis, Ferris E. The Story of the Knights Templars (1118-1315) 100p. 1994. reprint ed. pap. 14.95 (*1-56459-441-6*) Kessinger Pub.

Lewis, Fiona. Between Men. 1996. pap. 5.99 (*0-312-95861-7*) St Martin.

Lewis, Florence V. Fray: History & Genealogy of John Fray (Johannes Frey) of Culpeper County, Virginia: His Descendants & Their Related Families. (Illus.). 207p. 1995. reprint ed. pap. 37.00 (*0-8328-4914-6*); reprint ed. lib. bdg. 47.00 (*0-8328-4913-8*) Higginson Bk Co.

Lewis, Frances M., jt. ed. see Ward, William B.

***Lewis, Francesca.** Slave of Darkness. 256p. 2000. pap. 9.95 (*1-901388-50-6*, Pub. by Chimera Pubns) Firebird Dist.

Lewis, Francis A., Jr. Law Relating to Stocks, Bonds & Other Securities in the United States. LC 97-28831. xxxiv, 196p. 1997. reprint ed. 42.50 (*0-8377-2418-X*, Rothman) W S Hein.

Lewis, Frank & Bolton, Robert, eds. Form, Matter & Mixture in Aristotle. 290p. (Orig.). (C). 1997. pap. text 25.95 (*0-631-20092-4*) Blackwell Pubs.

Lewis, Frank C., ed. see Haight, Ada C.

Lewis, Frank L. Applied Optimal Control & Estimation. 656p. (C). 1992. text 59.20 (*0-13-040361-X*) P-H.

— Optimal Estimation with an introduction to Stachastic Control Theory. LC 85-26554. 400p. 1986. 130.00 (*0-471-83741-5*) Wiley.

Lewis, Frank L. & Syrmos, Vassilis L. Optimal Control. 2nd ed. LC 95-15649. 560p. 1995. 120.00 (*0-471-03378-2*) Wiley.

Lewis, Frank L., jt. auth. see Stevens, Brian L.

Lewis, Frank R., Jr. & Weigelt, John A. Surgical Critical Care. LC 94-44206. (Illus.). 416p. 1995. text 105.00 (*0-7216-3368-4*, W B Saunders Co) Harcrt Hlth Sci Grp.

Lewis, Frank W. Rumpah! 300p. pap. 14.95 (*0-614-25162-1*) Western Tales.

— Solving Cipher Problems: Cryptanalysis, Probabilities & Diagnostics. 250p. (Orig.). 1992. pap. 30.80 (*0-89412-178-2*) Aegean Park Pr.

***Lewis, Franklin.** Rumi - Past & Present, East & West: Life Teachings & Poetry of Jalalu L-Din Rumi. (Illus.). 686p. 2000. 35.95 (*1-85168-214-7*, Pub. by Onewrld Pubns) Penguin Putnam.

Lewis, Franklin & Yazdanfar, Farzin, eds. In a Voice of Their Own: A Collection of Stories by Iranian Women Written since the Revolution of 1979. LC 96-39171. (Bibliotheca Iranica Ser.: Vol. 4). 196p. (Orig.). 1996. pap. 13.95 (*1-56859-045-8*) Mazda Pubs.

Lewis, Fred. Young at Heart: Johnny Kelley. 208p. 1992. 16.95 (*0-915297-18-3*) Cedarwinds.

Lewis, Frederick P. The Context of Judicial Activism. LC 98-17901. 143p. 2000. pap. 21.95 (*0-8476-8992-1*) Rowman.

— The Context of Judicial Activism: The Endurance of the Warren Court Legacy in a Conservative Age. LC 98-17901. 143p. 2000. 53.00 (*0-8476-8991-3*) Rowman.

— The Nationalization of Liberty. 82p. (Orig.). (C). 1990. pap. text 13.50 (*0-8191-7763-6*) U Pr of Amer.

***Lewis, G.** Windrush Echoes Soundings 10. 1999. pap. text 19.50 (*0-85315-886-X*) Lawrence & Wishart.

Lewis, G., jt. auth. see Descartes, Rene.

Lewis, G., ed. see Trucks, H. E.

Lewis, G. Douglass. Meeting the Moment: Leadership & Well-Being in Ministry. 124p. 1997. pap. 12.95 (*0-687-07286-7*) Abingdon.

Lewis, G. E. Communication Services Via Satellite: A Handbook for Design, Installation & Service Engineers. 2nd ed. (Illus.). 400p. 1992. pap. text 82.95 (*0-7506-0437-9*) Buttrwrth-Heinemann.

— Service Engineer's Pocket Book. (Newnes Pocket Bks.). 256p. 1998. pap. text 29.95 (*0-7506-3448-0*, Newnes) Buttrwrth-Heinemann.

Lewis, G. L., jt. auth. see Spink, M. S.

Lewis, G. M. Neutrinos. (Wykeham Science Ser.: No. 12). 132p. 1971. pap. 18.00 (*0-85109-140-7*) Taylor & Francis.

Lewis, G. M. & Wheatley, G. A. Neutrinos. LC 73-135382. (Wykeham Science Ser.: No. 12). 132p. (C). 1970. 18.00 (*0-8448-1114-9*, Crane Russak) Taylor & Francis.

Lewis, G. Malcolm, ed. Cartographic Encounters. LC 97-49064. 318p. 1998. 60.00 (*0-226-47694-4*) U Ch Pr.

Lewis, G. Malcolm, ed. see Woodward, David.

Lewis, G. P. Caesalpinia: A Revision of the Poincianella-Erthrostemon Group. (Illus.). 233p. 1998. pap. 36.00 (*1-900347-32-6*, Pub. by Royal Botnic Grdns) Balogh.

— Legumes of Bahia. (Illus.). xvi, 369p. 1987. pap. 24.00 (*0-947643-05-2*, Pub. by Royal Botnic Grdns) Balogh.

Lewis, G. P. & Owen, P. E. Legumes of the Ilha de Maraca. (Illus.). xvi, 95p. 1989. pap. 15.00 (*0-947643-15-X*, Pub. by Royal Botnic Grdns) Balogh.

Lewis, G. W. Light of the Tittle. LC 99-191429. 285p. 1998. write for info. (*0-9657415-8-3*) Blue Planet Pubns.

Lewis, G. W. & Lewis, Diana. It's a Colorbe's Life! Vol. 1: Returning to Love. (Illus.). 1998. spiral bd., wbk. ed. 12.95 (*0-9657415-7-5*) Blue Planet Pubns.

Lewis, Gail. Forming Nation, Framing Welfare. LC 97-46855. (Social Policy--Welfare, Power & Diversity Ser.). 352p. (C). 1998. 80.00 (*0-415-18129-1*); pap. 22.99 (*0-415-18130-5*) Routledge.

***Lewis, Gail.** Race, Gender, Social Welfare: Encounters in a Postcolonial Society. LC 99-86007. 200p. 2000. text 59.95 (*0-7456-2284-4*, Pub. by Polity Pr); pap. text 27.95 (*0-7456-2285-2*, Pub. by Polity Pr) Blackwell Pubs.

Lewis, Gail & Hughes, Gordon. Unsettling Welfare: The Reconstruction of Social Policy. LC 97-48928. (Social Policy--Welfare, Power & Diversity Ser.). 496p. (C). 1998. 75.00 (*0-415-18133-X*); pap. 24.99 (*0-415-18134-8*) Routledge.

Lewis, Gail & Hughes, Gordon, eds. The University of Oxford College Histories: From Their Foundations to the Twentieth Century. 19 vols. fac. ed. (Social Policy--Welfare, Power & Diversity Ser.). 5472p. (C). (gr. 13). 1998. 2475.00 (*0-415-18632-3*, D6167) Routledge.

Lewis, Gareth. The Mentoring Manager: Strategies for Fostering Talent & Spreading Knowledge. (Institute of Management Ser.). (Illus.). 212p. (Orig.). 1996. pap. 47.50 (*0-273-62344-3*, Pub. by Pitman Pub) Trans-Atl Phila.

— The Mentoring Manager: Strategies for Fostering Talent & Spreading Knowledge. 2nd ed. (Smarter Solutions Ser.). 192p. (Orig.). 2000. pap. 22.50 (*0-273-64484-X*, Pub. by F T P-H) Trans-Atl Phila.

Lewis, Gareth. Understanding Business Statistics. LC 96-6541. (Barron's Business Success Ser.). 96p. 1997. pap. 6.95 (*0-7641-0257-5*) Barron.

Lewis, Gareth & Mathieu, Didier. Pharmaceutical Experimental Design. LC 98-37068. (Drugs & the Pharmaceutical Sciences Ser.). (Illus.). 552p. 1998. text 175.00 (*0-8247-9860-0*) Dekker.

Lewis, Gary, et al. Fly Casting for Everyone. LC 95-37129. (Illus.). 96p. 1996. pap. 7.95 (*0-8117-2525-1*) Stackpole.

Lewis, Gary A. The Clean-up of Codfish Cove. (Shamu & His Crew Adventure Ser.). (Illus.). 32p. (J). (gr. k-3). 1994. 5.95 (*1-884506-05-4*) Third Story.

— News from Somewhere: Connecting Health & Freedom at the Workplace, 151. LC 85-27269. (Contributions in Political Science Ser.: No. 151). (Illus.). 226p. 1986. 55.00 (*0-313-24869-9*, LNF/, Greenwood Pr) Greenwood.

— Shamu's Best Friend. (Shamu & His Crew Adventure Ser.). (Illus.). 32p. (J). (gr. k-4). 1994. 5.95 (*1-884506-04-6*) Third Story.

Lewis, Gary L., jt. auth. see Viessman, Warren, Jr.

Lewis, Gary L., jt. auth. see Viessman, Warren.

Lewis, Gary M. Oracle Reporting: Queries with SQL Objects. LC 95-94198. (Illus.). (Orig.). 1995. pap. 36.00 (*0-9644912-3-0*) Komenda Pub.

Lewis, Gary M. & Sirota, Alex. Oracle SQL: 101 Frequently Asked Questions. LC 96-94143. (Illus.). (Orig.). 1997. pap. 30.00 (*0-9644912-7-3*) Komenda Pub.

Lewis, Gaspar. Cabinetmaking, Patternmaking & Millwork. LC 79-50917. (Carpentry-Cabinetmaking Ser.). 438p. (C). 1981. teacher ed. 14.00 (*0-8273-1815-4*) Delmar.

— Carpentry. LC 83-71049. 544p. 1984. text 39.95 (*0-8273-1800-6*) Delmar.

— Carpentry. LC 83-71049. 544p. 1984. teacher ed. 13.50 (*0-8273-1801-4*) Delmar.

— Carpentry. LC 83-71049. 544p. 1984. student ed. 14.95 (*0-8273-1808-1*) Delmar.

— Carpentry. 2nd ed. LC 83-71049. (Illus.). 800p. 1995. pap. 67.95 (*0-8273-5979-9*) Delmar.

— Safety for Carpenters & Woodworkers. LC 80-66859. (Carpentry-Cabinetmaking Ser.). (C). 1980. mass mkt. 18.00 (*0-8273-1869-3*) Delmar.

— Safety for Carpenters & Woodworkers. LC 80-66859. (Carpentry-Cabinetmaking Ser.). (C). 1981. teacher ed. 13.50 (*0-8273-1870-7*) Delmar.

Lewis, Gaspar J. Carpentry. 800p. 1995. teacher ed. write for info. (*0-8273-7049-0*) Delmar.

Lewis, Gavin. Close-Ups of the Past Vol. 1: Case Studies in Western Civilization, Vol. 1. LC 96-77708. 257p. (C). 1996. pap. text 26.50 (*0-15-501507-9*, Pub. by Harcourt Coll Pubs) Harcourt.

— Tomas Masaryk-Czechoslovak: Philosopher & Statesman. (World Leaders Past & Present Ser.). (Illus.). 120p. (YA). (gr. 5 up). 1990. 17.95 (*1-55546-816-0*) Chelsea Hse.

Lewis, Gavin, jt. auth. see Greer, Thomas H.

Lewis, Geneva, jt. auth. see Weber, Valerie.

***Lewis, Geoff.** Communications Systems: Engineers' Choices. 3rd ed. LC 98-41625. 544p. 1998. text 79.95 (*0-240-51494-7*, Focal) Buttrwrth-Heinemann.

Lewis, Geoff. Communications Technology Handbook. (Illus.). 456p. 1994. text 76.95 (*0-7506-1729-2*) Buttrwrth-Heinemann.

— Communications Technology Handbook. 2nd ed. LC 96-28604. (Illus.). 480p. 1997. text 89.95 (*0-240-51461-0*, Focal) Buttrwrth-Heinemann.

Lewis, Geoff, jt. auth. see Sinclair, Ian.

Lewis, Geoff E. & Sinclair, Ian R. Servicing Electronics Systems, Vol. 1. 256p. 1991. pap. text 27.95 (*1-85628-171-X*, Pub. by Avebry) Ashgate Pub Co.

Lewis, Geoffrey. Behind the Walls: A Chelmsford Turnkey of the Nineteenth Century. unabridged ed. (Illus.). 64p. 1996. pap. 14.00 (*0-86025-467-4*, Pub. by I Henry Pubns) Empire Pub Srvs.

Lewis, Geoffrey. Corporate Strategy in Action: The Strategy Process in British Road Services. LC 88-30796. (Illus.). 271p. reprint ed. pap. 84.10 (*0-608-20391-2*, 207164400002) Bks Demand.

— Java Programming Sourcebook. LC 97-228822. 336p. 1997. pap. 34.99 (*0-471-24797-9*) Wiley.

— Lord Atkin. 288p. 1984. boxed set 50.00 (*0-406-27210-7*, UK, MICHIE) LEXIS Pub.

***Lewis, Geoffrey.** Lord Atkin. 264p. 1999. reprint ed. 54.00 (*1-84113-057-5*, Pub. by Hart Pub) Intl Spec Bk.

Lewis, Geoffrey. Lord Hailsham: A Life. (Illus.). 403p. 1998. 50.00 (*0-224-04252-1*, Pub. by Jonathan Cape) Trafalgar.

— The Turkish Language Reform: A Revolution in Language. LC 99-24289. (Illus.). 200p. 2000. text 60.00 (*0-19-823856-8*) OUP.

Lewis, Geoffrey E. & Sinclair, Ian R. Newnes Service Engineer's Pocket Book. LC 97-27320. 272p. 1998. text 29.95 (*0-7506-3789-7*, Newnes) Buttrwrth-Heinemann.

Lewis, Geoffrey E., jt. auth. see Sinclair, Ian R.

Lewis, Geoffrey L. Teach Yourself Turkish. (Teach Yourself Ser.). 1992. 15.95 (*0-8288-8407-2*); 45.00 incl. audio (*0-8288-8408-0*) Fr & Eur.

— Teach Yourself Turkish: A Complete Course for Beginners. (TUR.). 224p. 1994. pap. 13.95 (*0-8442-3840-6*, Teach Yrslf) NTC Contemp Pub Co.

— Turkish Grammar. 328p. 1985. pap. text 55.00 (*0-19-815838-6*) OUP.

Lewis, Geoffrey L., jt. auth. see Timperley, Stuart.

Lewis, Geoffrey L., tr. see Taner, Haldun.

Lewis, George. Encyclopedia of Massachusetts: A Reference Guide to the Bay State. (Encyclopedia of the United States Ser.). (Illus.). 601p. 1984. reprint ed. lib. bdg. 79.00 (*0-403-09983-8*) Somerset Pub.

Lewis, George. Power Stronger Itself. 1997. pap. 16.95 (*0-226-47696-0*); lib. bdg. 48.00 (*0-226-47695-2*) U Ch Pr.

Lewis, George C. An Essay on the Influence of Authority in Matters of Opinion. LC 73-14165. 440p. 1974. reprint ed. 28.95 (*0-405-05510-2*) Ayer.

— A Treatise on the Methods of Observation & Reasoning in Politics, 2 vols. LC 73-14166. (Perspectives in Social Inquiry Ser.). 984p. 1974. reprint ed. 59.95 (*0-405-05511-0*) Ayer.

Lewis, George C., tr. see Boeckh, Augustus.

Lewis, George E. The Indiana Company, 1763-1798: A Study in Eighteenth Century Frontier Land Speculation & Business Venture. LC 70-140363. (Select Bibliographies Reprint Ser.). 1977. reprint ed. 25.95 (*0-8369-5606-0*) Ayer.

Lewis, George H., ed. All That Glitters: Country Music in America. LC 92-74544. 340p. 1993. 44.95 (*0-87972-573-7*); pap. 21.95 (*0-87972-574-5*) Bowling Green Univ Popular Press.

Lewis, George K. Growing up in Wayland: Life in a Massachusetts Town During the Depression. (Illus.). 100p. 1997. pap. 15.95 (*1-882063-42-2*, Heritage Hse) Cottage Pr MA.

Lewis, George L., Jr. Casino Surveillance the Eye That Never Blinks. (Illus.). 116p. 1996. pap. 30.00 (*0-9666009-0-8*) G & G Surv Spec.

Lewis, George S. Black Heritage Unveiled. 2nd ed. LC 86-62546. (Illus.). 200p. 1987. text 15.95 (*0-937771-09-0*); pap. text 10.95 (*0-937771-08-2*); lib. bdg. 14.95 (*0-937771-10-4*) Spencers Intl.

— Israel, Egypt & the Blackman. LC 86-62542. 180p. (Orig.). 1986. text 15.95 (*0-937771-06-6*); pap. text 10.95 (*0-937771-05-8*); lib. bdg. 15.95 (*0-937771-07-4*) Spencers Intl.

— Space Age Laws of Success. LC 87-6009. (Orig.). 1987. text 15.95 (*0-937771-14-7*); pap. text 10.95 (*0-937771-15-5*) Spencers Intl.

— Space Age Marriage Techniques. LC 87-60010. (Orig.). 1987. text 15.95 (*0-937771-13-9*) Spencers Intl.

Lewis, George S. Space Age Marriage Techniques. LC 87-60010. (Orig.). 1987. pap. text 12.95 (*0-937771-12-0*) Spencers Intl.

Lewis, George S. Space Age Predictions. LC 86-90555. 71p. 1986. pap. text 10.95 (*0-937771-02-3*); lib. bdg. 10.95 (*0-937771-00-7*) Spencers Intl.

— Space Age Predictions. LC 90-91673. xvi, 54 p. 1990. write for info. (*0-937771-01-5*) Spencers Intl.

An Asterisk (*) at the beginning of an entry indicates that the title is appearing for the first time.

— The Wayward Wife. LC 86-62543. 25p. (Orig.). 1986. text 10.95 (*0-937771-03-1*); pap. text 8.95 (*0-937771-04-X*); lib. bdg. 10.95 (*0-937771-11-2*) Spencers Intl.

Lewis, George S., intro. Message to Adam's Children: The Book of Enoch. (Orig.). 1990. pap. 12.95 (*0-937771-17-1*); text 18.95 (*0-937771-16-3*) Spencers Intl.

Lewis, Geraint. Michael Tippett, O. M. A Celebration. (Illus.). 255p. 1985. 39.95 (*0-85936-140-3*, Pub. by The Baton Pr) Pro-Am Music.

Lewis, Gerald & Simmons, Bill. Profitable Roadside Retailing: Making It Happen. 131p. 10.00 (*0-685-65572-5*) Mkters Assn of Am.

Lewis, Gerald E. How to Talk Yankee. rev. ed. LC 88-38431. (Illus.). 58p. (Orig.). 1986. pap. 3.95 (*0-945980-07-8*) Nrth Country Pr.

— So Long, Scout, & Other Stories. LC 87-7104. (Illus.). 161p. (Orig.). 1988. pap. 9.95 (*0-945432-00-3*) Nrth Country Pr.

***Lewis, Gerald W. & Zare, Nancy C.** Workplace Hostility: Myth & Reality. LC 98-42983. 1998. boxed set 39.95 (*1-56032-535-6*) Hemisp Pub.

Lewis, Gerald W. & Zare, Nancy C. Workplace Hostility: Myth & Reality. LC 98-42983. xvi, 171p. 1999. pap. 17.95 (*1-56032-536-4*) Hemisp Pub.

Lewis, Gertrud J., ed. & tr. see Gertrude the Great of Helfta.

Lewis, Gertrude, ed. see Anschell, Helen & Malkin, Marsha.

Lewis, Gifford. Eva Gore-Boothe & Esther Roper: A Biography. 1988. pap. 13.00 (*0-86358-159-5*, Pub. by Rivers Oram) NYU Pr.

— The Yeats Sisters & the Cuala. (Illus.). 222p. 1994. 37.50 (*0-7165-2525-9*, Pub. by Irish Acad Pr) Intl Spec Bk.

***Lewis, Gilbert.** A Failure of Treatment. (Oxford Studies in Social & Cultural Anthropology). (Illus.). 296p. 2000. text 65.00 (*0-19-823408-2*); pap. text 24.95 (*0-19-823409-0*) OUP.

Lewis, Gilbert. Knowledge of Illness in a Sepik Society: A Study of the Gnau, New Guinea. (London School of Economics Monographs on Social Anthropology: No. 52). (Illus.). 379p. (C). 1975. text 55.00 (*0-485-19552-6*, Pub. by Athlone Pr) Humanities.

Lewis, Gilbert, jt. ed. see Frankel, Stephen.

Lewis, Gilbert Newton. Anatomy of Science. LC 75-156680. (Essay Index Reprint Ser.). 1977. reprint ed. 20.95 (*0-8369-2408-8*) Ayer.

Lewis, Gillian. Calvinism in Europe: 1540-1620. 296p. 1996. pap. text 19.95 (*0-521-57452-8*) Cambridge U Pr.

Lewis, Gillian & Pettegree, Andrew, eds. Calvinism in Europe, 1555-C. 1620: A Collection of Documents. Duke, Alastair et al, trs. 288p. (C). 1992. text 27.95 (*0-7190-3552-X*, Pub. by Manchester Univ Pr) St Martin.

***Lewis, Gladys S.** Loaves & Hyacinths: Tea Rooms in London & East Anglia. unabridged ed. LC 99-94360. (Illus.). 206p. 1999. 36.00 (*0-9669682-0-4*) Greystone.

Lewis, Glen. Australian Movies & the American Dream. LC 87-14590. (Illus.). 229p. 1987. 49.95 (*0-275-92675-3*, C2675, Praeger Pubs) Greenwood.

Lewis, Glen, jt. auth. see Osborne, Graeme.

Lewis, Gloria. The Informed Technical Reader: An Anthology. 266p. (C). 1996. per. 40.95 (*0-7872-2897-4*, 41289701) Kendall-Hunt.

Lewis, Gordon. Notes on the Puerto Rican Revolution: An Essay on American Dominance & Caribbean Resistance. LC 74-7791. 288p. 1976. pap. 10.00 (*0-85345-371-3*, Pub. by Monthly Rev) NYU Pr.

— Slavery, Imperialism, & Freedom: Studies in English Radical Thought. LC 78-2826. 346p. 1979. pap. 10.00 (*0-85345-501-5*, Pub. by Monthly Rev) NYU Pr.

Lewis, Gordon, ed. History of the Japanese Camera. 1990. 60.00 (*0-935398-16-3*); pap. 50.00 (*0-935398-17-1*) G Eastman Hse.

Lewis, Gordon D. & Kyrou, Emilios J. Handy Hints on Legal Practice. 2nd ed. 334p. 1993. pap. 45.00 (*0-455-21201-5*, Pub. by LawBk Co) Gaunt.

Lewis, Gordon H. & Michel, Richard C., eds. Microsimulation Techniques for Tax & Transfer Analysis. LC 89-24832. (Illus.). 262p. 1990. pap. text 25.50 (*0-87766-433-1*); lib. bdg. 50.50 (*0-87766-432-3*) Urban Inst.

Lewis, Gordon K. Grenada: The Jewel Despoiled. LC 86-46282. 251p. 1987. pap. 77.90 (*0-7837-7453-2*, 204917500010) Bks Demand.

— Growth of the Modern West Indies. LC 68-13657. 512p. 1970. pap. 15.00 (*0-85345-130-3*, Pub. by Monthly Rev) NYU Pr.

— Main Currents in Caribbean Thought: The Historical Evolution of Caribbean Society in Its Ideological Aspects, 1492-1900. LC 82-17128. (Johns Hopkins Studies in Atlantic History & Culture). 391p. reprint ed. pap. 121.30 (*0-608-06104-2*, 206643600008) Bks Demand.

— Puerto Rico: Freedom & Power in the Caribbean. LC 63-20065. 638p. 1963. reprint ed. pap. 197.80 (*0-7837-9607-2*, 206036400005) Bks Demand.

Lewis, Gordon P. Bookkeeping & Tax Preparation: Start & Build a Prosperous Bookkeeping, Tax, & Financial Services Business. LC 95-83817. (Illus.). 179p. (Orig.). 1996. pap. 18.95 (*0-9639371-7-0*) Acton Circle.

Lewis, Gordon R. Confronting the Cults. LC 66-26791. 1966. pap. 8.99 (*0-87552-323-4*) P & R Pubng.

— Decide for Yourself: A Theological Workbook. LC 71-116046. 174p. (Orig.). 1970. pap., wbk. ed. 13.99 (*0-87784-633-2*, 633) InterVarsity.

— Testing Christianity's Truth Claims: Approaches to Christian Apologetics. 363p. (C). 1990. reprint ed. pap. text 29.50 (*0-8191-7838-1*) U Pr of Amer.

Lewis, Gordon R. & Demarest, Bruce A. Integrative Theology, 3 vols. LC 96-214279. 1500p. 1996. boxed set 64.99 (*0-310-20915-3*) Zondervan.

***Lewis, Grace R.** 1,001 Chemicals in Everyday Products. 2nd ed. LC 98-6419. 400p. 1998. pap. 43.95 (*0-471-29212-5*, Wiley-Interscience) Wiley.

Lewis, Grace Ross, see Ross Lewis, Grace.

Lewis, Graham, et al, eds. Columbia Poetry Review, No. 2. 96p. (Orig.). 1989. pap. 8.00 (*0-932026-20-6*) Columbia College Chi.

Lewis, Graham, jt. auth. see Abraham, John.

Lewis, Greg, jt. auth. see Carson, Ben.

Lewis, Gregg. El Poder de una Pormesa Cumplida.Tr. of Power of a Promise Kept. (SPA.). 240p. 1995. 8.99 (*0-7899-0147-1*, 497272) Editorial Unilit.

— The Power of a Promise Kept. 1995. 17.99 (*1-56179-350-7*) Focus Family.

Lewis, Gregg, jt. auth. see Akers, Michelle.

Lewis, Gregg, jt. auth. see Jordan, Deloris.

Lewis, Gregg, jt. auth. see Landry, Tom.

Lewis, Gregg, jt. auth. see Lewis, Margie M.

Lewis, Gregg, jt. auth. see Lewis, Marjorie.

Lewis, Gregg, jt. auth. see Lewis, Ralph L.

Lewis, Gregg, jt. auth. see Morris, Debbie.

Lewis, Gregg, jt. auth. see Purl, Sandy.

Lewis, Gregg, jt. auth. see Wazeter, Mary.

Lewis, Gregg A., jt. photos by see Lewis, Deborah S.

Lewis, Gregory. Exoskeleton. 48p. 1999. pap. 8.00 (*0-8059-4702-7*) Dorrance.

— Le Moine. unabridged ed. (FRE.). Date not set. reprint ed. pap. 8.95 (*2-87714-358-9*, Pub. by Bookking Intl) Distribks Inc.

Lewis, Griffith L. Guide to Your Parenting Concerns. LC 95-95128. 334p. (Orig.). 1996. pap. 15.00 (*0-9648933-0-4*) Kindred Bks.

Lewis, Griselda. A Collector's History of English Pottery. 4th ed. (Illus.). 360p. 1987. 79.50 (*1-85149-056-6*) Antique Collect.

— Collector's History of English Pottery. 4th ed. LC 99-230173. (Illus.). 384p. 1999. 89.50 (*1-85149-291-7*) Antique Collect.

Lewis, Griselda, jt. auth. see Lewis, John.

Lewis, Guy & Appenzeller, Herb. Successful Sport Management. 377p. 1985. 60.00 (*0-87215-925-6*, 60183-10, MICHIE) LEXIS Pub.

Lewis, Gwendolyn R. Plant a Seed . . . Read! 101 Activities to Motivate Children to Read! (Illus.). 112p. (Orig.). 1995. pap., spiral bd. write for info. (*0-9649216-0-X*) Hold on to your Dreams.

Lewis, Gwyneth. Parables & Faxes. 80p. 1995. pap. 15.95 (*1-85224-319-8*, Pub. by Bloodaxe Bks) Dufour.

— Zero Gravity. LC 98-234173. 80p. 1998. pap. 16.95 (*1-85224-456-9*, Pub. by Bloodaxe Bks) Dufour.

Lewis, Gwyneth & Drife, James O. Why Mothers Die: Report on Confidential Enquiries into Maternal Deaths in the United Kingdom, 1994-1996. LC 98-234428. xvii, 282p. 1998. 34.00 (*0-11-322253-X*, Pub. by Statnry Office) Balogh.

Lewis, Gwynne. The French Revolution: Rethinking the Debate. LC 92-44015. (Historical Connections Ser.). 144p. (C). (gr. 13). 1993. pap. 16.99 (*0-415-05466-4*, A7868) Routledge.

— Pierre-Francois Tubeuf & the Advent of Capitalism in France, 1770-1840. (Illus.). 350p. 1993. text 65.00 (*0-19-822895-3*) OUP.

— The Second Vendee: The Continuity of Counter-Revolution in the Department of the Gard 1789-1815. (Illus.). 1978. 55.00 (*0-19-822544-X*) OUP.

Lewis, Gwynne, tr. see Soboul, Albert.

Lewis, H., jt. auth. see Bird, Martyn.

Lewis, H. D., ed. see Dumas, Alexandre.

Lewis, H. Elvit. Christ among the Welsh Miners. 1987. pap. 8.99 (*0-88019-221-6*) Schmul Pub Co.

Lewis, H. Gregg. Union Relative Wage Effects: A Survey. LC 85-8663. 240p. 1998. lib. bdg. 45.00 (*0-226-47721-5*) U Ch Pr.

— Unionism & Relative Wages in the United States. LC 63-20915. (Midway Reprint Ser.). 1973. reprint ed. pap. text 13.00 (*0-226-47720-7*) U Ch Pr.

Lewis, H. Spencer. Essays of a Modern Mystic. LC 63-12317. 195p. 1962. 16.95 (*0-912057-21-1*, 501820) GLELJ AMORC.

— Mental Poisoning. LC 59-55270. 84p. 1937. pap. 6.95 (*0-912057-49-1*, 502010) GLELJ AMORC.

— The Mystical Life of Jesus. LC 54-20988. (Illus.). 248p. 1929. pap. 14.95 (*0-912057-46-7*, 501980) GLELJ AMORC.

— Rosicrucian Principles for the Home & Business. LC 54-21694. 172p. 1929. pap. 12.95 (*0-912057-54-8*, 502030) GLELJ AMORC.

— The Secret Doctrines of Jesus. LC 37-22922. 183p. 1937. pap. 12.95 (*0-912057-91-2*, 501610) GLELJ AMORC.

— Self-Mastery & Fate with the Cycles of Life. LC 55-16785. (Illus.). 185p. 1929. pap. 14.95 (*0-912057-45-9*, 501970) GLELJ AMORC.

Lewis, H. Spencer. A Thousand Years of Yesterday: A Strange Story of Mystic Revelations. LC 20-9068. 119p. 1920. pap. 15.95 (*0-912057-99-8*) GLELJ AMORC.

Lewis, H. Spencer, ed. American Rosae Crucis: A Magazine of Life's Mysteries (1916) 432p. 1998. reprint ed. pap. 30.00 (*0-7661 0697-7*) Kessinger Pub.

— American Rosae Crucis: A Magazine of Life's Mysteries (1917) 296p. 1998. reprint ed. pap. 24.95 (*0-7661-0698-5*) Kessinger Pub.

— American Rosae Crucis: An Official Publication of Rosicrucian Mysticism (1920) 100p. 1998. reprint ed. pap. 14.95 (*0-7661-0699-3*) Kessinger Pub.

— Cromaat: A Monograph for the Members of Amorc (1918) 274p. 1998. reprint ed. pap. 24.95 (*0-7661-0219-X*) Kessinger Pub.

— The Mystic Triangle: A Modern Magazine of Rosicrucian Philosophy, 1925. 136p. 1998. reprint ed. pap. 17.95 (*0-7661-0702-7*) Kessinger Pub.

— The Mystic Triangle: A Modern Magazine of Rosicrucian Philosophy (1926) 310p. 1998. reprint ed. pap. 24.95 (*0-7661-0703-5*) Kessinger Pub.

— The Mystic Triangle: A Modern Magazine of Rosicrucian Philosophy (1927) 402p. 1998. reprint ed. pap. 29.95 (*0-7661-0704-3*) Kessinger Pub.

— The Mystic Triangle: A Modern Magazine of Rosicrucian Philosophy (1928) 416p. 1998. reprint ed. pap. 29.95 (*0-7661-0705-1*) Kessinger Pub.

— The Mystic Triangle: A Modern Magazine of Rosicrucian Philosophy (1929) 434p. 1998. reprint ed. pap. 29.95 (*0-7661-0706-X*) Kessinger Pub.

Lewis, H. W. The Foundations of Fuzzy Control. LC 97-14026. (IFSR International Series on Systems Science: Vol. 10). 318p. (C). 1997. 89.50 (*0-306-45452-1*, Plenum Trade) Perseus Pubng.

— Technological Risk. 368p. 1992. pap. 13.95 (*0-393-30829-4*) Norton.

— Why Flip a Coin? The Art & Science of Good Decisions. LC 96-29444. 224p. 1997. 22.95 (*0-471-16597-2*) Wiley.

***Lewis, H. W.** Why Flip a Coin? The Art & Science of Good Decisions. 206p. 1998. pap. 14.95 (*0-471-29645-7*) Wiley.

Lewis, H. W. Why Flip a Coin? The Art & Science of Good Decisions in Everyday Life. 1997. 24.95 (*0-614-28190-3*) Wiley.

Lewis, Hanna B., ed. from GER. A Year of Revolutions: Fanny Lewald's Recollections of 1848. LC 96-43633. (Illus.). 176p. 1997. 39.95 (*1-57181-099-4*) Berghahn Bks.

Lewis, Hanna B., ed. & tr. see Lewald, Fanny.

Lewis, Harold. Civil Rights & Employment Discrimination Law: Hornbook Series. LC 96-40335. (Paralegal). 551p. (C). 1997. text 29.25 (*0-314-20604-3*) West Pub.

— The Intellectual Base of Social Work Practice: Tools for Thought in a Helping Profession. LC 82-5593. (Saul Horowitz Jr. Memorial Ser.). 258p. 1982. text 39.95 (*0-86656-176-5*) Haworth Pr.

— The Intellectual Base of Social Work Practice: Tools for Thought in a Helping Profession. LC 82-5593. (Saul Horowitz Jr. Memorial Ser.). 258p. 1985. pap. text 19.95 (*0-86656-418-7*) Haworth Pr.

— Mathematics for Daily Living. rev. ed. 1979. 21.96 (*0-8009-1552-6*); text, teacher ed. 23.92 (*0-8009-1549-6*) Random.

Lewis, Harold G. Unionism & Relative Wages in the United States: An Empirical Inquiry. LC 63-20915. (Studies in Economics of the Economics Research Center of the University of Chicago). 325p. reprint ed. pap. 100.80 (*0-608-18243-5*, 205665700078) Bks Demand.

Lewis, Harold T. Yet with a Steady Beat: The African American Struggle for Recognition in the Episcopal Church. LC 95-46837. (Illus.). 272p. (Orig.). (C). 1996. pap. 20.00 (*1-56338-130-3*) TPI PA.

Lewis, Harry. Home Cooking. LC 75-20729. (Haystack Bks.). (Illus.). 76p. 1975. 6.00 (*0-913142-08-5*); pap. 3.50 (*0-913142-07-7*) Mulch Pr.

Lewis, Harry & Papadimitriou, Christos. Elements of the Theory of Computation. 2nd ed. LC 97-13879. 361p. (C). 1997. 73.00 (*0-13-262478-8*) P-H.

Lewis, Harry A., ed. Peter Geach: Philosophical Encounters. (Synthese Library). (C). 1991. lib. bdg. 160.50 (*0-7923-0823-9*, Pub. by Kluwer Academic) Kluwer Academic.

Lewis, Heather. House Rules. LC 95-69748. (High Risk Ser.). 321p. 1995. pap. 12.99 (*1-85242-413-3*, High Risk Bks) Serpents Tail.

Lewis, Hedwig. Body Language: A Guide for Professionals. LC 97-45131. 1998. pap. write for info. (*0-7619-9234-0*) Sage.

***Lewis, Helen.** Improving the Health of Children & Young People in Public Care: A Manual for Training Residential Social Workers & Foster Care. 372p. 2000. ring bd. 19.00 (*1-900990-51-2*, Pub. by Natl Childrens Bur) Paul & Co Pubs.

Lewis, Helen. A Time to Speak. 132p. 1993. pap. 15.95 (*0-85640-491-8*, Pub. by Blackstaff Pr) Dufour.

— A Time to Speak. 144p. 1998. pap. 9.95 (*0-7867-0486-1*) Carroll & Graf.

Lewis, Helen & Hudson, Hilary. The Don't Panic Guide to Annual Report Production. 95p. 1992. 24.95 (*0-644-24264-7*, Pub. by Aust Gov Pub) Accents Pubns.

Lewis, Helen B. Freud & Modern Psychology Vol. 2: The Emotional Basis of Human Behavior. (Emotions, Personality, & Psychotherapy Ser.). (Illus.). 246p. (C). 1983. 72.00 (*0-306-41329-9*, Plenum Trade) Perseus Pubng.

— Freud & Modern Psychology, Vol. 1: The Emotional Basis of Mental Illness. LC 80-20937. (Emotions, Personality, & Psychotherapy Ser.). 258p. 1981. 49.50 (*0-306-40525-3*, Plenum Trade) Perseus Pubng.

Lewis, Helen B., ed. The Role of Shame in Symptom Formation. 264p. 1987. text 49.95 (*0-89859-600-9*) L Erlbaum Assocs.

Lewis, Helen F. New York's Finger Lakes, Pioneer Families Especially Tompkins County: A Genealogical Notebook. LC 91-196260. 403p. 1991. lib. bdg. 69.95 (*1-56012-111-4*, 105) Kinship Rhinebeck.

— Southeastern Michigan Pioneer Families: Especially Jackson County & New York Origins. LC 98-208390. 446 p. 1998. lib. bdg. 76.95 (*1-56012-152-1*) Kinship Rhinebeck.

— Southeastern Michigan Pioneer Families: Especially Livingston County & New York Origins. 302p. 1995. lib. bdg. 51.95 (*1-56012-138-6*, 136) Kinship Rhinebeck.

Lewis, Helen F., ed. Southeastern Michigan Pioneer Families: Especially Lenawee County & New York Origins. LC 95-105152. 426p. 1994. lib. bdg. 73.95 (*1-56012-130-0*, 128) Kinship Rhinebeck.

Lewis, Helen N., ed. see Pincus, Robert, et al.

Lewis, Heloise. Vamos Amigos: A Beginning Spanish Course. 1986. pap. text 8.70 (*0-582-36225-3*, 74821) Longman.

Lewis, Henry. The Valley of the Mississippi Illustrated. Heilbron, Bertha L., ed. Poatgieter, A. Hermina, tr. from GER. LC 67-65590. (Illus.). 601p. 1967. reprint ed. pap. 186.40 (*0-608-06681-8*, 206687800009) Bks Demand.

Lewis, Henry C. Odd Leaves from the Life of a Louisiana Swamp Doctor. LC 96-54030. (Library of Southern Civilization). (Illus.). 240p. 1997. 24.95 (*0-8071-2185-1*); pap. 12.95 (*0-8071-2167-3*) La State U Pr.

***Lewis, Henry M.** Ancient Society. 560p. 2000. pap. 34.95 (*0-7658-0691-6*) Transaction Pubs.

Lewis, Herbert S. A Galla Monarchy: Jimma Abba Jifar, Ethiopia, 1830-1932. LC 65-24185. (Illus.). 168p. 1965. reprint ed. pap. 52.10 (*0-608-07442-X*, 2067669) Bks Demand.

— Jimma Abba Jifar: An Oromo Monarchy Ethiopia 1830-1932. 1998. pap. 19.95 (*1-56902-089-2*) Red Sea Pr.

— Jimma Abba Jifar: An Oromo Monarchy Ethiopia 1830-1932. (Illus.). 180p. 1998. 69.95 (*1-56902-088-4*) Red Sea Pr.

***Lewis, Herschell G.** Catalogue Copy That Sizzles: All the Hints, Tips & Tricks of the Trade You'll Ever Need to Write Copy That Sells. LC 99-26318. (Sizzles Ser.). 288p. 1999. 39.95 (*0-8442-2447-2*, 24472, Natl Textbk Co) NTC Contemp Pub Co.

— On the Art of Writing Copy. 2nd ed. LC 99-43415. 424p. 1999. pap. 29.95 (*0-8144-7031-9*) AMACOM.

Lewis, Herschell Gordon. Big Profits from Small Budget Advertising. (Illus.). 260p. 1992. ring bd. 79.95 (*0-85013-221-5*) Dartnell Corp.

— The Complete Advertising & Marketing Handbook. LC 98-4434. 291p. 1998. 59.95 (*1-56625-101-X*) Bonus Books.

— Copywriting Secrets & Tactics. (Illus.). 255p. 1994. ring bd. 91.50 (*0-85013-193-6*) Dartnell Corp.

— Direct Mail Copy That Sells. (Illus.). 258p. (C). 1984. pap. 14.95 (*0-13-214750-5*, Busn) P-H.

— Direct Marketing Strategies & Tactics. (Illus.). 356p. 1992. 39.95 (*0-85013-220-7*) Dartnell Corp.

— How to Make Your Advertising Twice As Effective at Half the Cost. LC 85-9573. 273p. 1986. 27.95 (*0-13-417882-3*, Busn) P-H.

— How to Write Powerful Fund Raising Letters. LC 88-64123. 210p. 1990. 40.00 (*0-944496-05-9*) Precept Pr.

— Open Me Now! (Illus.). 136p. 1995. 40.00 (*1-56625-036-6*) Bonus Books.

— Power Copywriting. 334p. 1992. pap. text 34.50 (*0-85013-187-1*) Dartnell Corp.

— Power Copywriting. 334p. 1994. pap. 34.50 (*0-85013-227-4*) Dartnell Corp.

— Sales Letters That Sizzle: All the Hooks, Lines & Sinkers You'll Ever Need to Close Sales. LC 94-16176. (Illus.). 224p. 1994. 29.95 (*0-8442-3547-4*, NTC Business Bks) NTC Contemp Pub Co.

— Sales Letters That Sizzle: All the Hooks, Lines & Sinkers You'll Ever Need to Close Sales. 2nd ed. LC 98-55946. 256p. 1999. 29.95 (*0-8442-2348-4*, 23484) NTC Contemp Pub Co.

— Silver Linings: Selling to the Expanding Mature Market. LC 96-21808. 165p. 1996. 40.00 (*1-56625-058-7*) Bonus Books.

Lewis, Herschell Gordon & Lewis, Margo. Everybody's Guide to Plate Collecting. 2nd rev. ed. LC 94-70119. (Illus.). 222p. 1994. pap. 12.95 (*1-56625-007-2*) Bonus Books.

Lewis, Herschell Gordon & Lewis, Robert D. Selling on the Net: The Complete Guide. LC 96-23087. (Illus.). 288p. 1996. 39.95 (*0-8442-3233-5*, NTC Business Bks); pap. 19.95 (*0-8442-3234-3*) NTC Contemp Pub Co.

Lewis, Herschell Gordon & Murphy, Jamie. Cybertalk That Sells. LC 97-50104. (...That Sell Ser.). 144p. 1998. pap. 14.95 (*0-8092-2923-4*, 292340, Contemporary Bks) NTC Contemp Pub Co.

Lewis, Herschell Gordon & Nelson, Carol. Advertising Age: Handbook of Advertising. 240p. 1999. pap. 24.95 (*0-8442-2448-0*) NTC Contemp Pub Co.

— The Advertising Age Handbook of Advertising. LC 98-8362. 240p. 1999. 39.95 (*0-8442-3670-5*, NTC Business Bks) NTC Contemp Pub Co.

— World's Greatest Direct Mail Sales Letters. LC 95-11303. (Illus.). 480p. 1995. 79.95 (*0-8442-3570-9*) NTC Contemp Pub Co.

Lewis, Hilary & O'Connor, John. Philip Johnson: The Architect in His Own Words. LC 94-16057. (Illus.). 208p. 1994. 50.00 (*0-8478-1823-3*, Pub. by Rizzoli Intl) St Martin.

Lewis, Hilda. Ship That Flew. LC 58-5903. (Illus.). (J). (gr. 3-7). 1958. 31.95 (*0-87599-067-3*) S G Phillips.

Lewis, Hilda, ed. Child Art: The Beginnings of Self-Affirmation. rev. ed. LC 73-75581. (Illus.). 124p. 1973. pap. 6.95 (*0-87297-005-1*) Diablo.

— Child Art: The Beginnings of Self-Affirmation. rev. ed. LC 73-75581. (Illus.). 124p. 1973. 7.95 (*0-87297-004-3*) Diablo.

Lewis, Hilda S. Deprived Children: The Mersham Experiment; a Social & Clinical Study. LC 77-27491. 163p. 1978. reprint ed. lib. bdg. 35.00 (*0-8371-9070-3*, LEDC, Greenwood Pr) Greenwood.

Lewis, Hilton, ed. Telescope Control Systems II, Vol. 3112. LC 98-122070. 360p. 1997. 80.00 (*0-8194-2534-6*) SPIE.

***Lewis, Hilton, ed.** Telescope Control Systems III. LC 99-160761. 494p. 1998. 99.00 (*0-8194-2798-5*) SPIE.

Lewis, Howard, III, jt. auth. see Richardson, J. David.

An Asterisk (*) at the beginning of an entry indicates that the title is appearing for the first time.

L

***Lewis, Hubert.** Ancient Laws of Wales Viewed Especially in Regard to the Light they Throw upon the Origin of Some English... xvi, 558p. 2000. reprint ed. 85.00 (*1-57588-641-3*) W S Hein.

Lewis, Hunter. A Question of Values: Six Ways We Make the Personal Choices that Shape Our Lives. 3rd unabridged ed. LC 90-56471. 283p. 1990. 9.95 (*0-9661908-0-7*, 101); pap. 9.95 (*0-9661908-1-5*, 101) Axios Pr.

***Lewis, Hunter.** A Question of Values: Six Ways We Make the Personal Choices That Shape Our Lives. 4th rev. unabridged ed. LC 99-60982. 300p. 1999. pap. 12.95 (*0-9661908-3-1*) Axios Pr.

Lewis, Hunter, ed. The Words of Jesus. LC 98-70605. 275p. 1998. pap. 9.95 (*0-9661908-2-3*) Axios Pr.

Lewis, Hylan. Blackways of Kent. 1955. pap. 13.95 (*0-8084-0064-9*) NCUP.

Lewis, Hyman. Self Hypnosis Dynamics. 1962. pap. 3.00 (*0-87505-334-3*) Borden.

Lewis, I., jt. auth. see Jenkins, Edgar N.

Lewis, I. M. The Anthropologist's Muse: An Inaugural Lecture. LC 74-171279. 28p. 1973. write for info. (*0-85328-013-4*) London Schl Econ.

***Lewis, I. M.** Arguments with Ethnography: Comparative Approaches to History, Politics & Religion. LC 98-54619. (Monographs on Social Anthropology). 288p. 1999. 90.00 (*0-485-19570-4*) Athlone Pr.

Lewis, I. M. Blood & Bone: The Call of Kinship in Somali Society. LC 93-47165. 286p. 1994. 49.95 (*0-932415-92-X*); pap. 16.95 (*0-932415-93-8*) Red Sea Pr.

— Ecstatic Religion: An Anthropological Study of Spirit Possession & Shamanism. 2nd ed. 224p. (Orig.). (C). 1988. pap. 24.99 (*0-415-00799-2*) Routledge.

***Lewis, I. M.** A Pastoral Democracy. 392p. 1999. 56.95 (*3-8258-3566-9*, Pub. by CE24); pap. 29.95 (*3-8258-3084-5*, Pub. by CE24) Transaction Pubs.

Lewis, I. M. A Pastoral Democracy: A Study of Pastoralism & Politics among the Northern Somali of the Horn of Africa. LC 81-4074. (Illus.). 349p. reprint ed. pap. 108.20 (*0-8357-3015-8*, 205710100010) Bks Demand.

— Peoples of the Horn of Africa: Somali, Afar & Saho. LC 99-163653. 424p. 1998. 89.95 (*1-56902-104-X*); pap. 24.95 (*1-56902-105-8*) Red Sea Pr.

— Peoples of the Horn of Africa: Somali, Afar & Saho. LC 55-4468. (Ethnographic Survey of Africa: North Eastern Africa Ser.: Pt. 1). 212p. reprint ed. pap. 65.80 (*0-8357-3014-X*, 205710000010) Bks Demand.

— Religion in Context: Cults & Charisma. 2nd ed. (Illus.). 213p. (C). 1996. text 54.95 (*0-521-56234-1*); pap. text 17.95 (*0-521-56634-7*) Cambridge U Pr.

— Social Anthropology in Perspective: The Relevance of Social Anthropology. 2nd ed. 386p. 1986. pap. text 18.95 (*0-521-31351-1*) Cambridge U Pr.

Lewis, I. M., ed. Nationalism & Self-Determination in the Horn of Africa. (Illus.). 229p. (Orig.). 1984. pap. 19.95 (*0-685-08758-1*) Evergreen Dist.

Lewis, I. M., et al. Women's Medicine: The Zar-Bori Cult in Africa & Beyond. 296p. 1991. text 68.00 (*0-7486-0261-5*, Pub. by Edinburgh U Pr) Col U Pr.

Lewis, I. Murphy. Why Ostriches Don't Fly & Other Tales from the African Bush. (World Folklore Ser.). 120p. 1997. lib. bdg. 21.50 (*1-56308-402-3*) Libs Unl.

Lewis, I. Murphy, ed. see Borie, Lysbeth B.

***Lewis, Ian.** Guerrilla TV: Low Budget Programme Making. LC 99-86969. (Illus.). 247p. 2000. pap. 39.95 (*0-240-51601-X*, Focal) Buttrwrth-Heinemann.

Lewis, Ian. Visual Basic 6 Core Requirements. 1536p. 1999. pap. text 64.99 (*0-7821-2568-9*) Sybex.

Lewis, Ian & Nielson, Bruce. Analyzing Requirements & Defining Solution Architectures. LC 99-61812. 336p. 1999. 24.99 (*0-7821-2430-5*) Sybex.

***Lewis, Ian & Reddihough, Alison.** How to Make Great Short Feature Films. (Illus.). 192p. 2000. pap. 24.95 (*0-240-51624-9*, Focal) Buttrwrth-Heinemann.

Lewis, Ian, jt. auth. see Rosenblatt, Jeremy.

Lewis, Ian C., et al. Consulting with Children. (Illus.). 144p. 1993. text 30.00 (*0-7295-0337-2*) Bailliere Tindall.

Lewis, Ida B. The Education of Girls in China. LC 78-176992. (Columbia University. Teachers College. Contributions to Education Ser.: No. 104). reprint ed. 37.50 (*0-404-55104-1*) AMS Pr.

Lewis-Idema, Deborah. Increasing Provider Participation: Strategies for Improving State Perinatal Programs. 75p. (Orig.). 1988. pap. text 15.00 (*1-55877-026-7*) Natl Governor.

— Monitoring Medicaid Provider Participation & Access to Care. Glass, Karen, ed. 42p. (Orig.). 1992. pap. text 15.00 (*1-55877-166-2*) Natl Governor.

Lewis, I.M. Modern History of Somalia: Nation & State in the Horn of Africa. 1980. pap. 10.95 (*0-582-64657-X*) Longman.

Lewis Inf. Sys. Staff. Saxs./Haw. International Non-Sub. 12th ed. 1997. 650.00 (*0-442-02364-2*, VNR) Wiley.

Lewis, Ioan M. A Modern History of Somalia: Nation & State in the Horn of Africa. rev. ed. LC 79-40569. 289p. reprint ed. pap. 89.60 (*0-608-13143-1*, 202523200043) Bks Demand.

— Saints & Somalis: Popular Islam in a Clan-Based Society. LC 98-46317. 284p. 1998. 69.95 (*1-56902-102-3*); pap. 19.95 (*1-56902-103-1*) Red Sea Pr.

Lewis, Ioan M., jt. ed. see Johoda, Gustav.

Lewis, Ira. Chinese Coffee. 1995. pap. 5.25 (*0-8222-1426-1*) Dramatists Play.

Lewis, Isabelle. Sadhana: A Safe Passage with Jean Klein. 120p. Date not set. pap. write for info. (*0-9678754-0-4*) Shakti.

Lewis, Ivor. Sahibs, Nabobs, & Boxwallahs: A Dictionary of the Words of Anglo-India. (Oxford India Paperbacks Ser.). 280p. 1998. reprint ed. pap. 16.95 (*0-19-564223-6*) OUP.

Lewis, J. Education, Industry & Technology. Waddington, D. J., ed. LC 87-2344. (Science & Technology Education & Future Human Needs Ser.: Vol. 3). (Illus.). 389p. 1987. 170.00 (*0-08-033913-1*, Pub. by Pergamon Repr) Franklin.

— Energy Resources in Science Education. Kirwan, D. F., ed. LC 87-2394. (Science & Technology Education & Future Human Needs Ser.: Vol. 7). (Illus.). 237p. 1987. 105.00 (*0-08-033950-6*, Pub. by Pergamon Repr) Franklin.

Lewis, J. Migraine Handbook. pap. 15.95 (*0-09-181666-1*, Pub. by Random) Trafalgar.

Lewis, J. Las Misiones Mundiales.Tr. of World Missions. (SPA.). 85p. 1985. pap. 3.50 (*1-56063-397-2*, 498547) Editorial Unilit.

— Primarily Speaking Vol. 2: Organizations. 1990. pap. 7.95 (*0-88494-751-3*) Bookcraft Inc.

— Science Education & Information Transfer. Taylor, C. A., ed. LC 86-25229. (Science & Technology Education & Future Human Needs Ser.: Vol. 9). (Illus.). 244p. 1987. 112.00 (*0-08-033954-9*, Pub. by Pergamon Repr) Franklin.

Lewis, J. El Toque Tierno de Dios.Tr. of Tender Touch of God. (SPA.). 9.99 (*0-7899-0331-8*, 497395) Editorial Unilit.

Lewis, J. Trabajando Tu Llamado a las Naciones.Tr. of Working Your Call to the Nations. (SPA.), 205p. 1995. 10.99 (*1-56063-975-X*, 498624) Editorial Unilit.

Lewis, J., jt. auth. see Shaw, T.

Lewis, J., tr. see De Gourmont, Remy.

Lewis, J., tr. see Kong, Shiu L. & Samuda, Ronald J.

Lewis, J. A. Economic Impact Analysis: A UK Literature Survey & Bibliography. (Progress in Planning Ser.: PRPL 30). 56p. 1990. pap. 38.50 (*0-08-036880-8*, Pergamon Pr) Elsevier.

Lewis, J. C. & Masatomi, H., eds. Crane Research Around the World. (Illus.). 259p. 1981. pap. 17.00 (*0-318-14550-2*) Intl Crane.

Lewis, J. D. Three of the Best. (C). 1989. 40.00 (*0-7223-2331-X*, Pub. by A H S Ltd) St Mut.

Lewis, J. David & Smith, Richard L. American Sociology & Pragmatism: Mead, Chicago Sociology, & Symbolic Interaction. LC 80-15489. (Illus.). 376p. 1998. 36.00 (*0-226-47697-9*) U Ch Pr.

Lewis, J. H., jt. auth. see Seeff, L. B.

Lewis, J. L. 125 Years: The Physical Society & the Institute of Physics. LC 99-10834. 256p. 1999. 25.00 (*0-7503-0609-2*) IOP Pub.

Lewis, J. L. & Kelly, P. J., eds. Science & Technology Education & Future Human Needs, Vol. 1. LC 87-7020. (STEF Ser.: No. 1). (Illus.). 130p. 1987. 93.00 (*0-08-033909-3*, Pub. by Pergamon Repr) Franklin.

Lewis, J. L., jt. ed. see Kelly, P. J.

Lewis, J. Lowell. Ring of Liberation: Deceptive Discourse in Brazilian Capoeira. (Illus.). 294p. 1992. pap. text 19.00 (*0-226-47683-9*); lib. bdg. 38.50 (*0-226-47682-0*) U Ch Pr.

Lewis, J. N., jt. auth. see Headley, Joseph C.

Lewis, J. Norman, jt. auth. see Lewis, C. J.

Lewis, J. O., intro. Johnson City: The Way We Were. (Illus.). 64p. 1989. reprint ed. pap. 4.95 (*0-932807-46-1*) Overmountain Pr.

Lewis, J. O., jt. auth. see Scorer, N.

Lewis, J. P. Manual of the Vanni Districts, Ceylon. (C). 1993. text 32.50 (*81-7013-113-8*, Pub. by Navarang) S Asia.

— Statistics Explained. LC 98-222904. (C). 1998. pap. text. write for info. (*0-201-17802-8*) Addison-Wesley.

Lewis, J. Patrick. Black Swan, White Crow. LC 94-34984. (Illus.). 32p. (J). (gr. 2-4). 1995. 15.00 (*0-689-31899-5*) Atheneum Yung Read.

— The Boat of Many Rooms. LC 95-581. (Illus.). 32p. (J). (gr. 1-5). 1997. 16.00 (*0-689-80118-1*) Atheneum Yung Read.

***Lewis, J. Patrick.** A Burst of Firsts: A Salute in Verse to First-Time Feats & Amazing Achievements. LC 99-44286. (Illus.). (J). 2001. 15.99 (*0-8037-2108-0*, Dial Yng Read) Peng Put Young Read.

Lewis, J. Patrick. Doodle Dandies: Poems at a Glance. LC 96-1920. (Illus.). 32p. (J). (ps-3). 1998. 16.00 (*0-689-81075-X*) Atheneum Yung Read.

— Earth Verses & Water Rhymes. LC 90-40709. (Illus.). 32p. (J). (gr. 2-5). 1991. lib. bdg. 13.95 (*0-689-31693-3*) Atheneum Yung Read.

***Lewis, J. Patrick.** Freedom Like Sunlight: Praisesongs for Black Americans. LC 98-50909. (Illus.). 32p. (J). 2000. 23.95 (*1-56846-163-1*, Creative Eds) Creative Co.

Lewis, J. Patrick. A Hippopotamusn't: And Other Animal Poems. (Illus.). 40p. (J). (ps-3). 1994. pap. 5.99 (*0-14-055273-1*, PuffinBks) Peng Put Young Read.

— Hippopotamusn't & Other Animal Verses. (Picture Puffin Ser.). (Illus.). (J). 1990. 10.19 (*0-606-05875-3*, Pub. by Turtleback) Demco.

— The House of Boo. LC 97-16937. (Illus.). 32p. (J). (gr. k-3). 1998. 16.00 (*0-689-80356-7*) Atheneum Yung Read.

— July Is a Mad Mosquito. LC 93-19743. (Illus.). 32p. (J). (gr. 2-5). 1994. 14.95 (*0-689-31813-8*) Atheneum Yung Read.

— The La-Di-Da Hare. LC 95-44674. (Illus.). 40p. (J). (gr. 1-4). 1997. 16.00 (*0-689-31925-8*) S&S Childrens.

— The Little Buggers: Insect & Spider Poems. LC 94-31900. (Illus.). 32p. (J). (gr. k up). 1998. 15.89 (*0-8037-1770-9*, Dial Yng Read) Peng Put Young Read.

***Lewis, J. Patrick.** The Little Buggers: Insect & Spider Poems. LC 94-31900. (Illus.). 32p. (J). (gr. 1-4). 1998. 15.99 (*0-8037-1769-5*, Dial Yng Read) Peng Put Young Read.

Lewis, J. Patrick. Night of the Goat Children. Foley, Michele, ed. LC 95-45186. (Illus.). 32p. (J). (ps-3). 1999. 15.99 (*0-8037-1870-5*, Dial Yng Read) Peng Put Young Read.

— One Dog Day. LC 92-24573. (Illus.). 64p. (J). (gr. 2-5). 1993. 12.95 (*0-689-31808-1*) Atheneum Yung Read.

— Riddle - Lightful: Oodles of Little Riddles. (Illus.). (J). 1998. 7.98 (*0-679-88766-0*, Pub. by Random Bks Yng Read) Random.

— Riddle-Icious. LC 93-43759. (Illus.). 40p. (J). (ps-4). 1996. write for info. (*0-679-84011-7*); lib. bdg. 16.99 (*0-679-94011-1*) Knopf.

— Riddle-Icious. (J). 1997. pap. 6.99 (*0-679-88545-5*) Knopf.

— Riddle-Icious. 1997. 12.19 (*0-606-11798-9*, Pub. by Turtleback) Demco.

— Riddle-icious. (Illus.). (J). (ps-3). 1997. reprint ed. pap. 6.99 (*0-614-28950-5*) Random Bks Yng Read.

— Riddle-Lightfull. LC 97-39083. (J). 1998. lib. bdg. 18.99 (*0-679-98760-6*, Pub. by Random Bks Yng Read) Random.

***Lewis, J. Patrick.** The Shoe Tree of Chagrin: A Christmas Story. LC 98-50908. (J). 2001. write for info. (*1-56846-173-9*, Creative Eds) Creative Co.

***Lewis, J. Patrick & Desimini, Lisa.** Good Mousekeeping: Animal Home Poems. LC 99-88259. (J). 2002. write for info. (*0-689-83161-7*) Atheneum Yung Read.

Lewis, J. R. & Mercer, A. D. Corrosion & Marine Growth on Offshore Structures. 156p. 1984. text 61.95 (*0-470-27506-5*) P-H.

Lewis, J. Slater. The Commercial Organization of Factories: A Handbook. Brief, Richard P., ed. LC 77-87274. (Development of Contemporary Accounting Thought Ser.). 1978. reprint ed. lib. bdg. 60.95 (*0-405-10902-4*) Ayer.

Lewis, J. W., jt. ed. see Akil, H.

Lewis, J. W., ed. see Sanders, Viola H.

***Lewis, Jack.** Face Down. LC 99-90722. 192p. 1999. 18.95 (*0-8034-9379-7*, Avalon Bks) Bouregy.

Lewis, Jack. Shotgun Digest. 4th ed. LC 74-80333. (Illus.). 256p. 1993. pap. 17.95 (*0-87349-137-8*, SD4, DBI Bks) Krause Pubns.

Lewis, Jack & Combs, Roger. Gun Digest Book of Knives. 5th ed. LC 73-83465. (Illus.). 256p. 1997. pap. 19.95 (*0-87349-188-2*, GDK5) Krause Pubns.

***Lewis, Jack & Steele, David E.** The Gun Digest Book of Assault Weapons. 5th ed. LC 85-73744. (Illus.). 256p. 2000. pap. 21.95 (*0-87341-778-X*) Krause Pubns.

Lewis, Jack, ed. & tr. see Gertrude the Great of Helfta.

Lewis, Jack P. The Gospel According to Matthew, Pt. 1. LC 75-21256. 1984. 12.95 (*0-915547-17-1*) Abilene Christ U.

— The Gospel According to Matthew, Pt. 2. LC 75-21256. 1984. 12.95 (*0-915547-18-X*) Abilene Christ U.

— Questions You've Asked about Bible Translations. 423p. (Orig.). 1991. 15.95 (*0-945441-04-5*) Res Pubns AR.

Lewis, Jack P., ed. Interpreting Second Corinthians 5:14-21: An Exercise in Hermeneutics. LC 89-34218. (Studies in Bible & Early Christianity: Vol. 17). 204p. 1989. lib. bdg. 89.95 (*0-88946-617-3*) E Mellen.

Lewis, Jack W. Modeling Engineering Systems: PC-Based Techniques & Design Tools. LC 93-40319. (Illus.). 288p. 1994. pap. 29.95 incl. cd-rom (*1-878707-08-6*) LLH Tech Pub.

Lewis, Jack W., ed. Studies in General & English Phonetics: Essays in Honour of Professor J. D. O'Connor. LC 94-4050. (Illus.). 384p. (C). (gr. 13). 1994. 165.00 (*0-415-08068-1*, C0285) Routledge.

Lewis, Jackie. Pathways to Learning in Rett Syndrome. LC 98-186005. 1998. pap. 26.95 (*1-85346-533-X*, Pub. by David Fulton) Taylor & Francis.

Lewis, Jackson. Winning NLRB Elections: Avoiding Unionization Through Preventive Employee Relations Programs. LC 98-122567. (Illus.). 280p. 1997. 75.00 (*0-8080-0195-7*, 5489) CCH INC.

Lewis, Jacquie J. & Warren, Dianne, selected by. Eureka! Seven One-Act Plays for Secondary Schools. (Florence James Ser.: No. 5). 184p. 1996. text 12.95 (*1-55050-059-7*, Pub. by Coteau) Genl Dist Srvs.

Lewis, James, Jr. Achieving Excellence in Our Schools...by Taking Lessons from America's Best Run Companies. LC 85-51152. 250p. 1986. 24.95 (*0-915253-03-8*) Wilkerson Pub Co.

***Lewis, James.** The Best Options for Treating & Diagnosing Prostate Cancer: Based on Research, Clinical Trials & Scientific & Investigational Studies. LC 99-37185. 1999. write for info. (*1-883257-04-2*) Hlth Edu Lit.

Lewis, James, Jr. Creating Excellence in Our Schools...by Taking More Lessons from America's Best Run Companies. LC 85-51533. 250p. 1986. 24.95 (*0-915253-04-6*) Wilkerson Pub Co.

***Lewis, James.** Development in Diaster-Prone Places. (Studies in Vulnerability). (Illus.). 224p. 1999. pap. 29.95 (*1-85339-472-6*, Pub. by Intermed Tech) Stylus Pub VA.

Lewis, James. Doomsday Prophecies. LC 99-50123. 269p. 1999. 49.95 (*1-57392-690-6*) Prometheus Bks.

— Everything You Always Wanted to Know about Drafting, Vol. 1, No. 1. (Illus.). 68p. 1987. pap. 10.00 (*0-9617322-1-0*) Flat Surface.

Lewis, James, Jr. Excellent Organizations: How to Develop & Organize Them Using Theory Z. LC 83-51208. (Illus.). 318p. 1985. 9.95 (*0-915253-00-3*) Wilkerson Pub Co.

***Lewis, James.** Herbal Remedy for Prostate Cancer. 2000. pap. write for info. (*1-883257-02-6*) Hlth Edu Lit.

Lewis, James. Horoscope Signs Illustrated, Vol. 1. (Illus.). 24p. 1987. pap. 2.00 (*0-9617322-5-3*) Flat Surface.

— How I Survived Prostate Cancer, & So Can You: A Guide for Diagnosing & Treating Prostate Cancer. (Illus.). 274p. 1994. pap. 18.95 (*1-883257-06-9*) Hlth Edu Lit.

— How to Advertise with No Money Down: No Credit-Bad Credit, Vol. 1, No. 1. (Illus.). 126p. 1987. pap. 15.00 (*0-9617322-0-2*) Flat Surface.

Lewis, James, Jr. Implementing Total Quality in Education to Produce Great Schools: Transforming the American School System. 320p. (C). 1993. 35.95 (*1-883257-00-X*) Hlth Edu Lit.

Lewis, James. Over Three Hundred Anxious Gift Catalogs, Vol. 1. 96p. 1987. pap. 5.00 (*0-9617322-6-1*) Flat Surface.

— Peculiar Prophets: A Biographical Dictionary of New Religions. LC 99-21563. (Illus.). 320p. 1999. pap. 19.95 (*1-55778-768-9*) Paragon Hse.

Lewis, James, Jr. Recreating Our Schools for the Twenty-first Century. 280p. 1987. 24.95 (*0-915253-10-0*) Wilkerson Pub Co.

— What Every Principal Should Know about Transforming Schools: The Mandate for New School Leadership. LC 95-26510. 1996. write for info. (*0-915253-49-6*) Wilkerson Pub Co.

Lewis, James, Jr. & Berger, E. Roy. New Guidelines for Surviving Prostate Cancer. LC 95-50596. (Illus.). 460p. 1997. pap. 22.95 (*1-883257-13-1*) Hlth Edu Lit.

Lewis, James, Jr. & Berger, Roy. New Guidelines for Surviving Prostrate Cancer. 1996. pap. 18.95 (*0-915253-47-X*) Wilkerson Pub Co.

Lewis, James & DuBois, Andre. Gastrointestinal Pharmacology, Vol. 1. (Illus.). 342p. 1997. 75.00 (*0-86542-521-3*) Blackwell Sci.

Lewis, James, et al. Applied Quantitative Methods for Health Services Management. LC 95-3855. 272p. (C). 1995. 42.00 (*1-878812-24-6*) Hlth Prof Pr.

— The Human Rights Encyclopedia, 3 vols. LC 99-48341. 900p. 2000. 275.00 (*0-7656-8023-8*, Sharpe Ref) M E Sharpe.

Lewis, James, ed. see Currier, Paul J., et al.

Lewis, James, jt. ed. see Krummenacker, Markus.

Lewis, James A. Humorous Poems with Illustrations, Vol. 1. (Illus.). 68p. 1987. pap. 10.00 (*0-9617322-2-9*) Flat Surface.

— The Miracle of Dr. George Washington Carver, Vol. 1. (Illus.). 68p. (Orig.). 1987. pap. 10.00 (*0-9617322-3-7*) Flat Surface.

***Lewis, James A.** Neptune's Militia: The Frigate South Carolina During the American Revolution. LC 99-20255. (Illus.). 288p. 1999. text 39.00 (*0-87338-632-9*) Kent St U Pr.

Lewis, James A. Southern Life, Vol. 1. (Illus.). 68p. 1987. pap. 10.00 (*0-9617322-4-5*) Flat Surface.

Lewis, James A., jt. auth. see Anderson, William L.

Lewis, James C. How to Think Like a Winner. 154p. (Orig.). 1989. pap. 7.95 (*0-942482-12-3*) Unity Church Denver.

— The Key to Spiritual Growth. LC 84-52070. 163p. 1985. 3.48 (*0-87159-004-2*) Unity Bks.

— Moving on to Greater Things. LC 88-50843. 294p. (Orig.). 1990. pap. 10.95 (*0-942482-11-5*) Unity Church Denver.

Lewis, James D. A Survey of the Hodge Conjecture. 2nd ed. LC 99-13391. (CRM Monograph Ser.). xvi, 368p. 1999. write for info. (*0-8218-0568-1*) Am Math.

Lewis, James E., Jr. The American Union & the Problem of Neighborhood: The United States & the Collapse of the Spanish Empire, 1783-1829. LC 97-48987. 320p. 1998. pap. 18.95 (*0-8078-4736-4*); lib. bdg. 49.95 (*0-8078-2429-1*) U of NC Pr.

Lewis, James F. & Novick, Richard J. Surfactant in Lung Injury & Lung Transplantation. (Medical Intelligence Unit Ser.). 218p. 1997. 99.00 (*1-57059-432-5*) Landes Bioscience.

***Lewis, James F. & Travis, William G.** Religious Traditions of the World. 424p. 1999. pap. 33.00 (*1-57910-230-1*) Wipf & Stock.

Lewis, James H. A Pharmacologic Approach to Gastrointestinal Disorders. LC 93-13185. (Illus.). 667p. 1994. 85.00 (*0-683-04970-4*) Lppncott W & W.

Lewis, James H., jt. auth. see Watkins, William H.

***Lewis, James Hamilton.** Removal of Causes from State to Federal Courts. 679p. 1999. reprint ed. 170.00 (*1-56169-571-8*, 18416) Gaunt.

Lewis, James K. Religious Life of Fugitive Slaves & Rise of the Coloured Baptist Churches, 1820-1865, in What Is Now Ontario. Gaustad, Edwin S., ed. LC 79-52574. (Baptist Tradition Ser.). 1980. lib. bdg. 23.95 (*0-405-12442-2*) Ayer.

Lewis, James P. Fundamentals of Project Management. LC 94-41740. (WorkSmart Ser.). 128p. 1995. pap. 10.95 (*0-8144-7835-2*) AMACOM.

— How to Build & Manage a Winning Project Team. 224p. 1993. 26.95 (*0-8144-5137-3*) AMACOM.

— Mastering Project Management: Applying Advanced Concepts of Project Planning, Control & Evaluation. LC 97-38133. 319p. 1998. 45.00 (*0-7863-1188-6*, Irwn Prfssnl) McGraw-Hill Prof.

— The Project Manager's Desk Reference: A Comprehensive Guide to Project Planning, Evaluation & Control. 525p. 1995. 29.95 (*1-55738-896-2*, Irwn Prfssnl) McGraw-Hill Prof.

— The Project Manager's Desk Reference: A Comprehensive Guide to Project Planning, Scheduling, Evaluation, Control & Systems. 475p. 1993. text 60.00 (*1-55738-461-4*, Irwn Prfssnl) McGraw-Hill Prof.

***Lewis, James P.** Project Planning, Scheduling & Control. 3rd ed. 350p. 2000. 50.00 (*0-07-136050-6*, Schaums Outlne) McGraw-Hill Prof.

Lewis, James P. Project Planning, Scheduling & Control: A Hands-on Guide to Bringing Projects in on Time & on Budget. 2nd rev. ed. 300p. 1995. 45.00 (*1-55738-869-5*, Irwn Prfssnl) McGraw-Hill Prof.

— Team-Based Project Management. LC 97-26629. 256p. 1997. 55.00 (*0-8144-0364-6*) AMACOM.

An Asterisk (*) at the beginning of an entry indicates that the title is appearing for the first time.

Lewis, James R. Angels A to Z. (Illus.). xxiv, 485 p. 1996. 17.95 (0-7876-0652-9) Visible Ink Pr.
— The Astrology Encyclopedia. 603p. 1994. 45.00 (0-8103-8900-2, 101561) Gale.
— The Astrology Encyclopedia. (Illus.). 630p. 1994. 19.95 (0-8103-9460-X) Visible Ink Pr.
— Cult - Anti-Cult: How a National Mindset & Government Incompetence Aided & Abetted the Waco Disaster. (Illus.). 300p. 1994. 25.00 (1-883322-03-0) Agamemnon Pr.
— Cults in America: A Reference Handbook. LC 98-29089. (Contemporary World Issues Ser.). 240p. 1998. lib. bdg. 45.00 (1-57607-031-X) ABC-CLIO.
— Doomsday Prophecies. 1999. mass mkt. 6.99 (0-425-16819-0) Berkley Pub.
— The Dream Encyclopedia. 416p. 1995. 60.00 (0-7876-0155-1) Gale.
— The Dream Encyclopedia, Vol. 1. LC 95-10759. (Illus.). 416p. 1995. 14.95 (0-7876-0156-X) Gale.
— Encyclopedia of Afterlife Beliefs & Phenomena. LC 94-29172. 420p. (YA). 1994. 45.00 (0-8103-4879-9) Gale.
***Lewis, James R.** Encyclopedia of Afterlife Beliefs & Phenomena. (Illus.). 420p. 2000. reprint ed. pap. text 16.00 (0-7881-9036-9) DIANE Pub.
Lewis, James R. The Encyclopedia of Cults, Sects & New Religions. LC 98-20192. (Illus.). 600p. 1998. 149.95 (1-57392-222-6) Prometheus Bks.
— Encyclopedia of UFOs: Abductions, Crashes, Cover-Ups - & More. LC 98-11155. (Illus.). 320p. 1998. 25.00 (0-8092-3108-5) NTC Contemp Pub Co.
— The Gods Have Landed: New Religions from Other Worlds. LC 94-10333. (Illus.). 343p. (C). 1995. text 59.50 (0-7914-2329-8); pap. text 21.95 (0-7914-2330-1) State U NY Pr.
***Lewis, James R.** Odd Gods: New Religions & the Cult Controversy. 395p. 2001. 33.00 (1-57392-842-9) Prometheus Bks.
Lewis, James R. Seeking the Light: Revealing the Truth about the Movement of Spiritual Inner Awareness & Its Founder John-Roger. 200p. 1997. 24.00 (0-914829-42-4) Mandeville LA.
— The Tales They Told Me. 120p. 1999. pap. 7.95 (0-7392-0170-0, 3127) Morris Pubng.
— Witchcraft Today: An Encyclopedia of Wiccan & Neopagan Traditions. LC 99-40345. 377p. 1999. lib. bdg. 75.00 (1-57607-134-0) ABC-CLIO.
Lewis, James R., ed. From the Ashes: Making Sense Out of Waco. 288p. (C). 1994. pap. text 22.95 (0-8476-7915-2); lib. bdg. 58.50 (0-8476-7914-4) Rowman.
— Magical Religion & Modern Witchcraft. LC 95-42351. 423p. (C). 1996. text 59.50 (0-7914-2889-3); pap. text 24.95 (0-7914-2890-7) State U NY Pr.
Lewis, James R. & Melton, J. Gordon, eds. Church Universal & Triumphant: In Scholarly Perspective. (Illus.). 174p. (C). 1994. pap. text 20.00 (0-8191-9634-7) U Pr of Amer.
— Perspectives on the New Age. LC 91-39093. (SUNY Series in Religious Studies). 369p. (C). 1992. text 59.50 (0-7914-1213-X); pap. text 19.95 (0-7914-1214-8) State U NY Pr.
Lewis, James R. & Oliver, Evelyn D. Angels A to Z. Sisung, Kelle, ed. LC 95-35403. (Illus.). 485p. 1995. 49.95 (0-7876-0489-5) Gale.
Lewis, James W. The Protestant Experience in Gary, Indiana, 1906-1975: At Home in the City. LC 91-24752. (Illus.). 304p. (C). 1992. text 41.00 (0-87049-737-5) U of Tenn Pr.
— Stewardship: Whole Life Discipleship. Kelly, Arthur, ed. (Bridges Ser.: Vol. 10). 50p. 1997. pap. 4.95 (0-87162-713-2, D5306) Warner Pr.
Lewis, James W., jt. ed. see Wind, James P.
***Lewis, Jan.** Cinderella Bunny. (Illus.). 16p. (J). (ps-1). 2000. pap. 6.99 (0-525-46324-0, Dutton Child) Peng Put Young Read.
Lewis, Jan. Fun with R. Drolet, Cindy & Anderson, Kirsteen, eds. (Illus.). 162p. (J). 1999. spiral bd. 39.95 (1-883315-45-X) Imaginart Intl.
***Lewis, Jan.** Jan Lewis' Nursery Rhymes. LC 99-23241. (Illus.). 90p. (J). (ps-1). 2000. 12.95 (1-57145-405-5, Silver Dolph) Advantage Pubs.
— Snow White Lamb. (Illus.). 16p. (J). (ps-1). 2000. pap. 6.99 (0-525-46325-9, Dutton Child) Peng Put Young Read.
***Lewis, Jan & Amery, Heather.** Jan Lewis' Bedtime Stories. LC 99-26985. (Illus.). 90p. (J). (ps-1). 2000. 12.95 (1-57145-406-3, Silver Dolph) Advantage Pubs.
— Jan Lewis' Fairy Tales. LC 99-28862. (Illus.). 90p. (J). (ps-1). 2000. 12.95 (1-57145-404-7, Silver Dolph) Advantage Pubs.
***Lewis, Jan & Onuf, Peter S.** Sally Hemings & Thomas Jefferson: History, Memory & Civic Culture. LC 99-33901. (Jeffersonian America Ser.). 1999. 59.50 (0-8139-1948-7) U Pr of Va.
— Sally Hemings & Thomas Jefferson: History, Memory, & Civic Culture. LC 99-33901. 1999. 59.50 (0-8139-1918-5) U Pr of Va.
Lewis, Jan, jt. auth. see Boydston, Jeanne.
Lewis, Jan, jt. auth. see Butterfield, Moira.
Lewis, Jan, jt. auth. see Marketing Graphics Corporation Staff.
Lewis, Jan E. & Onuf, Peter S., eds. Sally Hemings & Thomas Jefferson: History, Memory & Civic Culture. LC 99-33901. 1999. pap. 17.95 (0-8139-1919-3) U Pr of Va.
Lewis, Jan P. & Braunger, Jane. Building a Knowledge Base in Reading. 112p. 1997. pap. 12.95 (0-8141-0387-1) NCTE.
Lewis, Jan Patricia, jt. auth. see Braunger, Jane.
Lewis, Jane. Lone Motherhood in Twentieth-Century Britain: From Footnote to Front Page. (Illus.). 346p. 1998. pap. text (0-19-829069-1) OUP.
— The Voluntary Sector, the State & Social Work in Britain: The Charity Organisation Society/Family Welfare Association since 1869. 200p. 1995. 85.00 (1-85898-188-3) E Elgar.
— Women & Social Action in Victorian & Edwardian England. 352p. 1991. 95.00 (1-85278-023-1) E Elgar.
— Women & Social Action in Victorian & Edwardian England. LC 90-71680. 336p. 1991. 45.00 (0-8047-1905-5) Stanford U Pr.
— Women in England, 1870-1950: Sexual Divisons & Social Change. LC 84-48437. (Illus.). 288p. 1985. 27.50 (0-253-36608-9) Ind U Pr.
Lewis, Jane, ed. Gender, Social Care & Welfare State Restructuring in Europe. LC 98-73511. 296p. 1998. text 67.95 (1-84014-538-2, Pub. by Ashgate Pub) Ashgate Pub Co.
— Lone Mothers in European Welfare Regimes: Shifting Policy Logics. LC 97-206164. 224p. 1997. 69.95 (1-85302-448-1, Pub. by Jessica Kingsley); pap. 26.95 (1-85302-461-9, Pub. by Jessica Kingsley) Taylor & Francis.
— Women & Social Policies in Europe: Work, Family & the State. 264p. 1993. pap. text 30.00 (1-85278-918-2) E Elgar.
— Women & Social Policies in Europe: Work, Family & the State. 264p. 1993. 95.00 (1-85278-563-2) E Elgar.
Lewis, Jane & Glennerster, Howard. Implementing the New Community Care. LC 96-4760. 224p. 1996. 101.95 (0-335-19610-1); pap. 34.95 (0-335-19609-8) OpUniv Pr.
Lewis, Jane & Meredith, Barbara. Daughters Who Care: Daughters Caring for Mothers at Home. 200p. (C). 1988. lib. bdg. 54.00 (0-415-00681-3) Routledge.
Lewis, Jane, jt. auth. see Kalman, Bobbie.
Lewis, Jane E. & Meredith, Barbara. Daughters Who Care: Daughters Caring for Mothers at Home. LC 87-31671. 202p. reprint ed. pap. 62.70 (0-608-20359-9, 207161200002) Bks Demand.
Lewis, Janet. Birthday of the Infanta. 22p. 1981. 25.00 (0-936576-03-0) Symposium Pr.
— Ghost of Monsieur Scarron. LC 65-16520. 378p. 1959. pap. 11.95 (0-8040-0133-2, 82-70514) Swallow.
— Goodbye, Son & Other Stories. LC 85-27731. 221p. 1986. reprint ed. pap. 10.95 (0-8040-0868-X); reprint ed. text 19.95 (0-8040-0867-1) Swallow.
— Invasion. LC 99-55796. 1998. pap. 21.95 (0-87013-495-7) Mich St U Pr.
— The Legend: The Story of Neengay, a Libretto. LC 86-32863. 72p. (Orig.). 1987. pap. 8.95 (0-936784-26-1) J Daniel.
— Poems Old & New, 1918-1978. LC 80-26209. xvi, 112p. 1981. pap. 10.95 (0-8040-0372-6) Swallow.
***Lewis, Janet.** The Selected Poems of Janet Lewis. Barth, R. L., ed. LC 99-87448. 144p. 2000. 28.95 (0-8040-1023-4); pap. 14.95 (0-8040-1024-2) Ohio U Pr.
Lewis, Janet. Trial of Soren Qvist. LC 72-94405. 256p. 1959. pap. 12.95 (0-8040-0297-5) Swallow.
— The Wife: A Libretto (For an Opera in Three Acts) 2nd ed. LC 88-11720. 64p. 1988. pap. 8.95 (0-936784-63-6) J Daniel.
— Wife of Martin Guerre. LC 84-109. 109p. 1967. reprint ed. pap. 7.95 (0-8040-0321-1) Ohio U Pr.
Lewis, Janet R. Smart Trainers: Brilliant Dogs. (Illus.). 192p. (Orig.). 1997. pap. 19.95 (1-888119-01-2) Canine Spts.
Lewis, Janet T. & Plumb, Barbara L. Cooking with Zucchini. 3rd ed. 170p. (Orig.). 1980. pap. 8.00 (0-9611974-0-4) Country Garden.
Lewis, Jay. Other Men's Minds. LC 70-134108. (Essay Index Reprint Ser.). 1977. 19.95 (0-8369-1974-2) Ayer.
Lewis, Jayne E. The English Fable: Aesop & Literary Culture, 1651-1740. (Studies in Eighteenth-Century English Literature & Thought Ser.: No. 28). (Illus.). 247p. (C). 1996. text 59.95 (0-521-48111-2) Cambridge U Pr.
— Mary Queen of Scots: Romance & Nation. LC 98-17140. (Illus.). 256p. (C). 1998. 85.00 (0-415-11480-2); pap. 20.99 (0-415-11481-0) Routledge.
Lewis, Jean & Messerli, Joe. Bugs Bunny Rides Again. LC 86-80139. (A Golden Tell-a-Tale Book Ser.). 26p. (J). 1986. write for info. (0-307-07046-8, Whitman Coin) St Martin.
Lewis, Jeanne M., ed. Emergency Care of the Elder Person (Nurse's Edition) unabridged ed. (Regional Conference Ser.). (Illus.). Date not set. ring bd. 475.00 (0-935890-22-X) Emerg Nurses IL.
Lewis, Jeanne M., et al. Emergency Care of the Elder Person: Nurse's Edition. (Illus.). 351p. 1996. text, teacher ed. 40.00 (0-935890-10-6) Emerg Nurses IL.
***Lewis, Jed.** Deliberate Indifference. LC 99-91808. 296p. 2000. 18.95 (0-9674922-0-3) Laughing Fire.
Lewis, Jeff. Extremity of the Skies. 140p. (C). 1990. 40.00 (1-875184-01-5, Pub. by Pascoe Pub) St Mut.
— The Sweetheart of Sigma Chi: David Letterman, the College Years. 1997. pap. 14.95 (1-57860-021-9) Guild Pr IN.
— Treasures from the Beginning of the World. (Illus.). 140p. (Orig.). 1994. pap. 10.95 (1-886028-13-3) Savage Pr.
— The Writer's Manual: A Practical Guide to Creative & Vocational Writing. 120p. (C). 1990. 60.00 (0-7316-2314-2, Pub. by Pascoe Pub) St Mut.
Lewis, Jefferson. Something Hidden: A Biography of Wilder Penfield. 311p. 1981. mass mkt. 5.95 (0-88780-101-3, Pub. by Formac Publ Co) Formac Dist Ltd.
Lewis, Jeffrey, jt. auth. see Prasthofer, Thomas.
Lewis, Jei D. Most Beautiful Girl. 250p. 1998. pap. 12.95 (0-9639917-4-4) Writers Unltd.
Lewis, Jel D. The Black Virgin. 200p. (Orig.). 1996. pap. 16.95 (0-9639917-2-8) Writers Unltd.
— Indulge in Endless Romance. 200p. 1999. pap. 12.95 (0-9639917-5-2) Writers Unltd.
— The Man Pleaser. 200p. (Orig.). 1996. pap. 12.95 (0-9639917-3-6) Writers Unltd.
Lewis, Jennifer M. Endometriosis: One Woman's Journey. (Illus.). 192p. 1998. pap. 17.95 (1-882180-91-7) Griffin CA.
Lewis, Jennifer M., jt. auth. see Sammons, William A.
Lewis, Jeremy. Cyril Connolly: A Life. 1999. pap. 19.95 (0-7126-6635-4) Trafalgar.
Lewis, Jeremy. Kindred Spirits. 1996. mass mkt. 13.95 (0-00-654338-3, Pub. by HarpC) Trafalgar.
Lewis, Jeremy, jt. ed. see Lewis, Suzan.
Lewis, Jeremy, ed. see Wells, H. G.
Lewis, Jerre G. & Renn, Leslie. How to Start & Manage a Building Service Contracting Business: Step by Step Guide to Starting & Managing Your Own Businses. (Illus.). 125p. 1999. pap. 18.95 (1-57916-049-2) Lewis Renn.
— How to Start & Manage a Cosmetology Business: Step by Step Guide to Starting & Managing Your Own Business. (Illus.). 125p. 1999. pap. 18.95 (1-57916-053-0) Lewis Renn.
— How to Start & Manage a Crime Prevention Business: Step by Step Guide to Starting & Managing Your Own Business. (Illus.). 125p. 1999. pap. 18.95 (1-57916-065-4) Lewis Renn.
— How to Start & Manage a Desktop Publishing Business: Step by Step Guide to Starting & Managing Your Own Business. (Illus.). 125p. 1999. pap. 18.95 (1-57916-064-6) Lewis Renn.
— How to Start & Manage a Dry Cleaning Business: Step by Step Guide to Starting & Managing Your Own Business. (Illus.). 125p. 1999. pap. 18.95 (1-57916-041-7) Lewis Renn.
— How to Start & Manage a Fish Farming Business: Step by Step Guide to Starting & Managing Your Own Business. (Illus.). 125p. 1999. pap. 18.95 (1-57916-046-8) Lewis Renn.
— How to Start & Manage a Hardware Store Business: Step by Step Guide to Starting & Managing Your Own Business. (Illus.). 125p. 1999. pap. 18.95 (1-57916-042-5) Lewis Renn.
— How to Start & Manage a Marine Retailing Business: Step by Step Guide to Starting & Managing Your Own Business. (Illus.). 125p. 1999. pap. 18.95 (1-57916-043-3) Lewis Renn.
— How to Start & Manage a Personnel Referral Service Business: Step by Step Guide to Starting & Managing Your Own Business. (Illus.). 125p. 1999. pap. 18.95 (1-57916-047-6) Lewis Renn.
— How to Start & Manage a Pharmacy Business: Step by Step Guide to Starting & Managing Your Own Business. (Illus.). 125p. 1999. pap. 18.95 (1-57916-045-X) Lewis Renn.
— How to Start & Manage a Radio-Television Repair Shop Business: Step by Step Guide to Starting & Managing Your Own Business. (Illus.). 125p. 1999. pap. 18.95 (1-57916-040-9) Lewis Renn.
— How to Start & Manage a Retail Decorating Products Business: Step by Step Guide to Starting & Managing Your Own Business. (Illus.). 125p. 1999. pap. 18.95 (1-57916-050-6) Lewis Renn.
— How to Start & Manage a Retail Florist Business: Step by Step Guide to Starting & Managing Your Own Business. (Illus.). 125p. 1999. pap. 18.95 (1-57916-039-5) Lewis Renn.
— How to Start & Manage a Solar Energy Business: Step by Step Guide to Starting & Managing Your Own Business. (Illus.). 125p. 1999. pap. 18.95 (1-57916-048-4) Lewis Renn.
— How to Start & Manage an Apartment Preparation Business: Step by Step Guide to Starting & Managing Your Own Business. (Illus.). 125p. 1999. pap. 18.95 (1-57916-087-5) Lewis Renn.
— How to Start & Manage an Electronics Industry Consulting Business: Step by Step Guide to Starting & Managing Your Own Business. (Illus.). 125p. 1999. pap. 18.95 (1-57916-055-7) Lewis Renn.
— How to Start & Manage an Independent Trucking Business: Step by Step Guide to Starting & Managing Your Own Business. (Illus.). 125p. 1999. pap. 18.95 (1-57916-057-3) Lewis Renn.
Lewis, Jerre G. & Renn, Leslie D. How to Buy & Sell a Business: Step by Step Guide to Starting & Managing Your Own Business. (Illus.). 125p. 1999. pap. 18.95 (1-57916-096-4) Lewis Renn.
— How to Finance Your Business for the 21st Century: Step by Step Guide to Starting & Managing Your Own Business. (Illus.). 125p. 1999. pap. 18.95 (1-57916-099-9) Lewis Renn.
— How to Start a Participative Management Program: 10 Easy Steps. LC 91-90576. 93p. 1991. pap. 16.95 (0-9628759-1-0) Lewis Renn.
— How to Start & Manage a Bar & Cocktail Lounge Business: Step by Step Guide to Starting & Managing Your Own Business. (Illus.). 125p. 1999. pap. 18.95 (1-57916-061-1) Lewis Renn.
— How to Start & Manage a Bed & Breakfast Business: Step by Step Guide to Business Success. (Illus.). 125p. 1999. pap. 18.95 (1-57916-018-2) Lewis Renn.
— How to Start & Manage a Bookkeeping Service Business: Step by Step Guide to Business Success. (Illus.). 125p. 1999. pap. 18.95 (1-57916-016-6) Lewis Renn.
— How to Start & Manage a Bookstore Business: Step by Step Guide to Starting & Managing Your Own Business. 125p. 1999. pap. 18.95 (1-57916-037-9) Lewis Renn.
— How to Start & Manage a Carpentry Service Business. (Illus.). 125p. 1999. pap. 18.95 (1-57916-025-5) Lewis Renn.
— How to Start & Manage a Carpet-Cleaning Service: Step by Step Guide to Starting & Managing Your Own Business. (Illus.). 125p. 1999. pap. 18.95 (1-57916-084-0) Lewis Renn.
— How to Start & Manage a Catering Service Business: Step by Step Guide to Starting & Managing Your Own Business. (Illus.). 125p. 1999. pap. 18.95 (1-57916-083-2) Lewis Renn.
— How to Start & Manage a Children's Bookstore Business: Step by Step Guide to Starting & Managing Your Own Business. (Illus.). 125p. 1999. pap. 18.95 (1-57916-075-1) Lewis Renn.
— How to Start & Manage a Children's Clothing Store Business: Step by Step Guide to Starting & Managing Your Own Business. (Illus.). 125p. 1999. pap. 18.95 (1-57916-030-1) Lewis Renn.
— How to Start & Manage a Coin-Operated Laundries Business: Step by Step Guide to Starting & Managing Your Own Business. (Illus.). 125p. 1999. pap. 18.95 (1-57916-068-9) Lewis Renn.
— How to Start & Manage a Construction Electrician Business: Step by Step Guide to Business Success. (Illus.). 125p. 1999. pap. 18.95 (1-57916-013-1) Lewis Renn.
— How to Start & Manage a Convenience Food Store Business: Step by Step Guide to Starting & Managing Your Own Business. (Illus.). 125p. 1999. pap. 18.95 (1-57916-032-8) Lewis Renn.
— How to Start & Manage a Dairy Farming Business: Step by Step Guide to Starting & Managing Your Own Business. (Illus.). 125p. 1999. pap. 18.95 (1-57916-028-X) Lewis Renn.
— How to Start & Manage a Day Care Center Business: Step by Step Guide to Business Success. (Illus.). 125p. 1999. pap. 18.95 (1-57916-011-5) Lewis Renn.
— How to Start & Manage a Energy Specialist Business. (Illus.). 125p. 1999. pap. 18.95 (1-57916-019-0) Lewis Renn.
— How to Start & Manage a Farm Equipment Repair Service Business: Step by Step Guide to Starting & Managing Your Own Business. (Illus.). 125p. 1999. pap. 18.95 (1-57916-029-8) Lewis Renn.
— How to Start & Manage a Fertilizer & Pesticide Business: Step by Step Guide to Starting & Managing Your Own Business. (Illus.). 125p. 1999. pap. 18.95 (1-57916-063-8) Lewis Renn.
— How to Start & Manage a Flower & Plant Store Business: Step by Step Guide to Business Success. (Illus.). 125p. 1999. pap. 18.95 (1-57916-012-3) Lewis Renn.
— How to Start & Manage a Franchised Business: Step by Step Guide to Starting & Managing Your Own Business. (Illus.). 125p. 1999. pap. 18.95 (1-57916-054-9) Lewis Renn.
— How to Start & Manage a Garden Center Business: Step by Step Guide to Business Success. (Illus.). 135p. 1999. pap. 18.95 (1-57916-002-6) Lewis Renn.
— How to Start & Manage a Gift Basket Service Business: Step by Step Guide to Starting & Managing Your Own Business. (Illus.). 125p. 1999. pap. 18.95 (1-57916-080-8) Lewis Renn.
— How to Start & Manage a Gift Shop Business: Step by Step Guide to Starting & Managing Your Own Business. (Illus.). 125p. 1999. pap. 18.95 (1-57916-066-2) Lewis Renn.
— How to Start & Manage a Gift Speciality Store Business: Step by Step Guide to Starting & Managing Your Own Business. (Illus.). 125p. 1999. pap. 18.95 (1-57916-079-4) Lewis Renn.
— How to Start & Manage a Guard Service Business. (Illus.). 125p. 1999. pap. 18.95 (1-57916-020-4) Lewis Renn.
— How to Start & Manage a Hair Styling Salon Business: Step by Step Guide to Starting & Managing Your Own Business. (Illus.). 125p. 1999. pap. 18.95 (1-57916-094-8) Lewis Renn.
— How to Start & Manage a Hair Styling Shop Business: Step by Step Guide to Business Success. (Illus.). 125p. 1999. pap. 18.95 (1-57916-003-4) Lewis Renn.
— How to Start & Manage a Handcrafts Success Business: Step by Step Guide to Starting & Managing Your Own Business. (Illus.). 125p. 1999. pap. 18.95 (1-57916-067-0) Lewis Renn.
— How to Start & Manage a Health Spa Business: Step by Step Guide to Business Success. (Illus.). 125p. 1999. pap. 18.95 (1-57916-007-7) Lewis Renn.
— How to Start & Manage a Home Attentant Service Business: Step by Step Guide to Starting & Managing Your Own Business. (Illus.). 125p. 1999. pap. 18.95 (1-57916-026-3) Lewis Renn.
— How to Start & Manage a Home Based Business: Step-by-Step Guide to Business Success. LC 95-95310. (Illus.). 135p. (Orig.). 1996. pap. 16.95 (1-887005-11-0) Lewis Renn.
— How to Start & Manage a Home Furnishing Business: Step by Step Guide to Starting & Managing Your Own Business. 125p. 1999. pap. 18.95 (1-57916-038-7) Lewis Renn.
— How to Start & Manage a Home Health Care Business: Step by Step Guide to Starting & Managing Your Own Business. (Illus.). 125p. 1999. pap. 18.95 (1-57916-092-1) Lewis Renn.
— How to Start & Manage a Hospitality Management Business: Step by Step Guide to Starting & Managing Your Own Business. (Illus.). 125p. 1999. pap. 18.95 (1-57916-081-6) Lewis Renn.
— How to Start & Manage a Hotel: Step by Step Guide to Starting & Managing Your Own Business. (Illus.). 125p. 1999. pap. 18.95 (1-57916-082-4) Lewis Renn.

L

— How to Start & Manage a House Cleaning Service Business: Step by Step Guide to Business Success. (Illus.). 125p. 1999. pap. 18.95 (*1-57916-014-X*) Lewis Renn.
— How to Start & Manage a Janitorial Service Business: Step by Step Guide to Starting & Managing Your Own Business. (Illus.). 125p. 1999. pap. 18.95 (*1-57916-089-1*) Lewis Renn.
— How to Start & Manage a Kiosks & Cart Business: Step by Step Guide to Starting & Managing Your Own Business. (Illus.). 125p. 1999. pap. 18.95 (*1-57916-088-3*) Lewis Renn.
— How to Start & Manage a Mail Order Business: Step by Step Guide to Starting & Managing Your Own Business. (Illus.). 1999. pap. 18.95 (*1-57916-036-0*) Lewis Renn.
— How to Start & Manage a Medical Claims Processing: Step by Step Guide to Starting & Managing Your Own Business. (Illus.). 125p. 1999. pap. 18.95 (*1-57916-090-5*) Lewis Renn.
— How to Start & Manage a Men's Apparel Store: Step by Step Guide to Starting & Managing Your Own Business. (Illus.). 125p. 1999. pap. 18.95 (*1-57916-071-9*) Lewis Renn.
— How to Start & Manage a Nursery Business: Step by Step Guide to Starting & Managing Your Own Business. (Illus.). 125p. 1999. pap. 18.95 (*1-57916-059-X*) Lewis Renn.
— How to Start & Manage a Nursing Home Care Business: Step by Step Guide to Starting & Managing Your Own Business. (Illus.). 125p. 1999. pap. 18.95 (*1-57916-091-3*) Lewis Renn.
— How to Start & Manage a Nursing Service Business: Step by Step Guide to Business Success. (Illus.). 125p. 1999. pap. 18.95 (*1-57916-015-8*) Lewis Renn.
— How to Start & Manage a Pest Control Service Business: Step by Step Guide to Starting & Managing Your Own Business. (Illus.). 125p. 1999. pap. 18.95 (*1-57916-033-6*) Lewis Renn.
— How to Start & Manage a Plumbing Service Business. (Illus.). 125p. 1999. pap. 18.95 (*1-57916-023-9*) Lewis Renn.
— How to Start & Manage a Printing Business: Step by Step Guide to Starting & Managing Your Own Business. (Illus.). 125p. 1999. pap. 18.95 (*1-57916-034-4*) Lewis Renn.
— How to Start & Manage a Property Management Business: Step by Step Guide to Starting & Managing Your Own Business. (Illus.). 125p. 1999. pap. 18.95 (*1-57916-069-7*) Lewis Renn.
— How to Start & Manage a Referral Services Business: Step by Step Guide to Starting & Managing Your Own Business. (Illus.). 125p. 1999. pap. 18.95 (*1-57916-093-X*) Lewis Renn.
— How to Start & Manage a Restaurant Business: Step by Step Guide to Business Success. (Illus.). 125p. 1999. pap. 18.95 (*1-57916-008-5*) Lewis Renn.
— How to Start & Manage a Retail Grocery Store Business: Step by Step Guide to Starting & Managing Your Own Business. (Illus.). 125p. 1999. pap. 18.95 (*1-57916-052-2*) Lewis Renn.
— How to Start & Manage a Sandwich Shop/Deli Business: Step by Step Guide to Starting & Managing Your Own Business. (Illus.). 125p. 1999. pap. 18.95 (*1-57916-077-8*) Lewis Renn.
— How to Start & Manage a Secretarial Service Business: Step by Step Guide to Business Success. (Illus.). 125p. 1999. pap. 18.95 (*1-57916-017-4*) Lewis Renn.
— How to Start & Manage a Seminar Promotion Business: Step by Step Guide to Starting & Managing Your Own Business. (Illus.). 125p. 1999. pap. 18.95 (*1-57916-060-3*) Lewis Renn.
— How to Start & Manage a Sewing Service Business. (Illus.). 125p. 1999. pap. 18.95 (*1-57916-024-7*) Lewis Renn.
— How to Start & Manage a Software Design Business. (Illus.). 125p. 1999. pap. 18.95 (*1-57916-021-2*) Lewis Renn.
— How to Start & Manage a Specialty Food Store Business: Step by Step Guide to Business Success. (Illus.). 125p. 1999. pap. 18.95 (*1-57916-009-3*) Lewis Renn.
— How to Start & Manage a Sporting Goods Store Business: Step by Step Guide to Starting & Managing Your Own Business. (Illus.). 125p. 1999. pap. 18.95 (*1-57916-051-4*) Lewis Renn.
— How to Start & Manage a Travel Agency Business: Step by Step Guide to Business Success. (Illus.). 125p. 1999. pap. 18.95 (*1-57916-005-0*) Lewis Renn.
— How to Start & Manage a Tree Service Business: Step by Step Guide to Starting & Managing Your Own Business. (Illus.). 125p. 1999. pap. 18.95 (*1-57916-027-1*) Lewis Renn.
— How to Start & Manage a Used Bookstore Business: Step by Step Guide to Starting & Managing Your Own Business. (Illus.). 125p. 1999. pap. 18.95 (*1-57916-076-X*) Lewis Renn.
— How to Start & Manage a Welding Business: Step by Step Guide to Business Success. (Illus.). 125p. 1999. pap. 18.95 (*1-57916-010-7*) Lewis Renn.
— How to Start & Manage a Wheelchair Transportation Business: Step by Step Guide to Starting & Managing Your Own Business. (Illus.). 125p. 1999. pap. 18.95 (*1-57916-062-X*) Lewis Renn.
— How to Start & Manage a Window Washing Service: Step by Step Guide to Starting & Managing your Own Business. (Illus.). 125p. 1999. pap. 18.95 (*1-57916-085-9*) Lewis Renn.
— How to Start & Manage a Word Processing Business: Step by Step Guide to Business Success. (Illus.). 135p. 1999. pap. 18.95 (*1-57916-001-8*) Lewis Renn.
— How to Start & Manage an Accounting Service Business: Step by Step Guide to Starting & Managing Your Own Business. (Illus.). 125p. 1999. pap. 18.95 (*1-57916-058-1*) Lewis Renn.
— How to Start & Manage an Advertising Agency Business: Step by Step Guide to Starting & Managing Your Own Business. (Illus.). 125p. 1999. pap. 18.95 (*1-57916-073-5*) Lewis Renn.
— How to Start & Manage an Air Conditioning-Heating Business. (Illus.). 125p. 1999. pap. 18.95 (*1-57916-022-0*) Lewis Renn.
— How to Start & Manage an Answering Service Business: Step by Step Guide to Business Success. (Illus.). 125p. 1999. pap. 18.95 (*1-57916-006-9*) Lewis Renn.
— How to Start & Manage an Apparel Store Business: Step by Step Guide to Business Success. (Illus.). 140p. 1999. pap. 18.95 (*1-57916-000-X*) Lewis Renn.
— How to Start & Manage an Auto Supply Story Business: Step by Step Guide to Starting & Managing Your Own Business. (Illus.). 125p. 1999. pap. 18.95 (*1-57916-070-0*) Lewis Renn.
— How to Start & Manage an Ice Cream Business: Step by Step Guide to Starting & Managing Your Own Business. (Illus.). 125p. 1999. pap. 18.95 (*1-57916-035-2*) Lewis Renn.
— How to Start & Manage an Independent Consulting Practice Business: Step by Step Guide to Starting & Managing Your Own Business. (Illus.). 125p. 1999. pap. 18.95 (*1-57916-056-5*) Lewis Renn.
— How to Start & Manage an Innkeeping Service: Step by Step Guide to Starting & Managing Your Own Business. (Illus.). 125p. 1999. pap. 18.95 (*1-57916-086-7*) Lewis Renn.
— How to Start & Manage an Instant Print/Copy Shop: Step by Step Guide to Starting & Managing Your Own Business. (Illus.). 125p. 1999. pap. 18.95 (*1-57916-078-6*) Lewis Renn.
— How to Start & Manage an Office Products Business: Step by Step Guide to Starting & Managing Your Own Business. (Illus.). 125p. 1999. pap. 18.95 (*1-57916-044-1*) Lewis Renn.
— How to Start & Manage Your Own Business: A Practical Way to Start Your Own Business. LC 91-60125. (Illus.). 104p. (Orig.). 1991. pap. 18.95 (*0-9628759-0-2*) Lewis Renn.
— How to Start & Managing a Temporary Help Services Business: Step by Step Guide to Starting & Managing Your Own Business. (Illus.). 125p. 1999. pap. 18.95 (*1-57916-072-7*) Lewis Renn.
— How to Start & Managing a Women's Apparel Store Business: Step by Step Guide to Starting & Managing Your Own Business. (Illus.). 125p. 1999. pap. 18.95 (*1-57916-031-X*) Lewis Renn.
— How to Write a Successful Business Plan: Step by Step Guide to Starting & Managing Your Own Business. (Illus.). 125p. 1999. pap. 18.95 (*1-57916-098-0*) Lewis Renn.
— Top Eighteen Business Guides for the Twentieth Century: Step-by-Step Guides to Business Success. 300p. (Orig.). 1994. pap. 305.10 (*0-9628759-2-9*) Lewis Renn.
Lewis, Jerre G., jt. auth. see Renn, Leslie D.
Lewis, Jerry, intro. Great Achievers: Lives of the Physically Challenged. Incl. Ludwig Van Beethoven: The Composer Who Continued to Write Music after He Became Deaf. Balcavage, Dynise. (Illus.). 120p. (YA). (gr. 5 up). 1997. lib. bdg. 19.95 (*0-7910-2082-7*); Roy Campanella: The Baseball Star Who Became Paralyzed in a Car Accident. (Illus.). 120p. (YA). (gr. 5 up). 1995. lib. bdg. 19.95 (*0-7910-2083-5*); 1995. Set lib. bdg. 379.05 (*0-7910-2075-4*) Chelsea Hse.
— Mary Tyler Moore: The Award-Winning Actress Who Has Diabetes. (Great Achievers Ser.). (Illus.). 120p. (YA). (gr. 5 up). 1996. lib. bdg. 19.95 (*0-7910-2416-4*) Chelsea Hse.
— Vincent Van Gogh: The Painter Who Suffered from Depression. (Great Achievers Ser.). (Illus.). 120p. (YA). (gr. 5 up). 1995. lib. bdg. 19.95 (*0-7910-2422-9*) Chelsea Hse.
Lewis, Jerry A. Wings for the Heart: Montana's Upland Birds & Waterfowl. 352p. 1992. pap. write for info. (*0-9632227-0-8*) W River Pr.
Lewis, Jerry M. The Birth of the Family: An Empirical Inquiry. LC 89-9911. 224p. 1989. text 31.95 (*0-87630-550-8*) Brunner-Mazel.
— Marriage As a Search for Healing. LC 96-54242. 320p. 1997. 34.95 (*0-87630-831-0*) Brunner-Mazel.
— The Monkey Rope: A Psychotherapist's Reflections on Relationships. 186p. (Orig.). 1996. pap. 17.95 (*0-9641887-2-4*) Bernel Bks.
— Swimming Upstream: Teaching & Learning Psychotherapy in a Biological Era. LC 90-2671. 208p. 1991. text 31.95 (*0-87630-612-1*) Brunner-Mazel.
Lewis, Jerry M., 3rd & Blotcky, Mark J. Child Therapy: Concepts, Strategies, & Decision Making. LC 97-22378. (Basic Principles into Practice Ser.: No. 15). 270p. 1997. 37.95 (*0-87630-822-1*) Brunner-Mazel.
Lewis, Jerry M. & Gossett, John T. Disarming the Past: How an Intimate Relationship Can Heal Old Wounds. LC 98-33362. 221p. 1999. 35.95 (*1-891944-06-1*) Zeig Tucker.
Lewis, Jerry M. & Usdin, Gene, eds. Treatment Planning in Psychiatry. LC 82-3985. 453p. reprint ed. pap. 140.50 (*0-8357-7792-8*, 203615300002) Bks Demand.
Lewis, Jesse J. & Hayman, John. Empowerment of a Race: The Revitalization of Black Institutions. LC 99-21617. 192p. 1999. 24.95 (*1-57359-019-3*) Black Belt Communs.
Lewis, Jessica H. Comparative Hemostasis in Vertebrates. (Illus.). 446p. (C). 1996. text 95.00 (*0-306-44841-6*, Kluwer Plenum) Kluwer Academic.
Lewis, Jill. Academic Literacy: Readings & Strategies. (C). 1996. text, teacher ed. 2.66 (*0-669-33199-6*); pap. text 33.56 (*0-669-33197-X*) HM Trade Div.
— Fascism & the Working Class in Austria Nineteen Eighteen to Nineteen Thirty-Four. 246p. 1991. 30.00 (*0-85496-581-5*) Berg Pubs.
— Handbook for Academic Literacy. 360p. (C). 1996. pap. text 29.96 (*0-669-33198-8*) HM Trade Div.
Lewis, Jill, jt. auth. see Joseph, Gloria.
Lewis, Jim. Biblical Favorites. LC 85-50948. 134p. (Orig.). 1985. pap. 7.95 (*0-942482-08-5*) Unity Church Denver.
— The Great Commitment. LC 81-71542. 120p. (Orig.). 1982. pap. 7.50 (*0-942482-03-4*) Unity Church Denver.
— Mystical Teachings of Christianity. 150p. 1980. pap. 7.95 (*0-942482-01-8*) Unity Church Denver.
— Positive Thoughts for Successful Living. LC 80-50277. 138p. (Orig.). 1979. pap. 7.95 (*0-942482-00-X*) Unity Church Denver.
— Real Gone. (Illus.). 56p. 1994. 15.00 (*0-9631095-2-9*) Artspace Bks.
— Reincarnation & Translation. 31p. (Orig.). 1981. pap. 3.00 (*0-942482-02-6*) Unity Church Denver.
— Spiritual Gospel. LC 82-51231. 145p. (Orig.). 1982. pap. 8.95 (*0-942482-05-0*) Unity Church Denver.
— The Ten Commandments: Then & Now. LC 84-50912. 95p. (Orig.). 1984. pap. 5.95 (*0-942482-07-7*) Unity Church Denver.
— The Twelve Thrones. LC 83-91008. 85p. (Orig.). 1983. pap. 5.95 (*0-942482-06-9*) Unity Church Denver.
— The Upward Path. LC 82-60277. 150p. (Orig.). 1982. pap. 7.95 (*0-942482-04-2*) Unity Church Denver.
— Why the Tree Loves the Ax. 276p. 1999. reprint ed. pap. 12.95 (*0-425-16864-6*) Berkley Pub.
***Lewis, Jim & Hart, Charles.** Goldpanning Southwest B. C. & Vancouver Island: A Prospectors Treasure Trail to Creeks of Gold. (Illus.). 96p. 1998. pap. 9.95 (*1-895811-60-0*) Heritage Hse.
Lewis, Jim & Irving, Kenneth. The Psychology of Astrocartography. LC 97-223553. (Illus.). 341p. 1997. pap. 13.95 (*0-14-019512-2*) Viking Penguin.
Lewis, Jim & Lewis, Lorrie. I Am Independent Curriculum/Workbook Series, 8 vols., Vols. 1-8. (Illus.). 530p. 1993. student ed., spiral bd. 80.00 (*1-878110-02-0*) Abundant Answers.
— I Am Independent Instructors Guide. (I Am Independent Curriculum Ser.: Vol. 1). (Illus.). 40p. 1991. teacher ed. 12.00 (*1-878110-01-2*) Abundant Answers.
— I Can Help Myself. (I Am Independent Curriculum Ser.: Vol. 2). 82p. 1993. student ed. 12.00 (*1-878110-03-9*) Abundant Answers.
— I Can Live on My Own. (I Am Independent Curriculum Ser.: Vol. 7). (Illus.). 60p. 1993. student ed. 12.00 (*1-878110-08-X*) Abundant Answers.
— I Can Live Safely. (I Am Independent Curriculum Ser.: Vol. 3). 64p. 1992. 12.00 (*1-878110-05-5*) Abundant Answers.
— I Like Learning More. (I Am Independent Curriculum Ser.: Vol. 8). 64p. 1993. student ed. 12.00 (*1-878110-09-8*) Abundant Answers.
— I Like to Cook Good Food. (I Am Independent Curriculum Ser.: Vol. 5). 154p. 1991. student ed. 12.00 (*1-878110-04-7*) Abundant Answers.
— I Like Who I Am. (I Am Independent Curriculum Ser.: Vol. 4). (Illus.). 62p. 1991. student ed. 12.00 (*1-878110-06-3*) Abundant Answers.
— I Want Money. (I Am Independent Curriculum Ser.: Vol. 6). (Illus.). 128p. 1991. student ed. 12.00 (*1-878110-07-1*) Abundant Answers.
— Institute of Abundant Living: Instructional Guideline, Class Outlines & Teaching Guides. 70p. (Orig.). 1996. pap., teacher ed. 10.00 (*1-878110-17-9*) Abundant Answers.
— Institute of Abundant Living Catalogue - Discover Abilities: Institute of Abundant Living Class Catalogue. (Illus.). 70p. (Orig.). 1996. pap. write for info. (*1-878110-18-7*) Abundant Answers.
***Lewis, Joan.** Jubilee 2000 in Rome: Guide to Basilicas & Catacombs. 112p. 1999. pap. 6.95 (*1-889334-22-7*) Scepter Pubs.
Lewis, Joan, jt. auth. see Heymsfield, Carla.
Lewis, Joanna, jt. auth. see Wise, Gayla.
Lewis, Joe. The Beth Shalom Hagadah. Nelson, David A. & Nelson, Alicia, eds. (ENG & HEB., Illus.). 100p. (Orig.). 1997. pap. 12.95 (*1-888822-01-5*) Singlish Pub.
— A Book of Song & Prayer for Shabbat in the Jewish Home. (ENG & HEB., Illus.). 82p. (Orig.). 1997. pap. 12.95 (*1-888822-02-3*) Singlish Pub.
— Friday Night Alive! Service of the Heart: Shabbat Evening Service. Bernstein, Ellen, ed. (ENG & HEB., Illus.). 120p. 1997. pap. 12.95 (*1-888822-03-1*) Singlish Pub.
— Friday Night Alive! Service of the Heart: Shabbat Evening Service. Bernstein, Ellen, ed. (ENG & HEB., Illus.). 120p. 1998. pap. 11.95 (*1-888822-05-8*) Singlish Pub.
— Weekday Morning Service: A Simplified Version from Jewish Tradition. (ENG & HEB., Illus.). 72p. 1997. pap. 8.95 (*1-888822-04-X*) Singlish Pub.
— The World-Peacemaker. 1983. pap. 2.95 (*0-87505-329-7*) Borden.
***Lewis, Joe.** Zemirot from My Father's House. 28p. 1998. pap. 6.95 (*1-888822-06-6*) Singlish Pub.
***Lewis, Joe, ed.** The Join-In, Participate, Sing-Along Hagadah. 2nd ed. (HEB & ENG., Illus.). 128p. 2000. pap. 18.95 (*1-888822-08-2*) Singlish Pub.
Lewis, Joe & Beasley, Jerry. The Greatest Karate Fighter of All Time: Joe Lewis & His American Karate Systems. LC 98-228873. 104p. 1998. pap. 20.00 (*0-87364-981-8*) Paladin Pr.
Lewis, Joel. House Rent Boogie. 1992. pap. 5.95 (*0-916328-21-X*) Yellow Pr.
— Palookas of the Ozone. 1992. pap. 4.00 (*0-938979-38-8*) EG Bksellers.
— Vertical's Currency: New & Selected Poems. LC 99-18964. 144p. 1999. pap. 13.95 (*1-883689-83-X*) Talisman Hse.
— Vertical's Currency: Selected Poems. LC 99-18964. 136p. 1999. 32.95 (*1-883689-84-8*) Talisman Hse.
Lewis, Joel, ed. On the Level Everyday: Selected Talks on Poetry & the Art of Living. LC 97-6862. 128p. 1997. 32.95 (*1-883689-56-2*); pap. 12.95 (*1-883689-55-4*) Talisman Hse.
Lewis, Joel, ed. see Lowenfelt, Walter.
***Lewis, Joelle.** I'm Going to Give Myself Some Very Good Advice... And Then I'm Going to Take It! Real-Aid Not Band-Aid for When You've Hit the Potholes in the Road of Life. 64p. 2000. pap. 8.75 (*0-9533331-2-4*) CityScape Bks.
Lewis, Johanan. The Ancient Mysteries of Melchizedek, Vol. 1. rev. ed. Levi, Malkeyan & Levi, Makedah, eds. (Illus.). 192p. 1998. pap. 14.95 (*0-9665426-1-4*) M Y L Pub.
Lewis, Johanna M. Artisans in the North Carolina Backcountry. (Illus.). 224p. 1995. text 34.95 (*0-8131-1908-1*) U Pr of Ky.
Lewis, John. Godfather of the Brandywine. (Illus.). 298p. 1996. 24.95 (*1-878970-04-6*); pap. 7.95 (*1-878970-05-4*) Dyne-American.
— The History of the Life & Sufferings of the Revered & Learned John Wiclif, D. D. LC 74-178543. reprint ed. 52.50 (*0-404-56625-1*) AMS Pr.
— A House Esteemed: Building Esteem for God, for Ourselves & for the Church. 200p. (Orig.). 2000. pap. 12.95 (*1-878647-45-8*) APU Pub Grp.
Lewis, John. Java Software Solutions: Foundations of Program Design. LC 97-19400. 829p. (C). 1997. pap. text 68.00 (*0-201-57164-1*) Addison-Wesley.
— Java Software Solutions: Foundations of Program Design. 2nd ed. LC 99-51658. 780p. (C). 1999. pap. text 68.00 (*0-201-61271-2*) Addison-Wesley.
Lewis, John. Java Software Structures. (C). 1999. pap. text Price not set. (*0-201-35751-8*) Addison-Wesley.
— Marxism & the Irrationalists. LC 72-6687. 141p. 1973. reprint ed. lib. bdg. 55.00 (*0-8371-6494-X*, LEMB, Greenwood Pr) Greenwood.
— Marxism & the Open Mind. 222p. 1957. 34.95 (*0-87855-032-1*) Transaction Pubs.
— Printed Ephemera. (Illus.). 288p. 1990. 69.50 (*1-85149-116-3*) Antique Collect.
— Software Systems Using Java Preliminary Version. (C). 1997. pap. text. write for info. (*0-201-69588-X*) Addison-Wesley.
— Such Things Happen: The Life of a Typographer. (Illus.). 224p. 1998. 29.50 (*0-906290-06-6*) Antique Collect.
— Tales of the Eastern Shore. (Illus.). 136p. 1996. 18.95 (*1-878970-02-X*); pap. 11.95 (*1-878970-03-8*) Dyne-American.
— Tales of the Eastern Shore: The Boyhood Memoir of a Welsh-American Publisher. (Illus.). 132p. 1997. 24.95 (*0-9657328-0-0*, 50413); pap. 12.95 (*0-9657328-1-9*, 50414) Cedar Tree Bks.
— A Taste for Sailing. 240p. 1990. 48.00 (*0-86138-077-0*, Pub. by T Dalton) St Mut.
— A Treatise on the Law of Eminent Domain in the United States, 2 vols. LC 97-70482. cccx, 1,804p. 1997. reprint ed. 225.00 (*1-57588-209-4*, 311120) W S Hein.
— Uniqueness of Man. 1974. 24.95 (*0-8464-0948-8*) Beekman Pubs.
Lewis, John, ed. Eat No Evil Cookbook: There Is No Such Thing As a Bad, Evil or Forbidden Food! (Illus.). 1991. text 18.95 (*0-685-46316-8*) New Outlook.
Lewis, John, et al, eds. Christianity & the Social Revolution. LC 79-37892. (Select Bibliographies Reprint Ser.). 1977. reprint ed. 27.95 (*0-8369-6729-1*) Ayer.
Lewis, John & D'Orso, Michael. Walking on the Wind: A Memoir of the Movement. LC 98-3040. (Illus.). 496p. 1998. 25.50 (*0-684-81065-4*) S&S Trade.
— Walking with the Wind: A Memoir of the Movement. LC 99-28356. 496p. 1999. pap. 15.00 (*0-15-600708-8*, Harvest Bks) Harcourt.
Lewis, John & Lewis, Griselda. Pratt Ware. (Album Ser.: No. 296). (Illus.). 32p. (C). 1989. pap. 4.75 (*0-7478-0220-3*, Pub. by Shire Pubns) Parkwest Pubns.
— Pratt Ware, 1780-1840: English & Scottish Relief Decorated & Underglaze Coloured Earthenware, 1780-1840. (Illus.). 320p. 1993. 69.50 (*1-85149-191-0*) Antique Collect.
Lewis, John & Shreeves, Karl. Decompression Theory, Dive Tables & Dive Computers. Talley, Tonya, ed. (Illus.). 100p. (Orig.). (C). 1990. pap. text 14.95 (*1-878663-06-2*) PADI.
Lewis, John, et al. Success & Failure in Small Business. LC 83-16447. 304p. 1984. text 73.95 (*0-566-00645-6*, Pub. by Avebry) Ashgate Pub Co.
Lewis, John, jt. auth. see Green, David R.
Lewis, John, jt. auth. see Walker, Lydia.
Lewis, John, ed. see Shamos, Mike, et al.
Lewis, John, ed. see Sundermeyer, Velma & Sundermeyer, Colleen A.
Lewis, John E. Bruce Lee. LC 97-15064. (They Died Too Young Ser.). (Illus.). 48p. (YA). (gr. 4-7). 1999. lib. bdg. 15.95 (*0-7910-4635-4*) Chelsea Hse.
Lewis, John F. Thomas Spry, Lawyer & Physician: The First Attorney Admitted to Practice under English Law in the Delaware River Settlements Now Included in the States of Pennsylvania, New Jersey & Delaware. LC 96-75356. 140p. 1996. reprint ed. 45.00 (*1-56169-209-3*) Gaunt.
Lewis, John F. & Hastings, Susan C. Sexual Harassment in Education. 2nd ed. 57p. 1994. text 20.00 (*1-56534-064-7*) Ed Law Assn.
***Lewis, John F. & Merk, David, eds.** Marine Fire Fighting. (Illus.). 400p. 2000. pap. 30.00 (*087939-177-4*) IFSTA.
Lewis, John F., et al. Drug & Alcohol Abuse in Schools: A Practical Guide for Administrators & Educators for Combatting Drug & Alcohol Abuse. 2nd ed. 47p. 1992. text 13.00 (*1-56534-050-7*) Ed Law Assn.
Lewis, John G., jt. auth. see Miller, Virginia L.

An Asterisk (*) at the beginning of an entry indicates that the title is appearing for the first time.

Lewis, John G., ed. see SIAM Conference on Applied Linear Algebra Staff.

Lewis, John H. Recollections from 1860 to 1865: Incidents of Camp Life, Descriptions of Battles, The Life of the Southern Soldier, 9th Virginia Infantry. 2nd ed. (Illus.). 92p. 1983. pap. 12.50 (*0-89029-774-6*, Mrngside Press) Morningside Bkshop.

Lewis, John H. & Ewart, Gordon J. Jedburgh Abbey. (Society of Antiquaries of Scotland, Monograph Ser.: No. 10). (Illus.). 182p. 1995. pap. 48.00 (*0-903903-10-5*, Pub. by Soc Antiquaries) David Brown.

Lewis, John L. & Murray, Margaret A. The Method of Layer Potentials for the Heat Equation in Time-Varying Domains. LC 94-43211. (Memoirs Ser.: Vol. 545). 157p. 1995. pap. 38.00 (*0-8218-0360-3*, MEMO/114/545) Am Math.

Lewis, John L., et al. The CIO Files of John L. Lewis. LC 88-26194. (The Cio & Industrial Unionism in America). 45 p. 1988. write for info. (*1-55655-049-9*) U Pubns Amer.

Lewis, John M. & Fontrier, Tionette H. Near Misses in Anesthesia. 112p. 1988. pap. text 36.50 (*0-409-90111-3*) Buttrwrth-Heinemann.

Lewis, John P. Asian Development: The Role of Development Assistance. (Asian Agenda Reports: No. 7). (Illus.). 66p. (Orig.). 1987. pap. text 8.50 (*0-8191-6590-5*) U Pr of Amer.

— India's Political Economy: Governance & Reform. (Illus.). 414p. 1995. text 32.00 (*0-19-563515-9*) OUP.

— India's Political Economy: Governance & Reform. 412p. 1997. reprint ed. pap. text 17.95 (*0-19-564270-8*) OUP.

— Pro-Poor Aid Conditionality. LC 93-19137. (Policy Essay Ser.: No. 8). 72p. (C). 1993. pap. 13.95 (*1-56517-009-1*) Overseas Dev Council.

— Strengthening the Poor: What Have We Learned? Feinberg, Richard E. & Kallab, Valeriana, eds. (U. S. Third World Policy Perspectives Ser.: No. 10). 1988. pap. 21.95 (*0-88738-768-3*) Transaction Pubs.

— Strengthening the Poor: What Have We Learned? Feinberg, Richard E. & Kallab, Valeriana, eds. (U. S. Third World Policy Perspectives Ser.: No. 10). 256p. 1988. text 39.95 (*0-88738-267-3*) Transaction Pubs.

Lewis, John P., ed. Development Strategies: A New Synthesis. (U. S. Third World Policy Perspectives Ser.). 128p. 1985. 39.95 (*0-88738-044-1*); pap. 24.95 (*0-87855-991-4*) Transaction Pubs.

Lewis, John P., et al, eds. The World Bank: Its First Half Century. LC 97-21093. 1276p. 1997. text 79.95 (*0-8157-5234-2*) Brookings.

Lewis, John P. & Kallab, Valeriana, eds. U. S. Foreign Policy & the Third World: Agenda 1983. LC 83-3373. 293p. 1983. 69.50 (*0-275-91034-2*, C1034, Praeger Pubs) Greenwood.

Lewis, John P., et al. The World Bank: Its First Half Century. LC 97-21093. 2042p. 1997. write for info. (*0-8157-5230-X*); 79.95 (*0-8157-5236-9*) Brookings.

***Lewis, John-Paul.** Buffalo Gordon. 2001. write for info. (*0-312-87376-X*, Pub. by Forge NYC) St Martin.

Lewis, John R. Atlas of Aesthetic Plastic Surgery. (Illus.). 1973. 62.00 (*0-316-52335-6*, Little Brwn Med Div) Lppncott W & W.

— Dragons Are Lonely. LC 93-12977. (Illus.). 32p. (J). (gr. 1-3). 1993. 14.95 (*0-87797-239-7*) Cherokee.

Lewis, John R., Jr. Sussex Spaniel: AKC Rank #139. (Rare Breed Ser.). (Illus.). 96p. 1997. 19.95 (*0-7938-0776-X*, RX-126) TFH Pubns.

***Lewis, John S.** Comet & Asteroid Impact Hazard. LC 99-62311. 200p. (C). 1999. text 49.95 (*0-12-446760-1*) Acad Pr.

Lewis, John S. Mining the Sky. (Illus.). 288p. 1997. pap. 15.00 (*0-201-32819-4*) Addison-Wesley.

— Rain of Iron & Ice: The Very Real Threat of Comet & Asteroid Bombardment. LC 97-171126. (C). 1997. pap. 13.00 (*0-201-15494-3*) Addison-Wesley.

— Worlds Without End: The Exploration of Planets Known & Unknown. 1998. write for info. (*0-201-32825-9*) Addison-Wesley.

***Lewis, John S.** Worlds Without End: The Exploration of Planets Known & Unknown. 264p. 1999. pap. text 13.00 (*0-7382-0170-7*, Pub. by Perseus Pubng) HarpC.

Lewis, John S., ed. Physics & Chemistry of the Solar System. 2nd rev. ed. LC 97-207375. (Illus.). 591p. 1997. pap. text 69.95 (*0-12-446742-3*) Morgan Kaufmann.

Lewis, John S. & Lewis, Ruth A. Space Resources: Breaking the Bonds of the Earth. LC 86-32677. (Illus.). 384p. 1987. text 68.50 (*0-231-06498-5*) Col U Pr.

Lewis, John S. & Primm, Ronald G. Planets & Their Atmospheres: Origin & Evolution (Monograph) LC 83-10001. (International Geophysics Ser.). 1983. pap. text 77.00 (*0-12-446582-X*) Acad Pr.

Lewis, John S., et al. Resources of Near-Earth Space. LC 93-23753. (Space Science Ser.). (Illus.). 977p. 1993. 82.00 (*0-8165-1404-6*) U of Ariz Pr.

Lewis, John W. China's Strategic Seapower: The Politics of Force Modernization in the Nuclear Age. 1996. pap. 16.95 (*0-8047-2804-6*) Stanford U Pr.

— Leadership in Communist China. LC 77-25475. (Illus.). 305p. 1978. reprint ed. lib. bdg. 65.00 (*0-313-20119-6*, LELC, Greenwood Pr) Greenwood.

— Political Networks & the Chinese Policy Process. (Occasional Paper of the Northeast Asia-United States Forum on International Policy, Stanford University). 32p. (Orig.). pap. 6.00 (*0-935371-15-X*) CFISAC.

Lewis, John W., ed. The City in Communist China. LC 78-130828. 469p. 1971. reprint ed. pap. 30.00 (*0-8357-4633-X*, 203756200008) Bks Demand.

— Party Leadership & Revolutionary Power in China. LC 72-120056. (Contemporary China Institute Publications). 430p. reprint ed. pap. 122.60 (*0-608-16803-3*, 2027229) Bks Demand.

— Peasant Rebellion & Communist Revolution in Asia. LC 73-89860. xvi, 364p. 1974. pap. 17.95 (*0-8047-0924-6*) Stanford U Pr.

Lewis, John W. & Blacker, Coit D., eds. Next Steps on the Creation of an Accidental Nuclear War Prevention Center. (Special Report of the Center for International Security & Arms Control, Stanford University Ser.). 45p. (Orig.). 1983. pap. 8.00 (*0-935371-07-9*) CFISAC.

Lewis, John W. & Litai, Xue. China Builds the Bomb. LC 87-30404. (ISIS Studies in International Security & Arms Control: Vol. 3). (Illus.). 352p. 1988. 47.50 (*0-8047-1452-5*); pap. 16.95 (*0-8047-1841-5*) Stanford U Pr.

— China's Strategic Seapower: The Politics of Force Modernization in the Nuclear Age. LC 94-11688. (Studies in International Security & Arms Control). 440p. 1994. 55.00 (*0-8047-2303-6*) Stanford U Pr.

Lewis, John W., jt. ed. see Cowan, Alan.

Lewis, JoLinda & Lewis, Danny. Discover the Apocrypha. 25p. 1972. pap. 3.95 (*0-932807-02-X*) Overmountain Pr.

***Lewis, Jon.** Hollywood vs. Hardcore: How the Struggle over Censorship Created the Modern Film Industry. 2000. 26.95 (*0-8147-5142-3*) NYU Pr.

Lewis, Jon. Industrialization & Trade Union Organisation in South Africa, 1924-1955: The Rise & Fall of the South African Trades & Labour Council. (African Studies: No. 42). (Illus.). 256p. 1985. text 74.95 (*0-521-26312-3*) Cambridge U Pr.

— The New American Cinema. LC 97-35210. 1998. 59.95 (*0-8223-2087-8*); pap. write for info. (*0-8223-2115-7*) Duke.

— True Swamp: The Memoirs of Lenny the Frog. 144p. 1996. pap. 16.95 (*0-943151-10-4*) Slave Labor Bks.

— Whom God Wishes to Destroy... Francis Coppola & the New Hollywood. LC 94-44270. (Illus.). 216p. 1995. 29.95 (*0-8223-1602-1*) Duke.

— Whom God Wishes to Destroy... Francis Coppola & the New Hollywood. LC 94-44270. (Illus.). 208p. 1997. pap. 12.95 (*0-8223-1889-X*) Duke.

Lewis, Jon, ed. Permanent Book of Twentieth Century Eyewitness History: An Enthralling Kaleidoscope of the Great Moments of Our Century. (Illus.). 512p. 1995. pap. 11.95 (*0-7867-0161-7*) Carroll & Graf.

Lewis, Jon & Stempel, Penny. Cult TV: The Essential Critical Guide. (Illus.). 272p. 1996. pap. 19.95 (*1-85793-926-3*, Pub. by Pavilion Bks Ltd) Trafalgar.

Lewis, Jon, ed. see Sundermeyer, Colleen A.

Lewis, Jon E. Jim Morrison. LC 97-21940. (They Died Too Young Ser.). (Illus.). 48p. (YA). (gr. 4-7). 1997. lib. bdg. 15.95 (*0-7910-4631-1*) Chelsea Hse.

— Muhammad Ali. LC 97-26031. (Life & Times of...Ser.). (Illus.). 48p. (YA). (gr. 5 up). 1999. lib. bdg. 15.95 (*0-7910-4641-9*) Chelsea Hse.

— War: A Classic Collection of 56 Great War Stories of Our Time. 1995. 12.98 (*0-88365-909-3*) Galahad Bks.

***Lewis, Jon E.** The West: The Making of the American West. 528p. 2000. reprint ed. pap. text 10.00 (*0-7881-6861-4*) DIANE Pub.

Lewis, Jon E., ed. D-Day: Eyewitness Accounts of the Battle of Normandy. 352p. 1994. pap. 11.95 (*0-7867-0090-4*) Carroll & Graf.

***Lewis, Jon E., ed.** The Mammoth Book of Battles. (Mammoth Book Ser.). (Illus.). 512p. 1999. pap. text 10.95 (*0-7867-0689-9*) Carroll & Graf.

— The Mammoth Book of Endurance & Adventure. 512p. 2000. pap. 11.95 (*0-7867-0788-7*, Pub. by Carroll & Graf) Publishers Group.

— The Mammoth Book of Eyewitness History 2000. 608p. 2000. pap. 12.95 (*0-7867-0747-X*, Pub. by Carroll & Graf) Publishers Group.

— The Mammoth Book of Life Before the Mast: Sailors Eyewitness Stories from the Age of Fighting Ships. 512p. 2001. pap. 11.95 (*0-7867-0811-5*, Pub. by Carroll & Graf) Publishers Group.

Lewis, Jon E., ed. The Mammoth Book of Modern War Stories. 544p. 1993. pap. 9.95 (*0-88184-958-8*) Carroll & Graf.

***Lewis, Jon E., ed.** The Mammoth Book of Private Lives. 512p. 2000. pap. 11.95 (*0-7867-0748-8*, Pub. by Carroll & Graf) Publishers Group.

Lewis, Jon E., ed. The Mammoth Book of the West. (Mammoth Book Ser.). (Illus.). 512p. 1996. pap. 11.95 (*0-7867-0376-8*) Carroll & Graf.

— The Mammoth Book of True War Stories. (Mammoth Book Ser.). 1999. pap. 11.95 (*0-7867-0629-5*) Carroll & Graf.

— The Mammoth Book of War Diaries & Letters: A Collection of Letters & Diaries from the Battlefield. (Mammoth Book Ser.). 512p. 1999. pap. 10.95 (*0-7867-0589-2*) Carroll & Graf.

Lewis, Jon E. & Stempel, Penny. Cult TV: The Comedies. (Illus.). 256p. 1998. pap. 19.95 (*0-912333-65-0*, Pub. by BB&T Inc) Publishers Group.

***Lewis, Jon E. & Stempel, Penny.** Cult TV: The Detectives. (Illus.). 256p. 2000. pap. 24.95 (*1-86205-311-1*, Pub. by Pavilion Bks Ltd) Trafalgar.

Lewis, Jonathan. Mision Mundial, 3 vols., Set.Tr. of World Mission. (SPA.). 16.99 (*0-685-74961-4*, 498481) Editorial Unilit.

— Mision Mundial, Tomo 3.Tr. of World Mission. (SPA.). 47p. 1987. pap., teacher ed. 2.50 (*1-56063-538-X*, 498680) Editorial Unilit.

— Mision Mundial, Vol. I.Tr. of World Mission. (SPA.). 47p. 1987. pap. 5.99 (*1-56063-065-5*, 498478); pap., teacher ed. 2.50 (*1-56063-536-3*, 498678) Editorial Unilit.

— Mision Mundial, Vol. 2.Tr. of World Mission. (SPA.). 47p. 1987. pap. 5.99 (*1-56063-066-3*, 498479) Editorial Unilit.

— Mision Mundial, Vol. II.Tr. of World Mission. (SPA.). 40p. 1993. pap., teacher ed. 2.50 (*1-56063-537-1*, 498679) Editorial Unilit.

— Mision Mundial, Vol. 3.Tr. of World Mission. (SPA.). 47p. 1987. pap. 5.99 (*1-56063-067-1*, 498480) Editorial Unilit.

— Working Your Way to the Nations: A Guide to Effective Tentmaking. rev. ed. LC 96-47612. 208p. (Orig.). 1997. pap. 12.99 (*0-8308-1905-3*, 1905) InterVarsity.

Lewis, Jonathan. World Mission: An Analysis of the World Christian Movement. 160p. 1999. pap. 24.99 (*0-87808-237-9*, WCL237-9) William Carey Lib.

Lewis, Jordan D. The Connected Corporation: How Leading Companies Win Through Customer-Supplier Alliances. (Illus.). 368p. 1995. 29.50 (*0-02-919055-X*) Free Pr.

— Partnerships for Profit: Structuring & Managing Strategic Alliances. 1990. 35.00 (*0-02-919050-9*) Free Pr.

— Trusted Partners: How Companies Build Mutual Trust & Win Together. LC 99-42069. (Illus.). 336p. 2000. 29.50 (*0-684-83651-3*) Free Pr.

Lewis, Joseph. Atheism & Other Addresses. LC 72-161333. (Atheist Viewpoint Ser.). (Illus.). 510p. 1972. reprint ed. 35.95 (*0-405-03800-3*) Ayer.

— Atheism & Other Addresses. 160p. 1999. reprint ed. pap. 17.95 (*0-7661-0757-4*) Kessinger Pub.

— The Bible Unmasked. 236p. 1996. reprint ed. spiral bd. 16.50 (*0-7873-0557-X*) Hlth Research.

— The Bible Unmasked. 246p. 1996. reprint ed. pap. 12.95 (*1-56459-540-4*) Kessinger Pub.

— The Bible Unmasked, Vol. I. 122p. 1990. pap. text 15.00 (*0-916157-37-7*) African Islam Miss Pubns.

— The Bible Unmasked, Vol. II. 120p. 1990. pap. text 15.00 (*0-916157-38-5*) African Islam Miss Pubns.

— In the Name of Humanity. unabridged ed. (Classic Reprint Ser.). 158p. 1997. reprint ed. 28.00 (*0-936128-81-X*) De Young Pr.

— Ingersoll the Magnificent. (Illus.). 342p. (C). 1985. reprint ed. pap. 14.00 (*0-910309-12-4*, 5216) Am Atheist.

— Spain: A Land Blighted by Religion. (Illus.). 96p. (C). reprint ed. write for info. (*0-318-70299-1*) Hakims Pubs.

— Spain: A Land Blighted by Religion. (Illus.). 96p. (C). 1993. reprint ed. pap. 5.95 (*0-317-05574-7*) Hakims Pubs.

Lewis, Jr., Albert D. Then God Showed Up. (Illus.). 112p. 1998. pap. 22.99 (*0-9633356-0-X*) Harvest Time.

Lewis, Judith & Leviton, Richard. Complete Book of Reflexology Remedies. 312p. (C). 1996. 27.95 (*0-13-187469-1*) P-H.

Lewis, Judith, jt. auth. see Carlson, Jon.

Lewis, Judith A., ed. Addictions: Concepts & Strategies for Treatment. LC 94-9159. 414p. 1994. 56.00 (*0-8342-0563-7*) Aspen Pub.

Lewis, Judith A. & Bernstein, Judith. Women's Health. (Nursing Ser.). (C). 1996. pap. 49.95 (*0-86720-485-0*) Jones & Bartlett.

Lewis, Judith A. & Lewis, Michael D. Community Counseling. (Counseling, Human Services Ser.). 265p. (C). 1990. text 48.95 (*0-534-10248-4*) Brooks-Cole.

— Management of Human Service Programs. LC 82-14684. (Counseling Ser.). 228p. (C). 1983. pap. 31.00 (*0-534-01335-X*) Brooks-Cole.

Lewis, Judith A., et al. Community Counseling: Empowering Individuals & Communities in a Diverse Society. 2nd ed. LC 97-16993. (Counseling Ser.). 407p. 1997. pap. 60.95 (*0-534-25854-9*) Brooks-Cole.

Lewis, Judith A., et al. Counseling Women over the Life Span. LC 91-77048. 307p. 1992. pap. 34.95 (*0-89108-222-0*, 9203) Love Pub Co.

— Health Counseling. LC 92-37322. 291p. 1993. text 41.00 (*0-534-13446-7*) Brooks-Cole.

— Substance Abuse Counseling: An Individualized Approach. LC 87-24618. 281p. (C). 1987. pap. 34.50 (*0-534-08448-6*) Brooks-Cole.

— Substance Abuse Counseling: An Individualized Approach. 2nd ed. LC 93 8054. 243p. 1993. mass mkt. 46.75 (*0-534-20053-2*) Brooks-Cole.

Lewis, Judith A., jt. ed. see Carlson, Jon.

Lewis, Judith S. In the Family Way: Childbearing in the British Aristocracy, 1760-1860. 270p. (C). 1986. text 40.00 (*0-8135-1116-X*) Rutgers U Pr.

Lewis, Judy. Heart Beats & Soul Sounds. LC 93-93718. (Illus.). 112p. (Orig.). 1993. pap. 8.95 (*0-9639332-0-5*) Swamp Pond.

— Uncommon Knowledge. 1995. pap. 6.50 (*0-671-70020-0*) PB.

Lewis, Judy & Williams, Janice. NMS Introduction to Clinical Medicine. (National Medical Ser.). (Illus.). 260p. 1991. 24.00 (*0-683-06212-3*) Lppncott W & W.

Lewis, Julie. Mary Martin: A Double Life - Australia-India, 1915-1973. LC 98-146131. 280p. 1997. pap. 29.95 (*0-7022-2725-0*, Pub. by Univ Queensland Pr) Intl Spec Bk.

— Olga Masters: A Lot of Living. 1991. pap. 16.95 (*0-7022-2387-5*, Pub. by Univ Queensland Pr) Intl Spec Bk.

Lewis, June. Arkansas Criminal & Traffic Law Manual: 1993 Edition. (Illus.). 216p. 27.50 (*0-614-05784-1*, MICHIE) LEXIS Pub.

— The Cotswolds: Life & Traditions. (Illus.). 160p. 1998. pap. (*1-85799-955-X*) Phoenix Hse.

***Lewis, Justin.** Constructing Public Opinion: How Political Elites Do What they Like & Why We Seem to Go Along With It. 240p. 2001. text 49.50 (*0-231-11766-3*); pap. text 16.50 (*0-231-11767-1*) Col U Pr.

Lewis, Justin. The Ideological Octopus. (Studies in Culture & Communication). 192p. (C). (gr. 13). 1991. pap. 18.99 (*0-415-90288-6*, A4291) Routledge.

Lewis, Justin, jt. auth. see Jhally, Sut.

Lewis, Justus & Storz, Moni L. Switch on Your Mind: Accelerative Learning Strategies at Work. 1998. pap. 19.95 (*1-86448-256-7*, Pub. by Allen & Unwin Pty) IPG Chicago.

Lewis, K. E., jt. ed. see Limbaugh, Ronald H.

Lewis, K. R., jt. ed. see Riley, Ralph.

Lewis, Karen. From Arapesh to Zuni: A Book of Bibleless Peoples. (Illus.). 31p. (J). (gr. 1-6). 1986. pap. text 4.95 (*0-938978-07-1*) Wycliffe Bible.

Lewis, Karen & Hathersmith, June. Harvest of Trust. (Illus.). 200p. (Orig.). 1989. pap. 3.95 (*0-938978-12-8*) Wycliffe Bible.

Lewis, Karen, ed. see Packard, David.

Lewis, Karen B. & Henderson, Roxanne. Sign Language Made Simple. LC 97-9233. (Illus.). 256p. 1997. pap. 12.95 (*0-385-48857-2*) Doubleday.

***Lewis, Karen G.** With or Without a Man: Taking Control of Your Life as a Single Woman. 2000. pap. 18.95 (*0-923521-50-X*) Bull Pub.

Lewis, Karen G., ed. Family Systems Application to Social Work: Training & Clinical Practice. LC 91-26307. (Journal of Independent Social Work). 217p. 1991. pap. text 19.95 (*1-56024-194-2*) Haworth Pr.

— Family Systems Application to Social Work: Training & Clinical Practice. LC 91-26307. (Journal of Independent Social Work). 217p. 1992. lib. bdg. 6.95 (*1-56024-191-8*) Haworth Pr.

Lewis, Karen G., intro. Variations on Teaching & Supervising Group Therapy. LC 89-19970. (Journal of Independent Social Work: Vol. 3, No. 4). (Illus.). 151p. 1989. text 29.95 (*0-86656-921-9*) Haworth Pr.

Lewis, Karen G., jt. ed. see Kahn, Michael D.

Lewis, Karoki, jt. auth. see Lewis, Charles.

Lewis, Karron G., ed. The TA Experience: Preparing for Multiple Roles: Selected Readings from the 3rd National Conference on the Training & Employment of Graduate Teaching Assistants. 448p. (Orig.). 1993. pap. 42.95 (*0-913507-55-5*) New Forums.

***Lewis, Katherine J.** The Cult of St. Katherine of Alexandria in Late Medieval England. 296p. 2000. 75.00 (*0-85115-773-4*) Boydell & Brewer.

Lewis, Katherine J., jt. ed. see Hansen, Everett M.

***Lewis, Kathleen.** Celebrate Life: New Attitudes for Living with Chronic Illness. LC 99-65981. 356p. 2000. pap. 12.95 (*0-912423-24-2*) Arthritis Found.

Lewis, Kathleen S. Prayer Without Ceasing: Breath Prayers. LC 97-69269. 1998. pap. text 8.99 (*0-933451-37-7*) Prescott Pr.

Lewis, Kathryn, ed. see Evans-Tiller, Jan.

Lewis, Kathryn E. Here Comes the Rain! Big Book. large type ed. (Little Books & Big Bks.). (Illus.). 8p. (J). (ps-1). 1998. pap. text 19.89 (*0-8215-0864-4*) Sadlier.

— The Yellow Yarn Mystery: Big Book. large type ed. (Little Books & Big Bks.). (Illus.). 8p. (J). (ps-1). 1998. pap. text 19.89 (*0-8215-0874-1*) Sadlier.

Lewis, Kathryn R., jt. auth. see Hefner, Christine R.

Lewis, Kathy. Chatty Cathy Dolls. LC 94-163213. 142p. 1994. pap. 15.95 (*0-89145-579-5*, 3810) Collector Bks.

Lewis, Kathy & Lewis, Don. Talking Toys of the 20th Century. 288p. 1999. pap. text 15.95 (*1-57432-125-0*) Collector Bks.

Lewis, Keeta D. Infants & Children with Prenatal Alcohol & Drug Exposure: A Guide to Identification & Intervention. LC 94-47669. 367p. 1995. pap. 44.95 (*0-9624814-2-4*) Sunrise River Pr.

Lewis, Keeta D., jt. auth. see Thomson, Helen.

Lewis, Keith & Housden, Matthew. Introduction to International Marketing. (Marketing in Action Ser.). 160p. 1998. pap. 30.00 (*0-7494-2246-7*) Kogan Page Ltd.

Lewis, Keith, jt. auth. see Fifield, Paul.

***Lewis, Ken.** Software Pricing for Profit & Growth in [Name of Continents]: Benchmarks & Best Practices for Competitive Licensing & Pricing, Vols. 1-3. 2nd ed. LC 99 208213. (Culpepper Surveys Ser.). 1998. write for info. (*1-58128-040-8*) Culpepper.

Lewis, Ken. Writing Stories: The Nuts & Bolts of Writing Fiction. 186p. (Orig.). (YA). 1996. pap. text. write for info. (*1-55059-133-9*) Detselig Ents.

Lewis, Ken & Culpepper & Associates Staff. Selling Software in the Global Market: Benchmarks & Guidelines for Success in International Markets. (Illus.). 340p. 1996. 695.00 (*1-58128-005-X*, ZR) Culpepper.

Lewis, Kenneth B. Steel Wire in America. 2nd ed. 1989. 30.00 (*0-685-26880-2*) Wire Assn Intl.

Lewis, Kenneth E. The American Frontier: An Archaeological Study of Settlement Pattern & Process. LC 83-19725. (Studies in Historical Archaeology). 1984. text 79.95 (*0-12-446560-9*) Acad Pr.

Lewis, Kenneth H. & Bass, Joe R. Fiber Optic Fundamentals. (ABC of the Telephone Ser.: Vol. 17). (Illus.). 120p. 1991. spiral bd. 28.95 (*1-56016-064-0*) ABC TeleTraining.

Lewis, Kenrich M. & Rethwisch, David G., eds. Catalyzed Direct Reactions of Silicon. LC 93-34294. (Studies in Organic Chemistry: No. 49). 664p. 1993. 323.00 (*0-444-81715-8*) Elsevier.

***Lewis, Keren.** Tarot. 1999. pap. 4.95 (*965-494-039-6*) Astrolog Pub.

Lewis, Keren. The Tarot of Love. (Little Big Book Ser.). (Illus.). 72p. 1998. pap. 4.95 (*965-494-055-8*) Astrolog Pub.

***Lewis, Kevin.** Chugga Chugga Choo Choo. LC 98-42101. (Illus.). 32p. (J). 1999. lib. bdg. 13.49 (*0-7868-2379-8*, Pub. by Disney Pr) Little.

— Chugga Chugga Choo Choo. LC 98-42101. (Illus.). 32p. (J). (ps-k). 1999. 12.99 (*0-7868-0429-7*, Pub. by Disney Pr) Time Warner.

— Creating Effective JavaHelp. Posner, John & Loukides, Mike, eds. 200p. 2000. pap. 29.95 (*1-56592-719-2*) OReilly & Assocs.

Lewis, Kevin. Crown House Collection Vol. 1: The Printed Calicos of Manchester. (Illus.). 70p. 1990. boxed set. write for info. (*1-872669-00-X*) Crown House.

L

An Asterisk (*) at the beginning of an entry indicates that the title is appearing for the first time.

— Crown House Collection Vol. 2: Fleurs de France, Weaves, Prints & Original Designs, 1860-1905. (Illus.). 85p. 1991. boxed set. write for info. (1-872669-01-8) Crown House.

Lewis, Kevin. My Truck is Stuck. LC 99-31527. 32p. (J). Date not set. lib. bdg. 13.49 (0-7868-2465-4, Pub. by Disney Pr) Little.

— My Truck Is Stuck. LC 99-31527. (Illus.). 32p. (J). 2000. write for info. (0-7868-0534-X) Hyprn Child.

Lewis, Kevin, jt. ed. see Aldridge, Marion D.

Lewis, Kevin M. Standards-Based Procurement. 31p. (Orig.). 1993. pap. 10.00 (0-936593-19-9) UniForum.

Lewis, Kevin N. Downsizing Future USAF Fighter Forces: Living Within the Constraints of History. LC 94-48047. 130p. 1995. pap. text 15.00 (0-8330-1621-0, MR-480-AF) Rand Corp.

— Planning Future U. S. Fighter Forces. LC 93-23131. 1993. pap. 15.00 (0-8330-1416-1, MR-285-AF) Rand Corp.

Lewis, Kim. Emma's Lamb. 2nd ed. LC 97-27248. (Illus.). 32p. (J). 1998. 15.99 (0-7636-0424-0) Candlewick Pr.

— First Snow. LC 92-54413. (Illus.). 32p. (J). (ps up). 1993. 14.95 (1-56402-194-7) Candlewick Pr.

— First Snow. LC 92-54413. 1996. 11.19 (0-606-10186-1, Pub. by Turtleback) Demco.

— First Snow. LC 92-54413. (Illus.). 32p. (J). (ps-3). 1996. reprint ed. pap. 5.99 (1-56402-963-8) Candlewick Pr.

— Floss. LC 91-71853. (Illus.). 32p. (J). (ps up). 1992. 14.95 (1-56402-010-X) Candlewick Pr.

— Floss. LC 91-71853. (Illus.). 32p. (J). (ps-3). 1994. pap. 5.99 (1-56402-271-4) Candlewick Pr.

— Friends. LC 97-7046. 32p. (J). (ps-1). 1998. 15.99 (0-7636-0346-5) Candlewick Pr.

***Lewis, Kim.** Just Like Floss. LC 98-4954. (Illus.). 32p. (J). (ps-1). 2000. pap. 5.99 (0-7636-1079-8) Candlewick Pr.

Lewis, Kim. Just Like Floss. LC 98-4954. (Illus.). 32p. (J). (ps-1). 1998. 15.99 (0-7636-0684-7) Candlewick Press.

Lewis, Kim. The Last Train. LC 93-32370. 1996. 11.19 (0-606-10249-3, Pub. by Turtleback) Demco.

Lewis, Kim. The Last Train. LC 93-32370. (Illus.). 32p. (J). (ps-2). 1996. reprint ed. pap. 5.99 (1-56402-969-7) Candlewick Pr.

— Little Calf. LC 99-28784. 24p. (J). 2000. 9.99 (0-7636-0899-8) Candlewick Pr.

— Little Lamb. LC 99-28786. 24p. (J). 2000. 9.99 (0-7636-0900-5) Candlewick Pr.

***Lewis, Kim.** Little Puppy. LC 99-34817. (Illus.). 24p. (J). 2000. 9.99 (0-7636-0901-3) Candlewick Pr.

Lewis, Kim. My Friend Harry. LC 94-38903. (Illus.). 32p. (J). (ps-3). 1995. 15.95 (1-56402-617-5) Candlewick Pr.

— My Friend Harry. LC 94-38903. (Illus.). 32p. (J). (ps-1). 1997. reprint ed. pap. 5.99 (0-7636-0285-X) Candlewick Pr.

— One Summer Day. LC 95-20580. (Illus.). 32p. (J). (ps up). 1996. 15.99 (1-56402-883-6) Candlewick Pr.

— One Summer Day. LC 95-20580. (Illus.). 32p. (J). (ps). 1998. pap. 5.99 (0-7636-0508-5) Candlewick Pr.

— The Shepherd Boy. LC 89-23679. (Illus.). 32p. (J). (ps-1). 1990. lib. bdg. 13.95 (0-02-758581-6, Four Winds Pr) S&S Childrens.

Lewis, Klara K. The Adventures of Mr. Lewis in Russia. (Illus.). 1995. pap. 9.95 (1-886821-28-3) Pavleen.

— Adventures of Mr. Lewis in Russia: A Ten Act Situational Play. (In the Shoes of the Traveler Ser.). (RUS., Illus.). (Orig.). 1995. pap. 9.95 (1-886821-08-9); pap. 16.95 incl. audio (1-886821-09-7); pap. text 9.95 (1-886821-21-6) Pavleen.

— Audio-Visual Russian, 7 bks. & 7 cass., Set. (ENG & RUS., Illus.). (Orig.). 1996. pap. 119.95 incl. audio (1-886821-22-4); pap. 59.95 (1-886821-23-2) Pavleen.

— In the Shoes of the Traveler. (In the Shoes of the Traveler Ser.). (RUS., Illus.). (Orig.). 1995. pap. 119.95 incl. audio (1-886821-15-1); pap. text 119.95 incl. audio (1-886821-16-X) Pavleen.

— In the Shoes of the Traveler: Russian Language, Culture, Way of Life, 7 bks., Set. (In the Shoes of the Traveler Ser.). (RUS., Illus.). (Orig.). 1995. pap. 59.95 (1-886821-14-3) Pavleen.

— In the Shoes of the Traveler, Situational Russian Pt. I: Meeting People, Packing & Customs, at a Hotel, Shopping, at a Restaurant, 2 bks. (In the Shoes of the Traveler Ser.). (RUS., Illus.). (Orig.). 1995. pap. 27.95 (1-886821-04-6); pap. 36.95 incl. audio (1-886821-05-4); pap. text 27.95 (1-886821-19-4) Pavleen.

— In the Shoes of the Traveler, Situational Russian Pt. II: In a City Using Transportation, at the Post Office, Talking on the Telephone, at a Bank, at a Doctor's Office, When Things Go Wrong, Visiting Russian Friends & Toasting. (In the Shoes of the Traveler Ser.). (RUS., Illus.). (Orig.). 1995. pap. 7.95 (1-886821-06-2); pap. 14.95 incl. audio (1-886821-07-0); pap. text 7.95 (1-886821-20-8) Pavleen.

— Russian Culture Keys. 2nd ed. (In the Shoes of the Traveler Ser.). 1995. audio 14.95 (1-886821-13-5) Pavleen.

— Russian Instant Help Cards. (ENG & RUS., Illus.). 1995. pap. 14.95 incl. audio (1-886821-31-3) Pavleen.

— Russian Instant Help Cards: Everyday Expressions, Frequently Asked Questions, Gratitude, Apology, Agreement, Refusal, Regret, Congratulations & Good Wishes, Requests, Wants & Needs, Compliments, Toasts. (In the Shoes of the Traveler Ser.). (RUS., Illus.). (Orig.). 1995. pap. 7.95 (1-886821-10-0); pap. 14.95 incl. audio (1-886821-11-9) Pavleen.

— Russian Picture Alphabet. (In the Shoes of the Traveler Ser.). (RUS., Illus.). (Orig.). 1995. pap. 9.95 (1-886821-00-3); pap. 16.95 incl. audio (1-886821-01-1); pap. 16.95 incl. audio (1-886821-24-0); pap. text 9.95 (1-886821-18-6) Pavleen.

— Russian Picture Dictionary. (ENG & RUS., Illus.). 1995. pap. 21.95 incl. audio (1-886821-25-9) Pavleen.

— Russian Picture Dictionary: Things Around Me, Colors, Numbers, Pronouns, Professions, Days of the Week, Family, Fruits, Vegetables, Groceries, Parts of the Body, Weather, Clothing, Living Room, Kitchen, Bedroom, Office, Questions, Animals, Verbs, Time, Etc. (In the Shoes of the Traveler Ser.). (RUS., Illus.). (Orig.). 1995. pap. 15.95 (1-886821-02-X); pap. 21.95 incl. audio (1-886821-03-8); pap. text 15.95 (1-886821-17-8) Pavleen.

— Russian Restaurant Menu. (ENG & RUS., Illus.). 1995. pap. 5.95 (1-886821-29-1) Pavleen.

— Russian Restaurant Menu: Food & Drink Guide for Breakfast, Lunch & Dinner. (In the Shoes of the Traveler Ser.). (RUS., Illus.). (Orig.). 1995. pap. 5.95 (1-886821-12-7) Pavleen.

— Situational Russian, 2 bks., Pt. 1. (ENG & RUS., Illus.). 1995. pap. 36.95 incl. audio (1-886821-26-7) Pavleen.

— Situational Russian, 2 bks., Pt. 2. (ENG & RUS., Illus.). 1995. pap. 36.95 incl. audio (1-886821-27-5) Pavleen.

Lewis, Kristen N. Roses Are Red, Violets Are Blue, I Beat Cancer, So Can You! (Illus.). 24p. (J). 1998. write for info. (0-9666212-0-4) Meeko Tin Pr.

Lewis, L. A. & Berry, L. African Environments & Resources. (Illus.). 352p. 1988. 49.95 (0-04-916010-9); pap. 19.95 (0-04-916011-7) Routledge.

Lewis, L. A. & Opplt, J. J., eds. Handbook of Electrophoresis, CRC, 3 vols., III. 400p. 1983. lib. bdg. 185.00 (0-8493-0573-X, CRC Reprint) Franklin.

— Handbook of Electrophoresis, CRC, 3 vols., IV. 344p. 1983. lib. bdg. 163.00 (0-8493-0574-8, CRC Reprint) Franklin.

— Handbook of Electrophoresis, CRC, 3 vols., Vol. 1: Basic Principles & Concepts. 336p. 1980. 182.00 (0-8493-0571-3, QD117, CRC Reprint) Franklin.

— Handbook of Electrophoresis, CRC, 3 vols., Vol. 2: Lipoproteins in Disease. 400p. 1980. 217.00 (0-8493-0572-1, CRC Reprint) Franklin.

Lewis, L. G., et al. Equivariant Stable Homotopy Theory. (Lecture Notes in Mathematics Ser.: Vol. 1213). ix, 538p. 1986. 73.95 (0-387-16820-6) Spr-Verlag.

Lewis, L. H., et al, eds. Advanced Hard & Soft Magnetic Materials Vol. 577: Materials Research Society Symposium Proceedings. LC 99-43779. 629p. 1999. text 80.00 (1-55899-485-8) Materials Res.

Lewis, Larry. The Misfit: Haunting of the Human, Unveiling the Divine. LC 96-51865. 150p. (Orig.). 1997. pap. 13.00 (1-57075-122-6) Orbis Bks.

Lewis, Larry, et al. The Sunfish Bible. (Illus.). 368p. (Orig.). 1996. pap. 24.95 (0-9654005-0-6) Omega Cubed.

Lewis, Larry L. Manual para Plantar Iglesias.Tr. of Church Planter's Handbook. (SPA.). 176p. 1997. pap. text 6.99 (0-311-13863-2) Casa Bautista.

— Organizar para Evangelizar - Manual para el Crecimiento de la Iglesia (Organize to Evangelize - A Manual for Church Growth) Smith, Josie H., tr. from ENG. (SPA.). 112p. (Orig.). 1992. pap. 6.50 (0-311-13857-8) Casa Bautista.

— Proclaiming the Pro-Life Message: Christian Leaders Address the Abortion Issue. 192p. 1997. pap. 10.95 (0-929292-84-7) Hannibal Bks.

Lewis, Laura. 52 Ways to Live a Long & Healthy Life. Moyer, Ann & Towle, Mike, eds. 300p. 1993. pap. 8.95 (1-56530-066-1) Summit TX.

— 52 Ways to Live a Long & Healthy Life. LC 97-75634. 240p. 1998. reprint ed. 6.98 (1-56731-242-X, MJF Bks) Fine Comms.

Lewis, Laurel, jt. auth. see Nestingen, Signe L.

Lewis, Laurie. Campus Crime & Security at Postsecondary Education Institutions. 108p. 1997. pap. 13.00 (0-16-063606-X) USGPO.

— Institutional Perspective on Students with Disabilities in Postsecondary Education. 80p. 1999. pap. 7.50 (0-16-050127-X) USGPO.

— Remedial Education at Higher Education Institutions in Fall 1995. 82p. 1996. pap. 10.00 (0-16-048915-6) USGPO.

— Teacher Quality: A Report on the Preparation & Qualifications of Public School Teachers. 266p. 1999. pap. text 22.00 (0-16-049931-3) USGPO.

— What to Charge: Pricing Strategies for Freelancers & Consultants. LC 99-75382. 180p. 1999. pap. 19.95 (1-929129-00-9) Aletheia.

Lewis, Laurie, et al. Campus Crime & Security at Postsecondary Education Institutions. (Illus.). 94p. (C). 1997. reprint ed. pap. text 30.00 (0-7881-4002-7) DIANE Pub.

Lewis, LaVaughn G., jt. ed. see Stedman, W. David.

Lewis, LeDene. The Black Person's Guide to Adult Education & Economic Empowerment. (Illus.). 44p. 1992. pap. 5.95 (0-913543-30-6) African Am Imag.

Lewis, Lee A. The Trouble with Dreams. LC 91-27503. (Illus.). 160p. (Orig.). (J). (gr. 3-7). 1991. pap. 5.99 (0-8361-3571-7) Herald Pr.

Lewis, Leland. The Baja Sea Guide. LC 85-173041. (Sea Guide Ser.). (Illus.). 368p. Date not set. reprint ed. 37.50 (0-688-04314-3) Hearst Marine Bks.

Lewis, Leonard C., jt. auth. see Eickhoff, Randy Lee.

Lewis, Leonard C., jt. auth. see Eickoff, Randy L.

Lewis, Lesle, ed. see Longacre, Celeste.

Lewis, Lesley. The Private Life of a Country House, 1912-1939. LC 98-112897. (Illus.). 146p. 1998. pap. 17.95 (0-7509-1678-8, Pub. by Sutton Pub Ltd) Intl Pubs Mktg.

— The Private Life of a Country House, 1912-1939. 2nd large type ed. (Illus.). 237p. 1993. 24.95 (1-85695-001-8, Pub. by ISIS Lrg Prnt) Transaction Pubs.

***Lewis, Leslie.** Improving Army Planning, Programming, Budgeting & Execution System (PPBES) The Planning Phase. LC 00-26298. 2000. write for info. (0-8330-2818-9) Rand Corp.

Lewis, Leslie. Joint Warfighting Capabilities (JWCA) Integration: Report on Phase 1 Research. LC 97-17961. (Illus.). 71p. 1998. pap. 10.00 (0-8330-2518-X, MR-872-JS) Rand Corp.

Lewis, Leslie, et al. Analytic Architecture for Joint Staff Decision Support Activities: Final Report. LC 95-52611. (Illus.). 58p. 1996. pap. 13.00 (0-8330-2335-7, MR-651-JS) Rand Corp.

— Defining a Common Planning Framework for the Air Force. LC 99-26298. (Illus.). 75p. 1999. pap. 10.00 (0-8330-2730-1, MR-1006-AF) Rand Corp.

— Improving Army PPBS: The Programming Phase. LC 98-47651. (Illus.). 98p. 1999. pap. text 15.00 (0-8330-2670-4, MR-934-A) Rand Corp.

— New-Concept Development: A Planning Approach for the 21st Century Air Force. LC 96-50342. (Illus.). 75p. 1997. pap. 13.00 (0-8330-2478-7, MR-815-AF) Rand Corp.

— The United States Special Operations Command Resource Management Process: An Application of the Strategy-to-Tasks Framework. LC 94-17803. 1994. pap. 15.00 (0-8330-1557-5, MR-445-A/SOCOM) Rand Corp.

Lewis, Leslie L., jt. auth. see Altenbernd, Lynn.

Lewis, Leslie N. Waiter, There's a Fly in My Soup! How to Make Megabucks Waiting Tables. (Illus.). 128p. 1997. pap. 8.95 (1-880808-05-6) Bookmark NY.

Lewis, Linda. Cinderella & the Texas Prince. 1998. per. 3.50 (0-373-52070-0, 1-52070-9) Silhouette.

— Le Cow-Boy et la Danseuse. (Horizon Ser.: No. 481). (FRE.). 1998. mass mkt. 3.50 (0-373-39481-0, 1-39481-6) Harlequin Bks.

— Cowboy Seeks Perfect Wife. 1997. per. 3.25 (0-373-19226-6, 1-19226-9) Silhouette.

— Dedicated to That Boy I Love. (Linda Story Ser.). 168p. (J). (gr. 7 up). 1990. mass mkt. 2.75 (0-671-68244-X, Archway) PB.

— Honeymoon Suite. 1995. per. 2.99 (0-373-19113-8, 1-19113-9) Silhouette.

— The Husband Hunt. (Romance Ser.). 1996. per. 3.25 (0-373-19135-9, 1-19135-2) Silhouette.

— Is There Life after Boys? 165p. (YA). (gr. 6 up). 1990. per. 2.95 (0-671-69559-2, Archway) PB.

— Pre-Teen Means Inbetween. MacDonald, Pat, ed. 160p. (Orig.). (J). (gr. 3-6). 1993. per. 2.99 (0-671-74535-2, Minstrel Bks) PB.

— Secret Agent Santa. (Yours Truly Ser.). 1998. per. 3.50 (0-373-52082-4, 1-52082-4) Silhouette.

— Two Young Two Go Four Boys. (J). (gr. 2-5). 1990. pap. 2.75 (0-671-69560-6, Archway) PB.

— Water's Edge: Women Who Push the Limits in Rowing, Kayaking & Canoeing. LC 92-4361. (Illus.). 288p. (Orig.). 1992. pap. 14.95 (1-878067-18-4) Seal Pr WA.

— We Hate Everything but Boys. (YA). (gr. 5 up). 1990. mass mkt. 2.99 (0-671-72225-5, Archway) PB.

Lewis, Linda, jt. auth. see Ewing, Patrick.

Lewis, Linda F. Sister Songs: A Poetic Voyage. 66p. 1994. pap. 10.00 (1-888077-00-X) Akosua Visions.

Lewis, Linda G. The Devil, Me, & Jerry Lee. LC 98-66365. (Illus.). 160p. 1998. 20.00 (1-56352-526-7) Longstreet.

Lewis, Linda L., jt. ed. see Dan, Alice J.

Lewis, Linda M. Elizabeth Barrett Browning's Spiritual Progress: Face to Face with God. LC 97-35039. 272p. 1998. 34.95 (0-8262-1146-1) U of Mo Pr.

— The Promethean Politics of Milton, Blake, & Shelley. (Illus.). 240p. (C). 1992. text 34.95 (0-8262-0805-3) U of Mo Pr.

Lewis, Lionel S. The Cold War & Academic Governance: The Lattimore Case at Johns Hopkins. LC 92-24053. (SUNY Series, Frontiers in Education). 318p. (C). 1993. text 64.50 (0-7914-1493-0); pap. text 21.95 (0-7914-1494-9) State U NY Pr.

— Cold War on Campus: A Study of the Politics of Organizational Control. 314p. 1987. 44.95 (0-88738-178-2) Transaction Pubs.

— Cold War on Campus: A Study of the Politics of Organizational Control. 358p. 1997. pap. text 24.95 (1-56000-898-9) Transaction Pubs.

— Marginal Worth: Teaching & the Academic Labor Market. 163p. 1996. text 34.95 (1-56000-263-8) Transaction Pubs.

— Scaling the Ivory Tower: Merit & Its Limits in Academic Careers. LC 75-11358. 256p. 1975. reprint ed. pap. 79.40 (0-608-04031-2, 206476700011) Bks Demand.

***Lewis, Lionel S.** When Power Corrupts: Academic Governing Boards in the Shadow of the Adelphi Case. LC 00-37389. 248p. 2000. 39.95 (0-7658-0031-4) Transaction Pubs.

Lewis, Lionel S., intro. Scaling the Ivory Tower: Merit & Its Limits in Academic Careers. LC 97-7926. (Foundations of Higher Education Ser.). 250p. 1997. pap. text 24.95 (1-56000-958-6) Transaction Pubs.

Lewis, Lionel S., jt. ed. see Kingston, Paul W.

***Lewis, Lis.** Singers First Aid Kit - Female Voice: Problem Solving for Serious Singers. (Illus.). 40p. 1998. pap. 19.95 (1-56922-183-9, 07-1120) Creat Cncpts.

— Singers First Aid Kit - Male Voice: Problem Solving for Serious Singers. (Illus.). 40p. 1998. pap. 19.95 (1-56922-195-2, 07-1121) Creat Cncpts.

Lewis, Lisa. Silent Treatment: Poems. LC 97-42971. (National Poetry Ser.). 80p. 1998. pap. 14.95 (0-14-058902-3) Viking Penguin.

— Special Diets for Special Kids: Understanding & Implementing Special Diets to Aid in the Treatment of Autism & Related Developmental Disorders. 252p. 1998. pap. 24.95 (1-885477-44-9) Fut Horizons.

— The Unbeliever. LC 94-10661. (Brittingham Prize in Poetry Ser.). 72p. (C). 1994. pap. 11.95 (0-299-14404-6); text 18.95 (0-299-14400-3) U of Wis Pr.

Lewis, Lisa & Lewis, Dallas. The Box. 32p. (J). (gr. 2-4). 1997. 13.95 (0-9634087-6-3); pap. 6.95 (0-9634087-7-1) Silly Billys Bks.

— The Last Book. 32p. (J). (gr. 2-4). 1997. 13.95 (0-9634087-4-7); pap. 6.95 (0-9634087-5-5) Silly Billys Bks.

Lewis, Lisa, jt. auth. see Lewis, Dallas.

Lewis, Lisa, ed. see Kipling, Rudyard.

Lewis, Lisa, ed. & intro. see Kipling, Rudyard.

Lewis, Lisa A. The Adoring Audience: Fan Culture & Popular Media. 272p. 1992. 49.95 (0-04-445572-0, A8162); pap. 15.95 (0-04-445573-9, A8187) Routledge.

— Gender Politics & MTV: Voicing the Difference. 1991. pap. 22.95 (0-87722-942-2) Temple U Pr.

Lewis, Lisa A., ed. The Adoring Audience: Fan Culture & Popular Media. LC 91-37332. 272p. (C). 1992. pap. 22.99 (0-415-07821-0, A8187) Routledge.

Lewis, Lisa M., jt. auth. see Lewis, Dallas.

Lewis, Lloyd. The Assassination of Lincoln: History & Myth. LC 94-560. xviii, 367p. 1994. pap. 15.95 (0-8032-7949-3, Bison Books) U of Nebr Pr.

— Captain Sam Grant, 1822-1861. 1991. pap. 13.95 (0-316-52348-8) Little.

— It Takes All Kinds. LC 70-117328. (Biography Index Reprint Ser.). 1977. 25.95 (0-8369-8020-4) Ayer.

— Sherman: Fighting Prophet. LC 93-11132. (Illus.). xxi, 720p. 1993. reprint ed. pap. 20.00 (0-8032-7945-0, Bison Books) U of Nebr Pr.

Lewis, Lloyd & Smith, Henry J. Oscar Wilde Discovers America, 1882. LC 67-12459. (Illus.). 1972. reprint ed. 24.95 (0-405-08746-2) Ayer.

Lewis, Lloyd B. The Tainted War: Culture & Identity in Vietnam War Narratives, 44. LC 84-27926. (Contributions in Military History Ser.: No. 44). 193p. 1985. 52.95 (0-313-23723-9, LVW/, Greenwood Pr) Greenwood.

Lewis, Lloyd D. The Virginian Era. (Illus.). 60p. 1996. pap. 14.95 (0-9622003-9-5) TLC VA.

Lewis, Loel, ed. Bluestones & Salt Hay: An Anthology of New Jersey Poets. LC 89-36067. 210p. (Orig.). 1990. pap. 13.95 (0-8135-1486-X); text 35.00 (0-8135-1485-1) Rutgers U Pr.

Lewis, Loida N. How the Filipino Veteran of World War II Can Become a U. S. Citizen (According to the Immigration Act of 1990) LC 91-72022. 155p. 1991. pap. 19.95 (0-9629516-0-9) FR Pubns.

— One Hundred One Legal Ways to Stay in the U. S. A.: or How to Get a Green Card According to the Immigration Act of 1990, Bk. 1. Wiley, Elliott et al, eds. LC 91-77185. 222p. (Orig.). 1994. 29.95 (1-880808-01-3) Bookmark NY.

— One Hundred One Legal Ways to Stay in the U. S. A.: or How to Get a Green Card According to the Immigration Act of 1990, Bk. 1. Eakin, Sybil et al, eds. LC 91-77185. 308p. (Orig.). 1992. pap. 19.95 (1-880808-00-5) Bookmark NY.

Lewis, Lois F. Carlin School, A History Book: The Story of a School in Ravenna, Ohio, U. S. A. (Illus.). 28p. (Orig.). (J). (gr. 5). 1989. pap. text. write for info. (0-9620136-3-3) L F Lewis.

— Tappan School, a History Book: The Story of a School in Ravenna, Ohio, U. S. A. (Illus.). 28p. (Orig.). (J). (gr. 5). 1989. pap. text. write for info. (0-9620136-1-7) L F Lewis.

— West Main School, a History Book: The Story of a School in Ravenna, Ohio, U. S. A. (Illus.). (Orig.). (J). (gr. 5). 1988. pap. text 2.00 (0-9620136-0-9) L F Lewis.

Lewis, Lon D. Equine Clinical Nutrition. (Illus.). 650p. 1995. 105.00 (0-683-04962-3) Lppncott W & W.

— Feeding & Care of the Horse. 2nd ed. LC 94-18096. (Illus.). 446p. 1996. 29.95 (0-683-04967-4) Lppncott W & W.

Lewis, Lon D., et al. Alimentation Clinique des Petits Animoux, No. III. 3rd ed. Moreau, Philippe, tr. from ENG. (Illus.). 470p. (C). 1989. 18.00 (0-945837-00-3) M Morris Assocs.

— Feeding Dogs & Cats. rev. ed. 61p. (C). 1989. pap. text 1.50 (0-945837-01-1) M Morris Assocs.

— Guide to Dietary Management of Small Animals. rev. ed. 37p. (C). 1989. pap. text 1.50 (0-945837-02-X) M Morris Assocs.

Lewis, Lorene, jt. auth. see Lewis, Merrill.

Lewis, Lorrie. In Our Weakness. 96p. 1991. pap. 5.00 (1-878110-00-4) Abundant Answers.

Lewis, Lorrie, jt. auth. see Lewis, Jim.

Lewis, Lucinda. Porsche: Fine Art of the Sports Car. rev. ed. LC 97-29136. (Illus.). 312p. 1997. 39.98 (1-57145-135-8, Thunder Bay) Advantage Pubs.

***Lewis, Lucinda.** Roadside America: The Automobile & the American Dream. LC 00-21034. (Illus.). 271p. 2000. 49.50 (0-8109-4434-0, Pub. by Abrams) Time Warner.

Lewis, Lucius L. A Better Way of Taking Care of You. rev. ed. (Illus.). 55p. 1997. pap. write for info. (0-9653264-3-8, 1002) Noisemaker Pub.

***Lewis, Lundy.** Service Level Management for Enterprise Networks. LC 99-41775. (Telecommunications Library). 307p. 1999. 75.00 (1-58053-016-8) Artech Hse.

Lewis, LuVerne W., jt. auth. see McConnell, Edwina A.

Lewis, Lynette & Ross, Michael. A Select Body: The Gay Dance Party Subculture & the HIV/AIDS Pandemic. (AIDS Awareness Ser.). 256p. 1997. 69.95 (0-304-33510-X) Continuum.

— A Select Body: The Gay Dance Party Subculture & the HIV/AIDS Pandemic. (AIDS Awareness Ser.). 256p. 1997. pap. 21.95 (0-304-33511-8) Continuum.

Lewis, Lynne E., ed. see Akutagawa, Donald & Whitman, Terry.

An Asterisk (*) at the beginning of an entry indicates that the title is appearing for the first time.

Lewis, Lynne E., ed. see Black, Joanne C.

Lewis, Lynne E., ed. see Farebee, Gideon, Jr.

Lewis, Lynne E., ed. see Froelich, Craig.

Lewis, Lynne E., ed. see Kruger, Fred J.

Lewis, Lynne E., ed. see Price, R. N.

Lewis, Lynne E., ed. & intro. see Bolen, Steven J.

Lewis, M. Hay Esperanza-Padres Que Sufren (Hope for the Hurting Parent) (SPA.). 1.79 (*0-685-74943-6*, 497414) Editorial Unilit.

Lewis, M. & Feinman, S. Social Influences & Socialization in Infancy. LC 90-14308. (Genesis of Behavior Ser.: Vol. 6). (Illus.). 358p. (C). 1990. 70.00 (*0-306-43632-9*, Plenum Trade) Perseus Pubng.

Lewis, M. & Miller, S., eds. Handbook of Developmental Psychopathology. LC 89-23243. (Illus.). 556p. (C). 1990. 90.00 (*0-306-43190-4*, Plenum Trade) Perseus Pubng.

Lewis, M. & Saarni, C. The Socialization of Emotions. (Genesis of Behavior Ser.: Vol. 5). (Illus.). 334p. (C). 1985. 75.00 (*0-306-41851-7*, Plenum Trade) Perseus Pubng.

Lewis, M., et al. Crystal Structure Analysis for Chemists & Biologists. (Methods in Stereochemical Analysis Ser.). 872p. 1994. 98.95 (*0-471-18543-4*) Wiley.

***Lewis, M. A.** Bloody Bones in the Basement. 1999. pap. 9.95 (*1-55517-434-5*) CFI Dist.

Lewis, M. A. Stock Assessment of Anadromous Salmonids, 1994. (Illus.). 120p. 1997. reprint ed. 18.00 (*0-89904-686-X*, Cascade Geog Soc); reprint ed. pap. 13.00 (*0-89904-687-8*, Cascade Geog Soc) Crumb Elbow Pub.

— Stock Assessment of Salmonids, 1996. (Illus.). 76p. 1998. reprint ed. 13.60 (*0-89904-857-9*, Cascade Geog Soc); reprint ed. pap. 8.60 (*0-89904-858-7*, Cascade Geog Soc) Crumb Elbow Pub.

Lewis, M. E. Thematic Methods & Strategies in Learning Disabilities: A Textbook for Practitioners. LC 92-42082. (Illus.). 212p. (Orig.). (C). 1993. pap. 34.95 (*1-879105-95-0*, 0353) Thomson Learn.

Lewis, M. E., jt. ed. see Sharif, N. A.

Lewis, M. H., ed. Glasses & Glass-Ceramics. 416p. (gr. 13). 1989. text 104.95 (*0-412-27690-9*) Chapman & Hall.

Lewis, M. J. Millstone & Hammer: The Origins of Water Power. 200p. 1998. pap. 25.00 (*0-85958-657-X*, Pub. by Univ of Hull Pr) Paul & Co Pubs.

***Lewis, M. J. & Heppell, N. J.** Continuous Thermal Processing of Foods: Pasteurization & UHT Sterilization. LC 00-40601. (Food Engineering Ser.). 2000. write for info. (*0-8342-1259-5*) Aspen Pub.

Lewis, M. J. & Lloyd-Jones, Roger. Using Computers in History: A Practical Guide. LC 95-20050. (Illus.). 264p. (C). 1996. 85.00 (*0-415-10311-8*); pap. 25.99 (*0-415-10312-6*) Routledge.

Lewis, M. J., jt. auth. see Lloyd-Jones, Roger.

Lewis, M. J., jt. ed. see Grandison, A. S.

Lewis, M. K. & Lewis, Rosemary R. Your Film Acting Career: How to Break into the Movies & TV & Survive in Hollywood. 4th rev. ed. LC 97-94182. (Illus.). 320p. 1998. pap. 17.95 (*0-929149-02-5*, SAN 249-8960) Gorham Hse.

Lewis, M. Paul, jt. ed. see Kindell, Gloria.

Lewis, Madeline D., jt. auth. see Lewis, Thomas L.

Lewis, Madeline D., jt. auth. see Lewis, Thomas M.

Lewis, Madeline K., jt. auth. see Lewis, Thomas M.

Lewis, Magda. Rewriting the Gender Curriculum. Kincheloe, Joe & Steinberg, Shirley R., eds. (Critical Education Practice Ser.). 200p. Date not set. text 30.00 (*0-8153-1185-0*) Garland.

Lewis, Maggie. Morgy Makes His Move. LC 98-43245. (Illus.). 80p. (J). (gr. 1-4). 1999. 15.00 (*0-395-92284-4*) HM.

Lewis, Malcolm J. & Shah, Ajay M., eds. Endothelial Modulation of Cardiac Function. (Endothelial Cell Research Ser.: Vol. 2). 268p. 1997. text 62.00 (*90-5702-120-X*, Harwood Acad Pubs) Gordon & Breach.

Lewis, Marc. Jazz Trumpet Duets. 56p. 1996. pap. 8.95 (*0-7935-6396-8*) H Leonard.

***Lewis, Marc D. & Granic, Isabela, eds.** Emotion, Development & Self-Organization: Dynamic Systems Approaches to Emotional Development. LC 99-48061. (Studies in Social & Emotional Development). (Illus.). 448p. (C). 2000. 64.95 (*0-521-64089-X*) Cambridge U Pr.

Lewis, Marcia. The Private Lives of the Three Tenors. (Illus.). 224p. 1996. 21.95 (*1-55972-363-7*, Birch Ln Pr) Carol Pub Group.

— The Private Lives of the Three Tenors: Behind the Scenes with Placido Domingo, Luciano Pavarotti, & Jose Carreras. 1998. mass mkt. 6.99 (*1-57297-332-3*) Blvd Books.

Lewis, Marcia A. & Tamparo, Carol A. Medical Law, Ethics, & Bioethics for Ambulatory Health Care. 4th ed. LC 97-50565. (Illus.). 295p. (C). 1998. pap. text 22.95 (*0-8036-0348-7*) Davis Co.

Lewis, Marcia A., jt. auth. see Tamparo, Carol D.

Lewis, Margaret. Edith Pargeter: Ellis Peters. (Illus.). 156p. 1994. 30.00 (*1-85411-128-0*, Pub. by Seren Bks) Dufour.

— Edith Pargeter: Ellis Peters. 150p. 1995. pap. 15.95 (*1-85411-129-9*, Pub. by Seren Bks) Dufour.

— Edith Pargeter: Ellis Peters. large type ed. 232p. 1997. text 25.95 (*1-85089-255-5*, Pub. by ISIS Lrg Prnt) Transaction Pubs.

— Ngaio Marsh: A Life. 1995. 20.00 (*1-883402-86-7*) S&S Trade.

— Ngaio Marsh: A Life. 275p. 1998. reprint ed. 24.95 (*1-890208-05-1*) Poisoned Pen.

— Ngaio Marsh: A Life. 2nd large type ed. 448p. 1993. 24.95 (*1-85089-327-6*, Pub. by ISIS Lrg Prnt) Transaction Pubs.

Lewis, Margaret, et al, contrib. by. Wild Discovery Guide to Your Cat: Understanding & Caring for the Tiger Within. LC 99-31017. (Illus.). 224p. 1999. 24.95 (*1-56331-804-0*) Discovery.

***Lewis, Margaret, et al, contrib. by.** Wild Discovery Guide to Your Dog: Understanding & Caring for the Wolf Within. LC 99-31016. (Illus.). 224p. 1999. 24.95 (*1-56331-805-9*) Discovery.

Lewis, Margaret, jt. ed. see Peterson, Janice.

Lewis, Margie M. Hay Esperanza para los Padres Que Sufren. (Serie Enfoque a la Familia - Focus on the Family Ser.).Tr. of Hope for the Hurting Parent. (SPA.). 1991. 1.99 (*1-56063-057-4*, 497414) Editorial Unilit.

Lewis, Margie M. & Lewis, Gregg. The Hurting Parent. 160p. (Orig.). 1980. pap. 7.95 (*0-310-41731-7*, 11222P) Zondervan.

Lewis, Margo, jt. auth. see Lewis, Herschell Gordon.

Lewis, Marguerite. Hooked on Reading! LC 86-2629. 248p. 1986. pap. text 27.95 (*0-87628-406-3*) Ctr Appl Res.

— Hooked on the Caldecott Award Winners! 60 Crossword Puzzles Based on the Caldecott Gold Medal.. (Illus.). 112p. (gr. 4-7). 1997. pap. text 6.95 (*0-87628-424-1*) Ctr Appl Res.

— Hooked on the Newbery Award Winners: 75 Wordsearch Puzzles Based on the Newbery Gold Medal Books. (Illus.). 144p. (C). (gr. 4-7). 1996. pap. text 6.95 (*0-87628-398-9*) P-H.

— Randolph Caldecott: The Children's Illustrator. (Illus.). 48p. (J). (gr. 2-7). 1992. pap. 4.95 (*0-913853-22-4*, 32533, Alleyside) Highsmith Pr.

Lewis, Marguerite & Kudla, Pamela J. Hooked on Independent Study: A Programmed Approach to Library Skills for Grades 3-8. 256p. 1989. pap. text 18.95 (*0-87628-405-5*) Ctr Appl Res.

— Hooked on Library Skills: A Sequential Activities Program for Grades K - 6. 328p. 1988. pap. text 27.95 (*0-87628-408-X*) Ctr Appl Res.

Lewis, Maria C., tr. see Sargent, Dennis J., et al.

Lewis, Marilyn. Using Student-Centered Methods with Teacher-Centered ESL Students. 112p. 1996. pap. 16.00 (*0-88751-068-X*, Pub. by Dominie Pr Ltd) Alemany Pr.

Lewis, Marilyn, ed. New Ways in Teaching Adults. LC 96-61905. 266p. 1997. pap. 24.95 (*0-939791-68-4*) Tchrs Eng Spkrs.

Lewis, Marilyn Jaye. Neptune & Surf. 1999. pap. text 12.95 (*1-58419-001-9*) Masq Bks.

Lewis, Marion T. D. The Law School Rules: 115 Survival Strategies to Make the Challenges of Law School Seem Like "Small Stuff" LC 99-30266. 144p. 1999. 14.00 (*0-609-60528-3*) Harmony Bks.

Lewis, Marjorie & Lewis, Gregg. The Hurting Parent. rev. ed. 176p. (Orig.). 1988. reprint ed. pap. 10.99 (*0-310-41631-0*, 11224P) Zondervan.

Lewis, Mark. Birding in the San Juan Islands. LC 87-23997. (Illus.). 224p. (Orig.). 1996. pap. 10.95 (*0-89886-133-0*) Mountaineers.

— Casino Comics. LC 97-73566. 192p. 1997. pap. 6.99 (*0-914839-41-1*) Gollehon Pr.

— Forty-Five Programs for the TRS-80 Model 4 Computer. 96p. 1984. 8.95 (*0-86668-040-3*) ARCsoft.

— The Rough Guide to Singapore: The Gateway to Asia, Now in a New Rough Guide Edition. 2nd ed. (Illus.). 256p. 1998. pap. 14.95 (*1-85828-237-3*) Viking Penguin.

Lewis, Mark, jt. auth. see Dodd, Jan.

Lewis, Mark, jt. auth. see Frank, Jacob.

Lewis, Mark, jt. auth. see Rowley, Chris.

Lewis, Mark, jt. ed. see Rowley, Chris.

Lewis, Mark E. Sanctioned Violence in Early China. LC 88-37052. (SUNY Series in Chinese Philosophy & Culture). 374p. (C). 1989. pap. text 24.95 (*0-7914-0077-8*) State U NY Pr.

Lewis, Mark Edward. Writing & Authority in Early China. LC 98-43852. (SUNY Series in Chinese Philosophy & Culture). 544p. (C). 1999. pap. text 31.95 (*0-7914-4114-8*) State U NY Pr.

— Writing & Authority in Early China. LC 98-43852. (SUNY Series in Chinese Philosophy & Culture). 512p. (C). 1999. text 92.50 (*0-7914-4113-X*) State U NY Pr.

Lewis, Marla, jt. auth. see Falletta, Bernadette.

***Lewis, Marlyn, et al, eds.** The Ancestry of Elizabeth of York, 3 vols. LC 98-87887. 1600p. 1998. 139.95 (*1-892977-05-2*, 05-2) H T Commun.

Lewis, Martha W. The Official Priests of Rome under the Julio-Claudians: A Study of the Nobility from 44 B. C. to 68 A. D. LC 56-2111. (American Academy in Rome. Papers & Monographs: Vol. 16). 192p. pap. 59.60 (*0-608-16481-X*, 202673000051) Bks Demand.

Lewis, Martin. A-Z of Cars of the '80s. (Illus.). 160p. 1998. pap. 19.95 (*1-901432-10-6*, Bay View Bks) MBI Pubg.

***Lewis, Martin G.** Hearts of Elephants & Men: And Other Stories of Africa. 2nd ed. (Illus.). 160p. 1999. reprint ed. pap. 14.95 (*1-884707-88-2*) Lifestyles.

Lewis, Martin G. & Rowden, Geoffrey. Histopathology: A Step-by-Step-Approach. 250p. 1984. 40.95 (*0-316-52340-2*, Little Brwn Med Div) Lppncott W & W.

Lewis, Martin G., et al. Appleton & Lange's Review of General Pathology. 3rd ed. (Illus.) 197p. (C). 1995. pap. text 34.95 (*0-8385-0161-3*, A0161-8, Apple Lange Med) McGraw.

Lewis, Martin W. Green Delusions: An Environmentalist Critique of Radical Environmentalism. LC 92-5671. 298p. 1992. text 49.95 (*0-8223-1257-3*) Duke.

— Green Delusions: An Environmentalist Critique of Radical Environmentalism. LC 92-5671. 304p. 1994. pap. 16.95 (*0-8223-1474-6*) Duke.

— Wagering the Land: Ritual, Capital, & Environmental Degradation in the Cordillera of Northern Luzon, 1900-1986. LC 91-12307. (C). 1992. 48.00 (*0-520-07272-3*, Pub. by U CA Pr) Cal Prin Full Svc.

Lewis, Martin W. & Wigen, Karen. The Myth of Continents: A Critique of Metageography. LC 96-30294. (Illus.). 383p. 1997. 55.00 (*0-520-20742-4*, Pub. by U CA Pr); pap. 19.95 (*0-520-20743-2*, Pub. by U CA Pr) Cal Prin Full Svc.

Lewis, Martina E. Easy English: A Quick, Easy Guide to Standard English Usage. 110p. (Orig.). 1987. pap. 8.95 (*0-933109-00-8*) Probata Pr.

— Videodiscs for English Classes: Classroom Applications of Videodisc Technology: Secondary English. 120p. (Orig.). 1989. pap. text 26.95 (*0-933109-02-4*) Probata Pr.

Lewis, Marty & Moynier, John. Mammoth Area Rock Climbs. 2nd rev. ed. (Eastern Sierra Climbing Guides Ser.: Vol. 2). (Illus.). 96p. 1996. pap. 12.00 (*0-9676116-3-6*) Maximus Pr.

***Lewis, Martyn.** Owens River Gorge Climbs. 9th rev. ed. (Eastern Sierra Climbing Guides Ser.: Vol. 1). (Illus.). 134p. 2000. pap. 19.00 (*0-9676116-2-8*) Maximus Pr.

Lewis, Martyn, jt. auth. see Moynier, John.

Lewis, Marvin. From This High Hill. LC 94-34648. 228p. 1994. pap. 6.49 (*0-89084-786-X*, 082529) Bob Jones Univ.

Lewis, Marvin A. Afro-Argentine Discourse: Another Dimension of the Black Diaspora. 164p. (C). 1995. text 34.95 (*0-8262-1042-2*) U of Mo Pr.

— Ethnicity & Identity in Contemporary Afro-Venezuelan Literature: A Culturalist Approach. 136p. (C). 1992. text 24.95 (*0-8262-0840-1*) U of Mo Pr.

— From Lima to Leticia: The Peruvian Novels of Mario Vargas Llosa. LC 83-1057. 182p. (Orig.). (C). 1983. pap. text 23.00 (*0-8191-3050-8*); lib. bdg. 52.00 (*0-8191-3049-4*) U Pr of Amer.

— Treading the Ebony Path: Ideology & Violence in Contemporary Afro-Colombian Prose Fiction. LC 86-30901. 152p. 1988. text 24.95 (*0-8262-0638-7*) U of Mo Pr.

Lewis, Marvin E. & Sadoff, Robert L. Psychic Injuries, 3 vols., Vols. 12, 12a & 12b. (Courtroom Medicine Ser.). 1975. 580.00 (*0-8205-1256-7*) Bender.

Lewis, Mary. Antonio Gardano, Venetian Music Printer, 1538-1569, Vol. 3. (Music Reference Ser.). 1997. text 117.00 (*0-8240-8456-X*) Garland.

— Rewriting the Gender Curriculum. Kincheloe, Joe & Steinberg, Shirley R., eds. 200p. Date not set. pap. text 18.95 (*0-8153-2315-8*) Garland.

Lewis, Mary, ed. The Buglhat Motet Anthologies: Selections from Liber Cantus (Vocum Quatuor) Triginta Novem Motetos Habet. LC 95-5755. (Sixteenth-Century Motet Ser.: No. 14). 392p. 1995. text 116.00 (*0-8240-7914-0*) Garland.

— The Gardane Motet Anthologies: Selections from Parimus Liber Cum Quatuor Vocibus. Mottetti Del Frutto a Quatro (Venice, 1539) LC 93-36477. (Sixteenth-Century Motet Ser.: No. 13). 312p. 1994. text 99.00 (*0-8240-7913-2*) Garland.

Lewis, Mary, jt. auth. see Staf, Edie.

Lewis, Mary C. Herstory: Black Female Rites of Passage. (Illus.). 138p. 1988. pap. 10.95 (*0-913543-08-X*) African Am Imag.

Lewis, Mary E. The Layperson's Prophecy Handbook for Everyday Use: The Revelation of Jesus Christ & Seventy Weeks of Daniel. LC 94-77966. (Illus.). 193p. (Orig.). 1994. pap. text 17.95 (*0-9642873-0-7*) Lewis Pubng.

Lewis, Mary H. An Adventure with Children. Provenzo, Eugene F., Jr. & Provenzo, Therese M., eds. LC 85-15821. (Illus.). 124p. 1985. reprint ed. lib. bdg. 52.00 (*0-8191-4911-X*) U Pr of Amer.

Lewis, Mary L. Love Lives Here, Vol. 2. (Illus.). 98p. 1988. pap. 6.50 (*1-56770-185-X*) S Scheewe Pubns.

— Love Lives Here, Vol. 3. 100p. 1988. pap. text 6.50 (*1-56770-195-7*) S Scheewe Pubns.

Lewis, Mary S. Antonio Gardano, Venetian Music Printer, 1538-1569 Vol. 2: A Descriptive Bibliography & Historical Study, 1550-1559. LC 87-21202. (Music Reference Ser.: Vol. 2). 564p. 1997. text 132.00 (*0-8240-8455-1*) Garland.

— Antonio Gardano, Venetian Music Printer, 1538-1569 Vol. 2: A Descriptive Bibliography & Historical Study 1550-1559. Date not set. 120.00 (*0-8240-8457-8*) Garland.

***Lewis, Mary T.** Cezanne. 2000. pap. 19.95 (*0-7148-3515-3*) Phaidon Pr.

Lewis, Mary T. Cezanne's Early Imagery. 300p. (C). 1989. 55.00 (*0-520-06561-1*, Pub. by U CA Pr) Cal Prin Full Svc.

— Cezanne's Early Imagery. 1992. pap. 24.95 (*0-520-06563-8*, Pub. by U CA Pr) Cal Prin Full Svc.

Lewis, Mason. Instant Computer-Business Kit: Turn Any Home-Computer into a Cash-Spewing Machine - 51 Fool-Proof Ways. 128p. (Orig.). 1997. pap. 36.95 (*1-891039-00-8*) Kipp Pub.

Lewis, Matthew. Animaniacs in Sir Yaksalot & the Dragon. (Illus.). 96p. (J). (gr. 4-7). 1996. pap. text 3.99 (*0-590-53531-5*) Scholastic Inc.

— Journal of a West India Proprietor. Terry, Judith, ed. LC 98-31282. (Oxford World's Classics Ser.). (Illus.). 252p. 1999. pap. 12.95 (*0-19-283261-1*) OUP.

— The Monk. 1999. pap. 5.95 (*0-451-52577-9*, Sig Classics) NAL.

— The Monk. Anderson, Howard, ed. (Oxford World's Classics Ser.). 496p. 1998. pap. 8.95 (*0-19-283394-4*) OUP.

— Monk. LC 99-236098. 384p. 1999. pap. 9.95 (*0-14-043603-0*) Viking Penguin.

Lewis, Matthew G. Bravo of Venice, A Romance. LC 74-131327. (Gothic Novels Ser.). 1974. reprint ed. 51.95 (*0-405-00807-4*) Ayer.

— Journal of a West India Proprietor, Kept During a Residence in the Island of Jamaica. LC 74-89041. 408p. 1970. reprint ed. lib. bdg. 35.00 (*0-8371-1845-X*, LEJ&) Greenwood.

— The Monk. LC 92-38487. 368p. 1970. pap. 12.95 (*0-8021-5107-8*, Grove) Grove-Atltic.

Lewis, Matthew G., et al. Pelissier's Columbian Melodies: Music for the New York & Philadelphia Theaters. Kroeger, Karl, ed. (Recent Researches in American Music Ser.: No. RRAM13-14). (Illus.). 178, xxviiip. 1984. pap. 65.00 (*0-89579-199-4*) A-R Eds.

Lewis, Maureen, jt. auth. see Wray, David.

Lewis, Maurice. Electrical Installation Pt. 1: Theory & Practice; Studies. (Revision & Self Assessment Ser.). 228p. 1997. pap. text 23.95 (*0-340-67665-5*, TK3271, Pub. by Cassell) LPC InBook.

— Electrical Installation Guide. LC 98-118067. (Newnes Practitioner Ser.). (Illus.). 96p. 1997. spiral bd. 36.95 (*0-7506-3139-2*, Newnes) Buttrwrth-Heinemann.

— Electrical Installation Technology Pt. 1: Theory & Regulations. 3rd rev. ed. 168p. (C). 1992. pap. 35.00 (*0-7487-1542-8*, Pub. by S Thornes Pubs) Trans-Atl Phila.

***Lewis, Maxine.** Medicare Rules & Regulations 2000: A Survival Guide to Policies, Procedures & Payment Reform. annuals rev. ed. (Illus.). 404p. 2000. pap. text Price not set. (*1-57066-148-0*, 20043) Practice Mgmt Info.

Lewis, Maxine & Davison, Jan. Working with Insurance & Managed Care Plans. 2nd ed. LC 99-10591. (Illus.). 400p. 1999. pap. 49.95 (*1-57066-131-6*, ME125) Practice Mgmt Info.

Lewis, Maxine, jt. auth. see Davis, James B.

Lewis, Maxine, jt. auth. see Davison, Jan.

Lewis, Maybury D. Millennium. 1999. pap. 15.00 (*0-14-012432-2*, Viking) Viking Penguin.

Lewis, Maynah. The Other Side of Paradise. large type ed. 288p. 1985. 27.99 (*0-7089-1379-2*) Ulverscroft.

***Lewis-McCormick, Irene.** Aquatic Exercise. American Council on Exercise Staff, ed. (Illus.). 75p. 2000. 14.95 (*1-890720-06-2*) Am Coun Exer.

Lewis, Melanie, jt. auth. see Marek, Edmund A.

Lewis, Melvin. Child & Adolescent Psychiatry: A Comprehensive Textbook. (Illus.). 1318p. 1991. 139.00 (*0-683-04954-2*) Lppncott W & W.

— Child & Adolescent Psychiatry: A Comprehensive Textbook. 2nd ed. LC 95-23168. (Illus.). 1532p. 1996. 149.00 (*0-683-04955-0*) Lppncott W & W.

Lewis, Melvin & Volkmar, Fred R. Clinical Aspects of Child & Adolescent Development: An Introductory Synthesis of Developmental Concepts & Clinical Experience. 3rd ed. LC 89-7955. (Illus.). 475p. 1990. text 49.00 (*0-8121-1218-0*) Lppncott W & W.

Lewis, Meriwether & Clark, William. The History of the Lewis & Clark Expedition, 3 vols., 1. Coues, Elliot, ed. (Illus.). 1508p. 1979. pap. 10.95 (*0-486-21268-8*) Dover.

— The History of the Lewis & Clark Expedition, 3 vols., 2. 2nd ed. Coues, Elliot, ed. (Illus.). 1508p. 1979. pap. 10.95 (*0-486-21269-6*) Dover.

— The History of the Lewis & Clark Expedition, 3 vols., 3. 3rd ed. Coues, Elliot, ed. (Illus.). 1508p. 1979. pap. 10.95 (*0-486-21270-X*) Dover.

— Journals of Lewis & Clark: A New Selection. Bakeless, John, ed. (Orig.). 1964. mass mkt. 6.99 (*0-451-62670-2*, Ment) NAL.

— Journals of Lewis & Clark Expedition Vol. 10: The Journal of Patrick Gass, May 14, 1804-September 23, 1806. Moulton, Gary, ed. LC 82-8510. xxix, 300p. 1996. text 75.00 (*0-8032-2916-X*) U of Nebr Pr.

— The Journals of the Lewis & Clark Expedition Vol. 1: Atlas of the Lewis & Clark Expedition. Moulton, Gary E., ed. LC 82-675167. (Illus.). 192p. 1999. text 150.00 (*0-8032-2861-9*) U of Nebr Pr.

— The Journals of the Lewis & Clark Expedition Vol. 2: August 30, 1803-August 24, 1804. Moulton, Gary E., ed. LC 82-8510. (Illus.). x, 612p. 1986. text 75.00 (*0-8032-2869-4*) U of Nebr Pr.

— The Journals of the Lewis & Clark Expedition Vol. 3: August 25, 1804-April 6, 1805. Moulton, Gary E., ed. LC 82-8510. (Illus.). ix, 544p. 1987. text 75.00 (*0-8032-2875-9*) U of Nebr Pr.

— The Journals of the Lewis & Clark Expedition Vol. 4: April 7-July 27, 1805. Moulton, Gary E., ed. LC 82-8510. (Illus.). ix, 464p. 1987. text 75.00 (*0-8032-2877-5*) U of Nebr Pr.

— The Journals of the Lewis & Clark Expedition Vol. 5: July 28-November 1, 1805. Moulton, Gary E., ed. LC 82-8510. (Illus.). xii, 415p. 1988. text 75.00 (*0-8032-2883-X*) U of Nebr Pr.

— The Journals of the Lewis & Clark Expedition Vol. 6: November 2, 1805-March 22, 1806. Moulton, Gary E., ed. LC 82-8510. (Illus.). xii, 531p. 1990. text 75.00 (*0-8032-2893-7*) U of Nebr Pr.

— The Journals of the Lewis & Clark Expedition Vol. 7: March 23-June 9, 1806, Vol. 7. Moulton, Gary E., ed. LC 82-8510. (Illus.). x, 383p. 1991. text 75.00 (*0-8032-2898-8*) U of Nebr Pr.

— The Journals of the Lewis & Clark Expedition Vol. 8: June 10-September 26, 1806. Moulton, Gary E., ed. LC 82-8510. (Illus.). x, 456p. (C). 1993. text 75.00 (*0-8032-2903-8*) U of Nebr Pr.

— The Journals of the Lewis & Clark Expedition Vol. 9: The Journals of John Ordway, May 14, 1804-Sept. 23, 1806, & Charles Floyd, May 14-Aug. 18, 1804, Vol. 9. Moulton, Gary E., ed. LC 82-8510. xxii, 419p. 1996. text 75.00 (*0-8032-2914-3*) U of Nebr Pr.

— The Journals of the Lewis & Clark Expedition Vol. 11: The Journals of Joseph Whitehouse, May 14, 1804-April 2, 1806. Moulton, Gary E., ed. LC 82-8510. xx, 460p. 1997. text 65.00 (*0-8032-2918-6*) U of Nebr Pr.

— Lewis & Clark in the Three Rivers Valleys, Montana,

1805-1806: From the Original Journals of the Lewis & Clark Expedition. Nell, Donald F. & Taylor, John E., eds. LC 96-35318. 1996. pap. 16.95 (*1-880397-17-X*) Patrice Pr.

Lewis, Meriwether, et al. History of the Expedition under the Command of Captains Lewis & Clark, 3 vols., Set. LC 72-2820. (American Explorers Ser.). (Illus.). reprint ed. 165.00 (*0-404-54920-9*) AMS Pr.

— Lewis & Clark in the Three Rivers Valleys, Montana, 1805-1806: From the Original Journals of the Lewis & Clark Expedition (Includes Sheets Containing Six Full Color Maps) (Illus.). 1996. pap., suppl. ed. 20.90 (*1-880397-19-6*) Patrice Pr.

Lewis, Merrill. Robert Cantwell. LC 85-70130. (Western Writers Ser.: No. 70). (Illus.). 54p. (Orig.). 1985. pap. 4.95 (*0-88430-044-7*) Boise St U W Writ Ser.

Lewis, Merrill & Lee, L. L., eds. The Westering Experience in American Literature: Bicentennial Essays. LC 77-80814. 1977. pap. 4.95 (*0-930216-01-6*) West Wash Univ.

Lewis, Merrill & Lewis, Lorene. Wallace Stegner. LC 72-619569. (Western Writers Ser.: No. 4). (Illus.). 48p. (Orig.). (C). 1972. pap. 4.95 (*0-88430-003-X*) Boise St U W Writ Ser.

Lewis, Merv, jt. auth. see Lloyd-Jones, Roger.

Lewis, Mervyn K., ed. Financial Intermediaries. (International Library of Critical Writings in Economics: Vol. 43). 688p. 1995. 270.00 (*1-85278-791-0*) E Elgar.

— The Globalization of Financial Services. LC 98-55208. 672p. 1999. 245.00 (*1-85898-893-4*) E Elgar.

Lewis, Mervyn K. & Davis, Kevin T. Domestic & International Banking. 1987. 47.50 (*0-262-12126-3*) MIT Pr.

Lewis, Michael. Altering Fate: Why the Past Does Not Predict the Future. LC 96-52568. 238p. 1997. lib. bdg. 34.95 (*0-89862-856-3*, 2856) Guilford Pubns.

— Altering Fate: Why the Past Does Not Predict the Future. 238p. 1998. pap. text 15.95 (*1-57230-371-9*) Guilford Pubns.

***Lewis, Michael.** Between State & Empire: Local Politics & National Power in Prewar Toyama, 1868-1954. (Harvard East Asian Monographs: Vol. 192). 2000. text 45.00 (*0-674-00242-3*) HUP.

Lewis, Michael. The Culture of Inequality. 2nd ed. LC 77-24214. 240p. 1993. pap. 17.95 (*0-87023-857-4*) U of Mass Pr.

Lewis, Michael. Landform Dynamics: An Exercise Manual. 2nd ed. 78p. (C). per. 70.95 (*0-7872-6626-4*) Kendall-Hunt.

Lewis, Michael. Landform Dynamics: An Exercise Manual. 60p. (C). 1997. per. 47.50 (*0-7872-4332-9*) Kendall-Hunt.

— Liar's Poker. 1989. 21.95 (*0-393-02750-3*) Norton.

— Liar's Poker: Rising Through the Wreckage on Wall Street. 1990. pap. 12.95 (*0-14-014345-9*, Penguin Bks) Viking Penguin.

— The Money Culture. 304p. 1992. reprint ed. pap. 13.95 (*0-14-017318-8*, Penguin Bks) Viking Penguin.

— The New New Thing: A Silicon Valley Story. LC 99-43412. 256p. 1999. 25.95 (*0-393-04813-6*) Norton.

***Lewis, Michael.** The New New Thing: A Silicon Valley Story. 2001. pap. 13.00 (*0-14-029646-8*) Penguin Putnam.

Lewis, Michael. Poisoning the Ivy: The 7 Deadly Sins & Other Vices of Higher Education in America. LC 96-40284. 230p. (C). (gr. 13). 1997. 33.95 (*0-7656-0071-4*) M E Sharpe.

— Preparing a Business Plan for a Small-Scale Recycling Related Venture. 8p. 1994. 6.00 (*0-614-18037-6*) Inst Local Self Re.

— Recycling Economic Development Through Scrap-Based Manufacturing. LC 94-5188. (Illus.). 42p. 1994. pap. text 20.00 (*0-917582-97-7*) Inst Local Self Re.

— Shame: The Exposed Self. 276p. 1992. 29.95 (*0-02-918881-4*) Free Pr.

— Trail Fever: Spin Doctors, Rented Strangers, Thumb Wrestlers, Toe Suckers, Grizzly Bears, & Other Creatures on the Road to the White House. LC 97-5444. 299p. 1997. 3.99 (*0-679-44660-5*) Knopf.

— Trail Fever: Spin Doctors, Rented Strangers, Thumb Wrestlers, Toe Suckers, Grizzly Bears, & Other Creatures on the Road to the White House. 320p. 1998. pap. 14.00 (*0-679-76809-2*) Vin Bks.

— Urban America: Institutions & Experience. LC 72-10944. 526p. reprint ed. pap. 163.10 (*0-608-30206-6*, 201372300087) Bks Demand.

Lewis, Michael, ed. Beyond the Dyad. (Genesis of Behavior Ser.: Vol. 4). 346p. 1984. 65.00 (*0-306-41446-5*, Plenum Trade) Perseus Pubng.

— Manufacturing from Recyclables: 24 Case Studies of Successful Recycling Enterprises. (Illus.). 115p. (C). 1999. pap. text 25.00 (*0-7881-7605-6*) DIANE Pub.

— Origins of Intelligence: Infancy & Early Childhood. LC 75-31530. 423p. reprint ed. pap. 131.20 (*0-608-14054-6*, 202402000035) Bks Demand.

Lewis, Michael, ed. Origins of Intelligence: Infancy & Early Childhood. 2nd ed. 552p. 1983. 47.50 (*0-306-41225-X*, Plenum Trade) Perseus Pubng.

Lewis, Michael, et al, eds. Mothers, Babies, & Cocaine: The Role of Toxins in Development. 408p. 1995. pap. 37.50 (*0-8058-1584-8*); text 79.95 (*0-8058-1583-X*) L Erlbaum Assocs.

Lewis, Michael & Feiring, Candice, eds. Families, Risks, & Competence. LC 97-37790. 300p. 1997. write for info. (*0-8058-2344-1*); pap. write for info. (*0-8058-2345-X*) L Erlbaum Assocs.

Lewis, Michael & Haviland, Jeannette M., eds. Handbook of Emotions. LC 92-48999. 653p. 1993. lib. bdg. 69.95 (*0-89862-988-8*) Guilford Pubns.

***Lewis, Michael & Haviland-Jones, Jeannette M., eds.** Handbook of Emotions. 2nd ed. LC 99-86558. 694p. 2000. lib. bdg. 69.95 (*1-57230-529-0*, CO529) Guilford Pubns.

Lewis, Michael & Hill, Jimmie. Source Book for Teaching English As a Second Language. 136p. 1993. pap. text 22.00 (*0-435-24060-9*, 24060) Heinemann.

Lewis, Michael & Lacey, Debbi. The Cheapskate's Unauthorized Guide to Walt Disney World: Time Saving Techniques & the Best Values in Lodging, Food, & Shopping. LC 97-219. 224p. 1997. pap. 9.95 (*0-8065-1877-4*, Citadel Pr) Carol Pub Group.

Lewis, Michael & Michalson, Linda, eds. Children's Emotions & Moods: Developmental Theory & Measurement. LC 83-2456. 488p. 1983. 59.50 (*0-306-41209-8*, Plenum Trade) Perseus Pubng.

Lewis, Michael & Pfeiffer, Lee. The Ultimate James Bond Trivia Book. (Illus.). 128p. 1996. pap. 8.95 (*0-8065-1793-X*, Citadel Pr) Carol Pub Group.

Lewis, Michael & Ramsay, Douglas, eds. Soothing & Stress. LC 98-40680. 328p. 1999. 69.95 (*0-8058-2855-9*); pap. 29.95 (*0-8058-2856-7*) L Erlbaum Assocs.

Lewis, Michael & Rosenblum, Leonard A., eds. The Origins of Fear. LC 74-9565. (Origins of Behavior Ser.: Vol. 2). 298p. reprint ed. pap. 92.40 (*0-608-30793-9*, 201262100082) Bks Demand.

— The Uncommon Child. LC 80-20601. (Genesis of Behavior Ser.: Vol. 3). 354p. 1981. 65.00 (*0-306-40499-0*, Plenum Trade) Perseus Pubng.

Lewis, Michael & Saarni, Carolyn, eds. Lying & Deception in Everyday Life. LC 92-36145. 221p. 1993. lib. bdg. 32.00 (*0-89862-894-6*) Guilford Pubns.

Lewis, Michael & Sullivan, Margaret W., eds. Emotional Development in Atypical Children. 296p. 1996. 65.00 (*0-8058-1967-3*) L Erlbaum Assocs.

— Emotional Development in Atypical Children. 296p. 1996. pap. text 29.95 (*0-8058-1968-1*) L Erlbaum Assocs.

Lewis, Michael & Taft, Lawrence, eds. Developmental Disabilities: Theory, Assessment & Intervention. 288p. 1982. text 35.00 (*0-88331-134-8*) R B Luce.

Lewis, Michael & Worobey, John, eds. Infant Stress & Coping. LC 85-644581. (New Directions for Child Development Ser.: No. CD 45). 1989. pap. 25.00 (*1-55542-844-4*) Jossey-Bass.

Lewis, Michael, et al. Community Development Corporations & Reuse Operations: Four Case Studies of Working Relationships. 20p. 1996. 8.00 (*0-614-18034-1*) Inst Local Self Re.

— Financing Recycling-Related Ventures: Options for Community Development. LC 97-1335. (Illus.). 31p. 1995. pap. text 12.00 (*0-917582-94-2*) Inst Local Self Re.

— Reuse Operations: Community Development Through Redistribution of Used Goods. LC 95-31168. (Illus.). 60p. (Orig.). 1995. pap. text 12.00 (*0-917582-95-0*) Inst Local Self Re.

Lewis, Michael, jt. auth. see Hunt, Michael.

Lewis, Michael, jt. auth. see Pfeiffer, Lee.

Lewis, Michael, jt. auth. see Schmidt, Thomas.

Lewis, Michael, jt. auth. see U. S. Soccer Federation Staff.

Lewis, Michael A., et al, eds. Ecotoxicology & Risk Assessment for Wetlands. LC 98-5474. (Illus.). 1999. 98.00 (*1-880611-16-3*, SETAC Pr) SETAC.

Lewis, Michael A., jt. ed. see Suter, Glenn W., II.

Lewis, Michael C. To the Brink: Stockton, Malone, & the Utah Jazz's Climb to the Edge of Glory. (Illus.). 288p. 1998. 23.00 (*0-684-85686-7*) S&S Trade.

Lewis, Michael D., jt. auth. see Lewis, Judith A.

Lewis, Michael D., jt. auth. see Wallace, Sheri A.

Lewis, Michael J. Physical Properties of Foods & Food Processing Systems. 465p. 1987. reprint ed. pap. text 74.95 (*1-85573-272-6*) Technomic.

— The Politics of the German Gothic Revival: August Reichensperger. LC 92-38723. (Architectural History Foundation Ser.). (Illus.). 318p. 1993. 55.00 (*0-262-12177-8*) MIT Pr.

— Stout. (Classic Beer Style Ser.). (Illus.). 192p. 1996. pap. 11.95 (*0-937381-44-6*) Brewers Pubns.

Lewis, Michael J., jt. auth. see Johnson, Eugene J.

Lewis, Michael L., jt. auth. see Dodd, Carley H.

Lewis, Michael R., ed. & intro. see Lewis, Anna M.

Lewis, Mike & Kelly, Graham. Twenty Training Workshops for Developing Managerial Effectiveness, Vol. 1. 288p. 1986. text 253.95 (*0-566-02515-9*, Pub. by Gower) Ashgate Pub Co.

Lewis, Mike & Lacey, Debbi. Cheapskate's Guide to Walt Disney World: Time Saving Techniques & the Best Values in Lodging, Food, & Shopping. rev. ed. LC 98-52225. 224p. 1999. pap. 12.00 (*0-8065-2083-3*, Citadel Pr) Carol Pub Group.

Lewis, Mike, tr. see Pruyt, Hans.

***Lewis, Miles Marshall.** Four Days in February. 238p. (C). 1999. pap. 15.00 (*0-9675022-0-9*) Dream Fac.

Lewis, Milton, ed. see Lyons, Maryinez.

Lewis, Milton, jt. ed. see Macleod, Roy.

Lewis, Milton J., et al. Sex, Disease & Society: A Comparative History of Sexually Transmitted Diseases & HIV AIDS in Asia & the Pacific, 43. LC 96-28065. (Contributions in Medical Studies). 312p. 1997. 69.50 (*0-313-29442-9*, Greenwood Pr) Greenwood.

***Lewis, Miriam Striezheff.** Departures Bk. 1: Beyond Recognition. LC 00-190699. 2000. 25.00 (*0-7388-1934-4*); pap. 18.00 (*0-7388-1935-2*) Xlibris Corp.

Lewis, Monty & Lewis, Sara. Explorer Chartbook: Exumas. 2nd rev. ed. Drew, Erin & Fears, Kate, eds. (Illus.). 69p. 1998. pap. 34.95 (*0-9659842-0-6*) Lewis Offshore.

Lewis, Monty, jt. auth. see Lewis, Sara.

***Lewis, Morag.** A Love Betrayed. large type ed. 304p. 1999. pap. 18.99 (*0-7089-5579-7*, Linford) Ulverscroft.

Lewis, Morgan V. & Pratzner, Frank C., eds. Perspectives on Vocational Education: Purposes & Performance. 73p. 1984. 7.95 (*0-318-17788-9*, RD247) Ctr Educ Trng Employ.

Lewis, Morgan V., et al. Future Influences on Vocational Education. 17p. 1984. 2.75 (*0-318-22107-1*, SN46) Ctr Educ Trng Employ.

Lewis, Morris & Cooper, Mark B. Windows 98 MCSE Study Guide. LC 97-78220. (MCSE Certification Ser.). 816p. 1998. student ed. 49.99 incl. cd-rom (*0-7645-3113-1*) IDG Bks.

Lewis, Morris M. Infant Speech: A Study of the Beginnings of Language. LC 74-21420. (Classics in Child Development Ser.). 350p. 1978. reprint ed. 33.95 (*0-405-06470-5*) Ayer.

Lewis, Myrna I., jt. auth. see Butler, Robert N.

Lewis, Myron. History of the YMCA of San Diego County. Griffin, Pattie & Collato, Richard, eds. 162p. 1997. write for info. (*0-9657829-0-5*) YMCA CA.

Lewis, N. Exito! en la Vida. (Versos para Memorizar - Scripture Memory Ser.).Tr. of Success in Life. (SPA.). 2.99 (*0-7899-0220-6*, 498268) Editorial Unilit.

— Finanzas para las Misiones Mundiales.Tr. of Finances for World Missions. (SPA.). 72p. 1996. 4.50 (*0-7899-0193-5*, 498449) Editorial Unilit.

— Instant Word Power. 1982. mass mkt. 6.99 (*0-451-16647-7*) NAL.

— Thirty Days to Better English. 1985. mass mkt. 4.99 (*0-451-16191-2*) NAL.

Lewis, N. Douglas, jt. ed. see Campbell, David.

Lewis, Nancy, jt. auth. see Lewis, R. W. B.

Lewis, Nancy, ed. see Moorman, Chick.

Lewis, Nancy B., jt. auth. see Greenspan, Stanley I.

***Lewis, Nantawan B. & Fortune, Marie M., eds.** Remembering Conquest: Feminist/Womanist Perspectives on Religion, Colonization, & Sexual Violence. LC 99-46046. 91p. 1999. 24.95 (*0-7890-0796-7*, Haworth Pastrl) Haworth Pr.

Lewis, Naomi. Classic Fairy Tales to Read Aloud. 224p. (J). (gr. 1-9). 1998. pap. 7.95 (*0-7534-5164-6*, Kingfisher) LKC.

***Lewis, Naomi.** Elf Hill: Tales from Hans Christian Andersen. (Illus.). 72p. (J). (gr. k-3). 1999. 18.95 (*1-887734-70-8*) Star Brght Bks.

Lewis, Naomi. Proud Knight Fair. 1999. pap. 4.99 (*0-14-034038-6*) Viking Penguin.

***Lewis, Naomi.** Rocking Horse Land. (Illus.). 144p. (J). (gr. 3-7). 2000. write for info. (*0-7636-0897-1*, Pub. by Candlewick Pr) Penguin Putnam.

Lewis, Naomi. Where Will You Be in 2000 A. D.? (Illus.). 32p. (J). (ps-6). 1999. pap. 5.95 (*0-9673205-0-X*) Where Will You Be.

Lewis, Naomi, ed. East o' the Sun & West o' the Moon. Dasent, George W., tr. LC 91-58727. (Illus.). 48p. (J). (ps up). 1992. 15.95 (*1-56402-049-5*) Candlewick Pr.

— East o' the Sun & West o' the Moon. Dasent, George W., tr. (Illus.). (J). (ps-3). 1995. pap. 6.99 (*1-56402-437-7*) Candlewick Pr.

Lewis, Naomi, ed. see Andersen, Hans Christian.

Lewis, Naomi, tr. see Andersen, Hans Christian.

Lewis, Naomi, tr. see Grimm, Jacob W. & Grimm, Wilhelm K.

Lewis, Naphtali. Greeks in Ptolemaic Egypt. (Illus.). 224p. 1986. 49.95 (*0-19-814867-4*) OUP.

— The Interpretation of Dreams & Portents in Antiquity. LC 95-43401. 168p. 1996. reprint ed. pap. 15.00 (*0-86516-256-5*) Bolchazy-Carducci.

Lewis, Naphtali & Reinhold, Meyer. Roman Civilization, Vol. 2. 3rd ed. 1990. pap. text 55.50 (*0-231-07055-1*) Col U Pr.

— Roman Civilization, Vols. I & II. 3rd ed. 1990. text 162.00 (*0-231-07054-3*) Col U Pr.

— The Roman Empire. (Roman Civilization Ser.: Vol. 2). 736p. 1990. text 87.50 (*0-231-07132-9*); pap. text 30.50 (*0-231-07133-7*) Col U Pr.

— The Roman Republic & the Principate of Augustus. (Roman Civilization Ser.: Vol. 1). (Illus.). 696p. 1990. text 87.50 (*0-231-07130-2*); pap. text 30.50 (*0-231-07131-0*) Col U Pr.

Lewis, Natalie. Novel Extenders: African-American Collection. (ECS Think & Learn Activity Bks.). (Illus.). 128p. (Orig.). 1996. pap., teacher ed. 14.95 (*1-57022-050-6*) ECS Lrn Systs.

— Novel Extenders: Multicultural Collection, Grade 4-6. (ECS Think & Learn Activity Bks.). (Illus.). 112p. 1996. pap. text, teacher ed. 14.95 (*1-57022-078-6*, ECS0786) ECS Lrn Systs.

— Novel Extenders IV. (ECS Think & Learn Activity Bks.). 128p. 1994. pap. 15.95 (*1-57022-007-7*) ECS Lrn Systs.

— Novel Extenders, Grade 1-3: Multicultural Collection. (ECS Think & Learn Activity Bks.). (Illus.). 112p. 1996. pap. text, teacher ed. 14.95 (*1-57022-060-3*, ECS0603) ECS Lrn Systs.

— Novel Extenders I. (ECS Think & Learn Activity Bks.). 128p. 1994. pap., teacher ed. 15.95 (*1-57022-000-X*) ECS Lrn Systs.

— Novel Extenders III. (ECS Think & Learn Activity Bks.: Vol. 3). (Illus.). 128p. 1994. pap., teacher ed. 15.95 (*1-57022-006-9*, ECS:0069) ECS Lrn Systs.

— Novel Extenders II. (ECS Think & Learn Activity Bks.). (Illus.). 144p. 1994. pap., teacher ed. 16.95 (*1-57022-001-8*, ECS0018) ECS Lrn Systs.

Lewis, Natawan B., ed. Revolution of Spirit: Ecumenical Theology in a Global Context. 320p. 1998. pap. text 30.00 (*0-8028-4591-6*) Walker & Co.

Lewis, Neville, jt. auth. see Haag, Michael.

Lewis, Nigel. The Book of Babel: Words & the Way We See Things. LC 94-61461. 320p. 1995. pap. text 19.95 (*0-87745-496-5*) U of Iowa Pr.

Lewis, Nigel C. Road Pricing: Theory & Practice. 128p. 1993. 7.00 (*0-7277-1963-7*) Am Soc Civil Eng.

Lewis, Noelle, jt. auth. see Pogue, Pamela.

Lewis, Nolan D. Research in Dementia Precox. Grob, Gerald N., ed. LC 78-22572. (Historical Issues in Mental Health Ser.). 1980. reprint ed. lib. bdg. 25.95 (*0-405-11925-9*) Ayer.

Lewis, Norah. I Want to Join Your Club: Letters from Rural Children, 1900-1920. (Illus.). 216p. 1996. pap. 24.95 (*0-88920-260-5*) W Laurier U Pr.

Lewis, Norah L., ed. Dear Editor & Friends: Letters from Rural Women of the North-West, 1900-1920. LC 97-932474. (Illus.). 166p. 1998. pap. 29.95 (*0-88920-287-7*, HQ1453) W Laurier U Pr.

Lewis, Noreen, jt. auth. see Coulson, Arlene.

Lewis, Norm. Prioridad Uno.Tr. of Priority One. (SPA.). 177p. 1990. pap. 4.50 (*1-56063-079-5*, 498483) Editorial Unilit.

— Priority One/Faith Promise. LC 88-70157. 192p. 1988. reprint ed. pap. 7.95 (*0-87808-215-8*, WCL215-8) O M Lit.

Lewis, Norma. Going for the Gold. (YA). (gr. 7 up). 1996. pap. 9.99 (*0-88092-327-X*) Royal Fireworks.

Lewis, Norman. Choice & Legal Order: A Jurisprudence for Contemporary. LC 96-160201. 400p. 1995. pap. text 52.95 (*0-406-05050-3*, MICHIE) LEXIS Pub.

— An Empire of the East. 1995. 25.00 (*0-8050-1960-X*) H Holt & Co.

— Naples '44: An Intelligence Officer in the Italian Labyrinth. LC 94-27642. 88p. 1995. pap. 14.95 (*0-8050-3373-4*) H Holt & Co.

— Naples '44: An Intelligence Officer in the Italian Labyrinth. large type ed. 264p. 1997. text 20.95 (*1-85695-149-9*, Pub. by ISIS Lrg Prnt) Transaction Pubs.

— New Roget's Thesaurus: In Dictionary Form. 1978. 10.09 (*0-606-01133-1*, Pub. by Turtleback) Demco.

— The New Roget's Thesaurus in Dictionary Form. 512p. 1986. mass mkt. 5.99 (*0-425-09975-X*) Berkley Pub.

— The New Roget's Thesaurus in Dictionary Form. rev. ed. LC 77-24457. 552p. 1981. 13.95 (*0-399-12678-3*, G P Putnam); 15.95 (*0-399-12679-1*, G P Putnam) Peng Put Young Read.

— A Suitable Case for Corruption. large type ed. 352p. 1985. 27.99 (*0-7089-1390-3*) Ulverscroft.

— Twenty Days to Better Spelling. (Orig.). 1989. pap. 3.95 (*0-317-02802-2*) NAL.

— Word Power Made Easy. 544p. 1995. 9.98 (*0-88365-925-5*) Galahad Bks.

— Word Power Made Easy: The Complete Handbook for Building a Superior Vocabulary. 528p. 1991. per. 6.99 (*0-671-74190-X*) PB.

— The World, the World. LC 97-12711. 304p. 1997. 27.50 (*0-8050-5112-0*) H Holt & Co.

— The World, the World. large type ed. LC 98-13748. 4860p. 1998. 25.95 (*0-7862-1450-3*) Thorndike Pr.

Lewis, Norman, ed. Happy & Glorious: The Constitution in Transition. (Studies in Law & Politics Ser.). 112p. 1990. pap. 25.95 (*0-335-09487-2*) OpUniv Pr.

Lewis, Norman & Birkinshaw, Patrick. When Citizens Complain: Reforming Justice & Administration. LC 92-21161. (Law & Political Change Ser.). 240p. 1993. 118.00 (*0-335-15745-9*); pap. 37.95 (*0-335-15744-0*) OpUniv Pr.

Lewis, Norman, et al. Back to Mandalay: Burmese Life, Past & Present. (Illus.). 240p. 1996. 55.00 (*0-7892-0254-9*) Abbeville Pr.

Lewis, Norman, jt. auth. see Funk, Wilfred.

Lewis, Norman G. & Paice, Michael G., eds. Plant Cell Wall Polymers: Biogenesis & Biodegradation. LC 89-6926. (Symposium Ser.: No. 399). (Illus.). xi, 664p. 1989. 119.95 (*0-8412-1658-4*) Am Chemical.

— Plant Cell Wall Polymers: Biogenesis & Biodegradation. LC 89-17541. (ACS Symposium Ser.: No. 399). (Illus.). 688p. 1989. reprint ed. pap. 200.00 (*0-608-03199-2*, 206371800007) Bks Demand.

Lewis, Norman G. & Sarkanen, Simo, eds. Lignin & Lignan Biosynthesis. LC 98-6367. (Symposium Ser.: No. 697). (Illus.). 448p. 1998. text 130.95 (*0-8412-3566-X*, Pub. by Am Chemical) OUP.

Lewis, O. A. Plants & Nitrogen. (Studies in Biology: No. 166). 112p. (C). 1992. pap. text 15.95 (*0-521-42776-2*) Cambridge U Pr.

***Lewis, Ora M.** Seeds in the Wind. Franklin, Juanita L., ed. viii, 391p. 2000. 39.95 (*0-9642067-1-4*) Maranatha Pr.

Lewis, Orlando F. The Development of America Prisons & Prison Customs, 1776-1845 Definitive Edition. LC 93-39530. (Criminology, Law Enforcement, & Social Problems Ser.: No. 1). (Illus.). 1996. reprint ed. 30.00 (*0-87585-706-X*) Patterson Smith.

Lewis, Oscar. Bay Window Bohemia. (Illus.). 248p. 1983. reprint ed. pap. 9.95 (*0-911819-01-0*) Yosemite D.

— The Big Four. 1992. reprint ed. lib. bdg. 75.00 (*0-7812-5060-9*) Rprt Serv.

— The Big Four. rev. ed. 310p. (C). 1995. reprint ed. pap. 6.95 (*0-89174-042-2*) Comstock Edns.

— The Big Four: The Story of Huntington, Stanford, Hopkins, & Crocker, & of the Building of the Central Pacific. Bruchey, Stuart, ed. LC 80-1324. (Railroads Ser.). (Illus.). 1981. reprint ed. lib. bdg. 44.95 (*0-405-13799-0*) Ayer.

— Children of Sanchez. 1979. pap. 16.00 (*0-394-70280-8*) Vin Bks.

— The Effects of White Contact upon Blackfoot Culture. LC 84-45511. (American Ethnological Society Monographs: No. 6). 1988. reprint ed. 20.00 (*0-404-62906-7*) AMS Pr.

— Five Families: Mexican Case Studies in the Culture of Poverty. LC 59-10644. 364p. 1975. pap. 20.00 (*0-465-09705-7*, Pub. by Basic) HarpC.

— I Remember Christine. LC 88-37037. (Vintage West Ser.). 280p. 1989. reprint ed. pap. 11.00 (*0-87417-151-2*) U of Nev Pr.

An Asterisk (*) at the beginning of an entry indicates that the title is appearing for the first time.

— Sea Routes to the Gold Fields. 256p. 1987. reprint ed. 4.50 (0-89174-044-9) Comstock Edns.
— Tepoztlan Village in Mexico. 104p. (C). 1960. pap. text 23.50 (0-03-006050-8) Harcourt Coll Pubs.
Lewis, Oscar, et al. Four Men: Living the Revolution: An Oral History of Contemporary Cuba. LC 76-54878. 608p. 1976. text 44.95 (0-252-00628-3) U of Ill Pr.
— Four Women: Living the Revolution: An Oral History of Contemporary Cuba. LC 79-54878. 485p. 1977. text 39.95 (0-252-00639-9) U of Ill Pr.
Lewis, P. The High Hill. Date not set. 3.99 (1-871676-14-2, Pub. by Christian Focus) Spring Arbor Dist.
— Reason Wounded: An Experience of India's Emergency. 207p. 1978. 16.95 (0-318-36609-6) Asia Bk Corp.
— White Stone. Date not set. 3.99 (1-871676-20-7, Pub. by Christian Focus) Spring Arbor Dist.
Lewis, P. C. & Lewis, C. Student Manual for the Donut Franchise: A Microcomputer Simulation. 32p. 1985. pap. text 18.36 (0-07-037604-2) McGraw.
Lewis, P. D., jt. ed. see Symmers, W. S.
Lewis, P. R. & Knight, D. P. Cytochemical Staining Methods for Electron Microscopy. (Practical Methods in Electron Microscopy Ser.: Vol. 14). 322p. 1992. pap. 69.75 (0-444-89387-3) Elsevier.
Lewis, P. S. Essays in Later Medieval French History. 256p. (C). 1985. 55.00 (0-907628-41-9) Hambledon Press.
Lewis, Pamela S., et al. Management: Challenges in the 21st Century. LC 94-22667. (SWC-General Business). 724p. (C). 1994. mass mkt. 58.25 (0-314-04568-6) West Pub.
Lewis, Patrice P., jt. auth. see Horn, Carl.
Lewis, Patricia, ed. see Blinks, William, et al.
Lewis, Patrick D. A City Called Heaven. (J). 1995. 14.95 (0-8050-4716-6) H Holt & Co.
Lewis, Patrick Denise. The Longest Ride. LC 98-54828. 164p. (J). (gr. 5-7). 1995. 14.95 (0-8050-4715-8) H Holt & Co.
Lewis, Patrick J. Riddle-Lightful. LC 97-39083. 32p. (J). (ps-3). 1998. 17.00 (0-679-88760-1, Pub. by Random Bks Yng Read) Random.
Lewis, Paul. Akha-English Dictionary. LC 73-14371. (Cornell University, Southeast Asia Program, Data Paper Ser.: No. 70). 403p. reprint ed. pap. 125.00 (0-8357-5291-7, 201047500068) Bks Demand.
— Comic Effects: Interdisciplinary Approaches to Humor in Literature. LC 88-28227. 179p. (C). 1989. pap. text 21.95 (0-7914-0023-9) State U NY Pr.
— Cuarenta Maneras para Ensenar/Ninos Valores Morales.Tr. of Forty Ways to Teach Your Child Values. (SPA.). 189p. 1985. pap. 6.99 (1-56063-241-0, 498405) Editorial Unilit.
— Ensene a Su Hijo con Destreza. (Serie Guia de Bolsillo - Pocket Guides Ser.).Tr. of Terrific Tips for Parents. (SPA.). 1990. 2.79 (1-56063-023-X, 498055) Editorial Unilit.
— 40 Ways to Teach Your Child Values. LC 96-50965. 176p. 1997. pap. 9.99 (0-310-21699-0) Zondervan.
— The Successful Management of Redundancy. (Human Resource Management in Action Ser.). 272p. 1994. pap. 47.95 (0-631-18681-6) Blackwell Pubs.
***Lewis, Paul.** 30 Days to a Smart Family. (Illus.). 2000. pap. 9.99 (0-310-23518-9) Zondervan.
Lewis, Paul. Twenty Years of Statutory Redundancy Payments in Great Britain. (C). 1988. text 39.00 (0-7855-3173-4, Pub. by Univ Nottingham) St Mut.
— Twenty Years of Statutory Redundancy Payments in Great Britain . . . (Leeds-Nottingham Occasional Papers in Industrial Relations: No. 8). (C). 1985. 35.00 (0-900572-63-9) St Mut.
Lewis, Paul & Lewis, Elaine. Peoples of the Golden Triangle. LC 84-50047. (Illus.). 200p. (YA). 1980. pap. 24.95 (0-500-97472-1, Pub. by Thames Hudson) Norton.
— Peoples of the Golden Triangle: Six Tribes in Thailand. LC 84-50047. (Illus.). 1984. 40.00 (0-500-97314-8, Pub by Thames Hudson) Norton.
Lewis, Paul, et al. Pamphlet Architecture Vol. 21: Situation Normal. LC 98-39325. (Illus.). 80p. 1998. pap. 12.95 (1-56898-154-6) Princeton Arch.
Lewis, Paul, jt. auth. see McDowell, Josh.
Lewis, Paul, jt. auth. see McGrew, Anthony.
Lewis, Paul, jt. auth. see Pridham, Geoffrey.
Lewis, Paul G. Central Europe Since 1945. LC 93-32588. (Post War World Ser.). 352p. (C). 1995. pap. text 37.80 (0-582-03608-9) Addison-Wesley.
Lewis, Paul G. CENTRL EUROPE SINCE 1945. LC 93-32588. (Post War World Ser.). (C). 1994. text 68.95 (0-582-03609-7, Pub. by Addison-Wesley) Longman.
— Political Authority & Party Secretaries in Poland, 1975-1986. (Illus.). 368p. (C). 1989. text 69.95 (0-521-36369-1) Cambridge U Pr.
— Shaping Suburbia: How Political Institutions Organize Urban Development. LC 95-52088. (Pitt Series in Policy & Institutional). 208p. (C). 1996. pap. 19.95 (0-8229-5595-4); text 44.95 (0-8229-3938-X) U of Pittsburgh Pr.
Lewis, Paul G., ed. Party Structure & Organization in East-Central Europe. LC 96-13006. (Studies of Communism in Transition). 256p. 1996. 90.00 (1-85898-289-8) E Elgar.
Lewis, Paul G. & Sprague, Mary. Federal Transportation Policy & the Role of Metropolitan Planning Organizations in California. LC 97-14160. (Illus.). xxii, 165p. 1997. pap. 15.00 (0-9653184-5-1) Pub Policy Inst.
***Lewis, Paul George & Barbour, Elisa.** California Cities & the Local Sales Tax. LC 99-23683. (Illus.). xxviii, 145p. 1999. pap. 12.00 (1-58213-010-8) Pub Policy Inst.
Lewis, Paul H. The Crisis of Argentine Capitalism. LC 89-31350. xxviii, 573p. 1992. pap. 27.50 (0-8078-4356-3) U of NC Pr.
— Paraguay under Stroessner. LC 79-28554. 268p. reprint ed. pap. 83.10 (0-8357-3896-5, 203662800004) Bks Demand.
— Political Parties & Generations in Paraguay's Liberal Era, 1869-1940. LC 92-21164. xvi, 228p. 1992. 49.95 (0-8078-2078-4) U of NC Pr.
— Socialism, Liberalism, & Dictatorship in Paraguay. Hoover Institution Press Staff & Wesson, Robert, eds. LC 81-21092. (Politics in Latin America, A Hoover Institution Ser.). 154p. 1982. 49.95 (0-275-90847-X, C0847, Praeger Pubs) Greenwood.
Lewis, Paul H. & Yang, Chang. Basic Control & Systems Engineering. LC 96-53660. (Illus.). 450p. (C). 1997. 105.00 (0-13-597436-4) P-H.
Lewis, Paul L. Deep Roots: Local Government Structure in California. LC 98-36654. (Illus.). xxvi, 102p. 1998. pap. 12.00 (1-58213-001-9) Pub Policy Inst.
Lewis, Paul M. Beauty of America. LC 89-38286. (Illus.). 1991. pap. 9.95 (1-55988-002-3) Am Prods.
— Beauty of California. LC 88-37210. (Illus.). 80p. 1989. 19.95 (0-917630-71-8) Am Prods.
— Beauty of Florida. Shangle, Robert D., ed. (Illus.). 80p. 1990. 19.95 (0-917630-81-5) Am Prods.
— Beauty of Hawaii. Shangle, Robert D., ed. (Illus.). 80p. 1989. 19.95 (0-917630-58-0); pap. 9.95 (0-917630-57-2) Am Prods.
— Beauty of Massachusetts. Shangle, Robert D., ed. LC 89-12522. (Illus.). 80p. 1990. 19.95 (0-917630-83-1); pap. 9.95 (0-917630-82-3) Am Prods.
— Beauty of New Jersey. LC 91-25684. (Illus.). 80p. 1989. 19.95 (0-917630-85-8); pap. 9.95 (0-917630-84-X) Am Prods.
— The Beauty of the California Coast. LC 89-35182. (Illus.). 80p. (Orig.). 1990. 19.95 (0-917630-90-4) Am Prods.
— Beauty of Utah. LC 88-37209. 1989. 19.95 (1-55988-328-6); pap. 9.95 (1-55988-327-8) Renais Pubng.
— Beauty of Washington. rev. ed. 1992. pap. 9.95 (1-55988-316-2) Renais Pubng.
Lewis, Paul O. Ever Wondered? For Explorers, Inventors, & Artists of All Ages. (Illus.). 36p. (J). (gr. 3-6). 1991. pap. 5.95 (0-941831-67-1) Beyond Words Pub.
— Frog Girl. LC 98-21282. (Illus.). 32p. (J). (gr. 2 up). 1999. lib. bdg. 21.27 (0-8368-2228-5) Gareth Stevens Inc.
— The Starlight Bride. (Illus.). 40p. (J). (ps-6). 1988. 14.95 (0-941831-33-7); pap. 9.95 (0-941831-25-6) Beyond Words Pub.
Lewis, Paul Owen. Davy's Dream: A Young Boy's Adventures with Wild Orca Whales. 1999. 14.95 (1-58246-000-0); pap. text 8.95 (1-58246-001-9) Tricycle Pr.
— Grasper: A Young Crab's Discovery. (J). 1999. pap. text 7.95 (1-883672-98-8) Tricycle Pr.
— P. Bear's New Year's Party: A Counting Book. 1999. pap. text 6.95 (1-883672-99-6) Tricycle Pr.
— P. Bear's New Year's Party: A Counting Book. (J). 1999. 13.95 (1-58246-002-7) Tricycle Pr.
— Storm Boy. LC 98-21284. (Illus.). 32p. (J). (gr. 2 up). 1999. lib. bdg. 19.93 (0-8368-2229-3) Gareth Stevens Inc.
— Storm Boy. 1999. 14.95 (1-883672-96-1) Tricycle Pr.
Lewis, Paul W. & Bibo, Bai, compiled by. Hani-English/English-Hani Dictionary.Tr. of Haqniqdoq-Yilyidoq, Doqlo-Soqdaoq. 837p. 1996. 161.50 (0-7103-0564-8, Pub. by Kegan Paul Intl) Col U Pr.
Lewis, Paula G. The Aesthetics of Stephane Mallarme in Relation to His Public. LC 74-5898. 260p. (C). 1976. 25.00 (0-8386-1615-1) Fairleigh Dickinson.
Lewis, Paula G., ed. Traditionalism, Nationalism, & Feminism: Women Writers of Quebec, 53. LC 84-10854. (Contributions in Women's Studies: No. 53). (Illus.). 280p. 1985. 65.00 (0-313-24510-X, LTF/, Greenwood Pr) Greenwood.
Lewis, Peirce, jt. auth. see White, Marjorie L.
Lewis, Peirce F. New Orleans. The Making of an Urban Landscape. LC 76-4797. (Contemporary Metropolitan Analysis Ser.). (Illus.). 136p. 1976. text 16.95 (0-88410-433-8, HarpBusn) HarpInfo.
Lewis, Penny. Creative Transformation: The Healing Power of the Arts. LC 92-38693. (Illus.). 200p. (Orig.). 1993. pap. 19.95 (0-933029-66-7) Chiron Pubns.
***Lewis, Penny & Johnson, David Read.** Current Approaches in Drama Therapy. LC 00-32612. 2000. write for info. (0-398-07083-0) C C Thomas.
Lewis, Penny & Loman, Susan. The Kestenberg Movement Profile: Its Past, Present Applications & Future Directions. LC 90-81441. 176p. (C). 1990. pap. text 12.00 (1-881245-01-2) Antioch New Eng.
Lewis, Penny & Singer, David L. The Choreography of Object Relations. LC 82-73067. 196p. (C). 1982. pap. text 9.95 (1-881245-06-3) Antioch New Eng.
***Lewis, Pericles.** Modernism, Nationalism & the Novel. 247p. (C). 2000. 59.95 (0-521-66111-0) Cambridge U Pr.
Lewis, Peter. The Genius of Puritanism. 2nd ed. 144p. 1996. reprint ed. pap. 14.95 (1-57358-031-7) Soli Deo Gloria.
— The Glory of Christ. LC 97-147228. 512p. 1997. pap. 16.99 (0-8024-3029-5, 151) Moody.
***Lewis, Peter.** God's Hall of Fame: The Trials & Triumphs of Faith. 1999. pap. 10.99 (1-85792-529-7) Christian Focus.
Lewis, Peter. The Martial Arts: Origins, Philosophy, Practice. 192p. 1997. pap. 11.95 (1-85375-206-1) Prion.
— Media & Communication for Beginners. (Writers & Readers Documentary Comic Bks.). (Illus.). 176p. (Orig.). 1991. pap. 7.95 (0-86316-115-4) Writers & Readers.
— Myths & Legends of the Martial Arts. 192p. 1998. pap. 13.95 (1-85375-271-1) Prion.
— On Our Knees & in His Arms. LC 98-192706. (Foundations of the Faith). 1998. pap. 8.99 (0-8024-3051-1) Moody.
— Secret Art of the Ninja. 176p. 1997. pap. 13.95 (1-85375-270-3) Trafalgar.
— Top Roping. (How to Rock Climb Ser.). (Illus.). (Orig.). 1997. pap. 12.95 (1-57540-082-0) Falcon Pub Inc.
Lewis, Peter, ed. Africa: Dilemmas of Development & Change. LC 98-13688. 464p. (C). 1998. text 85.00 (0-8133-2754-7, Pub. by Westview); pap. text 35.00 (0-8133-2755-5, Pub. by Westview) HarpC.
Lewis, Peter & Booth, Jerry, eds. The Invisible Medium: Commercial, Public & Community Radio. LC 90-4357. 250p. (C). 1990. reprint ed. 24.95 (0-88258-032-9); reprint ed. pap. 14.95 (0-88258-106-6) Howard U Pr.
Lewis, Peter & Lynch, Margaret. Campanulas: A Gardener's Guide. rev. ed. LC 98-17830. (Illus.). 168p. 1998. 34.95 (0-88192-463-6) Timber.
Lewis, Peter A. Fielding's Burlesque Drama. (University of Durham Ser.: Vol. 2). (Illus.). 200p. 1988. 68.00 (0-85224-542-4, Pub. by Edinburgh U Pr) Col U Pr.
— Maps & Statistics. 336p. 1977. pap. 22.50 (0-416-65380-4, NO. 6180) Routledge.
Lewis, Peter A. Organic Pigments. 2nd ed. (Illus.). 43p. 1995. pap. 30.00 (0-934010-34-X) Fed Soc Coat Tech.
Lewis, Peter A., ed. Pigment Handbook, 3 vols. 3rd ed. 2000p. 1988. 995.00 (0-471-60021-0) Wiley.
— Pigment Handbook, 3 vols., Vol. 1. 2nd ed. LC 87-13358. 976p. 1988. 435.00 (0-471-82833-5) Wiley.
— Pigment Handbook: Applications & Markets, 3 vols., Vol. 2, Applications and Markets, 1st ed. 464p. 1973. 365.00 (0-471-67124-X) Wiley.
— Pigment Handbook: Characterization & Physical Relationships, 3 vols., Vol. 3, Characterization and Physical Relationship. 560p. 1973. 365.00 (0-471-67126-6) Wiley.
Lewis, Peter A., et al. Enhanced Simulation & Statistics Package. LC 89-4860. 96p. (C). (gr. 13). 1990. text 109.50 (0-534-10260-3) Chapman & Hall.
Lewis, Peter H., ed. see Hein, Peg.
Lewis, Peter J., et al, eds. Prostacyclin in Pregnancy. LC 83-42597. (Illus.). 246p. 1983. reprint ed. pap. 76.30 (0-7837-9559-9, 206030800005) Bks Demand.
Lewis, Peter J. & O'Grady, John, eds. Clinical Pharmacology of Prostacyclin. LC 80-83272. 274p. 1981. reprint ed. pap. 85.00 (0-608-00443-X, 206115800007) Bks Demand.
Lewis, Peter M., et al. Stabilizing Nigeria: Sanctions, Incentives, & Support for Civil Society. LC 98-23151. 120p. 1998. pap. 11.95 (0-87078-415-3) Century Foundation.
Lewis, Peter R., jt. auth. see Glauert, Audrey M.
Lewis, Philip. Islamic Britain: Religion, Politics & Identity among British Muslims. 1994. text 19.95 (1-85043-861-7, Pub. by I B T) St Martin.
— Life of Death: A Novel. 253p. 1993. 18.95 (0-932511-74-0); pap. 8.95 (0-932511-75-9) Fiction Coll.
***Lewis, Philip.** NATE. LC 99-79057. 430p. 2000. pap. 15.00 (0-9671951-0-1) Back House.
Lewis, Philip. Seeing Through the Mother Goose Tales: Visual Turns in the Writings of Charles Perrault. LC 95-18795. 312p. 1996. 39.50 (0-8047-2410-5) Stanford U Pr.
Lewis, Philip C. The American Dame. 1963. pap. 5.25 (0-8222-0028-7) Dramatists Play.
Lewis, Philip G. Approaching Precalculus Mathematics Discretely: Explorations in a Computer Environment. (Explorations in Logo Ser.). 574p. (Orig.). 1990. 60.00 (0-262-12138-7); pap. text 30.00 (0-262-62063-4) MIT Pr.
Lewis, Philip H. Tomorrow by Design: A Regional Design Process for Sustainability. LC 95-43871. (Series in Sustainable Design). (Illus.). 272p. 1996. 69.95 (0-471-10935-5) Wiley.
Lewis, Philip M., 2nd, et al. Compiler Design Theory. LC 75-9012. (Illus.). 672p. (C). 1976. text. write for info. (0-201-14455-7) Addison Wesley.
Lewis, Philip S., jt. ed. see Abel, Richard L.
Lewis, Philip V. & Baker, William H. Business Report Writing. 2nd ed. LC 82-15436. (Business Communications Ser.). 368p. (C). 1984. text 38.95 (0-471-84177-3) P-H.
Lewis, Philippa, jt. auth. see Cameron, Elisabeth.
Lewis, Philippa, jt. auth. see Drury, Elizabeth.
Lewis, Phillip H. The Social Context of Art in Northern New Ireland. LC 71-83764. (Field Museum of Natural History, Publication 1069: Vol. 58). 194p. 1969. reprint ed. pap. 60.20 (0-608-03767-2, 206459000009) Bks Demand.
Lewis, Phillip V. Organizational Communication: The Essence of Effective Management. 3rd ed. LC 86-5571. 345p. 1987. text 38.95 (0-471-84131-5) P-H.
— Transformational Leadership. 256p. (Orig.). 1996. pap. 19.99 (0-8054-1239-5, 4212-39) Broadman.
Lewis, Phyllis H., jt. ed. see McDade, Sharon A.
Lewis, Preston. The Demise of Billy the Kid. large type ed. LC 95-2476. 484p. 1995. lib. bdg. 20.95 (0-7838-1280-9) Thorndike Pr.
— The Redemption of Jesse James. large type ed. LC 95-35732. 496p. 1995. 20.95 (0-7838-1500-X, G K Hall Lrg Type) Mac Lib Ref.
Lewis Publishers Staff, et al. Geraghty & Miller's Groundwater Bibliography. 5th ed. 507p. 1991. per. 95.00 (0-87371-642-6, L642) Lewis Pubs.
Lewis, R. Show Me the MAC. (Show Me Ser.). (Illus.). 125p. 1993. 12.95 (1-56761-265-2, Alpha Ref) Macmillan Gen Ref.
Lewis, R. & Tagg, E. D. Computer for Each Student. 1987. 46.50 (0-318-32598-5) Elsevier.
Lewis, R., jt. auth. see Sax, I.
Lewis, R., jt. auth. see Wills, S.
Lewis, R. B. Light & Truth. 400p. 1998. reprint ed. pap. 45.00 (1-58073-004-3) BCP Bks.
— Light & Truth. 400p. 1998. reprint ed. pap. 45.00 (0-933121-73-3) Black Classic.
Lewis, R. Barry. The Hood Site: A Late Woodland Hamlet in the Sangamon Valley of Central Illinois. (Reports of Investigations: No. 31). (Illus.). 41p. 1975. pap. 2.00 (0-89792-057-0) Ill St Museum.
— Mississippian Exploitative Strategies: A Southeast Missouri Example. Wood, W. Raymond, ed. LC 73-620254. (Research Ser.: No. 11). (Illus.). 63p. (Orig.). 1974. pap. 5.00 (0-943414-12-1) MO Arch Soc.
— Mississippian Towns & Sacred Spaces: Searching for an Architectural Grammar. LC 98-19772. 1999. pap. text 29.95 (0-8173-0947-0) U of Ala Pr.
Lewis, R. Barry, ed. Kentucky Archaeology. (Illus.). 312p. 1995. text 29.95 (0-8131-1907-3) U Pr of Ky.
Lewis, R. E. & Tagg, E. D. A Computer for Each Student: Proceedings of the IFIP WG 3.2 Working Conference on A Computer for Each Student & Its Impact on Teaching & Curriculum in the University, Delft University, The Netherlands, April 21-23, 1987. xii, 180p. 1987. 70.00 (0-444-70301-2, North Holland) Elsevier.
Lewis, R. E., jt. ed. see Cruse, J. M.
Lewis, R. E., jt. ed. see Cruse, Julius M.
Lewis, R. F., Jr., jt. ed. see Cruse, J. M.
Lewis, R. H., ed. see Davidson, Harry X., et al.
Lewis, R. I. Turbomachinery Performance Analysis. (Illus.). 329p. 1996. pap. text 99.00 incl. disk (0-470-23596-9, Wiley-Interscience) Wiley.
— Vortex Element Methods for Fluid Dynamic Analysis of Engineering Systems. (Engine Technology Ser.). (Illus.). 588p. (C). 1991. text 155.00 (0-521-36010-2) Cambridge U Pr.
Lewis, R. R., jt. ed. see Zorn, J. C.
Lewis, R. T., jt. ed. see Everitt, W. Norrie.
***Lewis, R. W. B.** American Characters: Selections from the National Portrait Gallery, Accompanied by Literary Portraits. LC 98-53021. 1999. pap. write for info. (0-300-07945-1) Yale U Pr.
Lewis, R. W. B. A Century of Arts & Letters: The History of the National Institute of Arts & Letters & the American Academy of Arts & Letters As Told, Decade by Decade. Updike, John, ed. LC 97-40940. (Illus.). 346p. 1998. 39.95 (0-231-10248-8) Col U Pr.
— The City of Florence: Historical Vistas & Personal Sightings. LC 94-20160. (Illus.). 351p. 1995. text 27.50 (0-374-12404-3) FS&G.
— The City of Florence: Historical Vistas & Personal Sightings. (Illus.). 368p. 1995. pap. 14.95 (0-8050-4630-5, Owl) H Holt & Co.
— Edith Wharton: A Biography. LC 85-13035. (Illus.). 592p. (C). 1985. reprint ed. pap. 20.00 (0-88064-020-0) Fromm Intl Pub.
— The Jameses: A Family Narrative. (Illus.). 660p. 1991. text 35.00 (0-374-17861-5) FS&G.
— Literary Reflections: A Shoring of Images, 1960-1993. 288p. 1993. text 40.00 (1-55553-160-1) NE U Pr.
— Programming Industrial Control Systems Using IEC 1131-3. (IEE Control Engineering Ser.: No. 50). xiv, 281p. 1995. boxed set 77.00 (0-85296-827-2) INSPEC Inc.
Lewis, R. W. B., et al, eds. Numerical Methods in Coupled Systems. fac. ed. LC 82-24809. (Wiley Series in Numerical Methods in Engineering). (Illus.). 632p. 1984. reprint ed. pap. 196.00 (0-608-00958-X, 206180600011) Bks Demand.
***Lewis, R. W. B. & Lewis, Nancy.** American Characters: Selections from the National Portrait Gallery, Accompanied by Literary Portraits. LC 98-53021. (Illus.). 432p. 1999. 45.00 (0-300-07895-1) Yale U Pr.
Lewis, R. W. B. & Shrefler, B. A. The Finite Element Method in the Static & Dynamic Deformation & Consolidation of Porous Media, 2E. 2nd ed. LC 98-12080. 508p. 1998. 185.00 (0-471-92809-7) Wiley.
Lewis, R. W. B., et al. The Finite Element Method in Heat Transfer Analysis. LC 93-7789. 290p. 1996. 160.00 (0-471-93424-0); pap. 80.00 (0-471-94362-2) Wiley.
Lewis, R. W. B., jt. auth. see Woodberry, George E.
Lewis, R. W. B., jt. ed. see Schrefler, B. A.
Lewis, R. W. B., ed. see Technical Association of the Pulp & Paper Industry.
Lewis, R. W. B., ed. see Wharton, Edith.
Lewis, Ralph. By Dead Reckoning. (Illus.). 240p. 1994. 25.00 (0-9626483-6-1) Paladwr Pr.
— Team-Building Skills: Trainer's Guide. LC 94-13300. (One-Day Workshop Ser.). 1994. 110.00 (0-07-040831-9) McGraw.
Lewis, Ralph & Smith, Douglas. Total Quality in Higher Education. LC 93-23440. (Total Quality Ser.). (Illus.). 344p. 1993. boxed set 57.95 (0-9634030-7-9) St Lucie Pr.
Lewis, Ralph, jt. auth. see Lowe, Phil.
Lewis, Ralph L. & Lewis, Gregg. Inductive Preaching: Helping People Listen. LC 83-70321. 224p. 1983. pap. 10.99 (0-89107-287-X) Crossway Bks.
Lewis, Ralph M. The Conscious Interlude. LC 57-8541. 371p. 1957. 18.95 (0-912057-20-3, 501810) GLELJ AMORC.
— Cosmic Mission Fulfilled: The Life of Dr. H. Spencer Lewis - a 20th Century Mystic. LC 66-25243. (Illus.). 364p. 1976. pap. 18.95 (0-912057-90-4, 501790) GLELJ AMORC.
— Land Buying Checklist. 4th ed. 60p. 1990. pap. 20.00 (0-86718-358-6) Home Builder.
— Mental Alchemy. LC 79-66799. 270p. 1978. pap. 17.95 (0-912057-92-0, 501830) GLELJ AMORC.
— The Sanctuary of Self. LC 48-17673. 351p. 1948. pap. 14.95 (0-912057-53-X, 502040) GLELJ AMORC.
Lewis, Ralph M. Through the Mind's Eye. LC 81-84954. 213p. 1982. pap. 13.95 (1-893971-01-5) GLELJ AMORC.
Lewis, Ralph M., ed. The Immortalized Words of the Past. LC 85-63539. 293p. 1986. pap. 12.95 (0-912057-42-4, 501950) GLELJ AMORC.

L

Lewis, Ramana, ed. see Brendan-Brown, Sean, et al.

Lewis, Ramana, ed. see Kinney, Judy, et al.

Lewis, Ramon. The Discipline Dilemma. (C). 1990. 70.00 (0-86431-083-8, Pub. by Aust Council Educ Res) St Mut.

— The Discipline Dilemma. 2nd ed. 1997. pap. 25.00 (0-86431-203-2, Pub. by Aust Council Educ Res) Stylus Pub VA.

Lewis, Ramon & Lewis, Susan. The Parenting Puzzle. (C). 1989. pap. 60.00 (0-86431-036-6, Pub. by Aust Council Educ Res) St Mut.

Lewis, Rand C. A Nazi Legacy: Right-Wing Extremism in West Germany. LC 90-24277. 208p. 1991. 42.95 (0-275-93853-0, C3853, Praeger Pubs) Greenwood.

— The Neo-Nazis & German Unification. LC 96-2198. 136p. 1996. 49.95 (0-275-95638-5, Praeger Pubs) Greenwood.

Lewis, Randine A. Techniques of Medical Litigation: A Professional's Handbook for Plaintiffs, Defendants, & Medical Consultants. LC 96-32508. 320p. 1997. 75.00 (1-56720-088-5, Quorum Bks) Greenwood.

***Lewis, Randolph.** Emile de Antonio: Radical Filmmaker in Cold War America. 2000. 50.00 (0-299-16910-3); pap. 19.95 (0-299-16914-6) U of Wis Pr.

Lewis, Randolph, ed. see Gilbert, Stuart.

Lewis, Rebecca. Guide to Owning a Collie: AKC Rank #29. (Guide to Owning Ser.). (Illus.). 64p. 1995. pap. 6.95 (0-7938-1856-7, RE-306) TFH Pubns.

***Lewis, Regina.** Wired in a Week: Master the Internet in 10 Minutes a Day. 2000. pap. 6.95 (0-446-67736-1) Warner Bks.

Lewis, Reginald F. & Price, Hugh B. "Why Should White Guys Have All the Fun?" How Reginald Lewis Created a Billion-Dollar Business Empire. LC 94-17864. 318p. 1994. 22.95 (0-471-04227-7) Wiley.

— "Why Should White Guys Have All the Fun?" How Reginald Lewis Created a Billion-Dollar Business Empire. LC 94-17864. 318p. 1995. pap. 12.95 (0-471-14560-2) Wiley.

— "Why Should White Guys Have All the Fun?" How Reginald Lewis Created a Billion-Dollar Business Empire. LC 94-17864. 336p. 1996. pap. 6.99 (0-471-17689-3) Wiley.

Lewis, Reina. Gendering Orientalism: Race, Femininity & Representation. LC 95-16143. (Gender, Racism, Ethnicity Ser.). 328p. (C). 1995. pap. 24.99 (0-415-12490-5) Routledge.

Lewis, Reina, jt. ed. see Horne, Peter.

Lewis, Rena B. Special Education Technology: Practical Applications. LC 92-35860. 552p. 1993. 35.25 (0-534-20286-1) Brooks-Cole.

Lewis, Rena B. & Doorlag, Donald H. Teaching Special Students in General Education Classrooms. 5th ed. LC 98-4433. 519p. (C). 1998. pap. text 59.00 (0-13-095307-5, Merrill Coll) P-H.

Lewis, Rena B., jt. auth. see McLoughlin, James A.

Lewis, Renee. Talk the Talk! How to Master Verbal Etiquette & Use It to Your Advantage. LC 96-94617. Orig. Title: Talk & Go Talk. 100p. 1998. pap. write for info. (0-9653907-0-5) HLC.

Lewis, Richard. All of You Was Singing. LC 89-18263. (Illus.). 32p. (J). 1991. text, lib. bdg. 13.95 (0-689-31596-1) Atheneum Yung Read.

— Black Cop: The Real Deal, the True Stroy of New York's Most Decorated Black Cop. LC 97-131519. 264p. 1996. 10.99 (1-56043-583-6, Treasure Hse) Destiny Image.

— Compensation for Industrial Injuries. 1987. text 65.00 (0-86205-214-9, UK, MICHIE) LEXIS Pub.

— A Contemporary Approach to Fidelity & Surety Bonding. 255p. (Orig.). 1994. pap. 43.00 (1-56461-120-5, 26020) Rough Notes.

— The Contractor's Financial Statement: Accounting, Analysis & Underwriting. 88p. 1995. pap. 46.00 (1-56461-136-1, 26335) Rough Notes.

— It's a Wonderful Strife. 1999. write for info. (0-375-50218-1) Villard Books.

— Living by Wonder: The Imaginative Life of Childhood. LC 97-52573. x, 150 p. 1998. 18.95 (0-930407-38-5) Parabola Bks.

***Lewis, Richard.** The Other Great Depression: How I'm Overcoming, on a Daily Basis, at Least a Million Addictions & Dysfunctions & Finding a Spiritual (Sometimes) Life. 2001. 23.00 (1-891620-93-2) PublicAffairs NY.

Lewis, Richard. Symbols of Power Self-Healing System. (Illus.). 1998. pap. 49.95 (0-9664069-0-7, Symbols Power) Lewis Pub CA.

— There Will I Sing: The Making of a Tenor: A Biography of Richard Lewis CBE. (Illus.). 152p. 1997. 24.95 (1-871871-29-8, Pub. by Open Gate Pr) Paul & Co Pubs.

— When Thought Is Young: Reflections on Teaching & the Poetry of the Child. LC 91-61262. (Illus.). 69p. 1992. pap. 1.20 (0-89823-137-X) New Rivers Pr.

Lewis, Richard & Lewis, Susan. The Power of Art. (Illus.). 528p. (Orig.). (C). 1994. pap. text 65.50 (0-15-500320-8, Pub. by Harcourt Coll Pubs) Harcourt.

Lewis, Richard & Pendrill, David. Advanced Financial Accounting. 5th ed. 640p. (Orig.). 1996. pap. 67.50 (0-273-62291-9, Pub. by Pitman Pub) Trans-Atl Phila.

Lewis, Richard A., jt. auth. see Gold, Daniel.

***Lewis, Richard C.** Contract Suretyship: From Principle to Practice. LC 99-33864. 224p. 2000. 69.95 (0-471-37135-1) Wiley.

***Lewis, Richard D.** When Cultures Collide: Managing Successfully Across Cultures. LC 99-51394. (Illus.). 500p. 2000. pap. 19.95 (1-85788-087-0, Pub. by Nicholas Brealey) Natl Bk Netwk.

Lewis, Richard E., jt. ed. see Gregory, Robert G.

Lewis, Richard J. Hawley's Condensed Chemical Dictionary. 3rd ed. 1248p. 1997. 138.00 (0-471-29205-2, VNR) Wiley.

Lewis, Richard J., Sr. Hawley's Condensed Chemical Dictionary. 13th ed. LC 97-35762. (Illus.). 2500p. (C). 1997. 99.95 (0-442-02324-3, VNR) Wiley.

— Hazardous Chemicals: Desk Reference. 4th ed. LC 96-45239. 1760p. (C). 1997. text 125.95 (0-442-02322-7, VNR) Wiley.

— Hazardous Chemicals Desk Reference. 3rd rev. ed. LC 92-46784. 1600p. 1993. text 114.95 (0-442-01408-2, VNR) Wiley.

Lewis, Richard J. Hazardous Chemicals Desk Reference. 4th ed. 1680p. 1996. 149.00 (0-471-28779-2, VNR) Wiley.

— Rapid Guide to Hazardous Chemicals in the Workplace. 4th ed. 288p. 2000. pap. 34.95 (0-471-35542-9) Wiley.

Lewis, Richard J., Sr. Reproductively Active Chemicals. 864p. 1991. text 167.95 (0-442-31878-2, VNR) Wiley.

Lewis, Richard J. Reproductively Active Chemicals: A Reference Guide. (Sax/Lewis Program Ser.). 841p. 1991. 175.00 (0-471-28973-6, VNR) Wiley.

Lewis, Richard J., Sr. Sax's Dangerous Properties of Industrial Materials, 3 vols. 9th ed. LC 96-523. (Space Ser.: Vol. 56). 2454p. (J). (gr. 5-10). 1998. text 499.95 incl. digital audio (0-442-02025-2, VNR) Wiley.

Lewis, Richard J. Sax's Dangerous Properties of Industrial Materials, 3 Vols. 9th ed. 4320p. 1995. 500.00 (0-471-28694-X, VNR) Wiley.

— Sax's Dangerous Properties of Industrial Materials, 3 vols. Set. 10th ed. LC 99-39820. 4000p. 1999. 545.00 (0-471-35407-4) Wiley.

— Sax's Dangerous Properties of Industrial Materials, 3 vols., Vols. 1-3. 10th ed. 4000p. 1999. 985.00 (0-471-37858-5) Wiley.

Lewis, Richard J., Sr., ed. Rapid Guide to Hazardous Chemicals in the Workplace. 3rd ed. 288p. 1994. pap. 29.95 (0-442-01759-6, VNR) Wiley.

Lewis, Richard J. & Lisella, Frank S. Hawley's Condensed Chemical Dictionary & the VNR Dictionary of Environmental Health & Safety & Sax's Dangerous Properties of Industrial Materials. 8th ed. 1995. 150.00 (0-442-02044-9, VNR) Wiley.

Lewis, Richard L. Runic & Mediterranean Epigraphy. (NOWELE Ser.: Suppl. Vol. 4). 178p. (Orig.). 1988. pap. 42.50 (87-7492-683-7, Pub. by Odense Universitets Forlag) Coronet Bks.

Lewis, Richard L., jt. auth. see Simmons, H. Leslie.

Lewis, Richard O. Conventional Functions of Black English in American Literature. LC 96-39480. 88p. 1997. 69.95 (1-57292-033-5); pap. 49.95 (1-57292-032-7) Austin & Winfield.

Lewis, Richard P., ed. see American College of Cardiology Staff.

Lewis, Richard P., jt. ed. see Warren, James V.

Lewis, Richard S. Space in the Twenty-First Century. (Illus.). 240p. 1990. 40.00 (0-231-06304-0) Col U Pr.

— Voyages of Columbia. 1984. text 46.00 (0-231-05924-8) Col U Pr.

Lewis, Richard T. New York: A Geography. 1996. text 35.00 (0-86531-227-3) Westview.

— New York: A Geography. (C). 1996. pap. text 20.00 (0-86531-485-3) Westview.

Lewis, Richard W. Absolut Book: The Absolut Vodka Advertising Story. 1996. 60.00 (1-885203-32-2) Jrny Editions.

— Absolut Book: The Absolut Vodka Advertising Story. LC 95-53040. (Illus.). 288p. 1996. pap. 29.95 (1-885203-29-2) Jrny Editions.

— American Adam. LC 55-5133. 207p. 1959. pap. text 10.95 (0-226-47681-2, P38) U Ch Pr.

***Lewis, Rick.** The Perfection of Nothing: Reflections of Spiritual Practice. 180p. 2000. pap. 14.95 (1-890772-02-X, Pub. by Hohm Pr) SCB Distributors.

Lewis, Rick & Smith, Judy. Fighting Fair for Families Trainer's Implementation. Burke, James A., II, ed. (Illus.). (Orig.). 1996. pap. text 49.95 (1-878227-31-9) Peace Educ.

Lewis, Ricki. The Beginnings of Life. 2nd ed. (C). 1994. text, student ed. write for info. (0-697-26491-2, WCB McGr Hill) McGrw-H Hghr Educ.

— The Beginnings of Life: An Introduction to Cell, Molecular & Developmental Biology. 2nd ed. LC 93-74672. 550p. (C). 1994. per. 46.40 (0-697-13661-2, WCB McGr Hill) McGrw-H Hghr Educ.

— The Beginnings of Life: An Introduction to Cell, Molecular & Developmental Biology. 2nd ed. 136p. (C). 1994. text, student ed. write for info. (0-697-24806-2, WCB McGr Hill) McGrw-H Hghr Educ.

***Lewis, Ricki.** Discovery: Windows on the Life Sciences. LC 00-34229. (Illus.). 225p. 2000. pap. 32.95 (0-632-04452-7) Blackwell Sci.

Lewis, Ricki. Human Genetics. 2nd ed. 440p. (C). 1997. per. write for info. (0-07-114192-8, WCB McGr Hill) McGrw-H Hghr Educ.

— Human Genetics. 2nd ed. 192p. (C). 1997. text, student ed. 20.62 (0-697-24032-0, WCB McGr Hill) McGrw-H Hghr Educ.

***Lewis, Ricki.** Human Genetics. 2nd ed. 160p. (C). 2000. pap. 19.38 (0-07-232530-5) McGrw-H Hghr Educ.

Lewis, Ricki. Human Genetics: Concepts & Applications. 416p. (C). 1993. text, student ed. 23.12 (0-697-22287-X, WCB McGr Hill) McGrw-H Hghr Educ.

— Human Genetics: Concepts & Applications. 416p. (C). 1994. text, student ed. 20.62 (0-697-20817-6, WCB McGr Hill) McGrw-H Hghr Educ.

— Human Genetics: Concepts & Applications. 2nd ed. LC 96-85271. 427p. (C). 1996. text 56.55 (0-697-24030-4, WCB McGr Hill) McGrw-H Hghr Educ.

— Life. 832p. (C). 1991. text. write for info. (0-697-14187-X, WCB McGr Hill); text. write for info. (0-697-12059-7, WCB McGr Hill); text. write for info. (0-697-14193-4, WCB McGr Hill); text. write for info. (0-697-14197-7, WCB McGr Hill); text. write for info. (0-697-14199-3, WCB McGr Hill); text. write for info. (0-697-14201-9, WCB McGr Hill) McGrw-H Hghr Educ.

Lewis, Ricki & Jacklet, Alice C. Life. 3rd ed. 192p. (C). 1997. text, lab manual ed. write for info. (0-697-28568-5, WCB McGr Hill) McGrw-H Hghr Educ.

Lewis, Ricki & Moore, Randall C. Life. 2nd ed. (C). 1994. text, student ed. write for info. (0-697-26488-2, WCB McGr Hill) McGrw-H Hghr Educ.

— Life. 2nd ed. (C). 1995. text, student ed. write for info. (0-697-26487-4, WCB McGr Hill) McGrw-H Hghr Educ.

Lewis, Ricki & Moore, Randall c. Life, Lab Manual. 2nd ed. 192p. (C). 1994. text, student ed. write for info. (0-697-15942-6, WCB McGr Hill) McGrw-H Hghr Educ.

— Life, Study Art Notebook. 2nd ed. 232p. (C). 1994. text, student ed. write for info. (0-697-24548-9, WCB McGr Hill) McGrw-H Hghr Educ.

— Life, Study Guide. 2nd ed. 176p. (C). 1995. text, student ed. 18.75 (0-697-15945-0, WCB McGr Hill) McGrw-H Hghr Educ.

Lewis, Ricki, et al. Life. 2nd ed. (SPA.). 224p. (C). 1995. student ed. write for info. (0-697-28041-1, WCB McGr Hill) McGrw-H Hghr Educ.

— Life. 3rd ed. LC 97-15290. 976p. (C). 1997. text. write for info. (0-697-28563-4, WCB McGr Hill) McGrw-H Hghr Educ.

Lewis, Ricki, jt. auth. see Moore, Randall c.

Lewis, Rik. Dragonfly: Cycle of Fire. Black, Bill, ed. (Illus.). 52p. (Orig.). 1991. pap. 9.95 (1-56225-000-0) A C Comics.

Lewis, Rita. The Adobe PageMill 2.0 Handbook. LC 96-77656. 432p. 1996. 39.99 (1-56830-313-0) Hayden.

— Sams Teach Yourself iMac in 10 Minutes. LC 98-88376. 1999. pap. text 12.99 (0-672-31519-X) Sams.

***Lewis, Rita.** Sams Teach Yourself Mac OS 9 in 24 Hours. 488p. 1999. 19.99 (0-672-31775-3) Sams.

Lewis, Rita. Teach Yourself Mac OS 8 in 24 Hours. (Teach Yourself Ser.). 400p. 1998. pap. 19.99 (0-672-31335-9) Sams.

Lewis, Rita F. Mac OS in a Nutshell. Stone, Mark, ed. (In a Nutshell Ser.). (Illus.). 376p. 2000. pap. 24.95 (1-56592-533-5) OReilly & Assocs.

Lewis, Rob. Aquidneck Island & Her Neighbors. LC 97-158783. (Images of America Ser.). 1997. pap. 16.99 (0-7524-0532-2) Arcadia Publng.

— Fall River. (Images of America Ser.). 1999. pap. 16.99 (0-7524-0826-7) Arcadia Publng.

— Grandpa at the Beach. LC 97-11753. (Illus.). (J). (gr. 1-5). 1998. pap. 4.50 (1-57255-552-1) Mondo Pubng.

— Grandpa Comes to Stay. LC 95-50370. (Illus.). 48p. (J). (gr. 1-5). 1996. pap. 4.50 (1-57255-212-3) Mondo Pubng.

— Hide & Seek with Grandpa. LC 96-32108. (Illus.). (J). (gr. 1-5). 1997. pap. 4.50 (1-57255-226-3) Mondo Pubng.

— Newport. (Images of America Ser.). 128p. 1996. pap. 16.99 (0-7524-0405-9) Arcadia Publng.

— Ollie's Song. 1999. pap. 10.99 (0-8037-1102-6, NewStar Pr); pap. 10.89 (0-8037-1103-4, NewStar Pr) NewStar Media.

— Tidy up, Trevor. LC 92-30327. (Illus.). 32p. (J). (ps-2). 1993. 13.95 (0-15-200626-5) Harcourt.

— Too Much Trouble for Grandpa. LC 97-14197. (Illus.). (J). (gr. 1-5). 1998. pap. 4.50 (1-57255-551-3) Mondo Pubng.

— Try Again, Trevor. (Illus.). 32p. (J). (ps-k). 1996. 17.95 (0-370-31974-5, Pub. by Bodley Head) Trafalgar.

Lewis, Rob & Young, Ryan. Rhode Island's Amusement Parks. (Images of America Ser.). 1998. write for info. (0-7524-1302-3) Arcadia Publng.

Lewis, Robert. Advice to the Players. LC 79-3291. 192p. 1998. reprint ed. pap. 10.95 (1-55936-003-8) Theatre Comm.

Lewis, Robert, Jr. Hemingway on Love. LC 72-6772. (Studies in Fiction: No. 34). 1972. reprint ed. lib. bdg. 75.00 (0-8383-1650-6) M S G Haskell Hse.

Lewis, Robert. Method or Madness. 165p. 1958. 6.50 (0-573-69033-2) French.

— Raising a Modern-Day Knight. 1999. pap. 9.99 (1-56179-716-2) Focus Family.

— Raising a Modern-Day Knight: A Father's Role in Guiding His Son to Authentic Manhood. LC 96-52752. 1997. 16.99 (1-56179-534-8) Focus Family.

— Slings & Arrows: Theatre in My Life. (Illus.). 384p. 1996. pap. 19.95 (1-55783-244-7) Applause Theatre Bk Pubs.

***Lewis, Robert & Campbell, Rich.** Real Family Values: Keeping the Faith in an Age of Cultural Chaos. LC 99-50892. 2000. pap. 12.99 (1-57673-667-9, Pub. by Multnomah Pubs) GL Services.

Lewis, Robert & Hendricks, William. Rocking the Roles: Building a Win-Win Marriage. LC 91-61395. 252p. 1991. pap. 12.00 (0-89109-641-8) NavPress.

— Rocking the Roles: Building a Win-Win Marriage. LC 98-33948. 1999. 12.00 (1-57683-125-6) NavPress.

Lewis, Robert & Kaplan, Roger P. Responding to Union Organizing Campaigns. Vol. E6. text 82.00 (0-8205-2395-X) Bender.

Lewis, Robert & Mendelsohn, Patrick, eds. Lessons from Learning: Proceedings of the IFIP TC3 - WG3.3 Wording Conference on Lessons from Learning, Archamps, France. LC 94-7739. (IFIP Transactions Ser.). 256p. 1994. 94.00 (0-444-81832-4) Elsevier.

Lewis, Robert, jt. auth. see Spiess, Arthur.

Lewis, Robert A., ed. Dictionary of Toxicology. LC 96-35759. 1127p. 1996. 79.95 (1-56670-223-2, L1223) Lewis Pubs.

Lewis, Robert A., et al, eds. Environmental Specimen Banking & Monitoring As Related to Banking. 370p. 1983. text 211.50 (0-89838-621-7) Kluwer Academic.

Lewis, Robert A. & Rowland, Richard H. Population Redistribution in the U. S. S. R. Its Impact on Society, 1897-1977. LC 79-18076. (Praeger Special Studies). 485p. 1979. 95.00 (0-275-90382-6, C0382, Praeger Pubs) Greenwood.

Lewis, Robert A. & Salt, Robert E., eds. Men in Families. LC 85-14330. (Sage Focus Editions Ser.: No. 76). 288p. 1986. reprint ed. pap. 89.30 (0-608-01178-9, 205947600001) Bks Demand.

Lewis, Robert A., jt. ed. see Culp, Robert D.

Lewis, Robert C. Cases in Hospitality Marketing & Management. 2nd ed. 400p. 1997. pap. text, teacher ed. write for info. (0-471-17553-6) Wiley.

— Cases in Hospitality Marketing & Mangagement. 2nd ed. LC 96-37343. 504p. 1997. pap. 44.95 (0-471-16732-0) Wiley.

— Cases in Hospitality Strategy & Policy. 440p. 1998. pap. 59.95 (0-471-24012-5) Wiley.

— Marketing Leadership in Hospitality. 2nd ed. (Hospitality, Travel & Tourism Ser.). 860p. 1994. text 55.95 (0-442-01888-6, VNR) Wiley.

***Lewis, Robert C. & Chambers, Richard E.** Marketing Leadership in Hospitality: Foundations & Practices. 3rd ed. LC 99-19482. 960p. (C). 2000. 64.95 (0-471-33270-4) Wiley.

Lewis, Robert C., et al. Marketing Leadership in Hospitality: Foundations & Practices. 2nd ed. (Hospitality, Travel & Tourism Ser.). 880p. 1994. 59.95 (0-471-28646-X, VNR) Wiley.

Lewis, Robert C., jt. auth. see Leitritz, Earl.

Lewis, Robert D., jt. auth. see Lewis, Herschell Gordon.

Lewis, Robert E. How to Conduct a Sensitivity Analysis. Burke, Sarah A., ed. LC 91-22358. (Illus.). 64p. (Orig.). 1991. pap. text 55.00 (0-936742-83-6, 32461) Robt Morris Assocs.

Lewis, Robert E., ed. Middle English Dictionary. (Illus.). (C). 1952. pap. text 25.00 (0-472-01051-4, 01051) U of Mich Pr.

— Middle English Dictionary. (Illus.). (C). 1953. pap. text 25.00 (0-472-01052-2, 01052) U of Mich Pr.

— Middle English Dictionary. (Illus.). (C). 1953. pap. text 25.00 (0-472-01053-0, 01053) U of Mich Pr.

— Middle English Dictionary. (Illus.). (C). 1953. pap. text 25.00 (0-472-01061-1, 01061) U of Mich Pr.

— Middle English Dictionary. (Illus.). (C). 1954. pap. text 25.00 (0-472-01062-X, 01062) U of Mich Pr.

— Middle English Dictionary. (Illus.). (C). 1954. pap. text 25.00 (0-472-01063-8, 01063) U of Mich Pr.

— Middle English Dictionary. (Illus.). (C). 1954. pap. text 25.00 (0-472-01064-6, 01064) U of Mich Pr.

— Middle English Dictionary. (Illus.). (C). 1956. pap. text 25.00 (0-472-01013-1, 01013); pap. text 25.00 (0-472-01012-3, 01012) U of Mich Pr.

— Middle English Dictionary. (Illus.). (C). 1957. pap. text 25.00 (0-472-01022-0, 01022); pap. text 25.00 (0-472-01014-X, 01014); pap. text 25.00 (0-472-01023-9, 01023) U of Mich Pr.

— Middle English Dictionary. (Illus.). (C). 1958. pap. text 25.00 (0-472-01025-5, 01025); pap. text 25.00 (0-472-01024-7, 01024) U of Mich Pr.

— Middle English Dictionary. (Illus.). (C). 1959. pap. text 25.00 (0-472-01033-6, 01033); pap. text 25.00 (0-472-01032-8, 01032); pap. text 25.00 (0-472-01031-X, 01031) U of Mich Pr.

— Middle English Dictionary. (Illus.). (C). 1960. pap. text 25.00 (0-472-01034-4, 01034) U of Mich Pr.

— Middle English Dictionary. (Illus.). (C). 1960. pap. text 25.00 (0-472-01035-2, 01035); pap. text 25.00 (0-472-01036-0, 01036) U of Mich Pr.

— Middle English Dictionary. (Illus.). (C). 1961. pap. text 25.00 (0-472-01041-7, 01041); pap. text 25.00 (0-472-01042-5, 01042) U of Mich Pr.

— Middle English Dictionary. (Illus.). (C). 1961. pap. text 25.00 (0-472-01043-3, 01043) U of Mich Pr.

— Middle English Dictionary. (Illus.). (C). 1962. pap. text 25.00 (0-472-01044-1, 01044) U of Mich Pr.

— Middle English Dictionary. (Illus.). (C). 1962. pap. text 25.00 (0-472-01045-X, 01045) U of Mich Pr.

— Middle English Dictionary. (Illus.). (C). 1963. pap. text 25.00 (0-472-01071-9, 01071) U of Mich Pr.

— Middle English Dictionary. (Illus.). (C). 1963. pap. text 25.00 (0-472-01072-7, 01072) U of Mich Pr.

— Middle English Dictionary. (Illus.). (C). 1964. pap. text 25.00 (0-472-01073-5, 01073) U of Mich Pr.

— Middle English Dictionary. (Illus.). (C). 1966. pap. text 25.00 (0-472-01081-6, 01081) U of Mich Pr.

— Middle English Dictionary. (Illus.). (C). 1966. pap. text 25.00 (0-472-01082-4, 01082) U of Mich Pr.

— Middle English Dictionary. (Illus.). (C). 1966. pap. text 25.00 (0-472-01083-2, 01083) U of Mich Pr.

— Middle English Dictionary. (Illus.). (C). 1966. pap. text 25.00 (0-472-01084-0, 01084) U of Mich Pr.

— Middle English Dictionary. (Illus.). (C). 1967. pap. text 25.00 (0-472-01085-9, 01085) U of Mich Pr.

— Middle English Dictionary. (Illus.). (C). 1968. pap. text 25.00 (0-472-01091-3, 01091) U of Mich Pr.

— Middle English Dictionary. (Illus.). (C). 1968. pap. text 25.00 (0-472-01092-1, 01092) U of Mich Pr.

— Middle English Dictionary. (Illus.). (C). 1969. pap. text 25.00 (0-472-01101-4, 01101) U of Mich Pr.

— Middle English Dictionary. (Illus.). (C). 1969. pap. text 25.00 (0-472-01111-1, 01111) U of Mich Pr.

— Middle English Dictionary. (Illus.). (C). 1970. pap. text 25.00 (0-472-01121-9, 01121) U of Mich Pr.

— Middle English Dictionary. (Illus.). (C). 1970. pap. text 25.00 (0-472-01122-7, 01122) U of Mich Pr.

— Middle English Dictionary. (Illus.). (C). 1971. pap. text 25.00 (0-472-01123-5, 01123) U of Mich Pr.

An Asterisk (*) at the beginning of an entry indicates that the title is appearing for the first time.

— Middle English Dictionary. (Illus.). (C). 1972. pap. text 25.00 (*0-472-01124-3*, 01124) U of Mich Pr.
— Middle English Dictionary. (Illus.). (C). 1973. pap. text 25.00 (*0-472-01125-1*, 01125) U of Mich Pr.
— Middle English Dictionary. (Illus.). (C). 1973. pap. text 25.00 (*0-472-01126-X*, 01126) U of Mich Pr.
— Middle English Dictionary. (Illus.). (C). 1975. pap. text 25.00 (*0-472-01131-6*, 01131) U of Mich Pr.
— Middle English Dictionary. (Illus.). (C). 1975. pap. text 25.00 (*0-472-01132-4*, 01132) U of Mich Pr.
— Middle English Dictionary. (Illus.). (C). 1975. pap. text 25.00 (*0-472-01133-2*, 01133) U of Mich Pr.
— Middle English Dictionary. (Illus.). (C). 1977. pap. text 25.00 (*0-472-01134-0*, 01134) U of Mich Pr.
— Middle English Dictionary. (Illus.). (C). 1977. pap. text 25.00 (*0-472-01135-9*, 01135) U of Mich Pr.
— Middle English Dictionary. (Illus.). (C). 1978. pap. text 25.00 (*0-472-01136-7*, 01136) U of Mich Pr.
— Middle English Dictionary. (Illus.). (C). 1978. pap. text 25.00 (*0-472-01141-3*, 01141) U of Mich Pr.
— Middle English Dictionary. (Illus.). (C). 1979. pap. text 25.00 (*0-472-01142-1*, 01142) U of Mich Pr.
— Middle English Dictionary. (Illus.). (C). 1979. pap. text 25.00 (*0-472-01143-X*, 01143) U of Mich Pr.
— Middle English Dictionary. (Illus.). (C). 1980. pap. text 25.00 (*0-472-01151-0*, 01151) U of Mich Pr.
— Middle English Dictionary. (Illus.). (C). 1980. pap. text 25.00 (*0-472-01152-9*, 01152) U of Mich Pr.
— Middle English Dictionary. (Illus.). (C). 1981. pap. text 25.00 (*0-472-01153-7*, 01153) U of Mich Pr.
— Middle English Dictionary. (Illus.). (C). 1981. pap. text 25.00 (*0-472-01154-5*, 01154) U of Mich Pr.
— Middle English Dictionary. (Illus.). (C). 1982. pap. text 25.00 (*0-472-01161-8*, 01161) U of Mich Pr.
— Middle English Dictionary. (Illus.). (C). 1982. pap. text 25.00 (*0-472-01162-6*, 01162) U of Mich Pr.
— Middle English Dictionary. (Illus.). (C). 1982. pap. text 25.00 (*0-472-01163-4*, 01163) U of Mich Pr.
— Middle English Dictionary. (Illus.). (C). 1983. pap. text 25.00 (*0-472-01164-2*, 01164) U of Mich Pr.
— Middle English Dictionary. (Illus.). (C). 1983. pap. text 25.00 (*0-472-01165-0*, 01165) U of Mich Pr.
— Middle English Dictionary. (Illus.). (C). 1983. pap. text 25.00 (*0-472-01166-9*, 01166) U of Mich Pr.
— Middle English Dictionary. (Illus.). (C). 1983. pap. text 25.00 (*0-472-01167-7*, 01167) U of Mich Pr.
— Middle English Dictionary. (Illus.). (C). 1984. pap. text 25.00 (*0-472-01168-5*, 01168) U of Mich Pr.
— Middle English Dictionary. (Illus.). (C). 1985. pap. text 25.00 (*0-472-01171-5*, 01171); pap. text 25.00 (*0-472-01181-2*, 01181) U of Mich Pr.
— Middle English Dictionary. (Illus.). (C). 1985. pap. text 25.00 (*0-472-01182-0*, 01182) U of Mich Pr.
— Middle English Dictionary. (Illus.). (C). 1985. pap. text 25.00 (*0-472-01183-9*, 01183) U of Mich Pr.
— Middle English Dictionary. (Illus.). (C). 1985. pap. text 25.00 (*0-472-01184-7*, 01184) U of Mich Pr.
— Middle English Dictionary. (Illus.). (C). 1986. pap. text 25.00 (*0-472-01185-5*, 01185) U of Mich Pr.
— Middle English Dictionary. (Illus.). (C). 1986. pap. text 25.00 (*0-472-01186-3*, 01186) U of Mich Pr.
— Middle English Dictionary. (Illus.). (C). 1986. pap. text 25.00 (*0-472-01191-X*, 01191) U of Mich Pr.
— Middle English Dictionary. (Illus.). (C). 1986. pap. text 25.00 (*0-472-01192-8*, 01192) U of Mich Pr.
— Middle English Dictionary. (Illus.). (C). 1987. pap. text 25.00 (*0-472-01193-6*, 01193) U of Mich Pr.
— Middle English Dictionary. (Illus.). (C). 1987. pap. text 25.00 (*0-472-01194-4*, 01194) U of Mich Pr.
— Middle English Dictionary. (Illus.). (C). 1987. pap. text 25.00 (*0-472-01195-2*, 01195) U of Mich Pr.
— Middle English Dictionary. (Illus.). (C). 1988. pap. text 25.00 (*0-472-01196-0*, 01196); pap. text 25.00 (*0-472-01197-9*, 01197) U of Mich Pr.
— Middle English Dictionary. (Illus.). (C). 1988. pap. text 25.00 (*0-472-01198-7*, 01198) U of Mich Pr.
— Middle English Dictionary. (Illus.). (C). 1988. pap. text 25.00 (*0-472-01199-5*, 01199) U of Mich Pr.
— Middle English Dictionary. (Illus.). (C). 1989. pap. text 25.00 (*0-472-01200-2*, 01200) U of Mich Pr.
— Middle English Dictionary. (Illus.). (C). 1989. pap. text 25.00 (*0-472-01201-0*, 01201) U of Mich Pr.
— Middle English Dictionary. (Illus.). (C). 1990. pap. text 25.00 (*0-472-01202-9*, 01202) U of Mich Pr.
— Middle English Dictionary, Bk. 1. (Illus.). (C). 1957. pap. text 25.00 (*0-472-01021-2*, 01021) U of Mich Pr.
— Middle English Dictionary, W.3. (Illus.). 128p. (C). 2000. pap. text 17.50 (*0-472-01229-0*, 01229) U of Mich Pr.
— Middle English Dictionary, W.4. (Illus.). 128p. (C). 2000. pap. text 17.50 (*0-472-01230-4*, 01230) U of Mich Pr.
— Middle English Dictionary: Plan & Bibliography. (Illus.). (C). 1985. pap. text 25.00 (*0-472-01002-6*, 01002) U of Mich Pr.
— Middle English Dictionary: S.13. (Illus.). (C). 1990. pap. text 25.00 (*0-472-01203-7*, 01203) U of Mich Pr.
— Middle English Dictionary: S.14. (Illus.). (C). 1990. pap. text 25.00 (*0-472-01204-5*, 01204) U of Mich Pr.
— Middle English Dictionary: S.15. (Illus.). (C). 1991. pap. text 25.00 (*0-472-01205-3*, 01205) U of Mich Pr.
— Middle English Dictionary: S.16. (Illus.). (C). 1991. pap. text 25.00 (*0-472-01206-1*, 01206) U of Mich Pr.
— Middle English Dictionary: S.17. (Illus.). (C). 1992. pap. text 25.00 (*0-472-01207-X*, 01207) U of Mich Pr.
— Middle English Dictionary: S.18. (Illus.). (C). 1992. pap. text 25.00 (*0-472-01208-8*, 01208) U of Mich Pr.
— Middle English Dictionary: T.6. LC 53-62158. (Illus.). 128p. (C). 1995. pap. text 25.00 (*0-472-01216-9*, 01216) U of Mich Pr.
— Middle English Dictionary: U.4. (Illus.). 128p. (C). 1998. pap. text 17.50 (*0-472-01224-X*, 01224) U of Mich Pr.
— Middle English Dictionary: V.1. 184p. 1999. pap. text 17.50 (*0-472-01225-8*, 01225) U of Mich Pr.
— Middle English Dictionary: W.1. 128p. 1999. pap. text 17.50 (*0-472-01227-4*, 01227) U of Mich Pr.
Lewis, Robert E., ed. Middle English Dictionary: W.2. 128p. 1999. pap. text 17.50 (*0-472-01228-2*, 01228) U of Mich Pr.
Lewis, Robert E., et al, eds. Middle English Dictionary: Fascicle T.3. 128p. 1994. pap. text 25.00 (*0-472-01213-4*, 01213) U of Mich Pr.
— Middle English Dictionary: Fascicle T.4. 128p. 1994. pap. text 25.00 (*0-472-01214-2*, 01214) U of Mich Pr.
— Middle English Dictionary: Fascicle T.5. 128p. 1995. pap. text 25.00 (*0-472-01215-0*, 01215) U of Mich Pr.
Lewis, Robert E. & Williams, Mary J., eds. Middle English Dictionary: Fascicle T.1. (C). 1993. pap. text 25.00 (*0-472-01211-8*, 01211) U of Mich Pr.
— Middle English Dictionary: Fascicle T.10. 88p. (Orig.). 1997. pap. text 25.00 (*0-472-01220-7*, 01220) U of Mich Pr.
— Middle English Dictionary: Fascicle T.2. (C). 1993. pap. text 25.00 (*0-472-01212-6*, 01212) U of Mich Pr.
— Middle English Dictionary: Fascicle T.7. 128p. (Orig.). 1996. pap. text 25.00 (*0-472-01217-7*, 01217) U of Mich Pr.
— Middle English Dictionary: Fascicle T.8. 128p. (Orig.). 1996. pap. text 25.00 (*0-472-01218-5*, 01218) U of Mich Pr.
— Middle English Dictionary: Fascicle T.9. 112p. (Orig.). 1997. pap. text 25.00 (*0-472-01219-3*, 01219) U of Mich Pr.
— Middle English Dictionary: Fascicle U.1, Vol. U.1. 128p. (Orig.). 1997. pap. text 25.00 (*0-472-01221-5*, 01221) U of Mich Pr.
— Middle English Dictionary: Fascicle U.2, Vol. U.2. 128p. (Orig.). 1998. pap. text 25.00 (*0-472-01222-3*, 01222) U of Mich Pr.
— Middle English Dictionary: U.1. 128p. 1998. pap. text 25.00 (*0-472-01223-1*, 01223) U of Mich Pr.
Lewis, Robert E., et al. Fleas of the Pacific Northwest. LC 88-1612. (Illus.). 304p. 1988. text 59.95 (*0-87071-355-8*) Oreg St U Pr.
Lewis, Robert E., jt. ed. see Williams, Jerry M.
***Lewis, Robert G. & Heffernan, Maureen S.** Adolescents & Families for Life: A Toolkit for Supervisors. (Illus.). 218p. 2000. spiral bd., wbk. ed. 59.95 (*0-9659217-1-9*) High Popples.
Lewis, Robert J. Fire Station Location Studies Using a Microcomputer. 1986. pap. 5.35 (*0-318-22360-0*, TR 86-1) Society Fire Protect.
— Lewis Patriarchs of Early Virginia & Maryland. 3rd ed. LC 99-159785. (Illus.). 176p. 1998. pap. 27.00 (*0-7884-0906-9*, L183) Heritage Bk.
— Welsh Family Coats of Arms. (Illus.). 96p. (Orig.). 1995. pap. text 22.00 (*0-7884-0156-4*) Heritage Bk.
Lewis, Robert J., jt. auth. see Koohang, Alex A.
Lewis, Robert L. Real Estate Investing in New York City: A Handbook for the Small Investor. 128p. (Orig.). 1995. pap. 7.95 (*0-9647940-9-8*) Adventura Pubng.
Lewis, Robert M. & Picut, Catherine A. Veterinary Clinical Immunology: From Classroom to Clinics. LC 88-22624. 280p. reprint ed. pap. 86.80 (*0-7837-2851-4*, 205762100006) Bks Demand.
Lewis, Robert O. Independent Verification & Validation: A Life Cycle Engineering Process for Quality Software. LC 92-7792. (New Dimensions in Engineering Ser.). 384p. 1992. 125.00 (*0-471-57011-7*) Wiley.
Lewis, Robert S. Elements of Mining. 3rd ed. LC 64-14990. 782p. reprint ed. pap. 200.00 (*0-608-11230-5*, 201629800003) Bks Demand.
Lewis, Robert T. & Peterson, Hugh M. Human Behavior: An Introduction to Psychology. LC 71-190207. 469p. reprint ed. pap. 145.40 (*0-608-11248-8*, 201253900081) Bks Demand.
— Human Behavior: An Introduction to Psychology (Student Guide) LC 71-190207. (Illus.). 117p. reprint ed. pap. 36.30 (*0-608-11252-6*, 201254000081) Bks Demand.
Lewis, Robert W. A Farewell to Arms: The War of the Words. (Masterwork Studies). 170p. (C). 1992. 29.00 (*0-8057-8052-1*) Macmillan.
Lewis, Robert W., ed. Hemingway in Italy & Other Essays: Critical Approaches. LC 89-48747. 232p. 1990. 49.95 (*0-275-92916-7*, C2916, Greenwood Pr) Greenwood.
Lewis, Robyn, ed. The Legal Dictionary English - Welsh. 500p. 1992. 114.00 (*0-86383-534-1*, Pub. by Gomer Pr) St Mut.
Lewis, Roger. Color & the Edgar Cayce Readings. 48p. 1973. pap. 4.95 (*0-87604-068-7*, 264) ARE Pr.
— The Life & Death of Peter Sellers. (Illus.). 528p. 1996. 24.95 (*1-55783-248-X*) Applause Theatre Bk Pubs.
— The Life & Death of Peter Sellers. (Illus.). 528p. 1999. pap. 14.95 (*1-55783-357-5*) Applause Theatre Bk Pubs.
— The Real Life of Laurence Olivier. LC 97-31702. (Illus.). 288p. 1999. 25.95 (*1-55783-298-6*); pap. 18.95 (*1-55783-413-X*) Applause Theatre Bk Pubs.
Lewis, Roger & Trevitt, Roger. Advanced Business. 2nd ed. 700p. 1995. pap. 62.50 (*0-7487-2203-3*, Pub. by S Thornes Pubs) Trans-Atl Phila.
***Lewis, Roger & Trevitt, Roger.** Business for Advanced GNVQ. 3rd ed. (Illus.). 768p. 2000. pap. 49.50 (*0-7487-3506-2*, Pub. by S Thornes Pubs) Trans-Atl Phila.
Lewis, Roger C. Thomas James Wise & the Trial Book Fallacy. (Illus.). 260p. 1994. 83.95 (*1-85928-036-6*, Pub. by Scolar Pr) Ashgate Pub Co.
Lewis, Roger K. Architect? A Candid Guide to the Profession. rev. ed. LC 97-35747. (Illus.). 299p. 1998. 33.00 (*0-262-12208-1*) MIT Pr.
— Architect? A Candid Guide to the Profession. rev. ed. (Illus.). 299p. 1998. pap. text 16.50 (*0-262-62121-5*) MIT Pr.
Lewis, Roland. Learn to Make Videos in a Weekend. LC 92-54795. 1993. 16.00 (*0-679-42230-7*) Knopf.
Lewis, Roland W. Numerical Methods in Heat Transfer, Vol. 1. LC 80-49973. (Wiley Series in Numerical Methods in Engineering). 552p. reprint ed. pap. 171.20 (*0-7837-6553-3*, 204413100001) Bks Demand.
— Numerical Methods in Heat Transfer, Vol. 3. LC 80-49973. (Wiley Series in Numerical Methods in Engineering). (Illus.). 308p. reprint ed. pap. 95.50 (*0-7837-4391-2*, 204413100003) Bks Demand.
Lewis, Ron. Flashback: The Untold Story of Lee Harvey Oswald. Young-Coloma, Lessie R., ed. & intro. by. (Illus.). 272p. (Orig.). 1993. pap. 14.95 (*1-883305-00-4*) Lewcom Prods.
Lewis, Ronald & Hennen, John. West Virginia: Documents in the History of a Rural Industrial State. 2nd ed. 444p. (C). 1996. per. 45.95 (*0-7872-2540-1*, 41254001) Kendall-Hunt.
Lewis, Ronald J. Activity-Based Costing for Marketing & Manufacturing. LC 92-31710. 248p. 1993. 65.00 (*0-89930-801-5*, LYB, Quorum Bks) Greenwood.
— Activity-Based Models for Cost Management Systems. LC 94-37876. 296p. 1995. 69.50 (*0-89930-965-8*, Quorum Bks) Greenwood.
— Mackinaw - Honolulu Connection. LC 98-72209. 224p. 1998. pap. 12.95 (*0-9642436-2-8*) Agawa Pr.
— Murder in Mackinac. LC 94-72293. 238p. 1994. pap. 12.95 (*0-9642436-0-1*) Agawa Pr.
— Terror at the Soo Locks: A Novel. LC 96-85424. 250p. 1997. 12.95 (*0-9642436-1-X*) Agawa Pr.
Lewis, Ronald J., jt. auth. see Most, Kenneth S.
Lewis, Ronald L. Black Coal Miners in America: Race, Class, & Community Conflict, 1780-1980. LC 87-2086. (Illus.). 256p. 1987. 29.95 (*0-8131-1610-4*) U Pr of Ky.
— Coal, Iron, & Slaves: Industrial Slavery in Maryland & Virginia, 1715-1865. 6. LC 78-55333. (Contributions in Labor Studies: No. 6). (Illus.). 283p. 1979. 59.95 (*0-313-20522-1*, LCI/, Greenwood Pr) Greenwood.
— Transforming the Appalachian Countryside: Railroads, Deforestation, & Social Change in West Virginia, 1880-1920. LC 97-36616. (Illus.). 384p. 1998. 49.95 (*0-8078-2405-4*); pap. 18.95 (*0-8078-4706-2*) Univ of North Carolina at.
Lewis, Ros, jt. auth. see Howe, Renate.
Lewis, Rose A. I Love You Like Crazy Cakes. LC 99-34175. (Illus.). 32p. (J). (ps-3). 2000. 14.95 (*0-316-52538-3*) Little.
Lewis, Rosemary. GED Writing Skills No. Two: The Essay. 1989. pap. text, student ed. 14.95 (*1-56030-007-8*) Comex Systs.
— Review for the CLEP General English Composition. rev. ed. 164p. (C). 2000. pap. text 15.95 (*1-56030-001-9*) Comex Systs.
Lewis, Rosemary, et al. Our Children's Heritage: A History of Clarkston-Independence Township. (Illus.). 81p. (J). (gr. 2-4). 1995. 25.00 (*0-9621749-2-0*); text 8.79 (*0-9621749-1-2*) Clarkston CHS.
— Reviewbooks for the GED Test. (Reviewbooks for the GED Test Ser.). (Illus.). (YA). 1992. pap. text 90.65 (*1-56030-089-2*) Comex Systs.
Lewis, Rosemary R., jt. auth. see Lewis, M. K.
Lewis, Roy. Cock of the Walk: A Mid Victorian Rumpus. (Illus.). 154p. 1996. 32.00 (*0-7206-0942-9*, Pub. by P Owen Ltd) Dufour.
— Dispersion in Estuaries & Coastal Waters. LC 97-20298. 328p. 1997. 110.00 (*0-471-96162-0*) Wiley.
***Lewis, Roy.** Ghost Dancers. 1999. 27.00 (*0-00-232678-7*, Pub. by HarpC) Trafalgar.
— The Ghost Dancers. large type ed. 336p. 2000. write for info. (*0-7505-1538-4*, Pub. by Mgna Lrg Print) Ulverscroft.
Lewis, Roy. Men of Subtle Craft. 192p. 1988. 13.95 (*0-312-81789-4*) St Martin.
Lewis, Roy. Most Cunning Workmen. LC 85-25244. (Atlantic Ser.). 274 p. 1986. write for info. (*0-89340-966-9*) Chivers N Amer.
— Most Cunning Workmen. LC 84-23738. 182 p. 1985. 10.95 (*0-312-54907-5*) St Martin.
Lewis, Roy. On Reading French Verse: A Study of Poetic Form. 1982. 29.95 (*0-19-815775-4*) OUP.
Lewis, Roy A., jt. auth. see Maranjian, Selena.
Lewis, Roy H. A Cracking of Spines. large type ed. (Linford Mystery Library). 352p. 1987. pap. 16.99 (*0-7089-6459-1*, Linford) Ulverscroft.
— The Manuscript Murders. large type ed. (Linford Mystery Library). 304p. 1987. pap. 16.99 (*0-7089-6389-7*) Ulverscroft.
— A Pension for Death. large type ed. (Linford Mystery Library). 336p. 1987. pap. 16.99 (*0-7089-6395-1*) Ulverscroft.
— Theatre Ghosts. large type ed. (Lythway Ser.). 200p. 1992. 20.50 (*0-7451-1437-7*, G K Hall Lrg Type) Mac Lib Ref.
Lewis, Roy H. A Trout in the Milk: An Arnold Landon Novel. large type ed. LC 87-34335. (Atlantic Large Print Ser.). 285 p. 1988. write for info. (*1-55504-562-6*) Chivers N Amer.
Lewis, Roy H. A Wisp of Smoke. large type ed. 326p. 1992. 27.99 (*0-7505-0355-6*) Ulverscroft.
Lewis, Roy R. Creation & Restoration Of Coastal Plant Communities. Date not set. 55.00 (*0-87371-547-0*) Lewis Pubs.
Lewis, Roy R., III, ed. Creation & Restoration of Coastal Plant Communities. 232p. 1982. 132.00 (*0-8493-6573-2*, QK938, CRC Reprint) Franklin.
Lewis, Royce C., Jr. Primary Care Orthopaedics. (Illus.). 328p. 1987. text 54.95 (*0-443-08356-8*) Church.
Lewis, Rudolph, ed. see Christian, Marcus.
Lewis, Rudy. The International Trader's IntroGuide. LC 93-72321. (Illus.). 230p. 1993. pap. 18.00 (*1-878647-10-5*) APU Pub Grp.
Lewis, Rupert. Garvey: His Work & Impact. LC 91-70398. 1991. 49.95 (*0-86543-225-2*); pap. 14.95 (*0-86543-224-4*) Africa World.
— Marcus Garvey: Anti-Colonial Champion. LC 87-72598. 280p. 1988. 29.95 (*0-86543-061-6*); pap. 18.95 (*0-86543-062-4*) Africa World.
Lewis, Rupert & Warner-Lewis, Maureen, eds. Garvey: Africa, Europe, the Americas. 200p. 1994. 39.95 (*0-86543-415-8*); pap. 14.95 (*0-86543-416-6*) Africa World.
Lewis, Rupert C. A Study of Walter Rodney's Intellectual & Political Thought. LC 97-61422. (African American Life Ser.). 296p. 1998. 39.95 (*0-8143-2743-5*); pap. 19.95 (*0-8143-2744-3*) Wayne St U Pr.
Lewis, Russell. The New Service Society. LC 74-169688. 187p. reprint ed. pap. 58.00 (*0-608-10744-1*, 200588700056) Bks Demand.
— Recent Controversies in Political Economy. LC 91-45321. 1992. write for info. (*0-415-07979-9*) Routledge.
Lewis, Ruth. Memo to Self: Songs of Jewish Living. 1996. 14.95 (*1-56871-104-2*) Feldheim.
Lewis, Ruth A., jt. auth. see Lewis, John S.
***Lewis, S.** Topographical Dictionary of Ireland: Comprising the Several Counties, Cities, Boroughs, Etc... fac. ed. 1412p. 2000. reprint ed. 135.00 (*0-7404-0416-4*) Higginson Bk Co.
— What Is, Is! 1998. pap. 93.00 (*81-86982-00-0*, Pub. by Business Pubns) St Mut.
Lewis, S. & Beumer, J. The Branemark Implant System: Clinical & Laboratory Procedures. (Illus.). 250p. 1989. 95.00 (*0-912791-62-4*, Ishiyaku EuroAmerica) Med Dent Media.
Lewis, S. J. Anatomical Workbook. 134p. 1991. pap. text 17.50 (*0-7506-1023-9*) Buttrwrth-Heinemann.
— Forgotten Legions: German Army Infantry Policy, 1918-1941. LC 85-6601. 208p. 1985. 45.00 (*0-275-90235-8*, C0235, Praeger Pubs) Greenwood.
Lewis, S. M., jt. auth. see Dacie, John V.
Lewis, S. M., jt. ed. see Dacie, John V.
Lewis, S. Mark. Modes of Historical Discourse in J. G. Herder & N. M. Karamzin. LC 94-18326. (Studies on the Themes & Motifs in Literature: Vol. 12). IX, 125p. (C). 1995. text 38.95 (*0-8204-2576-1*) P Lang Pubng.
Lewis, S. Mark, tr. see Banti, Anna.
Lewis, S. Peter. Toproping. (Illus.). 86p. 1998. pap. 12.95 (*1-56044-753-2*) Falcon Pub Inc.
Lewis, S. Peter, jt. auth. see Cauthorn, Dan.
Lewis, Sadie & Hermes, Robert. ATM - SONET Explained. (Illus.). 145p. (Orig.). 1995. pap. 12.95 (*1-880548-53-4*) Numidia Pr.
Lewis, Samella S. African American Art & Artists. LC 93-40781. 1994. 65.00 (*0-520-08788-7*, Pub. by U CA Pr); pap. 32.50 (*0-520-08532-9*, Pub. by U CA Pr) Cal Prin Full Svc.
— Art: African American. 2nd rev. ed. (Illus.). 312p. (Orig.). (C). 1990. reprint ed. pap. text 25.00 (*0-941248-08-9*) Hancraft.
Lewis, Samella S., jt. auth. see Waddy, Ruth.
Lewis, Samuel. Lewis' Cork: A Topographical Dictionary of the Parishes, Towns & Villages of Cork City & County. LC 99-176130. (Illus.). 360p. 1998. pap. 31.95 (*1-898256-57-8*, Pub. by Collins Press) Irish Bks Media.
— A Topographical Dictionary of England, 4 vols. in 2, Set. LC 95-82368. (Illus.). 2464p. 1996. reprint ed. text 150.00 (*0-8063-1508-3*, 3360) Genealog Pub.
— A Topographical Dictionary of Ireland, 2 vols. LC 83-82827. 1480p. 1995. reprint ed. 85.00 (*0-8063-1063-4*) Genealog Pub.
Lewis, Samuel L. The Jerusalem Trilogy. Tessler, Sitara & Jablonski, Moineddin, eds. (Illus.). 336p. (Orig.). 1975. pap. 13.00 (*0-915424-03-7*, Prophecy Pressworks) PeaceWks Intl Ntwrk.
— Siva! Siva! Cresent & Heart: Selected Poetry of Murshid Samuel L. Lewis. (Bismillah Bks.: No. 1). (Illus.). 112p. (Orig.). 1980. pap. 8.95 (*0-915424-04-5*) PeaceWks Intl Ntwrk.
— Sufi Vision & Initiation: Meetings with Remarkable Beings. Douglas-Klotz, Neil, ed. LC 86-42579. (Illus.). 398p. (Orig.). 1986. pap. 14.95 (*0-915424-10-X*) PeaceWks Intl Ntwrk.
Lewis, Samuel L. & Douglas-Klotz, Neil. Spiritual Dance & Walk: An Introduction to the Dances of Universal Peace & Walking Meditations of Samuel L. Lewis. rev. ed. Demcho-Wagor, Marie, ed. (Illus.). 144p. 1990. pap. 9.95 (*0-915424-13-4*) PeaceWks Intl Ntwrk.
Lewis, Samuel L. & Khan, Hazrat I. The Bowl of Saki Commentary. Jablonski, Moineddin & Klotz, Saadi, eds. 180p. (Orig.). 1981. pap. 20.00 (*0-915424-08-8*) PeaceWks Intl Ntwrk.
Lewis, Sandra. My Health Record: Help the Doctor Help You. 2nd rev. ed. 80p. 2000. pap. 8.95 (*0-9662129-1-6*, Pub. by SDL Pubs) ACCESS Pubs Network.
***Lewis, Sandra, et al.** Seeing Eye to Eye: An Administrator's Guide to Students with Low Vision. LC 00-44747. 2000. write for info. (*0-89128-359-5*) Am Foun Blind.
Lewis, Sandra C. Elder Care in Occupational Therapy. LC 87-43265. 502p. 1989. pap. 36.00 (*1-55642-037-4*) SLACK Inc.
Lewis, Sanford, ed. see Seigel, Lenny, et al.
Lewis, Sangeeta P., jt. auth. see Sharma, Hari D.
Lewis, Sara. The Answer Is Yes. LC 97-46079. 272p. (C). 1998. 23.00 (*0-15-100326-2*) Harcourt.
— The Answer Is Yes. 272p. 1999. pap. 13.00 (*0-15-600564-6*, Harvest Bks) Harcourt.
— The Answer Is Yes. large type ed. LC 98-41759. 399p. Date not set. 30.00 (*0-7838-0392-3*, G K Hall Lrg Type) Mac Lib Ref.
— But I Love You Anyway. 272p. 1996. 22.00 (*0-15-100160-X*) Harcourt.

— But I Love You Anyway. 2nd ed. 272p. 1997. pap. 12.00 (*0-15-600504-2*) HUP.

— Cooking for Babies & Toddlers: Nutritious, Delicious & Easy-to-Prepare Recipes to Give Your Child. 1999. pap. text 24.95 (*1-85967-730-4*, Lorenz Bks) Anness Pub.

— Eating Well on a Budget. (C). 1992. 30.00 (*0-86242-120-9*, Pub. by Age Concern Eng) St Mut.

***Lewis, Sara.** First Food: Preparing Food For Babies & Toddlers. 256p. 2000. pap. 19.95 (*1-84215-076-6*) Anness Pub.

Lewis, Sara. Heart Conditions. large type ed. LC 94-8001. 370p. 1994. lib. bdg. 22.95 (*0-7862-0221-1*) Thorndike Pr.

— Heart Conditions. 2nd ed. 288p. 1997. pap. 12.00 (*0-15-600499-2*) HUP.

— Trying to Smile. 1992. 19.95 (*0-15-191312-9*) Harcourt.

— Trying to Smile: And Other Stories. 192p. 1996. pap. 13.00 (*0-15-600395-3*, Harvest Bks) Harcourt.

Lewis, Sara & Lewis, Monty. Explorer Chartbook: Near Bahamas. rev. ed. Drew, Erin & Fears, Kate, eds. (Illus.). 72p. 1998. pap. 34.95 (*0-9659842-1-4*) Lewis Offshore.

Lewis, Sara, jt. auth. see Lewis, Monty.

Lewis, Sara R. The Interior of a Heart. 1998. pap. write for info. (*1-57553-849-0*) Watermrk Pr.

Lewis, Sasha G. Sunday's Women: A Report on Lesbian Life Today. LC 78-53655. 229p. reprint ed. pap. 71.00 (*0-7837-1385-1*, 204156100021) Bks Demand.

Lewis, Saunders. Excelsior: A Play by Saunders Lewis. (WEL.). 64p. 1980. pap. 5.95 (*0-8464-4929-3*) Beekman Pubs.

— Monica. LC 98-104802. 107p. 1997. pap. 17.95 (*1-85411-195-7*, Pub. by Seren Bks) Dufour.

— Saunders Lewis: A Presentation of His Work. Jones, Harri P., ed. 228p. 1990. pap. 14.95 (*0-87243-187-8*) Templegate.

Lewis, Scott. Fitness Groove: How to Never Stop, Never Give up & Stay Fit Forever! 1999. pap. 12.95 (*0-9666224-1-3*, Pub. by Breakthrough Ent) Midpt Trade.

— The Rainforest Book. LC 90-70820. 112p. 1990. pap. 7.95 (*0-9626072-1-5*) Living Planet Pr.

Lewis, Scott, jt. auth. see Bratman, Fred.

Lewis, Scott, jt. auth. see Browning, Robert.

Lewis, Scott, ed. see Browning, Elizabeth Barrett.

Lewis, Scott, ed. see Browning, Elizabeth Barrett & Browning, Robert.

Lewis, Scott, ed. see Browning, Robert & Browning, Elizabeth Barrett.

Lewis, Selma S. A Biblical People in the Bible Belt: The Jewish Community of Memphis, Tennessee, 1840-1960. LC 98-22299. 320p. 1998. text 35.00 (*0-86554-602-9*, H454) Mercer Univ Pr.

Lewis, Sharen, jt. auth. see LaMorte, Kathy.

Lewis, Shari. Lamb Chop's Fables: The Lamb Who Could Featuring Aesop's The Tortoise & the Hare. Doyle, Robert A., ed. LC 93-46420. (Illus.). 32p. (J). 1994. 14.95 (*0-8094-7804-8*) Time-Life.

Lewis, Shari & Aesop. The Boat Contest: The Lion & the Mouse. Marshall, Blaine, ed. (Lamb Chop's Fables Ser.). (Illus.). 32p. (J). (ps-3). 1999. pap. 8.95 (*0-8094-7446-8*) Time-Life.

— You Can Do It, Lamb Chop! With Puppet, Set. (J). (ps-5). 1994. pap. 16.95 (*0-8094-7833-1*) Time-Life.

Lewis, Shari & Oppenheimer, Lillian. Folding Paper Puppets. rev. ed. LC 93-9285. 1995. pap. 11.95 (*0-8128-8541-4*, Scrbrough Hse) Madison Bks UPA.

— Folding Paper Toys. rev. ed. LC 63-20060. (Illus.). 100p. (J). (gr. 4 up). 1992. reprint ed. pap. 11.95 (*0-8128-1953-5*, Scrbrough Hse) Madison Bks UPA.

Lewis, Sharon. IBM Computerized Testbank to Acompany Medical-Surgical Nursing. 4th ed. 1996. write for info. (*0-8151-5297-3*) Mosby Inc.

— Macintosh Computerized Testbank T/A Medical-Surgical Nursing. 4th ed. 1996. write for info. (*0-8151-5320-1*) Mosby Inc.

Lewis, Sharon. Medical Surgical Nursing: Assessment & Management of Clinical Problems. 4th ed. 368p. 1996. student ed. write for info. (*0-8151-5524-7*) Mosby Inc.

Lewis, Sharon, et al. Medical-Surgical Nursing: Assessment & Management of Clinical Problems: Skidmore Drug Guide Package, 2 vols. 4th ed. 1996. write for info. (*0-323-00496-2*) Mosby Inc.

— Medical-Surgical Nursing: Assessment & Management of Clinical Problems: Text & Skidmore Drug Guide Package. 4th ed. (Illus.). 1996. write for info. (*0-323-00495-4*) Mosby Inc.

Lewis, Sharon M. Medical-Surgical Nursing: View Studies. 4th ed. (C). (gr. 13). 1997. pap. text 150.00 (*0-8151-9523-0*, 29394) Mosby Inc.

Lewis, Sharon M., et al, eds. Medical-Surgical Nursing: Assessment & Management of Clinical Problems. 4th ed. LC 95-30732. (Illus.). 2176p. (C). (gr. 13). 1995. text 75.00 (*0-8151-5301-5*, 24617) Mosby Inc.

Lewis, Sharon M., et al. Medical-Surgical Nursing: Assessment & Management of Clinical Problems. 4th ed. student ed. write for info. (*0-8151-5299-X*) Mosby Inc.

— Medical-Surgical Nursing: Assessment & Management of Clinical Problems, 2 vols. 4th ed. (Illus.). 2176p. (C). (gr. 13). 1996. text 81.00 (*0-8151-5373-2*, 28963) Mosby Inc.

***Lewis, Sharon M., et al.** Medical-Surgical Nursing: Assessment & Management of Clinical Problems. 5th ed. LC 99-23884. (Illus.). 2176p. (C). 1999. text 76.00 (*1-55664-430-2*) Mosby Inc.

— Medical Surgical Nursing: Assessment & Management of Clinical Problems. 5th ed. (Illus.). (C). 1999. student ed. write for info. (*0-323-00258-7*) Mosby Inc.

Lewis, Sheila. Destroy Not the Dream. (Rainbow Romances Ser.). 160p. 1993. 14.95 (*0-7090-4914-5*) Parkwest Pubns.

— Destroy Not the Dream. large type ed. 288p. 1994. pap. 16.99 (*0-7089-7544-5*) Ulverscroft.

— For Love of Lucia. large type ed. (Linford Romance Library). 272p. 1993. pap. 16.99 (*0-7089-7319-1*) Ulverscroft.

— Kenny, Come Home. large type ed. (Linford Romance Library). 304p. 1998. pap. 17.99 (*0-7089-5230-5*) Ulverscroft.

— A Promise for Tomorrow. large type ed. (Linford Romance Library). 304p. 1997. pap. 16.99 (*0-7089-5178-3*) Ulverscroft.

— Silver Bird of Prey. large type ed. 1996. 17.95 (*0-7838-1889-0*, G K Hall Lrg Type) Mac Lib Ref.

Lewis, Shelby. Delicious. 224p. 1996. mass mkt. 4.99 (*0-7860-0225-5*, Pinncle Kensgtn) Kensgtn Pub Corp.

***Lewis, Shelby.** Destiny. 2000. mass mkt. 5.99 (*1-58314-100-6*) BET Bks.

Lewis, Shelby. Sensation. 224p. 1997. mass mkt. 4.99 (*0-7860-0351-0*, Pinncle Kensgtn) Kensgtn Pub Corp.

Lewis, Sheldon, jt. auth. see Holland, Jimmie C.

Lewis, Sheri H. The Karl N. Llewellyn Papers: A Supplementary Guide to the Collection. vi, 44p. 1995. 38.50 (*0-89941-969-0*, 308740) W S Hein.

Lewis, Sherman L. Evaluating Corporate Investment & Financing Opportunities: A Handbook & Guide to Selected Methods for Managers & Finance Professionals. LC 86-623. 309p. 1986. 79.50 (*0-89930-144-4*, LCP/, Quorum Bks) Greenwood.

— The Improvement of Corporate Financial Performance: A Manager's Guide to Evaluating Selected Opportunities. LC 88-35684. 395p. 1989. 79.50 (*0-89930-432-X*, LIM/, Quorum Bks) Greenwood.

Lewis, Sherri Y., ed. see Brisson, Lynn.

Lewis, Sherri Y., ed. see Brown, Sam E.

Lewis, Sherri Y., ed. see Cochran, Judith.

Lewis, Sherri Y., ed. see Forte, Imogene & Schurr, Sandra.

Lewis, Sherry. Call Me Mom. LC 95-6955. (Women Who Dare Ser.). 296p. 1995. per. 3.50 (*0-373-70628-6*, 1-70628-2) Harlequin Bks.

***Lewis, Sherry.** Le Coeur Reconcilie. (Amours d'Aujourd'Hui Ser.: No. 347). (FRE.). 2000. mass mkt. 5.50 (*0-373-38347-9*, 1-38347-0, Harlequin French) Harlequin Bks.

Lewis, Sherry. For the Baby's Sake. (Superromance Ser.: Bk. 883). 1999. per. 4.25 (*0-373-70883-1*, 1-70883-3) Harlequin Bks.

— Keeping Her Safe. 1997. per. 3.99 (*0-373-70744-4*, 1-70744-7) Harlequin Bks.

— Let It Snow. (Harlequin Super Romance Ser.). 1998. per. 4.25 (*0-373-70816-5*) Silhouette.

— A Man for Mom. (Superromance Ser.: No. 826). 1999. per. 4.25 (*0-373-70826-2*, 1-70826-2) Harlequin Bks.

— No Place for Death. 256p. 1996. mass mkt. 5.99 (*0-425-15383-5*, Prime Crime) Berkley Pub.

— No Place for Memories. 1999. mass mkt. 5.99 (*0-425-16736-4*) Berkley Pub.

— No Place for Secrets. 256p. (Orig.). 1995. mass mkt. 4.99 (*0-425-14835-1*, Prime Crime) Berkley Pub.

— No Place for Sin. (Fred Vickery Novel Ser.). 1997. mass mkt. 5.99 (*0-425-16113-7*, Prime Crime) Berkley Pub.

— No Place for Tears. (Orig.). 1997. mass mkt. 5.99 (*0-425-15626-5*, Prime Crime) Berkley Pub.

— This Montana Home. (Superromance Ser.). 1996. per. 3.99 (*0-373-70692-8*, 1-70692-8) Harlequin Bks.

***Lewis, Sherry.** Time to Dream. 1999. mass mkt. 5.99 (*0-515-12729-9*, Jove) Berkley Pub.

Lewis, Sherry L. My Trip to the Big Chicken. LC 93-80806. 32p. (J). 1996. pap. 10.00 (*0-9639319-0-3*) K S Jewels.

Lewis, Shirley, jt. ed. see Dabney, Norma.

Lewis, Shon & Higgins, Nicholas, eds. Brain Imaging in Psychiatry. LC 96-6148. 312p. 1996. 99.95 (*0-632-03647-8*) Blackwell Sci.

Lewis, Sian. Cities in the Sea. LC 97-202613. (Illus.). 32p. (J). (gr. 2-6). 1998. 22.95 (*0-8464-4637-5*) Beekman Pubs.

— News & Society in the Greek Polis. (Studies in the History of Greece & Rome). 224p. (C). 1996. 55.00 (*0-8078-2309-0*); pap. 19.95 (*0-8078-4621-X*) U of NC Pr.

— Smoke in the Tunnel. 62p. (J). (gr. 4). 1992. pap. 7.95 (*0-8464-4876-9*) Beekman Pubs.

— The Story of St. David. 2nd ed. 16p. (J). (gr. 1). 1997. reprint ed. pap. 7.95 (*0-8464-4806-8*) Beekman Pubs.

Lewis, Sian & Morris, Jackie. Cities in the Sea. LC 97-202613. 30p. (J). 1996. 22.50 (*0-8464-4807-6*) Beekman Pubs.

Lewis, Simon A. The Art & Science of Small Talk. LC 94-45966. (Hewlett Packard Professional Bks.). 250p. 1995. pap. 50.00 (*0-13-371345-8*, Prentice Hall) P-H.

Lewis, Sinclair. Arrowsmith. 1976. 24.95 (*0-8488-0825-8*) Amereon Ltd.

— Arrowsmith. LC 25-78. (Modern Classic Ser.). 132p. 1990. 15.95 (*0-15-108216-2*) Harcourt.

— Arrowsmith. (Signet Classics Ser.). 440p. 1998. mass mkt. 6.95 (*0-451-52691-0*, Sig Classics) NAL.

Lewis, Sinclair. Arrowsmith. (Signet Classics). 1980. 11.05 (*0-606-00362-2*, Pub. by Turtleback) Demco.

— Arrowsmith. 1996. reprint ed. lib. bdg. 29.95 (*0-89966-402-4*) Buccaneer Bks.

Lewis, Sinclair. Arrowsmith. (Collected Works of Sinclair Lewis). 562p. 1998. reprint ed. lib. bdg. 118.00 (*1-58201-667-4*) Classic Bks.

— Babbit. 1998. mass mkt. 6.95 (*0-451-52708-9*, Sig Classics) NAL.

— Babbitt. (C). 1997. pap. text. write for info. (*0-321-02601-2*) Addson-Wesley Educ.

— Babbitt. 1976. 27.95 (*0-8488-0826-6*) Amereon Ltd.

— Babbitt. 480p. 1998. mass mkt. 5.95 (*0-553-21486-1*) Bantam.

— Babbitt. LC 84-254209. (Barron's Book Notes Ser.). 1985. pap. 2.50 (*0-8120-3504-6*) Barron.

— Babbitt. LC 22-14419. (Modern Classic Ser.). 408p. 1989. 17.00 (*0-15-110421-2*) Harcourt.

Lewis, Sinclair. Babbitt. (Signet Classics). 1961. 11.05 (*0-606-00369-X*, Pub. by Turtleback) Demco.

Lewis, Sinclair. Babbitt. LC 95-36188. 320p. 1996. pap. 9.95 (*0-14-018902-5*, Penguin Classics) Viking Penguin.

— Babbitt. large type ed. LC 97-32574. (Perennial Ser.). 516 p. 1998. 25.95 (*0-7838-8373-0*, G K Hall & Co) Mac Lib Ref.

— Babbitt. large type ed. LC 97-4346. 448p. 1997. text 24.95 (*1-56000-532-7*) Transaction Pubs.

— Babbitt. 408p. 1987. reprint ed. lib. bdg. 25.95 (*0-89966-622-1*) Buccaneer Bks.

— Babbitt. (Collected Works of Sinclair Lewis). 401p. 1998. reprint ed. lib. bdg. 98.00 (*1-58201-668-2*) Classic Bks.

***Lewis, Sinclair.** Babbitt, Set. unabridged ed. 1999. 53.95 incl. audio (*1-55685-433-1*) Audio Bk Con.

Lewis, Sinclair. Cass Timberlane. 1976. 19.95 (*0-8488-1411-8*) Amereon Ltd.

— Dodsworth. 1976. 27.95 (*0-8488-0565-8*) Amereon Ltd.

— Elmer Gantry. 1976. 29.95 (*0-8488-0827-4*) Amereon Ltd.

— Elmer Gantry. 1967. mass mkt. 7.95 (*0-451-52251-6*, CE1653, Sig Classics) NAL.

— Elmer Gantry. (Signet Classics). 1967. 12.05 (*0-606-00605-2*, Pub. by Turtleback) Demco.

— Free Air. LC 92-37702. xii, 370p. 1993. pap. 11.95 (*0-8032-7943-4*, Bison Books) U of Nebr Pr.

— Free Air. (Collected Works of Sinclair Lewis). 370p. 1998. reprint ed. lib. bdg. 98.00 (*1-58201-669-0*) Classic Bks.

— Free Air. reprint ed. lib. bdg. 69.00 (*0-7812-0766-5*) Rprt Serv.

— Free Air. 1971. reprint ed. 59.00 (*0-403-01071-3*) Scholarly.

— Hike & the Aeroplane. (Collected Works of Sinclair Lewis). 275p. 1998. reprint ed. lib. bdg. 88.00 (*1-58201-670-4*) Classic Bks.

— If I Were Boss: The Early Business Stories of Sinclair Lewis. Di Renzo, Anthony, ed. LC 96-52565. 352p. 1997. pap. 19.95 (*0-8093-2139-4*) S Ill U Pr.

— The Innocents. (Collected Works of Sinclair Lewis). 216p. 1998. reprint ed. lib. bdg. 88.00 (*1-58201-671-2*) Classic Bks.

— It Can't Happen Here. 366p. 1993. mass mkt. 6.95 (*0-451-52582-5*, Sig Classics) NAL.

— The Job. LC 93-43084. xvii, 327p. 1994. pap. 15.00 (*0-8032-7948-5*, Bison Books) U of Nebr Pr.

— The Job. (Collected Works of Sinclair Lewis). 326p. 1998. reprint ed. lib. bdg. 98.00 (*1-58201-672-0*) Classic Bks.

Lewis, Sinclair. Kingsblood Royal. lib. bdg. 26.95 (*1-56723-179-9*) Yestermorrow.

Lewis, Sinclair. Main Street. 544p. 1996. mass mkt. 5.95 (*0-553-21451-9*) Bantam.

— Main Street. 1920. 11.05 (*0-606-01015-7*, Pub. by Turtleback) Demco.

— Main Street. LC 95-16373. 448p. 1995. pap. 9.95 (*0-14-018901-7*, Penguin Classics) Viking Penguin.

— Main Street. 297p. 1984. reprint ed. lib. bdg. 31.95 (*0-89966-495-4*) Buccaneer Bks.

— Main Street. (Collected Works of Sinclair Lewis). 451p. 1998. reprint ed. lib. bdg. 108.00 (*1-58201-673-9*) Classic Bks.

— Main Street. unabridged ed. LC 99-11770. 384p. 1999. pap. text 2.50 (*0-486-40655-5*) Dover.

— Main Street: One of Modern Library's 100 Best Novels. 1976. 25.95 (*0-8488-0828-2*) Amereon Ltd.

— Main Street: One of Modern Library's 100 Best Novels. 496p. 1996. pap. 10.95 (*0-7867-0325-3*) Carroll & Graf.

— Main Street: One of Modern Library's 100 Best Novels. LC 98-31439. 1999. pap. 9.95 (*0-375-75314-1*) Modern Lib NY.

— Main Street: One of Modern Library's 100 Best Novels. (Signet Classics Ser.). 440p. 1998. mass mkt. 5.95 (*0-451-52682-1*, Sig) NAL.

— Main Street: One of Modern Library's 100 Best Novels. LC 96-4005. 463p. 1996. pap. text 8.95 (*1-57392-048-7*) Prometheus Bks.

— Main Street & Babbitt. Hersey, John, ed. 898p. 1992. 40.00 (*0-940450-61-5*, Pub. by Library of America) Penguin Putnam.

— Man Who Knew Coolidge: Being the Soul of Lowell Schmaltz, Constructive & Nordic Citizen. LC 79-157784. (Short Story Index Reprint Ser.). 1980. reprint ed. 23.95 (*0-8369-3896-8*) Ayer.

— Our Mr. Wrenn. (Collected Works of Sinclair Lewis). 254p. 1988. reprint ed. lib. bdg. 88.00 (*1-58201-674-7*) Classic Bks.

— The Trail of the Hawk. (Collected Works of Sinclair Lewis). 408p. 1998. reprint ed. lib. bdg. 108.00 (*1-58201-675-5*) Classic Bks.

Lewis, Sinclair & Graham, Tom. Hike & the Aeroplane. unabridged ed. Pastore, Stephen, ed. (Illus.). 250p. (YA). (gr. 5 up). 1999. 45.00 (*1-893173-06-2*) YaleBooks.

Lewis, Sinclair & Pastore, Stephen R. The Collectible Sinclair Lewis: A Catalogue of Books by & about Sinclair Lewis. (Illus.). 240p. 1998. pap. 24.95 (*1-893173-01-1*) YaleBooks.

Lewis, Sinclair & Schary, Dore. Storm in the West. rev. ed. LC 63-13228. (Illus.). 200p. (C). 1981. pap. 5.95 (*0-8128-6079-9*, Scrbrough Hse) Madison Bks UPA.

Lewis, Sinclair, jt. auth. see Monarch Notes Staff.

Lewis-Smith, Victor. Inside the Magic Rectangle: Letters & Reviews. 256p. 1996. 35.00 (*0-575-06119-7*, Pub. by V Gollancz) Trafalgar.

Lewis, Sol, ed. see Hyatt, Felicia B.

Lewis, Sol, ed. see Kaplan, Helene C.

Lewis, Sol, ed. see Stabholz, Thaddeus.

Lewis, Sondra K. & Blakley, Lonnett D. Allergy & Candida Cooking Made Easy. Orig. Title: Allergy & Candida Cooking - Rotational Style. (Illus.). 304p. (Orig.). 1996. pap. 29.95 (*0-9643462-1-4*) Canary Connect.

Lewis, Stanley X., Jr. The Auditor's Guide to Sampling. 79p. 1991. pap. text 60.00 (*0-933179-06-5*) Bus Account Pubns.

Lewis, Stanley X. & Glover, Robert I. Accounting for Social Responsibility: A Historical Perspective. 95p. (C). 1986. pap. text 19.50 (*0-933179-00-6*) Bus Account Pubns.

Lewis, Stanley X., Jr. & King, Jerry G. Community (Rural) Water Associations' Accountability. 30p. 1992. pap. text 19.50 (*0-614-04640-8*) Bus Account Pubns.

Lewis, Stanley X., Jr., et al. Developing & Implementing Business Information Systems for Small Businesses. 51p. 1990. pap. text 19.50 (*0-933179-04-9*) Bus Account Pubns.

***Lewis, Stephanie.** Novell's Guide to Troubleshooting TCP/IP. LC 99-33557. 1056p. 1999. pap. 59.99 (*0-7645-4562-0*) IDG Bks.

Lewis, Stephanie, ed. Health & Welfare Plans under the ERISA Act: Guidelines for States & Federal Regulation. 3rd rev. ed. 277p. (C). 1997. pap. 45.00 (*0-89382-482-8*, ERS-OM) Nat Assn Insurance.

***Lewis, Stephen.** Action Rhymes for You & Your Friends. LC 00-30301. 2000. pap. write for info. (*0-7894-4873-4*) DK Pub Inc.

— And Baby Makes None. 208p. 1991. 18.95 (*0-8027-5789-8*) Walker & Co.

— The Blind in Darkness. 272p. 2000. mass mkt. 5.99 (*0-425-17466-2*, Prime Crime) Berkley Pub.

Lewis, Stephen. The Dumb Shall Sing: A Mystery of Colonial Times. 262p. 1999. mass mkt. 5.99 (*0-425-16997-9*, Prime Crime) Berkley Pub.

Lewis, Stephen & Slawson, Evan. Sanctuary: The Path to Consciousness. LC 98-96537. 240p. 1998. 24.95 (*0-9664433-4-9*) HTTPress.

Lewis, Stephen, jt. auth. see Kleiman, Lowell.

Lewis, Stephen D., jt. auth. see Boyd, Daniel R.

Lewis, Stephen E., jt. auth. see Zuckerman, Howard A.

Lewis, Stephen J., et al. Undaunted Faith: Memorial Edition. 149p. 1995. 18.00 (*1-886826-04-8*) Manassas Mus.

Lewis, Stephen M., jt. auth. see Gill, Ann M.

Lewis, Stephen R., Jr., ed. Henry George & Contemporary Economic Development. 96p. 1985. pap. 5.00 (*0-911312-68-4*) Schalkenbach.

Lewis, Steve, jt. ed. see Fraser, George C.

Lewis, Steven. The ABC's of Real Family Values: What Politicians Do Not Understand about Family Life. 258p. 1999. pap. 23.95 (*0-525-94346-3*) NAL.

— Zen & the Art of Fatherhood: Lessons from a Master Dad. (Illus.). 272p. 1997. pap. 11.95 (*0-452-27651-9*, Plume) Dutton Plume.

***Lewis, Steven.** Zen & the Art of Fatherhood: Lessons from a Master Dad. 253p. 2000. reprint ed. text 20.00 (*0-7881-6880-0*) DIANE Pub.

***Lewis, Steven, ed.** Disaster Recovery Yellow Pages, 1999-2000. 8th ed. LC HV-5512-D57. 329p. 1999. 101.00 (*0-9677468-0-9*) Syst Audit Grp.

Lewis, Steven H. & Perrin, Eugene. Pathology of the Placenta. 2nd ed. LC 98-23008. (Contemporary Issues in Surgical Pathology Ser.: Vol. 23). (Illus.). 432p. (C). 1998. text 99.00 (*0-443-07586-7*) Church.

Lewis, Steven J. Aging & Health: Linking Research & Public Policy. (Illus.). 492p. 1989. lib. bdg. 119.00 (*0-87371-160-2*, L160) Lewis Pubs.

Lewis, Steven M. The ABCs of Real Family Values: The Simple Thing That Make Families Work. LC 97-49946. 170p. 1998. pap. 11.95 (*0-452-27860-0*, Plume) Dutton Plume.

***Lewis-Stratford, Lenora.** Mars, a Growing Nation. LC 00-90313. 2000. pap. 10.95 (*0-533-13532-X*) Vantage.

Lewis, Stuart M., jt. ed. see Kushner, Michael G.

Lewis, Sue, jt. auth. see Maio, Barbara.

Lewis, Sue, ed. see Martinez, Debby.

Lewis, Sue, ed. see Schwartz, David M.

Lewis, Sue, ed. see Shiotsu, Vicky.

Lewis, Suford. Noreascon 2 Memory Book. (Illus.). 56p. 1985. pap. text 2.00 (*0-9603146-3-6*) MA Convent Fandom.

Lewis, Suford, ed. see Bujold, Lois McMaster.

Lewis, Susan. Reinventing Ourselves after Motherhood. LC 98-30259. 272p. 1999. 19.95 (*0-8092-2906-4*, 290640, Contemporary Bks) NTC Contemp Pub Co.

***Lewis, Susan.** Reinventing Ourselves after Motherhood: How Former Career Women Refocus Their Personal & Professional Lives after the Birth of a Child. 272p. 2000. pap. 14.95 (*0-8092-2375-9*, 237590, Contemporary Bks) NTC Contemp Pub Co.

Lewis, Susan, compiled by. Handbook of Brownville History, with Records of Its Centennial Celebration, Incorporated 1824. (Illus.). 122p. 1997. reprint ed. pap. 17.50 (*0-8328-5820-X*) Higginson Bk Co.

Lewis, Susan, jt. auth. see Lewis, Ramon.

Lewis, Susan, jt. auth. see Lewis, Richard.

Lewis, Susan, jt. auth. see Perry, C. Michael.

Lewis, Susan, jt. ed. see Blumenreich, Patricia E.

Lewis, Susan A. Interior Design Sourcebook: A Guide to Resources on the History & Practice of Interior Design. LC 97-202133. (Design Reference Ser.: Vol. 3). 1997. lib. bdg. 45.00 (*0-7808-0198-9*) Omnigraphics Inc.

Lewis, Susan J., jt. auth. see Messner, Roberta L.

Lewis, Susanna. Knitting Lace: A Workshop with Patterns & Projects. LC 92-7457. (Illus.). 224p. 1992. pap. 24.95 (*0-942391-52-7*, 070096) Taunton.

Lewis, Suzan, et al, eds. Dual-Earner Families: International Perspectives. 256p. 1991. 55.00 (*0-8039-8382-4*); pap. 22.50 (*0-8039-8383-2*) Sage.

An Asterisk (*) at the beginning of an entry indicates that the title is appearing for the first time.

Lewis, Suzan & Lewis, Jeremy, eds. The Work Family Challenge: Rethinking Employment. LC 96-69551. 192p. 1996. 69.95 (*0-8039-7468-X*); pap. 26.95 (*0-8039-7469-8*) Sage.

Lewis, Suzan, jt. auth. see Cooper, Cary.

Lewis, Suzanne. Reading Images: Narrative Discourse & Reception in the Thirteenth-Century Illuminated Apocalypse. (Illus.). 489p. (C). 1995. text 90.00 (*0-521-47920-7*) Cambridge U Pr.

— The Rhetoric of Power in the Bayeux Tapestry. (Cambridge Studies in New Art History & Criticism). (Illus.). 208p. (C). 1998. text 50.00 (*0-521-63238-2*) Cambridge U Pr.

***Lewis, Sydney.** Help Wanted. 2001. 25.00 (*1-56584-369-X*, Pub. by New Press NY) Norton.

Lewis, Sydney. Hospital: An Oral History of Cook County Hospital. LC 96-209519. 368p. 1996. pap. 14.00 (*0-425-15452-1*) Berkley Pub.

— Hospital: An Oral History of Cook County Hospital. LC 94-21775. 1994. 25.00 (*1-56584-138-7*, Pub. by New Press NY) Norton.

— Totally Alien Life Form. 1997. pap. 15.95 (*1-56584-283-9*, Pub. by New Press NY) Norton.

— "A Totally Alien Life Form" - Teenagers. LC 96-5574. 320p. 1996. 25.00 (*1-56584-282-0*, Pub. by New Press NY) Norton.

Lewis, Sygall, ed. Loud, Proud & Passionate: Including Women with Disabilities in International Development Programming. (SPA.). 1997. 25.00 (*0-614-31254-X*) Mobility Intl.

Lewis, Sylvan R. Diet & Exercise Made Easy. (Illus.). 128p. (Orig.). 1980. pap. 2.00 (*0-936320-00-1*) Compact Books.

— Doctor's Cholesterol & Low Salt Diet Guide. (Illus.). 128p. (Orig.). 1980. pap. 2.00 (*0-936320-02-8*) Compact Books.

— Lose Ugly Fat Fast. (Illus.). 128p. 1980. pap. 2.00 (*0-936320-04-4*) Compact Books.

— Lose Weight Without Going Hungry. (Illus.). 128p. 1981. pap. 2.00 (*0-936320-10-9*) Compact Books.

Lewis, T., jt. auth. see Fry, Michael.

Lewis, T. D. The Law School Rules: How Not to Sweat the Small Stuff of Law School. Longden, Jennifer, ed. 190p. 1998. pap. 12.95 (*0-9663893-0-1*) Waterfall NY.

Lewis, Tahira. Decorative Painting: Techniques & Designs for Transforming Everyday Objects. (Illus.). 144p. 1998. pap. 25.99 (*0-9658248-2-9*) GUILDcom.

Lewis, Tamra W. A Mother's Things to Do Organizer: Balancing It All. abr. ed. write for info. (*0-9633508-0-3*); audio 10.95 (*0-9633508-1-1*) TRB & Assocs.

Lewis, Taylor, photos by. Chesapeake, the Eastern Shore: Gardens & Houses. LC 92-35045. (Illus.). 1993. 45.00 (*0-671-75857-8*) S&S Trade.

Lewis, Taylor & Heard, Virginia. Nantucket: Gardens & Houses. (Illus.). 230p. (gr. 8). 1990. 50.00 (*0-316-52334-8*) Little.

Lewis, Taylor, jt. auth. see Sinclair, Peg.

Lewis, Taylor, jt. auth. see Talbot, Elizabeth.

Lewis, Ted. Deploying Distributed Business Software. (Managing Object Technology Ser.: No. 5). 272p. (Orig.). (C). 1996. pap. 34.95 (*0-13-531906-4*) Cambridge U Pr.

Lewis, Ted. The Friction-Free Economy. Date not set. pap. 15.00 (*0-88730-926-7*, HarpBusn) HarpInfo.

— The Friction-Free Economy. LC 97-13811. 243p. 1997. 25.00 (*0-88730-847-3*, HarpBusn) HarpInfo.

— The Keep on Going Spirit, Vol. 1. unabridged ed. Shelley, R. Lee, ed. LC 97-77673. (Illus.). 196p. 1997. mass mkt. 14.95 (*0-9661682-0-8*) Business Mgmt.

***Lewis, Ted.** Microsoft Rising: And Other Tales of the Silicon Valley. 350p. 1999. pap. 29.95 (*0-7695-0200-8*) IEEE Comp Soc.

Lewis, Ted, jt. ed. see Zaky, Amr.

Lewis, Ted G. Foundations of Parallel Programming: A Machine-Independent Approach. LC 84-4873. 296p. 1994. 54.00 (*0-8186-5692-1*, BP05692) IEEE Comp Soc.

Lewis, Terence. Harrap's English-Brazilian Portuguese Business Dictionary. 283p. 1982. 125.00 (*0-8288-0118-5*, M14371) Fr & Eur.

Lewis, Terence, et al, eds. Mechanical Circulatory Support. (An Arnold Publication). 416p. 1995. text 135.00 (*0-340-57602-2*, Pub. by E A) OUP.

Lewis, Terrance L. A Climate for Appeasement. LC 90-6166. (Studies in History & Culture: Vol. 3). X, 263p. (C). 1991. text 44.95 (*0-8204-1314-3*) P Lang Pubng.

— Dorothy L. Sayers' Wimsey & Interwar British Society. LC 94-19556. 180p. 1994. text 79.95 (*0-7734-9102-3*) E Mellen.

Lewis, Terry. Conflict of Interest. 352p. 1998. pap. 5.99 (*0-7860-0539-4*, Pinncle Kensgtn) Kensgtn Pub Corp.

— Conflict of Interest. LC 96-52927. 328p. 1997. 18.95 (*1-56164-132-4*) Pineapple Pr.

Lewis, Tess, tr. see Handke, Peter.

Lewis, Thelma L. The Destructive Force of the Male Ego. LC 97-90355. (Orig.). 1997. pap. 8.95 (*0-533-12370-4*) Vantage.

Lewis, Thelma M. To Save My Soul: A Simple Guide to Christian Living. (Illus.). xv, 175p. 1998. pap. 10.00 (*0-9670652-0-8*, 100-2) Louisiana Images.

Lewis, Theodore G. Pascal for the IBM Personal Computer. LC 82-22750. 288p. 1983. pap. 15.95 (*0-201-05464-7*) Addison-Wesley.

Lewis, Theodore G., ed. History of Waterbury, 1763-1915. 286p. 1997. reprint ed. lib. bdg. 37.50 (*0-8328-6508-7*) Higginson Bk Co.

Lewis, Theresa. Caribbean Folk Legends. LC 89-81981. (Young Reader's Ser.). 90p. (YA). (gr. 6-12). 1990. 19.95 (*0-86543-158-2*); pap. 7.95 (*0-86543-159-0*) Africa World.

Lewis, Theresa, ed. see Berry, Mary.

***Lewis, Thomas.** Professional VB6 Com. 500p. 1999. pap. 39.99 (*1-86100-213-0*) Wrox Press.

Lewis, Thomas, ed. A Source Guide to the Music of Percy Grainger. (Illus.). 352p. 1991. pap. 35.00 (*0-912483-56-3*) Pro-Am Music.

***Lewis, Thomas, et al.** A General Theory of Love. 240p. 2000. 23.95 (*0-375-50389-7*) Random.

Lewis, Thomas, jt. auth. see Lewis, Cynthia C.

Lewis, Thomas, jt. auth. see Lewis, Walter.

Lewis, Thomas A. For King & Country: George Washington: the Early Years. LC 94-48700. 296p. 1995. pap. 14.95 (*0-471-10465-5*) Wiley.

— The Guns of Cedar Creek. 2nd rev. ed. LC 87-46153. (Illus.). 312p. 1997. 24.95 (*0-9659268-1-8*) Herit Assocs.

Lewis, Thomas H. Forgotten Battles along the Yellowstone. (Illus.). 1985. pap. 4.95 (*0-916552-31-4*) Acoma Bks.

— The Medicine Men: Oglala Sioux Ceremony & Healing. LC 89-22508. (Studies in the Anthropology of North American Indians). (Illus.). viii, 219p. 1990. reprint ed. pap. 10.95 (*0-8032-7939-6*, Bison Books) U of Nebr Pr.

Lewis, Thomas J., jt. auth. see Lewis, Cynthia C.

Lewis, Thomas L. & Fingeret, Murray. Primary Care of the Glaucomas. (Illus.). 410p. (C). 1993. pap. text 110.00 (*0-8385-7998-1*, A7998-6, Apple Lange Med) McGraw.

Lewis, Thomas L. & Lewis, Madeline D. The Prehistory of the Chickamauga Basin in Tennessee, 2 vols., Set, Vol. 1. (Illus.). 320p. (C). 1995. lib. bdg. 50.00 (*0-87049-861-4*) U of Tenn Pr.

Lewis, Thomas M. & Kneberg, Madeline. Hiwassee Island: An Archaeological Account of Four Tennessee Indian Peoples. LC 75-130688. (Illus.). 328p. 1970. pap. 18.95 (*0-87049-420-1*) U of Tenn Pr.

— Tribes That Slumber: Indians of the Tennessee Region. LC 58-12085. (Illus.). 208p. 1958. pap. 16.95 (*0-87049-021-4*) U of Tenn Pr.

Lewis, Thomas M. & Lewis, Madeline D. The Prehistory of the Chickamauga Basin in Tennessee, 2 vols., Set, Vol. 1. (Illus.). 320p. (C). 1995. pap. text 25.00 (*0-87049-863-0*) U of Tenn Pr.

— The Prehistory of the Chickamauga Basin in Tennessee, 2 vols., Set, Vol. 2. (Illus.). 432p. (C). 1995. pap. text 25.00 (*0-87049-864-9*); lib. bdg. 50.00 (*0-87049-862-2*) U of Tenn Pr.

Lewis, Thomas M. & Lewis, Madeline K. Eva: An Archaic Site. LC 61-18403. (University of Tennessee Study in Anthropology). 188p. reprint ed. pap. 58.30 (*0-7837-3027-6*, 204291300006) Bks Demand.

Lewis, Thomas P. Call for Mr. Sniff. LC 79-2679. (I Can Read Mystery Bks.). (Illus.). 64p. (J). (ps-3). 1981. 11.95 (*0-06-023814-3*) HarpC Child Bks.

— Clipper Ship. (I Can Read Bks.). (Illus.). 64p. (J). (gr. 2-4). 1978. 11.95 (*0-06-023808-9*) HarpC Child Bks.

— Clipper Ship. LC 77-11858. (I Can Read Bks.). (Illus.). 64p. (J). (ps-3). 1992. pap. 3.95 (*0-06-444160-1*, HarpTrophy) HarpC Child Bks.

— Frida's Office Day. LC 87-33488. (I Can Read Bks.). (Illus.). 64p. (J). (ps-3). 1989. 11.95 (*0-06-023843-7*) HarpC Child Bks.

— Hill of Fire. LC 70-121802. (I Can Read Bks.). (Illus.). 64p. (J). (ps-3). 1971. lib. bdg. 15.89 (*0-06-023804-6*) HarpC Child Bks.

— Hill of Fire. LC 70-121802. (I Can Read Bks.). (Illus.). 64p. (J). (ps-3). 1983. pap. 3.95 (*0-06-444040-0*, HarpTrophy) HarpC Child Bks.

— Hill of Fire. (I Can Read Bks.). (J). (gr. 2-4). 1987. 8.95 (*0-606-03198-7*, Pub. by Turtleback) Demco.

— Hill of Fire. unabridged ed. (I Can Read Bks.). (Illus.). (J). (gr. 2-4). 1990. 8.95 incl. audio (*1-55994-232-0*, TBC 2320) HarperAudio.

— La Montana de Fuego. 1997. 10.15 (*0-606-10858-0*, Pub. by Turtleback) Demco.

— The Pro - Am Book of Music & Mythology, Vol. 1. (Illus.). 892p. 1992. 59.95 (*0-912483-51-2*) Pro-Am Music.

— The Pro - Am Book of Music & Mythology, Vol. 2. 659p. 1992. 49.95 (*0-912483-82-2*) Pro-Am Music.

— The Pro Am Guide to U. S. Books about Music: Annotated Subject Guide to Current & Backlist Titles. (General Music Ser.: Gms-6). 211p. (Orig.). 1987. pap. 35.00 (*0-912483-03-2*) Pro-Am Music.

— Something about the Music, No. 2: Anthology of the Critical Opinions. 660p. 1991. 44.50 (*0-912483-66-0*); pap. 29.50 (*0-912483-54-7*) Pro-Am Music.

Lewis, Thomas P., ed. The Pro-Am Guide to U. S. Books about Music: Annotated Subject Guide to Current & Backlist Titles, 1987 Supplement. 173p. (Orig.). 1988. pap. 23.50 (*0-912483-14-8*) Pro-Am Music.

Lewis, Thomas P., ed. see Leppard, Raymond.

Lewis, Thomas R. Connecticut: A Geography. (Westview Geographies of the United States Ser.). (C). 1986. text 71.00 (*0-86531-484-5*) Westview.

— Organization, Training, Search & Recovery Procedures for the Underwater Unit. 2nd ed. LC 79-83668. (Illus.). 54p. 1979. 6.95 (*0-918616-04-2*) Northern Mich.

Lewis, Thomas S., ed. see Crane, Hart.

Lewis, Thomas T., ed. see Harley, Brilliana.

***Lewis Thompson, Vickie.** Side-by-Side: A Photographic History of American Women in Military Service. (Illus.). 160p. 1999. 29.95 (*1-55670-944-7*) Stewart Tabori & Chang.

Lewis Thompson, Vickie & Leclaire, Day. Mail-Order Grooms: Holding Out for a Hero; Mail-Order Bridegroom, 2 bks. (By Request 2's Ser.). 2000. mass mkt. 4.99 (*0-373-21711-0*, 1-21711-6) Harlequin Bks.

Lewis, Thrope, intro. The History of the Kings of Britain. (Classics Ser.). 384p. 1966. pap. 19.99 (*0-14-044170-0*, Penguin Classics) Viking Penguin.

Lewis, Timothy E. Environmental Chemistry & Toxicology of Aluminum. (Illus.). 350p. 1989. lib. bdg. 110.00 (*0-87371-194-7*, L194) Lewis Pubs.

— Tree Rings As Indicators of Ecosystem Health. 224p. 1994. lib. bdg. 110.00 (*0-8493-7651-3*, 7651) CRC Pr.

Lewis, Timothy J., jt. auth. see Sugai, George.

Lewis, Toby, jt. auth. see Barnett, Vic.

Lewis, Toby, jt. ed. see Goldstein, Harvey.

Lewis, Todd. Reader's Theatre 2: Two Scripts for Readers Theater. 59p. 1989. pap. 8.99 (*0-8341-9729-4*, MP-657) Nazarene.

Lewis, Todd T. The Himalayas: A Syllabus of the Region's History, Anthropology, & Religion. Riccardi, Theodore, Jr., ed. LC 95-24655. (Occasional Papers). 1995. pap. 25.00 (*0-924304-34-0*) Assn Asian Studies.

— Mahayana Buddhist Texts from Nepal: Narratives & Rituals of Newar Buddhism. LC 99-45350. (C). 2000. text 59.50 (*0-7914-4611-5*) State U NY Pr.

— Mahayana Buddhist Texts from Nepal: Popular Buudhist Texts from Nepal. LC 99-45350. (C). 2000. pap. text 19.95 (*0-7914-4612-3*) State U NY Pr.

Lewis, Todd V. Communicating Literature. 2nd ed. 256p. (C). 1995. per. 31.95 (*0-7872-1274-1*, 41127401) Kendall-Hunt.

Lewis, Todd V. & Harmin, Merrill. RT: A Readers Theater Ministry. 1987. 8.99 (*0-00-528656-5*, MP-641) Lillenas.

Lewis, Tom. Darwin Sayonara. 104p. (C). 1990. pap. 39.00 (*0-86439-133-1*, Pub. by Boolarong Pubns) St Mut.

— Divided Highways: Building the Interstate Highways, Transforming American Life. (Illus.). 354p. 2000. text 28.00 (*0-7881-6850-9*) DIANE Pub.

Lewis, Tom. Divided Highways: Building the Interstate Highways, Transforming American Life. (Illus.). 384p. 1999. pap. 13.95 (*0-14-026771-9*) Viking Penguin.

***Lewis, Tom & Sanchez, Francisco J., eds.** Culture & the State in Spain, 1550-1850. LC 99-16669. (Hispanic Issues Ser.: No. 20). (Illus.). 336p. 1999. 60.00 (*0-8153-3484-2*, H2169, Pub. by Garland) Taylor & Francis.

Lewis, Tom, jt. auth. see Lewis, Cynthia C.

Lewis, Tom G. Karate for Kids. 120p. (Orig.). (J). (gr. 2-10). 1980. pap. 5.95 (*0-89826-005-1*) Natl Paperback.

Lewis, Tom J. & Jungman, Robert E., eds. On Being Foreign: Culture Shock in Short Fiction: An International Anthology. LC 86-81109. 308p. (Orig.). (C). 1986. pap. text 17.95 (*0-933662-62-9*) Intercult Pr.

Lewis, Tommi. Movie Scrapbook. (Prince of Egypt Ser.). (J). 1998. pap. 8.99 (*0-8499-5900-4*) Tommy Nelson.

— Prince of Egypt: The Movie Scrapbook. LC 99-190555. (Illus.). 64p. 1998. pap. 8.99 (*0-14-056474-8*, PuffinBks) Peng Put Young Read.

Lewis, Tony. MCC Masterclass: The New MCC Coaching Book. (Illus.). 192p. 1995. 39.95 (*0-297-81431-1*, Pub. by Weidenfeld & Nicolson) Trafalgar.

Lewis, Trevor, ed. Insect Communication. 1984. text 136.00 (*0-12-447175-7*) Acad Pr.

— Thrips as Crop Pests. LC 97-24320. (A CAB International Publication). 764p. (C). 1998. text 175.00 (*0-85199-178-5*) OUP.

Lewis, Trudy. Private Correspondences. 180p. 1994. 19.95 (*0-8101-5033-6*, TriQuart) Northwestern U Pr.

— Private Correspondences. 198p. 1996. pap. 12.95 (*0-8101-5041-7*, TriQuart) Northwestern U Pr.

***Lewis, Valerie.** Medicaid Waivers: California's Use of a Federal Option. (Illus.). 27p. 2000. pap. write for info. (*1-929008-28-7*) CA HlthCare Fnd.

Lewis, Valerie, et al. Valerie & Walter's Best. LC 98-7711. 720p. 1998. pap. 15.95 (*0-380-79438-1*, Avon Bks) Morrow Avon.

Lewis, Vicki, et al. Be Mine, Valentine; To Have It All; Cupid's Task; Only with the Heart, 4 vols. in 1. (Romance Digest Ser.: Vol. 4, No. 4). 1995. pap. 2.75 (*0-373-82722-9*, 1-82722-9) Harlequin Bks.

Lewis, Victoria. The Know It All Book for Women, 4 vols. Lynn, Peny, ed. (Illus.). 2100p. 1998. 199.95 (*0-9645932-2-X*) Women Know It All.

— The Know It All Book for Women: Organizer. 1998. 199.95 (*0-9645932-3-8*) Women Know It All.

— The Night Before: A Cookbook. 1998. 16.00 (*0-207-18849-1*) HarpC.

Lewis, Victoria M. Colorado Home Owner's Guide to Paying Less Property Taxes: Complete Step by Step Instructions to Lower Current Year Property Taxes, Receive Refunds for Past Years, Plus Interest. 216p. (C). 1995. pap. text 24.95 (*0-9645932-0-3*) Women Know It All.

Lewis, Virgil. Life & Times of Ann Bailey: Pioneer Heroine of the Kanawha Valley. 2nd ed. LC 98-88393. Orig. Title: Life & Times of Anne Bailey. (Illus.). 96p. 1998. reprint ed. pap. 9.95 (*0-9667246-0-7*) Discovery WV.

Lewis, Virgil A. The Soldiery of West Virginia in the French & Indian War; Lord Dunmore's War; the Revolution; the Later Indian Wars; the Whiskey Insurrection; the Second War with England; the War with Mexico, & Addenda Relating to West Virginians in the Civil War. LC 67 28603. (Illus.). 227p. 1998. reprint ed. pap. 25.00 (*0-8063-0210-0*) Clearfield Co.

Lewis, Virginia, jt. auth. see Brown, Stephanie.

Lewis, Virginia A. & Brock, Robert A. Virginia & Virginians, 2 vols. (Illus.). 813p. 1996. reprint ed. pap. 65.00 (*0-8063-4633-7*, 9211) Clearfield Co.

Lewis, Virginia L. Flames of Passion - Flames of Greed: Acts of Arson in German Prose Fiction 1850-1900. LC 91-3807. (Studies on Themes & Motifs in Literature: Vol. 2). XVI, 251p. 1991. 47.95 (*0-8204-1500-6*) P Lang Pubng.

Lewis, Vivian. The Traveler's Atlas. (Illus.). 230p. (Orig.). (C). 1988. pap. 9.95 (*0-945332-13-0*) Agora Inc MD.

Lewis, W. Modern Problems in Gear Testing & a Proposed Testing Machine. (Technical Papers: Vol. P70). (Illus.). 8p. 1923. pap. text 30.00 (*1-55589-438-0*) AGMA.

Lewis, W. Arthur. Development Economics in the 1950s. LC 94-19438. (Occasional Papers). 1994. pap. 9.95 (*1-55815-354-3*) ICS Pr.

— Racial Conflict & Economic Development. (Illus.). 128p. 1985. 24.95 (*0-674-74579-5*) HUP.

Lewis, W. Cris, jt. auth. see Peterson, H. Craig.

***Lewis, W. David.** Airline Executives & Federal Regulation: Case Studies in American Enterprise from the Airmail & to the Dawn of the Jet Age. 288p. (C). 2000. text 60.00 (*0-8142-0833-9*) Ohio St U Pr.

— Hopewell Furnace: A Guide to Hopewell Village National Historic Site, Pennsylvania. 95p. 1984. pap. 96.00 (*0-16-003456-6*) USGPO.

Lewis, W. David. Iron & Steel in America. (Industry in America Ser.). (Illus.). 64p. 1975. reprint ed. pap. 5.95 (*0-914650-10-6*) Hagley Museum.

Lewis, W. H. In the Arms of Our Elders. 170p. 1995. pap. 10.95 (*0-932112-35-8*) Carolina Wren.

— The Splendid Century: Life in the France of Louis XIV. (Illus.). 306p. (C). 1997. reprint ed. pap. text 13.50 (*0-88133-921-0*) Waveland Pr.

Lewis, W. H., ed. see Lewis, C. S.

Lewis, W. M., Jr., et al. Eutrophication & Land Use. (Ecological Studies. Analysis & Synthesis: Vol. 46). (Illus.). 275p. 1984. 91.00 (*0-387-90961-3*) Spr-Verlag.

Lewis, W. S., ed. see Walpole, Horace.

Lewis, W. T. Genealogy of the Lewis Family in America. 458p. 1989. reprint ed. pap. 68.50 (*0-8328-0768-0*); reprint ed. lib. bdg. 76.50 (*0-8328-0767-2*) Higginson Bk Co.

Lewis, Walter & Lewis, Thomas. Modern Organ Building. (Illus.). xii, 164p. 1986. reprint ed. 90.00 (*0-913746-26-6*); reprint ed. pap. 68.00 (*0-913746-27-4*) Organ Lit.

Lewis, Walter D. & Trimble, William F. The Airway to Everywhere: A History of All American Aviation, 1937-1953. LC 87-25176. (Illus.). 240p. 1988. reprint ed. pap. 74.40 (*0-608-07695-3*, 206778500010) Bks Demand.

Lewis, Walter E. Yankee Ingenuity, Yankee Know-How. LC 97-90449. 343p. 1997. 35.00 (*0-533-12408-5*) Vantage.

Lewis, Walter H. Ecology Field Glossary: A Naturalist's Vocabulary. LC 77-71856. 153p. 1977. lib. bdg. 55.00 (*0-8371-9547-0*, LEF/, Greenwood Pr) Greenwood.

Lewis, Walter H. & Elvin-Lewis, Memory P. Medical Botany: Plants Affecting Man's Health. LC 76-44376. 544p. 1982. pap. 59.95 (*0-471-86134-0*) Wiley.

Lewis, Walter L. How to Keep More of What You Win: A Gambler's Guide to Taxes. Simon, Kelly, ed. LC 96-95259. 60p. 1996. pap. 9.95 (*0-9655716-0-2*) Impulse Pubng.

— How to Keep More of What You Win: A Gambler's Guide to Taxes. 1998. pap. text 11.95 (*0-9655716-1-0*) Impulse Pubng.

Lewis, Ward B. Eugene O'Neill: The German Reception of America's First Dramatist. LC 84-47881. (Germanic Studies in America: Vol. 50). 211p. (C). 1984. text 28.95 (*0-8204-0156-0*) P Lang Pubng.

— The Ironic Dissident: Frank Wedekind in the View of His Critics. (LCGERM Ser.). xiv, 166p. (C). 1997. 55.00 (*1-57113-023-3*) Camden Hse.

Lewis, Warfield. Just Around the Corner. unabridged ed. LC 97-94985. (Illus.). 380p. 1998. pap. 18.95 (*0-9661925-0-8*) Davidge Hse.

Lewis, Warren. Computer Site Integration Technique. (Illus.). 32p. 1993. 57.00 (*0-614-03636-4*) emf-emi Control.

Lewis, Warren, ed. see Simic, Marjorie R.

Lewis, Warren L. Franchises: Dollars & Sense. 556p. 1995. pap. text 49.95 (*0-8403-8963-9*) Kendall-Hunt.

Lewis, Warren W., ed. Whole Language: The Debate. 350p. (Orig.). 1994. pap. 24.95 (*0-927516-39-X*) ERIC-REC.

Lewis, Warren W., ed. see Behm, Richard & Behm, Mary.

Lewis, Warren W., ed. see Gottlieb, Stephen S.

Lewis, Warren W., ed. see Grusko, Robin & Kramer, Judy.

Lewis, Warren W., ed. see Katz, Kim & Katz, Claudia.

Lewis, Warren W., ed. see McAllister, Elizabeth.

Lewis, Warren W., ed. see McGowen, Carolyn S.

Lewis, Warren W., ed. see Measell, James S.

Lewis, Warren W., ed. see Newman, Anabel P. & Metz, Elizabeth.

Lewis, Warren W., ed. see Sproule, J. Michael.

Lewis, Wayne K. & Resnicoff, Steven H. The New Law of Negotiable Instruments. LC 96-76060. 1996. 95.00 (*1-55834-373-3*, 64238, MICHIE) LEXIS Pub.

— The New Law of Negotiable Instruments, 1998 Supplement. 90p. 1998. suppl. ed. 35.00 (*0-327-00342-1*, 6423911) LEXIS Pub.

Lewis, Wendi L. Montgomery: At the Forefront of a New Century. 384p. 1996. 39.00 (*1-885352-36-0*) Community Comm.

Lewis-Wild, Robin. One Hundred One Torchon Patterns. rev. ed. (Illus.). 132p. 1992. reprint ed. pap. 19.95 (*0-9633892-0-3*) Robins Bobbins.

Lewis, Wilfred, Jr. Federal Fiscal Policy in the Postwar Recessions. LC 80-16. (Brookings Institution, National Committee on Government Finance, Studies of Government Finance). (Illus.). 311p. 1980. reprint ed. lib. bdg. 38.50 (*0-313-22284-3*, LEFF) Greenwood.

***Lewis, William & Marks, Edward.** Searching for Partners: Regional Organizations & Peace Operations. (Illus.). 188p. (C). 1999. pap. text 30.00 (*0-7881-8390-7*) DIANE Pub.

Lewis, William & Schuman, Nancy. Fast Track Guide to the Highest Paying Jobs. LC 87-10045. 212p. 1987. pap. 14.95 (*0-471-83801-2*) Wiley.

Lewis, William, jt. auth. see Schuman, Nancy.

L

Lewis, William A. Politics in West Africa, Series X (1965) LC 81-13317. (Whidden Lectures for 1965). 90p. 1982. reprint ed. lib. bdg. 55.00 (*0-313-23202-4*, LEPW, Greenwood Pr) Greenwood.

Lewis, William A. & Molloy, Nancy H. How to Choose & Use Temporary Services. LC 90-53214. 260p. reprint ed. pap. 80.60 (*0-7837-7061-8*, 204687300004) Bks Demand.

Lewis, William B. Helping the Youthful Offender: Individual & Group Therapies That Work. 217p. 1991. pap. 24.95 (*1-56024-127-6*) Haworth Pr.

Lewis, William D. It's Called Making It Happen. (Illus.). 158p. (Orig.). 1997. pap. 9.95 (*1-57502-342-3*, PO1134) Morris Pubng.

— Miscellaneous Writings of the Late Hon. Joseph P. Bradley, Associate Justice of the Supreme Court of the United States: With a Sketch of His Life by His Son, Charles Bradley & a Review of His "Judicial Record" & an Account of His "Dissenting Opinions" Bradley, Charles, ed. & compiled by by. xii, 435p. 1986. reprint ed. 50.00 (*0-8377-0876-1*, Rothman) W S Hein.

***Lewis, William D.** Serious Players Only. 226p. 1999. pap. 14.95 (*0-7392-0498-X*, PO3645) Morris Pubng.

***Lewis, William E.** PDCA Test: A Quality Framework for Software Testing. 2nd ed. LC 99-86186. 656p. 2000. boxed set 69.95 (*0-8493-9833-9*) CRC Pr.

— Problem-solving Principles for Ada Programmers: Applied Logic, Psychology & Grit. LC 82-178782. 183p. 1982. write for info. (*0-8104-5211-1*) Sams.

— Problem-solving Principles for Fortran Programmers: Applied Logic, Psychology & Grit. LC 81-2070. 177 p. 1981. write for info. (*0-8104-5430-0*) Sams.

— Problem-solving Principles for Pascal Programmers: Applied Logic, Psychology & Grit. LC 81-2057. 179 p. 1981. write for info. (*0-8104-5767-9*) Sams.

— Problem-solving Principles for Programmers: Applied Logic, Psychology & Grit. LC 80-23834. 163p. 1980. write for info. (*0-8104-5138-7*) Sams.

Lewis, William E. Quality Standard for Instrument Air. LC 98-45186. 448p. 1998. ring bd. 285.00 (*0-8493-9980-7*) CRC Pr.

Lewis, William F. Soul Rebels: The Rastafari. (Illus.). 139p. (C). 1993. pap. text 10.95 (*0-88133-739-0*) Waveland Pr.

***Lewis, William H.** Searching for Partners: Regional Organizations & Peace Operations. 192p. 1998. per. 9.00 (*0-16-061218-7*) USGPO.

Lewis, William H. & Johnson, Stuart E., eds. Weapons of Mass Destruction: New Perspectives on Counterproliferation. (Illus.). 247p. (Orig.). (C). 1995. pap. text 40.00 (*0-7881-2127-8*) DIANE Pub.

Lewis, William J. Interpreting for Park Visitors. (Illus.). 160p. 1981. pap. 3.95 (*0-915992-11-6*) Eastern National.

***Lewis, William K.** Set a Course for Freedom: A Novel of the Revolutionary War. LC 00-190180. 231p. 2000. 25.00 (*0-7388-1498-9*); pap. 18.00 (*0-7388-1499-7*) Xlibris Corp.

Lewis, William L., jt. auth. see Beker, Jerome.

Lewis, William M. From a College Platform: Addresses. LC 68-29224. (Essay Index Reprint Ser.). (Illus.). 1977. reprint ed. 20.95 (*0-8369-0617-9*) Ayer.

Lewis, William M., et al. Wharton Assembly Addresses, 1937. LC 79-157969. (Essay Index Reprint Ser.). 1977. reprint ed. 15.95 (*0-8369-2258-1*) Ayer.

Lewis, William R. Cash - For Your Used Clothing. (Illus.). 64p. Date not set. pap. 25.00 (*0-9653626-2-0*) Client Valuation.

Lewis, William R. Cash - For Your Used Clothing. 10th ed. 60p. 1996. pap. 15.95 (*0-9653626-0-4*) Client Valuation.

***Lewis, William R.** Cash for Your Used Clothing, Vol. 11. rev. ed. (Illus.). 64p. 2000. pap. 25.00 (*0-9653626-1-2*) Client Valuation.

— John Gwilym Jones. LC 94-229473. (Writers of Wales Ser.). 109p. 1994. write for info. (*0-7083-1251-9*, Pub. by Univ Wales Pr) Paul & Co Pubs.

Lewis, William S. The Case of Spokane Garry. 139p. 1987. 14.95 (*0-87770-428-7*) Ye Galleon.

— Early Days in the Big Bend Country. fac. ed. (Shorey Historical Ser.). 35p. 1926. reprint ed. pap. 10.00 (*0-8466-0089-7*, S-89) Shoreys Bkstore.

Lewis, William S., ed. see MacDonald, Ranald.

Lewis-Williams, David & Dowson, Thomas A., eds. Rock Paintings of Natal Drakensberg. (Illus.). 68p. (Orig.). 1992. pap. 18.95 (*0-86980-869-9*, Pub. by Univ Natal Pr) Intl Spec Bk.

Lewis-Williams, J. David, jt. auth. see Clottes, Jean.

Lewis, Willie N. Willie, a Girl from a Town Called Dallas. LC 83-18081. (Illus.). 150p. 1984. 19.95 (*0-89096-175-1*) Tex A&M Univ Pr.

Lewis, Wilmarth S. Collector's Progress. LC 73-16738. (Illus.). 253p. 1974. reprint ed. lib. bdg. 65.00 (*0-8371-7219-5*, LECP, Greenwood Pr) Greenwood.

— Rescuing Horace Walpole. LC 78-7590. (Illus.). 1978. 52.50 (*0-300-02278-6*) Yale U Pr.

— Three Tours Through London in the Years 1748, 1776, 1797. LC 77-104252. (Illus.). 135p. 1971. reprint ed. lib. bdg. 55.00 (*0-8371-3977-5*, LETL, Greenwood Pr) Greenwood.

Lewis, Wilmarth S., ed. see Walpole, Horace.

Lewis, Winsome V., ed. see Wright-Lewis, Joan.

Lewis, Wyndham. America, I Presume. LC 72-2158. (American Literature Ser.: No. 49). 1972. reprint ed. lib. bdg. 75.00 (*0-8383-1476-7*) M S G Haskell Hse.

— The Apes of God. LC 81-7659. (Illus.). 642p. 1992. reprint ed. pap. 17.50 (*0-87685-512-5*) Black Sparrow.

— The Art of Being Ruled. LC 88-32776. (Illus.). 464p. (C). 1989. reprint ed. 25.00 (*0-87685-754-3*) Black Sparrow.

— The Art of Being Ruled. LC 88-32776. (Illus.). 464p. (C). 1989. reprint ed. pap. 15.00 (*0-87685-753-5*) Black Sparrow.

— The Art of Being Ruled. LC 72-39603. (English Literature Ser.: No. 33). 1972. reprint ed. lib. bdg. 75.00 (*0-8383-1376-0*) M S G Haskell Hse.

— Blast One. (Illus.). 167p. (C). 1997. reprint ed. pap. 17.50 (*0-87685-521-4*) Black Sparrow.

— Blast Two, Vol. 2. (Illus.). 111p. 1993. reprint ed. pap. 15.00 (*0-87685-523-0*) Black Sparrow.

— Blasting & Bombardiering. 350p. (Orig.). 1982. pap. 11.95 (*0-7145-0130-1*) Riverrun NY.

— Blasting & Bombardiering. 2nd rev. ed. LC 67-17112. (Illus.). 359p. (Orig.). reprint ed. pap. 111.30 (*0-8357-7313-2*, 202995400066) Bks Demand.

— The Caliph's Design: Architects! Where is Your Vortex? Edwards, Paul, ed. & afterword by by. LC 86-3560. (Illus.). 188p. 1986. pap. 12.50 (*0-87685-664-4*) Black Sparrow.

— The Childermass. LC 76-145141. (Literature Ser.). 328p. 1972. reprint ed. 49.00 (*0-403-01072-1*) Scholarly.

— The Complete Wild Body. Lafourcade, Bernard, ed. LC 82-4498. (Illus.). 418p. 1982. 25.00 (*0-87685-552-4*) Black Sparrow.

— Count Your Dead, They Are Alive. LC 72-82185. 1972. reprint ed. lib. bdg. 250.00 (*0-87968-007-5*) Gordon Pr.

— Creatures of Habit & Creatures of Change: Essays on Art, Literature & Society, 1914-1956. Edwards, Paul, ed. & intro. by. LC 89-14999. (Illus.). 430p. (C). 1989. pap. 15.00 (*0-87685-769-1*) Black Sparrow.

— Diabolical Principle & the Dithyrambic Spectator. LC 78-176495. (English Literature Ser.: No. 33). 1971. reprint ed. lib. bdg. 75.00 (*0-8383-1362-0*) M S G Haskell Hse.

— Doom of Youth. LC 72-2090. (English Literature Ser.: No. 33). 1972. reprint ed. lib. bdg. 75.00 (*0-8383-1475-9*) M S G Haskell Hse.

— The Enemy: A Review of Art & Literature, Vol. 1. (Illus.). 246p. (Orig.). (C). 1994. 25.00 (*0-87685-948-1*, 1355-820X); pap. 15.00 (*0-87685-947-3*, 1355-820X) Black Sparrow.

— The Enemy: A Review of Art & Literature, Vol. 1. deluxe ed. (Illus.). 246p. (Orig.). (C). 1994. 35.00 (*0-87685-949-X*, 1355-820X) Black Sparrow.

— The Enemy: A Review of Art & Literature, Vol. 2. (Illus.). 215p. (Orig.). (C). 1994. 25.00 (*0-87685-951-1*, 1355-280X); pap. 15.00 (*0-87685-950-3*, 1355-820X) Black Sparrow.

— The Enemy: A Review of Art & Literature, Vol. 2. deluxe ed. (Illus.). 215p. (Orig.). (C). 1994. 35.00 (*0-87685-952-X*, 1355-820X) Black Sparrow.

— The Enemy: A Review of Art & Literature, Vol. 3. (Illus.). 205p. (Orig.). (C). 1994. 25.00 (*0-87685-954-6*, 1355-820X); pap. 15.00 (*0-87685-953-8*, 1355-820X) Black Sparrow.

— The Enemy: A Review of Art & Literature, Vol. 3. deluxe ed. (Illus.). 205p. (Orig.). (C). 1994. 35.00 (*0-87685-955-4*, 1355-820X) Black Sparrow.

— Filibusters in Barbary. LC 72-2114. (English Literature Ser.: No. 33). 1972. reprint ed. lib. bdg. 75.00 (*0-8383-1477-5*) M S G Haskell Hse.

— Hitler. LC 72-82189. 1972. reprint ed. lib. bdg. 250.00 (*0-87968-005-9*) Gordon Pr.

— The Hitler Cult. LC 72-82187. 1972. reprint ed. lib. bdg. 250.00 (*0-87968-006-7*) Gordon Pr.

— Hitler, the Germans & the Jews, 5 vols, Set. 1522p. 1973. 1500.00 (*0-8490-0366-0*) Gordon Pr.

— The Jews, Are They Human? LC 72-82188. 1972. reprint ed. lib. bdg. 250.00 (*0-87968-008-3*) Gordon Pr.

— Journey into Barbary. Fox, C. J., ed. LC 82-20784. (Illus.). 238p. (Orig.). (C). 1983. 25.00 (*0-87685-519-2*); pap. 15.00 (*0-87685-518-4*) Black Sparrow.

— Left Wings over Europe. LC 72-82186. 1972. reprint ed. lib. bdg. 250.00 (*0-87968-004-0*) Gordon Pr.

— Men Without Art. Cooney, Seamus, ed. LC 87-733. 330p. (Orig.). 1987. pap. 15.00 (*0-87685-686-5*) Black Sparrow.

— Monstre Gai. (Orig.). 1981. pap. 9.95 (*0-7145-0386-X*) Riverrun NY.

— The Old Gang & the New Gang. LC 72-3159. (English Literature Ser.: No. 33). 1972. reprint ed. lib. bdg. 75.00 (*0-8383-1525-9*) M S G Haskell Hse.

— Paleface. 1973. lib. bdg. 250.00 (*0-87968-018-0*) Gordon Pr.

— Paleface. LC 73-95438. (English Biography Ser.: No. 31). 1970. reprint ed. lib. bdg. 75.00 (*0-8383-0990-9*) M S G Haskell Hse.

— Paleface, the Philosophy of the Melting Pot. 1971. reprint ed. 39.00 (*0-403-01073-X*) Scholarly.

— The Revenge for Love. LC 91-4269. (Illus.). 404p. (C). 1991. 25.00 (*0-87685-829-9*) Black Sparrow.

— The Revenge for Love. LC 91-4269. (Illus.). 404p. (C). 1991. pap. 18.00 (*0-87685-828-0*) Black Sparrow.

— The Roaring Queen. 184p. 1973. 10.00 (*0-87140-576-8*, Pub. by Liveright) Norton.

— Rotting Hill. Edwards, Paul, ed. LC 85-22834. 355p. 1986. reprint ed. pap. 15.00 (*0-87685-646-6*) Black Sparrow.

— Rude Assignment. Foshay, Toby, ed. LC 84-16837. (Illus.). 315p. (Orig.). 1984. 25.00 (*0-87685-604-0*); pap. 15.00 (*0-87685-603-2*) Black Sparrow.

— Self Condemned. LC 83-2836. (Illus.). 440p. (Orig.). 1983. 25.00 (*0-87685-576-1*) Black Sparrow.

— Self Condemned. LC 83-2836. (Illus.). 440p. (Orig.). 1983. pap. 15.00 (*0-87685-575-3*) Black Sparrow.

— Snooty Baronet. LC 83-22472. (Illus.). 350p. 1984. 25.00 (*0-87685-600-8*) Black Sparrow.

— Snooty Baronet. deluxe ed. LC 83-22472. (Illus.). 350p. 1984. 30.00 (*0-87685-601-6*) Black Sparrow.

— Snooty Baronet. LC 77-176492. (English Literature Ser.: No. 33). 1971. reprint ed. lib. bdg. 75.00 (*0-8383-1359-0*) M S G Haskell Hse.

— Tarr: The Nineteen Eighteen Version. LC 89-29842. (Illus.). 430p. (C). 1990. reprint ed. pap. 17.50 (*0-87685-784-5*) Black Sparrow.

— Time & Western Man. Edwards, Paul, ed. & intro. by. LC 93-1568. 617p. (C). 1993. 30.00 (*0-87685-879-5*); pap. 17.50 (*0-87685-878-7*) Black Sparrow.

— Time & Western Man. LC 78-64042. (Des Imagistes: Literature of the Imagist Movement Ser.). reprint ed. 36.00 (*0-404-17125-7*) AMS Pr.

— Volcanic Heaven: Essays on Wyndham Lewis. Edwards, Paul, ed. LC 96-4671. (Illus.). 200p. (C). 1996. pap. 17.50 (*1-57423-010-7*) Black Sparrow.

— Volcanic Heaven: Essays on Wyndham Lewis. deluxe ed. Edwards, Paul, ed. LC 96-4671. (Illus.). 200p. (C). 1996. 35.00 (*1-57423-012-3*) Black Sparrow.

— The Vulgar Streak. LC 85-6099. (Illus.). 273p. (Orig.). (C). 1985. 25.00 (*0-87685-629-6*); pap. 15.00 (*0-87685-628-8*) Black Sparrow.

— The Vulgar Streak. deluxe ed. LC 85-6099. (Illus.). 273p. (Orig.). (C). 1985. 30.00 (*0-87685-630-X*) Black Sparrow.

— Wild Body. LC 70-137666. (Studies in Poetry: No. 38). 1971. reprint ed. lib. bdg. 75.00 (*0-8383-1225-X*) M S G Haskell Hse.

— The Writer & the Absolute. LC 75-7240. 202p. 1975. reprint ed. lib. bdg. 59.50 (*0-8371-8098-8*, LEWR, Greenwood Pr) Greenwood.

— Wyndham Lewis the Artist. LC 74-173843. (English Literature Ser.: No. 33). 1971. reprint ed. lib. bdg. 75.00 (*0-8383-1348-5*) M S G Haskell Hse.

Lewis, Wyndham, ed. Enemy, 1927-1929, 2 vols., Set. (Illus.). 1968. reprint ed. 85.00 (*0-7146-2107-2*, Pub. by F Cass Pubs) Intl Spec Bk.

— Tyro: A Review of the Arts of Painting, Sculpture & Design, Nos. 1 & 2: 1921-22. (Illus.). 120p. 1970. 65.00 (*0-7146-2116-1*, Pub. by F Cass Pubs) Intl Spec Bk.

Lewis, Wyndham, jt. auth. see Pound, Ezra.

Lewis, Yohanan. The History of Edom & Khazaria: The Other Israel. rev. ed. Levi, Makeda, ed. 312p. 1998. pap. 17.95 (*0-9665426-0-6*) M Y L Pub.

Lewis, Zack, ed. Latin America on Bicycle. LC 87-62242. 160p. (Orig.). 1987. pap. 12.95 (*0-930016-07-6*) Pass Pr Trvl Line.

Lewis, Zack & Levesque, Jacques. Montreal & the Casino: The Gaming Guide to Montreal. (Illus.). 192p. (Orig.). 1994. pap. 12.95 (*0-930016-21-1*) Pass Pr Trvl Line.

Lewis, Zenrin R., tr. see Roshi, Shibayama Z., et al, eds.

Lewis, Zoe. Beauty & the Beast Teacup Mix-Up: A Sorting Book. LC 94-70049. (Illus.). 24p. (J). (ps-k). 1994. 10.95 (*0-7868-3013-1*, Pub. by Disney Pr) Little.

— Keisha Discovers Harlem. Bodnar, Judit, ed. LC 98-27014. (Magic Attic Club Ser.). (Illus.). 80p. (J). (gr. 2-6). 1998. 12.95 (*1-57513-130-7*); pap. 5.95 (*1-57513-129-3*) Magic Attic.

— Keisha Discovers Harlem. (Magic Attic Club Ser.). (Illus.). 74p. (J). (gr. 2-6). 1999. lib. bdg. 16.40 (*1-57513-144-7*) Magic Attic.

Lewis, Zoe, adapted by. Cinderella. LC 94-70524. (Illustrated Classics Ser.). (Illus.). 96p. (J). 1995. lib. bdg. 14.89 (*0-7868-5008-6*, Pub. by Disney Pr) Little.

Lewis, Zoe, jt. auth. see Hapka, Cathy.

Lewisehn, Leonard, jt. auth. see Nurbakhsh, Javad.

Lewishon, Leonard, tr. see Nurbakhsh, Javad.

Lewisohn, James. Lead Us Forth from Prison. 1977. 3.00 (*0-912678-34-8*, Greenfld Rev Pr) Greenfld Rev Lit.

Lewisohn, Leonard. Beyond Faith & Infidelity: The Sufi Poetry & Teachings of Mahmud Shabistari. (Sufi Ser.: No. 5). 360p. (C). 1995. pap. 29.95 (*0-7007-0343-8*, Pub. by Curzon Pr Ltd) Paul & Co Pubs.

***Lewisohn, Leonard.** Heritage of Sufism Vol. III: Late Classical Persianate Sufism, 1501-1750. 2000. pap. 42.95 (*1-85168-193-0*, Pub. by Onewrld Pubns) Penguin Putnam.

Lewisohn, Leonard, ed. Classical Persian Sufism: From Its Origins to Rumi. 620p. 1996. pap. 29.95 (*0-614-21259-6*, 137) Kazi Pubns.

— The Heritage of Sufism I Vol. I: Classical Persian Sufism from Its Origins to Rumi. 704p. 1999. pap. 29.95 (*1-85168-188-4*, Pub. by Onewrld Pubns) Penguin Putnam.

— The Heritage of Sufism II Vol. II: The Legacy of Medieval Persian Sufism. 448p. 1999. pap. 25.95 (*1-85168-189-2*, Pub. by Onewrld Pubns) Penguin Putnam.

— The Legacy of Medieval Persian Sufism. (Illus.). 434p. 1992. pap. 29.95 (*0-933546-46-7*) KNP.

— The Legacy of Medieval Persian Sufism. 434p. 1996. pap. 29.95 (*0-614-21301-0*, 707) Kazi Pubns.

Lewisohn, Leonard, tr. see Nurbakhsh, Javad.

Lewisohn, Ludwig. The Broken Snare. (Collected Works of Ludwig Lewisohn). 289p. 1998. reprint ed. lib. bdg. 88.00 (*1-58201-676-3*) Classic Bks.

— The Creative Life. (Collected Works of Ludwig Lewisohn). 210p. 1998. reprint ed. lib. bdg. 88.00 (*1-58201-677-1*) Classic Bks.

— Don Juan. (Collected Works of Ludwig Lewisohn). 305p. 1998. reprint ed. lib. bdg. 98.00 (*1-58201-678-X*) Classic Bks.

— Drama & the Stage. LC 71-84319. (Essay Index Reprint Ser.). 1977. 19.95 (*0-8369-1089-3*) Ayer.

— The Drama & the Stage. (Collected Works of Ludwig Lewisohn). 245p. 1998. reprint ed. lib. bdg. 88.00 (*1-58201-679-8*) Classic Bks.

— German Style: An Introduction to the Study of German Prose. (Collected Works of Ludwig Lewisohn). 215p. 1998. reprint ed. lib. bdg. 88.00 (*1-58201-680-1*) Classic Bks.

— The Island Within. LC 97-17834. (Library of Modern Jewish Literature). 266p. 1997. pap. 18.95 (*0-8156-0499-8*) Syracuse U Pr.

— The Island Within. LC 74-29503. (Modern Jewish Experience Ser.). 1975. reprint ed. 33.95 (*0-405-06730-5*) Ayer.

— Israel. (Collected Works of Ludwig Lewisohn). 279p. 1998. reprint ed. lib. bdg. 88.00 (*1-58201-681-X*) Classic Bks.

— Israel. LC 76-138122. 279p. (C). 1971. reprint ed. lib. bdg. 65.00 (*0-8371-5698-X*, LEIS, Greenwood Pr) Greenwood.

— Mid-Channel. LC 74-29502. (Modern Jewish Experience Ser.). 1975. reprint ed. 28.95 (*0-405-06729-1*) Ayer.

— The Modern Drama: An Essay in Interpretation. (Collected Works of Ludwig Lewisohn). 340p. 1998. reprint ed. lib. bdg. 98.00 (*1-58201-682-8*) Classic Bks.

— A Night in Alexandria: A Dramatic Poem in One Act. (Collected Works of Ludwig Lewisohn). 60p. 1998. reprint ed. lib. bdg. 98.00 (*1-58201-683-6*) Classic Bks.

— Permanent Horizon. LC 73-117818. (Essay Index Reprint Ser.). 1977. 21.95 (*0-8369-1811-8*) Ayer.

— The Poets of Modern France. (Collected Works of Ludwig Lewisohn). 199p. 1998. reprint ed. lib. bdg. 88.00 (*1-58201-684-4*) Classic Bks.

— The Spirit of Modern German Literature. (Collected Works of Ludwig Lewisohn). 145p. 1998. reprint ed. lib. bdg. 88.00 (*1-58201-685-2*) Classic Bks.

— Up Stream. (Collected Works of Ludwig Lewisohn). 248p. 1998. reprint ed. lib. bdg. 88.00 (*1-58201-686-0*) Classic Bks.

— Up Stream: An American Chronicle. LC 24-11220. reprint ed. 29.00 (*0-403-00655-4*) Scholarly.

Lewisohn, Ludwig, tr. see Sudermann, Hermann.

Lewisohn, Ludwig, tr. see Werfel, Franz.

***Lewisohn, Mark.** Complete Beatles Chronicle: The Only Definitive Guide to the Beatles' Entire Career. (Illus.). 2000. pap. 24.95 (*0-600-60033-5*) P HM.

Lewisohn, Sam A. Painters & Personality: A Collector's View of Modern Art. LC 70-152188. (Essay Index Reprint Ser.). 1977. reprint ed. 42.95 (*0-8369-2238-7*) Ayer.

Lewison. Marketing Management. (C). 1996. pap. text, teacher ed. 28.00 (*0-03-016227-0*) Harcourt Coll Pubs.

Lewison, Dale M. Retailing. 5th ed. (Illus.). 912p. (C). 1993. text 86.00 (*0-02-370530-2*, Macmillan Coll) P-H.

— Retailing. 6th ed. LC 96-36764. (Illus.). 800p. (C). 1996. text 84.00 (*0-13-461427-5*) P-H.

Lewison, Dana, ed. see Sullivan, Rick & Gaffikin, Lynne.

***Lewison, Helen.** Seduction of Silence: Journal of a Reluctant Widow. LC 99-66899. 300p. 2000. pap. 14.95 (*1-885003-26-9*, Pub. by R D Reed Pubs) Midpt Trade.

Lewison, Jeremy. Ben Nicholson. 277p. 1994. pap. 60.00 (*1-85437-130-4*) U of Wash Pr.

— A Genius of Industrial England: Edward Wadsworth, 1889-1949. (Illus.). 128p. (C). 1990. pap. 25.00 (*0-9505532-7-1*, Pub. by Lund Humphries) Antique Collect.

Lewison, Jeremy & McMillan, Duncan. Contemporary British Art in Print. 232p. 1995. 59.50 (*1-873968-63-9*) Dist Art Pubs.

Lewison-Singar, Rita, ed. see Lin, Jami.

Lewison, Wendy. Boo! Peekaboo! LC 90-83244. (Wee Pudgy Board Bks.). (Illus.). 24p. (J). (ps). 1991. bds. 2.95 (*0-448-40133-9*, G & D) Peng Put Young Read.

— Christmas Cookies. (Wee Pudgy Board Bks.). (Illus.). 24p. (J). (ps). 1993. bds. 2.95 (*0-448-40554-7*, G & D) Peng Put Young Read.

— Happy Thanksgiving! (Wee Pudgy Board Bks.). (Illus.). 24p. (J). (ps). 1993. bds. 2.95 (*0-448-40552-0*, G & D) Peng Put Young Read.

— Nighty-Night. (Poke & Look Bks.). (Illus.). 16p. (J). (ps-1). 1992. spiral bd., bds. 9.95 (*0-448-40391-9*, G & D) Peng Put Young Read.

***Lewison, Wendy C.** Big Snowball. (Illus.). 32p. (J). (ps-3). 2000. pap. 3.99 (*0-448-42184-4*, Planet Dexter) Peng Put Young Read.

Lewison, Wendy C. Buzz Said the Bee. LC 91-19610. (Illus.). 32p. (J). (ps-3). 1992. pap. 3.50 (*0-590-44185-X*, Cartwheel) Scholastic Inc.

Lewison, Wendy C. "Buzz", Said the Bee. (Hello, Reader! Ser.). (J). 1992. 8.70 (*0-606-01792-5*, Pub. by Turtleback) Demco.

— Buzz the Little Seaplane. LC 98-52434. (All Aboard Bks.). 32p. 1999. pap. 2.99 (*0-448-41997-1*) Putnam Pub Group.

Lewison, Wendy C. Don't Wake the Baby! (All Aboard Reading Picture Readers Ser.). (Illus.). 32p. (J). (ps-1). 1996. pap. 3.95 (*0-448-41293-4*, G & D) Peng Put Young Read.

— Hello, Snow! (All Aboard Bks.). (Illus.). 32p. (J). (ps-3). 1994. pap. 2.95 (*0-448-40486-9*, G & D) Peng Put Young Read.

— I Wear My Tutu Everywhere! LC 94-36629. (All Aboard Bks.). (Illus.). 32p. (J). (ps-3). 1996. pap. 2.99 (*0-448-40877-5*, G & D) Peng Put Young Read.

— Our New Baby. (All Aboard Bks.). (Illus.). 32p. (Orig.). (J). (ps-3). 1996. pap. 2.95 (*0-448-41147-4*, G & D) Peng Put Young Read.

— The Princess & the Potty. LC 93-7853. (Illus.). 32p. (J). (ps-k). 1998. per. 5.99 (*0-689-82253-7*) Aladdin.

— The Princess & the Potty. LC 93-7853. (Illus.). 40p. (J). (ps up). 1994. pap. 15.00 (*0-671-87284-2*) S&S Bks Yung.

— Shy Vi. LC 91-39658. (Illus.). 40p. (J). (ps-2). 1993. pap. 14.00 (*0-671-76968-5*) S&S Bks Yung.

— A Trip to the Firehouse. LC 97-41109. (All Aboard Bks.). (Illus.). 32p. (J). (ps-3). 1998. mass mkt. 2.99 (*0-448-41740-5*, G & D) Peng Put Young Read.

— Uh-Oh, Baby. 16p. (J). (ps). 1992. 4.95 (*0-590-45171-5*, Cartwheel) Scholastic Inc.

— Where's Baby? (J). 1992. 4.95 (*0-685-53516-9*) Scholastic Inc.

An Asterisk (*) at the beginning of an entry indicates that the title is appearing for the first time.

Lewison, Wendy C. & Greigo, Tony. So Many Boots. LC 99-30153. (My First Hello Reader Ser.). (J). Date not set. pap. write for info. (*0-439-09865-3*) Scholastic Inc.

Lewison, Wendy Cheyette. Going to Sleep on the Farm. LC 91-3737. 1996. 11.19 (*0-606-09334-6*, Pub. by Turtleback) Demco.

— Hello, Snow! (Grosset & Dunlap All Aboard Bks.). 1994. 8.15 (*0-606-07637-9*, Pub. by Turtleback) Demco.

— I Am a Flower Girl. LC 98-32219. (ps-3). 1999. pap. text 2.99 (*0-448-41956-4*, G & D) Peng Put Young Read.

***Lewison, Wendy Cheyette.** One Little Butterfly. (Illus.). 14p. (J). (ps-k). 2000. bds. 5.99 (*0-448-42160-7*, G & D) Peng Put Young Read.

— One Little Dragonfly. (Finger Puppet Collection Ser.). (Illus.). 14p. (J). (ps-k). 2000. bds. 5.99 (*0-448-42159-3*, G & D) Peng Put Young Read.

Lewison, Wendy Cheyette. Our New Baby. (All Aboard Bks.). (Orig.). (J). 1996. 8.15 (*0-606-11714-8*, Pub. by Turtleback) Demco.

— Snow Angels: A Glitter Tattoo Book. (Glitter Tattoos Ser.). (Illus.). 24p. (J). (ps-2). 1998. mass mkt. 3.99 (*0-448-41855-X*, G & D) Peng Put Young Read.

***Lewison, Wendy Cheyette.** A Trip to the Firehouse. (J). 1998. 8.19 (*0-606-13870-6*, Pub. by Turtleback) Demco.

***Lewison, Wendy Cheyette & Basso, Bill.** Mud. LC 00-35815. (Hello Reader! Ser.). (Illus.). (J). 2001. write for info. (*0-439-17932-7*) Scholastic Inc.

Lewiston, David, prod. Heart of Dharma: The Music & Lives of Exiled Tibetan Monks. (Illus.). 64p. 1996. pap. 16.95 (*1-55961-318-1*) Relaxtn Co.

— Heart of Dharma: The Music & Lives of Exiled Tibetan Monks. (Illus.). 64p. 1996. pap. 19.95 incl. cd-rom (*1-55961-317-3*) Relaxtn Co.

Lewit. Manipulative Therapy in Rehabilitation Locomotor System. 3rd ed. LC 98-54113. 320p. 1999. pap. text 70.00 (*0-7506-2964-9*) Buttrwrth-Heinemann.

Lewit, Jane. Record & Remember: Tracing Your Roots Through Oral History. 1993. pap. 10.95 (*0-8128-8550-3*, Scrbrough Hse) Madison Bks UPA.

Lewit, Karel. Manipulative Therapy in the Rehabilitation of the Motor System. 2nd ed. (Illus.). 320p. 1991. 70.00 (*0-7506-1123-5*) Buttrwrth-Heinemann.

LeWita, Beatrix. French Bourgeois Culture. Underwood, J. A., tr. (Illus.). 346p. (C). 1994. pap. text 19.95 (*0-521-46626-1*) Cambridge U Pr.

— French Bourgeois Culture. Underwood, J. A., tr. from FRE. LC 93-29766. 178p. (C). 1994. text 59.95 (*0-521-44099-8*) Cambridge U Pr.

Lewites, Deborah. How to Use Microsoft Outlook 97. 304p. 1997. pap. text 24.99 (*1-56276-550-7*, Ziff-Davis Pr) Que.

Lewith, George T. Clinical Research Methodology for Complementary Therapies. 486p. 1993. 144.50 (*1-56593-128-9*, 0449) Singular Publishing.

Lewith, George T., et al. Complementary Medicine: An Integrated Approach. (Oxford General Practice Ser.: No. 34). 288p. 1996. pap. text 49.50 (*0-19-262565-9*) OUP.

Lewitova, Iris U., tr. see Olbracht, Ivan.

Lewitt. Memento Mori. 1996. mass mkt. 5.99 (*0-8125-3481-6*) Tor Bks.

Lewitt, Jane & Epstein, Ellen. The Bar/Bat Mitzvah Planbook. rev. ed. 200p. 1996. pap. 14.95 (*0-8128-8546-5*, Scrbrough Hse) Madison Bks UPA.

Lewitt, P. A. Handbook of Movement Disorders. (Neurological Disease & Therapy Ser.). Date not set. write for info. (*0-8247-9495-8*) Dekker.

***LeWitt, Peter A. & Oertel, Wolfgang H., eds.** Parkinson's Disease: The Treatment Options. 260p. 1999. 125.00 (*1-85317-379-7*) Martin Dunitz.

Lewitt, S. N. Cybersong. (Star Trek: Voyager Ser.: No. 8). 288p. 1996. mass mkt. 5.99 (*0-671-56783-7*) S&S Trade.

Lewitt, Shariann. Memento Mori. 288p. 1995. 21.95 (*0-312-85625-3*) Tor Bks.

— Memento Mori. 1997. pap. 14.95 (*0-312-86294-6*, Pub. by Tor Bks) St Martin.

***Lewitt, Shariann.** Rebel Sutra. 352p. 2000. text 24.95 (*0-312-86451-5*) St Martin.

Lewitt, Sol. Hundred Cubes. 1996. pap. text 50.00 (*3-89322-753-9*, Pub. by Edition Cantz) Dist Art Pubs.

— Incomplete Open Cubes. 1974. pap. 8.50 (*0-686-46773-6*) J Weber Gall.

LeWitt, Sol. Isometric Drawings. 1981. pap. 10.00 (*0-686-43403-X*) J Weber Gall.

LeWitt, Sol, tr. see Pound, Ezra.

Lewitter, Sidney R. American Dreams: The Story of a Jewish Immigrant Family. Lehman, Sarah, ed. LC 94-70749. 300p. (YA). 1994. 16.95 (*1-56062-263-6*); pap. 13.95 (*1-56062-262-8*) CIS Comm.

Lewittes. Anne Frank: The Diary of a Young Girl, 2 vols., Set. large type ed. reprint ed. 10.00 (*0-89064-003-3*) NAVH.

Lewittes, Mendell. Principles & Development of Jewish Law. LC 87-11778. 298p. (Orig.). pap. 12.95 (*0-8197-0506-3*) Bloch.

— Religious Foundations of the Jewish State: The Concept & Practice of Jewish Statehood from Biblical Times to the Modern State of Israel. LC 94-17488. 284p. 1994. pap. 30.00 (*1-56821-301-8*) Aronson.

Lewittes, Mordecai H., jt. auth. see Blumberg, Harry.

Lewk, Karla, ed. see Pezzi, Kevin.

Lewke, Gillian, et al. Physician Assistant Pearls of Wisdom. (Pearls of Wisdom Ser.). 1998. pap. 32.00 (*1-890369-05-5*) Boston Medical.

Lewkenor, Samuel. A Discourse for Such As Are Desirous to Know...of All Those Cities Wherein Doe Flourish Priviledged Universities. LC 70-6110. (English Experience Ser.: No. 90). 1969. reprint ed. 22.00 (*90-221-0090-1*) Walter J Johnson.

***Lewkowicz, Adina B.** Teaching Emotional Intelligence: Making Informed Choices LC 98-61534. 227p. 1999. write for info. (*1-57517-127-9*) SkyLght.

Lewkowicz, David J. & Lickliter, Robert, eds. The Development of Intersensory Perception: Comparative Perspectives. 448p. 1994. text 99.95 (*0-8058-1217-2*) L Erlbaum Assocs.

Lewkowicz, John. The Complete MUMPS: An Introduction & Reference Manual for the MUMPS Programming Language. (Illus.). 500p. 1989. pap. text 51.00 (*0-13-162125-4*) P-H.

Lewkowitz, Albert. Das Judentum und die Geistigen Stroemungen des 19. Jahrhunderts. (Grundriss der Gesamtwissenschaft des Judentums Ser.). (GER.). xii, 570p. 1974. reprint ed. write for info. (*3-487-05252-0*) G Olms Pubs.

Lewkowski, J. P., jt. auth. see Mohr, V.

Lewman, David. Adventures with Young King Arthur - Musical. 1995. 5.95 (*0-87129-473-7*, A07) Dramatic Pub.

***Lewman, David.** The Case of the Missing Gold. (Rugrats Files: Vol. 1). 144p. (J). (gr. 3-7). 2000. 3.99 (*0-689-83334-2*) S&S Childrens.

— A Day in the Life of Angelica. (Rugrats Ser.). (Illus.). 48p. (J). (ps-3). 2000. pap. 2.99 (*0-689-83132-3*, Simon Spot) Litle Simon.

— A Day in the Life of Chuckie. (Rugrats Ser.). (Illus.). 48p. (J). (gr. k-4). 1999. pap. 2.99 (*0-689-82833-0*, Simon Spot) Litle Simon.

Lewman, David. A Day in the Life of Tommy. (Rugrats Ser.). (Illus.). 48p. (J). (ps-3). 1999. pap. 2.99 (*0-689-82542-0*) S&S Childrens.

***Lewman, David.** A Day in the Life of Tommy. (Rugrats Ser.). (J). (ps-3). 1999. per. 2.99 (*0-671-02872-3*) S&S Trade.

Lewman, David. Eat it First, Ask Questions Later! Trivia & Advice from the Rugrats. (Rugrats Ser.). (Illus.). 48p. (J). (ps-3). 1998. pap. 2.99 (*0-689-82184-0*) S&S Childrens.

— More Jokes! (Rugrats Ser.). (Illus.). 48p. (J). (ps-3). 1999. pap. 2.99 (*0-689-82538-2*) S&S Childrens.

***Lewman, David.** Rocky & Bullwinkle: Movie Joke Book. (Illus.). 48p. (J). (gr. 4-7). 2000. pap. 2.99 (*0-689-83326-1*, Simon Spot) Litle Simon.

— Rocky Bullwinkle Dudley Doorights Book of Manners. (Illus.). 48p. (J). (gr. 4-7). 1998. 2.99 (*0-689-82152-2*) S&S Childrens.

Lewman, David. The Rugrats Joke Book. (Rugrats Ser.). (Illus.). 48p. (J). (ps-3). 1998. mass mkt. 2.99 (*0-689-82037-2*) S&S Childrens.

— A Rugrats Night Before Christmas. (Rugrats Ser.). (Illus.). 32p. (J). (ps-3). 1999. pap. 9.99 (*0-689-82854-3*) S&S Childrens.

***Lewman, David.** A Rugrats Night Before Christmas. (Rugrats Ser.). (Illus.). (J). (ps-3). 1999. per. 9.99 (*0-671-03756-0*) S&S Childrens.

— Twin Talk: Phil & Lil's Guide to Life. (Rugrats Ser.). 48p. (J). (ps-3). 2000. 2.99 (*0-689-83129-3*, Simon Spot) Litle Simon.

— Twin Talk: Phil & Lil's Guide to Life. (Rugrats Ser.). (Illus.). (J). (ps-3). 2000. per. write for info. (*0-671-77395-X*) S&S Childrens.

Lewman, John. Fireplace & Mantel Ideas: Over 100 Classic Wood & Stone Fireplace Mantel Designs. (Illus.). 90p. 1999. pap. 19.95 (*1-56523-106-6*) Fox Chapel Pub.

Lewnes, George P. Tikla. (Illus.). 229p. (C). 1988. reprint ed. 13.95 (*0-9623211-0-9*); reprint ed. lib. bdg. 10.00 (*0-685-26168-9*) T Lewnes Pub.

Lewontin, Richard C. Biology As Ideology: The Doctrine of DNA. LC 92-54487. 144p. 1993. pap. 12.00 (*0-06-097519-9*, Perennial) HarperTrade.

— Human Diversity. (Illus.). 179p. 1995. pap. text 19.95 (*0-7167-6013-4*) W H Freeman.

— Inside & Outside: Gene, Environment, & Organism. LC 93-39598. (C). 1994. pap. write for info. (*0-914206-35-4*) Clark U Pr.

***Lewontin, Richard C.** It Ain't Necessarily So: The Dream of the Human Genome & Other Illusions. LC 99-56280. 356p. 2000. 24.95 (*0-940322-10-2*) NY Rev Bks.

— The Triple Helix: Gene, Organism & Environment. LC 99-53879. (Illus.). 192p. 2000. pap. text 22.95 (*0-674-00159-1*) HUP.

Lewontin, Richard C., jt. auth. see Levins, Richard.

Lewontin, Richard C., ed. see Dobzhansky, Theodosius.

Lewontin, Richard C., ed. see Suzuki, David T. & Griffiths, Tony.

Leworth, Shuttan. Ken & Em: A Biography of Kenneth Branagh & Emma Thompson. LC 95-4899. vii, 255 p. 1995. write for info. (*0-312-13531-9*) St Martin.

Lewrs, R. Camp Life of a Confederate Boy. 1976. 24.50 (*0-8488-1079-1*) Amereon Ltd.

Lewry, Osmund, ed. Robert Kilwardby O. P., on Time & Imagination: De Tempore, De Spiritu Fantastico. (Auctores Britannici Medii Aevi IX). 224p. 1987. text 175.00 (*0-19-726054-3*) OUP.

Lewry, P. Osmund, ed. The Rise of British Logic: Acts of the Sixth European Symposium on Medieval Logic & Semantics, Oxford, 1983. xii, 421p. pap. text 52.57 (*0-88844-807-4*) Brill Academic Pubs.

Lewry, Peter. Fleetwood Mac: The Complete Recording Sessions: 1967-1997. LC 99-208639. (Illus.). 1999. pap. 19.95 (*0-7137-2724-1*, Pub. by Blandford Pr) Sterling.

Lewry, Peter, jt. auth. see Goodall, Nigel.

Lewry, S., jt. auth. see Abbott, P.

Lewry, S., jt. auth. see Abbott, Pamela.

Lewsen, Phyllis. John X. Merriman: Paradoxical South African Statesman. LC 81-13097. 451p. reprint ed. pap. 139.90 (*0-7837-3323-2*, 205772800007) Bks Demand.

Lewsey, Jonathan. Who's Who & What's What in Wagner. LC 96-41353. 364p. 1997. text 69.95 (*1-85928-280-6*, Pub. by Scolar Pr) Ashgate Pub Co.

— Who's Who & What's What in Wagner. LC 96-41353. 364p. (C). 1997. pap. 29.95 (*1-85928-285-7*, Pub. by Scolar Pr) Ashgate Pub Co.

Lewthwaite, John, jt. auth. see Hodgson, John.

***Lewton, J. V.** Just Pretend. 2000. mass mkt. 3.99 (*0-7860-1251-X*, Pinncle Kensgtn) Kensgtn Pub Corp.

Lewton, Kathleen L., ed. Public Relations in Health Care: A Guide for Professionals. 2nd ed. 284p. (Orig.). 1995. pap. 69.00 (*1-55648-143-8*, 166123) AHPI.

Lewty, Marjorie. Deep Water. large type ed. (Harlequin Ser.). 1992. reprint ed. 18.95 (*0-263-12981-0*) Mac Lib Ref.

— Honeymoon Island. large type ed. (Magna Large Print Ser.). 256p. 1996. 27.99 (*0-7505-0994-5*, Pub. by Mgna Lrg Print) Ulverscroft.

— Little White Lies. large type unabridged ed. (Harlequin Ser.). 1994. pap. 19.95 (*0-263-13589-6*) Mac Lib Ref.

— Love Is a Dangerous Game. large type ed. (Linford Romance Library). 304p. 1985. pap. 16.99 (*0-7089-6064-2*, Linford) Ulverscroft.

— A Real Engagement. 1999. mass mkt. 3.50 (*0-373-17438-1*, 1-17438-2) Harlequin Bks.

— The Short Engagement. large type ed. 352p. 1984. 27.99 (*0-7089-1213-3*) Ulverscroft.

— Step in the Dark. large type ed. 1995. 23.99 (*0-263-14127-6*, Pub. by Mills & Boon) Ulverscroft.

Lewty, Peter J. Across the Columbia Plain: Railroad Expansion in the Interior Northwest, 1885-1893. LC 94-39630. (Illus.). 326p. (Orig.). 1995. 35.00 (*0-87422-115-3*); pap. 25.00 (*0-87422-114-5*) Wash St U Pr.

— To the Columbia Gateway: The Oregon Railway & the Northern Pacific, 1879-1884. LC 87-21041. (Illus.). 202p. 1987. pap. 20.00 (*0-87422-029-7*) Wash St U Pr.

Lewy, Arieh. The International Encyclopedia of Curriculum. (Advances in Education Ser.). 1991. 150.00 (*0-08-037762-9*, Pergamon Pr) Elsevier.

— Studies in Educational Evaluation. (Reviews in Educational Evaluation Ser.: Vol. 6, No. 2). (Illus.). 116p. 1980. pap. 21.00 (*0-08-026760-2*, Pergamon Pr) Elsevier.

— Studies in Educational Evaluation, ser. vol. 6. (Studies in Educational Evaluation). 1980. pap. 21.00 (*0-08-026116-7*, 1, Pergamon Pr) Elsevier.

Lewy, Arieh, ed. The International Encyclopedia of Curriculum. 1096p. 1991. write for info. (*0-08-041379-X*, Pergamon Pr) Elsevier.

Lewy, Guenter. America in Vietnam. 554p. 1980. pap. text 15.95 (*0-19-502732-9*) OUP.

***Lewy, Guenter.** The Catholic Church & Nazi Germany. LC 99-42093. 448p. 2000. pap. text 17.00 (*0-306-80931-1*, Pub. by Da Capo) HarpC.

Lewy, Guenter. False Consciousness: An Essay on Mystification. LC 82-1985. 192p. 1982. 39.95 (*0-87855-451-3*) Transaction Pubs.

— The Federal Loyalty-Security Program: The Need for Reform. LC 83-2711. (AEI Studies: No. 378). 104p. reprint ed. pap. 32.30 (*0-8357-4480-9*, 203733000008) Bks Demand.

— Peace & Revolution: The Moral Crisis of American Pacifism. LC 88-1374. 293p. reprint ed. pap. 90.90 (*0-8357-4364-0*, 203719300007) Bks Demand.

Lewy, Guenter, ed. The Nazi Persecution of the Gypsies. LC 98-52545. (Illus.). 320p. 2000. 30.00 (*0-19-512556-8*) OUP.

***Lewycka, Marina.** Caring for Someone with Diabetes. 128p. 1999. pap. 24.00 (*0-86242-282-5*, Pub. by Age Concern Eng) St Mut.

Lewyt, C., ed. see Broad, C. D.

Lex, Legion & Thompson, Robert S. Remedies: Damages, Equity & Restitution 1989. annuals 2nd ed. 1989. text 58.00 (*0-8205-2882-X*) Bender.

Lexander, Ren, jt. auth. see Soadhi, Geraldine.

Lexau, Joan M. Crocodile & Hen. LC 99-45410. 48p. (J). (gr. k-3). 2001. 14.95 (*0-06-028486-2*) HarpC Child Bks.

— The Crocodile & the Hen. LC 99-45410. 48p. (J). (gr. k-3). Date not set. 3.95 (*0-06-444263-2*) HarpC Child Bks.

— The Crocodile & the Hen. LC 99-45410. 48p. (J). (gr. k-3). 2001. lib. bdg. 14.89 (*0-06-028487-0*) HarpC Child Bks.

— Don't Be My Valentine: A Classroom Mystery. (I Can Read Bks.). (Illus.). 64p. (J). (gr. 1-3). 1985. 11.95 (*0-06-023872-0*) HarpC Child Bks.

— Don't Be My Valentine: A Classroom Mystery. (I Can Read Bks.). (Illus.). 64p. (J). (gr. 1-3). 1988. mass mkt. 3.50 (*0-06-444115-6*, HarpTrophy) HarpC Child Bks.

— Don't Be My Valentine: A Classroom Mystery. rev. ed. LC PZ7.L5895Dp 1999. (I Can Read Bks.). (Illus.). 64p. (J). (gr. 1-3). 1999. 14.95 (*0-06-028239-8*) HarpC Child Bks.

— Don't Be My Valentine: A Classroom Mystery. rev. ed. LC 85-42621. (I Can Read Bks.). (Illus.). 64p. (J). (ps-3). 1999. pap. 3.95 (*0-06-444254-3*, HarpTrophy); lib. bdg. 14.89 (*0-06-028240-1*) HarpC Child Bks.

— Striped Ice Cream. LC 68-10774. (Illus.). 96p. (J). (gr. k-3). 1968. lib. bdg. 15.89 (*0-397-31047-1*) HarpC Child Bks.

— Striped Ice Cream. LC 68-10774. 128p. (J). (gr. 2-5). 1992. 2.99 (*0-590-45729-2*, Little Apple) Scholastic Inc.

Lexau, Joan M. Striped Ice Cream. (J). 1968. 8.60 (*0-606-04060-9*, Pub. by Turtleback) Demco.

***Lexi-Comp Inc. Staff.** Drug Information Handbook for the Allied Health Professional 2000-2001. 7th ed. 2000. pap. 33.95 (*0-916589-96-X*) Lexi-Comp.

Lexicon, jt. auth. see Leibniz, Gottfried Wilhelm.

Lexicon, Lawrence. The New Webster's Crossword Dictionary. pap. 5.99 (*0-425-13096-7*) Berkley Pub.

Lexicon Publications Staff. The New Webster's Crossword Dictionary. 1991. mass mkt. 5.99 (*0-425-12882-2*) Berkley Pub.

Lexington. Businessman's Guide. 1985. lib. bdg. 93.50 (*0-86010-596-2*) Kluwer Academic.

Lexington School for the Deaf Staff. Auditory Skills Curriculum: Preschool Supplement. (Auditory Skills Instructional Planning System Ser.). 180p. 1988. ring bd. 35.00 (*0-943292-23-9*) Foreworks.

Lexington Who's Who, Inc. Staff. The Lexington Who's Who Registry, 1998-1999. Date not set. write for info. (*0-9672740-0-1*) Lex Whos Who.

***LEXIS Law Publishing Editors.** Arkansas Motor Vehicle & Traffic Laws & State Highway Commission Regulations: 1999 Edition. 440p. 1999. pap. 30.00 (*0-327-10217-9*, 2094013) LEXIS Pub.

— Delaware Corporation Laws: 1999-2000 Edition. annot. ed. 457p. 1999. pap. 28.00 incl. cd-rom (*0-327-10212-8*, 2213817) LEXIS Pub.

— Leyes y Reglamentos de Puerto Rico Municipal: 1999 Edition. (SPA.). 799p. 1999. pap. 80.00 (*0-327-10218-7*, 3183711) LEXIS Pub.

— North Carolina Court Rules: 2000 Edition. annot. ed. 1355p. 1999. pap. 47.50 (*0-327-10222-5*, 4648817) LEXIS Pub.

— North Carolina Criminal Law & Procedure: 1999 Edition. 1414p. 1999. pap. 43.00 incl. cd-rom (*0-327-10149-0*, 3051916) LEXIS Pub.

— North Carolina 2000 Rules of Civil Procedure & Evidence. 865p. 1999. pap. 45.00 (*0-327-10223-3*, 4649017) LEXIS Pub.

— Revenue Laws of North Carolina: 1999 Edition. 696p. 1999. pap. 40.00 (*0-327-10127-X*, 3052513) LEXIS Pub.

— Tennessee Accountancy Laws & Rules: 1999 Edition. 81p. 1999. pap. 10.00 (*0-327-10213-6*, 3320212) LEXIS Pub.

— Tennessee Auctioneer License Law & Regulations: 1999 Edition. 27p. 2000. pap. 12.00 (*0-327-10126-1*, 3320013) LEXIS Pub.

— Tennessee Election Laws: 1999 Edition. 400p. 2000. pap. 34.00 (*0-327-10125-3*, 3318013) LEXIS Pub.

— Tennessee Workers' Compensation Laws Annotated: 1999 Edition. 336p. 2000. pap. 25.00 (*0-327-10180-6*, 3319114) LEXIS Pub.

***LEXIS Law Publishing Editors, ed.** Alaska Administrative Code - Register 153 Replacement Title 20 (April 2000) 510p. 2000. write for info. (*0-327-13124-1*, 4049313) LEXIS Pub.

— Alcoholic Beverage Control Laws of North Carolina, 1999 Edition. 433p. 2000. pap. 28.00 (*0-327-10882-7*, 3059211) LEXIS Pub.

— Annotated Laws of Massachusetts 2000 Edition Index: A-D, E-O, P-Z, 3 vols. 3626p. 2000. write for info. (*0-327-11218-2*, 4308313) LEXIS Pub.

— Arkansas Code of 1987 Annotated Official Edition Court Rules, 2000 Edition. 1357p. 2000. write for info. (*0-327-11040-6*, 4077717) LEXIS Pub.

— California Fish & Game, 2000. 505p. 2000. pap. 15.00 (*0-327-11255-7*, 2126710) LEXIS Pub.

— Colorado Court Rules, 2000 Edition. 1180p. 2000. write for info. (*0-327-11042-2*, 4103312) LEXIS Pub.

— Delaware Rules Annotated, 2001 Edition, 2 vols. 1612p. 2000. write for info. (*0-327-11066-X*, 41504018) LEXIS Pub.

— District of Columbia Court Rules Annotated 2000 Edition, 2 vols. 1840p. 2000. 80.00 (*0-327-11070-8*, 4173917) LEXIS Pub.

— General Laws of Rhode Island, Rhode Island Court Rules Annotated 2000. 1350p. 2000. write for info. (*0-327-11143-7*, 4774517) LEXIS Pub.

— Georgia Rules of Court Annotated, 2001 Edition. 1300p. 2000. write for info. (*0-327-11080-5*, 4207218) LEXIS Pub.

— Georgia 2000 Replacement Index Vol. 43 & 44. 2500p. 2000. write for info. (*0-327-11077-5*, 4205716) LEXIS Pub.

— Idaho Code 2000 Replacement, Vol. 10A. 1060p. 2000. write for info. (*0-327-13139-X*, 4230112) LEXIS Pub.

— Illinois 2000 Index, 2 vols. 2145p. 2000. write for info. (*0-327-11093-7*, 4246417) LEXIS Pub.

— Massachusetts Criminal & Traffic Law Manual, 2000 Edition. 880p. 2000. write for info. (*0-327-10899-1*, 2520011) LEXIS Pub.

— Michie's Hawaii Revised Statutes Annotated 2000 Replacement Volume 5. 780p. 2000. write for info. (*0-327-13116-0*, 4212312) LEXIS Pub.

— Michie's Hawaii Revised Statutes Annotated 2000 Replacement 6A. 780p. 2000. write for info. (*0-327-13117-9*, 4212112) LEXIS Pub.

— Michie's Nevada Revised Statutes Annotated, Replacement Volume 16. 851p. 2000. write for info. (*0-327-13122-5*, 4548613) LEXIS Pub.

— Michie's Nevada Revised Statutes Annotated, Replacement Volume 17. 1392p. 2000. write for info. (*0-327-13123-3*, 4549112) LEXIS Pub.

— Michigan Statutes Annotated 2000 General Index. 3833p. 2000. write for info. (*0-327-11208-5*, 3767013) LEXIS Pub.

— Mississippi Wildlife, Fisheries & Parks Law Book, 1999 Cumulative Supplement. 363p. 2000. pap. 17.00 (*0-327-10660-3*, 2528010) LEXIS Pub.

— Mississippi Workers' Compensation Laws & Rules, 1999. annot. ed. 280p. pap. 30.00 (*0-327-19728-5*) LEXIS Pub.

— New Hampshire Revised Statutes Annotated Advance Code Service, February 2000. 86p. 2000. write for info. (*0-327-11115-1*, 4566114) LEXIS Pub.

— New York Consolidated Laws Service (NY CLS) 2000 General Indexes, 4 vols. 4423p. 2000. write for info. (*0-327-11216-6*, 4094613) LEXIS Pub.

— Revised Statutes of Nebraska Annotated 2000 Replacement Volume 21. 900p. 2000. write for info. (*0-327-13337-6*, 4523111) LEXIS Pub.

— Revised Statutes of Nebraska Annotated 2000 Replacement Volume 9. 920p. 2000. write for info. (*0-327-11110-0*, 4521911) LEXIS Pub.

— South Dakota Codified Laws Court Rules 2000. 2nd ed. 1200p. 2000. write for info. (*0-327-11149-6*, 4816117) LEXIS Pub.

— South Dakota Codified Laws 2000 Replacement, Vol. 11C. 500p. 2000. write for info. (*0-327-12995-6*, 4807412) LEXIS Pub.

— South Dakota Codified Laws 2000 Revised, Vol. 14A. 600p. 2000. write for info. (*0-327-12959-X*, 4809411) LEXIS Pub.

— South Dakota Rules of Evidence. 75p. 2000. write for info. (*0-327-13623-5*, 4810310) LEXIS Pub.

— South Dakota 2000 Index: Vol. 1: A-J; Vol. 2: K-Z, 2 vols. 2233p. 2000. write for info. (*0-327-11148-8*, 4815617) LEXIS Pub.

— Tennessee Court Rules Annotated 2000 Edition, 2 vols. 1398p. 2000. write for info. (*0-327-11151-8*, 4845317) LEXIS Pub.

— United States Code Service 2000 General Index, 4 vols. 5832p. 2000. write for info. (*0-327-11211-5*, 3770713) LEXIS Pub.

— Utah Court Rules Annotated 2000. 1427p. 2000. write for info. (*0-327-11156-9*, 4877217) LEXIS Pub.

— Vermont Court Rules 2000, 2 vols. 2300p. 2000. pap. write for info. (*0-327-11164-X*, 4888012) LEXIS Pub.

— Vermont Statutes Annotated 2000 Advance Code Service. 72p. 2000. write for info. (*0-327-11166-6*, 4894716) LEXIS Pub.

— Vermont Statutes Annotated 2000 Replacement Title 28-31. 904p. 2000. write for info. (*0-327-13064-4*, 4892611) LEXIS Pub.

— Virgin Islands 2000 Index: Virgin Islands Code Annotated. 516p. 2000. write for info. (*0-327-11168-2*, 4897216) LEXIS Pub.

— Virginia 2000 Replacement, Vol. 2. 900p. 2000. write for info. (*0-327-13074-1*, 4902111) LEXIS Pub.

— Washington Criminal & Traffic Law Manual, 2000 Edition. 1014p. 2000. 20.00 incl. cd-rom (*0-327-13137-3*, 3752511) LEXIS Pub.

— Washington Rules of Court 2000, 2 vols. 1900p. 2000. write for info. (*0-327-11180-1*, 4934516) LEXIS Pub.

— West Virginia 2000 Replacement Index: Vol. 18: A-K; Vol.19: L-Z. 2013p. 2000. write for info. (*0-327-11183-6*, 4964917) LEXIS Pub.

Lexis Law Publishing Staff. Alaska Children, Youth & Family Laws, Rules & Regulations: 1998-99 Edition. 423p. write for info. (*0-327-06552-4*, Lexis Law PR) LEXIS Pub.

— Alaska Criminal & Traffic Law Manual: 1998 Edition. LC 99-160569. 1003p. 1998. write for info. (*0-327-06666-0*) LEXIS Pub.

— Alaska Fish & Game Laws & Regulations Annotated, October: 1998 Supplement. 57p. 1998. write for info. (*0-327-06564-8*) LEXIS Pub.

— Alaska Workers' Compensation Laws & Regulations Annotated, 1998-99 Edition. 203p. 1998. pap. write for info. (*0-327-06596-6*) LEXIS Pub.

— Alaska 1999 Advance Code Service. 26p. 1999. pap. write for info. (*0-327-06675-X*) LEXIS Pub.

— Alcoholic Beverage Laws of Kentucky: 1998 Edition. 146p. 1998. pap. 15.00 (*0-327-06661-X*) LEXIS Pub.

— Annotated Rules of North Carolina, 1999. 950p. 1998. write for info. (*0-327-06652-0*) LEXIS Pub.

— Arizona Education Laws 1998-99 Edition. annot. ed. LC 99-163171. 478p. 1998. write for info. (*0-327-06541-9*) LEXIS Pub.

— Burns Indiana Statutes: 1998 Replacement Volume, 015. annot. ed. 800p. 1998. write for info. (*0-327-06531-1*, Lexis Law PR) LEXIS Pub.

— Burns Indiana Statutes: 1998 Replacement Volume, 033. annot. ed. 930p. 1998. write for info. (*0-327-06532-X*, Lexis Law PR) LEXIS Pub.

— Burns Indiana Statutes: 1998 Replacement Volume, 035. annot. ed. 1000p. 1998. write for info. (*0-327-06534-6*, Lexis Law PR) LEXIS Pub.

— Burns Indiana Statutes: 1998-1999 Advance Code Service, 002. annot. ed. 300p. 1999. pap. write for info. (*0-327-06537-0*, Lexis Law PR) LEXIS Pub.

— Deering's California Code Advance Legislative Service. 300p. 1998. pap. write for info. (*0-327-06587-7*); pap. write for info. (*0-327-06588-5*); pap. write for info. (*0-327-06589-3*) LEXIS Pub.

— Deering's California Code Advance Legislative Service, 006. 300p. 1998. pap. write for info. (*0-327-06586-9*) LEXIS Pub.

— Delaware Corporation Laws Annotated: 1998-99 Edition. 651p. 1998. write for info. (*0-327-06670-9*) LEXIS Pub.

— Delaware Corporations Laws 1998. annot. ed. 111p. 1998. pap., suppl. ed. write for info. (*0-327-06539-7*, Lexis Law PR) LEXIS Pub.

— Delaware Criminal & Traffic Law Manual 1998-1999. 845p. 1998. write for info. (*0-327-06533-8*, Lexis Law PR) LEXIS Pub.

— The Education of People with Disabilities Laws & Regulations. 2800p. 1998. write for info. (*0-327-06529-X*, Lexis Law PR) LEXIS Pub.

***Lexis Law Publishing Staff.** Florida Statues & Rules--Civil. (Code Ser.). 2115p. 1999. pap. 80.00 (*0-327-01590-X*, 6984011) LEXIS Pub.

— Georgia Worker's Compensation Laws, 1999 ALS. 58p. 1999. pap. 5.00 (*0-327-09174-6*, 2314510) LEXIS Pub.

Lexis Law Publishing Staff. Hawaii Court Rules Annotated: 1999 Edition. 1385p. 1998. write for info. (*0-327-06554-0*) LEXIS Pub.

— Hawaii Revised Statutes Annotated: 1998 Replacement, 001. 725p. 1998. write for info. (*0-327-06646-6*) LEXIS Pub.

— Hawaii Revised Statutes Annotated: 1998 Replacement, 006. 740p. 1998. write for info. (*0-327-06647-4*) LEXIS Pub.

Lexis Law Publishing Staff. Illinois Jurisprudence, 27 vols. 1500.00 (*0-327-00072-4*) LEXIS Pub.

Lexis Law Publishing Staff. Kentucky Banking & Related Laws & Rules Annotated: 1998 Edition. 420p. 1998. write for info. (*0-327-06637-7*) LEXIS Pub.

— Kentucky Criminal Law & Procedure, 1998-99 Edition. 1,195p. 1999. 47.00 (*0-327-06599-0*) LEXIS Pub.

— Laws of Virginia Relating to Adult Corrections: 1998 Editions. 332p. 1998. pap. 34.00 (*0-327-06650-4*) LEXIS Pub.

— Maryland Income Tax Laws & Regulations, 1998. 38p. 1998. suppl. ed. write for info. (*0-327-06585-0*) LEXIS Pub.

— Maryland 1999: Advance Code Service, 001. 60p. 1998. pap. write for info. (*0-327-06581-8*) LEXIS Pub.

— Michie's Alabama Code Replacement, 021. 1037p. 1998. write for info. (*0-327-06677-6*) LEXIS Pub.

— Michie's Alabama Motor Vehicle Laws Annotated with Commentaries: 1998 Replacement. LC 99-180271. 389p. 1999. write for info. (*0-327-06649-0*) LEXIS Pub.

— Motor Vehicle Laws of Vermont: 1998 Edition. 550p. 1998. write for info. (*0-327-06578-8*) LEXIS Pub.

— New Hampshire Education Laws Annotated: 1998-99 Edition. 954p. 1998. pap. write for info. (*0-327-06672-5*) LEXIS Pub.

— New Hampshire Juvenile Laws: 1998-99 Edition. 587p. 1999. write for info. (*0-327-06653-9*) LEXIS Pub.

— New Hampshire Selected Motor Vehicle, Boating & Related Laws Annotated: 1998-99 Edition. 487p. 1998. 49.50 (*0-327-06583-4*) LEXIS Pub.

— New York Consolidated Law Service Advance Legislative Service, 1999, No. 3. 100p. 1999. 77.50 (*0-327-08709-9*, 40983-12) LEXIS Pub.

— North Carolina 1999 Rules of Civil Procedure & Evidence. 880p. 1998. write for info. (*0-327-06651-2*) LEXIS Pub.

— Parker's California Business & Professions Code Advance Legislative Service. 611p. 1998. pap. write for info. (*0-327-06538-9*, Lexis Law PR) LEXIS Pub.

— Parker's California 1999 Civil Code. 777p. 1998. pap. 32.00 (*0-327-06558-3*) LEXIS Pub.

— Parker's California 1999 Evidence Code. 233p. 1998. pap. write for info. (*0-327-06555-9*, Lexis Law PR) LEXIS Pub.

— Parker's California 1999 Family Code. 739p. 1998. pap. 34.00 (*0-327-06559-1*) LEXIS Pub.

— Parker's California 1999 Insurance Code. 1,035p. 1998. pap. 35.00 (*0-327-06560-5*) LEXIS Pub.

— Parker's 1999 California Business & Professions Code, 2 vols. 2024p. 1998. pap. 65.00 (*0-327-06557-5*, Lexis Law PR) LEXIS Pub.

— Parker's 1999 California Civil Code Advance Legislative Service. 161p. 1998. pap. write for info. (*0-327-06530-3*, Lexis Law PR) LEXIS Pub.

***Lexis Law Publishing Staff.** Parker's 1999 California Code of Civil Procedure Advance Legislative Service. 293p. 1998. pap. write for info. (*0-327-06526-5*, Lexis Law PR) LEXIS Pub.

Lexis Law Publishing Staff. Parker's 1999 California Labor Code. 95p. 1998. pap. write for info. (*0-327-06527-3*) LEXIS Pub.

— Parker's 1999 California Labor Code. 496p. 1998. pap. 40.00 (*0-327-06561-3*, Lexis Law PR) LEXIS Pub.

— Parker's 1999 California Uniform Commerical Code. 274p. 1998. pap. write for info. (*0-327-06556-7*) LEXIS Pub.

— Parker's 1999 California Vehicle Code. 841p. 1998. pap. 27.00 (*0-327-06563-X*) LEXIS Pub.

— Parker's 1999 Larmac Index to California Laws. 1201p. 1998. pap. 90.00 (*0-327-06326-2*) LEXIS Pub.

— Primary Law Appendix For Employment In Oregon. 1300p. 1998. write for info. (*0-327-06641-5*) LEXIS Pub.

— Primary Law Appendix for Employment in Texas. 1300p. write for info. (*0-327-06656-3*) LEXIS Pub.

— Rhode Island 1998 Replacement Index: General Laws of Rhode Island Index. 838p. 1998. write for info. (*0-327-06524-9*, Lexis Law PR); write for info. (*0-327-06525-7*, Lexis Law PR) LEXIS Pub.

— Rhode Island Workers' Compensation Law; 1998-99 Edition. 340p. 1998. write for info. (*0-327-06582-6*) LEXIS Pub.

— South Dakota Rules 1999. annot. ed. 1550p. 1998. write for info. (*0-327-06535-4*, Lexis Law PR) LEXIS Pub.

— State of Tennessee Contractors' License Law & Rules & Regulations: 1998 Edition. 54p. 1998. pap. 8.50 (*0-327-06664-4*) LEXIS Pub.

— Statutes of Nebraska: 1999 Advance Code Service Pamphlet, 001. annot. rev. ed. 100p. 1998. pap. write for info. (*0-327-06521-4*, Lexis Law PR) LEXIS Pub.

— Tennessee Compilation of Selected Laws on Children, Youth & Families 1998 Edition. LC 99-172502. 488p. 1998. write for info. (*0-327-06520-6*, Lexis Law PR) LEXIS Pub.

— Tennessee Criminal Laws Annotated: 1998 Edition. 854p. 1998. 58.33 (*0-327-06579-6*) LEXIS Pub.

— Tennessee Motor Vehicle Laws 1998. annot. ed. 598p. 1998. write for info. (*0-327-06540-0*, Lexis Law PR) LEXIS Pub.

— Texas Municipal Zoning Law. 3rd rev. ed. LC 98-67070. 1998. ring bd. 25.00 (*0-327-00196-8*) LEXIS Pub.

— United States Code Service 1999 Tables Statutes at Large 1987 Through XX Replacement. 900p. 1999. 44.00 (*0-327-08710-2*, 47111-11) LEXIS Pub.

— Vermont Advance Reports, 167. 325p. 1999. pap. write for info. (*0-327-06519-2*) LEXIS Pub.

— Vermont Education Lawbook: 1998 Edition. LC 99-171372. 493p. 1998. 25.00 (*0-327-06665-2*) LEXIS Pub.

— Virgin Islands Code Annotated: 1998 Advanced Legislative Service. 200p. 1998. pap. write for info. (*0-327-06660-1*) LEXIS Pub.

— Virginia Islands Court Rules Annotated: 1999 Edition. 1250p. 1998. write for info. (*0-327-06642-3*) LEXIS Pub.

— Virginia Landlord-Tenant Laws & Rules Annotated, 1998 Edition. LC 99-170646. 654p. 1998. 35.00 (*0-327-06658-X*) LEXIS Pub.

— Virginia 1999 Advance Code Service, 002. 100p. 1998. write for info. (*0-327-06597-4*) LEXIS Pub.

— Virginia Retirement Systems: 1998 Edition. 118p. 1998. pap. write for info. (*0-327-06659-8*) LEXIS Pub.

— Virginia Unemployment Compensation Act: 1998 Edition. LC 99-183059. 167p. 1998. pap. write for info. (*0-327-06576-1*) LEXIS Pub.

— West Virginia Natural Resources Laws 1998 Edition. LC 99-163248. 290p. 1998. 27.00 (*0-327-06528-1*, Lexis Law PR) LEXIS Pub.

— Wyoming Court Rules Annotated November: 1998 Supplement. 168p. 1998. pap. write for info. (*0-327-06549-4*) LEXIS Pub.

Lexis Law Publishing Staff, compiled by. Administrative & Financial Laws for Local Government in North Carolina. 944p. (C). 1998. pap. text 60.00 (*1-56011-325-1*) Institute Government.

Lexis Law Publishing Staff, ed. Brandis & Broun on North Carolina Evidence 1998 Replacement Volumes, 2 vols. 5th ed. lib. bdg. 175.00 (*0-327-00500-9*) LEXIS Pub.

Lexis Law Publishing Staff, ed. C.A. Deering's Desktop Code 1999. 2100p. 1998. pap. write for info. (*0-327-06546-X*, Lexis Law PR) LEXIS Pub.

— CA Deering's Desktop Code 1999 Ed. 2100p. 1998. pap. write for info. (*0-327-06547-8*, Lexis Law PR) LEXIS Pub.

— Code of Virginia: 1998 Replacement Volume. rev. ed. (Code of Virginia, 1950 Ser.: No. 7). 1998. write for info. (*0-327-05022-5*, 49064-13) LEXIS Pub.

***Lexis Law Publishing Staff, ed.** Courtroom Criminal Evidence, 2 vols. 3rd ed. LC 98-88607. 1998. lib. bdg. write for info. (*0-327-00567-X*) LEXIS Pub.

Lexis Law Publishing Staff, ed. Illinois Compiled Statutes Annotated Advance Legislative Service Pamphlet, No. 1. annot. ed. 65p. 1998. pap. write for info. (*0-327-05017-9*, 4248015) LEXIS Pub.

— Illinois Jurisprudence: 1998 Cumulative Supplement, 23 vols. lib. bdg., suppl. ed. 235.00 (*0-327-00192-5*) LEXIS Pub.

— Kentucky Motor Vehicle Laws 1998-99 Edition. annot. ed. 569p. 1998. write for info. (*0-327-06518-4*) LEXIS Pub.

— Labor, Vol. 4. 1998. write for info. (*0-327-06457-9*) LEXIS Pub.

***Lexis Law Publishing Staff, ed.** Liability of Corporate Officers & Directors: 1998 Replacement Volumes, 2 vols. 6th ed. LC 98-88727. 1998. lib. bdg. 165.00 (*0-327-00730-3*) LEXIS Pub.

Lexis Law Publishing Staff, ed. Michie's Alabama Criminal Code Advance Legislative Service, 1998 Edition. 721p. 1998. write for info. (*0-327-06671-7*) LEXIS Pub.

— Michigan Law & Practice Encyclopedia: 1998 Cumulative Supplement, 31 vols. lib. bdg., suppl. ed. 240.00 (*0-327-00193-3*) LEXIS Pub.

— New Hampshire Court Rules Annotated June 1998 Replacement Pages. annot. ed. 1998. ring bd. write for info. (*0-327-05020-9*, 45657-14) LEXIS Pub.

— Official Code of Georgia Annotated No. 41: 1998 Edition Tables Volume. rev. ed. 1998. write for info. (*0-327-05090-X*, 41741-11) LEXIS Pub.

— Practica Forense Puertorriquena: Evidencia y Reglas Miscelaneas, Comentadas y Anotadas. (SPA.). 670p. 1998. pap. write for info. (*0-327-05127-2*, 47523-11) LEXIS Pub.

— Practica Forense Puertorriquena: Procedimiento Criminal, Comentado 7 Anotado. (SPA.). 670p. 1998. pap. write for info. (*0-327-05126-4*, 47522-11) LEXIS Pub.

— Practica Forense Puertorriquena No. 1: Procedimiento Civil, Comentado 7 Anotado. (SPA.). 810p. 1998. pap. write for info. (*0-327-05125-6*, 47521-11) LEXIS Pub.

Lexis Law Publishing Staff, ed. Products Liability, 3 vols. 3rd ed. lib. bdg. 240.00 (*0-327-00792-3*) LEXIS Pub.

Lexis Law Publishing Staff, ed. Rules of Virginia Supreme Court. (Code of Virginia Ser.: No. 11). 522p. 1998. pap. write for info. (*0-327-05018-7*, 49095-15) LEXIS Pub.

— Virginia Rules Annotated, 1998. annuals 1998. pap., suppl. ed. write for info. (*0-327-05019-5*, 49227-15) LEXIS Pub.

Lexis Law Publishing Staff, ed. Waters & Water Rights 1998 Cumulative Supplement: 1991 Edition, 6 vols. lib. bdg. write for info. (*0-327-00776-1*) LEXIS Pub.

Lexis Law Publishing Staff, jt. ed. see Dougherty, Dennis.

***Lexis Pub Editorial Staff.** Alabama Rules Annotated: 1999 - 2000 Edition, 2 vols., Set. annot. ed. 2210p. 1999. pap. 60.00 (*0-327-09502-4*, 4015513) LEXIS Pub.

— Arkansas Criminal Code Annotated ALS: 1999 Edition. 245p. 1999. pap. 20.00 (*0-327-09219-X*, 2094511) LEXIS Pub.

— Code of Virginia Annotation Citator. 960p. 1999. pap. 35.00 (*0-327-08895-8*, 4908010) LEXIS Pub.

— District of Columbia Criminal Law & Procedure Annotated: 1999 Edition. 918p. 1999. pap. 43.00 (*0-327-09102-9*, 2240517) LEXIS Pub.

— Georgia Criminal & Traffic Law Manual: 1999 Edition. 1031p. 1999. pap. 32.00 (*0-327-09446-X*, 2300216) LEXIS Pub.

— Georgia School Laws, 1999 Edition. 607p. 1999. 50.00 (*0-327-09718-3*) LEXIS Pub.

— Georgia Workers' Compensation Laws, Rules & Regulations Annotated: 1999 Edition. annot. ed. 569p. 1999. pap. 26.00 (*0-327-09401-X*, 2308215) LEXIS Pub.

— Official Code of Georgia Annotation Citator. 1500p. 1999. pap. 39.95 (*0-327-09179-7*, 4135210) LEXIS Pub.

— Official Manual of the Tennessee Real Estate Commission: 1998-99 Edition. 179p. 1999. pap. 15.00 (*0-327-09008-1*, 3318513) LEXIS Pub.

— Puerto Rico Seguros, 1998 Edition, 2 vols. pap. 75.00 (*0-327-06221-5*) LEXIS Pub.

— Tennessee Dealer-Manufacturer Licensing Laws, Rules & Regulations: 1998-1999 Edition. 90p. 1999. pap. 10.00 (*0-327-09004-9*, 3325010) LEXIS Pub.

— Virgin Islands Criminal, Vehicle & Traffic Laws Annotated: 2000 Edition. 31p. 2000. pap. write for info. (*0-327-08786-2*, 3422110) LEXIS Pub.

— Virginia's Internet Policy & Secretariat of Technology: 1999 Edition. 102p. 1999. pap. 15.00 (*0-327-09001-4*, 3446510) LEXIS Pub.

***LEXIS Publishing Staff.** Interactive Citation Workbook. LC 00-29616. 2000. write for info. (*0-8205-4369-1*) Bender.

Lexova, Irena. Ancient Egyptian Dances. LC 99-51617. 176p. 1999. pap. text 7.95 (*0-486-40906-6*) Dover.

Lextz, Gerald S. Lancaster County Architecture, 1700-1850. (Illus.). 176p. 1992. write for info. (*0-9635153-0-6*) Hist Preserv Trst.

Lexus, compiled by. German: A Rough Guides Phrasebook. LC 95-139081. (Rough Guide Phrasebooks Ser.). 224p. (Orig.). 1995. pap. 5.00 (*1-85828-146-6*, Penguin Bks) Viking Penguin.

— The Rough Guide Dictionary Phrasebook. 272p. 2000. pap. 6.50 (*1-85828-467-8*, Pub. by Rough Guides) Penguin Putnam.

— The Rough Guide French Dictionary Phrasebook. 2nd rev. ed. 240p. 2000. pap. 5.00 (*1-85828-576-3*, Pub. by Rough Guides) Penguin Putnam.

— The Rough Guide Italian Dictionary Phrasebook. 2nd rev. ed. 240p. 2000. pap. 5.00 (*1-85828-578-X*, Pub. by Rough Guides) Penguin Putnam.

— The Rough Guide Spanish Dictionary Phrasebook. 2nd rev. ed. 240p. 2000. pap. 5.00 (*1-85828-577-1*, Pub. by Rough Guides) Penguin Putnam.

Lexus (Firm), jt. see Mazza, Debora.

Lexus Limited Staff. Dutch at Your Fingertips. 1987. pap. 8.95 (*0-7102-0953-3*, Routledge Thoemms) Routledge.

— German at Your Fingertips. 1987. pap. 6.95 (*0-7102-0954-1*, Routledge Thoemms) Routledge.

— Harrap's Chinese Phrase Book. 128p. 1991. pap. 3.95 (*0-13-388729-4*) P-H.

— Harrap's Japanese Phrase Book. 128p. 1991. pap. 4.00 (*0-13-388737-5*) P-H.

— Harrap's Russian Phrase Book. 128p. 1991. per. 4.00 (*0-13-388745-6*) P-H.

— Italian at Your Fingertips. LC 86-21913. 1987. pap. 6.95 (*0-7102-0955-X*, Routledge Thoemms) Routledge.

Lexus Limited Staff & Mitchell, Carolyn B. Spanish Handy Dictionary. (ENG & SPA.). 1992. pap. 8.95 (*0-7818-0012-9*) Hippocrene Bks.

Lexus Limited Staff, et al. Harrap's Student German. 800p. 1991. per. 12.00 (*0-13-377623-9*, Harraps IN) Macmillan Gen Ref.

LEXUS Staff & Passport Books Editorial Staff, compiled by. Just Enough Business Spanish. LC 98-26322. (Just Enough Business Ser.). (SPA., Illus.). 192p. 1994. pap. 6.95 (*0-8442-9655-4*, 9655-4, Passprt Bks) NTC Contemp Pub Co.

Ley, Alice C. At Dark of the Moon. large type ed. 352p. 1995. 27.99 (*0-7089-3263-0*) Ulverscroft.

— A Conformable Wife. large type ed. 1994. 27.99 (*0-7089-3150-2*) Ulverscroft.

— The Georgian Rake. large type ed. 1994. 27.99 (*0-7089-3168-5*) Ulverscroft.

— The Intrepid Miss Haydon. large type ed. LC 94-29902. (Nightingale Ser.). 364p. 1995. pap. 17.95 (*0-8161-7491-1*, G K Hall Lrg Type) Mac Lib Ref.

— The Jewelled Snuffbox. large type ed. 368p. 1994. 27.99 (*0-7089-3114-6*) Ulverscroft.

— Masquerade of Vengeance. large type ed. (Large Print Ser.). 384p. 1996. 27.99 (*0-7089-3653-9*) Ulverscroft.

— The Master of Liversedge. large type ed. 1994. 11.50 (*0-7089-3203-7*) Ulverscroft.

— Tenant of Chesdene Manor. large type ed. (Ulverscroft Large Print Ser.). 352p. 1997. 27.99 (*0-7089-3851-5*) Ulverscroft.

Ley, Alice Chetwynd. A Conformable Wife. 1981. mass mkt. 2.50 (*0-345-28390-2*, Ballantine) Ballantine Pub Grp.

Ley, Alice Chetwynd. The Toast of the Town. large type ed. (Ulverscroft Large Print Ser.). 336p. 1998. 29.99 (*0-7089-3884-1*) Ulverscroft.

Ley, Beth M. Colostrum: Nature's Gift to the Immune System: Help for Auto-Immunity (Allergies, Arthritis, Multiple Sclerosis, Etc.) & Immune Deficiency. LC 97-12670. 80p. (Orig.). 1997. pap. 4.95 (*0-9642703-7-4*) B L Pubns.

— DHEA: Unlocking the Secrets to the Fountain of Youth. rev. ed. LC 95-96059. 208p. (Orig.). 1997. pap. 14.95 (*0-9642703-3-1*) B L Pubns.

— Dr. John Willard's Catalyst Altered Water. 64p. (Orig.). 1992. pap. 3.95 (*91-49-59100-2*) B L Pubns.

— How to Fight Osteoporosis & Win! The Miracle of Microcrystalline Hydroxyapitite (MCHC) 80p. (Orig.). 1996. pap. 6.95 (*0-9642703-5-8*) B L Pubns.

***Ley, Beth M.** Immune System Control: Colostrum & Lactoferrin. (Illus.). 200p. 2000. pap. 12.95 (*1-890766-11-9*, Pub. by B L Pubns) New Leaf Dist.

— Marvelous Memory Boosters. LC 99-47612. (Health Learning Handbook Ser.). 32p. 1999. pap. 3.95 (*1-890766-09-7*, Pub. by B L Pubns) Nutri-Books Corp.

Ley, Beth M. MSM: On Our Way Back to Health with Sulfur. 40p. 1998. pap. 3.95 (*1-890766-00-3*) B L Pubns.

An Asterisk (*) at the beginning of an entry indicates that the title is appearing for the first time.

— Natural Healing Handbook: Get Back to Health . . . Naturally. 2nd ed. 328p. 1995. pap. 14.95 (*0-9642703-1-5*) B L Pubns.
— Phyto Nutrients: Medicinal Nutrients Found in Foods. 40p. 1998. pap. 3.95 (*0-9642703-9-0*) B L Pubns.
— The Potato Antioxidant: Alpha Lipoic Acid. LC 96-44738. 80p. (Orig.). 1996. pap. 6.95 (*0-9642703-6-6*) B L Pubns.

***Ley, Beth M.** Vinpocetine: Boost Your Brain Power with Periwinkle Extract. LC 99-50632. (Health Learning Handbook Ser.). 56p. 1999. pap. 4.95 (*1-890766-08-9*, Pub. by B L Pubns) Nutri-Books Corp.

Ley, Beth M. & Ash, Richard N. DHEA: Unlocking the Secrets to the Fountain of Youth. 2nd rev. ed. LC 97-22004. (GER, JPN & SPA.). 256p. (Orig.). 1997. pap. 14.95 (*0-9642703-8-2*) B L Pubns.

Ley, Beth M. & Susser, Arnold J. How Did We Get So Fat? A Guide for Those Who Want to Safely Obtain Their Weight Goals Without Going Crazy. (Illus.). 96p. (Orig.). 1994. pap. 7.95 (*0-9642703-0-7*) B L Pubns.

Ley, Charles D. Spanish Poetry since 1939. LC 62-52819. 289p. reprint ed. pap. 89.60 (*0-608-18728-3*, 202951100061) Bks Demand.

Ley, D. Forbes. The Best Seller. LC 84-50560. 313p. 1997. reprint ed. pap. 14.95 (*0-9613319-2-5*) Sales Success.
— The Best Seller: Of Automobiles. LC 85-90516. 1986. 9.95 (*0-9613319-1-7*) Sales Success.

Ley, David. The New Middle Class & the Remaking of the Central City. LC 96-11424. (Oxford Geographical & Environmental Studies Series). (Illus.). 400p. (C). 1997. text 85.00 (*0-19-823292-6*) OUP.
— A Social Geography of the City. (Illus.). 449p. 1999. reprint ed. pap. text 20.00 (*0-7881-6437-6*) DIANE Pub.

Ley, David, jt. auth. see Duncan, James S.

Ley, David F. & Hasson, Shlomo. Neighbourhood Organizations & the Welfare State. (Illus.). 472p. (C). 1994. text 65.00 (*0-8020-2887-X*); pap. text 24.95 (*0-8020-7392-1*) U of Toronto Pr.

Ley, David F., jt. ed. see Bourne, Larry S.

Ley, Gary. Taking Ronnie to the Pictures, 1. LC 99-219541. 1999. pap. text 23.00 (*1-85411-193-0*) Seren Bks.

Ley, Gerd De, see De Ley, Gerd, ed.

Ley, Graham. From Mimesis to Interculturalism: Readings of Theatrical Theory Before & After 'Modernism' 352p. 1999. 85.00 (*0-85989-640-4*) Univ Exeter Pr.
— A Short Introduction to the Ancient Greek Theater. (Illus.). 118p. 1991. pap. 8.00 (*0-226-47760-6*) U Ch Pr.
— A Short Introduction to the Ancient Greek Theater. (Illus.). 118p. 1996. lib. bdg. 24.00 (*0-226-47759-2*) U Ch Pr.

Ley, Herbert De, see De Ley, Herbert.

Ley, J. W. The Dickens Circle. LC 72-573. (Studies in Dickens: No. 52). 1972. reprint ed. lib. bdg. 75.00 (*0-8383-1415-5*) M S G Haskell Hse.

Ley-Jacobs, Beth. Dha: The Magnificent Marine Oil. LC 99-13847. 120p. 1998. pap. 6.95 (*1-890766-01-1*) B L Pubns.
— Natures Road to Recovery: Nutritional Supplements for the Social Drinker, Alcoholic & Chemical Dependent. LC 99-19566. 72p. 1999. pap. text 5.95 (*1-890766-03-8*) B L Pubns.

***Ley, Klaus, ed.** Physiology of Inflammation. (Methods in Physiology Ser.). (Illus.). 496p. 2000. text 95.00 (*0-19-512829-X*) OUP.

Ley, L. & Cardona, M., eds. Photoemission in Solids II: Case Studies. LC 78-2503. (Topics in Applied Physics Ser.: Vol. 27). (Illus.). 1979. 89.95 (*0-387-09202-1*) Spr-Verlag.

Ley, Philip. Communicating with Patients: Improving Communication, Satisfaction & Compliance. 240p. 1989. 49.95 (*0-7099-4161-7*); pap. 17.95 (*0-7099-4174-9*) Routledge.

Ley, Ralph, jt. auth. see Hill, Claude.

Ley Robert & Johnson, Lowell E. Origins Modern Economics: Paradigmatic Approach. 218p. (C). 1990. text 49.00 (*0-536-57844-3*) Pearson Custom.

Ley, Ronald. A Whisper of Espionage: Wolfgang Kohler & the Apes of Tenerife. (Illus.). 264p. 1997. reprint ed. text 20.00 (*0-7881-5134-7*) DIANE Pub.

Ley, Ronald, jt. ed. see Timmons, Beverly H.

Ley, Rosamond, tr. see Busoni, Ferruccio.

Ley, S. V. Oxidation, Vol. 7. 1992. 445.00 (*0-08-040598-3*, Pergamon Pr) Elsevier.

Ley, S. V. & Low, C. M. Ultrasound in Synthesis. (Reactivity & Structure Ser.: Vol. 27). (Illus.). 185p. 1989. 119.95 (*0-387-51023-0*) Spr-Verlag.

Ley, Thomas W., jt. ed. see Williams, Kathleen M.

Ley, Willy. Rockets, Missiles & Space Travel. 1994. reprint ed. lib. bdg. 45.95 (*1-56849-302-9*) Buccaneer Bks.

Leybourne, Douglas M., Jr. Red Book Vol. 8: The Collector's Guide to Old Fruit Jars. LC 00-104038. (Illus.). 387p. 1997. pap. 30.00 (*0-9655558-1-X*) Altarfire Pub.

Leyburn, Ellen D. Satiric Allegory: Mirror of Man, Vol. 130--130. LC 78-5886. (Yale Studies in English: Vol. 130). 142p. 1978. reprint ed. lib. bdg. 49.50 (*0-313-20457-8*, LESM, Greenwood Pr) Greenwood.

Leyburn, James G. The Haitian People, 9. rev. ed. LC 80-476. (Caribbean Ser.: No. 9). (Illus.). 342p. 1980. reprint ed. lib. bdg. 48.50 (*0-313-22155-3*, LEHA, Greenwood Pr) Greenwood.
— The Scotch-Irish: A Social History. LC 62-16063. xx, 397p. (C). 1989. reprint ed. pap. 16.95 (*0-8078-4259-1*) U of NC Pr.
— The Way We Lived: Durham, 1900-1920. Savage, Lon K., ed. 220p. 1987. 16.95 (*0-9617256-1-3*) Northcross Hse.

Leyda, Jay. An Index to the Creative Work of Alexander Dovzhenko. (Film Ser.). 1980. lib. bdg. 59.95 (*0-8490-3094-3*) Gordon Pr.
— An Index to the Creative Work of V. I. Pudovkin. (Film Ser.). 1980. lib. bdg. 59.95 (*0-8490-3092-7*) Gordon Pr.
— The Melville Log, Vol. 1. 492p. Date not set. 30.95 (*0-8488-2355-9*) Amereon Ltd.
— The Melville Log, Vol. 2. 528p. Date not set. 31.95 (*0-8488-2356-7*) Amereon Ltd.

Leyda, Jay, ed. Eisenstein, No. 2: A Premature Celebration of Eisenstein's Centenary. Upchurch, Alan et al, trs. from RUS. (Illus.). 59p. (Orig.). (C). 1989. pap. write for info. (*0-413-19370-5*, AO346, Methuen Drama) Methn.

Leyda, Jay & Bertensson, Sergei, eds. The Musorgsky Reader: A Life of Modeste Petrovich Musorgsky in Letters & Documents. LC 70-87393. (Music Ser.). (Illus.). 1970. reprint ed. lib. bdg. 49.50 (*0-306-71534-1*) Da Capo.

Leyda, Jay, et al. Before Hollywood: Turn-of-the-Century American Film. (Illus.). 172p. (Orig.). 1987. pap. 25.00 (*0-917418-81-6*) Am Fed Arts.

Leyda, Jay, ed. see Eisenstein, Sergei.

Leydecker, G., jt. auth. see Henger, M.

Leyden, Andrew P. Gulf War Debriefing Book: An after Action Report. LC 97-5411. 318p. 1997. pap. 18.95 (*1-55571-396-3*, Hellgate Pr) PSI Resch.

Leyden, D. & Collins, W. Silyated Surfaces, Vol. 2. (Midland Macromolecular Monographs). viii, 380p. 1980. text 385.00 (*0-677-13370-7*) Gordon & Breach.

Leyden, D. E. & Collins, W. T., eds. Chemically Modified Oxide Surfaces: Proceedings of the Chemically Modified Surfaces Symposium, Midland, Michigan, June 28-30, 1989, Vol. 3. xii, 410p. 1990. text 156.00 (*2-88124-428-9*) Gordon & Breach.

Leyden, Dennis P. & Link, Albert N. Government's Role in Innovation. LC 92-20984. 224p. (C). 1992. lib. bdg. 116.50 (*0-7923-9261-2*) Kluwer Academic.

Leyden, Donald E., ed. Silanes, Surfaces & Interfaces Vol. 1: Proceedings of the Silanes, Surfaces & Interfaces Symposium, Snowmass, Colorado, June 19-21, 1985: Chemically Modified Surfaces, Vol. 1. xii, 600p. 1986. text 274.00 (*2-88124-085-2*) Gordon & Breach.

Leyden, Donald E. & Collins, Ward T., eds. Chemically Modified Surfaces in Science & Industry. (Chemically Modified Surfaces Ser.: Vol. 2). xiv, 686p. (C). 1988. text 249.00 (*2-88124-221-9*) Gordon & Breach.

Leyden, John. Introduction to Programming Using C Language. (C). 1998. text. write for info. (*0-673-98196-7*) Addison-Wesley.

Leyden-Rubenstein, Lori A. The Stress Management Handbook: Strategies for Health & Inner Peace. LC 97-39243. 208p. 1998. pap. 14.95 (*0-87983-794-2*, 37942K, Keats Publng) NTC Contemp Pub Co.

Leyden, Susan. Helping the Child of Exceptional Ability. large type ed. LC 85-4137. (Special Education Ser.). 102p. (Orig.). 1985. pap. 19.95 (*0-7099-1635-3*, Pub. by C Helm) Routldge.

Leydesdorf, Loet. Evolutionary Economics & Chaos Theory: New Directions in Technology Studies, Vol. 1. LC 94-1945. 1994. pap. 22.95 (*0-312-12218-7*) St Martin.

Leydesdorff, Loet, et al, eds. Evolutionary Economics & Chaos Theory: New Directions in Technology Studies. LC 94-1945. 1994. write for info. (*1-85567-198-0*); pap. write for info. (*1-85567-202-2*) St Martin.

Leydesdorff, Loet A., jt. auth. see Etzkowitz, Henry.

Leydesdorff, Selma. We Lived with Dignity: The Jewish Proleteriat of Amsterdam, 1900-1940. Heny, Frank, tr. from DUT. (Illus.). 288p. 1994. reprint ed. text 39.95 (*0-8143-2338-3*) Wayne St U Pr.

Leydesorff, Selma & Passerini, Luisa, eds. International Yearbook of Oral History & Life Stories Vol. 4: Gender & Memory, Vol. 4. LC 95-45259. (International Yearbook of Oral History & Life Stories Ser.: 4). (Illus.). 232p. (C). 1996. text 59.00 (*0-19-820251-2*) OUP.

Leydet, Francois. The Coyote: Defiant Songdog of the West. LC 87-40563. (Illus.). 224p. 1981. pap. 14.95 (*0-8061-2123-8*) U of Okla Pr.

Leydon, Michael & Lee, Leathea, eds. Market Research: A Guide to British Library Collections. 8th ed. (Key to British Library Holdings Ser.). 320p. 1994. pap. 59.95 (*0-7123-0804-0*, Pub. by SRIS) L Erlbaum Assocs.

Leyel, C. F. The Truth about Herbs. 106p. 1985. pap. 8.00 (*0-89540-145-2*, SB-145) Sun Pub.
— The Truth about Herbs. 106p. 1996. reprint ed. spiral bd. 11.00 (*0-7873-0558-8*) Hlth Research.

Leyel, C. F., ed. see Grieve, M.

Leyendecker, G., ed. see Stock, H. & Wildt, L.

Leyendekkers, J. V. Thermodynamics of Seawater As a Multicomponent Electrolyte Solution, Pt. 1: Entropy, Volume, Expansibility, Compressibility. LC 76-18422. (Marine Science Ser.: No. 3). (Illus.). 510p. reprint ed. pap. 158.10 (*0-7837-0788-6*, 204110200001) Bks Demand.

Leyens, Erich. Years of Estrangement. 128p. 1996. 12.95 (*0-8101-1166-7*) Northwestern U Pr.

Leyens, Erich & Andor, Lotte. Years of Estrangement. Goldstein, Brigitte, tr. from GER. LC 96-33080. (Jewish Lives Ser.). 128p. 1996. 39.95 (*0-8101-1181-0*) Northwestern U Pr.

Leyens, J. P., jt. auth. see Codol, J. P.

Leyens, Jacques-Philippe, et al. Stereotypes & Social Cognition. 256p. 1994. 69.95 (*0-8039-8583-5*); pap. 26.95 (*0-8039-8584-3*) Sage.

Leyerle, Anne L. & Leyerle, William D. Song Anthology One. 4th rev. ed. 159p. 1985. spiral bd. 12.95 (*1-878617-05-2*) Leyerle Pubns.

Leyerle, Anne L. & Leyerle, William D. Song Anthology Two. 2nd enl. rev. ed. iv, 205p. 1998. pap. 14.95 (*1-878617-17-6*) Leyerle Pubns.

Leyerle, Anne L. & Leyerle, William D., eds. French Diction Songs. 2nd rev. ed. 128p. 1990. pap. text 12.95 (*0-9602296-9-8*) Leyerle Pubns.

Leyerle, Betty. Moving & Shaking American Medicine: The Structure of a Socioeconomic Transformation, 57. LC 83-22646. (Contributions in Economics & Economic History Ser.: No. 57). 218p. 1984. 55.00 (*0-313-24020-5*, LIP/, Greenwood Pr) Greenwood.

Leyerle, Betty. The Private Regulation of American Health Care. LC 93-42516. 240p. (gr. 13). 1994. 70.95 (*1-56324-288-5*); pap. 34.95 (*1-56324-289-3*) M E Sharpe.

Leyerle, John & Quick, Anne, eds. Chaucer: A Selected Bibliography. (Medieval Bibliographies Ser.: No. 10). 352p. 1986. pap. text 10.95 (*0-8020-6408-6*) U of Toronto Pr.

Leyerle, John, jt. ed. see Damico, Helen.

Leyerle, William D. Vocal Development Through Organic Imagery. 2nd enl. rev. ed. LC 78-103579. (Illus.). 189p. (C). 1986. pap. 14.95 (*0-9602296-6-3*) Leyerle Pubns.

Leyerle, William D., jt. auth. see Leyerle, Anne L.

Leyerle, William D., jt. ed. see Ellingboe, Bradley.

Leyerle, William D., jt. ed. see Leyerle, Anne L.

Leyerzapf, James W., ed. see Eisenhower, Dwight D., et al.

Leyes, Maggie, ed. see Lin, Jami.

Leyes, Richard A., II & Fleming, William A. The History of North American Small Gas Turbine Aircraft Engines. LC 99-45475. 998p. 31.95 (*1-56347-332-1*) AIAA.

Leygraf, Christofer & Graedel, Thomas E. Atmospheric Corrosion. LC 99-57530. 256p. 2000. text 79.95 (*0-471-37219-6*) Wiley.

Leyh, ed. see Bacon, Jonathan P.

Leyh, ed. see Bacon, Jonathan P. & Sindt, Robert G.

Leyh, ed. see Barfield, Jesse T., et al.

Leyh, ed. see Bitter, Gary.

Leyh, ed. see Bitter, Gary G.

Leyh, ed. see Black, Ken.

Leyh, ed. see Clabaugh, Maurice G., Jr. & Forbes, Jesse L.

Leyh, ed. see Clabaugh, Maurice G., Jr., et al.

Leyh, ed. see Copeland, Cody T. & Bacon, Jonathan P.

Leyh, ed. see Fandt, Patricia M.

Leyh, ed. see Guay, E. Joseph.

Leyh, ed. see Harris, O. Jeff & Hartman, Sandra.

Leyh, ed. see Harrison, Jeffrey S. & St. John, Caron H.

Leyh, ed. see Heiman, Barbara & McGauley, Nancy.

Leyh, ed. see Jennings, Daniel F.

Leyh, ed. see Jennings, Marianne M.

Leyh, ed. see Lozuk, Larry & Ketcham, Emily M.

Leyh, ed. see Lund, Patsy H.

Leyh, ed. see McDaniel, Carl, Jr. & Gates, Roger H.

Leyh, ed. see Nelson, Debra L. & Quick, James C.

Leyh, ed. see Raiborn, Cecily A., et al.

Leyh, ed. see Ross, Paul W., et al.

Leyh, ed. see Ross, Steven C.

Leyh, ed. see Ross, Steven C. & Hutson, Stephen V.

Leyh, ed. see Ross, Steven C. & Maestas, Ronald W.

Leyh, ed. see Ross, Steven C., et al.

Leyh, ed. see Ruff, Laura B. & Weitzer, Mary K.

Leyh, ed. see Smith, Larry D.

Leyh, ed. see Zikmund, William G. & D'Amico, Michael.

Leyh, ed. see Zimmerman, Steven M. & Conrad, Leo.

Leyh, Gregory, intro. Legal Hermeneutics: History, Theory, & Practice. LC 90-19397. 335p. 1991. 55.00 (*0-520-07283-9*, Pub. by U CA Pr); pap. 18.95 (*0-520-07284-7*, Pub. by U CA Pr) Cal Prin Full Svc.

Leyi, Li. Tracing the Roots of Chinese Characters: 500 Cases. (Illus.). 500p. 1993. pap. 19.95 (*7-5619-0204-2*) China Bks.

Leylan, Thomas. Writing Applications with Clipper. LC 94-12561. 1994. pap. 39.95 incl. disk (*1-55851-382-5*, M&T Bks) IDG Bks.

Leyland, B. N., jt. ed. see Duz'minskii, A. S.

Leyland, Charles G. Fusang or the Discovery of America by Chinese Buddhist Priests in the Fifth Century. 212p. 1981. pap. 19.00 (*0-89540-094-4*, SB-094) Sun Pub.

Leyland, Francis A. Bronte Family, 2 vols., Set. LC 70-157554. (English Literature Ser.: No. 33). 1971. reprint ed. lib. bdg. 150.00 (*0-8383-1256-X*) M S G Haskell Hse.

Leyland, Peter & Woods, Terry. Textbook on Administrative Law. 2nd ed. LC 98-134501. 462p. 1997. pap. 42.00 (*1-85431-658-3*, Pub. by Blackstone Pr) Gaunt.

***Leyland, Peter & Woods, Terry.** Textbook on Administrative Law. 3rd ed. 500p. 1999. pap. 40.00 (*1-85431-891-8*, Pub. by Blackstone Pr) Gaunt.

Leyland, Peter & Woods, Terry, eds. Administrative Law Facing the Future: Old Constraints & New Horizons. 465p. 1997. pap. 54.00 (*1-85431-689-3*, Pub. by Blackstone Pr) Gaunt.

Leyland, Peter, et al. Textbook on Administrative Law. 398p. 1994. pap. 38.00 (*1-85431-318-5*, Pub. by Blackstone Pr) Gaunt.

Leyland, W. Eighteen & Over: True Gay Encounters, Vol. 10. 1991. pap. 12.95 (*0-943595-30-4*) Leyland Pubns.

Leyland, Winston. Lust: Licentious Underground Sexy True Gay Encounters, Vol. 1. (Illus.). 176p. (Orig.). 1994. reprint ed. pap. 14.95 (*0-943595-48-7*) Leyland Pubns.
— Meatmen: An Anthology of Gay Male Comics, Vol. 23. 1999. pap. text 16.95 (*0-943595-76-2*) Leyland Pubns.
— Meatmen: Anthology of Gay Male Comics, Vol. 2. (Anthology of Gay Male Comics Ser.). 1996. pap. text 16.95 (*0-943595-04-5*) Leyland Pubns.
— Meatmen: Special Edition, Vol. 24. 2000. pap. text 16.95 (*0-943595-77-0*) Leyland Pubns.

Leyland, Winston, ed. Angels of the Lyre: Anthology of Gay Poetry. LC 75-19135. (Illus.). 256p. (C). 1975. 12.95 (*0-915572-14-1*); pap. 6.95 (*0-915572-13-3*) Panjandrum.
— Basic Training: True Homosexual Military Stories, Vol. 5. 160p. (Orig.). 1995. pap. 14.95 (*0-943595-56-8*) Leyland Pubns.
— Gay Roots Vol. 1: Twenty Years of Gay Sunshine: An Anthology of Gay History, Sex, Politics, & Culture. (Illus.). 702p. 1991. pap. 22.95 (*0-940567-13-X*); lib. bdg. 75.00 (*0-940567-12-1*) Gay Sunshine.
— Gay Roots Vol. 2: An Anthology of Gay History, Sex, Politics & Culture. (Illus.). 320p. (Orig.). 1993. pap. 19.95 (*0-940567-15-6*); lib. bdg. 50.00 (*0-940567-14-8*) Gay Sunshine.
— Gay Sunshine Interviews, Vol. 1. (Illus.). 328p. (Orig.). 1984. 25.00 (*0-917342-60-7*); pap. 14.95 (*0-917342-61-5*) Gay Sunshine.
— Gay Sunshine Interviews, Vol. 2. (Illus.). 288p. (Orig.). 1982. 25.00 (*0-917342-62-3*); pap. 14.95 (*0-917342-63-1*) Gay Sunshine.
— Hot Studs, Vol. 3: True Homosexual Encounters First Hand. (Illus.). 192p. (Orig.). 1986. pap. 10.95 (*0-917342-15-1*) Leyland Pubns.
— Humongous: True Gay Encounters, Vol. 5. 192p. (Orig.). 1994. reprint ed. pap. 14.95 (*0-943595-14-2*) Leyland Pubns.
— Macho Marines: True Homosexual Military Stories, Vol. 6. 160p. 1997. pap. 14.95 (*0-943595-67-3*) Leyland Pubns.
— Manplay Vol. 3: True Gay Encounters. 192p. (Orig.). 1986. pap. 10.00 (*0-943595-06-1*) Leyland Pubns.
— Marine Biology: True Homosexual Military Stories. (Military Sex Stories Ser.: Vol. 4). 160p. (Orig.). 1994. pap. 14.95 (*0-943595-49-5*) Leyland Pubns.
— Meatmen: An Anthology of Gay Male Comics. (Meatmen Comics Ser.: Vol. 16). (Illus.). 160p. 1995. pap. 15.95 (*0-943595-44-4*) Leyland Pubns.
— Meatmen: An Anthology of Gay Male Comics. (Comics Antholoby Ser.: Vol. 17). (Illus.). 160p. 1995. pap. 16.95 (*0-943595-50-9*) Leyland Pubns.
— Meatmen: An Anthology of Gay Male Comics, 5. (Illus.). 1989. pap. 14.95 (*0-943595-15-0*) Leyland Pubns.
— Meatmen: An Anthology of Gay Male Comics, 6. (Illus.). 1989. pap. 14.95 (*0-943595-20-7*) Leyland Pubns.
— Meatmen: An Anthology of Gay Male Comics, 8. (Illus.). 1990. pap. 13.95 (*0-943595-23-1*) Leyland Pubns.
— Meatmen: An Anthology of Gay Male Comics, 9. (Illus.). 1990. pap. 14.95 (*0-943595-24-X*) Leyland Pubns.
— Meatmen: An Anthology of Gay Male Comics, 10. (Illus.). 1991. pap. 14.95 (*0-943595-27-4*) Leyland Pubns.
— Meatmen: An Anthology of Gay Male Comics, 11. (Illus.). 1991. pap. 14.95 (*0-943595-28-2*) Leyland Pubns.
— Meatmen: An Anthology of Gay Male Comics, 12. (Illus.). 1991. pap. 15.95 (*0-943595-29-0*) Leyland Pubns.
— Meatmen: An Anthology of Gay Male Comics, Vol. 1. 2nd ed. (Illus.). 192p. 1996. reprint ed. pap. 16.95 (*0-917342-23-2*) Leyland Pubns.
— Meatmen: An Anthology of Gay Male Comics, Vol. 14. (Illus.). 160p. 1993. pap. 15.95 (*0-943595-35-5*) Leyland Pubns.
— Meatmen: An Anthology of Gay Male Comics, Vol. 15. (Illus.). 160p. 1993. pap. 15.95 (*0-943595-38-X*) Leyland Pubns.
— Meatmen: An Anthology of Gay Male Comics, Vol. 18. (Illus.). 160p. 1996. pap. 16.95 (*0-943595-53-3*) Leyland Pubns.
— Meatmen: An Anthology of Gay Male Comics, Vol. 21. (Illus.). 160p. 1997. pap. 16.95 (*0-943595-68-1*) Leyland Pubns.
— Meatmen: Anthology of Gay Male Comics, Vol. 19. (Anthology of Gay Male Comics Ser.). 1996. pap. text 16.95 (*0-943595-60-6*) Leyland Pubns.
— Meatmen: Anthology of Gay Male Comics, Vol. 20. (Illus.). 160p. 1997. pap. 16.95 (*0-943595-63-0*) Leyland Pubns.
— Meatmen Vol. 22: An Anthology of Gay Male Comics. (Illus.). 160p. 1998. pap. 16.95 (*0 943595 75 4*) Leyland Pubns.
— Military Sex: True Homosexual Stories, Vol. 3. 160p. (Orig.). 1993. pap. 14.95 (*0-943595-41-X*) Leyland Pubns.
— My Deep Dark Pain Is Love: A Collection of Latin American Gay Fiction. Lacey, E. A., tr. from POR. (Illus.). 384p. (Orig.). 1983. pap. 14.95 (*0-917342-03-8*) Gay Sunshine.
— Orgasms: Homosexual Encounters from First Hand, Vol. 2. (Illus.). 192p. (Orig.). 1985. pap. 10.95 (*0-917342-12-7*) Leyland Pubns.
— Queer Dharma Vol. 1: Voices of Gay Buddhists. LC 97-27590. (Illus.). 416p. 1998. 50.00 (*0-940567-21-0*) Gay Sunshine.
— Queer Dharma Vol. 1: Voices of Gay Buddhists. LC 97-27590. (Illus.). 416p. 2000. pap. 19.95 (*0-940567-22-9*) Gay Sunshine.
— Queer Dharma Vol. 2: Voices of Gay Buddhists. (Illus.). 224p. 2000. 50.00 (*0-940567-24-5*); pap. 16.95 (*0-940567-23-7*) Gay Sunshine.
— Studflesh Vol. 8: True Gay Encounters. 160p. (Orig.). 1989. pap. 10.00 (*0-943595-25-8*) Leyland Pubns.
— Warriors & Lovers: True Homosexual Military Stories, Vol. 2. 160p. (Orig.). 1992. pap. 14.95 (*0-943595-37-1*) Leyland Pubns.

Leyland, Winston, intro. Teleny: Novel Attributed to Oscar Wilde. 184p. 1984. reprint ed. pap. 14.95 (*0-917342-33-X*); reprint ed. lib. bdg. 25.00 (*0-917342-32-1*) Gay Sunshine.

Leyland, Winston, ed. see Ginsberg, Allen & Orlovsky, Peter.

Leyland, Winston, ed. see Stoddard, Charles W.

Leyman, Jean. How Do You Feel? Koj Puas Xis Nyob (English-Hmong Medical Handbook) Ly, Xeng, tr. LC 82-91138. (Illus.). 36p. 1983. pap. 6.50 (*0-9610684-0-X*) Mulberry Tree.

Leymann. Socialization & Learning at Work. 320p. 1989. 87.95 (*0-566-05639-9*) Ashgate Pub Co.

L

L

Leymarie, Jean. The Jerusalem Windows of Marc Chagall. LC 62-18146. (Illus.). 96p. 1996. pap. 23.50 (0-8076-0807-6) Braziller.

Leyn, K. Russisch-Deutsches Woerterbuch. 11th ed. (GER & RUS.). 735p. 1991. 105.00 (0-7859-8548-4, 3894511117) Fr & Eur.

Leyn, P. De, see De Leyn, P.

Leyner, Mark. Et Tu, Babe. LC 93-15503. (Vintage Contemporaries Ser.). 1993. pap. 11.00 (0-679-74506-8) Vin Bks.

— I Smell Esther Williams: And Other Stories. LC 94-31359. 1995. pap. 11.00 (0-679-75045-2) Vin Bks.

***Leyner, Mark.** Leyner: Novel, Vol. 2. 2001. 20.00 (0-517-70102-2) Crown Pub Group.

Leyner, Mark. My Cousin, My Gastroenterologist. LC 93-15505. 1995. pap. 10.00 (0-679-74579-3) Vin Bks.

— The Tetherballs of Bougainville. 240p. 1998. pap. 12.00 (0-679-76349-X) Vin Bks.

— Tooth Imprints on a Corn Dog. 240p. 1996. pap. 11.00 (0-679-74521-1) Random.

Leyner, Mark, et al, eds. American Made. LC 86-4459. 214p. 1986. 15.95 (0-914590-98-7); pap. 8.95 (0-914590-99-5) Fiction Coll.

***Leypoldt, John K.** The Artificial Kidney: Physiological Modeling & Tissue Engineering. LC 99-33005. (Tissue Engineering Intelligence Unit Ser.: Vol. 3). 154p. 1999. 89.00 (1-57059-602-6) Landes Bioscience.

Leypoldt, Martha M. 40 Ways to Teach in Groups. (Orig.). 1967. pap. text 11.00 (0-8170-0376-2) Judson.

— Learning Is Change. LC 70-144082. (Illus.). 159p. 1971. reprint ed. pap. 49.30 (0-608-00215-1, 206100800006) Bks Demand.

Leys. Politics in Britain. 1983. 16.95 (0-435-83493-2) Ashgate Pub Co.

Leys, Brian D., jt. auth. see Kuhn, Kevin.

Leys, Colin & Mamdani, Mahmood. Crises & Reconstruction-- African Perspectives: Two Lectures LC 98-140475. (Discussion Papers). 26p. 1997. write for info. (91-7106-417-6) Nordisk Afrikainstitutet.

Leys, Colin, jt. ed. see Panitch, Leo.

Leys, Colin T. European Politics in Southern Rhodesia. LC 82-6176. 323p. 1982. reprint ed. lib. bdg. 65.00 (0-313-23548-1, LEEU, Greenwood Pr) Greenwood.

— Politics in Britain. 2nd ed. 400p. 1989. pap. text 19.95 (0-8020-6751-4) U of Toronto Pr.

— Politics in Britain: An Introduction. LC 83-213340. (Illus.). 360p. (Orig.). reprint ed. pap. 111.60 (0-8357-3645-8, 203637200003) Bks Demand.

— Politics in Britain: From Labourism to Thatcherism. 384p. 1989. 50.00 (0-86091-240-X, A3888); pap. 17.95 (0-86091-954-4, A3892) Routledge.

— The Rise & Fall of Development Theory. LC 95-39293. 1996. pap. text 14.95 (0-253-21016-X) Ind U Pr.

— The Rise & Fall of Development Theory. LC 95-39293. (C). 1996. 35.00 (0-253-33083-1) Ind U Pr.

— Underdevelopment in Kenya: The Political Economy of Neo-Colonialism, 1964-1971. LC 74-76387. 1975. pap. 18.95 (0-520-02770-1, Pub. by U CA Pr) Cal Prin Full Svc.

Leys, Colin T., ed. Politics & Change in Developing Countries: Studies in the Theory & Practice of Development. 301p. reprint ed. pap. 85.80 (0-608-30039-X, 2051389) Bks Demand.

Leys, Colin T. & Mendell, Marguerite, eds. Culture & Social Change, Vol. 2. LC 92-70625. 230p. 1992. 48.99 (1-895431-29-8, Pub. by Black Rose); pap. text 19.99 (1-895431-28-X, Pub. by Black Rose) Consort Bk Sales.

Leys, Colin T. & Saul, John S. Namibia's Liberation Struggle: The Two-Edged Sword. LC 94-8024. (Eastern African Studies). (Illus.). 224p. (C). 1994. text 44.95 (0-8214-1103-9); pap. text 19.95 (0-8214-1104-7) Ohio U Pr.

Leys, Colin T., jt. ed. see Berman, Bruce J.

***Leys, Marilyn.** Living with Wildlife. LC 00-101580. (Illus.). 232p. 2000. pap. 16.95 (0-87341-857-3, WILD) Krause Pubns.

Leys, Ruth. From Sympathy to Reflex: Marshall Hall & His Opponents. LC 90-19507. (Harvard Dissertations in the History of Science Ser.). 568p. 1991. reprint ed. text 40.00 (0-8240-0042-0) Garland.

***Leys, Ruth.** Trauma: A Genealogy. LC 99-52681. 1999. pap. text 19.00 (0-226-47766-5) U Ch Pr.

Leys, Ruth & Evans, Rand B., eds. Defining American Psychology: The Correspondence Between Adolph Meyer & Edward Brandord Titchener. LC 89-15315. 296p. 1990. text 49.95 (0-8018-3865-7) Johns Hopkins.

Leys, Simon. The Analects of Confucius. 256p. 1997. pap. 12.95 (0-393-31699-8) Norton.

— The Death of Napoleon. Clancy, Patricia, tr. 1992. 15.00 (0-374-13565-7) FS&G.

Leys, Simon, tr. & notes see Confucius.

Leysath, Scott. The Sporting Chef's Favorite Wild Game Recipes. Gazzaniga, Donald A., ed. (Illus.). 112p. (C). 1997. text 19.95 (1-886571-02-3) Sport Chef.

Leyser, Brady J. & Gosset, Pol, eds. Rock Stars - Pop Stars: A Comprehensive Bibliography, 1955-1994, 43. LC 94-28691. (Music Reference Collection: No. 43). 328p. 1994. lib. bdg. 65.00 (0-313-29422-4) Greenwood.

***Leyser, Conrad.** Authority & Asceticism from Augustine to Gregory the Great. (Oxford Historical Monographs). 220p. 2000. text 60.00 (0-19-820868-5) OUP.

Leyser, Karl J. Communications & Power in Medieval Europe: The Carolingian & Ottonian Centuries. Reuter, Timothy, ed. LC 94-20663. 1994. 55.00 (1-85285-013-2) Hambledon Press.

— Communications & Power in Medieval Europe: The Gregorian Revolution & Beyond. Reuter, Timothy, ed. LC 94-25531. 1994. 55.00 (1-85285-113-9) Hambledon Press.

— Medieval Germany & Its Neighbours, 900-1250. 300p. (C). 1982. 55.00 (0-907628-08-7); pap. 18.00 (0-907628-09-5) Hambledon Press.

Leyshon, Andrew, et al, eds. The Place of Music. LC 97-46480. (Mappings). 326p. 1998. pap. 24.95 (1-57230-314-X, C0314) Guilford Pubns.

Leyshon, Andrew & Thrift, Nigel. Money - Space: Geographies of Monetary Transformation. LC 96-18262. (International Library of Sociology Ser.). 424p. (C). 1997. 85.00 (0-415-13981-3); pap. 27.99 (0-415-03835-9) Routledge.

Leyshon, Andrew, et al. The Place of Music. LC 97-46480. (Mappings Ser.). 326p. 1998. 43.95 (1-57230-313-1) Guilford Pubns.

— The Rise of the British Provincial Financial Centre. (Progress in Planning Ser.: PRPL 31). 80p. 1990. pap. 38.50 (0-08-037384-4, Pergamon Pr) Elsevier.

Leyshon, Glynn A. The Coach & Sport Management. Zeigler, Earle F., ed. (Monograph Series on Sport & Physical Education Management). 48p. 1992. pap. text 4.80 (0-87563-425-7) Stipes.

Leyshon, Glynn A., ed. see Mikalachki, Albert.

Leyshon, Peter R. & Lisle, Richard J. Stereographic Projection Techniques in Structural Geology. LC 95-14960. (Illus.). 112p. 1995. pap. 36.95 (0-7506-2450-7) Buttrwrth-Heinemann.

Leyson, J. F. J., ed. Sexual Rehabilitation of the Spinal-Cord-Injured Patient. LC 90-4685. (Illus.). 572p. 1991. 125.00 (0-89603-145-4) Humana.

Leytham, Rob. Jazz & Blues Drumming. 40p. 1997. pap. 9.95 incl. audio compact disk (0-7866-2853-7, 96669BCD) Mel Bay.

— Progressive Rock Drumming & Soloing Methods. 36p. 1997. pap. 9.95 incl. audio compact disk (0-7866-2854-5, 96670BCD) Mel Bay.

— Rock Drumming & Soloing Methods. 40p. 1997. pap. 9.95 incl. audio compact disk (0-7866-2852-9, 96668BCD) Mel Bay.

Leyton-Brown, David, ed. Canadian Annual Review of Politics & Public Affairs. (Illus.). 344p. 1998. text 70.00 (0-8020-4369-0) U of Toronto Pr.

— Canadian Annual Review of Politics & Public Affairs. 88th ed. 352p. 1994. text 70.00 (0-8020-5849-3) U of Toronto Pr.

Leyton, Elliot, ed. Serial Murder: Modern Scientific Perspectives. (International Library of Criminology, Criminal Justice & Penology). 560p. 1999. text 175.95 (1-84014-452-1, Pub. by Ashgate Pub) Ashgate Pub Co.

Leyton, Elliott. Hunting Humans. 1990. mass mkt. 4.99 (0-671-73141-6) PB.

— Hunting Humans: The Rise of the Modern Multiple Murderer. rev. ed. 320p. 1995. pap. 17.99 (0-7710-5309-6) McCland & Stewart.

— Men of Blood: Murder in Everyday Life. 237p. 1998. text 30.00 (0-7881-5923-2) DIANE Pub.

— Men of Blood: Murder in Everyday Life. (Illus.). 264p. 1996. 29.99 (0-7710-5310-X) McCland & Stewart.

— Men of Blood: Murder in Everyday Life. 264p. 1997. pap. write for info. (0-7710-5306-1) McCland & Stewart.

— Touched by Fire: Doctors Without Borders in a Third World Crisis. LC 98-166663. (Illus.). 224p. 1998. 24.95 (0-7710-5305-3) McCland & Stewart.

Leyton, Lawrence. My First Magic Book. LC 93-22104. (Illus.). 48p. (J). (gr. k-4). 1993. 12.95 (1-56458-319-8) DK Pub Inc.

Leyton, Michael. Symmetry, Causality, Mind. 1992. pap. text 32.50 (0-262-62131-2) MIT Pr.

Leyva, Adolfo, ed. see Andrei, Moscovit.

Leyva, Adolfo, ed. see Llerena, Mario.

Leyva, Francisco & Coats, Andrew J. Hypertension & Co-Existing Disease. LC 98-32240. (Illus.). 241p. 2000. pap. 99.00 (0-632-05073-X) Blackwell Sci.

Leyva, Josefina. El Aullido de las Muchedumbres. (SPA.). 746p. (Orig.). 1994. pap. 24.95 (1-882721-04-7) Edit Ponce de Leon.

— Los Balseros de la Libertad. 105p. 1992. pap. 9.95 (1-882721-00-4); pap. 9.95 (1-882721-02-0) Edit Ponce de Leon.

— The Freedom Rafters. Smith, Dorothy J., tr. from SPA.Tr. of Balseros de la Libertad. 123p. 1993. pap. 9.95 (1-882721-03-9) Edit Ponce de Leon.

— Imagenes Desde Cuba. (SPA., Illus.). 147p. (Orig.). 1995. pap. 9.95 (1-882721-06-3) Edit Ponce de Leon.

— Operacion Pedro Pan: El Exodo de los Ninos Cubanos. (SPA.). 305p. 1993. pap. 19.95 (1-882721-01-2) Edit Ponce de Leon.

— El Tiempo Inagotado de Irene Marquina. (SPA.). 255p. (Orig.). 1994. pap. 14.95 (1-882721-05-5) Edit Ponce de Leon.

Leyva-Leon, Francisco & Coats, Andrew J. Practical Management of Hypertension. LC 98-32240. 1999. write for info. (0-632-05045-4) Blackwell Sci.

Leza, Richard L. Export Now: A Guide for Small Businesses. 3rd ed. (Illus.). 300p. 1993. pap. 24.95 (1-55571-167-7, Oasis Pr) PSI Resch.

Lezak, Muriel D. Neuropsychological Assessment. 3rd ed. (Illus.). 1056p. 1995. text 72.50 (0-19-509031-4) OUP.

Lezak, Roseann, ed. see Kubi, K. Appiah.

***Lezama Lima, Jose.** Paradiso. Rabassa, Gregory, tr. from SPA. LC 99-35090. 478p. 1999. reprint ed. pap. 14.50 (1-56478-228-X, Pub. by Dalkey Arch) Chicago Distribution Ctr.

Lezar, Ted. Making Government Work: A Conservative Agenda for the States. LC 93-47055. 1993. pap. 15.95 (0-89526-730-6) Regnery Pub.

Lezhnev, Abram. Pushkin's Prose. Orig. Title: Proza Pushkina. 300p. 27.95 (0-88233-627-4) Ardis Pubs.

— Pushkin's Prose. Orig. Title: Proza Pushkina. 225p. 1983. pap. 9.95 (0-88233-628-2) Ardis Pubs.

— Pushkin's Prose. Reeder, Roberta, tr. Orig. Title: Proza Pushkina. 225p. 1986. pap. 45.00 (0-7855-0906-2) St Mut.

Lezin, Arthur S. From Afghanistan to Zaire: Reflections on a Foreign Service Life. 1997. pap. 15.00 (0-9658696-0-1) Karakoram Pr.

Lezin, Katya. Finding Life on Death Row: Profiles of Six Inmates. LC 99-31731. 212p. 1999. text 30.00 (1-55553-405-8) NE U Pr.

***Lezin, Katya.** Finding Life on Death Row: Profiles of Six Inmates. 224p. 2000. pap. 16.95 (1-55553-457-0) NE U Pr.

Lezine, I., jt. auth. see David, M.

Leznoff, Clifford C. & Lever, A. B., eds. Phthalocyanines: Properties & Applications, Vol. 2. (Illus.). 640p. 1993. text 150.00 (1-56081-544-2, Wiley-VCH) Wiley.

Leznoff, Clifford C. & Lever, A. Phillip, eds. Phthalocyanines: Properties & Applications, 4 vols., Set. (Illus.). vii, 1046p. 1996. 499.00 (1-56081-951-0, Wiley-VCH) Wiley.

Leznoff, Clifford C. & Lever, Phillip, eds. Phthalocyanines: Properties & Applications, Vol. 1. LC 89-16518. 436p. 1989. 165.00 (0-89573-753-1, Wiley-VCH) Wiley.

Leznoff, Clifford C., jt. ed. see Lever, A. B.

Leznoff, Noah. Why We Go to Zoos. 112p. 1998. pap. 11.99 (1-895837-03-0) Insomniac.

Leznov, A. N. & Saveliev, Mikhail V. Group-Theoretical Methods for Integration of Nonlinear Dynamical Systems. Leites, D. A., tr. from RUS. (Progress in Physics Ser.: Vol. 15). 312p. 1992. 193.00 (0-8176-2615-8) Birkhauser.

Lezotte, Lawrence, ed. Effective Schools Research Abstracts Vol. 12: 1997-98 Series. 81p. 1997. text 100.00 (1-883247-09-8) Effect Schls.

Lezotte, Lawrence W. Creating the Total Quality Effective School. 110p. 1992. pap. 25.00 (1-883247-02-0) Effect Schls.

— Dear Colleague. 220p. 1998. pap. 14.98 (1-883247-11-X) Effect Schls.

— Effective Schools Practices That Work. Jacoby, Barbara C., ed. 93p. 1991. pap. 17.95 (1-883247-03-9) Effect Schls.

— Learning for All. 92p. 1997. pap. text 24.95 (1-883247-08-X) Effect Schls.

— Sustainable School Reform: The District Context. Jacoby, Barbara C., ed. 283p. 1992. pap. 32.50 (1-883247-01-2) Effect Schls.

Lezotte, Lawrence W. & Jacoby, Barbara C. A Guide to the School Improvement Process Based on Effective Schools Research. 165p. 1990. pap. 29.95 (1-883247-00-4) Effect Schls.

***Lezotte, Lawrence W. & Pepperl, Jo-Ann Cipriano.** The Effective Process: A Proven Path to Learning for All. 160p. 1999. 35.00 (1-883247-12-8) Effect Schls.

Lezotte, Lawrence W., jt. auth. see Pepperl, Jo-Ann Cipriano.

Lezra, Jacques. Depositions: Althusser, Balibar, Macherey & the Labor of Reading. pap. write for info. (0-300-06578-7) Yale U Pr.

— Unspeakable Subjects: The Genealogy of the Event in Early Modern Europe. LC 96-38471. 1997. write for info. (0-8047-2778-3) Stanford U Pr.

LFFEY, Alice L. First & Second Kings. (Collegeville Bible Commentary - Old Testament Ser.). 112p. 1985. pap. 4.95 (0-8146-1416-7) Liturgical Pr.

Lg Inc. Southeast Asia. 944p. 1999. pap. 23.99 (0-312-24528-9) St Martin.

***Lg Inc.** Washington, D. C. (Let's Go 2000 Ser.). (Illus.). 336p. 1999. pap. 16.99 (0-312-24486-X) St Martin.

Lhalungpa, Lobsang, tr. see Keegan, Marcia.

Lhalungpa, Lobsang P. The Life of Milarepa: A New Translation from the Tibetan. 256p. 1992. pap. 14.95 (0-14-019350-2, Arkana) Viking Penguin.

Lhamon, W. T., Jr. Deliberate Speed: The Origins of a Cultural Style in the American 1950s. LC 89-26197. 304p. 1993. reprint ed. pap. 16.95 (1-56098-316-7) Smithsonian.

Lhamon, W. T. Raising Cain: Blackface Performance from Jim Crow to Hip Hop. LC 97-28735. 288p. 1999. text 25.95 (0-674-74711-9) HUP.

***Lhamon, W. T.** Raising Cain: Blackface Performance from Jim Crow to Hip Hop. 2000. pap. text 16.95 (0-674-00193-1) HUP.

Lhamon, W. T., jt. auth. see Rourke, Constance.

Lhardy, Patricia, tr. see Ricard, Rene.

L'Harmet, Corine, jt. auth. see Bellet, Michel.

Lherbier, L. W. & Bhat, G. K., eds. Vacuum Metallurgy Conference on Specialty Metals Melting & Processing: Pittsburgh, Pennsylvania, June 9-11, 1986. fac. ed. LC 86-81028. (Illus.). 229p. 1987. pap. 71.00 (0-7837-8236-5, 204900000009) Bks Demand.

Lherbier, L. W., ed. see Vacuum Metallurgy Conference on the Melting & Proc.

L'Heritier, Philippe. Dictionnaire de Genetique. (FRE.). 272p. 1979. pap. 69.95 (0-7859-7824-0, 2225526575) Fr & Eur.

L'Hermine, C. Radiology of Liver Circulation. LC 85-8905. (Radiology Ser.). 1985. text 215.00 (0-89838-715-9) Kluwer Academic.

L'Hermite, M., ed. Update on Hormonal Treatment in the Menopause. (Progress in Reproductive Biology & Medicine Ser.: Vol. 13). (Illus.). viii, 108p. 1989. 85.25 (3-8055-4904-0) S Karger.

L'Hermite, P. L. Processing & Use of Organic Sludge & Liquid Agricultural Wastes. 1986. text 256.00 (90-277-2338-9) Kluwer Academic.

L'Hermite, P. L. & Handtschutter, J., eds. Copper in Animal Wastes & Sewage Sludge. xiv, 378p. 1981. text 112.50 (90-277-1293-X) Kluwer Academic.

L'Hermite, P. L. & Ott, H., eds. Characterization, Treatment & Use of Sewage Sludge. xviii, 803p. 1981. text 234.00 (90-277-1294-8) Kluwer Academic.

— Processing & Use of Sewage Sludge. 600p. 1984. text 252.50 (90-277-1727-3) Kluwer Academic.

L'Heureux, Conrad E., jt. auth. see Bybee, Howard C.

L'Heureux, John. The Handmaid of Desire. LC 96-20632. 256p. 1996. 23.00 (1-56947-073-1) Soho Press.

— The Handmaid of Desire. 256p. 1998. pap. 12.00 (1-56947-123-1) Soho Press.

— Having Everything. LC 99-28837. 240p. 1999. 24.00 (0-87113-763-1, Atlntc Mnthly) Grove-Atltic.

***L'Heureux, John.** Having Everything. 2000. reprint ed. pap. 12.00 (0-8021-3732-6, Grove) Grove-Atltic.

L'Heureux, John. Lies. 1999. text 18.95 (0-670-83908-6) Viking Penguin.

— The Shrine at Altamira. LC 99-27591. 272p. 1999. pap. 13.00 (0-8021-3655-9) Grove-Atltic.

— Tight White Collar. LC 93-13352. 224p. 1993. pap. 10.00 (0-14-015526-0, Penguin Bks) Viking Penguin.

***L'Heureux, John.** A Woman Run Mad. 2000. pap. 13.00 (0-8021-3731-8, Grove) Grove-Atltic.

L'Heureux, John. A Woman Run Mad. 1999. pap. write for info. (0-14-010194-2, Viking) Viking Penguin.

— A Woman Run Mad. 240p. 1989. reprint ed. mass mkt. 4.99 (0-380-70686-5, Avon Bks) Morrow Avon.

L'Heureux, Mother Aloysius G. Mystical Vocabulary of Venerable Mere Marie De L'Incarnation & Its Problems. LC 72-94190. (Catholic University of America. Studies in Romance Languages & Literatures: No. 53). (FRE.). reprint ed. 37.50 (0-404-50353-5) AMS Pr.

Lhevinne, Josef. Basic Principles in Pianoforte Playing. LC 74-157433. Orig. Title: The Etude. 50p. 1972. reprint ed. pap. 3.95 (0-486-22820-7) Dover.

***Lhevinne, Josef.** Basic Principles in Pianoforte Playing. (Music Book Index Ser.). Orig. Title: The Etude. 2000. reprint ed. lib. bdg. 59.00 (0-7812-9175-5) Rprt Serv.

L'Hevreux, Raymond. Cabinetmaking: Building Drawers. LC 81-730635. 1981. student ed. 7.00 (0-8064-0267-9, 705) Bergwall.

— Cabinetmaking: Rod Layout. LC 80-730671. 1981. student ed. 7.00 (0-8064-0265-2, 704) Bergwall.

Lho, Kyongsoo, jt. ed. see Henriksen, Thomas H.

L'Hoaste, Simon S., tr. see Carle, Eric.

L'Hoeste, Simon S., tr. see Carle, Eric.

Lhomeau, Franck & Coelho, Alain. Marcel Proust: Remembrance of Publishers Past. Destree, Sabine, tr. from FRE. 320p. 2000. 24.45 (1-55970-058-0, Pub. by Arcade Pub Inc) Time Warner.

L'Hommedieu, Art. Bats. (Information Ser.). (J). (ps-3). 1995. 6.99 (0-85953-956-3) Childs Play.

— Bats, Giant. (Information Ser.). (J). 1997. pap. 13.99 (0-85953-962-8) Childs Play.

— Butterfly: Butterfly. (Information Ser.). 8p. (J). (ps-3). 1994. 6.99 (0-85953-170-8) Childs Play.

— Egg, Tadpole, Frog: Egg, Tadpole, Frog. (Information Ser.). 8p. (J). (ps-3). 1994. 6.99 (0-85953-169-4) Childs Play.

— Spiders. LC 97-883. (Information Ser.). (J). (ps-5). 1997. pap. 6.99 (0-85953-957-1) Childs Play.

L'Hommedieu, Art. Spiders: Giant. large type ed. (Information Ser.). (J). 1997. pap. 13.99 (0-85953-960-1) Childs Play.

L'Hommedieu, Art. Time Tunnel. (J). (ps-3). 1995. 10.99 (0-85953-940-7) Childs Play.

Lhommedieu, Arthur J. Children of the Sun. 24p. (J). (ps-3). 1993. 10.99 (0-85953-931-8) Childs Play.

L'Hommedieu, Arthur J. Children of the Sun. (J). (gr. k-11). 10.99 (0-85953-939-3); 10.99 (0-85953-938-5) Childs Play.

Lhommedieu, Arthur J. Children of the Sun-Big Book. (J). 1996. pap. text 24.99 (0-85953-937-7) Childs Play.

— From Plant to Blue Jeans. LC 97-23610. (Changes Ser.). (J). (gr. 2-3). 1998. pap. text 6.95 (0-516-20366-5) Childrens.

— From Plant to Blue Jeans: A Photo Essay. LC 97-23610. (Changes Ser.). (Illus.). (J). (gr. 2-3). 1997. lib. bdg. 24.00 (0-516-20738-5) Childrens.

— Ocean Tide Pool. LC 97-17674. (Habitats Ser.). (Illus.). 32p. (gr. 2-3). 1997. lib. bdg. 24.00 (0-516-20740-7) Childrens.

— Ocean Tide Pool. LC 97-17674. (Habitats Ser.). (J). 1998. pap. text 6.95 (0-516-20373-8) Childrens.

L'Hommedieu, Arthur J. Working at a Museum. LC 98-13207. (Working Here Ser.). (Illus.). 32p. (J). (ps-5). 1998. 23.00 (0-516-20748-2) Childrens.

— Working at a Museum. (Illus.). 32p. (J). (gr. 2-4). 1999. pap. text 6.95 (0-516-20590-0) Childrens.

L'Hommedieu, P. H., jt. auth. see L'Hommedieu, William A.

L'Hommedieu, Toni. The Divorce Experience of Working & Middle Class Women. LC 83-17967. (Research in Clinical Psychology Ser.: No. 8). 178p. reprint ed. pap. 55.20 (0-8357-1478-0, 207040000088) Bks Demand.

L'Hommedieu, William A. & L'Hommedieu, P. H. L'Hommedieu Genealogy, 2 vols., Set. (Illus.). 930p. 1994. reprint ed. pap. 125.00 (0-8328-4342-3); reprint ed. lib. bdg. 135.00 (0-8328-4341-5) Higginson Bk Co.

***Lhoning, Karl & Zenger, Erich.** To Begin with, God Created... Biblical Theologies of Creation. LC 99-49576. 200p. 2000. 19.95 (0-8146-5937-3) Liturgical Pr.

Lhonnrot, Elias, jt. auth. see Magoun, Francis P.

Lhoscher, Wolfgang. Valproate. LC 99-18269. (Milestones in Drug Therapy Ser.). 1999. write for info. (0-8176-5836-X) Birkhauser.

Lhote, Gilles. Cowboys of the Sky. Clyman, Jacky & Clyman, Jeff, trs. from FRE. 160p. 1988. write for info. (0-9621229-0-4) Avirex Ltd.

L

Lhote, Pierre. Essai sur le Mouvement Cobra: L'Emploi de la Couleur Chez Asger Jorn, Karel Appel et Pierre Alechinsky. (Publications Universitaires Europeennes Ser.: Series 28, Vol. 244). (FRE.). 168p. 1996. 30.95 (*3-906754-16-2*, Pub. by P Lang) P Lang Pubng.

***Lhote, Pierre.** Recherches Sur la Technique Picturale de Vincent Van Gogh: Essai. xx, 134p. 1999. 26.95 (*3-906762-78-5*) P Lang Pubng.

***Lhotka, Edward R.** ABC of Leather Bookbinding: An Illustrated Manual on Traditional Bookbinding. LC 00-39996. (Illus.). 2000. write for info. (*1-58456-026-6*) Oak Knoll.

Lhotka, John F., Jr. Introduction to East Roman (Byzantine) Coinage. 2nd rev. ed. LC 88-72080. (Illus.). 128p. 1989. reprint ed. pap. 15.00 (*0-942666-53-4*) S J Durst.

— Introduction to Medieval Bracteates. 2nd rev. ed. LC 88-72318. (Illus.). 80p. 1989. reprint ed. pap. 12.00 (*0-942666-52-6*) S J Durst.

Lhotka, John F. Medieval Feudal French Coinage. 2nd ed. (Illus.). 1997. pap. 15.00 (*0-685-36401-1*) S J Durst.

Lhotka, John F. & Anderson, P. K. Survey of Medieval Iberian Coinages. 2nd rev. ed. LC 88-72079. 128p. 1989. reprint ed. pap. 15.00 (*0-942666-54-2*) S J Durst.

***Lhotka, Rockford.** Implementing Visual Basic 6 Distributed Objects. (Illus.). 500p. 1999. pap. 49.99 (*1-86100-207-6*) Wrox Pr Inc.

— Professional Visual Basic 6.0 Business Objects. 700p. 1998. pap. 59.99 (*1-86100-107-X*) Wrox Pr Inc.

***Lhotka, Rockford & Moniz, Joseph.** Wrox Visual Basic Enterprise Developer's Resource Kit. 2000p. 1999. 129.99 (*1-86100-345-5*) Wrox Pr Inc.

L'Hotte, Alexis F. Ein Offizier der Cavallerie. (GER., Illus.). 344p. 1979. write for info. (*3-487-08186-5*) G Olms Pubs.

— Reitfragen (Questions Equestres) 164p. 1977. write for info. (*3-487-08122-9*) G Olms Pubs.

Lhoyd, H., tr. see Caradoc Of Llancarfan.

***LHP Editorial Staff.** Fiji. 96p. 1999. pap. 14.95 (*1-86315-129-X*) Bilingual Bks.

Lhucke, Friedrich, jt. auth. see Schleiermacher, Friedrich Daniel Ernst.

Lhuillier, Alberto R. La Civilizacion de los Antiguos Mayas (Civilization of the Acient Mayas) 3rd ed. (SPA.). 95p. 1991. pap. 8.99 (*968-16-3514-0*, Pub. by Fondo) Continental Bk.

L'Huillier, Monique. Advanced French Grammar. LC 98-22110. 650p. (C). 1999. text 74.95 (*0-521-48228-3*); pap. text 32.95 (*0-521-48425-1*) Cambridge U Pr.

L'Huillier, Peter. The Church of the Ancient Councils: The Disciplinary Work of the First Four Ecumenical Councils. LC 95-50117. 352p. 1995. pap. 19.95 (*0-88141-007-1*) St Vladimirs.

L'Hygiene Populaire Staff. Dictionnaire Chinois-Francais des Termes Medicaux Usuels. (CHI & FRE.). 1990. write for info. (*0-7859-8702-9*, 7117006668) Fr & Eur.

Li. Taiwan Business Law. Date not set. write for info. (*90-6544-445-9*) Kluwer Law Intl.

Li, Jian, et al. Eternal China: Splendors from the First Dynasties. LC 98-70294. 196 p. 1998. write for info. (*0-937809-15-2*) Dayton Art.

Li, Xiao-bing, jt. auth. see Jung, Walter B.

Li, Xiao-bing, jt. ed. see Jung, Walter B.

Li, Alain W. Statistics for Pharmacists. LC 97-20887. 1997. pap. 34.95 (*0-632-04881-6*) Blackwell Sci.

Li, Alain Wan Po & Li, G. Wan Po. OTC Medications: Symptoms & Treatments of Common Illnesses. 2nd ed. LC 97-11878. 1997. pap. 34.95 (*0-632-04046-7*) Blackwell Sci.

Li, Albert P., ed. Advances in Pharmacology Vol. 43: Drug - Drug Interactions: Scientific & Regulatory Perspectives. (Illus.). 304p. 1997. text 89.95 (*0-12-032944-1*) Morgan Kaufmann.

— Genetic Toxicology. 1991. 84.95 (*0-685-48568-4*, RA1224, CRC Reprint) Franklin.

Li, Albert P., et al, eds. Toxicity Testing: New Approaches & Applications in Human Risk Assessment. fac. ed. LC 84-27634. 300p. pap. 93.00 (*0-7837-7281-5*, 204702500005) Bks Demand.

Li, Albert P. & Heflich, Robert H. Genetic Toxicology. 493p. 1991. lib. bdg. 139.00 (*0-8493-8815-5*, RA1224) CRC Pr.

— Genetic Toxicology: A Treatise. 500p. 1990. 65.00 (*0-936923-38-5*) Telford Pr.

Li, Allen. Intellectual Property: Fees Are Not Always Commensurate with the Costs of Services. (Illus.). 132p. (C). 1998. pap. text 30.00 (*0-7881-4745-5*) DIANE Pub.

Li, Allen, et al, eds. Aviation Safety: FAA Can Better Prepare General Aviation Pilots for Mountain Flying Risks. 68p. 1998. reprint ed. pap. text 20.00 (*0-7881-4155-4*) DIANE Pub.

Li, Andrea Yeo Lyn, ed. Second Mekong Tourism Forum: Proceedings from the Second Mekong Tourism Forum. 71p. 1997. pap. 35.00 (*981-04-0362-3*) Pac Asia Trvl.

Li Ang. The Butcher's Wife & Other Stories. Goldblatt, Howard, ed. & tr. by. from CHI. LC 95-24838. 245p. 1995. pap. text 18.95 (*0-88727-222-3*) Cheng & Tsui.

Li, Anita M. & Yeung, Chap-Yung. A Clinical Atlas of Chinese Infants. LC 97-178884. (Illus.). 97p. (Orig.). 1996. pap. 32.50 (*962-209-390-6*, Pub. by HK Univ Pr) Coronet Bks.

Li, B. H. & Deng, J. T., eds. Information Control Problems in Manufacturing 1995. (IFAC Postprint Ser.). 1996. pap. text. write for info. (*0-08-042380-9*, Pergamon Pr) Elsevier.

Li, B. Q., ed. Processing of Metals & Advanced Materials: Modeling, Design & Properties. LC 97-75877. (Illus.). 306p. 1998. 90.00 (*0-87339-395-3*, 3953) Minerals Metals.

Li, Barbara, jt. auth. see Christensen, Kathy.

Li, Bingren, et al, eds. Functional Analysis in China. LC 95-47761. (Mathematics & Its Applications Ser.: Vol. 356). 373p. (C). 1996. text 191.50 (*0-7923-3880-4*) Kluwer Academic.

***Li, Bingren, et al.** Quantitative Analysis, Trading Strategies & Risk Management for Fixed-Income Markets. 300p. 2000. 46.00 (*981-02-4079-1*) World Scientific Pub.

Li, Bingren, jt. auth. see Tsai, Jeffrey J.

Li, Bozhong. Agricultural Development in Jiangnan, 1620-1850. LC 97-9154. (Studies on the Chinese Economy). 224p. 1998. text 69.95 (*0-312-17529-9*) St Martin.

Li, C. K., et al. Children's Sexual Encounters with Adults: A Scientific Study. LC 92-43601. 343p. (C). 1993. 43.95 (*0-87975-820-1*) Prometheus Bks.

Li, C. Y. & Maser, Chris. New & Modified Techniques for Studying Nitrogen-Fixing Bacteria in Small Mammal Droppings. (Illus.). 8p. 1997. reprint ed. pap. 1.30 (*0-89904-650-9*, Wildlife Resrch Grp) Crumb Elbow Pub.

Li, C. Y., et al. Stress Induced Phenomena in Metallization. (AIP Conference Proceedings Ser.: No. 263). 288p. 1992. 95.00 (*1-56396-082-6*) Am Inst Physics.

Li, Can & Xin, Qin, eds. Spillover & Migration of Surface Species on Catalysts: Proceedings of the 4th International Conference on Spillover, Dalian, China, 15-18 September, 1997. LC 97-29219. (Studies in Surface Science & Catalysis: Vol. 112). 538p. 1997. 284.00 (*0-444-82333-6*) Elsevier.

Li, Carlos M., et al. Dynamic Cardiomyoplasty: The Mechanisms & Optimization of Programming. LC 97-29969. (Current Clinical Practices in Dynamic Cardiomyoplasty Ser.: Vol. 1). (Illus.). 67p. 1997. pap. 15.00 (*0-87993-686-X*) Futura Pub.

Li-Chan, Eunice, jt. auth. see Nakai, Shuryo.

Li, Chao-Jun & Chan, Tak-Hang. Organic Reactions in Aqueous Media. LC 96-29886. 216p. 1997. 64.95 (*0-471-16395-3*) Wiley.

Li, Charles. Invariant Manifolds & Fibrations for Perturbed Nonlinear Schrodinger Equations. LC 97-15251. 180p. 1997. 39.00 (*0-387-94925-9*) Spr-Verlag.

— The Origins of Language. 224p. 2001. 23.00 (*0-06-039196-0*, ReganBks) HarperTrade.

Li, Charles & Talania, Franquintin. Professional Engineers (Civil) License Reviewer (Solved Problems) LC 89-81648. (Illus.). 300p. 1990. pap. 34.00 (*0-929176-07-3*) Burdick & Landreth Co.

Li, Charles N. & Thompson, Sandra A. Mandarin Chinese: A Functional Reference Grammar. LC 80-6054. 1981. pap. 27.50 (*0-520-06610-3*, Pub. by U CA Pr) Cal Prin Full Svc.

Li, Charles N., jt. ed. see Hyman, Larry M.

Li, Chen. The Clever Fartuma. (Asian Folk Tales Ser.). (Illus.). 24p. (J). 1995. 9.95 (*983-9808-65-6*, Pub. by Delta Edits) Weatherhill.

— Fadilah & the Magic Men. (Asian Folk Tales Ser.). (Illus.). 24p. (J). 1995. 9.95 (*983-9808-64-8*, Pub. by Delta Edits) Weatherhill.

— Fairy Maiden Carved in Wood. (Asian Folk Tales Ser.). (Illus.). 24p. (J). 1995. 9.95 (*983-9808-69-9*, Pub. by Delta Edits) Weatherhill.

— A Gold Comb. (Asian Folk Tales Ser.). (Illus.). 24p. (J). 1995. 9.95 (*983-9808-71-0*, Pub. by Delta Edits) Weatherhill.

— Magic Bow & Silver Flute. (Asian Folk Tales Ser.). (Illus.). 24p. (J). 1995. 9.95 (*983-9808-67-2*, Pub. by Delta Edits) Weatherhill.

— Mansul. (Asian Folk Tales Ser.). (Illus.). 24p. (J). 1995. 9.95 (*983-9808-68-0*, Pub. by Delta Edits) Weatherhill.

— Three Gold Bricks. (Asian Folk Tales Ser.). (Illus.). 24p. (J). 1995. 9.95 (*983-9808-63-X*, Pub. by Delta Edits) Weatherhill.

— The Three Problems. (Asian Folk Tales Ser.). (Illus.). 24p. (J). 1995. 9.95 (*983-9808-66-4*, Pub. by Delta Edits) Weatherhill.

— Two Brothers. (Asian Folk Tales Ser.). (Illus.). 24p. (J). 1995. 9.95 (*983-9808-70-2*, Pub. by Delta Edits) Weatherhill.

— Wahab & His Animal Friends. (Asian Folk Tales Ser.). (Illus.). 24p. (J). 1995. 9.95 (*983-9808-72-9*, Pub. by Delta Edits) Weatherhill.

Li, Cheng. Rediscovering China: Dynamics & Dilemmas of Reform. LC 96-45616. (Illus.). 376p. 1996. pap. 19.95 (*0-8476-8338-9*); text 67.50 (*0-8476-8337-0*) Rowman.

Li Cheng Sen. Atlas of Fossil Plant Anatomy in China. (ENG & LAT.). 1995. 135.00 (*0-7855-0524-5*, Pub. by Wanhai Books) St Mut.

***Li Chengsen & Cui Jinzhong.** Global Karst Correlation. (Chinese Science Studies). 300p. 1999. 150.00 (*7-03-006837-8*) Intl Scholars.

Li, Chenyang. The Tao Encounters the West: Explorations in Comparative Philosophy. LC 98-31714. (SUNY Series in Chinese Philosophy & Culture). 256p. (C). 1999. text 59.50 (*0-7914-4135-0*, Suny Pr); pap. text 19.95 (*0-7914-4136-9*, Suny Pr) State U NY Pr.

***Li, Chenyang, ed.** The Sage & the Second Sex: Confucianism, Ethics & Gender. LC 00-29672. 300p. 2000. 24.95 (*0-8126-9418-X*); pap. 24.95 (*0-8126-9419-8*) Open Court.

Li Chi. Anyang. LC 75-40873. (Illus.). 324p. 1978. pap. 30.00 (*0-295-95490-6*) U of Wash Pr.

Li Chi & Johnson, Dale, eds. Two Studies in Chinese Literature. (Michigan Monographs in Chinese Studies: No. 3). (Illus.). 98p. 1968. pap. text 15.00 (*0-89264-003-0*) Ctr Chinese Studies.

Li, Chi-Wang, jt. auth. see Benjamin, Mark M.

Li Ch'iao-P'ing. The Chemical Arts of Old China. LC 75-36234. reprint ed. 37.50 (*0-404-14482-9*) AMS Pr.

Li Chih. Li Chih, Fifteen Twenty-Seven to Sixteen Hundred Two, in Contemporary Chinese Historiography: New Light on His LIfe & Works. LC 79-57496. 231p. reprint ed. pap. 71.70 (*0-608-18122-6*, 203277500081) Bks Demand.

Li Chih-Ch'ang. The Travels of an Alchemist. LC 75-36233. reprint ed. 24.50 (*0-404-14481-0*) AMS Pr.

Li, Chin-Yang, et al. Modern Modalities for the Diagnosis of Hematologic Neoplasms: Color Atlas-Text. LC 95-36945. (Illus.). 272p. 1996. 158.50 (*0-89640-292-4*) Igaku-Shoin.

Li-Ching-Chao. Li-Ch'ing-Chao: Complete Poems. Rexroth, Kenneth & Ling Chung, eds. LC 79-15596. 1980. pap. 8.95 (*0-8112-0745-5*, NDP492, Pub. by New Directions) Norton.

Li, Cho-ming. Economic Development of Communist China: An Appraisal of the First Five Years of Industrialization. LC 84-6517. 284p. 1984. reprint ed. lib. bdg. 89.50 (*0-313-24451-0*, LEDE, Greenwood Pr) Greenwood.

***Li, Choiao.** Wintry Night. LC 00-35882. (Modern Chinese Literature from Taiwan Ser.). 2001. pap. 22.95 (*0-231-12200-4*) Col U Pr.

Li, Chor-Shing. Beitrage Zur Kontrastiven Aspektologie: Das Asperktsystem Im Modernen Chinesisch. (Europaische Hochschulschriften Ser.: Reihe 21, Bd. 102). (GER.). VIII, 328p. 1991. 58.80 (*3-631-44176-2*) P Lang Pubng.

Li, Christine, et al. Real Estate Closing Procedures (1992) LC 84-153773. 147p. 1992. 35.00 (*0-685-10481-8*) NJ Inst CLE.

Li, Chu-tsing, tr. see Nai, Xia.

Li Chuan-Shih. Central & Local Finance in China. LC 68-57573. (Columbia University. Studies in the Social Sciences: No. 226). reprint ed. 20.00 (*0-404-51226-7*) AMS Pr.

Li, Chung. Chinese Astrology. LC 98-208084. (Illus.). 72p. 1998. 9.95 (*1-85368-950-5*, Pub. by New5 Holland) Sterling.

Li, Chung-Sheng, et al, eds. Electronic Imaging & Multimedia Systems, Vol. 2898. 336p. 1996. 46.00 (*0-8194-2299-1*) SPIE.

Li, Chung-Sheng, jt. ed. see Zhou, Liwei.

Li, Chung-Tze. Directory of Chinese-American Librarians. 2nd ed. 45p. 1986. pap. 6.00 (*0-937256-04-8*) Chinese Cult Serv.

Li-Chung Wang. Analytic Functions with Mathematical Philosophy. LC 89-90388. 104p. (Orig.). (C). 1989. pap. text 9.95 (*0-9624242-1-8*) L C Wang Pr.

Li, Chuni. Policy Deployment: Setting the Direction for Change. Hankinson, Mari-Lynn, ed. (AT&T Quality Library). (Illus.). 97p. (Orig.). 1992. pap. 24.95 (*0-932764-31-2*, 500-453) AT&T Customer Info.

Li, Conan K., ed. see Symposium on Electrochemical Sensors for Biomedica.

Li, Conghua. China: The Consumer Revolution. LC 97-35917. 300p. 1998. 27.95 (*0-471-24862-2*) Wiley.

Li Cunbao. The Wreath at the Foot of the Mountain. Hanming, Chen & Belcher, James O., trs. from CHI. LC 90-3019. (Library of World Literature in Translation: Vol. 6). 136p. 1991. text 20.00 (*0-8240-2992-5*) Garland.

Li, D. Y., et al, eds. The Second International Conference on Computational Physics. (Series in Applied Physics). 569p. (C). 1994. text 45.00 (*1-57146-010-1*) Intl Pr Boston.

Li, Daoping. Analysis, Design & Fabrication of Tapered Integrated Optical Structures: Implementation of the Fully Vectorial 3-D Beam Propagation Method. (Illus.). xi, 141p. (Orig.). 1995. pap. 59.50 (*90-407-1154-2*, Pub. by Delft U Pr) Coronet Bks.

Li, David C. Issues in Bilingualism & Biculturalism Vol. 21: A Hong Kong Case Study. (Berkeley Insights in Linguistics & Semiotics Ser.). XVIII, 205p. (C). 1996. text 46.95 (*0-8204-3036-6*) P Lang Pubng.

Li, David H. All-by-Yourself Self-Publishing. LC 96-94440. (Illus.). 254p. (Orig.). 1996. pap. 20.00 (*0-9637852-6-5*) Premier MD.

— Chess Detective: Kriegspiel Strategies, Endgames, & Problems. LC 95-68356. (Illus.). 191p. 1995. pap. 15.00 (*0-9637852-4-9*) Premier MD.

— First Syllabus on Xiangqi: Chinese Chess 1. LC 95-72620. (Illus.). 160p. 1996. pap. 15.00 (*0-9637852-5-7*) Premier MD.

— The Happy Game of Mah-Jong. LC 94-65637. (Illus.). 136p. 1994. pap. 9.95 (*0-9637852-3-0*) Premier MD.

— Kriegspiel: Chess under Uncertainty. LC 93-85826. (Illus.). 144p. 1994. pap. 9.95 (*0-9637852-1-4*) Premier MD.

— Our Town, 1993: A Daily Record of the Twenty Remaining Days of the Bush Administration & the First 100 Days of the Clinton Administration. LC 93-92769. 144p. (Orig.). 1993. pap. 10.00 (*0-9637852-0-6*) Premier MD.

— Xiangqi Syllabus on Cannon: Chinese Chess 2. LC 98-91439. (Illus.). 160p. 1998. pap. 25.00 (*0-9637852-7-3*) Premier MD.

***Li, David H., tr. from CHI.** The Analects of Confucius: A New Millennium Translation (Bilingual) LC 99-93035. (Illus.). 283p. 1999. 20.00 (*0-9637852-8-1*) Premier MD.

Li, David L. Imagining the Nation: Asian American Literature & Cultural Consent. LC 98-24578. (Asian America Ser.). 364p. 1998. 49.50 (*0-8047-3400-3*) Stanford U Pr.

Li, Dejie, jt. auth. see Chang, Keqian.

Li Ding. Acupuncture, Meridian Theory & Acupuncture Points. You Benlin & Wang Zhaorong, trs. from CHI. (Illus.). 414p. (C). 1992. reprint ed. text 60.00 (*0-8351-2143-7*) China Bks.

Li, Elizabeth & Wei, Betty P. Culture Shock! Hong Kong. LC 94-76070. (Illus.). 280p. 1994. pap. 12.95 (*1-55868-167-1*) Gr Arts Ctr Pub.

Li, Evelyn, tr. see Yuen Liao Fan.

Li, Fei-Kan. The Family. Pa, Chin, ed. 1976. lib. bdg. 59.95 (*0-8490-1800-5*) Gordon Pr.

Li, Feng. The Geography of Business Information: Corporate Network & the Spatial & Functional Corporation. LC 94-35284. (Belhaven Studies in the Information Economics). 264p. 1995. text 95.00 (*0-471-94939-6*) Wiley.

***Li, Feng & Li, Jing.** Foreign Investment in China. LC 98-45602. 1999. text 69.95 (*0-312-21913-X*) St Martin.

Li, G. Wan Po, jt. auth. see Li, Alain Wan Po.

Li, Gao-Xiang, jt. auth. see Peng, Jin-Sheng.

***Li, Gertraude Roth.** Manchu: A Textbook for Reading Documents. LC 99-58186. 416p. 2000. pap. text 29.00 (*0-8248-2206-4*) UH Pr.

Li, Gotami G. Tibet in Pictures: A Journey into the Past, 2 vols., Set. LC 79-21352. 210p. 1980. 85.00 (*0-913546-57-7*) Dharma Pub.

Li, H. P. Probabilities & Statistics. 300p. 1993. text 95.00 (*981-02-1650-5*) World Scientific Pub.

Li, Haibo, jt. auth. see Forchheimer, Robert.

Li, Hans. Ancient Ones: Sacred Monuments of the Inca, Maya & Cliffdwellers. 1994. 35.00 (*0-9639556-0-8*) City of Light.

Li, Hau, ed. see Gupta, Madan M.

Li He. Chinese Ceramics: The New Comprehensive Survey from the Asian Art Museum of San Francisco. LC 96-68511. (Illus.). 352p. 1996. 95.00 (*0-8478-1973-6*, Pub. by Rizzoli Intl) St Martin.

Li, He. Sino-Latin American Economic Relations. LC 91-19434. 192p. 1991. 57.95 (*0-275-93759-3*, C3759, Praeger Pubs) Greenwood.

Li He, tr. see Liu, Manni, et al.

Li Heng. Dictionary of Library & Information Sciences. (CHI & ENG.). 400p. 1984. 150.00 (*0-8288-0179-7*, M15588) Fr & Eur.

Li, Hengde. Machine Learning of Design Concepts. 180p. 1995. 91.00 (*1-85312-358-7*) Computational Mech MA.

***Li, Herbert, ed.** Semiconductor Quantum Well Intermixing: Material Properties & Optoelectronic Applications. (Optoelectronic Properties of Semiconductor Ser.: Vol. 8). 688p. 2000. text 159.00 (*90-5699-689-4*, G & B Science) Gordon & Breach.

Li Ho. Poems of Li Ho, 791-817. Frodsham, J. D., tr. (Oxford Library of East Asian Literature Ser.). 1970. 26.00 (*0-19-815436-4*) OUP.

Li, Hong-Chan. Social Work Education. LC 77-19339. 359p. 1978. lib. bdg. 27.50 (*0-8108-1108-1*) Scarecrow.

— Social Work Education II: A Bibliography, 1977-1987. LC 77-19339. 318p. 1989. 31.00 (*0-8108-2195-8*) Scarecrow.

Li, Hong-Xing & Yen, Vincent C. Fuzzy Sets & Fuzzy Decision-Making. LC 95-1571. 288p. 1995. boxed set 79.95 (*0-8493-8931-3*, 8931) CRC Pr.

***Li, Hong-Xing, et al.** Fuzzy Neural Intelligent Systems: Mathematical Foundation & the Applications in Engineering. LC 00-44485. (Illus.). 2000. write for info. (*0-8493-2360-6*) CRC Pr.

Li, Hongshan & Hong, Zhaohui. Image, Perception & the Making of U. S.-China Relations. LC 98-7510. 420p. (C). 1998. 67.00 (*0-7618-1157-5*); pap. 42.50 (*0-7618-1158-3*) U Pr of Amer.

Li, Hongshan, jt. ed. see Li, Xiaobing.

Li, Hongxing, jt. auth. see Wang, Peizhuang.

Li, Hua, jt. ed. see Koch, Christof.

Li, Hua Harry, et al. Video Data Compression for Multimedia Computing: Statistically Based & Biologically Inspired Techniques. LC 96-47147. (International Series in Engineering & Computer Science, Natural Language Processing & Machine Translation). 440p. (C). 1997. text 143.00 (*0-7923-9790-8*) Kluwer Academic.

Li Hui-Lin. Shade & Ornamental Trees: Their Origins & History. LC 96-26742. (Illus.). 288p. (Orig.). 1996. reprint ed. pap. 15.95 (*0-8122-1605-9*) U of Pa Pr.

Li i, B., et al, eds. Theory & Technology of Quenching: A Handbook. (Illus.). 512p. 1992. 326.95 (*0-387-52040-6*) Spr-Verlag.

Li, Itunda Y. Analysis of Bulk Flow of Materials under Gravity Caving Process: Pt. 1: Sublevel Caving in Relation to Flow in Bins & Bunkers. Raese, Jon W., ed. LC 81-129. (Colorado School of Mines Quarterly Ser.: Vol. 75, No. 4). (Illus.). 45p. 1981. pap. 8.00 (*0-686-74853-0*) Colo Sch Mines.

Li, Iun J. The Ageless Chinese: A History. 3rd ed. LC 73-159451. 629p. (C). 1978. pap. text 46.60 (*0-02-370550-7*, Macmillan Coll) P-H.

Li, J. C. Microstructure & Properties of Materials, Vol. 1. LC 96-225067. 500p. 1996. text 98.00 (*981-02-2403-6*) World Scientific Pub.

Li, J. C., ed. see International Symposium on Rate Processes in Plast.

***Li, J. C. M.** Microstructure & Properties of Materials, Vol. 2. 2000. 78.00 (*981-02-4180-1*) World Scientific Pub.

Li, J. J., et al, eds. Hormonal Carcinogenesis: Proceedings of the First International Symposia, March 19-21, 1991. (Illus.). 392p. 1992. 102.00 (*0-387-97797-X*) Spr-Verlag.

— Hormonal Carcinogenesis II: Proceedings of the Second International Symposium on Hormonal Carcinogenesis, No. II. 500p. 1995. 115.00 (*0-387-94469-9*) Spr-Verlag.

Li, J. K., jt. auth. see Wang, H. P.

Li, Jenni. Passport China: Your Pocket Guide to Chinese Business, Customs & Etiquette. Szerlip, Barbara, ed. LC 96-14389. (Passport to the World Ser.). (Illus.). 96p. (Orig.). 1996. pap. 6.95 (*1-885073-16-X*) Wrld Trade Pr.

Li, Jenny. Learning Chinese with Fun. (Illus.). (Orig.). 1967. pap. 3.75 (*0-910286-24-8*) Boxwood.

Li, Jiali & Bennett, Neil. One in Four: America's Youngest Poor. unabridged ed. LC 96-38526. (Illus.). 88p. 1996. pap. 16.95 (*0-926582-20-8*) NCCP.

***Li, Jiequan, et al.** The Two-Dimensional Reimann Problem for Systems of Conservation Laws. 312p. 1999. 89.95 (*0-8493-0693-0*) CRC Pr.

Li, Jing, jt. auth. see Li, Feng.

Li Jinxue & Wei Yuanping. Chinese Manipulation & Massage: Chinese Manipulative Therapy (CMT) (International Academic Publishers Ser.). 1990. text 70.00 (*0-08-037488-3*, Pergamon Pr) Elsevier.

Li, Jinyan. Taxation in the People's Republic of China. LC 90-19994. 208p. 1991. 62.95 (*0-275-93688-0*, C3688, Praeger Pubs) Greenwood.

Li, John K. Comparative Cardiovascular Dynamics of Mammals. 176p. 1995. boxed set 149.95 (*0-8493-0169-6*, 169) CRC Pr.

Li, John K., jt. ed. see Drzewiecki, Gary M.

***Li, John K. J.** The Arterial Circulation: Physical Principles & Clinical Applications. 288p. 2000. 125.00 (*0-89603-633-2*) Humana.

Li, John Papa. Fragments of Hawaiian History. rev. ed. Barrere, Dorothy B., ed. Pukui, Mary K., tr. (Special Publications: No. 70). (Illus.). 212p. 1983. pap. 19.95 (*0-910240-31-0*) Bishop Mus.

Li-Jost, Xianqing, jt. auth. see Jost, Jurgen.

Li, Jui. The Early Revolutionary Activities of Comrade Mao Tse-tung. Hsiung, James C., ed. LC 74-24422. (China Book Project Ser.). 399p. reprint ed. 123.70 (*0-608-17071-2*, 202762000055) Bks Demand.

Li, Junheng & Harrington, James A., eds. Biomedical Optics & Lasers: Diagnostics & Treatment. LC 98-233180. (Proceedings of SPIE Ser.: Vol. 3548). 250p. 1998. 80.00 (*0-8194-3009-9*) SPIE.

Li, K., jt. auth. see Liu, T. S.

***Li, K. S., et al, eds.** Slope Engineering in Hong Kong: Proceedings of the Annual Seminar, Hong Kong, 2 May 1997. LC 99-496426. (Illus.). 450p. 1998. 93.00 (*90-5410-935-1*, Pub. by A A Balkema) Ashgate Pub Co.

Li, K. S. & Lo, S. C., eds. Probabilistic Methods in Geotechnical Engineering: Proceedings of the Conference on Probabilistic Methods in Geotechnical Engineering Canberra - Australia - 10-12 February, 1993. (Illus.). 342p. (C). 1993. text 136.00 (*90-5410-303-5*, Pub. by A A Balkema) Ashgate Pub Co.

Li, K. T. The Economic Transformation of Taiwan. (Illus.). 448p. 1988. text 55.00 (*0-85683-108-5*, Pub. by Shepheard-Walwyn Pubs) Paul & Co Pubs.

— The Evolution of Policy Behind Taiwan's Development Success. 300p. 1995. text 46.00 (*981-02-1838-9*) World Scientific Pub.

Li, Kam W. Applied Thermodynamics: Availability Method & Energy Conversion. (Combustion: an International Ser.). 369p. 1995. 85.00 (*1-56032-349-3*) Taylor & Francis.

Li, Kam W. & Priddy, A. Paul. Power Plant System Design. LC 84-22177. 656p. 1985. text 111.95 (*0-471-88847-8*) Wiley.

Li, Ke-Zheng, ed. see Oort, Frans.

Li, Keqin, et al. Parallel Computing Using Optical Interconnections. LC 98-41635. (International Series in Engineering & Computer Science). 279p. 1998. write for info. (*0-7923-8296-X*) Kluwer Academic.

Li, Kevin, jt. auth. see Harris, James.

***Li, Kit-Man.** Western Civilization & Its Problems: A Dialogue between Weber, Elias & Habermas. (Avebury Series in Philosophy). 308p. 1999. text 69.95 (*1-84014-179-4*, Pub. by Inst Materials) Ashgate Pub Co.

Li, Kui Wai. Financial Repression & Economic Reform in China. LC 93-50074. 208p. 1994. 59.95 (*0-275-94801-3*, Praeger Pubs) Greenwood.

Li, Kui-Wai, ed. Financing China Trade & Investment. LC 96-20691. 304p. 1997. 75.00 (*0-275-95115-4*, Praeger Pubs) Greenwood.

Li, Kung-Lin, jt. auth. see Harrist, Robert E.

Li Kung Shaw. Purposive Biology. LC 81-90747. (Illus.). 359p. (C). 1982. text 20.00 (*0-9607806-0-2*); pap. text 15.00 (*0-9607806-1-0*) Li Kung Shaw.

Li, Kwok-sing. A Glossary of Political Terms of People's Republic of China. Lok, Mary, tr. from CHI. LC 96-228604. 680p. (Orig.). (C). 1997. pap. text 29.95 (*962-201-615-4*, Pub. by Chinese Univ) U of Mich Pr.

Li, L. Java: Data Structures & Programming. LC 98-25666. x, 350p. 1998. 49.95 (*3-540-63763-X*) Spr-Verlag.

Li, Leslie. Bittersweet. 512p. 1994. pap. 12.95 (*0-8048-3036-3*) Tuttle Pubng.

Li, Li. Deviant Fertility in China. LC 97-209464. 178p. (C). 1997. lib. bdg. 85.00 (*1-56072-445-5*) Nova Sci Pubs.

Li, Liangqing. Classification of Simple C* - Algebras: Inductive Limits of Matrix Algebras. LC 97-421. (Memoirs of the American Mathematical Society Ser.: Vol. 127/605). 123p. 1997. pap. 39.00 (*0-8218-0596-7*, MEMO/127/605) Am Math.

Li, Lillian M. China's Silk Trade: Traditional Industry in the Modern World, 1842-1937. (East Asian Monographs: No. 97). (Illus.). 309p. 1981. 32.50 (*0-674-11962-2*) HUP.

Li, Lillian M., jt. ed. see Rawski, Thomas G.

Li, Lincoln. The China Factor in Modern Japanese Thought: The Case of Tachibana Shiraki, 1881-1945. LC 96-3630. (Series in Chinese Philosophy & Culture). 171p. (C). 1996. text 65.50 (*0-7914-3039-1*); pap. text 21.95 (*0-7914-3040-5*) State U NY Pr.

— Student Nationalism in China, 1924-1949. LC 93-6639. (SUNY Series in Chinese Philosophy & Culture). 209p. (C). 1994. text 59.50 (*0-7914-1749-2*); pap. text 19.95 (*0-7914-1750-6*) State U NY Pr.

***Li, Linda C.** Centre & Provinces: China, 1978-1993: Power as Non-Zero-Sum. LC 97-39265. (Studies on Contemporary China). (Illus.). 360p. 1998. text 85.00 (*0-19-829361-5*) OUP.

Li, Ling-Fong, jt. auth. see Cheng, Ta-Pei.

Li Ling Hin. Privatization of Urban Land in Shanghai. 190p. (Orig.). 1997. pap. 39.50 (*962-209-421-X*, Pub. by HK Univ Pr) Coronet Bks.

Li, Liwu. The VisualAge for Smalltalk Primer. LC 98-229103. (Advances in Object Technology Ser.: No. 16). 320p. (C). 1998. pap. 44.95 (*0-521-64669-3*) Cambridge U Pr.

Li, Marjorie & Li, Peter, eds. Understanding Asian Americans: A Curriculum Resource Guide. 185p. (Orig.). 1990. pap. text 38.50 (*1-55570-047-0*) Neal-Schuman.

Li Mei-Ge, tr. see Jackins, Harvey.

Li, Min. NMDA Receptor Protocols. LC 98-53445. (Methods in Molecular Biology Ser.: Vol. 128). (Illus.). 208p. 1999. 79.50 (*0-89603-713-4*) Humana.

Li, Ming, et al, eds. Algorithmic Learning Theory: 8th International Workshop, ALT '97, Sendai, Japan, October 6-8, 1997 : Proceedings. LC 97-38160. (Lecture Notes in Computer Science Ser.: Vol. 1316). xi, 461p. 1997. pap. 69.00 (*3-540-63577-7*) Spr-Verlag.

Li, Ming & Vitanyi, Paul M. An Introduction to Kolmogorov Complexity & Its Applications. 2nd ed. LC 96-42357. (Graduate Texts in Computer Science Ser.). (Illus.). 637p. 1997. 49.95 (*0-387-94868-6*) Spr-Verlag.

Li, Ming, jt. auth. see International Conference on Production Research Staff.

Li, Ming, jt. auth. see Song, C. Charlie.

Li, Ming, jt. auth. see Vitanyi, Paul M.

Li, Ming-Fu. Modern Semiconductor Quantum Physics. (Solid State Electronics Ser.). 588p. 1995. text 84.00 (*981-02-1599-1*) World Scientific Pub.

Li Ming Yu, tr. see DuoDuo Staff.

Li, Mirok. The Yalu Flows: A Korean Childhood. Chung, Kyu-Hwa, ed. Hammelmann, H. A. & Gutensohn, Gertraud, trs. from KOR. (Illus.). 204p. 1987. 17.50 (*0-930878-75-2*) Hollym Intl.

Li, N. Recent Developments in Separation Science, 2 vols. LC 72-88417. 1982. 243.00 (*0-8493-5031-X*) CRC Pr.

Li, N., ed. see Fang, Z. Y., et al.

Li, Nian P. Old Tales of China. (Illus.). 206p. 1983. reprint ed. pap. 4.95 (*9971-947-34-X*) Heian Intl.

Li, Norman C., jt. ed. see Bunger, James W.

Li, Norman N. Recent Developments in Separation Science, Vol. VI. 208p. 1982. 113.00 (*0-8493-5487-0*, TP156, CRC Reprint) Franklin.

— Recent Developments in Separation Science, Vol. VII. 224p. 1982. 130.00 (*0-8493-5488-9*, CRC Reprint) Franklin.

Li, Norman N. & Calo, Joseph M., eds. Recent Developments in Separation Science, Vol. IX. 352p. 1986. 197.00 (*0-8493-5490-0*, TP156, CRC Reprint) Franklin.

— Separation & Purification Technology. LC 92-19323. (Illus.). 320p. 1992. text 155.00 (*0-8247-8721-8*) Dekker.

Li, Norman N. & Navratil, James D., eds. Recent Developments in Separation Science, Vol. VIII. 344p. 1986. 204.00 (*0-8493-5489-7*, TP156) CRC Pr.

Li, P., et al, eds. A Mathematician & His Mathematical Work - Selected Papers of S. S. Chern. (World Scientific Series in 20th Century Mathematics: Vol. 4). 700p. 1996. text 86.00 (*981-02-2385-4*) World Scientific Pub.

***Li, P., et al, eds.** Mineralization in Natural & Synthetic Biomaterials Vol. 599: Materials Research Society Symposium Proceedings. (Materials Research Society Symposium Proceedings Ser.). 2000. text 86.00 (*1-55899-507-2*) Materials Res.

Li, P. K., ed. A Text of Chinese Military Terms. (CHI & ENG.). 390p. 1972. pap. 12.95 (*0-7859-0792-0*, M-9577) Fr & Eur.

Li, Patrick. Fashion Publication: Creative Time In The Anchorage: Exposing Meaning In Fashion Through Present. 1999. pap. text 24.95 (*1-928570-00-3*) Creat Time.

Li, Paul H. Advances in Plant Cold Hardiness. 352p. 1992. lib. bdg. 199.00 (*0-8493-4950-8*, QK756) CRC Pr.

Li, Paul H., ed. Low Temperature Stress Physiology in Crops. 208p. 1988. 124.00 (*0-8493-6567-8*, SB781, CRC Reprint) Franklin.

Li, Paul H. & Chen, Tony H., eds. Plant Cold Hardiness: Molecular Biology, Biochemistry & Physiology: Proceedings of the 5th International Seminar Held in Corvallis, Oregon, August 4-8, 1996. LC 97-28663. (Illus.). 380p. (C). 1998. text 150.00 (*0-306-45712-1*, Kluwer Plenum) Kluwer Academic.

Li, Paul M., intro. California Judges' Benchbook: Criminal Posttrial Proceedings 1991, 4 vols., Set. LC 90-82513. 368p. 1991. pap. text 65.00 (*0-88124-382-5*, CR-31791) Cont Ed Bar-CA.

— California Judges' Benchbook: Criminal Pretrial Proceedings 1991, 4 vols., Set. LC 90-82514. 253p. 1991. pap. text 65.00 (*0-88124-380-9*, CR-31791) Cont Ed Bar-CA.

— California Judges' Benchbook: Criminal Trials 1991, Set. LC 90-82512. 266p. 1991. pap. text 65.00 (*0-88124-381-7*, CR-31791) Cont Ed Bar-CA.

— California Judges Benchbook: Nineteen Ninety-One Edition, 4 vols., Set. 1342p. 1991. pap. text 65.00 (*0-88124-379-5*, CR-31791) Cont Ed Bar-CA.

Li, Peter, et al. Culture & Politics in China: An Anatomy of Tiananmen Square. 250p. (C). 1990. 34.95 (*0-88738-353-X*) Transaction Pubs.

Li, Peter, jt. ed. see Li, Marjorie.

Li, Peter K., jt. auth. see Feit, Marvin D.

Li, Peter S. The Chinese in Canada. 2nd ed. LC 98-207038. 224p. 1998. pap. text 21.00 (*0-19-541271-0*) OUP.

— The Making of Post-War Canada. 200p. 1997. pap. text 24.00 (*0-19-540920-5*) OUP.

***Li, Peter S.** Race & Ethnic Relations in Canada. 2nd ed. LC 99-461879. 424p. 1999. pap. text 29.95 (*0-19-541477-2*) OUP.

Li Po. The Selected Poems of Li Po. Hinton, David, tr. from CHI. LC 96-5139. 160p. (Orig.). 1996. pap. 11.95 (*0-8112-1323-4*, NDP823, Pub. by New Directions) Norton.

Li Po, et al. Li Po & Tu Fu: Poems. Cooper, Arthur, tr. & intro. by. (Classics Ser.). (Illus.). 256p. (Orig.). 1973. pap. 10.95 (*0-14-044272-3*, Penguin Classics) Viking Penguin.

Li, Q. B., ed. High Energy Astrophysics: Compact Stars & Active Galaxies. 300p. (C). 1991. text 98.00 (*981-02-0697-6*) World Scientific Pub.

Li, Rex. A Theory of Conceptual Intelligence: Thinking, Learning, Creativity, & Giftedness. LC 95-37642. 256p. 1996. 55.00 (*0-275-95326-2*, Praeger Pubs) Greenwood.

***Li, Richard T.** Education & Career: An Immigrant's Journey in the Promise Land with Survival Tips. LC 99-96346. 164p. 1999. pap. 7.95 (*0-9675988-0-X*) R T Li.

Li-ron, Yael. How to Use the Microsoft Network. 1996. pap. 19.99 (*1-56276-375-X*, Ziff-Davis Pr) Que.

***Li, Ronghua, et al.** Generalized Difference Methods for Differential Equations: Numerical Analysis of Finite Volume Methods. LC 99-51331. (Monographs & Textbooks in Pure & Applied Mathematics). 442p. 2000. write for info. (*0-8247-0330-8*) Dekker.

Li, Rongxi, tr. see Numata Center for Buddhist Translation & Research.

Li, S., et al, eds. Recent Developments in Computer Vision: Proceedings, Second Asian Conference on Computer Vision, ACCV '95, Singapore, December 5-8, 1995. LC 96-4291. (Lecture Notes in Computer Science Ser.: Vol. 1035). 604p. 1996. pap. text 94.00 (*3-540-60793-5*) Spr-Verlag.

Li, S. & Yu, S. Culture & Capture of Fish in Chinese Reservoirs. LC 96-155919. 138p. 1995. pap. 17.50 (*0-88936-749-3*, Pub. by IDRC Bks) Stylus Pub VA.

Li, S. F. Capillary Electrophoresis: Principles, Practice, & Applications. LC 92-14151. (Journal of Chromatography Library: Vol. 52). 608p. 1993. reprint ed. 290.75 (*0-444-89433-0*) Elsevier.

— Capillary Electrophoresis: Principles, Practice, & Applications. (Journal of Chromatography Library: Vol. 52). 608p. 1993. reprint ed. pap. 134.00 (*0-444-81590-2*) Elsevier.

Li, S. S. Semiconductor Physical Electronics. (Microdevices: Physics & Fabrication Technologies Ser.). (Illus.). 524p. (C). 1992. text 85.00 (*0-306-44157-8*, Kluwer Plenum) Kluwer Academic.

Li, S. S., et al, eds. Long Wavelength Infrared Detectors & Arrays: Physics & Applications. LC 95-61601. (Proceedings Ser.: Vol. 95-28). (Illus.). 264p. 1995. 44.00 (*1-56677-124-2*) Electrochem Soc.

***Li, S. S., et al, eds.** Long Wavelength Infrared Detectors & Arrays: Physics & Applications VI. 242p. 1999. 46.00 (*1-56677-215-X*, PV 98-21) Electrochem Soc.

Li, S. S., et al, eds. Long Wavelength Infrared Detectors & Arrays V: Physics & Applications. LC 98-158678. (Proceedings Ser.: Vol. 97-33). 280p. 1998. 46.00 (*1-56677-186-2*) Electrochem Soc.

Li, S. X., jt. auth. see L-Z Fang.

Li, S. Z. Markov Random Field Modeling in Computer Vision. Kunii, Toshiyasu L., ed. LC 95-23304. (Computer Science Workbench Ser.). (Illus.). 280p. 1995. 135.00 (*0-387-70145-1*) Spr-Verlag.

Li, Shan. Analyzing Efficiency & Managerial Performance: Using Sensitivity Scores of DEA Models. rev. ed. LC 96-36712. (Studies on Industrial Productivity). (Illus.). 163p. 1996. text 46.00 (*0-8153-2753-6*) Garland.

Li, Shan L. Strategic Investment Planning & Technology Choice in Manufacturing Systems. rev. ed. LC 93-38434. (Studies on Industrial Productivity). 176p. 1994. text 20.00 (*0-8153-1594-5*) Garland.

Li, Shao-ch'Ang. Popular Buddhism in China. lib. bdg. 79.95 (*0-87968-539-5*) Krishna Pr.

Li, Sheng S. & Su Yan-Kuin. Intersubband Transitions in Quantum Wells: Physics & Devices. LC 98-22040. 1998. 145.00 (*0-7923-8164-5*) Kluwer Academic.

Li, Sheng S., jt. auth. see Cristoloveanu, Sorin.

***Li, Shi-zhen.** The Lakeside Master's Study of the Pulse: (Pin-hu Mo Hsueh) Flaws, Bob, tr. from CHI. LC 98-71824. 130p. 1998. pap. 15.95 (*1-891845-01-2*) Blue Poppy Pr.

Li, Shing T., et al. Microcomputer Tools for Communications Engineering. LC 83-71834. (Illus.). 279p. reprint ed. pap. 86.50 (*0-608-16024-5*, 203312300083) Bks Demand.

Li, Shiyou & Adair, Kent T. Camptotheca Acuminata Decaisne, Xi Shu, a Promising Anti-Tumor & Anti-Viral Tree for the Twenty-First Century. (Illus.). 268p. 45.00 (*0-938361-11-2*) Austin Univ Forestry.

— Species Pools of Seed Plants in Eastern Asia & North America. LC 97-35153. (Illus.). 375p. 1997. 79.95 (*0-938361-13-9*) Austin Univ Forestry.

***Li, Shoamin & Tse, David K., eds.** China Markets Yearbook 1999. (Illus.). 1200p. 2000. text 350.00 (*0-7656-0638-0*, East Gate Bk) M E Sharpe.

Li, Shuiang. Mythology & Folklore of the Hui, a Muslim Chinese People. 459p. 1996. pap. 19.95 (*0-614-21520-X*, 1356) Kazi Pubns.

Li, Shujiang & Luckert, Karl W. Mythology & Folklore of the Hui, a Muslim Chinese People. Yu, Fenglan et al, trs. LC 93-21529. (Illus.). 459p. (C). 1994. text 22.50 (*0-7914-1823-5*) State U NY Pr.

Li, Shujuan. Chinese Dictionary of Modern Chinese Slang. 262p. 1999. pap. 14.95 (*0-89346-879-7*) Heian Intl.

***Li, Shuo-Yen Robert.** Algebraic Switching Theory & Broadband Applications. 240p. 2000. 94.95 (*0-12-447181-1*) Acad Pr.

Li, Si M. & Tang, Wing S., eds. China's Regions, Polity & Economy: A Study of Spatial Transformation in the Post-Reform Era. (Illus.). 416p. (C). pap. text 25.00 (*962-201-854-8*, Pub. by Chinese Univ) U of Mich Pr.

Li, Sifa & Mathias, Jack, eds. Freshwater Fish Culture in China: Principles & Practice. LC 94-39744. (Developments in Aquaculture & Fisheries Science Ser.: Vol. 28). 462p. 1994. 227.25 (*0-444-88882-9*) Elsevier.

***Li, Sing.** Professional Jini & JavaSpaces Programming. 500p. 2000. pap. 49.99 (*1-86100-355-2*) Wrox Pr Inc.

Li, Sing & Economopolous, Panos. Professional COM Control Applications with ATL. LC 99-494991. 500p. 1998. pap. 49.99 (*1-86100-170-3*) Wrox Pr Inc.

Li, T-T, ed. Collection of Papers on Geometry, Analysis & Mathematical Physics. LC 97-159897. 250p. 1997. 38.00 (*981-02-3024-9*) World Scientific Pub.

***Li, T-T, et al, eds.** Nonlinear Evolution Equations & Their Applications. 332p. 1999. 58.00 (*981-02-4048-1*) World Scientific Pub.

Li, T. T. & De Mottoni, P. School on Qualitative Aspects & Applications of Nonlinear Evolution Equations. 250p. 1991. text 93.00 (*981-02-0504-X*) World Scientific Pub.

Li, Ta M., et al, eds. Mineral Resource Management by Personal Computer. LC 86-63422. 180p. (Orig.). reprint ed. pap. 55.80 (*0-8357-2566-9*, 204025600015) Bks Demand.

— Mineral Resources of the Pacific Rim: Proceedings of the Special Programming by the Minerals Resource Management Committee During the First International SME-AIME Fall Meeting, Honolulu, Hawaii, September 5-9, 1982. LC 82-71990. (Illus.). 237p. reprint ed. pap. 73.50 (*0-7837-1217-0*, 204174800023) Bks Demand.

Li, Ta-Tsien, ed. Problems & Solutions in Mathematics. LC 98-22020. 500p. 1998. 86.00 (*981-02-3479-1*); pap. 48.00 (*981-02-3480-5*) World Scientific Pub.

Li, Tai W. Marc-Francois Beche's Collection of Eleven Grands Motets by Esprit-Joseph-Antoine Blanchard (1696-1770) (American University Studies XX: Vol. 27). XV, 206p. (C). 1996. text 42.95 (*0-8204-2745-4*) P Lang Pubng.

***Li, Tania Murray.** Transforming the Indonesian Uplands: Marginality, Power & Production. 344p. 1999. text 48.00 (*90-5702-400-4*, Harwood Acad Pubs) Gordon & Breach.

Li-Teik Choo, Andrew. Hearsay & Confrontation in Criminal Trials. (Oxford Monographs on Criminal Law & Justice). (Illus.). 272p. 1996. text 65.00 (*0-19-825891-7*) OUP.

***Li, Thomas S. C.** Medicinal Plants: Culture, Utilization & Phytopharmacology. LC 00-104016. 544p. 2000. text 134.95 (*1-56676-903-5*) Technomic.

Li Tianchi & Wang Shumin, eds. Landslide Hazards & Their Mitigation in China. 100p. 1996. 29.50 (*7-03-003078-6*, Pub. by Sci Pr) Lubrecht & Cramer.

Li, Tien-Yi. Chinese Fiction: A Bibliography of Books & Articles in Chinese & English. 1968. 22.95 (*0-88710-017-1*) Yale Far Eastern Pubns.

— The History of Chinese Literature: A Selected Bibliography. enl. rev. ed. 1968. 16.95 (*0-88710-030-9*) Yale Far Eastern Pubns.

Li, Tien-Yi, compiled by. Selected Readings in Chinese Communist Literature. rev. ed. 1954. 11.95 (*0-88710-080-5*) Yale Far Eastern Pubns.

Li, Tien-Yi, compiled by. Selected Readings in Chinese Communist Literature. rev. ed. 1954. audio 8.95 (*0-88710-081-3*) Yale Far Eastern Pubns.

Li, Tien-Yi, ed. Selected Works of George A. Kennedy. 1964. 25.95 (*0-88710-082-1*) Yale Far Eastern Pubns.

Li, Tien-yi & Chang, Richard F. Advanced Chinese Reader. (CHI & ENG.). 442p. (Orig.). 1997. pap. text 27.95 (*962-201-533-6*, Pub. by Chinese Univ) U of Mich Pr.

Li, Tien-Yi & Liu Wu-Chi, eds. Readings in Modern Chinese Literature, 2 vols. Incl. Vol. 1. Readings in Modern Chinese Literature: Plays & Poems. 3rd ed. 1953. 8.95 incl. audio (*0-88710-071-6*); Vol. 11. Readings in Modern Chinese Literature: Stories. rev. ed. (C). 1953. pap. text 8.95 incl. audio (*0-88710-072-4*); write for info. (*0-88710-073-2*) Yale Far Eastern Pubns.

Li, Tiger, jt. ed. see Cavusgil, S. Tamer.

Li Tim-Oi, Florence. Raindrops of My Life. 118p. 1996. pap. 9.95 (*1-55126-128-6*, 1386) Forward Movement.

Li, Tze-Chung. An Introduction to Online Searching. 50. LC 84-6686. (Contributions in Librarianship & Information Science Ser.: No. 50). (Illus.). 289p. 1985. 49.95 (*0-313-24274-7*, LIO/, Greenwood Pr) Greenwood.

— A List of Doctoral Dissertations by Chinese Students in the United States, 1961-1964. LC 67-30284. 1967. pap. 5.95 (*0-686-24155-X*) Chinese Cult Serv.

— Mah Jong: The Rules for Playing the Chinese Game. 2nd ed. 79p. 1991. pap. 12.95 (*0-937256-02-1*) Chinese Cult Serv.

— Social Science Reference Sources
 A Practical Guide. 3rd ed. LC 99-31574. 488p. 2000. lib. bdg. 99.50 (*0-313-30483-1*) Greenwood.

Li, Victor H., ed. The Future of Taiwan: A Difference of Opinion, A Dialogue among Trong R. Chai et al. LC 80-50142. 200p. reprint ed. pap. 62.00 (*0-8357-2615-0*, 204010200014) Bks Demand.

— Law & Politics in China's Foreign Trade. LC 76-7790. (Asian Law Ser.: No. 4). 488p. 1977. 40.00 (*0-295-95512-0*) U of Wash Pr.

Li, W., jt. ed. see Billinton, Roy.

Li, W. C. Number Theory with Applications. LC 95-49001. (Series on University Mathematics: Vol. 7). 300p. 1996. 53.00 (*981-02-2226-2*) World Scientific Pub.

Li, Wai-yee. Enchantment & Disenchantment: Love & Illusion in Chinese Literature. LC 92-32032. 336p. (C). 1993. text 42.50 (*0-691-05684-6*, Pub. by Princeton U Pr) Cal Prin Full Svc.

Li, Weiping, jt. auth. see Slotine, Jean-Jacques E.

***Li, Wen-Chao.** A Diachronically-Motivated Segmental Phonology of Mandarin Chinese. LC 98-41902. (Berkeley Insights in Linguistics & Semiotics Ser.: Vol. 37). xiv, 267p. (C). 1999. text 54.95 (*0-8204-4293-3*) P Lang Pubng.

An Asterisk (*) at the beginning of an entry indicates that the title is appearing for the first time.

Li, Wen-Hsiung. Molecular Evolution. LC 96-38032. (Illus.). 432p. (C). 1997. text 62.95 (*0-87893-463-4*) Sinauer Assocs.

Li, Wen-Hsiung & Lam, Sau-Hai. Principles of Fluid Mechanics. 1964. write for info. (*0-201-04240-1*) Addison-Wesley.

Li, Wen-Hsiung, jt. auth. see Graur, Dan.

Li, Wen-Ren & Cramer, Frederick S., eds. Proceedings of the Eleventh International Congress on Hyperbaric Medicine. LC 95-77069. (Illus.). 306p. 1995. 49.50 (*0-941332-44-6*, B0787) Best Pub Co.

Li, Wen Y., jt. auth. see Lien, Eric J.

***Li, Wenhua, ed.** Agro-Ecological Farming Systems in China. LC 99-53873. (Man & the Biosphere Ser.: Vol. 27). (Illus.). 500p. 2000. 105.00 (*1-85070-631-X*) Prthnon Pub.

Li Wenyan & Lu Dadao. Atlas of Fossil Plant Anatomy in China. Cheng-Sen Li & Jin-Zhong Cui, eds. (Chinese Science Studies). 132p. 1998. 119.00 (*7-03-004900-4*, Pub. by Sci Pr) Intl Scholars.

Li, William D. Housing in Taiwan: Agency & Structure? LC 97-76949. (Illus.). 218p. 1998. text 59.95 (*1-84014-332-0*, Pub. by Ashgate Pub) Ashgate Pub Co.

Li, X. & Yong, J. M., eds. Control Theory of Distributed Parameter Systems & Applications: Proceedings of the IFIP WG 7.2 Working Conference, Shanghai, China, May 6-9, 1990. (Lecture Notes in Control & Information Sciences: Vol. 159). (Illus.). 227p. 1991. 54.95 (*0-387-53894-1*) Spr-Verlag.

Li, X. B., jt. auth. see Basu, A.

Li, X. S., jt. ed. see Low, I. M.

Li, Xia, ed. Essays, Interviews, Recollections & Unpublished Material of Gu Cheng, 20th Century Chinese Poet: The Poetics of Death. LC 99-13204. (Chinese Studies: Vol. 5). 488p. 1999. text 109.95 (*0-7734-8005-6*) E Mellen.

Li, Xia & Crane, Nancy. Electronic Style: A Guide to Citing Electronic Information. LC 93-24523. 65p. 1996. 14.95 (*0-88736-909-X*) Mecklermedia.

— Electronic Styles: A Handbook of Citing Electronic Information. 2nd ed. LC 96-25799. 214p. (Orig.). 1996. pap. 19.99 (*1-57387-027-7*) Info Today Inc.

Li, Xia & Crane, Nancy B. Electronic Style: A Guide to Citing Electronic Information. rev. ed. 100p. 1995. pap. 14.95 (*0-88736-998-7*) Mecklermedia.

Li, Xianoyuan, ed. Surface Physics. (China Center of Advanced Science & Technology (World Laboratory) Symposium - Workshop Proceedings Ser.). 243p. 1992. pap. text 87.00 (*2-88124-860-8*) Gordon & Breach.

Li, Xiao M., tr. from CHI. The Mending of the Sky & Other Chinese Myths. (Illus.). 54p. (Orig.). (YA). (gr. 5 up). 1989. pap. 10.00 (*0-9617481-3-3*) Oyster River Pr.

Li, Xiao-Rong. Probability & Random Signals with Electrical Engineering Applications. LC 99-25417. 1999. 69.95 (*0-8493-0433-4*) Chapman & Hall.

Li, Xiao-Rong, jt. auth. see Bar-Shalom, Yaakov.

Li, Xiaobing & Li, Hongshan, eds. China & the United States: A New Cold War History. LC 97-42758. 356p. (C). 1997. 62.00 (*0-7618-0977-5*); pap. 39.50 (*0-7618-0978-3*) U Pr of Amer.

Li, Xiaobing, et al. Interpreting U. S.-China-Taiwan Relations: China in the Post-Cold War Era. LC 98-16403. 384p. 1998. 48.00 (*0-7618-1121-4*) U Pr of Amer.

Li, Xiaoguang. Koalitionen & Verteilung: Eine Spieltheoretische Untersuchung. (GER., Illus.). 124p. 1996. 32.95 (*3-631-30821-3*) P Lang Pubng.

Li, Xiaoming. Disequilibria, Economic Reforms & Economic Policies: A Theoretical & Empirical Investigation for China. 256p. 1995. 72.95 (*1-85972-081-1*, Pub. by Avebry) Ashgate Pub Co.

Li Xiaoqi, jt. auth. see Liu, Irene.

Li Xingdong. Basics of Taiji Quan. (Illus.). 102p. 1995. pap. 6.95 (*7-119-00171-X*, Pub. by Foreign Lang) China Bks.

Li Xuemei & Jingyi, Zhao. Acupuncture Patterns & Practice. LC 92-85309. (Illus.). 205p. 1993. text 35.00 (*0-939616-16-5*) Eastland.

Li Xueqin. Chinese Bronzes: A General Introduction. (Illus.). 172p. 1995. 54.95 (*7-119-01387-4*, Pub. by Foreign Lang) China Bks.

Li Xueqin & Chang, K. C. Eastern Zhou & Qin Civilizations. LC 85-5387. 336p. 1986. 73.00 (*0-300-03286-2*) Yale U Pr.

Li, Xun, jt. auth. see Perry, Elizabeth.

Li, Xungjing & Yong, Jiongmin. Optimal Control Theory for Infinite Dimensional Systems. LC 94-37168. (Systems & Control Ser.). 1994. 115.00 (*0-8176-3722-2*) Birkhauser.

Li, Y. H., jt. ed. see Huang, C. T.

Li, Yen-Hui A., jt. auth. see Aoun, Joseph.

Li Ying-chang. Lao-Tzu's Treatise on the Response of the Tao to Human Actions: Tai-Shang Kan-Ying Pien. (Sacred Literature Ser.). 160p. 1994. 29.95 (*0-7619-8997-8*) AltaMira Pr.

Li, Yip F. Essence of Chinese Medical. 218p. 1995. pap. text 20.00 (*0-9649931-9-8*) Yip Fun Li.

Li Yongming & Zhao Yuqi, contrib. by. Practical Protocols in Molecular Biology. 312p. 1996. 49.95 (*7-03-005077-0*, Pub. by Sci Pr) Lubrecht & Cramer.

Li, You-Zheng. The Constitution of Han-Academic Ideology: The Archetype of Chinese Ethics & Academic Ideology. (Hermeneutico-Semiotic Study Ser.: Vol. 2). xxxiii, 309p. 1997. pap. 48.95 (*3-631-31385-3*) P Lang Pubng.

— The Constitution of Han-Academic Ideology: The Archetype of Chinese Ethics & Academic Ideology. LC 97-4334. (Hermeneutico-Semiotic Study Ser.: Vol. 2). XXXIII, 309p. 1997. pap. 48.95 (*0-8204-3249-0*) P Lang Pubng.

— Epistemological Problems of the Comparative Humanities: A Semiotic-Chinese Perspective. LC 97-34021. (Illus.). viii, 312p. 1997. pap. 57.95 (*3-631-31897-9*) P Lang Pubng.

— Epistemological Problems of the Comparative Humanities: A Semiotic/Chinese Perspective. LC 97-34021. (Illus.). VIII, 312p. 1997. pap. 57.95 (*0-8204-3288-1*) P Lang Pubng.

— The Structure of the Chinese Ethical Archetype: The Archetype of Chinese Ethics & Academic Ideology: A Hermeneutico-Semiotic Study. (Hermeneutico-Semiotic Study Ser.: Vol. 1). xxxvii, 419p. 1997. pap. 57.95 (*3-631-31386-1*) P Lang Pubng.

Li Yu. The Carnal Prayer Mat. Hanan, Patrick, tr. LC 95-40936. (Orig.). 1996. pap. 12.95 (*0-8248-1798-2*) UH Pr.

***Li Yu.** Tower for the Summer Heat. Hanan, Patrick, tr. LC 98-17764. 256p. 1998. reprint ed. pap. 15.50 (*0-231-11385-4*); reprint ed. lib. bdg. 39.50 (*0-231-11384-6*) Col U Pr.

Li, Yu-cheng & Chung, Jin S., eds. The Proceedings of the Special Offshore Symposium China: SOSC 1994 (PACOMS '94) 797p. 1994. 100.00 (*1-880653-15-X*) ISOPE.

Li, Yu-ning, ed. Chinese Women Through Chinese Eyes. LC 91-11313. 282p. (gr. 13). 1992. pap. 35.95 (*0-87332-597-4*, East Gate Bk) M E Sharpe.

Li, Yu-ning, ed. Chinese Women through Chinese Eyes. LC 91-11313. 282p. (C). (gr. 13). 1992. 68.95 (*0-87332-596-6*, East Gate Bk) M E Sharpe.

Li, Yu-Ning, ed. Shang Yang's Reforms & State Control in China. LC 76-4301. (China Book Project Ser.). 392p. 1977. reprint ed. pap. 121.60 (*0-8357-2621-5*, 204010900014) Bks Demand.

Li Yu-Ning, et al, eds. Images of Women in Chinese Literature. (Illus.). 232p. (C). 1994. text 35.50 (*0-614-14901-0*); pap. text 25.50 (*0-614-14902-9*) Outer Sky.

***Li, Yuan-Hui.** A Compendium of Geochemistry: From Solar Nebula to the Human Brain. LC 99-89467. (Illus.). 440p. 2000. 65.00 (*0-691-00938-4*) Princeton U Pr.

Li, Yuying, jt. ed. see Coleman, Thomas F.

Li, Z., et al, eds. Languages & Compilers for Parallel Computing: 10th International Workshop, LCPC '97, Minneapolis, Minnesota, U. S. A., August 7-9, 1997. Proceedings. (Lecture Notes in Computer Science Ser.: Vol. 1366). xii, 428p. 1998. pap. 67.00 (*3-540-64472-5*) Spr-Verlag.

Li, Z. C. Numerical Methods for Elliptic Problems with Singularities: Boundary Methods & Non-Conforming Combinations. 276p. (C). 1990. text 48.00 (*981-02-0292-X*) World Scientific Pub.

Li, Z. C., et al, eds. Computer Transformation of Digital Images & Patterns. 276p. (C). 1989. text 68.00 (*9971-5-0951-2*) World Scientific Pub.

Li, Z. P., et al. Retrospect & Prospect in Protein Research. 280p. 1991. text 61.00 (*981-02-0518-X*) World Scientific Pub.

Li, Zexiang & Canny, J. F., eds. Nonholonomic Motion Planning. LC 92-27560. (Kluwer International Series in Engineering & Computer Science). 1992. text 187.00 (*0-7923-9275-2*) Kluwer Academic.

Li, Zhixiong. The Dynamics of Export Channels from United Kingdom to People's Republic of China: A Network Approach. LC 96-83714. 280p. 1996. 72.95 (*1-85972-373-X*, Pub. by Avebry) Ashgate Pub Co.

Li, Zhong, et al, eds. Proceedings of the Conference on Complex Analysis. (Series in Analysis). 1994. 42.00 (*1-57146-017-9*) Intl Pr Boston.

Li, Zi-Cai. Combined Methods for Elliptic Equations with Singularities, Interfaces, & Infinities. LC 98-21543. (Mathematics & Its Applications Ser.). 476p. 1998. write for info. (*0-7923-5084-7*) Kluwer Academic.

Li, Zi M. Liang Zhen Pu Eight Diagram Palm. 154p. 1993. pap. 17.95 (*1-883175-00-3*) High View Pubns.

Li, Zongmin. Changes in the Role of Rural Women under the Household Responsibility System: A Case Study of the Impact of Agrarian Reform & Rural Industrialization in Dongyao Village, Hebei Province, North China. (Research Paper Ser.: Vol. 113). (Illus.). v, 53p. (C). 1993. pap. 7.00 (*0-934519-24-2*, RP113) U of Wis Land.

Lia, Brynjar. Society of the Muslim Brothers in Egypt: The Rise of an Islamic Mass Movement, 1928-1942. 1998. 45.00 (*0-86372-220-2*, Pub. by Garnet-Ithaca) LPC InBook.

Lia, Robert, jt. auth. see Gibert, Roland.

Lia, Robert, jt. auth. see Gilbert, Roland.

***Lia, Simone.** Red's Great Chase. LC 99-25588. (Illus.). 32p. (J). 2000. 14.99 (*0-525-46213-9*, Dutt) Dutton Plume.

***Liable, Don.** Wrestling Trivia Book. (Illus.). 2000. pap. 10.95 (*0-7407-1091-5*) Andrews & McMeel.

Liachowitz, Claire H. Disability As a Social Construct: Legislative Roots. LC 88-17153. 152p. (C). 1988. text 29.95 (*0-8122-8134-9*) U of Pa Pr.

Liacos, Paul J. Handbook of Massachusetts Evidence. 5th ed. 584p. 1981. 75.00 (*0-316-51813-1*, Aspen Law & Bus) Aspen Pub.

— Handbook of Massachusetts Evidence. 6th ed. LC 93-79760. xxxiii, 914 p. 1993. 125.00 (*0-316-52412-3*, Aspen Law & Bus) Aspen Pub.

— Massachusetts Evidence. 6th ed. 947p. 1994. 145.00 (*0-316-52410-7*, Aspen Law & Bus) Aspen Pub.

— Massachusetts Evidence Law, 1995. 1995. 65.00 (*0-316-52416-6*, Aspen Law & Bus) Aspen Pub.

— Massachusetts Evidence, 1994. 1994. suppl. ed. 60.00 (*0-316-52411-5*, Aspen Law & Bus) Aspen Pub.

***Liacos, Paul J., et al.** Handbook of Massachusetts Evidence. 7th ed. LC 99-52436. 1999. boxed set 165.00 (*0-7355-0532-2*) Panel Pubs.

Liacouras, Christopher A., jt. auth. see Altschuler, Steven M.

Liad. Engineering Applications. (West Engineering Ser.). 1988. text 70.95 (*0-534-93832-9*) PWS Pubs.

Liagin, Elizabeth, jt. auth. see Information Project for Africa Staff.

Liahona Research, Inc. Staff. Alabama Marriages, Early to 1825. Dodd, Jordan, ed. 158p. 1991. lib. bdg. 35.00 (*1-877677-36-1*) Herit Quest.

— Arkansas Marriages, Early to 1850. Dodd, Jordan, ed. 1990. lib. bdg. 60.00 (*1-877677-25-6*) Herit Quest.

— Georgia Marriages, Early to 1800. Dodd, Jordan, ed. 1990. lib. bdg. 25.00 (*1-877677-27-2*) Herit Quest.

— Illinois Marriages, Early to Eighteen Twenty-Five. Dodd, Jordan, ed. 87p. 1991. lib. bdg. 25.00 (*1-877677-31-0*) Herit Quest.

— Indiana Marriages, Early to Eighteen Twenty-Five. Dodd, Jordan, ed. 345p. 1991. lib. bdg. 80.00 (*1-877677-34-5*) Herit Quest.

— Kentucky Marriages, Early to 1800. Dodd, Jordan, ed. 1990. lib. bdg. 60.00 (*1-877677-30-2*) Herit Quest.

— Mississippi Marriages, Early to 1825. Dodd, Jordan, ed. 117p. 1991. lib. bdg. 35.00 (*1-877677-35-3*) Herit Quest.

— Missouri Marriages, Early to 1825. Dodd, Jordan, ed. 67p. 1991. lib. bdg. 25.00 (*1-877677-37-X*) Herit Quest.

— North Carolina Marriages, Early to Eighteen Hundred. Dodd, Jordan, ed. 523p. 1991. lib. bdg. 95.00 (*1-877677-28-0*) Herit Quest.

— Tennessee Marriages, Early to 1800. Dodd, Jordan, ed. 1990. lib. bdg. 25.00 (*1-877677-29-9*) Herit Quest.

— Texas Marriages, Early to 1850. Dodd, Jordan, ed. 1990. lib. bdg. 60.00 (*1-877677-26-4*) Herit Quest.

— Virginia Marriages, Early to 1800. Dodd, Jordan, ed. 1148p. 1991. lib. bdg. 145.00 (*1-877677-39-6*) Herit Quest.

Liahona Research Staff. District of Columbia Marriages Index: Early to 1825. 79p. lib. bdg. 31.50 (*1-877677-54-X*) Herit Quest.

— Georgia Marriages Index, 1826-1850. 613p. lib. bdg. 115.00 (*1-877677-63-9*); lib. bdg. 130.00 (*1-877677-96-5*) Herit Quest.

— Illinois Marriages Index, 1826-1850. 923p. lib. bdg. 150.00 (*0-945433-47-6*) Herit Quest.

— Indiana Marriages Index, 1826-1850. 1085p. lib. bdg. 195.00 (*0-945433-43-3*) Herit Quest.

— Iowa Marriages Index: Early to 1850. 373p. lib. bdg. 60.00 (*0-945433-42-5*) Herit Quest.

— Kentucky Marriages Index, 1801-1825. 797p. lib. bdg. 140.00 (*0-945433-44-1*) Herit Quest.

— Louisiana Marriages Index, Early to 1850. 185p. lib. bdg. 35.00 (*0-945433-45-X*) Herit Quest.

— Missouri Marriages Index, 1826-1850. 870p. lib. bdg. 145.00 (*1-877677-16-7*) Herit Quest.

— North Carolina Marriages Index, 1801-1825. 900p. lib. bdg. 145.00 (*1-877677-33-7*) Herit Quest.

— Tennessee Marriages Index, 1801-1825. 301p. lib. bdg. 50.00 (*1-877677-38-8*, Precision Index) Herit Quest.

Liaites, Bill & Naharo, Master. Reiki: A Practical Guide. (Healing Ser.). (Illus.). 128p. 1998. pap. 8.95 (*965-494-046-9*, Pub. by Astrolog Pub) Assoc Pubs Grp.

Liakishev, N. P. & Gasik, M. I. Metallurgy of Chromium. LC 97-8697. 1997. 245.00 (*0-89864-083-0*) Allerton Pr.

Liakopoulos, A., jt. ed. see Simpkins, P. G.

***Liakopoulos, Athanassios.** Intellectual Property Law in Greece. 152p. 1999. pap. text 51.00 (*90-411-1299-5*) Kluwer Law Intl.

Lial. Alg Col Stdnt Alg Col PK. (C). 1996. 81.00 (*0-321-80004-4*) Addison-Wesley.

— Beginning ALG Custom. 6th ed. (C). 1998. text 70.00 (*0-201-43515-2*) Addison-Wesley.

— Beginning Algebra. 7th ed. (C). 1998. student ed. 85.33 (*0-321-80114-8*) Addison-Wesley.

***Lial.** Beginning Algebra. 8th ed. 416p. (C). 1999. pap. text 21.00 (*0-321-06195-0*) Addison-Wesley.

Lial. Beginning Algebra Solutions Manual. 8th ed. 464p. (C). 1999. pap. text 28.00 (*0-321-06196-9*) Addison-Wesley.

— Beginning & Intermediate Algebra. (C). 1997. student ed. 84.00 (*0-321-80036-2*) Addison-Wesley.

— Calc w/ Appl Brf Ti Rebat. 6th ed. (C). 1998. 86.00 (*0-201-42243-3*) Addison-Wesley.

— Calculus with Applications & Calculus with Applications Brief. 6th ed. (C). 1998. pap. text 25.00 (*0-321-01626-2*) Addson-Wesley Educ.

— Col Mat Found Triton Col. 2nd ed. (C). 1997. pap. text 52.00 (*0-201-30471-6*) Addison-Wesley.

Lial. College Algebra. 1997. pap. text 12.60 (*0-201-30479-1*) Addison-Wesley.

Lial. Explorations in Finite Mathematics & Visual Calculus for Finite Mathematics & Calculus with Applications. 5th ed. (C). 1998. 11.60 (*0-321-03096-6*) Addison-Wesley.

— Finite Mathematics. 5th ed. (C). 1997. pap. text, teacher ed. 13.00 (*0-673-55080-X*) Addison-Wesley.

— Finite Mathematics: Instructor's Guide & Solutions. (C). 1997. pap. text, teacher ed. 24.00 (*0-673-55079-6*) Addison-Wesley.

— Finite Mathematics & Calculus. 4th ed. (C). 1997. pap. text, teacher ed. 13.00 (*0-673-55103-2*) Addison-Wesley.

— Finite Mathematics & Calculus with Applications. 4th ed. (C). 1997. student ed. 104.20 (*0-321-80043-5*) Addison-Wesley.

— Finite Mathematics & Calculus with Applications: Student Solutions Manual. 5th ed. (C). 1998. pap. text 25.00 (*0-321-01627-0*) Addison-Wesley.

— Finite Mathematics, Calculus & Applications: A Student's Solution Manual. 4th ed. (C). 1993. 96.00 (*0-673-78632-3*) Addison-Wesley.

Lial. Foundations of College Mathematics. 1997. text 79.00 (*0-201-30481-3*) Addison-Wesley.

Lial. Intermediate Algebra with Early Graph & Functions. 6th ed. (C). 1999. text. write for info. (*0-321-01599-1*) Addson-Wesley Educ.

Lial. Intermediate Algebra with Early Graphing. 5th ed. (C). 1997. pap. text, teacher ed. 12.00 (*0-673-55939-4*) Addison-Wesley.

— Introduction & Intermediate Algebra: Combined Approach. 1999. 84.37 (*0-201-66376-7*) Addison-Wesley.

Lial. Introduction To Algebra. 5th ed. 1995. student ed. 72.00 (*0-673-78952-7*) Addison-Wesley.

— Introduction To Algebra. 5th ed. (C). 1995. pap. 58.50 (*0-321-80048-6*) Addison-Wesley.

— Introductory Algebra. 5th ed. (C). 1997. pap. text, teacher ed. 24.00 (*0-673-55473-2*) Addison-Wesley.

— Introductory Algebra Worktext. 6th ed. (C). 1998. pap. text. write for info. (*0-201-41736-7*) Addison-Wesley.

***Lial.** Mathpass: Lial Basic College Mathematics. 5th ed. 1998. 29.00 (*0-201-44073-3*) Addison-Wesley.

— Mathpass: Lial Basic College Mathematics. 6th ed. 2001. 29.00 (*0-201-44077-6*) Addison-Wesley.

Lial. Precalculus Recover of College Algebra & Trigonometry. (C). 1997. text 84.00 (*0-321-00968-1*) Addson-Wesley Educ.

— Set Notation Kipolianni. (C). 1997. pap. text, suppl. ed. 3.95 (*0-201-33821-1*) Addison-Wesley.

Lial. Solutions Study Guide. 4th ed. 1997. student ed. 24.00 (*0-673-55358-2*, GoodYrBooks) Addson-Wesley Educ.

Lial. S/S/M Foundation Coll Math. (C). 1997. pap. text, student ed. 29.00 (*0-201-30143-1*) Addison-Wesley.

Lial. Trigonometry. 1997. pap. text, student ed. 22.00 (*0-673-38250-8*) Addison-Wesley.

Lial. Trigonometry: Objective Listing for Tutorials. 6th ed. (C). 1997. write for info. (*0-321-40245-6*) Addison-Wesley.

— Trigonometry with Applications. (C). 1997. 93.20 (*0-673-78584-X*) Addison-Wesley.

Lial, ed. Additional Exercise: First Edition (Int. Hardcover Book) (C). 1997. text 19.00 (*0-673-67641-2*) Addison-Wesley.

Lial, ed. Algebra: Tallahassee Edition. (C). 1988. text 43.66 (*0-673-38604-X*) Addison-Wesley.

Lial, ed. Calculus with Applications: Answer Manual. 5th ed. 128p. (C). 1997. pap. text 11.00 (*0-673-55074-5*) Addison-Wesley.

— Calculus with Applications: Student Solutions Manual. 4th ed. (C). 1989. pap. text, student ed. 20.66 (*0-673-38252-4*) Addison-Wesley.

— College Algebra. 5th ed. (C). 1989. pap. text, student ed. 19.33 (*0-673-38247-8*) Addson-Wesley Educ.

— College Algebra & Trigonometry. (C). 1997. text. write for info. (*0-321-40841-1*); text. write for info. (*0-321-40842-X*); text. write for info. (*0-321-40843-8*) Addson-Wesley Educ.

— Introductory, Intermediate & College Algebra. 980p. (C). 1997. text 74.00 (*0-673-99957-2*) Addison-Wesley.

— Mathematical Applications for Business CB. (C). 1997. text 68.00 (*0-673-67530-0*) Addison-Wesley.

— Study Guide. 4th ed. (C). 1997. pap. text, student ed. 21.00 (*0-673-38249-4*) Addson-Wesley Educ.

— Trigonometry. 5th ed. (C). 1995. text 48.66 (*0-673-67487-8*) Addison-Wesley.

— Trigonometry: Instructor's Solution Manual. (C). 1989. pap. text, teacher ed. 11.00 (*0-673-48892-6*) Addison-Wesley.

— Trigonometry with Additional Topics. 2nd ed. (C). 1996. text. write for info. (*0-673-67652-8*) Addison-Wesley.

Lial & Hestwood. Pre-Algebra: Instructor's Solutions Manual. 144p. 1999. 25.20 (*0-321-02989-5*) Addson-Wesley Educ.

***Lial & Hornsby.** Foundations of College Mathematics. 2nd ed. 1999. 74.00 (*0-201-38809-X*) Addison-Wesley.

— Intermediate Algebra, Alternate Version. 8th ed. 2000. pap. 28.00 (*0-321-08213-3*); pap., student ed. 23.00 (*0-321-08214-1*) Addison-Wesley.

Lial & Hornsby. Pitman Office Handbook. 4th ed. (C). 1999. pap. text, wbk. ed. write for info. (*0-201-38887-1*) Addison-Wesley.

***Lial & Hornsby.** Trigonometry. 1999. pap. text 9.20 (*0-201-66988-9*) Addison-Wesley.

Lial & Hornsby. Trigonometry Custom. (C). 1998. pap. text 71.00 (*0-201-43518-7*) Addison-Wesley.

Lial & Hungerford. Mathematics with Applications: Answer Book. 7th ed. 192p. 1998. 23.00 (*0-321-03955-6*) Addson-Wesley Educ.

Lial & Miller. Math with Applications. 4th ed. (C). 1987. pap. text 14.33 (*0-673-18469-2*) Addson-Wesley Educ.

Lial, et al. Algebra & Trigonometry. (C). 1990. pap. text, student ed. 22.00 (*0-673-38957-X*) Addson-Wesley Educ.

— Algebra & Trigonometry. 6th ed. (C). 1997. pap. text, student ed. 20.25 (*0-673-46990-5*) Addson-Wesley Educ.

— Basic College Math. 5th ed. (C). 1998. write for info. (*0-201-43517-9*) Addison-Wesley.

— Basic College Math Custm. 5th ed. (C). 1998. pap. text 71.00 (*0-201-43528-4*) Addison-Wesley.

— Basic College Mathematics: Instructor's Resource Manual. 5th ed. (Lial/Miller Paperback Ser.). 496p. 1998. 30.00 (*0-321-40342-8*) Addson-Wesley Educ.

— Basic College Mathematics: Teacher's Edition. 5th ed. (Lial/Miller Paperback Ser.). 832p. 1997. 61.00 (*0-321-40343-6*) Addson-Wesley Educ.

— Calculus with Applications. 6th ed. (C). 1998. teacher ed. 24.00 (*0-321-40739-3*) Addson-Wesley Educ.

— Essential Geometry for College Students: Study Guide. 176p. 1997. pap. 30.00 (*0-673-38963-4*) Addison-Wesley.

— Intermediate Algebra: Early Functions & Graphing Instructor's Manual. 6th ed. (The Lial/Miller Paperback Ser.). 848p. 1997. 61.00 (*0-321-40337-1*) Addson-Wesley Educ.

— Introductory Algebra: Instructor's Resource Manual. 6th ed. (Lial/Miller Paperback Ser.). 496p. 1998. 30.00 (*0-321-40331-2*) Addson-Wesley Educ.

— Introductory Algebra: Teacher's Edition. 6th ed. (Lial/Miller Paperback Ser.). 704p. 1997. 61.00 (*0-321-40332-0*) Addson-Wesley Educ.

— Trigonometry: Annotated Instructor's Edition. 6th ed. 54.75 (*0-673-97659-9*) Addson-Wesley Educ.
— Trigonometry: Instructor's Resource Manual. 6th ed. 18.00 (*0-673-97886-9*) Addson-Wesley Educ.
— Trigonometry: Instructor's Solutions Manual. 6th ed. 18.00 (*0-673-97883-4*) Addson-Wesley Educ.

Lial, jt. auth. see Hornsby.

Lial, Margaret. Intermediate Algebra with Early Graphs & Functions. 6th ed. 352p. (C). 1998. pap. text 21.00 (*0-321-01319-0*) Addson-Wesley Educ.
— Mathematics with Applications: Management of Natural Social Science. 7th ed. 1999. text 22.50 (*0-321-03954-8*) Addison-Wesley.

Lial, Margaret L. Algebra for College Students. 3rd ed. 880p. (C). 1997. teacher ed. 25.20 (*0-673-55955-6*) Addson-Wesley Educ.
— Algebra for College Students. 4th ed. LC 99-33179. 901p. (C). 2000. 83.00 (*0-321-03647-6*) Addison-Wesley.
— Algebra for College Students: Custom Reprint. (C). 1997. pap. text 48.00 (*0-201-30147-4*) Addison-Wesley.
— Beginning Algebra. 8th ed. LC 99-25871. 639p. (C). 1999. 83.00 (*0-321-03644-1*) Addison-Wesley.
— Beginning Algebra. 8th ed. (C). 1999. 67.00 (*0-321-06132-2*) Addison-Wesley.
— Beginning & Intermediate Algebra. (C). 1997. trans. 177.00 (*0-673-99982-3*) Addson-Wesley Educ.
— Beginning & Intermediate Algebra 2nd ed. LC 99-22008. 896p. (C). 1999. 89.00 (*0-321-04133-X*) Addson-Wesley Educ.
— Calculus with Applications. 6th ed. (C). 1998. text. write for info. (*0-321-02869-4*) Addison-Wesley.
— College Algebra: Solutions Manual. 7th ed. 496p. (C). 1997. pap. text, student ed. 25.00 (*0-673-98336-6*) Addison-Wesley.
— College Algebra in Simplest Terms: Study Guide for the Television Course. 288p. (C). 1997. pap. text, student ed. 37.00 (*0-673-46560-8*) Addison-Wesley.
— Finite Mathematics. 6th ed. (C). 1998. text. write for info. (*0-321-02868-6*) Addison-Wesley.
— Finite Mathematics & Calculus with Applications. 5th ed. (C). 1998. text. write for info. (*0-321-02871-6*) Addison-Wesley.
— Intermediate Algebra. (C). 1997. pap. text, student ed. 28.00 (*0-673-99858-4*) Addson-Wesley Educ.
— Intermediate Algebra: A Graphing Approach. 7th ed. (C). 1997. pap. text, student ed. 21.00 (*0-673-99840-1*) Addson-Wesley Educ.
— Intermediate Algebra - Beginner: Student's Solution Manual. (C). 1997. pap. text, student ed. 21.00 (*0-673-99859-2*) Addson-Wesley Educ.
— Intermediate Algebra - Study Guide: A Graphing Approach. 7th ed. (C). 1997. pap. text, student ed. 28.00 (*0-673-99841-X*) Addson-Wesley Educ.
— Intermediate Algebra with Early Graphs & Functions. 7th ed. (C). 1997. teacher ed. 24.00 (*0-673-97388-3*) Addson-Wesley Educ.
— Intermediate Algebra with Early Graphs & Functions. 8th ed. 738p. (C). 1999. 83.00 (*0-321-03646-8*) Addison-Wesley.
— Intermediate Algebra With Early Graphs & Functions. 8th ed. (C). 2000. text. write for info. (*0-321-02982-8*) Addison-Wesley.
— Introduction To Algebra. 6th ed. (C). 1998. write for info. (*0-321-05817-8*) Addison-Wesley.
— Mathematics with Applications: In the Management, Natural & Social Sciences. 7th ed. LC 98-21682. 880p. (C). 1998. 103.00 (*0-321-02294-7*) Addson-Wesley Educ.
— S/G College Algebra. 7th ed. 416p. (C). 1997. pap. text, student ed. 25.00 (*0-673-98430-3*) Addison-Wesley.
— Trigonometry: Solutions Manual. 6th ed. 352p. (C). 1997. pap. text, student ed. 25.00 (*0-673-98337-4*) Addison-Wesley.

Lial, Margaret L., ed. Algebra: A Brief Introduction. (C). 1997. text 51.00 (*0-673-67503-3*) Addison-Wesley.
— Calculus with Applications. 6th ed. LC 97-19170. (Illus.). 626p. (C). 1997. 97.66 (*0-321-01631-9*) Addson-Wesley Educ.
— Mathematics with Applications: A Graphing Approach. LC 98-21684. 864p. (C). 1998. 103.00 (*0-321-01621-1*) Addson-Wesley Educ.
— Trigonometry. 6th ed. (C). 1997. text. write for info. (*0-321-40186-7*) Addson-Wesley Educ.

Lial, Margaret L. & Hornsby, E. John. Algebra for College Students 4th ed. LC 99-33179. 1999. write for info. (*0-321-04131-3*) Addson-Wesley Educ.
— Intermediate Algebra with Early Graphs & Functions. 7th ed. (C). 1997. pap. text 24.00 (*0-673-97389-1*) Addson-Wesley Educ.

Lial, Margaret L. & Miller, Charles D. College Algebra. 5th ed. (C). 1989. cd-rom 73.00 (*0-673-38245-1*) Addson-Wesley Educ.
— Trigonometry. 4th ed. (C). 1997. pap. text 67.00 (*0-673-38248-6*) Addson-Wesley Educ.

Lial, Margaret L., et al. Algebra & Trigonometry. 5th ed. (C). 1990. text 63.33 (*0-673-38576-0*) Addson-Wesley Educ.
— Algebra & Trigonometry. 6th ed. LC 93-26181. 654p. (C). 1997. text 77.00 (*0-673-46739-2*) Addson-Wesley Educ.
— Algebra College Students. 3rd ed. (Illus.). 883p. (C). 1997. text 78.00 (*0-673-99061-3*) Addson-Wesley Educ.
— Algebra for College Student: Study Guide. 3rd ed. (C). 1996. pap. text, student ed. 26.25 (*0-673-99545-3*) Addson-Wesley Educ.
— Algebra for College Students: Student's Solution Manual. 3rd ed. 784p. (C). 1997. pap. text, student ed. 6.67 (*0-673-99547-X*) Addson-Wesley Educ.
— Beginning Algebra. 7th ed. (C). 1996. pap. text, student ed. 26.25 (*0-673-99542-9*) Addson-Wesley Educ.
— Beginning Algebra. 7th ed. (C). 1997. teacher ed. 24.00 (*0-673-55948-3*); text 78.00 (*0-673-99139-3*) Addson-Wesley Educ.
— Beginning & Intermediate Algebra. (C). 1997. teacher ed. 24.00 (*0-673-97338-7*) Addson-Wesley Educ.
— Beginning Intermediate Algebra. 992p. (C). 1997. text 84.00 (*0-673-99857-6*) Addson-Wesley Educ.
— Calculus With Applications. 5th ed. LC 92-27440. 688p. (C). 1997. text 88.15 (*0-673-46726-0*) Addson-Wesley Educ.
— Calculus with Applications: Brief Version. 6th ed. LC 97-14851. 608p. (C). 1997. 96.00 (*0-321-01630-0*) Addison-Wesley.
— College Alg Trigonometry. 7th ed. LC 96-653. 784p. (C). 1997. 91.00 (*0-673-98046-4*) Addson-Wesley Educ.
— College Algebra. 6th ed. LC 92-13866. (Illus.). (C). 1993. text 80.63 (*0-673-46648-5*) Addson-Wesley Educ.
— Early & Intermediate Algebra: Student Study Manual. 5th ed. (C). 1997. pap. text, student ed. 25.00 (*0-673-99538-0*) Addson-Wesley Educ.
— Essentials of Geometry for College Students. 431p. (C). 1997. 102.00 (*0-673-38419-5*) Addson-Wesley Educ.
— Finite Mathematics. 5th ed. LC 92-28348. (C). 1993. text 75.50 (*0-673-46727-9*) Addson-Wesley Educ.
— Finite Mathematics. 6th ed. LC 97-19171. (Illus.). 544p. (C). 1997. 96.00 (*0-321-01632-7*) Addson-Wesley Educ.
— Finite Mathematics & Calculus with Applications. 5th ed. LC 97-14862. (Illus.). 969p. (C). 1997. 103.00 (*0-321-01633-5*) Addson-Wesley Educ.
— Finite Mathematics & Calculus with Applications Student Solutions. 4th ed. (C). 1994. pap. text, student ed. 36.00 (*0-673-46764-3*) Addson-Wesley Educ.
— Intermediate Algebra. 6th ed. (C). 1991. text 57.50 (*0-673-46464-4*) Addson-Wesley Educ.
— Intermediate Algebra. 6th ed. LC 96-52939. 726p. (C). 1997. pap. text 78.00 (*0-321-01266-6*) Addson-Wesley Educ.
— Intermediate Algebra. 7th ed. LC 95-10263. 92p. (C). 1997. 83.00 (*0-673-99059-1*); pap. text, student ed. 28.00 (*0-673-99539-9*); pap. text, student ed. 21.00 (*0-673-99541-0*) Addson-Wesley Educ.
— Intermediate Algebra with Early Graph Functions. 7th ed. 816p. (C). 1997. 83.00 (*0-673-99575-5*) Addson-Wesley Educ.
— Introductory Algebra. 6th ed. LC 96-52940. (Illus.). 590p. (C). 1997. pap. text 78.00 (*0-321-01267-4*) Addson-Wesley Educ.
— Introductory & Intermediate Algebra. LC 97-16486. (Illus.). 820p. (C). 1998. pap. text 84.00 (*0-321-01926-1*) Addison-Wesley.
— Mathematics & Applications: Student's Solution Manual. 6th ed. LC 94-13576. (C). 1995. pap. text, student ed. 29.06 (*0-673-46944-1*) Addson-Wesley Educ.
— Mathematics with Applications: In the Management, Natural & Social Sciences. 4th ed. (C). 1995. teacher ed. write for info. (*0-673-55304-3*) Addson-Wesley Educ.
— Trigonometry. 5th ed. LC 92-22236. 560p. (C). 1997. 11.00 (*0-673-46753-8*, Scott Frsmn) Addson-Wesley Educ.

Lial, Margaret L., jt. auth. see Hornsby, E. John.

Lial, Margaret L., jt. auth. see Hornsby, E. John, Jr.

Lial, Margaret L., jt. auth. see Hornsby, E. John.

Lial, Margarget L. Calculus with Applications: Brief Edition. 6th ed. (C). 1998. text. write for info. (*0-321-02870-8*) Addson-Wesley.
— Intermediate Algebra: Solutions Manual. 8th ed. (C). 2000. pap. text 21.00 (*0-321-06200-0*) Addison-Wesley.

Lial, Marge. Algebra for College Students. 4th ed. (C). 2000. pap., student ed. 21.00 (*0-321-06212-4*) Addson-Wesley Educ.
— Introduction to Intermediate Algebra. (C). 1997. text, student ed. 24.00 (*0-673-99958-0*) Addison-Wesley.
— Introduction to Intermediate Algebra. 1p. (C). 1999. pap. text 29.00 (*0-321-06439-9*) Addison-Wesley.

Lialinger, Margaret. Intermediate Algebra Worktext. 6th ed. (C). 1998. pap. text. write for info. (*0-201-41737-5*) Addison-Wesley.

Liammoir, Micheal Mac, see Mac Liammoir, Micheal.

Lian, George J. & Marder, Richard A. Sports Injuries of the Ankle & Foot. LC 96-7605. (Illus.). 224p. 1996. 135.00 (*0-387-94687-X*) Spr-Verlag.

Lian, J. B., jt. ed. see Glimcher, M. J.

Lian, Shi Q. An Anonymous Girl on the Bank of the Seine River. (CHI.). pap. 9.95 (*7-5004-1702-0*, Pub. by China Intl Bk) Distribks Inc.

Lian, Tanja, ed. see Beares, Paul R.

Lian, Tongshu. Theory of Conjugation for Reflecting Prisms. (International Academic Publishers Ser.). (Illus.). 500p. 1991. 115.00 (*0-08-037935-4*, Pub. by IAP) Elsevier.

***Lian, Xinda.** The Wild & Arrogant: Expression of Self in Xin Qiji's Song Lyrics. LC 98-33829. (Asian Thought & Culture Ser.: Vol. 34). viii, 199p. (C). 1999. text 49.00 (*0-8204-4193-7*) P Lang Pubng.

Lian, Yang. Non-Person Singular: Selected Poems of Yang Lian. Holton, Brian & Lee, Mabel, trs. LC 95-233707. (WellSweep Chinese Poets Ser.; Vol. 6). 128p. (C). 1994. pap. 14.95 (*0-948454-15-6*) Cheng & Tsui.

***Lian, Yang.** Where the Sea Stands Still: New Poems. (Orig.). 1999. pap. 18.95 (*1-85224-471-2*, Pub. by Bloodaxe Bks) Dufour.
— Yi. 376p. 2000. pap. text 14.95 (*1-892295-68-7*) Green Integer.

Lianas, A. Taylor. Sunrise, Vol. 4. 1997. pap. write for info. (*0-17-555491-9*, Pub. by ITP Nelson) Thomson Learn.
— Sunrise: Activity Book. 1997. pap. write for info. (*0-17-555483-8*, Pub. by ITP Nelson) Thomson Learn.
— Sunrise: Activity Book, Vol. 4. 1997. pap. write for info. (*0-17-555492-7*, Pub. by ITP Nelson) Thomson Learn.

Liang, jt. auth. see Klippel.

Liang, Amy. The Living Art of Bonsai: Principles & Techniques of Cultivation & Propagation. (Illus.). 288p. 1995. pap. 24.95 (*0-8069-8781-2*) Sterling.

***Liang, Bryan A.** Health Law & Policy: A Survival Guide to Medicolegal Issue. LC 99-34309. 328p. 1999. pap. text 39.95 (*0-7506-7107-6*) Buttrwrth-Heinemann.
— A Zone of Twilight: Executive Orders in the Modern Policy State. LC 99-204884. 40p. 1999. write for info. (*0-937299-81-2*) Natl Legal Ctr Pub Interest.

Liang-Che & Tao. Cytopathology of Malignant Effusions: Cytomorphologic Interpretation. LC 95-35871. (ASCP Theory & Practice of Cytopathology Ser.: No. 5). (Illus.). 1996. 80.00 (*0-89189-395-4*) Am Soc Clinical.

Liang Chi-Chao. History of Chinese Political Thought. LC 70-100526. reprint ed. 34.50 (*0-404-03985-5*) AMS Pr.
— History of Chinese Political Thought During the Early Tsin Period. (Illus.). 300p. (C). 1996. reprint ed. text 55.00 (*0-7007-0354-3*, Pub. by Curzon Pr Ltd) UH Pr.

Liang, Chi-Shad. Burma's Foreign Relations: Neutralism in Theory & Practice. LC 90-31953. 288p. 1990. 62.95 (*0-275-93455-1*, C3455, Praeger Pubs) Greenwood.

Liang-Chi Tao. Guides to Clinical Aspiration Biopsy: Lung, Pleura, & Mediastinum. LC 87-29883. (Illus.). 512p. 1988. 95.00 (*0-89640-136-7*) Igaku-Shoin.

Liang, Congjie. The Great Thoughts of China: 3,000 Years of Wisdom That Shaped A Civilization. LC 95-30503. 278p. 1996. 24.95 (*0-471-02751-0*) Wiley.

Liang, Diana F., compiled by. Mathematical Journals: An Annotated Guide. LC 92-18459. 246p. 1992. 36.00 (*0-8108-2585-6*) Scarecrow.

Liang, Du, tr. see Ching-Yuen, Loy.

Liang, Edison P. & Petrosian, Vahe, eds. Gamma-Ray Bursts. LC 86-70761. (AIP Conference Proceedings Ser.: 141). 224p. 1986. lib. bdg. 60.00 (*0-88318-340-4*) Am Inst Physics.

Liang, Ernest P. China: Railways & Agricultural Development, 1875-1935. LC 82-4749. (University of Chicago, Department of Geography, Research Paper Ser.: No. 203). 201p. 1982. reprint ed. pap. 62.40 (*0-608-02290-X*, 206293100004) Bks Demand.

Liang, Foo S., jt. auth. see Meng, Low A.

Liang, Hsi-Huey. The Rise of Modern Police & the European State System from Metternich to the Second World War. 361p. (C). 1992. text 74.95 (*0-521-43022-4*) Cambridge U Pr.

Liang, J. Q., et al, eds. Proceedings of International Symposium on Advanced Topics of Quantum Physics Held in Taiyuan, Shanxi Province of China June 12-16, 1992. 493p. 1996. 59.95 (*7-03-003507-0*, Pub. by Sci Pr) Lubrecht & Cramer.

Liang, James. Pronunciation Exercises for Beginning Chinese. 1978. 1.75 (*0-88710-059-7*) Yale Far Eastern Pubns.

Liang, James. Pronunciation Exercises for Beginning Chinese. 1978. 8.95 incl. audio (*0-88710-060-0*) Yale Far Eastern Pubns.

Liang, Jin, jt. auth. see Tri-Jun Xiao.

Liang, K. S., et al, eds. Interface Dynamics & Growth. (Symposium Proceedings Ser.: Vol. 237). 689p. 1992. text 17.50 (*1-55899-131-X*) Materials Res.

Liang, Kiayang, jt. auth. see Irvine, Kip.

Liang, Peng, jt. ed. see Pardee, Arthur B.

Liang, Ping, jt. auth. see Bose, Nirmal K.

Liang, Pingzhi, et al, eds. Detectors, Focal Plane Arrays & Imaging Devices II, Vol. 3553. LC 98-226759. 48p. 1998. 89.00 (*0-8194-3014-5*) SPIE.

Liang, Robert Y., ed. see American Society of Civil Engineers Geotechnical E.

Liang, S. Y. & Wu, C. L., eds. Sensors & Signal Processing for Manufacturing. (PED Ser.: Vol. 55). 240p. 1992. 57.50 (*0-7918-0798-3*, G00692) ASME.

***Liang, Sheng.** Against Confucianism: Neo-Mohism. Heye, Sam, ed. LC 99-97293. (CHI.). 220p. 1999. pap. 15.00 (*1-930323-00-X*) Sayinga.

Liang, Sheng. Against Fatalism: Neo-Mohism. Heye, Sam, ed. (CHI.). 250p. 1999. pap. 15.00 (*0-9642790-9-6*) Sayinga.
— Against Offensive Warfare: Neo-Mohism. Heye, Sam, ed. (CHI.). 250p. 1998. pap. 15.00 (*0-9642790-8-8*) Sayinga.

***Liang, Sheng.** Cultivating Humanity: Neo-Mohism. Heye, Sam, ed. LC 00-131901. (CHI.). 250p. 2000. pap. 15.00 (*1-930323-02-6*) Sayinga.

Liang, Sheng. Java Native Interface: Programming Guide & Reference. LC 99-30384. (Java Ser.). 320p. (C). 1999. pap. text 39.95 (*0-201-32577-2*) Addison-Wesley.
— Neo-Mohism. (CHI.). 200p. (Orig.). 1995. pap. 20.00 (*0-9642790-2-9*) Sayinga.
— Seeking Commonalities: Neo-Mohism. Heye, Sam, ed. (CHI.). 250p. 1998. pap. 15.00 (*0-9642790-7-X*) Sayinga.

***Liang, Sheng.** Seeking Commonalities: Neo-Mohism. Heye, Sam, ed. LC 00-90023. (CHI.). 250p. 2000. pap. 15.00 (*1-930323-01-8*) Sayinga.

Liang, Sheng. Universal Love: Neo-Mohism. 2nd ed. (CHI.). 300p. 1996. pap. 20.00 (*0-9642790-4-5*) Sayinga.
— Universal Love: Neo-Mohism. 4th ed. Heye, Sam, ed. LC 97-72839. (CHI.). 300p. 1997. reprint ed. pap. 20.00 (*0-9642790-6-1*) Sayinga.
— Zhen Mo. (CHI.). 200p. (Orig.). 1995. pap. text 20.00 (*0-9642790-1-0*) Sayinga.

Liang, Shou-Yu & Wu, Wen-Ching. Qigong Empowerment: A Guide to Medical, Taoist, Buddhist, Wushu Energy Cultivation. Breiter-Wu, Denise, ed. & photos by by. LC 96-61197. (Illus.). 348p. 1996. pap. 34.95 (*1-889659-02-9*) Way of Dragon.

Liang, Shou-Yu & Wu, Wen-Ching. Xiaoyaoshuai: Wuji System Free Fighting Take down Routine. Breiter-Wu, Denise, ed. 117p. pap. 18.00 (*1-889659-12-6*) Way of Dragon.

Liang, Shou-Yu, et al. Tai Chi Chuan: 24 & 48 Postures with Martial Applications. rev. ed. LC 95-61982. (Illus.). 138p. (Orig.). 1996. pap. 15.95 (*1-886969-33-7*, B019R/337) YMAA Pubn.

Liang, Shou-Yu, jt. auth. see Yang, Jwing-Ming.

Liang, Shu-Jan, jt. auth. see Losman, Donald L.

Liang, T. T. T'ai Chi Ch'uan for Health & Self-Defense: Philosophy & Practice. 1977. pap. 10.00 (*0-394-72461-5*) Vin Bks.

Liang, Tan W., jt. auth. see Meng, Low A.

Liang, Ting-Peng & Lee, Jae K. Applied Knowledge Acquisition. 1998. 44.95 (*1-55860-202-X*); disk 25.00 (*1-55860-204-6*) Morgan Kaufmann.

Liang-tso, Hsieh. Shang-ts'ai Yh-lu (Recorded Sayings of Hsieh Liang-Tso) Chu, Ron G., tr. 1999. pap. 17.00 (*1-883058-48-1*, Consort Bilingual) Global Pubns.

Liang, Xiaoyan. Cultural & Economic Factors Influencing Children's Preschool Attendance. rev. ed. LC 98-35309. (Children of Poverty Ser.). 154p. 1998. 40.00 (*0-8153-3132-0*) Garland.

***Liang, Y. Daniel.** Introduction to Java Programming. 2nd ed. LC 98-88887. (Illus.). 598p. (C). 1999. pap. text. write for info. (*1-58076-255-7*) Que Educ & Trng.
— Introduction to Java Programming. 3rd ed. 700p. 2001. pap. 52.00 (*0-13-031997-X*, Prentice Hall) P-H.
— Introduction to Java Programming with JBuilder3. LC 99-53385. (Illus.). 700p. 2000. pap. 68.00 (*0-13-086911-2*) P-H.
— Introduction to Java Programming with Microsoft Visual J++6. LC 99-58866. 700p. 2000. pap. 68.00 (*0-13-086912-0*) P-H.
— Rapid Java Application Development Using Jbuilder 3. LC 99-53483. (Illus.). 784p. 1999. pap. 68.00 (*0-13-026161-0*) P-H.

Liang-Ying Hsu & Dainian, Fan. Science & Socialist Construction in China. Perrolle, Pierre M., ed. Hsu, John C., tr. LC 81-23250. (China Book Project). 253p. 1982. reprint ed. pap. 78.50 (*0-7837-9975-6*, 206070200006) Bks Demand.

Liang, Yun & Biaut, Alan. Theory & Design of Air Cushion Craft. 2nd ed. 640p. 2000. 190.00 (*0-470-23621-3*, Wiley-Interscience) Wiley.

Liang, Z., et al, eds. Flow Modeling & Turbulence Measurements. 800p. 1992. 175.00 (*1-56032-209-8*) Hemisp Pub.

Liang, Zhuge & Ji, Liu. Mastering the Art of War. Cleary, Thomas, ed. & tr. by. from CHI. LC 89-10264. (Dragon Editions Ser.). 152p. 1989. pap. 14.95 (*0-87773-513-1*, Pub. by Shambhala Pubns) Random.

Liang, Zhuge, et al. Mastering the Art of War. Cleary, Thomas, tr. 208p. 1995. pap. 6.00 (*1-57062-081-4*, Pub. by Shambhala Pubns) Random.

***Liang, Zi-Pei.** Principles of Magnetic Resonance Imaging: A Signal Processing Perspective. 1999. 90.00 (*0-8194-3516-3*) SPIE.

***Liangyong, Wu.** Rehabilitating the Old City of Beijing: A Project in the Ju'er Huting Neighbourhood. (Illus.). 256p. 2000. pap. 22.95 (*0-7748-0727-X*, Pub. by UBC Pr) U of Wash Pr.

Lianli, Liu, jt. ed. see Rickett, Adele A.

Lianos, Elias A., ed. Eicosanoid Protocols. LC 98-52322. (Methods in Molecular Biology Ser.: Vol. 120). (Illus.). 312p. 1999. 89.50 (*0-89603-667-7*) Humana.

Lianson. Contemporary Sociology - Critical Perspectives. 1993. pap. text. write for info. (*0-7730-5212-7*) Addison-Wes.

***Lianying, Wang, ed.** Chinese Tree Peony. (Illus.). 224p. 1998. 80.00 (*7-5038-2019-5*, Pub. by China Forest) Wellesley-Cambridge Pr.

Liao, David. The Unresponsive - Resistant or Neglected: Homogeneous Unit Principal Illustrated by the Hakka Chinese in Taiwan. LC 73-175494. 160p. 1979. reprint ed. pap. 6.95 (*0-87808-735-4*) William Carey Lib.

Liao, I-Chiu, jt. ed. see Lee, Cheng-Sheng.

Liao, Jenny, jt. auth. see Goldschmidt, Peter G.

***Liao, Jimmy.** A Chance of Sunshine. LC 99-45319. (Illus.). 128p. (J). 2000. 14.95 (*1-56846-133-X*, Creative Eds) Creative Co.

Liao Kaiming, ed. Chinese Modern Folk Paintings, Vol. I. 151p. 1996. 74.50 (*7-03-004210-7*, Pub. by Sci Pr) Lubrecht & Cramer.

Liao, Kang. Pearl S. Buck: A Cultural Bridge Across the Pacific, 77. LC 96-25016. (Contributions to the Study of World Literature Ser.). 200p. 1997. 52.95 (*0-313-30146-8*) Greenwood.

Liao, Ko-Kaung, jt. auth. see Sauerland, Eberhardt K.

Liao, S. T., et al. Dynamical Systems. (Nankai Series in Pure, Applied Mathematics & Theoretical Physics). 332p. 1993. text 95.00 (*981-02-1350-6*) World Scientific Pub.

***Liao, Sabrina.** Chinese Astrology: Ancient Secrets for Modern Life. 2001. mass mkt. write for info. (*0-446-60981-1*) Warner Bks.

Liao She. Humorous Novels. (CHI.). pap. 9.95 (*7-5321-0880-5*, Pub. by China Intl Bk) Distribks Inc.
— Stories of the Countryside. (CHI.). pap. 9.95 (*7-5321-0876-7*, Pub. by China Intl Bk) Distribks Inc.

Liao, Shu S., jt. auth. see Fremgen, James M.

Liao, Sung J., et al. Principles & Practices of Contemporary Acupuncture. LC 94-21951. (Illus.). 472p. 1994. text 69.75 (*0-8247-9291-2*) Dekker.

Liao, T. T., ed. Advanced Educational Technology: Research Issues & Future Potential. (NATO ASI Series F: Computer & Systems Science: Vol. 145). 256p. 1996. 79.00 (*3-540-59090-0*) Spr-Verlag.

Liao, Tim F. Interpreting Probability Models: Logit, Probit, & Other Generalized Models, No. 101. (Quantitative Applications in the Social Sciences Ser.: Vol. 101). 96p. 1994. pap. 10.95 (*0-8039-4999-5*) Sage.

Liao, Waysun. The Essence of T'ai Chi. LC 94-6790. (Pocket Consultant Ser.). 200p. (Orig.). 1995. pap. 6.95 (1-57062-039-3, Pub. by Shambhala Pubns) Random.
— T'ai Chi Classics. LC 89-43316. (Illus.). 296p. (Orig.). 1990. pap. 15.00 (0-87773-531-X, Pub. by Shambhala Pubns) Random.
Liao Wen-Kuei. The Individual & the Community. LC 73-14035. (International Library of Psychology, Philosophy & Scientific Method Ser.). 314p. (C). 1974. reprint ed. lib. bdg. 69.50 (0-8371-7142-3, LIIN, Greenwood Pr) Greenwood.
Liao, Woody M., et al. Cost Accounting for Managerial Planning, Decision Making & Control. 4th ed. LC 91-73135. 744p. 1992. 76.95 (0-87393-136-X) Dame Pubns.
Liapin, Lev, tr. see Frank-Kamenetskii, Maxim D.
Liapounoff, M. A. Probleme General de la Stabilite du Mouvement. (Annals of Mathematics Studies: No. 17). 1947. 28.00 (0-527-02733-2) Periodicals Srv.
Liapunov, Vadim, ed. & tr. see Bakhtin, Mikhail M.
Liapunova, Rosa G. Essays on the Ethnography of the Aleuts (at the End of the Eighteenth & First Half of the Nineteenth Century) Shelest, Jerry, tr. from RUS. (Rasmuson Library Historical Translation: Vol. IX). Orig. Title: Ocherki po Ethnografii Aleutov (Konets XVIII-per Vaia Polovina XIX v.). xx, 256p. (C). 1996. pap. 18.00 (0-912006-85-4) U of Alaska Pr.
Liard, Charleton Grant. New World Thesaurus. 1986. mass mkt. 9.95 (0-446-38412-7, Pub. by Warner Bks) Little.
Liard, P., et al. Schwindel. (Illus.). x, 102p. 1994. pap. 33.25 (3-8055-5814-7) S Karger.
— Le Vertige. (Illus.). xii, 96p. 1993. pap. 33.25 (3-8055-5822-8) S Karger.
Liardet, Frances, tr. see Al-Kharrat, Edwar.
Liardet, Frances, tr. see Ibrahim, Gamil A.
Liardet, Tim. Competing with the Piano Tuner. LC 99-199889. 64p. 1998. pap. 17.95 (1-85411-227-9, Pub. by Seren Bks) Dufour.
— Fellini Beach. 1995. 14.95 (0-614-07440-1, Pub. by Seren Bks) Dufour.
Liardet, Tim, et al. Fellini Beach. 72p. 1995. pap. 14.95 (1-85411-115-9) Dufour.
Liardon, Roberts. Breaking Controlling Powers. 112p. 1996. pap. 6.99 (1-880089-73-4, AP-973, Pub. by Albury Pub) Appalach Bk Dist.
— Breaking Controlling Powers: To Protect the Spirit, Soul & Body. 1998. pap. text 9.99 (1-57778-089-2) Albury Pub.
— Call to Action. pap. 6.99 (0-89274-894-X) Harrison Hse.
— A Call to Action: Killing Giants & Subduing Kingdoms. 112p. 1996. pap. 6.99 (1-880089-76-9, AP-976, Pub. by Albury Pub) Appalach Bk Dist.
— A Call to Action: Killing Giants & Subduing Kingdoms. rev. ed. 108p. 1985. pap. 6.00 (1-879993-12-0) Albury Pub.
— The Cry of the Spirit. rev. ed. 168p. 1989. pap. 8.00 (1-879993-10-4) Albury Pub.
— Cry of the Spirit: Unpublished Sermons by Smith Wigglesworth. 168p. 1996. pap. 8.99 (1-880089-74-2, AP-974, Pub. by Albury Pub) Appalach Bk Dist.
— Final Approach. 192p. 1993. pap. 10.99 (0-88419-338-1) Creation House.
— Forget Not His Benefits. 64p. 1996. pap. 4.99 (1-880089-78-5, Pub. by Albury Pub) Appalach Bk Dist.
— God's Generals: Why They Succeeded & Why Some Failed. LC 97-200971. 416p. 1996. 39.99 (1-880089-47-5, Pub. by Albury Pub) Appalach Bk Dist.
— God's Generals: Why They Succeeded & Why Some Failed. 88p. 1996. wbk. ed. 9.99 (1-880089-49-1, AP-949, Pub. by Albury Pub) Appalach Bk Dist.
— Haunted Houses, Ghost & Demons: What You Can Do about Them. 128p. 1996. pap. 7.99 (1-880089-79-3, Pub. by Albury Pub) Appalach Bk Dist.
— Holding to the Word of the Lord. 48p. 1996. pap. 4.99 (1-880089-80-7, Pub. by Albury Pub) Appalach Bk Dist.
— How to Survive an Attack. 112p. 1991. pap. 6.99 (1-879993-00-7) Albury Pub.
— How to Survive an Attack. 112p. 1996. pap. 7.99 (1-880089-64-5, Pub. by Albury Pub) Appalach Bk Dist.
— I Saw Heaven. 64p. 1996. pap. 5.99 (1-880089-75-0, Pub. by Albury Pub) Appalach Bk Dist.
***Liardon, Roberts.** I Saw Heaven-& More! 2000. pap. 9.99 (1-890900-24-9, Pub. by Insight Intl) BookWorld.
Liardon, Roberts. The Invading Force. 64p. 1996. pap. 5.99 (1-880089-67-X, AP-967, Pub. by Albury Pub) Appalach Bk Dist.
— The Invading Force. 63p. 1987. pap. 3.95 (0-88144-088-4) Christian Pub.
— The Invading Force. rev. ed. 64p. 1988. pap. 4.00 (1-879993-03-1) Albury Pub.
— Kathryn Kulman: A Spiritual Biography of God's Miracle Working Power. 160p. 1996. pap. 8.99 (1-880089-72-6, Pub. by Albury Pub) Appalach Bk Dist.
— Learning to Say No. rev. ed. 64p. (Orig.). 1988. pap. 4.00 (1-879993-05-8) Albury Pub.
— Learning to Say No: Without Feeling Guilty. 64p. (Orig.). 1996. pap. 5.99 (1-880089-69-6, AP-969, Pub. by Albury Pub) Appalach Bk Dist.
***Liardon, Roberts.** Maria Woodworth-Etter: The Complete Collection of Her Life Teachings. 1032p. 2000. 34.99 (1-57778-122-8) Albury Pub.
Liardon, Roberts. The Price of Spiritual Power. 48p. 1996. pap. 3.99 (1-880089-68-8, Pub. by Albury Pub) Appalach Bk Dist.
— The Price of Spiritual Power. 47p. 1987. pap. 2.95 (0-88144-090-6) Christian Pub.
— The Quest for Spiritual Hunger. 48p. 1996. pap. 3.99 (1-880089-77-7, Pub. by Albury Pub) Appalach Bk Dist.
— The Quest for Spiritual Hunger. 43p. 1987. pap. 2.95 (0-88144-089-2) Christian Pub.
***Liardon, Roberts.** Quest for Spiritual Hunger: Quest for Spiritual Hunger/Price of Spiritual Power, No. 3. 2000. pap. 10.99 (1-57778-129-5) Albury Pub.
Liardon, Roberts. Religious Politics: Men Pleasers or God Pleasers. 32p. 1996. pap. 12.50 (1-880089-66-1, AP-966, Pub. by Albury Pub) Appalach Bk Dist.
— Run to the Battle: Take Your Position in the Move of God. 144p. 1996. pap. 8.99 (1-880089-70-X, Pub. by Albury Pub) Appalach Bk Dist.
***Liardon, Roberts.** Run to the Battle Compilation: The Invading Force/ A Call to Action/ Run to the Battle. 1999. pap. text 12.99 (1-57778-115-5) Albury Pub.
Liardon, Roberts. The School of the Spirit. 1994. pap. 9.99 (0-88419-360-8) Creation House.
— Sharpen Your Discernment: Because When Life Looks Grey, It's Really Black & White. 240p. 1997. pap. 9.99 (1-57778-029-9, Pub. by Albury Pub) Spring Arbor Dist.
— Smith Wigglesworth: The Complete Collection of His Life Teachings. LC 97-205901. 864p. 1997. 29.99 (1-57778-024-8, Pub. by Albury Pub) Appalach Bk Dist.
— Smith Wigglesworth Speaks to Students of the Bible: Includes a One-of-a-Kind Question & Answer Session with Smith Wigglesworth. 368p. 1998. 19.99 (1-57778-058-2, Pub. by Albury Pub) Appalach Bk Dist.
— Spiritual Timing: Discerning Seasons of Change in the Realm of the Spirit. 64p. 1996. pap. 5.99 (1-880089-71-8, AP-971, Pub. by Albury Pub) Appalach Bk Dist.
— What Jesus Likes to Do Through You. 1995. pap. text 4.00 (1-879993-01-5) Albury Pub.
Lias, Edward, jt. auth. see Rondthaler, Edward.
Lias, Godfrey, tr. see Benes, Edvard.
Lias, Kai-Lung. From Yenan to Peking. 1976. lib. bdg. 59.95 (0-8490-1869-2) Gordon Pr.
Lias, Sharon G., jt. ed. see Aulsoos, Pierre.
***Liathain, Ide Ni.** The Life & Career of P. A. McHugh, 1859-1909: A Foot-Soldier of the Party. LC 99-29351. (Maynooth Studies in Local History). 64p. 1999. pap. 10.95 (0-7165-2677-8, Pub. by Irish Acad Pr) Intl Spec Bk.
Liatsos, Sandra. Bicycle Riding. LC 96-83924. (Illus.). 32p. (J). (ps-3). 1997. 15.95 (1-56397-235-2, Wordsong) Boyds Mills Pr.
— Poems to Count On: 30 Terrific Poems & Activities to Help Teach Math Concepts. (Illus.). 1995. pap. 9.95 (0-590-60340-X) Scholastic Inc.
***Liau, Linda M., et al, eds.** Brain Tumor Immunotherapy. 360p. 2000. 165.00 (0-89603-638-3) Humana.
***Liaupsin, Carl J., et al.** Functional Behavioral Assessment: An Interactive Training Module. (Illus.). 114p. 1999. pap. 79.00 incl. cd-rom (1-57035-262-3) Sopris.
— Functional Behavioral Assessment: An Interactive Training Module, Set. 2nd rev. ed. 105p. 2000. per. 79.00 incl. cd-rom (1-57035-274-7, 140FBA) Sopris.
Liaut, Jean-Noel. Cover Girls & Supermodels: 1945-1965. Buss, Robin, tr. from FRE. (Illus.). 271p. 1996. pap. 27.50 (0-7145-2998-2) M Boyars Pubs.
***Liautaud, Bernard.** E-Business Intelligence: Turning Information into Knowledge & Knowledge into Profit. 2000. 27.95 (0-07-136478-1) McGraw.
Liauwnardi, Leonard, et al. Measurement & Predictions of Plastic Gear Transmission Errors with Comparison to the Measured Noise of Plastic & Steel Gears. (Technical Papers: Vol. 97FTM4). (Illus.). 11p. 1977. pap. text 30.00 (1-55589-698-7) AGMA.
Liaw. Capital Markets. (SWC-Economics Ser.). 2001. pap. 64.00 (0-324-02420-7) Thomson Learn.
***Liaw, K. Thomas.** The Business of Investment Banking. LC 98-11641. 352p. 1999. 65.00 (0-471-29305-9) Wiley.
— Irwin Guide to Stocks, Bonds, Futures & Options: A Comprehensive Guide to Wall Street's Market. (Illus.). 388p. 2000. 27.95 (0-07-135947-8) McGraw.
Liaw, K. Thomas, jt. auth. see Lees, Francis A.
Liaw, P. K., et al, eds. First International Conference on Physical Properties of Composites. LC 96-80438. (Illus.). 233p. 1996. 80.00 (0-87339-329-5, 3295) Minerals Metals.
— Microstructure & Mechanical Properties of Aging Materials II. LC 96-80436. (Illus.). 458p. 1995. 100.00 (0-87339-339-2, 3392) Minerals Metals.
***Liaw, P. K., et al, eds.** Nondestructive Evaluation (NDE) & Materials Properties IV. LC 98-68629. (Illus.). 20p. 1999. 100.00 (0-87339-431-3, 4313) Minerals Metals.
Liaw, P. K., ed. see International Conference on Microstructures & Mech.
Liaw, P. K., ed. see Minerals, Metals & Materials Society Staff.
Liaw, Peter K., ed. see Metallurgical Society of AIME Staff.
Liaw, Peter K., ed. see Minerals, Metals & Materials Society Staff.
Liaw, Peter K., ed. see Morris E. Fine Symposium Staff.
Lib. Sanchez Staff. Spanish-English, English-Spanish Dictionary. 1704p. 1991. 55.00 (0-7859-6246-8, 8476300980) Fr & Eur.
Libai, A. & Simmonds, J. G. The Nonlinear Theory of Elastic Shells. 2nd rev. ed. LC 97-13643. (Illus.). 558p. (C). 1998. text 85.00 (0-521-47236-9) Cambridge U Pr.
Libaire, George, ed. see Caulaincourt, Armand A.
Libaire, George, tr. see Caulaincourt, Armand A.
***Libal, Joyce.** Lively Little Quilt Blocks: 26 Step-by-Step Patterns. Hearn, Debbie, ed. (Illus.). 32p. 2000. pap. 14.95 (1-885588-33-X) Chitra Pubns.
Libal, Joyce. Miniature Quilts with Vintage Style. Hearn, Debbie, ed. (Illus.). 32p. 1999. pap. 12.95 (1-885588-28-3) Chitra Pubns.
Libal, Joyce, ed. see Craig, Sharyn S.
Libal, Michael. Limits of Persuasion: Germany & the Yugoslav Crisis, 1991-1992. LC 97-2246. 224p. 1997. 59.95 (0-275-95798-5, Praeger Pubs) Greenwood.
Liban, Felicia. Cloisonne Enameling & Jewelry Making. (Illus.). 256p. 1989. pap. 9.95 (0-486-25971-4) Dover.
Libana, Susanaha, jt. auth. see Lee, Susan.
Libanio, J. B. Spiritual Discernment & Politics: Guidelines for Religious Communities. Morrow, Theodore, tr. from POR. LC 82-2257. Orig. Title: Discernment E politica. 143p. (Orig.). reprint ed. pap. 44.40 (0-8357-7034-6, 203354000086) Bks Demand.
Libanius. Concordantiae in Libanium, Pars Tertia: Declamationes Et Progymnasmata. write for info. incl. 3.5 hd (0-318-70964-3) G Olms Pubs.
— Opera, 12 vols. in 13. cxi, 6513p. 1985. reprint ed. write for info. (0-318-70965-1) G Olms Pubs.
— Selected Orations, 2 vols., I. Warmington, E. H., ed. (Loeb Classical Library: No. 451, 452). (ENG & GRE.). 590p. 1969. text 19.95 (0-674-99496-5) HUP.
— Selected Orations, 2 vols., II. Warmington, E. H., ed. (Loeb Classical Library: No. 451, 452). (ENG & GRE.). 556p. 1969. 19.95 (0-674-99497-3) HUP.
Libaridian, Gerard J., ed. Armenia at the Crossroads: Democracy & Nationhood in the Post-Soviet Era. LC 91-70342. 172p. 1991. 29.95 (0-9628715-1-6); pap. 14.95 (0-9628715-0-8) Blue Crane Bks.
Libaridian, Gerhard J. The Challenge of Statehood: Armenian Political Thinking Since Independence. LC 99-20499. (Human Rights & Democracy Ser.). 128p. 1999. pap. 14.95 (1-886434-10-7, Pub. by Blue Crane Bks) Paul & Co Pubs.
Libassi, Steve. Fundamentals of Placekicking. (Illus.). 256p. 1999. pap. 16.95 (1-58382-019-1) Coaches Choice.
***Libaw, William H.** How We Got to Be Human: Subjective Minds with Objective Bodies. 390p. 2000. 34.95 (1-57392-813-5) Prometheus Bks.
Libb, Melva, jt. auth. see Gregorino, Linda.
Libb, Melva, ed. see Bass-Foster, Cheryl.
Libb, Melva, ed. see Clinkscale, Lonnie.
Libb, Melva, ed. see Conningham, Jewell.
Libb, Melva, ed. see Ragland, Thomas E.
Libben, Gary, jt. auth. see Paradis, Michel.
Libberman, Cy. Mystique of the Tall Ships. 1989. 14.98 (0-88365-747-3) Galahad Bks.
Libbey, Elizabeth. All That Heat in a Cold Sky. LC 91-76615. (Poetry Ser.). (Orig.). 1992. pap. 11.95 (0-88748-145-0) Carnegie-Mellon.
— The Crowd Inside. LC 79-59801. (Poetry Ser.). 1978. 20.95 (0-915604-52-3); pap. 11.95 (0-915604-53-1) Carnegie-Mellon.
— Songs of a Returning Soul. LC 81-71587. 1982. pap. 11.95 (0-915604-67-1) Carnegie-Mellon.
Libbey, James K. Alexander Gumberg & Soviet-American Relations, 1917-1933. LC 77-73704. 241p. reprint ed. pap. 74.80 (0-7837-5777-8, 204544300006) Bks Demand.
— American-Russian Economic Relations, 1770s-1990s: A Survey of Issues & Literature, No. 4. (Guides to Historical Issues Ser.). 220p. 1989. 21.95 (0-941690-35-0); pap. text 11.95 (0-941690-36-9) Regina Bks.
Libbey, Kenneth R. I Forgot, Honey, Why Are We Democrats? LC 97-95062. (Illus.). vi, 196p. 1998. pap. 10.00 (0-9662206-0-9) MacLean & Clark.
Libbey, Mary, ed. see Kipper, Patrick V.
Libbey, Peter, jt. auth. see Hansson, Goran K.
Libbey, Robert. Signal & Image Processing Sourcebook. 512p. 1994. text 69.95 (0-442-30861-2, VNR) Wiley.
Libbey, Robert L., ed. Handbook of Circuit Mathematics for Technical Engineers. 384p. 1991. boxed set 94.95 (0-8493-7400-6) CRC Pr.
Libbey, Ted. The National Symphony Orchestra: The NSO History. (Illus.). 152p. (Orig.). Date not set. 39.95 (0-9649554-0-7); pap. 29.95 (0-9649554-1-5) Devon Jacklin.
— The NPR Guide to Building a Classical CD Collection. LC 92-50292. (Illus.). 496p. 1994. pap. 15.95 (1-56305-051-X, 3051) Workman Pub.
***Libbey, Ted.** NPR Guide to Building a Classical CD Collection: The 300 Essential Works. 2nd rev. ed. (Illus.). 528p. 1999. pap. 15.95 (0-7611-0487-9) Workman Pub.
Libbie, Frederick J. Tinker Family: Ancestors & Descendants of Joseph Wescot Tinker, Ellsworth, Maine, 1791-1868, a Descendant of John Tinker of Boston. 36p. 1994. reprint ed. pap. 7.50 (0-8328-4065-3) Higginson Bk Co.
Libbin, jt. auth. see Catlett.
Libbon, Robert P. Byte Me! Computing for the Terminally Frustrated. LC 97-106622. 224p. 1996. pap. 11.00 (1-57297-204-1) Blvd Books.
— Instant European History: From the French Revolution to the Cold War. (Illus.). 256p. 1996. pap. 10.00 (0-449-90702-3) Fawcett.
Libbrecht, Katrien. Hysterical Psychosis: A Historical Survey. LC 94-8720. 290p. (C). 1994. 44.95 (1-56000-181-X) Transaction Pubs.
Libbrecht, Liz, tr. see Flichy, Patrice.
Libbrecht, Liz, tr. see Hatchuel, Armand & Weil, Benoit.
Libby. Financial Account Win. Tutorial. 2nd ed. 1998. 19.06 (0-07-292414-4) McGraw.
— Financial Accounting. 2nd ed. 1997. pap. 30.00 (0-256-25433-8) McGraw.
— Financial Accounting. 2nd ed. 536p. 1998. pap. 28.13 (0-256-25434-6) McGraw.
— Financial Accounting. 3rd ed. 2001. 68.74 (0-07-230035-3) McGraw.
— Financial Accounting Ready Not. 2nd ed. 264p. 1997. pap. 25.31 (0-256-25435-4) McGraw.
— Using Art to Make Art. LC 99-54016. 250p. (C). 2000. pap. text 25.95 (0-7668-1505-6) Delmar.
Libby, Anthony. The Secret Turning of the Earth. LC 94-33242. (Wick Poetry Chapbook Ser.: No. 5). 32p. (Orig.). 1995. pap. 4.75 (0-87338-520-9) Kent St U Pr.
Libby, Bob. The Forgiveness Book. LC 91-38206. 149p. (Orig.). 1992. pap. 9.95 (1-56101-048-0) Cowley Pubns.
— Grace Happens: Stories of Everyday Encounters with Grace. LC 93-49859. 163p. 1994. pap. 10.95 (1-56101-091-X) Cowley Pubns.
Libby, Charles T. Libby Family in America, 1602-1881. (Illus.). 628p. 1990. reprint ed. pap. 93.50 (0-8328-1495-4); reprint ed. lib. bdg. 101.50 (0-8328-1494-6) Higginson Bk Co.
***Libby, Frederick.** Horses Don't Fly. 2000. 25.95 (1-55970-526-4, Pub. by Arcade Pub Inc) Time Warner.
Libby, Gary R. Coast to Coast: The Contemporary Landscape in Florida. (Illus.). 104p. 1998. write for info. (0-933053-14-2) Museum Art Sciences.
— Cuba: A History in Art. Martinez, Juan A., ed. LC 97-71251. (Illus.). 104p. 1997. 24.95 (0-933053-12-6) Museum Art Sciences.
— Salon & Picturesque Photography in Cuba, 1860-1920. Miller, Sandra L., ed. (Illus.). 50p. (C). 1988. pap. 5.00 (0-933053-02-9) Museum Art Sciences.
Libby, Gary R., ed. Celebrating Florida: Works of Art from the Vickers Collection. LC 95-79304. (Illus.). 144p. 1995. 65.00 (0-933053-09-6) Museum Art Sciences.
— Celebrating Florida: Works of Art from the Vickers Collection. (Illus.). 144p. 1996. 39.95 (0-8130-1477-8) U Press Fla.
Libby, Gary R., ed. see Poyner, Robin.
Libby, Herbert C., ed. see Hichborn, Faustina.
Libby, James A. Meat Hygiene. 4th ed. LC 73-14959. 670p. reprint ed. pap. 200.00 (0-608-16680-4, 205618900055) Bks Demand.
***Libby, Jean, ed.** John Brown & the Coming of the Civil War. 192p. 2000. pap. text. write for info. (1-881089-39-8) Brandywine Press.
— John Brown & the Coming of the Civil War. (Illus.). 180p. 2000. pap. text 14.50 (1-881089-42-8) Brandywine Press.
Libby, Jean, ed. see Cephas, Judith, et al.
Libby, John, Family Association Members Staff, ed. The Libby Family in America, 2 bks., Set, Vol. II. LC 87-125730. 1900p. 1993. 80.00 (0-9636308-1-4) Libby Homestead.
Libby, Kathryn. Cursive Connections: A Traditional Style. 84p. (J). (gr. 2-6). 1998. wbk. ed. 9.99 (0-9666572-0-9) KEL Pub.
***Libby, Kathryn.** Cursive Connections: Modern. 82p. (J). (gr. 2-6). 1999. pap. text, wbk. ed. 17.99 (0-9666572-1-7) KEL Pub.
Libby, L. M. Carbon Dioxide & Climate: Dedicated to Williard F. Libby & Hans E. Suss. (Illus.). 270p. 1980. pap. 48.00 (0-08-026240-6, Pergamon Pr) Elsevier.
Libby, Larry. Someone with You. LC 97-51805. (J). 1998. 14.99 (1-57673-317-3, Gold n Honey) Zondervan.
***Libby, Larry & Halliday, Steve.** No Matter What, No Matter Where: God's Presence on the Road Ahead. LC 99-88476. 128p. 2000. 11.95 (1-57856-314-3) Waterbrook Pr.
— Wonderful Counselor: A Fortnight of Christmas Meditations. 160p. 2000. 12.95 (1-57856-315-1) Waterbrook Pr.
Libby, Larry R. I Remember When I Was Afraid. 1996. 14.99 (0-88070-919-7, Gold n Honey) Zondervan.
— Someday Heaven. 48p. (J). 14.99 (0-945564-77-5, Gold n Honey) Zondervan.
— Someone Awesome. LC 96-128535. (Illus.). 48p. (J). 1995. 14.99 (0-88070-632-5, Gold n Honey) Zondervan.
— Somewhere Angels. (Illus.). 42p. (J). (ps up). 1994. 14.99 (0-88070-651-1, Gold n Honey) Zondervan.
Libby, Larry R., ed. see Mehl, Ron.
Libby, Larry R., ed. see Reeve, Pamela.
Libby, Larry R., ed. see Swindoll, Charles R.
Libby-Larson, Yvonne, jt. auth. see Herr, Judy.
Libby, Margaret S. Attitude of Voltaire to Magic & the Sciences. LC 35-10134. (Columbia University. Studies in the Social Sciences: No. 408). reprint ed. 27.50 (0-404-51408-1) AMS Pr.
***Libby, Megan M.** Postcards from France. LC 96-30924. 160p. 1998. mass mkt. 4.99 (0-06-101170-3) HarpC.
Libby, O. G. The Arikara Narrative of the Campaign Against the Hostile Dakotas: June 1876. (Illus.). Date not set. pap. 22.00 (0-914074-00-8, J M C & Co) Amereon Ltd.
Libby, Orin G., ed. The Arikara Narrative of Custer's Campaign & the Battle of the Little Bighorn. LC 98-23649. (Illus.). 240p. 1998. 9.95 (0-8061-3072-5) U of Okla Pr.
Libby, Patricia A., jt. auth. see Libby, Robert.
Libby, Paul A. An Introduction to Turbulence. (Combustion: an International Ser.). 341p. 1996. 75.00 (1-56032-100-8) Taylor & Francis.
Libby, Paul A., jt. ed. see Williams, F.
Libby, Peter, ed. see Peabody, Kathleen L. & Mooney, Margaret L.
Libby, Robert. Financial Accounting. 1995. pap. text, teacher ed. 27.50 (0-256-21592-8) McGraw.
— Financial Accounting. 336p. (C). 1995. text, student ed. 27.50 (0-256-19971-X, Irwn McGrw-H) McGrw-H Hghr Educ.
— Financial Accounting: Solutions Manual. 640p. (C). 1995. per. 22.50 (0-256-19978-7, Irwn McGrw-H) McGrw-H Hghr Educ.
— Financial Accounting: Working Papers. 584p. (C). 1996. text, suppl. ed. 27.50 (0-256-19976-0, Irwn McGrw-H) McGrw-H Hghr Educ.
Libby, Robert & Libby, Patricia A. Financial Accounting. 2nd ed. 1997. write for info. (0-07-092072-9) McGraw.
Libby, Robert & Libby, Patricia A. Financial Accounting. 2nd ed. LC 97-38002. (C). 1997. text. write for info. (0-256-24568-1, Irwn Prfssnl) McGraw-Hill Prof.
— Financial Accounting: Ready Notes. 304p. (C). 1996. text, suppl. ed. 23.12 (0-256-19977-9, Irwn McGrw-H) McGrw-H Hghr Educ.

L

An Asterisk (*) at the beginning of an entry indicates that the title is appearing for the first time.

Libby, Robert & Short, Daniel G. Financial Accounting: General Ledger Applications Software DOS. 24p. (C). 1996. text 16.50 incl. 3.5 hd (*0-256-21602-9*, Irwn McGrw-H) McGrw-H Hghr Educ.
— Financial Accounting: Wall Street Journal Edition. 864p. (C). 1995. text 82.20 (*0-256-21586-3*, Irwn McGrw-H) McGrw-H Hghr Educ.
— Financial Accounting Package: Wall Street Journal Edition, with Careers CD-ROM & Working Papers. (C). 1996. text, pap. text 92.00 incl. cd-rom (*0-256-24083-3*, Irwn McGrw-H) McGrw-H Hghr Educ.
Libby, Robert, et al. Financial Accounting. LC 95-36377. (Undergraduate Accounting Ser.). 1995. write for info. (*0-256-16053-8*, Irwn McGrw-H) McGrw-H Hghr Educ.
— Financial Accounting. 864p. (C). 1995. text 70.95 (*0-256-19969-8*, Irwn McGrw-H) McGrw-H Hghr Educ.
— Financial Accounting. 2nd ed. LC 97-38002. 784p. 1997. 99.69 (*0-07-289773-2*) McGraw.
***Libby, Ronald.** Eco-Wars: Political Campaigns & Social Movements. LC 98-39826. (Power, Conflict, & Democracy Ser.). 256p. 1999. pap. 21.50 (*0-231-11311-0*); lib. bdg. 49.50 (*0-231-11310-2*) Col U Pr.
Libby, Ronald T. Hawke's Law: The Politics of Mining & Aboriginal Land Rights in Australia. 208p. 1992. reprint ed. pap. text 19.95 (*0-271-00835-0*) Pa St U Pr.
— The Politics of Economic Power in Southern Africa. LC 87-2406. 391p. reprint ed. pap. 121.30 (*0-608-06431-9*, 206664400008) Bks Demand.
— Protecting Markets: U. S. Policy & the World Grain Trade. LC 91-55536. (Illus.). 176p. 1992. text 32.50 (*0-8014-2617-0*) Cornell U Pr.
Libby, Stephen E., Sr., jt. auth. see Martin, Ann Marie.
Libby, Susan, ed. see Levitine, George.
Libby, Terry. The Hunter's Table: The Countrysport Book of Wild Game Cuisine. LC 99-50065. 1999. 30.00 (*0-924357-80-0*) Countrysport Pr.
Libby, W. J., jt. ed. see Ahuja, M. R.
Libby, Willard Frank. Radiocarbon Dating. 2nd ed. LC 55-10246. 187p. reprint ed. pap. 58.00 (*0-608-30492-1*, 200539600053) Bks Demand.
Libecap, Gary. Advances in the Study of Entrepreneurship, Innovation & Economic Growth, Vol. 10. 1998. 78.50 (*0-7623-0357-3*) Jai Pr.
Libecap, Gary, ed. Advances in the Study of Entrepreneurship, Innovation, & Economic Growth, Vol. 7. 1996. 78.50 (*1-55938-728-9*) Jai Pr.
— Advances in the Study of Entrepreneurship, Innovation, & Economic Growth: Corporate Reorganization Through Mergers, Acquisitions, & Leverage Buyouts; Proceeding of the Third Annual Business - Academic Dialogue Held December 5-6, 1986, No. 1. 217p. 1989. suppl. ed. 78.50 (*0-89232-776-6*) Jai Pr.
— Advances in the Study of Entrepreneurship, Innovation, & Economic Growth: Entrepreneurship & Innovation. (Advances in the Study of Entrepreneurship, Innovation & Economic Growth Ser.: Vol. 1). 232p. 1987. 78.50 (*0-89232-703-0*) Jai Pr.
— Advances in the Study of Entrepreneurship, Innovation, & Economic Growth: Innovation in New Markets. (Advances in the Study of Entrepreneurship, Innovation & Economic Growth Ser.: Vol. 2). 304p. 1988. 78.50 (*0-89232-771-5*) Jai Pr.
— Advances in the Study of Entrepreneurship, Innovation, & Economic Growth Vol. 6: New Learning on Entrepreneurship. 192p. 1993. 78.50 (*1-55938-520-0*) Jai Pr.
— Advances in the Study of Entrepreneurship, Innovation, & Economic Growth, Vol. 3 Vol. 3: American International Competitiveness. 231p. 1989. 78.50 (*0-89232-944-0*) Jai Pr.
Libecap, Gary D. Contracting for Property Rights. (Political Economy of Institutions & Decisions Ser.). (Illus.). 142p. (C). 1990. text 59.95 (*0-521-36620-8*) Cambridge U Pr.
— Contracting for Property Rights. (Political Economy of Institutions & Decisions Ser.). (Illus.). 142p. (C). 1994. pap. text 16.95 (*0-521-44904-9*) Cambridge U Pr.
— The Evolution of Private Mineral Rights: Nevada's Comstock Lode. LC 77-14777. (Dissertations in American Economic History Ser.). 1978. 33.95 (*0-405-11047-2*) Ayer.
Libecap, Gary D., ed. Advances in the Study of Entrepreneurship, Innovation, & Economic Growth Vol. 4: Health Care Issues & American Economic Growth. 235p. 1990. 78.50 (*1-55938-191-4*) Jai Pr.
— Advances in the Study of Entrepreneurship, Innovation, & Economic Growth Vol. 9: Policy Constraints & Technological Opportunities for Entrepreneurial Mid-Sized Firms. 1997. 78.50 (*0-7623-0329-8*) Jai Pr.
— The Innovation Middle: Political & Economic Factors Affecting Mid-Size Business. (Advances in the Study of Entrepreneurship, Innovation & Economic Growth Ser.: Vol. 8). 1996. 78.50 (*0-7623-0185-6*) Jai Pr.
Libecap, Gary D., jt. auth. see Johnson, Ronald N.
Libecap, Gary D., jt. ed. see Goldin, Claudia D.
Libel Defense Resource Center Staff, ed. LDRC 50-State Survey: Current Developments in Media Libel Law. 12th ed. xviii, 938p. (C). 1995. pap. text 135.00 (*0-913269-09-3*) Libel Defense Resource Ctr.
Libel Defense Staff. LDRC 50-State Survey, 1999-00 Vol. 5: Media Privacy & Related Law. 1280p. 1999. pap. 125.00 (*0-913269-16-6*) Libel Defense Resource Ctr.
— LDRC 50-State Survey, 1999-00 Vol. 16: Media Libel Law. 1000p. 1999. pap. 125.00 (*0-913269-17-4*) Libel Defense Resource Ctr.
Libel Defense Staff, ed. LDRC 50-State Survey, 1999: Employment Libel & Privacy Law. 1000p. 1998. pap. 135.00 (*0-913269-18-2*) Libel Defense Resource Ctr.
Liben, Lynn, ed. Piaget & the Foundations of Knowledge. 272p. 1984. text 59.95 (*0-89859-248-8*) L Erlbaum Assocs.
Liben, Lynn S. Development & Learning: Conflict or Congruence? (Jean Piaget Symposia Ser.). 256p. 1987. 49.95 (*0-8058-0009-3*) L Erlbaum Assocs.
Libenson, Mikhail N., jt. ed. see Konov, Vitaly I.
Liber de Duobus Principiis Staff. Un Traite Neo-Manicheen du XIIIe Siecle. LC 78-63185. (Heresies of the Early Christian & Medieval Era Ser.: Second Ser.). 1979. reprint ed. 49.50 (*0-404-16224-X*) AMS Pr.
Liber Domicilii Regis Jacobi Quinti Staff. Excerpta E Libris Domicilii Domini Jacobi Quinti Regis Scotorum. LC 75-172317. (Bannatyne Club, Edinburgh. Publications: No. 54). reprint ed. 37.50 (*0-404-52764-7*) AMS Pr.
Liber, George O. Soviet Nationality Policy, Urban Growth, & Identity Change in the Ukrainian SSR, 1923-1934. (Cambridge Russian, Soviet & Post-Soviet Studies: No. 84). (Illus.). 314p. (C). 1992. text 69.95 (*0-521-41391-5*) Cambridge U Pr.
Liber Kartor AB Staff, jt. auth. see Maps International Staff.
Libera, Alain De, see Hoenen, Maarten J. & De Libera, Alain.
***Libera, Antoni.** Madame. Kolakowska, Agniewska, tr. from POL. LC 99-49705. 288p. 2000. 24.00 (*0-374-20006-8*) FS&G.
Libera, M. R., et al, eds. Crystallization & Related Phenomena in Amorphous Materials Vol. 321: Materials Research Society Symposium Proceedings. LC 94-2232. 753p. 1994. text 17.50 (*1-55899-220-0*) Materials Res.
Liberace, Maire. Life Career & Educational Planning. 150p. (C). 1990. 45.00 (*0-536-57807-9*) Pearson Custom.
— Life Career & Educational Planning. 2nd ed. 154p. (C). 1996. text 33.60 (*0-536-59615-8*) Pearson Custom.
Liberal Summer School Oxford Staff. Essays in Liberalism Being the Lectures & Papers Which Were Delivered at the Liberal Summer School at Oxford, 1922. 1977. 23.95 (*0-8369-0426-5*) Ayer.
Liberatore. Cpso Operations Mgmt Notebook. 1997. pap. text 18.25 (*0-07-292541-8*) McGraw.
— Liberatore's Women. 96p. 1998. 24.95 (*0-87816-617-3*) Kitchen Sink.
***Liberatore, Angela.** The Management of Uncertainty Learning from Chernobyl. 324p. 1999. text 55.00 (*90-5700-552-2*) Gordon & Breach.
Liberatore, E. K. Helicopters Before Helicopters. LC 97-40003. 310p. (C). 1998. text 69.50 (*1-57524-053-X*) Krieger.
Liberatore, M. J., ed. Selection & Evaluation of Advanced Manufacturing Technologies. (Illus.). vi, 324p. 1990. 95.95 (*0-387-52656-0*) Spr-Verlag.
Liberatore, Paul. The San Quentin Massacre: A True Story of Race & Violence in the Radical New Left. 1994. 22.95 (*1-879360-32-2*) Noble Pr.
Libercier, Marie-Helene & Schneider, Hartmut. Migrants: Partners in International Cooperation. LC 97-102597. 60p. (Orig.). 1996. pap. 12.00 (*92-64-14907-4*, 41-96-06-1, Pub. by Org for Econ) OECD.
Libercier, Marie-Helene, ed. see OECD Staff.
Liberles, Robert. Religious Conflict in Social Context: The Resurgence of Orthodox Judaism in Frankfurt Am Main, 1838-1877, 13. LC 84-27981. (Contributions to the Study of Religion Ser.: No. 13). 295p. 1985. 62.95 (*0-313-24806-0*, LRX/) Greenwood.
— Salo Wittmayer Baron: Architect of Jewish History. (Modern Jewish Masters Ser.). (C). 1995. text 45.00 (*0-8147-5088-5*) NYU Pr.
Liberman, Alvin M. Speech: A Special Code. (Learning, Development & Conceptual Change Ser.). (Illus.). 472p. 1996. 59.50 (*0-262-12192-1*, Bradford Bks) MIT Pr.
Liberman, Anatoly. Germanic Accentology, Vol. 1: The Scandinavian Languages. LC 80-27276. (Minnesota Publications in the Humanities). 392p. reprint ed. pap. 121.60 (*0-7837-2937-5*, 205751700006) Bks Demand.
Liberman, Anatoly, ed. see Propp, Vladimir.
Liberman, Anatoly, ed. & tr. see Trubetskoi, Nikolai Sergeevich.
Liberman, Anatoly, ed. & tr. see Trubetzkoy, N. S.
Liberman, Anatoly, tr. & intro. see Trubetzkoy, N. S.
Liberman, Cy & Liberman, Pat. The Crab Cook Book: How to Catch & Cook Crabs. LC 98-3260. 136p. 1998. 9.95 (*0-912608-96-X*) Mid Atlantic.
Liberman, David. The Eternal Torah: A Commentary upon the Books of Joshua-Judges-Smauel One, Samuel Two,, Pt. 2. 360p. 1983. 20.00 (*0-9609840-1-1*) Twin Pines Pr.
Liberman, Evsefi G. Economic Methods & the Effectiveness of Production. LC 70-183252. 195p. reprint ed. pap. 60.50 (*0-608-14593-9*, 202481300038) Bks Demand.
Liberman, Gail & Lavine, Alan. Love, Marriage & Money. LC 98-12784. 208p. 1998. pap. 15.95 (*0-7931-2661-4*) Dearborn.
Liberman, Gail, jt. auth. see Lavine, Alan.
Liberman, Hal, jt. auth. see Liberman, Rita T.
Liberman, Isabelle Y., jt. ed. see Shankweiler, Donald.
Liberman, Jacob. Light: A New Paradigm for Healing. Set. 142p. 1995. pap. 16.95 incl. audio (*1-879323-27-3*) Sound Horizons AV.
— Light: Medicine of the Future: How We Can Use It to Heal Ourselves Now. LC 90-748. (Illus.). 288p. (Orig.). 1993. pap. 16.95 (*1-879181-01-0*) Bear & Co.
Liberman, Jacob. Take off Your Glasses & See: A Mind - Body Approach to Expanding Your Eyesight & Insight. 288p. 1995. pap. 14.00 (*0-517-88604-9*) Crown Pub Group.
Liberman, Joan. The Busy World of Richard Scarry Busytown (an OMSI Exhibit) Activity Guide for Parents & Teachers. (SPA., Illus.). 72p. (Orig.). 1995. pap. 5.00 (*0-9617645-2-X*) Oreg Mus Sci & Indus.
Liberman, Jon C. SuperCharge Your Sales Force: Applying the Power of Computers to Get the Best from Your Sales Team. 225p. 1993. text 22.95 (*1-55738-441-X*, Irwn Prfssnl) McGraw-Hill Prof.
Liberman, Kenneth. Understanding Interaction in Central Australia. (Studies in Ethnomethodology). 352p. 1985. 67.50 (*0-7102-0473-6*, Routledge Thoemms) Routledge.
Liberman, Lee, ed. see Cohen, David.
Liberman, Lee, ed. see Wels, Susan.
Liberman, Leon, ed. see Avis, Kenneth E., et al.
Liberman, M., et al. Physics of High - Density Z - Pinch Plasmas. 350p. 1998. 79.00 (*0-387-98568-9*) Spr-Verlag.
Liberman, M. A. & Velikovich, A. L. Physics of Shock Waves in Gases & Plasmas. (Electrophysics Ser.: Vol. 19). (Illus.). 400p. 1986. 102.95 (*0-387-15605-4*) Spr-Verlag.
Liberman, Myron M. Katherine Anne Porter's Fiction. LC 73-107951. 115p. reprint ed. pap. 35.70 (*0-7837-3630-4*, 204349600009) Bks Demand.
Liberman, Pat, jt. auth. see Liberman, Cy.
Liberman, Peter. Does Conquest Pay? The Exploitation of Occupied Industrial Societies. (Princeton Studies in International History & Politics). 272p. 1996. pap. text 17.95 (*0-691-00242-8*, Pub. by Princeton U Pr) Cal Prin Full Svc.
— Does Conquest Pay? The Exploitation of Occupied Industrial Societies. LC 95-17925. (Studies in International History & Politics). 272p. 1996. text 37.50 (*0-691-02986-5*, Pub. by Princeton U Pr) Cal Prin Full Svc.
Liberman, R. P., et al. Handbook of Marital Therapy: A Positive Approach to Helping Troubled Relationships. LC 79-9103. (Applied Clinical Psychology Ser.). (Illus.). 278p. (C). 1980. 45.00 (*0-306-40235-1*, Plenum Trade) Perseus Pubng.
Liberman, Rita T. & Liberman, Hal. Tot's 'n Tension. 100p. (Orig.). 1985. pap. 5.95 (*0-9614923-0-9*) Tranquil Pr.
Liberman, Robert P., ed. Effective Psychiatric Rehabilitation. LC 87-646993. (New Directions for Mental Health Services Ser.: No. MHS 53). 120p. 1991. pap., student ed. 25.00 (*1-55542-757-X*) Jossey-Bass.
— Psychiatric Rehabilitation of Chronic Mental Patients. LC 87-1492. 319p. 1988. pap. text 28.00 (*0-88048-201-X*, 8201) Am Psychiatric.
Liberman, Robert P. & Yager, Joel, eds. Stress in Psychiatric Disorders. LC 93-41244. 208p. 1994. 34.95 (*0-8261-8310-7*) Springer Pub.
Liberman, Robert P., et al. The Handbook of Marital Therapy: A Positive Approach to Helping Troubled Relationships. LC 79-9103. (Applied Clinical Psychology Ser.). (Illus.). 278p. 1980. student ed. 15.00 (*0-685-04074-7*, Plenum Trade) Perseus Pubng.
Liberman, Robert Paul. Social Skills Training for Psychiatric. 272p. (C). 1989. pap. text 41.00 (*0-205-14406-3*, H4406) Allyn.
— Social Skills Training for Psychiatric. 272p. (C). 1992. pap. text 60.50 (*0-205-14407-1*, H4407) Allyn.
Liberman, Rosette, jt. auth. see Heyworth, Gregory.
Liberman, Susan, et al. Memorable Film Characters: An Index to Roles & Performers, 1915-1983, 1. LC 84-10844. (Bibliographies & Indexes in the Performing Arts Ser.: No. 1). 291p. 1984. lib. bdg. 69.50 (*0-313-23977-0*, LMF/, Greenwood Pr) Greenwood.
Liberman, Susan A., jt. auth. see Bartle, Nathalie A.
***Liberman, Tania.** Stop the Stress for Personal Growth. 1999. 24.99 (*965-222-915-6*) Maureen Mack.
Liberman, Yaacov. My China: Jewish Life in the Orient, 1900-1950. LC 97-36231. (Illus.). 248p. 1997. 24.95 (*965-229-171-4*, Pub. by Gefen Pub Hse) Gefen Bks.
Libermann, Y., jt. auth. see Van der Wolf, W.
***Libero, Chiara.** Florida. (Illus.). 2000. 9.99 (*0-7858-1238-5*) Bk Sales Inc.
Libero, Chiara. London. (Places & History Ser.). 272p. 1998. 24.95 (*1-55670-692-8*) Stewart Tabori & Chang.
Libersat, Henry. Miracles Today: True Stories of Divine Healing. LC 99-33944. 194p. 1999. pap. 10.99 (*1-56955-107-3*, Charis) Servant.
— We Believe: Growing Spiritually Through the Catechism of the Catholic Church, Vol. 1. LC 96-50958. (Catholic Confession of Faith Ser.). 90p. 1997. pap. 5.95 (*0-8198-8288-7*) Pauline Bks.
— We Celebrate the Mystery: Growing Spiritually Through the Catechism of the Catholic Church, Vol. 2. LC 96-50959. (Catholic Confession of Faith Ser.). 106p. (Orig.). 1997. pap. 5.95 (*0-8198-8289-5*) Pauline Bks.
— We Live the Good Life: Growing Spiritually Through the Catechism of the Catholic Church, Vol. 3. LC 96-50957. (Catholic Confession of Faith Ser.). 142p. 1997. pap. 5.95 (*0-8198-8290-9*) Pauline Bks.
— We Pray: Growing Spiritually Through the Catechism of the Catholic Church, Vol. 4. LC 96-37932. (Catholic Confession of Faith Ser.). 62p. (Orig.). 1997. pap. 5.95 (*0-8198-8291-7*) Pauline Bks.
Libersat, Henry, jt. auth. see McKenna, Briege.
Liberski, P. P. The Enigma of Slow Viruses: Facts & Artefacts. LC 92-48419. (Archives of Virology Ser.: No. 6). 1993. write for info. (*3-211-82427-8*); 196.95 (*0-387-82427-8*) Spr-Verlag.
Liberski, Pawel P., ed. Light & Electronmicroscopic Neuropathology - Slow Virus Diseases. 448p. 1992. lib. bdg. 239.00 (*0-8493-6725-5*, QR201) CRC Pr.
Liberson, Cathryn. W. T. Liberson Vol. 1: Collected Writings. 377p. 1998. 75.00 (*0-918266-35-1*) Smyrna.
Liberson, Cathryn, ed. see Liberson, Wladimir T.
Liberson, Wladimir T. Brains, Nerves, Muscles, & Electricity: My Life in Science. Cohen, Robert, ed. LC 99-7093. Date not set. pap. 15.00 (*0-918266-38-6*) Smyrna.
— Collected Writings of Wladimir T. Liberson Vol. I: 1940-1959. Liberson, Cathryn, ed. LC 96-71967. (Illus.). 400p. 1998. lib. bdg. 75.00 (*0-918266-34-3*) Smyrna.
Libert, Bo. The Environmental Heritage of Soviet Agriculture. (Sustainable Rural Development Ser.). (Illus.). 250p. 1995. text 80.00 (*0-85198-961-6*) OUP.
Libert, Jack. Brothers & Sisters of the January Moon. (Illus.). (Orig.). 1971. pap. 10.00 (*0-911732-58-6*) Irego.
— Children of the Twenty Third Century Beautiful As You Will Be I Know Your Hair. (Illus.). 73p. 1980. pap. 10.00 (*0-911732-08-X*) Irego.
— The Doorman. (Orig.). 1966. 20.00 (*0-911732-50-0*); pap. 10.00 (*0-911732-51-9*) Irego.
— Edasi. (Illus.). 96p. (Orig.). (C). 1986. pap. 10.00 (*0-9614148-0-4*) Edasi.
— Myself Exactly. (Illus.). (Orig.). 1971. pap. 10.00 (*0-911732-56-X*) Irego.
— Sun a Honeydew, Moon a Cantaloupe. (Illus.). (Orig.). 1970. pap. 10.00 (*0-911732-53-5*) Irego.
— Waiting for Me Waiting for the Train Hilda Dearwater. (Illus.). 1972. pap. 10.00 (*0-911732-59-4*) Irego.
— You. (Orig.). 1971. pap. 10.00 (*0-911732-57-8*) Irego.
Liberte, Barbra. Am I Guilty? LC 97-60960. 229p. 1997. pap. 14.95 (*0-931563-18-6*, P-aig) Wishing Rm.
Liberthson. Con Heart Disease. 1989. 85.00 (*0-316-52413-1*, Little Brwn Med Div) Lppncott W & W.
Liberti, Annamaria. Ancient Rome: History of a Civilization That Ruled the World. LC 60-69113. (Illus.). 292p. 1996. 60.00 (*1-55670-531-X*) Stewart Tabori & Chang.
Liberti, Lawrence E., jt. auth. see Der Marderosian, Ara H.
Liberti, Lorenzo & Millar, John R. Fundamentals & Applications of Ion Exchange. LC 85-18842. 1985. text 215.00 (*90-247-3229-8*) Kluwer Academic.
Libertine, Dan, tr. see Crary, Dan.
***Libertino, Dan.** The Ventures Pipline: 25 Surfin Hits for Solo Guitar. (Illus.). 128p. 1999. pap. 19.95 (*1-56922-199-5*, 07-4093) Creat Cncpts.
Libertino, John. Pediatric & Reconstructive Urologic Surgery. 3rd ed. (Illus.). 800p. (C). (gr. 13). 1997. text 165.00 (*0-8016-7802-1*, 07802) Mosby Inc.
Liberto, Nicholas, ed. Powder Coating: The Complete Finisher's Handbook. LC 94-78590. (Illus.). 1994. 75.00 (*0-9643091-0-6*) Powder Coat Inst.
Libertone, David. Windows NT Cluster Server Guidebook. LC 99-161354. 280p. (C). 1998. pap. text 49.95 (*0-13-096019-5*) P-H.
***Libertone, David.** Windows 2000 Cluster Server. 2nd ed. 336p. 2000. pap. 49.99 (*0-13-028469-6*) P-H.
***Libertone, David & Scoppa, Andrew.** Implementing an E-Commerce Web Site Using MS Site Server 3.0: Commerce Edition. LC 99-40079. (Series on Microsoft Technology). (Illus.). 252p. 1999. pap. text 39.99 (*0-13-085082-9*) P-H.
Libertson, Joseph. Proximity, Levinas, Blanchot, Bataille & Communication. (Phaenomenologica Ser.: No. 87). 361p. 1982. lib. bdg. 171.00 (*90-247-2506-2*, Pub. by M Nijhoff) Kluwer Academic.
Liberty, Anita. How to Heal the Hurt by Hating. LC 98-19072. 1998. pap. 10.95 (*0-345-42374-7*) Ballantine Pub Grp.
Liberty, Arthur L. Pewter & the Revival of Its Use. (Shorey Lost Arts Ser.). (Illus.). 44p. 1904. reprint ed. pap. 10.00 (*0-8466-6007-5*, U-7) Shoreys Bkstore.
Liberty, Franklin P. Computer Programming Ship's Business. LC 87-5231. (Illus.). 294p. (Orig.). 1987. reprint ed. pap. 91.20 (*0-7837-9064-3*, 204981300003) Bks Demand.
Liberty, Jesse. Beginning Object Oriented Analysis & Design. 400p. 1998. pap. 34.95 (*1-86100-133-9*, Pub. by Wrox Press) Wrox Pr Inc.
***Liberty, Jesse.** Creating & Deploying Web Databases Using WinDNA from Scratch. (From Scratch Ser.). 400p. 1999. pap. 39.99 (*0-7897-2126-0*) Que.
Liberty, Jesse. Sams Teach Yourself C++ in 21 Days. 3rd ed. LC 98-88869. (Teach Yourself Ser.). 1999. pap. text 29.99 (*0-672-31515-7*) Sams.
— Teach Yourself C++ in 21 Days: Complete Compiler Edition. (Teach Yourself Ser.). 1999. text 49.99 (*0-672-31564-5*) Sams.
— Teach Yourself C++ in 24 Hours. 2nd ed. LC 98-89565. (Teach Yourself Ser.). 1999. pap. text 19.99 (*0-672-31516-5*) Sams.
— Teach Yourself C++ in 21 Days. (Illus.). 815p. 1994. pap. 29.99 (*0-672-30541-0*) Sams.
— Teach Yourself C++ in 21 Days. 2nd ed. LC 97-65468. 800p. 1997. 29.99 (*0-672-31070-8*) Sams.
— Sams Teach Yourself C++ in 21 Days: Complete Complier Edition. 760p. 1998. pap. text 49.99 (*0-672-31261-1*) Sams.
***Liberty, Jesse & Kraley, Mike.** XML Web Documents from Scratch. (Illus.). 350p. 2000. 29.99 (*0-7897-2316-6*) Que.
Liberty, Jesse, et al. C++ Unleashed. LC 97-69859. 800p. 1998. 39.99 (*0-672-31239-5*, Pub. by Macmillan) S&S Trade.
Liberty, John. Journals of Dissent & Social Change. 7th ed. 554p. 1993. pap. 25.00 (*0-938847-01-5*) CSU Sacto Lib.
Liberty, Larry L. Leadership Wisdom: A Guide to Producing Extraordinary Results. LC 94-226132. 272p. (Orig.). 1994. pap. 19.95 (*0-9641669-0-9*) Liberty Cnslting.
Liberty, Margo, et al. Working Cowboy: Recollections of Ray Holmes. LC 94-29445. (Illus.). 288p. 1995. 24.95 (*0-8061-2692-2*) U of Okla Pr.
Liberty, Margot, jt. auth. see Stands in Timber, John.
Liberty, Margot, jt. auth. see Stands In Timber, John.
Liberty, Margot, jt. ed. see Wood, W. Raymond.
Liberty National Council for Civil Liberties Staff, ed. Liberating Cyberspace: Civil Liberties, Human Rights & the Internet. 256p. 1999. pap. 19.95 (*0-7453-1294-2*, Pub. by Pluto GBR) Stylus Pub VA.
— Liberating Cyberspace: Civil Liberties, Human Rights & the Internet. LC 97-44923. 256p. 1999. 59.95 (*0-7453-1299-3*, Pub. by Pluto GBR) Stylus Pub VA.
Liberty Publishing Staff. National Park Vacation: America's Best. 1991. pap. 9.95 (*0-89709-191-4*) Liberty Pub.

Libes, Don. Exploring Expect: A TCL-Based Toolkit for Automating Interactive Programs. O'Reilly, Tim, ed. LC 97-159228. (Illus.). 602p. (Orig.). 1994. pap. 32.95 (*1-56592-090-2*) Thomson Learn.

— Obfuscated C & Other Mysteries, Set. LC 92-17028. (Illus.). 432p. 1992. pap. 39.95 incl. disk (*0-471-57805-3*) Wiley.

Libes, Sol, et al. Digital Electronics: Concepts & Applications. (Illus.). 292p. 1988. reprint ed. pap. text 14.00 (*0-86657-007-1*) Lab-Volt.

Libes, Susan. An Introduction to Marine Biochemistry. LC 91-28299. 752p. (C). 1992. text 96.95 (*0-471-50946-9*) Wiley.

Libeskind, jt. auth. see Billstein.

***Libeskind, D.** The Jewish Museum in Berlin. (Illus.). 160p. 1999. text 38.00 (*90-5701-252-9*) Gordon & Breach.

— Das Judische Museum in Berlin. (GER., Illus.). 160p. 1998. text 36.00 (*90-5705-098-6*, Verlag Kunst) Gordon & Breach.

***Libeskind, Daniel.** Daniel Libeskind: The Space of Encounter. (Illus.). 224p. 2000. 50.00 (*0-7893-0483-X*); pap. 35.00 (*0-7893-0496-1*) Universe.

— Kein Ort An Seiner Stelle: Schriften Zur Architektur - Visionen Fur Berlin. (GER., Illus.). 248p. 1995. text 23.00 (*3-364-00360-2*, Verlag Kunst) Gordon & Breach.

Libeskind, Daniel. Radix-Matrix: Daniel Libeskind. Green, Peter, tr. from GER. LC 98-114166. (Illus.). 176p. 1996. 65.00 (*3-7913-1727-X*, Pub. by Prestel) te Neues.

Libeskind, Daniel & LeCuyer, Annette W. 1995 Raoul Wallenberg Lecture: Daniel Libeskind: Traces of the Unborn. (Illus.). 50p. (Orig.). (C). 1995. pap. text 11.50 (*0-9614792-1-3*) U Mich Arch.

Libeskind, Daniel, jt. auth. see Benjamin, Andrew.

Libeskind-Hadas, Ran. Fault Covering Problems in Reconfigurable VLSI Systems. (International Series in Engineering & Computer Science, VLSI, Computer Architecture, & Digital Screen Processing). 144p. (C). 1992. text 105.00 (*0-7923-9231-0*) Kluwer Academic.

Libeskind, Lanny. Advances in Metal-Organic Chemistry, Vol. 6. 1999. 109.50 (*0-7623-0206-2*) Jai Pr.

Libet, Benjamin. Neurophysiology of Consciousness: Selected Papers of Benjamin Libet. LC 93-16896. (Contemporary Neuroscientists Ser.). (Illus.). 424p. 1993. 109.00 (*0-8176-3538-6*) Birkhauser.

***Libet, Benjamin, et al.** The Volitional Brain: Towards a Neuroscience of Free Will. 1999. 32.95 (*0-907845-50-9*, Pub. by Imprint Acad) Philos Document.

— The Volitional Brain: Towards a Neuroscience of Free Will. xxi, 298p. 2000. pap. 24.95 (*0-907845-11-8*, Pub. by Imprint Acad) Philos Document.

Libet, Gayla, ed. see Ogbu, Ogbonna.

Libey, Don, et al. The Operations & Fulfillment Handbook. Evens, Judy, ed. (Illus.). 1996. 79.95 (*0-9652607-0-4*) Target Communicators.

Libgober, A., jt. auth. see Birman, J.

Libicki, Martin. Information Technology Standards: Quest for the Common Byte. 432p. 1995. text 69.95 (*1-55558-131-5*, Digital DEC) Buttrwrth-Heinemann.

***Libicki, Martin, et al.** Scaffolding the New Web: Standards & Standards Policy for the Digital Economy. xxiii, 123p. (C). 2000. pap. 15.00 (*0-8330-2858-8*) Rand Corp.

Libicki, Martin C. Defending Cyberspace & Other Metaphors. LC 96-53238. 1997. write for info. (*1-57906-031-5*) Natl Defense.

Libicki, Martin C. Mesh & the Net: Speculations on Armed Conflict in a Time of Free Silicon. 133p. 1994. per. 7.50 (*0-16-061161-X*) USGPO.

Libicki, Martin C. The Mesh & the Net: Speculations on Armed Conflict in a Time of Free Silicon. 127p. (C). 1996. reprint ed. pap. text 30.00 (*0-7881-3504-X*) DIANE Pub.

— Standards: The Rough Road to the Common Byte. (Illus.). 46p. (Orig.). 1994. pap. text. write for info. (*1-879716-15-1*, P-94-6) Ctr Info Policy.

— Standards: The Rough Road to the Common Byte. 75p. (Orig.). 1995. per. 4.25 (*0-16-042637-5*) USGPO.

— Standards: The Rough Road to the Common Byte. (Illus.). 61p. (Orig.). (C). 1997. reprint ed. pap. text 25.00 (*0-7881-4673-4*) DIANE Pub.

— What Makes Industries Strategic: A Perspective on Technology, Economic Development, & Defense. (Illus.). 89p. (Orig.). (C). 1996. reprint ed. pap. text 30.00 (*0-7881-3155-9*) DIANE Pub.

Libietis, Helmuts. True Devotion Consecration to Mary. LC 99-14060. 420p. 1981. pap. 12.95 (*0-935952-44-6*) Angelus Pr.

Libin, Laurence. Our Tuneful Heritage: American Musical Instruments from the Metropolitan Museum of Art. LC 94-42019. 103p. 1998. pap. 19.95 (*0-8425-2325-1*, Pub. by Brigham) U Ch Pr.

Libin, Laurence, et al. The Spanish Guitar. (ENG & SPA., Illus.). 210p. (C). reprint ed. pap. 65.00 (*0-933224-79-6*, 1150, Pub. by Opera Tres) Bold Strummer Ltd.

Libin, Nina. Tatted Lace of Beads: The Techniques of Beanile Lace. LC 98-228567. (Illus.). 112p. 1998. pap. 24.00 (*0-916896-93-5*, LE46) Lacis Pubns.

***Libis, Scott.** Air Force Legends Number 204 Lockhead NF-104A Aerospace Trainer. Ginter, Steve, ed. (Air Force Legends Ser.: 204). (Illus.). 44p. 1999. pap. 10.95 (*0-942612-97-3*, NFAF204) Naval Fighters.

Libis, Scott. Martin XB-51. Ginter, Steve, ed. (Air Force Legends Ser.: No. 201). (Illus.). 48p. 1998. pap. 10.95 (*0-942612-00-0*, NFAF201) Naval Fighters.

Libkind, Marcus. Ski Tours in Lassen Volcanic National Park. LC 89-92069. (Illus.). 128p. (Orig.). 1989. pap. 12.95 (*0-931255-04-X*) Bittersweet Pub.

— Ski Tours in the Sierra Nevada: Carson Pass, Bear Valley, Pinecrest, Vol. 2. LC 84-73452. (Illus.). 132p. (Orig.). 1985. pap. 12.95 (*0-931255-01-5*) Bittersweet Pub.

— Ski Tours in the Sierra Nevada: East of Sierra Crest, Vol. 4. LC 84-73452. (Illus.). 184p. (Orig.). 1986. pap. 14.95 (*0-931255-03-1*) Bittersweet Pub.

— Ski Tours in the Sierra Nevada: Lake Tahoe, Vol. 1. (Illus.). 266p. (Orig.). 1995. pap. 16.95 (*0-931255-08-2*) Bittersweet Pub.

— Ski Tours in the Sierra Nevada: Yosemite, Kings Canyon, Sequoia, Vol. 3. LC 84-73452. (Illus.). 136p. (Orig.). 1985. pap. 12.95 (*0-931255-02-3*) Bittersweet Pub.

Libliner, Murray, intro. International Brand Packaging Awards. (Illus.). 160p. 1993. 34.99 (*1-56496-059-5*, 30544) Rockport Pubs.

***Libman, Howard & Makadon, Harvey, eds.** HIV. LC 99-57890. (Key Diseases Ser.). (Illus.). 320p. 2000. pap. text 35.00 (*0-943126-84-3*, 330300890) Amer Coll Phys.

Libman, Howard & Witzburg, Robert A., eds. HIV Infection: A Primary Care Manual. 3rd ed. 732p. 1995. pap. text 44.00 (*0-316-51160-9*, Little Brwn Med Div) Lppncott W & W.

Libman, Lillian. Music at the Close: Stravinsky's Last Years. (Illus.). 1972. 34.95 (*0-8464-0659-4*) Beekman Pubs.

Libo, Kenneth & Howe, Irving. We Lived There Too: In Their Own Words & Pictures - Pioneer Jews & the Westward Movement of America 1630-1930. (Illus.). 4p. 1985. pap. 14.95 (*0-312-85867-1*) St Martin.

Liboff, Richard L. Introductory Quantum Mechanics. (Illus.). 672p. 1980. text 61.25 (*0-201-12221-9*) Addison-Wesley.

— Introductory Quantum Mechanics. 3rd ed. Davis, Linda, ed. LC 96-23160. 839p. (C). 1997. 100.00 (*0-201-87879-8*) Addison-Wesley.

— Kinetic Theory: Classical, Quantum & Relativistic Descriptions. 2nd ed. LC 97-18171. 548p. 1998. 89.95 (*0-471-15298-6*, Wiley-Interscience) Wiley.

Libonati, Gerald. The Adjuster. LC 94-71378. 292p. 1995. pap. 10.95 (*0-9640965-0-1*) Avant G Bks.

***Libonati, Gerald.** The Artist's Life. 150p. 2000. pap. 10.95 (*1-886383-40-5*) Pride & Imprints.

Libonati, Joseph. Excerise Physiology CPS 1615. 1998. text 12.90 (*1-56870-304-X*) RonJon Pub.

Libonati, Michael, jt. auth. see Sands, C.

Libonati, Michael E., jt. auth. see Martinez, John.

Libondi, T., jt. ed. see Vrensen, G. F.

Libov, Charlotte. Beat Your Risk Factors: A Woman's Guide to Reducing Her Risk for Cancer, Heart Disease, Stroke, Diabetes, & Osteoporosis. LC 99-22860. 370p. 1999. pap. 14.95 (*0-452-27832-5*, Plume) Dutton Plume.

— Conquer Odds. 1999. text 23.95 (*0-525-94166-5*) Viking Penguin.

Libov, Charlotte, jt. auth. see Pashkow, Frederic.

Libow, Judith A., jt. auth. see Schreier, Herbert A.

Libowitz, R., ed. Faith & Freedom: A Tribute to Franklin H. Littell. LC 87-15972. 268p. 1987. 47.00 (*0-08-035852-7*, Pergamon Pr) Elsevier.

Libowitz, Richard. Mordecai M. Kaplan & the Development of Reconstructionism. LC 83-923. (Studies in American Religion: Vol. 9). (Illus.). 266p. 1983. lib. bdg. 89.95 (*0-88946-651-3*) E Mellen.

Libr. du Liban Staff. Dictionary of English Idioms. (ARA & ENG.). 1989. 29.95 (*0-86685-512-2*) Intl Bk Ctr.

— How Science Works: Eyewitness Science Guides. (ARA., Illus.). 1996. 29.95 (*0-86685-668-4*, Pub. by Librairie du Liban) Intl Bk Ctr.

Libra, C. A. Astrology: Its Techniques & Ethics. (Arcana Ser.). (Illus.). 272p. 1981. reprint ed. pap. 5.95 (*0-87877-035-6*, P-35) Newcastle Pub.

Librach, Hank. Pocket Computer Primer. LC 82-80270. 96p. (Orig.). 1982. pap. 9.95 (*0-942412-00-1*); audio 8.95 (*0-686-87024-7*) Micro Text Pubns.

Librach, Hank & Behrendt, William. Using the Commodore 64 in the Home. (Illus.). 100p. 1984. pap. 10.95 (*0-685-06718-1*) P-H.

Librairie du Liban Staff. ABC Dictionary I: Arabic & English. (ARA & ENG.). (J). (ps-4). 1983. 6.00 (*0-86685-336-7*) Intl Bk Ctr.

— ABC Dictionary I: Arabic & French. (ARA & FRE.). (J). (ps-4). 1983. 6.00 (*0-86685-310-3*) Intl Bk Ctr.

— ABC Dictionary I: Arabic & German. (ARA & GER.). (J). (ps-4). 1983. 6.00 (*0-86685-309-X*) Intl Bk Ctr.

— ABC Dictionary Tamhidi: Arabic & French. (ARA & FRE.). (J). (ps-4). 1983. 6.00 (*0-86685-315-4*) Intl Bk Ctr.

— ABC Dictionary Tamhidi: Arabic & German. (ARA & GER.). (J). (ps-4). 1983. 6.00 (*0-86685-313-8*) Intl Bk Ctr.

— ABC Dictionary Tamhidi: Arabic & Italian. (ARA & ITA.). (J). (ps-4). 1983. 6.00 (*0-86685-316-2*) Intl Bk Ctr.

— ABC I: Arabic Italian Dictionary. (J). (ps-4). 1983. 6.00 (*0-86685-308-1*) Intl Bk Ctr.

— ABC Tamhidi Arabic-Spanish Dictionary. (ARA & SPA.). (J). (ps-4). 1983. 6.00 (*0-86685-312-X*) Intl Bk Ctr.

— A Comprehensive English-Arabic Dictionary. (ARA & ENG.). 1103p. 1983. 22.00 (*0-86685-356-1*, LDL3561, Pub. by Librairie du Liban) Intl Bk Ctr.

— Dictionary of Economics & Commerce: Arabic-English. (ARA & ENG.). 385p. 1983. 35.00 (*0-86685-573-4*, LDL5734, Pub. by Librairie du Liban) Intl Bk Ctr.

— English-Arabic Dictionary of Economics & Commerce. (Libraire du Liban). (ARA & ENG.). 385p. 1983. 35.00 (*0-86685-169-0*, LDL1690, Pub. by Librairie du Liban); pap. 8.95 (*0-86685-076-7*, LDL0767, Pub. by Librairie du Liban) Intl Bk Ctr.

— English Grammar Made Easy: English - Arabic. 1990. pap. 6.95 (*0-86685-458-4*, LDL4584, Pub. by Librairie du Liban) Intl Bk Ctr.

— Maroof the Cobbler. (J). 1986. 9.95 (*0-86685-566-1*) Intl Bk Ctr.

— The Mesopotamia. (J). 1991. 9.95 (*0-86685-489-4*) Intl Bk Ctr.

— My First Word Book: English-Arabic. (ARA., Illus.). 64p. (J). 1993. 19.95 (*0-86685-598-X*, LDL598X, Pub. by Librairie du Liban) Intl Bk Ctr.

— My Illustrated Dictionary. (ARA & ENG.). (J). (gr. 5-12). 1983. 11.95 (*0-86685-317-0*); 9.95 (*0-86685-318-9*); 9.95 (*0-86685-319-7*); 9.95 (*0-86685-320-0*); 9.95 (*0-86685-321-9*) Intl Bk Ctr.

— My Illustrated Dictionary: Arabic & English. (ARA & ENG., Illus.). 64p. (J). 1983. 9.95 (*0-86685-314-6*, LDL3146, Pub. by Librairie du Liban) Intl Bk Ctr.

— The Phoenicians. (J). 1991. 9.95 (*0-86685-570-X*) Intl Bk Ctr.

Librairie Grund Staff. Benezit-Dictionnaire des Peintres, Sculpteurs et Graveurs, 14 vols. rev. ed. (FRE.). 13500p. 1999. lthr. 2220.00 (*2-7000-3040-0*, Pub. by Lib Grund) New Eng Gallery.

Librairie Grund Staff, ed. Benezit-Dictionnaire des Peintres, Sculpteurs et Graveurs, 14 vols. rev. ed. (FRE.). 13500p. 1999. 945.00 (*2-7000-3019-2*, Pub. by Lib Grund); lib. bdg. 1590.00 (*2-7000-3025-7*, Pub. by Lib Grund) New Eng Gallery.

Librairie Larousse Staff, jt. ed. see Houghton Mifflin Company Staff.

Librarie du Liban Staff. Arabic English Pocket/Wortabet. 450p. 1997. pap. 8.95 (*1-56744-535-7*) Kazi Pubns.

— Arabic English/English Arabic Pocket Dictionary/ Wortabet. 900p. 1997. pap. 14.95 (*1-56744-538-1*) Kazi Pubns.

— English Arabic Pocket Dictionary/Wortabet. 450p. 1997. pap. 8.95 (*1-56744-534-9*) Kazi Pubns.

Libraries Unlimited Inc. Staff. Encyclopedia of Living Artists. 11th ed. 1999. pap. 11.95 (*0-940899-33-7*) ArtNetwork.

Library & Archives of New Hampshire's Political Tradition Staff. New Hampshire Political Troubadour. LC 98-68671. 112p. 1999. pap. 15.00 (*0-9637615-2-8*) Res N Hampshire.

Library Administration & Management Association Pr. Checklist of Library Building Design Considerations. 3rd ed. Sannwald, William W., ed. LC 96-31741. 110p. 1996. 30.00 (*0-8389-3466-8*) ALA.

— Library Buildings, Equipment, & the ADA: Compliance Issues & Solutions. Cirillo, Susan E. & Danford, Robert E., eds. LC 95-40196. 105p. 1996. pap. 27.00 (*0-8389-0673-7*, 0673-7-2045) ALA.

Library Administration & Management Association Pr & Dahlgren, Anders C. Planning the Small Library Facility. 2nd ed. LC 96-16226. (Small Library Publications Ser.: 23). 55p. 1996. pap. 15.00 (*0-8389-0681-8*, 0681-8-2045) ALA.

Library Administration & Management Association Pr, jt. auth. see Giesecke, Joan.

Library Assn., Working Party on Community Info. St. Community Information: What Libraries Can Do: a Consultative Document. fac. ed. LC 80-508485. (Illus.). 137p. 1980. reprint ed. pap. 42.50 (*0-7837-8204-7*, 204796200009) Bks Demand.

Library Association, Conference Staff. Preserving the Word: The Library Association Conference Proceedings, Harrogate, 1986. Palmer, R. E., ed. LC 87-16523. 159p. reprint ed. pap. 49.30 (*0-7837-5316-0*, 204505500005) Bks Demand.

Library Association of America. Ket Business of the U.S. Government. 1998. pap. text 21.95 (*0-8389-7949-1*) ALA.

Library Association Staff. Guidelines for Training in Libraries, 9 vols. LC 81-154916. 39p. reprint ed. pap. 30.00 (*0-7837-7071-5*, 204688300001) Bks Demand.

Library Association Staff. Local Studies Libraries: Library Association Guidelines for Local Studies Provision in Public Libraries. LC 91-105680. 31p. 1990. 14.00 (*1-85604-005-4*, Pub. by Library Association) Bernan Associates.

Library Committee Staff & Wilson, Doris L. Martin County, North Carolina Abstracts of Deed Book A, 1774-1787. 136p. 1993. pap. 25.00 (*0-9626609-2-2*) MCH Soc NC.

Library Information Technology Centre Staff, ed. European Directory of Software for Libraries & Information Services. 180p. 1993. 76.95 (*1-85742-092-6*, Pub. by Gower) Ashgate Pub Co.

***Library of America Staff.** American Poetry: The Twentieth Century: E. E. Cummings to May Swenson, Vol. 2. O'Brien, Geoffrey, ed. LC 99-43721. 1009p. 2000. 35.00 (*1-883011-78-7*, Pub. by Library of America) Penguin Putnam.

— American Poetry Vol. 1: The Twentieth Century: Henry Adams to Dorothy Parker. O'Brien, Geoffrey, ed. LC 99-43721. 986p. 2000. 35.00 (*1-883011-77-9*, Pub. by Library of America) Penguin Putnam.

— Reporting Vietnam: American Journalism, 1959-1975. LC 99-59744. 830p. 2000. pap. 17.95 (*1-883011-90-6*, Pub. by Library of America) Penguin Putnam.

Library of America Staff, ed. Reporting Vietnam Pt. 1: American Journalism, 1959-1969. LC 98-12267. 858p. 1998. 35.00 (*1-883011-58-2*, Pub. by Library of America) Penguin Putnam.

— Reporting Vietnam Pt. 2: American Journalism, 1969-1975. LC 98-12267. 857p. 1998. 35.00 (*1-883011-59-0*, Pub. by Library of America) Penguin Putnam.

Library of American Art Staff & Ballinger, James K. Frederic Remington. (Illus.). 160p. 1989. 45.00 (*0-8109-1573-1*, Pub. by Abrams) Time Warner.

***Library of Congress.** Civil War Diaries & Personal Narratives, 1960-1994: A Selected Bibliography of Books in the General Collections of the Library of Congress. LC 96-42144. (Illus.). 79p. 1998. pap. 4.25 (*0-8444-0910-3*) Lib Congress.

Library of Congress. Library of Congress Classification. A. General Works LC 98-49940. 1998. write for info. (*0-8444-0973-1*) Lib Congress.

Library of Congress. Revelations from the Russian Archives: Documents in English Translation. Koenker, Diane & Bachman, Ronald D., eds. LC 96-24752. (Illus.). 808p. 1997. 59.00 (*0-8444-0891-3*) Lib Congress.

Library of Congress, jt. auth. see National Institutes of Mental Health (U.S.).

Library of Congress Carson, Marian S., Collection, et al. Gathering History: The Marian S. Carson Collection of Americana. Day, Sara, ed. LC 98-51398. x, 124 p. 1999. 24.95 (*0-8444-0977-4*, Pub. by Lib Congress) U Pr of New Eng.

Library of Congress, Cataloging Policy & Support O, compiled by. Subject Cataloging Manual: Classification. 1992. 27.00 (*0-8444-0759-3*) Lib Congress.

— Subject Cataloging Manual: Shelflisting. 2nd ed. LC 94-41263. 1995. ring bd. 37.00 (*0-614-32184-0*) Lib Congress.

Library of Congress, Cataloging Policy & Support Office Staff, compiled by. Subject Cataloging Manual: Subject Headings, 4 vols. 5th ed. LC 96-30800. 1446p. 1996. 120.00 (*0-8444-0906-5*) Lib Congress.

Library of Congress, Collections Policy Office Sta, compiled by. Library of Congress Collections Policy Statements. LC 94-40681. 1994. write for info. (*0-614-32185-9*) Lib Congress.

***Library of Congress Copyright Office.** Report on Copyright & Digital Distance Education. LC 99-33196. 350p. 1999. pap. write for info. (*0-16-050067-2*) USGPO.

Library of Congress, Federal Research Div. Staff. Uganda: A Country Study. 2nd ed. Byrnes, Rita M., ed. LC 92-513. (Area Handbook Ser.: No. 550-74). 1992. write for info. (*0-8444-0749-6*) Lib Congress.

Library of Congress. Federal Research Division. Turkey: A Country Study. 498p. 1996. 28.00 (*0-8444-0864-6*, Pub. by Lib Congress) Bernan Associates.

Library of Congress. Federal Research Division, jt. see Curtis, Glenn E.

Library of Congress. Federal Research Division, jt. see Hudson, Rex A.

Library of Congress Federal Research Division Staff. Cyprus, a Country Study. 4th ed. Solsten, Eric, ed. LC 92-36090. (Area Handbook Ser.). 1993. write for info. (*0-8444-0752-6*) Lib Congress.

— Israel: A Country Study. 3rd ed. Metz, Helen C., ed. LC 90-6119. (Area Handbook Ser.). (Illus.). 454p. 1991. text 25.00 (*0-16-028017-6*, 008-020-01233-5) USGPO.

— Portugal Country Studies: Area Handbook. 2nd ed. Solsten, Eric, ed. LC 93-30722. (Area Handbook Ser.). 1994. 19.00 (*0-8444-0776-3*) Lib Congress.

— Saudi Arabia Country Studies: Area Handbook. Metz, Helen C., ed. LC 93-28506. (Area Handbook Ser.: No. 550-51). 1993. 20.00 (*0-8444-0791-7*) Lib Congress.

— Sudan: A Country Study. 4th ed. Metz, Helen C., ed. LC 92-21336. (Area Handbook Ser.). 1992. write for info. (*0-8444-0750-X*) Lib Congress.

Library of Congress Federal Research Division Staff, et al, eds. Zaire Country Studies: Area Handbook. 4th ed. LC 94-25092. (Area Handbook DA Pam Ser.: 550-67). 1994. 22.00 (*0-8444-0795-X*) Lib Congress.

Library of Congress Federal Research Division Staff & Hudson, Rex A. Chile: A Country Study. 3rd ed. LC 94-21663. (Area Handbook DA Pam Ser.: Vol. 550-77). 1994. 25.00 (*0-8444-0828-X*) Lib Congress.

Library of Congress Miniature Book Collection Staff, jt. auth. see Haley, Amanda.

Library of Congress National Library Service for the Blind & Physically Handicapped Staff. Coping Skills. LC 93-32178. 1993. write for info. (*0-08-440799-9*, Pergamon Pr) Elsevier.

— More Mysteries. LC 92-30160. 1992. write for info. (*0-8444-0763-1*) Lib Congress.

***Library of Congress Network Development and MARC Standards Office Staff, contrib. by.** MARC 21 Format for Bibliographic Data 2 vols. Including Guidelines for Content Designation (1999), 2 vols. LC 99-31117. 1999. 70.00 (*0-8444-0989-8*) Lib Congress.

Library of Congress, Network Development Departmen. Network Advisory Committee: Proceedings of the Library of Congress Network Advisory Committee Meeting, December 12-14, 1993. LC 94-33175. (Network Planning Paper: Vol. 26). 1994. write for info. (*0-8444-0824-7*) Lib Congress.

Library of Congress Prints Division Staff, jt. auth. see Beall, Karen F.

Library of Congress Staff. Addresses Near & Far. (Illus.). 96p. 1991. 15.95 (*1-55550-815-4*, Pub. by Universe) St Martin.

— Africa South of the Sahara: Index to Periodical Literature 1900-1970. 1981. 420.00 (*0-8161-1256-8*) Mac Lib Ref.

— An Album of Civil War Battle Art. 128p. 1988. reprint ed. pap. 12.95 (*1-55709-111-0*) Applewood.

— American Prints in the Library of Congress: A Catalog of the Collection. LC 73-106134. (Illus.). 590p. reprint ed. 182.90 (*0-8357-9262-5*, 205125300092) Bks Demand.

— Bibliographic Guide to Law, 1992, Set, vols. 2. 1993. 340.00 (*0-8161-1675-X*) Mac Lib Ref.

— Bibliographic Guide to Law, 1995, 2 vols. 1996. 410.00 (*0-7838-1332-5*) Macmillan.

— Bibliographic Guide to Law, 1995, Vol. 1. 1996. 210.00 (*0-7838-1333-3*, G K Hall & Co) Mac Lib Ref.

— Bibliographic Guide To Law, 1995, Vol. 2. 1996. 210.00 (*0-7838-1334-1*, G K Hall & Co) Mac Lib Ref.

— Bibliographic Guide to Law 1996, 2 vols. Incl. Vol. 1. Bibliographic Guide to Law 1996., 2 vols. 1997. 220.00 (*0-7838-1768-1*, G K Hall & Co); Vol. 2. Bibliographic Guide to Law 1996. 1997. 220.00 (*0-7838-1769-X*, G K Hall & Co); 1997. 440.00 (*0-7838-1767-3*, G K Hall & Co) Mac Lib Ref.

— Catalog of American Political Prints in the Library of Congress, 1766-1876. (Library Reference Ser.). (Illus.). 800p. 1991. 160.00 (*0-8161-0444-1*, G K Hall & Co) Mac Lib Ref.

— Catalog of Brazilian Acquisitions of the Library of Congress, 1964-1974. 1983. 175.00 (*0-8161-1373-4*, G K Hall & Co) Mac Lib Ref.

— Charles Fenderich: Lithographer of American Statesmen. Miller, Lillian B., ed. LC 76-24470. (Illus.). 78p. 1978. lib. bdg. 30.00 incl. fiche (*0-226-69243-4*) U Ch Pr.

— European Collections: An Illustrated Guide. LC 94-32368. (Illus.). 80p. 1994. pap. 9.50 (*0-8444-0841-7*) Lib Congress.

— I'll Be Home for Christmas: The Library of Congress Revisits the Spirit of Christmas During World War II. LC 99-35252. 240p. 1999. 24.00 (*0-385-33463-X*) Delacorte.

— Index to Latin American Legislation, First Supplement, 1961-1965, 2 vols., Set. 1970. 250.00 (*0-8161-0875-7*, G K Hall & Co) Mac Lib Ref.

— LC Classification Outline. 1991. pap. text 5.00 (*0-8444-0684-8*) Lib Congress.

***Library of Congress Staff.** Library of Congress: An Architectural Alphabet. LC 99-50105. (Illus.). 2000. 17.95 (*0-7649-1262-3*) Pomegranate Calif.

— Library of Congress Classification. M. Music, Books on Music. LC 99-11719. 1999. write for info. (*0-8444-0981-2*) Lib Congress.

— Library of Congress Classification. R. Medicine, 1999. LC 99-86967. 2000. write for info. (*0-8444-1004-7*) Lib Congress.

— Library of Congress Geography & Maps: An Illustrated Guide. (Illus.). 84p. pap. 22.00 (*0-8444-0817-4*) Lib Congress.

Library of Congress Staff. Library of Congress Luso-Hispanic Collection: An Illustrated Guide. LC 95-18095. (Illus.). 84p. 1995. pap. 13.00 (*0-8444-0881-6*) Lib Congress.

— Library of Congress Manuscripts: An Illustrated Guide. LC 93-2529. (Illus.). 64p. 1993. pap. 7.00 (*0-8444-0798-4*) Lib Congress.

— Library of Congress Music, Theater, & Dance: An Illustrated Guide. LC 93-27720. (Illus.). 80p. 1993. pap. 13.00 (*0-8444-0801-8*) Lib Congress.

— Many Nations: A Library of Congress Resource Guide for the Study of Indian & Alaska Native Peoples of the United States. Frazier, Patrick, ed. LC 96-42503. (Library of Congress Resource Guide Ser.). (Illus.). 334p. 1996. pap. 33.00 (*0-8444-0904-9*) Lib Congress.

— National Union Catalog: A Cumulative Author List, 1958-62. Incl. Pt. 1. Music & Phonorecords - Authors List. 40.00 (*0-87471-731-0*); Pt. 2. Music & Phonorecords - Subject Index. 40.00 (*0-87471-732-9*); Vol. 53. Motion Pictures & Film Strips Pt. 2: Titles. 40.00 (*0-87471-733-7*); Vol. 54. Motion Pictures & Film Strips Pt. 2: Subject Index. 40.00 (*0-87471-734-5*); write for info. (*0-318-55560-3*) Rowman.

— USMARC Code List for Relators, Sources, Description Conventions. LC 97-14263. 1997. pap. write for info. (*0-8444-0944-8*) Lib Congress.

***Library of Congress Staff.** Usmarc Concise Formats 1998. 98th ed. 1998. 69.44 (*0-8444-0955-3*) Lib Congress.

***Library of Congress Staff, ed.** Catalog of the Alfred Whital Stern Collection of Lincolniana in the Library of Congress. (Illus.). 498p. 2000. 85.00 (*1-57898-221-9*) Martino Pubng.

Library of Congress Staff, ed. Music Subject Headings Used in Printed Catalog Cards of the Library of Congress. (Library Science Ser.). 1980. lib. bdg. 59.95 (*0-8490-3178-8*) Gordon Pr.

Library of Congress Staff & Dershem, Larry D. Library of Congress Classification: Cumulative Schedule & Index. 1997th ed. LC 98-8004. (AALL Publications Ser.). 1998. 67.50 (*0-8377-9330-0*, Rothman) W S Hein.

***Library of Congress Staff & Dershem, Larry D.** Library of Congress Classification - Class KF Law of the United States: Cumulative Index. LC 00-27725. (AALL Publications). 2000. ring bd. write for info. (*0-8377-9340-8*, Rothman) W S Hein.

Library of Congress Staff & Dershem, Larry D. Library of Congress Classification, Class KD Law of the United Kingdom & Ireland: Cumulative Schedule & Index. LC 99-12103. (AALL Publications Ser.: No. 25). 1999. ring bd. 75.00 (*0-8377-9334-3*, Rothman) W S Hein.

***Library of Congress Staff & National Library of Canada Staff.** MARC 21 Concise Formats, 2000. LC 99-87123. 2000. write for info. (*0-8444-1002-0*) Lib Congress.

— MARC 21 Specifications for Record Structure, Character Sets & Exchange Media, 1999. LC 99-87122. 2000. write for info. (*0-8444-1006-3*) Lib Congress.

Library of Congress Staff & New York Public Library Staff. Bibliographic Guide to Business & Economics 1991, 3 vols., Vol. 3. (Bibliographic Guides Ser.). 1560p. 1992. 600.00 (*0-8161-7154-8*, G K Hall & Co) Mac Lib Ref.

— Bibliographic Guide to Maps & Atlases 1988. 675p. 1989. 315.00 (*0-8161-7105-X*, Hall Reference) Macmillan.

— Bibliographic Guide to Theatre Arts: 1991. (Bibliographic Guides Ser.). 203p. 1992. 215.00 (*0-8161-7170-X*, G K Hall & Co) Mac Lib Ref.

Library of Congress Staff & New York Public Library Staff, compiled by. Bibliographic Guide to East Asian Studies, 1991. 600p. 1992. 195.00 (*0-8161-7158-0*, G K Hall & Co) Mac Lib Ref.

— Bibliographic Guide to Middle Eastern Studies, 1991. 500p. 1992. 205.00 (*0-8161-7172-6*, G K Hall & Co) Mac Lib Ref.

— Bibliographic Guide to the Environment, 1991. 250p. 1992. 185.00 (*0-8161-7222-6*, G K Hall & Co) Mac Lib Ref.

Library of Congress Staff & Research Libraries of the New York Public Library. Bibliographic Guide to Conference Publications, 1991, 2 vols. (Bibliographic Guides Ser.). 1031p. 1992. 345.00 (*0-8161-7156-4*, G K Hall & Co) Mac Lib Ref.

Library of Congress Staff, et al. Bibliographic Guide to Music 1991. (Bibliographic Guides Ser.). 600p. 1992. 235.00 (*0-8161-7167-X*, G K Hall & Co) Mac Lib Ref.

— India: A Country Study, Vol. 550. 5th ed. LC 96-19266. 850p. 1996. 49.00 (*0-8444-0833-6*) Lib Congress.

***Library of Congress Staff, et al.** Library of Congress Classification Class KE Law of Canada: Cumulative Schedule & Index. LC 99-57328. (AALL Publications: No. 27). 1999. ring bd. 75.00 (*0-8377-9338-6*, Rothman) W S Hein.

— The Nation's Library: The Library of Congress, Washington, D.C. LC 00-24286. 2000. write for info. (*0-8444-1014-4*) Lib Congress.

Library of Congress Staff, jt. auth. see New York Public Library Staff.

Library of Congress Staff, jt. auth. see Research Libraries of the New York Public Library.

Library of the Peabody Museum of Archaeology & Eth. Tozzer Library. 2nd ed. (Library Reference Ser.). 1988. 7550.00 (*0-8161-1731-4*, G K Hall & Co) Mac Lib Ref.

Library of Tibetan Works & Archives Staff, jt. auth. see Noru, Namkhai.

Library of Virginia. The Common Wealth: Treasures from the Collections of the Library of Virginia. LC 97-61664. (Illus.). 1997. write for info. (*0-88490-186-6*) Library of VA.

Library of Virginia Staff, et al. The Common Wealth: Treasures from the Collections of the Library of Virginia. LC 97-8430. 293p. 1997. 65.00 (*0-88490-185-8*) Library of VA.

***Library Research Center, Graduate School of Librar.** ACRL University Library Statistics, 1996-97. 74p. 1998. 80.00 (*0-8389-7991-2*) Assn Coll & Res Libs.

Library Research Center, Graduate School of Librar. ACRL University Library Statistics, 1994-95. 84p. 1996. 79.95 (*0-8389-7831-2*) ALA.

Library Service for the Blind & Physically Handica. Classics. LC 94-9204. 1994. write for info. (*0-8444-0811-5*) Lib Congress.

***Library Service to Children Staff.** Guide to the Medal & Honor Books 2000. (Newbery & Caldecott Awards Ser.). 2000. pap. 21.25 (*0-8389-3500-1*) ALA.

Library Service to Children Staff. Newbery & Caldecott Awards: A Guide to the Medal & Honor Books 1998. 1998. pap. 16.00 (*0-8389-3473-0*) ALA.

Library Service to Impaired Elderly Forum Publicat. 101 Ideas for Serving the Impaired Elderly. 1990. 8.00 (*0-8389-7356-6*) ASCLA.

Library Services Task Force Staff. Substitute Natural Gas from Hydrocarbon Liquids (Oil Gasification) A Bibliography, 1960-1973. 62p. 1974. 7.00 (*0-318-12711-3*, H02074) Am Gas Assn.

Library Staff. Southeast Asia Subject Catalog. 1979. 750.00 (*0-8161-1234-7*, G K Hall & Co) Mac Lib Ref.

Library Staff, et al. Historical American Sketches: An Illustrated Guide to the Manuscript Collections of the American Philosophical Society. American Philosophical Society Staff, ed. 300p. 1984. 210.00 (*0-8161-0433-6*, G K Hall & Co) Mac Lib Ref.

Libreria Editrice Vaticana Staff. Catecismo de la Iglesia Catolica.Tr. of Catechism of the Catholic Church. (SPA.). 662p. (Orig.). 1993. pap. 9.95 (*0-89243-583-6*) Liguori Pubns.

Librescu, L., ed. Non-Classical Problems of the Theory & Behavior of Structures Exposed to Complex Environmental Conditions. LC 93-71578. (AMD Ser.: Vol. 164). 183p. 1993. pap. 50.00 (*0-7918-1143-3*, G00787) ASME.

***Librett, Jeffrey S.** Rhetoric of Cultural Dialogue: Jews & Germans from Moses Mendelssohn to Richard Wagner & Beyond. (Cultural Memory in the Present Ser.). 443p. 2000. 65.00 (*0-8047-3622-7*); pap. text 24.95 (*0-8047-3931-5*) Stanford U Pr.

Librett, Jeffrey S., tr. from FRE. Of the Sublime: Presence in Question: Essays by Jean-Francois Courtine, Michel Deguy, Eliane Escoubas, Philippe Lacoue-Labarthe, Jean-Francois Lyotard, Louis Marin, Jean-Luc Nancy, & Jacob Rogozinski. LC 91-9447. (SUNY Series, Intersections: Philosophy & Critical Theory). 255p. (C). 1993. text 64.50 (*0-7914-1379-9*); pap. text 21.95 (*0-7914-1380-2*) State U NY Pr.

— The Sense of the World. LC 97-11889. 1997. pap. 19.95 (*0-8166-2611-1*); text 49.95 (*0-8166-2610-3*) U of Minn Pr.

LiBretto, Ellen V., ed. High-Low Handbook: Encouraging Literacy in the 1990s. 3rd ed. (Serving Special Needs Ser.). 304p. 1990. 43.00 (*0-8352-2804-5*) Bowker.

Libri, Guillaume. Histoire Des Sciences Mathematiques en Italie, 4 vols., Set. xxviii, 1950p. 1967. reprint ed. write for info. (*0-318-71371-3*) G Olms Pubs.

Libro, Toni. The House at the Shore. 24p. (Orig.). 1997. pap. 4.00 (*1-885208-01-4*) Lincoln Springs Pr.

Libron, Kecia R. Poems from Me to You. Shultz, Gerald, ed. 1997. pap. 5.00 (*0-9659049-0-3*) K R Libron.

Libros Alianza Staff. Celebremos Su Gloria.Tr. of Celebrate His Glory. (SPA.). pap., spiral bd. 7.00 (*0-685-74912-6*, 490182); spiral bd., vinyl bd. 16.50 (*0-685-74913-4*, 490193) Editorial Unilit.

Libros Alianza Staff. Celebremos Su Gloria.Tr. of Celebrate His Glory. (SPA.). 7.50 (*958-9269-27-3*, 490195) Editorial Unilit.

Libros Alianza Staff. Celebremos Su Gloria.Tr. of Celebrate His Glory. (SPA.). 1990. 11.50 (*958-9269-09-5*, 490181); 20.00 (*958-9269-14-1*, 490194); pap. 14.50 (*958-9269-10-9*, 490191); vinyl bd. 15.50 (*958-9269-13-3*, 490183) Editorial Unilit.

Libros Alianza Staff. Celebremos Su Gloria: Gigante Musica.Tr. of Celebrate His Glory: Giant Music. (SPA.). 68.00 (*958-9269-21-4*, 490196) Editorial Unilit.

— Celebremos Su Gloria: Hojas Sueltas.Tr. of Celebrate His Glory: Professional. (SPA.). 55.00 (*958-9269-25-7*, 490197) Editorial Unilit.

Libros de Ecuador Staff. Gaceta Oficial del Acuerdo de Cartagena, 8 vols. in 11, \. LC 94-76807. 1994. reprint ed. 1900.00 (*0-89941-892-9*, 308330) W S Hein.

Libros Desafio Staff, ed. see Francen, Mike.

Libros, Harold. Hard-Core Liberals: A Sociological Analysis of the Philadelphia Americans for Democratic Action. 147p. 1975. boxed set 34.95 (*0-87073-148-3*) Transaction Pubs.

Libsch, R. R., et al, eds. Flat-Panel Displays & Sensors--Principles, Materials & Processes Vol. 558: Materials Research Society Symposium Proceedings. 615p. 1999. text 73.00 (*1-55899-465-3*) Materials Res.

Libster, Bernard. The Bonsai Bear. LC 98-42666. (Illus.). 32p. (J). (ps-7). 1999. 15.95 (*0-935699-15-5*) Illum Arts.

One day, Issa the bonsai master & his wife are given an orphan bear cub. Even though the emperor forbids the keeping of wild animals, they can't bring themselves to part with their adorable pet. After adapting bonsai techniques to keep the bear from growing, Issa finally learns that the greatest love is allowing him to return to his true nature. "A touching story that teaches the importance of giving loved ones the freedom to be themselves. My children love this book." Jack Canfield, co-author, Chicken Soup for the Kid's Soul. *Publisher Paid Annotation.*

***Libster, Bernard.** Demonstrating Care: Art of Integrated Nursing. (C). 2000. pap. 32.95 (*0-7668-1766-0*) Delmar.

Libucha, Mark, jt. ed. see No, Yongkyoon.

Libura, Krystyna & Burr, Claudia. What the Aztecs Told Us. (J). (gr. 5). 1997. 15.95 (*0-88899-305-6*) Publishers Group.

Libura, Krystyna, et al. Broken Shields. (Illus.). 32p. (J). (gr. 5). 1997. 15.95 (*0-88899-303-X*) Publishers Group.

Liburd Jordon, Sondra. How to Buy the Best Phone System: Getting Maximum Value Without Spending a Fortune. LC 98-24172. (Illus.). 120p. 1998. pap. 9.95 (*1-890154-06-7*, TC20) Aegis Pub Grp.

Liburdi, Joe & Sherman, Cara. The Complete Guide to Sea & Sea. (Illus.). 256p. (Orig.). 1994. pap. text 10.25 (*0-9621111-2-0*) Orca Pubns.

— How to Use Sea & Sea. (Illus.). 120p. (Orig.). 1988. pap. text. write for info. (*0-9621111-0-4*) Orca Pubns.

— The New Guide to Sea & Sea. LC 98-65719. (Illus.). 320p. 1998. mass mkt. 24.95 (*0-9621111-3-9*) Orca Pubns.

Libutti, L. Robert. Systems Application Architecture: The IBM - SAA Strategy. 1990. pap. 24.95 (*0-8306-3516-5*) McGraw-Hill Prof.

Libutti, Patricia O. & Gratch, Bonnie, eds. Teaching Information Retrieval & Evaluation Skills to Education Students & Practioners: A Casebook of Applications. 152p. (Orig.). (C). 1995. pap. 26.50 (*0-8389-7813-4*) Assn Coll & Res Libs.

Libutti, Patricia O'Brien, ed. Librarians As Learners, Librarians As Teachers: The Diffusion of Internet Expertise in the Academic Library. LC 99-13042. 308p. (C). 1999. pap. 27.00 (*0-8389-8003-1*) Assn Coll & Res Libs.

Libutti, Rebecca L. That's Unacceptable: Surviving a Brain Tumor - My Personal Story. (Illus.). 198p. 1997. pap. 19.95 (*0-9670397-0-3*) Krystal Pub.

Liby, Shirley. Around the World with Little Landscapes. (Illus.). 58p. 1996. spiral bd. 14.95 (*1-890952-15-X*) S Liby Pubns.

— Bargello Basics. (Illus.). 63p. 1993. spiral bd. 14.95 (*1-890952-08-7*) S Liby Pubns.

— Bible Blocks Old & New. (Illus.). 76p. 1991. spiral bd. 14.95 (*1-890952-04-4*) S Liby Pubns.

— Borders, Borders, Borders. (Illus.). 78p. 1990. spiral bd. 14.95 (*1-890952-02-8*) S Liby Pubns.

— Christmas Blocks, Borders, & Banners. (Illus.). 74p. (Orig.). 1990. spiral bd. 14.95 (*1-890952-03-6*) S Liby Pubns.

— Color Wash Workbook. (Illus.). 66p. 1993. spiral bd. 14.95 (*1-890952-06-0*) S Liby Pubns.

— Designing with Nine Patch. rev. ed. (Illus.). 69p. 1987. spiral bd. 14.95 (*1-890952-00-1*) S Liby Pubns.

— Even More Paper Piecing Patterns. (Illus.). 65p. 1995. spiral bd. 14.95 (*1-890952-13-3*) S Liby Pubns.

— Exploring Four Patch. (Illus.). 115p. 1988. spiral bd. 14.95 (*1-890952-01-X*) S Liby Pubns.

— Holiday Paper Piecing Patterns. (Illus.). 51p. 1995. spiral bd. 14.95 (*1-890952-12-5*) S Liby Pubns.

— Kids Can Paper Piece. (Illus.). 59p. (J). (gr. 4-6). 1995. spiral bd. 14.95 (*1-890952-14-1*) S Liby Pubns.

— Miniatrue Mania. (Illus.). 80p. 1992. spiral bd. 14.95 (*1-890952-05-2*) S Liby Pubns.

— More Paper Piecing Patterns. (Illus.). 76p. 1994. spiral bd. 14.95 (*1-890952-09-5*) S Liby Pubns.

— Paper Pieced A, B, C's & 1, 2, 3's. (Illus.). 70p. 1994. spiral bd. 14.95 (*1-890952-10-9*) S Liby Pubns.

— Paper Pieced Cats & Dogs. LC 97-206912. (Illus.). 62p. 1997. spiral bd. 14.95 (*1-890952-16-8*) S Liby Pubns.

***Liby, Shirley.** Paper Pieced Down on the Farm. (Illus.). 41p. 2000. spiral bd. 14.95 (*1-890952-20-6*, Pub. by S Liby Pubns) Hearts IN.

Liby, Shirley. Paper Pieced Houses & Gardens. (Illus.). 44p. 1998. spiral bd. 14.95 (*1-890952-18-4*) S Liby Pubns.

— Paper Pieced Little Landscapes. (Illus.). 54p. 1995. spiral bd. 14.95 (*1-890952-11-7*) S Liby Pubns.

— Paper Pieced Sea & Shore. 49p. 1999. spiral bd. 14.95 (*1-890952-19-2*, Pub. by S Liby Pubns) Hearts IN.

— Paper Piecing Old Favorites. LC 98-158292. (Illus.). 46p. 1998. spiral bd. 14.95 (*1-890952-17-6*) S Liby Pubns.

— Paper Piecing Patterns. (Illus.). 82p. 1993. spiral bd. 14.95 (*1-890952-07-9*) S Liby Pubns.

Licari, James J. The Learning Company. 381p. 1992. 60.00 (*0-07-037715-4*) McGraw.

Licari, James J. & Enlow, Leonard R. Hybrid Microcircuit Technology Handbook: Materials, Processes, Design, Testing & Production. LC 87-34701. (Illus.). 429p. 1989. 72.00 (*0-8155-1152-3*) Noyes.

— Hybrid Microcircuit Technology Handbook: Materials, Processes, Design, Testing & Production. 2nd ed. LC 98-6322. 578p. 1998. 125.00 (*0-8155-1423-9*) Noyes.

Licari, James J. & Hughes, Laura A. Handbook of Polymer Coatings for Electronics: Chemistry, Technology & Applications. 2nd ed. LC 89-70994. (Illus.). 392p. 1990. 109.00 (*0-8155-1235-X*) Noyes.

Licastro, Peter J. Birthplace of Legends: The Story of Corvette Production at the St. Louis Assembly Plant, 1953-1981. (Illus.). 146p. 1993. pap. 32.95 (*0-9630555-8-5*) Just The Facts.

— The Original 1973-1977 Corvette Fact Manual. 2nd ed. (Illus.). 148p. 1994. pap. 35.95 (*0-9630555-7-7*) Just The Facts.

Licata, David P. Basic Chemistry in Microscale. 30p. 1993. pap. text, student ed. 9.95 (*0-9636095-1-3*) Licatas Edutype.

— Chemistry Labs for Distance Learning: A Microscale Laboratory Manual. (Illus.). 64p. (C). 1994. pap. text, student ed. 16.65 (*0-9636095-2-1*) Licatas Edutype.

Licata, Elizabeth, jt. ed. see Ehmke, Ronald.

Licata, Jenni. Unveiled, 1. (Love Spell Ser.). 320p. 1999. mass mkt. 4.99 (*0-8439-4542-7*) Dorchester Pub Co.

Licata, Joseph W., jt. auth. see Willower, Donald J.

Licata, Renora. Everything You Need to Know about Anger. rev. ed. (Need to Know Library). (Illus.). 64p. (YA). (gr. 7-12). 1996. lib. bdg. 17.95 (*0-8239-2315-0*) Rosen Group.

— Princess Diana: Royal Ambassador. 1993. 13.15 (*0-606-12596-5*, Pub. by Turtleback) Demco.

***Licata, Renora.** Princess Diana: Royal Ambassador. rev. ed. LC 92-42255. (Library of Famous Women). (Illus.). 64p. (J). (gr. 4-7). 1998. lib. bdg. 17.95 (*1-56711-013-4*) Blackbirch.

Licata, Salvatore J. & Petersen, Robert P., eds. Historical Perspectives on Homosexuality. LC 80-6262. (Journal of Homosexuality: Vol. 6, Nos. 1-2). 224p. 1982. text 39.95 (*0-917724-27-5*) Haworth Pr.

— Historical Perspectives on Homosexuality. LC 80-6262. (Journal of Homosexuality: Vol. 6, Nos. 1-2). 224p. 1985. pap. 2.95 (*0-86656-436-5*) Haworth Pr.

Licata, Salvatore J., jt. ed. see Peterson, Robert.

Licate, Jack A. Creation of a Mexican Landscape: Territorial Organization & Settlement in the Eastern Puebla Basin, 1520-1605. LC 81-12941. (University of Chicago, Department of Geography, Research Paper Ser.: No. 201). 156p. 1981. reprint ed. pap. 48.40 (*0-608-02291-8*, 206293200004) Bks Demand.

Licavoli, Lisa & Brannon, Tami. Love Your Body: A Guide to Transforming Body Language. LC 96-86301. 200p. (Orig.). 1996. pap. 12.50 (*1-57502-304-0*, P01043) Morris Pubng.

***Liccione, Jean.** Great Big Book of Super-Fun Math Activities: A Jumbo Collection Packed with Fun-Filled Reproductions. (Illus.). 304p. (J). 2000. 24.95 (*0-439-07755-9*) Scholastic Inc.

Licensing Group Staff. The Bay Watch Cookbook. 1996. pap. write for info. (*0-8092-3163-8*) NTC Contemp Pub Co.

Lich, Glen E. Fred Gipson at Work. LC 89-39876. (Illus.). 152p. 1990. 31.95 (*0-89096-424-6*) Tex A&M Univ Pr.

— German Texans. rev. ed. (Illus.). 232p. 1996. pap. 16.95 (*0-86701-072-X*) U of Tex Inst Tex Culture.

Lich, Glen E., ed. Regional Studies: The Interplay of Land & People. LC 91-4133. (Elma Dill Russell Spencer Series in the West & Southwest: No. 12). (Illus.). 198p. 1992. 33.95 (*0-89096-477-7*) Tex A&M Univ Pr.

Lich, Glen E. & Reeves-Marquardt, Dona B., eds. Texas Country: The Changing Rural Scene. LC 86-40216. (Illus.). 280p. 1986. 24.95 (*0-89096-247-2*) Tex A&M Univ Pr.

Lichardus, B., ed. see Natriuretic Hormone Symposium Staff.

Lichauco, Alejandro. The Lichauco Paper: Imperialism in the Philippines. LC 73-7953. 127p. 1973. reprint ed. pap. 39.40 (*0-7837-9603-X*, 206036000005) Bks Demand.

Lichauco, Marcial P., jt. auth. see Storey, Moorfield.

Lichbach, Mark I. The Cooperator's Dilemma: Economics, Cognition, & Society. LC 95-4601. 336p. (C). 1996. text 42.50 (*0-472-10572-8*, 10572) U of Mich Pr.

— The Rebel's Dilemma. (Economics, Cognition, & Society Ser.). 544p. 1995. text 52.50 (*0-472-10532-9*, 10532) U of Mich Pr.

— The Rebel's Dilemma. (Economics, Cognition, & Society Ser.). 544p. 1998. pap. text 22.95 (*0-472-08574-3*, 08574) U of Mich Pr.

Lichbach, Mark I. & Zuckerman, Alan S., eds. Comparative Politics: Rationality, Culture, & Structure. (Cambridge Studies in Comparative Politics). 336p. (C). 1997. text 59.95 (*0-521-58369-1*); pap. text 18.95 (*0-521-58668-2*) Cambridge U Pr.

Lichbach, Mark I., jt. ed. see Kopstein, Jeffrey.

***Lichbach, Mark Irving & Seligman, A.** Market & Community: The Bases of Social Order, Revolution & Relegitimation. LC 00-35620. 2000. write for info. (*0-271-02081-4*) Pa St U Pr.

An Asterisk (*) at the beginning of an entry indicates that the title is appearing for the first time.

Lichello, Robert. How to Make One Million Dollars in the Stock Market - Automatically! 3rd rev. ed. 256p. 1992. mass mkt. 6.99 (*0-451-17453-4*, Sig) NAL.

Lichenberg, Frank R. Corporate Takeovers & Productivity. (Illus.). 168p. 1992. 32.50 (*0-262-12164-6*) MIT Pr.

Lichenstein, Carl, ed. see Clay, J. E.

Lichfield, et al. Community Impact Evaluation: Principles & Practice. 352p. 1995. 95.00 (*1-85728-237-X*, Pub. by UCL Pr Ltd); pap. 32.00 (*1-85728-238-8*, Pub. by UCL Pr Ltd) Taylor & Francis.

Lichfield, N. & Proudlove, A. Conservation & Traffic: Planning Problems in York. (C). 1988. 80.00 (*0-900657-23-5*, Pub. by W Sessions) St Mut.

Lichfield, Sylvia & Hall, Christine. How to Work in Retail: Practical Skills for Job Applicants & Trainees. (Illus.). 152p. 1996. pap. 19.95 (*1-85703-194-6*, Pub. by How To Bks) Trans-Atl Phila.

Lichine, Alexis. Encyclopedie des Vins et des Alcools de Tous les Pays. (FRE.). 945p. 1980. pap. 49.95 (*0-8288-1177-6*, M12622) Fr & Eur.

Lichius, Johannes J. Phytochemische Analyse Seltener Digitalisarten (Wie Digitalis Subalpina Br.-Bl.) und Reziproker Digitaliskreuzungen. (Dissertationes Botanicae Ser.: Band 172). (GER., Illus.). 298p. 1991. pap. 71.00 (*3-443-64084-2*, Pub. by Gebruder Borntraeger) Balogh.

Lichko, Joseph, jt. auth. see Freed, Shervin.

***Lichliter, Asselia S., et al.** 700 Years of the Beville Family. 2nd ed. (Illus.). 641p. 1999. 45.00 (*0-7884-1329-5*, P321) Heritage Bk.

Lichliter, Katherine M., tr. see Csokor, Franz T.

***Lichliter, Vernon.** The Girl in the Red Cadillac. 2000. pap. 17.95 (*0-87714-663-2*) Denlingers.

Lichnerowicz, Andre. Magnetohydrodynamics: Waves & Shock Waves in Curved Space-Time. (Mathematical Physics Studies). 292p. (C). 1994. text 140.00 (*0-7923-2805-1*) Kluwer Academic.

Lichnewsky, Alain, jt. ed. see Glowinski, Roland.

***Lichnowsky, Mechtilde.** Der Stimmer. Keith-Smith, Brian, tr. LC 99-58587. (German Woman Writers Ser.: Vol. 13). 120p. 2000. text 59.95 (*0-7734-7859-0*) E Mellen.

Lichnter, R. B. & Harkins, R. N. EGF Receptor in Tumor Growth & Progession. LC 96-41508. (Ernst Schering Research Foundation Workshop Ser.: Vol. 19). (Illus.). 255p. 1996. 65.00 (*3-540-61720-5*) Spr-Verlag.

Lichon, Chuck, ed. Waterfowling Boats, Blinds & Related Gear. LC 97-94138. (Illus.). 128p. 1997. pap. 17.95 (*0-9659784-0-0*) Outdoor Publns.

Lichstein, Kenneth L. Clinical Relaxation Strategies. LC 87-25296. (Personality Processes Ser.). 426p. 1988. 165.00 (*0-471-81592-6*) Wiley.

Licht. The Framers & Fundamental Rights. 100p. (C). 1992. 19.95 (*0-8447-3788-7*) Am Enterprise.

Licht, A. Lewis, jt. auth. see Ramsey, John T.

Licht, Chaim. The Legends of the Sages: The Image of the Sage in Rabbinic Literature. 25.00 (*0-88125-361-8*) Ktav.

Licht, Daniel S. Ecology & Economics of the Great Plains. LC 96-27203. (Our Sustainable Future Ser.: Vol. 10). (Illus.). xii, 227p. 1997. text 55.00 (*0-8032-2922-4*) U of Nebr Pr.

Licht, Fred. Canova. LC 82-16309. (Illus.). 280p. 1983. 125.00 (*0-89659-327-4*) Abbeville Pr.

***Licht, Fred, text.** Constantino Nivola. (Illus.). 20p. 1999. pap. 15.00 (*1-58821-051-0*) Salander OReilly.

Licht, Fred, et al. William Congdon. (Illus.). 358p. 1996. 75.00 (*0-8028-3818-9*) Eerdmans.

Licht, Fred, jt. auth. see Grand, Stanley I.

***Licht, Hans, pseud.** Sexual Life in Ancient Greece. 400p. 2001. text 110.00 (*0-7103-0702-0*) Col U Pr.

Licht, Hans, pseud. Sexual Life in Ancient Greece. Dawson, Lawrence H., ed. Freese, J. H., tr. from GER. LC 72-9622. (Illus.). reprint ed. 67.50 (*0-404-57417-3*) AMS Pr.

Licht, J. Storytelling in the Bible. 2nd ed. 154p. (C). 1986. text 15.00 (*965-223-542-3*, Pub. by Magnes Pr) Eisenbrauns.

Licht, Jacob S., ed. Time & Holy Days. (Biblical Encyclopaedia Library: Vol. III). (HEB.). 225p. 1988. pap. text 29.00 (*965-342-515-3*, Pub. by Bialik) Eisenbrauns.

Licht, Lilla M. & Moore, William B. McKnight Genealogy, 1754-1981. LC 81-85782. (Illus.). 476p. 1981. 25.00 (*0-9607184-0-0*); pap. 22.00 (*0-9607184-1-9*) Licht Pubns.

Licht, R. & De Villiers, B., eds. South Africa's Crisis of Constitutional Democracy Vol. 1: Can the U. S. Constitution Help? 261p. 1994. pap. text 20.00 (*0-7021-3143-1*, Pub. by Juta & Co) Gaunt.

Licht, Robert A. Is the Supreme Court the Guardian of the Constitution? LC 92-34511. (AEI Studies). 200p. (Orig.). 1993. 19.95 (*0-8447-3813-1*, AEI Pr) Am Enterprise.

— Old Rights & New. 213p. 1993. 19.95 (*0-8447-3775-5*, AEI Pr) Am Enterprise.

Licht, Robert A. & De Villiers, Bertus. South Africa's Crisis of Constitutional Democracy: Can the U. S. Constitution Help? Van Wyk, David et al, eds. LC 93-43191. 200p. 1994. 39.75 (*0-8447-3835-2*, AEI Pr) Am Enterprise.

Licht, Robert A., jt. auth. see De Villiers, Bertus.

Licht, Robert A., jt. auth. see Goldwin, Robert A.

Licht, Walter. Getting Work: Philadelphia, 1840-1950. 336p. 1992. text 45.00 (*0-674-35428-1*) HUP.

***Licht, Walter.** Getting Work: Philadelphia, 1840-1950. 2000. pap. text 19.95 (*0-8122-1719-5*) U of Pa Pr.

Licht, Walter. Industrializing America: The Nineteenth Century. (The American Moment Ser.). 224p. 1995. text 38.95 (*0-8018-5013-4*) Johns Hopkins.

Licht, William. Air Pollution Control Engineering: Basic Calculations for Particulate Collection. 2nd ed. (Illus.). 496p. 1988. text 170.00 (*0-8247-7898-7*) Dekker.

Lichtarovicz, A., ed. Jet Cutting Technology. LC 92-35068. (Fluid Mechanics & Its Applications Ser.: Vol. 13). 1992. text 396.50 (*0-7923-1979-6*) Kluwer Academic.

Lichtblau, Mina, intro. The Book of Psalms. LC 93-19316. 240p. 1993. 7.99 (*0-517-09116-X*) Random Hse Value.

Lichtblau, Myron I. The Argentine Novel: An Annotated Bibliography. LC 96-41916. 1136p. 1997. 99.50 (*0-8108-3242-9*) Scarecrow.

— Manuel Galvez. LC 71-169627. (Twayne's World Authors Ser.). 152p. (C). 1972. lib. bdg. 20.95 (*0-8290-1737-2*) Irvington.

— Rayuela y la Creatividad Artistica. LC 88-81377. (SPA.). 92p. (Orig.). 1989. pap. 12.00 (*0-89729-491-2*) Ediciones.

Lichtblau, Myron I., ed. Eduardo Mallea ante la Critica. LC 84-81478. (SPA.). 92p. (Orig.). 1985. pap. 10.00 (*0-89729-355-X*) Ediciones.

— La Emigracion y el Exilio en la Literatura Hispanica del Siglo Veinte. LC 87-81465. (ENG & SPA.). 156p. (Orig.). 1988. pap. 19.00 (*0-89729-445-9*) Ediciones.

Lichtblau, Myron I., tr. & anno. see Mallea, Eduardo.

***Lichte, Shannon McMahon.** Irish Wedding Traditions: A Guide to Creating the Perfect Irish Wedding. 2001. 20.00 (*0-7868-6671-3*, Pub. by Hyperion) Time Warner.

Lichten, Eric. Class, Power & Austerity: The New York City Fiscal Crisis. LC 85-22954. (Critical Studies in Work & Community). 272p. (Orig.). 1986. 59.95 (*0-89789-090-6*, Bergin & Garvey); pap. 16.95 (*0-89789-091-4*, Bergin & Garvey) Greenwood.

Lichten, Frances. Folk Art Motifs of Pennsylvania. LC 75-28849. (Pictorial Archive Ser.). (Illus.). 94p. 1976. reprint ed. pap. 7.95 (*0-486-23303-0*) Dover.

Lichten, Jan. Wyznania Niechrzescijanskie na Drugim Soborze Watykanskim. 24p. 1965. 2.50 (*0-940962-46-2*) Polish Inst Art & Sci.

***Lichten, Joanne V.** Dining Lean: How to Eat Healthy in Your Favorite Restaurants. 2nd ed. Craig, Christy, ed. 288p. 2000. pap. 14.95 (*1-880347-00-8*) Nutrifit Cnslt.

— How to Stay Healthy & Fit on the Road: The Ultimate Health Guide for Road Warriors. 2000. pap. 9.95 (*1-880347-53-9*) Nutrifit Cnslt.

Lichten, Joseph L., jt. auth. see Graham, Robert A.

Lichtenberg, jt. auth. see Troutman.

Lichtenberg, A. J. & Lieberman, M. A. Regular & Chaotic Dynamics. 2nd ed. John, F. & Marsden, Jerrold E., eds. (Applied Mathematical Sciences Ser.: Vol. 38). Orig. Title: Regular & Stochastic Motion. (Illus.). 656p. 1994. 79.95 (*0-387-97745-7*) Spr-Verlag.

— Regular & Stochastic Motion. (Applied Mathematical Sciences Ser.: Vol. 38). (Illus.). 499p. 1989. 56.00 (*0-387-90707-6*) Spr-Verlag.

Lichtenberg, Allan J., jt. auth. see Lieberman, Michael A.

Lichtenberg, Betty K., jt. auth. see Troutman, Andrai P.

Lichtenberg, Betty K., jt. auth. see Troutman, Andria P.

Lichtenberg, D. B., ed. see Conference on the Present Status of Weak Interacti.

Lichtenberg, Dierdre. Poems. (Illus.). 60p. (Orig.). pap. 5.00 (*0-9617811-0-6*) Chandrabala Pr.

Lichtenberg, Fran, ed. Polyurethanes, 1994: Proceedings of the Society of the Plastics Industry, Inc., Polyurethane Division's 35th Annual Technical/Marketing Conference, Boston, MA, October 9-12, 1994. LC 94-61290. 692p. 1994. pap. 149.95 (*1-56676-208-1*, 762081) Technomic.

Lichtenberg, Franz Von, see Von Lichtenberg, Franz.

Lichtenberg, Georg C. Lichtenberg's Visits to England. Mare, Margaret L. & Quarrell, W. H., trs. LC 71-91906. 130p. 1972. 24.95 (*0-405-08747-0*, Pub. by Blom Pubns) Ayer.

***Lichtenberg, Georg Christoph.** The Waste Books. Hollingdale, R. J., ed. & tr. by. (Classics). 256p. 2000. pap. 12.95 (*0-940322-50-1*, Pub. by NY Rev Bks) Midpt Trade.

Lichtenberg, Greg. Playing Catch with My Mother: A Memoir of Coming to Manhood When all the Rules Have Changed. LC 98-42355. 272p. 1999. 23.95 (*0-553-09982-5*) Bantam.

***Lichtenberg, Greg.** Playing Catch with My Mother: Coming to Manhood When All the Rules Have Changed. 256p. 2000. pap. 14.95 (*0-553-37802-3*) Bantam.

Lichtenberg, Jacqueline. The Biblical Tarot: Never Cross a Palm with Silver, Vol. 6. (Biblical Tarot Ser.: Vol. 1). (Illus.). 184p. (Orig.). 1997. pap. 14.95 (*0-9637498-5-4*) Toad Hall PA.

Lichtenberg, James, et al, eds. Chemical & Biological Characterization of Municipal Sludges, Sediments, Dredge Spoils, & Drilling Muds. LC 88-3295. (Special Technical Publication Ser.: No. 976). (Illus.). 510p. 1988. text 69.00 (*0-8031-0987-3*, STP976) ASTM.

Lichtenberg, James W. & Goodyear, Rodney K., eds. Scientist-Practitioner Perspectives on Test Interpretation. LC 98-20688. 192p. (C). 1998. pap. text 33.00 (*0-205-17481-7*) Allyn.

Lichtenberg, Joseph. Psychoanalysis & Infant Research. (Psychoanalytic Inquiry Bk.: Vol. 2). 280p. (C). 1991. pap. 24.95 (*0-88163-002-0*) Analytic Pr.

— Psychoanalysis & Infant Research. (Psychoanalytic Inquiry Bk.: Vol. 2). 280p. (C). 1991. reprint ed. pap. 29.95 (*0-88163-145-0*) Analytic Pr.

Lichtenberg, Joseph D. Psychoanalysis & Motivation. (Psychoanalytic Inquiry Bk.: Vol. 10). 440p. 1989. text 49.95 (*0-88163-084-5*) Analytic Pr.

— The Talking Cure: A Descriptive Guide to Psychoanalysis. (Psychoanalytic Inquiry Bk.). 166p. (C). 1994. reprint ed. pap. 24.95 (*0-88163-192-2*) Analytic Pr.

Lichtenberg, Joseph D., et al, eds. Empathy, 2 vols., Vol. 1. LC 84-2862. (Psychoanalytic Inquiry Bk.: No. 3). (Illus.). 372p. reprint ed. pap. 115.40 (*0-8357-4386-1*, 203721800001) Bks Demand.

— Empathy, 2 vols., Vol. 2. LC 84-2862. (Psychoanalytic Inquiry Book Ser.: No. 3). (Illus.). 391p. reprint ed. pap. 121.30 (*0-8357-4387-X*, 203721800002) Bks Demand.

Lichtenberg, Joseph D. & Kaplan, Samuel, eds. Reflections on Self Psychology. (Psychoanalytic Inquiry Bk.: Vol. 1). 448p. 1983. text 59.95 (*0-88163-001-2*) Analytic Pr.

Lichtenberg, Joseph D., et al. The Clinical Exchange: Techniques Derived from Self & Motivational Systems. LC 96-28332. (Psychoanalytic Inquiry Book Ser.: Vol. 16). 264p. 1996. 45.00 (*0-88163-220-1*) Analytic Pr.

— Self & Motivational Systems: Toward a Theory of Psychoanalytic Technique. (Psychoanalytic Inquiry Bk.: Vol. 13). 272p. 1992. 45.00 (*0-88163-154-X*) Analytic Pr.

Lichtenberg, Joseph D., jt. ed. see Castelnuovo-Tedesco, Pietro.

Lichtenberg, Judith. Foundations & Limits of Freedom of the Press. 1987. 1.50 (*0-318-33305-8*) IPPP.

— On Alternatives to Industrial Flight: The Moral Issues. Ezorsky, Gertrude, ed. 1987. 2.50 (*0-318-33306-6*) IPPP.

Lichtenberg, Judith, ed. Democracy & the Mass Media. (Cambridge Studies in Philosophy & Public Policy). 421p. (C). 1990. pap. text 24.95 (*0-521-38817-1*) Cambridge U Pr.

— Democracy & the Mass Media. 1990. 44.50 (*0-317-05240-3*); pap. 21.95 (*0-317-05241-1*) IPPP.

Lichtenberg, Kara. A Research Guide to Human Sexuality. LC 93-37236. 527p. 1994. text 20.00 (*0-8153-0867-1*, SS836) Garland.

Lichtenberg, Marc L., jt. auth. see Tarlow, David M.

Lichtenberg, Michael. Depression in Geriatric & Nursing Home Patients: A Treatment Manual. LC 98-36843. (William Beaumont Hospital Speech & Language Pathology Ser.). 1998. pap. text 15.95 (*0-8143-2801-6*) Wayne St U Pr.

Lichtenberg, Peter A. A Guide to Psychological Practice in Geriatric Long-Term Care. LC 92-48389. (Illus.). 210p. 1993. pap. 19.95 (*1-56024-411-9*); lib. bdg. 49.95 (*1-56024-410-0*) Haworth Pr.

***Lichtenberg, Peter A.** Handbook of Assessment in Clinical Gerontology. LC 98-51809. (Series on Adulthood & Aging). 672p. 1999. 85.00 (*0-471-28300-2*) Wiley.

Lichtenberg, Peter A. Mental Health Practice in Geriatric Health Care Settings. LC 97-21734. 212p. 1997. 49.95 (*0-7890-0117-9*); pap. 24.95 (*0-7890-0435-6*) Haworth Pr.

Lichtenberg, Philip. Community & Confluence: Undoing the Clinch of Oppression. (Gestalt Institute of Cleveland Press Book Ser.). 242p. 1990. pap. 22.50 (*0-88163-251-1*) Analytic Pr.

— Getting Even: The Equalizing Law of Relationship. 120p. (Orig.). (C). 1988. lib. bdg. 31.50 (*0-8191-6774-6*) U Pr of Amer.

— Undoing the Clinch of Oppression. LC 89-48239. (American University Studies: Psychology: Ser. VIII, Vol. 21). 235p. (C). 1990. text 52.95 (*0-8204-1301-1*) P Lang Pubng.

Lichtenberg, Robert M. The Role of Middleman Transactions in World Trade. (Occasional Papers: No. 64). 104p. 1959. reprint ed. 27.10 (*0-87014-378-6*) Natl Bur Econ Res.

***Lichtenberg, Ronna.** It's Not Business, It's Personal: The 9 Relationship Principles That Power Your Career. 256p. 2001. 23.95 (*0-7868-6594-6*, Pub. by Hyperion) Time Warner.

***Lichtenberg, Ronna & Stone, Gene.** Work Would Be Great If It Weren't for the People: Ronna & Her Evil Twin's Guide to Making Office Politics Work for You. LC 97-46836. 256p. (J). 1998. 22.45 (*0-7868-6371-4*, Pub. by Hyperion) Time Warner.

— Work Would Be Great If It Weren't for the People: Ronna & Her Evil Twin's Guide to Making Office Politics Work for You. 196p. 2000. reprint ed. 23.00 (*0-7881-9374-0*) DIANE Pub.

Lichtenberg, Ronna, jt. auth. see Stone, Gene.

Lichtenberger, Andre. Le Socialisme Au Dix-Huitieme Siecle: Etudes Sur les Idees Socialistes Dans les Ecrivains Francais due XVIII Siecle Avant la Revolution. LC 67-27835. viii, 471p. 1967. reprint ed. 57.50 (*0-678-00329-7*) Kelley.

***Lichtenberger, Andre.** We Come from Brazil. LC 99-14210. (We Come from Ser.). (Illus.). (J). 2000. 22.83 (*0-8172-5514-1*) Raintree Steck-V.

***Lichtenberger, Elisabeth.** Austria: Society & Regions. (Illus.). 492p. 2000. 45.00 (*3-7001-2775-8*) U of Wash Pr.

Lichtenberger, Elisabeth. Vienna: A Bridge Between Cultures. Mohlgassner, Dietlinde & Reisser, Craig, trs. LC 93-7361. (World Cities Ser.). 224p. 1993. 105.00 (*0-471-94705-9*) Wiley.

Lichtenberger, Elizabeth, jt. auth. see Kaufman, Alan S.

Lichtenberger, Elizabeth O., jt. auth. see Kaufman, Alan S.

Lichtenberger, F., jt. auth. see Kutzler, B.

Lichtenberger, Henri. Germany & Its Evolution in Modern Times. Ludovici, A. M., tr. 1977. lib. bdg. 59.95 (*0-8490-1887-0*) Gordon Pr.

— Third Reich. Pinson, Koppel S., tr. LC 73-102249. (Select Bibliographies Reprint Ser.). 1977. 35.95 (*0-8369-5134-4*) Ayer.

Lichtenberger, Hermann, jt. auth. see Eckstein, Hans-Joachim.

Lichtenberger, James P. Divorce: A Social Interpretation. LC 70-169392. (Family in America Ser.). 488p. 1979. reprint ed. 28.95 (*0-405-03869-0*) Ayer.

— Divorce: A Study in Social Causation. LC 72-76685. (Columbia University. Studies in the Social Sciences: No. 94). reprint ed. 34.50 (*0-404-51094-9*) AMS Pr.

Lichtenberger, John. Advertising Compliance Law: Handbook for Marketing Professionals & Their Counsel. LC 85-31248. 224p. 1986. 67.95 (*0-89930-122-3*, LAD/, Quorum Bks) Greenwood.

Lichtenegger, E., jt. auth. see Kutschera, L.

Lichtenegger, Herbert, jt. auth. see Hofmann-Wellenhof, B.

Lichtenfels, Alexander, jt. auth. see Rose, Steven.

Lichtenheld, Tom. Everything I Know about Pirates. LC 99-38576. (J). (gr. k-3). 2000. per. 16.00 (*0-689-82625-7*) S&S Childrens.

Lichtens, Claude. Streamlined: A Metaphor for Progress. 320p. 1996. pap. 29.95 (*1-56898-065-5*) Princeton Arch.

Lichtenstadter, Ilse. Islam & the Modern Age. 228p. 1958. text 32.00 (*0-8290-0179-4*) Irvington.

Lichtensteiger, Walter, jt. ed. see Schlumpf, M.

Lichtenstein. Articles of Faith, 2 vols. write for info. (*0-88125-672-2*) Ktav.

Lichtenstein. Beach Bunnies. 24p. 1993. 11.95 (*1-55550-892-8*, Pub. by Universe) St Martin.

Lichtenstein, jt. auth. see Ferrera.

Lichtenstein, Alex. Twice the Work of Free Labor: The Political Economy of Convict Labor in the New South. 240p. (C). 1996. 65.00 (*1-85984-991-1*, C0513, Pub. by Verso); pap. 20.00 (*1-85984-086-8*, C0514, Pub. by Verso) Norton.

Lichtenstein, Alexander C. & Kroll, Michael A. The Fortress Economy: The Economic Role of the U. S. Prison System. Kamel, Rachael, ed. 1990. pap. 2.00 (*0-910082-16-2*) Am Fr Serv Comm.

***Lichtenstein, Alice.** The Genius of the World. LC 99-89713. (Illus.). 272p. 2000. pap. 13.00 (*1-58195-018-7*) Zoland Bks.

Lichtenstein, Beverly, jt. auth. see Hanlin, Jayne.

***Lichtenstein, Charlene.** HerScopes: A Guide to Astrology for Lesbians. 224p. 2000. pap. 12.00 (*0-684-86867-9*, Fireside) S&S Trade Pap.

Lichtenstein, Claude. Luigi Snozzi. LC 97-13750. (Studio Paperback Ser.). (Illus.). 224p. 1997. pap. 29.95 (*3-7643-5439-9*, Pub. by Birkhauser) Princeton Arch.

***Lichtenstein, Claude & Haberli, Alfredo W., eds.** Air Made Visible: A Visual Reader on Bruno Munari. (Illus.). 320p. 2000. 60.00 (*3-907044-89-4*, Pub. by Lars Muller) Princeton Arch.

Lichtenstein, Claude, ed. see Fuller, R. Buckminster.

Lichtenstein, Claude, jt. ed. see Krausse, Joachim.

Lichtenstein, Conrad & Nellen, Wolfgang, eds. Antisense Technology: A Practical Approach, Vol. 185. LC 97-23434. (The Practical Approach Ser.: No. 185). (Illus.). 326p. 1998. text 105.00 (*0-19-963584-6*); pap. text 50.00 (*0-19-963583-8*) OUP.

Lichtenstein, Diane. Writing Their Nations: The Tradition of Nineteenth-Century American Jewish Women Writers. LC 91-47015. 196p. 1992. 27.50 (*0-253-33346-6*) Ind U Pr.

Lichtenstein, Diane, jt. ed. see Hyman, Colette A.

Lichtenstein, E. A. Labour Law. 200p. (C). 1991. pap. 85.00 (*1-85352-564-2*, Pub. by HLT Pubns) St Mut.

Lichtenstein, E. A. & Read, P. A., eds. Contract Law. 330p. (C). 1991. 60.00 (*1-85352-694-0*, Pub. by HLT Pubns); pap. 60.00 (*1-85352-832-3*, Pub. by HLT Pubns) St Mut.

Lichtenstein, Elissa C., ed. see Owens, Sabra.

Lichtenstein, Ellen. Doomsday: A Millenium Almanac. 384p. 1998. pap. 16.95 (*0-02-862179-4*) Macmillan.

— 10 Minute Guide to Applying to Graduate School. 1996. 10.95 (*0-02-861192-6*, Arco) Macmillan Gen Ref.

— 10 Minute Guide to Paying for Graduate School. LC 96-85371. 1996. 10.95 (*0-02-861165-9*, Arco) Macmillan Gen Ref.

Lichtenstein, Ellen, ed. see Princeton Institute Staff.

***Lichtenstein, Gary R., ed.** 2000 Year Book of Gastroenterology. (Illus.). 350p. 2000. 81.00 (*0-323-01503-4*) Mosby Inc.

Lichtenstein, Gaston, jt. auth. see Ezekiel, Herber T.

Lichtenstein, Howard & Freedman, Monroe H. Understanding Lawyers' Ethics, 1990. annuals 1990. text 30.00 (*0-8205-2866-8*) Bender.

Lichtenstein, Irving L. Hernia Repair Without Disability. 2nd ed. (Illus.). 268p. 1986. text 90.00 (*0-912791-30-6*, Ishiyaku EuroAmerica) Med Dent Media.

Lichtenstein, Jack. Field to Fabric: The Story of American Cotton Growers. 350p. 1990. 19.95 (*0-89672-238-4*) Tex Tech Univ Pr.

Lichtenstein, Jacqueline. The Eloquence of Color: Rhetoric & Painting in the French Classical Age. McVarish, Emily, tr. (New Historicism: Studies in Cultural Poetics: No. 18). (C). 1992. 55.00 (*0-520-06907-2*, Pub. by U CA Pr) Cal Prin Full Svc.

Lichtenstein, Laurence M. & Fauci, Anthony S. Current Therapy in Allergy, Immunology & Rheumatology. 5th ed. (Illus.). 464p. (C). (gr. 13). 1996. text 92.95 (*0-8151-5396-1*, 25697) Mosby Inc.

Lichtenstein, Lawrence M. Conversations about Asthma. LC 97-26218. 157p. 1997. pap. 14.95 (*0-683-30434-8*) Lppncott W & W.

Lichtenstein, Lawrence M., ed. see Collegium Internationale Allergologicum Staff.

Lichtenstein, Michael H., jt. auth. see Patitucci, Frank M.

Lichtenstein, Michael J. Vitamin Deficiencies: Index of Modern Information with Bibliography. LC 88-47794. 150p. 1988. 47.50 (*0-88164-888-4*); pap. 44.50 (*0-88164-889-2*) ABBE Pubs Assn.

Lichtenstein, Nelson. Labor's War at Home: The CIO in World War II. LC 82-4349. 332p. 1987. pap. text 20.95 (*0-521-33573-6*) Cambridge U Pr.

— Walter Reuther: The Most Dangerous Man in Detroit. LC 96-33058. 608p. 1997. 19.95 (*0-252-06626-X*) U of Ill Pr.

Lichtenstein, Nelson, ed. Political Profiles, Vol. 4. LC 76-20897. 765p. reprint ed. pap. 200.00 (*0-7837-6489-8*, 204508900004) Bks Demand.

Lichtenstein, Nelson & Harris, Howell J., eds. Industrial Democracy in America: The Ambiguous Promise. LC 92-28462. (Woodrow Wilson Center Ser.). 303p. (C). 1993. text 59.95 (*0-521-43121-2*) Cambridge U Pr.

— Industrial Democracy in America: The Ambiguous Promise. (Woodrow Wilson Center Press Ser.). 304p. 1996. pap. text 17.95 (*0-521-56622-3*) Cambridge U Pr.

Lichtenstein, Nelson & Meyer, Stephen, eds. On the Line: Essays in the History of Auto Work. (Working Class in American History Ser.). (Illus.). 280p. 1989. pap. 12.95 (*0-252-06015-6*) U of Ill Pr.

Lichtenstein, Nelson & Schoenebaum, Eleanora W., eds. Political Profiles Vol. 3: The Kennedy Years. LC 76-20897. 647p. reprint ed. pap. 200.00 (*0-7837-5346-2*, 204508900003) Bks Demand.

Lichtenstein, Nelson, jt. ed. see Boris, Eileen.

Lichtenstein, Peter M. China at the Brink: The Political Economy of Reform & Retrenchment in the Post-Mao Era. LC 91-9594. 176p. 1991. 52.95 (*0-275-94052-7*, C4052, Praeger Pubs) Greenwood.

***Lichtenstein, Rachel & Sinclair, Ian.** Rodinsky's Room. LC 99-487882. 376p. 2000. 29.95 (*1-86207-257-4*) Granta.

Lichtenstein, Robert, tr. from GER. The Nibelungenlied. LC 91-44798. (Studies in German Language & Literature: Vol. 9). 260p. 1992. lib. bdg. 89.95 (*0-7734-9470-7*) E Mellen.

Lichtenstein, Robert, et al. How to Prepare for & Respond to a Crisis. LC 95-41771. 1995. pap. 7.95 (*0-87120-258-1*) ASCD.

Lichtenstein, Robert, tr. see Koenig Rother.

Lichtenstein, Roy. Roy Lichtenstein: Brushstroke Sculptures. 16p. 1986. pap. 6.00 (*0-614-13073-5*) Tyler Graphics Ltd.

— Roy Lichtenstein: Nudes. 1994. pap. 10.00 (*0-614-13074-3*) Tyler Graphics Ltd.

Lichtenstein, Roy, et al. Roy Lichtenstein's ABC. (Illus.). 64p. 1999. 16.95 (*0-8212-2591-X*, Pub. by Bulfinch Pr) Little.

Lichtenstein, Shari. My Mom Has Cancer. (Illus.). 60p. (Orig.). (J). (gr. k-12). 1997. pap. 15.50 (*1-890867-00-4*) Justice Research.

Lichtenstein, Therese. Master of Light: Ansel Adams & His Influences. 1998. 24.98 (*1-57717-059-8*) Todtri Prods.

Lichtenthaler, Hartmut L., ed. Applications of Chlorophyll Fluorescence: In Photosynthesis Research, Stress Physiology, Hydrobiology & Remote Sensing. (C). 1988. text 185.00 (*90-247-3787-7*) Kluwer Academic.

Lichtenwalner, Charles, et al. Lichtenwalner Family History. (Illus.). 198p. 1996. reprint ed. pap. 32.00 (*0-8328-5412-3*); reprint ed. lib. bdg. 42.00 (*0-8328-5411-5*) Higginson Bk Co.

Lichtenwalter, J. J. Criticality Benchmark Guide for Light-water Reactor Fuel In Transportation & Storage Packages. 358p. 1997. per. 32.00 (*0-16-062824-5*) USGPO.

***Lichtenwalter, Larry L.** Well-Driven Nails How to Find Contentment in a Disappointing World. 1999. pap. 11.99 (*0-8280-1361-6*) Review & Herald.

Lichtenwanger, William, ed. Oscar Sonneck & American Music. LC 82-13670. (Music in American Life Ser.). 304p. 1983. text 29.95 (*0-252-01021-3*) U of Ill Pr.

Lichter, Barry D. His Father's Teacher: Reflections on the Life of Joel Carl Lichter. (Illus.). 119p. (Orig.). 1995. pap. 14.95 (*0-9643902-0-5*) B D Lichter.

Lichter, Carolyn, jt. auth. see Levine, Bobbie.

***Lichter, Daphne.** How to Protect Our Children in School - A Step by Step Guide for Busy Professionals: It Could Save Their Lives! (Illus.). 140p. 1999. per. 24.95 (*0-9674560-0-2*) N Millennium Publishing.

Lichter, Don & Copella, Sue. Pennsylvania Population Projections Background Report. Shoop, Diane, ed. 82p. 1998. pap. 40.00 (*1-58036-060-2*) Penn State Data Ctr.

Lichter, Ivan. Communication in Cancer Care. LC 86-20764. (Illus.). 209p. 1987. text 60.00 (*0-443-03698-5*) Church.

Lichter, Linda S. The Benevolence of Manners: Recapturing the Lost Art of Gracious Victorian Living. (Illus.). 336p. 1999. pap. 13.00 (*0-06-098745-6*) HarpC.

Lichter, Paul. E. P. (Elvis Presley) in Concert. (Illus.). 144p. 1997. 65.00 (*0-9616027-8-3*) Jesse Bks.

— Elvis - Behind Closed Doors. 135p. 1987. 45.00 (*0-9616027-4-0*) Jesse Bks.

— Elvis Magic Moments. 176p. 1994. 65.00 (*0-9616027-7-5*) Jesse Bks.

— Elvis Rebel Heart. (Illus.). 200p. 1992. 75.00 (*0-9616027-6-7*) Jesse Bks.

— Elvis Thank You Very Much. (Illus.). 144p. 1998. 65.00 (*0-9616027-9-1*) Jesse Bks.

***Lichter, Paul.** Millennium Elvis - As Good As It Gets - Larger Than Life. (Illus.). 140p. 2000. 65.00 (*1-929137-01-X*) Jesse Bks.

Lichter, Robert & Noyes, Richard. Good Intentions Make Bad News: Political Thought in the Novels of Jane Austen. LC 95-32349. 240p. (C). 1995. pap. text 22.95 (*0-8476-8096-7*); lib. bdg. 58.50 (*0-8476-8095-9*) Rowman.

Lichter, S., jt. auth. see Rothman, Stanley.

Lichter, S. Robert & Noyes, Richard E. Good Intentions Make Bad News: Why Americans Hate Campaign Journalism. 2nd ed. LC 96-32260. 328p. 1996. pap. 18.95 (*0-8476-8273-0*) Rowman.

Lichter, S. Robert & Rothman, Stanley. Environmental Cancer: A Political Disease? LC 98-25559. (Illus.). 208p. 1998. 35.00 (*0-300-07306-2*); pap. 17.00 (*0-300-07634-7*) Yale U Pr.

Lichter, S. Robert, et al. Prime Time: How TV Portrays American Culture. 336p. 1993. 22.95 (*0-89526-491-9*) Regnery Pub.

Lichter, S. Robert, jt. auth. see Sabato, Larry J.

Lichterman, Paul. The Search for Political Community: American Activists Reinventing Commitment. (Cambridge Cultural Social Studies). 288p. (C). 1996. pap. text 19.95 (*0-521-48343-3*) Cambridge U Pr.

— The Search for Political Community: American Activists Reinventing Commitment. (Cultural Social Studies). 288p. (C). 1996. text 59.95 (*0-521-48286-0*) Cambridge U Pr.

Lichtheim, George. Marxism: A Historical & Critical Study. rev. ed. 432p. 1964. pap. 13.95 (*0-7100-4645-6*, Routledge Thoemms) Routledge.

— Marxism: An Historical & Critical Study. LC 81-17066. 424p. 1982. reprint ed. pap. text 23.00 (*0-231-05425-4*) Col U Pr.

— Thoughts among the Ruins: Collected Essays on Europe & Beyond. 524p. 1986. reprint ed. pap. 44.95 (*0-88738-657-1*) Transaction Pubs.

Lichtheim, Miriam. Ancient Egyptian Autobiographies Chiefly of the Middle Kingdom: A Study & an Anthology. (Orbis Biblicus et Orientalis Ser.: Vol. 84). 171p. 1988. text 42.00 (*3-7278-0594-3*, Pub. by Presses Univ Fribourg) Eisenbrauns.

— Ancient Egyptian Literature: A Book of Readings, Vol. 3: The Late Period. LC 75-189225. (Near Eastern Center Series, UCLA: No. 12). 248p. 1980. pap. 15.95 (*0-520-04020-1*, Pub. by U CA Pr) Cal Prin Full Svc.

— Ancient Egyptian Literature Vol. 2: A Book of Readings: The New Kingdom. LC 75-189225. (Near Eastern Center Series, UCLA: No. 12). 1978. pap. 15.95 (*0-520-03615-8*, Pub. by U CA Pr) Cal Prin Full Svc.

— Ancient Egyptian Literature, a Book of Readings, Vol. 1: The Old & the Middle Kingdoms. LC 75-189225. (Near Eastern Center Series, UCLA: No. 12). 1975. pap. 15.95 (*0-520-02899-6*, Pub. by U CA Pr) Cal Prin Full Svc.

— Maat in Egyptian Autobiographies & Related Studies. (Orbis Biblicus et Orientalis Ser.: Vol. 120). 211p. 1992. text 45.00 (*3-7278-0846-2*, Pub. by Presses Univ Fribourg) Eisenbrauns.

— Moral Values in Ancient Egypt. LC 98-101349. 1997. text 26.75 (*3-7278-1138-2*, 155, Pub. by Presses Univ Fribourg) Eisenbrauns.

Lichti, Wayne P. Introduction to Micro Processor-Controller Design. (Illus.). 170p. (Orig.). 1991. pap. text 18.95 (*0-9629672-0-3*) Lassen Tech Pr.

Lichtlen, P. R. & Reale, A., eds. Adalat: A Comprehensive Review. (Illus.). 248p. 1991. 62.95 (*0-387-54033-4*) Spr-Verlag.

Lichtlen, P. R., jt. ed. see Engel, H. J.

***Lichtman.** Blood Work: Hematology. 1000p. 1999. 129.95 (*0-12-448510-3*) Morgan Kaufmann.

Lichtman, Allan J. The Keys to the White House: A Surefire Guide to Predicting the Next President. 224p. 1996. 22.95 (*1-56833-061-8*) Madison Bks UPA.

***Lichtman, Allan J.** The Keys to the White House: A Surefire Guide to Predicting the Next President. 216p. 2000. reprint ed. pap. 12.95 (*0-7391-0179-X*) Lxngtn Bks.

— Prejudice & the Old Politics: The Presidential Election of 1928. 400p. 2000. pap. 26.95 (*0-7391-0126-9*) Lxngtn Bks.

Lichtman, Allan J. Prejudice & the Old Politics: The Presidential Election of 1928. LC 78-26813. 380p. reprint ed. pap. 117.80 (*0-7837-0302-3*, 204062400018) Bks Demand.

Lichtman, Allan J. & Challinor, Joan R. Kin & Communities: Families in America. LC 78-24246. (Illus.). 336p. 1979. text 34.00 (*0-87474-608-6*, LIKC); pap. text 18.95 (*0-87474-609-4*, LIKCP) Smithsonian.

Lichtman, Allan J. & DeCell, Ken. The Thirteen Keys to the Presidency. 464p. 1992. pap. 14.95 (*0-8191-8751-8*) Madison Bks UPA.

— Thirteen Keys to the Presidency: A Radically New System for Determining the Winners & Losers of American Presidential Elections. 456p. 1990. 24.95 (*0-8191-7008-9*) Madison Bks UPA.

Lichtman, Allan J. & French, Valerie. Historians & the Living Past: The Theory & Practice of Historical Study. LC 77-86035. (C). 1978. reprint ed. pap. text 16.95 (*0-88295-773-2*) Harlan Davidson.

Lichtman, Allan J., jt. auth. see Langbein, Laura I.

Lichtman, Andrew H., jt. auth. see Abbas, Abul K.

Lichtman, Brenda. Innovative Games. LC 93-20454. (Illus.). 144p. 1993. pap. text 18.00 (*0-87322-488-4*, BLIC0488) Human Kinetics.

— More Innovative Games. LC 98-39169. (Illus.). 200p. 1999. pap. 18.00 (*0-88011-712-5*, BLIC0712) Human Kinetics.

Lichtman, David M. The Wrist & Its Disorders. 2nd ed. 1997. write for info. (*0-7216-6758-9*, W B Saunders Co) Harcrt Hlth Sci Grp.

— The Wrist & Its Disorders. 2nd ed. LC 96-7415. 1997. text 195.00 (*0-7216-4774-X*, W B Saunders Co) Harcrt Hlth Sci Grp.

Lichtman, Jeff W., jt. auth. see Purves, Dale.

Lichtman, Jim. The Lone Ranger's Code of the West: Action-Packed Adventure in Values & Ethics. LC 95-92728. 280p. 1996. pap. 15.00 (*0-9648591-0-6*) Scrblrs Ink.

***Lichtman, Kevin & Lynn, Duke.** The Stock Detective Investor: Beat the Online Hype & Unearth the Real Stock Market Winners. 2000. 24.95 (*0-471-38775-4*) Wiley.

Lichtman, Richard. Essays in Critical Social Theory: Toward a Marxist Critique of Liberal Ideology. LC 92-24510. (New Directions in Philosophy Ser.: Vol. 1). XXX, 308p. (C). 1993. pap. text 29.95 (*0-8204-1521-9*) P Lang Pubng.

Lichtman, Robert J. Biogas Systems in India. 130p. 1990. 19.25 (*0-86619-167-4*) Vols Tech Asst.

Lichtman, Ronnie. Gynecology: Well-Woman Care. 2nd ed. (C). 1999. text 84.95 (*0-8385-3514-3*) Appleton & Lange.

Lichtman, Ronnie & Papera, Susan. Gynecology: Well-Woman Care. (Illus.). 608p. (C). 1989. pap. text 84.95 (*0-8385-9682-7*, A9682-4) Appleton & Lange.

Lichtman, Susan A. The Female Hero in Women's Literature & Poetry. LC 95-43269. (Women's Studies: Ser. 10). 88p. 1996. 49.95 (*0-7734-8796-4*) E Mellen.

— Life Stages of Woman's Heroic Journey: A Study of the Origins of the Great Goddess Archetype. LC 91-31494. 112p. 1991. lib. bdg. 59.95 (*0-7734-9699-8*) E Mellen.

Lichtmann, Maria R. The Contemplative Poetry of Gerard Manley Hopkins. LC 88-39915. 241p. 1989. reprint ed. pap. 74.80 (*0-608-04636-1*, 206532300003) Bks Demand.

***Lichtmann, Tamas.** Angezogen und Abgestoβen: Juden in der Ungarischen Literatur. (Debrecener Studien zur Literatur Ser.). 408p. 1999. 52.95 (*3-631-35728-1*) P Lang Pubng.

Lichtmann, Tamas. Nicht (Aus, in, Uber, Von) Osterreich: Zur Osterreichischen Literatur, Zu Celan, Bachmann, Bernhard und Anderen 2., Unverand. Auflage. 2nd ed. (GER.). 319p. 1996. 57.95 (*3-631-30811-6*) P Lang Pubng.

Lichtmann, Tamas, jt. ed. see Schestag, Thomas.

Lichtnau, Bernfried, jt. ed. see Hartel, Brigitte.

Lichtner-Aix, Werner. Sinai: Farben einer Landschaft - Landschaft der Farbe. (GER., Illus.). 88p. (C). 1986. 48.00 (*3-8170-2007-4*, Pub. by Knstvrlag Weingrtn) Intl Bk Import.

Lichtner, Monique. La Cuisine Provencale. 5th ed. (GER., Illus.). 191p. (C). 1994. 40.00 (*3-8170-0001-4*, Pub. by Knstvrlag Weingrtn) Intl Bk Import.

— Knoblauch, Krauter und Oliven: Specialitaten der Provencalischen Kuche. 4th ed. (GER., Illus.). 175p. (C). 1992. 40.00 (*3-8170-0002-2*, Pub. by Knstvrlag Weingrtn) Intl Bk Import.

Lichtner, P. C., et al, eds. Reactive Transport in Porous Media. (Reviews in Mineralogy Ser.: Vol. 34). (Illus.). xiii, 438p. (Orig.). (C). 1996. pap. text 32.00 (*0-939950-42-1*) Mineralogical Soc.

Lichtner, Schomer. Alphabet Drawings. (Illus.). 88p. (Orig.). (J). (gr. k up). 1973. pap. 4.50 (*0-686-97176-0*) Lichtner.

— Ballerina's Holiday. (Illus.). 76p. (Orig.). (J). (gr. 5 up). 1979. pap. 4.95 (*0-941074-04-8*) Lichtner.

— Drawings from the Nude. (Illus.). 156p. 1974. bds. 12.00 (*0-941074-03-X*) Lichtner.

— The Fan, Ballet & Other Drawings. LC 81-81113. (Illus.). 56p. (Orig.). 1981. pap. 4.95 (*0-941074-05-6*) Lichtner.

— Schomer Lichtner Drawings. (Illus.). 72p. (Orig.). 1964. pap. 5.00 (*0-941074-00-5*) Lichtner.

— Schomer Lichtner Paintings. (Illus.). 14p. 1997. pap. write for info. (*0-941074-07-2*) Lichtner.

— Spotted Cow. LC 81-81117. (Illus.). 48p. (Orig.). 1969. pap. 4.50 (*0-941074-01-3*) Lichtner.

Lichtstein, Daniel. Preparing for Medical Practice Made Ridiculously Simple. 70p. 1998. pap. text 12.95 (*0-940780-38-0*) MedMaster.

Lichtwardt, Robert W., jt. auth. see Misra, J. K.

Lichty, Bob. The Official Book of the Antique Automobile Club of America: A 60-Year History of Dedication to the Automobile. LC 98-84624. (Illus.). 496p. 1999. 59.95 (*0-87341-481-0*, AACA) Krause Pubns.

Lichty, Lawrence W., jt. auth. see Webster, James G.

Lichty, Richard W., jt. auth. see Maki, Wilbur R.

Lichty, Robert. Collecting & Restoring Antique Fire Engines. (Illus.). 224p. 1981. pap. 9.95 (*0-8306-2099-0*) McGraw-Hill Prof.

Lichty, Ron, jt. auth. see Eyes, David.

Lichty, Tom. Design Principles for Desktop Publishers. 2nd ed. 226p. 1994. 23.50 (*0-534-23082-2*) Wadsworth Pub.

— International Yellow Pages for Boaters: The Online Guide to Nautical Adventure. LC 99-27964. 400p. (Orig.). 1999. pap. 19.95 (*0-07-134559-0*) McGraw.

Lichy, Roger. The Waterbirth Handbook: The Gentle Art of Waterbirthing. (Illus.). 216p. 1993. pap. write for info. (*0-946551-70-7*) ACCESS Pubs Network.

Lichy, Wolfgang. Besteuerung und Innenfinanzierung. (C). 1967. 67.70 (*3-11-000911-0*) De Gruyter.

Licina, Scott V., jt. auth. see Garton, Ray.

Licitka, Annette, jt. ed. see DeAngelis, James.

Lick, D. R. & Liu, J. Q. Graph Theory, Combinatorics, Algorithms & Applications. LC 95-137213. 500p. 1994. text 109.00 (*981-02-1855-9*) World Scientific Pub.

Lick, Dale W., jt. auth. see Murphy, Carlene U.

Lick, Sue F. Stories Grandma Never Told: Portuguese Women in California. LC 98-14247. (Illus.). 256p. 1998. pap. 17.50 (*1-890771-05-8*) Heyday Bks.

Licka, C. E., jt. auth. see Higby, Wayne.

Lickbarrow, Isabella. Poetical Effusions, 1814. LC 93-46504. (Revolution & Romanticism Ser.). 1994. 48.00 (*1-85477-167-1*) Continuum.

Licker, Paul S. The Art of Managing Software Development People. LC 84-25619. 280p. reprint ed. pap. 86.80 (*0-7837-2815-8*, 205765700006) Bks Demand.

— Management Information Systems: A Strategic Leadership Approach. 188p. (C). Date not set. pap. text 28.00 (*0-03-020314-7*) Dryden Pr.

— Management Information Systems: A Strategic Leadership Approach. LC 95-71897. 562p. (C). 1997. text 77.00 (*0-15-500244-9*) Dryden Pr.

— Management Information Systems: A Strategic Leadership Approach. (C). 1996. pap. text 33.50 (*0-03-020322-8*) Harcourt Coll Pubs.

Lickey, Marvin E. & Gordon, Barbara. Medicine & Mental Illness. Orig. Title: Drugs for Mental Illness. (C). 1991. text 24.00 (*0-7167-2195-3*); pap. text 22.95 (*0-7167-2196-1*) W H Freeman.

***Lickfett, Jay.** MP3 FYI: Digital Music Online. 240p. 2000. pap. 14.95 (*1-929685-05-X*, Pub. by Muska Lipman) IPG Chicago.

Licklider, Patricia. Your Command. 2nd ed. (C). 1997. text 30.00 (*0-673-39276-7*) Addson-Wesley Educ.

Licklider, Roy, ed. Stopping the Killing: How Civil Wars End. (Illus.). 354p. (C). 1993. text 50.00 (*0-8147-5070-2*) NYU Pr.

— Stopping the Killing: How Civil Wars End. (Illus.). 354p. (C). 1995. pap. text 18.50 (*0-8147-5097-4*) NYU Pr.

Lickliter, Robert, jt. ed. see Lewkowicz, David J.

Lickliter, Robert E., jt. auth. see Salmon, Terrell P.

Lickona, Thomas. Educating for Character: How Our Schools Can Teach Respect & Responsibility. 496p. 1992. pap. 15.95 (*0-553-37052-9*) Bantam.

— Raising Good Children. 464p. (Orig.). 1994. pap. 14.95 (*0-553-37429-X*) Bantam.

Lickona, Thomas, jt. ed. see Ryan, Kevin.

Lickona, Tom, et al. Sex, Love & You: Making the Right Decision. LC 94-71887. (Illus.). 192p. (YA). (gr. 9-12). 1994. pap. 8.95 (*0-87793-540-8*) Ave Maria.

Lickorish & Jefferson. Marketing Tourism. 1988. pap. text. write for info. (*0-582-03340-3*, Pub. by Addison-Wesley) Longman.

Lickorish, John R., jt. auth. see Howells, John G.

Lickorish, Leonard & Jenkins, Kit. An Introduction to Tourism. LC 95-163139. 256p. 1997. pap. 26.95 (*0-7506-1956-2*) Buttrwrth-Heinemann.

Lickorish, W. B. An Introduction to Knot Theory, Vol. 175. LC 97-16660. (Graduate Texts in Mathematics Ser.). 250p. 1997. 49.95 (*0-387-98254-X*) Spr-Verlag.

Lickson, Bryane, jt. auth. see Lickson, Charles P.

Lickson, Charles P. Ethics for Government Employees: Standards of Conduct for the "Public Sector" Keppler, Kay, ed. LC 92-75718. (Fifty-Minute Ser.). 113p. (Orig.). 1993. pap. 10.95 (*1-56052-208-9*) Crisp Pubns.

— Ironing It Out: Seven Simple Steps to Resolving Conflict. 2nd rev. ed. LC 95-71177. 170p. 1995. pap. 12.95 (*1-56052-379-4*) Crisp Pubns.

— A Legal Guide for Small Business. Manber, Beverly, ed. LC 93-72970. (Crisp Small Business & Entrepreneurship Ser.). 210p. 1996. pap. 15.95 (*1-56052-266-6*) Crisp Pubns.

Lickson, Charles P. & Lickson, Bryane. Finance & Tax Planning for the Home-Based Business. Preciado, Regina, ed. LC 96-85514. 150p. (Orig.). 1996. pap. 15.95 (*1-56052-397-2*) Crisp Pubns.

Lickson, J. The Continuously Improving Self: A Personal Guide to TQM. Keppler, Kay, ed. LC 91-77764. (Fifty-Minute Ser.). (Illus.). 101p. 1992. pap. 10.95 (*1-56052-151-1*) Crisp Pubns.

Lickteig, Mary J. Amelia Bloomer. LC 97-41512. (Read & Discover Photo-Illustrated Biographies Ser.). 24p. (J). 1998. lib. bdg. 13.75 (*1-56065-747-2*, Bridgestone Bks) Capstone Pr.

Lico, Laurie E. Resumes for Executive Women. 128p. (Orig.). 1984. pap. 7.95 (*0-671-49758-8*) S&S Trade.

Lictenberger, E. & Pecsi, Marton. Comtemporary Essays in Austrian & Hungarian Geography: Proceedings of the 1st Austro-Hungarian Geographical Seminar, Vienna, November 17-19, 1986. (Studies in Geography in Hungary: No. 22). 264p. (C). 1988. 84.00 (*963-05-4946-8*, Pub. by Akade Kiado) St Mut.

***Lictenberger, Elizabeth, et al.** Essentials of Cognitive Assessment with KAIT & Other Kaufman Measures. 256p. 2000. pap. 29.95 (*0-471-38317-1*) Wiley.

***LID Editorial Empresaria Staff.** Diccionario Bilingue de Negocios. (SPA.). 450p. 1999. pap. 24.95 (*0-7931-3369-6*) Dearborn.

Lid, J. Norwegian-Swedish-Finnish Flora: Norsk-Svensk-Finsk Flora. (FIN, NOR & SWE.). 837p. 1985. 195.00 (*0-8288-1248-9*, F22443) Fr & Eur.

***Lida, David.** Travel Advisory: Stories of Mexico. LC 99-23557. 224p. 2000. 24.00 (*0-688-17406-X*, Wm Morrow) Morrow Avon.

Lida, Keisuke. International Monetary Cooperation Among the United States, Japan, & Germany. LC 98-52217. 1999. write for info. (*0-7923-8459-8*) Kluwer Academic.

Lida, Kunihiro, et al, eds. Nondestructive Evaluation in the Nuclear Industry: Ninth International Conference Held April 25-28, 1988, Tokyo, Japan. LC 88-71719. (Illus.). 699p. 1988. reprint ed. pap. 200.00 (*0-608-02646-8*, 206330500004) Bks Demand.

Lidberg, Paul, et al. Steam Age. (Castle Falkenstein Ser.). (Illus.). 104p. (Orig.). 1995. pap. 14.00 (*0-937279-56-0*, CF6021) Talsorian.

***Lidbert, Pam A.** Kill the Commies Bastards!!! 2nd ed. (Illus.). 42p. 1999. reprint ed. 5.95 (*1-929332-00-9*, CFE0001) Crunchy Frog.

***Lidbert, Paul A.** Battle for Fruitcake Hell: Battle #1 of the Christmas Wars. Lincoln, D. B., ed. (Illus.). 24p. (J). 1999. 5.95 (*1-929332-11-4*, CFE0701) Crunchy Frog.

— Beer Bash. Lincoln, D. B., ed. (Illus.). 24p. (J). 1999. 5.95 (*1-929332-09-2*, CFE0203) Crunchy Frog.

— Big Damn Armies. (Illus.). 20p. 1999. 6.95 (*1-929332-05-X*, CFE0103) Crunchy Frog.

— Big Damn Range Wars. (Illus.). 12p. 1998. 4.95 (*1-929332-04-1*, CFE0102) Crunchy Frog.

— Big Damn Robots. (Illus.). 24p. (J). 1999. 5.95 (*1-929332-06-8*, CFE0104) Crunchy Frog.

— Big Damn Space Battles. (Illus.). 16p. (YA). 1998. 4.95 (*1-929332-03-3*, CFE0101) Crunchy Frog.

— Big Time Professional "Rasslin" 2nd rev. ed. (Illus.). 1999. 5.95 (*1-929332-01-7*, CFES102) Crunchy Frog.

— Full Metal Santa: Battle #3 of the Christmas Wars. Lincoln, D. B., ed. (Illus.). 24p. (J). 1999. 5.95 (*1-929332-13-0*, CFE0703) Crunchy Frog.

— Gimme a Stake - Medium Rare! An Adventure - Source Book for Vampire Hunters. (Illus.). 60p. (YA). 1999. pap. text 14.95 (*1-929332-17-3*, CFE1501) Crunchy Frog.

— A Line in the Snow: Battle #4 of the Christmas Wars. Lincoln, D. B., ed. (Illus.). 24p. (J). 1999. 5.95 (*1-929332-14-9*, CFE0704) Crunchy Frog.

— Madworld: The Battle Game. (Illus.). 20p. (J). 1998. 4.95 (*1-929332-07-6*, CFE0201) Crunchy Frog.

An Asterisk (*) at the beginning of an entry indicates that the title is appearing for the first time.

— 10 Minutes over Toyland: Battle #2 of the Crristmas Wars. (Illus.). 24p. (J). 1999. 5.95 (*1-929332-12-2*, CFE0702) Crunchy Frog.

*__Lidbert, Paul A., ed.__ Watch the Skies: An Adventure - Sourcebook for Hidden Invasion. (Illus.). 72p. (YA). 1999. pap. text 14.95 (*1-929332-20-3*, CFE1702) Crunchy Frog.

Lidbert, Paul A. & Arsenault, Mark. Hidden Invasion. (Illus.). 160p. (YA). 1995. pap. text 19.95 (*1-929332-18-1*, CFE1700) Crunchy Frog.

Lidbert, Paul A. & Greer, Ray. $tar Corp$ Call to Battle! (Illus.). 48p. (J). 1992. pap. text 9.95 (*1-929332-23-8*, CFE5000) Crunchy Frog.

*__Lidbert, Paul A. & Lincoln, D. B.__ Happy Farm. (Illus.). 12p. (J). 1999. 5.95 (*1-929332-08-4*, CFE0202) Crunchy Frog.

Lidbert, Paul A., et al. Hidden Invasion: Things to Come: GM Screen & Source Book for Hidden Invasion. (Illus.). 32p. (YA). 1995. 9.95 (*1-929332-19-X*, CFE1701) Crunchy Frog.

Lidbert, Paul A., ed. see Oines, Charles.

Lidbetter, Andrew. Company Investigations & Public Law: A Practical Guide to Government Investigations. 320p. 1999. 95.00 (*1-84113-074-5*, Pub. by Hart Pub) Intl Spec Bk.

Lidbetter, Ernest J. Heredity & the Social Problem Group. 1977. lib. bdg. 59.95 (*0-8490-1944-3*) Gordon Pr.

Lidbetter, H. Martin. The Friends Ambulance Unit, 1939-1943. 1999. pap. 21.00 (*1-85072-128-9*, Pub. by W Sessions) St Mut.

*__Lidbetter, Hubert.__ The Friends Meeting House. 1999. pap. 24.00 (*1-85072-179-3*, Pub. by W Sessions) St Mut.

Lidbetter, Hubert. The Friends Meeting House: Historical Survey of Friends' Places of Worship from the Beginning of Quakerism Including Plans & Photographs. (C). 1989. pap. 21.00 (*0-900657-50-2*, Pub. by W Sessions) St Mut.

Lidbury, Christine, jt. auth. see Maguire, Maria.

Lidchi-Grassi, Maggi. The Light That Shone into the Dark Abyss. 144p. 1994. pap. 7.95 (*81-7058-380-2*, Pub. by SAA) E-W Cultural Ctr.

Lidchi, Hentietta, jt. auth. see King, J. C.

Liddament, M. Building Air Tightness & Ventilation: An Overview of International Practice. 1986. pap. 25.00 (*0-86022-143-1*, Pub. by Build Servs Info Assn) St Mut.

Liddel, Alex. Madeira. 272p. 1998. pap. 21.95 (*0-571-19097-9*) Faber & Faber.

Liddell, Alex. Madeira. (Faber Books on Wine). (Illus.). 297p. 1998. 37.95 (*0-571-19096-0*) Faber & Faber.

Liddell, Andree, ed. The Practice of Clinical Psychology in Great Britain. LC 82-20030. 277p. reprint ed. pap. 85.90 (*0-7837-3219-8*, 204323700007) Bks Demand.

Liddell, Caroline. Frozen Desserts. 2nd ed. (Illus.). 192p. 1996. pap. 14.95 (*0-312-14343-5*) St Martin.

Liddell, F. D. & Miller, Klara. Mineral Fibers & Health. (Illus.). 376p. 1991. lib. bdg. 229.00 (*0-8493-6646-1*, RC1231) CRC Pr.

Liddell, Felix H., jt. ed. see Woods, Paula L.

Liddell, H., et al, eds. High Performance Computing & Networking: International Conference & Exhibition, Brussels, Belgium, April 15-19, 1996: Proceedings. LC 96-16991. 1040p. 1996. pap. 139.50 (*3-540-61142-8*) Spr-Verlag.

*__Liddell Hart, B. H.__ Thoughts on War. 352p. 1999. pap. 68.00 (*1-86227-059-7*, Pub. by Spellmnt Pubs) St Mut.

Liddell-Hart, Basil H. The Defence of Britain. LC 79-23041. 444p. 1980. reprint ed. lib. bdg. 75.00 (*0-313-22175-8*, LHDB, Greenwood Pr) Greenwood.

— Foch, the Man of Orleans. LC 79-22870. (Illus.). 480p. 1980. reprint ed. lib. bdg. 85.00 (*0-313-22171-5*, LHFO, Greenwood Pr) Greenwood.

— German Generals Talk. 1971. pap. 13.50 (*0-688-06012-9*, Quil) HarperTrade.

— The Ghost of Napoleon. LC 79-23039. 199p. 1980. reprint ed. lib. bdg. 35.00 (*0-313-22172-3*, LHGN, Greenwood Pr) Greenwood.

— Great Captains Unveiled. LC 67-23240. (Essay Index Reprint Ser.). 1977. 23.95 (*0-8369-0618-7*) Ayer.

— A Greater Than Napoleon, Scipio Africanus. LC 75-156735. 281p. 1927. 30.00 (*0-8196-0269-8*) Biblo.

— The Real War, 1914-1918. 508p. 1963. pap. 18.95 (*0-316-52505-7*) Little.

— The Remaking of Modern Armies. 1980. lib. bdg. 64.95 (*0-8490-3189-3*) Gordon Pr.

— Reputations Ten Years After. LC 68-8478. (Essay Index Reprint Ser.). (Illus.). 1977. reprint ed. 23.95 (*0-8369-0619-5*) Ayer.

— The Revolution in Warfare. LC 79-22632. 125p. 1980. reprint ed. lib. bdg. 38.50 (*0-313-22173-1*, LHRW, Greenwood Pr) Greenwood.

— Scipio Africanus: Greater Than Napoleon. 288p. 1992. 37.50 (*1-85367-132-0*) Stackpole.

— Sherman: Soldier, Realist, American. (Illus.). 480p. 1993. reprint ed. pap. 15.95 (*0-306-80507-3*) Da Capo.

— Sherman: Soldier, Realist, American. LC 78-536. 456p. 1978. reprint ed. lib. bdg. 52.50 (*0-313-20288-5*, LHSH, Greenwood Pr) Greenwood.

— Strategy. 2nd rev. ed. (Illus.). 432p. 1991. pap. 15.95 (*0-452-01071-3*, Mer) NAL.

Tanks: The History of the Royal Tank Regiment & Its Predecessors, 1914-1915, 2 vols., Set. 1980. reprint ed. 49.95 (*0-89201-079-7*) Zenger Pub.

Liddell-Hart, Basil H., intro. The Rommel Papers. (Quality Paperbacks Ser.). (Illus.). xxx, 544p. 1982. reprint ed. pap. 16.95 (*0-306-80157-4*) Da Capo.

Liddell, Henry G. & Scott, Robert, compiled by. Intermediate Greek-English Lexicon. (ENG & GRE.). 914p. 1945. text 39.95 (*0-19-910206-6*) OUP.

Liddell, Henry G. & Scott, Robert, eds. Abridged Greek-English Lexicon. (ENG & GRE.). 812p. 1935. text 35.00 (*0-19-910207-4*) OUP.

Liddell, Henry G., jt. auth. see Scott, R.

Liddell, J. E. & Symondson, W. O. C., eds. Ecology of Agricultural Pests: Biochemical Approaches. 532p. 1996. write for info. (*0-412-62190-8*) Kluwer Academic.

Liddell, J. E. & Weeks, I. Antibody Technology: A Comprehensive Overview. (Introduction to Biotechniques Ser.). 160p. (Orig.). 1995. pap. 48.50 (*1-872748-87-2*, Pub. by Bios Sci) Coronet Bks.

Liddell, J. Eryl & Cryer, A. A Practical Guide to Monoclonal Antibodies. LC 90-13056. 206p. 1991. pap. 147.00 (*0-471-92905-0*) Wiley.

Liddell, Janice. Arms Akimbo: African Women in Contemporary Literature. LC 99-38712. 1999. 49.95 (*0-8130-1728-9*) U Press Fla.

— Imani & the Flying Africans. (Illus.). 32p. (J). (gr. 3-8). 1993. 14.95 (*0-86543-365-8*); pap. 6.95 (*0-86543-366-6*) Africa World.

Liddell, Jill, jt. auth. see Patchwork Quilt Tsushin Staff.

*__Liddell, Knona C. & Chaiko, David J., eds.__ Metal Separation Technologies Beyond 2000: Integrating Novel Chemistry with Processing: Proceedings. 375p. 1999. 78.00 (*0-87339-442-9*) Minerals Metals.

Liddell, Louise A. Building Life Skills. LC 98-20147. (Home Economics Ser.). 1998. 45.28 (*1-56637-467-7*) Goodheart.

— Clothes & Your Appearance. (Goodheart-Willcox Home Economics Ser.). 496p. 1996. 45.28 (*1-56637-256-9*) Goodheart.

Liddell, Mary S. Gray. Hon. George Gray 4th of Philadelphia, His Ancestors & Descendants. (Illus.). 226p. 1997. reprint ed. pap. 34.00 (*0-8328-8829-X*); reprint ed. lib. bdg. 44.00 (*0-8328-8828-1*) Higginson Bk Co.

Liddell, Nona C., ed. see Minerals, Metals & Materials Society, Meeting (199.

Liddell, Robert. The Aunts. LC 87-60977. (Illus.). 192p. 1987. 24.95 (*0-7206-0665-9*, Pub. by P Owen Ltd) Dufour.

— The Deep End. 187p. 1996. pap. 18.95 (*0-7206-0919-4*, Pub. by P Owen Ltd) Dufour.

— The Deep End: A Novel. 187p. 1994. 29.00 (*0-7206-0903-8*, Pub. by P Owen Ltd) Dufour.

— Elizabeth & Ivy. LC 86-82059. 126p. 1986. 30.00 (*0-7206-0644-6*, Pub. by P Owen Ltd) Dufour.

— The Last Enchantments. 221p. 1991. 29.00 (*0-7206-0816-3*, Pub. by P Owen Ltd) Dufour.

— Mind at Ease: Barbara Pym & Her Novels. 144p. 1989. 30.00 (*0-7206-0731-0*, Pub. by P Owen Ltd) Dufour.

— The Novels of George Eliot. LC 77-366420. 193 p. 1977. write for info. (*0-7156-0992-0*) G Duckworth.

— The Rivers of Babylon. 288p. 1996. 30.00 (*0-7206-0929-1*) Dufour.

— Some Principles of Fiction. LC 73-433. 162p. 1974. reprint ed. lib. bdg. 9.50 (*0-8371-6764-7*, LIPF, Greenwood Pr) Greenwood.

— Stepsons. 228p. 1992. 32.00 (*0-7206-0853-8*, Pub. by P Owen Ltd) Dufour.

— A Treatise on the Novel. LC 83-45913. reprint ed. 21.00 (*0-404-20160-1*) AMS Pr.

— Twin Spirits: The Novels of Emily & Anne Bronte. LC 90-80795. 144p. 1990. 32.00 (*0-7206-0776-0*, Pub. by P Owen Ltd) Dufour.

— Unreal City. 238p. 1993. reprint ed. 30.00 (*0-7206-0884-8*, Pub. by P Owen Ltd) Dufour.

Liddell, Robert, et al. Kind Relations: A Novel. 288p. 1994. 30.00 (*0-7206-0947-X*, Pub. by P Owen Ltd) Dufour.

Liddell, Robert, tr. & intro. see Fabre, Ferdinand.

Liddell, Scott. Racing with the World: How States Can Build a 21st Century Workforce. 37p. 1994. 20.00 (*1-55516-807-8*, 3912) Natl Conf State Legis.

Liddell, Scott, jt. auth. see Ashley-Oehm, Dayna.

Liddell, Scott K. American Sign Language Syntax. (Approaches to Semiotics Ser.: No. 52). 194p. 1980. 50.00 (*90-279-3437-1*) Mouton.

Liddell, Sharen. Being Big. (NFS Canada Ser.). (Illus.). 24p. (J). (ps-3). 1994. pap. 5.95 (*0-929005-60-0*, Pub. by Sec Story Pr) LPC InBook.

Liddell, Sharen & Cathcart, Yvonne. Being Big. (FRE., Illus.). (J). pap. 7.99 (*0-590-24378-0*) Scholastic Inc.

Liddell, Sharon & Cathcart. Being Big. (Illus.). 24p. (J). (ps-3). 1995. 12.95 (*0-929005-62-7*, Pub. by Sec Story Pr) LPC InBook.

*__Liddell, Siobhan.__ An Young Girl Slipping. 82p. 1999. pap. 28.95 (*4-7713-3406-4*, Pub. by Korinsha) Dist Art Pubs.

Liddell, St. John R. Liddell's Record. Hughes, Nathaniel C., Jr., ed. LC 97-21424. (Illus.). 224p. 1997. pap. 11.95 (*0-8071-2218-1*) La State U Pr.

Liddell, Viola G. A Place of Springs. 192p. 1982. pap. 14.95 (*0-8173-0121-6*) U of Ala Pr.

— With a Southern Accent. LC 82-10893. (Library of Alabama Classics). 272p. 1982. pap. 15.95 (*0-8173-0130-5*) U of Ala Pr.

Liddell, W. E. & Howard, M. The Pickingill Papers: The Origin of the Gardnerian Craft. 1994. pap. 22.95 (*1-898307-10-5*, Pub. by Capall Bann Pubng) Holmes Pub.

Liddelow, Lorelei. Cook with Me: Language Development through Cooking Activities, Poems & Stories. (Illus.). 136p. (J). (gr. k-3). 1990. pap. 10.00 (*0-920541-95-X*) Peguis Pubs Ltd.

— Fly with Me: Language Development through Drama, Poems & Stories. (Ideas for Teachers). (Illus.). 112p. (J). (gr. k-3). 1990. pap., teacher ed. 10.00 (*0-920541-93-3*) Peguis Pubs Ltd.

— Talk with Me: Language Development through Drama, Poems & Stories. (Ideas for Teachers). (Illus.). 112p. (J). (gr. k-3). 1984. pap. 10.00 (*0-920541-97-6*) Peguis Pubs Ltd.

Liddiard, Jean, jt. auth. see Condell, Diana.

Liddiard, Nicola & Courtenay-Thompson, Fiona, eds. The Visual Dictionary of Buildings. LC 92-7673. (Eyewitness Visual Dictionaries Ser.). (Illus.). 64p. (J). (gr. 4 up). 1993. 16.95 (*1-56458-102-0*) DK Pub Inc.

Liddiard, Penny, jt. auth. see Howard, Cottia.

Liddick, Don. The Mob's Daily Number: Organized Crime & the Numbers Gambling Industry. LC 98-37050. 1998. write for info. (*0-7618-1266-0*); pap. write for info. (*0-7618-1267-9*) U Pr of Amer.

Liddick, Donald R., ed. An Empirical, Theoretical & Historical Overview of Organized Crime. LC 99-15792. (Criminology Studies: Vol. 6). 284p. 1999. pap. text 89.95 (*0-7734-7965-1*) E Mellen.

Liddicoat, Anthony. A Grammar of the Norman French of the Channel Islands: The Dialects of Jersey & Sark. LC 93-40684. (Grammar Library: No. 13). xii, 452p. (C). 1994. lib. bdg. write for info. (*3-11-012631-1*) Mouton.

Liddicoat, Richard T., Jr. Handbook of Gem Identification. 12th ed. (Illus.). 1987. 47.50 (*0-87311-012-9*) Gemological.

Liddicoat, Richard T., ed. GIA Diamond Dictionary. 1993. 99.50 (*0-87311-026-9*) Gemological.

Liddicoat, Richard T., jt. auth. see Keller, Alice.

Liddie, Bruce R. & Harbaugh, Paul, eds. Custer & Company: Walter Camp's Notes on the Custer Fight. LC 98-35169. (Illus.). 1998. pap. 13.00 (*0-8032-6393-7*, Bison Books) U of Nebr Pr.

Liddington, Jill. Female Fortune: Land, Gender & Authority. LC 98-211639. (Illus.). 304p. 1998. text 50.00 (*1-85489-088-3*) NYU Pr.

— Female Fortune: Land, Gender & Authority. LC 98-211639. (Illus.). 304p. 1998. pap. text 18.50 (*1-85489-089-1*) NYU Pr.

— One Hand Tied Behind Us: The Rise of the Women's Suffrage Movement, Revised Ed. 1999. pap. text 19.50 (*1-85489-111-1*, Pub. by Rivers Oram) NYU Pr.

Liddington, Jill & Norris, Jill. One Hand Tied Behind Us: The Rise of the Women's Suffrage Movement. 304p. 1999. 55.00 (*1-85489-110-3*) Rivers Oram.

Liddle. Labor & Employment in New York, Issue 1. 2nd ed. 151p. 1998. ring bd. write for info. (*0-327-00733-8*, 8218821) LEXIS Pub.

Liddle, Andrew. An Introduction to Modern Cosmology. LC 98-49130. 144p. 1999. 98.00 (*0-471-98757-3*); pap. 49.95 (*0-471-98758-1*) Wiley.

Liddle, Andrew R. & Lyth, David H. Cosmological Inflation & Large-Scale Structure. (Illus.). 430p. (C). 2000. pap. 34.95 (*0-521-57598-2*) Cambridge U Pr.

*__Liddle, Andrew R. & Lyth, David H.__ Cosmological Inflation & Large-Scale Structure. LC 99-14940. (Illus.). 430p. (C). 2000. 80.00 (*0-521-66022-X*) Cambridge U Pr.

Liddle, Art. Hot Tip Harry's 200 New & Improved AutoLISP Routines for AutoCAD 2000. 3rd ed. 150p. 1999. pap. 41.95 incl. cd-rom (*0-929870-53-0*) Advanstar Commns.

Liddle, Barry, compiled by. Dictionary of Sports Quotations. 1987. 24.95 (*0-7102-0785-9*, Routledge Thoemms) Routledge.

Liddle-Bhutt, Heidi, ed. see Abiva, Husryin.

Liddle-Bhutt, Heidi, ed. see Akhtar, Hina Naseem.

Liddle-Bhutt, Heidi, ed. see Ur-Rahman, Mushtaq & Rahman, Guljan.

Liddle, Heidi, ed. see Kolocotronis, Jamilah.

Liddle, Heidi, ed. see Shaikh, Khalid M.

Liddle, Howard A., et al, eds. Handbook of Family Therapy Training & Supervision. LC 87-24848. (Family Therapy Ser.). 432p. 1988. lib. bdg. 55.00 (*0-89862-073-2*) Guilford Pubns.

*__Liddle, James.__ Agility: Trails & Tribulations. (Illus.). 100p. 2000. pap. Price not set. (*1-888994-16-9*) Howln Moon.

Liddle, Jeff & Storck, Steve, eds. Adventure Program Risk Management Report 1995: Incident Data & Narratives from 1989 & 1990. 1995. 12.50 (*0-614-12914-1*) Assn Exper Ed.

Liddle, Jeffrey L. & Marino, Michael F. Labor & Employment in New York: Guide to New York Laws, Regulations & Practices. 2nd ed. 450p. 95.00 (*0-327-12476-8*) LEXIS Pub.

Liddle, Joanna & Joshi, Rama. Daughters of Independence: Gender, Caste, & Class in India. 264p. (C). 1989. text 40.00 (*0-8135-1435-5*) Rutgers U Pr.

Liddle, Matt. Make Your Own Book. LC 93-83466. (Discovery Kit Ser.). (Illus.). 64p. (Orig.). (J). (gr. 3 up). 1993. 18.95 (*1-56138-337-6*) Running Pr.

Liddle, Michel, ed. & tr. see Culioli, Antoine.

Liddle, Nancy, ed. see Feroleto, Mia.

Liddle, Peter. Eleventh Hour: The Eightieth Anniversary of Armistice Day. 1998. pap. text 39.95 (*0-85052-644-2*, Pub. by Leo Cooper) Trans-Atl Phila.

— Passchendaele in Perspective. (Illus.). 1998. pap. 45.00 (*0-85052-588-8*) Leo Cooper.

Liddle, Peter & Cecil, Hugh. The Eleventh Hour: The Eightieth Anniversary of Armistice Day. 1998. 65.00 (*0-85052-609-4*, 526094, Pub. by Leo Cooper) Combined Pub.

Liddle, Peter H. The Worst Ordeal. LC 95-204185. (Illus.). 232p. 1994. 31.95 (*0-85052-417-2*, Pub. by Leo Cooper) Trans-Atl Phila.

Liddle, R. William. Ethnicity, Party, & National Integration: An Indonesian Case Study. LC 70-99830. (Southeast Asia Studies: No. 7). (Illus.). 256p. reprint ed. 79.40 (*0-8357-9165-3*, 201108800074) Bks Demand.

— Leadership & Culture in Indonesian Politics. 320p. 1997. pap. 34.95 (*1-86448-196-X*, Pub. by Allen & Unwin Pty) Paul & Co Pubs.

Liddle, R. William, et al, eds. Political Participation in Modern Indonesia. LC 73-89521. (Monographs: No. 19). (Illus.). 206p. 1973. 9.50 (*0-938692-11-9*) Yale U SE Asia.

Liddle, William. Reading for Concepts: Bks. A-H, Bks. A-H. 2nd ed. (Illus.). (gr. 3-9). 1977. pap. text 7.40 (*0-07-037661-1*); pap. text 7.40 (*0-07-037662-X*); pap. text 7.40 (*0-07-037663-8*); pap. text 7.40 (*0-07-037664-6*); pap. text 7.40 (*0-07-037665-4*); pap. text 7.96 (*0-07-037666-2*); pap. text 7.96 (*0-07-037667-0*); pap. text 7.96 (*0-07-037668-9*) McGraw.

Liddon, Sim C. The Dual Brain, Religion & the Unconscious. LC 89-3765. 265p. 1989. 31.95 (*0-87975-523-7*) Prometheus Bks.

Liddy, G. Gordon. The Monkey Handlers. 352p. 1991. mass mkt. 4.50 (*0-312-92613-8*) St Martin.

— Out of Control. 352p. 1991. mass mkt. 5.99 (*0-312-92428-3*) St Martin.

— Will. 1995. mass mkt. 5.99 (*0-312-95617-7*, Pub. by Tor Bks) St Martin.

— Will: The Autobiography of G. Gordon Liddy. 5th ed. (Illus.). 416p. 1996. text 26.95 (*0-312-11915-1*) St Martin.

Liddy, James. Collected Poems. LC 94-71283. xv, 359p. 1994. 24.95 (*1-881871-09-6*); pap. 14.95 (*1-881871-08-8*) Creighton U Pr.

— Esau, My Kingdom for a Drink: Homage to James Joyce on His Eightieth Birthday. 1962. pap. 4.00 (*0-910664-10-2*) Gotham.

*__Liddy, James.__ Poets in a Frieze & a Valentine. (Poetry New York Pamphlet Ser.: No. 26). 1999. pap. 5.00 (*0-923389-36-9*) Meet Eyes Bind.

Liddy, Pat. Walking Dublin: Twenty-Five Original Walks in & Around Dublin. (Walking Ser.). (Illus.). 192p. 1998. pap. 14.95 (*0-8442-9479-9*, 94799) NTC Contemp Pub Co.

Liddy, Richard M. Transforming Light: Intellectual Conversion in the Early Lonergan. LC 96-31965. 248p. (Orig.). 1993. pap. text 14.95 (*0-8146-5839-3*, M Glazier) Liturgical Pr.

Lide. 1998 Freshman Achievement Award. 76th ed. ring bd. write for info. (*0-8493-0594-2*) CRC Pr.

Lide. Properties of Organic Compounds. 1995. cd-rom 179.00 (*0-8493-0449-0*); cd-rom 550.00 (*0-8493-0450-4*); cd-rom 2900.00 (*0-8493-0451-2*); cd-rom 3800.00 (*0-8493-0452-0*) CRC Pr.

— Properties of Organic Compounds: Pers Edition. 48p. 1996. 139.95 incl. cd-rom (*0-8493-0408-3*) CRC Pr.

Lide, jt. auth. see Lodge.

Lide, David R., Jr. Basic Laboratory & Industrial Chemicals. 384p. 1993. per. 78.95 (*0-8493-4498-0*, QP64) CRC Pr.

Lide, David R. CRC Handbook of Chemistry & Physics. 1997. student ed. 49.95 (*0-8493-0597-7*) CRC Pr.

— CRC Handbook of Chemistry & Physics. 78th ed. 2512p. 1997. boxed set 119.95 (*0-8493-0478-4*) CRC Pr.

— Handbook of Chemistry & Physics. 72nd ed. 2407p. 1991. lib. bdg. 99.50 (*0-8493-0472-5*, QD65, CRC Reprint) Franklin.

— Handbook of Chemistry & Physics. 72nd ed. 2407p. 1993. lib. bdg. 41.95 (*0-8493-0565-9*, CRC Reprint) Franklin.

Lide, David R., Jr. Handbook of Chemistry & Physics. 73rd ed. 1992. 99.50 (*0-8493-0473-3*, QD) CRC Pr.

— Handbook of Chemistry & Physics. 74th ed. 2624p. 1993. lib. bdg. 107.00 (*0-8493-0474-1*, QD) CRC Pr.

— Handbook of Chemistry & Physics. 80th ed. 2504p. 1999. boxed set 139.95 (*0-8493-0480-6*, 480) CRC Pr.

— Handbook of Chemistry & Physics. 81st ed. 2556p. 2000. boxed set 129.95 (*0-8493-0481-4*, 481) CRC Pr.

Lide, David R. Handbook of Chemistry & Physics, CRCnetBase 1999. (CRCNetBase Ser.). 2226p. 1998. 195.00 incl. cd-rom (*0-8493-9720-0*) CRC Pr.

Lide, David R., Jr. Handbook of Data on Organic Compounds, Vol. I. 2nd ed. 728p. 1989. lib. bdg. 323.95 (*0-8493-0421-0*) CRC Pr.

— Handbook of Data on Organic Compounds, Vol. III. 2nd ed. 784p. 1989. lib. bdg. 345.00 (*0-8493-0423-7*) CRC Pr.

— Handbook of Data on Organic Compounds, Vol. IV. 2nd ed. 720p. 1989. lib. bdg. 323.95 (*0-8493-0424-5*) CRC Pr.

— Handbook of Data on Organic Compounds, Vol. V. 2nd ed. 832p. 1989. lib. bdg. 323.95 (*0-8493-0425-3*) CRC Pr.

— Handbook of Data on Organic Compounds, Vol. VI. 2nd ed. 928p. 1989. lib. bdg. 323.95 (*0-8493-0426-1*) CRC Pr.

— Handbook of Data on Organic Compounds, Vol. VII. 2nd ed. 1032p. 1989. lib. bdg. 323.95 (*0-8493-0427-X*) CRC Pr.

— Handbook of Data on Organic Compounds, Vol. VIII. 2nd ed. 1232p. 1989. lib. bdg. 323.95 (*0-8493-0428-8*) CRC Pr.

— Handbook of Data on Organic Compounds, Vol. IX. 2nd ed. 764p. 1989. lib. bdg. 323.95 (*0-8493-0429-6*) CRC Pr.

— Handbook of Data on Organic Compounds, Vol. 10. 2nd ed. 840p. 1990. lib. bdg. 340.00 (*0-8493-0442-3*) CRC Pr.

Lide, David R. Handbook of Organic Solvents. 584p. 1994. boxed set 141.95 (*0-8493-8930-5*) CRC Pr.

Lide, David R., Jr. Handbook of Thermophysical & Thermochemical Data. 528p. 1994. boxed set 194.95 (*0-8493-0197-1*, QC173) CRC Pr.

Lide, David R., ed. CRC Handbook of Chemistry & Physics. 74th ed. 2624p. 1995. lib. bdg., student ed. 49.95 (*0-8493-0595-0*, 595) CRC Pr.

— CRC Handbook of Chemistry & Physics. 75th ed. 2624p. 1994. lib. bdg. 106.95 (*0-8493-0475-X*, 475) CRC Pr.

— CRC Handbook of Chemistry & Physics. 77th ed. (Illus.). 2608p. 1996. student ed., otabind 64.95 (*0-8493-0596-9*) CRC Pr.

— CRC Handbook of Chemistry & Physics. 77th ed. (Illus.). 2496p. 1996. boxed set 119.00 (*0-8493-0477-6*) CRC Pr.

An Asterisk (*) at the beginning of an entry indicates that the title is appearing for the first time.

L

— Handbook of Chemistry & Physics. 76th ed. 2576p. 1995. boxed set 119.95 (*0-8493-0476-8*, 476C2W) CRC Pr.

— Handbook of Chemistry & Physics, 1994 Special Student Edition. 2472p. 1994. lib. bdg. 41.95 (*0-8493-0566-7*, 566) CRC Pr.

Lide, David R. & Milne, G. W. Handbook of Data on Common Organic Compounds. 2796p. 1995. boxed set 1314.95 (*0-8493-0404-0*, 404) CRC Pr.

Lide, David R., Jr. & Milne, G. W. Names, Synonyms, & Structures of Organic Compounds: A CRC Reference Handbook. 3104p. 1994. boxed set 656.95 (*0-8493-0405-9*, 405) CRC Pr.

Lide, David R. & Milne, G. W., eds. Handbook of Data on Organic Compounds. 3rd ed. LC 93-40342. 6560p. 1993. per. 3675.95 (*0-8493-0445-8*) CRC Pr.

Lide, David R., Jr. & Milne, G. W., eds. Properties of Organic Compounds 5.0. 50p. 1995. 1049.95 incl. cd-rom (*0-8493-0447-4*, 447) CRC Pr.

Lide, Elizabeth. You Are What You See. 1993. pap. 25.00 (*0-932526-47-0*) Nexus Pr.

***Lide, Jr., David R.** Handbook of Chemistry & Physics. 79th ed. 2496p. 1998. boxed set 139.95 (*0-8493-0479-2*) CRC Pr.

Lide, Mary. Command of the King. large type ed. (General Ser.). 1993. 27.99 (*0-7089-2554-5*) Ulverscroft.

— Isobelle. LC 87-40414. 288p. 1989. pap. 12.95 (*0-446-38949-8*) Warner Bks.

— A Royal Quest. 1988. pap. 12.95 (*0-446-38791-6*) Warner Bks.

— The Sea Scape. large type ed. LC 92-26852. (Popular Ser.). 310p. 1993. reprint ed. lib. bdg. 17.95 (*1-56054-552-6*) Thorndike Pr.

— Tregaran. large type ed. (General Ser.). 300p. 1990. lib. bdg. 18.95 (*0-8161-4980-1*, G K Hall Lrg Type) Mac Lib Ref.

Lide, Vanessa, jt. ed. see Bleviss, Deborah L.

***Lidell, Lucy.** The Book of Massage: The Complete Step-by-step Guide to Eastern & Western Techniques. 2nd ed. LC 00-44046. 2001. write for info. (*0-7432-0390-9*) Simon & Schuster.

Lidell, Lucy & Cooke, Carola Beresford. The Book of Massage: The Complete Step-By-Step Guide to Eastern & Western Techniques. (Illus.). 191p. 1984. pap. 15.00 (*0-671-54139-0*, Fireside) S&S Trade Pap.

Liden, Elisabeth. Between Water & Heaven: Carl Milles' Search for American Commissions. (Illus.). 128p. 1986. 46.50 (*91-22-00815-2*) Coronet Bks.

Liden, M. & Andersson, L. Flora of Ecuador No. 69 & 70: Papaveraceae, Tovariaceae. (Opera Botanica Series B). 23p. 1995. pap. 20.00 (*87-88702-79-0*, Pub. by Coun Nordic Pubs) Balogh.

Liden, Robert. Advanced Engine Demonstration Project. 1987. pap. 4.95 (*0-685-24742-2*) Research Analysts.

Lider. Correlation of Forces. 1985. 38.95 (*0-566-00945-5*) Ashgate Pub Co.

Lider, Julian. British Military Thought after World War II. LC 83-20724. 621p. 1985. text 101.95 (*0-566-00638-3*, Pub. by Dartmth Pub) Ashgate Pub Co.

— Military Force. 360p. 1981. text 85.95 (*0-566-00296-5*) Ashgate Pub Co.

— On the Nature of War. 420p. 1978. text 109.95 (*0-566-00178-0*) Ashgate Pub Co.

— Origins & Development of West German Military Thought, 1949-1966, Vol. 1. 1986. text 133.95 (*0-566-00946-3*, Pub. by Dartmth Pub) Ashgate Pub Co.

— Origins & Development of West German Military Thought, 1966-1985, Vol. 2. 500p. 1988. text 133.95 (*0-566-05236-9*, Pub. by Dartmth Pub) Ashgate Pub Co.

Liderbach, Daniel. Christ in the Early Christian Hymns. LC 98-29762. 176p. 1998. pap. 14.95 (*0-8091-3809-3*, 3809-3) Paulist Pr.

— The Numinous Universe. 1989. pap. 9.95 (*0-8091-3060-2*) Paulist Pr.

— The Theology of Grace & the American Mind: A Representation of Catholic Doctrine. LC 83-22154. (Toronto Studies in Theology: Vol. 15). 170p. 1983. lib. bdg. 79.95 (*0-88946-761-7*) E Mellen.

— Why Do We Suffer? New Ways of Understanding. LC 92-12767. 160p. 1992. pap. 11.95 (*0-8091-3319-9*) Paulist Pr.

Lidhoo, Motilal. Child Rearing & Psycho-Social Development. (C). 1991. 12.50 (*81-7024-300-9*, Pub. by Ashish Pub Hse) S Asia.

Lidiak, Edward G. & Larue, D. K. Tectonics & Geochemistry of the Northeastern Caribbean. LC 97-51386. (Special Papers: Vol. 322). 1998. write for info. (*0-8137-2322-1*) Geol Soc.

Lidiak, Edward G. & Zietz, Isidore. Interpretation of Aeromagnetic Anomalies Between Latitudes 37 Degrees N & 38 Degrees N in the Eastern & Central United States. LC 76-12278. (Geological Society of America, Special Paper: No. 167). 59p. reprint ed. pap. 30.00 (*0-608-14463-0*, 202503200041) Bks Demand.

Lidiard, Alan, jt. auth. see Allnatt, Alan.

Lidicker, William Z., Jr., ed. Landscape Approaches in Mammalian Ecology & Conservation. 216p. 1995. 35.95 (*0-8166-2587-5*) U of Minn Pr.

— Rodents: A World Survey of Species of Conservation Concern. (Occasional Papers of the IUCN Species Survival Commission: No. 4). (Illus.). 64p. (Orig.). 1989. pap. 15.00 (*2-88032-971-X*, Pub. by IUCN) Island Pr.

Lidie, Stephen. Perl/Tk Pocket Reference. (Illus.). 104p. 1998. pap. 9.95 (*1-56592-517-3*) OReilly & Assocs.

Lidin, R. A. Handbook of Inorganic Chemistry. 2nd ed. LC 93-26771. 1993. write for info. (*0-8493-9343-4*) CRC Pr.

Lidin, Rostislav A. Inorganic Substances: Handbook. LC 96-6022. 1996. write for info. (*1-56700-065-7*) Begell Hse.

Lidin, Rostislav A., ed. Reactivity of Inorganic Substances Handbook. rev. ed. 938p. 1996. 165.00 (*1-56700-050-9*) Begell Hse.

Lidin, Rostislav A., et al. Constants of Inorganic Substances: Handbook. 2nd rev. ed. 444p. 1996. 97.50 (*1-56700-041-X*) Begell Hse.

Lidinsky, William & Vlack, David, eds. Perspectives on Packetized Voice & Data Communications. LC 90-32479. (Illus.). 304p. 1990. text 69.95 (*0-87942-263-7*, PC02527) Inst Electrical.

Lidis Staff. Dictionnaire Encyclopedique Lidis, 3 vols., Set. (FRE.). 1104p. 1977. 350.00 (*0-8288-5386-X*, M6138) Fr & Eur.

— Encyclopedie de l'Art, 6 vols, Set. (FRE.). 1976. 895.00 (*0-8288-5680-X*, M6189) Fr & Eur.

— Encyclopedie Medicale de la Famille, 4 vols., Set. (FRE.). 1200p. 1976. 650.00 (*0-8288-5688-5*, M6221) Fr & Eur.

— L' Encyclopedie Pour Tous: Everyone's Encyclopedia in French, 6 vols., Set. (FRE.). 1978. 695.00 (*0-8288-5234-0*, M6231) Fr & Eur.

— Encyclopedie Scientifique et Technique, 5 vols., Set. (FRE.). 2480p. 1975. 795.00 (*0-8288-5878-0*, M6233) Fr & Eur.

Lidke, Liza. Your Guide to Child Care Savings. 2nd rev. ed. 94p. 1995. pap. 8.95 (*1-888523-00-X*) Lidke & Assocs.

Lidl, Andreas. Six Sonatas for Solo Viola Da Gamba & Violoncello. Miloradovitch, Hazelle, ed. (Baroque Ser.: No. 5). 1997. pap. text 23.00 (*1-56571-095-9*) PRB Prods.

Lidl, Rudolf, ed. Papers in Algebra, Analysis & Statistics. LC 82-1826. (Contemporary Mathematics Ser.: Vol. 9). 400p. 1982. pap. 35.00 (*0-8218-5009-1*, CONM/9) Am Math.

Lidl, Rudolf & Mullen, G. L. Dickson Polynomials, 65. LC 92-30842. (Pitman Monographs & Surveys in Pure & Applied Mathematics). 216p. 1993. 85.95 (*0-582-09119-5*) Longman.

Lidl, Rudolf & Niederreiter, Harald. Finite Fields. 2nd ed. (Encyclopedia of Mathematics & Its Applications Ser.: No. 20). (Illus.). 769p. (C). 1997. text 110.00 (*0-521-39231-4*) Cambridge U Pr.

— Introduction to Finite Fields & Their Applications. rev. ed. LC 93-49020. (Illus.). 428p. (C). 1994. text 57.95 (*0-521-46094-8*) Cambridge U Pr.

Lidl, Rudolf & Pilz, G. Applied Abstract Algebra. LC 84-10576. (Undergraduate Texts in Mathematics Ser.). (Illus.). 450p. 1984. 49.00 (*0-387-96035-X*) Spr-Verlag.

Lidl, Rudolf & Pilz, Gunter. Applied Abstract Algebra. 2nd ed. Gehring, F. W. & Halmos, P. R., eds. LC 97-22883. (Undergraduate Texts in Mathematics Ser.). (Illus.). 400p. 1997. 49.00 (*0-387-98290-6*) Spr-Verlag.

Lidman, U., ed. Upgrading of Water & Wastewater Systems. (Water Science & Technology Ser.: No. 37-9). 260p. 1999. pap. 159.00 (*0-08-043385-5*, Pub. by Elsevier) Elsevier.

Lidman, Sara. Naboth's Stone. Tate, Joan, tr. from SWE. LC 89-81774. (Norvik Press Series B: No. 7). 262p. (Orig.). 1990. pap. 19.95 (*1-870041-12-7*, Pub. by Norvik Pr) Dufour.

Lidman, Sven. Audiovisual Combi, 8 vols., Set. 1991. 695.00 (*0-7859-6359-6*, 8485797302) Fr & Eur.

— Audiovisual Combi, Vol. 1. 312p. 1991. 95.00 (*0-685-70609-5*, 8485797310) Fr & Eur.

— Audiovisual Combi, Vol. 2. 312p. 1991. 95.00 (*0-7859-6361-8*, 8485797329) Fr & Eur.

— Audiovisual Combi, Vol. 3. 296p. 1991. 95.00 (*0-7859-6362-6*, 8485797337) Fr & Eur.

— Audiovisual Combi, Vol. 4. 304p. 1991. 95.00 (*0-7859-6363-4*, 8485797345) Fr & Eur.

— Audiovisual Combi, Vol. 5. 312p. 1991. 95.00 (*0-7859-6364-2*, 8485797353) Fr & Eur.

— Audiovisual Combi, Vol. 6. 296p. 1991. 95.00 (*0-7859-6365-0*, 8485797361) Fr & Eur.

— Audiovisual Combi, Vol. 7. 312p. 1991. 95.00 (*0-7859-6499-1*) Fr & Eur.

— Audiovisual Combi, Vol. 8. 304p. 1991. 95.00 (*0-7859-6366-9*, 8485797388) Fr & Eur.

— Enciclopedia Combi Visual, 10 vols. 7th ed. (SPA.). 2448p. 1989. write for info. (*0-7859-5075-3*) Fr & Eur.

— Enciclopedia Combi Visual, Vol. 1. 248p. 1989. 75.00 (*0-7859-6349-9*, 8485797191) Fr & Eur.

— Enciclopedia Combi Visual, Vol. 2. 248p. 1989. 75.00 (*0-7859-6351-0*, 8485797205) Fr & Eur.

— Enciclopedia Combi Visual, Vol. 3. 248p. 1989. 75.00 (*0-7859-6352-9*, 8485797213) Fr & Eur.

— Enciclopedia Combi Visual, Vol. 4. 248p. 1989. 75.00 (*0-7859-6353-7*, 8485797221) Fr & Eur.

— Enciclopedia Combi Visual, Vol. 5. 248p. 1989. 75.00 (*0-7859-6500-9*) Fr & Eur.

— Enciclopedia Combi Visual, Vol. 6. 248p. 1989. 75.00 (*0-7859-6354-5*, 8485797248) Fr & Eur.

— Enciclopedia Combi Visual, Vol. 7. 240p. 1989. 75.00 (*0-7859-6355-3*, 8485797256) Fr & Eur.

— Enciclopedia Combi Visual, Vol. 8. 240p. 1989. 75.00 (*0-7859-6356-1*, 8485797264) Fr & Eur.

— Enciclopedia Combi Visual, Vol. 10. 240p. 1989. 75.00 (*0-7859-6358-8*, 8485797280) Fr & Eur.

Lido, Serge. Ballet. 1991. lib. bdg. 15.00 (*0-8288-2636-6*) Fr & Eur.

— Ballet d'Aujourd'hui of Today. (ENG & FRE., Illus.). 1965. lib. bdg. 9.95 (*0-8288-3984-0*) Fr & Eur.

Lidoff, Lorraine, jt. ed. see Massof, Robert W.

Lidofsky, Lillian & Strnad, Ed. Cats & the People They Own. LC 94-5388. 144p. 1995. pap. 7.00 (*0-399-51908-4*, Perigee Bks) Berkley Pub.

— Dogs & the People They Own. LC 94-31192. 144p. (Orig.). 1995. pap. 9.00 (*0-399-51944-0*, Perigee Bks) Berkley Pub.

***Lidolt, Erwina.** Food Combining Cookbook: Over 200 Delicious Recipes. LC 99-490992. 192p. 1998. pap. 10.00 (*0-7225-3666-6*, Pub. by Thorsons MD) Natl Bk Netwk.

Lidor, Ronnie & Bar-Eli, Michael, eds. Sport Psychology: Linking Theory & Practice. 328p. 1999. text 34.00 (*1-885693-15-X*) Fit Info Tech.

Lidorenko, N. S., ed. see Koltun, M. M.

Lidov. Elements of Semiotics. LC 98-44712. (New in the Semaphores & Signs Ser.). 272p. 1999. text 45.00 (*0-312-21413-8*) St Martin.

Lidov, Aleksei, jt. ed. see Batalov, Andrei.

Lidova, Natalia. Drama & Ritual of Early Hinduism. (C). 1994. text 14.00 (*0-614-04134-1*, Pub. by Motilal Bnarsidass) S Asia.

***Lidow, Michael S.** Neurotransmitter Receptors in Actions of Antipsychotic Medications. LC 00-25387. (Pharmacology & Toxicology Ser.). 272p. 2000. boxed set 99.95 (*0-8493-0744-9*) CRC Pr.

***Lidsey, James E.** The Bigger Bang. (Illus.). 160p. (C). 2000. 19.95 (*0-521-58289-X*) Cambridge U Pr.

Lidsey, John. Light in Watercolour. (Learn to Paint Ser.). (Illus.). 1999. pap. 15.95 (*0-00-413343-9*, Pub. by HarpC) Trafalgar.

Lidskog, Rolf. Radioactive & Hazardous Waste Management in Sweden: Movements, Politics & Science. (Studia Sociologica Upsaliensia: No. 38). 195p. (Orig.). 1994. pap. 47.50 (*91-554-3298-0*) Coronet Bks.

Lidsky, Theodore I., jt. auth. see Schneider, Jay S.

Lidster, Angela. Chester & Daisy Move On. (Illus.). 1995. pap. 35.00 (*1-873868-19-7*, Pub. by BAAF) St Mut.

LIDSTONE. Making Effective Presentations. 1985. 78.95 (*0-566-02382-2*) Ashgate Pub Co.

— Training Salesmen on the Job: Second Edition. 1986. 78.95 (*0-566-02414-4*) Ashgate Pub Co.

Lidstone, John. Beyond the Pay-Packet: Proven Techniques for Leading, Motivating, & Inspiring Salespeople to Achieve Success. LC 92-21880. 1992. 24.95 (*0-07-707697-4*) McGraw.

— How to Recruit & Select Successful Salesmen. rev. ed. 320p. 1983. text 78.95 (*0-566-02325-3*, Pub. by Gower) Ashgate Pub Co.

— International Perspectives on Teaching about Hazards & Disasters. LC 96-24017. 139p. 1996. 39.00 (*1-873150-19-9*) Taylor & Francis.

— Marketing Planning for the Pharmaceutical Industry. 250p. 1987. text 109.95 (*0-566-02630-9*, Pub. by Gower) Ashgate Pub Co.

— Motivating Your Sales Force. 144p. 1978. text 46.95 (*0-566-02082-3*) Ashgate Pub Co.

— Motivating Your Sales Force. 144p. 1995. pap. 26.95 (*0-566-07617-9*, Pub. by Gower) Ashgate Pub Co.

— Profitable Selling. 240p. 1986. pap. text 22.95 (*0-7045-0524-X*, Pub. by Gower) Ashgate Pub Co.

Lidstone, John, ed. Global Issues of Our Time. LC 93-34256. (Illus.). 176p. (J). 1995. pap. text 22.95 (*0-521-42163-2*) Cambridge U Pr.

***Lidstone, John & MacLennan, Janice.** Marketing Planning for the Pharmaceutical Industry. 2nd ed. LC 98-41233. 200p. 1999. 160.00 (*0-566-08112-1*) Ashgate Pub Co.

Lidstone, John, jt. ed. see Gerber, Rodney.

Lidstone, Ken & Palmer, Clare. Bevan & Lidstone's Investigation of Crime - A Guide to Police Powers. 2nd ed. 584p. 1996. pap. write for info. (*0-406-04837-1*, MICHIE) LEXIS Pub.

Lidstone, Ronald A. Studies in Symbology. 93p. 1996. reprint ed. spiral bd. 10.00 (*0-7873-0559-6*) Hlth Research.

— Studies in Symbology: The Tarot, Astrology, the Bible, Numerology. 1991. lib. bdg. 79.95 (*0-8490-4990-3*) Gordon Pr.

— Studies in Symbology (1926) 94p. 1996. reprint ed. pap. 9.95 (*1-56459-861-6*) Kessinger Pub.

Lidstrom, Anders. Discretion: An Art of the Possible. 208p. (Orig.). 1991. pap. 58.50 (*0-685-62398-X*) Coronet Bks.

Lidstrom, Erik. Static & Dynamic Properties of Rare Earth Compounds. (Uppsala Dissertations from the Faculty of Science Ser.: No. 8). (Illus.). 117p. (Orig.). 1995. pap. 39.50 (*91-554-3587-4*) Coronet Bks.

Lidstrom, Mary E. & Tabita, F. Robert, eds. Microbial Growth on C1 Compounds: Proceedings of the 8th International Symposium on Microbial Growth on C1 Compounds, Held in San Diego, U. S. A., 27 August-1 September, 1995. LC 96-198. 376p. (C). 1996. text 166.00 (*0-7923-3938-X*) Kluwer Academic.

Lidtke, Vernon L. Outlawed Party: Social Democracy in Germany, 1878-1890. LC 66-14131. 388p. reprint ed. 120.30 (*0-8357-9506-3*, 201148000078) Bks Demand.

Lidz, B., jt. auth. see Rose, P. R.

Lidz, Carol S. Improving Assessment of Schoolchildren. LC 80-26130. (Jossey-Bass Social & Behavioral Science Ser.). 239p. reprint ed. pap. 74.10 (*0-8357-4993-2*, 203792600009) Bks Demand.

— Practitioner's Guide to Dynamic Assessment. LC 91-13657. (School Practitioner Ser.). 210p. 1991. pap. text 24.00 (*0-89862-242-5*); lib. bdg. 49.95 (*0-89862-363-4*) Guilford Pubns.

Lidz, Carol S., ed. Dynamic Assessment: An Interactional Approach to Evaluating Learning Potential. LC 86-19375. 511p. 1987. lib. bdg. 49.95 (*0-89862-695-1*) Guilford Pubns.

Lidz, Charles, ed. see Cowan, Penney.

Lidz, Charles, ed. see Cowan, Penney, et al.

Lidz, Charles W., et al. The Erosion of Autonomy in Long-Term Care. 216p. 1992. text 39.95 (*0-19-507394-0*) OUP.

— Informed Consent: A Study of Decisionmaking in Psychiatry. LC 83-8488. (Perspectives on Law & Behavior Ser.). 365p. 1984. lib. bdg. 47.00 (*0-89862-275-1*) Guilford Pubns.

Lidz, Jane. Zak: The One-of-a-Kind Dog. LC 96-79284. (Illus.). 32p. (J). 1997. pap. 12.95 (*0-8109-3995-9*, Pub. by Abrams) Time Warner.

Lidz, Jane, photos by. Water & Architecture: Architecture, History, & Myth. LC 93-27389. (Illus.). 224p. 1994. 60.00 (*0-8109-3975-4*, Pub. by Abrams) Time Warner.

Lidz, Ruth W., jt. auth. see Lidz, Theodore.

Lidz, Theodore. The Family & Human Adaptation. LC 63-20457. 126p. 1963. 27.50 (*0-8236-1880-3*); pap. 24.95 (*0-8236-8051-7*, 21880) Intl Univs Pr.

— Hamlet's Enemy: Madness & Myth in Hamlet. xii, 258p. 1990. reprint ed. pap. 24.95 (*0-8236-8067-3*) Intl Univs Pr.

— Origin & Treatment of Schizophrenic Disorders. 158p. 1990. reprint ed. pap. 26.95 (*0-8236-8206-4*, BN 23895) Intl Univs Pr.

— The Person: His & Her Development Throughout the Life Cycle. rev. ed. LC 76-22745. 625p. 1983. pap. 40.00 (*0-465-05541-9*, Pub. by Basic) HarpC.

— The Relevance of the Family to Psychoanalytic Theory. LC 92-1477. ix, 228p. (C). 1992. 37.50 (*0-8236-5784-1*) Intl Univs Pr.

Lidz, Theodore & Fleck, Stephen. Schizophrenia & the Family. rev. ed. LC 65-23613. x, 494p. 1985. 72.50 (*0-8236-6001-X*, 06001) Intl Univs Pr.

Lidz, Theodore & Lidz, Ruth W. Oedipus in the Stone Age: A Psychoanalytic Study of Masculinization in Papua New Guinea. LC 88-25796. 215p. 1989. 35.00 (*0-8236-3727-1*) Intl Univs Pr.

Lidz, Victor M., jt. ed. see Klausner, Samuel Z.

Lidzbarski, Mark. Handbuch der Nordsemitischen Epigraphik Nebst Ausgewahlten Inschriften, 2 vols., Set. 1969. reprint ed. write for info. (*0-318-72103-1*) G Olms Pubs.

— Die Neu-Aramaischen Handschriften der Koniglichen Bibliothek Zu Berlin. (Erganzungshefte Zur Zeitschrift Fur Assyriologie. Semitische Studien: Hefte 4/9, 1-2). (GER.). xliii, 1080p. 1973. reprint ed. write for info. (*3-487-04524-9*) G Olms Pubs.

Lidzey, John. Mix Your Own Watercolors. 64p. 1995. 6.98 (*0-7858-0265-7*) Bk Sales Inc.

— Mix Your Own Watercolors. (Artist's Library Ser.). (Illus.). 64p. 1997. pap. 7.95 (*1-56010-223-3*, AL27) W Foster Pub.

Lie. Introduction to Sociology. 3rd ed. 2000. pap. text 18.00 (*0-393-97337-9*) Norton.

Lie, Dix. Cultural Competency in the Practice of Social Work. (Social Work Ser.). 2002. text 28.00 (*0-534-54221-2*) Wadsworth Pub.

Lie, Hakon Wiun. Cascading Style Sheets. 2nd ed. 416p. (C). 1999. pap. text 39.95 (*0-201-59625-3*) Addison-Wesley.

Lie, Hakon Wiun & Bos, Bert. Cascading Style Sheets. LC 97-171203. 304p. 1997. pap. text 29.95 (*0-201-41998-X*) Addison-Wesley.

Lie, Herbert. Selected Papers on Quantum Well Intermixing for Phontonics. LC 98-10722. (Milestone Ser.). 1998. write for info. (*0-8194-2856-6*) SPIE.

Lie, Hiu. Die Mandschu-Sprachkunde in Korea. LC 70-635028. (Uralic & Altaic Ser.: Vol. 114). (Illus.). 304p. (Orig.). 1971. 19.00 (*0-87750-162-9*) Res Inst Inner Asian Studies.

Lie, J. T. Biopsy Diagnosis in Rheumatic Diseases. LC 96-29142. (Illus.). 256p. 1997. 98.50 (*0-89640-327-0*) Igaku-Shoin.

***Lie, J. T.** Management & Organizations. LC 99-41116. 2000. text 69.95 (*0-312-22841-4*) St Martin.

Lie, J. T., jt. ed. see Stehbens, William E.

***Lie, John.** Han Unbound: The Political Economy of South Korea. 2000. pap. text 17.95 (*0-8047-4015-1*) Stanford U Pr.

— Multiethnic Japan. 288p. 2001. 35.00 (*0-674-00299-7*) HUP.

Lie, John. The Political Economy of South Korea. LC 97-34019. 1998. 49.50 (*0-8047-3055-5*) Stanford U Pr.

Lie, John, ed. The Impoverished Spirit in Contemporary Japan: Selected Essays of Honda Katuichi. 320p. 1993. 34.00 (*0-85345-858-8*, Pub. by Monthly Rev); pap. 19.00 (*0-85345-859-6*, Pub. by Monthly Rev) NYU Pr.

Lie, John, jt. auth. see Abelmann, Nancy.

Lie, John, jt. auth. see Ablemann, Nancy.

Lie, Jonas. The Seer & Other Norwegian Tales. Morton, Brian & Trevor, Richard, trs. from NOR. 160p. (Orig.). 1990. pap. 19.95 (*0-948259-65-5*, Pub. by Forest Bks) Dufour.

— Weird Tales from Northern Seas: Norwegian Legends. 128p. 1996. pap. 10.95 (*1-57216-021-7*) Penfield.

— Weird Tales from Northern Seas, from the Danish of Jonas Lie. LC 79-81272. (Short Story Index Reprint Ser.). (Illus.). 1977. 17.95 (*0-8369-3024-X*) Ayer.

Lie, K. I., jt. ed. see Van der Wall, Ernst E.

***Lie, Lorinda.** Heart-Felt Wool Applique. (Illus.). 112p. 2000. pap. 22.95 (*1-57432-750-X*, Am Quilters Soc) Collector Bks.

Lie, Merete & Lund, Ragnhild. Renegotiating Local Values: Working Women & Foreign Industry in Malaysia. LC 95-122964. (SIAS Studies in Asian Topics: No. 15). 288p. (C). 1996. pap. text 35.00 (*0-7007-0280-6*, Pub. by Curzon Pr Ltd) UH Pr.

Lie, Merete & Sorensen, Knut, eds. Making Technology Our Own? Domesticating Technology into Everyday Life. 232p. (C). 1996. text 36.00 (*82-00-22758-8*) Scandnvan Univ Pr.

Lie, Nadia. Transicion y Transaccion: La Revista Cubana Casa de las Americas (1960-1976) (SPA.). 318p. (Orig.). (C). 1996. pap. 30.00 (*0-935318-23-2*) Edins Hispamerica.

Lie, O. S. H. The Middle Dutch Prose Lancelot: A Study of the Rotterdam Fragments & Their Place in the French, German & Dutch Lancelot in Prose Tradition. 232p. 1987. text 81.25 (*0-444-85647-1*) Elsevier.

An Asterisk (*) at the beginning of an entry indicates that the title is appearing for the first time.

Lie, Sophus. Differentialgleichungen. LC 66-12880. 39.50 (*0-8284-0206-X*) Chelsea Pub.

— Geometrie der Beruehrungstransformationen. LC 72-113134. (GER.). 1976. 39.50 (*0-8284-0291-4*) Chelsea Pub.

— Transformationsgruppen, 3 Vols. 2nd ed. LC 76-113135. 1970. 125.00 (*0-8284-0232-9*) Chelsea Pub.

— Vorlesungen Uber Continuierliche Gruppen Mit Geometrischen und Anderen Anwendungen. 2nd ed. LC 66-12879. 1971. text 59.95 (*0-8284-0199-3*) Chelsea Pub.

Lie, T. A., jt. ed. see Hardarson, G.

Lie, T. T., ed. Structural Fire Protection: Manual of Practice. 250p. 1992. text 61.00 (*0-87262-888-4*) Am Soc Civil Eng.

Lieb. Answer Key. 1995. teacher ed. 10.93 (*0-697-29409-9*, WCB McGr Hill) McGrw-H Hghr Educ.

— St. Louis Cardinals: Great Baseball Club. 1976. 24.95 (*0-8488-1579-3*) Amereon Ltd.

— Transportation. 4th ed. 1994. 61.95 (*0-87393-227-7*) Dame Pubns.

Lieb, Barbara, ed. Achieving World Class Standards: The Challenge for Educating Teachers. 53p. (Orig.). (C). 1994. pap. text 35.00 (*0-7881-1387-9*) DIANE Pub.

Lieb, Carl, et al. Lab Manual for Introductory Biology. 160p. (C). 1995. spiral bd. 16.95 (*0-7872-1696-8*) Kendall-Hunt.

Lieb, E. H., ed. see Bargmann, Valentine.

Lieb, Elliott H. The Stability of Matter: From Atoms to Stars: Selecta of Elliott H. Lieb. Thirring, W., ed. viii, 565p. 1991. 89.00 (*0-387-53039-8*) Spr-Verlag.

Lieb, Elliott H. & Loss, Michael. Analysis. LC 96-31605. (Graduate Studies in Mathematics: Vol. 14). 278p. 1996. text 35.00 (*0-8218-0632-7*, GSM/14) Am Math.

Lieb, Elliott H. & Mattis, D. C., eds. The Many-Body Problem: An Encyclopedia of Exactly Solved Models 1D. 2nd ed. 800p. 1994. text 109.00 (*981-02-0975-4*) World Scientific Pub.

Lieb, Elliott H. & Thirring, Walter E. The Stability of Matter: From Atoms to Stars: Selecta of Elliott H. Lieb. 2nd ed. LC 96-35788. 675p. 1997. 74.95 (*3-540-61565-2*) Spr-Verlag.

Lieb, Fred. Baseball As I Have Known It. LC 95-36384. (Illus.). vi, 288p. 1996. pap. 16.00 (*0-8032-7962-0*, Bison Books) U of Nebr Pr.

Lieb, Frederick G. Baseball As I Have Known It. 1976. 29.95 (*0-8488-1549-1*) Amereon Ltd.

— The Boston Red Sox. 276p. Date not set. 23.95 (*0-8488-2357-5*) Amereon Ltd.

— Detroit Tigers. 1976. 22.95 (*0-8488-1578-5*) Amereon Ltd.

Lieb, Hans-Heinrich. Integrational Linguistics, 6 vols., Vol. 1. (Current Issues in Linguistic Theory Ser.: No. 17). xxviii, 527p. 1984. 97.00 (*90-272-3508-2*) J Benjamins Pubng Co.

— Linguistic Variables: Towards a Unified Theory of Linguistic Variation. LC 93-5760. (Current Issues in Linguistic Theory Ser.: Vol. 108). xiv, 261p. 1993. 68.00 (*1-55619-562-1*) J Benjamins Pubng Co.

Lieb, Hans-Heinrich, ed. Prospects for a New Structuralism. LC 92-33520. (Current Issues in Linguistic Theory Ser.: No. 96). vii, 275p. 1992. 59.00 (*1-55619-158-8*) J Benjamins Pubng Co.

Lieb, Irwin C. Past, Present, & Future: A Philosophical Essay about Time. 272p. 1991. text 34.95 (*0-252-01804-4*); pap. text 14.95 (*0-252-06182-9*) U of Ill Pr.

Lieb, Julian. A Medical Solution to the Health Care Crisis. 129p. 1993. pap. 19.50 (*0-87527-512-5*) Green.

Lieb, Julian, jt. auth. see Hershman, D. Jablow.

Lieb, K., jt. ed. see Medrano, G.

Lieb, Michael. Children of Ezekiel: Aliens, UFOs, the Crisis of Race & the Advent of End Time. LC 98-27097. (Illus.). 344p. 1999. pap. 18.95 (*0-8223-2268-4*); lib. bdg. 54.95 (*0-8223-2137-8*) Duke.

— The Dialectics of Creation: Patterns of Birth & Regeneration in "Paradise Lost" LC 71-76047. 272p. 1970. 32.50 (*0-87023-049-2*) U of Mass Pr.

— Milton & the Culture of Violence. LC 93-32279. 288p. 1994. text 37.50 (*0-8014-2903-X*) Cornell U Pr.

— Poetics of the Holy: A Reading of "Paradise Lost" LC 80-29159. (Illus.). 464p. 1981. reprint ed. pap. 143.90 (*0-7837-7073-1*, 204688500004) Bks Demand.

— The Sinews of Ulysses: Form & Convention in Milton's Works. LC 88-25651. (Duquesne Studies: Language & Literature Ser.: Vol. 9). 190p. 1989. text 28.95 (*0-8207-0205-6*) Duquesne.

— The Visionary Mode: Biblical Prophecy, Hermeneutics & Cultural Change. LC 91-9439. 352p. 1991. text 42.50 (*0-8014-2273-6*) Cornell U Pr.

Lieb, Michael, jt. ed. see Benet, Diana T.

Lieb, Michael, jt. ed. see Labriola, Albert C.

Lieb, Robert C. Labor in the Transportation Industry. LC 73-13343. (Special Studies in U. S. Economic, Social & Political Issues). 1974. 50.50 (*0-275-28791-2*) Irvington.

Lieb, Sandra R. Mother of the Blues: A Study of Ma Rainey. LC 81-1168. (Illus.). 256p. 1983. pap. 17.95 (*0-87023-394-7*) U of Mass Pr.

Lieb, Thomas. Editing for Clear Communication. 464p. (C). 1995. text. write for info. (*0-697-23196-8*) Brown & Benchmark.

Liebaers, H., et al, eds. New Information Technologies & Libraries. 1985. text 167.00 (*90-277-2105-X*) Kluwer Academic.

Liebaers, Herman. Mostly in the Line of Duty: Thirty Years with Books. 1980. lib. bdg. 85.50 (*90-247-2228-4*) Kluwer Academic.

— Small Talk about Great Books. 1979. pap. 3.00 (*0-89073-062-8*, 256) Boston Public Lib.

Liebaert, Richard M. Biology: Concepts, Connections & Abnormal Psychology Pk. 2nd ed. 480p. (C). 1996. pap. text 25.00 (*0-8053-2023-7*) Addison-Wesley.

Lieban, Lindy. Unanswered Lives. LC 98-88476. 325p. 1998. 25.00 (*0-7388-0167-4*); pap. 15.00 (*0-7388-0168-2*) Xlibris Corp.

Liebau, H., ed. Mechanisms & Recent Advances in Therapy of Hypertension. (Contributions to Nephrology Ser.: Vol. 8). (Illus.). 1977. 29.75 (*3-8055-2671-7*) S Karger.

Liebau, H., jt. ed. see Bahlmann, J.

Liebb, Julius, jt. auth. see Bromberg, Murray.

Liebchen, Peter A. Kontum: Battle for the Central Highlands. 104p. 1993. reprint ed. pap. 15.00 (*0-923135-66-9*) Dalley Bk Service.

— MAP Aid to Laos, 1959-1972. 200p. 1993. reprint ed. pap. 22.00 (*0-923135-51-0*) Dalley Bk Service.

Liebe, jt. auth. see Splaver.

***Liebe, Frankie & Leibe, Frankie.** Miller's Ceramics of the '20s & '30s: A Collector's Guide. (Illus.). 100p. 1999. 11.95 (*1-84000-161-5*) Antique Collect.

Liebeault, Ambroise-Auguste. Le Sommeil Provoque et les Etats Anologues. LC 75-16716. (Classics in Psychiatry Ser.). 1976. reprint ed. 26.95 (*0-405-07444-1*) Ayer.

Liebeck, Helen, ed. see Pollard, Elaine.

Liebeck, Helen, jt. ed. see Pollard, Elaine.

***Liebeck, M. W.** A Concise Introduction to Pure Mathematics. LC 99-462376. 176p. (C). 2000. 34.95 (*1-58488-193-3*) CRC Pr.

Liebeck, Martin W. & Seitz, Gary M. Reductive Subgroups of Exceptional Algebraic Groups. LC 96-4542. (Memoirs of the American Mathematical Society Ser.: No. 580). 111p. 1996. pap. 36.00 (*0-8218-0461-8*, MEMO/121/580) Am Math.

Liebeck, Martin W., et al. The Maximal Factorizations of the Finite Simple Groups & Their Automorphism Groups. LC 90-31827. (Memoirs Ser.: Vol. 86/432). 151p. 1990. pap. 22.00 (*0-8218-2494-5*, MEMO/86/432) Am Math.

Liebeck, Martin W., jt. auth. see James, Gordon D.

Liebeck, Pamela. How Children Learn Mathematics. pap. 15.95 (*0-14-013488-3*, Pub. by Pnguin Bks Ltd) Trafalgar.

Liebecq, C., ed. Compendium of Biochemical Nomenclature & Related Documents. 2nd ed. 350p. (Orig.). (C). 1992. 36.00 (*1-85578-005-4*, Pub. by Portland Pr Ltd) Ashgate Pub Co.

Liebelt, Robert A. & Truitt, Edward B., Jr. Let's Talk about Alcoholism. (Illus.). 248p. (Orig.). 1989. pap. 15.95 (*0-926719-00-9*) Platte River Pr.

Liebeman, Dan. I Want to Be a Cowboy. (I Want to Be Ser.). (Illus.). 24p. (J). (gr. k-3). 1999. 14.95 (*1-55209-447-2*) Firefly Bks Ltd.

— I Want to Be a Firefighter. (I Want to Be Ser.). (Illus.). 24p. (J). (gr. k-3). 1999. 14.95 (*1-55209-448-0*) Firefly Bks Ltd.

Liebenau, Jonathan. Medical Science & Medical Industry: The Formation of the American Pharmaceutical Industry. LC 86-27346. 217p. 1987. reprint ed. pap. 67.30 (*0-608-07329-6*, 206755700009) Bks Demand.

Liebenau, Jonathan, et al, eds. Pill Peddlers: Essays on the History of the Pharmaceutical Industry. 133p. (Orig.). (C). 1990. pap. 10.95 (*0-931292-22-0*) Am Inst Hist Pharm.

Liebenau, Jonathan, jt. ed. see Davenport-Hines, R. P.

Liebenauer, Paul. Laboratory Manual for College Physics. 1995. pap. text 17.98 (*1-56581-084-8*) Tichenor Pub.

Liebenberg. Techniques for Geographers, Bk. 1. 160p. 1987. pap. 29.95 (*0-409-11147-3*) Buttrwrth-Heinemann.

Liebenow, J. Gus. African Politics: Crises & Challenges. LC 85-45469. (Illus.). 320p. 1986. pap. 14.95 (*0-253-20388-0*, MB-388) Ind U Pr.

— Colonial Rule & Political Development in Tanzania: The Case of the Makonde. LC 72-126898. 374p. reprint ed. pap. 116.00 (*0-8357-9449-0*, 201477700093) Bks Demand.

— Liberia: The Evolution of Privilege. LC 69-18359. (Africa in the Modern World Ser.). 269p. reprint ed. pap. 83.40 (*0-608-18811-5*, 203023000067) Bks Demand.

Liebenow, Mark. And Everyone Shall Praise: Resources for Multicultural Worship. LC 99-18722. 1999. pap. 19.95 (*0-8298-1318-7*) Pilgrim OH.

Liebenow, R. Mark. Prepare the Way: Daily Meditations for Advent & Lent. LC 99-41004. 144p. 1999. pap. 15.95 (*0-8298-1351-9*) Pilgrim OH.

— The Well Is Deep: Prayers to Draw Up Living Waters. LC 98-50327. 144p. 1999. pap. 14.95 (*0-8298-1325-X*) Pilgrim OH.

Liebenow, Todd. Superbook Olympics: Additional Quiz Questions, 2. 22p. 1997. pap. 10.00 (*1-58302-092-6*, BTU-03QB) One Way St.

Liebenow, Todd & Privett, Dave. Let There Be... Blacklight. VonSeggen, Liz, ed. (Illus.). 32p. 1998. pap. 15.00 (*1-58302-136-1*) One Way St.

Liebenson, Craig, ed. Rehabilitation of the Spine: A Practitioner's Manual. (Illus.). 464p. 1996. 75.00 (*0-683-05032-X*) Lppncott W & W.

Liebenstein, Meret, tr. see Ohlig, Adelheid.

Liebenthal, Andres, et al. Solar Energy: Lessons from the Pacific Island Experience. LC 94-13345. (Technical Paper, Energy Ser.: No. 244). 72p. 1994. pap. 22.00 (*0-8213-2802-6*, 12802) World Bank.

Liebenthal, Jean Z. Cottonwood Summer. 1992. pap. 6.95 (*0-88494-825-0*) Bookcraft Inc.

— Feathers & Rings. 1993. pap. 6.95 (*0-88494-870-6*) Bookcraft Inc.

Lieber, Albert J. Road to Scottsdale. LC 99-90648. (Illus.). 128p. 1999. pap. 21.95 (*0-9673020-0-5*) A J Lieber.

Lieber, Alex, ed. see Rodengen, Jeffrey L.

Lieber, Carol M. Making Choices about Conflict, Security & Peacemaking Pt. 1: Personal Perspectives. (Illus.). 399p. (Orig.). 1994. pap. 28.00 (*0-942349-08-3*) Eductrs Soc Respons.

Lieber, Carol Miller, see Miller Lieber, Carol.

Lieber, Charles S. Medical & Nutritional Complications of Alcoholism: Mechanisms & Management. (Illus.). 598p. (C). 1992. 132.00 (*0-306-43558-6*, Kluwer Plenum) Kluwer Academic.

— Medical Disorders of Alcoholism: Pathogenesis & Treatment. (Major Problems in Internal Medicine Ser.: Vol. 22). (Illus.). 608p. 1982. text 120.00 (*0-7216-5774-5*, W B Saunders Co) Harcrt Hlth Sci Grp.

Lieber, Charles S., ed. Recent Advances in the Biology of Alcoholism. LC 82-1033. (Advances in Alcohol & Substance Abuse Ser.: Vol. 1, No. 2). 123p. 1982. text 39.95 (*0-86656-104-8*) Haworth Pr.

Lieber, Constance L., ed. see Cannon, Martha H. & Cannon, Angus M.

***Lieber, Edvard.** Willem De Kooning: Reflections in the Studio. LC 99-56282. (Illus.). 138p. 2000. 35.00 (*0-8109-4560-6*, Pub. by Abrams) Time Warner.

Lieber, Francis. Notes on Fallacies of American Protectionists. (Neglected American Economists Ser.). 1974. lib. bdg. 61.00 (*0-8240-1018-3*) Garland.

***Lieber, Francis.** On Civil Liberty & Self-Government, 1859. fac. ed. LC 99-56928. 2000. write for info. (*1-58477-070-8*) Lawbk Exchange.

Lieber, James B. Rats in the Grain: The Dirty Tricks of the "Supermarket to the World" - Archer Daniels Midland. (Illus.). 326p. 1999. 24.00 (*1-56858-142-4*) FWEW.

Lieber, M. The Pirlei Avos Treasury - Ethics of the Fathers: The Sages Guide to Living with an Anthologized Commentary & Anecdotes. Scherman, Nosson, ed. (ArtScroll Mesorah Ser.). Date not set. 54.99 (*0-89906-374-8*) Mesorah Pubns.

Lieber, M., jt. auth. see Stein, M.

Lieber, M. R., jt. ed. see Jessberger, R.

Lieber, Maria, jt. auth. see Marri, Fabio.

Lieber, Michael. Street Scenes: Afro-American Culture in Urban Trinidad. 120p. 1981. pap. 11.95 (*0-87073-874-7*) Schenkman Bks Inc.

Lieber, Michael D., ed. Exiles & Migrants in Oceania. LC 77-10756. (ASAO Monograph Ser.: Vol. 5). 440p. 1977. reprint ed. pap. 136.40 (*0-608-00536-3*, 206141500008) Bks Demand.

Lieber, Phyllis, et al. Grown up Children, Grown up Parents: Opening the Door to Healthy Relationships Between Parents Adult Children. LC 94-16678. 240p. 1994. 18.95 (*1-55972-243-6*) Carol Pub Group.

— Stop Treating Me Like a Child (But First, Can You Lend Me Some Money?) Opening the Door to Healthy Relationships Between Parents & Adult Children. LC 97-75627. 224p. 1998. reprint ed. 8.98 (*1-56731-246-2*, MJF Bks) Fine Comms.

— Stop Treating Me Like a Child but First You Can Lend Me Some Money: Opening the Door to Healthy Relationships Between Parents & Adult Children. 224p. 1995. pap. 12.95 (*0-8065-1705-0*, Citadel Pr) Carol Pub Group.

Lieber, Ray. For Kids Sake - Teaching Tackle Football: The Youth Coach's Field Manual. Inneracity, Jacqueline, ed. LC 97-222052. (Illus.). 1997. 23.95 (*0-9659985-0-9*) Youth Sports Pr.

Lieber, Richard L. Skeletal Muscle Structure & Function. (Illus.). 314p. 1994. write for info. (*0-683-05026-5*) Lppncott W & W.

Lieber, Robert J. American Diplomatic Response to the 1973-1974 Energy Crisis. (Pew Case Studies in International Affairs). 50p. (C). 1988. pap. text 3.50 (*1-56927-148-8*) Geo U Inst Dplmcy.

— No Common Power. 3rd ed. LC 94-7217. 386p. (C). 1997. pap. text 57.00 (*0-673-52390-X*) Addson-Wesley Educ.

***Lieber, Robert J.** No Common Power: Understanding International Relations. 4th ed. 416p. 2000. pap. 34.67 (*0-13-011504-5*, Prentice Hall) P-H.

Lieber, Rochelle. Deconstructing Morphology: Word Formation in Syntactic Theory. (Illus.). 250p. 1992. pap. text 28.95 (*0-226-48063-1*); lib. bdg. 66.50 (*0-226-48062-3*) U Ch Pr.

— An Integrated Theory of Autosegmental Processes. LC 86-30049. (SUNY Series in Linguistics). 209p. (C). 1987. pap. text 29.95 (*0-88706-510-4*) State U NY Pr.

Lieber, Ron. Upstart Start-Ups! How 25 Young Entrepreneurs Overcame Youth, Inexperience & Lack of Money to Create Thriving Businesses. LC 98-17647. 240p. 1998. pap. 15.00 (*0-7679-0088-X*) Broadway BDD.

Lieber, Ron, jt. auth. see Hall, Colin.

Lieber, William M. Lieber on Pensions, 5 vols. 4200p. 1991. ring bd. 595.00 (*0-13-085821-8*) Aspen Law.

Lieberfeld, Daniel. Talking with the Enemy: Negotiation & Threat Perception in South Africa & Israel/Palestine. LC 98-56633. 192p. 1999. 55.00 (*0-275-96555-4*, C6555, Praeger Pubs) Greenwood.

Lieberg, Carolyn. Calling the Midwest Home: A Lively Look at the Origins, Attitudes, Quirks & Curiosities of America's Heartlanders. LC 96-32107. (Illus.). 240p. 1996. pap. 14.95 (*1-885171-12-9*) Wldcat Canyon.

— Little Sisters: The Last but Not the Least. LC 98-29819. 224p. 1998. pap. 13.95 (*1-885171-24-2*) PageMill Pr.

Lieberg, Godo. Poeta Creator: Studien Zu Einer Figur der Antiken Dichtung. (GER.). 189p. (C). 1982. pap. 40.00 (*90-70265-53-2*, Pub. by Gieben) J Benjamins Pubng Co.

Lieberg, Owen S. High Temperature Water Systems. 2nd ed. LC 63-24500. 237p. reprint ed. pap. 73.50 (*0-608-11492-8*, 200190800009) Bks Demand.

Liebergen, Patrick. Classic Canons II. (Classic Canons Ser.). 1999. pap. 3.95 (*0-7390-0035-7*, 18915) Alfred Pub.

— Favorite Christmas Classics for Solo Singers, Medium-High Voice. 1998. pap. 9.95 (*0-88284-886-0*, 17923); pap. 20.95 incl. audio (*0-88284-887-9*, 17926); pap. 20.95 incl. audio compact disk (*0-88284-888-7*, 17927); pap. 20.95 incl. audio compact disk (*0-88284-891-7*, 17932) Alfred Pub.

Liebergen, Patrick. Favorite Sacred Classics, Medium High. 1995. pap. 30.95 incl. audio compact disk (*0-7390-0114-0*, 11511) Alfred Pub.

Liebergen, Patrick. Favorite Sacred Classics, Medium High. 112p. 1995. pap. 19.95 (*0-7390-0113-2*, 11481) Alfred Pub.

Lieberherr, Karl J. Adaptive Object-Oriented Software: The Demeter Method with Propagation Patterns. LC 95-21469. 656p. 1995. pap. 81.95 (*0-534-94602-X*) PWS Pubs.

Lieberman. Chemistry & Public Policy. 11th ed. 1998. pap. text 39.00 (*0-536-01744-1*) Pearson Custom.

— Economic Principles, Economic Policy: Complete. LC 97-17927. (AB - Accounting Principles Ser.). (C). 1997. 92.95 (*0-538-84757-3*) S-W Pub.

— Economic Principles, Economic Policy: Complete. (AB - Accounting Principles Ser.). 1998. pap., wbk. ed. 19.25 (*0-538-85471-5*) S-W Pub.

— Economic Principles, Economic Policy: Macro Split. (AB - Accounting Principles Ser.). 1998. pap., wbk. ed. 16.75 (*0-538-85473-1*) S-W Pub.

— Economic Principles, Economic Policy: Micro Split. (AB - Accounting Principles Ser.). 1997. pap., wbk. ed. 16.75 (*0-538-85472-3*) S-W Pub.

***Lieberman.** In Praise of Public Life: The Honor & Purpose of Political Science. 2001. pap. write for info. (*0-684-86775-3*, Fireside) S&S Trade Pap.

Lieberman. International Economics. (SWC-Finance Ser.). 2001. pap. 55.00 (*0-324-00868-6*) Thomson Learn.

— International Finance. (SWC-Finance Ser.). 2002. 55.00 (*0-324-00869-4*) Thomson Learn.

— International Trade. (SWC-Finance Ser.). 2002. pap. 45.00 (*0-324-00870-8*) Thomson Learn.

***Lieberman.** Introduction to Economics. LC 99-30970. (SWC-Economics Ser.). 1999. pap. 82.95 (*0-324-00879-1*) Thomson Learn.

— Introduction to Economics. (SWC-Economics Ser.). 1999. pap. text, student ed. 16.00 (*0-324-00880-5*) Thomson Learn.

Lieberman. Macroeconomics: Principles & Applications. LC 97-17926. (AB - Accounting Principles Ser.). (C). 1997. 67.95 (*0-538-84759-X*) S-W Pub.

— Microeconomics: Principles & Applications. LC 97-17925. (AB - Accounting Principles Ser.). (C). 1997. 67.95 (*0-538-84758-1*) S-W Pub.

— Parental Bereavement. Date not set. 29.95 (*0-465-05444-7*, Pub. by Basic) HarpC.

— Public Speaking & the Multicultural Environment. 2nd ed. 59p. 1996. pap. text 3.00 (*0-205-26511-1*) Allyn.

Lieberman, et al, eds. Monoamine Oxidase Inhibitors in Neurological Diseases. (Neurological Disease & Therapy Ser.: Vol. 21). (Illus.). 400p. 1994. text 165.00 (*0-8247-9082-0*) Dekker.

— Pharmaceutical Dosage Forms: Disperse Systems, Vol. 3. 2nd ed. (Illus.). 584p. 1998. text 165.00 (*0-8247-9842-2*) Dekker.

— Pharmaceutical Dosage Forms Vol. 2: Disperse Systems, Vol. 2. 2nd ed. (Illus.). 528p. 1996. text 175.00 (*0-8247-9713-2*) Dekker.

Lieberman, et al. Pharmaceutical Dosage Forms: Tablets, Vol. 2. 2nd ed. (Illus.). 640p. 1990. text 167.50 (*0-8247-8289-5*) Dekker.

Lieberman, jt. auth. see Hall.

Lieberman, A. S., jt. auth. see Navch, Z.

Lieberman, A. S., jt. auth. see Naveh, Zev.

Lieberman, Abraham N., et al. Parkinson's Disease: The Complete Guide for Patients & Caregivers. 272p. (Orig.). 1993. per. 12.00 (*0-671-76819-0*) S&S Trade Pap.

Lieberman, Adrienne, jt. auth. see Kerns, Lawrence.

Lieberman, Adrienne B. Easing Labor Pain: The Complete Guide to a More Comfortable & Rewarding Birth. rev. ed. Rosenberg, Dan, ed. LC 92-382. (Illus.). 288p. 1992. 19.95 (*1-55832-044-X*); pap. 14.95 (*1-55832-043-1*) Harvard Common Pr.

Lieberman, Adrienne B., jt. auth. see Holt, Linda H.

Lieberman, Alice A. The Social Workout Book: Strength Building Exercises for the Pre-Professional. LC 97-33799. 288p. (Orig.). (C). 1998. pap. text 18.95 (*0-7619-8531-X*) Pine Forge.

Lieberman, Alicia F. Emotional Life of the Toddler. 256p. 1993. 24.95 (*0-02-919021-5*) Free Pr.

— The Emotional Life of the Toddler. 1995. per. 12.00 (*0-02-874017-3*) Free Pr.

Lieberman, Alicia F., et al, eds. The DC 0-3 Casebook: A Guide to the Use of Zero to Three's Diagnostic Classification of Mental Health & Developmental Disorders of Infancy & Early Childhood in Assessment & Treatment Planning. 350p. 1997. pap. 35.00 (*0-943657-38-5*) ZERO TO THREE.

Lieberman, Alvin. Contamination Control & Cleanrooms: Problems, Engineering Solutions, & Applications. (Illus.). 384p. (gr. 13). 1992. text 72.95 (*0-442-00574-1*) Chapman & Hall.

Lieberman, Ann, ed. Building a Professional Culture in Schools. (Series on School Reform). 248p. (C). 1988. text 32.95 (*0-8077-2901-9*); pap. text 18.95 (*0-8077-2900-0*) Tchrs Coll.

— The Changing Contexts of Teaching. (National Society for the Study of Education Publication Ser.). 250p. 1992. 27.50 (*0-226-60157-9*) U Ch Pr.

— Rethinking School Improvement: Research, Craft & Concept. 240p. 1986. pap. text 18.95 (*0-8077-2807-1*) Tchrs Coll.

— Work of Restructuring Schools: Building from the Ground Up. (Series on School Reform). 208p. (C). 1995. text 40.00 (*0-8077-3404-7*); pap. text 18.95 (*0-8077-3403-9*) Tchrs Coll.

L

Lieberman, Ann & McLaughlin, Milbrey W., eds. Policy Making in Education. LC 81-85130. (National Society for the Study of Education Publication Ser.: 81st; Pt. 1). 304p. (C). 1982. lib. bdg. 15.00 (0-226-60132-3) U Ch Pr.

Lieberman, Ann & Miller, Lynne. Teachers--Transforming Their World & Their Work. LC 99-13653. 103p. 1999. pap. 16.95 (0-87120-352-9, 199217) ASCD.

— Teachers, Their World & Their Work: Implications for School Improvement. 160p. (C). 1991. reprint ed. pap. text 14.95 (0-8077-3165-X) Tchrs Coll.

Lieberman, Ann & Miller, Lynne, eds. Staff Development for Education in the 90s: New Demands, New Realities, New Perspectives. 2nd ed. (Series on School Reform). 288p. (C). 1991. pap. text 20.95 (0-8077-3099-8) Tchrs Coll.

Lieberman, Annette & Lindner, Vicki. The Money Mirror: How Money Reflects Women's Dreams, Fears, & Desires. LC 96-83239. 232p. 1996. pap. 14.95 (1-880559-41-2) Allworth Pr.

Lieberman, Barbara B., jt. auth. see Allison, Martha B.

Lieberman, Ben. Environmental Audits: Colorado Carrots Versus Federal Sticks in Environmental Enforcement. (Issue Paper #1-98 Ser.). 18p. 1998. pap. text 8.00 (1-57655-163-6) Independ Inst.

— From Recovery to Catastrophe: Municipal Stabilization & Political Crisis in weimar Germany. LC 97-19436. (Monographs in German History: Vol. 3). 232p. (C). 1997. 42.00 (1-57181-104-4) Berghahn Bks.

Lieberman, Bernhardt. Social Choice. LC 75-132954. (Monographs & Texts in the Behavioral Sciences). (Illus.). xii, 426p. 1971. text 235.00 (0-677-14770-8) Gordon & Breach.

Lieberman, Bernhardt, ed. see Rader, Trout.

Lieberman, Betsy, ed. Financing AIDS Housing. 165p. (C). 2000. pap. text 25.00 (0-7881-4360-3) DIANE Pub.

Lieberman, Betsy & Chamberlain, Donald. Breaking New Ground: Developing Innovative AIDS Care Residences. LC 93-71111. 250p. 1993. pap. text 39.95 (0-9636595-0-2) AIDS Hse WA.

— Breaking New Ground: Developing Innovative AIDS Care Residences. 311p. 1993. pap. 39.95 (0-9639595-0-6) AIDS Hse WA.

***Lieberman, Bruce S.** Paleobiogeography: Using Fossils to Study Global Change, Plate Techtonics & Evolution. LC 99-55322. (Topics in Geobiology Ser.). 1999. write for info. (0-306-46277-X, Kluwer Plenum) Kluwer Academic.

Lieberman, Bruce S., jt. auth. see White, Russell D.

Lieberman, Carl. Educational Expenditures & Economics Growth in the American States. unabridged ed. LC 99-208793. 122p. 1998. pap. 22.95 (0-9646524-4-7) Midwest Pr.

Lieberman, Carl, ed. Government & Politics in Ohio. LC 84-15205. 340p. (Orig.). 1984. pap. text 27.00 (0-8191-4207-7) U Pr of Amer.

— Government, Politics & Public Policy in Ohio. LC 95-94293. 277p. (C). 1995. text 44.95 (0-9646524-0-4); pap. text 24.95 (0-9646524-1-2) Midwest Pr.

Lieberman, Carole. Bad Boys. 384p. 1998. mass mkt. 6.99 (0-451-19524-8, Sig) NAL.

Lieberman, Cheryl A. Creating Ceremonies: Innovative Ways to Meet Adoption Challenges. LC 98-30945. 141p. 1999. pap. 23.95 (1-891944-10-X) Zeig Tucker.

Lieberman-Cline, Nancy, et al. Basketball for Women: Becoming a Complete Player. LC 95-17945. (Illus.). 296p. (Orig.). 1995. pap. 16.95 (0-87322-610-0, PLIE0610) Human Kinetics.

Lieberman, Dale. Witness to the Covenant of Circumcision: Bris Milah. LC 96-48368. (Illus.). 104p. 1997. pap. 27.50 (1-56821-994-6) Aronson.

Lieberman, Dan. Renovating Your Home for Maximum Profit: Make up to 4,000 Dollars for Every 1,000 Dollars You Invest. 1991. pap. 14.95 (1-55958-097-6) Prima Pub.

Lieberman, Dan & Hoffman, Paul. Renovating Your Home for Maximum Profit: Make up to 4,000 Dollars for Every 1,000 Dollars You Invest. 390p. 1994. 21.95 (0-914629-93-X) Prima Pub.

Lieberman, Dan, jt. auth. see Hoffman, Paul.

Lieberman, David. The Eternal Torah: A Commentary Integrating All the Prophets into the Books of Kings, Bk. 3. 600p. (C). 1986. 25.00 (0-9609840-2-X) Twin Pines Pr.

— The Eternal Torah: A Commentary upon Torah Pentateuch Consolidating the Scholarship Throughout Hebrew Literature, Pt. 1. 570p. 1986. reprint ed. 25.00 (0-9609840-0-3) Twin Pines Pr.

— Learning: Behavior & Cognition, Test Items. 2nd ed. 1992. mass mkt. write for info. (0-534-17402-7) Brooks-Cole.

Lieberman, David A. Learning: Behavior & Cognition. 500p. (C). 1990. mass mkt. 45.50 (0-534-12318-X) Brooks-Cole.

— Learning: Behavior & Cognition. 2nd ed. (C). 1992. pap. 49.75 (0-534-17400-0) Brooks-Cole.

— Learning, Behavior & Cognition. 3rd ed. LC 99-36080. (Psychology Ser.). 595p. 1999. mass mkt. 81.95 (0-534-33925-5) Brooks-Cole.

***Lieberman, David J.** Get Anyone to Do Anything & Never Feel Powerless Again: Psychological Secrets to Predict, Control & Influence Every Situation. LC 00-27043. 208p. 2000. text 21.95 (0-312-20904-5) St Martin.

Lieberman, David J. Instant Analysis. LC 97-8968. 1997. text 22.95 (0-312-15554-9) St Martin.

— Instant Analysis. 320p. 1998. pap. 12.95 (0-312-19466-8) St Martin.

— Instant Analysis, Vol. 1. 1997. mass mkt. write for info. (0-312-96176-6) St Martin.

Lieberman, David J. Instant Analysis: How to Understand-& Change-the Most Common, Puzzling, Annoying, Self-Defeating Behaviors & Habits. abr. ed. 1997. audio 18.00 (0-694-51862-X, CPN 2676) HarperAudio.

Lieberman, David J. Never Be Lied to Again. LC 98-18634. 224p. 1998. text 19.95 (0-312-18634-7) St Martin.

— Never Be Lied to Again. 2nd ed. 204p. 1999. pap. 12.95 (0-312-20428-0) St Martin.

Lieberman, Deborah, jt. auth. see Fox, Perla G.

Lieberman, Devorah A. & Gurtov, Mel. Revealing the World: An Interdisciplinary Reader for International Studies. LC 92-82742. 304p. (C). 1994. per. 36.95 (0-8403-7951-X) Kendall-Hunt.

Lieberman, Donald. The Doctor in Your House: Dr. Lieberman's Unique Guide to Preventive Medicine & Sensible Money Saving Self Care. 80p. (Orig.). 1989. pap. 6.95 (0-317-93298-5) Jadon Pubns.

Lieberman, Donna H., ed. see Rudnick & Wolfe Staff.

Lieberman, E. James. Acts of Will: The Life & Work of Otto Rank. 2nd ed. LC 93-28227. (Illus.). 536p. 1993. reprint ed. pap. 21.95 (0-87023-871-X) U of Mass Pr.

Lieberman, E. James & Troccoli, Karen L. Like It Is: A Teen Sex Guide. LC 98-27176. (Illus.). 216p. (YA). (gr. 6 up). 1998. pap. 25.00 (0-7864-0526-0) McFarland & Co.

Lieberman, E. James, jt. auth. see Brenner, Marcella B.

Lieberman, Elias. American Short Story. LC 71-128995. reprint ed. 31.50 (0-404-03986-3) AMS Pr.

— The American Short Story: A Study of the Influence of Locality in Its Development. (BCL1-PS American Literature Ser.). 183p. 1992. reprint ed. lib. bdg. 69.00 (0-7812-6637-8) Rprt Serv.

Lieberman, Elizabeth T., jt. auth. see Lieberman, Norman.

Lieberman, Ellen, jt. auth. see Douglass, Catherine J.

Lieberman, Elli. Deterrence Theory: Success or Failure in Arab-Israeli Wars? 81p. (Orig.). (C). 1996. pap. text 25.00 (0-7881-2713-6) DIANE Pub.

Lieberman, Ellin, jt. auth. see Kaplan, Norman M.

Lieberman, Florence. Clinical Social Workers as Psychotherapists. LC 82-3109. 1982. 29.95 (0-89876-037-2) Gardner Pr.

— Social Work with Children. LC 78-23287. 344p. 1979. 45.95 (0-87705-255-7, Kluwer Acad Hman Sci); pap. 26.95 (0-87705-257-3, Kluwer Acad Hman Sci) Kluwer Academic.

Lieberman, Florence, et al, eds. The Foster Care Dilemma: A Special Issue of Child & Adolescent Social Work Journal. 134p. 1987. pap. 16.95 (0-89885-367-2, Kluwer Acad Hman Sci) Kluwer Academic.

Lieberman, Frederic, jt. auth. see Miller, Leta E.

Lieberman, Fredric, ed. A Chinese Zither Tutor: The Mei-an ch'in-p'u. LC 82-4895. (Illus.). 156p. 1982. 40.00 (0-295-95941-X) U of Wash Pr.

Lieberman, Fredric, jt. auth. see Hart, Mickey.

Lieberman, Gerald F. Three Thousand Five Hundred Good Jokes for Speakers. LC 74-29354. 480p. 1975. pap. 7.95 (0-385-00545-8) Doubleday.

— Three Thousand Five Hundred Good Quotes for Speakers. LC 81-43552. 288p. 1987. pap. 7.95 (0-385-17769-0) Doubleday.

Lieberman, Gerald J., jt. auth. see Hillier, Frederick S.

Lieberman, H. A., et al. Pharmaceutical Dosage Forms: Tablets, Vol. 1. 2nd ed. (Illus.). 576p. 1989. text 175.00 (0-8247-8044-2) Dekker.

Lieberman, Harvey. Decision Guides. (Simulation Game Ser.). 1974. 12.00 (0-89401-015-8) Didactic Syst.

— Decision Guides. (Simulation Game Ser.). 1974. pap. 35.00 (0-89401-013-1) Didactic Syst.

— Effective Supervision in Government. (Simulation Game Ser.). 1973. pap. 26.25 (0-89401-024-7) Didactic Syst.

— Women in Management. (Simulation Game Ser.). 1975. pap. 26.25 (0-89401-095-6) Didactic Syst.

Lieberman, Harvey & Rausch, Erwin. Managing & Allocating Time: Industrial. 1976. pap. 26.25 (0-89401-060-3) Didactic Syst.

— Managing & Allocating Time (Non-Industrial) (Simulation Game Ser.). 1976. pap. 26.25 (0-89401-061-1) Didactic Syst.

Lieberman, Herbert. Girl with the Botticelli Eyes. 1998. mass mkt. 6.99 (0-312-96406-4) St Martin.

Lieberman, Herbert A., et al, eds. Pharmaceutical Dosage Forms: Disperse Systems, Vol. 1. 2nd ed. LC 96-15604. (Illus.). 552p. 1996. text 175.00 (0-8247-9387-0) Dekker.

Lieberman, Herbert A., et al. Pharmaceutical Dosage Forms Vol. 3: Tablets. 2nd ed. (Illus.). 584p. 1990. text 165.00 (0-8247-8300-X) Dekker.

Lieberman, Herbert H. Shadow Dancers. 1990. reprint ed. mass mkt. write for info. (0-312-92288-4) St Martin.

— Shadow Dancers: A Novel. 416p. 1989. 18.95 (0-316-52417-4) Little.

Lieberman, Ira W., et al, eds. Between State & Market: Mass Privatization in Transition Economies. (Studies of Economies in Transformation: No. 23). 264p. 1997. pap. 30.00 (0-8213-3947-8, 13947) World Bank.

— Russia: Creating Private Enterprise & Efficient Markets. LC 94-49067. (Studies of Economies in Transformation: No. 15). 266p. 1995. pap. 22.00 (0-8213-3187-6, 13187) World Bank.

Lieberman, Ira W. & Kirkness, Christopher D. Privatization & Emerging Equity Markets. LC 98-9379. 160p. 1998. pap. 125.00 (0-8213-4187-1, 14187) World Bank.

***Lieberman, J. Ben.** NRC Enforcement Policy Review: July 1995-July 1997. 64p. 1998. pap. 5.50 (0-16-062737-0) USGPO.

Lieberman, J. Ben. Type & Typefaces. 2nd ed. LC 77-24401. (Illus.). 142p. 1978. 30.00 (0-918142-01-6); pap. 19.95 (0-918142-02-4) Oak Knoll.

Lieberman, Jack. Inherited Disease of the Lung. 1988. text 69.00 (0-7216-2763-3, W B Saunders Co) Harcrt Hlth Sci Grp.

***Lieberman, Jacob.** Light Years Ahead: The Illustrated Guide to Full Spectrum & Colored Light in Mindbody Healing. (Illus.). 424p. 1999. reprint ed. pap. text 20.00 (0-7881-6777-4) DIANE Pub.

Lieberman, James, tr. see Rank, Otto.

Lieberman, James L. A Practical Guide for Hazardous Waste Management, Administration, & Compliance. Gauiter, Gary, ed. LC 94-12877. 256p. 1994. lib. bdg. 75.00 (1-56670-115-5, L1115) Lewis Pubs.

— A Practical Guide for Hazardous Waste Management, Administration & Compliance: RCRA Compliance Guide. (Environmental Regulatory Compliance Ser.). 240p. (C). 1993. pap. text. write for info. (0-9638274-0-5) Envir Info Srvs.

Lieberman, Janet & Hungar, Julie. Transforming Students' Lives: How "Exploring Transfer" Works & Why. 128p. 1998. pap. 20.00 (1-56377-025-3, NO9801) Am Assn Higher Ed.

Lieberman, Janet E., ed. Collaborating with High Schools. LC 85-644753. (New Directions for Community Colleges Ser.: No. CC 63). 1988. pap. 22.00 (1-55542-882-7) Jossey-Bass.

Lieberman, Janice & Raff, Jason. Tricks of the Trade: A Consumer Survival Guide. LC 98-19624. 400p. 1998. pap. 11.95 (0-440-50825-8) Doubleday.

***Lieberman, Janice S.** Body Talk: Looking & Being Looked at in Psychotherapy. LC 99-88327. 2000. 40.00 (0-7657-0258-4) Aronson.

Lieberman, Janice S., jt. auth. see Gediman, Helen K.

Lieberman, Jeffrey A. & Kane, John M., eds. Predictors of Relapse in Schizophrenia. LC 86-10900. (Clinical Insights Ser.). 167p. reprint ed. pap. 51.80 (0-8357-7847-9, 203622300002) Bks Demand.

Lieberman, Jethro K. The Enduring Constitution. LC 86-32458. (Illus.). 493p. 1987. text 86.95 (0-314-32026-1) West Pub.

— The Enduring Constitution. limited ed. LC 86-32458. (Illus.). 483p. 1987. text 42.95 (0-314-32025-3) West Pub.

— The Evolving Constitution: How the Supreme Court Has Ruled on Issues from Abortion to Zoning. LC 98-18427. 1999. pap. 35.00 (0-520-21280-0, Pub. by U CA Pr) Cal Prin Full Svc.

— The 1995 Supplement to the Evolving Constitution. 55p. 1995. 14.95 (0-614-13519-2) Dialogue.

— The 1994 Supplement to the Evolving Constitution. 85p. (Orig.). 1994. pap. 16.95 (0-9630136-1-0) Dialogue.

Lieberman, Jethro K. & Siedel, George J., III. Business Law & the Legal Environment. 3rd ed. 1400p. (C). 1992. text 100.00 (0-15-505516-X) Dryden Pr.

Lieberman, Jethro K., jt. auth. see Goldstein, Tom.

Lieberman, Joe. Sentimental Journeys: Images from a Lifetime of Observation. LC 98-88955. (Illus.). 184p. 1999. pap. 14.95 (1-880404-19-2) Bkwrights.

— Those Amazing Tables: Teaching Multiplication Through Patterns & Color Strips. (J). (gr. 4-7). 1995. pap. 11.95 (0-201-48019-0) Addison-Wesley.

— Those Amazing Tables: Teaching Multiplication Through Patterns & Color Strips. 64p. (J). (gr. 3-8). 1983. pap. text 11.95 (0-914040-98-7) Cuisenaire.

Lieberman, Joseph A., III, jt. auth. see Stuart, Marian R.

***Lieberman, Joseph L. & D'Orso, Michael.** In Praise of Public Life. LC 99-59278. 176p. 2000. 21.00 (0-684-86774-5) S&S Trade.

Lieberman, Judy S. The Complete Off-Premise Caterer. 2nd ed. (Hospitality, Travel & Tourism Ser.). (Illus.). 480p. 1997. text 49.95 (0-442-02091-0, VNR) Wiley.

Lieberman, Julia R., ed. El Teatro Alegorico de Miguel (Daniel Levi) de Barrios. (Ediciones Criticas Ser.: Vol. 5). (SPA.). 234p. (Orig.). 1996. pap. 17.00 (0-936388-68-4) Juan de la Cuesta.

Lieberman, Julie L. Blues Fiddle. (Illus.). 112p. pap. 17.95 (0-8256-0308-0, OK64162, Oak) Music Sales.

— The Contemporary Violinist. 152p. 1999. lib. bdg. 23.95 incl. audio compact disk (1-879730-07-3, Pub. by Huiksi Music) IPG Chicago.

— The Creative Orchestra: Exercises & Games to Enliven Your Band or Orchestra. (Illus.). 64p. 1999. lib. bdg. 16.95 (1-879730-33-2, Pub. by Huiksi Music) IPG Chicago.

— Improvising Violin. rev. ed. (Illus.). 136p. (YA). (gr. 10 up). 1995. pap. 19.95 (1-879730-10-3) Huiksi Music.

— Planet Musician: The World Music Sourcebook for Musicians. 152p. 1998. otabind 22.95 incl. audio compact disk (0-7935-8695-X) H Leonard.

— You Are Your Instrument: The Definitive Musician's Guide to Practice & Performance. (Illus.). 152p. 1991. pap. 20.00 (1-879730-20-0) Huiksi Music.

Lieberman, Julie L., ed. see Deva, Jeannie.

Lieberman, Lauren J. & Cowart, Jim F. Games for People with Sensory Impairments: Strategies for Including Individuals of All Ages. LC 96-2010. (Illus.). 160p. (Orig.). 1996. pap. text 17.00 (0-87322-890-1, BLIE0890) Human Kinetics.

Lieberman, Laurence. Beyond the Muse of Memory: Essays on Contemporary American Poets. LC 95-36753. 304p. (C). 1995. text 49.95 (0-8262-1027-9); pap. text 24.95 (0-8262-1047-3) U of Mo Pr.

— Compass of the Dying: Poems by Lawrence Lieberman. LC 97-37473. 1998. pap. 16.00 (1-55728-510-1) U of Ark Pr.

***Lieberman, Laurence.** Compass of the Dying: Poems by Lawrence Lieberman. LC 97-37473. 1998. 24.00 (1-55728-509-8) U of Ark Pr.

Lieberman, Laurence. Dark Songs Slave House & Synagogue: Poems by Laurence Lieberman. LC 95-49128. 144p. 1996. 24.00 (1-55728-409-1) U of Ark Pr.

— Dark Songs Slave House & Synagogue: Poems by Laurence Lieberman. LC 95-49128. 144p. 1996. pap. 16.00 (1-55728-410-5) U of Ark Pr.

***Lieberman, Laurence.** Flight from the Mother Stone. LC 99-39102. 184p. 2000. pap. 20.00 (1-55728-585-3) U of Ark Pr.

Lieberman, Laurence. New & Selected Poems, 1962 to 1992. LC 92-45567. 232p. 1993. 16.95 (0-252-06314-7); text 34.95 (0-252-02010-3) U of Ill Pr.

— The Regatta in the Skies: Selected Long Poems. LC 98-20341. 192p. 1999. pap. 19.95 (0-8203-2035-8) U of Ga Pr.

Lieberman, Leo. Arco SAT II Writing: SAT II Writing. 2nd ed. LC 97-81130. 240p. 1998. pap. text 12.95 (0-02-862472-6, Arc) IDG Bks.

***Lieberman, Leo.** Memories of Laughter & Garlic: Jewish Wit, Wisdom & Humor to Warm Your Heart. Huberman, Rob, ed. 240p. 1999. write for info. (0-9674074-0-0) ComteQ Pubg.

Lieberman, Leo. What Can I Be? A Guide to Five Hundred Twenty-Five Liberal Arts & Business Careers. LC 75-26001. 1976. pap. 31.90 (0-935198-03-2) M M Bruce.

Lieberman, Leo & Spielberger, Jeffrey. College Board Achievement Test: English Composition. 2nd ed. 256p. 1991. pap. 11.00 (0-13-144965-6, Arco) Macmillan Gen Ref.

— Essential English Composition for College-Bound Students. 3rd ed. LC 93-2054. 240p. 1993. per. 10.00 (0-671-86401-7, Arc) IDG Bks.

Lieberman, Leo, et al. CLEP: College-Level Examination Program. 7th ed. LC 99-60542. 512p. 1999. 13.95 (0-02-862806-3, Arc) IDG Bks.

Lieberman, Leon, ed. see Avis, Kenneth E., et al.

Lieberman, Leonard, jt. ed. see Reynolds, Larry T.

Lieberman, Lillian. FolderGames for Math Plus. (Illus.). 144p. (J). (gr. 1-3). 1995. pap., teacher ed. 13.95 (1-878279-84-X, MM 2007) Monday Morning Bks.

— FolderGames for Phonics Plus. (Illus.). 144p. (J). (gr. 1-3). 1995. pap., teacher ed. 13.95 (1-878279-85-8, MM 2008) Monday Morning Bks.

— KinderFolders for Math Readiness. (Illus.). 144p. (J). (ps-1). 1995. pap., teacher ed. 13.95 (1-878279-82-3, MM 2005) Monday Morning Bks.

— Starting Points for Language Arts. (Illus.). 128p. (J). (gr. 1-3). 1999. pap. 14.95 (1-57612-069-4, MM2082) Monday Morning Bks.

— Starting Points for Reading. (Illus.). 128p. (J). (gr. 1-3). 1999. pap. 14.95 (1-57612-068-6, MM2083) Monday Morning Bks.

Lieberman, Linda. KinderFolders for Reading Readiness. (Illus.). 144p. (J). (ps-1). 1995. pap., teacher ed. 13.95 (1-878279-83-1, MM 2006) Monday Morning Bks.

Lieberman, M. A., jt. auth. see Lichtenberg, A. J.

Lieberman, M. Laurence. The Sexual Pharmacy: The Complete Guide to Drugs with Sexual Side Effects. 320p. 1988. 18.95 (0-317-66926-5) NAL.

Lieberman, Marc R. Your Rights As a Consumer: Legal Tips for Savvy Purchases of Goods, Service & Credit. Strohm, Richard L., ed. LC 96-37518. (Layman's Law Guides Ser.). 128p. 1999. 16.95 (0-7910-4445-9) Chelsea Hse.

Lieberman, Marcel S. Commitment, Value, & Moral Realism. LC 97-41740. (Studies in Philosophy). 216p. (C). 1998. 54.95 (0-521-63111-4) Cambridge U Pr.

Lieberman, Marcia. The Outdoor Traveler's Guide to the Alps. LC 91-3146. (Illus.). 360p. 1991. pap. 12.50 (1-55670-177-2) Stewart Tabori & Chang.

Lieberman, Marcia, photos by. When Divas Confess: Heroes, Friends, & Other Opera Characters. LC 99-11129. (Illus.). 160p. 1999. pap. 29.95 (0-7893-0259-4, Pub. by Universe) St Martin.

Lieberman, Marcia & Lieberman, Philip. Switzerland's Mountain Inns: A Walking Vacation in a World Apart. LC 97-46866. (Illus.). 256p. 1998. pap. 16.95 (0-88150-406-8, Pub. by Countryman) Norton.

Lieberman, Marcia, jt. auth. see Lieberman, Philip.

Lieberman, Martin. Apple Dining & Entertainment Club. rev. ed. (Illus.). 54p. 1988. pap. 6.95 (0-943711-01-0) Apple Dining.

Lieberman, Marvin & Warshaw, Leon J. New York Academy of Medicine, 1947-1997: Enhancing the Health of the Public. LC 97-29698. 428p. 1998. 69.50 (0-89464-984-1) Krieger.

Lieberman, Maurice. Ear Training & Sight Singing. (Illus.). (C). 1959. pap. text 32.75 (0-393-09519-3) Norton.

***Lieberman, Melissa, ed.** Girlfriends: A Celebration of the Unique Bond. (Illus.). 120p. 2000. 4.95 (1-930408-03-X) Lawrnce Teach.

— The Little Book of Women's Wit: A Bouquet of Quotations. (Illus.). 126p. 2000. 4.95 (1-930408-01-3) Lawrnce Teach.

Lieberman, Melvyn, jt. ed. see Nelson, Phillip G.

Lieberman, Michael. A History of the Sweetness of the World. LC 95-49074. (Texas Review Southern & Southwestern Poets Breakthrough Ser.). 80p. 1995. pap. 8.00 (1-881515-07-9); text 15.00 (1-881515-06-0) TX Review Pr.

— Sojourn at Elmhurst: A Poem Sequence. LC 97-69842. 96p. 1998. pap. 14.95 (0-89823-189-2) New Rivers Pr.

Lieberman, Michael & Dinkin, Michael. Get A Life: A Healthy Life. 114p. 1997. pap. 9.95 (1-929073-25-9) DL Prods.

Lieberman, Michael A. & Lichtenberg, Allan J. Principles of Plasma Discharges & Materials Processing. 600p. 1994. 89.95 (0-471-00577-0) Wiley.

Lieberman, Morris, ed. Post-Harvest Physiology & Crop Preservation. LC 82-3645. (NATO ASI Series A, Life Sciences: Vol. 46). 586p. 1983. 125.00 (0-306-40984-4, Plenum Trade) Perseus Pubng.

An Asterisk (*) at the beginning of an entry indicates that the title is appearing for the first time.

Lieberman, Morton. Doors Close, Doors Open: Widows, Grieving & Growing. 287p. 1998. text 24.00 (*0-7881-5925-9*) DIANE Pub.

Lieberman, Morton A., et al. Self-Help Groups for Coping with Crisis: Origins, Members, Processes, & Impact. LC 79-88772. (Jossey-Bass Social & Behavioral Science Ser.). 480p. reprint ed. pap. 148.80 (*0-8357-4903-7*, 203783300009) Bks Demand.

Lieberman, Morton A., jt. auth. see Tobin, Sheldon S.

Lieberman, Myron. The Future of Public Education. LC 59-15108. 1993. pap. text 1.95 (*0-226-48082-8*, P94) U Ch Pr.

— Public Education: An Autopsy. LC 92-46732. 400p. 1993. text 27.95 (*0-674-72232-9*) HUP.

— Public Education: An Autopsy. 400p. 1995. pap. 14.95 (*0-674-72234-5*, LIEPUX) HUP.

— Restoring School Board Options on Contracting Out: Will School Boards & State Legislatures Act to Reverse the Erosion of Management Authority in Public School Governance? 19p. 1996. pap. 10.00 (*1-886306-18-4*) Nevada Policy.

***Lieberman, Myron.** The Teacher Unions: How the NEA & AFT Sabotage Education. LC 97-2982. 300p. 2000. 16.95 (*1-893554-21-X*) Encounter Bks.

Lieberman, Myron. The Teacher Unions: How the NEA & AFT Suffocate Reform, Waste Money, & Hold Students, Teachers, & Parents Hostage to Politics. LC 97-2982. 320p. 1997. 24.50 (*0-684-84282-3*) Free Pr.

— Teachers Evaluating Teachers: Peer Review & the New Unionism. LC 98-13441. (Studies in Social Philosophy & Policy). 140p. 1998. 34.95 (*1-56000-381-2*); pap. 19.95 (*0-7658-0461-1*) Transaction Pubs.

***Lieberman, Myron.** Understanding the Teacher Union Contract: A Citizen's Handbook. LC 99-31392. 196p. 2000. 39.95 (*0-7658-0014-4*); pap. 21.95 (*0-7658-0681-9*) Transaction Pubs.

Lieberman, Myron, jt. auth. see Geisert, Gene.

Lieberman, Natalie K. & Goodman, Marilyn J. Learning Through Art: The Guggenheim Museum Collection. (Guggenheim Museum Publication Ser.). (Illus.). 64p. 1998. pap. 19.95 (*0-8109-6910-6*, Pub. by Abrams) Time Warner.

Lieberman, Nathaniel, photos by. Manhattan Lightscape. (Illus.). 124p. 2000. 45.00 (*1-55859-121-4*) Abbeville Pr.

Lieberman-Nissen, Karen. Nutrition & Disease: An Annotated Bibliography. LC 90-14114. 190p. 1991. text 10.00 (*0-8240-7977-9*, 548) Garland.

Lieberman, Norman & Lieberman, Elizabeth T. Working Guide to Process Equipment. LC 96-30959. (Illus.). 425p. 1996. 84.95 (*0-07-038075-9*) McGraw.

Lieberman, Norman P. Process Design for Reliable Operations. 2nd ed. LC 88-1463. (Illus.). 263p. 1988. reprint ed. pap. 81.60 (*0-608-07949-9*, 206792200012) Bks Demand.

— Troubleshooting Natural Gas Processing - Wellhead to Transmission. 208p. 1987. 69.95 (*0-87814-308-4*) PennWell Bks.

— Troubleshooting Process Operations. 3rd ed. 576p. 1991. 94.95 (*0-87814-348-3*) PennWell Bks.

Lieberman, Paul. West's Legal Forms: Business Organizations with Tax Analysis, Vol. 2A. 2nd rev. ed. text. write for info. (*0-314-02897-8*) West Pub.

— West's Legal Forms Vol. 2: Business Organizations with Tax Analysis. 2nd rev. ed. 800p. text. write for info. (*0-314-02102-7*) West Pub.

Lieberman, Phil. Understanding Asthma. LC 99-13753. (Understanding Health & Sickness Ser.). (Illus.). 120p. 1999. 28.00 (*1-57806-141-5*) U Pr of Miss.

***Lieberman, Phil.** Understanding Asthma. LC 99-13753. (Understanding Health & Sickness Ser.). (Illus.). 120p. 1999. pap. 12.00 (*1-57806-142-3*) U Pr of Miss.

Lieberman, Phil & Anderson, John A., eds. Allergic Diseases: Diagnosis & Treatment. LC 96-38857. (Current Clinical Practice Ser.). (Illus.). 416p. 1997. 89.50 (*0-89603-367-8*) Humana.

***Lieberman, Phil & Anderson, John A., eds.** Allergic Diseases: Diagnosis & Treatment. 2nd ed. (Current Clinical Practice Ser.). 496p. 2000. 99.50 (*0-89603-685-5*) Humana.

Lieberman, Philip. The Biology & Evolution of Language. (Illus.). 392p. 1984. pap. 19.50 (*0-674-07413-0*) HUP.

— The Biology & Evolution of Language. LC 83-22582. (Illus.). 392p. 1984. 47.50 (*0-674-07412-2*) HUP.

— Eve Spoke: Human Language & Human Evolution. LC 97-17100. (Illus.). 192p. 1998. 25.00 (*0-393-04089-5*) Norton.

***Lieberman, Philip.** Human Language & Our Reptilian Brain: The Subcortical Bases of Speech, Syntax & Thought. LC 99-86092. 2000. 39.95 (*0-674-00226-1*) HUP.

Lieberman, Philip. Speech Acoustics & Perception. LC 70-183114. (Studies in Communicative Disorders). (C). 1972. write for info. (*0-672-61293-3*, Bobbs) Macmillan.

— The Speech of Primates. (Janua Linguarum, Ser. Minor: No. 148). (Illus.). 133p. (Orig.). 1972. pap. text 46.95 (*90-279-2321-3*) Mouton.

Lieberman, Philip. Uniquely Human: The Evolution of Speech, Thought, & Selfless Behavior. LC 90-38130. (Illus.). 224p. 1991. 41.00 (*0-674-92182-8*, LIEUNI) HUP.

— Uniquely Human: The Evolution of Speech, Thought, & Selfless Behavior. (Illus.). 224p. (C). 1993. pap. 16.50 (*0-674-92183-6*) HUP.

Lieberman, Philip & Blumstein, Shelia E. Speech Physiology, Speech Perception, & Acoustic Phonetics. (Cambridge Studies in Speech Science & Communication). (Illus.). 272p. 1988. text 64.95 (*0-521-30866-6*); pap. text 23.95 (*0-521-31357-0*) Cambridge U Pr.

Lieberman, Philip & Lieberman, Marcia. Walking Switzerland - The Swiss Way: From Vacation Apartments, Hotels, Mountain Inns, & Huts. 2nd rev. ed. LC 96-6542. (Illus.). 288p. (Orig.). 1997. pap. 16.95 (*0-89886-511-5*) Mountaineers.

Lieberman, Philip, jt. auth. see Lieberman, Marcia.

Lieberman, Philip A. Radio's Morning Show Personalities: Early Hour Broadcasters & Deejays from the 1920's to the 1990's. LC 95-45032. (Illus.). 213p. 1996. lib. bdg. 35.00 (*0-7864-0037-4*) McFarland & Co.

Lieberman, Philip H. & Good, Robert A., eds. Diseases of Hematopoietic System: Proceedings of the 45th Annual Anatomic Pathology Slide Seminar of ASCP. LC 81-4946. (Anatomic Pathology Slide Seminar Ser.). (Illus.). 121p. 1981. pap. text 35.00 (*0-89189-085-8*, 50-1-046-00) Am Soc Clinical.

Lieberman, Rachel. A Leaf Falls...a Bud Blossoms: One Codependent's Journey to Heal the Wounded Soul. Baron, Arleen, ed. (Illus.). ix, 225p. (Orig.). 1997. pap. 13.95 (*0-9657142-0-9*) My Inner Child.

Lieberman, Ralph. Cornerstones: Twenty-Six Masterpieces of Western Architecture. 1989. 25.95 (*0-525-24461-1*, Dutt); pap. 15.95 (*0-525-48259-8*, Dutt) Dutton Plume.

— Renaissance Architecture in Venice. LC 82-22606. (Illus.). 144p. 1982. 60.00 (*0-89659-310-X*) Abbeville Pr.

Lieberman, Richard D. Elements of Contract Administration: Practical Advice on Performing Government Contracts. LC 96-79447. 127p. (Orig.). 1996. pap., per. 45.00 (*0-935165-55-X*) GWU Gov Contracts.

***Lieberman, Richard D. & O'Brien, Karen.** Elements of Contract Formation: Practical Advice on Winning Government Contracts. 176p. (C). 2000. pap. text 50.00 (*0-8080-0500-6*) CCH INC.

Lieberman, Richard K. Steinway & Sons. LC 95-17330. 384p. 1995. 37.00 (*0-300-06364-4*) Yale U Pr.

— Steinway & Sons. 384p. 1997. pap. 18.00 (*0-300-06850-6*) Yale U Pr.

Lieberman, Robbie. My Song Is My Weapon: People's Songs, American Communism, & the Politics of Culture, 1930-1950. (Music in American Life Ser.). (Illus.). 232p. 1989. text 24.95 (*0-252-01559-2*) U of Ill Pr.

— My Song Is My Weapon: People's Songs, American Communism, & the Politics of Culture, 1930-1950. (Music in American Life Ser.). (Illus.). 232p. (C). 1995. 16.95 (*0-252-06525-5*) U of Ill Pr.

***Lieberman, Robbie.** The Strangest Dream: Communism, Anti-Communism & the U.S. Peace Movement, 1945-1963. LC 99-86248. (Illus.). 272p. 2000. text 34.95 (*0-8156-2841-2*) Syracuse U Pr.

Lieberman, Robert A., ed. Chemical, Biochemical & Environmental Fiber Sensors IX. (Europto Ser.: Vol. 3105). 406p. 1997. 80.00 (*0-8194-2526-5*) SPIE.

— Chemical, Biochemical & Environmental Fiber Sensors VIII. 364p. 1996. 94.00 (*0-8194-2224-X*) SPIE.

***Lieberman, Robert A., ed.** Chemical, Biochemical & Environmental Fiber Sensors X. 268p. 1999. pap. text 59.00 (*0-8194-3001-3*) SPIE.

Lieberman, Robert A., ed. Chemical, Biochemical & Environmental Fiber Sensors X, Vol. 3540. 1999. 59.00 (*0-8194-3002-1*) SPIE.

Lieberman, Robert A. & Vo-Dinh, Tuan, eds. Biomedical Sensing & Imaging Technologies, Vol. 3253. 300p. 1998. 80.00 (*0-8194-2692-X*) SPIE.

Lieberman, Robert A., et al. Biomedical Sensing, Imaging & Tracking Technologies I: 29-31 January 1996, San Jose, California. LC 95-72271. (Proceedings Ser.). vii, 384 p. 1996. write for info. (*0-8194-2050-6*) SPIE.

Lieberman, Robert C. Shifting the Color Line: Race & the American Welfare State. LC 97-42373. (Illus.). 320p. 1999. 45.00 (*0-674-74562-0*) HUP.

Lieberman, Robert H. Goobersville Breakdown. (Illus.). 221p. 1979. 17.95 (*0-933124-01-5*) Gamma Bks.

— Goobersville Breakdown. (Illus.). 221p. 1979. reprint ed. pap. 9.95 (*0-933124-00-7*) Gamma Bks.

— The Physics Ferret: A Guide to Ferreting Out the Solution to Problems in Science, Math, &...Life. (Illus.). 32p. 1994. pap. 4.95 (*0-933124-02-3*) Gamma Bks.

Lieberman, Ron & Bush, Russell. Affectionate Men: A Photographic History of a Century of Male Couples. LC 98-22815. (Illus.). 112p. 1998. text 24.95 (*0-312-18299-6*) St Martin.

Lieberman, Ronald. Keystone Five - Pennsylvania Books in Print. 1978. pap. 5.00 (*0-934630-03-8*); lib. bdg. 12.00 (*0-934630-05-4*) Family Album.

— Keystone Tercentenary. 1983. 15.00 (*0-934630-12-7*); pap. 10.00 (*0-934630-14-3*); lib. bdg. 15.00 (*0-934630-13-5*) Family Album.

Lieberman, Ronald & Mukherjee, Asoke. Principles of Drug Development in Transplantation & Autoimmunity. LC 95-37929. (Medical Intelligence Unit Ser.). 874p. 1996. 130.00 (*1-57059-283-7*) Landes Bioscience.

Lieberman, S. A., jt. auth. see Schimmel, Warren T.

Lieberman, Sally T. The Mother & Narrative Politics in Modern China. LC 97-30291. (Feminist Issues Ser.). 300p. 1998. text 39.50 (*0-8139-1790-5*) U Pr of Va.

Lieberman, Shari. All about Vitamin C: Frequently Asked Questions. (FAQs All about Health Ser.). 96p. 1999. mass mkt. 2.99 (*0-89529-976-3*, Avery) Penguin Putnam.

— Get off the Menopause Roller Coaster: Natural Solutions for Mood Swings, Hot Flashes, Fatigue, Anxiety, Depression & Other Symptoms. 208p. 2000. pap. 13.95 (*1-58333-000-3*, Avery) Penguin Putnam.

Lieberman, Shari & Babal, Ken. Maitake: King of Mushrooms. LC 98-222773. pap. 3.95 (*0-87983-882-5*, 38825K, Keats Publng) NTC Contemp Pub Co.

Lieberman, Shari & Bruning, Nancy Pauline. The Real Vitamin & Mineral Book: Going Beyond the RDA for Optimum Health. LC 90-40460. 326p. (Orig.). 1990. pap. 9.95 (*0-89529-449-4*, Avery) Penguin Putnam.

— The Real Vitamin & Mineral Book: Using Supplements for Optimum Health. 2nd ed. 352p. 1996. pap. 12.95 (*0-89529-769-8*, Avery) Penguin Putnam.

— The Real Vitamin & Mineral Book: Using Supplements for Optimum Health. 2nd ed. 416p. 1999. mass mkt. 6.95 (*0-89529-690-X*, Avery) Penguin Putnam.

Lieberman, Sima. The Economic & Political Roots of the New Protectionism. 200p. 1988. 64.50 (*0-8476-7595-5*, JR 7595) Rowman.

— Growth & Crisis in the Spanish Economy: 1940-1993. LC 95-2227. (Studies in the European Economy Ser.). 377p. (C). (gr. 13). 1995. 100.00 (*0-415-12428-X*) Routledge.

— Labor Movements & Labor Thought: Spain, France, Germany & the United States. LC 85-16859. 302p. 1985. 69.50 (*0-275-90214-5*, C0214, Praeger Pubs) Greenwood.

— The Long Road to a European Monetary Union. 222p. (Orig.). (C). 1992. pap. text 26.50 (*0-8191-8591-4*); lib. bdg. 48.50 (*0-8191-8590-6*) U Pr of Amer.

Lieberman, Sima, ed. Europe & the Industrial Revolution. LC 74-189099. 487p. 1972. reprint ed. pap. 151.00 (*0-608-05327-9*, 206503300012) Bks Demand.

Lieberman, Stephen J. Sumerological Studies in Honor of Thorkild Jacobsen: On His Seventieth Birthday, June 7, 1974. LC 75-42584. (Assyriological Studies: No. 20). 332p. 1977. pap. text 24.00 (*0-226-62282-7*) U Ch Pr.

***Lieberman, Susan.** A Travel Guide for the Wandering Jew: United States Edition. 300p. 2000. pap. 15.00 (*0-9679808-0-1*) S Lieberman.

Lieberman, Susan, jt. auth. see Bartle, Nathalie.

Lieberman, Susan A. The Real High School Handbook: How to Survive, Thrive & Prepare for What's Next. LC 97-26558. 320p. 1997. pap. 9.95 (*0-395-79760-8*, Mariner Bks) HM.

Lieberman, Syd. Streets & Alleys: Stories with a Chicago Accent. (American Storytelling Ser.). 1995. 19.95 (*0-87483-424-4*) August Hse.

— The Wise Shoemaker of Studena. LC 93-43481. (Illus.). 32p. (J). (gr. 5-8). 1994. write for info. (*0-8276-0509-9*) JPS Phila.

Lieberman, Tanya. Storybooks Teach about World Cultures. (Illus.). 48p. (Orig.). 1995. pap., teacher ed. 6.95 (*1-878279-77-7*, MM1998) Monday Morning Bks.

Lieberman, Tanya & Suid, Annalisa. Literature Teaches about the U. S. A. 48p. (Orig.). (J). (gr. 3-6). 1996. pap. 6.95 (*1-878279-92-0*, MM2021) Monday Morning Bks.

Lieberman, Trudy. How to Plan for a Secure Retirement. LC 99-169478. viii, 374p. 2000. 29.95 (*0-89043-889-7*) Consumer Reports.

***Lieberman, Trudy.** Slanting the Story: The Forces That Shape the News. LC 99-55616. 160p. 2000. pap. 21.95 (*1-56584-577-3*) Norton.

***Lieberman, Trudy & Consumer Reports Editors.** Senior Security: Consumer Reports' Complete Guide to Finding & Financing Health Services for Seniors. 448p. 2000. pap. 18.00 (*0-8129-3147-5*, Times Bks) Crown Pub Group.

***Lieberman, Victor B.** Beyond Binary Histories: Re-Imagining Eurasia to CA., 1830. LC 99-29479. 336p. (C). 1999. pap. text 21.95 (*0-472-08633-2*, 08633) U of Mich Pr.

Lieberman, Victor B. Burmese Administrative Cycles: Anarchy & Conquest, c. 1580-1760. LC 83-13716. 357p. 1984. reprint ed. pap. 110.70 (*0-7837-9376-6*, 206012000004) Bks Demand.

Lieberman, William. Images. 1982. 12.50 (*0-934630-11-9*) Family Album.

— Images. deluxe limited ed. 1982. 25.00 (*0-934630-15-1*) Family Album.

Lieberman, William S. Edvard Munch: A Selection of His Prints from American Collections. LC 79-169306. (Museum of Modern Art Publications in Reprint). (Illus.). 42p. 1972. reprint ed. 12.95 (*0-405-01565-8*) Ayer.

— Matisse: Fifty Years of His Graphic Art. 150p. 1981. pap. 12.95 (*0-8076-1022-4*) Braziller.

— Matisse: 50 Years of His Graphic Art. 152p. 1956. reprint ed. 30.00 (*0-8076-0037-7*, Pub. by Braziller) Norton.

— Max Ernst. LC 72-169307. (Museum of Modern Art Publications in Reprint). (Illus.). 66p. 1972. reprint ed. 15.95 (*0-405-01566-6*) Ayer.

***Lieberman, William S.** Painters in Paris, 1895-1950. 144p. 2000. 45.00 (*0-8109-6548-8*, Pub. by Abrams) Time Warner.

Lieberman, William S. & Rewald, Sabine. Twentieth-Century Modern Masters: The Jacques & Natasha Gelman Collection. (Illus.). 336p. 1990. 60.00 (*0-8109-1037-3*, Pub. by Abrams) Time Warner.

Liebermann. Rapidly Solidified Alloys: Processes-Structures-Properties-Applications. (Materials Engineering Ser.: Vol. 3). (Illus.). 808p. 1993. text 250.00 (*0-8247-8951-2*) Dekker.

Liebermann, Alvin. Contamination Control. (Illus.). 182p. (C). 1990. student ed. 100.00 (*0-918247-09-8*) Tustin Tech.

Liebermann, Jude. Formerly Brandewyne. LC 98-139474. 150p. (Orig.). 1997. pap. 5.00 (*0-9660653-0-1*) Lee Bks FL.

***Liebermann, Jude.** Mexican Sunsets. 160p. 1999. pap. 10.95 (*0-9660653-1-X*) Lee Bks FL.

Liebermann, Loni & Bilger, Andrea. The Foldout Book of Tai Chi Chuan. LC 98-29550. (Illus.). 192p. 1998. 19.95 (*0-8348-0456-5*) Weatherhill.

Liebermann, M. Coloring Books on Events of the Jewish Months: Nisan. (Learn As You Color Ser.: No. II). (J). (ps-2). 1987. 3.50 (*0-914131-86-9*, D712) Torah Umesorah.

— Coloring Books on Events of the Jewish Months: Tishrei, Cheshvan. (Learn As You Color Ser.: No. II). (J). (ps-2). 1987. 3.25 (*0-914131-84-2*, D710) Torah Umesorah.

— Coloring Books on the Parshas Hashavua: Bereishis. (Learn As You Color Ser.: No. I). (J). (ps-2). 1987. 3.25 (*0-914131-79-6*, D700) Torah Umesorah.

— Coloring Books on the Parshas Hashavua: Devorim. (Learn As You Color Ser.: No. I). (J). (ps-2). 1987. 3.25 (*0-914131-83-4*, D704) Torah Umesorah.

— Coloring Books on the Parshas Hashavua: Shemos. (Learn As You Color Ser.: No. I). (J). (ps-2). 1987. 3.25 (*0-914131-80-X*, D701) Torah Umesorah.

— Coloring Books on the Parshas Hashavua: Vayikrah. (Learn As You Color Ser.: No. I). (J). (ps-2). 1987. 3.25 (*0-914131-81-8*, D702) Torah Umesorah.

— Learn As You Color Series III: Brachos. (J). (ps-2). 1987. 3.25 (*0-914131-88-5*, D720) Torah Umesorah.

Liebermann-Meffert, D., et al, eds. Greater Omentum: Anatomy, Physiology, Pathology, Surgery. (Illus.). 361p. 1983. 348.00 (*0-387-11882-9*) Spr-Verlag.

Liebermann-Meffert, Dorothea. Rudolf Nissen & the World Revolution of Fundoplication: A Picture Biography with 78 Mostly Unpublished Photographs Provides Unusual Insights into the Life of the Famous Surgeon: Dedicated to Tom R. Demeester's 60th Birthday. LC 99-163405. (Illus.). 88p. 1998. 18.50 (*1-57626-113-1*) Quality Med Pub.

Liebermann, R. C., jt. auth. see Plomerova, Jaroslava.

Liebermann, Robert C. & Sondergeld, Carl H., eds. Experimental Techniques in Mineral & Rock Physics: The Schreiber Volume. LC 94-8954. 1994. write for info. (*3-7643-5028-8*) Birkhauser.

— Experimental Techniques in Mineral & Rock Physics: The Schreiber Volume. LC 94-8954. (Pure & Applied Geophysics Ser.). 430p. 1994. 35.00 (*0-8176-5028-8*) Birkhauser.

Lieberoff, Allen. Climb Your Own Ladder: 101 Home Businesses that Can Make You Wealthy. 224p. 1982. pap. 7.95 (*0-671-45477-3*, Fireside) S&S Trade Pap.

***Liebers, Gerhard.** Funktion und Gestalt der Bibliothek. 2000. 52.95 (*3-631-32397-2*) P Lang Pubng.

Liebers, Reinhold. Wie Geschrieben Steht: Studien zu Einer Besonderen Art Fruehchristlichen Schriftbezuges. (GER.). viii, 445p. (C). 1993. lib. bdg. 136.95 (*3-11-013859-X*) De Gruyter.

Liebersohn, Harry. Aristocratic Encounters: European Travelers & North American Indians. LC 98-29057. (New Approaches to the Americas Ser.). (Illus.). 192p. (C). 1999. text 49.95 (*0-521-64090-3*) Cambridge U Pr.

— Fate & Utopia in German Sociology. (German Social Thought Ser.). 280p. 1988. 35.00 (*0-262-12133-6*) MIT Pr.

— Fate & Utopia in German Sociology. (Studies in Contemporary German Thought). 246p. 1990. reprint ed. pap. text 12.95 (*0-262-62079-0*) MIT Pr.

Lieberson, Alan D. Advance Medical Directives. LC 92-82793. 1992. 145.00 (*0-685-59919-1*) West Group.

— Healthcare Enterprise Liability. 1997. 110.00 (*1-55834-548-5*, 80979) LEXIS Pub.

— Healthcare Enterprise Liability, 1998 Supplement. 320p. 1998. suppl. ed. write for info. (*0-327-00559-9*, 8098010) LEXIS Pub.

— A Physician's Guide to Advance Medical Directives. Karaffa, Melanie C., ed. LC 92-48385. 350p. 1993. 69.95 (*1-878487-52-3*, ME223) Practice Mgmt Info.

Lieberson, Allan. Healthcare Enterprise Liability: 1997 Edition. LC 97-73504. 1146p. 1997. text 110.00 (*1-55834-559-0*, 80979-10, MICHIE) LEXIS Pub.

Lieberson, Stanley. Making It Count: The Improvement of Social Research & Theory. 1985. pap. 16.95 (*0-520-06037-7*, Pub. by U CA Pr) Cal Prin Full Svc.

— Making It Count: The Improvement of Social Research & Theory. LC 84-25285. 271p. reprint ed. pap. 84.10 (*0-7837-4843-4*, 204449000003) Bks Demand.

***Lieberson, Stanley.** A Matter of Taste: How Names, Fashions & Culture Change. (Illus.). 352p. 2000. 29.95 (*0-300-08385-8*) Yale U Pr.

Lieberson, Stanley. A Piece of the Pie: Blacks & White Immigrants since 1880. (Illus.). 420p. 1980. pap. 18.95 (*0-520-04362-6*, Pub. by U CA Pr) Cal Prin Full Svc.

Lieberson, Stanley, ed. Explorations in Sociolinguistics. 4th ed. LC 67-64323. (General Publications: Vol. 44). 1973. pap. text 18.00 (*0-933070-40-3*) Res Inst Inner Asian Studies.

Lieberson, Stanley & Waters, Mary C. From Many Strands: Ethnic & Racial Groups in Contemporary America. (Population of the United States in the 1980s: A Census Monograph Ser.). 304p. 1988. 45.00 (*0-87154-543-8*) Russell Sage.

— From Many Strands: Ethnic & Racial Groups in Contemporary America. LC 88-9651. (Population of the United States in the 1980s: A Census Monograph Ser.). (Illus.). 304p. (C). 1990. pap. 16.95 (*0-87154-527-6*) Russell Sage.

Lieberstein, Stanley H. Who Owns What Is in Your Head? A Guide for Entrepreneurs, Inventors & Creative Employees. 1995. pap. 14.95 (*0-941968-04-9*) Wildcat Pubs.

***Liebert.** A History of Scientific Psychology. (Psychology Ser.). 2001. 50.00 (*0-534-57825-X*) Wadsworth Pub.

***Liebert & Liebert.** Personality: Strategies & Issues. 9th ed. 2001. pap. 58.50 (*0-534-57987-6*) Wadsworth Pub.

Liebert & Siegler. Personality: Strategies & Issues. 7th ed. (Psychology Ser.). 1994. pap., teacher ed. write for info. (*0-534-17582-1*) Wadsworth Pub.

Liebert & Spiegler. Personality: Strategies & Issues. 7th ed. 1994. write for info. (*0-534-22652-3*); pap. write for info. (*0-534-22653-1*) Wadsworth Pub.

Liebert, jt. auth. see Liebert.

Liebert, Arthur. Mythus und Kultur (Myth & Culture) Bolle, Kees W., ed. (Mythology Ser.). (GER.). 1978. reprint ed. lib. bdg. 19.95 (*0-405-10549-5*) Ayer.

***Liebert, David.** The Long-Term Care Clinical Assessment: A Guide for the Social Worker. (Illus.). 100p. (C). 1999. pap. 29.50 (*0-929442-55-5*) Prof Prnting & Pub.

*__Liebert, Elizabeth.__ Changing Life Patterns: Adult Development in Spiritual Direction. expanded ed. 2000. pap. 23.99 (*0-8272-0479-5*) Chalice Pr.

Liebert, Georges. Nietzsche & Music. 1997. pap. text 17.50 (*0-226-48088-7*); lib. bdg. 44.00 (*0-226-48087-9*) U Ch Pr.

Liebert, Herman. Bibliography Old & New. LC 72-619564. (Bibliographical Monograph: No. 6). (Illus.). 1974. 10.00 (*0-87959-050-5*) U of Tex H Ransom Ctr.

Liebert, Herman W., contrib. by. The British Look at America During the Age of Samuel Johnson: With an Address by Herman W. Liebert. (Illus.). 55p. 1971. pap. 15.00 (*0-916617-07-6*) J C Brown.

Liebert, J., jt. auth. see Hayes, D. S.

Liebert, Mary A., ed. The Author's Guide to Biomedical Journals: Complete Manuscript Submission Instruction for 185 Leading Biomedical Periodicals. 628p. 1994. 164.00 (*0-913113-61-1*) M Liebert.

Liebert, Peter S. Color Atlas of Pediatric Surgery. 2nd ed. McGrew, Larry, ed. LC 95-33478. 268p. 1996. text 239.00 (*0-7216-5885-7*, W B Saunders Co) Harcrt Hlth Sci Grp.

Liebert, Robert, jt. auth. see Irwin, Louis Two Ravens.

Liebert, Robert M. The Early Window. 3rd ed. (C). 1992. pap. text 38.50 (*0-205-14408-X*, H4408) Allyn.

— Osage Life & Legends: Earth People - Sky People. LC 89-3359. (Illus.). 144p. 1987. pap. 8.95 (*0-87961-169-3*) Naturegraph.

— Personality: Strategies & Issues. 8th ed. LC 97-44686. (Psychology Ser.). 643p. 1997. pap. 81.95 (*0-534-26418-2*) Brooks-Cole.

Liebert, Robert M. & Spiegler, Michael D. Personality: Strategies & Issues. 5th ed. (C). 1987. pap. 39.00 (*0-534-10675-7*) Brooks-Cole.

— Personality: Strategies & Issues. 6th ed. LC 89-22097. 608p. (C). 1989. pap. 54.75 (*0-534-12228-0*) Brooks-Cole.

— Personality: Strategies & Issues. 7th ed. LC 93-36565. 1993. pap. 58.00 (*0-534-17580-5*) Brooks-Cole.

Liebert, Robert M., et al. The Early Window: Effects of Television on Children & Youth. 2nd ed. LC 82-5327. (General Psychology Ser.: No. 34). (Illus.). 280p. 1982. text 35.00 (*0-08-027548-6*, J125, Pergamon Pr); pap. text 12.95 (*0-08-027547-8*, Pergamon Pr) Elsevier.

Liebert, Robert M., jt. auth. see Houts, Arthur C.

Liebert, Robert M., jt. auth. see Johnson, Margaret H.

Liebert, Robert S., jt. auth. see Oldham, John M.

Liebert, Robert S., jt. ed. see Oldham, John M.

Liebert, U. G., ed. Virus Infections in Pregnancy. (Intervirology Ser.: Vol. 41, Nos. 4-5 (1998)). (Illus.). 90p. 1999. pap. 34.00 (*3-8055-6872-X*) S Karger.

Liebert, Ulrike & Cotta, Maurizio, eds. Parliament & Democratic Consolidation in Southern Europe: Italy, Spain, Portugal, Greece & Turkey in Comparison. 300p. 1990. text 55.00 (*0-86187-819-1*) St Martin.

Liebert, Ulrike, jt. ed. see Hirschmann, Nancy J.

Liebert, Wolf-Andreas, et al, eds. Discourse & Perspective in Cognitive Linguistics. LC 97-39411. (Amsterdam Studies in the Theory & History of Linguistic Science: Vol. 151). xiv, 270p. 1997. lib. bdg. 79.00 (*1-55619-866-3*) J Benjamins Pubng Co.

Lieberth, jt. auth. see Martin.

Lieberthal, Edwin M. The Complete Book of Fingermath. (Illus.). 1979. text 21.96 (*0-07-037680-8*) McGraw.

Lieberthal, Kenneth. Governing China. (C). 1996. pap. text 18.00 (*0-393-96987-8*) Norton.

— Governing China: From Revolution Through Reform. (Illus.). 512p. 1995. 30.00 (*0-393-03787-8*) Norton.

Lieberthal, Kenneth, et al, eds. Perspectives on Modern China: Four Anniversaries. LC 91-13410. (Studies on Modern China). 448p. (C). (gr. 13). 1991. pap. text 32.95 (*0-87332-890-6*, East Gate Bk) M E Sharpe.

Lieberthal, Kenneth & Dickson, Bruce. A Research Guide to Central Party & Government Meetings in China, 1949-1986. 2nd rev. ed. LC 88-18527. 392p. (C). (gr. 13). 1989. text 114.95 (*0-87332-492-7*, East Gate Bk) M E Sharpe.

Lieberthal, Kenneth, et al. Central Documents & Politburo Politics in China. LC 78-8740. (Michigan Monographs in Chinese Studies: No. 33). 201p. 1978. pap. text 15.00 (*0-89264-033-2*) Ctr Chinese Studies.

Lieberthal, Kenneth G. Revolution & Tradition in Tientsin, 1949-1952. LC 79-64215. xiv, 234p. 1980. 35.00 (*0-8047-1044-9*) Stanford U Pr.

Lieberthal, Kenneth G., et al, eds. Constructing China: The Interaction of Culture & Economics. LC 97-27317. (Michigan Monographs in Chinese Studies: No. 78). 1998. 60.00 (*0-89264-121-5*) Ctr Chinese Studies.

Lieberthal, Kenneth G. & Lampton, David M., eds. Bureaucracy, Politics, & Decision Making in Post-Mao China. LC 91-9476. (Studies on China: Vol. 14). (Illus.). 384p. 1992. 55.00 (*0-520-07356-8*, Pub. by U CA Pr) Cal Prin Full Svc.

Lieberthal, Kenneth G., jt. ed. see Lardy, Nicholas R.

Liebes, Tamar. Reporting the Arab Israeli Conflict: How Hegemony Works. LC 99-162387. (Research in Cultural & Media Studies). 184p. (C). 1997. 80.00 (*0-415-15465-0*) Routledge.

Liebes, Tamar & Curran, James. Media Ritual & Identity. LC 97-45502. (Communication & Society Ser.). (Illus.). 280p. (C). 1998. 75.00 (*0-415-15991-1*) Routledge.

Liebes, Tamar & Katz, Elihu. The Export of Meaning: Cross-Cultural Readings of Dallas. 2nd ed. 200p. 1994. pap. text 26.95 (*0-7456-1295-4*) Blackwell Pubs.

Liebes, Tamar, et al. Media, Ritual, & Identity. LC 97-45502. (Communication & Society Ser.). 296p. (C). 1998. pap. 24.99 (*0-415-15992-X*) Routledge.

Liebes, Yehuda. Studies in Jewish Myth & Messianism. Stein, Batya, tr. from HEB. LC 91-36470. (SUNY Series in Judaica: Hermeneutics, Mysticism, & Religion). 226p. (C). 1992. text 19.50 (*0-7914-1193-1*) State U NY Pr.

— Studies in the Zohar. Schwartz, Arnold & Nakache, Stephanie, trs. LC 91-36469. (SUNY Series in Judaica: Hermeneutics, Mysticism, & Religion). 262p. 1993. text 21.50 (*0-7914-1189-3*) State U NY Pr.

Liebeschuetz, J. H. Barbarians & Bishops: Army, Church, & State in the Age of Arcadius & Chrysostom. (Illus.). 326p. 1992. pap. text 45.00 (*0-19-814073-8*) OUP.

— Continuity & Change in Roman Religion. 374p. 1979. text 79.00 (*0-19-814822-4*) OUP.

*__Liebeschuetz, J. H.__ The Decline & Fall of the Roman City. (Illus.). 400p. 2000. text 105.00 (*0-19-815247-7*) OUP.

Liebeschuetz, J. H. From Diocletian to the Arab Conquest: Change in the Late Roman Empire. (Collected Studies: No. CS310). 288p. 1990. text 120.95 (*0-86078-258-1*, Pub. by Variorum) Ashgate Pub Co.

Liebeshutz, Hans. Mediaeval Humanism in the Life & Writings of John of Salisbury, with an Epilogue: John of Salisbury & the School of Chartres. (Warburg Institute Studies: Vol. 17). 1969. reprint ed. pap. 50.00 (*0-8115-1392-0*) Periodicals Srv.

Liebeskind, Claudia. Piety on Its Knees: Three Sufi Traditions in South Asia in Modern Times. LC 98-903530. (Illus.). 356p. 1998. text 35.00 (*0-19-564309-7*) OUP.

Liebeskind, J. C., jt. ed. see Fields, Howard L.

Liebeskind, Joseph, ed. see Von Dittersdorf, Karl D.

Liebeskind, Lanny S., ed. Advances in Metal-Organic Chemistry, Vol. 1. 393p. 1989. 109.50 (*0-89232-863-0*) Jai Pr.

— Advances in Metal-Organic Chemistry, Vol. 2. 300p. 1991. 109.50 (*0-89232-948-3*) Jai Pr.

— Advances in Metal-Organic Chemistry, Vol. 3. 321p. 1994. 109.50 (*1-55938-406-9*) Jai Pr.

— Advances in Metal-Organic Chemistry, Vol. 4. 1996. 109.50 (*1-55938-709-2*) Jai Pr.

— Advances in Metal-Organic Chemistry, Vol. 5. 1996. 109.50 (*1-55938-789-0*) Jai Pr.

Liebesman, Lawrence R. The Water Supplier's Guide to Wetlands Regulation & Management. LC 96-103917. (Illus.). 342p. 1995. 180.00 (*0-89867-780-7*, 20411) Am Water Wks Assn.

Liebesman, Sandford. Using ISO 9000 to Improve Business Processes. Wright, Robert K., ed. (AT&T Quality Library). (Illus.). 256p. (Orig.). 1994. pap. 24.95 (*0-932764-46-0*) AT&T Customer Info.

Liebesny, Herbert J., jt. ed. see Khadduri, Majid.

Liebetrau, Albert M. Measures of Association. LC 83-60229. (Quantitative Applications in the Social Sciences Ser.: Vol. 32). 95p. 1983. 10.95 (*0-8039-1974-3*) Sage.

Liebgott, Bernard. The Anatomical Basis of Dentistry. (Illus.). 511p. (C). 1986. 61.95 (*0-941158-88-8*) Mosby Inc.

Liebhaber, Josephine D. The Cat Fights Back. (Illus.). 118p. (Orig.). 1993. pap. 6.95 (*0-9635609-0-5*) Action Res.

Liebhaberg, Bruno. Industrial Relations & Multinational Corporations in Europe. LC 80-83365. 107p. 1981. 49.95 (*0-275-90670-1*, C0670, Praeger Pubs) Greenwood.

Liebhardt, Paul. Odyssey: Tales of the Universe. 224p. 1991. 60.00 (*0-9628861-0-6*) Inst Shipboard.

Liebhardt, Paul W. Discovery: The Adventure of Shipboard Education. Rogers, Judy S., ed. LC 85-50383. (Illus.). 1985. 50.00 (*0-9614403-0-9*) William & Allen.

Liebhart, Wilhelm. Bayerns Konige. 2nd ed. (Illus.). X, 365p. 1997. 32.95 (*3-631-31567-8*) P Lang Pubng.

Liebherr, James K. Cladistic Analysis of North American Platynini & Revision of the Agonum Extensicolle Species Group: Coleoptera: Carabidae. LC 85-29034. (University of California Publications in Entomology: No. 106). 210p. 1986. pap. 65.10 (*0-7837-7490-7*, 204921200010) Bks Demand.

Liebherr, James K., ed. Zoogeography of Caribbean Insects. LC 87-47868. (Illus.). 304p. 1988. text 49.95 (*0-8014-2143-8*) Cornell U Pr.

Liebich, Andre. From the Other Shore: Russian Social Democracy after 1921. LC 96-41417. (Historical Studies: Vol. 125). (Illus.). 464p. 1997. 48.00 (*0-674-32517-6*) HUP.

— From the Other Shore: Russian Social Democracy After 1921, 125. 1999. pap. text 19.95 (*0-674-32518-4*) HUP.

Liebich, Andre, et al, eds. Citizenship, East & West. LC 94-14172. (Publications de l'Institut Universitaire de Hautes Etudes Internationales, Geneve Ser.). 200p. 1995. 76.50 (*0-7103-0491-9*) Routledge.

Liebig, H., jt. auth. see Flik, T.

Liebig, James E. Business Ethics: Profiles in Civic Virtue. LC 89-29522. 260p. 1991. pap. 12.95 (*1-55591-101-3*) Fulcrum Pub.

— Merchants of Vision: People Bringing New Purpose & Values to Business. LC 93-43269. (Illus.). 256p. 1994. 24.95 (*1-881052-42-7*) Berrett-Koehler.

Liebig, Justus Von. The Natural Laws of Husbandry. LC 72-2852. (Use & Abuse of America's Natural Resources Ser.). 392p. 1972. reprint ed. 28.95 (*0-405-04541-7*) Ayer.

Liebig, Nelda J. Carrie & the Apple Pie. LC 99-19998. 128p. (J). (gr. 3-7). 1999. pap. 10.95 (*1-883953-30-8*, Pub. by Midwest Trad) Partners Pubs Grp.

— Carrie & the Crazy Quilt. LC 96-29722. 88p. (Orig.). (J). (gr. 3-7). 1997. pap. 7.50 (*1-883953-19-7*) Midwest Trad.

— Carrie & the Crazy Quilt. 96p. (Orig.). (J). 1996. pap. 7.50 (*1-883893-40-2*) WinePress Pub.

Liebig, Phoebe S., jt. ed. see Pynoos, Jon.

Liebing, Alison. Deaths in Custody: Caring for People at Risk. LC 97-175864. 226p. 1997. 79.00 (*1-871177-85-5*, Pub. by Whiting & Birch); pap. 34.50 (*1-871177-86-3*, Pub. by Whiting & Birch) Paul & Co Pubs.

Liebing, Alison & Ward, Tony. Deaths in Custody: International Perspectives. 196p. 1994. 90.00 (*1-871177-55-3*, Pub. by Whiting & Birch); pap. 34.95 (*1-871177-42-1*, Pub. by Whiting & Birch) Paul & Co Pubs.

Liebing, Ralph W. Architectural Working Drawings. 4th ed. LC 98-51777. 704p. 1999. 85.00 (*0-471-34876-7*) Wiley.

— Construction Contract Administration. LC 97-2167. 400p. (C). 1997. 73.00 (*0-13-381591-9*) P-H.

— Introduction to the Construction Industry. 224p. (C). 2000. pap. 46.67 (*0-13-863853-5*, Macmillan Coll) P-H.

Liebkind, Karmela. New Identities in Europe: Immigrant Ancestry & the Ethnic Identity of Youth. (Illus.). 1989. text 82.95 (*0-566-05741-7*, Pub. by Gower) Ashgate Pub Co.

Liebknecht, Karl. Militarism & Anti-Militarism. 1969. 29.50 (*0-86527-130-5*) Fertig.

— Militarism & Anti-Militarism. 1972. 59.95 (*0-8490-0635-X*) Gordon Pr.

Liebknecht, Wilhelm P. Karl Marx: Biographical Memoirs. Untermann, Ernest, tr. LC 69-10119. 181p. 1969. reprint ed. lib. bdg. 59.50 (*0-8371-0536-6*, LIKM, Greenwood Pr) Greenwood.

— Karl Marx, Biographical Memoirs. Date not set. 13.00 (*0-403-00200-1*) Scholarly.

Liebl, Ulrike. Die Illustrierten Flavius-Josephus-Handschriften des Hochmittelalters. (Europaische Hochschulschriften Ser.: Reihe 28, Bd. 304). (GER., Illus.). XII, 277p. 1997. 76.95 (*3-631-31548-1*) P Lang Pubng.

Liebl, W., jt. ed. see Wessely, G.

Liebler. Medical Records: Policies & Guidelines. annuals 1991. ring bd. 210.00 (*0-8342-0136-4*) Aspen Pub.

— Renaissance Female Tragic Hero. 1999. text. write for info. (*0-312-22059-6*) St Martin.

Liebler, Barbara. Hands on Weaving. LC 86-80911. (Illus.). 112p. 1986. pap. 12.95 (*0-934026-24-6*) Interweave.

Liebler, Joan, ed. see Aspen Reference Group Staff.

Liebler, Joan G. Management Principles for Health Professionals. 3rd ed. 448p. 1999. 55.00 (*0-8342-0798-2*) Aspen Pub.

*__Liebler, Joan G. & McConnell, Charles R.__ Management Principles for Health Professionals. 3rd ed. LC 99-34437. 524p. 1999. write for info. (*0-8342-1245-5*) Aspen Pub.

Liebler, Joan G., et al. Management Principles for Health Professionals. 2nd ed. 448p. (C). 1992. 55.00 (*0-8342-0287-5*) Aspen Pub.

Liebler, John. Frog Counts to Ten. LC 93-40116. (Illus.). 32p. (J). (gr. k-3). 1994. lib. bdg. 19.90 (*1-56294-436-3*) Millbrook Pr.

Liebler, M. L. Breaking the Voodoo: Poetry & Fiction. 2nd ed. LC 89-643744. 116p. (Orig.). pap. text 6.50 (*1-56439-038-1*) Ridgeway.

— Deliver Me: Christian Poems. (King Tree Little Bk.). (Illus.). 16p. (Orig.). (C). 1991. pap. text 3.00 (*1-56439-006-3*) Ridgeway.

— Stripping the Adult Century Bare: New & Selected Writings. (White Noise Poetry Ser.: No. 6). 88p. (Orig.). 1995. pap. 12.00 (*1-885215-09-6*, Viet Nam Gnrtn) Burning Cities Pr.

*__Liebler, M. L.__ Written in Rain: New & Selected Poems 1985-2000. Kaiser, Mifanwy, ed. LC 00-131212. (Illus.). 208p. (C). 2000. pap. 14.00 (*1-893670-09-0*) T Bach.

Liebler, M. L., ed. The Vision of Words: Poetry by Southeast Michigan Poets. (Illus.). 80p. (Orig.). 1992. per. 19.95 (*1-56439-022-5*) Ridgeway.

Liebler, M. L., intro. The Hollow Moon: Poetry by Five Young St. Clair Shores Poets. 40p. 1993. pap. text 6.00 (*1-56439-029-2*) Ridgeway.

Liebler, M. L., ed. see Daniels, Jim, et al.

Liebler, Naomi C. Shakespeare's Festive Tragedy: The Ritual Foundations of Genre. LC 95-9687. 280p. (C). 1995. pap. 29.99 (*0-415-13183-9*) Routledge.

Liebler, Scott. Funsical Fitness: A Comprehensive Movement & Health Education Experience for Ages 2 3/4ths to 7 5/6ths. Alexander, Frank, ed. (Illus.). 175p. (Orig.). 1996. pap., teacher ed. 17.00 (*0-915256-44-4*) Front Row.

Liebler, Sylvia. Der Einflub der Unabhangigkeit von Notenbanken auf die Stabilitat des Geldwertes. (GER., Illus.). XIX, 231p. 1996. 51.95 (*3-631-30315-7*) P Lang Pubng.

Lieblich, Amia. Conversations with Dvora: An Experimental Biography of the First Modern Hebrew Woman Writer. Seidman, Naomi, ed. & tr. by. from HEB. Kronfeld, Chana, ed. LC 96-37297. (Contraversions Ser.: Vol. 6). 294p. 1997. 48.00 (*0-520-08539-6*, Pub. by U CA Pr); pap. 17.95 (*0-520-08541-8*, Pub. by U CA Pr) Cal Prin Full Svc.

— Seasons of Captivity: The Inner World of POW's. 240p. (C). 1994. text 45.00 (*0-8147-5079-6*) NYU Pr.

— Seasons of Captivity: The Inner World of POW's. 240p. (C). 1995. pap. text 18.50 (*0-8147-5095-8*) NYU Pr.

— Transition to Adulthood During Military Service: The Israeli Case. LC 89-30041. (SUNY Series in Israeli Studies). 221p. (C). 1989. pap. text 21.95 (*0-7914-0147-2*) State U NY Pr.

Lieblich, Amia & Josselson, Ruthellen, eds. Exploring Identity & Gender: The Narrative Study of Our Lives. (Narrative Study of Lives Ser.: Vol. 2). 280p. Date not set. 52.00 (*0-8039-5568-5*) Sage.

— Exploring Identity & Gender: The Narrative Study of Our Lives. (Narrative Study of Lives Ser.: Vol. 2). 280p. 1994. pap. 24.00 (*0-8039-5569-3*) Sage.

— Narrative Study of Lives, Vol. 5. 244p. 1997. 52.00 (*0-7619-0324-0*); pap. 24.00 (*0-7619-0325-9*) Sage.

Lieblich, Amia, et al. Narrative Research: Reading, Analysis & Interpretation. LC 98-9071. (Applied Social Research Methods Ser.). 1998. 49.95 (*0-7619-1042-5*); pap. 21.95 (*0-7619-1043-3*) Sage.

Lieblich, Amia, jt. auth. see Josselson, Ruthellen.

Lieblich, Amia, jt. ed. see Josselson, Ruthellen.

Lieblich, Jerome H. Drawing Requirements Manual. 9th ed. Whitmire, Gary, ed. LC 96-168744. 1200p. 1995. per. 195.00 (*1-57053-033-5*); ring bd. 195.00 (*1-57053-034-3*) Global Eng Doc.

Lieblich, Jerome H., ed. Screw Thread Standards for Federal Services. 582p. 1978. ring bd. 125.00 (*0-912702-11-7*, FED-STD-H28) Global Eng Doc.

Lieblich, Ruthka. Ruthka: A Diary of War. Eibeshitz, Jehoshua & Eibeshitz, Anna, eds. & trs. by. (Illus.). 170p. 1993. 15.95 (*0-932351-42-5*); pap. 12.95 (*0-932351-43-3*) B P Marketing.

Liebling, et al. Geology 101. 62p. (C). 1997. spiral bd. 12.95 (*0-7872-4507-0*, 41450701) Kendall-Hunt.

Liebling, A. J. Between Meals: An Appetite for Paris. LC 94-26990. 210p. 1995. 13.50 (*0-679-60142-2*) Modern Lib NY.

— Between Meals: An Appetite for Paris. LC 85-73123. 208p. 1986. pap. 12.00 (*0-86547-236-X*) N Point Pr.

— The Earl of Louisiana. LC 76-130664. 252p. 1970. pap. 15.95 (*0-8071-0203-2*) La State U Pr.

— The Honest Rainmaker: The Life & Times of Colonel John R. Stingo. LC 89-8812. 176p. 1989. reprint ed. pap. 9.95 (*0-86547-396-X*) N Point Pr.

— Neutral Corner: Boxing Essays. Warner, Fred & Barbour, James, eds. 245p. 1996. pap. text 12.00 (*0-86547-495-8*) N Point Pr.

— A Neutral Corner: Boxing Essays. Warner, Fred & Barbour, James, eds. 256p. 1990. 19.95 (*0-86547-450-8*) N Point Pr.

— A Reporter at Large: Dateline: Pyramid Lake, Nevada. Rusco, Elmer, ed. & intro. by. LC 99-33548. (Illus.). 192p. 2000. pap. 21.95 (*0-87417-341-8*) U of Nev Pr.

Liebling, Alison & Cropwood Round-Table Conference. Security, Justice, & Order in Prison: Developing Perspectives. LC 98-127136. 1997. write for info. (*0-901382-18-3*) Cambs Criminology.

Liebling, E. Coloratura Cadenzas - Traditional & New Cadenzas: Vocal & Piano. 112p. 1986. per. 19.95 (*0-7935-5190-0*, 50327860) H Leonard.

— Liebling Vocal Course for Mezzo-Soprano & Contralto. 60p. 1981. pap. 9.95 (*0-7935-0635-2*, 00312243) H Leonard.

Liebling, Emil, jt. auth. see Mathews, William S.

Liebling, Henry E. Handbook for Personal Productivity. rev. ed. (Illus.). 128p. 1996. pap. 5.00 (*1-56327-131-1*, PP-305) Productivity Inc.

Liebling, Herman I. U. S. Corporate Profitability & Capital Formation: Are Rates of Return Sufficient? (Policy Studies). 1980. 58.00 (*0-08-024622-2*, Pergamon Pr) Elsevier.

Liebling, Jerome. Jerome Liebling: The Minnesota Photographs, 1949-1969. LC 97-7757. (Illus.). 129p. 1997. 45.00 (*0-87351-354-1*) Minn Hist.

— Jerome Liebling Photographs. LC 82-6919. (Illus.). 108p. 1982. 40.00 (*0-87023-371-8*) U of Mass Pr.

*__Liebling, Lawrence.__ The Most Precious Gift. LC 99-54867. (Illus.). 240p. 2000. 19.95 (*0-9642874-2-0*, Silent River Pr) Liebling Press.

Liebman, Arthur. The Politics of Puerto Rican University Students. LC 78-630381. (Latin American Monographs: No. 20). 217p. reprint ed. pap. 67.30 (*0-8357-7719-7*, 203607600002) Bks Demand.

Liebman, Arthur, et al. Latin American University Students: A Six Nation Study. LC 70-180152. (Center for International Affairs Ser.). (Illus.). 322p. 1972. 34.95 (*0-674-51275-8*) HUP.

Liebman, Charles, jt. auth. see Susser, Bernard.

Liebman, Charles S. Deceptive Images: Toward a Redefinition of American Judaism. 256p. 1988. 39.95 (*0-88738-218-5*) Transaction Pubs.

— Pressure Without Sanctions: The Influence of World Jewry on Israeli Policy. LC 75-18242. 304p. (C). 1976. 39.50 (*0-8386-1791-3*) Fairleigh Dickinson.

— Religion, Democracy & Israeli Society. (The Sherman Lecture Ser). 128p. 1997. text 13.00 (*90-5702-012-2*, Harwood Acad Pubs) Gordon & Breach.

— Religious & Secular: Conflict & Accommodation Between Jews in Israel. 238p. 1990. pap. 8.95 (*0-9623723-1-5*) AVI CHAI.

Liebman, Charles S., ed. Conflict & Accommodation Between Jews in Israel: Religious & Secular. 8.95 (*0-88125-374-X*) Ktav.

Liebman, Charles S. & Cohen, Steven M. Two Worlds of Judaism: The Israeli & American Experiences. LC 89-28455. 224p. (C). 1990. 37.50 (*0-300-04726-6*) Yale U Pr.

— Two Worlds of Judaism: The Israeli & American Experiences. 213p. (C). 1992. reprint ed. pap. 15.00 (*0-300-05231-6*) Yale U Pr.

Liebman, Charles S. & Don-Yehiya, Eliezer. Civil Religion in Israel: Traditional Judaism & Political Culture in the Jewish State. LC 82-17427. 270p. 1983. 55.00 (*0-520-04817-2*, Pub. by U CA Pr) Cal Prin Full Svc.

— Religion & Politics in Israel. LC 83-48172. (Jewish Political & Social Studies). 160p. 1984. reprint ed. pap. 49.60 (*0-7837-6104-X*, 205915000008) Bks Demand.

Liebman, Charles S. & Katz, Elihu, eds. The Jewishness of Israelis: Responses to the Guttman Report. LC 96-2904. (SUNY Series in Israeli Studies). 188p. (C). 1997. text 59.50 (*0-7914-3305-6*); pap. text 19.95 (*0-7914-3306-4*) State U NY Pr.

Liebman, Charles S., jt. auth. see Cohen, Steven M.

*__Liebman, Dan.__ I Want to Be a Doctor. LC R690.L53 2000. (I Want to Be Ser.). (Illus.). 42p. (J). (ps-2). 2000. pap. 3.99 (*1-55209-461-8*); lib. bdg. 14.95 (*1-55209-463-4*) Firefly Bks Ltd.

— I Want to Be a Doctor. (Illus.). (J). 2000. 9.44 (*0-606-18138-5*) Turtleback.

An Asterisk (*) at the beginning of an entry indicates that the title is appearing for the first time.

— I Want to Be a Police Officer. LC HV7922.L53 2000. (I Want to Be Ser.). (Illus.). 42p. (J). (ps-2). 2000. pap. 3.99 (*1-55209-465-0*); lib. bdg. 14.95 (*1-55209-467-7*) Firefly Bks Ltd.

— I Want to Be a Police Officer. (Illus.). (J). 2000. 9.44 (*0-606-18139-3*) Turtleback.

— I Want to Be a Vet. LC SF756.L53 2000. (Illus.). 42p. (J). (ps-2). 2000. pap. 3.99 (*1-55209-469-3*); lib. bdg. 14.95 (*1-55209-471-5*) Firefly Bks Ltd.

— I Want to Be a Veterinarian. (Illus.). (J). 2000. 9.44 (*0-606-18140-7*) Turtleback.

— Quiero Ser un Doctor (I Want to Be a Doctor) LC HV7922.L53 2000. (SPA., Illus.). 24p. (J). (ps-2). 2000. pap. 5.99 (*1-55209-473-1*) Firefly Bks Ltd.

— Quiero Ser un Oficial de Policia (I Want to Be a Police Officer) LC HV7922.L53 2000. (SPA., Illus.). 24p. (J). (ps-2). 2000. pap. 5.99 (*1-55209-475-8*) Firefly Bks Ltd.

— Quiero Ser un Veterinario (I Want to Be a Vet) LC SF756.L53 2000. (SPA., Illus.). 24p. (J). (ps-2). 2000. pap. 5.99 (*1-55209-477-4*) Firefly Bks Ltd.

Liebman, Dan, jt. ed. see Paulick, Raymond S.

Liebman, Dave, jt. auth. see Fisher, Larry.

Liebman, Glenn. Baseball Shorts; 1,000 of the Game's Funniest One-Liners. 240p. 1994. 11.95 (*0-8092-3644-3*) NTC Contemp Pub Co.

— Basketball Shorts. 256p. 1995. 12.95 (*0-8092-3350-9*, 335090, Contemporary Bks) NTC Contemp Pub Co.

— Football Shorts. LC 97-26159. 264p. 1997. 14.95 (*0-8092-3215-4*, 321540, Contemporary Bks) NTC Contemp Pub Co.

— Golf Shorts: Par 2. LC 98-12750. 256p. 1998. 14.95 (*0-8092-2865-3*, 286530, Contemporary Bks) NTC Contemp Pub Co.

— Golf Shorts: 1,001 of Golf's Funniest One-Liners. 256p. 1995. 12.00 (*0-8092-3489-0*, 348900, Contemporary Bks) NTC Contemp Pub Co.

— Hockey Shorts. LC 96-7985. 272p. 1996. 12.95 (*0-8092-3351-7*, 335170, Contemporary Bks) NTC Contemp Pub Co.

— Political Shorts. LC 98-54960. 256p. 1999. 14.95 (*0-8092-2780-0*, 278000, Contemporary Bks) NTC Contemp Pub Co.

— Sports Shorts. LC 93-2776. 432p. 1993. 14.95 (*0-8092-3768-7*, 376870, Contemporary Bks) NTC Contemp Pub Co.

— Tennis Shorts. LC 97-7162. 256p. 1997. 14.95 (*0-8092-3075-5*, 307550, Contemporary Bks) NTC Contemp Pub Co.

— 2000 Sports Quips & Quotes. LC 97-48989. 424p. 1998. 9.99 (*0-517-18934-8*) Random Hse Value.

*__Liebman, Glenn.__ Women's Sport Shorts: 1001 Slam Dunk One-Liners by & about Women in Sports. LC 99-55607. (Sports Shorts Ser.). 256p. 2000. 14.95 (*0-8092-2533-6*, 253360, Contemporary Bks) NTC Contemp Pub Co.

Liebman, Glenn. Yankee Shorts. LC 97-20726. 144p. 1997. 12.95 (*0-8092-2983-8*, 298380, Contemporary Bks) NTC Contemp Pub Co.

Liebman, Henry. Immigration Handbook. 2nd ed. LC 97-60647. 174p. 1997. 22.50 (*1-57588-440-2*, 311630) W S Hein.

*__Liebman, Henry G.__ Getting into America: The Immigration Guide to Finding a New Life in the U. S. A. (Illus.). 144p. (Orig.). 1999. pap. 19.95 (*1-85703-490-2*, Pub. by How To Bks) Trans-Atl Phila.

Liebman, Henry G. The Immigration Handbook for Work, Investment, Study & Retirement in the U. S. A. 2nd rev. ed. LC 97-60647. 176p. (Orig.). 1997. pap. 9.95 (*0-9629329-3-0*) Fairgreens Mda.

Liebman, Herbert. The Dramatic Art of David Storey: The Journey of a Playwright, 71. LC 95-45210. (Contributions in Drama & Theatre Studies: Vol. 71). 200p. 1996. 49.95 (*0-313-29865-3*, Greenwood Pr) Greenwood.

Liebman, J. Funk Bass. 96p. 1992. pap. 14.95 (*0-7935-1619-6*, 00699347) H Leonard.

— Funk Bass. 96p. 1992. pap. 17.95 (*0-7935-1620-X*, 00699348) H Leonard.

Liebman, J. F. & Greenberg, A., eds. Molecular Structure & Energetics: Advances in Boron & the Boranes, Vol. 5. 529p. 1988. 149.00 (*0-471-18680-5*, Wiley-VCH) Wiley.

Liebman, J. F. & Greenberg, A., eds. Molecular Structure & Energetics: Biophysical Aspects, 4. 405p. 1987. 149.00 (*0-471-18673-2*, Wiley-VCH) Wiley.

— Molecular Structure & Energetics: Chemical Bonding Models, 10. 360p. 1986. 149.00 (*0-471-18669-4*) Wiley.

— Molecular Structure & Energetics: Environmental Influences & Recognition in Enzyme Chemistry. 349p. 1989. 149.00 (*0-471-18713-5*, Wiley-VCH) Wiley.

— Molecular Structure & Energetics: Fluorine-Containing Molecules, Vol. 8. 346p. 1988. 149.00 (*0-471-18711-9*, Wiley-VCH) Wiley.

— Molecular Structure & Energetics: From Atoms to Polymers Isoelectronic Analogies, Vol. 11. 473p. 1989. 149.00 (*0-471-18721-6*, Wiley-VCH) Wiley.

— Molecular Structure & Energetics: Physical Measurements, 2. 388p. 1987. 149.00 (*0-471-18671-6*) Wiley.

Liebman, J. F. & Greenberg, A., eds. Molecular Structure & Energetics: Structure & Reactivity, Vol. 7. 385p. 1989. 149.00 (*0-471-18723-2*, Wiley-VCH) Wiley.

Liebman, J. F. & Greenberg, A., eds. Molecular Structure & Energetics: Studies of Organic Molecules, 3. 385p. 1986. 149.00 (*0-471-18672-4*, Wiley-VCH) Wiley.

Liebman, James S. & Hertz, Randy. Federal Habeas Corpus Practice & Procedure, 2 vols. 2nd ed. LC 94-73061. 1994. 180.00 (*1-55834-210-9*, 64330-11, MICHIE) LEXIS Pub.

— Federal Habeas Corpus Practice & Procedure. 2nd ed. 1995. suppl. ed. 45.00 (*0-614-25246-6*, 64329-12, MICHIE) LEXIS Pub.

— Federal Habeas Corpus Practice & Procedure, Vol. 1. 2000p. 1998. write for info. (*0-327-00662-5*, 6433012) LEXIS Pub.

— Federal Habeas Corpus Practice & Procedure, 2 vols., Vol. 1 & 2. 3rd ed. LC 98-89331. 2000p. 1998. 205.00 (*0-327-00661-7*, 6433012) LEXIS Pub.

— Federal Habeas Corpus Practice & Procedure, Vol. 2. 2000p. 1998. write for info. (*0-327-00663-3*, 6433012) LEXIS Pub.

Liebman, Jeffrey M. & Cooper, Steven J. The Neuropharmacological Basis of Reward. (Illus.). 448p. 1989. text 75.00 (*0-19-852176-6*) OUP.

Liebman, Jerome, et al, eds. Pediatric & Fundamental Eletrocardiography. (Developments in Cardiovascular Medicine Ser.). 1987. text 242.00 (*0-89838-815-5*) Kluwer Academic.

Liebman, Joel F. Molecular Structure & Energetics, Vols. 1-11. 4503p. 1989. 1425.00 (*0-471-18618-X*) Wiley.

— Molecular Structure & Energetics - Mechanistic Principles of Enzyme Activity, Vol. 9. 404p. 1989. 149.00 (*0-471-18712-7*) Wiley.

Liebman, Joel F. & Greenberg, Arthur. Molecular Structure & Energetics - Modern Models of Bonding & Delocalization, Vol. 6. 461p. 1988. 149.00 (*0-471-18722-4*) Wiley.

Liebman, John. Funk Bass. Lefferts, Michael, ed. (FRE.). 96p. (Orig.). (C). 1997. pap. text 40.95 incl. audio compact disk (*0-7692-1323-5*, 01010320) Wrner Bros.

Liebman, John R., et al. Export Controls in the United States. 1985. 75.00 (*0-317-29422-9*, #H43953) Harcourt.

Liebman, John R., jt. auth. see Root, William A.

*__Liebman, Jon.__ Blues Bass: The Complete Method. 80p. 1999. pap. 17.95 incl. audio compact disk (*0-7935-8668-2*) H Leonard.

Liebman, Judith, et al. Modeling & Optimization with GINO. (Illus.). 200p. (C). 1986. pap. text, mass mkt. 54.75 incl. 3.5 hd (*0-89426-157-6*) Course Tech.

Liebman, Lance, jt. auth. see Rothstein, Mark A.

Liebman, Lance M., ed. Ethnic Relations in America. LC 82-552. 184p. 1982. 11.95 (*0-13-291682-7*) Am Assembly.

Liebman, Lance M. & Heymann, Philip B. The Social Responsibilities of Lawyers: Case Studies. (University Casebook Ser.). 354p. (C). 1988. text 20.95 (*0-88277-645-2*) Foundation Pr.

Liebman, Lance M. & Rothstein, Mark A. Employment Law: Cases & Materials. 3rd ed. (University Casebook Ser.). 121p. 1994. teacher ed. write for info. (*1-56662-227-1*) Foundation Pr.

— Employment Law: Cases & Materials. 3rd ed. (University Casebook Ser.). 1327p. (C). 1994. pap. text 48.00 (*1-56662-158-5*) Foundation Pr.

— Employment Law, 1996 Supplement to Cases & Materials On. 3rd ed. (University Casebook Ser.). 107p. 1996. pap. text. write for info. (*1-56662-394-4*) Foundation Pr.

— 1995 Supplement to Cases & Materials on Employment Law, Suppl. 1. 3rd ed. (University Casebook Ser.). 50p. 1995. pap. text 3.95 (*1-56662-309-X*) Foundation Pr.

— Supplement to Cases & Materials on Employment Law, 1994 Statutory. (University Casebook Ser.). 271p. 1994. pap. text. write for info. (*1-56662-180-1*) Foundation Pr.

Liebman, Lance M., jt. auth. see Haar, Charles M.

Liebman, Lance M., ed. see American Assembly Staff.

Liebman, Lisa, jt. auth. see Kanjo, Kathryn.

Liebman, Malvina W. Jewish Cookery from Boston to Baghdad. LC 75-2186. (Illus.). 272p. 1975. 18.00 (*0-911389-02-4*) NightinGale Res.

Liebman, Marcel. Leninism under Lenin. (C). 1985. pap. 9.95 (*0-85036-261-X*, Pub. by MRLN) Paul & Co Pubs.

Liebman, Marcia C. & Camp-Sorrell, Dawn, eds. Multimodal Therapy in Oncology Nursing. LC 96-10353. (Illus.). 528p. (C). (gr. 13). 1996. pap. text 37.95 (*0-8151-5422-4*, 25466) Mosby Inc.

Liebman, Mary. A Fast Walk Through American History: 1492-1992. (Illus.). 400p. 1998. pap. 20.00 (*0-8059-4290-4*) Dorrance.

Liebman, Matthew Z., jt. ed. see Altieri, Miguel A.

Liebman, Michael N., ed. see American Chemical Society, Division of Agricultura.

Liebman, P., et al, eds. European Shortsea Shipping: Proceedings from the First & Second European Research Roundtable Conference on Shortsea Shipping 26-27 November 1992 & 2-3 June 1994, First Conference. 440p. 1993. 140.00 (*1-85044-560-5*) LLP.

Liebman, Robert C. & Wuthnow, Robert. The New Christian Right: Mobilization & Legitimation. (Social Institutions & Social Change Ser.). 264p. 1983. lib. bdg. 44.95 (*0-202-30307-1*) Aldine de Gruyter.

Liebman, Robert C. & Wuthnow, Robert, eds. The New Christian Right: Mobilization & Legitimation. (Social Institutions & Social Change Ser.). 264p. (C). 1983. pap. text 23.95 (*0-202-30308-X*) Aldine de Gruyter.

Liebman, Ronald S. Grand Jury. 1983. mass mkt. 2.95 (*0-345-29784-9*) Ballantine Pub Grp.

*__Liebman, Ronald S.__ Shark Tales: True (And Amazing) Stories from America's Lawyers. 288p. 2000. 24.50 (*0-684-85728-6*) Simon & Schuster.

Liebman, Roy. From Silents to Sound: A Biographical Encyclopedia of Performers Who Made the Transition to Talking Pictures. LC 97-41808. 319p. 1998. lib. bdg. 65.00 (*0-7864-0382-9*) McFarland & Co.

— Silent Film Performers: An Annotated Bibliography of Published, Unpublished & Archival Sources for over 350 Actors & Actresses. LC 95-20915. 391p. 1995. lib. bdg. 75.00 (*0-7864-0100-1*) McFarland & Co.

*__Liebman, Roy.__ The Wampas Baby Stars, 1922-1934. (Illus.). 256p. 2000. 45.00 (*0-7864-0756-5*) McFarland & Co.

Liebman, S. A. & Levy, E. J. Pyrolysis & GC in Polymer Analysis. (Chromatographic Science Ser.: Vol. 29). (Illus.). 576p. 1984. text 250.00 (*0-8247-7187-7*) Dekker.

Liebman, Seymour B. New World Jewry, 1493-1825: Requiem for the Forgotten. 25.00 (*0-87068-277-6*) Ktav.

Liebman, Wayne. Tending the Fire: The Ritual Men's Group. 64p. 1991. pap. 7.00 (*0-915408-45-7*) Ally Pr.

Liebman, Wayne, ed. see Scott, Jo.

Liebmann, George W. The Gallows in the Grove: Civil Society in American Law. LC 97-11083. 264p. 1997. 59.95 (*0-275-95886-8*, Praeger Pubs) Greenwood.

— The Little Platoons: Local Governments in Modern History. LC 95-5308. 192p. 1995. 57.95 (*0-275-95178-2*, Praeger Pubs) Greenwood.

*__Liebmann, George W.__ Solving Problems Without Large Government. 208p. 2000. 59.95 (*0-275-96852-9*, C6852, Praeger Pubs) Greenwood.

Liebmann, Hannah, ed. see Hillebrandt, Ina.

Liebmann, Hannah, jt. tr. see Kinnell, Galway.

Liebmann, Hannah, tr. see Rilke, Rainer Maria.

Liebmann, Lisa. Fauve Birds, Butterflies & Flowers. (Giftwraps by Artists Ser.). 1990. pap. 14.95 (*0-8109-2976-7*, Pub. by Abrams) Time Warner.

— Pat Steir: Waterfalls. (Illus.). 32p. (Orig.). 1990. pap. text 10.00 (*1-879293-01-3*) Contemp Art Mus.

— Southeast Bank Collects: A Corporation Views Contemporary Art. Perez, Esther, ed. 70p. (Orig.). 1990. write for info. (*0-943411-21-1*) Norton Gal Art.

Liebmann, Lisa I., jt. auth. see Trasobares, Cesar.

Liebmann, Louis & Wahl, Gustav. Katalog der Historischen Abteilung der Ersten Internationalen Luftschiffahrts Ausstellung. (GER., Illus.). xxi, 513p. 1997. reprint ed. 95.00 (*1-891396-00-5*) Pober Pub.

Liebmann, M. Western European Sculpture from Soviet Museums: 15th & 16th Centuries. (Illus.). 264p. (C). 1988. text 300.00 (*0-7855-5815-2*, Pub. by Collets) St Mut.

— Western European Sculpture from Soviet Museums, 15th-16th Centuries. 264p. (C). 1988. 275.00 (*0-7855-4503-4*, Pub. by Collets) St Mut.

Liebmann, Marian. Art Therapy for Groups: A Handbook of Themes, Games & Exercises. (Illus.). 226p. (Orig.). 1986. pap. text 19.95 (*0-914797-24-7*) Brookline Bks.

Liebmann, Marian, ed. Art Therapy in Practice. 176p. 1990. pap. 24.00 (*1-85302-058-3*) Taylor & Francis.

— Art Therapy with Offenders. 220p. 1994. pap. 29.95 (*1-85302-171-7*) Taylor & Francis.

— Arts Approaches to Conflict. LC 95-44815. 250p. 1996. 29.95 (*1-85302-293-4*, Pub. by Jessica Kingsley) Taylor & Francis.

— Community & Neighbour Mediation. xvii, 315p. 1998. pap. 36.00 (*1-85941-156-8*, Pub. by Cavendish Pubng) Gaunt.

Liebmann, R. Statistical Mechanics of Periodic Frustrated Ising Systems. (Lecture Notes in Physics Ser.: Vol. 251). vii, 142p. 1986. 29.95 (*0-387-16473-1*) Spr-Verlag.

Liebmann, Rosemarie M., jt. auth. see Costa, Arthur L.

Liebmann, Rosemarie M., jt. ed. see Costa, Arthur L.

Liebmann-Smith, Richard, ed. The Question of AIDS. 89p. 1985. pap. text 6.00 (*0-89766-302-0*) NY Acad Sci.

Liebnitz, Jennifer, et al. Rilke & the Visual Arts. Baron, Frank, ed. (Illus.). 150p. 1982. 15.00 (*0-87291-153-5*) Coronado Pr.

Liebo, Stephen L., ed. Minnesota Family Law Journal. 125.00 (*0-327-12455-5*) LEXIS Pub.

Liebo, Stephen L. & Cavel, Michael P. Workers' Compensation Forms, 1981-1988. (Nebraska Legal Forms Ser.). 16p. 1995. pap. text, suppl. ed. 95.00 (*0-86678-052-1*, 81841-10, MICHIE) LEXIS Pub.

Liebo, Stephen L., ed. see Winer, Edward L., et al.

Liebovich, Louis W. Bylines in Despair: Herbert Hoover, the Great Depression, & the U. S. News Media. LC 93-50679. 256p. 1994. 57.95 (*0-275-94843-9*, Praeger Pubs) Greenwood.

— The Press & the Modern Presidency: Myths & Mindsets from Kennedy to Clinton. LC 97-23010. 256p. 1998. 59.95 (*0-275-95926-0*, Praeger Pubs) Greenwood.

— The Press & the Origins of the Cold War, 1944-1947. LC 87-38478. 181p. 1988. 55.00 (*0-275-92999-X*, C2999, Praeger Pubs) Greenwood.

Liebovich, Louis W., jt. ed. see Bielawski, Shraga F.

Liebovitch, Larry S. Fractals & Chaos Simplified for the Life Sciences. LC 97-20874. 288p. (C). 1998. pap. 37.95 (*0-19-512024-8*) OUP.

Liebovitz, Annie, et al, photos by. Animal: Dolce & Gabbana. (Illus.). 160p. 1998. pap. 29.95 (*0-7892-0439-8*) Abbeville Pr.

Liebovitz, Annie, photos by. Stern Portfolio: Annie Leibovitz, 1968-1997. (Illus.). 112p. 1998. pap. 19.95 (*3-570-12300-6*) te Neues.

Liebow, Averill A., jt. auth. see Bloor, Colin M.

Liebow, Cynthia, tr. see Saumont, Annie.

Liebow, Elliot. Tally's Corner: A Study of Negro Streetcorner Men. 260p. 1968. pap. 11.95 (*0-316-52514-6*) Little.

— Tell Them Who I Am: The Lives of Homeless Women. 339p. 1993. 27.95 (*0-02-919095-9*) Free Pr.

— Tell Them Who I Am: The Lives of Homeless Women. 368p. 1995. pap. 13.95 (*0-14-024137-X*, Penguin Bks) Viking Penguin.

Liebow, Ely. Dr. Joe Bell: Model for Sherlock Holmes. LC 81-85520. 286p. 1982. 16.95 (*0-87972-197-9*) Bowling Green Univ Popular Press.

Liebow, Ely, ed. see Nieminski, John.

Liebow, Franette, jt. reader see Menken, Adam.

Liebowitz. Expert Systems World Congress Proceedings. 3074p. 1991. text 545.00 (*0-08-041445-1*, Prgamon Press) Buttrwrth-Heinemann.

— Structuring Expert Systems. 1989. 21.95 (*0-07-158631-8*) McGraw.

Liebowitz, Barry, jt. auth. see Light, Enid.

Liebowitz, Daniel. The Physician & the Slave Trade: John Kirk, the Livingstone Expeditions & the Crusade Against Slavery in East Africa. (Illus.). 375p. 1998. pap. text 27.95 (*0-7167-3098-7*) W H Freeman.

Liebowitz, Elsbeth. The Tomorrrow Book of Verse: Poems by Elsbeth Liebowitz. (Illus.). 1995. pap. 6.95 (*0-9636373-0-4*) OverBoard Pr.

Liebowitz, H., ed. Combined Nonlinear & Linear (Micro & Macro) Fracture Mechanics: Applications to Modern Engineering Structures - Selected Papers, U.S.-Japan Seminar. 1976. pap. 56.00 (*0-08-019982-8*, Pergamon Pr) Elsevier.

— Progress in Fatigue & Fracture, Vol. 8 No. 1. 1976. pap. 73.00 (*0-08-020866-5*, Pergamon Pr) Elsevier.

Liebowitz, H., jt. auth. see Eringen, A. Cemal.

Liebowitz, H., jt. ed. see Bodner, S. R.

Liebowitz, Harold. The Oriental Institute Excavations at Selenkahiye, Syria: Terra-Cotta Figurines & Model Vehicles. Van Loon, Maurits Nanning, ed. LC 81-71738. (Bibliotheca Mesopotamica Ser.: Vol. 22). (Illus.). xiv, 60p. 1988. 23.00 (*0-89003-105-3*); pap. 16.00 (*0-89003-104-5*) Undena Pubns.

Liebowitz, J., et al. Expert Systems World Congress Proceedings. 530.00 (*0-08-041446-X*, Pergamon Pr) Elsevier.

Liebowitz, Janet, jt. auth. see Prerau, David S.

*__Liebowitz, Jay.__ Building Organizational Intelligence: A Knowledge Management Primer. LC 99-29263. 160p. 1999. boxed set 49.95 (*0-8493-2036-4*) CRC Pr.

— Developing Your First Expert System: An Interactive Tutorial on CD-ROM. 5p. 1997. pap. 79.00 (*0-8493-3214-1*) CRC Pr.

Liebowitz, Jay. The Handbook of Applied Expert Systems. LC 97-13424. 736p. 1997. boxed set 104.95 (*0-8493-3106-4*) CRC Pr.

— The Handbook on Knowledge Management. LC 98-45326. 328p. 1999. boxed set 89.95 (*0-8493-0238-2*) CRC Pr.

*__Liebowitz, Jay.__ Information Technology Management: A Knowledge Repository. LC 98-29655. 224p. 1998. per. 44.95 (*0-8493-7167-8*) CRC Pr.

Liebowitz, Jay. Knowledge Organizations: What Every Manager Should Know. LC 98-12630. 208p. 1998. lib. bdg. 39.95 (*1-57444-196-5*) St Lucie Pr.

Liebowitz, Jay, ed. Moving Towards Expert Systems Globally in the 21st Century. LC 94-4689. (Illus.). 1573p. (C). 1994. 175.00 (*1-882345-00-2*) Cognizant Comm.

— Operational Expert System Applications in the United States. LC 91-2280. (Series in Operational Expert Systems Applications Worldwide). (Illus.). 165p. reprint ed. pap. 51.20 (*0-608-04553-5*, 206529500001) Bks Demand.

— Worldwide Expert Systems Activities & Trends. LC 94-4690. (Illus.). 178p. (C). 1994. 48.00 (*1-882345-02-9*) Cognizant Comm.

Liebowitz, Jay, ed. Hybrid Intelligent System Applications. LC 95-38349. (Illus.). 245p. (C). 1996. text 45.00 (*1-882345-05-3*) Cognizant Comm.

Liebowitz, Jay & Khosrowpour, Mehdi. Cases on Information Technology Management in Modern Organizations. LC 97-3865. (Series in Information Technology Management). (Illus.). 332p. 1997. pap. text 38.95 (*1-878289-37-3*) Idea Group Pub.

Liebowitz, Jay & Ragusa, James. Interactive Multimedia: Technologies, Applications & Trends. 1994. 129.00 (*0-9629217-7-7*) Lionheart Pub.

Liebowitz, Jay & Singh, I., eds. FAX-Net Electronic Mail Source Directory. (Illus.). 228p. 1986. pap. 96.00 (*0-08-033983-2*, K125, Pergamon Pr) Elsevier.

— Fax-Net Electronic Mail Source Directory. 220p. 1987. pap. 96.00 (*0-08-034495-X*, Pergamon Pr) Elsevier.

Liebowitz, Jay & Wilcox, Lyle C. Knowledge Management & Its Integrative Elements. LC 97-305. 224p. 1997. boxed set 69.95 (*0-8493-3116-1*) CRC Pr.

Liebowitz, Jay & Zelde, Janet S. Kids & Computers. 2nd ed. (Illus.). 70p. (J). (gr. 3-6). 1989. reprint ed. write for info. (*0-9623252-0-1*); reprint ed. pap. write for info. (*0-9623252-2-8*) J Liebowitz.

Liebowitz, Jay, et al. The Explosion of Intelligent Systems by the Year 2000. LC 96-5182. 41p. (Orig.). (YA). (gr. 6 up). 1996. pap. 9.95 (*1-882345-06-1*, 1-882345) Cognizant Comm.

Liebowitz, Jay, jt. ed. see Turban, Efraim.

Liebowitz, Jay, ed. see World Congress on Expert Systems Staff.

Liebowitz, Julie, jt. auth. see Williams, Deborah.

Liebowitz, Nathan. Daniel Bell & the Agony of Modern Liberalism, 124. LC 84-15690. (Contributions in Political Science Ser.: No. 124). 293p. 1985. 65.00 (*0-313-24279-8*, LID/, Greenwood Pr) Greenwood.

Liebowitz, Ronald D., ed. Gorbachev's New Thinking: Prospects for Joint Ventures. (Middlebury Center for Economic Studies Series in International Economic Affairs). 280p. 1988. text 29.95 (*0-88730-322-6*, HarpBusn) HarpInfo.

Liebowitz, Sol. Argentina: Major World Nations. (Major World Nations Ser.). (Illus.). 144p. (YA). (gr. 5 up). 1999. lib. bdg. 19.95 (*0-7910-4730-X*) Chelsea Hse.

Liebowitz, Stanley J. & Margolis, Stephen E. Winners, Losers & Microsoft: Competition & Antitrust in High Technology. (Illus.). 250p. 1999. 29.95 (*0-945999-80-1*, Pub. by Independent Inst) Seven Hills Bk.

Liebrand, W. G., et al, eds. Social Dilemmas: Theoretical Issues & Research Findings. (International Series in Experimental Social Psychology). 242p. 1992. 57.95 (*0-08-037775-0*, Prgamon Press) Buttrwrth-Heinemann.

Liebrand, Wim B. & Messick, David M. Frontiers in Social Dilemmas Research. LC 96-26104. 438p. 1996. 139.50 (*3-540-61299-8*) Spr-Verlag.

L

Liebrecht, Savyon. Apples from the Desert: Selected Stories. Institute for the Translation of Hebrew Staff, tr. from HEB. LC 98-22698. (Helen Rose Scheuer Jewish Women's Ser.). 240p. 1998. 22.95 (*1-55861-190-8*, Pub. by Feminist Pr) Consort Bk Sales.

***Liebrecht, Savyon.** Apples from the Desert: Selected Stories. unabridged ed. (Helen Rose Scheuer Jewish Women's Ser.). 240p. 2000. pap. 13.95 (*1-55861-235-1*, Pub. by Feminist Pr) Consort Bk Sales.

Liebs, Chester H. Main Street to Miracle Mile: American Roadside Architecture. LC 95-14226. (Illus.). 262p. 1995. pap. 24.95 (*0-8018-5095-9*) Johns Hopkins.

Liebsch, A. Electronic Excitations at Metal Surfaces: Applications of Local Density Theory. LC 97-16144. (Physics of Solids & Liquids Ser.). (Illus.). 348p. (C). 1997. text 85.00 (*0-306-45545-5*, Kluwer Plenum) Kluwer Academic.

***Liebsch, Bill & Liebsch, Janet.** It's a Disaster!... And What Are You Gonna Do about It? A Basic First Aid & Disaster Preparedness Manual from Fedhealth. (Illus.). 176p. 2000. pap. 19.95 (*1-930131-00-3*) Fedhealth.

Liebsch, Janet, jt. auth. see Liebsch, Bill.

Liebscher, Hans-Juergen, jt. auth. see Baumgartner, Albert.

Liebscher, J. J., jt. auth. see Baumgartner, A.

Liebschutz, David S., jt. auth. see Gold, Steven D.

Liebschutz, Sarah F. Bargaining under Federalism: Contemporary New York. LC 90-39852. (SUNY Series in Public Administration). 251p. (C). 1991. pap. text 19.95 (*0-7914-0635-0*) State U NY Pr.

Liebschutz, Sarah F. Bargaining under Federalism: Contemporary New York. LC 90-39852. (SUNY Series in Public Administration). 251p. (C). 1991. text, pap. text 59.50 (*0-7914-0634-2*) State U NY Pr.

Liebschutz, Sarah F. Federal Aid to Rochester. LC 83-73308. 58p. 1984. pap. 8.95 (*0-8157-5253-9*) Brookings.

***Liebschutz, Sarah F.** Managing Welfare Reform in Five States: The Challenge of Devolution. LC 00-42211. 2000. pap. write for info. (*0-914341-77-4*, Rockefeller Inst Pr) Nelson Rockefeller Inst Govt.

Liebschutz, Sarah F. New York Politics & Government: Competition & Compassion. LC 97-26898. (Politics & Governments of the American States Ser.). (Illus.). xxv, 235p. 1998. text 50.00 (*0-8032-2925-9*); pap. text 22.00 (*0-8032-7971-X*) U of Nebr Pr.

Liebson, David J. & Nowka, Richard H. The Uniform Commercial Code of Kentucky. 2nd ed. 1151p. 1992. 95.00 (*0-87473-852-0*, 64319-10, MICHIE) LEXIS Pub.

Liebson, John. Exploring Wordperfect 6 for DOS. 390p. (Orig.). 1993. pap. text 29.95 (*0-9626660-8-4*) Future Commns.

Liebson, Milt. Direct Stone Sculpture. LC 90-64436. (Illus.). 160p. 1991. text 29.95 (*0-88740-305-0*) Schiffer.

***Liebster, Simone Arnold.** Facing the Lion: Memoirs of a Young Girl in Nazi Europe. (Illus.). xvi, 408p. 2000. 29.95 (*0-9679366-5-9*) Grammaton Pr.

Lieburg, M. J. Van, see Van Lieburg, M. J.

Liechti, Elaine. The Complete Illustrated Guide to Shiatsu: The Japanese Healing Art of Touch for Health & Fitness. LC 98-6450. (Illustrated Health Bks.). (Illus.). 224p. 1998. pap. 24.95 (*1-86204-177-6*, Pub. by Element MA) Penguin Putnam.

— Shiatsu: Japanese Massage for Health & Fitness. (Health Essentials Ser.). 1993. pap. 9.95 (*1-85230-318-2*, Pub. by Element MA) Penguin Putnam.

Liechti, Kenneth M, jt. auth. see Bedford, Anthony M.

Liechty, Ann & Wezeman, Phyllis. Festival of Faith. (Illus.). 250p. 1993. ring bd. 39.95 (*1-877871-48-6*, 5236) Ed Ministries.

Liechty, Anna & Wezeman, Phyllis. The Christmas Story A-Z. (Illus.). 44p. 1992. pap. 7.95 (*1-877871-45-1*, 2569) Ed Ministries.

— The Easter Story A-Z. (Illus.). 52p. 1994. pap. 7.95 (*1-877871-78-8*, 2669) Ed Ministries.

Liechty, Anna L., et al. Hymn Stories for Children: The Apostles' Creed. LC 95-24907. 64p. 1995. pap. 8.99 (*0-8254-3985-X*) Kregel.

Liechty, Anna L., jt. auth. see Vos Wezeman, Phyllis.

Liechty, Anna L., jt. auth. see Wezeman, Phyllis V.

Liechty, Daniel. Andreas Fischer & the Sabbatarian Anabaptists: An Early Reformation Episode in East Central Europe, Vol. 29. LC 87-17727. (Studies in Anabaptist & Mennonite History: Vol. 29). 192p. 1988. 29.99 (*0-8361-1293-8*) Herald Pr.

— Early Anabaptist Spirituality: Selected Writings. LC 94-8478. (Classics of Western Spirituality Ser.). 1994. pap. 19.95 (*0-8091-3475-6*) Paulist Pr.

— Sabbatarianism in the Sixteenth Century: A Page in the History of the Radical Reformation. LC 93-71090. 104p. 1993. pap. 13.99 (*0-943872-99-5*) Andrews Univ Pr.

— Transference & Transcendence: Ernest Becker's Contribution to Psychotherapy. LC 94-39365. 224p. 1995. 45.00 (*1-56821-434-0*) Aronson.

Liechty, Daniel, ed. Early Anabaptist Spirituality: Selected Writings. LC 94-8478. (Classics of Western Spirituality Ser.). 1994. 29.95 (*0-8091-0466-0*) Paulist Pr.

Liechty, Elizabeth L., et al. Fitting & Pattern Alteration: A Multi-Method Approach. LC 85-82047. (Illus.). 344p. (C). 1992. pap. 39.00 (*0-87005-775-8*) Fairchild.

Liechty, Jay. America's State Church: Will It Be the Dominant Religion in the Twenty First Century? 197p. (Orig.). 1994. pap. 11.95 (*0-9624576-1-2*) Calder Pr.

— How to Avoid a Collision (Audit) with the IRS. 120p. (Orig.). 1990. pap. 9.95 (*0-9624576-0-4*) Calder Pr.

Lieck, Albert, ed. Trial of Benjamin Knowles, No. 1. (Notable British Trials Ser.). 215p. 1995. reprint ed. 69.00 (*1-56169-175-5*) Gaunt.

***Lied, Kate.** Potato: A Tale from the Great Depression. (Illus.). 48p. (J). (gr. k-5). 1998. 16.00 (*0-7922-3521-5*, Pub. by Natl Geog) Publishers Group.

Lieder, F. W., ed. Popular German Stories. (GER.). (Orig.). pap. text 9.95 (*0-89197-351-6*) Irvington.

Lieder, Michael. Wild Justice: The People of Geronimo vs. the United States. LC 98-43278. 1999. pap. text 16.95 (*0-8061-3133-0*) U of Okla Pr.

Lieder, Nancy. ZetaTalk: Direct Answers from the Zeta Reticuli People. LC 99-57714. 200p. 1999. pap. 14.95 (*1-893183-15-7*, Pub. by Granite Pub) ACCESS Pubs Network.

Lieder, Paul R., ed. Eminent British Poets of the Nineteenth Century: Tennyson to Housman, Vol. 2. LC 72-448. (Granger Index Reprint Ser.). 1977. reprint ed. 38.95 (*0-8369-6366-0*) Ayer.

— Eminent British Poets of the Nineteenth Century: Wordsworth to Landor, Vol. 1. LC 72-448. (Granger Index Reprint Ser.). 1977. reprint ed. 40.95 (*0-8369-6365-2*) Ayer.

Lieder, Ulrich. Crustacea: Cladocera, Bosminidae. (Suesswasserfauna von Mitteleuropa Ser.: Band 8, Heft 2 & 3). (GER., Illus.). 80p. 1996. pap. 90.00 (*3-437-25028-0*) Gustav Fischer.

Liederman, Erica. The Book of Eleanor. 216p. (Orig.). 1995. pap. 14.00 (*0-9646828-0-X*) N Fork Pr.

Liedholm, Carl & Mead, Donald C. Small Enterprises & Economic Development: The Dynamics of Micro & Small Enterprises. LC 98-34289. 1998. write for info. (*0-415-19351-6*) Routledge.

Liedke, Ulf. Naturgeschichte und Religion: Eine Theologische Studie Zum Religionsbegriff in der Philosophie Theodor W. Adornos. (Kontexte Ser.: Bd. 21). (GER.). 501p. 1996. 82.95 (*3-631-30937-6*) P Lang Pubng.

Liedl, Anthony. The Adventures of Shangri the Elephant: Shangri & the Rogue Elephant. (Illus.). 24p. (J). (gr. 5-6). 1997. pap. 8.00 (*0-8059-4037-5*) Dorrance.

Liedl, G. L. & Hobbs, L. W., eds. Frontiers in Materials Education, Vol. 66. (Materials Research Society Symposium Proceedings Ser.). 1986. text 17.50 (*0-931837-31-6*) Materials Res.

Liedl, R., et al, eds. Iteration Theory & Its Functional Equations. (Lecture Notes in Mathematics Ser.: Vol. 1163). viii, 231p. 1985. 37.95 (*0-387-16067-1*) Spr-Verlag.

Liedlich, Raymond D., jt. auth. see Smith, William F.

Liedloff, Helmut. Ohne Muhe!, 001. LC 79-84596. (German Sequential Readers Ser.). (Illus.). (J). (gr. 9-10). 1980. pap. 12.52 (*0-395-27931-3*) HM.

Liedloff, Helmut, et al. Kaleidoskop: Kultur, Literatur und Grammatik, 3 vols. 3rd ed. (C). 1991. text. write for info. (*0-395-43224-3*) HM Soft Schl Col Div.

Liedloff, Helmut, jt. auth. see Moeller, Jack R.

Liedloff, Jean. The Continuum Concept. 256p. 1985. pap. 13.00 (*0-201-05071-4*) Addison-Wesley.

— The Continuum Concept. 1990. 25.25 (*0-8446-6267-4*) Peter Smith.

Liedman, Jay W. Index to the 1865 Minnesota State Census for Chicago County: Indexed & Annotated. LC 97-50192. (Illus.). 64p. 1998. pap. write for info. (*0-915709-57-0*) Pk Geneal Bk.

Liedo, Pablo, jt. ed. see Aluja, Martin.

Liedtke. Embracing a Dictatorship. LC 97-12036. 256p. 1998. text 59.95 (*0-312-17492-6*) St Martin.

Liedtke, Boris N. Embracing a Dictatorship: U. S. Relations with Spain, 1945-1953. 272p. 1996. 65.00 (*1-898723-52-4*, Pub. by Sussex Acad Pr) Intl Spec Bk.

***Liedtke, Helmut.** Hope & Chaos: Philosophical Fragments, 1973 to 2000. Kautt, James Louis, tr. from GER. LC 00-9191. 48p. 2000. pap. 6.80 (*1-58750-602-5*) Fouque Pubs.

Liedtke, R. K. Dictionary of Clinical Pharmacology for Doctors & Pharmacists: Woerterbuch der Klinischen Pharmakologie Fuer Mediziner und Pharmazeuten. (ENG & GER.). 245p. 1980. 49.95 (*0-8288-1838-X*, M15389) Fr & Eur.

Liedtke, Rainer. Jewish Welfare in Hamburg & Manchester, c. 1850-1914. (Oxford Historical Monographs). 280p. 1998. text 69.00 (*0-19-820723-9*) OUP.

Liedtke, Walter. Royal Horse & Rider. 336p. 1989. lib. bdg. 65.00 (*0-89835-267-3*) Abaris Bks.

Liedtke, Walter, et al. Robert Lee Huber: A Collector Creates. (Illus.). 120p. 1996. write for info. (*0-9636759-2-3*) East Carolin Mus.

Liedtke, Walter A. Flemish Paintings in the Metropolitan Museum of Art, 2 vols. (Illus.). 488p. 1984. 25.00 (*0-87099-356-9*, 0-8109-6461-9) Metro Mus Art.

Lief, Alfred. Brandeis: The Personal History of an American Ideal. LC 72-169768. (Select Bibliographies Reprint Ser.). 1977. reprint ed. 35.95 (*0-8369-5988-4*) Ayer.

Lief, Alfred, compiled by. The Social & Economic Views of Mr. Justice Brandeis. 446p. 1996. reprint ed. 110.00 (*1-56169-201-8*) Gaunt.

Lief, Alfred, ed. The Dissenting Opinions of Mr. Justice Holmes. xviii, 314p. 1981. reprint ed. lib. bdg. 48.00 (*0-8377-0811-7*, Rothman) W S Hein.

— Public Control of Business. LC 96-77572. xx, 324p. 1996. reprint ed. 65.00 (*1-57588-121-7*, 310680) W S Hein.

Lief, Alfred, intro. Representative Opinions of Mr. Justice Holmes. xxii, 319p. 1997. reprint ed. 95.00 (*1-56169-347-2*) Gaunt.

Lief, Alfred. The Dissenting Opinions of Mr. Justice Holmes. xviii, 314p. 1996. reprint ed. 88.00 (*1-56169-199-2*) Gaunt.

Lief, Alfred, ed. see Meyer, Adolf.

Lief, Bert W. EURoad: The Complete Guide to Motoring in Europe. 24th ed. (Illus.). 64p. 1998. pap. 9.75 (*0-912693-12-6*) VLE Ltd.

— Walks Through London. 1998. pap. 3.00 (*0-912693-63-0*, 1043) VLE Ltd.

— Walks Through Munich. 1997. pap. 3.00 (*0-912693-65-7*, 1046) VLE Ltd.

Lief, Bert W. & Keely, L. M. Walks Through Amsterdam. 1998. pap. 3.00 (*0-912693-60-6*, 1054) VLE Ltd.

— Walks Through Barcelona. 1998. pap. 3.00 (*0-912693-62-2*, 1050) VLE Ltd.

— Walks Through Brussels. 1991. pap. 3.00 (*0-912693-61-4*, 1053) VLE Ltd.

— Walks Through Dublin. 1998. pap. 3.00 (*0-912693-71-1*, 1055) VLE Ltd.

— Walks Through Madrid. 1998. pap. 3.00 (*0-912693-64-9*, 1044) VLE Ltd.

— Walks Through Paris. 1998. pap. 3.00 (*0-912693-66-5*, 1045) VLE Ltd.

— Walks Through Rome. 1998. pap. 3.00 (*0-912693-67-3*, 1047) VLE Ltd.

— Walks Through Seville. 1998. pap. 3.00 (*0-912693-68-1*, 1051) VLE Ltd.

— Walks Through Stuttgart. 1988. pap. 3.00 (*0-912693-57-6*, 1048) VLE Ltd.

— Walks Through Vienna. 1992. pap. 3.00 (*0-912693-69-X*, 1052) VLE Ltd.

— Walks Through Zurich. 1992. pap. 3.00 (*0-912693-70-3*, 1049) VLE Ltd.

Lief, Greg, jt. auth. see Booth, Joe.

Lief, Harold I. & Hoch, Zwi. International Research in Sexology: Selected Papers from the Fifth World Congress, 1. LC 83-21146. 216p. 1984. 59.95 (*0-275-91442-9*, C1442, Praeger Pubs) Greenwood.

Lief, Jo. Notes from a Mother to Her Children on Getting, Being & Staying Married. LC 98-45947. 1999. 0.00 (*0-8362-7867-4*) Andrews & McMeel.

***Lief, Jo.** Notes to My Children on Getting, Being & Staying Married. 64p. 1999. 8.95 (*0-7407-0038-3*) Andrews & McMeel.

Lief, Judith L., ed. see Trungpa, Chogyam.

Lief, Michael S., et al. Ladies & Gentlemen of the Jury: Greatest Closing Arguments in Modern Law. LC 97-50267. 400p. 1998. 26.00 (*0-684-83661-0*) Scribner.

***Lief, Michael S., et al.** Ladies & Gentlemen of the Jury: The Greatest Closing Arguments in Modern Law. LC 97-50267. 400p. 2000. per. 15.00 (*0-684-85948-3*) S&S Trade.

Lief, Nina R. & Fahs, Mary E. The Early Childhood Development Center's Parenting Series: The First Year of Life. 288p. 1991. 24.95 (*0-8027-1153-7*); pap. 12.95 (*0-8027-7349-4*) Walker & Co.

— The Early Childhood Development Center's Parenting Series: The Second Year of Life. 288p. 1991. 24.95 (*0-8027-1154-5*); pap. 12.95 (*0-8027-7350-8*) Walker & Co.

— The Early Childhood Development Center's Parenting Series: The Third Year of Life. 288p. 1991. 24.95 (*0-8027-1155-3*); pap. 12.95 (*0-8027-7351-6*) Walker & Co.

Lief, Patricia. Fun with Fruits & Vegetables. 1991. 11.99 (*0-86653-994-8*) Fearon Teacher Aids.

Lief, Philip. French-English/English-French Dictionary. (FRE.). 480p. 1996. mass mkt. 5.99 (*0-440-22088-2*) Dell.

— Italian-English - English-Italian Dictionary. (ENG & ITA.). 480p. 1996. mass mkt. 5.99 (*0-440-22090-4*) Dell.

— Spanish-English, English-Spanish Dictionary. (ENG & SPA.). 464p. 1996. mass mkt. 5.99 (*0-440-22087-4*) Dell.

— Twenty First Century German-English English-German Dictionary. (ENG & GER.). 448p. 1996. mass mkt. 5.99 (*0-440-22089-0*) Dell.

Lief, Stephen J. Busy Lawyer's Guide to Microsoft Word for Windows 95, Vol. 1. Perlman, Alan, ed. LC 96-25093. 110p. 1996. pap. text. write for info. (*0-314-07716-2*) West Pub.

Liefde, Jacob de, see De Liefde, Jacob.

***Liefeld, Olive F. & Becker, Verne.** Unfolding Destinies: The Ongoing Story the Auca Mission. LC 98-27390. 256p. 1998. pap. 13.99 (*1-57293-041-1*) Discovery Hse Pubs.

Liefeld, Rob. Warchild, Vol. 1. Hawkins, Matt, ed. (Illus.). 104p. 1996. reprint ed. pap. 12.95 (*1-888610-03-4*) Mximum Pr.

Liefeld, Rob & Napton, Robert. Avengelyne, Vol. 1. Hankins, Matt, ed. (Illus.). Date not set. reprint ed. pap. 9.95 (*1-888610-02-6*) Mximum Pr.

— Battlestar Galactica: War of Eden, Vol. 1. Hankins, Matt, ed. (Illus.). 128p. 1995. reprint ed. pap. 12.95 (*1-888610-01-8*) Mximum Pr.

Liefeld, Walter L. 1 & 2 Timothy/Titus. LC 99-18861. 1999. 24.99 (*0-310-50110-5*) Zondervan.

— Interpreting the Book of Acts. LC 95-46099. (Guides to New Testament Exegesis Ser.). 144p. 1995. pap. 10.99 (*0-8010-2015-8*) Baker Bks.

— New Testament Exposition: From Text to Sermon. 176p. (C). 1984. 15.95 (*0-310-45910-9*, 12607) Zondervan.

***Lieferbar, Ebenfalls.** Die Franken und die Alemannen bis zur Schlacht bei Zulpich. (Illus.). 690p. 1998. 218.00 (*3-11-015826-4*) De Gruyter.

Lieferman, Henry. South Carolina. 2nd ed. LC 97-18958. (Compass American Guides Ser.). 324p. 1997. pap. 18.95 (*0-679-03599-0*, Compass Amrcn) Fodors Travel.

Lieff, Jonathan D. Computers & Other Technological Aids for Psychiatric Private Practice. LC 84-6286. (Private Practice Monograph Ser.). 123p. reprint ed. pap. 38.20 (*0-8357-7846-0*, 203622100002) Bks Demand.

Lieff, Morris & Stumpf, S. M., eds. Fire Resistive Coatings: The Need for Standards - STP 826. LC 83-71335. 162p. 1984. pap. text 22.00 (*0-8031-0214-3*, STP826) ASTM.

Liefferink, J., et al. European Integration & Environmental Policy. LC 93-14599. 1993. 105.00 (*1-85293-282-1*) Halsted Pr.

Liefferink, Duncan, jt. ed. see Andersen, Mikael Skou.

Liefferink, J. Duncan. The Making of European Environmental Policy: The Netherlands, the EU & Acid Rain. LC 96-28199. (Issues in Environmental Politics Ser.). 216p. 1997. text 69.95 (*0-7190-4924-5*, Pub. by Manchester Univ Pr) St Martin.

Liefkes, Reino. Glass. 1997. 45.00 (*1-85177-197-2*, Pub. by V&A Ent) Antique Collect.

Liefmann, Robert. Cartels, Concerns & Trusts. Wilkins, Mira, ed. LC 76-29997. (European Business Ser.). 1977. reprint ed. lib. bdg. 35.95 (*0-405-09755-7*) Ayer.

Lieftinck, Pieter. Water & Power Resources of West Pakistan, a Study in Sector Planning. Incl. Vol. 1. Main Report. 310p. 1968. 24.95 (*0-8018-1004-3*); Vol. 2. Development of Irrigation & Agriculture. 419p. 1969. 24.95 (*0-8018-1005-1*); (World Bank Research Publications). 1968. write for info. (*0-318-53787-7*) Johns Hopkins.

Liegel, Leon, jt. ed. see Campbell, Sally.

***Liegeois, Jean-Pierre.** School Provision for Ethnic Minorities: The Gypsy Paradigm. (Interface Collection: Vol. 11). 310p. 1998. pap. 19.95 (*0-900458-88-7*, Pub. by Univ of Herfordshire) Bold Strummer Ltd.

Liegey, G. M., jt. ed. see Hodgson, P.

Lieh-Lai, Mary. The Pediatric Acute Care Handbook. LC 95-9591. 258p. 1995. pap. text 32.00 (*0-316-09306-8*, Little Brwn Med Div) Lppncott W & W.

Lieh-Lai, Mary. Pocket Pediatrics. 200p. 24.95 (*0-7817-2567-4*) Lppncott W & W.

Lieh-Tzu. The Book of Lieh-Tzu: A Classic of the Tao. Graham, A. C., tr. from CHI. (Translations from the Oriental Classics Ser.). 208p. 1990. pap. text 19.00 (*0-231-07237-6*) Col U Pr.

Liehaus, Jacob L. Premenstrual Syndrome: Index of Modern Information. LC 88-47618. 150p. 1990. 47.50 (*1-55914-138-7*); pap. 44.50 (*1-55914-139-5*) ABBE Pubs Assn.

— Psychiatric Status Rating Scales: Index & Reference Book of New Information. 150p. 1996. 47.50 (*0-7883-0826-2*); pap. 44.50 (*0-7883-0827-0*) ABBE Pubs Assn.

— Sexology Encyclopedia Vol. 23: Premenstrual Syndromes: Index & Reference Books of New Information. (Illus.). 123p. 1996. 49.50 (*0-7883-0894-7*); pap. 39.95 (*0-7883-0895-5*) ABBE Pubs Assn.

Liehm, Antonin J. Closely Watched Films: The Czechoslovak Experience. LC 72-94987. 495p. reprint ed. 153.50 (*0-608-17067-4*, 202761900055) Bks Demand.

— The Milos Forman Stories. LC 73-92806. (Illus.). 201p. reprint ed. pap. 62.40 (*0-608-18128-5*, 203278200081) Bks Demand.

Liehm, Freddy. French & Dutch Lexicon of Economic & Commercial Terms: Lexique de Termes Economiques et Commerciaux. (DUT & FRE.). 104p. 1986. pap. 35.00 (*0-8288-0804-X*, M2365) Fr & Eur.

Liehm, Mira. Passion & Defiance: Italian Film from 1942 to the Present. LC 83-6667. (Illus.). 450p. (C). 1984. pap. text 18.95 (*0-520-05744-9*, Pub. by U CA Pr) Cal Prin Full Svc.

Liehr, M., et al, eds. Ultraclean Semiconductor Processing Technology & Surface Chemical Cleaning & Passivation. (Symposium Proceedings Ser.: Vol. 386). 411p. 1995. text 86.00 (*1-55899-289-8*) Materials Res.

Liell, Peter, et al, eds. Law of Education. ring bd. write for info. (*0-406-99895-7*, LE9ASET, MICHIE) LEXIS Pub.

Liell, Peter & Coleman, John. The Law of Education, 2 vols., Set. ring bd. 495.00 (*0-406-02647-5*, UK, MICHIE) LEXIS Pub.

Lielpeteris, J. & Moreau, R., eds. Liquid Metal Magnetohydrodynamics. (C). 1989. text 234.50 (*0-7923-0344-X*) Kluwer Academic.

Liem, Ann. Jacob Boehme: Insights into the Challenge of Evil. LC 77-79823. 32p. (Orig.). 1977. pap. 4.00 (*0-87574-214-9*) Pendle Hill.

Liem, Channing. The Korean War: An Unanswered Question. 93p. 1992. 7.00 (*0-317-04972-0*) Comm New Korea.

Liem, Tik L. Invitations to Science Inquiry. 2nd ed. (Illus.). 467p. 1991. reprint ed. 40.00 (*1-878106-00-7*) Sci Inquiry.

— Invitations to Science Inquiry: Supplement to First & Second Edition. (Illus.). 180p. 1992. pap. text 19.50 (*1-878106-01-5*) Sci Inquiry.

— Turning Kids on to Science in the Home: Forces & Motion, Vol. 3. (Illus.). 122p. 1992. pap. text 17.50 (*1-878106-06-6*) Sci Inquiry.

— Turning Kids on to Science in the Home: Living Things, Vol. 4. (Illus.). 67p. 1992. pap. text 12.50 (*1-878106-07-4*) Sci Inquiry.

— Turning Kids on to Science in the Home Vol. 2: Energy, Vol. 2. (Illus.). 168p. 1992. pap. text 20.00 (*1-878106-05-8*) Sci Inquiry.

— Turning Our Kids on to Science in the Home: Our Environment, 4 vols. (Illus.). 185p. 1992. pap. text 25.00 (*1-878106-08-2*) Sci Inquiry.

— Turning Our Kids on to Science in the Home: Our Environment, 4 vols., 1. (Illus.). 185p. 1992. write for info. (*1-878106-04-X*) Sci Inquiry.

Lieman, Yossi. My Pesach Book: Halachos of Pesach & the Seder. LC 98-165911. (Illus.). 69p. (J). (gr. 2-4). 1998. 8.00 (*0-9666133-0-9*) Yamban.

Liemant, A., et al. Equilibrium Distributions of Branching Processes. (C). 1988. text 140.50 (*90-277-2774-0*) Kluwer Academic.

Liemt, G. Van, see Van Liemt, G., ed.

Lien, Bhikkhuni T. Tin, see Tin Lien, Bhikkhuni T.

***Lien, Carsten.** Olympic Battleground: The Power Politics of Timber Preservation. 2nd ed. (Illus.). 464p. 2000. pap. 18.95 (*0-89886-736-3*) Mountaineers.

Lien, David A. The BASIC Handbook: Encyclopedia of the BASIC Computer Language. 3rd ed. LC 85-71338. 862p. (Orig.). 1986. pap. 24.95 (*0-932760-33-3*) CompuSoft.

— The IBM BASIC Handbook: The Encyclopedia of the BASIC Computer Language for All IBM Personal Computers & Compatibles. 2nd ed. LC 85-63823. 250p. (Orig.). 1986. pap. 16.95 (*0-932760-38-4*) CompuSoft.

— Learning IBM BASIC for the Personal Computer. rev. ed. LC 82-73471. (CompuSoft Learning Ser.). (Illus.). 494p. (Orig.). (gr. 7 up). 1984. pap. 19.95 (*0-932760-13-9*) CompuSoft.

— Learning Microsoft BASIC for the Macintosh: New Microsoft 2.X Version. LC 85-71339. (Illus.). 457p. (Orig.). 1985. pap. 19.95 (*0-932760-34-1*) CompuSoft.

— MS-DOS-the Advanced Course. 1989. pap. 27.95 (*0-932760-49-X*) CompuSoft.

— MS-DOS-the Basic Course. 1989. pap. 14.95 (*0-932760-48-1*) CompuSoft.

Lien, Eric J. Sar. (Medicinal Research Ser.: Vol. 11). (Illus.). 384p. 1987. text 199.00 (*0-8247-7686-0*) Dekker.

Lien, Eric J. & Li, Wen Y. Anticancer Chinese Drugs & Related Plants. Bensen, Don R., ed. 160p. 1996. pap. 10.95 (*0-941942-18-X*, Keats Publng) NTC Contemp Pub Co.

Lien, George E., ed. see American Society of Mechanical Engineers Staff.

Lien, Marianne. Marketing & Modernity. LC 98-119929. 1997. pap. 19.50 (*1-85973-996-2*, Pub. by Berg Pubs) NYU Pr.

Lien, Pei-te. The Political Participation of Asian Americans: Voting Behavior in Southern California. rev. ed. Ng, Franklin, ed. LC 97-33628. (Asian Americans). (Illus.). 200p. 1997. text 53.00 (*0-8153-2984-9*) Garland.

Lien-Teh, Wu, jt. auth. see Wong, Chi-Min.

Lien-Teh, Wu, jt. auth. see Wong, K. C.

Lien-Ying Kuo. The T'ai Chi Boxing Chronicle. Guttman, Dac, tr. from CHI. LC 93-40412. (Illus.). 141p. (C). 1994. pap. 14.95 (*1-55643-177-5*) North Atlantic.

Lienau, C. C., ed. see Richardson, Lewis F.

Lienesch, Michael. New Order of the Ages: Time, the Constitution, & the Making of Modern American Political Thought. 245p. (C). 1988. text 42.50 (*0-691-07779-7*, Pub. by Princeton U Pr) Cal Prin Full Svc.

— New Order of the Ages: Time, the Constitution, & the Making of Modern American Political Thought. LC 88-1503. 245p. 1988. reprint ed. pap. 76.00 (*0-608-04576-4*, 206534500003) Bks Demand.

— Redeeming America: Piety & Politics in the New Christian Right. LC 92-45782. xii, 332p. 1993. pap. 19.95 (*0-8078-4428-4*) U of NC Pr.

Lienesch, Michael, jt. ed. see Gillespie, Michael A.

Lienesch, William C. National Parks in Urban Areas. Corbett, Marjorie, ed. 29p. (Orig.). 1986. pap. 4.50 (*0-940091-17-8*) Natl Parks & Cons.

Lieng, Huang L., ed. Polymer Wear & Its Control. LC 85-15755. (ACS Symposium Ser.: Vol. 287). 432p. 1985. reprint ed. pap. 134.00 (*0-608-03915-2*, 206436200009) Bks Demand.

Liengme, Bernard V. COBOL by Command. (Illus.). 320p. (gr. 13). 1996. pap. text 24.95 (*0-340-65292-6*) Chapman & Hall.

— COBOL by Command. 300p. 1999. pap. 44.95 (*0-470-34541-1*) Halsted Pr.

***Liengme, Bernard V.** A Guide to Microsoft Excel for Business & Management. 256p. 2000. pap. 39.95 (*0-470-38436-0*) Wiley.

Liengme, Bernard V. A Guide to Microsoft Excel for Scientists & Engineers. 210p. 1997. pap. 44.95 (*0-470-24428-3*) Wiley.

***Lienhard, Heinrich, et al.** New Worlds to Seek: Pioneer Heinrich Lienhard in Switzerland & America, 1824-1846. Abbott, John Cushman, ed. Spahn, Raymond Jhurgen, tr. LC 99-21412. 352p. 2000. 39.95 (*0-8093-2233-1*) S Ill U Pr.

Lienhard, Janet. FrameMaker for Windows: Step-by-Step Calendar. Arias, Claire C., ed. & illus. by. (Trainers' Signature Ser.). 120p. (Orig.). 1993. pap. 11.95 (*1-880663-47-3*) Ellipsys Intl.

— FrameMaker for Windows: Step-by-Step Chart. Arias, Claire C., ed. & illus. by. (Trainers' Signature Ser.). 120p. (Orig.). 1993. pap. 11.95 (*1-880663-48-1*) Ellipsys Intl.

— FrameMaker for Windows: Step-by-Step Letter. 2nd ed. Arias, Claire C., ed. & illus. by. (Trainers' Signature Ser.). 120p. (Orig.). 1993. pap. 11.95 (*1-880663-42-2*) Ellipsys Intl.

Lienhard, John H., jt. auth. see Tien, Chang L.

Lienhard, Joseph T. The Bible, the Church, & Authority: The Canon of the Christian Bible in History & Theology. 120p. (Orig.). 1995. pap. text 9.95 (*0-8146-5536-X*, M Glazier) Liturgical Pr.

— Contra Marcellum: Marcellus of Ancyra & Fourth-Century Theology. LC 98-21261. 270p. 1999. lib. bdg. 59.95 (*0-8132-0901-3*) Cath U Pr.

— Ministry. Halton, Thomas, ed. LC 83-83154. (Message of the Fathers of the Church Ser.: Vol. 8). 183p. 1984. pap. 11.95 (*0-8146-5320-0*) Liturgical Pr.

***Lienhard, Joseph T.** St. Joseph in Early Christianity: Devotion & Theology: A Study & an Anthology of Patristic Texts. LC 99-29177. 1999. write for info. (*0-916101-29-0*) St Joseph.

Lienhard, Joseph T., et al. Augustine: Presbyter Factus Sum. LC 93-16709. XVIII, 590p. (C). 1994. text 69.95 (*0-8204-2199-5*) P Lang Pubng.

Lienhard, Joseph T., jt. auth. see Carey, Patrick W.

Lienhard, Joseph T., tr. see Origen.

Lienhard, M. The Origins & Characteristics of Anabaptism. (International Archives of the History of Ideas Ser.: No. 87). 1977. lib. bdg. 191.50 (*90-247-1896-1*) Kluwer Academic.

Lienhard, Marc. Un Temps, une Ville, une Reforme: La Reformation a Strasbourg. 310p. 1990. text 117.95 (*0-86078-268-9*, Pub. by Variorum) Ashgate Pub Co.

***Lienhard, Martin.** La Voz y Su Huella. (Rama Ser.: Vol. 10). 325p. (C). 1998. 35.00 (*0-910061-52-1*) Ediciones Norte.

Lienhard, Siegfried. Songs of Nepal: An Anthropology of Newar Folksongs & Hymns. 1992. 50.00 (*0-7855-0287-4*, Pub. by Ratna Pustak Bhandar) St Mut.

— Songs of Nepal - An Anthropology of Newar Folk Songs & Hymns. (C). 1991. text 30.00 (*0-7855-0155-X*, Pub. by Ratna Pustak Bhandar) St Mut.

Lienhardt, G. Antropologia Social. (SPA.). pap. 8.99 (*968-16-0978-6*, Pub. by Fondo) Continental Bk.

Lienhardt, Godfrey. Divinity & Experience: The Religion of the Dinka. (Illus.). 336p. 1988. pap. 23.00 (*0-19-823405-8*) OUP.

***Lienhardt, John.** The Engines of Our Ingenuity: An Engineer Looks at Technology & Culture. 288p. 2000. 25.00 (*0-19-513583-0*) OUP.

Lienhart, David A., jt. ed. see McElroy, Charles H.

***Lientz.** 2000 Strategic Planning Manual. Orig. Title: 1999 Budget & Planning Workbook. 2000. pap. text. write for info. (*0-15-607113-4*) Harcourt.

***Lientz, Bennet P.** Business Process Improvement, 2000. 1999. pap. 75.00 (*0-15-606966-0*) Acad Pr.

Lientz, Bennet P. Guide to Successful Project Management. 98th ed. (Illus.). 435p. (C). 1998. pap. 65.00 (*0-15-606300-X*, Pub. by Harcourt Coll Pubs) Harcourt.

— How to Plan & Implement Business Process Improvement: 2000. 1999. pap. text 75.00 (*0-15-606965-2*) Harcourt.

— How to Plan & Implement Business Process Improvement: 2000. 1998. pap. 65.00 (*0-15-606083-3*, Pub. by Harcourt Coll Pubs) Harcourt.

— 1999 Strategic Systems Planning & Management, 1999. 350p. 1999. pap. text 65.00 (*0-15-606075-2*) Harcourt.

— On Time Technology Implementation: How to Achieve Implementation Success with Limited Time. 285p. 1999. pap. text 44.95 (*0-12-449975-9*) Acad Pr.

***Lientz, Bennet P.** Strategic Systems Planning & Management, 1999 Ed. 1999. pap. text 65.00 (*0-15-606093-0*) Assessment Sys.

— 2001 Professional's Guide to Process Improvement. 500p. 2000. pap. 99.00 (*0-15-607239-4*) Harcourt.

Lientz, Bennet P. & Rea, Kathryn. Breakthrough Technology Project Management. LC 98-84983. (Illus.). 289p. (C). 1998. pap. 44.95 (*0-12-449970-8*) Acad Pr.

Lientz, Bennet P. & Rea, Kathryn, eds. Project Management for the 21st Century. 2nd ed. (Illus.). 339p. 1998. pap. text 44.95 (*0-12-449966-X*) Morgan Kaufmann.

***Lientz, Bennet P. & Rea, Kathryn P.** Dynamic E-Business Implementation Management: How to Effectively Manage E-Business Implementation. (Illus.). 266p. 2000. pap. 44.95 (*0-12-449980-5*) Acad Pr.

— Start Right in E-Business: A Step by Step Guide to Successful E-Business Implementation. 234p. 2000. pap. 44.95 (*0-12-449977-5*) Acad Pr.

Lientz, Bennett P. An Introduction to Distributed Systems: Contract Title: Network Services--Managerial Evaluation. (Computer-Business Interface Ser.). 1981. pap. text. write for info. (*0-201-04297-5*) Addison-Wesley.

Lientz, Bennett P. & Swanson, E. Burton. Software Maintenance Management. LC 80-12154. 160p. 1980. pap. text. write for info. (*0-201-04205-3*) Addison-Wesley.

Lientz, Rea. 2000 Guide to Successful Projects. 600p. (C). 1999. pap. text 75.00 (*0-15-607010-3*) Harcourt.

***Liep, John.** Locating Cultural Creativity. LC 00-9108. (Anthropology, Culture & Society Ser.). 2000. write for info. (*0-7453-1703-0*) Stylus Pub VA.

Liepa, Alex, ed. see MacDougall, Mary-Katherine.

Liepa, George U., et al, eds. Dietary Proteins: How They Alleviate Disease & Promote Better Health. 296p. 1992. 60.00 (*0-935315-41-1*) Am Oil Chemists.

Liepe, Anita, et al, eds. Castella Maris Baltici II. (Lund Studies in Medieval Archaeology: No. 18). (ENG & GER., Illus.). 247p. 1996. 97.50 (*91-87794-12-8*, Pub. by Almqvist Wiksell) Coronet Bks.

Liepins. Data Quality Control: Theory & Pragmatics. (Statistics: Textbooks & Monographs: Vol. 112). (Illus.). 304p. 1990. text 135.00 (*0-8247-8354-9*) Dekker.

Liepins, Raimond, jt. auth. see Ku, Chen C.

Liepitz, Susan. That Wilder Man. 1997. per. 3.50 (*0-373-25752-X*, 1-25752-6) Harlequin Bks.

Liepitz, Susan L. Mystic Memories. 1998. mass mkt. 5.99 (*0-515-12262-9*, Jove) Berkley Pub.

— This Time Together. (Time Passages Ser.). 352p. 1996. mass mkt. 5.99 (*0-515-11981-4*, Jove) Berkley Pub.

Liepkalns, Arturs, ed. see Latvian Evangelical Lutheran Church in America Sta.

Liepman, Ruth. Maybe Luck Isn't Just Chance. Broadwin, John, tr. LC 97-39708. 150p. 1998. 39.95 (*0-8101-1294-9*); pap. 15.95 (*0-8101-1295-7*) Northwestern U Pr.

Liepmann, Clara M., jt. auth. see Van de Wall, William.

Liepmann, Hans W. & Narashima, R., eds. Turbulence Management & Relaminarisation. (Illus.). xxiii, 550p. 1987. 99.00 (*0-387-18574-7*) Spr-Verlag.

Liepmann, Heinrich. Tariff Levels & the Economic Unity of Europe: An Examination of Tariff Policy Export Movements & the Economic Integration of Europe 1913-1931. Stenning, H., tr. from GER. LC 79-12741. (Studies in International Economics: No. 3). (Illus.). 424p. 1980. reprint ed. lib. bdg. 49.50 (*0-87991-852-7*) Porcupine Pr.

Liepmann, Kate K. The Journey to Work: Its Significance for Industrial & Community Life. LC 73-13403. 1973. lib. bdg. 65.00 (*0-8371-7051-6*, LIJW, Greenwood Pr) Greenwood.

Liepmann, Klaus. The Language of Music. LC 52-12521. 384p. reprint ed. pap. 119.10 (*0-608-10886-3*, AU0015100092) Bks Demand.

Liepmann, Lise. Winning Connections: A Program for On-Target Business Communications. LC 83-7052. (Illus.). 252p. 1984. write for info. (*0-672-52743-X*) Macmillan.

Liepmann, Moritz. Krieg und Kriminalitat in Deutschland. (Wirtschafts-Und Sozialgeschichte des Weltkrieges (Osterreichische Und Ungarische Serie)). (GER.). 1930. 100.00 (*0-317-27496-1*) Elliots Bks.

Liepsch, Dieter W., ed. Biofluid Mechanics: Blood Flow in Large Vessels: Proceeding of the Second International Symposium, June 25-18, 1989. (Illus.). 500p. 1991. 118.95 (*0-387-52730-3*) Spr-Verlag.

— Blood Flow in Large Arteries: Applications to Atherogenesis & Clinical Medicine. (Monographs on Atherosclerosis: Vol. 15). (Illus.). viii, 288p. 1989. 235.00 (*3-8055-4983-0*) S Karger.

Lier, A. Peter. Tax & EC Harmonization. 1993. pap. text 70.50 (*90-6544-709-1*) Kluwer Academic.

Lier, Aida W., jt. auth. see Barraza, Ruth A.

Lier, Bruno, et al. Bruno Lier: Ad Topica Carminum Amatorium Symbolae, Repr. of 1914 Ed. Commager, Steele, ed. LC 77-70837. (Latin Poetry Ser.). 1978. lib. bdg. 31.00 (*0-8240-2973-9*) Garland.

Lier, Hubert N. Van, see Van Lier, Hubert N., ed.

Lier, Hubert N. Van, see Cook, E. A. & Van Lier, Hubert N.

Lier, Leo Van, see Van Lier, Leo.

Lierde, S. Van, see Van Lierde, S.

Liere, Alan. Bear Heads & Fish Tales. (Illus.). 144p. (Orig.). 1989. pap. 9.95 (*0-916771-05-9*) Alaska Angler.

— Bear Heads & Fish Tales. Batin, Christopher M., ed. LC 88-70823. (Illus.). 140p. (Orig.). 1990. pap. 9.95 (*0-916771-25-3*, SK33.L5) Alaska Angler.

— Dancin' with Shirley. 202p. 1998. pap. 14.95 (*0-9652697-1-X*) Pease Mtn.

Liere, Alan W. And Pandemonium Rained. LC 96-92318. (Illus.). 208p. (Orig.). 1996. pap. 14.95 (*0-9652697-0-1*) Pease Mtn.

Liere, Eldon N. Van, see Van Liere, Eldon N.

Liere, Eldon N. Van, see Omoto, Sadayoshi & Van Liere, Eldon N.

Liere, R. Van, see de leeuw, W. C. & Van Liere, R., eds.

Liere, R. Van, see Mulder, J. D. & Van Liere, R., eds.

Lierena, Mario. La Honda de David. LC 94-72078. (Coleccion Cuba y sus Jueces). 208p. 1994. pap. 19.00 (*0-89729-747-4*) Ediciones.

Lierley, Joyce M. Affectionately Yours: Three English Immigrants, the American Civil War & a Michigan Family Saga. LC 99-182119. (Illus.). 400p. 1998. pap. 22.50 (*0-9631699-8-X*) Making Hist.

Lierman, Terry, ed. Building a Healthy America: Conquering Disease & Disability. 2nd rev. ed. 248p. 1987. 49.00 (*0-913113-12-3*) M Liebert.

Liermann, Sheila. Unconditional Love in Sun Valley: Pets & Their People. (Illus.). 160p. 1998. pap. 17.00 (*0-9649428-2-8*) Lost Trail.

Liermann, Sheila & Reid, Nancy. Austin & Hill Country Celebrity Cookbook. (Illus.). 160p. (Orig.). 1996. pap. 20.00 (*0-9649428-1-X*) Lost Trail.

— Utah Celebrity & Local Heroes Cookbook. (Illus.). 144p. (Orig.). 1995. pap. 20.00 (*0-9649428-0-1*) Lost Trail.

***Liersch, Anne.** A House Is Not a Home. LC 99-18978. (Illus.). 32p. (J). (ps-k). 1999. 15.95 (*0-7358-1156-3*, Pub. by North-South Bks NYC) Chronicle Bks.

***Liersch, Anne, et al.** A House Is Not a Home. LC 99-18978. 32p. (J). (gr. k-3). 1999. lib. bdg. 15.88 (*0-7358-1157-1*, Pub. by North-South Bks NYC) Chronicle Bks.

Lierse, W. Applied Anatomy of the Pelvis. (Illus.). 350p. 1987. 544.00 (*0-387-16750-1*) Spr-Verlag.

Lierse, W., ed. European Anatomical Congress: Sixth Congress Abstracts. (Journal: Acta Anatomica: Vol. 3, No. 1-2). 176p. 1981. pap. 137.50 (*3-8055-3463-9*) S Karger.

Lierse, W. & Beck, F., eds. Studies of the Normal & Abnormal Development of the Nervous System. (Bibliotheca Anatomica Ser.: No. 19). (Illus.). 1980. pap. 162.75 (*3-8055-1039-X*) S Karger.

Lies, Betty. My Ticket to Tomorrow: Activities for Exploring the Past, Present & Future. LC 97-225319. 1997. pap. 15.95 (*1-55591-285-0*) Fulcrum Pub.

Lies, Betty B. Earth's Daughters: Stories of Women in Classical Mythology. LC 98-47862. 1999. pap. 16.95 (*1-55591-414-4*) Fulcrum Pub.

Lies, Brian. Hamlet & the Enormous Chinese Dragon Kite. (Illus.). 32p. (J). 1994. 14.95 (*0-395-68391-2*) HM.

Lies, Eugene T. The New Leisure Challenges for the Schools. 1982. 24.95 (*0-8434-0425-6*) McGrath NH.

Lies, Jalon E. Friends in My Neighborhood, Vol. 1, Bk. 2. Holland, David, ed. (Illus.). (J). (ps-2). 1996. 7.50 (*1-889994-01-4*) For His Kingdom.

— God's Heart, Vol. 1, Bk. 1. Holland, David, ed. (Illus.). (J). (ps-2). 1996. 7.50 (*1-889994-00-6*) For His Kingdom.

— Jesus, Vol. 2, Bk. 1. Holland, David, ed. (Illus.). (J). (ps-2). 1996. 7.50 (*1-889994-02-2*) For His Kingdom.

— My Best Friend, Vol. 2, Bk. 2. Holland, David, ed. (Illus.). (J). (ps-2). 1996. 7.50 (*1-889994-03-0*) For His Kingdom.

Liesbrock, Heinz. Edward Hopper: Forty Masterworks. (Schirmer's Visual Library). (Illus.). 120p. 1998. pap. 13.95 (*0-393-30764-6*, Norton Paperbks) Norton.

Liesbrock, Heinz, jt. ed see Weski, Thomas.

Liesch, Barry. The New Worship: Straight Talk on Music & the Church. LC 95-2576. (Illus.). 272p. (Orig.). 1995. pap. 15.99 (*0-8010-9001-6*) Baker Bks.

Liesch, Peter. Government Mandated Countertrade: Deals of Arm Twisting. 186p. 1991. 82.95 (*1-85628-266-X*, Pub. by Avebry) Ashgate Pub Co.

Liese, Andreas. Industrial Biotransformations: A Collection of Processes. 276p. 1994. text 125.00 (*3-527-30094-5*) Wiley.

Liese, B., ed. Classical Swine Fever & Related Viral Infections. (Developments in Veterinary Virology Ser.). (C). 1987. text 159.00 (*0-89838-969-0*) Kluwer Academic.

Liesen, Dieter, ed. Physics with Multiply Charged Ions: Proceedings of a NATO ASI Held in Cargese, France, July 18-30, 1994, Vol. 348. (NATO ASI Ser.: Vol. 349). (Illus.). 376p. (C). 1995. text 125.00 (*0-306-45114-X*, Kluwer Plenum) Kluwer Academic.

***Liesen, Jan.** Full of Praise: An Exegetical Study of Sir 39, 12-35. LC 99-54802. (Supplements to the Journal for the Study of Judaism Ser.). 1999. write for info. (*90-04-11359-2*) Brill Academic Pubs.

Liesener, James W. Instruments for Planning & Evaluating Library Media Programs. rev. ed. 1991. pap. 10.00 (*0-911808-15-9*) U of Md Lib Serv.

Liesenfeld, Vincent J. The Licensing Act of 1737. LC 84-40153. (Illus.). 272p. 1984. text 29.95 (*0-299-09810-9*) U of Wis Pr.

— The Licensing Act of 1737. LC 84-40153. 275p. reprint ed. pap. 85.30 (*0-608-20449-8*, 207170200002) Bks Demand.

Lieser, K. H. Nuclear- & Radiochemistry: Fundamentals & Applications. LC 98-113375. 472p. 1997. 260.00 (*3-527-29453-8*, Wiley-VCH) Wiley.

Lieshout, Cornelis F. M. Van, see Van Lieshout, Cornelis F. M.

Lieshout, M. N. Van, see Van Lieshout, M. N.

Lieshout, Robert H. Between Anarchy & Hierarchy: A Theory of International Politics & Foreign Policy. LC 95-30786. (Illus.). 240p. 1995. 85.00 (*1-85898-196-4*) E Elgar.

— The Struggle for the Organization of Europe: The Foundations of the European Union. LC 99-13612. 224p. 1999. 75.00 (*1-85898-975-2*) E Elgar.

Lieske, Ewald & Myers, Robert. Coral Reef Fishes: Caribbean, Indian Ocean, & Pacific Ocean: Including the Red Sea. LC 96-10786. Orig. Title: Collins Pocket Guide to Coral Reef fishes. (Illus.). 400p. 1996. reprint ed. 35.00 (*0-691-02659-9*, Pub. by Princeton U Pr) Cal Prin Full Svc.

Lieske, Jay H. & Abalakin, Victor K., eds. Inertial Coordinate System on the Sky. (C). 1990. pap. text 86.00 (*0-7923-0787-9*); lib. bdg. 193.00 (*0-7923-0786-0*) Kluwer Academic.

Liess, B., et al, eds. Ruminant Pestivirus Infections: Virology, Pathogenesis, & Perspectives of Prophylaxis. (Archives of Virology Ser.: Supplementum 3). (Illus.). viii, 271p. 1993. 175.00 (*0-387-82279-8*) Spr-Verlag.

Liess, Otto. Conical Refraction & Higher Microlocalization. (Lecture Notes in Mathematics Ser.: Vol. 1555). x, 389p. 1993. pap. write for info. (*3-540-57105-1*) Spr-Verlag.

— Conical Refraction & Higher Microlocalization. LC 93-26024. (Lecture Notes in Mathematics Ser.: Vol. 1555). x, 389 p. 1993. 69.95 (*0-387-57105-1*) Spr-Verlag.

Liestman, Linda. 1993-1994 North American Horsemen's Association Safety (Risk Reduction) (NAHA Risk Reduction Ser.). 96p. 1993. pap. text 30.00 (*1-887811-06-0*) N Amer Horsemens.

— Welcome to the Wonderful World of Horses! What a Beginner Needs to Know. 56p. (YA). (gr. 5 up). 1994. pap. text 6.00 (*1-887811-09-5*) N Amer Horsemens.

Liestman, Linda, ed. North American Horsemen's Association Safety Progam Catalog. (NAHA Risk Reduction Ser.). 11p. 1987. pap. text 15.00 (*1-887811-00-1*) N Amer Horsemens.

— North American Horsemen's Association Safety Program Catalog. (NAHA Risk Reduction Ser.). 25p. 1990. pap. text 15.00 (*1-887811-01-X*) N Amer Horsemens.

— North American Horsemen's Association Safety Progam Catalog. (NAHA Risk Reduction Ser.). 34p. 1991. pap. text 15.00 (*1-887811-02-8*) N Amer Horsemens.

— North American Horsemen's Association Safety (Risk Management) Program Catalog. (NAHA Risk Reduction Ser.). 56p. 1992. pap. text 15.00 (*1-887811-04-4*) N Amer Horsemens.

— North American Horsemen's Association 1990 Yearbook. (NAHA Yearbook Ser.). 47p. 1991. pap. text 3.00 (*1-887811-03-6*) N Amer Horsemens.

— North American Horsemen's Association 1991 Yearbook. (NAHA Yearbook Ser.). 54p. 1992. pap. text 3.00 (*1-887811-05-2*) N Amer Horsemens.

— North American Horsemen's Association 1992-1993 Yearbook. (NAHA Yearbook Ser.). 68p. 1994. pap. text 4.00 (*1-887811-08-7*) N Amer Horsemens.

— North American Horsemen's Association 1994 Yearbook. (NAHA Yearbook Ser.). 62p. 1994. pap. text 4.00 (*1-887811-07-9*) N Amer Horsemens.

— North American Horsemen's Association 1995 Risk Reduction Programs & Contracts & Agreements. (NAHA Risk Reduction Ser.). 109p. 1995. pap. text 20.00 (*1-887811-10-9*) N Amer Horsemens.

— North American Horsemen's Association 1995 Yearbook. (NAHA Yearbook Ser.). 78p. 1995. pap. text 4.00 (*1-887811-11-7*) N Amer Horsemens.

L

L

Liestman, Vicki. Columbus Day. (Holiday on My Own Ser.). (Illus.). 56p. (J). (gr. k-3). 1991. lib. bdg. 18.60 (0-87614-444-X, Carolrhoda) Lerner Pub.
— Columbus Day. (Illus.). 56p. (J). (gr. k-3). 1992. pap. 5.95 (0-87614-559-4, Carolrhoda) Lerner Pub.
Liesz, ed. Principles of Managerial Finance: Student Lecture Notes. 7th ed. 448p. (C). 1997. pap. text 18.00 (0-06-502329-3) Addison-Wesley.
Lietaer, G., et al, eds. Client-Centered & Experiential Psychotherapy in the Nineties. 863p. (Orig.). 1990. pap. 77.50 (90-6186-364-3, Pub. by Leuven Univ) Coronet Bks.
Lietchi, Elaine. Health Essentials: Shiatsu: Japanese Massage for Health & Fitness. (Health Essentials Ser.). (Illus.). 128p. 1998. pap. 9.95 (1-86204-094-X, Pub. by Element MA) Penguin Putnam.
Lieten, G. K. Continuity & Change in Rural West Bengal. 1993. 38.00 (0-8039-9449-4) Sage.
— Dutch Multinational Corporations in India. (C). 1987. 32.50 (81-85054-33-9, Pub. by Manohar) S Asia.
Lieten, G. K., et al, eds. Women, Migrants & Tribals: Survival Strategies in Asia. (C). 1989. 22.50 (81-85054-77-0, Pub. by Manohar) S Asia.
Lieten, Georges K. Development, Devolution & Democracy: Village Discourse in West Bengal. LC 96-3336. (Indo-Dutch Studies on Development Alternatives). 1996. 32.50 (0-8039-9339-0) Sage.
— The First Communist Ministry in Kerala, 1957-1959. 1983. 15.00 (0-8364-0976-0, Pub. by KP Bagchi) S Asia.
Lieten, Georges K. & Srivastava, Ravi. Unequal Partners: Power Relations, Devolution & Development in Uttar Pradesh. LC 98-37837. (Indo-Dutch Studies on Development Alternatives). 1998. write for info. (0-7619-9289-8) Sage.
Lieter, Bernard A. European Multinationals in Latin America: A Positive Sum Game for the Exchange of Raw Materials & Technology in the 1980's. LC 79-91943. (Praeger Special Studies). 273p. 1980. 65.00 (0-275-90513-6, C0513, Praeger Pubs) Greenwood.
Lieth, H., ed. Effects of Atmospheric & Geophysical Variables in Biology & Medicine, Vol. 8. (Illus.). vii, 144p. 1991. pap. 45.00 (90-5103-061-4, Pub. by SPB Acad Pub) Balogh.
Lieth, H., et al, eds. Correlation Analyses Between Weatherclasses & Blood Sedimentation Rate Fluctuations of a Population Sample in Leiden, The Netherlands, Vol. 10. LC 96-209292. xxi, 120p. 1996. 50.00 (90-5103-120-3, Pub. by SPB Acad Pub) Balogh.
***Lieth, H., et al, eds.** Halophyte Uses in Different Climates I. (Ecological & Ecophysiological Studies). (Illus.). 270p. 1999. pap. 75.00 (90-5782-038-2, PiB 13, Pub. by Backhuys Pubs) Balogh.
Lieth, H. & Schwartz, M. D., eds. Progress in Biometeorology Vol. 12: Phenology in Seasonal Climates. LC 97-218588. (Illus.). 143p. (C). 1997. pap. 43.00 (90-73348-79-X, Pub. by Backhuys Pubs) Balogh.
Lieth, Helmut & Lohmann, Martina, eds. Restoration of Tropical Forest Ecosystems. LC 92-33607. (Tasks for Vegetation Science Ser.). 272p. 1993. text 233.00 (0-7923-1945-1) Kluwer Academic.
Lieth, Helmut & Massoum, Ahmed A., eds. Towards Rational Use of High Salinity Tolerant Plants: Agriculture & Forestry under Marginal Soil Water Conditions. LC 92-22601. No. 28. 1993. text 335.00 (0-7923-1866-8) Kluwer Academic.
— Towards Rational Use of High Salinity Tolerant Plants Vol. 1: Deliberations about High Salinity Tolerant Plants & Ecosystems. 1992. text 403.00 (0-7923-1865-X) Kluwer Academic.
Lieth, Helmut & Werger, Marinus J., eds. Tropical Rain Forest Ecosystems: Biogeographical & Ecological Studies. (Ecosystems of the World Ser.: Vol. 14B). 714p. 1989. 405.75 (0-444-42755-4) Elsevier.
Lieth, Helmut & Whittaker, R. H., eds. Primary Productivity of the Biosphere. LC 74-26627. (Ecological Studies: Vol. 14). (Illus.). 350p. 1975. 175.00 (0-387-07083-4) Spr-Verlag.
Lieth, Helmut, jt. ed. see Pandeya, S. C.
Lieth, Ronald M., ed. Preparation & Crystal Growth of Materials with Layered Structures. (Physics & Chemistry of Materials with Layered Structures Ser.: Vol. 1). 200p. 1977. text 176.50 (90-277-0638-7) Kluwer Academic.
Lietty Raventos de Pubillones Staff. Modales y Vida Social: Preguntas y Respuestas. (SPA.). 157p. (Orig.). 1994. pap. 9.95 (0-931839-19-X) Miami Herald.
***Lietz, Petra & Kotte, Dieter.** The Importance of Economic Literacy. xv, 142p. 2000. pap. 29.95 (0-8204-4740-4) P Lang Pubng.
Lietz, Robert. At Park & East Division. LC 81-8430. 76p. 1981. 7.95 (0-934332-33-9); pap. 4.25 (0-934332-32-0) LEpervier Pr.
— The Inheritance. LC 85-50682. (Plains Poetry Ser.: Vol. 5). 72p. (Orig.). 1988. pap. 6.95 (0-911015-15-9) Sandhills Pr.
— The Lindbergh Half-Century. (Poetry Ser.). 75p. (Orig.). (C). 1987. pap. 8.00 (0-934332-47-9) LEpervier Pr.
Lietz, Robert C., 3rd, ed. see Chestnut, Charles W.
Lietze, Ernst. Modern Heliographic Processes. 1974. pap. 7.95 (0-87992-000-9) Visual Studies.
Lietzman, Hans. Apollinaris von Laodicea und seine Schule: Texte und Untersuchungen. LC 82-45817. (Orthodoxies & Heresies in the Early Church Ser.). reprint ed. 37.50 (0-404-62390-5) AMS Pr.
Lietzmann, Hans. Apollinaris Von Laodicea und Seine Schule. xvi, 323p. 1970. reprint ed. write for info. (0-318-70966-X) G Olms Pubs.
— Geschichte der Alten Kirche, 4 vols. in 1. 1220p. (C). 1975. reprint ed. 167.70 (3-11-004625-3) De Gruyter.
Lietzmann, Kurt M., jt. ed. see Carius, Alexander.
Lietzmann, Sabina. New York. LC 81-7564. (Illus.). 80p. 1999. pap. 19.95 (0-86565-023-3) Vendome.
Lieu, Bing H. Digital Computer Programming: Principles, Techniques, & Applications. (Illus.). 1990. 7.75 (0-8446-5059-5) Peter Smith.
Lieu, Judith. The Jews among Pagans & Christians: In the Roman Empire. 216p. (C). 1992. text 60.00 (0-415-04972-5, Pub. by Tavistock) Routldge.
— The Second & Third Epistles of John. 280p. 1987. 47.95 (0-567-09443-X, Pub. by T & T Clark) Bks Intl VA.
— The Second & Third Epistles of John: History & Background. (Early Christianity & Patristics/New Testament Studies). 288p. 1998. pap. 29.95 (0-567-08630-5, Pub. by T & T Clark) Bks Intl VA.
— The Theology of the Johannine Epistles. (New Testament Theology Ser.). 142p. (C). 1991. text 54.95 (0-521-35246-0); pap. text 16.95 (0-521-35806-X) Cambridge U Pr.
Lieu, Judith, et al, eds. The Jews among Pagans & Christians: In the Roman Empire. 216p. (C). 1994. pap. 22.99 (0-415-11448-9, B4737) Routledge.
Lieu, Judith M. Image & Reality: The Jews in the World of the Christians in the Second Century. (Early Christianity & Patristics/New Testament Studies). 362p. 1998. 49.95 (0-567-08529-5, Pub. by T & T Clark) Bks Intl VA.
Lieu Quoc Nhi. Duong Tinh Doinga. 314p. (Orig.). 1994. pap. 14.00 (1-886535-02-7) Dong Van.
— Hoang Hon Cuoi Cung. 326p. (Orig.). 1994. pap. 14.00 (1-886535-01-9) Dong Van.
Lieu Quoc Nhi, tr. see Quynh Dao.
Lieu, Samuel & Montserrat, Dominic, eds. Constantine: History Historiography & Legend. LC 97-45571. 264p. (C). 1998. 75.00 (0-415-10747-4) Routledge.
Lieu, Samuel N. Manichaeism in Central Asia & China. LC 97-47631. (Nag Hammadi & Manichaean Studies). 1998. 97.00 (90-04-10405-4) Brill Academic Pubs.
— Manichaeism in Mesopotamia & the Roman East. LC BT1410.L46 1994. (Religions in the Graeco-Roman World Ser.: Vol. 118). 325p. 1994. 113.50 (90-04-09742-2) Brill Academic Pubs.
— Manichaeism in the Later Roman Empire & Medieval China. (WissUNT Neuen Testament Ser.: No. 63). 400p. 1992. 117.50 (3-16-145820-6, Pub. by JCB Mohr) Coronet Bks.
Lieu, Samuel N., ed. The Emperor Julian: Panegyric & Polemic. 2nd ed. (Translated Texts for Historians Ser.). 160p. (C). 1992. reprint ed. pap. text 16.95 (0-85323-376-4, Pub. by Liverpool Univ Pr) U of Pa Pr.
Lieu, Samuel N. & Montserrat, Dominic. From Constantine to Julian: A Source History. LC 95-283. 320p. (C). (gr. 13). 1995. 80.00 (0-415-09335-X) Routledge.
— From Constantine to Julian: A Source History. LC 95-283. 320p. (C). 1996. pap. 25.99 (0-415-09336-8) Routledge.
Lieu, Samuel N., jt. ed. see Dodgeon, Michael H.
***Lieurance, Suzanne.** Shoelaces. LC 99-23554. (Rookie Readers Ser.). (Illus.). (J). 2000. 17.50 (0-516-21613-9) Childrens.
— Shoelaces. (Rookie Readers Ser.). (Illus.). 32p. (J). (gr. 1-2). 2000. pap. 4.95 (0-516-26546-6) Childrens.
Lieurance, Suzanne, jt. auth. see Harkrader, Lisa.
Lieure, Jules. Callot's Graphic Work: A Catalogue Raisonne, 2 vols. (FRE., Illus.). 1989. reprint ed. 295.00 (1-55660-028-3) A Wofsy Fine Arts.
Lieuwen, Edwin. Mexican Militarism: The Political Rise & Fall of the Revolutionary Army, 1910-1940. LC 80-28937. (Illus.). 194p. 1981. reprint ed. lib. bdg. 59.50 (0-313-22911-2, LIMM, Greenwood Pr) Greenwood.
— Venezuela. LC 85-24781. 222p. 1986. reprint ed. lib. bdg. 59.50 (0-313-24979-2, LIVE, Greenwood Pr) Greenwood.
Lieux, Elizabeth. Exploring Food Production. 136p. (C). 1995. spiral bd. 15.95 (0-7872-1538-4) Kendall-Hunt.
***Lieux, Elizabeth M. & Luoto, Patricia K.** Exploring Quantity Food Production & Service. 2nd ed. 144p. 1999. pap. text 25.00 (0-13-083534-X, Prentice Hall) P-H.
Lievano, M. Francisco, tr. see Bennett, Rita & Bennett, Dennis.
Lievano, M. Francisco, tr. see Cho, David Y.
Lievano, M. Francisco, tr. see Foster, Richard.
Lievano, M. Francisco, tr. see Lindsey, Hal.
Lievano, M. Francisco, tr. see Ogilvie, Lloyd J.
***Lievanos, Daniel.** Pardon Me, But Aren't You... ? LC 99-96743. 2000. pap. 8.95 (0-533-13344-0) Vantage.
Lieve. Targeted Inactivation ("Knock-Out") of the Mouse Genes Coding for the Alpha-2-Macroglobulin & for the A2M Receptor Associated Protein. (Acta Biomedica Lovaniensia Ser.: No. 123). (Illus.). 137p. (Orig.). 1996. pap. 43.50 (90-6186-728-2, Pub. by Leuven Univ) Coronet Bks.
Lievegoed, B. C. Mystery Streams in Europe & the New Mysteries. Van Houten, J. M. et al, trs. from DUT. 87p. (Orig.). 1982. pap. 8.95 (0-88010-002-8) Anthroposophic.
Lievegoed, Bernard. Battle for the Soul: The Working Together of Three Great Leaders of Humanity. Mees, Philip, tr. 144p. 1995. 15.95 (1-869890-64-7, Pub. by Hawthorn Press) Anthroposophic.
— Developing Communities. 1991. 19.95 (1-869890-30-2, Pub. by Hawthorn Press) Anthroposophic.
— Eye of the Needle: His Life & Working Encounter with Anthroposophy. Mees, Philip, tr. 103p. 1995. pap. 14.95 (1-869890-50-7, Pub. by Hawthorn Press) Anthroposophic.
— Phases: The Spiritual Rhythms of Adult Life. 4th ed. Lake, H. S., tr. from GER. 1993. pap. 16.95 (1-85584-056-1, 388, Pub. by R Steiner Pr) Anthroposophic.
— Phases of Childhood: Growing in Body Soul & Spirit. 2nd ed. (Illus.). 204p. 1997. pap. 15.95 (0-88010-446-5, 644) Anthroposophic.
Lieven, Anatol. The Baltic Revolution: Estonia, Latvia, Lithuania & the Path to Independence. (Illus.). 496p. (C). 1994. pap. 18.00 (0-300-06078-5) Yale U Pr.
— Chechnya: Tombstone of Russian Power. LC 98-84479. (Illus.). 436p. 1998. 35.00 (0-300-07398-4) Yale U Pr.
— Chechnya: Tombstone of Russian Power. LC 98-84479. (Illus.). 436p. 1999. pap. text 16.95 (0-300-07881-1) Yale U Pr.
— Ukraine & Russia: A Fraternal Rivalry. LC 99-12974. (Illus.). 208p. 1999. pap. 19.95 (1-878379-87-9) US Inst Peace.
Lieven, Dominic C. The Aristocracy in Europe, 1815-1914. 308p. (C). 1994. pap. 19.00 (0-231-08113-8) Col U Pr.
— Nicholas II. 304p. 1996. pap. 16.95 (0-312-14379-6) St Martin.
— Russia's Rulers Before the Revolution. LC 88-38155. 384p. 1989. 50.00 (0-300-04371-6) Yale U Pr.
— Russia's Rulers under the Old Regime. (Illus.). 384p. (C). 1991. reprint ed. pap. 22.00 (0-300-04937-4) Yale U Pr.
Lieven, Michael. Senghennydd: The Universal Pit Village, 1890-1930. 387p. 1994. 52.95 (0-8464-4701-0) Beekman Pubs.
— Senghennydd: The Universal Pit Village, 1890-1930. LC 95-194795. 387p. 1994. 53.00 (1-85902-043-7, Pub. by Gomer Pr) St Mut.
Lieven, Richard Van, see Van Lieven, Richard.
***Lievense, Kathleen B.** Encore: A Collection of Poems. 1999. pap. write for info. (1-58235-360-3) Watermrk Pr.
Lievense, Kathleen B. A Potpourri of Poetry. 1998. pap. write for info. (1-57553-705-2) Watermrk Pr.
***Lievesley, Geraldine.** Democracy in Latin America. 240p. 1999. pap. 24.95 (0-7190-4311-5, Pub. by Manchester Univ Pr); text 69.95 (0-7190-4310-7, Pub. by Manchester Univ Pr) St Martin.
Lievesley, Geraldine, jt. ed. see Rai, Shirin M.
***Lieveuse, James D.** Sweat the Small Stuff: A Comprehensive Approach to Improving Your Independent Insurance Agency. LC 99-64738. (Illus.). 112p. (Orig.). 1999. pap. 18.85 (0-9674321-0-3) Metro MI.
Lievrouw, Leah A., jt. ed. see Ruben, Brent D.
Lievsay, John L. Elizabethan Image of Italy. LC 64-9036. (Folger Guides to the Age of Shakespeare Ser.). 1964. pap. 4.95 (0-918016-26-6) Folger Bks.
— The Sixteenth Century: Skelton Through Hooker. LC 68-15229. (Goldentree Bibliographies Series in Language & Literature). (C). 1968. pap. text 13.95 (0-88295-520-9) Harlan Davidson.
Lievsay, John L., ed. The Seventeenth-Century Resolve: A Historical Anthology of a Literary Form. fac. ed. LC 79-4004. 221p. 1980. pap. 68.60 (0-7837-7595-4, 204734800007) Bks Demand.
Lievsay, John L., ed. see Tuvill, Daniel.
Liew, F. Y., ed. Vaccination Strategies of Tropical Diseases. 304p. 1989. lib. bdg. 206.00 (0-8493-6189-3, RC119) CRC Pr.
Liew, Julian, jt. auth. see Von Wartberg, Walter P.
Liew, K. M. Vibration of Mindlin Plates: Programming the P-Version Ritz Method. LC 98-41634. 1998. 138.50 (0-08-043341-3) Elsevier.
Liew, Lana. Natural Estrogen Book: A Natural Treatment for the Symptoms of Menopause. 1998. pap. text 11.95 (0-7318-0702-2) Simon & Schuster.
Liew, Lana & Ojeda, Linda. The Natural Estrogen Diet: Healthy Recipes for Perimenopause & Menopause. LC 98-52737. (Illus.). 224p. 1999. reprint ed. pap. 13.95 (0-89793-246-3) Hunter Hse.
Liew, Leong. The Chinese Economy in Transition: From Plan to Market. LC 96-35860. 200p. 1997. 80.00 (1-85898-250-2) E Elgar.
Liew, Richard, jt. ed. see Severino, Sally K.
Liew Shih How. Creation of the Gods. 205p. 1996. 9.95 (981-3029-45-5, Pub. by Asiapac) China Bks.
Liew, Tat-Siong Benny. Politics of Parousia: Reading Mark Intercontextually. LC 99-19920. (Biblical Interpretation Ser.). 192p. 1999. 71.00 (90-04-11360-6) Brill Academic Pubs.
Liewellyn, John, et al. Economic Forecasting & Policy. (International Library of Economics). 256p. 1985. 22.00 (0-7102-0600-3, Routledge Thoemms) Routledge.
Liewes, E. W. Culture, Feeding & Diseases of Commercial Flatfish Species. 112p. 1984. 71.00 (90-6191-291-1, Pub. by A A Balkema) Ashgate Pub Co.
Lifanov, Ivan K. Singular Integral Equations & Discrete Vortices. (Illus.). 486p. 1996. 260.00 (90-6764-207-X, Pub. by VSP) Coronet Bks.
Lifanov, Ivan K., jt. auth. see Belotserkovsky, Sergei M.
Lifchez, Raymond, ed. The Dervish Lodge: Architecture, Art, & Sufism in Ottoman Turkey. 370p. 1996. 50.00 (0-614-21573-0, 196) Kazi Pubns.
— Dervish Lodge: The Architecture, Art, & Sufism in Ottoman Turkey. 370p. 1996. 50.00 (0-614-21263-4, 196) Kazi Pubns.
Lifchitz. Latin America: Its Music & Its People. 2000. 28.00 (0-02-864747-5) S&S Trade.
Life & Work of Christiaan Huygens Symposium Staff. Studies on Christiaan Huygens: Invited Papers of the Symposium, Amsterdam, August 22-25, 1979. Bos, H. J. et al, eds. vi, 321p. 1980. text 69.25 (90-265-0333-4) Swets.
Life Application Study Bible Staff. Biblia del Diario Vivir. (SPA.). 1997. 42.99 (0-89922-416-4); 68.99 (0-89922-421-0) Caribe Betania.
— Biblia Del Diario Vivir. 1997. 62.99 (0-89922-418-0); 62.99 (0-89922-420-2) Caribe Betania.
— Life Application Study Bible. 1997. 89.99 (0-8423-2099-7) Tyndale Hse.
— Life Application Study Bible. 2000. 39.99 (0-8423-4035-1); 64.99 (0-8423-4039-4); 64.99 (0-8423-4040-8) Tyndale Hse.
— Life Application Study Bible. 2000. 69.99 (0-8423-4041-6) Tyndale Hse.
— Life Application Study Bible. 2000. 74.99 (0-310-91101-X); 74.99 (0-310-91161-3) Zondervan.
— Life Application Study Bible. (Illus.). 2000. 84.99 (0-310-91172-9) Zondervan.
***Life Application Study Staff.** Life Appliation Study Bible. 2000. 84.99 (0-310-91164-8, Zondervan Bibles) Zondervan.
Life Applications Staff. Biblia Diario Vivir Negra Elaborada, Indice. 1997. 64.99 (0-89922-419-9) Caribe Betania.
— Biblia Diario Vivir Tapadura 1997. 34.99 (0-89922-415-6) Caribe Betania.
Life, Daniel H., jt. auth. see Friestad, Jennifer G.
***Life Editors.** Life: The Way We Were. (Illus.). 192p. 2000. 29.95 (0-8212-2634-7, Pub. by Bulfinch Pr) Little.
Life Editors. Life 60 Years: An Anniversary Celebration. 192p. 1996. 24.95 (0-8212-2335-6, Pub. by Bulfinch Pr) Little.
Life Extension Staff & Medical Advisary Board Staff & Faloon, William. Disease Prevention & Treatment. 3rd rev. ed. 946p. 2000. pap. 34.95 (0-9658777-4-4, Pub. by Life Ext Media) Midpt Trade.
Life Magazine Editors. The Beatles: From Yesterday to Today. 128p. 1996. 24.95 (0-8212-2317-8, Pub. by Bulfinch Pr) Little.
— The Beatles: From Yesterday to Today. 1995. 24.95 (0-614-96886-0) Little.
— A Dog's Life: A Book of Classic Photographs, Vol. 1. LC 95-77659. (Illus.). 96p. (gr. 8). 1995. 14.95 (0-316-52691-6) Little.
— Enciclopedia Life De la Fotografia, 16 vols., Set. 3650p. 1975. 495.00 (0-8288-5871-3, S50551) Fr & Eur.
— Life: The Millennium: The 100 Most Important Events & People of the Past 1,000 Years. (Illus.). 192p. 1998. 29.95 (0-8212-2557-X, Pub. by Bulfinch Pr) Little.
— Life Carries On: Still More Classic Photographs from the Pages of America's Favorite Magazine. (Illus.). 192p. 1993. pap. 14.00 (0-671-86852-7, Fireside) S&S Trade Pap.
***Life Magazine Editors.** Pope John Paul II. (Illus.). 128p. 2000. 29.95 (0-8212-2677-0, Pub. by Bulfinch Pr) Little.
Life Magazine Editors, ed. Life with Father. LC 94-46902. 96p. (gr. 8). 1995. 15.00 (0-316-52635-5) Little.
— Life with Mother. LC 94-46898. 96p. (gr. 8). 1995. 14.95 (0-316-52636-3) Little.
Life Magazine Editors, jt. auth. see Hirshberg, Charles.
***Life Magazine Staff.** Life Year in Pictures. (Illus.). 2000. 24.95 (1-883013-87-9) Tme Inc.
Life Magazine Staff. LIFE Year in Pictures, 1998. (Illus.). 160p. 1999. 29.95 (1-883013-60-7) Tme Inc.
Life Magazine Staff, ed. Life Legends. 176p. 1998. 27.95 (0-8212-2504-9, Pub. by Bulfinch Pr) Little.
Life Office Management Assn. Staff. Forms Used in Human Resources. Hale, Mary J., ed. LC 97-221189. (Illus.). 656p. 1997. ring bd. 114.95 (1-57444-076-4) St Lucie Pr.
***Life Publisher International Staff, prod.** La Guia, Tomo 3. (SPA., Illus.). 112p. 2000. pap., student ed. write for info. (0-7361-0152-7) Life Pubs Intl.
Life Publishers International Staff. El Companero Alumno, Vol. 9, Sept. 1999. (SPA., Illus.). 48p. (J). (gr. 4-6). 1999. pap. write for info. (0-7361-0064-4) Life Pubs Intl.
— El Companero Alumno, Dec. 1999-Feb. 2000, Vol. 9, Tomo. (SPA., Illus.). 48p. (J). (gr. 4-6). 1999. pap., student ed. write for info. (0-7361-0065-2) Life Pubs Intl.
— El Companero Ayudas Visuales, Sep. 1999-Feb. 2000, No. COM-05. (SPA.). 18p. 1999. pap., teacher ed. write for info. (0-7361-0066-0) Life Pubs Intl.
— El Companero Maestro, Sep. 1999-Feb. 2000, Vol. 9, Tomo. (SPA., Illus.). 112p. 1999. pap., teacher ed. write for info. (0-7361-0067-9) Life Pubs Intl.
***Life Publishers International Staff.** El Companero Alumno, Dec. 2000 to Feb. 2001, Vol. 10. (SPA., Illus.). 48p. (gr. 4-7). 2000. pap., student ed. write for info. (0-7361-0143-8) Life Pubs Intl.
Life Publishers International Staff. El Embajador Alumno, Dec. 1999-Feb. 2000, Vol 9, Tomo. (SPA., Illus.). 48p. (YA). (gr. 10-12). 1999. pap., student ed. write for info. (0-7361-0072-5) Life Pubs Intl.
— El Embajador Alumno, Sep. 1999-Nov. 1999, Vol. 9, Tomo. (SPA.). 48p. (YA). (gr. 10-12). 1999. pap., student ed. write for info. (0-7361-0071-7) Life Pubs Intl.
— El Embajador Maestro, Sept. 1999-, Vol. 9, Tomo. (SPA.). 112p. 1999. pap., teacher ed. write for info. (0-7361-0073-3) Life Pubs Intl.
***Life Publishers International Staff.** El Embajador Maestro, Sept. 2000 to Feb. 2001, Vol. 10. (SPA., Illus.). 112p. 2000. pap., teacher ed. write for info. (0-7361-0147-0) Life Pubs Intl.
Life Publishers International Staff. El Explorador Alumno, Dec. 1999-Feb. 2000, Vol 9, Tomo. (SPA., Illus.). 48p. (YA). (gr. 7-9). 1999. pap., student ed. write for info. (0-7361-0069-5) Life Pubs Intl.
— El Explorador Alumno, Sep. 1999-Nov. 1999, Vol. 9, Tomo. (SPA., Illus.). 48p. (YA). (gr. 7-9). 1999. pap., student ed. write for info. (0-7361-0068-7) Life Pubs Intl.
— El Explorador Maestro, Sep. 1999-Feb. 2000, Vol. 9, Tomo. (SPA., Illus.). 112p. 1999. pap., teacher ed. write for info. (0-7361-0070-9) Life Pubs Intl.
— La Guia, Sep. 1999-Feb. 2000, Tomo 1. (SPA., Illus.). 112p. 1999. pap., student ed. write for info. (0-7361-0076-8) Life Pubs Intl.
— El Maestro, Sep. 1999-Feb. 2000, Tomo 1. (SPA.). 112p. 1999. teacher ed. write for info. (0-7361-0075-X) Life Pubs Intl.

An Asterisk (*) at the beginning of an entry indicates that the title is appearing for the first time.

— El Maestro, Sep. 1999-Feb. 2000, Tomo 1. (SPA., Illus.). 1999. pap., teacher ed. write for info. (*0-7361-0074-1*) Life Pubs Intl.
— Mis Amigos Alumno, Dec 1999 a Feb 2000, Vol. 9 Tomo. (SPA., Illus.). 32p. (J). (gr. 1-3). 1999. pap., student ed. write for info. (*0-7361-0061-X*) Life Pubs Intl.
— Mis Amigos Alumno, Sep 99 a Nov 99, Vol. 9 Tomo. (SPA., Illus.). 32p. (J). (gr. 1-3). 1999. pap., student ed. write for info. (*0-7361-0060-1*) Life Pubs Intl.
— Mis Amigos Ayudas Visuales, Sep 1999 a Feb 2000, No. AMI-01. (SPA., Illus.). 26p. (J). (gr. 1-3). 1999. pap. write for info. (*0-7361-0062-8*) Life Pubs Intl.
— Mis Amigos Maestro, Vol. 9, Sept. 1999. (Illus.). 1999. pap., teacher ed. write for info. (*0-7361-0063-6*) Life Pubs Intl.
— Primeros Pasos II Ayudas Visuales Sep 98 a Feb 99, No. PP2-03. (SPA., Illus.). 28p. (J). (ps-k). 1999. pap. write for info. (*0-7361-0058-X*) Life Pubs Intl.
— Primeros Pasos II Maestro, Sept 99. (SPA., Illus.). 112p. 1999. pap., teacher ed. write for info. (*0-7361-0059-8*) Life Pubs Intl.
— Primeros Pasos II Trabajo Manual, Dec. 1999-Feb. 2000, (SPA., Illus.). 16p. (J). (ps-k). 1999. pap. write for info. (*0-7361-0057-1*) Life Pubs Intl.
— Primeros Pasos II Trabajo Manual, Sept. 99-Nov. 99. (SPA., Illus.). 16p. (J). (ps). 1999. pap. write for info. (*0-7361-0056-3*) Life Pubs Intl.
— Primeros Pasos I Ayudas Visuales, Sep. 1999-Feb. 2000, No. PP1-03. (SPA., Illus.). 28p. (J). 1999. pap. write for info. (*0-7361-0054-7*) Life Pubs Intl.
— Primeros Pasos I Trabajo Manual, Dec 1999-Feb 2000. (SPA., Illus.). 16p. (J). 1999. pap. write for info. (*0-7361-0053-9*) Life Pubs Intl.
— Primeros Pasos I Maestro, Vol. 9 Tomo. (SPA., Illus.). 112p. 1999. pap., teacher ed. write for info. (*0-7361-0055-5*) Life Pubs Intl.
Life Publishers International Staff, ed. Small Group Study Guide Russian Language: Bible Studies for Small Groups. (RUS., Illus.). 1999. pap. write for info. (*0-7361-0080-6*) Life Pubs Intl.
***Life Publishers International Staff, prod.** El Companero Alumno, Vol. 10, No. 3. (Vida Nueva Ser.). (SPA., Illus.). 48p. (J). (gr. 4-6). 2001. pap., student ed. write for info. (*0-7361-0183-7*) Life Pubs Intl.
— El Companero Alumno, Vol. 10, No. 4. (Vida Nueva Ser.). (Illus.). 48p. (J). (gr. 4-6). 2001. pap., student ed. write for info. (*0-7361-0184-5*) Life Pubs Intl.
— El Companero Alumno, Sept. 2000 to Nov. 2000, Vol. 10. (SPA., Illus.). 48p. (gr. 4-7). 2000. pap., student ed. write for info. (*0-7361-0142-X*) Life Pubs Intl.
— El Companero Ayudas Visuales, Vol. Com-2. (Vida Nueva Ser.). (SPA., Illus.). 26p. (J). (gr. 4-6). 2001. pap. write for info. (*0-7361-0182-9*) Life Pubs Intl.
— El Companero Ayudas Visuales, Sept. 2000 to Feb. 2001, Vol. 10. (SPA., Illus.). 18p. 2000. pap., teacher ed. write for info. (*0-7361-0141-1*) Life Pubs Intl.
— El Companero Maestro, Sept. 2000 to Feb. 2001, Vol. 10. (SPA., Illus.). 112p. 2000. pap., teacher ed. write for info. (*0-7361-0140-3*) Life Pubs Intl.
— El Embajador Alumno, Vol. 10, No. 3. (Vida Nueva Ser.). (SPA., Illus.). 48p. (YA). (gr. 10-13). 2001. pap., student ed. write for info. (*0-7361-0189-6*) Life Pubs Intl.
— El Embajador Alumno, Vol. 10, No. 4. (Vida Nueva Ser.). (SPA., Illus.). 48p. (YA). (gr. 10-12). 2001. pap., student ed. write for info. (*0-7361-0190-X*) Life Pubs Intl.
— El Embajador Alumno, Dec. 2000 to Feb. 2001, Vol. 10. (SPA., Illus.). 48p. (gr. 10-12). 2000. pap., student ed. write for info. (*0-7361-0149-7*) Life Pubs Intl.
— El Embajador Alumno, Sept. 2000 to Nov. 2000. (Illus.). 48p. (gr. 10-12). 2000. pap., student ed. write for info. (*0-7361-0148-9*) Life Pubs Intl.
— El Embajador Maestro, Vol. 10. (Vida Nueva Ser.). (SPA., Illus.). 112p. 2001. pap., teacher ed. write for info. (*0-7361-0188-8*) Life Pubs Intl.
— El Explorado Alumno, Vol. 10, No. 4. (Vida Nueva Ser.). (SPA., Illus.). 48p. (YA). (gr. 7-9). 2001. pap., student ed. write for info. (*0-7361-0187-X*) Life Pubs Intl.
— El Explorador Alumno, Vol. 10, No. 3. (Vida Nueva Ser.). (SPA., Illus.). 48p. (YA). (gr. 7-9). 2001. pap., student ed. write for info. (*0-7361-0186-1*) Life Pubs Intl.
— El Explorador Alumno, Dec. 2000 to Feb. 2001, Vol. 10. (SPA., Illus.). 48p. (gr. 7-9). 2000. pap. write for info. (*0-7361-0146-2*) Life Pubs Intl.
— El Explorador Alumno, Sept. 2000 to Nov. 2000, Vol. 10. (Illus.). 48p. (gr. 7-9). 2000. pap., student ed. write for info. (*0-7361-0145-4*) Life Pubs Intl.
— El Explorador Maestro, Vol. 10. (Vida Nueva Ser.). (SPA., Illus.). 112p. (YA). (gr. 7-9). 2001. pap. write for info. (*0-7361-0185-3*) Life Pubs Intl.
— El Explorador Maestro, Sept. 2000 to Feb. 2001, Vol. 10. (SPA., Illus.). 112p. 2000. pap., teacher ed. write for info. (*0-7361-0144-6*) Life Pubs Intl.
— La Guia. (Vida Nueva Ser.). (SPA., Illus.). 112p. 2001. pap. write for info. (*0-7361-0193-4*) Life Pubs Intl.
— El Maestro, Vol. 4. (Vida Nueva Ser.). (SPA., Illus.). 207p. 2001. teacher ed., boxed set. write for info. (*0-7361-0191-8*); pap., teacher ed. write for info. (*0-7361-0192-6*) Life Pubs Intl.
— El Maestro, Sept. 2000 to Feb. 2001, Tomo 3. (SPA., Illus.). 207p. 2000. teacher ed. write for info. (*0-7361-0151-9*); pap., boxed set. write for info. (*0-7361-0150-0*) Life Pubs Intl.
— Mis Amigos Alumno, Dec. 2000 to Feb. 2001, Vol. 10. (SPA., Illus.). 32p. (gr. 1-3). 2000. pap., student ed. write for info. (*0-7361-0139-X*) Life Pubs Intl.
— Mis Amigos Alumno, Sept. 2000 to Nov. 2000, Vol. 10. (SPA., Illus.). 32p. (gr. 1-3). 2000. pap., student ed. write for info. (*0-7361-0138-1*) Life Pubs Intl.
— Mis Amigos Ayudas Visuales, Vol. 10. (SPA., Illus.). 26p. 2000. pap., teacher ed. write for info. (*0-7361-0137-3*) Life Pubs Intl.
— Mis Amigos Maestro, Sept. 2000 to Feb. 2001, Vol. 10. (SPA., Illus.). 112p. 2000. pap., teacher ed. write for info. (*0-7361-0136-5*) Life Pubs Intl.
— Primeros Pasos I Ayudas Visuales, Vol. 10. (SPA., Illus.). 28p. 2000. pap., teacher ed. write for info. (*0-7361-0129-2*) Life Pubs Intl.
— Primeros Pasos I Maestro, Vol. 10. (SPA., Illus.). 112p. 2000. pap., teacher ed. write for info. (*0-7361-0128-4*) Life Pubs Intl.
— Primeros Pasos I Trabajo Manual, Dec. 2000 to Feb. 2001, Vol. 10. (SPA., Illus.). 16p. 2000. pap., student ed. write for info. (*0-7361-0131-4*) Life Pubs Intl.
— Primeros Pasos I Trabajo Manual, Sept. to Nov. 2000, Vol. 10. (SPA., Illus.). 16p. 2000. pap., student ed. write for info. (*0-7361-0130-6*) Life Pubs Intl.
— Tesoros del Rey Ayudas Visuals, Vol. 10. (SPA., Illus.). 28p. 2000. pap., teacher ed. write for info. (*0-7361-0133-0*) Life Pubs Intl.
— Tesoros del Rey Maestro, Vol. 10. (SPA., Illus.). 112p. 2000. pap., teacher ed. write for info. (*0-7361-0132-2*) Life Pubs Intl.
— Tesoros del Rey Trabajo Manual, Vol. 10. (SPA., Illus.). 16p. (ps-k). 2000. pap., student ed. write for info. (*0-7361-0134-9*); pap., student ed. write for info. (*0-7361-0135-7*) Life Pubs Intl.
***Life Publishers International Staff, tr.** Mis Amigos Alumno, Vol. 10, No. 3. (Vida Nueva Ser.). (SPA., Illus.). 32p. (J). (gr. 1-3). 2001. pap., student ed. write for info. (*0-7361-0179-9*) Life Pubs Intl.
— Mis Amigos Alumno, Vol. 10, No. 4. (Vida Nueva Ser.). (SPA., Illus.). 26p. (J). (gr. 1-3). 2001. pap., student ed. write for info. (*0-7361-0180-2*) Life Pubs Intl.
— Mis Amigos Ayudas Visuales, Vol. AMI-04. (Vida Nueva Ser.). (SPA., Illus.). 26p. (J). (gr. 1-3). 2001. pap. write for info. (*0-7361-0178-0*) Life Pubs Intl.
— Mis Amigos Maestro, Vol. 10, No. 3. (Vida Nueva Ser.). (SPA., Illus.). 112p. 2001. pap., teacher ed. write for info. (*0-7361-0177-2*) Life Pubs Intl.
— Primeros Pasos Ayudas Visales, Vol. PP-02. (Vida Nueva Ser.). (SPA., Illus.). 28p. 2001. pap. write for info. (*0-7361-0170-5*) Life Pubs Intl.
— Primeros Pasos Maestro, Vol. 10, No. 3. (Vida Nueva Ser.). (SPA., Illus.). 112p. 2001. pap., teacher ed. write for info. (*0-7361-0169-1*) Life Pubs Intl.
— Primeros Pasos Manual. (Vida Nueva Ser.). (SPA., Illus.). 16p. (J). (ps). 2001. pap., student ed. write for info. (*0-7361-0171-3*) Life Pubs Intl.
— Primeros Pasos Manual 2. (Vida Nueva Ser.). (SPA., Illus.). 16p. (J). (ps). 2001. pap., student ed. write for info. (*0-7361-0172-1*) Life Pubs Intl.
— Tesoros del Rey Ayudas Visuales, Vol. TES-02. (Vida Nueva Ser.). (SPA., Illus.). 28p. (J). (ps-k). 2001. pap. write for info. (*0-7361-0174-8*) Life Pubs Intl.
— Tesoros del Rey Maestro, Vol. 10, No. 3. (Vida Nueva Ser.). (SPA.). 112p. 2001. pap., teacher ed. write for info. (*0-7361-0173-X*) Life Pubs Intl.
— Tesoros del Rey Trabajo Manual, Vol. 10. (Vida Nueva Ser.). (SPA., Illus.). 16p. (J). 2001. pap., student ed. write for info. (*0-7361-0175-6*) Life Pubs Intl.
— Tesoros del Rey Trabajo Manual 2, Vol. 10. (Vida Nueva Ser.). (SPA., Illus.). 16p. (J). (ps-k). 2001. pap., student ed. write for info. (*0-7361-0176-4*) Life Pubs Intl.
Life Publishers International Staff, tr. see Brandt, William.
Life Publishers International Staff, tr. see Horton, Stanley.
Life Publishers International Staff, tr. see Mohr, Franz.
Life Publishers International Staff, tr. see Musgrove, Peggy.
Life Publishers International Staff, tr. see Peretti, Frank.
Life Publishers Staff. Ambassador Vol. 4, Bk. 1: Russian Language Sunday School. (RUS., Illus.). (YA). (gr. 10-12). 1999. pap., student ed. write for info. (*0-7361-0085-7*) Life Pubs Intl.
— Ambassador Vol. 4, Bk. 2: Russian Language Sunday School. (RUS., Illus.). (J). (gr. 10-12). 1999. pap., student ed. write for info. (*0-7361-0086-5*) Life Pubs Intl.
— Ambassador Vol 4, Bks. 1 & 2: Russian Language Sunday School. (RUS., Illus.). 1999. pap., teacher ed. write for info. (*0-7361-0084-9*) Life Pubs Intl.
— Companion Vol. 4, Bk. 1: Russian Language Sunday School. (RUS., Illus.). (J). (gr. 4-6). 1999. pap., student ed. write for info. (*0-7361-0091-1*) Life Pubs Intl.
— Companion Vol. 4, Bk. 2: Russian Language Sunday School. (RUS., Illus.). (J). (gr. 4-6). 1999. pap., student ed. write for info. (*0-7361-0092-X*) Life Pubs Intl.
— Companion Vol. 4, Bks. 1 & 2: Russian Language Sunday School. (RUS., Illus.). 1999. pap., teacher ed. write for info. (*0-7361-0090-3*) Life Pubs Intl.
— Explorer Vol. 4, Bk. 1: Russian Language Sunday School. (RUS., Illus.). (J). (gr. 7-9). 1999. pap., student ed. write for info. (*0-7361-0088-1*) Life Pubs Intl.
— Explorer Vol. 4, Bk. 2: Russian Language Sunday School. (RUS.). (YA). (gr. 7-9). 1999. pap., student ed. write for info. (*0-7361-0089-X*) Life Pubs Intl.
— Explorer Vol. 4, Bks. 1 & 2: Russian Language Sunday School. (RUS., Illus.). 1999. pap., teacher ed. write for info. (*0-7361-0087-3*) Life Pubs Intl.
— First Steps Vol. 1, Bks. 1 & 2: Russian Language Sunday School. (RUS.). 1999. pap., teacher ed. write for info. (*0-7361-0096-2*) Life Pubs Intl.
— First Steps - Visual Aids Vol. 1, Bks. 1 & 2: Russian Language Sunday School. (RUS., Illus.). (J). (ps-k). 1999. write for info. (*0-7361-0097-0*) Life Pubs Intl.
— My Friends Vol. 2, Bk. 1: Russian Language Sunday School. (RUS., Illus.). (J). (gr. 1-3). 1999. pap., student ed. write for info. (*0-7361-0094-6*) Life Pubs Intl.
— My Friends Vol. 2, Bk. 2: Russian Language Sunday School. (RUS., Illus.). (J). (gr. 1-3). 1999. pap., student ed. write for info. (*0-7361-0095-4*) Life Pubs Intl.
— My Friends Vol. 2, Bks. 1 & 2: Russian Language Sunday School. (RUS., Illus.). (J). (gr. 1-3). 1999. pap., teacher ed. write for info. (*0-7361-0093-8*) Life Pubs Intl.
***Life Publishers Staff, prod.** Ambassador - Student Manual Vol. 5, Bk. 1: Russian Language Sunday School. (RUS., Illus.). 48p. (YA). (gr. 10-12). 2000. pap., student ed. write for info. (*0-7361-0154-3*) Life Pubs Intl.
— Ambassador - Student Manual Vol. 5, Bk. 2: Russian Language Sunday School. (RUS., Illus.). 48p. (YA). (gr. 10-12). 2000. pap., student ed. write for info. (*0-7361-0155-1*) Life Pubs Intl.
— Ambassador - Teacher Manual Vol. 5: Russian Language Sunday School. (RUS., Illus.). 80p. 2000. pap., teacher ed. write for info. (*0-7361-0153-5*) Life Pubs Intl.
— Companion - Student Book Vol. 3: Russian Language Sunday School. (RUS., Illus.). 48p. (J). (gr. 4-7). 2000. pap., student ed. write for info. (*0-7361-0160-8*) Life Pubs Intl.
— Companion - Student Book Vol. 3: Russian Language Sunday School Student Book. (Illus.). 48p. (J). (gr. 4-7). 2000. pap., student ed. write for info. (*0-7361-0161-6*) Life Pubs Intl.
— Companion - Teacher Manual Vol. 3: Russian Language Sunday School Manual for Teachers. (RUS.). 112p. 2000. pap., teacher ed. write for info. (*0-7361-0159-4*) Life Pubs Intl.
— Explorer - Student Manual Vol. 5, Bk. 1: Russian Language Sunday School. (RUS., Illus.). 48p. (J). (gr. 7-9). 2000. pap., student ed. write for info. (*0-7361-0157-8*) Life Pubs Intl.
— Explorer - Student Manual Vol. 5, Bk. 2: Russian Language Sunday School. (RUS., Illus.). 48p. (YA). (gr. 7-9). pap., student ed. write for info. (*0-7361-0158-6*) Life Pubs Intl.
— Explorer - Teachers Manual Vol. 5: Russian Language Sunday School. (RUS., Illus.). 80p. 2000. pap., teacher ed. write for info. (*0-7361-0156-X*) Life Pubs Intl.
— First Steps - Teachers Manual Vol. 2: Russian Language Teachers Sunday School Manual. (RUS., Illus.). 80p. (J). (ps-k). 2000. pap., teacher ed. write for info. (*0-7361-0166-7*) Life Pubs Intl.
— First Steps - Visual Aids Vol. 2: Russian Language Sunday School Manual. (RUS., Illus.). 26p. (J). (ps-k). 2000. pap. write for info. (*0-7361-0167-5*) Life Pubs Intl.
— My Friends - Student Book Vol. 3: Russian Language Sunday School Manual. (RUS., Illus.). 48p. (J). (gr. 1-3). 2000. pap., student ed. write for info. (*0-7361-0163-2*) Life Pubs Intl.
— My Friends - Student Book Vol. 3: Russian Language Student Sunday School Manual. (RUS., Illus.). 48p. (J). (gr. 1-3). 2000. pap., student ed. write for info. (*0-7361-0165-9*) Life Pubs Intl.
— My Friends - Teachers Manual Vol. 3: Russian Language Sunday School. (RUS., Illus.). 80p. (J). (gr. 1-3). 2000. pap., teacher ed. write for info. (*0-7361-0162-4*) Life Pubs Intl.
— My Friends - Visual Aids Vol. 3: Russian Language Visual Aids for Sunday School. (RUS., Illus.). 24p. 2000. pap. write for info. (*0-7361-0164-0*) Life Pubs Intl.
Life Publishers Staff, tr. see Wigglesworth, Smith.
Life Span Editiorial Staff. The Planning Companion: Practical Guide for Pre-Retirement Planning -5-250 (Regular Edition) (LifeSystems Ser.). 1999. 13.95 (*0-927289-45-8*) LifeSpan Services.
Life-Study Fellowship Staff. With God All Things Are Possible. 304p. 1990. mass mkt. 6.50 (*0-553-26249-1*) Bantam.
***LifeCare.com, Inc. Staff.** A LifeCare Digest on Residential Cleaning Services. 4p. 2000. pap. 1.95 (*1-58559-073-8*) DCC Inc.
— A LifeCare Guide to Protecting Your Child. 8p. 2000. 2.50 (*1-58559-074-6*) DCC Inc.
Lifei Ji & Ji, Lifei. Chinese the Fast & Fun Way. (CHI & ENG.). 208p. 1998. pap. 39.95 incl. audio (*0-8120-8451-9*, 835975Q) Barron.
Lifeline Staff. Health Care Basics Mac Cd-Rom Multiple Site License. 352p. 1996. pap. text. write for info. (*0-8151-4559-4*) Mosby Inc.
— Health Care Basics Mac Cd-Rom Singlesite License. 352p. 1996. pap. text 195.00 (*0-8151-4558-6*) Mosby Inc.
Lifescapes Corporation Staff. Memory Lane: The Fun & Easy System for Writing about Your Life. 1995. 79.95 incl. reel tape, VHS (*1-886701-02-4*) Lifescapes.
***Lifeskills International Ltd. Staff.** Building a Service Culture LC 99-40392. 1999. write for info. (*0-566-08139-3*) Ashgate Pub Co.
— Exceptional Customer Service--Team Leader's Guide: A Condensed Team-Based Learning System (Manual & Team Leader's Guide) 186p. 1999. ring bd. 262.95 (*0-566-08266-7*, Pub. by Gower) Ashgate Pub Co.
— High Performance Teamworking. LC 99-40396. 1999. pap. write for info. (*0-566-08142-3*, Pub. by Gower) Ashgate Pub Co.
— Staying Healthy at Work LC 99-32843. 1999. write for info. (*0-566-08144-X*) Ashgate Pub Co.
***Lifeskills International Ltd. Staff, ed.** Developing Your Career. 180p. 1999. ring bd. 113.95 (*0-566-08267-5*, Pub. by Gower) Ashgate Pub Co.
— Exceptional Customer Service: A Condensed Team-Based Learning System. 304p. 1999. ring bd. 166.95 (*0-566-08265-9*, Pub. by Gower) Ashgate Pub Co.
Lifeskills International Ltd. Staff, jt. auth. see Hopson, Barrie.
Lifeskills International Staff, jt. auth. see Hopson, Barrie.
Lifetime Careers Wiltshire (London,Engalnd) Staff. Land & the Environment LC 98-150560. (Just the Job! Ser.). 112 p. 1997. write for info. (*0-340-68791-6*) Trafalgar.
Lifetime Guarantee Ministries Staff & Mars Hill Productions Staff. The Life Series. (Illus.). 62p. 1996. student ed., spiral bd. 8.00 (*0-9624056-6-3*) Mars Hill TX.
***LifeTime Media, Inc. Staff.** The Best Baby Names in the World, from Around the World. LC 99-87420. (Illus.). 320p. 2000. 24.95 (*0-8160-4131-8*, Checkmark); pap. 14.95 (*0-8160-4132-6*, Checkmark) Facts on File.
***Lifetime Television for Women Staff.** Love Letters of a Lifetime: Romance in America. 192p. 2001. 15.95 (*0-7868-6705-1*, Pub. by Hyperion) Time Warner.
Liff, Allen & Blanken, Rhea L. Embracing the Future: An Action Guide for Association Leaders. LC 99-18555. (Foundation Ser.). (Illus.). xxiii, 121p. 1999. pap. 90.00 (*0-88034-151-3*) Am Soc Assn Execs.
Liff, Alvin A. Color & Black & White Television Theory & Servicing. (Illus.). 1979. text 29.95 (*0-685-03795-9*) P-H.
Liff, Alvin A. & Wilson, Sam. Color & Black & White Television Theory & Servicing. 3rd ed. 608p. 1993. 97.00 (*0-13-150012-0*) P-H.
Liff, David M., et al. Corporate Advertising: The Business Response to Changing Public Attitudes. 67p. 1980. pap. 10.00 (*0-931035-56-2*) IRRC Inc DC.
Liff, Sharon R. No Place Else to Go: Homeless Mothers & Their Children Living in an Urban Shelter. rev. ed. LC 95-53203. (Children of Poverty Ser.). (Illus.). 192p. 1996. text 55.00 (*0-8153-2436-7*) Garland.
Lifficier, Randy, jt. auth. see Lofficier, Jean-Marc.
Liffick, Blaise W. Programming Techniques. LC 78-8649. 1978. write for info. (*0-931718-12-0*) Byte Pubns Inc.
Liffring-Zug, Joan. Men, 1950-1985. Zug, John & Crum, Dorothy, eds. LC 86-63007. (Illus.). 64p. 1986. pap. 20.95 (*0-941016-38-2*) Penfield.
Liffring-Zug, Joan, compiled by. The Amanas Yesterday: A Religious Communal Society. LC 74-26353. (Illus.). 48p. 1975. pap. 10.95 (*0-9603858-8-6*) Penfield.
Liffring-Zug, Joan, ed. The American Gothic Cookbook: From the Artist Grant Wood, His Family, Friends, Fans, Famous Colleagues. 158p. 1996. spiral bd. 6.95 (*1-57216-004-7*) Penfield.
Liffring-Zug, Joan, ed. see Kangas, Gerry.
Liffring-Zug, Joan, ed. see Martin, Pat.
Liffring-Zug, Joan, ed. see McDonald, Julie.
Lifland, William T. State Antitrust Law. 350p. 1984. ring bd. 95.00 (*0-318-12030-5*, 00583) NY Law Pub.
Liflander, Pamela, jt. auth. see Fitzsimmons, Tracy.
***Liflander, Robert.** Everything Online Business Book. LC 00-27194. 304p. 2000. pap. 12.95 (*1-58062-320-4*) Adams Media.
Lifschitz, Alexander E. Magnetohydrodynamics & Spectral Theory. (C). 1989. text 329.00 (*90-247-3713-3*) Kluwer Academic.
Lifschitz, Elena D., jt. auth. see Rosengrant, Sandra F.
Lifschitz, Leatrice, ed. Only Morning in Her Shoes: Poems about Old Women. 176p. (Orig.). 1990. pap. 4.00 (*0-87421-145-X*) Utah St U Pr.
Lifschitz, Marvin. Freedom from Memory, Desire, & Understanding: Psychoanalysis & Gestalt Psychology. LC 93-20971. (Frontiers of Consciousness Ser.). (Illus.). 260p. (C). 1995. text 34.95 (*0-8290-2452-2*) Ardent Media.
Lifschitz, Vladimir. Mechanical Theorem Proving in the U. S. S. R. The Leningrad School. Krafft, Rebecca, ed. (Illus.). 103p. (Orig.). 1986. pap. text 75.00 (*1-55831-026-6*) Delphic Associates.
Lifschitz, Vladimir, tr. see Maslov, S. Yu.
Lifschultz, Lawrence, et al. Bordering on Treason? The Trial & Conviction of Arif Durrani. 56p. 1991. 5.50 (*0-9630587-0-3*) Pamphleteers.
Lifschultz, Lawrence, jt. auth. see Bird, Kai.
Lifschultz, Lawrence, jt. ed. see Ali, Rabia.
Lifshin, Eric, ed. X-Ray Characterization of Materials. 278p. 1999. 180.00 (*3-527-29657-3*) Wiley.
Lifshin, Eric, jt. ed. see Cahn, Robert W.
Lifshin, Lyn. Before It's Light. LC 99-50179. 250p. 1999. 27.50 (*1-57423-115-4*); pap. 16.00 (*1-57423-114-6*); boxed set 35.00 (*1-57423-116-2*) Black Sparrow.
— Blue Tattoo. 80p. 1995. pap. 9.95 (*1-880391-12-0*) Event Horizon.
— Cold Comfort: Selected Poems 1970-1996. LC 97-26949. 225p. 1997. 25.00 (*1-57423-041-7*); pap. 14.00 (*1-57423-040-9*) Black Sparrow.
— Cold Comfort: Selected Poems 1970-1996. limited ed. LC 97-26949. 225p. 1997. 35.00 (*1-57423-042-5*) Black Sparrow.
— Dance Poems. (Dialogues on Dance Ser.: No. 7). 1986. pap. 6.00 (*0-941240-05-3*) Ommation Pr.
— Jesus Christ - Live & in the Flesh. 28p. 1997. pap. 3.00 (*0-9653194-5-8*) Future Tense.
— Leaning South. LC 76-58048. (Contemporary Poets Ser.). 1977. 10.95 (*0-87376-030-1*); pap. 4.95 (*0-87376-031-X*) Red Dust.
— The Mad Girl Drives in a Daze. (Illus.). 20p. (Orig.). 1995. 4.95 (*1-878116-37-1*) JVC Bks.
— Marilyn Monroe: Poems by Lyn Lifshin. Hamilton, Brian C. & DelMargo, Lynn D., eds. 143p. (Orig.). 1994. pap. 8.95 (*1-882550-02-1*) Quiet Lion Pr.
— Red Hair & the Jesuit. (Backpocket Poets Ser.). 36p. (Orig.). 1988. pap. 2.50 (*0-916155-05-6*) Trout Creek.
— Restrooms, Anyone? Plus: A Classic Lifshin Reader. limited ed. Carbone, Joyce, ed. 82p. (Orig.). 1997. pap. 8.95 (*1-878116-69-X*) JVC Bks.
— Thirty-Five Sundays. (Offset Offshoot Ser.: No. 3). 56p. 1979. pap. 4.00 (*0-317-06439-8*) Ommation Pr.
Lifshin, Lyn, ed. Tangled Vines: New Edition. 164p. 1992. pap. 11.00 (*0-15-688166-7*, Harvest Bks) Harcourt.
Lifshin, Lyn, et al. Eye of the Beast. Lovingood, Sut, ed. (Gypsy Ser.: No. 5). (Illus.). 64p. (Orig.). 1986. pap. 4.95 (*0-935839-02-X*) Virgin Press.
— Poor - A Rich Labial! The 1997 Dung Annual. (Illus.). 100p. 1997. lib. bdg. 13.30 (*0-9644321-6-1*) Camel Dung Writ.
— Vergin' Mary & Madonna. (Elite Chaps: No. 4). 62p. (Orig.). 1986. pap. 3.20 (*0-935839-01-1*) Virgin Press.

L

L

Lifshits, Evgenii M. & Andronikashvili, E. L. A Supplement of "Helium" LC 59-8465. 176p. reprint ed. pap. 54.60 (0-608-10078-1, 200336500021) Bks Demand.

Lifshits, M. A. Gaussian Random Functions. LC 95-3066. (Mathematics & Its Applications Ser.: Vol. 322). 352p. (C). 1995. text 180.50 (0-7923-3385-3) Kluwer Academic.

Lifshits, Tanya, jt. auth. see Lifshits, Yonatan.

Lifshits, V. G., et al. Surface Phases on Silicon: Preparation, Structures, & Properties. 462p. 1994. 260.00 (0-471-94846-2) Wiley.

Lifshits, Yonatan & Lifshits, Tanya. Uman, Uman, Rosh HaShanah: A Guide to Rebbe Nachmans Rosh HaShanah in Uman. Greenbaum, Avraham, ed. (Illus.). 96p. 1992. pap. 4.00 (0-930213-43-2) Breslov Res Inst.

Lifshitz. Course of Theoretical Physics Vol. 10: Physical Kinetics. 625p. 1981. pap. text 59.95 (0-7506-2635-6) Buttrwrth-Heinemann.

***Lifshitz, Aliza A.** Mama Sana, Bebe Sano: Una Guia en Espanol E ingles Sobre el Embarazo la Atencion Prenatal, el Nacimiento y el Cuidado. (ENG & SPA., Illus.). 464p. 1999. pap. 15.00 (0-380-79245-1, Avon Bks) Morrow Avon.

Lifshitz, Assa, ed. Shock Waves in Chemistry. LC 81-5375. (Illus.). 400p. reprint ed. pap. 124.00 (0-7837-0744-4, 204106400019) Bks Demand.

Lifshitz, E. M., jt. auth. see Landau, L. D.

Lifshitz, Fima, ed. Carbohydrate Intolerance in Infancy. LC 82-5107. (Clinical Disorders in Pediatric Nutrition Ser.: No. 1). 271p. reprint ed. pap. 84.10 (0-608-15920-4, 203087100071) Bks Demand.

— Childhood Nutrition. LC 94-14377. (Modern Nutrition Ser.). 288p. 1994. boxed set 104.95 (0-8493-2764-4, 2764) CRC Pr.

— Clinical Disorders in Pediatric Gastroenterology & Nutrition. LC 80-18516. (Pediatrics Ser.: No. 1). 480p. 1980. reprint ed. pap. 148.80 (0-608-01333-1, 206207700001) Bks Demand.

— Common Pediatric Disorders: Metabolism, Heart Disease, Allergies, Substance Abuse & Trauma. LC 84-14294. (Clinical Pediatrics Ser.: No. 1). (Illus.). 463p. reprint ed. pap. 143.60 (0-7837-0610-3, 204095800019) Bks Demand.

— Nutrition for Special Needs in Infancy: Protein Hydrolysates. LC 85-25288. (Clinical Disorders in Pediatric Nutrition Ser.: No. 4). 336p. 1985. reprint ed. pap. 104.20 (0-608-01305-6, 206205000001) Bks Demand.

— Pediatric Endocrinology: A Clinical Guide. 3rd expanded rev. ed. (Clinical Pediatrics Ser.: Vol. 8). (Illus.). 992p. 1995. text 215.00 (0-8247-9369-2) Dekker.

— Pediatric Nutrition: Infant Feedings, Deficiencies, Diseases. LC 82-14926. (Clinical Disorders in Pediatric Nutrition Ser.: No. 2). 647p. 1982. reprint ed. pap. 200.00 (0-608-01287-4, 206203300001) Bks Demand.

Lifshitz, Leatrice H., ed. Her Soul Beneath the Bone: Women's Poetry on Breast Cancer. LC 88-1348. 104p. 1988. 10.95 (0-252-06008-3); text 19.95 (0-252-01518-5) U of Ill Pr.

Lifshitz, Y. Y. Unser Buch, 2 vols. 10th ed. Incl. Vol. 1. 10th ed. (YID.). 64p. 1969. reprint ed. pap. text 2.00 (0-8266-0209-6, Merkos LInyonei Chinuch); Vol. 2. 10th ed. (YID.). 48p. 1969. reprint ed. pap. text 2.00 (0-8266-0210-X, Merkos LInyonei Chinuch); (YID.). Set pap. 2.00 (0-8266-0208-8) Kehot Pubn Soc.

Lifshitz, Ze'ev H. The Paradox of Human Existence: A Commentary on the Book of Jonah. LC 94-6287. 296p. 1995. pap. 30.00 (1-56821-219-4) Aronson.

Lifson, Ben. Eugene Atget. 2nd ed. (Masters of Photography Ser.). (Illus.). 96p. 1997. reprint ed. 18.95 (0-89381-750-3) Aperture.

Lifson, Ben, jt. auth. see Lebowitz, Fran.

Lifson, Ben, tr. see Nuridsany, Claude & Perennou, Marie.

Lifson, David S., tr. Epic & Folk Plays from the Yiddish Theatre. 224p. 1975. 36.50 (0-8386-1082-X) Fairleigh Dickinson.

Lifson, David S. & Aleichem, Sholem. Sholem Aleichem's Wandering Star & Other Plays of Jewish Life. LC 86-73240. 216p. 1988. 19.95 (0-8453-4810-8, Cornwall Bks) Assoc Univ Prs.

Lifson, Lawrence, ed. Understanding Therapeutic Action: Psychodynamic Concepts of Cure. (Psychoanalytic Inquiry Ser.: No. 15). 272p. 1996. text 45.00 (0-88163-205-8) Analytic Pr.

Lifson, Lawrence E. & Geist, Richard. The Psychology of Investing. LC 99-18529. (Investments Ser.). 208p. 1999. 34.95 (0-471-18339-3) Wiley.

Lifson, Lawrence E. & Simon, Robert I. The Mental Health Practitioner & the Law: A Comprehensive Handbook. LC 97-41510. 416p. 1999. 49.95 (0-674-69721-9) HUP.

Lifson, Thomas B., jt. auth. see Yoshino, M. Y.

Lifter. Writing & Desktop Publishing on the Computer. 80p. (J). (gr. 1-3). 1996. pap., wbk. ed. 9.95 (1-55734-922-3) Tchr Create Mat.

Lifter, Marsha. Integrating Technology into the Classroom. 1997. pap. text 11.95 (1-55734-933-9) Tchr Create Mat.

— Kid Pix Simple Projects (Primary) (Illus.). 144p. (J). (gr. 1-3). 1998. pap., teacher ed. 14.95 (1-57690-412-1, TCM2412) Tchr Create Mat.

— Print Shop for Terrified Teachers. (Terrified Teachers Ser.). (Illus.). 304p. pap., teacher ed. 19.95 (1-57690-189-0, TCM2189) Tchr Create Mat.

Lifter, Marsha & Adams, Marian E. Kid Pix Simple Projects (Intermediate) (Illus.). 144p. (J). (gr. 3-5). 1998. pap., teacher ed. 14.95 (1-57690-413-X, TCM2413) Tchr Create Mat.

— Make & Take Technology. LC 98-170771. 223 p. 1997. write for info. (1-57369-096-1) Visions Tech.

— The Print Shop: Simple Projects. (Illus.). 96p. 1998. pap., teacher ed. 14.95 (1-57690-414-8, TCM2414) Tchr Create Mat.

***Lifter, Marsha, et al.** Multimedia Projects for Kid Pix. (Illus.). 120p. 1998. ring bd. 29.95 (1-885830-49-1, MPI) Pixel Genius.

Lifter, Marsha, jt. auth. see Teacher Created Materials Staff.

Liftin, Elaine, jt. auth. see Hansen, John H.

Liftin, Hilary. Dear Exile: The True Story of Two Friends Separated (for a Year) by an Ocean. LC 98-47190. (Vintage Departures Ser.). 204p. 1999. pap. 11.00 (0-375-70367-5) Vin Bks.

Lifton. Destroying the World to Save. pap. write for info. (0-8050-5306-9) St Martin.

Lifton. Twice Born. LC 98-2896. 1998. pap. 13.95 (0-312-18766-1) St Martin.

Lifton, Bernice. Bug Busters: Poison-Free Controls for Your House & Garden. 2nd ed. LC 90-19678. (Illus.). 272p. 1991. pap. 9.95 (0-89529-451-6, Avery) Penguin Putnam.

Lifton, Betsy & Lifton, Karen. Five's a Crowd. (Not for Blondes Only Ser.). 176p. (J). (gr. 3-7). 1992. pap. 2.95 (0-590-45526-5, Apple Paperbacks) Scholastic Inc.

Lifton, Betty J. The Journey of the Adopted Self: A Quest for Wholeness. 336p. 1995. pap. 14.00 (0-465-03675-9, Pub. by Basic) HarpC.

— The King of Children. LC 97-2877. 1997. pap. 15.95 (0-312-15560-3) St Martin.

— Lost & Found: The Adoption Experience. LC 87-45636. 320p. 1988. reprint ed. pap. 9.95 (0-685-43848-1, PL-7132, Perennial) HarperTrade.

— A Place Called Hiroshima. LC 84-48127. (Illus.). 151p. 1985. 24.95 (0-87011-649-5) Kodansha.

— A Place Called Hiroshima. Pockell & Ichiba, eds. (Illus.). 152p. 1990. reprint ed. pap. 14.95 (0-87011-961-3) Kodansha.

***Lifton, David.** Final Charade. 2000. 25.50 (0-688-16562-1, Wm Morrow) Morrow Avon.

Lifton, Karen, jt. auth. see Lifton, Betsy.

Lifton, Paul. Vast Encyclopedia: The Theatre of Thornton Wilder, 61. LC 95-5675. (Contributions in Drama & Theatre Studies: Vol. 61). 240p. 1995. 59.95 (0-313-29356-2, Greenwood Pr) Greenwood.

Lifton, Robert J. America & the Asian Revolutions. 2nd ed. 178p. (C). 1973. reprint ed. 32.95 (0-87855-065-8); reprint ed. pap. text 19.95 (0-87855-562-5) Transaction Pubs.

— The Broken Connection: On Death & the Continuity of Life. 474p. 1996. pap. text 39.00 (0-88048-874-3, 8874) Am Psychiatric.

— Death in Life: Survivors of Hiroshima. LC 91-50248. xii, 594p. (C). 1991. reprint ed. pap. 27.50 (0-8078-4344-X) U of NC Pr.

— Thought Reform & the Psychology of Totalism: A Study of "Brainwashing" in China. LC 88-40534. xiv, 510p. (C). 1989. reprint ed. pap. 24.95 (0-8078-4253-2) U of NC Pr.

***Lifton, Robert J.** Who Owns Death: Capital Punishment, the American Conscience, & the End of Executions. LC 00-32464. 288p. 2000. 25.00 (0-380-97498-3, Wm Morrow) Morrow Avon.

Lifton, Robert J., ed. The Woman in America, No. 3--3. LC 77-11064. 293p. 1977. reprint ed. lib. bdg. 49.50 (0-8371-9810-0, LIWO, Greenwood Pr) Greenwood.

Lifton, Robert J. & Humphrey, Nicholas, eds. In a Dark Time. LC 84-10816. 160p. (Orig.). 1984. text 24.95 (0-674-44538-4); pap. text 8.50 (0-674-44539-2) HUP.

Lifton, Robert J. & Mitchell, Greg. Hiroshima in America: A Half Century of Denial. 448p. 1996. pap. 15.00 (0-380-72764-1, Avon Bks) Morrow Avon.

Lifton, Robert Jay. Destroying the World to Save It: Aum Shinrikyo, Apocalyptic Violence & the New Global Terrorism. LC 99-23905. 352p. 1999. 26.00 (0-8050-5290-9) H Holt & Co.

— Protean Self: Human Resilience in an Age of Fragmentation. LC 99-35389. 262p. 1999. pap. 15.00 (0-226-48098-4) U Ch Pr.

Lifton, Robert K. Practical Real Estate: Legal, Tax & Business Strategies. 702p. 1983. 60.00 (0-15-004280-9, H42809) Harcourt.

***Lifton, Robery Jay.** Destroying the World to Save It: Aum Shinrikyo, Apocalyptic Violence & the New Global Terrorism. 384p. 2000. pap. 16.00 (0-8050-6511-3, Owl) H Holt & Co.

Ligachev, Yegor. Inside Gorbachev's Kremlin: The Memoirs of Yegor Ligachev. (C). 1996. pap. 35.00 (0-8133-2887-X, Pub. by Westview) HarpC.

Ligas, J. R., jt. ed. see Epstein, M. A.

Liger, Louis. Le Jardinier Fleuriste et Historiographe. 679p. reprint ed. write for info. (0-318-71372-1) G Olms Pubs.

Ligertwood, A. L. Australian Evidence. 2nd ed. 1993. 107.00 (0-409-30487-5, MICHIE); pap. 83.00 (0-409-30488-3, Australia, MICHIE) LEXIS Pub.

— Australian Evidence: Cases & Materials. 944p. 1995. pap. write for info. (0-409-30721-1, MICHIE) LEXIS Pub.

Ligeti, Louis, ed. Proceedings of the Csoma de Koros Memorial Symposium: Held at Matrafured, Hungary, 24-30 September 1976. (Bibliotheca Orientalis Hungarica Ser.: Vol. 23). (FRE, GER & RUS.). 586p. (C). 1978. 153.00 (963-05-1568-7, Pub. by Akade Kiado) St Mut.

Ligget, Cathy, jt. auth. see Ligget, Mark.

Ligget, Mark & Ligget, Cathy. The Complete Handbook of Songwriting: An Insider's Guide to Making It in the Music Industry. LC 85-7197. 352p. 1985. pap. 9.95 (0-452-25687-9, Plume) Dutton Plume.

Liggett. Intermediate Fluid Mechanics. 1994. 22.81 (0-07-037806-1) McGraw.

Liggett, Barbara. Archaeology at New Market. 1978. pap. 5.00 (0-916530-09-4) Athenaeum Phila.

Liggett, Cathy, jt. auth. see Liggett, Mark.

Liggett, Diane T. & Mack, James A. Real Cool Colorado Places for Curious Kids. LC 97-48551. 160p. (YA). (gr. 5-12). 1998. pap. 15.95 (1-56579-293-9) Westcliffe Pubs.

***Liggett, Don.** Sport Hypnosis. LC 99-50149. (Illus.). 208p. 2000. pap. 17.95 (0-7360-0214-6) Human Kinetics.

Liggett, Helen & Perry, David C. Spatial Practices: Critical Explorations in Social - Spatial Theory. 264p. 1995. text 52.00 (0-8039-5114-0); pap. text 24.50 (0-8039-5115-9) Sage.

***Liggett, Hunter.** The Murder Maze. large type ed. 304p. 1999. pap. 18.99 (0-7089-5589-4, Linford) Ulverscroft.

— The Victim Died Twice. large type ed. 304p. 2000. pap. 18.99 (0-7089-5679-3, Linford) Ulverscroft.

Liggett, James A. Fluid Mechanics. LC 93-28418. (C). 1993. text 82.50 (0-07-037805-3) McGraw.

Liggett, Larry, jt. auth. see Welcher, Frank.

Liggett, Mark & Liggett, Cathy. The Complete Handbook of Songwriting: An Insider's Guide to Making It in the Music Industry. 2nd ed. 272p. 1993. pap. 13.95 (0-452-27011-1, Plume) Dutton Plume.

Liggett, Peter, jt. auth. see Alfaro, D. Virgil.

Liggett, Sarah, jt. auth. see Halpern, Jeanne W.

Liggett, Stephen B. & Meyers, Deborah, eds. The Genetics of Asthma, No. 96. LC 96-23405. (Lung Biology in Health & Disease Ser.: Vol. 96). (Illus.). 642p. 1996. text 215.00 (0-8247-9729-9) Dekker.

***Liggett, T.** Stochastic Interacting Systems: Contact, Voter & Exclusion Processes. LC 99-38162. (Grundlehren der Mathematischen Wissenschaften Ser.: Vol. 324). (Illus.). 330p. 1999. 99.00 (3-540-65995-1) Spr-Verlag.

Liggett, T. M. Interacting Particle Systems. (Grundlehren der Mathematischen Wissenschaften Ser.: Vol. 276). (Illus.). 500p. 1985. 117.00 (0-387-96069-4) Spr-Verlag.

Liggett, Twila C. & Benfield, Cynthia M. The "Reading Rainbow" Guide to Children's Books. rev. ed. (Illus.). 288p. 1996. pap. 14.95 (0-8065-1796-4, Citadel Pr) Carol Pub Group.

Liggett, Twila C. & Mayer, Cynthia. The Reading Rainbow Guide to Children's Books: The 101 Best Titles. LC 93-46695. 1994. 19.95 (1-55972-222-3, Birch Ln Pr); pap. 12.95 (0-8065-1493-0, Birch Ln Pr) Carol Pub Group.

Liggins-Hill, Patricia. Anthology African-American Literature, Vol. 2. (C). Date not set. pap. 32.76 (0-395-80964-9) HM.

— Anthology of African-American Literature, Vol. 1. (C). Date not set. pap. 32.76 (0-395-80962-2) HM.

— Anthology of African-American Literature, Vol. 2. (C). Date not set. text 34.76 (0-395-80963-0) HM.

Liggins-Hill, Patricia, ed. see Bell, Bernard W., et al.

Liggio, Ann, jt. auth. see Liggio, Joe.

***Liggio, Joe & Liggio, Ann.** Wild Orchids of Texas. LC 98-51720. (Corrie Herring Hooks Ser.). 240p. 1999. 29.95 (0-292-74712-8) U of Tex Pr.

Liggio, Leonard P. & Martin, James J., eds. Watershed of Empire: Essays on New Deal Foreign Policy. LC 76-4291. 1976. pap. 3.95 (0-87926-020-3) R Myles.

Light. Delicate Balance. 1997. pap. text 10.00 (0-312-15368-6) St Martin.

— A Delicate Balance. LC 95-73199. xx, 472p. 1997. pap. text 48.95 (0-312-08969-4) St Martin.

— Delicate Balance. 2nd ed. 1998. pap. text 42.95 (0-312-19049-2) St Martin.

***Light.** Delicate Balance. 2nd ed. 1999. pap. text 44.95 (0-312-24941-1) St Martin.

Light. Delicate Balance & Big Ideas. 1997. pap. text 35.00 (0-312-17124-2) St Martin.

— Delicate Balance & Real Thing. 1997. pap. text 35.00 (0-312-17132-3) St Martin.

— Delicate Balance/Online. 1997. pap. text 39.60 (0-312-17863-8) St Martin.

— Introduction to Criminal Justice. (Criminal Justice Ser.). 1999. text, student ed. 15.00 (0-534-55945-X) Wadsworth Pub.

— Odyssey of the Soul: Light: The Act of Creation. (Illus.). 151p. 2000. pap. 12.00 (0-9659891-1-9) Quick Bk Pub.

— Policing. (Criminal Justice Ser.). 2001. text 43.00 (0-534-54230-1) Wadsworth Pub.

— Starting Design & Communication. Date not set. pap. text. write for info. (0-582-00429-2, Pub. by Addison-Wesley) Longman.

— Understanding Criminal Justice. (Criminal Justice). 1998. mass mkt. 44.50 (0-534-55943-3) Wadsworth Pub.

— Understanding Criminal Justice with Infotrac. (Criminal Justice Ser.). 1998. pap. 44.50 (0-534-55944-1) Wadsworth Pub.

Light, ed. Environmental Pragmatism. 368p. 1996. text 65.00 (0-415-07687-0) Routledge.

Light & Groom, A. J. R., eds. International Relations: A Handbook of Current Theory. 244p. 1985. text 49.00 (0-86187-527-3) St Martin.

— International Relations: A Handbook of Current Theory. 244p. 1986. pap. text 17.50 (0-86187-683-0) St Martin.

Light & Lan-Ying. Contemporary World Issues. (J). 1991. pap. text 25.95 (0-8384-3328-6) Heinle & Heinle.

Light & Life Symposium Staff. Light & Life: Proceedings of the Symposium, Johns Hopkins University, 1960. McElroy, William D. & Glass, Bentley, eds. LC 60-16544. (Johns Hopkins University, McCollum-Pratt Institute, Contribution: No. 302). 938p. reprint ed. pap. 200.00 (0-608-12100-2, 202413900035) Bks Demand.

Light & Light Staff. Train Up a Child Cradle Roll: Child's Packet. 1982. pap. 11.95 (0-89367-207-6) Light & Life Comm.

***Light, A. R.** Delicate Balance Comprehensive. 2000. pap. text. write for info. (0-312-25628-0) St Martin.

Light, A. R. The Initial Processing of Pain & Its Descending Control: Spinal & Trigeminal Systems. (Pain & Headache Ser.: Vol. 12). (Illus.). xiv, 306p. 1992. 304.50 (3-8055-5569-5) S Karger.

Light, Alan, ed. see Vibe Magazine Staff.

Light, Andrew. Environmental Pragmatism. Katz, Eric, ed. 368p. 1996. pap. text 19.95 (0-415-07688-9) Routledge.

Light, Andrew, ed. Social Ecology after Bookchin. LC 98-35447. (Democracy & Ecology Ser.). 401p. 1998. pap. 19.95 (1-57230-379-4) Guilford Pubns.

Light, Andrew & Katz, Erick, eds. Environmental Pragmatism. LC 95-18536. (Environmental Philosophies Ser.). 368p. (C). 1996. 75.00 (0-415-12236-8); pap. 24.99 (0-415-12237-6) Routledge.

***Light, Andrew & Nagel, Mechtild.** Race Class & Community Identity. LC 99-58011. (Radical Philosophy Today Ser.). 210p. 2000. 54.95 (1-57392-816-X, Humanity Bks) Prometheus Bks.

***Light, Andrew & Smith, Jonathan, eds.** Aesthetics of Everyday Life. (Spaces, Places & Environments Ser.). 304p. 2000. pap. text 26.95 (1-889119-54-7) Seven Bridges.

Light, Andrew & Smith, Jonathan, eds. Philosophy & Geography II: The Production of Public Space. LC 97-27911. (Philosophy & Geography Ser.). 255p. 1997. 61.00 (0-8476-8809-7); pap. 24.95 (0-8476-8810-0) Rowman.

Light, Andrew & Smith, Jonathan M., eds. Philosophy & Geography III: Philosophies of Place. LC 98-34655. (Philosophy & Geography Ser.: No. 98). 320p. 1998. 68.00 (0-8476-9094-6); pap. 25.95 (0-8476-9095-4) Rowman.

— Space, Place, & Environmental Ethics: Philosophy & Geography I. LC 96-23667. (Philosophy & Geography Ser.: No. 98). 248p. 1996. 60.50 (0-8476-8220-X) Rowman.

— Space, Place & Environmental Ethics: Philosophy & Geography I. LC 96-23667. (Philosophy & Geography Ser.: No. 98). 248p. 1996. pap. 24.95 (0-8476-8221-8) Rowman.

Light, Arthur, et al. Opiate Addiction. Grob, Gerald N., ed. LC 80-1257. (Addiction in America Ser.). 1981. reprint ed. lib. bdg. 15.95 (0-405-13604-8) Ayer.

Light, Dale B. Rome & the New Republic: Conflict & Community in Philadelphia Catholicism Between the Revolution & the Civil War. LC 95-16520. (Notre Dame Studies in American Catholicism: Vol. 14). (C). 1996. text 48.95 (0-268-01652-6) U of Notre Dame Pr.

Light, Danielle. Remembering Me: A Journal for You & Your Loved Ones. 136p. 1986. pap. 7.95 (0-9616478-0-9) Mt Shasta Pubns.

Light, David. Treat Me Right: A Women's Guide to the Perfect Relationship. unabridged ed. (Illus.). 62p. 1998. write for info. (0-9660614-1-1) Light the Wrld.

Light, Diana, jt. auth. see Gilchrist, Paige.

Light, Donald, jt. auth. see Calhoun, Craig.

Light, Donald W. & Schuller, Alexander, eds. Political Values on Health Care: The German Experience. (Humanistic & Social Dimensions of Medicine Ser.). (Illus.). 550p. 1986. 65.00 (0-262-12109-3) MIT Pr.

Light, Duane R. Boats in Watercolor. (How to Draw & Paint Ser.). (Illus.). 32p. (Orig.). 1989. pap. 6.95 (0-929261-70-4, HT210) W Foster Pub.

— Felt Pen & Watercolor. (Artist's Library). (Illus.). 64p. (Orig.). 1992. pap. 7.95 (1-56010-123-7, AL20) W Foster Pub.

— Watercolor. (Artist's Library). (Illus.). 64p. (Orig.). 1989. pap. 7.95 (0-929261-02-X, AL02) W Foster Pub.

— Watercolor Painting Kit. (Illus.). 32p. (YA). (gr. 7 up). 1995. pap., student ed. 19.95 (1-56010-191-1, K04) W Foster Pub.

— Watercolor with Mixed Media. (Artist's Library). (Illus.). 64p. (Orig.). 1989. pap. 7.95 (1-56010-032-X, AL16) W Foster Pub.

***Light, Duncan & Phinnemore, David.** Post-Communist Romania. LC 00-42209. (Illus.). 2000. write for info. (0-333-79187-8) St Martin.

Light, Enid, et al, eds. Stress Effects on Family Caregivers of Alzheimer's & Related Dementias: Research & Interventions. 440p. 1994. 58.95 (0-8261-7890-1) Springer Pub.

Light, Enid & Lebowitz, Barry D., eds. The Elderly with Chronic Mental Illness. 384p. 1991. 49.95 (0-8261-7280-6) Springer Pub.

Light, Enid & Liebowitz, Barry. Alzheimer's Disease Treatment & Family Stress: Directions for Research. 500p. 1990. 60.95 (1-56032-137-7) Hemisp Pub.

Light, Fred R. CERCLA Law & Procedure. LC 91-26413. 416p. 1991. trans. 92.00 (0-87179-707-0, 0707) BNA Books.

— CERCLA Law & Procedure Compendium. 1284p. 1992. trans. 88.00 (0-87179-742-9, 0742) BNA Books.

— CERCLA Law & Procedure, '93 Supplement. 122p. 1993. suppl. ed. 38.00 incl. trans. (0-87179-802-6) BNA Books.

Light, G. S. & Higham, J. B. Theoretical Mechanics, Vol. 1. LC 74-81553. 93.00 (0-608-13132-6) Bks Demand.

— Theoretical Mechanics, Vol. 1. LC 74-81553. 372p. reprint ed. pap. 115.40 (0-608-10350-0, 202522700001) Bks Demand.

Light, G. S. & Kalsi, T. S. Theoretical Mechanics, Vol. 2. LC 74-81553. 110.00 (0-608-13133-4) Bks Demand.

— Theoretical Mechanics, Vol. 2. LC 74-81553. 440p. reprint ed. pap. 136.40 (0-608-10351-9, 202522700002) Bks Demand.

Light, H. Wayne. Light's Retention Scale, 1998. 80p. 1998. pap. 30.00 (0-87879-914-1, 914-1AN); pap. 22.00 (0-87879-915-X); pap., student ed. 75.00 (0-685-71873-5, 914-1AN) Acad Therapy.

— Light's Retention Scale, 1998. 80p. 1998. pap. 20.00 (0-87879-916-8) Acad Therapy.

An Asterisk (*) at the beginning of an entry indicates that the title is appearing for the first time.

Light, H. Wayne & Morrison, Pam. Beyond Retention: A Survival Guide for the Regular Classroom Teacher. Kratoville, Betty Lou, ed. (Illus.). 126p. (Orig.). 1990. pap. text 15.00 (*0-87879-900-1*) Acad Therapy.

Light, Ivan & Isralowitz, Richard E., eds. Immigrant Entrepreneurs & Immigrant Absorption in the United States & Israel. LC 97-70893. (Research in Ethnic Relations Ser.). 272p. 1997. text 73.95 (*1-85972-467-1*, Pub. by Ashgate Pub) Ashgate Pub Co.

Light, Ivan H., ed. Italians in America: Annotated Guide to New York Times Articles, 1890-1940, No. 824. 1975. 6.00 (*0-686-20359-3*, Sage Prdcls Pr) Sage.

Light, Ivan H. & Bahchu, Parminder, eds. Immigration & Entrepreneurship: Culture, Capital, & Ethnic Networks. LC 92-14137. 352p. (C). 1993. 44.95 (*1-56000-070-8*) Transaction Pubs.

Light, Ivan H. & Bonacich, Edna. Immigrant Entrepreneurs: Koreans in Los Angeles, 1965-1982. (Illus.). 506p. 1991. reprint ed. pap. 18.95 (*0-520-07656-7*, Pub. by U CA Pr) Cal Prin Full Svc.

Light, Ivan H. & Rosenstein, Carolyn. Race, Ethnicity, & Entrepreneurship in Urban America. LC 95-3418. (Sociology & Economics Ser.). 266p. 1995. lib. bdg. 49.95 (*0-202-30505-8*) Aldine de Gruyter.

— Race, Ethnicity & Entrepreneurship in Urban America. LC 95-3418. (Sociology & Economics Ser.). 266p. 1995. pap. text 25.95 (*0-202-30506-6*) Aldine de Gruyter.

Light, James F. John William De Forest. 192p. 1965. 49.50 (*0-685-63207-5*) Elliots Bks.

Light, Janice B. & Binger, Cathy. Building Communicative Competence with Individuals Who Use Augmentative & Alternative Communication. LC 97-33599. 1998. 36.95 (*1-55766-324-6*) P H Brookes.

Light, Jeremy, jt. auth. see Harper, Peter.

Light, Joanna R. Prayer, the Remedy That Always Works. Love, Leo, ed. 185p. 1997. pap. 13.00 (*1-891109-36-7*) Peace Mind.

Light, Joanne. Coastal Nova Scotia: An Outdoor Adventure Guide. (Illus.). 148p. (Orig.). 1993. pap. 9.95 (*1-55109-043-0*) Nimbus Publ.

— Hiking Nova Scotia: A Field Guide to Adventure. LC 96-133080. (Illus.). 148p. 1995. pap. 11.95 (*1-55109-108-9*) Nimbus Publ.

Light, Joey. Daddy for Hire. (Romance Ser.). 1997. per. 3.25 (*0-373-19215-0*, 1-192152) Silhouette.

Light, John. Beachcombers. (ITA.). (J). 1991. pap. 3.99 (*0-85953-605-X*) Childs Play.

— Beachcombers. LC 91-38130. (Light Reading Ser.). 24p. (J). (gr. 4 up). 1991. 1.99 (*0-85953-502-9*) Childs Play.

— Dig That Hole! (ITA.). (J). 1991. pap. 3.99 (*0-85953-606-8*) Childs Play.

— Dig That Hole! LC 91-39036. (Light Reading Ser.). 24p. (YA). (gr. 5 up). 1991. 1.99 (*0-85953-503-7*) Childs Play.

— It's Great Outdoors. LC 90-34353. (Light Reading Ser.). 24p. (YA). (gr. 5 up). 1991. 1.99 (*0-85953-338-7*) Childs Play.

— It's Great Outdoors. (ITA.). (J). 1991. pap. 3.99 (*0-85953-602-5*) Childs Play.

Light, John. Lines of Light. 67p. pap. write for info. (*3-7052-0414-9*, Pub. by Poetry Salzburg) Intl Spec Bk.

Light, John. Odd Jobs. (ITA.). (J). 1991. pap. 3.99 (*0-85953-603-3*) Childs Play.

— Odd Jobs. LC 90-34354. (Light Reading Ser.). 24p. (J). (gr. 4 up). 1991. 1.99 (*0-85953-339-5*) Childs Play.

— Playing at Home. (ITA.). (J). 1991. pap. 3.99 (*0-85953-600-9*) Childs Play.

— Playing at Home. LC 90-34356. (Light Reading Ser.). 24p. (J). (gr. 4 up). 1991. pap. 1.99 (*0-85953-336-0*) Childs Play.

— Race Ace Roger. (ITA.). (J). 1991. pap. 3.99 (*0-85953-604-1*) Childs Play.

— Race Ace Roger. LC 91-33417. (Light Reading Ser.). 24p. (J). (gr. 4 up). 1991. 1.99 (*0-85953-501-0*) Childs Play.

— Snap Happy. (ITA.). (J). 1991. pap. 3.99 (*0-85953-607-6*) Childs Play.

— Snap Happy. LC 91-36610. (Light Reading Ser.). 24p. (J). (gr. 4 up). 1991. 1.99 (*0-85953-504-5*) Childs Play.

— What's Cooking. LC 90-34355. (Light Reading Ser.). 24p. (J). (gr. 4 up). 1991. 1.99 (*0-85953-337-9*) Childs Play.

— What's Cooking? (ITA.). (J). 1991. 3.99 (*0-85953-601-7*) Childs Play.

Light, Jonathan F. The Cultural Encyclopedia of Baseball. LC 97-763. (Illus.). 896p. (YA). (gr. 7 up). 1997. boxed set 75.00 (*0-7864-0311-X*) McFarland & Co.

Light, Kate. Laws of Falling Bodies. LC 97-27243. (Roerich Poetry Prize Winner Ser.). 88p. 1997. pap. text 11.00 (*1-885266-55-3*) Story Line.

Light, Ken. Delta Time: Mississippi Photographs. Moses, Robert, ed. & intro. by. LC 94-25891. (Illus.). 144p. 1995. 65.00 (*1-56098-470-8*); pap. 34.95 (*1-56098-469-4*) Smithsonian.

***Light, Ken.** Witness in Our Times: Working Lives of Documentary Photographers. 2000. 45.00 (*1-56098-923-8*) Smithsonian.

— Witness in Our Times: Working Lives of Documentary Photographers. LC 00-20889. (Illus.). 2000. pap. 17.00 (*1-56098-948-3*) Smithsonian.

Light, Ken, photos by. Texas Death Row. LC 96-41256. (Illus.). 128p. 1997. 50.00 (*0-87805-950-4*) U Pr of Miss.

Light, Ken, et al. To the Promised Land. (Illus.). 90p. 1988. 37.95 (*0-89381-324-9*) Aperture.

Light, Laura, ed. Catalogue of Medieval & Renaissance Manuscripts in the Houghton Library, Harvard University Vol. 1: MSS3-179 Latin. LC 95-21800. (Medieval & Renaissance Texts & Studies: Vol. 145). (Illus.). 448p. 1997. reprint ed. 40.00 (*0-86698-185-3*, MR145) MRTS.

Light, Laura, ed. see Bingham, Mindy, et al.

Light, Leah L. & Burke, Deborah M., eds. Language, Memory, & Aging. (Illus.). 296p. (C). 1988. text 64.95 (*0-521-32942-6*) Cambridge U Pr.

— Language, Memory, & Aging. (Illus.). 293p. (C). 1993. pap. text 22.95 (*0-521-44876-X*) Cambridge U Pr.

Light, Linda. Passions & Prejudice: The Secrets of Spindletop. expanded rev. ed. (Illus.). 405p. 1997. 24.95 (*0-9645617-2-7*) Spindletop Prod.

Light, Luise, ed. Holistic Living: The Millenium Guide for a Healthy & Joyous Life. 400p. 1999. pap. 19.95 (*0-87983-973-2*, Keats Publng) NTC Contemp Pub Co.

Light, Margot, ed. Troubled Friendships: Moscow's Third World Venture. 288p. 1994. text 59.50 (*1-85043-649-5*) I B T.

Light, Margot, jt. ed. see Groom, A. J. R.

Light, Marilyn H. Hypoglycemia. Passwater, Richard A. & Mindell, Earl R., eds. (Good Health Guide Ser.). 31p. (Orig.). 1983. pap. 3.95 (*0-87983-302-5*, 33025K, Keats Publng) NTC Contemp Pub Co.

— Hypoglycemia: One of Man's Most Widespread & Misdiagnosed Diseases. 1.95 (*0-317-00895-1*) Hypoglycemia Foun.

— Psychology & Physiologic Findings in Psychosomatic Disorders. 3.00 (*0-317-05970-X*) Hypoglycemia Foun.

***Light, Michael.** Full Moon. (Illus.). 255p. 1999. 50.00 (*0-375-40634-4*) Knopf.

Light, Michael. Ranch. (Illus.). 96p. 1993. 45.00 (*0-944092-25-X*) Twin Palms Pub.

Light, Nathan. Qazaqs in the People's Republic of China: The Local Processes of History. Cuffel, Victoria J., ed. LC 93-655022. (MacArthur Scholar Series, Occasional Paper: No. 22). (Illus.). 107p. (Orig.). 1994. pap. 4.00 (*1-881157-24-5*) In Ctr Global.

Light, Paul & Butterworth, George, eds. Context & Cognition. 192p. 1993. pap. 24.50 (*0-8058-1393-4*) L Erlbaum Assocs.

— Context & Cognition. 192p. 1993. text 39.95 (*0-8058-1392-6*) L Erlbaum Assocs.

***Light, Paul & Littleton, Karen.** Social Processes in Children's Learning. LC 99-19464. (Cambridge Studies in Cognitive & Perceptual Development: No. 4). (Illus.). 130p. (C). 2000. 49.95 (*0-521-59308-5*) Cambridge U Pr.

— Social Processes in Children's Learning. LC 99-19464. (Cambridge Studies in Cognitive & Perceptual Development: Vol. 4). (Illus.). 130p. (C). 2000. pap. 17.95 (*0-521-59691-2*) Cambridge U Pr.

Light, Paul, jt. auth. see Littleton, Karen.

Light, Paul, jt. ed. see Butterworth, George.

***Light, Paul C.** Baby Boomers. 322p. 1999. 26.95 (*0-7351-0158-2*) Replica Bks.

— End of Public Service. LC 99-6972. 184p. 1999. pap. 12.95 (*0-8157-5243-1*) Brookings.

— Tides of Nonprofit Reform: A Report on the Nonprofit Public Service. 2000. pap. write for info. (*0-8157-5245-8*) Brookings.

Light, Paul Charles. Forging Legislation. 192p. (C). 1991. 22.95 (*0-393-03038-5*) Norton.

Light, Paul Charles. Monitoring Government: Inspectors General & the Search for Accountability. 268p. (C). 1993. 16.95 (*0-8157-5255-5*); pap. 16.95 (*0-8157-5256-3*) Brookings.

— The President's Agenda: Domestic Policy Choice from Kennedy to Clinton. 3rd ed. LC 98-34586. 1999. pap. 16.95 (*0-8018-6066-0*) Johns Hopkins.

***Light, Paul Charles.** The President's Agenda: Domestic Policy Choice from Kennedy to Clinton. 3rd ed. LC 98-34586. 1999. 49.95 (*0-8018-6065-2*) Johns Hopkins.

Light, Paul Charles. The President's Agenda: Domestic Policy Choice from Kennedy to Reagan. rev. ed. LC 91-3779. 304p. 1991. pap. text 15.95 (*0-8018-4279-4*) Johns Hopkins.

— The President's Agenda: Domestic Policy Choice from Kennedy to Reagan. 2nd rev. ed. LC 91-3779. 304p. 1991. text 49.95 (*0-8018-4278-6*) Johns Hopkins.

— Still Artful Work: The Continuing Politics of Social Security Reform. 2nd ed. LC 94-17594. 256p. (C). 1994. 28.75 (*0-07-037949-1*) McGraw.

— Sustaining Innovation: Creating Nonprofit & Government Organizations That Innovate Naturally. LC 97-40025. (Jossey-Bass Nonprofit & Public Management Ser.). 1998. 25.95 (*0-7879-4098-4*) Jossey-Bass.

— Thickening Government. 217p. (C). 1995. 34.95 (*0-8157-5250-4*); pap. 14.95 (*0-8157-5249-0*) Brookings.

— The Tides of Reform: Making Government Work, 1945-1995. LC 96-38557. 304p. 1997. 40.00 (*0-300-06987-1*); pap. 17.00 (*0-300-07657-6*) Yale U Pr.

— The True Size of Government LC 98-58143. 1999. 18.95 (*0-8157-5265-2*) Brookings.

***Light, Paul Charles.** True Size of Government. LC 98-58143. 1999. 44.95 (*0-8157-5266-0*) Brookings.

Light, Paul Charles. Vice-Presidential Power: Advice & Influence in the White House. LC 83-48050. 288p. 1983. text 45.00 (*0-8018-3058-3*) Johns Hopkins.

Light, Paul Charles, jt. auth. see Butterworth, George E.

Light, Paul Charles, jt. ed. see Richards, Martin.

Light, Phyllis B. Prince Charming Lives! Finding the Love of Your Life. LC 93-6409. 240p. 1994. pap. 12.95 (*0-931892 78 3*) Lght Unltd.

Light, Rebecca Campbell, ed. War at Our Doors: The Civil War Diaries & Letters of the Bernard Sisters. (Illus.). 165p. 1998. pap. 14.95 (*1-891722-02-6*) Am Hist Co.

Light, Richard. Presenting XML. LC 97-67511. 448p. 1997. pap. 24.99 (*1-57521-334-6*) Sams.

Light, Richard J. & Pillemer, David B. Summing up: The Science of Reviewing Research. LC 84-4506. (Illus.). 224p. 1984. 29.00 (*0-674-85430-6*); pap. 14.95 (*0-674-85431-4*) HUP.

Light, Richard J., et al. By Design: Planning Research on Higher Education. (Illus.). 288p. 1990. 42.00 (*0-674-08930-8*); pap. 17.50 (*0-674-08931-6*) HUP.

Light, Richard U. Focus on Africa. LC 73-150192. (Select Bibliographies Reprint Ser.). (Illus.). 1977. reprint ed. 60.95 (*0-8369-5705-9*) Ayer.

Light, Richard W. Pleural Diseases. 3rd ed. LC 94-44122. (Illus.). 408p. 1995. 79.00 (*0-683-05017-6*) Lppncott W & W.

Light, Roy. Criminalizing the Drunk-Driver. 224p. 1994. 77.95 (*1-85521-456-3*, Pub. by Dartmth Pub) Ashgate Pub Co.

Light, Roy, et al. Car Theft: The Offender's Perspective. (Home Office Research Studies: No. 130). 100p. 1993. pap. 15.00 (*0-11-341069-7*, HM10697, Pub. by Statnry Office) Bernan Associates.

Light, Roy, jt. auth. see Bottoms, Anthony E.

Light, Russel D. On Perspective. (Illus.). 160p. 1998. pap. 28.95 (*0-7506-1694-6*) Buttrwrth-Heinemann.

Light, Sally. Canals & Crossroads: An Illustrated History of the Albany, New York, Roman Catholic Diocese. Breig, James, ed. (Illus.). 280p. 1997. 25.00 (*0-9658982-0-2*) Albany Cath Pr.

— House Histories: A Guide to Tracing the Genealogy of Your Home: Including Chapters on How to Operate a Homebased "House Histories" Business. LC 88-83479. (Illus.). 302p. (Orig.). 1989. pap. text 14.95 (*0-9614876-1-5*) Golden Hl Pr NY.

Light, Sharon. Voting by Institutional Investors on Corporate Governance Issues - 1992. O'Hara, Peg, ed. 69p. (Orig.). 1992. pap. 25.00 (*1-879775-03-4*) IRRC Inc DC.

Light, Stephen. Shuzo Kuki & Jean Paul Sartre: Influence & Counter-Influence in the Early History of Existential Phenomenology. LC 86-11861. (Journal of the History of Philosophy Monograph Ser.). 168p. (Orig.). 1987. pap. text 15.95 (*0-8093-1271-9*) S Ill U Pr.

Light Technology Publishing Staff. Shining the Light Vol. 5: Humanity Is Going to Make It! 328p. 1998. pap. 14.95 (*1-891824-00-7*) Light Tech Pubng.

Light Technology Research Staff. Shining the Light Vol. 2: The Battle Continues. Vol. 1. 418p. 1995. pap. 14.95 (*0-929385-70-5*) Light Tech Pubng.

— Shining the Light Vol. 3: Humanity Gets a Second Chance. 460p. 1996. pap. 14.95 (*0-929385-71-3*) Light Tech Pubng.

— Shining the Light Vol. 4: Humanity's Greatest Challenge. 557p. 1996. pap. text 14.95 (*0-929385-93-4*) Light Tech Pubng.

***Light, Terry R. & American Society for Surgery of the Hand Staff.** Hand Surgery Update 2. 2nd ed. LC 99-42929. 1999. pap. write for info. (*0-89203-233-2*) Amer Acad Ortho Surg.

Light, Timothy & Yao, Tao-Chung. The Character Book: A Workbook to Accompany "Read Chinese", Bk. 1. (Mirror Ser.). (CHI.). 316p. (Orig.). 1985. pap. text 16.95 (*0-88710-137-2*) Yale Far Eastern Pubns.

Light, W. A. Introduction to Abstract Analysis. LC 99-24928. (Illus.). 208p. (gr. 13). 1990. per. 41.95 (*0-412-31090-2*, A5287, Chap & Hall CRC) CRC Pr.

Light, W. A. & Cheney, E. W. Approximation Theory in Tensor Product Spaces. (Lecture Notes in Mathematics Ser.: Vol. 1169). vii, 157p. 1985. 34.95 (*0-387-16057-4*) Spr-Verlag.

Light, W. A. & Marletta, M. Advances in Numerical Analysis Vol. 4: Theory & Numerics of Ordinary & Partial Differential Equations, Vol. 4. Ainsworth, M. et al, eds. LC 95-31855. (Illus.). 346p. (C). 1995. text 65.00 (*0-19-851193-0*) OUP.

Light, Will, ed. Advances in Numerical Analysis: Nonlinear Partial Differential Equations & Dynamical Systems, Vol. 1. (Illus.). 224p. 1991. 55.00 (*0-19-853438-8*) OUP.

— Advances in Numerical Analysis: Wavelets, Subdivision Algorithms, & Radial Basis Functions, Vol. 2. (Illus.). 224p. 1992. text 55.00 (*0-19-853439-6*) OUP.

Light, Will, jt. auth. see Cheney, E. W.

Light, William J. Spionidae: Invertebrates of the San Francisco Bay Estuary System, Vol. 1. Lee, Welton L., ed. (Illus.). 1978. text 12.50 (*0-910286-58-2*) Boxwood.

Light Work Staff & Gonchar, Nancy, eds. John Wood. (Illus.). 24p. 7.50 (*0-935445-01-3*) Light Work.

Light Years Ahead Productions Staff. Light Years Ahead: The Illustrated Guide to Full Spectrum & Colored Light MindBody Healing. Breiling, Brian & Argisle, Bethany, eds. LC 95-20046. (Illus.). 256p. 1995. pap. 19.95 (*0-89087-762-9*) Celestial Arts.

Lightbody, Andy. Angling Guide to Colorado's Blue Mesa Reservoir. (Illus.). 120p. (Orig.). 1995. pap. 14.95 (*1-882391-10-1*) N Cape Pubns.

Lightbody, Andy & Lightbody, Tari. Winter Trails of Colorado: The Best Cross Country & Snowshoe Trails. LC 98-38869. (Winter Trails Ser.: Vol. 2). (Illus.). 224p. 1998. pap. 11.95 (*0-7627-0303-2*) Globe Pequot.

Lightbody, Andy & Poyer, Joe. Milspeak: A Dictionary of International Military Acronyms & Abbreviations. 91p. (Orig.). 1986. pap. 5.95 (*1-882391-00-4*) N Cape Pubns.

Lightbody, Audrey. Faith Is the Journey. 144p. (Orig.). (YA). (gr. 7 up). 1987. pap. 5.95 (*0-939925-10-9*) R C Law & Co.

Lightbody, Audrey B. Reflections on Caring for an Aging Parent. LC 99-38526. 1999. pap. 12.99 (*0-8272-3220-9*) Chalice Pr.

***Lightbody, Heather & Sharp, Garry.** Corporate Finance; Self-Study Workbook. 3rd ed. 2000. 295.00 (*1-85564-820-2*, Pub. by Euromoney) Am Educ Systs.

Lightbody, Marcia, jt. ed. see Cohen, Samuel H.

Lightbody, Marcia L., jt. auth. see Cohen, Samuel H.

Lightbody, Mark & Talbot, Dorinda. Lonely Planet Canada. 5th ed. (Illus.). 976p. 1997. 21.95 (*0-86442-409-4*) Lonely Planet.

***Lightbody, Mark, et al.** Canada. 7th ed. (Illus.). 976p. 1999. pap. 24.95 (*0-86442-752-2*) Lonely Planet.

Lightbody, Nancy K. & Malley, Sarah H. Observa-Story: Portland to Cut & Color. LC 76-54460. (Illus.). (J). (gr. 1-4). 1976. pap. 1.25 (*0-9600612-5-8*) Greater Portland.

Lightbody, Tari, jt. auth. see Lightbody, Andy.

Lightbourne & Rankin. Physical Mathematics & Nonlinear Partial Differential Equations. (Lecture Notes in Pure & Applied Mathematics Ser.: Vol. 102). (Illus.). 280p. 1985. pap. text 135.00 (*0-8247-7343-8*) Dekker.

Lightbourne, ed. see Giesea, Roberta.

Lightbourne, Aleaa, ed. see Colon, Rafael.

Lightbourne, K. A. Grandfather Played the Trumpet: Sailors Fantasies. 375p. (Orig.). (J). 1988. pap. 12.50 (*0-9621212-0-7*) Sailors Fantasies Pub.

***Lightbourne, Kirk.** Sam's Secret. 2000. pap. 13.95 (*0-87714-628-4*) Denlingers.

Lightbown, R. W. Secular Goldsmiths' Work in Medieval France: A History. (Illus.). 230p. 1978. 19.98 (*0-85431-224-2*, Pub. by Soc Antiquaries) David Brown.

Lightbown, Ronald. Botticelli: Life & Work. (Illus.). 336p. 1989. 95.00 (*0-89659-931-0*) Abbeville Pr.

— Piero Della Francesca. (Illus.). 312p. 1992. 95.00 (*1-55859-168-0*) Abbeville Pr.

***Lightbulb Press Staff.** Guide to Choosing, Serving & Enjoying Wines. (Illus.). 160p. 2000. pap. 14.95 (*0-07-135905-2*) McGraw-Hill Pubng.

Lightburn, Anita, jt. auth. see Schamess, Gerald.

Lightburn, Ron & Lightburn, Sandra. Driftwood Cove. (Illus.). 32p. 1998. 19.95 (*0-385-25626-4*) Doubleday.

Lightburn, Sandra, jt. auth. see Lightburn, Ron.

Lighten Up Enterprises Staff. Going Home. (Places of the Heart Ser.). 366p. 1994. spiral bd. 8.50 (*1-879127-34-2*) Lighten Up Enter.

— Lessons from the Heart. (Places of the Heart Ser.). 366p. 1994. spiral bd. 8.50 (*1-879127-35-0*) Lighten Up Enter.

— Main Street Memories. (Places of the Heart Ser.). 366p. 1994. spiral bd. 8.50 (*1-879127-33-4*) Lighten Up Enter.

— Simple Treasures. (Places of the Heart Ser.). 366p. 1994. spiral bd. 8.50 (*1-879127-36-9*) Lighten Up Enter.

Lighten Up Enterprises Staff, jt. auth. see Estrem, Victoria L.

Lighten-Up Staff. A Mother's Love. (Small Wonders Ser.). 120p. 1994. spiral bd. 4.99 (*1-879127-47-4*) Lighten Up Enter.

— Special Angel. (Small Wonders Ser.). 120p. 1995. spiral bd. 4.99 (*1-879127-50-4*) Lighten Up Enter.

— Sunshine & Smiles. (Small Wonders Ser.). 120p. 1994. spiral bd. 4.99 (*1-879127-48-2*) Lighten Up Enter.

— With Love. (Small Wonders Ser.). 120p. 1994. spiral bd. 4.99 (*1-879127-49-0*) Lighten Up Enter.

Lighter, Dawn. Gentle Discipline: 50 Effective Techniques for Teaching Your Children Good Behavior. 1995. 6.00 (*0-671-52701-0*); pap. 6.00 (*0-88166-233-X*) Meadowbrook.

— Gentle Discipline: 50 Simple Ways to Teach Your Child Good Behavior. 1995. pap. 6.00 (*0-88116-233-7*) Meadowbrook.

Lighter, Jonathan E. Random House Historical Dictionary of American Slang, 3 vols., Vol. 1. 1080p. 1994. 65.00 (*0-394-54427-7*) Random.

— Random House Historical Dictionary of American Slang, 2 vols., Vol. 2. 768p. 1997. 65.00 (*0-679-43464-X*) Random.

— Random House Historical Dictionary of American Slang, Vol. II, H-O. 1997. 75.00 (*0-614-28230-6*) Random Ref & Info.

— Random House Historical Dictionary of American Slang, 3 vols., Vol. 3. 2002. 65.00 (*0-679-43465-8*) Random.

Lightfoot, C., et al, compiled by. Training Resource Book for Agro-Ecosystems Mapping. 55p. 1989. write for info. (*0-614-23053-5*, Pub. by ICLARM) Intl Spec Bk.

— Training Resource Book for Farming Systems Diagnosis. 62p. 1990. per. write for info. (*971-10-4222-3*, Pub. by ICLARM) Intl Spec Bk.

— Training Resource Book for Participatory Experimental Design. 73p. 1991. per. write for info. (*0-614-23054-3*, Pub. by ICLARM) Intl Spec Bk.

Lightfoot, C., et al. Households Agroecosystems & Rural Resources Management: A Guidebook for Broadening the Concepts of Gender & Farming System. (ICLARM Education Ser.: No. 12). 80p. 1997. reprint ed. pap. 19.95 (*971-10-2289-3*, Pub. by ICLARM) Intl Spec Bk.

Lightfoot, C. S. Recent Turkish Coin Hoards & Numismatic Studies. (Monographs: No. 12). (Illus.). 34p. 1991. pap. 60.00 (*0-946897-27-1*, Pub. by Brit Inst Arch) David Brown.

Lightfoot, Claude & Patterson, William L. Four Score Years in Freedom's Fight. 16p. 1972. pap. 0.35 (*0-87898-081-4*) New Outlook.

Lightfoot, Claude M. Human Rights U. S. Style: From Colonial Times Through the New Deal. LC 77-21113. 239p. reprint ed. pap. 74.10 (*0-608-17491-2*, 202999000067) Bks Demand.

— Racism & Human Survival: Lessons of Nazi Germany for Today's World. LC 72-82082. (Illus.). 304p. reprint ed. pap. 94.30 (*0-8357-3510-9*, 203425500089) Bks Demand.

Lightfoot, Cynthia. The Culture of Adolescent Risk-Taking. LC 96-47250. (Culture & Human Development Ser.). 187p. 1997. pap. text 21.00 (*1-57230-232-1*, 0232) Guilford Pubns.

Lightfoot, Cynthia, jt. ed. see Cox, Brian D.

Lightfoot, David. The Development of Language: Acquisition, Change & Evolution. LC 98-28674. (Blackwell/Maryland Lectures in Language & Cognition Ser.: Vol. 1). (Illus.). 352p. 1999. 59.95 (*0-631-21059-8*); pap. 29.95 (*0-631-21060-1*) Blackwell Pubs.

— How to Set Parameters: Arguments from Language Change. (Illus.). 226p. 1991. 35.00 (*0-262-12153-0*) MIT Pr.

— How to Set Parameters: Arguments from Language Change. (Illus.). 225p. 1993. pap. text 17.50 (*0-262-62090-1*, Bradford Bks) MIT Pr.

L

L

— Natural Logic & the Greek Moods. (Janua Linguarum, Series Practica: No. 230). 149p. 1975. pap. text 46.95 (*90-279-3061-9*) Mouton.

Lightfoot, David, jt. ed. see Webelhuth, Gert.

***Lightfoot, Freda.** Manchester Pride. large type ed. 448p. 2000. write for info. (*0-7505-1478-7*, Pub. by Mgna Lrg Print) Ulverscroft.

Lightfoot, Freda. Rhapsody Creek. 256p. 1999. 25.00 (*0-7278-5405-4*, Pub. by Severn Hse) Chivers N Amer.

***Lightfoot, Freda.** Wine & Roses. large type ed. 400p. 1999. 31.99 (*0-7505-1400-0*, Pub. by Mgna Lrg Print) Ulverscroft.

Lightfoot, Freda. Woman Beyond Price. 250p. 2000. 25.00 (*0-7278-5470-4*) Severn Hse.

Lightfoot, Frederick S. Nineteenth-Century New York in Rare Photographic Views. (New York City Ser.). (Illus.). 96p. (Orig.). 1981. pap. 12.95 (*0-486-24137-8*) Dover.

Lightfoot, Frederick S., et al, eds. Suffolk County, Long Island in Early Photographs. (Americana Ser.). (Illus.). 144p. 1998. pap. 10.95 (*0-486-24672-8*) Dover.

Lightfoot, Frederick S., jt. auth. see Johnson, Harry.

Lightfoot, J. B. Biblical Essays. 460p. 1994. 19.95 (*1-56563-077-7*) Hendrickson MA.

— J. B. Lightfoot's Commentary on the Epistles of St. Paul, 4 vols., Set. 1504p. 1993. 79.95 (*1-56563-016-5*) Hendrickson MA.

— Philippians. LC 94-18837. (Crossway Classic Commentaries Ser.). 224p. 1994. pap. 15.99 (*0-89107-800-2*) Crossway Bks.

Lightfoot, J. B. & Harmer, J. R. The Apostolic Fathers. 2nd ed. Holmes, Michael W., ed. LC 89-35173. 368p. (C). 1998. pap. 19.99 (*0-8010-2199-5*) Baker Bks.

Lightfoot, J. B., ed. see Mansel, Henry L.

Lightfoot, J. D., tr. see Ignatius.

Lightfoot, J. L., ed. Parthenius of Nicaea. LC PA4263.P3A2 1999. 622p. 1999. text 135.00 (*0-19-815253-1*) OUP.

Lightfoot, J. Timothy. Physiology Phil's True Life Lab Experiences. 2nd ed. LC 95-71158. (Illus.). 76p. (C). 1995. pap. 13.95 (*0-9629526-2-1*) Presyncopal.

Lightfoot, John. Agent Undercover. 256p. 1998. 24.95 (*1-85782-211-0*, Pub. by Blake Publng) Seven Hills Bk.

— A Commentary on the New Testament from the Talmud & Hebraica, 4 vols., Set. 1664p. 1989. 75.00 (*0-943575-26-5*) Hendrickson MA.

***Lightfoot, John.** The Spanish Connection: How I Smashed an International Drug Cartel. 2000. mass mkt. 6.99 (*1-85782-328-1*) Blake Publng.

Lightfoot, John. Whole Works of John Lightfoot, 13 vols. Pitman, John, ed. LC 79-172318. reprint ed. write for info. (*0-404-04010-1*) AMS Pr.

Lightfoot, Joseph B. Colossians & Philemon. abr. ed. LC 97-19164. (Classic Commentaries Ser.). 144p. 1997. pap. 12.99 (*0-89107-951-3*) Crossway Bks.

Lightfoot, Joseph B., tr. The Apostolic Fathers - Patres Apostolici, 5 vols. (GER.). lv, 2940p. 1973. reprint ed. write for info. (*0-318-70114-6*); reprint ed. write for info. (*0-318-70116-2*) G Olms Pubs.

— The Apostolic Fathers - Patres Apostolici, 5 vols., Set. (GER.). lv, 2940p. 1973. reprint ed. 518.70 (*3-487-04687-3*) G Olms Pubs.

— The Apostolic Fathers - Patres Apostolici, 5 vols., Vol. II. (GER.). lv, 2940p. 1973. reprint ed. write for info. (*0-318-70115-4*) G Olms Pubs.

Lightfoot, Judy. Calling the Crow. LC 99-161458. (Illus.). 36p. 1998. pap. 11.95 (*0-918116-99-6*) Brooding Heron Pr.

***Lightfoot, Judy.** Calling the Crow. LC 99-161458. (Illus.). 36p. 1998. 24.95 (*0-918116-98-8*) Brooding Heron Pr.

Lightfoot, K. G., et al. The Archaeology & Ethnohistory of Fort Ross, California Vol. 1: Introduction, Nos. 74-75. fac. ed. (Reports of the University of California Archaeological Survey: No. 49). (Illus.). 66p. 1991. reprint ed. pap. 19.00 (*1-55567-366-X*) Coyote Press.

Lightfoot, Kent G. Prehistoric Political Dynamics: A Case Study From the American Southwest. LC 83-25079. 193p. 1984. 30.00 (*0-87580-097-1*) N Ill U Pr.

Lightfoot-Klein, Hanny. A Woman's Odyssey into Africa: Tracks Across a Life. LC 91-18809. (Women's Studies). 150p. 1992. 69.95 (*1-56024-155-1*) Haworth Jrnl Co-Edits.

— A Woman's Odyssey into Africa: Tracks Across a Life. LC 91-18809. (Women's Studies). 150p. 1992. pap. 17.95 (*1-56023-007-X*, Harrington Park) Haworth Pr.

Lightfoot-Klein, Hanny, ed. Prisoners of Ritual: An Odyssey into Female Genital Circumcision in Africa. LC 89-15637. (Illus.). 306p. 1989. pap. text 14.95 (*0-918393-68-X*, Harrington Park) Haworth Pr.

Lightfoot-Klein, Hanny, pref. Prisoners of Ritual: An Odyssey into Female Genital Circumcision in Africa. LC 89-15639. (Haworth Series on Women: No. 2). (Illus.). 306p. 1989. text 39.95 (*0-86656-877-8*) Haworth Pr.

Lightfoot, Lynn O., jt. auth. see Ross, Robert R.

Lightfoot, Marge. Cartooning for Kids. (Illus.). 64p. (YA). (gr. 3 up). 1993. 16.95 (*1-895688-03-5*, Pub. by Greey dePencier); pap. 8.95 (*0-920775-84-5*, Pub. by Greey dePencier) Firefly Bks Ltd.

Lightfoot, Marise P., jt. auth. see Garrett, Jill K.

Lightfoot, Martin & Martin, Nancy, eds. The Word for Teaching Is Learning: Essays for James Britton. LC 88-5069. 300p. (C). 1988. pap. text 23.50 (*0-86709-237-8*, 0237, Pub. by Boynton Cook Pubs) Heinemann.

Lightfoot, N. F. & Maier, E. A. Microbiological Analysis of Food & Water: Guidelines for Quality Assurance. LC 98-13035. 1998. 210.00 (*0-444-82911-3*) Elsevier.

Lightfoot, N. F. & Maier, E. A., eds. Microbiological Analysis of Food & Water: Guidelines for Quality Assurance. 284p. 1998. 143.50 (*0-444-50203-3*) Elsevier.

Lightfoot, Neil R. How We Got the Bible. rev. ed. LC 86-71090. (Way of Life Ser.). 95p. 1986. reprint ed. pap. 6.95 (*0-89112-180-3*) Abilene Christ U.

— How We Got the Bible. 2nd ed. LC 62-22230. 168p. 1988. 16.99 (*0-8010-5644-6*) Baker Bks.

— Jesus Christ Today: A Commentary on the Book of Hebrews. 274p. (C). 1989. reprint ed. pap. 14.95 (*0-9623823-0-2*) Bible Guides.

— Parables of Jesus, Vol. 2. LC 86-71089. (Way of Life Ser.). 95p. 1986. reprint ed. pap. 6.95 (*0-89112-179-X*) Abilene Christ U.

Lightfoot, Ricky R. The Duckfoot Site Vol. 2: Archaeology of the House & Household. LC 94-68616. (Occasional Paper: No. 4). (Illus.). 192p. (Orig.). 1995. pap. 19.95 (*0-9624640-5-8*) Crow Canyon Archaeol.

Lightfoot, Ricky R. & Etzkorn, Mary C., eds. The Duckfoot Site Vol. 1: Descriptive Archaeology. LC 92-75597. (Occasional Paper: No. 3). (Illus.). 398p. (Orig.). 1993. pap. 29.95 (*0-9624640-2-3*) Crow Canyon Archaeol.

Lightfoot, Robert. Employment Game. 50p. 1994. pap. 5.00 (*0-939427-81-8*) Alpha Pubns OH.

— Obtaining Credit Fast & Easy. 79p. 1992. pap. 10.95 (*0-939427-73-7*) Alpha Pubns OH.

Lightfoot, Sara L. Good High School Portraits of Character & Culture. LC 83-70772. 416p. 1985. pap. 20.00 (*0-465-02696-6*, Pub. by Basic) HarpC.

Lightfoot, Sara L., jt. auth. see Carew, Jean V.

Lightfoot, Susanna & Thomas, Martha. Quaker Women Passing: Deathbed As Pulpit: The Memoirs of Susanna Lightfoot (1720-1781) & Martha Thomas (1805-1836) Rutherford, Anne, ed. LC 98-68490. 60p. (Orig.). 1999. reprint ed. pap. 10.95 (*1-889298-33-6*) Rhwymbooks.

Lighthall, J. I. The Indian Household Medicine Guide. 152p. 1996. pap. 14.95 (*0-9663702-0-1*) Fly Eagle.

— The Indian Household Medicine Guide. 1991. lib. bdg. 79.95 (*0-8490-4100-7*) Gordon Pr.

— The Indian Household Medicine Guide. 2nd ed. 152p. 1996. reprint ed. pap. 12.50 (*0-7873-0560-X*) Hlth Research.

Lighthall, Lynne, jt. ed. see Haycock, Ken.

Lighthill, Celia. Cinema Century Vol. 1: The First Fifty Years. LC 94-210342. 240p. (C). 1993. pap. text, per. 58.95 (*0-8403-8788-1*, 40878801) Kendall-Hunt.

Lighthill, J. Mathematical Biofluiddynamics. (CBMS-NSF Regional Conference Ser.: No. 17). vi, 281p. 1975. reprint ed. pap. text 53.00 (*0-89871-014-6*) Soc Indus-Appl Math.

Lighthill, James. An Informal Introduction to Theoretical Fluid Mechanics. (Institute of Mathematics & Its Applications Conference Series, New Ser.: No. 2). (Illus.). 272p. 1988. pap. text 45.00 (*0-19-853630-5*) OUP.

— Waves in Fluids. LC 77-8174. (Illus.). 504p. 1979. pap. text 52.95 (*0-521-29233-6*) Cambridge U Pr.

Lighthill, M. J. Introduction to Fourier Analysis & Generalized Functions. (Cambridge Monographs on Mechanics & Applied Mathematics). 80p. (C). 1958. pap. text 20.95 (*0-521-09128-4*) Cambridge U Pr.

Lighthill, M. James. Collected Papers of Sir James Lighthill, 4 vols., Set. Hussaini, M. Yousuff, ed. (Illus.). 2688p. 1996. text 395.00 (*0-19-509222-8*) OUP.

Lighthouse, Jack N., jt. ed. see Fishbane, Simcha.

Lighting Research Center Staff. The Lighting Pattern Book for Homes. 2nd ed. LC 96-41380. (Illus.). 208p. 1996. 74.95 (*0-07-038079-1*) McGraw.

— Outdoor Lighting Pattern Book. (Illus.). 208p. 1996. 59.95 (*0-07-037188-1*) McGraw.

Lightle. Blueprint Read Sketch. 3rd ed. 5.28 (*0-02-672010-8*) Macmillan Info.

Lightle, jt. auth. see Headley.

Lightle, Juliana & Doucet, Elizabeth H. Sexual Harassment in the Workplace: A Guide to Prevention. LC 91-68537. (Legal Issues in Business Ser.). (Illus.). 116p. (Orig.). 1995. pap. 10.95 (*1-56052-153-8*) Crisp Pubns.

Lightle, Steve. Exodus II. 1983. pap. 6.95 (*0-917726-56-1*) Hunter Bks.

***Lightle, Steve.** Operation Exodus II: Answers You Need to Know about Explosive Future Events. 272p. 1999. pap. 12.99 (*1-890900-05-2*) Insight Intl.

Lightley, John W. Jewish Sects & Parties in the Time of Jesus. 1980. lib. bdg. 75.00 (*0-8490-3150-8*) Gordon Pr.

Lightman. Great Ideas in Physics. 3rd ed. 250p. 2000. pap. 14.95 (*0-07-135738-6*) McGraw.

— Victorian Science in Context. LC 97-20789. 1997. lib. bdg. 70.00 (*0-226-48111-5*) U Ch Pr.

***Lightman, Alan.** The Diagnosis. LC 00-24543. 384p. 2000. 25.00 (*0-679-43615-4*) Pantheon.

Lightman, Alan P. Ancient Light: Our Changing View of the Universe. (Illus.). 192p. (C). 1991. text 18.95 (*0-674-03362-0*) HUP.

— Ancient Light: Our Changing View of the Universe. (Illus.). 192p. (C). 1993. pap. text 12.00 (*0-674-03363-9*) HUP.

— Dance for Two: Selected Essays. 192p. 1996. pap. 13.00 (*0-679-75877-1*) Pantheon.

Lightman, Alan P. Einstein's Dreams. LC 93-27403. (Illus.). 192p. 1994. mass mkt. 10.95 (*0-446-67011-1*, Pub. by Warner Bks) Little.

Lightman, Alan P. Good Benito. 224p. 1996. mass mkt. 8.99 (*0-446-67160-6*, Pub. by Warner Bks) Little.

— Great Ideas in Physics. 2nd ed. LC 96-7247. 304p. (C). 1996. pap. 38.75 (*0-07-038048-1*) McGraw.

Lightman, Alan P. Time for the Stars: Astronomy in the 1990's. 144p. 1994. mass mkt. 6.99 (*0-446-67024-3*, Pub. by Warner Bks) Little.

***Lightman, Alan P. & Atwan, Robert, eds.** The Best American Essays 2000. (Best American Ser.). 320p. 2000. 27.50 (*0-618-03578-8*); pap. 13.00 (*0-618-03580-X*) HM.

Lightman, Alan P. & Brawer, Roberta. Origins: The Lives & Worlds of Modern Cosmologists. (Illus.). 576p. 1990. text 42.00 (*0-674-64470-0*) HUP.

— Origins: The Lives & Worlds of Modern Cosmologists. (Illus.). 576p. 1992. pap. text 16.95 (*0-674-64471-9*) HUP.

Lightman, Alan P., jt. auth. see Rybicki, George B.

Lightman, Benjamin, jt. auth. see Lightman, Marjorie.

Lightman, Bernard. Victorian Science in Context. LC 97-20789. 1997. pap. text 22.50 (*0-226-48112-3*) U Ch Pr.

Lightman, Bernard, jt. ed. see Brown, Michael.

Lightman, Bernard V. The Origins of Agnosticism: Victorian Unbelief & the Limits of Knowledge. LC 87-2690. 264p. 1987. reprint ed. pap. 81.90 (*0-608-03722-2*, 206454700009) Bks Demand.

Lightman, Bernard V. & Helmstadter, Richard J., eds. Victorian Faith in Crisis: Essays on Continuity & Change in Nineteenth-Century Religious Belief. LC 88-63908. 403p. 1991. 49.50 (*0-8047-1602-1*) Stanford U Pr.

Lightman, Bernard V., jt. ed. see Eisen, Sydney.

***Lightman, Marjorie & Lightman, Benjamin.** Biographical Dictionary of Ancient Greek & Roman Women. LC 99-20682. (Illus.). 320p. 1999. 45.00 (*0-8160-3112-6*, Checkmark) Facts on File.

— Biographical Dictionary of Ancient Greek & Roman Women. (Illus.). 320p. 2000. pap. 18.95 (*0-8160-4436-8*, Checkmark) Facts on File.

Lightman, Marjorie & Negrin, Howard, eds. Outside Academe: New Ways of Working in the Humanities. LC 81-13463. 74p. 1982. pap. text 12.00 (*0-86656-132-3*) Haworth Pr.

Lightman, Marjorie, jt. ed. see Hoff-Wilson, Joan.

Lightman, Sam, jt. auth. see Patterson, Marvin L.

Lightman, Stafford L. Horizons in Medicine, Vol. 7. (Illus.). 608p. 1996. boxed set 99.95 (*0-86542-756-9*) Blackwell Sci.

Lightman, Stafford L., jt. auth. see Levy, Andrew.

Lightman, Susan, ed. HIV & the Eye. LC 99-29629. 300p. 1998. 58.00 (*1-86094-084-6*, Pub. by Imperial College) World Scientific Pub.

— Immunology of Eye Diseases. (Immunology & Medicine Ser.). (C). 1989. text 114.50 (*0-7923-8908-5*) Kluwer Academic.

Lightman, Susan & Towler, Hamish, eds. Uveitis. 163p. 1998. text 67.00 (*0-7279-1202-X*, Pub. by BMJ Pub) Login Brothers Bk Co.

Lightmark, Rondi, jt. auth. see Frost, April.

Lightner, Candy. Giving Sorrow Words: How to Cope with Grief & Get on with Your Life. 1991. mass mkt. 12.99 (*0-446-39290-1*, Pub. by Warner Bks) Little.

***Lightner, David A & Gurst, Jerome E.** Organic Conformational Analysis & Stereochemistry Form Circular Dichroism Spectroscopy. LC 99-38864. 480p. 2000. text 94.95 (*0-471-35405-8*, Wiley-VCH) Wiley.

Lightner, David L. Labor on the Illinois Central Railroad, 1852-1900: The Evolution of an Industrial Environment. Bruchey, Stuart, ed. LC 76-39834. (Nineteen Seventy-Seven Dissertations Ser.). (Illus.). 1977. lib. bdg. 36.95 (*0-405-09914-2*) Ayer.

Lightner, David L. & Lynde Dix, Dorothea. Asylum, Prison & Poorhouse: The Writings & Reform Work of Dorothea Dix in Illinois. LC 98-38579. 1999. pap. 19.95 (*0-8093-2163-7*) S Ill U Pr.

Lightner, Donald V., ed. A Handbook of Shrimp Pathology & Diagnostic Procedures for Diseases of Cultured Penaeid Shrimp. unabridged ed. (Illus.). xi, 256p. (C). 1996. ring bd. 80.00 (*0-9624529-9-8*) World Aquaculture.

Lightner, Helen. Class Voice & the American Art Song: A Source Book & Anthology. LC 91-7428. (Illus.). 191p. 1991. 34.50 (*0-8108-2381-0*) Scarecrow.

Lightner, Robert P. A Biblical Case for Total Inerrancy: How Jesus Viewed the Old Testament. LC 97-44684. 192p. 1997. pap. 11.99 (*0-8254-3110-7*) Kregel.

— The Death Christ Died: A Case for Unlimited Atonement. 2nd ed. LC 98-39124. 176p. 1998. pap. text 10.99 (*0-8254-3155-7*) Kregel.

— The God of the Bible & Other Gods: Is the Christian God Unique Among World Religions? LC 98-15293. 224p. 1998. pap. 11.99 (*0-8254-3154-9*) Kregel.

— Handbook of Evangelical Theology: A Historical, Biblical, & Contemporary Survey & Review. 312p. 1995. pap. 13.99 (*0-8254-3145-X*) Kregel.

— The Last Days Handbook. LC 97-28259. 256p. 1997. pap. 12.99 (*0-7852-1250-7*) Nelson.

— Manual de los Postreros Dias.Tr. of Last Days Handbook. (SPA.). 159p. 1995. 8.99 (*0-88113-193-8*, B001-1938) Caribe Betania.

***Lightner, Robert P.** Safe in the Arms of Jesus: God's Provision for the Death of a Child. 96p. 2000. pap. 6.99 (*0-8254-3156-5*) Kregel.

Lightner, Robert P. Sin, the Savior, & Salvation: The Theology of Everlasting Life. 320p. 1996. pap. 13.99 (*0-8254-3153-0*) Kregel.

Lightner, Robert Paul. Angels, Satan & Demons. LC 98-26782. (Swindoll Christian Leadership Library). 1998. 24.99 (*0-8499-1371-3*) Word Pub.

Lightner, Ted. Introduction to English Derivational Morphology. (Linguisticae Investigationes Supplementa Ser.: No. 6). xxxviii, 533p. 1983. 107.00 (*90-272-3116-8*) J Benjamins Pubng Co.

Lighton, Harriett V. Sandwich Cemeteries. 161p. 1997. reprint ed. pap. 19.50 (*0-8328-6023-9*) Higginson Bk Co.

Lighton, Merle. Addict to Yearning: Inspirational Philosophy & Religion. 1952. 5.00 (*0-910892-00-8*, 910892) Lighton Pubns.

***Lightsey, D., et al.** Healthy Start Initiative Vol. VI: A Community Driven Approach to Infant Mortality Reduction. LC 94-67194. 104p. 1999. pap. write for info. (*1-57285-050-7*) Nat Ctr Educ.

Lightsey, Harry M., Jr. Gems in a Crown: The People & Places of the College of Charleston - University of Charleston, South Carolina. 116p. 1993. 39.95 (*0-9638620-0-6*) Coll Charleston.

Lightship Software Staff. MacSheme: Users Guide & Language Reference Manual. 216p. 1990. pap. text 37.50 (*0-262-62077-4*) MIT Pr.

Lightstone, A. H. Mathematical Logic: An Introduction to Model Theory. LC 77-17838. (Mathematical Concepts & Methods in Science & Engineering Ser.: Vol. 9). (Illus.). 352p. 1978. 55.00 (*0-306-30894-0*, Plenum Trade) Perseus Pubng.

Lightstone, Jack N. The Rhetoric of the Babylonian Talmud, Its Social Meaning & Context. 330p. (C). 1994. pap. 22.95 (*0-88920-238-9*) W Laurier U Pr.

— Society, the Sacred & Scripture in Ancient Judaism: A Sociology of Knowledge. 148p. (C). 1988. pap. 15.95 (*0-88920-975-8*) W Laurier U Pr.

Lightstone, Jack N., et al. Ritual & Ethnic Identity: A Comparative Study of the Social Meaning of Liturgical Ritual in Synagogues. viii, 224p. (C). 1995. text 34.95 (*0-88920-247-8*) W Laurier U Pr.

Lightstone, Jack N., jt. ed. see Fishbane, Simcha.

Lightstone, James F., jt. ed. see Latman, Alan.

Lightstone, Susan, jt. auth. see Cork, David.

LightWavePro Magazine Editors. The Lightwave 3D Book: Tips, Techniques & Ready-to-Use Objects. (Illus.). 288p. 1997. pap. 39.95 incl. cd-rom (*0-87930-455-3*) Miller Freeman.

Lightweaver, Michael. A Day of Grace. Walker, Ron, ed. (Illus.). 96p. 1997. pap. 8.95 (*0-9666414-0-X*) Mount Light Pub.

Lightwood, James T. Charles Dickens & Music. LC 76-119084. (Studies in Music: No. 42). 1970. reprint ed. lib. bdg. 75.00 (*0-8383-1080-X*) M S G Haskell Hse.

— Samuel Wesley, Musician: The Story of His Life. LC 72-83745. 1972. reprint ed. 20.95 (*0-405-08748-9*) Ayer.

Lightwood, John M. Nature of Positive Law. xiv, 419p. 1982. reprint ed. 47.50 (*0-8377-0814-1*, Rothman) W S Hein.

Ligi, Elio E. Disturbances. Trusky, Tom, ed. LC 89-80858. (Ahsahta Press Modern & Contemporary Poets of the West Ser.). 60p. (Orig.). 1990. pap. 6.95 (*0-916272-40-0*) Ahsahta Pr.

***Ligibel, Ted.** The Toledo Zoo's First 100 Years: A Century of Adventure. LC 99-50338. (Illus.). 1999. write for info. (*1-57864-094-6*) Donning Co.

Ligibel, Ted & Wright, Richard T. Island Heritage: A Guided Tour to Lake Erie's Bass Islands. LC 87-5742. (Illus.). 82p. 1987. pap. 16.00 (*0-8142-0442-2*) Ohio St U Pr.

Ligibel, Ted J. Clark Lake: Images of a Michigan Tradition. (Illus.). 156p. 1991. 40.00 (*0-9630645-0-9*) Clark Lke HPC.

Ligne, Charles-Joseph De, see De Ligne, Charles-Joseph.

Lignell, Kathleen. Red Horses. LC 91-61223. 56p. 1991. pap. 7.95 (*0-9621570-1-5*) North Lights.

Lignell, Kathleen, ed. The Eloquent Edge: Fifteen Maine Women Writers. LC 89-38065. 176p. 1989. 6.95 (*0-934745-12-9*) Acadia Pub Co.

Lignor, Amy, jt. ed. see Mackenzie, Leslie.

Ligo, Larry L. The Concept of Function in Twentieth-Century Architectural Criticism. LC 84-44. (Studies in the Fine Arts - Architecture: No. 2). 233p. reprint ed. pap. 72.30 (*0-8357-1542-6*, 207033900085) Bks Demand.

Ligocki, Kenneth. Drug Testing: What We Will All Need to Know. LC 95-92591. 184p. (Orig.). 1996. pap. 12.95 (*0-9648741-9-9*) Scarbrgh Pub.

Ligon, Fred & Tannenbaum, Elizabeth. Picture Stories: Language & Literacy Activities for Beginners. (Illus.). 1990. pap. text 16.55 (*0-8013-0366-4*, 78145) Longman.

Ligon, Fred, et al. More Picture Stories: Language & Problem-Posing Activities for Beginners. 128p. 1991. pap. text 16.55 (*0-8013-0839-9*, 78905) Longman.

Ligon, Helen H. Successful Management Information Systems. rev. ed. LC 86-6979. (Research for Business Decisions Ser.: No. 78). 223p. reprint ed. pap. 69.20 (*0-8357-1703-8*, 207040100088) Bks Demand.

Ligon, J. David. Evolution of Avian Breeding Systems. (Oxford Ornithology Ser.). (Illus.). 526p. 1999. text 98.00 (*0-19-854913-X*) OUP.

Ligon, Linda C., ed. The Herb Companion Cooks: Recipes from the First Five Years of the Herb Companion Magazine. (Illus.). 128p. 1994. pap. 16.95 (*0-934026-95-5*) Interweave.

— Homespun, Handknit: Caps, Socks, Mittens & Gloves. LC 87-80522. (Illus.). 160p. (Orig.). 1987. pap. 15.00 (*0-934026-26-2*) Interweave.

— A Rug Weaver's Source Book. LC 84-82358. (Illus.). 176p. 1986. pap. 20.00 (*0-934026-16-5*) Interweave.

Ligon, Linda C., ed. see Atwater, Mary M.

Ligon, Linda C., ed. see Becker, Jim & Becker, Dotti.

Ligon, Linda C., ed. see Belsinger, Susan & Dille, Carolyn.

Ligon, Linda C., ed. see Cooper, Frank M.

Ligon, Linda C., ed. see DuBoff, Leonard D.

Ligon, Linda C., ed. see Van Stralen, Trudy.

Ligon, Lindon, ed. see Lovejoy, Sharon.

Ligon, Polly C., jt. ed. see Clubb, Deborah.

Ligon, Polly C., jt. ed. see Swegle, W. E.

Ligon, Richard. A True & Exact History of the Island of Barbadoes. (Cass Library of West Indian Studies: No. 11). (Illus.). 144p. 1970. reprint ed. 36.00 (*0-7146-1941-8*, Pub. by F Cass Pubs) Intl Spec Bk.

An Asterisk (*) at the beginning of an entry indicates that the title is appearing for the first time.

— A True & Exact History of the Island of Barbados. LC 98-134714. (Cass Library of West Indian Studies: No. 11). (Illus.). 144p. 1998. 42.50 (*0-7146-4886-8*, Pub. by F Cass Pubs) Intl Spec Bk.

Ligon, Terry, jt. auth. see Enns, Peter.

Ligon, Vicki, ed. see Freeman, Barry.

Ligon, W. V. The McGehee Papers: Southside Virginia in the 1850's. (Illus.). 120p. (Orig.). 1984. pap. 9.95 (*0-930051-00-9*) Green Creek Pub Co.

Ligon, William T., Sr. Imparting the Blessing to Your Children: What the Jewish Patriarchs Knew. 56p. 1989. student ed. 10.00 (*1-886327-00-9*) Fathers Blessing.

***Ligotti, Gene.** Dark Eagle: Six Crucial Years in the Life of Benedict Arnold. LC 99-91972. 2000. 25.00 (*0-7388-1454-7*); pap. 18.00 (*0-7388-1455-5*) Xlibris Corp.

— Swamp Fox: Southern Gentleman of the American Revolution. LC 99-91974. 2000. 25.00 (*0-7388-1458-X*); pap. 18.00 (*0-7388-1459-8*) Xlibris Corp.

— The Youngest Patriot: The Story of the British Occupation of Long Island. LC 99-69437. 2000. 25.00 (*0-7388-1270-6*); pap. 18.00 (*0-7388-1271-4*) Xlibris Corp.

Ligotti, Thomas. Grimscribe: His Lives & Works. 240p. 1994. mass mkt. 4.99 (*0-515-11471-5*, Jove) Berkley Pub.

— The Nightmare Factory. 576p. 1996. pap. 12.95 (*0-7867-0302-4*) Carroll & Graf.

— Noctuary. 208p. 1995. pap. 8.95 (*0-7867-0235-4*) Carroll & Graf.

— Songs of a Dead Dreamer. 288p. 1991. pap. 4.50 (*0-88184-721-6*) Carroll & Graf.

Ligou, Daniel. Dictionnaire de la Franc-Maconnerie, 2 vols., Set. 3rd ed. (FRE.). 1344p. 1991. 175.00 (*0-7859-4767-1*, M267) Fr & Eur.

— Dictionnaire Franc-Maconnerie. 4th ed. (FRE.). 1998. 195.00 (*0-320-00358-2*) Fr & Eur.

Ligou, Jacques P. Elements of Nuclear Engineering. xiv, 532p. (YA). (gr. 6 up). 1986. text 552.00 (*3-7186-0363-2*) Gordon & Breach.

Ligouri, Alphonsus. El Camino de la Cruz. (SPA.). 1991. pap. 0.60 (*0-89942-016-8*, 16/S) Catholic Bk Pub.

— The Way of the Cross: According to the Method of St. Alphonsus Liguori. 1995. reprint ed. pap. 1.00 (*0-89555-313-9*) TAN Bks Pubs.

Ligtelijn, Vincent, jt. auth. see Eyck, Aldo van.

***Ligtendag.** The Discovery of the Far South: The History of the Discovery of Antarctica As Revealed by Old Maps & Charts. 2000. 135.00 (*0-08-042812-6*, Pergamon Pr) Elsevier.

Ligthart, Ari, jt. ed. see Van Loo, Humphrey.

Liguori, Alfonso M., jt. auth. see Redemptorist Pastoral Pubns. Staff.

Liguori, Alphonsus. The Blessed Virgin Mary: Excerpt from the Glories of Mary. LC 82-50587. 96p. 1986. reprint ed. pap. 4.50 (*0-89555-177-2*) TAN Bks Pubs.

— The Glories of Mary. LC 90-33219. 215p. 1990. pap. 10.95 (*0-8189-0561-1*) Alba.

***Liguori, Alphonsus.** The Glories of Mary. LC 00-30949. 448p. 2000. pap. 18.95 (*0-7648-0664-5*) Liguori Pubns.

Liguori, Alphonsus. The Glories of Mary. large type ed. (Illus.). 1967. im. lthr. 6.75 (*0-89942-360-4*, 360/22) Catholic Bk Pub.

— Hail Holy Queen! 237p. 1995. pap. 8.00 (*0-89555-523-9*) TAN Bks Pubs.

— The Holy Eucharist. LC 93-5955. 1994. pap. 8.95 (*0-8189-0676-6*) Alba.

— Preparation for Death. abr. ed. LC 82-50596. 146p. 1991. reprint ed. pap. 8.00 (*0-89555-174-8*) TAN Bks Pubs.

— Selected Writings & Prayers of Saint Alphonsus Liguori. LC 97-71961. (A Leguori Classic Ser.). 192p. 1997. pap. 6.95 (*0-7648-0025-6*) Liguori Pubns.

— What Will Hell Be Like? Schaefer, John, ed. 24p. 1988. reprint ed. pap. 0.75 (*0-89555-341-4*) TAN Bks Pubs.

Liguori, Alphonsus & Ingram, Kristen Johnson. The Way of Mary: Praying & Living Her Words. LC 96-78940. 96p. 1997. pap. 4.95 (*0-7648-0033-7*) Liguori Pubns.

Liguori, Alphonsus & Redemptorist Pastoral Publication Staff. A Man of Vision: Saint Alphonsus Liguori. 48p. 1997. pap. 2.95 (*0-85231-157-5*) Liguori Pubns.

Liguori, Alphonsus. The Way of the Cross. 1987. pap. 0.60 (*0-89942-014-1*, 14/05) Catholic Bk Pub.

Liguori, Ann. A Passion for Golf: Celebrity Musings about the Game. LC 97-24658. 256p. 1997. 22.95 (*0-87833-972-8*) Taylor Pub.

Liguori, Salvatore, jt. auth. see Gray, Wiliam S.

Lih, D., jt. auth. see Arya, Pandit U.

Lih, D., jt. auth. see Arya, Pandit Usharbudh.

Lih, K. W., jt. ed. see Chang, M. K.

Lih, Lars T. Bread & Authority in Russia: 1914-1921. 1990. 50.00 (*0-520-06584-0*, Pub. by U CA Pr) Cal Prin Full Svc.

— Stalin's Letters to Molotov, 1925-1936. (Illus.). 308p. 1996. pap. 16.00 (*0-300-06861-1*) Yale U Pr.

Lih, Lars T., jt. ed. see Naumov, Oleg V.

Lihani, John. Manuscript Documents from Spain Dating from the 12th through the 18th Centuries Housed in the Special Collection of the Margaret I King Library, Univer. of Ky. LC 84-50663. (University of Kentucky Libraries Occasional Papers). 117p. (Orig.). 1984. lib. bdg. 7.00 (*0-917519-01-9*) U of KY Libs.

Lihani, John, ed. Global Demands on Language & the Mission of the Language Academies. LC 88-623526. xxxii, 219p. (Orig.). (C). 1988. pap. 14.95 (*0-929390-00-8*) KY Foreign Language Conference.

— Poema de Fernan Gonzalez. (Medieval Texts & Studies: No. 4). 188p. 1991. text 26.95 (*0-937191-21-3*) Mich St U Pr.

Liheng, Carol & Chan, Winnie S. Serials Cataloging Handbook: An Illustrative Guide to the Use of AACR2R & LC Rule Interpretations. 2nd ed. LC 98-2631. 470p. 1998. pap. 75.00 (*0-8389-0732-6*) American Library Association National Library.

Lihn, Enrique. Al Bello Aparecer de Este Lucero. (SPA.). 85p. 1983. pap. 10.00 (*0-910061-17-3*, 1403) Ediciones Norte.

— The Dark Room & Other Poems. Lerzundi, Patricio C., ed. Cohen, Jonathan et al, trs. from SPA. LC 77-12927. 1978. 8.95 (*0-8112-0676-9*, Pub. by New Directions) Norton.

Lihn, Enrique. The Dark Room & Other Poems. Lerzundi, Patricio C., ed. Cohen, Jonathan et al, trs. from SPA. LC 77-12927. 1978. pap. 2.45 (*0-8112-0677-7*, NDP452, Pub. by New Directions) Norton.

Liholm, Molly. The Adventurous Bride. 1998. per. 3.75 (*0-373-25806-2*, 1-25806-0) Harlequin Bks.

— Baby.Com. (Temptation Ser.). 1999. per. 3.75 (*0-373-25845-3*, 1-25845-8) Harlequin Bks.

— Boardroom Baby. (Temptation Ser.: No. 643). 1997. per. 3.50 (*0-373-25743-0*, 1-25743-5) Harlequin Bks.

— The Getaway Groom. (Temptation Ser.: No. 672). 1998. per. 3.75 (*0-373-25772-4*, 1-25772-4) Harlequin Bks.

— Tempting Jake. LC 96-325. (Temptation Ser.). 219p. 1995. per. 3.25 (*0-373-25652-3*, 1-25652-8) Harlequin Bks.

Lihs, Harriet R. Appreciating Dance: A Guide to the World's Livliest Art. (Illus.). 165p. 1998. pap. text 25.95 (*0-9665420-0-2*) H R Lihs.

— Jazz Dance. 2nd ed. 170p. 1993. pap. text 12.95 (*0-89641-259-8*) American Pr.

— Teaching Gymnastics. 2nd ed. 150p. (Orig.). 1994. pap. text 11.95 (*0-89641-226-1*) American Pr.

Lii, Battle, jt. auth. see Martin.

***Liiceanu, Gabriel.** The Paltinis Diary. (Library of Ideas). 250p. (C). 2000. 49.95 (*963-9116-88-2*); pap. 22.95 (*963-9116-89-0*) Ctrl Europ Univ.

Liindon, Jennie, jt. auth. see Bonel, Paul.

Liittschwager, David, jt. auth. see Middleton, Susan.

Liivaku, U. Stock Exchange Dictionary, Estonian-Finnish-English-German-Russian. (ENG, EST, FIN, GER & RUS.). 1994. 97.00 (*0-7859-9744-X*) Fr & Eur.

Lijklema, L., et al, eds. Interurba '92. (Water Science & Technology Ser.: Vol. 27). 256p. 1993. pap. 114.25 (*0-08-042350-7*, Pergamon Pr) Elsevier.

— Water Pollution Research & Control, Amsterdam 1984: Proceedings of the 12th Biennial Conference of the International Association on Water Pollution Research & Control Held in Amsterdam, The Netherlands, 17-20 September 1984. 1985. 330.00 (*0-08-033657-4*, Pub. by PPL) Elsevier.

Lijklema, L., ed. see IAPRC Programme Committee.

Lijn, Liliane. Crossing Map. (Illus.). (Orig.). 1983. pap. 14.95 (*0-500-97310-5*, Pub. by Thames Hudson) Norton.

Lijnen, H. R., et al, eds. Synthetic Substrates in Clinical Blood Coagulation Assays. (Developments in Hematology & Immunology Ser.: No. 1). 142p. 1980. text 73.50 (*90-247-2409-0*) Kluwer Academic.

Lijnzaad, Elizabeth. Reservations to UN-Human Rights Treaties: Ratify & Ruin? LC 94-40864. (International Studies in Human Rights: Vol. 38). 1995. lib. bdg. 136.50 (*0-7923-3256-3*, Pub. by M Nijhoff) Kluwer Academic.

Lijphart, Arend. Democracies: Patterns of Majoritarian & Consensus Government in Twenty-One Countries. LC 83-14639. 248p. 1984. pap. 15.00 (*0-300-03182-3*, Y 493) Yale U Pr.

— Democracy in Plural Societies: A Comparative Exploration. LC 77-76311. 1980. pap. 16.00 (*0-300-02494-0*) Yale U Pr.

— Electoral Systems & Party Systems: A Study of Twenty-Seven Democracies, 1945-1990. (Comparative Politics Ser.). (Illus.). 228p. 1995. reprint ed. pap. text 19.95 (*0-19-828054-8*) OUP.

— Institutional Design in New Democracies: Eastern Europe & Latin America. (C). 1996. pap. 26.00 (*0-8133-2109-3*, Pub. by Westview) HarpC.

Lijphart, Arend. Parliamentary vs. Presidential Government. (Oxford Readings in Politics & Government Ser.). 270p. 1992. pap. text 24.95 (*0-19-878044-3*) OUP.

— Patterns of Democracy: Government Forms & Performance in Thirty-Six Countries. LC 99-12365. (Illus.). 336p. 1999. pap. text 17.00 (*0-300-07893-5*) Yale U Pr.

Lijphart, Arend. Patterns of Democracy: Government Forms & Performance in Thirty-Six Countries. LC 99-12365. 336p. 1999. 40.00 (*0-300-07894-3*) Yale U Pr.

— The Politics of Accommodation: Pluralism & Democracy in the Netherlands. 2nd rev. ed. LC 68-11667. 255p. reprint ed. pap. 79.10 (*0-608-18025-4*, 202905100058) Bks Demand.

— Power Sharing in South Africa. LC 85-82195. (Policy Papers in International Affairs: No. 24). x, 179p. (C). 1985. pap. text 11.50 (*0-87725-524-5*) U of Cal IAS.

— The Trauma of Decolonization: The Dutch & West New Guinea. LC 66-12506. (Yale Studies in Political Science). 316p. reprint ed. pap. 98.00 (*0-608-11822-2*, 202201400024) Bks Demand.

Lijphart, Arend, ed. Conflict & Coexistence in Belgium: The Dynamics of a Culturally Divided Society. LC 81-7200. (Research Ser.: No. 46). (Illus.). ix, 171p. 1981. pap. text 10.50 (*0-87725-146-0*) U of Cal IAS.

Lijphart, Arend, jt. ed. see Grofman, Bernard N.

Lijphart, Arent & Grofman, Bernard N., eds. Choosing an Electoral System: Issues & Alternatives. LC 84-18283. (American Political Parties & Elections Ser.). 273p. 1984. 75.00 (*0-275-91216-7*, C1216, Praeger Pubs) Greenwood.

Likaka, Osumaka. Rural Society & Cotton in Colonial Zaire. LC 96-36690. (Illus.). 192p. 1997. 47.95 (*0-299-15330-4*); pap. 19.95 (*0-299-15334-7*) U of Wis Pr.

Likar, I. V. & Robinson, R. W. Atherosclerosis. (Monographs on Atherosclerosis: Vol. 12). (Illus.). viii, 176p. 1986. 118.50 (*3-8055-4069-8*) S Karger.

Like, E., ed. see Sheldon, J. G. M.

Like, Russel. After the Blue. unabridged ed. LC 97-97156. 256p. 1998. pap. 12.95 (*0-9661039-0-4*) Brunswick Galaxy.

Likely, John. The Thirsty Camel & the Big Fish. (J). (gr. 1-5). 1998. pap. 6.95 (*0-533-12609-6*) Vantage.

Likely, Newt A. & Courier, Herb. Day One: And Other Stories. (Illus.). iii, 131p. 1998. pap. 8.95 (*0-9671477-0-0*) Courier & Likely.

Liken, Shari, ed. Houston Medical Directory, 1990. 700p. 1990. 34.95 (*0-933745-06-0*) Med Prod.

— Houston Medical Directory, 1991. 710p. 1990. 39.95 (*0-933745-07-9*) Med Prod.

Likeness, James B. Crayons on the Wall. 128p. 1995. ring bd. 15.00 (*0-9629765-5-5*) Frederick Pubs.

Likens, Agnes. The Good Ol' Days. LC 93-91807. 162p. 1993. write for info. (*0-9639220-0-9*) A Likens.

Likens, Gene E., ed. An Ecosystem Approach to Aquatic Ecology. (Illus.). xiv, 516p. 1985. 120.00 (*0-387-96106-2*) Spr-Verlag.

— Long-Term Studies in Ecology. (Illus.). 210p. 1990. 101.95 (*0-387-96743-5*) Spr-Verlag.

Likens, Gene E. & Bormann, F. H. Biogeochemistry of a Forested Ecosystem. 2nd ed. LC 94-41866. (Illus.). 168p. 1995. 60.95 (*0-387-94502-4*) Spr-Verlag.

Likens, Gene E. & Bormann, F. Herbert. Biogeochemistry of a Forested Ecosystem. 2nd ed. LC 94-41866. (Illus.). 159p. 1995. 32.95 (*0-387-94351-X*) Spr-Verlag.

Likens, Gene E., et al. Biogeochemistry of a Forested Ecosystem. LC 76-50113. 1991. pap. 28.00 (*0-387-90225-2*) Spr-Verlag.

Likens, Gene E., jt. auth. see Bormann, F. H.

Likens, Gene E., jt. auth. see Wetzel, Robert G.

***Liker, Jeffrey, et al, eds.** Remade in America: Transplanting & Transforming Japanese Management Systems. LC 98-24205. (Japan Business & Economics Ser.). (Illus.). 432p. 1999. 39.95 (*0-19-511815-4*) OUP.

Liker, Jeffrey K., ed. Becoming Lean: Inside Stories of U. S. Manufacturers. LC 97-31995. (Illus.). 530p. 1998. 35.00 (*1-56327-173-7*) Productivity Inc.

Liker, Jeffrey K., et al. Engineered in Japan: Japanese Technology - Management Practices. (Illus.). 416p. 1995. 49.95 (*0-19-509555-3*) OUP.

Liker, Jeffrey K., jt. auth. see Fleischer, Mitchell.

Likert, Jane G., jt. auth. see Likert, Rensis.

Likert, Rensis & Likert, Jane G. New Ways of Managing Conflict. LC 75-23216. (Illus.). 383p. reprint ed. pap. 118.80 (*0-8357-3611-3*, AU0039600004) Bks Demand.

Likes, Homer C. & Likes, Phyllis C. Route 1 Mack, Colorado: A History of the Communities of Mack & New Liberty. unabridged ed. LC 97-94419. (Illus.). 850p. 1997. 69.95 (*0-9660635-0-3*) Likes Pub.

Likes, Phyllis C., jt. auth. see Likes, Homer C.

Likes, Robert C. & Day, Glenn R. From This Mountain-Cerro Gordo. LC 75-44236. (Illus.). 86p. 1975. pap. 8.95 (*0-912494-15-8*) Commun Print.

Likewise, Robert H. Introductory Saddlemaking. (Illus.). 108p. 1997. pap. 20.00 (*0-9659562-0-2*) Saddle Shed Pr.

Likhachev, A., ed. see International Agency for Research on Cancer Staff.

Likhachev, Dmitry S. Reflections on the Russian Soul: A Memoir. LC 00-31502. 350p. (C). 2000. 35.00 (*963-9116-46-7*) Ctrl Europ Univ.

Likhachev, N. I., et al. Design Handbook of Wastewater Systems, 4 vols., Set. Incl. Vol. 2. Methods of Wastewater Treatment. 500p. 1986. 185.00 (*0-89864-022-9*); Vol. 3. Municipal & Industrial Systems. 265p. 1986. 135.00 (*0-89864-023-7*); Vol. 4. Systems Integration & Ancillary Facilities. 150p. 1986. 100.00 (*0-89864-024-5*); (Illus.). 1986. 395.00 (*0-89864-025-3*) Allerton Pr.

— Wastewater Collection & Transportation, Vol. 1. 150p. 1986. 100.00 (*0-89864-021-0*) Allerton Pr.

Likhacheva, V. The Art of Byzantium. (RUS.). 310p. 1981. 35.00 (*0-7855-1502-X*) St Mut.

Likhachova, Liudmila, jt. auth. see Pleshanova, I.

Likhanov, Albert. Shadows Across the Sun. Lourie, Richard, tr. from RUS. LC 80-8440. 128p. (YA). (gr. 7 up). 1983. 10.50 (*0-06-023868-2*) HarpC Child Bks.

Likharev, Konstantin K. Dynamics of Josephson Junctions & Circuits. xx, 614p. 1986. text 336.00 (*2-88124-042-9*) Gordon & Breach.

Likhi, S. K. Hydraulics: Laboratory Manual. 1995. write for info. (*81-224-0516-9*, Pub. by Wiley Estrn) Franklin.

Likholobov, V., jt. ed. see Yermakov, Yu.

Likhtenshtefin, Gerktis. Spin Labeling Methods in Molecular Biology. LC 76-16500. 271p. reprint ed. pap. 84.10 (*0-608-13613-1*, 205515100008) Bks Demand.

Likhtenshtein, Gertz I. Biophysical Labeling Methods in Molecular Biology. LC 92-19487. (Illus.). 319p. (C). 1993. text 57.95 (*0-521-43132-8*) Cambridge U Pr.

Liking, Werewere. African Ritual Theatre: The Power of Um & A New Earth. Dingome, Jeanne N. et al, eds. (Illus.). 90p. 1997. 69.95 (*1-57309-067-0*, U Pr W Africa); pap. 49.95 (*1-57309-066-2*, U Pr W Africa) Intl Scholars.

***Liking, Werewere.** It Shall Be of Jasper & Coral & Love-Across-a-Hundred-Lives. De Jager, Marjolijin, tr. from FRE. LC 99-56677. 288p. 2000. 55.00 (*0-8139-1942-8*) U Pr of Va.

— It Shall Be of Jasper & Coral & Love-Across-a-Hundred-Lives. De Jager, Marjolijn, tr. from FRE. LC 99-56677. 288p. 2000. pap. 17.50 (*0-8139-1943-6*) U Pr of Va.

Likins, Stephen F. Playing Corners, Counting Points, Understanding Shape & Other Amateur Go Topics. (Illus.). 80p. Date not set. pap. 24.95 (*0-9671321-0-X*) Stevel Enterp.

— Simplified Winning Wagering System Vol. 1: Roulette. (Illus.). 58p. Date not set. pap. 25.95 (*0-9671321-1-8*) Stevel Enterp.

Likoudis, James & Whitehead, K. D. The Pope, the Council, & the Mass. 1981. 13.95 (*0-8158-0400-8*) Chris Mass.

Likoudis, James, et al. Ending the Byzantine Greek Schism: Containing: The 14th c. Apologia of Demetrios Kydones for Unity with Rome & St. Thomas Aquinas' Contra Errones Graecorum. rev. ed. (Illus.). 235p. (C). 1992. pap. text 14.95 (*1-879860-01-5*) Cath United Faith.

Liksen, H. J. Classical Circus Equitation Liberty, High School, Quadrilles & Vaulting. Coxe, Anthony H., tr. 240p. 1990. 120.00 (*0-85131-542-9*, Pub. by J A Allen) St Mut.

Liksom, Rosa. One Night Stands. (Masks Ser.). 128p. 1994. pap. 11.99 (*1-85242-292-0*) Serpents Tail.

Likta, Michael. Int'l Dim Of Legal Environment Of Bus. 2nd ed. (SWC-Business Law). 256p. (C). 1990. pap. 21.75 (*0-534-92505-7*) S-W Pub.

Lila, Kim. Simply Casseroles: Over 100 Quick & Delicious One-Dish Dinners. LC 97-37051. (Simply Cooking Ser.). 150p. 1998. pap. text 14.95 (*1-57284-013-7*) Surrey Bks.

***Lilac, Susan.** Your Chess Questions Answered. 144p. 1999. pap. text 12.95 (*0-7134-8406-3*, Pub. by B T B) Branford.

Lilburn, Pat & Rawson, Pam. Let's Talk Math: Encouraging Children to Explore Ideas. LC 93-44870. 120p. 1994. pap. text 16.00 (*0-435-08348-1*, 08348) Heinemann.

***Lilburn, Tim.** To the River. LC 99-205259. 88p. 2000. 12.95 (*0-7710-5323-1*) McCland & Stewart.

Lilburn, Tim, ed. Poetry & Knowing: Speculative Essays & Interviews. 192p. 1995. pap. 19.95 (*1-55082-116-4*, Pub. by Quarry Pr) LPC InBook.

Lilburn, Tim & Shantz, Susan. From the Great Above She Opened Her Ear to the Great Below. 48p. 1988. pap. 16.95 (*0-919626-39-4*, Pub. by Brick Bks) Genl Dist Srvs.

Lile, Laird A. & McEachern, William A. Florida Probate: Discussion & Commentary on Code, Rules & Forms. LC 94-73045. 1999. ring bd. 89.50 (*1-887024-32-8*) Bisel Co.

Lile, R. Kenneth. Thy Hand Hath Provided: A History of the Louisville Conference of the United Methodist Church. (Illus.). 480p. 1996. text 29.95 (*1-881576-92-2*) Providence Hse.

Lileks, James. Fresh Lies. 304p. 1995. per. 10.00 (*0-671-73704-X*, PB Trade Paper) PB.

— Mr. Obvious. 1995. pap. 5.50 (*0-671-73705-8*) S&S Trade.

— Notes of a Nervous Man. Chelius, Jane, ed. 240p. 1992. reprint ed. pap. 10.00 (*0-671-73702-3*) PB.

***Liles, Gerren.** On the Road to Damascus. vi, 96p. 2000. pap. 10.95 (*0-9671082-2-5*, Division of Wrds) Black Alchemist.

Liles, Glennis S. The W-Hollow Cookbook. Charles, Chuck D., ed. LC 95-45901. (Illus.). 310p. 1996. 24.00 (*0-945084-56-0*) J Stuart Found.

— W-Hollow Holidays & Holiday Recipes. LC 95-66858. 240p. 1995. write for info. (*1-886029-07-5*) Spider Hill Pr.

Liles, Glennis S. & Shultz, Helen. W-Hollow Kitchen Adventure: Cooking with Herbs & Hot Peppers. LC 99-51801. (Illus.). 224p. 1999. 24.00 (*0-945084-77-3*) J Stuart Found.

Liles, Hannah L. Inspired by the Light. LC 96-95371. 96p. (Orig.). 1997. pap. 11.95 (*1-890268-00-3*) Inspired Light.

Liles, J. N. The Art & Craft of Natural Dyeing: Traditional Recipes for Modern Use. LC 90-12045. 254p. 1990. 42.00 (*0-87049-669-7*); pap. 19.50 (*0-87049-670-0*) U of Tenn Pr.

***Liles, Janene L.** Wine Tasting in San Diego & Beyond. LC 99-75894. (Illus.). 160p. 1999. pap. 10.95 (*0-9674351-0-2*) Popcorn Pr CA.

Liles, Jason & Sokitch, Shiroko. Building a Successful Practice: A Step by Step Guide to Building Your Own Profitable Business. 3rd rev. ed. 60p. 1997. pap. text 19.95 (*0-9660950-0-6*) Hrt to Hrt Med.

Liles, Larry E. & Neimeyer, Robert A. Winning Racquetball. 192p. (C). 1993. text. write for info. (*0-697-13151-3*) Brown & Benchmark.

Liles, Marcia T., ed. see Taggard, Genevieve.

Liles, Maurine W. Kitty of Blossom Prairie. (Illus.). 128p. (J). (gr. 5-6). 1992. 14.95 (*0-89015-863-0*) Sunbelt Media.

— The Littlest Vaquero: A Story of the First Texas Cowboys, Longhorns, & the American Revolution. LC 96-24043. (Illus.). 120p. (J). (gr. 4-6). 1996. 14.95 (*1-57168-103-5*, Eakin Pr) Sunbelt Media.

— Rebecca of Blossom Prairie: Grandmother of a Vice President. Roberts, M., ed. (Illus.). 105p. (J). (gr. 5-6). 1990. 14.95 (*0-89015-754-5*) Sunbelt Media.

— Sam & the Speaker's Chair. LC 93-42374. 148p. (YA). (gr. 8-9). 1994. 14.95 (*0-89015-946-7*) Sunbelt Media.

— Sam & the Speaker's Chair: The Story of Sam Rayburn. (Illus.). 148p. (J). 1997. pap. 5.95 (*0-89015-978-5*, Eakin Pr) Sunbelt Media.

— Willer & the Piney Woods Doctor. LC 95-30740. (Illus.). 112p. (J). (gr. 6-7). 1995. 14.95 (*1-57168-058-6*, Eakin Pr) Sunbelt Media.

Liles, Necia D., ed. see Lord, Israel S.

Liles, Parker, et al. Typing Mailable Letters. 3rd ed. Rubin, Audrey S., ed. (Illus.). (J). (gr. 9-12). 1978. text 11.24 (*0-07-037855-X*) McGraw.

Liley, D. T., jt. auth. see Kingsford, D. P.

L

Liley, Peter E., et al. Properties of Inorganic & Organic Fluids. (CINDAS Data Series on Material Properties: Vol. V[00ad]1). 309p. 1988. 165.00 (0-89116-802-8) Hemisp Pub.

Liley, Peter E., ed. see Thermophysical Properties Symposium Staff.

***Liley, Vicki.** Asian Hot & Spicy. (Essential Kitchen Ser.). (Illus.). 112p. 2000. pap. 17.95 (962-593-933-4) Tuttle Pubng.

Liley, Vicki. Dim Sum. LC 99-60843. (Essential Kitchen Ser.). (Illus.). 111p. 1999. 17.95 (962-593-528-2, Periplus Eds) Tuttle Pubng.

***Liley, Vicki.** Essential Kitchen: Hors D Oeuvres. LC 99-50047. (Illus.). 112p. 2000. 17.95 (962-593-820-6, Pub. by Periplus) Tuttle Pubng.

Liley, Vicki. Noodles: Essential Kitchen. LC 98-37002. (Essential Kitchen Ser.). (Illus.). 112p. 1999. 17.95 (962-593-459-6) Periplus.

***Liley, Vicki.** Vegetables: Essential Kitchen. LC 99-50046. (Essential Kitchen Ser.). (Illus.). 112p. 2000. 17.95 (962-593-821-4, Pub. by Periplus) Tuttle Pubng.

Liley, Vicki. Wok: Essential Kitchen. LC 98-37003. (Essential Kitchen Ser.). (Illus.). 1999. 17.95 (962-593-264-X) Periplus.

Lilford, Richard J. & Setchell, Marcus E. MCQs in Gynaecology & Obstetrics. 3rd ed. 88p. pap. text 14.95 (0-340-58896-9, Pub. by E A) Routldge.

Lilford, Richard J., jt. auth. see Chard, Tim.

Lilie, Ralph-J. Byzantium & the Crusader States 1096-1204. rev. ed. Morris, J. C. & Ridings, Jean E., trs. (Illus.). 358p. 1994. text 75.00 (0-19-820407-8) OUP.

Lilie, Tish. The Knitting Problem Solver. Foster, Kim & Parkinson, Connie, eds. (Country Wisdom Bulletin Ser.). (Illus.). 32p. 1991. 2.95 (0-88266-696-7, Storey Pub) Storey Bks.

Lilien, Gary. Marketing Management & Strategy: Marketing Engineering Applications. 128p. (C). 1998. pap. text 33.00 (0-321-04640-4, Prentice Hall) P-H.

— Marketing Research: Marketing Engineering Applications. 152p. (C). 1998. pap. text 40.00 (0-321-04646-3, Prentice Hall) P-H.

— New Product & Brand Management: Marketing Engineering Applications. 144p. (C). 1998. pap. text 33.00 (0-321-04643-9, Prentice Hall) P-H.

Lilien, Gary L. Marketing Engineering: Computer-Assisted Marketing Analysis & Planning, Revised Edition, Compatible with Office 97. 400p. (C). 1998. text 123.00 incl. audio compact disk (0-321-03050-8, Prentice Hall) P-H.

— Marketing Mix Analysis with Lotus 1-2-3. 250p. 1986. 42.50 incl. 3.5 hd (0-89426-168-1) Course Tech.

— Marketing Models. LC 91-34512. 1995. pap. text 39.00 (0-13-545641-X, Pub. by P-H) S&S Trade.

Lilien, Gary L., jt. ed. see Eliashberg, J.

Lilienfeld, Abraham M. Epidemiology of Mongolism. LC 78-82451. (Illus.). 160p. reprint ed. 49.60 (0-8357-9270-6, 201155900078) Bks Demand.

Lilienfeld, Abraham M., et al. Cancer in the United States. LC 72-80658. (Vital & Health Statistics Monographs, American Public Health Association). (Illus.). 572p. 1972. 55.50 (0-674-09425-5) HUP.

Lilienfeld, Abraham M., jt. auth. see Levine, Sol.

***Lilienfeld, Jane.** Languages of Addiction. LC 99-22567. 1999. text 45.00 (0-312-21850-8) St Martin.

— Reading Alcoholisms: Theorizing Character & Narrative in Selected Novels of Hardy, Joyce, & Woolf. LC 99-21180. 272p. 1999. text 49.95 (0-312-21709-9) St Martin.

Lilienfeld, Pedro. Handbook of Methods for Optical Sensing of Airborne Particles. 2000. 79.95 (0-87371-489-X) Lewis Pubs.

***Lilienfeld, Robert.** Use Less Stuff. 1999. pap. 12.00 (0-449-45903-9) Fawcett.

Lilienfeld, Robert, jt. auth. see Bensman, Joseph.

Lilienfeld, Robert M. & Rathje, William L. Use Less Stuff: Environmentalism for Who We Really Are. LC 98-26903. 288p. 1999. pap. 12.00 (0-449-00168-7, Columbine) Fawcett.

Lilienfeld, Scott. Current Readings in Abnormal Psychology: Contemporary Questions & Debates in Psychopathology Research. LC 97-53041. (Psychology Ser.). 234p. (C). 1998. mass mkt. 40.95 (0-534-35416-5) Brooks-Cole.

Lilienfeld, Scott O. Seeing Both Sides: Classic Controversies in Abnormal Psychology. LC 94-18083. 512p. 1994. mass mkt. 43.95 (0-534-25134-X) Brooks-Cole.

Lilienfield, David E. & Stolley, Paul D. Foundations of Epidemiology. 3rd ed. (Illus.). 384p. 1994. text 55.00 (0-19-505035-5); pap. text 34.50 (0-19-505036-3) OUP.

Lilienheim, Henry. The Aftermath: A Survivor's Odyssey Through War-Torn Europe. LC 95-182940. 181p. 1994. pap. 12.95 (0-919688-44-6) ACCESS Pubs Network.

Lilienstein, Fred M. Magnetics Engineering Fundamentals & Computer-Aided Design Solutions. LC 92-26751. 1993. text 115.95 (0-442-00738-8, VNR) Wiley.

Lilienthal, Alfred M. The Zionist Connection II. 904p. 1986. pap. 29.00 (0-949667-33-1, 0310, Pub. by Veritas Pub) Legion Survival.

Lilienthal, B. Phosphates & Dental Caries. (Monographs in Oral Science: Vol. 6). (Illus.). 1977. 60.00 (3-8055-2677-6) S Karger.

Lilienthal, David E. Big Business: A New Era. LC 73-2517. (Big Business; Economic Power in a Free Society Ser.). 1973. reprint ed. 19.95 (0-405-05097-6) Ayer.

— Change, Hope & the Bomb. LC 63-16236. 178p. reprint ed. pap. 55.20 (0-8357-8827-X, 203338400085) Bks Demand.

Lilienthal, Meta. Dear Remembered World. (American Autobiography Ser.). 248p. 1995. reprint ed. lib. bdg. 79.00 (0-7812-8577-1) Rprt Serv.

Lilienthal, Nancy, et al. Tackling Toxics in Everyday Products: A Directory of Organizations. LC 91-29961. 192p. 1992. pap. 19.95 (0-918780-56-X) INFORM NY.

Lilienthal, Nancy, jt. auth. see Rohmann, Steven O.

Lilienthal, Philip E., tr. see Bousquet, Georges H.

Lilies, W. Conrad, Jr., jt. auth. see Larson, Eric B.

Liliuokalani. Hawaii's Story by Hawaii's Queen. (American Biography Ser.). 1991. reprint ed. lib. bdg. 89.00 (0-7812-8245-4) Rprt Serv.

— The Kumulipo: A Hawaiian Creation Myth. Campbell, James K. & Vorhies, Aleen, eds. LC 78-60923. (Illus.). 1978. reprint ed. pap. 7.95 (0-917850-02-5) Pueo Pr.

Lilja, David J. & Bird, Peter L., eds. The Interaction of Compilation Technology & Computer Architecture. LC 94-1648. 296p. (C). 1994. text 133.50 (0-7923-9451-8) Kluwer Academic.

Lilja, Dick, jt. auth. see Lilja, Irene.

Lilja, Irene & Lilja, Dick. Suislaw Forest Hikes: A Guide to Oregon's Coast Range. (Illus.). 64p. (Orig.). 1990. pap. 8.95 (0-910467-08-0) Heritage Assocs.

Lilja, R., et al. Unemployment & Labour Market Flexibility in Finland. vi, 222p. 1990. pap. 27.00 (92-2-107273-8) Intl Labour Office.

Lilja, Robert. International Equity Markets: The Art of the Deal. 600p. 1997. 240.00 (1-85564-368-5, Pub. by Euromoney) Am Educ Systs.

Lilja, Torsten & Hovdenakk, Per. Christo & Jean-Claude Projects: Works from the Lilja Collection. (Illus.). 192p. 1996. 50.00 (1-898592-06-3, Pub. by Art Bks Intl) Partners Pubs Grp.

Liljebald, Cynthia B. TV Toys & the Shows That Inspired Them. LC 95-82426. (Illus.). 224p. 1996. pap. 19.95 (0-87341-440-3, TTT) Krause Pubns.

Liljedahl, John B., et al. Tractors & Their Power Units. 4th ed. LC 96-83446. 463p. 1997. 76.25 (0-929355-72-5) Am Soc Ag Eng.

Liljedahl, Karen. Tom Cruise. LC 98-85415. (Little Bks.). (Illus.). 80p. 1998. 4.95 (0-8362-7155-6) Andrews & McMeel.

Liljegren, S. B. American Studies in Sweden. (Essays & Studies on American Language & Literature: Vol. 14). (Orig.). 1962. pap. 25.00 (0-8115-0194-9) Periodicals Srv.

— Bulwer-Lytton's Novels & Isis Unveiled. (Essays & Studies on English Language & Literature: Vol. 18). (Orig.). 1957. pap. 15.00 (0-8115-0216-3) Periodicals Srv.

— Joseph Conrad As a "Prober of Feminine Hearts" Notes on the Novel "The Rescue" (Essays & Studies on English Language & Literature: Vol. 27). (Orig.). 1968. pap. 25.00 (0-8115-0225-2) Periodicals Srv.

— Revolt Against Romanticism in American Literature: As Evidenced in the Work of S. L. Clemens. 59p. 1983. pap. 12.50 (0-87556-650-2) Saifer.

— The Revolt Against Romanticism in American Literature: As Evidenced in the Works of S. L. Clemens. (Essays & Studies on American Language & Literature: Vol. 1). 1974. reprint ed. pap. 25.00 (0-8115-0183-3) Periodicals Srv.

— Studies on the Origin & Early Tradition of English Utopian Fiction. (Essays & Studies on English Language & Literature: Vol. 23). (Orig.). 1961. pap. 25.00 (0-8115-0221-X) Periodicals Srv.

Liljegren, Sten. American & European in the Works of Henry James. LC 71-119080. (Studies in Henry James: No. 17). (C). 1970. reprint ed. lib. bdg. 75.00 (0-8383-1076-1) M S G Haskell Hse.

— The Revolt Against Romanticism in American Literature. (BCL1-PS American Literature Ser.). 60p. 1993. reprint ed. lib. bdg. 59.00 (0-7812-6951-2) Rprt Serv.

— The Revolt Against Romanticism in American Literature: As Evidenced in the Works of S. L. Clemens. LC 65-15896. (Studies in Fiction: No. 34). (C). 1969. reprint ed. lib. bdg. 75.00 (0-8383-0583-0) M S G Haskell Hse.

— Studies in Milton. LC 67-30816. (Studies in Milton: No. 22). 1969. reprint ed. lib. bdg. 75.00 (0-8383-0718-3) M S G Haskell Hse.

Liljegren, Steven K., jt. auth. see Chiauzzi, Emil.

Liljenberg, Sue. Heart to Heart Ministries: Help for Those Suffering from Post-Abortion Trauma. 128p. (Orig.). 1996. pap. 15.00 (1-883893-62-3) WinePress Pub.

Liljencrants, Johan. Spiritism & Religion. 1926. 19.50 (0-8159-6820-5) Devin.

Liljencrants, Jonathan. Memory Defects in Organic Psychoses. (Psychology Monographs General & Applied: Vol. 32). 1974. reprint ed. 55.00 (0-8115-1431-5) Periodicals Srv.

Liljendahl, Eva. Explosion & Other Poems. LC 94-71350. 104p. (Orig.). 1994. pap. write for info. (0-9637979-1-3) T Y Okosun.

— Un-Sheltered. 63p. 1996. pap. write for info. (0-9637979-3-X) T Y Okosun.

Liljenstolpe, Carl & Burke, Mary A. Recruiting Volunteers: A Guide for Non-Profits. Manber, Beverly, ed. LC 91-76308. (Fifty-Minute Ser.). (Illus.). 90p. (Orig.). 1992. pap. 10.95 (1-56052-141-4) Crisp Pubns.

Liljenstolpe, Carl, jt. auth. see Burke, Mary A.

Liljequist, Gosta H., ed. Weather & Weather Maps. (Contributions to Current Research in Geophysics Ser.: 10). 265p. (C). 1982. text 71.95 (0-8176-1192-4) Birkhauser.

Liljestrand, G., jt. ed. see Holmstedt, B.

Liljestrom, Rita & Rwebangira, Magdalena K., eds. Haraka, Haraka... Look before You Leap: Youth at the Crossroad of Custom & Modernity. LC 99-184914. 275p. 1999. pap. 31.95 (91-7106-429-X) Transaction Pubs.

Liljestrom, Rita, et al. Young Children in China. 262p. 1984. 79.00 (0-905028-30-9, Pub. by Multilingual Matters); pap. 29.95 (0-905028-29-5, Pub. by Multilingual Matters) Taylor & Francis.

Liljestrom, Rita, jt. ed. see Tumbo-Masabo, Z.

Lilker, Shalom. Kibbutz Judaism: A New Tradition in the Making. LC 80-70886. (Norwood Editions, Kibbutz, Cooperative Societies, & Alternative Social Policy Bks.: Vol. 7). 240p. 1983. 14.95 (0-8453-4740-3, Cornwall Bks) Assoc Univ Prs.

Lill, Debra. Music & Drum: Voices of War & Peace, Hope & Dreams. LC 92-39312. 32p. (J). (ps up). 1997. 16.95 (0-399-22024-0, Philomel) Peng Put Young Read.

Lill, Herbert F. An Early History of Mascoutah to & Including the Year 1850. 184p. 1997. reprint ed. lib. bdg. 29.00 (0-8328-5766-1) Higginson Bk Co.

Lill, Klaus, jt. auth. see Crowner, David.

Lill, Roland, jt. ed. see Neupert, Walter.

Lill, Wayne P., Jr. Decision Tables & Flowcharts: DEVA, the Decision Table Evaluation Program for Strategic Logic Design & Development. 200p. 1992. 34.95 (1-882619-08-0) Binary Triangles.

Lill, Wendy. All Fall Down. LC 94-197184. 108p. 1994. pap. 11.95 (0-88922-336-X, Pub. by Talonbks) Genl Dist Srvs.

Lill, Wendy. Corker. LC 99-191787. 1998. pap. text 11.95 (0-88922-394-7) Talon Pr.

Lill, Wendy. The Fighting Days. LC 86-115084. 96p. 1985. pap. 10.95 (0-88922-226-6, Pub. by Talonbks) Genl Dist Srvs.

Lill, Wendy. The Glace Bay Miners' Museum: A Stage Play Based on the Novel by Sheldon Currie. 128p. 1996. pap. 11.95 (0-88922-369-6, Pub. by Talonbks) Genl Dist Srvs.

Lilla, Mark. Arch in Public Space. 1986. pap. write for info. (0-02-919170-X) Free Pr.

— G. B. Vico: The Making of an Anti-Modern. (Illus.). 320p. (C). 1993. text 50.95 (0-674-33962-2) HUP.

— G. B. Vico: The Making of an Anti-Modern. LC 92-23388. (Illus.). 320p. 1993. text. write for info. (0-674-54305-X) HUP.

— G. B. Vico: The Making of an Anti-Modern. (Illus.). 272p. 1994. pap. text 20.50 (0-674-33963-0, LILVIX) HUP.

Lilla, Mark, jt. ed. see Glazer, Nathan.

***Lillard, Charles & Glavin, Terry.** A Voice Great Within Us. (Transmontanus Ser.: Vol. 7). (Illus.). 120p. 1998. pap. 12.00 (0-921586-56-6, Pub. by New Star Bks) Genl Dist Srvs.

***Lillard, David.** Hiking Maryland & Delaware. (Guide Ser.). (Illus.). 288p. 2000. pap. 16.95 (1-56044-721-4) Falcon Pub Inc.

Lillard, David & Hicks, Gwyn. Hikes in the Virginias. (Exploring the Appalachian Trail Ser.). (Illus.). 416p. 1998. pap. 19.95 (0-8117-2670-3) Stackpole.

Lillard, Jeremiah B., et al. An Introduction to the Archaeology of Central California. fac. ed. (Sacramento Junior College, Department of Anthropology Bulletin Ser.: No. 2). (Illus.). 130p. 1939. reprint ed. pap. text 14.38 (1-55567-556-5) Coyote Press.

Lillard, Jeremiah V. & Purves, William K. The Archaeology of the Deer Creek-Cosumnes Area, Sacramento Co., California. fac. ed. (Sacramento Junior College, Department of Anthropology Bulletin Ser.: No. 1). (Illus.). 60p. 1936. reprint ed. pap. text 7.19 (1-55567-555-7) Coyote Press.

Lillard, Paul T. Poems from the Alamo Saloon. LC 98-90154. 1998. pap. 10.95 (0-533-12728-9) Vantage.

Lillard, Paula P. Montessori: A Modern Approach. LC 78-163334. (Illus.). 192p. (C). 1988. pap. 12.00 (0-8052-0920-4) Schocken.

— Montessori in the Classroom: A Teacher's Account of How Children Really Learn. LC 97-3290. 1997. pap. 14.00 (0-8052-1087-3) Schocken.

— Montessori Today: A Comprehensive Approach to Education from Birth to Adulthood. (Illus.). 240p. 1996. pap. 12.00 (0-8052-1061-X) Schocken.

Lillard, Reshana, ed. see Marshall, Carl.

Lillard, Richard G. The Great Forest. LC 72-8129. (Illus.). 452p. 1973. reprint ed. lib. bdg. 49.50 (0-306-70534-6) Da Capo.

— My Urban Wilderness in the Hollywood Hills: A Year of Years on Quito Lane. (Illus.). 218p. (Orig.). (C). 1983. pap. text 24.00 (0-8191-3318-3); lib. bdg. 52.00 (0-8191-3317-5) U Pr of Amer.

Lillard, Stewart. Meigs County, Tennessee: A Documented Account of Its European Settlement & Growth. rev. ed. (Illus.). 202p. 1983. reprint ed. 20.00 (0-317-39990-X) Southern Hist Pr.

Lillberg, John & Oothoudt, Michael, eds. Computing for High Luminosity & High Intensity Facilities. LC 90-55634. (AIP Conference Proceedings Ser.: No. 209). (Illus.). 704p. 1990. 95.00 (0-88318-786-8) Am Inst Physics.

Lille, Eva L. & Petersen, Nils H., eds. Liturgy & the Arts in the Middle Ages: Studies in Honour of C. Clifford Flanigan. LC 97-162436. (Illus.). 304p. 1996. 56.00 (87-7289-361-3) Paul & Co Pubs.

Lillegard, Dee. The Big Bug Ball. LC 97-9614. (Illus.). 32p. (ps-3). 1999. 15.95 (0-399-23121-8, G P Putnam) Peng Put Young Read.

Lillegard, Dee. The Day the Daisies Danced. LC 93-30583. (Illus.). 32p. (J). (ps-3). 1996. 15.95 (0-399-22661-3, G P Putnam) Peng Put Young Read.

Lillegard, Dee. The Hee Haw River. (J). 1995. 14.95 (0-8050-2375-5) H Holt & Co.

— James A. Garfield. LC 87-18200. (Encyclopedia of Presidents Ser.). (Illus.). 100p. (J). (gr. 3 up). 1987. lib. bdg. 24.00 (0-516-01394-7) Childrens.

— James K. Polk. LC 87-35188. (Encyclopedia of Presidents Ser.). (Illus.). 100p. (J). (gr. 3 up). 1988. lib. bdg. 24.00 (0-516-01351-3) Childrens.

— John Tyler. LC 87-18202. (Encyclopedia of Presidents Ser.). (Illus.). 100p. (J). (gr. 3 up). 1987. lib. bdg. 24.00 (0-516-01393-9) Childrens.

— Papas el Martes, Level 1. (Let Me Read Ser.).Tr. of Potatoes on Tuesday. (SPA.). (J). 1996. 2.95 (0-673-36327-9, GoodYrBooks) Addson-Wesley Educ.

***Lillegard, Dee.** Poombah of Badoombah. (Illus.). (J). 2000. pap. 5.99 (0-698-11823-5) Putnam Pub Group.

Lillegard, Dee. Potatoes on Tuesday. 2nd ed. (Let Me Read Ser.). (Illus.). 8p. (J). (ps). 1995. pap. 2.95 (0-673-36235-3, GoodYrBooks) Addson-Wesley Educ.

— Richard Nixon. LC 87-35185. (Encyclopedia of Presidents Ser.). (Illus.). 100p. (J). (gr. 5-8). 1988. lib. bdg. 24.00 (0-516-01356-4) Childrens.

— Tiger Tiger. Date not set. 15.95 (0-399-22633-8) Putnam Pub Group.

— Where Is It? LC 84-7005. (Rookie Readers Ser.). (Illus.). 32p. (J). (gr. k-2). 1984. pap. 4.95 (0-516-42065-8) Childrens.

Lillegard, Dee & Stoker, Wayne. Nevada. rev. ed. LC 90-34665. (America the Beautiful Ser.). (Illus.). 144p. (J). (gr. 5-8). 1992. lib. bdg. 28.00 (0-516-00474-3) Childrens.

Lillegard, Dee, jt. auth. see Redfield, James.

Lillegard, Wade A. & Rucker, Karen S., eds. Handbook of Sports Medicine: A Symptom-Oriented Approach. (Illus.). 298p. 1993. text 70.00 (1-56372-052-3) Buttrwrth-Heinemann.

Lillegard, Wade A., et al. Handbook of Sports Medicine: A Symptom-Oriented Approach. 2nd ed. LC 98-26931. 448p. 1998. text 65.00 (0-7506-9041-0) Buttrwrth-Heinemann.

Lillegraven, Jason A., et al. Evolutionary Relationships of Middle Eocene & Younger Species of Centetodon (Mammalia, Insectivora, Geolabididae) with a Description of the Dentition of Ankylodon (Adapisoricidae) LC 81-53020. (Illus.). 116p. (C). 1981. pap. 12.50 (0-941570-00-2) U of Wyoming.

— Vertebrates, Phylogeny, & Philosophy. Flanagan, K., ed. LC 86-50857. (Illus.). 372p. 1986. lib. bdg. 30.00 (0-941570-02-9) U of Wyoming.

Lillehoj, Erik P., jt. ed. see Malik, Vedpal S.

Lillemoe, et al. Essentials of Surgery: Scientific Principles & Practice. Greenfield, Lazar J., ed. LC 97-2444. (Illus.). 700p. 1997. spiral bd. 49.95 (0-397-51532-4) Lppncott W & W.

Lillemoe, Keith D., et al. Review for Surgery: Scientific Principles & Practice. 2nd ed. Greenfield, Lazar J., ed. (Illus.). 528p. 1996. pap. text 39.95 incl. mac hd (0-397-51831-5) Lppncott W & W.

Liller, Tamara, ed. see Rapahango, Ana B. & Liller, William.

Liller, William. The Ancient Solar Observations of Rapanui: The Archaeoastronomy of Easter Island. LC 93-25642. (Easter Island Foundation Ser.). 1993. 12.00 (1-880636-01-8) Easter Isl Fnd.

— The Cambridge Guide to Astronomical Discovery. (Illus.). 269p. (C). 1992. 31.95 (0-521-41839-9) Cambridge U Pr.

Liller, William & Mayer, Ben S. The Cambridge Astronomy Guide: A Practical Introduction to Astronomy. (Illus.). 176p. (C). 1990. pap. 24.95 (0-521-39915-7) Cambridge U Pr.

Liller, William, jt. auth. see Rapahango, Ana B.

Lillesand, Thomas M. & Kiefer, Ralph W. Remote Sensing & Image Interpretation. 3rd ed. 768p. 1994. text 96.95 (0-471-57783-9) Wiley.

— Remote Sensing & Image Interpretation. 4th ed. LC 99-31327. 736p. 1999. text 99.95 (0-471-25515-7) Wiley.

Lillestol, Janne, ed. Keiserens Nye Klaer, Vol. 102B. 2nd ed. (Listen & Learn Language Audio Ser.: Vol. LL0399).Tr. of Emperor's New Clothes. (ENG & NOR., Illus.). 28p. 1999. pap. 9.95 (1-892623-09-9) Intl Book.

— Keiserens Nye Klaer: The Emperor's New Clothes, Vol. 102. 2nd ed. (Listen & Learn Language Ser.: Vol. LL0399). (ENG & NOR., Illus.). 28p. 1999. pap. 15.95 incl. audio (1-892623-08-0) Intl Book.

— Nattergalen, Vol.103B. 3rd ed. (Listen & Learn Language Audio Ser.: Vol. LL0399).Tr. of Nightingale. (ENG & NOR., Illus.). 32p. 1999. pap. 15.95 (1-892623-11-0) Intl Book.

— Nattergalen: The Nightingale, Vol. 103. 3rd unabridged ed. (Listen & Learn Language Ser.: Vol. LL0399). (ENG & NOR., Illus.). 32p. 1999. pap. 15.95 incl. audio (1-892623-10-2) Intl Book.

— Prestekragen, Vol. 101. (Listen & Learn Language Audio Ser.: Vol. LL0399).Tr. of Daisy. (ENG & NOR., Illus.). 28p. 1999. pap. 15.95 incl. audio (1-892623-06-4) Intl Book.

— Prestekragen, Vol. 101. unabridged ed. (Listen & Learn Language Audio Ser.: Vol. LL0399).Tr. of Daisy. (ENG & NOR., Illus.). 28p. 1999. pap. 15.95 incl. audio (1-892623-07-2) Intl Book.

Lillethorup, Galen K. Can Your Cat Do That? A Whimsical Aid to Expanding a Child's Imagination. Lillethorup, Kragh, ed. & illus. by. LC 95-92189. 32p. (J). (ps-3). 1995. pap. 8.95 (0-9646015-0-8) Sibling Pr.

— A Guide to Understanding ADF Navigation & NDB Instrument Approaches. 2nd ed. (Illus.). 54p. pap. text 12.95 (0-9646015-1-6) Sibling Pr.

Lillethorup, Kragh, ed. & illus. see Lillethorup, Galen K.

Lilley. The Almanac of State Legislatures. 1998. 95.00 (1-56802-178-X) Congr Quarterly.

Lilley, Alan A. A Handbook of Segmental Paving. (Illus.). 160p. 1991. 83.95 (0-442-31381-0) Chapman & Hall.

Lilley, D. M., jt. ed. see Eckstein, F.

Lilley, David M., ed. DNA-Protein: Structural Interactions: Frontiers in Molecular Biology. (Frontiers in Molecular Biology Ser.). (Illus.). 214p. 1995. text 115.00 (0-19-963454-8) OUP.

Lilley, David M., et al, eds. Structural Tools for the Analysis of Protein-Nucleic Acid Complexes. LC 92-30658. (Advances in Life Sciences Ser.). ix, 469p. 1992. 117.50 (0-8176-2776-6) Birkhauser.

An Asterisk (*) at the beginning of an entry indicates that the title is appearing for the first time.

An Asterisk (*) at the beginning of an entry indicates that the title is appearing for the first time.

L

— Criminological Theory: Context & Consequences. 2nd ed. 240p. 1994. 45.00 (0-8039-5900-1) Sage.

Lilly, Jeff. How to Restore Metal Auto Trim. LC 97-12211. (Illus.). 96p. 1997. pap. 14.95 (0-7603-0331-2) MBI Pubg.

Lilly, Joan, jt. auth. see Warren, Ann.

Lilly, John. Mountains of Music: West Virginia Traditional Music from Goldenseal. LC 99-6043. 224p. 1999. 49.95 (0-252-02499-0) U of Ill Pr.

Lilly, John, ed. Mountains of Music: West Virginia Traditional Music from Goldenseal. LC 99-6043. (Music in American Life Ser.). (Illus.). 224p. 1999. pap. 21.95 (0-252-06815-7) U of Ill Pr.

Lilly, John C. The Scientist: A Metaphysical Autobiography. 3rd rev. ed. LC 78-3545. (Illus.). 320p. 1997. pap. 14.95 (0-914171-72-0) Ronin Pub.

Lilly, John C., jt. auth. see Gold, E. J.

Lilly, Julie, ed. see Hagen, Ross.

Lilly, Kathryn W. Efficient Dynamic Simulation of Robotic Mechanisms. LC 92-33226. (International Series in Engineering & Computer Science, VLSI, Computer Architecture, & Digital Screen Processing: Vol. 203). 1992. text 116.50 (0-7923-9286-8) Kluwer Academic.

Lilly, Kenneth, jt. auth. see Pope, Joyce.

Lilly, Leonard. Pathophysiology of Heart Disease. (Illus.). 300p. 1992. pap. 26.00 (0-8121-1566-X) Lppncott W & W.

Lilly, Leonard S., ed. see Harvard Medical School Staff.

Lilly Library (Blomington Indiana University Staff, jt. auth. see Sites, Kriston.

Lilly, Mark. Gay Men's Literature in the Twentieth Century. LC 93-15241. 256p. (C). 1993. text 45.00 (0-8147-5071-0); pap. text 17.50 (0-8147-5081-8) NYU Pr.

Lilly, Mark, ed. Lesbian & Gay Writing: An Anthology of Critical Essays. 220p. 1990. 27.95 (0-87722-706-3) Temple U Pr.

Lilly, Mark, ed. see Bronte, Charlotte.

Lilly, Melinda. Eye Spy a Bear! LC 96-72504. (Illus.). 10p. (J). (ps up). 1997. pap. 6.99 (0-8431-7867-1, Price Stern) Peng Put Young Read.

— Eye Spy a Ladybug. (Illus.). 10p. (J). (ps up). 1997. pap. 6.99 (0-8431-7866-3, Price Stern) Peng Put Young Read.

***Lilly, Melinda.** Huatya Curi & the Five Condors. LC 99-12101. 1999. write for info. (1-57103-263-0) Rourke Pr.

Lilly, Melinda. Kwian & the Lazy Sun: African Tales & Myths. LC 98-22311. (Illus.). (J). (gr. 3-4). 1998. 22.60 (1-57103-243-6) Rourke Pr.

***Lilly, Melinda.** My Ultimate Pink Book. 12p. 1999. 10.99 (0-307-12158-5, Goldn Books) Goldn Bks Pub Co.

— The Snake's Toothache. LC 99-12098. (Latin American Tales & Myths Ser.). 1999. write for info. (1-57103-266-5) Rourke Pr.

Lilly, Melinda. Spider & His Son Find Wisdom: An Akan Tale. LC 98-20334. (African Tales & Myths Ser.). (Illus.). 31p. (J). (gr. 1-4). 1998. 16.95 (1-57103-244-4) Rourke Pr.

— Tamba & the Chief. LC 98-12827. (African Tales & Myths Ser.). (Illus.). (J). 1998. 16.95 (0-86625-634-2) Rourke Pubns.

— Tamba & the Chief: (A Temne Tale) LC 98-20326. (African Tales & Myths Ser.). (J). (gr. 3-4). 1998. 22.60 (1-57103-245-2) Rourke Pr.

— Wanyana & Matchmaker Frog: A Bagandan Tale. LC 98-23123. (African Tales & Myths Ser.). (Illus.). 31p. (J). (gr. 1-4). 1998. 16.95 (1-57103-247-9) Rourke Pr.

— Warrior Son of a Warrior Son: A Masai Tale. LC 98-23124. (African Tales & Myths Ser.). (Illus.). (J). 1998. (1-57103-246-0) Rourke Pr.

— Zimani's Drum. LC 98-12826. (African Tales & Myths Ser.). (Illus.). (J). 1998. write for info. (0-86625-633-4) Rourke Pub Grp.

— Zimani's Drum: A Malawian Tale. LC 98-20325. (African Tales & Myths Ser.). (Illus.). 31p. (J). (gr. 1-4). 1998. 16.95 (1-57103-248-7) Rourke Pr.

***Lilly, Melinda & Reasoner, Charles.** Aletbin & the Falling Sky. LC 99-12100. 1999. write for info. (1-57103-262-2) Rourke Pr.

— Mira & the Stone Tortoise. LC 99-12113. 1999. write for info. (1-57103-264-9) Rourke Pr.

— The Moon People. LC 99-12099. 1999. write for info. (1-57103-265-7) Rourke Pr.

Lilly, Melinda & Reasoner, Charles. Song of the Sun. LC 99-10321. 1999. write for info. (1-57103-267-3) Rourke Pr.

Lilly, Michael A. If You Die Tomorrow. 128p. 1990. pap. text 12.95 (0-9640614-0-6) KC Collins.

***Lilly, Mike.** West Virginia Jew. 128p. 2001. pap. write for info. (1-57197-245-5, Pub. by Pentland Pr) Assoc Pubs Grp.

Lilly, Paul R., Jr. Words in Search of Victims: The Achievement of Jerzy Kosinksi. LC 88-3021. 212p. 1988. 18.50 (0-87338-366-4) Kent St U Pr.

Lilly, Reginald, ed. The Ancients & the Moderns. LC 95-31887. (Studies in Continental Thought). 346p. 1996. 49.95 (0-253-33041-6) Ind U Pr.

Lilly, Reginald, tr. see Haar, Michel.

Lilly, Reginald, tr. see Heidegger, Martin.

Lilly, Reginald, tr. see Marx, Werner.

Lilly, Robert, jt. auth. see Nazzaro, Robin.

Lilly, Roy S., jt. auth. see Graham, John R.

Lilly, Sharon. Golf Course Tree Management. Skiera, Jim, ed. LC 98-49650. (Illus.). 220p. 1999. 45.00 (1-57504-117-0, Ann Arbor Press) Sleepng Bear.

— Tree Climber's Guide. 2nd ed. (Illus.). (C). 1998. pap. 40.00 (1-881956-08-3) Int Soc Arboricult.

***Lilly, Sharon & Zayas, Iris Magaly, eds.** Quick Reference Guide of Arboricultural Terms: English-Spanish & Spanish-English. (SPA & ENG., Illus.). 90p. 1999. pap. 12.50 (1-881956-24-5, P1245) Int Soc Arboricult.

Lilly, Simon. The Complete Illustrated Guide to Crystal Healing: The Therapeutic Use of Crystals for Health & Well-Being. (Complete Illustrated Guide Ser.). (Illus.). 224p. 1999. pap. 24.95 (1-86204-326-4, Pub. by Element MA) Penguin Putnam.

— Crystals & Crystal Healing: Placements & Techniques for Restoring Balance & Health. (New Life Library). 1998. 9.95 (1-85967-624-3, Lorenz Bks) Anness Pub.

Lilly, Simon & Lilly, Sue. Crystal Doorways. (Orig.). 1997. pap. 19.95 (1-898307-98-9, Pub. by Capall Bann Pubng) Holmes Pub.

Lilly, Simon, jt. auth. see Lilly, Sue.

***Lilly, Sue & Lilly, Simon.** Tree: Essence of Healing. (Illus.). 1999. pap. 29.95 (1-86163-081-6, Pub. by Capall Bann Pubng) Holmes Pub.

— Tree: Essence, Spirit & Teacher. (Illus.). 1999. pap. 29.95 (1-86163-084-0, Pub. by Capall Bann Pubng) Holmes Pub.

Lilly, Sue, jt. auth. see Lilly, Simon.

Lilly, Susan C., jt. auth. see Dale, Nell.

Lilly, Susan C., jt. auth. see Dale, Nell B.

Lilly, Teri Ann, et al. Work-Family Research: An Annotated Bibliography, 25. LC 97-24357. (Bibliographies & Indexes in Sociology: Vol. 25). 336p. 1997. lib. bdg. 75.00 (0-313-30322-3, Greenwood Pr) Greenwood.

Lilly, Willene J. The Petroleum Secretary's Handbook. 2nd ed. LC 84-27384. 352p. 1985. 25.00 (0-87814-278-9, P4369) PennWell Bks.

Lilly, William. Astrologer's Guide. 112p. 1970. 10.00 (0-86690-123-X, L1294-014) Am Fed Astrologers.

— Christian Astrology, 3 vols. Wiggers, Carol A., ed. (Illus.). 893p. (C). 1985. reprint ed. write for info. (1-878935-25-9) JustUs & Assocs.

— Christian Astrology, 3 vols., Set. Wiggers, Carol A., ed. (Illus.). 893p. (C). 1985. reprint ed. pap. text 80.00 (1-878935-03-8) JustUs & Assocs.

— Christian Astrology Vol. 1: Introduction to Astrology - The Basics. Wiggers, Carol A., ed. (Illus.). 147p. (C). 1985. reprint ed. pap. text 20.00 (1-878935-00-3) JustUs & Assocs.

— Christian Astrology Vol. II: Horary Astrology (Traditional Method) Wiggers, Carol A., ed. (Illus.). 367p. (C). 1985. reprint ed. pap. 30.00 (1-878935-01-1) JustUs & Assocs.

— Christian Astrology Vol. III: Natal Astrology & Predictive Astrology. Wiggers, Carol A., ed. (Illus.). 379p. (C). 1985. reprint ed. pap. 30.00 (1-878935-02-X) JustUs & Assocs.

— An Introduction to Astrology. 556p. 1996. reprint ed. pap. 33.00 (0-7873-0561-8) Hlth Research.

— An Introduction to the Study of Astrology: With Numerous Emendations, Adapted to the Improved State of Science. 575p. 1993. reprint ed. pap. 33.00 (1-56459-406-8) Kessinger Pub.

Lilly, William & Coley, Henry. The Astrologer's Guide: Anima Astrologia. Wiggers, Carol A., ed. (C). Date not set. text, wbk. ed. 18.00 (1-878935-24-0) JustUs & Assocs.

Lilly, William, ed. see Bonatus, Guido.

Lilly, William, ed. see Cardan, Joseph.

Lilly, William S. The Great Enigma (1892) 320p. 1998. reprint ed. pap. 19.95 (0-7661-0133-9) Kessinger Pub.

Lillya, Clifford. Trumpet Technic. expanded rev. ed. 96p. 1995. pap. 12.60 (0-9630856-3-8) Balquhidder.

Lillyman, William J. Reality's Dark Dream: The Narrative Fiction of Ludwig Tieck. (C). 1979. 100.00 (3-11-007710-8) De Gruyter.

Lillyman, William J., ed. Goethe's Narrative Fiction: The Irvine Goethe Symposium. LC 83-18848. viii, 299p. 1983. 83.85 (3-11-008734-0) De Gruyter.

Lillyman, William J., et al, eds. Critical Architecture & Contemporary Culture. LC 92-22185. (University of California Humanities Research Institute Ser.). (Illus.). 224p. (C). 1994. text 52.00 (0-19-507819-5) OUP.

Lillystone, Simon, ed. see Pecar, Branko.

Lilo & Cohen. A Shadow over My Life: A Holocaust Story. (Illus.). 92p. 1994. text 9.95 (965-229-110-2, Pub. by Gefen Pub Hse) Gefen Bks.

***Liloia, C. Tony.** The Appaloosa Kid. LC 00-190613. 275p. 2000. 25.00 (0-7388-1864-X); pap. 18.00 (0-7388-1865-8) Xlibris Corp.

— Father Anthony's Sin: . . . Beyond the Lure of Lust & Love. LC 99-91671. 2000. 25.00 (0-7388-1186-6); pap. 18.00 (0-7388-1187-4) Xlibris Corp.

Lilore, Joseph. Learnin' the Blues. Stang, Aaron, ed. 60p. (C). 1987. pap. text 8.95 (0-7692-1354-5, GF0303) Wrner Bros.

Lilore, Joseph R. 59 Days to the Guitar. 80p. 1987. pap. 10.95 (0-9646596-2-X) Lionhead Pubng.

— The Songwriter's Guide to Chords & Progressions. 48p. 1982. pap. 15.95 incl. audio (0-9646596-0-3) Lionhead Pubng.

— The Songwriter's Guide to Melodies. 80p. 1989. pap. 11.95 (0-9646596-1-1) Lionhead Pubng.

Lilwall-Smith, Andrew. Stenciling. LC 97-31117. 40p. 1997. 14.95 (0-8230-5632-5) Watsn-Guptill.

Lily, Don, ed. see Juray, G. John.

Lily, Melinda. Shapes for Lunch! (Mini Bites Ser.). (Illus.). 32p. (J). (ps-k). 1998. pap. 4.99 (0-8431-7822-1, Price Stern) Peng Put Young Read.

Lily, William. A Shorte Introduction of Grammar. LC 45-4059. 224p. 1977. reprint ed. 50.00 (0-8201-1208-9) Schol Facsimiles.

Lilya, Mary, ed. see Mayer, Steven E. & Scheie, David.

Lilya, Pann. Neskuchnyi Sad: Poety, Prozaiki, 1980-90-e. LC 98-21408. (RUS.). 220p. 1998. pap. 14.00 (1-55779-110-4) Hermitage Pubs.

Lilya, Wagner. Peer Teaching: Historical Perspective. 5. LC 82-939. (Contributions to the Study of Education Ser.: No. 5). 266p. 1982. 59.95 (0-313-23230-X, WPT/, Greenwood Pr) Greenwood.

Lilyquist, Christine. Egyptian Stone Vessels: Khian Through Tuthmosis IV. LC 95-26007. (Illus.). 128p. (Orig.). 1995. pap. 25.00 (0-87099-760-2) Metro Mus Art.

Lilyquist, Christine, et al. Studies in Early Egyptian Glass. LC 93-24451. (Illus.). 77p. 1993. pap. 20.00 (0-87099-683-5, 0-8109-6457-0) Metro Mus Art.

***Lilyquist, J. Gary.** Are Schools Really Like This? Factors Affecting Teacher Attitude Toward School Improvement. LC 97-40389. (Innovations in Science Education & Technology). (Illus.). 212p. (C). 1998. pap. 27.50 (0-306-45735-0, Plenum Trade) Perseus Pubng.

Lim. Growth & Transform 1960-1990. LC 97-49927. 257p. 1998. text 65.00 (0-312-21292-5) St Martin.

— World of Literature. (C). 1993. pap., teacher ed. 3.96 (0-395-58881-2) HM.

Lim & Smalzer. Noteworthy. 2nd ed. 1996. pap. text, teacher ed. 4.75 (0-8384-5011-3) Heinle & Heinle.

Lim & Soter, Nicholas A. Clinical Photomedicine. (Basic & Clinical Dermatology Ser.: Vol. 6). (Illus.). 428p. 1993. text 175.00 (0-8247-8862-1) Dekker.

Lim, C. T., jt. ed. see Chau, Fook S.

Lim, A. S., jt. auth. see Ratnam, S. Shan.

Lim, Arthur M. Patient's Interest First: The Nature of Medical Ethics & the Dilemma of a Good Doctor. 120p. pap. 20.00 (981-02-3548-8) World Scientific Pub.

Lim, Arthur M., ed. Fison's Retinal Detachment Surgery. (Illus.). 1978. 68.00 (3-8055-2862-0) S Karger.

Lim, Arthur S. A Colour Atlas of Posterior Chamber Implants. (Illus.). 692p. 1985. text 142.00 (0-7216-1573-2, W B Saunders Co) Harcrt Hlth Sci Grp.

Lim, Arthur S., ed. Ocular Microsurgery. (Developments in Ophthalmology Ser.: Vol. 1). (Illus.). viii, 96p. 1981. 43.50 (3-8055-1106-X) S Karger.

Lim, Arthur S. & Constable, Ian. Colour Atlas of Ophthalmology. 3rd ed. 170p. 1995. text 38.00 (981-02-2286-6) World Scientific Pub.

— Colour Atlas of Opthalmology. 3rd ed. 170p. 1995. pap. text 25.00 (981-02-2339-0) World Scientific Pub.

Lim, Arthur S., jt. auth. see Constable, Ian J.

Lim, B. S., ed. Computer Integrated Manufacturing (ICCIM '91) 800p. (C). 1991. text 118.00 (981-02-0684-4) World Scientific Pub.

Lim, Bill, ed. Control of the External Environment of Buildings in Tropical Climates. 170p. (Orig.). 1988. pap. 35.00 (9971-69-119-1, Pub. by Sngapore Univ Pr) Coronet Bks.

Lim, Bill B. Environmental Design Criteria of Tall Buildings. (Illus.). 249p. (C). 1994. pap. text 28.00 (0-939493-08-X) Coun Tall Bldg.

— Solar Energy Application in the Tropics. 1982. text 176.50 (90-277-1506-8) Kluwer Academic.

Lim, C. Introduction to Vortex Dynamics. 250p. 1999. 32.00 (981-02-3608-5) World Scientific Pub.

Lim, C. E. & Sessa, D. J., eds. Nutrition & Utilization Technology in Aquaculture. 288p. 1995. 70.00 (0-935315-54-3) Am Oil Chemists.

Lim, C. L., jt. auth. see Elias, O. A.

Lim, C. L., jt. auth. see Harding, Christopher.

Lim, Catherine. The Bondmaid. LC 97-9908. 384p. 1997. 24.95 (0-87951-790-5, Pub. by Overlook Pr) Penguin Putnam.

— The Bondmaid. 1998. pap. write for info. (0-446-67475-3); mass mkt. 6.99 (0-446-60734-7, Pub. by Warner Bks) Little.

— Little Ironies: Stories of Singapore. (Writing in Asia Ser.). 106p. (C). 1978. pap. 5.00 (0-435-00224-4, 00244) Heinemann.

— Or Else, the Lightning God & Other Stories. (Writing in Asia Ser.). 194p. (Orig.). (C). 1980. pap. 5.00 (0-435-00251-1, 00251) Heinemann.

— The Teardrop Story Woman. LC 98-16590. 330p. 1998. 24.95 (0-87951-901-0, Pub. by Overlook Pr) Penguin Putnam.

Lim, Ching S. & Lee, Gim. Mac-Graphics: A Designer's Visual Guide to Graphics for the Apple Macintosh. (Illus.). 288p. 1991. pap. 49.95 (0-8306-1072-3, 3864, Windcrest) TAB Bks.

***Lim, Chong-Yah.** Wages & Wages Policies: Tripartism in Singapore. LC 98-52734. 400p. 1999. 48.00 (981-02-3773-1) World Scientific Pub.

Lim, Chong-Yah, ed. Economic Policy Management in Singapore. LC 95-36403. 1996. write for info. (0-201-88902-1) Addison-Wesley.

Lim, Christina, et al. In the Shadow of the Tiger: The 407th Air Service Squadron, 14th Air Service Group, 14th Air Force, World War II. (Illus.). 225p. 1993. 32.00 (0-9637207-0-8) Lim & Lim.

Lim, Daniel V. Microbiology. 2nd ed. 720p. (C). 1997. text. write for info. (0-697-26186-7, WCB McGr Hill) McGrw-H Hghr Educ.

Lim, Daniel V., et al. Introduction to Microbiology: Lab Manual. (Illus.). 220p. (Orig.). (C). 1995. lab manual ed. 39.95 (0-89892-127-9) Contemp Pub Co of Raleigh.

Lim, David. Explaining Economic Growth: A New Analytical Framework. LC 95-42410. 272p. 1996. 95.00 (1-85898-119-0) E Elgar.

— Spiritual Gifts: A Fresh Look. LC 90-23950. 336p. 1991. pap. 8.95 (0-88243-636-8, 02-0636) Gospel Pub.

***Lim, David J.** Cell & Molecular Biology of the Ear. LC 00-36371. (Illus.). 2000. write for info. (0-306-46374-1) Plenum.

Lim, David J. Recent Advances in Otitis Media: Proceedings of the Sixth International Symposium. 1996. 115.00 (1-55009-028-3) DEKR.

Lim, Frank C. First Degree Murder: An Intellectual Journey. 40p. 1997. pap. write for info. (1-889534-11-0) Jay St Pubs.

Lim, Franklin, ed. Biomedical Applications of Microencapsulation. 192p. 1984. 101.00 (0-8493-5440-4, RS201, CRC Reprint) Franklin.

Lim, Genny. Winter Place. 1989. pap. 8.95 (0-9609630-4-9) Kearny St Wkshop.

Lim, H. A. & Cantor, C. R. Bioinformatics & Genome Research: Proceedings of the 3rd International Conference. (Series in Machine Perception & Artificial Intelligence: Vol. 20). 530p. 1995. text 128.00 (981-02-2401-X) World Scientific Pub.

Lim, H. A., et al. Bioinformatics, Supercomputing & Complex Genome Analysis: International Conference. 400p. 1993. text 118.00 (981-02-1157-0) World Scientific Pub.

Lim, H. A., jt. auth. see Kolchanov, N. A.

Lim, Hee-Kuk. Jesus Ist Sieger! Bei Christoph Friedrich Blumhardt: Keim Einer Kosmischen Christologie. (Basler und Berner Studien zur Historischen und Systematischen Theologie: Bd. 67). (GER.). 201p. 1996. 36.95 (3-906756-42-4, Pub. by P Lang) P Lang Pubng.

Lim, Henry. Pocket Guide to Digital Imaging. (Graphic Communications Ser.). 1996. pap. 11.95 (0-8273-7506-9) Delmar.

Lim-Hing, Sharon, ed. The Very Inside: An Anthology of Writings by Asian & Pacific Islander Lesbians. LC 95-163883. (Illus.). 488p. 1994. per. 19.95 (0-920813-97-6) Sister Vis Pr.

Lim, Irene & Singapore History Museum Staff. Secret Societies in Singapore: Featuring the William Stirling Collection LC 98-474015. 109 P. :p. 1999. write for info. (981-3018-79-8, Pub. by Arch Pr) Tuttle Pubng.

***Lim, Jes T.** Feng Shui & Your Health: A Guide to High Vitality. (Illus.). 250p. 1999. pap. 19.95 (0-89346-915-7) Heian Intl.

Lim, Jessie. China. rev. ed. (Focus On Ser.). (Illus.). 32p. (J). (gr. 4-8). 1992. write for info. (0-237-51660-8) EVN1 UK.

Lim, Joe S. Two-Dimensional Signal & Image Processing. 880p. (C). 1989. 94.00 (0-13-935322-4) P-H.

Lim, Joseph Y., et al. Initial Public Offerings: The Role of Venture Capitalists. LC 99-207585. xiv, 55 p. 1990. write for info. (0-943205-07-7) RFICFA.

Lim, Joyce, tr. 100 Parables of Zen. (Illus.). 201p. 1995. 14.95 (981-3029-49-8, Pub. by Asiapac) China Bks.

***Lim, Justin K.** Male Mid-Life Crisis: Psychological Dynamics, Theological Issues, & Pastoral Interventions. 184p. 2000. 46.00 (0-7618-1766-2); pap. 26.50 (0-7618-1767-0) U Pr of Amer.

Lim, Kean S. The Eye over the Golden Sands: The Memoirs of a Penang Family. LC 98-944715. 236p. 1997. write for info. (967-978-567-X) Pelanduk.

Lim, Kee Y. & Long, John. The MUSE Method for Usability Engineering. (Series in Human-Computer Interaction: No. 8). (Illus.). 350p. (C). 1995. text 54.95 (0-521-47494-9) Cambridge U Pr.

***Lim, Kim-anh.** Practical Guide to the I Ching. 304p. 2000. pap. 16.95 (90-74597-40-8, Pub. by Binkey Kok) Weiser.

Lim King, Betty. Girl on a Leash: The Healing Power of Dogs. Cuyugan, Ruben S., ed. LC 98-96447. (Illus.). 224p. 1999. pap. 19.95 (0-9665954-0-8) Sanct NC.

Lim, Kyung S., ed. How Products Are Made Vol. 2: An Illustrated Guide to Product Manufacturing, Vol. 2. 520p. 1995. 90.00 (0-8103-8952-5, 101637) Gale.

Lim, Levan, jt. auth. see Browder, Diane M.

Lim, Lida. How to Assess Student Work. LC 99-225809. (Illus.). 1997. write for info. (0-13-433908-8) P-H.

Lim, Lin L. More & Better Jobs for Women: An Action Guide. LC 97-103824. xii, 193p. 1996. pap. 22.50 (92-2-109459-6) Intl Labour Office.

Lim, Lin L., ed. The Sex Sector: The Economic & Social Bases of Prostitution in Southeast Asia. LC 98-176639. 228p. 1998. pap. 24.95 (92-2-109522-3) Intl Labour Office.

Lim, Linda & Fong, Pang Eng. Trade Employment & Industrialisation in Singapore. (Employment, Adjustment & Industrialisation Ser.: No. 2). vi, 110p. 1986. pap. 22.50 (92-2-105231-1) Intl Labour Office.

Lim, Lucy. Six Contemporary Chinese Women Artists. LC 91-74138. (Illus.). 102p. 1993. pap. 24.95 (0-9609784-1-0) CCF San Francisco.

Lim, Lucy, et al. Stories from China's Past: Han Dynasty Pictorial Tomb Reliefs & Archaeological Objects from Sichuan Province, People's Republic of China. LC 87-70422. (Illus.). 210p. 1988. reprint ed. pap. 35.00 (0-295-96797-8) U of Wash Pr.

— Wu Guanzhong: A Contemporary Chinese Artist. (Illus.). 185p. 1989. 30.00 (0-9609784-2-9) CCF San Francisco.

Lim, Patricia. Discovering Hong Kong's Cultural Heritage. LC 97-29015. (Illus.). 190p. 1998. pap. text 24.00 (0-19-590075-8) OUP.

Lim, Paul & Godin, Seth. If You're Clueless about Accounting & Finance & Want to Know More. LC 98-5446. 208p. 1998. pap. text 15.95 (0-7931-2881-1) Dearborn.

Lim, Paulino, Jr. Sparrows Don't Sing in the Philippines. 133p. (Orig.). 1994. pap. 10.75 (971-10-0527-1, Pub. by New Day Pub) Cellar.

— Tiger Orchids on Mount Mayon: A Novella. 94p. (Orig.). (C). 1990. pap. 10.00 (971-10-0410-0, Pub. by New Day Pub) Cellar.

Lim, Phyllis L. Noteworthy. 2nd ed. (College ESL Ser.). 230p. (J). 1996. pap. 28.95 (0-8384-5009-1) Heinle & Heinle.

Lim, Phyllis L. & Smalzer, William. Noteworthy. (J). 1990. audio 14.95 (0-8384-2949-1) Heinle & Heinle.

— Noteworthy. (J). 1990. audio 62.95 (0-8384-2948-3) Heinle & Heinle.

— Noteworthy. (J). 1991. pap. 17.50 (0-8384-2946-7) Heinle & Heinle.

Lim, Phyllis L., jt. auth. see Dunkel, Patricia.

Lim, R. P., et al, eds. Sustainable Clean Water: Proceedings of the Regional Workshop on Limnology & Water Resources Management in the Developing Countries of Asia & the Pacific, November 29-December 5, 1982,

An Asterisk (*) at the beginning of an entry indicates that the title is appearing for the first time.

University of Malaya, Kuala Lumpur, Malaysia. (Advances in Limnology Ser.: Vol. 28). (GER., Illus.). xvii, 571p. 1987. pap. text 142.00 (*3-510-47026-5*, Pub. by E Schweizerbartsche) Balogh.

Lim, Richard. Public Disputation, Power, & Social Order in Late Antiquity. LC 93-43761. (Transformation of the Classical Heritage Ser.: No. 23). 1995. 55.00 (*0-520-08577-9*, Pub. by U CA Pr) Cal Prin Full Svc.

Lim, Robin. After the Baby's Birth...a Woman's Way to Wellness: A Complete Guide for Postpartum Women. LC 90-1802. 272p. (Orig.). 1995. pap. 14.95 (*0-89087-590-1*) Celestial Arts.

***Lim, Robin.** Indonesia. LC 00-8034. (Globe-Trotters Club Ser.). (Illus.). 48p. (J). (gr. 3-12). 2000. 22.60 (*1-57505-150-8*, Carolrhoda) Lerner Pub.

— Indonesia. LC 00-8586. (Illus.). 48p. (J). (ps-3). 2000. 22.60 (*1-57505-175-3*, Carolrhoda) Lerner Pub.

***Lim, Shirley.** Asian-American Literature: An Anthology LC 99-16872. 2000. pap. write for info. (*0-8442-1729-8*) NTC Contemp Pub Co.

Lim, Shirley & Spencer, Norman K. One World of Literature. (C). 1992. pap. text 37.56 (*0-395-58880-4*) HM.

***Lim, Shirley, et al.** Power, Race & Gender in Academe: Strangers in the Tower? LC 99-44991. 1999. 18.00 (*0-87352-270-2*) Modern Lang.

Lim, Shirley, et al. Transnational Asia Pacific: Gender, Culture & the Public Sphere. LC 99-6055. 208p. 1999. pap. 14.95 (*0-252-06809-2*) U of Ill Pr.

Lim, Shirley G. Among the White Moon Faces: An Asian-American Memoir of Homelands. LC 95-25428. (Cross-Cultural Memoir Ser.). (Illus.). 248p. 1996. 22.95 (*1-55861-144-4*) Feminist Pr.

— Among the White Moon Faces: An Asian-American Memoir of Homelands. LC 95-25428. (Cross-Cultural Memoir Ser.). (Illus.). 248p. 1996. reprint ed. pap. 12.95 (*1-55861-179-7*) Feminist Pr.

— Nationalism & Literature: English-Language Writing from the Philippines & Singapore. 186p. (Orig.). 1994. pap. 15.00 (*971-10-0525-5*, Pub. by New Day Pub) Cellar.

— Two Dreams: New & Selected Stories. LC 96-52523. 240p. 1997. 24.00 (*1-55861-164-9*) Feminist Pr.

Lim, Shirley G., ed. Approaches to Teaching Kingston's The Woman Warrior. LC 91-27413. (Approaches to Teaching World Literature Ser.: No. 39). xi, 178p. 1991. pap. 18.00 (*0-87352-704-6*, AP39P); lib. bdg. 37.50 (*0-87352-703-8*, AP39C) Modern Lang.

Lim, Shirley Geok-lin, see Geok-lin Lim, Shirley.

Lim Siew Ming, A. Practical Ophthalmic Microsurgery. (Illus.). 1980. 34.00 (*3-8055-3036-6*) S Karger.

Lim, Sing. West Coast Chinese Boy. LC 79-67110. 64p. (J). (gr. 5 up). 1991. pap. 7.95 (*0-88776-270-0*) Tundra Bks.

Lim, T. E. & Niew, Bock C., eds. Quality Management Systems: Assessment to ISO 9000, 1994 Series. LC 95-35169. 420p. (C). 1997. pap. 48.00 (*0-13-240714-0*) P-H.

Lim, T. K., et al. Few Body Methods: Principles & Applications. (Proceedings of the International Symposium on Transport Phenomena, Dynamics & Design of Rotating Machinery Ser.). 900p. 1986. text 131.00 (*9971-5-0126-0*, Z0281P-P) World Scientific Pub.

***LIM, T T.** Flow Visualization: Techniques & Examples. 1999. 64.00 (*1-86094-193-1*) World Scientific Pub.

Lim, Timothy H. Holy Scripture in the Qur'an Commentaries & Pauline Letters. LC 97-10994. 236p. (C). 1997. text 75.00 (*0-19-826206-X*) OUP.

Lim, Walter S. The Arts of Empire: The Poetics of Colonialism from Raleigh to Milton. LC 97-39171. 280p. 1998. 43.50 (*0-87413-641-5*) U Delaware Pr.

Lim, Wayne C. Managing Software Reuse. LC 97-36429. 480p. (C). 1998. 57.00 (*0-13-552373-7*) P-H.

Lim, William S. & Beng, Tan H. The New Asian Architecture: Vernacular Traditions & Contemporary Style. (Illus.). 176p. 1998. 42.50 (*962-593-302-6*) Tuttle Pubng.

Lim-Wilson, Fatima. Crossing the Snow Bridge. LC 95-17599. 105p. 1995. pap. 13.00 (*0-8142-0681-6*) Ohio St U Pr.

Lim, Y. K. Introduction to Classical Electrodynamics. 433p. 1986. text 47.00 (*9971-978-51-2*); pap. text 30.00 (*9971-978-85-7*) World Scientific Pub.

— Problems & Solutions on Mechanics: Major American Universities Ph.d. Qualifying Questions & Solutions. 768p. 1994. text 99.00 (*981-02-1295-X*); pap. text 48.00 (*981-02-1298-4*) World Scientific Pub.

— Problems & Solutions on Optics: Major American Univ. PhD Qualifying Questions & Solutions. 204p. 1991. text 59.00 (*981-02-0438-8*); pap. text 30.00 (*981-02-0439-6*) World Scientific Pub.

— Problems & Solutions on Solid State Physics, Relativity & Miscellaneous Topics. 364p. 1994. text 99.00 (*981-02-1892-3*); pap. text 38.00 (*981-02-1893-1*) World Scientific Pub.

Lim, Y. K., ed. Problems & Solutions on Electromagnetism. 550p. (C). 1994. text 78.00 (*981-02-0625-9*); pap. text 39.00 (*981-02-0626-7*) World Scientific Pub.

— Problems & Solutions on Thermodynamics & Statistical Mechanics. 420p. (C). 1990. text 74.00 (*981-02-0055-2*); pap. text 36.00 (*981-02-0056-0*) World Scientific Pub.

Lim, Y. S., tr. see Johnson, Jerry A.

Lim, Youngil. Technology & Productivity: The Korean Way of Learning & Catching Up. LC 99-28634. (Illus.). 238p. 1999. 39.95 (*0-262-12221-9*) MIT Pr.

Lim, Yung K., ed. Problems & Solutions on Atomic, Nuclear & Particle Physics. 550p. 1999. 86.00 (*981-02-3917-3*) World Scientific Pub.

— Problems & Solutions on Atomic, Nuclear & Particle Physics. 550p. 1999. 42.00 (*981-02-3918-1*) World Scientific Pub.

Lima, Anthony K. The dBASE II for Beginners. LC 84-22897. (Personal Computing Ser.). (Illus.). 160p. 1986. 16.50 (*0-13-196080-6*); pap. text 24.33 (*0-13-196098-9*) P-H.

— Mastering dBASE III in Less Than a Day. (Illus.). 160p. 1986. 20.50 (*0-13-559816-8*) P-H.

Lima, Arthur De, see De Lima, Arthur.

Lima, C. L., et al, eds. Nuclear Physics: Proceedings of the 20th Brazilian Meeting Brazil 31 August - 4 September 1997. LC 98-8802. 467p. 1998. 86.00 (*981-02-3429-5*) World Scientific Pub.

Lima, Carolyn W. & Lima, John A. A to Zoo: Subject Access to Children's Picture Books. 5th ed. LC 98-11920. 1425p. 1998. 65.00 (*0-8352-3916-0*) Bowker.

***Lima, David R.** The Love Workbook: A Guide to Happiness in Your Personal Relationships. 192p. 2000. pap., wbk. ed. 14.95 (*1-893733-00-9*, DL01, Pub. by Super Six) ACCESS Pubs Network.

Lima-de-Faria, A. Biological Periodicity: Its Molecular Mechanism & Evolutionary Implications. 340p. 1996. 128.50 (*1-55938-412-3*) Jai Pr.

Lima-de-Faria, J. Structural Minerology: An Introduction. LC 94-10374. (Solid Earth Sciences Library: Vol. 7). 1994. text 213.00 (*0-7923-2821-3*) Kluwer Academic.

Lima-de-Faria, J., ed. Historical Atlas of Crystallography. (C). 1990. text 36.00 (*0-7923-0649-X*) Kluwer Academic.

Lima, Donald R. A Piece Is Missing. LC 98-85234. 192p. 1998. text 19.95 (*1-56167-427-3*) Noble House.

Lima, Eloisa L. Una Familia Habanera. LC 98-84327. (Coleccion Cuba y sus Jueces). (SPA., Illus.). 105p. 1998. pap. 12.00 (*0-89729-862-4*, 862-4) Ediciones.

— Fundamentos de la Lengua Espanola. 4th ed. (SPA.). 476p. (C). 1995. reprint ed. pap. text 18.95 (*1-56328-044-2*) Edit Plaza Mayor.

Lima, Eloisa L. & Tamargo, Paloma. Como Redactar Correctamente. 2nd ed. (SPA.). 144p. 1995. reprint ed. pap. text 8.95 (*1-56328-049-3*) Edit Plaza Mayor.

Lima, Elvira S. Conhecendo A Crianca Pequena. 2nd unabridged ed. (POR., Illus.). 24p. 1997. pap. 2.99 (*0-9663398-0-0*) Alba Bk Co.

— Learning & Development in School: Cultural, Neurological & Psychological Aspects. Lima, M. G., tr. 32p. 1999. pap. 3.25 (*0-9662298-4-3*) Alba Bk Co.

Lima Fontes, F., jt. auth. see Fontes, Lima F.

***Lima, Frank.** Beatitudes: Prose Poetry by Frank Lima. (Lingo Bks.). 2000. pap. 14.95 (*1-889097-44-6*) Hard Pr MA.

Lima, Frank. Inventory: New & Selected Poems. LC 97-8776. (Profile Ser.). 202p. 1997. 12.95 (*1-889097-10-1*) Hard Pr MA.

Lima, Gabriel S., tr. see Souza, Iza R.

***Lima, Joao A.** Diagnostic Imaging in Clinical Cardiology. (Illus.). 360p. 1998. write for info. (*1-85317-309-6*, Pub. by Martin Dunitz) Mosby Inc.

Lima, John A., jt. auth. see Lima, Carolyn W.

Lima, Jose L. La Expresion Americana (The American Expression) (SPA.). 184p. 1993. pap. 9.99 (*968-16-4007-1*, Pub. by Fondo) Continental Bk.

— Juego de las Decapitaciones. (SPA.). 93p. 1984. pap. 7.50 (*84-85859-90-1*, 2016) Ediciones Norte.

Lima, Joseph A. & Otterman, George R., eds. Manual on Selection & Use of Engine Coolants & Cooling System Chemicals. 4th ed. LC 89-342. (Manual Ser.: No. MNL 6). (Illus.). 16p. 1989. pap. text 12.00 (*0-8031-1265-3*, MNL6) ASTM.

Lima, Luiz C. The Dark Side of Reason: Fictionality & Power. Britto, Paulo H., tr. from POR. LC 91-24853. 360p. (C). 1992. 42.50 (*0-8047-1976-4*) Stanford U Pr.

Lima, M. G., tr. see Lima, Elvira S.

Lima, Manuel De Oliveira, see De Oliveira Lima, Manuel.

Lima, P. & Saridis, George N. Design of Intelligent Control Systems Based on Hierarchical Stochastic Automata. (Series on Intelligent Control & Intelligent Automation: Vol. 1). 200p. 1996. text 44.00 (*981-02-2255-6*) World Scientific Pub.

Lima, Patrick. The Art of Perennial Gardening: Creative Ways with Hardy Flowers. (Illus.). 176p. 1998. pap. 24.95 (*1-55209-219-4*) Firefly Bks Ltd.

— The Harrowsmith Illustrated Book of Herbs. (Illus.). 176p. 1986. pap. 19.95 (*0-920656-45-5*) Firefly Bks Ltd.

— The Harrowsmith Perennial Garden: Flowers for Three Seasons. (Illus.). 160p. 1987. pap. 19.95 (*0-920656-74-9*) Firefly Bks Ltd.

— Portraits of Flowers. LC 95-181015. (Illus.). 160p. 1995. pap. write for info. (*0-88984-157-8*) Porcup Quill.

Lima, Patrick & Scanlan, John. The Natural Food Garden: Growing Vegetables & Fruits Chemical-Free. (Illus.). 160p. 1992. pap. 19.95 (*1-55958-202-2*) Prima Pub.

Lima, R. F. Arco Motor Vehicle Dictionary.Tr. of Diccionario Arco Del Automotor. (ENG & SPA.). 362p. 1980. pap. 39.95 (*0-8288-0049-9*, S36349) Fr & Eur.

Lima, Robert. Dark Prisms: Occultism in Hispanic Drama. 208p. 1995. text 29.95 (*0-8131-1909-X*) U Pr of Ky.

— Ramon del Valle-Inclan. LC 72-186643. (Columbia Essays on Modern Writers Ser.: No. 59). 1972. pap. text 12.00 (*0-231-03499-7*) Col U Pr.

***Lima, Robert.** Sardinia. Sardegna. (VIA Folios Ser.: Vol. 24). 54p. 2000. pap. 10.00 (*1-884419-36-4*) Bordighera.

Lima, Robert. Valle-Inclan: The Theatre of His Life. LC 87-19119. (Illus.). 392p. 1988. text 37.50 (*0-8262-0661-1*) U of Mo Pr.

Lima, Robert, jt. ed. see Zatlin, Phyllis.

Lima, Robert, tr. see Del Valle-Inclan, Ramon.

Lima, Robert, tr. see Miller, Yvette E. & Tatum, Charles M., eds.

Lima, Sara N. Di, see Di Lima, Sara N.

Lima, Sara N. Di, see Beard, Shawn & Di Lima, Sara N.

Lima, Sara N. Di, see Di Lima, Sara N.

Lima, Sara N. Di, see Aspen Reference Group Staff & Di Lima, Sara N.

Lima, Sara N. Di, see Di Lima, Sara N., ed.

Lima, Sara N. Di, see Johns, Lisa T. & Di Lima, Sara N.

Lima, Susan D., et al, eds. The Reality of Linguistic Rules. LC 94-27030. (Studies in Language Companion Ser.: Vol. 26). xxiii, 480p. 1994. 115.00 (*1-55619-378-5*, JB1926) J Benjamins Pubng Co.

Lima, Tony. Developing Foxpro for Windows Applications. 512p. (C). 1993. pap. text 26.95 (*0-201-62456-7*) Addison-Wesley.

— Developing Paradox Applications. LC 92-31141. 560p. 1993. pap. text 29.95 (*0-201-63210-1*) Addison-Wesley.

— Inside dBASE IV. 1987. pap. 21.95 (*0-201-16638-0*) Addison-Wesley.

Liman, A. V. A Critical Study of the Literary Style of Ibuse Musuji: As Sensitive as Waters. LC 91-41402. 632p. 1992. lib. bdg. 129.95 (*0-7734-9614-9*) E Mellen.

Liman, Anthony. Castaways: Two Short Novels. 160p. 1993. pap. 8.00 (*4-7700-1744-8*) Kodansha.

Liman, Anthony, tr. see Ibuse, Masuji.

Liman, Arthur L. Lawyer: A Life of Cases, Counsel & Controversy. LC 98-27279. 416p. 1998. text 30.00 (*1-891620-04-5*, Pub. by PublicAffairs NY) HarpC.

***Liman, Ellen.** Baby Space: A Guide for Growing Families with Shrinking Space. (Illus.). 160p. 2000. pap. 16.00 (*0-06-095627-5*, HarpRes) HarpInfo.

Liman, Ellen. Regional Analysis of Tourism: The Economic Impact of Tourism in New Zealand, Auckland, Bay of Plenty & Canterbury Regions: Summary Report LC 94-111941. 149p. 1991. pap. write for info. (*0-478-02132-1*) Manaaki Whenua.

Limardo, Miguel. Luces Encendidas para Cada Dia: Lights for Each Day. 376p. 1985. reprint ed. 11.99 (*0-311-40038-8*) Casa Bautista.

Limato, Susan. Baby Basics for New Parents: Quick Answers When You Need Them. LC 93-90639. 160p. (Orig.). 1994. mass mkt. 4.99 (*0-380-77378-3*, Avon Bks) Morrow Avon.

Limaye, B. V., jt. ed. see Kulkarni, S. H.

***Limaye, Champa.** Women: Power & Progress. 1999. 34.00 (*81-7646-103-2*, Pub. by BR Pub) S Asia.

Limaye, Dilip R., ed. Industrial Cogeneration Applications. LC 85-45873. 300p. 1986. text 57.00 (*0-88173-022-X*) Fairmont Pr.

Limaye, Dilip R., jt. auth. see Gellings, Clark W.

Limaye, Madhu. Cabinet Government in India. 135p. 1989. text 35.00 (*81-7027-138-X*, Pub. by Radiant Pubs) S Asia.

— Contemporary Indian Politics. 400p. 1987. text 40.00 (*81-7027-104-5*, Pub. by Radiant Pubs) S Asia.

— Janata Party Experiment, 2 vols., Set. LC 93-911002. (C). 1994. 88.50 (*81-7018-711-7*, Pub. by BR Pub) S Asia.

— Mahatma Gandhi & Jawaharlal Nehru: A Historic Partnership since 1916-1948, Vol. II. 1989. 62.00 (*0-685-34763-X*, Pub. by BR Pub) S Asia.

— Mahatma Gandhi & Jawaharlal Nehru: A Historic Partnership, 1916-1948, Vol. 3. 1990. 50.00 (*81-7018-583-1*, Pub. by BR Pub) S Asia.

— Mahatma Gandhi & Jawaharlal Nehru Vol. I: A Historic Partnership, 1916-1948. (C). 1989. 27.50 (*81-7018-548-3*) S Asia.

— Mahatma Gandhi & Jawaharlal Nehru Vol. 3: A Historic Partnership, Set. (C). 1990. text 50.00 (*81-7018-547-5*, Pub. by BR Pub) S Asia.

— Prime Movers: Role of the Individual in History. xii, 448p. 1986. text 45.00 (*81-7027-087-1*, Pub. by Radiant Pubs) S Asia.

— Religious Bigotry: A Threat to Ordered State. LC 94-900789. (C). 1995. 18.00 (*81-202-0409-3*, Pub. by Ajanta) S Asia.

— Socialist Communist Interactions in India. (C). 1991. 36.00 (*81-202-0319-4*, Pub. by Ajanta) S Asia.

Limaye, Madhu, ed. Mahatma Gandhi & Jawaharlal Nehru, Vol. IV. (C). 1991. 40.00 (*0-685-49094-7*, Pub. by BR Pub) S Asia.

Limaye, Santosh Y., jt. ed. see Stinton, David P.

Limaye, Satu. South Asia & the United States after the Cold War. (Illus.). xxii, 86p. (Orig.). 1994. pap. 5.00 (*0-614-27187-8*, X88904) Asia Soc.

Limaye, Satu P. & Mukarram, Ahmed. India, Southeast Asia & the United States: New Opportunities & Prospects for Cooperation: Governance Issues: New York Conference Papers, September 6-7, 1996. LC 98-945932. 128p. 1998. write for info. (*0-87848-526-0*) Asia Soc.

Limaye, Surekha V., tr. Mahayanasutralamkara by 'Asanga' (Bibliotheca Indo-Buddhica Ser.: No. 94). (C). 1992. 54.00 (*81-7030-347-8*) S Asia.

Limb, Peter. The ANC & Black Workers in South Africa, 1912-1992: An Annotated Bibliography. LC 93-26607. 394p. 1993. 95.00 (*1-873836-95-3*, Pub. by H Zell Pubs) Seven Hills Bk.

Limb, Peter & Volet, Jean-Marie. Bibliography of African Literatures. LC 96-870. (Area Bibliographies Ser.: Vol. 10). 456p. 1996. 55.00 (*0-8108-3144-9*) Scarecrow.

Limb, Sue. Dulcie Domum's Bad Housekeeping. 224p. 1995. pap. 13.95 (*1-85702-066-9*) Fourth Estate.

***Limb, Sue.** Dulcie Goes Native. 472p. 2000. 31.99 (*0-7089-4218-0*) Ulverscroft.

Limb, Sue. More Bad Housekeeping. 176p. 1995. pap. 13.95 (*1-85702-151-7*) Trafalgar.

— Out on a Limb. LC 99-487841. 224p. 1999. 25.00 (*0-7278-2292-6*, Pub. by Severn Hse) Chivers N Amer.

Limb, Sue, jt. auth. see Cordingley, Pat.

Limbacher, James L. Four Aspects of the Film. Jowett, Garth S., ed. LC 77-11379. (Aspects of Film Ser.). (Illus.). 1978. reprint ed. lib. bdg. 30.95 (*0-405-11138-X*) Ayer.

— Keeping Score: Film Music, 1972-1979. LC 80-26474. 519p. 1981. 52.00 (*0-8108-1390-4*) Scarecrow.

— A Reference Guide to Audiovisual Information. LC 72-1737. 107p. reprint ed. pap. 33.20 (*0-608-11155-4*, 205019000078) Bks Demand.

— Sexuality in World Cinema, 2 vols. LC 83-3019. 1535p. 1983. 95.00 (*0-8108-1609-1*) Scarecrow.

Limbacher, James L., ed. Haven't I Seen You Somewhere Before? Remakes, Sequels & Series in Motion Pictures, Videos, & Television, 1896-1990. LC 79-84272. 454p. 1992. 65.00 (*0-87650-244-3*) Pierian.

— The Song List: A Guide to Contemporary Music from Classical Sources. LC 73-78293. 1973. 16.50 (*0-87650-041-6*) Pierian.

Limbacher, James L. & Wright, H. Stephen. Keeping Score: Film & Television Music, 1980-1988 (with Additional Coverage of 1921-1979) LC 91-21180. 928p. 1991. 97.50 (*0-8108-2453-1*) Scarecrow.

Limbaugh, Ronald H. John Muir's "Stickeen" & the Lessons of Nature. LC 96-5172. (Illus.). xviii, 185p. (C). 1996. 22.95 (*0-912006-84-6*) U of Alaska Pr.

Limbaugh, Ronald H. & Lewis, K. E., eds. The John Muir Papers, 1858-1957: Guide & Index to the Microfilm Edition. 190p. 1986. pap. write for info. (*0-89887-050-X*) Chadwyck-Healey.

Limbaugh, Rush H., III. See, I Told You So. large type ed. LC 94-1662. 539p. 1994. lib. bdg. 25.95 (*0-8161-7427-X*, G K Hall Lrg Type) Mac Lib Ref.

— See, I Told You So. large type ed. LC 94-1662. 539p. 1995. pap. 18.95 (*0-8161-7428-8*, G K Hall Lrg Type) Mac Lib Ref.

— See, I Told You So. LC 95-130873. 1994. reprint ed. mass mkt. 6.99 (*0-671-87121-8*, Pocket Star Bks) PB.

***Limbaugh, Rush H., III.** Way Things Ought to Be. 1999. 9.98 (*0-671-04597-0*) S&S Trade.

Limbaugh, Rush H., III. The Way Things Ought to Be. large type ed. LC 92-38202. (General Ser.). 456p. 1993. lib. bdg. 23.95 (*0-8161-5731-6*, G K Hall Lrg Type) Mac Lib Ref.

— The Way Things Ought to Be. Regan, Judith, ed. 336p. 1993. reprint ed. per. 6.99 (*0-671-75150-6*, Pocket Star Bks) PB.

***Limber, Jill.** Come What May. 2000. mass mkt. 4.99 (*0-8217-6529-9*, Zebra Kensgtn) Kensgtn Pub Corp.

Limber, T. Peter. Hellenika, Heritage & History. LC 97-77149. (Illus.). 267p. 1997. pap. 25.00 (*0-9660449-0-8*, 11527) Cosmos.

Limberg, Fred & Koppel, Ted. Estonian Army Uniforms & Insignia, 1936-44. 3rd rev. ed. (World War II Military Ser.: Vol. 10). (Illus.). 44p. 1997. 17.95 (*1-57638-076-9*, M10H); pap. 7.95 (*1-57638-029-7*, M10S) Merriam Pr.

***Limberhand, Dennis.** Cheyenne. (Indian Nations Ser.). (Illus.). 2000. 25.69 (*0-8172-5469-2*) Raintree Steck-V.

Limberis, Vasiliki. Divine Heiress: The Virgin Mary & the Creation of Christian Constantinople. LC 93-47960. 224p. (C). 1994. 65.00 (*0-415-09677-4*, B3246) Routledge.

Limbert, Charles P., & Co. Staff. Limbert Arts & Crafts Furniture: The Complete 1903 Catalog. (Illus.). 80p. 1992. reprint ed. pap. 7.95 (*0-486-27120-X*) Dover.

Limbert, Paul M. Denominational Policies in the Support & Supervision of Higher Education. LC 75-176994. (Columbia University. Teachers College. Contributions to Education Ser.: No. 378). reprint ed. 37.50 (*0-404-55378-8*) AMS Pr.

Limbird, Lee, jt. ed. see Lanier, Stephen M.

Limbird, Lee E. Cell Surface Receptors: A Short Course on Theory & Methods. 2nd ed. LC 95-42298. 256p. (C). 1996. text 97.00 (*0-7923-3839-1*) Kluwer Academic.

Limbird, Lee E., ed. The Alpha-2 Adrenergic Receptors. LC 88-6833. (Receptors Ser.). (Illus.). 377p. 1988. 125.00 (*0-89603-135-7*) Humana.

Limbird, Randy, ed. see Marcus, Hal.

Limbo, Rana K. & Wheeler, Sara R. When a Baby Dies: A Handbook for Healing & Helping. 168p. 1986. pap. 8.95 (*0-9612310-3-3*) Harsand Pr.

— When a Baby Dies: A Handbook for Healing & Helping. rev. ed. 184p. 1998. pap. 12.95 (*0-9607098-4-3*) Luth Hosp La Crosse.

Limbrick, Elaine & Thomson, Douglas F., eds. Franciscus Sanchez: That Nothing Is Known. LC 96-31602. 320p. 1989. text 89.95 (*0-521-35077-8*) Cambridge U Pr.

Limbrunner, Alfred, jt. auth. see Richardz, Klaus.

Limbrunner, George F., jt. auth. see Spiegel, Leonard.

Limburg, James. Hosea-Micah. LC 87-46293. (Interpretation: a Bible Commentary for Preaching & Teaching Ser.). 204p. 1988. 23.00 (*0-8042-3128-1*) Westminster John Knox.

— Jonah: A Commentary. Mays, James L. et al, eds. LC 93-17160. (Old Testament Library). 144p. 1993. text 21.00 (*0-664-21296-4*) Westminster John Knox.

***Limburg, James.** Psalms. (Bible Companion Ser.). 448p. 2000. pap. 29.95 (*0-664-25557-4*) Westminster John Knox.

Limburg, James, ed. Judaism: An Introduction for Christians. LC 87-9189.Tr. of Was jeder vom Judentum wissen muss. (Illus.). 288p. (Orig.). 1987. pap. 11.99 (*0-8066-2263-6*, 10-3610, Augsburg) Augsburg Fortress.

Limburg, K. E., et al. The Hudson River Ecosystem. (Environmental Management Ser.). (Illus.). xiv, 331p. 1986. 175.00 (*0-387-96220-4*) Spr-Verlag.

Limburg, Peter R. Deceived: The Story of the Donner Party. LC 98-14253. (Illus.). 296p. 1998. 29.95 (*1-890988-00-6*) Pacifica Military.

— Weird! The Complete Book of Halloween Words. 176p. (J). 1991. pap. 3.50 (*0-380-71172-9*, Avon Bks) Morrow Avon.

— Weird! The Complete Book of Halloween Words. LC 88-38678. (Illus.). 128p. (J). (gr. 4-10). 1989. lib. bdg. 13.95 (*0-02-759050-X*, Bradbury S&S) S&S Childrens.

Limburg, Val E. Electronic Media Ethics. 200p. 1994. pap. 34.95 (*0-240-80145-8*, Focal) Buttrwrth-Heinemann.

Limebeer, David J., jt. auth. see Green, Michael.

Limeburner, Grace, compiled by. Gravestone Inscriptions, Penobscot. (Illus.). 44p. 1997. reprint ed. pap. 9.00 (*0-8328-5893-5*) Higginson Bk Co.

Limeburner, Grace M., compiled by. Sedgewick Gravestone Inscriptions to 1892. (Illus.). 85p. 1997. reprint ed. pap. 15.50 (*0-8328-5912-5*) Higginson Bk Co.

— Sedgewick, Incorporated January 12, 1789: All Vital Statistics...(1789 to 1809) (Illus.). 84p. 1997. reprint ed. pap. 15.00 (*0-8328-5913-3*) Higginson Bk Co.

Limentani, Adam. Between Freud & Klein: The Psychoanalytic Quest for Knowledge & Truth. LC 90-104872. xiv, 281 p. 1989. write for info. (*1-85343-063-3*) Free Assoc Bks.

***Limentani, Adam.** Between Freud & Klein: The Psychoanalytic Quest for Knowledge & Truth. 304p. 1999. pap. text 33.00 (*1-85575-145-3*, Pub. by H Karnac Bks Ltd) Other Pr LLC.

Limeres, Rene & Pederson, Gunnar. Foghorn Outdoors: Alaska Fishing. 2nd ed. (Illus.). 560p. 1997. pap. text 20.95 (*0-935701-51-6*, Foghorn Outdoors) Avalon Travel.

Limerick, David & Cunnington, Bert. Managing the New Organization: A Blueprint for Networks & Strategic Alliances. (Management Ser.). 302p. 1993. text 32.95 (*1-55542-581-X*) Jossey-Bass.

Limerick, Patricia. Something in the Soil. pap. 16.95 (*0-393-32102-9*) Norton.

Limerick, Patricia N. Desert Passages: Encounters with the American Deserts. LC 84-28032. 224p. reprint ed. pap. 69.50 (*0-7837-5168-0*, 204489700004) Bks Demand.

— The Legacy of Conquest: The Unbroken Past of the American West. LC 86-23883. 1988. pap. 13.95 (*0-393-30497-3*) Norton.

— The Real West. (Illus.). 96p. 1996. 12.95 (*0-942576-36-5*) CO Hist Soc.

Limerick, Patricia N., et al, eds. Trails: Toward a New Western History. LC 91-25640. (Illus.). 250p. 1991. pap. 14.95 (*0-7006-0501-0*) U Pr of KS.

Limerick, Patricia N., jt. auth. see White, Richard.

Limerick, Patricia Nelson. Something in the Soil: Field-Testing the New Western History. LC 99-47246. 352p. 2000. 27.95 (*0-393-03788-6*) Norton.

LiMes. Italy & the Balkans. LC 98-20055. (Significant Issues Ser.). 108p. (C). 1998. pap. text 15.95 (*0-89206-344-0*) CSIS.

Liming, Gary. Working with Clarion. (Illus.). 304p. 1990. 29.95 (*0-8306-9403-X*, 3403) McGraw-Hill Prof.

***Liming, Sean D.** Windows NT Embedded Step-By-Step. (Illus.). 200p. 2000. pap. 44.95 (*0-929392-68-X*, Pub. by Annabooks) Coriolis Grp.

Limkemann, Will, et al. AudioFile: Catalog Your Recordings from A to Z. (Software-in-a-Book Ser.: No. 3). (Illus.). 192p. (Orig.). 1997. pap. 39.95 (*1-887155-02-3*) Doubleware Pubns.

— ScoreKeepers: Catalog Your Music from A to Z. (Software-in-a-Book Ser.: No. 4). (Illus.). 192p. (Orig.). 1997. pap. 49.95 (*1-887155-03-1*) Doubleware Pubns.

— VideoStore: Catalog Your Videos from A to Z. (Software-in-a-Book Ser.: No. 5). (Illus.). 192p. (Orig.). 1997. pap. 39.95 (*1-887155-04-X*) Doubleware Pubns.

Limkemann, William, et al. Celery, Cilantro & Computers: The Personal Recipe & Cook's Reference. (Software-in-a-Book Ser.). (Illus.). 192p. (Orig.). 1997. pap. 39.95 incl. disk (*1-887155-01-5*) Doubleware Pubns.

— Choirs Claviers & Computers: Church Music Cataloging & Musician's Desk Reference. (Software-in-a-Book Ser.). (Illus.). 320p. (Orig.). 1995. pap. 49.95 (*1-887155-00-7*) Doubleware Pubns.

Limmer. Emergency Care. 8th ed. O'Keefe, Michael F., ed. LC 97-14615. 912p. 1997. pap. text 57.00 (*0-8359-5089-1*) P-H.

— Emergency Care. 8th ed. O'Keefe, Michael F., ed. LC 97-14615. (Illus.). 912p. 1997. text 54.00 (*0-8359-5073-5*) P-H.

Limmer & Elling. Essentials Emergency Care. 2nd ed. LC 98-24803. 544p. 1998. pap. text 42.00 (*0-8359-5181-2*) P-H.

Limmer, Cliare, jt. ed. see Ullman, Montague.

Limmer, Daniel & Elling, Robert. First Responder Exam Preparation & Review. LC 97-165206. (Illus.). 212p. 1997. pap. text 24.60 (*0-8359-5021-2*) P-H.

***Limmer, Daniel & Grill, Michael.** Fire Service First Responder. Dickinson, Edward T., ed. LC 99-35632. (Illus.). 513p. 1999. pap. text 49.00 (*0-8359-5314-9*) Globe Fearon.

Limmer, Hans C. Controlling in Mode-Markenartikelunternehmen. (GER., Illus.). X, 238p. 1996. 44.95 (*3-631-30574-5*) P Lang Pubng.

Limmer, Milly J. Where Do Little Girls Grow? Levine, Abby, ed. LC 92-22936. (Illus.). 32p. (J). (ps-2). 1993. lib. bdg. 15.95 (*0-8075-8924-1*) A Whitman.

— Where Will You Swim Tonight? Fay, Ann, ed. LC 90-38938. (Illus.). 32p. (J). (ps-1). 1990. 15.95 (*0-8075-8949-7*) A Whitman.

Limmer, Ruth. Six Heritage Tours of the Lower East Side: A Walking Guide. LC 97-2074. (Illus.). 176p. 1997. pap. 13.95 (*0-8147-5130-X*) NYU Pr.

***Limnios, N. & Nikulin, M., eds.** Recent Advances in Reliability Theory: Methodology, Practice & Interference. (Statistics for Industry & Technology Ser.). (Illus.). 537p. 2000. 79.95 (*0-8176-4135-1*, Pub. by Birkhauser) Spr-Verlag.

Limnios, N., jt. auth. see Ionescu, D. C.

Limnios, N., jt. auth. see Janssen, Jacques.

Limnios, N., jt. ed. see Ionescu, D. C.

Limoge, Y. & Bocquet, J. L. Reactive Phase Formation at Interfaces & Diffusion Processes. (Materials Science Forum Ser.: Vols. 155-156). (Illus.). 598p. (C). 1994. text 206.00 (*0-87849-680-7*, Pub. by Trans T Pub) Enfield Pubs NH.

Limoges, Camille, jt. ed. see Coleman, William R.

Limoges, Camille, jt. ed. see Coleman, William.

Limoges, Raymonde. American Limoges: Identification & Value Guide. 208p. 1996. 24.95 (*0-89145-685-6*, 4630) Collector Bks.

Limoli, Howard, tr. see Duras, Marguerite.

Limon, Graciela. The Day of the Moon. LC 98-47015. 228p. 1999. pap. 12.95 (*1-55885-274-3*, Pub. by Arte Publico) SPD-Small Pr Dist.

— In Search of Bernabe. LC 93-12813. 166p. (C). 1993. pap. 10.95 (*1-55885-073-2*) Arte Publico.

— The Memories of Ana Calderon. LC 94-8663. 200p. 1994. 9.95 (*1-55885-116-X*) Arte Publico.

— Song of the Hummingbird. LC 95-37666. 217p. 1996. pap. 12.95 (*1-55885-091-0*) Arte Publico.

Limon, Janet, jt. auth. see Minear, Tish.

Limon, Jerzy. Gentlemen of a Company: English Players in Central & Eastern Europe, 1590 to 1660. (Illus.). 208p. 1985. text 57.95 (*0-521-26304-2*) Cambridge U Pr.

— The Masque of Stuart Culture. LC 89-40475. (Illus.). 240p. 1990. 40.00 (*0-87413-396-3*) U Delaware Pr.

Limon, Jerzy & Halio, Jay L., eds. Shakespeare & His Contemporaries: Eastern & Central European Studies. LC 92-53788. (International Studies in Shakespeare & His Contemporaries). 272p. (C). 1993. 39.50 (*0-87413-475-7*) U Delaware Pr.

Limon, John. The Place of Fiction in the Time of Science: A Disciplinary History of American Writing. (Cambridge Studies in American Literature & Culture: No. 39). 230p. (C). 1990. text 54.95 (*0-521-35251-7*) Cambridge U Pr.

***Limon, John.** Stand-Up Comedy in Theory or Abjection in America. LC 00-29446. 176p. 2000. pap. write for info. (*0-8223-2546-2*) Duke.

— Stand-Up Comedy in Theory, Or, Abjection in America. LC 00-29446. 176p. 2000. lib. bdg. 49.95 (*0-8223-2509-8*) Duke.

Limon, John. Writing after War: American War Fiction from Realism to Postmodernism. 272p. 1994. pap. text 24.95 (*0-19-508759-3*) OUP.

Limon, Jose. Jose Limon: An Unfinished Memoir. Garafola, Lynn, ed. LC 98-30941. (Studies in Dance History Ser.). (Illus.). 229p. 1998. 29.95 (*0-8195-6374-9*, Wesleyan Univ Pr) U Pr of New Eng.

Limon, Jose E. American Encounters: Greater Mexico, the United States & the Erotics of Culture. LC 98-17146. 264p. 1998. 27.00 (*0-8070-0236-4*) Beacon Pr.

— American Encounters: Greater Mexico, the United States & the Erotics of Culture. LC 98-17146. 264p. 1999. pap. 17.50 (*0-8070-0237-2*) Beacon Pr.

— Dancing with the Devil: Society & Cultural Poetics in Mexican-American South Texas. LC 93-39968. (New Directions in Anthropological Writing Ser.). 256p. 1994. pap. 19.95 (*0-299-14224-8*) U of Wis Pr.

— Mexican Ballads, Chicano Poems: History & Influence in Mexican-American Social Poetry. (New Historicism: Studies in Cultural Poetics: No. 17). (C). 1992. pap. 17.95 (*0-520-07633-8*, Pub. by U CA Pr) Cal Prin Full Svc.

Limon, Jose E., ed. see Gonzalez, Jovita & Raleigh, Eve.

Limon, Jose E., ed. & intro. see Gonzalez, Jovita.

Limon, Lynn, et al, eds. Nonprescription Products: Patient Assessment Handbook. LC 96-79456. (Illus.). 456p. (Orig.). 1996. pap. 42.00 (*0-917330-82-X*, T270) Am Pharm Assn.

Limon, Martin. Buddha's Money. 1999. mass mkt. 5.99 (*0-553-57610-0*) Bantam.

— Jade Lady Burning. LC 92-27572. 224p. 1992. 19.95 (*0-939149-71-0*) Soho Press.

— Jade Lady Burning. LC 92-27572. (Soho Crime Ser.). 224p. 1994. pap. 10.00 (*1-56947-020-0*) Soho Press.

Limon, Sharlene, jt. auth. see Waters, Verle.

Limongelli, Carla, jt. auth. see Calmet, Jacques.

Limonov, Eduard. Eto Ia - Edichka. 3rd ed. (RUS.). 290p. 1989. pap. 16.00 (*0-89830-132-7*) Russica Pubs.

— U Nas Byla Velikaia Epokha. (RUS.). 150p. (Orig.). 1989. pap. 15.50 (*0-89830-124-6*) Russica Pubs.

Limor, Yehiel, jt. auth. see Caspi, Dan.

Limouris, Gennadios, ed. Come, Holy Spirit - Renew the Whole Creation: An Orthodox Approach for the Seventh Assembly of the World Council of Churches (Canberra, Australia, 6-21 February, 1991) LC 90-25501. 263p. (J). (gr. 10-12). 1991. pap. 17.95 (*0-917651-31-6*) Holy Cross Orthodox.

Limouris, Gennadios & Vaporis, Nomikos M., eds. Orthodox Perspectives on Baptism, Eucharist & Ministry. LC 85-27298. Vol. 128. xii, 168p. (Orig.). 1985. pap. 6.95 (*0-917651-22-7*, Pub. by Holy Cross Orthodox) BookWorld.

Limousin, Odile. The Story of Paper. Matthews, Sarah, tr. from FRE. LC 87-31752. (Illus.). 38p. (J). (gr. k-5). 1988. 5.95 (*0-944589-16-2*, 162) Young Discovery Lib.

Limousin, Odile & Neumann, Daniele. TV & Films: Behind the Scenes. (Young Discovery Library). (Illus.). 40p. (J). (gr. k-6). 1993. lib. bdg. 2.99 (*1-56674-073-8*, HTS Bks) Forest Hse.

— TV & Films: Behind the Scenes. Bogard, Vicki, tr. from FRE. LC 92-966. (Illus.). (J). (gr. k-5). 1992. 5.95 (*0-944589-36-7*) Young Discovery Lib.

Limouze, Dorothy & Kuretsky, Susan D. The Felix M. Warburg Print Collection: A Legacy of Discernment. (Illus.). 189p. (Orig.). 1995. pap. 35.00 (*0-9644263-0-7*) F L Loeb Art Ctr.

Limouze, Henry S., jt. ed. see Cary, Cecile W.

Limouzy, Pierre. Manuel de Composition Francais. (FRE.). 1970. 14.00 (*0-394-30363-6*) Random.

Limouzy, Pierre & Bourgeacq, Jacques A. Manuel de Composition Francaise. 2nd ed. 288p. (C). 1990. 44.69 (*0-07-037903-3*) McGraw.

— Manuel de Composition Francaise. 2nd ed. (C). 1990. pap. text, teacher ed. 12.18 (*0-07-037904-1*) McGraw.

Limp, Fred & Harmon, Debbie. Inside Geomedia (V 2.1) LC 98-38548. 608p. (C). 1998. pap. 52.95 (*1-56690-185-5*) Thomson Learn.

Limp, Fredrick, et al. Gone to a Better Land: A Biohistory of a Rural Black Cemetery in the Post-Reconstruction South. Rose, Jerome C., ed. (Illus.). 216p. 1985. pap. 12.50 (*1-56349-050-1*, RS25) AR Archaeol.

Limp, W. Fredrick. Guidelines for Historic Properties Management, Southwestern Division Management Plan. (Illus.). 240p. 1989. pap. 10.00 (*1-56349-067-6*, SP01) AR Archaeol.

Limp, W. Fredrick, ed. The Use of Multispectral Digital Imagery in Archeological Investigations. (Illus.). 121p. 1989. pap. 16.00 (*1-56349-062-5*, RS34) AR Archaeol.

Limp, W. Fredrick, et al, eds. The Archeological Literature of the South-Central United States, 4 vols. 1049p. 1989. pap. 25.00 (*1-56349-064-1*, RS36) AR Archaeol.

Limper, Mary G., ed. see Mills, Kenneth G.

Limpert, Dana. Swan Flyway, the Tundra Swan. (Smithsonian Wild Heritage Collection). (J). 1993. 10.15 (*0-606-08216-6*, Pub. by Turtleback) Demco.

Limpert, E., jt. ed. see Wolfe, M. S.

***Limpert, Rudolf.** Brake Design & Safety. 2nd ed. LC 98-53284. 1999. 89.00 (*1-56091-915-9*) Soc Auto Engineers.

Limpert, Rudolf. Motor Vehicle Accident Reconstruction & Cause Analysis. 4th ed. LC 94-79932. 876p. 1994. 85.00 (*1-55834-207-9*, 64362-11, MICHIE) LEXIS Pub.

— Motor Vehicle Accident Reconstruction & Cause Analysis. 4th ed. 1995. suppl. ed. 20.00 (*0-614-25249-0*, 64363, MICHIE) LEXIS Pub.

***Limpert, Rudolf.** Motor Vehicle Accident Reconstruction & Cause Analysis. 5th ed. 1000p. 1999. write for info. (*0-327-04974-X*, 6436212) LEXIS Pub.

Limpert, Rudolf. Motor Vehicle Accident Reconstruction & Cause Analysis, 1998 Supplement. 4th ed. (Illus.). 100p. 1998. write for info. (*0-327-00846-6*, 6436311) LEXIS Pub.

Limpert, Rudolph. Brake Design & Safety. LC 92-25978. 468p. 1992. 39.00 (*1-56091-261-8*, R-120) Soc Auto Engineers.

— Motor Vehicle Accident Reconstruction & Cause Analysis. 3rd ed. (Illus.). 843p. 1989. boxed set 110.00 (*0-87473-462-2*, MICHIE) LEXIS Pub.

Limpic, T. Catalogo de Org. Mision Iberoamericanas.Tr. of Catalog of Spanish-American Mission Organization. (SPA.). 9.99 (*0-7899-0440-3*, 498656) Editorial Unilit.

Limpin, Juanita, jt. auth. see Forys, Edward.

Limpp, Marcie A. Oscar's Dreamland Yesteryear Museum: The Story of Oscar O. Cooke & His Collection. (Illus.). 144p. (Orig.). 1997. pap. 17.95 (*0-9656378-0-8*) Hayseed Pub.

Limprecht, Jane E. ConAgra Who? The Story of ConAgra's First 70 Years. Amsden, Don B., ed. (Illus.). 301p. 1990. 19.95 (*0-9627100-0-8*) Conagra.

Limpumba, N. Africa Beyond Adjustment. LC 94-36132. (Policy Essay Ser.: Vol. 15). 1994. pap. 13.95 (*1-56517-016-4*) Overseas Dev Council.

Limpus, Bruce. Lights! Camera! Action! A Guide to Using Video Production in the Classroom. 88p. 1994. pap. text 19.95 (*1-882664-08-6*) Prufrock Pr.

Limson, Stella G. Primary Health Care in Omaha Nebraska: A Case Study of Nine Primary Health Care Centers. (Illus.). 50p. (Orig.). 1986. pap. 3.50 (*1-55719-025-9*) U NE CPAR.

Limulus Inc. Staff. Fast Food & Quick Service Restaurant Franchises: The North American Directory. LC 94-76699. (Franchise Information Ser.). 136p. (Orig.). 1994. pap. 19.95 (*1-885177-00-3*) Limulus.

Lin. Basic Electric Circuit Analysis: Student Problem Set with Solutions. 5th ed. 240p. 1995. pap. 28.95 (*0-471-36587-4*) Wiley.

— China. 157.95 (*1-84014-483-1*) Ashgate Pub Co.

Lin. Craniofacial Surgery. 2001. text. write for info. (*0-7216-8701-6*, W B Saunders Co) Harcrt Hlth Sci Grp.

— Mastering DB2 400. 2000. text 46.92 (*0-13-262205-X*) P-H.

— Nonlinear & Convex Analysis: Proceedings in Honor of Ky Fan. Simons, Stephen, ed. (Lecture Notes in Pure & Applied Mathematics Ser.: Vol. 107). (Illus.). 320p. 1987. pap. text 165.00 (*0-8247-7777-8*) Dekker.

Lin. Pencil Sketching & Drawing & Designing with Confidence: A Step By Step Guide. 74.95 (*0-471-35777-4*) Wiley.

Lin & Stewart. AS 400: Systems, Utilities, Database & Programming. 2nd ed. LC 99-207391. 696p. 1998. 59.99 (*0-13-083067-4*) P-H.

Lin & Wildberger, eds. Soft Computing. 332p. 1995. pap. 80.00 (*1-56555-077-3*, SOFT-95) Soc Computer Sim.

Lin, jt. auth. see Johnson.

Lin, A. The Rural Economy of Guangdong, 1870-1937: A Study of the Agrarian Crisis & Its Origins in Southernmost China. LC 97-13959. xiii, 226p. 1997. text 69.95 (*0-312-17594-9*) St Martin.

Lin, A. M., jt. ed. see Krisch, Alan D.

Lin, A. N. & Carter, D. M., eds. Epidermolysis Bullosa: Basic & Clinical Aspects. (Illus.). xiv, 302p. 1992. 145.00 (*0-387-97796-1*) Spr-Verlag.

Lin, Adet, tr. see Pingying Hsieh.

Lin, Alice. Grandmother Had No Name. 1988. pap. 9.95 (*0-8351-2034-1*) China Bks.

Lin, Alvin C., et al. Guide to Federal Funding for Anti-crime Programs. 2nd ed. LC 97-216083. 1997. write for info. (*0-933544-94-4*) Gov Info Srvs.

Lin, Ann C., jt. ed. see Danziger, Sheldon.

Lin, Anna. Handbook of TCM Urology & Male Sexual Dysfunction. Flaws, Bob, ed. LC 92-73392. 240p. (Orig.). 1992. pap. 19.95 (*0-936185-36-8*) Blue Poppy Pr.

Lin, Anor, tr. see Pingying Hsieh.

Lin, B., ed. Banach Space Theory. LC 88-38106. (CONM Ser.: Vol. 85). 521p. 1989. pap. 59.00 (*0-8218-5092-X*, CONM/85) Am Math.

Lin, Bai. Lip Flexibilities: For All Brass Instruments. 40p. 1996. pap. text 14.00 (*0-9630856-6-2*) Balquhidder.

Lin, Ben C., jt. auth. see Dunphy, Robert T.

Lin, Bih-Jaw & Myers, James T. Forces for Change in Contemporary China. LC 93-15124. 400p. (C). 1993. text 34.95 (*0-87249-969-3*) U of SC Pr.

Lin, Bih-Jaw & Myers, James T., eds. Contemporary China & the Changing International Community. LC 94-11684. 390p. 1994. text 39.95 (*1-57003-024-3*) U of SC Pr.

— Contemporary China in the Post-Cold War Era. LC 95-11684. 430p. 1996. text 39.95 (*1-57003-093-6*) U of SC Pr.

Lin, Biing-Hwan, et al. Pesticide & Fertilizer Use & Trends in U. S. Agriculture. (Illus.). 47p. (Orig.). (C). 1995. pap. text 20.00 (*0-7881-2477-3*) DIANE Pub.

Lin, C. & Au-Yang, M. K., eds. Seismic Analysis of Power Plant Systems & Components. (PVP Ser.: Vol. 73). 200p. 1983. pap. text 12.00 (*0-317-02647-X*, H00259) ASME.

Lin, C. A., jt. auth. see Parallel CFD '98 Conference Staff.

Lin, C. C. & Segel, Lee A. Mathematics Applied to Deterministic Problems in the Natural Sciences. LC 88-62304. (Classics in Applied Mathematics Ser.: No. 1). xxi, 609p. 1988. pap. 39.50 (*0-89871-229-7*) Soc Indus-Appl Math.

Lin, C. C., jt. auth. see Bertin, G.

Lin, C. D. Fundamental Processes & Applications of Atoms & Ions, Review. 628p. 1993. text 164.00 (*981-02-1537-1*) World Scientific Pub.

Lin, C. W., ed. Natural Hazard Phenomena & Mitigation: Proceedings of the Pressure Vessels & Piping Conference, Minneapolis, MN, 1994. LC 94-71661. (PVP Ser.: Vol. 271). 163p. 1994. pap. 50.00 (*0-7918-1194-8*) ASME.

— Seismic Modal Analysis & System Interaction. (PVP Ser.: Vol. 249). 156p. 1993. 45.00 (*0-7918-0976-5*, H00808) ASME.

Lin, C. W., et al, eds. Natural Hazard Phenomena & Mitigation - 1995. LC 94-71661. (Proceedings of the 1995 ASME/JSME Pressure Vessels & Piping Conference Ser.: PVP-Vol. 308). 464p. 1995. 140.00 (*0-7918-1339-8*, H00971) ASME.

Lin, Cantian, jt. auth. see Gregory, John.

Lin, Catherine, et al. A Gathering Place: Art Making by Asian/Pacific Women in Traditional Contemporary Directions. (Illus.). 73p. 1995. pap. 19.95 (*1-877921-13-0*) Pacific Asia.

Lin-Chandler, Irene. Grievous Angel. 320p. 1996. pap. 11.95 (*0-7472-5081-2*, Pub. by Headline Bk Pub) Trafalgar.

Lin, Cheng-hung & Fu, Daiwie, eds. Philosophy & Conceptual History of Science in Taiwan. LC 92-12852. (Boston Studies in the Philosophy of Science: Vol. 141). 284p. (C). 1993. lib. bdg. 175.00 (*0-7923-1766-1*, Pub. by Kluwer Academic) Kluwer Academic.

Lin, Cheng-Yen & Lu, Chuanrong. Limit Theory for Mixing Dependent Random Variables. LC 96-34057. (Mathematics & Its Applications Ser.). 1997. text 160.50 (*0-7923-4219-4*) Kluwer Academic.

Lin, Chin-Chu, et al, eds. The High-Risk Fetus: Pathophysiology, Diagnosis, & Management. LC 92-2378. (Illus.). 696p. 1992. 149.00 (*0-387-97836-4*) Spr-Verlag.

Lin, Chin-Teng. Neural Fuzzy Control Systems with Structure & Parameter Learning. 150p. 1994. text 39.00 (*981-02-1613-0*) World Scientific Pub.

Lin, Chin-Ti. Perfect Sex: For Men & for the Women Who Love Them. LC 97-68873. 250p. 1998. 22.95 (*1-882792-51-3*); pap. 18.95 (*1-882792-73-4*) Proctor Pubns.

Lin, Ching-Fang. Modeling, Design, Analysis, Simulation & Evaluation. 640p. (C). 2001. 56.00 (*0-13-596388-5*) P-H.

— Modern Navigation, Guidance, & Control Processing. 560p. (C). 1991. text 63.75 (*0-13-596230-7*) P-H.

Lin, Ching-Yuan. Latin America vs. East Asia: A Comparative Development Perspective. LC 89-4128. 256p. (gr. 13). 1989. text 74.95 (*0-87332-526-5*, East Gate Bk) M E Sharpe.

Lin, D. Mposium & Fleming, Thomas R. Proceedings of the 1st Seattle Symposium in Biostatistics, Vol. 123. LC 97-13962. (Lecture Notes in Statistics Ser.). 1997. pap. 34.95 (*0-387-94992-5*) Spr-Verlag.

Lin, David. China Letters. 470p. (Orig.). 1993. pap. 9.95 (*0-923309-05-5*) Hartland Pubns.

Lin, David, ed. see Wang, Shengzhong.

Lin, Dong, photos by. One American Reality: A Photographic Essay. (Illus.). 90p. 1996. 35.00 (*0-8351-2577-7*) China Bks.

Lin, Doris, jt. auth. see Dugre, Donald.

Lin, Edmund C., et al. Bacteria, Plasmids, & Phages: An Introduction to Molecular Biology. LC 83-22784. (Illus.). 328p. 1984. reprint ed. pap. 101.70 (*0-7837-6077-9*, 205912300007) Bks Demand.

Lin, Emil T. & Sadee, Wolfgang, eds. Drug Level Monitoring, Vol. 2. LC 85-17833. 378p. 1986. reprint ed. pap. 117.20 (*0-7837-2814-X*, 205765800006) Bks Demand.

Lin, Enbing, jt. auth. see Aldroubi, Akram.

Lin, Forest. Active X & the Internet. (Illus.). 344p. (C). 1998. pap. text 36.10 (*1-57676-016-2*) Scott Jones Pubng.

— The Internet, HTML & VBScript Coursebook. (Illus.). 73p. (C). 1998. pap. text 7.22 (*1-57676-014-6*) Scott Jones Pubng.

— Quick Start in JavaScript. (Illus.). (C). 1998. pap. text 16.61 (*1-57676-018-9*) Scott Jones Pubng.

An Asterisk (*) at the beginning of an entry indicates that the title is appearing for the first time.

*__Lin, Forest.__ Quickstart to DOS in Windows 9X. (Illus.). 154p. 1999. pap. text 23.10 (*1-57676-032-4*) Scott Jones Pubng.

__Lin, Forest.__ A Short Course in HTML. (Illus.). 327p. (C). 1998. pap. text 23.10 (*1-57676-024-3*) Scott Jones Pubng.

— Visual Basic 5 Coursebook. (Illus.). 1020p. (Orig.). (C). 1997. pap. text 59.20 (*1-57676-004-9*) Scott Jones Pubng.

— Visual Basic 6 Coursebook. 2nd ed. (Illus.). 1000p. (C). Date not set. pap. text 64.98 (*1-57676-029-4*) Scott Jones Pubng.

__Lin, Freddie S. & Xu, Daxiong, eds.__ Holographic Optical Elements & Displays, Vol. 2885. 246p. 1996. 85.00 (*0-8194-2286-X*) SPIE.

__Lin-Geiger, Chao & Nguyen-Carr, Van.__ DOS 6.2: The Tutorial Guide. 167p. 1997. pap. text. write for info. (*1-880634-69-4*) Access Pubs.

__Lin, George.__ Mastering the AS/400 Control Language. 432p. (C). 1995. pap. 50.00 (*0-13-461955-2*) P-H.

__Lin, George C.__ Red Capitalism in South China. LC 98-113369. (Urbanization in Asia Ser.). (Illus.). 256p. 1997. text 75.00 (*0-7748-0616-8*) U of Wash Pr.

__Lin, Geraline C. & Erinoff, Lynda, eds.__ Anabolic Steroid Abuse. 249p. (Orig.). (C). 1996. reprint ed. pap. text 30.00 (*0-7881-2969-4*) DIANE Pub.

*__Lin, Grace.__ The Ugly Vegetables. LC 98-26863. (Illus.). 32p. (J). (ps-3). 1999. 15.95 (*0-88106-336-3*, Talewinds) Charlesbridge Pub.

__Lin, H. K. & Rao, P. Dharma.__ Ferric Chloride Leaching of the Delta Sulfide Ores & Gold Extraction from the Leaching Residue. (MIRL Reports: No. 84). (Illus.). 18p. (Orig.). (C). 1987. pap. 4.00 (*0-911043-08-X*) UAKF Min Ind Res Lab.

__Lin, Helen T.__ Beginning Standard Chinese. 188p. (Orig.). (C). 1992. pap. 17.95 (*0-8351-1940-8*) China Bks.

— Beginning Standard Chinese, Vol. 2. (Orig.). 1992. 17.95 (*0-8351-1941-6*) China Bks.

— Essential Grammar for Modern Chinese. 2nd ed. LC 81-67784. (C & T Language Ser.). (CHI.). 312p. (C). 1984. pap. 14.95 (*0-917056-10-8*) Cheng & Tsui.

*__Lin, Henry.__ The Art & Science of Feng Shui: The Ancient Chinese Tradition of Shaping Fate. LC 00-30970. 2000. pap. 17.95 (*1-56718-436-7*) Llewellyn Pubns.

__Lin, Henry.__ Wanted Certified by the Computer Industry. 135p. 1998. pap. 25.00 (*0-9668408-0-1*) FutuReady Pubng.

*__Lin, Henry B.__ Chinese Health Care Secrets: A Natural Lifestyle Approach. LC 99-45849. (Illus.). 528p. 2000. pap. 24.95 (*1-56718-434-0*) Llewellyn Pubns.

__Lin, Henry B.__ What Your Face Reveals: Chinese Secrets of Face Reading. LC 99-11653. (Illus.). 312p. (Orig.). 1999. pap. 17.95 (*1-56718-433-2*) Llewellyn Pubns.

__Lin, Herbert S., ed. see Denning, Dorothy E.__

__Lin, Hong-Hsin.__ Die Person Des Heiligen Geistes Als Thema der Pneumatologie in der Reformierten Theologie. VIII, 283p. 1998. 48.95 (*3-631-33853-8*) P Lang Pubng.

__Lin, Hsin H.__ In Bytes We Travel. LC 97-47136. 224p. 1998. 16.00 (*981-02-3359-0*) World Scientific Pub.

__Lin Hsin Hsin.__ Love at First Byte. 300p. 1992. pap. text 21.00 (*981-02-1026-4*) World Scientific Pub.

__Lin, Huaxin.__ C*-Algebra Extensions of C(X) LC 95-3280. (Memoirs Ser.: No. 550). 89p. 1995. pap. 33.00 (*0-8218-2611-5*, MEMO/115/550) Am Math.

__Lin, Huaxin & Phillips, N. Christopher.__ Classification of Direct Limits of Even Cuntz-Circle Algebras. LC 95-34454. (Memoirs of the American Mathematical Society Ser.: No. 565). 116p. 1995. pap. 35.00 (*0-8218-0403-0*, MEMO/118/565) Am Math.

__Lin, Hui, tr. see Lu, Zuyin.__

__Lin, Hui-Sheng, jt. auth. see Thornton, Arland.__

__Lin, Ian B., intro.__ MECH '91 Australia: Engineering for a Competitive World, Conference 1: Improving the Manufacturing Environment. (Illus.). 58p. (Orig.). 1991. pap. 38.50 (*0-85825-525-1*, Pub. by Inst Engrs Aust-EA Bks) Accents Pubns.

__Lin, J.__ Steenrod Connections & Connectivity in H Spaces. LC 87-12589. (Memoirs Ser.: No. 68-369). 87p. 1987. pap. 18.00 (*0-8218-2431-7*, MEMO/68/369) Am Math.

__Lin, J. C., jt. auth. see Michaelson, S. M.__

__Lin, James C., ed.__ Advances in Electromagnetic Fields in Living Systems, Vol. 1. (Illus.). 204p. (C). 1994. text 75.00 (*0-306-44738-X*, Kluwer Plenum) Kluwer Academic.

— Advances in Electromagnetic Fields in Living Systems, Vol. 2. (Illus.). 300p. (C). 1996. text 89.50 (*0-306-45508-0*, Kluwer Plenum) Kluwer Academic.

__Lin, James C., ed.__ Electromagnetic Interaction with Biological Systems. (Illus.). 292p. 1989. 85.00 (*0-306-43109-2*, Plenum Trade) Perseus Pubng.

__Lin, Jami.__ The Essence of Feng Shui: Balancing Your Home, Body & Life with Fragrance. LC 98-17035. 1998. pap. 12.95 (*1-56170-567-5*) Hay House.

— Feng Shui. (Good Health Guide Ser.). 48p. 1999. pap. 3.95 (*0-87983-953-8*, Keats Publng) NTC Contemp Pub Co.

— Feng Shui Anthology: Contemporary Earth Design. Leyes, Maggie & Lewison-Singar, Rita, eds. (EarthDesign Ser.: No. 2). (Illus.). 448p. (Orig.). 1997. pap. text 22.50 (*0-9643060-8-5*) Earth Design.

— Feng Shui Today: Earth Design: The Added Dimension. Lewison-Singar, Rita, ed. (EarthDesign Ser.: No. 1). (Illus.). 302p. (Orig.). 1995. pap. 18.00 (*0-9643060-9-3*) Earth Design.

__Lin, Jan.__ Reconstructing Chinatown: Ethnic Enclaves & Global Change. LC 98-10693. (Globalization & Community Ser.). 234p. 1998. write for info. (*0-8166-2904-8*); pap. 19.95 (*0-8166-2905-6*) U of Minn Pr.

__Lin, Jason Y. & Bailey, Mary L., eds.__ 9th Workshop on Parallel & Distributed Simulation (PADS '95) LC 95-76898. 212p. 1995. pap. 80.00 (*0-8186-7120-3*, PADS-95) Soc Computer Sim.

__Lin, Jason Yi-Bing, jt. auth. see Chlamtac, Imrich.__

__Lin, Jian H., jt. auth. see Grub, Phillip D.__

__Lin, Jiann I., tr. see Yu Xuanji.__

__Lin, Jiann I., tr. & intro. see Young, David & Yu Xuanji.__

__Lin, Jing.__ Education in Post-Mao China. LC 92-19593. 152p. 1992. 52.95 (*0-275-94270-8*, C4270, Praeger Pubs) Greenwood.

— The Opening of the Chinese Mind: Democratic Changes in China since 1978. LC 93-50073. 208p. 1994. 49.95 (*0-275-94594-4*, Praeger Pubs) Greenwood.

— The Red Guards' Path to Violence: Political, Educational, & Psychological Factors. LC 91-2272. 200p. 1991. 52.95 (*0-275-93872-7*, C3872, Praeger Pubs) Greenwood.

*__Lin, Jing.__ Social Transformation & Private Education in China. LC 98-56632. 248p. 1999. 69.50 (*0-275-95590-7*, Praeger Pubs) Greenwood.

__Lin, Jonathon & Shiue, Tony.__ CNC Programming Using Mastercam Version Four & Five. Sterzik, Karen L., ed. (Illus.). 880p. (C). 1995. pap. text 55.00 (*1-886552-00-2*) Scholars Intl.

*__Lin, Julia.__ Parasol Tree Village. LC 99-67354. 176p. 2000. pap. 14.95 (*1-56167-569-5*, Five Star Spec Ed) Am Literary Pr.

__Lin, Julia C.__ Essays on Contemporary Chinese Poetry. LC 85-2972. 210p. (C). 1985. text 28.50 (*0-8214-0804-6*) Ohio U Pr.

__Lin, Julie S.__ San Diego Penny-Wise Parent Guide. 116p. 1996. spiral bd. 8.95 (*0-9656708-0-5*) J Lin Creative.

__Lin, Justin Y., et al.__ The China Miracle: Development Strategy & Economic Reform. 1996. pap. text 24.95 (*962-201-748-7*, Pub. by Chinese Univ) U of Mich Pr.

__Lin, K. Y., et al.__ Computational Number Theory & Digital Signal Processing: Fast Algorithms & Error Control Techniques. 352p. 1994. boxed set 89.95 (*0-8493-7177-5*, 7177) CRC Pr.

__Lin, L. L., ed. see International Conference on Myopia Staff.__

__Lin, Lee H.__ Simply Vegetarian. Wolhardt, Connie, tr. (CHI., Illus.). 96p. 1997. pap. 19.95 (*0-941676-71-4*) Wei-Chuan Pub.

__Lin, Lee H., ed. see Weichuan.__

__Lin, Lee-Hwa.__ Appetizers Chinese Style. (CHI & ENG., Illus.). 96p. (Orig.). 1996. pap. 19.95 (*0-941676-69-2*) Wei-Chuan Pub.

— International Baking Delights. (CHI., Illus.). 96p. 1996. pap. 19.95 (*0-941676-68-4*) Wei-Chuan Pub.

__Lin, Lee-Hwa, ed.__ Chinese Cuisine: Cantonese Style. (Illus.). 96p. 1998. pap. 19.95 (*0-941676-74-9*, 11CT3) Wei-Chuan Pub.

— Chinese Home Cooking for Health. (CHI., Illus.). 96p. 1998. pap. 19.95 (*0-941676-75-7*, 11CF3) Wei-Chuan Pub.

__Lin, Lin, jt. auth. see Spaulding, Seth.__

__Lin, Liwei, et al, eds.__ Micro-Electro-Mechanical Systems (MEMS), 1998; Proceedings: ASME International Mechanical Engineering Congress & Exposition (1998: Anaheim, CA) LC 99-192238. 593p. 1998. pap. 180.00 (*0-7918-1596-X*) ASME Pr.

__Lin, Longwei & Yan, Tong.__ Existence of Global Solutions of Strictly Hyperbolic Laws. LC 96-31179. (Pitman Monographs & Surveys in Pure & Applied Mathematics). 1998. write for info. (*0-582-30405-9*) Longman.

__Lin, M. J., jt. auth. see Hwang, L.__

__Lin, Maria, ed. see Da Silva, Nicholas.__

__Lin, Maria, ed. see Da Silva, Nicholas & Taylor, Benito.__

__Lin, Marjorie, jt. auth. see Leonard, Schalk.__

__Lin, Marjorie, jt. ed. see Leonard, Schalk.__

*__Lin, Maya.__ Boundaries. (Illus.). 224p. 2000. 40.00 (*0-684-83417-0*) S&S Trade.

*__Lin, Maya Y., et al.__ Maya Lin: American Academy in Rome, 10 Dicembre 1998-21 Febbraio 1999. LC 99-197257. 99p. 1998. write for info. (*88-435-6832-9*, Pub. by Electa) Gingko Press.

__Lin, Michael C.__ Construction Technology for Tall Buildings. (Civil Engineering Ser.). (Illus.). 307p. (Orig.). 1999. pap. text 42.50 (*981-02-3568-2*, Pub. by World Scientific Pub) Coronet Bks.

__Lin, Mike W.__ Architectural Rendering Techniques: A Color Reference. 252p. 1985. 59.95 (*0-471-28939-6*, VNR) Wiley.

— Architectural Rendering Techniques: A Color Reference. LC 84-25812. (Illus.). 256p. 1985. text 54.95 (*0-442-25953-0*, VNR) Wiley.

— Drawing & Designing with Confidence. (Illus.). 224p. 1993. text 54.95 (*0-442-00176-2*, VNR) Wiley.

— Drawing & Designing with Confidence: A Step by Step Guide. 208p. 1993. 54.95 (*0-471-28390-8*, VNR) Wiley.

*__Lin, Min.__ Certainty as a Social Metaphor: The Social & Historical Production of Certainty in China & the West, 79. LC 00-27634. (Contributions in Philosophy Ser.: Vol. 79). 312p. 2000. 65.00 (*0-313-31417-9*, GM1417, Greenwood Pr) Greenwood.

__Lin, Ming C. & Galikowski, Maria.__ The Search for Modernity: Chinese Intellectuals & Cultural Discourse in the Post-Mao Era LC 99-20105. 1999. text 49.95 (*0-312-21758-7*) St Martin.

__Lin, Ming C. & Manocha, Dinesh N.__ Applied Computational Geometry: Towards Geometric Engineering, FCRC '96 Workshop, WACG '96, Philadelphia, PA, May 27-28, 1996 Selected Papers, Vol. 114. LC 96-35287. (Lecture Notes on Computer Science Ser.). viii, 223p. 1996. 39.00 (*3-540-61785-X*) Spr-Verlag.

__Lin, Moses, jt. auth. see Lao, He H.__

__Lin, Nan.__ The Struggle for Tiananmen: Anatomy of the 1989 Mass Movement. LC 92-15780. 232p. 1992. 52.95 (*0-275-93656-2*, C3656, Praeger Pubs) Greenwood.

__Lin, Nan, jt. ed. see Marsden, Pater V.__

__Lin, Nancy T., tr. see Chou, En-Lai.__

__Lin, Norman.__ Learn Linux 3-d Graphics Programming. 2000. pap. text 49.95 (*1-55622-723-X*) Wordware.

__Lin, P.__ Mangrove Vegetation. 150p. 1988. 29.50 (*0-387-15718-2*) Spr-Verlag.

__Lin, Patrick P., jt. ed. see Wilson, Frank C.__

__Lin, Paul J.__ A Translation of Lao Tzu's "Tao Te Ching" & Wang Pi's "Commentary." LC 77-623897. (Michigan Monographs in Chinese Studies: No. 30). 232p. (Orig.). 1977. pap. text 15.00 (*0-89264-030-8*) Ctr Chinese Studies.

__Lin, Pei-Jan P., et al, eds.__ Acceptance Testing of Radiological Imaging Equipment: Proceedings of the Symposium Held on October 1-2, 1981. (American Association of Physicists in Medicine Symposium Ser.: No. 1). 310p. 1982. 40.00 (*0-88318-400-1*, Pub. by Am Inst Physics) Med Physics Pub.

__Lin, Phylis L., et al, eds.__ Families: East & West. 241p. 1992. pap. 21.00 (*1-880938-00-6*) Univ Ind Pr.

__Lin, Phylis L. & Decker, David, eds.__ China (Mainland China & Taiwan) in Transition: Selected Essays. LC 96-61326. 103p. 1997. 20.00 (*1-880938-02-2*) Univ Ind Pr.

__Lin, Ray Y. & Fishman, Steven G., eds.__ Control of Interfaces in Metal & Ceramics Composites. LC 93-80902. (Illus.). 377p. 1994. 84.00 (*0-87339-259-0*, 2590) Minerals Metals.

__Lin, Ray Y., ed. see Minerals, Metals & Materials Society Staff.__

__Lin, Ray Y., ed. see Symposium on Interfaces in Metal-Ceramics Composit.__

__Lin, Robert I., ed.__ Garlic in Biology & Medicine: Proceedings Of The First World Congress On The Health Significance of Garlic & Garlic Constituents. (Illus.). 275p. (Orig.). 1995. pap. text 150.00 (*0-9640678-0-3*) Nutrit Intl.

__Lin, Rufa, jt. ed. see Corke, Harold.__

__Lin, S. C.__ Computer Numerical Control from Programming to Networking. 106p. 1993. teacher ed. 14.95 (*0-8273-4716-2*) Delmar.

__Lin, S. C. & Shiue, F. C.__ Mastercam Book for Windows. Sterzik, Karen L., ed. (Illus.). 900p. 1995. pap. 69.00 (*1-886552-01-0*) Scholars Intl.

__Lin, S. C., et al.__ CNC Process Modeling Using SmartCAM. Chou, Joy, ed. (Illus.). 700p. (C). 1995. pap. 65.00 (*1-886552-02-9*) Scholars Intl.

*__Lin, S. C. Jonathon.__ Engineering Design Graphics with CADKEY. Sterzik, Karen L., ed. (Illus.). 550p. 1998. pap. write for info. (*1-886552-10-X*) Scholars Intl.

— Mastercam Solids. Sterzik, Karen L., ed. (Illus.). 350p. (C). 1999. pap. 59.00 (*1-886552-13-4*) Scholars Intl.

*__Lin, S. C. Jonathon & Griess, Jerald A.__ Autodesk Mechanical Desktop Made Easy Release 2. Sterzik, Karen L., ed. (Illus.). 625p. (C). 1998. pap. 59.00 (*1-886552-07-X*) Scholars Intl.

__Lin, S. C. Jonathon & Lahidji, Behrooz.__ Maximizing Surfcam. Sterzik, Karen L., ed. (Illus.). 900p. (C). 1997. pap. 79.00 (*1-886552-05-3*) Scholars Intl.

*__Lin, S. C. Jonathon & Shiue, F. C. Tony.__ Mastercam Version 7. Sterzik, Karen L., ed. (Illus.). 1300p. (C). 1998. pap. 83.00 (*1-886552-11-8*) Scholars Intl.

— Mastering I-DEAS. Sterzik, Karen L., ed. (Illus.). 750p. (C). 1999. pap. 69.00 (*1-886552-12-6*) Scholars Intl.

*__Lin, S. C. Jonathon, et al.__ SmartCAM Production Milling & Turning. Sterzik, Karen L., ed. (Illus.). 700p. (C). 1998. pap. 65.00 (*1-886552-06-1*) Scholars Intl.

__Lin, S. H.__ Advances in Multiphoton Processes & Spectroscopy, Vol. 1. 532p. 1984. text 113.00 (*9971-966-17-4*) World Scientific Pub.

__Lin, S. H., abr.__ Advances in Multiphoton Processes & Spectroscopy, Vol 12. 300p. 1999. 74.00 (*981-02-3829-0*) World Scientific Pub.

__Lin, S. H., ed.__ Advances in Multiphoton Processes & Spectroscopy, Vol. 2. 408p. 1986. text 113.00 (*9971-5-0085-X*) World Scientific Pub.

— Advances in Multiphoton Processes & Spectroscopy, Vol. 3. 348p. 1987. text 98.00 (*9971-5-0289-5*) World Scientific Pub.

— Advances in Multiphoton Processes & Spectroscopy, Vol. 4. 324p. (C). 1988. text 85.00 (*9971-5-0577-0*) World Scientific Pub.

— Advances in Multiphoton Processes & Spectroscopy, Vol. 5. 384p. (C). 1989. text 101.00 (*981-02-0037-4*) World Scientific Pub.

— Advances in Multiphoton Processes & Spectroscopy, Vol. 6. 212p. (C). 1990. text 84.00 (*981-02-0446-9*) World Scientific Pub.

— Advances in Multiphoton Processes & Spectroscopy, Vol. 7. 320p. (C). 1991. text 98.00 (*981-02-0718-2*) World Scientific Pub.

__Lin, S. H., et al, eds.__ Advances in Multiphoton Processes & Spectroscopy, Vol. 11. 200p. 1998. 58.00 (*981-02-3284-5*) World Scientific Pub.

__Lin, S. H., et al.__ Advances in Multi-Photon Processes & Spectroscopy, Vol. 9. 324p. 1995. text 74.00 (*981-02-2169-X*) World Scientific Pub.

— Advances in Multiphoton Processes & Spectroscopy, Vol. 8. 408p. 1993. text 91.00 (*981-02-1543-6*) World Scientific Pub.

— Density Matrix Method & Femtosecond Processes. 228p. (C). 1991. text 36.00 (*981-02-0709-3*) World Scientific Pub.

__Lin, S. K., ed.__ Molecules Annual '96 Vol. 1: Organic & Natural Product CD-ROM & Print Archive Edition of Molecules - Journal of Synthic Chemistry, 1996. 220p. 1997. 145.00 incl. cd-rom (*3-540-14572-9*) Spr-Verlag.

__Lin, S. P., et al, eds.__ Nonlinear Instability of Nonparallel Flows. LC 94-19338. 1994. 202.95 (*0-387-57679-7*) Spr-Verlag.

__Lin, S. P. & Lai, W. Michael.__ Selected Papers of Chia-Shun Yih, 2 vols. (Advanced Series on Fluid Mechanics). 1064p. (C). 1991. text 193.00 (*981-02-0543-0*) World Scientific Pub.

__Lin, Sein, ed. see Lincoln Institute of Land Policy Staff.__

__Lin, Sharon C.__ Libraries & Librarianship in China. LC 97-49482. (Guides to Asian Librarianship Ser.). 272p. 1998. lib. bdg. 75.00 (*0-313-28937-9*, Greenwood Pr) Greenwood.

__Lin, Sharon C. & Leung, Martha C.__ Chinese Libraries & Librarianship: An Annotated Bibliography. 1986. pap. 14.95 (*0-937256-03-X*) Chinese Cult Serv.

__Lin, Shiow-Ching & Pearce, Eli M.__ High Performance Thermosets: Chemistry, Properties, Applications. LC 93-37466. 368p. 1993. 98.50 (*1-56990-155-4*) Hanser-Gardner.

__Lin, Shou-ying.__ College Chinese, 4 vols., Set. LC 93-72860. 1064p. (Orig.). 1993. pap. text 79.95 (*0-88727-188-X*) Cheng & Tsui.

__Lin, Shu.__ Introduction to Error-Correcting Codes. LC 76-124417. 1970. 32.95 (*0-685-03876-9*) P-H.

— Trellises & Trellis-Based Decoding Algorithms for Linear Block Codes. LC 98-14363. (International Series in Engineering & Computer Science). 1998. 86.50 (*0-7923-8151-3*) Kluwer Academic.

__Lin, Shuen-Fu & Owen, Stephen, eds.__ The Vitality of the Lyric Voice: Shih Poetry from the Late Han to the T'ang. LC 85-30755. (Studies in China: Vol. 6). 423p. 1986. reprint ed. pap. 131.20 (*0-608-07647-3*, 205996400010) Bks Demand.

__Lin, Shuen-Fu, tr. see Tung, Yueh.__

__Lin, Shwu Yeng T., jt. auth. see Lin, You-Feng.__

__Lin, Sophia, ed. see Wei Chuan Publishing Staff.__

__Lin, Su-Chen J.__ Computer Numerical Control: Essentials in Programming & Networking. 1994. pap. 83.95 (*0-8273-4715-4*) Delmar.

__Lin, Sun, et al, eds.__ UNEP's New Way Forward: Environmental Law & Sustainable Development. LC 96-981185. (Illus.). 420p. 80.00 (*92-807-1524-0*) UN.

__Lin, Sylvia Li-chun, tr. see Tien-Wen, Chu.__

__Lin, Szu-Chuan.__ Wundertaten und Mission: Dramatische Episoden in Apg 13-14. XVII, 327p. 1998. 51.95 (*3-631-33180-0*) P Lang Pubng.

__Lin, T. Y., ed.__ Rough Sets & Data Mining: Analysis of Imprecise Data. LC 96-27716. 448p. (C). 1996. text 169.50 (*0-7923-9807-6*) Kluwer Academic.

__Lin, T. Y. & Burns, Ned H.__ Design Concrete Structures 3e. 3rd ed. LC 80-20619. 656p. (C). 1981. text 106.95 (*0-471-01898-8*) Wiley.

*__Lin, T. Y. & Qian, Shelly, eds.__ Database Security XI: Status & Prospects: Proceedings of the 11th IFIP TC11/WG 11.3 International Conference on Database Security, 1997: Lake Tahoe, California. 388p. 1998. 150.50 (*0-412-82090-0*) Chapman & Hall.

__Lin, Tan.__ Lotion Bullwhip Giraffe. LC 95-51822. (New American Poetry Ser.: Vol. 26). 110p. 1996. pap. 10.95 (*1-55713-258-5*) Sun & Moon CA.

__Lin, Tan Y.__ Criminal Procedure, 2 vols. LC 98-945888. 1770p. 1996. ring bd. write for info. (*0-409-99794-3*, MICHIE) LEXIS Pub.

__Lin, Te-Hua, jt. ed. see Iturralde, Armando.__

*__Lin, Timothy.__ Recruiting the Overcomers. (Ministry Ser.). 187p. 1999. pap. 9.50 (*1-885216-25-4*) Evan Formosan.

__Lin, Timothy.__ The Secret of Church Growth. Taniguchi, Ruth W., tr. 118p. (Orig.). 1992. pap. write for info. (*0-945304-01-3*) FCBC.

__Lin, Timothy T.__ The Life & Thought of Soren Kierkegaard. (Masterworks of Literature Ser.). 1974. pap. 13.95 (*0-8084-0377-X*) NCUP.

__Lin, Tom.__ Losing Face & Finding Grace: Twelve Bible Studies for Asian-American. 80p. (Orig.). 1997. pap., student ed. 5.99 (*0-8308-1684-4*, 1684) InterVarsity.

__Lin, Tung-Hai.__ Development of the Agrarian Movement & Agrarian Legislation in China, 1912-1930. 1976. lib. bdg. 34.95 (*0-8490-1714-9*) Gordon Pr.

__Lin, V. A. & Popovic, D.__ Computer-Aided Process & Quality Control. (Quality & Reliability Ser.). Date not set. write for info. (*0-8247-9916-X*) Dekker.

__Lin, Vladimir & Pinchover, Yehuda.__ Manifolds with Group Actions & Elliptic Operators. LC 94-26456. (Memoirs of the American Mathematical Society Ser.: No. 540). 78p. 1994. pap. 31.00 (*0-8218-2604-2*, MEMO/112/540) Am Math.

__Lin, Vladimir, jt. ed. see Kuchment, Peter.__

__Lin, W., jt. auth. see Byrnes, C. I.__

__Lin, Wei-Ying.__ The Future of Foreign Business & Foreign Investments in China. LC 75-30068. (Institute of Pacific Relations Ser.). reprint ed. 39.50 (*0-404-59541-3*) AMS Pr.

__Lin, Wen C.__ Handbook of Digital Systems for Scientists & Engineers. 272p. 1981. 147.00 (*0-8493-0671-X*, TK868, CRC Reprint) Franklin.

__Lin, Wen C., ed.__ Handbook of Digital System Design. 2nd ed. 486p. 1990. lib. bdg. 89.95 (*0-8493-4272-4*, TK868) CRC Pr.

__Lin Wusun, tr. see Xu Zhigeng.__

__Lin, X.__ Numerical Computation of Stress Waves in Solids. 317p. 1996. 205.00 (*3-05-501725-0*) Wiley.

__Lin, X., ed.__ Computing Theory '98: Proceedings of the 4th Australasian Theory Symposium - CATS'98. 350p. 1998. pap. 59.95 (*981-3083-92-1*) Spr-Verlag.

__Lin, Xiannuan.__ China's Energy Strategy: Economic Structure, Technological Choices, & Energy Consumption. LC 95-11328. 224p. 1996. 67.95 (*0-275-95306-8*, Praeger Pubs) Greenwood.

__Lin, Xiao.__ Numerical Computation of Stress Waves in Solids. 317p. 1996. 170.00 (*3-527-40094-X*) Wiley.

L

Lin, Y. General Systems Theory: A Mathematical Approach. LC 98-42068. (IFSR International Series on Systems Science & Engineering: 12). (Illus.). 382p. (C). 1999. 115.00 (*0-306-45944-2*) Plenum.

Lin, Y. C., jt. auth. see Volakis, John L.

Lin, Y. K. Probabilistic Theory of Structural Dynamics. LC 75-42154. 380p. 1976. reprint ed. 41.00 (*0-88275-377-0*) Krieger.

Lin, Y. K., ed. Probabilistic Mechanics & Structural & Geotechnical Reliability: Proceedings of the Sixth Specialty Conference Sponsored by the Engineering Mechanics, Structural, & Geotechnical Engineering Divisions, American Society of Civil Engineers, Denver, Colorado, July 8-10, 1992. LC 92-15903. 616p. 1992. pap. text 61.00 (*0-87262-873-6*) Am Soc Civil Eng.

Lin, Y. K. & Cai, G. Q. Probabilistic Structure Dynamics: Advanced Theory & Applications. rev. ed. LC 94-13102. 496p. (C). 1994. 77.81 (*0-07-038038-4*) McGraw.

Lin, Y. K. & Elishakoff, Isaac, eds. Stochastic Structural Dynamics 1: New Theoretical Developments. xiii, 356p. 1991. 106.95 (*0-387-54167-5*) Spr-Verlag.

Lin, Y. K. & Schueller, G. I., eds. Stochastic Structural Mechanics. (Lecture Notes in Engineering Ser.: Vol. 31). xi, 507p. 1987. pap. 79.00 (*0-387-18463-5*) Spr-Verlag.

Lin, Y. K. & Su, T. C., eds. Engineering Mechanics: Proceedings of the 11th Conference. LC 96-16971. 1254p. 1996. 129.00 (*0-7844-0172-1*) Am Soc Civil Eng.

Lin, Y. K., jt. auth. see Cai, C. Q.

Lin, Y. K., jt. ed. see Elishakoff, Isaac.

Lin, Yan-Xia, jt. auth. see Lin, Zhensheng.

***Lin, Yi-Min.** Between Politics & Markets: Firms, Competition & Institutional Change in Post-Mao China. (Structural Analysis in the Social Sciences Ser.: Vol. 18). (Illus.). 240p. (C). 2000. Price not set. (*0-521-77130-7*) Cambridge U Pr.

Lin, You-Feng & Lin, Shwu Yeng T. Set Theory with Applications. (Illus.). ix, 221p. 1985. reprint ed. pap. text 29.50 (*0-931541-04-2*) Mancorp Pub.

Lin, You-Feng, jt. auth. see McWaters, Marcus M.

Lin, Yu-Chong & Niu, Alan K., eds. Hyperbaric Physiology & Medicine. (Illus.). 170p. (C). 1988. text 31.50 (*0-941332-11-X*, D272) Best Pub Co.

Lin, Yu-Chong & Shida, Kathleen K., eds. Man in the Sea, Vol. I. (Illus.). 330p. 1990. text 35.50 (*0-941332-12-8*, D312) Best Pub Co.

— Man in the Sea, Vol. II. (Illus.). 232p. 1990. text 33.00 (*0-941332-13-6*, D313) Best Pub Co.

Lin Yu Tang. Essay. (CHI.). pap. 9.95 (*7-5387-0667-4*, Pub. by China Intl Bk) Distribks Inc.

Lin Yu-T'ang. The Gay Genius: The Life & Times of Su Tungpo. LC 71-112327. (Illus.). 427p. 1971. reprint ed. lib. bdg. 35.00 (*0-8371-4715-8*, LIGG, Greenwood Pr) Greenwood.

— Widow, Nun & Courtesan: Three Novelettes from the Chinese. LC 75-112328. 266p. 1971. reprint ed. lib. bdg. 38.50 (*0-8371-4716-6*, LIWN, Greenwood Pr) Greenwood.

Lin Yu-T'ang, ed. The Importance of Understanding: Translations from the Chinese. (Essay Index Reprint Ser.). 1977. reprint ed. 29.95 (*0-518-10115-0*) Ayer.

Lin, Yuh-Ru, jt. auth. see Kim, Haksu.

Lin, Yunmei. Advances in Rock Mechanics. (Civil Engineering Ser.). 300p. 1998. 78.00 (*981-02-3621-2*) World Scientific Pub.

Lin, Yutang. Between Tears & Laughter. 216p. 1977. 18.95 (*0-8369-2957-8*) Ayer.

— The Importance of Living. 448p. 1996. 26.00 (*0-688-14717-8*, Wm Morrow) Morrow Avon.

Lin, Z. Jun, et al. Accounting & Auditing in China. LC 97-42933. 377p. 1998. text 110.95 (*1-84014-048-8*, Pub. by Ashgate Pub) Ashgate Pub Co.

***Lin, Zhensheng & Lin, Yan-Xia.** Linear Systems & Exponential Dichotomy Structure of Sets of Hyperbolic Points. 200p. 2000. 32.00 (*981-02-4283-2*) World Scientific Pub.

Lin, Zhi P. Secrets of China's Anti Japanese War. (CHI.). pap. 12.95 (*7-200-02664-6*, Pub. by China Intl Bk) Distribks Inc.

Lin, Zhiguang, jt. auth. see Zhang, Jiacheng.

Lin Zhiling & Robinson, Thomas G., eds. The Chinese & Their Future: Beijing, Taipei, & Hong Kong. LC 93-21227. 554p. 1994. pap. 19.95 (*0-8447-3804-2*, AEI Pr) Am Enterprise.

Lin, Zhiqiu, jt. auth. see Keith, Ronald C.

Linacre, Anthea, jt. auth. see Bowskill, Derek.

Linacre, Edward. Climate Data & Resources: A Reference & Guide. (Illus.). 384p. (C). 1992. pap. 35.00 (*0-415-05703-5*, A6539); text 89.95 (*0-415-05702-7*, A6535) Routledge.

— Climates & Weather Explained. LC 96-13601. (Illus.). 464p. (C). 1997. 150.00 (*0-415-12519-7*) Routledge.

Linacre, Edward & Geerts, Bart. Climates & Weather Explained: An Introduction from a Southern Perspective. 1996. write for info. (*0-415-12517-0*) Routledge.

— Climates & Weather Explained: An Introduction from a Southern Perspective. LC 96-13601. (Illus.). 464p. (C). 1997. pap. 50.00 (*0-415-12520-0*) Routledge.

— Climates & Weather Explained: An Introduction from a Southern Perspective: Instructor's Resource Pack (Includes Students' & Instructors' CD-ROM) (Illus.). (C). 1997. pap., teacher ed. 150.00 incl. cd-rom (*0-415-16368-4*) Routledge.

Linacre, John M. Many-Facet Rasch Measurement. 2nd ed. LC 94-76939. (Illus.). 157p. 1994. pap. text 30.00 (*0-941938-02-6*) Mesa Pr.

Linacre, John M., ed. Rasch Measurement Transactions, Pt. 1. (Illus.). 208p. (Orig.). (C). 1995. pap. 25.00 (*0-941938-06-9*) Mesa Pr.

— Rasch Measurement Transactions, Pt. 2. LC 95-80148. (Illus.). 240p. (Orig.). (C). 1996. pap. 25.00 (*0-941938-07-7*) Mesa Pr.

***Linafelt, Tod.** Surviving Lamentations: Catastrophe, Lament & Protest in the Afterlife of a Biblical Book. 200p. 2000. 31.95 (*0-226-48190-5*) U Ch Pr.

Linafelt, Tod & Beal, Timothy K., eds. God in the Fray: A Tribute to Walter Brueggemann. 320p. 1998. pap. 33.00 (*0-8006-3090-4*, 1-3090) Augsburg Fortress.

Linafelt, Tod, et al. Ruth & Esther. LC 99-11352. (Berit Olam Ser.). 1999. 34.95 (*0-8146-5045-7*) Liturgical Pr.

Linahan, L. North of England Ghost Trail. 1997. text 29.95 (*0-09-476910-9*, Pub. by Constable & Co) Trafalgar.

Linahon, Gail. Hancock County, IA. (Illus.). 417p. 1993. 57.50 (*0-88107-222-2*) Curtis Media.

***Linaker, Kathryn.** Nursery Activity Book, Bk. 1. (J). (ps). 1999. pap., wbk. ed. 15.00 (*0-7217-6500-9*, Pub. by Schofield) St Mut.

— Nursery Activity Book, Bk. 2. (J). (ps). 1999. pap., wbk. ed. 15.00 (*0-7217-6501-7*, Pub. by Schofield) St Mut.

— Nursery Activity Book, Bk. 3. (J). (ps). 1999. pap., wbk. ed. 15.00 (*0-7217-6502-5*, Pub. by Schofield) St Mut.

— Nursery Activity Book, Bk. 4. (J). 1999. pap., wbk. ed. 15.00 (*0-7217-6503-3*, Pub. by Schofield) St Mut.

— Nursery Activity Book, Bk. 5. (J). 1999. pap., wbk. ed. 15.00 (*0-7217-6504-1*, Pub. by Schofield) St Mut.

— Nursery Activity Book, Bk. 6. (J). 1999. pap., wbk. ed. 15.00 (*0-7217-6505-X*, Pub. by Schofield) St Mut.

— Nursery Writing Book, Bk. 1. (J). (ps). 1999. pap., wbk. ed. 19.00 (*0-7217-6512-2*, Pub. by Schofield) St Mut.

— Nursery Writing Book, Bk. 2. (J). (ps). 1999. pap., wbk. ed. 19.00 (*0-7217-6513-0*, Pub. by Schofield) St Mut.

— Nursery Writing Book, Bk. 3. (J). (ps). 1999. pap., wbk. ed. 19.00 (*0-7217-6514-9*, Pub. by Schofield) St Mut.

— Nursery Writing Book, Bk. 4. (J). (ps). 1999. pap., wbk. ed. 19.00 (*0-7217-6515-7*, Pub. by Schofield) St Mut.

— Nursery Writing Book, Bk. 5. (J). (ps). 1999. pap., wbk. ed. 19.00 (*0-7217-6516-5*, Pub. by Schofield) St Mut.

— Nursery Writing Book, Bk. 6. (J). (ps). 1999. pap., wbk. ed. 19.00 (*0-7217-6517-3*, Pub. by Schofield) St Mut.

Linaker, Mike. Darksiders. (Cade Ser.: No. 804). 1992. per. 3.50 (*0-373-63804-3*, 1-63804-8) Harlequin Bks.

— Hardcase. 1992. per. 3.50 (*0-373-63805-1*, 1-63805-5) Harlequin Bks.

Linam, Shawn L. & Jarvis, M. Todd. Biotechnology Sourcebook. LC 88-45788. 372p. 1989. pap. text 95.00 (*0-88173-073-4*) Fairmont Pr.

Linaman, Todd, jt. auth. see Sowers, Laura.

***Linamen, Karen.** Sometimes I Wake Up Grumpy. 2001. pap. 9.99 (*0-8007-5745-9*) Revell.

Linamen, Karen S. The Parent Warrior. 204p. 1993. pap. 10.99 (*1-56476-127-4*, 6-3127, Victor Bks) Chariot Victor.

— Pillow Talk: The Intimate Marriage from A to Z. LC 96-20791. 272p. 1998. pap. 9.99 (*0-8007-5655-X*) Revell.

Linamen, Karen S. & Holland, Linda. Working Women, Workable Lives: Creative Solutions for Managing Home & Career. 296p. 1993. reprint ed. pap. 9.99 (*0-87788-851-5*, H Shaw Pubs) Waterbrook Pr.

Linamen, Karen S. & Wall, Keith A. Broken Dreams. Edwards, Judith, ed. 256p. 1996. pap. text 8.99 (*1-56309-161-5*, N953180, New Hope) Womans Mission Union.

Linamen, Karen Scalf. Happily Ever After: And 21 Other Myths about Family Life. LC 97-14915. 272p. (C). (gr. 13). 1998. pap. 9.99 (*0-8007-5675-4*) Revell.

— Just Hand over the Chocolate & No One Will Get Hurt. LC 98-44926. 176p. (C). (gr. 13). 1999. pap. 9.99 (*0-8007-5694-0*) Revell.

Linamen, Larry. Guide for the College Bound: Everything You Need to Know. LC 98-23848. 208p. (C). (gr. 13). 1998. pap. 12.99 (*0-8007-5670-3*) Revell.

Linamin, Linda Scalf. The Parent Warrior: Protecting Your Children through Prayer. LC 98-31892. 224p. 1999. pap. 11.99 (*0-8007-5698-3*) Revell.

Linan, Amable. Dynamical Issues in Combustion Theory. Friedman, A. et al, eds. (IMA Volumes in Mathematics & Its Applications Ser.: Vol. 35). (Illus.). 272p. 1991. 62.95 (*0-387-97583-7*) Spr-Verlag.

Linan, Amable & Williams, Forman A. Fundamental Aspects of Combustion. LC 92-23050. (Oxford Engineering Science Ser.: No. 34). (Illus.). 192p. 1993. text 50.00 (*0-19-507626-5*) OUP.

Linard, Brian. A Way to the Heart of Christmas. 3rd ed. 104p. 1994. pap. 7.95 (*1-56548-025-2*) New City.

***Linardakis, Connie.** Baby Gourmet 1-2-3. 2000. pap. 16.00 (*0-7615-2790-7*) Prima Pub.

Linardakis, Constantina. The Baby Gourmet Cookbook. Linardakis, Nikos M., ed. (Illus.). Date not set. pap. 14.95 (*1-884084-16-8*) Michaelis Med.

— The Baby Gourmet Cookbook: The #1 Doctor-Recommended Baby Cookbook. Linardakis, Nikos & Jones, Rachel, eds. (Illus.). 250p. 1998. 22.95 (*1-891886-04-5*) Olive Recs.

Linardakis, Constantina & Linardakis, Nikos M. Recipes Sworn to Secrecy. (Illus.). 64p. (Orig.). 1995. pap. 12.95 (*1-884084-07-9*) Michaelis Med.

Linardakis, Linas M. Biochemistry: Digging up the Bones, Vol. 4. 2nd ed. (Digging Up the Bones Medical Review Ser.). (Illus.). 115p. 1997. pap. text 18.95 (*0-07-038217-4*) McGraw-Hill HPD.

— Pathology: Digging up the Bones, Vol. 3. 2nd ed. LC 97-49310. (Digging Up the Bones Medical Review Ser.). (Illus.). 44p. 1997. pap. text 18.95 (*0-07-038216-6*) McGraw-Hill HPD.

Linardakis, Linas M., ed. Microbiology & Immunology Vol. 2: Digging up the Bones, Vol. 2. 2nd ed. (Digging Up the Bones Medical Review Ser.). (Illus.). 122p. 1997. pap. text 18.95 (*0-07-038215-8*) McGraw-Hill HPD.

Linardakis, Nikos, ed. see Linardakis, Constantina.

Linardakis, Nikos M. Anatomy. LC 99-24495. (Digging Up the Bones Medical Review Ser.). (Illus.). 130p. 1999. pap. text 18.95 (*0-07-038415-0*) McGraw-Hill HPD.

— Cigar: The Novel - Instrument of Art & Science. (Illus.). 300p. 1998. 24.00 (*1-891886-02-9*); pap. 14.95 (*1-891886-03-7*) Olive Recs.

— Digging up the Bones: Pharmacology. 2nd ed. LC 96-157441. 1996. pap. 17.95 (*1-884084-23-0*) Michaelis Med.

— Digging up the Bones... Pharmacology, Microbiology, Pathology & Biochemistry, 4 vols., Set B. 400p. (Orig.). (C). 1994. pap. text 16.00 (*1-884084-00-1*); pap. text 16.00 (*1-884084-01-X*); pap. text 16.00 (*1-884084-02-8*); pap. text. write for info. (*1-884084-04-4*) Michaelis Med.

— Digging up the Bones... Pharmacology, Microbiology, Pathology & Biochemistry, 4 vols., Set B, Set. 400p. (Orig.). (C). 1994. pap. text 64.00 (*1-884084-10-9*) Michaelis Med.

— Digging up the Bones... Vol. 5: Behavioral Science. (Illus.). 80p. (C). 1995. pap. text 16.00 (*1-884084-11-7*) Michaelis Med.

***Linardakis, Nikos M.** Neuroscience. LC 99-31930. (Digging Up the Bones Medical Review Ser.). (Illus.). 130p. 1999. pap. text 18.95 (*0-07-038369-3*) McGraw-Hill HPD.

Linardakis, Nikos M. Physiology: Digging up the Bones, Vol. 8. LC 98-10208. (Digging Up the Bones Medical Review Ser.). (Illus.). 1998. pap. 18.95 (*0-07-038221-2*) McGraw-Hill HPD.

***Linardakis, Nikos M.** Surgery. (Digging Up the Bones Medical Review Ser.). (Illus.). 130p. 1999. pap. text 18.95 (*0-07-038367-7*) McGraw-Hill HPD.

Linardakis, Nikos M. & Khatchatryan, Armen. Biostatistics & Epidemiology: Digging up the Bones, Vol. 9. 2nd ed. LC 98-2834. (Digging Up the Bones Medical Review Ser.). (Illus.). 1998. pap. text 18.95 (*0-07-038222-0*) McGraw-Hill HPD.

Linardakis, Nikos M. & Lott, Sonia. Obstetrics & Gynecology: Digging up the Bones, Vol. 7. LC 98-10207. (Digging Up the Bones Medical Review Ser.). (Illus.). 1998. pap. 18.95 (*0-07-038220-4*) McGraw-Hill HPD.

Linardakis, Nikos M., jt. auth. see Golbin, Alexander Z.

Linardakis, Nikos M., jt. auth. see Linardakis, Constantina.

Linardakis, Nikos M., ed. see Linardakis, Constantina.

***Linarelli, John, et al.** Regulation Public Procurement - National & International Perspectives. 900p. 2000. 190.00 (*90-411-0636-7*) Kluwer Law Intl.

Linares, Enrique. A Scientific Approach to the Metaphysics of Astrology. Robertson, Arlene, ed. 170p. (Orig.). 1982. per. 7.95 (*0-930706-10-2*) Seek-It Pubns.

Linares, Filadelfo. Beitraege Zur Staats- und Geschichtsphilosophie. (Studien und Materialien Zur Geschichte der Philosophie Ser.: Bd. 28). (GER.). viii, 146p. 1988. write for info. (*3-487-09084-8*) G Olms Pubs.

Linares, Filadelfo. Einblicke in Hugo Grotius' Werk. (Studien und Materialien Zur Geschichte der Philosophie Ser.: Bd. 15). (GER.). viii, 82p. 1993. write for info. (*3-487-09730-3*) G Olms Pubs.

— Jean-Jacques Rousseaus Bruch Mit David Hume. (Studien und Materialien Zur Geschichte der Philosophie Ser.: No. 30). xi, 127p. 1991. write for info. (*3-487-09478-9*) G Olms Pubs.

— Max Stirner's Paradigmenwechsel. (Studien & Materialien zur Geschichte der Philosophie Ser.: Vol. 41). viii, 82p. 1996. pap. write for info. (*3-487-10053-3*) G Olms Pubs.

— Das Politische Denken Von David Hume. (Studien und Materialien Zur Geschichte der Philosophie Ser.: Vol. 24). (GER.). vi, 125p. 1984. write for info. (*3-487-07551-2*) G Olms Pubs.

Linares, Frederico Navarrete. A Day with a Maya. Dulin, Laura, tr. LC 99-17214. (Day with Ser.). (Illus.). 48p. (J). (gr. 5-7). 2000. 22.60 (*0-8225-1922-4*, Runestone Pr) Lerner Pub.

Linares, Rick & Lloyd, Chuck. Warfighters: A History of the USAF Weapons School & the 57th Wing. LC 95-72155. (Illus.). 264p. (C). (gr. 13). 1996. 49.95 (*0-7643-0044-X*) Schiffer.

Linari, F., et al, eds. Pathogenesis & Treatment of Nephrolithiasis. (Contributions to Nephrology Ser.: Vol. 58). x, 298p. 1987. 29.75 (*3-8055-4554-1*) S Karger.

Linaweaver, Brad. Moon of Ice. 288p. 1993. mass mkt. 4.99 (*0-8125-2020-3*) Tor Bks.

— Sliders: Parallel Universes. (Illus.). 288p. (Orig.). 1998. pap. 14.95 (*1-57500-053-9*, Pub. by TV Bks) HarpC.

— Sliders: The Novel. (Orig.). 1996. mass mkt. 5.99 (*1-57297-098-7*) Blvd Books.

Linaweaver, Brad, jt. ed. see Kramer, Edward E.

Linaweaver, F. Pierce, ed. Environmental Engineering. LC 92-23894. 688p. 1992. pap. text 61.00 (*0-87262-878-7*) Am Soc Civil Eng.

Linberg, G. & Heard, A. Dictionary of Names of Marine Food Fishes of World Fauna. 562p. (C). 1980. 135.00 (*0-89771-913-1*, Pub. by Collets) St Mut.

Linberg, John V. Oculoplastic & Orbital Emergencies. (Illus.). 237p. (C). 1992. pap. text 65.00 (*0-8385-3626-3*, A3626-7) McGraw.

Linberg, Tod, jt. ed. see Pruden, Wesley.

Linc, Deb, intro. Women's Wheels. 38p. (Orig.). 1982. pap. 7.95 (*0-9610084-0-7*) Amelia Pub.

Lincecum, Jerry B. Adventures of the Good Humor Man. LC 90-81801. (Illus.). 145p. (Orig.). 1990. pap. 15.00 (*0-9626851-0-0*) Big Barn Pr.

Lincecum, Jerry B., ed. Adventures of a Frontier Naturalist: The Life & Times of Dr. Gideon Lincecum. LC 94-11122. (Illus.). 360p. 1994. 35.00 (*0-89096-592-7*); pap. 16.95 (*0-89096-603-6*) Tex A&M Univ Pr.

Lincecum, Jerry B., et al, eds. Science on the Texas Frontier: Observations of Dr. Gideon Lincecum. LC 97-10939. (Illus.). 224p. 1997. 35.00 (*0-89096-768-7*); pap. 17.95 (*0-89096-790-3*) Tex A&M Univ Pr.

Lincecum, Jerry B. & Redshaw, Peggy A., eds. Texas Family Secrets. (Illus.). 212p. 1998. pap. 15.00 (*0-9626851-1-9*) Big Barn Pr.

***Lincecum, Jerry B. & Redshaw, Peggy A., eds.** Texas Millennium Book: The Way Things Used to Be. (Telling Our Stories Ser.: Vol. 3). (Illus.). 280p. 1999. pap. 20.00 (*0-9626851-3-5*) Big Barn Pr.

Linch. Haematology. 1996. pap. text 16.95 (*0-443-04615-8*, W B Saunders Co) Harcrt Hlth Sci Grp.

Linch, Adrian L. Evaluation of Ambient Air Quality by Personnel Monitoring, Vol. 1. 2nd ed. 384p. 1981. 209.00 (*0-8493-5293-2*, TD890, CRC Reprint) Franklin.

— Evaluation of Ambient Air Quality by Personnel Monitoring, Vol. 2. 2nd ed. 336p. 1981. 178.00 (*0-8493-5294-0*, CRC Reprint) Franklin.

Linch, David & Yates, A. P. Haematology. LC 85-16585. (Colour Aids Ser.). (Illus.). 124p. (Orig.). (C). 1986. pap. 19.95 (*0-443-02842-7*) Church.

Linch, Jennifer, jt. auth. see Gschwandtner, Gerhard.

***Linch, Tanya.** My Duck. (Illus.). 32p. (J). (ps-2). 2000. 14.95 (*0-439-20670-7*) Scholastic Inc.

Linch, Tanya. The Three Little Kittens. (J). 1999. write for info. (*0-316-56115-0*) Little.

Linch-Zadel, Lauri, ed. see Burbank, Doreen C.

Linche, Richard, tr. see Cartari, Vincenzo.

Lincicome, Mark E. Principle, Praxis, & the Politics of Educational Reform in Meiji Japan. LC 94-35279. (Illus.). 304p. (C). 1995. text 45.00 (*0-8248-1620-X*) UH Pr.

Linck, Charles E., ed. see Greenidge, Terence.

Linck, Charles E., ed. see Rye, Edgar.

Linck, Ernestine S. Eats: A Folk History of Texas Foods. LC 88-20158. (Illus.). 271p. 1989. pap. 12.95 (*0-87565-035-X*) Tex Christian.

— How the Cimarron River Got Its Name: And Other Stories About Coffee. LC 93-4973. 184p. 1994. pap. 12.95 (*1-55622-384-6*, Rep of TX Pr) Wordware Pub.

Linck, Madeleine H., jt. ed. see Compton, Donna C.

Linck, Orville F. A Passage Through Pakistan. LC 59-15364. 283p. reprint ed. 87.80 (*0-608-17034-8*, 202761000055) Bks Demand.

***Linck, Tony.** Napoleon's Generals of the Glory Years. (Illus.). 2000. 38.00 (*1-883476-21-6*, Pub. by Emperors Pr) Combined Pub.

Lincoff, A. Michael & Topol, Eric J., eds. Platelet Glycoprotein IIb/IIIa Inhibitors in Cardiovascular Disease. LC 99-30220. (Contemporary Cardiology Ser.). (Illus.). 384p. 1999. 125.00 (*0-89603-727-4*) Humana.

Lincoff, Gary, jt. auth. see Laess, Thomas E.

Lincoff, Gary H. Simon & Schuster's Guide to Mushrooms. (Illus.). 512p. 1982. per. 15.00 (*0-671-42849-7*) S&S Trade.

Lincoff, Gary H., jt. auth. see Audubon Society Staff.

Lincold, Roger N., ed. see Howe, Donald W.

Lincoln. American History Reader. 1998. 21.00 (*0-07-430609-X*) McGraw.

— Growing Collaboratively. 1993. pap. text 51.00 (*0-13-117292-1*) P-H.

— Key to Sacred Pattern. LC 98-14282. (Illus.). 225p. 1998. text 26.95 (*0-312-21484-7*) St Martin.

— Psychosexual Medicine: A Study of Underlying Themes. 230p. 1992. pap. 47.75 (*1-56593-049-5*, 0297) Thomson Learn.

***Lincoln & Bruce.** Sunlight at Midnight. 2000. mass mkt. 13.00 (*0-465-08324-2*, Pub. by Basic) HarpC.

Lincoln, jt. auth. see Heffernan.

Lincoln, Abraham. Abraham Lincoln: Autobiographical Narrative. (American Autobiography Ser.). 77p. 1995. reprint ed. lib. bdg. 69.00 (*0-7812-8578-X*) Rprt Serv.

— Abraham Lincoln: His Speeches & Writings. (History - United States Ser.). 843p. 1993. reprint ed. lib. bdg. 199.00 (*0-7812-4898-1*) Rprt Serv.

— Abraham Lincoln: Selected Writings. LC 97-60837. (Public Library Ser.). 192p. 1997. pap. 4.95 (*0-87243-232-7*) Templegate.

— Abraham Lincoln's An Introduction to Handwriting & Calligraphy: An Italic Calligraphy Workbook. (Illus.). 72p. (Orig.). (J). (gr. 3-12). 1995. pap. 13.95 (*0-942032-09-8*) Whiz Bang.

— Abraham Lincoln's Autobiography. (American Autobiography Ser.). 45p. 1995. reprint ed. lib. bdg. 69.00 (*0-7812-8579-8*) Rprt Serv.

— Calligraphy Is Fun. 80p. (Orig.). 1990. pap. 12.95 (*0-943295-13-0*) Graphics Plus FL.

— The Emancipation Proclamation. 32p. 1998. 9.95 (*1-55709-470-5*) Applewood.

— The Essential Lincoln. LC 93-3373. (Library of Freedom). 352p. 1993. 7.99 (*0-517-09345-6*) Random Hse Value.

— The Families from Gordon, Ohio - From 1849-1998. LC 98-213115. 84p. 1998. mass mkt. 15.00 (*0-942032-10-1*) Whiz Bang.

— Famous Speeches of Abraham Lincoln. LC 78-90652. (Essay Index Reprint Ser.). 1977. 18.95 (*0-8369-1207-1*) Ayer.

— The Gettysburg Address. (Illus.). 32p. (J). 1995. 14.95 (*0-395-69824-3*) HM.

— Gettysburg Address. (Illus.). 32p. 1998. pap. 6.95 (*0-395-88397-0*) HM.

— Great Speeches. (Thrift Editions Ser.). 128p. 1991. reprint ed. pap. 1.00 (*0-486-26872-1*) Dover.

— Italic. 60p. (Orig.). 1989. pap. 9.95 (*0-943295-11-4*) Graphics Plus FL.

***Lincoln, Abraham.** The Law Practice of Abraham Lincoln: Complete Documentary. Brenner, Martha L. et al, eds. 2000. pap. 2000.00 (*0-252-02566-0*) U of Ill Pr.

An Asterisk (*) at the beginning of an entry indicates that the title is appearing for the first time.

Lincoln, Abraham. The Life & Writings of Abraham Lincoln. Morris, Jeffrey, ed. LC 99-12661. 1999. 22.95 (*0-679-60329-8*) Random.

***Lincoln, Abraham.** Life & Writings of Abraham Lincoln. (Classics Ser.). 2000. pap. 14.95 (*0-679-78329-6*) Modern Lib NY.

Lincoln, Abraham. The Life & Writings of Abraham Lincoln. (History - United States Ser.). 863p. 1993. reprint ed. lib. bdg. 119.00 (*0-7812-4899-X*) Rprt Serv.

— The Lincoln Encyclopedia: The Spoken & Written Words of A. Lincoln Arranged for Ready Reference. Shaw, Archer H., ed. LC 80-12651. 395p. 1980. reprint ed. lib. bdg. 45.50 (*0-313-22471-4*, SHLE, Greenwood Pr) Greenwood.

— Lincoln's Legacy: The Emancipation Proclamation & the Gettysburg Address. (Illus.). 24p. 1994. pap. 2.95 (*0-87328-149-7*) Huntington Lib.

Lincoln, Abraham. Lincoln's Letters: The Private Man & the Warrior. unabridged ed. 1995. lib. bdg. 18.95 incl. audio (*1-883049-51-2*) Sound Room.

Lincoln, Abraham. Lincoln's Letters: The Private Man & the Warrior, Set. unabridged ed. 1995. 16.95 incl. audio (*1-883049-50-4*, Pub. by Sound Room) Penton Overseas.

Lincoln, Abraham. Lincoln's Prose: Major Works of a Great American Writer. unabridged ed. 1995. lib. bdg. 18.95 incl. audio (*1-883049-53-9*) Sound Room.

Lincoln, Abraham. Lincoln's Prose: Major Works of a Great American Writer, Set. unabridged ed. 1995. 16.95 incl. audio (*1-883049-52-0*, Pub. by Sound Room) Penton Overseas.

— Poems of Abraham Lincoln. 28p. 1991. 8.95 (*1-55709-133-1*) Applewood.

— Selected Speeches & Writings. LC 91-50227. (Vintage Books - the Library of America). 608p. 1992. pap. 15.00 (*0-679-73731-6*) Vin Bks.

— Selected Writings & Speeches. Williams, T. Harry, ed. (University Classics Ser.). 334p. 1980. pap. 12.95 (*0-87532-136-4*) Hendricks House.

— Speeches & Letters. 316p. 1993. pap. 6.95 (*0-460-87146-3*, Everyman's Classic Lib) Tuttle Pubng.

— Speeches & Writings: Presidential Messages & Proclamations, 1859-1865, Vol. 2. 1990. write for info. (*0-318-66783-5*, Penguin Bks) Viking Penguin.

— Speeches & Writings: The Lincoln-Douglas Debates, 1832-1858, Vol. 1. 1990. write for info. (*0-318-66782-7*, Penguin Bks) Viking Penguin.

— Speeches & Writings, 1859-1865, Vol. II. Fehrenbacher, Don E., ed. 788p. 1989. 35.00 (*0-940450-63-1*, Pub. by Library of America) Penguin Putnam.

— Speeches & Writings, 1832-1858, Vol. I. Fehrenbacher, Don E., ed. 898p. 1989. 35.00 (*0-940450-43-7*, Pub. by Library of America) Penguin Putnam.

Lincoln, Abraham & Douglas, Stephen. Lincoln-Douglas Debates of 1858. Johannsen, Robert W., ed. 336p. (Orig.). 1965. pap. 21.95 (*0-19-500921-5*) OUP.

Lincoln, Abraham, jt. auth. see Leidner, Gordon.

Lincoln, Adams W., ed. Sunlight & Shadow. LC 76-24669. (Sources of Modern Photography Ser.). (Illus.). 1979. reprint ed. lib. bdg. 19.95 (*0-405-09646-1*) Ayer.

Lincoln, Alan J. & Lincoln, Carol Z. Library Crime & Security: An International Perspective. LC 87-12059. (Library & Archival Security Ser.: Vol. 8, Nos. 1-2). 163p. 1987. text 39.95 (*0-86656-480-2*) Haworth Pr.

Lincoln, Andrew. Ephesians. (Biblical Commentary Ser.: Vol. 42). 29.99 (*0-8499-0241-X*) Word Pub.

— Spiritual History: A Reading of William Blake's the Four Zoas. 340p. 1996. text 82.00 (*0-19-818314-3*) OUP.

Lincoln, Andrew, ed. see Blake, William, et al.

Lincoln, Andrew T. & Wedderburn, A. J. The Theology of the Later Pauline Letters. LC 92-31674. (New Testament Theology Ser.). 197p. (C). 1993. text 54.95 (*0-521-36460-4*); pap. text 16.95 (*0-521-36721-2*) Cambridge U Pr.

Lincoln, Anna T. Wilmington Delaware: Three Centuries under Four Flags, 1609-1937. (Illus.). 411p. 1997. reprint ed. lib. bdg. 45.00 (*0-8328-7056-0*) Higginson Bk Co.

Lincoln, Anne T. There's a Place I Go: A Fantasy Adventure for Children & Adults. (Illus.). 40p. (J). (gr. 3-5). 1995. 24.95 incl. audio (*0-9649730-2-2*, TADCO TRIPLETT); audio 19.95 (*0-9649730-1-4*, TADCO TRIPLETT) TADCO.

— There's a Place I Go: A Fantasy Adventure for Children & Adults. (Illus.). 40p. (J). (gr. 3-5). 1997. 15.95 (*0-9649730-0-6*, TADCO TRIPLETT) TADCO.

Lincoln Beta Club Staff, jt. auth. see Marshall, Ed.

Lincoln, Betty W. Festschriften in Art History, 1960-1975: Bibliography & Index. LC 87-22767. 234p. 1987. text 20.00 (*0-8240-8497-7*) Garland.

Lincoln, Bill, et al. Encyclopedia of Wood: A Tree-by-Tree Guide to the World's Most Valuable Resource. (Illus.). 224p. 1989. 29.95 (*0-8160-2159-7*) Facts on File.

Lincoln, Brayton, et al. Mechanical Fastening of Plastics: An Engineering Handbook. (Mechanical Engineering Ser.: Vol. 26). (Illus.). 240p. 1984. text 99.75 (*0-8247-7078-1*) Dekker.

Lincoln, Bruce. Authority: Construction & Corrosion. 240p. 1994. 22.50 (*0-226-48197-2*) U Ch Pr.

— Death, War, & Sacrifice: Studies in Ideology & Practice. LC 90-26902. (Illus.). 312p. 1991. pap. text 19.95 (*0-226-48200-6*) U Ch Pr.

— Death, War, & Sacrifice: Studies in Ideology & Practice. LC 90-26902. (Illus.). 312p. 1991. lib. bdg. 52.00 (*0-226-48199-9*) U Ch Pr.

— Discourse & the Construction of Society: Comparitive Studies of Myth, Ritual & Classification. (Illus.). 256p. 1992. pap. text 21.00 (*0-19-507909-4*) OUP.

— Emerging from the Chrysalis: Rituals of Women's Initiation. 2nd ed. (Illus.). 184p. (C). 1991. pap. text 21.95 (*0-19-506910-2*) OUP.

— Emerging from the Chrysalis: Studies in Rituals of Women's Initiation. LC 80-24189. 167p. reprint ed. pap. 51.80 (*0-7837-2062-9*, 204233700004) Bks Demand.

— Theorizing Myth: Narrative, Ideology, & Scholarship. LC 99-13427. 320p. 2000. pap. text 24.00 (*0-226-48202-2*) U Ch Pr.

— Theorizing Myth: Narrative, Ideology & Scholarship. LC 99-13427. 320p. 2000. lib. bdg. 59.00 (*0-226-48201-4*) U Ch Pr.

Lincoln, C. Eric. The Avenue, Clayton City. LC 95-40002. 256p. 1996. pap. 15.95 (*0-8223-1745-1*) Duke.

— Black Muslims in America. 288p. 1996. pap. 20.00 (*0-614-21698-2*, 1360) Kazi Pubns.

— The Black Muslims in America. 3rd ed. 1996. 49.95 (*0-86543-399-2*) Africa World.

— Coming Through the Fire: Surviving Race & Place in America. LC 95-40107. 168p. 1996. 17.95 (*0-8223-1736-2*) Duke.

— Race, Religion, & the Continuing American Dilemma. rev. ed. LC 98-33377. 320p. 1999. pap. 14.00 (*0-8090-1623-0*) Hill & Wang.

— This Road since Freedom. 92p. (Orig.). 1990. 17.50 (*0-932112-30-7*); pap. 10.00 (*0-932112-31-5*) Carolina Wren.

Lincoln, C. Eric & Mamiya, Lawrence. The Black Church in the African American Experience. LC 90-34050. 536p. (C). 1990. pap. text 24.95 (*0-8223-1073-2*) Duke.

Lincoln, C. Eric, jt. auth. see Frazier, E. Franklin.

Lincoln, C. I., jt. auth. see Chalofsky, N.

Lincoln, Carol Z., jt. auth. see Lincoln, Alan J.

Lincoln, Charles H. Manuscript Records of the French & Indian War in the Library of the American Antiquarian Society. 267p. 1993. reprint ed. pap. text 20.00 (*1-55613-739-7*) Heritage Bk.

Lincoln, Charles H., ed. see Shirley, William.

Lincoln, Charles J. New England Town Affairs. 224p. (Orig.). 1995. pap. 12.95 (*0-924771-52-6*, Covered Brdge Pr) Douglas Charles Ltd.

Lincoln, Charles Z. Constitutional History of New York, 5 vols., Set. 1993. reprint ed. lib. bdg. 450.00 (*0-7812-5189-3*) Rprt Serv.

— Constitutional History of New York, 5 vols., Set. LC 94-78803. 3698p. 1994. reprint ed. 350.00 (*0-89941-910-0*, 308470) W S Hein.

Lincoln, D. A. Boston Cooking School Cook Book: A Reprint of the 1883 Classic. Orig. Title: Mrs. Lincoln's Boston Cook Book. (Illus.). 560p. 1996. reprint ed. pap. text 12.95 (*0-486-29196-0*) Dover.

Lincoln, D. B., jt. auth. see Lidbert, Paul A.

Lincoln, D. B., ed. see Lidbert, Paul A.

Lincoln, Dennis W., jt. ed. see Edwards, Christopher R.

Lincoln, E. Eric. Black Muslims in America. 1993. pap. 16.95 (*0-86543-400-X*) Africa World.

Lincoln, Edmond E., tr. see Du Pont De Nemours, Pierre S.

Lincoln, Edward J. Japan: Facing Economic Maturity. LC 87-18235. 298p. (C). 1988. 42.95 (*0-8157-5260-1*); pap. 18.95 (*0-8157-5259-8*) Brookings.

— Japan's Economic Role in Northeast Asia. LC 86-22439. (Asian Agenda Reports: No. 10). (Illus.). 86p. (Orig.). (C). 1987. pap. text 8.00 (*0-8191-5678-7*); lib. bdg. 25.50 (*0-8191-5677-9*) U Pr of Amer.

— Japan's New Global Role. (Integrating National Economies: Promise & Pitfalls Ser.). 320p. (Orig.). (C). 1995. 42.95 (*0-8157-5258-X*); pap. 18.95 (*0-8157-5257-1*) Brookings.

— Japan's Unequal Trade. 180p. 1990. 36.95 (*0-8157-5262-8*); pap. 16.95 (*0-8157-5261-X*) Brookings.

***Lincoln, Edward J.** Troubled Times: U. S. - Japan Trade Relations in the 1990s LC 98-58144. 5p. 1999. write for info. (*0-8157-5268-7*) Brookings.

Lincoln, Edward J. Troubled Times: U. S. Japan Trade Relations in the 1990s. LC 98-58144. 240p. 1999. pap. 18.95 (*0-8157-5267-9*) Brookings.

Lincoln, Edward J., ed. Japan & the Middle East. LC 90-53699. 82p. (C). 1990. pap. text 5.00 (*0-916808-38-6*) Mid East Inst.

Lincoln, Elverda. Udder Confusion: An Alaskan Homesteader True Life Adventure. (Illus.). 194p. 1992. pap. 12.95 (*1-888125-18-7*) Publ Consult.

Lincoln, Eugene. How Good is "Good Enough"? The CPR Treatment for an Ailing Christian Experience. LC 95-50281. 1995. pap. 0.89 (*0-8280-1080-3*) Review & Herald.

Lincoln, Evelyn. Art in Transition: Post-Impressionist Prints & Drawings from the Achenbach Foundation for Graphic Arts. LC 88-80186. (Illus.). 15p. (C). 1988. pap. 4.00 (*0-88401-058-9*) Fine Arts Mus.

***Lincoln, Evelyn.** The Invention of the Italian Renaissance Printmaker. LC 99-87337. (Illus.). 224p. 2000. 65.00 (*0-300-08041-7*) Yale U Pr.

Lincoln, Frances. A Family Treasury of Prayers: With Paintings from the Great Art Museums of the World. LC 95-51178. (Illus.). 96p. (J). 1996. 16.00 (*0-689-80956-5*) S&S Bks Yung.

— The Message of St. Francis with Frescoes from the Basilica of St. Francis of Assisi. 60p. 1999. 16.95 (*0-7112-1317-8*) F Lincoln.

— Stories from the Old Testament: With Masterwork Paintings Inspired by Stories. (Illus.). 48p. (J). 1996. 18.00 (*0-689-80955-7*) S&S Childrens.

Lincoln, Frances, ed. Stories from the New Testament: With Masterwork Paintings Inspired by the Stories. LC 96-46558. (Illus.). 48p. (J). 1997. 18.00 (*0-689-81297-3*) S&S Childrens.

Lincoln, Francis G. Mining Districts & Mineral Resources of Nevada. (Illus.). 1982. pap. 14.95 (*0-913814-48-2*) Nevada Pubns.

***Lincoln, Frederick C.** Migration of Birds. 117p. 1999. per. 8.00 (*0-16-061701-4*) USGPO.

Lincoln, George. History of the Town of Hingham, Vol. I. (Illus.). 805p. 1992. reprint ed. lib. bdg. 77.50 (*0-8328-2494-1*) Higginson Bk Co.

— History of the Town of Hingham, Vol. II. (Illus.). 915p. 1992. reprint ed. lib. bdg. 62.50 (*0-8328-2495-X*) Higginson Bk Co.

Lincoln, Harry B. The Italian Madrigal & Related Repertories: Indexes to Printed Collections. LC 87-51189. 1139p. (C). 1988. 110.00 (*0-300-03683-3*) Yale U Pr.

— Latin Motet: Indices to Printed Collections, 1500-1600. (Wissenschaftliche Abhandlungen-Musicological Studies: Vol. 59). xii, 835p. 1993. lib. bdg. 220.00 (*0-931902-80-0*) Inst Mediaeval Mus.

Lincoln, I. T. Revelations of an International Spy. 1972. 59.95 (*0-8490-0949-9*) Gordon Pr.

Lincoln Institute of Land Policy Staff. Agribusiness Education in Transition: Strategies for Change, Report of the National Agribusiness Education Commission, June 1989. Downey, W. David, ed. LC HD9006.. 80p. reprint ed. pap. 30.00 (*0-7837-2162-5*, 204246700004) Bks Demand.

— American Federalism in the 1980s: Changes & Consequences: Conference Summary & Papers May 19-20, 1981. LC JC0355.A6. (Lincoln Institute Monograph: No. 81-7). 86p. reprint ed. pap. 30.00 (*0-7837-2171-4*, 204249400004) Bks Demand.

— Land Management Issues & Development Strategies in Developing Countries, Vol. 2. Lin, Sein & Zaman, Wasin, eds. LC HD0111.L5. 134p. reprint ed. pap. 41.60 (*0-7837-3873-0*, 204371200002) Bks Demand.

— Land Policy in Developing Countries. LC HD1131.L34. (Lincoln Institute Monograph Ser.: No. 84-4). 78p. reprint ed. pap. 30.00 (*0-7837-2156-0*, 204245600004) Bks Demand.

Lincoln, J. D. & Lincoln, Rosemary. People of Portsmouth & Some Who Came to Town. LC 82-16543. (Illus.). 112p. 1982. pap. 13.95 (*0-914339-00-1*) P E Randall Pub.

Lincoln, Jack, ed. see Birch, Stephen & Ida, Junko.

Lincoln, Jack, ed. see Hacker, Edward.

Lincoln, James R. Prescription Filled. LC 81-51752. (Illus.). 202p. 1981. 12.50 (*0-88492-039-9*) W S Sullwold.

Lincoln, Jill, et al. Nitric Oxide in Health & Disease. (Biomedical Research Topics Ser.). (Illus.). 377p. (C). 1997. text 90.00 (*0-521-55038-6*); pap. text 39.95 (*0-521-55977-4*) Cambridge U Pr.

Lincoln, John. Rich Grass & Sweet Water: Ranch Life with the Koch Matador Cattle Company. LC 89-4434. (Centennial Series of the Association of Former Students: No. 32). (Illus.). 168p. 1989. 19.95 (*0-89096-387-8*) Tex A&M Univ Pr.

— Thank God & the Infantry. LC 99-178842. 1999. write for info. (*0-7509-0630-8*) A Sutton.

Lincoln, John C. Ground Rent, Not Taxes: The Natural Source of Revenue for the Government. LC HD1313.L55. 72p. reprint ed. pap. 30.00 (*0-7837-2170-6*, 204249200004) Bks Demand.

Lincoln, John E., jt. auth. see Heffernan, James A.

Lincoln, John E., jt. auth. see Heffernan, James W.

Lincoln, Jonathan T. The City of the Dinner-Pail. Stein, Leon, ed. LC 77-70511. 1977. reprint ed. lib. bdg. 23.95 (*0-405-10181-3*) Ayer.

Lincoln, Joseph C. Cape Cod Stories. 1976. reprint ed. lib. bdg. 23.95 (*0-88411-791-X*) Amereon Ltd.

— Cap'n Eri. 1976. reprint ed. lib. bdg. 27.95 (*0-88411-792-8*) Amereon Ltd.

— Christmas Days. 158p. 18.95 (*0-8488-2651-5*) Amereon Ltd.

— Partners of the Tide. LC 72-98402. reprint ed. 49.50 (*0-404-03987-1*) AMS Pr.

— Storm Girl. 1976. reprint ed. lib. bdg. 23.95 (*0-88411-793-6*) Amereon Ltd.

Lincoln Journal Star Staff. A Salute to Nebraska's Tom Osborne. (Illus.). 282p. 1998. 29.95 (*1-57167-230-3*) Sports Pub.

Lincoln Journal Star Staff, ed. The Best of the Big Red Running Backs. (Illus.). 200p. 1998. 29.95 (*1-58261-001-0*) Sports Pub.

Lincoln, Kelly, jt. auth. see Whitman, Theresa.

Lincoln, Kelly J. Let's Go Storyknifing. large type ed. (Illus.). 12p. (J). (gr. k-3). 1999. pap. text 17.00 (*1-58084-066-3*) Lower Kuskokwim.

— Making a Grass Basket. large type ed. (Illus.). 16p. (J). (gr. k-3). 1999. pap. text 21.00 (*1-58084-062-0*) Lower Kuskokwim.

— Mingqiileg. large type ed.Tr. of Making a Grass Basket. (ESK., Illus.). 16p. (J). (gr. k-3). 1999. pap. text 21.00 (*1-58084-063-9*) Lower Kuskokwim.

— Mingqiller Tapernarneg. large type ed.Tr. of Making a Grass Basket. (ESK., Illus.). 16p. (J). (gr. k-3). 1999. pap. text 21.00 (*1-58084-110-4*) Lower Kuskokwim.

***Lincoln, Kelly J.** Yaaruiyarciqukug. large type ed.Tr. of Let's Go Story Knifing. (ESK., Illus.). 12p. (J). (gr. k-3). 1999. pap. text 17.00 (*1-58084-108-2*) Lower Kuskokwim.

— Yaaruiyarluk. large type ed.Tr. of Let's Go Story Knifing. (ESK., Illus.). 12p. (J). (gr. k-3). 1999. pap. text 17.00 (*1-58084-067-1*) Lower Kuskokwim.

Lincoln, Kelly J., jt. auth. see Whitman, Theresa M.

Lincoln, Kenneth. Indi'n Humor: Bicultural Play in Native America. (Illus.). 416p. 1993. text 60.00 (*0-19-506887-4*) OUP.

— Men down West. LC 96-34543. 250p. (Orig.). 1997. pap. 15.95 (*0-88496-412-4*) Capra Pr.

— Native American Renaissance. LC 82-17450. 320p. 1983. pap. 17.95 (*0-520-05457-1*, Pub. by U CA Pr) Cal Prin Full Svc.

— Native American Renaissance. LC 82-17450. (Illus.). 323p. reprint ed. pap. 100.20 (*0-7837-4752-7*, 204449900003) Bks Demand.

***Lincoln, Kenneth.** Sing with the Heart of a Bear: Fusions of Native & American Poetry, 1890-1999. LC 99-11519. 454p. 1999. 50.00 (*0-520-21889-2*, Pub. by U CA Pr); pap. 19.95 (*0-520-21890-6*, Pub. by U CA Pr) Cal Prin Full Svc.

Lincoln, Kenneth. A Writer's China: Bridges East & West. LC 98-54859. (Illus.). 275p. 1999. pap. 15.95 (*0-88496-439-6*, Pub. by Capra Pr) SPD-Small Pr Dist.

Lincoln, Kenneth & Slagle, Al L. The Good Red Road: Passages into Native America. LC 97-20384. (Illus.). xxiv, 286p. 1997. pap. 13.00 (*0-8032-7974-4*, Bison Books) U of Nebr Pr.

Lincoln, Kenneth, ed. see TallMountain, Mary.

Lincoln, Kenneth R., jt. auth. see Arpad, Joseph J.

Lincoln, Key. Submission Holds. (Orig.). 1994. mass mkt. 4.95 (*1-56333-266-3*, Badboy) Masquerade.

Lincoln Land Conservation Trust Staff. A Guide to Conservation Land in Lincoln. 151p. (Orig.). 1992. pap. 11.00 (*0-614-11092-0*) Lincoln Land.

Lincoln, Louise, et al. An Assemblage of Spirits: Idea & Image in New Ireland. LC 87-15779. (Illus.). 168p. 1987. pap. 17.95 (*0-8076-1188-3*) Braziller.

Lincoln, Margaret. Amazing Boats. LC 92-3045. (Eyewitness Juniors Ser.: No. 21). (Illus.). 32p. (J). (ps-3). 1992. pap. 7.99 (*0-679-82770-6*, Pub. by Knopf Bks Yng Read) Random.

— The Most Excellent Book of Face Painting. LC 96-48466. (Illus.). 32p. (J). (gr. 4-6). 1997. lib. bdg. 19.90 (*0-7613-0551-3*, Copper Beech Bks) Millbrook Pr.

— The Most Excellent Book of Face Painting. LC 96-48466. (Most Excellent Book...Ser.). (Illus.). 32p. (J). (gr. 4-6). 1997. pap. 6.95 (*0-7613-0576-9*, Copper Beech Bks) Millbrook Pr.

Lincoln, Margarette. Amazing Boats. (Eyewitness Juniors Ser.: No. 21). (J). (ps-3). 1992. 13.19 (*0-606-01537-X*, Pub. by Turtleback) Demco.

— The Pirate's Handbook. (Illus.). (J). 15.99 (*0-590-24558-9*) Scholastic Inc.

— The Pirate's Handbook. (Puffin Book Ser.). 1998. 12.19 (*0-606-13711-4*, Pub. by Turtleback) Demco.

Lincoln, Margarette, ed. Science & Exploration: European Voyages to the Southern Oceans in the Eighteenth Century. LC 98-29021. (Illus.). 248p. 1998. 63.00 (*0-85115-721-1*) Boydell & Brewer.

***Lincoln, Maryanne.** Recipes from the Dye Kitchen. (Illus.). 56p. 1999. spiral bd. 17.95 (*1-881982-20-3*) Stackpole.

Lincoln, Patrick J. & Thomson, Jim, eds. Forensic DNA Profiling Protocols. LC 97-30911. (Methods in Molecular Biology Ser.: Vol. 98). (Illus.). 312p. 1998. 79.50 (*0-89603-443-7*) Humana.

Lincoln, Paul, jt. auth. see Southworth, Geoff.

Lincoln, R., jt. ed. see Tietze, S. L.

Lincoln, R. J. Dicc. de Ecologia, Evolucion y Taxonomia. (SPA.). 24.99 (*968-16-4877-3*, Pub. by Fondo) Continental Bk.

Lincoln, R. J. & Boxshall, G. A. The Cambridge Illustrated Dictionary of Natural History. (Illus.). 417p. (C). 1990. pap. 22.95 (*0-521-39941-6*) Cambridge U Pr.

Lincoln, R. J., et al. A Dictionary of Ecology, Evolution & Systematics. 2nd ed. LC 96-51626. (Illus.). 370p. (C). 1998. text 74.95 (*0-521-59139-2*); pap. text 29.95 (*0-521-43842-X*) Cambridge U Pr.

Lincoln, Ray. Puff of Smoke. (Illus.). 88p. (J). (gr. 2-6). 1989. pap., per. 10.00 (*0-9659447-0-0*) Three Friends.

Lincoln Residents, photos by. Five Roads: Photographic Essay by the Lincoln 1975 Bicentennial Commission. (Illus.). 34p. 1990. reprint ed. pap. 4.95 (*0-944856-02-0*) Lincoln Hist Soc.

Lincoln, Rosalie. Arnat Castun Pillerkat Assigeskuneng. large type ed.Tr. of What Girls Should Do When Eskimo Dancing. (ESK., Illus.). 16p. (J). (gr. k-3). 1999. pap. text 21.00 (*1-58084-111-2*) Lower Kuskokwim.

— Nasaurluum Yurallra. large type ed.Tr. of What Girls Should Do When Eskimo Dancing. (ESK., Illus.). 16p. (J). (gr. k-3). 1999. pap. text 21.00 (*1-58084-065-5*) Lower Kuskokwim.

***Lincoln, Rosalie.** What Girls Should Do When Eskimo Dancing. large type ed. (Illus.). 16p. (J). (gr. k-3). 1999. pap. text 21.00 (*1-58084-064-7*) Lower Kuskokwim.

Lincoln, Rosemary, jt. auth. see Lincoln, J. D.

Lincoln, Rufus, ed. Papers of Captain Rufus Lincoln of Wareham, Mass. LC 74-140872. (Eyewitness Accounts of the American Revolution Ser.). 1971. reprint ed. 23.95 (*0-405-01220-9*) Ayer.

Lincoln, Shirley H., jt. compiled by see Watlington, Roy A.

Lincoln, Solomon, Jr. History of the Town of Hingham Plymouth County, Massachusetts. 183p. 1996. pap. 17.00 (*0-7884-0434-2*, L351) Heritage Bk.

Lincoln, Stephen F., jt. auth. see Easton, Christopher J.

***Lincoln, Taylor, et al, eds.** Access 2000 Advanced. 256p. 2000. pap. 20.00 (*1-58264-103-X*) ActiveEd.

Lincoln, Victoria. Teresa - A Woman: A Biography of Teresa of Avila. LC 84-8561. (SUNY Series in Cultural Perspectives). 440p. (C). 1985. text 64.50 (*0-87395-936-1*); pap. text 21.95 (*0-87395-937-X*) State U NY Pr.

Lincoln, W. Genealogy of the Waldo Family: A Record of the Descendants of Cornelius Waldo of Ipswich, Massachusetts, from 1647 to 1900, 2 vols. in 1. (Illus.). 1129p. 1989. reprint ed. pap. 169.00 (*0-8328-1215-3*); reprint ed. lib. bdg. 177.00 (*0-8328-1214-5*) Higginson Bk Co.

Lincoln, W. Bruce. Between Heaven & Hell: The Story of a Thousand Years of Artistic Life in Russia. 528p. 1999. pap. 18.95 (*0-14-026773-5*) Viking Penguin.

— The Great Reforms: Autocracy, Bureaucracy, & the Politics of Change in Imperial Russia. 293p. (C). 1990. text 32.00 (*0-87580-155-2*); pap. text 15.00 (*0-87580-549-3*) N Ill U Pr.

— In the Vanguard of Reform: Russia's Enlightened Bureaucrats, 1825-1861. LC 82-6509. (Illus.). 297p. (C). 1986. pap. 16.00 (*0-87580-536-1*) N Ill U Pr.

— Nicholas I: Emperor & Autocrat of All the Russias. 424p. 1989. reprint ed. pap. text 16.00 (*0-87580-548-5*) N Ill U Pr.

— Red Victory: A History of the Russian Civil War, 1918-1921. LC DK265.L449 1999. (Illus.). 672p. 1999. reprint ed. mass mkt. 18.95 (*0-306-80909-5*, Pub. by Da Capo) HarpC.

— The Romanovs: Autocrats of All the Russias. LC 80-39902. (Illus.). 864p. 1983. pap. 22.00 (*0-385-27908-6*, Dial Pr) Dell.

Lincoln, W. Bruce, et al. Moscow: Treasures & Traditions. LC 90-30271. (Illus.). 320p. 1990. 50.00 (*0-295-96994-6*) U of Wash Pr.

Lincoln, W. E. Lincoln: Some Descendants of Stephen Lincoln of Wymondham, England; Edmund Larkin of England; Thomas Oliver of Bristol, England. 322p. 1993. reprint ed. pap. 49.50 (*0-8328-3704-0*); reprint ed. lib. bdg. 59.50 (*0-8328-3703-2*) Higginson Bk Co.

***Lincoln, Waldo.** History of the Lincoln Family: An Account of the Descendants of Samule Lincoln of Hingham, Massachusetts, 1637-1920. 752p. 2000. pap. 47.00 (*0-7884-1489-5*, 1489) Heritage Bk.

Lincoln, Wanda. Write Through the Year. (Illus.). 112p. (J). (gr. 2-6). 1989. pap., teacher ed. 9.95 (*0-912107-90-1*, MM 1907) Monday Morning Bks.

Lincoln, Wanda & Suid, Murray, eds. The Teacher's Quotation Book. 168p. 1997. 10.35 (*0-86651-316-7*) Seymour Pubns.

Lincoln, Wanda, jt. auth. see Suid, Murray.

Lincoln, Wanda, jt. auth. see Svid, Murray.

Lincoln, William. Alton Trials - of Winthrop S. Gilman, Enoch Long & Others. LC 70-125703. (American Journalists Ser.). 1978. reprint ed. 18.95 (*0-405-01684-0*) Ayer.

Lincoln, William A. The Complete Manual of Wood Veneering. rev. ed. LC 94-41869. (Illus.). 400p. 1995. pap. 21.95 (*0-941936-32-5*) Linden Pub Fresno.

— The Marquetry Manual. LC 94-41869. (Illus.). 272p. (Orig.). 1990. reprint ed. pap. 21.95 (*0-941936-19-8*) Linden Pub Fresno.

— World Woods in Color. LC 90-23574. (Illus.). 320p. 1991. reprint ed. 49.95 (*0-941936-20-1*) Linden Pub Fresno.

Lincoln, William F., jt. ed. see Huelsberg, Nancy A.

Lincoln, Yvonna S. Organizational Theory & Inquiry. (Focus Editions Ser.: Vol. 75). 320p. 1985. 59.95 (*0-8039-2494-1*); pap. 26.00 (*0-8039-2495-X*) Sage.

Lincoln, Yvonna S. & Guba, Egon G. Naturalistic Inquiry. LC 84-26295. 416p. 1985. 44.00 (*0-8039-2431-3*) Sage.

Lincoln, Yvonna S., jt. auth. see Denzin, Norman K.

Lincoln, Yvonna S., jt. auth. see Guba, Econ G.

Lincoln, Yvonna S., jt. auth. see Guba, Egon G.

Lincoln, Yvonna S., jt. ed. see Denzin, Norman K.

Lincoln, Yvonna S., jt. ed. see Tierney, William G.

Lincoln, Yvonne S., jt. auth. see Guba, Egon G.

Lincourt, John. Ethics Without a Net. 128p. (C). 1994. pap. text, spiral bd. 11.95 (*0-7872-0276-2*) Kendall-Hunt.

***Lincourt, Michel.** In Search of Elegance: Towards an Architecture of Satisfaction. LC 99-488472. (Illus.). 409p. 1999. write for info. (*0-85323-524-4*, Pub. by Liverpool Univ Pr) U of Pa Pr.

Lincourt, Michel. In Search of Elegance: Towards an Architecture of Satisfaction. (Illus.). 409p. 1998. 75.00 (*0-7735-1753-7*) McG-Queens Univ Pr.

***Lincourt, Michel.** In Search of Elegance: Towards an Architecture of Satisfaction. 1999. pap. 24.95 (*0-7735-1827-4*) McG-Queens Univ Pr.

***Lincove, David A., compiled by.** Reconstruction in the United States: An Annotated Bibliography, 43. LC 99-53148. (Bibliographies & Indexes in American History Ser.: Vol. 43). 664p. 2000. lib. bdg. 85.00 (*0-313-29199-3*, Greenwood Pr) Greenwood.

Linczy, E. Vampire Desire. (Illus.). mass mkt. 11.95 (*0-340-66576-9*, Pub. by Hodder & Stought Ltd) Trafalgar.

Lind. Exploring Science. 2nd ed. (Early Childhood Education Ser.). 1996. text, teacher ed. 14.95 (*0-8273-7310-4*) Delmar.

***Lind.** Exploring Science in Early Childhood. 3rd ed. LC 99-34455. (Early Childhood Education Ser.). 320p. (C). 1999. pap. 40.95 (*0-7668-0231-0*) Delmar.

— Intermediate Business Statistics. (Business Statistics Ser.). 2001. pap., student ed. 15.00 (*0-534-37124-8*) Brooks-Cole.

Lind & Jurs. Intermediate Business. 2001. pap. text 54.00 (*0-534-36229-X*) Thomson Learn.

Lind & Plendl. Hands-On Astronomy. 122p. (C). 1998. spiral bd. 29.95 (*0-7872-4828-2*) Kendall-Hunt.

Lind, et al. Fundamentals of Business Enterprise Taxation: 1998 Case Supplement. 1998. write for info. (*1-56662-659-5*) Foundation Pr.

— Fundamentals of Business Enterprise Taxation, 1997: Cases & Materials. LC 97-191322. (University Casebook Ser.). lxxxv, 846p. 1997. 50.95 (*1-56662-547-5*) Foundation Pr.

— Fundamentals of Corporate Taxation: 1998 Supplement. 1998. write for info. (*1-56662-674-9*) Foundation Pr.

Lind, jt. auth. see Dreke.

Lind, jt. auth. see Mason.

Lind, jt. auth. see Mason, Robert D.

Lind, A. Forsikerungs Ordbok. (ENG & NOR.). 57p. 1989. 59.95 (*0-8288-7876-5*) Fr & Eur.

Lind, A. R. Lyric Poetry of the Italian Renaissance: An Anthology with Verse Translations. 1954. 59.50 (*0-685-26673-7*) Elliots Bks.

Lind, Al. Black Bear Cub. (Smithsonian Wild Heritage Collection). 1994. 10.15 (*0-606-07291-8*, Pub. by Turtleback) Demco.

Lind, Alan. Black Bear Cub. LC 93-31130. (Smithsonian Wild Heritage Collection). (Illus.). 32p. (J). (gr. k-3). 1994. 11.95 (*1-56899-030-8*) Soundprints.

— Black Bear Cub. (Smithsonian Wild Heritage Collection). (Illus.). 32p. (J). (gr. k-3). 1995. pap. 4.95 (*1-56899-200-9*) Soundprints.

— Black Bear Cub, Incl. small toy. (Smithsonian Wild Heritage Collection). (Illus.). 32p. (J). (gr. k-3). 1995. pap. 15.95 (*1-56899-206-8*) Soundprints.

Lind, Andrew W., jt. auth. see Coman, Katherine.

Lind, Andrew W., ed. see Conference on Race Relations in World Perspective,.

Lind, Angus & Stahls, Paul F. New Orleans: Rollin' on the River. LC 96-36009. (Urban Tapestry Ser.). (Illus.). 256p. 1996. 44.95 (*1-881096-36-X*) Towery Pub.

Lind, Aulis O. Coastal Landforms of Cat Island, Bahamas: A Study of Holocene Accretionary Topography & Sea Level Change. LC 76-77892. (University of Chicago, Department of Geography, Research Paper Ser.: No. 122). (Illus.). 175p. reprint ed. pap. 54.30 (*0-7837-0399-6*, 204072000018) Bks Demand.

Lind, Beth B. Multicultural Children's Literature: An Annotated Bibliography, Grades K-8. LC 96-23847. 279p. (J). (gr. k-8). 1996. lib. bdg. 38.50 (*0-7864-0038-2*) McFarland & Co.

Lind, Brenda. The Conservation Easement Stewardship Guide: Designing, Monitoring, & Enforcing Conservation Easements. (Illus.). 72p. (Orig.). 1991. pap. 16.00 (*0-943915-07-4*) Land Trust DC.

Lind, Carl S., jt. auth. see Lind, Marilyn.

Lind, Carla. Frank Lloyd Wright's California Houses. (Wright at a Glance Ser.). (Illus.). 60p. 1996. 9.95 (*0-7649-0013-7*) Pomegranate Calif.

— Frank Lloyd Wright's Dining Rooms. LC 95-418. (Wright at a Glance Ser.). (Illus.). 60p. 1995. 9.95 (*0-87654-470-7*) Pomegranate Calif.

— Frank Lloyd Wright's Fallingwater. (Wright at a Glance Ser.). (Illus.). 60p. 1996. 9.95 (*0-7649-0015-3*) Pomegranate Calif.

— Frank Lloyd Wright's Fireplaces. LC 95-419. (Wright at a Glance Ser.). (Illus.). 60p. 1995. 9.95 (*0-87654-469-3*) Pomegranate Calif.

— Frank Lloyd Wright's First Houses. (Wright at a Glance Ser.). (Illus.). 60p. 1996. 9.95 (*0-7649-0014-5*) Pomegranate Calif.

— Frank Lloyd Wright's Furnishings. LC 95-420. (Wright at a Glance Ser.). (Illus.). 60p. 1995. 9.95 (*0-87654-471-5*) Pomegranate Calif.

— Frank Lloyd Wright's Glass Designs. LC 95-417. (Wright at a Glance Ser.). (Illus.). 60p. 1995. 9.95 (*0-87654-468-5*) Pomegranate Calif.

— Frank Lloyd Wright's Life & Homes. LC 94-7923. (Wright at a Glance Ser.). (Illus.). 60p. 1994. 9.95 (*1-56640-996-9*) Pomegranate Calif.

— Frank Lloyd Wright's Lost Buildings. LC 94-7935. (Wright at a Glance Ser.). (Illus.). 60p. 1994. 9.95 (*1-56640-999-3*) Pomegranate Calif.

— Frank Lloyd Wright's Prairie Houses. LC 94-7924. (Wright at a Glance Ser.). (Illus.). 60p. 1994. 9.95 (*1-56640-997-7*) Pomegranate Calif.

— Frank Lloyd Wright's Public Buildings. (Wright at a Glance Ser.). (Illus.). 60p. 1996. 9.95 (*0-7649-0016-1*) Pomegranate Calif.

— Frank Lloyd Wright's Usonian Houses. LC 94-7934. (Wright at a Glance Ser.). (Illus.). 60p. 1994. 9.95 (*1-56640-998-5*) Pomegranate Calif.

— Lost Wright: Frank Lloyd Wright's Vanished Masterpieces. (Illus.). 176p. 1996. 34.50 (*0-684-81306-8*) S&S Trade.

— Wright Style: Re-Creating the Spirit of Frank Lloyd Wright. (Illus.). 224p. 1992. 50.00 (*0-671-74959-5*) S&S Trade.

Lind, Dave & Wright, Meg. Building. (Visualized Songs Ser.). 20p. (J). (gr. 1-8). 1983. pap. 4.50 (*0-86508-135-2*) BCM Pubn.

Lind, David A. & Sanders, Scott P. The Physics of Skiing: Skiing at the Triple Point. (Illus.). 300p. 1997. pap. 24.95 (*1-56396-319-1*) Spr-Verlag.

Lind, Deborah W. Fishes Swim When Going Far: Tales of Rhyme & Reason. (Illus.). 32p. (J). (ps-3). 1997. pap. 9.95 (*0-9658862-0-4*) Step Into Yourself.

Lind, Douglas & Marcus, Brian. An Introduction to Symbolic Dynamics & Coding. (Illus.). 513p. (C). 1995. pap. text 30.95 (*0-521-55900-6*) Cambridge U Pr.

— An Introduction to Symbolic Dynamics & Coding. (Illus.). 513p. (C). 1996. text 74.95 (*0-521-55124-2*) Cambridge U Pr.

***Lind, Douglas, et al.** Basic Statistics for Business & Economics. 3rd ed. 320p. (C). 1999. pap., student ed. 24.06 (*0-07-233985-3*) McGrw-H Hghr Educ.

Lind, Douglas A. & Mason, Robert D. Basic Statistics for Business & Economics. LC 93-3530. 528p. (C). 1993. text 62.75 (*0-256-12222-9*, Irwn McGrw-H) McGrw-H Hghr Educ.

— Basic Statistics for Business & Economics. 2nd ed. LC 96-7837. 1996. teacher ed. write for info. (*0-256-21499-9*, Irwn McGrw-H) McGrw-H Hghr Educ.

— Statistical Techniques in Business & Economics. LC 95-16497. 1995. teacher ed. write for info. (*0-256-18904-8*, Irwn Prfssnl) McGraw-Hill Prof.

— Statistical Techniques in Business & Economics. 8th ed. 360p. (C). 1992. text 72.81 (*0-256-12680-1*, Irwn McGrw-H) McGrw-H Hghr Educ.

***Lind, Douglas A., et al.** Basic Statistics for Business & Economics. 3rd ed. LC 99-42855. 2000. write for info. (*0-07-366062-0*) McGraw.

Lind, Douglas A., jt. auth. see Mason, Robert D.

Lind, E. A. & Tyler, T. R. The Social Psychology of Procedural Justice. LC 87-38473. (Critical Issues in Social Justice Ser.). (Illus.). 280p. (C). 1988. 51.00 (*0-306-42726-5*, Plenum Trade) Perseus Pubng.

Lind, Earl, et al. Autobiography of an Androgyne. LC 75-12333. (Homosexuality Ser.). 1975. reprint ed. 23.95 (*0-405-07400-X*) Ayer.

— The Female Impersonators: A Sequel to "the Autobiography of an Androgyne" LC 75-12334. (Homosexuality Ser.). (Illus.). 1975. reprint ed. 23.95 (*0-405-07358-5*) Ayer.

Lind, Edna M. & Brook, Alan J. Desmids of the English Lake District. 1980. 39.00 (*0-7855-7278-3*) St Mut.

Lind, Edna M. & Morrison, M. E. S. East African Vegetation. LC 73-85206. 274p. 1974. reprint ed. pap. 85.00 (*0-608-08184-1*, 205126000094) Bks Demand.

Lind, Ekard. Exercises for Musicians: How to Control & Prevent Postural Stress. Plucked String Staff, ed. Harris, Keith, tr. from GER. LC 87-60423.Tr. of Bewegungsausgleich fur Musiker. (Illus.). 68p. (Orig.). 1987. pap. 10.00 (*0-9614120-1-1*) Plucked.

***Lind, Eva-Marie.** Aromatique: A Sensualist's Guide to Aromatic Oils. LC 99-37559. (Illus.). 128p. 1999. 16.00 (*1-57959-023-3*, SOMA) BB&T Inc.

Lind, Georg, et al. Moral Development & Social Environment: Studies in the Philosophy & Psychology of Moral Judgement & Education. Wakenhut, Roland & Hartman, Hans, eds. 314p. 1985. 39.95 (*0-913750-27-1*) Transaction Pubs.

Lind, Heidemarie. Mowgli Has a Party. (Illus.). 36p. (J). (ps-8). 1997. 15.95 (*1-891126-06-7*); pap. 7.95 (*1-891126-00-8*) Rocky Mtn W.

— Mowgli in Arches. (Illus.). 40p. (J). (ps-8). 1997. 15.95 (*1-891126-09-1*); pap. 7.95 (*1-891126-03-2*) Rocky Mtn W.

— Mowgli in Bryce Canyon. (Illus.). 44p. (J). (ps-8). 1997. 15.95 (*1-891126-07-5*); pap. 7.95 (*1-891126-01-6*) Rocky Mtn W.

— Mowgli in Grand Canyon. (Illus.). 38p. (J). (ps-8). 1997. 15.95 (*1-891126-11-3*); pap. 7.95 (*1-891126-05-9*) Rocky Mtn W.

— Mowgli in the Winter Sports. (Illus.). 64p. (J). (ps-8). 1997. 15.95 (*1-891126-08-3*); pap. 7.95 (*1-891126-02-4*) Rocky Mtn W.

— Mowgli in Yellowstone. (Illus.). 40p. (J). (ps-8). 1997. 15.95 (*1-891126-10-5*); pap. 7.95 (*1-891126-04-0*) Rocky Mtn W.

Lind, Henry C., ed. The Long Road for Home: The Civil War Experiences of Four Farmboy Soldiers of the Twenty-Seventh Massachusetts Regiment of Volunteer Infantry as Told by Their Personal Correspondence, 1861-1864. LC 91-58579. (Illus.). 216p. (C). 1992. 36.50 (*0-8386-3464-8*) Fairleigh Dickinson.

Lind, Hera. Das Weibernest. 1999. 22.00 (*3-596-13770-5*) Fischer Taschen.

Lind, Hope K. Apart & Together: Mennonites in Oregon & Neighboring States, 1876-1976. LC 90-30840. (Studies in Anabaptist & Mennonite History). (Illus.). 416p. 1990. 26.99 (*0-8361-3106-1*) Herald Pr.

Lind, Ingrid. The Spiritual Teachings of White Eagle. (Illus.). 80p. 1989. pap. 6.95 (*0-85030-791-0*, Pub. by Aqrn Pr) Harper SF.

Lind, J., et al, eds. Children & Parents in Hospitals. (Journal: Pediatrician: Vol. 9, No. 3-4). (Illus.). 120p. 1980. pap. 17.25 (*3-8055-1476-X*) S Karger.

— Surface Strength Terminology. 2nd rev. ed. (Illus.). 42p. 1993. pap. 29.00 (*0-89852-411-3*, 0101R111) TAPPI.

Lind, Jakov. The Stove. LC 82-10824. 77p. 1983. pap. 12.95 (*0-935296-27-1*, Pub. by Sheep Meadow) U Pr of New Eng.

Lind, Jane. Kids' Northwoods Activity Book with Glossary. (Illus.). 26p. (Orig.). 1987. pap. 4.95 (*0-910259-06-2*) Womens Times.

Lind, Jane, ed. see Holte, Ingeborg.

Lind, Jennifer, ed. see Cornesky, Robert A.

Lind, Jens & Moller, Iver H., eds. Inclusion & Exclusion: Unemployment & Non-Standard Employment in Europe. LC 98-73855. 6p. 1999. text 59.95 (*1-84014-849-7*) Ashgate Pub Co.

Lind, Judi. Jackson's Woman (Her Protector) Her Protector. (Intrigue Ser.: No. 504). 1999. per. 3.99 (*0-373-22504-0*, 1-22504-4) Harlequin Bks.

— Menace Sans Visage. (Rouge Passion Ser.: No. 498). (FRE.). 1999. mass mkt. 3.50 (*0-373-37498-4*, 1-37498-2) Harlequin Bks.

— Storm Warnings. 1997. per. 3.75 (*0-373-22433-8*, 1-22433-6) Harlequin Bks.

— To Save His Baby. (Intrigue Ser.). 1999. mass mkt. 3.99 (*0-373-22531-8*, 1-22531-7) Harlequin Bks.

— Undercover Vows. LC 96-3691. (Intrigue Ser.). 248p. 1996. per. 3.50 (*0-373-22355-2*, 1-22355-1) Harlequin Bks.

— Veil of Fear. LC 95-6900. (Intrigue Ser.). 248p. 1995. per. 3.50 (*0-373-22310-2*, 1-22310-6) Harlequin Bks.

— When Dreams Come True. 256p. 1997. mass mkt. 5.50 (*0-7860-0393-6*, Pinncle Kensgtn) Kensgtn Pub Corp.

— Without a Past. (Intrigue Ser.). 1994. per. 2.99 (*0-373-22260-2*, 1-22260-3) Harlequin Bks.

Lind, Karen K. Exploring Science in Early Childhood: A Developmental Approach. 352p. 1991. pap. 25.95 (*0-8273-4722-7*) Delmar.

— Exploring Science in Early Childhood: A Developmental Approach. 352p. 1991. pap., teacher ed. 8.00 (*0-8273-4723-5*) Delmar.

— Exploring Science in Early Childhood: A Developmental Approach. 2nd ed. (Early Childhood Education Ser.). (C). 1996. mass mkt. 29.50 (*0-8273-7309-0*) Delmar.

Lind, Karen K., ed. Water, Stones, & Fossil Bones. (CESI Sourcebook Ser.: Vol. VI). (Illus.). 140p. 1991. pap. text 18.50 (*0-87355-101-X*) Natl Sci Tchrs.

Lind, Kate. From Hazelbrush to Cornfields: Amish Mennonites of Iowa, 1846-1946. LC 95-106656. (Illus.). 765p. 1994. 40.00 (*0-9636151-3-0*) St Andrews IA.

Lind, L. R. Berengario da Carpi, on Fracture of the Skull or Cranium. LC 90-55267. (Transactions Ser.: Vol. 80, Pt. 4). (Illus.). 164p. (C). 1990. pap. 15.00 (*0-87169-804-8*, T804-LIL) Am Philos.

— An Epitaph Years After. LC 89-81153. 75p. 1990. 4.00 (*0-9624631-0-8*) Bennett & Kitchel.

— Gabriele Zerbi, Gerontocomia: On the Care of the Aged & Maximianus, Elegies on Old Age & Love. LC 87-72873. (Memoirs Ser.: Vol. 182). (Illus.). 346p. (C). 1988. 20.00 (*0-87169-182-5*, M182-LIL) Am Philos.

— The Letters of Giovanni Garzoni: Bolognese Humanist & Physician (1419-1505) (American Philological Association Philological Monographs). 600p. 1992. 69.95 (*1-55540-111-2*, 400033) OUP.

Lind, L. R., ed. Twentieth Century Italian Poetry: A Bilingual Anthology. LC 73-11343. (Library of Liberal Arts). 432p. 1974. pap. 10.50 (*0-672-61220-8*, Bobbs) Macmillan.

Lind, L. R., tr. see Virgil.

Lind, Laura J., jt. auth. see Haring, Joen I.

Lind, Lew. The Navy Day by Day: Historic Naval Events in Australia & Abroad. LC 97-114780. (Illus.). 272p. 1997. 42.95 (*0-86417-787-9*, Pub. by Kangaroo Pr) Seven Hills Bk.

Lind, Loren J. The Learning Machine: A Hard Look at Toronto Schools. 228p. (Orig.). 1974. pap. 9.95 (*0-88784-646-7*, Pub. by Hse of Anansi Pr) Genl Dist Srvs.

Lind, Louise. William Blackstone: Sage of the Wilderness. (Illus.). 108p. 1993. pap. text 11.00 (*1-55613-910-1*) Heritage Bk.

***Lind, Louise.** William Blackstone: Sage of the Wilderness. 2nd rev. ed. 110p. 1999. pap. 15.95 (*0-9655311-1-2*, JDS101) Jemtec Digital.

Lind, Louise, ed. see Rocheleau, Corinne.

Lind, Marilyn. Continuing Your Genealogical Research in Minnesota. LC 85-80942. (Illus.). 161p. 1986. pap. text 14.50 (*0-937463-09-4*) Linden Tree.

— Immigration, Migration & Settlement in the United States: A Genealogical Guidebook. LC 85-809040. (Illus.). 144p. (Orig.) (C). 1985. pap. 12.95 (*0-937463-08-6*) Linden Tree.

— Printing & Publishing Your Family History. LC 86-8100. (Illus.). 63p. (Orig.). 1986. pap. text 7.50 (*0-937463-10-8*) Linden Tree.

— Researching & Finding Your German Heritage. 2nd enl. rev. ed. LC 90-62026. (Illus.). 150p. (Orig.). 1991. reprint ed. pap. 13.25 (*0-937463-12-4*) Linden Tree.

— Researching Your Family & Heritage. LC 90-62025. (Illus.). 176p. (Orig.). (C). 1991. pap. 14.50 (*0-937463-13-2*) Linden Tree.

— Supplement to Using Maps & Aerial Photography in Your Genealogical Research. LC 85-80941. (Illus.). 43p. (Orig.). 1985. pap. text 5.50 (*0-937463-07-8*) Linden Tree.

— Thiem, Christoph & August-A Dream & a Promise. LC 81-90330. (Illus.). 187p. 1981. text 35.00 (*0-937463-01-9*); pap. text 30.00 (*0-937463-02-7*) Linden Tree.

— Trauungen: Marriages, 1825-1844, Evangelical Kirchengemeinde Zempelburg, Kreis Flatow, Provinz Westpreussen, German Kaiser Reich. large type ed. LC 97-75611. (Illus.). 104p. 1997. pap. 14.95 (*0-937463-15-9*) Linden Tree.

— Using Maps & Aerial Photography in Your Genealogical Research-With Supplement on Foreign Aerial Photography. rev. ed. LC 85-80941. (Illus.). 217p. (Orig.). 1985. pap. text 15.50 (*0-937463-06-X*) Linden Tree.

— Volkszahlung: Birth Census 1856-1878, Evangelical Kirchengemeinde Mrotschen, Kreis Wiristz, Provinz Posen German Kaiser Reich. LC 94-79225. (Illus.). 103p. (Orig.). 1995. pap. 14.95 (*0-937463-14-0*) Linden Tree.

Lind, Marilyn & Lind, Carl S. Looking Backward to Sweden: A Genealogical Research Book, & the Lind-Bure Family, 1000-1986. LC 86-81744. (Illus.). 154p. (Orig.). 1986. pap. text 14.50 (*0-937463-11-6*) Linden Tree.

Lind, Mary A. Asia: A Christian Perspective. rev. ed. 175p. 1994. pap. 9.99 (*0-927545-72-1*) YWAM Pub.

— The Compassionate Memsahibs: Welfare Activities of British Women in India, 1900-1947, 90. LC 87-24953. (Contributions in Women's Studies). 144p. 1988. 45.00 (*0-313-26059-1*, LRJ/, Greenwood Pr) Greenwood.

Lind, Mary B., jt. auth. see Myers, Sarah E.

Lind, Michael. The Alamo: An Epic. 1997. 22.95 (*0-614-27861-9*) HM.

***Lind, Michael.** The Alamo: An Epic. 376p. 1999. 29.95 (*0-7351-0133-7*) Replica Bks.

Lind, Michael. Hamilton's Republic: Readings in the American Democratic Nationalist Tradition. LC 97-33438. 320p. 1997. 24.50 (*0-684-83160-0*) Free Pr.

— The New Republic Guide to the Issues: The '96 Campaign. LC 96-24671. 272p. 1996. pap. 12.00 (*0-465-05086-7*, Pub. by Basic) HarpC.

— The Next American Nation: The New Nationalism & the Fourth American Revolution. 350p. 1995. 25.00 (*0-02-919103-3*) Free Pr.

— The Next American Nation: The New Nationalism & the Fourth American Revolution. LC 96-2144. 448p. 1996. per. 15.00 (*0-684-82503-1*) Free Pr.

— Powertown. 1997. mass mkt. write for info. (*0-06-101219-X*, Harp PBks) HarpC.

— The Sociocultural Dimensions of Mixtec Ceramics. Spores, Ronald M. & McNutt, Paula M., eds. (Vanderbilt University Publications in Anthropology: No. 33). (Illus.). 120p. (Orig.). 1987. pap. text 13.85 (*0-935462-24-4*) VUPA.

— Up from Conservatism: Why the Right Is Wrong for America. 1996. 25.00 (*0-02-874109-9*) Free Pr.

***Lind, Michael.** Vietnam, The Necessary War: A Reinterpretation of America's Most Disastrous Military Conflict. LC 99-28449. 336p. 1999. pap. 25.00 (0-684-84254-8) S&S Trade.

***Lind, Michael, ed.** Hamilton's Republic: Readings in the American Democratic Nationalist Tradition. 345p. 2000. reprint ed. 25.00 (0-7881-9255-8) DIANE Pub.

Lind, Micheal. Up from Conservatism. 1997. per. 13.00 (0-684-83186-4) S&S Trade.

Lind, Millard C. Ezekiel. LC 95-52499. (Believers Church Bible Commentary Ser.: Vol. 8). 416p. (Orig.). 1996. pap. 21.99 (0-8361-9016-5) Herald Pr.

— Monotheism, Power, - Justice: Collected Old Testament Essays. (Text-Reader Ser.: No. 3). 273p. 1990. pap. text 10.00 (0-936273-16-X) Inst Mennonite.

***Lind, Millard C.** Peace & Justice Shall Embrace: Power & Theopolitics in the Bible. unabridged ed. Grimsrud, Ted & Johns, Loren L., eds. LC 99-41416. 252p. 2000. pap. 22.95 (0-9665021-1-6, Pub. by Pandora PA) Herald Pr.

Lind, Millard C. Yahweh Is a Warrior. LC 80-16038. (Christian Peace Shelf Ser.). 248p. 1980. pap. 15.99 (0-8361-1233-4) Herald Pr.

Lind, Nancy S. & Elder, Ann, eds. The Small City & Regional Community Vol. 8: Proceedings of the 1988 Conference. vii, 295p. 1988. pap. text 19.00 (0-932310-10-9, 79-644450) U of Wis-Stevens Point.

Lind, Niels Christian, jt. ed. see Eggwertz, Sigge.

Lind, O. T., ed. Reservoir Eutrophication. (Water Science & Technology Ser.: Vol. 28). 112p. 1993. pap. 114.25 (0-08-042354-X, Pergamon Pr) Elsevier.

Lind, O. T., et al, eds. Proceedings of the International Conference on Reservoir Limnology & Water Quality, June 15 to 20, 1987 Teil 3: Key Factors of Reservoir Limnology, Eutrophication, Water Quality & Its Prediction. (Advances in Limnology Ser.: Vol. 33, Pt. 3). (GER., Illus.). iv, 333p. 1990. pap. text 109.00 (3-510-47034-6, Pub. by E Schweizerbartsche) Balogh.

Lind, Regina F. & Bachman, Debra H., eds. Fundamentals of Perinatal Social Work: A Guide for Clinical Practice with Women, Infants & Families. LC 97-6350. (Social Work in Health Care Monograph Ser.: Vol. 24, Nos. 3-4). 224p. (C). 1997. 44.95 (0-7890-0043-1); pap. text 24.95 (0-7890-0049-0) Haworth Pr.

***Lind, Richard.** The Seeking Self: The Search for Self Improvement & the Creation of Personal Suffering. 200p. 2000. pap. 14.95 (1-890482-76-5) Phanes Pr.

***Lind, Richard E.** The Devil's Due. unabridged ed. (Illus.). 204p. 1999. 29.99 (1-57529-025-1) Kabel Pubs.

Lind, Richard E., jt. auth. see Hall, Calvin S.

Lind, Richard W., jt. auth. see Hinkel, Arthur R.

***Lind, Robert C.** Copyright Law. 200p. 2000. pap., student ed. write for info. (0-89089-628-3) Carolina Acad Pr.

— Trademark Law. 192p. 2000. pap. write for info. (0-89089-629-1) Carolina Acad Pr.

Lind, Robert C., et al. Discounting for Time & Risk in Energy Policy. 468p. 1982. 42.50 (0-8018-2709-4) Resources Future.

Lind, Robin. Pedaling Northwards: A Father & Son's Bicycle Adventure from Virginia to Canada. 108p. 1993. pap. 8.95 (0-9639531-0-9) Hope Springs.

Lind, Robin, jt. auth. see Williams, Kitty.

Lind, Roger M., jt. auth. see Tropman, John E.

Lind, Stephen A. Fundamentals of Corporate Taxation: Cases & Materials. 4th ed. LC 97-130068. xvii, 760p. 1997. teacher ed. 50.00 (1-56662-450-9) Foundation Pr.

Lind, Stephen A., et al. Cases & Materials on Fundamentals of Partnership Taxation. 5th ed. LC 98-23389. (University Casebook Ser.). 425p. 1998. text. write for info. (1-56662-615-3) Foundation Pr.

— Fundamentals of Business Enterprise Taxation, Teachers Manual to Accompany Cases & Materials On. (University Casebook Ser.). 296p. (C). 1997. pap. text, teacher ed. write for info. (1-56662-579-3) West Pub.

— Fundamentals of Corporate Taxation: Cases & Materials On. 3rd ed. (University Casebook Ser.). 809p. 1991. text 39.95 (0-88277-877-3) Foundation Pr.

— Fundamentals of Corporate Taxation: Teacher's Manual to Accompany Case & Materils On. 3rd ed. (University Casebook Ser.). 297p. 1991. pap. text, teacher ed. write for info. (0-88277-905-2) Foundation Pr.

— Fundamentals of Corporate Taxation: Teacher's Manual to Accompany Cases & Materials On. 4th ed. (University Casebook Ser.). 215p. (C). 1996. pap. text, teacher ed. write for info. (1-56662-530-0) Foundation Pr.

— Fundamentals of Partnership Taxation: Cases & Materials. 4th ed. (University Casebook Ser.). 504p. 1994. text 39.00 (1-56662-169-0) Foundation Pr.

— Fundamentals of Partnership Taxation: 1997 Supplement to Cases & Materials On. 4th ed. (University Casebook Ser.). 54p. 1997. pap. text. write for info. (1-56662-509-2) Foundation Pr.

— 1996 Supplement to Cases & Materials on Fundamentals of Corporate Taxation. 3rd ed. (University Casebook Ser.). 71p. 1996. pap. text, suppl. ed. write for info. (1-56662-385-5) Foundation Pr.

— 1996 Supplement to Cases & Materials on Fundamentals of Partnership Taxation. 4th ed. (University Casebook Ser.). 33p. 1996. pap. text. write for info. (1-56662-410-X) Foundation Pr.

Lind, Stephen A., jt. auth. see Freeland, James J.

Lind, Stephen A., jt. auth. see Hudson, David M.

Lind, T. & Mackay, G. A. Norwegian Oil Policies. LC HD9575.N62L5. 158p. reprint ed. pap. 49.00 (0-7837-1170-0, 204169900022) Bks Demand.

Lind, T., jt. ed. see Huisjes, H. J.

Lind, Vibeke. Knitting in the Nordic Tradition. Jensen, Annette A., tr. from DAN. LC 84-81825. Orig. Title: Strek Med Nordisk Tradition. (Illus.). 128p. 1987. 24.95 (0-937274-15-1, Pub. by Lark Books) Sterling.

Lind, William S. Maneuver Warfare Handbook. (Replica Edition Ser.). 152p. (C). 1985. pap. 32.00 (0-86531-862-X, Pub. by Westview) HarpC.

Lind, Wolfgang, jt. auth. see Dreke, Michael.

Linda, C. Majka, jt. ed. see Voydanoff, Patricia.

Linda, Mary F., ed. see Zabel, Craig.

Lindabury, Richard V. Study of Patriotism in the Elizabethan Drama. LC 68-54170. (Studies in Drama: No. 39). 1969. reprint ed. lib. bdg. 75.00 (0-8383-0584-9) M S G Haskell Hse.

Lindabury, Tryon. One Magnificent Moment. 140p. (Orig.). 1991. pap. 6.95 (1-879366-09-6) Hearthstone OK.

Lindahl, Anders. Information Through Sherds: A Case Study of the Early Glazed Earthenware from Dalby Scania. (Illus.). xvi, 200p. (Orig.). 1987. pap. 93.00 (91-7810-717-2) Coronet Bks.

Lindahl, Anders & Stilborg, Ole, eds. The Aim of Laboratory Analyses of Ceramics in Archaeology. (Konferenser Ser.: No. 34). (Illus.). 172p. (Orig.). 1995. pap. 42.50 (91-7402-258-X) Coronet Bks.

Lindahl, Barry A., jt. auth. see Lee, J. D.

Lindahl, Carl. Contemporary Legend: A Reader. Bennett, Gillian & Smith, Paul, eds. LC 96-19857. (New Perspectives in Folklore Ser.: Vol. 4). (Illus.). 430p. 1996. reprint ed. text 77.00 (0-8153-1317-9, H1718) Garland.

— Earnest Games: Folkloric Patterns in the Canterbury Tales. LC 86-45469. 207p. reprint ed. pap. 64.20 (0-608-09347-5, 205409300002) Bks Demand.

***Lindahl, Carl.** Medieval Folklore: An Encyclopedia of Myths, Legends, Tales, Beliefs & Customs, 2 vols. (Illus.). 800p. 2000. lib. bdg. 150.00 (1-57607-121-9) ABC-CLIO.

Lindahl, Carl, et al, eds. Folktales of Newfoundland: The Resilience of the Oral Tradition, 2 vols., Set. LC 96-3648. (World Folktale Library: Vol. 3). (Illus.). 1288p. 1996. text 175.00 (0-8153-1736-0, H1856) Garland.

— Swapping Stories: Folktales from Louisiana. LC 96-41265. 352p. 1997. 45.00 (0-87805-930-X); pap. 20.00 (0-87805-931-8) U Pr of Miss.

Lindahl, Carl & Ware, Carolyn. Cajun Mardi Gras Masks. LC 97-11388. (Folk Art & Artists Ser.). 1997. pap. 22.50 (0-87805-969-5) U Pr of Miss.

— Cajun Mardi Gras Masks. LC 97-11388. (Folk Art & Artists Ser.). (Illus.). 96p. 1997. 22.50 (0-87805-968-7) U Pr of Miss.

Lindahl, Carl, et al. Encyclopedia of Medieval Folklore. 1000p. 1998. text 100.00 (0-8153-2758-7) Garland.

Lindahl, Carl, jt. ed. see Burlakoff, Nikolai.

Lindahl, Carl, ed. see Green, Thomas A., et al.

Lindahl, Carl, jt. ed. see Walker, Warren S.

Lindahl, Carol, ed. see Angelson, B.

Lindahl, Carol, ed. see Schomer, David C.

***Lindahl, Charles W., ed.** Standards in Mathematics & English for California High School Graduates. (Illus.). 108p. 1999. reprint ed. pap. text 20.00 (0-7881-8176-9) DIANE Pub.

Lindahl, Erik R. Studies in the Theory of Money & Capital. LC 70-117915. (Reprints of Economic Classics Ser.). (Illus.). 391p. 1970. reprint ed. 45.00 (0-678-00655-5) Kelley.

Lindahl, Hans. Welfare & Enlightenment: An Enquiry into the Rational Foundations of the Welfare State. 334p. (Orig.). 1995. pap. 72.50 (90-6186-671-5, Pub. by Leuven Univ) Coronet Bks.

Lindahl, Ingemar B., jt. ed. see Nordenfelt, Lennart.

Lindahl, Judy. Decorating with Fabric: An Idea Book. rev. ed. 128p. 1980. pap. 6.95 (0-9603032-1-9) Lindahl.

— Energy Saving Decorating. rev. ed. LC 81-90134. (Illus.). 128p. (Orig.). 1981. pap. 6.95 (0-9603032-3-5) Lindahl.

— The Shade Book. rev. ed. (Illus.). 148p. pap. 9.95 (0-9603032-2-7) Lindahl.

Lindahl-Kiessling, Kerstin & Landberg, Hans, eds. Population, Economic Development, & the Environment. (Illus.). 306p. 1998. reprint ed. pap. text 22.00 (0-19-829242-2) OUP.

Lindahl, Kristin, jt. ed. see Kerig, Patricia.

Lindahl, Lars-Ake & Poulsen, F., eds. Thin Sets in Harmonic Analysis: Seminars Held at Institute Mittag-Leffler, 1969-70. LC 79-163310. (Lecture Notes in Pure & Applied Mathematics Ser.: No. 2). 197p. reprint ed. pap. 61.10 (0-7837-3419-0, 205246500008) Bks Demand.

Lindahl, Laurel. Twin Cities' Best Seats. 80p. (Orig.). 1994. pap. text 14.95 (0-963451-2-9) MN Monthly.

Lindahl, Thomas, ed. Genetic Instability in Cancer. (Cancer Surveys Ser.: Vol. 28). (Illus.). 400p. (C). 1996. text 90.00 (0-87969-485-8) Cold Spring Harbor.

Lindahl, Wesley E. Strategic Planning for Fund Raising: How to Bring in More Money Using Strategic Resource Allocation. LC 92-25900. (Nonprofit Sector-Public Administration Ser.). 152p. 1992. text 37.95 (1-55542-495-3) Jossey-Bass.

***Lindal Cedar Homes Staff.** Discovering Your Dream. 2000. pap. 29.95 (0-9625396-4-3) Lindal Cedar.

Lindall, Robert J., et al. Minnesota Condemnation Law. 450p. 1992. suppl. ed. 35.00 (0-685-74268-7, MICHIE); ring bd. 115.00 (0-86678-646-5, MICHIE) LEXIS Pub.

Lindamood, Jean, ed. Road Trips, Head Trips, & Other Car-Crazed Writings: An Anthology. 272p. 1996. 22.00 (0-87113-654-6, Atlntc Mnthly) Grove-Atltic.

Lindamood, Phyllis, jt. auth. see Bell, Nanci.

Lindars, Barnabas. John. (New Testament Guides Ser.: No. 4). 106p. 1990. pap. 12.50 (1-85075-255-9, Pub. by Sheffield Acad) CUP Services.

Lindars, Barnabas. Judges 1-5. Mayes, Andrew A., ed. 352p. 1994. text 49.95 (0-567-09696-3, Pub. by T & T Clark) Bks Intl VA.

— Theology of the Letter to Hebrews. (New Testament Theology Ser.). 169p. 1991. pap. text 16.95 (0-521-35748-9) Cambridge U Pr.

— Theology of the Letter to the Hebrews. (New Testament Theology Ser.). 169p. (C). 1991. text 54.95 (0-521-35487-0) Cambridge U Pr.

Lindau, Buff, ed. see Casey, Eileen L.

Lindau, Gustav, ed. Kryptogamenflora Feur Anfaenger Bande 1: Die Hoeheren Pilze, Vol. 1. (GER.). xii, 497p. 1971. reprint ed. 112.20 (3-87429-021-2, 007117, Pub. by Koeltz Sci Bks) Lubrecht & Cramer.

— Kryptogamenflora Fuer Anfaenger Vol. 5: Die Laubmoose. 242p. 1971. reprint ed. 56.10 (3-87429-026-3, 007129, Pub. by Koeltz Sci Bks) Lubrecht & Cramer.

— Kryptogamenflora Fuer Anfaenger Vol. 6: Die Torf-und Lebermoose. 124p. 1971. reprint ed. 78.20 (3-87429-027-1, 007132, Pub. by Koeltz Sci Bks) Lubrecht & Cramer.

Lindau, Gustav, ed. Kryptogamenflora fuer Anfanger: Band 4:1-2Lindau, G. & H. Melchoir: die Algen. (GER., Illus.). 615p. 1970. 110.00 (3-87429-024-7, Pub. by Koeltz Sci Bks) Lubrecht & Cramer.

Lindau, Hans & Weber, Marianne. Schriften zu J. G. Fichtes Sozialphilosophie. (Fichteana Ser.). (GER.). vii, 235p. 1987. reprint ed. write for info. (3-487-07906-2) G Olms Pubs.

Lindau, Joan. Letting in the Night. LC 89-1331. 180p. (Orig.). 1989. pap. 8.95 (0-932379-59-1); lib. bdg. 18.95 (0-932379-60-5) Firebrand Bks.

Lindau, Juan D. & Cheek, Timothy, eds. Market Economics & Political Change: Comparing China & Mexico. LC 98-10415. 360p. 1998. 65.00 (0-8476-8732-5); pap. 24.95 (0-8476-8733-3) Rowman.

***Lindau, R.** Climate Atlas of the Atlantic Ocean: Derived from the Comprehensive Ocean Atmosphere Data Set (COADS) (Illus.). vii, 456p. 2000. 179.00 incl. cd-rom (3-540-66813-6) Spr-Verlag.

Lindauer, Anthony D. From Paths to Plats: The Development of Annapolis, 1651 to 1718. LC 99-489353. (Illus.). 32p. pap. 7.00 (0-942370-46-5, Pub. by MD St Archives) Cornell Maritime.

Lindauer, David & Nunberg, Barbara, eds. Rehabilitating Government: Pay & Employment Reform in Africa. (World Bank Ser.). 256p. 1996. 77.95 (1-85972-226-1, Pub. by Avebry) Ashgate Pub Co.

Lindauer, David L. & Nunberg, Barbara, eds. Rehabilitating Government: Pay & Employment Reform in Africa. LC 94-26924. (World Bank Regional & Sectoral Studies). 254p. 1994. pap. 22.00 (0-8213-3000-4, 13000) World Bank.

Lindauer, David L. & Roemer, Michael. Asia & Africa: Legacies & Opportunities. LC 94-7211. 1994. pap. 19.95 (1-55815-320-9) ICS Pr.

Lindauer, David L., et al. The Strains of Economic Growth: Labor Unrest & Social Dissatisfaction in Korea. LC 97-5513. (Harvard Institute for International Development Ser.). (Illus.). 194p. 1997. 30.00 (0-674-83981-1) HUP.

Lindauer, M. S. Perceptual Psychology. 1978. text 23.50 (0-685-04011-9, Pergamon Pr); pap. text 17.00 (0-685-04012-7, Pergamon Pr) Elsevier.

Lindauer, Margaret A. Devouring Frida: The Art History & Popular Celebrity of Frida Kahlo. LC 98-47641. (Illus.). 232p. 1999. pap. 19.95 (0-8195-6348-X, Wesleyan Univ Pr); text 45.00 (0-8195-6347-1, Wesleyan Univ Pr) U Pr of New Eng.

Lindauer, Martin. Communication among Social Bees. LC 61-5579. (Harvard Bks. in Biology: No. 2). (Illus.). 155p. 1961. reprint ed. pap. 48.10 (0-7837-1714-8, 205724300024) Bks Demand.

Lindauer, Martin S., ed. Interdisciplinarity, the Psychology of Art, & Creativity: A Special Issue of Creativity Research Journal. 81p. 1998. pap. write for info. (0-8058-9841-7) L Erlbaum Assocs.

Lindauer, Owen. Not for School, but for Life: Lessons from the Historical Archaeology of the Phoenix Indian School. LC 97-51619. (OCRM Report Ser.). 1998. write for info. (1-886067-15-5) AZ State Univ Anthro.

— Where the Rivers Converge: Roosevelt Platform Mound Study. LC 95-45382. (Anthropological Field Studies: No. 33). 1995. 24.50 (1-886067-04-X) ASU Office Cultural Res.

Lindauer, Owen, et al. The Archaeological of Schoolhouse Point Mesa: Roosevelt Platform Mound Study, Report on the Schoolhouse Point Mesa Sites, Schoolhouse Management Group, Pinto Creek Complex. LC 97-24183. (Anthropological Field Studies: Vol. 37). 724p. 1997. pap. 40.00 (1-886067-08-2) ASU Office Cultural Res.

— Archaeology of the Sabdo in the Livingston Area of Tonto Basin: Roosevelt Platform Mound Study, Pts. I & II. LC 94-32391. (Anthropological Field Studies: Vol. 32). 1058p. 1994. pap. 46.00 (1-886067-03-1) ASU Office Cultural Res.

— Historical Archaeology of the United States Industrial Indian School at Phoenix: Investigations of a Turn of the Century Trash Dump. LC 96-36561. (Anthropological Field Studies). 1996. 10.00 (1 886067 14 7) AZ State Univ Anthro.

— The Place of the Storehouses Pts. 1 & 2: Roosevelt Platform Mound Study, Report on the Schoolhouse. LC 96-28094. (Anthropological Field Studies: Vol. 35). 998p. 1996. pap. 58.00 (1-886067-06-6) ASU Office Cultural Res.

Lindauer, Steve. Secrets of a Satisfying Lovelife. LC 91-73491. 1991. 17.95 (0-9630158-1-8); pap. 14.95 (0-9630158-2-6) Baker-Hill.

— Secrets of a Satisfying Lovelife. 2nd rev. ed. LC 91-73491. 196p. 1992. pap. 9.95 (0-9630158-3-4) Baker-Hill.

Lindbeck, jt. auth. see Feirer.

Lindbeck, A. Nobel Lectures in Economic Sciences 1969-1980. 500p. 1992. text 86.00 (981-02-0833-2); pap. text 46.00 (981-02-0834-0) World Scientific Pub.

Lindbeck, Assar. Macroeconomics & Economic Policy Vol.1: The Selected Essays of Assar Lindbeck, Vol. 1. (Economists of the Twentieth Century Ser.). 352p. 1993. 100.00 (1-85278-720-1) E Elgar.

— The Selected Essays of Assar Lindbeck, 2 vols. (Economists of the Twentieth Century Ser.). 680p. 1993. 190.00 (1-85278-603-5) E Elgar.

— The Swedish Experiment: Economic & Social Policies in Sweden after WWII. LC 99-179971. (Center Business Studies). 104p. 1997. pap. 39.50 (91-7150-689-6, Pub. by Almqvist Wiksell) Coronet Bks.

— Unemployment & Macroeconomics. LC 92-29465. (Ohlin Lectures: Vol. 3). (Illus.). 213p. 1993. 27.50 (0-262-12175-1) MIT Pr.

— The Welfare State: The Selected Essays of Assar Lindbeck, Vol. II. (Economists of the Twentieth Century Ser.). 328p. 1993. 100.00 (1-85278-721-X) E Elgar.

Lindbeck, Assar, et al. Turning Sweden Around. (Illus.). 249p. 1994. 35.00 (0-262-12181-6) MIT Pr.

Lindbeck, George A. Infallibility. (Pere Marquette Lectures). 1972. 15.00 (0-87462-504-1) Marquette.

— The Nature of Doctrine: Religion & Theology in a Postliberal Age. LC 83-27332. 142p. 1984. pap. 19.95 (0-664-24618-4) Westminster John Knox.

***Lindbeck, Jennifer.** A Collector's Book of Willowware. LC 99-57142. (Illus.). 160p. 2000. pap. 29.95 (0-7643-1055-0) Schiffer.

***Lindbeck, Jennifer A.** Elegant Seneca Glass: Victorian,Depression & Modern. (Illus.). 192p. 2000. 29.95 (0-7643-1141-7) Schiffer.

— Fine Fashion Jewelry from Sarah Coventry. (Illus.). 176p. 2000. pap. 29.95 (0-7643-1142-5) Schiffer.

Lindbeck, John R. Manufacturing Technology. 640p. 1995. pap. text 100.00 (0-13-211690-1) P-H.

Lindbeck, John R. & Kruppa. Basic Manufacturing. (gr. 9-12). 1984. text 31.96 (0-02-662590-3) Glencoe.

Lindbeck, John R. & Wygant, Robert M. Product Design & Manufacture. LC 94-20422. 352p. 1994. 96.00 (0-13-034257-2) P-H.

Lindbeck, John R., et al. Basic Crafts. (gr. 7-12). 1979. text 43.56 (0-02-662430-3) Glencoe.

Lindbeck, John R., jt. auth. see Feirer, John L.

Lindbeck, Susan, jt. auth. see Amoriell, Amelia.

***Lindberg.** Novell Netware 5 Basics. LC 99-31810. 368p. 1999. pap. 29.99 (0-7645-4563-9) IDG Bks.

Lindberg, Alf, jt. ed. see Garegg, Per.

Lindberg, Barbro. Understanding Rett Syndrome: A Practical Guide for Parents, Teachers & Therapists. LC 90-34409. (Illus.), 184p. 1997. text 26.00 (0-88937-033-8) Hogrefe & Huber Pubs.

Lindberg, Becky T. Chelsea Martin Turns Green. Tucker, Kathy, ed. LC 92-31613. (Illus.). 144p. (J). (gr. 2-4). 1993. lib. bdg. 13.95 (0-8075-1134-X) A Whitman.

— Thomas Tuttle Just in Time. LC 93-38606. (Illus.). (J). (gr. 2-4). 1994. lib. bdg. 13.95 (0-8075-7898-3) A Whitman.

Lindberg, Bertil. Cross Stitch Motifs & Borders. 1998. 27.95 (0-7063-7679-X, Pub. by WrLock) Sterling.

— The Future for Telecommunications Equipment & Services. LC 98-120929. (Report Ser.: No. G-198). 150p. 1997. 2750.00 (1-56965-090-X) BCC.

— The Future of Communications Teleconferencing - Audio, Graphics, Data & Video. LC 99-483082. 122p. 1998. 2750.00 (1-56965-096-9, G-199) BCC.

— The Future of Communications Traffic Patterns. LC 98-124890. 114p. 1997. 3150.00 (1-56965-083-7, G-197) BCC.

Lindberg, Bertil C. Troubleshooting Communications Facilities. LC 89-31891. 321p. 1990. 129.00 (0-471-61286-3) Wiley.

Lindberg, Carter. Beyond Charity: Reformation Initiatives for the Poor. LC 92-29963. 208p. 1993. pap. 22.00 (0-8006-2569-2, 1-2569) Augsburg Fortress.

— The European Reformations. (Illus.). 464p. (C). 1996. pap. 33.95 (1-55786-575-2) Blackwell Pubs.

— The Third Reformation: Charismatic Movements & the Lutheran Tradition. LC 83-11371. x, 346p. 1983. 24.95 (0-86554-075-6, MUP/H083) Mercer Univ Pr.

***Lindberg, Carter, ed.** The European Reformations Sourcebook. LC 99-34524. 400p. 1999. text 62.95 (0-631-21361-9); pap. text 29.95 (0-631-21362-7) Blackwell Pubs.

Lindberg, Christer, ed. & intro. see Old Nordenski, Erland.

Lindberg, Christine A., ed. The Oxford American Desk Thesaurus. 528p. 1998. 12.95 (0-19-512674-2) OUP.

— The Oxford American Thesaurus of Current English. LC 99-31092. 863p. 1999. 17.95 (0-19-513375-7) OUP.

Lindberg, Conrad. The Earlier Version of the Wycliffite Bible Vol. 8: The Epistles etc. Edited from Ms. Christ Church 145. (Acta Universitatis Stockholmiensis/ Stockholm Studies in English: Vol. LXXXVII). 376p. (Orig.). 1997. pap. 69.50 (91-22-01745-3, Pub. by Almqvist Wiksell) Coronet Bks.

Lindberg, D. A., ed. see O'Moore, R. R., et al.

Lindberg, David C. The Beginnings of Western Science: The European Scientific Tradition in Philosophical, Religious, & Institutional Context, 600 B. C. to A. D. 1450. LC 91-37741. (Illus.). 474p. 1992. pap. text 22.50 (0-226-48231-6); lib. bdg. 66.00 (0-226-48230-8) U Ch Pr.

— A Catalogue of Medieval & Renaissance Optical Manuscripts. 142p. pap. text 18.29 (0-88844-353-6) Brill Academic Pubs.

Lindberg, David C., ed. John Pecham, Tractatus de Perspectiva. 110p. 1972. pap. 13.00 (1-57659-051-8) Franciscan Inst.

L

— Science in the Middle Ages. LC 78-5367. (Chicago History of Science & Medicine Ser.). (Illus.). 568p. 1980. pap. text 25.00 (0-226-48233-2, P870) U Ch Pr.
Lindberg, David C. & Numbers, Ronald L., eds. God & Nature: Historical Essays on the Encounter Between Christianity & Science. 1986. pap. 24.95 (0-520-05692-2, Pub. by U CA Pr) Cal Prin Full Svc.
— God & Nature: Historical Essays on the Encounter Between Christianity & Science. LC 85-7548. (Illus.). 528p. reprint ed. pap. 163.70 (0-7837-4751-9, 204449800003) Bks Demand.
Lindberg, David C., ed. & tr. see Bacon, Roger.
Lindberg, David C., tr. & intro. see Bacon, Roger.
Lindberg, David G. Theories of Vision from Al-Kindi to Kepler. LC 75-19504. 336p. 1981. reprint ed. pap. text 16.95 (0-226-48235-9) U Ch Pr.
Lindberg, David L., ed. see Pecham, John.
Lindberg, David R. Acmaeidae: Invertebrates of the San Francisco Bay Estuary System, Vol. 2. Lee, Welton L., ed. (Illus.). 1981. text 12.50 (0-910286-72-8) Boxwood.
Lindberg, David S., ed. see Williams, Margaret R.
Lindberg, Duane R. Men of the Cloth & the Social-Cultural Fabric of the Norwegian Ethnic Community in North Dakota. Cordasco, Francesco, ed. LC 80-877. (American Ethnic Groups Ser.). 1981. lib. bdg. 42.95 (0-405-13438-X) Ayer.
Lindberg, G. U. & Krasykova, Z. V., eds. Fishes of the Sea of Japan & the Adjacent Areas of the Sea of Okhotsk & the Yellow Sea, Pt. 4: Gobiodei (CXLV. Fam. Anarhichadidae - CLXXV. Fam. Periophthalmidae) (Russian Translation Ser.: No. 71). (Illus.). 628p. (C). 1990. 142.00 (90-6191-415-9, Pub. by A A Balkema) Ashgate Pub Co.
Lindberg, Gil, ed. 1996 PATA Annual Statistical Report. (Illus.). 133p. 1997. pap. 150.00 (1-882866-11-8) Pac Asia Trvl.
Lindberg, H. E. & Florence, A. L. Dynamic Pulse Buckling: Theory & Experiment. (C). 1987. text 218.00 (90-247-3566-1) Kluwer Academic.
Lindberg, Jan F., jt. auth. see Berliner, Marilyn J.
Lindberg, Jana H. Cross Stitch Animals: More Than 60 Captivating Designs from the World of Nature. (Illus.). 128p. (Orig.). 1996. pap. 16.95 (0-304-34835-X, Pub. by WrLock) Sterling.
***Lindberg, Jana Hauschild.** Cross Stitch Borders & Motifs: Endless Ways to Mix & Match Designs Creating Unique Cross Stitch. 128p. 1999. pap. text 19.95 (0-7063-7837-7) Ward & Ward.
Lindberg, Jana Hauschild. Scandinavian Cross Stitch Designs. (Illus.). 128p. 1998. pap. 19.95 (0-304-34951-8) Continuum.
Lindberg, Janice B. Introduction to Nursing: Concepts, Issues & Opportunities. 3rd ed. LC 97-35556. 448p. 1998. pap. text 29.95 (0-7817-9199-5) Lppncott W & W.
Lindberg, Jeff. Fright Night: Halloween Stories & Poems. 96p. (Orig.). (J). (gr. 3-7). 1996. pap. 2.95 (0-8167-4125-5) Troll Communs.
Lindberg, John. Foundations of Social Survival. LC 72-9590. 260p. 1973. reprint ed. lib. bdg. 65.00 (0-8371-6586-5, LIFS, Greenwood Pr) Greenwood.
Lindberg, John D., ed. see Weise, Christian.
***Lindberg, Jordan J.** Analytic Philosophy: Beginnings to the Present. LC 00-29225. 2000. write for info. (0-7674-1455-1) Mayfield Pub.
Lindberg, Judy. Every Fourth of July. 44p. 1995. pap. 5.00 (1-889806-11-0) Devils Millhopper.
Lindberg, Karen. Addition. Ryan, Shirley V., ed. (Step Ahead Workbooks Ser.). (Illus.). 32p. (J). (ps-3). wbk. ed. 2.09 (0-307-23539-4, 03539, Goldn Books) Gldn Bks Pub Co.
Lindberg, Kathryne V. & Kronick, Joseph G., eds. America's Modernisms: Revaluing the Canon: Essays in Honor of Joseph N. Riddel. LC 95-23249. (Horizons in Theory & American Culture Ser.). (Illus.). 240p. (C). 1996. text 45.00 (0-8071-2018-9) La State U Pr.
Lindberg, Kelley J. Managing Small Netware Networks. 2nd ed. 1996. pap. text 29.99 (0-7821-1906-9) Sybex.
— Novell's Intranetware Administrator's Handbook. LC 96-78238. 576p. 1996. pap. 39.99 incl. disk (0-7645-4517-5) IDG Bks.
— Novell's NetWare 5 Administrator's Handbook. LC TK5105.8.N65L565. 560p. 1999. pap. 39.99 (0-7645-4546-9) IDG Bks.
Lindberg, Kreg, et al, eds. Ecotourism Vol. II: A Guide for Planners & Managers. (Illus.). 244p. (C). 1998. pap. 25.00 (0-9636331-3-9) Ecotourism Soc.
Lindberg, Kreg & Hawkins, Donald E., eds. Ecotourism: A Guide for Planners & Managers, Vol. I. LC 93-70175. (Illus.). 176p. (Orig.). 1993. pap. 22.00 (0-9636331-0-4) Ecotourism Soc.
Lindberg, Kreg, et al. Attitudes, Concerns, & Priorities of Oregon Coast Residents Regarding Tourism & Economic Development: Results from Surveys of Residents in Eight Communities. 48p. 1994. pap. 6.00 (1-881826-04-X) OR Sea Grant.
Lindberg, Leon N. European Community. (Dilemmas in World Politics Ser.). (C). 1996. pap. text 10.95 (0-8133-1056-3) Westview.
— The Political Dynamics of European Economic Integration. LC 63-14129. 381p. 1963. reprint ed. pap. 30.00 (0-608-08293-7, 203097600073) Bks Demand.
Lindberg, Leon N. & Maier, Charles S., eds. The Politics of Inflation & Economic Stagnation. LC 84-23263. 612p. 1985. 44.95 (0-8157-5264-4); pap. 19.95 (0-8157-5263-6) Brookings.
Lindberg, Leon N. & Scheingold, Stuart A., eds. Regional Integration: Theory & Research. LC 77-139717. (Illus.). 439p. 1971. pap. 18.00 (0-674-75327-5) HUP.
Lindberg, Llyod M. Was the Whole World Covered? 16p. 1998. pap. 7.00 (0-8059-4487-7) Dorrance.
Lindberg, Michael, jt. auth. see Todd, Daniel.
Lindberg, Per, et al, eds. International Manufacturing Strategies: Context, Content & Change. LC 97-42288. 516p. 1998. lib. bdg. 154.00 (0-7923-8061-4) Kluwer Academic.
Lindberg, Peter, photos by. Stern Portfolio: Lindberg Smoking Women. (Illus.). 112p. 1998. pap. 19.95 (3-570-12281-6) te Neues.
— 10 Women. (Illus.). 144p. 1996. 35.00 (3-8238-1416-8) te Neues.
Lindberg Press Staff. Big Book of Floral Charted Designs. LC 96-44776. (Illus.). 96p. 1997. pap. 6.95 (0-486-29436-6) Dover.
— Butterfly Charted Designs. (Illus.). 48p. (Orig.). 1988. pap. 3.95 (0-486-25639-1) Dover.
— Charted Bird Designs. 48p. 1990. pap. 2.95 (0-486-26138-7) Dover.
— Children in Charted Designs. (Illus.). 48p. 1989. pap. 2.95 (0-486-25941-2) Dover.
Lindberg Press Staff, ed. Charted Designs for the Kitchen. 48p. (Orig.). 1987. pap. 2.95 (0-486-25496-8) Dover.
— Hearts & Flowers Charted Designs. 48p. (Orig.). 1986. pap. 2.95 (0-486-25111-X) Dover.
— Roses Charted Designs. (Illus.). 32p. (Orig.). 1987. pap. 3.50 (0-486-25523-9) Dover.
— Zodiac Charted Designs for Cross-Stitch Needlepoint & Other Techniques. 48p. 1985. pap. 3.50 (0-486-24932-8) Dover.
Lindberg, R. A. & Braton, N. R. Welding & Other Joining Processes. 1985. pap. text 30.00 (0-9606344-6-0) Blitz Pub Co.
Lindberg, Reeve. Benjamin's Barn. 1994. pap. 4.99 (0-14-054287-6) NAL.
Lindberg, Rich. Passport's Guide to Ethnic Chicago. (Illus.). 300p. 1995. pap. 14.95 (0-8442-9541-8, Passprt Bks) NTC Contemp Pub Co.
Lindberg, Rich & Williams, Biart. The Armchair Companion to Chicago Sports. LC 97-23285. 272p. (Orig.). 1997. pap. 10.95 (1-888952-60-1) Cumberland Hse.
Lindberg, Rich, et al, eds. Ethnic Chicago. 2nd ed. (Illus.). 400p. 1997. pap. 16.95 (0-8442-8994-9, 89949, Passprt Bks) NTC Contemp Pub Co.
Lindberg, Richard. Chicago by Gaslight: A History of Chicago's Underworld, 1880-1920. (Illus.). 236p. 1995. pap. 14.00 (0-89733-421-3) Academy Chi Pubs.
***Lindberg, Richard.** Return to the Scene of the Crime: A Guide to Infamous Places in Chicago. LC 99-27633. (Illus.). 304p. 1999. pap. 16.95 (1-58182-013-5) Cumberland Hse.
Lindberg, Richard. To Serve & Collect: Chicago Politics & Police Corruption from the Lager Beer Riot to the Summerdale Scandal, 1855-1960. LC 98-18571. (Illus.). 375p. 1998. reprint ed. 19.95 (0-8093-2223-4) S Ill U Pr.
Lindberg, Richard C. To Serve & Collect: Chicago Politics & Police Corruption from the Lager Beer Riot to the Summerdale Scandal. LC 90-38713. 384p. 1991. 55.00 (0-275-93415-2, C3415, Praeger Pubs) Greenwood.
— The White Sox Encyclopedia. LC 95-48446. (Baseball Encyclopedias of North America Ser.). 592p. (C). 1997. 59.95 (1-56639-449-X) Temple U Pr.
Lindberg, Richard C., ed. Quotable Chicago. 231p. (Orig.). 1996. pap. 9.95 (0-8294-0927-0, Wild Onion) Loyola Pr.
Lindberg, Rick. Stuck on the Sox. 192p. (Orig.). 1978. pap. 1.95 (0-930528-02-6) Sassafras Pr.
Lindberg, Rick & Brenner, Marty. Robust Aeroservoelastic Stability Analysis: Flight Test Applications. LC 98-52346. (Advances in Industrial Control Ser.). 1999. write for info. (1-85233-069-4) Spr-Verlag.
Lindberg, Roderick L. Cousin Eddy Motorhome & Towing Truck Performance. (Illus.). 126p. 1997. pap. 21.95 (0-9660859-0-6) Seamat Pub.
Lindberg, Roy A. Processes & Materials of Manufacture. 4th ed. (Illus.). 848p. (C). 1989. text 63.00 (0-205-11817-8, H18179) P-H.
— Processes & Materials of Manufacture. 4th ed. (Illus.). 848p. 1990. teacher ed. write for info. (0-318-63888-6, H18187); teacher ed. write for info. (0-318-63887-8, H18195) P-H.
Lindberg, Roy A., jt. auth. see Cohn, Theodore.
Lindberg, S. E., et al, eds. Acidic Precipitation. (Advances in Environmental Science Ser.: Vol. 3). (Illus.). xiv, 332p. 1989. 129.00 (0-685-31289-5, 2993) Spr-Verlag.
Lindberg, Sarah, ed. see Hoyland, Terri R.
Lindberg-Seyersted, Brita. Black & Female: Essays on Writings by Black Women in the Diaspora. 164p. 1994. 24.00 (82-00-03956-0) Scandnvan Univ Pr.
Lindberg-Seyersted, Brita, ed. A Literary Friendship: Correspondence Between Caroline Gordon & Ford Madox Ford. LC 98-40213. 152p. 1999. 22.50 (1-57233-046-5, Pub. by U of Tenn Pr) U Ch Pr.
Lindberg, Staffan & Sverrisson, Arni. Social Movements in Development: The Challenge of Globalization & Democratization. LC 96-9721. (International Political Economy Ser.). (Illus.). 296p. 1997. text 59.95 (0-312-16472-6) St Martin.
Lindberg, Stanley W. The Legacy of Erskine Caldwell. (Georgia Humanities Council Publications). (Illus.). 64p. 1991. pap. 9.95 (0-8203-1315-7) U of Ga Pr.
Lindberg, T., et al. Ecology of Arable Land: Organisms, Carbon & Nitrogen Cycling. Andren, O., ed. (Ecological Bulletins Ser.: No. 40). 221p. 1990. 300.00 (87-16-10605-9) Mosby Inc.
Lindberg, Thomas, ed. Strategies & Tactics in Organic Synthesis, Vol. 1. (Illus.). 370p. 1993. reprint ed. pap. text 48.00 (0-12-450275-X) Acad Pr.
— Strategies & Tactics in Organic Synthesis, Vol. 2. 507p. 1988. text 146.00 (0-12-450281-4) Acad Pr.
— Strategies & Tactics in Organic Synthesis, Vol. 3. (Illus.). 544p. 1991. text 161.00 (0-12-450282-2) Acad Pr.
Lindbergh. International Law Dictionary. 1993. lib. bdg. 77.50 (90-6544-697-4) Kluwer Academic.
— The Worry Week. (J). (gr. 3-7). 1988. pap. 2.95 (0-380-70394-7, Avon Bks) Morrow Avon.
Lindbergh, Anne M. Bailey's Window. LC 83-18360. (Illus.). 132p. (J). (gr. 3-7). 1984. 14.95 (0-15-205642-4, Harcourt Child Bks) Harcourt.
— Bailey's Window. 144p. (YA). 1991. pap. 3.50 (0-380-70767-5, Avon Bks) Morrow Avon.
— Bring Me a Unicorn: Diaries & Letters of Anne Morrow Lindbergh, 1922-1928. (Illus.). 288p. 1993. pap. 8.95 (0-15-614164-7) Harcourt.
— Dearly Beloved. 202p. 1991. reprint ed. lib. bdg. 37.95 (0-89966-790-2) Buccaneer Bks.
— Earth Shine. LC 77-84877. (Helen & Kurt Wolff Bk.). 1969. 6.95 (0-15-127236-0) Harcourt.
— Flower & the Nettle: Diaries & Letters of Anne Morrow Lindbergh, 1936-1939. (Illus.). 636p. 1994. pap. 15.95 (0-15-631942-X) Harcourt.
— Gift from the Sea. 132p. 1991. 16.00 (0-679-40683-2) Pantheon.
— Gift from the Sea. LC 90-50140. 144p. 1991. pap. 8.95 (0-679-73241-1) Vin Bks.
— Gift from the Sea. large type ed. 224p. 1995. 18.00 (0-679-44532-3) Random Hse Lrg Prnt.
— The Hunky-Dory Dairy. LC 85-16408. (Illus.). 160p. (J). (gr. 3-6). 1986. 14.95 (0-15-237449-3, Harcourt Child Bks) Harcourt.
— Hunky-Dory Dairy. 160p. (J). (gr. 3-7). 1987. pap. 2.75 (0-380-70320-3, Avon Bks) Morrow Avon.
***Lindbergh, Anne M.** Local Vertical. Perrin, Noel & Lindbergh, Reeve, eds. 96p. 2000. pap. 15.95 (1-56792-125-6) Godine.
Lindbergh, Anne M. Locked Rooms & Open Doors: Diaries & Letters of Anne Morrow Lindbergh, 1933-1935. (Illus.). 380p. 1993. pap. 12.95 (0-15-652956-4) Harcourt.
— Nobody's Orphan. (J). (gr. 3-7). 1987. pap. 2.95 (0-380-70395-5, Avon Bks) Morrow Avon.
— North to the Orient. LC 35-27279. 168p. 1966. pap. 10.00 (0-15-667140-9, Harvest Bks) Harcourt.
— The People in Pineapple Place. LC 82-47935. 153p. (J). (gr. 3-7). 1982. 14.95 (0-15-260517-7, Harcourt Child Bks) Harcourt.
— The People in Pineapple Place. 160p. (J). (gr. 4-5). 1990. pap. 2.95 (0-380-70766-7, Avon Bks) Morrow Avon.
— The Prisoner of Pineapple Place. LC 87-28815. 173p. (J). (gr. 3-7). 1988. 13.95 (0-15-263559-9, Harcourt Child Bks) Harcourt.
— The Prisoner of Pineapple Place. 192p. (J). 1990. pap. 2.95 (0-380-70765-9, Avon Bks) Morrow Avon.
— The Shadow on the Dial. LC 86-45783. 160p. (J). (gr. 5-8). 1987. 12.95 (0-06-023882-8) HarpC Child Bks.
— The Shadow on the Dial. (J). (gr. 3-7). 1988. pap. 2.75 (0-380-70545-1, Avon Bks) Morrow Avon.
— Three Lives to Live. (J). (gr. 3-6). 1995. reprint ed. per. 3.50 (0-671-86732-6, Minstrel Bks) PB.
— Tidy Lady. LC 88-10905. (Illus.). 50p. (J). (ps-3). 1989. 13.95 (0-15-287150-0) Harcourt.
— War Within & Without: Diaries & Letters, Nineteen Thirty-Nine to Nineteen Forty-Four. LC 79-21614. 536p. 1980. 14.95 (0-15-194661-2) Harcourt.
— The Worry Week. LC 84-19299. (Illus.). 144p. (J). (gr. 3-7). 1985. 12.95 (0-15-299675-3, Harcourt Child Bks) Harcourt.
Lindbergh, Charles A., Jr. The Autobiography of Values. (Illus.). 448p. 1992. pap. 14.95 (0-15-609402-9, Harvest Bks) Harcourt.
— Banking, Currency, the Money Trust & War, 3 vols. 1972. 300.00 (0-87968-704-5) Gordon Pr.
— Boyhood on the Upper Mississippi: A Reminiscent Letter. LC 72-75804. (Illus.). 50p. (J). (gr. 4-12). 1972. reprint ed. pap. 7.95 (0-87351-217-0) Minn Hist.
— Radio Speeches of Charles A. Lindbergh: 1939-1940. 1982. lib. bdg. 250.00 (0-87700-455-2) Revisionist Pr.
— The Spirit of St. Louis. LC 87-20352. (Illus.). 562p. 1975. 60.00 (0-684-14421-2) S&S Trade.
— The Spirit of St. Louis. (Scribner Classics). (Illus.). 576p. 1998. 34.50 (0-684-85277-2) S&S Trade.
— The Spirit of St. Louis. LC 97-77925. (Adventure Library: No. 15). (Illus.). 472p. 1998. reprint ed. lib. bdg. 35.00 (1-885283-13-X) Advent Library.
— The Spirit of St. Louis. LC 93-4148. xviii, 562p. 1993. reprint ed. pap. 14.95 (0-87351-288-X, Borealis Book) Minn Hist.
— The Wartime Journals of Charles A. Lindbergh. LC 78-124830. 1038p. 1970. 19.95 (0-15-194625-6) Harcourt.
— We. 1976. 25.95 (0-8488-1412-6) Amereon Ltd.
— We. (Illus.). 368p. 1991. reprint ed. lib. bdg. 37.95 (0-89966-832-1) Buccaneer Bks.
Lindbergh, E. Dictionary of International Law. (GER, ENG & FRE.). 440p. 1993. pap. 150.00 (0-320-03105-5) Fr & Eur.
Lindbergh, E. International Legal Dictionary. 440p. 1993. boxed set 75.00 (0-316-52633-9, Aspen Law & Bus) Aspen Pub.
Lindbergh, Ernest A. International Law Dictionary: English - French - German. 448p. (C). 1992. 72.00 (1-85431-119-0, Pub. by Blackstone Pr) Gaunt.
***Lindbergh, Peter.** Images of Women. (Illus.). 300p. 2000. pap. 55.00 (3-8238-5484-4) te Neues.
Lindbergh, Peter, photos by. Images of Women. (Illus.). 300p. 1997. 120.00 (3-8238-2120-2) te Neues.
Lindbergh, Reeve. The Awful Aardvarks Go to School. LC 97-8820. (Illus.). 32p. (J). 1997. 15.99 (0-670-85920-6) Viking Penguin.
***Lindbergh, Reeve.** Awful Aardvarks Go to School. (Picture Puffin Ser.). (Illus.). 32p. (J). 2000. pap. 5.99 (0-14-055488-2, PuffinBks) Peng Put Young Read.
— Awful Aardvarks Shop for School. (Illus.). (J). 2000. 15.99 (0-670-88763-3, Viking Child) Peng Put Young Read.
Lindbergh, Reeve. The Circle of Days. LC 96-49848. (Illus.). 32p. (J). (gr. k-7). 1998. 15.99 (0-7636-0357-0) Candlewick Pr.
— Day the Goose Got Loose. 1995. 10.19 (0-606-07420-1, Pub. by Turtleback) Demco.
— Grandfather's Lovesong. 1995. 10.19 (0-606-07591-7, Pub. by Turtleback) Demco.
— If I'd Known Then What I Know Now. LC 93-24058. 1996. 10.19 (0-606-09458-X, Pub. by Turtleback) Demco.
***Lindbergh, Reeve.** In Every Tiny Grain of Sand: A Child's Book of Prayers & Praise. LC 99-89379. (Illus.). 80p. (YA). (ps up). 2000. 21.99 (0-7636-0176-4) Candlewick Pr.
Lindbergh, Reeve. Johnny Appleseed. 32p. (J). (gr. k-3). 1993. pap. 5.95 (0-316-52634-7) Little.
— Johnny Appleseed: A Poem. (J). 1990. 11.15 (0-606-05893-1, Pub. by Turtleback) Demco.
— Midnight Farm. (J). 1995. 11.19 (0-606-07869-X) Turtleback.
— The Names of the Mountains. large type ed. LC 93-18466. 344p. 1993. reprint ed. lib. bdg. 21.95 (1-56054-695-6) Thorndike Pr.
— The Names of the Mountains: A Novel. 224p. 1992. 19.00 (0-671-73148-3) S&S Trade.
— Nobody Owns the Sky: The Story of "Brave Bessie" Coleman. LC 96-6901. (Illus.). 32p. (J). (gr. 1-4). 1996. 15.99 (1-56402-533-0) Candlewick Pr.
***Lindbergh, Reeve.** Nobody Owns the Sky: The Story of "Brave Bessie" Coleman. (J). 1998. 11.19 (0-606-13668-1, Pub. by Turtleback) Demco.
Lindbergh, Reeve. Nobody Owns the Sky: The Story of "Brave Bessie" Coleman. LC 96-6901. (Illus.). 32p. (J). (gr. 1-4). 1998. reprint ed. pap. 5.99 (0-7636-0361-9) Candlewick Pr.
— North Country Spring. LC 95-52366. (Illus.). 32p. (J). 1997. 15.95 (0-395-82819-8) HM.
— North Country Spring. LC 95-52366. (Illus.). (J). 1997. write for info. (0-316-52710-6) Little.
— Que es el Sol? Uribe, Veronica, tr.Tr. of What Is the Sun?. (SPA., Illus.). 32p. (J). (gr. k-2). 1998. 14.95 (1-880507-37-4) Lectorum Pubns.
— Under a Wing: A Memoir. 224p. 1999. pap. 12.95 (0-385-33444-3, Dell Trade Pbks) Dell.
— Under a Wing: A Memoir. LC 98-30111. (Illus.). 223p. (YA). (gr. 8 up). 1998. 23.00 (0-684-80770-X) Simon & Schuster.
***Lindbergh, Reeve.** Under a Wing: A Memoir. large type unabridged ed. 1999. 26.95 (0-7531-5733-0, 157330, Pub. by ISIS Lrg Prnt) ISIS Pub.
— Visit. (J). 1999. 14.95 (0-8037-1189-1, Dial Yng Read) Peng Put Young Read.
Lindbergh, Reeve. What Is the Sun? LC 93-3557. (Illus.). (J). (ps up). 1996. pap. 4.99 (1-56402-609-4) Candlewick Pr.
— What Is the Sun? LC 93-3557. 1996. 10.19 (0-606-10051-2, Pub. by Turtleback) Demco.
***Lindbergh, Reeve & Carter, Abby.** The Hippie Grandmother. LC 00-37964. (Illus.). (J). 2002. write for info. (0-7636-0671-5) Candlewick Pr.
Lindbergh, Reeve, ed. see Lindbergh, Anne M.
Lindblad, A. S., et al, eds. Continuous Ambulatory Peritoneal Dialysis in the U. S. A. (Developments in Nephrology Ser.). (C). 1989. text 207.50 (0-7923-0179-X) Kluwer Academic.
Lindblad, Carl & Druben, Laurel. Small Farm Grain Storage, Vol. I. (Illus.). 204p. 1976. 12.50 (0-86619-052-X) Vols Tech Asst.
— Small Farm Grain Storage, Vol. II. (Illus.). 170p. 1976. 12.50 (0-86619-053-8) Vols Tech Asst.
— Small Farm Grain Storage, Vol. III. (Illus.). 148p. 1976. 12.50 (0-86619-054-6) Vols Tech Asst.
— Small Farm Grain Storage: Almacenamiento del Grano. (SPA., Illus.). 331p. 1976. 19.95 (0-86619-072-4) Vols Tech Asst.
Lindblad, Carl, jt. auth. see Harris, Kenton.
Lindblad-Goldberg, Marion, et al. Creating Competence from Chaos: A Comprehensive Guide to Home-Based Services. LC 98-20695. 224p. 1998. 39.00 (0-393-70264-2) Norton.
Lindblad, Goran. Non-Equilibrium Entropy & Irreversibility. 1983. text 139.00 (90-277-1640-4) Kluwer Academic.
Lindblad, Ishrat & Ljung, Magnus, eds. Proceedings from the Third Nordic Conference for English Studies, 2 vols., Set. (Stokholm Studies in English: LXXIII). 806p. (Orig.). 1987. pap. text 108.00 (91-22-00870-5) Coronet Bks.
Lindblad, J. Historical Foundations of a National Economy in Indonesia. LC 97-103309. 436p. pap. 59.50 (0-444-85807-5) Elsevier.
Lindblad, K. E. Noah Webster's Pronunciation & Modern New England Speech. (Essays & Studies on American Language & Literature: Vol. 11). (Orig.). 1954. pap. 25.00 (0-8115-0191-4) Periodicals Srv.
Lindblad, Lisa. Bamboo. (J). 1996. write for info. (0-7868-0191-3) Hyperion.
— Bamboo. (J). 1996. lib. bdg. write for info. (0-7868-2162-0) Hyprn Child.
— The Serengeti Migration. LC 93-26338. (Illus.). 40p. (J). (gr. 3-7). 1994. 15.95 (1-56282-668-9, Pub. by Hyprn Child); lib. bdg. 15.89 (1-56282-669-7, Pub. by Hyprn Child) Little.
Lindblad, Owen. Full of Fair Hope: A History of St. Mary's Mission. (Illus.). 280p. (Orig.). 1997. pap. 19.95 (0-9652044-5-6) Park Pr MN.

An Asterisk (*) at the beginning of an entry indicates that the title is appearing for the first time.

Lindblad, Perolof & Sandqvist, Aage. Barred Galaxies & Circumnuclear Activity: Proceedings of the Nobel Symposium 98, Held at Stockholm Observatory, Saltsjobaden, Sweden, 30 November-3 December 1995. LC 96-30573. (Lecture Notes in Physics Ser.: Vol. 474). 1996. 78.00 (*3-540-61571-7*) Spr-Verlag.

Lindblad, Sven-Olof, et al. Baja: A Special Expedition to Baja & the Sea of Cortez. 64p. 1995. pap. write for info. (*0-9641652-1-X*) Spec Expedit.

***Lindblad, Thomas, et al, eds.** Virtual Intelligence/Dynamic Neural Networks. 610p. 1999. pap. text 111.00 (*0-8194-3202-4*) SPIE.

Lindblad, Thomas & Kinser, Jason M. Image Processing Using Pulse-Coupled Neural Networks. Taylor, J. G., ed. LC 98-13421. (Perspectives in Neural Computing Ser.). (Illus.). x, 150p. 1998. pap. 59.95 (*3-540-76264-7*) Spr-Verlag.

Lindblad, Thomas, jt. ed. see Padgett, Mary L.

Lindblad, Ulrika, tr. see Braulik, Georg.

Lindblade, Frank. The Spirit Which Is from God. (Illus.). 288p. (Orig.). 1995. reprint ed. pap. 9.95 (*0-9646289-1-0*) Christian Life Bks.

Lindblom. Group Actions & the Role of Courts - a European Perspective, Vol. FOIN 23. 1997. 24.50 (*90-411-0379-1*) Kluwer Law Intl.

Lindblom, Charles E. Inquiry & Change: The Troubled Attempt to Understand & Shape Society. 336p. (C). 1992. reprint ed. pap. 19.00 (*0-300-05667-2*) Yale U Pr.

— Politics & Markets: The World's Political-Economic Systems. LC 77-75250. 416p. 1980. pap. 20.00 (*0-465-05958-9*, Pub. by Basic) HarpC.

— The Science of "Muddling Through" (Reprint Series in Social Sciences). (C). 1993. reprint ed. pap. text 5.00 (*0-8290-3504-4*, PS-169) Irvington.

Lindblom, Charles E. & Woodhouse, Edward J. The Policy Making Process: Foundations of Modern Political Science Ser. 3rd ed. LC 92-28729. 176p. (C). 1992. pap. text 32.80 (*0-13-682360-2*) P-H.

Lindblom, Charles E., jt. auth. see Dahl, Robert A.

Lindblom, Johannes. Prophecy in Ancient Israel. LC 63-907. 480p. reprint ed. pap. 148.80 (*0-608-15450-4*, 202929800060) Bks Demand.

Lindblom, Steve. Flying the Hot Ones. (J). (gr. 3-7). 1990. write for info. (*0-318-66741-X*) HM.

Lindbloom, Carl G., jt. auth. see Moskowitz, Harvey S.

Lindbloom, Eric, photos by. Angels at the Arno. LC 93-50142. (Illus.). 1994. 35.00 (*0-87923-974-3*) Godine.

— Angels at the Arno. (Illus.). 84p. 1995. pap. 19.95 (*0-87923-994-8*) Godine.

Lindbloom, Erik, jt. auth. see McCahill, Margaret E.

Lindbom, Annie, jt. auth. see Venge, Per.

Lindbom, Annie, jt. ed. see Venge, Per.

Lindborg, Bonnie, ed. Home Owner's Guide to Free Heat. 2nd ed. (Illus.). 90p. 1991. reprint ed. pap., spiral bd. 14.95 (*0-9632945-0-4*) Sunstore Farms.

Lindborg, Henry J. The Basics of Cross-Functional Teams. LC 97-28136. (Illus.). 84p. 1997. pap. 7.95 (*0-527-76332-2*, 763322) Productivity Inc.

Lindborg, Kristina, tr. see Simic, Marjorie R.

Lindburg, jt. auth. see Strum.

Lindburg, Donald G., jt. ed. see Fa, John E.

Linde, Barbara M. The Color Purple: A Unit Plan. 160p. 1998. teacher ed., ring bd. 26.95 (*1-58337-215-6*) Teachers Pet Pubns.

— A Day No Pigs Would Die: A Unit Plan. 166p. 1997. teacher ed., ring bd. 26.95 (*1-58337-158-3*) Teachers Pet Pubns.

— Dr. Jekyll & Mr. Hyde: A Unit Plan. 158p. 1997. teacher ed., ring bd. 26.95 (*1-58337-159-1*) Teachers Pet Pubns.

— Flowers for Algernon: A Unit Plan. 170p. 1996. teacher ed., ring bd. 26.95 (*1-58337-151-6*) Teachers Pet Pubns.

— The Giver: A Unit Plan. 189p. 1997. teacher ed., ring bd. 26.95 (*1-58337-160-5*) Teachers Pet Pubns.

— Hatchet: A Unit Plan. 174p. 1996. teacher ed., ring bd. 26.95 (*1-58337-161-3*) Teachers Pet Pubns.

— The House on Mango Street: A Unit Plan. 160p. 1998. teacher ed., ring bd. 26.95 (*1-58337-210-5*) Teachers Pet Pubns.

— I Know Why the Caged Bird Sings: A Unit Plan. 168p. 1995. teacher ed., ring bd. 26.95 (*1-58337-150-8*) Teachers Pet Pubns.

— Johnny Tremain: A Unit Plan. 180p. 1996. teacher ed., ring bd. 26.95 (*1-58337-157-5*) Teachers Pet Pubns.

— Joy Luck Club: A Unit Plan. 160p. 1998. teacher ed., ring bd. 26.95 (*1-58337-214-8*) Teachers Pet Pubns.

— Light in the Forest: A Unit Plan. 166p. 1996. teacher ed., ring bd. 26.95 (*1-58337-155-9*) Teachers Pet Pubns.

— Maniac Magee: A Unit Plan. 208p. 1997. teacher ed., ring bd. 26.95 (*1-58337-162-1*) Teachers Pet Pubns.

— Merchant of Venice: A Unit Plan. 160p. 1999. teacher ed., ring bd. 26.95 (*1-58337-216-4*) Teachers Pet Pubns.

— Night: A Unit Plan. 158p. 1998. teacher ed., ring bd. 26.95 (*1-58337-166-4*) Teachers Pet Pubns.

— The River: A Unit Plan. 182p. 1996. teacher ed., ring bd. 26.95 (*1-58337-165-6*) Teachers Pet Pubns.

— Rumblefish: A Unit Plan. 168p. 1996. teacher ed., ring bd. 26.95 (*1-58337-163-X*) Teachers Pet Pubns.

— Scorpions: A Unit Plan. 160p. 1998. teacher ed., ring bd. 26.95 (*1 58337-209-1*) Teachers Pet Pubns.

— That Was Then; This Is Now: A Unit Plan. 172p. 1997. teacher ed., ring bd. 26.95 (*1-58337-164-8*) Teachers Pet Pubns.

— Their Eyes Were Watching God: A Unit Plan. 172p. 1995. teacher ed., ring bd. 26.95 (*1-58337-152-4*) Teachers Pet Pubns.

— Things Fall Apart: A Unit Plan. 166p. 1995. teacher ed., ring bd. 26.95 (*1-58337-154-0*) Teachers Pet Pubns.

— Where the Red Fern Grows: A Unit Plan. 178p. 1996. teacher ed., ring bd. 26.95 (*1-58337-153-2*) Teachers Pet Pubns.

Linde, Barbara M. & Anaya, Rudolfo A. Bless Me Ultima: A Unit Plan. 184p. 1996. teacher ed., ring bd. 26.95 (*1-58337-156-7*) Teachers Pet Pubns.

Linde, Barbara M., jt. auth. see Sherman, Janine.

Linde, A. Particle Physics & Inflationary Cosmology. Feshbach, Herman, ed. (Contemporary Concepts in Physics Ser.: Vol. 1). xviii, 362p. 1990. text 101.00 (*3-7186-0489-2*); pap. text 48.00 (*3-7186-0490-6*) Gordon & Breach.

Linde, Ada Van Der, see Van Der Linde, Ada.

Linde, Anders. Dentin & Dentinogenesis. 168p. 1984. 96.00 (*0-8493-5201-0*, QM569, CRC Reprint) Franklin.

— Dentin & Dentinogenesis, Vol. 1. LC 83-7714. 176p. 1984. 104.00 (*0-8493-5200-2*, QM569, CRC Reprint) Franklin.

Linde, Antonius Van Der, see Van Der Linde, Antonius.

Linde, Charlotte. Life Stories: The Creation of Coherence. LC 92-25763. (Oxford Studies in Sociolinguistics). 256p. 1993. pap. text 21.00 (*0-19-507373-8*) OUP.

Linde, D. Night Is Fallin' in My Heart. (Piano-Vocal-Guitar Ser.). 8p. 1994. pap. 3.95 (*0-7935-4285-5*, 00351047) H Leonard.

Linde, H. M., tr. from GER. The Recorder Player's Handbook. rev. ed. 1974. pap. 29.95 (*0-930448-11-1*, ST12322) Eur-Am Music.

Linde, Hans A., et al. Legislative & Administrative Processes. 2nd ed. LC 81-4738. (University Casebook Ser.). 887p. 1991. reprint ed. text 37.00 (*0-88277-026-8*) Foundation Pr.

Linde, Helmut. Baedeker's Istanbul. Hogarth, James, tr. (Baedeker's City Guides Ser.). (Illus.). 240p. (Orig.). 1988. pap. 12.95 (*0-13-058207-7*) P-H.

Linde, J., ed. The Ingredients Vol. 1: Fresh Pacific Northwest Cuisine. 111p. 1996. 12.95 (*1-888561-02-5*) Tools for Life.

Linde, Karen & Hoehn, Robert G. Girls' Softball: A Complete Guide for Players & Coaches. LC 85-3653. 208p. (C). 1985. text 27.95 (*0-13-356734-6*, Parker Publishing Co) P-H.

Linde, Laurel van der, see Van der Linde, Laurel.

Linde, Lavaun & Quishenberry, Mary. Daniel & the Big Cats: Level One. (Bible Stories for Early Readers Ser.: Bk. 5). (Illus.). 32p. (J). (gr. 1). 1986. pap. text 4.99 (*0-945107-04-8*) Bradshaw Pubs.

— God Adds Oil: Level Two. (Bible Stories for Early Readers Ser.: Bk. 1). (Illus.). 32p. (Orig.). (J). (gr. 1). 1988. pap. text 4.99 (*0-945107-05-6*) Bradshaw Pubs.

— I Will Help: Level One. (Bible Stories for Early Readers Ser.: Bk. 2). (Illus.). 32p. (Orig.). (J). (gr. 1). 1986. pap. text 4.99 (*0-945107-01-3*) Bradshaw Pubs.

— Jonah's Ride, No. 2. (Bible Stories for Early Readers Ser.: Bk. 5). (Illus.). 32p. (Orig.). (J). (gr. 1). 1988. pap. text 4.99 (*0-945107-09-9*) Bradshaw Pubs.

— The Lad's Bag: Level One. (Bible Stories for Early Readers Ser.: Bk. 4). (Illus.). 32p. (J). (gr. 1). 1986. pap. text 4.99 (*0-945107-03-X*) Bradshaw Pubs.

— Mom & the Lad, Level 1. (Bible Stories for Early Readers Ser.: Bk. 3). (Illus.). 32p. (J). (gr. 1). 1986. pap. text 4.99 (*0-945107-02-1*) Bradshaw Pubs.

— Not a Bed: Level One. (Bible Stories for Early Readers Ser.: Bk. 1). (Illus.). 32p. (Orig.). (J). (gr. 1). 1986. pap. text 4.99 (*0-945107-00-5*) Bradshaw Pubs.

— Seven Dips: Level Two. (Bible Stories for Early Readers Ser.: Bk. 4). (Illus.). 32p. (Orig.). (J). (gr. 1). 1988. pap. text 4.99 (*0-945107-08-0*) Bradshaw Pubs.

— Three Brave Men: Level Two. (Bible Stories for Early Readers Ser.: Bk. 3). (Illus.). 32p. (Orig.). (J). (gr. 1). 1988. pap. text 4.99 (*0-945107-07-2*) Bradshaw Pubs.

— Zacchaeus' Cash Bag, Level Two. (Bible Stories for Early Readers Ser.: Bk. 2). (Illus.). 32p. (Orig.). (J). (gr. 1). 1988. pap. text 4.99 (*0-945107-06-4*) Bradshaw Pubs.

Linde, Leonard M., jt. ed. see Kawaguchi, Akira T.

Linde, Nancy. The Orange Cat Bistro. 192p. 1996. 18.95 (*1-57566-050-4*, Knsington) Kensgtn Pub Corp.

— The Orange Cat Bistro. 1997. pap. 5.50 (*1-57566-132-2*, Knsington); pap. 12.00 (*1-57566-151-9*, Knsington) Kensgtn Pub Corp.

Linde, Peter. Numerical Modelling & Capacity Design of Earthquake-Resistant Reinforced Concrete Walls. LC 93-37013. (Report of the Institute of Structural Engineering ETH Zurich Ser.: No. 200). 236p. 1994. 76.00 (*0-8176-2968-8*) Birkhauser.

Linde, Polly Van der, see Van der Linde, Polly.

Linde, Richard M., jt. auth. see Wakita, Osamu A.

Linde, Shirley. The World's Most Intimate Cruises. (Illus.). 360p. 1998. pap. 16.95 (*1-883323-90-8*) Open Rd Pub.

Linde, Shirley & Carrow, Donald J., eds. The Directory of Holistic Medicine & Alternate Health Care Services in the U. S. LC 85-13193. 264p. 1986. pap. 6.95 (*0-932090-18-4*) Mosby Inc.

Linde, Shirley, jt. auth. see Allen, Robert F.

Linde, Shirley, jt. auth. see Hauri, Peter J.

Linde, Shirley, jt. auth. see Hoffstein, Victor.

Linde, Shirley M., jt. auth. see Breecher, Maury M.

Linde, Tasha Van der, see Van der Linde, Polly & Van der Linde, Tasha.

Linde, Terry. The Fat Monkey: The Final Edge to Metabolic Control. 70p. 1994. 19.95 incl. VHS (*1-888561-00-9*, IA Pubns) Tools for Life.

Linde, Werner. Infinitely Divisible & Stables Measures on Banach Spaces. 202p. (C). 1983. 75.00 (*0-7855-4986-2*, Pub. by Collets) St Mut.

Lindeberg, J. F., ed. Safety of Computer Control Systems, 1991: Proceedings of the IFAC-IFIP-EWICS-SRE Symposium, Trondheim, Norway, 30 October - 1 November 1991. (IFAC Symposia Ser.). 200p. 1991. 73.00 (*0-08-041697-7*, Pergamon Pr) Elsevier.

Lindeberg, Tony. Scale-Space Theory in Computer Vision. LC 93-23648. 440p. (C). 1993. lib. bdg. 130.00 (*0-7923-2636-9*) Kluwer Academic.

— Scale-Space Theory in Computer Vision. 440p. (C). 1994. text 197.00 (*0-7923-9418-6*) Kluwer Academic.

Lindeberry, Heather S. Benito Huerta: Preserve, Negate, Transcend. (Illus.). 32p. 1994. pap. write for info. (*1-879286-08-4*) AZ Bd Regents.

Lindeboom, G. A. Herman Boerhaave: The Man & His Work. (History of Science Ser.). (Illus.). 500p. 1999. 65.00 (*90-5235-137-6*, Pub. by Erasmus Pub) Balogh.

— The Letters of Jan Swammerdam to Melchisedec Thevenot, with English Translation & a Biographical Sketch. 202p. 1975. text 94.50 (*90-265-0222-2*) Swets.

Lindeburg, Michael R. Civil Engineering Reference Manual for the PE Exam. 7th ed. LC 99-15710. 1472p. 1999. student ed. 99.95 (*1-888577-40-1*, CERM7) Prof Pubns CA.

***Lindeburg, Michael R.** Civil Engineering Sample Examination. 5th ed. 88p. 2000. pap. 24.95 (*1-888577-60-6*) Prof Pubns CA.

Lindeburg, Michael R. Consolidated Gas Dynamics Tables. (Engineering Reference Manual Ser.). 88p. (C). 1989. pap. text 26.95 (*0-932276-96-2*) Prof Pubns CA.

— Engineer-in-Training Reference Manual. 8th ed. LC 91-66398. (Engineering Reference Manual Ser.). 1064p. (C). 1992. 69.95 (*0-912045-56-6*) Prof Pubns CA.

— Engineering Economic Analysis: An Introduction. (Engineering Reference Manual Ser.). (Illus.). 234p. (Orig.). 1993. pap. 24.95 (*0-912045-60-4*) Prof Pubns CA.

— Engineering Unit Conversions. 4th ed. LC 98-37575. 160p. (C). 1999. 29.95 (*1-888577-33-9*) Prof Pubns CA.

***Lindeburg, Michael R.** FE Review Manual: Rapid Preparation for the General Fundamentals of Engineering Exam. 850p. 2000. pap. 52.95 (*1-888577-53-3*) Prof Pubns CA.

Lindeburg, Michael R. FE/EIT Sample Examinations. LC 98-32100. 111p. 1999. pap. 28.95 (*1-888577-38-X*, FESE) Prof Pubns CA.

— Fire & Explosion Protection Systems: A Design Professional's Introduction. 2nd ed. LC 94-23456. (Engineering Reference Manual Ser.). (Illus.). 88p. 1995. pap. 34.95 (*0-912045-82-5*, FIRE2) Prof Pubns CA.

— Mechanical Engineering Reference Manual for the PE Exam. 10th ed. LC 97-7741. (Engineering Reference Manual Ser.). 1300p. 1997. 89.95 (*1-888577-13-4*, MERMIO) Prof Pubns CA.

— Mechanical Engineering Sample Exam. 3rd ed. LC 97-31464. 52p. 1997. pap. 29.95 (*1-888577-17-7*) Prof Pubns CA.

— 101 Solved Civil Engineering Problems. 3rd ed. LC 96-24168. 185p. 1999. pap. 39.95 (*1-888577-32-0*) Prof Pubns CA.

— 101 Solved Mechanical Engineering Problems. LC 98-113908. 130p. 1994. pap. 39.95 (*0-912045-77-9*) Prof Pubns CA.

— 1001 Solved Engineering Fundamentals Problems. 2nd ed. LC 96-51622. 760p. 1997. pap. 35.95 (*1-888577-09-6*, EFPRB2) Prof Pubns CA.

— Practice Problems for the Civil Engineering PE Exam: A Companion to the Civil Engineering Reference Manual. 7th ed. 592p. 1999. pap., student ed. 34.95 (*1-888577-41-X*, CESL7) Prof Pubns CA.

***Lindeburg, Michael R.** Practice Problems for the Mechanical Engineering PE Exam: A Companion to the Mechanical Engineering Reference Manual. 10th ed. 480p. 2000. pap. 29.95 (*1-888577-49-5*) Prof Pubns CA.

— Quick Reference for the Civil Engineering PE Exam. 2nd ed. LC 99-38595. 65p. 1999. pap. 29.95 (*1-888577-47-9*, CEQR2) Prof Pubns CA.

Lindeburg, Michael R. Quick Reference for the Mechanical Engineering PE Exam. 3rd ed. LC 97-7740. 72p. 1997. pap. 29.95 (*1-888577-14-2*) Prof Pubns CA.

— Solutions Manual for the Engineer-in-Training Reference Manual: English Units. 8th ed. (Engineering Reference Manual Ser.). 256p. 1992. pap. 25.95 (*0-912045-39-6*) Prof Pubns CA.

— Solutions Manual for the Engineer-in-Training Reference Manual: SI Units. 8th ed. (Engineering Reference Manual Ser.). 256p. 1992. pap. 25.95 (*0-912045-40-X*) Prof Pubns CA.

Lindeburg, Michael R. & University of Missouri-Columbia Dept. of Industrial Engineering Staff. Industrial Discipline-Specific Review for the FE/EIT Exam. LC 97-31945. 80p. 1998. pap. 29.95 (*1-888577-22-3*) Prof Pubns CA.

Lindecke, Fred W., ed. see Rose, Louis J. & Malone, Roy.

Lindee, M. Susan. Suffering Made Real: American Science & the Survivors at Hiroshima. LC 94-1832. (Illus.). 300p. 1994. 29.95 (*0-226-48237-5*) U Ch Pr.

— Suffering Made Real: American Science & the Survivors at Hiroshima. (Illus.). xii, 288p. 1997. pap. text 15.95 (*0-226-48238-3*) U Ch Pr.

Lindee, M. Susan, jt. auth. see Nelkin, Dorothy.

Lindegaard, Annette, jt. ed. see Dollerup, Cay.

Lindegger, Max O. & Tap, Robert, eds. The Best of Permaculture: A Collection. (Illus.). 136p. 1990. pap. text 16.99 (*0-9589585-1-3*, Pub. by Nascimanere Pty Ltd) Rodale Inst.

Lindeke, B., jt. ed. see Cho, Arthur K.

Lindeke, Wolfgang. Dictionary of Ventilation & Health. 186p. 1980. 65.00 (*0-569-08522-5*) St Mut.

— Technical Veterinary Dictionary. (ENG, GER, RUS & SLV.). 185p. 1972. 95.00 (*0-8288-6421-7*, M-9894) Fr & Eur.

Lindekugel, D. M. Shooters: TV News Photographers & Their Work. LC 93-23672. 192p. 1994. 55.00 (*0-275-94603-7*, Praeger Pubs) Greenwood.

Lindel, Albert, jt. auth. see Resling, Darlene E.

Lindell, Anne. Audio Tape Program: A Workbook. LC 83-. (Illus.). 160p. (C). 1983. audio 165.00 (*0-472-00212-0*, 00212) U of Mich Pr.

Lindell, Anne. Audio Tape Program: A Workbook. 160p. (C). 1983. pap. text, wbk. ed. 14.95 (*0-472-08573-5*, 08573) U of Mich Pr.

— Intensive English for Communication, Bk. 2. (Illus.). 352p. 1980. pap. text 14.95 (*0-472-08572-7*, 08572) U of Mich Pr.

Lindell, Anne & Hagiwara, M. Peter. Intensive English for Communication, Bk. 1. LC 78-58152. (Illus.). 264p. 1979. pap. text 14.95 (*0-472-08570-0*, 08570) U of Mich Pr.

— Intensive English for Communication: Workbook for Writing, Listening & Speaking, Bk. 1. LC 78-58152. (Illus.). 184p. 1979. pap. text, student ed., wbk. ed. 14.95 (*0-472-08571-9*, 08571) U of Mich Pr.

Lindell, Bo. How Safe Is Safe Enough? LC 88-22075. (Taylor Lectures: No. 12). 1988. pap. 25.00 (*0-913392-99-5*) NCRP Pubns.

Lindell, Colleen. Internet Medical & Health, Searching & Sources Guidebook: For Healthcare Consumers & Professionals Who Want to Know More. DeRose, Paulette, ed. LC 98-92026. (Illus.). 100p. 1998. pap. 7.95 (*0-9667080-4-0*) KC Press.

***Lindell, Colleen & Hersh, William R.** Internet Medical & Health Searching & Sources Guidebook II: For Healthcare Consumers & Professionals Who Want to Know More. 2nd rev. ed. DuRose, Paulette, ed. (Illus.). 275p. 1999. 7.95 (*0-9667080-3-2*) KC Press.

Lindell, Ethel B., jt. auth. see Lindell, John E.

Lindell, G. L. & Zines, Leslie. Sawyer's Australian Constitutional Cases. 4th ed. xxxv, 774p. 1982. pap. 73.00 (*0-455-20460-8*, Pub. by LawBk Co) Gaunt.

Lindell, Geoffrey, ed. Future Directions in Australian Constitutional Law: Essays in Honour of Professor Leslie Zines. 304p. 1994. 54.00 (*1-86287-147-7*, Pub. by Federation Pr) Gaunt.

Lindell, Ismo V. Electromagnetic Waves in Chiral & Bi-Isotropic Media. LC 94-7656. 1994. 10.00 (*0-89006-684-1*) Artech Hse.

— Methods for Electromagnetic Field Analysis. 332p. 1996. 69.95 (*0-7803-1154-X*, PC5625) Inst Electrical.

— Methods for Electromagnetic Field Analysis. (Oxford Engineering Science Ser.: No. 30). (Illus.). 304p. 1992. text 95.00 (*0-19-856239-X*) OUP.

Lindell, John E. & Lindell, Ethel B. Oh God, Help Me! A True Story of Faith in the Life of a Polio Survivor. LC 88-91189. (Illus.). 209p. 1988. pap. 10.00 (*0-9620643-0-0*) J E Lindell.

Lindell, Kristina. The Student Lovers. DeFrancis, John, ed. LC 70-189615. (PALI Language Texts, Chinese Ser.). (Illus.). 68p. (Orig.). (C). 1975. pap. text 8.00 (*0-8248-0225-X*) UH Pr.

Lindell, Kristina, et al. Folk Tales from Kammu: A Teller's Last Tales. (NIAS Monographs: Vol. 77). 190p. 1998. pap. text 20.00 (*0-7007-0624-0*, Pub. by Curzon Pr Ltd) UH Pr.

— Folk Tales from Kammu Vol. 5: A Young Story-Teller's Tales. (NIAS Monographs: No. 66). (Illus.). 220p. (C). 1996. pap. text 15.00 (*0-7007-0297-0*, Pub. by Curzon Pr Ltd) UH Pr.

Lindell, Kristina, jt. auth. see Tayanin, Damrong.

Lindell, Michael K., jt. auth. see Perry, Ronald W.

***Lindeman.** PianoLab: An Introduction to Classic Piano. 4th ed. LC 99-27834. (Music Ser.). 1999. pap. 51.95 (*0-534-53434-1*) Wadsworth Pub.

Lindeman, contrib. by. Agency in Real Estate. 256p. (C). 2001. pap. 22.60 (*0-13-079769-3*, Macmillan Coll) P-H.

Lindeman, Anne. State Concerns in the Future Development of Vocational Education. 22p. 1984. 3.00 (*0-318-22201-9*, OC98) Ctr Educ Trng Employ.

Lindeman, Bard. Be an Outrageous Older Man: Action Guide for Men 50 & Beyond. 272p. 1998. pap. 14.95 (*1-879198-24-X*) Knwldg Ideas & Trnds.

Lindeman, Bruce. Real Estate Brokerage Management. 4th ed. LC 97-21276. 347p. (C). 1997. 41.00 (*0-13-639634-8*) P-H.

Lindeman, Bruce J. & Friedman, Jack P. How to Prepare for Florida Real Estate Exams: Salesperson, Broker, Appraiser. LC 96-45154. 464p. 1997. pap. 13.95 (*0-8120-9809-9*) Barron.

Lindeman, Carl. The Valley Outfitter: Your Complete Recreational Guide to Montana's Flathead Valley. LC 94-60440. 1994. pap. write for info. (*0-9640756-0-1*) Whitefish Mag.

Lindeman, Carol. Instructor's Manual for Fundamentals of Contemporary Nursing Practice. 255p. Date not set. teacher ed. write for info. (*0-7216-8234-0*, W B Saunders Co) Harcrt Hlth Sci Grp.

— Study Guide for Fundamentals of Contemporary Nursing. (Illus.). 350p. Date not set. student ed. write for info. (*0-7216-8308-8*, W B Saunders Co) Harcrt Hlth Sci Grp.

— Test Manual for Fundamentals of Contemporary Nursing Practice. 175p. Date not set. write for info. (*0-7216-8237-5*, W B Saunders Co) Harcrt Hlth Sci Grp.

Lindeman, Carol A. Contemporary Nursing Procedures. 1999. pap. text. write for info. (*0-7216-4208-X*, W B Saunders Co) Harcrt Hlth Sci Grp.

Lindeman, Carol A., ed. Alternate Conceptions of Work & Society: Implications for Professional Nursing. 225p. (Orig.). 1988. pap. 20.00 (*0-922148-00-7*) AACN.

Lindeman, Carol A. & McAthie, Marylou. Fundamentals of Contemporary Nursing Practice. Eoyang, Thomas, ed. LC 98-36263. (Illus.). 1020p. 1999. text. write for info. (*0-7216-3527-X*, W B Saunders Co) Harcrt Hlth Sci Grp.

Lindeman, Carolynn A. PianoLab: An Introduction to Class Piano. 292p. (C). 1983. pap. write for info. (*0-534-01305-8*) Wadsworth Pub.

— PianoLab: An Introduction to Class Piano. 3rd ed. LC 95-23956. (C). 1995. 32.75 (*0-534-25140-4*) Wadsworth Pub.

Lindeman, Carolynn A., jt. auth. see Cutietta, Robert A.

Lindeman, Carolynn A., jt. auth. see Hackett, Patrica.

L

Lindeman, Carolynn A., jt. auth. see Hackett, Patricia.

Lindeman, Eduard. The Meaning of Adult Education. LC 89-61231. 150p. (C). 1989. pap. 24.95 (*0-9622488-1-9*) U OK PMC.

Lindeman, Eduard C. Wealth & Culture. 155p. 1987. 44.95 (*0-88738-170-7*) Transaction Pubs.

Lindeman, Eric D. & Blumenthal, Anita. Handbook: The International Nuclear Fuel Cycle. 80p. 1995. 8.25 (*0-9646545-0-4*) NY Nuclear.

Lindeman, J. Bruce. Microeconomics. LC 91-35214. (Barron's EZ-101 Study Keys Ser.). 144p. 1992. pap. 6.95 (*0-8120-4601-3*) Barron.

Lindeman, J. Bruce & Friedman, Jack P. How to Prepare for California Real Estate Salesperson, Broker, Appraiser Examinations: Salesperson, Broker, Appraiser. 450p. 1995. pap. 12.95 (*0-8120-9375-5*) Barron.

— How to Prepare for New York Real Estate Examinations: Salesperson, Broker, Appraiser. LC 95-40332. (Barron's Educational Ser.). 496p. 1996. pap. 13.95 (*0-8120-9376-3*) Barron.

— How to Prepare for Real Estate Licensing Examinations: Salesperson & Broker. 5th ed. 1995. pap., student ed. 13.95 (*0-8120-2994-1*) Barron.

Lindeman, J. C., jt. auth. see Cowan, R. S.

Lindeman, J. F., jt. ed. see Holman, B. L.

Lindeman, Jack. Twenty-One Poems. 1963. pap. 10.00 (*0-685-62609-1*) Atlantis Edns.

Lindeman, Peter V. Introductory Biology: Laboratory Manual. (Illus.). 85p. (C). 1991. write for info. (*0-944324-49-5*) Am Artist Pub.

Lindeman, Stephan D. Structural Novelty in the Early Romantic Piano Concerto. LC 98-28921. (Illus.). 348p. 1998. 76.00 (*1-57647-000-8*) Pendragon NY.

Lindeman, Stephan D., ed. see Mendelssohn, Felix.

Lindeman, Stephen P. Nutshells. 12p. (Orig.). 1994. pap. write for info. (*1-885206-05-4*, Iliad Pr) Cader Pubng.

Lindeman, William, tr. see Steiner, Rudolf.

Lindemann, A., jt. auth. see Conzelmann, H.

***Lindemann, Albert S.** Anti-Semitism Before the Holocaust. LC 99-47311. 160p. 2000. pap. 11.95 (*0-582-36964-9*) Longman.

— Esau's Tears: Modern Anti-Semitism & the Rise of the Jews. 568p. (C). 2000. pap. text Price not set. (*0-521-79538-9*) Cambridge U Pr.

Lindemann, Albert S. Esau's Tears: Modern Anti-Semitism & the Rise of the Jews, 1870-1933. 589p. (C). 1997. 36.95 (*0-521-59369-7*) Cambridge U Pr.

— A History of European Socialism. LC 82-40167. xxi, 386p. 1983. 20.00 (*0-300-02797-4*) Yale U Pr.

— A History of European Socialism. LC 82-40167. 406p. 1984. reprint ed. pap. 20.00 (*0-300-03246-3*, Y-505) Yale U Pr.

— The Jew Accused: Three Anti-Semitic Affairs - Dreyfus, Beilis, Frank - 1894-1915. (Illus.). 311p. (C). 1992. pap. 17.95 (*0-521-44761-5*) Cambridge U Pr.

— The Jew Accused: Three Anti-Semitic Affairs - Dreyfus, Beiliss, Frank - 1894-1915. (Illus.). 311p. (C). 1991. text 17.95 (*0-521-40302-2*) Cambridge U Pr.

Lindemann, Barbara & Grossman, Paul. Employment Discrimination Law: 1998 Supplement. 3rd ed. Jordan, W. Carl et al, eds. 802p. 1998. pap. 165.00 (*1-57018-127-6*, 1127-PR8) BNA Books.

Lindemann, Barbara & Grossmann, Paul. Employment Discrimination Law: 1998 Supplement, 2 vols. 3rd ed. Jordan, W. Carl et al, eds. LC 96-48048. 2356p. 1976. 445.00 (*0-87179-791-7*, 9127-PR8) BNA Books.

Lindemann, Barbara & Kadue, David D. Primer on Sexual Harassment. LC 92-25748. 319p. 1992. trans. 45.00 (*0-87179-764-X*, 0764) BNA Books.

— Sexual Harassment in Employment Law, with 1999 Supplement. LC 91-41340. 882p. 1999. trans. 128.00 (*0-87179-704-6*, 9896) BNA Books.

— Sexual Harassment in Employment Law, 1999 Supplement. Strubbe, Mary Rose, ed. 350p. (Orig.). 1999. pap., suppl. ed. 140.00 (*0-87179-896-4*, 0896-PR7) BNA Books.

Lindemann, Barbara, et al. Employment Discrimination Law: With 1998 Supplement. 2 vols. 3rd ed. LC 96-48048. ixx, 2236 p. 1996. pap. 525.00 (*1-57018-065-2*) BNA Books.

Lindemann, Bonnie, jt. auth. see Harstad, Peter T.

Lindemann, Carol, ed. Handbook of the Treatment of the Anxiety Disorders. 2nd expanded ed. 1996. 65.00 (*1-56821-805-2*) Aronson.

Lindemann, Constance. This Is How Seventy Looks: Stories of My Life. 147p. (Orig.). 1993. pap. 9.50 (*0-9637014-0-1*) Compage Pr.

Lindemann, Elizabeth B. Erich Lindemann: A Biographical Sketch. LC 87-80018. (Illus.). (Orig.). 1987. pap. 14.40 (*0-9618299-0-7*) E B Lindemann.

Lindemann, Eric. Crisis Intervention. LC 94-47404. 1995. pap. 50.00 (*1-56821-468-5*) Aronson.

Lindemann, Erika C. Longman Bibliography of Composition & Rhetoric, 1984 1985: Longman Series in College Composition & Communication, Vol. I, 1984-1985. 318p. 1987. text 44.76 (*0-582-28376-0*, 71409) Longman.

— A Rhetoric for Writing Teachers. 3rd ed. (Illus.). 328p. (C). 1995. pap. text 26.95 (*0-19-508844-1*) OUP.

Lindemann, Erika C., ed. LONGMN BIBLIO COMP&RHET2, Vol. II. 216p. (C). 1988. text 42.36 (*0-8013-0254-4*, 75907) Longman.

Lindemann, Erika C., et al, eds. CCCC Bibliography of Composition & Rhetoric 1987. 216p. (C). 1990. 31.95 (*0-8093-1647-1*) S Ill U Pr.

— CCCC Bibliography of Composition & Rhetoric 1987. 216p. (C). 1990. pap. 21.95 (*0-8093-1648-X*) S Ill U Pr.

Lindemann, Erika C. & Fleming, Sandra M., eds. CCCC Bibliography of Composition & Rhetoric, 1989. annot. ed. 224p. (C). 1991. 31.95 (*0-8093-1712-5*) S Ill U Pr.

Lindemann, Erika C. & Harding, Mary B., eds. CCCC Bibliography of Composition & Rhetoric, 1988. 224p. (C). 1990. pap. 21.95 (*0-8093-1670-6*) S Ill U Pr.

— CCCC Bibliography of Composition & Rhetoric, 1988. 224p. (C). 1991. 31.95 (*0-8093-1669-2*) S Ill U Pr.

Lindemann, Erika C. & Tate, Gary, eds. An Introduction to Composition Studies. (Illus.). 208p. (C). 1991. pap. text 24.95 (*0-19-506363-5*, 11255) OUP.

Lindemann, G. Lexikon der Kunststile, 2 vols., Set. (GER.). 360p. 1980. pap. 24.95 (*0-8288-1421-X*, M7251) Fr & Eur.

Lindemann, James & Nelson, Hilde L. Philosophy of Health Care Reader. LC 98-30800. 416p. (C). (gr. 13). 1999. 65.00 (*0-415-91915-0*); pap. 24.99 (*0-415-91916-9*) Routledge.

Lindemann, James E., et al. Psychological & Behavioral Aspects of Physical Disability: A Manual for Health Practitioners. LC 81-17885. 452p. (C). 1981. 59.50 (*0-306-40776-0*, Plenum Trade) Perseus Pubng.

Lindemann, Jeff W., jt. auth. see Cole, SuzAnne C.

Lindemann, Kelvin. The Red Umbrellas. LC 74-30367. 214p. 1975. reprint ed. lib. bdg. 59.50 (*0-8371-7521-6*, LIRU, Greenwood Pr) Greenwood.

***Lindemann, Marilee.** Willa Cather: Queering America. LC 98-29688. (Between Men - Between Women Ser.). 190p. 1998. pap. 16.50 (*0-231-11325-0*); lib. bdg. 45.00 (*0-231-11324-2*) Col U Pr.

Lindemann, Marilee, ed. see Cather, Willa.

Lindemann, Marilee, ed. & intro. see Cather, Willa.

Lindemann, Mary. Health & Healing in Eighteenth-Century Germany. LC 95-53137. (Johns Hopkins University Studies in Historical & Political Science: Vol. 114). (Illus.). 544p. 1996. text 49.95 (*0-8018-5281-1*) Johns Hopkins.

***Lindemann, Mary.** Medicine & Society in Early Modern Europe. LC 99-17819. (New Approaches to European History Ser.: No. 16). (Illus.). 249p. (C). 1999. 49.95 (*0-521-41254-4*); pap. 18.95 (*0-521-42354-6*) Cambridge U Pr.

Lindemann, Michael. UFOs & the Alien Presence: Six Viewpoints. 1998. pap. 12.00 (*0-926524-46-1*) Granite Pub.

Lindemans, Fred W., jt. ed. see Kappenberger, Lukas.

Lindemeyer, Nancy, jt. auth. see McCaffery, Janet.

Lindemeyer, Paul. Celebrating the Saxophone. 1996. 25.00 (*0-688-13518-8*, Hearst) Hearst Commns.

— Celebrating the Saxophone. (Illus.). 96p. 1997. reprint ed. pap. 15.00 (*0-688-15556-1*, Quil) HarperTrade.

Linden. George Ripleys Compound of Alchemy. 70.95 (*0-7546-0105-6*) Ashgate Pub Co.

Linden. Reconstruction Reader. LC 98-84958. (C). 1998. pap. text 26.50 (*0-15-508456-9*, Pub. by Harcourt Coll Pubs) Harcourt.

— Voices from House & Ordeal. 1994. 34.74 (*0-07-912134-9*) McGraw.

Linden, Alexandra, tr. see Andreyeu, Leonid.

Linden, Allen M. Canadian Tort Law. 5th ed. 864p. 1993. pap. text, student ed. 80.00 (*0-409-91429-0*, MICHIE) LEXIS Pub.

Linden, Allen M. & Firestone, S. E. Butterworths Ontario Motor Vehicle Law Practice & Procedure Manual. ring bd. 150.00 (*0-409-91920-9*, CN, MICHIE) LEXIS Pub.

Linden, Anne & Perutz, Kathrin. Mindworks: NLP Tools for Building a Better Life. LC 98-227920. 368p. 1998. pap. 6.99 (*0-425-16624-4*) Berkley Pub.

Linden, Blanche. Boston Freedom Trail. LC 96-96194. (Illus.). 50p. (Orig.). 1996. pap. 9.95 (*0-9643015-2-0*) Back Bay Boston.

Linden, Bobbie. The Maltese. LC 98-22378. (Owner's Guide to a Happy, Healthy Pet Ser.). (Illus.). 160p. 1998. 12.95 (*0-87605-237-5*) Howell Bks.

Linden, C. A. Van der, see Van der Linden, C. A.

Linden, Carl A. Khrushchev & the Soviet Leadership: With an Epilogue on Gorbachev. rev. ed. LC 89-43532. 299p. reprint ed. pap. 92.70 (*0-608-06053-4*, 206638500008) Bks Demand.

— Khrushchev & the Soviet Leadership, 1957-1964. LC 66-16035. 283p. 1966. reprint ed. pap. 87.80 (*0-8357-6909-7*, 203796700009) Bks Demand.

— Russia & China on the Eve of a New Millennium. LC 96-33083. 351p. 1996. text 44.95 (*1-56000-291-3*) Transaction Pubs.

— The Soviet Party-State: Aspects of Ideocratic Despotism. LC 83-13984. 174p. 1983. 45.00 (*0-275-91037-7*, C1037, Praeger Pubs) Greenwood.

Linden, D. Handbook of Batteries. 2nd ed. LC 94-29189. 1216p. 1995. 125.00 (*0-07-037921-1*) McGraw.

***Linden, Dana Wechsler, et al.** Preemies: A Companion Guide for Parents of Premature Babies. 2000. pap. write for info. (*0-671-02413-2*, PB Trade Paper) PB.

— Preemies: The Essential Guide for Parents of Premature Babies. (Illus.). 576p. 2000. 24.95 (*0-671-03491-X*) PB.

Linden, Erik-Jan Van Der, see Everaert, Martin.

Linden, Eugene. The Future in Plain Sight: Can We Control the Coming Chaos? LC 98-7080. 256p. 1998. 25.00 (*0-684-81133-2*) Simon & Schuster.

— The Parrot's Lament: And Other True Tales of Animal Intrigue, Intelligence, & Ingenuity. LC 99-23424. 256p. 1999. 23.95 (*0-525-94476-1*, Dutton Child) Peng Put Young Read.

***Linden, Eugene.** Parrot's Lament: And Other True Tales of Animal Intrigue, Intelligence & Ingenuity. 2000. pap. 12.95 (*0-452-28068-0*, Plume) Dutton Plume.

— The Parrot's Lament: And Other True Tales of Animal Intrigue, Intelligence, & Ingenuity. large type ed. LC 00-26274. (Core Ser.). 255p. 2000. 27.95 (*0-7838-9031-1*, G K Hall Lrg Type) Mac Lib Ref.

Linden, Eugene, jt. auth. see Wang, An.

Linden, F. Taschenlexikon der Logistik. (ENG & GER.). 130p. 1991. pap. 95.00 (*0-8288-3882-8*, F112511) Fr & Eur.

Linden, Fabian, et al. How We Spend Our Money. LC 98-188294. 99p. 1995. write for info. (*0-8237-0574-9*) Conference Bd.

Linden, Fabian, jt. auth. see Gates, Theodore R.

Linden, Frank Van Der, see Van Der Linden, Frank.

Linden, Frans P., ed. Transition of the Human Dentition. LC RK0525.. (Craniofacial Growth Monographs: Vol. 13). (Illus.). 150p. 1982. reprint ed. pap. 46.50 (*0-608-08519-7*, 203302200083) Bks Demand.

Linden, Franz-Karl Von, see Von Linden, Franz-Karl.

Linden, G., ed. Analytical Techniques for Foods & Agricultural Products. Dieter, Lance, tr. from FRE. LC 95-14991. (Analysis & Control Methods for Foods & Agricultural Products Ser.).Tr. of Principes des Techniques d'Analyse. (Illus.). 592p. 1995. 145.00 (*1-56081-687-2*, Wiley-VCH) Wiley.

***Linden, G. & Lorient, D.** New Ingredients in Food Processing: Biochemistry & Agriculture. 392p. 1999. pap. 207.00 (*1-85573-443-5*) Am Educ Systs.

***Linden, G. & Lorient, Denis.** New Ingredients in Food Processing. LC 99-32797. 1999. write for info. (*0-8493-0631-0*) CRC Pr.

Linden, Glenn M. Desegrating Schools in Dallas: Four Decades in the Federal Courts. (Illus.). 243p. 1995. 23.00 (*0-9637629-1-5*) Three Forks.

Linden, Glenn M. & Thomas, Milton. Voices from the House Divided: The United States Civil War as Personal Experience. LC 94-26795. 352p. (C). 1994. pap. 21.25 (*0-07-037934-3*) McGraw.

Linden, H. R. & Pettyjohn, E. S. Selection of Oils for High-Btu Oil Gas. (Research Bulletin Ser.: No. 12). iv, 48p. 1952. pap. 25.00 (*1-58222-043-3*) Inst Gas Tech.

Linden, H. R. & Schultz, E. B., Jr. High-Pressure Hydrogasification of Petroleum Oils. (Research Bulletin Ser.: No. 29). iv, 60p. 1960. pap. 25.00 (*1-58222-024-7*) Inst Gas Tech.

Linden, H. R., jt. auth. see Bair, W. G.

Linden, H. R., jt. auth. see Dirksen, H. A.

Linden, H. R., jt. auth. see Pettyjohn, E. S.

Linden, H. R., jt. auth. see Tarman, P. B.

Linden, Harry Van Der, see Van Der Linden, Harry.

Linden, Ingemar. The Last Trump. (IC-Studies in the Intercultural History of Christianity: Vol. 17). 372p. 1978. pap. 52.00 (*3-261-02370-8*) P Lang Pubng.

Linden, Jan Van Der, see Van Der Linden, Jan.

Linden, Jan Van Der, see Baken, Robert-Jan.

Linden, Jan Van Der, see Baken, Robert-Jan & Van Der Linden, Jan.

Linden, Jenni. Playing Away. 144p. (J). 1997. pap. 6.95 (*0-09-926322-X*, Pub. by Random) Trafalgar.

— The Red-Hot Love Hunt. 144p. (J). 1997. pap. 6.95 (*0-09-925112-4*, Pub. by Random) Trafalgar.

Linden, John H. Surrender The Dachau Concentration Camp, 29 April 45: The True Account. LC 98-60876. 158 p. 1997. write for info. (*0-9665151-0-2*) J H Linden.

Linden, Jonathan, ed. see CAD-CAM Alert Editors.

Linden, Jonathan, ed. see Johnson, Robert H.

Linden, Jonathan, ed. see Mayer, Ralph.

Linden, Kevin J. Making Movies on Your Own: Practical Talk from Independent Filmmakers. LC 98-16263. (Illus.). 200p. 1998. pap. 35.00 (*0-7864-0517-1*) McFarland & Co.

Linden, Kurt J., ed. Laser Diode & LED Applications III, Vol. 3000. 226p. 1997. 69.00 (*0-8194-2411-0*) SPIE.

Linden Lane Press Staff, ed. see Arango, Guillermo.

Linden, Lena. Development Change & Linear Structural Equations: Application of LISREL Models. (IEA Monograph Studies: No. 13). 114p. (Orig.). 1986. pap. text 38.00 (*91-22-00803-9*) Coronet Bks.

Linden, Marcel Van Der, see Montgomery, David & Van Der Linden, Marcel, eds.

Linden, Marcel Van Der, see Griffin, Larry & Van Der Linden, Marcel, eds.

Linden, Marcel Van der, see Amin, Shahid & Van der Linden, Marcel, eds.

Linden, Marcel Van Der, see Brass, Tom & Van Der Linden, Marcel, eds.

Linden, Marcel Van Der, see Van Der Linden, Marcel.

Linden, Marcel Van der, see Van der Linden, Marcel, ed.

Linden, Marcel Van der, see Van Holthoon, Frits & Van der Linden, Marcel, eds.

Linden, Marcel Van der, see Van der Linden, Marcel, ed.

Linden, Marcel Van der, see Brass, Tom & Van der Linden, Marcel, eds.

Linden, Mary A., jt. auth. see Bateman, Barbara D.

Linden, Michael. Kick the Square Wheels off Government: Emergent Hope in a Loving World. (Illus.). x, 148p. (Orig.). 1997. 22.95 (*0-9656575-0-7*) Empire of Ideas.

Linden, Millicent. Living in a State of Orgasm. LC 62-22285. (Illus.). (Orig.). 1967. pap. 5.00 (*0-912628-01-4*) M Linden NY.

— The Orgasm Is a Vacuum, Tension-in-Repose, the Fountain of Youth Foundation: Unifying the Body in the Universal Field of Unification Through Tension-in-Repose. (Illus.). 1985. 8.00 (*0-912628-11-1*) M Linden NY.

— Preparing Your Body to Fly, Vol. 1. 1977. pap. 7.00 (*0-912628-05-7*) M Linden NY.

— Tension-in-Repose: A Basic Home Series Course. (Illus.). 100p. 1971. 4.95 (*0-912628-08-1*) M Linden NY.

— Tension-in-Repose: An Introduction to Living in a State of Orgasm, Vol. 1. LC 62-22285. (Illus.). 1975. 5.00 (*0-912628-09-X*) M Linden NY.

— The Yawn, et Al: A Key to Reserve Buoyancy for Human Flight. LC 78-64375. (Evolutionary New Material from Tension in Repose Ser.). (Illus.). 1978. 7.00 (*0-912628-06-5*) M Linden NY.

Linden, Millicent, contrib. by. Be Weightless Courtesy of the Universe Via Tension-in-Repose. (Illus.). 46p. 1998. pap. 10.00 (*0-912628-02-2*) M Linden NY.

Linden, Myra J. & Whimbey, Arthur. Analytical Writing & Thinking: Facing the Tests. 472p. 1990. 79.95 (*0-8058-0908-2*); teacher ed. write for info. (*0-8058-0932-5*); pap. 34.50 (*0-8058-0648-2*) L Erlbaum Assocs.

— Why Johnny Can't Write: How to Improve Writing Skills. 136p. 1990. 29.95 (*0-8058-0852-3*) L Erlbaum Assocs.

— Why Johnny Can't Write: How to Improve Writing Skills. 136p. 1990. pap. 14.50 (*0-8058-0853-1*) L Erlbaum Assocs.

Linden, Pat, ed. see Cahill, Timothy.

Linden, Pat, ed. see Koury, Jen.

Linden, Paul. Comfort at Your Computer: Bosy Awareness Training for Pain-Free Computer Use. 2nd ed. LC 99-16526. (Illus.). 250p. 2000. pap. 14.95 (*1-55643-322-0*) North Atlantic.

Linden, Paul C. Van Der, see Piel, Robert J. & Van Der Linden, Paul C.

Linden, Paula & Gross, Susan. Taking Care of Mommy. (Family Bk. Ser.). 239p. 1983. pap. 7.95 (*0-318-19491-0*) M E Pinkham.

Linden, Philip Van, see Van Linden, Philip.

Linden, R. Ruth. Making Stories, Making Selves: Feminist Reflections on the Holocaust. LC 92-20410. (Helen Hooven Santmyer Prize in Women's Studies). 191p. (C). 1993. pap. text 16.95 (*0-8142-0584-4*) Ohio St U Pr.

Linden, Richard, jt. auth. see Newkirk, William.

Linden, Robert van der, see Van der Linden, Robert.

Linden, Robin R., et al, eds. Against Sadomasochism: A Radical Feminist Analysis. LC 81-15284. 224p. (Orig.). (C). 1981. pap. 7.95 (*0-9603628-3-5*) Frog in Well.

Linden, Roger W., ed. The Scientific Basis of Eating: Taste & Smell, Salivation, Mastication & Swallowing & Their Dysfunctions. LC 98-3604. (Frontiers of Oral Biology Ser.: Vol. 9). (Illus.). viii, 244p. 1998. 190.50 (*3-8055-6498-8*) S Karger.

Linden, Ronald H. Bear & Foxes: The International Relations of the East European States, 1965-1969. (East European Monographs: No. 50). 328p. 1979. text 68.50 (*0-914710-45-1*, Pub. by East Eur Monographs) Col U Pr.

Linden, Ronald H. & Rockman, Bert A., eds. Elite Studies & Communist Politics: Essays in Memory of Carl Beck. LC 83-21637. 366p. 1984. pap. 113.50 (*0-7837-8540-2*, 204935500011) Bks Demand.

Linden, Rozella F. Easy Tatting. LC 98-32402. (Illus.). 32p. 1999. spiral bd. 3.50 (*0-486-29986-4*) Dover.

Linden, Russell M. Seamless Government: A Practical Guide to Re-Engineering in the Public Sector. (Public Administration Ser.). 314p. 1994. text 27.95 (*0-7879-0015-X*) Jossey-Bass.

— Workbook for Seamless Government. LC 98-213919. (Nonprofit & Public Management Ser.). xx, 203p. 1998. pap. text 24.95 (*0-7879-4035-6*) Jossey-Bass.

***Linden, Ruth W.** The Time of My Life: A Memoir. Lora, Doris, ed. (Illus.). 140p. 1999. write for info. (*1-888069-21-X*) Biography For Everyone.

Linden, Scott. Fun Family Outdoor Ideas. 112p. 1998. pap. 9.95 (*0-9667880-0-1*) Linden Media.

Linden, Stanton J. Darke Hieroglyphicks: Alchemy in English Literature from Chaucer to the Restoration. (Illus.). 384p. 1996. text 45.00 (*0-8131-1968-5*) U Pr of Ky.

Linden, Stanton J., ed. see Abraham, Lyndy & Dee, Arthur.

Linden, Steven. Wager. large type unabridged ed. (Nightingale Ser.). 312p. 1989. 13.95 (*0-8161-4718-3*, G K Hall Lrg Type) Mac Lib Ref.

Linden, Toby, jt. ed. see Crocker, David A.

Linden, Tom & Kienholz, Michelle L. Dr. Tom Linden's Guide to Online Medicine. LC 95-31555. (Illus.). 304p. 1995. pap. 17.95 (*0-07-038055-4*) McGraw.

Linden van den Heuvell, H. B. van, et al, eds. Atomic Physics 15: Proceedings of the 15th International Conference on Atomic Physics, Zeeman-Effect Centenary, Amsterdam, The Netherlands, 5-9 August 1996. 450p. 1997. 96.00 (*981-02-3186-5*) World Scientific Pub.

Linden, W. Biological Barriers in Behavioral Medicine. LC 87-36137. (Behavioral Psychophysiology Ser.). (Illus.). 348p. (C). 1988. 75.00 (*0-306-42651-X*, Plenum Trade) Perseus Pubng.

— Psychological Perspectives of Essential Hypertension. (Biobehavioral Medicine Ser.: Vol. 3). (Illus.). x, 130p. 1984. pap. 60.00 (*3-8055-3662-3*) S Karger.

— Psychologiche Perspektiven des Bluthochdrucks. (Illus.). vii, 132p. 1983. 58.50 (*3-8055-3642-9*) S Karger.

Linden, W. J. Van Der, see Van Der Linden, W. J.

Linden-Ward, Blanche & Green, Carol H. American Women in the Nineteen Sixties: Changing the Future. LC 92-592. (American Women in the Twentieth Century Ser.). 608p. 1992. pap. 23.00 (*0-8057-9913-3*, Twyne); text 55.00 (*0-8057-9905-2*, Twyne) Mac Lib Ref.

Linden, Wilhelm Z. When a Child Is Born: The Natural Child Care Classic. LC 98-21689. 224p. 1998. pap. 12.95 (*0-89281-751-8*, Heal Arts VT) Inner Tradit.

Lindenauer, Isak. August Tiesselinck: A Lifetime in Metal, 1890-1972. (Illus.). 82p. 1990. pap. 20.00 (*0-9624994-0-4*) Lindenauer.

Lindenbauer, Leo. Diets, Diets, Diets Made You Fat, Fat, Fat: Diets Don't Work. (Health Ser.). 95p. 1992. reprint ed. pap. 9.95 (*0-9639616-0-8*) L Lindenbauer.

— Diets Only Solve Part of the Problem. (Health Ser.). 138p. 1995. pap. 9.95 (*1-55197-371-5*) L Lindenbauer.

— The Greatest Diet Book in the World. (Health Ser.). 70p. 1989. pap. 6.95 (*0-9639616-2-4*) L Lindenbauer.

— Health in Spite of Medicine. (Health Ser.). 240p. 1998. 17.95 (*0-9639616-3-2*) L Lindenbauer.

— Twenty Million Walking Dead. (Health Ser.). 145p. 1992. pap. 11.95 (*1-879331-30-6*) L Lindenbauer.

Lindenbaum, Pija. Boodil, My Dog. LC 92-13172. (Illus.). 48p. (J). (gr. k-2). 1995. pap. 5.95 (*0-8050-3940-6*, Owlet BYR) H Holt & Co.
— Boodil, My Dog. LC 92-13172. (Illus.). 48p. (J). (ps-2). 1995. 14.95 (*0-8050-2444-1*, Bks Young Read) H Holt & Co.
Lindenbaum, Richard H., jt. auth. see Papp, Zoltan.
Lindenbaum, S. J. Particle-Interaction Physics at High Energies. (International Series of Monographs on Physics). (Illus.). 1973. 65.00 (*0-19-851267-8*) OUP.
Lindenbaum, S. J., ed. Experimental Meson Spectroscopy, 1983: Seventh International Conference, Brookhaven. LC 84-70910. (AIP Conference Proceedings Ser.: No. 113). 506p. 1984. lib. bdg. 46.00 (*0-88318-312-9*) Am Inst Physics.
Lindenbaum, S. J., jt. ed. see Chung, S. U.
Lindenbaum, Samuel D. Analytical Dynamics - Course N. 316p. 1994. text 74.00 (*981-02-1467-7*) World Scientific Pub.
— Lecture Notes on Quantum Mechanics. 350p. 1999. 46.00 (*981-02-3839-8*) World Scientific Pub.
— Mathematical Methods in Physics. LC 96-31604. 450p. 1996. write for info. (*981-02-2760-4*) World Scientific Pub.
Lindenbaum, Shirley. Kuru Sorcery: Disease & Danger in the New Guinea Highlands. Edgerton, Robert B. & Langness, L. L., eds. LC 78-64596. xii, 174p. (C). 1979. pap. text 18.95 (*0-87484-362-6*, 362) Mayfield Pub.
Lindenbaum, Shirley & Lock, Margaret M., eds. Knowledge, Power, & Practice: The Anthropology of Medicine & Everyday Life. LC 92-28208. (Comparative Studies of Health Systems & Medical Care: Vol. 36). 1993. 58.00 (*0-520-07784-9*, Pub. by U CA Pr); pap. 18.95 (*0-520-07785-7*, Pub. by U CA Pr) Cal Prin Full Svc.
Lindenbaum, Shirley, jt. auth. see Herdt, Gilbert.
Lindenbaum, Shirley, jt. ed. see Herdt, Gilbert H.
Lindenberg, Charles W. The Academy. 288p. 1998. pap. 14.00 (*0-7392-0033-X*, PO2799) Morris Pubng.
Lindenberg, Christof-Andrea. Child's Praise of the Seasons: Festival Music to Sing. 1997. pap. text 18.00 (*1-889511-12-9*, WindRose Pub) Rose Harmony.
Lindenberg, Christof-Andreas. In Praise of the Seasons. pap. 20.00 (*1-889511-07-2*, 1967, WindRose Pub) Rose Harmony.
Lindenberg, Christoph. Teaching History: Suggested Themes of the Curriculum in Waldorf Schools. Luborsky, Peter, tr. from GER. 204p. (Orig.). 1989. pap. text 12.00 (*0-9623978-0-6*) Assn Waldorf Schls.
***Lindenberg, Greg & Giesen, Lauri, eds.** Directory of Online Banking & Financial Services. 726p. 1999. write for info. (*1-57987-155-0*) Faulkner & Gray.
Lindenberg, J., jt. ed. see Kolkman, P. A.
Lindenberg, K. & West, B. J. The Nonequilibrium Statistical Mechanics of Open & Closed Systems. 448p. 1990. 89.95 (*0-471-18683-X*) Wiley.
Lindenberg, Karen E., jt. auth. see Reese, Laura A.
Lindenberg, Katja, tr. see Honerkamp, Josef.
Lindenberg, Marc, jt. ed. see Dominguez, Jorge I.
Lindenberg, Marc M. The Human Development Race: Improving the Quality of Life in Developing Countries. LC 93-14619. 233p. 1993. pap. 19.95 (*1-55815-278-4*) ICS Pr.
Lindenberg, Marc M. & Crosby, Benjamin. Managing Development: The Political Dimension. LC 80-83345. (Library of Management for Development). 217p. (Orig.). 1981. 39.95 (*0-931816-49-1*) Transaction Pubs.
— Managing Development: The Political Dimension. fac. ed. LC 80-83345. (Illus.). 231p. (Orig.). 1994. pap. 71.70 (*0-7837-7579-2*, 204733200007) Bks Demand.
Lindenberg, Marc M. & Ramirez, Noel. Managing Adjustment in Developing Countries: Economic & Political Perspectives. LC 89-20119. 328p. 1990. 34.95 (*1-55815-053-6*); pap. 19.95 (*1-55815-054-4*) ICS Pr.
Lindenberg, Richard, et al. Neuropathology of Vision: An Atlas. LC 73-12319. 510p. reprint ed. pap. 158.10 (*0-608-13665-4*, 205543700022) Bks Demand.
Lindenberg, Richard, tr. see Duus, Peter.
Lindenberg, Siegwart M. & Schreuder, Hein, eds. Interdisciplinary Perspectives on Organization Studies. LC 92-33026. 366p. 1993. text 100.75 (*0-08-040814-1*, Pergamon Pr) Elsevier.
Lindenberger, Herbert. Georg Trakl. 166p. 1971. 49.50 (*0-685-63212-1*) Elliots Bks.
— Historical Drama: The Relation of Literature & Reality. LC 74-11630. xiv, 194p. 1992. lib. bdg. 14.00 (*0-226-48239-1*) U Ch Pr.
— Historical Drama: The Relationship of Literature & Reality. LC 74-11630. 1978. pap. text 3.45 (*0-226-48240-5*, P762) U Ch Pr.
— Opera: The Extravagant Art. LC 84-7092. 298p. 1984. 39.95 (*0-8014-1698-1*); pap. text 17.95 (*0-8014-9425-7*) Cornell U Pr.
Lindenberger, Herbert S. The History in Literature: On Value, Genre, & Institutions. 269p. 1992. pap. text 21.50 (*0-231-07253-8*) Col U Pr.
— On Wordsworth's Prelude. LC 75-25493. 316p. 1976. reprint ed. lib. bdg. 60.50 (*0-8371-8417-7*, LIOW, Greenwood Pr) Greenwood.
— Opera in History: From Monteverdi to Cage. LC 97-16405. 359p. 1998. 49.50 (*0-8047-3104-7*); pap. write for info. (*0-8047-3105-5*) Stanford U Pr.
— Saul's Fall: A Critical Fiction. LC 78-22003. (Illus.). 280p. reprint ed. pap. 86.80 (*0-608-06079-8*, 206641100008) Bks Demand.
Lindenberger, Jan. Black Memorabilia Around the House: A Handbook & Price Guide. LC 92-63106. (Illus.). 160p. (Orig.). 1993. pap. 16.95 (*0-88740-481-1*) Schiffer.
— Black Memorabilia for the Kitchen: A Handbook & Price Guide. LC 96-60635. (Illus.). 144p. 1992. pap. 15.95 (*0-88740-432-4*) Schiffer.
— Black Memorabilia for the Kitchen: A Handbook & Price Guide. 2nd rev. ed. LC 98-88134. (Illus.). 144p. 1999. pap. 16.95 (*0-7643-0763-0*) Schiffer.
— Cabbage Patch Kids Collectibles. LC 99-60308. (Illus.). 192p. 1999. pap. 16.95 (*0-7643-0835-1*) Schiffer.
— Care Bears Collectibles: An Unauthorized Handbook & Price Guide. LC 97-65939. (Schiffer Book for Collectors Ser.). (Illus.). 192p. 1997. pap. 19.95 (*0-7643-0310-4*) Schiffer.
— Clothing & Accessories from the 40s, 50s & 60s: A Handbook & Price Guide. LC 96-10490. 160p. 1996. pap. 16.95 (*0-7643-0023-7*) Schiffer.
***Lindenberger, Jan.** Collectible Ashtrays; Information & Price Guide. (Illus.). 160p. 1999. pap. 16.95 (*0-7643-0945-5*) Schiffer.
— Collecting Garfield, An Unauthorized Handbook & Price Guide. (Illus.). 144p. 1999. pap. 16.95 (*0-7643-0948-X*) Schiffer.
Lindenberger, Jan. Collecting Plastics: A Handbook & Price Guide. LC 91-65648. (Illus.). 114p. 1991. pap. 15.95 (*0-88740-335-2*) Schiffer.
— Collecting Plastics: A Handbook & Price Guide. 2nd rev. ed. LC 99-62134. (Illus.). 144p. 1999. pap. 15.95 (*0-7643-0904-8*) Schiffer.
— Collecting the 50s & 60s: A Handbook & Price Guide. rev. ed. (Illus.). 160p. 1997. pap. 16.95 (*0-7643-0131-4*) Schiffer.
— Encyclopedia of Cabbage Patch Kids: The 1980s. (Illus.). 176p. 1999. 29.95 (*0-7643-0967-6*) Schiffer.
— The Fifties & Sixties Kitchen: A Handbook & Price Guide. LC 93-87048. (Illus.). 160p. 1994. pap. 16.95 (*0-88740-591-6*) Schiffer.
— The '50s & '60s Kitchen: A Handbook & Price Guide. 2nd rev. ed. LC 98-89659. (Illus.). 160p. (Orig.). 1999. pap. 16.95 (*0-7643-0775-4*) Schiffer.
— Fun Kitchen Collectibles. (Illus.). 160p. 1996. pap. 16.95 (*0-7643-0022-9*) Schiffer.
— Lamps of the '50s & '60s. LC 97-68210. (Schiffer Book for Collectors Ser.). (Illus.). 144p. 1997. pap. 16.95 (*0-7643-0355-4*) Schiffer.
— More Black Collectibles: A Handbook & Price Guide. LC 94-37616. (Illus.). 160p. (Orig.). 1995. pap. 16.95 (*0-88740-733-1*) Schiffer.
— More Black Memorabilia: A Handbook & Price Guide. 2nd rev. ed. LC 99-61081. (Illus.). 160p. 1999. pap. 16.95 (*0-7643-0849-1*) Schiffer.
— More Smurf Collectibles: An Unauthorized Handbook & Price Guide. LC 97-80131. (Illus.). 144p. 1998. pap. 19.95 (*0-7643-0408-9*) Schiffer.
— Peanuts Gang Collectibles: An Unauthorized Handbook & Price Guide. LC 98-85649. 176p. 1998. pap. 29.95 (*0-7643-0671-5*) Schiffer.
— Planters Peanut Collectibles, 1906-1961: A Handbook & Price Guide. 2nd rev. ed. (Illus.). 160p. (Orig.). 1999. pap. 19.95 (*0-7643-0853-X*) Schiffer.
— Puppets & Marionettes. (Schiffer Book for Collectors Ser.). (Illus.). 176p. 1997. pap. 19.95 (*0-7643-0279-5*) Schiffer.
— Raggedy Ann & Andy Collectibles: A Handbook & Price Guide. LC 95-19703. (Illus.). 160p. (Orig.). 1995. pap. 19.95 (*0-88740-782-X*) Schiffer.
— Raggedy Ann & Andy Collectibles: A Handbook & Price Guide. 2nd rev. ed. LC 98-89344. (Illus.). 160p. (Orig.). 1999. pap. 19.95 (*0-7643-0773-8*) Schiffer.
— Strawberry Shortcake Collectibles: An Unauthorized Handbook & Price Guide. LC 97-80965. 144p. 1998. pap. 16.95 (*0-7643-0517-4*) Schiffer.
— Trolls. LC 99-60904. (Illus.). 136p. 1999. pap. 19.95 (*0-7643-0863-7*) Schiffer.
— An Unauthorized Guide to Rugrats Collectibles. LC 99-61131. (Illus.). 160p. 1999. pap. 16.95 (*0-7643-0877-7*) Schiffer.
— The Unauthorized Guide to Snoopy Collectibles. 2nd rev. ed. 160p. 1997. pap. 29.95 (*0-7643-0524-7*) Schiffer.
Lindenberger, Jan & Bowles, Jennifer. The Cream of Strawberry Shortcake Collectibles: An Unauthorized Handbook & Price Guide. LC 98-89926. (Illus.). 192p. 1999. pap. 16.95 (*0-7643-0812-2*) Schiffer.
***Lindenberger, Jan & Bowles, Jennifer.** More Strawberry Shortcake: An Unauthorized Handbook & Price Guide. LC 98-88721. (Books for Collectors Ser.). 160 p. 1999. write for info. (*0-7643-0762-2*) Schiffer.
Lindenberger, Jan & Cain, Dana. 501 Collectible Horses. 160p. 1996. pap. 19.95 (*0-88740-887-7*) Schiffer.
***Lindenberger, Jan & Cain, Dana.** 501 Collectible Horses, A Handbook & Price Guide. 2nd rev. ed. (Illus.). 160p. 2000. pap. 19.95 (*0-7643-0987-0*) Schiffer.
Lindenberger, Jan & Cain, Dana. Fun Collectibles of the 1950s, 1960s & 1970s. LC 95-37091. 160p. (YA). (gr. 10). 1996. pap. 19.95 (*0-88740-888-5*) Schiffer.
Lindenberger, Jan & Martone, Joel. Smurf Collectibles: A Handbook & Price Guide. LC 96-17120. (Illus.). 160p. 1996. pap. 19.95 (*0-7643-0031-8*) Schiffer.
***Lindenberger, Jan & Morris, Judy.** Encyclopedia of Cabbage Patch Kids, the 1990s. (Illus.). 176p. 1999. pap. 29.95 (*0-7643-1031-3*) Schiffer.
Lindenberger, Jan & Porges, Cher. More Peanuts Gang Collectibles. LC 98-88435. (Illus.). 160p. (Orig.). 1999. pap. 29.95 (*0-7643-0747-9*) Schiffer.
— More Snoopy Collectibles: An Unauthorized Guide with Values. LC 97-65475. (Schiffer Book for Collectors Ser.). (Illus.). 176p. 1997. pap. 29.95 (*0-7643-0283-3*) Schiffer.
***Lindenberger, Jan & Porges, Cher.** More Snoopy Collectibles, An Unauthorized Guide with Values. 2nd rev. ed. (Illus.). 176p. 1999. pap. 29.95 (*0-7643-0881-5*) Schiffer.
Lindenberger, Jan & Rosenthal, Jean. Collecting Plastic Jewelry: A Handbook & Price Guide. LC 95-53168. 160p. (gr. 10-13). 1996. pap. write for info. (*0-7643-0024-5*) Schiffer.
— More Plastics for Collectors: A Handbook & Price Guide. (Illus.). 160p. (YA). (gr. 10-13). 1996. pap. 19.95 (*0-88740-967-9*) Schiffer.
Lindenberger, Jan & Spontak, Joyce. Planters Peanut Collectibles, 1906-1961: A Handbook & Price Guide. LC 95-10515. (Illus.). 160p. (Orig.). 1995. pap. 19.95 (*0-88740-792-7*) Schiffer.
— Planters Peanut Collectibles since 1961: A Handbook & Price Guide. LC 95-31083. 160p. (gr. 10). 1996. pap. 19.95 (*0-88740-793-5*) Schiffer.
Lindenberger, Ruth. Beard Family History & Genealogy. (Illus.). 130p. 1997. reprint ed. pap. 21.00 (*0-8328-7453-1*); reprint ed. lib. bdg. 31.00 (*0-8328-7452-3*) Higginson Bk Co.
Lindenburg, Katja & West, Bruce J. The Nonequilibrium Statistical Mechanics of Open & Closed Systems. (Illus.). xi, 448p. 1990. 55.00 (*0-89573-347-1*, Wiley-VCH) Wiley.
Lindenbusch, John, ed. see Harris, NiNi.
***Lindencrona, Gustaf, et al, eds.** International Studies in Taxation: Law & Economics. (Series on International Taxation: Vol. 21).Tr. of Liber Amicorum Leif Muten. 417p. 1999. 150.00 (*90-411-9692-7*) Kluwer Law Intl.
Lindenfeld, David F. The Practical Imagination: The German Sciences of State in the Nineteenth Century. LC 96-43699. 1997. pap. text 19.95 (*0-226-48242-1*); lib. bdg. 57.00 (*0-226-48241-3*) U Ch Pr.
Lindenfeld, Frank, ed. Radical Perspectives on Social Problems: Readings in Critical Sociology. 3rd ed. 414p. (Orig.). 1987. lib. bdg. 39.95 (*0-930390-74-1*) Gen Hall.
Lindenfeld, Frank & Rothschild-Whitt, Joyce, eds. Workplace Democracy & Social Change. LC 82-80137. 456p. (C). 1982. 20.00 (*0-87558-101-3*); pap. 12.00 (*0-87558-102-1*) Porter Sargent.
***Lindenfeld, Jacqueline.** The French in the United States: An Ethnographic Study. LC 00-37815. 2000. write for info. (*0-89789-734-X*, Bergin & Garvey) Greenwood.
Lindenfeld, Jacqueline. Speech & Sociability at French Urban Marketplaces. LC 90-31713. (Pragmatics & Beyond New Ser.: Vol. 7). viii, 173p. 1990. 47.00 (*1-55619-109-X*) J Benjamins Pubng Co.
Lindenfeld, Jacqueline, tr. see Cohen, Daniel.
Lindenfeld, P., jt. auth. see Fillo, J. A.
Lindenfield, Gael. Build Your Self-Esteem: Adams,&Polly. 1997. audio 9.95 (*0-694-51873-5*, CPN10119) HarperAudio.
— Como Mantener la Calma. 1998. pap. text 10.95 (*84-08-02729-8*) Planeta.
— Confident Children: Help Children Feel Good about Themselves. 2000. pap. 13.00 (*0-7225-3956-8*, Pub. by Thorsons PA) HarpC.
Lindenfield, Gael. Emotional Confidence. 192p. 1998. pap. 11.00 (*0-7225-3245-8*) Thorsons PA.
***Lindenfield, Gael.** Increase Your Confidence: Adams,&Polly. 1998. audio 9.95 (*0-694-51906-5*, CPN10134) HarperAudio.
— Manage Your Anger: Adams,&Polly. abr. ed. 1998. audio 9.95 (*0-694-51910-3*, CPN10135) HarperAudio.
— Self Motivation: Simple Steps to Develop Self-Reliance & Perseverance. 2000. pap. 12.00 (*0-7225-4121-X*, Pub. by Thorsons PA) HarpC.
— Self Motivation: Simple Steps to Develop Self-Worth & Heal Emotional Wounds. 2000. pap. 12.00 (*0-7225-4021-3*) Thorsons PA.
— Success from Setbacks: Winning Strategies to Help You Respond Positively to Change. 1999. pap. 11.00 (*0-7225-3246-6*) Thorsons PA.
— Super Confidence: Simple Steps to Build Self-Assurance. 2000. pap. 12.00 (*0-7225-4011-6*) Thorsons PA.
***Lindenmann, Jean & Schleuning, Wolf-Dieter, eds.** Interferon: The Dawn of Recombinant Protein Drugs. LC 99-38273. (Ernst Schering Research Foundation Workshop Ser.: Suppl. 5). (Illus.). xiv, 138p. 1999. 48.00 (*3-540-66170-0*) Spr-Verlag.
Lindenmayer, A., jt. auth. see Prusinkiewicz, P.
Lindenmayer, Clem. Lonely Planet Trekking in the Patagonian Andes: A Walking Guide. 2nd ed. LC 98-130340. (Illus.). 224p. (Orig.). 1998. pap. 15.95 (*0-86442-477-9*) Lonely Planet.
— Lonely Planet Walking in Switzerland: Walking Guide. (Illus.). 352p. 1996. pap. 14.95 (*0-86442-327-6*) Lonely Planet.
Lindenmayer, David. Wildlife & Woodchips. (Illus.). 168p. 1996. pap. 29.95 (*0-86840-231-1*, Pub. by New South Wales Univ Pr) Intl Spec Bk.
Lindenmeyer, Kriste. A Right to Childhood: The U. S. Children's Bureau & Child Welfare, 1912-46. LC 96-10031. 384p. 1997. text 49.95 (*0-252-02275-0*); pap. text 21.95 (*0-252-06577-8*) U of Ill Pr.
***Lindenmeyer, Kriste, ed.** Ordinary Women, Extraordinary Lives: Women in American History. LC 00-25659. (Human Tradition in America Ser.: No. 6). 320p. 2000. 55.00 (*0-8420-2752-1*); pap. 18.95 (*0-8420-2754-8*, SR Bks) Scholarly Res Inc.
Lindenmeyr, Adele. Poverty Is Not a Vice: Charity, Society, & the State in Imperial Russia. 304p. 1996. text 49.50 (*0-691-04489-9*, Pub. by Princeton U Pr) Cal Prin Full Svc.
Lindenmuth, Evelyn D. Mom, I Need to Be a Girl. LC 98-8472. (Illus.). 128p. 1998. pap. 9.95 (*0-9663272-0-9*) W Trook Pubg.
Lindenschmidt, Louis, ed. see Bate Cabal Assocs. Staff.
Lindensmith, Mark. Short-Term Losses: Stories. LC 96-15669. 200p. 1996. 22.50 (*0-87074-406-2*); pap. 12.95 (*0-87074-407-0*) SMU Press.
Lindenstrauss, J. Classical Banach Spaces I & II: Sequence Spaces; Function Spaces. (Classics in Mathematics Ser.). 243p. 1996. reprint ed. pap. 35.00 (*3-540-60628-9*) Spr-Verlag.
Lindenstrauss, J. & Milman, V. D., eds. Geometric Aspects of Functional Analysis. (Lecture Notes in Mathematics Ser.: Vol. 1267). vii, 212p. 1987. 38.95 (*0-387-18103-2*) Spr-Verlag.
— Geometric Aspects of Functional Analysis. (Lecture Notes in Mathematics Ser.: Vol. 1376). vii, 288p. 1989. 41.95 (*0-387-51303-5*) Spr-Verlag.
— Geometric Aspects of Functional Analysis. (Lecture Notes in Mathematics Ser.: Vol. 1469). xi, 191p. 1991. 41.95 (*0-387-54024-5*) Spr-Verlag.
— Geometric Aspects of Functional Analysis: Israel Seminar (GAFA), 1992-94. LC 95-10775. (Operator Theory, Advances & Applications Ser.: Vol. 77). 337p. 1995. 123.00 (*0-8176-5207-8*) Birkhauser.
Lindenstrauss, J. & Tzafriri, L. Classical Banach Spaces II: Function Spaces. (Ergebnisse der Mathematik und Ihrer Grenzgebiete Ser.: Vol. 97). 1979. 84.00 (*0-387-08888-1*) Spr-Verlag.
Lindenstrauss, Joram. Extension of Compact Operators. LC 52-42839. (American Mathematical Society Ser.: No. 48). 114p. reprint ed. pap. 35.40 (*0-608-09174-X*, 205267800002) Bks Demand.
— Extension of Compact Operators. 4th ed. LC 52-42839. (Memoirs Ser.: No. 1/48). 112p. 1987. reprint ed. pap. 18.00 (*0-8218-1248-3*, MEMO/1/48) Am Math.
Lindenstrauss, Joram, jt. auth. see Benyamini, Yoav.
Lindenstrauss, Naomi, jt. ed. see Dershowitz, Nachum.
Lindenthal, Jacob J. The Health of the American Jew. write for info. (*0-275-90018-5*, C0018, Praeger Pubs) Greenwood.
Lindenthal, Jacob J. & Schneider, Mareleyn. Health Concerns of Hispanics in New York City. LC 91-21072. 256p. 1991. lib. bdg. 89.95 (*0-7734-9852-4*) E Mellen.
Lindenthal, Jacob J., jt. auth. see Thomas, Claudewell S.
Linder, jt. auth. see Cauley, Kathleen.
Linder, A. Planen und Auswerten von Versuchen. 3rd ed. (Reihe der Experimentellen Biologie Ser.: No. 13). (GER., Illus.). 344p. 1980. 111.00 (*0-8176-0248-8*) Birkhauser.
Linder, Amnon, ed. The Jews in Legal Sources in the Early Middle Ages. LC 97-7310. 676p. 1997. text 65.00 (*0-8143-2403-7*) Wayne St U Pr.
Linder, Ann. Princes of the Trenches: Narrating the German Experience of the First World War. (GERM Ser.). x, 206p. 1997. 55.00 (*1-57113-075-6*) Camden Hse.
***Linder-Aronson, Sten & Woodside, Donald G.** Excess Face Height Malocclusion: Etiology, Diagnosis & Treatment. LC 00-27818. (Illus.). 2000. write for info. (*0-86715-389-X*) Quint Pub Co.
Linder, Bert. Condemned Without Judgement: The Three Lives of a Holocaust Survivor. (GER., Illus.). 340p. 1994. 19.95 (*0-9655690-0-4*) B Linder.
Linder, Bonnie S. Dear Mr. President: When Parents Are Sent to War. (Children in the Military Ser.). (J). (ps-4). 1995. pap. text 4.95 (*0-9643966-2-9*) Sylvan Crest.
— Just a Toy: Dealing with Weapons. (Children in the Military Ser.). (J). (ps-4). 1995. pap. text 4.95 (*0-9643966-3-7*) Sylvan Crest.
— On My Way: Dealing with a Move. LC 94-92235. (Children in the Military Ser.). 20p. (J). (ps-4). 1994. pap. 4.95 (*0-9643966-0-2*) Sylvan Crest.
— Time Apart: Dealing with Family Separation. LC 94-92271. (Children in the Military Ser.). 18p. (J). (ps-4). 1994. pap. text 4.95 (*0-9643966-1-0*) Sylvan Crest.
Linder, David, ed. see Miller, Judy A.
Linder, Doris H. Crusader for Sex Education: Elisa Ottesen-Jensen, 1886-1973 in Scandinavia & on the International Scene. LC 96-15161. 328p. (C). 1996. lib. bdg. 46.50 (*0-7618-0333-5*) U Pr of Amer.
Linder, Eric V. First Principles of Cosmology. 1997. pap. 26.97 (*0-201-40395-1*) Addison-Wesley.
Linder, Erik H. Hjalmar Bergman. LC 74-23060. (Twayne's World Authors Ser.). 197p. (C). 1975. lib. bdg. 17.95 (*0-8057-2147-9*) Irvington.
Linder, Fredric, jt. auth. see Cauley, Kathleen.
Linder, Greg. Alexander Graham Bell. LC 98-31474. (Photo-Illustrated Biographies Ser.). (Illus.). 1999. 14.00 (*0-7368-0202-9*, Bridgestone Bks) Capstone Pr.
— Marie Curie. LC 98-46104. (Photo-Illustrated Biographies Ser.). (Illus.). 1999. write for info. (*0-7368-0206-1*, Bridgestone Bks) Capstone Pr.
— Marie Curie. 1999. 14.00 (*0-516-21764-X*) Capstone Pr.
— Thomas Edison. LC 98-31472. (Photo-Illustrated Biographies Ser.). (Illus.). 1999. write for info. (*0-7368-0207-X*, Bridgestone Bks) Capstone Pr.
— Thomas Edison. 1999. 14.00 (*0-516-21765-8*) Capstone Pr.
Linder, Greg, jt. auth. see Hartley, Bill.
Linder, Greg, ed. see Backes, David.
Linder, Greg, ed. see Breining, Greg.
***Linder, H. P. & Kurzweil, H.** Orchids of South Africa. (Illus.). 600p. (C). 1999. 97.50 (*90-5410-445-7*, Pub. by A A Balkema) Ashgate Pub Co.
Linder, Harry P. Techniques of Code Drafting: The Lively Art of Personal Weaving Drafts. LC 83-72938. (Illus.). 140p. (Orig.). 1983. 16.95 (*0-915113-00-7*) Bizarre Butterfly.
Linder, Harry P., jt. auth. see Linder, Olive.
Linder, James, jt. auth. see Damjanov, Ivan.
Linder, James, jt. auth. see Koss, Leopold G.
Linder, Laura R. Public Access Television: America's Electronic Soapbox. LC 98-56631. (Illus.). 192p. 1999. 55.00 (*0-275-96487-6*, C6487, Praeger Pubs); pap. 19.95 (*0-275-96488-4*, C6487, Praeger Pubs) Greenwood.
Linder, Leo & Dromberg, D. A. The Serpentine Rouletted Stamps of Finland: Issues of 1860 & 1866. Koplowitz, George B., ed. Aro, Kauko, tr. from FIN. (Illus.). 106p. (Orig.). 1983. pap. text 17.50 (*0-936493-00-3*) Scand Philatelic.

L

L

Linder, M. C. Biochemistry of Copper. (Biochemistry of the Elements Ser.: Vol. 10). (Illus.). 544p. (C). 1991. text 110.00 (*0-306-43658-2*, Kluwer Plenum) Kluwer Academic.

Linder, Marc. The Dilemmas of Laissez-Faire Population Policy in Capitalist Societies When the Invisible Hand Controls Reproduction, 183. LC 96-32978. (Contributions in Economics & Economic History Ser.). 416p. 1997. 69.50 (*0-313-30309-6*) Greenwood.

— The Employment Relationship in Anglo-American Law: An Historical Perspective, 54. LC 89-7492. (Contributions in Legal Studies: No. 54). 309p. 1989. 69.50 (*0-313-26824-X*, LER/, Greenwood Pr) Greenwood.

— Farewell to the Self-Employed: Deconstructing a Socioeconomic & Legal Solipsism, 41. LC 91-39643. (Contributions in Labor Studies: No. 41). 200p. 1992. 55.00 (*0-313-28466-0*, LFW/, Greenwood Pr) Greenwood.

— Labor Statistics & Class Struggle. LC 94-34677. 130p. 1994. pap. 7.50 (*0-7178-0711-8*) Intl Pubs Co.

— Projecting Capitalism: A History of the Internationalization of the Construction Industry, 158. LC 93-50546. (Contributions in Economics & Economic History Ser.). 288p. 1994. 65.00 (*0-313-29293-0*, Greenwood Pr) Greenwood.

***Linder, Marc.** Wars of Attrition: Vietnam, the Business Roundtable & the Decline of Construction Unions. LC 99-95101. 453p. 1999. pap. 15.00 (*0-9673899-0-9*, Pub. by Fanpihua Pr) Iowa Book.

Linder, Marc & Nygaard, Ingrid. Void Where Prohibited: Rest Breaks & the Right to Urinate on Company Time. LC 97-35049. 192p. 1997. 27.50 (*0-8014-3390-8*) Cornell U Pr.

Linder, Marc & Zacharias, Lawrence S. Of Cabbages & Kings County: Agriculture & the Formation of Modern Brooklyn. LC 98-51779. (Illus.). 512p. 1999. 32.95 (*0-87745-670-4*) U of Iowa Pr.

***Linder, Marc & Zacharias, Lawrence S.** Of Cabbages & Kings County: Agriculture & the Formation of Modern Brooklyn. LC 98-51779. (Illus.). 484p. 2000. reprint ed. pap. text 21.95 (*0-87745-714-X*) U of Iowa Pr.

Linder, Marc, ed. see Kirk, Hans.

Linder, Marc, tr. see Kirk, Hans.

Linder, Mats. The ECITC Guide to IT&T Testing & Certification. (Illus.). 110p. (Orig.). (C). 1994. pap. text 35.00 (*0-7881-1493-X*) DIANE Pub.

Linder, Mike. Play It As It Lies: Golf & the Spiritual Life. LC 98-50849. 144p. 1999. pap. 15.00 (*0-664-25822-0*) Westminster John Knox.

Linder, O. D. & Linder, Penny. Gibson & Related Families. LC 90-62622. 428p. 1991. 50.00 (*0-9627513-1-6*) Linder.
Some families traced to European Royalty. Related Families featured are Bennett, Burrell, Coburn, Crosby, Hall, Henry, Hughes, Jeffries, Lowther, Marsh, Means, Meek, Peterson, Smith. Many other Related Families are given in the book.The Research for this book was done in major depositories in Washington, DC, in Salt Lake City & in several states. *Publisher Paid Annotation.*

Linder, O. D., jt. auth. see Linder, Penny.

Linder, Olive & Linder, Harry P. Handspinning Cotton. (Illus.). 100p. 1985. pap. 8.95 (*0-915113-02-3*) Bizarre Butterfly.

— Handspinning Flax. (Illus.). 80p. 1986. 9.95 (*0-915113-04-X*) Bizarre Butterfly.

Linder, P. W., et al. Analysis Using Glass Electrodes. 160p. 1984. 65.00 (*0-335-10420-7*) OpUniv Pr.

Linder, Pamela, jt. auth. see Holstead, Christy.

Linder, Patrick, jt. ed. see Hall, Michael N.

Linder-Peiz, Susie, jt. auth. see Bates, Erica.

***Linder, Penny & Linder, O. D. Dever & Related Families. LC 98-65801. (Illus.). 984p. 1998. 50.00 (*0-9627513-2-4*) Linder.**
The result of several years research in major depositories in Washington, DC, in Salt Lake City & several states & five years assembling. There are 572 pages devoted to Dever families in early Maryland & their migration to Dever families in early Maryland & their migration to other states. The book also contains information on Other Dever families, including John Dever, Amos M. Dever, Simon Dever, Philip Peyton Dever & others. Related families are Barker, Current, Keener, Mason, Phillips, Robinson/Robison, Rogers. Many other related families are given in the book. *Publisher Paid Annotation.*

Linder, Penny & Linder, O. D. The Linder Family. LC 90-62412. (Illus.). 220p. 1991. 35.00 (*0-9627513-0-8*) Linder.
Switzerland-Canton of Bern; Meiringen, 1500-1800ds-Brienz, 1600-1900ds/Canada-Alberta,USA-KS, WIS, AK, CA, PA, NY, ILL, MT, WV. Some of the families included are: Heinrich Linder, wife Lucy Buehler, Robert Linder, wife Margaritha Stahi (Stohli), Herminia Linder, husband Edward Fagan, Alfred Linder, wife Rosa Borter, Hermann Linder, wife Marie Berger. Many related families are given the book. *Publisher Paid Annotation.*

Linder, Penny, jt. auth. see Linder, O. D.

Linder, Ray. Making the Most of Your Money: How to Develop a Personal Financial Strategy for Maximum Impact. 180p. 1995. pap. 10.99 (*1-56476-389-7*, 6-3389, Victor Bks) Chariot Victor.

— Seven Secrets to Reduce Financial Worry. LC 99-231491. 1999. pap. 11.99 (*0-8024-8196-5*) Moody.

***Linder, Ray.** What Will I Do with My Money? How Your Personality Affects Your Financial Behavior. 192p. 2000. pap. write for info. (*1-881273-33-4*) Northfield Pub.

Linder, Robert D. & Pierard, Richard V. Civil Religion & the Presidency. 252p. 1988. pap. 14.95 (*0-310-28331-0*, 11081P) Zondervan.

Linder, Ron. Animals on the Roof. 136p. (Orig.). 1993. pap. 9.95 (*0-9635886-3-X*) R Linder.

— Dancer Stay Out! 102p. (Orig.). 1995. pap. 9.95 (*0-9646098-6-X*) Linn Pub.

Linder, S. Wayne. Loan Review Deskbook: How to Establish, Maintain & Regulate an Effective Program. 276p. 1989. ring bd. 135.00 (*1-55520-203-9*, Irwn Prfssnl) McGraw-Hill Prof.

— Total Quality Loan Management: Applying the Principles of TQM for Superior Lending Performance. 1992. per. 50.00 (*1-55738-371-5*, Irwn Prfssnl) McGraw-Hill Prof.

Linder, Staffan B. The Pacific Century: Economic & Political Consequences of Asian-Pacific Dynamism. 168p. 1986. 27.50 (*0-8047-1294-8*); pap. 11.95 (*0-8047-1305-7*) Stanford U Pr.

Linder, Steven. The Measure of Justice. LC 92-11520. 194p. 1992. 19.95 (*0-8027-4134-7*) Walker & Co.

— Wager. 192p. 1986. 14.95 (*0-8027-4061-8*) Walker & Co.

Linder, Sune & Kellomaki, Seppo, eds. Management of Structure & Productivity of Boreal & Subalpine Forests. (Studia Forestalia Suecica: No. 191). (Illus.). 94p. (Orig.). 1994. pap. 38.50 (*91-576-4822-0*) Coronet Bks.

***Linder, Suzanne Cameron.** Anglican Churches in Colonial South Carolina: Their History & Architecture. LC 99-59040. (Illus.). 160p. 2000. 35.00 (*0-941711-45-5*, Pub. by Wyrick & Co) IPG Chicago.

***Linder, Toni W.** Teacher's Guide for Read, Play & Learn! Storybook Activities for Young Children. LC 99-31608. 1999. text 45.00 (*1-55766-400-5*) P H Brookes.

Linder, Toni W. Transdisciplinary Play-Based Assessment: A Functional Approach to Working with Young Children. rev. ed. LC 89-70795. 224p. (Orig.). 1993. spiral bd. 44.00 (*1-55766-162-6*, 1626) P H Brookes.

— Transdisciplinary Play-Based Assessment & Intervention: Child & Program Summary Forms. 58p. 1993. 27.00 (*1-55766-163-4*) P H Brookes.

— Transdisciplinary Play-Based Intervention: Guidelines for Developing a Meaningful Curriculum for Young Children. LC 93-426. 1993. 49.95 (*1-55766-130-8*) P H Brookes.

Linder, William, Jr. Andrew Murray. LC 95-25904. (Men of Faith Ser.). 144p. (Orig.). 1995. mass mkt. 4.99 (*1-55661-670-8*) Bethany Hse.

Linderer, Gary A. Eyes Behind the Lines. 1991. mass mkt. 5.99 (*0-8041-0819-6*) Ivy Books.

— The Eyes of the Eagle. 224p. (Orig.). 1991. mass mkt. 6.99 (*0-8041-0733-5*) Ivy Books.

— Phantom Warriors: LRRPs, LRPs & Rangers in Vietnam. 2000. mass mkt. 7.50 (*0-8041-1601-6*) Ivy Books.

— Six Silent Men: Silent & Deadly, Book 3, Bk. 3. LC 97-93362. 1997. mass mkt. 5.99 (*0-8041-1567-2*) Ivy Books.

Linderman, Alf. The Reception of Religious Television: Social Semeiology Applied to an Empirical Case Study. LC 96-233410. (Psychologia & Sociologia Religionum Ser.: No. 12). 229p. (Orig.). 1996. pap. 48.50 (*91-554-3809-1*) Coronet Bks.

Linderman, Becki. Complicated Child? Simple Options. (Illus.). 1996. pap. 10.00 (*0-941903-19-2*) Ransom Hill.

Linderman, Bill. Reading for Understanding: Grade 2. (Illus.). (J). 1997. pap. text 2.29 (*0-7647-0095-2*) Schaffer Pubns.

Linderman, Charles W., ed. International Technical Conference on Slurry Transportation, 2nd: Proceedings. LC 77-81416. (Illus.). 152p. 1977. pap. 100.00 (*0-932066-02-X*) Coal Slurry Tech.

— International Technical Conference on Slurry Transportation, 4th: Proceedings. LC 79-63397. (Illus.). 248p. 1971. pap. 100.00 (*0-932066-04-6*) Coal Slurry Tech.

Linderman, Charles W. & Skedgell, David W., eds. International Technical Conference on Slurry Transportation, 5th: Proceedings. 5th ed. LC 80-92621. (Illus.). 296p. (Orig.). 1980. pap. 100.00 (*0-932066-05-4*) Coal Slurry Tech.

Linderman, David A., et al. Alzheimer's Day Care: A Basic Guide. 152p. 1990. 66.95 (*0-89116-106-6*); pap. 29.95 (*1-56032-152-0*) Hemisp Pub.

Linderman, Earl. The True & Incredible Adventures of Doktor Thrill. LC 84-6. (Illus.). 155p. 1984. 40.00 (*0-87358-366-3*) Paradise Hse.

Linderman, Earl W. & Linderman, Marlene M. Arts & Crafts in the Classroom. 2nd ed. (Illus.). 528p. (C). 1984. 76.60 (*0-02-370860-3*, Macmillan Coll) P-H.

Linderman, Frank B. Indian Lodge-Fire Stories. LC 98-12660. (Illus.). 96p. (Orig.). 1998. pap. 12.95 (*0-943972-39-6*) Homestead WY.

— Indian Old-Man Stories: More Sparks from War Eagle's Lodge-Fire. LC 95-50129. (Illus.). xxvii, 169p. 1996. pap. 8.95 (*0-8032-7960-4*, Bison Books) U of Nebr Pr.

— Indian Why Stories. unabridged ed. LC 95-12885. (Illus.). 128p. 1995. reprint ed. pap. text 3.95 (*0-486-28800-5*) Dover.

— Indian Why Stories: Sparks from War Eagle's Lodge-Fire. LC 95-46963. (Illus.). xx, 236p. 1996. pap. 9.95 (*0-8032-7959-0*, Bison Books) U of Nebr Pr.

— Kootenai Why Stories: The Authorized Edition. LC 97-25922. (Illus.). xxiv, 173p. 1997. pap. 9.95 (*0-8032-7972-8*, Bison Books) U of Nebr Pr.

— Montana Adventure: The Recollections of Frank B. Linderman. Merriam, Harold G., ed. LC 85-1051. 236p. reprint ed. pap. 67.30 (*0-7837-4277-0*, 2043969) Bks Demand.

— The Montana Stories of Frank B. Linderman: The Authorized Edition. LC 97-17727. viii, 214p. 1997. pap. 9.95 (*0-8032-7970-1*, Bison Books) U of Nebr Pr.

— Old Man Coyote. LC 96-32438. (Illus.). v, 254p. 1996. pap. 11.95 (*0-8032-7964-7*, Bison Books) U of Nebr Pr.

— Plenty-Coups: Chief of the Crows. LC 30-11369. (Illus.). ix, 327p. 1962. pap. 14.95 (*0-8032-5121-1*, Bison Books) U of Nebr Pr.

— Pretty-Shield. (Native American Voices Ser.). (Illus.). 256p. 1993. reprint ed. 24.95 (*0-7835-1758-0*) Time-Life.

— Pretty-Shield: Medicine Woman of the Crows. LC 72-3273. (Illus.). 256p. 1974. reprint ed. pap. 9.95 (*0-8032-5791-0*, Bison Books) U of Nebr Pr.

— Recollections of Charley Russell. LC 63-18074. (Illus.). 196p. 1988. pap. 15.95 (*0-8061-2112-2*) U of Okla Pr.

— Wolf & the Winds. LC 86-40075. 224p. 1986. 19.95 (*0-8061-2007-X*) U of Okla Pr.

Linderman, Frank Bird. Henry Plummer: A Novel. LC 99-42663. (Illus.). 392p. 2000. pap. 16.95 (*0-8032-7989-2*, A Bison Orig) U of Nebr Pr.

Linderman, Gerald F. Embattled Courage: The Experience of Combat in the American Civil War. 357p. 1989. pap. 17.95 (*0-02-919761-9*) Free Pr.

— The World Within War: America's Combat Experience in World War II. 1997. 26.00 (*0-02-919115-7*) Free Pr.

— The World Within War: America's Combat Experience in World War II. LC 97-36361. 416p. 1997. 25.50 (*0-684-82797-2*) Free Pr.

— The World Within War: America's Combat Experience in World War II. 1999. pap. 15.95 (*0-674-96202-8*) HUP.

Linderman, Hank. Hot Tips for the Home Recording Studio. 160p. 1994. 18.99 (*0-89879-651-2*, Wrtrs Digest Bks) F & W Pubns Inc.

Linderman, Jennifer J., jt. auth. see Lauffenburger, Douglas A.

Linderman, Joan M. & Funk, Virginia. The New Complete Akita. (Illus.). 256p. 1994. 25.95 (*0-87605-031-3*) Howell Bks.

Linderman, Joan M. & Funk, Virginia B. The Complete Akita. LC 83-6180. (Complete Breed Bk.). (Illus.). 216p. 1983. pap. 25.00 (*0-87605-006-2*) Howell Bks.

Linderman, Leon & Goldwasser, Judy. Unstuck for Words Vol. 1: How to Start & Finish Any Writing Project. (Illus.). 58p. (Orig.). (YA). (gr. 9). 1994. pap. 13.95 (*0-9638780-0-X*) Writing Dynamics.

Linderman, Marlene G. Art in the Elementary School: Drawing, Painting, & Creating for the Classroom. 4th ed. 320p. (C). 1989. text. write for info. (*0-697-03341-4*) Brown & Benchmark.

— Art in the Elementary School: Drawing, Painting & Creating for the Classroom. 5th ed. LC 96-86033. 372p. (C). 1996. text. write for info. (*0-697-12500-9*) Brown & Benchmark.

Linderman, Marlene M., jt. auth. see Linderman, Earl W.

Linderman, Michael. Developing Visual Programming Applications Using SmallTalk. (Advances in Object Technology Ser.: No. 12). 349p. 1996. pap. 39.95 (*0-13-569229-6*) Cambridge U Pr.

Linderman, R. G., jt. ed. see Bethlenfalvay, G. J.

Linderman, R. G., jt. ed. see Pfleger, F. L.

Linderman, Sheila, jt. auth. see Hayot, Roger.

Linderman, Shelia. The New French Baker: Perfect Pastries & Beautiful Breads from Your Kitchen. LC 98-26185. (Illus.). 320p. 1998. 35.00 (*0-688-14325-3*, Wm Morrow) Morrow Avon.

Lindermeyer, Vivian & Howell, Leon, eds. Ethics in the Present Tense: Christianity & Crisis 1966-1991. 200p. (Orig.). 1991. pap. 12.95 (*0-377-00230-5*) Friendship Pr.

— Ethics in the Present Tense: Readings from Christianity & Crisis 1966-1991. 200p. 1991. 21.95 (*0-377-00239-9*) Friendship Pr.

Linders, B. E. Strategic Planning in South East England, 1968-78: A Case Study. (Illus.). 83p. 1985. pap. 22.00 (*0-08-032720-6*, Pergamon Pr) Elsevier.

Linders, Tullia. Studies in the Treasure Records of Artemis Brauronia Found in Athens. (Acta Instituti Atheniensis Regni Sueciae Ser.: Vol. XIX). (Illus.). 80p. 1972. pap. 29.50 (*91-85086-02-9*, Pub. by P Astroms) Coronet Bks.

Linders, Tullia, ed. Opuscula Atheniensia XVIII. (Acta Instituti Atheniensis Regni Sueciae Ser.: Series 4, XXXIX). (Illus.). 249p. (Orig.). 1990. pap. 97.50 (*91-7916-020-4*, Pub. by P Astroms) Coronet Bks.

Linders, Tullia, et al, eds. Opus Mixtum: Essays in Ancient Art & Society. (Acta Instituti Romani Regni Sueciae, Series in 4 Degrees). (Illus.). 176p. 1994. pap. 49.50 (*91-7042-150-1*, Pub. by P Astroms) Coronet Bks.

— Opuscula Romana XVIII. (Acta Instituti Romani Regni Sueciae Ser.: Series 4, XLVII). (Illus.). 239p. (Orig.). 1990. pap. 97.50 (*91-7042-136-6*, Pub. by P Astroms) Coronet Bks.

— Opuscula Romana XIX. (Acta Instituti Romani Regni Sueciae Ser.: Series 4, LI). (Illus.). 119p. (Orig.). 1993. pap. 57.50 (*91-7042-146-3*, Pub. by P Astroms) Coronet Bks.

Linders, Tullia & Alroth, Brita, eds. Economics of Cult in the Ancient Greek World: Proceedings of the Uppsala Symposium 1990. (Uppsala Studies in Ancient Mediterranean & Near Eastern Civilizations: No. 21). (Illus.). 99p. (Orig.). (C). 1993. pap. 41.50 (*91-554-3031-7*, Pub. by Uppsala Universitet) Coronet Bks.

Lindert, Kathy, jt. auth. see Tuck, Laura.

Lindert, Peter H. International Economics. 9th ed. 256p. (C). 1991. text, student ed. 23.12 (*0-256-07901-3*, Irwn McGrw-H) McGrw-H Hghr Educ.

— International Economics. 11th ed. LC 99-56092. 736p. 1999. 84.69 (*0-07-290387-2*) McGraw.

— Key Currencies & Gold, 1900-1913. LC 76-93955. (Princeton Studies in International Finance Ser.: no. 24). 89p. reprint ed. pap. 30.00 (*0-608-13561-5*, 202239100026) Bks Demand.

***Lindert, Peter H.** Shifting Ground: The Changing Agricultural Soils of China & Indonesia. (Illus.). 338p. 2000. 45.00 (*0-262-12227-8*) MIT Pr.

Lindert, Peter H. & Pugel, Thomas A. International Economics. 10th ed. LC 95-36376. 704p. (C). 1995. student ed. 34.50 (*0-256-20686-4*, Irwn McGrw-H); text 69.75 (*0-256-14026-X*, Irwn McGrw-H) McGrw-H Hghr Educ.

Lindert, Peter H., jt. auth. see Pugel, Thomas A.

Lindert, Peter H., jt. ed. see Eichengreen, Barry J.

Lindert, Wilgert Te, see Te Lindert, Wilgert.

***Lindesay, Guo.** Terracotta Army. 2nd ed. 1999. pap. 9.95 (*962-217-487-6*) China Guides.

Lindesay, Guo. Terracotta Army. 2nd ed. 1999. 14.95 (*962-217-600-3*) Norton.

Lindesay, James, ed. Neurotic Disorders in the Elderly. (Illus.). 260p. (C). 1995. text 79.50 (*0-19-262396-6*) OUP.

Lindesay, James, et al. Delirium & the Elderly. (Illus.). 132p. 1991. 45.00 (*0-19-261862-8*) OUP.

Lindesay, William. Alone on the Great Wall. LC 91-71367. 288p. 1991. pap. 14.95 (*1-55591-079-3*) Fulcrum Pub.

— Beijing. 4th ed. (China Guides Ser.). (Illus.). 208p. 1997. pap. 19.95 (*0-8442-4768-5*, 47685, Passprt Bks) NTC Contemp Pub Co.

***Lindesay, William.** Great Wall. 2nd ed. 1999. pap. 9.95 (*962-217-488-4*) China Guides.

Lindesay, William & Qi, Wu. Beijing. 5th ed. LC 98-53869. (Odyssey Passport Ser.). (Illus.). 203p. 1999. pap. 19.95 (*962-217-603-8*) Norton.

***Lindesay, William & Wu, Qingyun.** Beijing. 6th ed. 2000. pap. 19.95 (*962-217-622-4*, Pub. by China Guides) Norton.

***Lindesmith, Alfred R., et al.** Social Psychology. LC 98-58146. 475p. 1999. 65.00 (*0-7619-0745-9*) Sage.

Lindesmith, Alfred R., et al. Social Psychology. 8th ed. LC 98-58146. 1999. 29.95 (*0-7619-0746-7*) Sage.

Lindestrom, Peter. Geographia Americae with an Account of the Delaware Indians. Scott, Franklyn D., ed. LC 78-15195. (Scandinavians in America Ser.). (Illus.). 1979. reprint ed. lib. bdg. 40.95 (*0-405-11648-9*) Ayer.

Lindey, Alexancer. Separation Agreements & Ante-Nuptial Contracts, 3 vols. 1964. ring bd. write for info. (*0-8205-1360-1*) Bender.

Lindey, Alexander & Landau, Michael. Lindey on Entertainment, Publishing & the Arts: Agreements & the Law, 4 vols. 2nd ed. LC 80-10991. (Entertainment & Communication Law Ser.). 1980. ring bd. 580.00 incl. disk (*0-87632-005-1*) West Group.

***Lindey, Alexander & Parley, Louis I.** Lindey & Parley on Separation Agreements & Antenuptial Contracts. 2nd ed. LC 99-48711. 1999. 350.00 (*0-8205-4188-5*) Bender.

Lindey, Christine. Art in the Cold War. (Illus.). 224p. (C). 1991. 30.00 (*1-56131-010-7*, NAB) I R Dee.

Lindfield, G. R. Numerical Methods Using MATLAB. 2nd ed. LC 99-36536. 482p. 1999. pap. 56.00 (*0-13-012641-1*) Allyn.

Lindfield, G. R. & Penny, J. E. Microcomputers in Numerical Analysis. LC 93-23169. (Mathematics & Its Applications Ser.: Statistics, Operational Research, & Computational Mathematics Section). 1993. 23.95 (*0-13-336744-4*, Pub. by Tavistock-E Horwood) Routldge.

Lindfors, Bernth. African Textualities: Texts, Pre-Texts & Contexts of African Literature. LC 97-4365. 1997. write for info. (*0-86543-615-0*); pap. write for info. (*0-86543-616-9*) Africa World.

— Black African Literature in English, 1982-1986. 550p. 1989. lib. bdg. 85.00 (*0-905450-75-2*, Pub. by H Zell Pubs) Seven Hills Bk.

— Black African Literature in English, 1987-1991. LC 97-189537. (Bibliographical Research in African Literature Ser.: No. 3). 682p. 1995. 125.00 (*1-873836-16-3*, Pub. by H Zell Pubs) Seven Hills Bk.

— The Blind Men & the Elephant & Other Essays LC 98-55999. 1999. pap. write for info. (*0-86543-729-7*) Africa World.

— Loaded Vehicles: Studies in African Literary Media. LC 96-16371. 224p. 1996. 59.95 (*0-86543-542-1*); pap. 18.95 (*0-86543-543-X*) Africa World.

— Long Drums & Canons: Teaching & Researching African Literatures. LC 94-37182. 200p. 1994. 49.95 (*0-86543-436-0*); pap. 16.95 (*0-86543-437-9*) Africa World.

— Popular Literatures in Africa. per. 12.95 (*0-86543-221-X*) Africa World.

— Popular Literatures in Africa. 1996. 45.00 (*0-86543-220-1*) Africa World.

Lindfors, Bernth, ed. Africans on Stage: Studies in Ethnological Show Business. LC 98-50551. (Illus.). 1998. 35.00 (*0-253-33468-3*); pap. 16.95 (*0-253-21245-6*) Ind U Pr.

— Approaches to Teaching Achebe's Things Fall Apart. LC

An Asterisk (*) at the beginning of an entry indicates that the title is appearing for the first time.

91-26230. (Approaches to Teaching World Literature Ser.: No. 37). x, 145p. 1991. pap. 18.00 (*0-87352-548-5*, AP37P); lib. bdg. 37.50 (*0-87352-547-7*, AP37C) Modern Lang.

— Contemporary Black South African Literature: A Symposium. 2nd ed. LC 85-50381. (African Literature Association Annuals Ser.: No. 1). 145p. 1985. reprint ed. 22.00 (*0-89410-454-3*); reprint ed. pap. 14.00 (*0-89410-455-1*) Cornell AS&RC.

— Critical Perspectives on Amos Tutuola. LC 75-13706. (Illus.). 318p. (Orig.). 1975. 25.00 (*0-914478-05-2*, Three Contnts); pap. 17.95 (*0-914478-06-0*, Three Contnts) L Rienner.

— Critical Perspectives on Nigerian Literatures. LC 75-27391. 286p. 1976. boxed set 25.00 (*0-914478-27-3*, Three Contnts) L Rienner.

— Mazungumzo: Interviews with East African Writers, Publishers, Editors & Scholars. LC 80-25684. (Papers in International Studies: Africa Ser.: No. 41). 187p. reprint ed. pap. 58.00 (*0-7837-1327-4*, 204147500001) Bks Demand.

— South African Voices. 36p. 1975. pap. 10.00 (*0-87959-125-0*) U of Tex H Ransom Ctr.

Lindfors, Bernth & Kothandaraman, Bata, eds. South Asian Responses to Chinua Achebe. 200p. (C). 1993. text 27.50 (*81-85218-66-8*, Pub. by Prestige) Advent Bks Div.

Lindfors, Bernth & Sander, Reinhard W., eds. Twentieth-Century Caribbean & Black African Writers. LC 95-32083. (Dictionary of Literary Biography Ser.: Vol. 157). 400p. 1995. text 155.00 (*0-8103-9352-2*) Gale.

Lindfors, Bernth & Schild, Ulla. Neo-African Literature & Culture: Essays in Memory of Jahneinz Jahn. 352p. 1982. text 49.50 (*3-593-32821-6*) Irvington.

Lindfors, Bernth, et al. Black Africa. Gerard, Albert, ed. LC 77-126039. (Review of National Literature Ser.: Vol. 2, No. 2). 254p. 1972. pap. 6.95 (*0-918680-59-X*) Griffon House.

Lindfors, Bernth, ed. see Achebe, Chinua.

Lindfors, Bernth, ed. see Tutuola, Amos.

Lindfors, Bernth, ed. see Veit-Wild, Flora.

Lindfors, Bernth, jt. ed. see Wylie, Hal.

Lindfors, Berth. Early Nigerian Literature. LC 81-12719. 180p. 1982. 35.50 (*0-8419-0740-4*, Africana) Holmes & Meier.

Lindfors, Eula A., ed. Guild Musicianship. 64p. (gr. 3-12). 1974. pap. text 9.95 (*0-87487-638-9*) Summy-Birchard.

***Lindfors, Judith.** Children's Inquiry: Using Language to Make Sense of the World. LC 98-55069. 44. 288p. 1999. pap. 24.95 (*0-8077-3836-0*) Tchrs Coll.

Lindfors, Judith W. Children's Inquiry: Using Language to Make Sense of the World LC 98-55069. (Language & Literacy Ser.). 288p. 1999. text 53.00 (*0-8077-3837-9*) Tchrs Coll.

— Children's Language & Learning. 2nd ed. LC 86-22624. (Illus.). 512p. (C). 1987. 83.00 (*0-13-131962-0*) P-H.

***Lindfors, Judith Wells & Townsend, Jane S., eds.** Teaching Language Arts: Learning Through Dialogue. LC 99-35050. (Illus.). 335p. 1999. pap. 29.95 (*0-8141-5035-7*, 50357) NCTE.

Lindfors, Viveca & Austin, Paul, eds. I Am a Woman: The Play. 96p. 1990. pap. 7.95 (*1-55783-048-7*) Applause Theatre Bk Pubs.

Lindgaard, Gitte. Usability Testing & System Evaluation: A Guide for Designing Useful Computer Systems. LC 94-142590. (Computing Ser.). 416p. 1993. mass mkt. 59.95 (*0-412-46100-5*) Chapman & Hall.

Lindgre. Marketing: Interact with CD ROM. (C). 1995. student ed. 88.50 (*0-03-018563-7*) Harcourt.

Lindgren. Marketing. (C). 1995. pap. text, student ed. 54.50 (*0-03-017479-1*) Harcourt Coll Pubs.

Lindgren & Shrimp. Marketing: Media Guide. (C). 1995. pap. text, teacher ed., student ed. 28.00 (*0-03-017572-0*) Harcourt Coll Pubs.

Lindgren, jt. auth. see Berry.

Lindgren, Alice, jt. auth. see Hausheer, Peggy.

Lindgren, Alvin J. Foundations for Purposeful Church Administration. LC 65-16459. 1965. 17.95 (*0-687-13339-4*) Abingdon.

Lindgren, Alvin J. & Shawchuck, Norman. Let My People Go: Empowering Laity for Ministry. 144p. (Orig.). (C). 1989. reprint ed. pap. text 12.95 (*0-938180-15-0*) Spiritual Growth.

Lindgren, Alvin J., jt. auth. see Shawchuck, Norman.

Lindgren, Amy. Cracking the Hidden Job Market, Vol. 3. 2nd ed. (Pocket Job Ser.). 64p. 1995. reprint ed. pap. 2.95 (*0-9633008-3-0*) Prototype Career Media.

— Financial Survival Between Jobs, Vol. 6. 2nd ed. (Pocket Job Ser.). 64p. 1995. reprint ed. pap. 2.95 (*0-9633008-5-7*) Prototype Career Media.

— Five Steps to Your Next Job, Vol. I. 2nd ed. (Pocket Job Ser.). 64p. 1995. reprint ed. pap. 2.95 (*0-9633008-2-2*) Prototype Career Media.

— Job Interviews: 10 Steps to Success, Vol. 4. 2nd ed. (Pocket Job Ser.). 64p. 1995. reprint ed. pap. 2.95 (*0-9633008-6-5*) Prototype Career Media.

— Job Search over 40: Selling to Your Strengths, Vol. 5. 2nd ed. (Pocket Job Ser.). 64p. 1995. reprint ed. pap. 2.95 (*0-9633008-7-3*) Prototype Career Media.

— Job Search Problem-Solving Companion. (Pocket Job Ser.: Vol. 7). 64p. 1997. pap. 2.95 (*0-9633008-8-1*) Prototype Career Media.

— Resumes, Etc., Vol. 2. 2nd ed. (Pocket Job Ser.). 112p. 1995. reprint ed. pap. 2.95 (*0-9633008-4-9*) Prototype Career Media.

Lindgren, Amy, ed. see Kelnhofer, Guy, Jr.

Lindgren, Amy, ed. see Rask, Mark.

Lindgren, Anders. Major Anders Lindgren's Teaching Exercises: A Manual for Instructors & Riders. LC 98-31462. (Illus.). 160p. 1998. 24.95 (*0-939481-53-7*) Half Halt Pr.

Lindgren, Astrid. The Adventures of Pippi Longstocking. LC 97-20035. (Pippi Longstocking Ser.). (Illus.). 320p. (J). (gr. 2-5). 1997. 25.00 (*0-670-87612-7*, Viking) Viking Penguin.

— A Calf for Christmas. Lucas, Barbara, tr. LC 91-60168. (Illus.). 32p. (J). (ps up). 1991. bds. 13.95 (*91-29-59920-2*, Pub. by R & S Bks) FS&G.

— The Children of Noisy Village. (J). (gr. 3-7). 1988. pap. 5.99 (*0-14-032609-X*, PuffinBks) Peng Put Young Read.

— The Children of Noisy Village. (J). 1988. 9.09 (*0-606-03557-5*, Pub. by Turtleback) Demco.

— Christmas in the Stable. (Illus.). 32p. (J). (ps-3). 1998. pap. 5.99 (*0-698-11664-X*, PapStar) Peng Put Young Read.

***Lindgren, Astrid.** Do You Know Pippi Longstocking? Dyssegaard, Elisabeth Kallick, tr. from SWE. LC 99-70430. (Pippi Longstocking Ser.). (Illus.). 32p. (J). (ps-3). 1999. 9.95 (*91-29-64661-8*, Pub. by R&S Bks SW) FS&G.

Lindgren, Astrid. Emil in Soup. (J). 1999. pap. 3.95 (*0-14-034121-8*, Viking) Viking Penguin.

— Emil's Pranks. 1999. pap. 3.95 (*0-14-034122-6*, Viking) Viking Penguin.

— I Don't Want to Go to Bed. Lucas, Barbara, tr. from SWE. LC 88-4713. (Illus.). 32p. (J). (ps up). 1988. 12.95 (*91-29-59066-3*, Pub. by R & S Bks) FS&G.

— I Want to Go to School, Too! Lucas, Barbara, tr. from SWE. LC 87-45162. (Illus.). 32p. (J). (ps up). 1987. 10.95 (*91-29-58328-4*, Pub. by R & S Bks) FS&G.

— Lotta's Christmas Surprise. LC 90-60542. (Illus.). 32p. (J). (ps-3). 1990. 13.95 (*91-29-59782-X*, Pub. by R & S Bks) FS&G.

— Lotta's Easter Surprise. Lucas, Barbara, tr. LC 90-9054. (Illus.). 32p. (J). (ps-3). 13.95 (*91-29-59862-1*) FS&G.

— Pippi Goes on Board. (Pippi Longstocking Ser.). 172p. (J). (gr. 3-5). 1980. lib. bdg. 25.95 (*0-89967-014-8*, Harmony Rain) Buccaneer Bks.

— Pippi Goes on Board. (Pippi Longstocking Ser.). (Illus.). 144p. (J). (gr. 2-5). 1957. 14.99 (*0-670-55677-7*, Viking Child) Peng Put Young Read.

— Pippi Goes on Board. LC 76-54740. (Pippi Longstocking Ser.). 144p. (J). (gr. 3-7). 1977. pap. 4.99 (*0-14-030959-4*, PuffinBks) Peng Put Young Read.

— Pippi Goes on Board. (Pippi Longstocking Ser.). (J). (gr. 3-5). 1970. 9.09 (*0-606-04316-0*, Pub. by Turtleback) Demco.

Lindgren, Astrid. Pippi Goes on Board. (Pippi Longstocking Ser.). 140p. (J). (gr. 3-5). pap. 3.99 (*0-8072-1401-9*) Listening Lib.

Lindgren, Astrid. Pippi Goes to School. Lamborn, Frances, tr. LC PZ7.L6585Pgf 1998. (Pippi Longstocking Ser.). (Illus.). 32p. (J). (gr. 3-5). 1998. 13.99 (*0-670-88075-2*) Viking Penguin.

***Lindgren, Astrid.** Pippi Goes to the Circus. (Pippi Longstocking Ser.). (Illus.). 32p. (J). (ps-3). 2000. pap. 5.99 (*0-14-130243-7*, PuffinBks) Peng Put Young Read.

Lindgren, Astrid. Pippi in the South Seas. Bothmer, Gerry, tr. (Pippi Longstocking Ser.). (Illus.). 128p. (J). (gr. 2-5). 1959. 15.99 (*0-670-55711-0*, Viking Child) Peng Put Young Read.

— Pippi in the South Seas. Bothmer, Gerry, tr. LC 76-54802. (Pippi Longstocking Ser.). (Illus.). 128p. (J). (gr. 3-7). 1977. pap. 4.99 (*0-14-030958-6*, PuffinBks) Peng Put Young Read.

— Pippi in the South Seas. (Pippi Longstocking Ser.). (J). (gr. 3-5). 1998. 18.50 (*0-8446-6974-1*) Peter Smith.

Lindgren, Astrid. Pippi in the South Seas. (Pippi Longstocking Ser.). (J). (gr. 3-5). 1977. 9.09 (*0-606-04317-9*, Pub. by Turtleback) Demco.

— Pippi in the South Seas. (Pippi Longstocking Ser.). 125p. (J). (gr. 3-5). pap. 3.99 (*0-8072-1392-6*) Listening Lib.

Lindgren, Astrid. Pippi Longstocking. Lamborn, Florence, tr. LC 50-10396. (Pippi Longstocking Ser.). (Illus.). 158p. (J). (gr. 2-5). 1950. 15.99 (*0-670-55745-5*, Viking Child) Peng Put Young Read.

— Pippi Longstocking. Lamborn, Florence, tr. LC 77-1374. (Pippi Longstocking Ser.). (Illus.). 158p. (J). (gr. 3-7). 1977. pap. 4.99 (*0-14-030957-8*, PuffinBks) Peng Put Young Read.

Lindgren, Astrid. Pippi Longstocking. (Pippi Longstocking Ser.). (J). (gr. 3-5). 1969. 9.09 (*0-606-04318-7*, Pub. by Turtleback) Demco.

— Pippi Longstocking. (Pippi Longstocking Ser.). 160p. (J). (gr. 3-5). pap. 4.99 (*0-8072-1431-0*) Listening Lib.

Lindgren, Astrid. Pippi Longstocking. (Pippi Longstocking Ser.). 192p. (J). (gr. 3-5). 1980. reprint ed. lib. bdg. 25.95 (*0-89967-013-X*, Harmony Rain) Buccaneer Bks.

Lindgren, Astrid. Pippi Longstocking. unabridged ed. (Pippi Longstocking Ser.). (J). (gr. 3-5). 1990. audio 15.95 (*0-8072-7388-0*, YA 807 CXR) Listening Lib.

Lindgren, Astrid. The Pippi Longstocking Omnibus. (Pippi Longstocking Ser.). (Illus.). (J). 1997. write for info. (*0-614-29322-7*) Viking Penguin.

— Pippi Longstocking's After-Christmas Party. (Pippi Longstocking Ser.). (Illus.). 32p. (J). (gr. k-3). 1998. pap. 5.99 (*0-14-056425-X*, PuffinBks) Peng Put Young Read.

— Pippi Longstocking's After-Christmas Party. (Pippi Longstocking Ser.). (Illus.). 32p. (J). (gr. 3-5). 1996. 13.99 (*0-670-86790-X*) Viking Penguin.

***Lindgren, Astrid.** Pippi to the Rescue. LC 99-56111. (Pippi Longstocking Ser.). (Illus.). 32p. (J). (ps-3). 2000. 13.99 (*0-670-88074-4*, Viking Child) Peng Put Young Read.

Lindgren, Astrid. Pippi's Extraordinary Ordinary Day. LC 99-26986. (Pippi Longstocking Ser.). (Illus.). 64p. (J). (ps-3). 1999. pap. 13.99 (*0-670-88073-6*, Viking Child) Peng Put Young Read.

— Ronia, the Robber's Daughter. (Illus.). 176p. (J). (gr. 4-7). 1985. pap. 4.99 (*0-14-031720-1*, PuffinBks) Peng Put Young Read.

— Ronia, the Robber's Daughter. (J). (gr. 3-7). 1993. 18.50 (*0-8446-6649-1*) Peter Smith.

— Ronia, the Robber's Daughter. 1985. 10.09 (*0-606-03438-2*, Pub. by Turtleback) Demco.

— The Tomten. LC 97-217161. (Illus.). 32p. (J). (ps-3). 1997. pap. 5.99 (*0-698-11591-0*, PapStar) Peng Put Young Read.

— The Tomten & the Fox. LC 65-25501. (Illus.). 32p. (J). (ps-3). 1997. pap. 5.99 (*0-698-11592-9*, PapStar) Peng Put Young Read.

Lindgren, Astrid & Lamborn, Florence. Pippi Goes to the Circus. LC 98-8836. (Pippi Longstocking Ser.). (Illus.). 32p. (J). (ps-3). 1999. 13.99 (*0-670-88070-1*) Viking Penguin.

***Lindgren, Barbro.** Andrei's Search. LC 99-52905. (Illus.). 28p. (J). (ps-3). 2000. 14.00 (*91-29-64756-8*) R&S Bks SW.

— Benny's Had Enough! Dyssegaard, Elisabeth Kallick, tr. (Illus.). 28p. (J). (ps-3). 1999. 14.00 (*91-29-64563-8*, Pub. by R&S Bks SW) FS&G.

Lindgren, Barbro. Rosa: Perpetual Motion Machine. (Illus.). 32p. (J). (gr. k-1). 1996. 14.95 (*1-55054-241-9*) Publishers Group.

***Lindgren, Barbro.** Rosa Goes to Daycare. (Illus.). 32p. (J). (ps-1). 2000. 15.95 (*0-88899-391-9*) Grndwd Bks.

Lindgren, Barbro. Sam's Ball. LC 83-722. (Illus.). 32p. (J). (ps). 1983. mass mkt. 6.95 (*0-688-02359-2*, Wm Morrow) Morrow Avon.

— Sam's Bath. LC 83-724. (Illus.). 32p. (J). (ps). 1983. mass mkt. 6.95 (*0-688-02362-2*, Wm Morrow) Morrow Avon.

Lindgren, Barbro. Sam's Car. LC 82-3437. Orig. Title: Max Bil. (Illus.). 32p. (J). (gr. k-3). 1982. pap. 6.95 (*0-688-01263-9*, Wm Morrow) Morrow Avon.

Lindgren, Barbro. Sam's Cookie. LC 82-3419. (Illus.). 32p. (J). (gr. k-3). 1982. mass mkt. 6.95 (*0-688-01267-1*, Wm Morrow) Morrow Avon.

— Sam's Potty. LC 86-864.Tr. of Max Potta. (Illus.). 32p. (J). (ps). 1986. mass mkt. 6.95 (*0-688-06603-8*, Wm Morrow) Morrow Avon.

— Sam's Teddy Bear. LC 82-3418. (Illus.). 32p. (J). (gr. k-3). 1982. mass mkt. 6.95 (*0-688-01270-1*, Wm Morrow) Morrow Avon.

Lindgren, Bernard W., jt. auth. see Berry, Donald A.

Lindgren, Bernard W., jt. auth. see Berry, Donald L.

Lindgren, Brian J., ed. see Dailey, Franklyn E., Jr. & Rosenthal, Morris.

Lindgren, Brian J., ed. see Lahr, Christopher J.

Lindgren, Brian J., ed. see Varhol, Peter D. & Varhol, Pamela H.

Lindgren, Bruce, jt. auth. see Judd, Peter.

Lindgren, C. E. Spiritual Alchemists: Rosicrucians, the Brotherhood of Light. 70p. (Orig.). 1997. pap. 5.95 (*1-885591-18-7*, PO1351) Morris Pubng.

***Lindgren, C. E., ed.** Capturing the Aura: Integrating Science, Technology, & Metaphysics. LC 98-37105. (Progen - Aura Imaging Ser.). 368p. 2000. pap. 19.95 (*0-9652490-6-9*) B Dolphin Pub.

Lindgren, C. E. & Baltz, Jennifer, eds. Aura Awareness: What Your Aura Says about You. (Illus.). 168p. (Orig.). 1997. pap. 12.95 (*0-9652490-5-0*) Aura Imaging.

Lindgren, Charlotte H. Gerald Warner Brace: Writer, Sailor, Teacher. LC 99-171539. (Illus.). 280p. 1998. 29.95 (*1-884186-08-4*) Hollis Pub.

Lindgren, David T. Land Use Planning & Remote Sensing. 1984. text 154.50 (*90-247-3083-X*) Kluwer Academic.

***Lindgren, David T.** Trust but Verify: Imagery Analysis in the Cold War. LC 00-22464. (Illus.). 240p. 2000. 32.95 (*1-55750-518-7*) Naval Inst Pr.

Lindgren, Dorothy, jt. auth. see Crafton, Helen.

Lindgren, Douglas A. Venture Capital: An Authoritative Guide for Investors, Entrepreneurs & Managers. 300p. 1998. 65.00 (*0-7863-1051-0*) McGraw-Hill Prof.

Lindgren, Gary F. Managing Industrial Hazardous Waste: A Practical Handbook. (Illus.). 404p. 1989. lib. bdg. 99.95 (*0-87371-147-5*, L147) Lewis Pubs.

Lindgren, Gunilla W., ed. Growth As a Mirror of Conditions in Society. 116p. (Orig.). 1990. pap. 48.00 (*91-7656-224-7*) Coronet Bks.

Lindgren, H. Elaine. Land in Her Own Name: Women As Homesteaders in North Dakota. LC 96-20628. (Illus.). 320p. 1996. pap. 17.95 (*0-8061-2886-0*) U of Okla Pr.

Lindgren, Henry C. Featherweight Verses for Ticklish Tastes. LC 97-94854. 60p. 1997. pap. 10.00 (*0-9653126-1-5*) ChkeCherry Pr.

— The Happy Marriage: A Celebration in Verse. LC 97-94853. iii, 39p. 1997. pap. 10.00 (*0-9653126-2-3*) ChkeCherry Pr.

— Leadership, Authority & Powersharing. LC 81-18644. 186p. (Orig.). 1982. lib. bdg. 16.50 (*0-89874-251-X*) Krieger.

— Lindgren Three: Ancient Greek Bronze Coins from the Lindgren Collection. LC 93-74078. (Illus.). 228p. 1993. 90.00 (*0-9636738-1-5*) Classical Numismatic Grp.

— Mixed Messages: Light Heavyweight Verse. LC 96-85147. 48p. (Orig.). 1996. pap. 10.00 (*0-9653126-0-7*) ChkeCherry Pr.

— The Psychology of Money. 342p. (C). 1991. lib. bdg. 39.50 (*0-89464-399-1*) Krieger.

Lindgren, I. & Morrison, J. Atomic Many-Body Theory. 2nd ed. (Atoms & Plasmas Ser.: Vol. 3). (Illus.). xv, 469p. 1986. 73.95 (*0-387-16649-1*) Spr-Verlag.

Lindgren, I., et al. Heavy Ion Spectroscopy & QED Effects in Atomic Systems: Proceedings of the Nobel Symposium. 272p. 1993. text 95.00 (*981-02-1337-9*) World Scientific Pub.

Lindgren, J. Ralph & Knaak, Jay, eds. Ritual & Semiotics. LC 96-30662. (Critic of Institutions Ser.: No. 14). XIV, 226p. (C). 1997. text 46.95 (*0-8204-2805-1*) P Lang Pubng.

Lindgren, J. Ralph & Taub, Nadine. Law Of Sex Discrimination. 2nd ed. Hannan, ed. LC 93-25946. (Political Science). 550p. (C). 1993. 46.50 (*0-314-02708-4*) West Pub.

Lindgren, James M. Preserving Historic New England: Preservation, Progressivism & the Remaking of Memory. (Illus.). 256p. 1995. 45.00 (*0-19-509363-1*) OUP.

— Preserving the Old Dominion: Historic Preservation & Virginia Traditionalism. LC 92-46301. (Illus.). 400p. 1993. text 42.50 (*0-8139-1450-7*) U Pr of Va.

Lindgren, Joan, ed. & tr. see Gelman, Juan.

Lindgren, Joan, tr. see Morales, Jose Santos.

Lindgren, K. E. Time in the Performance of Contracts. 2nd ed. 1982. 62.00 (*0-409-30390-9*, A.T., MICHIE) LEXIS Pub.

Lindgren, Laura, ed. see Rugoff, Ralph.

Lindgren, Laura, tr. see Schumann, Charles.

Lindgren, Lisa, jt. auth. see Gurugbe, Anura.

Lindgren, Lowell E., ed. see Bononeini, Antonio.

Lindgren, Marcia, jt. auth. see Dettmer, Helena.

Lindgren, Mereth, et al. A History of Swedish Art. (Illus.). 278p. 1987. 125.00 (*91-85330-78-7*, Pub. by Signum) Coronet Bks.

Lindgren, Merri V., ed. see Cooperative Children's Book Center Staff.

Lindgren, Michael. Glory & Failure: The Difference Engines of Johann Muller, Charles Babbage, & Georg & Edvard Scheutz. McKay, Craig G., tr. (Illus.). 416p. 1990. 52.00 (*0-262-12146-8*) MIT Pr.

Lindgren, Nilo, jt. auth. see Wildes, Karl.

Lindgren, Ralph & Kevelson, Roberta, eds. Horizons of Justice. LC 95-11862. (Critic of Institutions Ser.: Vol. 8). XV, 232p. (C). 1996. text 55.95 (*0-8204-2802-7*) P Lang Pubng.

Lindgren, Ralph, jt. ed. see Pencak, William A.

Lindgren, Raymond E. Norway-Sweden: Union, Disunion, & Scandinavian Integration. LC 78-13451. 298p. 1979. reprint ed. lib. bdg. 38.50 (*0-313-21043-8*, LINS, Greenwood Pr) Greenwood.

Lindgren, S., jt. auth. see Jonsson, A.

Lindgren, Sue A. Justice Expenditure & Employment Extracts, 1992. (Illus.). 91p. (Orig.). (C). 1997. pap. text 30.00 (*0-7881-4019-1*) DIANE Pub.

***Lindgren, Torgny.** Sweetness. Geddes, Tom, tr. 144p. 2000. pap. text 13.00 (*1-86046-656-7*) Harvill Press.

Lindgren, Torgny. The Way of the Serpent. Geddes, Tom, tr. 104p. 1998. mass mkt. 10.00 (*1-86046-261-8*) Harvill Press.

Lindgrenson, Sonja, tr. see Hallberg, Peter.

Lindgrin. Student Handbook Custom. 1999. write for info. (*0-07-235686-3*) McGraw.

***Lindh.** Administrative Medical Assisting. 2nd ed. (C). 2002. pap. 35.00 (*0-7668-2423-3*); pap., wbk. ed. 16.75 (*0-7668-2425-X*) Delmar.

Lindh. Comprehensive Medical Assisting. (Medical Assisting Ser). (C). 1997. pap., wbk. ed. 19.25 (*0-8273-6765-1*) Thomson Learn.

— Comprehensive Medical Assisting. (Medical Assisting Ser.). 1997. teacher ed. 19.95 (*0-8273-6763-5*, VNR) Wiley.

Lindh & Tamparo. Delmar's Administrative Medical Assisting. 256p. (C). 1997. pap., wbk. ed. 17.95 (*0-8273-8529-3*) Delmar.

Lindh, E. & Thorell, Jan, eds. Clinical Impact of Bone & Connective Tissue Markers. 350p. 1989. text 104.00 (*0-12-450740-9*) Acad Pr.

Lindh, Lennart, jt. auth. see Sjoholm, Stefan.

Lindh, Thomas. Essays on Expectations in Economic Theory. (Studia Oeconomica Upsaliensia: No. 21). 112p. 1992. pap. text 40.00 (*91-554-2850-9*) Coronet Bks.

Lindh, Wilburta Q. & Pooler, Marilyn S. Delmar's Clinical Medical Assisting. LC 97-14957. 704p. (C). 1997. mass mkt. 48.95 (*0-8273-8525-0*) Delmar.

Lindh, Wilburta Q., et al. Delmar's Administrative Medical Assisting. LC 97-21697. 507p. (C). 1997. pap. 45.95 (*0-8273-8528-5*) Delmar.

Lindh, Wilburta Q., jt. auth. see Indovina, Theresa.

Lindh, Wilburta Q., jt. auth. see Tamparo, Carol D.

Lindh, Wilbuta Q. Comprehensive Medical Assisting. LC 96-45520. (Medical Assisting Ser.). (C). 1997. mass mkt. 61.95 (*0-8273-6764-3*) Delmar.

Lindhal, Erik, ed. see Wicksell, Knut.

Lindhardt, Jan. Martin Luther: Knowledge & Mediation in the Renaissance. LC 86-17940. (Texts & Studies in Religion: Vol. 29). 270p. 1986. lib. bdg. 89.95 (*0-88946-817-6*) E Mellen.

Lindheim, Ralph & Luckyj, George S., eds. Towards an Intellectual History of Ukraine: An Anthology of Ukrainian Thought from 1710 to 1993. 480p. 1996. text 65.00 (*0-8020-0871-2*); pap. text 24.95 (*0-8020-7855-9*) U of Toronto Pr.

Lindheim, Richard D., jt. auth. see Blum, Richard A.

Lindheim, Roslyn, et al. Changing Hospital Environments for Children. LC 75-188969. (Illus.). 218p. reprint ed. pap. 67.60 (*0-7837-1715-6*, 205724400024) Bks Demand.

Lindheimer, Elinor, jt. ed. see Jacobs, Christine.

Lindheimer, Marshall D., et al, eds. Chesley's Hypertensive Disorders in Pregnancy. 2nd ed. LC 98-49703. (Illus.). 650p. 1999. pap. text 135.00 (*0-8385-3970-X*, Apple Lange Med) McGraw.

Lindheimer, Marshall D., jt. auth. see Barron, John M.

Lindholdt, Paul J., ed. & intro. see Josselyn, John.

Lindholm. Culture & the Self. 2000. 33.50 (*0-07-037995-5*) McGraw.

Lindholm, Byron W., jt. ed. see Touliatos, John.

Lindholm, Charles. The Islamic Middle East: An Historical Anthropology. (Illus.). 288p. 1996. pap. 31.95 (1-55786-421-7) Blackwell Pubs.
— The Islamic Middle East: An Historical Anthropology. (Illus.). 288p. (C). 1996. 72.95 (1-55786-420-9) Blackwell Pubs.
Lindholm, Charles, jt. auth. see Hall, John A.
Lindholm, Dan. Encounters with Angels. pap. 11.95 (0-86315-137-X, 1409, Pub. by Floris Bks) Anthroposophic.
Lindholm, E. & Asbrink, L. Molecular Orbitals & Their Energies, Studied by the Semiempirical HAM Method. (Lecture Notes in Chemistry Ser.: Vol. 38). x, 288p. 1985. 38.95 (0-387-15659-3) Spr-Verlag.
Lindholm, Jan & Enger, Raymond. Excel & Fox Pro. 2nd ed. 92p. (C). 1995. text 22.60 (0-536-58849-X) Pearson Custom.
Lindholm, Megan, jt. auth. see Brust, Steven.
Lindholm, Paul E. A Slew of Stupid Criminals: Plus Some Spectacular Misspellings & Other Atrocious Crimes. LC 96-71108. 94p. (Orig.). 1996. pap. 7.95 (0-9653027-2-5) Paper Moon Pub.
Lindholm, Paul R. First Fruits: Stewardship Thoughts & Stories from Around the World. LC 93-15679. 128p. (Orig.). 1993. pap. 11.95 (0-932727-66-2); lib. bdg. 18.95 (0-932727-67-0) Hope Pub Hse.
Lindholm, Richard W. Money & Banking. (Quality Paperback Ser.: No. 19). 271p. (Orig.). 1969. pap. 8.00 (0-8226-0019-6) Littlefield.
Lindholm, Richard W., ed. Examination of Basic Weaknesses of Income As the Major Federal Tax Base. LC 86-518. 336p. 1986. 59.95 (0-275-92148-4, C2148, Praeger Pubs) Greenwood.
— Property Taxation & the Finance of Education. LC 73-2046. (Publications of the Committee on Taxation, Resources & Economic Development: Vol. 7). 345p. 1974. reprint ed. pap. 107.00 (0-608-01896-1, 206254800003) Bks Demand.
— Property Taxation, U. S. A. Proceedings of a Symposium Sponsored by the Committee on Taxation, Resources & Economic Development (TRED) at the University of Wisconsin, Milwaukee, 1965. LC 67-20762. 327p. 1969. reprint ed. pap. 101.40 (0-608-01929-1, 206258400003) Bks Demand.
Lindholm-Romantschuk, Ylva. Scholarly Book Reviewing in the Social Sciences & Humanities: The Flow of Ideas Within & among Disciplines, 91. LC 97-16126. (Contributions in Librarianship & Information Science: 91). 168p. 1998. 55.00 (0-313-29514-X, Greenwood Pr) Greenwood.
Lindholm, Roy. A Practical Approach to Sedimentology. (Illus.). 192p. 1987. text 45.00 (0-04-551131-4); pap. text 21.95 (0-04-551132-2) Routledge.
Lindholm, T. Sam. Bone Morphogenetic Proteins. LC 96-12937. (Tissue Engineering Intelligence Unit Ser.). 225p. 1996. 69.95 (0-12-450745-X) Acad Pr.
— Skeletal Reconstruction & Bioimplantation: Demineralized Bone Matrix, Non-Collagenous, Native & Recombinant Bonemorphogenetic Proteins. LC 97-34263. (Medical Intelligence Unit Ser.). 225p. 1998. 99.00 (1-57059-506-2) Landes Bioscience.
***Lindholm, Tim.** Java Virtual Machine Specification. 2nd ed. LC 99-18470. (Java Ser.). 496p. (C). 1999. pap. text 42.95 (0-201-43294-3) Addison-Wesley.
Lindholm, Tim & Yellin, Frank. The Java Virtual Machine Specification. LC 96-15897. (Java Ser.). 496p. 1996. pap. text 39.95 (0-201-63452-X) Addison-Wesley.
Lindholt, Lone. Questioning the Universality of Human Rights: The "African Charter on Human & People's Rights" in Botswana, Malawi & Mozambique. LC 97-7872. (Law, Social Change & Development Ser.). 320p. 1997. text 82.95 (1-85521-828-3, Pub. by Ashgate Pub) Ashgate Pub Co.
Lindhop, M. J., jt. ed. see Klinck, J. R.
***Lindhout, T., ed.** North Sea Conference on Thrombosis & Haemostasis: 1st Conference, Maasticht, The Netherlands, June 2000. (Haemostasis Ser.: Vol. 30). 102p. 2000. pap. 34.00 (3-8055-7106-2) S Karger.
Lindig, Carmen. The Path from the Parlor: Louisiana Women, 1879-1920. 195p. 1986. 17.50 (0-940984-30-X) Univ LA Lafayette.
Lindinger, Herbert, ed. Ulm Design: The Morality of Objects. Britt, David, tr. from GER. (Illus.). 288p. 1991. 50.00 (0-262-12147-6) MIT Pr.
Lindinger, W., et al, eds. Swarms of Ions & Electrons in Gases. (Illus.). 320p. 1984. 60.95 (0-387-81823-5) Spr-Verlag.
Lindio-McGovern, Ligaya. Filipino Peasant Women: Exploitation & Resistance. LC 97-19617. (C). (gr. 13). 1997. text 42.50 (0-8122-3410-3); pap. text 19.95 (0-8122-1624-5) U of Pa Pr.
***Lindisfarne, Nancy.** Dancing in Damascus: Stories. LC 99-49702. (C). 2000. text 44.50 (0-7914-4635-2) State U NY Pr.
— Dancing in Damascus: Stories. LC 99-49702. 2000. pap. 14.95 (0-7914-4636-0) State U NY Pr.
Lindisfarne, Nancy, jt. ed. see Cornwall, Andrea.
Lindisfarne-Tapper, Nancy & Ingham, Bruce, eds. Languages of Dress in the Middle East. LC 98-121076. 240p. 1997. 65.00 (0-7007-0670-4, Pub. by Curzon Pr Ltd); pap. 25.00 (0-7007-0671-2, Pub. by Curzon Pr Ltd) Paul & Co Pubs.
Lindkvist, K. G. Studies on the Local Sense of the Prepositions "in", "at", "on", "to" in Modern English. (Lund Studies in English: Vol. 20). 1974. reprint ed. pap. 50.00 (0-8115-0563-4) Periodicals Srv.
Lindkvist, Marian R. Bring White Beads When You Call on the Healer. (Illus.). 280p. 1997. 32.00 (1-878281-11-9) Rivendell Hse Ltd.
Lindkvist, R. G. Handbook of Materials Handling. 286p. 1985. text 83.95 (0-470-20098-7) P-H.
Lindl, John. Inertial Confinement Fusion: The Quest for Ignition & Energy Gain Using Indirect Drive. LC 97-48859. (Illus.). 322p. 1997. 50.00 (1-56396-662-X) Am Inst Physics.
Lindlahr, Henry. Natural Therapeutics, Vol. II. 108p. 1981. 17.95 (0-85207-148-5, Pub. by C W Daniel) Natl Bk Netwk.
— Natural Therapeutics, Vol. III. 108p. 1983. 12.95 (0-85207-155-8, Pub. by C W Daniel) Natl Bk Netwk.
— Natural Therapeutics, Vol. IV. 108p. 1985. pap. 17.50 (0-85207-171-X, Pub. by C W Daniel) Natl Bk Netwk.
— Natural Therapeutics: Iridiagnosis, Vol. 4. 284p. pap. 26.95 (0-685-71020-3) Beekman Pubs.
— Natural Therapeutics Vol. 1: Philosophy. 354p. (Orig.). pap. 35.95 (0-8464-4258-2) Beekman Pubs.
— Natural Therapeutics Vol. 2: Practice. 328p. 26.95 (0-8464-4259-0) Beekman Pubs.
— Natural Therapeutics Vol. 3: Natural Dietics. 184p. 19.95 (0-8464-4260-4) Beekman Pubs.
— Natural Therapeutics Vol. 4: Iridiagnosis. 284p. pap. 26.95 (0-8464-4261-2) Beekman Pubs.
— Natural Therapeutics Vol. 6: Iridiagnosis & Other Diagnostic Methods. 5th ed. 327p. 1996. reprint ed. spiral bd. 22.00 (0-7873-0563-4) Hlth.Research.
— Nature Cure 2000. Poesnecker, G. E., ed. LC 98-227357. 384p. 1998. pap. 15.00 (0-916285-60-X) Humanitarian.
— Philosophy Natural Therapeutics, Vol. I. (Natural Therapeutics Ser.). 327p. 1975. pap. 24.00 (0-85207-159-0, Pub. by C W Daniel) Natl Bk Netwk.
Lindlahr, Victor H. Eat & Reduce. (Illus.). 194p. 1972. pap. 4.95 (0-87877-015-1, H-15) Newcastle Pub.
— For Women After Forty. 1976. pap. 2.95 (0-87904-035-1) Lust.
— You Are What You Eat. LC 80-19722. 128p. 1990. reprint ed. pap. 17.00 (0-89370-990-5) Millefleurs.
Lindland, Frances K. Memories of the Morning Calm: A Modest Texas Bride's Experiences As She Merged into the Foreign Customs of Korea - the Land of the Morning Calm. Brown, Darlene, ed. (Illus.). 228p. 1992. pap. 13.95 (0-9617572-3-X) Times Journal Pub.
Lindlar, Heinrich. Rororo Musikhandbuch, 2 vols. (GER.). 1976. pap. 35.00 (0-8288-5753-9, M7605) Fr & Eur.
— Woerterbuch der Musik. (GER.). 331p. 1989. 59.95 (0-7859-8378-3, 3458160329) Fr & Eur.
Lindlarh, Henry. Acute Diseases, Pts. I-II: Their Uniform Treatment by Natural Methods: Mental, Emotional & Psychic Disorders. 54p. 1996. spiral bd. 9.00 (0-7873-0562-6) Hlth Research.
Lindlater, Magnus. People in a Landscape: The New Highlanders. (Illus.). 96p. 1997. pap. 19.95 (1-85158-958-9, Pub. by Mainstream Pubng) Trafalgar.
Lindle, Jane C. Surviving School Micropolitics: Strategies for Administrators. LC 94-60924. 168p. 1994. text 39.95 (1-56676-175-1) Scarecrow.
Lindle, Jane C., jt. auth. see Steffy, Betty E.
Lindley, Arthur. Hyperion & Hobbyhorse. LC 96-2971. (Studies in Carnivalesque Subversion). 200p. 1996. 33.50 (0-87413-588-5) U Delaware Pr.
***Lindley, Ashleigh.** Echoes from the Past. 1999. pap. write for info. (1-58235-203-8) Watermrk Pr.
Lindley, Ashleigh B. Through the Years. 1998. pap. write for info. (1-57553-911-X) Watermrk Pr.
Lindley, Betty & Lindley, Ernest K. A New Deal for Youth: The Story of the National Youth Administration. LC 72-172687. (FDR & the Era of the New Deal Ser.). (Illus.). 316p. 1972. reprint ed. lib. bdg. 39.50 (0-306-70382-3) Da Capo.
Lindley, Celeste M. & Deloatch, Kimberly H. Infusion Technology: A Self-Instructional Approach. 120p. 1993. pap. 219.00 incl. VHS (1-879907-40-2) Am Soc Hlth-Syst.
— Infusion Technology Manual: A Self-Instructional Approach. (Illus.). 120p. 1993. pap. 63.00 (1-879907-38-0) Am Soc Hlth-Syst.
Lindley, Charles. The Ghost Book: Of Charles Lindley, Viscount Halifax. 512p. 1994. pap. 10.95 (0-7867-0151-X) Carroll & Graf.
Lindley, Charlet R., tr. see Weissermel, K.
***Lindley, Craig A.** Digital Audio with Java. LC 99-58694. 512p. 1999. pap. 39.99 (0-13-087676-3) P-H.
Lindley, Craig A. Photographic Imaging Techniques in C++ for Windows3 & Windows NT. LC 94-49718. 432p. 1995. pap. 44.95 incl. disk (0-471-11568-1) Wiley.
— Practical Image Processing in C: Acquisition Manipulation Storage. Ep. 1990. disk 49.95 (0-471-53240-1) Wiley.
— Practical Image Processing in C: Acquisition Manipulation Storage. LC 90-41054. 553p. 1991. pap. 51.95 (0-471-53062-X); pap. text 94.90 incl. disk (0-471-54377-2) Wiley.
— Practical Ray Tracing in C. LC 92-30223. 528p. 1992. pap. 49.95 incl. disk (0-471-57301-9) Wiley.
Lindley, Curtis H. Treatise on the American Law Relating to Mines & Mineral Lands: Within the Public Land States & Territories & Governing the Acquisition & Enjoyment of Mining Rights in Lands of the Public Domain, 3 vols. 3rd ed. cclii, 2810p. 1988. reprint ed. 225.00 (0-8377-2411-2, Rothman) W S Hein.
— A Treatise on the American Law Relating to Mines & Mineral Lands Within the Public Land States & Territories & Governing the Acquisition & Enjoyment of Mining Rights in Lands of the Public Domain, 2 vols. 2nd ed. LC 72-2853. (Use & Abuse of America's Natural Resources Ser.). 1972. reprint ed. 145.95 (0-405-04517-4) Ayer.
— A Treatise on the American Law Relating to Mines & Mineral Lands Within the Public Land States & Territories & Governing the Acquisition & Enjoyment of Mining Rights in Lands of the Public Domain, 2 vols., 1. 2nd ed. LC 72-2853. (Use & Abuse of America's Natural Resources Ser.). 1972. reprint ed. 72.95 (0-405-04546-8) Ayer.
— A Treatise on the American Law Relating to Mines & Mineral Lands Within the Public Land States & Territories & Governing the Acquisition & Enjoyment of Mining Rights in Lands of the Public Domain, 2 vols., Vol. 2. 2nd ed. LC 72-2853. (Use & Abuse of America's Natural Resources Ser.). 1972. reprint ed. 72.95 (0-405-04547-6) Ayer.
Lindley, D. V. Bayesian Statistics, a Review. (CBMS-NSF Regional Conference Ser.: No. 2). v, 83p. 1971. reprint ed. pap. text 21.00 (0-89871-002-2) Soc Indus-Appl Math.
Lindley, D. V. & Scott, W. F. New Cambridge Elementary Statistical Tables. 2nd ed. (Illus.). 96p. (C). 1995. pap. text 15.95 (0-521-48485-5) Cambridge U Pr.
Lindley, Daniel. Ambrose Bierce Takes on the Railroad: The Journalist As Muckraker & Cynic. LC 99-21193. 168p. 1999. 55.00 (0-275-96696-8, C6696, Praeger Pubs) Greenwood.
Lindley, Daniel A. This Rough Magic: The Life of Teaching. LC 93-25009. 160p. 1993. 57.95 (0-89789-363-8, G366, Bergin & Garvey); pap. 17.95 (0-89789-366-2, H363, Bergin & Garvey) Greenwood.
***Lindley, David.** Boltzmann's Atom: The Great Debate That Launched a Revolution in Physics. LC 00-32167. 2001. 24.00 (0-684-85186-5) Free Pr.
Lindley, David. The End of Physics: The Myth of a Unified Theory. LC 92-54524. 320p. 1994. pap. 14.00 (0-465-01976-5, Pub. by Basic) HarpC.
— Thomas Campion. (Medieval & Renaissance Authors Ser.: Vol. 7). xii, 242p. 1986. 67.50 (90-04-07601-8) Brill Academic Pubs.
— The Trials of Frances Howard: Fact & Fiction in the Court of King James. 256p. (C). 1996. pap. 24.99 (0-415-14424-8) Routledge.
Lindley, David, ed. Court Masques: Jacobean & Caroline Entertainments, 1605-1640. (World's Classics Ser.). (Illus.). 336p. 1995. text 65.00 (0-19-812164-4) OUP.
Lindley, David, et al, eds. Cosmology & Particle Physics. 172p. 1991. per. 26.00 (0-917853-42-3, RB-58) Am Assn Physics.
Lindley, David & Moore, T. Harvey, eds. Webster's New World Dictionary of Science: The World Science from A to Z. LC 98-41247. 704p. 1998. pap. text 19.95 (0-02-862382-7, Pub. by Macmillan) S&S Trade.
Lindley, David, jt. auth. see De Salle, Rob.
Lindley, Dennis V. Making Decisions. 220p. 1991. pap. 89.95 (0-471-90808-8) Wiley.
Lindley, Denver, tr. see Hesse, Hermann.
Lindley, Denver, tr. see Mann, Thomas.
Lindley, Denver, tr. see Remarque, Erich-Maria.
Lindley, Dwight N., ed. see Mill, John Stuart.
Lindley, Ernest K. Franklin Delano Roosevelt: A Career in Progressive Democracy. rev. ed. LC 73-21771. (FDR & the Era of the New Deal Ser.). 366p. 1974. reprint ed. lib. bdg. 39.50 (0-306-70634-2) Da Capo.
— Half Way with Roosevelt. LC 75-8789. (FDR & the Era of the New Deal Ser.). x, 449p. 1975. reprint ed. lib. bdg. 49.50 (0-306-70706-3) Da Capo.
— The Roosevelt Revolution: First Phase. LC 74-637. (FDR & the Era of the New Deal Ser.). 328p. 1974. reprint ed. lib. bdg. 39.50 (0-306-70651-2) Da Capo.
Lindley, Ernest K., jt. auth. see Lindley, Betty.
***Lindley, G.** Analysis of Source Spectra, Attenuation & Site Effects from Central & Eastern United States Earthquakes. 100p. 1998. per. 8.00 (0-16-062886-5) USGPO.
Lindley, H., ed. New Harmony As Seen by Participants & Travelers Pts. 1-3: Letters of William Pelham; Diary & Recollections of Victor Colin Duclos; Report of a Visit to New Harmony by Karl Bernhard. LC 74-32002. (American Utopian Adventure Ser.). (Illus.). 128p. 1975. reprint ed. lib. bdg. 25.00 (0-87991-028-3) Porcupine Pr.
Lindley, Harlow. Indiana As Seen by Early Travelers. 596p. 1992. pap. 23.95 (1-885323-05-0) IN Hist Bureau.
Lindley, I. J., et al. The Chemokines: Biology of the Inflammatory Peptide Supergene Family II. (Advances in Experimental Medicine & Biology Ser.: Vol. 351). (Illus.). 244p. (C). 1993. text 95.00 (0-306-44710-X, Kluwer Plenum) Kluwer Academic.
Lindley, James A. & Whitaker, James H. Agricultural Buildings & Structures. rev. ed. LC 96-85566. 636p. 1997. 50.50 (0-929355-73-3) Am Soc Ag Eng.
Lindley, John. Contribution to the Orchidology of India. 100p. (C). 1982. 30.00 (0-7855-3286-2, Pub. by Scientific) St Mut.
— Folia Orchidacea. 400p. (C). 1983. 80.00 (0-7855-3285-4, Pub. by Scientific) St Mut.
— Folia Orchidacea: A Enumeration of the Known Species of Orchids, 2 vols. in 1. 1983. reprint ed. 50.00 (90-6123-088-8) S Asia.
— The Genera & Species of Orchidaceous Plants, 7 vols. in 1. 1984. reprint ed. 50.00 (90-6123-091-8) Lubrecht & Cramer.
— Medical & Economical Botany. (C). 1988. 50.00 (0-7855-2294-8, Pub. by Scientific) St Mut.
— Medicinal & Economical Botany. 274p. (C). 1984. 65.00 (0-7855-3299-4, Pub. by Scientific) St Mut.
— Orchidaceous Plants. 553p. (C). 1983. 80.00 (0-7855-3287-0, Pub. by Scientific) St Mut.
Lindley, Karen B., ed. Cave Research Foundation Annual Report, 1993. (Illus.). 68p. (Orig.). 1995. pap. 5.00 (0-939748-30-4) Cave Bks MO.
Lindley, Keith. The English Civil War & Revolution: A Sourcebook. LC 97-51158. (Illus.). 216p. (C). 1998. 65.00 (0-415-17418-X); pap. 19.99 (0-415-17419-8) Routledge.
— Popular Politics & Religion in Civil War London. LC 96-34695. 464p. 1997. text 86.95 (1-85928-343-8, Pub. by Ashgate Pub) Ashgate Pub Co.
***Lindley, Keith & Scott, David, eds.** The Journal of Thomas Juxon, 1644-1647. LC 99-28023. (Camden Fifth Ser.: No. 13). 224p. (C). 2000. 64.95 (0-521-65259-6) Cambridge U Pr.
Lindley, L. Flora Medica: Botanical Account of More Important Plants Used in Medicine. (C). 1988. 120.00 (0-7855-2295-6, Pub. by Scientific) St Mut.
— The Genera & Species of Orchideous Plants. (C). 1988. 60.00 (0-7855-3274-9, Pub. by Scientific) St Mut.
Lindley, Lester G. The Constitution Faces Technology: The Relationship of the National Government to the Telegraph, 1866-1884. LC 75-2586. (Dissertations in American Economic History Ser.). 1975. 28.95 (0-405-07206-6) Ayer.
— Contract, Economic Change, & the Search for Order in Industrialized America. LC 93-5722. (Distinguished Studies in American Legal & Constitutional History). 344p. 1993. text 15.00 (0-8153-0895-7, 93-5722) Garland.
Lindley, Lindsey, jt. ed. see Atrill, Peter.
Lindley, Mary E. A Manual on Investigating Child Custody Reports. 194p. 1988. pap. 29.95 (0-398-06241-2) C C Thomas.
— A Manual on Investigating Child Custody Reports. 194p. (C). 1988. text 45.95 (0-398-05487-8) C C Thomas.
Lindley, P. G., ed. see Gunn, S. J.
Lindley, Phillip, ed. Sculpture Conservation: Preservation or Interference. LC 96-4097. (Illus.). 272p. 1997. 69.95 (1-85928-254-7, Pub. by Scolar Pr) Ashgate Pub Co.
Lindley, Richard, tr. Mexico: Una Vision de Altura: Un Recorrido Aereo de Pasado al Presente. (SPA., Illus.). 192p. 1996. 35.00 (1-883051-08-8) ALTI Pub.
Lindley, Richard, jt. auth. see Holmes, Jeremy.
Lindley, Ricky. Refreshings: A Book of Renewal. 210p. (Orig.). 1990. pap. 9.95 (0-942727-18-5) NC Yrly Pubns Bd.
Lindley, Robert, ed. Higher Education & the Labor Market. 184p. 1981. 21.00 (0-900868-83-X) OpUniv Pr.
Lindley, Robert M. Economic Change & Employment Policy LC 80-513962. (Warwick Studies in the Economics of Employment). xvii, 395p. 1980. write for info. (0-333-28750-9) Macmillan.
Lindley, Susan H. You Have Stept Out of Your Place: A History of Women & Religion in America. 384p. 1996. 36.95 (0-664-22081-9) Westminster John Knox.
Lindley, William R. Hard Times, Good Times in Oregon: Recollections of the 1930s. (Illus.). 112p. 1994. pap. 14.95 (0-89745-186-4) Sunflower U Pr.
— Twentieth-Century American Newspapers. (Illus.). 116p. 1993. pap. 14.95 (0-89745-160-0) Sunflower U Pr.
Lindlof, Thomas R. Qualitative Communications Research Methods. (Current Communication: An Advanced Text Ser.: Vol. 3). 364p. 1994. 58.00 (0-8039-3517-X); pap. 26.95 (0-8039-3518-8) Sage.
Lindlof, Thomas R. & Voigt, Melvin J., eds. Natural Audiences: Qualitative Research of Media Uses & Effects. LC 86-17425. (Communication & Information Science Ser.). 288p. 1987. text 73.25 (0-89391-341-3) Ablx Pub.
Lindlof, Thomas R., jt. ed. see Grodin, Debra.
Lindman, B., et al, eds. Surfactants & Macromolecules: Self-Assembly at Interfaces & in Bulk. (Progress in Colloid & Polymer Science Ser.: Vol. 82). 200p. 1991. 148.00 (0-387-91367-X) Spr-Verlag.
Lindman, B., jt. ed. see Alexandridis, P.
Lindman, Bjorn, jt. ed. see Friberg, Stig E.
Lindman, H. R. Analysis of Variance in Experimental Designs. (Texts in Statistics Ser.). (Illus.). ix, 531p. 1991. 72.95 (0-387-97571-3) Spr-Verlag.
Lindman, H. R., et al, eds. Cognitive Theory, Vol. 1. LC 74-14293. 320p. 1975. text 69.95 (0-89859-436-7) L Erlbaum Assocs.
Lindman, Maj. Flicka, Ricka, Dicka & the Big Red Hen. LC 95-916. (J). (ps-2). 1995. pap. 6.95 (0-8075-2493-X) A Whitman.
— Flicka, Ricka, Dicka & the Little Dog. (J). (ps-3). 1995. pap. 6.95 (0-8075-2497-2) A Whitman.
— Flicka, Ricka, Dicka & the New Dotted Dresses. (Albert Whitman Prairie Bks.). (Illus.). 32p. (J). (ps-2). 1994. pap. 6.95 (0-8075-2494-8) A Whitman.
— Flicka, Ricka, Dicka & the Strawberries. LC 96-2705. (Illus.). 32p. (J). (ps-2). 1996. reprint ed. pap. 6.95 (0-8075-2499-9) A Whitman.
— Flicka, Ricka, Dicka & the Three Kittens. (Albert Whitman Prairie Bks.). (Illus.). 32p. (J). (ps-2). 1994. pap. 6.95 (0-8075-2500-6) A Whitman.
— Flicka, Ricka, Dicka & Their New Friend. LC 95-1050. (Illus.). (J). (ps-2). 1995. pap. 6.95 (0-8075-2498-0) A Whitman.
— Flicka, Ricka, Dicka Bake a Cake. (J). (ps-3). 1995. pap. 6.95 (0-8075-2492-1) A Whitman.
— Snapp, Snurr & the Yellow Sled. Date not set. lib. bdg. 11.95 (0-614-25288-1) Amereon Ltd.
— Snipp, Snapp, Snurr & Gingerbread. 1976. 11.95 (0-8488-1413-4) Amereon Ltd.
— Snipp, Snapp, Snurr & the Big Farm. (Illus.). 32p. (J). 1993. reprint ed. lib. bdg. 14.95 (1-56849-004-6) Buccaneer Bks.
— Snipp, Snapp, Snurr & the Big Surprise. LC 96-2706. (Snipp, Snapp, Snurr Ser.). (Illus.). 32p. (J). (ps-2). 1996. pap. 6.95 (0-8075-7490-2) A Whitman.
— Snipp, Snapp, Snurr & the Big Surprise. (Illus.). 32p. (J). 1993. reprint ed. lib. bdg. 14.95 (1-56849-003-8) Buccaneer Bks.
— Snipp, Snapp, Snurr & the Buttered Bread. (J). (ps-2). 1995. pap. 6.95 (0-8075-7491-0) A Whitman.
— Snipp, Snapp, Snurr & the Buttered Bread. (Illus.). 32p. (J). 1993. reprint ed. lib. bdg. 14.95 (1-56849-002-X) Buccaneer Bks.

An Asterisk (*) at the beginning of an entry indicates that the title is appearing for the first time.

— Snipp, Snapp, Snurr & the Gingerbread. (Albert Whitman Prairie Bks.). (Illus.). 32p. (J). (ps-2). 1994. pap. 6.95 (*0-8075-7493-7*) A Whitman.

— Snipp, Snapp, Snurr & the Gingerbread. (Illus.). 30p. (J). 1991. reprint ed. pap. 10.95 (*0-89966-829-1*) Buccaneer Bks.

— Snipp, Snapp, Snurr & the Magic Horse. (Illus.). 32p. (J). 1993. reprint ed. lib. bdg. 14.95 (*1-56849-001-1*) Buccaneer Bks.

— Snipp, Snapp, Snurr & the Red Shoes. (Albert Whitman Prairie Bks.). (Illus.). 32p. (J). (ps-2). 1994. pap. 6.95 (*0-8075-7496-1*) A Whitman.

— Snipp, Snapp, Snurr & the Red Shoes. (Illus.). 32p. (J). 1993. reprint ed. lib. bdg. 14.95 (*1-56849-000-3*) Buccaneer Bks.

— Snipp, Snapp, Snurr & the Reindeer. LC 95-1048. (Illus.). (J). (ps-2). 1995. pap. 6.95 (*0-8075-7497-X*) A Whitman.

— Snipp, Snapp, Snurr & the Reindeer. (Illus.). 32p. (J). 1993. reprint ed. lib. bdg. 14.95 (*1-56849-005-4*) Buccaneer Bks.

— Snipp, Snapp, Snurr & the Seven Dogs. (Illus.). 32p. (J). 1993. reprint ed. lib. bdg. 14.95 (*1-56849-007-0*) Buccaneer Bks.

— Snipp, Snapp, Snurr & the Yellow Sled. LC 95-1049. (J). (ps-2). 1995. pap. 6.95 (*0-8075-7499-6*) A Whitman.

— Snipp, Snapp, Snurr & the Yellow Sled. (Illus.). 30p. (J). 1991. reprint ed. pap. 10.95 (*0-89966-828-3*) Buccaneer Bks.

— Snipp, Snapp, Snurr Learn to Swim. (J). (ps-3). 1995. pap. 6.95 (*0-8075-7494-5*) A Whitman.

— Snipp, Snapp, Snurr Learn to Swim. (Illus.). 32p. (J). 1993. reprint ed. lib. bdg. 14.95 (*1-56849-006-2*) Buccaneer Bks.

Lindman, N., jt. ed. see Chadwick, M. J.

Lindmann, B., et al, eds. The Colloid Science of Lipids: New Paradigms for Self-Assembly in Science & Technology. (Progress in Colloid & Polymer Science Ser.: Vol. 108). 210p. 1998. 79.95 (*3-7985-1112-8*) Spr-Verlag.

Lindmier, Thomas A. & Mount, Steven R. I See by Your Outfit: Historic Cowboy Gear of the Northern Plains. (Illus.). 176p. (Orig.). 1995. pap. 16.95 (*0-931271-33-9*) Hi Plains Pr.

***Lindner.** Introduction Signals Systems. 2nd ed. 2001. 74.25 (*0-07-239369-6*, McGrw-H College) McGrw-H Hghr Educ.

Lindner. Introduction to Signals Systems. LC 98-50542. 969p. 1999. 74.25 (*0-256-25259-9*) McGraw.

Lindner, Al. Crappie Wisdom Handbook of Strategies. LC 85-81299. 1994. pap. text 11.95 (*0-929384-51-2*) In-Fisherman.

— Pike. LC 83-83060. 1994. pap. 11.95 (*0-929384-52-0*) In-Fisherman.

— Small Mouth Bass. LC 84-81854. 1994. pap. text 11.95 (*0-929384-50-4*) In-Fisherman.

— Walleye Wisdom. LC 82-82692. 1994. pap. text 11.95 (*0-929384-49-0*) In-Fisherman.

Lindner, Charles C. & Rodger, C. A. Design Theory. LC 97-7965. (Discrete Mathematics & Its Applications Ser.). 208p. 1997. boxed set 84.95 (*0-8493-3986-3*) CRC Pr.

***Lindner, Eileen W.** Yearbook of American & Canadian Churches, 1998 Edition. 1998. 29.95 (*0-687-05426-5*) Abingdon.

Lindner, Eileen W., ed. Yearbook of American & Canadian Churches: 1998. 300p. 1998. pap. 29.95 (*0-687-03092-7*) Abingdon.

— Yearbook of American & Canadian Churches, 1999. 382p. 1999. pap. 29.95 (*0-687-07474-6*) Abingdon.

Lindner, Erik. Patriotismus Deutscher Juden von der Napoleonischen Ara Bis Zum Kaiserreich: Zwischen Korporativem Loyalismus und Individueller Deutsch-Judischer Identitat. (Europaische Hochschulschriften Ser.: Reihe 3, Bd. 726). (GER., Illus.). 448p. 1996. 63.95 (*3-631-31356-X*) P Lang Pubng.

Lindner, G. & Nyberg, K., eds. Environmental Engineering: A Chemical Engineering Discipline. LC 73-75764. 1973. text 259.00 (*90-277-0347-7*) Kluwer Academic.

Lindner, Harold H. Clinical Anatomy. (Illus.). 690p. (C). 1992. pap. text 34.95 (*0-8385-1259-3*, A1259-9, Apple Lange Med) McGraw.

***Lindner, J. K. N., et al.** Ion Implantation into Semiconductors Oxides & Ceramics. LC 99-209818. (European Materials Research Society Monographs: Vol. 85). 454p. 1999. text 201.00 (*0-08-043613-7*) Elsevier.

Lindner, John B., ed. By Faith: Christian Students among the Cloud of Witnesses. (Orig.). 1991. pap. 9.95 (*0-377-00236-4*) Friendship Pr.

Lindner, Ken. Broadcasting Realities: Real Life Issues & Insights for Broadcast Journalists, Aspiring Journalists & Broadcasters. 317p. 1998. pap. 19.95 (*1-56625-114-1*) Bonus Books.

***Lindner, Klaus & Charlton, Eric Mark.** The King's Cat: A Fairy Tale. LC 00-9067. 2000. write for info. (*1-58750-001-9*) Fouque Pubs.

Lindner, Kurt. Bibliographie der Deutschen und der Niederlaendischen Jagdliteratur von 1480 bis 1850. (Illus.). (C). 1977. 384.60 (*3-11-006640-8*) De Gruyter.

***Lindner, Linda A.** Guide to Owning a Canary. (Illus.). 1999. pap. 6.95 (*0-7938-2001-4*) TFH Pubns.

Lindner, Lindy, jt. auth. see Means, Beth.

Lindner, M., jt. auth. see Buras, A. J.

Lindner, M., jt. ed. see Buras, A. J.

Lindner, P. & Zemb, T., eds. Neutron, X-Ray & Light Scattering: Introduction to an Investigative Tool for Colloidal & Polymeric Systems: Proceedings of the European School of Neutron, X-Ray & Light Scattering As an Investigative Tool for Colloidal & Polymeric Systems, Bombannes, Girone, France, 27 May-2 June, 1990. (North-Holland Delta Ser.). x, 376p. 1991. 131.50 (*0-444-88946-9*, NHD 8, North Holland) Elsevier.

***Lindner, Robert M.** The Fifty Minute Hour: A Collection of True Psychoanalytic Tales. LC 99-23368. (Illus.). 294p. 1999. reprint ed. pap. 14.95 (*1-892746-24-7*, 46247) Other Pr LLC.

Lindner, Rolf. The Reportage of Urban Culture: Robert Park & the Chicago School. (Ideas in Context Ser.: No. 43). (Illus.). 250p. (C). 1996. text 59.95 (*0-521-44052-1*) Cambridge U Pr.

Lindner, Rudi P. Explorations in Ottoman Prehistory. (Illus.). 170p. (C). text 44.50 (*0-472-09507-2*, 09507) U of Mich Pr.

Lindner, Rudi P. Nomads & Ottomans in Medieval Anatolia. LC 82-6127. (Uralic & Altaic Ser.: Vol. 144). 167p. 1983. pap. 20.00 (*0-933070-12-8*) Res Inst Inner Asian Studies.

Lindner, Thomas, jt. ed. see Lewerentz, Claus.

Lindner, Vicki, jt. auth. see Lieberman, Annette.

Lindner, William. John Calvin. (Men of Faith Ser.). 16p. 1998. mass mkt. 4.99 (*0-7642-2005-5*) Bethany Hse.

Lindner, William, Jr. & Unseth, Ben. John Paton. (Men of Faith Ser.). 16p. (Orig.). 1996. mass mkt. 4.99 (*1-55661-495-0*) Bethany Hse.

Lindnerer, Wolf-Volker, jt. auth. see Konig, Karl.

Lindo, jt. auth. see Turban.

Lindo, David K. Supervision Can Be Easy! LC 79-17682. 282p. reprint ed. pap. 87.50 (*0-608-12859-7*, 202358200033) Bks Demand.

Lindo, Elias H., tr. see Ben-Israel, Manasseh.

Lindo-Fuentes, Hector. Weak Foundations: The Economy of El Salvador in the Nineteenth Century, 1821-1898. (Illus.). 275p. 1990. 48.00 (*0-520-06927-7*, Pub. by U CA Pr) Cal Prin Full Svc.

Lindo-Fuentes, Hector, jt. auth. see Gudmundson, Lowell.

Lindo, Hugo. Only the Voice. Miller, Elizabeth G., tr. Orig. Title: Solo La Voz. 110p. (Orig.). 1984. pap. 8.00 (*0-939378-04-3*) Mundus Artium.

— The Ways of Rain: And Other Poems by Hugo Lindo. Miller, Yvette E., ed. Miller, Elizabeth G., tr. LC 86-18577. (Discoveries Ser.). (ENG & SPA.). 160p. 1986. pap. 14.95 (*0-935480-24-2*) Lat Am Lit Rev Pr.

Lindo, Laara, ed. see Russell, Walter & Russell, Lao.

Lindo Systems, Inc. Staff. Optimization Modeling with Lingo. 3rd rev. ed. (Illus.). 550p. (C). 1998. pap. text 71.95 (*1-893355-00-4*) Lindo Systs.

Lindofrs, Bernth & Gibbs, James, eds. Research on Wole Soyinka. 45.00 (*0-86543-218-X*); pap. 14.95 (*0-86543-219-8*) Africa World.

Lindon. Encyclopedia of Spectroscopy & Spectrometry. (C). 1999. text 310.00 (*0-12-226683-8*) Harcourt Coll Pubs.

Lindon, Jenni, et al. Caring for Young Children. 117p. 1997. pap. 28.95 (*0-7329-3199-1*, Pub. by Macmill Educ) Paul & Co Pubs.

Lindon, Jennie. Growing up: From Eight Years to Young Adulthood. LC 97-214974. 200p. 1996. pap. 31.50 (*1-874579-61-X*, Pub. by Natl Childrens Bur) Paul & Co Pubs.

Lindon, Jennie, jt. auth. see Bonel, Paul.

Lindon, John C. Encyclopedia of Spectroscopy & Spectrometry, 3 vols. Tranter, George E. & Holmes, John L., eds. 2500p. 1999. 925.00 (*0-12-226680-3*) Acad Pr.

Lindop. Athletes. 1996. write for info. (*0-8050-5256-9*) H Holt & Co.

— Political Leaders. 1996. write for info. (*0-8050-5257-7*) H Holt & Co.

— Political Parties. 1996. write for info. (*0-8050-5264-X*) H Holt & Co.

Lindop. Works of Thomas De Quincey, Vols. 15-21. 895.00 (*1-85196-520-3*) Ashgate Pub Co.

— Works of Thomas De Quincey, Vols.1-7) LC 99-58983. 1999. 895.00 (*1-85196-518-1*) Ashgate Pub Co.

— Works of Thomas De Quincey, Vol. 21. LC 99-58983. 1999. 2685.00 (*1-85196-054-6*) Ashgate Pub Co.

Lindop, Edmund. The Changing Supreme Court. LC 95-13842. (Democracy in Action Ser.). (Illus.). 128p. (YA). (gr. 7-12). 1995. lib. bdg. 24.00 (*0-531-11224-1*) Watts.

— Dwight D. Eisenhower, John F. Kennedy, Lyndon B. Johnson. (Presidents Who Dared Ser.). (Illus.). 64p. (J). (gr. 5-8). 1995. lib. bdg. 18.90 (*0-8050-3404-8*) TFC Bks NY.

— George Washington, Thomas Jefferson, Andrew Jackson. (Presidents Who Dared Ser.). (Illus.). 64p. (J). (gr. 5-8). 1995. lib. bdg. 18.90 (*0-8050-3401-3*) TFC Bks NY.

— Great Britain & the United States: Rivals & Partners. LC 98-12470. (Illus.). 127p. (YA). (gr. 7 up). 1999. lib. bdg. 24.40 (*0-7613-1471-7*) TFC Bks NY.

— James K. Polk, Abraham Lincoln, Theodore Roosevelt. (Presidents Who Dared Ser.). (Illus.). 64p. (J). (gr. 5-8). 1995. lib. bdg. 18.90 (*0-8050-3402-1*) TFC Bks NY.

— Political Parties. LC 96-11428. (J). 1995. lib. bdg. 15.98 (*0-8050-4618-6*) H Holt & Co.

— Presidents by Accident. LC 91-17056. (Non-Fiction Ser.). (Illus.). 160p. (YA). (gr. 9-12). 1991. lib. bdg. 24.00 (*0-531-11059-1*) Watts.

— Presidents vs. Congress: Conflict & Compromise. LC 93-30784. (Democracy in Action Ser.). (Illus.). 128p. (YA). (gr. 9-12). 1994. lib. bdg. 24.00 (*0-531-11165-2*) Watts.

— Richard M. Nixon, Jimmy Carter, Ronald Reagan. (Presidents Who Dared Ser.). (Illus.). 64p. (J). (gr. 5-8). 1995. lib. bdg. 18.90 (*0-8050-3405-6*) TFC Bks NY.

— Woodrow Wilson, Franklin D. Roosevelt, Harry S. Truman. LC 95-19526. (Presidents Who Dared Ser.). 64p. (J). (gr. 5-8). 1995. lib. bdg. write for info. (*0-8050-3403-X*) TFC Bks NY.

Lindop, George B., jt. auth. see Semple, P. F.

Lindop, George B., jt. auth. see Semple, Peter F.

***Lindop, Grevel.** Selected Poems. 128p. 2000. pap. 18.95 (*1-85754-465-X*, Pub. by Carcanet Pr) Paul & Co Pubs.

Lindop, Greves, ed. see Chatterton, Thomas.

Lindop, Laurie. Dynamic Modern Women Series, 4 vols. Incl. Political Leaders. LC 96-11431. (Illus.). 128p. (YA). (gr. 7 up). 1995. lib. bdg. 21.40 (*0-8050-4164-8*); Athletes. LC 96-11429. (Illus.). 128p. (YA). (gr. 7 up). 1996. lib. bdg. 21.40 (*0-8050-4167-2*); Scientists & Doctors. LC 96-41923. (Illus.). 128p. (YA). (gr. 7 up). 1995. lib. bdg. 21.40 (*0-8050-4166-4*); Champions of Equality. LC 96-39557. (Illus.). 128p. (YA). (gr. 7 up). 1997. lib. bdg. 21.40 (*0-8050-4165-6*); 57.53 (*0-8050-5383-2*) TFC Bks NY.

Lindor, Keith D., et al, eds. Primary Biliary Cirrhosis: From Pathogenesis to Clinical Treatment. 192p. 1998. 86.00 (*0-7923-8740-6*) Kluwer Academic.

Lindorf, W. Mountain Bike: Repair & Maintenance. (Illus.). 72p. 1995. pap. 14.95 (*0-7063-7420-7*, Pub. by WrLock) Sterling.

Lindow, C. W. & Blanchard, Homer D. A Little Organ Lexicon. (Little Organ Book Ser.: No. 2). 40p. 1981. pap. 7.50 (*0-930112-04-0*) Organ Lit.

Lindow, John. Comitatus, Individual & Honor: Studies in North Germanic Institutional Vocabulary. LC 75-620093. (University of California Publications in Social Welfare: Vol. 83). 193p. reprint ed. pap. 59.90 (*0-608-30832-3*, 201511100092) Bks Demand.

***Lindow, John.** Handbook of Norse Mythology. 2001. lib. bdg. 55.00 (*1-57607-217-7*) ABC-CLIO.

Lindow, John. Myths & Legends of the Vikings. (Illus.). 1980. pap. 3.95 (*0-88388-071-7*) Bellerophon Bks.

— Viking Ships. (J). (gr. 1-9). 1992. pap. 5.95 (*0-88388-078-4*) Bellerophon Bks.

Lindow, John, et al, eds. Structure & Meaning in Old Norse Literature: New Approaches to Textual Analysis & Literary Criticism. (Studies in Northern Civilization: No.3). 454p. 1986. pap. text 79.50 (*87-7492-607-1*, Pub. by Odense Universitets Forlag) Coronet Bks.

Lindow, Sandra. A Celebration of Bones. 64p. 1996. pap. 7.95 (*1-877655-18-X*) Wordcraft Oregon.

— Revision Quest. 24p. (Orig.). 1997. pap. 5.00 (*1-886895-09-0*) Poetry Harbor.

— Rooted in the Earth. Moore, Eugenia & Leiper, Esther M., eds. (Illus.). 32p. (Orig.). (YA). (gr. 9 up). 1989. pap. 3.95 (*0-9617284-8-5*) Sand & Silk.

Lindoy, Leonard F. The Chemistry of Macrocyclic Ligand Complexes. 288p. (C). 1989. text 95.00 (*0-521-25261-X*) Cambridge U Pr.

— The Chemistry of Macrocyclic Ligand Complexes. 277p. (C). 1991. pap. text 32.95 (*0-521-40985-3*) Cambridge U Pr.

Lindpaintner, K., jt. ed. see Ganten, D.

Lindquist. Answers to Milady's Standard Theory Workbook. 160p. 1991. pap. 26.95 (*1-56253-006-2*) Milady Pub.

— Cosmetology Review Exams. (Standard Texts of Cosmetology Ser.). 1991. pap. 16.95 (*1-56253-020-8*, VNR) Wiley.

— Milady's Standard Theory Workbook 91. 2nd ed. 160p. 1991. pap. 20.25 (*1-56253-005-4*) Milady Pub.

Lindquist, A., jt. auth. see Hanon.

Lindquist, Barbara, jt. auth. see Molnar, Alex.

Lindquist, C. Advances in Radiosurgery I. 124p. 1995. 107.00 (*3-211-82612-2*) Spr-Verlag.

Lindquist, Carol. The Banana Lover's Cookbook. LC 92-41399. 1993. pap. 10.95 (*0-312-08702-0*) St Martin.

Lindquist, Claude S. Active Network Design with Signal Filtering Applications. LC 76-14238. 1977. 59.95 (*0-917144-01-5*) Steward & Sons.

— Active Network Design with Signal Filtering Applications: Solutions Manual. 1978. 19.95 (*0-917144-02-3*) Steward & Sons.

— Adaptive & Digital Signal Processing with Digital Filtering Applications. 1988. 59.95 (*0-917144-03-1*) Steward & Sons.

Lindquist, David P. & Warren, Caroline C. Colonial Revival Furniture with Prices. LC 92-50671. (Illus.). 184p. 1993. pap. 14.95 (*0-87069-660-2*, Wllce-Homestd) Krause Pubns.

— English & Continental Furniture with Prices. LC 94-26750. (Illus.). 248p. 1994. pap. 18.95 (*0-87069-662-9*, Wllce-Homestd) Krause Pubns.

— Victorian Furniture with Prices. LC 95-10554. (Illus.). 208p. 1995. pap. 19.95 (*0-87069-664-5*, Wllce-Homestd) Krause Pubns.

Lindquist, Emory K. Bethany in Kansas: The History of a College. LC 75-18910. (Illus.). 320p. 1975. 5.00 (*0-916030-03-2*) Bethany Coll KS.

— Birger Sandzen: An Illustrated Biography. LC 92-23467. (Illus.). 200p. 1993. 29.95 (*0-7006-0575-4*) U Pr of KS.

— Hagbard Brase: Beloved Music Master. Pearson, A. John, ed. LC 84-16773. (Illus.). 166p. 1984. 10.00 (*0-916030-06-7*) Bethany Coll KS.

— An Immigrant's American Odyssey: A Biography of Ernst Skarstedt. LC 74-21137. (Augustana Historical Society Publications: No. 24). (Illus.). 240p. 1974. 5.95 (*0-910184-24-0*) Augustana.

— An Immigrant's Two Worlds: A Biography of Hjalmar Edgren. LC 72-80673. (Augustana Historical Society Publication Ser.: No. 23). (Illus.). 97p. 1972. 4.95 (*0-910184-23-2*) Augustana.

— Shepherd of an Immigrant People: The Story of Erland Carlsson. LC 78-108120. (Augustana Historical Society Publications: No. 26). 236p. 1978. 5.00 (*0-910184-26-7*) Augustana.

Lindquist, Emory K., et al. G. N. Malm: A Swedish Immigrant's Varied Career. Pearson, A. John, ed. LC 89-32481. (Illus.). 244p. 1989. 15.00 (*0-918331-01-3*) Smoky Valley Hist.

Lindquist, Eric N. The Origins of the Center for Hellenic Studies. (Illus.). 96p. 1991. text 16.95 (*0-691-03174-6*, Pub. by Princeton U Pr) Cal Prin Full Svc.

Lindquist, Evert E., et al, eds. Eriophyoid Mites: Their Biology, Natural Enemies, & Control. LC 96-26598. (World Crop Pests Ser.: Vol. 6). 822p. 1996. 296.50 (*0-444-88628-1*) Elsevier.

Lindquist, Galina. Shamanic Performances on the Urban Scene: Neoshamanism in Contemporary Sweden. (Stockholm Studies in Social Anthropology: No. 39). 325p. 1997. pap. 49.50 (*91-7153-691-4*, Pub. by Almqvist Wiksell) Coronet Bks.

Lindquist, Gustavus E. The Indian in American Life. LC 74-7977. reprint ed. 34.50 (*0-404-11867-4*) AMS Pr.

— The Red Man in the United States: An Intimate Study of the Social, Economic & Religious Life of the American Indian. LC 68-56243. (Illus.). xxvii, 461p. 1973. reprint ed. lib. bdg. 49.50 (*0-678-00798-5*) Kelley.

Lindquist, Hal, ed. see Groneman, Chris H.

Lindquist, Hal, ed. see Helsel, Jay D. & Urbanick, Byron.

Lindquist, Jack, ed. Designing Teaching Improvement Programs. LC 79-51475. 1979. reprint ed. pap. 8.00 (*0-937012-07-6*) Coun Indep Colleges.

Lindquist, Jennie D. The Crystal Tree. (Illus.). (J). (gr. 2-6). 1990. 20.00 (*0-8446-6287-9*) Peter Smith.

— The Little Silver House. (Illus.). (J). (gr. 2-6). 1990. 16.00 (*0-8446-6190-2*) Peter Smith.

Lindquist, John H. Misdemeanor Crime: Trivial Criminal Pursuit. LC 87-34664. (Studies in Crime, Law & Justice: No. 4). 197p. reprint ed. pap. 61.10 (*0-7837-6584-3*, 204614900011) Bks Demand.

Lindquist, Kenneth H., intro. Catalogue of the Permanent Collection. (Illus.). 175p. 1973. 7.95 (*1-877885-00-2*) Arnot Art.

— Transients: Paintings by Thomas S. Buechner. (Orig.). 1985. pap. 14.95 (*1-877885-04-5*) Arnot Art.

Lindquist, Lareau. Too Soon To Quit: The Daily Encouragement Factor. 192p. 1994. 17.95 (*1-885481-00-4*); pap. 9.95 (*1-885481-01-2*) Quadrus Media.

Lindquist, Linnea M. Teaching Tips for Cosmetology. 24p. (C). 1981. pap. text 16.00 (*0-314-63395-2*) West Pub.

***Lindquist, Mark.** Never Mind Nirvana. LC 99-88358. 256p. 2000. 21.95 (*0-679-46302-X*) Villard Books.

— Never Mind Nirvana: A Novel. 256p. 2000. 21.95 (*0-375-46302-X*) Villard Books.

Lindquist, Mark. Sculpting Wood: Contemporary Tools & Techniques. LC 86-70901. (Illus.). 292p. (YA). (gr. 9-12). 1986. pap. 31.15 (*0-87192-228-2*) Davis Mass.

Lindquist, Mark A. & Zanger, Martin N., eds. Buried Roots & Indestructible Seeds: The Survival of American Indian Life in Story, History, & Spirit. LC 93-39068. (Illus.). 160p. 1995. pap. text 17.95 (*0-299-14444-5*) U of Wis Pr.

— Buried Roots & Indestructible Seeds: The Survival of American Indian Life in Story, History, & Spirit. LC 94-39068. (Illus.). 160p. (C). 1995. lib. bdg. 45.00 (*0-299-14440-2*) U of Wis Pr.

Lindquist, Mary M., ed. Selected Issues in Mathematics Education. LC 80-82903. (National Society for the Education Series on Contemporary Education Issues). 276p. (C). 1981. 30.25 (*0-8211-1114-0*) McCutchan.

Lindquist, Mary M., et al. Making Sense of Data. LC 92-41881. (Curriculum & Evaluation Standards for School Mathematics Addenda Ser.: Grades K-6). (Illus.). 48p. 1992. pap. 12.95 (*0-87353-318-6*) NCTM.

***Lindquist, N. J.** Best of Friends. (Circle of Friends Ser.: Vol. 1). 192p. 2000. pap. 7.95 (*0-9685495-1-9*, Pub. by Thats Life Communs) Spring Arbor Dist.

— Friends Like These. (Circle of Friends Ser.: Vol. 2). 200p. 2000. pap. 7.95 (*0-9685495-2-7*, Pub. by Thats Life Communs) Spring Arbor Dist.

— In Time of Trouble. (Growing up, Taking Hold Ser.). 2000. pap. 6.95 (*0-9685495-0-0*, Pub. by Thats Life Communs) Spring Arbor Dist.

— Shaded Light. LC 99-45744. 337p. 1999. 24.95 (*0-9661879-4-6*, F-SKP99-47) St Kitts.

Lindquist, Patricia, jt. ed. see Azarnoff, Pat.

Lindquist, Patricia E. The Pictorial History of Fayetteville & Lincoln County, Tennessee. LC 94-22425. (Illus.). 1994. write for info. (*0-89865-926-4*) Donning Co.

Lindquist, Richard K., jt. auth. see Powell, Charles C.

Lindquist, Robert. Spinnin' 2000: The Ultimate Guide to Fun & Profit As a Mobile Disc Jockey. rev. ed. (Illus.). 160p. (Orig.). Date not set. pap. text 24.95 (*0-943047-01-3*) TNT Prodns.

Lindquist, Robert A. Spinnin' How to Score a Hit As a Mobile DJ for Fun & Profit. Warner, David & Dygert, Clare, eds. (Illus.). 110p. 1987. pap. 15.00 (*0-943047-00-5*) TNT Prodns.

Lindquist, Robert J., jt. auth. see Bologna, G. Jack.

Lindquist, Ruth, jt. auth. see Snyder, Mariah.

Lindquist, S., jt. ed. see Maresca, Bruno.

Lindquist, Scott. Before He Takes You Out: The Safe Dating Guide for the 90's. LC 89-51783. 172p. 1989. pap. 11.95 (*0-9623779-0-2*) Vigal Pubs.

***Lindquist, Scott.** The Date Rape Prevention Book: The Essential Guide for Girls & Women. LC 99-56824. 224p. 2000. pap. 12.95 (*1-57071-474-6*) Sourcebks.

Lindquist, Steven C., contrib. by. Car Buying Secrets; Tricks of the Trade. 50p. (Orig.). 1995. pap. 9.95 (*0-9650798-0-5*) Car Buying.

Lindquist, Susan H. Summer Soldiers. LC 98-47429. 178p. (YA). (gr. 5-9). 1999. 14.95 (*0-385-32641-6*) BDD Bks Young Read.

***Lindquist, Susan H.** Wander. 160p. 2000. pap. 4.50 (*0-440-41443-1*) Dell Yearling.

***Lindquist, Susan Hart.** Summer Soldiers. 192p. (YA). (gr. 5-9). 2000. pap. 4.50 (*0-440-41537-3*, Yearling) BDD Bks Young Read.

Lindquist, Tarry. Seeing the Whole Through Social Studies. LC 94-48190. 206p. 1995. pap. text 22.00 (*0-435-08902-1*, 08902) Heinemann.

An Asterisk (*) at the beginning of an entry indicates that the title is appearing for the first time.

L

— Ways That Work: Putting Social Studies Standards into Practice. LC 97-30027. 1997. pap. text 19.00 (*0-435-08907-2*) Heinemann.

*__Lindquist, Tarry, et al.__ Social Studies at the Center. LC 99-47993. 2000. pap. text 22.00 (*0-325-00168-5*) Heinemann.

Lindquist, Timothy & Koehnemann, Harry, eds. Proceedings of the PCTE '94 Conference. (PCTE Technical Journal Ser.: No. 2). 1994. pap. 50.00 (*0-9644599-0-6*) Mark V Systs.

Lindquist, Timothy M., jt. auth. see Abraham, Ronald J.

Lindquist, Tom, ed. see Pierce, Anne M.

Lindquist, W. Current Progress in Hyperbolic Systems: Riemann Problems & Computations. LC 89-17780. (Contemporary Mathematics Ser.: Vol. 100). 367p. 1989. pap. 49.00 (*0-8218-5106-3*, CONM/100) Am Math.

*__Lindquist, William J. & Olson, William H.__ A CPA's Guide to Marriage, Divorce & Family Taxation. 252p. 2000. pap. 45.00 (*0-87051-304-4*, 091004) Am Inst CPA.

Lindqvist, Gunilla. The Aesthetics of Play: A Didactic Study of Play & Culture in Preschools. (Uppsala Studies in Education: No. 62). 234p. 1995. pap. 46.50 (*91-554-3506-8*) Coronet Bks.

Lindqvist, Maria. Infant Multinationals: The Internationalization of Young, Technology-Based Swedish Firms. 274p. (Orig.). 1991. pap. 115.00 (*91-971005-8-7*) Coronet Bks.

Lindqvist, Mats, jt. ed. see Arvastson, Gosta.

*__Lindqvist, Ossi V.__ From Limnology to Fisheries: Lake Tanganyika & Other Large Lakes. LC 99-52685. (Developments in Hydrobiology Ser.). 1999. write for info. (*0-7923-6017-6*) Kluwer Academic.

Lindqvist, Svante, ed. Center on the Periphery: Historical Aspects of 20th-Century Swedish Physics. LC 93-32830. (Uppsala Studies in the History of Science: No. 17). (Illus.). 576p. (C). 1993. 50.00 (*0-88135-157-1*, Sci Hist) Watson Pub Intl.

Lindqvist, Sven. Exterminate All Brutes. 1996. 20.00 (*1-56584-334-7*) Norton.

— Exterminate All the Brutes. 1998. 24.00 (*0-8446-6950-4*) Peter Smith.

— Exterminate All the Brutes: A Modern Odyssey into the Heart of Darkness. Tate, Joan, tr. from SWE. (Illus.). 179p. 1996. 23.00 (*1-56584-002-X*) New Press NY.

— Exterminate All the Brutes: One Man's Odyssey into the Heart of Darkness & the Origins of European Genocide. 1997. pap. 12.00 (*1-56584-359-2*, Pub. by New Press NY) Norton.

*__Lindqvist, Sven.__ A History of Bombing. Rugg, Linda Haverty, tr. from SWE. 2001. 24.95 (*1-56584-625-7*, Pub. by New Press NY) Norton.

Lindqvist, Sven. The Skull Measurer's Mistake: And Other Portraits of Men & Women Who Spoke Out Against Racism. Tate, Joan, tr. from SWE. LC 96-40902. 1997. 22.00 (*1-56584-363-0*, Pub. by New Press NY) Norton.

Lindrall, Ella K. & Puckett, Kent. Parables Jesus Told. (Tell-Me Stories Ser.). 160p. (J). (gr. 1-6). 1998. 18.99 (*0-8024-7116-1*) Moody.

Lindroos & Cermakova, H. Finnish-Czech, Czech-Finnish Pocket Dictionary: Suomi-Tsekki-Suomi Taskusankirja. (CZE & FIN.). 447p. 1984. 95.00 (*0-8288-1688-3*, F12200) Fr & Eur.

*__Lindroos, Kia.__ Now-Time/Image-Space: Temporization of Politics in Walter Benjamin's Philosophy of History & Art. 303p. 1999. pap. 24.95 (*951-39-0341-9*, Pub. by SoPhi Academic) Intl Spec Bk.

Lindros, Eric. Fire on Ice. 1991. pap. 14.95 (*0-00-637747-5*) HarpC.

Lindros, Eric. Pursue Your Goals. LC 99-54410. 1999. 14.95 (*0-87833-167-0*) Taylor Pub.

Lindros, K. O. & Eriksson, C. J., eds. The Role of Acetaldehyde in the Actions of Ethanol: Satellite Symposium to the Sixth International Congress of Pharmacology. (Finnish Foundation for Alcohol Studies: Vol. 23). (Illus.). 1975. pap. 8.00 (*951-9191-23-2*) Rutgers Ctr Alcohol.

Lindroth, Carl H. The Carabidae (Coleoptera) of Fennoscandia & Denmark, Pt. 1. (Fauna Entomologica Scandinavica Ser.: No. 15-1). (Illus.). 226p. 1985. text 64.00 (*90-04-07727-8*) Lubrecht & Cramer.

— The Carabidae (Coleoptera) of Fennoscandia & Denmark, Pt. 2. (Fauna Entomologica Scandinavica Ser.: Vol. 15/2). (Illus.). 274p. 1986. 45.75 (*90-04-08182-8*) Lubrecht & Cramer.

Lindroth, Colette & Lindroth, James. Rachel Crothers: A Research & Production Sourcebook, 8. LC 94-41267. (Modern Dramatists Research & Production Sourcebooks Ser.: Vol. 8). 160p. 1995. lib. bdg. 65.00 (*0-313-27815-6*, Greenwood Pr) Greenwood.

Lindroth, Collette, jt. auth. see Lindroth, James R.

Lindroth, David, jt. auth. see Chapman, Victoria.

Lindroth, David, jt. ed. see Smith, Carter.

Lindroth, James, jt. auth. see Lindroth, Colette.

Lindroth, James, jt. auth. see Sweeney, John D.

Lindroth, James R. & Lindroth, Collette. Children of the Dream: Our Own Stories of Growing up Black in America. LC 98-50209. (Illus.). 384p. 1984. 1.95 (*0-671-00803-X*, PB Hardcover) PB.

Lindroth, S. E. & Rynaenen, S. S., eds. Food Technology in the Year Two Thousand. (Bibliotheca Nutritio et Dieta Ser.: No. 47). (Illus.). xiv, 22p. 1990. 115.00 (*3-8055-5243-2*) S Karger.

Lindrup, Garth. Butterworths Competition Law Handbook. 3rd ed. 826p. 1993. pap. 100.00 (*0-406-02280-1*, UK, MICHIE) LEXIS Pub.

Lindrup, Garth, ed. Butterworths Public Procurement & CCT Handbook. 1997. write for info. (*0-406-99913-9*, BPPC, MICHIE) LEXIS Pub.

Lindsau, Norene. Pathfinder Teacher's Guide. 56p. (J). (gr. 7-10). 1993. pap., teacher ed. 14.95 (*1-56370-121-9*) JIST Works.

Lindsay. The Child & Family. (C). 1995. pap. text 25.00 (*0-7020-1646-2*) Harcourt.

— Functional Human Anatomy. (C). 1995. text 283.12 (*0-8016-6472-1*) Mosby Inc.

— Great Wall. 2nd ed. 1999. 14.95 (*962-217-598-8*) Norton.

— Guide to Scientific Writing. 2nd ed. 1995. pap. text. write for info. (*0-582-80312-8*, Pub. by Addison-Wesley) Longman.

— High Performance Liquid Chromatography. 2nd ed. 104p. 1998. 890.00 (*0-471-98458-2*) Wiley.

*__Lindsay.__ High Performance Liquid Chromatography. 2nd ed. 104p. (C). 2000. write for info. (*0-471-98461-2*) Wiley.

Lindsay. Martin Luther. 1996. pap. 11.99 (*1-85792-261-1*, Pub. by Christian Focus); pap. 11.99 (*1-85792-262-X*, Pub. by Christian Focus) Spring Arbor Dist.

Lindsay. Study Guide T/A the Dissectable Human CD-ROM & Mosby's System Atlas. 144p. 1997. student ed. write for info. incl. cd-rom (*0-8151-4541-1*) Mosby Inc.

Lindsay. Working with Children in Grief. (C). 1996. pap. text 28.00 (*0-7020-1960-7*) Harcourt.

Lindsay, ed. Festi, Sexti, Pompei. (LAT.). 1997. 89.50 (*3-519-01349-5*, T1349, Pub. by B G Teubner) U of Mich Pr.

Lindsay, jt. auth. see Corbin.

Lindsay, jt. auth. see Evans.

Lindsay, A. A. New Psychology Complete: Mind the Builder & Scientific Man Building (1922) 446p. 1998. reprint ed. pap. 29.95 (*0-7661-0553-9*) Kessinger Pub.

Lindsay, A. A., jt. auth. see Sawyer, J. O.

Lindsay, A. D. Republic of Plato. 382p. 26.95 (*0-8488-2488-1*) Amereon Ltd.

Lindsay, A. D., ed. see Descartes, Rene.

Lindsay, A. D., tr. see Irwin, Terence, ed.

Lindsay-Abaire, David. A Devil Inside. Date not set. pap. 5.95 (*0-8222-1752-X*) Dramatists Play.

— Fuddy Meers. Date not set. pap. 5.95 (*0-8222-1751-1*) Dramatists Play.

Lindsay, Alan & Neumann, Ruth. The Challenge for Research in Higher Education: Harmonizing Excellence & Utility. Fife, Jonathan D., ed. & frwd. by. LC 89-83630. (ASHE-ERIC Higher Education Reports: No. 88-8). 150p. (Orig.). (C). 1989. pap. 24.00 (*0-913317-52-7*) GWU Grad Schl E&HD.

Lindsay, Alan E. & Budkin, Alberto. The Cardiac Arrhythmias: An Approach to Their Electrocardiographic Recognition. 2nd ed. (Illus.). 178p. 1975. pap. 26.50 (*0-8151-5428-3*) Mosby Inc.

Lindsay, Alan G. Death in the Funhouse Vol. 2: John Barth & Poststructuralist Aesthetics. (Studies in Literary Criticism & Theory). XIII, 180p. (C). 1995. pap. text 29.95 (*0-8204-2547-8*) P Lang Pubng.

Lindsay, Alexander. Index of English Literary Manuscripts Vol. III, Pt. 4: 1700-1800 Sterne-Young. (Illus.). 448p. 1996. 465.00 (*0-7201-2283-X*) Continuum.

Lindsay, Alexander D. Karl Marx's 'Capital' LC 73-7456. (Illus.). 128p. 1973. reprint ed. lib. bdg. 48.50 (*0-8371-6935-6*, LIMC, Greenwood Pr) Greenwood.

— Religion, Science, & Society in the Modern World. LC 70-37847. (Essay Index Reprint Ser.). 1977. reprint ed. 15.95 (*0-8369-2604-8*) Ayer.

Lindsay, Alexander D. & Erskine-Hill, Howard, eds. Congreve: The Critical Heritage. 496p. 1989. 112.00 (*0-415-02535-4*) Routledge.

Lindsay, Alexander J., Jr., et al. Survey & Excavations North & East of Navajo Mountain, Utah, 1959-1962. (Glen Canyon Ser.: No. 8). 400p. 1968. pap. 12.50 (*0-685-14708-8*, BS-45) Mus Northern Ariz.

Lindsay, Andrew. The Breadmaker's Carnival. LC 99-18560. 1999. write for info. (*0-88001-700-7*, Ecco Press) HarperTrade.

*__Lindsay, Andrew.__ The Breadmaker's Carnival. 2000. 25.00 (*0-06-019842-7*, Ecco Press) HarperTrade.

Lindsay, Ann K. Watercolor: A New Beginning: A Holistic Approach to Painting. LC 97-30967. (Illus.). 144p. 1997. pap. 24.95 (*0-8230-5638-4*) Watsn-Guptill.

Lindsay, Anne. American Cancer Society Cookbook. 1990. 9.98 (*0-671-07484-9*) S&S Trade.

— Guide to Owning a Rabbit. (Illus.). 64p. 1997. pap. 6.95 (*0-7938-2156-8*, RE-507) TFH Pubns.

Lindsay, Art & Berringer, Jan. One Final Pass. 160p. 1996. 19.95 (*1-887002-36-7*) Cross Trng.

Lindsay, Art, jt. auth. see Brown, Ron.

Lindsay, Arturo, ed. Santeria Aesthetics in Contemporary Latin American Art. LC 95-21186. 308p. 1996. pap. text 36.95 (*1-56098-615-8*) Smithsonian.

— Santeria Aesthetics in Contemporary Latin American Art. (Illus.). 308p. 1996. text 65.00 (*1-56098-644-1*) Smithsonian.

Lindsay, Barbara, ed. see Sanchez-Chew, Albert P.

Lindsay, Beverly, ed. Comparative Perspectives of Third World Women: The Impact of Race, Sex, & Class. LC 78-19793. (Praeger Special Studies). 318p. 1980. 38.50 (*0-275-90514-4*, C0514, Praeger Pubs) Greenwood.

Lindsay, Beverly, jt. ed. see Ginsburg, Mark B.

Lindsay, Bruce. Mixture Models: Theory, Geometry & Applications. LC 94-75430. (NSF-CBMS Regional Conference Series in Probability & Statistics: Vol. 5). (Illus.). 163p. (C). 1995. pap. 25.00 (*0-940600-32-3*) Inst Math.

*__Lindsay, C. H. Forbes.__ John Smith: Gentlemen Adventure. 2000. 19.99 (*1-887159-56-8*) Preston-Speed.

— John Smith: Gentlemen Adventurer. 2000. pap. 13.99 (*1-887159-57-6*) Preston-Speed.

Lindsay, Caroline H. Nothing Good Ever Happens to Me: An Adoption Love Story. 128p. 1996. pap. text 9.95 (*0-87868-601-0*) Child Welfare.

Lindsay, Cecile. Reflexivity & Revolution in the New Novel: Claude Ollier's Fictional Cycle. LC 90-39016. 225p. reprint ed. pap. 69.80 (*0-608-09852-3*, 206981700006) Bks Demand.

Lindsay, Cecile, tr. see Derrida, Jacques.

Lindsay, Charles. Mentawai Shaman: Shaman: Keeper of the Rain Forest. (Illus.). 120p. 1992. 60.00 (*0-89381-520-9*) Aperture.

*__Lindsay, Charles, photos by.__ Upstream: Fly-Fishing in the American West. (Illus.). 96p. 2000. 40.00 (*0-89381-889-5*) Aperture.

Lindsay, Charles L. Trident: A Trading Strategy. 234p. 1991. 50.00 (*0-930233-48-4*) Windsor.

Lindsay, Clare. Conquering Anorexia: The Route to Recovery. 208p. 1999. pap. 19.95 (*1-84024-096-2*, Pub. by Summers) Seven Hills Bk.

Lindsay, Cotton M. Equal Pay for Comparable Work: An Economic Analysis of a New Antidiscrimination Dotrine. 1980. pap. 2.50 (*0-916770-11-7*) Law & Econ U Miami.

— New Directions in Public Health Care: A Prescription for the 1980's. 308p. 1980. pap. 24.95 (*0-917616-37-5*) Transaction Pubs.

— New Directions in Public Health Care: A Prescription for the 1980's. 3rd ed. 308p. 1980. 39.95 (*0-87855-394-0*) Transaction Pubs.

Lindsay, Cynthia. Dear Boris: The Life of William Henry Pratt a.k.a. Boris Karloff. (Illus.). 288p. (Orig.). 1995. reprint ed. pap. 20.00 (*0-87910-076-1*) Limelight Edns.

Lindsay, D. C. The Macrolichens of South Georgia. (British Antarctic Survey Report Ser.: No. 89). 98p. 1974. 25.00 (*0-85665-028-5*, Pub. by Brit Antarctic Surv) Balogh.

Lindsay, D. Michael, jt. auth. see Gallup, George, Jr.

Lindsay, D. Steve, jt. ed. see Read, J. Don.

Lindsay, David. Ane Satyre of the Thrie Estaits. LC 75-26333. (English Experience Ser.: No. 137). 156p. 1969. reprint ed. 25.00 (*90-221-0137-1*) Walter J Johnson.

— Devil's Tor. Reginald, R. & Melville, Douglas, eds. LC 77-84249. (Lost Race & Adult Fantasy Ser.). 1978. reprint ed. lib. bdg. 44.95 (*0-405-10995-4*) Ayer.

— The Haunted Woman. (Classics Ser.). 193p. 1995. pap. 9.95 (*0-86241-162-9*, Pub. by Canongate Books) Interlink Pub.

*__Lindsay, David.__ House of Invention: The Secret Life of Everyday Products. LC 99-53253. 192p. 2000. 20.00 (*1-55821-740-1*) Lyons Pr.

Lindsay, David. Madness in the Making: The Triumphant Rise & Untimely Fall of America's Show Inventors. LC 97-39617. (Illus.). 384p. 1997. 27.00 (*1-56836-203-X*) Kodansha.

— The Patent Files: Dispatches from the Frontiers of Invention. LC 98-38808. 248p. 1999. 19.95 (*1-55821-741-X*) Lyons Pr.

*__Lindsay, David.__ Patent Files: Dispatches from the Frontiers of Invention. 2001. pap. 17.95 (*1-58574-072-1*) Lyons Pr.

Lindsay, David. The Three Estates: A Pleasant Satire in Commendation of Virtue & in Vituperation of Vice. Mace, Nigel, ed. LC 97-42175. (Illus.). 221p. 1998. 65.95 (*1-84014-204-9*, PR2659.L5A7, Pub. by Ashgate Pub) Ashgate Pub Co.

— A Voyage to Arcturus. (Classics Ser.). 304p. 1998. pap. 12.95 (*0-86241-377-X*, Pub. by Canongate Books) Interlink Pub.

— A Voyage to Arcturus. 248p. 1985. pap. 5.95 (*0-8065-0944-9*, Citadel Pr) Carol Pub Group.

— A Voyage to Arcturus. large type ed. 492p. 1998. reprint ed. lib. bdg. 24.00 (*0-939495-70-8*) North Bks.

— A Voyage to Arcturus. 1993. reprint ed. lib. bdg. 18.95 (*0-89968-406-8*, Lghtyr Pr) Buccaneer Bks.

— A Voyage to Arcturus. 302p. 1998. reprint ed. lib. bdg. 24.00 (*1-58287-091-8*) North Bks.

— The Warkis of the Famous & Worthie Knicht, Schir David Lyndesay. Newly Correctit & Augmentit. LC 75-171797. (English Experience Ser.: No. 352). 362p. 1971. reprint ed. 44.00 (*90-221-0352-8*) Walter J Johnson.

— Works, Pts. I-IV. Small, J. & Hall, F., eds. (EETS, OS Ser.: Nos. 11, 19, 35, 37). 1974. reprint ed. 55.00 (*0-527-00013-2*) Periodicals Srv.

Lindsay, David & Wenzel. Functional Human Anatomy. 448p. (C). 1996. text, student ed. 24.37 (*0-8151-5448-8*, WCB McGr Hill) McGrw-H Hghr Educ.

Lindsay, David, et al. Functional Human Anatomy. 400p. (C). 1996. text, lab manual ed. write for info. (*0-8151-5449-6*, WCB McGr Hill) McGrw-H Hghr Educ.

Lindsay, David W., ed. see Gay, John, et al.

Lindsay, Debra. Science in the Subarctic: Trappers, Traders, & the Smithsonian Institution. LC 92-29811. (Illus.). 192p. (C). 1993. text 34.00 (*1-56098-233-0*) Smithsonian.

Lindsay, Dennis. The Birth of the Planet Earth & the Age of the Universe. 2nd ed. (RUS., Illus.). (Orig.). 1997. reprint ed. mass mkt. write for info. (*1-890863-03-3*) Wrld Wide Print.

— The Dismantling of Evolution's Secret Code: Radiometric Dating. 2nd ed. (RUS., Illus.). (Orig.). 1997. reprint ed. mass mkt. write for info. (*1-890863-04-1*) Wrld Wide Print.

— Foundation for Creationism. 2nd ed. (RUS., Illus.). (Orig.). 1997. mass mkt. write for info. (*1-890863-00-9*) Wrld Wide Print.

— Harmony of Science & Scripture. 2nd ed. (RUS., Illus.). (Orig.). 1997. mass mkt. write for info. (*1-890863-01-7*) Wrld Wide Print.

— The Origins of Controversy. 2nd ed. (RUS., Illus.). (Orig.). 1997. mass mkt. write for info. (*1-890863-02-5*) Wrld Wide Print.

Lindsay, Dennis G. The ABCs of Evolutionism: Ape-Man, Batman & Catwoman & Other Evolutionary Fantasies (The Rest of the Story) (Creation Science Ser.: Vol. X). (Illus.). 392p. 1995. per. 9.95 (*0-89985-287-4*) Christ for the Nations.

— The Birth of Planet Earth & the Age of the Universe. (Creation Science Ser.: Vol. 8). 1993. per. 8.95 (*0-89985-285-8*) Christ for the Nations.

— The Canopied Earth: World That Was. (Creation Science Ser.: Vol. 9). 1991. per. 7.95 (*0-89985-281-5*) Christ for the Nations.

— The Dinosaur Dilemma: Fact or Fantasy. (Creation Science Ser.: Vol. 7). 1990. per. 11.95 (*0-89985-279-3*) Christ for the Nations.

— The Dismantling of Evolutionism's Sacred Cow: Radiometric Dating. (Creation Science Ser.: Vol. 9). 1992. per. 8.95 (*0-89985-286-6*) Christ for the Nations.

— Foundations for Creation Science. (Creation Science Ser.: Vol. 1). 1990. per. 9.95 (*0-89985-277-7*) Christ for the Nations.

— The Genesis Flood: Continents in Collision. (Creation Science Ser.: Vol. 5). 1992. per. 7.95 (*0-89985-282-3*) Christ for the Nations.

— Harmony of Science & Scripture. (Creation Science Ser.: Vol. 2). 1991. per. 9.95 (*0-89985-278-5*) Christ for the Nations.

— Joshua's Long Day & Jonah's Long Night: Fact or Fairytale. (Creation Ser.: Vol. XI). (Illus.). 408p. 1997. per. 9.95 (*0-89985-289-0*) Christ for the Nations.

— The Original Star Wars & the Age of Ice. (Creation Science Ser.: Vol. 6). 1992. per. 8.95 (*0-89985-284-X*) Christ for the Nations.

— The Origins Controversy: Creation or Chance. (Creation Science Ser.: Vol. 3). 1991. 6.95 (*0-89985-280-7*) Christ for the Nations.

Lindsay, Dennis R. Josephus & Faith: Pistis & Pisteuein As Faith Terminology in the Writings of Flavius Josephus & in the New Testament. LC 93-29156. (Arbeiten zur Geschichte des Antiken Judentums & des Urchristentums Ser.: Bd. 19). xiv, 212p. 1993. 82.00 (*90-04-09858-5*) Brill Academic Pubs.

Lindsay, Diana, jt. auth. see Lindsay, Lowell.

*__Lindsay, Diana E.__ Anza-Borrego A to Z: People, Places & Things. LC 00-41321. (Natural History Bks.). (Illus.). 2000. write for info. (*0-932653-38-3*) Sunbelt Pubns.

Lindsay, Dorothy & Lindsay, Steele. Destiny at Cracker Creek. LC 84-61590. 192p. 1984. pap. 8.50 (*0-88100-047-7*) Natl Writ Pr.

Lindsay, E. H., et al, eds. European Neogene Mammal Chronology. LC 89-26648. (NATO ASI Ser.: Vol. 180). (Illus.). 668p. (C). 1990. text 191.00 (*0-306-43391-5*, Kluwer Plenum) Kluwer Academic.

Lindsay, Elaine, ed. The Diaries of Barbara Hanrahan. LC 98-218124. 376p. 1998. pap. 34.95 (*0-7022-2892-3*, Pub. by Univ Queensland Pr) Intl Spec Bk.

Lindsay, Eldress B. Seasoned with Grace: My Generation of Shaker Cooking. Boswell, Mary R., ed. LC 87-19933. (Illus.). 192p. (Orig.). 1987. pap. 14.00 (*0-88150-099-2*, Pub. by Countryman) Norton.

Lindsay, Fay D. A Special Kind of Freedom. (Illus.). 99p. (Orig.). 1982. pap. 7.00 (*0-943980-01-1*) AIGA Pubns.

Lindsay, Forbes. Cuba & Her People of Today. 1976. lib. bdg. 59.95 (*0-8490-1689-4*) Gordon Pr.

— Panama, 2 vols. 1976. lib. bdg. 200.00 (*0-8490-2403-X*) Gordon Pr.

Lindsay, Franklin. Beacons in the Night: With the OSS & Tito's Partisans in Wartime Yugoslavia. (Illus.). 428p. 1995. pap. 14.95 (*0-8047-2588-8*) Stanford U Pr.

— Beacons in the Night: With the OSS & Tito's Partisans in Wartime Yugoslavia. LC 92-36774. (Illus.). 428p. (C). 1995. 45.00 (*0-8047-2123-8*) Stanford U Pr.

Lindsay, Franklin A., intro. Improving Management of the Public Work Force: The Challenge to State & Local Government. LC 78-11075. 138p. 1978. pap. 5.00 (*0-87186-067-8*) Comm Econ Dev.

— Jobs for the Hard-to-Employ: New Directions for a Private Partnership. LC 77-28272. (CED Statement on National Policy Ser.). 1978. pap. 3.00 (*0-87186-066-X*) Comm Econ Dev.

Lindsay, Frannie. The Aerial Tide Coming In. (Illus.). 16p. 1981. pap. 3.00 (*0-934714-24-X*); bds. 25.00 (*0-934714-23-1*) Swamp Pr.

— The Horse We Lie Down In: Eight Poems. (Poetry Chapbooks Ser.: No. 1). 10p. 1980. pap. 1.00 (*0-936044-02-0*) Pikestaff Pr.

Lindsay, Freda. A Book of Miracles: Providential Promised Provision Provided. (Illus.). 176p. 1996. per. 7.95 (*0-89985-200-9*) Christ for the Nations.

— My Diary Secrets. 1976. per. 9.95 (*0-89985-021-9*) Christ for the Nations.

Lindsay, G. C. Contract. 2nd ed. (LBC Nutshell Ser.). xiii, 157p. 1987. pap. 11.95 (*0-455-20767-4*, Pub. by LawBk Co) Gaunt.

— Guide to the Practice of the Supreme Court of New South Wales. xxv, 246p. 1989. pap. 39.50 (*0-455-20929-4*, Pub. by LawBk Co) Gaunt.

Lindsay, Gail F. & Lindsay-Sayre, Nancy. Within Hearts Reach: Hundreds of Fun Ways to Stay Close Across the Miles. (Illus.). 96p. 1998. pap. 13.95 (*0-9662016-3-9*) Millbarry Pub.

Lindsay, Geoff. Baseline Assessment: Practice, Problems & Possibilities. LC 98-203739. 154p. 1998. pap. text 27.95 (*1-85346-514-3*, Pub. by David Fulton) Taylor & Francis.

Lindsay, Geoff & Thompson, David. Values into Practice in Special Education. LC 98-149272. 160p. 1997. pap. 27.95 (*1-85346-466-X*, Pub. by David Fulton) Taylor & Francis.

Lindsay, Geoffrey A. & Singer, Kenneth D., eds. Polymers for Second-Order Nonlinear Optics. LC 95-30598. (ACS Symposium Ser.: Vol. 601). (Illus.). 560p. 1995. text 150.00 (*0-8412-3263-6*, Pub. by Am Chemical) OUP.

Lindsay, Geoffrey A., jt. auth. see Lewis, Anne.

*__Lindsay, George.__ In the Woods Who's Been Here. (Illus.). (J). 1999. 14.50 (*0-606-15588-0*) Turtleback.

An Asterisk (*) at the beginning of an entry indicates that the title is appearing for the first time.

Lindsay, Gertrude. Thought Chimes: Pure, Precious, Priceless (1914) 50p. 1998. reprint ed. pap. 7.95 (*0-7661-0564-4*) Kessinger Pub.

Lindsay, Gordon. The ABCs for Godly Living. 1992. 8.95 (*0-89985-283-1*) Christ for the Nations.

— Abraham, Friend of God. (Old Testament Ser.: Vol. 4). 1964. 1.95 (*0-89985-126-6*) Christ for the Nations.

— Adam & Eve. (Old Testament Ser.: Vol. 2). 1964. 0.95 (*0-89985-124-X*) Christ for the Nations.

— Alcohol - the Nationalized Sin. 1962. per. 2.95 (*0-89985-274-2*) Christ for the Nations.

— Amazing Discoveries in the Words of Jesus. 1960. per. 9.95 (*0-89985-112-6*) Christ for the Nations.

— Amazing Prophecies Prove The Bible. 1971. 2.95 (*0-89985-053-7*) Christ for the Nations.

— The Antichrist & His Forerunner. (End of the Age Ser.: Vol. 2). 1973. 1.95 (*0-89985-068-5*) Christ for the Nations.

— Apostles, Prophets & Administrators. 1960. per. 3.95 (*0-89985-121-5*) Christ for the Nations.

— Armageddon. (Revelation Ser.: Vol. 14). 1962. 1.95 (*0-89985-047-2*) Christ for the Nations.

— The Art of Successful Praying. 1967. 2.95 (*0-89985-079-0*) Christ for the Nations.

— The Astounding Diary of Dr. John G. Lake. 1987. mass mkt. 3.95 (*0-89985-273-4*) Christ for the Nations.

— The Beast from the Bottomless Pit. (Revelation Ser.: Vol. 10). 1962. 1.95 (*0-89985-043-X*) Christ for the Nations.

— Bible Days Are Here Again. 1960. per. 5.95 (*0-89985-194-0*) Christ for the Nations.

— The Bible Is a Scientific Book. 1971. per. 3.95 (*0-89985-117-7*) Christ for the Nations.

— The Bible Secret of Divine Health. 1960. 3.25 (*0-89985-023-5*) Christ for the Nations.

— Charismatic Ministry. 1968. per. 4.95 (*0-89985-122-3*) Christ for the Nations.

— Charles G. Finney, Vol. 5 of 7. (Men Who Changed the World Ser.: Vol. 5). 1972. 1.50 (*0-89985-258-0*) Christ for the Nations.

— Christ the Great Physician. 1960. 1.95 (*0-89985-024-3*) Christ for the Nations.

— D. L. Moody, Vol. 7 of 7. (Men Who Changed the World Ser.: Vol. 7). 1972. 1.50 (*0-89985-260-2*) Christ for the Nations.

— David Comes into the Kingdom. (Old Testament Ser.: Vol. 22). 1965. 1.95 (*0-89985-142-8*) Christ for the Nations.

— David Reaping the Whirlwind. (Old Testament Ser.: Vol. 23). 1966. 1.95 (*0-89985-143-6*) Christ for the Nations.

— Death & the Hereafter. 1972. 1.95 (*0-89985-096-0*) Christ for the Nations.

— The Death Cheaters. 1971. 2.95 (*0-89985-081-2*) Christ for the Nations.

— The Decline & Fall of Israel & Judah. (Old Testament Ser.: Vol. 33). 1967. 1.95 (*0-89985-153-3*) Christ for the Nations.

— Did Politics Influence Jesus? 1979. per. 3.95 (*0-89985-113-4*) Christ for the Nations.

— Difficult Questions About the Bible Answered. 1971. 1.95 (*0-89985-114-2*) Christ for the Nations.

— The Early Kings of Israel. (Old Testament Ser.: Vol. 27). 1966. 1.95 (*0-89985-147-9*) Christ for the Nations.

— The Early Kings of Judah & the Revolution. (Old Testament Ser.: Vol. 26). 1966. 1.95 (*0-89985-146-0*) Christ for the Nations.

— The Early Life of David. (Old Testament Ser.: Vol. 21). 1965. 1.95 (*0-89985-141-X*) Christ for the Nations.

— Elijah, the Man Who Did Not Die. (Old Testament Ser.: Vol. 29). 1967. 1.95 (*0-89985-149-5*) Christ for the Nations.

— Elijah, the Whirlwind Prophet. (Old Testament Ser.: Vol. 28). 1967. 1.95 (*0-89985-148-7*) Christ for the Nations.

— Elisha-Prophet of the Supernatural. (Old Testament Ser.: Vol. 31). 1967. 1.95 (*0-89985-151-7*) Christ for the Nations.

— Elisha-The Man Who Received the Double Portion. (Old Testament Ser.: Vol. 30). 1967. 2.95 (*0-89985-150-9*) Christ for the Nations.

— Enoch & Noah, Patriarchs of the Deluge. (Old Testament Ser.: Vol. 3). 1964. 1.95 (*0-89985-125-8*) Christ for the Nations.

— Evolution-The Incredible Hoax. 1961. 1.50 (*0-89985-115-0*) Christ for the Nations.

— Ezra & Nehemiah & the Return from Babylon. (Old Testament Ser.: Vol. 34). 1967. 1.95 (*0-89985-154-1*) Christ for the Nations.

— The Forgotten Miracles of the Bible, Vol. 6 of 7. (Miracles in the Bible Ser.: Vol. 6). 1977. 2.95 (*0-89985-183-5*) Christ for the Nations.

— Forty Signs of the Soon Coming of Christ. 1960. 3.95 (*0-89985-055-3*) Christ for the Nations.

— 450-Year Judgment Cycles. (Miracles in the Bible Ser.: Vol. 5). 1977. 2.95 (*0-89985-182-7*) Christ for the Nations.

— The 400 Silent Years. (Old Testament Ser.: Vol. 38). 1968. 1.95 (*0-89985-158-4*) Christ for the Nations.

— Francis, the Poor Man of Assisi, Vol. 1 of 7. (Men Who Changed the World Ser.: Vol. 1). 1972. 1.50 (*0-89985-254-8*) Christ for the Nations.

— Freda. 1984. per. 4.95 (*0-89985-268-8*) Christ for the Nations.

— George Muller & General Booth, Vol. 6 of 7. (Men Who Changed the World Ser.: Vol. 6). 1972. 1.50 (*0-89985-259-9*) Christ for the Nations.

— Gideon & the Early Judges. (Old Testament Ser.: Vol. 15). 1965. 2.95 (*0-89985-135-5*) Christ for the Nations.

— The Gifts of the Spirit. (Literature Crusade Ser.). 1965. pap. 0.95 (*0-89985-357-9*) Christ for the Nations.

— Gifts of the Spirit. (Gifts of the Spirit Ser.: Vol. 4). pap. 5.95 (*0-89985-198-3*) Christ for the Nations.

— Gifts of the Spirit. (Gifts of the Spirit Ser.: Vol. 1). 1963. pap. 5.95 (*0-89985-195-9*) Christ for the Nations.

— Gifts of the Spirit, 4 vols. (Gifts of the Spirit Ser.: Vol. 2). 1963. pap. 5.95 (*0-89985-196-7*) Christ for the Nations.

— Gifts of the Spirit, 4 vols. (Gifts of the Spirit Ser.: Vol. 3). 1963. pap. 7.95 (*0-89985-197-5*) Christ for the Nations.

— Gifts of the Spirit, 4 vols., 4. (Gifts of the Spirit Ser.). 1963. per. 5.95 (*0-89985-199-1*) Christ for the Nations.

— The Gifts of the Spirit (Dones Del Espirtu) (Literature Crusade Ser.). (SPA.). 1965. pap. write for info. (*0-89985-370-6*) Christ for the Nations.

— God's Master Key to Prosperity. 1960. per. 5.95 (*0-89985-001-4*) Christ for the Nations.

— God's Plan of the Ages. 1971. per. 6.95 (*0-89985-056-1*) Christ for the Nations.

— The Gordon Lindsay Story. Christ for the Nations Staff, ed. (Orig.). 1964. per. 6.95 (*0-89985-002-2*) Christ for the Nations.

— The Great Day of the Lord. (Revelation Ser.: Vol. 4). 1962. 1.95 (*0-89985-037-5*) Christ for the Nations.

— The Great Tribulation. (End of the Age Ser.: Vol. 4). 1973. 2.95 (*0-89985-070-7*) Christ for the Nations.

— The Great Trumpets & the Vial Judgments. (End of the Age Ser.: Vol. 6). 1973. 2.95 (*0-89985-072-3*) Christ for the Nations.

— The Great White Throne. (End of the Age Ser.: Vol. 9). 1974. 1.95 (*0-89985-075-8*) Christ for the Nations.

— Hades-Abode of the Unrighteous Dead. 1968. 1.95 (*0-89985-082-0*) Christ for the Nations.

— How to Be Enriched by Giving. 1974. per. 2.50 (*0-89985-012-X*) Christ for the Nations.

— How to Deal With Violence. (Powers of Darkness Ser.). per. 4.95 (*0-89985-087-1*) Christ for the Nations.

— How to Find the Perfect Will of God. 1967. 4.50 (*0-89985-003-0*) Christ for the Nations.

— How to Receive the Baptism of the Holy Spirit. (Literature Crusade Ser.). pap. 0.95 (*0-89985-354-4*) Christ for the Nations.

— How to Receive the Baptism of the Holy Spirit (Como Reciber El Bautismo Del Espiritu Santo) (Literature Crusade Ser.). (SPA.). 1965. pap. 0.95 (*0-89985-367-6*) Christ for the Nations.

— How You Can Be Healed. 1965. 2.95 (*0-89985-026-X*); pap. 0.95 (*0-89985-353-6*) Christ for the Nations.

— How You Can Be Healed (Como Puede Usted Ser Sanado) (Literature Crusade Ser.). (SPA.). 1965. pap. 0.95 (*0-89985-366-8*) Christ for the Nations.

— How You Can Have Divine Health. 1961. 2.50 (*0-89985-027-8*) Christ for the Nations.

— How You May Become a Successful Christian. (Literature Crusade Ser.). 1965. pap. 0.95 (*0-89985-359-5*) Christ for the Nations.

— How You May Become a Successful Christian (Como Vivar Una Vida) rev. ed. (Literature Crusade Ser.). (SPA.). 1965. pap. 0.95 (*0-89985-372-2*) Christ for the Nations.

— Increase Your Prayer Power Tenfold. 1972. 2.50 (*0-89985-080-4*) Christ for the Nations.

— Is Jesus the Son of God? (Literature Crusade Ser.). 1965. pap. 0.95 (*0-89985-360-9*) Christ for the Nations.

— Is Jesus the Son of God? (Es Jesus el Hijo de Dios?) (Literature Crusade Ser.). (SPA.). 1965. pap. 0.95 (*0-89985-373-0*) Christ for the Nations.

— Isaac & Rebekah. (Old Testament Ser.: Vol. 6). 1964. 1.95 (*0-89985-127-4*) Christ for the Nations.

Lindsay, Gordon. Isaiah & Jeremiah. (Old Testament Ser.: Vol. 35). 1967. 2.95 (*0-89985-155-X*) Christ for the Nations.

Lindsay, Gordon. Israel: Prophetic Signs. 1964. per. 3.95 (*0-89985-189-4*) Christ for the Nations.

— Israel, the False Prophet & the Two Witnesses. (End of the Age Ser.: Vol. 5). 1964. 1.95 (*0-89985-071-5*) Christ for the Nations.

— Israel's 48 Signs of Christ's Return. 1965. per. 3.00 (*0-89985-186-X*) Christ for the Nations.

— Jacob & His Son, Joseph. (Old Testament Ser.: Vol. 8). 1964. 1.95 (*0-89985-129-0*) Christ for the Nations.

— Jacob, the Supplanter Who Became a Prince with God. (Old Testament Ser.: Vol. 7). 1964. 1.95 (*0-89985-128-2*) Christ for the Nations.

— Jephthah & Samson. (Old Testament Ser.: Vol. 16). 1965. 1.95 (*0-89985-136-3*) Christ for the Nations.

— John Alexander Dowie: A Life of Tragedies & Triumphs. 1980. 6.95 (*0-89985-985-2*) Christ for the Nations.

— John G. Lake - Apostle to Africa. 1972. pap. 4.50 (*0-89985-011-1*) Christ for the Nations.

— John G. Lake Sermons on Dominion over Demons, Disease, & Death. 1960. per. 7.95 (*0-89985-028-6*) Christ for the Nations.

— John Wesley & William Carey, Vol. 4 of 7. (Men Who Changed the World Ser.: Vol. 4). 1972. 1.50 (*0-89985-257-2*) Christ for the Nations.

— Joseph & His Brethren. (Old Testament Ser.: Vol. 9). 1964. 2.95 (*0-89985-130-4*) Christ for the Nations.

— Joshua, Conqueror of Canaan. (Old Testament Ser.: Vol. 14). 1965. 1.95 (*0-89985-134-7*) Christ for the Nations.

— The Judgment Seat of Christ. (End of the Age Ser.: Vol. 7). 1973. 2.95 (*0-89985-073-1*) Christ for the Nations.

— The Judgment Throne & the Seven Seals. (Revelation Ser.: Vol. 3). 1962. pap. 1.95 (*0-89985-036-7*) Christ for the Nations.

— The Key to Israel's Future - The Forgotten Covenant. 1972. 3.95 (*0-89985-191-6*) Christ for the Nations.

— The Last Days of David & His Contemporaries. (Old Testament Ser.: Vol. 24). 1966. 1.95 (*0-89985-144-4*) Christ for the Nations.

— Life after Death. 1960. per. 3.95 (*0-89985-083-9*) Christ for the Nations.

— Life after Death. (Literature Crusade Ser.). 1965. pap. 0.95 (*0-89985-351-X*) Christ for the Nations.

— Life after Death (Vida Despues De la Muerta) (Literature Crusade Ser.). (SPA.). 1965. pap. 0.95 (*0-89985-364-1*) Christ for the Nations.

— Life & Teachings of Christ, Vol. 1. 1963. pap. 7.95 (*0-89985-967-4*) Christ for the Nations.

— Life & Teachings of Christ, Vol. 2. 1963. per. 7.95 (*0-89985-968-2*) Christ for the Nations.

— Life & Teachings of Christ, Vol. 3. 1963. reprint ed. per. 7.95 (*0-89985-969-0*) Christ for the Nations.

— The Lord, the Lion & Mutu (Cristo, el Leon y Pablo) (Literature Crusade Ser.). (SPA.). pap. 0.95 (*0-89985-377-3*) Christ for the Nations.

— Lot & Lot's Wife. (Old Testament Ser.: Vol. 5). 1964. pap. 1.95 (*0-89985-958-5*) Christ for the Nations.

— Martin Luther & George Fox, Vol. 3 of 7. (Men Who Changed the World Ser.: Vol. 3). 1965. 1.50 (*0-89985-256-4*) Christ for the Nations.

— Messiah Witness - Israel's Destiny & Coming Deliverer. 1.95 (*0-89985-187-8*) Christ for the Nations.

— The Millennium. (Revelation Ser.: Vol. 15). 1962. 2.50 (*0-89985-048-0*) Christ for the Nations.

— Ministry of Angels. 1964. 1.95 (*0-89985-018-9*) Christ for the Nations.

— The Minor Prophets: Hosea, Joel, Amos, Obadiah, Jonah, Micah. (Old Testament Ser.: Vol. 36). 1968. 1.95 (*0-89985-156-8*) Christ for the Nations.

— The Minor Prophets: Nahum, Habakkuk, Zephaniah, Haggai. Zechariah, Malachi. (Old Testament Ser.: Vol. 37). 1968. 1.95 (*0-89985-157-6*) Christ for the Nations.

— The Miracle of Israel. 3.95 (*0-89985-188-6*) Christ for the Nations.

— Miracles of Christ, Pt. I, Vol. 2. (Miracles in the Bible Ser.: Vol. 7). 1979. 2.95 (*0-89985-960-7*) Christ for the Nations.

— Miracles of Christ, Pt. II, Vol. 3. (Miracles in the Bible Ser.: Vol. 7). 1979. 2.95 (*0-89985-961-5*) Christ for the Nations.

— The Miracles of Divine Discipline, Vol. 7 of 7. (Miracles in the Bible Ser.: Vol. 7). 1977. 1.95 (*0-89985-184-3*) Christ for the Nations.

— Miracles of the Apostles, Vol. 4 of 7. (Miracles in the Bible Ser.: Vol. 4). 1977. 1.95 (*0-89985-181-9*) Christ for the Nations.

— Moses: The Lawgiver. (Old Testament Ser.: Vol. 11). 1964. pap. 1.95 (*0-89985-959-3*) Christ for the Nations.

— Moses & His Contemporaries. (Old Testament Ser.: Vol. 13). 1965. 1.95 (*0-89985-133-9*) Christ for the Nations.

— Moses & the Church in the Wilderness. (Old Testament Ser.: Vol. 12). 1964. 1.95 (*0-89985-132-0*) Christ for the Nations.

— Moses, the Deliverer. (Old Testament Ser.: Vol. 10). 1964. 1.95 (*0-89985-131-2*) Christ for the Nations.

— Mutu Finds the Way to Heaven (Pablo Encuentra el Camino al Cielo) (Literature Crusade Ser.). (SPA.). pap. 0.95 (*0-89985-376-5*) Christ for the Nations.

— The New Heavens & the New Earth. (Revelation Ser.: Vol. 16). 1962. 1.95 (*0-89985-049-9*) Christ for the Nations.

— The New John G. Lake Sermons. 1971. 3.95 (*0-89985-987-9*) Christ for the Nations.

— Old Testament Healings, Vol. 1 of 7. (Miracles in the Bible Ser.: Vol. 1). 1976. 2.95 (*0-89985-179-7*) Christ for the Nations.

— One Body, One Spirit, One Lord. 1982. per. 3.95 (*0-89985-991-7*) Christ for the Nations.

— The 144,000 on Mt. Zion. (Revelation Ser.: Vol. 11). 1962. 1.95 (*0-89985-044-8*) Christ for the Nations.

— Parables of Jesus Christ. (Life & Teachings of Christ Ser.: Vol. 1). (SPA.). 1973. 3.95 (*0-89985-261-0*) Christ for the Nations.

— Parables of Jesus Christ, Vol. 1. (Life & Teachings of Christ Ser.). (SPA.). 3.95 (*0 89985-980-1*) Christ for the Nations.

— Paradise - Abode of the Righteous Dead. 1967. 1.95 (*0-89985-085-5*) Christ for the Nations.

— Prayer & Fasting. 1960. 3.95 (*0-89985-076-6*) Christ for the Nations.

— Prayer That Moves Mountains. 1960. per. 5.95 (*0-89985-078-2*) Christ for the Nations.

— Prayer That Moves Mountains. (Literature Crusade Ser.). 1965. pap. 0.95 (*0-89985-352-8*) Christ for the Nations.

— Prayer That Moves Mountains (La Oracion Que Nueve las Montanas) (Literature Crusade Ser.). (SPA.). 1965. pap. 0.95 (*0-89985-365-X*) Christ for the Nations.

— Praying to Change the World. (School of Prayer Ser.). 200p. 1960. per. 6.95 (*0-89985-956-9*) Christ for the Nations.

— The Prophecies of Daniel. 1969. per. 4.95 (*0-89985-052-9*) Christ for the Nations.

— Red China in Prophecy. (Prophecy Ser.). 1972. per. 2.25 (*0-89985-059-6*) Christ for the Nations.

— The Revolution & After. (Old Testament Ser.: Vol.. 32). 1967. 1.95 (*0-89985-152-5*) Christ for the Nations.

— The Rise of the Antichrist. (Revelation Ser.: Vol. 9). 1962. 1.95 (*0-89985-042-1*) Christ for the Nations.

— Ruth, The Gleaner, & the Boy Samuel. (Old Testament Ser.: Vol. 17). 1965. 1.95 (*0-89985-137-1*) Christ for the Nations.

— Samuel, the Prophet. (Old Testament Ser.: Vol. 18). 1965. 1.95 (*0-89985-138-X*) Christ for the Nations.

— Satan & His Kingdom of Darkness. rev. ed. 1998. pap. 9.95 (*0-89985-952-6*) Christ for the Nations.

— Satan, Fallen Angels & Demons. (Literature Crusade Ser.: Vol. 2). 1965. pap. 0.95 (*0-89985-350-1*) Christ for the Nations.

— Satan, Fallen Angels & Demons (Los Angeles Caidos) (Literature Crusade Ser.). (SPA.). 1965. pap. 0.95 (*0-89985-363-3*) Christ for the Nations.

— Saul & Jonathan. (Old Testament Ser.: Vol. 20). 1965. 1.95 (*0-89985-140-1*) Christ for the Nations.

— Saul, Israel's First King. (Old Testament Ser.: Vol. 19). 1965. 2.95 (*0-89985-139-8*) Christ for the Nations.

— The Second Coming of Christ. (Literature Crusade Ser.). 1965. pap. 0.95 (*0-89985-358-7*) Christ for the Nations.

— The Second Coming of Christ. 1967. 1.95 (*0-89985-061-8*) Christ for the Nations.

— The Second Coming of Christ (La Segunda Venida de Cristo) (Literature Crusade Ser.). (SPA.). 1965. pap. 0.95 (*0-89985-371-4*) Christ for the Nations.

— The Seven Churches of Prophecy, Vol. 1. (Revelation Ser.: Vol. 2). 1962. 1.95 (*0-89985-977-1*) Christ for the Nations.

— The Seven Churches of Prophecy, 2 vols., Vol. 2. (Revelation Ser.: 2). 1962. 2.50 (*0-89985-978-X*) Christ for the Nations.

— Seven Master Keys to Triumphant Christian Living. 1967. 2.95 (*0-89985-006-5*) Christ for the Nations.

— Signs of the Coming of the Antichrist. (End of the Age Ser.: Vol. 1). 1.95 (*0-89985-067-7*) Christ for the Nations.

— Signs of the Soon Coming Christ (Senates De la Pronla Venida De Cristo) (Literature Crusade Ser.). (SPA.). 1960. pap. 0.95 (*0-89985-368-4*) Christ for the Nations.

— Signs of the Soon Coming of Christ. (Literature Crusade Ser.). 1965. pap. 0.95 (*0-89985-355-2*) Christ for the Nations.

— Signs of the Times in the Heavens. 1967. 1.95 (*0-89985-062-6*) Christ for the Nations.

— Solomon & Rehoboam. (Old Testament Ser.: Vol. 25). 1966. 1.95 (*0-89985-145-2*) Christ for the Nations.

— Spiritual Hunger (John G. Lake Sermons) 1960. per. 4.25 (*0-89985-020-0*) Christ for the Nations.

— Spiritualism, Vol. 3 of 4. (Sorcery in America Ser.: Vol. 3). 1969. 2.95 (*0-89985-093-6*) Christ for the Nations.

— The Sun-Clothed Woman & the Manchild. (Revelation Ser.: Vol. 7). 1962. 1.95 (*0-89985-040-5*) Christ for the Nations.

— They Saw It Happen. 1972. 2.95 (*0-89985-010-3*) Christ for the Nations.

— Thirty Bible Reasons Why Christ Heals Today. 1968. 3.50 (*0-89985-031-6*) Christ for the Nations.

— The Tribulation Temple. (Revelation Ser.: Vol. 5). 1962. 1.95 (*0-89985-038-3*) Christ for the Nations.

— Triunity of the Godhead. 1986. per. 3.95 (*0-89985-272-6*) Christ for the Nations.

— Twenty-Five Objections to Divine Healing & the Bible Answers. 1971. 1.95 (*0-89985-030-8*) Christ for the Nations.

— 21 Reasons Why Christians Should Speak in Other Tongues. 1971. 1.95 (*0-89985-269-6*) Christ for the Nations.

— 22 Questions Most Frequently Asked by the Unsaved. 1970. 2.95 (*0-89985-118-5*) Christ for the Nations.

— The Two Babylons. (Revelation Ser.: Vol. 13). 1962. 1.95 (*0-89985-046-4*) Christ for the Nations.

— The Two Witnesses. (Revelation Ser.: Vol. 6). 1962. 1.95 (*0-89985-039-1*) Christ for the Nations.

— Visitation: Key to Church Growth. 1966. 2.95 (*0-89985-119-3*) Christ for the Nations.

— Visitation (La Llave Al Crecimiento de Su Iglesia) (Literature Crusade Ser.). (SPA.). 1965. pap. 0.95 (*0-89985-375-7*) Christ for the Nations.

— The Way to Eternal Life (El Camino a la Vida Eterna) (SPA.). 1965. pap. 0.95 (*0-89985-374-9*) Christ for the Nations.

— Why Christians Are Sick. 1960. per. 3.95 (*0-89985-029-4*) Christ for the Nations.

— Why Do the Righteous Suffer? 1963. 2.95 (*0-89985-032-4*) Christ for the Nations.

— Why Some Are Not Healed. 1967. 1.95 (*0-89985-033-2*) Christ for the Nations.

— Why the Bible Is the Word of God. (Literature Crusade Ser.). 1965. pap. 0.95 (*0-89985-356-0*) Christ for the Nations.

— Why the Bible Is the Word of God (La Biblia el la Palabrade Dios Por Que? (Literature Crusade Ser.). (SPA.). 1965. pap. 0.95 (*0-89985-369-2*) Christ for the Nations.

— Will Christians Go Through the Great Tribulation? 1971. 2.95 (*0-89985-065-0*) Christ for the Nations.

Lindsay, Gordon, ed. see Davis, Marietta.

Lindsay, Gordon, ed. see Wright, Marilyn J.

Lindsay, Gordon B. Making a Killing: A Smoking Satire on Selling Cigarettes. 304p. 1997. pap. 19.98 (*0-88290-609-7*, 1982) Horizon Utah.

Lindsay, Grace M. & Gaw, Allan. Coronary Heart Disease: A Handbook for the Health Care Team. LC 96-25835. 1996. text 35.00 (*0-443-05460-6*) Church.

Lindsay, H. Suetonius: Tiberius. (Latin Texts Ser.). (LAT.). 1995. pap. 22.95 (*1-85399-387-5*, Pub. by Brist Class Pr) Focus Pub-R Pullins.

Lindsay, H., ed. Suetonius: Caligula. (Bristol Latin Texts Ser.). (LAT.). 197p. 1993. pap. 22.95 (*1-85399-375-1*, Pub. by Brist Class Pr) Focus Pub-R Pullins.

Lindsay, Howard & Crouse, Russel. The Great Sebastians. LC 56-7735. (Illus.). 177p. 1956. 16.95 (*0-910278-35-0*) Boulevard.

— Life with Father. 1948. pap. 5.25 (*0-8222-0661-7*) Dramatists Play.

— Life with Mother. 1950. pap. 5.25 (*0-8222-0662-5*) Dramatists Play.

Lindsay, Howard & Crouse, Russell. The Great Sebastians. 1956. pap. 5.25 (*0-8222-0484-3*) Dramatists Play.

Lindsay, Ian G. & Cosh, Mary. Inveraray & the Dukes of Argyll. (Illus.). 508p. 1988. pap. 35.00 (*0-85224-577-7*, Pub. by Edinburgh U Pr) Col U Pr.

Lindsay, Irene & Lindsay, Ralph. ABC Plates & Mugs. LC 97-217918. (Illus.). 224p. 1997. pap. 24.95 (*1-57432-000-9*, 4927) Collector Bks.

L

L

Lindsay, J. F. & Ramachandran, V. Modeling & Analysis of Linear Physical Systems. (Illus.). 780p. (C). 1990. text 69.95 (0-929704-19-3) Weber Systems.

Lindsay, Jack. Gainsborough: His Life & Art. (Illus.). 244p. 1983. pap. 7.95 (0-586-05613-0) Academy Chi Pubs.

— Turner: His Life & Work. (Illus.). 379p. 1980. reprint ed. pap. 8.95 (0-586-03852-3) Academy Chi Pubs.

— William Blake: Creative Will & the Poetic Image. LC 70-118005. (Studies in Blake: No. 3). 1970. reprint ed. lib. bdg. 75.00 (0-8383-1061-3) M S G Haskell Hse.

Lindsay, Jack, tr. see Apuleius, Lucius.

Lindsay, Jack, tr. see Bruno, Giordano.

Lindsay, James A. Annual & Semiannual Promotion, with Special Reference to the Elementary School. LC 72-176996. (Columbia University. Teachers College. Contributions to Education Ser.: No. 570). reprint ed. 37.50 (0-404-55570-5) AMS Pr.

Lindsay, James F. & Katz, Silas. Dynamics of Physical Circuits & Systems. (Illus.). 480p. 1978. 59.95 (0-916460-21-5, Matrix Pubs Inc) Weber Systems.

Lindsay, James H., ed. Coatings & Coating Processes for Metals. (Materials Data Ser.). 400p. 1998. 158.00 (0-87170-613-X, 06587G) ASM.

Lindsay, James J., jt. auth. see Wildman, John B.

Lindsay, James M. Congress & Nuclear Weapons. LC 90-49522. 223p. reprint ed. pap. 69.20 (0-608-06080-1, 206641200008) Bks Demand.

— Congress & the Politics of U. S. Foreign Policy. LC 94-1246. 228p. 1994. text 45.00 (0-8018-4881-4) Johns Hopkins.

— Gottfried Keller: Life & Works. LC 69-14390. 1968. 30.00 (0-8023-1205-5) Dufour.

— Techniques in Human Geography. LC 97-7185. (Contemporary Human Geography Ser.). (Illus.). 224p. (C). 1997. 60.00 (0-415-15475-8); pap. 17.99 (0-415-15476-6) Routledge.

Lindsay, James M., jt. auth. see Squire, Peverill.

Lindsay, James M., jt. ed. see Ripley, Randall B.

Lindsay, Janice. The Milly Stories: Corpses, Carnations, the Weirdness Index, and, of Course, Aunt Gloria. LC 97-36066. 131p. (J). (gr. 4-7). 1998. 15.95 (0-7894-2491-6) DK Pub Inc.

Lindsay, Jean. Miss Elizabeth B. Mitchell. (C). 1989. pap. text 40.00 (1-85821-023-2, Pub. by Pentland Pr) St Mut.

Lindsay, Jeanne. Organizing TAPP: Useful Forms for Teen Parenting Programs. (YA). 1997. pap. 4.95 (1-885356-23-4) Morning Glory.

***Lindsay, Jeanne.** Teen Dads. 1999. pap. 17.95 (0-7857-2434-6) Econo-Clad Bks.

Lindsay, Jeanne W. Challenge of Toddlers: For Teen Parents - Parenting Your Child from One to Three. 2nd rev. ed. LC 98-35683. (Illus.). 192p. 1998. 18.95 (1-885356-38-2); pap. 12.95 (1-885356-39-0); pap., wbk. ed. 2.50 (1-885356-40-4) Morning Glory.

— Parents, Pregnant Teens, & the Adoption Option: Help for Families. LC 88-8359. 208p. (Orig.). 1988. pap. 8.95 (0-930934-28-8) Morning Glory.

— Pregnant? Adoption Is an Option. (Illus.). 192p. 1996. pap. 11.95 (1-885356-08-0, 56080) Morning Glory.

— School-Age Parents: The Challenge of Three-Generation Living. LC 90-6039. 32p. 1990. pap., teacher ed. 2.50 (0-930934-56-3) Morning Glory.

— School-Age Parents: The Challenge of Three-Generation Living. LC 90-6039. (Illus.). 224p. 1990. 15.95 (0-930934-37-7); pap. 10.95 (0-930934-36-9) Morning Glory.

— Teen Dads: Rights, Responsibilities & Joys. 28p. (Orig.). (YA). (gr. 7 up). 1993. pap., teacher ed. 2.50 (0-930934-80-6); pap., student ed., wbk. ed. 2.50 (0-930934-79-2) Morning Glory.

— Teen Dads: Rights, Responsibilities & Joys. (Illus.). 192p. (Orig.). (YA). (gr. 7 up). 1993. 15.95 (0-930934-77-6); pap. 9.95 (0-930934-78-4) Morning Glory.

— Teenage Couples - Expectations & Reality: Teens' Views on Living Together, Roles, Work, Children, Jealousy, & Partner Abuse. LC 95-46209. (Illus.). 192p. (Orig.). (YA). (gr. 9 up). 1996. 21.95 (0-930934-99-7); pap. 14.95 (0-930934-98-9) Morning Glory.

Lindsay, Jeanne W. Teenage Couples: Caring, Commitment & Change: How to Build a Relationship That Lasts. LC 94-37983. (Teenage Couples Ser.). (Illus.). 208p. (Orig.). (YA). (gr. 7 up). 1996. 15.95 (0-930934-92-X) Morning Glory.

Lindsay, Jeanne W. Teenage Couples: Caring, Commitment & Change: How to Build a Relationship That Lasts. (Teenage Couples Ser.). 36p. (Orig.). (YA). (gr. 7 up). 1995. pap., student ed., wbk. ed. 2.50 (0-930934-96-2) Morning Glory.

— Teenage Couples: Caring, Commitment & Change: How to Build a Relationship That Lasts. LC 94-37983. (Teenage Couples Ser.). (Illus.). 208p. (Orig.). (YA). (gr. 7 up). 1996. pap. 9.95 (0-930934-93-8) Morning Glory.

— Teenage Couples: Coping with Reality: Dealing with Money, In-Laws, Babies & Other Details of Daily Life. (Teenage Couples Ser.). 32p. (Orig.). (YA). (gr. 7 up). 1995. pap., student ed., wbk. ed. 2.50 (0-930934-88-1) Morning Glory.

— Teenage Couples: Coping with Reality: Dealing with Money, In-Laws, Babies & Other Details of Daily Life. LC 94-36860. (Teenage Couples Ser.). (Illus.). 188p. (Orig.). 1996. pap. 9.95 (0-930934-86-5) Morning Glory.

— Teenage Couples: Coping with Reality: Dealing with Money, In-Laws, Babies & Other Details of Daily Life. LC 94-36860. (Teenage Couples Ser.). (Illus.). 188p. (Orig.). (YA). (gr. 7 up). 1996. 15.95 (0-930934-87-3) Morning Glory.

— Teenage Couples Series Curriculum Guide. (Teenage Couples Ser.). 136p. 1995. pap. 19.95 (0-930934-89-X) Morning Glory.

— Teens Parenting Curriculum Guide. 264p. 1999. pap. 29.95 (1-885356-41-2) Morning Glory.

— Teens Parenting Series Teacher's Guide. 128p. 1998. pap., teacher ed. 9.95 (1-885356-42-0) Morning Glory.

— Yo Tengo Papa? Do I Have a Daddy? Un Cuento Sobre Un Nino de Madre Soltera, A Story about a Single-Parent Child. Palacios, Argentina, tr. from SPA. (SPA., Illus.). 48p. (Orig.). (J). (ps-3). 1994. 12.95 (0-930934-83-0); pap. 5.95 (0-930934-82-2) Morning Glory.

— Your Baby's First Year: A Guide for Teenage Parents. 2nd rev. ed. LC 98-7746. (Teens Parenting Ser.). (Illus.). 192p. 1998. 18.95 (1-885356-32-3); pap. 12.95 (1-885356-33-1); pap., wbk. ed. 2.50 (1-885356-34-X) Morning Glory.

Lindsay, Jeanne W. & Brunelli, Jean. Adolescentes Como Padres - La Jornada de tu Embarazo y el Nacimiento de tu Bebe: Como Cuidar de ti Misma y de tu Recien Nacido si Eres una Adolescente Embarazada. Palacios, Argentina, tr. from ENG. LC 92-43626.Tr. of Teens Parenting - Your Pregnancy & Newborn Journey. (SPA.). 24p. 1993. pap., teacher ed. 2.50 (0-930934-72-5); pap., student ed., wbk. ed. 2.50 (0-930934-71-7) Morning Glory.

— Adolescentes Como Padres - La Jornada de tu Embarazo y el Nacimiento de tu Bebe: Como Cuidar de ti Misma y de tu Recien Nacido si Eres una Adolescente Embarazada. Palacios, Argentina, tr. from ENG. LC 92-43626.Tr. of Teens Parenting - Your Pregnancy & Newborn Journey. (SPA., Illus.). 192p. 1993. pap. text 9.95 (0-930934-69-5) Morning Glory.

— Nurturing Your Newborn: Young Parent's Guide to Baby's First Month Teacher Guide. 20p. 1999. pap., teacher ed. 2.00 (1-885356-60-9) Morning Glory.

— Nurturing Your Newborn: Young Parent's Guide to Baby's First Month Workbook. 24p. 1999. pap., wbk. ed. 2.00 (1-885356-61-7) Morning Glory.

— Teens Parenting - Your Pregnancy & Newborn Journey (Easier Reading) How to Take Care of Yourself & Your Newborn When You're a Pregnant Teen - Easy Reading Edition. LC 91-3712. 24p. (YA). (gr. 3 up). 1992. pap., teacher ed. 2.50 (0-930934-68-7); pap., student ed., wbk. ed. 2.50 (0-930934-63-6) Morning Glory.

— Teens Parenting - Your Pregnancy & Newborn Journey (Easier Reading) How to Take Care of Yourself & Your Newborn When You're a Pregnant Teen - Easy Reading Edition. LC 91-3712. (Illus.). 192p. (YA). (gr. 3 up). 1992. text 15.95 (0-930934-62-8); pap. text 9.95 (0-930934-61-X) Morning Glory.

— Your Pregnancy & Newborn Journey: A Guide for Pregnant Teens. 2nd rev. ed. LC 98-7616. (Illus.). 192p. 1998. 18.95 (1-885356-29-3); pap. 12.95 (1-885356-30-7); pap., wbk. ed. 2.50 (1-885356-31-5) Morning Glory.

Lindsay, Jeanne W. & Enright, Sharon G. Books, Babies & School-Age Parents: How to Teach Pregnant & Parenting Teens to Succeed. LC 97-5793. (Illus.). 225p. 1997. 21.95 (1-885356-21-8); pap. 14.95 (1-885356-22-6) Morning Glory.

Lindsay, Jeanne W. & McCullough, Sally. Discipline from Birth to Three: How Teen Parents Can Prevent & Deal with Discipline Problems with Babies & Toddlers. 2nd rev. ed. LC 98-27894. (Illus.). 192p. 1998. 18.95 (1-885356-35-8); pap. 12.95 (1-885356-36-6); pap., wbk. ed. 2.50 (1-885356-37-4) Morning Glory.

Lindsay, Jeanne W., ed. see Arthur, Shirley M.

Lindsay, Jeanne W., ed. see Pollock, Sudie.

Lindsay, Jeanne W., ed. see Reynolds, Marilyn & Doty, David.

***Lindsay, Jeanne Warren.** Do I Have a Daddy? A Story about a Single-Parent Child. LC 99-41556. (Illus.). 48p. (J). (ps). 1999. 14.95 (1-885356-62-5) Morning Glory.

— Do I Have a Daddy? A Story about a Single-Parent Child with a Special Section for Single Mothers & Fathers. rev. ed. LC 99-41556. (Illus.). 48p. (J). (ps-1). 1999. pap. 7.95 (1-885356-63-3) Morning Glory.

Lindsay, Jeanne Warren. Nurturing Your Newborn: A Young Parent's Guide to Baby's First Month. LC 99-25877. 1999. pap. 7.95 (1-885356-58-7) Morning Glory.

***Lindsay, Jeanne Warren.** Teen Dads: Rights, Responsibilities & Joys. 2nd ed. 224p. 2000. 18.95 (1-885356-67-6, Pub. by Morning Glory); pap. 12.95 (1-885356-68-4, Pub. by Morning Glory) IPG Chicago.

Lindsay, Jeffery P., jt. auth. see Hemingway, Hilary.

Lindsay, Jeffrey P., jt. auth. see Hemingway, Hilary.

Lindsay, Jeffry P., jt. auth. see Hemingway, Hilary.

Lindsay, Joan. Picnic at Hanging Rock. 1976. 18.95 (0-8488-1415-0) Amereon Ltd.

— Picnic at Hanging Rock. 1988. pap. 5.50 (0-87129-248-3, P62) Dramatic Pub.

— Picnic at Hanging Rock. 192p. 1999. reprint ed. 29.95 (0-89966-560-8) Buccaneer Bks.

Lindsay, Joan V. Chicago from the River. (Illus.). 48p. (Orig.). 1996. pap. 14.95 (0-9647350-0-8) J V & D Lindsay.

Lindsay, Joe. The Record Label Guide for Domestic LPs. (Illus.). 200p. (Orig.). 1986. pap. 25.00 (0-9617347-0-1) BIODISC.

— Up Shit Creek: A Collection of Horrifyingly True Toilet Misadventures. LC 97-9464. (Illus.). 79p. 1997. pap. 5.95 (0-89815-939-3) Ten Speed Pr.

Lindsay, John & Ellis, Norman. Staff Pensions in General Practice. LC 98-155951. (Business Side of General Practice Ser.). 102 p. 1998. write for info. (1-85775-222-8, Radcliffe Med Pr) Scovill Paterson.

Lindsay, John & Ellis, Norman, eds. Making Sense of Pensions & Retirement. LC 95-14243. 1995. write for info. (1-85775-090-X, Radcliffe Med Pr) Scovill Paterson.

Lindsay, John W. & Steele, D. Whedon's Commentary on the Old Testament Vol. 2: Leviticus-Deuteronomy. 25.99 (0-88019-129-5) Schmul Pub Co.

Lindsay, Joseph. Diseases of the Aorta. (Illus.). 370p. 1993. 75.00 (0-8121-1694-1) Lppncott W & W.

— In Wake of a Dream. 70p. 1998. pap. 9.95 (0-9617347-8-7) BIODISC.

Lindsay, Joyce & Lindsay, Maurice. A Pleasure of Gardens: A Literary Companion. (Aberdeen University Press Bks.). (Illus.). 224p. 1991. pap. text 16.95 (0-08-041209-2, Pub. by Aberdeen U Pr) Macmillan.

Lindsay, Joycey H. Marriages of Henrico County, Virginia, 1680-1808. 96p. 1983. reprint ed. pap. 15.00 (0-89308-364-X) Southern Hist Pr.

Lindsay, Karen, ed. see Ryan, Gary & Ryan, Bob.

Lindsay, Kathleen. Forever You'll Be Mine. large type ed. 393p. 1982. 27.99 (0-7089-0792-X) Ulverscroft.

Lindsay, Kenneth. European Assemblies: The Experimental Period, 1949 to 1959. LC 81-6877. 267p. 1981. reprint ed. lib. bdg. 65.00 (0-313-20846-8, LIEA, Greenwood Pr) Greenwood.

Lindsay, Kenneth C., tr. see Kandinsky, Wassily.

Lindsay, Kenneth L. Three-D & the MAFIA Club. viii, 228p. (Orig.). 1981. pap. 10.00 (0-943980-00-3) AIGA Pubns.

Lindsay, Kenneth W. & Bone, Ian. Neurology & Neurosurgery Illustrated. 3rd ed. LC 97-16820. 1997. pap. text 45.00 (0-443-05061-9) Church.

Lindsay, Kenneth W., jt. auth. see Jennett, Bryan J.

Lindsay, Laura L., jt. auth. see Rasberry, Robert W.

Lindsay, Len. Captain COMAL Gets Organized. (Amazing Adventures of Captain COMAL Ser.). (Illus.). 102p. 1984. pap. 14.95 (0-928411-01-X) COMAL Users.

Lindsay, Lord & Gillin, Donald G. Chinese Communism & the U. S. Proceedings of a Mini-Symposium, 1935-1936. 69p. 1975. pap. 6.00 (0-939252-03-1) ASU Ctr Asian.

Lindsay, Lowell. Geology & Geothermal Resources of the Imperial & Mexicali Valleys. Hample, William, ed. & illus. by. LC 98-48897. (SDAG Annual Field Trip Guides Ser.). 192p. 1998. pap. 19.95 (0-916251-50-0) Sunbelt Pubns.

Lindsay, Lowell & Lindsay, Diana. Anza-Borrego Desert Region. 4th ed. LC 98-10340. (Illus.). 224p. 1998. pap. 15.95 (0-89997-187-3) Wilderness Pr.

Lindsay, Lowell, jt. auth. see Remeika, Paul.

Lindsay, Lowell, ed. see Clifford, H. J., et al.

Lindsay, Lowell, ed. see Crosby, Harry.

Lindsay, Lowell, ed. see Mackintosh, Graham.

Lindsay, Lowell, ed. see Pepper, Choral.

Lindsay, Lowell, ed. see Peterson, Lee.

Lindsay, Margie. Developing Capital Markets in Eastern Europe: A Business Reference. 336p. (C). 1992. text 65.00 (0-8147-5067-2) NYU Pr.

Lindsay, Maurice. Collected Poems, 1940-1990. 270p. 1990. pap. text 25.00 (0-08-040910-5, Pub. by Aberdeen U Pr) Macmillan.

— History of Scottish Literature. 1977. 42.00 (0-7091-5642-1) Dufour.

— News of the World: Last Poems. 1990. pap. 21.00 (1-898218-32-3) St Mut.

— Speaking Likenesses Postcript. LC 99-216602. 64p. 1990. pap. 21.00 (1-898218-96-X) St Mut.

Lindsay, Maurice, jt. auth. see Lindsay, Joyce.

Lindsay, Mela M. Shukar Balan: The White Lamb. 1976. 20.00 (0-914222-02-3) Am Hist Soc Ger.

— The Story of Johann: The Boy Who Longed to Come to America. LC 90-85324. (Illus.). 190p. (YA). 1991. 15.00 (0-914222-18-X) Am Hist Soc Ger.

Lindsay, Michael, et al. Notes on Educational Problems in Communist China, 1941-47. LC 77-10962. 194p. 1977. reprint ed. lib. bdg. 55.00 (0-8371-9815-1, LINE, Greenwood Pr) Greenwood.

***Lindsay, Nick.** And I'm Glad: An Oral History of Edisto Island. (Illus.). 192p. 1999. 29.99 (0-7385-0170-0, Pub. by Tempus Pubng) Arcadia Publng.

Lindsay, Norene. Dream Catchers: Developing Career & Educational Awareness in the Intermediate Grades. Hall, Sara, ed. (Illus.). 80p. 1993. teacher ed. 14.95 (1-56370-086-7, DCTG); pap., student ed. 3.00 (1-56370-085-9, DCP) JIST Works.

— Dreamcatchers. 2nd ed. 72p. (J). 1998. pap., student ed. 4.95 (1-56370-514-1) JIST Works.

***Lindsay, Norene.** Pathfinder: Exploring Career & Educational Paths. 2nd rev. ed. 1999. pap. text 6.95 (1-56370-524-9) JIST Works.

Lindsay, Norene. Pathfinder: Exploring Career & Educational Paths & Career Plan Portfolio. 1997. pap. text 24.95 (1-56370-122-7) JIST Works.

— Pathfinder - Exploring Career & Educational Paths: Career & Educational Planning for Junior High & High School Students. Hall, Sara, ed. (Illus.). 112p. (YA). (gr. 8-12). 1994. pap., student ed. 5.99 (1-56370-120-0, J1200) JIST Works.

Lindsay, Norman. Saturdee. LC 75-41175. (Illus.). reprint ed. 39.50 (0-404-14716-X) AMS Pr.

Lindsay, P. A., et al. Mural: A Formal Development Support System. Ritchie, B. & Wills, A. C., eds. (Illus.). xiii, 421p. 1991. 98.95 (0-387-19651-X) Spr-Verlag.

Lindsay, Patressa, jt. auth. see Lindsay, Terry.

Lindsay, Paul. Code Name: Gentkill. large type ed. (Niagara Large Print Ser.). 401p. 1996. 29.50 (0-7089-5839-7) Ulverscroft.

— Freedom to Kill: A Novel of the FBI. 1998. mass mkt. 6.99 (0-449-14994-3, GM) Fawcett.

***Lindsay, Paul.** The Fuhrer's Reserve: A Novel of the FBI. LC 99-86656. 384p. 2000. 24.50 (0-684-85403-1) S&S Childrens.

Lindsay, Paul. The Synagogues of London. LC 92-21435. (Illus.). 144p. 1992. pap. 19.50 (0-85303-258-0, Pub. by M Vallentine & Co); text 35.00 (0-85303-241-6, Pub. by M Vallentine & Co) Intl Spec Bk.

***Lindsay, Paul.** Teaching English Worldwide: A Practice Guide to Teaching English. LC 00-100923. (Illus.). 416p. 2000. pap. text. write for info. (1-882483-77-4) Alta Bk Ctr.

Lindsay, Paula. Charity Child. large type ed. 1990. 27.99 (0-7089-2238-4) Ulverscroft.

— Country Doctor. large type ed. (Linford Romance Library). 1988. pap. 10.95 (0-7089-6540-7, Linford) Ulverscroft.

— Dream of Destiny. large type ed. (Linford Romance Library). 288p. 1993. pap. 16.99 (0-7089-7409-0) Ulverscroft.

— The Golden Girl. large type ed. (Linford Romance Library). 320p. 1997. pap. 16.99 (0-7089-7984-X, Linford) Ulverscroft.

— Magic in the Rain. large type ed. (Linford Romance Library). 304p. 1993. pap. 16.99 (0-7089-7337-X, Linford) Ulverscroft.

***Lindsay, Paula.** No Sunshine without Shadow. 392p. 2000. 18.99 (0-7089-5698-X) Ulverscroft.

Lindsay, Paula. Once upon a Dream. large type ed. (Linford Romance Library). 240p. 1997. pap. 16.99 (0-7089-5083-3, Linford) Ulverscroft.

— Promise of Happiness. large type ed. 288p. 1988. 27.99 (0-7089-1868-9) Ulverscroft.

— Suddenly a Stranger. large type ed. (Linford Romance Library). 288p. 1996. pap. 16.99 (0-7089-7926-2) Ulverscroft.

***Lindsay, Paula.** Swift Enchantment. large type ed. 352p. 2000. pap. 20.99 (1-85389-984-4, Dales) Ulverscroft.

Lindsay, Paula. This Bright Mantle. large type ed. 1990. 27.99 (0-7089-2141-8) Ulverscroft.

***Lindsay, Paula.** This Precious Gift. large type ed. 352p. 2000. 20.99 (1-85389-985-2, Pub. by Dales Lrg Prnt) Ulverscroft.

Lindsay, Penelope A. Placement Art: A Beginner's Guide to Feng-Shui. LC 97-51963. (Illus.). 144p. 1998. pap. 14.95 (0-8348-0413-1) Weatherhill.

Lindsay, Peter, Jr. Creative Individualism: The Democratic Vision of C. B. Macpherson. LC 95-44255. (SUNY Series in Political Theory). 176p. (C). 1996. text 49.50 (0-7914-3055-3); pap. text 16.95 (0-7914-3056-1) State U NY Pr.

Lindsay, Peter, et al. Pass the Summative Assessment & MRCGP: All the Techniques You Need. 110p. 1996. pap. text 19.95 (0-7020-2194-6, Pub. by W B Saunders) Saunders.

Lindsay, Philip. The Haunted Man: A Portrait of Edgar Allan Poe. 1976. 22.95 (0-89190-968-0) Amereon Ltd.

— Mirror for Ruffians. LC 72-303. (Essay Index Reprint Ser.). 1977. reprint ed. 23.95 (0-8369-2799-0) Ayer.

Lindsay-Poland, John, jt. auth. see Barry, Tom.

Lindsay, R. B. Introduction of Physical Statistics. 1990. 16.00 (0-8446-2471-3) Peter Smith.

Lindsay, R. B., ed. Journal of the Acoustical Society of America: Cumulative Index, Vols. 21-30. 952p. 1956. pap. 75.00 (0-318-19080-X) Acoustical Soc Am.

Lindsay, R. B., et al. Steelhead Production Factors, 1994. (Illus.). 48p. 1997. spiral bd. 6.00 (0-89904-599-5, Cascade Geog Soc) Crumb Elbow Pub.

— Steelhead Production Factors, 1994. (Illus.). 48p. 1997. reprint ed. 11.00 (0-89904-708-4, Cascade Geog Soc) Crumb Elbow Pub.

— Steelhead Production Factors, 1994: Influences of Pre-1900 Fires & Fire Exclusion. (Illus.). 48p. 1997. reprint ed. pap. 6.00 (0-89904-690-8, Cascade Geog Soc) Crumb Elbow Pub.

Lindsay, R. Bruce & Margenau, Henry. Foundations of Physics. LC 80-84973. 1981. pap. 19.50 (0-918024-17-X) Ox Bow.

Lindsay, R. C., jt. auth. see Kaylegian, K. E.

Lindsay, R. W., ed. Quality Requirements of Super-Duty Steels. LC 59-14904. (Metallurgical Society Conference Ser.: Vol. 3). 319p. reprint ed. pap. 98.90 (0-608-11551-7, 200066600038) Bks Demand.

Lindsay, Rachel. Mask of Gold. large type ed. 405p. 1981. 27.99 (0-7089-0706-7) Ulverscroft.

Lindsay, Rae. Left Is Right: The Survival Guide for Living Lefty in a Right-Handed World. LC 96-94650. (Illus.). 96p. (Orig.). 1996. pap. 9.95 (0-9653753-0-7, Gilmour Hse) R&R Writers.

Lindsay, Ralph, jt. auth. see Lindsay, Irene.

Lindsay, Richard P. The War to Save Our Kids: Raising G-rated Children in an X-rated World. LC 98-73705. 1998. pap. 12.98 (0-88290-623-2, 1082) Horizon Utah.

Lindsay, Robert. A Guide to Diagnosis, Prevention & Treatment: A General Guide to Diagnosis & Treatment. LC 92-14302. 52p. 1992. pap. text 19.00 (0-88167-941-0) Lppncott W & W.

Lindsay, Robert, jt. ed. see Stevenson, John C.

Lindsay, Robert B. The Nature of Physics: A Physicist's Views on the History & Philosophy of Science. LC 68-10642. 220p. reprint ed. 68.20 (0-608-16567-0, 202751300055) Bks Demand.

— Readings at the Blue Lamp. 77p. 1997. pap. text 9.50 (0-9660658-0-8) Other World Pr.

Lindsay, Robert G. This High Name: Public Relations & the U. S. Marine Corps. LC 57-5238. (Illus.). 126p. reprint ed. pap. 39.10 (0-608-30809-9, 202114000021) Bks Demand.

Lindsay, Robert O. & Neu, John. French Political Pamphlets, 1547-1648: A Catalog of Major Collections in American Libraries. LC 78-84953. 522p. 1969. reprint ed. pap. 161.90 (0-608-06997-3, 206720500009) Bks Demand.

Lindsay, Sandie. High Performance Liquid Chromatography. 2nd ed. LC 91-42823. (Analytical Chemistry by Open Learning Ser.). 360p. 1992. pap. 84.95 (0-471-93115-2) Wiley.

— High Performance Liquid Chromatography. 2nd ed. 104p. (C). 1998. 1485.00 (0-471-98459-0) Wiley.

An Asterisk (*) at the beginning of an entry indicates that the title is appearing for the first time.

Lindsay, Sarah. Bodies of Water. 48p. 1986. pap. 8.00 (*0-87775-186-2*) Unicorn Pr.
— Insomniac's Lullaby. (Illus.). 48p. (Orig.). 1989. pap. 8.00 (*0-87775-221-4*) Unicorn Pr.
— Primate Behavior. 112p. 1997. 20.00 (*0-8021-1619-1*, Grove) Grove-Atltic.
— Primate Behavior. 112p. 1998. reprint ed. pap. 11.00 (*0-8021-3557-9*, Grove) Grove-Atltic.
Lindsay-Sayre, Nancy, jt. auth. see Lindsay, Gail F.
Lindsay, Shannon. Caveats Against Dealings in Australia & New Zealand. 329p. 1995. 65.00 (*1-86287-194-9*, Pub. by Federation Pr) Gaunt.
Lindsay, Stace, jt. auth. see Fairbanks, Michael.
Lindsay, Stan & Powell, Graham. An Introduction to Clinical Child Psychology. 1988. text 78.95 (*0-566-05103-6*, Pub. by Avebry) Ashgate Pub Co.
Lindsay, Stan & Powell, Graham, eds. The Handbook of Clinical Adult Psychology. 2nd ed. LC 93-33181. 832p. (C). 1994. pap. 49.99 (*0-415-07216-6*, B3734) Routledge.
Lindsay, Stan A. Implicit Rhetoric: Kenneth Burke's Extension of Aristotle's Concept of Entelechy. LC 98-23713. 212p. (C). 1998. 49.00 (*0-7618-1168-0*); pap. 29.50 (*0-7618-1169-9*) U Pr of Amer.
— Twenty-One Sales in a Sale: What Sales Are You Missing? LC 98-9506. 160p. 1998. pap. 19.95 (*1-55571-448-X*, TOMSP) PSI Resch.
Lindsay, Steele, jt. auth. see Lindsay, Dorothy.
Lindsay, Steve. Handbook of Applied Dog Behavior & Training Vol. 1: Adaptation & Learning. LC 99-52013. (Illus.). 584p. 2000. 79.95 (*0-8138-0754-9*) Iowa St U Pr.
***Lindsay, Steven.** Handbook of Applied Dog Behavior & Training Vol. 2: Etiology & Assessment of Behavior Problems. (Illus.). 304p. 2000. 39.95 (*0-8138-2868-6*) Iowa St U Pr.
Lindsay, Suzanne G. Mary Cassatt & Philadelphia. LC 84-29623. (Illus.). 100p. 1985. pap. 18.95 (*0-87633-061-8*) Phila Mus Art.
Lindsay, Sylvia, jt. ed. see Altschul, Jeffrey H.
Lindsay, T. F., tr. see Dalbiez, Roland.
Lindsay, Terry & Lindsay, Patressa. Birds of Shenandoah National Park: A Naturalist's View. (Illus.). 94p. 1997. pap. 10.95 (*0-931606-19-5*) Shenandoah Nat Assn.
***Lindsay, Thomas M.** A History of the Reformation, 2. 544p. 1999. pap. 65.00 (*1-57910-283-2*) Wipf & Stock.
Lindsay, Thomas M. A History of the Reformation, 2 vols., Set. LC 83-45664. reprint ed. 105.00 (*0-404-19814-7*) AMS Pr.
— A History of the Reformation, 2 Vols., Set. LC 72-37893. (Select Bibliographies Reprint Ser.). 1977. reprint ed. 78.95 (*0-8369-6730-5*) Ayer.
— Luther & the Germany Reformation. LC 71-133524. (Select Bibliographies Reprint Ser.). 1977. reprint ed. 20.95 (*0-8369-5556-0*) Ayer.
Lindsay, Vachel. Adventures, Rhymes & Designs. LC 68-27399. (Illus.). 1968. 40.00 (*0-87130-011-7*); pap. 30.00 (*0-87130-012-5*) Eakins.
— Adventures While Preaching the Gospel of Beauty. (Collected Works of Vachel Lindsay). 186p. 1998. reprint ed. lib. bdg. 88.00 (*1-58201-687-9*) Classic Bks.
***Lindsay, Vachel.** The Art of the Moving Picture. Scorsese, Martin, ed. LC 99-42461. 320p. 2000. pap. 14.95 (*0-375-75613-2*) Modern Lib NY.
— Art of the Moving Picture. LC 75-114381. 1970. reprint ed. pap. 3.45 (*0-87140-204-1*, Pub. by Liveright) Norton.
Lindsay, Vachel. The Art of the Moving Picture. (Collected Works of Vachel Lindsay). 209p. 1998. reprint ed. lib. bdg. 98.00 (*1-58201-688-7*) Classic Bks.
— The Chinese Nightingale & Other Poems. (Collected Works of Vachel Lindsay). 127p. 1998. reprint ed. lib. bdg. 88.00 (*1-58201-689-5*) Classic Bks.
— Collected Poems. (Collected Works of Vachel Lindsay). 390p. 1998. reprint ed. lib. bdg. 98.00 (*1-58201-690-9*) Classic Bks.
— The Congo & Other Poems. alternate unabridged ed. 96p. 1992. reprint ed. pap. text 1.00 (*0-486-27272-9*) Dover.
— The Congo & Other Poems. (Collected Works of Vachel Lindsay). 159p. 1998. reprint ed. lib. bdg. 88.00 (*1-58201-691-7*) Classic Bks.
— The Daniel Jazz & Other Poems. (Collected Works of Vachel Lindsay). 94p. 1998. reprint ed. lib. bdg. 88.00 (*1-58201-692-5*) Classic Bks.
— General William Booth Enters into Heaven & Other Poems. (Collected Works of Vachel Lindsay). 1998. reprint ed. lib. bdg. 88.00 (*1-58201-693-3*) Classic Bks.
— God Help Us to Be Brave. (Collected Works of Vachel Lindsay). 300p. 1998. reprint ed. lib. bdg. 88.00 (*1-58201-694-1*) Classic Bks.
— Going-to-the-Sun. (Collected Works of Vachel Lindsay). 101p. 1998. reprint ed. lib. bdg. 88.00 (*1-58201-695-X*) Classic Bks.
— The Golden Book of Springfield. (Collected Works of Vachel Lindsay). 329p. 1998. reprint ed. lib. bdg. 98.00 (*1-58201-696-8*) Classic Bks.
***Lindsay, Vachel.** The Golden Book of Springfield. 2nd ed. (Illus.). 1999. reprint ed. 38.00 (*0-88286-243-X*); reprint ed. pap. 22.00 (*0-88286-242-1*, Pub. by C H Kerr) SPD-Small Pr Dist.
Lindsay, Vachel. The Golden Whales of California & Other Rhymes in the American Language. (Collected Works of Vachel Lindsay). 300p. 1998. reprint ed. lib. bdg. 88.00 (*1-58201-697-6*) Classic Bks.
— A Handy Guide for Beggars, Especially Those of the Poetic Fraternity. (Collected Works of Vachel Lindsay). 205p. 1998. reprint ed. lib. bdg. 98.00 (*1-58201-698-4*) Classic Bks.
— The Heroes of Time. (Collected Works of Vachel Lindsay). 300p. 1998. reprint ed. lib. bdg. 88.00 (*1-58201-699-2*) Classic Bks.
— Johnny Appleseed & Other Poems. 138p. (J). 1981. lib. bdg. 21.95 (*0-89967-039-3*, Harmony Rain) Buccaneer Bks.
— Johnny Appleseed & Other Poems. 129p. (YA). 1981. reprint ed. lib. bdg. 23.95 (*0-89966-365-6*) Buccaneer Bks.
— The Poetry of Vachel Lindsay, Vol. 1. Camp, Dennis, ed. (Illus.). 408p. 1984. 39.95 (*0-933180-45-4*) Spoon Riv Poetry.
— The Poetry of Vachel Lindsay, Vol. 2. Camp, Dennis, ed. (Illus.). 408p. 1984. 39.95 (*0-933180-67-5*) Spoon Riv Poetry.
— The Progress & Poetry of the Movies: A Second Book of Film Criticism, No. 2. Lounsbury, Myron, ed. & comment by. LC 94-16749. 490p. 1995. 92.00 (*0-8108-2917-7*) Scarecrow.
— The Prose of Vachel Lindsay, Vol. 1. Camp, Dennis, ed. 340p. 1989. 24.95 (*0-944024-08-4*) Spoon Riv Poetry.
— Una Tortuga Encantadora (Turtle Magic) LC 90-62625. (Illus.). 12p. (J). 1991. bds. 5.95 (*1-877779-22-9*) Schneider Educational.
***Lindsay, Vachel.** Tramping Across America: Travel Writings of Vachel Lindsay. (Illus.). 235p. 1999. pap. 19.95 (*0-9646037-8-0*) Rosehill Pr IL.
Lindsay, Vachel. Vachel. Barker, R-Lou & Victor, Roanna, eds. (Illus.). 54p. (C). 1995. lib. bdg. 9.95 (*0-9648065-0-9*) V Lindsay Assn.
Lindsay, Verna D., ed. see Deneen, Robert N.
Lindsay, W. A., ed. see Brenan, Gerald.
Lindsay, W. M., ed. Comoediae. 2nd ed. (Oxford Classical Texts Ser.). 342p. 1926. text 29.95 (*0-19-814636-1*) OUP.
— Comoediae, 2 vols., Vol. 1. 530p. 1922. text 59.00 (*0-19-814628-0*) OUP.
— Comoediae, 2 vols., Vol. 2. 590p. 1922. text 55.00 (*0-19-814629-9*) OUP.
— Epigrammata. 2nd ed. (Oxford Classical Texts Ser.). 490p. 1922. text 38.00 (*0-19-814625-6*) OUP.
Lindsay, Wallace M. The Codex Turnebi of Plautus & Plaui Codicis Senonsensis. (GER., Illus.). 59p. 1972. reprint ed. write for info. (*3-487-04312-2*) G Olms Pubs.
— Early Irish Minuscule Script. (St. Andrews University Publications: No. 6). 74p. 1971. reprint ed. 32.37 (*3-487-04026-3*) G Olms Pubs.
— Die Lateinische Sprache. xiii, 747p. 1984. reprint ed. write for info. (*3-487-07484-2*) G Olms Pubs.
— Notae Latinae. xxiv, 500p. 1972. reprint ed. write for info. (*0-318-71161-3*) G Olms Pubs.
— Notae Latinae: An Account of Abbreviation in Latin MSS. of the Early Minuscule Period. xxiv, 500p. 1972. reprint ed. write for info. (*0-318-72042-6*); reprint ed. suppl. ed. write for info. (*0-318-72043-4*) G Olms Pubs.
— Palaeographia Latina, 6 pts. in 1. (St. Andrews University Publications: Nos. 14, 16, 19, 20, 23, 28). 456p. 1989. reprint ed. 128.70 (*3-487-05308-X*) G Olms Pubs.
— Studies in Early Medieval Latin Glossaries. Lapidge, Michael, ed. LC 95-30954. (Collected Studies: Vol. 467). 416p. 1996. 138.95 (*0-86078-353-7*, Pub. by Variorum) Ashgate Pub Co.
Lindsay, Wallace M., ed. Nonius Marcellus: Dictionary of Republican Latin. (St. Andrews University Publications: No. 1). 120p. 1985. reprint ed. 25.87 (*3-487-01092-5*) G Olms Pubs.
— Plautus: Captivi. (Bristol Latin Texts Ser.). (LAT.). 120p. 1981. reprint ed. pap. 16.95 (*0-906515-95-5*, Pub. by Brist Class Pr) Focus Pub-R Pullins.
Lindsay, Wallace M., ed. see Festus, Sextus P.
Lindsay, Wallace M., ed. see Marcellus, Nonius.
Lindsay, William. AMNH Tyrannosaurus. 32p. 1999. 7.95 (*0-7894-4272-8*) DK Pub Inc.
— Prehistoric Life. (Eyewitness Books). (Illus.). (J). (gr. 4-7). 2000. 19.99 (*0-7894-6601-5*) DK Pub Inc.
— Prehistoric Life. (Eyewitness Books). (J). (gr. 4-7). 2000. 15.95 (*0-7894-5868-3*) DK Pub Inc.
Lindsay, William. Prehistoric Life. LC 93-32076. (Eyewitness Books). (Illus.). (J). (gr. 5 up). 1994. lib. bdg. 20.99 (*0-679-96001-5*, Pub. by Knopf Bks Yng Read) Random.
Lindsay, William, ed. On the Trail of Incredible Dinosaurs. LC 98-26396. 96p. (J). (gr. k-3). 1998. pap. 14.95 (*0-7894-3628-0*) DK Pub Inc.
Lindsay, William & Petrick, Joseph A. Total Quality & Organization Development. (Total Quality Ser.). 408p. 1996. boxed set 54.95 (*1-884015-22-0*) St Lucie Pr.
Lindsay, William, jt. auth. see Clark, Neil.
Lindsay, William A. The Journals of William A. Lindsay: An Ordinary Nineteenth-Century Physician's Surgical Cases. McDonell, Katherine M., ed. LC 88-32003. (Illus.). xlix, 216p. 1989. 27.50 (*0-87195-029-4*) Ind Hist Soc.
Lindsay, William M., jt. auth. see Evans, James R.
Lindsay, William S. History of Merchant Shipping & Ancient Commerce, 4 vols. LC 05-41460. reprint ed. 385.00 (*0-404-04030-6*) AMS Pr.
Lindsell, Harold. When You Pray - Chinese Edition. Liu, Jonathan, tr. (CHI.). 288p. 1991. pap. 6.50 (*1-56582-092-4*) Christ Renew Min.
Lindsell, Harold, intro. see Clark, Gordon H.
Lindsell, Robert M. The Rail Lines of Northern New England. (New England Rail Heritage Ser.). (Illus.). 375p. (Orig.). 1999. pap. write for info. (*0-942147-06-5*) Branch Line Pr.
Lindsell-Roberts, Sheryl. Business Letter Writing. 201p. 1994. pap. 11.95 (*0-02-860014-2*, Arc) IDG Bks.
— Business Letter Writing. LC 94-18524. 1994. pap. 12.00 (*0-671-88637-1*) Macmillan.
***Lindsell-Roberts, Sheryl.** Business Professional's Kit for Dummies. (For Dummies Ser.). 384p. 2000. pap. 24.99 (*0-7645-5273-2*) IDG Bks.
Lindsell-Roberts, Sheryl. Business Writing for Dummies. LC 99-61119. (For Dummies Ser.). 384p. 1999. pap. 16.99 (*0-7645-5134-5*) IDG Bks.
— Goofy Government Grants & Wacky Waste. LC 96-21075. (Illus.). 96p. 1996. pap. 5.95 (*0-8069-3858-7*) Sterling.
— Loony Laws & Silly Statutes. LC 93-42066. (Illus.). 128p. (J). 1994. pap. 5.95 (*0-8069-0472-0*) Sterling.
— Mastering Computer Typing: Learning the ABCs of the Computer Keyboard. LC 94-41777. (Illus.). 208p. 1995. 14.00 (*0-395-71406-0*) HM.
— The Office Professional's Quick Reference Handbook. 4th ed. 288p. 1995. 7.95 (*0-02-860027-4*, Arc) IDG Bks.
— The Office Professional's Quick Reference Handbook. 5th rev. ed. LC 94-32827. 1995. pap. 9.00 (*0-671-89919-8*, Arco) Macmillan Gen Ref.
— The Secretary's Quick Reference Handbook. 3rd ed. (Illus.). 304p. 1992. pap. 8.00 (*0-13-799396-X*, Arco) Macmillan Gen Ref.
***Lindsell-Roberts, Sheryl.** Writing Business Letters for Dummies. 384p. 1999. pap. 19.99 (*0-7645-5207-4*) IDG Bks.
Lindseth, Martina & Hanks, Steven. Formal Approaches to Slavic Linguistics: The Indiana Meeting, 1996. LC 97-10054. (Michigan Slavic Materials Ser.: Vol. 42). 1997. 18.00 (*0-930042-81-6*) Mich Slavic Pubns.
Lindseth, Roy O. Digital Processing of Geophysical Data: A Review. rev. ed. (Course Notes Ser.: No. 1). (Illus.). 282p. 1982. pap. text 61.00 (*0-931830-50-8*, 251A) Soc Expl Geophys.
Lindsey. Fitness for the Health of Individual. 6th ed. 1988. 14.06 (*0-697-07272-X*) McGraw.
— John Owen. 1996. mass mkt. 11.99 (*1-85792-267-0*, Pub. by Christian Focus) Spring Arbor Dist.
***Lindsey.** LOVE ME FOREVER (HC) 2000. 22.00 (*0-380-97263-8*) Morrow Avon.
Lindsey. Medical Language Specialist. (Medical Assisting Ser.). 1995. pap., teacher ed. 12.00 (*0-8273-6053-3*) Delmar.
— Medical Language Specialist. (Medical Assisting Ser.). 1997. pap. 21.95 (*0-8273-6052-5*) Delmar.
— Plant Biotechnology in Agriculture. 1991. pap. text 101.00 (*0-471-93238-8*) Wiley.
— Sociology. LC 99-27557. 736p. 1999. 70.00 (*0-13-488793-X*) P-H.
Lindsey, jt. auth. see Corbin.
Lindsey, jt. auth. see Zakahi.
Lindsey & Fairmont Press, Staff. Applied Illumination Engineering. 2nd ed. LC 96-36419. 528p. (C). 1997. 79.00 (*0-13-742800-6*) P-H.
Lindsey, A. A. Natural Features of Indiana. 1976. 18.00 (*1-883362-06-7*) IN Acad Sci.
Lindsey, A. W. The Science of Animal Life. 656p. 1984. pap. 175.00 (*0-7855-0389-7*, Pub. by Intl Bks & Periodicals) St Mut.
***Lindsey, Alfred J. & Deblois, Michael A.** Sunset of America: How the Golden Dream Can Be Saved. 2000. pap. 14.95 (*0-9675772-0-9*) Cedar Street.
Lindsey, Almont. Pullman Strike. LC 64-32413. 1994. pap. text 12.00 (*0-226-48383-5*, P165) U Ch Pr.
Lindsey, Alton A. The Bicentennial of John James Audubon: With Chapters by Mary Durant. LC 84-47791. (Illus.). 188p. Date not set. reprint ed. pap. 58.30 (*0-608-20558-3*, 205447200002) Bks Demand.
— Naturalist on Watch. (Illus.). 228p. (Orig.). 1983. 10.00 (*0-913859-00-1*); pap. 4.75 (*0-913859-01-X*) Goshen Coll.
Lindsey, Alton A., et al. The Bicentennial of John James Audubon. LC 84-47791. (Illus.). 192p. 1985. 14.95 (*0-253-10650-8*) Ind U Pr.
Lindsey, Anne H., jt. auth. see Bell, C. Ritchie.
Lindsey, Beate T., tr. see Tepoot, Pabloo.
Lindsey, Ben B. & Borough, Rube. The Dangerous Life. LC 73-11938. (Metropolitan America Ser.). 468p. 1974. reprint ed. 33.95 (*0-405-05400-9*) Ayer.
Lindsey, Ben B. & Evans, Wainwright. The Companionate Marriage. LC 73-169393. (Family in America Ser.). 400p. 1977. reprint ed. 21.95 (*0-405-03870-4*) Ayer.
Lindsey, Betina. The Serpent Beguiled. Tolley, Carolyn, ed. 256p. (Orig.). 1992. mass mkt. 4.99 (*0-671-74467-4*) PB.
— Swan Bride. Tolley, Carolyn, ed. 288p. (Orig.). 1990. mass mkt. 5.50 (*0-671-68914-2*) PB.
— Swan Star. 1994. mass mkt. 5.50 (*0-671-79939-8*) PB.
— Swan Witch. Tolley, Carolyn, ed. 256p. (Orig.). 1993. mass mkt. 4.99 (*0-671-75171-9*) PB.
Lindsey, Bill & Lindsey, Sandy. Camper's Roasting on an Open Fire: An Outdoor Cookbook with a Dash of Humor. 132p. 1999. pap. 8.95 (*1-893841-02-2*) Brookstone.
Lindsey, Bonnie J. The Professional Medical Assistant: Clinical Practice CTB. (Medical Assisting Ser.). 1993. 62.95 (*0-8273-5901-2*) Delmar.
Lindsey, Bonnie J. & Rayburn, Francis M. The Professional Medical Assistant: Clinical Practice. LC 92-18589. 316p. 1990. pap. 34.95 (*0-8273-4150-4*) Delmar.
— The Professional Medical Assistant Clinical Practice: Instructor's Resource Guide. 216p. 1990. pap., teacher ed. 18.00 (*0-8273-4151-2*) Delmar.
— The Professional Medical Assistant Clinical Practice: Workbook. 134p. 1991. pap., wbk. ed. 16.95 (*0-8273-4155-5*) Delmar.
Lindsey, Byron, jt. ed. see Goscilo, Helena.
Lindsey, Byron, tr. see Makanin, Vladimir.
Lindsey, Cecilee, tr. see Kennedy, Phanis.
Lindsey, Cordell. Step-by-Step Across the Pond. 122p. 1996. pap. 11.00 (*0-8059-3848-6*) Dorrance.
Lindsey, Crawford W., Jr. Teaching Students to Teach Themselves. 148p. 1988. pap. 27.95 (*0-89397-315-7*) Nichols Pub.
Lindsey, Dana. The Honeymoon Quest. (Romance Ser.). 1996. per. 3.25 (*0-373-19172-3*, 1-19172-5) Silhouette.
— Julie's Garden. (Romance Ser.). 1995. per. 2.99 (*0-373-19071-9*, 1-19071-9) Silhouette.
— Second Thoughts. (Temptation Ser.: No. 398). 1992. per. 2.99 (*0-373-25498-9*, 1-25498-6) Harlequin Bks.
Lindsey, Darryl. Electromechanical Package Design. 1992. text. write for info. (*0-07-037877-0*) McGraw.
***Lindsey, Dave & Lindsey, Matt.** Ultimate Stock Car Trivia Book. LC 98-24916. 224p. 1998. pap. 7.95 (*1-55853-665-5*) Rutledge Hill Pr.
Lindsey, David C. Bye Bye Backache. LC 81-67080. (Illus.). 256p. 1981. 17.95 (*0-939342-00-6*); pap. 10.95 (*0-939342-01-4*) DCarlin Pub.
Lindsey, David E., jt. auth. see Dolan, Edwin G.
Lindsey, David L. An Absence of Light. 576p. 1995. mass mkt. 6.99 (*0-553-56941-4*) Bantam.
— Black Gold, Red Death. 256p. 1986. mass mkt. 5.99 (*0-449-13121-1*, GM) Fawcett.
— Body of Truth. 480p. 1993. mass mkt. 6.99 (*0-553-28964-0*) Bantam.
— A Cold Mind. 368p. 1994. mass mkt. 6.99 (*0-553-56081-6*) Bantam.
— A Cold Mind. 352p. 1990. mass mkt. 5.99 (*0-671-73338-9*) PB.
— The Color of Night. LC 98-30770. 496p. 1999. 25.00 (*0-446-52361-5*, Pub. by Warner Bks) Little.
***Lindsey, David L.** The Color of Night. 496p. 2000. mass mkt. write for info. (*0-446-60803-3*, Warner Vision) Warner Bks.
— The Color of Night. large type ed. LC 99-25637. 1999. pap. 27.95 (*0-7862-1995-5*) Mac Lib Ref.
Lindsey, David L. Heat from Another Sun. 352p. 1996. mass mkt. 6.50 (*0-553-56790-X*) Bantam.
— Heat from Another Sun. 1985. mass mkt. 5.95 (*0-671-54632-5*) PB.
— In the Lake of the Moon. 400p. 1990. mass mkt. 6.50 (*0-553-28344-8*) Bantam.
— Mercy. 608p. 1991. mass mkt. 6.99 (*0-553-28972-1*) Bantam.
— Requiem for a Glass Heart. 448p. 1997. mass mkt. 6.99 (*0-553-57594-5*) Bantam.
— Requiem for a Glass Heart. large type ed. 684p. 1996. lib. bdg. 26.95 (*0-7838-1885-8*, G K Hall Lrg Type) Mac Lib Ref.
— Spiral. (Orig.). 1990. pap. 5.99 (*0-671-73337-0*) S&S Trade.
Lindsey, David M. Creating a Happier Life. 1990. pap. 11.00 (*1-878040-00-6*) Personal Growth.
— Discovering Life's Purpose. 1990. pap. 8.95 (*1-878040-01-4*) Personal Growth.
— Understanding Death & Grief. 1991. pap. 9.95 (*1-878040-03-0*) Personal Growth.
— The Woman & the Dragon: A History of Mary's Battle with the Devil. LC 98-92120. (Illus.). 450p. 1999. pap. write for info. (*0-9668981-0-9*) Quintus Augustus.
***Lindsey, David Michael.** The Woman & the Dragon: Apparitions of Mary. LC 99-54131. (Illus.). 400p. 2000. 21.95 (*1-56554-731-4*) Pelican.
***Lindsey, Dawn.** Nabob's Daughter. (Regency Romance Ser.). 224p. 2000. mass mkt. 4.99 (*0-451-20045-4*, Sig) NAL.
Lindsey, Dawn. The Reluctant Heroine. large type ed. LC 93-37451. 337p. 1994. lib. bdg. 19.95 (*0-7862-0097-9*) Thorndike Pr.
Lindsey, Deborah, jt. auth. see Christiana, Anna.
***Lindsey, Desiree.** Prisoner of Passion. 296p. 2000. pap. 14.99 (*0-9677336-1-8*) Lindsey Promo.
Lindsey, Donal F. Indians at Hampton Institute, 1877-1923. LC 93-45510. 336p. 1994. text 39.95 (*0-252-02106-1*) U of Ill Pr.
Lindsey, Doug, ed. see Vigil, Joe I.
Lindsey, Doug, ed. see Vigil, John J.
Lindsey, Duncan. The Scientific Publication System in Social Science. LC 78-62570. (Jossey-Bass Social & Behavioral Science Ser.). 189p. reprint ed. pap. 58.60 (*0-8357-4994-0*, 203792700009) Bks Demand.
— The Welfare of Children. (Illus.). 416p. 1994. text 39.95 (*0-19-508518-3*) OUP.
Lindsey, Edmon. Mastering Word Problems the Easy Way. 170p. 1991. pap. text 15.25 (*0-9634346-0-8*) S Paul Pub.
Lindsey, Forrest. Pipefitters Handbook. 3rd ed. (Illus.). 464p. 1967. 22.95 (*0-8311-3019-9*) Indus Pr.
Lindsey, G., et al. The CGNET Story: A Case Study in International Computer Networking. LC 94-201641. 140p. 1994. pap. write for info. (*0-88936-678-0*) IDRC Bks.
Lindsey, Hal. La Agonia del Gran Planeta Tierra. Lievano, M. Francisco, tr. from ENG. (SPA.). 255p. 1985. mass mkt. 4.95 (*0-8297-1413-8*) Vida Pubs.
— Amazing Grace. LC 97-142911. 303p. 1996. pap. 12.99 (*0-9641058-4-5*) Western Front.
— Apocalypse Code. LC 97-60814. 320p. 1997. pap. 12.99 (*1-888848-21-9*) Western Front.
— Blood Moon: A Novel. LC 96-60757. 358p. (J). 1996. 21.99 (*1-888848-07-3*) Western Front.
***Lindsey, Hal.** Combat Faith: Unshakable Faith for Every Day. 1999. pap. text 12.99 (*1-888848-33-2*) Western Front.
Lindsey, Hal. Facing Millennial Midnight, 1. 1999. pap. text 13.99 (*1-888848-29-4*) Western Front.
— The Final Battle. LC 97-144417. 286p. (Orig.). 1995. pap. 12.99 (*0-9641058-2-9*) Western Front.
***Lindsey, Hal.** Greatest Gift: God's Amazing Grace. 1999. pap. text 12.99 (*1-888848-34-0*) Western Front.
Lindsey, Hal. Greatest Works of Hal Lindsey. 1994. 10.98 (*0-88486-104-X*) Arrowood Pr.
— The Guilt Trip: How to Realize God's Forgiving Love. 47p. 1973. pap. 3.99 (*0-310-27762-0*, 18192P) Zondervan.
***Lindsey, Hal.** Late Great 20th Century. 1999. 19.99 (*1-888848-36-7*) Western Front.
Lindsey, Hal. The Messiah: Amazing Prophecies Fulfilled in Jesus. 1996. pap. 9.99 (*1-56507-460-2*) Harvest Hse.

L

— Planet Earth: The Final Chapter. 295p. 1998. pap. 12.99 (1-888848-25-1) Western Front.

— Planet Earth, 2000 A. D. rev. ed. LC 96-60756. 314p. 1996. pap. 12.99 (1-888848-05-7) Western Front.

***Lindsey, Hal.** The Promise of Bible Prophecy. 192p. 1999. pap. 9.99 (0-7369-0310-0) Harvest Hse.

Lindsey, Hal. There's a New World Coming: An In-Depth Analysis of the Book of Revelation. 288p. 1984. pap. 10.99 (0-89081-440-6) Harvest Hse.

***Lindsey, Hal.** Vanished into Thin Air: The Hope of Every Believer. 1999. pap. text 13.99 (1-888848-43-X) Western Front.

Lindsey, Hal & Carlson, C. C. The Late Great Planet Earth. 1970. pap. 9.99 (0-310-27771-X, 18089P) Zondervan.

— Satan Is Alive & Well on Planet Earth. 256p. 1974. pap. 4.70 (0-310-27792-2, 18195P) Zondervan.

Lindsey, Hal & Carlson, Carole C. Satan Is Alive & Well on Planet Earth. 255p. 1972. pap. 12.99 (0-310-27791-4, 18189P) Zondervan.

Lindsey, Hal, et al. Steeling the Mind of America, Vol. I. Perkins, Bill, ed. LC 95-69891. 304p. 1995. pap. 11.95 (0-89221-294-2) New Leaf.

Lindsey, Howard. History of Black America. 1994. 17.98 (1-55521-960-8) Bk Sales Inc.

Lindsey, Howard & Crouse, Russel. The Prescott Proposals. 1954. pap. 5.25 (0-8222-0909-8) Dramatists Play.

— State of the Union. 1947. pap. 5.25 (0-8222-1074-6) Dramatists Play.

Lindsey, Howard, ed. see Nemerov, Howard.

Lindsey, J. K. Introductory Statistics: The Modelling Approach. (Illus.). 232p. 1995. text 70.00 (0-19-852346-7); pap. text 38.00 (0-19-852345-9) OUP.

— Modelling Frequency & Count Data. (Oxford Statistical Science Ser.: No. 15). (Illus.). 300p. 1995. text 65.00 (0-19-852331-9) OUP.

— Models for Repeated Measurements. (Oxford Statistical Science Ser.: No. 10). (Illus.). 432p. 1993. text 69.00 (0-19-852299-1) OUP.

***Lindsey, J. K.** Models for Repeated Measurements. 2nd ed. LC 99-33069. 19. (Illus.). 528p. 1999. text 75.00 (0-19-850559-0) OUP.

Lindsey, J. K. Parametric Statistical Inference. LC 97-109161. (Illus.). 508p. 1996. text 65.00 (0-19-852359-9) OUP.

Lindsey, J. P. & Gilbertson, R. L. Basidiomycetes That Decay Aspen in North America. (Bibliotheca Mycologica Ser.: No. 63). 1978. lib. bdg. 78.00 (3-7682-1193-2) Lubrecht & Cramer.

Lindsey, Jack L. Applied Illumination Engineering. LC 88-45787. 500p. 1990. text 69.00 (0-88173-060-2) Fairmont Pr.

— Applied Illumination Engineering. 2nd ed. LC 96-36419. 514p. 1996. 74.00 (0-88173-212-5) Fairmont Pr.

Lindsey, Jack L., et al. Worldly Goods: The Arts of Early Pennsylvania, 1680-1758. LC 99-37645. (Illus.). 240p. 1999. 65.00 (0-87633-130-4) Phila Mus Art.

— Worldly Goods: The Arts of Early Pennsylvania, 1680-1758. LC 99-37645. (Illus.). 240p. 1999. pap. write for info. (0-87633-129-0) Phila Mus Art.

Lindsey, James K. Applying Generalized Linear Models. LC 97-6926. (Texts in Statistics Ser.). 280p. 1997. 54.95 (0-387-98218-3) Spr-Verlag.

Lindsey, Jason, jt. auth. see Shaw, Robert.

***Lindsey, Jennifer.** The Great Apes. LC 99-18039. (Illus.). 144p. 1999. text 19.98 (1-56799-734-1) M Friedman Pub Grp Inc.

Lindsey, Jim. Revealing Statistics Principles. LC 99-230986. 132p. 1999. pap. text 24.95 (0-340-74120-1, Pub. by E A) OUP.

Lindsey, Jim, tr. see Sosa, Robert.

***Lindsey, Jimmy D.** Technology & Exceptional Individuals. 3rd ed. LC 98-44790. 1999. write for info. (0-89079-790-0) PRO-ED.

Lindsey, Jimmy D., ed. Computers & Exceptional Individuals. 2nd ed. LC 91-48182. 430p. 1993. pap. text 36.00 (0-89079-547-9, 6548) PRO-ED.

Lindsey, Johanna. All I Need Is You. LC 97-27864. 384p. 1997. mass mkt. 22.00 (0-380-97534-3, Avon Bks) Morrow Avon.

— All I Need Is You. large type ed. LC 97-43272. (Basic Ser.). 1998. 28.95 (0-7862-1284-5) Mac Lib Ref.

— All I Need Is You. LC 97-27864. 416p. 1998. reprint ed. mass mkt. 6.99 (0-380-76260-9, Avon Bks) Morrow Avon.

— Angel. 416p. 1992. mass mkt. 6.99 (0-380-75628-5, Avon Bks) Morrow Avon.

— Angel. large type ed. (Romance Ser.). 362p. 1993. lib. bdg. 24.95 (0-8161-5760-X, G K Hall Lrg Type) Mac Lib Ref.

— Angel. large type ed. 362p. 1994. pap. 17.95 (0-8161-5761-8) Thorndike Pr.

— Brave the Wild Wind. 352p. 1984. mass mkt. 6.99 (0-380-89284-7, Avon Bks) Morrow Avon.

***Lindsey, Johanna.** El Camino del Amor. (SPA.). 320p. 2000. pap. 9.50 (0-553-06123-2) Bantam.

Lindsey, Johanna. Captive Bride. (Five Star Romance Ser.). 1996. lib. bdg. 23.95 (0-7862-0880-5) Five Star.

***Lindsey, Johanna.** Captive Bride. 384p. 1999. mass mkt. 6.99 (0-380-01697-4, 88799-1, Avon Bks) Morrow Avon.

Lindsey, Johanna. Captive Bride. large type ed. (General Ser.). 342p. 1992. 17.95 (0-8161-5292-6, G K Hall Lrg Type); lib. bdg. 19.95 (0-8161-5291-8, G K Hall Lrg Type) Mac Lib Ref.

***Lindsey, Johanna.** La Cautiva del Amor. 1998. pap. 6.95 (84-01-51124-0) Lectorum Pubns.

Lindsey, Johanna. Defy Not the Heart. 416p. (Orig.). 1989. mass mkt. 6.99 (0-380-75299-9, Avon Bks) Morrow Avon.

— Fires of Winter. 368p. 1980. reprint ed. mass mkt. 6.99 (0-380-75747-8, Avon Bks) Morrow Avon.

— A Gentle Feuding. 352p. 1984. mass mkt. 6.99 (0-380-87155-6, Avon Bks) Morrow Avon.

***Lindsey, Johanna.** A Gentle Feuding. 1999. 26.00 (0-7278-5487-9, Pub. by Severn Hse) Chivers N Amer.

Lindsey, Johanna. Gentle Rogue. LC 90-93175. 432p. 1990. mass mkt. 6.99 (0-380-75302-2, Avon Bks) Morrow Avon.

— Glorious Angel. 320p. 1982. mass mkt. 6.99 (0-380-79202-8, Avon Bks) Morrow Avon.

— Glorious Angel. large type ed. LC 93-46126. 317p. 1994. 23.95 (0-8161-5285-3, G K Hall Lrg Type) Mac Lib Ref.

***Lindsey, Johanna.** Heart of Thunder. 384p. 1999. mass mkt. 6.99 (0-380-85118-0, Avon Bks) Morrow Avon.

Lindsey, Johanna. Heart of Thunder. large type ed. LC 93-35910. 399p. 1994. 23.95 (0-8161-5293-4, G K Hall Lrg Type) Mac Lib Ref.

— Heart of Thunder. large type ed. LC 93-35910. 399p. 1994. 18.95 (0-8161-5294-2, G K Hall Lrg Type) Mac Lib Ref.

— Heart So Wild. 368p. 1986. mass mkt. 6.99 (0-380-75084-8, Avon Bks) Morrow Avon.

— Hearts Aflame. 368p. 1987. reprint ed. mass mkt. 6.99 (0-380-89982-5, Avon Bks) Morrow Avon.

***Lindsey, Johanna.** The Heir. LC 00-22025. 384p. 2000. 24.00 (0-380-97536-X) Morrow Avon.

— The Heir. large type ed. 464p. 2000. 24.00 (0-06-019752-8) HarpC.

— Home for the Holidays. 224p. 2000. 18.00 (0-380-97856-3, Wm Morrow) Morrow Avon.

— Home For the Holidays. large type ed. 2000. 20.00 (0-06-019909-1, HarpCollins) HarperTrade.

— Joining. LC 99-21612. 384p. 1999. 24.00 (0-380-97535-1, Avon Bks) Morrow Avon.

— Joining. LC 99-21612. 400p. 2000. mass mkt. 7.50 (0-380-79333-4, Avon Bks) Morrow Avon.

— Joining. large type ed. LC 99-38387. 1999. 26.95 (1-56895-771-8, Wheeler) Wheeler Pub.

Lindsey, Johanna. Keeper of the Heart. LC 93-90387. 416p. (Orig.). 1993. mass mkt. 6.99 (0-380-77493-3, Avon Bks) Morrow Avon.

— Keeper of the Heart. large type ed. 426p. (Orig.). 1998. 27.95 (0-7838-1840-8, G K Hall Lrg Type) Mac Lib Ref.

— Love Me Forever. 348p. 1996. mass mkt. 6.99 (0-380-72570-3, Avon Bks) Morrow Avon.

Lindsey, Johanna. Love Only Once. 352p. 1985. mass mkt. 6.99 (0-380-89953-1, Avon Bks) Morrow Avon.

Lindsey, Johanna. The Magic of You. large type ed. LC 96-17262. (Romc-Hall Ser.). 366p. 1997. 26.95 (0-7838-1839-4, G K Hall Lrg Type) Mac Lib Ref.

— Magic of You. large type ed. LC 92-97517. 416p. 1993. mass mkt. 6.99 (0-380-75629-3, Avon Bks) Morrow Avon.

— Man of My Dreams. 432p. 1992. mass mkt. 6.99 (0-380-75626-9, Avon Bks) Morrow Avon.

— Man of My Dreams. 405p. 1999. 26.00 (0-7278-2214-4, Pub. by Severn Hse) Chivers N Amer.

Lindsey, Johanna. Once a Princess. 432p. 1991. mass mkt. 6.99 (0-380-75625-0, Avon Bks) Morrow Avon.

Lindsey, Johanna. Once a Princess. large type ed. (General Ser.). 403p. 1992. 18.95 (0-8161-5313-2, G K Hall Lrg Type) Mac Lib Ref.

— Paradise Wild. 320p. 1981. mass mkt. 6.99 (0-380-77651-0, Avon Bks) Morrow Avon.

— Paradise Wild. large type ed. LC 93-19644. 427p. 1993. 23.95 (0-8161-5287-X, G K Hall Lrg Type) Mac Lib Ref.

— Paradise Wild. large type ed. LC 93-19644. 1994. lib. bdg. 17.95 (0-8161-5288-8, G K Hall Lrg Type) Mac Lib Ref.

— A Pirate's Love. LC 96-54265. (Star-Romance Ser.). 373p. 1997. 23.95 (0-7862-0953-4) Five Star.

— A Pirate's Love. 384p. 1978. mass mkt. 6.99 (0-380-40048-0, Avon Bks) Morrow Avon.

— A Pirate's Love. large type ed. LC 96-12830. 1996. 25.95 (0-7862-0724-8) Thorndike Pr.

***Lindsey, Johanna.** The Present. LC 98-35230. (Malory Holiday Novel Ser.). (Illus.). 352p. 1999. mass mkt. 6.99 (0-380-80438-7, Avon Bks) Morrow Avon.

Lindsey, Johanna. The Present. LC 98-48909. (Wheeler Large Print Book Ser.). 189 p. 1998. write for info. (1-56895-592-8) Wheeler Pub.

— The Present: A Malory Holiday Novel. LC 98-35230. (Malory Novels Ser.). 192p. 1998. 16.00 (0-380-97725-7, Avon Bks) Morrow Avon.

— Prisoner of My Desire. 400p. (Orig.). 1991. mass mkt. 6.99 (0-380-75627-7, Avon Bks) Morrow Avon.

— Savage Thunder. 416p. 1989. mass mkt. 6.99 (0-380-75300-6, Avon Bks) Morrow Avon.

— Savage Thunder. large type ed. LC 90-38576. 490p. 1990. reprint ed. 19.95 (1-56054-029-X) Thorndike Pr.

— Say You Love Me. large type ed. LC 96-42002. (Core Ser.). 477p. 1997. lib. bdg. 26.95 (0-7838-1928-5, G K Hall Lrg Type) Mac Lib Ref.

— Say You Love Me. large type ed. LC 96-42002. 477p. 1998. pap. 24.95 (0-7838-1927-7, G K Hall Lrg Type) Mac Lib Ref.

— Say You Love Me. large type ed. LC 96-28812. 400p. 1997. mass mkt. 6.99 (0-380-72571-1, Avon Bks) Morrow Avon.

— Secret Fire. 416p. 1987. mass mkt. 6.99 (0-380-75087-2, Avon Bks) Morrow Avon.

— Secret Fire. large type ed. 517p. 1996. lib. bdg. 25.95 (0-7862-0725-6) Thorndike Pr.

***Lindsey, Johanna.** Silver Angel. 448p. (Orig.). 1999. mass mkt. 6.99 (0-380-75294-8, Avon Bks) Morrow Avon.

Lindsey, Johanna. So Speaks the Heart. 384p. 1983. mass mkt. 6.99 (0-380-81471-4, Avon Bks) Morrow Avon.

— Surrender My Love. 432p. (Orig.). 1994. mass mkt. 6.50 (0-380-76256-0, Avon Bks) Morrow Avon.

— Surrender My Love. large type ed. LC 94-34502. 403p. (Orig.). 1994. 23.95 (0-7838-1124-1, G K Hall Lrg Type) Mac Lib Ref.

— Tender Is the Storm. 336p. 1985. mass mkt. 6.99 (0-380-89693-1, Avon Bks) Morrow Avon.

— Tender Rebel. LC 87-91458. 400p. 1988. mass mkt. 6.99 (0-380-75086-4, Avon Bks) Morrow Avon.

— Until Forever. 416p. (Orig.). 1995. mass mkt. 6.50 (0-380-76259-5, Avon Bks) Morrow Avon.

***Lindsey, Johanna.** Warrior's Woman. 448p. (Orig.). 1999. mass mkt. 6.99 (0-380-75301-4, Avon Bks) Morrow Avon.

Lindsey, Johanna. When Love Awaits. 368p. 1986. mass mkt. 6.99 (0-380-89739-3, Avon Bks) Morrow Avon.

— You Belong to Me. 432p. (Orig.). 1994. mass mkt. 6.99 (0-380-76258-7, Avon Bks) Morrow Avon.

— You Belong to Me. large type ed. LC 95-15707. (Large Print Bks.). (Orig.). 1995. 25.95 (1-56895-213-9) Wheeler Pub.

***Lindsey, John, compiled by.** Brits Speak Out: British Soldiers Impressions of the Northern Ireland Conflict. LC 99-198529. (Illus.). 158p. 1999. pap. text 17.95 (0-946451-51-6, Pub. by Guildhall Pr) Irish Bks Media.

Lindsey, Jonathan A., ed. Performance Evaluation: A Management Basic for Librarians. LC 86-42746. 232p. 1986. 39.50 (0-89774-313-X) Oryx Pr.

Lindsey, K., ed. Plant Tissue Culture Manual, Suppl. 5. 164p. (Orig.). 1995. ring bd., suppl. ed. 86.00 (0-7923-3319-5) Kluwer Academic.

— Plant Tissue Culture Manual, Supplement 2. (Looseleaf Product Code: LS Ser.). 75p. (Orig.). (C). 1992. ring bd. 32.00 (0-7923-1516-2) Kluwer Academic.

— Plant Tissue Culture Manual B - W. 585p. (C). 1991. lib. bdg. 143.00 (0-7923-1115-9) Kluwer Academic.

Lindsey, Karen. Divorced, Beheaded, Survived. 272p. 1996. pap. 15.00 (0-201-40823-6) Addison-Wesley.

— Divorced, Beheaded, Survived: A Feminist Reinterpretation of the Wives of Henry VIII. LC 94-34505. (Illus.). 320p. 1995. 25.00 (0-201-60895-2) Addison-Wesley.

— Falling off the Roof. LC 75-21788. 64p. 1975. pap. 3.95 (0-914086-08-1) Alice James Bks.

— 1997 Waste Treatment Technology Industry Review. 286p. 1998. 1500.00 (1-56965-515-4) BCC.

Lindsey, Karen & Kochummen, Sara, eds. High Tech Separations Industry Review. 1996. 1500.00 (1-56965-334-8) BCC.

Lindsey, Karen, jt. auth. see Love, Susan M.

Lindsey, Karen, jt. auth. see Tobin, Daniel R.

Lindsey, Keith, ed. Transgenic Plant Research. (Illus.). 304p. 1998. text 50.00 (90-5702-326-1, Harwood Acad Pubs) Gordon & Breach.

Lindsey, Lawrence B. Economic Puppetmasters: Lessons from the Halls of Power. 215p. 1999. 24.95 (0-8447-4081-0) Am Enterprise.

Lindsey, Lewis T. Student Guide to America's 100 Best College Buys, 1997-1998. 270p. 1997. pap. text 17.95 (1-887269-26-6) J Culler & Sons.

Lindsey, Libby, ed. World's Greatest Brain Bogglers: All The Best Puzzles, Games And Fun from The Pages of Creative Kids. 81p. 1996. pap. 14.95 (1-882664-19-1) Prufrock Pr.

Lindsey, Linda, jt. auth. see Schimelpfenig, Tod.

Lindsey, Linda L. Gender Roles: A Sociological Perspective. 3rd ed. LC 96-38322. 452p. 1996. pap. text 45.00 (0-13-533621-X) P-H.

Lindsey, Margaret. Training Teachers of the Gifted & Talented. Tannenbaum, Abraham J., ed. LC 80-11867. (Perspectives on Gifted & Talented Education Ser.). 60p. (Orig.). 1980. pap. text 8.95 (0-8077-2590-0) Tchrs Coll.

— Training Teachers of the Gifted & Talented. LC 80-11867. (Perspectives on Gifted & Talented Education Ser.). 72p. (Orig.). 1980. reprint ed. pap. 30.00 (0-608-00540-1, 206141900008) Bks Demand.

Lindsey, Margaret, jt. auth. see Stratemeyer, Florence B.

Lindsey, Marilyn L. The Little Lost Sheep. (Happy Day Bks.). (Illus.). 24p. (J). (ps). 1995. 1.99 (0-7847-0352-3, 04232) Standard Pub.

Lindsey, Marion. Writing Online Help. Date not set. 39.99 (0-672-30807-X, Bobbs) Macmillan.

Lindsey, Matt, jt. auth. see Lindsey, Dave.

Lindsey, Michael, et al. Cambio Es la Tercer Alternativa: Un Libro de Ejercicins para Terminar el Comportamiento Abusivo y Violento. Moscoso, Americo, tr.Tr. of Change Is the Third Path. (SPA., Illus.). 150p. (Orig.). 1996. pap. 14.95 (1-880197-13-8) Gylantic Pub.

— Change Is the Third Path: A Workbook for Ending Abusive & Violent Behavior. (Illus.). 130p. (Orig.). 1996. pap. 14.95 (1-880197-14-6) Gylantic Pub.

Lindsey, Myrna K. Divine Inspirations: (Inspired by the Holy Spirit) (Illus.). 75p. 1998. pap. 5.95 (0-9642764-4-5) E Pitt.

Lindsey, Neil M. Tales of a Wilderness Trapper. 66p. 1973. pap. 3.00 (0-936622-21-0) A R Harding Pub.

Lindsey, Randall B., et al. Cultural Proficiency: A Manual for School Leaders. LC 98-51236. 272p. 1999. 65.95 (0-8039-6762-4); pap. 29.95 (0-8039-6763-2) Corwin Pr.

Lindsey, Robert. Edward the Second. 2nd ed. (New Mermaids Ser.). (C). 1997. pap. text 8.00 (0-393-90083-5) Norton.

Lindsey, Robert L. Jesus, Rabbi & Lord: The Hebrew Story of Jesus Behind Our Gospels. LC 89-62723. 228p. (Orig.). 1990. pap. 12.95 (0-9623950-0-5) Cornerstn Pub.

Lindsey, Ruth & Gorrie, Douglas D. Survival Kit for Those Who Sit: Simple Office Exercises to Boost Your Energy & Productivity. LC 89-10211. (Illus.). 128p. (Orig.). 1989. pap. 8.95 (0-913581-10-0) Publitec.

Lindsey, Ruth, et al. Fitness for the Health of It. 6th ed. 192p. (C). 1988. text. write for info. (0-697-07282-7) Brown & Benchmark.

Lindsey, Ruth, jt. auth. see Corbin, Charles B.

Lindsey, Ruth, jt. auth. see Forey, Pamela.

Lindsey, S. & Miller, K. Dental Health Psychology. 122p. 1993. pap. text 51.00 (3-7186-5398-2, Harwood Acad Pubs) Gordon & Breach.

Lindsey, Sandy. Doggone Funny: A Book of Canine Humor. LC 98-71818. (Animal Ser.). (Illus.). 60p. 1998. pap. 6.95 (1-891210-86-6, DF14) Bartlett Pub.

***Lindsey, Sandy.** Powerboating. (Woman's Guides Ser.). (Illus.). 160p. 2000. pap. 14.95 (0-07-135702-5) McGraw.

Lindsey, Sandy. Quick & Easy Boat Maintenance: 1,001 Time-Saving Tips. LC 98-45846. 144p. (Orig.). 1999. pap. 15.95 (0-07-134325-3) McGraw.

— Seven Out of Ten Missing Fishhooks Will Eventually Be Found in an Angler's Thumb: A Fishing Humor Book. LC 97-36642. 1998. pap. 9.95 (0-8362-5209-8) Andrews & McMeel.

Lindsey, Sandy, jt. auth. see Lindsey, Bill.

Lindsey, Scott. Norfolk Southern, 1995 Review iew. Sanders, Dale, ed. (Illus.). 144p. 1995. per. 36.95 (0-945434-24-3) Hundman Pub.

— The Wisdom of Proverbs. LC 94-69839. 128p. (Orig.). 1995. pap. 6.95 (0-89221-284-5) New Leaf.

Lindsey, Sharon, jt. ed. see Orsund-Gassiot, Cindy A.

Lindsey, Stephen W., et al. Guide to GAAP. 1997. 55.00 (0-7646-0299-3) Prctnrs Pub Co.

***Lindsey, Stephen W., et al.** Guide to GAAP. 1998. ring bd. 63.00 (0-7646-0611-5) Prctnrs Pub Co.

Lindsey, Stephen W., et al. Guide to Nonprofit GAAP. 1997. ring bd. 48.00 (0-7646-0298-5) Prctnrs Pub Co.

***Lindsey, Stephen W., et al.** Guide to Nonprofit GAAP. 1998. ring bd. 63.00i (0-7646-0640-9) Prctnrs Pub Co.

— Guide to Nonprofit GAAP. 1999. ring bd. 63.00 (0-7646-0951-3, NPGP 99) Prctnrs Pub Co.

— Guide to Write-Up Services. 1998. ring bd. 105.00i (0-7646-0590-9) Prctnrs Pub Co.

— Guide to Write-Up Services. 1999. ring bd. 105.00i (0-7646-0946-7) Prctnrs Pub Co.

Lindsey, Stephen W., et al. Guide to Write-Up Services, Vol. 1. 1997. 90.00 (0-7646-0064-8) Prctnrs Pub Co.

***Lindsey, Stephen W., et al.** PPC'S Business Solutions, Vol. 1. 1999. ring bd. write for info. (0-7646-0947-5) Prctnrs Pub Co.

Lindsey, Susan Lyndaker, et al. The Okapi: Mysterious Animal of Congo-Zaire. LC 98-28740. 176p. 1999. 30.00 (0-292-74706-3) U of Tex Pr.

Lindsey, Terri. Dream Bride: Wedding Month. 1995. per. 2.99 (0-373-19106-5) Harlequin Bks.

— Going My Way. (Romance Ser.: No. 865). 1992. per. 2.69 (0-373-08865-5, 5-08865-3) Silhouette.

— Going My Way? large type ed. 261p. 1992. reprint ed. lib. bdg. 13.95 (1-56054-490-2) Thorndike Pr.

Lindsey, Timothy. The Romance of K'tut Tantri & Indonesia: Texts, Scripts, History & Identity. LC 96-33013. (Illus.). 382p. 1997. text 60.00 (983-56-0018-X) OUP.

Lindsey, Wallace M., jt. auth. see Isidori.

Lindsey, Wallace M., ed. see Plautus.

Lindsey, William, jt. auth. see Cable, Sandra.

Lindsey, William C., jt. auth. see Hinedi, Sami.

Lindsey, William C., jt. auth. see Simon, Marvin K.

Lindsey, William D. Shailer Mathews' Lives of Jesus: The Search for a Theological Foundation for the Social Gospel. LC 96-52290. 318p. (C). 1997. text 59.50 (0-7914-3507-5); pap. text 19.95 (0-7914-3508-3) State U NY Pr.

— Singing in a Strange Land: Praying & Acting with the Poor. LC 90-63488. 120p. (Orig.). (C). 1991. pap. 8.95 (1-55612-415-5, LL1415) Sheed & Ward WI.

Lindsey, William H. & Quint, Bruce. The Oasis Technique. 91p. 1986. 15.00 (0-317-01541-9) Fla Atlantic.

Lindsjoo, Christine, jt. auth. see Wohlin, Anna.

Lindskog, B. I. & Zetterberg, B. L. Lexicon of Medical Terminology: Medicinsk Terminologi Lexikon. 620p. 1981. 250.00 (0-8288-1884-3, F22400) Fr & Eur.

Lindskog, Per & Lundqvist, Jan. Why Poor Children Stay Sick: The Human Ecology of Child Health & Welfare in Rural Malawi. (Research Report Ser.: No. 85). 111p. 1989. write for info. (91-7106-284-X, Pub. by Nordic Africa) Transaction Pubs.

Lindskold, Jane. Brother to Dragons, Companion to Owls. 224p. (Orig.). 1994. mass mkt. 4.99 (0-380-77527-1, Avon Bks) Morrow Avon.

— Changer: A Novel of the Anthanor. 512p. 1998. mass mkt. 5.99 (0-380-78849-7, Eos) Morrow Avon.

***Lindskold, Jane.** Legends Walking: A Novel of the Athanor. 416p. 1999. mass mkt. 6.99 (0-380-78850-0, Avon Bks) Morrow Avon.

Lindskold, Jane. Marks of Our Brothers. 256p. (Orig.). 1995. mass mkt. 4.99 (0-380-77847-5, Avon Bks) Morrow Avon.

— The Pipes of Orpheus. 256p. (Orig.). 1995. mass mkt. 4.99 (0-380-77848-3, Avon Bks) Morrow Avon.

— Roger Zelazny. LC 93-29505. (Twayne's United States Authors Ser.). 192p. 1993. 28.95 (0-8057-3953-X, Twyne) Mac Lib Ref.

Lindskold, Jane. Roger Zelazny & Jane Lindskold's Chronomaster: A Novel. 360p. 1996. mass mkt., per. 5.99 (0-7615-0422-2) Prima Pub.

Lindskold, Jane. Roger Zelazny & Jane Lindskold's Chronomaster: The Official Strategy Guide. LC 95-72404. (Illus.). xiv, 176p. 1996. pap. 19.95 (0-7615-0413-3) Prima Pub.

— Smoke & Mirrors. 256p. (Orig.). 1996. mass mkt. 5.50 (0-380-78290-1, Avon Bks) Morrow Avon.

***Lindskold, Jane.** Through the Wolf's Eyes. 2000. text 25.95 (0-312-87427-8) St Martin.

Lindskold, Jane. When the Gods Are Silent. 1997. mass mkt. 5.99 (0-380-78848-9, Avon Bks) Morrow Avon.

Lindskold, Jane, jt. auth. see Zelazny, Roger.

Lindskoog, Donald. The Idea of Psychology: Reclaiming the Discipline's Identity. LC 98-15118. 1998. pap. 14.95 (0-88258-200-3) Howard Univ.

Lindskoog, John & Lindskoog, Kathryn. How to Grow a Young Reader: A Parent's Guide to Books for Kids. LC 88-23205. 182p. (Orig.). 1989. pap. 9.99 (0-87788-353-X, H Shaw Pubs) Waterbrook Pr.

Lindskoog, Kathryn. C. S. Lewis, Mere Christian. 4th rev. ed. LC 97-9967. 292p. (Orig.). 1997. reprint ed. pap. 14.95 (0-940895-36-6) Cornerstone IL.

— Creative Writing: For People Who Can't Not Write. 288p. 1989. pap. 24.99 (0-310-25321-7) Zondervan.

Lindskoog, Kathryn. Dante's Divine Comedy Vol. 2: Purgatory. (C). 1997. 22.95 (0-86554-573-1, MUP/H420) Mercer Univ Pr.

Lindskoog, Kathryn. Journey into Narnia: C. S. Lewis's Tales Explored. expanded ed. LC 97-18312. (Illus.). 256p. 1997. pap. 15.95 (0-932727-89-1) Hope Pub Hse.

***Lindskoog, Kathryn.** Words to the Wise: Collected Essays. 142p. 2000. pap. 12.95 (0-932727-95-6) Hope Pub Hse.

Lindskoog, Kathryn, retold by. Dante's Divine Comedy. LC 97-4270. 144p. 1997. 22.95 (0-86554-543-X, H420) Mercer Univ Pr.

Lindskoog, Kathryn & Dante Alighieri. Dante's Divine Comedy: Paradise. 192p. 1998. 24.95 (0-86554-584-7, MUP/H410) Mercer Univ Pr.

Lindskoog, Kathryn & Lewis, C. S. Finding the Landlord: A Guidebook to C. S. Lewis's Pilgrim's Regress. LC 95-34102. (Illus.). 165p. (Orig.). 1995. pap. 9.95 (0-940895-35-8, 58) Cornerstone IL.

Lindskoog, Kathryn, jt. auth. see Lindskoog, John.

Lindskoog, Kathryn Ann & Hunsicker, Ranelda Mack. How to Grow a Young Reader: Books from Every Age for Readers of Every Age. rev. ed. LC 98-51648. 392p. 1999. pap. 14.99 (0-87788-408-0, H Shaw Pubs) Waterbrook Pr.

Lindskoog, Nils. Long-Term Greedy: The Triumph of Goldman Sachs. LC 96-76405. (Illus.). 159p. 1998. 24.95 (0-9652153-3-4) McCrossen Pub.

***Lindskoog, Nils.** Long-Term Greedy: The Triumph of Goldman Sachs. 2nd ed. LC 99-74730. 192p. 1999. 24.95 (0-9652153-7-7) McCrossen Pub.

Lindsley, A. L. Sketches of an Excursion to Southern Alaska. fac. ed. (Shorey Historical Ser.). 76p. pap. 10.00 (0-8466-0091-9, S91) Shoreys Bkstore.

Lindsley, D. H., ed. Oxide Minerals: Petrologic & Magnetic Significance. (Reviews in Mineralogy Ser.: Vol. 25). 509p. 1991. per. 28.00 (0-939950-30-8) Mineralogical Soc.

Lindsley, Dan L. & Grell, E. H. Genetic Variations of Drosophila Melanogaster. LC 68-15915. (Illus.). 472p. 1968. 15.00 (0-87279-638-8, 627) Carnegie Inst.

Lindsley, Dan L. & Zimm, Georgianna G. Genome of Drosophila Melanogst. 1992. pap. text 24.00 (0-12-450991-6) Acad Pr.

— The Genome of Drosophilia Melanogaster. (Illus.). 1133p. 1992. text 99.00 (0-12-450990-8) Acad Pr.

***Lindsley, David.** Power-Plant Control & Instrumentation: The Control of Boilers & Heat-Recovery Steam Generator Systems (HRSGs) (IEE Control Engineering Ser.: No. 58). 240p. 1999. boxed set 65.00 (0-85296-765-9) INSPEC Inc.

Lindsley, Donald B., ed. see Blinkov, Samuil Mikha'ilovich & Smirnov, N. A.

Lindsley, E. F. Electric & Gas Welding. LC 77-26479. (Popular Science Skill Bks.). 1980. pap. 4.95 (0-06-090723-1) HarpC.

Lindsley, Evangeline & Diggs, Nancy. My Century: An Outspoken Memoir. (Illus.). 192p. (Orig.). 1996. pap. 10.00 (0-913428-79-5) Landfall Pr.

Lindsley, H. Hays. Hankerings, 1995. 76p. 1995. pap. write for info. (0-9662664-1-2) Rd Dog Ink.

— In the Rainforest. (Illus.). 44p. (J). (ps-1). 1998. pap. 14.95 (0-9662664-0-4) Rd Dog Ink.

Lindsley, James E. The Church Club of New York: The First Hundred Years. 256p. 1994. 20.00 (0-9638146-0-5) Church Club.

Lindsley, John B., ed. The Military Annals of Tennessee Vols. I & II: Confederate, 2 vols. (Illus.). 1634p. 1996. 100.00 (1-56837-310-4) Broadfoot.

Lindsley, Karen B., ed. Cave Research Foundation Annual Report, 1981. (Illus.). 55p. (Orig.). 1984. pap. 5.00 (0-939748-04-5) Cave Bks MO.

— Cave Research Foundation Annual Report, 1984. (Illus.). 60p. (Orig.). 1985. pap. 5.00 (0-939748-17-7) Cave Bks MO.

— Cave Research Foundation Annual Report, 1985. (Illus.). 48p. (Orig.). 1986. pap. 5.00 (0-939748-19-3) Cave Bks MO.

— Cave Research Foundation Annual Report, 1986. (Illus.). 51p. (Orig.). 1987. pap. 5.00 (0-939748-22-3) Cave Bks MO.

— Cave Research Foundation Annual Report 1987. (Illus.). 74p. 1988. pap. 5.00 (0-939748-23-1) Cave Bks MO.

— Cave Research Foundation Annual Report, 1988. (Illus.). 91p. (Orig.). 1989. pap. 5.00 (0-939748-24-X) Cave Bks MO.

— Cave Research Foundation Annual Report, 1989. (Illus.). 85p. (Orig.). 1990. pap. 5.00 (0-939748-26-6) Cave Bks MO.

— Cave Research Foundation Annual Report, 1990. (Illus.). 80p. (Orig.). 1991. pap. 5.00 (0-939748-34-7) Cave Bks MO.

— Cave Research Foundation Annual Report, 1991. (Illus.). 76p. (Orig.). 1992. pap. 5.00 (0-939748-35-5) Cave Bks MO.

— Cave Research Foundation Annual Report, 1992. (Illus.). 68p. (Orig.). 1993. pap. 5.00 (0-939748-38-X) Cave Bks MO.

— Cave Research Foundation Annual Report, 1994 & 1995 & 1996 & 1997. (Illus.). 80p. 2000. pap. 5.00 (0-939748-43-6) Cave Bks MO.

Lindsley, Karen B., jt. ed. see Bridgemon, Rondal R.

Lindsley, Lawrence, tr. see Lindsley, Margaret H.

Lindsley, Margaret H. Major Andrew Henry in Idaho. Lindsley, Lawrence & Campbell, Bruce, trs. (Illus.). 24p. 1985. pap. 4.00 (1-890535-03-6) H & J Spec.

***Lindsley, Mark A.** Oren's World. 296p. 1999. pap. 16.95 (0-7414-0184-3) Buy Books.

Lindsley, Michelle L. Bridging the Gap Between MIL-STD-810 & MIL-STD-781 - A Tutorial. LC 62-38584. 221p. 1990. pap. text 100.00 (0-915414-32-5) IEST.

— The Environmental Engineering Specialist's Role in Procurement - A Systems Acquisition Primer - A Tutorial. LC 62-38584. 93p. 1988. pap. text 75.00 (0-915414-39-2) IEST.

Lindsley, Steven. New Orleans: An Artist's Sketchbook. (Illus.). 86p. 1997. pap. 18.00 (1-884824-03-X) Tryon Pubng.

Lindsley, Thomas. Building a Workforce Investment System for America. 42p. 1992. pap. text 9.95 (0-88713-654-0) Nat Alliance.

Lindsted, Rob. The Cost of Revival. 40p. (Orig.). 1994. pap. 2.95 (1-879366-46-0) Hearthstone OK.

— The Sound of the Trumpet. 50p. (Orig.). 1994. pap. 2.95 (1-879366-57-6) Hearthstone OK.

Lindsted, Rob & Gaverluk, Emil. Why the Church Will Not Go Through the Great Tribulation. 40p. (Orig.). 1994. pap. 2.95 (1-879366-58-4) Hearthstone OK.

Lindsted, Rob & Werner, Earl. End-Time Prophetic Chronology. 242p. (Orig.). 1994. pap. 2.95 (1-879366-59-2) Hearthstone OK.

Lindsted, Rob, et al. Years That Changed the World. 92p. (Orig.). 1995. pap. 7.95 (1-879366-92-4) Hearthstone OK.

Lindsted, Rob, jt. auth. see Gaverluk, Emil.

Lindsted, Robert. Can You Really Know Your Future? 100p. (Orig.). 1992. pap. 7.95 (1-879366-32-0) Hearthstone OK.

— Travel Guide to Israel. LC 96-154227. (Illus.). 126p. (Orig.). (C). 1990. pap. 5.95 (0-9624517-5-4) Hearthstone OK.

***Lindstedt, Dave, ed.** The Christian Bed & Breakfast Directory, 2000-2001. 624p. 2000. pap. 4.97 (1-57748-662-5) Barbour Pub.

Lindstedt, David, ed. & intro. see Barbour Publishing, Inc. Editors.

Lindsten, J. Nobel Lectures in Physiology or Medicine 1971-1980. 690p. 1992. text 122.00 (981-02-0790-5); pap. text 61.00 (981-02-0791-3) World Scientific Pub.

— Nobel Lectures in Physiology or Medicine 1981-1990. 640p. 1993. text 118.00 (981-02-0792-1); pap. text 55.00 (981-02-0793-X) World Scientific Pub.

Lindsten, Jan & Pettersson, Ulf, eds. Etiology of Human Disease at the DNA Level. LC 91-8911. (Nobel Symposium Ser.: Vol. 80). 332p. 1991. reprint ed. pap. 103.00 (0-608-04676-0, 206539700004) Bks Demand.

Lindstrand, Doug. Alaska Sketchbook. LC 94-96881. (Illus.). 200p. 1995. pap. 25.00 (0-9608290-8-3) Sourdough Studio.

— Doug Lindstrand's Alaska Sketchbook #2, No. 2. LC 94-96881. (Illus.). 200p. (Orig.). 1995. pap. text 25.00 (0-9608290-9-1) Sourdough Studio.

— Drawing Alaska's "Big Game" LC 95-95214. (Illus.). 104p. 1995. pap. text 15.00 (0-9608290-7-5) Sourdough Studio.

— Drawing America's Wildlife. LC 98-66822. (Illus.). 216p. 1998. pap. text 25.00 (0-9608290-6-7) Sourdough Studio.

***Lindstrand, Douglas.** Drawing Mammals: Wildlife of North America. LC 99-94353. (Illus.). 208p. 1999. pap. text 25.00 (1-928722-00-8, Pub. by Sourdough Studio) Partners Pubs Grp.

Lindstrm, Tom, et al, eds. Stochastic Analysis & Application: Proceedings Oslo-Silivri, July 1992. LC 93-28190. (Stochastics Monographs: Vol. 8). 288p. 1993. text 112.00 (2-88124-948-5) Gordon & Breach.

Lindstrom, Ann-Marie. Common Embarrassing Mistakes in English: And How to Correct Them. LC 98-61611. 280p. 1999. pap. 12.95 (1-887053-12-3) United Res CA.

***Lindstrom, Ann-Marie.** The Rosacea Handbook: A Self-Help Guide. LC 00-131566. (Illus.). 200p. 2000. pap. 12.95 (1-887053-14-X) United Res CA.

Lindstrom, B., jt. ed. see Hedegaard, L.

Lindstrom, Bengt & Spencer, Nick, eds. Social Pediatrics. (Illus.). 628p. 1995. text 135.00 (0-19-262179-3) OUP.

Lindstrom, Carl, jt. auth. see Lindstrom, Virginia.

Lindstrom, Catarina. Atrial Fibrillations. (Orig.). 1997. pap. 8.00 (0-614-32421-1) Blckstone Pr.

Lindstrom, Christina, jt. auth. see Schaffer, Judith.

Lindstrom, Dan, jt. ed. see Moses, Leon N.

Lindstrom, Eva. The Cat Hat. Croall, Stephen, tr. from SWE. (Illus.). 40p. (J). (gr. 1-4). 1989. pap. 6.95 (0-916291-24-3) Kane-Miller Bk.

Lindstrom, Florence M. Adventures in Phonics Level A. (Adventures in Phonics Ser.). (J). 1991. 7.00 (1-930092-75-X, CLP29810) Christian Liberty.

— Adventures in Phonics Level A. (Adventures in Phonics Ser.: Vol. 1). (Illus.). 214p. (J). (gr. k-1). 1991. pap. text 8.00 (1-930092-74-1, CLP29810) Christian Liberty.

— Adventures in Phonics Level B. (Adventures in Phonics Ser.). 1996. teacher ed. 7.00 (1-930092-78-4) Christian Liberty.

— Adventures in Phonics Level B. (Adventures in Phonics Ser.: Vol. 2). (Illus.). 230p. (J). (gr. 1-2). 1996. pap. text 8.00 (1-930092-77-6, CLP29815) Christian Liberty.

— Adventures in Phonics Level C. (Adventures in Phonics Ser.). 2000. teacher ed. 7.00 (1-930092-80-6) Christian Liberty.

— Adventures in Phonics Level C. (Adventures in Phonics Ser.: Vol. 3). (Illus.). (J). (gr. 3-4). 2000. pap. text 8.00 (1-930092-79-2, CLP29820) Christian Liberty.

— It Is a Joy to Learn, Vol. 4. (Illus.). 60p. (J). (gr. k-1). 1998. pap. text 11.00 (1-930092-30-X) Christian Liberty.

— It Is Fun to Read, Vol. 1. (Illus.). 28p. (J). (gr. k). 1998. pap. text 11.00 (1-930092-27-X, CLP29931) Christian Liberty.

— Meeting New Friends. 150p. (J). (gr. 1-2). 1992. pap. text 6.00 (1-930092-26-1, clp29610) Christian Liberty.

— Pals & Pets, Vol. 2. (Illus.). 28p. (J). (gr. k-1). 1998. pap. text 11.00 (1-930092-28-8, CLP29931) Christian Liberty.

— A Time at Home, Vol. 3. (Illus.). 60p. (J). 1998. pap. text 11.00 (1-930092-29-6) Christian Liberty.

Lindstrom, Fred B., et al, eds. Kimball Young on Sociology in Transition, 1912-1968: An Oral Account by the 35th President of the ASA. (Illus.). 184p. (C). 1995. pap. text 29.50 (0-8191-9789-0); lib. bdg. 47.00 (0-8191-9788-2) U Pr of Amer.

Lindstrom, Fredrik. God & the Origin of Evil: A Contextual Analysis of Alleged Monistic Evidence in the Old Testament. (Coniectanea Biblica. Old Testament Ser.: No. 21). (Orig.). 1983. pap. 49.50 (0-317-65797-6) Coronet Bks.

— Suffering & Sin: Interpretations of Illness in the Individual Complaint Psalms. (Coniectanea Biblica Old Testament Ser.: No. 37). 500p. (Orig.). 1994. pap. 72.50 (91-22-01580-9) Coronet Bks.

Lindstrom, Gaell. Thomas Moran in Utah. 26p. 1983. pap. 1.00 (0-87421-146-8) Utah St U Pr.

Lindstrom, Harald. Wesley & Sanctification. LC 83-17025. 256p. 1984. pap. 12.95 (0-310-75011-3, 17025P) Zondervan.

— Wesley & Sanctification: A Study in the Doctrine of Salvation. 2nd ed. 228p. 1996. reprint ed. pap. 15.00 (0-916035-72-7) Evangel Indiana.

Lindstrom, Hildegard Schmidt, see Schmidt Lindstrom, Hildegard.

Lindstrom, Joyce. Bullitt County, Kentucky Marriages, 1797-1876. 171p. 1988. pap. 18.00 (1-889221-03-1) Ancestral Trails.

Lindstrom, Joyce. Handcarts West. pap. 13.95 (1-55517-391-8) CFI Dist.

Lindstrom, Lamont. Cargo Cult: Strange Stories of Desire from Melanesia & Beyond. LC 93-5399. (Illus.). 288p. (C). 1993. text 36.00 (0-8248-1526-2); pap. text 14.95 (0-8248-1563-7) UH Pr.

— Knowledge & Power in a South Pacific Society. LC 90-53172. (Series in Ethnographic Inquiry). (Illus.). 240p. 1990. text 45.00 (0-87474-365-6); pap. text 17.95 (0-87474-357-5) Smithsonian.

Lindstrom, Lamont, jt. auth. see White, Geoffrey M.

Lindstrom, Lamont, jt. ed. see White, Geoffrey M.

Lindstrom, Lars. Managing Alcoholism: Matching Clients to Treatment. (Illus.). 390p. 1992. text 69.50 (0-19-261902-0) OUP.

Lindstrom, Lars G. Christian Spiritual Healing: A Psychological Study. Ideology & Experience in the British Healing Movement. (Psychologia & Sociologica Religionum Ser.: No. 7). 207p. (Orig.). 1992. pap. text 46.50 (91-554-2962-9) Coronet Bks.

Lindstrom, Lauren E., jt. auth. see Benz, Michael R.

Lindstrom, Lisa M. Adequate Justice: Beginning Healing Through Poetry. (Illus.). 60p. (Orig.). 1996. pap. 11.00 (0-9650823-0-X) Leo Publishing.

Lindstrom, Lisa M., ed. see Humphries, Christy.

Lindstrom, Lorel L. & Kirkland, Shari L. Red Hot Relationships: How to Defuse the Anger & Keep the Romance. LC 98-66167. 180p. 1998. pap. 13.95 (0-88282-168-7, Pub. by New Horizon NJ) Natl Bk Netwk.

Lindstrom, Marilyn. The Voice from Inner Space: Answers Who Am I? Why Am I Here? Beckman, Jean, ed. LC 90-35087. 112p. (J). 1990. pap. (0-941992-20-9) Los Arboles Pub.

Lindstrom, Mary E., et al, eds. Hydrocarbons & Methylotrophy. (Methods in Enzymology Ser.: Vol. 188). 504p. 1990. text 115.00 (0-12-182089-0) Acad Pr.

Lindstrom, Meg. The Joy of Flow. 1998. pap. write for info. (0-609-80020-5, Crown) Crown Pub Group.

Lindstrom, Naomi. Jorge Luis Borges. (Twayne's Studies in Short Fiction). 208p. (C). 1990. 23.95 (0-8057-8327-X, Twyne) Mac Lib Ref.

— Literary Expressionism in Argentine Literature: The Presentation of Incoherence. LC 77-24558. 89p. 1978. pap. 10.00 (0-87918-038-2) ASU Lat Am St.

— Macedonio Fernandez. LC 80-53826. 138p. (Orig.). 1981. pap. 18.00 (0-89295-018-8) Society Sp & Sp-Am.

— The Social Conscience of Latin American Writing. LC 97-30035. (Texas Pan American Ser.). 200p. (C). 1998. 25.00 (0-292-74698-9, LINSOC); pap. 12.95 (0-292-74699-7, LINSCP) U of Tex Pr.

— Women's Voice in Latin American Literature. LC 86-51313. 153p. (Orig.). 1989. 26.00 (0-89410-295-8, Three Contnts); pap. 14.00 (0-89410-296-6, Three Contnts) L Rienner.

Lindstrom, Naomi, ed. see Alencar, Jose de.

Lindstrom, Naomi, tr. see Agosin, Marjorie.

Lindstrom, Naomi, tr. see Parente Cunha, Helena.

Lindstrom, P. Aspects of Incompleteness. LC 97-25726. (Lecture Notes in Logic Ser.: Vol. 10). x, 133p. 1997. pap. 42.00 (3-540-63213-1) Spr-Verlag.

Lindstrom, Paul D. & McHugh, Michael J., eds. Christian Liberty Nature Reader, Bk. 3. (Illus.). 160p. (J). (gr. 3-4). 1988. pap. text 6.00 (1-930092-53-9, CLP29955) Christian Liberty.

— Christian Liberty Nature Reader, Bk. 4. (Illus.). 218p. (J). 1992. reprint ed. pap. text 4.00 (1-930092-54-7, CLP29965) Christian Liberty.

Lindstrom, Paul D., jt. auth. see Parent, Tom.

Lindstrom, Robert L. & Collyer, Glenn. Business Weeks Guide to Multimedia Presentations. 448p. 1994. pap. text 39.95 incl. cd-rom (0-07-882057-X) Osborne-McGraw.

Lindstrom, Sandra C., ed. Fifteenth International Seaweed Symposium. 576p. (C). 1996. text 184.00 (0-7923-3997-5) Kluwer Academic.

Lindstrom, Sandra C. & Gabrielson, P. W., eds. Thirteenth International Seaweed Symposium. (Developments in Hydrobiology Ser.). (C). 1990. text 463.00 (0-7923-0763-1) Kluwer Academic.

Lindstrom, Sandra C., jt. auth. see O'Clair, Rita M.

***Lindstrom, Sieg, contrib. by.** The Big Green Book. 175p. 2000. spiral bd. 16.50 (0-911521-55-0) Tafnews.

Lindstrom, Talbot & Tighe, Kevin P. Trade Regulation by Negotiation: Federal Trade Commission Consent Decrees. LC 73-93919. 1181p. reprint ed. pap. 200.00 (0-608-12745-0, 202434100037) Bks Demand.

Lindstrom, Tom. Brownian Motion on Nested Fractals. LC 89-18138. (Memoirs of the American Mathematical Society Ser.: Vol. 420). 128p. 1990. pap. 22.00 (0-8218-2484-8, MEMO/83/420C) Am Math.

Lindstrom, Ulf. Euro-Consent, Euro-Contract, or Euro-Coercion? Scandinavian Social Democracy, the European Impasse. 168p. (C). 1993. pap. 24.00 (82-00-21918-6, Pub. by Scand Univ Pr) IBD Ltd.

Lindstrom, Ulf. Proceedings of the Symposium the Oskar Klein Centenary. 225p. 1995. text 58.00 (981-02-2332-3) World Scientific Pub.

***Lindstrom, Ursula.** Ten Secrets for Success with Beautiful Women: A/Complete How to Guide for Pursuing the Women of Your Dreams. LC 99-93604. (Illus.). 344p. 1999. pap. 19.95 (0-9669697-0-7, Pub. by Samarkand) ACCESS Pubs Network.

Lindstrom, Virginia & Lindstrom, Carl. Golden Cocoon: Myths & Realities of Lifecare Communities; One Couple's Experience. LC 95-33330. 148p. 1995. 19.95 (0-942597-88-5, Ragged Edge) White Mane Pub.

Lindstrom, Wendell D., jt. auth. see Finkbeiner, Daniel T.

Lindstromberg, Seth. English Prepositions Explained. LC 97-39938. xii, 309p. 1998. lib. bdg. 75.00 (1-55619-525-7) J Benjamins Pubng Co.

— English Prepositions Explained. LC 97-39938. xii, 309p. 1998. pap. 29.95 (1-55619-526-5) J Benjamins Pubng Co.

— English Prepositions Explained LC 97-39938. viii, 309 p. 1998. pap. write for info. (90-272-2172-3) J Benjamins Pubng.

— Planning from Lesson to Lesson. (Pilgrims Longman Resource Bks.). 1995. pap. text 22.39 (0-582-08959-X, Pub. by Addison-Wesley) Longman.

Lindstromberg, Seth, ed. Recipe Book. (Pilgrims Resource Bks.). 91p. 1990. pap. 22.39 (0-582-03764-6, 78673) Addison-Wesley.

Lindt, Carson Van, see Van Lindt, Carson.

Lindt, Gillian, ed. Religion in America. LC 75-54571. (Great Contemporary Issues Ser.). 1977. lib. bdg. 27.95 (0-405-09865-0) Ayer.

Lindt, J. T. The Paper-Mills of Berne. (Monumenta Chartae Papyraceae Ser.). (Illus.). 468p. (C). 1964. text 134.50 (90-5356-202-8, Pub. by Amsterdam U Pr) U of Mich Pr.

Lindt, Peggy. Buddies: Children's Thoughts on Friendship. 32p. (YA). (gr. 2 up). 1995. 9.95 (0-87905-663-0) Gibbs Smith Pub.

Lindtner, Christian, tr. from CHI. Master of Wisdom: Writings of the Buddhist Master Nagarjuna. LC 86-29111. (Tibetan Translation Ser.: Vol. 14). 413p. 1986. 40.00 (0-89800-139-0) Dharma Pub.

— Master of Wisdom: Writings of the Buddhist Master Nagarjuna. LC 86-29111. (Tibetan Translation Ser.: Vol. 14). 413p. 1997. pap. 19.95 (0-89800-286-9) Dharma Pub.

***Linduff, Katheryn M., et al, eds.** The Beginnings of Metallurgy in China. LC 99-58582. (Chinese Studies: Vol. 11). 440p. 2000. text 109.95 (0-7734-7853-1) E Mellen.

Lindup, Mike, jt. auth. see Evans, Dewi.

L'Industrie Aeronautique Staff. Dictionnaire Francais-Chinois de l'Aeronautique & de l'Espa. (CHI & FRE.). 1991. write for info. (0-7859-8707-X, 7800463672) Fr & Eur.

Lindvall, Ella K. Read-Aloud Bible Stories, Vol. 1. (Illus.). 160p. (J). (ps-2). 18.99 (0-8024-7163-3, 555) Moody.

— Read-Aloud Bible Stories, Vol. 2. (Illus.). (J). (ps up). 18.99 (0-8024-7164-1, 556) Moody.

— Read-Aloud Bible Stories, Vol. 3. (Illus.). (J). (ps-2). 18.99 (0-8024-7165-X, 557) Moody.

— Read-Aloud Bible Stories, Vol. 4. (Illus.). (J). (ps up). 18.99 (0-8024-7166-8, 558) Moody.

Lindvall, Joran, ed. The Swedish Art of Building. (Illus.). 255p. 1992. 99.50 (91-520-0287-X, Pub. by Almqvist Wiksell) Coronet Bks.

Lindvall, Michael L. The Good News from North Haven. Rubenstein, Julie, ed. 192p. 1992. reprint ed. pap. 9.00 (0-671-79200-8) PB.

Lindvall, O., ed. Restoration of Brain Function by Tissue Transplantation. LC 92-49462. (Basic & Clinical Aspects of Neuroscience Ser.: Vol. 5). 1993. 38.95 (0-387-55823-3) Spr-Verlag.

Lindvall, Terry. Surprised by Laughter. 432p. 1996. 22.99 (0-7852-7689-0) Nelson.

Lindvall, Torgny. Lectures on the Coupling Method. LC 92-12811. (Probability & Mathematical Statistics Ser.). 272p. 1992. 115.00 (0-471-54025-0) Wiley.

Lindwall, Bo, jt. ed. see Cavalli-Bojorkman, Gorel.

L

An Asterisk (*) at the beginning of an entry indicates that the title is appearing for the first time.

Lindway, Russ. The Superior Person's Guide to Everyday Irritations. Carle, Cliff, ed. (Illus.). 224p. (Orig.). 1990. pap. 4.95 (0-918259-23-1) CCC Pubns.

Lindwer, Willy. Classic Jewish Postcards for All Occasions. 1996. pap. 14.95 (0-8052-1073-3) Schocken.

— The Last Seven Months of Anne Frank. 256p. 1992. pap. 12.95 (0-385-42360-8, Anchor NY) Doubleday.

Lindworsky, Johann. The Training of the Will. Steiner, A. & Fitzpatrick, E. A., trs. 192p. 1995. reprint ed. text 19.95 (0-912141-31-X) Roman Cath Bks.

Lindy, Jacob D., et al, eds. Vietnam: A Casebook. LC 87-15062. (Psychosocial Stress Ser.: No. 10). 384p. 1987. text 53.95 (0-87630-471-4) Brunner-Mazel.

Lindy, Jacob D., jt. ed. see Wilson, John P.

***Lindy, Julie & McKenna, Jon, eds.** Recruiting & Retaining Accounting Professionals: Winning Strategies - Innovative Solutions - Ideas Worth Stealing. (Illus.). 200p. 1999. pap. 167.00 (1-887986-12-X) Strafford Pubns.

Lindzen, Richard S. Dynamics in Atmospheric Physics. (Illus.). 320p. (C). 1990. text 52.95 (0-521-36101-X) Cambridge U Pr.

Lindzen, Richard S., et al, eds. The Atmosphere - A Challenge: The Science of Jule Gregory Charney. (Illus.). 320p. 1990. 65.00 (1-878220-03-9) Am Meteorological.

Lindzen, Richard S., jt. auth. see Chapman, S.

Lindzey, G., jt. auth. see Hall, C. S.

Lindzey, Gardner. Projective Techniques & Cross-Cultural Research. LC 61-15951. (Century Psychology Ser.). 1976. reprint ed. 32.75 (0-89197-361-3); reprint ed. pap. text 12.95 (0-89197-908-5) Irvington.

Lindzey, Gardner, ed. History of Psychology in Autobiography, Vol. VIII. LC 30-20129. (Illus.). 504p. 1989. 57.50 (0-8047-1492-4) Stanford U Pr.

Lindzey, Gardner & Aronson, E. Handbook of Social Psychology, 5 vols. 2nd ed. Incl. Vol. 1. LINDZEY VOL 1HANDBOOK. 2nd ed. 1968. 23.25 (0-201-04262-2); Vol. 2. LINDZEY VOL 2HANDBOOK. 2nd ed. 1968. 23.25 (0-201-04263-0); Vol. 3. LINDZEY VOL 3HANDBOOK. 2nd ed. 1968. 23.25 (0-201-04264-9); Vol. 4. LINDZEY VOL 4HANDBOOK. 2nd ed. 1968. 23.25 (0-201-04265-7); Vol. 5. Handbook of Social Psychology: Applied Social Psychology. 2nd ed. 1968. 23.25 (0-201-04266-5); 1968. write for info. (0-318-50120-1) Addison-Wesley.

Lindzey, Gardner & Aronson, Elliot, eds. Handbook of Social Psychology, 2 vols., Set. 3rd ed. (C). 1985. text 150.00 (0-89859-720-X) L Erlbaum Assocs.

— Handbook of Social Psychology Vol. I: Theory & Methods. 3rd ed. 832p. (C). 1985. text 70.00 (0-89859-718-8) L Erlbaum Assocs.

Lindzey, Gardner & Thiessen, Delbert D., eds. Contributions to Behavior - Genetic Analysis. LC 73-92661. (Century Psychology Ser.). 1970. 34.50 (0-89197-109-2) Irvington.

Lindzey, Gardner, et al. Introduction to Theories of Pe. LC 84-29919. 672p. 1985. text 84.95 (0-471-08906-0) Wiley.

— An Introduction to Theories of Personality. LC 84-29919. 217p. 1985. pap. text, teacher ed. 15.00 (0-471-82459-3) Wiley.

— Psychology. 3rd ed. (C). 1988. text 55.95 (0-87901-361-3) Worth.

— Psychology. 3rd ed. (C). 1988. pap., student ed. 12.95 (0-87901-354-0) Worth.

Lindzey, Gardner, jt. ed. see Boring, Edwin G.

Line, Bonnie L. Family Ties. LC 98-60292. 96p. 1998. pap. 7.99 (1-57921-107-0) WinePress Pub.

— The Nativity. LC 97-60778. 80p. 1997. pap. 8.95 (1-57921-029-5) WinePress Pub.

Line, Dave. The Big Book of Brewing. (Illus.). 254p. (Orig.). pap. 12.95 (0-9619072-9-0) G W Kent.

— Brewing Beer Like Those You Buy. (Illus.). 158p. (Orig.). 1993. reprint ed. pap. 10.95 (0-9619072-3-1) G W Kent.

— Brewing Beers Like Those You Buy. 2nd ed. (Illus.). 158p. 1995. pap. 19.95 (1-85486-125-5) Nexus Special Interests.

Line, David & Line, Julia. The Wheel of Fortune: How to Control Your Future. (Illus.). 304p. (Orig.). 1989. pap. 16.95 (0-85030-618-3) Aqrn Pr.

Line, Francis R. Adventure Unlimited: Searching the Globe with Francis Raymond Line. (Illus.). 206p. (Orig.). 1988. pap. 8.95 (0-938109-05-7) Wide Horiz Pr.

— Scrapbook on America. (Orig.). 1990. pap. 8.95 (0-938109-07-3) Wide Horiz Pr.

— Sheep, Stars, & Solitude: Adventure Saga of a Wilderness Trail. LC 86-11154. (Illus.). 166p. (Orig.). 1986. pap. 8.95 (0-938109-02-2) Wide Horiz Pr.

— Super Seniors, Their Stories & Secrets. (Illus.). 175p. (Orig.). 1989. pap. 8.95 (0-938109-06-5) Wide Horiz Pr.

Line, Francis R. & Line, Helen E. Grand Canyon Love Story: A True Living Adventure. 2nd ed. (Illus.). 300p. 1988. reprint ed. pap. 8.95 (0-938109-04-9) Wide Horiz Pr.

Line, Francis R. & Line, Winfield H. Foot by Foot Through the U. S. A. A High Adventure Odyssey to Every State in the Union. LC 86-28939. (Illus.). 312p. (Orig.). 1987. pap. 8.95 (0-938109-03-0) Wide Horiz Pr.

Line, Helen E., jt. auth. see Line, Francis R.

***Line, Joanne Larsen & Tubesing, Nancy Loving.** Quilts from "The Quiltmaker's Gift" 20 Traditional Patterns for a New Generation of Generous Quiltmakers. (Illus.). 144p. 2000. pap. 26.95 (1-57025-203-3) Pfeifer-Hamilton.

Line, Julia, jt. auth. see Line, David.

Line, Julie. The Numerology Workbook: Understanding & Using the Powers of Numbers. (Illus.). 224p. 1997. reprint ed. pap. 14.95 (0-8069-9763-X) Sterling.

Line, Lee E., et al. Austin Vol. 1: The Pictorial. Hudspeth, Patrick D. & Cooke, Barbara V., eds. 68p. (Orig.). 1989. pap. 8.00 (0-317-93914-9) Pictorial Publishing.

Line, Les, ed. see National Audubon Society Staff.

***Line, Libby.** The Quilt. 82p. 1999. pap. write for info. (0-7392-0461-0, PO3768) Morris Pubng.

***Line, Lorie.** Just Me. Ruth, Anita, ed. (Illus.). 92p. 2000. pap. text 30.00 (1-891195-08-5) Time Line Prods.

Line, Lorie. Selections from Sharing the Season, Vol. 2. Maybery, Paul, ed. (Illus.). 36p. (YA). 1993. pap. text 9.95 (0-9638000-0-0) Time Line Prods.

***Line, Lorie.** The Silver Album. Ruth, Anita, ed. 100p. 2000. pap. text 30.00 (1-891195-09-3) Time Line Prods.

— Simply Grand. Ruth, Anita, ed. (Illus.). 96p. 1999. pap., student ed. 29.99 (1-891195-07-7, Lorie Line) Time Line Prods.

***Line, Maurice, et al, eds.** Librarianship & Information Work Worldwide, 1999. 353p. 1999. 175.00 (1-85739-297-3) Bowker-Saur.

Line, Maurice B. Lines of Thought: Selected Papers of Maurice B. Line. Anthony, L. J., ed. LC 88-24376. 354p. 1988. reprint ed. pap. 109.80 (0-7837-9269-7, 206000600004) Bks Demand.

Line, Maurice B., jt. ed. see MacKenzie, G.

Line, Shirly. Oysters: A True Delicacy. (Illus.). 64p. 1995. 12.95 (0-02-860376-1) Macmillan.

Line, Winfield H., jt. auth. see Line, Francis R.

Lineaweaver. Complex Wound Reconstruction: Elements & Strategies. (C). 1998. text 225.00 (0-8385-1399-9) Appleton & Lange.

Lineaweaver, Marion. The Season Within. 1967. 5.95 (0-87233-836-3) Bauhan.

Lineaweaver, Thomas H., III & Backus, Richard H. The Natural History of Sharks. LC 97-132421. (Illus.). 256p. 1986. pap. 14.95 (0-8052-0766-X) Lyons Pr.

Lineback, Kent L. Being the Boss: The Craft of Managing People. LC 86-27751. 192p. 1987. 34.95 (0-87942-212-2, PCO2055) Inst Electrical.

Lineback, Kent L., jt. auth. see Komisar, Randy.

Lineback, Mark. Corporate Madness. LC 94-76284. (Illus.). 104p. (Orig.). 1994. pap. 9.95 (0-9641121-0-8) Madness.

Lineback, Neal G. Geography in the News. (Illus.). 388p. (Orig.). (C). 1995. pap. text 48.00 (0-9641628-4-9) Karo Hollow.

Lineback, Richard H., ed. The Philosopher's Index: A Retrospective Index to Non-U. S. English Language Publications from 1940, 3 vols., Set. 1265p. 1980. 375.00 (0-912632-12-7) Philosophers Info Ctr.

— The Philosopher's Index: A Retrospective to U. S. Publications from 1940, 3 vols. 1619p. 1978. 395.00 (0-912632-09-7) Philosophers Info Ctr.

— The Philosopher's Index: Cumulative Edition, 1987, Vol. XXI. 672p. 1988. 130.00 (0-912632-22-4) Philosophers Info Ctr.

— The Philosopher's Index: Cumulative Edition, 1988, Vol. XXII. 649p. 1989. 140.00 (0-912632-24-0) Philosophers Info Ctr.

— The Philosopher's Index: Cumulative Edition, 1989, Vol. XXIII. 695p. 1990. 140.00 (0-912632-51-8) Philosophers Info Ctr.

— The Philosopher's Index: Cumulative Edition, 1990, Vol. 24. 774p. 1991. 150.00 (0-912632-52-6) Philosophers Info Ctr.

— The Philosopher's Index: Cumulative Edition, 1991, Vol. 25. 750p. 1992. 155.00 (0-912632-53-4) Philosophers Info Ctr.

— The Philosopher's Index: Cumulative Edition, 1992, Vol. 26. 534p. 1993. 162.00 (0-912632-54-2) Philosophers Info Ctr.

— The Philosopher's Index: Cumulative Edition, 1993, Vol. 27. 779p. 1994. 172.00 (0-912632-55-0) Philosophers Info Ctr.

— The Philosopher's Index: Cumulative Edition 1998, Vol. 32. 1075p. 1999. 239.00 (0-9656743-3-9) Philosophers Info Ctr.

— The Philosopher's Index Vol. 28: Cumulative Edition, 1994, Vol. 28. 791p. 1995. 181.00 (0-912632-56-9) Philosophers Info Ctr.

***Lineback, Richard H., ed.** The Philosopher's Index Vol. 33: 1999 Cumulative Edition. 1075p. (C). 2000. lib. bdg. 249.00 (0-9656743-4-7) Philosophers Info Ctr.

Lineback, Richard H., ed. The Philosopher's Index, 1996: Cumulative Edition, Vol. 30. 1019p. 1997. 205.00 (0-9656743-0-4) Philosophers Info Ctr.

— The Philosopher's Index, 1997: Cumulative Edition, Vol. 31. 1000p. 1998. 225.00 (0-9656743-2-0) Philosophers Info Ctr.

— The Philospher's Index: Cumulative Edition, 1995, Vol. 29. 704p. 1996. 189.00 (0-9656743-1-2) Philosophers Info Ctr.

Linebarger, Paul M. The Political Doctrines of Sun Yat-Sen, No. 24--24. LC 73-3926. 278p. 1973. lib. bdg. 38.50 (0-8371-6855-4, LISY, Greenwood Pr) Greenwood.

— The Political Doctrines of Sun Yat-Sen: An Exposition of the San Min Chu I. LC 78-64293. (Johns Hopkins University. Studies in the Social Sciences. Thirtieth Ser. 1912: 24). reprint ed. 27.50 (0-404-61393-4) AMS Pr.

— Psychological Warfare. LC 72-4671. (International Propaganda & Communications Ser.). (Illus.). 318p. 1977. reprint ed. 27.95 (0-405-04755-X) Ayer.

— Sun Yat Sen & the Chinese Republic. LC 70-96469. 1969. reprint ed. 34.50 (0-404-03989-8) AMS Pr.

Linebaugh, Donald W. & Robinson, Gary C., eds. Spatial Patterning in Historical Archaeology: Selected Studies of Settlement. (Occasional Papers in Archaeology: No. 2). (Illus.). 144p. (Orig.). (C). 1994. pap. 17.00 (0-9615670-6-6, King & Queen Pr) Soc Alu Wm.

Linebaugh, Peter. The London Hanged: Crime & Civil Society in the Eighteenth Century. (Illus.). 512p. (C). 1992. text 64.95 (0-521-41842-9) Cambridge U Pr.

— The London Hanged: Crime & Civil Society in the Eighteenth Century. (Illus.). 511p. (C). 1993. pap. 21.95 (0-521-45758-0) Cambridge U Pr.

***Linebaugh, Peter & Rediker, Marcus.** The Many-Headed Hydra: The Hidden History of the Revolutionary Atlantic. LC 00-8881. (Illus.). 352p. 2000. pap. 30.00 (0-8070-5006-7) Beacon Pr.

Lineberger, Kathryn. The Rock Band Handbook: Everything You Need to Know to Get a Band Together & Take It on the Road. LC 96-11444. 160p. 1996. pap. 10.00 (0-399-52237-9, Perigee Bks) Berkley Pub.

Lineberry. American Public Policy. 2000. 109.20 (1-57259-729-1) St Martin.

Lineberry. American Public Policy Choices & Challenges. pap. text. write for info. (0-312-15252-3) St Martin.

Lineberry, Heather S. & Gilbert-Rolfe, Jeremy, contrib. by. Art on the Edge of Fashion. 64p. (Orig.). 1997. pap. 19.50 (0-9644646-3-2) Ariz St U Art Mus.

Lineberry, Joseph L., Jr., jt. auth. see Sanes, Richard.

Lineberry, Robert L. Equality & Urban Policy: The Distribution of Municipal Public Services. LC 76-53962. (Sage Library of Social Research: No. 39). 207p. 1977. reprint ed. pap. 64.20 (0-7837-1127-1, 204165700022) Bks Demand.

— Government in America: Brief Edition. (C). 1993. 41.40 (0-06-500721-2) Addson-Wesley Educ.

Lineberry, Robert L. & Edwards, George C., III. Government in America. 5th ed. (C). 1997. pap. text, student ed. 25.20 (0-673-52136-2) Addson-Wesley Educ.

Lineberry, Robert L. & Masotti, Louis H. Urban Problems & Public Policy. 240p. 1985. reprint ed. lib. bdg. 37.50 (0-8191-5142-4) U Pr of Amer.

Lineberry, Robert L. & Masotti, Louis H., eds. Urban Policy Problems. (C). 1975. pap. 15.00 (0-918592-11-9) Pol Studies.

— Urban Problems & Public Policy. 240p. 1976. boxed set 34.95 (0-669-00017-5) Transaction Pubs.

Lineberry, Robert L., et al. Government in America. 6th ed. 724p. (C). 1994. pap. 57.25 (0-673-52323-3) Addson-Wesley Educ.

— Government in America Brief. 2nd ed. Date not set. pap., teacher ed. write for info. (0-673-97071-X) Addson-Wesley Educ.

Lineberry, Tommy. Twice a Champion: The Toney Lineberry Story. 2nd ed. Talbolt, Frederick, ed. 200p. 1988. 14.95 (0-685-23257-3); pap. 8.95 (0-685-23258-1) T Lineberry.

Lineburgh, Nancy E. Integrating Music into the Preprimary, Montessori Classroom. 165p. (Orig.). 1996. pap. text 30.00 (0-9652371-9-2) Gldn Clef.

Linecar, Howard W., ed. The Milled Coinage of England, 1662-1946. 1971. 22.00 (0-932106-61-7) S J Durst.

Linedecker, Clifford L. Babyface Killers: Hoffifying True Stories of America's Youngest Murderers. (Illus.). 320p. 1999. mass mkt. 6.50 (0-312-97032-3, St Martins Paperbacks) St Martin.

***Linedecker, Clifford L.** Blood in the Sand: A Shocking True Story of Murder, Revenge & Greed in Las Vegas. 264p. 2000. mass mkt. 6.50 (0-312-97509-0, St Martins Paperbacks) St Martin.

Linedecker, Clifford L. Blood Money. (Illus.). 384p. 1993. mass mkt. 4.99 (1-55817-773-6, Pinncle Kensgtn) Kensgtn Pub Corp.

***Linedecker, Clifford L.** Deadly Obsession: A True Story of Mutilation & Murder in the Backwood of Wisconsin. 352p. 1998. mass mkt. 5.99 (0-7860-0551-3, Pinncle Kensgtn) Kensgtn Pub Corp.

Linedecker, Clifford L. Deadly Obsessions. 1995. mass mkt. 4.99 (0-7860-0112-7, Pinncle Kensgtn) Kensgtn Pub Corp.

— Death of a Model. LC 97-165018. 1997. mass mkt. 5.99 (0-312-96163-4) St Martin.

— Gun for Hire: The Soldier of Fortune Killings. 392p. (Orig.). 1992. mass mkt. 4.99 (0-380-76204-8, Avon Bks) Morrow Avon.

— Hell Ranch Vol. 1: The Nightmare Tale of Voodoo, Drugs & Death in Matamoros. (Illus.). 180p. 1996. 19.95 (1-877858-45-5, HR) Amer Focus Pub.

— Killer Kids: Shocking True Stories of Children Who Murdered Their Parents. (Illus.). 304p. 1993. mass mkt. 4.99 (0-312-95006-3) St Martin.

— Marcia Clark. 1995. pap. 5.99 (0-7860-0218-2) Kensgtn Pub Corp.

— Massacre at Waco: The Shocking True Story of Cult Leader David Koresh & the Branch Davidians. 1993. mass mkt. 4.99 (0-312-95226-0) St Martin.

— Poisoned Vows. 1995. mass mkt. 5.50 (0-312-95513-8, Pub. by Tor Bks) St Martin.

— Smooth Operator. LC 98-100897. (True Crime Library). 1997. mass mkt. 5.99 (0-312-96400-5, St Martins Paperbacks) St Martin.

— Vampire Killers, Vol. 1. LC 98-217133. 1998. 6.50 (0-312-96672-5, Pub. by Tor Bks) St Martin.

Linedecker, Clifford L. & Osanka, Frank M. Deadly Obsessions. 352p. 1995. mass mkt. 4.99 (0-8217-0112-6, Zebra Kensgtn) Kensgtn Pub Corp.

***Linehan, Fergus.** The Safest Place LC 99-190915. 261 p. 1998. write for info. (1-86059-088-8) Roberts Rinehart.

Linehan, John C. The Irish Scots & the "Scotch-Irish" LC 98-117889. 138p. 1998. reprint ed. pap. 15.00 (0-7884-0788-0, L352) Heritage Bk.

***Linehan, Margaret.** Senior Female International Managers: Why So Few? LC 99-75558. 216p. 2000. text 69.95 (0-7546-1200-7, Pub. by Ashgate Pub) Ashgate Pub Co.

Linehan, Marsha M. Cognitive-Behavioral Treatment of Borderline Personality Disorder. LC 93-20483. (Diagnosis & Treatment of Mental Disorders Ser.). 558p. 1993. lib. bdg. 49.00 (0-89862-183-6) Guilford Pubns.

— Skills Training Manual for Treating Borderline Personality Disorder. LC 93-15216. (Diagnosis & Treatment of Mental Disorders Ser.). (Illus.). 180p. 1993. pap., student ed. 29.00 (0-89862-034-1) Guilford Pubns.

Linehan, Patricia & Landreth, Patrick. Mayas. deluxe ed. 160p. 1995. 25.00 (0-614-04527-4) Donald R Hoflin.

Linehan, Peter. The Ladies of Zamora. LC 96-41252. (Illus.). 208p. 1997. 35.00 (0-271-01682-5) Pa St U Pr.

— The Ladies of Zamora. (Illus.). 208p. 1999. pap. 18.95 (0-271-01835-6) Pa St U Pr.

— Past & Present in Medieval Spain. (Collected Studies: No. CS384). 360p. 1992. 115.95 (0-86078-341-3, Pub. by Variorum) Ashgate Pub Co.

Linehan, Thomas P. East London for Mosley: The Membership & Branches of the British Union of Fascists in East London & South-West Essex, 1933-40. LC 96-18660. 256p. 1996. 57.50 (0-7146-4568-0, Pub. by F Cass Pubs); pap. 26.50 (0-7146-4268-1, Pub. by F Cass Pubs) Intl Spec Bk.

Linehard, Marc, jt. ed. see Krieger, Christian.

Linek, V., et al. Measurement of Oxygen by Membrane-Covered Probes. (Analytical Chemistry Ser.). 328p. 1988. text 92.00 (0-470-21061-3) P-H.

Linek, Wayne M. & Sturtevant, Elizabeth G., eds. Exploring Literacy: The Nineteenth Yearbook of the College Reading Association 1997. 300p. (Orig.). (C). 1997. pap. text 20.00 (1-883604-03-6) Coll Read Assn.

— Generations of Literacy: The Seventeenth Yearbook of the College Reading Association 1995. annuals (Reading & Literacy Education Ser.). 325p. (Orig.). (C). 1995. pap. 15.00 (1-883604-00-1) Coll Read Assn.

— Growing Literacy: The Eighteenth Yearbook of the College Reading Association 1996. 325p. (Orig.). 1996. pap. 15.00 (1-883604-02-8) Coll Read Assn.

Lineker & Hey. Gary Linker's Golden Boots. (Illus.). (J). text 40.00 (0-340-70846-8, Pub. by Hodder & Stought Ltd) Trafalgar.

Lineker, Gary. The Young Soccer Player. LC 93-41145. (Illus.). 32p. (J). (gr. 2-6). 1994. 9.95 (1-56458-592-1) DK Pub Inc.

***Lineker, Gary.** Young Soccer Player. (Young Enthusiast Ser.). (Illus.). (J). (gr. 3). 2000. 9.95 (0-7894-5425-4) DK Pub Inc.

Linell, Per. Approaching Dialogue: Talk, Interaction & Contexts in Dialogical Perspectives. LC 98-39787. (Impact: Studies in Language & Society: No. 3). xvii, 322p. 1998. 85.00 (1-55619-852-3) J Benjamins Pubng Co.

Linell, Per, jt. ed. see Bergmann, Jorg R.

Lineman, Rose. Eclipse Interpretation Manual. 147p. 1986. 16.00 (0-86690-301-1, L2356-014) Am Fed Astrologers.

— Eclipses: Astrological Guideposts. LC 83-72326. 128p. 1984. 16.00 (0-86690-258-9, L2403-014) Am Fed Astrologers.

Lineman, Rose & Popelka, Jan. The Compendium of Astrology. LC 83-63067. 304p. 1993. pap. 24.95 (0-914918-43-5, Whitford) Schiffer.

Linenger, Jerry M. Off the Planet: Surviving Five Perilous Months Aboard the Space Station Mir. LC 99-31203. (Illus.). 256p. 1999. 22.50 (1-55972-516-8, Birch Ln Pr) Carol Pub Group.

***Linenger, Jerry M.** Off the Planet: Surviving Five Perilous Months Aboard the Space Station Mir. (Illus.). 256p. 1999. 24.95 (0-07-136112-X) McGraw.

Linenthal, Amy, jt. ed. see Sharp, Robert V.

Linenthal, Arthur J. First A Dream: The History of Boston's Jewish Hospitals, 1896-1928. LC 90-82277. (Illus.). xxii, 727p. 1990. 33.00 (0-9626606-0-4) A J Linenthal.

— Two Academic Lives: George Herbert Palmer & Alice Freeman Palmer a Compilation. LC 94-96814. (Illus.). 630p. 1995. 25.00 (0-9626606-1-2) A J Linenthal.

Linenthal, Edward T. Changing Images of the Warrior Hero in America: A History of Popular Symbolism. LC 82-22885. (Studies in American Religion: Vol. 6). 296p. 1983. lib. bdg. 89.95 (0-88946-921-0) E Mellen.

— Sacred Ground: Americans & Their Battlefields. 2nd ed. (Illus.). 320p. 1991. text 34.95 (0-252-01783-8) U of Ill Pr.

— Sacred Ground: Americans & Their Battlefields. 2nd ed. LC 93-23925. (Illus.). 320p. 1993. 24.95 (0-252-06171-3) U of Ill Pr.

— Symbolic Defense: The Cultural Significance of the Strategic Defense Initiative. LC 88-32111. (Illus.). 176p. 1989. text 21.95 (0-252-01619-X) U of Ill Pr.

— Symbolic Defense: The Cultural Significance of the Strategic Defense Initiative. fac. ed. LC 88-32111. (Illus.). 160p. 1989. reprint ed. pap. 49.60 (0-7837-8076-1, 204782900008) Bks Demand.

Linenthal, Edward T., jt. ed. see Chidester, David.

Linenthal, Mark. The Man I Am Watching. 1987. pap. 5.95 (0-938979-02-7) EG Bksellers.

***Linenthal, Peter.** Indonesian Folk Motifs. LC 97-48770. (Pictorial Archives Ser.). 48p. 1998. pap. 5.95 (0-486-40040-9) Dover.

Linenthal, Peter. Masks Book. 1999. pap. 12.99 (0-525-45837-9) NAL.

— Russian Folk Motifs. LC 98-34138. (Illus.). 48p. 1998. pap. text 5.95 (0-486-40275-4) Dover.

Liner. Scientific & Common Names for the Amphibians & Reptiles of Mexico. 1994. pap. write for info. (0-916984-32-X) SSAR.

Liner, Amon. The Far Journey & Final End of Dr. Faustwitz, Spaceman, Vol. II. 200p. (Orig.). 1988. pap. 10.00 (0-932112-19-6) Carolina Wren.

— Rose, a Color of Darkness. 100p. (Orig.). 1981. pap. 5.00 (0-932112-09-9) Carolina Wren.

Liner, Charles D., ed. State & Local Government Relations in North Carolina: Their Evolution & Current Status. 2nd ed. LC 95-219399. 251p. (C). 1995. pap. text 30.00 (1-56011-244-1) Institute Government.

***Liner, Christopher L.** Elements of 3-D Seismology. LC 99-37449. 1999. 79.95 (0-87814-768-3) PennWell Bks.

Liner, E. Blaine, ed. Compacts & Coalitions in Metropolitan Governance. fac. ed. LC JS0348.C65. (Lincoln Institute of Land Policy Monograph: No. 86-6). 54p. 1986. reprint ed. pap. 30.00 (0-7837-7825-2, 204758100007) Bks Demand.

— A Decade of Devolution: Perspectives on State & Local Relations. LC 89-31871. (Illus.). 260p. (Orig.). 1989. pap. text 35.50 (0-87766-463-3) Urban Inst.

— Intergovernmental Land Management Innovations. 57p. 1985. 12.00 (0-317-01540-0) Fla Atlantic.

— Intergovernmental Land Management Innovations. LC HD1261.I67. (Lincoln Institute of Land Policy Monograph: No. 85-7). 67p. reprint ed. pap. 30.00 (0-7837-5760-3, 204542200006) Bks Demand.

— Local Agenda Setting Processes. fac. ed. LC JF1525.D4L63. (Lincoln Institute of Land Policy Monograph: No. 85-10). 61p. 1985. reprint ed. pap. 30.00 (0-7837-7827-9, 204758300007) Bks Demand.

Liner, Tom & Butler, Deborah. Rooms to Grow: Natural Language Arts in the Middle School. LC 93-74700. (Illus.). 456p. (C). 1995. per. 27.95 (0-89089-577-5) Carolina Acad Pr.

Liner, Tom, jt. auth. see Butler, Deborah A.

Linerode, Darla. An Introduction to Art. (Illus.). 18p. (Orig.). 1991. pap. text 49.50 (1-56762-329-8) Modern Learn Pr.

— An Introduction to Art. (Illus.). (Orig.). (J). (gr. 3-6). 1992. pap. 63.00 (0-935493-29-8) Modern Learn Pr.

— Let's Look at Art. (Illus.). (Orig.). (J). (gr. 1-6). 1992. pap. write for info. (0-935493-30-1) Modern Learn Pr.

— Let's Look at Art, 9 vols., Set. (Illus.). 168p. (Orig.). pap. text 410.00 (1-56762-044-2) Modern Learn Pr.

— Let's Look at Faces. (Illus.). 18p. 1991. pap. text 49.50 (1-56762-042-6) Modern Learn Pr.

— Let's Look at Landscapes. (Illus.). 18p. 1991. pap. text 49.50 (1-56762-043-4) Modern Learn Pr.

— Let's Look at Line. (Illus.). 18p. 1991. pap. text 49.50 (1-56762-039-6) Modern Learn Pr.

— Let's Look at Portraits. (Illus.). 18p. 1991. pap. text 49.50 (1-56762-041-8) Modern Learn Pr.

— Let's Look at Transportation. (Illus.). 18p. 1991. pap. text 49.50 (1-56762-040-X) Modern Learn Pr.

Lines, Anni M. Vitamins & Minerals: The Health Connection. LC 85-7638. 188p. 1985. pap. 6.95 (0-932090-14-1) Health Plus.

Lines, Anni M., jt. auth. see Airola, Paavo O.

***Lines, David.** Jonathan Livingston Trafalger. (J). 1998. pap. 11.95 (0-09-927839-1, Pub. by Random) Trafalgar.

Lines, David. Power Supplies. 2nd ed. (Illus.). 124p. 1997. pap. 19.95 (0-7906-1120-1) Prompt Publns.

Lines, Eliza J. Bethany & Its Hills: Glimpses of the Town of Bethany As It Was Before the Railroads & the Fire... (Illus.). 65p. 1997. reprint ed. pap. 13.00 (0-8328-5624-X) Higginson Bk Co.

Lines, Kathleen. Lavender's Blue. (Illus.). 180p. (J). (ps-7). 1990. pap. 15.00 (0-19-272208-5) OUP.

Lines, Kathleen, ed. The Faber Book of Greek Legends. (Illus.). 268p. (J). (gr. 4 up). 1973. pap. 13.00 (0-571-13920-5) Faber & Faber.

Lines, Larry, ed. see Klem-Musatov, Kamill.

Lines, Larry R., jt. auth. see Bording, Ralph Phillip.

Lines, Malcolm E. A Number for Your Thoughts: Facts & Speculations about Numbers from Euclid to the Latest Computers. LC 86-183277. (Illus.). 220p. 1986. pap. 26.00 (0-85274-495-1) IOP Pub.

Lines, Malcolm E. Think of a Number. (Illus.). 172p. 1990. pap. 26.00 (0-85274-183-9) IOP Pub.

Lines, Malcom E. On the Shoulders of Giants. (Illus.). 296p. 1994. 110.00 (0-7503-0104-X); pap. 34.00 (0-7503-0103-1) IOP Pub.

Lines, Marianna. Sacred Stones, Sacred Places. (Illus.). 128p. (C). 1991. text 95.00 (0-7855-6550-7, Pub. by St Andrew) St Mut.

— Sacred Stones, Sacred Places. (Illus.). 160p. (C). 1992. 65.00 (0-7855-6813-1, Pub. by St Andrew) St Mut.

— Sacred Stones, Sacred Places. (Illus.). 176p. 1993. 39.90 (0-7152-0652-4, Pub. by St Andrew) St Mut.

Lines, Richard & Hellstrom, Lief. Frog Model Aircraft, 1932-1976: The Complete History of the Flying Aircraft & the Plastic Kits. (Illus.). 272p. 1989. 50.00 (0-904568-63-6) Pincushion Pr.

Lines, Timothy A. Functional Images of the Religious Educator. 540p. (Orig.). 1992. pap. 25.95 (0-89135-087-X) Religious Educ.

— Systemic Religious Education. LC 86-20383. 264p. (Orig.). 1987. pap. 24.95 (0-89135-057-8) Religious Educ.

Lines, William J. An All Consuming Passion: Origins, Modernity, & the Australian Life of Georgiana Molloy. LC 95-41403. (Illus.). 398p. (C). 1996. pap. 16.95 (0-520-20422-0, Pub. by U CA Pr) Cal Prin Full Svc.

— False Economy: Australia in the 20th Century. 1998. pap. 22.95 (1-86368-209-0, Pub. by Fremantle Arts) Intl Spec Bk.

— Taming the Great South Land: A History of the Conquest of Nature in Australia. 1992. 42.50 (0-520-07830-6, Pub. by U CA Pr) Cal Prin Full Svc.

— Taming the Great South Land: A History of the Conquest of Nature in Australia. LC 98-32383. (Illus.). 375p. 1999. pap. 18.95 (0-8203-2056-0) U of Ga Pr.

***Linesch, Debra.** Celebrating Family Milestones: By Making Art Together. (Illus.). 112p. 2000. pap. 18.95 (1-55209-505-3) Firefly Bks Ltd.

Linesch, Debra G. Adolescent Art Therapy. LC 87-21866. 256p. 1988. text 37.95 (0-87630-486-2) Brunner-Mazel.

Linesch, Debra G., ed. Art Therapy with Families in Crisis: Overcoming Resistance Through Nonverbal Expression. LC 92-27839. (Illus.). 192p. 1993. text 29.95 (0-87630-638-5) Brunner-Mazel.

Linetsky, Michael, ed. Rabbi Abraham Ibn Ezra's Commentary on the Creation. LC 97-23850. 176p. 1998. 30.00 (0-7657-9982-0) Aronson.

Linetsky, Michael, jt. auth. see ben Joseph, Sa'adia.

***Linett, Deena.** Rare Earths. 96p. 2001. pap. 12.50 (1-880238-99-3) BOA Edns.

Lineweaver, C. H., et al, eds. The Cosmic Microwave Background: Proceedings of the NATO Advanced Study Institute on the Cosmological Background Radiation, Strasbourg, France, May27-June 7, 1996. LC 97-42013. (NATO Advanced Science Institutes Ser.: No. 502). 484p. 1997. text 240.50 (0-7923-4815-X) Kluwer Academic.

Lineweber, David C., ed. The Industrial Customer: A Special Issue of Energy Services Journal, Vol. 2, No. 1. 64p. 1996. pap. 20.00 (0-8058-9922-7) L Erlbaum Assocs.

Linfert, Carl. Bosch. (Masters of Art Ser.). (Illus.). 128p. 1989. 24.95 (0-8109-0719-4, Pub. by Abrams) Time Warner.

Linffors, Bernth, jt. ed. see Sander, Reinhard W.

Linfield, Eva, ed. see Buxtehude, Dieterich.

Linfield, George & Penny, John. Numerical Methods Using MATLAB. 250p. 1995. pap. 50.00 (0-13-030966-4) P-H.

Linfield, J. & Krevisky, J. Words of Love: Romantic Quotations from Plato to Madonna. LC 96-48094. 1996. pap. 18.00 (0-679-77719-9) Random Ref & Info.

Linfield, Jordan L. & Kay, Joe. Your Mother Wears Army Boots! A Treasure Trove of Insults, Slurs & Putdowns. 288p. (Orig.). 1992. pap. 9.00 (0-380-76591-8, Avon Bks) Morrow Avon.

Linfield, Jordan L., jt. auth. see Krevisky, Joseph.

Linfield, Michael. Freedom under Fire: U. S. Civil Liberties in Times of War. 282p. (C). 1990. 40.00 (0-89608-375-6); pap. 14.00 (0-89608-374-8) South End Pr.

Linfield, Rachel Sparks, jt. auth. see Warwick, Paul.

Linfield, Robert F. Telecommunications: Present Status & Future Trends. LC 94-31267. (Advanced Computing & Telecommunications Ser.). (Illus.). 169p. 1995. 42.00 (0-8155-1368-2) Noyes.

Linfield, Warner A., ed. Anionic Surfactants, Pt. 1. LC 75-22777. (Surfactant Science Ser.: No. 7). (Illus.). 328p. reprint ed. pap. 101.70 (0-8357-5490-1, 203299000082) Bks Demand.

Linfoot, Ken, ed. Communication Strategies for People with Developmental Disabilities: Issues from Theory & Practice. LC 93-50222. 208p. 1994. 37.00 (1-55766-170-7, Pub. by MacLennan & Petty) P H Brookes.

Linford, Jenny. Writing about Food. pap. write for info. (0-7136-4216-5, Pub. by A & C Blk) Midpt Trade.

Linford, John. Planned Community Living: Handbook for California Homeowners Associations. LC 96-96606. 309p. (Orig.). 1996. pap. 19.95 (0-9652973-0-6) BenchMark Ent.

Linford, Laurance D. Archaeological Investigations in West-Central Arizona: The Cyprus-Bagdad Project. (Archaeological Ser.: No. 136). (Illus.). 220p. 1979. pap. 9.95 (1-889747-10-6) Ariz St Mus.

***Linford, Laurance D.** Navajo Places: History, Legend, Landscape. 314p. 2000. 60.00 (0-87480-623-2) U of Utah Pr.

— Navajo Places: History, Legend, Landscape. LC 99-53553. (Illus.). 314p. 2000. pap. 24.95 (0-87480-624-0) U of Utah Pr.

Linford, Marilynne T. Give Mom a Standing Ovation. 1996. pap. 9.95 (1-57008-237-5) Bookcraft Inc.

***Linford, Monica.** Awaken Your Body, Balance Your Mind: Perfect Health Using the Chi Ball Method. (Illus.). 2000. pap. 18.95 (0-7225-3993-2, Pub. by Thorsons PA) HarpC.

Linfors, Bernth, ed. Black African Literature in English, 1977-1981. LC 86-1021. 412p. 1986. 45.00 (0-8419-0962-8, Africana) Holmes & Meier.

Linforth, Ivan M. The Arts of Orpheus. LC 72-9296. (Philosophy of Plato & Aristotle Ser.). 1977. reprint ed. 35.95 (0-405-04847-5) Ayer.

Ling. Advanced Physics. 1995. pap. text. write for info. (0-582-35596-6, Pub. by Addison-Wesley) Longman.

— Flood Water. large type ed. 1995. 11.50 (0-7505-0757-8, Pub. by Mgna Lrg Print) Ulverscroft.

— History of Religion East & West. 1997. text 23.95 (0-333-10172-3, Pub. by Macmillan) St Martin.

***Ling.** Study Guide for Obstetrics & Gynecology. 1999. pap. text 55.00 (0-8385-8683-X) Appleton & Lange.

Ling, Agnes H., jt. auth. see Ling, Daniel.

Ling, Alex. Twilight of the White Rajahs. LC 98-945636. xxiv, 444 p. 1997. write for info. (981-00-8938-4) AgBe Pub.

Ling, Amy. Between Worlds: Women Writers of Chinese Ancestry. (Athene Ser.). 292p. 1990. text 37.50 (0-08-037464-6, Pub. by PPI); pap. text 16.95 (0-08-037463-8, Pub. by PPI) Elsevier.

Ling, Amy, ed. Yellow Light: The Flowering of Asian American Arts. LC 98-29511. (Asian American History & Culture Ser.). (Illus.). 448p. 1999. 44.50 (1 56639 670 0) Temple U Pr.

***Ling, Amy, ed.** Yellow Light: The Flowering of Asian American Arts. (Asian American History & Culture Ser.). (Illus.). 384p. 2000. pap. 22.95 (1-56639-817-7) Temple U Pr.

Ling, Amy, jt. ed. see Brown, Wesley.

Ling, Amy, jt. ed. see Geok-Lin Lim, Shirley.

Ling, Amy, ed. see Sui Sin Far.

Ling, Amy, jt. ed. see White-Parks, Annette.

Ling, Barbara. The Internet Recruiting Edge: Finding, Attracting & Networking Quality Candidates. (Illus.). x, 260p. 1998. ring bd. 149.00 (0-9663452-0-7) Lingstar.

***Ling, Barbara.** The Internet Recruiting Edge: Finding, Attracting & Networking with Quality Candidates, 2 vols. 4th rev. ed. 430p. 2000. 197.00 (0-9663452-5-8) Lingstar.

— Poor Richard's Internet Recruiting: How to Promote Yourself, Your Business, Your Ideas Online. 400p. 2000. pap. 29.95 (1-930082-01-0, Pub. by Top Floor Pub) IPG Chicago.

Ling, Barbara. The Real Estate Pro's Internet Edge - Agent's Edition: Maximizing Your Business on the World Wide Web. (Internet Edge Ser.). (Illus.). 270p. 1999. ring bd. 149.00 (0-9663452-1-5) Lingstar.

— The Real Estate Pro's Internet Edge - Broker's Edition: Maximizing Your Business on the World Wide Web. (Internet Edge Ser.). (Illus.). 370p. 1999. ring bd. 495.00 (0-9663452-2-3) Lingstar.

Ling, Bettina. Aung San Suu Kyi: Standing up for Democracy in Burma. LC 98-44109. 112p. 1998. pap. text 9.95 (1-55861-197-5, Pub. by Feminist Pr) Consort Bk Sales.

— Aung San Suu Kyi: Standing up for Democracy in Burma. LC 98-44109. 1999. 19.95 (1-55861-196-7, Pub. by Feminist Pr) Consort Bk Sales.

— The Fattest, Tallest, Biggest Snowman Ever. LC 96-20478. (Hello Math Reader Ser.). (Illus.). (J). 1997. 3.50 (0-590-97284-7) Scholastic Inc.

Ling, Bettina. The Fattest, Tallest, Biggest Snowman Ever. (Hello, Reader! Ser.). 1997. 8.70 (0-606-11315-0, Pub. by Turtleback) Demco.

Ling, Bettina. Jose Canseco. (J). (gr. 4-8). 1996. pap. 5.95 (0-8114-9790-9) Raintree Steck-V.

— Jose Canseco. (Contemporary Hispanic Americans Ser.). (Illus.). 48p. (J). (gr. 4-8). 1996. lib. bdg. 24.26 (0-8172-3983-9) Raintree Steck-V.

— Jose Canseco. large type ed. 54p. (J). (gr. 4-8). pap. 13.50 (0-614-20572-7, L-86293-00 APHB) Am Printing Hse.

— Lemonade for Sale. LC 97-31370. (Real Kids Readers Ser.). (Illus.). 48p. (J). (gr. 1-3). 1998. pap. 3.99 (0-7613-2035-0); lib. bdg. 17.90 (0-7613-2010-5) Millbrook Pr.

— The Little Mermaid: Flounder to the Rescue. LC PZ7.L66245Dl 1997. (Disney Chapters Ser.). (Illus.). 64p. (J). (gr. 2-4). 1997. pap. 3.50 (0-7868-4139-7, Pub. by Disney Pr) Time Warner.

— Maya Lin. LC 96-45935. (Contemporary Asian Americans Ser.). (Illus.). 48p. (J). 1997. lib. bdg. 24.26 (0-8172-3992-8) Raintree Steck-V.

— Where's Flit, Level 1. LC 96-85712. (Disney's First Readers Ser.). (Illus.). 24p. (J). (gr. k-1). 1997. pap. 2.95 (0-7868-4075-7, Pub. by Disney Pr) Time Warner.

Ling, Bettina & Buscher, Sarah. Mairead Corrigan & Betty Williams: Making Peace in Northern Ireland. LC 98-774. 112p. (YA). (gr. 7 up). 1999. 19.95 (1-55861-200-9, Pub. by Feminist Pr); pap. 9.95 (1-55861-201-7, Pub. by Feminist Pr) Consort Bk Sales.

Ling, C. Clifton, et al, eds. Computed Tomography in Radiation Therapy. LC 81-48496. 284p. 1983. reprint ed. pap. 88.10 (0-608-04737-6, 206545800004) Bks Demand.

***Ling-chi, Wang.** The Little Phoenix. 2000. pap. 13.95 (0-533-13296-7) Vantage.

Ling-chi, Wang & Gungwu, Wang, eds. The Chinese Diaspora: Selected Essays, Vol. 1. 304p. 1998. 39.00 (981-210-092-X) Intl Spec Bk.

— The Chinese Diaspora: Selected Essays, Vol. 2. LC 99-912479. 312p. 1998. 39.00 (981-210-093-8) Intl Spec Bk.

Ling Chung, ed. see Li-Ching-Chao.

Ling, Cindy. Case Management Handbook. 250p. (C). 1999. ring bd. 99.95 (1-56930-080-1) Skidmore Roth Pub.

Ling, Curtis C. An Integrated 94GHz Monopulse Tracking Receiver. LC TK7871.6. (University of Michigan Reports: No. RL900). 188p. reprint ed. pap. 58.30 (0-7837-6782-X, 204661200003) Bks Demand.

Ling, Cyril C., jt. auth. see Hilgert, Raymond L.

Ling, Daniel. Cumulative Record of Speech Skill Acquisition. LC 77-93949. 1977. pap. text 12.50 (0-88200-115-9, A1983) Alexander Graham.

— Speech & the Hearing Impaired Child: Theory & Practice. LC 76-21920. (Illus.). 1976. text 27.95 (0-88200-074-8, A0669) Alexander Graham.

— Teacher-Clinician Planbook & Guide to the Development of Speech Skills. LC 77-93949. 1978. pap. text 12.50 (0-88200-116-7, A2092) Alexander Graham.

Ling, Daniel & Ling, Agnes H. Aural Habilitation: The Foundations of Verbal Learning in Hearing-Impaired Children. LC 78-56077. 1978. pap. text 26.95 (0-88200-121-3, C2441) Alexander Graham.

— Basic Vocabulary & Language Thesaurus for Hearing-Impaired Children. LC 76-52826. 1977. 11.50 (0-88200-078-0, C1437) Alexander Graham.

Ling, Ding. I Myself Am a Woman: Selected Writings of Ding Ling. Barlow, Tani E., ed. Bjorge, Gary, ed. & tr. by. from CHI. LC 88-43313. (Asian Voices Ser.). 364p. 1990. reprint ed. pap. 19.00 (0-8070-6747-4) Beacon Pr.

Ling, Dorothy. The Original Art of Music. LC 88-19117. 190p. 1990. 38.50 (0-8191-7117-4); pap. 20.00 (0-8191-7118-2) U Pr of Amer.

Ling, Dwight L. Tunisia: From Protectorate to Republic. LC 67-63013. (Indiana University International Studies). (Illus.). 284p. reprint ed. pap. 88.10 (0-608-11802-8, 205523200011) Bks Demand.

Ling, Edwin R. One Family, Many Animals. LC 88-18580. 166p. 1988. 13.75 (0-930950-21-6); pap. 8.75 (0-930950-22-4) Nopoly Pr.

Ling, Evan, ed. see Metallurgical Society of AIME Staff.

Ling, Evelyn R. Archives in the Church or Synagogue Library. LC 81-7650. (Guide Ser.: No. 10). 20p. 1996. pap. 8.25 (0-915324-18-0) CSLA.

Ling, F. F., ed. see Berthelot, Jean M. & Cole, J. M.

Ling, F. F., ed. see Costello, George A.

Ling, F. F., ed. see Fischer-Cripps, Anthony C.

Ling, F. F., ed. see Gawronski, Wodek K.

Ling, F. F., ed. see Kaviany, Massoud.

Ling, F. F., ed. see Ladeveze, P. & Simmonds, J. G.

Ling, F. F., ed. see Madhusudana, C. V.

Ling, F. F., ed. see Miannay, D. P.

Ling, F. F., ed. see Shabana, A. A.

Ling, F. F., ed. see Yu, Yi-Yuan.

Ling, Frank & Duff, Patrick. Obstetrics & Gynecology: Principles for Practice. (C). 2000. 135.00 (0-8385-7201-4) Appleton & Lange.

— Pocket Guide to Obstetrics & Gynecology. (C). 2000. 30.00 (0-8385-8134-X) Appleton & Lange.

Ling, Frank W. & Laube. Comprehensive Gynecology Review. 3rd ed. LC 97-163936. (Illus.). 288p. (C). (gr. 13). 1997. pap. text 33.95 (0-8151-5512-3, 28451) Mosby Inc.

Ling, Frank W., et al. Primary Care in Gynecology. LC 95-42303. (Illus.). 512p. 1996. 75.00 (0-683-05057-5) Lppncott W & W.

Ling, Frank W., jt. auth. see Smith, Roger P.

Ling, Frank W., jt. auth. see Stovall, Thomas G.

Ling, Frederick F. Surface Mechanics. LC 72-10012. 336p. reprint ed. pap. 104.20 (0-608-11655-6, 200649200059) Bks Demand.

Ling, Frederick F., ed. Springer Texts in Mechanical Engineering. 1991. text. write for info. (0-318-68929-4) Spr-Verlag.

Ling, Frederick F. & Pan, C. H., eds. Approaches to Modeling of Friction & Wear. (Illus.). xiii, 173p. 1987. 98.95 (0-387-96656-0) Spr-Verlag.

Ling, Frederick F., et al. Boundary Lubrication: An Appraisal of World Literature. LC 70-79165. 586p. reprint ed. pap. 181.70 (0-8357-7367-1, 201684700006) Bks Demand.

Ling, Frederick F., ed. see American Society of Mechanical Engineers Staff.

Ling, Frederick F., ed. see Chryssolouris, G. & Sheng, P.

Ling, Frederick F., ed. see Costello, G. A.

Ling, Frederick F., ed. see DeVries, W. R.

Ling, Frederick F., ed. see Kuznetsov, E. N.

Ling, Frederick F., ed. see Miu, Denny K.

Ling, Georgia Curtis. What's in the Bible for... Women. Richards, Larry, ed. (What's in the Bible for... Ser.). 258p. 2000. pap. 16.95 (1-892016-10-9, Pub. by Starburst) Natl Bk Netwk.

Ling, Gerald V. Lower Urinary Tract Diseases of Dogs & Cats. LC 94-41538. (Illus.). 256p. (C). (gr. 13). 1995. text 90.00 (0-8151-5446-1, 23970) Mosby Inc.

Ling, Gilbert N. In Search of the Physical Basis of Life. LC 83-26919. 822p. 1984. 150.00 (0-306-41409-0, Plenum Trade) Perseus Pubng.

— A Revolution in the Physiology of the Living Cell & Beyond. LC 89-11068. 404p. 1992. lib. bdg. 64.50 (0-89464-398-3) Krieger.

Ling, H., ed. see Symposium on Materials & Processes for Wireless Co, et al.

***Ling, H. U. & Tyler, Peter A.** Australian Freshwater Algae (Exclusive of Diatoms) (Bibliotheca Phycologica Ser.: Vol. 105). (Illus.). xii, 644p. 2000. 102.59 (3-443-60032-8, Pub. by Gebruder Borntraeger) Balogh.

Ling-hin, Li. Appraisal Development in Hong Kong. LC 98-111591. 1997. pap. text 39.50 (962-201-776-2, Pub. by Chinese Univ) U of Mich Pr.

Ling-hsia Yeh. Practical Chinese Reader II: Patterns & Exercises, Simplified Character Edition. expanded ed. (C & T Asian Language Ser.). 171p. (Orig.). (C). 1995. pap. text, student ed. 14.95 (0-88727-208-8) Cheng & Tsui.

— Practical Chinese Reader II: Patterns & Exercises, Traditional Character Edition. expanded rev. ed. LC 93-74711. (C & T Asian Language Ser.). 171p. (Orig.). (C). 1995. pap., student ed. 14.95 (0-88727-200-2) Cheng & Tsui.

Ling, Hsin Yi, see Yi Ling, Hsin.

Ling, Hung C., et al, eds. Materials in Microelectronic & Optoelectronic Packaging. LC 93-11050. (Ceramic Transactions Ser.: Vol. 33). 471p. 1993. 74.00 (0-944904-63-7, CT033) Am Ceramic.

Ling, Huping. Surviving on the Gold Mountain: A History of Chinese American Women & Their Lives. LC 97-50217. (Illus.). 256p. (C). 1998. text 59.50 (0-7914-3863-5); pap. text 19.95 (0-7914-3864-3) State U NY Pr.

Ling, Jan. A History of European Folk Music. Schenck, Linda & Schenck, Robert, trs. from SWE. LC 97-1136. (Illus.). 256p. 1998. 50.00 (1-878822-77-2) Univ Rochester Pr.

Ling, Jinqi. Rereading Cultural Nationalism: Transformative Interventions in Asian American Literature, 1957-1980. LC 97-34558. (Illus.). 224p. 1998. text 45.00 (0-19-511116-8) OUP.

Ling, Josh. Star Wars: The Action Figure Archives. Sansweet, Stephen J., ed. LC 98-26349. (Star Wars Ser.). (Illus.). 184p. 1999. pap. 29.95 (0-8118-2279-6) Chronicle Bks.

Ling, Josh, jt. auth. see Windham, Ryder.

Ling, Julius. Guiding Stars. LC 99-22132. (Illus.). 370p. 1999. 19.95 (1-58141-031-X) Rivercross Pub.

Ling Lee, Theresa M. Politics & Truth: Political Theory & the Postmodernist Challenge. LC 97-3267. (SUNY Series in Political Theory). 243p. (C). 1997. text 54.50 (0-7914-3503-2) State U NY Pr.

Ling Li. Son of Heaven. Kwan, David, tr. from CHI. 672p. 1995. 16.95 (0-8351-3147-5) China Bks.

***Ling, Lincoln & Pierce, Renae.** WINsight: Nurturing Your Mind - Body - Spirit for Vitality, Fulfillment & Reality Based Self-Esteem. 360p. 2000. pap. 15.95 (0-9675753-9-7) V I A CA.

Ling, Linzho. Goldfish for Those Who Care. (Illus.). 32p. 1994. pap. 4.95 (0-7938-1378-6, B103) TFH Pubns.

Ling, Lorraine, jt. auth. see Burman, Eva.

Ling, M., ed. see Shabana, A. A.

L

Ling, Margaret S., jt. auth. see Humphris, Gerry.

Ling, Mary. Amazing Crocodiles & Reptiles. LC 90-19239. (Eyewitness Juniors Ser.: No. 10). (Illus.). 32p. (J). (ps-3). 1991. pap. 9.99 (*0-679-80689-X*, Pub. by Knopf Bks Yng Read) Random.

— Amazing Crocodiles & Reptiles. LC 90-19239. (Eyewitness Juniors Ser.: No. 10). (Illus.). 32p. (J). (ps-3). 1991. lib. bdg. 11.99 (*0-679-90689-4*, Pub. by Knopf Bks Yng Read) Random.

Ling, Mary. Amazing Crocodiles & Reptiles. (Eyewitness Juniors Ser.: No. 10). (J). (ps-3). 1991. 15.19 (*0-606-04862-6*, Pub. by Turtleback) Demco.

Ling, Mary. Amazing Fish. LC 90-49651. (Eyewitness Juniors Ser.: No. 11). (Illus.). 32p. (J). (ps-3). 1991. pap. 9.99 (*0-679-81516-3*, Pub. by Knopf Bks Yng Read) Random.

— Amazing Fish. LC 90-49651. (Eyewitness Juniors Ser.: No. 11). (Illus.). 32p. (J). (ps-3). 1991. lib. bdg. 11.99 (*0-679-91516-8*, Pub. by Knopf Bks Yng Read) Random.

Ling, Mary. Amazing Fish. (Eyewitness Juniors Ser.: No. 11). (J). (ps-3). 1991. 13.19 (*0-606-04863-4*, Pub. by Turtleback) Demco.

Ling, Mary. Amazing Wolves, Dogs, & Foxes. LC 91-6514. (Eyewitness Juniors Ser.: No. 16). (Illus.). 32p. (J). (ps-3). 1991. pap. 9.99 (*0-679-81521-X*, Pub. by Knopf Bks Yng Read); lib. bdg. 11.99 (*0-679-91521-4*, Pub. by Knopf Bks Yng Read) Random.

— Amazing Wolves, Dogs, & Foxes. (Eyewitness Juniors Ser.: No. 16). (J). (ps-3). 1991. 15.19 (*0-606-00270-7*, Pub. by Turtleback) Demco.

— Butterfly. LC 92-52808. (See How They Grow Ser.). (Illus.). 16p. (J). (ps-1). 1992. 9.95 (*1-56458-112-8*) DK Pub Inc.

— Calf. LC 92-53486. (See How They Grow Ser.). (Illus.). 16p. (J). (ps-1). 1993. 9.95 (*1-56458-205-1*) DK Pub Inc.

— Foal. LC 92-52809. (See How They Grow Ser.). (Illus.). 16p. (J). (ps-1). 1992. 9.95 (*1-56458-113-6*) DK Pub Inc.

— Fox. LC 92-52810. (See How They Grow Ser.). (Illus.). 16p. (J). (ps-3). 1992. 9.95 (*1-56458-114-4*) DK Pub Inc.

— Giraffe. LC 93-3041. (See How They Grow Ser.). (Illus.). 16p. (J). (ps-1). 1993. 9.95 (*1-56458-311-2*) DK Pub Inc.

— Owl. LC 92-52811. (See How They Grow Ser.). (Illus.). 16p. (J). (ps-1). 1992. 19.95 (*1-56458-115-2*) DK Pub Inc.

— Penguin. LC 93-22105. (See How They Grow Ser.). (Illus.). 16p. (J). (ps-1). 1993. 9.95 (*1-56458-312-0*) DK Pub Inc.

— Pig. LC 92-53487. (See How They Grow Ser.). (Illus.). 16p. (J). (ps-1). 1993. 9.95 (*1-56458-204-3*) DK Pub Inc.

— Wild Animal Go-Round. (Illus.). 18p. (J). 1995. 12.95 (*0-7894-0213-0*, 5-70626) DK Pub Inc.

Ling, Nam. Specification & Verification of Systolic Arrays. 150p. 1999. 28.00 (*981-02-3867-3*) World Scientific Pub.

Ling, Oiki. The Changing Role of the British Protestant Missionaries in China, 1945-1952. LC 98-8766. 303 p. 1999. write for info. (*0-8386-3776-0*) Fairleigh Dickinson.

Ling, Ooi G. Town Councils in Singapore: Self-Determination for Public Housing Estates. (Institute for Policy Studies Occasional Papers: No. 4). 48p. 1990. 6.30 (*981-210-000-8*, Pub. by Times Academic) Intl Spec Bk.

Ling, Ooi G., ed. Environment & the City: Sharing Singapore's Experience & Future Challenges. LC 97-946363. 344p. 1997. pap. 27.50 (*981-210-080-6*, Pub. by Times Academic) Intl Spec Bk.

***Ling, Ooi Giok & Rajan, Ramkishen S., eds.** Singapore: The Year in Review 1998. 138p. 1999. pap. 10.90 (*981-210-147-0*, Pub. by Times Academic) Intl Spec Bk.

Ling, Peter. Crown Wars. 320p. 1996. 24.00 (*0-7278-4926-3*) Severn Hse.

— Halfway to Heaven. 592p. 1994. 25.95 (*1-85797-076-4*) Orion Pubng Grp.

— Happy Tomorrow. large type ed. (Magna Large Print Ser.). 580p. 1996. 27.99 (*0-7505-0944-9*, Pub. by Mgna Lrg Print) Ulverscroft.

— High Water. large type ed. 580p. 1995. 27.99 (*0-7505-0755-1*, Pub. by Mgna Lrg Print) Ulverscroft.

— Storm Water. large type ed. 1996. 11.50 (*0-7505-0756-X*, Pub. by Mgna Lrg Print) Ulverscroft.

***Ling, Peter J. & Monteith, Sharon.** Gender in the Civil Rights Movement LC 99-36955. (Reference Library of the Humanities). 1999. write for info. (*0-8153-3079-0*) Garland.

Ling, Qui G. & Kwok, Kenson. City & the State: Singapore's Built Environment Revisited. LC 97-214687. (Illus.). 256p. 1997. 32.00 (*0-19-588263-6*) OUP.

Ling Rein, Mei, et al, eds. Death & Dying: Who Decides. 4th rev. ed. (Information Plus Reference Ser.). (Illus.). 180p. 1998. pap. text 26.95 (*1-57302-074-5*) Info Plus TX.

Ling, Richard C. & Goddard, Walter E. Orchestrating Success: Improve Control of the Business with Sales & Operations Planning. LC 88-50483. 157p. 1988. 116.00 (*0-939246-11-2*) Wiley.

— Orchestrating Success: Improve Control of the Business with Sales & Operations Planning. 176p. 1995. 55.00 (*0-471-13227-6*) Wiley.

Ling, Robert V., jt. auth. see Farmer, Randolph W.

Ling, Roger. Ancient Mosaics. LC 98-66086. (Illus.). 144p. 1998. pap. 19.95 (*0-691-00404-8*, Pub. by Princeton U Pr) Cal Prin Full Svc.

— The Insula of the Menander at Pompeii: The Structures, Vol. 1. (The Structures Ser.). (Illus.). 412p. 1997. text 160.00 (*0-19-813409-6*) OUP.

— Roman Painting. (Illus.). 261p. (C). 1991. text 95.00 (*0-521-30614-0*); pap. text 34.95 (*0-521-31595-6*) Cambridge U Pr.

— Romano-British Wall Painting. (Archaeology Ser.: No. 42). (Illus.). 64p. 1989. pap. 10.50 (*0-85263-715-2*, Pub. by Shire Pubns) Parkwest Pubns.

— Stuccowork & Painting in Roman Italy. LC 99-12301. (Variorum Collected Studies). 251p. 1999. text 107.95 (*0-86078-786-9*, Pub. by Ashgate Pub) Ashgate Pub Co.

Ling, Roger, ed. Fifth International Colloquium on Ancient Mosaics: Held at Bath, England, on September 5-12, 1987. (JRA Supplementary Ser.: No. 9, Pt. 2). (FRE, GER & ITA., Illus.). 300p. 1995. 149.00 (*1-887829-00-8*) Jour Roman Arch.

Ling, Roger, et al, eds. Roman Art. (Pelican History of Art Ser.). (Illus.). 406p. (C). 1988. reprint ed. pap. 25.00 (*0-300-05293-6*) Yale U Pr.

Ling, Roger, jt. auth. see Strong, Donald.

Ling, Sally. Fund Raising with Golf: Organizing & Conducting a Successful Fund Raising Event. abr. ed. 90p. 1997. pap. 50.00 (*1-57701-042-6*) Natl Golf.

Ling, Shao-Wen. Aquaculture in Southeast Asia: A Historical Overview. Mumaw, Laura, ed. LC 77-3828. (Washington Sea Grant Ser.). (Illus.). 108p. 1977. pap. 10.00 (*0-295-95563-5*) U of Wash Pr.

Ling, Sheilah W. St. Anthony of Padua: Friend of All the World. 158p. 1994. pap. 30.00 (*0-85439-503-2*, Pub. by St Paul Pubns) St Mut.

— Saints Alive! 240p. (C). 1990. 17.50 (*0-85439-367-6*, Pub. by St Paul Pubns) St Mut.

— Your Glory Reflected: Twenty Outstanding Christians of the Twentieth Century. 288p. 1996. pap. 39.95 (*0-85439-457-5*, Pub. by St Paul Pubns) St Mut.

Ling, Shen, jt. auth. see Craze, Richard.

Ling, Tok W., et al, eds. Deductive & Object-Oriented Databases: Proceedings; Fourth International Conference, DOOD 95, Singapore, December 1995. LC 95-45666. (Lecture Notes in Computer Science Ser.: No. 1013). 558p. 1995. 87.00 (*3-540-60608-4*) Spr-Verlag.

Ling, Tok-Wang, ed. see International Conference on Database Systems for A.

Ling, Tom. The British State since 1945: An Introduction. LC 97-39510. 280p. (C). 1998. 57.95 (*0-7456-1140-0*, Pub. by Polity Pr); pap. 26.95 (*0-7456-1141-9*, Pub. by Polity Pr) Blackwell Pubs.

Ling, Trevor. Buddhism & Mythology of Evil: A Study in Theravada Buddhism. LC 97-221644. 180p. 1997. pap. 17.95 (*1-85168-132-9*, Pub. by Onewrld Pubns) Penguin Putnam.

— The Significance of Satan: New Testament Demonology & Its Contemporary Relevance. LC 79-8110. (Satanism Ser.). 120p. 1985. reprint ed. 21.50 (*0-404-18424-3*) AMS Pr.

Ling, Vivian. The Girl in Red: A Study Guide for the Film. 304p. 1994. pap. text 25.00 (*0-89264-116-9*) Ctr Chinese Studies.

— A Reader in Post-Cultural Revolution Chinese Literature. 3rd ed. 534p. (Orig.). (C). 1997. pap. text 29.95 (*962-201-607-3*, Pub. by Chinese Univ) U of Mich Pr.

— Under the Bridge: A Study Guide for the Film. 325p. 1994. pap. text 25.00 (*0-89264-113-4*) Ctr Chinese Studies.

Ling, Vivian & Dew, James E. Studying in China: A Practical Text for Spoken Chinese. LC 93-74518. 144p. 1993. pap. text 14.95 (*0-88727-196-0*) Cheng & Tsui.

***Ling, W. & Ram, S.** Conceptual Modeling - ER '98: 17th International Conference on Conceptual Modeling, Singapore, November 16-19, 1998, Proceedings. Lee, M. L., ed. LC 98-44477. 482p. 1998. pap. 69.00 (*3-540-65189-6*) Spr-Verlag.

Ling, Yang, jt. ed. see Chengxiang, Li.

Ling Yeouruenn. A New Compendium of Materials Medica (Pharmaceutical Botany & China Medicinal Plants) 292p. 1996. 69.00 (*7-03-003789-8*, Pub. by Sci Pr) Lubrecht & Cramer.

Ling-Yun, Nora, jt. auth. see Avril, Ellen.

Ling, Zhu & Zhongyi, Jiang. Public Works & Poverty Alleviation in Rural China. 237p. (C). 1996. lib. bdg. 95.00 (*1-56072-395-5*) Nova Sci Pubs.

Ling, Zhu, et al. Credit Systems for the Rural Poor in China. LC 97-196088. (C). 1997. lib. bdg. 85.00 (*1-56072-442-0*) Nova Sci Pubs.

Lingam, Lakshmi, ed. see Kali for Women Publishing Staff.

Lingam, S., jt. auth. see Hall, C. M.

LIngappa, B. T., jt. auth. see Lingappa, Yamuna.

***Lingappa, Vishwanath R.** Physiological Medicine. (Illus.). 550p. 1999. pap. text. write for info. (*0-07-038128-3*) McGraw-Hill HPD.

Lingappa, Yamuna & LIngappa, B. T. Wholesome Nutrition for Microflora Body: The Goal of Lacto-Vegetarianism (Recipes of Udipi Cuisine Included) 416p. 1992. pap. 14.99 (*0-9634999-0-4*) Ecobiol Fnd.

Lingard, Ann. Figure in a Landscape. large type ed. 576p. 31.50 (*0-7089-3705-5*) Ulverscroft.

Lingard, Bob, et al, eds. Schooling Reform in Hard Times. LC 92-38081. 324p. 1993. 99.95 (*0-7507-0119-6*, Falmer Pr); pap. 37.95 (*0-7507-0120-X*, Falmer Pr) Taylor & Francis.

***Lingard, Bob & Douglas, Peter.** Men Engaging Feminisms: Pro-Feminism, Backlashes & Schooling. LC 98-41548. (Feminist Education Thinking Ser.). 192p. 1999. pap. 28.95 (*0-335-19817-1*) OpUniv Pr.

Lingard, Bob & Douglas, Peter. Men Engaging Feminisms: Pro-Feminism, Backlashes & Schooling. LC 98-41548. 9p. 1999. 95.00 (*0-335-19818-X*) Taylor & Francis.

Lingard, J. Tom & the Tree House. (Illus.). (J). text 22.95 (*0-340-71663-0*, Pub. by Hodder & Stought Ltd) Trafalgar.

Lingard, James R. Corporate Rescues & Insolvencies. 2nd ed. 268p. 1989. boxed set 87.00 (*0-406-10601-0*, U.K., MICHIE) LEXIS Pub.

— Lingard: Bank Security Documents. 1993. write for info. (*0-406-00491-9*, LBSD3, MICHIE) LEXIS Pub.

— Tolley's Commercial Loan Agreements. 136p. 1990. 105.00 (*0-85459-453-1*, Pub. by Tolley Pubng) St Mut.

Lingard, Jeanette, compiled by. Diverse Lives: Contemporary Stories from Indonesia. 134p. (C). 1996. pap. 18.95 (*967-65-3100-6*) OUP.

***Lingard, Joan.** The Same Only Different. (Illus.). 32p. (J). (ps-1). 2000. pap. write for info. (*1-871512-64-6*) Glowworm Bks.

Lingard, Paul, et al. Metrowest, Time, Place & Possibility. LC 97-16065. 128p. 1997. 39.00 (*1-885352-62-X*) Community Comm.

Lingard, Tim, ed. see Marion, Dawn D.

Lingas, A., et al, eds. Automata, Languages & Programming: Proceedings of the 20th International Colloquium, ICALP 93, Lund, Sweden, July 5-9, 1993. (Lecture Notes in Computer Science Ser.: Vol. 700). vii, 697p. 1993. 102.95 (*0-387-56939-1*) Spr-Verlag.

Lingat, Robert. The Classic Law of India. Derrett, J. D., tr. from FRE. 323p. 1993. 43.50 (*81-215-0610-7*, Pub. by M Manoharial) Coronet Bks.

— The Classical Law of India. Derret, J. Duncan, tr. LC 99-158405. (Law in India Ser.). Orig. Title: Sources Du Droit Dans le Systeme Traditionnel De L'inde. (Illus.). 322p. 1998. reprint ed. pap. text 16.95 (*0-19-564535-9*) OUP.

Linge, Godfrey, ed. China's New Spatial Economy: Heading Towards 2020. 2nd ed. (Illus.). 248p. 1998. 62.00 (*0-19-587666-0*) OUP.

Linge, Godfrey J. Spatial Analysis, Industry & the Industrial Environment: Progress in Research & Applications, Regional Economies & Industrial Systems, Vol. 3. 2nd ed. Hamilton, F. E., ed. 272p. 1995. pap. text 30.95 (*0-471-10434-5*) Wiley.

Linge, Godfrey J., ed. Peripheralisation & Industrial Change Impacts on Nations, Regions, Firms, & People. 272p. (C). 1988. text 57.50 (*0-7099-4865-4*, Pub. by C Helm) Routldge.

Linge, Godfrey J. & Forbes, D. K., eds. China's Spatial Economy: Recent Developments & Reforms. (Illus.). 240p. 1991. text 49.95 (*0-19-585296-6*) OUP.

Linge, Godfrey J. & Van Der Knaap, G. A., eds. Labour, Environment & Industrial Change. 256p. 1989. 57.50 (*0-415-00928-6*) Routledge.

Linge, Godfrey J., jt. auth. see Porter, Doug.

Linge, Lars, ed. Cypern: I Historiens Spegel. (Aktuellt om Historia Ser.). (ENG & ITA., Illus.). 63p. 1997. pap. 27.50 (*91-7081-138-5*, Pub. by P Astroms) Coronet Bks.

Lingelbach, Jenepher. Before Life Hurries On. LC 98-51450. (Illus.). 43p. 1999. 16.95 (*0-87451-911-X*) U Pr of New Eng.

Lingelbach, Jenepher R., ed. Hands-on Nature: Information & Activities for Exploring the Environment with Children. LC 86-28268. (Illus.), 233p. 1987. pap. 19.95 (*0-9617627-0-5*) VT Inst Nat Sci.

***Lingelbach, Karl Christoph & Zimmer, Hasko.** Jahrbuch fur Padagogik 1999 das Jahrhundert des Kindes? 394p. 2000. 32.95 (*3-631-35311-1*) P Lang Pubng.

Lingelbach, William E. Austria-Hungary: Based on the Work of Paul Louis Leger, College De France. LC 70-135846. (Eastern Europe Collection). 1971. reprint ed. 33.95 (*0-405-02788-5*) Ayer.

Lingeman, Henk & Underberg, Willy J.M. Detection-Oriented Derivatization Techniques in Liquid Chromatography. (Chromatographic Science Ser.: Vol. 48). (Illus.). 432p. 1990. text 170.00 (*0-8247-8287-9*) Dekker.

***Lingeman, James E., ed.** Endourology Techniques. 350p. 2000. 99.50 (*0-89603-778-9*) Humana.

Lingeman, James E. & Newman, D. M., eds. Shock Wave Lithotripsy Vol. 1: State of the Art. (Illus.). 432p. 1988. 110.00 (*0-306-43112-2*, Plenum Trade) Perseus Pubng.

— Shock Wave Lithotripsy Vol. 2: Urinary & Biliary Lithotripsy. LC 89-70948. (Illus.). 476p. 1989. 110.00 (*0-306-43416-4*, Plenum Trade) Perseus Pubng.

Lingeman, James E. & Preminger, Glenn M., eds. New Developments in the Management of Urolithiasis. LC 95-32960. (Topics in Clinical Urology Ser.). (Illus.). 216p. 1996. 69.50 (*0-89640-287-8*) Igaku-Shoin.

Lingeman, James E., et al. Urinary Calculi: ESWL, Endourology, & Medical Therapy. Moster, Mary B., ed. LC 88-38144. 476p. reprint ed. pap. 147.60 (*0-7837-2725-9*, 204310500006) Bks Demand.

Lingeman, Larry W. Mental Status Schedules & Psychiatric Rating Scales: Index of New Information for Reference & Research. 160p. 1997. 47.50 (*0-7883-1326-6*); pap. 44.50 (*0-7883-1327-4*) ABBE Pubs Assn.

Lingeman, Richard. Theodore Dreiser: An American Journey. abr. ed. LC 92-40559. 672p. 1993. pap. 19.95 (*0-471-57426-0*) Wiley.

Lingemann, Linda. Beluga Passage. (Smithsonian Oceanic Collection). (Illus.). 32p. (J). (ps-2). 1996. 15.95 (*1-56899-314-5*); 19.95 incl. audio (*1-56899-318-8*, BC4012) Soundprints.

— Beluga Passage, Incl. large toy. (Smithsonian Oceanic Collection). (Illus.). 32p. (J). (ps-2). 1996. 29.95 (*1-56899-316-1*) Soundprints.

— Beluga Passage, Incl. Sm. & Lg. Plush Toy. LC 96-12642. (Smithsonian Oceanic Collection). (Illus.). 32p. (J). (ps-2). 1996. 38.95 incl. audio (*1-56899-636-5*) Soundprints.

— Beluga Passage, Micro bk. (Smithsonian Oceanic Collection). (Illus.). 32p. (J). (ps-2). 1996. 4.95 (*1-56899-315-3*) Soundprints.

— Beluga Passage, Micro bk. & micro toy. (Smithsonian Oceanic Collection). (Illus.). 32p. (J). (ps-2). 1996. 9.95 (*1-56899-317-X*) Soundprints.

— Survival in the Sea: The Story of a Hammerhead Shark. LC 99-25918. (Smithsonian Oceanic Collection: No. 18). (Illus.). 32p. (J). (ps-2). 1999. 15.95 (*1-56899-769-8*); 19.95 incl. audio (*1-56899-771-X*, BC4018) Soundprints.

— Survival in the Sea: The Story of a Hammerhead Shark, Includes toy. (Smithsonian Oceanic Collection: Vol. 18). (Illus.). 32p. (J). (ps-2). 1999. 9.95 (*1-56899-772-8*); 29.95 incl. audio (*1-56899-773-6*) Soundprints.

— Survival in the Sea: The Story of a Hammerhead Shark-Micro Edition. LC 99-25918. (Smithsonian Oceanic Collection: Vol. 18). (Illus.). 32p. (J). (ps-2). 1999. 4.95 (*1-56899-770-1*) Soundprints.

***Lingen, Bert.** Coaching Soccer: The Official Coaching Book of the Dutch Soccer Association. (Illus.). 218p. 1998. pap. 14.95 (*1-890946-04-4*) Reedswain.

Lingen, G. J. Van der, see Van der Lingen, G. J.

Lingen, L. Russian-German Legal Dictionary: Juristisches Woerterbuch: Russisch-Deutsch. (GER & RUS.). 608p. 1985. 85.00 (*0-8288-0982-8*, M8601) Fr & Eur.

Lingenberg, R., jt. auth. see Scherk, Peter.

Lingenfelter, John. John Lingenfelter on Modifying Small-Block Chevy Engines: High Performance Engine Building & Tuning for Street & Racing. 1996. pap. 17.95 (*1-55788-238-X*, HP Books) Berkley Pub.

Lingenfelter, Mary R. Vocations in Fiction: An Annotated Bibliography. LC 74-3102. (Studies in Fiction: No. 34). 1974. lib. bdg. 75.00 (*0-8383-2052-X*) M S G Haskell Hse.

Lingenfelter, R. E., et al, eds. Gamma-Ray Transients & Related Astrophysical Phenomena: La Jolla Institute. LC 81-715443. (AIP Conference Proceedings Ser.: No. 77). 500p. 1982. lib. bdg. 37.00 (*0-88318-176-2*) Am Inst Physics.

Lingenfelter, Richard E. Death Valley & the Amargosa: A Land of Illusion. (Illus.). 622p. 1986. pap. 22.50 (*0-520-06356-2*, Pub. by U CA Pr) Cal Prin Full Svc.

— Steamboats on the Colorado River, 1852-1916. LC 78-16241. (Illus.). 211p. reprint ed. pap. 65.50 (*0-7837-1908-6*, 204211200001) Bks Demand.

Lingenfelter, Richard E., ed. Dan De Quille, The Washoe Giant: A Biography & Anthology. LC 89-16584. (Western Literature Ser.). 464p. (Orig.). 1990. pap. 19.95 (*0-87417-152-0*) U of Nev Pr.

Lingenfelter, Richard E. & Gash, Karen R. The Newspapers of Nevada: A History & Bibliography, 1854-1979. LC 83-16790. (Illus.). 368p. 1984. 50.00 (*0-87417-075-3*) U of Nev Pr.

Lingenfelter, Richard E., jt. auth. see Dwyer, Richard A.

Lingenfelter, Richard E., ed. see Wright, James W.

Lingenfelter, Sherwood G. Agents of Transformation: A Guide for Effective Cross-Cultural Ministry. LC 95-47638. 256p. 1996. pap. 17.99 (*0-8010-2068-9*) Baker Bks.

— Transforming Culture: A Challenge for Christian Missions. 2nd ed. 192p. (Orig.). (C). 1998. pap. 14.99 (*0-8010-2178-2*) Baker Bks.

Lingenfelter, Sherwood G. & Mayers, Marvin K. Ministering Cross-Culturally: An Incarnational Model for Personal Relationships. LC 86-71157. 128p. 1986. pap. 9.99 (*0-8010-5632-2*) Baker Bks.

Lingens, Hans. German Higher Education: Issues & Challenges. LC 97-75466. 79p. 1998. pap. 9.50 (*0-87367-397-2*) Phi Delta Kappa.

Linger, Christina. Die Chronologie Mittelalterlicher Keramik In Sudniedersachsen Aufgrund Nichtkomparativer Methoden. (Illus.). 182p. 1995. 46.95 (*3-631-48311-2*) P Lang Pubng.

Linger, Daniel T. Dangerous Encounters: Meanings of Violence in a Brazilian City. LC 91-28599. (Illus.). 300p. (C). 1993. 42.50 (*0-8047-1926-8*) Stanford U Pr.

— Dangerous Encounters: Meanings of Violence in a Brazilian City. (Illus.). 300p. 1995. pap. 14.95 (*0-8047-2589-6*) Stanford U Pr.

Linger, Juyne, ed. see Bosek, Rita.

Linger, Juyne, ed. see Malone, Lawrence.

Linger, Juyne, ed. see Rosenblum, Joseph.

Linger, M. The Motor & Generator Industry. 235p. 2000. 1350.00 (*0-318-00533-6*) Busn Trend.

— The U. S. Industrial Fastener Industry: Past Performance, Current Trends & Opportunities for Growth. 300p. 1999. 1350.00 (*0-317-55203-1*) Busn Trend.

— The U. S. Pasta Market. 370p. 2000. 1295.00 (*0-318-00493-3*) Busn Trend.

Linger, Richard C. & Poore, Jesse H. Cleanroom Software Engineer: Technology Process. LC 98-38520. 416p. (C). 1999. 49.95 (*0-201-85480-5*) Addison-Wesley.

Lingerfelt, Gene. You, Me & God: The Three-Fold Cord is Not Easily Broken. 1999. pap. text 7.99 (*1-57794-166-7*) Harrison Hse.

Lingerm, jt. auth. see Lingerman, Hal A.

Lingerman, Hal A. The Book of Numerology: Taking a Count of Your Life. LC 94-16826. (Illus.). 160p. (Orig.). 1994. reprint ed. pap. 9.95 (*0-87728-804-6*) Weiser.

— Healing Energies of Music. 2nd ed. LC 94-36151. 300p. 1995. pap. 16.00 (*0-8356-0722-4*, Quest) Theos Pub Hse.

— Life Streams: Journeys into Meditation & Music. LC 87-40522. (Illus.). 309p. 1988. pap. 7.95 (*0-8356-0629-5*, Quest) Theos Pub Hse.

— Living Your Destiny. LC 92-7903. 224p. (Orig.). 1992. pap. 10.95 (*0-87728-746-5*) Weiser.

Lingerman, Hal A. & Lingerm. Journeys into Meditation & Music, 2 cass. 1994. audio 14.95 (*0-8356-2094-8*, Quest) Theos Pub Hse.

Linggard, Robert. Electronic Synthesis of Speech. (Illus.). 159p. 1985. text 52.95 (*0-521-24469-2*) Cambridge U Pr.

An Asterisk (*) at the beginning of an entry indicates that the title is appearing for the first time.

L

*Linggard, Robert. Investing for the Long Term. (Orig.). 1999. pap. 27.50 (1-873668-76-7, Pub. by Take That Bks) Trafalgar.
Lingham, Brian, ed. Harry Truman: The Man-His Music. LC 85-80165. (Illus.). 100p. 1985. 19.95 (0-913504-98-X); pap. 12.95 (0-913504-97-1) Lowell Pr.
Lingham, Gretchen, ed. see Murray, Cindy C.
Lingham, Sundara & Harvey, David R. Manual of Child Development. LC 87-15861. (Manual Ser.). (Illus.). 120p. 1988. pap. text 24.95 (0-443-03784-1) Church.
Lingis, Alphonso. Abuses. LC 93-40254. 1994. 40.00 (0-520-08631-7, Pub. by U CA Pr) Cal Prin Full Svc.
— Abuses. LC 93-40254. 268p. 1995. pap. 15.95 (0-520-20344-5, Pub. by U CA Pr) Cal Prin Full Svc.
— The Community of Those Who Have Nothing in Common. LC 93-23955. (Studies in Continental Thought). 1994. 35.00 (0-253-33438-1); pap. 14.95 (0-253-20852-1) Ind U Pr.
*Lingis, Alphonso. Dangerous Emotions. LC 99-45371. 195p. 2000. 45.00 (0-520-21629-6) U CA Pr.
— Dangerous Emotions. LC 99-45371. (Illus.). 195p. 2000. pap. text 16.95 (0-520-22559-7) U CA Pr.
Lingis, Alphonso. Deathbound Subjectivity. LC 88-45450. (Studies in Phenomenology & Existential Philosophy). 222p. 1989. 13.95 (0-253-31660-X) Ind U Pr.
— Foreign Bodies. LC 93-49537. 256p. (C). 1994. pap. 20.99 (0-415-90990-2) Routledge.
— Foreign Bodies. LC 93-49537. 256p. (C). (gr. 13). 1994. 75.00 (0-415-90989-9) Routledge.
— The Imperative. LC 98-20003. (Studies in Continental Thought). (Illus.). 256p. 1998. 35.00 (0-253-33442-X); pap. 15.95 (0-253-21231-6) Ind U Pr.
— Libido: The French Existential Theories. LC 84-48483. (Studies in Phenomenology & Existential Philosophy). 144p. reprint ed. pap. 44.70 (0-7837-3715-7, 205789300009) Bks Demand.
— Phenomenological Explanations. (Phaenomenologica Ser.: Vol. 96). 122p. 1986. lib. bdg. 73.00 (90-247-3332-4, Pub. by M Nijhoff) Kluwer Academic.
— Sensation: Intelligibility in Sensibility. LC 95-21456. (Contemporary Studies in Philosophy & the Human Sciences). (Illus.). 136p. (C). 1996. 35.00 (0-391-03899-0) Humanities.
Lingis, Alphonso, ed. see Levinas, Emmanuel.
Lingis, Alphonso, tr. see Levinas, Emmanuel.
Lingis, Alphonso, tr. see Merleau-Ponty, Maurice.
Lingis, Alphonso, tr. & intro. see Klossowski, Pierre.
Lingl, James P. The California Community Association Reference Guide, 1993. 356p. 1993. text 40.00 (0-9629533-2-6) CAPCO.
— The California Community Association Reference Guide, 1993. 2nd ed. 360p. 1993. text 40.00 (0-9629533-3-4) CAPCO.
— The California Community Association Reference Guide, 1994. 366p. 1994. text 40.00 (0-9629533-4-2) CAPCO.
Lingle, Christopher. The Rise & Decline of the Asian Century: False Starts on the Path to the Global Millennium. 3rd rev. ed. LC 98-168429. 305p. 1998. pap. 18.95 (962-7160-63-6, Pub. by Asia) U of Wash Pr.
Lingle, Gary R. Birding Crane River: Nebraska's Platte. 124p. 1994. spiral bd. 11.95 (0-9641219-0-5) Harrier Pubng.
Lingle, John H., jt. auth. see Schiermann, William A.
Lingle, Ted R. The Basics of Cupping Coffee. 2nd unabridged ed. Date not set. pap. 20.00 (1-882552-01-6) Spec Coffee.
— The Coffee Brewing Handbook: A Systematic Guide to Coffee Preparation. (Illus.). 60p. 1996. pap. 47.00 (1-882552-02-4) Spec Coffee.
Lingle, Walter. Memories of Davidson College. (American Autobiography Ser.). 157p. 1995. reprint ed. lib. bdg. 69.00 (0-7812-8580-1) Rprt Serv.
Lingle, Walter L. & Kuykendall, John W. Presbyterians, Their History & Beliefs. LC 77-15750. 1958. reprint ed. pap. 14.95 (0-8042-0985-5) Westminster John Knox.
Lingle, Wilbur. Approaching Jehovah's Witnesses in Love: How to Witness Effectively Without Arguing. 250p. (Orig.). 1994. pap. 11.99 (0-87508-702-7) Chr Lit.
— 20 Important Questions for Jehovah's Witnesses. (Vital Ser.). 1997. pap. 0.75 (0-87508-474-5) Chr Lit.
Lingley, Charles R. Transition in Virginia from Colony to Commonwealth. LC 10-14656. (Columbia University. Studies in the Social Sciences: No. 96). reprint ed. 37.50 (0-404-51096-5) AMS Pr.
Lingley, William S., Jr., jt. auth. see Palmer, Stephen P.
Lingner, Michael. Franz Erhard Walther Kunsthalle Ritter. 1997. pap. text 24.95 (3-7757-0644-5, Pub. by Gerd Hatje) Dist Art Pubs.
Lingner, Michael, ed. see Von Bismarck, Beatrice.
Lingo, Susan. Bible Message Make-n-Takes: 50 Devotional Talks with Crafty Reminders for Kids. Frederick, Ruth, ed. LC 99-165754. (Illus.). 112p. 1998. pap. 12.99 (0-7847-0838-X, 14-42062) Standard Pub.
— Kids-Tell-'Em Bible Stories: Active Lessons Kids Can Lead. Frederick, Ruth, ed. LC 99-208224. (Illus.). 112p. 1999. pap. text 12.99 (0-7847-0940-8, 03579) Standard Pub.
— Larger - Than - Life Activities: Colossal Crafts That Teach & Serve. LC 98-123020. (Illus.). 112p. (J). 1998. per. 12.99 (0-7847-0782-0, 03082) Standard Pub.
— "Show Me!" Devotions for Leaders to Teach Kids. LC 96-43493. (J). (ps-6). 1997. pap. 14.99 (0-7644-2022-4) Group Pub.
— 200 Plus Activities for Children's Ministry. Frederick, Ruth, ed. LC 99-207447. (Illus.). 144p. 1999. 14.99 (0-7847-0939-4, 03577) Standard Pub.
— Worship Wow! 30 Activities for Children's Worship, 18 Complete Services Kids Can Lead. Frederick, Ruth, ed. (Illus.). 128p. 1998. pap., teacher ed. 14.99 (0-7847-0833-9, 14-42060) Standard Pub.
Lingo, Susan & Kershner, Jan, eds. Hands-On Service Ideas for Children's Ministry. LC 97-47216. 128p. 1998. per. 15.99 (0-7644-2040-2) Group Pub.
Lingo, Susan & Wolf, Beth, eds. More Than Mud Pies: Bible Learning Crafts & Games for Preschoolers. LC 97-37795. 112p. 1998. per. 15.99 (0-7644-2044-5) Group Pub.
Lingo, Susan, ed. see Goings, Nanette.
Lingo, Susan L. Affordable Family Fun: Family Fun for under $5. Buller, Bob, ed. LC 97-40097. 112p. 1998. per. 14.99 (0-7644-2032-1) Group Pub.
— Age-Right Play. LC 97-12084. 96p. (Orig.). 1997. pap. 14.99 (0-7644-2014-3) Group Pub.
*Lingo, Susan L. Bedtime for Night-Light. (Illus.). (J). 2000. pap. text. write for info. (0-7847-1106-2) Standard Pub.
— Disciple Makers: 13 Fun Filled Bible Lessons about Following Jesus. (Power Builders Ser.). (Illus.). 128p. (J). (gr. 1-5). 2000. pap. 14.99 (0-7847-1148-8, 42114) Standard Pub.
— Edible Object Talks That Teach about Jesus. (Illus.). 48p. 2000. pap. 4.99 (0-7847-1184-4, 02825) Standard Pub.
— Edible Object Talks That Teach about Values. (Illus.). 48p. 2000. pap. 4.99 (0-7847-1183-6, 02824) Standard Pub.
Lingo, Susan L. Eye-Popping 3-D Bulletin Boards. LC 96-3133. 128p. 1996. 16.99 (1-55945-904-2) Group Pub.
*Lingo, Susan L. Faith Finders: 13 Fun Filled Bible Lessons about Faith. (Power Builders Ser.). (Illus.). 128p. (J). (gr. 1-5). 2000. pap. 14.99 (0-7847-1146-1, 42112) Standard Pub.
— God's Friends. Ring, Laura, ed. (Illus.). 10p. (J). (ps-1). 2000. bds. 4.99 (0-7847-1057-0, 03550) Standard Pub.
Lingo, Susan L. Instant Games for Children's Ministry: Play 101 New Children's Games - Using Just 14 Everyday Items! LC 95-18765. 96p. 1995. 14.99 (1-55945-695-7) Group Pub.
*Lingo, Susan L. Making Scripture Memorable: Over 150 Fun Bible Memory Activities for Families at Home or Church. (Illus.). 128p. 2000. pap. text 14.99 (0-7847-1110-0, 02826) Standard Pub.
Lingo, Susan L. My Good Night Bible. Ring, Laura, ed. LC 99-22435. (Illus.). 208p. (J). (ps-1). 1999. 12.99 (0-7847-0406-6, Bean Sprouts) Standard Pub.
*Lingo, Susan L. 101 Simple Service Projects Kids Can Do. (Illus.). 128p. 2000. pap. text 14.99 (0-7847-1154-2, 02270) Standard Pub.
— Servant Leaders: 13 Fun Filled Bible Lessons about Serving God. (Power Builders Ser.). (Illus.). 128p. (J). (gr. 1-5). 2000. pap. text 14.99 (0-7847-1147-X, 42113) Standard Pub.
— Sleepy Animals. Ring, Laura, ed. (Illus.). 10p. (J). (ps-1). 2000. bds. 4.99 (0-7847-1056-2, 03549) Standard Pub.
— Value Seekers: 13 Fun Filled Bible Lessons about Values. (Power Builders Ser.). (Illus.). 128p. (J). (gr. 1-5). 2000. pap. 14.99 (0-7847-1145-3, 42111) Standard Pub.
Lingoes, J., jt. auth. see Borg, I.
Lingpa, Dudjom. Buddhahood Without Meditation: A Visionary Account Known As Refining Apparent Phenomena, Nangjang. Barron, Richard, tr. LC 93-34038. (TIB., Illus.). 251p. 1997. reprint ed. pap. 21.95 (1-881847-07-1) Padma Pub CA.
Lingquist, David G. & Page, Lawrence M., eds. Environmental Biology of Darters. (Developments in Environmental Biology of Fishes Ser.). 1984. text 147.50 (90-6193-506-7) Kluwer Academic.
Lingren, Art. Dean River, BC. (Steelhead River Journal Ser.: Vol. 3, No. 3). (Illus.). 48p. 2000. pap. 15.95 (1-57188-116-6) F Amato Pubns.
Lingren, Arthur J. Fly Patterns of British Columbia. 104p. 1996. 39.95 (1-57188-069-0); pap. 29.95 (1-57188-068-2) F Amato Pubns.
— Irresistable Waters: Fly Fishing in B. C. Throughout the Year. 176p. 1998. pap. 13.95 (1-55192-148-0) Raincoast Bk.
— Thompson River, BC. (River Journal Ser.: Vol. 2, No. 3). (Illus.). 48p. 1994. pap. 14.95 (1-878175-47-5) F Amato Pubns.
Lingren, Minnie. Hops Cultivation in Lewis County. 54p. 1989. reprint ed. pap. 7.50 (0-685-30404-3) Fernwood Pr.
Lings, Brian. Information Structures: A Uniform Approach Using Pascal. 250p. 1986. 52.50 (0-412-26490-0, 9565) Chapman & Hall.
Lings, Martin. Ancient Beliefs & Modern Superstitions. 84p. 1996. pap. 9.95 (0-614-21616-8, 34) Kazi Pubns.
— Ancient Beliefs & Modern Superstitions. 111p. 1991. reprint ed. pap. 6.95 (1-870196-09-0, Pub. by Islamic Texts) Intl Spec Bk.
— Collected Poems. (Orig.). 1996. pap. 15.95 (0-614-21637-0, 140) Kazi Pubns.
— Collected Poems. (Illus.). 51p. (Orig.). 1987. pap. 14.95 (0-900588-28-4) S Perennis.
— The Eleventh Hour: The Spiritual Crisis of the Modern World in the Light of Tradition & Prophecy. 124p. 1987. 22.95 (0-946621-07-1, Pub. by Islamic Texts) Intl Spec Bk.
— Eleventh Hour: The Spiritual Crisis of the Modern World in the Light of Tradition & Prophecy. 124p. 1996. 18.50 (0-614-21270-7, 1400) Kazi Pubns.
— Muhammad: His Life Based on the Earliest Sources. 368p. 1987. pap. 16.95 (0-89281-170-6) Inner Tradit.
— Muhammad: His Life Based on the Earliest Sources. 361p. 1995. reprint ed. write for info. (0-946621-25-X, Pub. by Islamic Texts) Intl Spec Bk.
— The Sacred Art of Shakespeare: To Take upon Us the Mystery of Things. rev. expanded ed. LC 98-31015. 224p. 1998. pap. 14.95 (0-89281-717-8) Inner Tradit.
— The Secret of Shakespeare: His Greatest Plays Seen in the Light of Sacred Art. 3rd ed. LC 98-115604. 224p. 1996. 39.95 (1-870196-15-5, Pub. by Islamic Texts) Intl Spec Bk.
— The Secret of Shakespeare: His Greatest Plays Seen in the Light of Sacred Art. 3rd rev. ed. 224p. 1996. pap. 24.95 (1-870196-14-7, Pub. by Islamic Texts) Intl Spec Bk.
— A Sufi Saint of the Twentieth Century. 242p. 1996. pap. 15.95 (0-614-21360-6, 1189) Kazi Pubns.
— A Sufi Saint of the Twentieth Century: Shaikh Ahmad Al-'Alawi. 3rd ed. (Golden Press Ser.). (Illus.). 132p. 1995. pap. 21.95 (0-946621-50-0, Pub. by Islamic Texts) Intl Spec Bk.
— Symbol & Archetype: A Study in the Meaning of Existence. viii, 141p. 1991. 26.95 (1-870196-04-X, Pub. by Islamic Texts) Intl Spec Bk.
— Symbol & Archetype: A Study in the Meaning of Existence, Vol. 1. 138p. 1991. pap. 14.95 (1-870196-05-8, Pub. by Islamic Texts) Intl Spec Bk.
— Symbol & Archetype: A Study of the Meaning of Existence. 142p. 1996. pap. 14.95 (0-614-21243-X, 1206) Kazi Pubns.
— What Is Sufism? 135p. 1996. pap. 21.95 (0-614-21381-9, 1308) Kazi Pubns.
— What Is Sufism? LC 97-179248. (Golden Palm Ser.). 134p. 1996. reprint ed. pap. text 19.95 (0-946621-41-1, Pub. by Islamic Texts) Intl Spec Bk.
Lings, Martin, ed. see Guenon, Rene.
Lingua, Franca. Real Guide to Grad School: What You Better Know Before You Choose. 524p. 1997. pap. text 24.95 (0-9630238-0-2) Lingua Franca.
Lingua Press Staff. Lingua Press Collection One Catalogue, Vol. 1. Gaburo, Kenneth, ed. (Illus.). 44p. 1976. 1.50 (0-939044-00-5) Lingua Pr.
— Lingua Press Collection Three Catalogue, Vol. 3. Gaburo, Kenneth, ed. (Illus.). 150p. pap. 8.50 (0-939044-23-4) Lingua Pr.
— Lingua Press Collection Two Catalogue, Vol. 2. Gaburo, Kenneth, ed. (Illus.). 132p. 1978. pap. 3.95 (0-939044-17-X) Lingua Pr.
LinguaFranca Language Services Staff, tr. see Degauque, Pierre & Hamelin, Joel, eds.
Linguaphone Staff. Linguaphone Afrikaans Course for English Speakers: Beginner's Course. (AFR & ENG.). 1991. student ed. 250.00 incl. digital audio (0-8288-4050-4, F60960) Fr & Eur.
Linguaphone Staff. Linguaphone American Course for Japanese Speakers: Beginner's Course. (ENG & JPN.). 1991. student ed. 395.00 incl. cd-rom (0-8288-4287-6) Fr & Eur.
Linguaphone Staff. Linguaphone Arabic Course for English Speakers: Beginner's Course. (ARA & ENG.). 1991. student ed. 295.00 incl. digital audio (0-8288-4051-2, F127355) Fr & Eur.
— Linguaphone Arabic Course for French Speakers: Beginner's Course. (ARA & FRE.). 1991. student ed. 295.00 incl. digital audio (0-8288-4052-0, F43160) Fr & Eur.
— Linguaphone Business English Course for Dutch Speakers: Beginner's Course. (DUT & ENG.). 1991. student ed. 295.00 incl. digital audio (0-8288-4053-9) Fr & Eur.
Linguaphone Staff. Linguaphone Business English Course for Finnish Speakers: Beginner's Course. (ENG & FIN.). 1991. student ed. 250.00 incl. digital audio (0-8288-4057-1) Fr & Eur.
Linguaphone Staff. Linguaphone Business English Course for French Speakers: Beginner's Course. (ENG & FRE.). 1991. student ed. 250.00 incl. digital audio (0-8288-4054-7) Fr & Eur.
— Linguaphone Business English Course for German Speakers: Beginner's Course. (ENG & GER.). 1991. student ed. 250.00 incl. digital audio (0-8288-4055-5) Fr & Eur.
— Linguaphone Business English Course for Mandarin-Chinese Speakers: Beginner's Course. (CHI & ENG.). 1991. student ed. 250.00 incl. digital audio (0-8288-4056-3) Fr & Eur.
— Linguaphone Continental Spanish Course for Danish Speakers: Beginner's Course. (DAN & SPA.). 1991. student ed. 295.00 incl. audio, digital audio (0-8288-4077-6) Fr & Eur.
— Linguaphone Continental Spanish Course for Dutch Speakers: Beginner's Course. (DUT & SPA.). 1991. student ed. 295.00 incl. digital audio (0-8288-4078-4) Fr & Eur.
— Linguaphone Continental Spanish Course for Finnish Speakers: Beginner's Course. (FIN & SPA.). 1991. student ed. 295.00 incl. digital audio (0-8288-4063-6) Fr & Eur.
— Linguaphone Continental Spanish Course for French Speakers: Beginner's Course. (FRE & SPA.). 1991. student ed. 295.00 incl. digital audio (0-8288-4062-8) Fr & Eur.
— Linguaphone Continental Spanish Course for Italian Speakers: Beginner's Course. (ITA & SPA.). 1991. student ed. 295.00 incl. digital audio (0-8288-4065-2) Fr & Eur.
— Linguaphone Continental Spanish Course for Japanese Speakers: Beginner's Course. (JPN & SPA.). 1991. student ed. 295.00 incl. digital audio (0-8288-4066-0) Fr & Eur.
— Linguaphone Continental Spanish Course for Norwegian Speakers: Beginner's Course. (NOR & SPA.). 1991. student ed. 295.00 incl. digital audio (0-8288-4067-9) Fr & Eur.
— Linguaphone Czech Course for English Speakers: Beginner's Course. (CZE & ENG.). 1991. student ed. 95.00 incl. digital audio (0-8288-3272-2) Fr & Eur.
— Linguaphone Danish Course for English Speakers: Beginner's Course. (DAN & ENG.). 1991. student ed. 250.00 incl. digital audio (0-8288-4068-7) Fr & Eur.
— Linguaphone Danish Course for Icelandic Speaking People: Beginner's Course. (DAN & ICE.). 1991. student ed. 250.00 incl. digital audio (0-8288-4069-5) Fr & Eur.
— Linguaphone Dutch Course for English Speakers: Beginner's Course. (DUT & ENG.). 1991. student ed. 250.00 incl. digital audio (0-8288-4070-9) Fr & Eur.
— Linguaphone Dutch Course for French Speakers: Beginner's Course. (DUT & FRE.). 1991. student ed. 295.00 incl. digital audio (0-8288-3284-6) Fr & Eur.
— Linguaphone English Course for Arabic Speakers: Beginner's Course. (ARA & ENG.). 1991. student ed. 295.00 incl. digital audio (0-8288-4074-1) Fr & Eur.
— Linguaphone English Course for Arabic Speakers: Intermediate Course. (ARA & ENG.). 1991. student ed. 225.00 incl. digital audio (0-8288-4079-2) Fr & Eur.
Linguaphone Staff. Linguaphone English Course for Cantonese Speakers: Beginner's Course. (CHI & ENG.). 1991. student ed. 225.00 incl. audio, digital audio (0-8288-4080-6); pap., student ed. 395.00 incl. cd-rom (0-685-52090-0) Fr & Eur.
Linguaphone Staff. Linguaphone English Course for Czech Speakers: Beginner's Course. (CZE & ENG.). 1991. student ed. 225.00 incl. digital audio (0-8288-4087-3) Fr & Eur.
Linguaphone Staff. Linguaphone English Course for Danish Speakers: Beginner's Course. (DAN & ENG.). 1991. student ed. 295.00 incl. audio, digital audio (0-8288-4088-1); pap., student ed. 395.00 incl. cd-rom (0-8288-4089-X) Fr & Eur.
Linguaphone Staff. Linguaphone English Course for Dutch Speakers: Beginner's Course. (DUT & ENG.). 1991. student ed. 295.00 incl. digital audio (0-8288-3280-3) Fr & Eur.
— Linguaphone English Course for Dutch Speakers: Intermediate Course. (DUT & ENG.). 1991. student ed. 225.00 incl. digital audio (0-8288-4091-1) Fr & Eur.
Linguaphone Staff. Linguaphone English Course for English Speakers: Beginner's Course. 1991. pap., student ed. 395.00 incl. cd-rom (0-685-52093-5) Fr & Eur.
— Linguaphone English Course for Finnish Speakers: Beginner's Course. (ENG & FIN.). 1991. pap., student ed. 395.00 incl. cd-rom (0-8288-4094-6) Fr & Eur.
Linguaphone Staff. Linguaphone English Course for Finnish Speakers: Intermediate Course. (ENG & FIN.). 1991. student ed. 225.00 incl. audio, digital audio (0-8288-4093-8) Fr & Eur.
— Linguaphone English Course for French Speakers: Advanced Course. (ENG & FRE.). 1991. student ed. 225.00 incl. digital audio (0-8288-3285-4) Fr & Eur.
Linguaphone Staff. Linguaphone English Course for French Speakers: Beginner's Course. (ENG & FRE.). 1991. student ed. 295.00 incl. audio, digital audio (0-8288-4072-5); pap., student ed. 395.00 incl. cd-rom (0-8288-4097-0) Fr & Eur.
Linguaphone Staff. Linguaphone English Course for French Speakers: Intermediate Course. (ENG & FRE.). 1991. student ed. 225.00 incl. digital audio (0-8288-4073-3) Fr & Eur.
Linguaphone Staff. Linguaphone English Course for German Speakers: Beginner's Course. (ENG & GER.). 1991. 295.00 incl. audio, digital audio (0-8288-4098-9); pap., student ed. 395.00 incl. cd-rom (0-8288-4100-4) Fr & Eur.
Linguaphone Staff. Linguaphone English Course for German Speakers: Intermediate Course. (ENG & GER.). 1991. student ed. 225.00 incl. digital audio (0-8288-4099-7) Fr & Eur.
— Linguaphone English Course for Greek Speakers: Beginner's Course. (ENG & GRE.). 1991. student ed. 295.00 incl. digital audio (0-8288-4101-2) Fr & Eur.
— Linguaphone English Course for Greek Speakers: Intermediate Course. (ENG & GRE.). 1991. student ed. 225.00 incl. digital audio (0-8288-4102-0) Fr & Eur.
— Linguaphone English Course for Hebrew Speakers: Beginner's Course. (ENG & HEB.). 1991. student ed. 295.00 incl. digital audio (0-8288-4103-9) Fr & Eur.
— Linguaphone English Course for Hungarian Speakers: Beginner's Course. (ENG & HUN.). 1991. student ed. 225.00 incl. digital audio (0-8288-4105-5) Fr & Eur.
— Linguaphone English Course for Icelandic Speakers: Beginner's Course. (ENG & ICE.). 1991. student ed. 295.00 incl. digital audio (0-8288-4104-7) Fr & Eur.
— Linguaphone English Course for Italian Speakers: Beginner's Course. (ENG & ITA.). 1991. student ed. 295.00 incl. digital audio (0-8288-4106-3) Fr & Eur.
— Linguaphone English Course for Italian Speakers: Intermediate Course. (ENG & ITA.). 1991. student ed. 225.00 incl. digital audio (0-8288-4107-1) Fr & Eur.
— Linguaphone English Course for Japanese Speakers: Intermediate Course. (ENG & JPN.). 1991. student ed. 295.00 incl. digital audio (0-8288-4108-X) Fr & Eur.
— Linguaphone English Course for Malay Speakers: Beginner's Course. (ENG & MAY.). 1991. student ed. 295.00 incl. digital audio (0-8288-4109-8) Fr & Eur.
Linguaphone Staff. Linguaphone English Course for Mandarin Speakers: Beginner's Course. (CHI & ENG.). 1991. student ed. 295.00 incl. audio, digital audio (0-8288-4110-1); pap., student ed. 395.00 incl. cd-rom (0-8288-4112-8) Fr & Eur.
Linguaphone Staff. Linguaphone English Course for Mandarin Speakers: Intermediate Course. (CHI & ENG.). 1991. student ed. 225.00 incl. digital audio (0-8288-4111-X) Fr & Eur.
Linguaphone Staff. Linguaphone English Course for Norwegian Speakers: Beginner's Course. (ENG & NOR.). 1991. student ed. 295.00 incl. audio, digital audio (0-8288-4113-6); pap., student ed. 395.00 incl. cd-rom (0-8288-4115-2) Fr & Eur.
Linguaphone Staff. Linguaphone English Course for Norwegian Speakers: Intermediate Course. (ENG & NOR.). 1991. student ed. 225.00 incl. digital audio (0-8288-4114-4) Fr & Eur.
— Linguaphone English Course for Persian Speakers: Beginner's Course. (ENG & PER.). 1991. student ed. 225.00 incl. digital audio (0-8288-4116-0) Fr & Eur.

An Asterisk (*) at the beginning of an entry indicates that the title is appearing for the first time.

— Linguaphone English Course for Polish Speakers: Beginner's Course. (ENG & POL.). 1991. student ed. 225.00 incl. digital audio (*0-8288-4117-9*, F127355) Fr & Eur.

— Linguaphone English Course for Portuguese Speakers: Beginner's Course. (ENG & POR.). 1991. student ed. 295.00 incl. digital audio (*0-8288-3307-9*) Fr & Eur.

— Linguaphone English Course for Portuguese Speakers: Intermediate Course. (ENG & POR.). 1991. student ed. 225.00 incl. digital audio (*0-8288-3308-7*) Fr & Eur.

— Linguaphone English Course for Russian Speakers: Beginner's Course. (ENG & RUS.). 1991. student ed. 295.00 incl. digital audio (*0-8288-4118-7*, F60960) Fr & Eur.

— Linguaphone English Course for Serbian Speakers: Beginner's Course. (ENG & SER.). 1991. student ed. 295.00 incl. digital audio (*0-8288-4119-5*, F43160) Fr & Eur.

— Linguaphone English Course for Serbo-Croatian Speakers: Beginner's Course. (ENG & SER.). 1991. student ed. 295.00 incl. digital audio (*0-8288-4121-7*) Fr & Eur.

— Linguaphone English Course for Slovenian Speakers: Beginner's Course. (ENG & SLV.). 1991. student ed. 295.00 incl. digital audio (*0-8288-4120-9*) Fr & Eur.

— Linguaphone English Course for Spanish Speakers: Beginner's Course. (ENG & SPA.). 1991. student ed. 295.00 incl. digital audio (*0-8288-4085-7*) Fr & Eur.

— Linguaphone English Course for Spanish Speakers: Intermediate Course. (ENG & SPA.). 1991. student ed. 225.00 incl. digital audio (*0-8288-4086-5*) Fr & Eur.

Linguaphone Staff. Linguaphone English Course for Swedish Speakers: Beginner's Course. (ENG & SWE.). 1991. student ed. 295.00 incl. audio, digital audio (*0-8288-4122-5*); pap., student ed. 395.00 incl. cd-rom (*0-8288-4124-1*) Fr & Eur.

Linguaphone Staff. Linguaphone English Course for Swedish Speakers: Intermediate Course. (ENG & SWE.). 1991. student ed. 225.00 incl. digital audio (*0-8288-4123-3*) Fr & Eur.

— Linguaphone English Course for Thai Speakers: Beginner's Course. (ENG & THA.). 1991. student ed. 295.00 incl. digital audio (*0-8288-4125-X*) Fr & Eur.

— Linguaphone English Course for Thai Speakers: Intermediate Course. (ENG & THA.). 1991. student ed. 225.00 incl. digital audio (*0-8288-4126-8*) Fr & Eur.

— Linguaphone English Course for Turkish Speakers: Beginner's Course. (ENG & TUR.). 1991. student ed. 295.00 incl. digital audio (*0-8288-4127-6*) Fr & Eur.

— Linguaphone English Course for Turkish Speakers: Intermediate Course. (ENG & TUR.). 1991. student ed. 225.00 incl. digital audio (*0-8288-4128-4*) Fr & Eur.

— Linguaphone English Course for Vietnamese Speakers: Beginner's Course. (ENG & VIE.). 1991. student ed. 225.00 incl. digital audio (*0-8288-4129-2*) Fr & Eur.

— Linguaphone Finnish Course for English Speakers: Beginner's Course. (ENG & FIN.). 1991. student ed. 225.00 incl. digital audio (*0-8288-4130-6*) Fr & Eur.

— Linguaphone Finnish Course for Swedish Speakers: Beginner's Course. (FIN & SWE.). 1991. student ed. 225.00 incl. digital audio (*0-8288-4131-4*) Fr & Eur.

— Linguaphone French Course for Arabic Speakers: Beginner's Course. (ARA & FRE.). 1991. student ed. 225.00 incl. digital audio (*0-8288-4132-2*) Fr & Eur.

Linguaphone Staff. Linguaphone French Course for Cantonese-Chinese Speakers: Beginner's Course. (CHI & ENG.). 1991. student ed. 395.00 incl. cd-rom (*0-8288-4260-4*) Fr & Eur.

Linguaphone Staff. Linguaphone French Course for Czech Speakers: Beginner's Course. (CZE & FRE.). 1991. student ed. 225.00 incl. digital audio (*0-8288-4137-3*) Fr & Eur.

Linguaphone Staff. Linguaphone French Course for Danish Speakers: Beginner's Course. (DAN & FRE.). 1991. student ed. 295.00 incl. audio, digital audio (*0-8288-4138-1*); pap., student ed. 395.00 incl. cd-rom (*0-8288-4139-X*) Fr & Eur.

Linguaphone Staff. Linguaphone French Course for Dutch Speakers: Beginner's Course. (DUT & FRE.). 1991. student ed. 295.00 incl. digital audio (*0-8288-3281-1*) Fr & Eur.

— Linguaphone French Course for Dutch Speakers: Intermediate Course. (DUT & FRE.). 1991. student ed. 225.00 incl. digital audio (*0-8288-3282-X*) Fr & Eur.

Linguaphone Staff. Linguaphone French Course for English Speakers: Beginner's Course. (ENG & FRE.). 1991. student ed. 295.00 incl. audio, digital audio (*0-8288-4142-X*); pap., student ed. 395.00 incl. cd-rom (*0-8288-4144-6*) Fr & Eur.

Linguaphone Staff. Linguaphone French Course for English Speakers: Intermediate Course. (ENG & FRE.). 1991. student ed. 225.00 incl. digital audio (*0-8288-4143-8*) Fr & Eur.

Linguaphone Staff. Linguaphone French Course for Finnish Speakers: Beginner's Course. (FIN & FRE.). 1991. student ed. 295.00 incl. audio, digital audio (*0-8288-4145-4*); pap., student ed. 395.00 incl. cd-rom (*0-8288-4147-0*) Fr & Eur.

Linguaphone Staff. Linguaphone French Course for Finnish Speakers: Intermediate Course. (FIN & FRE.). 1991. student ed. 225.00 incl. digital audio (*0-8288-4146-2*) Fr & Eur.

Linguaphone Staff. Linguaphone French Course for German Speakers: Beginner's Course. (FRE & GER.). 1991. student ed. 295.00 incl. audio, digital audio (*0-8288-4148-9*); pap., student ed. 395.00 incl. cd-rom (*0-8288-4149-7*) Fr & Eur.

Linguaphone Staff. Linguaphone French Course for German Speakers: Intermediate Course. (FRE & GER.). 1991. student ed. 225.00 incl. digital audio (*0-8288-4150-0*) Fr & Eur.

— Linguaphone French Course for Greek Speakers: Beginner's Course. (FRE & GRE.). 1991. student ed. 295.00 incl. digital audio (*0-8288-4151-9*) Fr & Eur.

— Linguaphone French Course for Greek Speakers: Intermediate Course. (FRE & GRE.). 1991. student ed. 225.00 incl. digital audio (*0-8288-4152-7*) Fr & Eur.

— Linguaphone French Course for Italian Speakers: Beginner's Course. (FRE & ITA.). 1991. student ed. 295.00 incl. digital audio (*0-8288-4153-5*) Fr & Eur.

— Linguaphone French Course for Italian Speakers: Intermediate Course. (FRE & ITA.). 1991. student ed. 225.00 incl. audio, digital audio (*0-8288-4154-3*) Fr & Eur.

— Linguaphone French Course for Japanese Speakers: Beginner's Course. (FRE & JPN.). 1991. student ed. 295.00 incl. digital audio (*0-8288-4155-1*) Fr & Eur.

Linguaphone Staff. Linguaphone French Course for Mandarin-Chinese Speakers: Beginner's Course. (CHI & ENG.). 1991. student ed. 395.00 incl. cd-rom (*0-8288-4259-0*) Fr & Eur.

— Linguaphone French Course for Norwegian Speakers: Beginner's Course. (FRE & NOR.). 1991. student ed. 295.00 incl. audio, digital audio (*0-8288-3298-6*); pap., student ed. 395.00 incl. cd-rom (*0-8288-4158-6*) Fr & Eur.

Linguaphone Staff. Linguaphone French Course for Norwegian Speakers: Intermediate Course. (FRE & NOR.). 1991. student ed. 225.00 incl. digital audio (*0-8288-3299-4*) Fr & Eur.

— Linguaphone French Course for Persian Speakers: Beginner's Course. (FRE & PER.). 1991. student ed. 225.00 incl. digital audio (*0-8288-4159-4*) Fr & Eur.

— Linguaphone French Course for Portuguese Speakers: Beginner's Course. (FRE & POR.). 1991. student ed. 295.00 incl. digital audio (*0-8288-3303-6*) Fr & Eur.

— Linguaphone French Course for Portuguese Speakers: Intermediate Course. (FRE & POR.). 1991. student ed. 225.00 incl. digital audio (*0-8288-3304-4*) Fr & Eur.

— Linguaphone French Course for Serbian Speakers: Beginner's Course. (FRE & SER.). 1991. student ed. 295.00 incl. digital audio (*0-8288-4160-8*) Fr & Eur.

— Linguaphone French Course for Slovenian Speakers: Beginner's Course. (FRE & SLV.). 1991. student ed. 295.00 incl. digital audio (*0-8288-4161-6*) Fr & Eur.

— Linguaphone French Course for Spanish Speakers: Beginner's Course. (FRE & SPA.). 1991. student ed. 295.00 incl. digital audio (*0-8288-4134-9*) Fr & Eur.

— Linguaphone French Course for Spanish Speakers: Intermediate Course. (FRE & SPA.). 1991. student ed. 225.00 incl. digital audio (*0-8288-3311-7*) Fr & Eur.

Linguaphone Staff. Linguaphone French Course for Swedish Speakers: Beginner's Course. (FRE & SWE.). 1991. student ed. 295.00 incl. audio, digital audio (*0-8288-4163-2*); student ed. 395.00 incl. cd-rom (*0-8288-4164-0*) Fr & Eur.

Linguaphone Staff. Linguaphone French Course for Swedish Speakers: Intermediate Course. (FRE & SWE.). 1991. student ed. 225.00 incl. digital audio (*0-8288-4162-4*) Fr & Eur.

— Linguaphone French Course for Turkish Speakers: Beginner's Course. (FRE & TUR.). 1991. student ed. 295.00 incl. digital audio (*0-8288-4165-9*) Fr & Eur.

Linguaphone Staff. Linguaphone German Course for Cantonese Chinese Speakers: Beginner's Course. (CHI & GER.). 1991. student ed. 395.00 incl. cd-rom (*0-8288-4187-X*) Fr & Eur.

— Linguaphone German Course for Chinese-Mandarin Speakers: Beginner's Course. (CHI & GER.). 1991. student ed. 395.00 incl. cd-rom (*0-8288-4261-2*) Fr & Eur.

— Linguaphone German Course for Danish Speakers: Beginner's Course. (DAN & GER.). 1991. student ed. 295.00 incl. audio, digital audio (*0-8288-3279-X*); student ed. 395.00 incl. cd-rom (*0-8288-4170-5*) Fr & Eur.

Linguaphone Staff. Linguaphone German Course for Dutch Speakers: Beginner's Course. (DUT & GER.). 1991. student ed. 295.00 incl. digital audio (*0-8288-4171-3*) Fr & Eur.

— Linguaphone German Course for Dutch Speakers: Intermediate Course. (DUT & GER.). 1991. student ed. 225.00 incl. digital audio (*0-8288-4172-1*) Fr & Eur.

Linguaphone Staff. Linguaphone German Course for English Speakers: Beginner's Course. (ENG & GER.). 1991. student ed. 295.00 incl. audio, digital audio (*0-8288-4173-X*); student ed. 395.00 incl. cd-rom (*0-8288-4175-6*) Fr & Eur.

Linguaphone Staff. Linguaphone German Course for English Speakers: Intermediate Course. (ENG & GER.). 1991. student ed. 225.00 incl. digital audio (*0-8288-4174-8*) Fr & Eur.

Linguaphone Staff. Linguaphone German Course for Finnish Speakers: Beginner's Course. (FIN & GER.). 1991. student ed. 295.00 incl. audio, digital audio (*0-8288-4176-4*); student ed. 395.00 incl. cd-rom (*0-8288-4178-0*) Fr & Eur.

Linguaphone Staff. Linguaphone German Course for Finnish Speakers: Intermediate Course. (FIN & GER.). 1991. student ed. 225.00 incl. digital audio (*0-8288-4177-2*) Fr & Eur.

Linguaphone Staff. Linguaphone German Course for French Speakers: Beginner's Course. (FRE & GER.). 1991. student ed. 295.00 incl. audio, digital audio (*0-8288-4179-9*); student ed. 395.00 incl. cd-rom (*0-8288-4181-0*) Fr & Eur.

Linguaphone Staff. Linguaphone German Course for French Speakers: Intermediate Course. (FRE & GER.). 1991. student ed. 225.00 incl. digital audio (*0-8288-4180-2*) Fr & Eur.

— Linguaphone German Course for Greek Speakers: Beginner's Course. (GER & GRE.). 1991. student ed. 295.00 incl. digital audio (*0-8288-4182-9*) Fr & Eur.

— Linguaphone German Course for Greek Speakers: Intermediate Course. (GER & GRE.). 1991. student ed. 225.00 incl. digital audio (*0-8288-4183-7*) Fr & Eur.

— Linguaphone German Course for Italian Speakers: Beginner's Course. (GER & ITA.). 1991. student ed. 295.00 incl. digital audio (*0-8288-4184-5*) Fr & Eur.

— Linguaphone German Course for Italian Speakers: Intermediate Course. (GER & ITA.). 1991. student ed. 225.00 incl. digital audio (*0-8288-4185-3*) Fr & Eur.

— Linguaphone German Course for Japanese Speakers: Beginner's Course. (GER & JPN.). 1991. student ed. 295.00 incl. digital audio (*0-8288-4186-1*) Fr & Eur.

— Linguaphone German Course for Mandarin Chinese Speakers: Beginner's Course. (CHI & GER.). 1991. student ed. 295.00 incl. digital audio (*0-8288-4188-8*) Fr & Eur.

Linguaphone Staff. Linguaphone German Course for Norwegian Speakers: Beginner's Course. (GER & NOR.). 1991. student ed. 395.00 incl. cd-rom (*0-8288-4293-0*) Fr & Eur.

Linguaphone Staff. Linguaphone German Course for Portuguese Speakers: Beginner's Course. (GER & POR.). 1991. student ed. 295.00 incl. digital audio (*0-8288-3305-2*) Fr & Eur.

— Linguaphone German Course for Serbian Speakers: Beginner's Course. (GER & SER.). 1991. student ed. 295.00 incl. digital audio (*0-8288-4189-6*) Fr & Eur.

— Linguaphone German Course for Slovenian Speakers: Beginner's Course. (GER & SLV.). 1991. student ed. 295.00 incl. digital audio (*0-8288-4190-X*) Fr & Eur.

— Linguaphone German Course for Spanish Speakers: Beginner's Course. (GER & SPA.). 1991. student ed. 295.00 incl. digital audio (*0-8288-4167-5*) Fr & Eur.

— Linguaphone German Course for Spanish Speakers: Intermediate Course. (GER & SPA.). 1991. student ed. 225.00 incl. digital audio (*0-8288-4168-3*) Fr & Eur.

Linguaphone Staff. Linguaphone German Course for Swedish Speakers: Beginner's Course. (GER & SWE.). 1991. student ed. 295.00 incl. audio, digital audio (*0-8288-4192-6*); student ed. 395.00 incl. cd-rom (*0-8288-4193-4*) Fr & Eur.

Linguaphone Staff. Linguaphone German Course for Swedish Speakers: Intermediate Course. (GER & SWE.). 1991. student ed. 225.00 incl. digital audio (*0-8288-4191-8*) Fr & Eur.

— Linguaphone German Course for Turkish Speakers: Beginner's Course. (GER & TUR.). 1991. student ed. 295.00 incl. digital audio (*0-8288-4194-2*) Fr & Eur.

— Linguaphone Greek Course for English Speakers: Beginner's Course. (ENG & GRE.). 1991. student ed. 250.00 incl. digital audio (*0-8288-4195-0*) Fr & Eur.

— Linguaphone Greek Course for French Speakers: Beginner's Course. (FRE & GRE.). 1991. student ed. 225.00 incl. digital audio (*0-8288-4196-9*) Fr & Eur.

— Linguaphone Greek Course for German Speakers: Beginner's Course. (GER & GRE.). 1991. student ed. 250.00 incl. digital audio (*0-8288-4197-7*) Fr & Eur.

— Linguaphone Hebrew Course for English Speakers: Beginner's Course. (ENG & HEB.). 1991. student ed. 250.00 incl. digital audio (*0-8288-4198-5*) Fr & Eur.

— Linguaphone Hebrew Course for French Speakers: Beginner's Course. (FRE & HEB.). 1991. student ed. 250.00 incl. digital audio (*0-8288-4199-3*) Fr & Eur.

— Linguaphone Hindi Course for English Speakers: Beginner's Course. (ENG & HIN.). 1991. student ed. 225.00 incl. digital audio (*0-8288-3273-0*) Fr & Eur.

— Linguaphone Icelandic Course for English Speakers: Beginner's Course. (ENG & ICE.). 1991. student ed. 225.00 incl. digital audio (*0-8288-4200-0*) Fr & Eur.

— Linguaphone Italian Course for Danish Speakers: Beginner's Course. (DAN & ITA.). 1991. student ed. 295.00 incl. digital audio (*0-8288-4207-8*) Fr & Eur.

— Linguaphone Italian Course for Dutch Speakers: Beginner's Course. (DUT & ITA.). 1991. student ed. 295.00 incl. audio (*0-8288-3283-8*) Fr & Eur.

— Linguaphone Italian Course for Spanish Speakers: Beginner's Course. (ITA & SPA.). 1991. student ed. 295.00 incl. digital audio (*0-8288-4206-X*) Fr & Eur.

— Linguaphone Persian Course for English Speakers: Beginner's Course. (ENG & PER.). 1991. student ed. 95.00 incl. digital audio (*0-8288-4254-X*) Fr & Eur.

— Linguaphone Portuguese Course for Danish Speakers: Beginner's Course. (DAN & POR.). 1991. student ed. 225.00 incl. digital audio (*0-8288-4059-8*) Fr & Eur.

— Linguaphone Portuguese Course for Dutch Speakers: Beginner's Course. (DUT & POR.). 1991. student ed. 225.00 incl. digital audio (*0-8288-4058-X*) Fr & Eur.

— Linguaphone Portuguese Course for French Speakers: Beginner's Course. (FRE & POR.). 1991. student ed. 250.00 incl. digital audio (*0-8288-4060-1*) Fr & Eur.

— Linguaphone Portuguese Course for Norwegian Speakers: Beginner's Course. (NOR & POR.). 1991. student ed. 225.00 incl. digital audio (*0-8288-4076-8*) Fr & Eur.

Linguistic Society of the Philippines Staff, jt. auth. see Quakenbush, John S.

Linguistic Symposium on Romance Languages Staff. Contemporary Research in Romance Linguistics: Papers from the 22nd Linguistics Symposium on Romance Languages, El Paso/Juarez, February 22-24 1992. Amastae, Jon et al, eds. LC 95-15320. (Current Issues in Linguistic Theory Ser.: No. 123). viii, 381p. 1995. 95.00 (*1-55619-577-X*) J Benjamins Pubng Co.

— Contemporary Studies in Romance Linguistics. fac. ed. Suner, Margarita, ed. LC 78-13028. (Illus.). 414p. 1978. reprint ed. pap. 128.40 (*0-7837-7786-8*, 204754100007) Bks Demand.

***Linguistic Symposium on Romance Languages Staff.** Formal Perspectives of Romance Linguistics: Selected Papers from the 28th Linguistic Symposium on Romance Languages (LSRL XVIII): University Park, 16-19 April 1998. Authier, J. Marc et al, eds. LC 99-22266. (Current Issues in Linguistic Theory Ser.: Vol. 185). xii, 334p. 1999. 85.00 (*1-55619-962-7*) J Benjamins Pubng Co.

Linguistic Symposium on Romance Languages Staff. Linguistic Studies in Romance Languages: Proceedings of the Third Linguistic Symposium on Romance Languages. Campbell, R. Joe et al, eds. LC 74-76135. 271p. reprint ed. pap. 84.10 (*0-7837-6310-7*, 204602500010) Bks Demand.

Linguistic Symposium on Romance Languages Staff & Ashby, William J. Linguistic Perspectives on the Romance Languages: Selected Papers from the 21st Linguistic Symposium on Romance Languages (ISRL XXI), Santa Barbara, California, 21-24 February 1991. LC 93-18384. xxii, 404 p. 1993. write for info. (*90-272-3605-4*) J Benjamins Pubng.

Lingwood, James, ed. Erik Bulatov: Moscow. 96p. (Orig.). 1989. pap. 25.00 (*3-907509-03-X*, Pub. by Parkett Verlag AG) Dist Art Pubs.

— Ilya Kabakov: Ten Characters. 72p. (Orig.). 1989. pap. 22.50 (*0-905263-47-2*, Pub. by Parkett Verlag AG) Dist Art Pubs.

Lingwood, James, ed. see Bird, Jon, et al.

Linh Duy Vo. Dear Daddy. (Illus.). 80p. 1996. reprint ed. text 25.00 (*0-9654498-0-7*) Voco Pub.

Linhai. Essentials of Qigong. Date not set. pap. 19.95 (*0-8488-1817-2*) Amereon Ltd.

— Keep Your Wife Happy Qigong. Date not set. pap. 19.95 (*0-8488-1822-9*) Amereon Ltd.

— Qigong Therapy & How to Use It. Date not set. pap. 14.95 (*0-8488-1821-0*) Amereon Ltd.

— Sea of Trees, Qigong Adventure. Date not set. lib. bdg. 23.95 (*0-8488-1820-2*) Amereon Ltd.

Linhart, J. F., ed. Plasma Physics: Proceedings of the EUR-CNEN Association Meeting, 1969. 1975. pap. 16.25 (*0-08-020450-3*, Pergamon Pr) Elsevier.

Linhart, Letty. Clues for the Clueless: Personal Experiences with Spiritual Transformation. Adams, Deborah B., ed. LC 96-68914. 100p. (Orig.). 1996. pap. 12.95 (*0-9652420-0-5*) Write Perspect.

Linhart, Robert. The Assembly Line. Crosland, Margaret, tr. from FRE. LC 81-1703. Orig. Title: L'Etabli. 160p. (Orig.). 1981. pap. text 15.95 (*0-87023-322-X*) U of Mass Pr.

Linhart, Sepp & Fruhstuck, Sabine, eds. The Culture of Japan As Seen Through Its Leisure. LC 97-37508. (SUNY Series in Japan in Transition). (Illus.). 398p. (C). 1998. pap. text 27.95 (*0-7914-3792-2*) State U NY Pr.

— The Culture of Japan As Seen Through Its Leisure. LC 97-37508. (SUNY Series in Japan in Transition). (Illus.). 398p. (C). 1998. text 83.50 (*0-7914-3791-4*) State U NY Pr.

Linhoff, Aimee, jt. auth. see Jay, Bill.

Linial, Andrew V., jt. auth. see Gerhardt, John J.

Linial, Michal, ed. Secretory Systems & Toxins. (Illus.). 475p. 1998. text 95.00 (*90-5702-335-0*) Gordon & Breach.

Linick, Andrew S. Nunchaku, Karate's Deadliest Fighting Sticks. 3rd ed. LC 75-6144. (Illus.). 240p. 1982. reprint ed. 29.95 (*0-917098-01-3*); reprint ed. pap. 17.95 (*0-917098-00-5*) LKA Inc.

— Picture Profits: Let Your Camera Make Money for You. 4th ed. 1981. pap. 7.95 (*0-917098-02-1*) LKA Inc.

Liniger, C., jt. ed. see Assal, J. P.

Liniger-Goumaz, Max. Historical Dictionary of Equatorial Guinea. 2nd ed. LC 88-11409. (African Historical Dictionaries Ser.: No. 21). (Illus.). 270p. 1999. 34.50 (*0-8108-2120-6*) Scarecrow.

***Liniger-Goumaz, Max.** Historical Dictionary of Equatorial Guinea. 3rd ed. (African Historical Dictionaries Ser.: No. 21). (Illus.). 656p. 2000. 115.00 (*0-8108-3394-8*) Scarecrow.

Liniger-Goumaz, Max. Small Is Not Always Beautiful: The Story of Equatorial Guinea. 200p. (C). 1989. lib. bdg. 50.00 (*0-389-20861-2*, N8419) B&N Imports.

Lininer, jt. auth. see Edye.

Lininger, Clarence. Best War at the Time. 1964. 15.00 (*0-8315-0068-9*) Speller.

***Lininger, Linda.** 10 Steps to Writing a Selling Book Proposal. 32p. 2000. pap. 19.95 (*0-9678605-1-2*) InfoHi.

Lininger, Linda, jt. auth. see Anderson, Jean.

Lininger, Skye, Jr. The Natural Pharmacy: From the Top Experts in the Field, Your Essential Guide to Herbs, Vitamins, Minerals & Homeopathic Remedies. LC 97-43106. 400p. 1998. per. 19.99 (*0-7615-1227-6*) Prima Pub.

Lininger, Skye W., et al. A-Z Guide to Drug-Herb-Vitamin Interactions: How to Improve Your Health & Avoid Problems When Using... LC 99-39218. 208p. 2000. pap. 19.95 (*0-7615-1599-2*) Prima Pub.

— The Natural Pharmacy: From the Top Experts in the Field, Your Essential Guide to Vitamins, Herbs, Minerals & Homeopathic Remedies. rev. ed. LC 99-56624. 480p. 1999. pap. 24.95 (*0-7615-1967-X*) Prima Pub.

Linington, George E. & Gardlund, Sharon L. Experiments & Exercises for General Chemistry. rev. ed. 208p. (C). 1994. spiral bd. 18.95 (*0-8403-9443-8*) Kendall-Hunt.

Linington, S. & Wiens, D. Mistletoes of Africa. (Illus.). 370p. 1998. 130.00 (*1-900347-56-3*, Pub. by Royal Botnic Grdns) Balogh.

Linington, S., ed. see De Kok, Luit J.

Linington, S., ed. see Hall, Robert.

Linjama, T. Internet with Explorer 4.0. LC 98-16074. 1998. write for info. (*0-7638-0019-8*) Paradigm MN.

Link. Conflicting Visions, Vol. 1. LC 98-87545. 1999. pap. text 32.95 (*0-312-13357-X*) St Martin.

An Asterisk (*) at the beginning of an entry indicates that the title is appearing for the first time.

— The South in the History of the Nation, 2 vols. LC 98-87545. 1999. pap. 32.95 (*0-312-15787-8*) St Martin.

Link, jt. auth. see Ramanathan.

LInk, Aaron, jt. auth. see Snead, John.

Link, Albert N. Evaluating Economic Damages: A Handbook for Attorneys. LC 91-47571. 256p. 1992. 65.00 (*0-89930-763-9*, LV#, Quorum Bks) Greenwood.

— Evaluating Public Sector Research & Development. LC 95-43771. 160p. 1996. 52.95 (*0-275-95368-8*, Praeger Pubs) Greenwood.

— A Generosity of Spirit: The Early History of the Research Triangle Park. (Illus.). 136p. 1995. 19.95 (*0-9648051-0-3*) Resrch Triangle.

— Public Accountability: Evaluating Technology-Based Institutions. 5p. 1998. 95.00 (*0-7923-8312-5*) Kluwer Academic.

— Research & Development in U. S. Manufacturing. LC 80-21542. 124p. 1981. 47.95 (*0-275-90672-8*, C0672, Praeger Pubs) Greenwood.

— Technological Change & Productivity Growth. (Fundamentals of Pure & Applied Economics Ser.: Vol. 13). viii, 78p. 1987. pap. text 46.00 (*3-7186-0347-0*) Gordon & Breach.

Link, Albert N., ed. Cooperative Research & Development: The Industry, University, Government Relationship. (C). 1989. lib. bdg. 95.50 (*0-89838-303-X*) Kluwer Academic.

Link, Albert N. & Boger, Michael B. The Art & Science of Business Valuation. LC 99-10383. (Illus.). 152p. 1999. 55.00 (*1-56720-171-7*, Q171, Quorum Bks) Greenwood.

Link, Albert N., et al. Economics: A Study of Markets. 2nd ed. 429p. (C). 1992. text 97.00 (*1-878907-70-0*) TechBooks.

Link, Albert N., jt. auth. see Bozeman, Barry.

Link, Albert N., jt. auth. see Hebert, Robert F.

Link, Albert N., jt. auth. see Leyden, Dennis P.

Link, Alice L. A Woman Called Easter: Easter Straker: Broadcasting Pioneer. LC 96-85324. 156p. 1996. pap. 16.50 (*0-7880-0695-9*, Fairway Pr) CSS OH.

Link, Andrew J. 2-D Proteome Analysis Protocols. LC 98-38677. (Methods in Molecular Biology Ser.). (Illus.). 608p. 1998. 89.50 (*0-89603-524-7*) Humana.

Link, Ann L. Group Work with Elders: 50 Therapeutic Exercises for Reminiscence, Validation, & Remotivation. LC 97-11591. (Illus.). 142p. (Orig.). 1997. pap. 28.95 (*1-56887-030-2*, GWWBP, Prof Resc Pr) Pro Resource.

Link, Arthur S. Woodrow Wilson: Revolution, War & Peace. LC 79-50909. 152p. (C). 1979. pap. text 11.95 (*0-88295-798-8*) Harlan Davidson.

Link, Arthur S., ed. The Deliberations of the Council of Four, March 24-June 28, 1919: Notes of the Official Interpreter, Paul Mantoux, 2 vols., Set. (Papers of Woodrow Wilson). (Illus.). 1283p. 1992. text 125.00 (*0-691-04793-6*, Pub. by Princeton U Pr) Cal Prin Full Svc.

— The Papers of Woodrow Wilson: April 8, 1922-February 6, 1924, Vol. 69. 375p. 1993. text 75.00 (*0-691-04812-6*, Pub. by Princeton U Pr) Cal Prin Full Svc.

— The Papers of Woodrow Wilson: December 24, 1920-April 7, 1922, Vol. 67. (Illus.). 655p. 1993. text 75.00 (*0-691-04799-5*, Pub. by Princeton U Pr) Cal Prin Full Svc.

— The Papers of Woodrow Wilson: September 14 to November 8, 1918, Vol. 51. LC 66-10880. (Illus.). 648p. 1985. text 75.00 (*0-691-04730-8*, Pub. by Princeton U Pr) Cal Prin Full Svc.

— The Papers of Woodrow Wilson Vol. 60: June 1 - June 17, 1919. 752p. 1989. text 75.00 (*0-691-04762-6*, Pub. by Princeton U Pr) Cal Prin Full Svc.

— The Papers of Woodrow Wilson Vol. 61: June 18 - July 25, 1919. 620p. (C). 1989. text 75.00 (*0-691-04766-9*, Pub. by Princeton U Pr) Cal Prin Full Svc.

— The Papers of Woodrow Wilson Vol. 62: July 26 September 3, 1919. (Illus.). 688p. 1990. text 75.00 (*0-691-04767-7*, Pub. by Princeton U Pr) Cal Prin Full Svc.

— The Papers of Woodrow Wilson Vol. 63: September 4-November 5, 1919. (Illus.). 546p. 1990. text 75.00 (*0-691-04775-8*, Pub. by Princeton U Pr) Cal Prin Full Svc.

— The Papers of Woodrow Wilson Vol. 65: February 28-July 31, 1920. (Illus.). 673p. 1992. text 75.00 (*0-691-04792-8*, Pub. by Princeton U Pr) Cal Prin Full Svc.

— The Papers of Woodrow Wilson Vol. 66: August 2-December 23, 1920. (Illus.). 583p. 1992. text 75.00 (*0-691-04798-7*, Pub. by Princeton U Pr) Cal Prin Full Svc.

— Woodrow Wilson & a Revolutionary World, 1913-1921. fac. ed. LC 82-2565. (Supplementary Volumes to The Papers of Woodrow Wilson). 249p. 1982. reprint ed. pap. 77.20 (*0-7837-8053-2*, 204780600008) Bks Demand.

Link, Arthur S., et al, eds. The Papers of Woodrow Wilson: January 11-February 7, 1919, Vol. 54. (Illus.). 616p. 1986. text 75.00 (*0-691-04736-7*, Pub. by Princeton U Pr) Cal Prin Full Svc.

— The Papers of Woodrow Wilson: November 6, 1919 - February 27, 1920, Vol. 64. 565p. 1991. text 75.00 (*0-691-04791-X*, Pub. by Princeton U Pr) Cal Prin Full Svc.

— The Papers of Woodrow Wilson Vol. 52: Contents & Index, Vol. 40-49, 51. 240p. 1987. text 75.00 (*0-691-04744-8*, Pub. by Princeton U Pr) Cal Prin Full Svc.

— The Papers of Woodrow Wilson Vol. 56: March 17 - April 4, 1919. (Illus.). 696p. 1987. text 75.00 (*0-691-04742-1*, Pub. by Princeton U Pr) Cal Prin Full Svc.

— The Papers of Woodrow Wilson Vol. 58: April 23 to May 9, 1919. (Illus.). 696p. 1988. text 75.00 (*0-691-04748-0*, Pub. by Princeton U Pr) Cal Prin Full Svc.

— The Papers of Woodrow Wilson Vol. 59: May 10 - May 31, 1919. (Illus.). 744p. 1988. text 75.00 (*0-691-04754-5*, Pub. by Princeton U Pr) Cal Prin Full Svc.

Link, Arthur S. & Hirst, David W., eds. The Papers of Woodrow Wilson: November 9, 1918-January 11, 1919, Vol. 53. LC 66-10880. (Illus.). 736p. 1985. text 75.00 (*0-691-04731-6*, Pub. by Princeton U Pr) Cal Prin Full Svc.

Link, Arthur S. & McCormick, Richard L. Progressivism. Eisenstadt, A. S. & Franklin, John H., eds. LC 82-15857. (American History Ser.). 164p. (C). 1983. pap. text 11.95 (*0-88295-814-3*) Harlan Davidson.

Link, Arthur S., et al. A Concise History of the American People. LC 83-23184. (Illus.). 622p. (C). 1984. pap. text 25.95 (*0-88295-817-8*) Harlan Davidson.

— The Papers of Woodrow Wilson: February 8-March 16, 1919, Vol. 55. Hirst, David W. et al, eds. (Illus.). 604p. 1986. text 75.00 (*0-691-04737-5*, Pub. by Princeton U Pr) Cal Prin Full Svc.

— The Papers of Woodrow Wilson Vol. 57: April 5 - April 22, 1919. Aandahl, Frederick, ed. (Illus.). 704p. 1987. text 75.00 (*0-691-04743-X*, Pub. by Princeton U Pr) Cal Prin Full Svc.

Link, Arthur S., jt. auth. see Link, William A.

Link, Arthur S., ed. see Axson, Stockton.

Link, Beulah, jt. auth. see Link, Eugene.

Link, Charles E. Jesus' Epilogue to the Sermon on the Mount: A Study of the Lord's Prayer. LC 94-24369. 88p. (Orig.). 1995. pap. 9.50 (*0-7880-0374-7*) CSS OH.

— A Meal for the Road: 14 Sermons on the Lord's Prayer. LC 93-30840. 92p. 1994. pap. 9.75 (*1-55673-702-5*) CSS OH.

— Out of the Mouths of Gentiles: Biblical Ingredients for an Inclusive Theology. 84p. (Orig.). 1995. pap. 7.25 (*0-7880-0619-3*) CSS OH.

Link, David & McDonnell, Ed, eds. Current Issues in Medical Device Quality Systems. 5th ed. LC 97-221321. 1996. pap. 225.00 (*1-57020-075-0*, GMP4-209) Assn Adv Med Instrn.

Link, David & Soderquist, Larry D. Law of Federal Estate & Gift Taxation, 1978-1990. rev. ed. 100.00 (*0-317-11947-8*) West Group.

Link, Dorothea. The National Court Theatre in Mozart's Vienna: Sources & Documents 1783-1792. (Illus.). 560p. 1998. text 125.00 (*0-19-816673-7*) OUP.

***Link Editorial Staff, contrib. by.** Link: A Critical Journal on the Arts in Baltimore & the World: "This Place Meant/Displacement" (Illus.). 176p. 2000. pap. 10.00 (*1-892813-03-3*, Pub. by Link) Bernhard DeBoer Inc.

LINK Editors. LINK No. 1: A Critical Journal on the Arts in Baltimore & the World: Inaugural Issue. (Illus.). 136p. 1996. pap. 7.00 (*1-892813-00-9*) Link.

— LINK No. 2: A Critical Journal on the Arts in Baltimore & the World: "You Are Here" (Illus.). 186p. 1997. pap. 8.00 (*1-892813-01-7*) Link.

— LINK No. 3: A Critical Journal on the Arts in Baltimore & the World: "RE:Visionary Art" 1998. pap. 10.00 (*1-892813-02-5*) Link.

Link, Edward P. An Audit of the System, Not of the People: A QS-9000 Pocket Guide for Every Employee. (Illus.). 136p. 1998. pap. text. write for info. (*0-9668699-1-5*) Qual Pursuit.

— An Audit of the System, Not of the People: An ISO 14000 Pocket Guide for Every Employee. Nguyen, Mary-Rose, ed. (Illus.). 90p. 1999. pap. text. write for info. (*0-9668699-4-X*) Qual Pursuit.

— An Audit of the System, Not of the People: An ISO-9000 Pocket Guide for Every Employee. (Illus.). 84p. 1997. pap. text. write for info. (*0-9668699-0-7*) Qual Pursuit.

— Una Auditoria del Sistema, No de la Gente: Guia de Bolsillo de ISO 9000 para Cada Empleado. (SPA., Illus.). 87p. 1997. pap. text. write for info. (*0-9668699-2-3*) Qual Pursuit.

— Una Auditoria del Sistema No de la Gente: Guia de Bolsillo QS-9000 para Cada Empleado. Rolleri-Freire, Liliana, tr. (SPA., Illus.). 155p. 1998. pap. text. write for info. (*0-9668699-3-1*) Qual Pursuit.

Link, Eric C., jt. ed. see Thompson, G. R.

Link, Eugene & Link, Beulah. The Tale of Three Cities: Gran Quivira in the Southwest. LC 97-90704. 1998. pap. 12.95 (*0-533-12461-1*) Vantage.

Link, Eugene P. Democratic-Republican Societies, 1790-1800. (History - United States Ser.). 256p. 1993. reprint ed. lib. bdg. 79.00 (*0-7812-4881-7*) Rprt Serv.

— The Social Ideas of American Physicians, 1776-1976: Studies of the Humanitarian Tradition in Medicine. LC 91-50603. (Illus.). 320p. 1993. 46.50 (*0-945636-34-2*) Susquehanna U Pr.

Link, Eugene P., ed. Stubborn Weeds: Popular & Controversial Chinese Literature after the Cultural Revolution. LC 82-48268. (Chinese Literature in Translation Ser.). 302p. 1983. reprint ed. pap. 93.70 (*0-7837-9658-7*, 205929100005) Bks Demand.

Link, Frances R., ed. Essays on the Intellect. fac. ed. LC 84-81488. (Illus.). 159p. (Orig.). 1985. reprint ed. pap. 49.30 (*0-608-01030-8*, 208250600011) Bks Demand.

Link, Frances R. & Almquist, S. Thinking to Write: A Work Journal Program. 62p. (Orig.). 1987. pap. 2.50 (*0-86631-120-3*); teacher ed. 5.00 (*0-317-62982-4*) Curriculum Dev Assocs.

Link, Frederick M., ed. see Behn, Aphra.

Link, Frederick M., ed. see Cather, Willa.

Link, Frederick M., ed. see Dryden, John.

Link, Frederick M., ed. see Scott, Sir Walter.

Link, Gail. All I Ask of You. 448p. 1997. mass mkt. 5.99 (*0-8439-4293-2*, Leisure Bks) Dorchester Pub Co.

— Encantadora. 448p. (Orig.). 1997. mass mkt. 5.99 (*0-8439-4181-2*) Dorchester Pub Co.

— Forsaking All Others. 368p. (Orig.). 1997. mass mkt. 5.50 (*0-8439-4151-0*) Dorchester Pub Co.

— Lone Star Lover. 1997. per. 3.99 (*0-373-24121-6*, 1-24121-5) Silhouette.

— Marriage-to-Be? 1996. per. 3.99 (*0-373-24035-X*, 1-24035-7) Silhouette.

***Link, Gail.** Sullivan's Child. 2000. mass mkt. 4.50 (*0-373-24325-1*) Harlequin Bks.

Link, Gail. Texan's Bride. 1998. per. 4.25 (*0-373-24163-1*, 1-24163-7) Silhouette.

Link, Geoffrey & Beggs, Marjorie. Serving Families, Building Partnerships. Seiderman, Ethel & Lee, Lisa, eds. (Illus.). 72p. (Orig.). 1996. pap. 10.00 (*0-936434-97-X*, PSP-SF) SF Study Ctr.

Link, Geoffrey, ed. see Lucas, Alice.

Link, George, ed. see Luther, Martin.

Link, George K. & Einarson, Benedict, eds. Theophrastus: De Causis Plantarum, Vols. 2-3, Vol. 2. LC 76-370781. (Loeb Classical Library: Nos. 474-475). 361p. 1990. text 18.95 (*0-674-99523-6*) HUP.

— Theophrastus: De Causis Plantarum, Vols. 2-3, Vol. 3. LC 76-370781. (Loeb Classical Library: Nos. 474-475). 465p. 1990. text 18.95 (*0-674-99524-4*) HUP.

Link, George K., tr. see Einarson, Benedict, ed.

Link, Godehard. Algebraic Semantics in Language & Philosophy. LC 97-46523. (Lecture Notes Ser.). 350p. (C). 1998. text 64.95 (*1-57586-091-0*); pap. text 24.95 (*1-57586-090-2*) CSLI.

***Link, Gunther.** Eugenische Zwangssterilisationen Und Schwangerschaftsaruche Im Nationalsozialismus: Dargestellt Am Beispiel Der Universitatsfrauenklinik Freiburg. (Illus.). XV, 614p. 1999. 73.95 (*3-631-33871-6*) P Lang Pubng.

Link, H., et al. The Costs of Road Infrastructure & Congestion in Europe. LC 99-25664. (Contributions to Economic Ser.). (Illus.). xii, 137p. 1999. pap. 47.00 (*3-7908-1201-3*) Spr-Verlag.

Link, Hans-Georg, ed. The Roots of Our Common Faith: Faith in the Scriptures & in the Early Church. LC BT0771.2.R66. (Faith & Order Papers: No. 119). (Illus.). 143p. reprint ed. pap. 44.40 (*0-7837-6002-7*, 204581200008) Bks Demand.

Link-Heer, Ursula. Prousts "A la Recherche du Temps Perdu" und die Form der Autobiographie: Zum Verhaltnis und Pragmatischer Erzahltexte. (Beihefte zu Poetica Ser.: Vol. 18). (GER.). 348p. 1988. 56.00 (*90-6032-214-2*, Pub. by B R Gruner) Humanities.

Link, Howard A. The Art of Shibata Zeshin: The Mr. & Mrs. James E. O'Brien Collection at the Honolulu Academy of Arts. LC 79-24341. (Illus.). 196p. (C). 1979. 14.99 (*0-937426-23-7*) Honolu Arts.

— Prints by Utagawa Hiroshige: The James A. Michener Collection, 2 vols., Vol. 1. (ENG & JPN., Illus.). 167p. (Orig.). (C). 1991. pap. 32.50 (*0-937426-13-X*, 6222) Honolu Arts.

— Prints by Utagawa Hiroshige Vol. 2: The James A. Michener Collection, 2 vols., Set. (ENG & JPN., Illus.). 167p. (Orig.). (C). 1991. boxed set 49.95 (*0-937426-18-0*) Honolu Arts.

— Waves & Plagues: The Art of Masami Teraoka. (Illus.). 96p. 1988. pap. 16.95 (*0-87701-590-2*) Chronicle Bks.

— Waves & Plagues: The Art of Masami Teraoka. (Illus.). 96p. 1989. 29.95 (*0-87701-602-X*) Chronicle Bks.

Link, Howard A. & Kobayashi, Tadashi. Edo Beauties in Ukiyo-e: The James A. Michener Collection. (Illus.). 183p. (Orig.). 1995. pap. 17.50 (*0-937426-30-X*) Honolu Arts.

Link, Howard A., jt. auth. see YuHo, Tseng.

Link, Howard A., ed. see Ecke, Tseng Y.

Link, J., et al. In-Vivo Magnetic Resonance Spectroscopy I: Probesheads & Radiofrequency Pulses, Spectrum Analysis. LC 91-30593. 284p. 1992. 119.00 (*0-387-54547-6*, QP519) Spr-Verlag.

***Link, Jay.** Linux Graphics Programming with SVGalib: An Easy to Use Reference for Linux Graphics Programmers. LC 99-53503. (Illus.). 600p. 2000. pap. 49.99 (*1-57610-524-5*) Coriolis Grp.

Link, Joe. Insurance. 350p. 1990. pap. 125.00 (*0-85297-386-1*, Pub. by Chartered Bank) St Mut.

Link, John. The Breast Cancer Survival Manual: A Step-by-Step Guide for the Woman with Newly Diagnosed Breast Cancer. LC 97-38722. (Illus.). 208p. 1998. pap. 15.95 (*0-8050-5515-0*) H Holt & Co.

***Link, John.** The Breast Cancer Survival Manual: A Step-by-Step Guide for the Woman with Newly Diagnosed Breast Cancer. 2nd ed. LC 99-47515. 2000. pap. 15.00 (*0-8050-6400-1*, Owl) H Holt & Co.

Link, John E., jt. auth. see Bailey, John J.

***Link, John F.** Elliott Carter: A Guide to Research LC 99-42718. (Garland Reference Library of the Humanities). 2000. 70.00 (*0-8153-2432-4*, Garland Publ) Taylor & Francis.

Link, Julie, ed. How to Live the Victorious Life. 112p. 1986. pap. 6.99 (*0-310-33481-0*, 6660P) Zondervan.

Link, Julie, ed. see Chambers, Oswald.

Link, Luther. The Devil: The Archfiend in Art from the Sixth to the Sixteenth Century. LC 95-30181. (Illus.). 208p. 1996. 29.95 (*0-8109-3226-1*, Pub. by Abrams) Time Warner.

Link, M. De Pascua A Pentecostes - Ano B. (SPA.). 64p. 1997. pap. 1.95 (*0-88347-377-1*) Res Christian Liv.

Link, M. & Crowley, Kate. Love of Loons. (Voyageur Wilderness Ser.). (Illus.). 96p. (Orig.). 1990. pap. 16.95 (*0-89658-072-5*) Voyageur Pr.

Link, Mae M. & Coleman, Hubert A. Medical Support: Army Air Forces in World War II. 1027p. 1992. pap. text. write for info. (*0-912799-69-2*) AFH & MP.

Link, Mardi, ed. see Jenkins, Jerrold R.

Link, Margaret S. The Pollen Path: A Collection of Navajo Myths. LC 98-66271. (Illus.). 240p. 1998. pap. 14.95 (*1-885772-09-2*) Kiva Pubng.

Link, Margaret S., retold by. The Pollen Path: A Collection of Navajo Myths. LC 56-7272. (Illus.). xiv, 210p. 1956. 32.50 (*0-8047-0473-2*) Stanford U Pr.

Link, Marion, jt. auth. see Van Hock, Susan.

Link, Mark. Action 2000: Praying Scripture in a Contemporary Way, Cycle C. 412p. 1994. pap. 8.95 (*0-88347-396-8*) Res Christian Liv.

— Advent 2000 - Year C. 64p. 1998. pap. 1.95 (*0-88347-375-5*) Res Christian Liv.

— Bible 2000: Genesis to Revelation - for Busy People. (Vision 2000 Ser.). 358p. (Orig.). (YA). 1994. pap. 8.95 (*0-7829-0459-9*, 22048) Res Christian Liv.

— Biblia, 2000: Bible, 2000 in Spanish. 358p. 1997. pap. text 8.95 (*0-7829-0612-5*) Tabor Pub.

***Link, Mark.** Celebration of Hope: Reflections for the Jubilee Year. 64p. 1999. pap. 4.95 (*0-88347-444-1*, Pub. by T More) BookWorld.

Link, Mark. Challenge, 2000: Daily Meditations Based on the Spiritual Exercises of St. Ignatius. (Mark Link, S. J., Library). 385p. 1993. pap. 8.95 (*0-7829-0363-0*, 22049) Res Christian Liv.

— Cuaresma - Ano B. 64p. 1997. pap. 1.95 (*0-88347-376-3*) Res Christian Liv.

— Cuaresma 2000/Ano C. (SPA.). 64p. 1998. pap. 1.95 (*0-88347-354-2*, 7354) T More.

— De Pascua a Pentecostes. 1997. pap. 1.95 (*0-88347-356-9*) Tabor Pub.

Link, Mark. Desafio, 2000. (SPA.). 386p. 8.95 (*0-88347-442-5*, 661-715, Pub. by T More) BookWorld.

Link, Mark. Desafio, 2000. 386p. 1997. pap. text 8.95 (*0-7829-0611-7*) Tabor Pub.

— Easter to Pentecost 2000. 64p. 1997. pap. 1.95 (*0-88347-355-0*) Tabor Pub.

— Easter to Pentecost 2000, Year B. 64p. 1997. pap. text 1.95 (*0-88347-374-7*) Res Christian Liv.

— Espiritu, 2000. 60p. 1994. pap. text 1.95 (*0-7829-0478-5*) Tabor Pub.

— God the Father. (Meditations for the Millennium Ser.: Vol. 3). (Illus.). 168p. 1998. pap. 9.95 (*0-88347-423-9*) T More.

— Holy Spirit. rev. ed. (Meditations for the Millennium Ser.: l. 2). 168p. 1998. pap. 9.95 (*0-88347-422-0*) T More.

— Jesus. 2nd rev. ed. (Meditations for the Millennium Ser.: Vol. 1). (Illus.). 176p. 1998. pap. 9.95 (*0-88347-421-2*) T More.

— Jesus, 2000. 416p. 1997. 8.95 (*0-88347-381-X*) Res Christian Liv.

— Lent, 2000. 64p. 1997. pap. text 1.95 (*0-88347-353-4*) Tabor Pub.

— Lent, 2000/Year B. 64p. 1997. pap. text 1.95 (*0-88347-373-9*) Res Christian Liv.

— Med. for the Millennium: Set. 1998. pap. 27.95 (*0-88347-420-4*, 661-025 7420) T More.

— Mission 2000 - Year B: Daily Meditations Based on the Lectionary, Cycle B. (Mark Link, S. J., Library). 412p. 1993. pap. 8.95 (*0-7829-0048-8*, 22046) Res Christian Liv.

— Psalms Beyond, 2000. (Illus.). 200p. (Orig.). 1996. pap. 12.95 (*0-88347-360-7*, 7360) Res Christian Liv.

— Psalms, 2000. 246p. 1996. pap. 8.95 (*0-7829-0633-8*) Res Christian Liv.

— Vision 2000: Year A-Praying Scripture in a Contemporary Way. 1998. pap. 8.95 (*0-88347-432-8*) T More.

Link, Mark J. Spirit 2000: Meditations on Discipleship. 1997. pap. 1.95 (*0-88347-398-4*, 661-125 7398) T More.

Link, Mark S. Advent - Christmas - Year. 1998. pap. 1.95 (*0-88347-400-X*, 661-127 7400) T More.

— Cuaresma - Ano A: Lent in Spanish. 1998. pap. 1.95 (*0-88347-414-X*, 661-129 7414) T More.

— Easter to Pentecost 2000, Year A. 1999. 1.95 (*0-88347-402-6*, 661-132 7402) T More.

— Lent 2000 - Year A. 1998. pap. 1.95 (*0-88347-401-8*, 661-139 7401) T More.

***Link, Mark S. J.** Mission Year Book. 1999. pap. 8.95 (*0-88347-457-3*, Pub. by T More) BookWorld.

Link, Martin, jt. auth. see Blood, Charles L.

Link, Martin A., ed. Navajo: A Century of Progress, 1868-1968. LC 68-15787. (Illus.). 110p. 1968. 6.00 (*0-318-19652-2*) Navajo.

Link, Matthew. Rainbow Handbook Hawaii: The Islands' Ultimate Gay Guide. LC 98-92014. (Illus.). 247p. 1999. pap. 14.95 (*0-9665805-0-8*) Missing Link Prod.

Link, Mike. Black Hills - Badlands: The Web of the West. (Voyageur Wilderness Ser.). (Illus.). 120p. 1980. reprint ed. pap. 14.95 (*0-89658-017-2*) Voyageur Pr.

Link, Mike & Crowley, Kate. Romancing Minnesota: Intimate Places to Stay & Dine. (Orig.). 1995. pap. 12.95 (*1-57025-043-X*) Pfeifer-Hamilton.

Link, Mike & Crowley, Kathleen. Hiking Minnesota. LC 98-48170. (America's Best Day Hiking Ser.). (Illus.). 216p. 1999. pap. 19.95 (*0-88011-900-4*) Human Kinetics.

Link, Mike, jt. auth. see Bireda, Martha R.

Link, Mike, jt. auth. see Crowley, Kate.

Link, Nelle W. Smocking & Gathering for Fabric Manipulation. Kliot, Jules & Kliot, Kaethe, eds. (Illus.). 112p. 1987. pap. 10.00 (*0-916896-25-0*) Lacis Pubns.

Link, O. Winston. Steam, Steel & Stars: America's Last Steam Railroad. (Illus.). 216p. 1994. pap. 19.95 (*0-8109-2587-7*, Pub. by Abrams) Time Warner.

— Steam, Steel & Stars: America's Last Steam Railroad. (Illus.). 144p. 1998. pap. 19.98 (*0-8109-8185-8*, Pub. by Abrams) Time Warner.

***Link, O. Winston, photos by.** The Last Steam Railroad in America. (Illus.). 144p. 2000. 19.98 (*0-8109-8201-3*, Pub. by Abrams) Time Warner.

Link, O. Winston & Garver, Thomas H. The Last Steam Railroad in America: From Tidewater to Whitetop. LC 95-7406. (Illus.). 144p. 1995. 49.50 (*0-8109-3575-9*, Pub. by Abrams) Time Warner.

Link, P. K., et al, eds. Regional Geology of Eastern Idaho & Western Wyoming. (Memoir Ser.: No. 179). (Illus.). 1992. 44.38 (0-8137-1179-7) Geol Soc.

Link, P. S., ed. Middle East Imbroglio: Status & Prospects. 298p. (C). 1996. lib. bdg. 95.00 (1-56072-391-2) Nova Sci Pubs.

Link, Paul. A Time to Sow & a Time to Reap. (Illus.). 178p. 1990. pap. text. write for info. (0-318-66612-X) P Link.

— A Time to Sow & a Time to Reap. rev. ed. 182p. 1991. pap. text. write for info. (0-9625216-1-2) P Link.

Link, Paul & Phoenix, E. Chilton. Rocks, Rails & Trails. 194p. 1996. reprint ed. pap. text 25.00 (0-939696-01-0) Idaho Mus Nat Hist.

Link, Perry. Evening Chats in Beijing. 336p. 1993. pap. 14.95 (0-393-31065-5) Norton.

Link, Perry, ed. see Binyan, Liu.

Link, Perry, ed. see Liu Binyan.

Link, Perry, ed. see Liu, Pin-Yen.

Link, Peter K. Basic Petroleum Geology. 2nd rev. ed. LC 81-83909. 425p. 1987. 55.00 (0-930972-10-4, P7140) Oil & Gas.

Link, Phil. Another Time: A Fictional Story of the Truth about Fraternities at Chapel Hill in the Thirties. 200p. 1990. pap. 9.95 (0-9628079-0-7) Carolina Cerulean.

***Link, R. E.** Dynamic Fracture Initiation: Toughness of ASTM A533, Grade B Steel Plate. 92p. 1998. pap. 7.50 (0-16-062977-2) USGPO.

Link, Robert G. English Theories of Economic Fluctuations, 1815-1848. LC 68-54282. (Columbia University. Studies in the Social Sciences: No. 598). reprint ed. 27.50 (0-404-51598-3) AMS Pr.

Link, Russell. Landscaping for Wildlife in the Pacific Northwest. LC 99-14300. (Illus.). 250p. 1999. pap. 29.95 (0-295-97820-1) U of Wash Pr.

Link, S. Gordden. Personal Journal for Yesterday, Now, & Tomorrow: And Other Selected Poems. 128p. 1992. 12.50 (0-9634744-0-5) B Souders.

Link, S. W., ed. The Wave Theory of Difference & Similarity. (Scientific Psychology Ser.). 384p. (C). 1992. text 79.95 (0-8058-0926-0) L Erlbaum Assocs.

Link-Salinger, Ruth. Jewish Law in Our Time. 183p. 17.95 (0-8197-0486-5); pap. 12.95 (0-8197-0487-3) Bloch.

Link-Salinger, Ruth, et al, eds. A Straight Path: Studies in Medieval Philosophy & Culture. LC 87-18403. (Essays in Honor of Arthur Hyman Ser.). 309p. 1988. 35.00 (0-8132-0648-0) Cath U Pr.

Link-Salinger, Ruth & Herrera, Robert, eds. Scholars, Savants & Their Texts: Studies in Philosophy & Religious Thought: Essays in Honor of Arthur Hyman. 271p. (C). 1989. text 48.95 (0-8204-0834-4) P Lang Pubng.

Link, Stephen W. & Perkins, Daniel. Psychology from a Personal Perspective. 4th ed. 168p. (C). 1993. text 32.00 (0-536-58455-9) Pearson Custom.

Link, Stephen W., ed. see Redding, Gordon M. & Wallace, Benjamin.

Link, Terry & Beggs, Marjorie, eds. Exploring Empowerment: Myths & Realities. LC 94-224232. 35p. (Orig.). 1994. pap. 5.00 (0-936434-74-0, Pub. by Zellerbach Fam Fund) Intl Spec Bk.

Link, Terry, ed. see Berson, Misha.

Link, Terry, ed. see Manian, Padma.

***Link, Thomas.** Die Politische (Un-)Person: Politisches Denken Am Ubergang Vom Jugendlichen Zum Erwachsenen. (GER.). 184p. 1999. 37.95 (3-631-34459-7) P Lang Pubng.

Link, Tom. Universal City & North Hollywood. 1991. 27.95 (0-89781-393-6) Am Historical Pr.

Link, Valerie & Skerritt, Linda. The Petit Basset Griffon Vendeen (PBGV) A Definitive Breed Study. Anderson, Mark, ed. LC 99-60315. (Pure Breds Ser.). (Illus.). 286p. 2000. 26.95 (0-944875-58-0) Doral Pub.

Link, Werner, jt. auth. see Kahler, Miles.

Link, William. A Fatherless Country. LC 78-26468. 1979. pap. 8.95 (0-87233-049-4) Bauhan.

Link, William, jt. auth. see Levinson, Richard.

Link, William A. A Hard Country & a Lonely Place: Schooling, Society, & Reform in Rural Virginia, 1870-1920. LC 86-1412. (Fred W. Morrison Series in Southern Studies). xvi, 275p. (C). 1986. 39.95 (0-8078-1706-6) U of NC Pr.

— The Paradox of Southern Progressivism, 1880-1930. LC 92-1328. (Fred W. Morrison Series in Southern Studies). (Illus.). xviii, 440p. (C). 1993. text 55.00 (0-8078-2040-7) U of NC Pr.

— The Paradox of Southern Progressivism, 1880-1930. LC 92-1328. (Illus.). 458p. (C). 1997. pap. 19.95 (0-8078-4589-2) U of NC Pr.

— The Rebuilding of Old Commonwealths: Documents of Social Reform in the Progressive Era South. 166p. 1996. pap. text 15.95 (0-312-10590-8) St Martin.

— William Friday: Power, Purpose & American Higher Education. 512p. 1997. pap. 18.95 (0-8078-4680-5) U of NC Pr.

— William Friday: Power, Purpose, & American Higher Education. LC 94-5723. (Illus.). 512p. 1995. 34.95 (0-8078-2167-5) U of NC Pr.

Link, William A., ed. The Rebuilding of Old Commonwealths: And Other Documents of Social Reform in the Progressive Era South. 166p. 1996. text 39.95 (0-312-12251-9) St Martin.

Link, William A. & Link, Arthur S. American Epoch: A History of the United States since 1900. 7th ed. LC 92-16975. 448p. (C). 1992. 43.75 (0-07-037951-3) McGraw.

— American Epoch - A History of the United States since 1900: Affluence & Anxiety, 1940-1992, Vol. 2. 7th ed. 448p. (C). 1993. pap. 42.50 (0-07-037952-1) McGraw.

Linke, Anita. French for Business. unabridged ed. 137p. 1989. pap. text 185.00 incl. audio (0-88432-267-X, SFR225) Audio-Forum.

Linke, Don, Jr., jt. auth. see Howard, Pam.

Linke, Don, Jr., jt. auth. see Mullican, Judy.

Linke, Esther, ed. see West, John R.

Linke, Frances. Space Patrol Comics. (Space Patrol Ser.: No. 2). 70p. (Orig.). 1977. pap. 15.00 (0-933276-05-2) Nin-Ra Ent.

— Space Patrol III. Linke, Ray, ed. (Space Patrol Ser.: No. 3). (Illus.). 205p. 1980. 30.00 (0-933276-06-0); lib. bdg. 40.00 (0-933276-07-9) Nin-Ra Ent.

— Space Patrol Memories, by Tonga. Wahle, Ted, ed. (Space Patrol Ser.: No. 1). (Illus.). 173p. (Orig.). 1976. 35.00 (0-933276-00-1); pap. 30.00 (0-933276-03-6); lib. bdg. 40.00 (0-933276-01-X) Nin-Ra Ent.

Linke, H. & Borner, J. Differences in the Local Stress of the Gear Tooth Root Based on Hobbing Cutters & Pinion Cutters. (Nineteen Ninety-Two Fall Technical Meeting Ser.: Vol. 92FTM7). (Illus.). 10p. 1992. pap. text 30.00 (1-55589-587-5) AGMA.

Linke, Heinz & Jahn, Claudia. Bending Load on Internal Gears of Planetary Gear Sets. (Technical Papers: Vol. 97FTM7). 10p. 1997. pap. text 30.00 (1-55589-701-0) AGMA.

Linke, Horst. Labyrinth Fish: The Bubble Nest Builders. (Illus.). 170p. 1991. 21.95 (3-89356-137-4, 16071) Tetra Pr.

Linke, Horst & Staeck, Wolfgang. African Cichlids Vol. I: Cichlids from West Africa: A Handbook for Their Identification, Care & Breeding. (Illus.). 200p. 1995. 28.95 (1-56465-166-5, 16755) Tetra Pr.

— American Cichlids I: Dwarf Cichlids: A Handbook for Their Identification, Care & Breeding. (Illus.). 232p. Date not set. 28.95 (1-56465-168-1, 16757) Tetra Pr.

— Large Cichlids: American Cichlids 2: A Handbook for Their Identification, Care & Breeding. (Illus.). 200p. 1995. 28.95 (1-56465-169-X, 16758) Tetra Pr.

Linke, Jorg. Untersuchungen Zu Vegetationsoekologie und Stoffhaushalt der Sekundaersukzession Auf Einer Meliorationsflaeche Im Solling. (Dissertationes Botanicae Ser.: Band 224). (Illus.). xi, 308p. 1994. pap. 65.00 (3-443-64136-9, Pub. by Gebruder Borntraeger) Balogh.

Linke, Lilo. Ecuador: Country of Contrasts. 1976. lib. bdg. 59.95 (0-8490-1750-5) Gordon Pr.

Linke, Pam, ed. Practical Parenting: 1-5 Years, Child & Youth Health, SA. 1996. 75.00 (0-86431-199-0, Pub. by Aust Council Educ Res); teacher ed. 110.00 (0-86431-198-2, Pub. by Aust Council Educ Res) St Mut.

Linke, Pam, jt. ed. see Bowler, Peter.

Linke, Paul. Time Flies When You're Alive: A Love Story. LC 92-37589. 1993. 16.95 (1-55972-183-9, Birch Ln Pr) Carol Pub Group.

Linke, Ray, ed. see Linke, Frances.

Linke, Uli. Blood & Nation: The European Aesthetics of Race. LC 98-41467. (Contemporary Ethnography Ser.). 1999. 37.50 (0-8122-3477-4) U of Pa Pr.

— German Bodies: Race & Representation after Hitler. LC 98-44572. 1999. 90.00 (0-415-92121-X); pap. 18.99 (0-415-92122-8) Routledge.

Linke, Uli, jt. ed. see Shapiro, Warren.

Linke, William F. Solubilities: Inorganic & Metal-Organic Compounds: A Compilation of Solubility Data from the Periodical Literature, Vol. 1. 4th ed. LC 65-6490. 1491p. reprint ed. pap. 200.00 (0-8357-4124-9, 205233500001) Bks Demand.

— Solubilities - Inorganic & Metal-Organic Compounds Vol. 2: A Compilation of Solubility Data from the Periodical Literature. 4th ed. LC 65-6490. 1918p. 1965. reprint ed. pap. 200.00 (0-608-04425-3, 205233500002) Bks Demand.

Linke, William F., ed. Seidell's Solubilities: Inorganic & Metal-Organic Compounds, 2 vols. 4th ed. Incl. A-J. 1486p. 1958. 39.95 (0-8412-0097-1); write for info. (0-318-50483-9) Am Chemical.

Linkemer, Bobbi. How to Write an Effective Resume. LC 86-47813. (Successful Office Skills Ser.). 64p. 1987. pap. 4.00 (0-8144-7669-4) AMACOM.

— Polishing Your Professional Image. LC 86-47814. (Successful Office Skills Ser.). 64p. 1987. pap. 4.00 (0-8144-7670-8) AMACOM.

Linkemer, Bobbi. Solving People Problems. LC 98-34030. 204p. 1998. pap. 57.95 incl. cd-rom (1-890003-03-4) AMACOM.

***Linkemer, Bobbi.** Solving People Problems. LC 99-53921. (Self-Development for Success Ser.: Vol. 15). 96p. 2000. pap. 12.95 (0-8144-7069-6) AMACOM.

Linkemer, Bobbi, jt. auth. see Weiss, Donald H.

Linkenback, Sean. An Unauthorized Guide to Godzilla Collectibles. LC 98-84391. 176p. 1998. pap. 29.95 (0-7643-0544-1) Schiffer.

Linkens, D. A. & Nicholson, R. I., eds. Trends in Information Technology. (Control Engineering Ser.: No. 43). 312p. 1990. 95.00 (0-86341-231-9, CE043) INSPEC Inc.

Linkens, Derek A. CAD for Control Systems. (Illus.). 600p. 1993. text 199.00 (0-8247-9060-X) Dekker.

Linkens, Derek A. & Atherton, D. P. Trends in Control & Measurement Education. (IFAC Symposia Ser.: Vol. 8905). 258p. 1989. 127.25 (0-08-035736-9, Pergamon Pr) Elsevier.

Linkens, Derek A., jt. auth. see Wang, Hang.

Linkens, Derek A., jt. ed. see Carson, E.

Linker, David T. Pediatric Echocardiography. (Illus.). 315p. 1998. text. write for info. (0-443-07640-5) Church.

Linker, Kate. Love for Sale: The Words & Pictures of Barbara Kruger. (Illus.). 96p. 1996. pap. 16.95 (0-8109-2651-2, Pub. by Abrams) Time Warner.

— Vito Acconci. LC 92-37681. (Illus.). 224p. 1994. 50.00 (0-8478-1645-1, Pub. by Rizzoli Intl) St Martin.

Linker, Robert W. A Bibliography of Old French Lyrics. LC 79-11948. (Romance Monographs: No. 31). 1979. 52.00 (84-499-2809-5) Romance.

— Music of the Minnesinger & Early Meistersinger. LC 73-181946. (North Carolina. University. Studies in the Germanic Languages & Literatures: No. 32). reprint ed. 35.00 (0-404-50932-0) AMS Pr.

Linker, Sue. Sunbonnet Sue All Through the Year. LC 94-6365. 1994. pap. 21.95 (1-56477-058-3, B182) Martingale & Co.

Linkert, Lo. Golf Epidemic. 96p. 1992. pap. 9.95 (0-929097-02-5) Spect Ln Pr.

— Golf Fever: Cartoons. (Illus.). 96p. (Orig.). 1993. pap. 9.95 (0-930753-16-X) Spect Ln Pr.

— Golf Nuts. (Illus.). 96p. 1992. pap. 9.95 (0-929097-00-9, 12955) Spect Ln Pr.

— Golfers - Enough Is Enough! (Illus.). 96p. 1992. pap. 9.95 (0-929097-01-7, 17988) Spect Ln Pr.

Linkert, Lo, jt. auth. see Olson, Bill.

Linkh, Richard M. American Catholicism & European Immigrants (1900-1924) LC 74-79914. (Illus.). 200p. 1975. 5.00 (0-913256-17-X) CMS.

Linkhart, Douglas K. Microwave Circulator Design. LC 89-6550. (Artech House Microwave Library). (Illus.). 206p. 1989. reprint ed. pap. 63.90 (0-608-03159-3, 206361200007) Bks Demand.

Linkhart, Luther & White, Michael James Denham. The Trinity Alps: A Hiking & Backpacking Guide. 3rd ed. LC 94-27756. 240p. 1994. pap. 15.95 (0-89997-176-8) Wilderness Pr.

Linkhorn, Renee. La Belgique Telle Qu'elle S'ecrit: Perspectives Sur les Lettres Belges de Langue Francaise, Vol. 4. (Belgian Francophone Library). (FRE.). XII, 404p. (C). 1995. 65.95 (0-8204-2744-6) P Lang Pubng.

***Linkhorn, Renee & Cochran, Judy, eds.** Belgian Women Poets: An Anthology. LC 98-53633. (Belgian Francophone Library: No. 11). 512p. 2000. text 72.95 (0-8204-4456-1) P Lang Pubng.

Linkhorn, Renee, ed. & tr. see Chedid, Andree.

Linkhorn, Renee, tr. see Wilwerth, Evelyne.

Linkin, Harriet K. & Behrendt, Stephen C., eds. Romanticism & Women Poets: Opening the Doors of Reception. LC 98-48349. (Illus.). 336p. 1999. 34.95 (0-8131-2107-8) U Pr of Ky.

Linkin, Harriet K., jt. ed. see Behrendt, Stephen C.

Linkin, Jim. The Link to Senior Golf: How to Play Better & Have More Fun. (Illus.). 150p. 1998. pap. 12.95 (1-57167-241-9) Sports Pub.

Linklater. Color Atlas of Diseases & Disorders of Sheep. (Illus.). 256p. (gr. 13). 1993. text 115.00 (0-8151-5438-0, 22882) Mosby Inc.

Linklater, Andrew. The Transformation of Political Community: Ethical Foundations of the Post-Westphalian Era. LC 97-45264. (Studies in International Relations). 269p. 1998. text 39.95 (1-57003-257-2); pap. text 19.95 (1-57003-258-0) U of SC Pr.

Linklater, Andrew, jt. ed. see MacMillan, John.

Linklater, Andro. Wild People: Travels with Borneo's Head Hunters. LC 91-9047. 216p. 1992. pap. 10.95 (0-87113-477-2, Atlntc Mnthly) Grove-Atltic.

Linklater, Beth V. Und Immer Zugellose Wird die Lust: Constructions of Sexuality in East German Literatures: With Special Reference to Irmtraud Morgner & Gabriele Stotzer-Kachold. 248p. (C). 1998. pap. text 39.95 (0-8204-3426-4) P Lang Pubng.

Linklater, Clive. Reflections from a Bookshop Window. 1996. 10.95 (0-947533-01-X, Pub. by Breese Bks) Firebird Dist.

Linklater, Elizabeth. A Child under Sail. (C). 1987. 60.00 (0-85174-302-1) St Mut.

***Linklater, Eric.** The Dark of Summer. 288p. 1999. pap. 11.95 (0-86241-894-1, Pub. by Canongate Books) Interlink Pub.

Linklater, Eric. Fanfare for a Tin Hat: A Third Essay in Autobiography. LC 72-556200. 328p. 1970. write for info. (0-333-11705-0) Macmillan.

— Magnus Merriman. (Classics Ser.). 308p. 1995. pap. 9.95 (0-86241-313-3, Pub. by Canongate Books) Interlink Pub.

— The Men of Ness. (C). 1986. 50.00 (0-907618-03-0, Pub. by Orkney Pr) St Mut.

— Private Angelo. (Classics Ser.). 262p. 1995. pap. 11.95 (0-86241-376-1, Pub. by Canongate Books) Interlink Pub.

— Seaskin Trousers. large type ed. (Illus.). 200p. 1991. 22.95 (1-85290-021-0) ISIS Lrg Prnt.

— A Spell for Old Bones. Reginald, R. & Melville, Douglas, eds. LC 77-84250. (Lost Race & Adult Fantasy Ser.). 1978. reprint ed. lib. bdg. 23.95 (0-405-10996-2) Ayer.

Linklater, Kristin. Freeing the Natural Voice. LC 75-28172. (Illus.). 224p. (C). 1985. pap. 19.95 (0-89676-071-5, Drama Pubs) QSMG Ltd.

Linklater, Magnus, jt. auth. see Prior, Colin.

Linklater, Peter, ed. Education & the World of Work: Positive Partnerships. 220p. 1987. 123.00 (0-335-15602-9) OpUniv Pr.

Linklater, Richard. Slacker. 1992. pap. 14.95 (0-312-07797-1) St Martin.

Linklater, Scott, jt. auth. see Burchill.

Linkletter, Art. The New Kids Say the Darndest Things. (Illus.). 180p. 1996. pap. 8.95 (0-915463-72-5) Jameson Bks.

Linkletter, Eve. Collin-O. LC 84-52307. (Illus.). 183p. (Orig.). 1985. 8.95 (0-931683-02-5, Pub. by Oracle Bks); pap. 4.95 (0-931683-00-9, Pub. by Oracle Bks) St Mut.

Linkletter, Jack. Breakthrough Leadership. (C). 1997. 24.95 (0-13-757113-5, Macmillan Coll) P-H.

— Breakthrough Leadership. (C). 1998. pap. 14.95 (0-13-757121-6, Macmillan Coll) P-H.

Linkman, Audrey. The Victorians: A Photographic Portrait. (Illus.). 192p. 1993. 39.95 (1-85043-738-6, Pub. by I B T) St Martin.

Linko, P., et al, eds. Extrusion Cooking. LC 89-83945. (Illus.). 471p. 1989. 110.00 (0-913250-67-8) Am Assn Cereal Chem.

— Food Process Engineering Vol. 1: Food Processing Systems. (Illus.). xii, 981p. 1980. 255.75 (0-85334-896-0) Elsevier.

Linkogle, Stephanie. Gender, Practice & Faith in Nicaragua. 280p. 1996. 72.95 (1-85972-298-9, Pub. by Avebry) Ashgate Pub Co.

Linkogle, Stephanie, jt. auth. see Lee-Treweek, Geraldine.

Linkon, Sherry & Mullen, Bill, eds. Radical Revisions: Rereading 1930s Culture. (Illus.). 280p. 1996. 15.95 (0-252-06505-0); text 39.95 (0-252-02206-8) U of Ill Pr.

Linkon, Sherry L. In Her Own Voice: Nineteenth-Century American Women Essayists. Bowen, Barbara, ed. LC 97-16446. (Gender & Genre in Literature Ser.: No. 9). 192p. 1997. text 41.00 (0-8153-2652-1) Garland.

Linkon, Sherry L., ed. Teaching Working Class. LC 98-32258. 336p. 1999. 60.00 (1-55849-187-2); pap. 19.95 (1-55849-188-0) U of Mass Pr.

***Linkov, Igor & Schell, W. R.** Contaminated Forests: Recent Developments in Risk Identification & Future Perspectives. LC 99-25675. (NATO Science Series 2). 1999. write for info. (0-7923-5738-8) Kluwer Academic.

Linkov, Igor & Wilson, Richard. Air Pollution in the Ural Mountains: Environmental, Health & Policy Aspects. LC 97-51760. (NATO ASI Series). 455p. 1998. 214.00 (0-7923-4967-9) Kluwer Academic.

Linkow, Leonard I. Implant Dentistry Today: A Multidisciplinary Approach, 3 vols. (Illus.). 1624p. 1990. text 732.00 (88-299-0739-1, Pub. by Piccin Nuova) Gordon & Breach.

Linkow, Leonard I. Implant Dentistry Today: A Multidisciplinary Approach, 3 vols., Set. 1624p. 1990. text 665.00 (1-57235-001-6) Piccin Nuova.

***Linkow, Leonard I. & Mangin.** Color Atlas of Implant Techniques & Implant Prostheses. (Illus.). 280p. 1998. text 150.00 (88-299-1435-5, Pub. by Piccin Nuova) Gordon & Breach.

Links, Bo. Follow the Wind. 256p. 1996. per. 12.00 (0-684-81575-3, Scribner Pap Fic) S&S Trade Pap.

Links Editors. Commercial Spaces. (Architectural Design Ser.). (Illus.). 238p. 1997. 85.00 (84-921606-7-5, Pub. by Links Inter) Bks Nippan.

***Links Editors.** Design Hotels. (Architectural Design Ser.). 1998. 85.00 (84-89861-03-X, Pub. by Links Inter) Bks Nippan.

Links Editors. Domestic Interiors. (Architectural Design Ser.). (Illus.). 238p. 1997. 85.00 (84-921606-8-3, Pub. by Links Inter) Bks Nippan.

***Links Editors.** New Houses in Old Buildings. (Architectural Design Ser.). 1998. 85.00 (84-89861-01-3, Pub. by Links Inter) Bks Nippan.

Links Editors. Rehabilitated Buildings. (Architectural Design Ser.). (Illus.). 238p. 1997. 85.00 (84-921606-9-1, Pub. by Links Inter) Bks Nippan.

***Links Editors.** Residential Complexes. (Architectural Design Ser.). 1998. 85.00 (84-89861-02-1, Pub. by Links Inter) Bks Nippan.

Links Editors. Urbanism. (Illus.). 238p. 1997. 85.00 (1-56970-548-8, Pub. by Links Inter) Bks Nippan.

Links, J. G. Canaletto. 1999. pap. 35.00 (0-7148-3843-8) Phaidon Press.

— Canaletto. rev. ed. (Illus.). 240p. (C). 1994. reprint ed. text 55.00 (0-7148-3170-0, Pub. by Phaidon Press) Phaidon Pr.

— Venice for Pleasure. 6th rev. ed. (Pallas for Pleasure Ser.). (Illus.). 272p. 1997. pap. 19.95 (1-873429-59-2, XC3710) Cimino Pub Grp.

***Links, J. G.** Venice for Pleasure. 7th ed. (Illus.). 2000. pap. 24.95 (1-873429-40-1) Pallas Athene.

Links, J. G. & Baetjer, Katherine. Canaletto. (Illus.). 384p. 1990. pap. 55.00 (0-87099-561-8) Metro Mus Art.

Links, J. G., ed. see Ruskin, John.

***Links, J.G.** Venice for Pleasure. 6th ed. 272p. 1999. pap. 19.95 (1-873429-27-4) Cimino Pub Grp.

Links Magazine Editors & Borton, Brett. The Golfer's Guide to the Carolinas. 176p. 1994. 15.00 (0-671-74335-X, Fireside) S&S Trade Pap.

Links, Martin, tr. see Guenon, Rene.

Links, Marty. There's No Such Thing As Too Much Love. LC 83-71146. (Illus.). 1984. 5.95 (0-915696-84-3) Determined Prods.

— Yes I Can: Yes I Did. Lins, Barbara, ed. (Illus.). 32p. (Orig.). (J). (ps). 1990. pap. write for info. (1-878079-00-X) Arts Pubns.

Links, Marty & Knight, Marilyn. Yes I Can. (Illus.). (J). 1990. 4.95 (0-685-57229-3) Arts Pubns.

Links, Marty, jt. auth. see Linse, Barbara B.

Links, Paul & Stockwell, Michelle. Couple Therapy with Personality Disordered Patients. LC 98-15005. 1999. 40.00 (0-7657-0022-0) Aronson.

Links, Paul S., ed. Clinical Assessment & Management of Severe Personality Disorders. (Clinical Practice Ser.: No. 35). 256p. 1995. text 35.00 (0-88048-488-8, 8488) Am Psychiatric.

Linksman, Ricki. How to Learn Anything Quickly: An Accelerated Program for Rapid Learning. LC 96-46094. (Illus.). 224p. 1996. pap. 12.95 (0-8065-1792-1, Citadel Pr) Carol Pub Group.

— How to Learn Anything Quickly: An Accelerated Program for Rapid Learning. 242p. 1999. reprint ed. 29.95 (0-7351-0117-5) Replica Bks.

— How to Solve Your Child's Reading Problems. 292p. 1995. pap. 12.95 (0-8065-1618-6, Citadel Pr) Carol Pub Group.

An Asterisk (*) at the beginning of an entry indicates that the title is appearing for the first time.

— How to Teach Accelerated Phonics Through Learning Styles: K-12, College & Adult. (Illus.). 160p. 1993. pap. 20.00 (*1-928997-12-0*) Natl Read Diag.

— How to Teach Literal & Inferential Comprehension Through Learning Styles. 120p. 1993. pap. 20.00 (*1-928997-13-9*) Natl Read Diag.

— How to Teach Memory, Note-Taking, Study, & Test-Taking Skills Through Learning Styles. 60p. 1993. pap. 20.00 (*1-928997-14-7*) Natl Read Diag.

— The Linksman Learning Style Preference Assessment & Brain Hemispheric Preference Assessment: Assessment Booklet. 24p. 1993. pap. 10.00 (*1-928997-10-4*) Natl Read Diag.

— The Linksman Learning Style Preference Assessment & Brain Hemispheric Preference Assessment: Instruction Manual. 1993. pap., teacher ed. 30.00 (*1-928997-09-0*) Natl Read Diag.

— Linksman Passage Reading Tests to Diagnose Reading Skills: Grades 1-12. 1993. pap. 20.00 (*1-928997-11-2*) Natl Read Diag.

— Linksman Phonics Diagnostic Test. (Illus.). 28p. 1993. pap. 30.00 (*1-928997-08-2*) Natl Read Diag.

— Linksman Phonics Diagnostic Test: Instruction Manual. 50p. 1993. pap. 30.00 (*1-928997-07-4*) Natl Read Diag.

— Solving Your Child's Reading Problems. LC 97-75628. 368p. 1998. reprint ed. 8.98 (*1-56731-245-4*, MJF Bks) Fine Comms.

— Superlinks Reading: Accelerated Phonics & Comprehension Program - Parent Kit. 1073p. 1993. 220.00 (*1-928997-03-1*) Natl Read Diag.

— Superlinks to Reading Success: Accelerated Phonics & Comprehension Program for Schools. (Illus.). 1073p. 1993. pap. 280.00 (*1-928997-01-5*) Natl Read Diag.

— Superlinks to Reading Success: Accelerated Phonics & Reading Comprehension Program. 1074p. 1999. ring bd. 225.00 (*1-928997-00-7*) Natl Read Diag.

— Superlinks to Reading Success: Accelerated Reading Program for Tutors, After-School & Summer School Programs. (Illus.). 1073p. 1993. pap. 280.00 (*1-928997-02-3*) Natl Read Diag.

— The Vowel & Consant Guide: For Parents, Teachers & Students. (Illus.). 80p. 1993. pap. 20.00 (*1-928997-05-8*) Natl Read Diag.

— The Vowel & Consonant Dictionary. (Illus.). 50p. 1993. pap. 10.00 (*1-928997-06-6*) Natl Read Diag.

— Your Child Can Be a Great Reader: Improving Skills & Developing a Lifetime Love of Books. LC 98-38162. (Illus.). 344p. 1998. pap. 14.95 (*0-8065-2009-4*) Carol Pub Group.

Linksman, Ricki, jt. auth. see Scotti, Juliet.

Linkugel, Wil A. & Pappas, Edward J. They Tasted Glory: Among the Missing at the Baseball Hall of Fame. LC 98-12340. (Illus.). 255p. 1998. pap. 28.50 (*0-7864-0484-1*) McFarland & Co.

Linkugel, Wil A. & Solomon, Martha. Anna Howard Shaw: Suffrage Orator & Social Reformer, 10. LC 90-38414. (Great American Orators: Critical Studies, Speeches & Sources: No. 10). 256p. 1990. lib. bdg. 55.00 (*0-313-26345-0*, LKA, Greenwood Pr) Greenwood.

Linkwitz, K., et al, eds. Applications of Geodesy to Engineering. LC 93-34455. (International Association of Geodesy Symposia Ser.: No. 108). 448p. 1993. 174.95 (*0-387-56233-8*) Spr-Verlag.

Linkwitz, K. & Hangleiter, U., eds. High Precision Navigation. (Illus.). 650p. 1989. 128.95 (*0-387-50921-6*) Spr-Verlag.

Linky, Donald. The New Jersey Directory: The Insider Guide to New Jersey Leaders (1996 Edition) 506p. Date not set. pap. 86.00 (*1-879171-06-6*) Joshua Comns.

Linky, Donald, ed. The New Jersey Directory: The Insider Guide to New Jersey Leaders. 5th ed. 578p. 1998. pap. 86.00 (*1-879171-22-8*) Joshua Comns.

— The New Jersey Directory: The Insider Guide to New Jersey Leaders, 1992-1993 Edition. 456p. 1992. pap. 86.00 (*1-879171-00-7*) Joshua Comns.

— The New Jersey Directory, 1993-94: The Insider Guide to New Jersey Leaders. 3rd ed. 486p. pap. 86.00 (*1-879171-02-3*) Joshua Comns.

Linky, Donald, et al, eds. The New Jersey Almanac. 369p. 1997. pap. 85.00 (*0-9658857-0-4*) Pub Affairs Res.

Linley, David. Classical Furniture. LC 93-603. (Illus.). 192p. 1993. 65.00 (*0-8109-3188-5*, Pub. by Abrams) Time Warner.

***Linley, David.** Design & Detail in the Home. (Illus.). 224p. 2000. 49.50 (*0-8109-4053-1*, Pub. by Abrams) Time Warner.

Linley, David. Extraordinary Furniture. LC 96-10862. (Illus.). 192p. 1996. 60.00 (*0-8109-3257-1*, Pub. by Abrams) Time Warner.

Linley, Eliza, jt. ed. see Welch, Marni.

Linley, John. The Georgia Catalog, Historic American Buildings Survey: A Guide to the Architecture of the State. LC 81-19856. (Wormsloe Foundation Publications: No. 15). (Illus.). 432p. 1982. 50.00 (*0-8203-0613-4*); pap. 24.95 (*0-8203-0614-2*) U of Ga Pr.

***Linley, Mark.** Anyone Can Draw - It's Child's Play. 160p. 2000. pap. 6.95 (*0-7160-2064-5*, Pub. by Elliot RW Bks) Midpt Trade.

— The Right Way to Draw. 2nd ed. (Illus.). 128p. 2001. pap. 6.95 (*0-7160-2070-X*, Pub. by Elliot RW Bks) Midpt Trade.

— The Right Way to Draw Caricatures. 160p. 2000. pap. 6.95 (*0-7160-2103-X*, Pub. by Elliot RW Bks) Midpt Trade.

— The Right Way to Draw Flowers. 160p. 2000. pap. 6.95 (*0-7160-2107-2*, Pub. by Elliot RW Bks) Midpt Trade.

— The Right Way to Draw People. 160p. 2000. pap. 6.95 (*0-7160-2086-6*, Pub. by Elliot RW Bks) Midpt Trade.

— The Right Ways to Draw Animals. 160p. 2000. pap. 6.95 (*0-7160-2085-8*, Pub. by Elliot RW Bks) Midpt Trade.

— The Right Ways to Draw Landscapes. 160p. 2000. pap. 6.95 (*0-7160-2095-5*, Pub. by Elliot RW Bks) Midpt Trade.

***Linley, Mark & Gibbs, Jon.** Start Calligraphy. (Illus.). 224p. 2001. pap. 9.95 (*0-7160-2097-1*, Pub. by Elliot RW Bks) Midpt Trade.

Linley, Neil, ed. see At-Tayyib, Ibn.

Linley, Thomas, Jr. Thomas Linley, Jr. Anthem: Let God Arise. Beechey, Gwilym, ed. (Recent Researches in Music of the Classic Era Ser.: Vol. RRC7). (Illus.). ix, 100p. 1977. pap. 40.00 (*0-89579-096-3*, RRC7) A-R Eds.

***Linley, Thomas, Jr.** Thomas Linley, Jr. The Song of Moses. Overbeck, Peter, ed. (Recent Researches in the Music of the Classical Era Ser.: Vol. C58). (Illus.). xii, 265p. 2000. pap. 85.00 (*0-89579-451-9*) A-R Eds.

Linmark, R. Zamora. Rolling the R's. LC 94-75595. 168p. 1996. 21.00 (*1-885030-02-9*) Kaya Prod.

— Rolling the R's. LC 94-75595. 168p. 1997. pap. 12.95 (*1-885030-03-7*) Kaya Prod.

Linn. Edu Psy Test CTB IBM. 2000. write for info. (*0-02-370633-3*) P-H.

— Edu Psy Test IM. 2000. write for info. (*0-02-370631-7*) P-H.

— Education, a Psychological Testing. 1999. text 40.68 (*0-02-370630-9*) P-H.

— Measurement &... 8th ed. 1999. pap. text, student ed. 14.25 (*0-13-878976-2*) P-H.

— Measurement & Assessment in Teaching. 8th ed. LC 98-51928. (Illus.). 574p. 1999. 72.00 (*0-13-878356-X*) P-H.

— Measurement & Authentic Assess. 7th ed. 1999. 81.60 (*0-13-012487-7*, Pub. by P-H) S&S Trade.

Linn, Beth. The Niche Series. (Illus.). 48p. 1991. pap. 16.95 (*0-89822-066-1*) Visual Studies.

Linn, Bill, jt. auth. see Drury, Kiny.

Linn, Brian M. Guardians of Empire: The U. S. Army & the Pacific, 1902-1940. LC 96-24200. 360p. (gr. 13). 1997. 45.00 (*0-8078-2321-X*) U of NC Pr.

— Guardians of Empire: The U.S. Army & the Pacific, 1902-1940. LC 96-24200. (Illus.). 360p. 1999. pap. 18.95 (*0-8078-4815-8*) U of NC Pr.

— The United States Army & Counterinsurgency in the Philippine War, 1899-1902. LC 88-20741. (Illus.). 276p. 1989. reprint ed. pap. 85.60 (*0-7837-9038-4*, 204978900003) Bks Demand.

Linn, Brian McAllister. The Philippine War, 1899-1902. LC 99-33549. (Modern War Studies). (Illus.). 424p. 2000. 39.95 (*0-7006-0990-3*) U Pr of KS.

Linn, Carl E. Brand Dynamics: Factors & Trade-Offs Affecting Value Development in Branded Goods & Services. Bergstrom, Alan J., ed. LC 98-70513. 100p. 1998. pap. 19.95 (*0-9661526-0-3*) Inst for Brand.

Linn, Charles F. Probability. LC 79-171006. (Young Math Ser.). (Illus.). 40p. (J). (gr. 1-4). 1972. lib. bdg. 10.89 (*0-690-65602-5*) HarpC Child Bks.

Linn, D. M., ed. Sorption & Degradation of Pesticides & Organic Chemicals in Soil. LC 93-25573. (Special Publications: No. 32). 260p. 1993. pap. 30.00 (*0-89118-803-7*) Soil Sci Soc Am.

***Linn, Denise.** Altars: Bringing Sacred Shrines into Your Everyday Life. LC 99-28074. (Illus.). 160p. 1999. pap. 24.95 (*0-345-43446-3*, Ballantine) Ballantine Pub Grp.

— Feng-Shui for the Soul: How to Create a Harmonious Environment That Will Nurture & Sustain You. 2nd ed. LC 99-48222. 256p. 2000. reprint ed. pap. 13.95 (*1-56170-731-7*, 5026) Hay House.

Linn, Denise. Past Lives, Present Dreams. LC 97-92906. 1997. pap. 12.00 (*0-345-40002-X*) Ballantine Pub Grp.

— A Pocketful of Dream. LC 97-93661. 1997. pap. 12.00 (*0-345-40003-8*) Ballantine Pub Grp.

— Quest. 288p. 1999. pap. 12.00 (*0-345-42544-8*) Ballantine Pub Grp.

— Sacred Legacies: Healing Your Past & Creating a Positive Future. LC 98-37037. 214p. 1999. 23.00 (*0-345-42515-4*) Ballantine Pub Grp.

— Sacred Space: Clearing & Enhancing the Energy of Your Home. LC 95-94469. 320p. 1996. pap. 12.00 (*0-345-39769-X*) Ballantine Pub Grp.

— The Secret Language of Signs: How to Interpret the Coincidences & Symbols in Your Life. LC 96-96538. 352p. 1996. pap. 12.00 (*0-345-40693-1*, Del Rey) Ballantine Pub Grp.

***Linn, Denise.** Space Clearing: How to Purify & Create Harmony in Your Home. LC 00-31409. (Illus.). 128p. 2000. 27.95 (*0-8092-9739-6*, Contemporary Bks) NTC Contemp Pub Co.

— Space Clearing A-Z. (Illus.). 156p. 2001. 19.95 (*1-56170-750-3*, L471, Hay Hse Lifestyles) Hay House.

Linn, Dennis & Linn, Matthew. Healing Life's Hurts: Healing Memories Through the Five Stages of Forgiveness. LC 77-14794. 324p. 1978. pap. 12.95 (*0-8091-2059-3*) Paulist Pr.

Linn, Dennis, et al. Belonging: Bonds of Healing & Recovery. LC 92-29855. 288p. 1993. pap. 9.95 (*0-8091-3365-2*) Paulist Pr.

— Don't Forgive Too Soon: Extending the Two Hands That Heal. LC 96-50101. (Illus.). 144p. (Orig.). 1997. pap. 10.95 (*0-8091-3704-6*) Paulist Pr.

— Good Goats: Healing Our Image of God. LC 93-41067. 1994. pap. 14.95 (*0-8091-3463-2*) Paulist Pr.

— Healing the Greatest Hurt: Healing Grief & the Family Tree. LC 85-60407. 258p. (Orig.). 1985. pap. 12.95 (*0-8091-2714-8*) Paulist Pr.

— Healing the Purpose of Your Life. LC 98-46198. (Illus.). 96p. 1999. pap. 10.95 (*0-8091-3853-0*) Paulist Pr.

— Praying with One Another for Healing. 1984. pap. 11.95 (*0-8091-2619-2*) Paulist Pr.

— Sleeping with Bread: Holding What Gives You Life. LC 95-2305. (Illus.). 80p. (Orig.). 1995. pap. 12.95 (*0-8091-3579-5*) Paulist Pr.

Linn, Dennis, jt. auth. see Linn, Matthew.

Linn-Desmond, Nancy. Men Just Don't Understand: A Womans Dating Dictionary. LC 95-22289. (Illus.). 160p. 1995. pap. 8.95 (*0-8065-1666-6*, Citadel Pr) Carol Pub Group.

— Men Who Hate Women & the Women Who Hate Them: The Masochistic Art of Dating. (Illus.). 160p. 1992. pap. 4.50 (*0-8216-2518-7*, Carol Paperbacks) Carol Pub Group.

Linn, Don. Detail & Scale, Av-8 Harrier, Vol. 28, pt. 1. (Illus.). 72p. 1987. pap. 10.95 (*0-8306-8038-1*, 25038) McGraw-Hill Prof.

Linn, Ed. Hitter: The Life & Turmoils of Ted Williams. LC 93-42460. 1993. 23.95 (*0-15-193100-3*, Harvest Bks) Harcourt.

— Hitter: The Life & Turmoils of Ted Williams. (Illus.). 448p. 1994. pap. 15.00 (*0-15-600091-1*) Harcourt.

Linn, Ed & Durslag, Mel. The One Hundred Million Dollar Game. 320p. 1985. 16.95 (*0-671-47054-X*) S&S Trade.

Linn, Elbridge B. That They May All Be One. 1969. 4.50 (*0-88027-020-9*) Firm Foun Pub.

Linn, Erin. Children Are Not Paper Dolls: A Visit with Bereaved Siblings. (Illus.). 121p. (Orig.). (J). 1982. pap. 8.95 (*0-9614636-0-0*) Pub Mark.

— I Know Just How You Feel... Avoiding the Cliches of Grief. Erickson, Claire L., ed. LC 85-90509. (Illus.). 128p. (Orig.). 1986. pap. 7.00 (*0-9614636-1-9*) Pub Mark.

— One Hundred Fifty Facts about Grieving Children. 96p. (Orig.). 1990. pap. 6.00 (*0-9614636-3-5*) Pub Mark.

— Premonitions, Visitations & Dreams of the Bereaved. Saulisbury, Jo, ed. (Orig.). 1991. pap. 6.95 (*0-9614636-4-3*) Pub Mark.

Linn, George W. Linn's History of a Fragment of the Clan Linn & a Genealogy of the Linn & Related Families. 204p. 1996. reprint ed. pap. 31.00 (*0-8328-5334-8*); reprint ed. lib. bdg. 41.00 (*0-8328-5333-X*) Higginson Bk Co.

Linn, Henry H. Safeguarding School Funds. LC 76-176997. (Columbia University. Teachers College. Contributions to Education Ser.: No. 387). reprint ed. 37.50 (*0-404-55387-7*) AMS Pr.

Linn, Ian. Application Refused: Employment Vetting by the State. 96p. (C). 1991. pap. text 25.00 (*0-900137-33-9*, Pub. by NCCL) St Mut.

Linn, James R. The Little Green Hummingbird. Huston, Dwayne L., ed. LC 92-75969. (Illus.). 44p. (J). (gr. 3). 1993. pap. 7.98 (*1-882798-01-5*) Erth & Sky Pub.

***Linn, James Weber.** Jane Addams: A Biography. LC 99-88394. (Illus.). 512p. 2000. pap. 15.95 (*0-252-06904-8*) U of Ill Pr.

Linn, Jan G. The Jesus Connection: A Christian Spirituality. LC 96-6503. 120p. (Orig.). 1997. pap. 11.99 (*0-8272-1709-9*) Chalice Pr.

— Living Inside Out: Learning How to Pray the Serenity Prayer. LC 94-12023. 176p. (Orig.). 1994. pap. 9.99 (*0-8272-2123-1*) Chalice Pr.

— Reclaiming Evangelism: A Practical Guide for Mainline Churches. LC 97-44095. 144p. 1998. pap. 14.99 (*0-8272-3216-0*) Chalice Pr.

— What Church Members Wish Ministers Knew. 160p. (Orig.). 1995. pap. 12.99 (*0-8272-4234-4*) Chalice Pr.

— What Ministers Wish Church Members Knew. LC 92-32944. 144p. (Orig.). 1993. pap. 12.99 (*0-8272-4230-1*) Chalice Pr.

Linn, Jo W. Abstracts of the Minutes of the Court of Pleas & Quarter Sessions, Rowan Co., N. C., 1753-1762. 177p. 1978. 35.00 (*0-918470-02-1*) J W Linn.

— Abstracts of the Minutes of the Court of Pleas & Quarter Sessions, Rowan Co., N.C., 1763-1774. 208p. 1979. 30.00 (*0-918470-03-X*) J W Linn.

— Abstracts of the Minutes of the Court of Pleas & Quarter Sessions, Rowan County, N.C., 1775-1789. LC 81-84591. 250p. 1982. 35.00 (*0-918470-13-7*) J W Linn.

— Abstracts of the Wills & Estates Records of Rowan County, N.C., 1753-1805 & Tax Lists of 1759-1778. 216p. 1980. 30.00 (*0-918470-04-8*) J W Linn.

— Ancestry of Sims-Hallman Families with Related Lines of Jernigan, Boon, Bryan. LC 94-73561. (Illus.). 148p. 1995. pap. 25.00 (*0-918470-22-6*) J W Linn.

— Census of Rowan County, North Carolina, 1850: A Genealogical Compilation of the Schedules. LC 91-77702. (Illus.). 158p. 1992. pap. 26.00 (*0-918470-21-8*); lib. bdg. 28.00 (*0-918470-20-X*) J W Linn.

— Davie County, North Carolina, Tax Lists of 1843 & 1847. LC 95-81870. 60p. 1996. pap. 15.00 (*0-918470-25-0*) J W Linn.

— The Diary of Elizabeth Dick Lindsay, 1831-1861: Guilford County, N. C. (Illus.). 110p. 1975. 18.50 (*0-918470-10-2*) J W Linn.

***Linn, Jo W.** Diary of Johann Gottfried Arends, 1740-1807: Annotated Transcription. LC 99-94475. (GER., Illus.). 168p. 1999. lib. bdg. 25.00 (*0-918470-30-7*) J W Linn.

Linn, Jo W. Drake, Arrington, White, Turner, Linn, Brown: And Two Dozen Related Southern Lines. LC 84-81760. (Illus.). 1984. 35.00 (*0-918470-17-X*) J W Linn.

— First Presbyterian Church, Salisbury, North Carolina, & Its People, 1821-1995. LC 96-75125. 560p. 1996. 45.00 (*0-918470-26-9*) J W Linn.

— The Gray Family & Allied Lines: Bowman, Lindsay, Millis, Disk, Peebles, Wiley, Shannon, Lamar, McGee. 607p. 1994. reprint ed. pap. 75.00 (*0-8328-4323-7*); reprint ed. lib. bdg. 85.00 (*0-8328-4322-9*) Higginson Bk Co.

— A Holmes Family of Rowan & Davidson Counties, NC. LC 88-91003. (Illus.). 316p. 1988. 25.00 (*0-918470-19-6*) J W Linn.

— Iredell County, NC, Earliest Extant Tax Lists, 1800, 1815, 1837: Annotated Transcriptions. LC 97-70146. (Illus.). 159p. 1997. 27.00 (*0-918470-27-7*) J W Linn.

— People Named Hanes. LC 80-52426. (Illus.). 281p. 1980. 25.00 (*0-918470-12-9*) J W Linn.

— Rowan County, N. C., Tax List, 1815. LC 87-92111. (Illus.). 1987. pap. 12.00 (*0-918470-18-8*) J W Linn.

— Rowan County, North Carolina, Tax Lists, 1757-1800: Annotated Transcriptions. LC 95-81908. 458p. 1996. 40.00 (*0-918470-24-2*) J W Linn.

— Stokes County, North Carolina, 1815 Tax List: Annotated Transcriptions. LC 97-70145. (Illus.). x, 66p. 1997. pap. 20.00 (*0-918470-28-5*) J W Linn.

Linn, Jo W. & Gray, Gordon. The Ancestry of Nathalie Fontaine Lyons: Lyons, Nunes Miranda, Luria, Cohen, Hart, Clayland, Maffitt, Beach. LC 81-84236. (Illus.). 265p. 1981. 25.00 (*0-918470-14-5*) J W Linn.

***Linn, Jo White.** Rowan County, North Carolina Divisions of Estates: 1807-1848, Bk. A. (Illus.). v, 83p. 2000. 26.00 (*0-918470-32-3*) J W Linn.

Linn, John B. Annals of Buffalo Valley, 1755-1855. (Illus.). 612p. 1997. reprint ed. lib. bdg. 65.00 (*0-8328-6395-5*) Higginson Bk Co.

— History of Centre & Clinton Counties, Pennsylvania. (Illus.). 1052p. 1990. reprint ed. 75.00 (*1-887315-00-4*) Centre Cty Hist Soc.

— History of Centre & Clinton Counties, Pennsylvania. (Illus.). 672p. 1994. reprint ed. lib. bdg. 69.50 (*0-8328-3621-4*) Higginson Bk Co.

Linn, John B. & Egle, William H. Lists of Officers of the Colonies on the Delaware & the Province of Pennsylvania, 1614-1776. 221p. 1992. reprint ed. pap. 25.00 (*0-8063-5000-8*, 9284) Clearfield Co.

— Muster Rolls of the Pennsylvania Volunteers in the War of 1812-1814: (From the Pennsylvania Archives, Second Series, Vol. XII, 1890) LC 67-30758. 560p. 1994. reprint ed. pap. 39.95 (*0-8063-0211-9*) Clearfield Co.

— Persons Naturalized in the Province of Pennsylvania, 1740-1773: With an Added Index (From the "Pennsylvania Archives," Second Series, Vol. 2, 1890) 139p. 1997. reprint ed. pap. 16.00 (*0-8063-0213-5*, 3395) Clearfield Co.

— Record of Pennsylvania Marriages Prior to 1810, 2 vols. 1391p. 1987. reprint ed. 75.00 (*0-8063-0214-3*, 3400) Genealog Pub.

Linn, John R. & Blumenthal, Stephen. Finding the Extra Target: The Ultimate Training Guide for All the Clay Target Sports. (Illus.). 126p. (Orig.). Date not set. pap. 14.95 (*0-925012-00-9*) Shotgun Sports.

***Linn, Jonathan.** Dadah Means Death. LC 99-91759. 2000. 25.00 (*0-7388-1234-X*); pap. 18.00 (*0-7388-1235-8*) Xlibris Corp.

Linn, Joseph. Bound for the Kingdom. 150p. 1992. 7.99 (*0-8341-9279-9*, MB-636); 7.00 (*0-685-71338-5*, L-9139C); cd-rom 85.00 (*0-685-71340-7*, MU-9139T) Lillenas.

— Can You Imagine? 128p. (J). 1983. 5.99 (*0-8341-9273-X*, BCMB-519) Lillenas.

— Find Us Faithful. 156p. 1988. spiral bd. 7.99 (*0-8341-9162-8*, MB-598) Lillenas.

— Glorybound. 128p. 1985. 6.99 (*0-8341-9286-1*, MB-552) Lillenas.

— Heart Songs. 131p. 1991. 6.99 (*0-8341-9008-7*, MB-632); 7.00 (*0-685-68447-4*, L-9137C); audio 75.00 (*0-685-68448-2*, MU-9137C); cd-rom 75.00 (*0-685-68449-0*, MU-9137T) Lillenas.

Linn, Joseph. Kidz of the Neighborhood: Songs to Change the World -- Arranged for Young Voices. 128p. 1992. pap. 9.99 (*0-8341-9888-6*) Lillenas.

Linn, Joseph, contrib. by. Instrumental Solotrax Vol. 2: B Flat Trumpet. 64p. 1987. 15.99 (*0-8341-9263-2*, MB-572) Lillenas.

Linn, Joseph, des. Lift High the Lord: Songs & Sketches for Contemporary Praise. 140p. 1993. 6.99 (*0-8341-9028-1*, MB-678); pap. 7.00 (*0-685-72856-0*, L-9164C); pap. 250.00 (*0-685-72859-5*, OR-9164); audio compact disk 75.00 (*0-685-72858-7*, MU-9164T) Lillenas.

— Soldiers of the Cross: Flexible Voicings for Men's Choir or Ensemble. 1994. suppl. ed. 7.00 (*0-614-01737-8*, L-9170C) Lillenas.

Linn, Judy, photos by. Terry Winters: Computation of Chains. (Illus.). 60p. 1997. 34.95 (*1-880146-18-5*) M Marks.

Linn, Julius, intro. Guide to UAB Medical Center: And Other Health Related Resources Available to the General Public. 511p. 1988. 5.00 (*0-685-22958-0*) UAB Med Ctr.

Linn, Karen. That Half-Barbaric Twang: The Banjo in American Popular Culture. (Music in American Life Ser.). (Illus.). 208p. 1991. 29.95 (*0-252-01780-3*) U of Ill Pr.

— That Half-Barbaric Twang: The Banjo in American Popular Culture. 208p. 1994. 12.95 (*0-252-06433-X*) U of Ill Pr.

Linn, Louis. Handbook of Hospital Psychiatry: A Practical Guide to Therapy. LC 55-8237. 1955. pap. 24.95 (*0-8236-8069-X*, 22300) Intl Univs Pr.

Linn, Louis, ed. Frontiers in General Hospital Psychiatry. LC 61-10147. 483p. 1961. 72.50 (*0-8236-2080-8*) Intl Univs Pr.

Linn, Marcia C. & Hsi, Sherry. Computers, Teachers, Peers: Science Learning Partners. 304p. 1999. pap. 29.95 (*0-8058-3343-9*) L Erlbaum Assocs.

Linn, Marcia C., jt. auth. see Clancy, Michael J.

Linn, Marcia C., jt. ed. see Hyde, Janet S.

Linn, Margot. A Trip to the Dentist. LC 87-14884. (Illus.). 20p. (J). (ps). 1988. 9.95 (*0-06-025829-2*) HarpC Child Bks.

— A Trip to the Doctor. LC 87-15004. (Illus.). 20p. (J). (ps). 1988. 9.95 (*0-06-025839-X*) HarpC Child Bks.

Linn, Mary J., et al. Healing the Dying. LC 79-53111. 128p. 1979. pap. 7.95 (*0-8091-2212-X*) Paulist Pr.

L

Linn, Matthew & Linn, Dennis. Healing of Memories: Prayers & Confession-Steps to Inner Healing. LC 74-17697. 112p. (Orig.). 1974. pap. 7.95 (*0-8091-1854-8*) Paulist Pr.

Linn, Matthew, et al. Healing Spiritual Abuse & Religious Addiction. LC 94-13408. 160p. 1994. pap. 8.95 (*0-8091-3488-8*) Paulist Pr.

— Healing the Eight Stages of Life. 272p. 1988. pap. 12.95 (*0-8091-2980-9*) Paulist Pr.

— Simple Ways to Pray for Healing. LC 97-30789. (Illus.). 128p. 1998. pap. 9.95 (*0-8091-3762-3*) Paulist Pr.

Linn, Matthew, jt. auth. see Linn, Dennis.

Linn, Michael D., ed. Handbook of Dialects & Language Variation. 2nd ed. LC 97-80821. (Illus.). 697p. (C). 1998. boxed set 149.95 (*0-12-451070-1*) Morgan Kaufmann.

Linn, Michael D. & Cleary, Linda M. Linguistics for Teachers. LC 92-26665. (C). 1992. pap. text 52.50 (*0-07-037946-7*) McGraw.

Linn, Michael D., jt. auth. see Allen, Harold E.

Linn, Nancy. Early Photography. (Illus.). 64p. (Orig.). 1994. pap. 6.00 (*0-9613812-0-5*) A White Pub.

— Madonna & Child. (Illus.). 160p. 1984. pap. 5.00 (*0-9613812-1-3*) A White Pub.

Linn, Ray. A Teacher's Introduction to Postmodernism. (Teacher's Introduction Ser.). 161p. 1996. pap. 12.95 (*0-8141-5009-8*) NCTE.

Linn, Richard. Guinness. Pedigree of Magennis (Guinness) Family of New Zealand & Dublin, Ireland. (Illus.). 58p. 1997. reprint ed. pap. 11.50 (*0-8328-8858-3*); reprint ed. lib. bdg. 21.50 (*0-8328-8857-5*) Higginson Bk Co.

Linn, Richard J. & Uyar, M. Umit, eds. Conformance Testing Methodologies & Architecture for OSI Protocols. LC 93-45664. 544p. 1994. 60.00 (*0-8186-5352-3*, 5352) IEEE Comp Soc.

Linn, Robert L., ed. Educational Measurement. (American Council on Education - Oryx Press Series on Higher Education). 624p. (C). 1998. reprint ed. pap. 65.00 (*1-57356-221-1*) Oryx Pr.

— Educational Measurement. 3rd ed. (Ace-Macmillan Series on Higher Education). 784p. 1988. write for info. (*0-318-41133-4*) Macmillan.

— Intelligence: Measurement, Theory, & Public Policy--Proceedings of a Symposium in Honor of Lloyd G. Humphreys. 240p. 1989. text 24.95 (*0-252-01535-5*) U of Ill Pr.

Linn, Rolf N. Schiller's Junge Idealisten. LC 71-182546. (University of California Publications in Social Welfare: Vol. 106). 96p. reprint ed. pap. 30.00 (*0-608-14167-4*, 202125800021) Bks Demand.

Linn, Ruth. Conscience at War: The Israeli Soldier As a Moral Critic. LC 95-40640. (SUNY Series in Israeli Studies). 245p. (C). 1996. text 54.50 (*0-7914-2777-3*); pap. text 17.95 (*0-7914-2778-1*) State U NY Pr.

— Not Shooting & Not Crying: Psychological Inquiry into Moral Disobedience, 85. LC 88-24720. (Contributions in Military Studies Ser.: No. 85). 174p. 1989. 52.95 (*0-313-26497-X*, LNS, Greenwood Pr) Greenwood.

Linn, S. L., et al. Monte Carlo Simulation in High Energy & Nuclear Physics: Proceedings of the 93 International Conference. 400p. 1994. text 112.00 (*981-02-1621-1*) World Scientific Pub.

Linn, S. P., compiled by. Golden Gleams of Thought. LC 74-121925. (Granger Index Reprint Ser.). 1977. 21.95 (*0-8369-6166-8*) Ayer.

Linn, Sandra. Contemporary's Put English to Work: Interaction & Competencies for Job Success. LC 96-30152. 100p. 1996. pap. 11.93 (*0-8092-3354-1*) NTC Contemp Pub Co.

Linn, Sheila F., et al. Remembering Home: Healing Hurts & Receiving Gifts from Conception to Birth. LC 99-37726. 160p. 1999. pap. 14.95 (*0-8091-3901-4*) Paulist Pr.

Linn, Stuart M. & Roberts, Richard J., eds. Nucleases. LC 85-9653. (Cold Spring Harbor Monographs: No. 14). 402p. reprint ed. pap. 124.70 (*0-7837-2004-1*, 204227800002) Bks Demand.

Linn, W. A. Story of Mormonism. 637p. 1993. reprint ed. lib. bdg. 109.00 (*0-7812-5311-X*) Rprt Serv.

Linn-Watson, TerriAnn. Radiographic Pathology. LC 95-13455. (Illus.). 256p. 1995. text 45.00 (*0-7216-4129-6*, W B Saunders Co) Harcrt Hlth Sci Grp.

— Radiographic Pathology. (Illus.). 315p. 1996. teacher ed. write for info. (*0-7216-4134-2*, W B Saunders Co) Harcrt Hlth Sci Grp.

— Radiographic Pathology Exams. 1996 195.00 (*0-7216-4172-5*, W B Saunders Co) Harcrt Hlth Sci Grp.

— Radiographic Pathology Workbook. 1995. pap. text, wbk. ed. 22.00 (*0-7216-4169-5*, W B Saunders Co) Harcrt Hlth Sci Grp.

Linn, William A. Horace Greeley, Founder & Editor of the New York Tribune. 1977. 18.95 (*0-8369-7115-9*, 7949) Ayer.

Linnaeus, Carl. Bibliotheca Botanica. 1968. 12.00 (*0-934454-13-2*) Lubrecht & Cramer.

— Hortus Cliffortianus. (Illus.). 1968. reprint ed. 162.50 (*3-7682-0543-6*) Lubrecht & Cramer.

— Mantissa Plantarum, 1767-71, 2 Vols. in 1. 1960. 97.50 (*3-7682-0037-X*) Lubrecht & Cramer.

— Miscellaneous Tracts Relating to Natural History, Husbandry, & Physick: Calender of Flora Is Added. Egerton, Frank N., 3rd, ed. LC 77-74237. (History of Ecology Ser.). 1978. reprint ed. lib. bdg. 31.95 (*0-405-10406-5*) Ayer.

— Philosophia Botanica. (Illus.). 1966. reprint ed. 97.50 (*3-7682-0350-6*) Lubrecht & Cramer.

— Select Dissertations from the Amoenitates Academicae: Supplement to Mr. Stillingfleet's Tracts, Relating Natural History. Egerton, Frank N., 3rd, ed. Brand, F. J., tr. LC 77-74238. (History of Ecology Ser.). 1978. reprint ed. lib. bdg. 42.95 (*0-405-10407-3*) Ayer.

— Systema Naturae: Tomus II, Vegetabilia. 10th ed. 1964. reprint ed. 112.50 (*3-7682-0219-4*) Lubrecht & Cramer.

— Systema Naturae, 1735. 30p. 1964. reprint ed. text 55.00 (*90-6004-104-6*, Pub. by B De Graaf) Coronet Bks.

— A Tour in Lapland. Date not set. 45.95 (*0-405-01717-0*) Arno Press.

Linnaeus, Carl, ed. see Artedi, P.

Linnainmaa, S., jt. ed. see Jaakkola, H.

Linnard, W. Forestry & Wood Dictionary: Russian-English. 109p. 1966. 49.95 (*0-8288-6717-8*, M-9709) Fr & Eur.

Linnard, W., tr. see Mattheck, C.

Linnard, William & Darrah-Morgan, D., trs. Russian-English, English-Russian Forestry & Wood Dictionary. 2nd ed. (CABI Publishing Ser.). 272p. 1999. text 75.00 (*0-85199-321-4*) OUP.

Linnartz, Jean-Paul. Narrowband Land-Mobile Radio Networks. LC 92-32244. (Artech House Mobile Communication Library). (Illus.). 363p. 1993. reprint ed. pap. 112.60 (*0-608-03158-5*, 206361100007) Bks Demand.

***Linne.** Lab Science Basics. 4th ed. 1999. text 26.00 (*0-323-00759-7*) Mosby Inc.

Linne, Carl Von, see Von Linne, Carl.

Linne, Eric B., ed. Home Care & Managed Care: Strategies for the Future. LC 95-24529. 264p. 1995. pap. 55.00 (*1-55648-145-4*, 079201) AHPI.

Linne, Eric B., ed. see Donaho, Barbara A., et al.

Linne, Eric B., jt. ed. see Lerman, Dan.

Linne, Jean J. & Ringsrud, Karen M. Basic Techniques in Clinical Laboratory Science. 3rd ed. (Illus.). 600p. (gr. 13). 1991. text 39.95 (*0-8016-2864-4*, 02864) Mosby Inc.

***Linne, Jean J. & Ringsrud, Karen M.** Clinical Laboratory Science: Basic & Routine Laboratory Techniques. 4th ed. (Illus.). 448p. (C). 1999. text. write for info. (*1-55664-505-8*) Mosby Inc.

***Linne, Mark R., et al.** A Guide to Appraisal Valuation Modeling. 150p. 2000. write for info. (*0-922154-59-7*) Appraisal Inst.

Linne, Olga, jt. ed. see Hamelink, Cees J.

Linnea, Ann. Deep Water Passage. 1997. pap. 12.00 (*0-671-00282-1*, PB Trade Paper) PB.

Linnea, Sharon. Princess K'iulani: Hope of a Nation, Heart of a People. LC 97-14260. (Illus.). 224p. (YA). (gr. 5 up). 1999. 18.00 (*0-8028-5145-2*, Eerdmans Bks); pap. 10.00 (*0-8028-5088-X*, Eerdmans Bks) Eerdmans.

— Raoul Wallenberg: The Man Who Stopped Death. (Illus.). 168p. 1993. pap. 9.95 (*0-8276-0448-3*) JPS Phila.

Linnea, Sharon, ed. see Shakespeare, William.

***Linneham, Genevieve.** Maggie Davis: The Poetry of Falling: Works on Paper. (Illus.). 2000. pap. 1.00 (*0-9619219-8-6*) Polk Mus Art.

Linnekin, Jocelyn. Sacred Queens & Women of Consequence: Rank, Gender, & Colonialism in the Hawaiian Islands. (Women & Culture Ser.). (Illus.). 308p. 1990. pap. text 18.95 (*0-472-06423-1*, 06423) U of Mich Pr.

Linnekin, Jocelyn & Poyer, Lin, eds. Cultural Identity & Ethnicity in the Pacific. 336p. 1990. pap. text 24.00 (*0-8248-1891-1*) UH Pr.

Linnell, Andrew & Auer, Varvara. The Dance of the Elves. (Illus.). 32p. (Orig.). (J). (ps). 1984. pap. 15.50 (*0-936132-68-X*) Merc Pr NY.

Linnell, Dennis. SAA Handbook. (C). 1990. pap. text 24.95 (*0-201-51786-8*) Addison-Wesley.

Linneman, Robert E. & Stanton, John L. Marketing Planning in a Total Quality Environment. LC 94-48363. (Illus.). 461p. 1995. lib. bdg. 79.95 (*1-56024-938-2*) Haworth Pr.

***Linnemann, Eta.** Is There a Synoptic Problem? Rethinking the Literary Dependence of the First Three Gospels. 220p. 1999. pap. 22.00 (*1-57910-267-0*) Wipf & Stock.

Linnemann, Hans. South-South Trade Preferences: The GSTP & Trade in Manufactures. (Illus.). 236p. (C). 1992. text 29.95 (*0-8039-9421-4*) Sage.

Linnemann, Hans, et al, eds. Export-Oriented Industrialization in Developing Countries. 456p. (Orig.). 1987. pap. 47.50 (*9971-69-112-4*, Pub. by Sngapore Univ Pr) Coronet Bks.

Linnemann, Hans, jt. ed. see Rao, C. Hanumantha.

Linnenkohl, Susan. Basic Nutrition Workbook. 160p. (C). 1993. spiral bd. 17.95 (*0-8403-8388-6*) Kendall-Hunt.

Linner, John H. Surgery for Morbid Obesity. (Illus.). 275p. 1984. 138.00 (*0-387-90888-9*) Spr-Verlag.

Linnert, G. E. Welding Metallurgy Vol. 1: Fundamentals. 4th ed. (Illus.). 940p. 1995. 99.00 (*0-87171-457-4*, wM1) Am Welding.

Linnert, Peter. Lexikon Angloamerikanischer und Deutscher Managementbegriffe: Lexicon of Anglo-American & german Management Terminology. (GER.). 1972. 45.00 (*0-8288-6406-3*, M-7286) Fr & Eur.

Linney, Barbara J. Hope for the Future: A Career Development Guide for Physician Executives. LC 96-86461. 142p. (Orig.). 1996. pap. 48.00 (*0-924674-47-4*) Am Coll Phys Execs.

Linney, Barbara J., jt. auth. see Linney, George E., Jr.

Linney, Bob & Wilson, Bruce, eds. The Copy Book: Copyright Free Illustrations for Development. (Illus.). 102p. 1988. pap. 21.00 (*0-946688-44-3*, Pub. by Intermed Tech) Stylus Pub VA.

Linney, George E., Jr. & Linney, Barbara J. Medical Directors: What, Why, How. LC 92-74400. 44p. (Orig.). (C). 1993. pap. text 20.00 (*0-924674-19-9*) Am Coll Phys Execs.

Linney, Jean A. & Wandersman, Abraham. Prevention Plus III: Assessing Alcohol & Other Drug Prevention Programs at the School & Community Level: A Four-Step Guide to Useful Program Assessment. (Illus.). 461p. (Orig.). (C). 1993. pap. text 50.00 (*0-7881-0085-8*) DIANE Pub.

Linney, Romulus. Ambrosio. 1993. pap. 5.25 (*0-8222-1320-6*) Dramatists Play.

— The Captivity of Pixie Shedman. 1981. pap. 5.25 (*0-8222-0180-1*) Dramatists Play.

— Childe Byron. 1981. pap. 5.25 (*0-8222-0201-8*) Dramatists Play.

— The Death of King Philip. 1984. pap. 3.25 (*0-8222-0291-3*) Dramatists Play.

— Democracy. 1976. pap. 5.25 (*0-8222-0299-9*) Dramatists Play.

— El Hermano. 1981. pap. 3.25 (*0-8222-0355-3*) Dramatists Play.

Linney, Romulus. Gint. pap. 5.95 (*0-8222-1711-2*) Dramatists Play.

Linney, Romulus. Heathen Valley. 1988. pap. 5.25 (*0-8222-0508-4*) Dramatists Play.

— Holy Ghosts. 1989. pap. 5.25 (*0-8222-0526-2*) Dramatists Play.

— Juliet - Yancey - April Snow. 1989. pap. 5.25 (*0-8222-0063-5*) Dramatists Play.

— Laughing Stock: Three Short Plays. 1984. pap. 5.25 (*0-8222-0643-9*) Dramatists Play.

— The Love Suicide at Schofield Barracks: Full Length. 1972. pap. 5.25 (*0-8222-0702-8*) Dramatists Play.

Linney, Romulus. The Love Suicide at Schofield Barracks: One-Act. Date not set. pap. 5.95 (*0-8222-1773-2*) Dramatists Play.

Linney, Romulus. The Love Suicide at Schofield Barracks: One-Act. 1985. pap. 3.25 (*0-8222-0701-X*) Dramatists Play.

— Mountain Memory. LC 98-178025. 1996. pap. 5.25 (*0-8222-1538-1*) Dramatists Play.

— Old Man Joseph & His Family. 1978. pap. 5.25 (*0-8222-0841-5*) Dramatists Play.

— Pops. 65p. 1987. pap. 5.25 (*0-8222-0906-3*) Dramatists Play.

***Linney, Romulus.** Romulus Linney: Adaptations for the American Stage: Cather, Chekhov, Gaines, Ibsen, Stringberg, Tolstoy, Trask & Wilde. 416p. 2000. 35.00 (*1-57525-260-0*) Smith & Kraus.

— Romulus Linney: 9 Adaptations for the American Stage: Cather, Chekhov, Gaines, Ibsen, Stringberg, Tolstoy, Trask & Wilde. 416p. 2000. pap. 19.95 (*1-57525-203-1*) Smith & Kraus.

Linney, Romulus. Romulus Linney, Seventeen Short Plays. LC 92-27781. (Contemporary Playwrights Ser.). 276p. 1994. pap. 16.95 (*1-880399-21-0*) Smith & Kraus.

— Sand Mountain. 1985. pap. 5.25 (*0-8222-0985-3*) Dramatists Play.

— The Sorrows of Frederick. 1976. pap. 5.25 (*0-8222-1058-4*) Dramatists Play.

— The Sorrows of Frederick & Holy Ghosts. LC 76-47904. 192p. 1977. pap. 3.95 (*0-15-683848-6*, Harvest Bks) Harcourt.

— Spain. 1994. pap. 5.25 (*0-8222-1376-1*) Dramatists Play.

— Tennessee. 1980. pap. 3.25 (*0-8222-1119-X*) Dramatists Play.

— Three Poets. 1990. pap. 5.25 (*0-8222-1141-6*) Dramatists Play.

— True Crimes. 1996. pap. 5.25 (*0-8222-1537-3*) Dramatists Play.

— 2. 1993. pap. 5.25 (*0-8222-1486-5*) Dramatists Play.

— Unchanging Love. 1991. pap. 5.25 (*0-8222-1188-2*) Dramatists Play.

— A Woman Without a Name. 57p. 1986. pap. 5.25 (*0-8222-1269-2*) Dramatists Play.

Linney, Romulus & Dickens, Charles. A Christmas Carol: Based on the Story by Charles Dickens. 1996. pap. 5.25 (*0-8222-1539-X*) Dramatists Play.

Linnhoff-Popien, Claudia & Meyer, Bernd E. Trends in Distributed Systems: Corba & Beyond - International Workshop Treds '96, Aachen, Germany, October 1-2, 1996 : Proceedings. LC 96-41958. (Lecture Notes in Computer Science Ser.: Vol. 1161). 289p. 1996. text 49.00 (*3-540-61842-2*) Spr-Verlag.

Linnik, E. F., jt. auth. see Bolotina, A. I.

Linnik, I. V. Dutch Paintings in the Museums of the Soviet Union: Gollandskaia Zhivopis'v Muzeiakh Sovetskogo Soiuza. (RUS., Illus.). 520p. 1984. 295.00 (*0-7855-1597-6*) St Mut.

— Old Master Paintings in Soviet Museums. (Illus.). 211p. (C). 1989. text 235.00 (*0-569-09217-5*, Pub. by Collets) St Mut.

Linnik, Iuril V. & Ostrovskii, I. V. Decomposition of Random Variables & Vectors. Israel Program for Scientific Translations Staff, tr. from RUS. LC 76-51345. (Translations of Mathematical Monographs: No. 48). 390p. reprint ed. pap. 120.90 (*0-608-07820-4*, 205266500010) Bks Demand.

Linnik, Jurii V. Dispersion Method in Binary Additive Problems. Schuur, S., tr. LC 63-15660. (Translations of Mathematical Monographs: Vol. 4). 186p. 1963. reprint ed. pap. 55.00 (*0-8218-1554-7*, MMONO/4) Am Math.

— Ergodic Properties of Algebraic Fields. (Ergebnisse der Mathematik und ihrer Grenzgebiete: Vol. 45). 1968. 65.00 (*0-387-04101-X*) Spr-Verlag.

— Statistical Problems with Nuisance Parameters. Technica, S., tr. LC 67-30101. (Translations of Mathematical Monographs: Vol. 20). 258p. 1968. text 44.00 (*0-8218-1570-9*, MMONO/20) Am Math.

Linnik, Jurii V., ed. Articles on Mathematical Statistics & the Theory of Probability. LC 66-26640. (Proceedings of the Steklov Institute of Mathematics Ser.: No. 79). 259p. 1967. pap. 75.00 (*0-8218-1879-1*, STEKLO/79) Am Math.

— Theoretical Problems of Mathematical Statistics: Proceedings. LC 72-5245. (Proceedings of the Steklov Institute of Mathematics Ser.: No. 111). 316p. 1973. pap. 75.00 (*0-8218-3011-2*, STEKLO/111) Am Math.

Linnik, Jurii V. & Ostrovskii, Iosif V. Decomposition of Random Variables & Vectors. LC 76-51345. (Translations of Mathematical Monographs: Vol. 48). 380p. 1977. text 89.00 (*0-8218-1598-9*, MMONO/48) Am Math.

Linnik, Jurii V., ed. Studies in Mathematical Statistics: Proceedings. (Proceedings of the Steklov Institute of Mathematics Ser.: No. 104). 260p. 1971. pap. 58.00 (*0-8218-3004-X*, STEKLO/104) Am Math.

Linnik, P., jt. auth. see Aizerman, M.

Linnman, Paul. Oregon Golf. LC 99-25224. 1999. 29.95 (*1-55868-474-3*) Gr Arts Ctr Pub.

Linnoila, Markku, jt. ed. see Davidson, Lucy.

***Linnros, J.** Light Emission from Silicon: Progress Towards Si-Based Optoelectronics of the E-MRS 1998 Spring Conference, Strasbourg, France, June 16-19, 1998. LC 99-228690. 546p. 1999. 177.50 (*0-08-043604-8*) Elsevier.

Linoff, Gordon, jt. auth. see Berry, Michael.

Linoner, Richard. How Do You Expect Me to Be Your Wife When I'm So Busy Being Your Mother. Portaro, Ron, ed. & reader by. (Illus.). 215p. 1995. pap. 12.95 (*0-9658644-0-5*) Total Qual.

Linosay, T. J. Capt. Gougar & His Steamboats. 1987. pap. 5.95 (*0-917914-67-8*) Lindsay Pubns.

Linowes, David F. Creating Public Policy: The Chairman's Memoirs of Four Presidential Commissions. LC 97-28855. 248p. 1998. 59.95 (*0-275-96002-1*, Praeger Pubs) Greenwood.

***Linowes, David F.** Living Through Fifty Years of Economic Progress with Ten Presidents: The Most Productive Generation in History, 1946-1996. LC 00-29643. (Industrial Development & the Social Fabric Ser.). (Illus.). 2000. write for info. (*0-7623-0590-8*) Jai Pr.

Linowes, David F. Managing Growth Through Acquisition. LC 68-31542. 192p. reprint ed. pap. 59.60 (*0-608-10731-X*, 205039400078) Bks Demand.

— Privacy in America: Is Your Private Life in the Public Eye? LC 88-20645. 206p. 1989. 19.95 (*0-252-01604-1*) U of Ill Pr.

Linowes, David F., ed. Privatization: Toward More Effective Government--Report of the President's Commission on Privatization. 304p. 1988. pap. text 15.95 (*0-252-06058-X*) U of Ill Pr.

Linowitz, Sol M. World Hunger: A Challenge to American Policy. LC 80-85486. (Headline Ser.: No. 252). (Illus.). 64p. 1980. pap. 5.95 (*0-87124-065-3*) Foreign Policy.

Linowitz, Sol M. & Mayer, Martin. The Betrayed Profession: Lawyering at the End of the Twentieth Century. LC 95-43782. 288p. (C). 1996. reprint ed. pap. 15.95 (*0-8018-5329-X*) Johns Hopkins.

Linquist, Luann. Secret Lovers: Affairs Happen - How to Cope. 221p. 1991. pap. 17.95 (*0-669-27666-9*) Jossey-Bass.

— Secret Lovers: Affairs Happen - How to Cope. LC 98-33868. 1999. 17.95 (*0-7879-4641-9*) Jossey-Bass.

***Linrothe.** Ruthless Compassion: Wrathful Deities in Early Indo-Tibetan Esoteric Buddist Art, 1. LC 99-13944. (Illus.). 368p. 1999. 55.00 (*1-57062-439-9*, Pub. by Shambhala Pubns) Random.

Lins, Barbara, ed. see Links, Marty.

Lins, Cathy, ed. see Jess, Denise.

Lins, Charles. The Modula-2 Software Component Library. (Compass International Ser.). (Illus.). xix, 450p. 1989. 59.95 (*0-387-97074-6*) Spr-Verlag.

— The Modula-2 Software Component Library, Vol. 1. (Compass International Ser.). (Illus.). xvi, 312p. 1988. 65.95 (*0-387-96867-9*) Spr-Verlag.

— The Modula-2 Software Component Library, Vol. 2. (Compass International Ser.). (Illus.). xviii, 368p. 1989. 65.95 (*0-387-96939-X*) Spr-Verlag.

— The Modula-2 Software Component Library, Vol. 4. Muchnik, S. S. & Schnupp, Peter, eds. (Compass International Ser.). (Illus.). xvii, 371p. 1990. 59.95 (*0-387-97255-2*) Spr-Verlag.

Lins, Gerald T., et al. Regulation of Investment Companies, 3 vols. ring bd. 355.00 (*0-8205-2005-5*) Bender.

Lins, Gerald T., jt. auth. see Lemke, Thomas.

Lins, Gerald T., jt. auth. see Lemke, Thomas P.

Lins, Osman. Avalovara. Rabassa, Gregory, tr. from SPA. (Texas Pan American Ser.). 344p. 1990. reprint ed. pap. 14.95 (*0-292-70416-X*) U of Tex Pr.

— Nine, Novena, Vol. 104. Frizzi, Adria, tr. from POR. LC 95-35738. (Sun & Moon Classics Ser.: No. 104). 250p. (Orig.). 1995. pap. 12.95 (*1-55713-229-1*) Sun & Moon CA.

— The Queen of the Prisons of Greece. Frizzi, Adria, tr. from POR. LC 94-7326. 192p. (Orig.). 1995. pap. 12.95 (*1-56478-056-2*) Dalkey Arch.

***Lins, Paolo.** City of God. 2000. text (*0-374-12407-8*) FS&G.

Linsay, Art. I Can: Coach Ron Brown's Search for Success. 162p. (Orig.). (YA). 1992. pap. 8.95 (*1-887002-01-4*) Cross Trng.

Linscheid, Adolph. In-Service Improvement of the State Teachers College Faculty: A Study of the Efforts at in-Service Improvement of the Faculties of State Teachers Colleges in the United States. LC 70-176998. (Columbia University. Teachers College. Contributions to Education Ser.: No. 309). reprint ed. 37.50 (*0-404-55309-5*) AMS Pr.

Linscheid, R. L., et al. The Wrist. Cooney, William Patrick, ed. LC 97-14867. (Illus.). 1424p. (C). (gr. 13). 1997. text 275.00 (*0-8016-6644-9*, 06644) Mosby Inc.

Linschoten, Jan H. Van, see Van Linschoten, Jan H.

***Linscomb, Shadrach.** Brother Status. 189p. 2000. pap. 12.99 (*0-9663420-4-6*) View Hse Pubg.

Linscomb, Shadrach. One Day in the Life of Zechariah. (Illus.). 1998. pap. 9.95 (*0-9663420-3-8*) View Hse Pubg.

An Asterisk (*) at the beginning of an entry indicates that the title is appearing for the first time.

Linscott, Caroline. The Art of the American West. (Illus.). 144p. 1998. 29.99 (*1-56496-473-6*) Rockport Pubs.

Linscott, Eloise H. Folk Songs of Old New England. 368p. 1993. reprint ed. pap. text 9.95 (*0-486-27827-1*) Dover.

Linscott, Eloise H., ed. Folk Songs of Old New England. 2nd ed. LC M 1629.L64F. 370p. reprint ed. pap. 114.70 (*0-608-10691-7*, 201021700068) Bks Demand.

Linscott, Gillian. Absent Friends. LC 99-13681. 288p. 1999. text 22.95 (*0-312-20765-4*) St Martin.

***Linscott, Gillian.** Absent Friends. large type ed. 368p. 2000. write for info. (*0-7505-1488-4*, Pub. by Mgna Lrg Print) Ulverscroft.

Linscott, Gillian. Crown Witness. large type ed. (Dales Large Print Ser.). 383p. 1997. pap. 18.99 (*1-85389-712-4*) Ulverscroft.

— Dance on Blood. LC 98-12778. 256p. 1998. text 22.95 (*0-312-18075-6*, 853567) St Martin.

— Dead Man's Sweetheart. LC 96-27973. 272p. 1996. 21.95 (*0-312-14579-9*) St Martin.

— An Easy Day for a Lady. large type ed. LC 94-39578. 326p. 1995. pap. 19.95 (*0-7862-0362-5*) Thorndike Pr.

— Hanging on the Wire. large type ed. LC 94-19730. 378p. 1995. pap. 18.95 (*0-7862-0309-9*) Thorndike Pr.

— Murder, I Presume. large type ed. (Keating's Choice Ser.). 312p. 1992. 21.95 (*1-85089-428-0*, Pub. by ISIS Lrg Prnt) Transaction Pubs.

Linscott, John D., jt. auth. see Wilson, Robert G.

Linscott, Robert N., ed. State of Mind. LC 72-8483. (Essay Index Reprint Ser.). 1977. reprint ed. 28.95 (*0-8369-7321-6*) Ayer.

Linscott, William D. Linscott's Directory of Immunological & Biological Reagents. 10th rev. ed. 377p. 1998. pap. 85.00 (*0-9604920-9-7*) Linscotts Direct.

Linse, jt. auth. see Yeldin.

Linse, A. R., jt. ed. see Stein, J. K.

Linse, Barbara B. The Art of the Mexican Folk. (Illus.). 78p. 1991. text 7.95 (*1-878079-03-4*) Arts Pubns.

— Arts & Crafts for All Seasons. LC 68-57698. 1969. pap. 7.99 (*0-8224-0490-7*) Fearon Teacher Aids.

***Linse, Barbara B.** Live Again Our Mission Past for Kids. (California Mission Ser.). (SPA.). 108p. (J). (gr. 4-6). 2000. pap. write for info. (*1-878079-26-3*) Arts Pubns.

Linse, Barbara B. & Judd, Dick. Fiesta! Mexico & Central America: A Global Awareness Program for Children in Grades 2-5. 240p. (J). (gr. 2-5). 16.99 (*1-56417-799-8*, FE4232B) Fearon Teacher Aids.

— Fiesta! Mexico & Central America for Children in Grades 2-5. (J). (gr. 2-5). 1993. pap. 27.99 (*0-8224-4232-9*) Fearon Teacher Aids.

Linse, Barbara B. & Knight, Marilyn. Love the Earth! Dresser, Ginny, ed. (Illus.). 32p. (J). 1991. pap. write for info. (*0-318-68833-6*) Arts Pubns.

Linse, Barbara B. & Kuska, George, eds. Live Again Our Mission Past: California Missions Through Children's Eyes. (Story of Spanish California through the Missions Ser.). (Illus.). 200p. (YA). (gr. 7-12). 1984. pap. 13.95 (*0-9607458-1-5*) Arts Pubns.

Linse, Barbara B. & Links, Marty. Love the Earth! An Ecology Resource Book. (Illus.). (J). 1991. 5.95 (*1-878079-01-8*); 4.95 (*0-685-59046-1*) Arts Pubns.

Linse, Barbara B., ed. see Andrews, Janice H.

Linse, Barbara B., ed. see Christensen, Kathy.

Linse, C., tr. see Maffesoli, Michel.

Linse, Caroline. Exploring English Placement Test. 1995. spiral bd. 27.56 (*0-201-89880-2*) Addison-Wesley.

— The Treasured Mailbox: How to Use Authentic Correspondence with Children, K-6. LC 97-600. 1997. pap., teacher ed. 14.95 (*0-435-08139-X*) Heinemann.

Linse, Caroline T., jt. auth. see Yeldin, Jane.

Linse, D. Dictionary Computer Technology: French/German/French. 2nd ed. (FRE & GER.). 261p. 1994. 150.00 (*0-320-00561-5*) Fr & Eur.

Linse, Doris. Woerterbuch der Datentechnik: German-French, French-German. 2nd ed. (FRE & GER.). 394p. 1993. 125.00 (*0-7859-7068-1*) Fr & Eur.

***Linsebardt, Mark.** SQL Server 2000 Administration. (Database Professional's Library). (Illus.). 2000. pap. 44.99 (*0-07-212618-3*) Osborne-McGraw.

Linsell, Stewart. Hickling Broad. 200p. 1990. 56.85 (*0-86138-072-X*, Pub. by T Dalton) St Mut.

Linsell, Tony. Anglo-Saxon: Mythology, Migration & Magic. LC 95-122348. (Illus.). 167p. 29.95 (*1-898281-09-2*, Pub. by Anglo-Saxon Bks) Paul & Co Pubs.

— Rune Cards. (Illus.). 30p. 19.95 (*0-9516209-7-5*, Pub. by Anglo-Saxon Bks) Paul & Co Pubs.

Linsenbach, Sherri. Creative Thinking. 1997. 4.95 (*1-55708-582-X*, McR349) McDonald Pub Co.

***Linsenbard, Gail.** An Investigation of Jean-Paul Sartre's Posthumously Published Notebooks for an Ethics. LC 00-20755. (Studies in French Literature : 40). 176p. 2000. 79.95 (*0-7734-7793-4*) E Mellen.

***Linsenbradt, Mark.** Iplanet Web Server Administrator's Handbook. (Illus.). 2000. pap. text 29.99 (*0-7645-4658-9*) IDG Bks.

***Linsenbradt, Mark & Stigler, Shane.** Windows 2000 Administrators Handbook. LC 00-22242. (Administrator's Handbook). 620p. 2000. pap. 24.99 (*0-7645-3345-2*) IDG Bks.

***Linsenman, Bob.** Michigan Blue-Ribbon Fly Fishing Guide. (Illus.). 96p. 2000. pap. 24.95 (*1-57188-160-3*) F Amato Pubns.

Linsenman, Bob. River Journal Vol. 5, No.3: Au Sable. (River Journal Ser.: Vol. 5, No. 3). (Illus.). 48p. 1998. pap. 15.95 (*1-57188-093-3*) F Amato Pubns.

Linsenman, Bob & Galloup, Kelly. Modern Streamers for Trophy Trout: New Techniques, Tactics, & Patterns. LC 99-29642. (Illus.). 224p. 1999. text 34.95 (*0-88150-466-1*, Pub. by Countryman) Norton.

Linsenman, Bob & Nevala, Steve. Great Lakes Steelhead: A Guided Tour for Fly-Anglers. LC 95-30537. (Illus.). 312p. (Orig.). 1995. pap. 22.00 (*0-88150-312-6*, Pub. by Countryman) Norton.

— Michigan Trout Streams: A Fly-Angler's Guide. LC 93-6118. (Illus.). 272p. (Orig.). 1993. pap. 17.00 (*0-88150-271-5*, Pub. by Countryman) Norton.

Linsey, Adrian & Fieldhouse, Ken. Landscape Design Guide Vol. I: Soft Landscape. Dodd, Jeremy, ed. 224p. 1990. text 73.95 (*0-566-09017-1*, Pub. by Gower) Ashgate Pub Co.

Linsk, Joseph A., et al. Clinical Aspiration Cytology. 2nd ed. Franzen, Sixten, ed. LC 65-9913. (Illus.). 432p. 1989. text 125.00 (*0-397-50826-3*, Lppncott) Lppncott W & W.

Linsk, Nathan, et al, eds. Wages for Caring: Compensating Family Care of the Elderly. LC 91-37512. 296p. 1992. 65.00 (*0-275-93635-X*, C3635, Praeger Pubs) Greenwood.

Linskens, H. F., et al, eds. Gas Chromatography-Mass Spectrometry. (Modern Methods of Plant Analysis Ser.: Vol. 3). (Illus.). 330p. 1986. 222.95 (*0-387-15911-8*) Spr-Verlag.

— Nuclear Magnetic Resonance. (Modern Methods of Plant Analysis Ser.: Vol. 2). (Illus.). 215p. 1986. 152.95 (*0-387-15910-X*) Spr-Verlag.

Linskens, H. F. & Heslop-Harrison, J., eds. Cellular Interactions. (Encyclopedia of Plant Physiology Ser.). (Illus.). 850p. 1984. 344.95 (*0-387-12738-0*) Spr-Verlag.

Linskens, H. F. & Jackson, J. F. Essential Oils & Waxes: With the Assistance of Numerous Experts. (Modern Methods of Plant Analysis Ser.: Vol. 12). (Illus.). xviii, 337p. 1991. 228.95 (*0-387-51915-7*) Spr-Verlag.

Linskens, H. F. & Jackson, J. F., eds. Analysis of Non-Alcoholic Beverages. (Modern Methods of Plant Analysis Ser.: Vol. 8). (Illus.). 450p. 1988. 277.95 (*0-387-18820-7*) Spr-Verlag.

— Analysis of Plant Waste Materials. (Modern Methods of Plant Analysis Ser.: Vol. 20). (Illus.). 210p. 1999. 164.00 (*3-540-64669-8*) Spr-Verlag.

— Cell Components. (Modern Methods of Plant Analysis Ser.: Vol. 1). (Illus.). 430p. 1986. 262.95 (*0-387-15822-7*) Spr-Verlag.

— Fruit Analysis. (Modern Methods of Plant Analysis Ser.: Vol. 18). 176p. 1995. 148.95 (*3-540-59118-4*) Spr-Verlag.

— Gases in Plant & Microbial Cells. (Modern Methods of Plant Analysis, New Ser.: Vol. 9). (Illus.). 385p. 1989. 248.95 (*0-387-18821-5*) Spr-Verlag.

— High Performance Liquid Chromatography in Plant Sciences. (Modern Methods of Plant Analysis Ser.: Vol. 5). (Illus.). 255p. 1987. 155.95 (*0-387-17243-2*) Spr-Verlag.

— Immunology in Plant Sciences. (Modern Methods of Plant Analysis Ser.: Vol. 4). (Illus.). 305p. 1986. 196.95 (*0-387-16842-7*) Spr-Verlag.

— Physical Methods in Plant Sciences. (Modern Methods of Plant Analysis Ser.: Vol. 11). (Illus.). 320p. 1990. 206.95 (*0-387-50332-3*) Spr-Verlag.

— Plant Cell Wall Analysis. (Modern Methods of Plant Analysis Ser.: Vol. 17). (Illus.). 224p. 1996. 179.00 (*3-540-59406-X*) Spr-Verlag.

— Plant Fibers. (Modern Methods of Plant Analysis Ser.: Vol. 10). (Illus.). 420p. 1989. 284.95 (*0-387-18822-3*) Spr-Verlag.

— Plant Toxin Analysis. (Modern Methods of Plant Analysis Ser.: Vol. 13). (Illus.). 368p. 1992. 251.95 (*0-387-52328-6*) Spr-Verlag.

— Plant Volatile Analysis. (Modern Methods of Plant Analysis: Vol. 19). 200p. 1997. 157.00 (*3-540-61589-X*) Spr-Verlag.

— Seed Analysis. (Modern Methods of Plant Analysis Ser.: Vol. 14). (Illus.). 384p. 1992. 294.95 (*0-387-52737-0*) Spr-Verlag.

— Vegetables & Vegetable Products. (Modern Methods of Plant Analysis Ser.: Vol. 16). 208p. 1994. 188.95 (*0-387-55843-8*) Spr-Verlag.

Linskens, H. F., jt. ed. see Jackson, J. F.

Linskey, Tom. Race Winning Strategies: Smart Lessons with Deep Dakron. (Illus.). 250p. 1995. pap. 17.95 (*0-924486-88-0*) Sheridan.

Linskie, Rosella. The Learning Process: Theory & Practice. LC 83-16882. 320p. 1983. reprint ed. pap. text 25.00 (*0-8191-3591-7*) U Pr of Amer.

Linskill, Joseph, ed. see Raimbaut de Vaqueiras.

Linsky, Arnold S. & Straus, Murray A. Social Stress in the United States: Links to Regional Patterns in Crime & Illness. LC 86-14192. 186p. 1986. 57.95 (*0-86569-149-5*, Auburn Hse) Greenwood.

Linsky, Arnold S., et al. Stress, Culture, & Aggression. LC 94-48643. 200p. 1995. 30.00 (*0-300-05706-7*) Yale U Pr.

Linsky, Benjamin, ed. Chicago Association of Commerce & Industry, Committee of Investigationon Smoke Abatement. Chicago Report on Smoke Abatement: A Landmark Survey of the Technology & History of Air Pollution Control. write for info. (*0-318-61059-0*, Pergamon Pr) Elsevier.

Linsky, Bernard. Russell's Metaphysical Logic. LC 99-31299. (Lecture Notes Ser.: Vol. 101). 176p. 1999. 64.95 (*1-57586-209-3*, Pub. by CSLI); pap. 22.95 (*1-57586-210-7*, Pub. by CSLI) Cambridge U Pr.

Linsky, Jeffrey L. & Serio, Salvatore, eds. Physics of Solar & Stellar Coronae - G. S. Vaiana Memorial Symposium: Proceedings of a Conference Held in Palermo, Italy, 22-26 June 1992. LC 93-17752. (Astrophysics & Space Science Library: Vol. 183). 1993. text 353.00 (*0-7923-2346-7*) Kluwer Academic.

Linsky, Jeffrey L. & Stencel, R. E., eds. Cool Stars, Stellar Systems & the Sun. (Lecture Notes in Physics Ser.: Vol. 291). 537p. 1988. 73.95 (*0-387-18653-0*) Spr-Verlag.

Linsky, Jeffrey L., jt. ed. see Strassmeier, Klaus G.

Linsky, Leonard. Names & Descriptions. LC 76-8093. 1993. reprint ed. pap. text 4.50 (*0-226-48442-4*, P871) U Ch Pr.

— Oblique Contexts. LC 82-23825. (C). 1995. lib. bdg. 30.00 (*0-226-48439-4*) U Ch Pr.

Linsky, Leonard, ed. Semantics & the Philosophy of Language. 2nd ed. LC 52-10465. 304p. 1952. reprint ed. pap. text 14.95 (*0-252-00093-5*) U of Ill Pr.

Linsky, Martin, et al. Impact: How the Press Affects Federal Policy Making. (C). 1988. pap. text 14.00 (*0-393-95793-4*) Norton.

Linsley. Hydrology for Engineers. 3rd ed. 1982. student ed. 21.75 (*0-07-037957-2*) McGraw.

***Linsley, Clyde.** Death Spiral. LC 00-190022. 192p. 2000. 18.95 (*0-8034-9419-X*, Avalon Bks) Bouregy.

Linsley, E. Gordon & Chemsak, John A. The Cerambycidae of North America, Vol. "Vol. 117, Pt. VIII" 544p. 1997. pap. 55.00 (*0-520-09819-6*, Pub. by U CA Pr) Cal Prin Full Svc.

Linsley, E. Gorton & Chemsak, John A. The Cerambycidae of North America Pt. VII, No.2: Taxonomy & Classification of the Subfamily Lamiinae, Tribes Acanthocinini Through Hemilophini. (Illus.). 304p. 1995. pap. 42.50 (*0-520-09795-5*, Pub. by U CA Pr) Cal Prin Full Svc.

Linsley, E. Gorton, jt. auth. see Chemsak, John A.

Linsley, Earle G. Nesting Biology & Associates of Melitoma (Hymenoptera, Anthophoridae) LC 80-12433. (University of California Publications in Social Welfare: No. 90). 53p. reprint ed. pap. 30.00 (*0-608-18314-8*, 203158600075) Bks Demand.

Linsley, Earle G. & Chemsak, John A. Taxonomy & Classification of the Subfamily Lamiinae: Tribes Parmenini Through Acanthoderini. (Publications in Entomology: Vol. 102). 1985. pap. 32.50 (*0-520-09690-8*, Pub. by U CA Pr) Cal Prin Full Svc.

Linsley, Earle G. & Sterling, Keir B., eds. Beetles from the Early Russian Explorations of the West Coast of North America: 1815-1857. (Biologists & Their World Ser.). (FRE, GER & LAT., Illus.). 1978. lib. bdg. 58.95 (*0-405-10691-2*) Ayer.

— The Principal Contributions of Henry Walter Bates to a Knowledge of the Butterflies & Longicorn Beetles of the Amazon Valley: Original Anthology. LC 77-81106. (Biologists & Their World Ser.). (Illus.). 1978. lib. bdg. 72.95 (*0-405-10690-4*) Ayer.

Linsley, Horace E. Broaching: Tooling & Practice. LC 61-9128. 224p. reprint ed. pap. 69.50 (*0-8357-7437-6*, 200190900008) Bks Demand.

— Machine Tools, What They Are & How They Work: An Introduction to the Fundamentals of Mass Production. Hall, Herbert D., ed. LC 57-7456. 448p. reprint ed. pap. 138.90 (*0-608-11573-8*, 200190700008) Bks Demand.

Linsley, Judith, jt. auth. see Foy, Jessica.

Linsley, Leslie. Crafts for Dummies. (For Dummies Ser.). (Illus.). 384p. 1999. pap. 19.99 (*0-7645-5140-X*, Dummies Trade Pr) IDG Bks.

— First Home: A Decorating Guide & Sourcebook. Hoeny, Pam, ed. LC 97-37174. 240p. 1998. pap. 20.00 (*0-688-15137-X*, Quil) HarperTrade.

— Key West Houses. LC 91-28698. (Illus.). 96p. (Orig.). 1992. pap. 19.95 (*0-8478-1494-7*, Pub. by Rizzoli Intl) St Martin.

— Leslie Linsley's Country Christmas Crafts: More Than 70 Quick & Easy Projects. (Illus.). 160p. 1995. pap. 18.95 (*0-312-13535-1*) St Martin.

— Leslie Linsley's 15-Minute Decorating Ideas. (Illus.). 269p. 1996. pap. 12.95 (*0-312-14117-3*, St Martin Griffin) St Martin.

— Leslie Linsley's High-Style, Low-Cost Decorating Ideas. LC 99-26230. 237p. 1999. pap. 12.95 (*0-312-19908-2*, St Martin Griffin) St Martin.

— Leslie Linsley's Quick Christmas Decorating Ideas. LC 96-18925. (Illus.). 160p. 1996. pap. 9.95 (*0-312-14643-4*) St Martin.

— Nantucket Style. (Illus.). 228p. 1994. pap. 29.95 (*0-8478-1830-6*, Pub. by Rizzoli Intl) St Martin.

Linsley, Ray K. Water Resources Engineering. 4th ed. (C). 1993. pap. text, student ed., lab manual ed. 26.87 (*0-07-038012-0*) McGraw.

Linsley, Ray K., et al. Hydrology for Engineers. 3rd ed. (Water Resources & Environmental Engineering Ser.). (Illus.). 512p. (C). 1982. 101.56 (*0-07-037956-4*) McGraw.

— Water Resources Engineering. 4th ed. 768p. (C). 1991. 82.19 (*0-07-038010-4*) McGraw.

Linsley, Robin. Railways in Camera, 1860-1913: Archive Photographs of the Great Age of Steam from the Public Record Office. LC 97-158879. (Illus.). 256p. 1997. 44.95 (*0-7509-1060-7*, Pub. by Sutton Pub Ltd) Intl Pubs Mktg.

— Railways in Camera, 1860-1913: Archive Photographs of the Great Age of Steam from the Public Record Office. (Illus.). 256p. 1997. pap. 22.95 (*0-7509-1515-3*, Pub. by Sutton Pub Ltd) Intl Pubs Mktg.

Linsmaier-Bednar, Elfriede M., tr. see Uhlig, Helmut.

Linsner, Joseph Michael. Angry Christ Comix: The Angry Works of Joseph Michael Linsner. (Cry for Dawn Ser.: Vol. 1). (Illus.). 144p. 1994. pap. 12.95 (*1-57989-000-8*) Sirius Ent.

— Crypt of Dawn. 2000. pap. 19.95 (*1-57989-035-0*) Sirius Ent.

Linsner, Joseph Michael. Dawn Vol. 1: Lucifer's Halo. (Illus.). 208p. 1997. pap. 19.95 (*1-57989-014-8*) Sirius Ent.

Linson, Art. A Pound of Flesh: Perilous Tales of How to Produce Movies in Hollywood. 208p. 1998. reprint ed. pap. 12.00 (*0-8021-3551-X*, Grove) Grove-Atltic.

— A Pound of Flesh: Producing in Hollywood--Perilous Tales from the Trenches. 208p. 1995. pap. 9.00 (*0-380-72401-4*, Avon Bks) Morrow Avon.

***Linson, William.** Inspirational Concepts. 2000. write for info. (*1-58235-536-3*) Watermrk Pr.

Linss, Wilhelm C., tr. see Luz, Ulrich.

Linssen, Adrian. Tapas. 1995. 6.98 (*0-7858-0491-9*) Bk Sales Inc.

Linssen, Linda. Las Vegas Cooks! Recipes from Popular Restaurants on the Strip, Downtown, & Across the Las Vegas Valley. LC 97-73358. (Illus.). 123p. 1997. pap. 10.95 (*0-9658172-0-2*) All She Wrote.

Linssen, Robert. Living Zen. Abrahams-Curiel, Diana, tr. from FRE. LC 60-198. 352p. 1988. pap. 14.00 (*0-8021-3136-0*, Grove) Grove-Atltic.

Linstead, Stephen, et al. Understanding Management. 256p. 1996. 69.95 (*0-8039-8912-1*); pap. 26.95 (*0-8039-8913-X*) Sage.

Linstead, Stephen, jt. auth. see Brewis, Joanna.

Linsted, Robert. Certainty of Bible Prophecy. 72p. (Orig.). 1991. pap. 7.50 (*1-879366-07-X*) Hearthstone OK.

Linster, Tom. Blue Food: A Case of National Indigestion. (Illus.). 90p. (Orig.). 1992. pap. 8.95 (*1-881631-00-1*) Byfor Fnd.

L'Institut Roeher Institute for the National Clear. Violence & People with Disabilities: A Review of the Literature. 85p. 1994. pap. write for info. (*0-662-22712-3*, Pub. by Can7 Govern Pub) Intl Spec Bk.

***Linstone, Harold A.** Decision-Making for Technology Executives: Using Multiple Perspectives to Improve Performance. LC 99-19222. (Technology Management & Professional Development Library). 315p. 1999. 69.00 (*0-89006-403-2*) Artech Hse.

Linstone, Harold A. Multiple Perspectives for Decision Making: Bridging the Gap Between Analysis & Action. 400p. 1984. 41.00 (*0-444-00803-9*) P-H.

Linstone, Harold A. & Mitroff, Ian I. The Challenge of the 21st Century: Managing Technology & Ourselves in a Shrinking World. LC 93-296698. (Illus.). 406p. (C). 1994. pap. text 23.95 (*0-7914-1950-9*) State U NY Pr.

Linstone, Harold A., jt. auth. see Mitroff, Ian I.

Linstromberg, Lillian. Taking Time. LC 89-61707. (Illus.). 96p. (Orig.). 1989. pap. 7.95 (*0-9623452-0-2*) Oregon Coast Cmnty Col.

***Linstromberg, Lillian.** Wild Is the Word. 64p. 1999. pap. 6.95 (*0-938911-17-1*, Pub. by Indiv Ed - Poppy Ln) Amer West Books.

Linstromberg, Walter W. & Baumgarten, Henry E. Organic Chemistry: A Brief Course. 5th ed. 448p. (C). text 71.96 (*0-669-05525-5*) HM Trade Div.

— Organic Chemistry: A Brief Course. 6th ed. LC 86-81385. 517p. (C). 1987. text 71.96 (*0-669-12660-8*); pap. text, student ed. 28.76 (*0-669-12661-6*); 2.66 (*0-669-17411-4*) HM Trade Div.

— Organic Experiments. 6th ed. 404p. (C). 1987. pap. text 37.96 (*0-669-12662-4*); teacher ed. 2.66 (*0-669-12663-2*) HM Trade Div.

Linstrum, Helen. Taking Your Show on the Road: A Guide for New Student Recruiters. 49p. 1990. 10.00 (*0-89964-274-8*, 27101) Coun Adv & Supp Ed.

Lint, Charles De, see De Lint, Charles.

Lint, G. Edwin. Gone: A Novel about the Rapture. 200p. (Orig.). 1996. pap. 15.00 (*1-877858-96-X*) Amer Focus Pub.

Lint, Gregg L. Papers of John Adams: March 1780 - December 1780, 2 vols., Vols. 9 & 10. Revelas, Joanna M. et al, eds. (Illus.). 1192p. 1996. 130.00 (*0-674-65445-5*) HUP.

Lint, Gregg L. & Taylor, Robert J., eds. The Papers of John Adams Vols. 7 & 8: September 1778-February 1780, Set. LC 77-4707. (Adams Papers: General Correspondence & Other Papers of the Adams Statesmen Ser.). (Illus.). 480p. 1989. 100.00 (*0-674-65444-7*) Belknap Pr.

Lint, Gregory A. & Rogers, Brian D., eds. Great Revival Sermons. LC 97-62046. (Complete Biblical Library Christian Classic: Vol. 1). 450p. 1997. 29.95 (*1-884642-12-8*) World Library.

Lint, J. H. Van, see Van Lint, J. H.

Lint, J. H. Van, see Cameron, P. J. & Van Lint, J. H.

Lint, J. H. Van, see Van Lint, J. H., ed.

Lint, J. Van, see Van Lint, J.

Lintas, Claudia, jt. ed. see Fabriani, Giuseppe.

Linteau, Paul-Ande, et al. Quebec: A History: 1867-1929. 602p. 49.95 (*0-88862-605-3*, Pub. by J Lorimer) Formac Dist Ltd.

— Quebec: A History: 1867-1929. 602p. reprint ed. pap. 29.95 (*0-88862-604-5*, Pub. by J Lorimer) Formac Dist Ltd.

— Quebec since 1930. LC 89-94964. (FRE., Illus.). 632p. 49.95 (*1-55028-298-0*, Pub. by J Lorimer) Formac Dist Ltd.

— Quebec since 1930, Vol. 2. 632p. pap. 29.95 (*1-55028-296-4*, Pub. by J Lorimer) Formac Dist Ltd.

***Linten, Allison J.** The Internet: A Bibliography with Indexes. 289p. 2000. lib. bdg. 49.00 (*1-56072-813-2*) Nova Sci Pubs.

Linten, Claudia S. Orangerien in Westfalen. (Europaische Hochschulschriften Ser.: Reihe 28, Vol. 327). (Illus.). 382p. 1998. pap. 56.95 (*3-631-33087-1*) P Lang Pubng.

Lintermans, Gloria. Cheap Chic: A Guide to LA's Resale Boutiques. (Illus.). 218p. (Orig.). 1990. pap. 12.95 (*0-9625807-0-8*) A Lintermans Pubs.

— The Newly Divorced Book of Protocol: How to Be Civil When You Hate Their Guts. LC 94-44570. 272p. 1995. 17.95 (*1-56980-037-5*) Barricade Bks.

Lintermans, J. P. Two-Dimensional Echocardiography in Infants & Children. 1986. text 281.00 (*0-89838-778-7*) Kluwer Academic.

Lintern, Gavan, ed. Cognitive Engineering: A Special Issue of the International Journal of Aviation Psychology. 120p. 1999. pap. 24.50 (*0-8058-9783-6*) L Erlbaum Assocs.

L

***Linthecome, Donnell.** Living. 1999. pap. write for info. (1-58235-401-4) Watermrk Pr.

Linthic. MCSE NT Server 4 in the E-W/CD. LC 98-25127. 456p. 1998. 49.99 (1-57610-253-X) Coriolis Grp.

Linthicum, Bob, ed. see Boyland, Anita W.

Linthicum, D. S. & Farid, Nadir R., eds. Anti-Idiotypes, Receptors, & Molecular Mimicry. 345p. 1987. 156.00 (0-387-96548-3) Spr-Verlag.

***Linthicum, David.** Enterprise Application Integration. LC 99-46633. (Information Technology Ser.). 352p. 1999. pap. text 39.95 (0-201-61583-5) Addison-Wesley.

Linthicum, David S. David Linthicum's Guide to Client Server & Intranet Development. LC 97-3995. 326p. 1997. pap. 34.99 (0-471-17467-X) Wiley.

Linthicum, Dorothy S. The Dry Pipeline: Increasing the Flow of Minority Faculty. LC LB2835.25.L4. 62p. reprint ed. pap. 30.00 (0-7837-5163-X, 204489200004) Bks Demand.

Linthicum, Fred H., Jr. & Schwartzman, Jorge A. An Atlas of Micropathology of the Temporal Bone. (Illus.). 104p. (C). 1994. text 125.00 (1-56593-377-X, 0755) Thomson Learn.

Linthicum, Robert C. Empowering the Poor. 128p. 1991. pap. 8.95 (0-912552-75-1) MARC.

— Signs of Hope in the City. 95p. 1996. pap. 7.95 (0-912552-95-6) MARC.

Linthorst, Ann T. A Gift of Love: Marriage As a Spiritual Journey. 166p. 1995. reprint ed. pap. 15.00 (0-913105-17-1) PAGL Pr.

— Mothering As a Spiritual Journey: Learning to Let God Nurture Your Children & You along with Them. 140p. (Orig.). 1993. pap. 12.95 (0-8245-1250-2) Crossroad NY.

— Soul-Kissed. 180p. 1996. pap. 15.95 (0-8245-1492-0) Crossroad NY.

— Thus Saith the Lord: Giddyap!: Metapsychiatric Commentaries on Human Experience & Spiritual Growth. 106p. (Orig.). 1986. pap. 10.00 (0-913105-18-X) PAGL Pr.

Linthurst, Rick A., et al, eds. Methods to Assess the Effects of Chemicals on Ecosystems. LC 95-219002. (SCOPE Ser.). 446p. 1995. 275.00 (0-471-95911-1) Wiley.

Linthwaite, Illona. Ain't I a Woman! Classic Poetry by Women from Around the World. LC 99-43286. 288p. 1999. pap. 12.95 (0-8092-2534-4, 253440, Contemporary Bks) NTC Contemp Pub Co.

Linthwaite, Illona, compiled by. Ain't I a Woman! A Book of Women's Poetry from Around the World. LC 87-35577. 214p. 1991. pap. 8.95 (0-87226-209-X, P Bedrick Books) NTC Contemp Pub Co.

Linthwaite, Illona, ed. Ain't I a Woman! A Book of Women's Poetry from Around the World. LC 93-13201. 224p. 1993. 7.99 (0-517-09365-0) Random Hse Value.

Lintilhac, John-Paul & Lintilhac, Simone. Aging Well: Using Eugeria to Stay Young & Healthy. Tinnon, Robert, ed. LC 99-73043. (Illus.). 272p. 1999. 23.95 (0-9649635-5-8, Pub. by Belle Pubng CA) Seven Locks Pr.

Lintilhac, Simone, jt. auth. see Lintilhac, John-Paul.

Lintinen, Hannu. Finnish/Portuguese/Finnish Dictionary. (FIN & POR.). 788p. 1992. 69.95 (0-320-00084-2) Fr & Eur.

***Lintner, Bertil.** Burma in Revolt: Opium & Insurgency since 1948. (Illus.). 604p. 2000. 29.95 (974-7100-78-9, Pub. by Silk Worm Bks) U of Wash Pr.

Lintner, Bertil. The Rise & Fall of the Communist Party of Burma (CPB) (Southeast Asia Program Ser.: No. 6). (Illus.). 124p. (Orig.). 1990. pap. 12.00 (0-87727-123-2) Cornell SE Asia.

Lintner, Grace. Bond & Free. LC 79-38656. (Black Heritage Library Collection). 1977. reprint ed. 22.95 (0-8369-9014-5) Ayer.

Lintner, John. Economic Research - Retrospect & Prospect Vol. 2: Finance & Capital Markets. (General Ser.: No. 96). 87p. 1972. reprint ed. 22.70 (0-87014-252-6) Natl Bur Econ Res.

Lintner, Mildred D., jt. auth. see Lauckner, Kurt F.

Lintner, Valerio. A Traveller's History of Italy. 5th ed. (Traveller's History Ser.). 1998. pap. text 14.95 (1-56656-296-1) Interlink Pub.

Linton. Introduction to Nursing Care for Adults. 1995. 125.00 (0-7216-6012-6) Harcourt.

— Introductory Nursing Care. (C). 1995. pap. text, student ed. 19.95 (0-7216-3318-8) Harcourt.

***Linton.** Introductory Nursing Care of Adults. 2nd ed. LC 99-19721. (C). 1999. text 49.00 (0-7216-8069-0, W B Saunders Co) Harcrt Hlth Sci Grp.

— Introductory Nursing Care of Adults: Study Guide. 2nd ed. (Illus.). 315p. (C). 1999. pap. text, student ed. write for info. (0-7216-8167-0, W B Saunders Co) Harcrt Hlth Sci Grp.

Linton. Manufacturing Processes. (Mechanical Technology Ser.). 1996. pap. text 41.95 (0-8273-7710-X) Delmar.

— Methods of Display of Ocean Survey Data, Vol. 1. pap. 24.25 (0-901875-51-1, Pergamon Pr) Elsevier.

— Methods of Display of Ocean Survey Data, Vol. 2. pap. 24.25 (90-70310-10-4, Pergamon Pr) Elsevier.

Linton, ed. The Ultimate Multi-Ethnic Resource for Chicago. (Ethnic Resources Ser.). 140p. 1997. pap. 29.50 (0-9658445-1-X) IL Ethnic.

Linton, Adelin, jt. auth. see Linton, Ralph.

Linton, Adelin, jt. ed. see Linton, Ralph.

Linton, Adrianne D., et al, eds. Introductory Nursing Care of Adults. (Illus.). 1995. teacher ed. write for info. (0-7216-4752-9, W B Saunders Co) Harcrt Hlth Sci Grp.

— Introductory Nursing Care of Adults. (Illus.). 1271p. 1995. text, student ed. 63.00 (0-7216-6216-1, W B Saunders Co) Harcrt Hlth Sci Grp.

Linton, Adrianne D., jt. auth. see Maebius, Nancy K.

Linton, Alan H. Microbes, Man & Animals: The Natural History of Microbial Interactions. LC 81-14719. (Illus.). 358p. reprint ed. pap. 111.00 (0-608-17651-6, 203050900069) Bks Demand.

— Topley & Wilson's Principles of Bacteriology, Virology & Immunity. 8th ed. 484p. text. write for info. (0-7131-4589-7, Pub. by E A) Routldge.

Linton, Anthony. Newes of the Complement of the Art of Navigation & of the Mightie Empire of Cataia. LC 72-215. (English Experience Ser.: No. 204). 1969. reprint ed. 30.00 (90-221-0204-1) Walter J Johnson.

***Linton, Bruce.** Finding Time for Fatherhood: Men's Concerns as Parents. 192p. 2000. pap. text 15.00 (1-893163-18-0) Berkeley Hills.

Linton, Bruce. Finding Time for Fatherhood: The Important Considerations Men Face When They Become Parents. LC 98-96047. 106p. 1998. pap. 12.95 (0-9649441-0-3) Fathers Forum.

— Wife, Son, Daughter: A Father's Poems. 24p. (Orig.). 1995. pap. 6.95 (0-9649441-3-8) Fathers Forum.

***Linton, Cathy.** Performance Recording of Animals State of the Art, 1998. (Illus.). 352p. 1998. 96.00 (90-74134-54-8) Wageningen Pers.

Linton, Clarence. A Study of Some Problems Arising in the Admission of Students As Candidates for Professional Degrees in Education. LC 73-176999. (Columbia University. Teachers College. Contributions to Education Ser.: No. 285). reprint ed. 37.50 (0-404-55285-4) AMS Pr.

Linton, Cynthia, ed. The Ethnic Handbook: A Guide to the Cultures & Traditions of Chicago's Diverse Communities. 1996. reprint ed. mass mkt. 39.95 (0-9658445-0-1) IL Ethnic.

Linton, Cynthia, ed. The Ultimate 2000: Directory of Ethnic Organizations, Media & Scholars for Chicago Metro Area. 2nd ed. 140p. Date not set. pap. 40.00 (0-9658445-2-8) IL Ethnic.

Linton, David. More Profit from Your PC: How to Turn Your PC into a Share Investment Powerhouse. 1998. pap. text 21.95 (0-7134-8388-1, Pub. by B T B) Branford.

— Profit from Your PC: How to Use a Personal Computer to Buy & Sell Shares. 1998. pap. text 19.95 (0-7134-8397-0, Pub. by B T B) Branford.

Linton, David & Boston, Ray. The Twentieth-Century Newspaper Press in Britain: An Annotated Bibliography. 416p. 1995. 120.00 (0-7201-2159-0) Continuum.

Linton, Derek S. Who Has the Youth, Has the Future: The Campaign to Save Young Workers in Imperial Germany. 331p. (C). 1991. text 74.95 (0-521-38537-7) Cambridge U Pr.

Linton, Fred E., tr. see Caratheodory, Constantin.

Linton, George, jt. auth. see Hanson, V.

***Linton, Gordon J., ed.** Data Tables for the 1995 National Transit Database Report Year. 17th ed. 480p. (C). 1999. reprint ed. pap. text 45.00 (0-7881-8310-9) DIANE Pub.

— Transit Profiles: Agencies in Urbanized Areas with a Population of Less Than 200,000. (Illus.). 210p. (C). 1999. reprint ed. pap. text 45.00 (0-7881-8314-1) DIANE Pub.

— Transit Profiles: The Thirty Largest Agencies. 90p. (C). 1999. reprint ed. pap. text 20.00 (0-7881-8315-X) DIANE Pub.

Linton, Harold. Architectural Sketching in Markers. 223p. 1990. pap. text 39.95 (0-442-31883-9, VNR) Wiley.

Linton, Harold. Architectural Sketching in Markers. (Illus.). 223p. 1990. pap. 44.95 (0-471-28974-4, VNR) Wiley.

Linton, Harold. Color Forecasting: A Survey of International Color Marketing. 1994. text 66.95 (0-442-01160-1, VNR) Wiley.

Linton, Harold. Color Forecasting: A Survey of International Color Marketing. 240p. 1994. 66.95 (0-471-28491-2, VNR) Wiley.

Linton, Harold. Portfolio Design. (Illus.). 144p. 1996. 30.00 (0-393-73008-5) Norton.

***Linton, Harold.** Portfolio Design. 2nd ed. (Illus.). 2000. 34.95 (0-393-73059-X) Norton.

Linton, I. The Business of Design. (Illus.). 124p. (C). 1987. text 60.00 (0-7476-0007-4) Chapman & Hall.

Linton, Ian. Database Marketing: How to Manage Customer Information for Profit. (Financial Times Management Ser.). 300p. 1995. pap. 62.50 (0-273-61179-8, Pub. by Pitman Pub) Trans-Atl Phila.

— 40 Activities for Improving Customer Service. 250p. 1996. ring bd. 195.00 (0-566-07587-3, Pub. by Gower) Ashgate Pub Co.

— Marketing Training Services. LC 97-3420. 210p. 1997. text 74.95 (0-566-07549-0, Pub. by Gower) Ashgate Pub Co.

Linton, Ian. Twenty-Five Tips for Excellent Customer Service: An Action Plan for Service Success. (Institute of Management Ser.). 192p. 1997. pap. 39.50 (0-273-60974-2, Pub. by Pitman Pub) Trans-Atl Phila.

Linton, Ian & Morley, Kevin. Integrated Marketing Communications. LC 95-153478. (Marketing Ser.). 144p. reprint ed. pap. 44.70 (0-608-09070-0, 206970400005) Bks Demand.

Linton, Isobel. The Counterfeit Heiress. 256p. 1997. mass mkt. 4.99 (0-8217-5690-7, Zebra Kensgtn) Kensgtn Pub Corp.

— False Pretenses. 256p. 1996. mass mkt. 4.50 (0-8217-5198-0, Zebra Kensgtn) Kensgtn Pub Corp.

— An Impromptu Charade. 256p. 1996. mass mkt. 4.50 (0-8217-5411-4, Zebra Kensgtn) Kensgtn Pub Corp.

Linton, James M., jt. auth. see Jowett, Garth.

Linton, Joan P. The Romance of the New World: Gender & the Literary Formations of English Colonialism. LC 97-30145. (Cambridge Studies in Renaissance Literature & Culture: No. 27). 282p. (C). 1998. text 59.95 (0-521-59454-5) Cambridge U Pr.

Linton, John, compiled by. Athwart the Storm: Prose & Poems. 1995. pap. 45.00 (1-85072-153-X, Pub. by W Sessions) St Mut.

Linton, Karin. The Temporal Horizon: A Study of the Theme of Time in Anne Tyler's Major Novels. (Studia Anglistica Upsaliensia Ser.: No. 68). 143p. (Orig.). 1989. pap. 40.00 (91-554-2339-6) Coronet Bks.

Linton, Marilyn. Just Desserts: And Other Treats for Kids to Make. (Illus.). 64p. (J). (gr. 1 up). 1998. pap. 5.95 (0-921103-02-6, Pub. by Kids Can Pr) Genl Dist Srvs.

Linton, Marilyn & Fairfield, Lesley. The Maple Syrup Book. unabridged ed. (Illus.). 48p. (J). (gr. 3-7). 1983. pap. 9.95 (0-919964-52-4, Pub. by Kids Can Pr) Genl Dist Srvs.

***Linton, Mary Fox.** Window Style: Blinds, Curtains, Screens, & Shutters. Dow, ed. (Illus.). 160p. 2000. 29.95 (0-8212-2659-2) Bulfinch Pr.

Linton, Meg. Avatars: The Watercolors of Walton Ford. Glenn, Constance, ed. (Illus.). 25p. 1999. pap. 14.95 (0-936270-38-1) CA St U LB Art.

***Linton, Meg.** The Infant Griffin & Other Recent Drawings by Tom Knechtel. (Illus.). 20p. 2000. 3.00 (1-880658-14-3) San Barb CAF.

***Linton, Meg, frwd.** Big Country: Recent Paintings by Elizabeth Olbert. (Illus.). 16p. 1999. pap. 2.00 (1-880658-13-5) San Barb CAF.

Linton, Nancy, jt. auth. see Frank, Marge.

Linton, Otha W. The American College of Radiology: The First 75 Years. LC 97-24700. 1997. write for info. (1-55903-140-9) Am Coll Radiology.

Linton, Patricia, jt. auth. see Bussell, Darcy.

Linton, Ralph. Age & Sex Categories. (Reprint Series in Social Sciences). (C). 1993. reprint ed. pap. text 1.00 (0-8290-2710-6, S-173) Irvington.

— Archaeology of the Marquesas Islands. (BMB Ser.: No. 23). 1972. reprint ed. 30.00 (0-527-02126-1) Periodicals Srv.

***Linton, Ralph.** Color In Architecture. 288p. 1999. 69.95 (0-07-038119-4) McGraw.

Linton, Ralph. The Cultural Background of Personality. LC 80-29240. 157p. 1981. reprint ed. lib. bdg. 35.00 (0-313-22783-7, LICU, Greenwood Pr) Greenwood.

— Tanala, a Hill Tribe of Madagascar. (Chicago Field Museum of Natural History Fieldiana Anthropology Ser.). 1974. 40.00 (0-527-01882-1) Periodicals Srv.

Linton, Ralph & Linton, Adelin. We Gather Together: The Story of Thanksgiving. (Illus.). 100p. 1990. reprint ed. lib. bdg. 38.00 (1-55888-883-7) Omnigraphics Inc.

Linton, Ralph & Linton, Adelin, eds. Lore of Birthdays. LC 97-20032. (Illus.). 116p. 1997. reprint ed. lib. bdg. 40.00 (0-7808-0265-9) Omnigraphics Inc.

Linton, Ralph & Wingert, Paul. Arts of the South Seas. LC 76-169308. (Museum of Modern Art Publications in Reprint). (Illus.). 200p. 1980. reprint ed. 29.95 (0-405-01567-4) Ayer.

Linton, Rupert, jt. auth. see Ballard, Sebastian.

Linton, Rupert, jt. ed. see Ballard, Sebastian.

Linton, Simi. Claiming Disability. LC 97-21218. 203p. 1998. text 45.00 (0-8147-5133-4); pap. text 17.00 (0-8147-5134-2) NYU Pr.

Linton, Steven J. & Rust, Damon. Ice Rescue. 1982. pap. text 2.00 (0-943717-13-2) Concept Sys.

Linton, Steven J., et al. Dive Rescue Specialist Training Manual. 81p. 1986. pap. text 14.95 (0-943717-42-6) Concept Sys.

Linton, Thomas, ed. The Linton Register, 1990-1991: The Trainer's Resource Directory. 2000p. (C). 1992. 125.00 (0-9626607-0-1) Linton Pub Co.

Linton, Virginia. Heading Out. LC 80-23182. 1981. 10.95 (0-87233-054-0) Bauhan.

Linton, William A., Jr. A Primer on Computer System Interoperability. (Orig.). pap. 19.95 (0-939547-00-7) SMC.

Linton, William J. Memories. LC 69-13753. vi, 236p. 1970. reprint ed. 39.50 (0-678-00596-6) Kelley.

Lintott, Andrew. Imperium Romanum: Politics & Administration. 272p. (C). 1993. pap. 24.99 (0-415-09375-9) Routledge.

— Violence, Civil Strife, & Revolution in the Classical City. 288p. (C). 1987. pap. text 14.95 (0-7099-4170-6, Pub. by C Helm) Routldge.

— Violence in Republican Rome. 2nd rev. ed. 272p. 1999. pap. 24.95 (0-19-815282-5) OUP.

Lintott, Andrew William. The Constitution of the Roman Republic. LC 98-30456. 310p. 1999. text 80.00 (0-19-815068-7) OUP.

Lints, F. A. Genetics & Aging. (Interdisciplinary Topics in Gerontology Ser.: Vol. 14). (Illus.). 1978. pap. 51.50 (3-8055-2891-4) S Karger.

Lints, F. A., ed. Non-Mammalian Models for Research on Ageing. (Interdisciplinary Topics in Gerontology Ser.: Vol. 21). (Illus.). viii, 288p. 1985. 172.25 (3-8055-4019-1) S Karger.

Lints, F. A., et al. Aging in Drosophila. (Aging Ser.). 179p. 1977. text 24.50 (0-8422-7244-5) Irvington.

***Lints, Richard.** The Fabric of Theology: A Prolegomenon to Evangelical Theology. 359p. 1999. pap. 35.00 (1-57910-326-X) Wipf & Stock.

Lintz, Christopher R. Architecture & Community Variability Within the Antelope Creek Phase of the Texas Panhandle. (Studies in Oklahoma's Past: Vol. 14). (Illus.). 433p. (C). 1986. pap. text 13.00 (1-881346-07-2) Univ OK Archeol.

Lintz, Christopher R. & Anderson, Jane L. Temporal Assessment of Diagnostic Materials from the Pinon Canyon Maneuver Site: Towards the Development of a Cultural Chronology for Southeastern Colorado. (Memoir Ser.: No. 4). 475p. 1989. pap. text 15.00 (1-888400-01-3) Colo Archaeol.

Lintzenich, Robert. Exodus. LC 97-37021. (Shepherd's Notes Ser.). 1997. 5.95 (0-8054-9056-6) Broadman.

***Lintzenich, Robert.** Hosea/Obadiah. LC 98-48097. (Shepherd's Notes Ser.). 1999. pap. 5.95 (0-8054-9326-3) Broadman.

Lintzenich, Robert. Ruth, Esther. LC 97-32781. (Shepherd's Notes Ser.). 1998. 5.95 (0-8054-9057-4) Broadman.

Linux Documentation Project Staff. The Linux Bible: The GNU Testament. 4th ed. LC 96-25216. (Illus.). 1850p. Date not set. pap. 39.95 incl. cd-rom (1-883601-20-7) Yggdrasil Comput.

Linux Documentation Project Staff & Yggdrasil Computing, Inc. Staff. The Linux Bible: The GNU Testament. (Illus.). 764p. 1994. pap. 39.95 (1-883601-07-X) Yggdrasil Comput.

— The Linux Bible: The GNU Testament. 2nd ed. (Illus.). 1000p. 1994. pap. 34.95 (1-883601-11-8) Yggdrasil Comput.

Linver, Sandy. The Leader's Edge: How to Use Communication to Grow Your Business & Yourself. 176p. 1994. 19.50 (0-671-88179-5) S&S Trade.

Linver, Sandy & Mengert, Jim. Speak & Get Results: The Complete Guide to Speeches & Presentations That Work in Any Business Situation. rev. ed. LC 93-46040. 1994. 22.00 (0-671-88996-6) S&S Trade.

***Linville.** Vocal Aging. 2000. pap. 35.25 (1-56593-902-6) Thomson Learn.

Linville, Bill, ed. Reservoir Characterization III. LC 92-43076. 1056p. 1993. 35.00 (0-87814-392-0) PennWell Bks.

***Linville, Dorothy.** Graph-X. (Illus.). 33p. (YA). (gr. 5-8). 2000. pap. 5.95 (0-9701551-0-7) D Linville.

Linville, Dorothy & Manning-Weber, Claudia. Every Woman's Guide to Looking Great. (Illus.). 139p. 1983. pap. 6.95 (0-9701551-1-5) D Linville.

***Linville, James Richard.** Israel in the Book of Kings: The Past as a Project of Social Identity. LC 98-170973. (JSOT Supplement Ser.: No. 272). 331p. 1998. 85.00 (1-85075-859-X, Pub. by Sheffield Acad) CUP Services.

Linville, Jim L., ed. see Brannigan, Francis L.

Linville, Jim L., ed. see Bryan, John L.

Linville, Jim L., ed. see Carter, Harry & Rausch, Erwin.

Linville, Linda K. Academic Skills Achievement Program. LC 93-14480. 352p. (C). 1993. text 19.60 (0-256-14219-X, Irwn McGrw-H) McGrw-H Hghr Educ.

Linville, Robert L. CI Boot Camp. 57p. 1996. pap. 15.00 (0-9621241-7-6) SCIP.

Linville, Susan E. Feminism, Film, Fascism: Women's Autobiographical Film in Postwar Germany. LC 97-3076. (Illus.). 208p. (C). 1998. 30.00 (0-292-74696-2, LINFEM); pap. 14.95 (0-292-74697-0, LINFEP) U of Tex Pr.

Linville, William. Boothery 1-2-3. 48p. 1995. pap. 7.95 (0-944754-32-5) Pudding Hse Pubns.

Linworth Publishing, Inc. Staff. Computers & the School Library. (Illus.). 125p. 1990. pap. text 24.95 (0-87436-607-0) ABC-CLIO.

Linworth Publishing, Inc. Staff, ed. The Book Report & Library Talk Author Profile Collection. (Professional Growth Ser.). (Illus.). 109p. 1992. student ed., ring bd. 29.95 (0-938865-12-9) Linworth Pub.

— Reading Motivation. 2nd ed. (Professional Growth Ser.). (Illus.). 120p. 1993. pap. text 19.95 (0-938865-26-9) Linworth Pub.

Linxwiler, Julie, ed. see Pilar, Jacquelin.

Linz. Continental Lover. large type ed. Date not set. 30.00 (0-7862-1722-7) Thorndike Pr.

Linz, Cathie. Abbie & the Cowboy. 1996. per. 3.50 (0-373-76036-1, 1-76036-2) Silhouette.

— Algo Mas Que Deseo: Husband Needed. (Silhouette Deseo Ser.: Vol. 239).Tr. of Something More Than Desire. (SPA.). 1998. per. 3.50 (0-373-35239-5, 1-35239-2) Harlequin Bks.

— Baby Wanted. (Montana Mavericks Ser.). 1995. per. 3.99 (0-373-50174-9, 1-50174-1) Harlequin Bks.

— Bridal Blues. 1994. per. 2.99 (0-373-05894-2, 1-05894-0) Harlequin Bks.

***Linz, Cathie.** Daddy in Dress Blues. (Silhouette Romance Ser.: Vol. 1470). 2000. mass mkt. 3.50 (0-373-19470-6, 1-19470-3) Harlequin Bks.

Linz, Cathie. Embrujo Gitano: Michael's Baby. (Deseo Ser.: Vol. 117).Tr. of Gypsy Enchantment. (SPA.). 1998. per. 3.50 (0-373-35247-6, 1-35247-5) Harlequin Bks.

— Escapades. (Desire Ser.). 1993. per. 2.99 (0-373-05804-7, 5-05804-5) Silhouette.

***Linz, Cathie.** A Handful of Trouble. large type ed. LC 99-27635. (Large Print Americana Ser.). 1999. 25.95 (0-7862-2021-X) Thorndike Pr.

Linz, Cathie. Husband Needed. 1997. per. 3.50 (0-373-76098-1, 1-76098-2) Silhouette.

— A Mi Lado (Close to Me), No. 133. (Harlequin Deseo Ser.). (SPA.). 1998. mass mkt. 3.50 (0-373-35263-8, 1-35263-2) Harlequin Bks.

— Michael's Baby. (Desire Ser.). 1996. per. 3.50 (0-373-76023-X, 1-76023-0) Silhouette.

— Midnight Ice. (Desire Ser.). 1994. per. 2.99 (0-373-05846-2, 5-05846-6) Silhouette.

***Linz, Cathie.** Pride & Joy, Vol. 1. LC 98-15557. 1998. pap. text 23.95 (0-7862-1494-5) Mac Lib Ref.

Linz, Cathie. Seduccion Magica: Seducing Hunter. (Deseo Ser.: Vol. 125). (SPA.). 1998. per. 3.50 (0-373-35255-7, 1-35255-8) Harlequin Bks.

— Seducing Hunter (Three Wedding & a Gift) (Desire Ser.). 1996. per. 3.50 (0-373-76029-9, 1-76029-7) Silhouette.

— Tiempo de Amor: A Wife in Time. (Deseo Ser.: Vol. 116).Tr. of Love Time. (SPA.). 1998. per. 3.50 (0-373-35246-8, 1-35246-7) Harlequin Bks.

— Too Sexy for Marriage. (Love & Laughter Ser.). 1998. mass mkt. 3.50 (0-373-44039-1, 1-44039-5) Harlequin Bks.

— Too Smart for Marriage. (Love & Laughter Ser.: Vol. 51). 1998. per. 3.50 (0-373-44051-0, 1-44051-0) Harlequin Bks.

An Asterisk (*) at the beginning of an entry indicates that the title is appearing for the first time.

— Too Stubborn to Marry: The Marriage Makers. (Love & Laughter Ser.). 185p. 1998. mass mkt. 3.50 (*0-373-44045-6*, 1-44045-2) Harlequin Bks.

Linz, Cathie & Hall, Marissa. The Rancher Gets Hitched; An Affair of Convenience. 2 bks. in 1. (Duets Ser.). 1999. per. 5.99 (*0-373-44075-8*, 1-44075-9) Harlequin Bks.

Linz, Cathie & Sharpe, Isabel. The Cowboy Finds a Bride; The Way We Weren't. (Duets Ser.: Bk. 17). 2000. per. 5.99 (*0-373-44083-9*, 1-44083-3) Harlequin Bks.

***Linz, Cathie & Sharpe, Isabel.** The Lawman Gets Lucky - Beauty & the Bet. (Duets Ser.: No. 26). 2000. mass mkt. 5.99 (*0-373-44092-8*) Harlequin Bks.

Linz, Daniel & Malamuth, Neil M. Pornography. (Communication Concepts Ser.: Vol. 5). 88p. (C). 1993. text 28.00 (*0-8039-4480-2*); pap. text 11.95 (*0-8039-4481-0*) Sage.

Linz, David G., et al. Environmentally Acceptable Endpoints in Soil: Risk-Based Approach to Contaminated Site Management Based on Availability of Chemicals in Soil. LC 96-23981. (Illus.). 632p. 1997. 134.95 (*1-883767-14-8*) Am Acad Environ.

Linz, Ed. Life Row: A Case Study of How a Family Can Survive a Medical Crisis. LC 97-600095. (Illus.). ix, 351p. (Orig.). 1997. pap. 16.00 (*0-9656895-0-6*, 02-00097) Exchange Pub WA.

Linz, James R. Art Deco Chrome. LC 98-88343. (Illus.). 192p. (Orig.). 1999. pap. 29.95 (*0-7643-0744-4*) Schiffer.

***Linz, Jim.** Electrifying Time: Deco Through the 50s. LC 00-9618. 2000. pap. write for info. (*0-7643-1190-5*) Schiffer.

***Linz, Juan J.** Totalitarian & Authoritarian Regions. LC 00-28259. 340p. 2000. pap. 22.50 (*1-55587-890-3*) L Rienner.

— Totalitarian & Authoritarian Regions. LC 00-28259. 340p. 2000. lib. bdg. 59.95 (*1-55587-866-0*) L Rienner.

Linz, Juan J., ed. Breakdown of Democratic Regimes: Crisis, Breakdown, & Requalibrium. LC 78-571. (BDR Ser.: Vol. 1). 144p. (Orig.). 1978. pap. text 11.95 (*0-8018-2009-X*) Johns Hopkins.

Linz, Juan J. & Stepan, Alfred. Problems of Democratic Transition & Consolidation: Southern Europe, South America, & Post-Communist Europe. LC 95-43462. (Illus.). 616p. (C). 1996. text 55.00 (*0-8018-5157-2*); pap. text 18.95 (*0-8018-5158-0*) Johns Hopkins.

Linz, Juan J. & Stepan, Alfred, eds. Breakdown of Democratic Regimes Vol. 2: Southern Europe. 249p. 1978. pap. text 13.95 (*0-8018-2022-7*) Johns Hopkins.

— Latin America. LC 78-594. (Breakdown of Democratic Regimes Ser.). (Illus.). 226p. 1978. reprint ed. pap. 70.10 (*0-608-07334-2*, 206756200009) Bks Demand.

Linz, Juan J. & Valenzuela, Arturo, eds. The Failure of Presidential Democracy. LC 93-27221. 454p. 1994. text 65.00 (*0-8018-4639-0*) Johns Hopkins.

— The Failure of Presidential Democracy Vol. 1: Comparative Perspectives. LC 93-27222. 1994. pap. text 14.95 (*0-8018-4640-4*) Johns Hopkins.

Linz, Juan J., jt. auth. see Shain, Yossi.

Linz, Juan J., jt. ed. see Chehabi, H. E.

Linz, Kathi & Linz, Lester. The Coin Hunting Book. (Illus.). 24p. (YA). (gr. 4-7). 1999. pap. 3.79 (*1-57532-131-9*) Press-Tige Pub.

Linz, Lester, jt. auth. see Linz, Kathi.

Linz, Mary, jt. auth. see Linz, William.

Linz, Peter. Analytical & Numerical Methods for Volterra Equations. LC 84-51968. (Studies in Applied Mathematics: No. 7). xiii, 227p. 1985. text 51.00 (*0-89871-198-3*) Soc Indus-Appl Math.

— Introduction to Formal Language & Automata. 2nd ed. (Computer Science Ser.). 72p. 1996. pap. 10.00 (*0-7637-0317-6*) Jones & Bartlett.

— An Introduction to Formal Languages & Automata. 2nd ed. LC 95-80417. 400p. 1996. 61.25 (*0-7637-0296-X*) Jones & Bartlett.

Linz, Susan, ed. The Impact of World War II on the Soviet Union. (Illus.). 312p. 1985. 62.00 (*0-8476-7378-2*); pap. 25.00 (*0-8476-7379-0*) Rowman.

Linz, Susan J. & Moskoff, William, eds. Reorganization & Reform in the Soviet Economy. LC 87-35630. 150p. (C). (gr. 13). 1988. text 70.95 (*0-87332-472-2*) M E Sharpe.

Linz, Werner. The Pilgrim's Guide to the Holy Land. (Illus.). 224p. 1998. text 17.95 (*0-670-87749-2*) Viking Penguin.

Linz, Werner A. Doggerel. (Illus.). 154p. (Orig.). 1996. pap. 16.00 (*1-887774-02-5*) Canmore Pr.

Linz, Werner M., ed. see Gentry, Francis G.

Linz, Wes, ed. see MacLean, Mrs. Alistair, pseud.

Linz, William & Linz, Mary. Maine Forts. LC 97-60844. (Illus.). 58p. (Orig.). 1997. pap. 5.00 (*1-883650-41-0*) Windswept Hse.

Linzee, J. W. Parker: The History of Peter Parker & Sarah Ruggles. (Illus.). 609p. 1991. reprint ed. pap. 89.50 (*0-8328-2893-9*); reprint ed. lib. bdg. 99.50 (*0-8328-2894-7*) Higginson Bk Co.

Linzee, Jill & Chaney, Michael P. Deeply Rooted: New Hampshire Traditions in Wood. LC 97-74494. (Illus.). 64p. 1998. pap. 14.95 (*0-9648953-1-5*) U NH Art Gallery.

Linzell, J. L., jt. auth. see Peaker, M.

Linzer. Philosophy of Contract. 59.95 (*1-85521-233-1*) Ashgate Pub Co.

Linzer, Anna. Ghost Dancing. LC 98-29648. 192p. 1998. text 21.00 (*0-312-19548-6*) St Martin.

— Ghost Dancing. LC 98-29648. 192p. 1999. pap. 12.00 (*0-312-20410-8*) St Martin.

Linzer, Anna, jt. auth. see Linzer, Richard.

***Linzer, Deborah Hansen.** Cameo Life Stories Writing Guide for Everywoman: Penning Your Portrait in Words. deluxe ed. 272p. 1999. pap. 14.95 (*0-9674820-0-3*) Blue Moon AZ.

Linzer, Estelle, ed. Guide to Albert Schweitzer Collections. 2nd ed. 64p. (Orig.). 1992. pap. text 7.50 (*1-881815-25-0*) Albert Schweitzer.

Linzer, Judith. Torah & Dharma: Jewish Seekers in Eastern Religions. LC 96-13676. 360p. 1996. pap. 40.00 (*1-56821-916-4*) Aronson.

Linzer, Lila. Once Upon an Island. LC 98-12935. (Illus.). 76p. (J). (gr. 3-7). 1999. 15.95 (*1-886910-10-3*) Front Str.

Linzer, M., ed. see International Conference on Hot Isostatic Pressing.

Linzer, Norman. Ethical Dilemmas in Jewish Communal Service. LC 95-35866. 1995. 39.50 (*0-88125-516-5*) Ktav.

— Ethical Dilemmas in Jewish Communal Service. LC 95-35866. 1996. pap. 19.95 (*0-88125-532-7*) Ktav.

— The Jewish Family: Authority & Tradition in Modern Perspectives. 317p. 1984. 43.95 (*0-89885-149-1*, Kluwer Acad Hman Sci); pap. 20.95 (*0-89885-191-2*, Kluwer Acad Hman Sci) Kluwer Academic.

— Suicide: The Will to Live vs the Will to Die. 240p. 1984. 35.95 (*0-89885-156-4*, Kluwer Acad Hman Sci); pap. 20.95 (*0-89885-190-4*, Kluwer Acad Hman Sci) Kluwer Academic.

Linzer, Norman, et al, eds. Crisis & Continuity: The Jewish Family in the 21st Century. LC 94-42914. 1995. pap. text 19.95 (*0-88125-508-4*) Ktav.

Linzer, Norman & Wurzweiler School of Social Work Staff. Resolving Ethical Dilemmas in Social Work Practice. LC 98-17573. 234p. 1998. pap. text 30.00 (*0-205-29041-8*) Allyn.

Linzer, Norman J., ed. see Chanes, Jerome.

Linzer, Peter, ed. A Contracts Anthology. 2nd ed. LC 96-102881. 459p. 1995. pap. 27.95 (*0-87084-418-0*) Anderson Pub Co.

***Linzer, Richard & Linzer, Anna.** It's Simple! Money Matters for the Nonprofit Member. LC 99-90178. 71p. 1999. pap. 21.00 (*0-9669792-0-6*) Port Madison Pr.

Linzer Schwartz, Lita, jt. auth. see Rich, Phil.

Linzey. Political Theory & Animal Rights. 256p. (C). 49.95 (*0-7453-0386-2*, Pub. by Pluto GBR); pap. 18.95 (*0-7453-0391-9*, Pub. by Pluto GBR) Stylus Pub VA.

Linzey, Alicia V. & Linzey, Donald W. Mammals of Great Smoky Mountains National Park. LC 74-111048. 148p. (Orig.). reprint ed. pap. 45.90 (*0-608-15466-0*, 202937700060) Bks Demand.

Linzey, Andrew. Animal Gospel. 1998. 10.99 (*0-340-62150-8*, Pub. by Hodder & Stought Ltd) Trafalgar.

***Linzey, Andrew.** Animal Gospel. LC 99-33963. 180p. 1999. pap. 16.95 (*0-664-22193-9*) Westminster John Knox.

— Animal Rites: Liturgies of Animal Care. 1998. pap. 15.00 (*0-334-02760-8*) TPI PA.

Linzey, Andrew. Animal Theology. LC 94-35580. 224p. 1995. 14.95 (*0-252-06467-4*) U of Ill Pr.

Linzey, Andrew, ed. The Saying Of Jesus. LC 98-4039. 64p. 1998. reprint ed. pap. 5.95 (*0-88001-640-X*) HarpC.

Linzey, Andrew & Clarke, Paul A. Dictionary of Ethics, Theology & Society. LC 95-238078. 960p. (C). (gr. 13). 1995. 165.00 (*0-415-06212-8*, B0385) Routledge.

Linzey, Andrew & Cohn-Sherbok, Dan. After Noah: Animals & the Liberation of Theology. 128p. 1997. pap. 17.95 (*0-264-67450-2*) Bks Intl VA.

Linzey, Andrew & Yamamoto, Dorothy. Animals on the Agenda: Questions about Animals for Theology & Ethics. LC 98-7118. 1998. pap. 21.95 (*0-252-06761-4*) U of Ill Pr.

Linzey, Donald W. Mammals of Great Smoky Mountains National Park. (Illus.). 152p. (Orig.). 1995. pap. text 14.95 (*0-939923-48-3*) M & W Pub Co.

— Mammals of Virginia. (Illus.). 500p. 1998. 59.95 (*0-939923-36-X*) M & W Pub Co.

***Linzey, Donald W.** Vertebrate Biology. LC 00-23088. (Illus.). 2000. write for info. (*0-697-36387-2*, WCB McGr Hill) McGrw-H Hghr Educ.

Linzey, Donald W. & Clifford, Michael J. Snakes of Virginia. LC 81-12951. (Illus.). 224p. (C). 1995. pap. 24.95 (*0-8139-0826-4*) U Pr of Va.

— Snakes of Virginia. LC 81-12951. 207p. reprint ed. pap. 64.20 (*0-7837-1244-8*, 204138100020) Bks Demand.

Linzey, Donald W., jt. auth. see Linzey, Alicia V.

***Linzey, James F.** A Divine Appointment in Washington, D.C. Sharing the Gospel in Cyberspace. LC 99-61666. 176p. 1999. pap. 10.99 (*1-56384-169-X*, Pub. by Huntington Hse) BookWorld.

Linzey, Sharon, et al, eds. The East-West Christian Organizations: A Directory of Western Christian Organizations Working in East Central Europe & the Former Soviet Union. 240p. 1993. pap. text 15.00 (*0-9635856-0-6*) Berry Pub Srv.

Linzey, Sharon & Kaisch, Ken. God in Russia: The Challenge of Freedom. 112p. 1999. 69.95 (*1-57309-399-8*); pap. 44.95 (*1-57309-398-X*) Intl Scholars.

***Linzey, Sharon & Kaisch, Ken, eds.** God in Russia: The Challenge of Freedom. 456p. 1999. 64.00 (*0-7618-1548-1*); pap. 44.50 (*0-7618-1549-X*) U Pr of Amer.

Linzmayer, Owen W. Apple Confidential: The Real Story of Apple Computer, Inc. LC 98-49132. (Illus.). 268p. 1999. pap. 17.95 (*1-886411-28-X*) No Starch Pr.

— The Mac Bathroom Reader. LC 94-67199. 320p. 1994. pap. 12.99 (*0-7821-1531-4*) Sybex.

Linzmeier, Joseph. Political Analysis. 120p. 1997. pap., teacher ed. 6.95 (*1-57087-299-6*) Prof Pr NC.

Linzner, Gordon. The Spy Who Drank Blood. LC 84-14127. 144p. (Orig.). 1984. pap. 5.95 (*0-917053-01-X*) Space And.

***Linzy, Jan.** Affenpincher Champions, 1968-1998. (Illus.). 79p. 1999. pap. 36.95 (*1-55893-058-2*) Camino E E & Bk.

Linzy, Jan. American Foxhound Champions, English Foxhound Champions, Harrier Champions, 1952-1992. (Illus.). 150p. 2001. pap. 36.95 (*1-55893-010-8*) Camino E E & Bk.

— American Water Spaniel Champions, 1952-1992. (Illus.). 70p. 2000. pap. 36.95 (*1-55893-018-3*) Camino E E & Bk.

***Linzy, Jan.** American Water Spaniel Champions, 1968-1999. (Illus.). 138p. 2000. 36.95 (*1-55893-062-0*) Camino E E & Bk.

Linzy, Jan. Basset Hound Champions, 1952-1992. (Illus.). 200p. 2001. pap. 36.95 (*1-55893-014-0*) Camino E E & Bk.

***Linzy, Jan.** Basset Hound Champions, 1968-1999. (Illus.). 125p. 2000. pap. 36.95 (*1-55893-065-5*) Camino E E & Bk.

— Bedlington Terrier Champions, 1968-1998. (Illus.). 101p. 2000. pap. 36.95 (*1-55893-060-4*) Camino E E & Bk.

Linzy, Jan. Belgian Malinois Champions, 1965-1994. (Illus.). 150p. 1998. pap. 36.95 (*1-55893-015-9*) Camino E E & Bk.

***Linzy, Jan.** Black & Tan Coonhound Champions, 1968-1999. (Illus.). 115p. 2000. pap. 36.95 (*1-55893-064-7*) Camino E E & Bk.

Linzy, Jan. Border Terrier Champions, 1952-1994. (Illus.). 180p. 1995. pap. 36.95 (*1-55893-041-8*) Camino E E & Bk.

***Linzy, Jan.** Brussels Griffon Champions, 1991-1999. (Illus.). 58p. 1999. pap. 32.95 (*1-55893-061-2*) Camino E E & Bk.

— Cairn Terrier Champions, 1987-1998. 90p. 1998. pap. 32.95 (*1-55893-053-1*) Camino E E & Bk.

Linzy, Jan. Dachshund (Longhaired) Champions, 1974-1994. (Illus.). 245p. 1996. pap. 36.95 (*1-55893-049-3*) Camino E E & Bk.

***Linzy, Jan.** Dandi Dinmont Terrier Champions, 1968-1998. (Illus.). 125p. 2000. pap. 36.95 (*1-55893-059-0*) Camino E E & Bk.

Linzy, Jan. German Shorthaired Pointer Champions, 1987-1994. (Illus.). 101p. 1996. pap. 32.95 (*1-55893-042-6*) Camino E E & Bk.

***Linzy, Jan.** Irish Water Spaniel Champions, 1968-1999. (Illus.). 125p. 2000. lib. bdg. 36.95 (*1-55893-063-9*) Camino E E & Bk.

Linzy, Jan. Labrador Retriever Champions, 1989-1994. (Illus.). 105p. 1998. pap. 32.95 (*1-55893-050-7*) Camino E E & Bk.

— Miniature Pinscher Champions, 1952-1992. (Illus.). 175p. 2001. pap. 36.95 (*1-55893-008-6*) Camino E E & Bk.

— Norwegian Elkhound Champions, 1952-1992. (Illus.). 175p. 2000. pap. 36.95 (*1-55893-011-6*) Camino E E & Bk.

— Rottweiler Champions, 1987-1996. (Illus.). 160p. 1999. pap. text 32.95 (*1-55893-025-6*) Camino E E & Bk.

— Weimaraner Champions, 1988-1994. LC 98-139396. (Illus.). 105p. 1996. pap. 32.95 (*1-55893-043-4*) Camino E E & Bk.

Linzy, Jan & Camino Staff. American Staffordshire Terrier Champions, 1988-1995. (Illus.). 98p. (Orig.). 1998. pap. 32.95 (*1-55893-054-X*) Camino E E & Bk.

Linzy, Stanford E., Jr. God Was at Midway. Knox, Dahk, ed. (Illus.). 135p. 1996. pap. 14.95 (*1-881116-80-8*, Pub. by Black Forest Pr) Epic Bk Promo.

Lio, Frederick F. A Military History of Modern China, 1924 to 1949. LC 81-6577. 312p. 1981. reprint ed. lib. bdg. 59.75 (*0-313-23012-9*, LIMH, Greenwood Pr) Greenwood.

***Lioger, Richard & Barber, Noel.** Les Industries Jurassiennes: Savoir-Faire et Cooperation. (Illus.). xii, 440p. 1999. 51.95 (*3-906762-27-0*, Pub. by P Lang) P Lang Pubng.

Liogier, Alain H. Flora of Puerto Rico & Adjacent Islands: A Systematic Synopsis. 2nd ed. LC 98 32420. (Orig.). 1999. pap. write for info. (*0-8477-0369-X*) U of PR Pr.

Liogier, Henri A. Descriptive Flora of Puerto Rico, Vol. 3. 462p. 1994. pap. 20.00 (*0-8477-2336-4*) U of PR Pr.

— Descriptive Flora of Puerto Rico, Vol. 4. (Illus.). 624p. 1995. pap. write for info. (*0-8477-2337-2*) U of PR Pr.

— Descriptive Flora of Puerto Rico & Adjacent Islands: Spermatophyta, Vol. I. LC 84-22668. 352p. 1985. pap. 20.00 (*0-8477-2334-8*) U of PR Pr.

— Descriptive Flora of Puerto Rico & Adjacent Islands Vol. II: Leguminosae to Anacardiaceae. LC 84-25668. 481p. 1988. pap. 23.00 (*0-8477-2333-X*) U of PR Pr.

Liogier, Henri A. & Martorell, Luis F. Flora of Puerto Rico & Adjacent Islands: A Systematic Synopsis. LC 82-16431. 342p. (Orig.). 1982. pap. 15.00 (*0-8477-2329-1*) U of PR Pr.

***Lion.** Christmas Angels. 1998. pap. 3.95 (*0-7459-4030-7*, Pub. by Lion Pubng) Trafalgar.

— Christmas Gifts. 1998. pap. 3.95 (*0-7459-4027-7*, Pub. by Lion Pubng) Trafalgar.

— Christmas Joy. 1998. pap. 3.95 (*0-7459-4028-5*, Pub. by Lion Pubng) Trafalgar.

— Christmas Stars. 1998. pap. 3.95 (*0-7459-4029-3*, Pub. by Lion Pubng) Trafalgar.

— Hooray for the World. 1993. 6.95 (*0-7459-2633-9*, Pub. by Lion Pubng) Trafalgar.

— Love Poetry Across the Centuries. 1995. 7.50 (*0-7459-3363-7*, Pub. by Lion Pubng) Trafalgar.

Lion, ed. Mi Primera Biblia. (Biblias para Ninos Ser.).Tr. of My First Bible. (SPA., Illus.). (J). 1999. 12.99 (*0-7899-0402-0*, 490299) Editorial Unilit.

Lion, Edgar. Shopping Centers: Planning, Development & Administration. LC 75-33374. 208p. reprint ed. pap. 64.50 (*0-608-16948-X*, 205629500056) Bks Demand.

Lion House Staff, jt. auth. see Davis, Melba.

Lion, John R., et al, eds. Creating a Secure Workplace: Effective Policies & Practices in Health Care. LC 96-27340. (Illus.). 340p. (Orig.). 1996. pap. 69.95 (*1-55648-167-5*, 181150) AHPI.

Lion Publishing Staff. Andy Tells the Truth. (J). (gr. 2 up). 1994. pap. text 2.29 (*0-7814-1537-3*) Chariot Victor.

— The Gospel of St. John: The Story of the Son of God. LC 99-23288. 160p. 1999. pap. 11.95 (*0-312-22077-4*) St Martin.

— Great Sayings of Jesus: Proverbs, Parables, & Prayers. LC 99-23289. 320p. 1999. pap. 12.95 (*0-312-22078-2*) St Martin.

— Hebrew Prophets: Visionaries of the Ancient World. LC 99-27857. 224p. 1999. pap. 12.95 (*0-312-22076-6*) St Martin.

— O Little Town of Bethlehem: Tree Ornament Book. 8p. (J). (gr. 1 up). 1992. 1.99 (*0-7814-0766-4*, Lion) Chariot Victor.

Lion Staff. Animales en Pareja. (Serie Despegables - According Puzzle Bks.).Tr. of Animals Two by Two. (SPA.). 10p. (J). 1987. 4.99 (*1-56063-204-6*, 494004) Editorial Unilit.

— Animales Grandes y Chicos. (Serie Libros Despegables - Accordian Puzzle Bks.).Tr. of All the Animals. (SPA.). 10p. (J). 1987. 4.99 (*1-56063-205-4*, 494005) Editorial Unilit.

— El Bebe de Navidad. (Serie Libros Despegables - Accordian Puzzle Books Ser.).Tr. of Christmas Baby. (SPA.). 10p. (J). 1987. 4.99 (*1-56063-203-8*, 494003) Editorial Unilit.

— Dios Cuida de Mi. (Serie Libros Despeglabes - Accordian Puzzle Bks.).Tr. of God Cares for Me. (SPA.). 10p. (J). 1987. 4.99 (*1-56063-206-2*, 494006) Editorial Unilit.

— Dios Cuida de Su Creacion. (Serie Libros Despegables - Accordian Puzzle Bks.).Tr. of God Cares for the Earth. (SPA.). 10p. (J). 1987. 4.99 (*1-56063-201-1*, 494001) Editorial Unilit.

— Libro Despegable (Concertina Puzzle Book) Regalos en la Primera Navidad (The First Christmas Present) (SPA.). 4.99 (*1-56063-202-X*, 494002) Editorial Unilit.

Lion, Thomas. Book of Prayers for first Years of Marriage. 1995. 12.95 (*0-7459-3359-9*, Pub. by Lion Pubng) Trafalgar.

— Book of Prayers for New Parents. 1995. 12.95 (*0-7459-3357-2*, Pub. by Lion Pubng) Trafalgar.

— Book of Prayers for those Who Grieve. 1995. 12.95 (*0-7459-3356-4*, Pub. by Lion Pubng) Trafalgar.

Lion, Thomas. Chelan. LC 97-212882. 419p. 1997. pap. 14.00 (*0-9658515-0-8*) Leobrand Bks.

Lion, Thomas. Faith to Live By. 1995. 7.50 (*0-7459-3361-0*, Pub. by Lion Pubng) Trafalgar.

Lion, Thomas. I Was an Unsolved Mystery: A Fugitive's Story. (Illus.). 360p. (Orig.). 1997. pap. 14.00 (*0-9658515-2-4*) Leobrand Bks.

Lion, Thomas. Prayers & Journey of Faith. 1995. 12.95 (*0-7459-3358-0*, Pub. by Lion Pubng) Trafalgar.

— Step of Faith Record Book. 1995. 10.95 (*0-7459-3366-1*, Pub. by Lion Pubng) Trafalgar.

Lionarons, Joyce T. The Medieval Dragon: The Nature of the Beast in Germanic Literature. LC 98-215530. 256p. 1998. 59.95 (*1-874312-33-8*, Pub. by Hisarlik Pr) Intl Spec Bk.

Lione, Armand, et al. Reproductive Effects of Chemical, Physical, & Biologic Agents: REPROTOX. LC 95-76708. 891p. 1995. text 150.00 (*0-8018-5183-1*) Johns Hopkins.

Lionel. Challenge. 183p. 1980. 9.00 (*0-85435-354-2*, Pub. by C W Daniel) Natl Bk Netwk.

Lionel. Peekaboo Babies: A Counting Book. LC 96-70373. (Illus.). 12p. (J). (ps-1). 1997. 12.95 (*0-531-30016-1*) Orchard Bks Watts.

Lionel Corporation Staff. How to Operate & Maintain Lionel Trains & Accessories. LC 92-70952. (Illus.). 60p. 1992. reprint ed. pap. 10.00 (*0-930429-02-8*) Bibliographic Pr.

— Instructions for Operating Lionel Trains: An Investment in Happiness. rev. ed. (Illus.). 50p. 1997. reprint ed. pap. 9.00 (*0-930429-05-2*) Bibliographic Pr.

Lionel, Frederic. Challenge. 164p. pap. 13.95 (*0-8464-4200-0*) Beekman Pubs.

— Mirrors of Truth: Reflections of Living Mastery. Wise Thinking Staff, tr. from FRE. 128p. (Orig.). 1991. pap. 10.95 (*0-944135-10-2*) Archedigm Pubns.

Lionel Sawyer & Collins Staff. Nevada Gaming Law. 2nd ed. LC 94-72895. xl, 442p. 1995. write for info. (*0-9644121-0-1*) L Sawyer & Collins.

Lionel Sawyer & Collins Staff, et al. Nevada Environmental Law Handbook. 3rd ed. LC 98-119332. (State Environmental Law Ser.). 351p. 1997. pap. text 89.00 (*0-86587-567-7*) Gov Insts.

Lionells, Marylou, et al, eds. Handbook of Interpersonal Psychoanalysis. LC 95-4323. 928p. 1995. text 180.00 (*0-88163-120-5*) Analytic Pr.

Lionetti, Harold E., jt. auth. see De Castells, Matilda O.

Lionetti, Mike. The Game We Know: Hockey in the Sixties. (Illus.). 128p. 1998. 24.95 (*1-55192-198-7*) Raincoast Bk.

— My Leafs Sweater. (Illus.). 32p. (J). (ps-3). 1998. 15.95 (*1-55192-194-4*) Raincoast Bk.

Lionheart Bks Ltd. Dinner & a Movie Cookbook, 1 vol. LC 99-37548. 1999. pap. text 14.95 (*0-7407-0321-8*) Andrews & McMeel.

— Guardians: The Secret Life of Goalies, 1 vol. LC 99-44726. (Illus.). 1999. pap. 19.95 (*0-7407-0322-6*) Andrews & McMeel.

***Lionheart Books Ltd. Staff.** Dinner & a Movie Cookbook. (Illus.). 1999. pap. 14.95 (*0-7407-0314-5*) Andrews & McMeel.

Lionheart Books Ltd. Staff. The Hand of God: A Collection of Thoughts & Images on the Wonders of the Universe Reflecting the Spirit of God. 160p. 1999. pap. 24.95 (*0-7407-0323-4*) Andrews & McMeel.

***Lionheart Books Ltd. Staff.** Have Yourself a Merry Little Christmas: The Illustrated Lyrics. (Illus.). 2000. pap. 4.95 (*0-7407-1052-4*) Andrews & McMeel.

L

— I Love How You Love Me: The Illustrated Lyrics. (Illus.). (J). 2000. pap. 4.95 (*0-7407-1053-2*) Andrews & McMeel.

— Ilia Kulik. (Illus.). (J). 2000. pap. 4.95 (*0-7407-1055-9*) Andrews & McMeel.

— Katia Gordeeva. (Illus.). (J). 2000. pap. 4.95 (*0-7407-1051-6*) Andrews & McMeel.

— Kristi Yamaguchi. (Illus.). (J). 2000. pap. 4.95 (*0-7407-1056-7*) Andrews & McMeel.

— Scott Hamilton. (Illus.). (J). 2000. pap. 4.95 (*0-7407-1057-5*) Andrews & McMeel.

— Silent Night: The Illustrated Lyrics. (Illus.). (J). 2000. pap. 4.95 (*0-7407-1050-8*) Andrews & McMeel.

— Still the One: The Illustrated Lyrics. (Illus.). 2000. pap. 4.95 (*0-7407-1058-3*) Andrews & McMeel.

— The Way We Were: The Illustrated Lyrics. (Illus.). (J). 2000. pap. 4.95 (*0-7407-1059-1*) Andrews & McMeel.

Lionheart Books Ltd. Staff, et al. They Changed the Game: Sports Pioneers of the Twentieth Century, 1 vol. LC 99-40398. 160p. 1999. 29.95 (*0-7407-0340-4*) Andrews & McMeel.

Lionheart, John H., ed. see Porter, John T.

Lionnet, Francoise. Autobiographical Voices: Race, Gender, Self-Portraiture. LC 88-43236. (Reading Women Writing Ser.). 280p. 1989. text 42.50 (*0-8014-2091-1*) Cornell U Pr.

— Autobiographical Voices: Race, Gender, Self-Portraiture. LC 88-43236. (Reading Women Writing Ser.). 280p. 1991. reprint ed. pap. text 15.95 (*0-8014-9927-5*) Cornell U Pr.

— Post - Colonial Conditions: Exiles, Migrations, & Nomadisms, Vol. 2. Scharfman, Ronnie, ed. (Yale French Studies: No. 83). 272p. (C). 1993. pap. 18.00 (*0-300-05397-5*) Yale U Pr.

— Postcolonial Representations: Women, Literature, Identity. (Reading Women Writing Ser.). 208p. 1995. text 35.00 (*0-8014-2984-6*); pap. text 13.95 (*0-8014-8180-5*) Cornell U Pr.

Lionnet, G., jt. auth. see D'Offay, Danielle.

Lionnett, Francoise. Post - Colonial Conditions: Exiles, Migrations, & Nomadisms, Vol. 1. Scharfman, Ronnie, ed. (Yale French Studies: No. 82). 272p. (C). 1993. pap. 18.00 (*0-300-05270-7*) Yale U Pr.

Lionni, Jane, ed. see Kaplan, Mira.

Lionni, Leo. Alexander & the Wind-up Mouse. LC 74-2088. (J). 1969. 11.19 (*0-606-03693-8*, Pub. by Turtleback) Demco.

Lionni, Leo. Alexander & the Wind-up Mouse. LC 74-2088. (Pinwheels Ser.). (Illus.). 32p. (J). (ps-3). 1974. reprint ed. pap. 5.99 (*0-394-82911-5*) Pantheon.

— Between Worlds: The Autobiography of Leo Lionni. LC 97-7379. (Illus.). 295p. 1997. 35.00 (*0-679-42393-1*) Knopf.

— The Biggest House in the World. LC 68-12646. (Children's Paperbacks Ser.). (Illus.). 32p. (J). (ps-6). 1973. pap. 5.99 (*0-394-82740-6*, Pub. by Knopf Bks Yng Read) Random.

— A Busy Year. 1992. pap. 10.99 (*0-685-52501-5*) McKay.

— A Color of His Own. (J). 1997. 12.19 (*0-606-12661-9*, Pub. by Turtleback) Demco.

***Lionni, Leo.** Color of His Own. (Illus.). (J). 2000. 6.99 (*0-375-81091-9*, Pub. by Knopf Bks Yng Read) Random.

Lionni, Leo. A Color of His Own. (Illus.). 32p. (J). (ps-k). 1997. reprint ed. pap. 6.99 (*0-679-88785-7*, Pub. by Knopf Bks Yng Read) Random.

— Cornelius. LC 82-6442. (Dragonfly Bks.). (Illus.). (J). (ps-2). 1994. pap. 5.99 (*0-679-86040-1*, Pub. by Knopf Bks Yng Read) Random.

Lionni, Leo. Cornelius: A Fable. LC 82-6442. 1994. 11.19 (*0-606-06959-3*, Pub. by Turtleback) Demco.

Lionni, Leo. An Extraordinary Egg. LC 93-28565. (Illus.). 40p. (J). (ps-2). 1994. 16.00 (*0-679-85840-7*, Pub. by Knopf Bks Yng Read); lib. bdg. 16.99 (*0-679-95840-1*, Pub. by Knopf Bks Yng Read) Random.

— An Extraordinary Egg. (J). (ps-3). 1998. pap. 6.99 (*0-679-89385-7*, Pub. by Random Bks Yng Read) Random.

— Fish Is Fish. LC 78-117452. (Knopf Children's Paperbacks Ser.). 32p. (J). (ps-6). 1974. pap. 5.99 (*0-394-82799-6*) Knopf.

— Fish Is Fish. (Illus.). (J). (ps-3). 1970. 17.00 (*0-394-80440-6*, 577664) Pantheon.

— Fish Is Fish. (J). 1970. 11.19 (*0-606-04222-9*, Pub. by Turtleback) Demco.

— A Flea Story: I Want to Stay Here! I Want to Go There! LC 77-4322. (Illus.). (J). (ps-2). 1977. 15.00 (*0-394-83498-4*); lib. bdg. 15.99 (*0-394-93498-9*) Pantheon.

— Frederick. LC 66-10355. (Illus.). 40p. (J). (gr. 4-7). 1967. lib. bdg. 18.99 (*0-394-91040-0*, Pub. by Knopf Bks Yng Read) Random.

— Frederick. LC 66-10355. (Illus.). 40p. (J). (ps-3). 1967. 17.00 (*0-394-81040-6*, Pub. by Knopf Bks Yng Read) Random.

— Frederick. LC 66-10355. (Pinwheel Bks.). (Illus.). 32p. (J). (ps-3). 1987. pap. 5.99 (*0-394-82614-0*, Pub. by Knopf Bks Yng Read) Random.

Lionni, Leo. Frederick. 1996. write for info. (*84-264-3529-7*) Lectorum Pubns.

Lionni, Leo. Frederick. (SPA., Illus.). (ps-3). 1998. pap. 5.50 (*84-264-4651-5*) Lectorum Pubns.

— Frederick. 1967. 11.19 (*0-606-00466-1*, Pub. by Turtleback) Demco.

— Frederick's Fables: A Treasury of 16 Favorite Leo Lionni Stories. LC 97-9906. (Illus.). 176p. (J). (ps-3). 1997. 29.00 (*0-679-88826-8*, Pub. by Knopf Bks Yng Read) Random.

— Frederick's Fables: A Treasury of 16 Favorite Leo Lionni Stories. rev. ed. LC 97-9906. (Illus.). 176p. (J). (ps-3). 1997. lib. bdg. 29.99 (*0-679-98826-2*, Pub. by Knopf Bks Yng Read) Random.

— Inch by Inch. (Illus.). (J). (gr. k-1). 1962. 15.95 (*0-8392-3010-9*) Astor-Honor.

— Inch by Inch. 1995. 19.00 (*0-606-07704-9*, Pub. by Turtleback) Demco.

Lionni, Leo. Inch By Inch. LC 94-6483. (Illus.). 32p. (J). (ps up). 1995. reprint ed. mass mkt. 5.95 (*0-688-13283-9*, Wm Morrow) Morrow Avon.

Lionni, Leo. It's Mine. (Illus.). 32p. (J). (ps-2). 1996. pap. 5.99 (*0-679-88084-4*) Random.

— It's Mine! LC 85-190. 1996. 11.19 (*0-606-09481-4*, Pub. by Turtleback) Demco.

— Little Blue & Little Yellow. (Illus.). (J). (gr. k-1). 1959. 14.95 (*0-8392-3018-4*) Astor-Honor.

— Little Blue & Little Yellow. (J). 1995. 10.15 (*0-606-07792-8*, Pub. by Turtleback) Demco.

— Little Blue & Little Yellow. LC 94-7324. (Illus.). 48p. (J). (ps-3). 1995. reprint ed. mass mkt. 5.95 (*0-688-13285-5*, Wm Morrow) Morrow Avon.

— Matthew's Dream. (Illus.). 1995. pap. 5.99 (*0-679-87318-X*) Random.

— Matthew's Dream. (J). 1995. 11.44 (*0-606-07847-9*) Turtleback.

— Mr. McMouse. LC 92-8963. (Illus.). 40p. (J). (ps-1). 1992. 15.00 (*0-679-83890-2*, Pub. by Knopf Bks Yng Read) Random.

— Nadarin. 1998. pap. 5.50 (*84-264-4650-7*) Lectorum Pubns.

— Nadarin - Swimmy. 1996. 15.95 (*84-264-3527-0*, Pub. by Editorial Lumen) Lectorum Pubns.

— On My Beach There Are Many Pebbles. (Illus.). (J). (gr. k-1). 1961. 15.95 (*0-8392-3024-9*) Astor-Honor.

— On My Beach There Are Many Pebbles. (J). 1995. 10.15 (*0-606-07966-1*, Pub. by Turtleback) Demco.

Lionni, Leo. On My Beach There Are Many Pebbles. LC 94-6484. (Illus.). 32p. (J). (ps up). 1995. reprint ed. mass mkt. 6.95 (*0-688-13284-7*, Wm Morrow) Morrow Avon.

— Una Piedra Extraordinaria. (SPA., Illus.). (J). (ps-3). 1999. pap. 6.95 (*980-257-239-X*) Ediciones Ekare.

Lionni, Leo. Pouce par Pouce. (FRE., Illus.). (J). (gr. k-1). 1961. 15.95 (*0-8392-3028-1*) Astor-Honor.

— Pulgada a Pulgada. (SPA., Illus.). (J). (gr. k-1). 1961. 15.95 (*0-8392-3030-3*) Astor-Honor.

— Swimmy. LC 63-8504. (Illus.). 40p. (J). (ps-2). 1963. 17.00 (*0-394-81713-3*, Pub. by Knopf Bks Yng Read) Random.

— Swimmy. LC 63-8504. (Illus.). 40p. (J). (ps-2). 1963. lib. bdg. 18.99 (*0-394-91713-8*, Pub. by Knopf Bks Yng Read) Random.

— Swimmy. LC 63-8504. (Children's Paperbacks Ser.). (Illus.). 30p. (J). (ps-3). 1987. pap. 5.99 (*0-394-82620-5*, Pub. by Knopf Bks Yng Read) Random.

— Swimmy. (J). 1963. 11.19 (*0-606-00346-0*, Pub. by Turtleback) Demco.

— Tillie & the Wall. 1989. 11.19 (*0-606-05033-7*, Pub. by Turtleback) Demco.

Lionni, Paolo. The Leipzig Connection. (Basics of Education Ser.: No. 1). (Illus.). xii, 119p. (Orig.). (C). 1980. pap. 4.95 (*0-89739-001-6*) Heron Bks OR.

Lions, J. L. Optimal Control of Systems Governed by Partial Differential Equations. Mitter, S. K., tr. LC 78-113638. (Grundlehren der Mathematischen Wissenschaften Ser.: Vol. 170). (Illus.). 1971. 86.95 (*0-387-05115-5*) Spr-Verlag.

— Some Aspects of the Optimal Control of Distributed Parameter Systems. (CBMS-NSF Regional Conference Ser.: No. 6). vi, 92p. 1972. pap. text 22.00 (*0-89871-004-9*) Soc Indus-Appl Math.

— Some Methods in Mathematical Analysis of Systems & Their Control. xxvi, 542p. 1981. text 467.00 (*0-677-60200-6*) Gordon & Breach.

— Vistas in Applied Mathematics. Balakrishnan, A. V. et al, eds. xii, 384p. 1986. 160.95 (*0-387-96376-6*) Spr-Verlag.

Lions, J. L. & Lagnese, John E. Modelling Analysis & Control of Thin Plates. (Recherches en Mathematiques Appliquees Ser.: Vol. 6). 185p. 1990. 45.95 (*0-387-51550-X*) Spr-Verlag.

Lions, J. L. & Magenes, E. Non-Homogeneous Boundary Value Problems & Applications, Vol. 1. Kenneth, P., tr. LC 71-151407. (Grundlehren der Mathematischen Wissenschaften Ser.: Vol. 181). 355p. 1972. 127.95 (*0-387-05363-8*) Spr-Verlag.

— Non-Homogeneous Boundary Value Problems & Applications, Vol. 3. Kenneth, P., tr. from FRE. LC 71-151407. (Grundlehren der Mathematischen Wissenschaften Ser.: Vol. 183). 330p. 1973. 103.95 (*0-387-05832-X*) Spr-Verlag.

Lions, J. L., jt. auth. see Ciarlet, P. G.

Lions, J. L., jt. auth. see Dautray, R.

Lions, J. L., jt. auth. see Duvant, G.

Lions, J. L., jt. ed. see Benoussan, Alain.

Lions, J. L., jt. ed. see Bensoussan, A.

Lions, J. L., jt. ed. see Brezis, Haim.

Lions, J. L., ed. see Ciarlet, P. G.

Lions, J. L., jt. ed. see Ciarlet, P. G.

Lions, J. L., jt. ed. see Cioranescu, D.

Lions, J. L., ed. see Crouzeix, M. & Rappaz, J.

Lions, J. L., ed. see Grisvard, P.

Lions, J. L., ed. see Le Tallec, P. V.

Lions, J. L., ed. see Rabier, P. J. & Oden, J. Tinsley.

Lions, John. Lions' Commentary on UNIX: Including Source Code. 6th ed. 264p. 1996. pap. 29.95 (*1-57398-013-7*) Annabooks.

Lions of Illinois Foundation Staff. Illinois Directory of Services for the Visually Impaired. large type ed. 1985. 10.00 (*0-317-01849-3*) Lions IL Foun.

Lions, P. L., jt. ed. see Fleming, W.

Lions, P. L., ed. see Kollar, Janos.

Lions, Pierre-Louis. Mathematical Topics in Fluid Mechanics: Compressible Models, Vol. 2. (Oxford Lecture Series in Mathematics & Its Applications: No. 10). 362p. 1998. text 75.00 (*0-19-851488-3*) OUP.

— Mathematical Topics in Fluid Mechanics Vol. 3: Incompressible Models, Vol. 1. LC 96-4085. (Oxford Lecture Series in Mathematics & Its Applications). 252p. 1996. text 55.00 (*0-19-851487-5*, Clarendon Pr) OUP.

Liontas, John, jt. auth. see Baginski, Thomas.

Lior, N. & Tanasawa, I., eds. Heat & Mass Transfer Materials Processing. 700p. 1991. 120.00 (*1-56032-192-X*) Hemisp Pub.

Liorzou, G. Knee Ligaments: Clinical Examination. Finlayson, D., tr. from FRE. (Illus.). xii, 108p. 1991. 158.00 (*0-387-53761-9*) Spr-Verlag.

Liothke, Werner, jt. auth. see Arbuckle, James L.

Liotta, Christine. Every Picture Tells a Story. (Global City Review Ser.: Vol. 9). 1997. pap. text 9.00 (*1-887369-07-4*) Global Cty Pr.

Liotta, Dennis, ed. Advances in Molecular Modeling, Vol. 1. 213p. 1987. 109.50 (*0-89232-871-1*) Jai Pr.

— Advances in Molecular Modeling, Vol. 2. 165p. 1990. 109.50 (*0-89232-949-1*) Jai Pr.

— Advances in Molecular Modeling, Vol. 3. 224p. 1996. 109.50 (*1-55938-326-7*) Jai Pr.

— Advances in Molecular Modeling, Vol. 4. 1999. 109.50 (*0-7623-0065-5*) Jai Pr.

Liotta, Dennis C. Organoselenium Chemistry. LC 86-5582. 422p. 1987. 215.00 (*0-471-88867-2*) Wiley.

Liotta, Dennis C. & Volmer, Mark. Organic Syntheses: Reaction Guide. (Organic Syntheses Collective Volumes Ser.). 872p. 1991. 98.95 (*0-471-54261-X*) Wiley.

Liotta, Lance A., ed. Influence of Tumor Development on the Host. (Cancer Growth & Progression Ser.). (C). 1988. text 211.50 (*0-89838-992-5*) Kluwer Academic.

Liotta, Lance A. & Hurt, I. R. Tumor Invasion & Metastasis. 1982. text 366.50 (*90-247-2611-5*) Kluwer Academic.

Liotta, Mary A., ed. see Brady, Joan.

Liotta, Mary A., ed. see Clark, Carolyn C.

Liotta, Mary A., ed. see Farese, Susan J.

Liotta, Mary A., ed. see Zagury, Carolyn S., et al.

Liotta, P. H. Rules of Engagement. (CSU Poetry Ser.: No. XXXIV). 137p. (Orig.). 1991. 15.00 (*0-914946-88-9*); pap. 10.00 (*0-914946-89-7*) Cleveland St Univ Poetry Ctr.

— The Wreckage Reconsidered: Five Oxymorons from Balkan Deconstruction. LC 98-50948. 240p. 1998. 50.00 (*0-7391-0012-2*) Lxngtn Bks.

Liotta, Peter. The Ruins of Athens. 68p. (Orig.). 1998. pap. 14.95 (*1-882329-08-2*) Garden St Pr.

Liotti, G., jt. auth. see Guidano, Vittorio F.

Liotti, Robert C. The Equine Consumer Compendium. 135p. 1996. pap. 16.95 (*0-9650327-1-X*) Equine Consumer.

— The Equine Prepurchase Compendium: The Consumer Guide to Ownership & Purchase. Beougher, Pamela D., ed. LC 95-90408. (Illus.). 240p. (Orig.). 1996. pap. 27.95 (*0-9650327-0-1*) Equine Consumer.

***Liou, Caroline.** China: Lonely Planet. 7th ed. (Travel Guides Ser.). (Illus.). 1208p. 2000. pap. 29.95 (*0-86442-755-7*) Lonely Planet.

Liou, J. J., jt. auth. see Yuan, J. S.

Liou, Juin J. Principles & Analysis of AlGaAs/GaAs Heterojuntion Bipolar Transistors. LC 95-53772. 227p. 1996. 85.00 (*0-89006-587-X*) Artech Hse.

Liou, Juin J., et al. Analysis & Design of Mosfets: Modeling, Simulation, & Parameter Extraction. LC 98-35564. 1998. 136.00 (*0-7923-8251-X*) Kluwer Academic.

— Analysis & Design of Mosfets: Modeling, Simulation & Parameter Extraction LC 98-35564. xiv, 349 p. 1998. write for info. (*0-412-14601-0*) Kluwer Academic.

***Liou, Koutsai T.** Handbook of Economic Development. LC 98-7446. (Public Administration & Public Policy Ser.). (Illus.). 768p. 1998. text 225.00 (*0-8247-0181-X*) Dekker.

Liou, Kuo-Nan. Radiation & Cloud Processes in the Atmosphere: Theory, Observation & Modeling. (Oxford Monographs on Geology & Geophysics: No. 21). (Illus.). 504p. 1992. text 115.00 (*0-19-504910-1*) OUP.

Liou, Kuotsai T. Managing Economic Reforms in Post-Mao China. LC 97-34754. 184p. 1998. 59.95 (*0-275-95792-6*, Praeger Pubs) Greenwood.

***Liou, Kuotsai T., ed.** Administrative Reform & National Economic Development. LC 99-75556. (Policy Studies Organization Ser.). 303p. 2000. text 79.95 (*1-84014-421-1*, Pub. by Ashgate Pub) Ashgate Pub Co.

Lip, Evelyn. Chinese Numbers: Significance, Symbolism & Traditions. (CHI., Illus.). 121p. (Orig.). 1992. pap. 9.95 (*0-89346-376-0*) Heian Intl.

— Chinese Temple Architecture in Singapore. (Illus.). 114p. (Orig.). 1983. pap. 49.50 (*9971-69-064-0*, Pub. by Sngapore Univ Pr) Coronet Bks.

— Choosing Auspicious Chinese Names. 172p. 1997. reprint ed. pap. 12.95 (*0-89346-847-9*) Heian Intl.

— The Design & Feing Shui of Logos, Trademarks & Signboards. (Illus.). 91p. 1998. pap. 12.95 (*0-89346-864-9*) Heian Intl.

— Feng Shui: A Layman's Guide to Chinese Geomancy. (Illus.). 132p. 1987. pap. 9.95 (*0-89346-286-1*) Heian Intl.

— Feng Shui: Environments of Power, a Study of Chinese Architecture. LC 96-143702. (Illus.). 129p. (Orig.). 1995. pap. 38.00 (*1-85490-427-2*, Pub. by Wiley) Wiley.

— Feng Shui for Business. (Illus.). 112p. 1990. pap. 9.95 (*0-89346-326-4*) Heian Intl.

— Feng Shui for the Home. (Illus.). 91p. 1990. pap. 9.95 (*0-89346-327-2*) Heian Intl.

— Fun with Astrology. (Illus.). 84p. (Orig.). 1983. pap. 8.95 (*981-218-033-8*) Heian Intl.

— Fun with Chinese Horoscopes. rev. ed. (Illus.). 104p. 1987. reprint ed. pap. 8.95 (*981-218-034-6*) Heian Intl.

— Out of China: Culture & Traditions. LC 93-23966. (Illus.). 1993. 29.90 (*0-685-65618-7*) Addison-Wesley.

Lip, Evelyn. What Is Feng Shui? (What Is? Ser.: Vol. VI). (Illus.). 64p. (Orig.). 1997. pap. 16.95 (*1-85490-491-4*) Academy Ed UK.

— What Is Feng Shui? 64p. (Orig.). 1997. pap. 16.95 (*0-471-97751-9*) Wiley.

Lip, G. Y., ed. ABC of Atrial Fibrillation. 48p. 1996. pap. text 19.00 (*0-7279-1070-1*, Pub. by BMJ Pub) Login Brothers Bk Co.

Lipack, Richard W. Epoch Moments & Secrets: John Lennon & the Beatles at the Mirror of Man's Destiny. LC 96-96003. (Beatles' Trilogy Ser.). (Illus.). 357p. 1996. 31.95 (*0-9650959-1-6*, 0007) Barrister Pubs.

Lipack, Richard W. Epoch Moments & Secrets: John Lennon & the Beatles at the Mirror of Man's Destiny. 1996. 31.95 (*1-886894-55-8*) Mus Bk Servs.

Lipanov, Aleksei, ed. Theory of Combustion of Powder & Explosives. (Illus.). 407p. (C). 1996. lib. bdg. 135.00 (*1-56072-398-X*) Nova Sci Pubs.

Lipanov, Aleksei M., ed. Theory of Combustion of Powder & Explosives. 407p. (C). 1996. lib. bdg. 89.00 (*0-614-21809-8*) Nova Sci Pubs.

Lipanovich, Marianne, ed. see Godwin, Sara.

Lipanovich, Marianne, ed. see Hodges, Larry & Powell, Charles C.

Lipanovich, Marianne, ed. see Hodgson, Larry & Lammers, Susan M.

Lipanovich, Marianne, ed. see Hodgson, Larry, et al.

Lipari, Joseph & Jobin, Leonard. Isn't That Romantic: Imaginative Ways to Express Your Love. LC 94-21294. 224p. 1995. pap. 9.95 (*0-89529-634-9*, Avery) Penguin Putnam.

Lipartito, Kenneth. The Bell System & Regional Business: The Telephone in the South, 1877-1920. LC 89-32037. (Johns Hopkins - AT & T Series in Telephone History). (Illus.). 301p. reprint ed. pap. 93.40 (*0-608-06081-X*, 206641300008) Bks Demand.

Lipartito, Kenneth J. & Pratt, Joseph A. Baker & Botts in the Development of Modern Houston. (Illus.). 276p. 1991. 24.95 (*0-292-70782-7*) U of Tex Pr.

Lipatov, Yuri S. & Nesterov, Anatoly E. Thermodynamics of Polymer Blends. LC 97-62285. (Polymer Thermodynamics Library: No. 1). 465p. 1997. 179.95 (*1-56676-624-9*) Technomic.

Lipay, Raymond J. Accounting Services for Your Small Business: A Guide for Evaluating Company Performance, Obtaining Financing, Selling Your Business. LC 82-13647. 270p. reprint ed. pap. 83.70 (*0-7837-3512-X*, 205784500008) Bks Demand.

— Keys to Choosing a Financial Specialist. (Barron's Business Keys Ser.). 160p. (Orig.). 1992. pap. text 4.95 (*0-8120-4545-9*) Barron.

Lipchitz, Leslie & McDonald, Donogh, eds. German Unification: Economic Issues. LC 90-26503. (Occasional Paper Ser.: No. 75). xiii, 171p. (Orig.). 1991. pap. 10.00 (*1-55775-200-1*) Intl Monetary.

Lipcon, Charles R. Seaman's Rights in the United States When Involved in an Accident. Professional Translating Services, Inc. Staff, tr. (FRE, GER, GRE, ITA & KOR.). 50p. (Orig.). 1989. pap. 9.95 (*0-932557-01-5*) Adels Inc.

Lipe, Belle N. Pieces of My Heart. (Illus.). 120p. 1996. 19.95 (*1-888366-03-6*) Dixie Pr.

Lipe, Betty & Lipe, Robert E. Clean Your Shells & Other Sealife. 36p. (Orig.). 1993. pap. 5.00 (*0-9637681-1-5*) Shell Store.

Lipe, David, jt. auth. see Andre, Lee.

Lipe, Karen. The Big Book of Boat Canvas: A Complete Guide to Fabric Work on Boats. 1988. pap. 19.95 (*0-07-038000-7*) Intl Marine.

Lipe, Riki. Color at Ricena's Pond, Bk. 2. (Illus.). 24p. (Orig.). (J). (ps-6). 1997. pap. 5.95 (*0-9659381-1-5*) Hoot N Cackle.

***Lipe, Riki.** The Mystery at Ricena's Pond. Spears-Stewart, Reta, ed. (Illus.). 36p. (J). (ps-6). 2000. 10.00 (*0-9659381-2-3*, Pub. by Hoot N Cackle) Booksource.

Lipe, Riki. The Secret of Ricena's Pond, Bk. 1. Spears-Stewart, Reat, ed. 32p. (J). (ps-6). 1992. pap. 9.95 (*0-9659381-0-7*) Hoot N Cackle.

— Sooty. Spears-Stewart, Reta, ed. (Illus.). 34p. (J). (ps-6). 1998. 10.00 (*0-9659381-3-1*) Hoot N Cackle.

Lipe, Robert E. Marginellas. 40p. (Orig.). 1991. pap. 15.95 (*0-9637681-0-7*) Shell Store.

Lipe, Robert E., jt. auth. see Lipe, Betty.

***Lipe, Roger.** Varsity Letters No. 2: Devotions for Athletes, Coaches & Fans. 88p. 1999. pap. 6.95 (*1-887002-99-5*) Cross Trng.

Lipe, William D. Excavations, Glen Canyon Area, 1958. (Glen Canyon Ser.: No. 11). reprint ed. 47.50 (*0-404-60644-X*) AMS Pr.

Lipe, William D., ed. The Sand Canyon Archaeological Project: A Progress Report. LC 91-76231. (Occasional Paper: No. 2). (Illus.). 160p. (Orig.). 1992. pap. 21.95 (*0-9624640-1-5*) Crow Canyon Archaeol.

Lipe, William D. & Hegmon, Michelle, eds. The Architecture of Social Integration in Prehistoric Pueblos. LC 89-81117. (Occasional Paper: No. 1). (Illus.). 189p. (Orig.). 1990. pap. 21.95 (*0-9624640-0-7*) Crow Canyon Archaeol.

Lipe, William D., et al. Excavations, Glen Canyon Area, 1959. (Glen Canyon Ser.: No. 13). reprint ed. 47.50 (*0-404-60649-0*) AMS Pr.

Lipeck, Udo W. & Thalheim, Bernhard. Modelling Database Dynamics: Selected Papers from the 4th International Workshop on Foundations of Models & Languages for Data & Objects, Volkse, Germany 19-22 October 1992. 4th ed. LC 93-3307. (Workshops in Computing Ser.). 1993. 66.95 (*0-387-19803-2*) Spr-Verlag.

Lipeles, Maxine I., jt. auth. see Battle, Jackson B.

An Asterisk (*) at the beginning of an entry indicates that the title is appearing for the first time.

L

Lipenius, Martin. Bibliotheca Realis Iuridica, 6 vols., Set. 1967. reprint ed. write for info. (*0-318-71838-3*) G Olms Pubs.
— Bibliotheca Realis Philosophica, 2 vols., Set. 1967. reprint ed. write for info. (*0-318-71839-1*) G Olms Pubs.
— Bibliotheca Realis Theologica, 2 vols., Set. 1973. reprint ed. write for info. (*3-487-04594-X*) G Olms Pubs.
Lipetz, Ben-Ami. Guide to Case Studies of Scientific Activity. LC 65-23580. 1965. 20.00 (*0-910788-02-2*) Intermedia.
— Measurement of Efficiency of Scientific Research. LC 65-23581. 1965. 20.00 (*0-910788-01-4*) Intermedia.
Lipetz, Marcia J. Routine Justice: Processing Cases in Women's Court. (New Observations Ser.). 128p. 1983. 32.95 (*0-87855-483-1*) Transaction Pubs.
Lipetz, Philip. The Good Calorie Diet. 288p. 1996. mass mkt. 5.99 (*0-06-109403-X*) HarpC.
— Naturally Slim & Powerful: The Natural Way to Boost Serotonin Levels Without Drugs. 240p. 1998. pap. text 11.95 (*0-8362-5284-5*) Andrews & McMeel.
Lipfert, Frederick W. Air Pollution & Community Health: A Critical Review & Data Sourcebook. LC 93-1364. 556p. 1994. text 81.95 (*0-442-01444-9*, VNR) Wiley.
Lipfert, Frederick W. Air Pollution & Community Health: A Critical Review & Data Sourcebook. (Industrial Health & Safety Ser.). 556p. 1994. 110.00 (*0-471-28560-9*, VNR) Wiley.
Lipfert, Helmut & Girbig, Werner. The War Diary of Hauptmann Helmut Lipfert: JG 52 on the Russian Front, 1943-1945. Johnston, David, tr. LC 92-61775. (Illus.). 224p. 1993. 29.95 (*0-88740-446-4*) Schiffer.
Lipfert, Nathan R., jt. auth. see Martin, Kenneth R.
Lipgens, Walter, ed. Documents on the History of European Integration Vol. 1: Continental Plans for European Union 1939-1945. LC 84-19842. (European University Institute, Series B (History)). (Illus.). xxiv, 823p. 1984. 290.80 (*3-11-009724-9*) De Gruyter.
— Documents on the History of European Integration Vol. 2: Plans for European Union in Great Britain & in Exile, 1939-1945. (European University Institute, Series B (History): Vols. 1/2). xxiv, 852p. 1986. 261.55 (*3-11-010338-9*) De Gruyter.
Lipgens, Walter & Loth, Wilfried, eds. Documents on the History of European Integration Vol. 3: The Struggle for the European Union by Political Parties & Pressure Groups in Western European Countries, 1945-1950. xliv, 824p. (C). 1988. lib. bdg. 284.65 (*3-11-011429-1*) De Gruyter.
Lipgens, Walter, et al. A History of European Integration: Nineteen Forty-Five to Nineteen Forty-Seven, the Formation of the European Unity Movement, Vol. 1. 740p. 1982. text 135.00 (*0-19-822587-3*) OUP.
Lipham, James M. Effective Principal, Effective School. LC 81-154085. 36p. (Orig.). reprint ed. pap. 30.00 (*0-608-18140-4*, 203279500081) Bks Demand.
Lipham, James M., et al. The Principalship. 335p. (C). 1985. text 32.95 (*0-582-28581-X*, 71607) Longman.
Lipiec, Jerzy, jt. ed. see Glinski, Jan.
Lipietz, Alain. Green Hopes: The Future of Political Ecology. Slater, Malcolm, tr. from FRE. LC 95-10787. 169p. 1995. 55.95 (*0-7456-1325-X*, Pub. by Polity Pr); pap. 28.95 (*0-7456-1327-6*, Pub. by Polity Pr) Blackwell Pubs.
— Towards a New Economic Order: Postfordism, Ecology & Democracy. LC 92-11305. (Europe & the International Order Ser.). 224p. (C). 1992. text 55.95 (*0-19-520961-3*) OUP.
Lipin, Lawrence M. Producers, Proletarians, & Politicians: Workers & Party Politics in Evansville & New Albany, Indiana, 1850-87. LC 92-41298. 336p. 1993. text 42.50 (*0-252-02019-7*) U of Ill Pr.
Lipin, R. B. & McKay, G. A., eds. Geochemistry & Mineralogy of Rare Earth Elements. (Reviews in Mineralogy Ser.: Vol. 21). 348p. 1989. per. 28.00 (*0-939950-25-1*) Mineralogical Soc.
Lipincot, Don & Treverton, Gregory F. Negotiations Concerning the Falklands - Maldives Dispute: Breakdown of Negotiations & the Haig Mediation Effort. (Pew Case Studies in International Affairs). 56p. (C). 1994. pap. text 3.50 (*1-56927-406-1*) Geo U Inst Dplmcy.
Lipiniski, Klaus. Lexikon der Datenkommunikation. (GER.). 380p. 1994. 185.00 (*0-7859-8541-7*, 3892380732) Fr & Eur.
Lipinski, Edward R. The New York Times Home Repair Almanac: A Season-by-Season Guide for Maintaining Your Home. LC 99-10048. (Illus.). 308p. 1999. pap. 19.95 (*0-86730-759-5*, Pub. by Lebhar Friedman) Natl Bk Netwk.
Lipinski, Alex. The Directory of Jobs & Careers Abroad. 8th ed. 352p. 1993. pap. 16.95 (*1-85458-025-6*, Pub. by Vac Wrk Pubns) Petersons.
Lipinski, Arlene L. Work, Jobs & Occupations--Distress, Dangers & Diseases: Index of New Information. (Illus.). 150p. 1994. 47.50 (*0-7883-0014-8*); pap. 44.50 (*0-7883-0015-6*) ABBE Pubs Assn.
Lipinski, Barbara. In the Best Interest of the Patient: Ethical & Legal Issues in the Practice of Psychotherapy. LC 99-90292. 1999. pap. text 23.95 (*1-928702-02-3*) Pacific Meridian.
Lipinski, Bob & Lipinski, Kathie. The Complete Beverage Dictionary. 2nd ed. (Culinary Arts Ser.). 458p. 1996. 49.95 (*0-471-28746-6*, VNR) Wiley.
— Professional Beverage Management. (Culinary Arts Ser.). 496p. 1996. 54.95 (*0-471-28737-7*, VNR) Wiley.
— Professional Beverage Management. (Culinary Arts Ser.). 500p. 1996. text 46.95 (*0-442-02176-3*, VNR) Wiley.
Lipinski, Boguslaw, ed. Electronic Conduction & Mechanoelectrical Transduction in Biological Materials. LC 82-12998. (Illus.). 319p. reprint ed. pap. 98.90 (*0-7837-0888-2*, 204119400019) Bks Demand.
Lipinski, Edouard. Dictionnaire de la Civilisation Phenicienne et Punique. (FRE.). 501p. 1993. 285.00 (*0-7859-7902-6*, 2503500331) Fr & Eur.
Lipinski, Edward. Tile Book. 1998. write for info. (*0-8069-6115-5*) Sterling.
Lipinski, Hubert & Adler, Richard. The HUB Project: Computer-Based Support for Group Problem Solving. 218p. 1982. 15.00 (*0-318-19196-2*, R-51) Inst Future.
Lipinski, Kathie, jt. auth. see Lipinski, Bob.
Lipinski, Kathleen A. & Lipinski, Robert A. Professional Guide to Alcoholic Beverages. (Illus.). 548p. (C). 1989. text 55.95 (*0-442-25837-2*, VNR) Wiley.
Lipinski, Martha E., ed. Role of the Civil Engineer in Highway Safety. 215p. 1983. pap. 5.00 (*0-87262-374-2*) Am Soc Civil Eng.
Lipinski, Miroslav, tr. see Sienkiewicz, Henryk.
Lipinski, Miroslaw, ed. Dictionary of 1,000 Polish Proverbs. LC 97-20024. (POL.). 141p. (Orig.). 1997. pap. 11.95 (*0-7818-0482-5*) Hippocrene Bks.
— Treasury of Classic Polish Love Short Stories in Polish & English: Short Stories. LC 97-15376. (ENG & POL.). 128p. 1997. 11.95 (*0-7818-0513-9*) Hippocrene Bks.
— Treasury of Polish Love Poems, Quotations & Proverbs. 128p. 1995. 11.95 (*0-7818-0297-0*) Hippocrene Bks.
Lipinski, Miroslaw, ed. & tr. see Sienkiewicz, Henryk.
Lipinski, Mivoslaw, tr. see Grabinski, Stefan.
Lipinski, Rick, tr. & intro. see Cernuda, Luis.
Lipinski, Robert A., jt. auth. see Lipinski, Kathleen A.
Lipinski, Tara. Tara Lipinski, Triumph on Ice. LC 97-18219. (Illus.). 128p. (J). (gr. 3-7). 1997. 15.95 (*0-553-09775-X*) Bantam.
— Totally Tara: An Olympic Journal. (Illus.). 146p. 1998. pap. 25.00 (*0-7893-0142-3*, Pub. by Universe) St Martin.
Lipinski, Tara, jt. auth. see Costello, Emily.
***Lipinski, Thomas.** Death in the Steel City. (Carroll Dorsey Mystery Ser.: 4). 224p. 2000. mass mkt. 5.99 (*0-380-79432-2*, Avon Bks) Morrow Avon.
Lipinski, Thomas. The Fall-Down Artist. (Carroll Dorsey Mystery Ser.). 304p. 1994. 20.95 (*0-312-10461-8*) St Martin.
— Picture of Her Tombstone. (Carroll Dorsey Mystery Ser.: 2). 224p. 1998. mass mkt. 5.99 (*0-380-73024-3*, Avon Bks) Morrow Avon.
— Steel City Confessions: A Mystery. LC 98-93547. (Carroll Dorsey Mystery Ser.: 3). 224p. 1999. mass mkt. 5.99 (*0-380-79431-4*, Avon Bks) Morrow Avon.
Lipinsky, Edward S. Handbook Bisolar Resources. McClure, Thomas A., ed. (Handbook of Biosolar Resources Ser.: Vol. 2). 608p. 1981. 321.00 (*0-8493-3473-X*, TP360, CRC Reprint) Franklin.
Lipinsky, Miroslaw, tr. see Sienkiewicz, Henryk.
LiPira, Benedict S. Giuseppe Garibaldi: A Biography of the Father of Modern Italy. LC 98-84760. (Illus.). 128p. 1998. 15.95 (*1-56167-432-X*) Noble Hse MD.
Lipis, Joan R. The Y'shua Challenge: Answers for Those Who Say Jews Can't Believe in Jesus. Gould, Elijah et al, eds. LC 93-18254. 40p. 1993. pap. 2.00 (*1-881022-03-X*, BT030) Purple Pomegranate.
Lipitakis, A. Computer Mathematics, Lecture Notes: Advances on Computer Mathematics & Its Applications. 384p. 1993. text 74.00 (*981-02-1292-5*) World Scientific Pub.
Lipka, Charles, ed. see Jud, Brian.
Lipka, Jerry & Mohatt, Gerald. Transforming the Culture of Schools: Yup'ik Eskimo Examples. LC 97-39258. (Sociocultural, Political, & Historical Studies in Education Ser.). 256p. 1998. write for info. (*0-8058-2820-6*); pap. 24.00 (*0-8058-2821-4*) L Erlbaum Assocs.
Lipka, Leonard. Semantic Structure & Word Formation: Verb-Particle Constructions in Contemporary English. 1973. bds. 47.75 (*3-7705-0947-1*) Adlers Foreign Bks.
Lipka, Richard P. & Brinthaupt, Thomas M., eds. The Role of Self in Teacher Development. LC 98-8361. (SUNY Series, Studying the Self). 256p. (C). 1998. text 65.50 (*0-7914-4015-X*); pap. text 21.95 (*0-7914-4016-8*) State U NY Pr.
— Self-Perspectives Across the Life Span. LC 91-16383. (SUNY Series, Studying the Self). 282p. (C). 1992. pap. text 21.95 (*0-7914-1004-8*) State U NY Pr.
Lipka, Richard P. & National Middle School Association Staff. The Eight-Year Study Revisited: Lessons from the Past for the Present. LC 98-22483. 1998. pap. write for info. (*1-56090-153-5*) Natl Middle Schl.
Lipka, Richard P., jt. auth. see Beane, James A.
Lipka, Richard P., jt. auth. see Le Tendre, Brenda G.
Lipka, Richard P., jt. ed. see Brinthaupt, Thomas M.
Lipke, Barbara. Figures, Facts & Fables: Telling Tales in Science & Math. LC 96-22037. 1996. pap. text 25.00 (*0-435-07105-X*) Heinemann.
***Lipke, Howard.** EMDR & Psychotherapy Integration: Theoretical & Clinical Suggestions with Focus on Traumatic Stress. LC 99-38186. (Innovations in Psychology Ser.). 176p. 1999. boxed set 39.95 (*0-8493-0630-2*) CRC Pr.
Lipke, Ken & Swiatek, Frank. The American Leader. (Illus.). 250p. (C). 1989. write for info. (*0-318-65231-5*) Gibraltar LIF.
Lipke, Paul, ed. see Ansel, Willits D.
Lipke, William C. Thomas Waterman Wood, PNA, 1823-1903. (Illus.). 1970. pap. 4.00 (*0-89073-032-6*, 136) Boston Public Lib.
Lipkes, Jeff. Politics, Religion & Classical Political Economy in Britain: John Stuart Mill & His Followers. LC 98-23640. (Studies in the History of Economics). 240p. 1999. text 79.95 (*0-312-21741-2*) St Martin.
Lipkin, Arthur. Understanding Homosexuality: Changing Schools. 256p. 1999. pap. 18.95 (*0-8133-2535-8*) Westview.
— Understanding Homosexuality: Changing Schools. LC 99-21973. 504p. 1999. text 69.00 (*0-8133-2534-X*, Pub. by Westview) HarpC.
Lipkin, Barbara, ed. see Charischak, Ihor.
Lipkin, Bernice S. Latex for Linux. LC 98-51994. 530p. 1999. pap. 44.95 (*0-387-98708-8*) Spr-Verlag.
Lipkin, David P., jt. auth. see Nolan, James.
Lipkin, Gladys B. & Cohen, Roberta G. Effective Approaches to Patients' Behavior. 4th ed. LC 91-4806. 312p. (C). 1992. pap. text 33.95 (*0-8261-1496-2*) Springer Pub.
— Effective Approaches to Patients Behavior: A Guide Book for Health Care Professionals, Patients & Their Caregivers. 5th ed. LC 97-52092. 360p. 1998. 56.95 (*0-8261-1497-0*) Springer Pub.
— Effective Approaches to Patient's Behavior: A Guide Book for Health Care Professionals, Patients, & Their Caregivers. 5th ed. LC 97-52092. 1998. pap. 34.95 (*0-8261-1498-9*) Springer Pub.
Lipkin, H. J. Quantum Mechanics: New Approaches to Selected Topics. LC 72-79733. (North-Holland Personal Library). xvi, 466p. 1992. reprint ed. pap. 71.00 (*0-444-87010-5*, North Holland) Elsevier.
***Lipkin, Lisa.** Bringing the Story Home: The Complete Guide to Storytelling for Parents. 192p. 2000. 19.95 (*0-393-04775-X*) Norton.
Lipkin, M., Jr., ed. see White, K. L.
Lipkin, Mack, Jr. Psychosocial Factors Affecting Health. LC 82-11249. 374p. 1982. 75.00 (*0-275-91371-6*, C1371, Praeger Pubs) Greenwood.
Lipkin, Mack, Jr. & Lybrand, William A., eds. Population-Based Medicine. LC 81-21116. 198p. 1982. 55.00 (*0-275-91370-8*, C1370, Praeger Pubs) Greenwood.
Lipkin, Mack, Jr., et al. The Medical Interview. LC 94-6511. 1994. 138.00 (*3-540-94257-2*) Spr-Verlag.
— The Medical Interview. LC 94-6511. 1996. 99.00 (*0-387-94257-2*) Spr-Verlag.
Lipkin, Mack, Jr., ed. see Tahir-Kheli, Shirin.
Lipkin, Marjorie B. The School Search Guide to Private Schools in the Northeast. 351p. 1988. pap. text 12.95 (*0-9620326-0-3*) Schoolsearch Pr.
Lipkin, Martin, et al. Calcium, Vitamin D, & Prevention of Colon Cancer. (Illus.). 416p. 1991. lib. bdg. 129.00 (*0-8493-4264-3*, RC280) CRC Pr.
Lipkin, Martin, jt. ed. see Zedeck, Morris S.
***Lipkin, Midge.** Colleges with Programs or Services for Students with Learning Disabilities. 3rd ed. 1999. pap. text. write for info. (*0-9620326-7-0*) Schoolsearch Pr.
Lipkin, Midge. The Schoolsearch Guide to Colleges with Programs or Services for Students with Learning Disabilities. 928p. (Orig.). 1993. pap. text 34.95 (*0-9620326-5-4*) Schoolsearch Pr.
— The Schoolsearch Guide to Private Schools with Programs or Services for Students with Learning Disabilities. 650p. (Orig.). 1992. pap. 34.95 (*0-9620326-4-6*) Schoolsearch Pr.
Lipkin, Randie. Untitled (A Skier) LC 94-72274. 188p. (Orig.). (C). 1995. pap. text 8.00 (*1-879193-03-5*) Fugue State.
— Without. LC 97-90992. 152p. 1998. per. 7.00 (*1-879193-06-X*) Fugue State.
Lipkin, Robert. Biker. 132p. 1982. reprint ed. pap. 7.95 (*0-9662182-1-3*) FTW Pub.
— Brotherhood of Outlaws. 234p. 1978. reprint ed. pap. 7.95 (*0-9662182-0-5*) FTW Pub.
***Lipkin, Robert J.** Constitutional Revolutions: Pragmatism & the Revolutionary Role of Judicial Review in American Constitutionalism. LC 99-45639. 2000. text 49.95 (*0-8223-2429-6*) Duke.
Lipkin, W. I., jt. ed. see Koprowski, Hilary.
Lipkind, William. Days to Remember. (Illus.). (J). (gr. 3 up). 1961. 10.95 (*0-8392-3006-0*) Astor-Honor.
Lipkind, William & Mordinoff, Nicolas. Finders Keepers. LC 51-12326. (Illus.). 32p. (J). (gr. k-4). 1951. 14.95 (*0-15-227529-0*, Harcourt Child Bks) Harcourt.
Lipkind, William, jt. auth. see Mordinoff, Nicolas.
Lipking, Joanna, ed. Oroonoko or, The Royal Slave. LC 96-47186. (Norton Critical Editions Ser.). (C). 1997. pap. text 9.25 (*0-393-97014-0*) Norton.
Lipking, Lawrence. The Life of the Poet: Beginning & Ending Poetic Careers. LC 81-1067. (Illus.). (C). 1995. lib. bdg. 26.50 (*0-226-48450-5*) U Ch Pr.
— The Life of the Poet: Beginning & Ending Poetic Careers. LC 81-1067. (Illus.). 260p. (C). 1997. pap. text 9.95 (*0-226-48451-3*) U Ch Pr.
Lipking, Lawrence, ed. High Romantic Argument: Essays for M. H. Abrams. 192p. 1981. 35.00 (*0-8014-1307-9*) Cornell U Pr.
Lipking, Lawrence I. The Ordering of the Arts in Eighteenth-Century England. LC 76-90953. 523p. reprint ed. pap. 162.20 (*0-8357-2780-7*, 203990600014) Bks Demand.
Lipking, Lawrence I. Samuel Johnson: The Life of an Author. LC 98-18526. 352p. 1998. 35.00 (*0-674-78777-3*) HUP.
***Lipking, Lawrence I.** Samuel Johnson: The Life of an Author. 2000. pap. text 16.95 (*0-674-00198-2*) HUP.
Lipkov, Alexander, jt. auth. see Konchalovsky, Andrei.
Lipkowitz, Brenda, ed. see Dickens, Nathaniel A.
Lipkowitz, Kenneth B. & Boyd, Donald B., eds. Reviews in Computational Chemistry, Vol. 1. LC 89-21466. (Illus.). xix, 419p. 1990. 115.00 (*0-89573-754-X*, Wiley-VCH) Wiley.
— Reviews in Computational Chemistry, Vol. 2. 520p. 1991. 110.00 (*1-56081-515-9*, Wiley-VCH) Wiley.
— Reviews in Computational Chemistry, Vol. 6. (Illus.). 566p. 1995. 110.00 (*1-56081-667-8*, Wiley-VCH) Wiley.
Lipkowitz, Kenneth B., jt. auth. see Boyd, Donald B.
Lipkowitz, Kenneth B., jt. ed. see Boyd, Donald B.
***Lipkowitz, Kenny B. & Boyd.** Reviews in Computational Chemistry, Vol. 14. 560p. 1999. 135.00 (*0-471-35495-3*) Wiley.
Lipkowitz, Kenny B. & Boyd, Donald B. Reviews in Computational Chemistry, Vol. 11. 431p. 1997. 139.00 (*0-471-19248-1*, Wiley-VCH) Wiley.
***Lipkowitz, Kenny B. & Boyd, Donald B.** Reviews in Computational Chemistry, Vol. 15. 368p. 2000. 134.95 (*0-471-36168-2*) Wiley.
— Reviews in Computational Chemistry, Vol. 16. 384p. 2000. 134.95 (*0-471-38667-7*) Wiley.
Lipkowitz, Kenny B. & Boyd, Donald B., eds. Reviews in Computational Chemistry, Vol. 1. 419p. 1990. 139.00 (*0-471-18728-3*) Wiley.
— Reviews in Computational Chemistry, Vol. 2. 527p. 1991. 139.00 (*0-471-18810-7*) Wiley.
— Reviews in Computational Chemistry, Vol. 3. 271p. 1992. 139.00 (*0-471-18853-0*) Wiley.
— Reviews in Computational Chemistry, Vol. 4. 280p. 1993. 139.00 (*0-471-18854-9*) Wiley.
— Reviews in Computational Chemistry, Vol. 5. 458p. 1993. 139.00 (*0-471-18866-2*) Wiley.
***Lipkowitz, Kenny B. & Boyd, Donald B., eds.** Reviews in Computational Chemistry, Vol. 13. 426p. 1999. 139.00 (*0-471-33135-X*) Wiley.
Lipkowitz, Kenny B., ed. see Boyd, Donald B.
Lipkowitz, Marcel. French Royal & Administrative Acts, Twelve Fifty-Six to Seventeen Ninety-Four: A Subject Guide to the New York Public Library Collection of Sixteen Thousand Pamphlets Now on Microfilm. LC 78-8497. 206p. 1978. 200.00 (*0-89235-011-3*) Primary Srce Media.
Lipkowitz, Myron, jt. auth. see Navarra, Tova.
Lipkowitz, Myron A. & Navarra, Tova. Allergies A-Z. (Illus.). 368p. 1997. pap. 19.95 (*0-8160-3654-3*) Facts on File.
***Lipkowski, Jacek & Ross, Philip N.** Electrocatalysis. LC 97-39798. (Frontiers of Electrochemistry Ser.). 400p. 1998. 159.00 (*0-471-24673-5*, Wiley-VCH) Wiley.
Lipkowski, Jacek & Ross, Philip N., eds. Adsorption of Molecules at Metal Electrodes. LC 92-19438. (Frontiers of Electrochemistry Ser.: Vol. 1). 1992. 145.00 (*0-89573-786-8*, Wiley-VCH) Wiley.
— The Eletrochemistry of Novel Materials. LC 93-40037. 1994. 145.00 (*0-89573-788-4*, Wiley-VCH) Wiley.
***Lipkowski, Jacek & Ross, Philip N., eds.** Imaging of Surfaces & Interfaces. LC 98-38181. (Frontiers of Electrochemistry Ser.: Vol. 5). 342p. 1999. 145.00 (*0-471-24672-7*) Wiley.
Lipley, Grey, tr. see Orton, Ray.
***Lipman.** Understanding Criminal Behavior. (Criminal Justice Ser.). 2002. pap. 24.50 (*0-534-53292-6*) Wadsworth Pub.
Lipman, Arthur G., jt. ed. see Battin, Margaret P.
***Lipman-Blumen, Jean.** The Connective Leadership: Managing in a Changing World. LC 99-40400. (Illus.). 432p. 2000. pap. 16.95 (*0-19-513469-9*) OUP.
Lipman, Bradford C. & Cascio, Toni. ECG Assessment & Interpretation. (Illus.). 295p. 1994. pap. 26.95 (*0-8036-5646-7*) Davis Co.
Lipman, Burton E. The Executive Job Search Program. LC 82-90123. (Illus.). 175p. (Orig.). 1982. pap. 24.95 (*0-943064-01-5*) Bell Pub.
— How to Become a Vice-President in Two Weeks (More or Less) (Illus.). 130p. 1982. pap. 24.95 (*0-943064-04-X*) Bell Pub.
— How to Control & Reduce Inventory. rev. ed. LC 72-4485. (Illus.). 210p. 1988. pap. 49.50 (*0-943064-02-3*) Bell Pub.
— Successful Cost Reduction & Control. 267p. 1978. 29.50 (*0-13-860460-6*) Bell Pub.
Lipman, Daniel G. Living Hints to Health. LC 97-5733. 96p. 1997. pap. 10.95 (*965-229-170-6*) Gefen Bks.
Lipman, Derek. Snoring from A to Zzzz. (Illus.). 256p. 1997. pap. 12.95 (*0-9650708-1-6*) Spencer Press.
Lipman, Derek S. Snoring from A to ZZZZ: Proven Cures for the Night's Worse Nuisance. (Illus.). 236p. 1998. pap. text 14.00 (*0-7881-5867-8*) DIANE Pub.
— Snoring from A to ZZZZ: Proven Cures for the Night's Worst Nuisance. 3rd rev. ed. (Illus.). 248p. 2001. pap. 14.95 (*0-9650708-2-4*, Pub. by Spencer Press) BookWorld.
***Lipman, Don.** Easter Sunday. 1999. pap. 12.95 (*0-9671205-0-0*) Jerdon Pubg.
Lipman, Doug. Improving Your Storytelling: Beyond the Basics for All who Tell Stories in Work or Play. LC 99-26088. 219p. 1999. pap. 14.95 (*0-87483-530-5*) August Hse.
— The Storytelling Coach. (American Storytelling Ser.). 1995. 24.95 (*0-87483-435-X*); pap. 14.95 (*0-87483-434-1*) August Hse.
— Storytelling Games: Creative Activities for Language, Communication, & Composition across the Curriculum. LC 94-38939. (Illus.). 192p. 1994. pap. 26.50 (*0-89774-848-4*) Oryx Pr.
— We All Go Together: Creative Activities for Children to Use with Multicultural Folksongs. LC 93-34071. (Illus.). 232p. 1993. pap. 26.50 incl. audio (*0-89774-764-X*) Oryx Pr.
Lipman, Ed. No Capital Crime. 1975. pap. 5.00 (*0-915016-04-4*) Second Coming.
Lipman, Elinor. The Inn at Lake Devine. 1998. 23.00 (*0-676-54572-6*) Random.
— The Inn at Lake Devine. 253p. 1999. pap. 12.00 (*0-375-70485-X*) Vin Bks.
— Into Love & Out Again. 208p. 1988. pap. 11.00 (*0-671-65676-7*) PB.
— Into Love & Out Again. 208p. 1996. pap. 10.00 (*0-671-00224-4*) PB.
— Isabel's Bed. 1996. mass mkt. 5.99 (*0-671-88161-2*) PB.

An Asterisk (*) at the beginning of an entry indicates that the title is appearing for the first time.

L

— Isabel's Bed. large type ed. LC 95-16428. 515p. 1995. 23.95 (*0-7862-0495-8*) Thorndike Pr.

— Isabel's Bed: A Novel. (Illus.). 387p. 1998. per. 14.00 (*0-671-01564-8*, PB Trade Paper) PB.

— The Ladies' Man. LC 98-56450. 240p. 1999. 23.95 (*0-679-45694-5*) Random House.

***Lipman, Elinor.** The Ladies Man. (Contemporaries Ser.). 272p. 2000. 12.00 (*0-375-70731-X*) Vin Bks.

— The Ladies' Man. large type ed. LC 99-59452. 2000. 25.95 (*1-56895-837-4*) Wheeler Pub.

Lipman, Elinor. Then She Found Me. Rosenman, Jane, ed. 320p. 1991. reprint ed. pap. 14.00 (*0-671-68615-1*, WSP) PB.

Lipman, Eva, jt. photos by see Graves, Ken.

Lipman, Frederick. Grow Your Business with Venture Capital: Strategies to Grow Your Business with Outside Investors. LC 98-33965. 368p. 1998. boxed set 25.00 (*0-7615-1460-0*) Prima Pub.

Lipman, Frederick D. Being Public. 3rd ed. 26p. 1987. pap. text 15.00 (*0-936093-06-4*) Packard Pr Fin.

***Lipman, Frederick D.** The Complete Going Public Handbook: Everything You Need to Know to Turn a Private Enterprise into a Publicly Traded Company. LC 00-28563. (Illus.). 464p. 2000. 30.00 (*0-7615-2406-1*) Prima Pub.

— Going Public: Everything You Need to Know to Succeed. 2nd rev. ed. 400p. 1997. pap. 20.00 (*0-7615-0831-7*) Prima Pub.

Lipman, Frederick D. Going Public: Everything You Need to Know to Successfully Turn a Private Enterprise into a Publicly Traded Company. (Illus.). 382p. (C). 1998. text 30.00 (*0-7881-5254-8*) DIANE Pub.

— Going Public: Everything You Need to Know to Successfully Turn a Private Enterprise into a Publicly Traded Company. LC 93-23557. 400p. 1994. boxed set 29.95 (*1-55958-425-4*) Prima Pub.

— How Much Is Your Business Worth? A Step-by-Step Guide to Selling. LC 96-610. 320p. 1996. boxed set 29.95 (*0-7615-0432-X*) Prima Pub.

— Venture Capital & Junk Bond Financing. 62p. 1996. lab manual ed. 20.00 (*0-8318-0761-X*); text 85.00 (*0-8318-0712-1*) Am Law Inst.

Lipman, Frederick D., et al. Audit Committee. 2nd ed. (Corporate Practice Ser.: No. 49). 1995. ring bd. 95.00 (*1-55871-315-8*) BNA.

***Lipman, Frederick D., et al.** Audit Committees. 3rd ed. (Corporate Practice Ser.: Vol. 49). 2000. pap. 95.00 (*1-55871-429-4*) BNA.

Lipman, Henry & Blazey, Mark. Students of the Third Age: University - College Programs for Retired Adults. Fischer, Richard B. et al, eds. (ACE-Oryx Series on Higher Education). (Illus.). 192p. 1992. 29.95 (*0-02-897143-4*) Oryx Pr.

Lipman, Ira A. How to Protect Yourself from Crime. LC 96-52242. 1997. write for info. (*0-89577-989-7*) RD Assn.

Lipman, Ira A., ed. The Private Security Industry: Issues & Trends. (Annals Ser.: Vol. 498). 1988. 26.00 (*0-8039-3102-6*); pap. 17.00 (*0-8039-3103-4*) Sage.

Lipman, J. & Gau, Y. Topological Invariants of Quasi-Ordinary Singularities & Embedded Topological Classification of Quasi-Ordinary Singularities. LC 88-10559. (Memoirs Ser.: No. 74/388). 129p. 1989. reprint ed. pap. 22.00 (*0-8218-2451-1*, MEMO/74/388) Am Math.

Lipman, J. & Teissier, B., eds. Oscar Zariski - Collected Papers Vol. 4: Equisingularity on Algebraic Varieties. (Mathematicians of Our Time Ser.). 1979. 85.00 (*0-262-24022-X*) MIT Pr.

Lipman, Jacob. Soap, Water, & Sex: A Lively Guide to the Benefits of Sexual Hygiene & to Coping with Sexually Transmitted Diseases. LC 97-31405. 191p. 1998. pap. text 18.95 (*1-57392-193-9*) Prometheus Bks.

Lipman, Jean. American Folk Art in Wood, Metal & Stone. (Illus.). 193p. 1972. pap. 8.95 (*0-486-22816-9*) Dover.

— Calder's Universe. (Illus.). 352p. 1999. 40.00 (*0-7624-0592-9*) Running Pr.

Lipman, Jean & Aspinwall, Margaret. Alexander Calder & His Magical Mobiles. LC 81-1811. (Illus.). 96p. (J). (ps up). 1981. 19.95 (*0-933920-17-2*) Hudson Hills.

Lipman, Jean & Mevlendyke, Eve. American Folk Decoration. (Illus.). xii, 163p. 1972. reprint ed. pap. 10.95 (*0-486-22217-9*) Dover.

Lipman, Jean & Winchester, Alice. The Flowering of American Folk Art, 1776-1876. (Illus.). 288p. 1997. 15.98 (*0-7624-0189-3*, Courage) Running Pr.

— Primitive Painters in America, 1750-1950: An Anthology. LC 70-179732. (Biography Index Reprint Ser.). 1980. reprint ed. 16.95 (*0-8369-8100-6*) Ayer.

Lipman, Joel. Provacateur. (Bloody Twin Press Ser.). (Illus.). 24p. (Orig.). 1988. pap. 25.00 (*1-886350-33-7*) Bloody Twin Pr.

— The Real Ideal: Poems. (Illus.). 23p. (Orig.). 1996. pap. 6.00 (*0-935350-59-4*) Luna Bisonte.

Lipman, John C., ed. Quick Reference to Radiology. LC 94-33452. 447p. (C). 1995. pap. text 44.95 (*0-8385-8196-X*, A8196-6, Apple Lange Med) McGraw.

Lipman, Jonathan. Frank Lloyd Wright & the Johnson Wax Buildings. LC 85-43489. (Illus.). 1991. pap. 29.95 (*0-8478-0706-1*, Pub. by Rizzoli Intl) St Martin.

Lipman, Jonathan, jt. auth. see Levine, Neil.

Lipman, Jonathan N. Familiar Strangers: A History of Muslims in Northwest China. LC 97-10814. (Studies on Ethnic Groups in China). (Illus.). xxxvi, 266p. 1998. per. 22.50 (*0-295-97644-6*) U of Wash Pr.

Lipman, Jonathan N. & Harrell, Stevan, eds. Violence in China: Essays in Culture & Counterculture. LC 88-32411. (SUNY Series in Chinese Local Studies). 249p. (C). 1990. text 64.50 (*0-7914-0113-8*); pap. text 21.95 (*0-7914-0115-4*) State U NY Pr.

Lipman, Jonathan N., et al. Imperial Japan: Expansion & War. (Humanities Approach to Japanese History Ser.). (Illus.). 188p. (Orig.). (YA). (gr. 9-12). 1995. pap. 37.95 (*0-89994-382-9*) Soc Sci Ed.

Lipman, Joseph. Residues & Traces of Differential Forms Via Hochschild Homology. LC 86-28698. (Contemporary Mathematics Ser.: Vol. 61). 95p. 1987. pap. 22.00 (*0-8218-5070-9*, CONM/61) Am Math.

Lipman, Ken. Bad News Babysitting! (Secret World of Alex Mack Ser.: No. 3). (J). (gr. 3-6). 1995. pap. 3.99 (*0-671-53446-7*, Minstrel Bks) PB.

Lipman, Kennard, ed. see Norbu, Namkhai.

Lipman, Linda. Real Estate Advertising That Works! (Illus.). 298p. 1992. reprint ed. pap. 19.95 (*1-887145-01-X*) Argyle Pr NV.

Lipman, M., et al. An Atlas of Differential Diagnosis in HIV Disease. LC 94-21470. (Encyclopedia of Visual Medicine Ser.). 140p. 1994. 78.00 (*1-85070-474-0*) Prthnon Pub.

Lipman, M. C., et al. Illlustrated Handbook of Skin Disease in HIV Infection. LC 97-12646. (Illus.). 64p. 1997. pap. 24.95 (*1-85070-976-9*) Prthnon Pub.

***Lipman, M. C. I.** An Atlas of Differential Diagnosis in HIV Disease. 2nd ed. (Illus.). 2001. write for info. (*1-84214-026-4*) Prthnon Pub.

Lipman, M. C. I., jt. auth. see Wilson, P. L.

Lipman, Marc & Thomas, Paul. Visual Diagnosis Self-Tests on HIV Medicine. (Visual Diagnosis Self-Tests Ser.). (Illus.). 86p. 1997. pap. 12.95 (*1-873413-41-6*) Merit Pub Intl.

Lipman, Marc E., jt. ed. see Dickson, Robert B.

Lipman, Matthew. Deciding What to Do: Instructional Manual to Accompany Nous. 154p. 1997. spiral bd. 35.00 (*0-916834-31-X*) Inst Advncmnt Philos Child.

— Elfie, Set. (Philosophy for Children Ser.). 184p. 1987. pap. 10.50 (*0-916834-24-7*) Inst Advncmnt Philos Child.

— Harry Prime. 213p. 1991. pap. 8.00 (*0-916834-23-9*) Inst Advncmnt Philos Child.

— Harry Stottlemeier's Discovery. rev. ed. LC 76-9315. (Philosophy for Children Ser.). 96p. (J). (gr. 5-6). 1982. pap. 10.50 (*0-916834-06-9*, TX516-633) Inst Advncmnt Philos Child.

— Kio & Gus. LC 79-9315. (Philosophy for Children Ser.). 77p. (J). (gr. 3-4). 1982. pap. 10.50 (*0-916834-19-0*, TX942-173) Inst Advncmnt Philos Child.

— Lisa. (Philosophy for Children Ser.). 96p. (YA). (gr. 7-10). 1983. pap. 10.50 (*0-916834-21-2*) Inst Advncmnt Philos Child.

— Mark. LC 80-80849. (Philosophy for Children Ser.). 86p. (gr. 11-12). 1980. pap. 10.50 (*0-916834-13-1*, TX 752-903) Inst Advncmnt Philos Child.

— Natasha: Vygotskian Dialogues. LC 95-52526. 168p. (C). 1996. text 44.00 (*0-8077-3517-5*); pap. text 19.95 (*0-8077-3516-7*) Tchrs Coll.

— Nous. (Philosophy for Children Ser.). 77p. 1997. 10.50 (*0-916834-30-1*) Inst Advncmnt Philos Child.

— Philosophy Goes to School. LC 87-18071. 250p. (C). 1988. 34.95 (*0-87722-537-0*); pap. 19.95 (*0-87722-555-9*) Temple U Pr.

— Pixie. LC 81-67706. (Philosophy for Children Ser.). 98p. (Orig.). (J). (gr. 3-4). 1981. pap. 10.50 (*0-916834-17-4*, TX782-682) Inst Advncmnt Philos Child.

— Suki. (Philosophy for Children Ser.). 153p. (Orig.). (gr. 9-10). 1978. pap. 10.50 (*0-916834-08-5*, TX86-788) Inst Advncmnt Philos Child.

— Thinking Children & Education. 768p. 1993. per. 42.95 (*0-8403-8584-6*) Kendall-Hunt.

— Thinking in Education. 292p. (C). 1991. text 59.95 (*0-521-40032-5*); pap. text 22.95 (*0-521-40911-X*) Cambridge U Pr.

— What Happens in Art? LC 66-27473. (Century Philosophy Ser.). (Orig.). 1967. pap. text 12.95 (*0-89197-470-9*) Irvington.

Lipman, Matthew, ed. Contemporary Aesthetics. LC 73-76197. 1973. 39.50 (*0-89197-711-2*); pap. text 15.95 (*0-89197-712-0*) Irvington.

Lipman, Matthew & Gazzard, Ann. Getting Our Thoughts Together: Instructional Manual to Accompany Elfie. 600p. 1988. 45.00 (*0-685-25529-8*) Inst Advncmnt Philos Child.

Lipman, Matthew & Sharp, A. M. Ethical Inquiry: Instructional Manual to Accompany Lisa. rev. ed. LC 76-9316. 1985. spiral bd. 45.00 (*0-916834-05-0*, TX 508-097) Inst Advncmnt Philos Child.

— Looking for Meaning: Instructional Manual to Accompany Pixie. LC 81-71564. 390p. 1982. teacher ed., spiral bd. 45.00 (*0-916834-18-2*, TX932-050) Inst Advncmnt Philos Child.

Lipman, Matthew & Sharp, Ann M. Social Inquiry: Instructional Manual to Accompany Mark. 396p. 1980. teacher ed. 45.00 (*0-916834-15-8*, TX 758-975) Inst Advncmnt Philos Child.

— Wondering at the World: Instructional Manual to Accompany KIO & GUS. (Philosophy for Children Ser.). 500p. 1986. 45.00 (*0-916834-20-4*) Inst Advncmnt Philos Child.

— Writing How & Why: Instructional Manual to Accompany Suki. 384p. 1980. teacher ed. 45.00 (*0-916834-14-X*, TX 726-631) Inst Advncmnt Philos Child.

Lipman, Matthew, et al. Philosophical Inquiry: Instructional Manual to Accompany Harry Stottlemeier's Discovery. 2nd ed. LC 76-9315. 1979. spiral bd. 45.00 (*0-916834-12-3*, TX467-188) Inst Advncmnt Philos Child.

— Philosophy in the Classroom. 2nd ed. 248p. 1980. pap. 22.95 (*0-87722-183-9*) Temple U Pr.

Lipman, Maureen. You Can Read Me Like a Book. 1997. 26.95 (*0-86051-979-1*, Robson-Parkwest) Parkwest Pubns.

Lipman, Michel. Medical Law & Ethics. LC 93-1344. 139p. (C). 1993. pap. 19.60 (*0-13-064585-0*) P-H.

— True Stories of the Wild West. 1997. pap. text 8.95 (*0-912517-29-8*) Bluewood Bks.

— You Are the Justice. 80p. 1993. pap. 14.00 (*0-87879-982-6*) High Noon Bks.

Lipman, Michel & Furniss, Cathy. Legal Eagle Series, 5 novels, Set. Kratoville, Betty Lou, ed. (Illus.). 240p. (Orig.). (J). (gr. 4-12). 1988. pap. 17.00 (*0-87879-594-4*) High Noon Bks.

— You Are the Boss. 80p. (J). 1981. pap. 12.00 (*0-87879-356-9*) Acad Therapy.

— You Are the Driver. 80p. (J). 1981. pap. 12.00 (*0-87879-542-1*) Acad Therapy.

— You Are the Judge, Bk. 2. 80p. (J). 1981. pap. 12.00 (*0-87879-281-3*) Acad Therapy.

— You Are the Judge, No. 1. 80p. (J). 1981. pap. 12.00 (*0-87879-280-5*) Acad Therapy.

— You Are the Mayor. 80p. (J). 1981. pap. 12.00 (*0-87879-888-9*) Acad Therapy.

— You Are the School Counselor. 80p. (J). 1981. pap. 12.00 (*0-87879-675-4*) Acad Therapy.

Lipman, Michel, et al. You Are the Banker. 80p. (J). 1981. pap. 12.00 (*0-87879-676-2*) Acad Therapy.

Lipman, Pauline. Race, Class & Power in School Restructuring. LC 97-26328. (SUNY Series, Restructuring & School Change). 320p. (C). 1998. pap. text 20.95 (*0-7914-3770-1*) State U NY Pr.

Lipman, Peter W. & Mullineaux, Donal R., eds. The 1980 Eruptions of Mount St. Helens, Washington: Early Results of Studies of Volcanic Events in 1980, Geophysical Monitoring of Activity, & Studies of Volcanic Deposits, Effects, & Potential Hazards. LC 81-600142. (Illus.). 872p. 1997. 35.00 (*0-295-97623-3*) U of Wash Pr.

Lipman, Samuel. Music & More: Essays, 1968-1991. 318p. (Orig.). 1994. 35.00 (*0-8101-1051-2*); pap. 14.95 (*0-8101-1076-8*) Northwestern U Pr.

Lipman, Samuel, ed. see Arnold, Matthew.

Lipman, Steve. Laughter in Hell: The Use of Humor During the Holocaust. LC 90-28101. 296p. 1993. pap. 30.00 (*1-56821-112-0*) Aronson.

Lipman, Steve, ed. & intro. see Ozarowski, Joseph S., et al.

***Lipman, Timothy E.** Electric Vehicles Cost Studies. (Electric Vehicle Information Ser.: Vol. 30). (Illus.). 120p. 1999. pap. 85.00 (*0-89934-379-1*); lib. bdg. 135.00 (*0-89934-380-5*) Bus Tech Bks.

Lipman, V. D. History of the Jews in Britain since 1858. LC 90-4865. 255p. 1990. 48.00 (*0-8419-1288-2*) Holmes & Meier.

Lipman, Victoria. Leaving Alva. LC 97-23021. 1998. 21.50 (*0-684-83415-4*) S&S Trade.

Lipman-Wulf, Peter. Period of Internment: Letters & Drawings from Les Milles 1939-1940. LC 91-73296. (Illus.). 98p. (Orig.). 1993. pap. 15.00 (*0-9630164-5-8*) Canios Edit.

Lipman, Zada, ed. Local Government & Environmental Control in New South Wales. 160p. 1991. pap. 35.00 (*1-86287-074-8*, Pub. by Federation Pr) Gaunt.

Lipmann, Joel. Sweet Home Chicago. 1980. pap. 2.00 (*0-686-70612-9*) Quixote.

Lipmanson, Don, tr. see Crepin, Joseph.

Lipnack, Jessica & Stamps, Jeffrey. The TeamNet Factor: Bringing the Power of Boundary Crossing into the Heart of Your Business. 400p. 1995. 29.95 (*0-471-13188-1*) Wiley.

— The TeamNet Factor: Bringing the Power of Boundary-Crossing Teams into the Heart of Your Business. LC 92-85207. 256p. 1993. 27.50 (*0-939246-34-1*) Wiley.

***Lipnack, Jessica & Stamps, Jeffrey.** Virtual Teams: People Working Across Boundaries with Technology. 2nd ed. (Illus.). 352p. 2000. 29.95 (*0-471-38825-4*) Wiley.

Lipnack, Jessica & Stamps, Jeffrey. Virtual Teams: Reaching Across Space, Time & Organizations with Technology. LC 96-40505. 288p. 1997. 29.95 (*0-471-16553-0*) Wiley.

Lipner, jt. auth. see Fredericks, Robert F.

Lipner, Julius. The Face of Truth: A Study of Meaning & Metaphysics in the Vedantic Theology of Ramanuja. LC 84-24075. 183p. (C). 1986. pap. text 19.95 (*0-88706-039-0*) State U NY Pr.

— Hindus: Their Religious Beliefs & Practices. LC 93-3813. 400p. (C). (gr. 13). 1993. 90.00 (*0-415-05181-9*) Routledge.

Lipner, Julius J. Brahmabandhab Upadhyay: The Life & Thought of a Revolutionary. LC 99-932091. 434p. 1999. text 26.00 (*0-19-564264-3*) OUP.

— Hindus: Their Religious Beliefs & Practices. (Library of Religious Beliefs & Practices). 396p. (C). 1998. pap. 25.99 (*0-415-05182-7*) Routledge.

Lipner, Seth E. The Legal & Economic Aspects of Gray Market Goods. LC 90-30008. 240p. 1990. 65.00 (*0-89930-466-4*, LLC/, Quorum Bks) Greenwood.

Lipniacka, Ewa. To Bed... or Else! (ARA., Illus.). 32p. (J). (ps-2). 1996. write for info. (*1-85430-388-0*, Pub. by MAGI1 UK); write for info. (*1-85430-389-9*, Pub. by MAGI1 UK); write for info. (*1-85430-390-2*, Pub. by MAGI1 UK); write for info. (*1-85430-391-0*, Pub. by MAGI1 UK); write for info. (*1-85430-392-9*, Pub. by MAGI1 UK); write for info. (*1-85430-393-7*, Pub. by MAGI1 UK) Midpt Trade.

— To Bed...or Else! LC 91-22118. (Illus.). 32p. (J). (ps-3). 1996. pap. 7.95 (*1-56656-214-7*, Crocodile Bks) Interlink Pub.

***Lipniacka, Ewa.** The Xenophobe's Guide to the Poles. (Xenophobe's Guides Ser.). 64p. 2000. pap. 5.95 (*1-902825-40-3*) Oval Bks.

***Lipnick, Robert L., et al, eds.** Persistent, Bioaccumulative, Toxic Chemicals: Fate & Exposure. (ACS Symposium Ser.: Vol. 772). 2000. 120.00 (*0-8412-3674-7*, Pub. by Am Chemical) OUP.

— Persistent, Bioaccumulative, Toxic Chemicals Assessment & Emerging Chemicals. (ACS Symposium Ser.: No. 773). (Illus.). 464p. 2000. text 130.00 (*0-8412-3675-5*, Pub. by Am Chemical) OUP.

Lipnick, Robert L., ed. see Overton, Charles E.

Lipo, Carl P., jt. auth. see Dales, George F.

Lipo, Carl P., ed. see Sterling, Sarah L.

Lipo, T. A., jt. auth. see Novotny, D. W.

Lipoff, Elise, ed. see Institute of Medicine Staff.

Lipoprotein Research Group Staff & Vance, Dennis E., eds. Phosphatidylcholine Metabolism. 248p. 1989. lib. bdg. 191.00 (*0-8493-6338-1*, QP752) CRC Pr.

Lipori, Daniel, ed. see Ritter, George Wenzel.

Lipovetsky, Gilles. The Empire of Fashion: Dressing Modern Democracy. Porter, Catherine, tr. LC 94-4830. (New French Thought Ser.). 288p. 1994. text 29.95 (*0-691-03373-0*, Pub. by Princeton U Pr) Cal Prin Full Svc.

Lipovetsky, Mark. Russian Postmodernist Fiction: Dialogue with Chaos. Borenstein, Eliot, ed. LC 98-7649. 352p. 1999. text 70.95 (*0-7656-0176-1*) M E Sharpe.

***Lipovetsky, Mark.** Russian Postmodernist Fiction: Dialogue with Chaos. Borenstein, Eliot, ed. LC 98-7649. 352p. 1999. pap. text 28.95 (*0-7656-0177-X*) M E Sharpe.

***Lipovski, G. Jack.** Embedded Microcontroller Interfacing for M-COR Systems. (Engineering Ser.). 450p. 2000. 79.95 (*0-12-451832-X*) Acad Pr.

***Lipovski, Jack.** Introduction to Microcontroller Architecture, Programming & Interfacing. 1999. 59.95 (*0-12-451831-1*) Acad Pr.

Lipovski, Jack. Single & Multichip Microcontroller Interfacing: For the Motorola 6812. (Academic Press Engineering Ser.). (Illus.). 512p. (C). 1999. 69.95 incl. cd-rom (*0-12-451830-3*) Morgan Kaufmann.

Lipovsky, Igor P. The Socialist Movement in Turkey, 1960-1980. LC 92-18122. (Social, Economic & Political Studies of the Middle East: Vol. 45). 190p. 1992. 68.00 (*90-04-09582-9*) Brill Academic Pubs.

Lipovsky, James. A Historiographical Study of Livy. rev. ed. Connor, W. R., ed. LC 80-2657. (Monographs in Classical Studies). 1981. lib. bdg. 24.95 (*0-405-14043-6*) Ayer.

Lipovszky, G., et al. Vibration Testing of Machines & Their Maintenance. (Studies in Mechanical Engineering: No. 10). 312p. 1990. 189.50 (*0-444-98808-4*) Elsevier.

Lipow, Anne G., ed. Rethinking Reference in Academic Libraries. (Illus.). 242p. (Orig.). 1993. pap. text 32.00 (*1-882208-02-1*) Library Solns.

Lipow, Anne G. & Creth, Sheila D., eds. Building Partnerships: Computing & Library Professionals. xii, 102p. 1995. pap. text 29.00 (*1-882208-18-8*) Library Solns.

Lipow, Anne G., et al. Crossing the Internet Threshold: An Instructional Handbook. 2nd ed. LC 94-192824. (Illus.). 175p. (Orig.). 1995. reprint ed. spiral bd. 45.00 (*1-882208-07-2*) Library Solns.

Lipow, Anne G., ed. see LAMA Development Committee Staff.

Lipow, Arthur. Political Parties & Democracy: Explorations in History & Theory. LC 95-52788. 256p. 1996. 59.95 (*0-7453-1099-0*) Pluto GBR.

— Political Parties & Democracy: Explorations in History & Theory. 256p. 1996. pap. 22.95 (*0-7453-1098-2*, Pub. by Pluto GBR) Stylus Pub VA.

Lipow, Arthur, jt. ed. see Haberkern, Ernest E.

Lipow, Arthur, jt. ed. see MacGregor, Susanne.

Lipow, Hershel & Price, Erica J. Unlocking Doors to Opportunity: A Report on Affordable Housing Programs. (Illus.). 165p. (C). 1998. reprint ed. pap. text 45.00 (*0-7881-7478-9*) DIANE Pub.

Lipow, Valerie. Retailing Career Starter. LC 98-37939. (Career Starters Ser.). 208p. 1998. pap. 14.95 (*1-57685-149-4*) LrningExprss.

Lipowitz, Alan J., et al, eds. Complications in Small Animal Surgery: Diagnosis, Management, Prevention. (Illus.). 500p. 1996. 79.95 (*0-683-05047-8*) Lppncott W & W.

Lipowitz, K. B. & Boyd, Donald B., eds. Reviews in Computational Chemistry, Vol. 6. (Reviews in Computational Chemistry Ser.). 504p. 1995. 139.00 (*0-471-18596-5*) Wiley.

— Reviews in Computational Chemistry, Vol. 7. 414p. 1995. 139.00 (*0-471-18628-7*) Wiley.

— Reviews in Computational Chemistry, Vol. 8. 324p. 1996. 139.00 (*0-471-18638-4*) Wiley.

— Reviews in Computational Chemistry, Vol. 9. 282p. 1996. 139.00 (*0-471-18639-2*) Wiley.

— Reviews in Computational Chemistry, Vol. 10. 360p. 1996. 139.00 (*0-471-18648-1*) Wiley.

Lipowitz, Myron A., jt. auth. see Navarra, Tova.

Lipowski, Adam, jt. auth. see Kulig, Jan.

Lipowski, J. & Ross, P. N., eds. Frontiers of Electrochemistry: Adsorption of Molecules at Metal Electrodes, Vol. 1. (Frontiers of Electrochemistry Ser.). 414p. 1992. 199.95 (*0-471-18774-7*) Wiley.

Lipowski, J. & Ross, P. N., eds. Frontiers of Electrochemistry: Structure of Electrified Interfaces, Vol. 2. (Frontiers of Electrochemistry Ser.). 406p. 1993. 205.00 (*0-471-18816-6*) Wiley.

— Frontiers of Electrochemistry: The Electrochemistry of Novel Materials, Vol. 3. (Frontiers of Electrochemistry Ser.). 387p. 1994. 205.00 (*0-471-18775-5*) Wiley.

Lipowski, Jacek & Ross, Philip N., eds. Structure of Electrified Interfaces. LC 92-44292. (Frontiers of Electrochemistry Ser.). 406p. 1993. 125.00 (*0-89573-787-6*, Wiley-VCH) Wiley.

Lipowski, Zbigniew J. Delirium: Acute Confusional States. 512p. 1990. text 79.00 (*0-19-506150-0*) OUP.

An Asterisk (*) at the beginning of an entry indicates that the title is appearing for the first time.

— Psychosomatic Medicine & Liaison Psychiatry: Selected Papers. LC 85-12474. (Illus.). 470p. (C). 1985. text 108.00 (0-306-42038-4, Kluwer Plenum) Kluwer Academic.

***Lipowsky, Frank.** Offene Lernsituationen Im Grundschulunterricht: Eine Empirische Studie zur Lernzeitnutzung Von Grundschulern Mit Unterschiedlicher Konzentrationsfahigkeit. (Europaische Hochschulschriften: Reihe 11, Padagogik Ser.). X, 244p. 1999. 42.95 (3-631-35075-9) P Lang Pubng.

Lipowsky, Reinhard & Sackmann, Erich, eds. Structure & Dynamics of Membranes: From Cells to Vesicles; Generic & Specific Interactions, 2 vols. LC 95-8846. (Handbook of Biological Physics Ser.: Vol. 1A). 1036p. 1995. 353.25 (0-444-81975-4) Elsevier.

Lipp-Biesterfeld, Irene Van, see Van Lipp-Biesterfeld, Irene.

Lipp, Frank J. The Mixe of Oaxaca: Religion, Ritual, & Healing. (Illus.). 275p. 1998. pap. 16.95 (0-292-74705-5) U of Tex Pr.

Lipp, Frank J., Jr., jt. auth. see Von Reis, Siri V.

Lipp, Frederick. That Cat Is Not for Sale. (Illus.). 24p. (J). (ps-3). 1998. pap. 5.99 (0-9664248-0-8) Sloane Prtlnd ME.

Lipp, G. Douglas, jt. auth. see Clarke, Clifford H.

***Lipp, Hans P.** Anticancer Drug Toxicity: Prevention, Management & Clinical Pharmocokinetics LC 99-22837. (Illus.). 576p. 1999. text 195.00 (0-8247-1930-1) Dekker.

Lipp, Markus D. Local Anesthesia. (Illus.). 166p. 1993. text 198.00 incl. VHS (0-86715-273-7) Quint Pub Co.

Lipp, Markus D., et al. Local Anesthesia. Coldwell, Mark et al, trs. from GER. LC 93-12264. (Illus.). 166p. 1993. text 60.00 (0-86715-263-X) Quint Pub Co.

Lipp, Martin. Medical Landmarks, U. S. A. A Travel Guide to Historical Sites, Architectural Gems, Remarkable. 384p. 1990. pap. text 45.00 (0-07-037974-2) McGraw-Hill HPD.

Lipp, Martin R., jt. auth. see Whitten, David N.

Lipp, Reiner, jt. ed. see Brogyanyi, Bela.

Lipp, Solomon. Crucible of Ideas. (Wor(l)ds of Change Ser.: Vol. 19). XII, 310p. (C). 1996. text 54.95 (0-8204-2838-8) P Lang Pubng.

— U. S. A. - Spanish America: Challenge & Response. (Monagrafias A Ser.: No. 154). 166p. (C). 1994. 54.00 (1-85566-033-4, Pub. by Tamesis Bks Ltd) Boydell & Brewer.

Lipp, Susan R., et al, eds. 1998 New York City Apartment Management Checklist. 14th rev. ed. (Illus.). 355p. 1997. pap. 72.50 (0-913828-00-9) Brownstone NYC.

Lipp, Sylvia E., tr. see Delgado, Ana M.

Lipp, Sylvia E., tr. see Levinson, Luisa M.

Lipp, Thomas. Das Addision-Wesley Druckerbuch. (GER.). (C). 1990. text. write for info. (0-201-55914-5) Addison-Wesley.

Lippa. Introduction to Social Psychology. (Psychology Ser.). 1990. student ed. 17.50 (0-534-11773-2) Brooks-Cole.

Lippa, Erik A. Mathematics for Freshman in the Life Sciences. (Illus.). 319p. (Orig.). (C). 1977. pap. text 30.00 (0-9607980-0-5) E A Lippa.

***Lippa, Louis.** Sacco & Vanzetti. 37p. 1999. pap. 10.00 (0-929741-48-X) Playsmith.

Lippa, Louis. The Welfare Lady. 22p. (C). 1985. pap. 3.50 (0-87129-786-8, W31) Dramatic Pub.

Lippa, Richard A. Introduction to Social Psychology. 643p. (C). 1989. mass mkt. 54.75 (0-534-11772-4) Brooks-Cole.

— Introduction to Social Psychology. 2nd ed. 1993. mass mkt., teacher ed. write for info. (0-534-17391-8) Brooks-Cole.

— Introduction to Social Psychology. 2nd ed. LC 93-35816. 1994. mass mkt. 54.25 (0-534-17388-8) Brooks-Cole.

Lippard, Bernhard, ed. 30 Years of Cisplatin: Chemistry & Biochemistry of a Leading Anticancer Drug. 576p. 1999. 225.00 (3-906390-20-9) Wiley.

Lippard, Chris. By Angels Driven: The Films of Derek Jarman, 58. LC 96-23744. (Contributions to the Study of Popular Culture Ser.). 208p. 1996. 65.00 (0-313-30219-7, Greenwood Pr) Greenwood.

Lippard, Chris, ed. By Angels Driven: The Films of Derek Jarman. LC 96-23744. 208p. 1996. pap. 23.95 (0-275-95765-9, Praeger Pubs) Greenwood.

Lippard, George. Blanche of Brandywine. LC 77-76926. (American Fiction Reprint Ser.). 1977. 18.95 (0-8369-7005-5) Ayer.

— Empire City. LC 70-76927. (American Fiction Reprint Ser.). 1977. 18.95 (0-8369-7006-3) Ayer.

— New York: Its Upper Ten & Lower Million. LC 70-104514. 1989. reprint ed. pap. text 19.95 (0-8290-1855-7) Irvington.

— The Quaker City: or The Monks of Monk Hall: A Romance of Philadelphia Life, Mystery, & Crime. Reynolds, David S., ed. & intro. by. LC 94-44599. 632p. 1995. pap. 22.95 (0-87023-971-6) U of Mass Pr.

— Washington & His Generals: or Legends of the American Revolution. LC 70-164570. (American Fiction Reprint Ser.). Orig. Title: The Legends of the American Revolution, 1776. 1977. reprint ed. 35.95 (0-8369-7047-0) Ayer.

Lippard, Karl. Fabbri Shotguns. (Illus.). 66p. 1998. pap. 19.95 (0-9611880-4-9) Vietnam Mar.

Lippard, Karl C. Perazzi Shotguns. LC 93-61609. (Illus.). 121p. 1993. pap. 14.95 (0-9611880-2-2) Vietnam Mar.

— The Warriors, the United States Marines. LC 83-90360. (Illus.). 239p. 1983. 34.95 (0-9611880-0-6); lthr. 250.00 (0-9611880-1-4) Vietnam Mar.

Lippard, Lucy. Eva Hesse. (Illus.). 251p. 1992. reprint ed. pap. 18.95 (0-306-80484-0) Da Capo.

— Florence Pierce: In Touch with Light. (Illus.). 1998. 50.00 (0-9663199-5-8) Smith Bk Fund.

— Lure of the Local: The Sense of Place in a Multicentered Society. LC 96-23879. (Illus.). 150p. 1997. 40.00 (1-56584-247-2, Pub. by New Press NY) Norton.

— Overlay: Contemporary Art & the Art of Prehistory. 296p. 1995. pap. 20.00 (1-56584-238-3, Pub. by New Press NY) Norton.

Lippard, Lucy, contrib. by. Six Years: The Dematerialization of the Art Object from 1966 to 1972. LC 96-47552. (Illus.). 280p. 1997. pap. 19.95 (0-520-21013-1, Pub. by U CA Pr) Cal Prin Full Svc.

Lippard, Lucy & Middlebrook, Diane W. Backtalk. (Illus.). 48p. (Orig.). 1993. pap. 10.00 (1-880658-06-2) San Barb CAF.

Lippard, Lucy, et al. Distant Relations: Chicano, Irish, Mexican Art & Critical Writing. Ziff, Trisha, ed. (Illus.). 286p. 1995. pap. 25.00 (0-9646426-1-1) Smart Art Pr.

— Ethics of Change. Fetscher, Elmar, ed. (Proceedings of the February Forum Ser.). 150p. (Orig.). 1992. pap. text. write for info. (1-882070-07-0) Atlantic Ctr Arts.

— Jimmie Durham: The Bishop's Moose & the Pinkerton Men. Colo, Papo, ed. (Illus.). 36p. (Orig.). 1990. pap. 15.00 (0-913263-31-1) Exit Art.

Lippard, Lucy, jt. auth. see Lahs-Gonzales, Olivia.

Lippard, Lucy R. A Different War: Vietnam in Art. LC 89-70103. (Illus.). 120p. (Orig.). 1990. pap. 18.95 (0-941104-43-5) Real Comet.

— Lure of the Local: Senses of Place in a Multicentered Society. 1998. pap. 19.95 (1-56584-248-0, Pub. by New Press NY) Norton.

***Lippard, Lucy R.** Mixed Blessings: New Art in a Multicultural America. 2000. pap. 27.95 (1-56584-573-0, Pub. by New Press NY) Norton.

— On the Beaten Track: Tourism, Art & Place. (Illus.). 2000. reprint ed. pap. 17.95 (1-56584-639-7, Pub. by New Press NY) Norton.

Lippard, Lucy R. Partial Recall: Photographs of Native North Americans. LC 92-53737. (Illus.). 200p. (Orig.). 1993. 35.00 (1-56584-016-X, Pub. by New Press NY); pap. 19.95 (1-56584-041-0, Pub. by New Press NY) Norton.

— The Pink Glass Swan: Selected Feminist Essays on Art. LC 94-23406. 352p. 1995. pap. 20.00 (1-56584-213-8, Pub. by New Press NY) Norton.

— Pop Art. (World of Art Ser.). (Illus.). 216p. 1985. pap. 14.95 (0-500-20052-1, Pub. by Thames Hudson) Norton.

Lippard, Lucy R., et al, contrib. by. Mike Glier Vol. 1: Garden Court. unabridged ed. (Illus.). 56p. (Orig.). (C). 1995. pap. 15.00 (0-614-13762-4) Temple U Tyler Gal.

Lippard, Lucy R., contrib. by. On the Beaten Track: Tourism, Art, & Place. (Illus.). 192p. 1999. 25.00 (1-56584-454-8, Pub. by New Press NY) Norton.

Lippard, Lucy R., intro. Voices of Women: Three Critics on Three Poets on Three Artist-Heroines. 2nd rev. ed. LC 80-80281. (Illus.). 1990. pap. text 8.00 (0-9602476-1-0) Midmarch Arts.

Lippard, Lucy R. & Desmett, Don, contrib. by. Partial Recall: Photographs of Native North Americans, Vol. 1. unabridged ed. (Illus.). 32p. (Orig.). (C). 1993. pap. 10.00 (0-614-13761-6) Temple U Tyler Gal.

Lippard, Lucy R. & Goldman, Shifra M. Juan Sanchez: Rican-Structed Convictions. (Illus.). 32p. (Orig.). 1989. pap. 15.00 (0-913263-28-1) Exit Art.

Lippard, Lucy R. & Huerta, Benito. Inescapable Histories: Mel Chin. LC 97-217962. (Illus.). 62p. 1997. pap. 18.95 (1-882603-04-4) Mid Am Arts.

Lippard, Lucy R. & Nakane, Kazuko. Roger Shimomura: Delayed Reactions. 1995. 16.00 (0-913689-40-8) Spencer Muse Art.

Lippard, Lucy R., et al. The Submuloc Show - Columbus Wohs: A Visual Commentary on the Columbus Quincentennial from the Perspective of America's First People. Roberts, Carla A., ed. LC 92-71363. (Illus.). 80p. (Orig.). 1992. pap. 12.50 (1-881388-04-2) Atlatl.

Lippard, Lucy R., jt. auth. see Wylder, Vicki D. Thompson.

Lippard, Stephen J. Progress in Inorganic Chemistry, 8 vols., Vol. 35. (Progress in Inorganic Chemistry Ser.). 660p. 1987. 275.00 (0-471-84291-5, Wiley-Interscience) Wiley.

— Progress in Inorganic Chemistry, 8 vols., Vol. 37. (Progress in Inorganic Chemistry Ser.). 613p. 1989. 275.00 (0-471-62297-4) Wiley.

— Progress in Inorganic Chemistry, 8 vols., Vol. 38. (Progress in Inorganic Chemistry Ser.). 535p. 1991. pap. 98.95 (0-471-52945-1) Wiley.

— Progress in Inorganic Chemistry, Vol. 33, 8 vols., Vol. 33. (Progress in Inorganic Chemistry Ser.). 533p. 1985. 275.00 (0-471-80334-0, Wiley-Interscience) Wiley.

— Progress in Inorganic Chemistry, Vol. 34, 8 vols., Vol. 34. (Progress in Inorganic Chemistry Ser.). 701p. 1986. 275.00 (0-471-81948-4, Wiley-Interscience) Wiley.

— Progress in Inorganic Chemistry, Vol. 39, 8 vols., Vol. 39. (Progress in Inorganic Chemistry Ser.). 544p. 1991. 275.00 (0-471-54489-2) Wiley.

Lippard, Stephen J., ed. Platinum, Gold, & Other Metal Chemotherapeutic Agents. LC 82-24333. (Symposium Ser.: No. 209). 453p. 1983. lib. bdg. 65.95 (0-8412-0758-5) Am Chemical.

— Platinum, Gold, & Other Metal Chemotherapeutic Agents: Chemistry & Biochemistry. LC 82-24333. (ACS Symposium Ser.: No. 209). (Illus.). 464p. 1983. reprint ed. pap. 143.90 (0-608-03221-2, 206374000007) Bks Demand.

— Progress in Inorganic Chemistry, Vol. 40. LC 59-13035. 608p. 1992. 275.00 (0-471-57191-1) Wiley.

Lippard, Stephen J. & Berg, Jeremy. Principles of Bioinorganic Chemistry. LC 91-67871. (Illus.). 411p. (C). 1994. text 56.00 (0-935702-72-5) Univ Sci Bks.

Lipparo, Lucy & Cottingham, Laura. Hot Potato: From Formalism to Feminism. 1996. 35.00 (90-5701-011-9, Pub. by G & B); pap. 18.95 (90-5701-001-1, Pub. by G & B) Dist Art Pubs.

Lippart, Lucy. Michelle Stuart: The Elements, 1973-1979. 1992. pap. 15.00 (0-9634941-0-4) Fanbush.

Lippe, Anna L. von der, see Skoe, Eva & Von Der Lippe, Anna L.

Lippe, Aschwin. The Freer Indian Sculptures. (Occasional Studies: No. 8). 1970. 15.00 (0-934686-12-2) Freer.

Lippe, George B. Von Der, see Von Der Lippe, George B.

Lippe, Toinette, ed. see Dass, Ram & Gorman, Paul.

Lippencott, J. Daryl. My Life at a Glance. Fisher, Gail B., ed. 170p. 1995. write for info. (1-885001-09-6) Via Press.

***Lippens, Ronnie.** Chaohybrids: Five Uneasy Peaces. 168p. 2000. 36.50 (0-7618-1740-9) U Pr of Amer.

Lipper Analytical Services International Corporati. Lipper International Closed-End Funds Service, 2 vols., Set. McKinney, Cherie, ed. Orig. Title: Lipper Directory of Emerging Funds. 1200p. 1994. 4200.00 (0-9640376-4-5) Lipper Analytical.

Lipper, Ari. Buy, Buy, Baby: The Complete Sourcebook for Your New Baby. (Illus.). 256p. 1996. pap. 12.95 (0-8092-3201-4) NTC Contemp Pub Co.

Lipper, Arthur, III & Ryan, George. Thriving up & down the Free Market Food Chain. 224p. 1991. 20.00 (0-88730-518-0, HarpBusn) HarpInfo.

Lipper, Robert & Henry, Jacqueline, eds. International Trade Desk Manual: An Export Reference Guide. 6th ed. 1996. pap. write for info. (0-9619832-9-9) Island-Metro Pubns.

Lipper, Robert, ed. see Henry, Jacqueline.

Lipper, Robert, jt. ed. see Zurblis, Valerie.

***Lipper, Susan.** Nurturing Our Children to Succeed: A Guide for Helping Parents & Teachers Understand & Address the Emotional & Academic Challenges Facing Our Early Childhood Students. unabridged ed. LC 99-90403. (Illus.). xviii, 154p. (Orig.). 1999. pap. 14.95 (0-9674865-0-5) Budding Self.

Lipper, Susan. Trip: Photographs by Susan Lipper. LC 99-32084. (Illus.). 112p. 1999. 45.00 (1-57687-051-0) pwerHse Cultrl.

Lipper, Susan, photos by. Grapevine. (Illus.). 112p. 1995. 50.00 (0-948797-13-4) Dist Art Pubs.

Lipperheide, Frieda. Old Italian Patterns for Linen Embroidery. rev. ed. Epstein, Kathleen A., ed. & tr. by. from GER. (Illus.). 60p. 1996. 45.00 (0-9633331-7-8) Curious Works.

Lipperheide, Richard, jt. auth. see Frobrich, Peter.

Lippert, ed. see Ferdico, John N.

Lippert, Barbara, et al. Britain, Germany & EU Enlargement: Partners or Competitors? LC 98-52852. 160p. 1999. 44.95 (1-85567-612-5); pap. 15.95 (1-85567-613-3) Continuum.

— German Unification & EC Integration: German & British Perspectives. LC 93-15273. 1993. 14.95 (0-87609-147-8) Coun Foreign.

Lippert, Catherine B. Eighteenth Century English Porcelain in the Collection of the Indianapolis Museum of Art. LC 82-84076. (Indianapolis Museum of Art: Centennial Catalogue Ser.). (Illus.). 320p. 1987. 47.50 (0-936260-11-4); pap. 32.50 (0-936260-12-2) Ind Mus Art.

Lippert, Donald F. Mister B. (Illus.). 32p. (J). (ps). 1989. write for info. (0-318-64642-0) Pastel Pubns.

— Polly Popcan. (Illus.). 32p. (J). (ps). 1989. write for info. (0-318-64640-4) Pastel Pubns.

— Shag & the Bouncing Ball. (Illus.). 32p. (J). (ps). 1989. write for info. (0-318-64643-9) Pastel Pubns.

— The Tale of the Two Golden Doves. 64p. (Orig.). 1989. pap. 7.95 (0-925737-00-3) Pastel Pubns.

Lippert, E. Dictionary of Political Psychology: Handwoerterbuch der Politischen Psychologie. (ENG & GER.). 380p. 1983. 65.00 (0-8288-2256-5, M15264) Fr & Eur.

Lippert, E. & Macomber, J. D., eds. Dynamics During Spectroscopic Transitions: Relaxation Processes in Condensed Matter. LC 94-41054. 1995. write for info. (0-387-58703-9) Spr-Verlag.

— Dynamics During Spectroscopic Transitions: Relaxation Processes in Condensed Matter. LC 94-41054. 1995. 97.95 (3-540-58703-9) Spr-Verlag.

Lippert, G. Mitchel. Avoiding Taxes & Ohio Probate: Taking the Mystery Out of Probate in Ohio. LC 95-71768. (Illus.). 176p. (Orig.). 1995. pap. 12.95 (0-9649260-0-8) ProLaw.

Lippert, Julius. The Evolution of Culture, 2 vols. 1975. 500.00 (0-87968-158-6) Gordon Pr.

Lippert, Laurel, ed. see Frohlich, Robert & Humphries, S. E.

Lippert, Laurel H., ed. see Frohlich, Robert.

Lippert, Laurel H., ed. see Huggins, Ellie.

Lippert, Laurel H., ed. see Prosor, Larry & Moreno, Richard.

Lippert, Laurel H., ed. see Prosor, Larry & Popoff, Leo.

Lippert, Laurel H., ed. see Rose, Gene.

Lippert, Lynn S. Clinical Kinesiology for Physical Therapist Assistants. 3rd ed. (Illus.). 492p. 2000. pap. text 36.95 (0-8036-0453-X) Davis Co.

Lippert, Margaret, jt. auth. see Paye, Won-Ldy.

Lippert, Margaret H. Finist the Falcon: A Russian Legend. (Legends of the World Ser.). (Illus.). 32p. (J). (gr. 2-5). 1998. pap. 4.95 (0-8167-4025-9) Troll Communs.

— Finist the Falcon: A Russian Legend. (Legends of the World Ser.). 1996. 10.15 (0-606-09276-5, Pub. by Turtleback) Demco.

— La Hija de la Serpiente Marina - the Sea Serpent's Daughter: Una Leyenda Brasilena. LC 92-21438. (SPA.). (J). (gr. 4-7). 1997. pap. 4.95 (0-8167-3074-1) Troll Communs.

— La Hija de la Serpiente Marina - the Sea Serpent's Daughter: Una Leyenda Brasilena. LC 92-21438. (J). (gr. 4-7). 1997. lib. bdg. 18.60 (0-8167-3124-1) Troll Communs.

— The Sea Serpent's Daughter: A Brazilian Legend. LC 92-21438. (Legends of the World Ser.). (Illus.). 32p. (J). (gr. 2-5). 1997. pap. 4.95 (0-8167-3054-7) Troll Communs.

— The Sea Serpent's Daughter: A Brazilian Legend. LC 92-21438. (Legends of the World Ser.). (Illus.). 32p. (J). (gr. 2-5). 1997. lib. bdg. 16.65 (0-8167-3053-9) Troll Communs.

— Sea Serpent's Daughter: A Brazilian Legend. (Legends of the World Ser.). (J). 1993. 10.15 (0-606-05582-7, Pub. by Turtleback) Demco.

Lippert, Marion. Walking on Central Boulevard, Vol. 1. 128p. 1998. 19.95 (1-878398-10-5) Blue Note Pubns.

Lippert, Raymond & Segal, Richard A., Jr. Traditions: A Tribute to Wedding Cake Decorating. (Orig.). 1990. write for info. (0-9627704-0-X) Bakery Crafts.

Lippert, T., et al. Science on the Connection Machine: Proceedings of the 1st European Users Meeting. 236p. 1992. text 81.00 (981-02-1206-2) World Scientific Pub.

Lippert, T. H., ed. see Lippert, T. H., Ary Workshop Staff.

Lippert, T. H., Ary Workshop Staff. Sex Steroids & Cardiovascular System: The Proceedings of the 1st Interdisciplinary Workshop, Tubingen, Germany, October 1996. Lippert, T. H. et al, eds. LC 97-7110. (Illus.). 256p. 1998. 55.00 (1-85070-956-4) Prthnon Pub.

Lippert, W. & Podlech, D. Wild Flowers. (Illus.). 254p. 1994. 14.95 (0-00-219996-3, Pub. by HarpC) Trafalgar.

Lippert, Wayne R. Stay Alive: How to Street Fight with a Pistol. LC 95-90017. (Illus.). 270p. (Orig.). pap. text. write for info. (0-9645362-0-X) Fair Winds.

Lippert, Werner. Gunther Forg: The Large Drawings. (Illus.). 154p. 1992. 45.00 (1-56466-016-8) Archer Fields.

Lippett, Ingrid, ed. Trust Your Feelings: A Protective Behaviours Resource Manual for Primary School Teachers. (Illus.). (C). 1989. pap. text 80.00 (0-89771-037-1, Pub. by Essence Pubns) St Mut.

Lipphardt, Walter. Die Geistlichen Spiele des Sterzinger Spielarchivs Bd. 1: Debs-Codex. 2nd rev. ed. (Mittlere Deutsche Literatur in Neu- und Nachdrucken Ser.: Bd. 14). (GER.). 542p. 1986. 126.80 (3-261-03550-1) P Lang Pubng.

Lippi, Filippino, et al. The Drawings of Filippino Lippi & His Circle. LC 97-28294. 1997. 65.00 (0-87099-828-5) Metro Mus Art.

Lippi, Francesco. Central Bank Independence, Targets & Credibility: Political & Economic Aspects of Delegation Arrangements for Monetary Policy. LC 98-31058. 176p. 1999. 70.00 (1-85898-915-9) E Elgar.

Lippi-Green, Rosina L. English with an Accent. LC 96-33234. (Illus.). 304p. (C). 1997. 75.00 (0-415-11476-4); pap. 21.99 (0-415-11477-2) Routledge.

— Language Ideology & Language Change in Early Modern German: A Sociolinguistic Study of the Consonantal System of Nuremburg. LC 94-31088. (Current Issues in Linguistic Theory Ser.: No. 119). xiv, 150p. 1994. lib. bdg. 48.00 (1-55619-573-7) J Benjamins Pubng Co.

Lippi-Green, Rosina L., ed. Recent Developments in Germanic Linguistics. LC 92-34480. (Current Issues in Linguistic Theory Ser.: No. 93). xii, 163p. 1992. 47.00 (1-55619-154-5) J Benjamins Pubng Co.

Lippi-Green, Rosina L. & Salmons, Joseph C., eds. Germanic Linguistics: Syntactic & Diachronic. LC 96-21612. (Current Issues in Linguistic Theory Ser.: Vol. 137). viii, 192p. 1996. lib. bdg. 65.00 (1-55619-592-3) J Benjamins Pubng Co.

Lippi, Marco, jt. auth. see Forni, Mario.

Lippi, Robert. How to Buy Good Printing & Save Money: A Printing Buyers Guide. (Illus.). 144p. 1987. 17.95 (0-88108-041-1); pap. 14.95 (0-88108-042-X) Art Dir.

***Lippi, Rosina.** Homestead: A Novel. LC 97-35269. 224p. 1998. 21.00 (1-883285-14-3) Delphinium.

Lippi, Rosina. Homestead: A Novel. LC 99-22726. 224p. 1999. pap. 12.00 (0-395-97771-1) HM.

Lippiatt, Arthur & Wright, Graham. Architecture of Small Computer Systems. 2nd ed. (Illus.). 240p. (C). 1986. pap. text 19.95 (0-13-044744-7) P-H.

Lippiatt, Thomas F., et al. Postmobilization Traning Resource Requirements: Army National Guard Heavy Enhanced Brigades. LC 96-20308. (Illus.). 192p. 1997. pap. 15.00 (0-8330-2379-9, MR-662-A) Rand Corp.

— Time & Resources Required for Post-Mobilization Training of AC ARNG Integrated Heavy Divisions. LC 98-6320. (Illus.). 56p. 1998. pap. 15.00 (0-8330-2606-2) Rand Corp.

Lippiello, Patrick M., et al, eds. The Biology of Nicotine: Current Research Issues. LC 91-33820. 240p. 1992. reprint ed. pap. 74.40 (0-608-04707-4, 206542800004) Bks Demand.

Lippin, Tobi, ed. Working Women. (Southern Exposure Ser.). (Illus.). 128p. (Orig.). (C). 1981. pap. 4.00 (0-943810-12-4) Inst Southern Studies.

Lippincott, Benjamin E. Democracy's Dilemma: The Totalitarian Party in a Free Society. LC 65-12755. 303p. reprint ed. pap. 94.00 (0-608-30279-1, 201242000081) Bks Demand.

Lippincott, Catherine. Well Rounded. 1998. per. 14.00 (0-671-54509-4, PB Trade Paper) PB.

— Well Rounded: Eight Simple Steps for Changing Your Life...Not Your Size. LC 96-41486. 272p. 1997. 22.00 (0-671-54508-6) PB.

Lippincott, David, jt. auth. see Philyaw, Chuck.

Lippincott, E. P., jt. ed. see Farrar, Harry, IV.

Lippincott, Isaac. A History of Manufactures in the Ohio Valley to the Year 1860. LC 73-2518. (Big Business; Economic Power in a Free Society Ser.). 1977. reprint ed. 19.95 (0-405-05098-4) Ayer.

— A History of Manufactures in the Ohio Valley to the Year 1860. LC 73-19608. (Perspectives in American History Ser.: No. 14). viii, 214p. 1974. reprint ed. lib. bdg. 35.00 (0-87991-340-1) Porcupine Pr.

Lippincott, Joe. Care & Repair of Classic Cameras for Photographers & Collectors: How to Buy, Maintain, Repair, Modify Cameras, Lenses, Accessories & More. Krause, Karen, ed. (Illus.). 144p. (Orig.). 1999. pap. 29.95 (*0-9672079-0-8*) Joe Lippincott.

Lippincott, Joseph W. Old Bill, the Whooping Crane. (Illus.). (YA). (gr. 7-9). 1958. 10.95 (*0-397-30429-3*) HarpC Child Bks.

— Phantom Deer. (Illus.). (YA). (gr. 7-9). 1954. 11.95 (*0-397-30278-9*) HarpC Child Bks.

— Wilderness Champion: The Story of a Great Hound. LC 44-9586. (Illus.). 192p. (YA). (gr. 7-9). 1944. 11.95 (*0-397-30099-9*); lib. bdg. 11.89 (*0-397-31320-9*) HarpC Child Bks.

Lippincott, Kristen. Astronomy. LC 94-18479. (Eyewitness Books). (J). (gr. 4-7). 1994. 15.95 (*1-56458-680-4*) DK Pub Inc.

***Lippincott, Kristen, ed.** The Story of Time. 304p. 1999. 45.00 (*1-85894-072-9*, Pub. by Merrell Holberton) U of Wash Pr.

Lippincott, Lillian. A Bibliography of the Writings & Criticisms of Edwin Arlington Robinson. LC 74-1423. (American Literature Ser.: No. 49). 1974. lib. bdg. 75.00 (*0-8383-2049-X*) M S G Haskell Hse.

Lippincott, Louise. Edvard Munch, Starry Night. LC 88-13061. (Getty Museum Studies on Art). (Illus.). 98p. 1988. pap. 17.50 (*0-89236-139-5*, Pub. by J P Getty Trust) OUP.

— Lawrence Alma Tadema: Spring. LC 90-49669. (Getty Museum Studies on Art). (Illus.). 100p. 1991. pap. 17.50 (*0-89236-186-7*, Pub. by J P Getty Trust) OUP.

Lippincott, Louise W. & Boyle, Richard J. Young America: A Selection of Paintings from the Collection of the Penn. Academy of the Fine Arts. (Illus.). 80p. (Orig.). 1975. pap. 12.95 (*0-614-30568-3*) Penn Acad Art.

Lippincott-Raven Staff. Lippincott's Nursing Drug Guide, 2000. 1,456p. pap. text 32.95 (*0-7817-1985-2*) Lppncott W & W.

Lippincott-Raven Staff, ed. The Only EKG Book You'll Ever Need. 3rd ed. 1999. 29.95 (*0-7817-1667-5*) Lppncott W & W.

Lippincott, Robin. Mr. Dalloway. LC 98-31006. 232p. 1999. pap. 13.95 (*1-889330-29-9*, Pub. by Sarabande Bks) Consort Bk Sales.

***Lippincott, Robin.** Our Arcadia. 2000. 21.95 (*0-670-89273-4*) Viking Penguin.

Lippincott, Robin. The Real, True Angel, Vol. 1. unabridged ed. LC 96-84722. (Fleur-de-lis Ser.). 150p. 1996. pap. 12.00 (*0-9652520-0-0*) Fleur-de-lis Pr.

Lippincott, Sara J. Haps & Mishaps of a Tour in Europe. (American Biography Ser.). 437p. 1991. reprint ed. lib. bdg. 89.00 (*0-7812-8246-2*) Rprt Serv.

Lippincott, Sharon M. Meetings: Do's, Don'ts & Donuts: The Complete Handbook for Successful Meetings. 2nd rev. ed. LC 98-83112. 224p. 1999. pap. 16.95 (*0-9637966-6-6*) Lghthse Pt Pr.

Lippincott, W. T., ed. Essays in Physical Chemistry: A Sourcebook for Physical Chemistry Teachers. (Illus.). v, 174p. 1988. pap. 39.95 (*0-8412-1478-6*) Am Chemical.

Lippincott Williams & Wilkens Staff. Complete Preparation for the AHPAT, 2001: Allied Health Professions Admission Test. 320p. pap. text 28.95 (*0-7817-2836-3*) Lppncott W & W.

— Complete Preparation for the DAT, 2001: Dental Admission Test. 256p. pap. text 28.95 (*0-7817-2838-X*) Lppncott W & W.

— Complete Preparation for the MCAT, 2001: Medical College Admission Test. 688p. pap. text 49.95 (*0-7817-2839-8*) Lppncott W & W.

— Complete Preparation for the OAT, 2001: Optometry Admission Test. 248p. pap. text 28.95 (*0-7817-2840-1*) Lppncott W & W.

— Complete Preparation for the PCAT, 2001: Pharmacy College Admission Test. 320p. pap. text 28.95 (*0-7817-2841-X*) Lppncott W & W.

— Complete Preparation for the VETS, 2001: Veterinary Entrance Tests. 280p. pap. text 28.95 (*0-7817-2842-8*) Lppncott W & W.

***Lippincott Williams & Wilkens Staff, ed.** Stedman's Medical Dictionary. (Illus.). 2000. 59.95 (*0-7817-2728-6*, Lippnctt) Lppncott W & W.

Lippisch, Alexander. The Delta Wing: History & Development. Lippisch, Gertrude L., tr. LC 81-8166. 136p. reprint ed. pap. 42.20 (*0-608-13262-4*, 202513000042) Bks Demand.

Lippisch, Gertrude L., tr. see Lippisch, Alexander.

***Lippit, Akira M.** Electric Animal: Toward a Rhetoric of Wildlife. (Illus.). 2000. 22.95 (*0-8166-3485-8*) U of Minn Pr.

***Lippit, Akira Mizuta.** Electric Animal: Toward a Rhetoric of Wildlife. LC 99-86532. 2000. pap. write for info. (*0-8166-3486-6*) U of Minn Pr.

Lippit, Norika M. & Selden, Kyoko I., eds. Japanese Women Writers: Twentieth Century Short Fiction. LC 91-2924. (Japan in the Modern World Ser.). 312p. (gr. 13). 1991. pap. 24.95 (*0-87332-860-4*, East Gate Bk) M E Sharpe.

Lippit, Noriko M. Reality & Fiction in Modern Japanese Literature. LC 79-67859. 231p. 1980. reprint ed. pap. 71.70 (*0-7837-9925-X*, 206065200006) Bks Demand.

Lippit, Noriko M., et al, eds. Stories by Contemporary Japanese Women Writers. LC 82-10270. 245p. 1982. reprint ed. pap. 76.00 (*0-7837-9924-1*, 206065100006) Bks Demand.

Lippit, Noriko M., jt. ed. see Selden, Kyoko I.

Lippit, Victor D. The Economic Development of China. LC 86-20410. 280p. (gr. 13). 1987. pap. text 35.95 (*0-87332-404-8*) M E Sharpe.

Lippit, Victor D. Land Reform & Economic Development in China: A Study of Institutional Change & Development Finance. LC 74-15391. 194p. reprint ed. pap. 60.20 (*0-8357-2614-2*, 204010500014) Bks Demand.

Lippit, Victor D., ed. Radical Political Economy: Explorations in Alternative Economic Analysis. LC 95-16934. 402p. (C). (gr. 13). 1995. text 87.95 (*0-87332-606-7*); pap. text 39.95 (*0-87332-607-5*) M E Sharpe.

Lippit, Victor D., jt. ed. see Selden, Mark.

Lippitt. Nietzsche's Futures. LC 98-21080. 1998. text 55.00 (*0-312-21559-2*) St Martin.

Lippitt, Jill, ed. The National Women's Information Exchange Directory. LC 93-41914. 192p. (Orig.). 1994. pap. 10.00 (*0-380-77570-0*, Avon Bks) Morrow Avon.

***Lippitt, John M.** Humour & Irony in Kierkegaard's Thought. LC 00-26984. 2000. write for info. (*0-312-23474-0*) St Martin.

***Lippitt, John M., et al.** Hazardous Waste Handbook. 3rd ed. 320p. 1999. 39.95 (*0-7506-7135-1*) Buttrwrth-Heinemann.

Lippitt, John M., jt. ed. see Urpeth, Jim.

Lippitt, Lawrence L. Preferred Futuring: Envision the Future You Want & Unleash the Energy to Get There. LC 98-35916. 292p. 1998. pap. 24.95 (*1-57675-041-8*) Berrett-Koehler.

Lippitt, Peggy, et al. Cross-Age Helping Program: Orientation, Training & Related Materials. LC 78-164709. 242p. reprint ed. pap. 75.10 (*0-7837-5274-1*, 204501200005) Bks Demand.

Lippitt, Ronald, et al. Futuring. 176p. 1986. pap. text. write for info. (*0-201-15792-6*) Addison-Wesley.

***Lippke Fretwell, Holly.** Public Lands: Forests. Platts, Linda E., ed. (Illus.). 32p. 1999. pap. 5.00i (*0-9668243-3-4*) Pol Econo Res.

Lippke, Richard L. Radical Business Ethics. 240p. (C). 1995. pap. text 22.95 (*0-8476-8070-3*); lib. bdg. 58.50 (*0-8476-8069-X*) Rowman.

Lippke, Wolfgang, jt. ed. see Boireau, Nicole.

Lippman. A C++ Primer. 2nd ed. (C). 1992. pap. text. write for info. (*0-201-55690-1*) Addison-Wesley.

Lippman, Anna. The Babies. 36p. 1969. pap. 3.50 (*0-87129-154-1*, B10) Dramatic Pub.

Lippman, Carlee. Representations of Innocence in Literatures of the World: Strategies of Multicultural Narrative. LC 93-34509. 196p. 1993. text 79.95 (*0-7734-9394-8*) E Mellen.

Lippman, David B. A CPA's Guide to High-Risk Investment Strategies. 1998. pap. 45.00 (*0-87051-228-5*, 090447) Am Inst CPA.

Lippman, Deborah & Colin, Paul. How to Make Amulets & Charms: What They Mean & How to Use Them. LC 94-17781. (Illus.). 208p. 1994. 12.95 (*0-8065-1572-4*) Carol Pub Group.

Lippman, Edward A. A History of Western Musical Aesthetics. LC 91-47076. viii, 551p. 1992. pap. text 35.00 (*0-8032-7951-5*, Bison Books) U of Nebr Pr.

— Musical Thought in Ancient Greece. LC 74-23415. (Music Reprint Ser.). 1975. reprint ed. lib. bdg. 32.50 (*0-306-70669-5*) Da Capo.

Lippman, Edward A., contrib. by. The Philosophy & Aesthetics of Music. LC 98-43967. 1999. text 60.00 (*0-8032-2912-7*); pap. text 25.00 (*0-8032-7984-1*) U of Nebr Pr.

Lippman, Edward A., ed. Musical Aesthetics: A Historical Reader - The Nineteenth Century. LC 85-28415. (Aesthetics in Music Ser.: No. 4, Vol.II). 450p. 1988. lib. bdg. 73.00 (*0-918728-90-8*) Pendragon NY.

— Musical Aesthetics: A Historical Reader - The Twentieth Century. LC 85-28415. (Aesthetics in Music Ser.: No. 4, Vol. 3). 350p. 1990. lib. bdg. 73.00 (*0-945193-10-6*) Pendragon NY.

Lippman, Helen & Reardon, Patricia. Enjoying New Jersey Outdoors: A Year-Round Guide to Outdoor Recreation in the Garden State & Nearby. LC 90-44574. (Illus.). 216p. (C). 1991. pap. 11.95 (*0-8135-1655-2*); text 34.00 (*0-8135-1654-4*) Rutgers U Pr.

***Lippman, Jack C.** AlphaBet Cards: Games for Teaching Phonics: Grades K-2. Mitchell, Judy, ed. (Illus.). 80p. 1999. pap., teacher ed. 15.95 (*1-57310-196-6*) Teachng & Lrning Co.

Lippman, Kennard, tr. see Longchenpa.

Lippman, Laura. Baltimore Blues. 352p. 1997. mass mkt. 5.99 (*0-380-78875-6*, Avon Bks) Morrow Avon.

***Lippman, Laura.** Butchers Hill. LC 97-94929. (Tess Monaghan Mysteries Ser.: Vol. 3). 288p. 1998. mass mkt. 5.99 (*0-380-79846-8*, Avon Bks) Morrow Avon.

Lippman, Laura. Charm City. LC 97-93019. Vol. 2. 304p. 1997. mass mkt. 6.50 (*0-380-78876-4*, Avon Bks) Morrow Avon.

— In Big Trouble. 352p. 1999. mass mkt. 6.50 (*0-380-79847-6*, Avon Bks) Morrow Avon.

— Merchant of Venice. (C). 3.95 (*0-671-00637-1*, Arco) Macmillan Gen Ref.

***Lippman, Laura.** The Sugar House: A Tess Monaghan Mystery. 320p. 2000. 24.00 (*0-380-97817-2*, Wm Morrow) Morrow Avon.

— Urban Schools: The Challenge of Location & Poverty. 230p. (Orig.). 1996. pap. 15.00 (*0-16-048669-6*) USGPO.

— Urban Schools: The Challenge of Location & Poverty, Executive Summary. 17p. 1996. pap. 1.00 (*0-16-048671-8*) USGPO.

Lippman, Laura, et al. Urban Schools: The Challenge of Location & Poverty. (Illus.). 196p. (Orig.). (C). 1996. pap. text 35.00 (*0-7881-3632-1*) DIANE Pub.

Lippman, Leopold D. & Goldberg, I. Ignacy. Right to Education: Anatomy of the Pennsylvania Case & Its Implications for Exceptional Children. LC 73-78038. (Teachers College Series in Special Education). 153p. reprint ed. pap. 47.50 (*0-608-18801-8*, 203017200067) Bks Demand.

Lippman, M. E., ed. see Dickson, Robert B.

Lippman, Marc E. & Dickson, Robert B., eds. Regulatory Mechanisms in Breast Cancer: Advances in Cellular & Molecular Biology of Breast Cancer. (Cancer Treatment & Research Ser.). (C). 1991. text 237.00 (*0-7923-0868-9*) Kluwer Academic.

Lippman, Marc E., et al. Diagnosis & Management of Breast Cancer. (Illus.). 480p. 1988. text 98.00 (*0-7216-1958-4*, W B Saunders Co) Harcrt Hlth Sci Grp.

Lippman, Marc E., jt. auth. see Thompson, E. Brad.

Lippman, Marc E., jt. ed. see Dickson, Robert B.

Lippman, Marcia. Marcia Lippman's Angels. 1995. pap. 8.95 (*0-8118-1191-3*) Chronicle Bks.

***Lippman, Marcia, photos by.** Marcia Lippman: Sacred Encounters, East & West. (Illus.). 2000. 70.00 (*3-908163-26-9*, Pub. by Edit Stemmle) Abbeville Pr.

Lippman, Marcia Z., et al. Developmental Psychology: Childhood & Adolescence. 4th ed. 1995. pap., teacher ed. write for info. (*0-534-26437-9*) Brooks-Cole.

Lippman, Marcia Z., jt. auth. see Clark, Nancy P.

Lippman, Matthew, et al. Islamic Criminal Law & Procedure: An Introduction. LC 88-4037. 183p. 1988. 55.00 (*0-275-93009-2*, C3009, Praeger Pubs) Greenwood.

Lippman, Paul. American Typewriters: A Collector's Encyclopedia. 288p. 1992. 55.00 (*0-9633201-0-6*) Orig & Copy.

Lippman, Paul, jt. auth. see Fryman, Joseph.

Lippman, Paul, ed. see Arnold, Lyle.

Lippman, Peter. The ABC Doghouse. (Mini House Bks.). (Illus.). 20p. (YA). 1999. bds. 9.95 (*0-7611-0947-1*) Workman Pub.

— Busy Trains. LC 77-86145. (Pictureback Ser.). (Illus.). 32p. (J). (ps-3). 1981. pap. 3.25 (*0-394-83748-7*, Pub. by Random Bks Yng Read) Random.

— The Enchanted Castle. (Mini House Bks.). (Illus.). 20p. (J). (ps-1). 1995. bds. 9.95 (*0-7611-0109-8*, 10109) Workman Pub.

— Firehouse Co. No. 1. (Mini House Bks.). (Illus.). 20p. (J). (ps up). 1994. bds. 9.95 (*1-56305-663-1*, 3663) Workman Pub.

— From Here to There. LC 75-19947. (Illus.). 48p. (J). (gr. 1 up). 1975. pap. 5.00 (*0-912846-11-9*) Bookstore Pr.

— The Haunted House. (Mini House Bks.). (Illus.). 20p. (J). (ps-1). 1994. bds. 9.95 (*1-56305-731-X*, 3731) Workman Pub.

— Mother Goose's House. (Mini House Bks.). (Illus.). 20p. (J). (ps-1). 1996. bds. 9.95 (*0-7611-0536-0*, 10536) Workman Pub.

— Noah's Ark. (Mini House Bks.). (Illus.). 20p. (J). (ps-1). 1994. bds. 9.95 (*1-56305-662-3*, 3662) Workman Pub.

— Old MacDonald's Barn. (Mini House Bks.). (Illus.). 20p. (J). (ps). 1993. bds. 9.95 (*1-56305-500-7*, 3500) Workman Pub.

— Santa's Workshop. (Mini House Bks.). (Illus.). 20p. (J). (ps-1). 1993. bds. 9.95 (*1-56305-499-X*, 3499) Workman Pub.

***Lippman, Peter.** 3 Pigs' Garage. LC 99-229407. 20p. 1998. bds. 9.95 (*0-7611-1361-4*) Workman Pub.

Lippman, Stanley B. A-C Plus Plus Primer. (Illus.). 448p. (C). 1989. pap. text 23.96 (*0-201-16487-6*) Addison-Wesley.

— C++ Gems: Programming Pearls from the C++ Report. (SIGS Reference Library: No. 5). 625p. (Orig.). (C). 1996. pap. 44.95 (*0-13-570581-9*) Cambridge U Pr.

— C++ Primer. 2nd ed. (Illus.). 640p. (C). 1991. pap. 42.95 (*0-201-54848-8*) Addison-Wesley.

— The C++ Primer. 2nd ed. (C). 1993. pap. text. write for info. (*0-201-59482-X*) Addison-Wesley.

— Inside the C++ Program & Object Models. 304p. (C). 1996. pap. 39.95 (*0-201-83454-5*) Addison-Wesley.

***Lippman, Stanley B.** Shortcuts to C++ LC 99-46613. 304p. 1999. pap. text 33.95 (*0-201-48518-4*) Addison-Wesley.

Lippman, Stanley B. & Lajoie, Jose. C++ Primer. 3rd ed. LC 98-9464. 1264p. (C). 1998. pap. text 45.95 (*0-201-82470-1*) Addison-Wesley.

Lippman, Steven A., jt. ed. see Levine, David K.

Lippman, Susannah, ed. see Weiss, Bonnie.

***Lippman, Thomas W.** Madeleine Albright & the New American Diplomacy. LC 00-27464. 288p. 2000. 27.00 (*0-8133-9767-7*, Pub. by Westview) HarpC.

Lippman, Thomas W. Understanding Islam: An Introduction to the Muslim World. 2nd rev. ed. 208p. 1995. pap. 12.95 (*0-452-01160-4*, Plume) Dutton Plume.

Lippman, Thomas W., compiled by. The Washington Post Deskbook on Style. 2nd ed. (C). 1990. text 9.95 (*0-07-068414-6*) McGraw.

Lippman, Walter. A Preface to Morals. LC 82-2035. (Social Science Classics Ser.). 375p. 1982. reprint ed. pap. 21.95 (*0-87855-907-8*) Transaction Pubs.

— Public Opinion. LC 97-5340. 1997. per. 13.00 (*0-684-83327-1*) S&S Trade.

Lippmann. Environmental Toxicants. 2nd ed. (Environmental Health Ser.). 1998. pap. 114.95 (*0-442-02670-6*, VNR) Wiley.

***Lippmann, Edward.** Architecture for a New Millennium. 2000. pap. 25.00 (*88-7838-075-X*) L'Arca IT.

Lippmann, Edward A., ed. Musical Aesthetics: A Historical Reader - The Eighteenth Century, 1 of 3 vols., Vol. I. LC 85-28415. (Aesthetics in Music Ser.: Vol. 1, No. 4). 430p. 1986. text 73.00 (*0-918728-41-X*) Pendragon NY.

Lippmann, H., ed. see CISM (International Center for Mechanical Sciences.

Lippmann, John. Deeper into Diving. (Illus.). 610p. (Orig.). 1991. pap. 45.00 (*0-9590306-3-8*) Aqua Quest.

— The Essentials of Deeper Sport Diving. LC 91-71776. (Illus.). 320p. (Orig.). 1992. pap. 21.95 (*0-9623389-3-1*) Aqua Quest.

***Lippmann, Morton.** Environmental Toxicants: Human Exposures & Their Health Effects. 2nd ed. LC 99-21927. 1008p. 1999. text 185.00 (*0-471-29298-2*) Wiley.

Lippmann, Morton, ed. Environmental Toxicants: Human Exposures & Their Health Effects. 699p. 1991. text 120.95 (*0-442-00549-0*, VNR) Wiley.

Lippmann, Richard P., et al, eds. Advances in Neural Information Processing Systems, Vol. 3. 1060p. (C). 1991. text 51.95 (*1-55860-184-8*) Morgan Kaufmann.

Lippmann, Walter. American Inquisitors. LC 92-16068. 142p. (C). 1992. pap. 24.95 (*1-56000-635-8*) Transaction Pubs.

— Drift & Mastery. LC 85-40764. 192p. 1986. reprint ed. pap. 17.95 (*0-299-10604-7*) U of Wis Pr.

— Force & Ideas: The Early Writings. LC 99-46898. 366p. 1999. pap. 29.95 (*0-7658-0620-7*) Transaction Pubs.

— An Inquiry into the Principles of the Good Society. LC 72-7871. 402p. 1973. reprint ed. lib. bdg. 70.00 (*0-8371-6522-9*, LIGS, Greenwood Pr) Greenwood.

— Liberty & the News. LC 94-44023. 92p. 1995. pap. 21.95 (*1-56000-809-1*) Transaction Pubs.

— The Method of Freedom. 146p. (C). 1991. pap. text 21.95 (*1-56000-559-9*) Transaction Pubs.

— The Phantom Public: Library of Conservative Thought. rev. ed. LC 92-41593. 225p. (C). 1993. pap. text 24.95 (*1-56000-677-3*) Transaction Pubs.

— Public Opinion. LC 97-28875. 463p. 1997. pap. text 24.95 (*1-56000-999-3*) Transaction Pubs.

— Public Persons. Harrison, Gilbert A., ed. 189p. 1976. 7.95 (*0-87140-620-9*, Pub. by Liveright) Norton.

— The Public Philosophy. 209p. 1989. pap. 24.95 (*0-88738-791-8*) Transaction Pubs.

Lippner, Alice Jane. The Managed Care Course: The Easy Way to Learn What You Can't Afford Not to Know. (Illus.). 304p. 1997. pap. 65.00 (*0-9662096-0-5*) Infobriefings.

Lippold. Nonverbal Communication. 2nd ed. 1988. teacher ed. 16.00 (*0-07-553824-5*) McGraw.

Lippoldt, Douglas, ed. Labour Market Dynamics in the Russian Federation. LC 98-136141. 161p. 1997. pap. 15.00 (*92-64-15979-7*, 14-97-12-1, Pub. by Org for Econ) OECD.

Lippoldt, Douglas, jt. auth. see Fay, Robert.

Lipponer, George. The End of Forever. 200p. 1993. write for info. (*0-89962-624-6*) Dove Pub NY.

— Mending Fences. 350p. (Orig.). 1989. pap. write for info. (*0-9624158-0-4*) Dove Pub NY.

Lipps. Our Oceans. (C). 1997. teacher ed. write for info. (*0-02-371042-X*, Macmillan Coll) P-H.

Lipps, Gottlob F. Mythenbildung und Erkenntnis: Eine Abhandlung Uber die Grundlagen der Philosophie. Bolle, Kees W., ed. LC 77-79141. (Mythology Ser.). 1978. lib. bdg. 30.95 (*0-405-10550-9*) Ayer.

Lipps, J. H. & Signor, P. W. Origin & Early Evolution of the Metazoa. (Topics in Geobiology Ser.: Vol. 10). (Illus.). 578p. (C). 1992. text 120.00 (*0-306-44067-9*, Kluwer Plenum) Kluwer Academic.

Lipps, Jere H. Our Oceans. (C). 1997. 61.00 (*0-02-371041-1*, Macmillan Coll) P-H.

Lipps, Jere H., et al. Foraminiferal Ecology & Paleoecology. LC 79-112303. (SEPM Short Course Ser.: Vol. 6). (Illus.). 205p. 1979. reprint ed. pap. 63.60 (*0-608-05676-6*, 206619200006) Bks Demand.

Lipps, Oscar H. The Case of the California Indians. fac. ed. (Illus.). 49p. (C). 1932. reprint ed. pap. text 5.31 (*1-55567-794-0*) Coyote Press.

Lipps, Theodor. Psychological Studies. 2nd ed. LC 73-2972. (Classics in Psychology Ser.). 1974. reprint ed. 23.95 (*0-405-05145-X*) Ayer.

Lipps, Theodore. Consonance & Dissonance in Music. LC 94-62085. 142p. 1995. 21.00 (*0-940459-18-3*) Everett Bks.

Lippson, Alice J., ed. The Chesapeake Bay in Maryland: An Atlas of Natural Resources. LC 72-12352. 64p. 1973. 30.00 (*0-8018-1467-7*) Johns Hopkins.

Lippson, Alice J., et al, eds. Environmental Atlas of the Potomac Estuary. (Illus.). 285p. 1981. 35.00 (*0-8018-2618-7*) Johns Hopkins.

Lippson, Alice J. & Lippson, Robert L. Life in the Chesapeake Bay. LC 83-11278. 240p. 1984. text 39.95 (*0-8018-3012-5*); pap. text 16.95 (*0-8018-3013-3*) Johns Hopkins.

— Life in the Chesapeake Bay. 2nd ed. LC 96-27103. (Illus.). 304p. 1997. pap. 19.95 (*0-8018-5475-X*); text 39.95 (*0-8018-5476-8*) Johns Hopkins.

Lippson, Robert L., jt. auth. see Lippson, Alice J.

Lippucci, Alessandra, jt. auth. see Edwards.

Lippucci, Alessandra, jt. auth. see Edwards, David.

Lippucci, Alessandra, jt. auth. see Edwards, David V.

Lippy. Encyclopedia of the American Religious Experience, Vol. 1. 1988. 110.00 (*0-684-18861-9*) Mac Lib Ref.

— Encyclopedia of the American Religious Experience, Vol. 2. 1987. 110.00 (*0-684-18862-7*) Mac Lib Ref.

— Encyclopedia of the American Religious Experience, Vol. 3. 1987. 110.00 (*0-684-18863-5*) Simon & Schuster.

Lippy, Charles H. Being Religious, American Style: A History of Popular Religiosity in the United States. LC 93-50545. 296p. 1994. pap. 21.95 (*0-275-94901-X*, Praeger Pubs) Greenwood.

— Being Religious, American Style: A History of Popular Religiosity in the United States, 37. LC 93-50545. (Series Contributions to the Study of Religion: Vol. 37). 296p. 1994. 75.00 (*0-313-27895-4*, Greenwood Pr) Greenwood.

— The Christadelphians in North America. (Studies in American Religion: Vol. 43). 320p. 1989. write for info. (*0-88946-647-5*) E Mellen.

— Modern American Popular Religion: A Critical Assessment & Annotated Bibliography, 37. LC 95-46009. (Bibliographies & Indexes in Religious Studies: No. 37). 264p. 1996. lib. bdg. 75.00 (*0-313-27786-9*, Greenwood Pr) Greenwood.

An Asterisk (*) at the beginning of an entry indicates that the title is appearing for the first time.

***Lippy, Charles H.** Pluralism Comes of Age: American Religious Culture in the Twentieth Century. LC 99-88431. 264p. 2000. text 34.95 (*0-7656-0150-8*) M E Sharpe.

Lippy, Charles H., ed. Religion in South Carolina. LC 92-46310. 247p. 1993. text 24.95 (*0-87249-891-3*) U of SC Pr.

— Religious Periodicals of the United States: Academic & Scholarly Journals. LC 85-9861. (Historical Guides to the World's Periodicals & Newspapers Ser.). 626p. 1986. lib. bdg. 85.00 (*0-313-23420-5*, LRP/, Greenwood Pr) Greenwood.

— Twentieth-Century Shapers of American Popular Religion. LC 88-15487. 519p. 1989. lib. bdg. 99.50 (*0-313-25356-0*, LTW/, Greenwood Pr) Greenwood.

Lippy, Charles H. & Williams, Peter W., eds. Encyclopedia of the American Religious Experience, 3 vols., Set. 1872p. 1987. 350.00 (*0-684-18062-6*, Scribners Ref) Mac Lib Ref.

Lippy, Charles H., et al. Christianity Comes to the Americas, 1492-1776. (Illus.). 384p. 1992. 24.95 (*1-55778-234-2*) Paragon Hse.

— Christianity Comes to the Americas, 1492-1776. LC 92-8490. 400p. 1992. pap. 18.95 (*1-55778-501-5*) Paragon Hse.

Lippy, Charles H., jt. auth. see Krapohl, Robert H.

Lippy, Charles H., jt. ed. see Fackler, Mark P.

Lippy, Elsie. God's Story. (Illus.). 10p. (J). (gr. k-6). 1989. pap. text 2.50 (*1-55976-128-8*) CEF Press.

Lippy, John. Chemical Magic. 164p. pap. 4.00 (*0-913022-32-2*) Angriff Pr.

***Lippy, Tod.** Projections, Vol. 11. Vol. 11. (Illus.). 304p. 2000. pap. 20.00 (*0-571-20591-7*) Faber & Faber.

Lips, Christine Hart. The White Stone. LC 98-83082. 220p. 2000. pap. 14.95 (*0-88739-242-3*) Creat Arts Bk.

Lips, Hilary M. A New Psychology of Women: Gender, Culture & Ethnicity. LC 98-19271. xviii, 413p. 1999. pap. text 40.00 (*1-55934-334-6*, 334-6) Mayfield Pub.

— A New Psychology of Women: Instructor's Manual. (C). 1999. pap. text. write for info. (*0-7674-1047-5*, 1047-5) Mayfield Pub.

— Sex & Gender: An Introduction. 3rd rev. ed. LC 96-21490. 513p. (C). 1996. pap. text 41.95 (*1-55934-630-2*, 1630) Mayfield Pub.

— Sex & Gender: Instructor's Manual. 3rd ed. 143p. (C). 1996. pap. text, teacher ed. write for info. (*1-55934-631-0*, 1631) Mayfield Pub.

— Women, Men, & Power. LC 90-41065. 245p. (C). 1991. pap. text 31.95 (*0-87484-916-0*, 916) Mayfield Pub.

Lips, J. M., jt. auth. see Duivenvoorden, J. F.

Lipscher, Randolph B., jt. auth. see Donnelly, Joseph L.

Lipschitz, Chaim U. Franco, Spain, the Jews & the Holocaust. 1983. 25.00 (*0-88125-025-2*) Ktav.

Lipschitz, Leslie, et al. Federal Republic of Germany: Adjustment in a Surplus Country. (Occasional Papers: No. 64). ix, 103p. 1989. pap. 7.50 (*1-55775-088-2*) Intl Monetary.

Lipschitz, O., jt. ed. see Bron, H.

Lipschitz, Y. Y., ed. Movo Lekrioh. large type ed.Tr. of Introduction to Reading. (HEB.). 32p. (J). (gr. k-2). 1997. pap. 3.00 (*0-8266-0176-6*, Merkos LInyonei Chinuch) Kehot Pubn Soc.

***Lipschultz, Andy.** How the Grinch Stole Hollywood: The Making of the Movie. (Illus.). 2000. pap. 14.95 (*0-375-80629-6*) Random.

***Lipschultz, Jeremy & Holtzman, Stan.** Classic American Semi-Trucks. LC 00-28175. (Illus.). 156p. 2000. pap. 24.95 (*0-7603-0825-X*, 130718AP, Pub. by MBI Pubg) Motorbooks Intl.

Lipschultz, Jeremy H. Broadcast Indecency: FCC Regulation & the First Ammendment. 2nd ed. (Broadcasting & Cable Ser.). 261p. 1996. pap. 35.95 (*0-240-80208-X*, Focal) Buttrwrth-Heinemann.

***Lipschultz, Jeremy H.** Free Expression in the Age of the Internet. LC 99-41536. 1999. pap. 25.00 (*0-8133-9113-X*) Westview.

Lipschultz, Seymour. Schaum's Probability. 160p. (C). 1968. pap. 14.95 (*0-07-037982-3*) McGraw.

Lipschutz, Barbara. Contractions. 1974. pap. 2.50 (*0-912786-28-0*) Know Inc.

Lipschutz, Kurt. The Good Neighbor Policy. (End of the Century Bks.). 88p. 1989. pap. 5.95 (*0-926664-03-4*) Bay Area Ctr Art & Tech.

Lipschutz, Martin. Differential Geometry. (Schaum's Outline Ser.). 288p. (C). 1969. pap. 12.95 (*0-07-037985-8*) McGraw.

***Lipschutz, Ronnie D.** After Authority: War, Peace & Global Politics in the 21st Century. LC 99-38551. (C). 2000. pap. text 19.95 (*0-7914-4562-3*) State U NY Pr.

— After Authority: War, Peace & Global Politics in the 21st Century. LC 99-38551. (C). 2000. text 59.50 (*0-7914-4561-5*) State U NY Pr.

Lipschutz, Ronnie D. When Nations Clash: Raw Materials, Ideology, & Foreign Policy. 336p. 1989. text 34.95 (*0-88730-366-8*, HarpBusn); pap. text 19.95 (*0-88730-390-0*, HarpBusn) HarpInfo.

Lipschutz, Ronnie D., ed. On Security. LC 95-16627. (New Directions in World Politics Ser.). 1995. 57.50 (*0-231-10270-4*) Col U Pr.

— On Security. LC 95-16627. (New Directions in World Politics Ser.). 240p. 1995. pap. 19.50 (*0-231-10271-2*) Col U Pr.

Lipschutz, Ronnie D. & Conca, Ken, eds. The State & Social Power in Global Environmental Politics. LC 93-15878. (New Directions in World Politics Ser.). 363p. 1993. 57.50 (*0-231-08106-5*); pap. 22.00 (*0-231-08107-3*) Col U Pr.

Lipschutz, Ronnie D. & Mayer, Judith. Global Civil Society & Global Environmental Governance: The Politics of Nature from Place to Planet. LC 95-52245. (SUNY Series in International Environmental Policy & Theory). 365p. (C). 1996. text 57.50 (*0-7914-3117-7*); pap. text 20.95 (*0-7914-3118-5*) State U NY Pr.

Lipschutz, Ronnie D., jt. ed. see Crawford, Beverly.

Lipschutz, Seymour. General Topology. 256p. (Orig.). (C). 1968. pap. 14.95 (*0-07-037988-2*) McGraw.

— Schaum's Outline of Beginning Linear Algebra. LC 96-9004. (Illus.). 473p. (C). 1996. pap. 15.95 (*0-07-038037-6*) McGraw.

— Schaum's Outline of Essential Computer Mathematics. 256p. (C). 1982. pap. 15.95 (*0-07-037990-4*) McGraw.

— Schaum's Outline of Finite Mathematics: Including Hundreds of Solved Problems. 2nd ed. (Schaum's Outline Ser.). 483p. (C). 1995. pap. 15.95 (*0-07-038002-3*) McGraw.

— Schaum's Outline of Linear Algebra. 2nd ed. (Schaum's Outline Ser.). 368p. (C). 1991. pap. 15.95 (*0-07-038007-4*) McGraw.

***Lipschutz, Seymour.** Schaum's Outline of Linear Algebra. 3rd ed. (Schaum's Outlines Ser.). (Illus.). 2000. pap. 15.95 (*0-07-136200-2*) McGraw.

— Schaum's Outline of Theory & Problems of Probability. 2nd ed. LC 99-59283. (Schaum's Outlines Ser.). 311p. 2000. pap. 15.95 (*0-07-135203-1*) McGraw.

Lipschutz, Seymour. Schaum's Three Thousand Solved Problems in Linear Algebra. 750p. (C). 1989. pap. 24.95 (*0-07-038023-6*) McGraw.

— Set Theory & Related Topics. 240p. (Orig.). (C). 1967. pap. 14.95 (*0-07-037986-6*) McGraw.

— Set Theory & Related Topics. 2nd ed. LC 98-8685. (Schaum's Outline Ser.). (Illus.). 200p. (Orig.). 1998. pap. 15.95 (*0-07-038159-3*) McGraw.

— Two Thousand Solved Problems in Discrete Mathematics. (Schaum's Solved Problems Ser.). 404p. (C). 1992. pap. 19.95 (*0-07-038031-7*) McGraw.

Lipschutz, Seymour & Lipson, Marc. Schaum's Outline of Discrete Mathematics. 2nd ed. LC 97-19341. (Schaum's Outline Ser.). (Illus.). 528p. (C). 1997. pap. 15.95 (*0-07-038045-7*) McGraw.

Lipschutz, Seymour & Poe, Arthur C. Schaum's Outline of Programming with FORTRAN IV. (Schaum's Outline Ser.). 314p. (C). 1978. pap. 12.95 (*0-07-037984-X*) McGraw.

Lipschutz, Seymour & Schiller, John. Introduction to Probability & Statistics. LC 98-11816. (Schaum's Outline Ser.). (Illus.). 256p. 1998. pap. 15.95 (*0-07-038084-8*) McGraw.

Lipschutz, Yacov. Kashruth: A Comprehensive Reference to the Principles of Kosher. (ArtScroll Ser.). (Illus.). 168p. 1988. 18.99 (*0-89906-558-9*); pap. 15.99 (*0-89906-559-7*) Mesorah Pubns.

Lipscomb, Adrian, et al. Lonely Planet Papua/New Guinea. 6th ed. (Illus.). 380p. 1998. pap. 17.95 (*0-86442-402-7*) Lonely Planet.

Lipscomb, Anne S. & Hutchison, Kathleen. Tracing Your Mississippi Ancestors. LC 94-13812. (Illus.). 160p. 1994. pap. 14.95 (*0-87805-698-X*); text 32.50 (*0-87805-697-1*) U Pr of Miss.

***Lipscomb, Carolyn E.** Widow's Might. 1999. 24.95 (*0-9665175-3-9*) Magnolia Mansions.

Lipscomb, Carolyn E., ed. Information Access & Delivery in Health Sciences Libraries. LC 95-42302. (Current Practice in Health Sciences Librarianship Ser.: No. 3). 280p. 1996. 39.50 (*0-8108-3050-7*) Scarecrow.

Lipscomb, Claire, jt. ed. see Exley, Helen.

Lipscomb, David M., ed. Hearing Conservation in Industry, Schools, & the Military. LC 94-26675. (Illus.). 344p. 1994. pap. text 49.95 (*1-56593-380-X*, 0768) Thomson Learn.

Lipscomb, Diana. Organic Evolution. 200p. (C). 1994. spiral bd. 26.95 (*0-8403-9478-0*) Kendall-Hunt.

Lipscomb, Elizabeth J., et al, eds. The Several Worlds of Pearl S. Buck: Essays Presented at a Centennial Symposium, Randolph-Macon Woman's College, March 26-28, 1992, 144. LC 93-43752. (Contributions in Women's Studies: No. 144). 184p. 1994. 57.95 (*0-313-29152-7*, Greenwood Pr) Greenwood.

Lipscomb, Ernest B., III. Walker on Patents, 11 vols. 3rd ed. LC 84-81078. (IP Ser.). 1984. 950.00 (*0-685-65399-4*) West Group.

— Walker on Patents, 11 vols., Set. annuals 3rd rev. ed. LC 84-81078. (IP Ser.). 1984. 950.00 (*0-685-59817-9*) West Group.

Lipscomb, Ernest B., 3rd, jt. auth. see Deller, Anthony W.

Lipscomb, Joseph, ed. Physician Staffing for the VA, Vol. I. 432p. 1991. pap. text 39.95 (*0-309-04549-5*) Natl Acad Pr.

Lipscomb, Mance. Mance Lipscomb Texas Blues Guitar Solos. Bowden, Dan, tr. 80p. 1994. pap. 10.95 (*0-7866-0087-X*, 95239) Mel Bay.

Lipscomb, Robert E. Church of the White Light. (Illus.). 320p. 1998. 23.95 (*0-9661926-5-6*) Eagles MO.

— "Comrade Clinton - The President, the KGBs Tales of High Treason" With Special Info on the Chi Com Connection. 384p. 1998. pap. 14.95 (*0-9661926-0-5*) Eagles MO.

— The Second Soviet Union. Communist Resurgence & the New Global Threat. 300p. 1998. 19.95 (*0-9661926-2-1*) Eagles MO.

Lipscomb, Scott D., jt. auth. see Stuessy, Joe.

Lipscomb, Stephen. Symmetric Inverse Semigroups. LC 96-26968. (Mathematics Surveys & Monographs: Vol. 46). 166p. 1996. text 49.00 (*0-8218-0627-0*, SURV/46) Am Math.

Lipscomb, Susan D. & Zuanich, Margaret A. BASIC Fun: Computer Games, Puzzles & Problems Children Can Write. 176p. (J). (gr. k-7). 1982. pap. 2.95 (*0-380-80606-1*, Avon Bks) Morrow Avon.

Lipscomb, Terry W. The Carolina Lowcountry April 1775-June 1776 & the Battle of Fort Moultrie. rev. ed. Andrews, Judith M., ed. LC 94-621657. (South Carolina Revolutionary War Studies: No. 1). 54p. 1994. pap. 6.00 (*1-880067-25-0*) SC Dept of Arch & Hist.

— South Carolina Becomes a State: The Road from Colony to Independence, 1765-1775. (Illus.). 56p. 1976. pap. 5.00 (*1-880067-00-5*) SC Dept of Arch & Hist.

— South Carolina in 1791: George Washington Tours the State. Andrews, Judith M., ed. 112p. 1993. pap. 9.00 (*1-880067-21-8*) SC Dept of Arch & Hist.

Lipscombe, Geoff. The Monetary & Financial System. 1997. pap. 30.00 (*0-85297-414-0*, Pub. by Chartered Bank) St Mut.

Lipscombe, Geoff, jt. auth. see Pond, Keith.

Lipscombe, R. J., jt. auth. see Tariq, A. S.

Lipsedge, Maurice, jt. auth. see Ball, Chris.

Lipsedge, Maurice, jt. auth. see Littlewood, Roland.

Lipsedge, Maurice, jt. auth. see Littlewood, Ronald.

Lipset, David. Mangrove Man: Dialogics of Culture in the Sepik Estuary. LC 96-50213. (Studies in Social & Cultural Anthropology: Vol. 106). (Illus.). 358p. (C). 1997. text 59.95 (*0-521-56434-4*); pap. text 23.95 (*0-521-56435-2*) Cambridge U Pr.

Lipset, Seymour M. American Exceptionalism: A Double-Edged Sword. 320p. 1996. 27.50 (*0-393-03725-8*) Norton.

— American Exceptionalism: A Double-Edged Sword. 352p. 1997. pap. 13.95 (*0-393-31614-9*) Norton.

— American Exceptionalism: A Double Edged Sword. 354p. 1998. reprint ed. lib. bdg. 32.95 (*0-7351-0026-8*) Replica Bks.

— Consensus & Conflict in Political Sociology. (Illus.). 275p. 1985. 44.95 (*0-88738-051-4*); pap. 24.95 (*0-88738-608-3*) Transaction Pubs.

— Continental Divide: The Values & Institutions of the United States & Canada. 352p. (C). (gr. 13). 1990. pap. 20.99 (*0-415-90385-8*, A5389) Routledge.

— The Emergence of the One-Party South: The Election of 1860. (Irvington Reprint Series in American History). (C). 1991. reprint ed. pap. text 1.00 (*0-8290-2608-8*, H-130) Irvington.

— Emerging Coalitions in American Politics. 530p. 1978. pap. text 24.95 (*0-917616-22-7*) Transaction Pubs.

— It Didn't Happen Here: Why Socialism Failed in the United States. 384p. 2000. 26.95 (*0-393-04098-4*) Norton.

— Jews & the New American Scene. 256p. 1997. pap. text 16.00 (*0-674-47494-5*) HUP.

— Political Man: The Social Bases of Politics. LC 80-8867. 608p. (C). 1981. reprint ed. pap. text 17.95 (*0-8018-2522-9*) Johns Hopkins.

— The Radical Right: A Problem for American Democracy. (Reprint Series in Social Sciences). (C). 1993. reprint ed. pap. text 5.00 (*0-8290-2661-4*, S-445) Irvington.

— Rebellion in the University. LC 92-14855. (Foundations of Higher Education Ser.). 372p. (C). 1992. pap. 24.95 (*1-56000-596-3*) Transaction Pubs.

— Revolution & Counterrevolution: Change & Persistence in Social Structure. rev. ed. 436p. 1987. pap. 24.95 (*0-88738-694-6*) Transaction Pubs.

— Some Social Requisites of Democracy: Economic Development & Political Legitimacy. (Reprint Series in Social Sciences). (C). 1993. reprint ed. pap. text 2.90 (*0-8290-3810-8*, S-175) Irvington.

— The Third Century: America As a Post-Industrial Society. 478p. 1996. pap. text 10.00 (*0-226-48458-0*, P884) U Ch Pr.

Lipset, Seymour M., ed. American Pluralism & the Jewish Community. 220p. 1989. 39.95 (*0-88738-286-X*) Transaction Pubs.

— Party Coalitions in the Nineteen Eighties. LC 81-83095. 464p. 1981. text 39.95 (*0-917616-45-6*); pap. text 24.95 (*0-917616-43-X*) Transaction Pubs.

— Unions in Transition: Entering the Second Century. LC 86-10256. 506p. 1986. 29.95 (*0-917616-74-X*); pap. 19.95 (*0-917616-73-1*) ICS Pr.

— Who's Who in Democracy. LC 96-48342. 247p. (YA). 1997. text 89.95 (*1-56802-121-6*) Congr Quarterly.

Lipset, Seymour M., et al, eds. The Encyclopedia of Democracy, 4 vols., Set. LC 95-34217. (Illus.). 1900p. (C). 1995. text 425.00 (*0-87187-675-2*) Congr Quarterly.

Lipset, Seymour M. & Bendix, Reinhard. Social Mobility in Industrial Society. 316p. (C). 1991. pap. text 24.95 (*1-56000-606-4*) Transaction Pubs.

Lipset, Seymour M. & Congressional Quarterly, Inc., Staff. Democracy in Asia & Africa. LC 97-42289. 237p. (C). (gr. 11). 1998. text 89.00 (*1-56802-123-2*) Congr Quarterly.

Lipset, Seymour M. & Congressional Quarterly Staff. Democracy in Europe & the Americas. LC 97-42922. 280p. (C). (gr. 11). 1998. text 89.00 (*1-56802-122-4*) Congr Quarterly.

Lipset, Seymour M. & Raab, Earl. Jews & the New American Scene. LC 94-32358. 256p. 1995. pap. text 22.95 (*0-674-47493-7*, LIPJEW) HUP.

— The Politics of Unreason: Right Wing Extremism in America. 2nd ed. LC 77-92800. 1993. pap. text 7.95 (*0-226-48457-2*, P750) U Ch Pr.

— The Politics of Unreason: Right-Wing Extremism in America. 2nd ed. LC 77-92800. (Phoenix Book Ser.: Vol. P75). 608p. reprint ed. pap. 188.50 (*0-608-09465-X*, 205426500005) Bks Demand.

Lipset, Seymour M. & Schneider, William. The Confidence Gap: Business, Labor & Government in the Public Mind. rev. ed. LC 86-27416. 480p. 1987. pap. text 16.95 (*0-8018-3044-3*) Johns Hopkins.

Lipset, Seymour M., et al. Politics in Developing Countries: Comparing Experiences with Democracy. 2nd ed. 500p. 1995. pap. text 23.50 (*1-55587-541-6*) L Rienner.

Lipset, Seymour M., ed. see Martineau, Harriet.

Lipsett, Laurence. Back to Work: How to Rejoin the Workforce after an Absence. 135p. (Orig.). 1993. pap. 15.95 (*0-9637107-0-2*) Curtice Pub.

— How to Test Sales Applicants Legally. 101p. 1994. pap. 29.95 (*0-9637107-1-0*) Curtice Pub.

Lipsett, Laurence, jt. auth. see McKie, W. Gilmore.

Lipsett, Lewis P. & Rovee-Collier, Carolyn, eds. Advances in Infancy Research, Vol. 3. 296p. 1984. text 78.50 (*0-89391-208-5*) Ablx Pub.

Lipsett, Linda O. Elizabeth Roseberry Mitchell's Graveyard Quilt: An American Pioneer Saga. LC 95-41580. (Illus.). 288p. (Orig.). 1996. pap. 18.95 (*0-9629399-2-7*) Halstead Meadows.

— Pieced from Ellen's Quilt: Ellen Spaulding Reed's Letters & Story. LC 91-16329. (Illus.). 224p. (Orig.). 1991. pap. 13.95 (*0-9629399-0-0*) Halstead Meadows.

— Remember Me: Women & Their Friendship Quilts. (Illus.). 144p. 1997. pap. 26.95 (*0-8442-2650-5*, Quilt Dgst Pr) NTC Contemp Pub Co.

— To Love & to Cherish: Brides Remembered. 2nd ed. LC 96-33616. (Illus.). 513p. 1997. pap. 26.95 (*0-8442-2651-3*, Quilt Dgst Pr) NTC Contemp Pub Co.

Lipsett, Linda O., jt. auth. see Price, Esther.

Lipsett, Mortimer B., ed. see Workshop on Gas-Liquid Chromatography of Steroids.

Lipsett-Rivera, Sonya. To Defend Our Water with the Blood of Our Veins: The Struggle for Resources in Colonial Puebla. LC 98-58046. 224p. 1999. 49.95 (*0-8263-2034-1*) U of NM Pr.

Lipsett-Rivera, Sonya, jt. auth. see Johnson, Lyman L.

Lipsett-Riviera, Sonya, tr. see Albban, Juan Pedro Viqueira.

Lipsett, Roger, et al. VHDL: Hardware Description & Design. 320p. (C). 1989. text 116.50 (*0-7923-9030-X*) Kluwer Academic.

Lipsett, Suzanne, ed. see Rascon, Armando.

Lipsett, Suzanne, ed. see Roads, Michael J.

Lipsett, Suzanne, ed. see Silva, Jose & Stone, Robert B.

***Lipsey.** Economics. 10th ed. 420p. (C). 2000. pap., student ed. 26.95 (*0-201-66468-2*) Addison-Wesley.

— Macroeconomics. 10th ed. 260p. (C). 2000. pap., student ed. 22.95 (*0-201-66472-0*) Addison-Wesley.

Lipsey. Macroeconomics. 12th ed. 560p. (C). 1998. pap. text 70.00 (*0-201-36012-8*) Addison-Wesley.

***Lipsey.** Macroeconomics. 12th ed. 320p. (C). 1999. pap. text, student ed. 23.20 (*0-201-45841-1*) Addison-Wesley.

Lipsey. Microeconomics. 10th ed. 250p. (C). 2000. pap., student ed. 22.95 (*0-201-66470-4*) Addison-Wesley.

***Lipsey.** Microeconomics. 12th ed. 512p. (C). 1998. pap. text 70.00 (*0-201-36011-X*) Addison-Wesley.

Lipsey. Microeconomics: Study Guide. 12th ed. 336p. (C). 1999. pap. text, student ed. 23.20 (*0-201-45842-X*) Addison-Wesley.

Lipsey, B. An Art of Our Own: The Spiritual in 20th Century Art. (C). 1990. 320.00 (*0-7855-4478-X*, Pub. by Collets) St Mut.

— Art of the Avant-Garde in Russia - Selections from the G. Costakis-Solomon Guggenheim Museum Exhibition. (C). 1990. pap. 170.00 (*0-7855-4477-1*, Pub. by Collets) St Mut.

Lipsey, Mark W. Design Sensitivity: Statistical Power for Experimental Research. (Illus.). 224p. (C). 1989. text 52.00 (*0-8039-3062-3*); pap. text 24.50 (*0-8039-3063-1*) Sage.

***Lipsey, Mark W. & Wilson, David B.** Practical Meta-Analysis. LC 00-35379. (Applied Social Research Methods Ser.). 2000. write for info. (*0-7619-2168-0*) Sage.

Lipsey, Richard A. Sports Market Place. 16th ed. 1350p. 1996. pap. 199.00 (*0-935644-02-4*) Sportsguide.

— Sports Market Place Register, 1995. 600p. 1996. pap. 59.00 (*0-935644-03-2*) Sportsguide.

Lipsey, Richard G. Economics. 10th ed. (C). 1997. pap. 74.00 (*0-06-501022-1*); pap., student ed. 27.66 (*0-06-501093-0*) Addson-Wesley Educ.

Lipsey, Richard G. Macroeconomic Theory & Policy Vol. 2: The Selected Essays of Richard G. Lipsey, Vol. 2. LC 96-35916. (Economists of the Twentieth Century Ser.). 480p. 1997. 110.00 (*1-85278-127-0*) E Elgar.

Lipsey, Richard G. Macroeconomics. 592p. (C). 1993. pap. 51.33 (*0-06-501023-X*) Addson-Wesley Educ.

— Microeconomics. (C). 1993. pap. 51.33 (*0-06-501024-8*); pap., student ed. 26.00 (*0-06-501095-7*) Addson-Wesley Educ.

Lipsey, Richard G. Microeconomics, Growth & Political Economy Vol. 1: The Selected Essays of Richard G. Lipsey, Vol. 1. LC 96-35917. (Economists of the Twentieth Century Series). 528p. 1997. 110.00 (*1-85278-126-2*) E Elgar.

***Lipsey, Richard G. & Chrystal, K. Alec.** Principles of Economics. 9th ed. LC 98-48332. 1999. write for info. (*0-19-877589-X*); write for info. (*0-19-877588-1*) OUP.

Lipsey, Richard G. & Courant, Paul N. Economics. 11th ed. LC 95-34901. (Illus.). 896p. (C). 1996. text 77.81 (*0-673-99476-7*) Addson-Wesley Educ.

— Macroeconomics. 11th ed. LC 95-35432. (Illus.). 560p. (C). 1996. text 56.25 (*0-673-99478-3*) Addson-Wesley Educ.

— Microeconomics. 11th ed. LC 95-34895. (Illus.). 528p. (C). 1997. text 63.00 (*0-673-99477-5*) Addson-Wesley Educ.

Lipsey, Richard G. & York, Robert C. Evaluating the Free Trade Deal: A Guided Tour Through the Canada-U.S. Agreement. LC 88-94376. (Policy Study Ser.: No. 6). 154p. 1988. reprint ed. pap. 47.80 (*0-608-01381-1*, 206213400002) Bks Demand.

Lipsey, Richard G., et al. Economics. 8th ed. (C). 1994. pap. text, student ed. 15.00 (*0-673-46984-0*) Addson-Wesley Educ.

— Economics. 9th ed. 1040p. (C). 1990. text 58.00 (*0-06-043908-4*) Addson-Wesley Educ.

***Lipsey, Richard G., et al.** Economics. 12th ed. LC 98-42665. 986p. (C). 1999. text 102.00 (*0-201-34739-3*) Addison-Wesley.

Lipsey, Richard G., et al. Microeconomics. 9th ed. 540p. (C). 1990. pap. 38.66 (*0-06-044113-5*) Addison-Wesley Educ.

Lipsey, Richard G., jt. see Chrystal, K. Alec.

Lipsey, Richard G., jt. auth. see Harbury, Colin D.

Lipsey, Robert E. Price & Quantity Trends in the Foreign Trade of the United States. (Studies in International Economic Relations: No. 2). 505p. 1963. reprint ed. 131.30 (*0-87014-154-6*) Natl Bur Econ Res.

Lipsey, Robert E. & Preston, Doris. Source Book of Statistics Relating to Construction. (General Ser.: No. 82). 319p. 1966. reprint ed. 83.00 (*0-87014-082-5*) Natl Bur Econ Res.

Lipsey, Robert E. & Tice, Helen S., eds. The Measurement of Saving, Investment, & Wealth. LC 88-4669. (National Bureau of Economic Research Studies in Income & Wealth: Vol. 52). (Illus.). 874p. 1989. lib. bdg. 99.50 (*0-226-48468-8*) U Ch Pr.

Lipsey, Robert E., jt. auth. see Cagan, Phillip.

Lipsey, Robert E., jt. auth. see Fabricant, Solomon.

Lipsey, Robert E., jt. auth. see Kravis, Irving B.

Lipsey, Roderick K. von, see Von Lipsey, Roderick K.

Lipsey, Roger. An Art of Our Own: The Spiritual in Twentieth-Century Art. (Illus.). 544p. 1997. pap. 35.00 (*1-57062-268-X*, Pub. by Shambhala Pubns) Random.

***Lipsey, Roger.** Have You Been to Delphi? Tales of the Ancient Oracle for Modern Minds. (C). 2000. pap. text 19.95 (*0-7914-4782-0*) State U NY Pr.

— Have You Been to Delphi? Tales of the Ancient Oracle for Modern Minds. (C). 2001. text 59.50 (*0-7914-4781-2*) State U NY Pr.

Lipsey, Roger, ed. see Coomaraswamy, Ananda K.

Lipsey, Sally I. & Ignatavicius, Donna D. Math for Nurses: A Problem Solving Approach. (Illus.). 256p. 1993. pap. text 28.00 (*0-7216-6481-4*, W B Saunders Co) Harcrt Hlth Sci Grp.

— Math for Nurses: A Problem Solving Approach. (Illus.). (C). 1993. pap. text, teacher ed. write for info. (*0-7216-6496-2*, W B Saunders Co) Harcrt Hlth Sci Grp.

***Lipsey, Shelia E.** Always, Now & Forever. 340p. 2000. pap. 12.95 (*0-615-11265-X*) tigbs Pubng.

Lipsher, Steve, jt. auth. see Castrone, Linda.

Lipshitz, Abe. Studies on Abraham Ibn Ezra. 118p. (C). 1969. 7.95 (*0-935982-43-4*, AL-01) Spertus Coll.

Lipshitz, Abe, intro. The Commentary of Abraham Ibn Ezra on Hosea. 190p. 1988. 19.95 (*0-87203-127-6*) Hermon.

Lipshitz, Arye. We Built Jerusalem: Tales of Pioneering Days. Louvish, Misha, tr. LC 84-45016. 176p. 1985. 14.95 (*0-8453-4787-X*, Cornwall Bks) Assoc Univ Prs.

Lipshitz, Gabriel. Core versus Periphery: Migration to & Within Israel, 1948-1995. LC 97-44283. (GeoJournal Library: No. 42). 180p. 1997. text 95.00 (*0-7923-4850-8*) Kluwer Academic.

Lipshitz, Howard D. Localized RNAs. LC 95-16554. (Molecular Biology Intelligence Unit Ser.). 318p. 1995. 99.00 (*1-57059-276-4*) Landes Bioscience.

— Localized RNAs LC 95-16554. (Molecular Biology Intelligence Unit Ser.). 322p. 1995. write for info. (*3-540-60005-1*) Spr-Verlag.

Lipshitz, Hymie. X-Rated Drinks. 152p. 1998. pap. 8.95 (*0-9617655-0-X*) Foley Pub.

Lipshultz. Webmastering Live Wire Pro. 1996. pap. text 39.99 incl. audio compact disk (*0-7821-1933-6*) Sybex.

Lipshultz, Larry I. Infertility in the Male. 3rd ed. Howards, Stuarts, ed. (Illus.). 576p. (C). (gr. 13). 1996. text 119.00 (*0-8151-5501-8*, 25776) Mosby Inc.

Lipshultz, Larry I., et al, eds. Surgery of the Male Reproductive Tract. (Clinics in Andrology Ser.: No. 2). (Illus.). 275p. 1980. text 211.50 (*90-247-2315-9*) Kluwer Academic.

Lipshultz, Larry I. & Kleinman, Isaac. Primary Care Urology: A Practitioner's Guide. 1996. mass mkt. 43.95 (*0-7234-2482-9*, Pub. by Martin Dunitz) Mosby Inc.

Lipshultz, Steven E. Cardiology in AIDS. LC 97-42609. (Current Topics in Cardiology Ser.). (Illus.). 256p. 1998. text 98.50 (*0-412-08861-4*, Pub. by E A) OUP.

Lipshutz, Nelson R. The Regulatory Economics of Title Insurance. LC 93-5440. 168p. 1994. 59.95 (*0-275-94742-4*, Praeger Pubs) Greenwood.

Lipsig, Ethan. Downsizing: Law & Practice: Including the 1999 Supplement, 2 vols. LC 96-20949. 2163p. 1998. suppl. ed. 365.00 incl. disk (*1-57018-007-5*, 9125) BNA Books.

— Downsizing: Law & Practice, 1998 Supplement. 953p. 1998. pap., suppl. ed. 145.00 (*1-57018-125-X*, 1125) BNA Books.

Lipsinski, Bob & Lapinski, Kathie. The Complete Beverage Dictionary. 2nd ed. (Culinary Arts Ser.). 420p. 1996. text 39.95 (*0-442-02208-5*, VNR) Wiley.

Lipsite, Edmond. Hebrew, Olam Shalem, 3 cass., Set. unabridged ed. (HEB.). 66p. 1985. 59.50 incl. audio (*0-88432-579-2*, AFHE10) Audio-Forum.

Lipsitt, Don R., jt. ed. see Starcevic, Vladen.

Lipsitt, Lewis P. & Field, Tiffany M., eds. Perinatal Risk & Newborn Behavior. LC 82-8909. 208p. (C). 1982. text 73.25 (*0-89391-123-2*) Ablx Pub.

Lipsitt, Lewis P. & Mitnick, Leonard L., eds. Self-Regulatory Behavior & Risk Taking: Causes & Consequences. 432p. (C). 1991. text 82.50 (*0-89391-818-0*) Ablx Pub.

Lipsitt, Lewis P. & Rovee-Collier, Carolyn, eds. Advances in Infancy Research, Vol. 1. (Advances in Infancy Research Ser.). 290p. 1981. text 78.50 (*0-89391-045-7*) Ablx Pub.

— Advances in Infancy Research, Vol. 2. (Advances in Infancy Research Ser.). 344p. 1983. text 78.50 (*0-89391-113-5*) Ablx Pub.

— Advances in Infancy Research, Vol. 4. 300p. 1986. text 78.50 (*0-89391-309-X*) Ablx Pub.

— Advances in Infancy Research, Vol. 7. LC 90-49579. 448p. 1992. text 78.50 (*0-89391-666-8*, RJ131) Ablx Pub.

— Advances in Infancy Research, Vol. 10. 270p. 1996. 78.50 (*1-56750-274-1*) Ablx Pub.

— Advances in Infancy Research, Vol. 11. 281p. 1997. text 78.50 (*1-56750-287-3*) Ablx Pub.

Lipsitt, Lewis P., ed. see Moerk, Ernst L.

Lipsitt, Lewis P., ed. see Plooij, Frans X.

Lipsitt, Lewis P., jt. ed. see Rovee-Collier, Carolyn.

Lipsitz, Alexis, jt. auth. see Burke, Delta.

Lipsitz-Bem, Sandra. The Lenses of Gender: Transforming the Debate on Sexual Inequality. 256p. 1994. pap. 16.00 (*0-300-06163-3*) Yale U Pr.

Lipsitz, Gail J. Practical Parenting: A Jewish Perspective. LC 96-40372. 1997. 29.50 (*0-88125-538-6*); pap. 17.95 (*0-88125-536-X*) Ktav.

Lipsitz, George. Dangerous Crossroads: Popular Music, Postmodernism & the Poetics of Place. LC 94-20455. 320p. (gr. 13). 1994. 35.00 (*1-85984-935-0*, B4542, Pub. by Verso) Norton.

— Dangerous Crossroads: Popular Music, Postmodernism & the Poetics of Place. 1997. pap. 19.00 (*1-85984-035-3*, Pub. by Verso) Norton.

— A Life in the Struggle: Ivory Perry & the Culture of Opposition. 2nd ed. (Illus.). 320p. 1995. pap. 22.95 (*1-56639-321-3*) Temple U Pr.

— The Possessive Investment in Whiteness: How White People Profit from Identity Politics. LC 97-53204. 320p. (C). 1998. text 59.95 (*1-56639-634-4*); pap. text 19.95 (*1-56639-635-2*) Temple U Pr.

— Rainbow at Midnight: Labor & Culture in the 1940s. LC 93-36425. 376p. (C). 1994. 16.95 (*0-252-06394-5*); text 49.95 (*0-252-02094-4*) U of Ill Pr.

— The Sidewalks of St. Louis: Places, People & Politics in an American City. (Illus.). 152p. (C). 1991. 19.95 (*0-8262-0814-2*) U of Mo Pr.

— Time Passages: Collective Memory & American Popular Culture. 323p. 1990. pap. 19.95 (*0-8166-1806-2*) U of Minn Pr.

Lipsitz, Jacquelyn, ed. Beginning Basic, Bk. 2. 1985. 4.95 (*1-55708-042-9*, MCR902) McDonald Pub Co.

Lipsitz, Joan. Growing up Forgotten. LC 79-67002. 267p. (Orig.). 1980. pap. text 24.95 (*0-87855-792-X*) Transaction Pubs.

— Successful Schools for Young Adolescents. 240p. 1983. 34.95 (*0-87855-487-4*); pap. text 21.95 (*0-87855-947-7*) Transaction Pubs.

Lipsitz, Lawrence, ed. Technology & Education: Articles from Educational Technology Magazine. LC 79-125873. 192p. 1971. 29.95 (*0-87778-011-0*) Educ Tech Pubns.

— The Test Score Decline: Meaning & Issues. LC 76-13169. (Illus.). 240p. 1977. 34.95 (*0-87778-095-1*) Educ Tech Pubns.

Lipsitz, Lawrence, jt. ed. see Ackerman, Jerrold.

Lipsitz, Lewis. American Democracy. 3rd ed. 1991. pap. text, student ed. 44.40 (*0-312-06697-X*) St Martin.

— American Democracy. 3rd ed. 1993. pap. text, teacher ed. 10.00 (*0-312-08081-6*) St Martin.

— Seeking the Hook: New & Selected Poems. LC 98-14087. 154p. 1998. pap. 12.00 (*0-930095-16-2*) Signal Bks.

Lipsitz, Lewis & Speak, David M. American Democracy. 3rd ed. LC 92-50017. (Illus.). 818p. (C). 1993. pap. text 48.95 (*0-312-06663-5*) St Martin.

— American Democracy. 3rd ed. LC 92-50017. (Illus.). 736p. (C). 1993. pap. text, student ed. 21.95 (*0-312-08080-8*) St Martin.

***Lipsius, J. G. & Leitzmann, J. J.** Bibliotheca Numaria: Numismatic Bibliography. fac. ed. 1002p. 2000. 85.00 (*1-57898-227-8*) Martino Pubng.

Lipsius, Justus. A Direction for Travailers for the Behoofe of the Young Earle of Bedford, Being Now Ready to Travell. LC 77-7414. (English Experience Ser.: No. 878). 1977. reprint ed. lib. bdg. 15.00 (*90-221-0878-3*) Walter J Johnson.

— Opera Omnia, 4 vols., Set. (GER.). xii, 5010p. reprint ed. write for info. (*0-318-70500-1*) G Olms Pubs.

— Principles of Letter-Writing: A Bilingual Text of Justi Lipsii Epistolica Institutio. Young, R. V. & Hester, M. Thomas, eds. & trs. by. from LAT. LC 93-41720. (Library of Renaissance Humanism: Vol. 3). (ENG & LAT.). 136p. (C). 1995. 34.95 (*0-8093-1958-6*) S Ill U Pr.

— The Roman Colosseum: De Amphitheatro Liber, 1584, 2 vols. (Printed Sources of Western Art Ser.). (LAT., Illus.). 1981. reprint ed. pap. 55.00 (*0-915346-58-3*) A Wofsy Fine Arts.

— Sixe Bookes of Politickes or Civil Doctrine. Jones, W., tr. LC 79-25633. (English Experience Ser.: No. 287). 1970. reprint ed. 22.00 (*90-221-0287-4*) Walter J Johnson.

Lipsius, Justus H. Das Attische Recht und Rechtsverfahren, 3 vols. in 1. iv, 1041p. 1984. reprint ed. write for info. (*3-487-01434-3*) G Olms Pubs.

Lipsius, Richard A. Acta Apostolorum Apocrypha, 2 vols. in 3. Bonnet, Max, ed. (GER.). cxc, 1174p. 1990. reprint ed. write for info. (*3-487-00044-X*) G Olms Pubs.

Lipska, Ewa. Poet? Criminal? Madman? Poems. Plebanek, B. & Howard, T., trs. from POL. LC 91-72165. 96p. (Orig.). 1991. pap. 16.95 (*1-85610-011-1*, Pub. by Forest Bks) Dufour.

Lipski, Alexander. Life & Teaching of Anandmayi Ma. 1977. 9.95 (*0-89684-484-6*, Pub. by Motilal Bnarsidass) S Asia.

— Life & Teaching of Sri Anandamayi Ma. (C). 1995. reprint ed. 12.00 (*81-208-0530-5*, Pub. by Motilal Bnarsidass) S Asia.

Lipski, Elizabeth. Digestive Wellness. 400p. 1999. pap. 17.95 (*0-87983-984-8*, 39848K, Keats Publng) NTC Contemp Pub Co.

Lipski, Elizabeth. Leaky Gut Syndrome. LC 98-204448. pap. 3.95 (*0-87983-824-8*, 38248K, Keats Publng) NTC Contemp Pub Co.

Lipski, John M. Language of the Islenos: Vestigial Spanish in Louisiana. LC 89-13508. 144p. 1990. text 25.00 (*0-8071-1534-7*) La State U Pr.

— Latin American Spanish. LC 93-31346. (Linguistics Library). 1994. write for info. (*0-582-08761-9*, Pub. by Addison-Wesley) Longman.

— Latin American Spanish. LC 93-31346. (Linguistics Library). 1995. pap. text 31.31 (*0-582-08760-0*) Addison-Wesley.

— The Speech of the Negros Congos of Panama. LC 88-7617. (Creole Language Library: Vol. 4). vii, 159p. (C). 1989. 59.00 (*1-55619-049-2*) J Benjamins Pubng Co.

Lipski, John M., jt. auth. see Neale-Silva, Eduardo.

Lipski, John M., jt. ed. see Roca, Ana.

Lipski, Jozef. Diplomat in Berlin, 1933-1939: Papers & Memoirs of Jozef Lipski, Ambassador of Poland. Jedrzejewicz, Waclaw, ed. LC 67-25871. 727p. reprint ed. pap. 200.00 (*0-608-30108-6*, 200610900060) Bks Demand.

Lipski, Liz. Digestive Wellness. Davis, Susan, ed. LC 95-49689. 320p. 1996. pap. 14.95 (*0-87983-679-2*, Keats Publng) NTC Contemp Pub Co.

Lipski, Thomas. Hans Henny Jahnns Einflu? auf den Orgelbau. (Studien und Materialien Zur Musikwissenschaft Ser.: Bd. 12). (Illus.). 376p. 1997. 98.00 (*3-487-10321-4*) G Olms Pubs.

Lipskier, D., et al, eds. Sefer Kovetz Raza"sh. (HEB.). 270p. 1987. 12.00 (*0-8266-5428-2*) Kehot Pubn Soc.

Lipskin, Beth A. The Eighth National Space Symposium Proceedings Report. 300p. 1992. text 50.00 (*0-9616962-6-5*) US Space Found.

— The Eleventh National Space Symposium Proceedings Report: Space-Vision & Reality, Face to Face. 214p. 1995. text 50.00 (*0-9616962-9-X*) US Space Found.

— The Ninth National Space Symposium Proceedings Report. 236p. 1993. text 50.00 (*0-9616962-7-3*) US Space Found.

Lipskin, Beth A., et al, eds. The Tenth National Space Symposium Proceedings Report. LC 96-222181. 244p. 1994. pap. 50.00 (*0-9616962-8-1*) US Space Found.

— The 12th National Space Symposium Proceedings Report: Space - Enhancing Life on Earth. 222p. 1996. pap. 50.00 (*1-889475-00-9*) US Space Found.

Lipsky. Rheumatoid Arthritis. 1997. write for info. (*0-397-51589-8*, L1216) Lppncott W & W.

Lipsky, Abram. John Wesley: A Portrait. LC 76-155619. reprint ed. 32.50 (*0-404-03994-4*) AMS Pr.

Lipsky, Daniel & Lipton, David A. A Student's Guide to Accounting for Lawyers. 3rd ed. LC 97-43524. (Student Guide Ser.). 1997. 24.00 (*0-8205-3054-9*) Bender.

Lipsky, David. The Pallbearer. 200p. (Orig.). (J). 1996. pap. 9.70 (*0-7868-8184-4*, Pub. by Hyperion) Time Warner.

Lipsky, David B., et al, eds. Advances in Industrial & Labor Relations, Vol. 1. 283p. 1983. 78.50 (*0-89232-250-0*) Jai Pr.

— Advances in Industrial & Labor Relations, Vol. 2. 377p. 1985. 78.50 (*0-89232-444-9*) Jai Pr.

— Advances in Industrial & Labor Relations, Vol. 3. 316p. 1986. 78.50 (*0-89232-642-5*) Jai Pr.

Lipsky, Dorothy K. Inclusion & School Reform: Transforming America's Classrooms. LC 96-37325. 414p. 1997. pap. text 36.95 (*1-55766-273-8*) P H Brookes.

Lipsky, George A., et al. Ethiopia. LC 62-13515. (Area & Country Surveys Ser.). 392p. 1962. 15.00 (*0-87536-917-0*) HRAFP.

— Saudi Arabia. LC 59-8227. (Area & Country Surveys Ser.). 381p. 1959. 15.00 (*0-87536-907-3*) HRAFP.

Lipsky, Jon. Call of the Wild. 1997. pap. 10.00 (*0-929741-38-2*) Playsmith.

Lipsky, Louis. Thirty Years of American Zionism, Vol.1. Davis, Moshe, ed. LC 77-70718. (America & the Holy Land Ser.). 1977. reprint ed. lib. bdg. 29.95 (*0-405-10263-1*) Ayer.

Lipsky, Martin S. Gastroenterology: Quick Reference Guides for Family Physicians. (The Academy Collection Ser.). 200p. pap. text. write for info. (*0-7817-2054-0*) Lppncott W & W.

Lipsky, Michael. Street-Level Bureaucracy: Dilemmas of the Individual in Public Services. LC 79-7350. 275p. 1983. pap. 12.95 (*0-87154-526-8*) Russell Sage.

Lipsky, Michael, ed. Law & Order: Police Encounters. LC 72-91468. 144p. 1970. reprint ed. pap. text 18.95 (*0-87855-563-3*) Transaction Pubs.

Lipsky, Michael & Olson, David J. Commission Politics: The Processing of Racial Crisis in America. LC 74-20192. 492p. 1977. 44.95 (*0-87855-078-X*) Transaction Pubs.

— Commission Politics: The Processing of Racial Crisis in America. LC 74-20192. 490p. reprint ed. pap. 151.90 (*0-608-15599-3*, 205658400077) Bks Demand.

Lipsky, Michael, jt. auth. see Rathgeb, Steven.

Lipsky, Michael, jt. auth. see Smith, Steven R.

Lipsky, Peter E., et al, eds. Structure, Function, & Regulation of Molecules Involved in Leukocyte Adhesion: Proceedings of the Second International Conferences on "Structure & Function of Molecules Involved in Leukocyte Adhesion II" Held in Titisee, Germany, October 2-6, 1991. LC 92-2337. (Illus.). 567p. 1992. 144.00 (*0-387-97870-4*) Spr-Verlag.

Lipsky, Stephen. Microwave Passive Direction Finding. LC 86-33995. 320p. 1987. 160.00 (*0-471-83454-8*) Wiley.

Lipsky, Suzanne. Internalized Racism. 1978. pap. 2.00 (*0-913937-24-X*) Rational Isl.

Lipsman, Samuel L., jt. auth. see Doyle, Edward G.

Lipson & Wixson. Assessment & Instruction of Reading Disabilities. 735p. (C). 1997. 79.00 (*0-673-18335-1*) Addison-Wesley Educ.

Lipson, Abigail & Perkins, David N. Block: Getting out of Your Own Way. 1990. 18.95 (*0-8184-0516-3*) Carol Pub Group.

Lipson, Alexander. A Russian Course, Pt. 1. (Illus.). ix, 338p. (Orig.). (C). 1981. pap. text 16.95 (*0-89357-080-X*) Slavica.

— A Russian Course, Pt. 2. (Illus.). 343p. (Orig.). (C). 1981. pap. text 16.95 (*0-89357-081-8*) Slavica.

— A Russian Course, Pt. 3. (Illus.). iv, 105p. (Orig.). 1981. pap. text 12.95 (*0-89357-082-6*) Slavica.

Lipson, Ashley S. Art of Advocacy: Demonstrative Evidence. 1988. ring bd. 160.00 (*0-8205-1082-3*) Bender.

— Art of Advocacy: Documentary Evidence. (Art of Advocacy Ser.). 1986. ring bd. 160.00 (*0-8205-1028-9*) Bender.

— Is It Admissible? 1998. pap. 89.98 (*1-58012-024-5*) James Pub Santa Ana.

— Law Office Automation for Paralegals, Administrators & Legal Secretaries. 384p. 1989. text 59.95 (*0-13-526583-5*) P-H.

Lipson, Charles. Standing Guard: Protecting Foreign Capital in the 19th & 20th Centuries. LC 83-24260. (Studies in International Political Economy: Vol. 11). 330p. 1985. pap. 16.95 (*0-520-05327-3*, Pub. by U CA Pr) Cal Prin Full Svc.

Lipson, Charles & Cohen, Benjamin J., eds. Theory & Structure in International Political Economy: An International Organization Reader. LC 98-50265. (Illus.). 432p. 1999. 50.00 (*0-262-12215-4*) MIT Pr.

— Theory & Structure in International Political Economy: An International Organization Reader. LC 98-50265. (Illus.). 432p. 1999. pap. 25.00 (*0-262-62127-4*) MIT Pr.

Lipson, Charles, jt. ed. see Cohen, Benjamin J.

Lipson, Debra J., et al. Approaches for Providing/Financing Health Care for the Uninsured: An Assessment of State Options & Experiences. 57p. 1997. pap. write for info. (*1-929008-01-5*) CA HlthCare Fnd.

Lipson, E. History of the Woolen & Worsted Industries. 273p. 1965. reprint ed. 30.00 (*0-7146-2339-3*, Pub. by F Cass Pubs) Intl Spec Bk.

Lipson, Eden R. The New York Times Parent's Guide to the Best Books for Children. (Illus.). 448p. 1988. 22.50 (*0-8129-1649-2*, Times Bks); pap. 12.95 (*0-8129-1688-3*, Times Bks) Crown Pub Group.

Lipson, Eden R. New York Times Parent's Guide to the Best Books for Children. (Illus.). 1991. 15.00 (*0-8129-1943-2*, Times Bks) Crown Pub Group.

Lipson, Eden R. The New York Times Parent's Guide to the Best Books for Children. rev. ed. LC 91-2675. (Illus.). 464p. 1991. pap. 17.00 (*0-8129-1889-4*, Times Bks) Crown Pub Group.

Lipson, Eden Ross. The New York Times Parent's Guide to the Best Books for Children. 3rd ed. (Illus.). 560p. 2000. pap. 18.00 (*0-8129-3018-5*, Three Riv Pr) Crown Pub Group.

Lipson, Edward D., jt. ed. see Cerda-Olmedo, Enrique.

Lipson, Ephraim. Europe in the Nineteenth Century, 1815-1914. 11th ed. LC 78-16548. (Illus.). 298p. 1979. reprint ed. lib. bdg. 59.75 (*0-313-20593-0*, LIEN, Greenwood Pr) Greenwood.

Lipson, Eric. Passover Haggadah: A Messianic Celebration. LC 85-82168. (Illus.). 128p. 1986. pap. 8.00 (*0-9616148-5-4*) Purple Pomegranate.

Lipson, Eric, jt. auth. see Lipson, Greta B.

Lipson, Fran, jt. auth. see Molyneux, Lynn.

Lipson, Great B. & Bolkosky, Sidney. Mighty Myth. 152p. (J). (gr. 5-12). 1982. 13.99 (*0-86653-064-9*, GA 419) Good Apple.

Lipson, Greta B. Audacious Poetry. (Illus.). 128p. (J). (gr. 6-12). 1992. student ed. 12.99 (*0-86653-683-3*, 1417) Good Apple.

— A Book for All Seasons. 160p. 1990. 12.99 (*0-86653-540-3*, GA1153) Good Apple.

— Fact, Fantasy, Folklore. 160p. (J). (gr. 3-12). 1977. 12.99 (*0-916456-11-0*, GA71) Good Apple.

— Famous Fables for Little Troupers. (Illus.). 168p. (J). (gr. k-6). 1984. 12.99 (*0-86653-202-1*, GA 554) Good Apple.

— Fast Ideas for Busy Teachers. 160p. 1989. 12.99 (*0-86653-504-7*, GA1082) Good Apple.

— A Leash on Love: A Book for All Ages. LC 93-176359. (Illus.). 32p. (J). 1992. 9.95 (*0-9630637-0-7*) Barclay Bks.

— Manners, Please! Poems & Activities That Teach Responsible Behavior. Mitchell, Judy, ed. (Illus.). 96p. (Orig.). (J). (gr. k-3). 1995. pap., teacher ed. 9.95 (*1-57310-014-5*) Teachng & Lrning Co.

***Lipson, Greta B.** Mind over Manners: Poems, Discussion & Activities about Responsible Behavior: Grades 4-6. Mitchell, Judy, ed. (Illus.). 112p. 1999. pap., teacher ed. 10.95 (*1-57310-186-9*) Teachng & Lrning Co.

Lipson, Greta B. More Fast Ideas for Busy Teachers: One Hundred Productive Activities for Teachers, Substitutes, & Parents. (Illus.). 144p. 1994. 13.99 (*0-86653-821-6*, GA1513) Good Apple.

— Poetry Writing Handbook: Definitions, Examples, Lessons. Mitchell, Judy, ed. (Illus.). 112p. (J). (gr. 4-6). 1998. pap., teacher ed. 10.95 (*1-57310-108-7*) Teachng & Lrning Co.

— Self-Esteem: Concepts for Activities, Discussion & Insights. Mitchell, Judy, ed. (Illus.). 96p. (Orig.). (J). (gr. k-3). 1997. pap. 9.95 (*1-57310-080-3*) Teachng & Lrning Co.

— Tales with a Twist. 160p. (J). (gr. 5-9). 1991. 12.99 (*0-86653-609-4*, GA1328) Good Apple.

Lipson, Greta B. & Greenberg, Bernice. Extra! Extra! Read All about It! 160p. (J). (gr. 4-8). 1981. 12.99 (*0-86653-006-1*, GA234) Good Apple.

An Asterisk (*) at the beginning of an entry indicates that the title is appearing for the first time.

Lipson, Greta B. & Lipson, Eric. Everyday Law for Young Citizens. 160p. (J). (gr. 5 up). 1988. student ed. 12.99 (*0-86653-447-4*, GA1056) Good Apple.
— The Scoop on Frogs & Princes. 128p. teacher ed. 12.99 (*0-86653-740-6*, GA1455) Good Apple.
Lipson, Greta B. & Romantowski, Jane. Calliope. 160p. (gr. 4-8). 1981. 12.99 (*0-86653-025-8*, GA230) Good Apple.
— Ethnic Pride. (Illus.). 152p. (J). (gr. 4-9). 1983. student ed. 13.99 (*0-86653-121-1*, GA 464) Good Apple.
Lipson, Greta B., jt. auth. see Solomon, Susan.
Lipson, H., ed. see Bragg, Lawrence.
Lipson, John D. Elements of Algebra & Algebraic Computing. 342p. (C). 1981. text 39.95 (*0-201-04115-4*) Addison-Wesley.
Lipson, Joseph I. Educational Technology in Voc Ed. 28p. 1984. 3.25 (*0-318-22085-7*, IN268) Ctr Educ Trng Employ.
Lipson, Juliene & Steiger, Nancy. Self-Care Nursing in a Multicultural Context. LC 96-4508. 352p. 1996. 49.95 (*0-8039-7054-4*); pap. 24.00 (*0-8039-7055-2*) Sage.
Lipson, Juliene G. Jews for Jesus: An Anthropological Study. LC 89-45372. (Studies in Anthropology: No. 5). 1990. 42.50 (*0-404-62605-X*) AMS Pr.
Lipson, Lawrence, tr. see Gleijeses, Piero.
Lipson, Lesley, tr. & intro. see De Cervantes Saavedra, Miguel.
Lipson, Leslie. The Ethical Crises of Civilization: Moral Meltdown or Advance. (Illus.). 416p. 1993. 62.00 (*0-8039-5242-2*); pap. 28.00 (*0-8039-5243-0*) Sage.
— I Do Not Itch to Etch: Views in Verse. 112p. (Orig.). 1987. pap. 7.95 (*0-9618591-0-5*) Davro Press.
Lipson, Linda R., jt. auth. see Henderson, Tim M.
Lipson, Marc, jt. auth. see Lipschutz, Seymour.
Lipson, Marjorie Y. & Wixson, Karen K. Assessment & Instruction of Reading & Writing Disability: An Interactive Approach. 2nd ed. LC 96-19727. (C). 1997. pap. 60.25 (*0-673-99057-5*) HarpC.
Lipson, Michael. How the Wind Plays. LC 93-11742. (Illus.). 32p. (J). (ps-1). 1994. lib. bdg. 15.49 (*1-56282-326-4*, Pub. by Hyprn Child) Little.
***Lipson, Michael.** How the Wind Plays. (Illus.). 28p. (ps-1). 1999. reprint ed. text 15.00 (*0-7881-6652-2*) DIANE Pub.
Lipson, Michael, tr. see Kuhlewind, Georg.
Lipson, Michael, tr. see Rudnicki, Konrad.
Lipson, Michael, tr. see Steiner, Rudolf.
Lipson, Michelle, et al. The Fantastic Costume Book: Forty Complete Patterns to Amaze & Amuse. LC 92-11365. (Illus.). 128p. (J). (gr. 4 up). 1992. 24.95 (*0-8069-8376-0*) Sterling.
Lipson, Ruth. Modeh Ani Means Thank You. (Illus.). (J). (ps-2). 1986. 10.95 (*0-87306-392-9*) Feldheim.
— Shabbos Is Coming. (Sifrei Rimon Ser.). 1985. pap. 2.95 (*0-87306-383-X*) Feldheim.
Lipson, S. G., et al. Optical Physics. (Illus.). 515p. (C). 1995. pap. text 39.95 (*0-521-43631-1*) Cambridge U Pr.
— Optical Physics. 3rd ed. (Illus.). 515p. (C). 1995. text 95.00 (*0-521-43047-X*) Cambridge U Pr.
Lipson, Stanley H. Westfield in the Golden Age of Postcards. (Images of America Ser.). 128p. 1996. pap. 16.99 (*0-7524-0406-7*) Arcadia Publng.
Lipson, Stefan B., jt. auth. see Furlong, Mary.
***Lipson, Susan L.** Knock on Wood. (Illus.). 135p. (J). (gr. 3-6). 2000. pap. 12.95 (*0-9677902-0-4*) Leba Hse Pubs.
Lipstadt, Deborah E. Beyond Belief: The American Press & the Coming of the Holocaust 1933-1945. 336p. (C). 1985. 35.00 (*0-02-919160-2*) Free Pr.
— Beyond Belief: The American Press & the Coming of the Holocaust 1933-1945. 370p. 1993. per. 14.95 (*0-02-919161-0*) Free Pr.
— Denying the Holocaust: The Growing Assault on Truth & Memory. LC 93-45586. 288p. 1994. pap. 13.95 (*0-452-27274-2*, Plume) Dutton Plume.
— Denying the Holocaust: The Growing Assault on Truth & Memory. LC 93-45586. 278p. 1993. 24.95 (*0-02-919235-8*) Free Pr.
— The Zionist Career of Louis Lipsky, 1900-1921. 1981. 38.95 (*0-405-14086-X*) Ayer.
Lipstein, Kurt. Principles of the Conflict of Laws: National & International. 160p. 1981. 21.50 (*90-286-0750-1*) Kluwer Academic.
— Principles of the Conflict of Laws: National & International. 160p. 1981. pap. text 75.50 (*90-247-2544-5*) Kluwer Academic.
Lipstein, Morissa. Lessons from Our Living Past, No. 1. (J). (gr. 2-3). 1995. pap., wbk. ed. 3.95 (*0-87441-087-8*) Behrman.
— Lessons from Our Living Past, No. 2. (J). (gr. 2-3). 1995. pap., wbk. ed. 3.95 (*0-87441-088-6*) Behrman.
Lipstein, Norman J., ed. see ASME Staff.
Lipstein, Sherman, ed. see Palmer, Paul M.
Lipsyte, Robert. Assignment Sports. LC 83-48436. (Trophy Bk.). 192p. (YA). (gr. 7 up). 1984. pap. 6.95 (*0-06-440138-3*, HarpTrophy) HarpC Child Bks.
— The Brave. LC 90-25396. (Charlotte Zolotow Bk.). 208p. (YA). (gr. 7 up). 1993. pap. 4.95 (*0-06-447079-2*, HarpTrophy) HarpC Child Bks.
— Brave. (J). 1993. 10.05 (*0-606-02539-1*, Pub. by Turtleback) Demco.
— The Chemo Kid. LC 91-55500. (Trophy Keypoint Bk.). 176p. (YA). (gr. 7 up). 1992. 14.00 (*0-06-020284-X*) HarpC Child Bks.
— The Chief. LC 92-54502. (Trophy Bk.). 240p. (J). (gr. 7 up). 1995. pap. 4.95 (*0-06-447097-0*) HarpC Child Bks.
— Chief. 1995. 9.60 (*0-606-07362-0*, Pub. by Turtleback) Demco.
— The Contender. LC 67-19623. 190p. (J). (gr. 4-7). 1967. lib. bdg. 15.89 (*0-06-023920-4*) HarpC Child Bks.
— The Contender. LC 67-19623. (Trophy Keypoint Bk.). 176p. (YA). (gr. 7-12). 1987. pap. 4.95 (*0-06-447039-3*, HarpTrophy) HarpC Child Bks.
— The Contender. (YA). 1987. 10.05 (*0-606-02525-1*, Pub. by Turtleback) Demco.
— In the Country of Illness: Comfort & Advice for the Journey. LC 97-31245. 272p. 1998. 24.00 (*0-679-43182-9*) Knopf.
— Jim Thorpe: Twentieth-Century Jock. LC 92-44069. 112p. (J). (gr. 4-7). 1995. pap. 3.95 (*0-06-446141-6*) HarpC Child Bks.
— Jim Thorpe: 20Th-Century Jock. (Superstar Lineup Ser.). 1995. 9.15 (*0-606-07741-3*, Pub. by Turtleback) Demco.
— Michael Jordan: A Life Above the Rim. LC 93-50561. (Superstar Lineup Ser.). (Illus.). 96p. (J). (gr. 5-9). 1994. lib. bdg. 14.89 (*0-06-024235-3*) HarpC Child Bks.
— One Fat Summer. LC 76-49746. (Trophy Bk.). 240p. (YA). (gr. 7-12). 1991. pap. 4.95 (*0-06-447073-3*, HarpTrophy) HarpC Child Bks.
— One Fat Summer. 1991. 10.05 (*0-606-01085-8*, Pub. by Turtleback) Demco.
— Summer Rules. LC 79-2816. (Trophy Keypoint Bk.). 208p. (YA). (gr. 7 up). 1992. mass mkt. 3.95 (*0-06-447071-7*, HarpTrophy) HarpC Child Bks.
— The Summerboy. LC 82-47578. (Charlotte Zolotow Bk.). 160p. (YA). (gr. 7 up). 1982. 12.95 (*0-06-023888-7*) HarpC Child Bks.
Lipsyte, Robert & Brown, Gene. Sports & Society. (Great Contemporary Issues Ser.). 35.00 (*0-405-13143-7*) Ayer.
Lipsyte, Robert, jt. auth. see Gregory, Dick.
***Lipsyte, Sam.** Venus Drive. LC 99-68410. 178p. 2000. pap. 13.00 (*1-890447-25-0*) Open City Bks.
Liptak, jt. auth. see Hudson, F. Parker.
Liptak, Andras, et al. Handbook of Oligosaccharides: Trisaccharides, 2 vols., 1. 256p. 1990. lib. bdg. 219.00 (*0-8493-2901-9*, QP702) CRC Pr.
— Handbook of Oligosaccharides: Trisaccharides, 2 vols., 2. 256p. 1990. lib. bdg. 219.00 (*0-8493-2902-7*) CRC Pr.
Liptak, B. Instrument Engineers Handbook: Process Measurement & Analysis. (Illus.). 1400p. 1995. 180.95 (*0-7506-2254-7*) Buttrwrth-Heinemann.
— Instrument Engineers Handbook Vol. 2: Process Control. (Illus.). 1558p. 1995. 180.95 (*0-7506-2255-5*) Buttrwrth-Heinemann.
Liptak, Bela G. Analytical Instrumentation. LC 93-48731. 432p. 1994. lib. bdg. 84.95 (*0-8019-8397-5*) Nichols Pub.
— Environmental Engineers' Handbook: Water Pollution, 1. 1999. cd-rom 129.00 (*0-8493-2157-3*) CRC Pr.
— Optimization of Industrial Unit Processes. 2nd ed. LC 98-20091. 432p. 1998. boxed set 94.95 (*0-8493-9873-8*, CH9873) CRC Pr.
— Optimization of Unit Operations. LC 86-47960. 432p. 1987. lib. bdg. 79.95 (*0-8019-7706-1*) NP-Chilton.
Liptak, D., ed. see Dennehy, R. & Grisez, G.
Liptak, D., ed. see Lawler, R. & May, W.
Liptak, David Q. Preaching Mary's Praises - Homilies on the Mother of the Lord. 105p. 1992. 3.95 (*1-56036-013-5*, 38608) AMI Pr.
— Sacramental & Occasional Homilies. LC 80-29287. 96p. (Orig.). 1981. pap. 5.95 (*0-8189-0408-9*) Alba.
Liptak, Diana. And Thy House. 123p. (Orig.). 1985. pap. 3.00 (*0-9615057-0-2*) D Liptak.
Liptak, Dolores. European Immigrants & the Catholic Church in Connecticut, 1870-1920. LC 86-6859. (CMS Migration & Ethnicity Ser.). 199p. 1987. 19.50 (*0-913256-79-X*); pap. text 14.50 (*0-913256-80-3*) CMS.
Liptak, Dolores, ed. A Church of Many Cultures: Selected Historical Essays on Ethnic American Catholicism. (Heritage of American Catholicism Ser.). 416p. 1988. lib. bdg. 20.00 (*0-8240-4081-3*) Garland.
Liptak, John J. Treatment Planning in Career Counseling. LC 00-20257. (Counseling Ser.). 159p. 2000. pap. text 41.95 (*0-534-54985-3*) Wadsworth Pub.
Liptak, Jphn. The Career Exploration Inventory Professional Manual: A Guide for Exploring Work, Leisure, & Learning. 150p. 1993. pap. 29.95 (*1-56370-198-7*, 397CEIPM) JIST Works.
Liptak, Karen. Astronomy Basics. (Illus.). 48p. (J). (gr. 3-7). 1986. 10.95 (*0-13-049966-8*) P-H.
— Indians of the Pacific Northwest. (First Americans Ser.). (Illus.). 96p. (J). (gr. 5-9). 1991. 21.95 (*0-8160-2384-0*) Facts on File.
— Indians of the Southwest. (First Americans Ser.). (Illus.). 96p. (J). (gr. 5-9). 1991. 21.95 (*0-8160-2385-9*) Facts on File.
— North American Indian Ceremonies. (First Time Bks.). 1992. 11.15 (*0-606-05512-6*, Pub. by Turtleback) Demco.
— North American Indian Ceremonies. Mathews, V., ed. LC 90-12337. (First Bks.). (Illus.). 64p. (J). (gr. 4-6). 1992. lib. bdg. 22.00 (*0-531-20100-7*) Watts.
— North American Indian Sign Language. (First Time Bks.). 1992. 12.15 (*0-606-05514-2*, Pub. by Turtleback) Demco.
— North American Indian Sign Language. LC 90-12336. (First Bks.). (Illus.). 64p. (J). (gr. 4-6). 1990. lib. bdg. 22.00 (*0-531-10869-4*) Watts.
— North American Indian Survival Skills. LC 90-12354. (First Bks.). (Illus.). 64p. (J). (gr. 4-6). 1990. lib. bdg. 22.00 (*0-531-10870-8*) Watts.
— North American Indian Tribal Chiefs. (First Time Bks.). 1992. 11.15 (*0-606-05516-9*, Pub. by Turtleback) Demco.
— Saving Our Wetlands & Their Wildlife. (First Bks.). (J). 1992. 11.15 (*0-606-05578-9*, Pub. by Turtleback) Demco.
— Saving Our Wetlands & Their Wildlife. LC 91-4682. (First Bks.). (Illus.). 64p. (J). (gr. 5-8). 1991. lib. bdg. 22.00 (*0-531-20092-7*) Watts.
Liptak, Pal. Avars & Ancient Hungarians. 208p. (C). 1983. 75.00 (*963-05-2956-4*, Pub. by Akade Kiado) St Mut.
Liptbak, Bela G., jt. auth. see Liu, David H.
Lipton, Alfred. Cinderella, Vol. 512. rev. ed. Caban, Janice, ed. & illus. by. (Once upon a Tale Ser.). 10p. (J). (gr. k). 1989. pap. 2.00 (*1-878501-01-1*) Ntrl Science Indus.
— Goldilox & the Three Bears, Vol. 514. rev. ed. Caban, Janice, ed. & illus. by. (Once upon a Tale Ser.). 10p. (J). (gr. k). 1989. pap. 2.00 (*1-878501-02-X*) Ntrl Science Indus.
— Jack & the Beanstalk, Vol. 510. rev. ed. Caban, Janice, ed. & illus. by. (Once upon a Tale Ser.). 10p. (J). (gr. k). 1989. pap. 2.00 (*1-878501-00-3*) Ntrl Science Indus.
— Little Red Riding Hood, Vol. 520. rev. ed. Caban, Janice, ed. & illus. by. (Once upon a Tale Ser.). 10p. (J). (gr. k). 1989. pap. 2.00 (*1-878501-05-4*) Ntrl Science Indus.
— Pinocchio, Vol. 516. rev. ed. Caban, Janice, ed. & illus. by. (Once upon a Tale Ser.). 10p. (J). (gr. k). 1989. pap. 2.00 (*1-878501-03-8*) Ntrl Science Indus.
— Sleeping Beauty, Vol. 518. rev. ed. Caban, Janice, ed. & illus. by. (Once upon a Tale Ser.). 10p. (J). (gr. k). 1989. pap. 2.00 (*1-878501-04-6*) Ntrl Science Indus.
Lipton, Barbara & Ragnubs, Nima D. Treasures of Tibetan Art: The Collections of the Jacques Marchais Museum of Tibetan Art. LC 95-34638. (Illus.). 320p. 1996. pap. 32.50 (*0-19-509714-9*) OUP.
Lipton, Carolee, jt. auth. see Lipton, Chet.
Lipton, Charles, jt. auth. see Haynes, J. H.
Lipton, Chet & Lipton, Carolee. Walking Easy in the French Alps: A Hiking Guide for Active Adults. (Walking Easy Ser.). (Illus.). 224p. (Orig.). 1995. pap. 11.95 (*0-933469-21-7*) Globe Pequot.
— Walking Easy in the Italian Alps: A Hiking Guide for Active Adults. (Walking Easy Ser.). (Illus.). 224p. 1995. pap. 11.95 (*0-933469-22-5*) Globe Pequot.
— Walking Easy in the Swiss & Austrian Alps. 2nd ed. LC 99-17101. (Illus.). 288p. 1999. pap. text 14.95 (*0-7627-0422-5*) Globe Pequot.
Lipton, David. A Visit to Portland. 39p. (J). 1990. 3.50 (*0-9643034-0-X*) White Truffle Bks.
Lipton, David A. Broker-Dealer Regulation. (Securities Law Ser.). 1988. ring bd. 145.00 (*0-87632-599-1*) West Group.
Lipton, David A., jt. auth. see Lipsky, Daniel.
***Lipton, David L.** Cherry Picking the Time Tree: Essays on Being an Historian. LC 99-90820. 1999. 25.00 (*0-7388-0540-8*); pap. 18.00 (*0-7388-0541-6*) Xlibris Corp.
Lipton, David R. Ernst Cassirer: The Dilemma of a Liberal Intellectual in Germany, 1914-1933. LC 78-6945. 226p. reprint ed. pap. 70.10 (*0-8357-8119-4*, 203399200088) Bks Demand.
Lipton, Diana. Revisions of the Night: Politics & Promises in the Patriarchal Dreams of Genesis. (JSOTS Ser.: Vol. 288). 250p. 1999. 75.00 (*1-85075-958-8*, Pub. by Sheffield Acad) CUP Services.
Lipton, Douglas S. Effectiveness of Treatment for Drug Abusers under Criminal Justice Supervision. (Illus.). 64p. (C). 1996. reprint ed. pap. text 20.00 (*0-7881-3514-7*) DIANE Pub.
Lipton, Douglas S., jt. ed. see Friedman, Samuel R.
Lipton, Douglas W. & Strand, Ivar E. Maryland's Ocean Fisheries: A Bioeconomic Assessment. 1983. pap. 1.50 (*0-943676-22-3*) MD Sea Grant Col.
Lipton, Eunice. Alias Olympia: A Woman's Search for Manet's Notorious Model & Her Own Desire. LC 98-49414. 1999. pap. 11.95 (*0-8014-8609-2*) Cornell U Pr.
— Looking into Degas: Uneasy Images of Women & Modern Life. (Illus.). 1986. 60.00 (*0-520-05604-3*, Pub. by U CA Pr) Cal Prin Full Svc.
Lipton, Gladys C. Beginning French Bilingual Dictionary. 3rd rev. ed. LC 98-70225. (ENG & FRE., Illus.). 180p. (J). (gr. 3 up). 1998. pap. 8.95 (*0-7641-0279-6*) Barron.
— Beginning Spanish Bilingual Dictionary: A Beginner's Guide in Words & Pictures. (ENG & SPA., Illus.). (J). 1989. 12.05 (*0-606-04541-4*, Pub. by Turtleback) Demco.
— Elementary Foreign Language Programs (FLES*) An Administrator's Handbook. 288p. 1998. pap. 16.95 (*0-8442-9366-0*, VS9366-0) NTC Contemp Pub Co.
— Practical Handbook of Elementary Foreign Language Programs. 2nd ed. 1991. pap. text 19.95 (*0-8442-9338-5*) NTC Contemp Pub Co.
— Practical Handbook to Elementary Foreign Language Programs. 2nd ed. 224p. 1995. pap. 19.95 (*0-8442-9332-6*, Natl Textbk Co) NTC Contemp Pub Co.
— Practical Handbook to Elementary Foreign Language Programs (FLES*) (FLES) Including FLES, FLEX & IMM. 3rd ed. LC 97-69971. 288p. 1998. pap. 19.95 (*0-8442-9330-X*, VS9330-X) NTC Contemp Pub Co.
***Lipton, Gladys C. & American Association of Teachers of French Staff.** A Celebration of Fles: Sequential Fles, Flex & Immersion. LC 98-91257. x, 226 p. 1998. write for info. (*0-8442-9343-1*) NTC Contemp Pub Co.
Lipton, Gladys C. & Colaneri, John. Beginning Italian Bilingual Dictionary. 3rd rev. ed. LC 98-70227. (ENG & ITA.). 180p. (J). (gr. 3 up). 1998. pap. 8.95 (*0-7641-0282-6*) Barron.
Lipton, Gladys C. & Losoncy, Renata. Beginning German Bilingual Dictionary. LC 98-70229. (ENG & GER., Illus.). 180p. (J). (gr. 4-7). 1998. pap. 8.95 (*0-7641-0340-7*) Barron.
Lipton, Gladys C. & Munoz, Olivia. Beginning Spanish Bilingual Dictionary. 3rd ed. LC 98-70224. (ENG & SPA., Illus.). 180p. (J). (gr. 3). 1998. pap. 8.95 (*0-7641-0281-8*) Barron.
Lipton, Helene L. & Lee, Philip R. Drugs & the Elderly: Clinical, Social, & Policy Perspectives. LC 87-33574. 280p. 1988. 39.50 (*0-8047-1295-6*) Stanford U Pr.
Lipton, Howard L., jt. ed. see Gilden, Donald H.
Lipton, James. An Exaltation of Larks: The Ultimate Edition. (Illus.). 336p. 1993. reprint ed. pap. 14.95 (*0-14-017096-0*, Penguin Bks) Viking Penguin.
Lipton, James A., jt. auth. see Glock, Martha H.
Lipton, Judith E., jt. auth. see Barash, David P.
Lipton, June, jt. auth. see O'Donnell, Asta.
Lipton, Karen S. & Wolf, Edward, eds. Emerging Legal Issues in Blood Banking & Transfusion Medicine. LC 98-3649. 202p. 1998. pap. text. write for info. (*1-56395-079-0*) Am Assn Blood.
Lipton, Kathryn L. Dictionary of Agriculture: From Abaca to Zoonosis. LC 94-25260. 375p. 1995. lib. bdg. 75.00 (*1-55587-523-8*) L Rienner.
Lipton, Ken. Yellow Sky: An Alternative Perspective about the Human Condition & History. Spinney, Jonathon, ed. 1998. pap. text 12.95 (*1-891850-03-2*) Med Bear.
Lipton, Laura & Hubble, Deborah. More Than 50 Ways to Learner-Centered Literacy. LC 96-80016. 224p. (Orig.). 1997. pap. 21.95 (*1-57517-069-8*, 1445) SkyLght.
Lipton, Leah. A Truthful Likeness: Chester Harding & His Portraits. (Illus.). 196p. 1985. pap. 19.95 (*0-87474-613-2*) Smithsonian.
Lipton, Lenny. Independent Filmmaking. (Illus.). 448p. 1983. 12.95 (*0-686-46243-2*, Fireside) S&S Trade Pap.
Lipton, M. Agriculture-Health Linkages. (WHO Offset Publications: No. 104). 111p. 1988. 17.00 (*92-4-170104-8*) World Health.
Lipton, Martin & Steinberger, Erica H. Takeovers & Freezeouts, 5 vols., Set. 2000p. 1978. 290.00 (*0-317-01347-5*, 00551) NY Law Pub.
Lipton, Martin, jt. auth. see Oakes, Jeannie.
Lipton, Martin J. & Lanzer, Peter. Vascular Diagnostics: Principles & Technology. LC 96-41507. 1996. write for info. (*0-387-61541-5*) Spr-Verlag.
— Vascular Diagnostics: Principles & Technology. LC 96-41507. (Illus.). xii, 288p. 1996. 159.00 (*3-540-61541-5*) Spr-Verlag.
Lipton, Martin J., jt. auth. see Funaki, Brian.
Lipton, Merrill I. Posttraumatic Stress Disorder: Additional Perspectives. LC 93-37142. 258p. 1994. pap. 34.95 (*0-398-06242-0*) C C Thomas.
— Posttraumatic Stress Disorder: Additional Perspectives. LC 93-37142. 258p. (C). 1994. text 52.95 (*0-398-05899-7*) C C Thomas.
Lipton, Michael. Successes in Anti-Poverty. LC 98-205885. 224p. 1998. pap. 24.75 (*92-2-110848-1*) Intl Labour Office.
Lipton, Michael & Longhurst, Richard. New Seeds & Poor People. LC 88-23079. (Johns Hopkins Studies in Development). 489p. reprint ed. pap. 151.60 (*0-608-06082-8*, 206641400008) Bks Demand.
Lipton, Michael & Van der Gaag, Jacques. Including the Poor. LC 93-34793. (Regional & Sectoral Studies). 624p. 1993. pap. 50.00 (*0-8213-2674-0*, 12674) World Bank.
Lipton, Michael, jt. auth. see Payne, Philip.
Lipton, Michael, jt. auth. see Pearlberg, Robert L.
Lipton, Mimi, ed. The Tiger Rugs of Tibet. LC 88-51136. (Illus.). 1989. 60.00 (*0-500-97369-5*, Pub. by Thames Hudson) Norton.
Lipton, Mimi & Dueser, Thorsten, photos by. Stacking Wood. LC 92-62137. (Illus.). 124p. 1993. pap. 19.95 (*0-500-97407-1*, Pub. by Thames Hudson) Norton.
***Lipton, Nigel.** Music Contracts. 350p. 2000. pap. 62.75 (*1-85811-215-X*, Pub. by CLT Prof) Gaunt.
Lipton, Peter, ed. Theory, Evidence, & Explanation. (International Research Library of Philosophy: Vol. 11). (Illus.). 544p. 1995. 184.95 (*1-85521-633-7*, Pub. by Dartmth Pub) Ashgate Pub Co.
Lipton, Phillip & Herzberg, Abe. Essential Corporations Legislation. (Essential Legislation Ser.). 600p. 1995. pap. 30.00 (*0-455-21307-0*, Pub. by LawBk Co) Gaunt.
— Understanding Company Law. 4th ed. 590p. 1991. pap. 49.00 (*0-455-21022-5*, Pub. by LawBk Co) Gaunt.
— Understanding Company Law: Supplement, July, 1992. 4th ed. 1992. 15.00 (*0-455-21155-8*, Pub. by LawBk Co) Gaunt.
— Understanding Company Law: With Computer Tutorials. 5th ed. 730p. 1993. pap. 69.00 incl. disk (*0-455-21215-5*, Pub. by LawBk Co) Gaunt.
Lipton, Richard J., et al. DNA Based Computers: DIMACS Workshop, April 4, 1995. LC 96-8191. (DIMACS Series in Discrete Mathematics & Theoretical Computer Science: Vol. 27). 221p. 1996. text 49.00 (*0-8218-0518-5*, DIMACS/27) Am Math.
Lipton, Rose C., jt. auth. see Provence, Sally.
Lipton, Russell C. Users Guide to FOCUS. 2nd ed. (Illus.). 320p. 1988. pap. text 24.95 (*0-07-038013-9*) McGraw.
Lipton, Sampson. Persistent Pain: Modern Methods of Treatment. Incl. Vol. 1. 282p. 1977. 43.50 (*0-8089-1017-5*, 792571, W B Saunders Co); Vol. 2. 416p. 1980. 69.50 (*0-8089-1018-3*, 792572, W B Saunders Co); write for info. (*0-318-56571-4*, Grune & Strat) Harcrt Hlth Sci Grp.
Lipton, Sampson, et al, eds. The Pain Clinic. LC 89-10878. (Advances in Pain Research & Therapy Ser.: Vol. 13). (Illus.). 435p. 1990. reprint ed. pap. 134.90 (*0-608-05865-3*, 205983200007) Bks Demand.
Lipton, Sara. Images of Intolerance: The Representation of Jews & Judaism in the Bible Moralisbee. LC 99-11009. (S. Mark Taper Foundation Imprint in Jewish Studies). 260p. 1999. 60.00 (*0-520-21551-6*, Pub. by U CA Pr) Cal Prin Full Svc.
Lipton, Sydney & Lynch, Jeremiah. Handbook of Health Hazard Control in the Chemical Process Industry. rev. ed. 1003p. 1994. 125.00 (*0-471-55464-2*) Wiley.
Lipton, Werner J. Fragments of a Childhood & Youth: Autobiographical Memories. (Illus.). 68p. 1998. pap. 15.00 (*0-9663011-1-0*) W J Lipton.

L

— The Science Editor's Soapbox: An Aid for Writers of Scientific & Technical Reports. (Illus.). 93p. (C). 1998. pap. text 18.00 (*0-9663011-0-2*) W J Lipton.

Lipton, Zelda, jt. auth. see Vadakin, Charles E.

Liptser, R. S. & Shiryayev, A. N. Theory of Martingales. (C). 1989. text 447.00 (*0-7923-0395-4*) Kluwer Academic.

***Liptser, Robert & Shiryaev, A. N.** Statistics of Random Processes Vol. 1: General Theory. 2nd rev. expanded ed. Karatzas, I. & Yor, M., eds. (Applications of Mathematics Ser.: 5). (Illus.). 400p. 2000. 69.95 (*3-540-63929-2*) Spr-Verlag.

— Statistics of Random Processes Vol. 2: Applications. 2nd rev. expanded ed. (Applications of Mathematics Ser.: Vol. 6). (Illus.). x, 402p. 2000. 72.00 (*3-540-63928-4*) Spr-Verlag.

Liptzin, Solomon. Arthur Schnitzler. LC 94-48728. (Studies in Austrian Literature, Culture, & Thought). 196p. 1995. pap. 19.95 (*1-57241-013-2*) Ariadne CA.

— Biblical Themes in World Literature. LC 84-19457. 316p. 1985. 25.00 (*0-88125-063-5*) Ktav.

— Germany's Stepchildren. LC 75-167378. (Essay Index Reprint Ser.). 1977. reprint ed. 24.95 (*0-8369-2462-2*) Ayer.

— Historical Survey of German Literature. LC 72-89407. (Illus.). xiii, 300p. 1972. reprint ed. lib. bdg. 53.50 (*0-8154-0441-7*) Cooper Sq.

— Lyric Pioneers of Modern Germany. LC 28-5277. reprint ed. 27.50 (*0-404-03995-2*) AMS Pr.

Liptzin, Solomon, ed. & tr. see Peretz, Isaac L.

Lipuma, Anthony, jt. auth. see Rooney, Robert.

Lipuma, Edward S. Encompassing Others: The Magic of Modernity in Melanesia. LC 99-51001. 368p. (C). 1999. text 49.50 (*0-472-11068-3*, 11068) U of Mich Pr.

Lipuma, Edward S., jt. auth. see Meltzoff, Sarah K.

Lipumba, Nguyuru H. & World Institute for Development Economics Research. The Liberalization of Foreign Exchange Markets & Economic Growth in Sub-saharan Africa. LC 98-178575. (Research for Action Ser.). viii, 60p. 1997. write for info. (*952-9520-52-2*) UN.

Lipunov, M. Astrophysics of Neutron Stars. Borner, Gerhard et al, eds. Wadhwa, R. S., tr. from RUS. (Astronomy & Astrophysics Library). 344p. (C). 1992. 98.00 (*0-387-53568-3*) Spr-Verlag.

Liquian, E. & Sobrevinas, Irene. Filipino Cooking: Here & Abroad. 194p. 1970. 12.95 (*0-318-36288-0*) Asia Bk Corp.

Liquid Chromatography Symposium Staff. Biological - Biomedical Applications of Liquid Chromatography. Hawk, Gerald L. et al, eds. LC 78-26628. (Chromatographic Science Ser.: No. 10). (Illus.). 756p. reprint ed. pap. 200.00 (*0-7837-0794-0*, 204110800019) Bks Demand.

— Biological - Biomedical Applications of Liquid Chromatography, No. II. Hawk, Gerald L. et al, eds. LC 79-18918. (Chromatographic Science Ser.: No. 12). (Illus.). 520p. reprint ed. pap. 161.20 (*0-7837-0798-3*, 204111200019) Bks Demand.

Liquid Scintillation Counting Symposium Staff. Liquid Scintillation Counting: Proceedings of a Symposium on Liquid Scintillation Counting, 5th, Bath, England, September 13-16, 1977, Vol. 3. Crook, M. A. & Johnson, P., eds. LC 70-156826. 321p. 1974. reprint ed. pap. 99.60 (*0-608-14248-4*, 2024009) Bks Demand.

— Liquid Scintillation Counting: Proceedings of a Symposium on Liquid Scintillation Counting, 5th, Bath, England, September 13-16, 1977, Vol. 4. Crook, M. A. & Johnson, P., eds. LC 70-156826. 279p. 1977. reprint ed. pap. 86.50 (*0-608-14249-2*, 202401000004) Bks Demand.

— Liquid Scintillation Counting: Proceedings of a Symposium on Liquid Scintillation Counting, 5th, Bath, England, September 13-16, 1977, Vol. 5. Crook, M. A. & Johnson, P., eds. 232p. 1978. reprint ed. pap. 72.00 (*0-608-14099-6*, 2024011) Bks Demand.

***Liquorman, Wayne.** Acceptance of What Is. Asche, Catherine, ed. LC 99-66782. 280p. 1999. pap. 16.00 (*0-929448-19-7*) Advaita Pr CA.

— Acceptance of What Is: A Book about Nothing. Asche, Catherine, ed. LC 99-66782. 300p. 2000. pap. 30.00 (*0-929448-20-0*) Advaita Pr CA.

Liquorman, Wayne, ed. see Balsekar, Ramesh S.

Lira, jt. auth. see Elliott.

Lira, David M. Bankruptcy. 184p. 1988. text 29.95 (*0-13-056532-6*, Busn) P-H.

Lira, Francisco M. El Encanto de las Superficies. (Ciencia para Todos Ser.). (SPA.). pap. 6.99 (*968-16-3947-2*, Pub. by Fondo) Continental Bk.

Lira, Gloria G. Maria Luisa Bombal: Realidad y Fantasia. 28.50 (*0-916379-25-6*) Scripta.

Lira, Gonzalo. Counterparts. 400p. 1999. reprint ed. mass mkt. 6.99 (*0-515-12429-X*, Jove) Berkley Pub.

Lira, Jorge. La Percepcion Remota. (Ciencia para Todos Ser.). (SPA.). pap. 6.99 (*968-16-2568-4*, Pub. by Fondo) Continental Bk.

Lira-Powell, Julianne H. Fifty Things You Can Do to Promote World Peace. Moran, Ran, ed. (Illus.). 144p. (Orig.). 1991. pap. 9.95 (*0-9629881-8-9*) Adelitas Pubs.

Lira, Solange de Azambuja. The Subject in Brazilian Portuguese. XII, 102p. (C). 1996. 39.95 (*0-8204-2763-2*) P Lang Pubng.

Liren, Huang. Second-Order Directional Derivatives in Nonsmooth Optimization. LC 97-153542. 102p. (Orig.). (C). 1997. pap. text 21.95 (*962-201-664-2*, Pub. by Chinese Univ) U of Mich Pr.

Lires, William J. A Long Walk in the Australian Bush. LC 98-21240. 208p. 1998. pap. 16.95 (*0-8203-2055-2*) U of Ga Pr.

Liria, Pilar, tr. see Garcia-Godoy, Cristian.

Liria, Yauka A. Bougainville Campaign Diary. 199p. 1993. pap. 20.95 (*0-9587718-4-7*, Pub. by Indra Pub) Intl Spec Bk.

Liria, Yauka Aluambo. Vote for the Future. LC 98-183596. 1997. write for info. (*0-19-554121-9*) OUP.

Liritzis, Y., ed. Radioactivity Alert: A Guide to Radiation Effects. (Illus.). 129p. 1992. pap. 9.95 (*960-220-069-3*) Paul & Co Pubs.

Liroff, Richard A. A National Policy for the Environment: NEPA & Its Aftermath. LC 75-28910. 284p. reprint ed. pap. 88.10 (*0-608-17408-4*, 205642900067) Bks Demand.

Liroff, Sylvia R., jt. ed. see Tozier, Carolyn D.

Lirov. Multi-Platform Systems Management. (C). 1999. text 45.00 (*0-13-915786-7*, Macmillan Coll) P-H.

Lirov, Yuval. Mission Critical Systems Management. LC 97-3634. 640p. (C). 1997. 33.80 (*0-13-240292-0*) P-H.

Lirtzman, Sidney I., jt. ed. see O'Connor, Charles J.

Lis, Catharina. Social Change & the Labouring Poor: Antwerp, 1770-1860. LC 85-52070. 224p. 1986. 37.50 (*0-300-03610-8*) Yale U Pr.

Lis, Catharina & Soly, Hugo. Disordered Lives: Eighteenth-Century Families & Their Unruly Relatives. Brown, Alexander, tr. (Illus.). 240p. 1996. 58.95 (*0-7456-1514-7*) Blackwell Pubs.

Lis, Halina, jt. auth. see Sharon, Nathan.

Lis-Turlejska, Maya, tr. see Jackins, Harvey.

Lisa-Bellecci-St. Romain. Building Family Faith Through Advent: Cycle B. LC 96-75881. (Illus.). 32p. (Orig.). 1996. pap. 3.95 (*0-89243-922-X*) Liguori Pubns.

Lisa, Bruce. Fran's Flower. LC 99-71630. 32p. (J). (ps-2). pap. 4.95 (*0-06-443610-1*) HarpC Child Bks.

Lisa, Bruce. Fran's Flower. LC 99-71630. (Illus.). 32p. (J). (ps-2). 2000. 14.95 (*0-06-028621-0*) HarpC Child Bks.

Lisa, Jeannette De, see De Lisa, Jeannette, ed.

Lisa, Kopper. Daisy Is a Mummy. (Illus.). 32p. (J). pap. 9.95 (*0-14-055565-X*, Pub. by Pnguin Bks Ltd) Trafalgar.

Lisa, M. P., ed. see Osho.

Lisa, Nikola. Hallelujah. LC 97-49121. (J). 2000. 16.00 (*0-689-81673-1*) S&S Childrens.

Lisa, Philip, jt. auth. see Pfeiffer, Lee.

LiSacchi, James. Activities for Effective Communication: Through Listening, Speaking, Reading & Writing. 96p. 1992. pap., student ed., wbk. ed. 6.99 (*0-8442-5192-5*) NTC Contemp Pub Co.

Lisagore, W. Barry, ed. see Leis, Brian N.

Lisak, Janet M. & Morgan, Marlene J. The Safe Home Checkout: A Professional Guide to Safe Independent Living. 2nd ed. 70p. 1997. pap. text 29.95 (*0-9658127-0-7*) GELL.

Lisak, Robert P. Handbook of Myasthenia Gravis & Myasthenic Syndromes. (Neurological Disease & Therapy Ser.: Vol. 23). (Illus.). 448p. 1994. text 190.00 (*0-8247-8825-7*) Dekker.

Lisandrelli, Elaine, jt. auth. see Bartoletti, Susan.

Lisandrelli, Elaine S. Bob Dole: Legendary Senator. LC 96-43570. (People to Know Ser.). (Illus.). 128p. (YA). (gr. 6 up). 1997. lib. bdg. 20.95 (*0-89490-825-1*) Enslow Pubs.

— Ida B. Wells-Barnett: Crusader Against Lynching. LC 97-34253. (African-American Biographies Ser.). (Illus.). 128p. (YA). (gr. 6 up). 1998. lib. bdg. 20.95 (*0-89490-947-9*) Enslow Pubs.

— Ignacy Jan Paderewski: Polish Pianist & Patriot. LC 98-37784. (Champions of Freedom Ser.). (Illus.). 112p. (J). (gr. 5 up). 1999. lib. bdg. 18.95 (*1-883846-29-3*) M Reynolds.

— Maya Angelou: More Than a Poet. (African-American Biographies Ser.). 128p. (YA). (gr. 6 up). 1996. lib. bdg. 20.95 (*0-89490-684-4*) Enslow Pubs.

Lisann, Maury. Broadcasting to the Soviet Union: International Politics & Radio. LC 74-14046. (Illus.). 224p. 1975. 34.95 (*0-275-05590-6*, Praeger Pubs) Greenwood.

Lisano, Michael. Lab Manual for Physiology. 1993. spiral bd. 15.65 (*0-88252-124-1*) Paladin Hse.

Lisansky, Edith S., jt. auth. see Schilit, Rebecca.

Lisansky, S. G., jt. ed. see Macmillan, R.

Lisante, James P. Personally Speaking. 144p. 2000. pap. 8.95 (*1-878718-51-7*, Resurrection Pr) Catholic Bk Pub.

Lisanti, Joseph, jt. auth. see Tigue, Joseph.

Lisanti, Suzana, jt. auth. see Melin, Nancy J.

***Lisath, Roy B., contrib. by.** God's Woman--The Power, the Authority--A Tribute the Life of the Woman. LC 99-97025. 2000. pap. 10.95 (*0-533-13366-1*) Vantage.

Lisboa, Eugenio, ed. Dedalus Book of Portuguese Fantasy. (Dedalus Anthology Ser.). (POR.). 384p. (Orig.). 1995. pap. 16.95 (*0-7818-0386-1*) Hippocrene Bks.

— Portuguese Short Fiction, Vol. I. LC 97-164484. 320p. 1997. pap. text 19.95 (*1-85754-206-1*, Pub. by Carcanet Pr) Paul & Co Pubs.

— Portuguese Short Fiction, Vol. II. 320p. 1997. pap. text 19.95 (*1-85754-241-X*, Pub. by Carcanet Pr) Paul & Co Pubs.

Lisboa, Eugenio & Macedo, Helder, eds. The Dedalus Book of Portuguese Fantasy. 3rd ed. Costa, Margaret F., tr. from POR. LC 95-188705. 291p. 2000. reprint ed. pap. 16.95 (*1-873982-66-6*, Pub. by Dedalus) Subterranean Co.

Lisboa, J. C. List of Bombay Grasses & Their Uses. 142p. 1979. reprint ed. 95.00 (*0-7855-3116-5*, Pub. by Intl Bk Distr) St Mut.

Lisboa, J. C., ed. List of Bombay Grasses & Their Uses. 142p. (C). 1979. text 125.00 (*0-89771-579-9*, Pub. by Intl Bk Distr) St Mut.

Lisboa, Maria M. Machado de Assis & Feminism: Re-Reading the Heart of the Companion. LC 96-4911. (Women's Studies: Vol. 11). 284p. 1996. 89.95 (*0-7734-8828-6*) E Mellen.

Lisboa, P. G. Neural Networks: Current Applications. (ITCP-UK Computer Science Ser.). 279p. (C). 1992. mass mkt. 84.95 (*0-412-42790-7*) Chapman & Hall.

Lisboa, P. G., ed. Neural Networks: Current Applications. 288p. 1992. pap. 59.95 (*0-442-31564-3*) Chapman & Hall.

***Lisboa, P. J., et al, eds.** Artificial Neural Networks in Biomedicine. LC 99-29082. (Perspectives in Neural Computing Ser.). 275p. 2000. pap. 79.95 (*1-85233-005-8*, Pub. by Spr-Verlag) Spr-Verlag.

***Lisboa, Paolo J., et al.** Business Applications of Neural Networks. 180p. 2000. 28.00 (*981-02-4089-9*) World Scientific Pub.

Lisboa, Rosendo C. Diccionari Castella-Valencia, Valencia-Castella. (CAT & SPA.). 1100p. 1989. 19.95 (*0-7859-6400-2*, 8486488036) Fr & Eur.

Lisbon, Alan, jt. ed. see Fink, Mitchell P.

Lisby, Gregory C. Mass Communication Law in Georgia. 2nd ed. (State Law Ser.). 120p. (C). 1996. pap. text 14.95 (*0-913507-66-0*) New Forums.

Lisca, Peter. The Wide World of John Steinbeck. 338p. (C). 1981. 50.00 (*0-87752-217-0*) Gordian.

Lisca, Peter, ed. see Steinbeck, John.

Liscam, Gary, jt. auth. see Zong Xiao-Fan.

***Liscano, Carlos.** Road to Ithaca. 2000. pap. 15.95 (*1-891270-08-7*) Lat Am Lit Rev Pr.

Lisch, W. Hereditary Vitreoretinal Degeneration. (Developments in Ophthalmology Ser.: Vol. 8). (Illus.). viii, 92p. 1983. 56.75 (*3-8055-3615-1*) S Karger.

Lischer, Henry J., Jr. Gifts to Minors. 3rd ed. (Tax Management Portfolio Ser.: No. 403). 1988. ring bd. 50.00 (*1-55871-074-4*) BNA.

Lischer, Richard. The Preacher King: Martin Luther King, Jr. & the Word That Moved America. 360p. 1995. 30.00 (*0-19-508779-8*) OUP.

— The Preacher King: Martin Luther King, Jr. & the Word That Moved America. 368p. 1997. reprint ed. pap. 15.95 (*0-19-511132-X*) OUP.

Lischer, Richard, jt. ed. see Willimon, William H.

***Lischi, Sandra.** Invideo 99. 1999. pap. text 25.00 (*88-8158-215-5*) Charta.

***Lischinski, D., et al, eds.** Rendering Techniques '99: Proceedings of the Eurographics Workshop in Granada, Spain, June 21-23, 1999. (Eurographics Ser.). (Illus.). xi, 382p. 1999. pap. 74.95 (*3-211-83382-X*) Spr-Verlag.

Lischke-McNab, Ute. Lily Braun (1865-1916) German Writer, Feminist, Socialist. LC 99-59147. (Studies in German Literature, Linguistics, & Culture). 190p. 2000. 55.00 (*1-57113-169-8*) Camden Hse.

***Lischner, Ray.** Delphi in a Nutshell. Hayes, Simon, ed. (Illus.). 600p. 2000. pap. 24.95 (*1-56592-659-5*) OReilly & Assocs.

Lischner, Ray. Hidden Paths of Delphi 3: Wizards, Experts & the Open Tools API. Coffey, Jerry & Ash, Lori, eds. (Illus.). 300p. (Orig.). 1997. pap. 39.99 (*0-9657366-0-1*) Informant Comm.

Lischner, Ray, et al. Secrets of Delphi 2, No. 2. (Illus.). 890p. 1996. 59.99 (*1-57169-026-3*) Sams.

Lischner, Ray, jt. auth. see Doyle, John.

Lisciandro, Frank. Jim Morrison: An Hour for Magic: A Photojournal. 2nd ed. (Illus.). 160p. 1996. pap. text 19.95 (*0-85965-246-7*, Pub. by Plexus) Publishers Group.

Liscomb, Delores. Reading & Writing Across the Curriculum. 125p. (YA). (gr. 5-12). 1988. wbk. ed. 15.65 (*0-941484-06-8*) Urban Res Pr.

Liscomb, Kathlyn M. Learning from Mt. Hua: A Chinese Physician's Illustrated Travel Record & Painting Theory. LC 96-32050. (RES Monographs on Anthropology & Aesthetics). (Illus.). 245p. (C). 1993. text 95.00 (*0-521-41112-2*) Cambridge U Pr.

Liscombe, Rhodri W. The Church Architecture of Robert Mills. (Illus.). 160p. 1985. 30.00 (*0-89308-542-1*) Southern Hist Pr.

— The New Spirit: Modern Architecture in Vancouver, 1938-1963. LC 96-37595. (Illus.). 208p. 1997. pap. 35.00 (*0-262-62115-0*) MIT Pr.

Liscombe, Rhodri W., jt. auth. see Wadell, Gene.

Liscouski, Joseph G. Laboratory & Scientific Computing: A Strategic Approach. (Wiley-Interscience Series on Laboratory Automation: Vol. 1). 224p. 1994. 59.95 (*0-471-59422-9*) Wiley.

Liscouski, Joseph G., ed. Computers in the Laboratory: Current Practice & Future Trends. LC 84-18518. (Symposium Ser.: No. 265). 136p. 1984. lib. bdg. 43.95 (*0-8412-0867-0*) Am Chemical.

— Computers in the Laboratory: Current Practice & Future Trends. LC 84-18518. (ACS Symposium Ser.: No. 265). 136p. 1984. reprint ed. pap. 42.20 (*0-608-03257-3*, 206377600007) Bks Demand.

Liscum, Gary, et al. Chinese Medicinal Teas: Simple, Proven, Folk Formulas for Common Diseases & Promoting Health. Flaws, Bob, ed. 190p. 1996. pap. 19.95 (*0-936185-76-7*) Blue Poppy Pr.

Liseau, Rene, jt. ed. see Yun, Joao L.

Lisech, Bonnie, jt. auth. see Lisech, Howard.

Lisech, Howard & Lisech, Bonnie. Abide in the Vine: A Biblical Focus for Spiritual Growth - 14 Day Edition. Madsen, Rick, ed. (Illus.). 76p. 1995. student ed., spiral bd. 5.50 (*1-930547-19-6*) Deeper Roots.

— Abide in the Vine: A Biblical Focus for Spiritual Growth - 21 Day Edition. Madsen, Rick, ed. (Illus.). 108p. 1995. student ed., spiral bd. 7.50 (*1-930547-18-8*) Deeper Roots.

— Abide in the Vine: A Biblical Focus for Spiritual Growth - 50 Day Edition. Madsen, Rick, ed. (Illus.). 218p. 1995. student ed., spiral bd. 10.50 (*1-930547-16-1*) Deeper Roots.

— Abide in the Vine: A Biblical Focus for the Spiritual Growth - 30 Day Edition. Madsen, Rick, ed. (Illus.). 130p. 2000. student ed., spiral bd. 8.50 (*1-930547-17-X*) Deeper Roots.

— Abide in the Vine - Fishers of Men: Combined Edition (14/14) 2nd ed. Madsen, Rick, ed. (Illus.). 150p. 1996. student ed., spiral bd. 10.00 (*1-930547-33-1*) Deeper Roots.

— Abide in the Vine - Fishers of Men: Combined Edition (21/14) 2nd ed. Madsen, Rick, ed. (Illus.). 182p. 1996. student ed., spiral bd. 12.00 (*1-930547-32-3*) Deeper Roots.

— Abide in the Vine - Fishers of Men: Combined Edition (30/14) 2nd rev. ed. Madsen, Rick, ed. (Illus.). 214p. 1996. spiral bd. 13.00 (*1-930547-31-5*) Deeper Roots.

— Abide in the Vine - Fishers of Men: Combined Edition (50/14) 2nd ed. Madsen, Rick, ed. (Illus.). 300p. 2001. student ed., spiral bd. 15.00 (*1-930547-30-7*) Deeper Roots.

— Fishers of Men (Overseas Returnee Edition) ReEntry Guide - 14 Day Devotional Bible Study. 2nd ed. Madsen, Rick, ed. (Illus.). 78p. 1993. student ed., spiral bd. 5.50 (*1-930547-12-9*) Deeper Roots.

— Fishers of Men (Stateside Ministry Returnee Edition) ReEntry Guide - 14 Day Devotional Bible Study. 2nd ed. Madsen, Rick, ed. (Illus.). 78p. 1995. student ed., spiral bd. 5.50 (*1-930547-13-7*) Deeper Roots.

— Ripe for Harvest: A Biblical Focus for Spiritual Growth 14 Day Edition. Madsen, Rick, ed. (Illus.). 94p. 2000. spiral bd. 5.50 (*1-930547-07-2*) Deeper Roots.

— Ripe for Harvest: A Biblical Focus for Spiritual Growth 21 Day Edition. Madsen, Rick, ed. (Illus.). 130p. 2000. spiral bd. 7.50 (*1-930547-06-4*) Deeper Roots.

— Rooted & Grounded - Curriculum: Unit Tests & Answer Keys. Madsen, Rick, ed. (Illus.). 40p. 1999. spiral bd. 2.95 (*1-930547-49-8*) Deeper Roots.

— Walk as He Walked: A Biblical Focus for Spiritual Growth - 14 Day Edition. 2nd ed. Madsen, Rick, ed. 78p. 1994. student ed., spiral bd. 5.50 (*1-930547-03-X*) Deeper Roots.

— Walk as He Walked: A Biblical Focus for Spiritual Growth - 21 Day Edition. 2nd ed. Madsen, Rick, ed. 102p. 1994. student ed., spiral bd. 7.50 (*1-930547-02-1*) Deeper Roots.

— Walk as He Walked: A Biblical Focus for Spiritual Growth - 30 Day Edition. 2nd ed. Madsen, Rick, ed. 136p. 1994. student ed., spiral bd. 8.50 (*1-930547-01-3*) Deeper Roots.

— Walk as He Walked: A Biblical Focus for Spiritual Growth - 50 Day Edition. 2nd ed. Madsen, Rick, ed. 216p. 1994. student ed., spiral bd. 10.50 (*1-930547-00-5*) Deeper Roots.

— Walk as He Walked - Fishers of Men: Combined Edition (14/14) 2nd ed. (Illus.). 150p. 1995. student ed., spiral bd. 10.00 (*1-930547-27-7*) Deeper Roots.

— Walk as He Walked - Fishers of Men: Combined Edition (21/14) 2nd ed. (Illus.). 184p. 1995. student ed., spiral bd. 12.00 (*1-930547-26-9*) Deeper Roots.

— Walk as He Walked - Fishers of Men: Combined Edition (30/14) (Illus.). 226p. 1995. student ed., spiral bd. 13.00 (*1-930547-25-0*) Deeper Roots.

— Walk as He Walked - Fishers of Men: Combined Edition (50/14) (Illus.). 300p. 2001. student ed., spiral bd. 15.00 (*1-930547-24-2*) Deeper Roots.

***Lisech, Howard, et al.** Rooted & Grounded - Student Workbook: A Guide for Spiritual Growth Curriculum. Madsen, Rick, ed. (Illus.). 232p. (YA). (gr. 11-12). 1999. student ed., spiral bd. 19.95 (*1-930547-48-X*) Deeper Roots.

— Rooted & Grounded - Teachers Guide: A Guide for Spiritual Growth Curriculum. Madsen, Rick, ed. (Illus.). 316p. 1999. teacher ed., spiral bd. 37.50 (*1-930547-47-1*) Deeper Roots.

Lisech, Howard, ed. & photos by see Chinn, Lisa Espineli.

***Liseikin, V. D.** Grid Generation Methods. Chattot, J. J. et al, eds. LC 99-14666. (Scientific Computation Ser.). (Illus.). xvi, 367p. 1999. 87.00 (*3-540-65686-3*) Spr-Verlag.

Lisella, Frank S. The VNR Dictionary of Environmental Health & Safety. 356p. 1993. 90.00 (*0-471-28410-6*, VNR) Wiley.

Lisella, Frank S., ed. Van Nostrand Reinhold Dictionary of Environmental Health & Safety. LC 93-25838. 384p. 1994. text 70.95 (*0-442-00508-3*, VNR) Wiley.

Lisella, Frank S., jt. auth. see Lewis, Richard J.

Lisenby, Foy. Charles Hillman Brough: A Biography. LC 95-25687. (Illus.). 192p. 1996. text 26.00 (*1-55728-411-3*) U of Ark Pr.

Lisensky, Robert P., jt. auth. see Ewell, Peter T.

Lish, Gordon. Arcade: or How to Write a Novel. LC 98-26693. 192p. 1998. 22.00 (*1-56858-115-7*) FWEW.

— Dear Mr. Capote. 3rd ed. LC 96-25820. 252p. 1996. reprint ed. pap. 12.95 (*1-56858-079-7*) FWEW.

— Epigraph. LC 96-19753. 162p. 1996. 22.00 (*1-56858-076-2*) FWEW.

— Extravaganza: A Joke Book. 190p. 1990. pap. 10.00 (*1-877727-05-9*) White Pine.

— Extravaganza: A Joke Book. 2nd rev. ed. LC 97-23122. 158p. 1997. pap. 12.95 (*1-56858-097-5*) FWEW.

***Lish, Gordon.** Krupp's Lulu: Short Stories & a Novella. 208p. 2000. 22.00 (*1-56858-154-8*, Pub. by FWEW) Publishers Group.

Lish, Gordon. Mourner at the Door. 3rd ed. LC 96-51153. 220p. 1997. reprint ed. pap. 12.95 (*1-56858-084-3*) FWEW.

— Peru. 3rd ed. LC 96-37673. 192p. 1997. reprint ed. pap. 12.95 (*1-56858-085-1*) FWEW.

Lish, Gordon. Selected Stories of Gordon Lish. 250p. pap. 19.95 (*1-895897-74-2*) Somerville Hse.

Lish, Gordon. Self-Imitation of Myself. LC 97-163200. 336p. 1997. 22.00 (*1-56858-098-3*) FWEW.

An Asterisk (*) at the beginning of an entry indicates that the title is appearing for the first time.

— What I Know So Far. 2nd ed. LC 96-28631. 234p. 1996. reprint ed. pap. 10.95 (*1-56858-080-0*) FWEW.
— Zimzum. 2nd ed. LC 97-32894. 98p. 1998. reprint ed. pap. 12.95 (*1-56858-109-2*) FWEW.
***Lishak, Anthony.** Row Your Boat. LC 98-30652. (Illus.). 12p. (J). (ps-k). 1999. 14.95 (*0-7894-3489-X*, D K Ink) DK Pub Inc.
Lisherness, Sara, jt. ed. see Basham, Beth.
Lishing, L. I. Job Notes: Cover Letters. LC 97-208385. 1997. pap. 4.95 (*0-679-77873-X*) Random.
— Job Smart. LC 97-208382. 1997. pap. 12.00 (*0-679-77355-X*) Random.
Lishing, L. L. C. Cracking the CBEST. LC 99-200852. (Princeton Review Ser.). 1999. pap. 18.00 (*0-375-75187-4*) Random.
Lishing, L.L.C. Cracking the ACT, '99: 1999-2000 Edition. (Princeton Review Ser.). 1999. pap. 18.00 (*0-375-75282-X*) Random.
— Cracking the AP: Biology, '99: 1999-2000 Edition. (Princeton Review Ser.). 1999. pap. 16.00 (*0-375-75286-2*) Random.
— Cracking the AP: Calculus AB & BC: 1999-2000 Edition. (Princeton Review Ser.). 1999. pap. 17.00 (*0-375-75285-4*) Random.
— Cracking the AP: Chemistry: 1999-2000 Edition. (Princeton Review Ser.). 1999. pap. 17.00 (*0-375-75287-0*) Random.
— Cracking the AP: English Literature: 1999-2000 Edition. (Princeton Review Ser.). 1999. pap. 16.00 (*0-375-75283-8*) Random.
— Cracking the AP: European History: 1999-2000 Edition. LC 98-51172. (Princeton Review Ser.). 272p. 1999. pap. 16.00 (*0-375-75290-0*) Random.
— Cracking the AP: U.S. Government: 1999-2000 Edition. (Princeton Review Ser.). 1999. pap. 16.00 (*0-375-75288-9*) Random.
— Cracking the AP: U.S. History. (Princeton Review Ser.). 1999. pap. 16.00 (*0-375-75284-6*) Random.
— Cracking the Regents: Math. (Princeton Review Ser.). 1999. pap. 5.95 (*0-375-75272-2*) Random.
— Cracking the Regents: Math I: 1999-2000 Edition. (Princeton Review Ser.). 1999. pap. 5.95 (*0-375-75271-4*) Random.
— Cracking the Regents: Math III: 1999-2000 Edition. (Princeton Review Ser.). 1999. pap. 5.95 (*0-375-75273-0*) Random.
— Cracking the SAT 2: Biology: 1999-2000 Edition. (Princeton Review Ser.). 1999. pap. 17.00 (*0-375-75297-8*) Random.
— Cracking the SAT 2: Chemistry: 1999-2000 Edition. (Princeton Review Ser.). 1999. pap. 17.00 (*0-375-75298-6*) Random.
— Cracking the SAT 2: English: 1999-2000 Edition. (Princeton Review Ser.). 1999. pap. 17.00 (*0-375-75295-1*) Random.
— Cracking the SAT 2: French: 1999-2000 Edition. (Princeton Review Ser.). 1999. pap. 17.00 (*0-375-75299-4*) Random.
— Cracking the SAT 2: History: 1999-2000 Edition. (Princeton Review Ser.). 1999. pap. 17.00 (*0-375-75300-1*) Random.
— Cracking the SAT 2: Math, '99: 1999-2000 Edition. (Princeton Review Ser.). 1999. pap. 18.00 (*0-375-75296-X*) Random.
— Cracking the SAT 2: Physics: 1999-2000 Edition. (Princeton Review Ser.). 1999. pap. 17.00 (*0-375-75302-8*) Random.
— Cracking the SAT 2: Spanish: 1999-2000 Edition. (Princeton Review Ser.). 1999. pap. 17.00 (*0-375-75301-X*) Random.
— Job Notes: Office Politics. (Princeton Review Ser.). 1999. pap. write for info. (*0-375-75303-6*) Random.
— Job Notes: Office Presentations. (Princeton Review Ser.). 1999. pap. write for info. (*0-375-75304-4*) Random.
— NCLEX Q & A. (Princeton Review Ser.). 1999. pap. write for info. (*0-375-75188-2*) Random.
Lishing L.L.C. Pr Pub. America's Top Internships 2000. 1999. pap. 21.00 (*0-375-75413-X*) Random.
— Internship Bible 2000. 1999. pap. 25.00 (*0-375-75415-6*) Random.
— Pocket Guide to Colleges, 2000 Edition. 1999. pap. 9.95 (*0-375-75416-4*) Random.
Lishka, Gerald R. Darkness Is Light Enough: Mystery & Enlightenment at Lake Geneva, Wisconsin. LC 96-8002. (Illus.). 224p. (Orig.). 1996. pap. 14.95 (*1-880090-28-7*) Galde Pr.
— A Handbook for the Ballet Accompanist. LC 78-2051. 148p. reprint ed. pap. 45.90 (*0-7837-6105-8*, 205915100008) Bks Demand.
— Jenny: A Father's Story. LC 96-31037. (Illus.). 256p. 1998. pap. 16.95 (*1-880090-38-4*) Galde Pr.
Lishman. Communication in Social Work. 1997. text 26.95 (*0-333-54412-9*, Pub. by Macmillan) St Martin.
Lishman, Bill. Father Goose & His Goslings. (Illus.). 72p. (Orig.). (J). (gr. k-8). 1992. pap. 10.95 (*0-9623072-8-9*) S Ink WA.
Lishman, J. Working with Children. 1983. 24.50 (*1-85302-007-9*, Pub. by Jessica Kingsley) Taylor & Francis.
Lishman, Joyce, ed. Evaluation. 2nd ed. (Research Highlights in Social Work Ser.: Vol. 8). 144p. 1988. 29.95 (*1-85302-006-0*, Pub. by Jessica Kingsley) Taylor & Francis.
— Handbook of Theory for Accredited Practice Teachers in Social Work. 200p. 1991. pap. 24.95 (*1-85302-098-2*) Taylor & Francis.
— Social Work Departments As Organisations. (Research Highlights in Social Work Ser.: Vol. 4). 112p. 1982. pap. 26.95 (*1-85302-008-7*, Pub. by Jessica Kingsley) Taylor & Francis.
Lishman, William A. Organic Psychiatry: The Psychological Consequences of Cerebral Disorder. 3rd ed. LC 97-7107. 1997. pap. 99.95 (*0-86542-820-4*) Blackwell Sci.
— Organic Psychiatry: The Psychological Consequences of Cerebral Disorder. 3rd ed. LC 97-7107. (Illus.). 1998. 99.95 (*0-86542-842-5*) Blackwell Sci.
Lishner, Kris M. & Bruya, Margaret A. Creating a Health Camp Community: A Nurse's Role. LC 94-4060. 258p. 1994. pap. 21.95 (*0-87603-135-1*) Am Camping.
***Lisi, Albert.** Central Park. 2001. pap. 9.95 (*1-930185-04-9*, 105) Joan of Arc Pubng.
— A Fairytale for Fairies: Adventures of a Manly Mouse. 150p. 2001. pap. 10.95 (*1-930185-06-5*, 107) Joan of Arc Pubng.
Lisi, Albert. Jungle Trips. 325p. 1990. per. 11.95 (*0-89697-349-2*) Intl Univ Pr.
Lisi, Patrick. Wisconsin Waterfalls: A Touring Guide. LC 98-8215. (Illus.). 140p. 1998. pap. 19.95 (*1-879483-50-5*) Prairie Oak Pr.
Lisick, Beth. Monkey Girl: Swinging Stories. LC 97-4728. 160p. 1997. pap. text 11.95 (*0-916397-49-1*) Manic D Pr.
Lisicky, Paul. Lawnboy. 386p. 1999. pap. 13.95 (*1-885983-40-9*) Turtle Point Pr.
Lisiecki, Johannes F. An Adventrenuer's Odyssey: A 70,000 Kilometer Sojourn of the Americas. LC 97-77790. (Illus.). 396p. 1998. pap. 21.95 (*1-883697-26-3*) Hara Pub.
Lisiewicz, M., et al. Destiny Can Wait: The Polish Air Force in World War II. (Aviation Ser.). (Illus.). 401p. 1988. reprint ed. 39.95 (*0-89839-113-X*) Battery Pr.
Lisiewski, Joseph, ed. see Zalewski, Patrick.
Lisio, Donald J. The President & Protest: Hoover, MacArthur, & the Bonus March. 2nd ed. xviii, 246p. 1994. reprint ed. 32.00 (*0-8232-1571-7*) Fordham.
— The President & Protest: Hoover, MacArthur & the Bonus March. 2nd ed. LC 94-19465. xviii, 246p. 1994. reprint ed. pap. 17.95 (*0-8232-1572-5*) Fordham.
Lisitsa, V. S. Atoms & Plasmas. LC 93-46645. (Atoms & Plasmas Ser.: Vol. 14). 1994. 107.95 (*0-387-57580-4*) Spr-Verlag.
Lisitzin, Alexander P. Sedimentation in the World Ocean with Emphasis on the Nature, Distribution & Behavior of Marine Suspensions. Rodolfo, Kelvin S., ed. LC 72-172081. (Society of Economic Paleontologists & Mineralogists, Special Publication Ser.: No. 17). 232p. reprint ed. pap. 72.00 (*0-608-12950-X*, 202474400038) Bks Demand.
Lisius, James D., ed. see Technical Association of the Pulp & Paper Industry.
Lisk, Anna L., jt. auth. see Traister, Robert J.
Lisk, Anna L., jt. auth. see Traister, Robert J., Sr.
Lisk, Edward S. The Creative Director: Alternative Rehearsal Techniques. 3rd ed. LC 87-90906. (Illus.). 221p. 1987. pap. text 24.95 (*0-9624308-0-3*) Meredith Music.
Lisk, Eunice A., jt. auth. see Rosen, Marcia.
Lisk, Mark, photos by. Idaho Impressions. LC 97-70194. (Illus.). 144p. 1997. 39.95 (*1-55868-314-3*) Gr Arts Ctr Pub.
Lisk, Thom. Become Number One in Selling: Beyond Success to Significance. LC 96-94021. 1996. 40.00 (*0-7880-0666-5*, Express Pr) CSS OH.
Liska. Drugs & the Human Body. 5th ed. 1997. pap. text, teacher ed. write for info. (*0-13-598152-2*) P-H.
— Drugs & the Human Body. 6th ed. LC 99-27197. 498p. 1999. pap. 53.00 (*0-13-040172-2*) P-H.
Liska, Allen E., ed. Social Threat & Social Control. LC 91-7550. (SUNY Series in Deviance & Social Control). (Illus.). 288p. (C). 1992. text 59.50 (*0-7914-0903-1*); pap. text 19.95 (*0-7914-0904-X*) State U NY Pr.
Liska, Allen E. & Messner, Steven F. Perspectives on Crime & Deviance. 3rd ed. LC 98-6254. 260p. 1998. 38.60 (*0-13-235771-2*) P-H.
Liska, David, jt. auth. see Holahan, John.
Liska, David W., et al. State-Level Databook on Health Care Access & Financing. 3rd ed. LC 98-9660. 249p. 1998. pap. 42.50 (*0-87766-677-6*) Urban Inst.
Liska, F., jt. auth. see Volke, J.
Liska, George. Alliances & the Third World. LC 68-17254. (Washington Center of Foreign Policy Research. Studies in International Affairs: No. 5). 71p. reprint ed. pap. 30.00 (*0-8357-5320-4*, 202312800032) Bks Demand.
— Beyond Kissinger: Ways of Conservative Statecraft. LC 75-10838. (Washington Center of Foreign Policy Research. Studies in International Affairs: No. 26). 170p. reprint ed. pap. 52.70 (*0-8357-7158-X*, 202312700031) Bks Demand.
— Career of Empire: America & Imperial Expansion over Land & Sea. LC 78-4576. (Studies in International Affairs). 376p. 1978. reprint ed. pap. 116.60 (*0-608-04040-1*, 206477600011) Bks Demand.
— Expanding Realism: A Geohistorical Theory of World Politics. LC 97-22607. 336p. 1997. 68.00 (*0-8476-8679-5*) Rowman.
— Expanding Realism: The Historical Dimension of World Politics. LC 97-22607. 336p. 1997. pap. 24.95 (*0-8476-8680-9*) Rowman.
— Imperial America: The International Politics of Primacy. LC E 0840.L5. (Washington Center of Foreign Policy Research, Studies in International Affairs: Vol. 2). 128p. (Orig.). reprint ed. pap. 39.70 (*0-608-06083-6*, 206641500008) Bks Demand.
— In Search of Poetry in the Politics of Power: Perspectives on Expanding Realism. LC 98-34777. 320p. 1998. 70.00 (*0-7391-0004-1*); pap. 24.95 (*0-7391-0005-X*) Lxngtn Bks.
— Nations in Alliance: The Limits of Interdependence. LC 62-14359. 313p. reprint ed. pap. 97.10 (*0-8357-8242-5*, 203414600088) Bks Demand.
— Quest for Equilibrium: America & the Balance of Power on Land & Sea. LC 77-4780. 278p. reprint ed. pap. 86.20 (*0-608-06163-8*, 206649600008) Bks Demand.
— The Restoration of Politics: Interrogating History about a Civilization in Crisis. 144p. (C). 1996. pap. 23.95 (*0-8476-8213-7*); lib. bdg. 55.50 (*0-8476-8212-9*) Rowman.
— Resurrecting a Discipline: Enduring Scholarship for Evolving World Politics / LC 99-21500. 1999. write for info. (*0-7391-0067-X*) Lxngtn Bks.
— Resurrecting a Discipline: Enduring Scholarship for Evolving World Politics. LC 99-21500. 384p. 1999. 75.00 (*0-7391-0066-1*) Lxngtn Bks.
— Russia & the Road to Appeasement: Cycles of East-West Conflict in War & Peace. LC 81-48188. 277p. reprint ed. pap. 85.90 (*0-608-06164-6*, 206649700008) Bks Demand.
— Russia & World Order: Strategic Choices & the Laws of Power in History. LC 79-22872. 208p. reprint ed. pap. 64.50 (*0-608-11993-8*, 202300100030) Bks Demand.
— War & Order: Reflections on Vietnam & History. LC 68-9697. (Washington Center of Foreign Policy Research. Studies in International Affairs: No. 11). 127p. reprint ed. pap. 39.40 (*0-608-11901-6*, 202312600032) Bks Demand.
Liska, Julie, jt. auth. see Dowding, Robert L.
Liska, Ken. The Pharmacist's Guide to the Most Misused & Abused Drugs in America: Prescription Drugs - Over-the-Counter Drugs - Designer Drugs. 1988. 23.99 (*0-02-572970-5*) Macmillan.
Liska, Roger W. Means Facilities Maintenance Standards. (Illus.). 600p. (C). 1988. 159.95 (*0-87629-096-9*, 67246) R S Means.
Liska, Roger W., jt. auth. see Schuette, Stephen D.
Liskar, Nancy, ed. see Oliver, Marcelo.
Liskar, Nancy, ed. see Sweeney, Kate.
Liske, Craig, et al, eds. Comparative Public Policy: Issues, Theories, & Methods. LC 73-91354. (Comparative Political Economy & Public Policy Ser.: Vol. 1). 302p. reprint ed. pap. 93.70 (*0-608-14203-4*, 202186800026) Bks Demand.
Lisker, Carol, ed. see Trotsky, Leon, et al.
Lisker, Emily. Judy with Punch. LC 92-27157. 192p. (J). (gr. 5-9). 1993. lib. bdg. 14.95 (*0-02-707755-1*, Bradbury S&S) S&S Childrens.
Lisker, Emily, jt. illus. see Spinelli, Eileen.
Lisker, Leigh. Spoken Telugu, Bk. 1, Units 1-30. LC 63-12992. (Spoken Language Ser.). xxvii, 345p. (gr. 9-12). 1976. pap. 20.00 (*0-87950-376-9*) Spoken Lang Serv.
Lisker, Leigh. Spoken Telugu, Vol. 1. LC 63-12992. (Spoken Language Ser.). xxvii, 345p. (gr. 9-12). 1976. audio 100.00 (*0-87950-377-7*) Spoken Lang Serv.
Lisker, Leigh. Spoken Telugu, Vol. 1. LC 63-12992. (Spoken Language Ser.). xxvii, 345p. (YA). (gr. 9-12). 1976. pap. 120.00 incl. audio (*0-87950-378-5*) Spoken Lang Serv.
— Spoken Telugu, Vol. 2. LC 63-12992. (Spoken Language Ser.). xxvii, 345p. (YA). (gr. 9-12). 1976. audio 55.00 (*0-87950-379-3*) Spoken Lang Serv.
Lisker, Tom. Terror in the Tropics: The Army Ants. (Great Unsolved Mysteries Ser.). 1997. pap. 4.95 (*0-8114-6866-6*) Raintree Steck-V.
Liskevych, Terry & Patterson, Don. Youth Volleyball: Championship Skills. (Illus.). 128p. (Orig.). 1995. pap. 12.95 (*1-57028-028-2*, 80282H, Mstrs Pr) NTC Contemp Pub Co.
Liskin-Gasparro, Judith. Entradas. 2nd ed. (College Spanish Ser.). (SPA.). (C). 1993. mass mkt., suppl. ed. 21.95 (*0-8384-2526-7*) Heinle & Heinle.
— Entradas 2e-student Text. 2nd ed. (College Spanish). (SPA.). (C). 1995. mass mkt., student ed. 57.95 (*0-8384-2536-4*) Heinle & Heinle.
— Testing & Teaching for Oral Proficiency: ETS Familiarization Kits. (C). 1987. pap. 57.95 (*0-8384-1897-X*); mass mkt. 57.95 (*0-8384-1896-1*) Heinle & Heinle.
Liskin-Gasparro, Judith E., ed. Building Bridges & Making Connections. (Reports of the Northeast Conference on the Teaching of Foreign Languages). 190p. 1991. pap. 10.95 (*0-915432-91-9*) NE Conf Teach Foreign.
***Liskin, Jack.** Moving Medicine. 2000. pap. 17.95 (*1-58177-065-0*) Barrytown Ltd.
Liskin, Jack. Moving Medicine: The Life Work of Milton Trager, M. D. LC 96-31343. 1996. 24.95 (*0-88268-196-6*) Station Hill Pr.
Liskin, Miriam. HELP! Microsoft Access. (Help! Ser.). 1006p. 1993. pap. 29.95 incl. disk (*1-56276-099-8*, Ziff-Davis Pr) Que.
— PC Magazine Programming Access 97. 1190p. 1997. 49.99 (*1-56276-437-3*, Ziff-Davis Pr) Que.
— PC Magazine Programming FoxPro for Windows. pap. 39.95 (*1-56276-173-0*, Ziff-Davis Pr) Que.
— PC Magazine Programming FoxPro 2.0. (Programming Ser.). (Illus.). 1516p. (Orig.). 1992. pap. 39.95 incl. disk (*1-56276-038-6*, Ziff-Davis Pr) Que.
Liskofsky, Sidney. U. N. Declaration on the Elimination of Religious Intolerance & Discrimination. 20p. 1982. pap. 2.00 (*0-87495-041-4*) Am Jewish Comm.
Liskov, Ellen. Eat Smart. 2nd rev. ed. (Illus.). 320p. 1995. pap. 6.99 (*0-679-76422-4*) Random.
Lisky & Andzel. Fitness for the New Millennium. 178p. (C). 1998. spiral bd. 25.95 (*0-7872-5237-9*, 41523701) Kendall-Hunt.
Lisle. Imaging Surgeon. (Orig.). 1993. text 95.00 (*0-340-55170-4*, Pub. by E A) Routldge.
***Lisle.** Petrified. (J). 2000. pap. 6.95 (*0-552-52964-8*, Pub. by Transworld Publishers Ltd) Trafalgar.
L'Isle-Adam, Auguste de Villiers De, see Villiers De L'Isle-Adam, Auguste de.
L'Isle-Adam, Villers De, see De L'Isle-Adam, Villers.
Lisle, Charles-Rene-Marie Leconte De, see Leconte De Lisle, Charles-Rene-Marie.
Lisle, Clifton. Diamond Rock: A Tale of the Paoli Massacre. 1993. reprint ed. lib. bdg. 89.00 (*0-7812-5483-3*) Rprt Serv.
— Lenape Trails. 1993. reprint ed. lib. bdg. 89.00 (*0-7812-5482-5*) Rprt Serv.
Lisle, David. Imaging for Surgeons: A Clinical Guide. 2nd ed. LC 98-27855. (Arnold Publications). (Illus.). 232p. (Orig.). 1998. pap. text 55.00 (*0-340-69267-7*) OUP.
Lisle, David A. Imaging for Students. (Illus.). 192p. 1996. pap. text 34.50 (*0-340-61383-1*) OUP.
Lisle, George. Accounting in Theory & Practice. LC 75-18475. (History of Accounting Ser.). (Illus.). 1979. reprint ed. 34.95 (*0-405-07557-X*) Ayer.
Lisle, George & Brief, Richard P., eds. Selections from Enclyclopaedia of Accounting, 1903: Original Anthology. LC 77-87310. (Contemporary Accounting Thought Ser.). 1978. lib. bdg. 41.95 (*0-405-10923-7*) Ayer.
Lisle, Harvey. The Enlivened Rock Powders. LC 94-71840. 208p. 1994. pap. 15.00 (*0-911311-48-3*) Acres USA.
Lisle, Holly. Bones of the Past. 336p. 1993. mass mkt. 5.99 (*0-671-72160-7*) Baen Bks.
***Lisle, Holly.** Courage of Falcons. 2000. pap. 12.95 (*0-446-67397-8*, Aspect) Warner Bks.
Lisle, Holly. Curse of the Black Heron. 1998. per. 5.99 (*0-671-87868-9*) Baen Bks.
***Lisle, Holly.** Diplomacy of Wolves. (Secret Texts Ser.: Bk. I). 416p. 1999. mass mkt. 6.50 (*0-446-60746-0*, Pub. by Warner Bks) Little.
Lisle, Holly. Diplomacy of Wolves, 3 vols., Vol. 1. LC 98-13712. (Secret Texts Ser.: Bk. 1). 352p. 1998. mass mkt. 12.99 (*0-446-67395-1*, Pub. by Warner Bks) Little.
— Fire in the Mist. 304p. 1992. mass mkt. 5.99 (*0-671-72132-1*) Baen Bks.
— Hunting the Corrigan's Blood. 320p. 1997. mass mkt. 5.99 (*0-671-87768-2*) Baen Bks.
— Mind of the Magic. 320p. 1995. per. 5.99 (*0-671-87654-6*) Baen Bks.
— Minerva Wakes. 288p. 1994. per. 4.99 (*0-671-72202-6*) Baen Bks.
— Sympathy for the Devil. 256p. 1996. mass mkt. 5.99 (*0-671-87703-8*) Baen Bks.
Lisle, Holly. Vengeance of Dragons. LC 99-19719. (Secret Texts Ser.: Bk. 2). 379p. 1999. mass mkt. 12.99 (*0-446-67396-X*, Pub. by Warner Bks) Little.
***Lisle, Holly.** Vengeance of Dragons. 464p. 2000. mass mkt. 6.50 (*0-446-60885-8*, Aspect) Warner Bks.
Lisle, Holly & Allston, Aaron. Thunder of the Captains: A Bard's Tale. 6p. 1996. pap., mass mkt., per. 5.99 (*0-671-87731-3*) Baen Bks.
— Wrath of the Princes. (Bard's Tale Novel Ser.). 352p. 1997. per. 5.99 (*0-671-87771-2*) Baen Bks.
Lisle, Holly & Guin, Chris. Mall, Mayhem & Magic. 1995. per. 5.99 (*0-671-87678-3*) Baen Bks.
Lisle, Holly & Spence, Walter. The Devil & Dan Cooley: A Devil's Point Novel. 256p. 1996. mass mkt. 5.99 (*0-671-87756-9*) Baen Bks.
Lisle, Holly, jt. auth. see Bradley, Marion Zimmer.
Lisle, Holly, jt. auth. see Lackey, Mercedes.
Lisle, Holly, jt. auth. see Stirling, S. M.
Lisle, Ian G., jt. ed. see Vassiliou, Peter J.
***Lisle, J.** Journeys from Home. 1999. pap. 13.00 (*0-7472-5555-5*, Pub. by Headline Bk Pub) Trafalgar.
Lisle, James De, see De Lisle, James, ed.
Lisle, Janet T. Afternoon of the Elves. LC 88-35099. 128p. (J). (gr. 4-6). 1989. 15.95 (*0-531-05837-9*); lib. bdg. 16.99 (*0-531-08437-X*) Orchard Bks Watts.
— Forest. LC 93-9630. 160p. (YA). (gr. 5 up). 1993. 15.95 (*0-531-06803-X*) Orchard Bks Watts.
Forest. 160p. (J). (gr. 4-7). 1995. pap. 3.50 (*0-590-48680-2*) Scholastic Inc.
— The Gold Dust Letters. LC 93-11806. 128p. (J). (gr. 3-5). 1994. 15.95 (*0-531-06830-7*) Orchard Bks Watts.
— The Gold Dust Letters. LC 93-11806. Vol. 1. 128p. (J). (gr. 4-7). 1994. lib. bdg. 16.99 (*0-531-08680-1*) Orchard Bks Watts.
— Gold Dust Letters. LC 93-11806. 128p. (J). (gr. 4-7). 1996. mass mkt. 3.99 (*0-380-72516-9*, Avon Bks) Morrow Avon.
— The Lampfish of Twill. LC 91-8279. (Illus.). 176p. (YA). (gr. 5 up). 1991. 16.95 (*0-531-05963-4*) Orchard Bks Watts.
— The Lampfish of Twill. (Illus.). 176p. (J). (gr. 4-7). 1993. pap. 3.50 (*0-590-46040-4*, Apple Paperbacks) Scholastic Inc.
— Lampfish of Twill. (J). 1991. 8.60 (*0-606-05409-X*, Pub. by Turtleback) Demco.
— Looking for Juliette. LC 94-6922. 128p. (J). (gr. 3-5). 1994. lib. bdg. 16.99 (*0-531-08720-4*) Orchard Bks Watts.
— Looking for Juliette. LC 94-6922. Vol. 2. 128p. (J). (gr. 4-7). 1994. 15.95 (*0-531-06870-6*) Orchard Bks Watts.
— A Message from the Match Girl. 128p. 1997. pap. 3.99 (*0-380-72518-5*, Avon Bks) Morrow Avon.
— A Message from the Match Girl. LC 95-6036. (Investigators of the Unknown Ser.: Bk. 3). (Illus.). 128p. (J). (gr. 4-6). 1996. 15.95 (*0-531-09487-1*); lib. bdg. 16.99 (*0-531-08787-5*) Orchard Bks Watts.
***Lisle, Janet Taylor.** Afternoon of the Elves. 66p. 2000. pap. 5.50 (*0-87129-959-3*, A86) Dramatic Pub.
Lisle, Janet Taylor. Afternoon of the Elves. LC 88-35099. 122p. (YA). (gr. 5-9). 1999. pap. 4.99 (*0-698-11806-5*, PapStar) Peng Put Young Read.
— Afternoon of the Elves. 1991. 9.09 (*0-606-04856-1*, Pub. by Turtleback) Demco.
— Angela's Aliens. LC 96-12991. (IOU Ser.: Bk. 4). 128p. (J). (gr. 4-6). 1996. 14.95 (*0-531-09541-X*); lib. bdg. 15.99 (*0-531-08891-X*) Orchard Bks Watts.

L

Lisle, Janet Taylor. Angela's Aliens. (Investigators of the Unknown Ser.). 1997. 9.09 (0-606-11043-7, Pub. by Turtleback) Demco.

Lisle, Janet Taylor. Gold Dust Letters. LC 93-11806. 1996. 9.09 (0-606-09336-2, Pub. by Turtleback) Demco.

— The Great Dimpole Oak. LC 99-21456. (Puffin Novels Ser.). (Illus.). 144p. (J). (gr. 3-7). 1999. reprint ed. pap. 5.99 (0-698-11805-7, PuffinBks) Peng Put Young Read.

— Looking for Juliette. LC 94-6922. (Investigators of the Unknown Ser.). 1996. 9.09 (0-606-10255-8, Pub. by Turtleback) Demco.

— The Lost Flower Children. LC 98-34912. (Illus.). 122p. (J). (gr. 3-6). 1999. 16.99 (0-399-23393-8, Philomel) Peng Put Young Read.

— A Message from the Match Girl. (Investigators of the Unknown Ser.). 1997. 9.09 (0-606-11621-4, Pub. by Turtleback) Demco.

Lisle, Jeff, tr. see Giardino, Vittorio.

Lisle, Jennifer. Chic Simple Storage. Gross, Kim Johnson & Stone, Jeff, eds. (Chic Simple Components Ser.). 104p. 1994. 12.50 (0-679-43222-1) Knopf.

Lisle, John, tr. see Del Vecchio, Giorgia.

Lisle, John, tr. see Del Vecchio, Giorgio.

Lisle, John, tr. see Miraglia, Luigi.

Lisle, Laurie. Portrait of an Artist: A Biography of Georgia O'Keeffe. 1997. per. 15.00 (0-671-01666-0) PB.

— Without Child: Challenging Stigma of Childlessness. LC 99-20815. 273p. 1999. pap. 15.99 (0-415-92493-6) Routledge.

Lisle, Leanda De, see De Lisle, Leanda.

Lisle, Richard J. Geological Strain Analysis. (Illus.). 108p. 1985. text 48.25 (0-08-032590-4, Pub. by PPL); pap. text 30.25 (0-08-032589-0, Pub. by PPL) Elsevier.

— Geological Structures & Maps: A Practical Guide. LC 88-5807. (Illus.). 160p. 1988. pap. text 23.00 (0-08-034853-X, Pergamon Pr) Elsevier.

— Geological Structures & Maps: A Practical Guide. 2nd ed. LC 95-20186. (Illus.). 160p. 1996. pap. 34.95 (0-7506-2588-0) Buttrwrth-Heinemann.

Lisle, Richard J., jt. auth. see Leyshon, Peter R.

Lisle, Richard J., jt. auth. see Ramsay, John G.

Lisle, Robert. Photography Remembered: A Selective View from the Robert W. Lisle Collection. LC 90-84178. 66p. 1990. pap. 19.95 (0-940744-61-9) Chrysler Museum.

Lisle, Rufus. Laughing at Ourselves: The Verses of Rufus Lisle. Houlihan, Edward T., ed. LC 97-34960. (Illus.). 128p. 1997. 24.80 (0-87642-015-3) Henry Clay.

Lisman, C. David. The Curricular Integration of Ethics: Theory & Practice. LC 95-34419. 192p. 1996. 57.95 (0-275-95304-1, Praeger Pubs) Greenwood.

— Toward a Civil Society: Civic Literacy & Service Learning. LC 98-11067. 192p. 1998. 55.00 (0-89789-566-5, Bergin & Garvey); pap. 19.95 (0-89789-567-3, Bergin & Garvey) Greenwood.

Lismore. Here We Go, Level 4. 3rd ed. 128p. 1995. pap. text, student ed. 14.20 (0-13-186065-8) P-H.

— Here We Go, Vol. 6. 3rd ed. 1998. pap. text 21.27 (0-13-186974-4) P-H.

Lisnek, Paul. Quality Mind, Quality Life. LC 95-76817. 220p. 1995. 19.95 (0-916990-35-4) META Pubns.

— Winning the Mind Game. LC 96-77198. 300p. 1996. pap. 19.95 (0-916990-39-7) META Pubns.

Lisnek, Paul & Kaufman, Michael J. Depositions: Procedure, Strategy & Technique. 2nd ed. 275p. 1994. text. write for info. (0-314-04475-2) West Pub.

Lisnek, Paul M. A Lawyer's Guide to Effective Negotiation & Mediation: CLE Edition. 225p. 1992. pap. text. write for info. (0-314-01679-1) West Pub.

— Practice Made Perfect: The Seven Secrets of Successful Lawyering. 208p. 1998. pap. 9.95 (0-15-900392-X, Pub. by Harcourt Legal) Natl Bk Netwk.

— Practice Makes Perfect. 120p. 1995. pap. text 10.00 (0-910095-02-7) Law Bulletin.

Lisnek, Paul M. & Kaufman, Michael J. Depositions: Procedure, Strategy & Technique. LC 95-176630. 230p. (C). 1995. pap. write for info. (0-314-06262-9) West Pub.

— Depositions: Procedure, Strategy, & Technique. LC 89-27265. 1990. write for info. (0-314-73923-8) West Pub.

Lisners, John, jt. auth. see Foreman, Freddie.

Lisney, Adrian & Fieldhouse, Ken. Landscape Design Guide Vol. II: Hard Landscape: The Design of Paved Spaces, Landscape Enclosure & Landscape Furniture. 224p. 1990. text 71.95 (0-566-09019-8, Pub. by Gower) Ashgate Pub Co.

Lisney, M. I., tr. see Makrakis, Apostolos.

Lison, Karen C., jt. auth. see Poston, Carol.

Lison Tolosana, Carmelo. La Imagen del Rey. Monarquia, Realeza y Poder Ritual en la Casa de los Austrias. (Nueva Austral Ser.: Vol. 249). (SPA.). 1991. pap. text 24.95 (84-239-7249-6) Elliots Bks.

Lisoskie, Pete. Profits Hidden, Profits Found: 12 Steps to Making a Big Fortune in Any Business. (Orig.). 1995. pap. 14.95 (1-879141-13-2) Busn Toolbox.

Lisoskie, Pete & Lisoskie, Shelly. Customers for Keeps: The Network System to Smash Your Profit Barrier. LC 93-90414. (Illus.). 352p. 1994. pap. 19.95 (1-879141-10-8) Busn Toolbox.

Lisoskie, Pete, jt. auth. see Lisoskie, Shelly.

Lisoskie, Shelly & Lisoskie, Pete. Your IIGS Guide. (Illus.). 308p. (Orig.). 1990. pap. 21.95 (1-879141-01-9) Busn Toolbox.

Lisoskie, Shelly, jt. auth. see Lisoskie, Pete.

***Lisovskii, A. F.** Development of Gradient Structures in Composite Materials. 220p. 1999. boxed set 108.00 (1-898326-52-5, Pub. by CISP) Balogh.

Lisovskii, F. & Kalugin, I. English-Russian Dictionary of Radio-Electronics. 752p. (C). 1987. 125.00 (0-7855-6462-4, Pub. by Collets) St Mut.

Lisovskis, Marjorie, jt. auth. see Fruehling, Rosemary T.

Lisovskis, Marjorie, ed. see Delisle, Jim & Delisle, Deb.

Lisowski, F. P. A Guide to Dissection of the Human Body. LC 98-53306. 424p. 1999. 87.50 (981-02-3528-3); pap. text 49.50 (981-02-3569-0) World Scientific Pub.

Lisowski, Joseph. Near the Narcotic Sea. 64p. (Orig.). 1992. pap. 10.00 (0-9624155-4-5) Cottage Wordsmiths.

Lisowski, Joseph, ed. Caribbean Perspectives: The Social Structure of a Region. 224p. (C). 1990. pap. 24.95 (0-88738-838-8) Transaction Pubs.

— Environment & Labor in the Caribbean Vol. 2: Caribbean Perspectives. 128p. (C). 1992. pap. 24.95 (1-56000-584-X) Transaction Pubs.

Lisowski, Marylin & Williams, Robert A. Wetlands. LC 96-25739. (Exploring Ecosystems Ser.). (J). 1997. lib. bdg. 23.00 (0-531-11311-6) Watts.

Lisowski, P., jt. auth. see Ho, P. Y.

Lispector, Clarice. An Apprenticeship or The Book of Delights. Mazzara, Richard A. & Parris, Lorri A., trs. from POR. (Texas Pan American Ser.). 140p. 1986. text 18.95 (0-292-79030-9) U of Tex Pr.

— Family Ties. Pontiero, Giovanni, tr. from POR. (Texas Pan American Ser.). 156p. 1984. pap. 11.95 (0-292-72448-9) U of Tex Pr.

— The Foreign Legion. Pontiero, Giovanni, tr. from POR. & afterword by by. LC 91-29992. 224p. 1992. reprint ed. pap. 10.95 (0-8112-1189-4, NDP732, Pub. by New Directions) Norton.

— The Hour of the Star. Pontiero, Giovanni, tr. from POR. & afterword by by. LC 91-29995. Vol. 733. 96p. 1992. reprint ed. pap. 8.95 (0-8112-1190-8, NDP733, Pub. by New Directions) Norton.

— Near to the Wild Heart. Pontiero, Giovanni, tr. from POR. & afterword by by. LC 90-33455. 192p. 1990. reprint ed. pap. 10.95 (0-8112-1140-1, NDP698, Pub. by New Directions) Norton.

— The Passion According to G. H. Sousa, Ronald W., tr. from POR. LC 88-4763. (Emergent Literatures Ser.).Tr. of A/Paixao Segundo G. H.. ix, 173p. (Orig.). 1988. pap. 13.95 (0-8166-1712-0) U of Minn Pr.

— Selected Cronicas. Pontiero, Giovanni, tr. from POR. LC 96-23768. 212p. (Orig.). 1996. pap. 12.95 (0-8112-1340-4, NDP834, Pub. by New Directions) Norton.

— Soulstorm: Stories. Levitin, Alexis, tr. from POR. LC 89-2938. 160p. 1989. 19.95 (0-8112-1090-1, Pub. by New Directions) Norton.

— Soulstorm: Stories. Levitin, Alexis, tr. from POR. LC 89-2938. 160p. 1989. pap. 11.95 (0-8112-1091-X, NDP671, Pub. by New Directions) Norton.

— The Stream of Life. Lowe, Elizabeth & Fitz, Earl, trs. from POR. (Emergent Literatures Ser.). Orig. Title: Agua Viva. 128p. (Orig.). 1989. pap. 12.95 (0-8166-1782-1) U of Minn Pr.

Lisper, B. Synthesizing Synchronous Systems by Static Scheduling in Space-Time. (Lecture Notes in Computer Science Ser.: Vol. 362). vi, 263p. 1989. 37.00 (0-387-51156-3) Spr-Verlag.

Liss, Andrea. Trespassing Through Shadows: Memory, Photography & the Holocaust. LC 98-14151. 1998. 49.95 (0-8166-3059-3); pap. 19.95 (0-8166-3060-7) U of Minn Pr.

Liss, Andrea, contrib. by. Original Accounts of the Lone Women of San Nicholas Island. (Illus.). 16p. 1998. pap. 9.95 (0-9666963-2-8) Side Street Pr.

Liss, Andrea & Snyder, Jill. Impossible Evidence: Contemporary Artists View the Holocaust. (Illus.). 40p. (Orig.). 1994. pap. 20.00 (0-614-01852-8) Freedman.

Liss, Andrea, jt. auth. see Atkinson, Karen.

***Liss, David.** A Conspiracy of Paper. LC 99-20691. 435p. 2000. 25.00 (0-375-50292-0) Random.

— A Conspiracy of Paper: A Novel. LC 00-37767. 2000. pap. write for info. (0-7862-2665-X) Thorndike Pr.

***Liss, Helene.** Demolition: The Art of Demolishing, Dismantling, Imploding, Toppling & Razing. 128p. 2000. 17.98 (1-57912-149-7) Blck Dog & Leventhal.

Liss, Howard. Great Drivers, Great Races. LC 73-6656. 160p. (YA). (gr. 7 up). 1973. 11.95 (0-397-31278-4) HarpC Child Bks.

Liss, Howard, jt. auth. see Graziano, Rocky.

Liss, Jeffrey G. & Chapman, Glenn H., eds. Annual International Space Development Conference Proceedings, 8th. (Illus.). 636p. 1992. pap. text 60.00 (0-912183-09-8) Univelt Inc.

Liss-Levinson, Nechama. When a Grandparent Dies: A Kid's Own Remembering Workbook for Dealing with Shiva & the Year Beyond. LC 95-5379. 48p. (J). (gr. 2 up). 1995. 15.95 (1-879045-44-3) Jewish Lights.

Liss, Peggy K. Atlantic Empires: The Network of Trade & Revolution, 1713-1826. LC 82-13099. (Johns Hopkins Studies in Atlantic History & Culture Ser.). 364p. reprint ed. pap. 112.90 (0-8357-6908-9, 203796600009) Bks Demand.

— Mexico under Spain, Fifteen Twenty One-Fifteen Fifty Six: Society & the Origins of Nationality. LC 74-33507. xvi, 230p. 1994. pap. text 9.95 (0-226-48496-3) U Ch Pr.

— Mexico under Spain, Fifteen Twenty One-Fifteen Fifty Six: Society & the Origins of Nationality. LC 74-33507. xvi, 230p. 1994. lib. bdg. 21.00 (0-226-48495-5) U Ch Pr.

— Origenes de la Nacionalidad Mexicana (Origins of the Mexican Nationality) (SPA.). 273p. 1986. pap. 13.99 (968-16-1937-4, Pub. by Fondo) Continental Bk.

Liss, Peggy K., jt. ed. see Knight, Franklin W.

Liss, Per-Erik. Health Care Needs: Meaning & Measurement. 147p. 1993. 61.95 (1-85628-453-0, Pub. by Avebry) Ashgate Pub Co.

Liss, Peter S., ed. Air-Sea Exchange of Gases & Particles. 1983. text 285.50 (90-277-1610-2) Kluwer Academic.

Liss, Peter S. & Duce, Robert A., eds. The Sea Surface & Global Change. LC 96-9377. (Illus.). 535p. (C). 1997. text 100.00 (0-521-56273-2) Cambridge U Pr.

Liss, Susan M. & Taylor, William L., eds. New Opportunities: Civil Rights at a Crossroads. LC 92-56191. 300p. 1993. pap. 20.00 (0-9622865-2-4) CCCR.

Liss, Susan M., ed. see Citizens' Commission on Civil Rights.

Lissa, Zofia, ed. see Feicht, Hieronim.

Lissack, Michael & Roos, Johan. The Next Common Sense: Mastering Corporate Complexity Through Coherence. LC 98-32271. 256p. 1999. 25.00 (1-85788-240-7) Nicholas Brealey.

***Lissack, Michael & Roos, Johan.** The Next Common Sense: Mastering Corporate Complexity Through Coherence. (Illus.). 256p. 2000. pap. 16.00 (1-85788-235-0, Pub. by Nicholas Brealey) Natl Bk Netwk.

Lissack, Michael R. & Gunz, Hugh P., eds. Managing Complexity in Organizations: A View in Many Directions. LC 99-13621. 424p. 1999. 75.00 (1-56720-285-3, Quorum Bks) Greenwood.

Lissak, K. Neural & Neurohumoral Organization of Motivated Behaviour: The 4th Conference in Interbrain Held in Pecs, Hungary, May 19-23, 1975. 267p. (C). 1978. 60.00 (963-05-1316-1, Pub. by Akade Kiado) St Mut.

— Results in Neuroanatomy, Motor Organization, Cerebral Circulation & Modelling: Recent Developments of Neurobiology in Hungary, Vol. 8. (Recent Developments of Neurobiology in Hungary Ser.: No. 8). 242p. (C). 1979. 63.00 (963-05-1594-6, Pub. by Akade Kiado) St Mut.

— Results in Neuroanatomy, Neurochemistry, Neurophysiology & Neuropathology: Recent Developments of Neurobiology in Hungary, Vol. 9. (Recent Developments of Neurobiology in Hungary Ser.: No. 9). 232p. (C). 1982. 72.00 (963-05-2947-5, Pub. by Akade Kiado) St Mut.

— Results in Neuroendocrinology, Neurochemistry & Sleep Research. (Recent Developments of Neurobiology in Hungary Ser.: No. 7). 189p. (C). 1978. 50.00 (963-05-1587-3, Pub. by Akade Kiado) St Mut.

Lissak, K. & Molnar, P., eds. Motivation & the Neural & Neurohumoral Factors in Regulation of Behaviour: Recent Development of Neurobiology in Hungary, Vol. 10. (Recent Developments of Neurobiology in Hungary Ser.: No. 10). 331p. (C). 1982. 145.00 (963-05-2993-9, Pub. by Akade Kiado) St Mut.

Lissak, Moshe. Social Mobility in Israeli Society. 136p. 1969. 39.95 (0-87855-176-X) Transaction Pubs.

Lissak, Moshe, ed. Israeli Society & Its Defense Establishment: The Social & Political Impact of a Protracted Violent Conflict. (Illus.). 162p. 1984. 42.50 (0-7146-3235-X, BHA-03235, Pub. by F Cass Pubs) Intl Spec Bk.

Lissak, Moshe, jt. auth. see Horowitz, Dan.

Lissak, Rivka S. Pluralism & Progressives: Hull House & the New Immigrants, 1890-1919. (Illus.). 264p. 1989. 42.00 (0-226-48502-1) U Ch Pr.

Lissakers, Karin. Money & Politics: The Iranian Asset Freeze. (Pew Case Studies in International Affairs). 50p. (C). 1995. pap. text 3.50 (1-56927-210-7, GU Schl Foreign) Geo U Inst Dplmcy.

Lissale, Keith, ed. see Swartz, David & Harris, Norman.

Lissaman, P. B., jt. auth. see Wilson, R. F.

Lissant, Kenneth J. Emulsions & Emulsion Technology, Pt. I. (Surfactant Science Ser.: Vol. 6). (Illus.). 456p. 1974. text 215.00 (0-8247-6097-2) Dekker.

— Emulsions & Emulsion Technology, Pt. II. (Surfactant Science Ser.: Vol. 6). (Illus.). 544p. 1974. text 215.00 (0-8247-6098-0) Dekker.

— Emulsions & Emulsion Technology, Pt. III. (Surfactant Science Ser.: Vol. 6). (Illus.). 272p. 1984. text 160.00 (0-8247-7083-8) Dekker.

Lissau, Rudi. Rudolf Steiner: Life, Work, Inner Path & Social Initiatives. 192p. 1987. pap. 14.95 (1-869890-06-X, 1230, Pub. by Hawthorn Press) Anthroposophic.

Lissauer. Pocket Examiner Paediatrics. 1985. pap. text 22.00 (0-443-03815-5, W B Saunders Co) Harcrt Hlth Sci Grp.

***Lissauer.** Texto Ilustrado de Pediatria. (C). 1998. text 32.58 (84-8174-288-0) Mosby Inc.

Lissauer, Robert. Lissauer's Encyclopedia of Popular Music in America: 1888 to the Present. 2nd ed. 1584p. 1996. 185.00 (0-8160-3238-6) Facts on File.

Lissauer, Tom & Clayden, Graham. Textbook of Pediatrics. (Illus.). 330p. 1996. pap. 42.95 (0-7234-1657-5) Mosby Inc.

Lisse, G. Barany, jt. ed. see Kiraly, B. K.

Lissette, Andrea, jt. auth. see Kraus, Richard L.

Lissfelt, J. Fred. The Dutchman Died & Other Tales of Pittsburgh's Southside. LC 92-11734. (Illus.). 152p. (C). 1992. pap. 10.95 (0-8229-5483-4); text 29.95 (0-8229-3726-3) U of Pittsburgh Pr.

Lissi-Caronna, Elisa. Il Mitreo dei Castra Peregrinorum: S. Stefano Rotondo. (Etudes Preliminaires aux Religions Orientales dans l'Empire Romain Ser.: Vol. 104). (Illus.). viii, 52p. 1986. pap. 71.00 (90-04-07493-7) Brill Academic Pubs.

Lissitzky, El. Boxed-Vesc Objet Gegenstand. (RUS, GER & ENG., Illus.). 276p. 1996. 75.00 (1-56898-067-1) Princeton Arch.

Lissitzky, El & Arp, Hans. Kunstismen: The Isms of Art. LC 69-9230. (Contemporary Art Ser.). (ENG, FRE & GER., Illus.). 1979. reprint ed. 15.95 (0-405-00710-8) Ayer.

Lissitzky, El, jt. auth. see Mayakovsky, Vladimir.

Lissitzky-Kuppers, Sophie. El Lissitzky. (GER., Illus.). 412p. 1992. text 50.00 (3-364-00226-6) Gordon & Breach.

— El Lissitzky. LC 79-83561. (Illus.). 410p. 1992. 70.00 (0-500-23090-0, Pub. by Thames Hudson) Norton.

Lissitzyn, Oliver J. International Air Transport & National Policy. (Airlines History Project Ser.). reprint ed. 52.00 (0-404-19327-7) AMS Pr.

— The International Court of Justice: Its Role in the Maintenance of International Peace & Security, Vol. 6. LC 78-2885. (Carnegie Endowment for International Peace, United Nations Studies: No. 6). 118p. 1978. reprint ed. lib. bdg. 45.00 (0-313-20333-4, LICJ) Greenwood.

Lisska, Anthony J. Aquinas's Theory of Natural Law: An Analytical Reconstruction. 336p. 1998. pap. text 24.95 (0-19-826967-6) OUP.

Lissner, tr. see Jackins, Harvey & Meyer.

Lissner, Andrew, jt. ed. see Blake, James A.

Lissner, David. Laboratory Manual for the TI-81 Graphing Calculator. Pullins, ed. (Illus.). 145p. (C). pap. text 18.50 (0-314-02386-0) West Pub.

Lissner, Dorothy B., ed. see Bremner, Robert H.

Lissner, Dorothy B., ed. see Lawrence, Elwood P., et al.

Lissner, Dorothy B., jt. ed. see Lissner, Will.

Lissner, Dorothy Burnham, ed. see Silagi, Michael.

Lissner, Will & Lissner, Dorothy B., eds. George & the Scholars: A Century of Scientific Research Reveals the Reformer Was an Original Economist & a World-Class Social Philosopher. LC 91-1901. (George Studies Program: Vol. 1). 528p. (Orig.). (C). 1991. pap. 12.00 (0-911312-86-2) Schalkenbach.

Lissner, Will, ed. see Bremner, Robert H.

Lissner, Will, ed. see Lawrence, Elwood P., et al.

Lissner, Will B., ed. see Silagi, Michael.

Lissok, Charlotte. Teste Dein Wirtschaftsdeutsch. (GER.). 112p. 1983. pap. 11.25 (3-468-38527-7) Langenscheidt.

Lissovs. Designing Israels Landscapes. 45.00 (1-888931-16-7) Spacemkr Pr.

Lissovsky, F. V. & Kalugin, J. K. English-Russian Dictionary of Electronics. (ENG & RUS.). 718p. 1984. 95.00 (0-8288-0302-1, F17530) Fr & Eur.

List. Introduction to Information Research. 128p. (C). 1997. per. 16.19 (0-7872-4305-1) Kendall-Hunt.

List. List of Members '89. 1990. 91.00 (90-6191-982-7) Ashgate Pub Co.

List, Charles J. & Plum, Stephen H., eds. Library Research Guide to Philosophy: Illustrated Search Strategy & Sources. (Library Research Guides Ser.: No. 9). 104p. 1991. pap. 18.00 (0-87650-264-8) Pierian.

List, Christine. Chicano Images: Refiguring Ethnicity in Mainstream Film. rev. ed. LC 95-53204. (Studies in American Popular History & Culture). 192p. 1996. text 61.00 (0-8153-2060-4) Garland.

List, E. John & Jirka, Gerhard H., eds. Stratified Flows. LC 90-41159. 1120p. 1990. pap. text 107.00 (0-87262-775-6) Am Soc Civil Eng.

List, Eugene, ed. see Gottschalk, Louis M.

List, Gary R., jt. ed. see King, Jerry W.

List, Gary R., jt. ed. see Szuhaj, B. F.

List, George. Stability & Variation in Hopi Song. LC 92-73156. (Memoirs Ser.: Vol. 204). 205p. 1993. 28.00 (0-87169-204-X, M204-LIG) Am Philos.

***List, Gloria.** The Journey: A Young Swallows Flight to the Mission of San Juan Capistrano. Ramirez, Ivan D., ed. (Illus.). 32p. (J). (gr. 2-4). 1999. 14.95 (1-57159-006-4) Los Andes Pub.

List, Gloria A. The Journey. unabridged ed. (Illus.). 32p. (J). (gr. k-4). 1998. pap. 12.95 (1-891168-01-0) U CA Riverside.

List, Harvey L., jt. auth. see Schmidt, Alois X.

List, Herbert, photos by. Herbert List: Junge Maenner. (Illus.). 112p. 1988. 60.00 (0-944092-03-9) Twin Palms Pub.

List, Ian, ed. see Genetsky, Barry & Anderson, Philip W.

List, Ian, ed. see Ingraham, John L., et al.

List, J. H., ed. Large Scale Coastal Behavior (1993) (Illus.). 238p. (Orig.). (C). 1995. pap. text 60.00 (0-7881-2542-7) DIANE Pub.

List, Lynn M. Little Green Friend. (Illus.). 36p. (J). (gr. k-5). 1998. 14.95 (0-9662900-0-3) Skinny Lamb Publ.

List, M., jt. auth. see Hofmann, M.

List, P. H. & Schmidt, P. C. Phytopharmaceutical Technology. 1990. 105.00 (0-8493-7709-9) CRC Pr.

***List, Peter, ed.** Environmental Ethics & Forestry: A Reader. (Environmental Ethics, Values, & Policy Ser.). 416p. 2000. 89.50 (1-56639-784-7); pap. 29.95 (1-56639-785-5) Temple U Pr.

List, Robert N. Merlin's Secret: The African & Near Eastern Presence in the Ancient British Isles. 432p. 1999. 64.00 (0-7618-1395-0); pap. 47.50 (0-7618-1396-9) U Pr of Amer.

List, W., ed. see Clark, R.

List, W. F., jt. ed. see Steinbereithner, K.

Lista, Giovanni. Balla (Giacomo) Catalogue of the Work. limited ed. (Illus.). 540p. 1982. 225.00 (1-55660-165-4) A Wofsy Fine Arts.

Liste-Ghoode Peace Foundation Women's Delegation S. Indian Women Spirituality, & Social Change. (Common Ground Ser.: Vol. 5). (Illus.). 54p. (Orig.). 1990. pap. 5.00 (1-884478-04-2) Common Grnd.

Listen & Enjoy Staff. Listen & Enjoy French Poetry. (Listen & Enjoy Cassettes Ser.). 1991. pap. 9.95 incl. audio (0-486-99927-0) Dover.

— Listen & Enjoy German Poetry. (Listen & Enjoy Cassettes Ser.). 1991. pap. 9.95 incl. audio (0-486-99929-7) Dover.

— Listen & Enjoy Italian Poetry. (Listen & Enjoy Cassettes Ser.). 1998. pap. 9.95 incl. audio (0-486-99930-0) Dover.

Listen & Learn Staff. Listen & Learn French. 8.95 incl. audio (0-486-99914-9) Dover.

— Listen & Learn Italian. 9.95 incl. audio (0-486-99916-5) Dover.

L

L

***Liszt, Franz.** The Complete Schwanengesang. (The Schubert Song Transcriptions for Solo Piano Ser.: Series III). 192p. 1999. pap. 12.95 (0-486-40622-9) Dover.

Liszt, Franz. Franz Liszt: Selected Letters. Williams, Adrian, ed. & tr. by. (Illus.). 1,104p. 1999. text 125.00 (0-19-816688-5) OUP.

— The Gipsy in Music, 2 vols. 1990. reprint ed. lib. bdg. 140.00 (0-7812-9069-4) Rprt Serv.

— Letters of Franz Liszt, 2 vols. 1990. reprint ed. lib. bdg. 140.00 (0-7812-0410-0) Rprt Serv.

— Letters of Franz Liszt, 2 Vols, Set. LC 68-25294. (Studies in Music: No. 42). 1969. reprint ed. lib. bdg. 150.00 (0-8383-0307-2) M S G Haskell Hse.

— Letters of Franz Liszt, 2 vols., Set. 1980. reprint ed. lib. bdg. 95.00 (0-403-00360-1) Scholarly.

— Letters of Franz Liszt to Marie Zu Sayn-Wittgenstein. Hugo, Howard E., ed. & tr. by. from FRE. LC 71-142931. 376p. 1971. reprint ed. lib. bdg. 69.50 (0-8371-1428-4, LILM, Greenwood Pr) Greenwood.

— The Letters of Franz Liszt to Olga von Meyendorff, 1871-1886: In the Mildred Bliss Collection at Dumbarton Oaks. Tyler, William R., tr. (Illus.). 553p. (C). 1979. text 32.50 (0-685-02129-7) HUP.

— The Letters of Franz Liszt to Olga Von Meyendorff, 1871-1886: In the Mildred Bliss Collection at Dumbarton Oaks. 553p. (C). 1979. 32.50 (0-88402-078-9) HUP.

Liszt, Franz. Liebestraume No3 A Flat Major. 12p. 1997. per. 4.95 (0-7935-8322-5) H Leonard.

Liszt, Franz. Liszt: Sonata in B Minor. Hamilton, Kenneth, ed. (Cambridge Music Handbks.). 101p. (C). 1996. text 39.95 (0-521-46570-2) Cambridge U Pr.

— Liszt's Complete Piano Transcriptions from Wagner's Operas. Suttoni, Charles, ed. (Illus.). 176p. 1981. pap. 9.95 (0-486-24126-2) Dover.

— Mephisto Waltz & Other Works for Solo Piano. 192p. 1994. pap. 10.95 (0-486-28147-7) Dover.

— Organ Works. 176p. 1996. pap. 13.95 (0-486-29083-2) Dover.

— The Piano Concerti in Full Score. 144p. 1987. pap. 8.95 (0-486-25221-3) Dover.

— Piano Concertos No. 1 & No. 2. 112p. 1996. pap. 10.95 (0-486-29238-X) Dover.

— Piano Transcriptions from French & Italian Operas. (Illus.). 247p. 1982. pap. 13.95 (0-486-24273-0) Dover.

— Les Preludes & Other Symphonic Poems in Full Score. 320p. 1994. pap. 13.95 (0-486-28322-4) Dover.

— The Schubert Song Transcriptions for Solo Piano Series I: "Ave Maria," "Erlkonig" & Ten Other Great Songs. 144p. 1996. pap. 10.95 (0-486-28865-X) Dover.

— The Schubert Song Transcriptions for Solo Piano Series II: The Complete Winterreise & Seven Other Great Songs. 192p. 1996. pap. 11.95 (0-486-28876-5) Dover.

— Selected Piano Pieces I, 1. (Music Scores Ser.). 1998. pap. text 7.95 (963-9059-97-8) Konemann.

— Selected Piano Pieces II, 1. (Music Scores Ser.). 1998. pap. text 7.95 (963-9059-98-6) Konemann.

— Sonata in B Minor & Other Works for Piano. 208p. 1990. pap. 9.95 (0-486-26182-4) Dover.

— Thirty Songs, for High Voice. Armbruster, Carl, ed. 1979. 15.50 (0-8446-5502-3) Peter Smith.

— Thirty Songs for High Voice. Armbruster, Carl, ed. LC 75-17172. 144p. 1975. reprint ed. pap. 9.95 (0-486-23197-6) Dover.

Liszt, Franz & La Mara. Letters, 2 vols., Set. Bache, Constance, tr. LC 69-13973. 1970. reprint ed. lib. bdg. 65.00 (0-8371-1104-8, LILE) Greenwood.

— Letters, 2 vols., Vol. 1. Bache, Constance, tr. LC 69-13973. 1970. reprint ed. lib. bdg. 45.00 (0-313-21285-6, LILA) Greenwood.

— Letters, 2 vols., Vol. 2. Bache, Constance, tr. LC 69-13973. 1970. reprint ed. lib. bdg. 45.00 (0-8371-1105-6, LILB) Greenwood.

***Liszt, Franz, et al.** Franz Liszt & Agnes Street-Klindworth: A Correspondence LC 99-32944. 1999. write for info. (1-57647-006-7) Pendragon NY.

Liszt, Rudolph. The Last Word in Make-Up: A Practical Illustrated Handbook: Manuscript Edition. (Illus.). 1964. pap. 13.00 (0-8222-0640-4) Dramatists Play.

Litai, Xue. Digital Imaging Of Photograph. 1999. pap. text 20.00 (0-8389-8005-8) ALA.

Litai, Xue, jt. auth. see Lewis, John W.

Litaize, Alain, jt. auth. see Lanher, Jean.

Litak, Bob. 101 Questions about Santa Claus. Hilt Muehlenberg, Christine, ed. LC 99-189814. (Illus.). 128p. (gr. 4-7). 1998. 12.95 (0-911493-23-9) Blue Sky.

Litak, Bob, et al. Reflections of a Small Town Santa: A True Story about Santa Claus. LC 98-230243. (Illus.). 94p. 1998. 12.95 (0-911493-22-0) Blue Sky.

L'Italien, J. J. Proteins: Structure & Function. 810p. 1987. 135.00 (0-306-42299-9, Plenum Trade) Perseus Pubng.

Litalien, Theresa L. The Secret of the Tooth Fairy. LC 98-96244. (Illus.). 26p. (J). (ps-6). 1998. pap. 3.99 (0-9664625-1-3) Twinkle Toes.

Litamoi, J., et al. Quality Control Testing of Contagious Bovine Pleuropneumonia Live Attenuated Vaccine. LC 97-204943. (Animal Production & Health Papers: No. 128). 53p. 1996. pap. 11.00 (92-5-103796-5, F37965, Pub. by FAO) Bernan Associates.

Litan, jt. auth. see Hahn.

Litan, Robert, et al. Physical Damage & Human Loss: The Economic Impact of Earthquake Mitigation Measures. LC 92-28616. (Insurance & Society Ser.). 98p. (Orig.). 1992. pap. 15.00 (0-932387-35-7) Insur Info.

Litan, Robert E. The Revolution in U. S. Finance. 55p. (C). 1991. pap. 7.95 (0-8157-5279-2) Brookings.

— What Should Banks Do? LC 87-18235. 207p. 1987. 29.95 (0-8157-5270-9) Brookings.

Litan, Robert E., ed. Verdict: Assessing the Civil Jury System. 542p. (C). 1993. 52.95 (0-8157-5282-2); pap. 24.95 (0-8157-5281-4) Brookings.

Litan, Robert E. & Lawrence, Robert Z., eds. American Living Standards: Threats & Challenges. LC 88-26238. 250p. 1988. 38.95 (0-8157-5274-1); pap. 16.95 (0-8157-5273-3) Brookings.

Litan, Robert E. & Niskanen, William A. Going Digital! LC 97-45317. 90p. 1997. pap. 9.95 (0-8157-5285-7) Brookings.

Litan, Robert E. & Rauch, Jonathan. American Finance for the 21st Century. LC 98-8988. 211p. 1998. 22.95 (0-8157-5288-1) Brookings.

— American Finance for the 21st Century. (Illus.). 162p. (C). 1999. reprint ed. pap. text 30.00 (0-7881-7713-3) DIANE Pub.

Litan, Robert E. & Santomero, Anthony M., eds. Brookings-Wharton Papers on Financial Services, 1998. 300p. 1998. pap. text 39.95 (0-8157-1185-9) Brookings.

— Brookings-Wharton Papers on Financial Services, 1999. 1999. pap. 39.95 (0-8157-5287-3) Brookings.

Litan, Robert E. & Winston, Clifford M., eds. Liability: Perspectives & Policy. LC 88-7254. 248p. 1988. 36.95 (0-8157-5272-5); pap. 16.95 (0-8157-5271-7) Brookings.

Litan, Robert E., jt. auth. see Herring, Richard J.

Litan, Robert E., jt. auth. see Lawrence, Robert Z.

Litan, Robert E., jt. auth. see Swire, Peter P.

Litan, Robert E., jt. ed. see Boltuck, Richard.

Litan, Robert E., jt. ed. see Huber, Peter W.

Litan, Robert E., jt. ed. see Kaufman, George G.

Litchfield, Ada B. A Button in Her Ear. Rubin, Caroline, ed. LC 75-28390. (Albert Whitman Concept Bks.). (Illus.). 32p. (J). (gr. 2-4). 1976. lib. bdg. 14.95 (0-8075-0987-6) A Whitman.

— A Cane in Her Hand. Rubin, Caroline, ed. LC 77-14255. (Albert Whitman Concept Bks.). (Illus.). (J). (gr. 1-3). 1977. lib. bdg. 14.95 (0-8075-1056-4) A Whitman.

— Words in Our Hands. Tucker, Kathleen, ed. LC 79-28402. (Albert Whitman Concept Bks.: Level 2). (Illus.). (J). (gr. 2-4). 1980. lib. bdg. 14.95 (0-8075-9212-9) A Whitman.

Litchfield, Barbara. The Battlefield. 160p. 1998. pap. 10.00 (1-57502-919-7, PO2535) Morris Pubng.

— From the Slime: To the Sublime. 126p. 1998. pap. 10.00 (1-57502-977-4, PO2672) Morris Pubng.

— Israel My Love. 160p. 1998. pap. 10.00 (1-57502-913-8, PO2521) Morris Pubng.

— Jesus in First Century Israel. Orig. Title: Jesus & the Socio Religious Milieu. 124p. 1998. 8.00 (1-57502-738-0, PO2054) Morris Pubng.

— A Scriptural View of World Religions. 123p. 1998. pap. 8.00 (1-57502-835-2, PO2297) Morris Pubng.

— A Sheep's Eye View of the Sheepfold. 120p. 1998. pap. 8.00 (1-57502-920-0, PO2538) Morris Pubng.

Litchfield, Barbara S. A Sheep's Eye View of the Shepherd. (Illus.). 110p. 1998. pap. 8.00 (1-57502-924-3, PO2549) Morris Pubng.

Litchfield, C. D. & Seyfried, P. L., eds. Methodology for Biomass Determinations & Microbial Activities in Sediments-STP 673. 199p. 1979. 22.50 (0-8031-0511-8, STP673) ASTM.

Litchfield, Carolyn, jt. auth. see Vorndran, Barbara S.

Litchfield, Carter. History of Oleomargarine Tax Stamps & Licenses in the United States. LC 86-21799. (Illus.). 128p. 1988. 27.50 (0-917526-03-1) Olearius Edns.

Litchfield, Carter, et al. The Bethlehem Oil Mill Seventeen Forty-Five to Nineteen Thirty-Four: German Technology in Early Pennsylvania. LC 82-61069. (Illus.). 128p. 1984. 25.00 (0-917526-02-3) Olearius Edns.

Litchfield, Grace D. As a Man Sows, & Other Stories. LC 77-160940. (Short Story Index Reprint Ser.). 1977. reprint ed. 23.95 (0-8369-3919-0) Ayer.

— Little Venice & Other Stories. LC 72-98583. (Short Story Index Reprint Ser.). 1977. 20.95 (0-8369-3157-2) Ayer.

Litchfield, Harry R. Live & Be Well. LC 72-76583. 300p. 1972. 12.95 (0-87212-022-8) Libra.

Litchfield, Hugh. Visualizing the Sermon: Preaching Without Notes. 1996. pap. 10.95 (0-7880-0909-5) CSS OH.

Litchfield, Jack. The Canadian Jazz Discography. 945p. 1982. 40.00 (0-8020-2448-3) U of Toronto Pr.

***Litchfield, Jo.** Animals. (First Words Board Bks.). (Illus.). 12p. (YA). (ps up). 2000. bds. 4.95 (0-7460-4093-8, Usborne) EDC.

Litchfield, Jo. Everyday Words. (Illus.). 48p. (ps-3). 1999. 20.95 (1-58086-190-3) EDC.

— Everyday Words in French. (Everyday Words Ser.). (FRE., Illus.). 48p. 1999. 12.95 (0-7460-2768-0, Usborne) EDC.

— Everyday Words in German. (Everyday Words Ser.). (GER., Illus.). 48p. 1999. 12.95 (0-7460-2770-2, Usborne) EDC.

— Everyday Words in Spanish. (Everyday Words Ser.). (SPA., Illus.). 48p. 1999. 12.95 (0-7460-2772-9, Usborne) EDC.

— Everyday Words in Spanish. (Illus.). 48p. (ps-3). 1999. 20.95 (1-58086-191-1) EDC.

***Litchfield, Jo, ed.** Very First Words. (Illus.). 20p. (ps up). 2000. bds. 6.95 (0-7460-3827-5, Pub. by Usbrne Pbng UK) EDC.

Litchfield, Jo, jt. auth. see Brooke, Felicity.

Litchfield, Jo, jt. auth. see Brooks, Felicity.

Litchfield, Jo, jt. ed. see Brooks, Felicity.

Litchfield, Michael. Decorating with Architectural Details. LC 95-24616. (For Your Home Ser.). 72p. 1995. 12.95 (1-56799-268-4, Friedman-Fairfax) M Friedman Pub Grp Inc.

Litchfield, Nathaniel. Evaluation in Planning: Facing the Challenge of Complexity. LC 98-24604. (Geojournal Library). 383p. 1998. write for info. (0-7923-5177-0) Kluwer Academic.

Litchfield, R. B. Tom Wedgwood, the First Photographer. LC 72-9217. (Literature of Photography Ser.). 1979. reprint ed. 21.95 (0-405-04924-2) Ayer.

Litchfield, R. Burr. Emergence of a Bureaucracy: The Florentine Patricians, 1530-1790. LC 86-12226. (Illus.). 421p. 1986. reprint ed. pap. 130.60 (0-608-02537-2, 206318100004) Bks Demand.

Litchfield, R. Burr, tr. from ITA. History of the Italian Agricultural Landscape. LC 96-47543. (Giovanni Agnelli Foundation Series in Italian History). 408p. 1997. text 55.00 (0-691-01216-4, Pub. by Princeton U Pr) Cal Prin Full Svc.

Litchfield, R. Burr, tr. see Sereni, Emilio.

Litchfield, R. Burr, tr. see Venturi, Franco.

Litchfield, R. M. Blood Will Have Blood. large type ed. (Linford Western Large Print Ser.). 240p. 1996. pap. 16.99 (0-7089-7821-5, Linford) Ulverscroft.

***Litchfield, Robert L., Jr.** To Be a Graceful Giant: A Living Expression of Grace. 315p. 2000. 14.95 (0-9702427-0-0, 01) Wings of Angels.

Litchfield, W. J. The Litchfield Family in America, Pt. 1, Nos. 1-5. 384p. 1989. reprint ed. pap. 57.00 (0-8328-0772-9); reprint ed. lib. bdg. 65.00 (0-8328-0771-0) Higginson Bk Co.

Litchford. Medical Nutrition Therapy: Case Studies for the Dietary Manager. 166p. 1997. spiral bd. 21.00 (0-7872-3605-5) Kendall-Hunt.

— Nutrition Through the Life Cycle: Case Studies for the Dietary Manager. 136p. 1997. spiral bd. 21.00 (0-7872-3604-7) Kendall-Hunt.

Litchford, Mary. Lab Assessment of Nutritional Status. 119p. 1998. spiral bd. 110.00 (1-879575-82-5) Acad Med Sys.

Litchford, Mary, et al. Nutrition Case Management of Diabetes: User's Manual. (C). 1997. pap. 7.00 (1-880989-56-5) Case Sftware.

Litchford, Mary D. Job Descriptions for Healthcare, Vol. 1. 143p. 1997. spiral bd. 95.00 (1-879575-67-1) Acad Med Sys.

— Job Descriptions for Nursing, Vol. 2. 175p. 1997. spiral bd. 95.00 (1-879575-73-6) Acad Med Sys.

Litchford, Mary D. & Yordy, Laura. Diabetes. (C). 1995. pap. 6.00 (1-880989-53-0) Case Sftware.

— Diabetes: Instructor's Guide. (C). 1991. teacher ed. 139.00 incl. 5.25 hd (1-880989-10-7); teacher ed. 139.00 incl. 3.5 hd (1-880989-11-5); teacher ed. 139.00 incl. 3.5 hd (1-880989-09-3); teacher ed. 139.00 incl. 5.25 hd (1-880989-08-5) Case Sftware.

— Hypertension. (C). 1995. pap. 6.00 (1-880989-54-9) Case Sftware.

— Reading the Medical Record. 1995. 139.00 (1-880989-40-9); 139.00 (1-880989-41-7); 139.00 (1-880989-42-5); 139.00 (1-880989-43-3) Case Sftware.

— Reading the Medical Record. rev. ed. 1995. pap. 6.00 (1-880989-45-X) Case Sftware.

***Litchford, Mary D., et al.** Case Studies in Food Safety. 1998. pap. text 7.00 (1-880989-60-3) Case Sftware.

Litchford, Mary D., et al. Food Menu Systems & Applications User's Manual. rev. ed. (C). 1997. pap. 7.00 (1-880989-28-X) Case Sftware.

— Hypertension User's Manual. rev. ed. (C). 1995. pap. 7.00 (1-880989-22-0) Case Sftware.

— Nutrition Through the Lifecycle I: User's Guide. 1994. 139.00 (1-880989-30-1); 139.00 (1-880989-31-X); 139.00 (1-880989-32-8); 139.00 (1-880989-33-6); pap., teacher ed. 6.00 (1-880989-35-2) Case Sftware.

— Nutrition Through the Lifecycle I: User's Guide. (C). 1997. pap., student ed. 7.00 (1-880989-34-4) Case Sftware.

— Nutrition Through the Lifecycle II. 1995. 139.00 (1-880989-46-8); 139.00 (1-880989-47-6); 139.00 (1-880989-48-4); 139.00 (1-880989-49-2) Case Sftware.

— Nutrition Through the Lifecycle II. (C). 1995. pap., student ed. 7.00 (1-880989-50-6) Case Sftware.

— Nutritional Assessment in Malnutrition & Stress. 1994. 139.00 (1-880989-36-0); 139.00 (1-880989-37-9); 139.00 (1-880989-38-7); 139.00 (1-880989-39-5) Case Sftware.

— Nutritional Assessment in Malnutrition & Stress. (C). 1994. pap. 6.00 (1-880989-44-1) Case Sftware.

— Nutritional Assessment of Malnutrition & Stress User's Manual. (C). 1994. pap. 7.00 (1-880989-20-4) Case Sftware.

— Reading the Medical Record User's Manual. rev. ed. (C). 1995. pap. 7.00 (1-880989-26-3) Case Sftware.

Litchford, Mary D., jt. auth. see Hogue, Mary A.

Litchford, Mary D., jt. auth. see Yordy, Laura.

Litchman, Kristin. All Is Well. 1999. pap. 3.99 (0-440-41488-1) BDD Bks Young Read.

Litchman, Kristin E. The Wrong Side of the Pattern. LC 98-119380. 154p. (YA). (gr. 9-12). 1998. pap. 9.99 (0-88092-381-4) Royal Fireworks.

Litchman, Kristin Embry. All Is Well. LC 97-31623. 128p. (J). (gr. 4-6). 1998. 14.95 (0-385-32592-4) Delacorte.

Litchman, William M., compiled by. An Every-Name Index for Agricultural Schedules, Industry Other Than Agriculture Schedules, Marriages, Deaths, & Civil War Soldier Deaths in the 1865 New York State Census for Jefferson County. LC 96-79332. (An Every-Name Index of the 1865 New York State Census for Jefferson County Ser.). 218p. (Orig.). 1996. pap. 35.00 (1-890034-10-X) Medley.

— An Every-Name Index of the 1865 New York State Census for Jefferson County Vol. 1: Town of Watertown. LC 96-79624. 345p. (Orig.). 1996. pap. 40.00 (1-890034-00-2) Medley.

— An Every-Name Index of the 1865 New York State Census for Jefferson County Vol. 2: Towns of Adams & Alexandria. LC 96-79915. 310p. (Orig.). 1996. pap. 35.00 (1-890034-01-0) Medley.

— An Every-Name Index of the 1865 New York State Census for Jefferson County Vol. 3: Towns of Antwerp & Brownville. LC 96-79916. 294p. (Orig.). 1997. pap. 35.00 (1-890034-02-9) Medley.

— An Every-Name Index of the 1865 New York State Census for Jefferson County Vol. 4: Towns of Cape Vincent & Leray. LC 96-79917. 289p. (Orig.). 1997. pap. 35.00 (1-890034-03-7) Medley.

— An Every-Name Index of the 1865 New York State Census for Jefferson County Vol. 5: Champion & Clayton. LC 96-79918. 289p. (Orig.). 1997. pap. 35.00 (1-890034-04-5) Medley.

— An Every-Name Index of the 1865 New York State Census for Jefferson County Vol. 6: Ellisburg & Lorraine. LC 96-79919. 306p. (Orig.). 1997. pap. 35.00 (1-890034-05-3) Medley.

— An Every-Name Index of the 1865 New York State Census for Jefferson County Vol. 7: Henderson, Rodman & Theresa. LC 96-79920. 281p. (Orig.). 1997. pap. 35.00 (1-890034-06-1) Medley.

— An Every-Name Index of the 1865 New York State Census for Jefferson County Vol. 8: Hounsfield, Lyme & Worth. LC 96-79921. 261p. (Orig.). 1997. pap. 35.00 (1-890034-07-X) Medley.

— An Every-Name Index of the 1865 New York State Census for Jefferson County Vol. 9: Orleans & Wilna. LC 96-79922. 301p. (Orig.). 1997. pap. 35.00 (1-890034-08-8) Medley.

— An Every-Name Index of the 1865 New York State Census for Jefferson County Vol. 10: Pamelia, Philadelphia & Rutland. LC 96-79923. 282p. (Orig.). 1997. pap. 35.00 (1-890034-09-6) Medley.

Litchten, William. Data & Error Analysis. 2nd ed. LC 98-33710. 192p. 1998. pap. 27.80 (0-13-368580-2) P-H.

Lite, Hyppo. Li, Konprann, Ekri: Read, Understand & Write. 244p. Date not set. wbk. ed. 17.00 (1-881839-63-X) Educa Vision.

Lite, Lori. The Affirmation Web: A Believe in Yourself Adventure. LC 97-26752. (Illus.). 34p. (J). 1997. pap. 9.00 (1-886941-25-4, 0942) Spec Pr FL.

— A Boy & a Bear: The Children's Relaxation Book. LC 96-33818. (Illus.). 32p. (Orig.). (J). (gr. 1-4). 1996. pap. 11.00 (1-886941-07-6, 0941) Spec Pr FL.

Litecky, Charles R., jt. auth. see Davis, Gordon B.

Litecky, Larry. Creating Active Learning. LC 99-163564. (Strategies & Solutions Ser.: No. 2). (Illus.). 100p. 1998. pap. 33.00 (0-87117-310-7, 1426) Comm Coll Pr Am Assn Comm Coll.

Litehiser, Joe J., ed. Observation Seismology: A Centennial Symposium for the Berkeley Seismographic Stations. 1990. 65.00 (0-520-06582-4, Pub. by U CA Pr) Cal Prin Full Svc.

Litell, Julia. Building Strong Foundations: Evaluation Strategies for Family Resource Programs. 148p. 1986. pap. 30.00 (1-885429-00-2) Family Resource.

Litely. Gardener's Collage. 1997. 6.00 (0-7667-0670-2) Gibson.

Literacy for Life Staff. We Have Something to Say: Our Words in Print. (Illus.). x, 197p. 1998. pap. 7.00 (0-9663115-0-7) Literacy for Life.

Literacy Volunteers Computer Task Force Staff. Computer Assisted Instruction (CAI) Review. Lawson, V. K. & Carlin, Chip, eds. 1986. pap. text 3.00 (0-318-41221-7) Lit Vol Am.

Literacy Volunteers of America Staff. ESL Tutor Training Workshop. 1980. student ed. 550.00 incl. audio, sl. (0-930713-43-5) Lit Vol Am.

Literacy Volunteers of New York City Staff, ed. Bars Coming Near: An Anthology by New Writers in Prison. (New Writers' Voices Ser.). 64p. (Orig.). 1992. pap. text 3.50 (0-929631-64-1, Signal Hill) New Readers.

— From My Imagination: An Anthology of Poetry & Short Stories by New Writers. (New Writers' Voices Ser.). 64p. (Orig.). 1990. pap. text 3.50 (0-929631-17-X, Signal Hill) New Readers.

— My Native Land: An Anthology by New Writers. 64p. (Orig.). 1992. pap. text 3.50 (0-929631-65-X, Signal Hill) New Readers.

— Speaking from the Heart: An Anthology of Writing by New Writers. (New Writers' Voices Ser.). 64p. (Orig.). 1990. pap. text 3.50 (0-929631-16-1, Signal Hill) New Readers.

— Speaking Out on Health: An Anthology. (New Writers' Voices Ser.). 64p. (Orig.). 1989. pap. text 3.50 (0-929631-05-6, Signal Hill) New Readers.

— Speaking Out on Home & Family: An Anthology of Writing by New Writers. (New Writers' Voices Ser.). (Illus.). 64p. (Orig.). 1990. pap. text 3.50 (0-929631-08-0, Signal Hill) New Readers.

— Speaking Out on Work: An Anthology of Writing by New Writers. (New Writers' Voices Ser.). (Illus.). 64p. (Orig.). 1991. pap. text 3.15 (0-929631-35-8, Signal Hill) New Readers.

— Taking Charge of My Life: An Anthology of Writing by New Writers. (New Writers' Voices Ser.). 64p. (Orig.). 1991. pap. text 3.50 (0-929631-37-4, Signal Hill) New Readers.

Literacy Volunteers of New York City Staff, suppl. Selected from Bless Me, Ultima. abr. ed. (Writers' Voices Ser.). (Illus.). 64p. (Orig.). 1989. pap. text 3.95 (0-929631-06-4, Signal Hill) New Readers.

Literacy Volunteers of New York City Staff, ed. see Benchley, Peter.

Literacy Volunteers of New York City Staff, ed. see Carbone, Sonny.

Literacy Volunteers of New York City Staff, ed. see Clark, Mary Higgins.

Literacy Volunteers of New York City Staff, ed. see Fargo, Jean.

Literacy Volunteers of New York City Staff, ed. see Feiffer, Jules, et al.

Literacy Volunteers of New York City Staff, ed. see Fulghum, Robert.

Literacy Volunteers of New York City Staff, ed. see Goodall, Jane.

An Asterisk (*) at the beginning of an entry indicates that the title is appearing for the first time.

L

Literacy Volunteers of New York City Staff, ed. see Gum, Lori.

Literacy Volunteers of New York City Staff, ed. see Henley, Beth, et al.

Literacy Volunteers of New York City Staff, ed. see Hijuelos, Oscar.

Literacy Volunteers of New York City Staff, ed. see Jackson, Katherine & Wiseman, Richard.

Literacy Volunteers of New York City Staff, ed. see King, Stephen.

Literacy Volunteers of New York City Staff, ed. see Kingston, Maxine H.

Literacy Volunteers of New York City Staff, ed. see Knobler, Peter & Abdul-Jabbar, Kareem.

Literacy Volunteers of New York City Staff, ed. see Krantz, Judith.

Literacy Volunteers of New York City Staff, ed. see Lynn, Loretta.

Literacy Volunteers of New York City Staff, ed. see McMurtry, Larry.

Literacy Volunteers of New York City Staff, ed. see Miles, Calvin.

Literacy Volunteers of New York City Staff, ed. see Millay, Edna St. Vincent, et al.

Literacy Volunteers of New York City Staff, ed. see Monette, Paul.

Literacy Volunteers of New York City Staff, ed. see Moore, Mamie.

Literacy Volunteers of New York City Staff, ed. see Sanservino, Theresa.

Literacy Volunteers of New York City Staff, ed. see Tan, Amy.

Literacy Volunteers of New York City Staff, ed. see Underwood, John & Williams, Ted.

Literacy Volunteers of New York City Staff, ed. see Walker, Alice.

Literary & Philosophical Society of New York Staff, Jr. & Clinton, DeWitt. An Introductory Discourse: Proceedings of the Literary & Philosophical Society of New York, May 1814. Albritton, Claude C., ed. LC 77-6515. (History of Geology Ser.). 1978. reprint ed. lib. bdg. 19.95 (*0-405-10437-5*) Ayer.

Literary Foundation Staff. The Complete Guide to Literary Contests, 2000. LC 99-50118. 658p. 1999. pap. 23.95 (*1-57392-770-8*) Prometheus Bks.

***Literary Fountain Staff, compiled by.** The Complete Guide to Literary Contests, 2001. 825p. 2000. pap. 30.00 (*1-57392-850-X*) Prometheus Bks.

Literary Fountain Staff, compiled by. The Complete Guide to Literary Contests. LC 98-52969. 550p. 1999. 69.95 (*1-57392-262-5*) Prometheus Bks.

— The Complete Guide to Literary Contests, 1999. LC 98-52969. 525p. 1999. pap. 22.95 (*1-57392-261-7*) Prometheus Bks.

Literary Volunteers of America Staff. Intercultural Communications - Trainer's Guide. 1980. student ed. 90.00 incl. audio, sl. (*0-930713-50-8*) Lit Vol Am.

Lites, Emily & Lehman, Jean. Visions: A Low Intermediate Grammar. 256p. (C). 1990. pap. text 23.80 (*0-13-328816-1*) P-H.

— Visions: Writing One. 164p. (C). 1989. pap. text 19.60 (*0-13-946070-5*) P-H.

Lites, Emily & Thorpe, Kathy. Doing Business Globally: American Business English Skills Book 1. (Illus.). (C). pap. text. write for info. (*0-472-08486-0*) U of Mich Pr.

— Doing Business Globally: American Business English Skills, Book 1. (Illus.). (C). write for info. (*0-472-08496-8*) U of Mich Pr.

— Doing Business Globally: American Business English Skills, Book 3. (Illus.). (C). write for info. (*0-472-08498-4*); pap. text. write for info. (*0-472-08488-7*) U of Mich Pr.

— English for Global Business: Intermediate Level, American Business English Skills. (Illus.). 180p. (C). write for info. (*0-472-08497-6*) U of Mich Pr.

— English for Global Business: Text 1: Intermediate Level, American Business English Skills. (Illus.). 180p. (C). pap. text 17.95 (*0-472-08487-9*, 08487) U of Mich Pr.

Lites, Emily, jt. auth. see Lehman.

Litewka, Albert. Warsaw: A Novel of Resistance. 512p. 1989. 21.95 (*0-685-31318-2*) IMA NYC.

Litext, Inc. Staff & Solorzano, Porfirio R., intros. The Nirex Collection: Nicaraguan Revolution Extracts. (Collection of Documents Ser.: Vols. 1-10). (Illus.). 9440p. (C). 1989. pap. 425.00 (*0-685-27216-8*) LITEXT Inc.

Litfin, Dave. Real-Life Handicapping: An Eclectic Horseplayers Year at the Track. LC 97-195777. (Illus.). 190p. (Orig.). 1997. pap., per. 25.00 (*0-933944-18-7*) City Miner Bks.

Litfin, Duane. Public Speaking: A Handbook for Christians. 2nd ed. LC 91-42786. 368p. 1992. pap. 24.99 (*0-8010-5675-6*) Baker Bks.

Litfin, Karen. Ozone Discourse: Science & Politics in Global Environmental Cooperation. LC 94-8867. (New Directions in World Politics Ser.). (Illus.). 296p. 1994. 52.50 (*0-231-08136-7*) Col U Pr.

— Ozone Discourses: Science & Politics in Global Environmental Cooperation. Milner, Helen V. & Ruggie, John G., eds. (New Directions in World Politics Ser.). 296p. 1995. pap. 19.50 (*0-231-08137-5*) Col U Pr.

Litfin, Karen T., ed. The Greening of Sovereignty in World Politics. LC 98-24300. (Global Environmental Accord Ser.). (Illus.). 344p. 1998. 50.00 (*0-262-12211-1*) MIT Pr.

— The Greening of Sovereignty in World Politics. LC 98-24300. (Global Environmental Accord Ser.). (Illus.). 360p. 1998. pap. text 25.00 (*0-262-62123-1*) MIT Pr.

Litherland, Caren, tr. see Paganini, Maria.

***Litherland, Donna. The Great Flood of California. 122p. 2000. 24.95 (*0-9607888-5-9*) Barney Press.**

The dam breaks. In a catastrophe reminiscent of the Johnstown Flood, this novel reveals the panic & devastation which inundates most of California. It might be termed Utopian. Many people are destroyed & the more rigorous survivors cluster at the Central Pacific Coast above Santa Barbara, close to Morro Bay. Our heroine, Sally, tries to pick up the pieces together with Charlie, a generally tough ex-seal & together, they take care of the neediest on that narrow strip of Neuva California. They are not to rest, however, as an invading force of strangers, not Russian, not Mongolian, arrive in large carriers & they destroy Los Angeles. Sally is in a quandary about which of two suitors she should choose; then, when she decides, she can't find him for a day & a half. Finally, the region gets restored in a way satisfying to all. $r24.95 hardback, include $3.00 for shipping & tax. 3807 Noel Place, Bakersfield, California 93306. donnajl@juno.com. *Publisher Paid Annotation.*

Litherland, Donna. Learning & Remembering from Text: Buttonhole Your Buddy. (Illus.). 14p. 1983. pap. text 1.50 (*0-9607888-1-6*) Barney Pr.

— Reading for Executives. (Illus.). 100p. (Orig.). (C). 1982. pap. text 12.50 (*0-9607888-0-8*) Barney Pr.

— Speed Reading for Progressive Adults. (Illus.). 134p. (C). 1993. pap. text 14.95 (*0-9607888-3-2*) Barney Pr.

— Speed Reading for Progressive Adults. (Illus.). 128p. 1993. pap. 14.95 (*1-56474-075-7*) Fithian Pr.

— Walker Pass Lodge. 220p. (Orig.). 1996. pap. 11.95 (*0-9607888-4-0*) Barney Pr.

Litherland, Janet. Absolutely Unforgettable Parties: Great Ideas for Party People. Zapel, Arthur L., ed. LC 89-13519. (Illus.). 192p. (Orig.). 1990. pap. 14.95 (*0-916260-63-1*, B135) Meriwether Pub.

Litherland, Janet. Clown Ministry Handbook: The Original Book of Clown Ministry Basics with Skits for Service & Worship. 4th ed. Pijanowski, Kathy & Zapel, Arthur L., eds. LC 82-61091. (Illus.). 160p. (YA). (gr. 9 up). 1982. pap. 12.95 (*0-916260-16-8*, B163) Meriwether Pub.

Litherland, Janet. The Complete Banner Handbook: A Creative Guide for Banner Design & Construction. Zapel, Arthur L. & Gallardo, Michelle, eds. LC 87-71778. (Illus.). 122p. 1987. pap. 14.95 (*0-916260-48-8*, B172) Meriwether Pub.

— Everything New & Who's Who in Clown Ministry: With 75 Skits for Special Days. Zapel, Arthur L. & Wray, Rhonda, eds. LC 93-14652. (Illus.). 280p. 1993. pap. 12.95 (*0-916260-99-2*, B126) Meriwether Pub.

— Storytelling from the Bible: Make Scripture Live for All Ages Through the Art of Storytelling. Zapel, Arthur L. & Wray, Rhonda, eds. LC 91-29871. 192p. (Orig.). 1991. pap. 12.95 (*0-916260-80-1*, B145) Meriwether Pub.

Litherland, Janet & McAnally, Sue. Broadway Costumes on a Budget: Big Time Ideas for Amateur Producers. Zapel, Theodore O., ed. (Illus.). 160p. (Orig.). (YA). (gr. 9 up). 1996. pap. 14.95 (*1-56608-021-5*, B166) Meriwether Pub.

***Lithgow, John.** The Remarkable Farkle McBride. LC 99-89157. (Illus.). (J). 2000. per. 16.00 (*0-689-83340-7*) S&S Childrens.

***Lithgow, Lynette.** Special Blend: Fusion Management from Asia & the West. LC 99-462326. 240p. 2000. 29.95 (*0-471-84550-7*, Wiley Heyden) Wiley.

Lithgow, R. A., ed. Dictionary of American Indian Place & Proper Names in New England. 400p. 2000. reprint ed. lib. bdg. 42.00 (*0-7808-0392-2*) Omnigraphics Inc.

Lithgow, Scott. Training & Working Dogs: For Quiet Confident Control of Stock. 2nd ed. (Orig.). 1991. pap. 18.95 (*0-7022-2394-8*, Pub. by Univ Queensland Pr) Intl Spec Bk.

Lithman, Adella. Horses of a Lifetime. 1998. 75.00 (*0-85131-728-6*, Pub. by J A Allen) Trafalgar.

***Lithman, Alan.** The Savitri Legend: A Transformational Tale. 244p. (C). 1999. pap. 17.95 (*1-879041-25-1*) Sigo Pr.

Lithman, Yngve G. The Community Apart: A Case Study of a Canadian Indian Reserve Community. LC 85-107602. 192p. Date not set. reprint ed. pap. 59.60 (*0-608-20626-1*, 207206200003) Bks Demand.

Lithmond, Greta T. Child Welfare & Foster Home Care: Index of Modern Information. LC 88-47999. 150p. 1990. 47.50 (*1-55914-078-X*); pap. 44.50 (*1-55914-079-8*) ABBE Pubs Assn.

— Psychiatric Nursing: International Subject Analysis with Reference Bibliography. LC 85-48185. 150p. 1987. 37.50 (*0-88164-482-X*); pap. 34.50 (*0-88164-483-8*) ABBE Pubs Assn.

Lithographic Technical Foundation Staff. How To Run an Offset Press. (Illus.). 300p. 1994. reprint ed. pap. 19.95 (*1-57002-008-6*) Univ Publng Hse.

Lithuanian Educational Council of the USA Staff. Easy Way to Lithuanian. unabridged ed. 292p. 1992. pap. 135.00 incl. audio (*0-88432-458-3*, AFLT10) Audio-Forum.

Lithuanian European Institute Staff, jt. auth. see Altvater, Elmara.

Lithuanian Philatelic Societies of New York & Toro. Postage Stamps of Lithuania. 237p. 1978. 18.00 (*0-912574-33-X*) Collectors.

Lithuanian Photographers Staff. Lithuanian Celebrations: Lietuviu Sventes a Collection of Photographs. Kezys, Algimantas, ed. LC 90-84748. (Illus.). 1991. pap. 20.00 (*0-9617756-4-5*) Galerija.

— Lithuanian Ethnographic Crafts. Kezys, Algimantas, ed. LC 98-72196. (LIT., Illus.). 180p. 1998. pap. 15.00 (*1-886060-12-6*) Galerija.

***Lithuanian Photographers Staff.** Lithuanian Photography '98: A Juxtaposition of Traditional & Computer-Generated Works. Kezys, Algimantas, ed. LC 99-71655. (ENG & LIT., Illus.). 250p. 1999. pap. 20.00 (*1-886060-15-0*) Galerija.

Lithwick, Harvey, jt. ed. see Bruins, Hendrik J.

Lithwick, Harvey, jt. ed. see Gradus, Yehuda.

Litiche, John M., ed. International Economic Policies & Their Theoretical Foundations: A Sourcebook. 2nd ed. (Economic Theory, Econometrics & Mathematical Economics Ser.). (Illus.). 988p. 1992. pap. text 79.95 (*0-12-444281-1*) Acad Pr.

Litigation Section Staff. Proposed Amendments to the Federal Rules of Evidence. 155p. 1985. 25.00 (*0-685-14430-5*, 531-0047) Amer Bar Assn.

Litka, Michael P. Int'l Dimensions Of The Legal Env Of Bus. (SWC-Management). 250p. (C). 1988. pap. 14.00 (*0-534-87208-5*) PWS Pubs.

Litka, Michael P. & Blodgett, Mark S. International Dimensions of the Legal Environment of Business. 3rd ed. LC 94-11693. (C). 1994. mass mkt. 43.95 (*0-538-84492-2*) S-W Pub.

Litke, Richard L. A Reconstruction of the Assyro-Babylonian God-Lists AN. Hallo, William W., ed. (Texts from the Babylonian Collection: Vol. 3). 358p. 1998. 55.00 (*0-9667495-0-2*) Yale Babylonian.

Litke, Robert, jt. ed. see Curtin, Deane.

Litke, Ronald. Ice Hockey. (Successful Sports Ser.). (J). 1998. 21.36 (*1-57572-074-4*) Heinemann Lib.

Litkei, Andrea F. Crossings. (Illus.). 60p. 1990. reprint ed. 9.95 (*1-880165-01-5*) Hanlit Pubns.

— ESP (Extrasensory Perception) 144p. 1967. pap. 6.95 (*1-880165-04-X*) Hanlit Pubns.

— Horn of the Unicorn. (Illus.). 121p. 1985. 9.95 (*1-880165-02-3*) Hanlit Pubns.

— Plums from a Tree. (Illus.). 102p. 1978. 9.95 (*1-880165-03-1*) Hanlit Pubns.

— Psychological Territories. 176p. 1992. 14.95 (*1-880165-00-7*) Hanlit Pubns.

— Thalassa. (Illus.). 61p. 1967. pap. 6.95 (*1-880165-05-8*) Hanlit Pubns.

Litkowski, Mary P. Father Damien, Loving Neighbor. LC 94-77541. 64p. (Orig.). 1994. pap. 5.95 (*0-916927-20-2*) Growth Unltd.

— A Friend to All - St. John Nepomucene Neumann C. SS. R. LC 87-80716. 64p. 1987. pap. 5.95 (*0-916927-07-5*) Growth Unltd.

— Kateri Tekakwitha: Joyful Lover. LC 89-84104. (Illus.). 64p. 1989. pap. 5.95 (*0-916927-10-5*) Growth Unltd.

Litman, Barry R. The Motion Picture Mega-Industry. LC 97-22703. 336p. 1998. pap. text 34.67 (*0-205-20026-5*) Allyn.

Litman, G. W., jt. ed. see Du Pasquier, L.

Litman, Jane R., jt. ed. see Orenstein, Debra.

***Litman, Judy.** People, Places & Things. LC 99-95230. (Illus.). 114p. 2000. reprint ed. pap. 25.00 (*0-9672800-0-1*) J Litman Pubn.

— The Wonder of the World. LC 00-91798. (Illus.). 65p. 2000. 40.00 (*0-9672800-2-8*); pap. 25.00 (*0-9672800-1-X*) J Litman Pubn.

Litman, Robert. Wynnefield & Limer. 237p. 1983. pap. 4.95 (*0-918921-00-7*) Ivy League Pr.

Litman, Robert B. Allergy Shots. LC 92-70081. 254p. (Orig.). 1993. pap. text 9.95 (*0-918921-04-X*) Ivy League Pr.

— The Treblinka Virus. LC 90-82034. 289p. 1991. pap. 8.95 (*0-918921-02-3*) Ivy League Pr.

Litman, Robert E., ed. Psychoanalysis in the Americas. LC 66-24394. 328p. 1966. 50.00 (*0-8236-5200-9*) Intl Univs Pr.

Litman, Theodor J. Health Politics & Policy. 2nd ed. 1991. text 48.50 (*0-8273-4555-0*) Delmar.

— Health Politics & Policy. 3rd ed. LC 96-39278. (Health Services Administration Ser.). 1997. mass mkt. 75.95 (*0-8273-6776-7*) Delmar.

Litman, Theodor J. & Robins, Leonard S. Health Politics & Policy. LC 83-26042. (Health Services Ser.: No. 1-456). 403p. (C). 1989. text 46.25 (*0-8273-4289-6*) Delmar.

Litman, Todd. Efficient Electric Motor Systems Handbook. 1995. 59.95 (*0-87814-631-8*) PennWell Bks.

Litman, Todd & Kart, Suzanne. Washington: Off the Beaten Path: A Guide to Unique Places. 3rd ed. Brown, Jo, ed. LC 98-36358. (Off the Beaten Path Ser.). (Illus.). 192p. 1999. pap. 12.95 (*0-7627-0280-X*) Globe Pequot.

Litman, Todd & Kort, Suzanne. The Best Bike Rides in the Pacific Northwest: British Columbia, Idaho, Oregon, & Washington. 2nd ed. LC 95-39188. (Best Bike Rides Ser.). (Illus.). 288p. (Orig.). 1996. pap. 12.95 (*1-56440-750-0*) Globe Pequot.

***Litman, Todd & Kort, Suzanne.** Washington: A Guide to Unique Places. 4th ed. (Off the Beaten Path Ser.). (Illus.). 2000. pap. 12.95 (*0-7627-0812-3*) Globe Pequot.

Litman, Viqui. The Ladies' Farm. LC 99-13508. 1999. 23.00 (*0-609-60380-9*) Crown Pub Group.

***Litnivov, W. G.** Optimization in Elliptic Problems with Applications to Mechanics of Deformable Bodies & Fluid Mechanics. (Operator Theory: Vol. 119). 544p. 2000. 145.00 (*3-7643-6199-9*, Pub. by Birkhauser) Spr-Verlag.

Litoff, Judy B. The American Midwife Debate: A Sourcebook on Its Modern Origins, 18. LC 85-17694. (Contributions in Medical Studies: No. 18). (Illus.). 251p. 1986. 59.95 (*0-313-24191-0*, LMD/, Greenwood Pr) Greenwood.

— American Midwives: Eighteen Sixty to Present, 1. LC 77-83893. (Contributions in Medical History Ser.: No. 1). 197p. 1978. 45.00 (*0-8371-9824-0*, LAM/) Greenwood.

Litoff, Judy B. & McDonnell, Judith, eds. European Immigrant Women in the United States: A Biographical Dictionary. LC 94-29001. (Biographical Directories of Minority Women Ser.: Vol. 3). (Illus.). 384p. 1994. text 20.00 (*0-8240-5306-0*, SS651) Garland.

Litoff, Judy B. & Smith, David C., eds. American Women in a World at War: Contemporary Accounts from World War II. LC 96-8148. (Worlds of Women Ser.: No. 1). (Illus.). 237p. 1996. pap. 18.95 (*0-8420-2571-5*) Scholarly Res Inc.

— American Women in a World at War: Contemporary Accounts from World War II. LC 96-8148. (Worlds of Women Ser.: No. 1). (Illus.). 237p. 1996. 55.00 (*0-8420-2570-7*) Scholarly Res Inc.

— Since You Went Away: World War II Letters from American Women on the Home Front. (Illus.). 312p. 1991. 27.50 (*0-19-506795-9*) OUP.

— Since You Went Away: World War II Letters from American Women on the Home Front. (Illus.). 310p. 1995. pap. 16.95 (*0-7006-0714-5*) U Pr of KS.

Litoff, Judy B., jt. auth. see Berman, Ruth.

Litoff, Judy B., ed. see Somerville, Keith.

***Litoff, Judy Barrett & Smith, David C.** What Kind of World Do We Want? American Women Plan for Peace. LC 00-37047. (World of Women: 6). (Illus.). 266p. 2000. 55.55 (*0-8420-2883-8*) Scholarly Res Inc.

***Litoff, Judy Barrett & Smith, David C., eds.** What Kind of World Do We Want? American Women Plan for Peace. LC 00-37047. (Worlds of Women Ser.: 6). (Illus.). 266p. 2000. 18.95 (*0-8420-2884-6*) Scholarly Res Inc.

Litonjua, D. Liberation Theology: The Paradigm Shift. LC 97-39632. 84p. (C). 1997. 32.00 (*0-7618-0928-7*); pap. 17.50 (*0-7618-0929-5*) U Pr of Amer.

Litovchenko, V. G., jt. auth. see Dobrovolsky, V. N.

Litovich, E. & Power, H. W. Parent-Offspring Conflict & Its Resolution in the European Starling. (Ornithological Monographs: Vol. 47). (Illus.). 71p. 1992. 15.00 (*0-935868-58-5*) Am Ornithologists.

Litovsky, Haydee. Sephardic Playwrights of the Seventeenth & Eighteenth Centuries in Amsterdam. 184p. (Orig.). (C). 1990. lib. bdg. 41.00 (*0-8191-7843-8*) U Pr of Amer.

Litowinski, Olga. The Pawloined Paper. LC 97-74831. (Adventures of Wishbone Ser.: No. 11). (Illus.). 137p. (J). (gr. 3-7). 1998. pap. 3.99 (*1-57064-276-1*, Big Red) Lyrick Pub.

Litowinsky, Olga. Boats for Bedtime. LC 98-26158. (Illus.). 32p. (J). 1999. 12.00 (*0-395-89128-0*, Clarion Bks) HM.

***Litowinsky, Olga.** Bug Blast! (Groovy Tube Bks.). (Illus.). 24p. (J). (gr. 1-5). 2000. 16.99 (*1-58476-018-4*) Innovative Kids.

Litowinsky, Olga. Short Circuit. LC 96-107223. (Illus.). 80p. (J). (gr. 5-9). 1996. pap. text 2.95 (*0-8114-9323-7*) Raintree Steck-V.

— Writing & Publishing Books for Children in the 1990s: The Inside Story, from the Editor's Desk. 144p. (Orig.). 1992. 17.95 (*0-8027-8130-6*); pap. 11.95 (*0-8027-7375-3*) Walker & Co.

Litowitz, Bonnie E. & Epstein, Phillip S., eds. Semiotic Perspectives on Clinical Theory & Practice: Medicine, Neuropsychiatry & Psychoanalysis. (Approaches to Semiotics Ser.: No. 98). (Illus.). xii, 206p. (C). 1991. lib. bdg. 90.80 (*3-11-012632-X*, 140 91) Mouton.

Litowitz, Douglas E. Postmodern Philosophy & Law: Douglas E. Litowitz. LC 97-14922. 240p. 1997. 35.00 (*0-7006-0857-5*) U Pr of KS.

***Litowitz, Douglas E.** Postmodern Philosophy & Law: Douglas E. Litowitz. 240p. 1999. reprint ed. pap. 15.95 (*0-7006-0999-7*) U Pr of KS.

Litpher, Markus. Auswirkungen der Ersten Markenrechtsrichtlinie auf die Merkmale der Verwechslungsgefahr und der Erschopfung im Deutschen Markenrecht, Vol. LVI. (Europaische Hochschulschriften: Reihe 2: Bd. 2048). (GER., Illus.). LVI, 285p. 1996. pap. 57.95 (*3-631-31029-3*) P Lang Pubng.

Litrides, Carol A. & Axler, Bruce H. Restaurant Service: Beyond the Basics. 384p. 1994. 59.95 (*0-471-51476-4*) Wiley.

Litrides, Carol A., jt. auth. see Axler, Bruce H.

Litritzis, Veronica M. The Role & Development of Metallurgy in the Late Neolithic & Early Bronze Age of Greece. (Studies in Mediterranean Archaeology & Literature: No. 122). (Illus.). 560p. 1996. pap. 122.50 (*91-7081-088-5*, Pub. by P Astroms) Coronet Bks.

Litschauer, R. Vocabularium Polyglottum Vitae Silvarum. (ENG, FRE, GER, LAT & RUM.). 126p. 1955. 55.00 (*0-8288-6869-7*, M-7679) Fr & Eur.

Litschel, David R., jt. auth. see Rand, Glenn M.

Litscher, Karen K., et al. Reflections from the Heart: A Collection of Short Stories & Poems. 84p. 1998. pap. 7.50 (*0-9664185-0-6*) K Litscher.

Litschgi, M., ed. Genitalendometriose. (Illus.). viii, 112p. 1985. 51.50 (*3-8055-3984-3*) S Karger.

Litsinger, J. A., jt. auth. see Barrion, A. T.

Litt, D., et al. The English Parliament in the Middle Ages. 560p. (C). 1981. 70.00 (*0-9506882-1-5*) Hambledon Press.

Litt, D., jt. auth. see Harris, Errol E.

Litt, D., jt. tr. see Thomas, Edward J.

Litt, Iris F. Taking Our Pulse: The Health of America's Women. LC 97-9512. 308p. 1997. 45.00 (*0-8047-2828-3*); pap. 15.95 (*0-8047-3137-3*) Stanford U Pr.

Litt, Iris F., ed. Evaluation of the Adolescent Patient. LC 90-81222. (Illus.). 211p. 1990. pap. text 23.95 (*0-932883-98-2*) Hanley & Belfus.

Litt, J. Z. Drug Eruption Reference Manual, 1999. expanded ed. (Illus.). 588p. 1999. pap. 149.00 (*1-85070-076-1*) Prthnon Pub.

***Litt, J. Z.** Pocketbook of Drug Eruptions & Interactions. 2001. write for info. (*1-84214-031-0*) Prthnon Pub.

Litt, J. Z. Pocketbook of Drug Eruptions & Interactions: Millennium Edition. 328p. 1999. pap. 32.00 (*1-85070-077-X*) Prthnon Pub.

***Litt, Jacquelyn S.** Medicalized Motherhood: Perspectives from the Lives of African American & Jewish Women. LC 99-43560. 224p. 2000. text 50.00 (*0-8135-2781-3*) Rutgers U Pr.

— Medicalized Motherhood: Perspectives from the Lives of African American & Jewish Women. LC 99-43560. 224p. (C). 2000. pap. 20.00 (*0-8135-2782-1*) Rutgers U Pr.

Litt, Jerome Z. Drug Eruption Reference Manual, 1998. (Illus.). 592p. 1998. pap. 149.00 (*1-85070-030-3*) Prthnon Pub.

— Drug Eruption Reference Manual, '97. 6th ed. (Illus.). 536p. 1997. pap. 149.00 (*1-85070-907-6*) Prthnon Pub.

***Litt, Jerome Z.** Drug Eruption Reference Manual 2000. LC 99-58758. (Illus.). 600p. 2000. pap. 149.50 (*1-85070-788-X*) Prthnon Pub.

Litt, Jerome Z. Physicians' Guide to Drug Eruptions. LC 97-36824. 278p. 1997. 68.00 (*1-85070-003-6*) Prthnon Pub.

Litt, Jerome Z. & Pawlak, Walter A., Jr. Drug Eruption Reference Manual. 400p. 1992. ring bd. 100.00 (*0-9634973-0-8*); ring bd. 100.00 (*0-9634973-1-6*) Wal-Zac Ent.

— Drug Eruption Reference Manual. 470p. 1993. write for info. (*0-9634973-2-4*); write for info. (*0-9634973-3-2*) Wal-Zac Ent.

— Drug Eruption Reference Manual. 5th ed. 1996. pap. 125.00 (*0-9634973-5-9*) Wal-Zac Ent.

Litt, M. A., jt. auth. see Dobbie, A. M.

***Litt, Paul.** Isotopes & Innovation: MDS Nordion's First Fifty Years, 1946-1996. 256p. 2000. pap. 40.00 (*0-7735-2082-1*, Pub. by McG-Queens Univ Pr) CUP Services.

Litt, Paul. The Muses, the Masses, & the Massey Commission. (Illus.). 336p. (Orig.). 1992. text 50.00 (*0-8020-5003-4*); pap. text 19.95 (*0-8020-6932-0*) U of Toronto Pr.

Litt, Thomas. Palaeoekologie, Palaeobotanik und Stratigraphie des Jungquartaers Im Nordmitteleuropaeischen Tiefland: Unter Besonderer Beruecksichtigung Des Elbe-Saale-Gebietes. (Dissertationes Botanicae Ser.: Band 227). (Illus.). ii, 1855p. 1994. pap. 65.00 (*3-443-64139-3*, Pub. by Gebruder Borntraeger) Balogh.

Litta, Pompeo. Celebrated Families of Italy: The Vitelli Family. Vitelli, Tom, ed. & tr. by. LC 95-60157. (Illus.). 120p. 1995. 50.00 (*1-883696-03-8*) EveryWare Bks.

Littauer, F. Liberando la Mente de los Recuerdos Que Atan.Tr. of Freeing Your Mind from Memories That Bind. (SPA.). 330p. 1993. 8.99 (*1-56063-402-2*, 498513) Editorial Unilit.

Littauer, Florence. El Arbol de Tu Personalidad.Tr. of Your Personality Tree. (SPA.). 256p. 1995. pap. 8.99 (*0-7899-0111-0*, 497267) Editorial Unilit.

— Blow Away the Black Clouds. LC 79-50380. 1986. pap. 8.99 (*0-89081-285-3*) Harvest Hse.

— Blow Away the Black Clouds: A Woman's Answer to Depression. large type ed. 1988. pap. 14.95 (*0-8027-2606-2*) Walker & Co.

— Enriquezca Su Personalidad.Tr. of Personality Plus. (SPA.). 211p. 1983. pap. 6.99 (*1-56063-317-4*, 498498) Editorial Unilit.

— How to Get Along with Difficult People. expanded rev. ed. LC 98-43195. 224p. 1998. pap. 9.99 (*1-56507-932-9*) Harvest Hse.

— Personality Plus: How to Understand Others by Understanding Yourself. 2nd expanded rev. ed. LC 92-13275. 208p. (gr. 11). 1994. pap. 9.99 (*0-8007-5445-X*) Revell.

***Littauer, Florence.** Personality Plus for Parents: Understanding What Makes Your Child Tick. 2000. pap. 11.99 (*0-8007-5737-8*) Revell.

Littauer, Florence. Put Power in Your Personality: Match Your Potential with America's Leaders. LC 95-6912. 288p. (YA). (gr. 10). 1995. pap. 9.99 (*0-8007-5563-4*) Revell.

— Raising the Curtain on Raising Children. 305p. 1988. pap. 10.99 (*0-8499-3133-9*) Word Pub.

— Regalos en Cofres de Plata.Tr. of Silver Boxes. (SPA.). 7.99 (*1-56063-759-5*, 498618) Editorial Unilit.

— Silver Boxes. 154p. 1989. 14.99 (*0-8499-0720-9*) Word Pub.

— Silver Boxes: The Gift of Encouragement. LC 94-150946. 1994. 4.99 (*0-8499-5073-2*) Word Pub.

— Taking Charge of Your Life: And Sometimes Women Need to Wake Up. LC 98-143718. 208p. 1999. pap. 9.99 (*0-8007-5682-7*) Revell.

— Your Personality Tree. 237p. 1989. pap. 10.99 (*0-8499-3169-X*) Word Pub.

Littauer, Florence & Littauer, Fred. Why Do I Feel the Way I Do? LC 98-8351. 208p. 1998. pap. 11.99 (*0-8007-5671-1*, Get a Life With) Revell.

Littauer, Florence & Littauer, Marita. Getting along with Almost Anybody: The Complete Personality Book. LC 98-5014. 352p. 1998. pap. 12.99 (*0-8007-5659-2*) Revell.

— Personality Puzzle: Understanding the People You Work With. LC 92-5608. 208p. (gr. 11). 1992. pap. 9.99 (*0-8007-1676-0*) Revell.

— Talking So People Will Listen: You Can Communicate with Confidence. LC 98-11847. 220p. 1998. pap. 10.99 (*1-56955-081-6*, Vine Bks) Servant.

Littauer, Florence, jt. auth. see Littauer, Fred.

Littauer, Francis. Atrevete a Sonar.Tr. of Dare to Dream. (SPA.). 398p. 1991. pap. 8.99 (*1-56063-143-0*, 498516) Editorial Unilit.

Littauer, Fred. Touched by the Master: Discover the Healing Power of a Face-to-Face Encounter with the Lord. LC 96-85042. 200p. 1999. pap. 10.99 (*0-88419-440-X*) Dake Pub.

Littauer, Fred & Littauer, Florence. After Every Wedding Comes a Marriage. expanded rev. ed. LC 96-45430. 224p. 1997. pap. 9.99 (*1-56507-552-8*) Harvest Hse.

— Daily Marriage Builder. LC 97-37391. 368p. 1997. 16.99 (*0-8499-1420-5*) Word Pub.

Littauer, Fred, jt. auth. see Littauer, Florence.

Littauer, Joel. Manual of Motivational Strategies: Text & Transparencies in Composition & Grammar. 4th ed. Ashkenas, Joan, ed. & intro. by. 60p. 1999. ring bd. 45.00 (*0-943327-05-9*) JAG Pubns.

Littauer, M. A. Chariots & Related Equipment from the Tomb of Tutankhamun. (Tutankhamun Tomb Ser.: Vol. 8). 118p. 1986. 115.00 (*0-900416-39-4*, Pub. by Aris & Phillips) David Brown.

***Littauer, Marita.** Looking Back, Moving Forward. LC 99-6613. 2000. pap. text 10.99 (*0-7642-2275-9*) Bethany Hse.

Littauer, Marita, jt. auth. see Littauer, Florence.

Littauer, Mary, tr. see Spruytte, J.

Littauer, Stephen. How to Buy Mutual Funds the Smart Way. 2nd ed. 208p. (Orig.). 1997. pap. 17.95 (*0-7931-2446-8*, 5608-7302) Dearborn.

***Littauer, Stephen.** Online Investing the Smart Way. LC 99-29569. 1999. pap. 19.95 (*0-7931-3424-2*) Dearborn.

Littauer, Stephen L. How to Buy Mutual Funds the Smart Way. LC 89-90240. 224p. 1989. pap. 9.95 (*0-9622593-1-4*, Montebello Pr) You Can Do It.

— How To Buy Stocks the Smart Way. 2nd ed. 348p. 1997. pap. 17.95 (*0-7931-1090-4*, 568008-01) Dearborn.

— How to Invest the Smart Way in Stocks, Bonds & Mutual Funds. LC 97-40867. 256p. 1998. pap. 19.95 (*0-7931-2695-9*, 5680-6001) Dearborn.

Littauer, Susan H. How to Start Your Business the Smart Way: 20 Common Mistakes to Avoid. 64p. (Orig.). 1989. pap. 6.95 (*0-9622593-0-6*) You Can Do It.

Littauer, U. Z., et al, eds. Neurotransmitters & Their Receptors: Based on a Workshop Sponsored by the European Molecular Biology Organisation & the Weizmann Institute of Science, Rehovot, February, 1980. LC 80-41130. (Illus.). 576p. reprint ed. pap. 178.60 (*0-608-17652-4*, 203051000069) Bks Demand.

Littek, W. & Charles, T., eds. The New Division of Labour: Emerging Forms of Work Organization in International Perspective. LC 95-30413. (Studies in Organization: No. 67). xiv, 514p. (C). 1995. lib. bdg. 98.95 (*3-11-013972-3*) De Gruyter.

Littel, Franklin H., et al, eds. In Answer... Is the Story True? 409p. 1988. write for info. (*0-318-68671-6*) Sylvan PA.

— In Answer . . . The Holocaust: Is the Story True. Foster, Claude R. & Van Sice, Mildred M., trs. 410p. 1989. text 24.95 (*0-926193-02-3*); lib. bdg. 24.95 (*0-926193-01-5*) Sylvan PA.

— In Answer . . . The Holocaust: Is the Story True. Foster, Claude R. et al, trs. 410p. 1989. 24.95 (*0-926193-00-7*) Sylvan PA.

Littel, Phil. Introduction to Biology: Lab Manual. 2nd ed. 304p. (C). 1999. lab manual ed. 38.95 (*0-7872-5620-X*, 41562001) Kendall-Hunt.

Litteljohn, Bruce, et al. Superior: The Haunted Shore. rev. ed. LC 96-117602. (Illus.). 176p. 1995. pap. 24.95 (*1-895565-58-8*) Firefly Bks Ltd.

***Littell, David A. & Tacchino, Kenn B.** The Practitioner's Guide to Advanced Pension Topics. 2nd ed. LC 99-73063. 375p. (C). 1999. text 56.00 (*1-57996-015-4*) Amer College.

Littell, David A., et al. Financial Decision Making at Retirement. 4th ed. LC 99-73326. 475p. 1999. text 60.00 (*1-57996-016-2*) Amer College.

Littell, David A., jt. auth. see Tacchino, Kenn B.

Littell, Franklin H. The Crucifixion of the Jews: The Failure of Christians to Understand the Jewish Experience. (Reprints of Scholarly Excellence Ser.: No. 12). 160p. (C). 1986. reprint ed. pap. text 10.95 (*0-86554-227-9*, MUP/P031) Mercer Univ Pr.

— The German Phoenix: Men & Movements in the Church in Germany. Garber, Zev, ed. (Studies in the Shoah: Vol. 2). 242p. (Orig.). (C). 1992. pap. text 27.50 (*0-8191-8584-1*); lib. bdg. 52.50 (*0-8191-8583-3*) U Pr of Amer.

— Religious Liberties in the Crossfire of Creeds. 169p. (Orig.). 1978. 5.00 (*0-931214-01-7*) Ecumenical Phila.

Littell, Franklin H., ed. A Half Century of Religious Dialogue, 1939-1989: Making the Circles Larger. LC 89-49749. (Toronto Studies in Theology: Vol. 46). 356p. 1990. lib. bdg. 99.95 (*0-88946-926-1*) E Mellen.

Littell, Franklin H., et al, eds. What Have We Learned? Telling the Story & Teaching the Lessons of the Holocaust. LC 93-24623. (Symposium Ser.: Vol. 30). 400p. 1994. text 109.95 (*0-7734-9336-0*) E Mellen.

Littell, Franklin H. & Locke, Hubert G., eds. The German Church Struggle & the Holocaust. LC 90-34203. 336p. 1990. lib. bdg. 99.95 (*0-7734-9995-4*) E Mellen.

Littell, Franklin H., jt. auth. see Shur, Irene G.

Littell, Franklin H., ed. see Fostter, Claude R. & Shur, Irene G.

Littell, John, jt. auth. see Caleel, Richard T.

***Littell, John S.** French Impressions: The Adventures of an American Family. 2000. 22.95 (*0-451-20098-5*) NAL.

Littell, John S., ed. see Graydon, Alexander.

Littell, Joseph F. The Man Who Found the Loch Ness Monster: And Other Fables for Grown-Ups. LC 91-90212. (Illus.). 128p. 1991. 12.95 (*1-880243-00-8*) New World.

Littell, Marcia S., ed. Holocaust Education: A Resource Book for Teachers & Professional Leaders. LC 85-2919. (Symposium Ser.: Vol. 13). 128p. 1985. lib. bdg. 59.95 (*0-88946-704-8*) E Mellen.

— The Holocaust Forty Years After. LC 89-12980. (Symposium Ser.: Vol. 22). 1989. lib. bdg. 79.95 (*0-88946-714-5*) E Mellen.

— Liturgies on the Holocaust. LC 86-23507. 208p. 1986. lib. bdg. 89.95 (*0-88946-030-2*) E Mellen.

Littell, Marcia S. & Gutman, Sharon W., eds. Liturgies on the Holocaust: An Interfaith Anthology. LC 96-1862. 216p. 1996. pap. 20.00 (*1-56338-138-9*) TPI PA.

Littell, Marcia S., jt. ed. see Colign, G. Jan.

Littell, Marcia S., jt. ed. see Colijn, G. Jan.

Littell, Marcia S., jt. ed. see Knight, Henry F.

Littell, Marcia S., jt. ed. see Locke, Hubert G.

Littell, Mary A. LSD. LC 96-6864. (Drug Library Ser.). (Illus.). 112p. (YA). (gr. 6 up). 1996. lib. bdg. 20.95 (*0-89490-739-5*) Enslow Pubs.

Littell, Mary Ann. Heroin Drug Dangers. LC 98-30743. (Drug Dangers Ser.). (Illus.). 64p. (YA). (gr. 4-10). 1999. lib. bdg. 19.95 (*0-7660-1156-9*) Enslow Pubs.

***Littell, Mary Ann.** Heroin Drug Dangers. LC 98-30743. (Drug Dangers Ser.). (Illus.). 64p. (YA). (gr. 4-10). 1999. pap. 10.95 (*0-7660-1738-9*) Enslow Pubs.

— Speed & Methamphetamine Drug Dangers. LC 99-10723. (Drug Dangers Ser.). (Illus.). 64p. (YA). (gr. 4-10). 1999. lib. bdg. 19.95 (*0-7660-1157-7*) Enslow Pubs.

***Littell, Mary Ann.** Speed & Methamphetamine Drug Dangers. LC 99-10723. (Drug Dangers Ser.). (Illus.). 64p. (YA). (gr. 4-10). 1999. pap. 10.95 (*0-7660-1741-9*) Enslow Pubs.

Littell, Norman M. My Roosevelt Years. Dembo, Jonathan, ed. LC 87-10523. (Illus.). 436p. 1987. 35.00 (*0-295-96525-8*) U of Wash Pr.

Littell, Philip. Books & Things. LC 71-90653. (Essay Index Reprint Ser.). 1977. 21.95 (*0-8369-1221-7*) Ayer.

Littell, Ramon C., et al. SAS System for Mixed Models. 656p. (C). 1999. pap. 44.95 (*1-55544-779-1*, BR55235) SAS Publ.

Littell, Ramon C., jt. auth. see Schlotzhauer, Sandra D.

Littell, Richard, ed. Controlled Wildlife Vol. 1: Federal Permit Procedures. 2nd ed. (Orig.). 1993. pap. 40.00 (*0-942924-16-9*) Assn Syst Coll.

Littell, Robert. Read America First. LC 68-16947. (Essay Index Reprint Ser.). 1977. reprint ed. 23.95 (*0-8369-0620-9*) Ayer.

— Walking Back the Cat. LC 96-49507. 218p. 1997. 23.95 (*0-87951-764-6*, Pub. by Overlook Pr) Penguin Putnam.

— Walking Back the Cat. 1996. write for info. (*0-614-09426-7*) Random.

— Walking Back the Cat. 1997. 21.00 (*0-679-43567-0*) Random.

Littell, Robert, jt. auth. see Peres, Shimon.

Littell, Robert S. & McSpadden, Larry. Crossing the Line: Sales Strategies for Life & Health in the P & C Agency. LC 98-115247. xii, 164 p. 1997. write for info. (*0-87218-361-0*) Natl Underwriter.

Litten, Clark W. Family & the Law. (Contemporary Legal Issues Ser.). (Illus.). 225p. 1997. lib. bdg. 39.50 (*0-87436-860-X*) ABC-CLIO.

Litten, Harold. Harold Litten's Best Erotic Fantasies: How to Enjoy & Understand the Sex in Your Head. LC 99-232062. (Illus.). 286p. 1999. pap. 12.95 (*1-887650-16-4*, Pub. by Factor Pr) BookWorld.

— The Joy of Solo Sex. Orig. Title: Solo Sex: Advanced Techniques. 193p. 1993. reprint ed. pap. 12.95 (*0-9626531-4-4*, Pub. by Factor Pr) BookWorld.

— More Joy... An Advanced Guide to Solo Sex. (Illus.). 200p. 1996. pap. 12.95 (*0-9626531-8-7*, Pub. by Factor Pr) BookWorld.

Litten, Raye Z. & Allen, John P., eds. Measuring Alcohol Consumption: Psychosocial & Biochemical Methods. LC 92-1536. 256p. 1992. 99.50 (*0-89603-231-0*) Humana.

Litter, Jonathan. There Were These Two Guys. (Orig.). 1988. pap. 3.50 (*0-945926-01-4*) Paradigm RI.

Litteral, Linda L. Boobies, Iguanas, & Other Critters: Nature's Story in the Galapagos. (Biosphere Reserve Ser.). (Illus.). 71p. (J). (gr. 5-9). 1994. 23.00 (*1-883966-01-9*) Am Kestrel Pr.

Litteral, Thomas R. Mountain Biking in the High Country of Steamboat Springs, Colorado. 104p. 1993. pap. 10.95 (*1-883966-00-0*) Am Kestrel Pr.

Litterer, Joseph A. Organizations: Structure & Behavior. 3rd ed. LC 80-15645. (Series in Management). 638p. 1980. pap. text 37.50 (*0-471-07786-0*) Krieger.

— Organizations: Structure & Behavior, Vol. 1. 2nd ed. LC 77-88314. 510p. 1969. reprint ed. pap. 158.10 (*0-608-13611-5*, 205516000001) Bks Demand.

— Organizations: Structure & Behavior, Vol. 2. 2nd ed. LC 77-88314. (Wiley Series in Management & Administration). (Illus.). 431p. 1969. reprint ed. pap. 133.70 (*0-7837-3421-2*, 205516000002) Bks Demand.

Litterer, Joseph A., jt. auth. see Lewicki, Roy J.

***Litterio, Francis.** Linux Programming for Dummies. (For Dummies Ser.). 384p. 2000. pap. 24.99 (*0-7645-0691-9*) IDG Bks.

***Littger, Klaus Walter.** Garden at Eichstatt: The Book of Plants. 1999. 49.99 (*3-8228-6527-3*) Benedikt Taschen.

Littig, M. D., et al. Littig: Descendants of Peter Littig, Godfrey Rogge & Others. 40p. 1994. reprint ed. pap. 8.00 (*0-8328-4125-0*) Higginson Bk Co.

***Littin, Miguel.** El Bandido De Los Ojos Transparentes. 1999. pap. 18.95 (*84-322-0768-3*) Planeta.

Littke, Lael. Haunted Sister. LC 98-12144. (J). (gr. 6-9). 1998. 16.95 (*0-8050-5729-3*) H Holt & Co.

Littke, Lael J. The Bridesmaids' Dress Disaster. LC 94-30487. (Bee There Ser.: Bk. 5). viii, 155p. (Orig.). (J). (gr. 3-7). 1994. pap. 4.95 (*0-87579-940-X*, Cinnamon Tree) Deseret Bk.

— Getting Rid of Rhoda. LC 92-25016. (Bee There Ser.: No. 1). 156p. (Orig.). (J). (gr. 3-7). 1992. pap. 5.95 (*0-87579-636-2*, Cinnamon Tree) Deseret Bk.

— Loydene in Love. LC 86-12000. 160p. (YA). (gr. 7 up). 1986. 13.95 (*0-15-249888-5*, Harcourt Child Bks) Harcourt.

— The Mystery of Ruby's Ghost. LC 92-25015. (Bee There Ser.: No. 2). 166p. (Orig.). (J). (gr. 3-7). 1992. pap. 5.95 (*0-87579-656-7*, Cinnamon Tree) Deseret Bk.

— The Phantom Fair. LC 96-26246. (Bee There Ser.: Bk. 7). 156p. (J). (gr. 3-7). 1996. pap. 6.95 (*1-57345-200-9*, Cinnamon Tree) Deseret Bk.

— Prom Dress. 176p. (YA). (gr. 7-9). 1989. pap. 3.50 (*0-590-44237-6*) Scholastic Inc.

— Run, Ducky, Run. LC 95-48820. (Bee There Ser.: Bk. 6). 168p. (Orig.). (J). (gr. 3-7). 1996. pap. 6.95 (*1-57345-134-7*, Cinnamon Tree) Deseret Bk.

— Shanny on Her Own. LC 85-8451. 179p. (J). (gr. 7 up). 1985. 12.95 (*0-15-273531-3*, Harcourt Child Bks) Harcourt.

— Star of the Show. LC 93-27258. (Bee There Ser.: Bk. 3). 162p. (Orig.). (J). (gr. 3-7). 1993. pap. 4.95 (*0-87579-785-7*, Cinnamon Tree) Deseret Bk.

— There's a Snake at Girls' Camp. LC 94-751. (Bee There Ser.: No. 4). (Orig.). (J). (gr. 3-7). 1994. pap. 4.95 (*0-87579-845-4*, Cinnamon Tree) Deseret Bk.

— Trish for President. LC 84-4587. 160p. (J). (gr. 7 up). 1984. 13.95 (*0-15-290512-X*, Harcourt Child Bks) Harcourt.

— Watcher. 208p. (YA). (gr. 7-9). 1994. pap. 3.50 (*0-590-47088-4*) Scholastic Inc.

Littke, Ralf. Deposition, Diagenesis, & Weathering of Organic Matter-Rich Sediments. LC 93-17490. (Lecture Notes in Earth Sciences Ser.: Vol. 47). (Illus.). ix, 216p. 1993. 70.95 (*0-387-56661-9*) Spr-Verlag.

Little. Beginner's Bible: Bath Time on Noah's Ark. LC 96-222549. (Illus.). (J). 1996. 4.99 (*0-679-87541-7*) McKay.

Little. Beginner's Bible: Who's Who in the New Testament. LC 95-79893. (Illus.). (J). 1996. 9.99 (*0-679-87741-X*) McKay.

— Beginner's Bible: Who's Who in the Old Testament. (Illus.). (J). 1996. 9.99 (*0-679-87740-1*) McKay.

— Cases & Materials on Workers Compensation. 4th ed. (Paralegal Ser.). (C). 1999. pap. 36.50 (*0-314-23188-9*) West Pub.

— Development Ethics. 2000. pap. 16.95 (*0-8133-1642-1*, Pub. by Westview) HarpC.

Little. The End of Change. 224p. 2000. 24.95 (*0-07-135700-9*) McGraw.

— No Car, No Radio, No Liquor. LC 99-177999. (Illus.). 320p. 1998. pap. text 26.50 (*0-19-541150-1*) OUP.

— Tax: One Payment. 1995. 1595.00 (*0-316-52807-2*, Aspen Law & Bus) Aspen Pub.

— Torts: The Civil Law of Reparation for Harm Done by Wrongful Act. 1985. teacher ed. write for info. (*0-8205-0507-2*) Bender.

— Tratamiento Odontologico. 5th ed. (C). 1998. text 70.34 (*84-8174-320-8*, Pub. by Mosby-Doyma Libros) Mosby Inc.

Little. Use of Quantitative Methods in Social. pap. 15.95 (*1-85521-463-6*) Ashgate Pub Co.

Little & Manis, Vincent C. Schematics Computation. 1995. pap. text, lab manual ed. 19.20 (*0-13-834714-X*) P-H.

Little & Mitchell. For King & Country. Date not set. pap. text. write for info. (*0-582-70603-3*, Pub. by Addison-Wesley) Longman.

Little, jt. ed. see Campbell, Jim.

Little, ed. see De Duras.

Little, A. D., ed. Study on State-of-the-Art of Dioxin from Combustion Sources. 1981. 6.00 (*0-686-34520-7*, H00180) ASME.

Little, A. H. Water Supplies & the Treatment & Disposal of Effluents. 71p. 1975. 60.00 (*0-7855-7234-1*) St Mut.

— Water Supplies & the Treatment & Disposal of Effluents. 71p. (C). 1975. pap. text 75.00 (*0-900739-21-5*, Pub. by Textile Inst) St Mut.

Little, A. J. Planning Controls & Their Enforcement. 1982. pap. 180.00 (*0-7219-0492-0*, Pub. by Scientific) St Mut.

Little, A. J., ed. Schofield's Election Law. (C). 1982. ring bd. 650.00 (*0-7219-0344-4*, Pub. by Scientific) St Mut.

Little, Adrian. The Political Thought of Andre Gorz. LC 96-7013. (Studies in Social & Political Thought). 224p. (C). 1996. 80.00 (*0-415-13866-3*) Routledge.

— Post Industrial Socialism: Towards a New Politics of Welfare. LC 98-169364. 232p. (C). 1998. 85.00 (*0-415-17193-8*); pap. 25.99 (*0-415-17194-6*) Routledge.

Little, Alan. Decor, Drama, & Design. 1977. 6.50 (*0-89679-007-X*) Moretus Pr.

— Roman Bridal Drama. 1978. 6.50 (*0-89679-009-6*) Moretus Pr.

— Roman Perspective Painting. 1976. 6.50 (*0-686-75219-8*) Moretus Pr.

***Little, Alastair.** Italian Kitchen: Recipes from la Cacciata. (Illus.). 2p. 2000. pap. 24.95 (*0-09-186584-0*, Pub. by Ebury Pr) Trafalgar.

— Soho Cooking. LC 99-490235. (Illus.). 256p. 2000. 45.00 (*0-09-186422-4*, Pub. by Ebury Pr) Trafalgar.

Little, Alastair & Whittington, Richard. The Daily Mail Modern British Cookbook: Over 500 Recipes, Advice & Kitchen Know-How. LC 99-232613. (Illus.). 320p. 1999. 29.95 (*1-85702-772-8*, Pub. by Fourth Estate) Trafalgar.

An Asterisk (*) at the beginning of an entry indicates that the title is appearing for the first time.

— Food of the Sun. LC 95-21929. (Illus.). 192p. 1996. 25.95 (*0-87951-635-6*, Pub. by Overlook Pr) Penguin Putnam.
— Keep It Simple: A Fresh Look at Classic Cooking. (Illus.). 192p. 1994. 29.95 (*0-87951-547-3*, Pub. by Overlook Pr) Penguin Putnam.
Little, Allan, jt. auth. see Silber, Laura.
Little, Amy, jt. ed. see Burger, Dan.
Little, Anastazia, tr. see Andersen, Hans Christian.
Little, Andrew G., et al. Essays in Medieval History Presented to Thomas Frederick Tout. 1977. 26.95 (*0-8369-0427-3*) Ayer.
***Little, Angela.** Labouring to Learn: Towards a Political Economy of Plantations, People & Education in Sri Lanka LC 98-28307. (International Political Economy Ser.). xxiv, 324p. 1999. write for info. (*0-333-71110-6*) St Martin.
Little, Angela. Labouring to Learn: Towards a Political Economy of Plantations, People, & Education in Sri Lanka. LC 98-28307. (International Political Economy Ser.). (Illus.). 270p. 1999. text 72.00 (*0-312-21842-7*) St Martin.
Little, Angela & Wolf, Alison, eds. Assessment in Transition: Learning, Monitoring & Selection in International Perspective. LC 96-13521. 286p. 1996. text 77.00 (*0-08-042767-7*, Pergamon Pr) Elsevier.
Little, Angela W. & Leach, Fiona E., eds. Education, Cultures, & Economics: Dilemmas for Development. LC 99-32544. (Reference Books in International Education: No. 48). 392p. 1999. 65.00 (*0-8153-2783-8*, SS1152) Garland.
Little, Anne C., jt. ed. see Evans, Robert C.
***Little, Anne Colclough & Paul, Susie, eds.** Denise Levertov: New Perspectives. LC 00-35705. (Literary Studies: Vol. 28). (Illus.). 2000. lib. bdg. 45.00 (*0-933951-87-6*) Locust Hill Pr.
Little, Anthony L. Faith, Reason & the Reality of God: A Search for Honesty. LC 98-96918. 192p. 1999. pap. 10.95 (*0-9669231-0-3*) Empower.
Little, Arthur D., jt. auth. see CommerceNet Staff.
Little, Arthur D., Inc. Staff. DSD Development Program Report. 1988. write for info. (*0-318-50035-3*) Uniform Code.
— Evaluation of LNG Vapor Control Methods. 150p. 1974. pap. 7.00 (*0-318-12609-5*, M19875) Am Gas Assn.
Little, Arthur W. From Harlem to the Rhine. LC 74-31101. (Studies in Black History & Culture: No. 54). 1974. lib. bdg. 75.00 (*0-8383-2033-3*) M S G Haskell Hse.
Little, Barbara J. Text-Aided Archaeology. 240p. 1991. lib. bdg. 79.95 (*0-8493-8853-8*, E159) CRC Pr.
Little, Barbara J., jt. auth. see Hardesty, Donald L.
Little, Barbara J., jt. ed. see Shackel, Paul A.
Little, Barbara V. Frederick County Virginia, Militia Records, 1755-61. 68p. (Orig.). 1991. pap. text 10.00 (*0-9624041-3-6*) Dominion Market.
— Orange County, Virginia, Order Book One 1734-1739, Pt. 1. 114p. (Orig.). 1990. pap. 15.00 (*0-9624041-2-8*) Dominion Market.
— Orange County, Virginia, Tithables, 1734-1782. rev. ed. 281p. (Orig.). 1990. pap. text 29.50 (*0-9624041-1-X*) Dominion Market.
Little Bear, Leroy, et al, eds. Pathways to Self Determination: Canadian Indians & the Canadian State. 192p. (Orig.). 1984. pap. text 15.95 (*0-8020-6539-2*) U of Toronto Pr.
— Pathways to Self-Determination: Canadian Indians & the Canadian State. LC 84-162255. (Illus.). 223p. reprint ed. pap. 69.20 (*0-8357-4729-8*, 203764500009) Bks Demand.
Little, Benilde. Good Hair. LC 96-26013. 240p. 1996. 22.00 (*0-684-80176-0*) S&S Trade.
— Good Hair: A Novel. 240p. 1997. per. 11.00 (*0-684-83557-6*) S&S Trade Pap.
— The Itch: A Novel. LC 98-14836. 288p. 1998. 22.50 (*0-684-83834-6*) S&S Trade.
— Itch: A Novel. 288p. 1999. per. 11.00 (*0-684-85430-9*) S&S Trade Pap.
***Little, Bentley.** The Revelation. 1999. mass mkt. 6.99 (*0-451-19225-7*, Sig) NAL.
Little, Bentley. The Store. 208p. 1998. mass mkt. 6.99 (*0-451-19219-2*, Sig) NAL.
— The Summoning. 544p. 1993. mass mkt. 4.50 (*0-8217-4221-3*, Zebra Kensgtn) Kensgtn Pub Corp.
***Little, Bentley.** The Town. 384p. 2000. mass mkt. 6.99 (*0-451-20015-2*, Sig) NAL.
Little, Bill. Eight Ways to Take an Active Role in Your Health. LC 95-2546. 224p. 1995. pap. 9.99 (*0-87788-382-3*, H Shaw Pubs) Waterbrook Pr.
— Fire Walking: Secrets for Surviving Life's Pressures. LC 96-37187. 128p. 1997. pap. 12.00 (*1-57312-152-5*) Smyth & Helwys.
Little, Billie. Recipes for Diabetics. rev. ed. 288p. 1991. mass mkt. 7.50 (*0-553-29378-8*) Bantam.
— Recipes for Diabetics. rev. ed. 288p. 1990. pap. 12.00 (*0-399-51643-3*, Perigee Bks) Berkley Pub.
***Little, Billie.** Recipes for Diabetics. rev. ed. LC 98-53075. 288p. 1999. pap. 12.95 (*0-399-52528-9*, Perigee Bks) Berkley Pub.
Little, Blake, photos by. Dichotomy: Photography of Blake Little. (Illus.). 100p. 1996. 50.00 (*1-880777-39-8*) State Man.
***Little Blessings Staff.** Little Blessings New Testament & Psalms. (Little Blessings Ser.). 2000. 14.99 (*0-8423-3517-X*) Tyndale Hse.
Little, Brenda J., et al. Microbiologically Influenced Corrosion. (Corrosion Testing Made Easy Ser.: Vol. 5). 120p. 1997. 127.00 (*1-57590-035-1*) NACE Intl.
Little, Brenda J., jt. ed. see Kearns, Jeffrey R.
Little, Brian & Snell, Ned. Microsoft Office 98 for Macintosh: The Comprehensive Guide. LC 98-3884. 600p. 1998. 39.99 (*1-57610-279-3*) Coriolis Grp.
Little, Brian A., jt. ed. see Tulchinsky, Dan.
Little, Brown & Company Staff. Empty Large. 1994. write for info. (*0-316-38193-4*) Little.
***Little, Brown & Company Staff.** Look-Alikes. (Illus.). 2000. 13.95 (*0-316-89077-4*) Little.
Little, Brown & Company Staff. Titanic. 1998. 12.95 (*0-7868-8365-0*, Pub. by Hyperion) Little.
***Little, Brown & Company Staff, ed.** Cock Roach. 2000. 15.99 (*0-7868-2565-0*) Hyperion.
Little, Brown & Company Staff, ed. Little, Brown & Company Rights Guide: Including Atlantic Monthly Press Books & New York Graphic Society Books. 1984. write for info. (*0-318-57553-1*, Aspen Law & Bus) Aspen Pub.
Little, Bruce, tr. see Fest, Joachim C.
Little, Bruce, tr. see Fridenson, Patrick, ed.
Little, Bruce, tr. see Kaelble, Hartmut.
Little, Bruce, tr. see Muller, Rolf-Dieter & Ueberschar, Gerd R.
Little, Bruce, tr. see Ziebura, Gilbert.
Little, Bruce E., ed. Secondary Art Education: An Anthology of Issues. 252p. (C). 1990. pap. text 22.00 (*0-937652-53-9*, 244) Natl Art Ed.
Little, C., et al. Vascular Morphogenesis in Vivo, in Vitro, in Mente: In Vivo, In Vitro, In Mente. LC 97-37689. (Illus.). 325p. 1998. 90.00 (*0-8176-3920-9*) Birkhauser.
Little, C. B., jt. ed. see Blitz, J.
Little, C. E., ed. see Ivanov, I. G., et al.
Little, Carl. Art of the Maine Islands. Skolnick, Arnold, ed. LC 97-27605. (Illus.). 96p. 1997. 30.00 (*0-89272-426-9*) Down East.
— Beverly Hallam: An Odyssey in Art. unabridged ed. Candage, Mellen, ed. LC 97-39962. (Illus.). 144p. 1998. 44.50 (*0-929590-18-X*) Whalesback Bks.
— Edward Hopper's New England. LC 93-17447. (Essential Paintings Ser.). (Illus.). 88p. 1993. 24.95 (*1-56640-315-4*) Pomegranate Calif.
— Paintings of New England. Skolnick, Arnold, ed. (Illus.). 128p. 1996. 30.00 (*0-89272-384-X*) Down East.
— The Watercolors of John Singer Sargent. LC 98-31212. 160p. 1999. 45.00 (*0-520-21969-4*, Pub. by U CA Pr); pap. 24.95 (*0-520-21970-8*, Pub. by U CA Pr) Cal Prin Full Svc.
— Winslow Homer: His Art, His Light, His Landscapes. Skolnick, Arnold, ed. (Illus.). 180p. 1997. 19.95 (*1-885440-04-9*) First Glance.
— Winslow Homer & the Sea. LC 95-31391. (Illus.). 80p. 1995. pap. 19.95 (*0-87654-479-0*) Pomegranate Calif.
Little, Carl, ed. see Farrar, Susan C.
Little, Carl, ed. see Gjelfriend, George E.
Little, Carl, ed. see May, Daryl & Bansemer, Roger.
Little, Carl, ed. see McMahon, James.
Little, Carol M. A Comprehensive Guide to Outdoor Sculpture in Texas. LC 95-41828. (Illus.). 430p. (C). 1996. 34.95 (*0-292-76034-5*); pap. 14.95 (*0-292-76036-1*) U of Tex Pr.
Little, Catherine J., jt. auth. see Morris, Libby V.
Little, Charles D., et al. Vascular Morphogenesis: In Vivo, In Vitro, In Mente. LC 97-37689. (Molecular Biology of Cardiovascular Development Ser.). 1997. write for info. (*3-7643-3920-9*) Birkhauser.
Little, Charles E. Cyclopedia of Classified Dates, with Exhaustive Index. 1992. reprint ed. 87.00 (*1-55888-952-3*) Omnigraphics Inc.
— Discover America: The Smithsonian Book of the National Parks. LC 95-33596. (Illus.). 224p. 1996. 29.97 (*0-89599-050-4*) Smithsonian.
— The Dying of the Trees: The Pandemic in America's Forests. 1997. pap. 11.95 (*0-14-015872-3*) Viking Penguin.
— Greenways for America. LC 90-34149. (Creating the North American Landscape Ser.). (Illus.). 288p. 1990. 38.00 (*0-8018-4066-X*) Johns Hopkins.
— Greenways for America. (Creating the North American Landscape Ser.). (Illus.). 288p. 1995. pap. 18.95 (*0-8018-5140-8*) Johns Hopkins.
— Hope for the Land. LC 91-33963. 288p. 1992. 24.95 (*0-8135-1802-4*) Rutgers U Pr.
Little, Charles E., ed. Louis Bromfield at Malabar: Writings on Farming & Country Life. LC 88-37841. 256p. 1988. 30.00 (*0-8018-3674-3*) Johns Hopkins.
Little, Charles H., jt. auth. see Bonnington, C. Paul.
Little, Charles T., jt. auth. see Parker, Elizabeth C.
Little, Chris E. & Sabotinov, Nikola V., eds. Pulsed Metal Vapour Lasers: Proceedings of the NATO Advanced Research Workshop on Pulsed Metal Vappur Lasers-Physics & Emerging Applications. (NATO ASI Ser.: Vol. 5). 496p. (C). 1996. text 247.00 (*0-7923-4002-7*) Kluwer Academic.
Little, Christopher. Rockbound Coast: Travels in Maine. 1994. 39.95 (*0-393-03635-9*) Norton.
Little, Christopher E. Metal Vapour Lasers: Physics, Engineering & Applications. LC 98-26739. 620p. 1999. 335.00 (*0-471-97387-4*) Wiley.
Little, Christopher H., jt. auth. see Circo, Carl J.
***Little, Colin.** The Biology of Soft Shores & Estuaries. (Biology of Habitats Ser.). (Illus.). 272p. 2000. text 70.00 (*0-19-850427-6*); pap. text 35.00 (*0-19-850426-8*) OUP.
Little, Colin. The Colonisation of Land: Origins & Adaptations of Terrestrial Animals. LC 83-1787. (Illus.). 308p. 1984. text 155.00 (*0-521-25218-0*) Cambridge U Pr.
— The Terrestrial Invasion: An Ecophysiological Approach to the Origins of Land Animals. (Cambridge Studies in Ecology). (Illus.). 314p. (C). 1990. text 110.00 (*0-521-33447-0*); pap. text 38.95 (*0-521-33669-4*) Cambridge U Pr.
Little, Colin & Holmes, Robert. Apple & Pear Storage. 208p. 1996. write for info. (*0-909605-83-1*) Intl Spec Bk.
Little, Colin & Kitching, J. A. The Biology of Rocky Shores. (Biology of Habitats). (Illus.). 250p. 1996. pap. text 32.00 (*0-19-854935-0*) OUP.
Little, Constance & Little, Gwenyth. The Black Gloves. Schantz, Tom & Schantz, Enid, eds. (Classic Mystery Ser.). 192p. 1998. reprint ed. pap. 14.00 (*0-915230-20-8*) Rue Morgue.
***Little, Constance & Little, Gwenyth.** The Black-Headed Pins. 156p. 1999. pap. 14.00 (*0-915230-25-9*) Rue Morgue.
Little, Constance & Little, Gwenyth. The Black Honeymoon. 2nd ed. Schantz, Tom & Schantz, Enid, eds. 187p. 1998. reprint ed. pap. 14.00 (*0-915230-21-6*) Rue Morgue.
***Little, Constance & Little, Gwenyth.** The Black Stocking. 154p. 2000. reprint ed. pap. 14.00 (*0-915230-30-5*) Rue Morgue.
Little, Constance & Little, Gwenyth. Great Black Kanba. 157p. 1998. reprint ed. pap. 14.00 (*0-915230-22-4*) Rue Morgue.
— The Grey Mist Murders. 153p. 1999. reprint ed. pap. 14.00 (*0-915230-26-7*) Rue Morgue.
Little, Craig B. Deviance & Control: Theory, Research & Social Policy. 3rd ed. LC 94-69685. 411p. (C). 1995. pap. text 37.50 (*0-87581-395-X*, DC3) F E Peacock Pubs.
Little, Craig B., jt. ed. see Traub, Stuart H.
Little Crow. From the Gathering: The Wisdom of Little Crow. Clark, C. F., ed. LC 92-63392. 168p. 1993. 29.95 (*0-9635440-0-4*); pap. 12.95 (*0-9635440-1-2*) One Wrld Pub.
Little, D. Richard. Governing Soviet Union. 416p. (C). 1989. pap. text 17.56 (*0-582-28484-8*, 71515) Longman.
Little, Daniel. Microfoundations, Methods & Causation on the Philosophy of Social Science. LC 97-46819. 231p. 1998. text 34.95 (*1-56000-369-3*) Transaction Pubs.
— Understanding Peasant China: Case Studies in the Philosophy of Social Science. (Illus.). 333p. (C). 1992. reprint ed. pap. 22.00 (*0-300-05477-7*) Yale U Pr.
— Varieties of Social Explanation: An Introduction to the Philosophy of Social Science. 272p. (C). 1990. pap. 28.00 (*0-8133-0566-7*, Pub. by Westview) HarpC.
Little, Daniel, ed. On the Reliability of Economic Models: Essays in the Philosophy of Economics. (Recent Economic Thought Ser.). 304p. (C). 1995. lib. bdg. 127.00 (*0-7923-9494-1*, Pub. by Kluwer Academic) Kluwer Academic.
Little, Danity. How Women Executives Succeed: Experiences & Lessons from the Federal Government. LC 93-37027. 208p. 1994. 55.00 (*0-89930-867-8*, Quorum Bks) Greenwood.
Little, Dave. Catching the Wind in a Net: The Religious Vision of Robertson Davies. LC 96-156254. 300p. 1996. pap. 20.00 (*1-55022-264-3*, Pub. by ECW) Genl Dist Srvs.
Little, David. Ancient Arts: Mosaics. (Ancient Arts! Ser.). (Illus.). 24p. (J). 1998. 16.95 (*0-7624-0348-9*) Running Pr.
— Religion, Order, & Law: A Study in Pre-Revolutionary England. LC 84-2611. 284p. (C). 1984. pap. text 13.50 (*0-226-48546-3*) U Ch Pr.
— Sri Lanka: The Invention of Enmity. LC 94-1061. 1994. pap. text 14.95 (*1-878379-15-1*) US Inst Peace.
— The Tabernacle in the Wilderness. 2nd ed. LC 89-36832. 59p. 1989. pap. 2.99 (*0-87213-520-9*) Loizeaux.
— Ukraine: The Legacy of Intolerance. LC 91-20695. 1991. pap. text 14.95 (*1-878379-12-7*) US Inst Peace.
Little, David, et al. Adult Learning in Vocational Education. 137p. (C). 1991. 65.00 (*0-7300-1279-4*, Pub. by Deakin Univ) St Mut.
Little, David, jt. auth. see Hibbard, Scott W.
Little, David, ed. see French, Allen.
Little, David, jt. ed. see Khare, R. S.
Little, David M., Jr. Classical Anesthesia Files. LC 85-12088. 335p. 1985. 35.00 (*0-9614932-0-8*) Wood Lib-Mus.
Little, Denise. Irish Magic. 384p. 1996. pap. 5.99 (*0-8217-5226-X*) NAL.
— Twice upon a Time. 320p. 1999. mass mkt. 6.99 (*0-88677-883-2*) DAW Bks.
Little, Denise, ed. Alien Pets. 320p. 1998. pap. 5.99 (*0-88677-822-0*, Pub. by DAW Bks) Penguin Putnam.
— A Dangerous Magic. 320p. 1999. mass mkt. 6.99 (*0-88677-825-5*, Pub. by DAW Bks) Penguin Putnam.
***Little, Denise, ed.** Perchance to Dream. 2000. 6.99 (*0-88677-888-3*, Pub. by DAW Bks) Penguin Putnam.
Little, Denise, ed. see Yolen, Jane, et al.
Little, Derek. Read This Before You Go Out in the Yard. (Illus.). 88p. (Orig.). 1996. pap. 12.95 (*1-888321-04-0*) Semco Bks.
Little, Donald M. Catalytic Reforming. 256p. 1985. 84.95 (*0-87814-281-9*) PennWell Bks.
Little, Donald P. History & Historiography of the Mamluks. (Collected Studies: No. CS240). (Illus.). 328p. (C). 1986. reprint ed. lib. bdg. 117.95 (*0-86078-188-7*, Pub. by Variorum) Ashgate Pub Co.
Little, Donald P., jt. ed. see Hallaq, Wael B.
Little, Dorothy, ed. Cross-Border Practice Compendium. 1991. ring bd. 100.00 (*90-6544-948-5*) Kluwer Law Intl.
Little, Douglas. Electric Boats: The Handbook of Clean, Quiet Boating. (Illus.). 160p. 1994. pap. 17.95 (*0-07-038104-6*) Intl Marine.
— Malevolent Neutrality: The United States, Great Britain, & the Origins of the Spanish Civil War. LC 84-19930. 288p. (C). 1985. 37.50 (*0-8014-1769-4*) Cornell U Pr.
Little, E. E., et al, eds. Environmental Toxicology & Risk Assessment, Vol. 7. (Special Technical Publications: Vol. 1333). (Illus.). 416p. 1998. text 71.00 (*0-8031-2479-1*, STP1333) ASTM.
Little, Eddie. Another Day in Paradise. 263p. 1999. pap. 12.95 (*0-14-026772-7*) Penguin Putnam.
Little, Edward H., jt. auth. see Foster, Mary N.
Little, Elbert L., Jr. Forest Trees of the United States & Canada & How to Identify Them. LC 79-52527. (Illus.). 1980. pap. text 5.95 (*0-486-23902-0*) Dover.
Little, Elbert L., Jr., jt. auth. see Audubon Society Staff.
Little, Elbert L., Jr., jt. auth. see Viereck, Leslie A.
Little, Emily. David & the Giant. LC 86-22079. (Step into Reading Ser.: A Step 1 Book). (Illus.). 48p. (J). (ps-1). 1987. pap. 3.99 (*0-394-88867-7*, Pub. by Random Bks Yng Read) Random.
— David & the Giant. (Step into Reading Ser.: A Step 1 Book). (J). (ps-1). 1987. 9.19 (*0-606-12238-9*, Pub. by Turtleback) Demco.
— The Trojan Horse: How the Greeks Won the War. LC 87-43118. (Step into Reading Ser.: A Step 4 Book). (Illus.). 48p. (J). (gr. 4-7). 1988. pap. 3.99 (*0-394-89674-2*, Pub. by Random Bks Yng Read) Random.
Little, Emily. The Trojan Horse: How the Greeks Won the War. (Step into Reading Ser.: A Step 4 Book). (J). (gr. 2-4). 1988. 9.19 (*0-606-03940-6*, Pub. by Turtleback) Demco.
Little, Eric E. Pools of Ancient Evil. 446p. mass mkt. 4.99 (*1-55197-008-2*) Picasso Publ.
Little, Frank. The Little Trapshooting Book. (Illus.). 168p. Date not set. pap. 19.95 (*0-925012-02-5*) Shotgun Sports.
Little, Frank A. Little Notes from the Office: Some Do's, Don'ts & Basic Observations That Have Made a Difference. LC 94-94159. (Illus.). (Orig.). 1994. pap. 5.95 (*0-9641206-3-1*) E W Franklin.
— More Little Notes: On Management, Motivation & . . . Living. (Illus.). 140p. (Orig.). 1996. pap. 5.95 (*0-9641206-5-8*) E W Franklin.
Little, G. T. The Descendants of George Little Who Came to Newbury, Mass., in 1640. (Illus.). 638p. 1989. reprint ed. pap. 80.00 (*0-8328-0774-5*); reprint ed. lib. bdg. 90.00 (*0-8328-0773-7*) Higginson Bk Co.
— Little: Genealogy of the Little Family: Descendants of George Little, Who Came to Newbury, Massachusetts, in 1640. (Illus.). 82p. 1993. reprint ed. pap. 16.50 (*0-8328-3366-5*); reprint ed. lib. bdg. 26.50 (*0-8328-3365-7*) Higginson Bk Co.
Little, Gary B. Exploring Apple ProDos: Programming with ProDos 8 & ProDos 16. 384p. 1989. pap. 21.95 (*0-201-15008-5*) Addison-Wesley.
— Inside the Apple IIe. (Illus.). 18.95 (*0-685-09669-6*) P-H.
Little Gems Publishing Staff. Golf Course Memory Aid. 5th ed. (Illus.). 76p. 1996. reprint ed. pap. 5.95 (*0-9613410-1-7*) Lttle Gems FL.
Little, George. The Many Deaths of George Robertson. 137p. 1990. pap. 10.95 (*0-86492-124-1*, Pub. by Goose Ln Edits) Genl Dist Srvs.
Little, Geraldine. No Home to Return to but This. 40p. 1994. pap. 5.00 (*1-880286-19-X*) Singular Speech Pr.
Little, Geraldine C. Contemplations Contemplations Contemplations. (Chickadee Ser.: Vol. 11). 17p. 1997. pap. 7.00 (*1-55780-176-2*) Juniper Pr ME.
— Contrasts in Keening: Ireland. LC 82-60038. 50p. (Orig.). 1982. pap. 4.00 (*0-943710-00-6*) Silver App Pr.
— More Light, Larger Vision. (Orig.). 1992. pap. 9.00 (*0-944676-38-3*) AHA Bks.
— Out of Darkness. LC 92-32571. 110p. (C). 1993. lib. bdg. 32.00 (*0-8191-8907-3*) U Pr of Amer.
— Star-Mapped. 72p. 1989. 6.00 (*0-943710-02-2*) Silver App Pr.
— A Well-Tuned Harp. LC 87-28838. (Illus.). 72p. (Orig.). 1988. pap. 7.00 (*0-938158-09-0*) Saturday Pr.
— Woman in a Special House & Other Stories. LC 96-9812. 176p. (Orig.). 1997. pap. 10.95 (*1-56474-196-6*) Fithian Pr.
— Women: In the Mask & Beyond. (QRL Poetry Bks.: Vol. XXX). 1991. pap. 10.00 (*0-614-06437-6*) Quarterly Rev.
Little, Geraldine C., ed. see Mandel, Charlotte.
Little Gift Books Staff. Friends. (Little Bks.). (Illus.). 1995. 4.95 (*0-8362-0861-7*) Andrews & McMeel.
Little, Gilbert. Como Vencer la Tension Nerviosa. Orig. Title: Nervous Christians. 128p. 1987. mass mkt. 4.99 (*0-8254-1443-1*, Edit Portavoz) Kregel.
Little Golden Books Staff. Addition & Subtraction No. 2. (Step Ahead Plus Workbks.). (Illus.). 64p. (J). (ps-3). pap., wbk. ed. 3.49 (*0-307-03654-5*, 03654, Goldn Books) Gldn Bks Pub Co.
— Bambi. (Illus.). (J). (ps-2). pap. 2.29 (*0-307-01061-9*, 98071) Gldn Bks Pub Co.
Little, Gordon, ed. Selected Papers on Fundamentals of Optoelectronics. LC 93-38813. 1993. 45.00 (*0-8194-1498-0*, MS 90/HC); pap. 35.00 (*0-8194-1497-2*, MS 90) SPIE.
Little, Gregory L. Grand Illusions: The Spectral Reality Underlying Sexual UFO Abductions, Crashed Saucers, Afterlife Experiences, Sacred Ancient Ritual Sites, & Other Enigmas. (Illus.). 271p. (Orig.). 1994. pap. 19.95 (*0-940829-10-X*) Eagle Wing Bks.
— People of the WEB. Robinson, Kenneth D., ed. (Illus.). 300p. 1989. pap. 19.95 (*0-940829-03-7*) Eagle Wing Bks.
— People of the WEB: What Indian Mounds, Ancient Rituals, & Stone Circles Tell Us about Modern UFO Abductions, Apparitions, & the Near Death. Robinson, Kenneth D., ed. LC 89-85686. (Illus.). 229p. 1990. pap. 19.95 (*0-940829-02-9*) Eagle Wing Bks.
— Psychopharmacology: Basics for Counselors. (Illus.). 279p. (C). 1996. pap. text 24.95 (*0-9655392-0-2*) Advanced Trnging.
— Relapse Prevention. 40p. 1996. pap., wbk. ed. 10.00 (*0-9655392-1-0*) Advanced Trnging.
Little, Gregory L. & Robinson, Kenneth D. Bringing Peace to Relationships: An MRT Educational Workbook. (Illus.). 119p. 1995. pap. 25.00 (*0-940829-14-2*) Eagle Wing Bks.

An Asterisk (*) at the beginning of an entry indicates that the title is appearing for the first time.

L

— Character Development. (Illus.). 54p. 1991. pap. 15.00 (*0-940829-04-5*) Eagle Wing Bks.
— Coping with Anger. 49p. 1997. pap. 10.00 (*0-940829-18-5*) Eagle Wing Bks.
— Discovering Life & Liberty in the Pursuit of Happiness: An MRT Educational Workbook. (Illus.). 109p. 1996. pap. 25.00 (*0-940829-16-9*) Eagle Wing Bks.
— Family Support: Responsibly Fulfilling a Life's Obligation. (Illus.). 26p. 1994. pap. 9.00 (*0-940829-13-4*) Eagle Wing Bks.
— Filling the Inner Void: An MRT Workbook. (Illus.). 120p. 1991. pap., wbk. ed. 25.00 (*0-940829-06-1*) Eagle Wing Bks.
— How to Escape Your Prison. (Illus.). 129p. (Orig.). 1989. reprint ed. pap., student ed. 25.00 (*0-940829-01-0*) Eagle Wing Bks.
— Job Readiness. (Illus.). 26p. 1994. pap. 9.00 (*0-940829-11-8*) Eagle Wing Bks.
— Juvenile MRT: How to Escape Your Prison. (Illus.). 117p. (J). (gr. 6). 1997. pap. 25.00 (*0-940829-21-5*) Eagle Wing Bks.
— Making Changes for Good: A Cognitive Behavioral Approach for Sex Offender Relapse Prevention. 58p. 1998. pap. 18.00 (*0-940829-22-3*) Eagle Wing Bks.
— Parenting & Family Values: A Cognitive-Behavioral MRT Workbook. (Illus.). 75p. 1995. pap. 15.00 (*0-940829-15-0*) Eagle Wing Bks.
— Understanding & Treating Antisocial Personality Disorder: Criminals, Chemical Abusers, & Batterers. 65p. 1997. pap. 10.00 (*0-940829-17-7*) Eagle Wing Bks.
— Untangling Relationships: Coping with Codependent Relationships Using the MRT Model. 28p. 1998. pap. 10.00 (*0-940829-24-X*) Eagle Wing Bks.
— Your Inner Enemy. (Illus.). 105p. (Orig.). 1989. pap. 8.95 (*0-940829-00-2*) Eagle Wing Bks.
Little, Gregory L., et al. Crisis Intervention Strategies: For Chemical Abusers & Offenders. 68p. (C). 1998. pap. 10.00 (*0-940829-20-7*) Eagle Wing Bks.
— Effective Counseling Approaches for Chemical Abusers & Offenders. 104p. (C). 1997. pap. 12.00 (*0-940829-19-3*) Eagle Wing Bks.
***Little, Gregory L., et al.** SmartLoss - MRT Group Workbook for Fitness & Weight Control. 60p. 2000. wbk. ed. 12.95 (*0-940829-29-0*) Eagle Wing Bks.
— Thinking for Good: Changing Antisocial & Criminal Thoughts with the MRT Model. (Illus.). 38p. 2000. wbk. ed. 10.00 (*0-940829-28-2*) Eagle Wing Bks.
Little, Gregory L., ed. see Robinson, Kenneth D.
Little, Greta D., jt. ed. see Montgomery, Michael B.
Little, Gwenyth, jt. auth. see Little, Constance.
Little, H. Ganse, Jr. Decision & Responsibility: A Wrinkle in Time. LC 74-24729. (American Academy of Religion. Studies in Religion: No. 8). (Illus.). 82p. reprint ed. pap. 30.00 (*0-7837-5488-4*, 204525300005) Bks Demand.
Little, Harry A. Potential Economies in the Reorganization of Local School Attendance Units. LC 72-177900. (Columbia University. Teachers College. Contributions to Education Ser.: No. 628). reprint ed. 37.50 (*0-404-55628-0*) AMS Pr.
Little, Helen. Association Chapters: How to Reinvent Your Local Organizations. (Illus.). 96p. 2000. pap. 24.95 (*1-928892-03-5*, 0001) Panacea Press.
— Members: How to Get Them, How to Keep Them. (Illus.). 96p. 1999. pap. 24.95 (*1-928892-02-7*, 9902) Panacea Press.
— Volunteers: How to Get Them, How to Keep Them. (Illus.). 128p. 1999. pap. 24.95 (*1-928892-01-9*, 9901) Panacea Press.
Little, Henry G. Early Days in Newington, CT, 1833-1836. 122p. 1994. reprint ed. pap. 17.50 (*0-8328-4402-0*) Higginson Bk Co.
Little Hills Press Editorial Board Staff. The Sydney Pocket Guidebook. (Illus.). 128p. 1996. pap. 9.95 (*1-86315-082-X*) Pelican.
Little Hills Press Editors. The Melbourne Pocket Guidebook. (Illus.). 64p. pap. 3.95 (*1-86315-033-1*) Pelican.
***Little Hills Press Editors, ed.** Hong Kong & Macau. (Illus.). 1999. pap. 14.95 (*1-86315-115-X*) Little Hills.
***Little Hills Press Staff.** Inland Australia. (Illus.). 2000. 14.95 (*1-86315-140-0*) Little Hills.
— Melbourne Pocket Guidebook. 1994. pap. 3.95 (*1-86315-090-0*) Pelican.
— Rome. (Shorter Stay Guides Ser.). (Illus.). 2000. pap. 9.95 (*1-86315-091-9*) Little Hills.
Little, I. M., jt. auth. see Joshi, V.
Little, I. M., jt. auth. see Joshi, Vijay.
Little, I. M., jt. ed. see Ahluwalia, Isher Judge.
Little, I. M. D. Collection & Recollections: Economic Papers & Their Provenance. LC 98-40743. 390p. 1999. text 85.00 (*0-19-829524-3*) OUP.
Little, Ian M. Macroeconomic Analysis & the Developing Countries, 1970-1990. LC 93-19069. 1993. pap. 9.95 (*1-55815-257-1*) ICS Pr.
Little, Ian M., et al. Boom, Crisis & Adjustment: The Macroeconomic Experience of Developing Countries, 1970-90. (World Bank Publication Ser.). 468p. 1993. text 60.00 (*0-19-520891-9*, 60891, Pub. by World Bank) OUP.
— Small Manufacturing Enterprises: A Comparative Study of India & Other Economies. (World Bank Research Publications Ser.). 376p. 1989. reprint ed. pap. text 19.95 (*0-19-520779-3*) OUP.
Little, Ian M., jt. auth. see Rayner, Anthony C.
Little, Ida & Walsh, Michael. Beachcruising & Coastal Camping. Wiiensky, Julius M., ed. LC 92-60226. (Illus.). 352p. 1992. pap. 17.95 (*0-918752-15-9*) Wescott Cove.
Little, J. Diaries of George Bird, Victorian Wheelwright, 1862-83. (C). 1980. text 35.00 (*0-7855-3213-7*, Pub. by Univ Nottingham) St Mut.
Little, J., et al. Ideals, Varieties, & Algorithms: An Introduction to Computational Algebraic Geometry & Communtative Algebra. 2nd ed. (Illus.). 536p. 1996. 45.00 (*0-387-94680-2*) Spr-Verlag.
Little, J. A., jt. ed. see Newcomb, S. B.
Little, J. B. Understanding Wall Street. 3rd ed. 272p. 1991. pap. 11.95 (*0-07-038102-X*) McGraw.
Little, J. I. Crofters & Habitants: Settler Society, Economy & Culture in a Quebec Township, 1848-1881. 392p. 1991. 55.00 (*0-7735-0807-4*, Pub. by McG-Queens Univ Pr) CUP Services.
— Nationalism, Capitalism, & Colonization in Nineteenth-Century Quebec: The Upper Saint Francis District. 336p. (C). 1989. text 55.00 (*0-7735-0699-3*, Pub. by McG-Queens Univ Pr) CUP Services.
— State & Society in Transition: The Politics of Institutional Reform in the Eastern Townships, 1838-1852. LC 98-123934. (Studies on the History of Quebec/Etudes d'Histoire du Quebec). (Illus.). 352p. 1997. 60.00 (*0-7735-1544-5*, Pub. by McG-Queens Univ Pr); pap. 24.95 (*0-7735-1545-3*, Pub. by McG-Queens Univ Pr) CUP Services.
Little, J. I., ed. The Child Letters: Public & Private Life in a Canadian Merchant-Politician's Family, 1841-1845. LC 96-108133. (Illus.). 200p. 1995. 55.00 (*0-7735-1260-8*, Pub. by McG-Queens Univ Pr) CUP Services.
Little, J. Wesley & Brigham, Arthur J. Emerging Strategies in Early Childhood Education. (Illus.). (C). 1973. 29.50 (*0-8422-5089-1*) Irvington.
Little, Jack. Business Writing for Adults. 137p. 1983. pap. 5.00 (*0-934768-02-1*) Altair Pr.
— Love Songs & Graffiti. 82p. (Orig.). pap. 7.00 (*0-913057-08-8*) Confront Mag Pr.
— Love Songs & Graffiti. deluxe limited ed. 82p. (Orig.). 20.00 (*0-913057-07-X*) Confront Mag Pr.
— Moon of Isis. LC 76-8728. (J). (gr. 5 up). 1976. pap. 5.00 (*0-934768-00-5*) Altair Pr.
— Thunder Egg. LC 77-94288. (J). (gr. 5 up). 1978. pap. 5.00 (*0-934768-01-3*) Altair Pr.
Little, James A. Jacob Hamblin. LC 72-164615. (Select Bibliographies Reprint Ser.). 1977. reprint ed. 19.95 (*0-8369-5899-3*) Ayer.
Little, James J., jt. auth. see Manis, Vincent C.
***Little, James R.** Wheelchair Field Events. LC 97-19256. 1998. write for info. (*1-56065-617-4*) W S Hein.
Little, James R. Wheelchair Road Racing. LC 97-15071. (Wheelchair Sports Ser.). (J). 1998. lib. bdg. write for info. (*1-56065-615-8*) Capstone Pr.
Little, James W., ed. see Falace, Donald A.
Little, Jan. If It Weren't for the Honor - I'd Rather Have Walked: Previously Untold Tales of the Journey to the ADA. LC 96-17461. 262p. 1996. pap. 15.95 (*1-57129-026-5*) Brookline Bks.
Little, Janet, jt. auth. see Gilles, Katie.
Little, Jason. Jack's Luck Runs Out. (Illus.). 24p. 1998. 3.50 (*0-9666243-0-0*) Beekeeper Cartoon.
Little, Jean. The Belonging Place. LC 97-214079. 128p. (J). (gr. 3-7). 1997. 13.99 (*0-670-87593-7*, Viking Child) Peng Put Young Read.
Little, Jean. Different Dragons. (Illus.). 144p. (J). (gr. 3-7). 1989. pap. 4.99 (*0-14-031998-0*, PuffinBks) Peng Put Young Read.
— Different Dragons. 1989. 9.60 (*0-606-12251-6*, Pub. by Turtleback) Demco.
Little, Jean. Emma's Magic Winter. LC 97-49667. (I Can Read Bks.). (Illus.). 64p. (J). (ps-3). 1998. 14.95 (*0-06-025389-4*); lib. bdg. 14.89 (*0-06-025390-8*) HarpC.
***Little, Jean.** Emma's Magic Winter. LC 97-49667. (I Can Read Bks.). (Illus.). 64p. (J). (gr. 2-4). 2000. pap. 3.95 (*0-06-443706-X*, HarpTrophy) HarpC Child Bks.
— Emma's Yucky Brother. LC 99-34515. 64p. (gr. k-3). pap. 3.95 (*0-06-444258-6*) HarpC.
Little, Jean. Emma's Yucky Brother. LC 99-34515. (Illus.). 64p. (J). (gr. k-3). 2000. 14.95 (*0-06-028348-3*); lib. bdg. 14.89 (*0-06-028349-1*) HarpC Child Bks.
— From Anna. (J). 1972. 9.60 (*0-606-02117-5*, Pub. by Turtleback) Demco.
— From Anna. LC 72-76505. (Trophy Bk.). (Illus.). 208p. (J). (gr. 4-7). 1973. reprint ed. pap. 4.95 (*0-06-440044-1*, HarpTrophy) HarpC Child Bks.
— Hey World, Here I Am! LC 88-10987. (Illus.). 96p. (J). (gr. 5-9). 1989. 13.00 (*0-06-023989-1*); lib. bdg. 13.89 (*0-06-024006-7*) HarpC Child Bks.
— Hey World, Here I Am! LC 88-10987. (Trophy Bk.). (Illus.). 96p. (J). (gr. 4-7). 1990. mass mkt. 4.95 (*0-06-440384-X*, HarpTrophy) HarpC Child Bks.
Little, Jean. Hey World, Here I Am! (Illus.). 96p. (J). 1986. pap. 4.95 (*1-55074-036-9*) Kids Can Pr.
Little, Jean. Hey World, Here I Am! 1990. 9.60 (*0-606-03525-7*, Pub. by Turtleback) Demco.
— His Banner over Me. 1999. mass mkt. 4.99 (*0-14-037761-1*) Viking Penguin.
— Jess Was the Brave One. 1994. 10.19 (*0-606-07738-3*, Pub. by Turtleback) Demco.
— KATE. LC 20-148419. (Trophy Bk.). 174p. (J). (gr. 5-8). 1973. pap. 3.95 (*0-06-440037-9*, HarpTrophy) HarpC Child Bks.
Little, Jeffrey B. Dean Witter: Understanding Wall Street. 1991. 3.25 (*0-8306-5326-0*) McGraw-Hill Prof.
— The Great Index Mania: The Stock Market (1997-2002) (Illus.). 130p. 1997. pap. 16.95 (*0-89709-216-3*) Liberty Pub.
— Investing & Trading. (Basic Investor's Library). (Illus.). 48p. 1988. lib. bdg. 12.95 (*1-55546-627-3*) Chelsea Hse.
— Reading the Financial Pages. (Basic Investor's Library). (Illus.). 48p. 1988. lib. bdg. 12.95 (*1-55546-623-0*) Chelsea Hse.
— Understanding a Company. (Basic Investor's Library). (Illus.). 48p. 1988. lib. bdg. 12.95 (*1-55546-622-2*) Chelsea Hse.
Little, Jeffrey B. & Rhodes, Lucien. Stock Options. 32p. 1977. pap. 2.95 (*0-89709-009-8*, 30009P) McGraw-Hill Prof.
— Understanding Wall Street. 3rd rev. ed. 240p. 1991. 21.95 (*0-8306-0482-0*, 3686) McGraw-Hill Prof.
— Understanding Wall Street. 3rd rev. ed. (Illus.). 259p. 1991. pap. 9.95 (*0-8306-0479-0*) McGraw-Hill Prof.
— Understanding Wall Street. 4th ed. (Illus.). 304p. 1997. pap. text 12.95 (*0-07-038111-9*) McGraw.
Little, Jeffrey B., jt. auth. see Leftwich, Jim.
Little, Jerrell. Cowboy Cap Guns & Guitars. (Illus.). 87p. (Orig.). 1996. pap. 12.00 (*0-89538-047-1*) L-W Inc.
Little, Jim. Wheelchair Field Events. (Wheelchair Sports Ser.). (Illus.). 48p. (J). (gr. 3-7). 1997. lib. bdg. 19.00 (*0-531-11474-0*, Rivr Front Bks) Capstone Pr.
— Wheelchair Road Racing. (Wheelchair Sports Ser.). (Illus.). 48p. (J). (gr. 3-7). 1997. lib. bdg. 19.00 (*0-531-11475-9*, Rivr Front Bks) Capstone Pr.
Little, Jim, jt. auth. see Labanowich, Stan.
Little, Jo. Gender, Planning & the Policy Process. LC 93-49389. (Policy, Planning & Critical Theory Ser.). 256p. 1994. pap. text 34.95 (*0-08-040480-4*, Prgamon Press) Buttrwrth-Heinemann.
Little, Jo, jt. auth. see Cloke, Paul J.
Little, Jocelyn. Weird People: We Are Stranger Than We Think. LC 95-51256. (Illus.). 128p. 1996. pap. 7.95 (*0-8069-3850-1*) Sterling.
— World's Strangest Animal Facts. (Illus.). 96p. (J). (gr. 4 up). 1995. pap. 5.95 (*0-8069-8521-6*) Sterling.
Little, John. Clinical Neurosurgery, Vol. 34. (Illus.). 718p. 1987. 64.95 (*0-683-02029-3*) Lppncott W & W.
— Learning & Using Communication Theory. 4th ed. (Speech & Theater Ser.). 1992. pap., student ed. 12.25 (*0-534-16135-9*) Wadsworth Pub.
— The Warrior Within. (Illus.). 160p. 1996. pap. 14.95 (*0-8092-3194-8*, 319480, Contemporary Bks) NTC Contemp Pub Co.
— Words of the Dragon: Bruce Lee's Interviews with the Press from, 1959-1973. (Bruce Lee Library). (Illus.). 160p. 1997. pap. text 14.95 (*0-8048-3133-5*) Tuttle Pubng.
***Little, John, ed.** Bruce Lee: The Celebrated Life of the Golden Dragon. (Illus.). 2000. pap. 24.95 (*0-8048-3230-7*) Tuttle Pubng.
Little, John & Sisco, Peter. Precious Training: The New Method to Achieve Optimum Muscularity. 241p. 1995. 14.95 (*1-886691-18-5*) Power Factor.
— Precision Training - The Science of Strength. 1995. 9.95 (*1-886691-19-3*) Power Factor.
Little, John & Williamson, Kenneth L. Microscale Chemical Experiments. (C). 1997. pap. text, teacher ed. 11.96 (*0-669-41607-X*) HM Trade Div.
— Microscale Chemical Experiments. (C). 1997. pap. text 43.96 (*0-669-41606-1*) HM Trade Div.
Little, John, jt. auth. see Sisco, Peter.
Little, John, ed. see Lee, Bruce.
Little, John, ed. & anno. see Lee, Bruce.
Little, John, ed. & contrib. by see Lee, Bruce.
Little, John B. History of Butler County: From 1815 to 1885, with Sketches of Some of Her Most Distinguished Citizens & Glances at Her Rich & Varied Resources. 256p. 1997. reprint ed. lib. bdg. 32.00 (*0-8328-6593-1*) Higginson Bk Co.
Little, John B., ed. Possible Health Effects of Exposure to Residential Electric & Magnetic Fields. (Illus.). 356p. (Orig.). (C). 1997. text 60.00 (*0-7881-4516-9*) DIANE Pub.
Little, John B., jt. auth. see Damiano, David B.
Little, John R. Bruce Lee: Words from a Master. 160p. 1999. pap. 10.95 (*0-8092-2501-8*, 250180, Contemporary Bks) NTC Contemp Pub Co.
— Clinical Neurosurgery: Proceedings of the Congress of Neurological Surgeons, Vol. 33. (Illus.). 702p. 1986. write for info. (*0-683-02028-5*) Lppncott W & W.
— Sacred Places. 347p. 1998. pap. 15.00 (*0-9667881-1-7*) J R Little.
***Little, John R.** Ultimate Paintball Field Guide. (Illus.). 2000. pap. 19.95 (*0-8092-2549-2*, Contemporary Bks) NTC Contemp Pub Co.
Little, John R., ed. Bruce Lee. LC 98-6795. 160p. 1999. 14.95 (*0-8092-2856-4*, 285640, Contemporary Bks) NTC Contemp Pub Co.
— Clinical Neurosurgery: Proceedings of the Congress of Neurological Surgeons, Vol. 32. (Illus.). 680p. 1985. 54.00 (*0-683-02027-7*) Lppncott W & W.
Little, John R. & Awad, Issam A. Reoperative Neurosurgery. (Illus.). 379p. 1992. 135.00 (*0-683-05080-X*) Lppncott W & W.
***Little, John R. & Wong, Curtis.** Ultimate Martial Arts Encyclopedia. LC 99-89715. (Best of Inside Kung-Fu Magazine Ser.). (Illus.). 128p. 2000. pap. 18.95 (*0-8092-2835-1*, 283510, Contemporary Bks) NTC Contemp Pub Co.
Little, John R. & Wong, Curtis, eds. Jackie Chan. LC 98-17958. (Illus.). 128p. 1998. pap. 12.95 (*0-8092-2837-8*, 283780, Contemporary Bks) NTC Contemp Pub Co.
Little, John R. & Wong, Curtis F., eds. Ultimate Guide to Tae Kwon Do. LC 99-48923. (Best of Inside Kung-Fu Magazine Ser.). 208p. 1999. pap. 18.95 (*0-8092-2831-9*, Contemporary Bks) NTC Contemp Pub Co.
— Ultimate Guide to Tai Chi. LC 98-54248. (Best of Inside Kung-Fu Magazine Ser.). (Illus.). 320p. 1999. pap. 18.95 (*0-8092-2833-5*, 283350, Contemporary Bks) NTC Contemp Pub Co.
Little, John R., jt. auth. see Sisco, Peter.
Little, John R., jt. auth. see Sisco, Peter N.
Little, John W., et al. OS/2 Warp Professional Reference. LC 95-34180. (Professional Ser.). 900p. 1995. pap. 55.00 (*1-56205-502-X*) New Riders Pub.
Little, John W., jt. auth. see Spear, Scott L.
Little, Jonathan. Charles Johnson's Spiritual Imagination. LC 97-33392. (Illus.). 192p. 1998. 39.95 (*0-8262-1147-X*); pap. 19.95 (*0-8262-1151-8*) U of Mo Pr.
Little, Joseph R., et al, eds. Micros for Managers: A Software Guide for School Administrators. rev. ed. LC 84-62050. xxi, 298p. (Orig.). 1984. pap. 25.00 (*0-912337-05-2*) NJ Schl Bds.
Little, Joseph W. Administration of Justice in Drunk Driving Cases. LC 75-11643. (University of Florida Monographs: Social Sciences: No. 53). (Illus.). 238p. reprint ed. pap. 73.80 (*0-7837-4956-2*, 204462200004) Bks Demand.
Little, Joseph W. Torts: The Civil Law of Reparation for Harm Done by Wrongful Act 1997. annuals 2nd ed. 1997. text 56.00 (*0-8205-2884-6*) Bender.
Little, Joseph W., et al. Cases & Materials on Workers Compensation. 3rd ed. (American Casebook Ser.). 537p. (C). 1992. text 42.00 (*0-314-00965-5*) West Pub.
Little, Joyce. The Church & the Culture War: Secular Anarchy or Sacred Order. 207p. (Orig.). 1995. pap. 12.95 (*0-89870-547-9*) Ignatius Pr.
Little, Joyce A. The Significance of Mary for Women. (Queen of Apostles Ser.: Vol. III). 26p. 1995. 0.65 (*0-911988-86-6*, 49716) AMI Pr.
— Toward a Thomist Theology. LC 87-34963. (Toronto Studies in Theology: Vol. 34). 576p. 1988. lib. bdg. 119.95 (*0-88946-779-X*) E Mellen.
Little, Joyce Currie, jt. auth. see ACM Committee on Curriculum for Community and Junior College Education Staff.
Little, Judith W. & McLaughlin, Milbrey W., eds. Teacher's Work: Individuals, Colleagues & Contexts. LC 92-34794. (Series on School Reform). 208p. (C). 1993. text 39.00 (*0-8077-3229-X*); pap. text 17.95 (*0-8077-3228-1*) Tchrs Coll.
Little, Judith W. & Nelson, Linda, eds. A Leader's Guide to Mentor Training. LC 89-80829. viii, 323p. (Orig.). 1990. ring bd. 20.00 (*0-86552-099-2*) U of Oreg ERIC.
Little, Judith W., jt. auth. see Siskin, Leslie S.
Little, Judy. Comedy & the Woman Writer: Woolf, Spark, & Feminism. LC 82-19999. xii, 224p. 1983. text 40.00 (*0-8032-2859-7*) U of Nebr Pr.
— The Experimental Self: Dialogic Subjectivity in Woolf, Pyn, & Brooke-Rose. LC 95-53744. 196p. (C). 1996. 29.95 (*0-8093-2061-4*) S Ill U Pr.
— Keats As a Narrative Poet: A Test of Invention. LC 74-81365. 175p. reprint ed. pap. 54.30 (*0-7837-6015-9*, 204582600008) Bks Demand.
Little, Julian. Epidemiology of Childhood Cancer. (IARC Scientific Publications: 149). (Illus.). 400p. (Orig.). 1999. pap. text 60.00 (*92-832-2149-4*) OUP.
Little, Karen. Frank Bridge: A Bio-Bibliography, 36. LC 90-23779. (Bio-Bibliographies in Music Ser.: No. 36). 280p. 1991. lib. bdg. 62.95 (*0-313-26232-2*, LFB/, Greenwood Pr) Greenwood.
Little, Karen, jt. auth. see Konicek, Joel.
Little, Karen E. & Thomas, A. Things That Fly. (Explainers Ser.). (Illus.). 24p. (J). (gr. 2-4). 1987. text 4.95 (*0-7460-0104-5*) EDC.
Little, Karen E. & Thomas, A. Wings, Wheels & Water. (Explainers Ser.). (Illus.). 72p. (J). (gr. 2-4). 1988. 12.95 (*0-7460-0106-1*) EDC.
Little, Karen R. Notes Vols. 1-50: An Index. LC 95-6324. 1995. write for info. (*0-914954-50-4*) Music Library Assn.
***Little, Kate.** The Determined Groom. (Desire Ser.: Bk. 1302). 2000. per. 3.99 (*0-373-76302-6*, 1-76302-8) Silhouette.
Little, Kate. Finding Out about Things That Fly. (Usborne Kid Kits Ser.). (Illus.). (J). (gr. 2-4). 1997. 14.95 (*0-88110-957-6*, Usborne) EDC.
***Little, Kate.** Husband for Keeps. (Desire Ser.). 2000. mass mkt. 3.99 (*0-373-76276-3*) Silhouette.
Little, Kate. Jingle Bell Baby. 1996. per. 3.50 (*0-373-76043-4*, 1-76043-8) Silhouette.
Little, Keith, jt. ed. see Robertson, Colin E.
***Little, Keith R.** The Survivor's Guide to MicroStation J: Making the Most of MicroStation. (Survivor's Guide to MicroStation Ser.: Vol. SRV-11). (Illus.). 665p. 1999. pap. 44.95 (*1-885315-73-2*) Adage Bks.
***Little, Kenneth E.** Fathering Our Daughters. LC 00-9405. 2000. write for info. (*1-57153-029-0*) Curriculm Presbytrn KY.
— Teach Yourself Investing in 24 Hours. (Illus.). 304p. 1900. 19.99 (*0-02-863898-0*) Simon & Schuster.
Little, Kenneth L. The Sociology of Urban Women's Image in African Literature. 174p. 1980. 42.00 (*0-8476-6290-X*) Rowman.
— West African Urbanization: A Study of Voluntary Associations in Social Change. LC 65-14349. 187p. reprint ed. pap. 53.30 (*0-608-12081-2*, 2024579) Bks Demand.
Little, Kevin. Nuclear Theology. 80p. 1999. pap. 8.00 (*0-8059-4540-7*) Dorrance.
Little, Kimberley G. Breakaway. 160p. (J). (gr. 3-7). 1998. pap. 3.99 (*0-380-79225-7*, Avon Bks) Morrow Avon.
Little, Kimberley Griffiths. Enchanted Runner. LC 98-54849. 160p. (J). (gr. 5-7). 1999. 15.00 (*0-380-97623-4*, Avon Bks) Morrow Avon.
Little, Kristen, ed. see Ross, Ann & Olsen, Karen D.
Little, L. P. Imprisoned Preachers & Religious Liberty in Virginia. 1987. reprint ed. 28.00 (*0-317-60755-3*) Church History.
Little, Larry. Larry Little's "Learn Bass Guitar Book" (Illus.). 40p. 1996. pap. 9.95 (*1-884208-10-X*, LL-18800) Larry Little Co.
— Larry Little's "Learn Guitar Book" LC 99-172152. (Illus.). 36p. 1996. pap. 9.95 (*1-884208-08-8*, LL-17800) Larry Little Co.

An Asterisk (*) at the beginning of an entry indicates that the title is appearing for the first time.

Little, Larry & Beyer, Dave. Larry Little's "Learn Drums Book" (Illus.). 40p. 1996. pap. 9.95 (*1-884208-09-6*, LLB-15800) Larry Little Co.

***Little, Laura E.** Advocacy Before Appellate Courts. LC 99-162549. 1998. pap. 30.95 (*1-55681-499-2*) Natl Inst Trial Ad.

Little, Laura E. Advocacy Before Appellate Courts, Vol. II. 1998. pap. 25.95 (*1-55681-608-1*) Natl Inst Trial Ad.

Little, Laurie & Gwyer, Mary Beth. White Grass Cafe. 192p. 1997. spiral bd. 13.95 (*0-87012-570-2*) McClain. Out of a tiny kitchen in the heart of West Virginia snow country comes some of the best food in the land. The cafe is part of White Grass Ski touring, one of the most unique cross country ski centers in the East. This collection is a sampling of the incredible foods you will find at White Grass & now you can create them for yourself at home. *Publisher Paid Annotation.*

Little, Lawrence C. Wider Horizons in Christian Adult Education. LC 62-14381. 348p. reprint ed. pap. 107.90 (*0-8357-9763-5*, 201787100010) Bks Demand.

***Little, Lawrence S.** Disciples of Liberty: The African Methodist Episcopal Church in the Age of Imperialism, 1884-1916. LC 99-50910. 264p. (C). 2000. text 32.00 (*1-57233-085-6*, Pub. by U of Tenn Pr) U Ch Pr.

Little, Lawson, jt. auth. see Wells, Sharon.

Little, Lessie J., jt. auth. see Greenfield, Eloise.

***Little, Lessie Jones.** Children of Long Ago. LC 99-56100. (Illus.). 32p. (YA). (ps up). 2000. 15.95 (*1-58430-008-6*, Pub. by Lee & Low Bks); pap. 6.95 (*1-58430-009-4*, Pub. by Lee & Low Bks) Publishers Group.

— Children of Long Ago: Poems. (Illus.). (J). 2000. 12.40 (*0-606-18246-2*) Turtleback.

Little, Lester K. Benedictine Maledictions: Liturgical Cursing in Romanesque France. (Illus.). 312p. 1993. text 45.00 (*0-8014-2876-9*) Cornell U Pr.

— Benedictine Maledictions: Liturgical Cursing in Romanesque France. (Illus.). 320p. 1996. pap. text 17.95 (*0-8014-8113-9*) Cornell U Pr.

— Liberty, Charity, Fraternity: Lay Religious Confraternities at Bergamo in the Age of the Commune. LC 89-154929. (Studies in History: Vol. 51). (Illus.). 228p. 1989. pap. 25.00 (*0-87391-040-0*) Smith Coll.

— Religious Poverty & the Profit Economy in Medieval Europe. LC 78-58630. xi, 267p. 1978. write for info. (*0-8014-1213-7*) Cornell U Pr.

— Religious Poverty & the Profit Economy in Medieval Europe. LC 78-58630. 268p. 1983. pap. text 16.95 (*0-8014-9247-5*) Cornell U Pr.

***Little, Lester K., et al.** Monks & Nuns, Saints & Outcasts: Religion in Medieval Society: Essays in Honor of Lester K. Little. LC 99-56454. 2000. pap. 21.95 (*0-8014-8656-4*) Cornell U Pr.

Little, Lester K., ed. see Rosenwein, Barbara H.

Little, Lester K., ed. & tr. see Chenu, M. D.

Little, Linda & Greenberg, Ingrid. Problem Solving: Critical Thinking & Communication Skills. 128p. 1991. pap. text 18.23 (*0-8013-0603-5*, 78533) Longman.

Little, Linda F., jt. auth. see Uram, Maggie.

Little, Linda F., ed. see Uram, Maggie.

Little, M., et al, eds. Becoming a Family Physician. (Illus.). 288p. 1989. 54.00 (*0-387-96949-7*, 2588) Spr-Verlag.

***Little, M. P.** Probabilistic Accident Consequence Uncertainty Analysis: Late Health Effects Uncertainty Assessment, Appendices. 232p. 1998. per. 19.00 (*0-16-062878-4*) USGPO.

— Probabilistic Accident Consequence Uncertainty Analysis: Late Health Effects Uncertainty Assessment, Main Report. 63p. 1998. pap. 5.50 (*0-16-062877-6*) USGPO.

Little, M. Ruth. Sticks & Stones: Three Centuries of North Carolina Gravemarkers. LC 97-32589. (Richard Hampton Jenrette Series in Architecture & the Decorative Arts). (Illus.). 352p. 1998. 45.00 (*0-8078-2417-8*) U of NC Pr.

Little, M. Ruth & Jones, Robbie D. Coastal Plain & Fancy: The Historic Architecture of Lenoir County & Kinston, North Carolina. LC 98-89604. ix, 480 p. 1998. write for info. (*0-9668319-0-X*) Lenoir Cty Hist Assn.

Little, Manon. Essays on Robert Browning. LC 73-21773. (Studies in Browning: No. 4). 1974. lib. bdg. 75.00 (*0-8383-1819-3*) M S G Haskell Hse.

Little, Margaret I. Miss Alice M & Her Dragon: Recovery of a Hidden Talent. (Illus.). 68p. 1998. pap. text 14.95 (*1-883881-30-7*, 30-7) S Freud RT&PF.

— Transference Neurosis & Transference Psychosis. LC 80-66925. 350p. 1980. 40.00 (*0-87668-421-5*) Aronson.

— Transference Neurosis & Transference Psychosis. LC 80-66925. 352p. 1993. pap. 50.00 (*1-56821-074-4*) Aronson.

Little, Marie, jt. auth. see Little, Paul.

Little, Marie, jt. auth. see Little, Paul E.

Little, Marilyn. Family Breakup. LC 82-48068. (Jossey-Bass Social & Behavioral Science Ser.). 251p. reprint ed. pap. 77.90 (*0-8357-4904-5*, 203783400009) Bks Demand.

Little, Marjorie. Diabetes. (Encyclopedia of Health Ser.). (Illus.). 116p. (YA). (gr. 7 up). 1991. lib. bdg. 19.95 (*0-7910-0061-3*) Chelsea Hse.

— The Endocrine System. (Encyclopedia of Health Ser.). (Illus.). 1161p. (YA). (gr. 7 up). 1990. lib. bdg. 19.95 (*0-7910-0016-8*) Chelsea Hse.

***Little, Marjorie.** Endocrine System. (Twenty-First Century Health & Wellness Ser.). (Illus.). 2000. 24.95 (*0-7910-5982-0*) Chelsea Hse.

— Sexually Transmitted Diseases. LC 99-51966. (Illus.). 128p. 1999. 24.95 (*0-7910-5528-0*) Chelsea Hse.

Little, Mark, ed. New French Thought: Political Philosophy. LC 94-8848. (New French Thought Ser.). 232p. 1994. text 55.00 (*0-691-03434-6*, Pub. by Princeton U Pr); pap. text 15.95 (*0-691-00105-7*, Pub. by Princeton U Pr) Cal Prin Full Svc.

Little, Mary A. Learning about Chores: Beginning the Process of Learning about Chores. (Competent Kids Ser.). 16p. (J). 1995. 19.95 (*1-887514-03-1*) Three Bears.

— Learning More about Being a Dad: Beginning the Process of Learning about Being a Dad. (Competent Kids Ser.). 16p. (J). 1995. 19.95 (*1-887514-06-6*) Three Bears.

— Learning More about Chores: Continuing the Process of Learning about Chores. (Competent Kids Ser.). 16p. (J). 1995. 19.95 (*1-887514-04-X*) Three Bears.

— Learning the Nighttime Routine: Beginning the Process of Learning the Nighttime Routine. (Competent Kids Ser.). 16p. (J). 1995. 19.95 (*1-887514-02-3*) Three Bears.

— Learning to Be a More Nurturing Parent: Beginning the Process of Learning to Become a Nurturing Parent. (Competent Kids Ser.). 16p. (J). 1995. 19.95 (*1-887514-05-8*) Three Bears.

— Learning to Get Dressed: Beginning the Process of Learning to Get Dressed. (Competent Kids Ser.). 16p. (J). 1995. 19.95 (*1-887514-00-7*) Three Bears.

— Learning to Go to Sleep Alone: Beginning the Process of Learning to Go to Sleep Alone. (Competent Kids Ser.). 16p. (J). 1995. 19.95 (*1-887514-01-5*) Three Bears.

Little, Mary E. Julian's Cat: An Imaginary History of a Cat of Destiny. LC 88-31750. 132p. 1993. reprint ed. pap. 8.95 (*0-8192-1609-7*) Morehouse Pub.

Little, Meredith & Jenne, Natalie. Dance & the Music of J. S. Bach. LC 90-42362. (Music Ser.). (Illus.). 264p. 1991. 39.95 (*0-253-33514-0*) Ind U Pr.

— Dance & the Music of J. S. Bach. LC 90-42362. (Music Ser.). (Illus.). 264p. 1998. pap. 17.95 (*0-253-21211-1*) Ind U Pr.

Little, Meredith, jt. auth. see Foster, Steven.

Little, Meredith, jt. auth. see Foster, Steven M.

Little, Meredith E. & Marsh, Carol G., eds. La Danse Noble: An Inventory of Dances & Sources. (Illus.). 1993. lib. bdg. 95.00 (*0-8450-0092-6*) Broude.

Little Mermaid, see Ariel, pseud.

Little, Michael. A Life Without Problems? The Achievements of a Therapeutic Community. 240p. 1995. 64.95 (*1-85742-317-8*, Pub. by Arena); pap. 28.95 (*1-85742-316-X*, Pub. by Arena) Ashgate Pub Co.

— Young Men in Prison: The Criminal Identity Explored Through the Rules of Behaviour. 174p. 1990. pap. text 24.95 (*1-85521-093-2*, Pub. by Dartmth Pub) Ashgate Pub Co.

Little, Michael & Leslie, Paul. Turkana Herders of the Dry Savana: Ecology & Biobehavioral Response of Nomads to an Uncertain Environment. LC 99-219983. (Research Monographs on Human Population Biology). (Illus.). 436p. 1999. text 115.00 (*0-19-854921-0*) OUP.

***Little, Michael & Mount, Kevin.** Prevention & Early Intervention with Children in Need. (Dartington Social Research Ser.). 166p. 1999. text 52.95 (*0-7546-2074-3*, Pub. by Ashgate Pub) Ashgate Pub Co.

Little, Michael, jt. auth. see Bullock, Roger.

Little, Michael A. & Haas, Jere D., eds. Human Population Biology: A Transdisciplinary Science. (Research Monographs on Human Population Biology). (Illus.). 352p. 1989. text 75.00 (*0-19-505016-9*) OUP.

Little, Michael R. A War of Information: The Conflict Between Public & Private U. S. Foreign Policy on El Salvador, 1979-1992. (Illus.). 210p. (C). 1993. lib. bdg. 42.00 (*0-8191-9311-9*) U Pr of Amer.

Little, Mickey. Camper's Guide to Colorado Parks, Lakes & Forests. (Camper's Guides Ser.). 156p. 1990. pap. 14.95 (*0-87201-124-0*, 1124) Gulf Pub.

— Camper's Guide to Florida Parks, Lakes, Forests, & Beaches: Where to Go & How to Get There. 2nd ed. LC 94-11410. (Camper's Guides Ser.). 160p. 1994. pap. 15.95 (*0-88415-180-8*, 5180) Gulf Pub.

— Camper's Guide to Indiana & Ohio Parks, Lakes, & Forests: Where to Go & to Get There. LC 92-31304. (Camper's Guides Ser.). 160p. 1993. pap. 15.95 (*0-87201-223-9*, 1223) Gulf Pub.

— Camper's Guide to Northern California Parks, Lakes, Forests & Beaches, Vol. 1. 2nd ed. LC 96-40263. (Camper's Guide Ser.). (Illus.). 180p. 1997. pap. 18.95 (*0-88415-245-6*, 5245) Gulf Pub.

— Camper's Guide to Southern California Parks, Lakes, Forests, & Beaches, Vol. 2. 2nd ed. LC 97-1214. (Camper's Guide Ser.). (Illus.). 184p. 1997. pap. 18.95 (*0-88415-246-4*, 5246) Gulf Pub.

— Camper's Guide to Texas Parks, Lakes, & Forests. 4th rev. ed. LC 98-13471. (Camper's Guide Ser.). 216p. 1998. pap. 18.95 (*0-88415-248-0*, 5248) Gulf Pub.

Little, Mickey & Morava, Lillian B. Camper's Guide to U. S. National Parks: East of the Rockies, Vol. 2. (Camper's Guide Ser.). 162p. 1994. pap. 18.95 (*0-88415-064-X*, 5064) Gulf Pub.

Little, Mickey, jt. auth. see Morava, Lillian B.

Little, Mildred J. Camper's Guide to Delaware, Maryland, Virginia, & West Virginia Parks, Lakes, & Forests. (Camper's Guide Ser.). (Illus.). 192p. 1996. pap. 17.95 (*0-88415-028-3*, 5028) Gulf Pub.

— Hiking & Backpacking Trails of Texas. 5th ed. LC 98-51177. 220p. 1999. 18.95 (*0-88415-325-8*) Gulf Pub.

Little, Miles. Humane Medicine. (Illus.). 207p. (C). 1995. pap. text 17.95 (*0-521-49863-5*) Cambridge U Pr.

— Humane Medicine: A Leading Surgeon Examines What Doctors Do, What Patients Expect of Them, & How the Expectations of Both Are Not Being Met. (Illus.). 207p. (C). 1995. text 49.95 (*0-521-49513-X*) Cambridge U Pr.

Little, Mindy M. Spellbound, a Musical Play on Words. 60p. (J). (gr. 1 up). 1999. pap. 5.50 (*0-87129-893-7*, SD3) Dramatic Pub.

Little Moorings Staff. Daniel & the Lions. LC 96-221707. 1996. 5.99 (*0-679-87745-2*) Random.

— David & Goliath. LC 97-119002. 1996. 5.99 (*0-679-87746-0*) Random.

— In the Beginning. (J). 1996. 4.99 (*0-679-87540-9*, Pub. by Random Bks Yng Read) Random.

— Jonah & the Whale. LC 97-119001. 1996. 5.99 (*0-679-87747-9*) Random.

— Noah & the Ark. LC 96-221710. 1996. 5.99 (*0-679-87748-7*) Random.

— Old Testament Read-Along Video. 1995. 9.99 incl. VHS (*0-679-87639-1*) Random.

Little, Nanci. First Resort. LC 98-71170. 323p. 1998. pap. 11.00 (*1-887237-01-1*) Odd Girls Pr.

Little, Nina F. Early Years of the McLean Hospital, Recorded in the Journal of George William Folsom, Apothecary at the Asylum in Charlestown. LC 72-181085. (Countway Library Associates Historical Publication Ser.: No. 1). (Illus.). 176p. 1972. 9.95 (*0-686-05704-X*) F A Countway.

— Little by Little: Six Decades of Collecting American Decorative Arts. LC 97-62560. (Illus.). 308p. 1998. pap. 35.00 (*0-87451-866-0*) U Pr of New Eng.

Little, Nina F., jt. auth. see Cummings, Abbott L.

Little, Nina F., jt. ed. see Smith, Philip C.

***Little, Nina Fletcher.** Country Arts in Early American Homes. LC 99-71082. (Illus.). 239p. 1999. reprint ed. pap. 17.95 (*1-58465-025-7*) U Pr of New Eng.

Little, Otis. State of Trade in the Northern Colonies Considered. LC 79-141124. (Research Library of Colonial Americana). 1972. reprint ed. 20.95 (*0-405-03336-2*) Ayer.

Little Oxford Staff. Little Oxford Bible. 1184p. 1997. 59.99 (*0-19-110147-8*) OUP.

***Little Oxford Staff.** Little Oxford Bible. 1999. 24.99 (*0-19-112476-1*) OUP.

***Little, Pat.** Penn State Then & Now. (Illus.). 192p. 1999. 30.00 (*0-9670580-0-7*) Pa St U Pr.

Little, Pat. Simone Weil. LC 87-37397. (Women's Ser.). 170p. 1989. pap. 14.50 (*0-85496-347-2*) Berg Pubs.

Little, Patrick, jt. auth. see Dym, Clive L.

Little, Paul. All the Way. 2nd ed. (Orig.). 1997. reprint ed. mass mkt. 6.95 (*1-56333-509-3*) Masquerade.

— The Best of Paul Little. 1996. mass mkt. 6.50 (*1-56333-469-0*) Masquerade.

— Captive Maidens. 3rd ed. 1996. mass mkt. 5.95 (*1-56333-440-2*) Masquerade.

— Chinese Justice. 1998. mass mkt. 6.95 (*1-56333-596-4*) Masquerade.

— Double Novel: The Metamorphosis of Lisette Joyaux. 3rd ed. Date not set. reprint ed. mass mkt. 7.95 (*1-56333-647-2*) Masquerade.

— Fit for a King/Beginner's Lust. (Orig.). 1997. pap. 8.95 (*1-56333-571-9*) Masquerade.

— How to Give Away Your Faith. rev. ed. LC 88-12809. (Illus.). 192p. 1988. pap. 10.99 (*0-8308-1217-2*, 1217) InterVarsity.

— Lust of the Cossacks. 2nd ed. 1998. reprint ed. mass mkt. 6.95 (*1-56333-664-2*) Masquerade.

— Passion in Rio. 2nd ed. 1998. reprint ed. mass mkt. 6.95 (*1-56333-663-4*) Masquerade.

— The Prisoner. 2nd ed. 1995. mass mkt. 5.95 (*1-56333-330-9*) Masquerade.

— Roomate's Secret. 1997. pap. 8.95 (*1-56333-557-3*) Masquerade.

— Sentenced to Servitude. (Orig.). 1997. pap. 9.95 (*1-56333-565-4*) Masquerade.

— Slave Island. 3rd ed. 1998. reprint ed. mass mkt. 6.95 (*1-56333-655-3*) Masquerade.

— Tears of the Inquisition. 2nd ed. (Orig.). 1998. reprint ed. mass mkt. 6.95 (*1-56333-612-X*) Masquerade.

— Tutored in Lust. 3rd ed. (Orig.). 1997. reprint ed. mass mkt. 6.95 (*1-56333-547-6*) Masquerade.

Little, Paul & Little, Marie. Know Why You Believe. 3rd ed. LC 88-12810. 168p. 1988. pap. 8.99 (*0-8308-1218-0*, 1218) InterVarsity.

Little, Paul E. Affirming the Will of God - Chinese Edition. Chen, Y. P., tr. (CHI.). 42p. 1988. pap. 1.50 (*1-56582-074-6*) Christ Renew Min.

— The Answer to Life. LC 86-72378. Orig. Title: Faith is for People. 96p. 1987. reprint ed. pap. 6.99 (*0-89107-429-5*) Crossway Bks.

— Certainty: Know Why You Believe. (Christian Basics Bible Studies). 64p. (Orig.). 1996. pap., wbk. ed. 4.99 (*0-8308-2013-2*, 2013) InterVarsity.

— Know What You Believe. expanded ed. LC 98-43448. 1999. pap. text 9.99 (*1-56476-755-8*, Victor Bks) Chariot Victor.

***Little, Paul E.** Know Why You Believe: Updated & Expanded Ed. LC 98-53688. 1999. pap. text 9.99 (*1-56476-754-X*, Chariot Bks) Chariot Victor.

Little, Paul E. Witnessing: How to Give Away Your Faith. (Christian Basics Bible Studies). 64p. (Orig.). 1996. pap., wbk. ed. 4.99 (*0-8308-2012-4*, 2012) InterVarsity.

***Little, Paul E. & Little, Marie.** Know Why You Believe. 2nd rev. ed. LC 99-59908. 189p. 2000. pap. 9.99 (*0-8308-2250-X*) InterVarsity.

***Little, Peter.** Britain at a Glimpse, 2001. (Illus.). 120p. 2000. pap. 18.95 (*1-901449-11-4*, Pub. by P Little Pub) Irish Bks Media.

— Ireland at a Glimpse, 2001. rev. ed. (Illus.). 120p. 2000. pap. 14.95 (*1-901449-10-6*, Pub. by P Little Pub) Irish Bks Media.

Little, Peter. The Law of Company Takeovers. 569p. 1997. pap. 100.00 (*0-455-21458-1*, Pub. by LawBk Co) Gaunt.

Little, Peter D. & Watts, Michael, eds. Living under Contract: Contract Farming & Agrarian Transformation in Sub-Saharan Africa. LC 93-6315. 288p. 1994. 68.95 (*0-299-14060-1*); pap. 27.95 (*0-299-14064-4*) U of Wis Pr.

Little, Phil, jt. auth. see Long, Harold.

***Little, Portia M.** Recipes, Roses & Rhyme: A Collection of Loverly Recipes. (Illus.). 89p. 1999. mass mkt. 6.95 (*0-9663066-0-0*) Panntree Pr.

Little, R. A. Injury in the Young. Platt, M. P., ed. LC 97-11815. (Illus.). 330p. (C). 1998. text 95.00 (*0-521-48117-1*) Cambridge U Pr.

Little, R. Daniel & Weinberg, Norman L., eds. Electroorganic Synthesis: Fetschrift for Manuel M. Baizer. (Illus.). 472p. 1991. text 225.00 (*0-8247-8584-3*) Dekker.

Little, R. E. & Ekvall, J. C., eds. Statistical Analysis of Fatigue Data - STP 744. 151p. 1981. 16.50 (*0-8031-0716-1*, STP744) ASTM.

Little, R. John, ed. Madrono: A West American Journal of Botany, an Eighty Year Index Vols. 1-43, 1916-1996: A Publication of the California Botanical Society. LC 97-62196. 202p. (Orig.). 1997. pap. 45.00 (*0-9661882-0-9*) Sycamore CA.

Little, R. Pat. Web Design for Health Professionals. (Informatics Ser.: No. 2). (Illus.). 1999. pap. 15.00 (*1-893549-12-7*) Biomed Genl.

Little, Randall D., rev. Economics: Applications to Agriculture & Agribusiness. 4th ed. LC 96-75234. 574p. 1997. text 58.75 (*0-8134-2949-8*, 2949) Interstate.

Little, Reg & Reed, Warren, eds. The Confucian Renaissance. 110p. (C). 1990. text 20.00 (*1-86287-007-1*, Pub. by Federation Pr) Gaunt.

Little, Rhodes. Fidelity: Understanding Wall Street. 1991. 2.20 (*0-8306-5327-9*) McGraw-Hill Prof.

Little, Richard & Smith, Michael, eds. Perspectives on World Politics. 2nd ed. LC 90-44301. 496p. (C). 1991. pap. 27.99 (*0-415-05624-1*, A5502) Routledge.

Little, Richard, jt. auth. see Buzan, Barry.

Little, Richard, ed. see White, Brian.

Little, Richard G., ed. see National Research Council Staff.

Little, Richard L. Diesel Mechanics: An Introduction. (Automotive Technology Ser.). 1982. pap. 37.95 (*0-8273-3906-2*) Delmar.

***Little, Rob, et al.** Gamebirds of Southern Africa. 2000. 49.95 (*1-86872-318-6*, Pub. by Struik Pubs) BHB Intl.

Little, Robert, jt. auth. see Eckert, Kenneth.

Little, Robert D., jt. auth. see Kim, Choong H.

Little, Robert E. Tables for Estimating Median Fatigue Limits. LC 80-69062. (ASTM Special Technical Publication: No. 731). 184p. reprint ed. pap. 57.10 (*0-8357-5555-X*, 203518500093) Bks Demand.

Little, Robert L., jt. ed. see Crumbley, Joseph.

Little, Robert W. Elasticity. LC 72-13136. (Civil Engineering & Engineering Mechanics Ser.). xvi, 431p. 1973. 55.01 (*0-13-246884-0*) P-H.

Little, Roderick. Statistical Analysis with Missing Data. 9th ed. LC 86-19075. 304p. 1987. 99.95 (*0-471-80254-9*) Wiley.

Little, Roderick A., jt. ed. see Horan, Michael A.

Little, Roger. The Shaping of Modern French Poetry: Reflections on Unrhymed Poetic Form, 1840-1990. 144p. 1996. pap. 18.95 incl. Apple II (*0-614-09904-8*, Pub. by Carcanet Pr); pap. 18.95 (*1-85754-189-8*, Pub. by Carcanet Pr) Paul & Co Pubs.

Little, Roger, jt. auth. see Bosquet, Alain.

Little, Roger, jt. auth. see Devlin, Denis.

Little, Roger, jt. auth. see Gaspar, Lorand.

Little, Roger, ed. see De Duras, Madame.

Little, Roger, ed. see De Saint-Lambert, Jean-Francois.

Little, Roger, ed. see De Saint-Pierre, Bernardin.

Little, Roger, ed. see Perse, Saint-John, pseud.

Little, Rosemarie, jt. auth. see Grey, Paul.

Little, Ruth. Food for Thought: A Potpourri of Delicious Recipes. LC 89-85755. (Illus.). 224p. 1990. lib. bdg. 15.95 (*0-9624294-4-9*) Brack Pubns.

— The Heart That Gives Gathers. (Illus.). 16p. 1994. 10.95 (*0-9624294-5-7*) R Little.

— Old Lamps & New: Restoring & Decorating. LC 64-17394. (Illus.). 1964. 15.00 (*0-9624294-2-2*) R Little.

— Painting China for Pleasure & Profit. (Illus.). 290p. 1962. 20.00 (*0-9624294-1-4*) R Little.

Little Simon Staff. Crossword Puzzle Adventures. (Activity Bks.). (J). (gr. 4-7). 1987. pap. 1.99 (*0-671-64356-8*) Litle Simon.

Little Simon Staff, ed. A Little ABC Book. (Chubby Board Bks.). 16p. (J). 1980. pap. 3.50 (*0-671-41342-2*) Litle Simon.

Little, Smith. Studying for Chemistry. LC 94-37734. (Studying for Ser.). (Illus.). 192p. (C). 1995. pap. text 16.88 (*0-06-500651-8*) Addson-Wesley Educ.

***Little, Soutas.** Engineering Mechanics: Dynamic & Mathematica Manual Package. 1999. 86.00 (*0-13-011371-9*) P-H.

Little, Stephen. Realm of the Immortals: Daoism in the Arts of China. LC 87-35473. 76p. 1988. 14.95 (*0-910386-92-7*) Cleveland Mus Art.

— Spirit Stones of China. 112p. 1999. 29.95 (*0-520-22045-5*, Pub. by U CA Pr) Cal Prin Full Svc.

— Spirit Stones of China: The Ian & Susan Wilson Collection of Chinese Stones, Paintings & Related Scholars Objects. LC 98-74881. (Illus.). 112p. 1999. pap., boxed set 29.95 (*0-86559-173-3*) Art Inst Chi.

— Visions of the Dharma: Japanese Buddhist Paintings & Prints in the Honolulu Academy of Arts. (Illus.). 200p. (Orig.). (C). 1991. pap. 17.50 (*0-937426-14-8*) Honolu Arts.

***Little, Stephen & Shipper, Kristofer.** Taoism & the Arts of China. (Illus.). 352p. 2000. pap. 39.95 (*0-520-22785-9*) U CA Pr.

***Little, Stephen, et al.** Taoism & the Arts of China. (Illus.). 352p. 2000. 60.00 (*0-520-22784-0*) U CA Pr.

Little, Stephen, jt. auth. see Pal, Pratapaditya.

***Little, Steve.** Samba Unleashed. (Unleashed Ser.). (Illus.). 900p. 2000. pap. 49.99 (*0-672-31862-8*, Waite Grp Pr) Sams.

An Asterisk (*) at the beginning of an entry indicates that the title is appearing for the first time.

L

Little, Stuart. After the Fact. 1975. 15.95 (*0-405-06661-9*) Ayer.

Little, Stuart W., jt. auth. see Cantor, Arthur.

Little, Susan N., et al. Predicting Duff Consumption from Prescribed Burns on Conifer Clearcuts in Western Oregon & Western Washington. (Illus.). 38p. 1998. reprint ed. pap. 8.40 (*0-89904-934-6*, Ecosytems Resrch) Crumb Elbow Pub.

Little, T. A. Handbook of Designed Experiments for Engineers. (Statistics Ser.: Vol. 807). Date not set. write for info. (*0-8247-9076-6*) Dekker.

Little, T. E. The Fantasts: Studies in J. R. R. Tolkien, Lewis Carroll, Mervyn Peake, Nikolay Gogol & Kenneth Grahame. LC 84-181608. viii, 136 p. 1984. write for info. (*0-86127-212-9*) Avebury.

Little, T. E., ed. Pushkin: The Bronze Horseman. (Bristol Russian Texts Ser.). (RUS.). 80p. (C). 1991. reprint ed. pap. 16.95 (*1-85399-245-3*, Pub. by Brist Class Pr) Focus Pub-R Pullins.

Little, T. M. Agricultural Experimentation Design & Analysis: Design & Analysis. Hills, F. J., ed. 368p. (C). 1978. pap. 87.95 (*0-471-02352-3*) Wiley.

***Little, T. Vance.** When Cotton Was King on Concord Road: A History of Brentwood Subdivisions. (Illus.). 120p. 1999. pap. 15.00 (*0-9671974-0-6*) T V Little.

Little, T. W., jt. ed. see Ellis, W. A.

Little, Thomas, ed. Psychedelics Reimagined. 256p. 1999. pap. 14.00 (*1-57027-065-1*) Autonomedia.

Little, Thomas & Gusella, Riccardo, eds. Network & Operating System Support for Digital Audio & Video: Proceedings, 5th International Workshop, NOSSDAV '95, Durham, New Hampshire, April 19-21, 1995. LC 95-47131. (Lecture Notes in Computer Science Ser.: No. 1018). 357p. 1995. 62.00 (*3-540-60647-5*) Spr-Verlag.

Little, Todd D., et al, eds. Modeling Longitudinal & Multiple-Group Data: Practical Issues, Applied Approaches & Specific Examples. LC 99-52417. 300p. 1999. 65.00 (*0-8058-3054-5*) L Erlbaum Assocs.

Little, Tony. Technique! Target Training for a Fat-Free Body. 240p. 1994. mass mkt. 13.99 (*0-446-67072-3*, Pub. by Warner Bks) Little.

Little, Viv, jt. ed. see Mortimore, Peter.

Little, W. A. Conductivity & Magnetism: The Legacy of Felix Bloch. 176p. (C). 1990. text 74.00 (*981-02-0194-X*) World Scientific Pub.

Little, W. A., jt. ed. see Kresin, Vladimir Z.

Little-Walker, Roma. A Cousin's View of Adelle Moss McCall. 92p. 1998. pap. 12.50 (*1-57502-839-5*, PO2304) Morris Pubng.

Little, Wallace H. & Goodman, Charles. Tiger Sharks! (Illus.). 246p. 1987. pap. 17.95 (*0-916693-08-2*) Castle Bks.

Little, Wallace H., ed. see Chennault, Max, et al.

Little, Wayne A. Shared Expectations: Sustaining Customer Relationships. LC 95-12450. (Management Master Ser.). (Illus.). 64p. 1995. 15.95 (*1-56327-149-4*) Productivity Inc.

— Shared Expectations: Sustaining Customer Relationships. LC 95-12450. (Management Master Ser.). (Illus.). 88p. 1996. pap. 12.95 (*1-56327-096-X*) Productivity Inc.

Little, William. The History of Wannen, a Mountain Hamlet Located among the White Hills of New Hampshire. (Illus.). iii, 592p. 1993. reprint ed. pap. text 35.00 (*1-55613-774-5*) Heritage Bk.

— History of Warren, a Mountain Hamlet Located among the White Hills of New Hampshire. (Illus.). 594p. 1995. reprint ed. lib. bdg. 59.50 (*0-8328-4611-2*) Higginson Bk Co.

— The History of Weare, New Hampshire, 1735-1888. (Illus.). 1064p. 1988. reprint ed. lib. bdg. 106.00 (*0-8328-0079-1*, NH0048) Higginson Bk Co.

Little, William T., tr. Garci Rodriguez de Montalvo, The Labors of the Very Brave Knight Esplandian. (Medieval & Renaissance Texts & Studies: Vol. 92). 584p. 1992. 40.00 (*0-86698-106-3*, MR92) MRTS.

***Little, Windee A.** Reminiscent: A Pictorial History of Eatonton/Putnam County, Georgia. LC 99-51821. 1999. write for info. (*1-57864-085-7*) Donning Co.

Littlebird, Harold. On Mountains' Breath. (Illus.). 72p. 1982. pap. 6.00 (*0-940510-03-0*) Tooth of Time.

Littlebury, F. E. & Praeger, D. K. Invisible Combat - C3CM: A Guide for the Tactical Commander. LC 86-28853. (AIP Monograph Ser.: Vol. II). (Illus.). 90p. (Orig.). 1986. pap. text 8.95 (*0-916159-11-6*) AFCEA Intl Pr.

Littlebury, Isaac, tr. see Herodotus.

Littlechild, George. This Land Is My Land. LC 93-12932. (Illus.). 32p. (YA). (gr. 1 up). 1993. 16.95 (*0-89239-119-7*) Childrens Book Pr.

Littlechild, George, frwd. We Are All Related: A Celebration of Our Cultural Heritage. (Illus.). 57p. (Orig.). (J). (gr. 4-7). 1997. pap. 15.95 (*0-9680479-0-4*) Polstar Bk.

Littlechild, Michael. Chemicals, Vol. I-5. (Single Market Review Ser.). 1998. 80.00 (*0-7494-2309-9*) Kogan Page Ltd.

Littlechild, Stephen C., ed. Austrian Economics, 3 vols., Set. (Schools of Thought in Economics Ser.: No. 10). (Illus.). 1456p. 1990. text 560.00 (*1-85278-120-3*) E Elgar.

Littledale, A., tr. see Von Balthasar, Hans U.

Littledale, Freya. The Elves & the Shoemaker. LC 75-12500. 32p. (J). (ps-3). 1991. pap. 4.95 (*0-590-44855-2*, Blue Ribbon Bks.) Scholastic Inc.

— The Elves & the Shoemaker. (Blue Ribbon Bks.). (J). 1975. 10.15 (*0-606-03776-4*, Pub. by Turtleback) Demco.

— The Magic Fish. LC 86-189345. (Easy-to-Read Folktales Ser.). (Illus.). 32p. (J). (ps-3). 1986. pap. 2.99 (*0-590-41100-4*) Scholastic Inc.

— The Magic Fish. (Easy-to-Read Folktale Ser.). (J). 1985. 8.19 (*0-606-01145-5*, Pub. by Turtleback) Demco.

— Stories of Ghosts, Witches, & Demons. 80p. (J). (gr. 4-7). 1992. pap. 2.95 (*0-590-45556-7*) Scholastic Inc.

— Stories of Ghosts, Witches, & Demons. (J). 1971. 8.15 (*0-606-01953-7*, Pub. by Turtleback) Demco.

Littledale, Harold. Essays on Lord Tennyson's Idylls of the King. 1977. lib. bdg. 59.95 (*0-8490-1786-6*) Gordon Pr.

Littledale, Richard F. Offices from the Service Books of the Holy Eastern Church. LC 77-133819. 1970. reprint ed. 42.50 (*0-404-03996-0*) AMS Pr.

Littledog, Pat. In Search of the Holy Mother of Jobs. LC 91-61487. 128p. 1991. pap. 9.95 (*0-938317-15-6*) Cinco Puntos.

***Littledyke, Michael.** Science Knowledge & the Environment: A Guide for Students & Teachers in Primary Education. 2000. pap. 28.95 (*1-85346-625-5*) David Fulton.

***Littledyke, Michael & Huxford, Laura.** Teaching the Primary Curriculum for Constructive Learning LC 98-214574. x, 198p. 1998. 24.95 (*1-85346-515-1*) Taylor & Francis.

Littlefield, Alice & Gates, Hill, eds. Marxist Approaches in Economic Anthropology. (Monographs in Economic Anthropology: No. 9). 280p. 1991. 50.00 (*0-8191-7926-4*) U Pr of Amer.

Littlefield, Alice & Knack, Martha C., eds. Native Americans & Wage Labor: Ethnohistorical Perspectives. LC 95-31899. (Illus.). 368p. 1996. 32.95 (*0-8061-2816-X*) U of Okla Pr.

***Littlefield, Bill.** Baseball Days: From the Sandlots to the Show. rev. ed. (Illus.). 118p. 2000. pap. 22.95 (*0-9666776-2-5*, Pub. by Pond Press) Consort Bk Sales.

Littlefield, Bill. Champions: Stories of Ten Remarkable Athletes. (J). 1998. 15.05 (*0-606-13262-7*, Pub. by Turtleback) Demco.

— Champions: Stories of Ten Remarkable Athletes. large type ed. 1995. 37.50 (*0-614-09545-X*, L-81858-00) Am Printing Hse.

— Chapions: Stories of Ten Remarkable Athletes. (Illus.). 144p. (J). (gr. 3 up). 1998. pap. 10.95 (*0-316-55849-4*) Little.

— Keepers: Radio Stories from "Only a Game" & Elsewhere. LC 97-80875. 248p. 1998. 23.00 (*1-883684-18-8*) Peninsula MA.

Littlefield, Bill, ed. The Best American Sports Writing, 1998. (Best American Sports Writing Ser). 320p. 1998. pap. 13.00 (*0-395-79764-0*) HM.

Littlefield, Bruce, jt. auth. see Hanselman, Duane C.

Littlefield, Bruce C., jt. auth. see Hanselman, Duane C.

Littlefield, Carroll D. Birds of Malheur National Wildlife Refuge, Oregon. LC 89-77930. (Illus.). 304p. 1990. pap. 18.95 (*0-87071-361-2*); text 29.95 (*0-87071-360-4*) Oreg St U Pr.

Littlefield, Charles W. Man, Minerals, & Masters. (Illus.). 172p. 1980. pap. 9.50 (*0-89540-059-6*, SB-059) Sun Pub.

— Man, Minerals, & Masters. (Illus.). 175p. 1996. reprint ed. pap. 9.00 (*1-56459-571-4*) Kessinger Pub.

Littlefield, Daniel. Revolutionary Citizens: African Americans, 1776-1804. (The Young Oxford History of African Americans Ser.). (YA). (gr. 12 up). 1997. 21.00 (*0-614-25377-2*) OUP.

Littlefield, Daniel, ed. see La Flesche, Francis.

Littlefield, Daniel C. Rice & Slaves: Ethnicity & the Slave Trade in Colonial South Carolina. (Blacks in the New World Ser.). 216p. 1991. pap. text 12.95 (*0-252-06214-0*) U of Ill Pr.

— Rice & the Making of South Carolina: An Introductory Essay. LC 95-622446. 40p. 1995. pap. 5.00 (*1-880067-29-3*) SC Dept of Arch & Hist.

Littlefield, Daniel F., Jr. Africans & Creeks: From the Colonial Period to the Civil War, 47. LC 78-75238. (Contributions in Afro-American & African Studies: No. 47). (Illus.). 286p. 1979. 55.00 (*0-313-20703-8*, LAF/, Greenwood Pr) Greenwood.

— Africans & Seminoles: From Removal to Emancipation, 32. LC 77-86. (Contributions in Afro-American & African Studies: No. 32). 278p. 1977. 49.95 (*0-8371-9529-2*, LAS/, Greenwood Pr) Greenwood.

— Alex Posey: Creek Poet, Journalist, & Humorist. LC 91-14538. (American Indian Lives Ser.). (Illus.). x, 330p. 1992. pap. 16.95 (*0-8032-7968-X*, Bison Books) U of Nebr Pr.

— Alex Posey: Creek Poet, Journalist, & Humorist. LC 91-14538. (American Indian Lives Ser.). (Illus.). x, 330p. 1992. text 55.00 (*0-8032-2899-6*) U of Nebr Pr.

— The Cherokee Freedmen: From Emancipation to American Citizenship, 40. LC 78-53659. (Contributions in Afro-American & African Studies: No. 40). 281p. 1978. 59.95 (*0-313-20413-6*, LCH/, Greenwood Pr) Greenwood.

— The Chickasaw Freedmen: A People Without a Country, 54. LC 79-6192. (Contributions in Afro-American & African Studies: No. 54). 248p. 1980. 59.95 (*0-313-22313-0*, LCF/, Greenwood Pr) Greenwood.

— Native American Writing in the Southeast: An Anthology, 1875-1935. LC 95-18038. 232p. 1995. 40.00 (*0-87805-827-3*); pap. 16.95 (*0-87805-828-1*) U Pr of Miss.

Littlefield, Daniel F., Jr., et al, eds. Selections from Walt Whitman & Emily Dickinson: Health Anthology of American Literature. 2nd ed. 212p. (C). 1990. pap. text 7.56 (*0-669-24998-X*) HM Trade Div.

Littlefield, Daniel F., Jr. & Parins, James W. American Indian & Alaska Native Newspapers & Periodicals, 1826-1924. LC 83-1483. (Historical Guides to the World's Periodicals & Newspapers Ser.). 482p. 1984. lib. bdg. 115.00 (*0-313-23426-4*, LNA/01) Greenwood.

— A Biobibliography of Native American Writers 1772-1924: A Supplement. LC 85-2045. (Native American Bibliography Ser.: No. 5). 350p. 1985. 35.00 (*0-8108-1802-7*) Scarecrow.

Littlefield, Daniel F., Jr. & Parins, James W., eds. American Indian & Alaska Native Newspapers & Periodicals, 1925-1970. LC 83-1483. (Historical Guides to the World's Periodicals & Newspapers Ser.). 577p. 1986. lib. bdg. 115.00 (*0-313-23427-2*, LNA/02) Greenwood.

— American Indian & Alaska Native Newspapers & Periodicals, 1971-1985. LC 83-1483. (Historical Guides to the World's Periodicals & Newspapers Ser.). 629p. 1986. lib. bdg. 115.00 (*0-313-24834-6*, LNA/03/) Greenwood.

Littlefield, Daniel F., Jr., ed. see Posey, Alexander.

Littlefield, Daniel L., Jr. Seminole Burning: A Story of Racial Vengeance. LC 96-16413. 240p. 1996. 26.00 (*0-87805-923-7*) U Pr of Miss.

Littlefield, Daniel R., Jr., ed. see Tubbee, Okah.

***Littlefield, Holly.** Children of the Indian Boarding Schools. LC 00-9456. (Picture the American Past Ser.). 2001. lib. bdg. write for info. (*1-57505-467-1*, Carolrhoda) Lerner Pub.

Littlefield, Holly. Children of the Trail West. LC 98-29732. (Picture the American Past Ser.). 48p. (J). (gr. 3-6). 1999. 22.60 (*1-57505-304-7*, Carolrhoda) Lerner Pub.

— Colors of Germany. LC 96-29457. (Colors of the World Ser.). (J). (gr. 2-5). 1997. 19.93 (*0-87614-887-9*, Lerner Publctns) Lerner Pub.

— Colors of Germany. LC 96-29457. (Colors of the World Ser.). (Illus.). 24p. (J). (gr. 2-5). 1997. pap. 5.95 (*1-57505-214-8*, Carolrhoda) Lerner Pub.

***Littlefield, Holly.** Colors of Ghana. LC 98-49496. (Colors of the World Ser.). 24p. (J). (gr. 1-4). 1999. pap. 5.95 (*1-57505-374-8*, Carolrhoda) Lerner Pub.

Littlefield, Holly. Colors of Ghana. LC 98-49496. (Colors of the World Ser.). 24p. (J). (gr. 1-4). 1999. 19.93 (*1-57505-354-3*, Carolrhoda) Lerner Pub.

***Littlefield, Holly.** Colors of India. (Colors of the World Ser.). (Illus.). 24p. (J). (gr. 1-4). 1999. pap. 5.95 (*1-57505-368-3*, Carolrhoda) Lerner Pub.

Littlefield, Holly. Colors of India. LC 98-30079. (Illus.). 24p. (J). (gr. 1-4). 1999. 22.60 (*1-57505-344-6*, Carolrhoda) Lerner Pub.

— Colors of Japan. LC 96-44297. (Colors of the World Ser.). (Illus.). 24p. (J). (gr. 3-4). 1997. 14.95 (*0-87614-885-2*, Carolrhoda) Lerner Pub.

— Colors of Japan. (Colors of the World Ser.). (Illus.). 24p. (J). (gr. k-3). 1997. pap. text 5.95 (*1-57505-215-6*, Carolrhoda) Lerner Pub.

Littlefield, Holly. Fire at the Triangle Factory. (Illus.). 48p. (J). (gr. k-3). 1996. pap. 5.95 (*0-87614-970-0*, Carolrhoda) Lerner Pub.

Littlefield, Holly. Fire at the Triangle Factory. (Illus.). 48p. (J). (gr. k-3). 1996. lib. bdg. 18.60 (*0-87614-868-2*, Carolrhoda) Lerner Pub.

Littlefield Hoopes, Lyn. Condor Magic. (Illus.). 32p. (J). (gr. k-5). 1997. 12.95 (*1-882728-95-5*) Benefactory.

Littlefield Hoopes, Lyn, ed. Condor Magic. (Illus.). 32p. (J). (gr. k-5). 1997. pap. text 5.95 (*1-882728-96-3*) Benefactory.

Littlefield, John W., jt. auth. see Commonwealth Fund Staff.

Littlefield, Kathy M. & Littlefield, Robert S. Let's Debate! (Illus.). 36p. (Orig.). (J). (gr. 3-6). 1989. pap. text 8.95 (*1-879340-03-8*, K0104) Kidspeak.

— Let's Work Together! (Illus.). 32p. (Orig.). (J). (gr. 3-6). 1991. pap. text 8.95 (*1-879340-08-9*, K0109) Kidspeak.

— Read to Me! (Illus.). 28p. (Orig.). (J). (gr. 3-6). 1990. pap. text 8.95 (*1-879340-04-6*, K0105) Kidspeak.

— Speak Up! (Illus.). 32p. (Orig.). (J). (gr. 3-6). 1989. pap. text 8.95 (*1-879340-00-3*, K0101) Kidspeak.

— Tell Me a Story! (Illus.). 32p. (Orig.). (J). (gr. 3-6). 1989. pap. text 8.95 (*1-879340-02-X*, K0103) Kidspeak.

— What Did You Say? (Illus.). 32p. (Orig.). (J). (gr. 3-6). 1989. pap. text 8.95 (*1-879340-01-1*, K0102) Kidspeak.

— What's Your Point? (Illus.). 32p. (Orig.). (J). (gr. 3-6). 1990. pap. text 8.95 (*1-879340-05-4*, K0106) Kidspeak.

Littlefield, Keith E., jt. ed. see Jones, Richard H.

Littlefield, Kinney & Morgan, Kitty. Dine Orange County: The Orange County Register Guide to Great Eating. (Register Bookshelf Ser.). (Illus.). 128p. (Orig.). 1994. pap. text 1.37 (*0-9635868-9-0*) OC Register.

Littlefield, Mark G. A Bibliographic Index to Romance Philology, Vols. 1-25. LC 73-76118. 274p. reprint ed. pap. 85.00 (*0-8357-7167-9*, 203153700075) Bks Demand.

— Escorial Bible I.I.7. (Spanish Ser.: No. 111). 1996. 40.00 (*1-56954-049-7*) Hispanic Seminary.

Littlefield, Mark G., ed. Biblia Romanceada I.I.8: The Thirteenth-Century Spanish Bible Contained in Escorial MS. I. I. 8. (Dialect Ser.: No. 4). (Illus.). xiv, 334p. 1983. 35.00 (*0-942260-34-1*) Hispanic Seminary.

Littlefield, Mark G., jt. ed. see Hauptmann, Oliver H.

Littlefield, Natalie. Las Vegas Child Care Resource Guide: A-Z Childrens Directory. 168p. 1998. spiral bd. 10.95 (*0-9669726-0-0*) Child Care Connection.

Littlefield, Neil. Metropolitan Area Problems & Municipal Home Rule. LC 63-62226. (Michigan Legal Publications). vi, 83p. 1985. reprint ed. lib. bdg. 34.00 (*0-89941-383-8*, 303530) W S Hein.

Littlefield, Robert C. Free Enterprise: Creating a Marketplace in the Classroom. (Illus.). 1996. teacher ed., ring bd. 19.95 (*1-57091-145-2*) Charlesbridge Pub.

Littlefield, Robert S. Voices on the Prairie: Bringing Speech & Theatre to North Dakota. LC 98-71520. 367p. 1998. pap. 29.95 (*0-911042-50-4*) NDSU Inst Reg.

Littlefield, Robert S. & Ball, Jane A. The Teacher's Guide to Kidspeak. (Illus.). 24p. (C). 1991. pap. text 8.95 (*1-879340-09-7*, K0110) Kidspeak.

— Tell Me the Way It Was . . . (Illus.). 32p. (Orig.). (J). (gr. 3-6). 1990. pap. text 8.95 (*1-879340-07-0*, K0108) Kidspeak.

— Who Am I? Who Are They? (Illus.). 28p. (Orig.). (J). (gr. 3-6). 1990. pap. text 8.95 (*1-879340-06-2*, K0107) Kidspeak.

Littlefield, Robert S., jt. auth. see Littlefield, Kathy M.

Littlefield, S. Shane. Proclaim My Word: Insights to Inspire Confidence in Members & Missionaries. LC 95-61399. 140p. 1995. 9.95 (*0-9647847-1-8*) Timpanogos UT.

Littlefield, Susan, jt. auth. see Schinz, Marina.

Littlefield, Thomson, ed. see Robbins, Daniel.

Littlefield, Warren M. dBASE - From the Dot Prompt: An Introduction to Structured Programming Using dBASE IV. LC 93-18937. 591p. (C). 1993. pap. text 24.95 (*0-7914-1780-8*) State U NY Pr.

Littleford, Alan. Java Commerce & Security Programming. 1997. pap. text 39.99 (*1-57610-101-0*) Coriolis Grp.

Littlegreen, Inc. Think Tank Staff. Transfiguration Diet. LC 85-91090. (Illus.). 176p. (Orig.). 1986. pap. 7.95 (*0-936863-04-8*, Littlegreen) Chris Pub UT.

Littlehales, Bates, photos by. The Smithsonian Guides to Natural America: The Atlantic Coast & Blue Ridge-Maryland, Washington, D. C., Virginia, & North Carolina. LC 95-1486. (Illus.). 304p. 1995. pap. 19.95 (*0-679-76314-7*, Pub. by Smithsonian Bks) Random.

Littlehales, Henry, ed. English Fragments from Latin Medieval Service-Books. (EETS, ES Ser.: No. 90). 1972. reprint ed. pap. 25.00 (*0-527-00294-1*) Periodicals Srv.

— St. Mary at Hill Church: The Medieval Records of a London City Church A.D. 1420-1559, Set, Pts. 1 & 2. (EETS, OS Ser.: Nos. 125, 128). 1974. reprint ed. 80.00 (*0-527-00121-X*) Periodicals Srv.

Littlehales, Lillian. Pablo Casals. rev. ed. LC 72-97385. 232p. 1970. reprint ed. lib. bdg. 49.50 (*0-8371-3010-7*, LIPC, Greenwood Pr) Greenwood.

Littlejohn. Learing/Using Communication Theories. 6th ed. (Speech & Theater Ser.). 1998. pap. 15.75 (*0-534-54824-5*) Wadsworth Pub.

— Theories of Human Communication. 6th ed. LC 98-7919. (Speech & Theater Ser.). 1998. pap. 75.95 (*0-534-54819-9*) Wadsworth Pub.

***Littlejohn.** Theories of Human Communication. 7th ed. 2001. text 52.00 (*0-534-54957-8*) Thomson Learn.

Littlejohn, Alice C., jt. auth. see Womack, Carol L.

Littlejohn, Andrew & Hicks, Diana. Cambridge English for Schools Starter: Teacher's Book. 132p. 1997. pap. text, teacher ed. 16.95 (*0-521-56793-9*) Cambridge U Pr.

— Cambridge English for Schools Starter: Workbook. 72p. 1997. pap. text 7.95 (*0-521-56794-7*) Cambridge U Pr.

Littlejohn, Beth, ed. see Russell, Ching Y.

Littlejohn, Bruce. Littlejohn's Half Century at the Bench & Bar (1936-1986) (Illus.). 232p. 1987. 25.00 (*0-318-23731-8*) SC Bar Found.

— Littlejohn's Political Memoirs, 1934-1988. (Illus.). 244p. 1989. 1.95 (*0-9625077-0-9*) B Littlejohn.

— Littlejohn's Political Memoirs, 1934-1988. 256p. (C). 1990. 19.95 (*0-685-30008-0*) B Littlejohn.

Littlejohn, Bruce, jt. ed. see Beck, Gregor G.

***Littlejohn, Carolyn.** Keep Talking That Book! Vol. 2: Booktalks to Promote Reading. LC 00-23064. (Professional Growth Ser.: Vol. 2). 155p. 2000. pap. 36.95 (*0-938865-92-7*) Linworth Pub.

— Talk That Book: Booktalks to Promote Reading. 166p. 1999. pap. 36.95 (*0-938865-75-7*) Linworth Pub.

Littlejohn, D. & Thorburn, D., eds. Reviews on Analytical Chemistry: Euroanalysis VIII. 376p. 1994. 168.00 (*0-85186-982-3*, R6982) CRC Pr.

Littlejohn, David. The Fate of the English Country House. (Illus.). 360p. 1997. 30.00 (*0-19-508876-X*) OUP.

— The Hitler Youth. LC 87-73304. (Illus.). 377p. 1987. 35.00 (*0-934870-21-7*) Johnson Ref Bks.

— The SA 1921-45: Hitler's Stormtroopers. (Men-at-Arms Ser.: No. 220). (Illus.). 48p. 1990. pap. 11.95 (*0-85045-944-3*, 9177, Pub. by Ospry) Stackpole.

— The Ultimate Art: Essays Around & about Opera. 1992. 40.00 (*0-520-07608-7*, Pub. by U CA Pr) Cal Prin Full Svc.

— The Ultimate Art: Essays Around & about Opera. (Illus.). 320p. (C). 1994. pap. 16.95 (*0-520-07609-5*, Pub. by U CA Pr) Cal Prin Full Svc.

Littlejohn, David, ed. The Real Las Vegas: Life Beyond the Strip. LC 98-43830. (Illus.). 352p. 1999. 30.00 (*0-19-513070-7*) OUP.

Littlejohn, David, jt. auth. see Angolia, J. R.

Littlejohn, Duffy. Hopping Freight Trains in America. (Illus.), 372p. (Orig.). 1993. pap. 13.95 (*0-944627-34-X*) Sand River Pr.

Littlejohn, Frances J. The Duodenary System of Astrology. 1967. 14.00 (*0-86690-371-2*, L2241-074) Am Fed Astrologers.

Littlejohn, G. S., ed. Ground Anchorages & Anchored Structures. 644p. 1997. 165.00 (*0-7277-2607-2*, 2607, Pub. by T Telford) RCH.

Littlejohn, G. S., jt. ed. see Thorburn, S.

Littlejohn, Gary, jt. ed. see Cox, Terry.

Littlejohn, Geoffrey. Rheumatism: A Consumer's Guide. large type ed. (Illus.). 218p. 1992. 21.95 (*1-85695-005-0*, Pub. by ISIS Lrg Prnt) Transaction Pubs.

Littlejohn, Henry. Learning Enrichments: A Parent's & Teacher's Handbook. LC 96-70431. (Illus.). 192p. (Orig.). 1996. pap. 21.95 (*1-56167-337-4*) Noble Hse MD.

Littlejohn, M. J. & Ladiges, Pauline Y., eds. Ecological Gradients & Boundaries. 178p. (C). 1981. text 75.00 (*0-909436-04-5*, Pub. by Surrey Beatty & Sons) St Mut.

Littlejohn, Ronnie L. Ethics: Studying the Art of Moral Appraisal. LC 92-2481. 190p. (Orig.). (C). 1992. pap. text 22.50 (*0-8191-8918-9*) U Pr of Amer.

An Asterisk (*) at the beginning of an entry indicates that the title is appearing for the first time.

— Exploring Christian Theology. 542p. (Orig.). 1985. pap. text 34.00 (*0-8191-4460-6*); lib. bdg. 70.00 (*0-8191-4459-2*) U Pr of Amer.

Littlejohn, Stephen W. Theories of Human Communication. 2nd ed. 340p. (C). 1983. pap. write for info. (*0-534-01280-9*) Wadsworth Pub.

— Theories of Human Communication. 3rd ed. 315p. (C). 1988. pap. write for info. (*0-534-09534-8*) Wadsworth Pub.

— Theories of Human Communication. 4th ed. 417p. (C). 1992. pap. 45.95 (*0-534-16134-0*) Wadsworth Pub.

— Theories of Human Communication. 5th ed. LC 95-4224. 399p. 1995. pap. 48.00 (*0-534-26052-7*) Wadsworth Pub.

— Theories of Human Communication. 5th ed. (Speech & Theater Ser.). 1995. pap., student ed. 15.75 (*0-534-26054-3*) Wadsworth Pub.

***Littlejohn, Stephen W. & Domenici, Kathy.** Engaging Communication in Conflict: Systemic Practice. LC 00-9056. 2000. pap. write for info. (*0-7619-2187-7*) Sage.

Littlejohn, Stephen W., jt. auth. see Jabusch, David M.

Littlejohn, Stephen W., jt. auth. see Pearce, W. Barnett.

Littlejohns, Andrew & McGaivl, Stephen, eds. Aircraft Financing. 3rd ed. 477p. 1997. 215.00 (*1-85564-554-8*, Pub. by Euromoney) Am Educ Systs.

Littlejohns, Peter & Victor, Christina R. Making Sense of a Primary Care Led Health Service. LC 96-25406. 1996. write for info. (*1-85775-048-9*, Radcliffe Med Pr) Scovill Paterson.

Littlemeyer, Mary H., ed. see Conference on the Optimal Preparation for the Stud.

Littlepage, Dean. The Alaska Gold Rush: Gold Fever in the North, One Hundred Year Celebration. Ellington, Darcy & Tripp, Angela, eds. (Illus.). 32p. 1995. pap. 10.95 (*1-880352-39-7*) Albion Pub.

— Hiking Alaska. LC 96-53934. (Illus.). 400p. 1997. pap. 16.95 (*1-56044-551-3*) Falcon Pub Inc.

Littlepage, John D. & Bess, Demaree. In Search of Soviet Gold. LC 75-115558. (Russia Observed, Series I). 1970. reprint ed. 20.95 (*0-405-03044-4*) Ayer.

Littler, et al. How to Manage Your Contingent Workforce: Part-Timers, Temps, Leased Employees & Independent Contractors. LC 97-30716. 68p. 1997. spiral bd. 47.00 (*0-925773-40-9*) M Lee Smith.

Littler, C. R. Technology & the Organisation of Work. 1992. pap. 45.00 (*0-7300-1309-X*, Pub. by Deakin Univ) St Mut.

Littler, Craig R., jt. auth. see Fosh, Patricia.

Littler, D. J., ed. Thermal Stresses & Thermal Fatigue. LC 72-182668. (Proceedings of the International Conferences on Basement Tectonics Ser.). 586p. reprint ed. pap. 181.70 (*0-608-14722-2*, 205583100038) Bks Demand.

Littler, Dale & Lewis, Barbara R., eds. The Blackwell Encyclopedic Dictionary of Marketing. LC 96-32587. (Blackwell Encyclopedia of Management Ser.). (Illus.). 256p. 1997. 105.95 (*1-55786-939-1*) Blackwell Pubs.

Littler, Dale & Wilson, Dominic, eds. Marketing Reader. (Management Reader Ser.). 300p. 1995. pap. text 41.95 (*0-7506-0662-2*) Buttrwrth-Heinemann.

Littler, Dale, jt. ed. see Lewis, Barbara.

Littler, Diane S., et al. Marine Plants of the Caribbean: A Field Guide from Florida to Brazil. LC 88-43157. (Illus.). 272p. (C). 1989. pap. 24.95 (*0-87474-607-8*) Smithsonian.

Littler, Diane S., jt. ed. see Littler, Mark M.

Littler, J. G., jt. auth. see Hancock, C. J.

Littler, Jody. The Little Goat on the Roof. (Illus.). 32p. (J). (ps-3). 1998. pap. 8.95 (*1-57534-029-1*) Skandisk.

Littler, John & Thomas, Randall. Design with Energy: The Conservation & Use of Energy in Buildings. (Cambridge Urban & Architectural Studies: 8). (Illus.). 378p. 1984. text 115.00 (*0-521-24562-1*); pap. text 49.95 (*0-521-28787-1*) Cambridge U Pr.

Littler, Margaret. Alfred Andersch (1914-1980) & the Reception of French Thought in the Federal Republic of Germany. LC 91-26228. (Studies in German Language & Literature: Vol. 8). 390p. 1991. lib. bdg. 109.95 (*0-7734-9679-3*) E Mellen.

Littler, Mark M. & Littler, Diane S., eds. Handbook of Phycological Methods: Ecological Field Methods: Macroalgae. (Illus.). 631p. 1986. text 105.00 (*0-521-24915-5*) Cambridge U Pr.

Littler, Mendelson, Fastiff, Tichy & Mathiason Sta. An Employer's Guide to Employee Leave. LC 97-17750. 48p. 1997. spiral bd. 47.00 (*0-925773-38-7*) M Lee Smith.

Littler, Mendelson, Fastiff, Tichy & Mathiason Sta, et al. Bringing ADR into Workplace 2000. LC 97-25266. vi, 84 p. 1997. spiral bd. 47.00 (*0-925773-36-0*) M Lee Smith.

Littler, William A. Clinical Ambulatory Monitoring. (Illus.). 174p. 1981. 60.00 (*0-8151-5482-8*, ACT-1) Mosby Inc.

Littler, William A., et al. Illustrated Case Histories in Cardiovascular Medicine. LC 93-15158. 128p. (C). (gr. 13). 1994. pap. text 29.00 (*0-8151-5484-4*, 23043) Mosby Inc.

Littlesugar, Amy. Jonkonnu: A Story from the Sketchbook of Winslow Homer. LC 95-46637. (Illus.). 32p. (J). (ps-3). 1997. 15.95 (*0-399-22831-4*, Philomel) Peng Put Young Read.

— Marie in Fourth Position: The Story of Degas's "The Little Dancer" LC 95-40827. (Illus.). 32p. (J). (ps-3). 1996. 15.99 (*0-399-22794-6*, Philomel) Peng Put Young Read.

— Marie in Fourth Position: The Story of Degas's "The Little Dancer" (gr. k up). 1999. pap. 6.99 (*0-698-11769-7*, PapStar) Peng Put Young Read.

— A Portrait of Spotted Deer's Grandfather. LC 96-2704. (Illus.). 32p. (J). (gr. 2-7). 1997. lib. bdg. 15.95 (*0-8075-6622-5*) A Whitman.

— The Rag Baby. LC 96-8583. (J). 2000. mass mkt. 16.00 (*0-689-80183-1*) S&S Bks Yung.

— Shake Rag: From the Life of Elvis Presley. LC 97-9618. (Illus.). 40p. (J). (gr. 1-4). 1998. 16.99 (*0-399-23005-X*, Philomel) Peng Put Young Read.

— The Spinner's Daughter. (Illus.). 40p. (J). (gr. 1-4). 1994. lib. bdg. 14.95 (*0-945912-22-6*) Pippin Pr.

— Tree of Hope. LC 98-12853. (Illus.). 40p. (J). (gr. k-3). 1999. 16.99 (*0-399-23300-8*, Philomel) Peng Put Young Read.

***Littlesugar, Amy & Cooper, Floyd.** Freedom School, Yes! LC 99-49706. (Illus.). (J). 2001. 15.99 (*0-399-23006-8*) Peng Put Young Read.

***Littlesugar, Amy & Ginsburg, Max.** Lisette's Angel. LC 99-87549. 2001. write for info. (*0-8037-2435-7*) Peng Put Young Read.

Littleton. Maternal Child Nursing. (C). 2001. 50.50 (*0-7668-0121-7*) Delmar.

Littleton, Ananias C. Structure of Accounting Theory. (Monograph No. 5). 234p. 1953. 12.00 (*0-86539-026-6*) Am Accounting.

Littleton, Ananias C., et al, eds. Studies in the History of Accounting. LC 77-87275. (Development of Contemporary Accounting Thought Ser.). 1978. reprint ed. lib. bdg. 34.95 (*0-405-10903-2*) Ayer.

Littleton, Ananias C., jt. auth. see Paton, W. A.

Littleton, C. Scott, ed. The Sacred East: An Illustrated Guide to Buddhism, Hinduism, Confucianism, Taoism & Shinto. LC 99-62079. (Illus.). 176p. 1999. pap. text 17.95 (*1-56975-200-1*) Ulysses Pr.

Littleton, C. Scott & Malcor, Linda A. From Scythia to Camelot: A Radical Reassessment of the Legends of King Arthur, the Knights of the Round Table, & the Holy Grail. LC 94-8776. (Illus.). 440p. 1994. text 77.00 (*0-8153-1496-5*, H1795) Garland.

Littleton, C. Scott, ed. see Wilson, Blakely.

Littleton, Christine & Hembacher, Brian. EEO Update: Sexual Harassment. (Current Issues Ser.: No. 5). 48p. 1987. pap. 7.50 (*0-89215-142-0*) U Cal LA Indus Rel.

Littleton, Christine A. In Whose Name? Feminist Legal Theory & the Experience of Women. (New Perspectives on Law, Culture & Society Ser.). 256p. 1999. 60.00 (*0-8133-1160-8*); pap. 22.00 (*0-8133-1161-6*) Westview.

Littleton, J. T. & Durizch, M. L. Chest Atlas: Correlated Thin-Section Anatomy in Five Planes. LC 92-49474. 336p. 1993. 285.00 (*0-387-97928-X*); write for info. (*3-540-97928-X*) Spr-Verlag.

Littleton, Jeanette G., jt. auth. see Littleton, Mark.

Littleton, Jeanette Gardner, jt. auth. see Littleton, Mark R.

Littleton, Karen, et al, eds. Making Sense of Social Development. LC 98-25642. (Illus.). vi, 278p. (C). (gr. 13). 1999. pap. 22.99 (*0-415-17374-4*, D6390) Routledge.

Littleton, Karen & Light, Paul. Learning with Computers: Analysing Productive Interactions. LC 98-17805. (Illus.). 216p. (C). 1998. 85.00 (*0-415-14285-7*); pap. 25.99 (*0-415-14286-5*) Routledge.

Littleton, Karen, jt. auth. see Light, Paul.

Littleton, Lucy. Al Fresco in Athens: The Owl Bay Guide to Georgia Bulldog Tailgating. (Illus.). 128p. 1994. pap. 8.95 (*0-9638568-6-3*) Owl Bay Pubs.

— In the Grove at Oxford: The Owl Bay Guide to Ole Miss Tailgating. (Illus.). 128p. 1994. pap. 8.95 (*1-885623-05-4*) Owl Bay Pubs.

— Picnics on the Plains: The Owl Bay Guide to Auburn Tiger Tailgating. (Illus.). 128p. 1994. pap. 8.95 (*0-9638568-3-9*) Owl Bay Pubs.

— Rocky Top Saturdays: The Owl Bay Guide to Tennessee Volunteer Tailgating. (Illus.). 128p. 1994. pap. 8.95 (*0-9638568-7-1*) Owl Bay Pubs.

— South Bend Saturdays: A Recipe Guide to Notre Dame Tailgating. 1995. pap. 8.95 (*1-885623-06-2*) Owl Bay Pubs.

— Sunshine Sensations: The Owl Bay Guide to Florida Gator Tailgating. (Illus.). 128p. 1994. pap. 8.95 (*0-9638568-5-5*) Owl Bay Pubs.

— Tailgating at Texas: A Recipe Guide to Texas Longhorn Tailgating. (Illus.). 1995. pap. 8.95 (*1-885623-07-0*) Owl Bay Pubs.

— Tailgating in T-Town: The Owl Bay Guide to Crimson Tide Tailgating. (Illus.). 128p. 1994. pap. 8.95 (*0-9638568-4-7*) Owl Bay Pubs.

Littleton, Mark. The Abdominable Snowbeast. (Get a Clue Mysteries Puzzles Ser.). 16p. (J). (gr. 4-7). 1997. 12.99 (*0-7847-0732-4*, 04112) Standard Pub.

— Aliens among Us. (Get a Clue Mysteries Puzzles Ser.). 16p. (J). (gr. 5-9). 1997. 12.99 (*0-7847-0733-2*, 04113) Standard Pub.

— Baseball, Vol. 1. (Sports Heroes Ser.). 112p. 1995. pap. 4.99 (*0-310-49551-2*) Zondervan.

Littleton, Mark. Baseball 2, Vol. 2. 2nd ed. (Sports Heroes Ser.). 112p. 1996. pap. 4.99 (*0-310-20263-9*) Zondervan.

Littleton, Mark. The Basics: Nailing down What Builds You Up. LC 93-74751. (Illus.). 200p. 1994. pap. 9.99 (*0-87509-549-6*) Chr Pubns.

— Basketball, Vol. 1. (Sports Heroes Ser.). 112p. 1995. pap. 4.99 (*0-310-49561-X*) Zondervan.

Littleton, Mark. Basketball 2, Vol. 2. 2nd ed. (Sports Heroes Ser.). 112p. (J). (gr. 3-7). 1996. pap. 4.99 (*0-310-20265-5*) Zondervan.

— Jesus: Everything You Need to Know to Figure Him Out. 224p. 2000. pap. 16.95 (*0-664-22245-5*) Westminster John Knox.

— NIrV Kids' Books of Devotions: A 365-Day Adventure in God's Word. LC 98-22806. 208p. (J). 1998. pap. 9.99 (*0-310-22130-7*) Zondervan.

Littleton, Mark. The Phantom Custodian. (Get a Clue Mystery Puzzles Ser.). 16p. (J). (gr. 4-7). 1997. 12.99 (*0-7847-0731-6*, 04111) Standard Pub.

— Soccer. (Sports Heroes Ser.). 112p. 1996. pap. 4.99 (*0-310-20264-7*) Zondervan.

— Tree Fort Wars. LC 56-94101. 208p. (J). (gr. 4 up). 1993. pap. 5.99 (*1-55513-764-4*, Chariot Bks) Chariot Victor.

— When They Invited Me to Fellowship I Thought They Meant a Cruise. LC 92-81349. 166p. (Orig.). (YA). 1992. pap. 9.99 (*0-87509-496-1*) Chr Pubns.

Littleton, Mark & Littleton, Jeanette G. Light the Torch Pass the Flame: Lessons from Our Fathers. LC 98-2671. 44p. 1998. pap. 2.99 (*0-8341-1710-X*) Beacon Hill.

Littleton, Mark, jt. auth. see Minirth, Frank B.

Littleton, Mark, jt. auth. see Peterson, Steve.

Littleton, Mark R. Conversations with God the Father. LC 97-80891. 256p. 1998. 17.95 (*0-914984-19-5*) Starburst.

— God Is! LC 96-72293. (Illus.). 192p. 1997. 14.95 (*0-914984-92-6*) Starburst.

— Trouble down the Creek. Norton, LoraBeth, ed. 208p. (J). (gr. 4-6). 1994. pap. 5.99 (*0-7814-0082-1*, Chariot Bks) Chariot Victor.

Littleton, Mark R. & Littleton, Jeanette Gardner. What's in the Bible for... Teens: The Bible Made Easy! Richards, Larry, ed. (What's in the Bible for... Ser.). (Illus.). 352p. (J). (gr. 8-12). 2000. pap. 16.95 (*1-892016-05-2*) Starburst.

Littleton, Sue. Ranch on the Pecos: Microcosm U. S. A. (Illus.). 104p. pap. 13.95 (*0-911051-88-0*) Plain View.

Littleton, Taylor. Al Fresco in Ann Arbor: The Owl Bay Guide to Michigan Wolverines Tailgating. (Illus.). 128p. 1994. pap. text 8.95 (*1-885623-04-6*) Owl Bay Pubs.

— Happy Valley Saturdays: The Owl Bay Guide to Penn State Nittany Lions Tailgating. (Illus.). 128p. 1994. pap. 8.95 (*1-885623-01-1*) Owl Bay Pubs.

— Picnics in Paradise: The Owl Bay Guide to Miami Hurricanes Tailgating. (Illus.). 128p. 1994. pap. 8.95 (*1-885623-03-8*) Owl Bay Pubs.

Littleton, Taylor, ed. The Rights of Memory: Essays on History, Science, & American Culture. LC 85-13972. (Franklin Lectures in the Sciences & Humanities). (Illus.). 238p. 1986. pap. 73.80 (*0-608-05136-5*, 206569700005) Bks Demand.

***Littleton, Taylor D.** The Color of Silver: William Spratling: His Life & Art. LC 99-53775. (Southern Biography Ser.). (Illus.). 312p. 2000. 34.95 (*0-8071-2533-4*) La State U Pr.

Littleton, Thomas, jt. ed. see Wambaugh, Eugene.

Littleton, Wesley. Northern Pass Book. 88p. 1998. pap. 23.00 (*0-7487-2401-X*) St Mut.

Littlewood, ed. Pselli, Michaelis: Orationes Forenses et Acta. (GRE.). 1994. 75.00 (*3-8154-1667-1*, T1667, Pub. by B G Teubner) U of Mich Pr.

— Pselli, Michaelis: Oratoria Minora. (GRE.). 1985. 75.00 (*3-322-00183-0*, T1660, Pub. by B G Teubner) U of Mich Pr.

Littlewood, A. B., ed. see International Symposium on Gas Chromatography Staf.

Littlewood, A. R., ed. Originality in Byzantine Literature, Art & Music. (Oxbow Monographs in Archaeology: No. 50). (Illus.). 240p. 1995. 45.00 (*0-946897-87-5*, Pub. by Oxbow Bks) David Brown.

Littlewood, Audrey, tr. see Catteau, Jacques.

Littlewood, Ian. The Idea of Japan: Western Images, Western Myths. LC 96-24432. (Illus.). 264p. 1996. text 26.00 (*1-56663-117-3*, Pub. by I R Dee) Natl Bk Netwk.

— A Literary Companion to Venice. 3rd ed. LC 95-5220. 1995. pap. 14.95 (*0-312-13113-5*) St Martin.

— The Writings of Evelyn Waugh. LC 82-18513. 256p. (C). 1983. text 58.50 (*0-389-80350-2*, 07208) B&N Imports.

Littlewood, Ian, ed. Jane Austen: Critical Assessments, 4 vols. (Critical Assessments Ser.). 2400p. (C). 1999. 535.00 (*1-873403-29-1*) Routledge.

Littlewood, J., ed. Current Issues in Community Nursing Vol. 1: Primary Health Care in Practice. (Illus.). 324p. 1995. pap. write for info. (*0-443-05185-2*) Church.

Littlewood, John. The Stock Market: 50 Years of Capitalism at Work. 480p. 1998. 50.00 (*0-273-63872-6*, Pub. by Pitman Pbg) Trans-Atl Phila.

Littlewood, Karin. Science Fiction Stories. LC 92-26453. (Story Library). 260p. (J). (gr. 1 up). 1993. 7.95 (*1-85697-889-3*, Kingfisher) LKC.

Littlewood, Kevin & Butler, Beverley. Of Ships & Stars: Maritime Heritage & the Founding of the National Maritime Museum, Greenwich. LC 98-37234. 340p. 1999. 70.00 (*0-485-11537-9*, Pub. by Athlone Pr) Transaction Pubs.

***Littlewood, Kevin & Butler, Beverley.** Of Ships & Stars: Maritime Heritage & the Founding of the National Maritime Museum, Greenwich. 20p. 1999. pap. 33.95 (*0-485-12146-8*, Pub. by Athlone Pr) Transaction Pubs.

Littlewood, Mary L. Women's Fastpitch Softball the Path to the Gold: An Historical Look at Women's Fastpitch in the United States. LC 98-66286. 274 p. 1998. write for info. (*0-9664310-0-6*) Natl Fastpitch.

Littlewood, Michael. How to Create a Competitive Market in Pensions: The International Lessons. (Choices in Welfare Ser.: No. 45). (Illus.). 264p. 1998. pap. 25.00 (*0-255-36437-7*, Pub. by Inst Economic Affairs) Coronet Bks.

— Landscape Detailing: Enclosures, 2 vols., 1. 3rd ed. LC 92-34847. (Illus.). 208p. 1993. pap. text 64.95 (*0-7506-1304-1*) Buttrwrth-Heinemann.

— Landscape Detailing: Structures, Vol. III. 3rd ed. (Illus.). 240p. 1997. pap. text 49.95 (*0-7506-2320-9*) Buttrwrth-Heinemann.

Littlewood, Paul. Chess Tactics. (Crowood Chess Library). 136p. 1989. pap. 17.95 (*0-946284-95-4*, Pub. by Cro1wood) Trafalgar.

***Littlewood, Paul, ed.** Social Exclusion in Europe: Problems & Paradigms. 254p. 1999. text 69.95 (*1-84014-717-2*, Pub. by Ashgate Pub) Ashgate Pub Co.

Littlewood, R., jt. auth. see Kareem, J.

Littlewood, Roland. The Butterfly & the Serpent: Essays in Psychiatry, Race & Religion. LC 99-490212. 320p. 1998. 55.00 (*1-85343-399-3*, Pub. by Free Assoc Bks); pap. 23.50 (*1-85343-400-0*, Pub. by Free Assoc Bks) NYU Pr.

— Pathology & Identity: The Work of Mother Earth in Trinidad. LC 92-18251. (Cambridge Studies in Social & Cultural Anthropology: No. 90). (Illus.). 348p. (C). 1993. text 95.00 (*0-521-38427-3*) Cambridge U Pr.

***Littlewood, Roland & Dein, Simon.** Readings in Cultural Psychiatry. LC 99-44634. 2000. pap. write for info. (*0-485-11527-1*, Pub. by Athlone Pr) Transaction Pubs.

Littlewood, Roland & Lipsedge, Maurice. Aliens & Alienists: Ethnic Minorities & Psychiatry. 3rd ed. LC 96-47567. 368p. (C). 1997. 85.00 (*0-415-15724-2*); pap. 24.99 (*0-415-15725-0*) Routledge.

Littlewood, Roland, jt. auth. see Kareem, Jafar.

Littlewood, Ronald & Lipsedge, Maurice. Aliens & Alienists: Ethnic Minorities & Psychiatry. 2nd ed. 256p. 1989. 40.00 (*0-04-445317-5*); pap. 15.95 (*0-04-445316-7*) Routledge.

Littlewood, Thomas B. Arch: A Promoter, Not a Poet: The Story of Arch Ward. LC 89-24456. (Illus.). 239p. 1990. reprint ed. pap. 74.10 (*0-608-00095-7*, 206086000006) Bks Demand.

— Calling Elections: The History of 'Horse-Race' Journalism. LC 98-39984. 1999. 30.00 (*0-268-00833-7*) U of Notre Dame Pr.

***Littlewood, Thomas B.** Calling Elections: The History of Horse-Race Journalism. LC 98-39983. 224p. 2000. reprint ed. pap. 15.00 (*0-268-02253-4*, Pub. by U of Notre Dame Pr) Chicago Distribution Ctr.

Littlewood, Trevor D. & Evan, Gerard I. Helix-Loop-Helix Transcription Factors. 3rd ed. LC 97-39870. (Protein Profile Ser.). (Illus.). 162p. 1998. pap. text 46.95 (*0-19-850248-6*) OUP.

Littlewood, William. Communicative Language Teaching: An Introduction. LC 80-41563. (Cambridge English Language Learning Ser.). (Illus.). 124p. 1981. pap. text 19.95 (*0-521-28154-7*) Cambridge U Pr.

— Foreign & Second Language Learning. (Cambridge Language Teaching Library). 120p. 1984. pap. text 19.95 (*0-521-27486-9*) Cambridge U Pr.

Littleworth, Arthur L. & Garner, Eric L. California Water. (Orig.). 1995. pap. 47.50 (*0-923956-25-5*) Solano Pr.

Littman. Advertising & Promotion. (General Business & Business Education Ser.). 1996. pap. 13.00 (*0-8273-6260-9*) Delmar.

Littman, Barbara. Everyday Ways to Raise Smart, Strong, Confident Girls: Successful Teens Tell Us What Works. LC 99-31472. 176p. 1999. pap. 12.95 (*0-312-20973-8*, Thomas Dunne) St Martin.

— The Women's Business Resource Guide. (Illus.). 208p. 1996. pap. 18.95 (*0-8092-3166-2*, 316620, Contemporary Bks) NTC Contemp Pub Co.

Littman, Barbara & Ray, Michael. The Women's Business Resource Guide: A National Directory. 144p. 1994. pap. 21.95 (*1-884565-01-8*, Resource Group) Informat Design.

Littman, D. R., ed. Current Topics in Microbiology & Immunology Vol. 205: The CD4 Molecule. (Illus.). 224p. 1995. 141.95 (*3-540-59344-6*) Spr-Verlag.

Littman, David, tr. see Yeor, Bat.

Littman, Ian D., jt. auth. see Carr, David K.

Littman, Jennifer. Matzo Ball Soup: The Balls That Bobbed in the Broth That Bubbe Brewed. (Illus.). 32p. (Orig.). (J). (ps-2). 1997. pap. 7.95 (0-9656431-0-7) Brickford Ln.

It is a cumulative story written with the rhythm, rhyme & repetition that children love. It is beautifully illustrated, & it is designed to support multicultural programs, family studies, Grandparents' Day, Shabbat, & cooking activities. In the book Bubbe prepares for Shabbat (Jewish Sabbath) dinner by making her family's favorite soup. First, Bubbe makes a broth, & with each new page she adds something else to her soup. Finally, dinner is ready, & all of her grandchildren are there to eat her special soup. The book includes a children's recipe for matzo ball soup & a glossary for Yiddish words. Pre-K to Grade 2. *Publisher Paid Annotation.*

***Littman, Jonathan.** The Beautiful Game: Sixteen Girls & the Soccer Season That Changed Everything. LC 99-14875. 304p. (YA). (gr. 7 up). 1999. 23.00 (*0-380-97796-6*, Avon Bks) Morrow Avon.

— The Beautiful Game: Sixteen Girls And The Soccer Season That Changed Everything. 304p. 2000. pap. 14.00 (*0-380-80860-9*) Morrow Avon.

Littman, Jonathan. The Fugitive Game. LC 97-162983. 288p. 1997. pap. 13.95 (*0-316-52869-2*) Little.

— The Watchman. LC 96-47168. 304p. (gr. 8). 1997. 24.95 (*0-316-52857-9*) Little.

***Littman, Mark.** Social Statistics of the United States 2000. (Illus.). 2000. pap. 65.00 (*0-89059-215-2*) Bernan Pr.

Littman, Mark & Gaquin, Deirdre A. County & City Extra: Annual Metro, City & County Data Book, 1999 Edition. 8th ed. 1000p. 1999. 109.00 (*0-89059-161-X*, BP161X) Bernan Pr.

Littman, Mark, et al. Totality: Eclipses of the Sun. 2nd ed. LC QB541.L69 1999. (Illus.). 296p. 1999. 35.00 (*0-19-513178-9*); pap. 18.95 (*0-19-513179-7*) OUP.

Littman, Mark S., ed. Statistical Portrait of the United States: Social Conditions & Trends. LC 98-72991. 350p. 1998. 89.00 (*0-89059-076-1*) Bernan Pr.

An Asterisk (*) at the beginning of an entry indicates that the title is appearing for the first time.

L

***Littman, Mark S. & Gaquin, Deirdre A.** County & City Extra, 2000. 9th ed. 2000. 109.00 (*0-89059-251-9*, BP2519) Bernan Pr.

Littman, Robert J., jt. auth. see Pasachoff, Naomi.

Littman, Ruth. Deadly Prayers. 224p. (Orig.). 1996. pap. 14.95 (*1-886094-40-3*) Chicago Spectrum.

Littman, Sol. Quebec's Jews: Vital Citizens or Eternal Strangers. (Special Reports). (Illus.). 35p. (Orig.). pap. write for info. (*0-943058-11-2*) S Wiesenthal Ctr.

— War Criminal on Trial: Rauca of Kaunas. LC 98-199396. (Illus.). 256p. 1999. pap. 14.95 (*1-55013-967-3*, Pub. by Key Porter) Firefly Bks Ltd.

Littman, Sol, ed. Holocaust Denial: Bigotry in the Guise of Scholarship. (Special Reports). (Illus.). 66p. (Orig.). 1994. pap. 6.95 (*0-943048-19-2*) S Wiesenthal Ctr.

Littman, W., jt. auth. see Friedman, A.

Littmann, Enno, ed. Schulthess, Friedrich - Enno Littmann: Grammatik des Christlich - Palastinischen Aramaisch. (GER.). xvi, 159p. 1983. reprint ed. 48.00 (*3-487-01136-0*) G Olms Pubs.

Littmann, Helene. Peripheries. 272p. 1998. pap. 14.95 (*1-896951-08-2*) Cormor Bks.

Littmann, Mark. The Heavens on Fire: The Great Leonid Meteor Storms. LC 99-161352. (Illus.). 288p. (C). 1998. 39.95 (*0-521-62405-3*) Cambridge U Pr.

***Littmann, Mark.** The Heavens on Fire: The Great Leonid Meteor Storms. (Illus.). 359p. 1999. pap. 19.95 (*0-521-77979-0*) Cambridge U Pr.

Littmann, Mark & Yeomans, Donald K. Comet Halley: Once in a Lifetime. 190p. 1985. text 24.95 (*0-8412-0905-7*, Pub. by Am Chemical) OUP.

— Comet Halley: Once in a Lifetime. 190p. 1985. pap. 14.95 (*0-8412-0911-1*) Am Chemical.

— Comet Halley: Once in a Lifetime. LC 85-4012. (Illus.). 184p. 1985. reprint ed. pap. 57.10 (*0-608-04349-4*, 206512900001) Bks Demand.

Littner, Jakob & Grubler, Kurt. Journey Through the Night: A Holocaust Memoir. 240p. 1999. 24.50 (*0-8264-1197-5*) Continuum.

Litto, Fredric M. American Dissertations on the Drama & the Theatre: A Bibliography. LC 71-76761. 529p. reprint ed. pap. 164.00 (*0-8357-5362-X*, 202730600055) Bks Demand.

Litto, Vittorio Del, see Stendhal, pseud & Del Litto, Vittorio.

Litton. Win Lose & Drew. 1987. pap. 7.95 (*0-914807-06-4*) Denver Pub Co.

Litton, Brougham. The Fallen Star: History of a False Religion. 129p. 1996. reprint ed. spiral bd. 14.00 (*0-7873-0564-2*) Hlth Research.

Litton, Burt. Double Bogey. DeBoy, Jill, ed. (Illus.). 106p. (Orig.). 1995. pap. 8.95 (*0-9647839-0-8*) Curtis Pubng.

Litton, Drew. Win, Lose & Drew: Greatest Hits. 1997. pap. text 9.00 (*0-914807-15-3*) Denver Pub Co.

Litton, Edmundo F., jt. ed. see Brainard, CeCilia Manguerra.

Litton, Evie. Hiking Hot Springs of the Pacific Northwest. 2nd rev. ed. LC 98-20202. (Illus.). 344p. 1998. pap. 16.95 (*1-56044-677-3*) Falcon Pub Inc.

Litton, Freddie W., jt. auth. see Love, Harold D.

Litton, Gaston, jt. auth. see Dale, Edward.

Litton, Gerry M. PC Magazine Guide to Ami Pro 2.0 & 3.0. (Guide to...Ser.). (Illus.). 753p. (Orig.). 1992. pap. 24.95 (*1-56276-090-4*, Ziff-Davis Pr) Que.

— PC Magazine Guide to Professional Write Plus. (Guide to...Ser.). (Illus.). 422p. (Orig.). 1991. pap. 24.95 (*1-56276-027-0*, Ziff-Davis Pr) Que.

— Take Ami Pro 3.0 to the Edge. (Customizing Ser.). (Illus.). 560p. (Orig.). 1993. pap. 29.95 incl. disk (*1-56276-089-0*, Ziff-Davis Pr) Que.

Litton, Glenn, jt. auth. see Smith, Cecil.

Litton, Helen. The Celts: An Illustrated History. LC 98-102051. (Illus.). 138p. 1997. pap. 11.95 (*0-86327-577-X*, Pub. by Wolfhound Press) Irish Amer Bk.

— The Irish Civil War: An Illustrated History. LC 96-101839. (Illus.). 156p. 1997. pap. 11.95 (*0-86327-480-3*, Pub. by Wolfhound Press) Irish Amer Bk.

— The Irish Famine: An Illustrated History. LC 94-76754. (Illus.). 128p. (Orig.). 1994. pap. 11.95 (*0-937702-14-5*) Irish Bks Media.

— Irish Rebellions 1798-1916: An Illustrated History. (Illustrated Histories Ser.). (Illus.). 144p. 1998. pap. 11.95 (*0-86327-634-2*, Pub. by Wolfhound Press) Irish Amer Bk.

Litton, Helen, jt. auth. see Clarke, Kathleen.

Litton, Melvin. Geminga: Sword of the Shining Path. 256p. (Orig.). 1993. pap. 9.95 (*0-9622937-4-1*) III Pub.

Litton, Nancy. Getting Your Math Message Out to Parents. LC 98-18969. (Illus.). 144p. 1998. pap. 14.95 (*0-941355-20-9*, MSP 5112-118) Math Solns Pubns.

Litton, Pamela. Dance with the Devil. (Historical Ser.: No. 722). 1992. mass mkt. 3.99 (*0-373-28722-4*, 1-28722-6) Harlequin Bks.

— Stardust & Whirlwinds. (Historical Ser.: No. 69). 1991. mass mkt. 3.95 (*0-373-28669-4*) Harlequin Bks.

Littre, Paul-Emile. Dictionnaire de la Langue Francaise. (FRE.). 6809p. 1983. lib. bdg. 1150.00 (*0-7859-4626-8*) Fr & Eur.

Littrell, David A., ed. String Syllabus Vol. 1: For Violin, Viola, Cello, Double Bass Ensembles. rev. ed. 95p. 1997. pap. text 25.00 (*0-89917-490-6*, 1908S) Am String Tchrs.

Littrell, David A., ed. String Syllabus Vol. 2: For Harp & Guitar. rev. ed. 62p. 1997. pap. text 25.00 (*1-883026-14-8*, 1916S) Am String Tchrs.

Littrell, Helen E., ed. Stedman's OB-GYN Words: Including Neonatology, Pediatrics, Genetics. 2nd ed. LC 95-4488. 480p. 1995. pap. 34.95 (*0-683-07967-0*) Lppncott W & W.

Littrell, Helen E. & Stedman, Thomas L. Stedman's Cardiology & Pulmonary Words. 2nd ed. LC 96-45978. (Stedman's Word Bks.). 640p. 1997. 35.95 (*0-683-40081-9*) Lppncott W & W.

Littrell, J. Understanding & Treating Alcoholism, 2 vols. (C). 1991. text 99.95 (*0-8058-0872-8*) L Erlbaum Assocs.

— Understanding & Treating Alcoholism, Vol. I. 408p. (C). 1991. text 75.00 (*0-8058-0870-1*) L Erlbaum Assocs.

— Understanding & Treating Alcoholism, Vol. II. 296p. (C). 1991. text 49.95 (*0-8058-0871-X*) L Erlbaum Assocs.

Littrell, Jay. Colony Wars: Prima's Official Strategy Guide. LC 98-65453. 96p. 1998. per. 12.99 (*0-7615-1579-8*) Prima Pub.

Littrell, John M. Brief Counseling in Action. LC 97-39263. 256p. 1998. 32.00 (*0-393-70265-0*) Norton.

Littrell, Joseph J., et al. From School to Work. LC 99-11553. 550p. 2000. 46.64 (*1-56637-655-6*) Goodheart.

Littrell, Mary Ann & Dickson, Marsha Ann. Social Responsibility in the Global Market: Fair Trade of Cultural Products. LC 99-6228. 1999. write for info. (*0-7619-1464-1*) Sage.

Littrell, W. Boyd, et al, eds. Bureaucracy As a Social Problem. LC 89-9383. (Contemporary Studies in Applied Behavioral Science: Vol. 1). 295p. 1983. 73.25 (*0-89232-368-X*) Jai Pr.

Littrup, Lisbeth, ed. Identity in Asian Literature. (NIAS Studies in Asian Topics: No. 21). 280p. (C). 1995. text 45.00 (*0-7007-0367-5*, Pub. by Curzon Pr Ltd); pap. text 23.95 (*0-7007-0368-3*, Pub. by Curzon Pr Ltd) UH Pr.

Liturgical Commission Publishings Diocese of Lansi. Server at the Lord's Table. Gilliland, Mary J., ed. (Illus.). 28p. (Orig.). 1995. pap. text 4.00 (*1-878268-00-7*) Lit Comm Pubs.

— Special Minister of the Eucharist Vol. 1: First Steps in Ministry. Gilliland, Mary J., ed. 25p. (Orig.). (C). 1995. pap. text 3.00 (*1-878268-04-X*) Lit Comm Pubs.

— To Love & to Honor: A Pre-Marriage Ministry Resource Manual. Hawkins, Myron, ed. 235p. (Orig.). (C). 1983. ring bd. 25.00 (*0-685-28963-X*) Lit Comm Pubs.

***Liturgical, Press.** The Jubilee Guide to Rome: The Four Basilicas: The Great Pilgrimage. 1999. 39.95 (*0-8146-2536-3*) Liturgical Pr.

Liturgical Press Staff. Canon Law: Letter & Spirit. 1088p. 1996. 99.95 (*0-8146-5516-5*) Liturgical Pr.

— Lectionary for Mass Vol. II: Chapel. 1999. 49.95 (*0-8146-2565-7*) Liturgical Pr.

— Lectionary for Mass Vol. II: Classic. abr. ed. 1999. 59.95 (*0-8146-2564-9*) Liturgical Pr.

***Liturgical Press Staff, ed.** Celebrant's Ritual: Marriage. 1999. pap. 14.95 (*0-8146-0999-6*) Liturgical Pr.

Liturgy Training Publications. Plenty Good Room: The Spirit & Truth of American Catholic Worship. LC 92-125332. 1998. pap. 9.95 (*1-55586-385-X*) US Catholic.

***Liturgy Training Publications Staff.** At Home with the Word 2000. 1999. pap. 7.00 (*1-56854-291-7*) Liturgy Tr Pubns.

Liturgy Training Publications Staff. Evening Prayer: Commemorating the Birthday of Dr. Martin Luther King Jr. 24p. 1993. pap. text 5.00 (*1-56854-019-1*) Liturgy Tr Pubns.

— Keeping Advent & Christmastime. 48p. 1998. pap. 3.00 (*1-56854-027-2*) Liturgy Tr Pubns.

***Liturgy Training Publications Staff.** Keeping Lent Triduum & Eastertime. LC 96-77207. 48p. 1998. pap. 3.00 (*1-56854-033-7*) Liturgy Tr Pubns.

— Prayers for Jubilee. 1999. pap. 3.00 (*1-56854-282-8*) Liturgy Tr Pubns.

— Tell Me Your Name: Images of God in the Bible. 2000. pap. 12.00 (*1-56854-167-8*) Liturgy Tr Pubns.

Litva, J. & Lo, Titus K. Digital Beamforming in Wireless Communications. LC 96-27151. 301p. 1996. 83.00 (*0-89006-712-0*) Artech Hse.

Litvack, David. CPS Marketing Notes. 268p. (C). 1995. text 6.50 (*0-256-21178-7*, Irwn McGrw-H) McGrw-H Hghr Educ.

Litvack, Jennie I., et al. Rethinking Decentralization in Developing Countries. LC 98-44529. vii, 40 p. 1998. 22.00 (*0-8213-4350-5*) World Bank.

Litvack, Leon. J. M. Neale & the Quest for Sobornost. 310p. 1994. text 55.00 (*0-19-826351-1*) OUP.

Litvack, Leon, jt. ed. see Hooper, Glenn.

Litvak, A. G., ed. High-Frequency Plasma Heating. 450p. 1991. 189.95 (*0-88318-765-5*) Spr-Verlag.

Litvak, Barry. Slow Memories. 1972. pap. 3.25 (*0-8222-1044-4*) Dramatists Play.

Litvak, Dianna. Travel Smart: Colorado. 2nd rev. ed. (Travel Smart Ser.). (Illus.). 256p. 1999. pap. 15.95 (*1-56261-451-7*, Travel Smart) Avalon Travel.

Litvak, Eugene. Soviet Telecommunications Systems Reliability Theory. Possehl, Suzanne R., ed. (Illus.). 102p. (Orig.). 1989. pap. 75.00 (*1-55831-111-4*) Delphic Associates.

Litvak, Jaime, et al, eds. Una Definicion de Mesoamerica. 2nd ed. 192p. 1992. pap. 8.50 (*968-36-2731-5*, UN038) UPLAAP.

Litvak, Jennie I., jt. ed. see Rondinelli, Dennis A.

Litvak, Jorge, jt. auth. see Grant, Marcus.

Litvak, Joseph. Caught in the Act: Theatricality in the Nineteenth-Century English Novel. LC 91-10222. (C). 1992. 50.00 (*0-520-07452-1*, Pub. by U CA Pr); pap. 16.95 (*0-520-07454-8*, Pub. by U CA Pr) Cal Prin Full Svc.

— Strange Gourmets: Sophistication, Theory, & the Novel. LC 96-54812. (Series Q). x, 181p. 1997. pap. 15.95 (*0-8223-2016-9*); lib. bdg. 45.95 (*0-8223-2007-X*) Duke.

Litvak, Lawrence. Pension Funds & Economic Renewal. Barker, Michael, ed. (Studies in State Development Policy: Vol. 11). 136p. (C). 1981. pap. 16.95 (*0-934842-10-8*) CSPA.

Litvak, Lawrence, et al. South Africa: Foreign Investment & Apartheid. 100p. 1978. write for info. (*0-318-59935-X*); pap. 3.95 (*0-685-43367-6*) Inst Policy Stud.

Litvak, Lily. A Dream of Arcadia: Anti-Industrialism in Spanish Literature. LC 74-22463. 300p. reprint ed. pap. 93.00 (*0-8357-7751-0*, 203610800002) Bks Demand.

Litvak, Meir. Shi'i Scholars of Nineteenth-Century Iraq: The Ulama of Najaf & Karbala. LC 97-35821. (Middle East Studies: Vol. 10). 264p. (C). 1998. 59.95 (*0-521-62356-1*) Cambridge U Pr.

Litvak, Simon. Retroviral Reverse Transcriptases. (Molecular Biology Intelligence Unit Ser.). 205p. 1996. 99.00 (*1-57059-369-8*) Landes Bioscience.

Litvak, Stuart & Senzee, A. Wayne. Toward a New Brain: Evolution & the Human Mind. 250p. 1985. 17.95 (*0-13-926056-0*) P-H.

Litvan, G. G., jt. ed. see Sereda, P. J.

Litvan, Gyorgy. The Hungarian Revolution of 1956: Form, Revolution, Repression, 1953-1963. Bak, Janos M. & Legters, Lyman H., trs. from HUN. LC 95-45648. 272p. (C). 1996. text 80.00 (*0-582-21505-6*) Addison-Wesley.

Litvan, Gyorgy, ed. see Jaszi, Oscar.

Litvan, Irene & Agid, Yves, eds. Progressive Supranuclear Palsy: Clinical & Research Approaches. (Illus.). 304p. 1992. text 67.50 (*0-19-507229-4*) OUP.

Litvan, Irene, et al. Corticobasal Degeneration, Vol. 82. 288p. text 139.00 (*0-7817-2124-5*) Lppncott W & W.

Litvin, Baruch & Litvin, Jeanne. The Sanctity of the Synagogue. 1987. 24.95 (*0-88125-113-5*) Ktav.

Litvin, D. B. & Wike, T. R. Character Tables & Compatibility Relations of the Eighty Layer Groups & Seventeen Plane Groups. (Illus.). 250p. (C). 1991. text 89.50 (*0-306-43917-4*, Kluwer Plenum) Kluwer Academic.

Litvin, Faydor, et al. Computerized Design & Generation of Low-Noise Gears with Localized Bearing Contact. (Nineteen Ninety-Four Fall Technical Meeting Ser.: Vol. 94FTM10). (Illus.). 10p. 1994. pap. text 30.00 (*1-55589-645-6*) AGMA.

— Face Gear Drives: Design, Analysis & Testing for Helicopter Transmission Applications. (Nineteen Ninety-Two Fall Technical Meeting Ser.: Vol. 92FTM2). (Illus.). 11p. 1992. pap. text 30.00 (*1-55589-582-4*) AGMA.

Litvin, Faydor L. Gear Geometry & Applied Theory. 752p. (C). 1994. pap. text 93.00 (*0-13-211095-4*) P-H.

Litvin, Faydor L. & Kin, Vadim. Simulation of Meshing, Transmission Errors & Bearing Contact for Single-Enveloping Worm-Gear Drives. (Nineteen Ninety Fall Technical Meeting Ser.: Vol. 90FTM3). (Illus.). 10p. 1990. pap. text 30.00 (*1-55589-555-7*) AGMA.

Litvin, Faydor L. & Zhang, J. Crowned Spur Gears: Optimal Geometry & Generation. (Nineteen Eighty-Seven Fall Technical Meeting Ser.: Vol. 87FTM7). (Illus.). 8p. 1987. pap. text 30.00 (*1-55589-483-6*) AGMA.

Litvin, Faydor L., et al. Design, Generation, Stress Analysis & Test of Low-Noise, Increased Strength Face-Milled Spiral Bevel Gears. (Technical Papers: Vol. 97FTM15). (Illus.). 15p. 1997. pap. text 30.00 (*1-55589-709-6*) AGMA.

— Generation of Conjugate Spiral Bevel Gears & Their Tooth Contact Analysis. (Nineteen Eighty-Six Fall Technical Meeting Ser.: Vol. 86FTM2). (Illus.). 11p. 1986. pap., pap. text 30.00 incl. audio compact disk (*1-55589-466-6*, 86FTM2) AGMA.

— Helical Gears with Pinion Circular Arc Teeth & Gear Screw Involute Teeth. (Nineteen Eighty-Six Fall Technical Meeting Ser.: Vol. 86FTM3). (Illus.). 5p. 1986. pap. 30.00 (*1-55589-467-4*, 86FTM3) AGMA.

— Hypoid Gear Drive with Face-Milled Teeth: Conditions of Pinion Nonundercutting & Fillet Generation. (Nineteen Eighty-Nine Fall Technical Meeting Ser.: Vol. 89FTM7). (Illus.). 8p. 1989. pap. text 30.00 (*1-55589-533-6*) AGMA.

Litvin, Gary, jt. auth. see Litvin, Maria.

Litvin, Jay, jt. auth. see Salk, Lee.

Litvin, Jeanne, jt. auth. see Litvin, Baruch.

***Litvin, Maria.** Be Prepared for the AP Computer Science Exam. 280p. 1999. pap. 15.95 (*0-9654853-6-6*) Skylight Pub.

Litvin, Maria & Litvin, Gary. C++ for You++ An Introduction to Programming & Computer Science. LC 97-91876. (Illus.). 536p. 1997. pap. text 55.00 (*0-9654853-4-X*) Skylight Pub.

— C++ for You++, AP Edition: An Introduction to Programming & Computer Science. LC 97-91209. (Illus.). 584p. 1997. text 47.50 (*0-9654853-9-0*) Skylight Pub.

— Workbook to Accompany C++ for You++, AP Edition. (Illus.). 144p. 1997. pap. text, wbk. ed. 12.00 (*0-9654853-8-2*) Skylight Pub.

— Workbook to Accompany C++ for You++ (Illus.). 144p. 1997. spiral bd., wbk. ed. 12.00 (*0-9654853-2-3*) Skylight Pub.

Litvin, Martin. I'm Going to Be Somebody! A Biography of George Fitch. LC 91-65514. (Illus.). viii, 153p. (Orig.). 1991. pap. 9.50 (*0-938463-05-5*) Western Bks.

— Mary Allen West: A Lady of Grit, Grace & Gumption. LC 96-62022. (Illus.). 160p. (Orig.). 1997. pap. 9.95 (*0-9654930-0-8*) Zephyr IL.

Litvin, S. Gerald & McHugh, Gerald A. Pennsylvania Torts: Law & Advocacy. LC 96-174233. (West's Pennsylvania Practice Ser.). 1996. write for info. (*0-314-08113-5*) West Pub.

Litvin, Valentin. The Soviet Agro-Industrial Complex: Structure & Performance: From Research to Production. McSharry, Patra, ed. (Illus.). 158p. (Orig.). 1985. pap. text 75.00 (*1-55831-027-4*) Delphic Associates.

Litvinchievici, Claudia, tr. see Cesereanu, Ruxandra.

Litvinchuk, G. & Spitkovskii, I. Factorization of Measurable Matrix Functions. (Operator Theory Ser.: No. 25). 384p. 1988. 118.00 (*0-8176-1883-X*) Birkhauser.

Litvinchuk, Georgii S., jt. auth. see Kravchenko, Victor G.

Litvinne, Felia. Ma Vie et Mon Art Souvenirs. Farkas, Andrew, ed. LC 76-29950. (Opera Biographies Ser.).Tr. of My Life & My Art. (FRE., Illus.). 1977. reprint ed. lib. bdg. 28.95 (*0-405-09691-7*) Ayer.

Litvinoff, Barnet. Fourteen Ninety-Two: The Decline of Medievalism & the Rise of the Modern Age. 296p. 1992. reprint ed. pap. 11.00 (*0-380-71917-7*, Avon Bks) Morrow Avon.

— The Letters & Papers of Chaim Weizmann, 1898-1931, Vol. I. (Series B Papers). 700p. 1984. 59.95 (*0-87855-279-0*) Transaction Pubs.

— The Letters & Papers of Chaim Weizmann, 1931-1952, Vol. II. (Series B Papers). 750p. 1984. 64.95 (*0-87855-297-9*) Transaction Pubs.

— A Very British Subject: Telling Tales. LC 96-1903. (Illus.). 216p. (Orig.). 1996. pap. 25.00 (*0-85303-293-9*, Pub. by M Vallentine & Co) Intl Spec Bk.

Litvinoff, Barnet, ed. The Essential Chaim Weizmann: The Man, the Statesman, the Scientist. 292p. 1983. 29.75 (*0-8419-0823-0*) Holmes & Meier.

Litvinoff, Barnet, jt. ed. see Weisgal, Meyer W.

Litvinoff, Emanuel. Journey Through a Small Planet: Jewish Childhood in East London. large type ed. (Reminiscence Ser.). 23.95 (*1-85695-171-5*, Pub. by ISIS Lrg Prnt) Transaction Pubs.

Litvinoff, Emanuel, ed. Penguin Book of Jewish Short Stories. 352p. 1979. pap. 13.95 (*0-14-004728-X*, Penguin Bks) Viking Penguin.

Litvinoff, Miles. The Young Gaia Atlas of Earthcare. LC 96-31417. (Illus.). 192p. (J). (gr. 5-9). 1996. 24.95 (*0-8160-3470-2*) Facts on File.

Litvinoff, Saul. The Law of Obligations in the Louisiana Jurisprudence: A Coursebook. 3rd ed. 928p. 1991. text 50.00 (*0-940448-21-1*) LSU Law Pubns.

— Sale & Lease in the Louisiana Jurisprudence: A Coursebook. 2nd ed. LC 86-62791. 730p. 1986. lib. bdg. 38.00 (*0-940448-14-9*) LSU Law Pubns.

Litvinov, I., jt. tr. see Miller, Arthur.

Litvinov, Ivy, jt. tr. see Pisemskii, Aleksei F.

Litvinov, Ivy, tr. see Turgenev, Ivan Sergeevich.

Litvinov, Ju. V., tr. see Vakhrameev, V. A.

Litvinov, Tatiana, tr. see Turgenev, Ivan Sergeevich.

Litvinov, V. Vicinal Heteroaromatic Hydroxy, Mercapto & Hydroseleno, Vol. 11. (Sulfur Reports). 389p. 1992. pap. text 275.00 (*3-7186-5271-4*, Harwood Acad Pubs) Gordon & Breach.

***Litvinov, William G.** Optimization in Elliptic Problems with Applications to Mechanics of Deformable Bodies & Fluid Mechanics. LC 00-30398. 2000. write for info. (*0-8176-6199-9*) Birkhauser.

Litvinsky, A., et al, eds. The Crossroads of Civilizations: AD 250 to 750. (History of the Civilizations of Central Asia Ser.: Vol. III). (Illus.). 550p. 1999. text 42.00 (*1-85043-871-4*) St Martin.

Litwack, jt. auth. see Shekleton, S.

Litwack, David M., jt. auth. see Blum, Daniel J.

***Litwack, Gerald.** Vitamins & Hormones. (Illus.). 520p. 2000. 99.00 (*0-12-709858-5*) Acad Pr.

— Vitamins & Hormones, Vol. 59. Vol. 59. 392p. 2000. 99.95 (*0-12-709859-3*) Acad Pr.

Litwack, Gerald. Vitamins & Hormones Vol. 53: Cell Death Proteins, Vol. 53. (Illus.). 198p. 1997. text 89.95 (*0-12-709853-4*) Morgan Kaufmann.

Litwack, Gerald, ed. Biochemical Actions of Hormones, Vol. 8. 1981. text 106.00 (*0-12-452808-2*) Acad Pr.

— Biochemical Actions of Hormones, Vol. 9. LC 70-107567. 374p. 1982. text 85.00 (*0-12-452809-0*) Acad Pr.

— Biochemical Actions of Hormones, Vol. 13. 426p. 1986. text 134.00 (*0-12-452813-9*) Acad Pr.

— Biochemical Actions of Hormones, Vol. 14. 384p. 1987. text 75.00 (*0-12-452814-7*) Acad Pr.

— Receptor Purification Vol. 1: Receptors for CNS Agents, Growth Factors, Hormones & Related Substances. LC 90-4689. (Illus.). 514p. 1990. 139.50 (*0-89603-167-5*) Humana.

— Receptor Purification Vol. 2: Receptors for Steroid Hormones, Thyroid Hormones, Water-Balancing Hormones & Others. LC 90-4689. (Illus.). 430p. 1990. 139.50 (*0-89603-183-7*) Humana.

— Vitamins & Hormones, Vol. 5. (Illus.). 496p. 1995. text 90.00 (*0-12-709850-X*) Acad Pr.

— Vitamins & Hormones, Vol. 48. (Illus.). 306p. 1994. text. write for info. (*0-12-709848-8*) Acad Pr.

— Vitamins & Hormones, Vol. 51. (Illus.). 468p. 1995. text 90.00 (*0-12-709851-8*) Acad Pr.

— Vitamins & Hormones, Vol. 52. (Illus.). 202p. 1996. text 74.95 (*0-12-709852-6*) Acad Pr.

— Vitamins & Hormones, Vol. 55. (Illus.). 522p. (C). 1998. boxed set 89.95 (*0-12-709855-0*) Acad Pr.

— Vitamins & Hormones, Vol. 57. (Illus.). 400p. 1999. 89.95 (*0-12-709857-7*) Acad Pr.

— Vitamins & Hormones Vol. 49: Steroids. (Illus.). 512p. 1994. text. write for info. (*0-12-709849-6*) Acad Pr.

— Vitamins & Hormones Vol. 54: Advances in Research & Applications, Vol. 54. (Illus.). 234p. 1998. text 84.95 (*0-12-709854-2*) Acad Pr.

— Vitamins & Hormones Vol. 56, Nos. 30-55: Cumulative Subject Index. (Illus.). 240p. (C). 1999. text 89.95 (*0-12-709856-9*) Acad Pr.

Litwack, Gerald, jt. auth. see Norman, Anthony W.

An Asterisk (*) at the beginning of an entry indicates that the title is appearing for the first time.

Litwack, Kim, ed. Core Curriculum for Post Anesthesia Nursing Practice. 3rd ed. LC 94-13579. (Illus.). 706p. (C). 1994. pap. text 49.00 (*0-7216-5051-1*, W B Saunders Co) Harcrt Hlth Sci Grp.

Litwack, Larry. Special Education & Quality Inclusion. 1998. text 31.87 (*1-56870-309-0*) RonJon Pub.

Litwack, Larry, ed. Journal of Reality Therapy: A Compendium of Articles, 1981-1993. (Illus.). 392p. (Orig.). 1994. pap. 24.00 (*0-944337-19-8*, 198) New View Pubns.

Litwack, Leon & Meier, August. Black Leaders of the Nineteenth Century. (Blacks in the New World Ser.). (Illus.). 360p. 1991. 14.95 (*0-252-06213-2*) U of Ill Pr.

Litwack, Leon F. Been in the Storm So Long: The Aftermath of Slavery. LC 80-11073. 672p. 1980. pap. 19.95 (*0-394-74398-9*) Vin Bks.

— North of Slavery: The Negro in the Free States, 1790-1860. LC 61-10869. 332p. 1965. pap. text 15.00 (*0-226-48586-2*, P179) U Ch Pr.

— Trouble in Mind: Black Southerners in Age of Jim Crow. LC 97-49465. 576p. 1998. 40.00 (*0-394-52778-X*) Knopf.

***Litwack, Leon F.** Trouble in Mind: Black Southerners in the Age of Jim Crow. (Illus.). 624p. 1999. pap. 17.00 (*0-375-70263-6*) Vin Bks.

Litwack, Leon F. & Meier, August, eds. Black Leaders of the Nineteenth Century. LC 87-19439. (Blacks in the New World Ser.). 360p. 1988. text 29.95 (*0-252-01506-1*) U of Ill Pr.

Litwack, Leon F., jt. auth. see Jordan, Winthrop D.

Litwack, Leon F., jt. ed. see Stampp, Kenneth M.

Litwak, Anthony B. Glaucoma Handbook. 336p. 2000. text 85.00 (*0-7506-9776-8*) Buttrwrth-Heinemann.

Litwak, Barbara A., jt. auth. see Lizotte, Ken.

Litwak, Eugene. Helping the Elderly: The Complementary Roles of Informal Networks & Formal Systems. LC 85-7985. (Perspectives on Marriage & the Family Ser.). (Illus.). 320p. 1985. reprint ed. pap. 99.20 (*0-608-07576-0*, 205989000010) Bks Demand.

Litwak, Eugene & Meyer, Henry J. School, Family & Neighborhood: The Theory & Practice of School-Community Relations. LC 73-17274. 316p. reprint ed. pap. 98.00 (*0-8357-4275-X*, 203707300007) Bks Demand.

***Litwak, Kenneth.** Pure Java 2. 700p. 1999. 24.99 (*0-672-31654-4*) Sams.

Litwak, Leo. Waiting for the News. LC 89-5577. (Great Lakes Bks.). 332p. 1990. reprint ed. pap. 19.95 (*0-8143-2275-1*); reprint ed. text 39.95 (*0-8143-2274-3*) Wayne St U Pr.

***Litwak, Mark.** Contracts for the Film & Television Industry. 2nd expanded ed. LC 98-54341. 4p. 1999. pap. 35.95 (*1-879505-46-0*) Silman James Pr.

Litwak, Mark. Dealmaking in the Film & Television Industry: From Negotiations Through Final Contracts. LC 94-1939. 406p. (Orig.). 1993. pap. 26.95 (*1-879505-15-0*) Silman James Pr.

— Litwak's Multimedia Producer's Handbook: A Legal & Distribution Guide. LC 97-29963. xix, 334p. 1998. pap. text 29.95 (*1-879505-35-5*) Silman James Pr.

— Reel Power: The Struggle for Influence & Success in The New Hollywood. LC 94-2909. 336p. 1994. pap. 14.95 (*1-879505-19-3*) Silman James Pr.

***Litwak, Robert.** Rogue States & U.S. Foreign Policy: Containment after the Cold War. LC 99-50562. 300p. 1999. 49.95 (*0-943875-98-6*) W Wilson Ctr Pr.

Litwak, Robert. Sources of Inter-State Conflict. LC 80-28448. (Security in the Persian Gulf Ser.: Vol. 2). 100p. 1981. pap. text 19.50 (*0-86598-045-4*) Rowman.

Litwak, Robert S. & Wells, Samuel F., Jr., eds. Superpower Competition & Security in the Third World. LC 87-24187. (Wilson Center Series on International Security Studies). 296p. 1987. 32.00 (*0-88730-253-X*, HarpBusn) HarpInfo.

Litwak, Robert S., jt. ed. see Bullock, Mary B.

Litwak, Robert S., jt. ed. see Reiss, Mitchell.

Litwak, Robert S., jt. ed. see Wells, Samuel F.

Litweiler, John. The Freedom Principle: Jazz after 1958. (Quality Paperbacks Ser.). (Illus.). 324p. 1990. reprint ed. pap. 13.95 (*0-306-80377-1*) Da Capo.

***Litwicki, Ellen M.** America's Public Holidays, 1865-1920. LC 99-462086. (Illus.). 2000. 39.95 (*1-56098-863-0*) Smithsonian.

Litwiller, Bonnie H., jt. auth. see Duncan, David R.

Litwiller, Daniel J. Essential Publisher 97 Book: The Get-It-Done Tutorial. LC 97-66858. 592p. 1997. per. 24.99 (*0-7615-1136-9*) Prima Pub.

Litwin. Genetic Determinants of Pulmonary Disease. (Lung Biology in Health & Disease Ser.: Vol. 11). (Illus.). 304p. 1978. text 165.00 (*0-8247-6608-3*) Dekker.

Litwin, Bennett. Where Exactly Is Heaven: Science, God & Common Sense. LC 89-69867. (Illus.). 184p. (Orig.). 1990. pap. 8.95 (*0-9615743-7-2*) SunShine CO.

Litwin, Bob, et al. The Last Bookmaker. 288p. 24.95 (*1-880325-18-7*, Pub. by Borderlnds NH) Baker & Taylor.

Litwin, Howard. Uprooted in Old Age: Russian Jews & Their Social Networks in Israel, 25. LC 94-29825. (Contributions to the Study of Aging Ser.: Vol. 25). 208p. 1995. 57.95 (*0-313-29280-9*, Greenwood Pr) Greenwood.

Litwin, Howard, ed. The Social Networks of Older People: A Cross-National Analysis. LC 96-16265. 272p. 1996. 65.00 (*0-275-95327-0*, Praeger Pubs) Greenwood.

***Litwin, Mark, et al.** Prostate Cancer Patient Outcomes & Choice of Providers: Development of an Infrastructure for Quality Assessment. 205p. (C). 2000. pap. 25.00 (*0-8330-2873-1*) Rand Corp.

Litwin, Mark S. How to Measure Survey Reliability & Validity. (Survey Kit Ser.: Vol. 7). 96p. 1995. pap. 11.95 (*0-8039-5704-1*) Sage.

Litwin, Paul, et al. Access 97 Developer's Handbook. 3rd ed. LC 96-70747. (Illus.). 1584p. 1997. pap. 59.99 incl. cd-rom (*0-7821-1941-7*) Sybex.

— Access 97 Developer's Set. 2560p. 1997. 89.99 (*0-7821-2207-8*) Sybex.

— Access 7 Developer's Handbook. 4th ed. 1552p. 1998. 59.99 (*0-7821-2323-6*) Sybex.

Litwin, Stephen D. Human Immunogenetics: Basic Principles & Clinical Relevance. (Immunology Ser.: Vol. 43). (Illus.). 856p. 1989. text 250.00 (*0-8247-7899-5*) Dekker.

Litwin, W., et al, eds. Advances in Databases & Information Systems: Second East European Symposium, ADBIS '98, Poznan, Poland, September 7-10, 1998, Proceedings, Vol. 147. LC 98-30695. (Lecture Notes in Computer Science Ser.: Vol. 1475). xiv, 369p. 1998. pap. 59.00 (*3-540-64924-7*) Spr-Verlag.

Litwin, Witold. Introduction to Interoperable Multidatabase Systems. 400p. (C). 2002. 25.50 (*0-13-497918-4*) P-H.

Litwin, Witold & Risch, Tore, eds. Applications of Databases: First International Conference, ADB-94, Vadstena, Sweden, June 1994, Proceedings. LC 94-21761. (Lecture Notes in Computer Science Ser.: Vol. 819). 1994. 65.95 (*0-387-58183-9*) Spr-Verlag.

Litwin, Witold & Schek, H. J., eds. Foundations of Data Organization & Algorithms. (Lecture Notes in Computer Science Ser.: Vol. 367). viii, 531p. 1989. 55.00 (*0-387-51295-0*) Spr-Verlag.

Litz. American Writers Selected Authors, 3 vol. set. LC 98-36810. 1998. 180.00 (*0-684-80604-5*) S&S Trade.

Litz, A. Walton. American Writers, Supp. 2, Pt. 1. 1981. 100.00 (*0-684-17592-4*) Mac Lib Ref.

— American Writers, Supp. 2, Pt. 2. 1981. 100.00 (*0-684-17593-2*) Mac Lib Ref.

— American Writers, Supp. 4, Pt. 1. 1996. 100.00 (*0-684-19786-3*) Mac Lib Ref.

— American Writers, Supp. 4, Pt. 2. 1996. 100.00 (*0-684-19787-1*) Mac Lib Ref.

— Major American Short Stories. 3rd ed. (Illus.). 896p. (C). 1994. pap. text 34.95 (*0-19-507899-3*) OUP.

Litz, A. Walton, ed. American Writers: Supplement I, 2 vols. LC 73-1759. 1979. 225.00 (*0-684-15797-7*, Scribners Ref) Mac Lib Ref.

— American Writers Supplement II, 2 vols., Set. LC 73-1759. 1981. 225.00 (*0-684-16482-5*, Scribners Ref) Mac Lib Ref.

— Poets, Poems, Movements. LC 86-30910. (Studies in Modern Literature: No. 64). 340p. reprint ed. pap. 105.40 (*0-8357-1783-6*, 207074800004) Bks Demand.

***Litz, A. Walton, et al, eds.** The Cambridge History of Literary Criticism Vol. 7: Modernism & the New Criticism. 550p. 2000. 110.00 (*0-521-30012-6*) Cambridge U Pr.

Litz, A. Walton & Weigel, Molly. American Writers, 2 vols. 911p. 1996. suppl. ed. 225.00 (*0-684-19785-5*) Mac Lib Ref.

Litz, A. Walton, jt. auth. see Unger, Leonard.

Litz, A. Walton, ed. see Agha, Shahid A.

Litz, A. Walton, jt. ed. see Baechler, Lea.

Litz, A. Walton, ed. see Baker, Paul G.

Litz, A. Walton, ed. see Bishop, George.

Litz, A. Walton, ed. see Boren, Lynda S.

Litz, A. Walton, ed. see Butterworth, Keen.

Litz, A. Walton, ed. see Callander, Marilyn B.

Litz, A. Walton, ed. see Davidson, Arnold E.

Litz, A. Walton, ed. see Dobrinsky, Joseph.

Litz, A. Walton, ed. see Emerson, O. B.

Litz, A. Walton, ed. see Fogelman, Bruce.

Litz, A. Walton, ed. see Fraser, Gail.

Litz, A. Walton, ed. see Fryer, Sarah B.

Litz, A. Walton, ed. see Gladstein, Mimi R.

Litz, A. Walton, ed. see Halper, Nathan.

Litz, A. Walton, ed. see Hardy, Thomas.

Litz, A. Walton, ed. see Hooker, Joan F.

Litz, A. Walton, ed. see Jones, Michael P.

Litz, A. Walton, ed. see Joyce, James.

Litz, A. Walton, ed. see MacDonald, Bonney.

Litz, A. Walton, ed. see Maika, Patricia.

Litz, A. Walton, ed. see Maini, Darshan S.

Litz, A. Walton, ed. see Malamud, Randy.

Litz, A. Walton, ed. see McArthur, Murray.

Litz, A. Walton, ed. see Meyers, Jeffrey.

Litz, A. Walton, ed. see Powers, Lyall H.

Litz, A. Walton, ed. see Ragan, David P.

Litz, A. Walton, ed. see Schnitzer, Deborah.

Litz, A. Walton, ed. see Sensibar, Judith L.

Litz, A. Walton, ed. see Serafin, Joan M.

Litz, A. Walton, ed. see Soldo, John J.

Litz, A. Walton, ed. see Tintner, Adeline R.

Litz, A. Walton, ed. see Tobin, David N.

Litz, A. Walton, ed. see Whelan, P. T.

Litz, A. Walton, ed. see Williams, William Carlos.

***Litz, Brian.** Colorado Hut to Hut Vol. 1: Northern & Central Regions. rev. ed. 244p. 2000. pap. 22.95 (*1-56579-384-6*) Westcliffe Pubs.

— Colorado Hut to Hut Vol. 2: Southern Region. rev. ed. 244p. 2000. pap. 22.95 (*1-56579-385-4*) Westcliffe Pubs.

Litz, Richard E., ed. The Mango: Botany, Production & Uses. LC 96-48881. (A CAB International Publication). 601p. 1997. text 140.00 (*0-85199-127-0*) OUP.

Litz, Walton. Jane Austen Handbook. Grey, David J. & Southam, Brian, eds. (C). 1986. text 75.00 (*0-485-11301-5*, Pub. by Athlone Pr) Humanities.

Litz'en, U., jt. auth. see Thorne, A.

Litzenberg, Corinne M. Close Duck Calls: The Adventures of Hanna Flats, Captain Can & Their Favorite Feathered Friends from the Flats. LC 95-70929. (Illus.). 36p. 1995. pap. 12.95 (*0-614-14105-2*) Decoy Mag.

Litzenberger, Caroline. The English Reformation & the Laity: Gloucestershire, 1540-1580. LC 97-1361. (Cambridge Studies in Early Modern British History). (Illus.). 230p. (C). 1998. text 54.95 (*0-521-47545-7*) Cambridge U Pr.

Litzenberger, Caroline, jt. ed. see Wabuda, Susan.

Litzenberger, Robert H., jt. auth. see Huang, Chi-Fu.

Litzenburg, Thomas V., Jr., jt. auth. see Diamond, Malcolm L.

Litzinger, Boyd & Buscemi, Santi V. The Heath Reader. 3rd ed. LC 89-81685. 602p. (C). 1990. pap. text 31.96 (*0-669-20597-4*); teacher ed. 2.66 (*0-669-24382-5*) HM Trade Div.

Litzinger, Boyd & Knickerbocker, K. L. The Browning Critics. LC 65-27008. (Kentucky Paperbacks Ser.). 448p. reprint ed. pap. 138.90 (*0-8357-7448-1*, 203152300075) Bks Demand.

***Litzinger, Ralph A.** Other Chinas: The Yao & the Politics of National Belonging. LC 99-87369. (Illus.). 344p. 2000. pap. 21.95 (*0-8223-2549-7*) Duke.

— Other Chinas: The Yao & the Politics of National Belonging. LC 99-87369. (Illus.). 344p. 2000. lib. bdg. 64.95 (*0-8223-2525-X*) Duke.

Litzinger, Rosanne. The Old Woman & Her Pig. LC 91-38227. (Illus.). 32p. 1997. pap. 5.00 (*0-15-201490-X*) Harcourt.

— The Old Woman & Her Pig: An Old English Tale. LC 91-38227. (Illus.). 32p. (J). (ps-1). 1993. 13.95 (*0-15-257802-1*) Harcourt.

Litzinger, Rosanne. Old Woman & Her Pig, an Old English Tale. 1997. 10.20 (*0-606-11699-0*, Pub. by Turtleback) Demco.

— Wheels on the Bus. (Illus.). 10p. (J). (gr. k-1). 1999. 15.95 (*0-7613-1276-5*, Copper Beech Bks) Millbrook Pr.

Litzinger, Rosanne, jt. illus. see Cohen, Caron Lee.

***Litzinger, Sandra L.** Word, Wisdom & Worship: Womanchurch Celebrates the Seasons. 1999. pap. 13.00 (*0-9658137-6-2*) Woven Word.

Litzky, Tsarah. Blessing Poems. (Chapbook Ser.: Vol. 5). (Illus.). 10p. 1996. pap. 10.00 (*0-9652505-4-7*) Synaesthesia.

— Easy Life: A Memoir, 1. 1999. mass mkt. 12.95 (*1-58419-016-7*) Masq Bks.

Litzman, Warren, et al. Church Unity. LC 91-76171. 87p. 1991. pap. 14.95 (*0-940232-47-2*) Seedsowers.

Litzmann, Berthold. Clara Schumann, 3 vols., Set. 1971. reprint ed. write for info. (*0-318-71925-8*) G Olms Pubs.

— Clara Schumann: An Artist's Life, 2 vols., Set. LC 79-20823. (Music Reprint Ser.). 1979. reprint ed. lib. bdg. 95.00 (*0-306-79582-5*) Da Capo.

Litzmann, Berthold, ed. see Schumann, Clara (Wieck) & Brahms, Johannes.

Liu. Elementary Discrete Mathematics. 2nd ed. 1985. student ed. 28.75 (*0-07-038130-5*) McGraw.

— Fundamentals Solutions Manual. 1999. pap. text. write for info. (*0-471-36276-X*) Wiley.

— Uncertain Programming. LC 99-28988. 249p. 1999. 79.95 (*0-471-35994-7*) Wiley.

Liu, jt. ed. see Chow.

Liu, A. Unity & Diversity: Local Cultures & Identities in China. 328p. (Orig.). 1996. pap. 39.50 (*962-209-402-3*, Pub. by HK Univ Pr) Coronet Bks.

Liu, A. Y., et al, eds. Transcription Factors & Cell Aging. (Journal: Biological Signals: Vol. 5, No. 3, 1996). (Illus.). 70p. 1996. pap. 28.00 (*3-8055-6366-3*) S Karger.

Liu, A. Y., jt. ed. see Chen, K. Y.

Liu, Aimee E. Cloud Mountain. 1998. mass mkt. write for info. (*0-446-60544-1*) Warner Bks.

— Cloud Mountain. 672p. 1998. mass mkt. 14.99 (*0-446-67434-6*, Pub. by Warner Bks) Little.

— Face. 368p. 1995. mass mkt. 10.99 (*0-446-67135-5*, Pub. by Warner Bks) Little.

Liu, Aimee E., jt. auth. see Katz, Stan J.

Liu, Alan. Wordsworth: The Sense of History. (Illus.). 742p. 1989. 67.50 (*0-8047-1373-1*); pap. 24.95 (*0-8047-1893-8*) Stanford U Pr.

***Liu, Alan F.** Structural Life Assessment Methods. LC 98-14143. (Illus.). 419p. 1998. 98.00 (*0-87170-653-9*, 06592G) ASM.

Liu, Albert Z., tr. see Tang, Sun L.

Liu, Anita, jt. auth. see Fellows, Richard.

***Liu, Athena Ngar Chee.** Family Law for the Hong Kong SAR. 492p. 1999. pap. (*962-209-492-9*) HK Univ Pr.

Liu, B., et al, eds. Large Scale Systems: Theory & Applications: Selected Papers from the 6th IFAC-FORS-IMACS Symposium, Beijing, PRC, 23-25 August 1992. LC 93-33127. (IFAC Symposia Ser.: Vol. 1993, No. 10). 430p. 1993. 142.00 (*0-08-041895-3*, Pergamon Pr) Elsevier.

Liu, B., ed. see IFAC Symposium on Transportation Systems (1994: Ti.

Liu Baimao. History of Textile Technology of Ancient China. (Illus.). 1996. 93.45 (*7-03-000548-1*, Pub. by Sci Pr) Lubrecht & Cramer.

Liu, Bang S., et al. A New English-Chinese Dictionary. 2nd rev. ed. 1613p. 1985. pap. 64.95 (*0-471-80897-0*) Wiley.

Liu, Bao-Lin & Fiala, Alan D. Canon of Lunar Eclipses, 1500 B.C. to 3000 A.D. LC 92-429. (Illus.). 1992. 24.95 (*0-943396-37-9*) Willmann-Bell.

Liu, Bea E. Remembering China, 1935-1945: A Memoir. LC 95-71165. (Minnesota Voices Project Ser.: No. 76). 192p. 1996. 22.95 (*0-89823-170-1*) New Rivers Pr.

Liu, Bede, jt. auth. see Peled, Abraham.

Liu, Ben-Hui. Statistical Genomics: Linkage, Mapping & QTL Analysis. LC 97-1863. 648p. 1997. boxed set 79.95 (*0-8493-3166-8*) CRC Pr.

Liu, Benjamin, jt. auth. see O'Connor, John.

Liu, Benjamin M. & Monroe, James T. Ten Hispano-Arabic Strophic Songs in the Modern Oral Tradition: Music & Texts. (Publications in Modern Philology: Vol. 125). (Illus.). 101p. 1990. pap. 15.00 (*0-520-09751-3*, Pub. by U CA Pr) Cal Prin Full Svc.

Liu Binyan. People or Monsters? And Other Stories & Reportage from China after Mao. Link, Perry, ed. LC 82-48594. (Chinese Literature in Translation Ser.). 160p. 1983. 20.00 (*0-253-34329-1*) Ind U Pr.

***Liu, Bolian & Lai, Hong-Jian.** Matrices in Combinatorics & Graph Theory. LC 00-42808. (Network Theory & Applications Ser.). 2000. write for info. (*0-7923-6469-4*) Kluwer Academic.

Liu, C. C., jt. ed. see Seymour, Richard K.

Liu, C. Q., jt. auth. see Huston, R.

Liu, C. S. & Tripathi, V. K. Interaction of Electromagnetic Wave with Electron Beams & Plasma. 180p. 1994. text 68.00 (*981-02-1577-0*) World Scientific Pub.

Liu, C. S. & Wagner, F. Nuclear Fusion & Plasma Physics. 400p. 1995. text 106.00 (*981-02-2151-7*) World Scientific Pub.

Liu, C. T., et al, eds. High-Temperature Ordered Intermetallic Alloys III Vol. 133: Materials Research Society Symposium Proceedings. 772p. 1989. text 17.50 (*1-55899-006-2*) Materials Res.

Liu, C. T., et al, eds. Ordered Intermetallics - Physical Metallurgy & Mechanical Behaviour: Proceedings of the NATO Advanced Research Workshop, Irsee, Germany, June 23-28, 1991. LC 92-10360. (NATO Advanced Study Institutes Series E, Applied Sciences: Vol. 213). 712p. (C). 1992. text 332.00 (*0-7923-1726-2*) Kluwer Academic.

Liu, C. T., et al, eds. Shape-Memory Materials & Phenomena - Fundamental Aspects & Applications. (Symposium Proceedings Ser.: Vol. 246). 435p. 1992. text 30.00 (*1-55899-140-9*) Materials Res.

Liu, C. Y., ed. Laparoscopic Hysterectomy & Pelvic Floor Reconstruction. (Minimally Invasive Gynecology Ser.). (Illus.). 240p. 1995. 125.00 (*0-86542-383-0*) Blackwell Sci.

Liu, C. Y. & Chien, Shu, eds. Fibrinogen, Thrombosis, Coagulation & Fibrinolysis. LC 90-14299. (Advances in Experimental Medicine & Biology Ser.: Vol. 281). (Illus.). 460p. (C). 1990. text 162.00 (*0-306-43726-0*, Kluwer Plenum) Kluwer Academic.

***Liu, Cary Y., et al.** Character & Context in Chinese Calligraphy LC 98-83210. 295 p. 1999. write for info. (*0-943012-29-5*) Prince U Art.

***Liu, Catherine.** Copying Machines: Taking Notes for the Automaton. LC 00-8066. 2000. pap. write for info. (*0-8166-3503-X*) U of Minn Pr.

Liu, Catherine. Oriental Girls Desire Romance. LC 94-74872. 280p. 1997. pap. 13.95 (*1-885030-24-X*) Kaya Prod.

Liu, Cengdian & Nichols, R. W., eds. Pressure Vessel Technology: Proceedings of the International Conference, 6th, Beijing, People's Republic of China, 11-15 September 1988, 2 vols. (Illus.). 1750p. 1989. 789.00 (*0-08-035896-9*, Pub. by Pergamon Repr); 260.00 (*0-08-035897-7*, Pub. by Pergamon Repr) Franklin.

Liu, Charles, ed. Artists of Taiwan. (Illus.). 312p. 1994. 75.00 (*1-885594-01-1*) Pt Fine Arts.

— Ting Shao Kuang Serigraphs. (Illus.). 110p. 1991. 30.00 (*0-9623747-4-1*) Segal Fine Art.

Liu, Charles, jt. ed. see Zhen, Sheng T.

***Liu, Cheng.** Soils & Foundations. 5th ed. LC 00-39195. (Illus.). 400p. 2000. 80.00 (*0-13-025517-3*) P-H.

Liu, Cheng, jt. auth. see Evett, Jack B.

Liu, Cheng, jt. auth. see Giles, Ranald V.

Liu, Cho-Teng, ed. Space Remote Sensing of Subtropical Oceans (SRSSO), Vol. 8. LC 97-211663. (COSPAR Colloquia Ser.). 272p. 1997. 215.00 (*0-08-042850-9*, Pergamon Pr) Elsevier.

Liu, Chongyun, et al. Encyclopedia of Chinese & U. S. Patent Herbal Medicine. LC 99-26881. 304p. 1999. 35.00 (*0-87983-891-4*, 38914K, Keats Publng) NTC Contemp Pub Co.

Liu, Christine. More Nutritional Chinese Cooking with Christine Liu. 3rd ed. LC 81-90263. (Illus.). 452p. 1996. 27.95 (*0-9610566-5-7*) Graphique Pubs.

— Nutrition & Diet with Chinese Cooking. 6th rev. ed. (Illus.). 338p. 1985. pap. 16.95 (*0-9610566-1-4*, A837797) Graphique Pubs.

— Nutritional Cooking with Tofu. 2nd rev. ed. LC 83-32385. (Illus.). 168p. 1992. pap. 12.95 (*0-9610566-8-1*) Graphique Pubs.

Liu Chun-Jo. Controversies in Modern Chinese Intellectual History: An Analytical Bibliography of Periodical Articles, Mainly of the May Fourth & Post-May Fourth Era. LC 64-56634. (East Asian Monographs: No. 15). 214p. 1964. pap. 20.00 (*0-674-17000-8*) HUP.

Liu Chun-Jo, ed. Building Bridges: University of Minnesota Alumni in China. LC 95-31527. (C). 1995. pap. write for info. (*0-9631087-1-9*) U MN China Ctr.

Liu, Chung L. Elements of Discrete Mathematics. 2nd ed. (Computer Science Ser.). 433p. (C). 1985. 96.88 (*0-07-038133-X*) McGraw.

Liu, Cricket & Albitz, Paul. Dns & Bind. 2nd ed. (Illus.). 438p. 1996. pap. 32.95 (*1-56592-236-0*) Thomson Learn.

— Dns & Bind. 3rd ed. Loukides, Mike, ed. (Illus.). 502p. 1998. pap. 37.95 (*1-56592-512-2*) OReilly & Assocs.

Liu, Cricket, et al. DNS on Windows NT. Loukides, Mike, ed. (Illus.). 348p. 1998. pap. 34.95 (*1-56592-511-4*) OReilly & Assocs.

— Managing Internet Information Services: World Wide Web, Gopher, FTP, & More. (Illus.). 400p. (Orig.). 1995. pap. 29.95 (*1-56592-062-7*) Thomson Learn.

Liu, Da. T'ai Chi Ch'uan & Meditation. LC 85-25071. (Illus.). 192p. 1991. pap. 14.00 (*0-8052-0993-X*) Schocken.

L

Liu Da. The Tao of Health & Longevity. (Illus.). 224p. 1997. pap. text 10.95 (*1-56924-718-8*) Marlowe & Co.

— Taoist Health Exercise Book. rev. expanded ed. 188p. 1994. pap. 10.95 (*1-56924-901-6*) Marlowe & Co.

Liu, Dalin, et al. Sexual Behavior in Modern China: The Report on the Nationawide Survey of 20,000 Men & Women. (Illus.). 556p. (C). 1997. 95.00 (*0-8264-0886-9*) Continuum.

Liu, Darrell T. Tao Te Ching. 1988. pap. 11.95 (*0-14-019060-0*, Penguin Bks) Viking Penguin.

Liu, Darrell T., jt. ed. see Marshak, Daniel R.

***Liu, David H. & Liptbak, Bela G.** Air Pollution. LC 99-52749. 244p. 1999. write for info. (*1-56670-513-4*) Lewis Pubs.

— Groundwater & Surface Water Pollution. LC 99-55330. 150p. 1999. write for info. (*1-56670-511-8*) Lewis Pubs.

— Hazardous Waste & Solid Waste. LC 99-55324. 273p. 1999. write for info. (*1-56670-512-6*) Lewis Pubs.

— Wastewater Treatment. LC 99-52047. 457p. 1999. write for info. (*1-56670-515-0*) Lewis Pubs.

Liu, David T., ed. A Practical Guide to Chorion Villus Sampling. (Illus.). 168p. 1991. 62.00 (*0-19-262006-1*) OUP.

Liu, Dean-Mo & Dixit, Vivek, eds. Porous Materials for Tissue Engineering. (Materials Science Forum Ser.: Vol. 250). (Illus.). 252p. (C). 1998. text 94.00 (*0-87849-773-0*, Pub. by Trans T Pub) Enfield Pubs NH.

Liu, Derong & Michel, Anthony N. Dynamical Systems with Saturation Nonlinearities: Analysis & Design. LC 94-12280. (Lecture Notes in Control & Information Sciences). 1994. 40.00 (*0-387-19888-1*) Spr-Verlag.

Liu, Dickson & Dutka. Toxicity Screening Procedures Using Bacterial Systems. (Drug & Chemical Toxicology Ser.: Vol. 1). (Illus.). 496p. 1984. text 199.00 (*0-8247-7171-0*) Dekker.

Liu, Doris. Best Chinese Names. Jingyu, Wu, tr. (Illus.). 152p. 1996. pap. 14.95 (*981-3068-30-2*, Pub. by Asiapac) China Bks.

Liu, E. The Travels of Lao Ts'an. Shadick, Harold, tr. from CHI. & intro. by. LC 86-1867.Tr. of Lao-ts'an Yu Chi. 300p. 1986. reprint ed. lib. bdg. 65.00 (*0-313-25164-9*, LITR, Greenwood Pr) Greenwood.

Liu, Edison T., ed. Current Topics in BRCA 1: A Breast Disease Book. 140p. 1998. pap. 99.00 (*90-5199-394-3*, Pub. by IOS Pr) IOS Press.

Liu, Edison T., jt. ed. see Benz, Christopher C.

Liu, Eric. The Accidental Asian: Notes of a Native Speaker. 224p. 1999. pap. 12.00 (*0-375-70486-8*) Knopf.

— Next: Young American Writers on the New Generation. LC 93-38794. 1994. pap. 12.95 (*0-393-31191-0*) Norton.

Liu, Eric S. Frequency Dictionary of Chinese Words. (Linguistic Structures, First Ser.). (CHI.). 1973. pap. text 70.80 (*90-279-2627-1*) Mouton.

Liu, F. C. & Liu, T. P., eds. Nonlinear Analysis, 1989 Conference. 384p. (C). 1991. text 113.00 (*981-02-0136-2*) World Scientific Pub.

Liu, F. C. & Mau, L. Y. Chinese Medical Terminology: English to Chinese. (CHI & ENG.). 262p. 1980. 39.95 (*0-8288-0559-8*, M9399) Fr & Eur.

Liu, Fan. The Story of Beijing. (CHI.). 128p. (Orig.). 1996. pap. 7.95 (*0-9644818-4-7*) Waymont Intl.

Liu, Fangtong, et al, eds. Philosophy & Modernization in China. LC 97-19303. (Cultural Heritage & Contemporary Change Series III: Vol. 13). 220p. 1997. pap. 17.50 (*1-56518-066-6*) Coun Res Values.

Liu, Felix & EFC Los Angeles Staff. Living Spring: Collected True Stories & Messages. 238p. 1996. pap. 9.95 (*1-885216-08-4*) Evan Formosan.

***Liu, Feng.** Environmental Justice & Equity Analysis: Theories, Methods & Practice. LC 00-41232. 2000. write for info. (*1-56670-403-0*) Lerner Pub.

Liu, Feng. Tackling Environmental Problems Across the Media of Land, Water, & Air. LC 93-379. (CPL Bibliographies Ser.: No. 289). 20p. 1993. pap. 10.00 (*0-86602-289-9*, Sage Prdcls Pr) Sage.

Liu, Feng-hsi. Scope & Specificity. LC 97-16442. (Linguistik Aktuell/Linguistics Today Ser.: Vol. 16). viii, 187p. 1997. lib. bdg. 84.00 (*1-55619-900-7*) J Benjamins Pubng Co.

Liu, Frank, et al. Integrated Multi-Media Research Guide to Pennsylvania Law. 1999. write for info. (*1-57588-453-4*, 311770) W S Hein.

Liu, Frank, tr. see Guan, Zenyzhu.

Liu, Frank, tr. see Tai, Shuangyuan.

Liu, Frank, tr. see Zhang, Yaoning.

***Liu, G. P. & Patton, Ron.** Eigenstructure Assignment for Control System Design. LC 97-35150. 248p. 1998. 149.95 (*0-471-97549-4*) Wiley.

Liu, Gillian. At the Seaside. (Early Words Ser.). (Illus.). 24p. (J). (gr. 1-3). 1996. write for info. (*0-237-51428-1*) EVN1 UK.

— The Funfair. (Early Words Ser.). (Illus.). 24p. (J). (gr. 1-3). 1996. write for info. (*0-237-51430-3*) EVN1 UK.

— How Do You Feel? (Early Words Ser.). (Illus.). 24p. (J). (gr. 1-3). 1996. write for info. (*0-237-51432-X*) EVN1 UK.

— Where Are My Stripes? (Early Words Ser.). (Illus.). 24p. (J). (gr. 1-3). 1996. write for info. (*0-237-51431-1*) EVN1 UK.

— Where's Our Dinner? (Early Words Ser.). (Illus.). 24p. (J). (gr. 1-3). 1996. write for info. (*0-237-51427-3*) EVN1 UK.

Liu, Gretchen. Pastel Portraits. (Illus.). 156p. 1995. 40.00 (*9971-88-020-2*, Pub. by Select Bks) Weatherhill.

Liu, H., ed. see Lu, H. J.

***Liu, H. C.** Intersubband Transitions in Quantum Wells: Physics & Device Applications. (Semiconductors & Semimetals Ser.: Vol. 62). 1999. 120.00 (*0-12-752171-2*) Acad Pr.

Liu, H. C., et al, eds. Quantum Well Intersubband Transition Physics & Devices: Proceedings of the NATO Advanced Research Workshop, Whistler, Canada, September 7-10, 1993. LC 94-12285. (NATO ASI Series E: Applied Sciences: Vol. 270). 588p. (C). 1994. text 336.00 (*0-7923-2877-9*) Kluwer Academic.

Liu, H. C. & Yeh, S. Y., eds. Fisheries Education & Training in Asia: Second Workshop Proceedings. (Asian Fisheries Society Spec. Publications: No. 8). 191p. 1993. per. write for info. (*971-8709-47-9*, Pub. by ICLARM) Intl Spec Bk.

Liu, Haiping & Swortzell, Lowell, eds. Eugene O'Neill in China: An International Centenary Celebration, 44. LC 91-28744. (Contributions in Drama & Theatre Studies: No. 44). 360p. 1992. 62.95 (*0-313-27379-0*, LEO/, Greenwood Pr) Greenwood.

Liu, Hans. Swimmer's Ear: The Diagnosis, Treatment: Management of Otitis Externa. (Illus.). 41p. 1998. spiral bd. 16.95 (*0-9668202-0-7*) S Dawson Pubs.

***Liu, Haoming.** Memory & History in George Elliot: Transfiguring the Past. LC 99-46744. 2000. text 55.00 (*0-312-22834-1*) St Martin.

Liu, Haws, et al. Shesffield Dawson Guide to Management of Infectious Disease. 157p. 1998. ring bd. 34.95 (*0-9668202-3-1*) S Dawson Pubs.

Liu, Henry. Wind Engineering: A Handbook for Structural Engineering. 224p. (C). 1990. text 46.20 (*0-13-960279-8*) P-H.

Liu, Herman C. Non-Verbal Intelligence Tests for Use in China. LC 76-177001. (Columbia University. Teachers College. Contributions to Education Ser.: No. 126). reprint ed. 37.50 (*0-404-55126-2*) AMS Pr.

Liu, Hong & Perry, Paul. The Healing Art of Qi Gong: Ancient Wisdom from a Modern Master. Orig. Title: Mastering Miracles. 320p. 1999. mass mkt. 14.00 (*0-446-67347-1*, Pub. by Warner Bks) Little.

Liu, Hongtan, jt. auth. see Kakacs, S.

Liu, Hua-Yih. Concordance of Proverbs. 250p. 1993. pap. 14.95 (*0-9631789-5-4*) Evan Formosan.

Liu, Huan & Motoda, Hiroshi. Feature Extraction, Construction & Selection: A Data Mining Perspective. LC 98-24450. (International Series in Engineering & Computer Science). 1998. 140.00 (*0-7923-8196-3*) Kluwer Academic.

— Feature Selection for Knowledge Discovery & Data Mining, Vol. 454. LC 98-25204. (International Series in Engineering & Computer Science). 1998. 125.00 (*0-7923-8198-X*) Kluwer Academic.

***Liu, Hui H.** Signal Processing Applications in CDMA Communications. 2000. 79.00 (*1-58053-042-7*) Artech Hse.

Liu, Huimin. Science & Engineering of Droplets: Fundamentals & Applications. LC 99-27324. 225p. 1999. 139.00 (*0-8155-1436-0*) Noyes.

Liu, Huimin & Dandy, David S. Diamond Chemical Vapor Deposition: Nucleation & Early Growth Stages. LC 95-30332. (Illus.). 188p. 1996. 109.00 (*0-8155-1380-1*) Noyes.

Liu, I-ching. A New Account of Tales of the World. Mather, Richard B., tr. & intro. by. LC 75-22650. 758p. 1976. reprint ed. pap. 200.00 (*0-608-00792-7*, 205934100010) Bks Demand.

Liu I-Ming. Awakening to the Tao. Cleary, Thomas, tr. from CHI. LC 88-17478. 96p. (Orig.). 1988. pap. 12.00 (*0-87773-447-X*, Pub. by Shambhala Pubns) Random.

Liu, Irene & Li Xiaoqi. A Chinese Text for a Changing China. rev. ed. (C & T Asian Language Ser.). 285p. (Orig.). 1995. pap. text 18.95 (*0-88727-232-0*) Cheng & Tsui.

Liu, J. P., jt. ed. see Hu, Z. X.

Liu, J. Q., jt. auth. see Lick, D. R.

Liu, J. Y., tr. see Carlson, Dwight L.

***Liu, Jack.** Surveying Review for the Civil Engineer: For the Professional Engineer's Exam, No. 3. (Illus.). 122p. 2000. pap. 28.50 (*1-57645-058-9*, 589) Engineering.

Liu, James C. The Road. 509p. 1994. pap. 16.95 (*0-9631789-8-9*) Evan Formosan.

Liu, James J. The Art of Chinese Poetry. LC 62-7475. xii, 176p. 1966. pap. text 10.95 (*0-226-48687-7*) U Ch Pr.

— The Art of Chinese Poetry. LC 62-7475. (Midway Reprint Ser.). xii, 164p. 1983. pap. text 11.00 (*0-226-48685-0*) U Ch Pr.

— The Art of Chinese Poetry. LC 62-7475. (Midway Reprint Ser.). 176p. reprint ed. pap. 54.60 (*0-608-09466-8*, 205426600005) Bks Demand.

— The Chinese Knight Errant. LC 66-14112. 256p. reprint ed. pap. 79.40 (*0-608-13420-1*, 202409700035) Bks Demand.

— Essentials of Chinese Literary Art. 150p. 1979. 4.95 (*0-318-36953-2*) Asia Bk Corp.

— The Interlingual Critic: Interpreting Chinese Poetry. LC 81-47010. 154p. reprint ed. pap. 47.80 (*0-608-18255-9*, 205670700081) Bks Demand.

— Language, Paradox, Poetics: A Chinese Perspective. LC 88-6013. 191p. reprint ed. pap. 59.30 (*0-608-06423-8*, 206663600008) Bks Demand.

Liu, James T. China Turning Inward: Intellectual-Political Changes in the Early Twelfth Century, Vol. 132. LC 80-3579. (East Asian Monographs). 225p. 1987. 30.00 (*0-674-11755-7*) HUP.

— Reform in Sung China: Wang An-Shih, 1021-1086, & His New Policies. LC 59-9281. (East Asian Monographs: No. 3). 1959. 5.00 (*0-674-75300-3*) HUP.

Liu, James T. & Tu, Wei-Ming. Traditional China: A Spectrum Book. LC 77-104855. (Asian Civilization Ser.). viii, 179 p. 1970. write for info. (*0-13-926014-5*) Prntice Hall Bks.

Liu, James T., jt. tr. see McKnight, Brian E.

***Liu, Jane W. S.** Real-Time Systems. LC 99-51522. 624p. 2000. 63.00 (*0-13-099651-3*) P-H.

Liu, Jen-Pei, jt. auth. see Chow, Shein-Chung.

Liu, Jen-Pei, jt. ed. see Chow, Shein-Chung.

Liu, Jennifer L. & Yan, Margaret M. Interactions II: A Cognitive Approach to Beginning Chinese. 1997. 39.95 (*0-253-33289-3*) Ind U Pr.

Liu, Jennifer L., jt. auth. see Yan, Margaret M.

Liu, Jennifer Li-Chia. Interactions II: A Cognitive Approach to Beginning Chinese. 1997. pap. text 18.95 (*0-253-21123-9*) Ind U Pr.

Liu, Jenny, jt. auth. see Chaio-Hui.

Liu, Jialiu & Blumert, Michael. Jiaogulan - China's "Immortality Herb" Unlocking the Secret of Nature's Powerful Adaptogen & Antioxidant. LC 98-51697. (Illus.). 80p. 1999. pap. 7.95 (*1-887089-16-0*) Torchlght Pub.

Liu, Jianguo, contrib. by. Telecommunications Market Opportunities in China. 187p. 1995. 2650.00 (*1-56965-072-1*, G-188) BCC.

***Liu, Jiming.** Autonomous Agents & Multi-Agent Systems. 320p. 2000. 58.00 (*981-02-4282-4*) World Scientific Pub.

***Liu, Jiming & Zhong, Ning, eds.** Inteligent Agent Technology. 520p. 2000. 96.00 (*981-02-4054-6*) World Scientific Pub.

Liu, John, tr. see Boice, James M.

***Liu, John J.** Manufacturing Innovations & Technological Operations: Theory & Application. 2000. 74.00 (*981-02-4179-8*) World Scientific Pub.

Liu, John J., tr. see Morgan, G. Campbell.

Liu, Jonathan, tr. see Lindsell, Harold.

Liu, Judith & Ross, Heidi A. Education in the People's Republic of China: An Ethnography. Beauchamp, Edward R., ed. LC 99-39740. (Reference Books in International Education: No. 47). 224p. 1999. text 55.00 (*0-8153-1471-X*, SS0922) Garland.

Liu, Juhne, jt. auth. see Narayanan, S. Naru.

Liu, Julius L., jt. auth. see Wang, Simon.

Liu, K. F., ed. Chiral Solitons. 578p. 1987. pap. 47.00 (*9971-5-0323-9*); text 131.00 (*9971-5-0322-0*) World Scientific Pub.

Liu, K. F., jt. auth. see Wagner, A.

Liu, K. F., jt. ed. see Wagner, A.

Liu, K. Ray & Yao, Kung. High Performance VLSI Signal Processing. LC 97-23776. 720p. 1997. write for info. (*0-7803-3468-X*); pap. write for info. (*0-7803-3469-8*) IEEE Standards.

***Liu, Kang.** Aesthetics & Marxism: Chinese Aesthetic Marxists & Their Western Contemporaries. LC 99-43220. (Post-Contemporary Interventions Ser.). 296p. 2000. 19.95 (*0-8223-2448-2*) Duke.

Liu Kang. Chop Suey. 96p. 1991. pap. text 5.00 (*981-00-2730-3*) World Scientific Pub.

Liu Kang & Tang, Xiaobing, eds. Politics, Ideology, & Literary Discourse in Modern China: Theoretical Interventions & Cultural Critique. LC 93-4448. (Illus.). 328p. 1994. text 49.95 (*0-8223-1403-7*) Duke.

— Politics, Ideology, & Literary Discourse in Modern China: Theoretical Interventions & Cultural Critique. LC 93-4448. (Illus.). 328p. 1994. pap. text 19.95 (*0-8223-1416-9*) Duke.

***Liu, Kecheng.** Semiotics in Information Systems Development. (Illus.). 240p. (C). 2000. text 49.95 (*0-521-59335-2*) Cambridge U Pr.

Liu, Keh-Fei, et al, eds. Medium & High-Energy Nuclear Physics. 816p. (C). 1989. text 141.00 (*9971-5-0658-0*) World Scientific Pub.

Liu, Keshun. Soybeans: Chemistry, Technology, & Utilization. 532p. 1997. 90.00 (*0-8342-1299-4*) Aspen Pub.

Liu, Kim C. & Zhang, Wei G. Accounting Issues in China: An Analytical Appraoch. LC 96-24387. 170p. (C). 1997. pap. 33.00 (*0-13-577065-3*) P-H.

Liu, Kwang-Ching. Anglo-American Steamship Rivalry in China, 1862-1874. LC 62-9426. (Harvard East Asian Studies: No. 8). (Illus.). 244p. 1962. reprint ed. pap. 75.70 (*0-7837-1716-4*, 205724500024) Bks Demand.

Liu Kwang-Ching, ed. American Missionaries in China: Papers from Harvard Seminars. LC 66-31226. (East Asian Monographs: No. 21). 316p. 1966. pap. 20.00 (*0-674-02600-4*) HUP.

Liu Kwang-Ching, jt. ed. see Chu, Samuel C.

Liu, Lawrence S., jt. ed. see Cheng, Chia-Jui.

Liu-Lengyel, Hongying, jt. auth. see Lengyel, Alfonz.

***Liu, Leping, et al, eds.** Information Technology in Educational Research & Statistics. LC 99-51388. (Computers in the Schools Monograph Ser.: Vol. 15, Nos. 3/4 & Vol. 16, No. 1). 258p. 1999. 59.95 (*0-7890-0958-7*) Haworth Pr.

— Information Technology in Educational Research & Statistics. LC 99-51388. (Computers in the Schools Monograph Ser.: Vol. 15, Nos. 3/4 & Vol. 16, No. 1). 258p. (C). 1999. pap. text 39.95 (*0-7890-0976-5*) Haworth Pr.

Liu, Lesley, jt. auth. see Chang, Monica.

Liu, Lewis-Guodo. The Internet & Library & Information Services: A Review, Analysis, & Annotated Bibliography. (Occasional Papers: No. 202). 90p. (Orig.). 1995. pap. 8.00 (*0-614-15033-7*) U of Ill Grad Sch.

Liu, Lewis-Guodo. The Internet & Library & Information Services: Issues, Trends & Annotated Bibliography, 1994-1995, 10. LC 96-8936. (Bibliographies & Indexes in Library & Information Science: No. 10). 320p. 1996. lib. bdg. 72.95 (*0-313-30019-4*, Greenwood Pr) Greenwood.

Liu, Lewis-Guodo. Internet Resources & Services for International Business: A Global Guide. LC 98-21251. 248p. 1998. pap. 49.95 (*1-57356-119-3*) Oryx Pr.

***Liu, Lewis-Guodo & Premus, Robert.** Global Economic Growth: Theories, Research, Studies & Annotated Bibliography, 1950-1997, 19. LC 99-53866. (Bibliographies & Indexes in Economics & Economic History Ser.: Vol. 19). 360p. 2000. lib. bdg. 85.00 (*0-313-30738-5*, Greenwood Pr) Greenwood.

Liu Li-Gang, et al. Global Economic Effects of the Asian Currency Devaluations. LC 98-6033. (Policy Analysis in International Economics Ser.: No. 56). 1998. pap. 15.95 (*0-88132-260-1*) Inst Intl Eco.

The Asian financial crisis has precipitated significant changes in real exchange rates in the region that will substantially alter the volume & pattern of international trade. The crisis countries will increase their exports & especially, reduce their imports. Japan, China & other non-crisis countries will experience more complex changes. The trade balances of the United States & Western Europe will deteriorate by about $40-50 billion as a result of the currency movements in Asia. This study quantifies the impact of the currency changes on the individual countries in Asia, on the United States, on Europe & on other regions on a sector-by-sector basis. It analyzes the additional impact that might occur if China, thus far a relative bystander in the crisis, were to devalue its currency as well. It then examines potential trade policy responses to these developments including the risk of an upsurge in protectionist pressure in the United States.
Publisher Paid Annotation.

Liu, Liangdong. Intelligent Autonomous Control in Aerospace: A Postprint Volume from the IFAC Conference, Beijing, PRC, 14-16 August 1995. LC 97-8926. (IFAC Proceedings Volumes Ser.). 1997. pap. text 83.00 (*0-08-042373-6*, Pergamon Pr) Elsevier.

Liu Lianshou. Proceedings of the International Symposium on Multiparticle Dynamics, XXI: Wu-han, China, 23-27 September, 1991. Wu Yuanfang, ed. LC 92-11996. 700p. 1992. text 137.00 (*981-02-0949-5*) World Scientific Pub.

Liu, Lily. The American Dream. Peng, H. L., ed. 240p. (Orig.). pap. 14.98 (*0-9639426-0-3*) Think Big Pubng.

Liu, Lin. Cartographic Design Using Arc View GIS & ARC/INFO. LC 99-58421. (Illus.). 432p. (C). 2000. pap. text 54.95 (*1-56690-187-1*) Thomson Learn.

Liu, Lydia H. Translingual Practice: Literature, National Culture, & Modernity - China, 1900-1937. LC 94-45961. (Illus.). 368p. 1995. 60.00 (*0-8047-2534-9*) Stanford U Pr.

***Liu, Lydia H., ed.** Tokens of Exchange: The Problem of Translation in Global Circulations. LC 99-28628. (Illus.). 384p. 1999. 64.95 (*0-8223-2401-6*) Duke.

Liu, Lydia He. Tokens of Exchange: The Problem of Translation in Global Circulations. LC 99-28628. (Post-Contemporary Interventions Ser.). 384p. 1999. pap. 21.95 (*0-8223-2424-5*) Duke.

Liu, M. C., jt. auth. see Chan, K. Y.

Liu, Manni, et al. Shiwan Ceramics: Beauty, Color, & Passion. Li He, tr. from ENG. LC 94-71002. (CHI., Illus.). 110p. (Orig.). 1995. pap. 28.00 (*0-9609784-0-2*); text 38.00 (*0-9609784-6-1*) CCF San Francisco.

Liu Mau-Tsai. Chinesisch-Deutsches Stilwoerterbuch fuer Konversation. (CHI & GER.). 816p. 1980. 185.00 (*0-8288-1007-9*, F34990) Fr & Eur.

Liu, Max M. Principles & Applications of Optical Communications. (C). 1993. text 44.95 (*0-256-16541-6*, Irwn McGrw-H) McGrw-H Hghr Educ.

Liu, Michael T., ed. Chemistry of Diazirines, 2 vols., Set. 352p. 1987. 189.00 (*0-8493-5047-6*, QD341, CRC Reprint) Franklin.

Liu, Micheal T., ed. Chemistry of Diazirines, Vol. I. 176p. 1987. 105.00 (*0-8493-5048-4*, CRC Reprint) Franklin.

Liu, Ming-Wood. Madhyamaka Thought in China. LC 94-953. (Sinica Leidensia Ser.: Vol. 30). 1994. 126.00 (*90-04-09984-0*) Brill Academic Pubs.

Liu, Nancy, tr. see Qing, Dai.

Liu, Oianhong & Ng, Peter A. Document Processing & Retrieval: Textpros. LC 95-39610. 312p. (C). 1995. text 127.00 (*0-7923-9644-8*) Kluwer Academic.

Liu, P. D. & Qian, Min. Smooth Ergodic Theory of Random Dynamical Systems. Dold, A. & Takens, F., eds. (Lecture Notes in Mathematics Ser.: Vol. 1606). xi, 221p. 1995. pap. 44.95 (*3-540-60004-3*) Spr-Verlag.

Liu, Pan-Tai & Roxin, Emilio D. Differential Games & Control Theory III: Proceedings of the Third Kingston Conference, Pt. A. (Lecture Notes in Pure & Applied Mathematics Ser.: Vol. 44). (Illus.). 256p. 1979. pap. text 145.00 (*0-8247-6845-0*) Dekker.

Liu, Pan-Tai, ed. see Kingston Conference on Differential Games & Contro.

Liu, Pan-Tai, ed. see Kingston Confererence on Differential Games & Contr.

Liu, Paul I. Introduction to Energy & the Environment. LC 93-7906. 208p. 1993. text 60.95 (*0-442-01557-7*, VNR) Wiley.

Liu, Pei-Dong & Qian, Min. Smooth Ergodic Theory of Random Dynamical Systems. LC 95-21996. (Lecture Notes in Mathematics Ser.: Vol. 1606). 1995. write for info. (*0-387-60004-3*) Spr-Verlag.

Liu, Peyia & Ghafoor, Arif. Multimedia Document Systems in Perspectives. LC 98-49293. 1999. write for info. (*0-7923-8416-4*) Kluwer Academic.

Liu, Philip. Advances in Coastal & Ocean Engineering, Vol. 2. 350p. 1996. text 78.00 (*981-02-2410-9*) World Scientific Pub.

An Asterisk (*) at the beginning of an entry indicates that the title is appearing for the first time.

Liu, Philip L. Advances in Coastal & Ocean Engineering, Vol. 4. 250p. 1998. 48.00 (981-02-3310-8) World Scientific Pub.

Liu, Philip L., ed. Principles & Procedures in Anesthesiology. LC 91-42092. (Illus.). 446p. 1992. reprint ed. pap. 138.30 (0-608-07263-X, 206749100009) Bks Demand.

***Liu, Philip L.** Advances in Coastal & Ocean Engineering, 5. 1999. 67.00 (981-02-3859-2) WSC Inst MA Studies.

Liu, Pin-Yen. People or Monsters? Other Stories & Reportage from China after Mao. Link, Perry, ed. LC 82-48594. (Chinese Literature in Translation Ser.). 157p. Date not set. reprint ed. pap. 48.70 (0-608-20559-1, 205447300002) Bks Demand.

Liu Qian. Panda Bear Goes Visiting. (Illus.). 22p. (J). (gr. 3-4). 1982. 3.95 (0-8351-1108-3); pap. 3.95 (0-8351-1139-3) China Bks.

Liu, Qingshan. Chinese Fitness - A Mind/Body Approach: Qigong for Healthy Joyful Living. Murray, Andrew, ed. LC 96-61428. (Qigong-Health & Healing Ser.).Tr. of Qi Gong-Der Chinesische Weg fur ein Gesundes Langes Leben. (Illus.). 144p. 1997. pap. 14.95 (1-886969-37-X, B029) YMAA Pubn.

Liu, Ray H. & Gadzala, Daniel E. Handbook of Drug Analysis: Applications in Forensic & Clinical Laboratories. LC 96-38029. 385p. 1997. text 135.00 (0-8412-3448-5, Pub. by Am Chemical) OUP.

Liu, Ray H. & Goldberger, Bruce A., eds. Handbook of Workplace Drug Testing. 2nd ed. 390p. 1995. reprint ed. pap. 49.00 (0-915274-77-9, 202638) Am Assn Clinical Chem.

Liu, Robert K. Collectible Beads: A Universal Aesthetic. LC 94-68696. (Illus.). 256p. 2000. 44.95 (0-9641023-0-7, Pub. by Ornament) Antique Collect.

Liu, Ruey-Wen, ed. Testing & Diagnosis of Analog Circuits & Systems. LC 90-45217. (Illus.). 240p. 1991. text 64.95 (0-442-25932-8, VNR) Wiley.

Liu, S. C., ed. Smart Structures & Materials, 1998: Smart Systems for Bridges, Structures & Highways. LC 98-227312. (Proceedings of SPIE Ser.: Vol. 3325). 302p. 1998. 80.00 (0-8194-2769-1) SPIE.

***Liu, S. C., ed.** Smart Systems for Bridges, Structures & Highways. 358p. 1999. pap. text 84.00 (0-8194-3145-1) SPIE.

Liu, S. C., et al, eds. Materials Symposium Vol. 3: Materials Symposium. LC 82-70515. (1995 Offshore Mechanics & Arctic Engineering Conference Ser.: Vol. III). 604p. 1995. 180.00 (0-7918-1309-6, H00940) ASME.

Liu, S. C. & Ilic, M, D. Hierarchical Power Systems Control: Its Value in a Changing Industry. (Advances in Industrial Control Ser.). 250p. 1996. 64.95 (3-540-76031-8) Spr-Verlag.

Liu, Samuel M., ed. Hymns of Praise: The Hymnal of the True Jesus Church. 608p. 1993. 12.00 (0-9638077-0-6) Genl Assem True.

Liu Sanders, Tao T. Dragons, Gods & Spirits from Chinese Mythology. LC 94-8354. (World Mythology Ser.). (Illus.). 152p. 1994. lib. bdg. 24.95 (0-87226-922-1, 69221B, P Bedrick Books) NTC Contemp Pub Co.

***Liu, Sandra & Hamamoto, Darrell Y., eds.** Countervisions: Asian American Film Criticism. (Asian American History & Culture Ser.). (Illus.). 288p. 2000. 74.50 (1-56639-775-8); pap. 24.95 (1-56639-776-6) Temple U Pr.

Liu, Sarah & Vittitow, Mary L. Learning Games Without Losers. (Illus.). 96p. (J). (gr. k-6). 1985. pap. text, student ed. 10.95 (0-86530-039-9, IP 39-9) Incentive Pubns.

Liu, Scott X. Foreign Direct Investment & the Multinational Enterprise: A Re-Examination Using Signaling Theory. LC 96-40533. 200p. 1997. 55.00 (0-275-95483-8, Praeger Pubs) Greenwood.

Liu, Shao. Study of Human Abilities. (American Oriental Ser.: Vol. 11). 1937. 25.00 (0-527-02685-9) Periodicals Srv.

Liu, Sheng, et al, eds. Thermo-Mechanical Characterization of Evolving Packaging Materials & Structures: Proceedings ASME International Mechanical Engineering Congress & Exposition 1998, Anaheim, CA. LC 98-74430. (EEP Ser.: Vol. 24). 141p. 1998. 90.00 (0-7918-1591-9) ASME.

Liu, Shih S. Extraterritoriality: Its Rise & Decline. LC 72-82238. (Columbia University. Studies in the Social Sciences: No. 263). reprint ed. 32.50 (0-404-51263-1) AMS Pr.

Liu, Shih S., tr. see Chen, Liu F.

Liu-Shing-I. Dictionary of Legal & Commercial Terms: Woerterbuch der Rechtssprache & Wirtschaftssprache. (CHI & GER.). 410p. 1984. 250.00 (0-8288-0974-7, M15021) Fr & Eur.

Liu, Shu-Hsien. Surveying Review for the Civil Engineer Exam. 3rd ed. 112p. 1996. pap. 28.50 (1-57645-017-1) Engineering.

— Understanding Confucian Philosophy: Classical & Sung-Ming. LC 97-52294. 288p. 1998. pap. 24.95 (0-275-96317-9, Praeger Pubs) Greenwood.

— Understanding Confucian Philosophy: Classical & Sung-Ming, 61. LC 97-52294. (Contributions in Philosophy Ser.: Vol. 61). 288p. 1998. 69.50 (0-313-30154-9, Greenwood Pr) Greenwood.

Liu, Shu-Zheng, et al, eds. International Symposium of Biological Effects of Low Level Exposure to Radiation & Related Agents: International Symposium of the Princess Takamatsu Cancer Research Fund (24th: 1994: Tokyo, Japan) (International Journal of Occupational Medicine, Immunology, & Toxicology Ser.: Vol. 3, No. 2). (Illus.). 357p. 1994. pap. text 60.00 (0-911131-78-7) Specialist Journals.

Liu, Sifeng & Liu, Yi. An Introduction to Grey Systems: Foundations, Methodology & Application. LC 98-88395. 425p. 1998. 80.00 (0-9665908-0-5); pap. 60.00 (0-9665908-1-3) Intl Institute.

Liu, Sola C. Blue Sky Green Sea: And Other Stories. Cheung, Martha, tr. from CHI. & intro. by. xxv, 145p. (Orig.). 1993. pap. 14.95 (962-7255-12-2, Pub. by Renditions Papbk) SPD-Small Pr Dist.

Liu, Song H., jt. auth. see He, Guang S.

Liu, Stella, ed. Holdings of the Haverhill Public Library: John Greenleaf Whittier Collection. (Illus.). 68p. (Orig.). 1976. pap. 10.00 (1-878651-02-1) HPL Pr.

Liu, Stephen S. My Father's Martial Art: Poems. LC 99-36762. (Western Literature Ser.). 80p. 2000. pap. 11.00 (0-87417-342-6) U of Nev Pr.

Liu, Stephen S., jt. auth. see Chen, Thomas M.

Liu, T. Discord in Zion: The Puritan Divines & the Puritan Revolution, 1640-1660. (International Archives of the History of Ideas Ser.: No. 61). 211p. 1973. lib. bdg. 106.00 (90-247-5156-X, Pub. by M Nijhoff) Kluwer Academic.

— Nonlinear Stability of Shock Waves for Viscous Conservation Laws. LC 85-9153. (Memoirs of the AMS Ser.: No. 56/328). 109p. 1988. reprint ed. pap. 21.00 (0-8218-2329-9, MEMO/56/328) Am Math.

Liu, T. P., jt. ed. see Liu, F. C.

Liu, T. S. & Li, K. Accelerator Mass Spectrometry. Chen, C. E. et al, eds. (Beijing Inst of Modern Phys Ser.: Vol. 4). 350p. 1992. text 94.00 (981-02-0493-0) World Scientific Pub.

Liu, Ta J. U. S. - China Relations, 1784-1992. LC 96-46100. 480p. 1996. 68.50 (0-7618-0598-2); pap. 46.50 (0-7618-0599-0) U Pr of Amer.

Liu, Tai. Puritan London: A Study of Religion & Society in the City Parishes. LC 85-40534. 256p. 1986. 45.00 (0-87413-283-5) U Delaware Pr.

Liu, Tai-Ping. Admissible Solutions of Hyperbolic Conservation Laws. LC 80-28506. (Memoirs Ser.: No. 30/240). 78p. 1981. pap. 16.00 (0-8218-2240-3, MEMO/30/240) Am Math.

***Liu, Tai-Ping.** Hyperbolic & Viscous Conservation Laws. LC 99-49815. (CBMS-NSF Regional Conference Series in Applied Mathematics: No. 72). (Illus.). viii, 73p. 2000. pap. 29.50 (0-89871-436-2, CB0072) Soc Indus-Appl Math.

Liu, Tai-Ping, jt. auth. see Ting, Hsia-Hsi.

Liu, Tessie P. The Weaver's Knot: The Contradictions of Class Struggle & Family Solidarity in Western France, 1750-1914. (Illus.). 296p. 1994. text 45.00 (0-8014-2738-X); pap. text 18.95 (0-8014-8019-1) Cornell U Pr.

Liu, Tien-Lung. The Chameleon State: Global Culture & Policy Shifts in Britain & Germany, 1914-1933. LC 98-16240. 192p. 1999. 39.95 (1-57181-174-5) Berghahn Bks.

Liu, Timothy. Burnt Offerings. LC 95-32454. 84p. (Orig.). 1995. pap. 12.00 (1-55659-104-7) Copper Canyon.

— Say Goodnight. LC 98-8918. 102p. 1998. pap. 14.00 (1-55659-085-7) Copper Canyon.

— Vox Angelica. LC 92-10732. 72p. (Orig.). 1992. pap. 11.95 (0-914086-97-9) Alice James Bks.

***Liu, Timothy.** Word of Mouth: An Anthology of Gay American Poetry. 2000. 49.95 (1-58498-007-9) Talisman Hse.

***Liu, Timothy, ed.** Word of Mouth: An Anthology of Gay American Poetry. 2000. pap. 28.95 (1-58498-006-0) Talisman Hse.

Liu, Ts-ui-jung, ed. Asian Population History. (International Studies in Demography). (Illus.). 496p. 2000. 115.00 (0-19-829443-3) OUP.

Liu, Ts'ui-jung, jt. ed. see Elvin, Mark.

Liu Tungsheng, ed. Loess, Environment & Global Change. 288p. 1996. 20.00 (7-03-002660-8, Pub. by Sci Pr) Lubrecht & Cramer.

— Quaternary Geology & Environment in China. 504p. 1996. 30.00 (7-03-002538-5, Pub. by Sci Pr) Lubrecht & Cramer.

Liu, Victoria & Durra, Joseph. Let's Talk Cantonese. (CHI & ENG., Illus.). 251p. 1994. pap. 49.95 incl. audio (1-881906-04-3) JBD Pub.

Liu, Victoria & Durra, Joseph B. Let's Talk Advanced American English. (Let's Talk Ser.). 100p. 1992. 108.00 incl. audio (1-881906-02-7) JBD Pub.

— Let's Talk American English: Beginning & Intermediate. rev. ed. (Let's Talk Ser.). (CHI & ENG.). 100p. 1992. reprint ed. 218.00 incl. VHS (1-881906-01-9) JBD Pub.

— Let's Talk Cantonese. (CHI & ENG., Illus.). 251p. 1994. pap. 16.95 (1-881906-03-5) JBD Pub.

Liu, W. C. Aging Management of Nuclear Power Plant Containments for License Renewal. 66p. 1997. pap. 6.00 (0-16-054744-X) USGPO.

Liu, W. K. & Santos, M. B., eds. Thin Films: Heteroepitaxial Systems. 700p. 1998. 82.00 (981-02-3390-6) World Scientific Pub.

Liu Wei-ping, et al, eds. Readings in Modern Chinese. 162p. 1990. pap. text 25.00 (0-9590735-4-X, Pub. by Wild Peony Pty) UH Pr.

Liu, Wensheng & Sussmann, Hector J. Shortest Paths for Sub-Riemannian Metrics on Rank-Two Distributions. LC 95-34455. (Memoirs of the American Mathematical Society Ser.: No. 564). 104p. 1995. pap. 35.00 (0-8218-0404-9, MEMO/118/564) Am Math.

***Liu, William.** Fundamentals of III-V Devices: HBTs, MESFETs, & HEMTs. LC 98-38918. 505p. 1999. 96.50 (0-471-29700-3) Wiley.

— Handbook of III-V Heterojunction Bipolar Transistors, 1. LC 97-36772. 1284p. 1998. 265.00 (0-471-24904-1, Wiley-Interscience) Wiley.

— MOSFET Models for SPICE Simulation Including BSIM3v3 & BSIM4. 544p. 2001. 98.00 (0-471-39697-4) Wiley.

***Liu, William & Kendig, Hal, eds.** Who Should Give Care to the Elderly: An East-West Value Divide. 380p. 2000. 65.00 (9971-69-232-5, Pub. by Sngapore Univ Pr) Coronet Bks.

Liu, William, jt. auth. see Cooper, Eleanor.

Liu, William T., ed. China Social Statistics, 1986. (China Statistics Ser.). 294p. 1989. 99.50 (0-275-93273-7, C3273, Praeger Pubs) Greenwood.

— China Statistical Abstract, 1988. LC 88-28571. 142p. 1988. 55.00 (0-275-93214-1, C3214, Praeger Pubs) Greenwood.

Liu, William T., et al, eds. Modernization in East Asia: Political, Economic, & Social Perspectives. LC 92-9117. 200p. 1992. 57.95 (0-275-93222-2, C3222, Praeger Pubs) Greenwood.

***Liu, William T. & Kendig, Hal L., eds.** Who Gives Care to the Elder? 400p. 2000. 48.00 (981-02-4259-X) World Scientific Pub.

Liu, William T., ed. see Notre Dame Conference on Population Staff.

Liu Wu-Chi. Confucius, His Life & Time. LC 73-138159. 189p. (C). 1972. reprint ed. lib. bdg. 35.00 (0-8371-5616-5, LICO, Greenwood Pr) Greenwood.

— An Introduction to Chinese Literature. LC 66-12729. 349p. reprint ed. pap. 108.20 (0-608-17039-9, 205624600056) Bks Demand.

Liu, Wu-Chi. K'uei Yeh Chi: Li Tai Tz'u Ch'hu Hshuan Chi - Sunflower Splendor: Three Thousand Years of Chinese Poetry. LC 76-12366. 310p. reprint ed. pap. 96.10 (0-7837-3716-5, 205789400009) Bks Demand.

Liu, Wu-Chi & Lo, Irving Y., eds. Sunflower Splendor: Three Thousand Years of Chinese Poetry. LC 90-39420. 696p. 1990. reprint ed. pap. 19.95 (0-253-20607-3, MB-607) Ind U Pr.

Liu Wu-Chi, jt. ed. see Li, Tien-Yi.

Liu, X., ed. see Cohen, P.

Liu, X. Drew, jt. ed. see Can, Wu X.

Liu, X. L., jt. auth. see Chen, Wai-Fah.

Liu, Xiaofeng. Personwerdung: Eine Theologische Untersuchung Zu Max Schelers Phanomenologie der "Person-Gefuhle" Mit Besonderer Berucksichtigung Seiner Kritik an der Moderne. (Basler und Berner Studien zur Historischen und Systematischen Theologie: Bd. 64). (GER.). 245p. 1996. 44.95 (3-906752-84-4, Pub. by P Lang) P Lang Pubng.

***Liu, Xiaohai.** Rechtsschutz von Unternehmensgeheimnissen: Vergleichende Untersuchung Zum Schutzniveau des Chinesischen Rechts im Vergleich Mit Dem Deutschen und Amerikanischen Recht. (Europaische Hochschulschriften Ser.: Bd. 2717). 243p. 1999. 42.95 (3-631-35443-6) P Lang Pubng.

Liu, Xiaolian. The Odyssey of the Buddhist Mind: The Allegory of the Later Journey to the West. 336p. (C). 1994. lib. bdg. 54.00 (0-8191-9670-3) U Pr of Amer.

***Liu, Xin.** In One's Own Shadow: An Ethnographic Account of the Condition of Post-reform Rural China. LC 99-31248. (Illus.). 281p. 2000. 45.00 (0-520-21993-7, Pub. by U CA Pr); pap. 15.95 (0-520-21994-5, Pub. by U CA Pr) Cal Prin Full Svc.

Liu, Xinru. Ancient India & Ancient China: Trade & Religious Exchanges AD 1-600. (Oxford India Paperbacks Ser.). (Illus.). 252p. 1995. pap. text 10.95 (0-19-563587-6) OUP.

— The Silk Road: Overland Trade & Cultural Interactions in Eurasia. LC 98-22781. (Essays on Global & Comparative History Ser.). 56p. 1998. pap. 6.00 (0-87229-106-5) Am Hist Assn.

Liu, Xinzhi & Siegel, David, eds. Comparison Methods & Stability Theory. LC 94-20391. (Lecture Notes in Pure & Applied Mathematics Ser.: Vol. 162). (Illus.). 384p. 1994. pap. text 165.00 (0-8247-9270-X) Dekker.

Liu, Xiufeng. Mathematics & Science Curriculum Change in the People's Republic of China. LC 95-42603. (Mellen Studies in Education: Vol. 27). 204p. 1996. 89.95 (0-7734-8863-4) E Mellen.

Liu, Xiuwu R. Western Perspectives on Chinese Higher Education: A Model for Cross-Cultural Inquiry. LC 96-22432. 192p. 1996. 33.50 (0-8386-3709-4) Fairleigh Dickinson.

Liu, Xuecheng. The Sino-Indian Border Dispute & Sino-Indian Relations. 236p. (C). 1994. lib. bdg. 46.50 (0-8191-9699-1) U Pr of Amer.

Liu, Xuejie, jt. auth. see O'Rourke, Michael.

Liu, Y. A. Physical Cleaning of Coal: Present & Developing Methods. (Energy, Power & Environment Ser.: Vol. 15). (Illus.). 576p. 1982. text 215.00 (0-8247-1862-3) Dekker.

Liu, Y. A., et al, eds. Recent Developments in Chemical Process & Plant Design. LC 87-17610. 509p. 1987. 240.00 (0-471-84780-1) Wiley.

Liu, Y. A., jt. auth. see Baughman, D. Richard.

Liu, Y. A., jt. auth. see Quantrille, Thomas E.

Liu, Yameng, jt. ed. see Young, Richard E.

Liu, Yang. The Costimulatory Pathway for T Cell Responses. LC 93-45549. (Molecular Biology Intelligence Unit Ser.). 128p. 1994. 99.00 (1-57059-052-4) Landes Bioscience.

Liu, Yanpei. Enumerative Theory of Maps. LC 99-10162. (Mathematics & Its Applications Ser.). 1999. write for info. (0-7923-5599-7) Kluwer Academic.

Liu, Yi, jt. auth. see Liu, Sifeng.

Liu, Ying. A Pattern Directed Approach Towards an Object Adaptive Decision Support Environment for Water Resources Management. (Illus.). 201p. (Orig.). 1995. pap. 59.50 (90-407-1311-1, Pub. by Delft U Pr) Coronet Bks.

Liu, Yong-chuan. Patterns & Results of the 3rd Democratization Wave. 142p. (C). 1993. lib. bdg. 39.50 (0-8191-9124-8) U Pr of Amer.

Liu, Yongping. Origins of Chinese Law: Penal & Administrative Law in Its Early Development. 374p. 1999. text 45.00 (0-19-590344-7) OUP.

Liu Yongqing. Stability Analysis & Stabilization Synthesis of Stochastic Large Scale Systems. Fang Zhaoshui, ed. 180p. 1996. 40.00 (7-03-004497-5, Pub. by Sci Pr) Lubrecht & Cramer.

Liu, Yongquan, jt. ed. see Mair, Victor H.

Liu, Yu. Poetics & Politics: The Revolutions of Wordsworth. LC 98-26877. (Studies in Nineteenth-Century British Literature: Vol. 12). IX, 138p. (C). 1999. text 39.95 (0-8204-4168-6) P Lang Pubng.

Liu, Yu-Cheng & Gibson, Glenn A. Microcomputer Systems: The 8086-8088 Family Architecture, Programming & Design. 2nd ed. (Illus.). 640p. (C). 1986. text 66.80 (0-13-580499-X) P-H.

Liu, Yu-Tung. Restructuring Shapes: Design Cognition & Computation. rev. ed. (Illus.). 320p. (C). 1998. pap. text 39.95 (1-882792-70-X) Proctor Pubns.

***Liu, Yuan & Hunt, W. A.** The Drunken Synapse: Studies of Alcohol-Related Disorders. LC 99-23706. (C). 1999. text. write for info. (0-306-46111-0, Kluwer Plenum) Kluwer Academic.

Liu Yuehua, jt. auth. see Teng Shou-Hsin.

***Liu, Yuzeng.** Wudang Qigong: China's Wudang Mountain Daoist Breath Exercises. Morgan, Terri, tr. (CHI & ENG.). 244p. (C). 1999. pap. 18.50 (0-9672889-0-8) Int Wudang.

Liu, Z. Q. & Caelli, T. Picture Interpretation: A Symbolic Approach. Vol. 20. LC 96-113789. (Series in Machine Perception & Artificial Intelligence). 152p. 1995. text 28.00 (981-02-2402-8) World Scientific Pub.

***Liu, Z.-Q. & Miyamoto, Sadaaki.** Soft Computing & Human-Centered Machines. LC 00-21951. (Computer Science Workbench Ser.). (Illus.). 2000. write for info. (4-431-70279-2) Spr-Verlag.

Liu, Zhenhai, jt. auth. see Hatakeyama, T.

Liu, Zhenyu. The Economic Analysis of the Growth of Network Products: The Case of Interorganizational Systems. LC 99-211748. (European University Studies: Vol. 28). xx, 182 p. (Orig.). 1998. 37.95 (3-631-33255-6) P Lang Pubng.

— The Economic Analysis of the Growth of Network Products: The Case of Interorganizational Systems. LC 99-211748. (European University Studies: Vol. 28). (Illus.). XX, 182p. (Orig.). (C). 1998. pap. text 37.95 (0-8204-3587-2) P Lang Pubng.

Liu, Zhi, jt. auth. see Stares, Stephen.

Liu, Zhuangyi. Semigroups Associated with Dissipative Systems. LC 98-51412. (Pitman Research Notes in Mathematics Ser.: Vol. 398). 218p. 1999. pap. text 74.95 (0-8493-0615-9) CRC Pr.

Liu, Ziaxing. The Economic Geography of China. Jingshi, Sun, ed. (Illus.). 424p. 1988. text 55.00 (0-19-584079-8) OUP.

Liu Zongren. Hard Time: Thirty Months in a Chinese Labor Camp. LC 95-69930. 280p. 1996. pap. 12.95 (0-8351-2542-4, DS778) China Bks.

— Two Years in the Melting Pot. rev. ed. 1988. reprint ed. 16.95 (0-8351-2048-1) China Bks.

— Two Years in the Melting Pot. rev. ed. (Illus.). 213p. 1988. reprint ed. pap. 9.95 (0-8351-2035-X) China Bks.

Liubimov, D. V., jt. auth. see Gershuni, G. Z.

Liubimov, G. A., et al, eds. Fluid Mechanics. (Series in Mechanical Engineering & Applied Mechanics: Vol. 2). 400p. 1991. 181.00 (0-89116-725-0) Hemisp Pub.

Liubimov, Nikolai. Nesgoraemye Slova. 304p. 1983. 50.00 (0-7855-5985-X) St Mut.

Liudmila, Pozhar, ed. Mori-Xwanzig Theory in Statistical Mechanics: Fundamentals & Applications. LC 94-37468. (Series in Contemporary Chemical Physics). 184p. 1995. text 53.00 (981-02-1750-1) World Scientific Pub.

Liukkonen, J., jt. ed. see Hofmann, K. H.

Liuksila, Claire, ed. External Assistance & Policies for Growth in Africa. LC 95-52025. 1995. write for info (1-55775-525-6) Intl Monetary.

Liulevicius, Arunas. The Factorization of Cyclic Reduced Powers by Secondary Cohomology Operations. LC 52-42839. (Memoirs Ser.: No. 1/42). 112p. 1989. reprint ed. pap. 17.00 (0-8218-1242-4, MEMO/1/42) Am Math.

Liulevicius, Arunas, ed. see Pure Mathematics Symposium Staff.

***Liulevicius, Vejas Gabriel.** War Land on the Eastern Front: Culture, National Identity & German Occupation in World War I. (Studies in the Social & Cultural History of Modern Warfare: Vol. 9). (Illus.). 320p. (C). 2000. text 59.95 (0-521-66157-9) Cambridge U Pr.

Liungman, C. Thought Signs: The Semiotics of Symbols - Western Ideograms. LC 94-79555. 660p. (gr. 12). 1994. 49.00 (90-5199-197-5) IOS Press.

Liungman, Carl G. Dictionary of Symbols. 608p. 1995. pap. 20.95 (0-393-31236-4) Norton.

— The Dictionary of Symbols: Western Ideograms. LC 91-36657. 596p. 1991. lib. bdg. 67.50 (0-87436-610-0) ABC-CLIO.

Liusc, Barbara. California's Hispanic Roots for Kids. LC 95-75811. (ENG & SPA., Illus.). 95p. (Orig.). (J). (gr. 2-5). 1995. pap. 9.95 (1-878079-21-2) Arts Pubns.

***Liuzza, R. M., ed.** Beowulf. (Literary Texts Ser.). 280p. 1999. pap. 7.95 (1-55111-189-6) Broadview Pr.

— The Old English Version of the Gospels, Vol. 2. (Early English Text Society Original Ser.: Vol. 314). 381p. 2000. text 74.00 (0-19-722313-3) OUP.

Liuzza, Roy M., ed. The Old English Versions of the Gospels Vol. I: Text & Introduction. (Early English Text Society-Original Ser.: No. 304). (Illus.). 280p. 1994. text 55.00 (0-19-722306-0) OUP.

***Liuzzi, Peter J.** With Listening Hearts: Understanding the Voices of Lesbian & Gay Catholics. 144p. 2001. pap. 9.95 (0-8091-3983-9) Paulist Pr.

Liv, Leang Hy, tr. see Catalla, Rebecca, et al.

Liva, E. & Germain, J. Mentally Sharp Naturally. 1999. pap. 15.00 (0-7615-1473-2) Prima Pub.

L

L

Livadas, Panos E. & Ward, Christopher. Computer Organization & the MC68000. LC 92-24684. 720p. 1993. 66.00 (*0-13-158940-7*) P-H.

Livadeas, Themistocles & Charitos, Minas. The Real Truth Concerning Apostolos Makrakis. Orthodox Christian Educational Society Staff, ed. Cummings, Denver, tr. 230p. (Orig.). 1952. pap. 5.95 (*0-938366-30-0*) Orthodox Chr.

Livadic, P. Dizionario Italiano-Serbocroato-Italiano. (ITA & SER.). 554p. 1980. 9.95 (*0-8288-1640-9*, M9180) Fr & Eur.

Livaditakis, Petros. Hameni Anioxi. Pagoulaton, Regina, ed. (GRE.). 144p. (Orig.). 1997. pap. 9.95 (*1-885778-28-7*) Seaburn.

Livanov, M. N. & Rusinov, V. S., eds. Mathematical Analysis of the Electrical Activity of the Brain. Barlow, John S., tr. LC 68-17621. (Illus.). 113p. 1968. 22.95 (*0-674-55400-0*) HUP.

Livanova, Anna. Landau: A Great Physicist & Teacher. Sykes, J. B., tr. 226p. 1980. 77.00 (*0-08-023076-8*, Pergamon Pr) Elsevier.

Livdahl, Barbara S., et al. Stories from Response-Centered Classrooms. 160p. (C). 1995. text 38.00 (*0-8077-3458-6*); pap. text 17.95 (*0-8077-3457-8*) Tchrs Coll.

Live, Anna H. Yesterday & Today in the U. S. A. Intermediate ESL Reader. 2nd ed. (Illus.). 288p. (C). 1988. pap. text. write for info. (*0-318-62497-4*) P-H.

Live, Anna Harris. Yesterday & Today in U. S. A. 2nd ed. 277p. (C). 1988. pap. text 31.40 (*0-13-971888-5*) P-H.

Live Oak Media Staff, jt. auth. see Auch, Mary J.

Livelsberger, Dean. Strange, Outlandish, Crude & Sometimes Funny Jokes. LC 96-48097. 1997. pap. 9.95 (*1-56980-097-9*) Barricade Bks.

Livelton, Trevor. Archival Theory, Records, & the Public. LC 95-26792. 192p. 1996. text 38.50 (*0-8108-3051-5*) Scarecrow.

Lively. Bridging the Gap: 2 Advanced French Title. (College French Ser.). (FRE.). (C). 1994. mass mkt., teacher ed. 21.95 (*0-8384-4609-4*) Heinle & Heinle.

— Bridging the Gap: 3 Interim French Title. (College French Ser.). (FRE.). (C). 1994. mass mkt., teacher ed. 21.95 (*0-8384-4608-6*) Heinle & Heinle.

***Lively.** Modern American Pharmacy. 316p. 1999. pap. text 33.00 (*0-536-02510-X*) Pearson Custom.

Lively, et al. Liens: En Paroles. (Bridging the Gap Ser.). (FRE.). (C). 1994. mass mkt. 36.95 (*0-8384-4607-8*) Heinle & Heinle.

Lively, Adam & Lively, Jack, eds. Democracy in Britain: A Reader. 360p. 1994. pap. 32.95 (*0-631-18831-2*) Blackwell Pubs.

Lively, Adams. Masks: Blackness, Race & the Imagination. LC 99-88632. 304p. 2000. 30.00 (*0-19-513370-6*) OUP.

Lively, Bob. Simple Steps...Costly Choices: A Guide to Inner Peace. 194p. (Orig.). 1995. pap., teacher ed. 5.00 (*0-9647272-6-9*); pap., wbk. ed. 10.00 (*0-9647272-5-0*) Riverbend Pr.

Lively, C. E. & Taeuber, Conrad. Rural Migration in the United States. LC 71-165601. (Research Monographs: Vol. 19). 1971. reprint ed. 25.00 (*0-306-70351-3*) Da Capo.

Lively, Chauncy. Chauncy Lively's Flybox. 1991. pap. 18.95 (*0-8117-2078-0*) Stackpole.

Lively, Donald E. The Constitution & Race. LC 91-30280. 208p. 1992. 55.00 (*0-275-93914-6*, C3914, Praeger Pubs); pap. 17.95 (*0-275-94228-7*, B4228, Praeger Pubs) Greenwood.

— Dissenting Judicial Opinions: Foreshadows of Constitutional Law. LC 92-19827. 200p. 1992. 65.00 (*0-275-94382-8*, C4382, Praeger Pubs); pap. 21.95 (*0-275-94383-6*, B4386, Praeger Pubs) Greenwood.

— Essential Principles of Communication Law. LC 91-6303. 336p. 1991. text 55.00 (*0-275-93912-X*, C3912, Praeger Pubs) Greenwood.

— Landmark Supreme Court Cases: A Reference Guide. LC 98-44220. 384p. 1999. 59.95 (*0-313-30602-8*) Greenwood.

— Modern Communications Law. LC 90-7504. 592p. 1991. 65.00 (*0-275-93735-6*, C3735, Praeger Pubs) Greenwood.

Lively, Donald E., et al, eds. First Amendment Anthology. LC 94-9984. 505p. 1994. pap. 29.95 (*0-87084-265-X*) Anderson Pub Co.

Lively, Donald E., et al. Communications Law: Media, Entertainment, & Regulation. 866p. 1997. 59.95 (*0-87084-158-0*) Anderson Pub Co.

***Lively, Donald E., et al.** Constitutional Law: Cases, History & Dialogues. 2nd ed. 1450p. 1999. 59.95 (*0-87084-319-2*) Anderson Pub Co.

— First Amendment Law: Cases, Readings & Dialogues. pap. write for info. (*1-58360-752-8*) Anderson Pub Co.

Lively, Edwin, jt. auth. see Lively, Virginia.

Lively, Frazer, ed. & tr. see Rachilde, et al.

***Lively, Harper W.** Themes. (C). 1999. pap., wbk. ed., lab manual ed. 28.00 (*0-8384-8208-2*) Heinle & Heinle.

Lively, Jack & Reeve, Andrew. Modern Political Theory from Hobbes to Marx: Key Debates. 320p. 1989. pap. 14.95 (*0-415-01351-8*) Routledge.

Lively, Jack, jt. ed. see Lively, Adam.

Lively, Ken & Pirtle, Caleb, 3rd, eds. Germania's Old Fashion Harvest Time Cookbook. 192p. 1995. write for info. (*0-614-07782-6*) Herit Pub TX.

Lively, Ken & Pirtle, Caleb, eds. Recipes for Today's Menus. 100p. 1996. write for info. (*1-879234-43-2*) Herit Pub TX.

Lively, Ken, ed. see Magid, Lynn H. & Kahn, Beth F.

Lively, Lynne. The Procrastinator's Guide to Success. LC 99-14473. 254p. 1999. pap. 12.95 (*0-07-038307-3*) McGraw.

Lively, Patricia A. Sweet Dreams . . . Bitter Awakenings. LC 96-94676. 176p. 1997. pap. 9.95 (*1-889808-00-8*) Lively Pubns.

Lively, Penelope. The Cat, the Crow, & the Banyan Tree. LC 93-22355. (Illus.). 32p. (J). (ps up). 1994. 14.95 (*1-56402-325-7*) Candlewick Pr.

— City of the Mind. large type ed. 319p. 1992. 22.95 (*1-85089-342-X*, Pub. by ISIS Lrg Prnt) Transaction Pubs.

— Cleopatra's Sister. large type ed. 1993. 23.95 (*1-56895-039-X*) Wheeler Pub.

— Cleopatra's Sister: A Novel. LC 92-54424. 288p. 1994. pap. 12.00 (*0-06-092217-6*, Perennial) HarperTrade.

— The Five Thousand & One Nights. LC 97-15212. (European Short Stories Ser.: No. 4). 156p. 1997. pap. 12.00 (*0-940242-73-7*) Fjord Pr.

Lively, Penelope. The Ghost of Thomas Kempe. 1995. 9.09 (*0-606-07563-1*, Pub. by Turtleback) Demco.

Lively, Penelope. Good Night, Sleep Tight. (Illus.). (J). (ps-2). reprint ed. pap. 5.99 (*0-614-15564-9*) Candlewick Pr.

— Heat Wave: A Novel. 224p. 1997. pap. 13.00 (*0-06-092855-7*, Perennial) HarperTrade.

— House Inside Out. large type ed. 176p. (J). (gr. 4-7). 1989. 17.50 (*0-7451-0957-8*, G K Hall Lrg Type) Mac Lib Ref.

— Moon Tiger. 224p. 1997. pap. 12.00 (*0-8021-3533-1*, Grove) Grove-Atltic.

— Oleander, Jacaranda: A Childhood Perceived. LC 93-39760. 160p. 1995. pap. 12.00 (*0-06-092622-8*, Perennial) HarperTrade.

— One, Two, Three, Jump! LC 99-76297. (Illus.). 32p. (J). (ps-1). 1999. per. 16.00 (*0-689-82201-4*) S&S Childrens.

— Pack of Cards: Stories. 336p. 1999. reprint ed. pap. 13.00 (*0-8021-3624-9*, Grove) Grove-Atltic.

— Passing On. large type ed. 342p. 1990. 19.95 (*1-85089-329-2*, Pub. by ISIS Lrg Prnt) Transaction Pubs.

— Passing On. 224p. 1999. reprint ed. pap. 12.00 (*0-8021-3626-5*, Grove) Grove-Atltic.

— Passing On. LC 90-55666. 224p. 1991. reprint ed. pap. 12.00 (*0-06-097370-6*, Perennial) HarperTrade.

— The Road to Lichfield. 224p. 1999. reprint ed. pap. 12.00 (*0-8021-3625-7*, Grove) Grove-Atltic.

***Lively, Penelope.** Spiderweb. large type unabridged ed. 2000. 25.95 (*0-7531-5996-1*, 159961, Pub. by ISIS Lrg Prnt) ISIS Pub.

Lively, Penelope. Spiderweb: A Novel. LC 98-45696. 224p. 1999. 22.00 (*0-06-019233-X*, HarperFlamingo) HarpC.

***Lively, Penelope.** Spiderweb: A Novel. 224p. 2000. pap. 13.00 (*0-06-092972-3*, Perennial) HarperTrade.

— Two Bears & Joe. (Illus.). 32p. (J). pap. 9.95 (*0-14-055551-X*, Pub. by Pnguin Bks Ltd) Trafalgar.

Lively, Robert D. Simple Steps...Costly Choices: A Guide to Inner Peace. 194p. (Orig.). 1995. pap. 14.95 (*0-9647272-4-2*) Riverbend Pr.

Lively, Scott. The Poisoned Stream: Gay Influence in Human History. (Germany 1900-1945 Ser.: Vol. 1). 136p. 1997. pap. 9.95 (*0-9647609-2-4*) Fndrs Pubng.

— Seven Steps to Recruit-Proof Your Child: A Parent's Guide to Protecting Children from Homosexuality & the "Gay" Movement. (Illus.). 224p. 1998. pap. 11.95 (*0-9647609-5-9*) Fndrs Pubng.

Lively, Scott & Abrams, Kevin. The Pink Swastika: Homosexualtiy in the Nazi Party. 3rd rev. ed. (Illus.). 280p. 1998. pap. 11.95 (*0-9647609-3-2*) Fndrs Pubng.

Lively, Scott, jt. auth. see Mabon, Lon T.

Lively, Virginia & Lively, Edwin. Sexual Development of Young Children. (C). 1991. mass mkt. 24.50 (*0-8273-4198-9*) Delmar.

— Sexual Development of Young Children. 1991. pap., teacher ed. 8.50 (*0-8273-4199-7*) Delmar.

Livengood, Roy. Powder River: 91st Infantry Division. LC 94-60146. (Illus.). 408p. 1994. 29.95 (*1-56311-135-7*) Turner Pub KY.

Livens, Leslie. Share Valuation Handbook: Techniques for the Valuation of Shares in Private Companies. 207p. (C). 1986. 150.00 (*0-906840-98-8*, Pub. by Fourmat Pub) St Mut.

— Share Valuation Handbook: Techniques for the Valuation of Shares in Private Companies. 2nd ed. 250p. 1993. 96.00 (*0-85459-811-1*, Pub. by Tolley Pubng) St Mut.

Livera, Giovanni & Raucherbaumer, Jon. The Amazing Cigar: The Cigar Connoisseur's Secrets to Smoke Rings, Mystifications & Other Cool Things. LC 97-76613. (Illus.). 160p. 1997. 24.95 (*0-9660567-2-8*) Magic Mktg.

***Liverakos, L. A.** The Shadows Between. (Poltergeist Ser.: No. 2). 2000. mass mkt. 5.99 (*0-441-00703-1*) Ace Bks.

Liveramento, Jan D. Dynamic Modelling for Analysis & Design of Bottle Conveying Systems in High-Speed Bottling Lines. (Illus.). 318p. 1998. pap. 57.50 (*90-407-1668-4*, Pub. by Delft U Pr) Coronet Bks.

Liverani, P., ed. see Andreade, B., et al.

Liverett, David, jt. auth. see Stephens, Christie S.

Liveright, A. A. National Trends in Higher Adult Education. 1960. 2.50 (*0-87060-020-6*, OCP 2) Syracuse U Cont Ed.

— University Adult Education: The Career for Experiment in Education. 1961. 2.50 (*0-87060-080-X*, PUC 21) Syracuse U Cont Ed.

Liveright, James. Simple Methods for Detecting Buying & Selling Points in Securities. LC 68-21699. 1968. reprint ed. pap. 12.00 (*0-87034-028-X*) Fraser Pub Co.

Liveris, Gwen, jt. auth. see Johnson, Nancy.

Liverman, Catharyn T. Internet Access to the National Library of Medicine's Toxicology & Environmental Health Databases. LC 99-169728. 35 p. 1998. write for info. (*0-309-06299-3*) Natl Acad Pr.

Liverman, Catharyn T., et al, eds. Toxicology & Environmental Health Information Resources: The Role of the National Library of Medicine. (Illus.). 160p. (Orig.). (C). 1998. pap. text 40.00 (*0-7881-7141-0*) DIANE Pub.

— Toxicology & Environmental Health Information Resources: The Role of the National Library of Medicine. LC 97-135062. 176p. (Orig.). 1997. pap. 32.00 (*0-309-05686-1*, Joseph Henry Pr) Natl Acad Pr.

Liverman, Diana & Solem, Michael. The Geography of Greenhouse Gas Emissions. (Active Learning Modules on the Human Dimensions of Global Change Ser.). (Illus.). 175p. (C). 1997. teacher ed. 20.00 (*0-89291-229-4*); pap., student ed., wbk. ed. 8.75 (*0-89291-230-8*) Assn Am Geographers.

Liverman, H. J. High Days & Holidays: Scenes from a Tyrrell County Childhood. 1994. pap., per. 9.95 (*0-9643396-0-9*) Sweet Bay Tree.

***Liverman, H. Joe.** High Days & Holidays: Scenes from a Tyrrell County Childhood. rev. ed. (Carolina Childhood Ser.). 136p. 2000. pap. 10.95 (*0-9643396-2-5*) Sweet Bay Tree.

Livermore, Abiel A. The War with Mexico Reviewed. Cortes, Carlos E., ed. LC 76-1287. (Chicano Heritage Ser.). 1977. reprint ed. 26.95 (*0-405-09511-2*) Ayer.

Livermore, Alton D. Zidovudine in Therapeutic Uses: Index of New Information. 150p. 1994. 47.50 (*0-7883-0104-7*); pap. 44.50 (*0-7883-0105-5*) ABBE Pubs Assn.

Livermore, Ann. Artists & Aesthetics in Spain. (Monografias A Ser.). (Illus.). 81p. 1990. 45.00 (*0-7293-0294-6*) Boydell & Brewer.

— A Short History of Spanish Music. LC 72-196469. 272p. reprint ed. pap. 84.40 (*0-608-14948-9*, 202611600048) Bks Demand.

Livermore, Donald R. Hands-On History: Projects & Activities to Accompany One-Eyed Charley, the California Whip. Bergez, John, ed. (History & Happenings of California Ser.). 48p. (J). (gr. 3-6). 1991. pap. 7.95 (*0-933818-63-7*) Ghost Town.

— Hands-On History: Projects & Activities to Accompany Stagecoach Santa. Bergez, John, ed. (History & Happenings of California Ser.). 48p. (J). (gr. 3-6). 1990. pap. 7.95 (*0-933818-60-2*) Ghost Town.

Livermore, George. An Historical Research Respecting the Opinion of the Founders of the Republic on Negroes As Slaves, As Citizens & As Soldiers. LC 68-18599. xviii, 184p. 1970. reprint ed. 12.50 (*0-678-00547-8*) Kelley.

— Historical Research Respecting the Opinions of the Founders of the Republic on Negroes As Slaves, As Citizens, & As Soldiers. LC 69-18541. (American Negro: His History & Literature. Series 2). 1968. reprint ed. 13.95 (*0-405-01878-9*) Ayer.

Livermore, Gordon. Soviet Foreign Policy Today, 1986-1989. 3rd ed. Current Digest of the Soviet Press Staff, tr. from RUS. 192p. (Orig.). (C). 1989. pap. 10.00 (*0-913601-62-4*) Current Digest.

— Soviet Foreign Policy Today, 1989-1990. 4th ed. Current Digest of the Soviet Press Staff, tr. 220p. (Orig.). 1990. pap. 10.00 (*0-913601-63-2*) Current Digest.

Livermore, Gordon, ed. Russian Foreign Policy Today: The Soviet Legacy & Post-Soviet Beginnings. 5th ed. (Current Digest Foreign Policy Readers Ser.). 228p. (Orig.). (C). 1992. pap. 15.00 (*0-913601-64-0*) Current Digest.

— Russia's Evolving Foreign Policy, 1992-1994: A Supplement to the 5th Edition of Russian Foreign Policy Today. (Foreign Policy Readers Ser.). 120p. 1994. pap. 21.00 (*0-913601-65-9*) Current Digest.

— Soviet Foreign Policy Today, 1983-1986. 2nd ed. 200p. (Orig.). (C). 1986. 10.00 (*0-913601-61-6*) Current Digest.

Livermore, Gordon, et al, eds. The U. S. S. R. Today: Perspectives from the Soviet Press, 1989-1991. 8th ed. 180p. 1991. pap. 18.00 (*0-913601-78-0*) Current Digest.

Livermore, Gordon, jt. ed. see Schulze, Fred.

Livermore, Harold U., ed. University of British Columbia Hispanic Studies. (Monagrafias A Ser.: Vol. XL). (ENG & SPA.). 250p. (Orig.). (C). 1974. pap. 51.00 (*0-900411-82-1*, Pub. by Tamesis Bks Ltd) Boydell & Brewer.

Livermore, Harold V., tr. see De La Vega, Garcilaso.

Livermore, Jesse L. How to Trade in Stocks: The Livermore Formula for Combining Time Element & Price. 116p. 1991. reprint ed. pap. 19.95 (*0-934380-20-1*, 277) Traders Pr.

Livermore, John, jt. auth. see Clark, E. Eugene.

Livermore, Marlin, jt. auth. see Smirnov, Mark.

Livermore, Mary A. My Story of the War: A Woman's Narrative of Four Year's Personal Experience As Nurse in the Union Army. LC 72-2612. (American Women Ser.: Images & Realities). (Illus.). 704p. 1975. reprint ed. 44.95 (*0-405-04466-6*) Ayer.

— My Story of the War: A Women's Narrative of Four Years Personal Experience As Nurse in the Union Army. 700p. 1978. reprint ed. 39.95 (*0-87928-100-6*) Corner Hse.

— My Story of the War: The Civil War Memoirs of the Famous Nurse, Relief Organizer, & Suffragette. (Illus.). 710p. 1995. reprint ed. pap. 19.95 (*0-306-80658-4*) Da Capo.

— The Story of My Life. (American Biography Ser.). 730p. 1991. reprint ed. lib. bdg. 119.00 (*0-7812-8247-0*) Rprt Serv.

— The Story of My Life: or The Sunshine & Shadow of Seventy Years...to Which Is Added Six of Her Most Popular Lectures. LC 74-3960. (Women in America Ser.). (Illus.). 760p. 1974. reprint ed. 57.95 (*0-405-06108-0*) Ayer.

Livermore, Paul. The God of Our Salvation: Christian Theology from the Wesleyan Perspective. 402p. (Orig.). (C). 1995. pap. text 14.95 (*0-89367-199-1*) Light & Life Comm.

Livermore, Putnam, jt. auth. see Barrett, Thomas S.

Livermore, Robert. Bostonians & Bullion: The Journal of Robert Livermore, 1892-1915. Gressley, Gene M., ed. LC 68-12703. (Illus.). 222p. reprint ed. pap. 68.90 (*0-8357-5608-4*, 205684800093) Bks Demand.

Livermore, S. T. Block Island: I, Map & Guide; II, History. 137p. 1997. reprint ed. pap. 19.00 (*0-8328-6475-7*) Higginson Bk Co.

— Condensed History of Cooperstown, with a Biographical Sketch of J. Fenimore Cooper. (Illus.). 276p. 1997. reprint ed. lib. bdg. 35.00 (*0-8328-6124-3*) Higginson Bk Co.

Livermore, Samuel & Reams, Bernard D., Jr. Treatise on the Law of Principal & Agent: And of Sales by Auction. 2 vols. Helmholz, R. H., ed. LC 86-62943. (Historical Writings in Law & Jurisprudence Ser.: No. 11). 1986. reprint ed. lib. bdg. 100.00 (*0-89941-526-1*, 304620) W S Hein.

Livermore, Shaw. Twilight of Federalism: The Disintegration of the Federalist Party - 1815-1830. LC 73-150413. 302p. 1972. reprint ed. 75.00 (*0-87752-137-9*) Gordian.

— The Twilight of Federalism: The Disintegration of the Federalist Party, 1815-1830. LC 62-7410. 305p. reprint ed. pap. 94.60 (*0-608-10917-7*, 200059300033) Bks Demand.

Livermore, Thomas L. Numbers & Losses in the Civil War in America, 1861-65. fac. ed. Kallmann, John D., ed. & intro. by. 160p. 1996. 24.95 (*0-9650926-0-7*, L-1001) J Kallmann.

Livernash, E. Robert, ed. Comparable Worth: Issues & Alternatives. 2nd ed. LC 84-81267. 299p. 1984. pap. 11.00 (*0-937856-08-8*) Equal Employ.

Livernash, E. Robert, jt. auth. see Foulkes, Fred K.

Livernash, E. Robert, jt. auth. see Peach, David A.

Livernash, Robert. Environmental Quality: Along the American River. (Illus.). 408p. 1998. pap. 19.00 (*0-16-049791-4*) USGPO.

***Livernash, Robert.** Environmental Quality: The 1997 Report of the Council on Environmental Quality. 368p. 1999. per. 21.00 (*0-16-050151-2*) USGPO.

Livernois, Jay, ed. Shadow of Perfection: Eranos Yearbook, 1996. 110p. 1995. pap. 15.00 (*1-882670-08-6*) Spring Pubns.

Livernois, Jay & Donat, James, eds. Chroniclers & Shamans. (Eranos Yearbook Ser.: Vol. 67). 160p. 2000. pap. 15.00 (*1-882670-18-3*, Pub. by Spring Jrnl) Continuum.

Livernois, Jay & Pollack, Rachel. Archetypal Sex: Spring 57. Hillman, James & Boer, Charles, eds. (Spring Journal: Vol. 57). 176p. (Orig.). 1995. pap. 17.50 (*1-882670-05-1*) Spring Jrnl.

Livernois, Jay, jt. ed. see Donat, James.

Livernois, Jay, ed. see Hillman, James & Giegerich, Wolfgang.

Livernois, Jay, ed. see Hillman, James, et al.

Livernois, Jay, tr. see Petrarch, Francis.

Liverpool, Charles J. A Collection of All the Treaties of Peace, Alliance & Commerce Between Great Britain & Other Powers, 3 vols. LC 69-16554. 1969. reprint ed. 150.00 (*0-678-00486-2*) Kelley.

— A Treatise on the Coins of the Realm: In a Letter to the King. LC 67-29513. (Reprints of Economic Classics Ser.). xii, 295p. 1968. reprint ed. 45.00 (*0-678-00412-9*) Kelley.

Liverpool, N. J., jt. ed. see Hewlett, Cecil E.

Livers, Eileen. The Unofficial Guide to Planning Your Wedding. 400p. 1998. pap. 22.95 (*0-02-862459-9*, Pub. by Macmillan) S&S Trade.

Liversage, David. Material & Interpretation: The Archaeology of Sjaelland in the Early Roman Iron Age. (Publications of the National Museum: No. 1, Pt. 20). (Illus.). 204p. (C). 1980. pap. 21.00 (*87-480-0311-5*, Pub. by Aarhus Univ Pr) David Brown.

***Liversain, Patricia.** Modeling in Clay. (Illus.). 80p. 2000. pap. 19.95 (*0-233-99549-8*, Pub. by Andre Deutsch) Trafalgar.

Liversay, Ed, Jr. Secrets of Accident Investigation. 64p. (C). 1995. pap. 35.00 (*0-918487-82-X*) Thomas Investigative.

Liversedge, Stan. Forever Everton: Thirty-Five Years of Triumphs & Trials. (Illus.). 224p. 1996. 34.95 (*1-85158-813-2*, Pub. by Mainstream Pubng) Trafalgar.

— Liverpool from the Inside. (Illus.). 224p. 1996. 34.95 (*1-85158-758-6*, Pub. by Mainstream Pubng) Trafalgar.

Liversidge, Michael, et al, eds. Imagining Rome: British Artists & Rome in the Nineteenth Century. LC 96-225686. (Illus.). 160p. pap. 29.95 (*1-85894-030-3*, Pub. by Merrell Holberton) U of Wash Pr.

Liversidge, Michael, et al. Canaletto & England. (Illus.). 192p. 1994. 50.00 (*1-85894-002-8*) U of Wash Pr.

Liversidge, Peggy, jt. ed. see Blake, Marcia.

Liverwright, A. A. & Goldmann, Freda H. Significant Developments in Continuing Higher Education. 1965. 2.50 (*0-87060-016-8*, OCP 12) Syracuse U Cont Ed.

Liverziani, Filippo. Reincarnation & Its Phenomena. 192p. (C). 1989. pap. 50.00 (*0-7212-0789-8*, Pub. by Regency Pr GBR) St Mut.

Livesay & Wilson. Frommer's France. 1997. 18.95 (*0-02-861579-4*) Macmillan.

Livesay, Ann. Death in the Amazon. LC 98-90555. (Barry Ross International Mystery Ser.). 326p. 1998. per. 12.95 (*0-9662817-1-3*) Silver River.

Livesay, Ann. The Chala Project. 326p. per. 12.95 (*0-9662817-3-X*) Silver River.

— The Madman of Mount Everest. 326p. per. 12.95 (*0-9662817-2-1*) Silver River.

Livesay, Anthony, jt. auth. see MacDonald, John.

Livesay, Billy R., jt. auth. see Mandel, C. E., Jr.

Livesay, Corinne R. Getting & Staying Organized. 112p. (Orig.). 1994. text 10.95 (*0-7863-0254-2*, Irwn Prfssnl) McGraw-Hill Prof.

An Asterisk (*) at the beginning of an entry indicates that the title is appearing for the first time.

Livesay, Dennis. Proper Care of Labrador Retrievers. (Illus.). 256p. (J). (gr. 5). 1995. 16.95 (*0-7938-1969-5*, TW140) TFH Pubns.

Livesay, Dorothy. Les Ages de l'Amour. (FRE.). 108p. 1989. pap. 10.00 (*2-89135-019-7*) Guernica Editions.

— Beginnings. 1997. pap. 12.95 (*0-920541-94-1*) Peguis Pubs Ltd.

***Livesay, Dorothy.** Journey with My Selves: A Memoir 1909-1963. 217p. 2000. reprint ed. text 27.00 (*0-7881-6875-4*) DIANE Pub.

Livesay, Harold. A History of the US. (C). pap. text. write for info. (*0-393-97418-9*) Norton.

Livesay, Harold C. American Made: Men Who Shaped the American Economy. LC 79-15971. (C). 1997. reprint ed. pap. text 21.20 (*0-673-39346-1*) Addson-Wesley Educ.

***Livesay, Harold C.** Andrew Carnegie & the Rise of Big Business. 2nd ed. LC 99-33825. (Library of American Biography). 228p. 1999. pap. text 20.20 (*0-321-04373-1*) Longman.

Livesay, Harold C. Samuel Gompers & Organized Labor in America. (Library of American Biography). (C). 1978. pap. text 16.80 (*0-673-39345-3*) Addson-Wesley Educ.

— Samuel Gompers & Organized Labor in America. 195p. (C). 1993. reprint ed. pap. text 11.95 (*0-88133-751-X*) Waveland Pr.

Livesay, Harold C., ed. Entrepreneurship & the Growth of Firms, 2 vols. LC 95-11872. (International Library of Critical Writings in Business History: Vol. 12). 1312p. 1995. 470.00 (*1-85278-768-6*) E Elgar.

Livesay, Harold C., jt. auth. see Porter, Glenn.

Livesay, June. A Candle in Darkness: A Novel. LC 90-70126. 280p. 1990. pap. 8.95 (*0-914984-22-5*) Starburst.

Livesay, Marguerite. Prairie Memories from the Bauhs House. (Illus.). 247p. 1991. pap. 14.95 (*0-9662144-0-4*) Shuab Bks.

Livesay, S. Survey of Legal Literature on Woman Offenders. i, 16p. 1975. pap. 2.00 (*0-938876-01-5*) Entropy Ltd.

Livesey & Proctor. Barron's Diccionario Juvenil Ilustrado-Ingles para Hispanos. LC 98-25562. (SPA.). 1998. pap. 14.95 (*0-7641-0806-9*) Barron.

Livesey, Claire. Our Polliwogs. (Books for Young Learners). (Illus.). 12p. (J). (gr. k-2). 1999. pap. text 5.00 (*1-57274-276-3*) R Owen Pubs.

***Livesey, Claire.** Los Renacuajos. Romo, Alberto, tr. (Books for Young Learners).Tr. of Our Polliwogs. (SPA., Illus.). 12p. (J). (gr. k-2). 1999. pap. text 5.00 (*1-57274-340-9*, A2897) R Owen Pubs.

Livesey, A., jt. auth. see Robinson, A.

Livesey, Anthony. The Historical Atlas of World War I. 192p. 1995. 45.00 (*0-8050-2651-7*) H Holt & Co.

Livesey, Brian, jt. auth. see Allan, Barbara.

Livesey, F., jt. ed. see Hunt, S.

Livesey, Frank. Dictionary of Economics. 320p. (Orig.). 1993. pap. 42.50 (*0-273-60034-6*, Pub. by Pitman Pub) Trans-Atl Phila.

— Textbook of Economics. 4th ed. LC 94-30854. 1995. write for info. (*0-582-23867-6*) Longman.

***Livesey, Herbert.** Frommer's Montreal & Quebec City 2001. (Illus.). 2000. pap. 14.99 (*0-7645-6172-3*) IDG Bks.

***Livesey, Herbert B.** Frommer's Montreal & Quebec City 2000. (Illus.). 288p. 2000. pap. text 14.99 (*0-02-863506-X*, Frommer) Macmillan Gen Ref.

Livesey, Herbert B. Frommer's New England 99. 704p. 1998. pap. 18.95 (*0-02-862226-X*) Macmillan.

Livesey, Herbert B., jt. auth. see Hamlin, Ron.

Livesey, Margot. Criminals. 1997. pap. 11.95 (*0-14-026277-6*) Viking Penguin.

***Livesey, Margot.** The Missing World. LC 99-35785. 352p. 2000. 23.00 (*0-375-40581-X*) Knopf.

Livesey, P. J. Learning & Emotion: A Biological Synthesis. 328p. (C). 1986. text 59.95 (*0-89859-552-5*) L Erlbaum Assocs.

Livesey, Peter. Rock Climbing. (Illus.). 160p. 1990. 21.95 (*0-938567-22-5*) Mountaineers.

Livesey, Peter G. The GP Consultation: A Registrar's Guide. LC 96-290. 138p. 1997. pap. text 37.50 (*0-7506-3130-9*) Buttrwrth-Heinemann.

Livesey, R. Dictionary of Automobile Engineering. (Illus.). 286p. 1996. pap. 15.95 (*0-948549-66-1*, Pub. by Peter Collin) IBD Ltd.

Livesey, Robert. The Fur Traders. LC 99-232199. (Discovering Canada Ser.). (Illus.). 96p. (YA). (gr. 3 up). 1989. pap. 11.95 (*0-7737-5304-4*) STDK.

— The Loyal Refugees. (Discovering Canada Ser.). 1999. pap. text 9.95 (*0-7737-6043-1*) STDK.

Livesey, Robert. Native Peoples. (Discovering Canada Ser.). (Illus.). 90p. (J). (gr. 3-6). 1993. pap. (*0-7737-5602-7*) STDK.

— New France. LC 99-162686. (Discovering Canada Ser.). (Illus.). (YA). (gr. 3 up). 1990. pap. write for info. (*0-7737-5341-9*) STDK.

— Railways. unabridged ed. (Discovering Canada Ser.). (Illus.). 90p. (J). (gr. 3-7). 1998. pap. 9.95 (*0-7737-5901-8*) STDK.

— The Vikings. (Discovering Canada Ser.). (Illus.). 96p. (YA). (gr. 3 up). 1989. pap. write for info. (*0-7737-5209-9*) STDK.

Livesey, Robert & Smith, A. G. The Defenders. LC 99-162699. (Discovering Canada Ser.). (Illus.). 96p. (YA). (gr. 3 up). 1994. pap. write for info. (*0-7737-5665-5*) STDK.

Livesey, Steven J. Antonius de Carlenis O. P. Four Questions on the Subalternation of the Sciences. LC 94-72415. (Transactions Ser.: Vol. 84, Pt. 4). 125p. (C). 1994. pap. 15.00 (*0-87169-844-7*, T844-LIS) Am Philos.

— Theology & Science in the Fourteenth Century: Three Questions on the Unity & Subalternation of the Sciences from John of Reading's Commentary on the Sentences. LC 89-909. (Studien und Texte zur Geistesgeschichte des Mittelalters Ser.: Vol. XXV). viii, 229p. (Orig.). 1989. pap. text 89.50 (*90-04-09023-1*) Brill Academic Pubs.

Livesley, R. K. Mathematical Methods for Engineers. 1989. text 74.95 (*0-470-21468-6*) P-H.

— Matrix Methods of Structural Analysis. 2nd ed. 208p. 1975. 176.00 (*0-08-018888-5*, Pub. by Pergamon Repr) Franklin.

Livesley, W. J. & Bromley, D. B. Person Perception in Childhood & Adolescence. LC 72-8606. 332p. reprint ed. pap. 103.00 (*0-608-12452-4*, 202520400042) Bks Demand.

Livesley, W. John, ed. The DSM-IV Personality Disorders. LC 94-25319. 516p. 1995. lib. bdg. 56.00 (*0-89862-257-3*, 2257) Guilford Pubns.

Liveson, Jay. Hanging On: Poems. LC 98-45062. 64p. 1998. pap. 14.95 (*0-7734-3096-2*) E Mellen.

***Liveson, Jay.** Peripheral Neurology: Case Studies in Electrodiagnosis. 3rd ed. (Illus.). 512p. 2000. pap. text 57.50 (*0-19-513563-6*) OUP.

Liveson, Jay. To Skim the Smoke: Poems. LC 96-53097. 92p. 1997. pap. 14.95 (*0-7734-2707-4*, Mellen Poetry Pr) E Mellen.

— To Slay the Dragon. LC 95-51017. 92p. 1996. pap. 14.95 (*0-7734-2676-0*, Mellen Poetry Pr) E Mellen.

***Liveson, Jay.** What Counts: Poems. 80p. 2000. pap. 12.00 (*1-56474-345-4*) Fithian Pr.

Liveson, Jay A. Peripheral Neurology: Case Studies in Electrodiagnosis. 2nd ed. LC 90-14135. (Illus.). 496p. (C). 1991. text 60.00 (*0-8036-5652-1*) OUP.

Liveson, Jay A. & Ma, Dong M. Laboratory Reference for Clinical Neurophysiology. (Illus.). 528p. 1992. text 69.50 (*0-19-512924-5*) OUP.

Livet, Charles L. Lexique de la Langue de Moliere, 3 vols., Set. xiii, 2022p. 1970. reprint ed. write for info. (*0-318-71373-X*) G Olms Pubs.

Livett, Anne, jt. auth. see Crane, Ralph.

Livett, Richard K. Shopping for God: A Guide to Your Spiritual Evolution. 250p. (Orig.). 1996. pap. 15.95 (*0-9654201-0-8*) Soul Star.

Livezeanu, Irina. Cultural Politics in Greater Romania: Regionalism, Nation Building, & Ethnic Struggle, 1918-1930. (Illus.). 356p. 1995. text 45.00 (*0-8014-2445-3*) Cornell U Pr.

***Livezeanu, Irina.** Cultural Politics in Greater Romania: Regionalism, Nation Building, & Ethnic Struggle, 1918-1930. 2000. reprint ed. pap. 19.95 (*0-8014-8688-2*) Cornell U Pr.

Livezey, Auriel W. Bird. LC 96-183496. (Illus.). 75p. 1995. 10.95 (*0-9642628-2-7*) Mtntop Pubng.

— Numberland. LC 95-175314. 160p. 1995. pap. 9.95 (*0-9642628-1-9*) Mtntop Pubng.

Livezey, Bradley C. & Humphrey, Philip S. Taxonomy & Identification of Steamer-Ducks: Anatidae: Tachyeres. (Monographs: No. 8). 210p. 1992. pap. 14.95 (*0-89338-042-3*) U KS Nat Hist Mus.

Livezey, Bradley C., jt. auth. see Humphrey, Philip S.

Livezey, Lowell W. Nongovernmental Organizations & the Ideas of Human Rights. (World Order Studies Program Occasional Paper: No. 15). 199p. (Orig.). 1988. pap. text 11.00 (*0-945101-00-7*) Princeton CIS.

— Nongovernmental Organizations & the Ideas of Human Rights. LC 87-34939. (World Order Studies Program Occasional Paper: No. 15). 201p. (Orig.). reprint ed. pap. 62.40 (*0-8357-8527-0*, 203482500091) Bks Demand.

***Livezey, Lowell W.** Public Religion & Urban Transformation. LC 99-50622. 280p. 1999. pap. text 18.50 (*0-8147-5158-X*) NYU Pr.

***Livezey, Lowell W., ed.** Public Religion & Urban Transformation. LC 99-50622. (Religion, Race, & Ethnicity Ser.). 280p. 1999. text 65.00 (*0-8147-5157-1*) NYU Pr.

Livgren, Kerry, jt. auth. see Boa, Kenneth.

Livi-Bacci, M. A Concise History of World Population. 2nd rev. ed. Ipsen, Carl, tr. LC 96-34353. (Illus.). 256p. (C). 1997. text 66.95 (*0-631-20454-7*); pap. text 22.95 (*0-631-20455-5*) Blackwell Pubs.

Livi Bacci, Massimo. A History of Italian Fertility During the Last Two Centuries. LC 76-3271. 334p. 1977. reprint ed. pap. 103.60 (*0-608-02882-7*, 206394600007) Bks Demand.

Livi-Bacci, Massimo. The Populations of Europe: A History. Shaw, Ian, tr. from ITA. LC 99-29297. (Making of Europe Ser.).Tr. of Popolazione Nella Storia D'Europa. (Illus.). 288p. 1999. 59.95 (*0-631-20078-9*); pap. 26.95 (*0-631-21881-5*) Blackwell Pubs.

Livi-Bacci, Massimo & De Santis, Gustavo, eds. Population & Poverty in the Developing World. LC 98-28485. (International Studies in Demography). (Illus.). 316p. 1999. text 70.00 (*0-19-829300-3*) OUP.

Livi, Roberto, et al, eds. Chaos & Complexity: Proceedings of the Workshop on Chaos & Complexity. 452p. (C). 1988. pap. 46.00 (*9971-5-0568-1*); text 125.00 (*9971-5-0567-3*) World Scientific Pub.

— Complex Dynamics. 320p. (C). 1994. text 145.00 (*1-56072-018-2*) Nova Sci Pubs.

Livi, Roberto & Politi, A., eds. Advances in Nonlinear Dynamics & Stochastic Processes: Proceedings of the meeting on Nonlinear Processes Arcetri, Florence, January 7-8 1985. 232p. 1985. 41.00 (*9971-5-0018-3*) World Scientific Pub.

Livia, Anna. Bruised Fruit: A Novel. LC 99-10943. 256p. 1999. 26.95 (*1-56341-107-5*); pap. 13.95 (*1-56341-106-7*) Firebrand Bks.

— Incidents Involving Mirth. LC 90-42348. 216p. 1990. 22.95 (*0-933377-14-2*, Pub. by Eighth Mount Pr); pap. 9.95 (*0-933377-13-4*, Pub. by Eighth Mount Pr) Consort Bk Sales.

— Minimax. LC 90-42350. 224p. 1991. pap. 9.95 (*0-933377-11-8*, Pub. by Eighth Mount Pr); lib. bdg. 22.95 (*0-933377-12-6*, Pub. by Eighth Mount Pr) Consort Bk Sales.

***Livia, Anna.** Pronoun Envy: Literary Uses of Linguistic Gender. (Studies in Language & Gender). 272p. 2000. pap. 29.95 (*0-19-513853-8*); text 55.00 (*0-19-513852-X*) OUP.

Livia, Anna & Hall, Kira, eds. Queerly Phrased: Language, Gender & Sexuality. LC 97-6284. (Oxford Studies in Sociolinguistics). (Illus.). 480p. 1997. pap. 29.95 (*0-19-510471-4*); text 75.00 (*0-19-510470-6*) OUP.

Livia, Anna, tr. see Barney, Natalie C.

Livia, Anna, tr. see Delarue-Mardrus, Lucie.

Livian, Yves F. & Burgoyne, John G., eds. Middle Managers in Europe. LC 96-12600. (Advances in Management & Tourism Ser.). 232p. (C). 1997. 80.00 (*0-415-13902-3*) Routledge.

Liviano, David. The Official Guide to Adoptions in Eastern Europe, 1994-1995, 3 vols., Set. 2820p. 1994. pap. 200.00 incl. VHS (*0-9640536-0-8*) Melador Pubng.

Liviatan, Nissan, ed. Proceedings of a Conference on Currency Substitution & Currency Boards. LC 93-26386. (Discussion Papers: No. 207). 128p. 1993. pap. 22.00 (*0-8213-2521-3*, 12521) World Bank.

Livick, Lester. Fluffy the Little White Rabbit with Pink Eyes. (Illus.). 16p. (J). (gr. k-3). 1997. pap. 5.00 (*0-8059-3986-5*) Dorrance.

***Living Art Seminars Staff.** Teaching the Middle Ages with Magnificent Art Masterpieces. (Illus.). 64p. (J). (gr. 4-8). 2000. pap. 22.99 (*0-590-64435-1*) Scholastic Inc.

Living Books. Arthur Adventures Library. 1998. cd-rom 119.95 (*1-57404-434-6*) Living Bks.

— Dr. Seuss Library. 1998. cd-rom 119.95 (*1-57404-435-4*) Living Bks.

Living Books, Inc., Staff. Dr. Seuss's ABC. 1995. 29.50 (*1-57135-136-1*) Living Bks.

Living Books, Inc. Staff. Frameworks, Vol. 2. 1995. 299.95 (*1-57135-175-2*) Living Bks.

Living Books, Inc., Staff. Living Books Library #2: Contains Complete Programs for Harry & the Haunted House, Just Grandma. 1997. pap. write for info. (*1-57135-334-8*) Rand McNally.

Living Books Staff. Creation. 1997. 7.50 (*1-57135-312-7*) Living Bks.

— Daniel & the Lion's Den. 1997. 7.50 (*1-57135-305-4*) Living Bks.

Living Books Staff. Living Books Library #1: Contains Complete Programs for Little Monster At School, Ruff's Bone. 1997. pap. write for info. (*1-57135-332-1*) Rand McNally.

Living Earth Foundation Staff, compiled by. The Rainforests: A Celebration. (Illus.). 224p. 1990. 35.00 (*0-87701-790-5*) Chronicle Bks.

— The Rainforests: A Celebration. (Illus.). 224p. 1992. pap. 22.95 (*0-8118-0155-1*) Chronicle Bks.

***Living Faith Staff.** Living Faith Bible. 2000. 26.99 (*0-8423-7358-6*); 44.99 (*0-8423-7359-4*); pap. 19.99 (*0-8423-7357-8*) Tyndale Hse.

Living Language. Living Language Complete Course: French. (Living Language Ser.). (ENG & FRE.). 1998. 30.00 incl. cd-rom (*0-609-60275-6*, 903601) Liv Lang.

— Living Language Complete Course: German. (Living Language Ser.). (ENG & GER.). 1998. 30.00 incl. cd-rom, audio compact disk (*0-609-60277-2*, 903603) Liv Lang.

— Living Language Complete Course: Italian. (ENG & ITA.). 1998. 30.00 incl. cd-rom, audio compact disk (*0-609-60272-1*, 903604) Liv Lang.

— Living Language Complete Course: Japanese. (ENG & JPN.). 1998. 30.00 incl. cd-rom, audio compact disk (*0-609-60279-9*, 903607) Liv Lang.

— Living Language Complete Course: Spanish. (ENG & SPA.). 30.00 incl. cd-rom, audio compact disk (*0-609-60267-5*, 903608) Liv Lang.

Living Language, jt. auth. see Weiman, Ralph.

Living Language Staff. American English Pronunciation Program: A Simple Approach to Speaking English Clearly, Set. 1999. audio 34.95 (*0-609-60419-8*) Liv Lang.

***Living Language Staff.** Bravissimo! Book of Italian Wit & Wisdom. (Living Language Ser.). 2000. 4.95 (*0-609-60618-2*) Liv Lang.

— English for New Americans: Health & Safety. 128p. 1999. pap. 9.95 (*0-609-80622-X*) Liv Lang.

— English for New Americans: Work & School. 128p. 1999. pap. 9.95 (*0-609-80621-1*) Liv Lang.

Living Language Staff. Espanol Rapido y Facil. (SPA & ENG.). 1998. 9.95 incl. audio (*0-609-60337-X*) Liv Lang.

***Living Language Staff.** Fantastico! Book of Spanish Wit & Wisdom. (Living Language Ser.). 2000. 4.95 (*0-609-60617-4*) Liv Lang.

Living Language Staff. Fast & Easy French. 1999. audio compact disk 13.95 (*0-609-80455-3*) Liv Lang.

— Fast & Easy German. 1999. audio compact disk 13.95 (*0-609-80456-1*) Liv Lang.

— Fast & Easy Italian. 1999. audio compact disk 13.95 (*0-609-80457-X*) Liv Lang.

— Fast & Easy Japanese. 1999. audio compact disk 13.95 (*0-609-80458-8*) Liv Lang.

— Fast & Easy Spanish. 1999. audio compact disk 13.95 (*0-609-80459-6*) Liv Lang.

— Fodor's Italian for Travelers. (Languages for Travelers Ser.). (ITA & ENG.). 288p. 1997. pap. 16.95 incl. audio (*0-679-03412-9*) Fodors Travel.

— Fodor's Spanish for Travelers. LC 97-157969. (Languages for Travelers Ser.). (SPA & ENG.). 288p. 1997. pap. 16.95 incl. audio (*0-679-03416-1*) Fodors Travel.

— French for Travelers. (Languages for Traveler's Ser.). (FRE & ENG.). 288p. 1997. pap. 16.95 incl. audio (*0-679-03410-2*) Fodors Travel.

— French in the Kitchen. LC 97-47768. (The Living Language Ser.). (FRE & ENG.). 1998. pap. 18.95 incl. audio (*0-609-60215-2*) Liv Lang.

— German All the Way II. (GER.). 1995. audio 65.00 (*0-517-70270-3*) Crown Pub Group.

— German for Travelers. (Languages for Trvelers Ser.). (GER & ENG.). 288p. 1997. pap. 16.95 incl. audio (*0-679-03414-5*) Fodors Travel.

***Living Language Staff.** Getting Started in Signing. 2000. 24.95 (*0-609-60567-4*) Crown Pub Group.

Living Language Staff. Ingles Rapido y Facil. (SPA & ENG.). 1998. 9.95 incl. audio (*0-609-60336-1*) Liv Lang.

— Interview Smart. 1998. 15.95 incl. audio (*0-609-60154-7*) Liv Lang.

— Italian in the Kitchen. LC 97-47432. (ITA & ENG.). 1998. 18.95 incl. audio (*0-609-60216-0*) Liv Lang.

— Living Language Chinese: Basic-Intermediate: Mandarin. LC 99-22778. (Living Language Ser.). (C). 2000. pap. 75.00 incl. audio (*0-517-70877-9*) Liv Lang.

— Living Language English for the Real World Russian. 1999. 29.95 incl. audio (*0-609-60510-0*, Crown) Crown.

— Living Language Fast & Easy Arabic. (ENG.). 1998. 9.95 incl. audio (*0-609-60350-7*) Liv Lang.

— Living Language Fast & Easy Czech. (ENG.). 1998. 9.95 incl. audio (*0-609-60349-3*) Liv Lang.

— Living Language Fast & Easy French. (FRE & ENG.). 1998. 9.95 incl. audio (*0-609-60348-5*) Liv Lang.

— Living Language Fast & Easy German. (GER & ENG.). 1998. 9.95 incl. audio (*0-609-60347-7*) Liv Lang.

— Living Language Fast & Easy Hebrew. (ENG.). 1998. 9.95 incl. audio (*0-609-60346-9*) Liv Lang.

— Living Language Fast & Easy Hungarian. (ENG.). 1998. 9.95 incl. audio (*0-609-60345-0*) Liv Lang.

— Living Language Fast & Easy Italian. (ITA & ENG.). 1998. 9.95 incl. audio (*0-609-60343-4*) Liv Lang.

— Living Language Fast & Easy Japanese. (JPN & ENG.). 1998. 9.95 incl. audio (*0-609-60342-6*) Liv Lang.

— Living Language Fast & Easy Korean. (KOR & ENG.). 1998. 9.95 incl. audio (*0-609-60344-2*) Liv Lang.

— Living Language Fast & Easy Mandarin. (CHI & ENG.). 1998. 9.95 incl. audio (*0-609-60341-8*) Liv Lang.

— Living Language Fast & Easy Polish. (POL & ENG.). 1998. 9.95 incl. audio (*0-609-60340-X*) Liv Lang.

— Living Language Fast & Easy Portuguese. (POR & ENG.). 1998. 9.95 incl. audio (*0-609-60339-6*) Liv Lang.

— Living Language Fast & Easy Russian. (RUS & ENG.). 1998. 9.95 incl. audio (*0-609-60338-8*) Liv Lang.

***Living Language Staff.** Living Language Ultimate Portuguese: Basic-Intermediate. (ENG & POR.). 2000. pap. 75.00 incl. audio (*0-609-60422-8*) Liv Lang.

— Mais Oui! Book of French Wit & Wisdom. (Living Language Ser.). 2000. 4.95 (*0-609-60619-0*) Liv Lang.

Living Language Staff. Negotiate Smart. 1998. 15.95 incl. audio (*0-609-60152-0*) Liv Lang.

***Living Language Staff.** Oy, Gevalt! Book of Yiddish Wit & Wisdom. (Living Language Ser.). 2000. 4.95 (*0-609-60616-6*) Liv Lang.

Living Language Staff. Spanish in the Kitchen. LC 98-11277. (SPA & ENG.). 1998. 18.95 incl. audio (*0-609-60217-9*) Liv Lang.

***Living Language Staff.** Terra Cognita Guide to China. 2000. write for info. (*0-609-60555-0*) Liv Lang.

— Ultimate Chinese: Basic-Intermediate: Mandarin. LC 99-22778. (Living Language Ultimate Courses Ser.). 416p. 2000. pap. 18.00 (*0-609-80065-5*) Liv Lang.

Living Language Staff. Ultimate French: Basic Intermediate. 1998. 75.00 incl. audio (*0-609-60175-X*) Liv Lang.

— Ultimate French Advanced Manual, Set. (Living Language Ser.). (FRE.). 1998. 75.00 incl. audio (*0-609-60194-6*) Crown Pub Group.

— Ultimate German: Basic Intermediate. 1998. 75.00 incl. audio (*0-609-60197-0*) Liv Lang.

— Ultimate German Advanced: Learn to Speak, Read, & Write German More Fluently. (Living Language Ser.). (GER.). 1998. 75.00 incl. audio (*0-609-60202-0*) Crown Pub Group.

— Ultimate Ingles: Basic - Intermediate. 1998. 75.00 incl. audio (*0-609-60173-3*) Liv Lang.

— Ultimate Ingles Advanced. (Living Language Ser.). (SPA & ENG.). 1998. 75.00 incl. audio (*0-517-70231-2*) Liv Lang.

— Ultimate Italian: Basic Intermediate. 1998. 75.00 incl. audio (*0-609-60199-7*) Liv Lang.

— Ultimate Italian Advanced. 1998. 75.00 incl. audio, cd-rom (*0-517-70234-7*) Liv Lang.

— Ultimate Japanese: Basic - Intermediate. 1998. 75.00 incl. audio (*0-609-60171-7*) Liv Lang.

— Ultimate Japanese Advanced. (Living Language Ser.). 1998. pap. 75.00 incl. audio (*0-517-70235-5*) Liv Lang.

***Living Language Staff.** Ultimate Portuguese: Basic-Intermediate. 448p. 2000. pap. 18.00 (*0-609-80407-3*) Liv Lang.

Living Language Staff. Ultimate Russian Advanced, Set. (Living Language Ser.). (RUS.). 1998. pap. 75.00 incl. audio (*0-517-70237-1*) Liv Lang.

— Ultimate Spanish: Basic Intermediate. 1998. 75.00 incl. audio (*0-609-60200-4*) Liv Lang.

— Ultimate Spanish - Basic Intermediate. (Ultimate Courses Ser.). (ENG & SPA.). 1998. 75.00 incl. audio, cd-rom (*0-609-60254-3*) Liv Lang.

— Word Smart: How to Build an Erudite Vocabulary. 1997. 25.00 incl. audio (*0-517-70816-7*) Liv Lang.

— Word Smart Plus Grammar Smart: Living Language Princeton Review, Set. 1999. 39.95 incl. audio (*0-609-60351-5*) Liv Lang.

L

***Living Oceans Society Staff.** Fish for Thought: The Living Oceans Cookbook. (Illus.). 2000. pap. 17.95 (*1-55152-081-8*) Arsenal Pulp.

Living Springs Retreat Staff & Weeks, Sherry. Nature's Banquet. LC 95-61139. 144p. 1997. reprint ed. otabind 12.95 (*1-57258-039-9*) Teach Servs.

Living Stream Ministry Staff. A Concordance of the Recovery Version New Testament. 398p. 1994. per. 18.75 (*0-87083-819-9*, 01-024-001) Living Stream Ministry.

***Living Stream Ministry Staff.** El Espiritu Santo y la Realidad. (SPA.). 1999. pap. write for info. (*0-7363-0701-X*) Living Stream Ministry.

Living Stream Ministry Staff. Himnos. (SPA.). 629p. 1996. per. 12.00 (*0-87083-969-1*, 02-023-002) Living Stream Ministry.

***Living Stream Ministry Staff.** Holy Bible. 1999. 50.00 (*0-7363-0632-3*) Living Stream Ministry.

— New Covenant. 1999. pap. write for info. (*0-7363-0088-0*) Living Stream Ministry.

— El Plan Eterno de Dios. (SPA.). 1999. pap. write for info. (*0-7363-0415-0*) Living Stream Ministry.

— Poder Preservador de Dios. 1999. pap. 10.00 (*0-7363-0333-2*) Living Stream Ministry.

***Living Stream Ministry Staff, ed.** Los Vencedores Que Dios Busca. 1999. pap. 8.25 (*0-7363-0651-X*) Living Stream Ministry.

Living Street Ministry Staff. And He Loved Us! 32p. 1991. pap. 3.00 (*0-87083-602-1*, 17-009-001) Living Stream Ministry.

— And The Little Child Grew. 32p. 1992. pap. 3.00 (*0-87083-673-0*, 17-012-001) Living Stream Ministry.

— Character - Color 'N Work Book. 32p. 1987. pap. 3.00 (*0-87083-369-3*, 17-001-001) Living Stream Ministry.

— Childrens Character Book. 32p. 1987. pap. 3.00 (*0-87083-370-7*, 17-002-001) Living Stream Ministry.

— Emmanuel: God With Us! 32p. 1992. pap. 3.00 (*0-87083-656-0*, 17-008-001) Living Stream Ministry.

— Fellowship With The Young People. 36p. 1989. pap. 3.25 (*0-87083-429-0*, 16-003-001) Living Stream Ministry.

— Hymns Jr. 142p. 1983. per. 7.00 (*0-87083-101-1*, 17-003-001) Living Stream Ministry.

— Lesson Book Level 1: God's Full Salvation. 113p. 1990. per. 6.00 (*0-87083-521-1*, 16-018-001) Living Stream Ministry.

— Lesson Book Level 2: Triune God & the Person & Work of Christ. 131p. 1990. per. 6.25 (*0-87083-522-X*, 16-019-001) Living Stream Ministry.

— Lesson Book Level 3: 2 Spirits - Divine Spirit & the Human Spirit. 181p. 1990. per. 7.50 (*0-87083-523-8*, 16-020-001) Living Stream Ministry.

— Lesson Book Level 5: Vision & Building of the Church. 294p. 1990. per. 10.50 (*0-87083-525-4*, 16-022-001) Living Stream Ministry.

— Lesson Book Level 6 - Bible: The Word of God. 342p. 1991. per. 11.75 (*0-87083-594-7*, 16-023-001) Living Stream Ministry.

— New Testament Recovery Version. 450p. 1985. 7.50 (*0-87083-697-8*, 01-001-901) Living Stream Ministry.

— New Testament Recovery Version. 450p. 1993. per. 5.00 (*0-87083-698-6*, 01-002-001) Living Stream Ministry.

— Nuevo Testamento, Version Recobro, Black.Tr. of New Testament, Recovery Version. (SPA.). 1338p. 1994. boxed set, lthr. 65.00 (*0-87083-801-6*, 01-013-002) Living Stream Ministry.

— Nuevo Testamento, Version Recobro, Edicion Economica en Rustica (Black)Tr. of NEW TESTAMENT, RECOVERY VERSION (ECONOMY BLACK, 6 3/4. (SPA.). 1368p. 1994. per. 15.00 (*0-87083-804-0*, 01-018-002) Living Stream Ministry.

— Nuevo Testamento, Version Recobro, Edicion Economica en Rustica (Maroon)Tr. of NEW TESTAMENT, RECOVERY VERSION (ECONOMY BURGUNDY, 6 3/4. (SPA.). 1368p. 1994. per. 15.00 (*0-87083-803-2*, 01-019-002) Living Stream Ministry.

— Nuevo Testamento, Version Recobro, Maroon.Tr. of NEW TESTAMENT, RECOVERY VERSION. (SPA.). 1338p. 1994. boxed set, lthr. 65.00 (*0-87083-802-4*, 01-014-002) Living Stream Ministry.

— Wonderfully! 32p. 1991. pap. 3.00 (*0-87083-601-3*, 17-010-001) Living Stream Ministry.

— Yes, We Love God's Word! 32p. 1991. pap. 3.00 (*0-87083-603-X*, 17-011-001) Living Stream Ministry.

— You Are My Son, the Beloved. 32p. 1993. pap. 3.00 (*0-87083-742-7*, 17-013-001) Living Stream Ministry.

— You Shall Not Test The Lord Your God! 32p. 1994. pap. 3.00 (*0-87083-784-2*, 17-016-001) Living Stream Ministry.

***Living Water Anglicized Staff.** Living Water Bible. 2000. 20.99 (*0-8423-4027-0*); pap. 14.99 (*0-8423-4026-2*) Tyndale Hse.

***Living Waters Pubns. Staff.** Living Water Bible. 2000. 19.99 (*0-8423-4029-7*); 39.99 (*0-8423-4033-5*); 39.99 (*0-8423-4034-3*); pap. 14.99 (*0-8423-4031-9*) Tyndale Hse.

Living Waters Pubns. Staff, ed. see Comfort, Ray.

Living Wellness Staff. Living Wellness: Directory & Journal of Holistic Practices & Providers Los Angeles 1998-1999, 1. (Illus.). 127p. 1998. pap. 4.95 (*0-9666402-0-9*) Liv Wellness.

Living Word Christian Center Staff. The Table of Blessing: Recipes from the Families & Friends of Living Word Christian Center. 1998. 15.00 (*1-57399-076-0*) Mac Hammond.

***Livinggood, Lee.** Retired Racing Greyhounds. 1999. pap. 14.95 (*1-58245-147-8*) Howell Bks.

Livingood, J., et al, eds. Christmas I Remember Best. (Illus.). (Orig.). write for info. (*0-910901-00-7*); pap. 5.95 (*0-910901-01-5*) Deseret News.

Livingood, James W. Chattanooga Country: Gateway to History: The Nashville to Atlanta Rail Corridor in the 1860's. LC 95-68156. (Illus.). 705p. (C). 1995. text. write for info. (*0-9648328-0-1*) Chttanooga Hist Assn.

— Philadelphia-Baltimore Trade Rivalry, 1780-1860. LC 70-112557. (Rise of Urban America Ser.). (Illus.). 1976. reprint ed. 21.95 (*0-405-02463-0*) Ayer.

Livingood, James W., jt. auth. see Govan, Gilbert E.

Livingood, James W., jt. auth. see Raulston, J. Leonard.

Livingood, Jay K. Development & Operation Manual for a Golf Practice Range Facility. (Illus.). 300p. 1992. 195.00 (*0-9645721-0-9*) Livingood Consult.

***Livingood, Lee.** Retired Racing Greyhounds for Dummies. (For Dummies (Lifestyles) Ser.). (Illus.). 334p. 2000. pap. 15.99 (*0-7645-5276-7*) IDG Bks.

Livings, Henry. Eh? 1968. pap. 5.25 (*0-8222-0351-0*) Dramatists Play.

***Livings, Henry.** Livings: Play One. (Oberon Bks.). 2000. pap. 20.95 (*1-84002-044-X*) Theatre Comm.

Livings, Henry, tr. see Garcia Lorca, Federico.

Livingston. Crime & Criminology. 2nd ed. 1995. text, teacher ed. write for info. (*0-13-375114-7*); text, teacher ed. write for info. (*0-13-375122-8*) Allyn.

Livingston. UA Fund Adjust Life Majr. 312p. 1999. pap. text 21.70 (*0-536-02366-2*) Pearson Custom.

Livingston & Straub. Windows 95 Secrets. 4th ed. 1008p. 1997. boxed set 59.99 (*0-7645-3094-1*) IDG Bks.

Livingston, jt. auth. see Butler.

Livingston, jt. auth. see Katzer.

Livingston, A. Dictionnaire du Graphisme. (FRE.). 1998. 49.95 (*0-320-00176-8*) Fr & Eur.

Livingston, A., tr. see Croce, Benedetto.

Livingston, A. D. Bass Cookbook. 160p. 1996. pap. 12.95 (*0-8117-2509-X*) Stackpole.

— Cast Iron Cooking. 224p. 1991. pap. 12.95 (*1-55821-115-2*) Lyons Pr.

— Cold Smoking & Salt Curing Meat, Fish, & Game. (Illus.). 168p. (Orig.). pap. 14.95 (*1-55821-422-4*, 315-5) Lyons Pr.

— Complete Fish & Game Cookbook. 488p. 1996. 29.95 (*0-8117-0428-9*) Stackpole.

— Duck & Goose Cookbook. LC 97-10729. 176p. 1997. pap. 12.95 (*0-8117-2742-4*) Stackpole.

— Good Vittles: One Man's Meat, a Few Vegetables & a Drink or Two. 224p. 1990. pap. 13.95 (*1-55821-079-2*) Lyons Pr.

— Guide to Edible Plants & Animals. (Reference Library). 1998. pap. 6.95 (*1-85326-377-X*, 377XWW, Pub. by Wrdsworth Edits) NTC Contemp Pub Co.

— Luremaking: The Art & Science of Spinnerbaits, Buzzbaits, Jigs, & Other Leadheads. 161p. 1993. pap. 16.95 (*0-07-038152-6*) McGraw.

— Luremaking: The Art & Science of Spinnerbaits, Buzzbaits, Jigs, & Other Leadheads. (Illus.). 192p. 1993. pap. 16.95 (*0-87742-372-5*, Ragged Mntain) McGraw-Hill Prof.

***Livingston, A. D.** On the Grill. LC 99-20143. Orig. Title: Grilling, Smoking & Barbecuing. (Illus.). 208p. 1999. pap. 14.95 (*1-55821-806-8*) Lyons Pr.

— Poker Strategy: Proven Principles for Winning Play. 240p. 2000. pap. 14.95 (*1-58574-064-0*) Lyons Pr.

Livingston, A. D. Saltwater Fish Cookbook. LC 96-47102. (Illus.). 288p. 1997. pap. 19.95 (*0-8117-2924-9*) Stackpole.

— Sausage. LC 97-17151. (Illus.). 208p. 1998. pap. 14.95 (*1-55821-526-3*) Lyons Pr.

— Shellfish Cookbook. LC 97-32159. 224p. 1998. pap. 14.95 (*0-8117-2923-0*) Stackpole.

***Livingston, A. D.** Strictly Steak. LC 99-59657. (Illus.). 160p. 2000. pap. 14.95 (*1-58080-048-3*) Burford Bks.

Livingston, A. D. The Trout Cookbook. 160p. 1996. pap. 12.95 (*0-8117-2581-2*) Stackpole.

— Venison Cookbook. LC 93-4400. (Illus.). 128p. 1993. pap. 12.95 (*0-8117-2594-4*) Stackpole.

***Livingston, A. D.** The Whole Grain Cookbook: Delicious Recipes for Wheat, Barley, Oats, Rye, Amaranth, Spelt, Corn, Millet, Quinoa & More with Instructions for Milling Your Own. LC 00-38062. (Illus.). 320p. 2000. pap. 18.95 (*1-58574-047-0*) Lyons Pr.

Livingston, A. D. Wild Turkey Cookbook. LC 94-20652. 192p. 1995. pap. 12.95 (*0-8117-3097-2*) Stackpole.

Livingston, A. D. & Livingston, Helen. Edible Plants & Animals: A Compendium of Unusual Foods from Aardvark to Zamia. 304p. 1993. 29.95 (*0-8160-2744-7*) Facts on File.

***Livingston, A. D. & Livingston, Helen.** The Wordsworth Guide to Edible Plants & Animals: An Omnivorous Feast of Unusual Meat & Vegetables. (Illus.). 292p. 2000. reprint ed. pap. text 17.00 (*0-7881-9154-3*) DIANE Pub.

Livingston, A. W. Livingston & the Tomato. LC 98-4410. (Illus.). 273p. 1998. pap. text 18.95 (*0-8142-5009-2*, LIVLIX) Ohio St U Pr.

Livingston, Alan & Livingston, Isabella. The Thames & Hudson Encyclopaedia of Graphic Design & Designers. LC 92-70862. (World of Art Ser.). (Illus.). 216p. 1992. pap. 14.95 (*0-500-20259-1*, Pub. by Thames Hudson) Norton.

***Livingston, Alice, contrib. by.** Moses Wrote about Me. 1999. pap. 7.95 (*1-56794-184-2*) Star Bible.

Livingston, Andrew. Hydrology & Water Resources Symposium, 23rd, 1996: Water & the Environment, 2 vols. (National Conference Proceedings Ser.: Vol. 96/05). (Illus.). 744p. 1996. pap. 144.00 (*0-85825-649-5*, Pub. by Inst Engrs Aust-EA Bks) Accents Pubns.

Livingston, Anne H. Nancy Shippen, Her Journal Book: The International Romance of a Young Lady of Fashion of Colonial Philadelphia. (American Biography Ser.). 348p. 1991. reprint ed. lib. bdg. 79.00 (*0-7812-8248-9*) Rprt Serv.

Livingston, Arthur. Essays on Modern Italian Literature. (ITA.). 197p. (C). 1950. 15.00 (*0-913298-74-3*) S F Vanni.

Livingston, Arthur, ed. see Mosca, Gaetano.

Livingston, Arthur, ed. see Pareto, Vilfredo.

Livingston, Barbara D. Four Seasons of Racing: A Year in Photographs. Duke, Jacqueline, ed. (Illus.). 144p. 1998. 39.95 (*1-58150-012-2*) Blood-Horse.

***Livingston, Billie.** Going down Swinging. 336p. 2000. write for info. (*0-679-31000-2*) Random.

— Going down Swinging. 2000. pap. write for info. (*0-679-31073-8*) Random.

Livingston, Bob. The Best of Tech Topics, Vol. I. 104p. 1997. pap. text 12.95 (*0-934798-55-9*) TL Enterprises.

— RV Repair & Maintenance. 3rd rev. ed. (Illus.). 336p. 1997. pap. 34.95 (*0-934798-45-1*, Trailer Life Bks) TL Enterprises.

Livingston, Bob, ed. see Estes, Bill.

Livingston, Bradford. Unions' Rights to Company Information. 3rd ed. (Labor Relations & Public Policy Ser.: Vol. 21). 150p. 1998. 37.50 (*1-891496-11-5*) J M Olin.

Livingston, Brian. InfoWorld Technical Books: Windows 3 Secrets. 838p. 1991. pap. 39.95 (*1-878058-23-1*) IDG Bks.

— More Windows 98 Secrets. LC 99-28102. (Secrets Ser.). 816p. 1999. pap. 34.99 (*0-7645-3360-6*) IDG Bks.

Livingston, Brian. More Windows 3.1 Secrets. 700p. 1993. pap. 39.95 (*1-56884-019-5*) IDG Bks.

— Windows 95 Secrets. 3rd ed. LC 95-78408. 984p. 1995. pap. 39.99 (*1-56884-453-0*) IDG Bks.

— Windows 95 Secrets. 4th ed. 1997. pap. 19.99 (*0-7645-3122-0*) IDG Bks.

— Windows 3.1 Secrets. 2nd ed. LC 92-70931. (InfoWorld Technical Bks.). 1024p. 1992. pap. 39.95 (*1-878058-43-6*) IDG Bks.

***Livingston, Brian.** Windows 98 Secrets Gold O-Wrap. (Secrets Ser.). 1154p. 1998. pap. text 69.99 (*0-7645-3207-3*); pap. text 69.99 (*0-7645-3208-1*) IDG Bks.

Livingston, Brian & Gruman, Galen. Windows Gizmos. (Illus.). 624p. 1992. pap. 39.95 incl. 5.25 hd (*1-878058-66-5*) IDG Bks.

Livingston, Brian & IDG Books Staff. Windows 98 Secrets. LC 97-78218. (Secrets Ser.). 1248p. 1998. pap. 49.99 (*0-7645-3186-7*) IDG Bks.

Livingston, Brian & Straub, Davis. Windows 95 Secrets. 4th ed. LC 96-80029. 1176p. 1997. pap. 49.99 (*0-7645-3070-4*) IDG Bks.

— Windows 95 Secrets. 4th ed. 1008p. 1997. 59.99 (*0-7645-3124-7*) IDG Bks.

— Windows 98 Secrets Bonus Pack. (Secrets Ser.). 1998. 19.99 (*0-7645-3194-8*) IDG Bks.

***Livingston, Brian, et al.** Microsoft Windows 2000 Secrets. LC 99-48112. (Secrets Ser.). (Illus.). 744p. 2000. pap. 39.99 incl. cd-rom (*0-7645-3413-0*) IDG Bks.

Livingston, Bruce & Morewitz, Stephen. The Medical Malpractice Handbook: The Plaintiff. 113p. 1996. 64.95 (*1-880921-66-9*); pap. 44.95 (*1-880921-65-0*) Austin & Winfield.

Livingston, Carl. A Laywoman's Primer of Breast Cancer. (Illus.). 24p. (Orig.). 1980. pap. 2.50 (*0-937816-03-5*) Tech Data.

Livingston, Carol. Gecko Tails: A Journey Through Cambodia. 256p. 1997. pap. 11.95 (*0-7538-0005-5*, Pub. by Orion Pubng Grp) Trafalgar.

— Teachers As Leaders: Evolving Roles. 176p. 1992. pap. 15.95 (*0-8106-1848-6*) NEA.

Livingston, Carol & Castle, Shari, eds. Teachers & Research in Action. 104p. 1989. pap. 10.95 (*0-8106-3004-4*) NEA.

Livingston, Carole. I'll Never Be Fat Again. LC 91-40267. 272p. 1992. pap. 12.95 (*0-942637-49-6*) Barricade Bks.

— I'll Never Be Fat Again. 3rd ed. 271p. 2000. pap. 16.95 (*1-56980-148-7*) Barricade Bks.

— Why Was I Adopted? (Illus.). (J). (gr. 1 up). 1978. text 12.00 (*0-8184-0257-1*) Carol Pub Group.

— Why Was I Adopted? (Illus.). 48p. 1986. pap. 8.95 (*0-8184-0400-0*) Carol Pub Group.

— Why Was I Adopted? (Illus.). 1997. pap. 9.95 (*0-8184-0588-0*, L Stuart) Carol Pub Group.

Livingston, Carole & Ciliotta, Claire. Why Am I Going to the Hospital? (Illus.). (J). (gr. 1 up). 1981. 12.00 (*0-8184-0316-0*) Carol Pub Group.

Livingston, Carole, jt. auth. see Ciliotta, Claire.

Livingston, Carole R. British Broadside Ballads of the Sixteenth Century Vol. I: A Catalogue of the Extant Sheets & an Essay. LC 90-48731. 928p. 1991. text 10.00 (*0-8240-7226-X*, 1390) Garland.

Livingston, Charles. Knot Theory. (Carus Monograph). 264p. 1993. text 41.50 (*0-88385-027-3*, CAM-24) Math Assn.

— She Died Young. LC 96-70174. 250p. (Orig.). 1996. pap. 8.95 (*1-889120-04-9*) StarsEnd Creations.

Livingston County Historical & Genealogical Societ, jt. auth. see Turner Publishing Company Staff.

Livingston County History Project Staff, compiled by. A History of Livingston County, Illinois. 343p. 1991. 60.00 (*0-88107-185-4*) Curtis Media.

Livingston, D. I., jt. ed. see Fleming, R. A.

Livingston, Dan & Brown, Micah. Essential CSS & DHTML for Web Masters. LC 99-32973. (Essential Series for Web Professionals Ser.). (Illus.). 208p. 1999. pap. text 29.99 (*0-13-012760-4*) P-H.

Livingston, Dan, jt. auth. see Eigen, Brad.

Livingston, Dennis. Maintaining a Lead Safe Home: A Do-It-Yourself Manual for Homeowners & Property Managers. LC 97-94481. (Illus.). 79p. 1997. pap. 14.95 (*0-9659833-0-7*) Commun Res Projs.

Livingston, Dick. Beauty of Horses. (Illus.). 128p. 1995. write for info. (*1-57215-088-2*) World Pubns.

Livingston, Donald W. Hume's Philosophy of Common Life. LC 83-18227. xiv, 378p. 1984. 30.00 (*0-226-48714-8*) U Ch Pr.

— Hume's Philosophy of Common Life. LC 83-18227. xiv, 392p. 1998. pap. text 17.00 (*0-226-48715-6*) U Ch Pr.

— Philosophical Melancholy & Delirium: Hume's Pathology of Philosophy. LC 97-35175. 456p. 1998. pap. text 25.00 (*0-226-48717-2*); lib. bdg. 68.00 (*0-226-48716-4*) U Ch Pr.

Livingston, Donald W. & King, James T., eds. Hume: A Re-Evaluation. LC 76-13968. 431p. reprint ed. pap. 133.70 (*0-8357-6874-0*, 203557200095) Bks Demand.

Livingston, Donald W. & Martin, Marie, eds. Hume as Philosopher of Society, Politics & History. (Library of the History of Ideas: No. IV). 188p. 1991. 70.00 (*1-878822-03-9*) Univ Rochester Pr.

Livingston, Donald W., jt. ed. see Capaldi, Nicholas.

Livingston, Donald W., ed. see Hume, David.

Livingston, E. A. President Lincoln's Third Largest City: Brooklyn & the Civil War. 187p. (Orig.). 1993. pap. 13.95 (*0-9638981-0-8*) E A Livingston.

— Studia Patristica, 1902 Vol. 2: Critica-Classica-Ascetica-Liturgica Papers of the 1983 Oxford Patristics Conference. (Cistercian Studies). 416p. (Orig.). 1989. pap. 55.00 (*0-87907-351-9*) Cistercian Pubns.

Livingston, E. A., ed. Studia Patristica, 1903 Vol. 3: Second Century-Tertullian to Nicaea in the West- Clement & Origen-The Cappadocian Fathers. Papers of the 1983 Oxford Patristics Conference. (Cistercian Studies). 584p. 1989. pap. 55.00 (*0-87907-352-7*) Cistercian Pubns.

Livingston, E. B. The Livingstones of Livingston Manor, Being the History of the Branch Which Settled in the Province of New York with an Account of Robert Livingston & Albany & His Principal Descendants. (Illus.). 623p. 1989. reprint ed. pap. 93.50 (*0-8328-0778-8*); reprint ed. lib. bdg. 101.50 (*0-8328-0777-X*) Higginson Bk Co.

Livingston, Edward. Complete Works on Criminal Jurisprudence: Consisting of Systems of Penal Law for the State of Louisiana & for the United States of America, with Introductory Reports to the Same, 2 vols., Set. LC 68-55775. (Criminology, Law Enforcement, & Social Problems Ser.: No. 7). 1968. reprint ed. 45.00 (*0-87585-007-3*) Patterson Smith.

***Livingston, Edward.** A System of Penal Law for the State of Louisiana: Consisting of a Code of Crimes & Punishments...: Prepared under the Authority of a Law of the Said State, 1833. LC 99-11403. 1999. 95.00 (*1-886363-83-8*) Lawbk Exchange.

— A System of Penal Law for the United States of America: Consisting of a Code of Crimes & Punishments, a Code of Procedure in Criminal Cases, a Code of Prison Discipline, & a Book of Definitions, Prepared & Presented to the House of Representatives of the United States. LC 00-33591. 2000. write for info. (*1-57588-644-8*) W S Hein.

Livingston, Edwin B. The Livingstons of Livingston Manor: Being a History of That Branch of the Scottish House of Callendar... 2nd ed. LC 98-74849. (Illus.). xxxiii, 590p. 1999. reprint ed. 30.00 (*0-9669674-0-2*) Curtis Hse.

Livingston, Elizabeth & Starbuck, Carol. Miami for Kids: A Family Guide to Greater Miami Including Everglades National Park & the Florida Keys. LC 81-65980. (Illus.). 80p. 1981. pap. 4.95 (*0-916224-63-5*) Banyan Bks.

Livingston, Eric. An Anthropology of Reading. LC 94-39577. 192p. 1995. 27.95 (*0-253-33509-4*) Ind U Pr.

— The Ethnomethodological Foundations of Mathematics. (Studies in Ethnomethodology). 256p. 1986. 49.95 (*0-7102-0335-7*, Routledge Thoemms) Routledge.

— Making Sense of Ethnomethodology. 160p. (C). 1988. pap. write for info. (*0-7102-1262-3*, Routledge Thoemms); text 55.00 (*0-7102-1261-5*, Routledge Thoemms) Routledge.

***Livingston-Fairley, Margaret.** All We Need Is Love: An Anthology of Poetry, Homilies & Prose. 64p. 2000. 22.50 (*1-85776-496-X*, Pub. by Book Guild Ltd) Trans-Atl Phila.

Livingston, Felix R., ed. see Hazlitt, Henry.

Livingston, G. E., ed. Nutritional Status Assessment of the Individual. 479p. 1989. 125.00 (*0-917678-25-7*) Food & Nut Pr.

Livingston, G. E., et al. The Role of Food Product Development in Implementing Dietary Guidelines. 212p. 1982. 50.00 (*0-685-67749-4*) Food & Nut Pr.

Livingston, Gary. Cradled in Glory: Georgia Military Institute 1851-1865. Livingston, Theresa, ed. LC 96-93011. (Illus.). 218p. 1997. 25.00 (*1-928724-02-7*) Caisson Pr.

— The Fall of Fort McAllister: "Among the Best Men the South Could Boast" Livingston, Theresa, ed. LC 96-92895. (Illus.). 156p. 1997. 25.00 (*1-928724-01-9*) Caisson Pr.

— Fields of Gray: Battle of Griswoldville, November 22, 1864. LC 96-85419. (Illus.). 223p. 1996. 25.00 (*1-928724-00-0*) Caisson Pr.

Livingston, Georgetta. The Tenacious Terrier Caper. LC 97-93731. (Jennifer Gray Veterinarian Mystery Ser.: Bk. 6). 192p. 1997. 18.95 (*0-8034-9249-9*, Avalon Bks) Bouregy.

Livingston, Georgette. The Black Cat Caper. LC 95-96225. (Jennifer Gray Veterinarian Mystery Ser.: Bk. 4). 192p. 1996. 18.95 (*0-8034-9168-9*, Avalon Bks) Bouregy.

— The Chattering Chimp Caper. LC 97-97219. (Jennifer Gray Veterinarian Mystery Ser.: Bk. 12). 192p. 1998. 18.95 (*0-8034-9289-8*, Avalon Bks) Bouregy.

— A Choice of Love. 256p. 1995. pap. 4.99 (*0-7860-0159-3*, Pinncle Kensgtn) Kensgtn Pub Corp.

— The Deadly Dog-Bone Caper. LC 95-95221. (Jennifer Gray Veterinarian Mystery Ser.: Bk. 3). 192p. 1996. 18.95 (*0-8034-9158-1*, Avalon Bks) Bouregy.

An Asterisk (*) at the beginning of an entry indicates that the title is appearing for the first time.

— The Dog Named Elvis Caper. LC 95-94891. (Jennifer Gray Veterinarian Mystery Ser.: Bk. 2). 192p. (YA). 1995. 18.95 (*0-8034-9149-2*, Avalon Bks) Bouregy.
— The Mischievous Monkey Caper. LC 96-97013. (Jennifer Gray Veterinarian Mystery Ser.: Bk. 7). 192p. 1996. 18.95 (*0-8034-9183-2*, Avalon Bks) Bouregy.
— The Pink Rabbit Caper. LC 97-97118. (Jennifer Gray Veterinarian Mystery Ser.: Bk. 11). 192p. 1998. 18.95 (*0-8034-9279-0*, Avalon Bks) Bouregy.
— The Potbellied Pig Caper. LC 97-97275. (Jennifer Gray Veterinarian Mystery Ser.: Bk. 10). 192p. 1997. 18.95 (*0-8034-9269-3*, Avalon Bks) Bouregy.
— The Precocious Parrot Caper. LC 96-96401. (Jennifer Gray Veterinarian Mystery Ser.: Bk. 6). 192p. 1996. 18.95 (*0-8034-9213-8*, Avalon Bks) Bouregy.
— The Telltale Turkey Caper. LC 96-96148. (Jennifer Gray Veterinarian Mystery Ser.: Bk. 5). 192p. 1996. 18.95 (*0-8034-9203-0*, Avalon Bks) Bouregy.
— The Unlucky Collie Caper. (Jennifer Gray Veterinarian Mystery Ser.: Bk. 1). 192p. 1995. 18.95 (*0-8034-9139-5*, Avalon Bks) Bouregy.
— The White Elephant Caper. LC 97-94021. 192p. 1997. 18.95 (*0-8034-9259-6*, Avalon Bks) Bouregy.

Livingston, Gordon. Only Spring: On Mourning the Death of My Son. LC 99-30985. 256p. 1999. pap. 12.95 (*1-56924-659-9*) Marlowe & Co.

Livingston, Guy. Happiness Is...A Celebration of Life & Love: Memoirs of a Francophile, 1935-1995. LC 96-75081. 218p. (Orig.). 1996. pap. 12.95 (*1-888592-27-3*) Eli Gilde.

Livingston, Harold. No Trophy, No Sword: An American Volunteer in the Israeli Air Force During the 1948 War of Independence. LC 93-49571. (Illus.). 224p. 1994. 21.95 (*1-883695-03-1*) Edition Q.

Livingston, Helen. Hampshire & the Isle of Wight. LC 95-72829. (Illus.). 128p. 1997. 12.95 (*0-8442-4877-0*, Passprt Bks) NTC Contemp Pub Co.

Livingston, Helen, jt. auth. see Livingston, A. D.

Livingston Hill, Grace. Grace Livingston Hill: Collection, No. 1. 450p. 1998. pap. 4.97 (*1-57748-443-6*) Barbour Pub.

***Livingston Hill, Grace.** Grace Livingston Hill: Collection, No. 2. Vol. 2. 450p. 1998. pap. 4.97 (*1-57748-444-4*) Barbour Pub.
— The Story of the Lost Star: A Christmas Tale. gif. ed. 48p. 2000. 11.99 (*0-7369-0371-2*) Harvest Hse.

Livingston, Ira. Arrow of Chaos: Romanticism & Postmodernity. (Theory Out of Bounds Ser.: No. 9). (Illus.). 320p. (C). 1997. pap. 22.95 (*0-8166-2795-9*); text 57.95 (*0-8166-2794-0*) U of Minn Pr.

Livingston, Ira, jt. ed. see Halberstam, Judith.

Livingston, Isabella, jt. auth. see Livingston, Alan.

Livingston, Ivor L., ed. Handbook of Black American Health: The Mosaic of Conditions, Issues, Policies, & Prospects. LC 93-4852. 496p. 1994. lib. bdg. 99.50 (*0-313-28640-X*, LHB/, Greenwood Pr) Greenwood.

Livingston, Ivor L. & Livingston, Shaffiran. Understanding Stress Using Pointed Illustrations. (Illus.). 143p. 1994. pap. write for info. (*0-9631535-0-1*) I L Livingston.

Livingston, J., et al, eds. Songs of the Siskiyous: Cowboys Poems from the Top of California. (Illus.). 80p. 1999. pap. 10.00 (*0-9651377-4-0*) Liv Gold Pr.

Livingston, J. B. If I Were a Teenager: Pupil Book, 4 vols. (J). 1966. pap. 3.00 (*0-685-74307-1*) Quality Pubns.
— If I Were a Teenager: Teacher's Manual, 4 vols. 1966. pap., teacher ed. 3.85 (*0-685-47447-X*) Quality Pubns.
— Love Yourself. 1972. 4.95 (*0-89137-421-3*) Quality Pubns.
— Today's Victorious Woman, Vol. I. 1983. pap. 5.80 (*0-89137-426-4*) Quality Pubns.
— Today's Victorious Woman, Vol. 2. 1983. pap. 5.80 (*0-89137-427-2*) Quality Pubns.

Livingston, James. Origins of the Federal Reserve System: Money, Class, & Corporate Capitalism, 1890-1913. LC 85-48199. 272p. 1986. pap. text 16.95 (*0-8014-9681-0*) Cornell U Pr.
— Pragmatism & the Political Economy of Cultural Revolution, 1850-1940. 416p. (C). 1994. pap. 19.95 (*0-8078-4664-3*) U of NC Pr.
— Pragmatism & the Political Economy of Cultural Revolution, 1850-1940. LC 94-5736. (Cultural Studies of the United States). 416p. 1997. 49.95 (*0-8078-2157-8*) U of NC Pr.

Livingston, James, jt. auth. see Kestner, Franklin D., Sr.

Livingston, James A., et al. Accountability & Objectives for Music Education. LC 49-626. (Contemporary Music Education Ser.). 29p. (Orig.). 1972. reprint ed. pap. 4.95 (*0-930424-00-X*) Music Educ Pubns.

Livingston, James C. Anatomy of the Sacred: An Introduction to Religion. 2nd ed. LC 92-32308. (Illus.). 480p. (C). 1992. pap. text 48.00 (*0-02-371401-8*, Macmillan Coll) P-H.

Livingston, James C. Anatomy of the Sacred: An Introduction to Religion. 3rd ed. LC 97-33464. 460p. 1997. pap. text 45.00 (*0-13-744269-6*) P-H.

Livingston, James C. Modern Christian Thought, Vol. 1. 2nd ed. 480p. (C). 1996. pap. text 61.00 (*0-02-371423-9*, Macmillan Coll) P-H.
— Modern Christian Thought Vol. 2: The Twentieth Century. 2nd ed. 544p. (C). 1999. pap. text 42.00 (*0-02-371410-7*, Macmillan Coll) P-H.

Livingston, James D. Driving Force: The Natural Magic of Magnets. LC 95-39595. (Illus.). 320p. 1996. 24.95 (*0-674-21644-X*) HUP.
— Driving Force: The Natural Magic of Magnets. (Illus.). 336p. 1997. pap. 14.95 (*0-674-21645-8*) HUP.

***Livingston, James D.** Electronic Properties of Engineering Materials. LC 98-24461. (MIT Series in Materials Science & Engineering). 336p. 1998. text 106.95 (*0-471-31627-X*) Wiley.

Livingston, Jane. The Art of Richard Diebenkorn. LC 96-52338. (Illus.). 1997. pap. write for info. (*0-87427-107-X*) Whitney Mus.
— Lee Miller Photographs. 1989. 50.00 (*0-500-55413-7*) Thames Hudson.

Livingston, Jane, contrib. by. Thomas Chimes: The Hermes Cycle. (Illus.). 52p. 1992. pap. 20.00 (*1-879173-11-5*) Locks Gallery.

Livingston, Jane & Elderfield, John. The Art of Richard Diebenkorn. LC 96-52338. 240p. 1997. pap. 45.00 (*0-520-21258-4*, Pub. by U CA Pr) Cal Prin Full Svc.
— The Art of Richard Diebenkorn. LC 96-52338. (Illus.). 240p. 1997. 65.00 (*0-520-21257-6*, Pub. by U CA Pr) Cal Prin Full Svc.

Livingston, Jay. Crime & Criminology. 2nd ed. LC 95-36406. 590p. 1995. 75.00 (*0-13-328006-3*) P-H.

Livingston, Jean. Tears for the Smaller Dragon: The Story of Jim & Jean Livingston. (Jaffray Collection of Missionary Portraits: No. 18). 1997. pap. 3.99 (*0-87509-717-0*) Chr Pubns.
— Tears for the Smaller Dragon: The Story of Jim & Jean Livingston. LC 97-181164. (Jaffray Collection of Missionary Portraits: Vol. 18). 1997. pap. 9.99 (*0-87509-703-0*) Chr Pubns.

Livingston, Jill. That Ribbon of Highway: Highway 99 from the Oregon Border to the State Capital. (Illus.). 176p. (Orig.). 1996. pap. 14.99 (*0-9651377-0-8*) Liv Gold Pr.

***Livingston, Jill.** That Ribbon of Highway Vol. 1: Highway 99 from the Oregon Border to the State Capitol. 2nd ed. (Illus.). 216p. 2000. pap. 15.99 (*0-9651377-3-2*) Liv Gold Pr.

Livingston, Jill. That Ribbon of Highway II: Highway 99 from the State Capital to the Mexican Border. (Illus.). 216p. (Orig.). 1998. pap. 15.99 (*0-9651377-2-4*) Liv Gold Pr.

Livingston, John & Rischin, Moses, eds. Jews of the American West. LC 90-44864. (American Jewish Civilization Ser.). 228p. 1992. pap. 16.95 (*0-8143-2171-2*) Wayne St U Pr.

Livingston, John, jt. auth. see Largay, James A.

Livingston, John, jt. ed. see Rischin, Moses.

Livingston, John A. Rogue Primate: An Exploration of Human Domestication. LC 95-69270. 236p. 1995. 22.95 (*1-57098-058-6*) Roberts Rinehart.

Livingston, John A., et al. Skinned: Activists Condemn the Horrors of the Fur Trade. 256p. (Orig.). (C). 1989. pap. text 6.95 (*0-685-26109-3*) Intl Wildlife.

***Livingston, Julian.** The Anonymous North American Tour of Franz Liszt. LC 99-91262. 150p. 2000. 18.00 (*0-7388-0710-9*); pap. 18.00 (*0-7388-0711-7*) Xlibris Corp.

Livingston, Julie, ed. see Kawasaki, Guy.

Livingston, Julie, ed. see Menuez, Doug & Kounalakis, Markos.

Livingston, Julie, ed. see Sollie, Eddie C.

Livingston, Julie, ed. see Strauss, Susan.

Livingston, Julie, ed. see Wang, Rosalind C.

Livingston, Julie, ed. see Wood, Wendy A.

Livingston, K. C. & Graham, T. C., eds. Manufacturing Processes in Canada. LC 60-4680. (Illus.). 308p. reprint ed. pap. 95.50 (*0-608-11643-2*, 201430100095) Bks Demand.

Livingston, Kathryn. Chic Simple Bed Linens. 1994. 13.95 (*0-679-43216-7*) Knopf.
— Eclectic Interiors. (Room by Room Ser.). (Illus.). 160p. 1998. 35.00 (*1-56496-426-4*, Pub. by Rockport Pubs) F & W Pubns Inc.
— Victorian Interiors. (Room by Room Ser.). (Illus.). 160p. 1999. 35.00 (*1-56496-424-8*) Rockport Pubs.

Livingston, Kathryn E., ed. Fashion Photography: Patrick Demarchelier. (American Photographer Master Ser.: Vol. 2). (Illus.). 144p. 1989. pap. 24.95 (*0-8212-1736-4*) Bulfinch Pr.

Livingston, Kevin. The Wired Nation Continent. The Communication Revolution & Federating Australia. 2nd ed. LC 97-106416. (Illus.). 232p. 1997. text 75.00 (*0-19-553633-9*) OUP.

Livingston, Kimball. Sailing the Bay. 2nd ed. LC 98-60545. 128 p. (Orig.). 1998. write for info. (*0-9663808-0-0*) White Bridge.

Livingston, Leon R. From Coast to Coast with Jack London by (A-No. 1) LC 74-101741. (Illus.). 1969. reprint ed. 12.00 (*0-912382-01-5*) Black Letter.

Livingston, Lili C. American Indian Ballerinas. LC 96-32307. (Illus.). 348p. 1997. 34.95 (*0-8061-2896-8*) U of Okla Pr.

Livingston, Lili Cockerille. American Indian Ballerinas. 328p. 1999. pap. 17.95 (*0-8061-3134-9*) U of Okla Pr.

Livingston, Linda, jt. auth. see Livingston, Richard.

Livingston, Margit, jt. auth. see Butler, Lynda L.

Livingston, Marius H., ed. International Terrorism in the Contemporary World, 3. LC 77-84773. (Contributions in Political Science Ser.: No.3). (Illus.). 522p. 1978. 45.00 (*0-8371-9884-4*, LIT/, Greenwood Pr) Greenwood.

Livingston, Marjorie. The New Nuctemeron: The Twelve Hours of Apollonius of Tyana. 143p. 1996. reprint ed. pap. 16.95 (*1-56459-522-6*) Kessinger Pub.

Livingston, Martin S. Near & Far: Closeness & Distance in Psychotherapy. LC 91-40451. 225p. 1992. 18.95 (*0-944957-34-X*) Rivercross Pub.

***Livingston, Mary E.** San Antonio in the 1920s & 1930s. (Voices of America Ser.). (Illus.). 128p. 1999. pap. 19.99 (*0-7385-0152-2*) Arcadia Publng.

Livingston, Mary P. A Civil War Marine at Sea: The Diary of Medal of Honor Recipient Miles M. Oviatt. LC 97-50177. 197p. 1998. 24.95 (*1-57249-076-4*) White Mane Pub.

Livingston, Michael. Common Whiplash Injury: A Modern Epidemic. LC 98-38332. (Illus.). 224p. 1999. text 47.95 (*0-398-06911-5*); pap. text 34.95 (*0-398-06912-3*) C C Thomas.

Livingston, Michael A. Taxation: A Skills Approach. 2000. text. write for info. (*0-87084-333-8*) Anderson Pub Co.

Livingston, Michael K. Mental Discipline: The Pursuit of Peak Performance. LC 88-34807. (Illus.). 280p. 1989. reprint ed. pap. 86.80 (*0-608-07067-X*, 206727300009) Bks Demand.

Livingston, Michael M. Beyond Backache: A Personal Guide to Back & Neck Pain Relief. LC 87-92101. 1988. 12.95 (*0-87212-212-3*) Libra.

Livingston, Michele. Visions from Mary. LC 99-60251. (Illus.). 190p. 1999. pap. 18.95 (*0-9665485-1-5*, 9901) Blue Mantle Pub.

Livingston, Mike, ed. User Conference Proceedings 1994, Vol. 1. (Illus.). 872p. (Orig.). (C). 1994. pap. text 25.00 (*1-879102-22-6*) ESR Inst.
— User Conference Proceedings 1994, Vol. 2. (Illus.). 808p. (Orig.). (C). 1994. pap. text 25.00 (*1-879102-23-4*) ESR Inst.
— User Conference Proceedings 1994 & 1994 User Conference Technical Handouts, 3 vols. (Illus.). 590p. (Orig.). (C). 1994. pap. text 25.00 (*1-879102-19-6*); cd-rom 30.00 (*1-879102-20-X*) ESR Inst.
— User Conference Proceedings 1994 & 1994 User Conference Technical Handouts, 3 vols., Set. (Illus.). (Orig.). (C). 1994. pap. text 75.00 (*1-879102-21-8*) ESR Inst.

Livingston, Miles. Bonds & Bond Derivatives. LC 98-22988. 288p. 1999. 64.95 (*0-631-20755-4*); pap. 32.95 (*0-631-20756-2*) Blackwell Pubs.
— Money & Capital Markets. 1996. pap. text 62.95 (*1-55786-884-0*) Blackwell Pubs.

Livingston, Milton S. Particle Accelerators: A Brief History. LC 69-18038. (Illus.). 128p. reprint ed. pap. 39.70 (*0-7837-4167-7*, 205901600012) Bks Demand.

Livingston, Myra. I Am Writing a Poem About. LC 97-4098. 64p. (YA). (gr. 5-9). 1997. 15.00 (*0-689-81156-X*) S&S Childrens.

Livingston, Myra C. B Is for Baby: An Alphabet of Verses. LC 95-44784. (Illus.). 32p. (J). (ps-3). 1996. 15.00 (*0-689-80950-6*) McElderry Bks.
— Celebrations. LC 84-19216. (Illus.). 32p. (J). (gr. k-3). 1985. pap. 6.95 (*0-8234-0654-7*); lib. bdg. 16.95 (*0-8234-0550-8*) Holiday.
— The Child As Poet: Myth or Reality? 356p. 1984. 24.95 (*0-87675-287-3*) Horn Bk.
— A Circle of Seasons. LC 81-20305. (Illus.). 32p. (J). (gr. k-3). 1982. pap. 5.95 (*0-8234-0656-3*) Holiday.
— Climb into the Bell Tower: Essays on Poetry. LC 89-36412. 256p. (J). 1990. 18.95 (*0-06-024015-6*) HarpC Child Bks.
— Cricket Never Does: A Collection of Haiku & Tanka. LC 96-30528. (Illus.). 48p. (YA). (gr. 5-9). 1997. 15.00 (*0-689-81123-3*) McElderry Bks.
— Festivals. (Illus.). 32p. (J). (gr. k-3). 1996. 16.95 (*0-8234-1217-2*) Holiday.

Livingston, Myra C. Flights of Fancy & Other Poems. LC 94-14476. 48p. (J). (gr. 3-7). 1994. pap. 13.95 (*0-689-50613-9*) McElderry Bks.
— I Like You, If You Like Me: Poems of Friendship. LC 86-21108. 160p. (YA). (gr. 4-7). 1987. 14.95 (*0-689-50408-X*) McElderry Bks.

Livingston, Myra C. I Never Told: And Other Poems. LC 91-20475. 48p. (J). (gr. 4-7). 1992. 12.95 (*0-689-50544-2*) McElderry Bks.
— If the Owl Calls Again: A Collection of Owl Poems. LC 89-27659. (Illus.). 128p. (YA). (gr. 5 up). 1990. 13.95 (*0-689-50501-9*) McElderry Bks.
— Keep on Singing: A Ballad of Marian Anderson. LC 93-46909. (Illus.). 32p. (J). (gr. k-3). 1994. lib. bdg. 15.95 (*0-8234-1098-6*) Holiday.
— Poem-Making: Ways to Begin Writing Poetry. LC 90-5012. (Charlotte Zolotow Bk.). 176p. (J). (gr. 4-8). 1991. 16.95 (*0-06-024019-9*) HarpC Child Bks.
— Remembering & Other Poems. LC 89-2654. 64p. (J). (gr. 3-7). 1989. lib. bdg. 13.95 (*0-689-50489-6*) McElderry Bks.
— A Song I Sang to You: A Selection of Poems. LC 84-4585. (Illus.). 84p. (J). (ps-3). 1984. 12.95 (*0-15-277105-0*, Harcourt Child Bks) Harcourt.
— A Time to Talk: Poems of Friendship. LC 91-42234. (Illus.). 128p. (YA). (gr. 7 up). 1992. mass mkt. 14.00 (*0-689-50558-2*) McElderry Bks.
— Up in the Air. LC 88-23293. (Illus.). 32p. (J). (gr. k-3). 1989. lib. bdg. 14.95 (*0-8234-0736-5*) Holiday.
— Valentine Poems. LC 85-31723. (Illus.). 32p. (J). (gr. k-3). 1987. lib. bdg. 15.95 (*0-8234-0587-7*) Holiday.

Livingston, Myra C., ed. Roll Along: Poems on Wheels. LC 92-32714. 80p. (J). (gr. 4 up). 1993. 11.95 (*0-689-50585-X*) McElderry Bks.

Livingston, Myra C., selected by. Call Down the Moon: Poems of Music. LC 95-8283. 144p. (YA). (gr. 5 up). 1995. 16.00 (*0-689-80416-4*) McElderry Bks.

Livingston, Myra C. & Dominguez, Joseph F., trs. Platero y Yo. LC 92-11634. (ENG & SPA., Illus.). 64p. (YA). (gr. 3-7). 1994. 14.95 (*0-395-62365-0*, Clarion Bks) HM.

Livingston, Myra C., ed. see Carroll, Lewis, pseud.

Livingston, Myra C., jt. ed. see Farber, Norma.

Livingston, Myra C., tr. see Jimenez, Juan Ramon.

Livingston, Nancy. Incident at Parga. 1993. mass mkt. 3.99 (*0-373-28001-7*, 1-28001-5) Harlequin Bks.
— Incident at Parga. mass mkt. 2.95 (*0-312-91389-3*, Pub. by Tor Bks) St Martin.
— Quiet Murder. LC 96-3735. 253p. 1995. per. 3.99 (*0-373-26186-1*, 1-26186-6, Wrldwide Lib) Harlequin Bks.

Livingston, P. Gullible the Seagull. (Illus.). (Orig.). (J). (gr. k-6). 1992. pap. 9.95 (*0-9629860-2-X*) Sound Pub WA.

Livingston, P., et al. Disorder Order: Proceedings of the Stanford International Symposium. (Stanford Literature Studies: Vol. 1). 302p. 1984. pap. 56.50 (*0-915838-01-X*) Anma Libri.

Livingston, Paisley. Literary Knowledge: Humanistic Inquiry & the Philosophy of Science. LC 87-47821. 296p. 1988. pap. 15.95 (*0-8014-9422-2*) Cornell U Pr.
— Literature & Rationality: Ideas of Agency in Theory & Fiction. 266p. (C). 1992. text 69.95 (*0-521-40540-8*) Cambridge U Pr.
— Models of Desire: Rene Girard & the Psychology of Mimesis. LC 91-39339. 232p. 1992. reprint ed. pap. 72.00 (*0-608-06724-5*, 206692100009) Bks Demand.

Livingston, Patricia H. Lessons of the Heart: Celebrating the Rhythms of Life. LC 92-72924. 128p. (Orig.). 1992. pap. 7.95 (*0-87793-486-X*) Ave Maria.

***Livingston, Patricia H.** This Blessed Mess: Finding Hope Amidst Life Chaos. LC 00-101264. 144p. 2000. pap. 11.95 (*1-893732-15-0*) SORIN BKS.

Livingston, Patricia H., jt. auth. see Mitchell, David.

Livingston, Phil. Team Penning. (Illus.). 144p. 1991. 12.95 (*0-911647-24-4*) Western Horseman.

Livingston, Philip A., ed. see West, Franklin H., et al.

Livingston, Ray F. The Traditional Theory of Literature. LC 62-10830. 198p. reprint ed. pap. 61.40 (*0-608-14723-0*, 205588900039) Bks Demand.

***Livingston, Richard & Livingston, Linda.** Smart & Caring: A Donor's Guide to Major Gifting. (Illus.). 216p. 1999. pap. 24.95 (*0-9674130-0-1*) R D L Pubg.

Livingston, Rik. Mr. Verlin's Zono Comix. LC 87-50993. (Showcase Comic Ser.: No. 2). (Illus.). 128p. (Orig.). 1988. pap. 7.95 (*0-917976-76-2*) Thunder Baas Pr.

Livingston, Robert. Resource Atlas of the Apalachicola Estuary: SGR-55. 64p. 1983. write for info. (*0-318-60283-0*) U Fla Law.

Livingston, Robert A. Artist/Artist's Rep Directory. (Livingston's Complete Music Business Directory Ser.). 209p. 1996. pap. 59.95 (*0-932303-20-X*) GLGLC Music.
— Label/A&R/Record Producer Directory. (Livingston's Complete Music Business Directory Ser.). 290p. 1996. pap. 44.95 (*0-932303-22-6*) GLGLC Music.
— Livingston's Complete Music Business Reference, Vol. I. 260p. 1996. pap. 69.95 (*0-932303-14-5*) GLGLC Music.
— Livingston's Complete Music Business Reference, Vol. II. 255p. 1996. pap. 69.95 (*0-932303-16-1*) GLGLC Music.
— Music Business Inside Out. 1997. 97.15 (*0-932303-30-7*) GLGLC Music.
— The Music Publisher Directory. (Livingston's Complete Music Business Directory Ser.). 94p. 1995. pap. 29.95 (*0-932303-21-8*) GLGLC Music.
— Promo/Distribution/Services Directory. (Livingston's Complete Music Business Directory Ser.). 114p. 1995. pap. 29.95 (*0-932303-23-4*) GLGLC Music.
— The Recording Contract. 1988. pap. 20.00 (*0-932303-07-2*) GLGLC Music.
— The Recording Studio/Production Directory. 1996. pap. 34.95 (*0-932303-25-0*) GLGLC Music.
— The Songwriter-Publisher Contract. 1985. pap. 20.00 (*0-932303-04-8*) GLGLC Music.

Livingston, Robert B., ed. Lung Cancer. (Cancer Treatment & Research Ser.: No. 1). (Illus.). 320p. 1981. text 175.50 (*90-247-2394-9*) Kluwer Academic.

Livingston, Robert G., ed. see Radunski, Peter, et al.

Livingston, Robert J. Marine Eutrophication. (Marine Science Ser.). 2000. 89.95 (*0-8493-9062-1*) CRC Pr.

Livingston, Robert R. Essay on Sheep: Their Varieties - Account of the Merinoes of Spain, France, Etc. 186p. (Orig.). 1994. reprint ed. pap. 12.00 (*0-9633659-1-6*) US Hist Res Srv.

Livingston, Shaffiran, jt. auth. see Livingston, Ivor L.

***Livingston, Stoney.** AMG'S Key Word Bible Studies on Prophecy. 1999. pap. text 14.99 (*0-89957-331-2*) AMG Pubs.
— AMG'S Key Word Bible Studies on Salvation. 1999. pap. text 14.99 (*0-89957-330-4*) AMG Pubs.

Livingston, Sue. Rethinking the Education of Deaf Students: Theory & Practice from a Teacher's Perspective. LC 97-3501. 180p. 1997. pap. text 22.50 (*0-435-07236-6*, 07236) Heinemann.

Livingston, Theresa, ed. see Livingston, Gary.

Livingston, Valerie A. W. Elmer Schofield: Proud Painter of Modest Lands. (Illus.). 64p. (Orig.). (C). 1988. pap. 15.00 (*0-9621345-0-3*) Moravian Coll.

Livingston-Wheeler, Virginia & Addeo, Edmond G. The Conquest of Cancer: Vaccines & Diet. 1993. pap. 9.95 (*0-9627145-1-8*, Cyrus Pr) Waterside Prodns.

Livingston, William. Letter to the Right Reverend Father in God, John, Lord Bishop of Landatt. (Notable American Authors Ser.). 1999. reprint ed. lib. bdg. 125.00 (*0-7812-3798-X*) Rprt Serv.
— Philosophic Solitude. (Notable American Authors Ser.). 1999. reprint ed. lib. bdg. 125.00 (*0-7812-3797-1*) Rprt Serv.
— A Solioquy. (Notable American Authors Ser.). 1999. reprint ed. lib. bdg. 125.00 (*0-7812-3799-8*) Rprt Serv.

Livingston, William, ed. Selected Papers on Instrumentation in Astronomy. LC 93-23374. (Milestone Ser.: Vol. MS 87). 1993. pap. 35.00 (*0-8194-1395-X*) SPIE.
— Selected Papers on Instrumentation in Astronomy. LC 93-23374. (Milestone Ser.: Vol. MS 87/HC). 1993. 45.00 (*0-8194-1396-8*) SPIE.

Livingston, William, et al. Independent Reflector or, Weekly Essays on Sundry Important Subjects More Particularly Adapted to the Province of New York. Klein, Milton M., ed. LC 62-13268. (John Harvard Library). 469p. 1963. 37.00 (*0-674-44850-2*) HUP.

Livingston, William K. Pain & Suffering. LC 98-40341. (Illus.). 268p. 1998. 48.00 (*0-931092-24-8*) Intl Assn Study Pain.

Livingston, William S. Federalism & Constitutional Change. LC 74-9226. 380p. 1974. reprint ed. lib. bdg. 75.00 (*0-8371-7623-9*, LIFC, Greenwood Pr) Greenwood.

— The Legacy of the Constitution: An Assessment for the Third Century. (Symposia Ser.). 164p. 1987. pap. 12.00 (*0-89940-421-9*) LBJ Sch Pub Aff.

Livingston, William S., ed. A Prospect of Liberal Democracy. LC 79-63171. 239p. reprint ed. pap. 74.10 (*0-7837-1015-1*, 204132600020) Bks Demand.

Livingston, William S. & Louis, W. Roger, eds. Australia, New Zealand, & the Pacific Islands since the First World War. 261p. 1979. text 20.00 (*0-292-70344-9*) U of Tex Pr.

Livingston, William S., et al. The Presidency & the Congress: A Shifting Balance of Power? 450p. 1979. pap. 7.00 (*0-89940-407-3*) LBJ Sch Pub Aff.

Livingstone & Louis. Australia & New Zealand Since the First World War. (Australian National University Press Ser.). 1996. text. write for info. (*0-08-033005-3*, Pergamon Pr) Elsevier.

Livingstone, Alasdair. Mystical & Mythological Explanatory Works of Assyrian & Babylonian Scholars. 280p. 1986. 85.00 (*0-19-815462-3*) OUP.

Livingstone, Alasdair, et al, eds. Muster Roll of Prince Charles Edward Stuart's Army, 1745-1746. 228p. 1984. 29.50 (*0-08-030385-4*, Pergamon Pr) Elsevier.

Livingstone, Angela, ed. Salome: Her Life & Work. (Illus.). 256p. 1987. pap. 9.95 (*0-918825-61-X*) Moyer Bell.

Livingstone, Angela, ed. see Schweitzer, Viktoria.

Livingstone, Angela, tr. see Platonov, Andrei.

Livingstone, Carol. Role Play in Language Learning. Byrne, Donn, ed. (Handbooks for Language Teachers Ser.). (Illus.). 94p. (Orig.). 1983. pap. 13.50 (*0-582-74611-6*) Longman.

Livingstone, Churchill. Dictionary of Nursing. 17th ed. 1996. pap. text 7.95 (*0-443-05534-3*) Church.

— The Medical Directory, 1994. (Illus.). 4672p. 1994. text 295.00 (*0-582-23418-2*) Church.

Livingstone Corp. Staff, jt. auth. see Barbour Publishing, Inc. Editors.

***Livingstone Corporation Staff, compiled by.** The One Year Book of Bible Prayers. 2000. 14.99 (*0-8423-3646-X*) Tyndale Hse.

— The One Year Book of Bible Promises. 2000. 14.99 (*0-8423-3553-6*) Tyndale Hse.

Livingstone, D. R., jt. auth. see Walker, C. H.

Livingstone, David. Darwin's Forgotten Defenders. (Illus.). 210p. 1984. pap. 17.50 (*1-57383-093-3*) Regent College.

— Data Analysis for Chemists: Applications to QSAR & Chemical Product Design. (Illus.). 256p. 1996. text 70.00 (*0-19-855728-0*) OUP.

— Family Letters: 1841-1856, 2 vols., Set. LC 75-17198. (Illus.). 1975. reprint ed. lib. bdg. 65.00 (*0-8371-8290-5*, LIFL) Greenwood.

— Family Letters: 1841-1856, 2 vols., Vol. 1. LC 75-17198. (Illus.). 1975. reprint ed. lib. bdg. 45.00 (*0-8371-8355-3*, LIFM) Greenwood.

— Family Letters: 1841-1856, 2 vols., Vol. 2. LC 75-17198. (Illus.). 1975. reprint ed. lib. bdg. 45.00 (*0-8371-8356-1*, LIFN) Greenwood.

— Livingstone's Africa. LC 70-138340. (Black Heritage Library Collection). 1977. 52.95 (*0-8369-8732-2*) Ayer.

— Missionary Travels & Researches in South Africa. LC 72-5439. (Select Bibliographies Reprint Ser.). 1977. reprint ed. 68.95 (*0-8369-6918-9*) Ayer.

Livingstone, David N. Darwin's Forgotten Defenders: The Encounter Between Evangelical Theology & Evolutionary Thought. LC 87-13469. 220p. (Orig.). reprint ed. pap. 68.20 (*0-7837-3186-8*, 204279000006) Bks Demand.

— The Geographical Tradition: Episodes in the History of a Contested Enterprise. LC 92-15681. 1992. pap. 28.95 (*0-631-18586-0*) Blackwell Pubs.

— Geography & Enlightenment. LC 98-52359. 336p. 2000. lib. bdg. 52.00 (*0-226-48720-2*) U Ch Pr.

— Nathaniel Southgate Shaler & the Culture of American Science. LC 85-28982. (History of American Science & Technology Ser.). 416p. 1987. text 39.95 (*0-8173-0305-7*) U of Ala Pr.

— The Preadamite Theory & the Marriage of Science & Religion. LC 92-76986. (Transactions Ser.: Vol. 82, Pt. 3). 89p. (C). 1992. pap. 16.00 (*0-87169-823-4*, T821-LID) Am Philos.

Livingstone, David N., et al, eds. Evangelicals & Science in Historical Perspective. (Religion in America Ser.). (Illus.). 360p. 1999. text 45.00 (*0-19-511557-0*) OUP.

***Livingstone, David N. & Wells, Ronald.** Ulster-American Religion: Episodes in the History of a Cultural Connection. LC 99-22331. (The Irish in America Ser.). 216p. 2000. reprint ed. pap. 15.00 (*0-268-04304-3*) U of Notre Dame Pr.

Livingstone, David N. & Wells, Ronald A. Ulster-American Religion: Episodes in the History of a Cultural Connection. LC 99-22331. (Irish in America Ser.). 208p. 1999. 30.00 (*0-268-04303-5*, Pub. by U of Notre Dame Pr) Chicago Distribution Ctr.

Livingstone, David N. & Withers, Charles W. Geography & Enlightenment. LC 98-52359. 336p. 1999. pap. text 25.00 (*0-226-48721-0*) U Ch Pr.

Livingstone, David N., jt. ed. see Noll, Mark A.

Livingstone, David W. Class Ideologies & Educational Futures. LC 83-8514. 250p. 1983. 36.00 (*0-905273-40-0*, Falmer Pr); pap. 20.00 (*0-905273-39-7*, Falmer Pr) Taylor & Francis.

— Critical Pedagogy & Cultural Power. LC 86-17176. (Critical Studies in Education). 358p. 1986. 65.00 (*0-89789-112-0*, Bergin & Garvey); pap. 24.95 (*0-89789-116-3*, Bergin & Garvey) Greenwood.

Livingstone, Dewey. Saving the Marin-Sonoma Coast: The Battles for Audubon Canyon Ranch, Point Reyes, & California's Russian River. 275p. 1998. 45.00 (*0-9661680-2-X*); pap. 29.95 (*0-9661680-1-1*) Sweetwater Sprngs.

Livingstone, Dinah, tr. see Beyerlin, Walter.

Livingstone, Dinah, tr. see Bloom, Anthony & LeFebvre, George.

Livingstone, Dinah, tr. see Camara, Helder.

Livingstone, Dinah, tr. see Cardenal, Ernesto.

***Livingstone, E. A.** The Concise Oxford Dictionary of the Christian Church. 2nd ed. (Oxford Paperback Reference Ser.). 620p. 2000. pap. 15.95 (*0-19-280057-4*) OUP.

Livingstone, E. A., ed. Studia Biblica 1978. III: Papers on Paul & Other New Testament Authors. (JSNT Supplement Ser.: Vol. 3). 468p. 1980. 99.00 (*0-905774-27-2*, Pub. by Sheffield Acad) CUP Services.

Livingstone, E. A., ed. Studia Biblica 1978 II - Papers on the Gospels. (JSNT Supplement Ser.: No. 2). 350p. 1980. 85.00 (*0-905774-22-1*, Pub. by Sheffield Acad) CUP Services.

Livingstone, E. A., jt. ed. see Cross, F. L.

Livingstone Editorial Group, et al. Mysteries & Intrigues of the Bible. LC 97-17546. 250p. 1997. pap. 12.99 (*0-8423-4674-0*) Tyndale Hse.

Livingstone, Elizabeth A., ed. Studia Patristica XVII. 3 vols., Set. 1520p. 1982. 642.00 (*0-08-025779-8*, Pub. by Pergamon Repr) Franklin.

Livingstone, Frank B. Data on the Abnormal Hemoglobins & Glucose-Six-Phosphate Dehydrogenase Deficiency in Human Populations. (Technical Reports Ser.: No. 3). 1973. pap. 2.00 (*0-932206-12-3*) U Mich Mus Anthro.

Livingstone, Greg. Planting Churches in Muslim Cities: A Team Approach. LC 93-6623. 272p. (C). 1993. pap. 17.99 (*0-8010-5682-9*) Baker Bks.

Livingstone, Harrison E. Baltimore. LC 98-19331. (Illus.). 480p. 1998. 27.00 (*0-941401-09-X*) Conservatory.

— Harvard, John. 1987. 10.00 (*0-941401-00-6*) Conservatory.

— Killing the Truth: Deceit & Deception in the JFK Case. (Illus.). 752p. 1994. pap. 15.95 (*0-7867-0154-4*) Carroll & Graf.

Livingstone, Harrison E., jt. auth. see Groden, Robert J.

Livingstone, Harrison E., ed. see Moore, Gilbert.

Livingstone, Harrison Edward. High Treason 2: The Great Cover-Up: The Assassination of President John F. Kennedy. (Illus.). 656p. 1993. pap. 16.95 (*0-7867-0017-3*) Carroll & Graf.

Livingstone, Harrison Edward & Groden, Robert J. High Treason: The Assassination of JFK & the Case for Conspiracy. rev. ed. (Illus.). 672p. 1998. pap. 17.95 (*0-7867-0578-7*) Carroll & Graf.

Livingstone, Ian. Aeolian Geomorphology: An Introduction. (C). 1996. pap. 52.00 (*0-582-08704-X*) Addison-Wesley.

— Darkmoon's Curse. 1995. pap. 3.99 (*0-14-036939-2*) Viking Penguin.

Livingstone, J. M. The British Economy in Theory & Practice. LC 75-300866. 230p. 1974. write for info. (*0-333-17848-3*) Macmillan.

Livingstone, J. M., jt. auth. see Branton, N.

Livingstone, James. The Contenders: The Growth of the Pacific Rim Powers. LC 98-163039. (Illus.). 320p. 1998. 90.00 (*0-304-70112-2*); pap. 33.95 (*0-304-70113-0*) Continuum.

Livingstone, John, ed. see Bryan-Day, Lisa & Day, Ashley M.

Livingstone, John L. The Portable MBA in Finance & Accounting. 2nd ed. LC 97-14095. 640p. 1997. 34.95 (*0-471-18425-X*) Wiley.

Livingstone, Ken. Livingstone's Labour: A Programme for the Nineties. 299p. 1990. text 24.95 (*0-04-440346-1*) Routledge.

Livingstone, Kimball, ed. see Valdury, J. P.

Livingstone, Marco. Buckley, Stephen Many Angles. 84p. 1985. pap. 28.00 (*0-905836-49-9*, Pub. by Museum Modern Art) St Mut.

— David Hockney. rev. ed. LC 95-61697. (World of Art Ser.). (Illus.). 280p. 1996. pap. 14.95 (*0-500-20291-5*, Pub. by Thames Hudson) Norton.

— David Hockney Faces. LC 86-83167. (Illus.). 96p. 1987. pap. 19.95 (*0-500-27464-9*, Pub. by Thames Hudson) Norton.

— Essential Duane Michals. (Illus.). 224p. 1997. 50.00 (*0-8212-2463-8*, Pub. by Bulfinch Pr) Little.

— Hockney Etchings & Lithographs. (Illus.). 1989. pap. 24.95 (*0-500-27546-7*, Pub. by Thames Hudson) Norton.

— Jim Dine: Botanical Drawings. LC 93-25858. (Illus.). 144p. 1994. 49.50 (*0-8109-3214-8*, Pub. by Abrams) Time Warner.

— Jim Dine: The Alchemy of Images. LC 98-7172. 352p. 1997. 85.00 (*1-885254-79-2*, Pub. by Monacelli Pr) Penguin Putnam.

***Livingstone, Marco.** Kitaj. 3rd ed. 224p. 1999. pap. 39.95 (*0-7148-3891-8*) Phaidon Pr.

— Pop Art: A Continuing History. 2nd ed. LC 00-100788. (Illus.). 272p. 2000. reprint ed. pap. 29.95 (*0-500-28240-4*, Pub. by Thames Hudson) Norton.

Livingstone, Marco. Tress, Arthur: Talisman. (Illus.). 156p. (C). 1986. pap. 48.00 (*0-905836-55-3*, Pub. by Museum Modern Art) St Mut.

Livingstone, Marco, contrib. by. Allen Jones: Prints. (Illus.). 144p. 1995. 45.00 (*3-7913-1481-5*, Pub. by Prestel) te Neues.

Livingstone, Marco, text. Farthing, Stephen: Mute Accomplices. (Illus.). 70p. 1987. pap. 32.00 (*0-905836-58-8*, Pub. by Museum Modern Art) St Mut.

Livingstone, Marco & Hanson, Duane. Duane Hanson. (Illus.). 74p. 1997. pap. 25.00 (*0-9527453-4-8*) Dist Art Pubs.

Livingstone, Marco, jt. auth. see Compton, Michael.

Livingstone, Neil C. & Halevy, David. Inside the PLO: Covert Units, Secret Funds, & the War Against Israel & the U. S. (Illus.). 336p. 1998. text 25.00 (*0-7881-5552-0*) DIANE Pub.

Livingstone, Neil C., et al. Cbw: The Poor Man's Atomic Bomb. LC 84-47502. (National Security Papers: No. 1). 36p. 1984. pap. 7.50 (*0-89549-057-9*) Inst Foreign Policy Anal.

Livingstone, Niall, jt. ed. see Too, Yun L.

Livingstone, R. Six-Membered Monoheterocyclic Compounds with a Hetero-Atom from Groups IV, VI, or VII of the Periodic Table, Vol. 4. 2nd ed. 682p. 453.25 (*0-444-82753-6*) Elsevier.

Livingstone, Richard W. Greek Ideals & Modern Life. LC 72-82814. 1969. reprint ed. pap. 21.00 (*0-8196-0245-0*) Biblo.

— History of the Peloponnesian War. (Illus.). 402p. 1960. pap. text 23.95 (*0-19-500218-0*) OUP.

Livingstone, Robin. Road: Memories of the Falls. LC 98-231198. 1999. pap. text 22.95 (*0-85640-632-5*) Blackstaff Pr.

Livingstone, Rodney, ed. & tr. see Marx, Karl & Engels, Friedrich.

Livingstone, Rodney, tr. see Adorno, Theodor W.

Livingstone, Rodney, tr. see Lukacs, Georg.

Livingstone, Rodney, tr. see Marx, Karl.

Livingstone, Sandy & SL Discovery Consulting Services Staff. Dealing with Anger. 2nd rev. ed. Johnson, Judith, ed. (Illus.). 168p. 1997. pap. 14.95 (*0-9681793-1-2*) SL Discovery Consult.

***Livingstone, Sheila.** Litany of Evil: Crime & Punishment in Scotland. (Orig.). 1999. pap. 19.95 (*1-84158-002-3*) Birlinn Ltd.

Livingstone, Sheila. Scottish Customs. LC 98-130838. (Traditional Scotland Ser.). 160p. pap. 13.95 (*1-874744-41-6*, Pub. by Birlinn Ltd) Dufour.

— Scottish Festivals. LC 98-187893. 218p. 1998. pap. 13.95 (*1-874744-78-5*, Pub. by Birlinn Ltd) Dufour.

Livingstone, Sonia M. Making Sense of Television: The Psychology of Audience Interpretation. (International Series in Experimental Social Psychology). (Illus.). 226p. 1990. 54.00 (*0-08-036760-7*, 2605; 2704, Prgamon Press) Buttrwrth-Heinemann.

— Making Sense of Television: The Psychology of Audience Interpretation. 226p. 1996. pap. 31.95 (*0-7506-2744-1*) Buttrwrth-Heinemann.

— Making Sense of Television: The Psychology of Audience Interpretation. 2nd ed. LC 97-51630. (International Series in Social Psychology). 224p. (C). 1998. pap. 25.99 (*0-415-18536-X*) Routledge.

— Making Sense of Television: The Psychology of Audience Interpretation. 2nd ed. LC 97-51630. (International Series in Social Psychology). (Illus.). 224p. (C). 1998. 85.00 (*0-415-18623-4*) Routledge.

Livingstone, Sonia M. & Lunt, Peter. Talk on Television: Audience Participation & Public Debate. LC 93-15440. (Communication & Society Ser.). 208p. (C). 1993. pap. 22.99 (*0-415-07738-9*) Routledge.

Livingstone, Stephen & Morison, John. Law, Society, & Change. 206p. 1990. text 78.95 (*1-85521-105-X*, Pub. by Dartmth Pub) Ashgate Pub Co.

Livingstone, Stephen & Owen, Tim. Prison Law. 2nd ed. 788p. 1999. text 120.00 (*0-19-876512-6*) OUP.

Livingstone, Stephen, jt. ed. see Harris, David J.

Livingstone, W. P. The Loneliest Woman in Africa: Christina Forsyth of Fingoland. Orig. Title: Christina Forsyth of Fingoland. 160p. 1994. pap. 10.99 (*0-88019-318-2*) Schmul Pub Co.

— Mary Slessor of Calabar. LC 83-9286. 352p. 1984. 7.95 (*0-310-27451-6*, 9286P) Zondervan.

Livinstone, Dinah, tr. see Aquino, Maria P.

***Livio, Mario.** The Accelerating Universe: Infinite Expansion, the Cosmological Constant, & the Beauty of the Cosmos. LC 99-22278. (Illus.). 288p. 2000. 27.95 (*0-471-32969-X*) Wiley.

Livio, Mario. Beautiful Number. text. write for info. (*0-471-36307-3*) Wiley.

***Livio, Mario, ed.** Unsolved Problems in Stellar Evolution. LC 99-88290. (Space Telescope Science Institute Symposium Ser.: No. 12). (Illus.). 350p. (C). 2000. text 69.95 (*0-521-78091-8*) Cambridge U Pr.

Livio, Mario, et al, eds. The Extragalactic Distance Scale. (Space Telescope Science Institute Symposium Ser.: Vol. 10). (Illus.). 337p. (C). 1997. text 69.95 (*0-521-59164-3*) Cambridge U Pr.

— The Hubble Deep Field. LC 98-34542. (Space Telescope Science Institute Symposium Ser.: No. 11). (Illus.). 300p. (C). 1998. 69.95 (*0-521-63097-5*) Cambridge U Pr.

***Livio, Mario, et al, eds.** Supernovae & Gamma-ray Bursts. (Space Telescope Science Institute Symposium Ser.). (Illus.). 300p. 2000. write for info. (*0-521-79141-3*) Cambridge U Pr.

Livio, Mario & Shaviv, Giori, eds. Cataclysmic Variables & Related Objects. 1983. text 155.50 (*90-277-1570-X*) Kluwer Academic.

Livio, Mario, et al. Interacting Binaries. Nujssbaumer, H. & Orr, A., eds. LC 93-29279. (Saas-Fee Advanced Course Twenty-Two Lecture Notes Ser.: Vol. 1992). 1994. 59.00 (*0-387-57014-4*) Spr-Verlag.

Livio, Mario, jt. ed. see Williams, Robert E.

Livnat, Joshua, jt. auth. see Hackel, Kenneth S.

***Livnat, Limor.** Limor Livnat: The Leading Lady in Israeli Politics Speaks Her Mind. LC 99-35018. 135p. 1999. 16.95 (*965-229-222-2*) Gefen Pub Hse.

Livneh, Hanoch & Antonak, Richard F. Psychosocial Adaptation to Chronic Illness & Disability. LC 97-14138. 576p. 1997. 49.00 (*0-8342-0967-5*) Aspen Pub.

Livneh, Hanoch, jt. auth. see Antonak, Richard F.

***Livni, Michael.** Reform Zionism: Twenty Years: An Educator's Perspective. LC 99-31958. 320p. 1999. 24.95 (*965-229-206-0*) Gefen Bks.

Livo, George O., jt. auth. see Livo, Norma J.

Livo, Norma, jt. auth. see Cha, Dia.

***Livo, Norma J.** Celebrating the Earth: Stories, Experiences & Activities. LC 99-59963. 2000. pap. 24.50 (*1-56308-776-6*) Libs Unl.

Livo, Norma J. Who's Afraid . . . ? Facing Children's Fears with Folktales. (Learning Through Folklore Ser.). (Illus.). xxxii, 176p. 1994. pap. text 18.50 (*0-87287-950-X*) Teacher Ideas Pr.

Livo, Norma J., ed. Moon Cakes to Maize: Delicious World Folk Tales. LC 98-33373. 181p. (J). (gr. 3-8). 1999. pap. 16.95 (*1-55591-973-1*) Fulcrum Pub.

Livo, Norma J., ed. Troubadour's Storybag: Musical Folktales of the World. LC 96-10188. 160p. 1996. 15.95 (*1-55591-953-7*) Fulcrum Pub.

Livo, Norma J. & Cha, Dia. Folk Stories of the Hmong: Peoples of Laos, Thailand, & Vietnam. (World Folklore Ser.). xii, 135p. 1991. lib. bdg. 22.00 (*0-87287-854-6*) Libs Unl.

Livo, Norma J. & Livo, George O. The Enchanted Wood & Other Tales from Finland. LC 98-23358. (Illus.). 150p. 1999. pap. 27.50 (*1-56308-578-X*) Libs Unl.

Livo, Norma J. & Rietz, Sandra A. Storytelling Activities. LC 86-33727. xiv, 140p. 1987. pap. text 17.50 (*0-87287-566-0*) Libs Unl.

— Storytelling Folklore Sourcebook. xiv, 384p. 1991. pap. text 34.00 (*0-87287-601-2*) Libs Unl.

Livo, Norma J., ed. see Miller, Teresa & Pellowski, Anne.

Livolsi, Virginia A. Pathology of the Thyroid. 2nd ed. 1999. text. write for info. (*0-7216-6324-9*) Harcourt.

— Pathology of the Thyroid MPP. (Illus.). 448p. 1990. text 92.00 (*0-7216-5782-6*, W B Saunders Co) Harcrt Hlth Sci Grp.

LiVolsi, Virginia A., et al, eds. Pathology. 3rd ed. LC 93-16371. (National Medical Series for Independent Study). (Illus.). 530p. 1994. pap. 26.00 (*0-683-06243-3*) Lppncott W & W.

LiVolsi, Virginia A. & DeLellis, Ronald A., eds. Pathology of the Parathyroid & Thyroid Glands. LC 92-48313. (Monographs in Pathology: No. 35). (Illus.). 203p. 1993. 90.00 (*0-683-04817-1*) Lppncott W & W.

Livolsi, Virginia A. & Logerfo, Paul. Thyroiditis. 224p. 1981. 126.00 (*0-8493-5705-5*, RC657, CRC Reprint) Franklin.

Livonen, Jyrki. The Changing Soviet Union in the New Europe. (Studies of Communism in Transition). 256p. 1991. text 80.00 (*1-85278-532-2*) E Elgar.

Livoni, Cathy. Element of Time. LC 82-48761. 192p. (J). (gr. 7 up). 1983. 12.95 (*0-15-225369-6*, Harcourt Child Bks) Harcourt.

Livoni, Phil. Russell's Standard Fashions, 1915-1918. LC 96-10939. (Illus.). 160p. 1996. reprint ed. pap. 11.95 (*0-486-29122-7*) Dover.

Livoti, Sandy & Kiesa, Jon. Adventures in Stone Artifacts: A Young Beginners Guide to Arrowheads & Other Artifacts. (Illus.). 300p. (Orig.). 1997. pap. 15.95 (*1-885061-15-3*) Adventure Pubns.

Livov, M. R. Dictionary of Antonyms of the Russian Language. (ENG & RUS.). 381p. 1984. 19.95 (*0-8288-2005-8*, M15178) Fr & Eur.

Livraga, Giorgio. Thebes. Scott, Julian, tr. from SPA. 163p. (Orig.). 1986. pap. 12.95 (*975-7502-00-6*) New Leaf Dist.

Livre De Poche Staff. L' Opera, Dictionnaire Chronologique de 1597 a Nos Jours. (FRE.). 1986. pap. 16.95 (*0-7859-7852-6*, 2253038687) Fr & Eur.

Livrea, M. A. Retinoids: Progress in Research & Clinical Applications. Packer, Lester, ed. (Basic & Clinical Dermatology Ser.: Vol. 5). (Illus.). 672p. 1993. text 250.00 (*0-8247-8758-7*) Dekker.

Livrea, M. A. & Vidali, G., eds. Retinoids: From Basic Science to Clinical Applications. LC 94-16145. (Molecular & Cell Biology Updates Ser.). 1994. write for info. (*0-8176-2812-6*) Birkhauser.

***Livrea, Maria A., ed.** Vitamin A & Retinoids: An Update of Biological Aspects & Clinical Applications. LC 99-36144. (Molecular & Cell Biology Updates Ser.). (Illus.). 350p. 1999. 175.00 (*3-7643-5882-3*, Pub. by Birkhauser) Spr-Verlag.

Livrea, P. & Thompson, E. CSF Analysis in Multiple Sclerosis. LC 96-26146. 160p. 1996. 89.50 (*3-540-75018-5*) Spr-Verlag.

Livsey, Karen E. Western New York Land Transactions, 1825-1835: Extracted from the Archives of the Holland Land Company. LC 96-77329. 812p. 1996. text 60.00 (*0-8063-1522-9*) Genealog Pub.

— Western New York Land Transactions, 1804-1824: Extracted from the Archives of the Holland Land Company. 472p. 1991. 35.00 (*0-8063-1294-7*, 3422) Genealog Pub.

Livsey, Larry. The Steve Young Story. LC 95-31504. 1995. 22.95 (*0-7615-0194-0*) Prima Pub.

Livsey, Laury. The Steve Young Story. (Illus.). 272p. 1996. pap. 13.00 (*0-7615-0756-6*) Prima Pub.

Livshits, Benedikt. The One & a Half-Eyed Archer. Bowlt, John E., ed. (Illus.). 1977. 35.00 (*0-89250-102-2*) Orient Res Partners.

Livshitz, August. Surgery of the Spinal Cord. Tatarchenko, V. E., tr. from RUS. LC 90-4997. 440p. 1991. 72.50 (*0-8236-6257-8*) Intl Univs Pr.

— Test Your Chess I. Q., Bk. 2. 2nd ed. Neat, Kenneth P., tr. (Russian Chess Ser.). (Illus.). 125p. 1988. 33.90 (*0-08-032072-4*, Pergamon Pr) Elsevier.

— Test Your Chess I. Q. First Challenge. 1997. pap. text 19.95 (*1-85744-139-7*) S&S Trade.

— Test Your Chess I. Q. Grandmaster Challenge, Bk. 3. 3rd ed. 1993. pap. 19.95 (*1-85744-002-1*, Maxwell Macmillan) Macmillan.

An Asterisk (*) at the beginning of an entry indicates that the title is appearing for the first time.

— Test Your Chess I. Q. Master Challenge. 1997. text 19.95 (*1-85744-144-3*) S&S Trade.

Livshitz, August & Neat, Kenneth P., eds. Test Your Chess I. Q., 2 bks. Incl. Bk. 1. LC 80-41072. 128p. 1981. 20.00 (*0-08-023120-9*); Bk. 1. LC 80-41072. 128p. 1981. pap. 11.50 (*0-08-024118-2*); Bk. 2. LC 80-41072. 233p. 1981. 26.00 (*0-08-026881-1*); Bk. 2. LC 80-41072. 233p. 1981. pap. 17.25 (*0-08-026880-3*); LC 80-41072. (Russian Chess Ser.). (Illus.). 1981. pap. write for info. (*0-318-55234-5*) Elsevier.

Livsic, M. S. Theory of Commuting Nonselfadjoint Operators. (Mathematics & Its Applications Ser.). 332p. (C). 1995. text 174.00 (*0-7923-3588-0*) Kluwer Academic.

Livsic, M. S., tr. Operators, Oscillations, Waves. LC 72-11580. (Translations of Mathematical Monographs: Vol. 34). 274p. (Orig.). 1973. 66.00 (*0-8218-1584-9*, MMONO/34) Am Math.

Livsic, M. S. & Waksman, L. L. Commuting Nonselfadjoint Operations in Hilbert Space. (Lecture Notes in Mathematics Ser.: Vol. 1272). iii, 115p. 1987. 30.95 (*0-387-18316-7*) Spr-Verlag.

Livvermore, Harold V., tr. see De La Vega, Garcilaso.

Livy. Ab Urbe Condiata: Latin Text with Apparatus Criticus, Vol. VI. Walsh, P. G., ed. (Oxford Classical Texts Ser.). (Illus.). 424p. 1999. text 45.00 (*0-19-814664-7*) OUP.

***Livy.** A Commentary on Livy Books VI-X: An Introduction, Bks. 6-10, Vol. 1. Oakley, Stephen, ed. (Illus.). 822p. 1999. pap. text 52.00 (*0-19-815277-9*) OUP.

— The Dawn of the Roman Empire, Bks. 31-40. Heckel, Waldemar, ed. Yardley, J. C., tr. (Oxford World's Classics). (Illus.). 528p. 2000. pap. 12.95 (*0-19-283293-X*) OUP.

Livy. Early History of Rome. De Selincourt, Aubrey, tr. (Classics Ser.). (Orig.). 1960. pap. 11.95 (*0-14-044104-2*, Penguin Classics) Viking Penguin.

— Livy, Bk. XXXVI. Walsh, P. G., ed. (Classical Texts Ser.). 144p. (C). 1991. 59.99 (*0-85668-523-2*, Pub. by Aris & Phillips) David Brown.

— Livy: Book XL, Bk. XL. Walsh, P. G., ed. & tr. by. from LAT. (Classical Texts Ser.). 196p. 1996. 59.99 (*0-85668-672-7*, Pub. by Aris & Phillips); pap. 28.00 (*0-85668-673-5*, Pub. by Aris & Phillips) David Brown.

— Livy: Book XXXVI. Walsh, P. G., ed. (Classical Texts Ser.). 144p. (C). 1991. pap. 22.00 (*0-85668-524-0*, Pub. by Aris & Phillips) David Brown.

— The Rise of Rome: Books I-V. Luce, T. James, Jr., ed. & tr. by. LC 98-11367. (World's Classics Ser.). (Illus.). 406p. 1999. pap. 10.95 (*0-19-282296-9*) OUP.

— Rome & Italy. Radice, Betty, tr. & anno. by. 400p. (Orig.). 1982. pap. 12.95 (*0-14-044388-6*, Penguin Classics) Viking Penguin.

— Rome & the Mediterranean. Bettenson, Henry, tr. (Classics Ser.). 704p. 1976. pap. 13.95 (*0-14-044318-5*, Penguin Classics) Viking Penguin.

— Stories of Rome. Nichols, Roger, tr. LC 81-10227. (Translations from Greek & Roman Authors Ser.). (Illus.). 112p. 1982. pap. text 14.95 (*0-521-22816-6*) Cambridge U Pr.

— War with Hannibal. De Selincourt, Aubrey, tr. (Classics Ser.). (Orig.). 1965. pap. 14.95 (*0-14-044145-X*, Penguin Classics) Viking Penguin.

Livy, Bryan. Management & People in Banking. 2nd ed. 1985. 75.00 (*0-85297-143-5*, Pub. by Chartered Bank) St Mut.

LIW. Electron & Laser Beam Welding. 1986. 28.43 (*0-08-034339-2*, Pergamon Pr) Elsevier.

Liwschitz-Garik, Michael & Gentilini, Celso. Winding Alternating Current Machines: A Book for Winders, Repairmen, & Designers of Electric Machines. 772p. 1950. 93.00 (*0-911740-03-1*) Datarule.

Liwschitz, Y., jt. ed. see Reinhold, L.

Lixfeld, Hannjost, jt. ed. see Dow, James R.

Lixi, Christian. Dictionnaire de Mathematiques. (FRE.). 239p. 1988. 42.95 (*0-7859-7726-0*, 2091889512) Fr & Eur.

Lixing Zhou, jt. ed. see Xuchang Xu.

Lixl-Purcell, Andreas. Ruckblick: Texte und Bilder Nach, 1945. (GER.). 305p. (C). 1994. pap. text 33.96 (*0-395-69904-5*) HM.

— Stimmen Eines Jahrhunderts. LC 89-77885. (Illus.). 304p. (C). 1991. pap. text 37.50 (*0-03-049182-7*) Harcourt Coll Pubs.

Lixl-Purcell, Andreas, ed. Women of Exile: German-Jewish Autobiographies Since Nineteen Thirty-Three, 91. LC 87-24952. (Contributions in Women's Studies: No. 91). 241p. 1988. 55.00 (*0-313-25921-6*, LXP/, Greenwood Pr) Greenwood.

Liyong, Taban Lo. Carrying Knowledge Up a Palm Tree: Poetry. LC 97-18101. 106p. 1997. 29.95 (*0-86543-593-6*); pap. 12.95 (*0-86543-594-4*) Africa World.

Liyuan, Zhu & Blocker, H. Gene, eds. Contemporary Chinese Aesthetics. (Asian Thought & Culture Ser.: Vol. 17). IX, 350p. (C). 1995. text 55.95 (*0-8204-2527-3*) P Lang Pubng.

Lizano, Eduardo. Desarrollo Economico e Integracion Regional en Centroamerica, Vol. 11. (SPA.). 52p. 1994. pap. text 8.00 (*0-940602-86-5*) IADB.

Economic Policy Making: Lessons from Costa Rica. 32p. 1991. pap. 9.95 (*1-55815-117-6*) ICS Pr.

Lizardi-Rivera, Carmen, tr. see Loya, Olga.

Lizardlover, Henry. Iguana: An Owner's Guide to a Happy Healthy Pet. LC 96-20450. 128p. 1996. 12.95 (*0-87605-478-5*) Howell Bks.

Lizardos, Georgia, jt. tr. see Papadopulos, Leonidas J.

Lizardos, Georgia, tr. see St. Nictarios Press Staff, ed.

Lizarraga, Angelica, tr. see Behm, Richard & Behm, Mary.

Lizarraga Valencia, Romulo, jt. auth. see Cumes, Carol.

Lizaso, Felix. Marti, Martyr of Cuban Independence. LC 73-20502. (Illus.). 260p. 1974. reprint ed. lib. bdg. 60.00 (*0-8371-7329-9*, LIMA, Greenwood Pr) Greenwood.

Lizatovic, Josip, jt. auth. see Donovan, Anna.

Lizatovic, Josip, jt. auth. see Murphy, Frank.

***Lizee.** Peace , Power & Resistence in Cambodia. LC 99-15386. 240p. 1999. text 65.00 (*0-312-22406-0*) St Martin.

Lizeng, Gong, tr. see Zehou, Li.

Lizhi, Fang. Bringing Down the Great Wall. 1991. 20.00 (*0-685-41162-1*) McKay.

— Bringing Down the Great Wall: Writings on Science, Culture, & Democracy in China. 384p. 1992. pap. 10.95 (*0-393-30885-5*) Norton.

— Galaxies, Quasars & Cosmology. Ruffini, Remo, ed. (Advanced Series in Astrophysics & Cosmology: Vol. 2). 232p. 1985. pap. 36.00 (*9971-5-0083-3*); text 48.00 (*9971-978-93-8*) World Scientific Pub.

— Selected Speeches & Writings by Fang Lizhi, Vol. 1. 176p. 1989. text 18.00 (*962-362-003-9*); pap. text 9.00 (*962-362-004-7*) World Scientific Pub.

— Selected Speeches & Writings by Fang Lizhi, Vol. 2. 267p. 1989. pap. text 11.00 (*962-362-006-3*) World Scientific Pub.

Lizhi, Fang, ed. Origin, Structure & Evolution of Galaxies: Proceedings of the Yellow Mountain Summer School of Astrophysics. 344p. (Orig.). (C). 1988. pap. 47.00 (*9971-5-0522-3*); text 108.00 (*9971-5-0521-5*) World Scientific Pub.

Lizhi, Fang & Chu, Y. Q. From Newton's Laws to Einstein's Theory of Relativity. 120p. (C). 1987. text 58.00 (*9971-978-36-9*) World Scientific Pub.

Lizhi, Fang & Ruffini, Remo. Cosmology of the Early Universe. (Advanced Series in Astrophysics & Cosmology: Vol. 1). 316p. (C). 1984. 54.00 (*9971-950-92-8*); pap. 30.00 (*9971-950-93-6*) World Scientific Pub.

Lizhi, Fang & Ruffini, Remo, eds. Basic Concepts in Relativistic Astrophysics. 230p. 1983. text 47.00 (*9971-950-66-9*) World Scientific Pub.

— Quantum Cosmology. (Advanced Series in Astrophysics & Cosmology: Vol. 3). 340p. (C). 1987. text 98.00 (*9971-5-0293-3*); pap. text 47.00 (*9971-5-0312-3*) World Scientific Pub.

Lizieri. A Change of Skin. 2001. write for info. (*0-15-100459-5*) Harcourt.

Lizieri, Colin, jt. auth. see Ball, Michael.

***Lizieri, Michelle.** Awaiting a Lover. LC 99-46668. 2000. 14.95 (*0-670-88999-7*, Viking) Viking Penguin.

Lizon, Lulu. Travel & Tourism Careers Guide Book. Parkerson, Janet, ed. (Illus.). 133p. (Orig.). (C). 1987. pap. 19.95 (*0-935423-05-2*) Educ Pubns.

Lizon, Peter. Villa Tugendhat: Svetovy Meznik Modernism V Brne. LC 97-9220. (Illus.). 80p. (Orig.). 1996. pap. write for info. (*0-9642219-4-2*) U TN Ofc U Relations.

— Villa Tugendhat in Brno: International Landmark of Modernism. LC 97-9220. (Illus.). 80p. (Orig.). 1996. pap. 20.00 (*0-9642219-3-4*) U TN Ofc U Relations.

Lizot, Jacques. Tales of the Yanomami: Daily Life in the Venezuelan Forest. (Canto Book Ser.). (Illus.). 214p. (C). 1991. pap. 12.95 (*0-521-40672-2*) Cambridge U Pr.

Lizotte, Ken & Litwak, Barbara A. Balancing Work & Family. LC 95-19855. (WorkSmart Ser.). 130p. (Orig.). 1995. pap. 10.95 (*0-8144-7837-9*) AMACOM.

— From Secretary Track to Fast Track: The Get Ahead Guide for Administrative Assistants, Secretaries, Office Managers, Receptionists & Everyone Who Wants More! 192p. 1996. pap. 15.95 (*0-8144-7902-2*) AMACOM.

Lizotte, Michael P. & Arrigo, Kevin R. Antarctic Sea Ice Biological Processes: Interactions & Variability. LC 97 53111. (Antarctic Research Ser.: Vol. 73). 198p. 1998. 45.00 (*0-87590-901-9*) Am Geophysical.

Lizuka, Keigo. Photonics for Fiber & Integrated Optics. LC 98-15244. (Pure & Applied Optics Ser.). 1168p. 1998. 175.00 (*0-471-83938-8*, Wiley-Interscience) Wiley.

***Lizza, Christopher.** Cedar or Soda. 1999. pap. write for info. (*1-58235-176-7*) Watermrk Pr.

Lizza, Michael. Better Days Journal, 3. unabridged ed. (Illus.). 45p. (Orig.). 1996. pap. 10.00 (*1-929326-52-1*) Hal Bar Pubg.

— Good Writer's Almanac, 4. unabridged ed. (Illus.). 86p. (Orig.). 1997. pap. 15.00 (*1-929326-53-X*) Hal Bar Pubg.

— Hopes & Dreams, 7. unabridged ed. (Illus.). 86p. (Orig.). 1998. pap. 20.00 (*1-929326-54-8*) Hal Bar Pubg.

— The Life & Times of Michael Lizza, Vol. 8. unabridged ed. (Illus.). 410p. 1998. write for info. (*1-929326-51-3*) Hal Bar Pubg.

— The Long & Winding Road, 1. unabridged ed. (Illus.). 20p. (Orig.). 1994. pap. 5.00 (*1-929326-50-5*) Hal Bar Pubg.

— Long & Winding Road II, 9. unabridged ed. (Illus.). 120p. (Orig.). 1999. pap. 25.00 (*1-929326-57-2*) Hal Bar Pubg.

— Off the Wall, Vol. 10. unabridged ed. (Illus.). 120p. 2000. lib. bdg. 25.00 (*1-929326-63-7*) Hal Bar Pubg.

— Photographs & Memories, Vol. 6. (Illus.). 134p. 1998. 20.00 (*1-929326-56-4*) Hal Bar Pubg.

— Poetry Gazzette, 2. unabridged ed. (Illus.). 38p. 1996. pap. 7.50 (*1-929326-58-0*) Hal Bar Pubg.

Lizza, Richard W. & Joyaux, Alain G. Byron Browne: Studies in Gouache from the 1940's. 16p. (Orig.). 1987. pap. 3.50 (*0-915511-06-1*) Ball St U Mus Art.

***Ljadov.** Ljadov: Complete Piano Works I. 1999. pap. 7.95 (*963-9155-40-3*) Kone Music.

— Ljadov: Complete Piano Works II. 1999. pap. 7.95 (*963-9155-41-1*) Kone Music.

— Ljadov: Complete Piano Works III. 1999. pap. 7.95 (*963-9155-42-X*) Kone Music.

Ljapin, E. S. Semigroups. 4th ed. Brown, A. et al, trs. LC 63-15659. (Translations of Mathematical Monographs: Vol. 3). 519p. 1975. reprint ed. pap. 62.00 (*0-8218-1553-9*, MMONO/3) Am Math.

Ljapin, E. S. & Evseev, A. E. The Theory of Partial Algebraic Operations. Cole, Michael, tr. LC 97-2589. (Mathematics & Its Applications Ser.: Vol. 414). 1997. text 151.00 (*0-7923-4609-2*) Kluwer Academic.

Ljubic, Tone, jt. ed. see Kaltnekar, Zdravko.

Ljung, Ellen J. Writing with Appleworks. (EC - HS Communication/English Ser.). 1991. mass mkt. 19.95 (*0-538-61212-6*) S-W Pub.

— Writing with Microsoft Works on the Macintosh. (EC - HS Communication/English Ser.). 1995. mass mkt. 20.95 (*0-538-62669-0*) S-W Pub.

— Writing with Microsoft Works on the Macintosh. large type ed. 300p. 74.50 (*0-614-20560-3*, L-85332-00 APHB) Am Printing Hse.

Ljung, Lennart. System Identification: Theory for the User. 2nd ed. LC 98-18554. 672p. (C). 1998. 89.00 (*0-13-656695-2*) P-H.

Ljung, Lennart & Glad, Torkel. Modeling of Dynamic Systems. 368p. 1994. 63.80 (*0-13-597097-0*) P-H.

Ljung, Lennart, et al. Stochastic Approximation & Optimization of Random Systems. LC 92-10322. (DMV Seminar Ser.: No. Bd. 17). 120p. 1992. 24.50 (*3-7643-2733-2*); 34.00 (*0-8176-2733-2*, Pub. by Birkhauser) Princeton Arch.

Ljung, Lennart, jt. auth. see Glad, Torkel.

Ljung, Lennart, jt. ed. see Anderson, B. D.

Ljung, Magnus, jt. ed. see Lindblad, Ishrat.

***Ljungberg, Christina.** To Join, to Fit, & to Make: The Creative Craft of Margaret Atwood's Fiction. LC 99-40571. (European University Studies: Vol. 361, Series 14). 202p. (C). 1999. pap. text 30.95 (*0-8204-4617-3*) P Lang Pubng.

***Ljungberg, Gert & Ljungberg, Inger A.** Carving & Whittling: The Swedish Style. LC 97-44387. (Illus.). 168p. 1998. pap. 19.95 (*1-887374-40-X*, Pub. by Lark Books) Random.

Ljungberg, Inger A., jt. auth. see Ljungberg, Gert.

Ljungberg, M. & King, M. A., eds. Monte Carlo Calculations in Nuclear Medicine: Applications in Diagnostic Imaging. LC 98-11380. (Medical Science Ser.). (Illus.). 256p. 1998. 99.00 (*0-7503-0479-0*) IOP Pub.

Ljunggren, Anna. At the Crossroads of Russian Modernism: Studies in Innokentij Annenskij's Poetics. LC 97-156214. (Acta Universitatis Stockholmiensis Ser.: Vol. 32). 144p. 1997. pap. 42.50 (*91-22-01744-5*, Pub. by Almqvist Wiksell) Coronet Bks.

Ljunggren, Anna & Gourianova, Nina, eds. Elena Guro: Selected Writings from the Archives. (Stockholm Studies in Russian Literature: No. 28). 134p. (Orig.). 1995. pap. 37.50 (*91-22-01688-0*) Coronet Bks.

Ljunggren, Borje, ed. The Challenge of Reform in Indochina, Vol. 2. LC 92-26516. (Studies in International Development). 416p. 1993. text 30.00 (*0-674-10712-8*) HUP.

Ljunggren, G. & Dornic, S., eds. Psychophysics in Action. (Illus.). 170p. 1989. 77.95 (*0-387-50686-1*) Spr-Verlag.

Ljunggren, Magnus. The Dream of Rebirth: A Study of Andrej Belyj's Novel Petersburg. (Stockholm Studies in Russian Literature). (Illus.). 180p. (Orig.). 1982. pap. 34.50 (*91-22-00586-2*) Coronet Bks.

— The Russian Mephisto: A Study of the Life & Work of Emilii Medtner. (Stockholm Studies in Russian Literature: No. 27). (Illus.). 240p. 1994. pap. 49.50 (*91-22-01656-2*) Coronet Bks.

Ljungmark, Lars. Swedish Exodus. Westerberg, Kermit B., tr. 192p. (C). 1996. pap. 14.95 (*0-8093-2047-9*) Swedish-Am.

Ljungquist, Kent P. The Grand & the Fair: Poe in the American Landscape. 1982. pap. 2.95 (*0-910556-20-2*) Enoch Pratt.

— The Grand & the Fair: Poe's Landscape Aesthetic & Pictorial Techniques. 1985. 27.50 (*0-916379-20-5*) Scripta.

***Ljungquist, Kent P.** Nineteenth-Century American Fiction Writers. LC 98-49304. (Dictionary of Literary Biography Ser.). 400p. 1999. text 155.00 (*0-7876-3096-9*) Gale.

Ljungqvist, Alexander, jt. auth. see Jenkinson, Tim.

Ljungqvist, Bengt & Reinmuller, Berit. Clean Room Design: Minimizing Contamination Through Proper Design. (Illus.). 124p. 1996. 89.00 (*1-57491-032-9*) Interpharm.

***Ljungqvist, Lars & Sargent, Thomas J.** Recursive Macroeconomic Theory. (Illus.). 650p. (C). 2000. 60.00 (*0-262-19451-1*) MIT Pr.

Ljungstedt, Milnor, ed. County Court Notebook & Ancestral Proofs & Probabilities. LC 77-173265. 788p. 1995. reprint ed. pap. 50.00 (*0-8063-0505-3*) Clearfield Co.

Ljungstedt, N., jt. ed. see Bostrom, H.

Ljunguist, Bengt. Practical Dressage Manual. (Illus.). 164p. 1983. 22.95 (*0-939481-36-7*) Half Halt Pr.

Ljusternik, L. A. The Topology of Function Spaces & the Calculus of Variations in the Large. LC 66-25298. (Translations of Mathematical Monographs: Vol. 16). 96p. 1967. reprint ed. pap. 31.00 (*0-8218-1566-0*, MMONO/16) Am Math.

Llabador, Y. & Moretto, P. H. Applications of Nuclear Microprobe in the Life Sciences: An Efficient Analytical Technique for the Research in Biology & Medicine. LC 95-43473. 300p. 1997. text 58.00 (*981-02-2362-5*) World Scientific Pub.

Llabres De Charneco, Amalia, jt. auth. see Charneco Babilonia, Efrain.

Llaire, Paul E. Industrial Conference & Exhibition on Magnetic Bearings: Proceedings. LC 97-61365. 353p. 1997. pap. 189.95 (*1-56676-599-4*) Technomic.

Llamas, Andreu. Birds Conquer the Sky. LC 95-3967. (Development of the Earth Ser.).Tr. of Aves Conquistan el Cielo. (ENG & SPA., Illus.). 32p. (J). (gr. 3 up). 1996. lib. bdg. 15.95 (*0-7910-3455-0*) Chelsea Hse.

Llamas, Andreu. The Development of the Earth. 32p. (gr. 3). 1996. 95.70 (*0-7910-3450-X*) Chelsea Hse.

Llamas, Andreu. The Era of Dinosaurs. LC 95-3963. (Development of the Earth Ser.).Tr. of Era de los Dinosaurios. (ENG & SPA., Illus.). 32p. (J). (gr. 3 up). 1996. lib. bdg. 15.95 (*0-7910-3452-6*) Chelsea Hse.

— The First Amphibians. LC 95-3964. (Development of the Earth Ser.).Tr. of Primeros Anfibios. (ENG & SPA., Illus.). 32p. (J). (gr. 3 up). 1996. lib. bdg. 15.95 (*0-7910-3453-4*) Chelsea Hse.

Llamas, Andreu. The Five Senses of the Animal World. (Illus.). 32p. (gr. 3). 1996. 79.75 (*0-7910-3489-5*) Chelsea Hse.

Llamas, Andreu. The Great Sea Reptiles. LC 95-3965. (Development of the Earth Ser.).Tr. of Grandes Reptiles Marinos. (ENG & SPA., Illus.). 32p. (J). (gr. 3 up). 1996. lib. bdg. 15.95 (*0-7910-3454-2*) Chelsea Hse.

— The Human Body, 4 bks. Incl. Digestion & Reproduction. LC 98-16719. (Illus.). 32p. (J). (gr. 2 up). 1998. lib. bdg. 21.27 (*0-8368-2111-4*); Muscles & Bones. LC 98-6601. (Illus.). 32p. (J). (gr. 2 up). 1998. lib. bdg. 21.27 (*0-8368-2112-2*); Nervous System. LC 98-6645. (Illus.). 32p. (J). (gr. 2 up). 1998. lib. bdg. 21.27 (*0-8368-2113-0*); Respiration & Circulation. LC 98-16720. (Illus.). 32p. (J). (gr. 2 up). 1998. lib. bdg. 21.27 (*0-8368-2110-6*); (Human Body Ser.). (Illus.). (J). 1998. Set lib. bdg. 85.07 (*0-8368-2109-2*) Gareth Stevens Inc.

— Life Starts in the Sea. LC 95-3962. (Development of the Earth Ser.).Tr. of Vida Empieza en el Mar. (ENG & SPA., Illus.). 32p. (J). (gr. 3-12). 1996. lib. bdg. 15.95 (*0-7910-3451-8*) Chelsea Hse.

— Mammals Dominate the Earth. LC 95-3966. (Edades de la Tierra Ser.).Tr. of Mamiferos Dominan la Tierra. (ENG & SPA., Illus.). 32p. (J). (gr. 3-12). 1996. lib. bdg. 15.95 (*0-7910-3456-9*) Chelsea Hse.

— Plants of the Forest. (Incredible World of Plants Ser.). (Illus.). 32p. (J). (gr. 3-12). 1995. lib. bdg. 15.95 (*0-7910-3467-4*) Chelsea Hse.

— Sight. LC 95-10514. (Five Senses of the Animal World Ser.). (Illus.). 32p. (J). (gr. 3 up). 1996. lib. bdg. 15.95 (*0-7910-3491-7*) Chelsea Hse.

— Touch. LC 95-14781. (Five Senses of the Animal World Ser.).Tr. of El Tacto. (Illus.). 32p. (J). (gr. 3 up). 1996. lib. bdg. 15.95 (*0-7910-3494-1*) Chelsea Hse.

Llamas, Andrew, jt. auth. see Chelsea House Publishing Staff.

Llamas, M. Ramon, jt. auth. see Rogers, Peter.

Llamazares, Julio. Mi tio Mario: Level D Books. 8.95 (*0-8219-1473-1*) EMC-Paradigm.

— Yellow Rain. 2000. write for info. (*0-15-100598-2*) Harcourt.

Llamzon, Teodoro A. Modern Tagalog: A Functional-Structural Description. LC 78-88212. (Janua Linguarum, Series Practica: No. 122). (Orig.). 1976. pap. text 43.10 (*90-279-3493-2*) Mouton.

***Llana, Andres, Jr.** Convergence of Wireless Technology & Enterprise Networks: Integrating the Internet. LC 99-40465. (Illus.). 225p. 2000. pap. 285.00 (*1-56607-079-1*) Comput Tech Res.

Llana, Christopher B. & Wisneskey, George P. Handbook of the Nautical Rules of the Road. 2nd ed. LC 90-46486. (Illus.). 244p. 1991. 29.95 (*1-55750-504-7*) Naval Inst Pr.

Llanes. Houses of Old Cuba. Date not set. 45.00 Thames Hudson.

Llanes, Eduardo, tr. see Johns, Helen.

Llanes, Flor A., ed. see Uceda, Mario A.

Llang, Henry R. Das Liederbuch des Konigs Denis von Portugal. (GER.). cxviii, 174p. 1972. reprint ed. write for info. (*3-487-04245-2*) G Olms Pubs.

Llano, jt. auth. see Schinke.

Llano, jt. auth. see Shinke.

Llano, George A., ed. Antarctic Terrestrial Biology. LC 72-92709. (Antarctic Research Ser.: Vol. 20). (Illus.). 322p. 1972. 39.00 (*0-87590-120-4*) Am Geophysical.

— Biology of the Antarctic Seas Two. LC 64-60030. (Antarctic Research Ser.: Vol. 5). (Illus.). 280p. 1965. 15.00 (*0-87590-105-0*) Am Geophysical.

Llano, George A. & Schmitt, Waldo L., eds. Biology of the Antarctic Seas Three. LC 64-60030. (Antarctic Research Ser.: Vol. 11). (Illus.). 261p. 1967. 17.00 (*0-87590-111-5*) Am Geophysical.

Llano, George A. & Wallen, I. Eugene, eds. Biology of the Antarctic Seas 4. LC 64-60030. (Antarctic Research Ser.: Vol. 17). (Illus.). 362p. 1971. 39.00 (*0-87590-117-4*) Am Geophysical.

Llano Restrepo, Maria C. & Campuzano Cifuentes, Marcela. La Chicha: Una Bebida Fermentada a Traves de la Historia. (SPA.). 160p. 1994. pap. 11.00 (*958-9061-79-6*, IC002) UPLAAP.

Llanos, Bernardita. Re-Descubrimiento y Re-Conquista de America en la Ilustracion Espanola. LC 93-2313. (Sociocritism Ser.: Vol. 6). 217p. (C). 1994. text 47.95 (*0-8204-2269-X*) P Lang Pubng.

Llanos, Hector. Presencia de la Cultura de San Agustin en la Depresion Calida del Valle del Rio Magdalena Garzon-Huila. (SPA., Illus.). 100p. (Orig.). (C). 1993. pap. 9.50 (*1-877812-35-8*, BR035, Pub. by Banco de la Repub) UPLAAP.

— Proceso Historico Prehispanico de San Agustin en el Valle de Laboyos (Pitalito-Huila) (SPA., Illus.). 122p. 1990. pap. 8.50 (*1-877812-31-5*, BR029) UPLAAP.

Llanos, Hector, jt. auth. see Pinto, Maria.

Llanos, Primitivo N., ed. see Urton, Gary.

Llanso, Steven L., jt. auth. see Laur, Timothy M.

Llarch, Juan. Dali's Universal Tarot. 44p. pap. 100.00 (*0-88079-090-3*) US Games Syst.

Llarena, Alicia. Realismo Magico y Lo Real Maravilloso: Una Cuestion de Verosimilitud. LC 97-74543. (SPA.). 360p. (C). 1997. pap. 30.00 (*0-935318-24-0*) Edins Hispamerica.

***Llarena, Ray.** Founded on the Rock: Finding God's Order for Your Family. 168p. 1998. pap. 9.99 (*1-884369-91-X*) McDougal Pubng.

Llarena, Ray. In Search of Significance: Why You Are Important to God. 1997. pap. text 9.99 (*1-884369-67-7*) McDougal Pubng.

Llast, Robin. Discover a New World of Healing: Answers for Successful Living in These Times. (Illus.). 234p. (Orig.). 1992. pap. text 12.95 (*0-929240-52-9*) EMIS.

***Llave, Rafael De, et al, eds.** Dynamics of Algorithms. LC 99-42675. (IMA Volumes in Mathematics & Its Applications Ser.: Vol.118). (Illus.). 156p. 1999. 59.95 (*0-387-98920-X*) Spr-Verlag.

Lleonart, Augusti B. Dictionary of Mythology: Diccionario de Mitologia. 2nd ed. (ENG & SPA.). 216p. 1985. 29.95 (*0-7859-4963-1*, S39844) Fr & Eur.

Llera, Humberto P. Idea, Sentimiento y Sensibilidad de Jose Marti. LC 79-56227. (Coleccion Cuba y sus Jueces). (SPA.). 490p. (Orig.). 1982. pap. 25.00 (*0-89729-242-1*) Ediciones.

Lleras, Agustin R., ed. see Martinez, Rodolfo V.

Lleras, Roberto. Arqueologia del Alto Valle de Tenza. (SPA., Illus.). 148p. 1989. pap. 8.50 (*1-877812-12-9*, BR002) UPLAAP.

Llerena, Mario. The Myth & the Mirage: Six Essays on Revolution. Leyva, Adolfo, ed. LC 95-83543. 217p. 1995. pap. 15.00 (*1-884619-07-X*) Endowment CAS.

— The Unsuspected Revolution: The Birth & Rise of Castroism. LC 77-3119. (Illus.). 327p. reprint ed. pap. 101.40 (*0-608-08541-3*, 206906400002) Bks Demand.

Llerena, P., ed. see Cohendet, Patrick.

Lleu, J. English-French Glossary of Marketing Terms. 2nd ed. 533p. 1983. pap. 95.00 (*0-8288-0084-7*, M8908) Fr & Eur.

Llevada, E. Jerry. Florida's High School Competency Test (Math) Llevada's Handbook. 2nd rev. ed. (Illus.). 145p. (YA). (gr. 9-12). 1996. pap. text 15.00 (*1-890953-00-8*, 94HSCTM) LS Pr.

Llewellyn. The Law Life & Society. 1996. 29.95 (*0-226-48791-1*) U Ch Pr.

— Lost Scrolls Medallion: Solid Brass Medallion, 1. 1999. pap. text 10.00 (*1-56718-058-2*) Llewellyn Pubns.

Llewellyn, jt. auth. see Tipler.

Llewellyn & Co. Staff. Puget Sound Catechism: A Convenient Compendium of Useful Information Respecting the State of Washington. (Shorey Historical Ser.). 33p. 1990. reprint ed. pap. 10.00 (*0-8466-0078-1*, S78) Shoreys Bkstore.

Llewellyn, Ann, jt. auth. see Swyer, P. R.

Llewellyn, Briony, jt. auth. see Guiterman, Helen.

Llewellyn, Caroline. False Light. large type ed. LC 96-50227. (Large Print Bks.). 1997. pap. 22.95 (*1-56895-403-4*) Wheeler Pub.

— Life Blood. 1994. mass mkt. 5.99 (*0-8041-1263-0*) Ivy Books.

— Life Blood. large type ed. LC 93-46458. 571p. 1994. lib. bdg. 21.95 (*0-8161-5940-8*, G K Hall Lrg Type) Mac Lib Ref.

— The Masks of Rome. large type ed. (General Ser.). 432p. 1989. lib. bdg. 21.95 (*0-8161-4752-3*, G K Hall Lrg Type) Mac Lib Ref.

Llewellyn, Charles. The Mill's Life: From the Domesday Book to the Millenium. LC 98-70056. (Illus.). 198p. 1999. 29.95 (*1-86105-105-0*, Pub. by Robson Bks) Parkwest Pubns.

Llewellyn, Chris. Steam Dummy & Fragments from the Fire: Poems. rev. ed. (Midwest Writers Ser.). (Illus.). 124p. (Orig.). 1991. pap. 8.95 (*0-933087-29-2*) Bottom Dog Pr.

Llewellyn, Claire. Animal Atlas. LC 97-48459. (Illus.). 48p. (J). (gr. 3-8). 1999. write for info. (*0-7166-9602-9*) World Bk.

— The Best Book of Bugs. LC 97-39700. (Best Book of . . . Ser.). (J). (ps-4). 1998. 12.95 (*0-7534-5118-2*) LKC.

***Llewellyn, Claire.** Best Book of Sharks. LC QL638.9.L57 1999. 31p. (J). (gr. 3-5). 1999. 12.95 (*0-7534-5173-5*) LKC.

Llewellyn, Claire. The Big Book of Bones: An Introduction to Skeletons. LC 97-48329. (Illus.). 48p. (YA). (gr. 5 up). 1998. 17.95 (*0-87226-546-3*, 65463B, P Bedrick Books) NTC Contemp Pub Co.

— Bread. LC 99-25904. (What's for Lunch? Ser.). 32p. (J). (gr. k-2). 1999. 20.50 (*0-516-21546-9*) Childrens.

— Chimps Use Tools: And Other Amazing Facts about Apes & Monkeys. LC 98-28527. (I Didn't Know That... Ser.). (Illus.). 32 p. (J). 1999. 8.95 (*0-7613-0786-9*, Copper Beech Bks); lib. bdg. 21.90 (*0-7613-0874-1*, Copper Beech Bks) Millbrook Pr.

— Chocolate. LC 97-34943. (What's for Lunch? Ser.). (J). 1998. 20.00 (*0-516-20837-3*) Childrens.

— Chocolate. (What's for Lunch? Ser.). (Illus.). 32p. (J). (ps). 1998. pap. 6.95 (*0-516-26218-1*) Childrens.

Llewellyn, Claire. Day & Night. (Why Do We Have? Ser.). 1995. 10.15 (*0-606-08904-7*, Pub. by Turtleback) Demco.

Llewellyn, Claire. Deserts & Rainforests. LC 96-52381. (Illus.). (J). 1998. 19.92 (*1-57572-196-1*) Heinemann Lib.

— Disguises & Suprises. LC 96-4228. (Supersmarts Ser.). (Illus.). 24p. (J). (gr. 2-5). 1998. pap. 4.99 (*0-7636-0288-4*) Candlewick Pr.

— Disguises & Surprises. LC 96-4228. (SuperSmarts Ser.). (Illus.). 24p. (J). (gr. 4-7). 1996. 11.99 (*0-7636-0037-7*) Candlewick Pr.

— Eggs. LC 99-28943. (What's for Lunch? Ser.). 32p. (J). (gr. k-2). 1999. 20.50 (*0-516-21547-7*) Childrens.

— The Encyclopedia of Awesome Animals. LC 98-28540. 192p. (J). (gr. 1-3). 1998. 16.95 (*0-7613-0781-8*, Copper Beech Bks) Millbrook Pr.

— Milk. LC 97-39803. (What's for Lunch? Ser.). (J). 1998. 20.00 (*0-516-20840-3*) Childrens.

— Milk. Cohen, Helaine, ed. (What's for Lunch? Ser.). (Illus.). 32p. (J). 1998. pap. 6.95 (*0-516-26221-1*) Childrens.

— My First Book of Time. LC 91-58194. (Illus.). 32p. (J). (ps-3). 1992. 14.95 (*1-879431-78-5*) DK Pub Inc.

— Only Some Big Cats Can Roar: And Other Amazing Facts about Wild Cats. LC 98-28524. (I Didn't Know That... Ser.). (Illus.). 32p. (J). 1999. 8.95 (*0-7613-0787-7*, Copper Beech Bks); lib. bdg. 21.90 (*0-7613-0900-4*, Copper Beech Bks) Millbrook Pr.

— Oranges. LC 99-28942. (What's for Lunch? Ser.). 32p. (J). (gr. k-2). 1999. 20.50 (*0-516-21548-5*) Childrens.

— Our Planet Earth. LC 97-12561. (Scholastic First Encyclopedia Ser.). (Illus.). 80p. (J). (gr. k-3). 1997. pap. 14.95 (*0-590-87929-4*, Scholastic Ref) Scholastic Inc.

— Peanuts. LC 97-34925. (What's for Lunch? Ser.). (J). (gr. k-2). 1998. 20.00 (*0-516-20839-X*) Childrens.

— Peanuts. Cohen, Helaine, ed. LC 97-34925. (What's for Lunch? Ser.). (Illus.). 32p. (J). 1998. pap. 6.95 (*0-516-26222-X*) Childrens.

— Peas. LC 99-25903. (What's for Lunch? Ser.). 32p. (J). (gr. k-2). 1999. 20.50 (*0-516-21549-3*) Childrens.

— Potatoes. LC 97-34924. (What's for Lunch? Ser.). (J). 1998. lib. bdg. 20.00 (*0-516-20838-1*) Childrens.

— Potatoes. Cohen, Helaine, ed. (What's for Lunch? Ser.). (Illus.). 32p. (J). (ps-2). 1998. pap. 6.95 (*0-516-26223-8*) Childrens.

— Rivers & Seas. (Why Do We Have? Ser.). 1995. 10.15 (*0-606-08905-5*, Pub. by Turtleback) Demco.

— Rocks & Mountains. LC 95-19701. (Why do We Have? Ser.). (Illus.). 24p. (gr. 1-3). 1995. 9.95 (*0-8120-6524-7*) Barron.

Llewellyn, Claire. Rocks & Mountains. (Why Do We Have? Ser.). 1995. 10.15 (*0-606-08906-3*, Pub. by Turtleback) Demco.

Llewellyn, Claire. Sharks Keep Losing Their Teeth: And Other Amazing Facts about Sharks. LC 97-41606. (I Didn't Know That... Ser.). (Illus.). 32p. (J). (gr. 1). 1998. lib. bdg. 19.90 (*0-7613-0712-5*, Copper Beech Bks) Millbrook Pr.

— Sharks Keep Losing Their Teeth: And Other Amazing Facts about Sharks. LC 97-41606. (I Didn't Know That... Ser.). (Illus.). 32p. (J). (gr. 1-3). 1998. 8.95 (*0-7613-0646-3*, Copper Beech Bks) Millbrook Pr.

— Sizes. Anness Publishing Staff, ed. (Fun to Learn Ser.). (Illus.). 32p. (J). 1999. 7.95 (*0-7548-0209-4*, Lorenz Bks) Anness Pub.

— Some Birds Hang Upside Down: And Other Amazing Facts about Birds. LC 97-10033. (I Didn't Know That... Ser.). (Illus.). 32p. (J). (gr. 1-3). 1997. 8.95 (*0-7613-0597-1*, Copper Beech Bks); lib. bdg. 19.90 (*0-7613-0608-0*, Copper Beech Bks) Millbrook Pr.

— Some Bugs Glow in the Dark: And Other Amazing Facts about Insects. LC 96-43331. (I Didn't Know That... Ser.). (Illus.). 32p. (J). (gr. 1-3). 1997. 8.95 (*0-7613-0587-4*, Copper Beech Bks); lib. bdg. 19.90 (*0-7613-0562-9*, Copper Beech Bks) Millbrook Pr.

— Some Plants Grow in Mid-Air: And Other Amazing Facts about the Rainforest. LC 97-41608. (I Didn't Know That... Ser.). (Illus.). 32p. (J). 1998. 8.95 (*0-7613-0644-7*, Copper Beech Bks) Millbrook Pr.

— Some Plants Grow in Mid-Air: And Other Amazing Facts about the Rainforest. LC 97-41608. (I Didn't Know That... Ser.). (Illus.). 32p. (J). (gr. 1-3). 1998. lib. bdg. 19.90 (*0-7613-0714-1*, Copper Beech Bks) Millbrook Pr.

— Some Snakes Spit Poison: And Other Amazing Facts about Snakes. (I Didn't Know That... Ser.). (Illus.). 32p. (J). (gr. 1-3). 1997. 8.95 (*0-7613-0586-6*, Copper Beech Bks); lib. bdg. 19.90 (*0-7613-0561-0*, Copper Beech Bks) Millbrook Pr.

— Spiders Have Fangs: And Other Amazing Facts about Arachnids. LC 97-1256. (I Didn't Know That... Ser.). (Illus.). 32p. (J). (gr. 1-3). 1997. 8.95 (*0-7613-0599-8*, Copper Beech Bks) Millbrook Pr.

— Spiders Have Fangs: And Other Amazing Facts about Arachnids. LC 97-1256. (I Didn't Know That... Ser.). (Illus.). 32p. (J). (gr. 1-3). 1997. lib. bdg. 19.90 (*0-7613-0610-2*, Copper Beech Bks) Millbrook Pr.

— Sums. Anness Publishing Staff, ed. (Fun to Learn Ser.). (Illus.). 32p. (J). 1999. 7.95 (*0-7548-0210-8*, Lorenz Bks) Anness Pub.

— Towns & Cities. LC 96-52728. (Illus.). (J). 1998. (*1-57572-197-X*) Heinemann Lib.

— Tractor. LC 94-24403. (Mighty Machines Ser.). (Illus.). 24p. (J). (ps-3). 1995. 9.95 (*1-56458-515-8*) DK Pub Inc.

— Truck. LC 94-38034. (Mighty Machines Ser.). (Illus.). 24p. (J). (ps-3). 1995. 9.95 (*1-56458-516-6*) DK Pub Inc.

— Trucks. LC 95-10739. (Worldwise Ser.). (Illus.). 48p. (J). (gr. 4-6). 1995. lib. bdg. 23.00 (*0-531-14378-3*) Watts.

— Trucks. LC 95-10739. (Worldwise Ser.). (Illus.). 48p. (J). (gr. 4-6). 1996. pap. 7.00 (*0-531-15285-5*) Watts.

— Wild, Wet & Windy. LC 96-44371. (Supersmarts Ser.). (Illus.). 24p. (J). (gr. 3-6). 1997. 11.99 (*0-7636-0304-X*) Candlewick Pr.

— Wild, Wet & Windy. LC 96-44371. (Supersmarts ser.). (Illus.). 24p. (J). (gr. 2-5). 1998. pap. text 4.99 (*0-7636-0630-8*) Candlewick Pr.

— Wind & Rain. LC 94-39686. (Why Do We Have? Ser.). (Illus.). 24p. (J). (gr. 1-3). 1995. 9.95 (*0-8120-6508-5*) Barron.

Llewellyn, Claire. Wind & Rain. (Why Do We Have? Ser.). 1995. 10.15 (*0-606-08907-1*, Pub. by Turtleback) Demco.

Llewellyn, Claire & Lewis, Anthony. Day & Night. LC 94-45156. (Why Do We Have? Ser.). (Illus.). 24p. (J). (gr. 1-3). 1995. 9.95 (*0-8120-6509-3*) Barron.

— Rivers & Seas. LC 95-17382. (Why Do We Have? Ser.). (Illus.). 24p. (J). (gr. 1-3). 1995. pap. 4.95 (*0-8120-9396-8*) Barron.

***Llewellyn, Claire, et al.** How Things Work. (First Encyclopedia Ser.). (Illus.). 96p. (J). (ps-3). 2000. pap. 7.95 (*0-590-47530-4*) Scholastic Inc.

Llewellyn, Claire, jt. auth. see Jeunesse, Gallimard.

Llewellyn, D. J., jt. ed. see Dennis, E. S.

Llewellyn, D. T. & Hudd, R. C. Steels: Metallurgy & Applications. 3rd ed. LC 97-48771. 400p. 1998. pap. text 95.00 (*0-7506-3757-9*) Buttrwrth-Heinemann.

Llewellyn, David T. The Evolution of the British Financial System. 1985. 65.00 (*0-85297-136-2*, Pub. by Chartered Bank) St Mut.

— The Regulation & Supervision of Financial Institutions. 1986. 50.00 (*0-85297-174-5*, Pub. by Chartered Bank) St Mut.

***Llewellyn, Don W. & Fisher, Julia B.** Tax Planning for Lifetime & Testamentary Dispoitions--Prototype Plans--2000 Supplement. LC 99-76722. 124p. 2000. pap. 25.00 (*0-8318-0810-1*, B810) Am Law Inst.

Llewellyn, Don W. & Richmond, Gail L. Tax Planning for Lifetime & Testamentary Dispositions: Prototype Plans. LC 97-77082. xxxviii, 630p. 1997. 175.00 (*0-8318-0758-X*, B758) Am Law Inst.

Llewellyn, G. C. & O'Rear, C. E., eds. Biodeterioration Research, Vol. 1. LC 87-25494. (Illus.). 406p. 1988. 95.00 (*0-306-42764-8*, Plenum Trade) Perseus Pubng.

— Biodeterioration Research: Mycotoxins, Biotoxins, Wood Decay, Air Quality, Cultural Properties, General Deterioration & Degradation, Vol. 3. (Illus.). 714p. (C). 1990. 186.00 (*0-306-43697-3*, Plenum Trade) Perseus Pubng.

Llewellyn, G. C., et al. Biodeterioration Research 4: Mycotoxins, Wood Decay, Plant Stress, Biocorrosion, & General Biodeterioration. (Illus.). 704p. (C). 1994. 186.00 (*0-306-44638-3*, Plenum Trade) Perseus Pubng.

Llewellyn, G. C., jt. ed. see O'Rear, C. E.

Llewellyn, Geoffrey. Homeopathic Remedies for Dogs. (Illus.). 128p. 1998. 19.95 (*1-85279-086-5*, GB046) TFH Pubns.

Llewellyn, Grace. The Teenage Liberation Handbook: How to Quit School & Get a Real Life & Education. LC 97-19785. 192p. 1997. pap. 9.95 (*1-86204-104-0*, Pub. by Element MA) Penguin Putnam.

— The Teenage Liberation Handbook: How to Quit School & Get a Real Life & Education. 2nd rev. ed. (Illus.). 448p. (YA). (gr. 7-12). 1998. pap. 19.00 (*0-9629591-7-0*) Lowry Hse.

Llewellyn, Grace, ed. Freedom Challenge: African American Homeschoolers. (Illus.). 320p. (Orig.). 1996. pap. 16.95 (*0-9629591-1-1*) Lowry Hse.

Llewellyn, Grace, ed. Real Lives: Eleven Teenagers Who Don't Go to School. (Illus.). 320p. (Orig.). (YA). (gr. 7-12). 1993. pap. 17.00 (*0-9629591-3-8*) Lowry Hse.

Llewellyn, J. Bells & Bell Founding. 20.00 (*0-87556-208-6*) Saifer.

Llewellyn, J. Bells & Bell-Founding. (Illus.). 57p. 1987. reprint ed. pap. 25.00 (*0-87556-696-0*) Saifer.

Llewellyn, J A., jt. auth. see Gilbert, Richard A.

Llewellyn, J. E. Arya Samaj as a Fundamentalist Movement: A Study in Comparative Fundamentalism. (C). 1994. 30.00 (*81-7304-015-X*) S Asia.

— The Legacy of Women's Uplift in India: Contemporary Women Leaders in the Arya Samaj. LC 98-5351. 1998. write for info. (*0-7619-9252-9*); pap. write for info. (*0-7619-9253-7*) Sage.

***Llewellyn, Jack.** Coming in First: Keys to Being a Winner Every Day. LC 00-105068. 224p. 2000. 22.00 (*1-56352-630-1*) Longstreet.

Llewellyn, John F. A Cemetary Should Be Forever: The Challenge to Managers & Directors. LC 98-96589. (Illus.). 320p. 1999. pap. 19.95 (*0-9665801-2-5*) Tropico Pr.

***Llewellyn, John R.** Murder of a Prophet: The Dark Side of Utah Polygamy. LC 99-68880. 192p. 2000. pap. 13.95 (*1-888106-93-X*) Agreka Bks.

Llewellyn-Jones, Derek. The A-Z of Women's Health. 2nd ed. (Oxford Paperback Reference Ser.). (Illus.). 272p. 1990. pap. 16.95 (*0-19-286112-3*) OUP.

***Llewellyn-Jones, Derek.** Every Man. 4th ed. LC 98-8550. (Illus.). 320p. 1999. pap. 14.95 (*0-19-288090-X*) OUP.

Llewellyn-Jones, Derek. Everybody: The Healthy Eating Handbook. LC 92-19159. 1993. 5.99 (*0-19-286155-7*) OUP.

— Fundamentals of Obstetrics & Gynecology. 6th ed. 1994. text 36.00 (*0-7234-2000-9*) Mosby Inc.

Llewellyn-Jones, Derek, jt. auth. see Abraham, Suzanne.

Llewellyn-Jones, Margaret, ed. Spectacle, Silence & Subversion: Women's Performance Language & Strategies, Vol. 2, Part 1. 118p. 1994. pap. text 15.00 (*3-7186-5515-2*, Harwood Acad Pubs) Gordon & Breach.

Llewellyn-Jones, Margaret, jt. auth. see Griffiths, Trevor R.

Llewellyn-Jones, Margaret, jt. ed. see Carson, Bruce.

Llewellyn-Jones, Rosie. A Fatal Friendship: The Nawabs, the British & the City of Lucknow. (Illus.). 1986. 29.95 (*0-19-561706-1*) OUP.

— A Very Ingenious Man: Claude Martin in Early Colonial India. (Illus.). 276p. 1993. 24.00 (*0-19-563131-5*) OUP.

Llewellyn, K. N. The Constitution As an Institution. (Reprint Series in Social Sciences). (C). 1993. reprint ed. pap. text 5.00 (*0-8290-2737-8*, PS-171) Irvington.

Llewellyn, Karl N. Bramble Bush: On Our Law & Its Study. LC 51-1727. 192p. 1981. reprint ed. text 35.00 (*0-379-20738-9*); reprint ed. pap. text 35.00 (*0-379-00073-3*) Oceana.

— The Case Law System in America. Ansaldi, Michael, tr. LC 89-32341. 166p. 1998. 29.95 (*0-226-48790-3*) U Ch Pr.

— The Common Law Tradition: Deciding Appeals. 565p. 1960. 45.00 (*0-316-52935-4*, Aspen Law & Bus) Aspen Pub.

— Common Law Tradition: Deciding Appeals. LC 96-75737. xii, 565p. 1996. reprint ed. 85.00 (*1-57588-076-8*, 310520) W S Hein.

***Llewellyn, Karl N.** Jurisprudence: Realism in Theory & Practice, 1962. fac. ed. LC 99-56923. 2000. 95.00 (*1-58477-067-8*) Lawbk Exchange.

Llewellyn, Karl N. & Hoebel, E. Adamson. The Cheyenne Way: Conflict & Case Law in Primitive Jurisprudence. LC 41-23735. (Civilization of the American Indian Ser.: Vol. 21). (Illus.). 374p. 1983. reprint ed. 37.95 (*0-8061-0099-0*) U of Okla Pr.

— The Cheyenne Way: Conflict & Case Law in Primitive Jurisprudence. LC 41-23735. (Civilization of the American Indian Ser.: Vol. 21). (Illus.). 374p. 1983. reprint ed. pap. 19.95 (*0-8061-1855-5*) U of Okla Pr.

Llewellyn, Keith R., jt. ed. see Chekaluk, Eugene.

Llewellyn, Marc, jt. auth. see Kruger, Natalie.

Llewellyn, Marilyn, jt. auth. see Ellis, Angele M.

Llewellyn, Michael. Twelfth Night. 480p. 1998. mass mkt. 5.99 (*1-57566-253-1*, Knsington) Kensgtn Pub Corp.

Llewellyn, Nigel. The Art of Death: Visual Culture in the English Death Ritual, c. 1500-1800. (Illus.). 160p. 1991. pap. 22.95 (*0-948462-16-7*, Pub. by Reaktion Bks) Consort Bk Sales.

***Llewellyn, Nigel.** Funeral Moments in Post-Reformation England. LC 99-86298. (Illus.). 370p. (C). 2001. text Price not set. (*0-521-78257-0*) Cambridge U Pr.

Llewellyn Publications Staff. The Truth about Creative Visualization. (Llewellyn's Truth about Ser.). 32p. (Orig.). 1999. pap. 1.99 (*0-87542-353-1*) Llewellyn Pubns.

Llewellyn, Richard. How Green Was My Valley. LC 86-28621. (Hudson River Editions Ver.). 512p. 1987. 40.00 (*0-02-573420-2*, Scribners Ref) Mac Lib Ref.

— How Green Was My Valley. LC 97-10174. 1997. per. 14.00 (*0-684-82555-4*) S&S Trade.

— How Green Was My Valley. 1997. 19.10 (*0-606-12728-3*, Pub. by Turtleback) Demco.

— How Green Was My Valley. 1983. reprint ed. lib. bdg. 30.95 (*0-88411-936-X*) Amereon Ltd.

Llewellyn, Robert. Boston. Patrick, James B., ed. (Scenic Discovery Ser.). (Illus.). 128p. 1984. 30.00 (*0-89909-046-X*) Foremost Pubs.

Llewellyn, Robert, photos by. The Cathedral of St. Peter & St. Paul. LC 88-80088. (Illus.). 120p. 1988. 19.95 (*0-943231-07-8*) Howell Pr VA.

Llewellyn, S. & Greer, A. Mathematics - the Basic Skills. 5th ed. 320p. 1996. pap. 27.50 (*0-7487-2509-1*, Pub. by S Thornes Pubs) Trans-Atl Phila.

Llewellyn, S. & Greer, D. A. Mathematics-The Basic Skills. 304p. (C). 1991. 32.00 (*0-7478-0598-9*, Pub. by S Thornes Pubs) Trans-Atl Phila.

Llewellyn, S. P., jt. ed. see Broome, Annabel K.

Llewellyn, Sam. Blood Knot. Chelius, Jane, ed. 336p. (Orig.). 1993. reprint ed. mass mkt. 4.99 (*0-671-86951-5*) PB.

— Blood Orange. large type ed. 1990. 27.99 (*0-7089-2174-4*) Ulverscroft.

— Clawhammer. Chelius, Jane, ed. 384p. 1995. mass mkt. 5.50 (*0-671-78994-5*) PB.

— Clawhammer. large type ed. LC 94-10666. 516p. 1994. pap. 19.95 (*0-8161-7401-6*, G K Hall Lrg Type) Mac Lib Ref.

— Clawhammer. large type ed. 548p. 1994. 27.99 (*0-7505-0684-9*) Ulverscroft.

— Dead Reckoning. 1989. pap. 3.50 (*0-685-25346-5*) PB.

— Dead Reckoning. large type ed. 400p. 1988. 11.50 (*0-7089-1916-2*) Ulverscroft.

— Deadeye. Chelius, Jane, ed. 288p. 1992. reprint ed. mass mkt. 4.99 (*0-671-67044-1*) PB.

— Death Roll. Chelius, Jane, ed. 256p. 1991. reprint ed. pap. 3.95 (*0-671-67043-3*) PB.

— Gurney's Release. large type ed. 555p. 1981. 27.99 (*0-7089-0727-X*) Ulverscroft.

— Gurney's Revenge. large type ed. 403p. 1981. 27.99 (*0-7089-0655-9*) Ulverscroft.

— Gurney's Reward. large type ed. 467p. 1981. 11.50 (*0-7089-0699-0*) Ulverscroft.

— Maelstrom. 1996. mass mkt. 5.99 (*0-671-78997-X*, PB Trade Paper) PB.

— Riptide. Chelius, Jane, ed. 288p. 1994. mass mkt. 5.50 (*0-671-89307-6*) PB.

— Riptide. large type ed. (Charnwood Ser.). 416p. 1994. 27.99 (*0-7089-8754-0*, Charnwood) Ulverscroft.

— The Shadow in the Sands. LC 99-33913. (Illus.). 288p. 1999. pap. 14.95 (*1-57409-089-5*) Sheridan.

***Llewellyn, Sam.** Storm Force from Navarone. 248p. 1998. pap. 10.95 (*0-00-649625-3*, Pub. by HarpC) Trafalgar.

Llewellyn, Sam. Storm Force from Navarone. large type ed. 352p. 1997. pap. 22.95 (*0-7862-1068-0*) Thorndike Pr.

***Llewellyn, Sam.** Thunderbolt from Navarone. 272p. 1998. 27.00 (*0-00-225712-2*, Pub. by HarpC) Trafalgar.

— Thunderbolt from Navarone. large type ed. LC 99-45073. 1999. 26.95 (*0-7862-2162-3*) Thorndike Pr.

***Llewellyn Staff.** Daily Planetary Guide 1999: Llewellyn's Astrology Datebook. 208p. 1999. 9.95 (*1-56718-943-1*) Llewellyn Pubns.

Llewellyn Staff. Llewellyn's 1998 Magical Almanac. Ahlquist, Cynthia, ed. (Illus.). 384p. (Orig.). 1997. pap. 6.95 (*1-56718-935-0*) Llewellyn Pubns.

An Asterisk (*) at the beginning of an entry indicates that the title is appearing for the first time.

— Llewellyn's 1997 Astrological Pocket Planner: Daily Ephemeris & Aspectarian, 1996-1998. 208p. 1996. pap. text 7.95 (*1-56718-927-X*) Llewellyn Pubns.

*Llewellyn, William.** Anabolics 2000. 212p. 2000. pap. 42.95 (*0-9679304-0-5*) W Llewellyn.

Llewellyn-Williams, Hilary. Animaculture. LC 97-227970. 72p. 1997. pap. 17.95 (*1-85411-202-3*, Pub. by Seren Bks) Dufour.

— Book of Shadows. 104p. (Orig.). 1990. pap. 17.95 (*1-85411-041-1*, Pub. by Seren Bks) Dufour.

***Llewelyn-Bowen, Laurence.** Fantasy Rooms: Inspirational Designs from the BBC Series. (Illus.). 192p. 1999. 34.95 (*0-7522-1735-6*, Pub. by Boxtree) Trans-Atl Phila.

Llewelyn-Bowen, Laurence, jt. auth. see Hall, Katrina.

Llewelyn-Davies, R. & Macaulay, H. M. Hospital Planning & Administration. (Monographs: No. 54). (ENG, FRE, RUS & SPA., Illus.). 215p. 1966. pap. text 32.00 (*92-4-140054-4*, 1140054) World Health.

Llewelyn, J. Debrett's Wedding Guide: The Planning & Etiquette of a Modern Wedding. rev. ed. (Illus.). 280p. 1999. pap. 14.95 (*0-7472-5664-0*, Pub. by Headline Bk Pub) Trafalgar.

Llewelyn, John. Beyond Metaphysics? The Hermeneutic Circle in Contemporary Philosophy. LC 84-4638. 256p. (C). 1989. pap. 18.50 (*0-391-03619-X*) Humanities.

— Emmanuel Levinas: The Genealogy of Ethics. LC 94-33895. (Warwick Studies in European Philosophy Ser.). 248p. (C). 1995. pap. 22.99 (*0-415-10730-X*, C0129) Routledge.

— Emmanuel Levinas: The Genealogy of Ethics. LC 94-33895. (Warwick Studies in European Philosophy Ser.). 248p. (C). (gr. 13). 1995. 75.00 (*0-415-10729-6*, C0128) Routledge.

***Llewelyn, John.** The Hypocritical Imagination: Between Kant & Levinas LC 99-30340. (Warwick Studies in European Philosophy Ser.). 272p. 1999. pap. 25.99 (*0-415-21362-2*) Routledge.

— Hypocritical Imagination: Kant & Levinas. (Warwick Studies in European Philosophy Ser.). 272p. (C). 1999. text 75.00 (*0-415-21361-4*) Routledge.

Llewelyn, John, ed. see King-Hall, Magdalen.

Llewelyn, John, tr. see Dastur, Francoise.

Llewelyn, Morgan & Scott, Michael. Ireland: A Graphic History. 1995. pap. 16.95 (*1-85230-627-0*, Pub. by Element MA) Penguin Putnam.

Llewelyn, Robert. The Joy of the Saints: Spiritual Readings Throughout the Year. 1992. pap. 16.95 (*0-87243-191-6*) Templegate.

Llewelyn, Robert, ed. Daily Readings from the Cloud of Unknowing. (Daily Readings Ser.). 1986. pap. 4.95 (*0-87243-149-5*) Templegate.

— The Fire of Divine Love: Readings from Jean-Pierre de Caussade. LC 95-16616. (Liguori Classic Ser.). 128p. (Orig.). 1995. pap. 10.95 (*0-89243-827-4*, Liguori Triumph) Liguori Pubns.

Llewelyn, Robert, ed. The Fire of Divine Love: Readings from Jean Pierre de Causade. 128p. 1994. pap. 21.00 (*0-86012-238-7*, Pub. by Srch Pr) St Mut.

Llewelyn, Robert, ed. see Augustine, Saint.

Llewelyn, Robert, ed. see Brother Lawrence.

LLewelyn, Robert, ed. see De Caussade, Jean-Pierre.

Llewelyn, Robert, ed. see Julian of Norwich.

Llewelyn, Robert, ed. see Law, William.

LLewelyn, Robert, ed. see St. Francis de Sales.

Llewelyn, Robert, ed. see St. Francis of Assisi.

Llewelyn, Robert, ed. see St. John of the Cross.

LLewelyn, Robert, ed. see St. Teresa of Avila.

Llewelyn, Robert, ed. see St. Therese of Lisieux.

Llewelyn, S. R., ed. A Review of the Greek Inscriptions & Papyri in 1980-1981, Vol. 6. 235p. 1997. pap. 35.00 (*0-8028-4516-9*) Eerdmans.

— A Review of the Greek Inscriptions & Papyri in 1982-1983, Vol. 7. 292p. 1997. pap. 35.00 (*0-8028-4517-7*) Eerdmans.

— Review of the Greek Inscriptions & Papyri in 1984-1985, Vol. 8. 208p. 1997. pap. text 35.00 (*0-8028-4518-5*) Eerdmans.

Llewelyn, Sue, jt. ed. see Broome, Annabel K.

Llibkin, L., jt. ed. see Thalheim, B.

Lliboutry, Louis A. Very Slow Flows of Solids: Basics of Modeling in Geodynamics & Glaciology. (C). 1987. text 326.50 (*90-247-3482-7*) Kluwer Academic.

***Lliboutry, Luis.** Quantitative Geophysics & Geology. LC 99-34589. (Praxis Series in Geophysics). 415p. 1999. pap. 59.95 (*1-85233-115-1*, Pub. by Spr-Verlag) Spr-Verlag.

Llibre, J., jt. auth. see Lacomba, E. A.

Llibre, Jaume & Nunes, Ana. Separatrix Surfaces & Invariant Manifolds of a Class of Integrable Hamiltonian Systems & Their Perturbations. LC 93-39026. (Memoirs of the American Mathematical Society Ser.: No. 513). 191p. 1994. pap. 36.00 (*0-8218-2581-X*, MEMO/107/513) Am Math.

Llibre, Jaume, jt. auth. see Casasayas, Josefina.

Llibre, Juan. Mastering Visual InterDev 6. (Mastering Ser.). 1999. pap. text 39.99 (*0-7821-2454-2*) Sybex.

***Llibre, Juan T.** Professional ASP 3 Performance Tuning. 600p. 2000. pap. 49.99 (*1-86100-309-9*) Wrox Pr Inc.

***Llic, Z.** Sicilian with QB6: Dynamic Surprise Weapons. 1999. pap. text 14.95 (*0-7134-8238-9*) B T B.

***Llimbos, Anna & Sadurni, Laia.** Christmas Creations. LC 00-8583. (Illus.). 32p. 2000. 18.95 (*1-56711-437-7*) Blackbirch.

Llinares, Rick & Lloyd, Chuck. Adversary: America's Aggressor Fighter Squadrons. LC 98-86277. (Illus.). 144p. 1999. 29.95 (*0-7643-0688-X*) Schiffer.

— Warfighters No. 2: The Story of the U. S. Marine Corps Aviation Weapons & Tactics Squadron One (MAWTS-1) LC 97-68044. 352p. 1997. 59.95 (*0-7643-0329-5*) Schiffer.

***Llinas, Rodolfo.** I of the Vortex: From Neurons to Self. (Illus.). 264p. 2000. 24.95 (*0-262-12233-2*, Bradford Bks) MIT Pr.

Llinas, J. Jujol. (SPA.). 1996. pap. 24.99 (*3-8228-8770-6*) Taschen Amer.

Llinas, Jose. Jujol. 1995. pap. 24.99 (*3-8228-9760-4*) Taschen Amer.

Llinas, Josep. Josep Llinas. (Illus.). 176p. 1997. 37.50 (*0-8230-2563-2*, Whitney Lib) Watsn-Guptill.

Llinas, Rodolfo R. The Squid Giant Synapse: A Model for Chemical Transmission. LC 98-38419. (Illus.). 240p. 1999. text 85.00 (*0-19-511652-6*) OUP.

— The Workings of the Brain: Development, Memory & Perception. 171p. (C). 1989. pap. text 14.95 (*0-7167-2071-X*) W H Freeman.

Llinas, Rodolfo R. & Churchland, Patricia S., eds. The Mind-Brain Continuum: Sensory Processes. (Illus.). 329p. (C). 1996. 52.50 (*0-262-12198-0*, Bradford Bks) MIT Pr.

Llinas, Rodolfo R. & Sotelo, C., eds. The Cerebellum Revisited. (Illus.). 320p. 1992. 125.00 (*0-387-97693-0*) Spr-Verlag.

Llinas, Salvador O. Diccionari Catala-Angles. 3rd ed. (CAT & ENG.). 1088p. 1991. 59.95 (*0-7859-6498-3*) Fr & Eur.

Llines, Salvador O. & Buxton, A. English-Catalan Dictionary: Diccionari Angles-Catala. 3rd ed. (CAT & ENG.). 1088p. 1991. write for info. (*0-7859-4903-8*) Fr & Eur.

Llistosella-Matzky, I., jt. auth. see Von Kunhardt, A.

Lliteras, D. S. Half Hidden by Twilight: A Novel. LC 95-141122. 176p. (Orig.). 1994. pap. 9.95 (*1-57174-000-7*) Hampton Roads Pub Co.

— In a Warrior's Romance. (Illus.). 208p. 1991. pap. 11.95 (*1-878901-05-2*) Hampton Roads Pub Co.

Lliteras, D. S. In the Heart of Things. 176p. 1992. pap. 8.95 (*1-878901-22-2*) Hampton Roads Pub Co.

Lliteras, D. S. Into the Ashes. 208p. 1993. pap. 9.95 (*1-878901-77-X*) Hampton Roads Pub Co.

— Judas the Gentile. LC 99-71617. 240p. 1999. text 19.95 (*1-57174-144-5*) Hampton Roads Pub Co.

— The Thieves of Golgotha. LC 98-72215. 192p. 1998. 19.95 (*1-57174-085-6*) Hampton Roads Pub Co.

Lllingworth, Mark. Real-Life Math Problems. LC 96-214357. 136p. 1996. pap. 15.95 (*0-590-48804-X*) Scholastic Inc.

Llobera, Jose, jt. auth. see Brambilla, Massimo.

Llobera, Josep R. The God of Modernity: The Development of Nationalism in Western Europe. Nelson, Brian, ed. (European Studies Ser.). 229p. 1994. 49.50 (*0-85496-921-7*, Pub. by Berg Pubs); pap. 19.50 (*0-85496-940-3*, Pub. by Berg Pubs) NYU Pr.

Llombar, Felipe V. Garin, see Garin Llombar, Felipe V.

Llombart, Felipe V. Treasures of the Prado. (Tiny Folios Ser.). (Illus.). 312p. 1996. pap. 11.95 (*1-55859-558-9*) Abbeville Pr.

Llompart, Gabriel. Pintura Gotica en Mallorca. (SPA., Illus.). 128p. 1993. 100.00 (*84-343-0477-5*) Elliots Bks.

Llompart, Miguel F. Diccionario de l'Art I Els Oficis de la Construccion. 5th ed. (SPA.). 440p. 1988. pap. 69.95 (*0-7859-5107-5*) Fr & Eur.

Llopis, A., jt. auth. see Buck, C.

Llorach, E. Alarcos. Gramatica de la Lengua Espanola. (SPA.). 389p. 1994. pap. 49.95 (*0-7859-9178-6*) Fr & Eur.

Llorenc, jt. auth. see Castellanos, Isabel.

Llorens, Lela A. & Rubin, Eli Z. Developing Ego Functions in Disturbed Children: Occupational Therapy in Milieu. LC 66-24385. (Lafayette Clinic Monographs in Psychiatry: No. 1). (Illus.). 147p. (Orig.). reprint ed. pap. 45.60 (*0-7837-3638-X*, 204350500009) Bks Demand.

Llorens, Paula A., ed. see Jones, Deena M.

Llorens, Paula A., ed. see Sanders, Pamelaia.

***Llorens, Thomas.** Manolo Valdes. (SPA.). 2000. text 75.00 (*958-9393-79-9*, Pub. by Villegas Ed) St Martin.

Llorens, Washington. Humor, Epigram & Satire in Puerto Rican Literature. (Puerto Rico Ser.). 1979. lib. bdg. 59.95 (*0-8490-2941-4*) Gordon Pr.

— La Magia de la Palabra. LC 80-19972. (Coleccion Mente y Palabra). (SPA.). x, 171p. 1981. 6.00 (*0-8477-0576-5*); pap. 5.00 (*0-8477-0577-3*) U of PR Pr.

Llorente, Jorge. La Distr. de los Seres Vivos. (Ciencia para Todos Ser.). (SPA.). pap. 6.99 (*968-16-5088-3*, Pub. by Fondo) Continental Bk.

Llorente, Pilar M. The Apprentice. (Illus.). 112p. (YA). (gr. 4-7). 1994. pap. 4.95 (*0-374-40432-1*) FS&G.

Llorente, Segundo. Memoirs of a Yukon Priest. LC 89-27434. (Illus.). 236p. 1990. pap. 17.95 (*0-87840-494-5*) Georgetown U Pr.

Llosa, J., ed. Relativistic Action at a Distance: Classical & Quantum Aspects, Barcelona, Spain 1981, Proceedings. (Lecture Notes in Physics Ser.: Vol. 162). 263p. 1982. 31.95 (*0-387-11573-0*) Spr-Verlag.

Llosa, Ricardo P. Rafael Soriano & the Poetics of Light. (Illus.). 204p. 1998. 60.00 (*0-939193-24-8*) Edit Concepts.

Llove, T. R. How to Be Macho. 328p. (Orig.). 1984. pap. 14.95 (*0-918483-09-3*) Galahad Pub.

— How to Satisfy a Woman. 123p. (Orig.). 1985. pap. 9.95 (*0-918483-17-4*) Galahad Pub.

Llover, Claudia Cordova de, see de Llover, Claudia Cordova, ed.

Llowarch, Tina, tr. see DeJong-Kramer, E.

Lloy, Owen, et al. An Atlas of Mortality in Scotland: Including the Geography of Selected Socio-Economic Characteristics. (Illus.). 192p. 1987. 140.00 (*0-7099-4122-6*, Pub. by C Helm) Routldge.

Lloyd. Building Law Reports. 1989. pap. text. write for info. (*0-582-04039-6*, Pub. by Addison-Wesley) Longman.

— Building Law Reports. 46th ed. 1990. pap. text. write for info. (*0-582-04038-8*, Pub. by Addison-Wesley) Longman.

— Building Law Reports, Vol. 144. 1989. pap. text. write for info. (*0-582-04040-X*, Pub. by Addison-Wesley) Longman.

— Communication Skills for Medicine. 1996. pap. text 17.95 (*0-443-05168-2*, W B Saunders Co) Harcrt Hlth Sci Grp.

— Secured Transactions. 1988. teacher ed. write for info. (*0-318-67319-3*) Bender.

— Secured Transactions. (C). 1993. 48.00 (*0-8205-0486-6*, 721) Bender.

— Typing 75. 5th ed. 1983. 24.36 (*0-07-038325-1*) McGraw.

— World Regional Geography: Patterns & Issues. 256p. 1998. pap. text 17.00 (*0-536-01883-9*) Pearson Custom.

Lloyd & Freeman, M. C. Lloyd's Introduction to Jurisprudence. 6th ed. 1994. pap. text 55.00 (*0-421-45680-9*, Pub. by Sweet & Maxwl) Gaunt.

Lloyd & Jackiewicz. World Regional Geography. 264p. 1998. pap. text 69.00 (*0-536-01653-4*) Pearson Custom.

Lloyd, jt. auth. see Seiber.

Lloyd, ed. see de Vega, Lope.

Lloyd, A. B. Herodotus Bk. II: Commentary 1-98. iv, 397p. 1994. 154.00 (*90-04-04182-6*, EPRO, 43/2) Brill Academic Pubs.

— Herodotus Bk. II: Commentary 99-182. viii, 330p. 1993. 134.00 (*90-04-07737-5*, EPRO, 43/3) Brill Academic Pubs.

— Herodotus Bk. II: Introduction. xv, 194p. 1994. 87.00 (*90-04-04181-8*, EPRO, 43/1) Brill Academic Pubs.

Lloyd, A. C. The Anatomy of Neoplatonism. 208p. 1998. reprint ed. pap. text 24.95 (*0-19-823806-1*) OUP.

Lloyd, A. L., ed. see Brailoiu, Constantin.

Lloyd, A. L., tr. see Fallada, Hans.

Lloyd, A. L., tr. see Garcia Lorca, Federico.

Lloyd, A. R. Sea Keeping Ship Behavior in Rough Weather. 550p. 1989. text 99.95 (*0-470-21232-2*) P-H.

— Wingfoot. large type ed. 1994. 27.99 (*0-7089-3188-X*) Ulverscroft.

Lloyd, Al. Enter to Face the Dragon: Exercising Proper Discernment As Your Christian Circles Develop. 266p. 1999. pap. 14.99 (*0-7392-0159-X*, PO3109) Morris Pubng.

Lloyd, Alan. The Hundred Years War. LC 77-379172. 176 p. 1977. write for info. (*0-246-10869-X*) Grfton HrprCllns.

Lloyd, Alan, ed. Battle in Antiquity. 250p. 1996. 49.50 (*0-7156-2695-7*, Pub. by Classical Pr) David Brown.

— What Is a God? Essays on the Nature of Greek Divinity. LC 98-124501. 181p. 1997. 49.50 (*0-7156-2779-1*, Pub. by Classical Pr) David Brown.

Lloyd, Alan B., ed. see Blackman, Alyward M.

Lloyd, Alan C. The Anatomy of Neoplatonism. 208p. 1990. 65.00 (*0-19-824229-8*) OUP.

Lloyd, Alan C. & Krevolin, R. You Learn to Type. 1966. text 26.52 (*0-07-038160-7*) McGraw.

Lloyd, Alan C., et al. Gregg College Typing. 5th ed. (Gregg Typing Ser.: No. 5, Kit 3). 1984. text 51.06 (*0-07-038324-3*) McGraw.

— Gregg College Typing: Complete Course. 5th ed. (College Typing Ser.: No. 5). 368p. 1984. text 61.05 (*0-07-038320-0*); 23.19 (*0-07-038327-8*) McGraw.

— Gregg College Typing: Keyboarding Course. 6th ed. (Series 6). (C). 1989. teacher ed. 14.21 (*0-07-048114-8*) McGraw.

— Gregg College Typing: Typing 75, Basic Kit. 5th ed. (Series 5). 320p. 1983. text 66.60 (*0-07-038322-7*) McGraw.

— Gregg Typing, Complete Course. 8th ed. (Series Eight). 1986. text 20.32 (*0-07-038342-1*); pap. text 25.24 (*0-07-038344-8*); pap. text 20.32 (*0-07-038343-X*) McGraw.

— Gregg Typing, Personal Keyboarding & Applications. (Series Eight). 160p. 1987. pap. text 15.96 (*0-07-038341-3*) McGraw.

— Personal Typing. 4th ed. (Illus.). 1978. text 19.96 (*0-07-038208-5*) McGraw.

— Selective Practice Typing Drills. 1974. text 10.88 (*0-07-038147-X*) McGraw.

— Series Seven Typing Complete Course, Gregg Typing. 496p. (gr. 11-12). 1982. text 27.96 (*0-07-038280-8*) McGraw.

— Typing One: General Course Gregg Typing. LC 81-15629. (Gregg Typing Ser.: No. 7). (Illus.). 288p. 1982. text 21.96 (*0-07-038281-6*) McGraw.

— Typing Power Drills. 3rd ed. LC 83-8592. (Illus.). 96p. 1984. text 12.96 (*0-07-038176-3*) McGraw.

— Typing Skill Drives. 2nd ed. 1974. text 13.96 (*0-07-038161-5*) McGraw.

— Typing Two: Advanced Course Gregg Typing. LC 81-15629. (Gregg Typing Ser.: No. 7). (Illus.). 288p. 1982. text 21.96 (*0-07-038282-4*) McGraw.

Lloyd, Albert. Etymologisches Woerterbuch des Althochdeutschen, 8 vols., Set. (GER.). 350.00 (*0-7859-8411-9*, 3525207670) Fr & Eur.

Lloyd, Albert L. Anatomy of the Verb: The Gothic Verb As a Model for a Unified Theory of Aspect, Actional Types, & Verbal Velocity. (Studies in Language Companion Ser.: No. 4). x, 351p. 1979. 71.00 (*90-272-3003-X*, 4) J Benjamins Pubng Co.

Lloyd, Alexander. The Jedera Adventure. 160p. (J). 1994. pap. 3.99 (*0-440-91004-8*) Dell.

Lloyd, Alfred H. Dynamic Idealism. LC 75-3243. reprint ed. 32.50 (*0-404-59233-3*) AMS Pr.

Lloyd, Alison, ed. The Painter in Glass. 74p. 1993. pap. 37.95 (*0-8464-4680-4*) Beekman Pubs.

— The Painter in Glass. 74p. 1993. pap. 38.00 (*0-86383-976-2*, Pub. by Gomer Pr) St Mut.

***Lloyd, Alwyn T.** A Cold War Legacy: A Tribute to the Strategic Air Command, 1946-1992. LC 99-85940. (Illus.). 760p. 2000. 55.00 (*1-57510-052-5*, 129961AE, Pub. by Pictorial Hist) Motorbooks Intl.

Lloyd, Alwyn T. Detail & Scale: B-52 Stratofortress, Vol. 27. (Illus.). 72p. 1988. pap. 10.95 (*0-8306-8037-3*, 25037) McGraw-Hill Prof.

— Details & Scale, the B-29 Superfortress, Pt. 2 Derivatives Vol. 25. (Illus.). 78p. (Orig.). 1987. pap. 10.95 (*0-8306-8035-7*, 25035) McGraw-Hill Prof.

***Lloyd, Ann.** Just 'Til I Finish This Chapter... Tips, Quotes & Practical Advice for Nurturing Young Readers. LC 00-104192. 148p. 2000. pap. 12.95 (*0-9701182-9-5*, JTI-01) Know More.

Lloyd, Ann. Principles of Health Care Ethics. Gillon, Raanan, ed. LC 92-23746. 1152p. 1994. 477.50 (*0-471-93033-4*) Wiley.

***Lloyd, Ann W. & Wegman, William.** Strange but True: William Wegman. Keough, Jeffrey, ed. LC 98-74606. (Illus.). 45p. 1998. pap. 20.00 (*0-9628905-7-X*) MA Collge Art.

Lloyd, Annie. Beginning Welsh Research. rev. ed. 188p. 1996. pap. text 20.00 (*0-9644567-4-5*) A Lloyd.

— Beginning Welsh Research. 3rd rev. ed. 155p. 1998. pap. 20.00 (*0-9644567-6-1*) A Lloyd.

— How to Plan a Research Trip to Wales. 100p. (Orig.). 1995. pap. text 15.00 (*0-9644567-1-0*) A Lloyd.

— Welsh Place & Farm Names. 52p. 1998. pap. 12.00 (*0-9644567-5-3*) A Lloyd.

— Welsh Surnames & Given Names & Their Meanings. 144p. (Orig.). 1996. 15.00 (*0-9644567-3-7*) A Lloyd.

Lloyd, Arnold. Quaker Social History: Sixteen Sixty-Nine to Seventeen Thirty-Eight. LC 79-4398. 207p. 1979. reprint ed. lib. bdg. 59.50 (*0-313-20943-X*, LLQU, Greenwood Pr) Greenwood.

Lloyd, Arthur. The Creed of Half Japan: Historical Sketches of Japanese Buddhism. LC 78-70095. reprint ed. 40.50 (*0-404-17344-6*) AMS Pr.

***Lloyd, B. E.** Lights & Shades in San Francisco. LC 99-41095. (Illus.). 544p. 1999. pap. 45.00 (*1-893163-10-5*) Berkeley Hills.

Lloyd, B. M. Not a Total Waste: The True Story of a Mother, a Son & AIDS. LC 93-93482. (Illus.). 270p. 1994. pap. 16.95 (*0-88962-540-9*) Mosaic.

Lloyd, Barbara. The Colours of Southern India. LC 99-70865. (Illus.). 160p. 1999. pap. 27.50 (*0-500-28134-3*) Norton.

— The Colours of Thailand. LC 96-61172. (Illus.). 160p. (Orig.). 1997. pap. 19.95 (*0-500-27930-6*, Pub. by Thames Hudson) Norton.

Lloyd, Barbara, jt. auth. see Archer, John.

Lloyd, Barbara, jt. ed. see Duveen, Gerard.

Lloyd, Barbara B., et al. Smoking in Adolescence: Images & Identities. LC 97-37982. (Illus.). 232p. (C). 1998. 75.00 (*0-415-17859-2*); pap. 24.99 (*0-415-17860-6*) Routledge.

Lloyd, Barbara B., jt. ed. see Rosch, Eleanor.

Lloyd, Beth. Explore Jersey. 128p. 1987. pap. 30.00 (*0-86368-007-0*) St Mut.

Lloyd, Beverly. Magic of Christmas. 16p. (J). 1996. pap. 3.95 (*0-87718-051-2*, 12007E) Willis Music Co.

Lloyd-Bostock, Sally M. & Clifford, Brian R., eds. Evaluating Witness Evidence: Recent Psychological Research & New Perspectives. LC 82-7107. 315p. reprint ed. pap. 97.70 (*0-7837-4410-2*, 204415300012) Bks Demand.

Lloyd, Brian. Left Out: Pragmatism, Exceptionalism, & the Poverty of American Marxism, 1890-1922. LC 96-47995. (New Studies in American Intellectual & Cultural History). 456p. 1997. text 45.00 (*0-8018-5541-1*) Johns Hopkins.

Lloyd, Bruce, ed. Creating Value Through Acquisitions, Demergers, Buyouts & Alliances. LC 97-13599. (Best of Long Range Planning Ser.: No. 2). 440p. 1997. 74.00 (*0-08-043055-4*, Pergamon Pr) Elsevier.

— Entrepreneurship: Creating & Managing New Ventures. (Best of Long Range Planning Ser.: Vol. 1, No. 2). 190p. 1989. pap. text 48.25 (*0-08-037407-7*) Elsevier.

— Entrepreneurship: Creating & Managing New Ventures. (Best of Long Range Planning Ser.: Vol. 1, No. 2). 190p. 1989. text 100.75 (*0-08-037108-6*, Pergamon Pr) Elsevier.

Lloyd, Bryant. Baseball: Batting. (Play It Like a Pro Ser.). 32p. (J). (gr. 2-5). 1997. lib. bdg. 20.50 (*1-57103-184-7*) Rourke Pr.

— Baseball: Field & Equipment. (Play It Like a Pro Ser.). 32p. (J). (gr. 2-5). 1997. lib. bdg. 20.60 (*1-57103-185-5*) Rourke Pr.

— Baseball: Pitching. (Play It Like a Pro Ser.). 32p. (J). (gr. 2-5). 1997. lib. bdg. 20.60 (*1-57103-186-3*) Rourke Pr.

— Baseball: Rules of the Game. LC 97-17456. (Baseball Ser.). 1997. lib. bdg. 17.27 (*1-57103-188-X*) Rourke Pr.

— Baseball: Rules of the Game, 6 bks., Set, Reading Level 3. (Play It Like a Pro-Baseball Ser.). (Illus.). 24p. (J). (gr. 2-5). 1989. lib. bdg. 12.95 (*0-86625-188-X*) Rourke Pubns.

— Baseball: Run, Throw & Catch. (Baseball Ser.). 32p. (J). (gr. 2-5). 1997. lib. bdg. 20.60 (*1-57103-189-8*) Rourke Pr.

— Baseball: The Positions. (Play It Like a Pro Ser.). 32p. (J). (gr. 2-5). 1997. lib. bdg. 20.60 (*1-57103-187-1*) Rourke Pr.

— Basketball: Court & Equipment. LC 97-13009. (Play It Like a Pro-Basketball Ser.). (Illus.). 24p. (J). (gr. 2-5). 1997. lib. bdg. 18.60 (*1-55916-224-4*) Rourke Bk Co.

— Basketball: Pass, Shoot & Dribble. LC 97-8438. (Play It Like a Pro-Basketball Ser.). (Illus.). 24p. (J). (gr. 2-5). 1997. lib. bdg. 18.60 (*1-55916-227-9*) Rourke Bk Co.

— Basketball: Rules of the Game. LC 97-8437. (Play It Like a Pro-Basketball Ser.). (Illus.). 24p. (J). (gr. 2-5). 1997. lib. bdg. 18.60 (*1-55916-228-7*) Rourke Bk Co.

— Basketball: The Defense. LC 97-13012. (Play It Like a Pro-Basketball Ser.). (Illus.). 24p. (J). (gr. 2-5). 1997. lib. bdg. 18.60 (*1-55916-225-2*) Rourke Bk Co.

— Basketball: The Fundamentals. LC 97-8439. (Play It Like a Pro-Basketball Ser.). (Illus.). 24p. (J). (gr. 2-5). 1997. lib. bdg. 18.60 (*1-55916-226-0*) Rourke Bk Co.

— Basketball: The Offense. LC 97-8436. (Play It Like a Pro-Basketball Ser.). (Illus.). 24p. (J). (gr. 2-5). 1997. lib. bdg. 18.60 (*1-55916-229-5*) Rourke Bk Co.

— Football: Equipment. LC 97-766. (Play It Like a Pro-Football Ser.). (Illus.). 24p. (J). (gr. 2-5). 1997. lib. bdg. 18.60 (*1-55916-212-0*) Rourke Bk Co.

— Football: Pass, Punt & Kick. LC 97-767. (Play It Like a Pro-Football Ser.). (Illus.). 24p. (J). (gr. 2-5). 1997. lib. bdg. 18.60 (*1-55916-210-4*) Rourke Bk Co.

— Football: Rules of the Game. LC 97-4238. (Play It Like a Pro Ser.). (J). 1997. lib. bdg. 18.60 (*1-55916-214-7*) Rourke Bk Co.

— Football: Rules of the Game. (Play It Like a Pro-Football Ser.). (Illus.). 24p. (J). (gr. 2-5). 1997. lib. bdg. 18.60 (*1-55916-209-0*) Rourke Bk Co.

— Football: The Defense. LC 97-778. (Play It Like a Pro-Football Ser.). (Illus.). 24p. (J). (gr. 2-5). 1997. lib. bdg. 18.60 (*1-55916-211-2*) Rourke Bk Co.

— Football: The Fundamentals. LC 97-777. (Play It Like a Pro-Football Ser.). (Illus.). 24p. (J). (gr. 2-5). 1997. lib. bdg. 18.60 (*1-55916-215-5*) Rourke Bk Co.

— Football: The Offense. LC 97-765. (Play It Like a Pro-Football Ser.). (Illus.). 24p. (J). (gr. 2-5). 1997. lib. bdg. 18.60 (*1-55916-213-9*) Rourke Bk Co.

— Martial Arts - Physical Development. LC 98-22411. (Martial Arts Ser.). (J). 1998. (*1-57103-231-2*) Rourke Pr.

— Martial Arts - Techniques. LC 98-22415. (Martial Arts Ser.). (J). 1998. (*1-57103-230-4*) Rourke Pr.

— Martial Arts... Personal Development. LC 98-22413. (Martial Arts Ser.). (J). 1998. (*1-57103-229-0*) Rourke Pr.

— Martial Arts... The Class: The Class. LC 98-22420. (Martial Arts Ser.). (J). 1998. 18.60 (*1-57103-226-6*) Rourke Pr.

— Martial Arts... The History. LC 98-20430. (Martial Arts Ser.). (J). 1998. (*1-57103-228-2*) Rourke Pr.

— Martial Arts... The Student. LC 98-22412. (Martial Arts Ser.). (J). 1998. (*1-57103-227-4*) Rourke Pr.

Lloyd, C. Forensic Psychiatry for Health Professionals. 232p. 1994. pap. text 47.75 (*1-56593-183-1*, 0498) Thomson Learn.

Lloyd, C., jt. auth. see Geffner, Robert.

Lloyd, Camille, jt. ed. see Hendrie, Hugh C.

Lloyd, Carol. Creating a Life Worth Living. LC 97-6822. 336p. 1997. pap. 14.00 (*0-06-095243-1*, Perennial) HarperTrade.

***Lloyd, Carol.** Shadows of Me. 1999. pap. write for info. (*1-58235-263-1*) Watermrk Pr.

Lloyd, Catherine. Discourses of Antiracism in France. (Research in Ethnic Relations Ser.). 284p. 1998. text 67.95 (*1-84014-345-2*, Pub. by Ashgate Pub) Ashgate Pub Co.

Lloyd, Charles. Edmund Oliver, 1798. LC 90-31305. (Revolution & Romanticism Ser.). 568p. 1990. reprint ed. 65.00 (*1-85477-051-9*) Continuum.

Lloyd, Charles, ed. The Roman Family: A Bridge to Roman Culture, Values & Literature. 191p. 1991. spiral bd. 13.75 (*0-939507-35-8*, B308) Amer Classical.

Lloyd, Charles W. Arts & Crafts Movement. 144p. 1995. 19.98 (*0-7858-0456-0*) Bk Sales Inc.

Lloyd, Charlotte, tr. see Fallada, Hans.

Lloyd, Chris & Beard, Jeff. Managing Classroom Collaboration. (Cassell Practical Handbooks Ser.). (Illus.). 128p. 1995. pap. 39.95 (*0-304-32988-6*) Continuum.

Lloyd, Christoper. Fra Angelico. (Color Library). (Illus.). 128p. (C). 1994. reprint ed. pap. 14.95 (*0-7148-2785-1*, Pub. by Phaidon Press) Phaidon Pr.

Lloyd, Christopher. The Adventurous Gardener. (Illus.). 256p. 1998. reprint ed. pap. 16.95 (*1-55821-757-6*, 17576) Lyons Pr.

***Lloyd, Christopher.** Ayme: Uranus/la Tete Des Autres. 80p. 1999. pap. 35.00 (*0-85261-445-4*, Pub. by U of Glasgow) St Mut.

Lloyd, Christopher. British Seaman. LC 76-118123. (Illus.). 319p. 1975. 32.50 (*0-8386-7708-8*) Fairleigh Dickinson.

— A Catalogue of the Earlier Italian Paintings in the Ashmolean Museum. (Illus.). 1977. 39.00 (*0-19-817342-3*) OUP.

***Lloyd, Christopher.** Christopher Lloyd's Garden Flowers: Perennials, Bulbs, Grasses, Ferns. (Illus.). 448p. 2000. 39.95 (*0-88192-492-X*) Timber.

— Christopher Lloyd's Gardening Year. (Illus.). 224p. 1999. 45.00 (*0-7112-1533-2*, Pub. by F Lincoln) Antique Collect.

Lloyd, Christopher. Gardener Cook. (Illus.). 256p. 1998. 29.50 (*1-57223-136-X*, 136X) Willow Creek Pr.

— In My Garden. 1995. pap. 22.00 (*0-671-51106-8*) S&S Trade.

— J-K Huysmans & the Fin-de-Siecle Novel. 1991. text 68.00 (*0-7486-0171-6*, Pub. by Edinburgh U Pr) Col U Pr.

— J-K Huysmans & the Fin-de-Siecle Novel. 192p. 1992. pap. 25.00 (*0-7486-0234-8*, Pub. by Edinburgh U Pr) Col U Pr.

— Lord Cochrane: Seaman, Radical, Liberator. LC 98-6484. 1998. 25.00 (*0-8050-5986-5*); pap. 14.00 (*0-8050-5569-X*, Owl) H Holt & Co.

— Observer's Good Gardening Guide. 1983. 25.95 (*0-03-063261-7*) Holt R&W.

Lloyd, Christopher. Other Peoples' Gardens. 224p. 1997. pap. 22.95 (*0-14-023860-3*, Pub. by Pnguin Bks Ltd) Trafalgar.

Lloyd, Christopher. Pacific Horizons, the Exploration of the Pacific Before Captain Cook. LC 75-41177. reprint ed. 37.50 (*0-404-14710-0*) AMS Pr.

— The Paintings in the Royal Collection. LC 99-70868. (Royal Collection). (Illus.). 320p. 1999. pap. 18.95 (*0-500-97480-2*, Pub. by Thames Hudson) Norton.

— Pissarro. (Color Library). (Illus.). 128p. (C). 1994. reprint ed. pap. 14.95 (*0-7148-2729-0*, Pub. by Phaidon Press) Phaidon Pr.

— The Quest for Albion: Monarchy & the Patronage of British Painting. LC 98-61116. (Illus.). 128p. 1999. pap. 27.50 (*0-500-97476-4*, Pub. by Thames Hudson) Norton.

— The Structures of History. LC 92-32022. (Studies in Social Discontinuity). 272p. 1993. 59.95 (*0-631-18464-3*) Blackwell Pubs.

— The Well-Tempered Garden. LC 97-10927. (Horticulture Garden Classics Ser.). 479p. 1997. pap. 18.95 (*1-55821-593-X*, 1593X) Lyons Pr.

— The Year at Great Dixter. 1999. pap. 12.95 (*0-14-046744-0*) Viking Penguin.

Lloyd, Christopher, ed. Studies on Camille Pissarro. (Illus.). 192p. 1986. pap. 37.50 (*0-7102-0928-2*, 09882, Routledge Thoemms) Routledge.

Lloyd, Christopher & Bird, Richard. The Cottage Garden. LC 98-51595. (Living Ser.). 192p. 1999. pap. text 13.95 (*0-7894-4305-8*) DK Pub Inc.

Lloyd, Christopher & Remington, Vanessa. Masterpieces in Little Portrait Miniatures: From the Collection of Her Majesty Queen Elizabeth II. LC 97-117011. (Illus.). 192p. 1997. 99.00 (*0-85115-694-0*) Boydell & Brewer.

Lloyd, Christopher & Rice, Graham. Garden Flowers from Seed. (Illus.). 312p. 1994. pap. 22.95 (*0-88192-296-X*) Timber.

Lloyd, Christopher & Thurley, Simon. Henry VIII: Images of a Tudor King. LC 96-140902. (Illus.). 128p. 1996. pap. text 14.95 (*0-7148-2699-5*, Pub. by Phaidon Press) Phaidon Pr.

Lloyd, Christopher, et al. Italian Paintings before 1600 in the Art Institute of Chicago: A Catalogue of the Collection. LC 93-12237. (Illus.). 312p. 1993. 95.00 (*0-86559-110-5*) Art Inst Chi.

Lloyd, Christopher, jt. auth. see Chatto, Beth.

Lloyd, Christopher, ed. see Popham, A. E.

Lloyd, Christopher J. The Statistical Analysis of Categorical Data. LC 98-39058. (Series in Probability & Statistics). 468p. 1999. 99.95 (*0-471-29008-4*) Wiley.

Lloyd, Chuck, jt. auth. see Linares, Rick.

Lloyd, Chuck, jt. auth. see Llinares, Rick.

Lloyd, Claire. Sensual Living. (Illus.). 160p. 1998. 35.00 (*1-85029-934-X*, Pub. by Conran Octopus) Antique Collect.

Lloyd, Clare S., et al. The Status of Seabirds in Britain & Ireland. (Illus.). 384p. 1991. text 39.00 (*0-85661-061-5*, 784661) Acad Pr.

Lloyd, Clive W., ed. The Cytoskeletal Basis of Plant Growth & Form. (Illus.). 344p. 1991. text 104.00 (*0-12-453770-7*) Acad Pr.

Lloyd, Clive W., jt. ed. see Hyams, Jeremy S.

Lloyd, Colin, jt. auth. see Sujita, Etsuko.

***Lloyd, Craig.** Eugene Bullard: Black Expatriate in Jazz-Age Paris. LC 99-55336. 2000. 26.95 (*0-8203-2192-3*) U of Ga Pr.

Lloyd, Cynthia B., ed. Fertility, Family Size & Structure: Consequences for Families & Children. 522p. 1993. pap. 18.00 (*0-87834-077-7*) Population Coun.

Lloyd, Cynthia B. & Marquette, Catherine M. Directory of Surveys in Developing Countries: Data on Families & Households, 1975-1992. LC 92-62578. 1992. pap. 25.00 (*0-87834-074-2*) Population Coun.

Lloyd, D., et al, eds. Biochemistry & Molecular Biology of "Anaerobic" Protozoa. xii, 290p. 1989. pap. text 156.00 (*3-7186-4943-8*) Gordon & Breach.

Lloyd, D., jt. auth. see Evans, Harold J.

Lloyd, D., jt. ed. see Boffey, S. A.

Lloyd, D. A. Electrostatic Precipitator Handbook. (Illus.). 232p. 1988. 132.00 (*0-85274-492-7*) IOP Pub.

Lloyd, D. H. Dreams, Myths & Other Realities. 32p. (Orig.). 1984. pap. 3.00 (*0-917554-24-8*) Maelstrom.

Lloyd, D. Myrddin, tr. see Gruffydd, W. J.

Lloyd, Dan. Simple Minds. 280p. 1989. 35.00 (*0-262-12140-9*, Bradford Bks) MIT Pr.

Lloyd, Dan S. Leading Today's Funerals: A Pastoral Guide for Improving Bereavement Ministry. LC 96-1639. 128p. (Orig.). 1997. pap. 12.99 (*0-8010-9032-6*) Baker Bks.

Lloyd, David. Anomalous States: Irish Writing & the Post-Colonial Moment. LC 93-3105. (Post-Contemporary Interventions Ser.). 184p. 1993. text 49.95 (*0-8223-1326-X*); pap. text 17.95 (*0-8223-1344-8*) Duke.

— Duck. LC 87-26200. (Illus.). 32p. (J). (ps). 1988. lib. bdg. 12.89 (*0-397-32275-5*) HarpC Child Bks.

— The I AM Discourses. LC 85-61043. (Saint Germain Ser.: Vol. 10). (Illus.). 417p. 1980. 26.00 (*1-878891-44-8*) St Germain Press Inc.

***Lloyd, David.** Ireland after History. LC 99-32217. (Critical Conditions Ser.: Vol. 9). 240p. 2000. pap. 25.00 (*0-268-01218-0*, Pub. by U of Notre Dame Pr) Chicago Distribution Ctr.

— Polly Molly Woof Woof: A Book about Being Happy. LC 99-34808. (Illus.). (J). 2000. 13.99 (*0-7636-0755-X*) Candlewick Pr.

Lloyd, David. The Sneeze. LC 85-46022. (Illus.). 32p. (J). (ps-2). 1986. lib. bdg. 11.89 (*0-397-32196-1*) HarpC Child Bks.

— The Stopwatch. LC 85-23847. (Illus.). 32p. (J). (ps-2). 1986. lib. bdg. 11.89 (*0-397-32193-7*) HarpC Child Bks.

Lloyd, David, ed. Flow Cytometry in Microbiology. LC 92-38958. 1993. 119.00 (*0-387-19796-6*) Spr-Verlag.

— The Urgency of Identity: Contemporary English-Language Poetry from Wales. (TriQuarterly Bks.). 200p. (Orig.). 1994. 39.95 (*0-8101-5032-8*); pap. 14.95 (*0-8101-5007-7*) Northwestern U Pr.

Lloyd, David & Lowe, Lisa, eds. The Politics of Culture in the Shadow of Capital. LC 97-8900. (Post-Contemporary Interventions Ser.). 1997. lib. bdg. 69.95 (*0-8223-2033-9*) Duke.

Lloyd, David & Lowe, Lisa, eds. The Politics of Culture in the Shadow of Capital. LC 97-8900. (Post-Contemporary Interventions Ser.). 593p. 1997. pap. text 23.95 (*0-8223-2046-0*) Duke.

Lloyd, David & Rosenfeld, Sydney. The Senator. Meserve, Walter J. & Meserve, Mollie A., eds. (When Conscience Trod the Stage Ser.). 1998. pap., spiral bd. 4.95 (*0-937657-43-3*) Feedbk Theabks & Prospero.

Lloyd, David & Rossi, Ernest L., eds. Ultradian Rhythms in Life Processes: An Inquiry into Fundamental Principles of Chronobiology & Psychobiology. LC 92-2298. xiii, 419p. 1992. 227.95 (*0-387-19746-X*) Spr-Verlag.

***Lloyd, David, et al.** Practical Equine Dermatology. (Illus.). 160p. 2001. pap. text 76.95 (*0-632-04807-7*, Pub. by Blckwell Science) Iowa St U Pr.

Lloyd, David, jt. auth. see Moore, Alan.

Lloyd, David, jt. auth. see Thomas, Paul.

Lloyd, David W. Battlefield Tourism: Pilgrimage & the Commemoration of the Great War in Britain, Australia & Canada. LC 98-230627. (Legacy of the Great War Ser.). 192p. 1998. 65.00 (*1-85973-174-0*, Pub. by Berg Pubs); pap. 16.50 (*1-85973-179-1*, Pub. by Berg Pubs) NYU Pr.

— The Making of English Towns. (Illus.). 290p. 1998. pap. 35.00 (*0-575-06576-1*, Pub. by V Gollancz) Trafalgar.

Lloyd, David W., ed. Traditional Native American Healing & Child Sexual Abuse. 62p. (Orig.). (C). 1994. pap. text 30.00 (*0-7881-1306-2*) DIANE Pub.

Lloyd, David W., jt. auth. see Clancy, Kevin J.

Lloyd-Davies, R. W. A Color Atlas of Urology. 2nd ed. 288p. (C). (gr. 13). 1993. 97.00 (*0-7234-1912-4*, Pub. by Wolfe Pub) Mosby Inc.

Lloyd-Davies, Victoria, jt. auth. see Dettmer, Anne.

Lloyd, Debbie. Time Management Skills. Edwards, Judith, ed. 72p. 1994. pap. text 5.95 (*1-56309-102-X*, N943116, New Hope) Womans Mission Union.

Lloyd, Dennis. Idea of Law. 1992. pap. 19.95 (*0-14-013830-7*, Pub. by Pnguin Bks Ltd) Trafalgar.

Lloyd, Dennis, ed. see Coupe, Ray & Parish, Roberta.

Lloyd, Diane V. & Stavrou, Marta B. The Physician's Assistant, No. 1210-1211. 1977. 10.00 (*0-686-19685-6*, Sage Prdcls Pr) Sage.

Lloyd, Donna H. The Confessions of a Heretic. LC 95-71961. 286p. Date not set. 24.95 (*0-9627291-4-0*) Deltaran Pub.

— The Physics of Metaphysics: Everything You Wanted to Know about the Universe & Your Place in It, but Did Not Know What to Ask. (Illus.). 300p. (C). 1993. pap. 13.95 (*0-9627291-3-2*) Deltaran Pub.

— The View from Olympus: Evolution of Consciousness Through Astrological - Historical Ages. (Illus.). 300p. (C). 1992. pap. 13.95 (*0-9627291-1-6*) Deltaran Pub.

Lloyd, Dorothy B. Genesis 2000. 1997. pap. write for info. (*1-57553-474-6*) Watermrk Pr.

Lloyd, Douglas. The Chemistry of Cyclic Conjugated Compounds: To Be or Not to Be Like Benzene? LC 89-22416. (Illus.). 197p. reprint ed. pap. 61.10 (*0-608-20221-5*, 207148000012) Bks Demand.

Lloyd, Douglas, ed. & tr. see Beyer, Hans & Walter, Wolfgang.

Lloyd, Douglas R., ed. Materials Science of Synthetic Membranes. LC 84-21652. (ACS Symposium Ser.: No. 269). 494p. 1984. lib. bdg. 87.95 (*0-8412-0887-5*) Am Chemical.

— Materials Science of Synthetic Membranes. LC 84-21652. (ACS Symposium Ser.: No. 269). 504p. 1985. reprint ed. pap. 156.30 (*0-608-03261-1*, 206378000007) Bks Demand.

— Topics in Carbocyclic Chemistry, Vol. 1. LC 74-80937. 383p. reprint ed. pap. 118.80 (*0-608-16727-4*, 202631000049) Bks Demand.

Lloyd, Douglas R., et al, eds. Inverse Gas Chromatography: Characterization of Polymers & Other Materials. LC 89-15. (ACS Symposium Ser.: No. 391). (Illus.). xi, 358p. 1989. 69.95 (*0-8412-1610-X*) Am Chemical.

— Inverse Gas Chromatography: Characterization of Polymers & Other Materials. LC 89-6628. (ACS Symposium Ser.: No. 391). (Illus.). 344p. 1989. reprint ed. pap. 106.70 (*0-608-03202-6*, 206372100007) Bks Demand.

Lloyd, Edward. Metal-Forming: An Introduction to Some Theory, Principles & Practice. (C). 1989. 300.00 (*0-7855-4925-0*, Pub. by Fuel Metallurgical Jrnl) St Mut.

Lloyd-Eley, Lesley. Tolley's VAT Penalty & Compliance Provisions. 3rd ed. 200p. 1994. 175.00 (*0-85459-805-7*, Pub. by Tolley Pubng) St Mut.

Lloyd, Elisabeth. The Structure & Confirmation of Evolutionary Theory. 247p. 1993. pap. text 16.95 (*0-691-00046-8*, Pub. by Princeton U Pr) Cal Prin Full Svc.

Lloyd, Elisabeth A. The Structure & Confirmation of Evolutionary Theory, 37. LC 88-3123. (Contributions in Philosophy Ser.: No. 37). 243p. 1988. 49.95 (*0-313-25563-6*, LVY/, Greenwood Pr) Greenwood.

Lloyd, Elisabeth A., jt. ed. see Keller, Evelyn F.

Lloyd, Elizabeth, jt. auth. see Smith, Ray.

Lloyd, Elizabeth A., jt. ed. see Keller, Evelyn F.

Lloyd, Elizabeth J. Gift Baskets for All Seasons: Seventy-Five Fun & Easy Craft Projects. LC 97-170675. (Illus.). 96p. 1997. pap. 15.95 (*0-7892-0295-6*) Abbeville Pr.

— Watercolor Still Life. LC 93-47008. (DK Art School Ser.). (Illus.). 72p. 1994. 16.95 (*1-56458-490-9*) DK Pub Inc.

Lloyd-Elliot, Martin. Secrets of Sexual Body Language. LC 95-62401. 144p. 1996. pap. 17.95 (*1-56975-060-2*) Ulysses Pr.

Lloyd-Elliott, Martin. City Ablaze: Life with the World's Busiest Firefighters. 2nd large type ed. 273p. 1993. 23.95 (*1-85695-085-9*, Pub. by ISIS Lrg Prnt) Transaction Pubs.

Lloyd, Emily. Catch of the Day: The Case of the Helpless Humpbacks. LC 97-209956. (Kinetic City Super Crew Ser.: No. 4). (Illus.). 163p. (J). (gr. 5-8). 1998. pap. 4.25 (*0-07-006390-7*, Lrning Triangle) McGraw.

— Forest Slump: The Case of the Pilfered Pine Needles. LC 97-17975. (Kinetic City Super Crew Ser.: No. 1). (Illus.). 150p. (J). (gr. 3-5). 1997. pap. 4.25 (*0-07-006388-5*, Lrning Triangle) McGraw.

— Home Run Has-Been: The Case of the Sluggish Slugger. (Kinetic City Super Crew Ser.: No. 11). (Illus.). 160p. (J). (gr. 3-5). 1998. pap. text 4.25 (*0-07-007066-0*) McGraw.

— Tall Tales: The Case of the Growing Suspicions. LC 97-46915. (Kinetic City Super Crew Ser.: No. 6). (Illus.). 160p. (J). (gr. 3-5). 1998. pap. 4.25 (*0-07-079062-0*) McGraw.

— Truffle Trouble: The Case of Fungus Among Us. (Kinetic City Super Crew Ser.: No. 10). (Illus.). 160p. (J). (gr. 3-5). 1998. pap. 4.25 (*0-07-079397-2*) McGraw.

Lloyd, Ernest, ed. Scrapbook Stories: Character Building Stories from Yesteryear. (Pioneer Ser.). (Illus.). 96p. (YA). (gr. 5 up). 1990. reprint ed. pap. 5.95 (*0-945460-08-2*) Upward Way.

Lloyd, Ernest M. A Review of the History of Infantry. LC 70-84277. 1982. reprint ed. lib. bdg. 100.50 (*0-8371-5015-9*, LLHI, Greenwood Pr) Greenwood.

Lloyd, Errol. Nine at Carnival. LC 78-4776. (Illus.). (J). (ps-2). 1979. 11.95 (*0-690-03891-7*) HarpC Child Bks.

Lloyd, Evan. The Methodist: A Poem. LC 92-1718. (Augustan Reprints Ser.: No. 151-152). 1972. reprint ed. 21.50 (*0-404-70151-5*, PR3541) AMS Pr.

Lloyd-Evans, Barbara, jt. auth. see Lloyd-Evans, Gareth.

Lloyd-Evans, Barbara, ed. see Bronte, Emily Jane.

Lloyd-Evans, Ceridwen. Margiad Evans. LC 98-212231. (Border Lines Ser.). (Illus.). 156p. 1998. 39.95 (*1-85411-219-8*, Pub. by Seren Bks); pap. 19.95 (*1-85411-220-1*, Pub. by Seren Bks) Dufour.

Lloyd-Evans, Gareth & Lloyd-Evans, Barbara. Everyman's Companion to Shakespeare. LC 78-324626. xiv, 368p. 1978. write for info. (*0-460-12028-X*, Everyman's Classic Lib) Tuttle Pubng.

Lloyd-Evans, Robert. Wide Area Networks: Performance & Optimization. LC 96-229035. 352p. (C). 1996. 44.95 (*0-201-42270-0*) Addison-Wesley.

Lloyd, Everett. Law West of the Pecos: The Story of Roy Bean. 106p. 1996. reprint ed. 35.00 (*1-56169-195-X*) Gaunt.

Lloyd, Eyre. Succession Laws of Christian Countries: With Special Reference to the Law of Primogeniture As It Exists in England. xi, 108p. 1985. reprint ed. 32.00 (*0-8377-0816-8*, Rothman) W S Hein.

Lloyd, Francis E. Guayule (Parthenium Argentatum Gray) A Rubber-Plant of the Chihuahuan Desert. (Illus.). 213p. 1911. pap. 10.00 (*0-87279-140-8*, 139) Carnegie Inst.

— Guayule (Parthenium Argentatum Gray) A Rubber-Plant of the Chihuahuan Desert. LC SB0291.G8L61. (Carnegie Institution of Washington Publication Ser.: Vol. 139). 250p. reprint ed. pap. 77.50 (*0-608-06213-8*, 206654100008) Bks Demand.

Lloyd, Frank W., jt. auth. see Ferris, Charles D.

Lloyd, Frederick E., ed. Lloyd's Church Musicians Directory. LC 72-1733. reprint ed. 37.50 (*0-404-08319-6*) AMS Pr.

Lloyd, G. A. Egypt Since Cromer, 2 Vols, Set. LC 68-9625. 1970. reprint ed. 95.00 (*0-86527-056-2*) Fertig.

Lloyd, G. A., jt. auth. see Phelps, P. D.

Lloyd, G. E. Adversaries & Authorities: Investigations into Ancient Greek & Chinese Science. (Ideas in Context Ser.: No. 42). 267p. (C). 1996. text 59.95 (*0-521-55331-8*); pap. text 19.95 (*0-521-55695-3*) Cambridge U Pr.

— Aristotelian Explorations. LC 95-50624. 251p. (C). 1996. text 54.95 (*0-521-55422-5*) Cambridge U Pr.

— Aristotelian Explorations. (Illus.). 256p. 1999. pap. 19.95 (*0-521-55619-8*) Cambridge U Pr.

— Aristotle: Growth & Structure of His Thought. LC 68-21195. 324p. (Orig.). (C). 1968. pap. text 22.95 (*0-521-09456-9*) Cambridge U Pr.

— Early Greek Science: Thales to Aristotle. Finley, Moses I., ed. (Ancient Culture & Society Ser.). (Illus.). (C). 1974. pap. 11.25 (*0-393-00583-6*) Norton.

— Greek Science after Aristotle. LC 72-11959. (Ancient Culture & Society Ser.). (Illus.). 208p. (C). 1975. pap. 11.95 (*0-393-00780-4*) Norton.

— The Insull Chicago Interurbans - CA&E, CNS&M, CSS&SB - in Color. (Illus.). 1996. 49.95 (*1-878887-61-0*) Morning NJ.

— Polarity & Analogy: Two Types of Argumentation in Early Greek Thought. LC 92-17832. 512p. (C). 1992. reprint ed. pap. text 16.95 (*0-87220-140-6*) Hackett Pub.

— The Revolution of Wisdom: Studies in the Claims & Practice of Ancient Greek Science. 1988. pap. 17.95 (*0-520-06742-8*, Pub. by U CA Pr) Cal Prin Full Svc.

Lloyd, G. E., ed. Hippocratic Writings. Chadwick, J. et al, trs. (Classics Ser.). 384p. 1984. pap. 13.95 (*0-14-044451-3*, Penguin Classics) Viking Penguin.

Lloyd, Gary A. & Kuszelewicz, Mary A., eds. HIV Disease: Lesbians, Gays, & the Social Services. 1995. 17.95 (*1-56023-070-3*, Harrington Park); 39.95 (*1-56024-749-5*) Haworth Pr.

Lloyd, Gary G. The Bibee Family. unabridged ed. LC 91-76099. (Illus.). 322p. (Orig.). 1991. pap. 32.00 (*0-9622972-3-2*) G G Lloyd.

— The Lewis Families of Putnam County, Missouri Vol. 2: Lewis Ancestors, Research Data, Maps & Obituaries. LC 89-91322. (Illus.). 166p. 1989. pap. 15.00 (*0-9622972-2-4*) G G Lloyd.

— The Lloyd (Loyd) Family of Putnam County, Missouri. unabridged ed. LC 96-75998. (Illus.). 285p. (Orig.). 1996. pap. 23.00 (*0-9622972-4-0*) G G Lloyd.

Lloyd, Genevieve. Being in Time: Self-Consciousness, Time & Narrative in Philosophy & Literature. LC 92-44132. (Ideas Ser.). 224p. (C). 1993. pap. 22.99 (*0-415-07196-8*, B2365) Routledge.

— The Man of Reason: "Male" & "Female" in Western Philosophy. 2nd ed. LC 93-17468. 166p. 1993. pap. 13.95 (*0-8166-2414-3*) U of Minn Pr.

— Part of Nature: Self-Knowledge in Spinoza's Ethics. LC 94-3195. 192p. 1994. text 32.50 (*0-8014-2999-4*) Cornell U Pr.

— Routledge Philosophy Guidebook to Spinoza & The Ethics. LC 96-6392. (Philosophy Guidebooks Ser.). 176p. (C). 1996. 60.00 (*0-415-10781-4*) Routledge.

— Routledge Philosophy Guidebook to Spinoza & the Ethics. LC 96-6392. (Philosophy Guidebooks Ser.). x, 163p. (C). 1996. pap. 12.99 (*0-415-10782-2*) Routledge.

Lloyd, Genevieve, jt. auth. see Gatens, Moira.

Lloyd, Geoffrey E. The Revolutions of Wisdom: Studies in the Claims & Practice of Ancient Greek Science. LC 86-16055. (Sather Classical Lectures: No. 52). 480p. reprint ed. pap. 148.80 (*0-7837-4847-7*, 204449400003) Bks Demand.

Lloyd, Geoffrey E. R., ed. see Pellegrin, Pierre.

Lloyd, George, ed. see Gerard, Alexander.

Lloyd, George A. Egypt Since Cromer, 2 vols. LC 75-107074. reprint ed. 45.00 (*0-404-04024-1*) AMS Pr.

Lloyd George, David. War Memoirs of David Lloyd George, 6 vols., Set. LC 75-41179. reprint ed. 450.00 (*0-404-15040-3*) AMS Pr.

Lloyd, George I. Cutlery Trades. (Illus.). 493p. 1968. reprint ed. 37.50 (*0-7146-1403-3*, Pub. by F Cass Pubs) Intl Spec Bk.

Lloyd, Germanischer, jt. auth. see Ihlenburg, Frank.

Lloyd, Gill & Jefferis, David. The History of Optics. (Science Discovery Ser.). (Illus.). 48p. (J). (gr. 5-10). 1995. lib. bdg. 24.26 (*1-56847-255-2*) Raintree Steck-V.

Lloyd, Gordon & Lloyd, Margien, eds. The Essential Bill of Rights: Original Arguments & Fundamental Documents. LC 98-12804. 384p. 1998. 64.00 (*0-7618-1075-7*); pap. 44.50 (*0-7618-1076-5*) U Pr of Amer.

Lloyd, Gordon B. Don't Call It "Dirt"! Improving Your Garden Soil. (Illus.). 128p. 1976. 6.95 (*0-916302-12-1*); pap. 3.95 (*0-916302-02-4*) Bookworm Pub.

Lloyd, Gordon E. Illinois Terminal in Color, Vol. 1. (Illus.). 128p. 1998. 49.95 (*1-58248-000-1*) Morning NJ.

Lloyd, Grahame. Jan the Man. (Illus.). 224p. 1998. 40.00 (*0-575-06561-3*, Pub. by V Gollancz) Trafalgar.

Lloyd, Grant & Lloyd, Mary L. Faith Blossoms at Cherry Hill. 128p. 1993. 7.98 (*0-88290-473-6*, 2016) Horizon Utah.

Lloyd, Greg, jt. auth. see Seed, Philip.

Lloyd, H. Evans, tr. see Von Feuchtersleben, Ernst F.

Lloyd, Harold C. & Stout, Wesley W. An American Comedy. LC 75-91907. (Illus.). 210p. 1972. 20.95 (*0-405-08749-7*, Pub. by Blom Pubns) Ayer.

Lloyd, Harvey. Sacred Lands of the Southwest. LC 95-30602. (Illus.). 224p. 1995. 60.00 (*1-885254-11-3*, Pub. by Monacelli Pr) Penguin Putnam.

— Sacred Lands of the Southwest, 4 vols., Set. LC 95-30602. (Illus.). 224p. 1995. 240.00 (*1-885254-18-0*) Monacelli Pr.

— Voyages: The Romance of Cruising. LC 99-15272. 272p. 1999. 40.00 (*0-7894-4617-0*) DK Pub Inc.

***Lloyd, Heather.** Sagan: Bonjour Tristesse. 64p. 1999. pap. text 35.00 (*0-85261-469-1*, Pub. by U of Glasgow) St Mut.

Lloyd, Henry D. Labour Copartnership. (Notable American Authors Ser.). 1999. reprint ed. lib. bdg. 125.00 (*0-7812-3802-1*) Rprt Serv.

— Lords of Industry. LC 73-2519. (Big Business; Economic Power in a Free Society Ser.). 1973. reprint ed. 24.95 (*0-405-05099-2*) Ayer.

— Man: The Social Creator. (Notable American Authors Ser.). 1999. reprint ed. lib. bdg. 125.00 (*0-7812-3804-8*) Rprt Serv.

— Men, the Workers. Withington, Anne & Stallbohen, Caroline, eds. LC 79-89751. (American Labor, from Conspiracy to Collective Bargaining Ser., No. 1). 280p. 1974. reprint ed. 21.95 (*0-405-02138-0*) Ayer.

— Newest England: A County Without Strikes. (Notable American Authors Ser.). 1999. reprint ed. lib. bdg. 125.00 (*0-7812-3803-X*) Rprt Serv.

— A Sovereign People. (Notable American Authors Ser.). 1999. reprint ed. lib. bdg. 125.00 (*0-7812-3805-6*) Rprt Serv.

— A Strike of Millionairs Against Miners. (Notable American Authors Ser.). 1999. reprint ed. lib. bdg. 125.00 (*0-7812-3800-5*) Rprt Serv.

— Wealth Aginst Commonwealth. (Notable American Authors Ser.). 1999. reprint ed. lib. bdg. 125.00 (*0-7812-3801-3*) Rprt Serv.

Lloyd, Henry D., ed. Wealth Against Commonwealth. LC 76-7. 184p. 1976. reprint ed. lib. bdg. 45.00 (*0-8371-8726-5*, LLWA, Greenwood Pr) Greenwood.

Lloyd, Hollis. How to Draw Cartoons & Animation. 96p. (J). 1994. 12.98 (*0-7858-0040-9*) Bk Sales Inc.

Lloyd House Staff. Obituary Notices from the Alexandria Gazette, 1784-1915. rev. ed. 220p. 1997. pap. 21.00 (*1-888265-20-5*) Willow Bend.

Lloyd, Howell A., ed. see Loyseau, Charles.

Lloyd, Humphrey. The Moving Balance System: A New Technique for Stock & Option Trading. (Illus.). 221p. 1988. pap. 50.00 (*0-930233-28-X*, Pub. by Windsor) Natl Bk Netwk.

Lloyd, Humphrey E. High Profit-Low Risk Options Strategies. 1984. pap. 34.95 (*0-930233-31-X*) Windsor.

— RSL Market Timing Method. 1990. 50.00 (*0-930233-45-X*) Windsor.

— Trading S&P Futures & Options: A Survival Manual & Study Guide. LC 97-184439. (Illus.). 135p. 1997. reprint ed. pap. 49.00 (*0-934380-34-1*, 1111) Traders Pr.

Lloyd, I. Simply the Best: Dunfermline Athletic. 180p. 1996. pap. 75.00 (*0-85976-448-6*, Pub. by J Donald) St Mut.

Lloyd, Ian. Law on the Electronic Frontier. (Hume Papers on Public Policy 2.4). 96p. 1995. pap. 16.00 (*0-7486-0594-0*, Pub. by Edinburgh U Pr) Col U Pr.

Lloyd, Idwal. Celtic Word Craft. (C). 1989. 30.00 (*1-85022-008-5*, Pub. by Dyllansow Truran) St Mut.

***Lloyd, Ivan.** Tahirh: A Poetic Vision. unabridged ed. Hedayati, Hamid & Yazdani, Bijan, trs. from PER. LC 99-98017. (Illus.). 68p. 2000. pap. text 15.95 (*0-9657967-1-X*, Pub. by Day Spring) Desert Rose Bahai.

Lloyd, J. Full Circle Summer. 50p. 1995. pap. 6.95 (*1-887589-01-5*) Sea Lore Pub.

— I Found My Porpoise. 50p. 1995. pap. 6.95 (*1-887589-00-7*) Sea Lore Pub.

Lloyd, J. & Herman, E. EMT: Race for Life. LC 98-96100. 1998. mass mkt. 5.99 (*0-8041-1545-1*) Ivy Books.

Lloyd, J. A. Dostoevsky. LC 75-30857. (Studies in Russian Literature & Life: No. 100). 1975. lib. bdg. 75.00 (*0-8383-2099-6*) M S G Haskell Hse.

Lloyd, J. Gordon. Alexander the Great: Selections from Arrian. LC 81-9453. (Translations from Greek & Roman Authors Ser.). 112p. 1982. pap. text 14.95 (*0-521-28195-4*) Cambridge U Pr.

Lloyd, J. M. Thermal Imaging Systems. LC 75-9635. (Optical Physics & Engineering Ser.). (Illus.). 456p. (C). 1975. text 110.00 (*0-306-30848-7*, Kluwer Plenum) Kluwer Academic.

Lloyd, J. R., et al, eds. Materials Reliability Issues in Microelectronics Vol. 225: Materials Research Society Symposium Proceedings. 354p. 1991. text 70.00 (*1-55899-119-0*) Materials Res.

Lloyd, J. R., ed. see Symposium on Electromigration of Metals Staff.

Lloyd, J. R., jt. ed. see Thompson, C. V.

Lloyd, J. W. Foundations of Logic Programming. (Symbolic Computation Ser.). xii, 212p. 1993. 72.95 (*0-387-18199-7*) Spr-Verlag.

Lloyd, J. W., ed. Computational Logic: Symposium Proceedings, Brussels, November 13-14, 1990. (ESPRIT Basic Research Ser.). (Illus.). xi, 211p. 1990. 37.95 (*0-387-53437-7*) Spr-Verlag.

Lloyd, J. W., et al, eds. The Regular Education Initiative: Alternative Perspectives on Concepts, Issues, & Methods. (Illus.). 320p. (C). 1991. text 36.95 (*0-9625233-3-X*) Sycamore Pub.

Lloyd, J. William. The Karezza Method: or Magnetation, the Art of Connubial Love. 64p. 1996. reprint ed. spiral bd. 12.00 (*0-7873-0565-0*) Hlth Research.

Lloyd, James, ed. see de Vega, Lope.

Lloyd-James, D. Martyn. Romans 11: Expositions of Chapter 11 to God's Glory. 290p. 1998. 29.99 (*0-85151-748-X*) Banner of Truth.

Lloyd, James G., ed. Lives of Mississippi Authors, 1817-1967. LC 81-2515. 513p. reprint ed. pap. 159.10 (*0-8357-4346-2*, 203714900007) Bks Demand.

***Lloyd, James T.** Lloyd's Steamboat Directory & Disasters on the Western Waters. Poole, Gregory G., ed. (Illus.). 360p. 2000. reprint ed. pap. 22.00 (*0-9650513-4-X*) Land Yacht Pr.

Lloyd, Janet. Joy & Wonder in All God's Works: Year A. 132p. (Orig.). (J). 1995. pap. 14.95 (*0-9646362-5-5*) Via Media.

— Joy & Wonder in All God's Works: Year C. 142p. (J). 1994. pap. 14.95 (*0-9646362-4-7*) Via Media.

Lloyd, Janet, jt. auth. see Calame, Claude.

Lloyd, Janet, jt. auth. see Hutchinson, Amelia P.

Lloyd, Janet, tr. see Aries, Philippe.

Lloyd, Janet, tr. see Aycoberry, Pierre.

Lloyd, Janet, tr. see Bergere, Marie-Claire.

Lloyd, Janet, tr. see Burrin, Philippe.

Lloyd, Janet, tr. see De Planhol, Xavier.

Lloyd, Janet, tr. see De Polignac, Francois.

Lloyd, Janet, tr. see De Romilly, Jacqueline.

Lloyd, Janet, tr. see Descola, Philippe.

Lloyd, Janet, tr. see Detienne, Marcel.

Lloyd, Janet, tr. see Detienne, Marcel & Vernant, Jean-Pierre.

Lloyd, Janet, tr. see Detienne, Marcel & Vidal-Naquet, Pierre.

Lloyd, Janet, tr. see Hartog, Francois.

Lloyd, Janet, tr. see Jullien, Francois.

Lloyd, Janet, tr. see Svenbro, Jesper.

Lloyd, Janet, tr. see Vernant, Jean-Pierre.

Lloyd, Janet, tr. see Vernant, Jean-Pierre & Vidal-Naquet, Pierre.

Lloyd, Janet, tr. see Vidal-Naquet, Pierre.

Lloyd, Janet E. Joy & Wonder in All God's Works: Year B. 132p. (Orig.). (J). Date not set. pap. 14.95 (*0-9646362-6-3*) Via Media.

Lloyd, Jeremy. The Are You Being Served? Stories: "Camping In" & Other Fiascoes. LC 97-366. Orig. Title: Are You Being Served?. (Illus.). 224p. 1997. reprint ed. pap. 12.95 (*0-912333-02-2*) BB&T Inc.

— Listen Very Carefully, I Shall Say This Only Once: An Autobiography. (Illus.). 170p. 1995. 21.95 (*0-563-36203-0*, BBC-Parkwest) Parkwest Pubns.

— Woodland Gospels: According to Captain Beaky & His Band. LC 83-20790. (Illus.). 63p. (J). (gr. k up). 1991. pap. 4.95 (*0-571-14285-0*) Faber & Faber.

Lloyd, Jill. German Expressionism: Primitivism & Modernity. LC 90-31786. (Illus.). 272p. (C). 1991. 70.00 (*0-300-04373-2*) Yale U Pr.

Lloyd, Joan. The Career Decisions Planner: When to Move, When to Stay, & When to Go Out on Your Own. 272p. 1992. pap. 17.95 (*0-471-54732-8*) Wiley.

— Guatemala, Land of the Mayas. LC 74-2557. (Illus.). 175p. 1974. reprint ed. lib. bdg. 55.00 (*0-8371-7415-5*, LLGU, Greenwood Pr) Greenwood.

Lloyd, Joan E. Bedtime Stories for Lovers. 128p. (Orig.). 1996. mass mkt. 9.99 (*0-446-67139-8*, Pub. by Warner Bks) Little.

— Come Play with Me: Games & Toys for Creative Lovers. 272p. (Orig.). 1994. mass mkt. 13.95 (*0-446-39538-2*, Pub. by Warner Bks) Little.

— Nice Couples Do: How to Turn Your Secret Dreams into Sensational Sex. 1991. mass mkt. 13.99 (*0-446-39258-8*, Pub. by Warner Bks) Little.

— Now & Forever - Let's Make Love. LC 97-7016. 256p. (Orig.). 1997. mass mkt. 12.99 (*0-446-67279-3*, Pub. by Warner Bks) Little.

Lloyd, Joan E. & Herman, Edwin B. Dial 911. 1995. mass mkt. 5.99 (*0-8041-1315-7*) Ivy Books.

Lloyd, Joan Elizabeth. Black Satin. 256p. 1995. pap. 8.95 (*0-7867-0236-2*) Carroll & Graf.

***Lloyd, Joan Elizabeth.** 52 Saturday Nights: Heat up Your Sex Life Even More with a Year of Creative Lovemaking. LC 99-44620. 288p. 2000. mass mkt. 12.95 (*0-446-67629-2*, Pub. by Warner Bks) Little.

Lloyd, Joan Elizabeth. The Love Flower. 224p. 1998. pap. 10.95 (*0-7867-0531-0*) Carroll & Graf.

***Lloyd, Joan Elizabeth.** Midnight Butterfly. 224p. 2000. pap. 11.95 (*0-7867-0761-5*, Pub. by Carroll & Graf) Publishers Group.

Lloyd, Joan Elizabeth. The Pleasures of JessicaLynn: An Erotic Novel. 208p. 1996. pap. 8.95 (*0-7867-0327-X*) Carroll & Graf.

— Slow Dancing. LC 97-4260. 224p. 1997. pap. 9.95 (*0-7867-0436-5*) Carroll & Graf.

— Velvet Whispers. 224p. 1999. pap. 11.95 (*0-7867-0640-6*) Carroll & Graf.

Lloyd, John. Flammability of Materials. 1989. 49.50 (*0-89116-289-5*) CRC Pr.

— The Pimm's Book of Polo. (Illus.). 240p. 1989. 35.00 (*0-943955-17-3*, Trafalgar Sq Pub) Trafalgar.

Lloyd, John, ed. Logic Programming: Proceedings of the 1995 International Symposium, Dec. 4-7, Portland, Oregon. (Logic Programming Ser.). (Illus.). 800p. (C). 1995. pap. text 75.00 (*0-262-62099-5*) MIT Pr.

Lloyd, John, et al. Plant Health Care for Woody Ornamentals: A Professional's Guide to Preventing & Managing Environmental Stresses & Pests. (Illus.). 256p. (Orig.). 1997. pap. 45.00 (*1-883097-17-7*) U Ill Ofc Agricult.

Lloyd, John, jt. auth. see Hill, Patricia.

Lloyd, John, jt. ed. see Morton, Ron.

Lloyd, John B. Eighteen Miles of History on Long Beach Island. 2nd rev. ed. (Illus.). 204p. 1994. 38.00 (*0-945582-17-X*) Down the Shore Pub.

— Six Miles at Sea: A Pictorial History of Long Beach Island. (Illus.). 176p. 1990. 35.00 (*0-945582-03-X*) Down the Shore Pub.

Lloyd, John B., et al, eds. Subcellular Biochemistry Vol. 27: Biology of the Lysosome. (Illus.). 435p. (C). 1997. text 129.50 (*0-306-45440-8*, Kluwer Plenum) Kluwer Academic.

Lloyd, John K., ed. see Navratil, Sidney J., et al.

Lloyd, John S. Leaving Flat Iron Creek. LC 98-96779. (Illus.). 300p. 1998. pap. 18.95 (*0-9668164-3-9*, 001-98) Spalding & Wallace.

Lloyd, John S., ed. How to Evaluate Residents. LC 86-72620. 400p. 1986. lib. bdg. 39.95 (*0-934277-09-5*) Am Bd Med Spec.

— Residency Director's Role in Specialty Certification. LC 85-70465. (Illus.). 255p. 1985. lib. bdg. 34.95 (*0-934277-05-2*) Am Bd Med Spec.

Lloyd, John S. & Langsley, Donald G., eds. Computer Applications in the Evaluation of Physician Competence. 241p. 1984. lib. bdg. 29.95 (*0-934277-04-4*) Am Bd Med Spec.

Lloyd, John S., jt. ed. see Langsley, Donald G.

Lloyd, John U. Etidorhpa or the End of Earth. 386p. 1974. pap. 30.00 (*0-89540-004-9*, SB-004) Sun Pub.

— Etidorhpa: or The End of Earth: The Strange History of a Mysterious Being & the Account of a Remarkable Journey. (Illus.). 375p. 1992. reprint ed. pap. 24.95 (*1-56459-243-X*) Kessinger Pub.

— Etidorpha & the Account of a Remarkable Journey: The End of the Earth, the Strange History of a Mysterious Being. 5th ed. 397p. 1966. pap. 32.00 (*0-7873-0566-9*) Hlth Research.

Lloyd, John U., ed. see King, John, III.

Lloyd, John W., et al, eds. Issues in Educating Students with Disabilities. LC 97-1095. (Special Education Ser.). 384p. 1997. write for info. (*0-8058-2201-1*); pap. write for info. (*0-8058-2202-X*) L Erlbaum Assocs.

Lloyd-Jones, Antonia, tr. see Huelle, Pawel.

Lloyd-Jones, D. Martyn. Alive in Christ: A 30 Day Devotional. LC 96-49545. (30-Day Devotional Ser.). 144p. 1997. pap. 8.99 (*0-89107-932-7*) Crossway Bks.

— Authority. 94p. 1992. reprint ed. pap. 5.99 (*0-85151-386-7*) Banner of Truth.

— Children of God. LC 92-21507. (Studies in First John: Vol. 3). 144p. 1993. pap. 9.99 (*0-89107-777-4*) Crossway Bks.

— The Cross. LC 85-72911. 192p. 1986. pap. 11.99 (*0-89107-382-5*) Crossway Bks.

— Cross: The Vindication of God. 1976. pap. 2.00 (*0-85151-266-6*) Banner of Truth.

— Depression Espiritual. (SPA.). 378p. 1998. pap. 12.00 (*0-939125-61-7*) CRC Wrld Lit.

— Evangelistic Sermons. 294p. (Orig.). 1983. pap. 15.99 (*0-85151-362-X*) Banner of Truth.

— Exposition of Ephesians, 8. 1p. (C). (gr. 13). 1998. reprint ed. pap. 150.00 (*0-8010-5793-0*) Baker Bks.

— Faith Tried & Triumphant. 218p. (Orig.). (gr. 10). 1988. pap. 9.99 (*0-8010-5649-7*) Baker Bks.

— Fellowship with God. LC 92-21507. (Studies in First John). 160p. 1992. pap. 10.99 (*0-89107-705-7*) Crossway Bks.

— God the Father, God the Son. LC 96-31333. (Great Doctrines of the Bible Ser.: Vol. 1). 384p. 1996. 25.00 (*0-89107-910-6*) Crossway Bks.

***Lloyd-Jones, D. Martyn.** God's Way Not Ours: Isaiah 1. 192p. 1999. pap. 12.99 (*0-8010-5995-X*) Baker Bks.

Lloyd-Jones, D. Martyn. I Am Not Ashamed: Advice to Timothy. 224p. (gr. 11). 1986. pap. 9.99 (*0-8010-5634-9*) Baker Bks.

— Joy Unspeakable: Power & Renewal in the Holy Spirit. LC 85-1929. 282p. 1985. pap. 9.99 (*0-87788-441-2*, H Shaw Pubs) Waterbrook Pr.

— The Kingdom of God. LC 92-5768. 224p. 1992. 13.99 (*0-89107-648-4*) Crossway Bks.

— Knowing the Times. 400p. 1989. 33.99 (*0-85151-556-8*) Banner of Truth.

— Letters of D. Martyn Lloyd-Jones. 248p. 1994. 25.99 (*0-85151-674-2*) Banner of Truth.

— Life in God. LC 92-2507. (Studies in First John: Bk. 5). 208p. 1994. pap. 10.99 (*0-89107-829-0*) Crossway Bks.

— The Love of God. LC 94-15386. (Studies in First John: Bk. 4). 208p. 1994. pap. 10.99 (*0-89107-814-2*) Crossway Bks.

— Old Testament Evangelistic Sermons. 268p. 1995. 27.99 (*0-85151-683-1*) Banner of Truth.

— Out of the Depths: Restoring Fellowship with God. LC 94-33867. 112p. 1995. pap. 8.99 (*0-89107-838-X*) Crossway Bks.

***Lloyd-Jones, D. Martyn.** Path to True Happiness: John 2. 224p. 1999. pap. 16.99 (*0-8010-5978-X*) Baker Bks.

Lloyd-Jones, D. Martyn. Por Que Lo Permite Dios?Tr. of Why Does God Allow War?. (SPA.). 96p. 1992. mass mkt. 3.99 (*0-8254-1448-2*, Edit Portavoz) Kregel.

— The Puritans: Their Origins & Successors. 436p. (C). 1987. 35.99 (*0-85151-496-0*) Banner of Truth.

— Reflections: A Treasury of Daily Readings. 384p. 1995. 14.99 (*0-529-10251-X*, REFL) World Publng.

— Revival. LC 86-72057. 320p. 1987. pap. 12.99 (*0-89107-415-5*) Crossway Bks.

— Romans: God's Sovereign Purpose. 328p. 1991. 31.99 (*0-85151-579-7*) Banner of Truth.

— Romans: The Gospel of God. 394p. 1985. 33.99 (*0-85151-467-7*) Banner of Truth.

— Romans: The Law (Chapter 7: 1 to 8: 4) 368p. 1989. 143.60 (*0-310-27948-8*, 10575) Zondervan.

— Romans: The Law: Its Functions & Limits. 359p. 1995. reprint ed. 35.99 (*0-85151-180-5*) Banner of Truth.

— Romans: The New Man. 313p. 1992. reprint ed. 33.99 (*0-85151-158-9*) Banner of Truth.

— Romans: The Righteous Judgment of God. 228p. 1989. 23.99 (*0-85151-545-2*) Banner of Truth.

— Romans: The Sons of God. 438p. 1995. reprint ed. 33.99 (*0-85151-207-0*) Banner of Truth.

— Romans Vol. 10: Savings Faith. 400p. 1997. 35.99 (*0-85151-737-4*) Banner of Truth.

— El Sermon Del Monte, 1. 1978. 10.99 (*0-85151-631-9*) Banner of Truth.

— El Sermon Del Monte, 2. 1978. 7.99 (*0-85151-509-6*) Banner of Truth.

— Spiritual Depression: Its Causes & Cure. 300p. 1965. pap. 15.00 (*0-8028-1387-9*) Eerdmans.

— Studies in the Sermon on the Mount. 1971. pap. 25.00 (*0-8028-0036-X*) Eerdmans.

— Truth Unchanged, Unchanging. 2nd ed. LC 93-376. 128p. 1993. reprint ed. pap. 9.99 (*0-89107-706-5*) Crossway Bks.

Unity in Truth. 1991. pap. 11.99 (*0-85234-288-8*, Pub. by Evangelical Pr) P & R Pubng.

— Walking with God. LC 92-21507. (Studies in First John: Vol. 2). 144p. (C). 1993. pap. 10.99 (*0-89107-735-9*) Crossway Bks.

— What Is an Evangelical? 91p. 1993. pap. 3.99 (*0-85151-626-2*) Banner of Truth.

— Why Does God Allow Suffering? 128p. 1994. pap. 8.99 (*0-89107-776-6*) Crossway Bks.

***Lloyd-Jones, D. Martyn, ed.** Puritan Papers: 1956-1959. 332p. 2000. pap. 14.99 (*0-87552-466-4*) P & R Pubng.

***Lloyd-Jones, Dadiva.** Of Tears & Flowers. 1999. pap. write for info. (*1-58235-117-1*) Watermrk Pr.

Lloyd-Jones, David, ed. & tr. see Mussorgsky, Modest.

Lloyd-Jones, David, tr. see Mussorgsky, Modest.

Lloyd-Jones, David Martyn. Romans: An Exposition of Chapter 8, 17-39: The Final Perseverance of the Saints. LC 76-377166. 1999. 37.99 (*0-85151-231-3*) Banner of Truth.

Lloyd-Jones, Hugh. Blood for the Ghosts: Classical Influences in the Nineteenth & Twentieth Centuries. LC 82-49061. 312p. 1982. reprint ed. pap. 96.80 (*0-608-06723-7*, 206692000009) Bks Demand.

— Greek Comedy, Hellenistic Literature, Greek Religion, & Miscellanea: Academic Papers of Sir Hugh Lloyd-Jones. (Illus.). 440p. 1991. 130.00 (*0-19-814745-7*) OUP.

— Greek Epic, Lyric, & Tragedy: Academic Papers of Sir Hugh Lloyd-Jones. 488p. 1991. 150.00 (*0-19-814680-9*) OUP.

— Greek in a Cold Climate. 248p. (C). 1991. text 70.00 (*0-389-20967-8*) B&N Imports.

Lloyd-Jones, Hugh, ed. The Greeks. (New Reprints in Essay & General Literature Index Ser.). 1977. reprint ed. 29.95 (*0-518-10204-1*, 10204) Ayer.

Lloyd-Jones, Hugh & Wilson, N. G., eds. Sophoclea: Studies in the Text of Sophocles. 288p. 1990. 65.00 (*0-19-814041-X*) OUP.

Lloyd-Jones, Hugh, ed. see Sophocles.

L

Lloyd-Jones, Hugh, ed. & tr. see Sophocles.

Lloyd-Jones, Hugh, tr. see Aeschylus.

Lloyd-Jones, Kenneth, jt. ed. see Beer, Jeanette M.

***Lloyd-Jones, Martyn.** The Assurance of Our Salvation: Exploring the Depth of Jesus' Prayer for His Own - Studies in John 17, 4 bks. in 1. LC 99-45041. 656p. 2000. reprint ed. 25.00 (*1-58134-140-7*) Crossway Bks.

— Authentic Christianity, Vol. 1. LC 99-53554. Vol. 1. 288p. 2000. 22.00 (*1-58134-036-2*) Crossway Bks.

Lloyd-Jones, Martyn. Church & the Last Things. LC 98-27041. (Great Doctrines of the Bible Ser.: Vol. 3). 1998. 22.00 (*1-58134-024-9*) Crossway Bks.

— God the Holy Spirit. LC 97-25586. (Great Doctrines of the Bible Ser.). 256p. 1997. 22.00 (*0-89107-959-9*) Crossway Bks.

***Lloyd-Jones, Martyn.** Jesus Christ & Him Crucified. 32p. 2000. pap. 2.50 (*0-85151-780-3*) Banner of Truth.

— My Soul Magnifies the Lord: Discovering the Riches of the Magnificant. 112p. 2000. pap. 9.99 (*1-58134-209-8*) Crossway Bks.

Lloyd-Jones, Martyn. Romans, 11 vols. 1998. 329.99 (*0-85151-756-0*) Banner of Truth.

— Romans 5: Assurance. 1998. 33.99 (*0-85151-050-7*) Banner of Truth.

— Romans 3:20-4:25 Atonement: Atonement. 1998. 25.99 (*0-85151-034-5*) Banner of Truth.

***Lloyd-Jones, Martyn.** 2 Peter: Expository Sermons. 263p. 1999. pap. 19.99 (*0-85151-771-4*) Banner of Truth.

Lloyd Jones, Peter. Taste Today: The Role of Appreciation in Consumerism & Design. (Illus.). 318p. 1991. 86.50 (*0-08-040251-8*, Pergamon Pr) Elsevier.

Lloyd-Jones, Roger & Lewis, M. J. Manchester in the Age of the Factory: The Business Structure of Cottonopolis in the Industrial Revolution. 272p. 1988. lib. bdg. 75.00 (*0-7099-4158-7*, Pub. by C Helm) Routldge.

Lloyd-Jones, Roger & Lewis, Merv. British Industrial Capitalism since the Industrial Revolution. LC 98-134664. 275p. 1998. 75.00 (*1-85728-408-9*, Pub. by UCL Pr Ltd); pap. 21.95 (*1-85728-409-7*, Pub. by UCL Pr Ltd) Taylor & Francis.

***Lloyd-Jones, Roger, et al.** Raleigh & the British Bicycle Industry: An Economic & Business History, 1870-1960. LC 99-45176. (Modern Social & Economic History Ser.). (Illus.). 224p. 2000. text 70.95 (*1-85928-457-4*, Pub. by Ashgate Pub) Ashgate Pub Co.

Lloyd-Jones, Roger, jt. auth. see Lewis, M. J.

Lloyd-Jones, Vernon. A-Z of Good Health. Date not set. pap. 9.95 (*0-8464-4868-8*) Beekman Pubs.

— Three Ways to Total Health. Date not set. pap. 11.95 (*0-8464-4895-5*) Beekman Pubs.

— Why Grow Old? How to Stay Young, Healthy & Confident. 100p. 1986. reprint ed. pap. 14.95 (*0-8464-4928-5*) Beekman Pubs.

***Lloyd, Josie.** Come Together. 2000. mass mkt. 6.99 (*0-425-17605-3*) Berkley Pub.

Lloyd, Josie, jt. auth. see Rees, Emlyn.

Lloyd, Julius A. Anderson. Family History, Containing a Brief Account of the Families of Anderson, Davies, Wersler. 80p. 1997. reprint ed. pap. 15.00 (*0-8328-7269-5*); reprint ed. lib. bdg. 25.50 (*0-8328-7268-7*) Higginson Bk Co.

Lloyd, Justin. The Possession of Tony Saurian. LC 86-70176. (Illus.). 242p. (YA). (gr. 10). 1986. pap. 10.00 (*0-937059-00-5*) AM to PM.

Lloyd, K. M., ed. Kew Index for 1987: Names of Seed-Bearing Plants, Ferns, & Fern Allies at the Rank of Family & Below Published During 1987 with Some Omissions from Earlier Years. 174p. 1988. pap. text 55.00 (*0-19-854245-3*) OUP.

Lloyd, K. M., jt. ed. see Davies, R. A.

Lloyd, Kathleen. Times One-Thousand Mots pour Parler. (FRE., Illus.). 95p. (Orig.). (J). (gr. 2-6). 1992. pap. 12.95 (*88-85148-54-9*, Pub. by Europ Lang Inst) Midwest European Pubns.

— Times One-Thousand Words to Talk About. (Illus.). 95p. (Orig.). (J). (gr. 2-6). 1992. pap. 12.95 (*981-01-0384-0*, Pub. by Europ Lang Inst) Midwest European Pubns.

— Times One-Thousand Worter Zum Sprechen. (GER., Illus.). 95p. (Orig.). (J). (gr. 2-6). 1992. reprint ed. pap. 12.95 (*88-85148-55-7*, Pub. by Europ Lang Inst) Midwest European Pubns.

Lloyd-Kemble, Quiche. Perchance to Dream. 40p. 1997. pap. 3.25 (*0-87440-048-1*) Bakers Plays.

Lloyd, Ken. Jerks at Work: How to Deal with People Problems & Problem People. LC 98-44917. 224p. 1999. pap. 15.99 (*1-56414-396-1*) Career Pr Inc.

Lloyd, Kenneth, jt. auth. see Moine, Donald J.

Lloyd, Kenneth L. Sexual Harassment: How to Keep Your Company Out of Court. 88p. 1992. 45.00 (*1-878375-47-4*, 75474) Panel Pubs.

Lloyd, Kent, et al. Reclaiming Our Nation at Risk: Lessons Learned-Reforming Our Public Schools. unabridged ed. LC 97-185008. (Illus.). xxiv, 570p. 1997. pap. 20.00 (*0-9634636-3-2*) T H Bell.

–Reclaiming Our Nation at Risk: Lessons Learned-Reforming Our Public Schools. unabridged ed. (Illus.). 600p. 1997. 30.00 (*0-9634636-4-0*) T H Bell.

RECLAIMING OUR NATION AT RISK: LESSONS LEARNED: REFORMING OUR PUBLIC SCHOOLS is Ted Bell's last school reform study & is a well-researched & highly-readable resource book. The result of in depth interviews with 44 of the nation's top school reformers & educational leaders, this new resource book is a guide to improving public schools everywhere, but especially schools with "at risk" children. It illustrates dramatic successes already in place in schools across the nation citing more than 20 effective reform models & 35 "best practices" in 15 states & 18 cities. This case study of "public engagement" describes how a small fictional Citizens' Commission of teacher, parent & community representatives together learn how to reform a struggling elementary school. The lively narrative maintains reader interest & is intertwined with issues of race & class that complicate & enrich public debate in our democracy today. In the dramatic climax, the group takes ownership & attempts to sell their reform plan for operating an "in-district, independent-public school to a skeptical school board. RECLAIMING also contains an "Elementary School Reform Inventory," which helps readers compare their own neighborhood public school with successful high-performance schools." To order: 1-800-610-9120. *Publisher Paid Annotation.*

Lloyd-Kolkin, Donna & Tyner, Kathleen R. Media & You: An Elementary Media Literacy Curriculum. LC 90-42205. (Illus.). 170p. 1991. pap. 34.95 (*0-87778-226-1*) Educ Tech Pubns.

***Lloyd, Kristina.** Asking for Trouble. (Black Lace Ser.). 1999. mass mkt. 10.99 (*0-352-33362-6*) Virgin Bks.

Lloyd, Kristina. Darker Than Love. (Black Lace Ser.). 1998. mass mkt. 6.95 (*0-352-33279-4*, Pub. by BLA4) London Brdge.

Lloyd, L. S. The Musical Ear. LC 88-31967. 104p. 1990. reprint ed. lib. bdg. 49.50 (*0-313-26666-2*, LLME, Greenwood Pr) Greenwood.

Lloyd, Les, ed. Administrative Computing in Higher Education: Issues in Enterprise-Wide Networks & Systems. 212p. 1996. 39.50 (*1-57387-007-2*) Info Today Inc.

— Teaching with Technology: Rethinking Tradition. LC 99-12230. 390p. 1999. 39.50 (*1-57387-068-4*) Info Today Inc.

— Technology & Teaching. LC 96-45083. 366p. 1997. 42.50 (*1-57387-014-5*) Info Today Inc.

Lloyd, Lewis E. Tariffs: The Case for Protectionism. 9.50 (*0-8159-6902-3*) Devin.

Lloyd, Linda. Classroom Magic: Amazing Technology for Teachers & Homeschoolers. 4th ed. (Illus.). 160p. (Orig.). 1990. reprint ed. pap. 15.95 (*1-55552-014-6*) Metamorphous Pr.

— Journey to Joy: A Day by Day Guide to Getting in Touch with Your Inner Child. (Illus.). (Orig.). 1994. pap. 10.00 (*0-914003-04-6*) Twiggs Comm.

Lloyd, Llewelyn S. Music & Sound. LC 70-107815. (Select Bibliographies Reprint Ser.). 1977. 20.95 (*0-8369-5188-3*) Ayer.

— Music & Sound. (Music Book Index Ser.). 181p. 1992. reprint ed. lib. bdg. 69.00 (*0-7812-9477-0*) Rprt Serv.

— Peasant Life in Sweden. LC 77-87710. 496p. reprint ed. 47.50 (*0-404-16501-X*) AMS Pr.

Lloyd, Lorna. Peace Through Law: Britain & the International Court in the 1920s. LC 96-46636. (Royal Historical Society Studies in History: No. 74). 320p. 1997. 75.00 (*0-86193-235-8*) Boydell & Brewer.

Lloyd, Louise, ed. see Chesman, Andrea.

Lloyd, Louise, ed. see Garden Way Publishing Editors.

Lloyd, Lucy C., jt. auth. see Bleek, Whilhelm H.

Lloyd, Lyle L., et al. Augmentative & Alternative Communication: A Handbook of Principles & Practices. LC 97-26195. 615p. 1997. 79.00 (*0-205-19884-8*) Allyn.

***Lloyd, Maggie.** Ferrets: Health, Husbandry & Diseases. LC 99-35580. 208p. 1999. 44.95 (*0-632-05178-7*, Pub. by Blckwell Science) Iowa St U Pr.

Lloyd, Maggie, jt. auth. see Wolfensohn, Sarah.

Lloyd, Margaret. This Particular Earthly Scene. LC 92-38198. 80p. (Orig.). 1993. pap. 9.95 (*0-914086-99-5*) Alice James Bks.

Lloyd, Margaret A., et al. Psychology Applied to Modern Life: Adjustment in the 90s. 3rd ed. 500p. (C). 1990. pap. 46.00 (*0-534-09708-1*) Brooks-Cole.

Lloyd, Margaret A., jt. auth. see Weiten, Wayne.

Lloyd, Margaret G. William Carlos William's Paterson: A Critical Appraisal. LC 77-89775. (Illus.). 305p. 1979. 35.00 (*0-8386-2152-X*) Fairleigh Dickinson.

Lloyd, Margien, jt. ed. see Lloyd, Gordon.

Lloyd, Marjorie L. It Must Have Been an Angel. LC 79-23418. (Redwood Ser.). 1980. pap. 7.99 (*0-8163-0363-0*) Pacific Pr Pub Assn.

Lloyd, Mark. Combat Uniforms of the Civil War. 1995. 17.98 (*0-7858-0457-9*) Bk Sales Inc.

— Combat Uniforms of the Civil War, 4 vols. (Illus.). (YA). (gr. 7 up). 1998. lib. bdg. 74.95 (*0-7910-4992-2*) Chelsea Hse.

— The Confederate Army, 4 vols., Set. LC 98-18187. (Illus.). 64p. 1998. 17.98 (*0-7910-4995-7*) Chelsea Hse.

— The Confederate Army, 4 vols., Set. (Illus.). 64p. (YA). 1998. 17.98 (*0-7910-4996-5*) Chelsea Hse.

— The Federal Army, 4 vols., Set. LC 98-18187. (Illus.). 64p. 1998. 17.98 (*0-7910-4993-0*); 17.98 (*0-7910-4994-9*) Chelsea Hse.

— The Guinness Book of Espionage. LC 94-8562. (Illus.). 256p. 1994. reprint ed. pap. 16.95 (*0-306-80584-7*) Da Capo.

— Military Badges & Insignia. (Illus.). 46p. (gr. 8-12). 1999. text 20.00 (*0-7881-6443-0*) DIANE Pub.

— Modern Combat Uniforms. (Illus.). 215p. 1988. pap. 19.95 (*0-89747-226-8*) Squad Sig Pubns.

Lloyd, Mark F. & Moak, Jefferson M., eds. Pennsylvania Society of Sons of the Revolution: Centennial Register, 1888-1988. LC 90-61497. (Illus.). x, 994p. 1990. 35.00 (*0-9626507-0-6*) PA Soc Sons Rev.

Lloyd, Mary. Pepsi-Cola Collectibles: The Everett Lloyd Book. LC 93-85216. (Illus.). 160p. 1993. pap. 29.95 (*0-88740-533-9*) Schiffer.

Lloyd, Mary F., jt. auth. see DeAngelis, Robert.

Lloyd, Mary L., jt. auth. see Lloyd, Grant.

Lloyd, Matthew, intro. First Run 3: New Plays by New Writers. 326p. 1991. pap. 19.95 (*1-85459-059-6*, Pub. by N Hern Bks) Theatre Comm.

Lloyd, Megan. Baba Yaga: A Russian Folktale. LC 90-39215. 32p. (J). (ps-3). 1991. lib. bdg. 16.95 (*0-8234-0854-X*) Holiday.

— The Gingerbread Man. 32p. (J). (gr. k-3). 1993. lib. bdg. 16.95 (*0-8234-0824-8*) Holiday.

— The Gingerbread Man. 32p. (J). (gr. k-3). 1993. pap. 6.95 (*0-8234-1137-0*) Holiday.

— The Gingerbread Man. (J). (gr. k-3). 24.95 incl. audio (*0-87499-319-9*); pap. 15.95 incl. audio (*0-87499-318-0*) Live Oak Media.

— The Gingerbread Man, 4 bks., Set. (J). (gr. k-3). pap. 37.95 incl. audio (*0-87499-320-2*) Live Oak Media.

Lloyd, Michael. The Agon in Euripides. 152p. 1992. text 55.00 (*0-19-814778-3*) OUP.

Lloyd, Michael, ed. Turner. LC 95-61908. (Illus.). 250p. (Orig.). 1996. pap. 24.95 (*0-500-97437-3*, Pub. by Thames Hudson) Norton.

Lloyd, Michael E., et al. 401(K) Plans: A Comprehensive Planning & Compliance Guide. 2nd ed. LC 96-7677. (CPA's Practice Guide Ser.). 528p. 1996. 135.00 (*0-471-15314-1*) Wiley.

Lloyd-Morris, Caroline, tr. see Kogon, Eugen, et al, eds.

Lloyd, N. G., et al, eds. Nonlinear Diffusion Equations & Their Equilibrium States 3: Proceedings from a Conference Held August 20-29, 1980 in Gregynog, Wales. (Progress in Nonlinear Differential Equations & Their Applications Ser.: Vol. 7). x, 572p. 1992. 146.00 (*0-8176-3531-9*) Birkhauser.

Lloyd, Nancy. Simple Money Solutions: 10 Ways You Can Stop Feeling Overwhelmed & Start Making it Work for You. LC 99-53930. 288p. 2000. 23.00 (*0-8129-3175-0*, Times Bks) Crown Pub Group.

Lloyd, Nathaniel. Garden Craftsmanship in Yew & Box. (Illus.). 104p. 1995. 29.50 (*1-870673-14-X*) Antique Collect.

— A History of English Brickwork. (Illus.). 464p. 1983. 89.50 (*0-907462-36-7*) Antique Collect.

— A History of English Brickwork. LC 72-87653. (Illus.). 449p. 1972. reprint ed. lib. bdg. 36.95 (*0-405-08750-0*, Pub. by Blom Pubns) Ayer.

Lloyd, Nelson M. Six Stars. LC 75-125229. (Short Story Index Reprint Ser.). 1977. 20.95 (*0-8369-3596-9*) Ayer.

Lloyd, Noppe, jt. auth. see Fergus, Hughes.

Lloyd, Norma. Utah Publicity Source Book, 1996. rev. ed. 1995. lib. bdg. 100.00 (*1-884689-05-1*) Orton Grp.

Lloyd, Norma & Brown, James W. Utah Publicity Source Book, 1996. 15th rev. ed. 1995. 130.00 (*1-884689-04-3*) Orton Grp.

Lloyd, Norman. Stages: Norman Lloyd. LC 89-77810. (Directors Guild of American Oral History Ser.: No. 9). (Illus.). 296p. 1990. 38.00 (*0-8108-2290-3*) Scarecrow.

— Stages: Of Life in Theatre, Film & Television. LC 92-30285. (Illus.). 278p. 1993. reprint ed. pap. 14.95 (*0-87910-166-0*) Limelight Edns.

Lloyd, Norman, jt. auth. see Fish, Arnold.

Lloyd, Owen L., et al. Atlas of Disease Mortalities in Hong Kong for the Three Five-Year Periods in 1979-93. (C). 1997. 134.00 (*962-201-732-0*, Pub. by Chinese Univ) U of Mich Pr.

Lloyd, P. & Beveridge, Michael. Information & Meaning in Child Communication. (Applied Language Studies). 1981. text 125.00 (*0-12-453520-8*) Acad Pr.

Lloyd, P. & Whitehead, R., eds. Transforming Organizations Through Groupware, Lotus Notes in Action: Lotus Notes in Action. 216p. 1996. pap. text 39.95 (*3-540-19961-6*) Spr-Verlag.

***Lloyd, P. J. & Zhang, Xiaoguang.** China in the Global Economy. LC 00-34828. 2000. write for info. (*1-84064-290-4*) E Elgar.

Lloyd, Pamela. Fortune Telling. 96p. 1996. 12.99 (*1-57215-207-9*, JG1206) World Pubns.

— How Writers Write. 149p. (C). 1990. pap. 16.00 (*0-435-08512-3*, 08512) Heinemann.

— Tarot. 96p. 1996. 12.99 (*1-57215-208-7*, JG1207) World Pubns.

Lloyd, Pat, jt. auth. see Moulton, Ron.

Lloyd, Patti. Acuenergy. 208p. 1982. 12.95 (*0-89557-060-2*) Woodland UT.

Lloyd, Paul. From Latin to Spanish. LC 87-72873. (Memoirs Ser.: Vol. 173). 346p. (C). 1987. pap. 30.00 (*0-87169-173-6*, M173-PAP) Am Philos.

Lloyd, Peta. Literacy Hour & Language Knowledge: Developing Literacy Through Fiction & Poetry. 1999. pap. text 26.95 (*1-85346-578-X*) Taylor & Francis.

Lloyd, Peter. The French Are Coming! The Invasion Scare, 1803-5. 240p. (C). 1991. 125.00 (*0-946771-77-4*, Pub. by Spellmnt Pubs) St Mut.

— Perspectives & Identities: The Elizabethan Writer's Search to Know His World. 1989. 35.00 (*0-948695-11-0*) Intl Spec Bk.

— San Francisco. (Architecture in Context Ser.). (ENG, FRE & GER., Illus.). 80p. 1997. pap. 9.95 (*3-89508-271-6*, 810088) Konemann.

— San Francisco. (Architecture Guides Ser.). (Illus.). 320p. 1998. pap. 5.95 (*3-89508-643-6*, 520202) Konemann.

— The Scam. 72p. 1996. pap. 15.95 (*1-85411-150-7*, Pub. by Seren Bks) Dufour.

Lloyd, Peter, ed. Groupware in the 21st Century: Computer Supported Cooperative Working Toward the Milennium. LC 94-28284. (Praeger Studies on the 21st Century). 336p. 1994. 69.50 (*0-275-95091-3*, Praeger Pubs); pap. 23.95 (*0-275-95092-1*, Praeger Pubs) Greenwood.

Lloyd, Peter & Fermyhough, Charles, eds. Lev Vygotsky: Critical Assessment, 4 vols. (Critical Assessments Ser.). (Illus.). 1536p. (C). (gr. 13). 1999. 700.00 (*0-415-11156-0*, D6205) Routledge.

Lloyd, Peter & Fernyhough, Charles. Lev Vygotsky: Critical Assessments. LC 98-9488. 1998. write for info. (*0-415-11152-8*); write for info. (*0-415-11153-6*); write for info. (*0-415-11154-4*); write for info. (*0-415-11155-2*) Routledge.

Lloyd, Peter & Milner, Chris, eds. The World Economy: Global Trade Policy 1998. (Global Trade Policy Ser.). 208p. 1999. pap. 34.95 (*0-631-21183-7*) Blackwell Pubs.

***Lloyd, Peter & Milner, Chris, eds.** The World Economy: Global Trade Policy 1999. 208p. 1999. pap. text 34.95 (*0-631-21810-6*) Blackwell Pubs.

Lloyd, Peter & Williams, Lynne, eds. International Trade & Migration in the APEC Region. (Illus.). 288p. 1997. 85.00 (*0-19-553763-7*) OUP.

Lloyd, Peter, jt. auth. see Phillips-Pulverman, Dian.

Lloyd, Peter, jt. ed. see King.

Lloyd, Peter C. A Third World Proletariat? (Controversies in Sociology Ser.: No. 11). 144p. 1982. pap. text 11.95 (*0-04-301141-1*) Routledge.

Lloyd, Peter E., jt. auth. see Dicken, Peter.

Lloyd, Peter J. International Trade Problems of Small Nations. LC 67-28850. 146p. reprint ed. pap. 45.30 (*0-608-11987-3*, 202342000033) Bks Demand.

Lloyd, Peter John. International Trade Opening & the Formation of the Global Economy: Selected Essays of Peter J. Lloyd. 20th ed. LC 98-46606. (Economists of the Twentieth Century Ser.). 584p. 1999. 120.00 (*1-85898-956-6*) E Elgar.

***Lloyd, Peter John & Vautier, Kerrin M.** Promoting Competition in Global Markets: A Multi-National Approach. LC 98-53418. 224p. 1999. 75.00 (*1-85898-803-9*) E Elgar.

Lloyd, Peter John, ed. see Particle Size Analysis Conference Staff.

Lloyd-Prichard, M. F., ed. see Keymer, John.

Lloyd, R., jt. auth. see Muller, R.

Lloyd, Ricardo V. Endocrine Pathology. (Illus.). 256p. 1990. 114.00 (*0-387-97166-1*) Spr-Verlag.

— Surgical Pathology of the Pituitary Gland. (Illus.). 271p. 1992. text 70.00 (*0-7216-6459-8*, W B Saunders Co) Harcrt Hlth Sci Grp.

Lloyd, Richard. The Christmas Cavalier: A Pantomime LC 91-192359. x, 41 p. 1990. write for info. (*0-573-06510-1*) S French Trade.

— Pollution & Freshwater Fish. (Illus.). 1992. 59.95 (*0-85238-187-5*) Blackwell Sci.

— Sixty Spins of a Lopsided Wheel: Selected Poems, 1957-1997. LC 98-3216. 300p. 1998. 20.00 (*1-889059-12-9*, DimeADozen) Regent Pr.

Lloyd, Richard & Stevenson, Robert Louis. Treasure Island, the Panto: A Pantomime. LC 99-165507. 79p. 1997. write for info. (*0-573-06496-2*) S French Trade.

Lloyd, Richard, jt. ed. see Davidson, Joan.

Lloyd, Richard M. Conventional Warhead Systems Physics & Engineering Design. LC 98-194777. 636p. 1998. 104.95 (*1-56347-255-4*) AIAA.

Lloyd, Richmond M., et al, eds. Strategy & Force Planning. 2nd ed. (Illus.). 676p. (C). 1997. pap. text. write for info. (*1-884733-08-5*) Naval War Coll.

***Lloyd, Richmond M. & Naval War College, Strategy & Force Planning Faculty Staff.** Strategy & Force Planning. 3rd ed. LC 00-27477. 2000. write for info. (*1-884733-13-1*) Naval War Coll.

Lloyd, Richmond M., et al. Strategy & Force Planning. LC 95-2794. 1995. write for info. (*1-884733-05-0*) Naval War Coll.

Lloyd, Robert. Spatial Cognition: Of Geographic Environments. LC 96-52349. (GeoJournal Library). 316p. (C). 1997. lib. bdg. 145.00 (*0-7923-4375-1*) Kluwer Academic.

— You Got Me!--Florida. LC 99-20444. 1999. pap. 14.95 (*1-56164-183-9*) Pineapple Pr.

Lloyd, Robert C., jt. auth. see Carey, Raymond G.

Lloyd, Robert M. Systematics of the Onocleoid Ferns. LC 72-170330. (University of California Publications in Social Welfare: Vol. 61). (Illus.). 99p. reprint ed. pap. 30.70 (*0-608-18053-X*, 201470400093) Bks Demand.

Lloyd-Roberts, G. C. & Fixsen, John A. Orthopedics in Infancy & Childhood. 2nd ed. 226p. 1990. pap. text 180.00 (*0-7506-1030-1*) Buttrwrth-Heinemann.

Lloyd, Roger B. Golden Middle Age. LC 75-90654. (Essay Index Reprint Ser.). 1977. 20.95 (*0-8369-1208-X*) Ayer.

— Revolutionary Religion: Christianity, Fascism, & Communism. LC 78-63686. (Studies in Fascism: Ideology & Practice). reprint ed. 32.50 (*0-404-16903-1*) AMS Pr.

Lloyd, Roseann. Tap Dancing for Big Mom. 106p. 1990. pap. 4.50 (*0-89823-073-X*) New Rivers Pr.

— War Baby Express: Poems. 96p. 1996. pap. 10.95 (*0-930100-68-9*) Holy Cow.

Lloyd, Roseann, tr. see Wassmo, Herbjorg.

Lloyd, Rosemary. Baudelaire et Hoffmann: Affinites et Influences. LC 78-58796. 403p. reprint ed. pap. 114.90 (*0-8357-5999-7*, 2031683) Bks Demand.

— Closer & Closer Apart: Jealousy in Literature. 224p. 1995. text 35.00 (*0-8014-3151-4*) Cornell U Pr.

— The Land of Lost Content: Children & Childhood in Nineteenth-Century French Literature. (Illus.). 286p. 1992. text 75.00 (*0-19-815173-X*) OUP.

— Madame Bovary. (Unwin Critical Library). 336p. 1989. 44.95 (*0-04-800084-1*) Routledge.

An Asterisk (*) at the beginning of an entry indicates that the title is appearing for the first time.

L

*Lloyd, Rosemary. Mallarme: The Poet & His Circle. LC 99-35644. 296p. 1999. 35.00 (0-8014-3662-1) Cornell U Pr.

Lloyd, Rosemary, tr. Revolutions in Writing: Readings in Nineteenth-Century French Prose. (Indiana Masterpiece Editions Ser.). 448p. 1996. pap. 18.95 (0-253-21069-0); text 49.95 (0-253-33054-8) Ind U Pr.

Lloyd, Rosemary, ed. & tr. see Baudelaire, Charles.

Lloyd, Rosemary, ed. & tr. see Mallarme, Stephane.

Lloyd, Rosemary, tr. see Sand, George.

Lloyd, Russell F. & Rehg, Virgil R. Quality Circles: Applications in Vocational Education. 47p. 1983. 4.95 (0-318-22183-7, IN249) Ctr Educ Trng Employ.

Lloyd, S. The Ruined Cities of Iraq. (Illus.). 72p. 1980. pap. 15.00 (0-89005-375-8) Ares.

Lloyd, S. A. Ideals As Interests in Hobbes's Leviathan: The Power of Mind over Matter. 410p. (C). 1992. text 85.00 (0-521-39243-8) Cambridge U Pr.

Lloyd, S. D., jt. ed. see Coss, P. R.

Lloyd, S. D., jt. ed. see Ross, P. R.

Lloyd, S. L., et al. Electron Positron Physics at the Z. LC 98-3929. (Illus.). 300p. 1998. 150.00 (0-7503-0383-2) IOP Pub.

Lloyd, Sally A., jt. ed. see Cahn, Dudley D.

Lloyd, Sam & Berthelot, Christine. Self-Empowerment: Getting What You Want from Life. Keppler, Kay, ed. LC 91-76251. (Fifty-Minute Ser.). 90p. (Orig.). 1992. pap. 10.95 (1-56052-128-7) Crisp Pubns.

Lloyd, Sam R. Developing Positive Assertiveness: Practical Techniques for Personal Success. rev. ed. Crisp, Michael, ed. LC 94-72612. (Fifty-Minute Ser.). (Illus.). 90p. 1995. pap. 9.95 (1-56052-313-1) Crisp Pubns.

— Leading Teams: The Skills for Success. LC 95-83968. (How-to Book Ser.). 103p. (Orig.). 1996. pap. 12.95 (1-884926-51-7, LEADT) Amer Media.

*Lloyd, Sampson. London. 160p. 1999. 35.00 (1-85585-676-X) Collins & Br.

Lloyd, Sampson, jt. auth. see Moore, Rowan.

Lloyd, Sandra J., jt. auth. see Lamit, Louis G.

Lloyd, Sarah. An Indian Attachment. (Eland Travel Classics Ser.). 272p. 1992. pap. 14.95 (0-7818-0018-8) Hippocrene Bks.

— Indian Attachment. 244p. 1992. pap. 14.95 (0-907871-12-7) Hippocrene Bks.

Lloyd, Scott, jt. auth. see Blake, Scott.

Lloyd, Selwyn J. The Mute Horseman of Dragon's Bay. (J). (gr. 4). 1992. pap. 7.95 (0-8464-4877-7, Gomer Pr) Beekman Pubs.

*Lloyd, Seton. Ancient Turkey: A Traveller's History of Anatolia. 240p. 1999. pap. 19.95 (0-520-22042-0, Pub. by U CA Pr) Cal Prin Full Svc.

Lloyd, Seton. Foundations in the Dust: A Story of Mesopotamian Exploration. LC 76-46179. reprint ed. 21.50 (0-404-15364-X) AMS Pr.

Lloyd, Seton, jt. auth. see Jacobsen, Thorkild.

Lloyd, Sharon. Clipping Horses & Ponies: A Complete Illustrated Manual. (Illus.). 128p. 1995. 34.95 (1-872082-77-7, Pub. by Kenilworth Pr) Half Halt Pr.

Lloyd, Siobhan, jt. auth. see Hall, Liz.

Lloyd, Siobhan, jt. ed. see Chapman, Polly.

Lloyd-Smith, Alan, ed. see James, Henry.

Lloyd, Stephen. H. Balfour Gardiner. LC 83-14227. (Illus.). 260p. 1984. text 80.00 (0-521-25609-7) Cambridge U Pr.

— Richard & Maria Cosway. (Illus.). 143p. 1996. pap. 29.95 (0-903598-53-1) Natl Galleries.

*Lloyd, Stephen & Perry, Melissa. Annotated Native Title Act. 400p. 1999. pap. write for info. (0-455-21680-0, Pub. by LBC Info Servs) Gaunt.

*Lloyd, Steve K. Farallon: Shipwreck & Survival on the Alaska Shore. 192p. 2000. 35.00 (0-87422-193-5); pap. 18.95 (0-87422-194-3) Wash St U Pr.

Lloyd, Steven. Ivory Diptych Sundials, 1570 1750. (Illus.). 150p. 1992. text 50.00 (0-685-53271-2) Contigo Pubns.

— Ivory Diptych Sundials, 1570-1750. (Illus.). 150p. 1992. text 50.00 (0-674-46977-1) HUP.

*Lloyd, Steven. Selling from the Heart: In the New Millennium, Selling Is Everyone's Job! East, Bill, ed. LC 00-100493. 240p. 2000. pap. 15.95 (0-9678616-0-8) S & P Pubng.

*Lloyd-Still, J. D. Family Violence. LC 00-27984. (Current Controversies Ser.). 2000. pap. write for info. (0-7377-0452-7) Greenhaven.

Lloyd, Sue. The Phonics Handbook. (Illus.). 218p. (J). (ps-3). 1993. pap. 22.50 (1-870946-08-1, Pub. by Jolly Lrning) Am Intl Dist.

Lloyd, Sue & Keys, Jacquie. Passion for Pasta: Delicious New Recipes for Fresh Pasta. (Illus.). 137p. 1994. 24.95 (0-85572-222-3, Pub. by Hill Content Pubng) Seven Hills Bk.

Lloyd, Sue & Wernham, Sara. Finger Phonics, 7 bks., Set. (Illus.). (J). (ps-2). 1994. pap. 45.50 (1-870946-31-6, Pub. by Jolly Lrning) Am Intl Dist.

— Finger Phonics Bk. 1: S, A, T, I, P, N. (Illus.). 14p. (J). (ps-2). 1994. pap. 6.50 (1-870946-24-3, Pub. by Jolly Lrning) Am Intl Dist.

— Finger Phonics Bk. 2: CK, E, H, R, M, D. (Illus.). 14p. (J). (ps-2). 1994. pap. 6.50 (1-870946-25-1, Pub. by Jolly Lrning) Am Intl Dist.

— Finger Phonics Bk. 3: G, O, U, L, F, B. (Illus.). 14p. (J). (ps-2). 1994. pap. 6.50 (1-870946-26-X, Pub. by Jolly Lrning) Am Intl Dist.

— Finger Phonics Bk. 4: AI, J, OA, IE, EE, OR. (Illus.). 14p. (J). (ps-2). 1994. pap. 6.50 (1-870946-27-8, Pub. by Jolly Lrning) Am Intl Dist.

— Finger Phonics Bk. 5: Z, W, NG, V, OO, OO. (Illus.). 14p. (J). (ps-2). 1994. pap. 6.50 (1-870946-28-6, Pub. by Jolly Lrning) Am Intl Dist.

— Finger Phonics Bk. 6: Y, X, CH, SH, TH, TH. (Illus.). 14p. (J). (ps-2). 1994. pap. 6.50 (1-870946-29-4, Pub. by Jolly Lrning) Am Intl Dist.

— Finger Phonics Bk. 7: QU, OU, OI, UE, ER, AR. (Illus.). 14p. (J). (ps-2). 1994. pap. 6.50 (1-870946-30-8, Pub. by Jolly Lrning) Am Intl Dist.

— Jolly Phonics. (Jolly Phonics Ser.). (Illus.). (Orig.). (J). (ps-2). 1997. boxed set 177.80 (1-870946-74-X, JL74X, Pub. by Jolly Lrning) Am Intl Dist.

— Jolly Phonics, Vols. 1-7. (Jolly Phonics Ser.). (Illus.). (Orig.). (J). (ps-2). 1996. pap., wbk. ed. 13.93 (1-870946-50-2, JL502, Pub. by Jolly Lrning) Am Intl Dist.

— Jolly Phonics Wall Frieze. (Illus.). (J). (ps-2). 1994. 8.95 (1-870946-32-4, Pub. by Jolly Lrning) Am Intl Dist.

— Jolly Phonics Workbook Vol. 1: S A T I P N. (Illus.). 24p. (Orig.). (J). (gr. k-3). 1995. wbk. ed. 1.99 (1-870946-51-0, JL510, Pub. by Jolly Lrning) Am Intl Dist.

— Jolly Phonics Workbook Vol. 2: C K E H R M D. (Illus.). 24p. (Orig.). (J). (gr. k-3). 1995. wbk. ed. 1.99 (1-870946-52-9, JL529, Pub. by Jolly Lrning) Am Intl Dist.

— Jolly Phonics Workbook Vol. 3: G O U L R B. (Illus.). 24p. (Orig.). (J). (gr. k-3). 1995. wbk. ed. 1.99 (1-870946-53-7, FL537, Pub. by Jolly Lrning) Am Intl Dist.

— Jolly Phonics Workbook Vol. 4: AI J OA LE EE OR. (Illus.). 24p. (J). (gr. k-3). 1995. wbk. ed. 1.99 (1-870946-54-5, JL545, Pub. by Jolly Lrning) Am Intl Dist.

— Jolly Phonics Workbook Vol. 5: Z W NG V OO OO. (Illus.). 24p. (J). (gr. k-3). 1995. wbk. ed. 1.99 (1-870946-55-3, FL553, Pub. by Jolly Lrning) Am Intl Dist.

— Jolly Phonics Workbook Vol. 6: Y X CH SH TH TH. (Illus.). 24p. (J). (gr. k-3). 1995. wbk. ed. 1.99 (1-870946-56-1, FL561, Pub. by Jolly Lrning) Am Intl Dist.

— Jolly Phonics Workbook Vol. 7: QU OU OI UE ER AR. (Illus.). 24p. (J). (gr. k-3). 1995. wbk. ed. 1.99 (1-870946-57-X, JL57X, Pub. by Jolly Lrning) Am Intl Dist.

— Using Jolly Phonics: A Guide for Teaching Reading & Writing. (Jolly Phonics Ser.). 1997. 14.99 (1-870946-72-3, JL723, Pub. by Jolly Lrning) Am Intl Dist.

Lloyd, Susan M. Roget's Thesaurus of English Words & Phrases. 1250p. 1989. 9.95 (0-582-55635-X, TV2782) Longman.

Lloyd, Susette H. Sketches of Bermuda. (Illus.). 1977. text 18.95 (0-8369-9228-8, 9082) Ayer.

Lloyd, T. O. The British Empire, 1558-1995. 2nd ed. LC 97-188661. (Short Oxford History of the Modern World). (Illus.). 468p. 1997. pap. text 22.00 (0-19-873133-7) OUP.

Lloyd, T. O. Empire, Welfare State, Europe: English History, 1906-1992. 4th ed. (Short Oxford History of the Modern World Ser.). (Illus.). 598p. 1993. pap. text 26.00 (0-19-873111-6) OUP.

*Lloyd, Tanya. Alaska. 2000. 14.95 (1-55285-025-0) Carlton Bks Ltd.

— Alberta. LC 96-910743. (Illus.). 96p. 17.95 (1-55110-529-2) Whitecap Bks.

Lloyd, Tanya. Atlantic Canada. LC 96-910744. (America Ser.). (Illus.). 96p. 1999. text 17.95 (1-55110-530-6) Whitecap Bks.

— British Columbia. LC 96-910742. (The America Ser.). (Illus.). 96p. text 14.95 (1-55110-521-7, Pub. by WCBI) Gr Arts Ctr Pub.

*Lloyd, Tanya. Calgary. (Illus.). 96p. 2000. 14.95 (1-55285-018-8) Carlton Bks Ltd.

— California. 2000. 14.95 (1-55285-028-5) Carlton Bks Ltd.

— Canada. LC 96-910739. (Illus.). 96p. 17.95 (1-55110-524-1) Whitecap Bks.

— Canada's National Parks. LC 96-910738. (Illus.). 96p. 17.95 (1-55110-525-X) Whitecap Bks.

— Chicago. 2000. 14.95 (1-55285-026-9) Carlton Bks Ltd.

— Colorado. (America Ser.). (Illus.). 96p. 1999. 14.95 (1-55110-946-8) Whitecap Bks.

Lloyd, Tanya. Montreal. (America Ser.). (Illus.). 96p. 1999. text 14.95 (1-55110-753-8) Whitecap Bks.

*Lloyd, Tanya. New England. (America Ser.). (Illus.). 96p. 1999. 14.95 (1-55110-947-6) Whitecap Bks.

— Niagara. Whitecap Books Staff, ed. (Illus.). 96p. 2000. 14.95 (1-55285-019-6) Carlton Bks Ltd.

— North Carolina. (Illus.). 96p. 2000. 14.95 (1-55285-027-7) Carlton Bks Ltd.

— Ontario. LC 96-910740. (Illus.). 96p. 17.95 (1-55110-523-3) Whitecap Bks.

— Ottawa. LC 96-910736. (Illus.). 96p. 17.95 (1-55110-527-6) Whitecap Bks.

— The Prairies. LC 96-910741. (Illus.). 96p. 14.95 (1-55110-522-5) Whitecap Bks.

— Texas. LC 99-910829. (Illus.). 96p. 1999. 14.95 (1-55110-949-2) Whitecap Bks.

— Toronto. LC 96-910737. (Illus.). 96p. 17.95 (1-55110-526-8) Whitecap Bks.

— The Twin Cities: Minneapolis & St. Paul. (Illus.). 96p. 1999. 14.95 (1-55110-948-4) Whitecap Bks.

— Vancouver. LC 96-910735. (Illus.). 96p. 17.95 (1-55110-528-4) Whitecap Bks.

— Vancouver Island. (Illus.). 96p. 2000. 14.95 (1-55285-017-X) Carlton Bks Ltd.

*Lloyd, Tanya & Cowden, Steve. Cheese Louise. (Illus.). 32p. (J). 2000. 16.95 (1-55110-965-4) Whitecap Bks.

Lloyd, Tim & Morrissey, Oliver, eds. Poverty, Inequality, & Rural Development. LC 93-47023. 1994. text 75.00 (0-312-12099-0) St Martin.

*Lloyd, Tim, et al. The Blue Plate Diner Cookbook. LC 99-28535. (Illus.). 128p. 1999. 16.95 (1-879483-59-9) Prairie Oak Pr.

Lloyd, Timothy & Glatt, Hillary. Folklife Resources in the Library of Congress. LC 93-36504. (Publications of the American Folklife Center: Vol. 8). 1993. write for info. (0-8444-0371-7) Lib Congress.

Lloyd, Timothy C. & Mullen, Patrick B. Lake Erie Fisherman: Work, Identity & Tradition. (Illus.). 216p. 1990. text 19.95 (0-252-01662-9) U of Ill Pr.

Lloyd, Tom. Crisis of Realism: Representing Experience in the British Novel, 1816-1910. LC 97-24000. 240p. 1997. 37.50 (0-8387-5359-0) Bucknell U Pr.

Lloyd, Tracey. The Old Man & the Rabbit. (Junior African Writers Ser.). (Illus.). 80p. (J). (gr. 3 up). 1992. pap. 4.95 (0-7910-2917-4) Chelsea Hse.

Lloyd, Trevor, jt. auth. see Perham, Michael.

Lloyd, Vicki, ed. see Stenger, Alma G.

Lloyd, W. Eugene, ed. Safety Evaluation of Drugs & Chemicals. LC 84-12912. (Illus.). 487p. (C). 1986. text 140.00 (0-89116-352-2) Hemisp Pub.

Lloyd, W. Francis, jt. auth. see Austin, Bertram, Jr.

Lloyd-Watts, Valery, jt. auth. see Bigler, Carole L.

Lloyd Webber, Andrew. Andrew Lloyd Webber. LC 95-753721. 64p. 1993. pap. 12.95 (0-7935-1503-3, 00292001) H Leonard.

— The Best of Andrew Lloyd Webber. 64p. 1991. pap. 14.95 (0-7935-0603-4, 00290333) H Leonard.

*Lloyd Webber, Andrew. The Best of Andrew Lloyd Webber. 64p. 1999. otabind 12.95 (0-634-00029-2) H Leonard.

Lloyd Webber, Andrew. The Best of Andrew Lloyd Webber: Composers Easy Piano. 64p. 1996. per. 10.95 (0-7935-6191-4) H Leonard.

— Cats: Vocal Selection. (Easy Piano Ser.). 64p. 1983. pap. 12.95 (0-7935-2955-7, 00359467) H Leonard.

Lloyd Webber, Andrew. Evita: Easy Piano. 56p. 1997. pap. 10.95 (0-7935-8289-X) H Leonard.

Lloyd Webber, Andrew. Joseph & the Amazing Technicolor Dreamcoat. 128p. 1991. per. 20.00 (0-7935-0839-8, 00362641) H Leonard.

— Joseph & the Amazing Technicolor Dreamcoat. rev. ed. 56p. 1994. otabind 15.95 (0-7935-3427-5, 00312505) H Leonard.

— Joseph & the Amazing Technicolor Dreamcoat: Abridged Vocal Score. 56p. 1991. pap. 5.95 (0-7935-0893-2, 00362042) H Leonard.

— Joseph & the Amazing Technicolor Dreamcoat: Easy Piano. (Easy Play Ser.). 28p. 1992. pap. 7.95 (0-7935-1957-8, 00222558) H Leonard.

— The New Starlight Express. 56p. 1994. per. 12.95 (0-7935-3367-8, 00312500) H Leonard.

— The Phantom of the Opera: Intermediate Piano Solos. 56p. 1993. pap. 12.95 (0-7935-1655-2, 00290386) H Leonard.

— The Phantom of the Opera: Piano Solos. 48p. 1993. pap. 12.95 (0-7935-1657-9, 00292005) H Leonard.

— Piano Duets of Andrew Lloyd Webber: 1 Piano, 4 Hands. 64p. 1991. pap. 9.95 (0-7935-0638-7, 00290332) H Leonard.

— Requiem. (Vocal Score Ser.). 80p. 1985. pap. 12.95 (0-88188-473-1, 00362640) H Leonard.

*Lloyd Webber, Andrew. Songs of Andrew Lloyd Webber. 48p. 1999. pap. 10.95 (0-7935-6564-2) H Leonard.

Lloyd Webber, Andrew. Still More Songs of the '60s. (Decade Ser.). 224p. 1995. per. 14.95 (0-7935-3588-3, 00311680) H Leonard.

— Sunset Boulevard Highlights. 24p. 1993. pap. 9.95 (0-7935-2779-1, 00312486) H Leonard.

— Variations for Piano. 64p. 1988. pap. 9.95 (0-7935-1939-X, 00361447) H Leonard.

— Variations 1-4 for Cello & Piano. 12p. 1992. 6.95 (0-7935-1784-2, 00312481) H Leonard.

Lloyd, William. Music in Sequence. 1997. pap. write for info. (0-8081-5416-8) Bonus Books.

Lloyd, William, jt. auth. see Salter, Christopher.

Lloyd-Williams, Paul, et al. Chemical Approaches to the Synthesis of Peptides & Proteins. LC 97-7644. (New Directions in Organic & Biological Chemistry Ser.). 304p. (C). 1997. boxed set 104.95 (0-8493-9142-3) CRC Pr.

Lloyd's Aviation Department Staff, compiled by. Aircraft Types & Price Guidelines, 1994-1995. pap. 100.00 (1-85044-562-1) LLP.

— Aircraft Types & Price Guidelines, 1995-1996. 1995. 110.00 (1-85044-977-5) Lloyds of London Pr.

Lloyds Bank Staff, ed. Monetarism & Keynesians. 1991. text 49.00 (0-86187-121-9, Pub. by P P Pubs) Cassell & Continuum.

Lloyds, Darren, jt. auth. see Hallett, Maurice B.

Lloyd's of London Press, Inc. Staff. Lloyd's Ports of the World 1995. 1995. 310.00 (1-85044-325-4) LLP.

— Lloyd's Survey Handbook. 6th ed. 337p. 1991. 89.00 (1-85044-395-5) LLP.

— Mediterranean Shipping Directory, 1993. 1993. pap. 130.00 (1-85044-332-7) LLP.

Lloyd's of London Press Staff. Capital for Shipping. 7th ed. 1995. pap. 90.00 (1-85044-504-4) LLP.

— Guide to International Ship Registers, Ship Managers & Manning Agents, 95/96. 1995. 90.00 (1-85044-360-2) LLP.

— Lloyd's Cruise Industry Direct 1996. (Illus.). 104p. 1996. pap. 90.00 (1-85044-478-1) LLP.

— Lloyd's Law Reports Citator, 1919-1986. 1988. 300.00 (1-85044-170-7) LLP.

— Lloyd's Law Reports Subject Index, 1919-1986. 1988. 445.00 (1-85044-171-5) LLP.

— Lloyd's Nautical Year Book 1996. 1995. 90.00 (1-85044-421-8) LLP.

— Lloyd's Shipping Connections 1996. 1995. 60.00 (1-85044-493-5) LLP.

— Lloyd's War Losses - The First World War, 1919-1918. 1990. 170.00 (1-85044-314-9) LLP.

— Lloyd's War Losses - The Second World War, 1939-1945. 1989. 170.00 (1-85044-217-7) LLP.

— Marine Equipment Buyers' Guide, 1995. 1995. pap. 185.00 (1-85044-553-2) LLP.

Lloyd's Ship Manager Staff. Guide to Worldwide Marine Training, 1996. 1996. pap. 90.00 (1-85044-378-5) LLP.

Lloyd's Shipping Economist Staff. Shipping & the Environment. (Orig.). 1991. pap. 30.00 (0-685-66240-3) LLP.

Lloyd's Training Centre Staff, ed. An Introduction to Lloyd's Market Procedures & Practices. 121p. (C). 1987. 105.00 (0-948691-22-0, Pub. by Witherby & Co) St Mut.

LLP Staff. Oregon Uniform Trial Court Rules. 431p. 1998. ring bd. write for info. (0-327-00584-X, 8229821) LEXIS Pub.

LLP Staff, ed. Local Rules of the Superior Court, Washinngton State, No. 62. 101p. 1998. ring bd. write for info. (0-327-00676-5, 8282720) LEXIS Pub.

— New Hampshire Practice: Index, 1999 Edition, 22 vols. 550p. 1998. write for info. (0-327-00721-4, 8206414) LEXIS Pub.

*LLP Staff, ed. New Mexico Local & Federal Rules. 2nd ed. 894p. 1999. write for info. (0-327-04917-0, 8215011) LEXIS Pub.

— New Mexico Local & Federal Rules, Issue 60. 100p. 1999. ring bd. write for info. (0-327-01380-X, 8215423) LEXIS Pub.

— Oregon Uniform Trial Court Rules, Issue 33. 600p. 1999. ring bd. write for info. (0-327-01283-8, 8229822) LEXIS Pub.

LLP Staff, ed. Practica Forense Puertorriquena, Vols. 1-3. (SPA.). 2260p. 1998. pap. 125.00 (0-327-05128-0, 47526-11) LEXIS Pub.

Lluch, Alex & Lluch, Elizabeth. Wedding Party Responsibility Cards: Christian Edition. 48p. 1994. pap. 6.95 (0-9639654-9-2) Wedding Solns.

— Your Rehearsal Day. (Illus.). 128p. 1999. pap. 12.95 (1-887169-07-5) Wedding Solns.

Lluch, Alex & Lluch, Elizabeth, eds. Naughty Games for the Honeymoon... And Beyond. 212p. 1999. pap. 17.95 (1-887169-06-7) Wedding Solns.

Lluch, Alex, jt. ed. see Lluch, Elizabeth.

*Lluch, Alex A. & Lluch, Elizabeth H. Easy Wedding Planner: With Free Planning Software. 248p. 2000. 17.95 incl. cd-rom (1-887169-15-6, Pub. by Wedding Solns) Natl Bk Netwk.

Lluch, Alex A. & Lluch, Elizabeth H. Easy Wedding Planner, Organizer & Keepsake: Unique & Inspirational Ideas for the Wedding of Your Dreams. (Illus.). 369p. 2000. 29.95 (1-887169-09-1, Pub. by Wedding Solns) Natl Bk Netwk.

*Lluch, Alex A. & Lluch, Elizabeth H. Easy Wedding Planning. 3rd rev. ed. 304p. 2000. pap. 9.95 (1-887169-12-1, Pub. by Wedding Solns) Natl Bk Netwk.

Lluch, Alex A. & Lluch, Elizabeth H. Easy Wedding Planning Plus. 2nd rev. ed. (Illus.). 288p. 1998. pap. 19.95 (1-887169-05-9) Wedding Solns.

*Lluch, Alex A. & Lluch, Elizabeth H. Easy Wedding Planning Plus. 3rd rev. ed. 310p. 2000. pap. 19.95 (1-887169-11-3, Pub. by Wedding Solns) Natl Bk Netwk.

— Easy Wedding Workbook & Organizer: Greatly Simplifies Your Wedding Planning Process. 204p. 2000. wbk. ed. 24.95 (1-887169-14-8, Pub. by Wedding Solns) Natl Bk Netwk.

Lluch, Alex A., et al. Indispensable Groom's Guide. 2nd rev. ed. (Illus.). 192p. 1997. pap. 6.95 (1-887169-02-4) Wedding Solns.

Lluch, Elizabeth & Lluch, Alex, eds. Naughty Games for Lovers. 2000. pap. 17.95 (1-887169-08-3) Wedding Solns.

Lluch, Elizabeth, jt. auth. see Lluch, Alex.

Lluch, Elizabeth, jt. ed. see Lluch, Alex.

Lluch, Elizabeth H., jt. auth. see Lluch, Alex A.

Lluch-Velez, Amalia. La Decima Culta en la Literatura Puertorriquena. LC 85-22643. 1988. pap. 10.00 (0-8477-3804-3) U of PR Pr.

Lluelles Cardona, Victor. Diccionari Politic de Catalunya. (CAT.). 344p. 1977. pap. 24.95 (0-8288-5306-1, S50183) Fr & Eur.

Lluelles, Manuel F. Diccionari de Sinonims. 5th ed. (CAT.). 1234p. 1986. 59.95 (0-7859-5117-2) Fr & Eur.

Lluesma, Elisa. Communication for Business. 2nd ed. 304p. (C). 1996. pap. text, per. 30.39 (0-7872-1822-7) Kendall-Hunt.

Llull, Ramon. The Book of the Lover & the Beloved: An English Translation with the Old Catalan & Latin Texts. Johnston, Mark D., ed. & tr. by. from CAT. (Illus.). 140p. 1995. 59.95 (0-85668-633-6, Pub. by Aris & Phillips); pap. 22.00 (0-85668-634-4, Pub. by Aris & Phillips) David Brown.

— Tree of Love: Ramon Llull's "Tree of the Philosophy of Love" (Historical & Scholarly Resources Ser.). 100p. 1997. pap. 19.95 (1-883938-11-2) Dry Bones Pr.

Llull, Ramon, jt. auth. see Johnson, Peter C.

Llwellyn, Michael. Twelfth Night. LC 96-77847. 384p. (YA). 1997. 21.95 (1-57566-082-2, Knsington) Kensgtn Pub Corp.

Llyinsky, M. Afghanistan: Onward March of the Revolution. 88p. 1982. 11.95 (0-318-37223-1) Asia Bk Corp.

Llyne, Jennifer, ed. see Batik, Albert L.

Llyod, Frank W. Cable Television Law Nineteen Ninety-Two: Cable Faces Congress, the Courts & Competition, 2 vols., Set. (Patents, Copyrights, Trademarks, & Literary Property Ser.). 1743p. 1992. pap. text 80.00 (0-685-56909-8, G4-3877) PLI.

Llywelyn, Morgan. Bard: The Odyssey of the Irish. 480p. 1995. 5.99 (0-8125-8515-1, Pub. by Tor Bks) St Martin.

An Asterisk (*) at the beginning of an entry indicates that the title is appearing for the first time.

L

— Brian Boru: Emperor of the Irish. 1997. mass mkt. 4.99 (*0-8125-4461-7*, Pub. by Tor Bks) St Martin.
— The Druids. 1993. mass mkt. 5.99 (*0-8041-0844-7*) Ivy Books.
— The Elementals. 1994. pap. 5.99 (*0-312-51815-3*) Tor Bks.
— The Elementals. 384p. 1994. mass mkt. 5.99 (*0-8125-1815-2*, Pub. by Tor Bks) St Martin.
— Essential Library for Irish American. LC 98-46785. 320p. 1999. 24.95 (*0-312-86914-2*, Pub. by Forge NYC) St Martin.
***Llywelyn, Morgan.** The Essential Library for Irish Americans. 320p. 2000. pap. 15.95 (*0-312-86913-4*, Pub. by Forge NYC) St Martin.
Llywelyn, Morgan. Finn Mac Cool. 528p. 1995. 6.99 (*0-8125-2401-2*, Pub. by Tor Bks) St Martin.
— Horse Goddess. 1998. mass mkt. 6.99 (*0-8125-5503-1*, Pub. by Tor Bks) St Martin.
— Lion of Ireland. 1996. mass mkt. 6.99 (*0-8125-5399-3*, Pub. by Tor Bks) St Martin.
***Llywelyn, Morgan.** 1916: A Novel of the Irish Rebellion. LC 97-29838. 447p. 1998. text 24.95 (*0-312-86101-X*) St Martin.
Llywelyn, Morgan. 1916: A Novel of the Irish Rebellion. 544p. 1999. pap. 6.99 (*0-8125-7492-3*, Pub. by Tor Bks) St Martin.
— 100 Essential Books for Irish-American Readers. (Illus.). 256p. 1998. 24.95 (*0-8065-1957-6*, Citadel Pr) Carol Pub Group.
***Llywelyn, Morgan.** A Pocket History of Irish Rebels. 112p. 2000. pap. 7.95 (*0-86278-580-4*, Pub. by OBrien Pr) IPG Chicago.
Llywelyn, Morgan. The Pride of Lions. 352p. 1996. 23.95 (*0-312-85700-4*) Forge NYC.
— The Pride of Lions. 1997. mass mkt. 6.99 (*0-8125-3650-9*, Pub. by Tor Bks) St Martin.
— Red Branch. 528p. 1990. mass mkt. 5.95 (*0-8041-0591-X*) Ivy Books.
— Star Dancer. 160p. 1997. pap. 6.95 (*0-86278-331-3*, Pub. by OBrien Pr) Irish Amer Bk.
— Strongbow. LC 95-53841. 160p. 1996. 15.95 (*0-312-86150-8*) Tor Bks.
— Strongbow: The Story of Richard & Aoife. 1997. mass mkt. 4.99 (*0-8125-4462-5*, Pub. by Tor Bks) St Martin.
— The Vikings in Ireland. (Illus.). 96p. 1997. pap. 12.95 (*0-86278-421-2*, Pub. by OBrien Pr) Irish Amer Bk.
— Wind from Hastings. 288p. 1998. mass mkt. 5.99 (*0-8125-5502-3*, Pub. by Tor Bks) St Martin.
— The Wind from Hastings. 1995. reprint ed. lib. bdg. 25.95 (*1-56849-613-3*) Buccaneer Bks.
***Llywelyn, Morgan & Scott, Michael.** Etruscans: Beloved of the Gods. 320p. 2000. 24.95 (*0-312-86627-5*, Pub. by Tor Bks) St Martin.
Llywelyn, Morgan & Scott, Michael. Silverhand: The Arcana. (Arcana Ser.: Bk. I). 432p. (Orig.). 1995. 22.00 (*0-671-87652-X*) Baen Bks.
— Silverhand No. 1: The Arcana, Bk. I. 432p. 1996. mass mkt. 5.99 (*0-671-87714-3*) Baen Bks.
— Silverlight. (Arcana Ser.: Vol. 2). 432p. 1997. per. 5.99 (*0-671-87790-9*) Baen Bks.
— Silverlight Bk. 2: The Arcana, II. 416p. 1996. 21.00 (*0-671-87728-3*) Baen Bks.
Llywelyn, Morgan, et al. Iris Magic: Four Unforgettable Novellas of Love & Enchantment, Vol. II. 320p. 1998. pap. 5.99 (*1-57566-272-8*) Kensgtn Pub Corp.
— Irish Magic II. 352p. 1997. 22.00 (*1-57566-140-3*, Knsington) Kensgtn Pub Corp.
Llywelyn, Robin. From Empty Harbour to White Ocean. LC 97-189757. 158p. 1997. pap. 11.95 (*0-9521558-2-6*) Dufour.
***Lm, Adam & Zhang, Qiao.** Advanced Chinese Reader. (Language & Linguistics Ser.). (CHI & ENG.). 208p. 1999. pap. 29.95 (*1-877133-64-7*, Pub. by Univ Otago Pr) Intl Spec Bk.
LMP, Inc. Staff & Love, Joe. Starting Your Own Business. LC 96-211346. 140p. 1996. pap. text, per. 29.95 (*0-7872-1873-1*) Kendall-Hunt.
LMS Associate Staff. Library Media & Information Skills. (School Library Media Ser.). 1992. pap. text 24.95 (*0-87436-665-8*) ABC-CLIO.
LMS Staff. Children's Literature: Promotion, Use, & Teaching in the School Media Center. (School Library Media Ser.). 1992. lib. bdg. 24.95 (*0-87436-666-6*) ABC-CLIO.
Lnades, William-Alan, ed. see **Corrie, Joe.**
Lnag, James. Anglo-Saxon Sculpture. (Archaeology Ser.: No. 52). (Illus.). 60p. 1989. pap. 10.50 (*0-85263-927-9*, Pub. by Shire Pubns) Parkwest Pubns.
Lo, S-Y & Bonavida, B., eds. Physical, Chemical & Biological Properties of Stable Water Clusters: Proceedings of the 1st International Symposium. LC 98-222277. 224p. 1998. 36.00 (*981-02-3509-7*) World Scientific Pub.
— Physical, Chemical & Biological Properties of Stable Water Clusters: Proceedings of the 1st International Symposium. LC 98-222277. 224p. 1998. pap. 18.00 (*981-02-3515-1*) World Scientific Pub.
***Lo, Amy.** The Book of Mahjong: An Illustrated Guide. (Illus.). 2000. pap. 15.95 (*0-8048-3302-8*) Tuttle Pubng.
Lo, Andrew W., ed. The Industrial Organization & Regulation of the Securities Industry. LC 95-18033. (National Bureau of Economic Research Conference Report Ser.). 386p. 1995. 59.95 (*0-226-48847-0*) U Ch Pr.
— Market Efficiency: Stock Market Behavior in Theory & Practice, 2 vols. LC 97-3805. (International Library of Critical Writings in Economics Ser.: No. 3). 1224p. 1997. 430.00 (*1-85898-161-1*) E Elgar.
Lo, Andrew W., et al. A Non-Random Walk down Wall Street. LC 98-31390. (Illus.). 424p. 1999. text 45.00 (*0-691-05774-5*, Pub. by Princeton U Pr) Cal Prin Full Svc.
Lo, Arlene, jt. ed. see **Ford, Donis W.**
Lo Bello, Francesco. The Story of Architecture. (Masters of Art Ser.). 64p. (J). 1999. lib. bdg. 22.50 (*0-87226-528-5*, 65285B, P Bedrick Books) NTC Contemp Pub Co.
Lo Bello, Nino. Travel Trivia Handbook of Oddball European Sights. (Illus.). 224p. 1992. pap. 12.95 (*0-8065-1333-0*, Citadel Pr) Carol Pub Group.
Lo, Bernard. Resolving Ethical Dilemmas: A Guide for Clinicians. LC 93-44523. (Illus.). 368p. 1994. 35.00 (*0-683-05138-5*) Lppncott W & W.
Lo, Bernard. Resolving Ethical Dilemmas: A Guide for Clinicians. 2nd ed. 352p. pap. text 39.95 (*0-7817-2219-5*) Lppncott W & W.
***Lo, Bobo.** Soviet Labour Ideology & the Collapse of the State. LC 99-48279. 2000. text 65.00 (*0-312-22984-4*) St Martin.
Lo Bosco, Rocco. Across a Distance of Knives. Taylor, Chuck, ed. (Orig.). 1982. pap. 4.95 (*0-941720-08-X*) Slough Pr TX.
Lo Bue, Erberto, jt. auth. see **Ricca, Franco.**
Lo, C. H. Ten Thousand - A Dictionary of New Chinese-English-Chinese. (CHI & ENG.). 474p. 1980. 25.00 (*0-8288-1606-9*, M9266) Fr & Eur.
Lo, Carlos Wing-Hung, jt. ed. see **Lee, Peter Nan-Shong.**
Lo Cascio, Thomas S. Alcohol Sellers & Servers: Professionals, Not Professional Servants. 153p. (C). 1993. teacher ed. write for info. (*0-9636613-0-2*); student ed. write for info. (*0-9636613-1-0*) Adv Desgn & Concept.
Lo, Cecilia W., jt. ed. see **Tuan, Rocky S.**
Lo Chai Chen. Aquaculture in Taiwan. (Illus.). 273p. 1990. 65.00 (*0-85238-165-4*) Blackwell Sci.
***Lo, Chi Y.** Boundary Value Problems. 300p. 2000. 48.00 (*981-02-4300-6*) World Scientific Pub.
Lo, Chi Y., tr. see **Yan-Qian, Ye, et al.**
Lo Cicero. Conservation in Thoracic Surgery. 2000. text. write for info. (*0-7216-4842-8*) Harcourt.
— Craft of General Thoracic Surgery. 2000. text. write for info. (*0-7216-4844-4*) Harcourt.
Lo, Clarence Y. Small Property vs. Big Government: Social Origins of the Property Tax Revolt. 1990. 45.00 (*0-520-05971-9*, Pub. by U CA Pr) Cal Prin Full Svc.
Lo, Clarence Y. & Schwartz, Michael, eds. Social Policy & the Conservative Agenda. LC 97-19087. 416p. 1998. pap. text 31.95 (*1-57718-120-4*) Blackwell Pubs.
— Social Policy & the Conservative Agenda. LC 97-19087. 416p. 1998. text 62.95 (*1-57718-119-0*) Blackwell Pubs.
Lo, Clarence Y.H. Small Property vs. Big Government: Expanded & Updated Edition. 306p. 1995. pap. 16.95 (*0-520-20028-4*, Pub. by U CA Pr) Cal Prin Full Svc.
Lo, Dic. Market & Institutional Regulation in Chinese Industrialization, 1978-94. LC 96-27846. (Illus.). 280p. 1997. text 69.95 (*0-312-16422-X*) St Martin.
Lo-dro of Drepung. Prince Who Became a Cuckoo: A Tale of Liberation. Geshe Wangyal, tr. (Bhaisajaguru Ser.). 1982. pap. 12.95 (*0-87830-574-2*, Thtre Arts Bks) Routledge.
Lo Duca, Joseph M. Bayard. Bunnell, Peter C. & Sobieszek, Robert A., eds. LC 76-23069. (Sources of Modern Photography Ser.). (FRE., Illus.). 1979. reprint ed. lib. bdg. 15.95 (*0-405-09634-8*) Ayer.
Lo, Eileen Y. Chinese Healthy Cooking. LC 96-43587. 1997. 24.95 (*0-02-860381-8*) Macmillan.
— The Chinese Kitchen: Recipes, Techniques & Ingredients, History & Memories from Americas Leading Authority on Chinese Cooking. LC 99-30746. (Illus.). 464p. 1999. 35.00 (*0-688-15826-9*, Wm Morrow) Morrow Avon.
***Lo Faro, Antonio.** Regulating Social Europe: Reality & Myth of Collective Bargaining in the EC Legal Order. 288p. 2000. 55.00 (*1-901362-90-6*, Pub. by Hart Pub) Intl Spec Bk.
Lo Fu-Chen & Yeung, Yue-Man. Globalization & the World of Large Cities. LC 98-19736. 360p. 1998. 34.95 (*92-808-0999-7*) UN Univ Pr.
Lo Gerfo, Paul & Ditkoff, Beth Ann. The Thyroid Guide. LC 99-34742. 192p. 2000. pap. 13.95 (*0-06-095260-1*, HarpRes) HarpInfo.
Lo, H. M. British Diplomatic & Consular Establishments, Vol. 2. 632p. 1988. 70.00 (*957-638-019-7*) Oriental Bk Store.
Lo, Hoi-Kwong, et al. Introduction to Quantum Computation & Information. LC 98-31095. 348p. 1998. 58.00 (*981-02-3399-X*) World Scientific Pub.
Lo Hui-Min, ed. see **Morrison, G. E.**
Lo, Irving Y. & Schultz, William, eds. Waiting for the Unicorn: Poems & Lyrics of China's Last Dynasty, 1644-1911. LC 85-42816. (Chinese Literature in Translation Ser.). (Illus.). 456p. (C). 1986. 37.95 (*0-253-36321-7*) Ind U Pr.
— Waiting for the Unicorn: Poems & Lyrics of China's Last Dynasty, 1644-1911. LC 85-42816. (Chinese Literature in Translation Ser.). 456p. 1987. pap. 8.95 (*0-253-20403-8*) Ind U Pr.
— Waiting for the Unicorn: Poems & Lyrics of China's Last Dynasty, 1644-1911. LC 85-42816. (Chinese Literature in Translation Ser.). (Illus.). 456p. (C). 1990. pap. 8.95 (*0-253-20575-1*, MB-575) Ind U Pr.
Lo, Irving Y., jt. ed. see **Liu, Wu-Chi.**
***Lo, Jack & Pressman, David.** How to Make Patent Drawings Yourself. 2nd ed. Harolde, Stephanie, ed. LC 98-25849. (Illus.). 256p. 1999. pap. 29.95 (*0-87337-491-6*) Nolo com.
Lo, Jeannie. Office Ladies/Factory Women: Life & Work at a Japanese Company. LC 89-70365. 140p. (C). (gr. 13). 1990. text 44.95 (*0-87332-598-2*, East Gate Bk) M E Sharpe.
— Office Ladies/Factory Women: Life & Work at a Japanese Company. LC 89-70365. 140p. (C). (gr. 13). 1993. pap. text 22.95 (*0-87332-599-0*, East Gate Bk) M E Sharpe.
Lo, Jenny, jt. auth. see **Lo, Vivienne.**
***Lo, Jim.** The Compassion of Missions. 100p. 2000. pap. text 9.95 (*0-89827-212-2*) Wesleyan Pub Hse.
— Showing Love to Other. (Illus.). 30p. (J). (gr. 1-3). 2000. pap. text 6.99 (*0-89827-208-4*) Wesleyan Pub Hse.
Lo, Jim. What Is Furlough? (Illus.). 28p. (Orig.). (J). (gr. 3-5). 1988. pap. 3.25 (*0-89827-060-X*, BKF99) Wesleyan Pub Hse.
Lo-Johansson, Ivar. Breaking Free (Godnatt, Jord) Wright, Rochelle, tr. & afterword by by. LC 89-24971. 486p. 1990. reprint ed. pap. 150.70 (*0-608-02384-1*, 206302600004) Bks Demand.
— Only a Mother - Bara en Mor. Bjork, Robert E., tr. & afterword by by. LC 90-13059. (Modern Scandinavian Literature in Translation Ser.). 513p. 1991. reprint ed. pap. 159.10 (*0-608-01838-4*, 206248700003) Bks Demand.
— Peddling My Wares. Wright, Rochelle, tr. & intro. by. LC 94-42896. (SCAND Ser.). xi, 229p. 1995. 60.00 (*1-57113-015-2*) Camden Hse.
Lo, K. Christmas Memories with Recipes. LC 94-10843. (Illus.). 320p. 1994. 9.99 (*0-517-10190-4*) Random Hse Value.
Lo, K. S. The Stonewares of Yixing: From the Ming Period to the Present Day. LC 85-50363. (Illus.). 288p. 1986. 125.00 (*0-85667-181-9*, Pub. by P Wilson) Scala Books.
Lo, Kenneth H. Chinese Vegetable & Vegetarian Cooking LC 75-311487. 172p. 1974. write for info. (*0-571-09889-4*) Faber & Faber.
— Encyclopedia of Chinese Cooking. 1996. pap. text 12.95 (*0-88486-147-3*, Bristol Park Bks) Arrowood Pr.
— Encyclopedia of Chinese Cooking. 1992. 10.98 (*0-88365-532-2*) Galahad Bks.
— The Encyclopedia of Chinese Cooking. (Illus.). 380p. Date not set. pap. 14.95 (*0-88486-158-9*, Bristol Park Bks) Arrowood Pr.
— Peking Cooking. LC 75-882821. 176p. 1971. write for info. (*0-571-09493-7*) Faber & Faber.
— Peking Cooking. LC 72-11556. 176p. 1973. write for info. (*0-394-48502-5*) Pantheon.
***Lo, Koua & Lo, Pa Houa.** Hmong & English Dictionary. Etzell, Lynne, ed. 150p. 2000. pap. 29.95 (*0-9701655-0-1*) Lomation Inc.
Lo Kuan-Chung. Au Bord de l'Eau: Epilogue Chapitre 47-92, Vol. 2. (FRE.). 1978. lib. bdg. 89.98 (*0-8288-3523-3*, M5576) Fr & Eur.
— Au Bord de l'Eau: Prologue Chapitre 1-46, Vol. 1. (FRE.). 1978. lib. bdg. 95.00 (*0-8288-3522-5*, F120800) Fr & Eur.
— Three Kingdoms: A Historical Novel. 1096p. 1994. pap. 45.00 (*0-520-08930-8*, Pub. by U CA Pr) Cal Prin Full Svc.
Lo Kuan-Chung & Roberts, Moss. Three Kingdoms: A Historical Novel. LC 98-39516. 488p. 1999. 50.00 (*0-520-21584-2*, Pub. by U CA Pr); pap. 19.95 (*0-520-21585-0*, Pub. by U CA Pr) Cal Prin Full Svc.
Lo Kuan-Chung, jt. auth. see **Shi, Nai'an.**
Lo Kuan-Chung, jt. auth. see **Shi Nai'an.**
Lo, Laotou, tr. see **Mattison, Wendy & Scareth, Thomas, eds.**
Lo, Lauri. Beginnings. Johnson, Macia, ed. LC 97-75419. 128p. 1997. pap. 14.95 (*0-89716-888-7*, Peanut Btr Pubng) Elton-Wolf Pub.
Lo, Lee. Traumatology As Treated by Traditional Chinese Medicine: A Comprehensive Text. 80p. (Orig.). (C). 1989. pap. text 24.95 (*0-685-29019-0*) Zee Lo.
Lo, Pa Houa, jt. auth. see **Lo, Koua.**
Lo Po Hu. The Tao of Silence. 128p. 1998. pap. 8.95 (*965-494-006-X*, Pub. by Astrolog Pub) Assoc Pubs Grp.
Lo, R. E., ed. Earth Observation & Remote Sensing by Satellites: Proceedings of the Symposium on Earth Observation & Remote Sensing by Satellites, Hannover, West Germany, 21 May 1982. 56p. 1984. pap. 45.00 (*0-08-031152-0*, Pergamon Pr) Elsevier.
Lo Re, A. G. Essays on the Periphery of the Quijote. (Documentacion Cervantina Ser.: Vol. 10). 124p. 1991. pap. 8.50 (*0-936388-47-1*) Juan de la Cuesta.
Lo Romer, David. Merchants & Reform in Livorno, 1814-1868. 1987. 65.00 (*0-520-05649-3*, Pub. by U CA Pr) Cal Prin Full Svc.
Lo Russo, Andrew P. Sing & Cook Italian. 2nd rev. ed. Cook, Jim, ed. 160p. (Orig.). 1993. reprint ed. pap. 19.95 (*0-9622020-1-0*) Happy Heart.
***Lo Russo, Andy.** Andy Lo Russo's "Singing Sauces" Recipe Book. (Illus.). 2000. pap. 3.95 (*0-9622020-2-9*) Happy Heart.
Lo, Ruth E. & Kinderman, Katharine S. In the Eye of the Typhoon: An American Woman in China During the Cultural Revolution. (Illus.). 312p. 1987. pap. 10.95 (*0-306-80283-X*) Da Capo.
Lo, S. C., jt. ed. see **Li, K. S.**
Lo, S. S. Glossary of Hydrology. 1770p. 1992. 110.00 (*0-918334-74-8*) WRP.
Lo, S. Y., ed. Geometrical Pictures in Hadronic Collisions. 412p. 1987. reprint ed. text 108.00 (*9971-978-48-2*); reprint ed. pap. text 60.00 (*9971-978-59-8*) World Scientific Pub.
Lo, Sai-Lai. A Modular & Extensible Network Storage Architecture. (Distinguished Dissertations in Computer Science Ser.: No. 11). (Illus.). 152p. (C). 1995. text 49.95 (*0-521-55115-3*) Cambridge U Pr.
Lo San Ross, Rosa. Beyond Bok Choy: With 70 Recipes. (Illus.). 192p. 1996. 25.00 (*1-885183-23-2*) Artisan.
Lo, Sara D., ed. Catalog of the Gerhard Mayer Collection of Rilkeiana. 400p. 1988. 115.00 (*0-8161-0468-9*, G K Hall & Co) Mac Lib Ref.
Lo Schiavo, Fulvia. Nuragic Sardinia in Its Mediterranean Setting: Some Recent Advances. 42p. 1985. pap. 7.00 (*0-614-21829-2*) David Brown.
Lo, Sonny S., jt. ed. see **Cheng, Joseph Y.**
Lo, T. Wing. Corruption & Politics in Hong Kong & China. LC 92-20666. (New Directions in Criminology Ser.). 176p. 1994. pap. 41.95 (*0-335-19385-4*) OpUniv Pr.
Lo, Tec C., et al, eds. Handbook of Solvent Extraction. 1006p. (C). 1991. reprint ed. lib. bdg. 169.00 (*0-89464-546-3*) Krieger.
Lo-Tien, F. Beginner's Translation Handbook: English-Chinese. (CHI & ENG.). 364p. 1974. pap. 14.95 (*0-8288-5974-4*, M9581) Fr & Eur.
Lo, Tien-When & Inderwiesen, Philip L. Fundamentals of Seismic Tomography. (Geophysical Monographs: No. 6). 178p. (C). 1994. pap. 33.00 (*1-56080-028-3*, 146A) Soc Expl Geophys.
Lo, Titus K., jt. auth. see **Litva, J.**
***Lo, Vivienne & Lo, Jenny.** Secrets from a Chinese Kitchen. (Secrets from a Kitchen Ser.). (Illus.). 2000. 27.50 (*1-86205-366-9*, Pub. by Pavilion Bks Ltd) Trafalgar.
Lo, Wingkwong. Das Werk des Menschen und die Gnade Gottes in Karl Barths Sakramentstheologie. (Regensburger Studien Zur Theologie Ser.: Bd. 44). (GER.). 229p. 1994. 39.95 (*3-631-47315-X*) P Lang Pubng.
Lo, Winston W. The Life & Thought of Yeh Shih. LC 73-92410. 216p. reprint ed. pap. 67.00 (*0-7837-5014-5*, 204468100004) Bks Demand.
Lo, Y. M. Dennis, ed. Clinical Applications of PCR. LC 97-51264. (Methods in Molecular Medicine Ser.: Vol. 16). (Illus.). 364p. 1998. 99.50 (*0-89603-499-2*) Humana.
Lo, Y. M. Dennis & Wainscoat, J. S., eds. Clinical Applications of PCR. LC 97-51264. (Methods in Molecular Medicine Ser.: Vol. 16). (Illus.). 364p. 1998. spiral bd. 79.00 (*0-89603-359-7*) Humana.
Lo, Y. T. & Lee, S. W., eds. The Antenna Handbook, Vol. 2: Antenna Theory. LC 93-6502. 1993. text 49.95 (*0-442-01593-3*, VNR) Wiley.
— The Antenna Handbook: Theory, Applications, & Design. (Illus.). 2162p. 1988. text 189.95 (*0-442-25843-7*, VNR) Wiley.
Lo Yang, G., jt. auth. see **Le Cam, Lucien M.**
Lo Zi Li. Best Writings. (CHI.). 1995. pap. 12.95 (*7-80590-354-9*, Pub. by China Intl Bk) Distribks Inc.
Loach, A. Orthopaedic Anaesthesia. 2nd ed. 192p. 1994. text 75.00 (*0-340-56438-5*, Pub. by E A) OUP.
***Loach, Jennifer.** Edward VI. LC 99-35554. (Illus.). 256p. 1999. 27.50 (*0-300-07992-3*) Yale U Pr.
Loach, Ken. Loach on Loach. Fuller, Graham, ed. (Illus.). 160p. 1999. 16.00 (*0-571-17918-5*) Faber & Faber.
Load-Curve Coverage in Future Electrical Power Gen. Electrical Load-Curve Coverage: Proceedings of the Symposium, Rome, Oct. 1977. United Nations. Economic Commission for Europe, ed. LC 78-40342. (Illus.). 1979. 244.00 (*0-08-022422-9*, Pub. by Pergamon Repr) Franklin.
Loader. Man Who Made Diamonds. (Longman Originals Ser.). 1995. pap. text. write for info. (*0-582-08144-0*, Pub. by Addison-Wesley) Longman.
Loader, Anne, jt. compiled by see **National Childbirth Trust Staff.**
Loader, Brian. Cyberspace Divide: Equality, Agency, & Policy in the Information Society. LC 97-39491. 272p. (C). 1998. pap. 25.99 (*0-415-16969-0*) Routledge.
— Cyberspace Divide: Equality, Agency, & Policy in the Information Society. LC 97-39491. (Illus.). 288p. (C). 1998. 85.00 (*0-415-16968-2*) Routledge.
Loader, Brian, jt. auth. see **Hague, Barry N.**
Loader, Brian D. The Governance of Cyberspace. LC 96-27222. 264p. (C). 1997. 85.00 (*0-415-14723-9*); pap. 22.99 (*0-415-14724-7*) Routledge.
Loader, Brian D., jt. ed. see **Burrows, Roger.**
Loader, C. Local Regression & Likelihood. Chambers, J. et al, eds. LC 99-14732. (Statistics & Computing Ser.). (Illus.). 304p. 1999. 54.95 (*0-387-98775-4*) Spr-Verlag.
Loader, J. A. Ecclesiastes: A Practical Commentary. Vriend, John, tr. LC 86-4266. (Text & Interpretation Ser.). 142p. reprint ed. pap. 44.10 (*0-7837-3190-6*, 204279400006) Bks Demand.
Loader, Jamer A. Polar Structures in the Book of Qohelet. (Beiheft zur Zeitschrift fuer die Alttestamentliche Wissenschaft Ser.). 150p. (C). 1979. text 65.40 (*3-11-007636-5*) De Gruyter.
***Loader, James A. & Kieweler, Hans V.** Vielseitigkeit des Alten Testaments: Festschrift Fur Georg Sauer Zum 70. Geburtstag. (Illus.). 475p. 1999. 67.95 (*3-631-32557-6*) P Lang Pubng.
Loader, Jeff. Fun to Make Wooden Toys & Games. LC 97-222428. (Illus.). 176p. 1997. pap. text 17.95 (*1-86108-049-2*, Pub. by Guild Master) Sterling.
Loader, Mandy. Great Discovery Stage Four. (Longman Originals Ser.). 1996. pap. text 7.35 (*0-582-05763-9*, Pub. by Addison-Wesley) Longman.
Loader, N. Claire. Building in Cyclopean Masonry: With Special Reference to the Mycenean Fortifications on Mainland Greece. (Pocket-Book Ser.: No. 148). (Illus.). 235p. 1998. pap. 69.50 (*91-7081-140-7*, Pub. by P Astroms) Coronet Bks.
Loader, William. The Christology of the Fourth Gospel: Structure & Issues. 2nd rev. ed. LC 92-19502. (Baitr Age Zur Biblischen Exegese und Theologie Ser.: Bd. 23). 303p. 1992. 50.00 (*3-631-44943-7*) P Lang Pubng.
Loader, William. Johannine Epistles. (Commentary Ser.). 1997. pap. text 14.00 (*0-7162-0480-0*) Epworth Pr.
Loader, William R. Jesus' Attitude Towards the Law: A Study of the Gospels. LC 97-226718. (WissUNT Zum Neuen Testament Ser.: Vol. 2, No. 97). 563p. 1997. pap. 87.50 (*3-16-146517-2*, Pub. by JCB Mohr) Coronet Bks.
Loades. Power in Tudor England. LC 96-25754. 256p. 1996. pap. 18.95 (*0-312-16392-4*); text 49.95 (*0-312-16391-6*) St Martin.
***Loades, Ann.** Evelyn Underhill. 1999. pap. write for info. (*0-00-628028-5*) HarpC.

An Asterisk (*) at the beginning of an entry indicates that the title is appearing for the first time.

Loades, Ann. For God & Clarity: New Essays in Honor of Austin Farrer. Eaton, Jeffrey C., ed. LC 83-2451. (Pittsburgh Theological Monographs, New Ser.: No. 4). 206p. 1983. pap. 12.00 (*0-915138-52-2*) Pickwick.

— Searching for Lost Coins: Explorations in Christianity & Feminism. LC 88-1056. (Princeton Theological Monographs: No. 14). 128p. (Orig.). 1988. reprint ed. pap. 12.00 (*1-55635-000-7*) Pickwick.

Loades, Ann, ed. Feminist Theology: A Reader. 324p. (Orig.). 1990. pap. 29.95 (*0-664-25129-3*) Westminster John Knox.

Loades, Ann & McLain, Michael, eds. Hermeneutics, the Bible & Literary Criticism. LC 91-24686. 199p. 1992. text 49.95 (*0-312-06881-6*) St Martin.

Loades, Ann, jt. ed. see Brown, David.

***Loades, D.** John Foxe: An Historical Perspective. LC 98-36991. (Illus.). 2p. 1999. 91.95 (*1-84014-678-8*) Ashgate Pub Co.

Loades, D. M. John Foxe & the English Reformation. LC 96-37218. (St. Andrews Studies in Reformation History). 352p. 1997. 96.95 (*1-85928-351-9*, Pub. by Scolar Pr) Ashgate Pub Co.

— The Papers of George Wyatt. (Camden Fourth Ser.: No. 5). 200p. 27.00 (*0-901050-01-6*) David Brown.

— Politics & Nation: England, 1450-1660. LC 98-51868. 512p. 1999. 62.95 (*0-631-21459-3*); pap. 28.95 (*0-631-21460-7*) Blackwell Pubs.

Loades, David. Henry VIII & His Queens. (Illus.). 192p. 1996. pap. 19.95 (*0-7509-1247-2*, Pub. by Sutton Pub Ltd) Intl Pubs Mktg.

Loades, David. John Dudley, Duke of Northumberland, 1504-1553. LC 97-108604. 334p. (C). 1996. text 80.00 (*0-19-820193-1*) OUP.

— Political & Military Transformation Of England, 1490-1690 - Rise Of England' The Rise of England's Maritime Empire. 224p. 2000. 69.95 (*0-582-35629-6*) Longman.

— The Rise of England's Maritime Empire: Sea Power & the Commercial, Political, & Military Transformation of England, 1490-1690. 224p. 2000. pap. 17.00 (*0-582-35628-8*) Longman.

Loades, David. Tudor Government: Structures of Authority in the Sixteenth Century. LC 96-54621. 304p. (C). 1997. pap. 28.95 (*0-631-19157-7*); text 72.95 (*0-631-19156-9*) Blackwell Pubs.

— The Tudor Navy: An Administrative Political & Military History. (Studies in Naval History). 304p. 1992. 69.95 (*0-85967-922-5*, Pub. by Scolar Pr) Ashgate Pub Co.

Loades, David M. The Reign of Mary Tudor: Politics, Government & Religion in England, 1553-58. (Illus.). 448p. (C). 1991. pap. text 34.50 (*0-582-05759-0*, 78831) Longman.

Loades, David M., ed. Politics, Censorship & the English Reformation. 227p. 1992. text 65.00 (*0-86187-861-2*, Pub. by P P Pubs) Cassell & Continuum.

Loague, K., jt. auth. see Corwin, D. L.

Loan, C. Van, see Van Loan, C.

Loan, Charles E. Van, see Van Loan, Charles E.

Loan, Charles F. Van, see Golub, Gene H. & Van Loan, Charles F.

Loan, Charles F. Van, see Coleman, T. & Van Loan, Charles F.

Loan, Linda B. The Edge of Survival: Vietnam, the Other Side. 270p. (Orig.). 1993. pap. 8.95 (*0-9637167-0-0*) Ashley Pub.

Loan, Raymond W., ed. Bovine Respiratory Disease: A Symposium. LC 83-40491. (Illus.). 544p. 1984. 34.95 (*0-89096-187-5*) Tex A&M Univ Pr.

Loan, Schuyler Van, see Van Loan, Schuyler.

Loan, Sharon Van, see Van Loan, Sharon.

***Loan, Shirley K. & Karolak, Robert.** Throwaway Kids: Story of a Foster Child. (Illus.). 88p. 1998. pap. 10.00 (*0-8059-4465-6*) Dorrance.

Loane, Helen. Industry & Commerce of the City of Rome. LC 78-64171. (Johns Hopkins University. Studies in the Social Sciences. Thirtieth Ser. 1912: 2). reprint ed. 37.50 (*0-404-61280-6*) AMS Pr.

Loane, Helen J. Industry & Commerce of the City of Rome: (50 B. C.-200 A. D.) Finley, Moses, ed. LC 79-4990. (Ancient Economic History Ser.). 1979, reprint ed. lib. bdg. 22.95 (*0-405-12378-7*) Ayer.

Loane, Marcus. Grace & the Gentiles. 149p. (Orig.). 1981. pap. text 10.99 (*0-85151-327-1*) Banner of Truth.

Loannides, N. S. Dinoflagellate Cysts from Upper Cretaceous-Lower Tertiary Sections, Bylot & Devon Islands, Arctic Archipelago LC 87-157420. (Bulletin/Geological Survey of Canada Ser.). 99p. 1986. 9.00 (*0-660-12198-0*, Pub. by Can7 Govern Pub) Intl Spec Bk.

Loar, Steve & DuBois, Alan. Moving Beyond Traditon: A Turned-Wood Invitational. LC 97-77091. (Illus.). 80p. 1997. pap. 12.95 (*1-884240-15-1*) Arkansas Art Ctr.

Loarca, Carlos, tr. see Chapline, Claudia.

Loarer, Even, et al. Peut-On Eduquer l'Intelligence? L'Evaluation d'Une Methode d'Education Cognitive. (Exploration Ser.). (FRE.). x, 216p. 1995. 36.95 (*3-906754-01-4*, Pub. by P Lang) P Lang Pubng.

Loasby, Brian J. Choice, Complexity, & Ignorance: An Inquiry into Economic Theory & the Practice of Decision-Making. LC 75-22558. 252p. reprint ed. pap. 71.90 (*0-608-17520-X*, 2030606) Bks Demand.

— Knowledge, Institutions, & Evolution in Economics. LC 98-33940. (Graz Schumpeter Lectures). 5p. 1999. write for info. (*0-415-20537-9*) Routledge.

Loasby, Wren. Stencilling on Fabric. Date not set. write for info. (*0-8069-3816-1*) Sterling.

— Stencilling on Fabric: Patterns & Possibilities. (Illus.). 128p. 1998. pap. 14.95 (*0-8069-8657-3*) Sterling.

Loase, John. Sigfluence: The Earthly Connection to Immortality. 96p. 1997. pap. 14.95 (*0-933025-61-0*) Blue Bird Pub.

Loase, John F. Sigfluence: Long-Term Positive Influence. LC 93-48962. 168p. (Orig.). lib. bdg. 48.00 (*0-8191-9449-2*) U Pr of Amer.

— Sigfluence: Long-Term Positive Influence. LC 93-48962. 168p. (Orig.). 1994. pap. text 27.50 (*0-8191-9450-6*) U Pr of Amer.

— Sigfluence III: The Key to: "It's a Wonderful Life" LC 95-43442. 114p. (C). 1996. lib. bdg. 26.50 (*0-7618-0207-X*) U Pr of Amer.

Loates, M., jt. auth. see Miller, P.

Loats, Jim, jt. auth. see Amdahl, Kenn.

Loayza, Luis. El Sol de Lima (The Lima Sun) (SPA.). 192p. 1993. pap. 10.99 (*968-16-4169-8*, Pub. by Fondo) Continental Bk.

Loba, Mark. Developments in Soviet Coking Technology. Gross, Janna, ed. (Institute of Minerals Fuels IGA Ser.). 159p. (Orig.). 1986. pap. text 75.00 (*1-55831-028-2*) Delphic Associates.

Lobanoff, Val S. & Ross, Robert R. Centrifugal Pumps. 2nd ed. 592p. 1992. 75.00 (*0-87201-200-X*) Gulf Pub.

— Centrifugal Pumps: Design & Application. LC 84-15769. 384p. reprint ed. pap. 119.10 (*0-8357-2578-2*, 204026900015) Bks Demand.

Lobanov, Grace, tr. see Leon-Portilla, Miguel.

Lobanov, L. Welded Structures Pt. 1-3, Vol. 8. (Welding & Surfacing Reviews Ser.). 300p. 1997. pap. text 52.00 (*90-5702-240-0*, Harwood Acad Pubs) Gordon & Breach.

***Lobanov, L., ed.** Welding & Related Technologies for the 21st Century, Vol. 12, Part 1. (Welding & Surfacing Reviews Ser.: Vol. 12, Issue 1). 400p. 1998. pap. text 80.00 (*90-5702-440-3*, Harwood Acad Pubs) Gordon & Breach.

Lobanov-Rostovsky, Andrei A. Russia & Asia. 1951. 20.00 (*0-911586-18-0*) Wahr.

— Russia & Europe, 1825-1878. 1954. 20.00 (*0-911586-19-9*) Wahr.

Lobanov, Y. Yu & Zhidkov, E. P. Programming & Mathematical Techniques in Physics. 324p. 1994. text 109.00 (*981-02-1706-4*) World Scientific Pub.

***Lobanova, Marina.** Musical Style & Genre: History & Modernity. Cook, Kate, tr. (Illus.). 220p. 2000. text 50.00 (*90-5755-067-9*, Harwood Acad Pubs) Gordon & Breach.

Lobao, Linda M. Locality & Inequality: Farm & Industry Structure & Socioeconomic Conditions. LC 90-30748. (SUNY Series, the New Inequalities). 291p. (C). 1990. pap. text 21.95 (*0-7914-0476-5*) State U NY Pr.

Lobas, Vladimir. Taxi from Hell: Confessions of a Russian Hack. LC 91-5680. 304p. 1992. pap. 12.00 (*0-939149-86-9*) Soho Press.

Lobato, Arcadio. Paper Bird. LC 93-24469.Tr. of Papiervogel. (Illus.). (J). (ps-3). 1994. lib. bdg. 19.95 (*0-87614-817-8*, Carolrhoda) Lerner Pub.

***Lobato, Arcadio.** Valley of Mist. 2000. 16.95 (*0-86315-312-7*) Floris Bks.

Lobato, Monteiro. Brazilian Short Stories. 1977. lib. bdg. 59.95 (*0-8490-1550-2*) Gordon Pr.

Lobaw, G. A Genealogy of the Warne Family in America, Principally the Descendants of Thomas Warne 1652-1722, One of the Proprietors of East N. J. (Illus.). 701p. 1989. reprint ed. pap. 99.00 (*0-8328-1227-7*); reprint ed. lib. bdg. 107.00 (*0-8328-1226-9*) Higginson Bk Co.

Lobay, Douglas. Amazing Natural Medicines: A Modern & Scientific Guide. 1998. pap. 13.95 (*0-9695681-3-4*) Vitl Communs.

— Creating Vibrant Health. 1999. pap. 11.95 (*0-9695681-2-6*) Vitl Communs.

Lobay, Douglas. Unlimited Health Vol. 1: A Modern & Scientific Guide to the Use of Food, Nutrition & Diet Therapy. 1994. pap. 16.95 (*0-9695681-1-8*) Vitl Communs.

Lobb, Fred H., ed. from CHI. The Wonderful Treasure Horse: Manchu, Mongolian & Turkic Folktales from China. (Illus.). xii, 180p. (J). (gr. 4-8). 1998. pap. text 21.95 (*0-9662833-0-9*) Cal-Asia Pub.

***Lobb, Janice.** At Home With Science: Bump! Thump! How Do We Jump? Experiments Outside. (Illus.). 32p. (J). 2000. 10.95 (*0-7534-5247-2*) LKC.

— At Home With Science: Munch! Crunch! What's for Lunch? Experiments in the Kitchen. (Illus.). 32p. (J). 2000. 10.95 (*0-7534-5246-4*) LKC.

***Lobb, Janice & Utton, Peter.** Dig & Sow! How Do Plants Grow? Experiments in the Garden. LC 99-49919. (At Home with Science Ser.). (Illus.). 32p. (J). (gr. k-2). 2000. 10.95 (*0-7534-5245-6*, Kingfisher) LKC.

— Splish! Splosh! Why Do We Wash? Experiments in the Bathroom. LC 99-49920. (At Home with Science Ser.). (Illus.). 32p. (J). (gr. k-2). 2000. 10.95 (*0-7534-5244-8*, Kingfisher) LKC.

Lobb, Michael L. & Watts, Thomas D. Native American Youth & Alcohol: An Annotated Bibliography, 16. LC 88-32345. (Bibliographies & Indexes in Sociology Ser.: No. 16). 210p. 1989. lib. bdg. 55.00 (*0-313-25618-7*, WNY/, Greenwood Pr) Greenwood.

Lobb, Nancy. 16 Extraordinary American Entrepreneurs. LC 99-183812. vi, 137 p. 1998. write for info. (*0-8251-3795-0*) J W Walch.

— 16 Extraordinary Native Americans. LC 98-212801. 134 p. 1997. write for info. (*0-8251-3342-4*) J W Walch.

Lobb, Roger. Eighth Row Center. Mitchell, John D., ed. (Illus.). 190p. 1997. pap. 14.95 (*1-884953-08-5*, ERC-0006) Eaton St Pr.

Lobban, Chirstopher S. & Schefter, Maria. Tropical Pacific Island Environments. LC 97-225315. (Illus.). 450p. (C). 1997. 70.00 (*1-881629-04-X*); pap. 50.00 (*1-881629-05-8*) Univ Guam Pr.

Lobban, Christopher S. & Harrison, Paul J. Seaweed Ecology & Physiology. LC 93-21306. (Illus.). 380p. (C). 1994. text 80.00 (*0-521-40334-0*) Cambridge U Pr.

— Seaweed Ecology & Physiology. LC 93-21306. (Illus.). 380p. (C). 1996. pap. text 31.95 (*0-521-40897-0*) Cambridge U Pr.

Lobban, Christopher S. & Schefter, Marla. Successful Lab Reports: A Manual for Science Students. (Illus.). 116p. (C). 1992. text 49.95 (*0-521-40404-5*); pap. text 14.95 (*0-521-40741-9*) Cambridge U Pr.

Lobban, J. H., ed. English Essays. LC 72-320. (Essay Index Reprint Ser.). 1977. reprint ed. 23.95 (*0-8369-2800-8*) Ayer.

Lobban, Michael. Common Law & English Jurisprudence, 1760-1850. (Illus.). 332p. 1991. text 65.00 (*0-19-825293-5*) OUP.

Lobban, Michael. White Man's Justice: South African Political Trials in the Black Consciousness Era. (Illus.). 298p. 1996. text 65.00 (*0-19-825809-7*) OUP.

Lobban, Richard, ed. Middle Eastern Women & the Invisible Economy. LC 98-12588. (Illus.). 416p. 1998. 49.95 (*0-8130-1577-4*) U Press Fla.

***Lobban, Richard A., Jr.** Cape Verde: Crioulo Colony to Independent Nation. 1998. pap. text 24.00 (*0-8133-3562-0*, Pub. by Westview) HarpC.

Lobban, Richard A. & Forrest, Joshua. Historical Dictionary of the Republic of Guinea-Bissau. 2nd ed. LC 87-32298. (African Historical Dictionaries Ser.: No. 22). (Illus.). 233p. 1988. 29.00 (*0-8108-2086-2*) Scarecrow.

Lobban, Richard A. & Lopes, Marlene. Historical Dictionary of the Republic of Cape Verde. 3rd ed. LC 94-17116. (African Historical Dictionaries Ser.: No. 62). (Illus.). 404p. 1995. 52.00 (*0-8108-2918-5*) Scarecrow.

Lobban, Richard A., Jr. & Mendy, Peter K. Historical Dictionary of the Republic of Guinea-Bissau. 3rd ed. LC 87-32298. (African Historical Dictionaries Ser.: No. 22). (Illus.). 432p. 1996. 79.00 (*0-8108-3226-7*) Scarecrow.

Lobban, Richard A., jt. auth. see Coli, Waltraud B.

Lobbert, Heribert. Zusammenhang: Die Theologie Hermann Kardinal Volks. (Europaische Hochschulschriften Ser.: Reihe 23, Bd. 524). (GER.). 436p. 1994. 62.95 (*3-631-47267-6*) P Lang Pubng.

Lobbrecht, A. H. Dynamic Water-System Control: Design & Operation of Regional Water-Resources Systems. LC 99-496422. (Illus.). 300p. (C). 1997. text 97.00 (*90-5410-431-7*, Pub. by A A Balkema) Ashgate Pub Co.

Lobby, Ted. Jessica & the Wolf: A Story for Children Who Have Bad Dreams. LC 89-29688. (Illus.). 32p. (J). (ps-3). 1990. 11.95 (*0-945354-22-3*); pap. 8.95 (*0-945354-21-5*) Am Psychol.

Lobdell, David, tr. see Blais, Marie-Claire.

Lobdell, David, tr. see Brault, Jacques.

Lobdell, J. H. Simon Lobdell, 1646 of Milford, Connecticut, & His Descendants, Also of Nicholas Lobden (Lobdell), 1635 of Hingham, Mass., & Some Descendants. (Illus.). 425p. 1989. reprint ed. pap. 63.50 (*0-8328-0780-X*); reprint ed. lib. bdg. 71.50 (*0-8328-0779-6*) Higginson Bk Co.

Lobdell, Jared. England & Always: Tolkien's World of the Rings. LC 81-12651. 108p. reprint ed. pap. 33.50 (*0-608-11915-6*, 202321900032) Bks Demand.

Lobdell, Jared C., ed. Further Materials on Lewis Wetzel & the Upper Ohio Frontier: The Historical Narrative of George Edgington Peter Henry's Account, the Narrative of Spencer Records, the Reminiscences of Stephen Burkam. 111p. (Orig.). 1994. pap. text 17.00 (*0-7884-0073-8*) Heritage Bk.

— Indian Warfare in Western PA & North WV at the Time of the American Revolution: Including the Narrative of Indian & Tory Depredations by John Crawford, the Military Reminiscences of Capt. Henry Jolly, & the Narrative of Lydia Boggs Shepherd Cruger. 155p. (Orig.). 1992. pap. 16.50 (*1-55613-653-6*) Heritage Bk.

Lobdell, Jared C., ed. & intro. see Draper, Lyman C.

Lobdell, Jared C., tr. & intro. see Larison, C. W.

Lobdell, Jared C., tr. & intro. see Larison, Cornelius W.

Lobdell, Richard A., jt. ed. see Forget, Evelyn L.

Lobdell, Scott. Askani'Son. (Illus.). 96p. 1997. pap. text 12.95 (*0-7851-0565-4*) Marvel Entrprs.

— Onslaught: Pyarmic Victory, Vol. 6. (Illus.). 144p. 1997. pap. text 12.95 (*0-7851-0285-X*) Marvel Entrprs.

— Onslaught: The Awakening, Vol. 1. (Illus.). 144p. 1997. pap. text 12.95 (*0-7851-0280-9*) Marvel Entrprs.

— Tales of the Age of Apocalypse. (Illus.). 48p. 1997. pap. 5.95 (*0-7851-0289-2*) Marvel Entrprs.

— The Ultimate Astonishing X-Men. (Illus.). 96p. 1995. pap. 8.95 (*0-7851-0127-6*) Marvel Entrprs.

— The Ultimate Generation Next. (Illus.). 96p. 1995. pap. 8.95 (*0-7851-0130-6*) Marvel Entrprs.

— X-Men: The Adventures of Cyclops & Phoenix. (Illus.). 96p. 1996. pap. text 12.95 (*0-7851-0171-3*) Marvel Entrprs.

— X-Men: Twilight of the Age of Apocalypse. 128p. 1996. pap. 8.95 (*0-7851-0181-0*) Marvel Entrprs.

Lobdell, Scott & Maggin, Elliot S. Generation X. 288p. 1997. mass mkt. 5.99 (*1-57297-223-8*) Blvd Books.

***Lobdell, Scott & Robinson, James.** X-Men: Zero Tolerance. (Marvels Finest Ser.). (Illus.). 336p. 2000. pap. 24.95 (*0-7851-0738-X*, Pub. by Marvel Entrprs) LPC Group.

Lobdell, Scott, et al. Wild C. A. T.s/X-Men Trade Paperback. (Illus.). 184p. 1998. pap. 19.95 (*1-58240-022-9*) Image Comics.

Lobdell, Terri, jt. auth. see Watahara, Alan.

Lobe, Matthias. Die Prinzipien der Ethik Emanuel Hirschs. (Theologische Bibliothek Toepelmann Ser.: Band 68). (GER.). xi, 295p. (C). 1995. lib. bdg. 121.55 (*3-11-014429-8*) De Gruyter.

Lobe, Mira. Christoph Wants a Party. LC 95-8395.Tr. of Christoph Will Ein Fest. (Illus.). 32p. (J). (ps-3). 1995. 15.95 (*0-916291-59-6*) Kane-Miller Bk.

Lobe, Tamara A. Let's Make a Garden. LC 95-78436. (Illus.). 40p. (Orig.). (J). (ps-3). 1995. pap. 7.99 (*0-8361-9021-1*) Herald Pr.

Lobe, Thom E. Tracheal Reconstruction in Infancy. 1991. text 115.00 (*0-7216-5779-6*, W B Saunders Co) Harcrt Hlth Sci Grp.

Lobe, Thom E. & Schropp, Kurt P. Pediatric Laparoscopy & Thoracoscopy. (Illus.). 272p. 1993. text 102.00 (*0-7216-4610-7*, W B Saunders Co) Harcrt Hlth Sci Grp.

Lobe, Thomas. United States National Security Policy & Aid to the Thailand Police. (Monograph Series in World Affairs: Vol. 14, 1976-77 Ser., Bk. 2). 161p. (Orig.). 1977. pap. 5.95 (*0-87940-051-X*) Monograph Series.

***Lobeck, Anne.** Discovering Grammar: An Introduction to English Sentence Grammar. LC 99-35472. (Illus.). 384p. (C). 2000. text 52.95 (*0-19-512984-9*) OUP.

Lobeck, Anne. Ellipsis: Functional Heads, Licensing & Identification. (Illus.). 224p. 1995. text 65.00 (*0-19-509181-7*) OUP.

Lobeck, Armin K. Things Maps Don't Tell Us: An Adventure into Map Interpretation. (Illus.). xiv, 174p. (C). 1993. pap. text 19.95 (*0-226-48877-2*) U Ch Pr.

Lobeck, C. August. Pathologiae Graeci Sermonis Elementa, 2 vols. xxv, 1099p. 1966. reprint ed. write for info. (*0-318-70968-6*) G Olms Pubs.

— Phrynichi Eclogae Nominum et Verborum Atticorum. lxxx, 841p. 1965. reprint ed. write for info. (*0-318-70969-4*) G Olms Pubs.

Lobeck, Christian A. Paralipomena Grammaticae Graecae, 2 vols. in 1. xii, 622p. 1967. reprint ed. write for info. (*0-318-70967-8*); reprint ed. write for info. (*0-318-72044-2*) G Olms Pubs.

— Phrynichi Eclogae Nominum et Verborum Atticorum. lxxx, 841p. 1965. reprint ed. write for info. (*0-318-72045-0*) G Olms Pubs.

Lobel. The Adventures of Frog & Toad. (Illus.). (J). 1998. 12.95 (*0-06-028043-3*) HarpC.

Lobel, Adrianne. A Small Sheep in a Pear Tree. LC 76-58721. (Illus.). 32p. (J). (gr. k-3). 1977. 12.95 (*0-06-023952-2*) HarpC Child Bks.

Lobel, Anita. Alison's Zinnia. LC 89-23700. (Illus.). 32p. (J). (ps-3). 1990. 16.00 (*0-688-08865-1*, Grenwillow Bks) HarpC Child Bks.

— Alison's Zinnia. (J). (ps up). pap. 4.95 (*0-614-15678-5*, Wm Morrow) Morrow Avon.

— Alison's Zinnia. LC 89-23700. 32p. (J). 1996. mass mkt. 5.95 (*0-688-14737-2*, Wm Morrow) Morrow Avon.

Lobel, Anita. Alison's Zinnia. LC 89-23700. 1996. 10.15 (*0-606-08979-9*, Pub. by Turtleback) Demco.

— Away from Home. LC 93-36521. (Illus.). 32p. (J). (ps-3). 1994. 15.89 (*0-688-10355-3*, Grenwillow Bks) HarpC Child Bks.

Lobel, Anita. Away from Home. LC 93-36521. (Illus.). 32p. (J). (ps up). 1994. 16.00 (*0-688-10354-5*, Grenwillow Bks) HarpC Child Bks.

— The Dwarf Giant. LC 95-6790. (Illus.). 32p. (J). (gr. k up). 1996. 16.00 (*0-688-14407-1*, Grenwillow Bks) HarpC Child Bks.

— The Dwarf Giant. 32p. (J). (ps-8). 1996. mass mkt. 4.95 (*0-688-14408-X*, Wm Morrow) Morrow Avon.

— Dwarf Giant. LC 95-6790. 1996. 10.15 (*0-606-09219-6*, Pub. by Turtleback) Demco.

Lobel, Anita. King Rooster, Queen Hen. LC 75-9787. (Read-Alone Bks.). 48p. (J). 1975. write for info. (*0-688-80008-4*, Grenwillow Bks) HarpC Child Bks.

Lobel, Anita. The Night Before Christmas. 32p. 1988. mass mkt. 3.95 (*0-552-52384-4*) Bantam.

***Lobel, Anita.** No Pretty Pictures: A Child of War. LC 97-48392. (Illus.). 208p. (YA). (gr. 5-9). 1998. 15.95 (*0-688-15935-4*, Grenwillow Bks) HarpC Child Bks.

— No Pretty Pictures: A Child of War. LC 97-48392. (Illus.). 208p. (YA). (gr. 5-9). 2000. mass mkt. 4.99 (*0-380-73285-8*, Avon Bks) Morrow Avon.

— On Market Street. (J). 1981. 10.15 (*0-606-04290-3*, Pub. by Turtleback) Demco.

Lobel, Anita. One Lighthouse, One Moon. LC 98-50790. (Illus.). 40p. (J). (ps-3). 2000. 15.95 (*0-688-15539-1*, Grenwillow Bks); lib. bdg. 15.89 (*0-688-15540-5*, Grenwillow Bks) HarpC Child Bks.

Lobel, Anita. The Cat & the Cook & Other Fables of Krylov. LC 94-4116. 32p. (J). (gr. k up). 1995. 15.00 (*0-688-12310-4*, Grenwillow Bks); lib. bdg. 14.93 (*0-688-12311-2*, Grenwillow Bks) HarpC Child Bks.

Lobel, Arnold. An Arnold Lobel Book of Mother Goose Fairytails. LC 97-1762. (l). (Illus.). 176p. 1997. 21.00 (*0-679-88736-9*, Pub. by Random Bks Yng Read) Random.

— Bk of Pigericks. LC 82-47730. (Illus.). 48p. (J). (gr. k-3). 1983. lib. bdg. 14.89 (*0-06-023983-2*) HarpC Child Bks.

— Bk of Pigericks. LC 82-47730. (Trophy Picture Bk.). (Illus.). 48p. (J). (gr. k-3). 1988. pap. 5.95 (*0-06-443163-0*, HarpTrophy) HarpC Child Bks.

— Book of Mother Goose. LC 97-1762. (Illus.). 176p. (J). 1997. lib. bdg. 22.99 (*0-679-98736-3*, Pub. by Random Bks Yng Read) Random.

— The Book of Pigericks: Pig Limericks. LC 82-47730. (Illus.). 48p. (J). (gr. k-3). 1983. 15.00 (*0-06-023982-4*) HarpC Child Bks.

— Days with Frog & Toad. LC 78-21786. (I Can Read Bks.). (Illus.). 64p. (J). (ps-3). 1979. 15.95 (*0-06-023963-8*); lib. bdg. 15.89 (*0-06-023964-6*) HarpC Child Bks.

— Days with Frog & Toad. (I Can Read Bks.). (Illus.). 64p. (J). (gr. 1-3). 1984. pap. 3.95 (*0-06-444058-3*, HarpTrophy) HarpC Child Bks.

— Days with Frog & Toad. (I Can Read Bks.). (J). (gr. 1-3). 1979. 8.95 (*0-606-03401-3*, Pub. by Turtleback) Demco.

— Days with Frog & Toad. unabridged ed. LC 78-21786. (I Can Read Bks.). (Illus.). 64p. (J). (ps-3). 1990. pap. 8.95 incl. audio (*1-55994-227-4*) HarperAudio.

— Days with Frog & Toad: (Dias con Sapo y Sepo) (SPA.). (J). (gr. 1-6). 8.95 (*84-204-3743-3*) Santillana.

— Dias con Sapo y Sepo (Days with Frog & Toad) (SPA.). (J). (gr. 2-4). 1995. pap. 10.95 (*1-56014-588-9*) Santillana.

Lobel, Arnold. Dias con Sapo y Sepo (Days with Frog & Toad) 1995. 15.15 (*0-606-10401-1*, Pub. by Turtleback) Demco.

Lobel, Arnold. Fables. LC 79-2004. (Illus.). 48p. (J). (ps-3). 1980. 15.95 (*0-06-023973-5*); lib. bdg. 15.89 (*0-06-023974-3*) HarpC Child Bks.

— Fables. LC 79-2004. (Trophy Picture Bk.). (Illus.). 48p. (J). (ps-3). 1983. pap. 6.95 (*0-06-443046-4*, HarpTrophy) HarpC Child Bks.

— Fables. (J). 1983. 11.15 (*0-606-02131-0*, Pub. by Turtleback) Demco.

— Fables: (Fabulas) (SPA.). (J). (gr. 1-6). 21.95 (*84-204-4552-5*) Santillana.

— Frog & Toad. LC 85-45373. (Pop-Up Bk.). (Illus.). 12p. (J). (ps-3). 1986. 9.95 (*0-06-023986-7*) HarpC Child Bks.

— Frog & Toad All Year. LC 76-2343. (I Can Read Bks.). (Illus.). 64p. (J). (ps-3). 1976. 15.95 (*0-06-023950-6*, HarpTrophy); lib. bdg. 15.89 (*0-06-023951-4*, HarpTrophy) HarpC Child Bks.

— Frog & Toad All Year. (I Can Read Bks.). (Illus.). 64p. (J). (gr. 1-3). 1984. pap. 3.95 (*0-06-444059-1*, HarpTrophy) HarpC Child Bks.

Lobel, Arnold. Frog & Toad All Year. (I Can Read Bks.). (J). (gr. 1-3). 1984. 8.70 (*0-606-03379-3*, Pub. by Turtleback) Demco.

Lobel, Arnold. Frog & Toad All Year. unabridged ed. LC 76-2343. (I Can Read Bks.). (Illus.). 64p. (J). (ps-3). 1990. pap. 8.95 incl. audio (*1-55994-228-2*) HarperAudio.

— Frog & Toad Are Friends. (I Can Read Bks.). (Illus.). 64p. (J). (gr. 1-3). 1970. 15.95 (*0-06-023957-3*, HarpTrophy) HarpC Child Bks.

— Frog & Toad Are Friends. LC 73-105492. (I Can Read Bks.). (Illus.). 64p. (J). (ps-3). 1970. lib. bdg. 15.89 (*0-06-023958-1*, HarpTrophy) HarpC Child Bks.

— Frog & Toad Are Friends. (I Can Read Bks.). (Illus.). 64p. (J). (gr. 1-3). 1979. pap. 3.95 (*0-06-444020-6*, HarpTrophy) HarpC Child Bks.

Lobel, Arnold. Frog & Toad Are Friends. (I Can Read Bks.). (J). (gr. 1-3). 1979. 8.70 (*0-606-01901-4*, Pub. by Turtleback) Demco.

Lobel, Arnold. Frog & Toad Are Friends. unabridged ed. LC 73-105492. (I Can Read Bks.). (Illus.). 64p. (J). (ps-3). 1990. pap. 8.95 incl. audio (*1-55994-229-0*) HarperAudio.

— Frog & Toad Are Friends: (Sapo y Sepo Son Amigos) (SPA.). (J). (gr. 1-6). 9.95 (*84-204-3043-9*) Santillana.

— Frog & Toad Together. (I Can Read Bks.). (Illus.). 64p. (J). (gr. 1-3). 1972. 15.95 (*0-06-023959-X*) HarpC Child Bks.

— Frog & Toad Together. LC 73-183163. (I Can Read Bks.). (Illus.). 64p. (J). (ps-3). 1972. lib. bdg. 15.89 (*0-06-023960-3*) HarpC Child Bks.

— Frog & Toad Together. LC 73-183163. (I Can Read Bks.). (Illus.). 64p. (J). (ps-3). 1979. pap. 3.95 (*0-06-444021-4*, HarpTrophy) HarpC Child Bks.

— Frog & Toad Together. LC PZ7.L7795Fp 1999. (I Can Read Bks.). (Illus.). 64p. (J). (gr. 1-3). 1999. 12.95 (*0-694-01298-X*) HarpC Child Bks.

— Frog & Toad Together. (I Can Read Bks.). (J). (gr. 1-3). 1979. pap. 1.95 (*0-590-06198-4*) Scholastic Inc.

— Frog & Toad Together. (I Can Read Bks.). (J). (gr. 1-3). 1979. 9.60 (*0-606-01900-6*, Pub. by Turtleback) Demco.

— Frog & Toad Together. unabridged ed. LC 73-183163. (I Can Read Bks.). (Illus.). 64p. (J). (ps-3). 1990. pap. 8.95 incl. audio (*1-55994-230-4*, Caedmon) HarperAudio.

— Frog & Toad Together: (Sapo y Sepo Inseparables) (SPA.). (J). 8.95 (*84-204-3047-1*) Santillana.

— Giant John. LC 64-16639. (Illus.). 32p. (J). (gr. k-3). 1964. lib. bdg. 14.89 (*0-06-022946-2*) HarpC Child Bks.

— Grasshopper on the Road. (I Can Read Bks.). (Illus.). 64p. (J). (gr. 1-3). 1978. 14.00 (*0-06-023961-1*); lib. bdg. 15.89 (*0-06-023962-X*) HarpC Child Bks.

— Grasshopper on the Road. LC 77-25653. (I Can Read Bks.). (Illus.). 64p. (J). (ps-3). 1986. pap. 3.95 (*0-06-444094-X*, HarpTrophy) HarpC Child Bks.

Lobel, Arnold. Grasshopper on the Road. (I Can Read Bks.). (J). (gr. 1-3). 1986. 8.95 (*0-606-01850-6*, Pub. by Turtleback) Demco.

— Grasshopper on the Road. abr. ed. (I Can Read Bks.). (Illus.). 64p. (J). (gr. 1-3). 1991. audio 8.95 (*1-55994-436-6*, TBC 4366) HarperAudio.

Lobel, Arnold. Gregory Griggs: And Other Nursery Rhyme People. LC 77-22209. (Illus.). 48p. (J). (ps up). 1987. pap. 3.95 (*0-688-07042-6*, Wm Morrow) Morrow Avon.

— Holiday for Mr. Muster. LC 63-15323. (Illus.). 32p. (J). (gr. k-3). 1963. lib. bdg. 12.89 (*0-06-023956-5*) HarpC Child Bks.

— Lucille. LC 64-11616. (I Can Read Bks.). (Illus.). 64p. (J). (gr. k-3). 1964. lib. bdg. 12.89 (*0-06-023966-2*) HarpC Child Bks.

Lobel, Arnold. Ming Lo Moves the Mountain. (J). 1993. 10.15 (*0-606-05926-1*, Wm Morrow) Morrow Avon.

— Ming Lo Moves the Mountain. LC 92-47364. (Illus.). 32p. (J). (ps-3). 1993. mass mkt. 5.95 (*0-688-10995-0*, Wm Morrow) Morrow Avon.

Lobel, Arnold. Mouse Soup. LC 76-41517. (I Can Read Bks.). (Illus.). 64p. (J). (ps-3). 1977. 15.95 (*0-06-023967-0*); lib. bdg. 15.89 (*0-06-023968-9*) HarpC Child Bks.

— Mouse Soup. (I Can Read Bks.). (Illus.). 64p. (J). (gr. 1-3). 1983. pap. 3.95 (*0-06-444041-9*, HarpTrophy) HarpC Child Bks.

— Mouse Soup. (I Can Read Bks.). (J). (gr. 1-3). 1977. pap. 3.95 (*0-590-20804-7*) Scholastic Inc.

Lobel, Arnold. Mouse Soup. (I Can Read Bks.). (J). (gr. 1-3). 1977. 8.95 (*0-606-03215-0*, Pub. by Turtleback) Demco.

— Mouse Soup. abr. ed. (I Can Read Bks.). (J). (gr. 1-3). 1990. 8.95 incl. audio (*1-55994-237-1*, TBC 2371) HarperAudio.

Lobel, Arnold. Mouse Tales. LC 66-18654. (I Can Read Bks.). (Illus.). 64p. (J). (ps-3). 1972. 15.95 (*0-06-023941-7*); lib. bdg. 15.89 (*0-06-023942-5*) HarpC Child Bks.

— Mouse Tales. LC 72-76511. (I Can Read Bks.). (Illus.). 64p. (J). (gr. 1-3). 1978. pap. 3.95 (*0-06-444013-3*, HarpTrophy) HarpC Child Bks.

Lobel, Arnold. Mouse Tales. (I Can Read Bks.). (J). (gr. 1-3). 1972. 8.95 (*0-606-02189-2*, Pub. by Turtleback) Demco.

— Mouse Tales. abr. ed. (I Can Read Bks.). (J). (gr. 1-3). 1990. 8.95 incl. audio (*1-55994-239-8*, TBC 2398) HarperAudio.

— On Market Street. LC 80-21418. (Illus.). 40p. (J). (ps-3). 1981. 16.89 (*0-688-84309-3*, Grenwillow Bks) HarpC Child Bks.

Lobel, Arnold. On Market Street. LC 80-21418. (Illus.). 40p. (J). (ps-2). 1981. 17.00 (*0-688-80309-1*, Grenwillow Bks) HarpC Child Bks.

— On Market Street. LC 80-21418. (Illus.). 40p. (J). (ps-3). 1989. mass mkt. 6.95 (*0-688-08745-0*, Wm Morrow) Morrow Avon.

— On Market Street. large type ed. (J). (ps-2). 1993. 19.95 (*0-590-71697-2*) Scholastic Inc.

— Owl at Home. (I Can Read Bks.). (Illus.). 64p. (J). (gr. 1-3). 1975. lib. bdg. 15.89 (*0-06-023949-2*) HarpC Child Bks.

— Owl at Home. LC 74-2630. (I Can Read Bks.). (Illus.). 64p. (J). (gr. 1-3). 1982. pap. 3.95 (*0-06-444034-6*, HarpTrophy) HarpC Child Bks.

— Owl at Home. (I Can Read Bks.). (J). (gr. 1-3). 1982. 8.95 (*0-606-01963-4*, Pub. by Turtleback) Demco.

— Owl at Home. abr. ed. (I Can Read Bks.). (Illus.). 64p. (J). (gr. 1-3). 1990. 8.95 incl. audio (*1-55994-240-1*, TBC 2401) HarpC.

— The Rose in My Garden. LC 83-14097. (Illus.). 40p. (J). (ps-3). 1984. 16.00 (*0-688-02586-2*, Grenwillow Bks) HarpC Child Bks.

— The Rose in My Garden. (J). 1993. 10.15 (*0-606-02880-3*, Pub. by Turtleback) Demco.

— The Rose in My Garden. LC 92-24588. (Illus.). 40p. (J). (ps-3). 1993. reprint ed. mass mkt. 6.95 (*0-688-12265-5*, Wm Morrow) Morrow Avon.

— Saltamontes Va Da Viage. Date not set. pap. text 9.95 (*84-204-3053-6*) Santillana.

— Sapo y Sepo Inseparables. 1996. 15.15 (*0-606-10501-8*, Pub. by Turtleback) Demco.

— Sapo y Sepo Son Amigos. 1995. 15.15 (*0-606-10502-6*, Pub. by Turtleback) Demco.

— Sapo y Sepo un Ano Entero. Date not set. pap. text 11.50 (*84-204-3052-8*) Santillana.

— Sapo y Sepo un Ano Entero. 1992. 15.15 (*0-606-10503-4*, Pub. by Turtleback) Demco.

— Small Pig. LC 69-10213. (I Can Read Bks.). (Illus.). 64p. (J). (ps-3). 1969. lib. bdg. 15.89 (*0-06-023932-8*) HarpC Child Bks.

— Small Pig. LC 69-10213. (I Can Read Bks.). (Illus.). 64p. (J). (ps-3). 1988. pap. 3.95 (*0-06-444120-2*, HarpTrophy) HarpC Child Bks.

— Small Pig. (I Can Read Bks.). (J). (gr. 1-3). 1988. 8.95 (*0-606-03922-8*, Pub. by Turtleback) Demco.

Lobel, Arnold. A Treeful of Pigs Lf. LC 78-1810. (Illus.). 32p. (J). (ps-3). 1979. 16.89 (*0-688-84177-5*, Grenwillow Bks) HarpC Child Bks.

Lobel, Arnold. The Turnaround Wind. LC 87-45293. (Illus.). 32p. (J). (ps-3). 1988. 12.95 (*0-06-023987-5*); lib. bdg. 14.89 (*0-06-023988-3*) HarpC Child Bks.

— Uncle Elephant. (I Can Read Bks.). (Illus.). 64p. (J). (gr. 1-3). 1981. 14.95 (*0-06-023979-4*) HarpC Child Bks.

— Uncle Elephant. LC 80-8944. (I Can Read Bks.). (Illus.). 64p. (J). (ps-3). 1981. lib. bdg. 15.89 (*0-06-023980-8*) HarpC Child Bks.

— Uncle Elephant. LC 80-8944. (I Can Read Bks.). (Illus.). 64p. (J). (ps-3). 1986. pap. 3.95 (*0-06-444104-0*, HarpTrophy) HarpC Child Bks.

Lobel, Arnold. Uncle Elephant. (I Can Read Bks.). (J). (gr. 1-3). 1986. 8.95 (*0-606-03276-2*, Pub. by Turtleback) Demco.

Lobel, Arnold. Uncle Elephant (Tio Elefante) (SPA.). (J). 9.95 (*84-204-3716-6*) Santillana.

— Whiskers & Rhymes. LC 83-25424. (Illus.). 48p. (J). (ps-3). 1985. 13.00 (*0-688-03835-2*, Grenwillow Bks) HarpC Child Bks.

— Whiskers & Rhymes. LC 83-25424. (Illus.). 48p. (J). 1988. mass mkt. 4.95 (*0-688-08291-2*, Wm Morrow) Morrow Avon.

— Whiskers & Rhymes. (J). 1985. 10.15 (*0-606-04365-9*, Pub. by Turtleback) Demco.

— Zoo for Mr. Muster. LC 62-7313. (Illus.). 32p. (J). (ps-3). 1962. lib. bdg. 13.89 (*0-06-023991-3*) HarpC Child Bks.

Lobel, Arnold & Addison, Donna. Frog & Toad All Year. (I Can Read Bks.). (J). (gr. 1-3). 1982. 33.26 incl. audio (*0-394-69358-2*) Random.

Lobel, Arnold & House Subsc Read a. The Book of Pigericks: Pig Limericks. (J). 1984. 13.00 (*0-676-30765-5*) Ballantine Pub Grp.

Lobel, Arnold, jt. auth. see Benchley, Nathaniel.

Lobel, Arnold, jt. auth. see Brookes, Diane.

Lobel, Arnold, jt. auth. see Parish, Peggy.

Lobel, Diana. Between Mysticism & Philosophy: Sufi Language of Religious Experience in Judah Ha-levi's Kuzari. LC 99-31812. (C). 2000. text 71.50 (*0-7914-4451-1*); pap. text 23.95 (*0-7914-4452-X*) State U NY Pr.

Lobel, Edgar. Medieval Latin Poetics. (Studies in Comparative Literature: No. 35). 1972. reprint ed. pap. 39.95 (*0-8383-0051-0*) M S G Haskell Hse.

Lobel, Eli, jt. auth. see Kodsy, Ahmad El.

Lobel, Ira B. & Manchise, Louis J. Training Russian Mediators: Advent of a New Era? (Current Issues Ser.: No. 19). 1993. 5.00 (*0-89215-182-X*) U Cal LA Indus Rel.

Lobel, J., jt. auth. see Grefen, K.

Lobel, Leon, et al. Prime Time: The Lobels' Guide to Great Grilled Meats. (Illus.). 224p. 1999. 25.00 (*0-02-862333-9*, Pub. by Macmillan) S&S Trade.

Lobel, Mary D., ed. British Atlas of Historic Towns Vol. III: The City of London from Prehistoric Times to c. 1520. (Illus.). 114p. 1990. text 160.00 (*0-19-822979-8*) OUP.

Lobel, Sharon A., jt. ed. see Kossek, Ellen.

***Lobell, John.** Between Silence & Light: Spirit in the Architecture of Louis I. Kahn. 128p. (Orig.). 2000. pap. 16.95 (*1-57062-582-4*, Pub. by Shambhala Pubns) Random.

Lobello, Peter, jt. auth. see Dyer, Angela.

Loben Sels, Robin E. Van, see Van Loben Sels, Robin E.

Lobene, Ralph & Kerr, Alix. The Forsyth Experiment: An Alternative System for Dental Care. (Illus.). 162p. (C). 1979. 25.95 (*0-674-31035-7*) HUP.

Lobenstein-Reichmann, Anja. Freiheit bei Martin Luther: Lexikographische Textanalyse als Methode Historischer Semantik. 560p. 1998. 153.00 (*3-11-016076-5*) De Gruyter.

Lobenthal, Joel. Radical Rags: Fashions of the Sixties. (Illus.). 256p. 1990. pap. 14.95 (*0-89659-930-2*) Abbeville Pr.

Lober, Irene. Promoting Your School: A Public Relations Handbook. LC 92-62396. 325p. 1997. text 39.95 (*0-87762-687-1*) Scarecrow.

Loberg, T. Addictive Behaviors: Prevention & Early Intervention. 304p. 1989. 58.00 (*90-265-0934-0*) Swets.

***Lobevero, Michael Anthony.** Out on the Balcony for 365 Days. LC 00-190167. (Balcony Ser.: Bk. 1). 402p. 2000. 25.00 (*0-7388-1597-7*); pap. 18.00 (*0-7388-1598-5*) Xlibris Corp.

Lobin, Wolfram, et al. The Ferns & Fern-Allies (Pteridophyta) of the Cape Verde Islands, West Africa. LC 99-166359. (Nova Hedwigia, Beihefte/ Supplementary Issues Ser.: Beih 115). 99p. 1998. pap. 60.00 (*3-443-51037-X*, Pub. by Gebruder Borntraeger) Balogh.

Lobingier, Charles S. The Ancient & Accepted Scottish Rite of Freemasonry. 170p. 1992. reprint ed. pap. 19.95 (*1-56459-289-8*) Kessinger Pub.

— Evolution of the Roman Law: From Before the Twelve Tables to the Corpus Juris. 2nd ed. iii, 319p. 1987. reprint ed. 55.00 (*0-8377-2409-0*, Rothman) W S Hein.

Lobinski, R. & Marczenko, Z. Spectrochemical Trace Analysis for Metals & Metalloids. LC 96-5734. (Comprehensive Analytical Chemistry Ser.: No. 30). 838p. 1996. text 293.25 (*0-444-82368-9*) Elsevier.

— Spectrochemical Trace Analysis for Metals & Metalloids. (Comprehensive Analytical Chemistry Ser.: Vol. XXX). 838p. 1997. pap. 163.75 (*0-444-82879-6*, North Holland) Elsevier.

Lobiondo-Wood, Geri & Haber, Judith. Nursing Research: Methods, Critical Appraisal & Utilization. 4th ed. LC 97-33347. (Illus.). 624p. (C). (gr. 13). 1997. pap. text 36.00 (*0-8151-2390-6*, 31043) Mosby Inc.

***LoBiondo-Wood, Geri & Haber, Judith.** Nursing Research: Methods, Critical Appraisal & Utilization. 4th ed. (Illus.). (C). 1998. teacher ed. write for info. (*1-55664-431-0*) Mosby Inc.

***Lobko, Hryhoriy.** The Provisional Postage Stamps of Ukraine 1992-1995. 2nd ed. Martyniuk, Andrew O., tr. from UKR. LC 00-131213. (Illus.). 272p. 2000. pap. 30.00 (*1-889581-13-5*) Ukrnian Phltlc.

Lobko, Mikhail A. The Methodical Notes: The Method & Technique of the First Violin Lessons. (Illus.). 32p. 1998. pap. 8.00 (*0-8059-4502-4*) Dorrance.

Lobkowicz, N. Marxismus-Leninismus in der CSR: Die tschechoslowakische Philosophie seit 1945. (Sovietica Ser.: No. 8). (GER.). 267p. 1962. lib. bdg. 85.50 (*90-277-0058-3*) Kluwer Academic.

— Das Widerspruchsprinzip in der neueren sowjetischen Philosophie. (Sovietica Ser.: No. 4). (GER.). 89p. 1960. lib. bdg. 106.00 (*90-277-0059-1*) Kluwer Academic.

Lobl, T. J. & Hafez, E. S. Male Fertility & It's Regulation. (Advances in Reproductive Health Care Ser.). 1985. text 322.00 (*0-85200-805-8*) Kluwer Academic.

***Lobley, G. E.** Protein Metabolism & Nutrition. (Illus.). 284p. 1999. 85.00 (*90-74134-69-6*) Wageningen Pers.

Lobmire, Daniel J. & Flattre, Dennis K. P. L. 94-142-The Idea Handbook. (SPA.). 129p. 1995. 39.95 (*0-9648200-1-3*) Talking Textbks.

Lobmire, Daniel S. & Flattre, Dennis K. P. L. 94-142-The Idea Handbook. 129p. 1995. 39.95 (*0-9648200-0-5*) Talking Textbks.

Lobo Antunes, Antonio. The Inquisitors Manual. Date not set. write for info. (*0-8050-5932-6*) H Holt & Co.

***Lobo Antunes, Antonio.** The Inquisitors Manual. 1999. text, teacher ed. 25.00 (*0-8050-5931-8*) St Martin.

— The Natural Order of Things. Zenith, Richard, tr. LC 99-40063. 320p. 2000. 25.00 (*0-8021-1658-2*, Pub. by Grove-Atltic) Publishers Group.

Lobo Antunes, Antonio. The Natural Order of Things. Zenith, Richard, tr. Date not set. pap. 14.00 (*0-8050-5761-7*, Owl) H Holt & Co.

— The Natural Order of Things. Zenith, Richard, tr. 1998. 25.00 (*0-8050-5760-9*) H Holt & Co.

Lobo-Cobb, Angela. The Water & the Leaf: Oriental Poems for Meditation. (Illus.). pap. write for info. (*0-318-57646-5*) Bloomsberry Pr.

Lobo-Cobb, Angela, ed. A Confluence of Colors: The First Anthology of Wisconsin Minority Poets, Vol. I. 79p. (C). 1984. pap. text 5.00 (*0-916783-04-9*) Blue Reed.

— Winter Nest: A Poetry Anthology of Midwestern Women Poets of Color. (Poetics of Color Ser.). 110p. (Orig.). 1987. pap. text 5.00 (*0-916783-05-7*) Blue Reed.

Lobo, Crispino & Orfer-Lucius, Gudrun K. The Rain Decided to Help Us: Participatory Watershed Management in the State of Maharashtra, India. LC 95-31209. (EDI Learning Resources Ser.). 80p. 1996. pap. 22.00 (*0-8213-3414-X*, 13414) World Bank.

Lobo, Elisa J., jt. auth. see Loustaunau, Martha O.

Lobo, Jeronimo. A Voyage to Abyssinia. Gold, Joel J., ed. Johnson, Samuel, tr. from FRE. LC 57-11918. (Works of Samuel Johnson Ser.: Vol. XV). (Illus.). 400p. 1985. 60.00 (*0-300-03003-7*) Yale U Pr.

— A Voyage to Abyssinia. Gold, Joel J., ed. Johnson, Samuel, tr. LC 74-15064. reprint ed. 55.00 (*0-404-12105-5*) AMS Pr.

Lobo, Jorge, et al. Foundations of Disjunctive Logic Programming. (Illus.). 300p. 1992. 50.00 (*0-262-12165-4*) MIT Pr.

Lobo, Lance C., ed. see Nadi, Aldo.

Lobo, Michael. Time Marching: A Step-by-Step Guide to a Flow Solver. LC 96-85547. 164p. 1997. 73.95 (*0-291-39826-X*, Pub. by Avebury Technical) Ashgate Pub Co.

Lobo Montalvo, Maria Luisa. Havana: History & Architecture of a Romantic City. (Illus.). 320p. 2000. text 75.00 (*1-58093-052-2*, Pub. by Monacelli Pr) Penguin Putnam.

Lobo, Rebecca, jt. auth. see Lobo, RuthAnn.

Lobo, Rogerio, ed. see U. S. A. Serono Symposia Staff.

Lobo, Rogerio A., ed. Treatment of the Postmenopausal Woman: Basic & Clinical Aspects. 464p. 1993. text 152.00 (*0-7817-0113-9*) Lppncott W & W.

***Lobo, Rogerio A., et al, eds.** Menopause: Biology & Pathology. 700p. 2000. 159.95 (*0-12-453790-1*) Acad Pr.

Lobo, Rogerio A., et al. Mishell's Textbook of Infertility, Contraception & Reproductive Endocrinology. 4th ed. LC 96-52003. (Illus.). 896p. 1997. 175.00 (*0-86542-385-7*) Blackwell Sci.

Lobo, RuthAnn & Lobo, Rebecca. The Home Team. Baker, Deborah, ed. (Illus.). 192p. 1996. 19.00 (*1-56836-140-8*) Kodansha.

— The Home Team: Of Mothers, Daughters, & American Champions. 192p. (Orig.). 1997. pap. 9.95 (*1-56836-199-8*) Kodansha.

Lobo, Susan. A House of My Own: Social Organization in the Squatter Settlements of Lima, Peru. LC 81-16275. 190p. (C). 1982. pap. 15.95 (*0-8165-0761-9*) U of Ariz Pr.

Lobo, Susan, ed. Native American Voices: A Reader. LC 97-23820. 448p. (C). 1997. pap. 39.80 (*0-321-01131-7*, Prentice Hall) P-H.

***Lobo, Susan & Peters, Kurt, eds.** American Indians & the Urban Experience. (Contemporary Native American Communities Ser.). 320p. 2000. 69.00 (*0-7425-0274-0*); pap. 25.95 (*0-7425-0275-9*) AltaMira Pr.

Lobo, Tatiana. Assault on Paradise. Zatz, Asa, tr. from SPA. LC 97-47572. Orig. Title: Asalto al Paradiso. 298p. 1998. pap. 15.95 (*1-880684-46-2*, Pub. by Curbstone) Consort Bk Sales.

Lobo, V. M. Handbook of Electrolyte Solutions, Set, Pts. A & B. (Physical Sciences Data Ser.: Nos. 41A & 41B). 2354p. 1990. 1135.25 (*0-444-98847-5*) Elsevier.

Lobodzinska, Barbara, ed. Family, Women & Employment in Central-Eastern Europe, 112. LC 94-25155. (Contributions in Sociology Ser.: Vol. 112). 344p. 1995. 75.00 (*0-313-29402-X*, Greenwood Pr) Greenwood.

Lobodzinski, Suave & Tomek, Ivan, eds. WebNet World Conference of the WWW, Internet, & Intranet: Proceedings of WebNet 97. unabridged ed. (Illus.). 829p. 1997. pap. 60.00 (*1-880094-27-4*, 1-880094) Assn Advan Comput Educ.

Lobos, Gabriela. Seaspring. (Illus.). 112p. (Orig.). (J). (gr. 4-6). 1996. pap. 9.95 (*1-880284-19-7*) J Daniel.

Lobosco, Michael L. Mental Math Challenges, 1. LC 99-18586. 1999. 16.95 (*1-895569-50-8*) Tamos Bks.

***Lobosco, Michael L.** Mental Math Challenges. (Illus.). 2000. pap. 9.95 (*1-895569-60-5*) Tamos Bks.

Lobosco, Michael L. Mental Math Workout. 1999. pap. 9.95 (*1-895569-56-7*) Strlng Pub CA.

***Lobprise, Heidi B. & Wiggs, Robert B.** The Veterinarian's Companion for Common Dental Procedures. LC 99-59463. (Illus.). 189p. 1999. pap. write for info. (*1-58326-006-4*, AAHA Pr) Am Animal Hosp Assoc.

Lobran, Michael, jt. auth. see Brooks, Christopher W.

Lobrano, Gustav, jt. auth. see Flick, Alexander C.

Lobrecht, jt. auth. see English.

Lobrutto. Elia Kazan. 1998. per. 14.95 (*0-8057-4508-4*) Macmillan.

— Elia Kazan. 1999. 26.95 (*0-8057-4507-6*) Macmillan.

LoBrutto, Vincent. By Design: Interviews with Film Production Designers. LC 92-5849. 296p. 1992. 65.00 (*0-275-94030-6*, C4030, Praeger Pubs); pap. 22.95 (*0-275-94031-4*, B4031, Praeger Pubs) Greenwood.

— Principal Photography: Interviews with Feature Film Cinematographers. LC 98-46797. 264p. 1999. 65.00 (*0-275-94954-0*, Praeger Pubs); pap. 22.95 (*0-275-94955-9*, Praeger Pubs) Greenwood.

— Selected Takes: Film Editors on Editing. LC 90-24262. 264p. 1991. 59.95 (*0-275-93378-4*, C3378, Praeger Pubs); pap. 21.95 (*0-275-93395-4*, B3395, Praeger Pubs) Greenwood.

Lobrutto, Vincent. Sound-On-Film: Interviews with Creators of Film Sound. LC 93-50686. 320p. 1994. 75.00 (*0-275-94442-5*, Praeger Pubs); pap. 24.95 (*0-275-94443-3*, Praeger Pubs) Greenwood.

LoBrutto, Vincent. Stanley Kubrick: A Biography. LC 96-35737. (Illus.). 480p. 1997. pap. 29.95 (*1-55611-492-3*, Pub. by D I Fine) Penguin Putnam.

An Asterisk (*) at the beginning of an entry indicates that the title is appearing for the first time.

— Stanley Kubrick: A Biography. LC 98-47434. (Illus.). 608p. 1999. reprint ed. mass mkt. 17.95 (*0-306-80906-0*, Pub. by Da Capo) HarpC.

Lobsenz, Janet S. Dollars & Sense. (School Board Library Ser.: Vol. 8). 1998. 29.90 (*0-912337-14-1*) NJ Schl Bds.

Lobsenz, Johanna. The Older Woman in Industry. LC 74-3961. (Women in America Ser.). (Illus.). 298p. 1974. reprint ed. 24.95 (*0-405-06110-2*) Ayer.

Lobsenz, Norman, jt. auth. see Weisinger, Hendrie.

Lobsenz, Norman M., jt. auth. see Fox, Isabelle.

Lobst, Richard. Civil War Macon. LC 99-22455. (Civil War Georgia Ser.). 500p. 1999. 35.00 (*0-86554-634-7*) Mercer Univ Pr.

Lobstein, Tom, jt. auth. see Whiting, Mary.

Lobster, Laura. Lobster Tales. LC 96-75799. (Illus.). 70p. (YA). (gr. 5 up). 1996. pap. 10.00 (*0-9652028-0-1*) Infinite Possibilities.

LoBue, Andrea & Marcus, Marsea. Don't Diet, Live-It! A Workbook for Healing: Food, Weight, & Body Issues. 215p. 1999. pap., wbk. ed. 17.95 (*0-936077-33-6*) Gurze Bks.

LoBue, Tony. Take My Hand: Physical Guided Action. Burke, Barbara, ed. (Illus.). (Orig.). 1989. pap. text 5.95 (*0-9625492-0-7*) T LoBue.

LoBuglio, Albert F., ed. Clinical Immunotherapy. LC 80-15386. (Immunology Ser.: No. 11). (Illus.). 351p. reprint ed. pap. 108.90 (*0-8357-6057-X*, 203454600090) Bks Demand.

Lobus, Catherine O. Careers As a Flight Attendant. rev. ed. Rosen, Ruth C., ed. (Careers Ser.). (Illus.). (YA). (gr. 7-12). 1995. lib. bdg. 16.95 (*0-8239-1953-6*) Rosen Group.

Loca, La, see La Loca.

Local Birds Editors. Local Birds of San Diego County: Pocket Size. (Illus.). 1995. 7.95 (*1-886403-07-4*) Local Birds.

— Local Birds of the Salton Sea: Pocket Size. (Illus.). 1997. 7.95 (*1-886403-33-3*) Local Birds.

Local Birds, Inc. Editors. Local Birds of Los Angeles County: Pocket Size. (Illus.). 1995. 7.95 (*1-886403-06-6*) Local Birds.

— Local Birds of Marin County: Pocket Size. (Illus.). 1995. 7.95 (*1-886403-02-3*) Local Birds.

— Local Birds of Orange County: Pocket Size. (Illus.). 1995. 7.95 (*1-886403-14-7*) Local Birds.

— Local Birds of Santa Barbara: Pocket Size. (Illus.). 1996. 7.95 (*1-886403-00-7*) Local Birds.

— Local Birds of the Monterey Penninsula: Pocket Size. (Illus.). 1995. 7.95 (*1-886403-11-2*) Local Birds.

— Local Birds of the San Francisco Bay Area: Pocket Size. (Illus.). 1995. 7.95 (*1-886403-01-5*) Local Birds.

— Trifold Checklist of San Diego County Birds. (Illus.). 1996. 7.95 (*1-886403-24-4*) Local Birds.

Local Examinations Syndicate Staff. Trends & Patterns. (Modular Sciences Ser.). 80p. 1997. pap. text 14.95 (*0-521-42206-X*) Cambridge U Pr.

Local Government Commission Staff, ed. The County Code, 1985. rev. ed. 125p. 1995. pap. 3.05 (*0-8182-0063-4*) Commonweal PA.

Local History Coordination Project Staff. Locating Australia's Past: A Practical Guide to Writing Local History. 1989. pap. 22.95 (*0-86840-211-7*, Pub. by New South Wales Univ Pr) Intl Spec Bk.

Localio, S. Arthur, et al. Anorectal, Presacral & Sacral Tumors: Anatomy, Physiology, Pathogenesis & Management. (Illus.). 378p. 1987. text 135.00 (*0-7216-1982-7*, W B Saunders Co) Harcrt Hlth Sci Grp.

Locarek-Junge, H., jt. ed. see Gaul, W.

LoCascio, Catherine H., jt. auth. see Stafford, Alan D.

Locatelli, Paul, jt. auth. see Gainen, Joanne.

Locche, Daniel, jt. auth. see Alesii, Brenda C.

Locche, Daniel, ed. see Stedler, Richard.

Locche, Daniel A. & Alesii, Brenda C. Buffalo Jock Rap: The "Settle Your Bet" Pro Sports Trivia Book. 264p. (Orig.). 1989. 8.95 (*1-877697-00-1*) Brendan Ventures.

Loce, Robert P. & Dougherty, Edward R. Enhancement & Restoration of Digital Documents: Statistical Design of Nonlinear Algorithms. LC 96-38287. (SPIE/IEEE Series on Imaging Science & Engineering). 1997. 65.00 (*0-8194-2109-X*, PM29) SPIE.

Loch, C. S. Poor Relief in Scotland: Its Statistics & Development, 1791-1891. LC 75-38137. (Demography Ser.). 1976. reprint ed. 17.95 (*0-405-07990-7*) Ayer.

Loch, D. S. & Ferguson, J. E., eds. Forage Seed Production: Tropical & Subtropical Species, Vol. 2. (CABI Publishing Ser.). (Illus.). 504p. 1999. text 160.00 (*0-85199-191-2*) OUP.

Loch, E. G. Ultrasonic Tomography in Obstetrics & Gynecology. (Advances in Obstetrics & Gynaecology Ser.: Vol. 51). (Illus.). 1973. 35.00 (*3-8055-1585-5*) S Karger.

Loch, Karen, jt. ed. see Khosrowpour, Mehdi.

Loch, Sydney. Three Predatory Women. LC 70-125230. (Short Story Index Reprint Ser.). 1977. 19.95 (*0-8369-3597-7*) Ayer.

Loch, Sylvia. The Classical Rider: Being at One with Your Horse. LC 96-62094. (Illus.). 373p. 1997. 29.95 (*1-57076-084-5*, Trafalgar Sq Pub) Trafalgar.

— Dressage: The Art of Classical Riding. (Illus.). 224p. 1990. 39.95 (*0-948253-46-0*, Trafalgar Sq Pub) Trafalgar.

— The Royal Horse of Europe. 256p. 1990. 110.00 (*0-85131-422-8*, Pub. by J A Allen) Trafalgar.

Lochak, P. & Meunier, C. Averaging in Classical Dynamical Systems. (Applied Mathematical Sciences Ser.: Vol. 72). (Illus.). 370p. 1988. 64.95 (*0-387-96778-8*) Spr-Verlag.

Lochak, Pierre, jt. ed. see Schneps, Leila.

Lochbaum, David. Nuclear Waste Disposal Crisis. 192p. 1995. 34.95 (*0-87814-463-3*) PennWell Bks.

Loche, A. I Can Say Apple. LC 99-160980. (Illus.). (J). (ps). 1998. pap. 2.95 (*1-84089-017-7*, 868278) Zero to Ten.

Loche, John. The Selected Writings of John Locke. Sigmund, Paul E., ed. (Critical Editions Ser.). (C). 1999. pap. 16.75 (*0-393-96451-5*, Norton Paperbks) Norton.

Lochead, Richard, ed. Beyond the Printed Word: The Evolution of Canada's Broadcast News Heritage. Vol. 1. (FRE & ENG.). 400p. 1992. 39.95 (*1-55082-014-1*, Pub. by Quarry Pr); pap. 29.95 (*1-55082-016-8*, Pub. by Quarry Pr) LPC InBook.

Locher, ed. Marii Victorini: Opera Theologica. (LAT.). 1976. 39.50 (*3-322-00185-7*, T1929, Pub. by B G Teubner) U of Mich Pr.

— Marii VictoriniCommentarii in Epistulas Pauli: Ad Galatas, Ad Philippenses, Ad Ephesios. (LAT.). 1972. 36.50 (*3-322-00186-5*, T1928, Pub. by B G Teubner) U of Mich Pr.

Locher, Adrian, tr. see Steiner, Rudolf.

Locher, Albert. Nomadic Architecture. 1998. 65.00 (*3-907044-44-4*) Lars Muller.

Locher, Dick. The Daze of Whine & Neurosis. LC 95-8974. (Editorial Cartoonists Ser.). (Illus.). 160p. (Orig.). 1995. pap. 8.95 (*1-56554-156-1*) Pelican.

Locher, Dick, jt. compiled by see Collins, Max Allan.

Locher, Ernst L. Arithmetik und Algebra. 4th ed. (GER.). 72p. 1980. 12.00 (*0-8176-0774-9*) Birkhauser.

Locher, Frances C. & Evory, Ann, eds. American Novelists. (Contemporary Authors Bibliographical Ser.: Vol. 1). 431p. 1986. 122.00 (*0-8103-2225-0*) Gale.

— Contemporary Authors Bibliographical Series, Vol. 2. 387p. 1986. 122.00 (*0-8103-2226-9*) Gale.

Locher, Hans. Piet Mondrian: Colour, Structure & Symbolism. Latcham, Michael, tr. (Illus.). 100p. 1995. 35.00 (*3-906127-44-3*) Dist Art Pubs.

Locher, J. C., jt. auth. see Escher, M. C.

***Locher, J. L.** The Magic of M. C. Escher. (Illus.). 200p. 2000. 39.95 (*0-8109-6720-0*, Pub. by Abrams) Time Warner.

Locher, J. L., ed. M. C. Escher: His Life & Complete Graphic Work. (Illus.). 352p. 1982. 65.00 (*0-8109-0858-1*) Abrams.

— M. C. Escher: His Life & Complete Graphic Work. (Illus.). 352p. 1992. pap. 29.98 (*0-8109-8113-0*, Pub. by Abrams) Time Warner.

Locher, Kees & Van Der Brug, Jos. Workways - Seven Stars to Steer By: Biography Workbook for Building an Enterprising Life. Langham, Tony & Peters, Plym, trs. (Biography & Self Development Ser.). (Illus.). 352p. 1997. 44.95 (*1-869890-89-2*, Pub. by Hawthorn Press) Anthroposophic.

Locher, Nancy C. College -- A Complete Guide for Parents & Students. 172p. (Orig.). 1989. pap. 8.95 (*0-89709-166-3*) Liberty Pub.

Locher, R. C., Jr. The Complete DX'er. 2nd ed. (Illus.). (Orig.). 1989. pap. 12.00 (*0-9617577-0-1*) Idiom Pr.

***Locher-Scholten, Elsbeth.** Women & the Colonial State: Essays on Gender & Modernity in the Netherlands Indies 1940-1942. (Illus.). (C). 2000. pap. text 27.50 (*90-5356-403-9*, Pub. by Amsterdam U Pr) U of Mich Pr.

Locher, Theo, jt. auth. see Harsch-Fischbach, Maggy.

***Lochery, Neill.** The Difficult Road to Peace: Netanyahu, Israel & the Middle East Peace. 376p. 2000. (*0-86372-248-2*) Garnet-Ithaca.

Lochery, Neill. The Israeli Labour Party: In the Shadow of the Likud. 272p. 1997. 45.00 (*0-86372-217-2*, Pub. by Garnet-Ithaca) LPC InBook.

Lochhaas, Philip H. Como Responder a... La Nueva Era. (Serie Respuesta). (SPA.). 1990. pap. 2.95 (*0-570-09905-6*) Concordia.

Lochhaas, Philip H. How to Respond to Secular Humanism. 40p. 1991. pap. 2.79 (*0-570-04549-5*, 12-3149) Concordia.

— The New Age Movement. LC 95-8596. (How to Respond Ser.). 64p. 1995. 3.99 (*0-570-04679-3*, 12-6012) Concordia.

Lochhaas, Thomas. Business Communications. 257p. (C). 1991. pap. text, student ed. 24.00 (*0-15-505670-0*) Harcourt Coll Pubs.

Lochhead, David. The Dialogical Imperative: A Christian Reflection on Interfaith Encounter. LC 88-1570. (Faith Meets Faith Ser.). 112p. reprint ed. pap. 34.80 (*0-608-20243-6*, 207150200012) Bks Demand.

Lochhead, Douglas. Breakfast at Mel's & Other Poems of Love & Places. LC 97-165040. (Illus.). 120p. 1997. pap. 10.95 (*0-86492-228-0*, Pub. by Goose Ln Edits) Genl Dist Srvs.

— Dykelands. (Illus.). 72p. (C). 1989. 85.00 (*0-7735-0722-1*, Pub. by McG-Queens Univ Pr) CUP Services.

— High Marsh Road. 136p. 1996. pap. 12.95 (*0-86492-192-6*, Pub. by Goose Ln Edits) Genl Dist Srvs.

— Homage to Henry Alline & Other Poems. 120p. 1992. pap. 10.95 (*0-86492-125-X*, Pub. by Goose Ln Edits) Genl Dist Srvs.

— Tiger in the Skull. 130p. 1986. 10.95 (*0-86492-072-5*, Pub. by Goose Ln Edits) Genl Dist Srvs.

— Upper Cape Poems. 130p. 1989. pap. 10.95 (*0-86492-100-4*, Pub. by Goose Ln Edits) Genl Dist Srvs.

***Lochhead, Ian.** Dream of Spires: B. W. Mountfort & the Gothic Revival. 320p. 1999. 79.95 (*0-908812-85-X*, Pub. by Canterbury Univ) Accents Pubns.

Lochhead, Ian. The Spectator & the Landscape in the Art Criticism of Diderot & His Contemporaries. Kuspit, Donald, ed. LC 82-4770. (Studies in the Fine Arts: Criticism: No. 13). 184p. 1982. reprint ed. pap. 41.30 (*0-8357-1323-7*, 207002700063) Bks Demand.

***Lochhead, Jack.** Thinkback: A User's Guide to Minding the Mind. LC 00-24518. 176p. 2000. pap. write for info. (*0-8058-3342-0*) L Erlbaum Assocs.

Lochhead, Jack & Clement, John, eds. Cognitive Process Instruction: Research on Teaching Thinking Skills. LC 78-22122. (Illus.). 339p. 1979. pap. 59.95 (*0-89859-729-3*) L Erlbaum Assocs.

Lochhead, Jack, jt. auth. see Whimbey, Arthur.

Lochhead, Jack, jt. auth. see Whimby, Arthur.

Lochhead, Liz. Dreaming Frankenstein... 1987. 14.95 (*0-7486-6158-1*, Pub. by Polygon) Subterranean Co.

***Lochhead, Liz.** Perfect Days. LC 99-487837. 96p. 1999. pap. 14.95 (*1-85459-437-0*, Pub. by Theatre Comm) Consort Bk Sales.

— Perfect Days. 2nd ed. 1999. pap. 16.95 (*1-85459-419-2*) Theatre Comm.

Lochhead, Liz. True Confessions . . . 1987. 16.00 (*0-7486-6156-5*, Pub. by Polygon) Subterranean Co.

***Lochhead, Liz & Moxley, Gina.** Cuba/Dog House. (Connections Ser.). (Illus.). 112p. (YA). 2000. pap. 17.95 (*0-7487-4291-3*, Pub. by S Thornes Pubs) Trans-Atl Phila.

Lochhead, Liz, et al. Three Scottish Poets: MacCaig, Morgan & Lochhead. (Classics Ser.). (Illus.). 96p. 1996. pap. 11.95 (*0-86241-400-8*, Pub. by Canongate Books) Interlink Pub.

Lochman, Jan M. Encountering Marx: Bonds & Barriers between Christians & Marxists. Robertson, Edwin H., tr. LC 76-55827. 156p. reprint ed. pap. 48.40 (*0-608-16773-8*, 202691700053) Bks Demand.

Lochman, Jiri. Melbourne & Victoria's Splendor. (Panoramic Ser.). (Illus.). 128p. 1999. 24.95 (*1-86436-371-1*, Pub. by New Holland) BHB Intl.

***Lochman, Jiri.** Western Australia's Wildflowers. 1999. 39.95 (*1-86436-329-0*) New Holland.

Lochman, Jiri & Lochman, Marie. Portrait of Perth. (Panoramic Ser.). (Illus.). 128p. 1999. 24.95 (*1-86436-374-6*, Pub. by New Holland) BHB Intl.

Lochman, John Nilic. The Faith We Confess. 1997. 49.95 (*0-567-09367-0*, Pub. by T & T Clark) Bks Intl VA.

Lochman, Marie, jt. auth. see Lochman, Jiri.

Lochmandy, Paula. What Come Out Dah Bottle. limited ed. Miller, Jeffrey A., ed. (Illus.). 30p. (J). (gr. 2-6). 1998. ring bd. 12.00 (*0-9639890-5-1*) Tattersall Pr.

— What Come Out Dah Bottle. 2nd ed. Miller, Jeffrey A., ed. (Illus.). 35p. (J). (gr. 2-6). 1998. pap. text 13.50 (*0-9639890-9-X*) Tattersall Pr.

Lochmandy, Paula J. Beauty Knows No Pain: The Anatomy of a Successful Facelift. LC 93-61905. (Illus.). 128p. (Orig.). 1994. pap. 20.00 (*0-9639890-7-3*) Tattersall Pr.

Lochmann, Christina & Chin, Soo-Young. Pop-N Kimchi. LC 98-12049. (J). 1998. write for info. (*1-879965-17-8*) Polychrome Pub.

Lochmann, W. J. & Indig, M., eds. Materials & Corrosion Problems in Energy Systems. (Illus.). 211p. 1980. pap. 10.00 (*0-915567-57-1*) NACE Intl.

Lochnan, Katharine. Seductive Surfaces: The Art of Tissot. LC 99-65333. (Studies in British Art: Vol. 6). 224p. 1999. 60.00 (*0-300-08184-7*) Yale U Pr.

Lochnan, Katharine A. The Etchings of James McNeil Whistler. LC 84-40185. (Illus.). 320p. 1984. 60.00 (*0-300-03275-7*) Yale U Pr.

Lochner, David. Twice As Funny . . . Twins Vol. 1: A Book of Cartoons. LC 97-169862. (Illus.). (Orig.). 1996. pap. 10.95 (*0-9655442-1-4*) Busn Word.

— Twice As Funny... Twins: A Book of Cartoons, Vol. II. (Illus.). 104p. (Orig.). (J). 1998. pap. 10.95 (*1-891846-04-3*) Busn Word.

Lochner, Louis P. Fritz Kreisler. 1988. reprint ed. lib. bdg. 69.00 (*0-7812-0138-1*) Rprt Serv.

— Fritz Kreisler. LC 76-181203. 1951. reprint ed. 24.00 (*0-403-01613-4*) Scholarly.

Lochner, Louis P., tr. see Goebbels, Joseph.

Lochner, Robert H. & Matar, Joseph E. Designing for Quality: An Introduction to the Best of Taguchi & Western Methods of Statistical Experimental Design. (Illus.). 250p. 1990. 41.00 (*0-527-91633-1*, 916331) Productivity Inc.

Lochner, W. K., ed. see Simonds, John O.

Lochray, Paul I. The Financial Planner's Guide to Estate Planning. 3rd ed. 364p. (C). 1991. 36.95 (*0-13-318502-8*) P-H.

Lochrie, Karma. Covert Operations: Medieval Uses of Secrecy. LC 98-11694. (Middle Ages Ser.). 304p. 1998. 45.00 (*0-8122-3473-1*) U of Pa Pr.

— Margery Kempe & Translations of the Flesh. 1994. pap. text 16.95 (*0-8122-1557-5*) U of Pa Pr.

Lochrie, Karma, et al. Constructing Medieval Sexuality. LC 97-9425. (Medieval Cultures Ser.). xviii, 205p. 1997. pap. 18.95 (*0-8166-2829-7*); text 47.95 (*0-8166-2828-9*) U of Minn Pr.

***Lochte, Dick.** Lucky Dog & Other Tales of Murder. LC 00-34753. (First Edition Mystery Ser.). 2000. write for info. (*0-7862-2688-9*) Five Star.

Lochte, Dick. The Neon Smile. 1995. 20.50 (*0-671-74712-6*) S&S Trade.

Lochte, Dick, jt. auth. see Darden, Christopher A.

Lochte-Holtgreven, W. Plasma Diagnostics. (AVS Classics Ser.). (Illus.). 945p. (C). 1995. text 64.95 (*1-56396-388-4*) Spr-Verlag.

***Lochtefeld, James.** The Illustrated Encyclopedia of Hinduism, 2 vols., Set. Incl. Illustrated Encyclopedia of Hinduism. LC 99-27747. (Illus.). 500p. 2000. lib. bdg. 150.00 (*0-8239-3180-3*); Illustrated Encyclopedia of Hinduism. LC 99-27747. (Illus.). 500p. 2000. lib. bdg. (*0-8239-3179-X*); (Illus.). 1000p. 2000. Set lib. bdg. 150.00 (*0-8239-2287-1*) Rosen Group.

***Locisano, Karen.** Selected Stories by O. Henry. LC 99-189768. (Pacemaker Classic Ser.). 80 p. 1999. write for info. (*0-8359-3586-8*) Globe Fearon.

***Lock.** Job Search: Career Planning Guide, Book 2. 4th ed. LC 99-16350. 336p. 1999. pap. 29.95 (*0-534-35618-4*) Thomson Learn.

Lock. Taking Charge Career. (Counseling Ser.). 1987. pap. write for info. (*0-534-08221-1*) Brooks-Cole.

— Taking Charge of Your Career Direction: Career Planning Guide, Bk. 1. 4th ed. LC 99-16348. (Counseling Ser.). 1999. pap. text 37.95 (*0-534-35617-6*) Wadsworth Pub.

— To Fight with Intrepidity. LC 99-200322. 1998. per. 6.99 (*0-671-01528-1*, Pocket Books) PB.

***Lock, Andrew & Peters, Charles.** The Handbook of Human Symbolic Evolution. LC 99-37853. 928p. 1999. pap. 49.95 (*0-631-21690-1*) Blackwell Pubs.

Lock, Andrew J. & Peters, Charles R., eds. Handbook of Human Symbolic Evolution. (Illus.). 936p. 1997. text 225.00 (*0-19-852153-7*) OUP.

Lock, Charles. Thomas Hardy. LC 92-22237. (Criticism in Focus Ser.). 1992. text 29.95 (*0-312-08604-0*) St Martin.

Lock, Corey R., jt. auth. see Churukian, George A.

Lock, D. Project Management. 300p. (C). 1989. 115.00 (*0-7855-6110-2*, Pub. by Inst Pur & Supply) St Mut.

Lock, D., ed. Project Management Handbook. 625p. (C). 1987. 475.00 (*0-7855-5711-3*, Pub. by Inst Pur & Supply) St Mut.

Lock, David W., photos by. Warpaint, Vol. I. (Illus.). 48p. 1992. 19.95 (*1-930607-34-2*, VPI 0693) Verlinden Prod.

— Warpaint, Vol. II. (Illus.). 48p. 1993. 21.95 (*1-930607-35-0*, VPI 0800) Verlinden Prod.

— Warpaint, Vol. III. (Illus.). 48p. 1994. 22.95 (*1-930607-36-9*, VPI 0900) Verlinden Prod.

Lock, Dennis. The Essentials of Project Management. 272p. 1996. pap. 26.95 (*0-566-07745-0*, Pub. by Gower) Ashgate Pub Co.

***Lock, Dennis.** The Essentials of Project Management. 2nd ed. LC 99-57306. 300p. 2000. 29.95 (*0-566-08224-1*, Pub. by Gower) Ashgate Pub Co.

Lock, Dennis. The Gower Handbook of Management. 3rd ed. 1002p. 1992. 109.95 (*0-566-02974-X*, Pub. by Gower) Ashgate Pub Co.

— The Gower Handbook of Management. 3rd ed. 1044p. 1993. pap. 42.95 (*0-566-07477-X*, Pub. by Gower) Ashgate Pub Co.

— Gower Handbook of Quality Management. 2nd ed. 1994. 131.95 (*0-566-07451-6*, Pub. by Gower) Ashgate Pub Co.

— Project Management. 6th ed. LC 96-29673. 522p. 1996. pap. 69.95 (*0-470-23723-6*) Wiley.

***Lock, Dennis.** Project Management. 7th ed. LC 99-57302. 592p. 2000. 87.95 (*0-566-08223-3*, Pub. by Gower); pap. 43.95 (*0-566-08225-X*, Pub. by Gower) Ashgate Pub Co.

Lock, Dennis. Project Planner. (Illus.). 168p. 1990. text 189.95 (*0-566-02845-X*, Pub. by Gower) Ashgate Pub Co.

Lock, Dennis, ed. The Gower Handbook of Management. 4th ed. LC 97-32768. 1050p. 1998. 131.95 (*0-566-07938-0*, Pub. by Gower) Ashgate Pub Co.

— Gower Handbook of Project Management. 2nd ed. LC 93-11068. 671p. 1994. 113.95 (*0-566-07391-9*, Pub. by Gower) Ashgate Pub Co.

— Handbook of Engineering Management. 2nd ed. LC 93-14758. (Illus.). 852p. 1993. text 145.00 (*0-7506-0786-6*) Buttrwrth-Heinemann.

Lock, E. A., jt. ed. see Bach, Peter H.

Lock, F. P. Swift's Tory Politics. LC 83-8155. 100p. 1984. 32.50 (*0-87413-252-5*) U Delaware Pr.

Lock, F. P., jt. ed. see Rawson, Claude.

Lock, Fred & Lawson, Alan. Australian Literature: A Reference Guide. 2nd ed. (Australian Bibliographies Ser.). 1980. pap. text 12.95 (*0-19-554214-2*) OUP.

Lock, Frederick. Edmund Burke Vol. I: 1730 to 1784. LC 98-7147. (Illus.). 616p. 1999. text 135.00 (*0-19-820676-3*) OUP.

Lock, G. S. The Growth & Decay of Ice. (Studies in Polar Research). (Illus.). 452p. (C). 1991. text 115.00 (*0-521-33133-1*) Cambridge U Pr.

— Latent Heat Transfer: An Introduction to Fundamentals. (Oxford Engineering Science Ser.: No. 43). (Illus.). 310p. 1996. reprint ed. pap. text 49.95 (*0-19-856284-5*) OUP.

Lock, G. S. The Tubular Thermosyphon: Variations on a Theme. (Oxford Engineering Science Ser.: No. 33). (Illus.). 342p. 1992. text 110.00 (*0-19-856247-0*) OUP.

Lock, Gary & Stancic, Zoran, eds. Archaeology & Geographic Information Systems: A European Perspective. 400p. 1995. 99.50 (*0-7484-0208-X*, Pub. by Tay Francis Ltd) Taylor & Francis.

Lock, Gary & Wilcock, John. Computer Archaeology. 1989. pap. 25.00 (*0-85263-877-9*, Pub. by Shire Pubns) St Mut.

Lock, Gary, jt. auth. see Fletcher, Mike.

***Lock, Graham.** Blutopia: Visions of the Future & Revisions of the Past in the Work of Sun Ra, Duke Ellington & Anthony Braxton. LC 99-34402. 336p. 2000. pap. 18.95 (*0-8223-2440-7*) Duke.

— Blutopia: Visions of the Future & Revisions of the Past in the Work of Sun Ra, Duke Ellington & Anthony Braxton. LC 99-34402. (Illus.). 336p. 2000. 54.95 (*0-8223-2404-0*) Duke.

Lock, Graham. Forces in Motion: The Music & Thoughts of Anthony Braxton. (Quality Paperbacks Ser.). (Illus.). 446p. 1989. pap. 15.95 (*0-306-80342-9*) Da Capo.

— Functional English Grammar: An Introduction for Second Language Teachers. (Cambridge Language Education Ser.). (Illus.). 310p. (C). 1995. pap. text 20.95 (*0-521-45922-2*) Cambridge U Pr.

— Functional English Grammar: An Introduction for Second Language Teachers. (Cambridge Language Education Ser.). (Illus.). 310p. (C). 1995. text 54.95 (*0-521-45305-4*) Cambridge U Pr.

Lock, Graham, ed. Mixtery: A Festschrift for Anthony Braxton. 1995. pap. 19.95 (*1-873012-97-7*, Pub. by Stride Pubns) SPD-Small Pr Dist.

L

Lock, Helen. A Case of Mistaken Identity Vol. 9: Detective Undercurrents in Recent African American Fiction. (Studies on Themes & Motifs in Literature: Vol. 9). IX, 147p. (C). 1994. text 35.95 (0-8204-2382-3) P Lang Pubng.

Lock, J. & McElhinny, Michael W., eds. The Global Paleomagnetic Database: Design, Installation & Use with Oracle. (C). 1991. text 122.00 (0-7923-1327-5) Kluwer Academic.

***Lock, J. M.** Flora of Tropical East Africa: Xyridaceae. 24p. 1999. pap. 10.00 (90-6191-385-3, Pub. by A A Balkema) Ashgate Pub Co.

Lock, J. M. Legumes of Africa: A Check-List. vii, 619p. 1989. pap. 30.00 (0-947643-10-9, Pub. by Royal Botnic Grdns) Balogh.

Lock, J. M. & Heald, J. Legumes of Indo-China: A Check-List. vi, 164p. 1994. pap. 22.00 (0-947643-66-4, Pub. by Royal Botnic Grdns) Balogh.

Lock, J. M. & Simpson, K. Legumes of West Asia: A Check-List. xi, 263p. 1991. pap. 30.00 (0-947643-29-X, Pub. by Royal Botnic Grdns) Balogh.

Lock, James E., et al. Diagnostic & Interventional Catherization in Cogenital Heart Disease. 208p. (C). 1987. text 139.00 (0-89838-831-7) Kluwer Academic.

***Lock, James E., et al.** Treatment Manual for Adolescents with Anorexia Nervosa: A Family-Based Approach. 278p. 2000. lib. bdg. 35.00 (1-57230-607-6) Guilford Pubns.

Lock, John & Dixon, Canon. A Man of Sorrow: The Life, Letters & Times of the Reverend Patrick Bronte. 566p. 1979. reprint ed. lib. bdg. 93.50 (0-313-27686-2) Greenwood.

***Lock, K. M.** Lakes Tie In. 256p. 1998. pap. 13.95 (0-14-026965-7, Pub. by Pnguin Bks Ltd) Trafalgar.

***Lock, Kate.** Eastenders: The Life & Loves of Grant Mitchell. 376p. 1999. pap. text 8.99 (0-563-38483-2, BBC-Parkwest) Parkwest Pubns.

Lock, Lee H. Central Banking in Malaysia. 520p. 1987. 167.00 (0-409-99533-9, MICHIE) LEXIS Pub.

Lock, M. J., jt. auth. see Pickersgill, B.

***Lock, Margaret.** Living & Working with New Biomedical Technologies: Intersections of Inquiry. Young, Allan & Cambrosio, Alberto, eds. (Cambridge Studies in Medical Anthropology: No. 8). (Illus.). 314p. (C). 2000. pap. 22.95 (0-521-65568-4) Cambridge U Pr.

***Lock, Margaret, et al, eds.** Living & Working with New Biomedical Technologies: Intersections of Inquiry. (Cambridge Studies in Medical Anthropology: No. 8). (Illus.). 314p. (C). 2000. 59.95 (0-521-65210-3) Cambridge U Pr.

Lock, Margaret & Kaufert, Patricia, eds. Pragmatic Women & Body Politics. LC 97-10263. (Studies in Medical Anthropology: No. 5). 376p. (C). 1998. text 64.95 (0-521-62099-6); pap. text 22.95 (0-521-62929-2) Cambridge U Pr.

Lock, Margaret M. East Asian Medicine in Urban Japan: Varieties of Medical Experience. (Comparative Studies of Health Systems & Medical Care: Vol. 3). (Illus.). 1979. pap. 19.95 (0-520-05231-5, Pub. by U CA Pr) Cal Prin Full Svc.

— Encounters with Aging: Mythologies of Menopause in Japan & North America. LC 93-21379. 1995. 45.00 (0-520-08221-4, Pub. by U CA Pr); pap. 17.95 (0-520-20162-0, Pub. by U CA Pr) Cal Prin Full Svc.

Lock, Margaret M. & Gordon, Deborah, eds. Biomedicine Examined. 558p. (C). 1988. lib. bdg. 175.00 (1-55608-071-9, Pub. by Kluwer Academic) Kluwer Academic.

Lock, Margaret M. & Gordon, Deborah R., eds. Biomedicine Examined. (Culture, Illness & Healing Ser.: No. 13). 558p. 1988. pap. text 73.50 (1-55608-072-7) Kluwer Academic.

Lock, Margaret M., jt. ed. see Lindenbaum, Shirley.

Lock, Maurice A. & Williams, D. D., eds. Perspectives in Running Water Ecology. LC 81-17838. 440p. 1981. 95.00 (0-306-40898-8, Plenum Trade) Perseus Pubng.

Lock, Michael D., jt. auth. see Tarter, Michael E.

Lock, Norman. Clothes & Costumes. (Information Activity Ser.). 24p. (J). 3.50 (0-7214-3449-5, Ladybrd) Penguin Putnam.

— House of Correction. 1988. pap. 6.95 (0-88145-061-8) Broadway Play.

Lock, Penelope, jt. auth. see Cela, Camilo Jose.

Lock, Peter. The Franks in the Aegean, 1204-1500. LC 94-39822. 400p. (C). 1995. pap. 47.00 (0-582-05139-8) Longman.

Lock, Peter & Sanders, Guy, eds. The Archaeology of Medieval Greece. (Monographs in Archaeology: Vol. 59). (Illus.). 192p. 1996. pap. 40.00 (1-900188-03-1, Pub. by Oxbow Bks) David Brown.

Lock, Robert D. Job Search, Bk. 2. LC 87-15838. (Career Planning Guidebooks Ser.). 248p. (C). 1987. pap. 12.00 (0-534-08222-X) Brooks-Cole.

— Job Search: Career Planning Guide, Bk. 2. 2nd ed. LC 91-17843. 256p. (C). 1992. pap. 14.75 (0-534-13657-5) Brooks-Cole.

— Job Search: Career Planning Guide, Bk. II. 3rd ed. (Counseling Ser.). 320p. 1995. pap. 18.84 (0-534-34001-6) Brooks-Cole.

— Student Activities for Lock's Job Search. 3rd ed. LC 87-15838. (Counseling Ser.: Bk. 2). 150p. 1996. pap., suppl. ed. 15.64 (0-534-34046-6) Brooks-Cole.

— Student Activities for Taking Charge of Your Career Direction & Job Search: Career Planning Guide, Bk. 3. 2nd ed. 136p. (YA). 1992. pap., wbk. ed. 13.20 (0-534-13659-1) Brooks-Cole.

— Taking Charge of Your Career Direction, Bk. 1. LC 87-11637. (Career Planning Guidebooks Ser.). 377p. (C). 1987. mass mkt. 18.75 (0-534-08220-3) Brooks-Cole.

— Taking Charge of Your Career Direction, Vols. I-III. 3rd ed. 1996. pap., teacher ed. write for info. (0-534-34045-8) Brooks-Cole.

— Taking Charge of Your Career Direction: Career Planning Guide, Bk. I. 3rd ed. LC 95-43468. (Counseling Ser.: Bk. 1). 350p. 1995. pap. 24.40 (0-534-34000-8) Brooks-Cole.

Lock, Ron. Blood on the Painted Mountain: Zulu Victory & Defeat, Hlobane & Kambula, 1879. (Illus.). 208p. 1995. 35.00 (1-85367-201-7, Pub. by Greenhill Bks) Stackpole.

***Lock, Samuel.** Nothing but the Truth. 232p. 1999. pap. 17.95 (0-224-05084-2, Pub. by Jonathan Cape) Trafalgar.

Lock, Shmuel. Crime, Public Opinion & Civil Liberties: The Tolerant Public. LC 98-33606. 280p. 1999. 59.95 (0-275-96432-9, Praeger Pubs) Greenwood.

***Lock, Stephen, et al, eds.** Oxford Illustrated Companion to Medicine. (Illus.). 1024p. 2001. 60.00 (0-19-262950-6) OUP.

Lock, Stephen & Wells, Frank, eds. Fraud & Misconduct in Medical Research. 202p. 1993. text 45.00 (0-7279-0757-3, Pub. by BMJ Pub) Login Brothers Bk Co.

— Fraud & Misconduct in Medical Research. 2nd ed. 1996. text 53.00 (0-7279-0996-7, Pub. by BMJ Pub) Login Brothers Bk Co.

Lock, Sylvia. The Classical Rider: Being at One with Your Horse. 337p. 1997. pap. (0-85131-683-2) J A Allen.

Lock, Walter. Pastoral Epistles: Critical & Exegetical Commentary. Driver, Samuel R. et al, eds. (International Critical Commentary Ser.). 212p. 1928. 39.95 (0-567-05033-5, Pub. by T & T Clark) Bks Intl VA.

Lockamy, Archie. Global Logistics: Managing the Product - Delivery System. 2nd ed. 292p. (C). 1995. text 60.00 (0-256-20336-9, Irwn McGrw-H) McGrw-H Hghr Educ.

Lockamy, Archie, III & Cox, James F., III. Reengineering Performance Measurement: How to Align Systems to Improve Processes, Products, & Profits. LC 93-30788. 312p. 1993. 47.50 (1-55623-916-5, Irwn Prfssnl) McGraw-Hill Prof.

— Reengineering Performance Measurement CPS-Chapter 4. (Loyola College Edition Ser.). (C). 1995. per. 5.95 (0-7863-0470-7, Irwn Prfssnl) McGraw-Hill Prof.

Lockard, Allen. Design Drawing. 280p. 1999. 50.00 (0-393-73040-9) Norton.

— Design Drawing Experiences. LC 99-86189. (Illus.). 144p. 1999. pap. 34.50 (0-393-73041-7, Norton Paperbks) Norton.

Lockard, Allen & Swanson, Alice Q. A Digger's Guide to Medicinal Plants. LC 98-84753. (Illus.). 96p. 1998. pap. 9.95 (0-9663398-1-9) Ameri Botan.

Lockard, Anna-Marie. The Quest for a Child. 120p. (Orig.). 1993. pap. 6.95 (0-89228-081-6) Impact Christian.

Lockard, Craig A. Dance of Life: Popular Music & Politics in Southeast Asia. LC 96-39802. (Illus.). 328p. 1998. text 48.00 (0-8248-1848-2); pap. text 29.95 (0-8248-1918-7) UH Pr.

— From Kampong to City: A Social History of Kucing, Malaysia, 1820-1970. LC 87-11237. (Monographs in International Studies, Southeast Asia Ser.: No. 75). 325p. 1986. pap. text 20.00 (0-89680-136-5) Ohio U Pr.

— Reflections of Change: Sociopolitical Commentary & Criticism in Malaysian Popular Music since 1950. (Crossroads Ser.: Ser. 6.1). 144p. 1991. pap. 12.00 (1-877979-92-9) SE Asia.

Lockard, Duane. Coal: A Memoir & Critique. LC 98-5196. 272p. 1998. 29.95 (0-8139-1784-0) U Pr of Va.

Lockard, I. Desk Reference for Neuroscience. 2nd ed. (Illus.). 344p. 1991. pap. 56.00 (0-387-97715-5) Spr-Verlag.

Lockard, James. Instructional Software: Practical Design & Development. 368p. (C). 1992. text. write for info. (0-697-13233-1) Brown & Benchmark.

Lockard, James L. Survival Thinking: For Police & Corrections Officers. 260p. 1991. pap. 35.95 (0-398-06243-9) C C Thomas.

— Survival Thinking: For Police & Corrections Officers. 260p. (C). 1991. text 52.95 (0-398-05728-1) C C Thomas.

Lockard, Joan S. & Ward, Arthur A., Jr., eds. Epilepsy: A Window to Brain Mechanisms. fac. ed. LC 79-5503. (Illus.). 296p. pap. 91.80 (0-7837-7167-3, 204713000005) Bks Demand.

Lockard, John R. Bee Hunting. 72p. pap. 3.00 (0-936622-00-8) A R Harding Pub.

Lockard, Karen, jt. auth. see Bigler, Philip.

Lockard, Nathan. The Good, the Bad & the Bogus: Nathan Lockard's Complete Guide to Video Games. LC 94-78034. 270p. 1994. pap. 14.95 (1-881583-04-X) Advent Pr WA.

Lockard, William K. Design Drawing. rev. ed. LC 79-65405. 280p. 1993. pap. 27.95 (1-56052-376-X) Crisp Pubns.

— Drawing As a Means to Architecture. 2nd ed. LC 76-47137. (Illus.). 112p. 1995. reprint ed. pap. 23.95 (1-56052-223-2) Crisp Pubns.

Lockart, G. W. The Scots & Their Oats. LC 99-231776. (Illus.). 94p. 1998. pap. 11.95 (1-874744-80-7, Pub. by Birlinn Ltd) Dufour.

Lockart, William B., et al. Constitutional Law, Cases-Comments-Questions. 7th ed. (American Casebook Ser.). 1643p. 1991. text 58.50 (0-314-86319-2) West Pub.

Lockborn, Paul, et al. Blood & Lust. Shirley, Sam, ed. (Pendragon Roleplaying Game System Ser.). (Illus.). 128p. (Orig.). (YA). (gr. 7 up). 1991. pap. 18.95 (0-933635-84-2, 2711) Chaosium.

Locke. College Administration. 1988. pap. text. write for info. (0-582-90117-0, Pub. by Addison-Wesley) Longman.

Locke, A. I Can Say Blanket. LC 98-222975. (Illus.). (J). (ps). 1998. pap. 2.95 (1-84089-020-7, 868278) Zero to Ten.

— I Can Say Boat. LC 99-179175. (Illus.). (J). (ps). 1998. pap. 2.95 (1-84089-018-5, 868246) Zero to Ten.

— I Can Say Teddy. LC 99-179032. (Illus.). (J). (ps). 1998. pap. 2.95 (1-84089-019-3, 868241) Zero to Ten.

Locke, A. H. A History & Genealogy of Captain John Locke, 1627-1696, of Portsmouth & Rye, New Hammpshire, & His Descendants, Also of Nathaniel Locke of Portsmouth & a Short Account of the Lockes in England. (Illus.). 730p. 1989. reprint ed. pap. 109.50 (0-8328-5167-1); reprint ed. lib. bdg. 119.50 (0-8328-5166-3) Higginson Bk Co.

Locke, Alain. The New Negro. 1999. per. 15.00 (0-684-83831-1) Simon & Schuster.

Locke, Alain L. The Negro & His Music. LC 69-18592. (American Negro His History & Literature, Ser. 2). 1979. reprint ed. 27.95 (0-88143-078-1) Ayer.

— The Negro & His Music: Negro Art: Past & Present. Lee, Ulysses, ed. LC 69-18592. (American Negro: His History & Literature. Series 2). 122p. 1988. pap. 22.95 (0-88143-079-X) Ayer.

— Plays of Negro Life: A Sourcebook of Native American Drama. LC 77-132077. 430p. 1971. reprint ed. lib. bdg. 35.00 (0-8371-5037-X, IPN&, Greenwood Pr) Greenwood.

— Race Contacts & Interracial Relations. Stewart, Jeffrey, ed. LC 91-43415. 114p. 1992. 22.95 (0-88258-137-6); pap. 14.95 (0-88258-158-9) Howard U Pr.

Locke, Alain L., ed. The New Negro: An Interpretation. LC 68-29008. (American Negro: His History & Literature. Series 1). 1968. reprint ed. 57.98 (0-405-01826-6) Ayer.

— Survey Graphic. 92p. 1980. reprint ed. pap. 14.95 (0-933121-05-9) Black Classic.

Locke, Arthur H. A History & Genealogy of Captain John Locke, 1627-1696. (Illus.). 720p. 1993. reprint ed. pap. text 40.00 (1-55613-889-X) Heritage Bk.

Locke, Arthur W. Music & the Romantic Movement in France. 184p. 1977. 15.95 (0-8369-6859-X) Ayer.

— Music & the Romantic Movement in France. LC 72-83508. 184p. 1977. reprint ed. 24.95 (0-405-08751-9, Pub. by Blom Pubns) Ayer.

— Selected List of Choruses for Women's Voices. 2nd ed. 253p. 1993. reprint ed. lib. bdg. 79.00 (0-7812-9691-9) Rprt Serv.

Locke, Baden. Chrysanthemums: The Complete Guide. (Illus.). 192p. 1995. pap. 22.95 (1-85223-890-9, Pub. by Crolwood) Trafalgar.

***Locke, Barbara S.** Blood on the Yangtze. 40p. 2000. pap. 8.00 (0-8059-4845-7) Dorrance.

Locke, Barry & Garrison, Rebecca. Generalist Social Work Practice: Context, Story & Partnerships. LC 97-17469. (Social Work Ser.). 448p. 1997. mass mkt. 63.95 (0-534-21876-8) Brooks-Cole.

Locke, Bette, ed. Great Register of Stanislaus County, California, 1890. LC 92-75212. 110p. (Orig.). 1992. pap. 15.00 (0-9635514-0-X) Geneal Soc.

— Great Register of Stanislaus County, California, 1890. LC 92-75212. 110p. (Orig.). 1993. reprint ed. pap. 15.00 (0-9635514-2-6) Geneal Soc.

***Locke, Billie Hughes.** More Than One Angel. LC 99-64804. 266p. 2000. pap. 15.99 (1-57921-244-1, Pub. by WinePress Pub) BookWorld.

Locke, Carl E., jt. auth. see Riggs, Olen L., Jr.

Locke, Christopher. How to Burn. limited ed. 26p. (Orig.). 1995. pap. 8.00 (0-938566-70-9) Adastra Pr.

Locke, David. Drum Damba: Talking Drum Lessons. Aynesmith, Lawrence, ed. LC 88-20455. (Performance in World Music Ser.: No. 2). (Illus.). 228p. 1989. pap. 17.95 (0-941677-10-9, Pub. by White Cliffs Media) Words Distrib.

— Drum Gahu: An Introduction to African Rhythm. LC 98-14750. (Performance in World Music Ser.: No. 1). 152p. 1998. pap. 29.95 (0-941677-90-7) White Cliffs Media.

— Kpegisu: A War Drum of the Ewe. LC 92-3213. (Performance in World Music Ser.: No. 8). 192p. 1992. 19.95 (0-941677-39-7) White Cliffs Media.

— Science As Writing. LC 92-7824. 256p. (C). 1992. 35.00 (0-300-05452-1) Yale U Pr.

Locke, David R. The Demagogue: A Political Novel. LC 73-104515. 465p. reprint ed. lib. bdg. 32.50 (0-8398-1163-2) Irvington.

— The Demagogue: A Political Novel. 465p. (C). 1986. reprint ed. pap. text 9.95 (0-8290-1912-X) Irvington.

— The Morals of Abou Ben Adhem. LC 76-91086. (American Humorists Ser.). reprint ed. lib. bdg. 25.50 (0-8398-1164-0) Irvington.

— Nasby in Exile. LC 77-104516. (Illus.). reprint ed. lib. bdg. 22.50 (0-8398-1165-9) Irvington.

— A Paper City. LC 68-57539. (Muckrakers Ser.). 431p. reprint ed. lib. bdg. 42.00 (0-8398-1166-7) Irvington.

— A Paper City. (Muckrakers Ser.). 431p. (C). 1986. reprint ed. pap. text 10.95 (0-8290-1861-1) Irvington.

— Swingin' Round the Cirkle. LC 72-91085. (American Humorists Ser.). (Illus.). 307p. reprint ed. lib. bdg. 29.50 (0-8398-1167-5) Irvington.

Locke, David R. & Maurer, Kent L. Defense Strategy for Women: Be Your Own Risk Manager. Runyon, Daniel V., ed. (Illus.). 136p. (Orig.). 1991. pap. 9.50 (1-878559-02-8) Saltbox Pr.

Locke, Doina N. City Smart: Pittsburgh. (City Smart Ser.). (Illus.). 208p. 1999. pap. 12.95 (1-56261-349-9, City Smart) Avalon Travel.

Locke, Don. Multicultural Understanding: A Comprehensive Model. (Multicultural Aspects of Counseling Ser.: Vol. 1). 220p. (C). 1992. text 42.00 (0-8039-4593-0); pap. text 18.95 (0-8039-4594-9) Sage.

Locke, Don, jt. ed. see Weinreich-Haste, Helen.

Locke, Don C. Increasing Multicultural Understanding: A Comprehensive Model. 2nd ed. LC 97-33920. (Multicultural Aspects of Counseling Ser.). 1998. 46.00 (0-7619-1118-9); pap. 21.95 (0-7619-1119-7) Sage.

Locke, Don C., jt. ed. see Pedersen, Paul B.

Locke, Duane. Watching Wisteria: Poems by Duane Locke. LC 95-60912. 80p. 1995. 19.95 (0-9632547-4-X); pap. 9.95 (0-9632547-5-8) Vida Pub.

Locke, Duane, ed. The Immanentist Anthology: Art of the Superconscious. LC 72-96447. (Illus.). 120p. 1973. pap. 10.00 (0-912292-30-X) Smith.

Locke, Duane, et al. Yefief 3: The Force of Good. limited ed. Alindogan-Medina, Noemi, tr. (Illus.). 179p. (C). 1996. pap. 24.95 (1-884434-03-7) Images For Media.

Locke, Edward. Advancing Back. 76p. (Orig.). 1995. pap. 7.00 (0-9646587-1-2) Harlequinade.

— Anointing the Tide. 78p. 1996. pap. 7.00 (0-9646587-3-9) Harlequinade.

— Names for the Self. 76p. 1997. pap. 7.00 (0-9646587-5-5) Harlequinade.

— Parings. 76p. (Orig.). 1995. pap. 7.00 (0-9646587-0-4) Harlequinade.

— Swimming in the Gene Pool. LC 97-211716. 74p. 1997. pap. 7.00 (0-9646587-4-7) Harlequinade.

— To the Lighter House. LC 99-192643. 78p. 1998. pap. 7.00 (0-9646587-7-1) Harlequinade.

— What Time Is It? 66p. 1998. pap. 7.00 (0-9646587-6-3) Harlequinade.

— Where We Park. 78p. (Orig.). 1996. pap. 7.00 (0-9646587-2-0) Harlequinade.

***Locke, Edwin, ed.** The Blackwell Handbook of Principles of Organizational Behavior. 2000. 125.00 (0-631-21505-0) Blackwell Pubs.

***Locke, Edwin A.** The Prime Movers: Traits of the Great Wealth Creators. LC 99-89272. 228p. 2000. 27.95 (0-8144-0570-3) AMACOM.

Locke, Edwin A. Study Methods & Motivation: A Practical Guide to Effective Study. 2nd ed. LC 98-20428. Orig. Title: A Guide to Effective Study. (Illus.). 188p. 1998. reprint ed. pap. 16.95 (1-56114-444-4) Second Renaissance.

***Locke, Edwin A., et al.** The Essence of Leadership: The Four Keys to Leading Successfully. LC 91-3705. 144p. 1999. reprint ed. pap. 22.95 (0-7391-0054-8) Lxngtn Bks.

Locke, Elsie Violet & Paul, Janet, eds. Mrs. Hobson's Album. (Illus.). 168p. 1990. 39.95 (1-86940-035-6) OUP.

Locke, Emma P. Colonial Amherst, the Early History, Customs & Homes. (Illus.). 122p. 1997. reprint ed. pap. 16.00 (0-8328-5972-9) Higginson Bk Co.

Locke, Flora M. Electronic Calculators for Business Use. LC 78-1852. 264p. 1978. pap. text 36.95 (0-471-03579-3) P-H.

Locke, Frederick W. Quest for the Holy Grail. LC 70-181948. (Stanford University. Stanford Studies in Language & Literature: No. 21). reprint ed. 32.50 (0-404-51831-1) AMS Pr.

Locke, G. Malcom. Experiences & Memories of G. Malcom Locke. Burtt, M. Edward, ed. Kareff, Roburt, tr. 46p. (Orig.). 1996. pap. write for info. (1-888913-19-3) M E Burtt.

Locke, George, ed. see Sakwa, Richard.

Locke, George H. Builders of the Canadian Commonwealth. LC 67-28755. (Essay Index Reprint Ser.). 1977. 21.95 (0-8369-0621-7) Ayer.

Locke, Grace. You're a Beary Special Friend. (Pocket Gift Editions Ser.). (Illus.). 50p. 1998. 4.95 (0-88088-097-X) Peter Pauper.

Locke, Harvey J., jt. auth. see Sutherland, Edwin H.

Locke, Hubert G. The Black Anti-Semitism Controversy: Protestant Views & Perspectives. LC 93-50999. 144p. 1994. text 29.50 (0-945636-51-2) Susquehanna U Pr.

— The Detroit Riot of Nineteen Sixty-Seven. LC 76-79479. (Illus.). 168p. reprint ed. pap. 52.10 (0-7837-3816-1, 204363600010) Bks Demand.

***Locke, Hubert G.** Learning from History: A Black Christian's Perspective on the Holocaust, 63. LC 00-22304. (Contributions to the Study of Religion Ser.: Vol. 63). 150p. 2000. 58.00 (0-313-31569-8, GM1569, Greenwood Pr) Greenwood.

Locke, Hubert G., ed. The Barmen Confession: Papers from the Seattle Assembly. LC 86-23874. (Toronto Studies in Theology: Vol. 26). 370p. 1987. lib. bdg. 99.95 (0-88946-770-6) E Mellen.

— The Church Confronts the Nazis: Barmen Then & Now. LC 84-10556. (Toronto Studies in Theology: Vol. 16). 248p. 1984. lib. bdg. 89.95 (0-88946-762-5) E Mellen.

Locke, Hubert G. & Littell, Marcia S., eds. Holocaust & Church Struggle: Religion, Power & the Politics of Resistance. LC 96-17780. (Studies in the Shoah: No. XVI). 366p. 1996. lib. bdg. 54.00 (0-7618-0375-0) U Pr of Amer.

— Remembrance & Recollection: Essays on the Centennial Year of Martin Niemoller & Reinhold Niebuhr & the Fiftieth Year of the Wannsee Conference, Vol. XII. (Study in the Shoah). 138p. 1995. lib. bdg. 32.50 (0-7618-0157-X) U Pr of Amer.

Locke, Hubert G., jt. ed. see Littell, Franklin H.

Locke, Hubert G., ed. see Niemoller, Martin.

Locke, Ian. The Wheel & How It Changed the World. LC 94-15228. (History & Invention Ser.). (Illus.). 48p. 1995. 16.95 (0-8160-3143-6) Facts on File.

Locke, J. Courtenay. First Englishmen in India. (C). 1995. 44.00 (81-206-1035-0, Pub. by Asian Educ Servs) S Asia.

— First Englishmen in India. (C). 1997. 44.00 (81-215-0768-5, Pub. by M Manoharial) Coronet Bks.

Locke, J. Courtney, tr. see De Grillot, Givry.

Locke, J. S. Shores of Saco Bay: Historical Guide to Biddeford Pool, Old Orchard Beach, Pine Point, Prout's Neck. (Illus.). 107p. 1997. reprint ed. pap. 15.00 (0-8328-5882-X) Higginson Bk Co.

Locke, Jane T., jt. auth. see Locke, Joseph H.

Locke, Jim. The Well-Built House. rev. ed. 320p. 1992. pap. 14.00 (*0-395-62951-9*, R Todd) HM.

Locke, John. The Correspondence of John Locke, Vol. 7, Letters 2665-3286. DeBeer, E. S., ed. (Clarendon Edition of the Works of John Locke Ser.). 800p. 1982. text 135.00 (*0-19-824564-5*) OUP.

Locke, John. The Correspondence of John Locke: Letters 1242-1701, Covering the Years 1690-1693, Vol. 4. De Beer, E. S., ed. (Clarendon Edition of the Works of John Locke Ser.). (Illus.). 814p. 1979. text 150.00 (*0-19-824561-0*) OUP.

— The Correspondence of John Locke: Letters 3287-3648, Vol. 8. De Beer, E. S., ed. 472p. 1989. text 130.00 (*0-19-824565-3*) OUP.

Locke, John. The Correspondence of John Locke: Vol. 5, Letters 1702-2198 Covering the Years 1694-1697, Vol. 5. DeBeer, E. S., ed. (Clarendon Edition of the Works of John Locke Ser.). 808p. (C). 1980. text 135.00 (*0-19-824562-9*) OUP.

— The Correspondence of John Locke Vol. 3: Letters 849-1241, Covering the Years 1686-1689, Vol. 3. De Beer, Gavin R., ed. (Clarendon Edition of the Works of John Locke Ser.). 810p. 1978. text 125.00 (*0-19-824560-2*) OUP.

— The Correspondence of John Locke Vol. 6: Letters 2199 to 2664, Vol. 6. De Beer, E. S., ed. (Clarendon Edition of the Works of John Locke Ser.). 806p. (C). 1981. text 160.00 (*0-19-824563-7*) OUP.

— Correspondence of John Locke & Edwin Clarke. LC 72-10623. (Select Bibliographies Reprint Ser.). 1977. reprint ed. 36.95 (*0-8369-7116-7*) Ayer.

— Discourses: Translated from Nicole's Essays 1828 Edition. 274p. 1996. reprint ed. 48.00 (*1-85506-115-5*) Bks Intl VA.

— Dos Ensayos Sobre el Gobierno Civil. Abellan, Joaquin, ed. Jimenez Gracia, F., tr. (Nueva Austral Ser.: Vol. 240). (SPA.). 1991. pap. text 29.50 (*84-239-7240-2*) Elliots Bks.

— Drafts for the Essay Concerning Human Understanding & Other Philosophical Writings, Vol. 1, Drafts A & B. Nidditch, Peter H. & Rogers, G. A., eds. (Clarendon Edition of the Works of John Locke Ser.). (Illus.). 326p. 1990. text 110.00 (*0-19-824545-9*) OUP.

— An Essay Concerning Human Understanding. Winkler, Kenneth, ed. LC 96-26935. (HPC Classics Ser.). 416p. (C). 1996. lib. bdg. 34.95 (*0-87220-217-8*) Hackett Pub.

— An Essay Concerning Human Understanding, 2 vols. Fraser, Alexander C., ed. 1959. 41.50 (*0-8446-2478-0*) Peter Smith.

— An Essay Concerning Human Understanding. LC 94-32887. (Great Books in Philosophy). 644p. (C). 1995. pap. 9.95 (*0-87975-917-8*) Prometheus Bks.

— An Essay Concerning Human Understanding. Goldie, Mark, ed. 420p. 1993. pap. 8.95 (*0-460-87355-5*, Everyman's Classic Lib) Tuttle Pubng.

— An Essay Concerning Human Understanding, 2 vols., Vol. 1. Fraser, Alexander C., ed. (Illus.). 1959. pap. 14.95 (*0-486-20530-4*) Dover.

— An Essay Concerning Human Understanding, 2 vols., Vol. 2. 2nd ed. Fraser, Alexander C., ed. (Illus.). 1959. pap. 12.95 (*0-486-20531-2*) Dover.

— An Essay Concerning Human Understanding: Abridged, with Introduction & Notes. abr. ed. Winkler, Kenneth, ed. LC 96-26935. (HPC Classics Ser.). 416p. (C). 1996. pap. text 9.95 (*0-87220-216-X*) Hackett Pub.

— Essay Concerning Humanity. 1974. pap. 13.95 (*0-452-01019-5*, Mer) NAL.

— Isometric Perspective Designs & How to Create Them. (Illus.). 52p. (Orig.). 1981. pap. 4.50 (*0-486-24123-8*) Dover.

— A Letter Concerning Toleration. 91p. 1997. pap. 15.00 (*0-9627423-6-8*, LCT) Candlestick.

— A Letter Concerning Toleration. Tully, James, ed. LC 83-281. (HPC Classics Ser.). 72p. (C). 1983. pap. text 4.95 (*0-915145-60-X*); lib. bdg. 24.95 (*0-87220-100-7*) Hackett Pub.

— A Letter Concerning Toleration. LC 89-64199. (Great Books in Philosophy). 78p. (C). 1990. reprint ed. pap. 5.95 (*0-87975-598-9*) Prometheus Bks.

— Locke on Money, 2 vols., Vol. 1. Kelly, Patrick H., ed. (Clarendon Edition of the Works of John Locke Ser.). (Illus.). 358p. 1991. text 130.00 (*0-19-824546-7*) OUP.

— Locke on Money, 2 vols., Vol. 2. Kelly, Patrick H., ed. (Clarendon Edition of the Works of John Locke Ser.). (Illus.). 330p. 1991. text 110.00 (*0-19-824837-7*) OUP.

— Of the Conduct of the Understanding. Garforth, Francis W., ed. LC 66-20498. (Classics in Education Ser.: Vol. 31). 144p. 1966. reprint ed. pap. 44.70 (*0-7837-8878-9*, 204958900001) Bks Demand.

— Of the Conduct of the Understanding: 1706 Edition. (Key Texts Ser.). 160p. 1996. reprint ed. pap. 19.95 (*1-85506-225-9*) Bks Intl VA.

Locke, John. A Paraphrase & Notes on the Epistles of St. Paul, 2 vols., Vol. 1. Wainright, Arthur W., ed. (Clarendon Edition of the Works of John Locke Ser.). (Illus.). 496p. 1988. text 110.00 (*0-19-824801-6*) OUP.

Locke, John. A Paraphrase & Notes on the Epistles of St. Paul, 2 vols., Vol. 2. Wainright, Arthur W., ed. (Clarendon Edition of the Works of John Locke Ser.). (Illus.). 368p. 1988. text 89.00 (*0-19-824806-7*) OUP.

— Political Essays. Goldie, Mark, ed. (Cambridge Texts in the History of Political Thought Ser.). 456p. (C). 1997. text 59.95 (*0-521-47269-5*); pap. text 19.95 (*0-521-47861-8*) Cambridge U Pr.

— Political Writings of John Locke. 592p. (Orig.). 1993. mass mkt. 6.99 (*0-451-62861-6*, Ment) NAL.

— Questions Concerning the Law of Nature. Clay, Diskin et al, eds. Clay, Jenny S., tr. LC 89-46178. (Illus.). 256p. 1990. text 39.95 (*0-8014-2348-1*) Cornell U Pr.

— The Reasonableness of Christianity. LC 97-36155. 224p. 1998. pap. 12.95 (*0-89526-402-1*, Gateway Editions) Regnery Pub.

— The Reasonableness of Christianity: As Deliverred in the Scriptures. Higgins-Ciddle, John C., ed. LC 98-26343. (Clarendon Edition of the Works of John Locke Ser.). (Illus.). 402p. 2000. text 95.00 (*0-19-824525-4*) OUP.

— Reasonableness of Christianity, & a Discourse of Miracles. Ramsey, I. T., ed. 104p. 1958. pap. 10.95 (*0-8047-0341-8*) Stanford U Pr.

Locke, John. The Reasonableness of Christianity As Delivered in the Scriptures, 1794 Edition. (Key Texts Ser.). 440p. 1997. pap. 30.00 (*1-85506-522-3*) Thoemmes Pr.

Locke, John. Second Treatise of Government. Macpherson, C. B., ed. LC 80-15052. (HPC Classics Ser.). 148p. (C). 1980. pap. text 4.95 (*0-915144-86-7*); lib. bdg. 24.95 (*0-915144-93-X*) Hackett Pub.

— Second Treatise of Government. Cox, Richard H., ed. LC 82-25160. (Crofts Classics). 200p. 1982. pap. text 4.95 (*0-88295-125-4*) Harlan Davidson.

— The Second Treatise on Civil Government. LC 86-60141. (Great Books in Philosophy). 132p. 1986. pap. 5.95 (*0-87975-337-4*) Prometheus Bks.

— Several Papers Relating to Money, Interest & Trade, Etc. LC 87-17243. (Reprints of Economic Classics Ser.). 328p. 1989. reprint ed. 57.50 (*0-678-00334-3*) Kelley.

— Some Thoughts Concerning Education. Yolton, John W. & Yolton, Jean, eds. (Clarendon Edition of the Works of John Locke Ser.). (Illus.). 346p. 1989. text 110.00 (*0-19-824582-3*) OUP.

***Locke, John.** Some Thoughts Concerning Education. Yolton, John W. & Yolton, Jean S., eds. (Clarendon Edition of the Works of John Locke Ser.). (Illus.). 348p. 2000. pap. 26.95 (*0-19-825016-9*) OUP.

Locke, John. Some Thoughts Concerning Education & of the Conduct of the Understanding. Grant, Ruth W. & Tarcov, Nathan, eds. LC 96-23832. (HPC Classics Ser.). 256p. 1996. pap. text 12.95 (*0-87220-334-4*); lib. bdg. 34.95 (*0-87220-335-2*) Hackett Pub.

— Treatise of Civil Government & a Letter Concerning Toleration. Sherman, Charles L., ed. 1965. pap. text 12.95 (*0-89197-519-5*) Irvington.

— Two Letters Concerning Toleration. 209p. 1997. lib. bdg. 50.00 (*0-9627423-7-6*, LCT) Candlestick.

— Two Treatises of Government. Goldie, Mark, ed. 298p. 1993. pap. 6.95 (*0-460-87356-3*, Everyman's Classic Lib) Tuttle Pubng.

— Two Treatises of Government. 3rd rev. ed. Laslett, Peter, ed. (Cambridge Texts in the History of Political Thought Ser.). 200p. 1988. 27.95 (*0-521-35448-X*); pap. text 10.95 (*0-521-35730-6*) Cambridge U Pr.

— Works, 10 Vols, Set. 1963. reprint ed. 800.00 (*3-511-02600-8*) Adlers Foreign Bks.

— Works of John Locke, 2 Vols, 1. LC 74-94275. (Select Bibliographies Reprint Ser.). 1977. 30.95 (*0-8369-9980-0*) Ayer.

— Works of John Locke, 2 Vols, Set. LC 74-94275. (Select Bibliographies Reprint Ser.). 1977. 61.95 (*0-8369-5049-6*) Ayer.

— Works of John Locke, 2 Vols, Vol. 2. LC 74-94275. (Select Bibliographies Reprint Ser.). 1977. 30.95 (*0-8369-9981-9*) Ayer.

Locke, John, et al. The Empiricists. Incl. Enquiry Concerning Human Understanding. 1961. Essay Concerning Human Understanding. abr. ed. 1961. Principles of Human Knowledge. 1961. Three Dialogues. 1961. 528p. 1960. Set pap. 14.95 (*0-385-09622-4*, Anchor NY) Doubleday.

Locke, John, et al. Locke - Berkeley - Hume: Macintosh. (Past Masters Ser.). (C). write for info. incl. cd-rom (*1-57085-025-9*) Intelex.

— Locke - Berkeley - Hume: Windows. (Past Masters Ser.). (C). write for info. incl. cd-rom (*1-57085-100-X*) Intelex.

Locke, John C., ed. First Englishmen in India. LC 75-43767 reprint ed. 37.50 (*0-404-06615-1*) AMS Pr.

Locke, John F., tr. see Maquet, Jacques P.

Locke, John L. The Child's Path to Spoken Language. LC 92-34661. (Illus.). 480p. (Orig.). 1993. text 49.95 (*0-674-11640-2*) HUP.

— The Child's Path to Spoken Language. (Illus.). 536p. (Orig.). (C). 1995. pap. text 22.50 (*0-674-11639-9*) HUP.

— The De Voicing of Society. LC 98-14921. 256p. 1998. 24.50 (*0-684-84333-1*) S&S Trade.

— Sketches of the History of the Town of Camden, Maine. (Illus.). 282p. 1998. reprint ed. pap. 24.00 (*0-7884-0925-5*, L515) Heritage Bk.

— Why We Don't Talk to Each Other Anymore: The De-Voicing of Society. 256p. 1999. pap. 14.00 (*0-684-85574-7*, Touchstone) S&S Trade Pap.

Locke, Jonathan & Richter, Jeffrey M. Windows 95: A Developer's Guide. 89p. 1995. pap. 39.95 incl. cd-rom (*1-55851-418-X*, M&T Bks) IDG Bks.

Locke, Joseph. Ben There, Done That. (Sabrina, the Teenage Witch Ser.: No. 6). 160p. (YA). (gr. 7-12). 1998. per. 3.99 (*0-671-01680-6*, Archway) PB.

— Good Burger Movie Tie In. (J). (gr. 3-7). 1997. per. 4.50 (*0-671-01692-X*) PB.

— Hocus Pocus! (Secret World of Alex Mack Ser.: No. 19). (J). (gr. 3-6). 1997. pap. 3.99 (*0-671-00707-6*) PB.

The Troll Bride. (Sabrina, the Teenage Witch Ser.: No. 4). (Illus.). 32p. (J). (gr. 1-6). 1998. pap. 3.99 (*0-689-81880-7*, Simon Spot) Litle Simon.

Locke, Joseph H. & Locke, Jane T. Locke Art Glass: A Guide for Collectors with Photographic Illustrations of 190 Examples. 64p. (Orig.). 1987. pap. 9.95 (*0-486-25400-3*) Dover.

Locke, Karen D., jt. auth. see Golden-Biddle, Karen.

Locke, Kathy, jt. auth. see Buzby, Beth M.

***Locke, Lawrence F.** Proposals That Work: A Guide for Planning Dissertations & Grant Proposals. 4th ed. LC 99-6594. 350p. 2000. 59.95 (*0-7619-1706-3*) Sage.

Locke, Lawrence F., et al. Proposals That Work: A Guide for Planning Dissertations & Grant Proposals. 3rd ed. (Illus.). 320p. (C). 1993. text 52.00 (*0-8039-5066-7*); pap. text 22.95 (*0-8039-5067-5*) Sage.

— Reading & Understanding Research. LC 97-45243. 1998. write for info. (*0-7619-0306-2*); pap. write for info. (*0-7619-0307-0*) Sage.

Locke, Lee J., ed. Essentials of Upholstery & Trim, for Vintage & Classic. (Illus.). 176p. 1970. pap. 9.95 (*0-911160-48-5*) Post Group.

Locke, Marianne, et al. Being in Motion. 75p. 1994. teacher ed. 59.95 (*0-9643923-0-5*) Young Imag.

Locke, Marie & Montgomery, P. Nancy. Memories of a Maine Island: Turn-of-the-Century Tales & Photographs. LC 97-75498. (Northeast Folklore Ser.: Vol. XXXIII). (Illus.). 112p. 1998. pap. 18.00 (*0-943197-25-2*) ME Folklife Ctr.

Locke, Mary, jt. auth. see Felts, Teri.

Locke, Mary E., ed. see Burghardt, Raymond F., et al.

Locke, Maryel & Warren, Charles, eds. Jean-Luc Godard's Hail Mary: Women & the Sacred in Film. LC 92-29569. (Illus.). 280p. (C). 1993. 21.95 (*0-8093-1824-5*) S Ill U Pr.

Locke, Matthew. The Present Practice of Musick Vindicated. fac. ed. (Monuments of Music & Music Literature in Facsimile Ser., Series II: Vol. 16). (Illus.). 1974. lib. bdg. 37.50 (*0-8450-2216-4*) Broude.

Locke, Mattie. Care Planning with the MDS+ for the Geriatric Nurse. 258p. (Orig.). (C). 1995. 48.00 (*1-877735-46-9*, 2268PP) Prof Prnting & Pub.

— Inservice Manual Continuing Education Program for LTC. (Illus.). 120p. (C). 1986. 34.50 (*1-877735-12-4*, 2115PP) Prof Prnting & Pub.

— Nursing Management in the 90's - An OBRA Guide for DON's. 224p. (C). 1991. 18.00 (*1-877735-31-0*, 2176PP) Prof Prnting & Pub.

— Quality Assurance with Care Planning. 290p. (C). 1992. 42.00 (*1-877735-36-1*, 2185PP) Prof Prnting & Pub.

— Texas Policies & Procedures. 6th ed. 383p. (C). 1993. 65.00 (*1-877735-01-9*, 2102PP) Prof Prnting & Pub.

Locke, Mattie, et al. Care Plans That Work with MDS. 3rd ed. 214p. (C). 1996. 49.50 (*1-877735-03-5*, 2104PP) Prof Prnting & Pub.

Locke, May S. Anti-Slavery in America from the Introduction of African Slaves to the Prohibition of the Slave Trade (1619-1808) 1988. 16.50 (*0-8446-1284-7*) Peter Smith.

Locke, Michael, jt. auth. see Harrison, Frederick W.

Locke, Norton. The Land of Milk & Honey. Costa, Gwen, ed. LC 90-40784. (Illus.). 350p. 1992. 29.95 (*0-87949-343-7*) Ashley Bks.

Locke, P. Harvey, et al, eds. Manual of Small Animal Dermatology. (Illus.). 280p. 1994. pap. text 72.95 (*0-905214-20-X*, Pub. by BSAVA) Iowa St U Pr.

***Locke, Peggy & Levin, Jackie.** Making Connections: A Practical Guide for Bringing the World of Voice Output Communication to Students with Severe Disabilities. (Illus.). 111p. 1998. pap. 27.00 (*0-9666667-1-2*) AbleNet Inc.

Locke, Philip, jt. auth. see Downing, Angela.

Locke, Ralph G., jt. auth. see Kelly, Edward F.

Locke, Ralph P. Music, Musicians, & the Saint-Simonians. LC 85-20915. (Illus.). xviii, 418p. (C). 1986. pap. text 24.95 (*0-226-48902-7*); lib. bdg. 55.00 (*0-226-48901-9*) U Ch Pr.

Locke, Ralph P. & Barr, Cyrilla, eds. Cultivating Music in America: Women Patrons & Activists since 1860. LC 97-25716. (Illus.). 385p. 1997. 48.00 (*0-520-08395-4*, Pub. by U CA Pr) Cal Prin Full Svc.

Locke, Ray. Seldom Sung Songs. LC 83-63200. 192p. 1984. 13.95 (*0-915677-02-4*) Roundtable Pub.

— Sweet Salt. LC 89-60774. 224p. (Orig.). 1990. pap. 12.95 (*0-915677-43-1*) Roundtable Pub.

Locke, Raymond F. James Beckwourth: Mountain Man. (Black American Ser.). (Illus.). 208p. (YA). 1995. mass mkt. 4.95 (*0-87067-590-7*, Melrose Sq) Holloway.

— Joaquin Murieta: The California Gold Rush "Robin Hood" 256p. 1980. mass mkt. 2.25 (*0-87067-009-3*, BH009) Holloway.

Locke, Raymond F., jt. auth. see Ruth, Marianne.

Locke, Reginald. A Naturalists Book of Poetry. 64p. 1984. 45.00 (*0-905418-85-9*, Pub. by Gresham Bks) St Mut.

Locke, Ricahrd M. Remaking the Italian Economy. (Cornell Studies in Political Economy). 256p. 1996. pap. text 14.95 (*0-8014-8421-9*) Cornell U Pr.

Locke, Richard. Global Supply Management: A Guide to International Purchasing. 304p. 1996. text 45.00 (*0-7863-0797-8*, Irwn Prfssnl) McGraw-Hill Prof.

— Locke Out: The Collected Writings of Richard Locke. (Illus.). 192p. (Orig.). 1993. pap. 12.95 (*0-943383-06-4*) FirstHand Ltd.

Locke, Richard, et al, eds. Employment Relations in a Changing World Economy. 427p. 1995. 49.00 (*0-262-12191-3*); pap. text 24.50 (*0-262-62098-7*) MIT Pr.

Locke, Richard A. Moon Walk, 1835: Was Neil Armstrong Really the First Man on the Moon? 5th ed. Tazewell, Calvert W., ed. LC 90-81467. (Illus.). 80p. 1990. pap. 10.00 (*1-878515-34-9*) W S Dawson.

Locke, Robert R. The Collapse of the American Management Mystique. (Illus.). 366p. (C). 1996. text 42.00 (*0-19-877406-0*) OUP.

— The End of the Practical Man: Higher Education & the Institutionalization of Entrepreneurial Performance in Germany, France, & Great Britain - 1880 to 1940. McKay, John, ed. LC 83-48094. (Industrial Development & the Social Fabric Ser.: Vol. 7). 250p. 1986. 73.25 (*0-89232-433-3*) Jai Pr.

— Management Education. LC 98-9491. (History of Management Thought Ser.). 8p. 1998. text 198.95 (*1-85521-990-5*, Pub. by Ashgate Pub) Ashgate Pub Co.

Locke, Sam. Fair Game. 1958. pap. 5.25 (*0-8222-0379-0*) Dramatists Play.

Locke, Saul R., ed. see Southern Metals/Materials Conference on Advances i.

Locke, Shirley A. Coping with Loss: A Guide for Caregivers. LC 94-7441. 238p. 1994. pap. 35.95 (*0-398-06244-7*) C C Thomas.

— Coping with Loss: A Guide for Caregivers. LC 94-7441. 238p. (C). 1994. text 51.95 (*0-398-05912-8*) C C Thomas.

Locke, Simon. Constructing "The Beginning" Discourses of Creation Science. LC 98-13598. (Communication Ser.). 248p. 1998. 59.95 (*0-8058-2346-8*); pap. 27.50 (*0-8058-2347-6*) L Erlbaum Assocs.

Locke, Steven & Hornig-Rohan, Mady. Mind & Immunity: Behavioral Immunology. LC 83-81107. 258p. 1983. 79.50 (*0-275-91400-3*, C1400, Praeger Pubs) Greenwood.

Locke, Tates & Ibach, Bob. Caught in the Net. LC 81-36382. (Illus.). 176p. (Orig.). 1982. reprint ed. pap. 54.60 (*0-608-07083-1*, 206731200009) Bks Demand.

Locke, Thomas. The Delta Factor. LC 94-19918. 24p. 1994. pap. 8.99 (*1-55661-501-9*) Bethany Hse.

— The Delta Factor. LC 98-10149. (Thomas Locke Mystery Ser.). 1998. 21.95 (*0-7862-1418-X*) Five Star.

— Dream Voyager. (Spectrum Chronicles Ser.: Bk. 2). 176p. (YA). (gr. 7-10). 1995. pap. 5.99 (*1-55661-433-0*) Bethany Hse.

— Heart Chaser. LC 96-45837. (Spectrum Chronicles Ser.). 16p. (YA). (gr. 7-10). 1997. pap. 5.99 (*1-55661-921-9*) Bethany Hse.

— Light Weaver. LC 94-19919. (Spectrum Chronicles Ser.). 176p. (YA). 1994. pap. 5.99 (*1-55661-432-2*) Bethany Hse.

— The Omega Network. (Thomas Locke Mystery Ser.: Bk. 2). 256p. 1995. pap. 8.99 (*1-55661-502-7*) Bethany Hse.

— Path Finder. LC 95-473. (Spectrum Chronicles Ser.: Bk. 3). 16p. (YA). (gr. 7-10). 1995. pap. 5.99 (*1-55661-434-9*) Bethany Hse.

***Locke, Tim, ed.** Europe 2000: The Budget Travel Guide. (Thomas Cook Independent Traveler's Guides Ser.). (Illus.). 1999. pap. 19.95 (*0-7627-0672-4*) Globe Pequot.

Locke, Virginia O., jt. auth. see Stevenson, Russell.

Locke, W. N. Pronunciation of the French Spoken at Brunswick, Maine. (Publications of the American Dialect Society: No. 12). 201p. 1949. pap. text 8.25 (*0-8173-0612-9*) U of Ala Pr.

Locke, William H., Jr. & Novak, Ralph M., Jr. Texas Foreclosure Manual. LC 91-65392. 484p. 1991. ring bd. 150.00 (*0-938160-63-X*, 6207) State Bar TX.

Locke, William J. Town of Tombarel. LC 71-150548. (Short Story Index Reprint Ser.). 1977. reprint ed. 20.95 (*0-8369-3845-3*) Ayer.

Locke, William N. Scientific French: A Concise Description of the Structural Elements of Scientific & Technical French. LC 78-11669. 124p. 1978. reprint ed. pap. 9.50 (*0-88275-771-7*) Krieger.

Locke, William N. & Booth, E. Donald, eds. Machine Translation of Languages: Fourteen Essays. LC 75-29339. 243p. 1976. reprint ed. lib. bdg. 38.50 (*0-8371-8434-7*, LOMT, Greenwood Pr) Greenwood.

Lockemann, P. C., jt. ed. see Bracchi, G.

Lockemann, P. C., jt. ed. see Encarnacao, Jose L.

Locker. Business & Administrative Communication. 4th ed. 1997. pap. text, teacher ed. write for info. (*0-256-26982-3*) McGraw.

— Foundations of Business Communications. 2000. 45.00 (*0-07-230598-3*) McGraw.

***Locker.** Mountain Dance: And Other Stories. 2001. write for info. (*0-15-202622-3*) Harcourt.

Locker & Stoddard. Business Communications & Effective Writing. 3rd ed. 1994. 67.00 (*0-256-18882-3*) McGraw.

***Locker, Ed & Zoloty, Donald.** Touchdown: The New Approach to Scholarships & the College Football Decision. (Illus.). v, 115p. 2000. pap. 24.95 (*0-9659347-6-4*) New Direct OH.

Locker, J., ed. Transcription Factors: Essential Data. (Essential Data Ser.). 160p. 1996. pap. 39.95 (*0-471-95339-3*) Wiley.

***Locker, John.** Spectral Theory of Non-Self-Adjoint Two-Point Differential Operators. LC 99-44328. (Mathematical Surveys & Monographs: Vol. 73). 252p. 1999. 65.00 (*0-8218-2049-4*) Am Math.

***Locker, Joseph.** Transcription Factors. (Human Molecular Genetics Ser.). 300p. 2000. 115.00 (*0-12-454345-6*) Acad Pr.

Locker, Kitty O. Business & Administrative Communication. 3rd ed. LC 94-17702. 720p. (C). 1994. text 64.50 (*0-256-14064-2*, Irwn McGrw-H) McGrw-H Hghr Educ.

— Business & Administrative Communication. 4th ed. LC 97-10359. 704p. (C). 1997. text 62.50 (*0-256-22057-3*, Irwn McGrw-H) McGrw-H Hghr Educ.

***Locker, Kitty O.** Business & Administrative Communication. 5th ed. LC 99-34639. 2000. write for info. (*0-07-229392-6*) McGraw.

Locker, Kitty O. The Irwin Business Communication Handbook. 128p. (C). 1993. text 13.00 (*0-256-14586-5*, Irwn McGrw-H) McGrw-H Hghr Educ.

***Locker, Sari.** The Complete Idiot's Guide to Being Sexy. (Complete Idiot's Guide Ser.). 352p. 2001. pap. 18.95 (*0-02-863916-2*, Alpha Ref) Macmillan Gen Ref.

***Locker, Thomas.** Cloud Dance. LC 99-42642. (Illus.). 32p. (J). (ps up). 2000. 16.00 (*0-15-202231-7*, Harcourt Child Bks) Harcourt.

Locker, Thomas. Family Farm. LC 87-19645. (Picture Puffin Ser.). (J). 1988. 11.19 (*0-606-06367-6*, Pub. by Turtleback) Demco.

— Home: A Journey Through America. LC 97-18206. (Illus.). 32p. (J). (gr. 1-5). 1998. 16.00 (*0-15-201473-X*, Harcourt Child Bks) Harcourt.

L

***Locker, Thomas.** Home: A Journey Through America. (Illus.). 32p. (J). (ps-3). 2000. pap. 6.00 (*0-15-202452-2*, Harcourt Child Bks) Harcourt.
— In Blue Mountains: An Artist's Return to America's First Wilderness. LC 99-40197. (Illus.). 32p. (J). 2000. 18.00 (*0-88010-471-6*, Bell Pond) Anthroposophic.
Locker, Thomas. The Land of Gray Wolf. LC 90-3915. (J). 1996. 11.19 (*0-606-09525-X*, Pub. by Turtleback) Demco.
— The Man Who Paints Nature. LC 98-21666. (Meet the Author Ser.). (Illus.). 32p. (J). (gr. 2-5). 1999. 14.95 (*1-57274-328-X*, 722) R Owen Pubs.
— Mare on the Hill. (J). 1995. 11.19 (*0-606-07840-1*) Turtleback.
— Sailing with the Wind. 1991. 15.00 (*0-07-158539-7*) McGraw.
— Sailing with the Wind. 1986. 11.19 (*0-606-04789-1*, Pub. by Turtleback) Demco.
***Locker, Thomas.** Sky Tree. (J). 2001. pap. write for info. (*0-06-443750-7*, HarpTrophy) HarpC Child Bks.
Locker, Thomas. Sky Tree: Seeing Science Through Art. LC 94-38342. (Illus.). 40p. (J). (ps-3). 1995. 16.95 (*0-06-024883-1*) HarpC Child Bks.
— Water Dance. (J). (ps-5). 1997. 16.00 (*0-614-28814-2*) Harcourt.
— Water Dance. LC 95-47861. (Illus.). 32p. (J). (ps-5). 1997. 16.00 (*0-15-201284-2*) Harcourt.
— Where the River Begins. (Picture Puffin Ser.). (Illus.). (J). 1993. 11.19 (*0-606-02990-7*, Pub. by Turtleback) Demco.
— Young Artist. (Picture Puffin Ser.). 1989. 10.19 (*0-606-06112-6*, Pub. by Turtleback) Demco.
Lockerbie. Voting Behavior. (C). 2000. 21.00 (*0-205-28098-6*, Macmillan Coll) P-H.
Lockerbie & Olson. Daktar. (SPA.). 1.95 (*0-685-74926-6*, 540099) Editorial Unilit.
Lockerbie, D. Bruce. Dismissing God: Modern Writers' Struggle Against Religion. LC 98-17390. 256p. 1998. pap. 15.99 (*0-8010-5804-X*) Baker Bks.
Lockerbie, D. Bruce & Fonseca, Donald R. College: Getting in & Staying In. LC 90-32755. 208p. reprint ed. pap. 64.50 (*0-7837-5559-7*, 204533400005) Bks Demand.
Lockerbie, D. Bruce, jt. auth. see Bell, Robert.
Lockerbie, Jeanette. A Cup of Sugar Neighbor. (Quiet Time Books for Women). 128p. pap. 4.99 (*0-8024-1681-0*, 409) Moody.
— Morning Glories. (Quiet Time Books for Women). (Orig.). pap. 4.99 (*0-8024-6861-6*, 413) Moody.
— Salt in My Kitchen. (Quiet Time Books for Women). pap. 4.99 (*0-8024-7500-0*, 416) Moody.
— Time Out for Coffee. (Quiet Time Books for Women). pap. 4.99 (*0-8024-8759-9*, 419) Moody.
Lockerbie, Jeannie. On Duty in Bangladesh: The Story the Newspapers Didn't Publish... 2nd ed. LC 72-95513. (Illus.). 191p. (Orig.). 1980. reprint ed. pap. text 6.95 (*1-888796-01-4*) ABWE Pubng.
Lockerbie, Jeannie, jt. ed. see Cuthbert, Melbourne E.
Lockerby, Susan C., ed. see International SAMPE Electronics Conference Staff.
Lockerd, Benjamin G., Jr. Aethereal Rumours: T. S. Eliot's Physics & Poetics. LC 97-32662. 320p. 1998. 48.50 (*0-8387-5373-6*) Bucknell U Pr.
— The Sacred Marriage: Psychic Integration in the Faerie Queene. LC 85-48293. (Illus.). 216p. 1987. 35.00 (*0-8387-5106-7*) Bucknell U Pr.
Lockeretz, William, ed. Environmentally Sound Agriculture. LC 83-4231. 426p. 1983. 44.95 (*0-275-91401-1*, C1401, Praeger Pubs) Greenwood.
— Proposed 1985 Farm Bill Changes: Taking the Bias Out of Farm Policy: Symposium Proceedings. 54p. 1985. pap. 6.00 (*1-893182-12-6*) H A Wallace Inst.
***Lockeretz, William, ed.** Visions of American Agriculture. LC 99-56718. (Illus.). 255p. 2000. pap. 24.95 (*0-8138-2709-4*) Iowa St U Pr.
Lockeretz, William & Anderson, Molly D. Agricultural Research Alternatives. LC 92-47113. (Our Sustainable Future Ser.: Vol. 3). x, 248p. 1993. text 45.00 (*0-8032-2901-1*) U of Nebr Pr.
Lockeretz, William, jt. auth. see Anderson, Molly D.
Lockeridge, Frances & Lockeridge, Richard. The Norths Meet Murder. 19.95 (*0-89190-916-8*) Amereon Ltd.
Lockeridge, Richard, jt. auth. see Lockeridge, Frances.
Lockert, Jan. An Infinite Journey. Shaw, Pat, tr. from NOR. 230p. (Orig.). 1993. pap. 12.95 (*0-9631750-2-5*) Muse Pubns.
Lockert, Lacy, tr. Chief Rivals of Corneille & Racine. LC 56-14366. 605p. 1956. 29.95 (*0-8265-1047-7*) Vanderbilt U Pr.
— Moot Plays of Corneille. LC 59-15968. 486p. 1959. 29.95 (*0-8265-1053-1*) Vanderbilt U Pr.
— More Plays by Rivals of Corneille & Racine. LC 68-17282. 694p. 1968. 29.95 (*0-8265-1110-4*) Vanderbilt U Pr.
Lockert, Lucia, ed. see Fox, Lucia.
Lockery, Glen, ed. Songs of Idaho. 94p. 1988. 25.00 (*0-9619700-0-6*); pap. 8.00 (*0-9619700-1-4*) Univ ID Alumni Assn.
Lockery, Shirley A. & Schoenrock, Susan A., eds. Ethnicity & Aging: Mental Health Issues. LC 90-71303. 73p. (C). 1990. pap. text 8.00 (*1-879167-00-X*) SDSU Coll Hlth Hum Servs.
Lockett, A. G. & Islei, G., eds. Improving Decision Making in Organizations. (Lecture Notes in Economics & Mathematical Systems Ser.: Vol. 335). (Illus.). ix, 606p. 1989. 77.95 (*0-387-51795-2*) Spr-Verlag.
Lockett, Brian. Construction Craft Jurisdiction Agreements, 1995. LC 94-43299. 1995. pap. 45.00 (*0-87179-851-4*) BNA Books.
Lockett, Hattie G. The Unwritten Literature on the Hopi. LC 76-43767. (Arizona Univ. Social Science Bulletin Ser.: No. 2). reprint ed. 36.00 (*0-404-15621-5*) AMS Pr.
Lockett, Hazel, ed. see Charles, Melvin.
Lockett, Keith. Physics in the Real World. 208p. (C). 1990. pap. text 23.95 (*0-521-36690-9*) Cambridge U Pr.
Lockett, Martin & Spear, Roger, eds. Organizations As Systems. 244p. 1980. pap. 38.00 (*0-335-00263-3*) OpUniv Pr.
Lockett, Matt, ed. see Young, David.
Lockett, Nick. Environmental Liability Insurance. (Environmental Law Ser.). 280p. 1996. 150.00 (*1-874698-65-1*, Pub. by Cameron May) Gaunt.
Lockett, Nick, ed. Digest of Environmental Law. (Environmental Law Ser.). 230p. 1996. pap. 45.00 (*1-874698-20-1*, Pub. by Federation Pr) Gaunt.
Lockett, R., jt. auth. see Fish, W. F.
Lockett, Raymond. World Civilization Readings. 304p. (C). 1992. pap. text 34.20 (*0-536-58217-3*) Pearson Custom.
Lockett, Reginald. Where the Birds Sing Bass. LC 88-93046. (Illus.). 109p. (Orig.). 1995. pap. 10.95 (*0-932693-05-9*) Jukebox Press.
Lockett, Richard. Samuel Prout, 1783-1852: Painter in Water-Colours to King George IV. (British Watercolour Ser.). (Illus.). 192p. 1985. pap. 25.00 (*0-7134-3491-0*) Wittenborn Art.
Lockett, Terence A. Collecting Victorian Tiles. (Illus.). 240p. 1979. 29.50 (*0-902028-82-0*) Antique Collect.
Lockett, Tony. Evidence-Based & Cost-Effective Medicine for the Uninitiated. LC 97-49. 1997. write for info. (*1-85775-235-X*, Radcliffe Med Pr) Scovill Paterson.
— Health Economics for the Uninitiated. LC 95-52776. 1996. write for info. (*1-85775-069-1*, Radcliffe Med Pr) Scovill Paterson.
Lockett-Wormsley, Robin E. Dottie Goes to Daycare. (Illus.). 16p. (J). (gr. k-2). 1999. pap. 7.00 (*0-8059-3831-1*) Dorrance.
Lockette, Kevin F. & Keyes, Ann M. Conditioning with Physical Disabilities. LC 93-47606. 288p. 1994. pap. 22.95 (*0-87322-614-3*, PLOC0614) Human Kinetics.
Lockey, Joseph B. Pan-Americanism: Its Beginnings. LC 79-111723. (American Imperialism: Viewpoints of United States Foreign Policy, 1898-1941 Ser.). 1970. reprint ed. 28.95 (*0-405-02034-1*) Ayer.
Lockey, Paul, ed. Studies in Thomistic Theology. 365p. (C). 1996. 32.00 (*0-268-01755-7*); pap. 19.95 (*0-268-01756-5*) Ctr Thomistic.
Lockey, Richard F. & Bukantz, Samuel C. Allergen Immunotherapy. 2nd ed. LC 98-39465. (Illus.). 632p. 1998. text 225.00 (*0-8247-0188-7*) Dekker.
— Fundamentals of Immunology & Allergy. (Illus.). 352p. 1987. pap. text 41.00 (*0-7216-2054-X*, W B Saunders Co) Harcrt Hlth Sci Grp.
Lockey, Richard F., jt. ed. see Kemp, Stephen F.
Lockhart. Latin American Jewish Literature. 1998. 22.95 (*0-8057-7803-9*, Twyne) Mac Lib Ref.
Lockhart, et al, eds. Out Loud: A Collection of New Songs by Women. LC 77-86751. (Illus.). 1979. pap. text 7.50 (*0-930712-00-5*) Inkworks.
Lockhart, Alexander. The Portable Pep Talk: Motivational Morsels for Inspiring You to Succeed. 256p. (Orig.). 1997. pap. 8.95 (*0-9643035-7-4*) Zander Pr.
— Positive Charges: 544 Ways to Stay Upbeat During Downbeat Times. 224p. (Orig.). 1994. pap. 6.95 (*0-9643035-5-8*) Zander Pr.
— School Teaching in Canada. 224p. 1991. text 40.00 (*0-8020-2748-2*); pap. text 19.95 (*0-8020-6788-3*) U of Toronto Pr.
Lockhart, Audrey. Some Aspects of Irish Emigration from Ireland to the North American Colonies Between 1660-1775. LC 76-6351. (Irish Americans Ser.). 1976. 23.95 (*0-405-09345-4*) Ayer.
Lockhart-Ball, H., jt. auth. see Norton, B.
Lockhart, Barbara & Lockhart, Lynne N. Once a Pony Time at Chincoteague. (Illus.). 30p. (J). (gr. k-5). 1992. 8.95 (*0-87033-436-0*, Tidewtr Pubs) Cornell Maritime.
Lockhart, Barbara M. Read to Me, Talk with Me. rev. ed. 260p. 1992. pap. text 44.00 (*0-7616-7165-X*) Commun Skill.
Lockhart, Barbara M., jt. auth. see Lockhart, Lynne N.
Lockhart, Betty A. A Calf Grows Up: The Story of Dairying with a Guide to Teaching & Learning. Lockhart, Donald G., ed. (Illus.). 1992. teacher ed. 7.00 (*1-880327-23-6*) Perceptions.
— The Maple Sugaring Story: A Guide for Teaching & Learning the Maple Industry. Lockhart, Donald G., ed. (Illus.). 84p. 1990. teacher ed. 4.50 (*1-880327-04-X*) Perceptions.
— Visiting a Farm? "Be Safe & Sound" Says Safety Hound: A Guide to Teaching & Learning about Farm Visit Safety. Lockhart, Donald G., ed. (Illus.). 1994. teacher ed. 2.50 (*1-880327-32-5*) Perceptions.
***Lockhart, Betty Ann, et al.** The Official Vermont Maple Cookbook. 2nd ed. Lockhart, Donald, ed. (Illus.). 65p. 1999. pap. write for info. (*1-880327-43-0*) Perceptions.
Lockhart, Bruce M. The End of the Vietnamese Monarchy. LC 93-60072. (Lax-Viet Series - Yale University Southeast Asia Studies: No. 15). 242p. (Orig.). 1993. pap. 15.00 (*0-938692-50-X*) Yale U SE Asia.
Lockhart, Charles. Gaining Ground: Tailoring Social Programs to American Values. 1989. 35.00 (*0-520-06437-2*, Pub. by U CA Pr) Cal Prin Full Svc.
Lockhart, Charles, jt. auth. see Crothers, Lane.
Lockhart, Charles, jt. auth. see Richards, Jack C.
Lockhart, Charles, jt. ed. see Utter, Glenn H.
Lockhart, Charlotte F. Adult Education Intensive Phonics Manual. LC 87-70692. 214p. 1987. teacher ed. 61.00 incl. audio (*0-9605654-5-0*) Char-L.
— Discover Intensive Phonics for Yourself. rev. ed. LC 83-71502. 452p. (J). 1983. teacher ed. 49.95 (*0-9605654-1-8*) Char-L.
— Discover Intensive Phonics for Yourself. 4th rev. ed. LC 88-91180. 420p. reprint ed. teacher ed. 70.00 incl. audio (*0-9605654-6-9*) Char-L.
— Intensive Phonics Mini Manual. LC 86-70531. 95p. (Orig.). 1986. pap. text 30.00 (*0-9605654-3-4*) Char-L.
— Intermediate & Adult Education Intensive Phonics Manual. LC 90-81351. 288p. 1990. teacher ed., ring bd. 109.00 (*0-9605654-7-7*) Char-L.
— Intermediate & Adult Education Intensive Phonics Workpack. LC 90-73112. 288p. 1990. student ed., ring bd. 39.00 (*0-9605654-8-5*) Char-L.
— Parents Intensive Phonics Mini Manual. LC 91-91750. 187p. (Orig.). 1991. pap. 34.00 (*0-9605654-9-3*) Char-L.
***Lockhart, Christy.** Amanecer en Tus Brazos. Vol. 223. (SPA.). 2000. per. 3.50 (*0-373-35353-7*) S&S Trade.
— The Cowboy's Christmas Baby, No. 126. (Desire Ser.). 1999. mass mkt. 3.75 (*0-373-76260-7*) Silhouette.
Lockhart, Christy. Hart's Baby. 1998. per. 3.75 (*0-373-76193-7*, 1-76193-1, Mira Bks) Harlequin Bks.
— Let's Have a Baby! Wed in the West. 1999. per. 3.75 (*0-373-76212-7*, 1-76212-9) Silhouette.
***Lockhart, Christy.** Obscures Intentions. (FRE.). 2000. mass mkt. 3.99 (*0-373-37543-3*) Harlequin Bks.
— One Snowbound Weekend... (Desire Ser.). 2000. mass mkt. 3.99 (*0-373-76314-X*, 1-76314-3) Silhouette.
— Un Padre de Verdad (The Real Father) Let's Have a Baby! (Deseo Ser.: No. 187). (SPA.). 156p. 1999. per. 3.50 (*0-373-35317-0*, 1-35317-6) Harlequin Bks.
Lockhart, Colin, ed. Misleading or Deceptive Conduct: Issues & Trends. 312p. 1996. 79.00 (*1-86287-154-X*, Pub. by Federation Pr) Gaunt.
Lockhart, Darrell B. Jewish Writers of Latin America: A Dictionary. Foster, David W., ed. LC 96-24191. (Latin American Studies: Vol. 9). 618p. 1997. text 83.00 (*0-8153-1495-7*) Garland.
Lockhart, Donald, ed. see Lockhart, Betty Ann, et al.
Lockhart, Donald G., ed. see Lockhart, Betty A.
Lockhart, Douglas. The Dark Side of God: A Quest for the Lost Heart of Christianity. 384p. 1999. text 27.50 (*1-86204-458-9*, Pub. by Element MA) Penguin Putnam.
— Jesus the Heretic: Freedom & Bondage in a Religious World. LC 97-25235. 464p. 1997. 24.95 (*1-86204-001-X*, Pub. by Element MA) Penguin Putnam.
— Paradise Complex: An Exploration of the Forbidden. LC 96-41674. 368p. 1997. pap. 24.95 (*1-85230-809-5*, Pub. by Element MA) Penguin Putnam.
— Sabazius: The Teachings of a Greek Magus. LC 97-1807. 304p. 1997. pap. 17.95 (*1-85230-970-9*, Pub. by Element MA) Penguin Putnam.
Lockhart, Douglas & Smith, David W., eds. Island Tourism: Trends & Prospects. LC 96-13734. (Tourism, Leisure & Recreation Ser.). (Illus.). 320p. (C). 1997. text 115.00 (*1-85567-416-5*) Bks Intl VA.
Lockhart, Earl G., compiled by. My Vocation, by Eminent Americans: or What Eminent Americans Think of Their Callings. LC 72-5602. (Essay Index Reprint Ser.). 1977. reprint ed. 35.95 (*0-8369-2997-7*) Ayer.
Lockhart, Estes J. Communicating with Kids: A Practical Guide to the Forgotten Language. 224p. (Orig.). 1990. 21.95 (*0-9623538-2-5*); pap. 16.95 (*0-9623538-0-9*) Undercurrents Pr.
Lockhart, Eugene. Simple Annals. 132p. (Orig.). 1987. pap. 7.65 (*0-9618581-3-3*) E Lockhart.
***Lockhart, G. W.** Fiddles & Folk: A Celebration of the Re-Emergence of Scotland's Musical Heritage. (Illus.). 192p. 1999. pap. 12.95 (*0-946487-38-3*, Pub. by Luath Pr Ltd) Midpt Trade.
Lockhart, G. W. Highland Balls & Village Halls. (Illus.). 128p. 1989. 12.95 (*0-946487-12-X*) Luath Pr Ltd.
***Lockhart, G. W.** On the Trail of Robert Service. (On the Trail of... Ser.). (Illus.). 160p. 1999. pap. 14.95 (*0-946487-24-3*, Pub. by Luath Pr Ltd) Midpt Trade.
Lockhart, G. W. The Scot & His Oats: A Survey of the Part Played by Oats & Oatmeal in Scottish History, Legend, Romance, & the Scottish Character. 72p. 1989. pap. write for info. (*0-946487-05-7*) Luath Pr Ltd.
— The Scots & Their Fish. LC 98-212245. (Illus.). 98p. 1998. pap. 11.95 (*1-874744-81-5*, Pub. by Birlinn Ltd) Dufour.
***Lockhart, Gary.** Natural Earth: The ENglish Standard Reference on Herbal Substances. (Illus.). 280p. 1999. pap. 29.95 (*1-890693-02-2*) EarthPulse Pr.
Lockhart, Gary. The Weather Companion: An Album of Meteorological History, Science, Legend, & Folklore. LC 88-6884. (Illus.). 240p. 1988. pap. 17.95 (*0-471-62079-3*) Wiley.
Lockhart, Greg. Nation in Arms: The Origins of the People's Army of Vietnam. 314p. 1991. 38.95 (*0-04-301294-9*, Pub. by Allen & Unwin Pty); pap. 24.95 (*0-04-324012-7*, Pub. by Allen & Unwin Pty) Paul & Co Pubs.
Lockhart, Harold. Osf Dce: Guide to Developing Distributed Applications. 1994. pap. 59.95 (*0-07-911481-4*) McGraw.
Lockhart, J. A. & Wiseman, A. J. Introduction to Crop Husbandry. 5th ed. (Illus.). 300p. 1983. text 48.00 (*0-08-029793-5*, Pergamon Pr); pap. text 19.25 (*0-08-029792-7*, Pergamon Pr) Elsevier.
Lockhart, James. The Nahuas after the Conquest: A Social & Cultural History of the Indians of Central Mexico. xx, 650p. 1994. pap. 29.95 (*0-8047-2317-6*) Stanford U Pr.
— The Nahuas after the Conquest: A Social & Cultural History of the Indians of Central Mexico, Sixteenth Through Eighteenth Centuries. LC 91-29972. (Illus.). 672p. (C). 1992. 75.00 (*0-8047-1927-6*) Stanford U Pr.
— Nahuas & Spaniards: Postconquest Central Mexican History & Philology. LC 91-9895. 320p. 1991. 47.50 (*0-8047-1953-5*); pap. 18.95 (*0-8047-1954-3*) Stanford U Pr.
***Lockhart, James.** Of Things of The Indies: Essays Old & New in Early Latin American History. LC 99-16980. 1999. pap. text 22.95 (*0-8047-3810-6*) Stanford U Pr.
Lockhart, James. Spanish Peru, 1532-1560: A Social History. 2nd ed. LC 93-23338. 342p. 1994. pap. 21.95 (*0-299-14164-0*) U of Wis Pr.
Lockhart, James, ed. We People Here: Nahuatl Accounts of the Conquest of Mexico. (Repertorium Columbianum Ser.: No. 1). 304p. 1994. 50.00 (*0-520-07875-6*, Pub. by U CA Pr) Cal Prin Full Svc.
Lockhart, James & Altman, Ida, eds. Provinces of Early Mexico: Variants of Spanish American Regional Evolution. LC 76-620055. (UCLA Latin American Studies: Vol. 36). (Illus.). 291p. 1984. pap. 17.95 (*0-87903-110-7*) UCLA Lat Am Ctr.
Lockhart, James & Otte, E. Letters & People of the Spanish Indies. LC 75-6007. (Cambridge Latin American Studies: No. 22). 267p. 1976. pap. text 19.95 (*0-521-09990-0*) Cambridge U Pr.
Lockhart, James & Schwartz, Stuart. Early Latin America: A History of Colonial Spanish America & Brazil. LC 82-23506. (Cambridge Latin American Studies: No. 46). (Illus.). 495p. 1983. pap. text 21.95 (*0-521-29929-2*) Cambridge U Pr.
Lockhart, James, jt. auth. see Karttunen, Frances.
Lockhart, Joan S. Unit-Based Nursing Staff Development: A Handbook for Clinical Nurses. 300p. 2000. pap. 39.00 (*0-8342-0887-3*, 20887) Aspen Pub.
Lockhart, John G. Life of Robert Burns. Douglas, William S., ed. LC 70-144515. reprint ed. 52.50 (*0-404-08517-2*) AMS Pr.
— Life of Sir Walter Scott, 10 vols. LC 73-144426. (Illus.). 7536p. 1983. reprint ed. 950.00 (*0-404-07700-5*) AMS Pr.
— Peacemakers, 1814 to 1815. LC 68-8479. (Essay Index Reprint Ser.). 1977. reprint ed. 21.95 (*0-8369-0622-5*) Ayer.
— Reginald Dalton: A Story of English University Life, 3 vols., 2 bks. LC 79-8157. reprint ed. 84.50 (*0-404-61987-8*) AMS Pr.
Lockhart, John G., ed. Ancient Spanish Ballads, Historical & Romantic. LC 69-13245. (Illus.). 242p. 1972. reprint ed. 24.95 (*0-405-08752-7*, Pub. by Blom Pubns) Ayer.
Lockhart, Julie, jt. auth. see Devin, Mary.
Lockhart, Julie, ed. see Alexander, Skye.
Lockhart, Julie, ed. see Bunker, Dusty.
Lockhart, Julie, ed. see Javane, Faith.
Lockhart, Julie, ed. see Kelynda.
Lockhart, Julie, ed. see Neville, E. W.
Lockhart, Julie, ed. see Steiger, Brad & Steiger, Francie.
Lockhart, Kimball, tr. see Haineault, Doris-Louise & Roy, Jean-Yves.
Lockhart, Laura, jt. auth. see Duncan, Donna.
Lockhart, Laurence. Nadir Shah: A Critical Study Based Mainly upon Contemporary Sources. LC 78-180358. reprint ed. 36.00 (*0-404-56290-6*) AMS Pr.
Lockhart, Lisa, jt. auth. see Smith, Jodi T.
Lockhart, Lynn. Date with an Outlaw. (American Romance Ser.). 1993. per. 3.50 (*0-373-16498-X*, 1-16498-7) Harlequin Bks.
— Nickie's Ghost. (American Romance Ser.). 1994. per. 3.50 (*0-373-16527-7*, 1-16527-3) Harlequin Bks.
Lockhart, Lynne N. & Lockhart, Barbara M. Rambling Raft. LC 89-50761. (Illus.). 30p. (J). (gr. k-5). 1989. 7.95 (*0-87033-392-5*, Tidewtr Pubs) Cornell Maritime.
Lockhart, Lynne N., jt. auth. see Lockhart, Barbara.
Lockhart, Melissa Fitch, jt. auth. see Foster, David William.
Lockhart, Olive. The Mortgage-Lifter & Other Stories. 145p. (C). 1995. pap. 16.95 (*1-875560-54-8*) Intl Spec Bk.
Lockhart, Paul D. Denmark in the Thirty Years' War, 1618-1648: King Christian IV & the Decline of the Oldenburg State. LC 95-35090. (Illus.). 348p. 1996. 48.50 (*0-945636-76-8*) Susquehanna U Pr.
Lockhart, Pennon & Henderson, Aaron. Scientific & Technological Genius: The Contributions of Peoples of African Descent. (Illus.). 61p. 1997. pap. 39.95 (*0-9649795-3-5*, Glovis Tech) Visions Three-Thousand.
Lockhart, Peter. Oral Medicine & Hospital Practice. 4th rev. ed. Orig. Title: A Practical Guide to Hospital Dental Practice. (Illus.). 550p. 1997. pap. text 30.00 (*0-9657191-0-3*) FSCOD.
Lockhart, R. H. Two Revolutions: An Eye-Witness Account of Russia, 1917. LC 67-24887. 144p. 1967. 18.95 (*0-8023-1124-5*) Dufour.
Lockhart, Robert H. Comes the Reckoning. LC 72-4672. (International Propaganda & Communications Ser.). 392p. 1972. reprint ed. 23.95 (*0-405-04756-8*) Ayer.
Lockhart, Robert S. Introduction to Data Analysis. LC 97-31126. 750p. (C). 1997. pap. text 69.95 (*0-7167-2974-1*) W H Freeman.
— Introduction to Statistics & Data Analysis: For the Behavioral Sciences - Instructor's Manual. 1997. teacher ed. 20.00 (*0-7167-3244-0*) W H Freeman.
Lockhart, Robert S. & Groff, Philip. Introduction to Statistics & Data Analysis: For the Behavioral Sciences - Student Study Guide & Workbook. 1997. pap. text, student ed., wbk. ed. 22.95 (*0-7167-3197-5*) W H Freeman.
***Lockhart, Robin Bruce.** Halfway To Heaven. (Cistercian Studies: Vol. CS186). 1999. pap. 15.95 (*0-87907-786-7*) Cistercian Pubns.
Lockhart, Russell A. Psyche Speaks: A Jungian Approach to Self & World. LC 87-18260. 130p. 1987. 29.95 (*0-933029-28-4*) Chiron Pubns.
— Psyche Speaks: A Jungian Approach to Self & World. LC 87-18260. 130p. 1987. pap. 15.95 (*0-933029-22-5*) Chiron Pubns.
Lockhart, S. F. To My Pocket. 1984. 39.00 (*0-946270-09-0*, Pub. by Pentland Pr) St Mut.

An Asterisk (*) at the beginning of an entry indicates that the title is appearing for the first time.

Lockhart, Sally. I Feel a Symphony. deluxe ed. (Illus.). 16p. (Orig.). 1986. pap. 4.00 (*0-9616899-1-9*) Anapauo Farm.
— Random & Rainbow Feelings. deluxe ed. (Illus.). 16p. (Orig.). 1986. pap. 4.00 (*0-9616899-0-0*) Anapauo Farm.
***Lockhart, Sharon.** Sharon Lockhart: Teatro Amazonas. 2000. pap. 29.95 (*90-5662-139-4*) NAi Uitgevers.
Lockhart, Sharon L. Educational Malpractice: A Pathfinder. LC 95-5749. (Legal Research Guides Ser.: Vol. 23). x, 54p. 1995. 38.50 (*0-89941-926-7*, 308660) W S Hein.
Lockhart, Shawna. A Tutorial Guide to AutoCAD Release 14. (CAD Ser.). 604p. (C). 1997. pap. text 37.50 (*0-201-82371-3*) Addison-Wesley.
***Lockhart, Shawna D.** Engineering Design Communication: Preliminary Edition. 400p. (C). 1998. pap. text 28.66 (*0-201-38042-0*, Prentice Hall) P-H.
Lockhart, Shawna D. & Johnson, Cindy M. Engineering Design Communication. LC 99-41992. 719p. (C). 2000. pap. 78.00 (*0-201-33151-9*, Prentice Hall) P-H.
Lockhart, Ted. Moral Uncertainty & its Consequences. LC 99-17331. (Illus.). 232p. 2000. text 45.00 (*0-19-512610-6*) OUP.
Lockhart, Vickie, ed. Catalog of California State Funding Sources, 1993. 426p. 1993. pap. text 17.50 (*0-929722-53-1*) CA State Library Fndtn.
Lockhart, William B., et al. The American Constitution, Cases, Comments & Questions. 7th ed. (American Casebook Ser.). 1193p. (C). 1991. text 52.00 (*0-314-88939-6*) West Pub.
— AMERICAN CONSTITUTION:CASES & MATERIALS 8E. 8th ed. LC 96-199254. (Paralegal). lix, 1454 p. (C). 1996. text 49.50 (*0-314-20471-7*) West Pub.
— Constitutional Law - the American Constitution - Constitutional Rights & Liberties, 1994: Cases - Comments. 265p. 1994. pap. text, suppl. ed. 14.00 (*0-314-04417-5*) West Pub.
— Constitutional Law, Cases, Comments, Questions. 8th ed. (American Casebook Ser.). xi, 1581 p. 1996. pap. text 15.50 (*0-314-06867-8*) West Pub.
— CONSTITUTIONAL LAW:CASES-COMMENTS-QUESTIONS 8E. 8th ed. (Paralegal). 1650p. (C). 1996. text 48.00 (*0-314-07208-X*) West Pub.
— Constitutional Rights & Liberties, Cases - Comments - Questions. 7th ed. (American Casebook Ser.). 1333p. (C). 1991. text 52.00 (*0-314-88940-X*) West Pub.
Lockhart, William E. English & Pre-Test: Placement Tests. (Michigan Prescriptive Program Ser.). (gr. 10). 1996. teacher ed. 3.00 (*0-87879-840-4*, Ann Arbor Div); student ed. 1.50 (*0-87879-838-2*, Ann Arbor Div) Acad Therapy.
— English Response Sheets & Prescription Sheets. (Michigan Prescriptive Program, High School Equivalency-GED Ser.). 1996. 8.00 (*0-87879-839-0*, Ann Arbor Div) Acad Therapy.
— Michigan Prescriptive Program in English. rev. ed. Martin, Nancy, ed. 72p. 1996. pap., wbk. ed. 10.00 (*1-57128-031-6*, 031-6) Acad Therapy.
— Michigan Prescriptive Program in Math. 1996. pap. 8.00 (*1-57128-037-5*); pap., student ed. 15.00 (*1-57128-036-7*); 3.00 (*1-57128-038-3*) Acad Therapy.
— Michigan Prescriptive Program in Math. Martin, Nancy, ed. (Illus.). 200p. 1996. pap., wbk. ed. 14.00 (*1-57128-035-9*) Acad Therapy.
Lockhart, William J., jt. auth. see Martin, Terri.
***Lockhart, Zelda.** Untitled First Novel. 2002. pap. 13.00 (*0-8050-6426-5*) H Holt & Co.
— Untitled First Novel. 2001. text 22.00 (*0-8050-6425-7*) St Martin.
Lockhead, Gregory R. & Pomerantz, James R., eds. The Perception of Structure. 338p. 1994. pap. 19.95 (*1-55798-263-5*) Am Psychol.
Lockhead, Jack, et al, eds. Thinking Through Math Word Problems: Strategies for Intermediate Elementary School Students. (C). 1990. teacher ed. write for info. (*0-8058-0912-0*); pap. 16.50 (*0-8058-0603-2*) L Erlbaum Assocs.
Lockhead, Jack, jt. auth. see Whimbey, Arthur.
***Lockhead, Sheila.** Outside-In. 1999. pap. 21.00 (*1-85072-121-1*, Pub. by W Sessions) St Mut.
Lockheed Aircraft Corporation Staff. Of Men & Stars: A History of Lockheed Aircraft Corporation. Gilbert, James B., ed. LC 79-7280. (Flight: Its First Seventy-Five Years Ser.). (Illus.). 1980. reprint ed. lib. bdg. 26.95 (*0-405-12189-X*) Ayer.
Lockheed, Marlaine E., jt. auth. see Jimenez, Emmanuel.
Lockheed, Marlaine E., jt. ed. see Hannaway, Jane.
Lockheed, Marlaine E., jt. ed. see Levin, Henry M.
Lockheed Martin Advanced Concepts Center Staff & Rational Software Corporation Staff. Succeeding with the Booch & OMT Methods: A Practical Approach. LC 96-8640. 400p. (C). 1996. pap. 40.95 (*0-8053-2279-5*) Benjamin-Cummings.
Lockheed Research Symposium on Space Science Staff. Auroral Phenomena: Experiments & Theory, Proceedings of the Lockheed Research Symposium on Space Science, 1st, Palo Alto, Calif., 1964. Walt, Martin, ed. LC 78-17993. 180p. reprint ed. pap. 55.80 (*0-8357-5885-0*, 201552800094) Bks Demand.
Lockheed Symposium on Magnetohydrodynamics Staff. The Plasma in a Magnetic Field: A Symposium on Magnetohydrodynamics, 2nd, 1957, Palo Alto. LC 58-11698. 139p. reprint ed. pap. 43.10 (*0-608-30253-8*, 200031700025) Bks Demand.
— Propagation & Instabilities in Plasmas: Proceedings of the Lockheed Symposium on Magnetohydrodynamics, Palo Alto, Calif., 1962. 7th ed. LC 63-19236. 155p. reprint ed. pap. 48.10 (*0-608-11828-1*, 200031800025) Bks Demand.
— Radiation & Waves in Plasmas: Proceedings of the Lockheed Symposium on Magnetohydrodynamics, 5th, Palo Alto, California, 1960. Mitchner, Morton, ed. LC 61-14651. 167p. reprint ed. pap. 51.80 (*0-608-30262-7*, 200031900025) Bks Demand.
***Lockie, Andrew.** Complete Guide to Homeopathy: The Priniciples & Practice of Treatment. 2000. 29.95 (*0-7894-5953-1*) DK Pub Inc.
— Encyclopedia of Homeopathy. 2000. 40.00 (*0-7894-5633-8*) DK Pub Inc.
Lockie, Andrew. The Family Guide to Homeopathy: Symptoms & Natural Solutions. (Illus.). 464p. 1993. per. 16.00 (*0-671-76771-2*, Fireside) S&S Trade Pap.
Lockie, Andrew & Geddes, Nicola. The Complete Guide to Homeopathy: The Principles & Practice of Treatment with a Comprehensive Range of Self-Help Remedies for Common Ailments. LC 95-6746. (Illus.). 240p. 1995. 29.95 (*0-7894-0148-7*, 6-70479) DK Pub Inc.
— The Women's Guide to Homeopathy. 352p. (Orig.). 1994. pap. 15.95 (*0-312-09944-4*) St Martin.
Lockitch, Gillian. Handbook of Diagnostic Biochemistry & Hematology. 256p. 1992. boxed set 145.95 (*0-8493-3518-3*, RG558) CRC Pr.
Lockitch, Gillian, contrib. by. Control of Pre-Analytical Variation in Trace Element Determinations: Proposed Guideline (1994) 1994. 75.00 (*1-56238-262-4*, C38-P) NCCLS.
Locklair, D. Fantasy Brings the Day: For Harpsichord. 16p. 1991. pap. 8.95 (*0-7935-1398-7*) H Leonard.
Locklair, Margaret, ed. see Cerny, Ed.
Locklair, Paula W. Quilts, Coverlets, & Counterpanes: Bedcoverings from the Museum of Early Southern Decorative Arts & Old Salem Collections. (Old Salem Series Frank L. Horton Series, Museum for Early Southern Decorative Arts). (Illus.). 72p. (C). 1997. pap. 18.95 (*0-8078-4725-9*) U of NC Pr.
Locklair, Paula W., et al. Quilts, Coverlets, & Counterpanes: Bedcoverings from the Museum of Early Southern Decorative Arts & Old Salem Collections. LC 97-18405. (Illus.). 72p. 1997. pap. 16.95 (*1-879704-04-8*) Old Salem NC.
Locklear, Edmond, Jr. How God Sees Princess Diana. (Illus.). 130p. 1997. pap. 16.95 (*0-9614336-5-5*) WFCPr.
— What the Hidden Monster Did to O. J. & Nicole. LC 95-60789. 164p. 1995. pap. 12.95 (*0-9614336-6-3*) WFCPr.
Locklear, Elliot. Arnold Schwarzenegger's "Fitness for Kids" 56p. (J). (gr. k-6). 1994. student ed. 2.95 (*1-885453-00-0*) Chldrns Better Hlth.
***Lockledge, Ann & Haynes, Judith L.** Using Portfolios Across the Curriculum. LC 00-28361. (Illus.). 2000. pap. write for info. (*1-56090-162-4*) Natl Middle Schl.
Lockley. Carpentry Workbook. 2nd ed. (Construction/ Building Trades Ser.). 1995. wbk. ed. 25.95 (*0-8273-6701-5*) Delmar.
Lockley, Andrew. The Pursuits of Quality: A Guide for Lawyers. 150p. 1993. 80.00 (*0-85459-751-4*, Pub. by Tolley Pubng) St Mut.
Lockley, Fred. Alaska's First Free Mail Delivery in 1900. (Shorey Historical Ser.). 20p. reprint ed. pap. 10.00 (*0-8466-0136-2*, S136) Shoreys Bkstore.
— A Bit of Verse Vol. 4: Poems from the Lockley Files. Helm, Mike, ed. & intro. by. LC 81-50845. 164p. (Orig.). 1983. pap. 7.95 (*0-931742-13-7*) Rainy Day Oreg.
— Conversations with Pioneer Men. Helm, Mike, ed. LC 81-50845. (Oregon Country Library: Vol. 2). (Illus.). 364p. (Orig.). 1996. reprint ed. pap. 22.00 (*0-931742-18-8*) Rainy Day Oreg.
— Conversations with Pioneer Women, Vol. 1. Hlem, Mike, ed. LC 81-50485. (Illus.). 310p. (Orig.). 1981. pap. 17.95 (*0-931742-08-0*) Rainy Day Oreg.
— Recollections of Benjamin Franklin Bonney. 1971. reprint ed. pap. 4.95 (*0-87770-060-5*) Ye Galleon.
— Reminiscences of Col. Henry Ernst Dosch. 19p. 1972. pap. 4.95 (*0-87770-081-8*) Ye Galleon.
— Vigilante Days at Virginia City. 21p. reprint ed. pap. 10.00 (*0-8466-0146-X*, SJS146) Shoreys Bkstore.
Lockley, M. G. & Rice, Alan, eds. Volcanism & Fossil Biotas. (Special Papers: No. 244). (Illus.). 136p. 1990. 14.00 (*0-8137-2244-6*) Geol Soc.
Lockley, Martin. Dinosaur Tracks of Western North America. LC 99-462640. 1999. pap. text 19.50 (*0-231-07927-3*) Col U Pr.
— The Eternal Trail: A Tracker Looks at Evolution. LC 99-64158. 352p. 1999. 26.00 (*0-7382-0165-0*, Pub. by Perseus Pubng) HarpC.
***Lockley, Martin.** The Eternal Trail: A Tracker Looks at Evolution. 352p. 2000. reprint ed. pap. text 17.50 (*0-7382-0362-9*, Pub. by Perseus Pubng) HarpC.
Lockley, Martin. Tracking Dinosaurs: A New Look at an Ancient World. (Illus.). 252p. (C). 1991. pap. 20.95 (*0-521-42598-0*) Cambridge U Pr.
— Tracking Dinosaurs: A New Look at an Ancient World. (Illus.). 252p. (C). 1991. text 59.95 (*0-521-39463-5*) Cambridge U Pr.
Lockley, Martin & Hunt, Adrian. Dinosaur Tracks & Other Fossil Footprints of the Western United States. (Illus.). 280p. 1995. 39.00 (*0-231-07926-5*) Col U Pr.
***Lockley, Martin & Meyer, Christian.** Dinosaur Tracks & Other Fossil Footprints of Europe. LC 99-31154. (Illus.). 360p. 1999. 35.00 (*0-231-10710-2*) Col U Pr.
Lockley, Martin, jt. ed. see Gillette, David D.
Lockley, Paul. Counselling Heroin & Other Drug Users. 315p. (C). 1995. 50.00 (*1-85343-312-8*, Pub. by Free Assoc Bks); pap. 25.00 (*1-85343-304-7*, Pub. by Free Assoc Bks) NYU Pr.
— Counselling Women in Violent Relationships. 200p. 1999. 55.00 (*1-85343-451-5*); pap. 24.95 (*1-85343-452-3*, Pub. by Free Assoc Bks) Intl Spec Bk.
— Working with Drug Family Support Groups. LC 97-187552. 312p. (C). 1996. 55.00 (*1-85343-336-5*, Pub. by Free Assoc Bks); pap. 20.00 (*1-85343-337-3*, Pub. by Free Assoc Bks) NYU Pr.
Lockley, R. M. Birds & Islands: The Nature Diaries of Ronald Lockley. 224p. (C). 1989. 110.00 (*0-7855-4686-3*, Pub. by Witherby & Co) St Mut.
— Grey Seal, Common Seal. (Illus.). 1966. 12.50 (*0-8079-0060-5*) October.
— The Private Life of the Rabbit. (Illus.). 1995. reprint ed. lib. bdg. 29.95 (*1-56849-614-1*) Buccaneer Bks.
Lockley, Ronald. Dear Islandman. Mark, Ann, ed. 250p. 1996. pap. write for info. (*0-8464-4608-1*) Beekman Pubs.
Lockley, Ronald M. Puffins. 15.00 (*0-8159-6511-7*) Devin.
— Saga of the Grey Seal. 8.50 (*0-8159-6801-9*) Devin.
***Lockley, Timothy James.** Lines in the Sand: Race & Class in Lowcountry Georgia, 1750-1860. LC 00-36461. 2000. write for info. (*0-8203-2228-8*) U of Ga Pr.
***Locklin, Allen C.** The Depths of Thought. LC 00-90306. 2000. pap. 8.95 (*0-533-13525-7*) Vantage.
Locklin, D. W. & Hazard, H. R. Power Plant Utilization of Coal. LC TK1191.L6. (Battelle Energy Program Report Ser.: No. 3). 109p. reprint ed. pap. 33.80 (*0-608-10895-2*, 200513500050) Bks Demand.
***Locklin, Gerald.** Candy Bars: Selected Stories. LC 00-20772. 200p. 2000. pap. 16.95 (*0-934953-69-4*) Water Row Pr.
Locklin, Gerald. The Chase. LC 76-5706. (Illus.). 1976. pap. 3.00 (*0-916918-00-9*) Duck Down.
— The Criminal Mentality. 1976. pap. 2.50 (*0-88031-031-6*) Invisible-Red Hill.
— The Death of Jean-Paul Sartre & Other Poems. 32p. 1988. pap. 4.50 (*0-941160-10-6*) Ghost Pony Pr.
— Down & Out. LC 98-74013. (Illus.). 370p. 1999. 34.95 (*1-880391-20-1*) Event Horizon.
— Frisco Epic. 1978. 3.00 (*0-917554-07-8*) Maelstrom.
— Gerald Haslam. LC 87-70032. (Western Writers Ser.: No. 77). (Illus.). 51p. (Orig.). 1987. pap. 4.95 (*0-88430-076-5*) Boise St U W Writ Ser.
***Locklin, Gerald.** Go West, Young Toad Selected Writings. LC 98-42574. 1998. pap. write for info. (*0-934953-55-4*) Water Row Pr.
— Go West, Young Toad: Selected Writings. LC 98-42574. 1998. 25.00 (*0-934953-54-6*) Water Row Pr.
Locklin, Gerald. The Hospital Poems. LC 99-195829. (Illus.). 90p. 1998. pap., per. 14.95 (*1-888832-06-1*) Kings Estate.
— Locked In. 1973. 5.00 (*0-917554-18-3*) Maelstrom.
— The Old Mongoose & Other Poems. 35p. (Orig.). 1993. pap. 6.00 (*0-9628094-6-2*) Pearl Edit.
— On the Rack. 24p. (Orig.). 1988. pap. 4.00 (*0-916155-09-9*) Trout Creek.
— Running into Ger: Poems. Brimm, Mark, ed. 1998. 4.00 (*1-889717-02-9*, RVP4) Royal Vagrant.
— Son of Poop. 1973. 5.00 (*0-917554-14-0*) Maelstrom.
***Locklin, Gerald.** This Sporting Life & Other Poems. Metzger, Joyce, ed. 56p. 1999. pap. 7.95 (*1-878116-92-4*) JVC Bks.
Locklin, Gerald. Two Summer Sequences. 1979. 4.00 (*0-917554-10-8*) Maelstrom.
Locklin, Gerald & Stetler, Charles, eds. A New Geography of Poets. LC 91-46003. 376p. 1992. 34.00 (*1-55728-240-4*); pap. 22.00 (*1-55728-241-2*) U of Ark Pr.
Locklin, Gerald & Zepeda, Rafael. By Land, Sea & Air. (Illus.). 60p. (Orig.). 1982. pap. 3.00 (*0-917554-21-3*) Maelstrom.
Locklin, Gerald, et al. Tarzan & Shane Meet the Toad. limited ed. 1975. 4.00 (*0-917554-01-9*) Maelstrom.
Locklin, Gerald, jt. auth. see Hilbert, Donna.
Lockman, Barbara. A Century's Child: The Story of Thompson Children's Home. Dixon, Stern, ed. LC 85-52345. (Illus.). 145p. 1986. 10.00 (*0-912081-02-3*) Delmar Co.
***Lockman, Darcy.** Computer Animation. LC 99-58310. (Kaleidoscope Ser.). (Illus.). 2000. 22.79 (*0-7614-1048-1*) Marshall Cavendish.
— Kaleidoscope Technology, 4 vols. 2001. 91.16 (*0-7614-1044-9*, Benchmark NY) Marshall Cavendish.
— Robots. LC 99-58311. (Kaleidoscope Ser.). 2000. 22.79 (*0-7614-1047-3*) Marshall Cavendish.
Lockman, David. SamsTeach Yourself Oracle 8 Database Development in 21 Days. LC 97-65457. (Teach Yourself Ser.). 665p. 1997. 49.99 (*0-672-31078-3*) Sams.
Lockman, F. J., jt. ed. see Blitz, Leo.
***Lockman Foundation Staff.** La Biblia de Las Americas. (SPA., Illus.). 1696p. 2000. pap. 13.99 (*1-58135-089-9*) Foun Pubns.
***Lockman Foundation Staff, contrib. by.** New Standard Bible. (Illus.). 960p. 1999. 7.99 (*1-58135-075-9*) Foun Pubns.
***Lockman Foundation Staff, ed.** La Biblia de las Americas: Gift & Award. 2nd rev. ed. (SPA., Illus.). 896p. 1998. im. lthr. 7.99 (*1-58135-062-7*) Foun Pubns.
***Lockman Foundation Staff, ed. from ARC.** La Biblia de las Americas: Handy Size Large Print. large type rev. ed. (SPA., Illus.). 1696p. 1998. 17.99 (*1-58135-007-4*, 7113); 17.99 (*1-58135-005-8*, 7119); bond lthr. 32.99 (*1-58135-013-9*, 7141); bond lthr. 32.99 (*1-58135-015-5*, 7143); im. lthr. 22.99 (*1-58135-009-0*, 7131); im. lthr. 22.99 (*1-58135-011-2*, 7133) Foun Pubns.
Lockman Foundation Staff, ed. from ARC. La Biblia de las Americas: Indexed Edition Handy Size Large Print. large type rev. ed. (SPA., Illus.). 1696p. 1998. im. lthr. 28.99 (*1-58135-012-0*, 7133-I) Foun Pubns.
***Lockman Foundation Staff, ed. from ARC.** La Biblia de las Americas: Indexed Edition Handy Size Large Print. large type rev. ed. (SPA., Illus.). 1696p. 1998. 23.99 (*1-58135-006-6*, 7119-I); 23.99 (*1-58135-008-2*, 7113-I); bond lthr. 38.99 (*1-58135-014-7*, 7141-I); bond lthr. 38.99 (*1-58135-016-3*, 7143-I); im. lthr. 28.99 (*1-58135-010-4*, 7131-I) Foun Pubns.
— La Biblia de las Americas: Readers Pew Edition. rev. ed. (SPA., Illus.). 896p. 1998. 7.99 (*1-58135-061-9*) Foun Pubns.
Lockman Foundation Staff, ed. from ARC. La Biblia de las Americas: Side Column Reference Bible. rev. ed.Tr. of Bible of the Americas. (SPA.). 1752p. 1998. im. lthr. 26.99 (*1-885217-99-4*, 6833); im. lthr. 26.99 (*1-885217-98-6*, 6831); lthr. 59.99 (*1-885217-97-8*, 6863) Foun Pubns.
— La Biblia de las Americas Plan de la Vida. rev. ed. (SPA.). 96p. 1997. pap. 0.75 (*1-885217-89-7*) Foun Pubns.
— New American Standard Bible: Giant Print. large type rev. ed. 1824p. 1997. im. lthr. 24.99 (*1-885217-90-0*, 1033) Foun Pubns.
— New American Standard Bible: Giant Print Bible. large type rev. ed. 1824p. 1997. im. lthr. 24.99 (*1-885217-91-9*, 1031) Foun Pubns.
— New American Standard Bible: Gift & Award. rev. ed. 960p. 1997. im. lthr. 7.99 (*1-885217-70-6*, 931) Foun Pubns.
— New American Standard Bible: Reader's Pew Edition. 2nd rev. ed. 960p. 1997. 7.99 (*1-885217-68-4*, 912) Foun Pubns.
— New American Standard Bible: Reader's Pew Edition Bible. 2nd rev. ed. 960p. 1997. 7.99 (*1-885217-69-2*, 919) Foun Pubns.
— New American Standard Bible Update: Side Column Reference Bible. 2nd rev. ed. 1856p. 1997. bond lthr. 55.99 (*1-885217-80-3*, 841-I) Foun Pubns.
***Lockman Foundation Staff, ed. from ARC.** New American Standard Bible Update Ultrathin. rev. ed. (Illus.). 1184p. 1998. bond lthr. 29.99 (*1-58135-020-1*, 1241); bond lthr. 29.99 (*1-58135-022-8*, 1243); lthr. 39.99 (*1-58135-024-4*, 1261); lthr. 39.99 (*1-58135-026-0*, 1263) Foun Pubns.
— New American Standard Bible Update Ultrathin: Indexed Edition. rev. ed. (Illus.). 1184p. 1998. bond lthr. 35.99 (*1-58135-023-6*, 1243-I); lthr. 45.99 (*1-58135-025-2*, 1261-I); lthr. 45.99 (*1-58135-027-9*, 1263-I) Foun Pubns.
Lockman Foundation Staff, ed. from GRE. New American Standard Plan of Life: Gospel of John. rev. ed. 96p. 1997. pap. 0.75 (*1-885217-88-9*) Foun Pubns.
***Lockman Foundation Staff, ed. from HEB.** New American Standard Update: In Touch Ministries Edition. (Illus.). 1568p. 1999. lthr. 149.99 (*1-58135-071-6*, 1473, Pub. by Foun Pubns) Riverside-World.
— New American Standard Update: In Touch Ministries Edition. 2nd rev. ed. (Illus.). 1568p. 1999. 39.99 (*1-58135-073-2*, 1410, Pub. by Foun Pubns) Riverside-World.
— New American Standard Update: In Touch Ministries Edition. 2nd rev. ed. (Illus.). 1568p. 1999. lthr. 149.99 (*1-58135-072-4*, 1479, Pub. by Foun Pubns); lthr. 99.99 (*1-58135-069-4*, 1463, Pub. by Foun Pubns); lthr. 99.99 (*1-58135-068-6*, 1461, Pub. by Foun Pubns); lthr. 149.99 (*1-58135-070-8*, 1471, Pub. by Foun Pubns) Riverside-World.
Lockman Foundation Staff, ed. from ARC. New American Standard Update Bible. rev. ed. 960p. 1997. pap. 4.99 (*1-885217-72-2*, 900) Foun Pubns.
***Lockman Foundation Staff, ed. from ARC.** New American Standard Update (La Biblia de las Americas) Bilingual Bible. (ENG & SPA., Illus.). 1856p. 1998. bond lthr. 41.99 (*1-58135-034-1*, 7341) Foun Pubns.
— New American Standard Update (La Biblia de las Americas) Bilingual Bible. rev. ed. (SPA & ENG., Illus.). 1856p. 1998. 24.99 (*1-58135-028-7*, 7313); bond lthr. 41.99 (*1-58135-036-8*, 7343); im. lthr. 29.99 (*1-58135-030-9*, 7331); im. lthr. 29.99 (*1-58135-032-5*, 7333) Foun Pubns.
— New American Standard Update (La Biblia de las Americas) Bilingual Bible, Indexed Edition. rev. ed. (SPA & ENG., Illus.). 1856p. 1998. 30.99 (*1-58135-029-5*, 7313-I); bond lthr. 47.99 (*1-58135-035-X*, 7341-I); im. lthr. 35.99 (*1-58135-031-7*, 7331-I); im. lthr. 35.99 (*1-58135-033-3*, 7333-I) Foun Pubns.
— New American Standard Update Ultrathin: Indexed Edition. rev. ed. (Illus.). 1184p. 1998. bond lthr. 35.99 (*1-58135-021-X*, 1241-I) Foun Pubns.
Lockman Foundation Staff, ed. from HEB. New American Standard UpDate/La Biblia de las Americas: Bilingual Bible. 2nd rev. ed. (SPA & ENG., Illus.). 1856p. 1999. lthr. 54.99 (*1-58135-064-3*, 7361); lthr. 54.99 (*1-58135-066-X*, 7363) Foun Pubns.
— New American Standard UpDate/La Biblia de las Americas: Bilingual Bible - Indexed Edition. 2nd rev. ed. (SPA & ENG., Illus.). 1856p. 1999. lthr. 60.99 (*1-58135-065-1*, 7361-I); lthr. 60.99 (*1-58135-067-8*, 7363-I) Foun Pubns.
***Lockman Foundation Staff, tr. from GRE.** La Biblia de las Americas: Jesus Salva Nuevo Testamento. (SPA.). 256p. 1999. mass mkt. 1.25 (*1-58135-076-7*) Foun Pubns.
Lockman Foundation Staff, tr. from HEB. La Biblia de Las Americas: Nuevo Testamento con Salmos y Proverbios.Tr. of Bible of the Americas. (SPA.). 1998. pap. 4.99 (*1-58135-019-8*, 8093) Foun Pubns.
— La Biblia de Las Americas: Nuevo Testamento con Salmos y Proverbios, No. 8043.Tr. of Bible of the Americas. (SPA.). 1998. bond lthr. 27.99 (*1-58135-017-1*) Foun Pubns.
— La Biblia de Las Americas: Nuevo Testamento con Salmos y Proverbios, No. 8091. (Biblia de Las Americas Ser.).Tr. of Bible of the Americas. (SPA.). 1998. pap. 4.99 (*1-58135-018-X*) Foun Pubns.
***Lockman Foundation Staff, tr. from GRE.** The New American Standard Bible: Jesus Saves New Testament. 256p. 1999. mass mkt. 1.25 (*1-58135-077-5*) Foun Pubns.
— New Standard Bible: Gospel of John. 96p. 1999. pap. 0.75 (*1-58135-074-0*) Foun Pubns.

Lockman, J. Travels of the Jesuits, 2 vols., Set. (C). 1995. reprint ed. 72.00 (*81-206-1060-1*, Pub. by Asian Educ Servs) S Asia.

Lockman, J. J. & Hazen, N. L., eds. Action in Social Context: Perspectives on Early Development. (Perspectives in Developmental Psychology Ser.). (Illus.). 326p. (C). 1989. 65.00 (*0-306-43139-4*, Plenum Trade) Perseus Pubng.

Lockman, J. N. Meinertzhagen's Diary Ruse: False Entries on T. E. Lawrence. 114p. 1995. 12.00 (*0-9648897-0-6*) Falcon Books.

— Parallel Captures: Lord Jim & Lawrence of Arabia. LC 98-145095. (Illus.). 44p. 1997. pap. 5.00 (*0-9648897-2-2*) Falcon Books.

— Scattered Tracks on the Lawrence Trail: Twelve Essays on T. E. Lawrence. LC 96-85429. (Illus.). xix, 208p. 1996. 24.00 (*0-9648897-1-4*) Falcon Books.

Lockman, Vic. Biblical Economics in Comics. (Illus.). 112p. (Orig.). 1985. pap. 9.00 (*0-936175-00-1*) V Lockman.

— The Big Book of Cartooning, Bk. I. (Illus.). 104p. (Orig.). 1990. pap., spiral bd. 15.00 (*0-936175-08-7*) V Lockman.

— The Big Book of Cartooning, Bk. II: Animals. (Illus.). 48p. 1991. spiral bd. 8.00 (*0-936175-15-X*) V Lockman.

— The Book of Revelation: A Cartoon Illustrated Commentary. 60p. 1993. 6.00 (*0-936175-24-9*) V Lockman.

— Cartooning for Young Children, Bk. I. (Illus.). 48p. 1991. spiral bd. 7.00 (*0-936175-16-8*) V Lockman.

— Cartooning for Young Children, Vol. II. (Illus.). 48p. (J). (ps-8). 1992. spiral bd. 7.00 (*0-936175-23-0*) V Lockman.

— The Catechism for Young Children with Cartoons, Bk. 1. (Illus.). 45p. (Orig.). (J). (ps-6). 1984. pap. 1.75 (*0-936175-01-X*) V Lockman.

— The Catechism for Young Children with Cartoons, Bk II. (Illus.). 45p. (Orig.). 1985. pap. 1.75 (*0-936175-02-8*) V Lockman.

— Church History for Young Children with Cartoons: The Reformation, 2 vols. (Illus.). 45p. (J). (ps-4). 1998. 1.75 (*0-936175-36-2*) V Lockman.

— God's Law for Modern Man. (Illus.). 60p. (YA). 1993. 6.00 (*0-936175-25-7*) V Lockman.

— In These Last Days. (Illus.). 60p. 1994. 6.00 (*0-936175-27-3*) V Lockman.

— Infant Baptism. (Illus.). 24p. 1998. pap. 3.00 (*0-936175-34-6*) V Lockman.

— Machines. (Big Book of Cartooning: No. 5). (Illus.). 48p. (Orig.). (YA). (gr. 8 up). 1992. pap. 6.00 (*0-936175-20-6*) V Lockman.

— Miracle Art: Trick Cartoons. (Illus.). 48p. (Orig.). (YA). (gr. 8 up). 1992. pap. 6.00 (*0-936175-19-2*) V Lockman.

— Money, Banking, & Usury. (Illus.). 36p. 1991. 4.00 (*0-936175-09-5*) V Lockman.

— Reading & Understanding the Bible. (Illus.). 56p. (J). (gr. 6). 1992. 6.00 (*0-936175-18-4*) V Lockman.

— Super Bug Leads Tim Burr to the Gospel in the Woods. (Biblical Educational & Recreational Story Book Ser.). (Illus.). 24p. (Orig.). (J). (gr. 8 up). 1991. pap. 3.00 (*0-936175-14-1*) V Lockman.

— Water, Water . . . Everywhere. 36p. 1992. 4.00 (*0-936175-17-6*) V Lockman.

— The Westminster Shorter Catechism with Cartoons. (Illus.). 140p. (Orig.). 1996. pap. 19.95 (*0-936175-28-1*) V Lockman.

— Who Stopped the Clock? The Seventy Weeks of Daniel. (Illus.). 24p. 1993. 3.00 (*0-936175-21-4*) V Lockman.

Lockman, Vic, et al. How Shall We Worship God? A Catechism for the Family. (Catechism for Young Children with Cartoons Ser.). (Illus.). 46p. (J). (gr. 1-8). 1996. 1.75 (*0-936175-30-3*) V Lockman.

Lockman, Vic, jt. auth. see Schiff, Irwin A.

Lockman, Vic, jt. auth. see Spurgeon, Charles H.

Lockman, Zachary. Comrades & Enemies: Arab & Jewish Workers in Palestine, 1906-1948. LC 95-22264. 443p. 1996. 60.00 (*0-520-20259-7*, Pub. by U CA Pr); pap. 27.50 (*0-520-20419-0*, Pub. by U CA Pr) Cal Prin Full Svc.

Lockman, Zachary, ed. Workers & Working Classes in the Middle East: Struggles, Histories & Historiographies. 360p. 1996. pap. 19.95 (*0-614-21503-X*, 1359) Kazi Pubns.

— Workers & Working Classes in the Middle East: Struggles, Histories, Historiographies. LC 92-42701. (SUNY Series in the Social & Economic History of the Middle East). 341p. (C). 1993. text 21.50 (*0-7914-1665-8*) State U NY Pr.

Lockman, Zachary & Beinin, Joel, eds. Intifada: The Palestinian Uprising Against Israeli Occupation. LC 89-11595. 423p. 1989. 35.00 (*0-89608-365-9*); pap. 15.00 (*0-89608-363-2*) South End Pr.

Lockman, Zachary, jt. auth. see Beinin, Joel.

Lockmiller, David A. Scholars on Parade. 290p. 1993. pap. 15.95 (*1-57087-002-0*) Prof Pr NC.

Lockridge, Elaine. The Needs of a Woman Book of Poems: Understanding the True Needs of a Woman. Printers, Franz, ed. 72p. 1997. pap. 8.00 (*0-9657213-2-9*) Trammella.

— Window of Life Book of Poems: The Things We See & Do in Life. Printers, Franz, ed. 60p. 1997. 4.00 (*0-9657213-1-0*) Trammella.

— The World Within a World. 1998. pap. write for info. (*1-57553-775-3*) Watermrk Pr.

— The World Within a World: Reaching for the Stars. Printers, Franz, ed. 56p. 1997. pap. 6.00 (*0-9657213-0-2*) Trammella.

Lockridge, Ernest, ed. Twentieth Century Interpretations of The Great Gatsby. (YA). (gr. 9-12). 1968. pap. 2.95 (*0-13-363812-X*, Spectrum IN) Macmillan Gen Ref.

Lockridge, Frances & Lockridge, R. Death Takes a Bow. (Mr. & Mrs. North Mystery Ser.). 21.95 (*0-89190-918-4*) Amereon Ltd.

Lockridge, Frances & Lockridge, Richard. And Left for Dead. (Mr. & Mrs. North Mystery Ser.). 20.95 (*0-89190-912-5*) Amereon Ltd.

— Catch As Catch Can. 1976. 20.95 (*0-89190-913-3*) Amereon Ltd.

— Cats & People. Rao, Maya & Turner, Philip, eds. (Kodansha Globe Ser.). (Illus.). 286p. 1996. pap. 13.00 (*1-56836-115-7*, Kodansha Globe) Kodansha.

— A Client Is Cancelled. large type ed. (Popular Ser.). 280p. 1993. reprint ed. lib. bdg. 17.95 (*1-56054-299-3*) Thorndike Pr.

— Curtain for a Jester. (Mr. & Mrs. North Ser.). 222p. 1975. reprint ed. lib. bdg. 21.95 (*0-89190-904-4*, Rivercity Pr) Amereon Ltd.

— Dead As a Dinosaur. (Mr. & Mrs. North Ser.). 185p. 1975. reprint ed. lib. bdg. 21.95 (*0-89190-903-6*, Rivercity Pr) Amereon Ltd.

— Dead As a Dinosaur. 1993. reprint ed. lib. bdg. 17.95 (*1-56849-208-1*) Buccaneer Bks.

— Death Has a Small Voice. 1993. reprint ed. lib. bdg. 17.95 (*1-56849-209-X*) Buccaneer Bks.

— Death of an Angel. (Mr. & Mrs. North Ser.). 1975. reprint ed. lib. bdg. 21.95 (*0-89190-907-9*, Rivercity Pr) Amereon Ltd.

— The Dishonest Murderer. 223p. 1975. reprint ed. lib. bdg. 21.95 (*0-89190-901-X*) Amereon Ltd.

— The Judge Is Reversed. 1975. reprint ed. lib. bdg. 21.95 (*0-89190-910-9*, Rivercity Pr) Amereon Ltd.

— A Key to Death. 224p. 1975. reprint ed. lib. bdg. 21.95 (*0-89190-906-0*, Rivercity Pr) Amereon Ltd.

— Long Skeleton. 1975. reprint ed. lib. bdg. 21.95 (*0-89190-909-5*, Rivercity Pr) Amereon Ltd.

— Murder Comes First. 192p. 1975. reprint ed. lib. bdg. 22.95 (*0-89190-902-8*, Rivercity Pr) Amereon Ltd.

— Murder out of Turn. 18.95 (*0-89190-914-1*) Amereon Ltd.

— A Pinch of Poison. 18.95 (*0-89190-917-6*) Amereon Ltd.

— Untidy Murder. large type ed. LC 92-23912. 333p. 1992. reprint ed. lib. bdg. 17.95 (*1-56054-298-5*) Thorndike Pr.

— Voyage into Violence: A Mr. & Mrs. North Mystery. large type ed. LC 93-12738. 305p. 1993. 17.95 (*1-56054-300-0*) Thorndike Pr.

— Voyage into Violence: A Mr. & Mrs. North Mystery. 1975. reprint ed. lib. bdg. 21.95 (*0-89190-908-7*, Rivercity Pr) Amereon Ltd.

Lockridge, Frances, jt. auth. see Lockridge, Richard.

Lockridge, Francis Louis Davis, jt. auth. see Lockridge, Richard.

Lockridge, Kenneth A. The Diary & Life of William Byrd II of Virginia, 1674-1744. LC 86-40425. (Institute of Early American History & Culture Ser.). xiv, 202p. 1987. 34.95 (*0-8078-1736-8*) U of NC Pr.

— Literacy in Colonial New England: An Inquiry into the Social Context of Literacy in the Early Modern West. (Illus.). 164p. (C). 1974. 9.75 (*0-393-05522-1*) Norton.

— Literacy in Colonial New England: An Inquiry into the Social Context of Literacy in the Early Modern West. (Illus.). 164p. (C). 1975. pap. text 5.50 (*0-393-09263-1*) Norton.

— A New England Town: The First Hundred Years. 2nd ed. (Essays in American History Ser.). 220p. (C). 1985. pap. text 15.50 (*0-393-95459-5*) Norton.

— On the Sources of Patriarchal Rage: The Commonplace Books of William Byrd II & Thomas Jefferson & the Gendering of Power in the Eighteenth Century. (Illus.). 133p. (C). 1993. text 42.50 (*0-8147-5069-9*) NYU Pr.

— On the Sources of Patriarchal Rage: The Commonplace Books of William Byrd II & Thomas Jefferson & the Gendering of Power in the Eighteenth Century. (Illus.). 133p. (C). 1994. pap. text 15.50 (*0-8147-5089-3*) NYU Pr.

Lockridge, Laurence. Shade of the Raintree: The Life & Death of Ross Lockridge, Jr. LC 93-26712. 1999. pap. 23.00 (*0-670-84136-6*); text 23.00 (*0-7139-9111-9*) Viking Penguin.

Lockridge, Laurence S., et al, eds. Nineteenth-Century Lives: Essays Presented to Jerome Hamilton Buckley. LC 91-15552. (Illus.). 240p. (C). 1989. text 69.95 (*0-521-34181-7*) Cambridge U Pr.

Lockridge, Patricia A., jt. auth. see Lander, James F.

Lockridge, R., jt. auth. see Lockridge, Frances.

Lockridge, Randall T., jt. auth. see Hopkins, Martha A.

Lockridge, Richard. Darling of Misfortune: Edwin Booth, 1833-1893. LC 79-91908. 368p. 1972. 30.95 (*0-405-08753-5*, Pub. by Blom Pubns) Ayer.

Lockridge, Richard & Lockridge, Frances. Accent on Murder: A Captain Heimrich Mystery. large type ed. LC 93-13220. 307p. 1993. pap. 19.95 (*1-56054-301-9*) Thorndike Pr.

— Death by Association. large type ed. LC 94-25980. 322p. 1995. pap. 18.95 (*1-56054-306-X*) Thorndike Pr.

— I Want to Go Home. large type ed. LC 93-13224. 344p. 1993. lib. bdg. 17.95 (*1-56054-302-7*) Thorndike Pr.

— Killing the Goose. 22.95 (*0-89190-911-7*) Amereon Ltd.

— Let Dead Enough Alone: A Captain Heimrich Mystery. large type ed. LC 94-33676. 232p. 1995. pap. 18.95 (*0-7838-1159-4*, G K Hall Lrg Type) Mac Lib Ref.

— Show Red for Danger: A Captain Heimrich Mystery. large type ed. LC 93-31000. (Popular Ser.). 287p. 1994. lib. bdg. 17.95 (*1-56054-303-5*) Thorndike Pr.

— Stand up & Die: A Captain Heimrich Mystery. large type ed. LC 94-19359. 296p. 1994. lib. bdg. 17.95 (*1-56054-305-1*) Thorndike Pr.

Lockridge, Richard & Lockridge, Francis Louis Davis. Death Has a Small Voice. 1976. 20.95 (*0-89190-905-2*) Amereon Ltd.

Lockridge, Richard, jt. auth. see Lockridge, Frances.

Lockridge, Ross, Jr. Raintree County. 1066p. 1991. reprint ed. lib. bdg. 49.95 (*0-89966-865-8*) Buccaneer Bks.

Locks, Doris C. Multistate Sales & Use Tax Compliance Forms Manual, 2 vols. 1993. ring bd. 295.00 (*0-685-69588-3*, CSTC) Warren Gorham & Lamont.

Locks, Gutman G. Spice of Torah Gematria. 318p. 1985. 17.95 (*0-910818-58-4*) Judaica Pr.

Locks, Marian, contrib. by. Thomas Chimes. LC 90-60705. (Orig.). 1990. pap. text 20.00 (*0-9623799-2-1*) Locks Gallery.

Locks, Mitchell O. Reliability, Maintainability, & Availability Assessment. 2nd ed. LC 94-40648. 348p. 1995. 68.00 (*0-87389-293-3*, H0849) ASQ Qual Pr.

Lockshin, Jane R., jt. auth. see Dollinger, Susan B.

Lockshin, Martin I., tr. see Ben Meir, Samuel.

Lockshin, Michael D. Guarded Prognosis. LC 98-10735. 260p. 1998. 23.00 (*0-8090-5345-4*) Hill & Wang.

Lockshin, R., jt. auth. see Bowen, I. D.

Lockshin, Richard A., et al, eds. When Cells Die: A Comprehensive Evaluation of Apoptosis & Cell Death. 50th ed. LC 97-23884. 528p. 1998. 98.95 (*0-471-16569-7*) Wiley.

Lockshin, Stephanie, jt. auth. see Romanczyk, Raymond G.

Lockshiv, Jane R., jt. auth. see Dollinger, Susan B.

Lockton, Deborah. Employment Law. (Student Statutes Ser.). 352p. 1993. pap. text 18.00 (*0-406-02302-6*, UK, MICHIE) LEXIS Pub.

Lockton, Deborah, ed. Employment Law. 2nd ed. (Butterworths Student Statutes Ser.). 1997. pap. write for info. (*0-406-89099-4*, LELB2, MICHIE) LEXIS Pub.

Lockton, Deborah J. Effective Contracts of Employment. 165p. 1992. 60.00 (*1-85190-159-0*, Pub. by Tolley Pubng) St Mut.

— Employment Law. (Questions & Answers Ser.). 332p. 1996. 18.00 (*1-85941-143-6*, Pub. by Cavendish Pubng) Gaunt.

Lockton, Deborah J., ed. Children & the Law. 112p. 1994. 32.00 (*1-85941-111-8*, Pub. by Cavendish Pubng) Gaunt.

Lockton, Deborah J. & Ward, Richard. Domestic Violence. 218p. 1997. pap. 54.00 (*1-85941-136-3*, Pub. by Cavendish Pubng) Gaunt.

Locktov, JoAnn & Clagett, Leslie P. The Art of Mosaic Design: A Collection of Contemporary Artists. (Illus.). 144p. 1998. 29.99 (*1-56496-420-5*, Quarry Bks) Rockport Pubs.

Lockward, A. Nuevo Diccionario Biblico.Tr. of New Bible Dictionary. (SPA.). 24.99 (*0-7899-0389-X*, 490258) Editorial Unilit.

Lockward, Alfonso. Algunas Cruces Altas.Tr. of Some High Crosses. (SPA.). 298p. 1991. pap. 6.99 (*1-56063-159-7*, 490218) Editorial Unilit.

— La Responsabilidad Social del Creyente.Tr. of Christian's Social Responsibility. (SPA.). 117p. 1992. pap. 4.50 (*1-56063-303-4*, 498523) Editorial Unilit.

Lockwood. Aesthetic Body Contour Surgery. 1999. text. write for info. (*0-7216-5608-0*, W B Saunders Co) Harcrt Hlth Sci Grp.

— The Math Connection. (C). 1991. pap. text, teacher ed. 2.76 (*0-395-57742-X*) HM.

Lockwood, jt. auth. see Korwin.

Lockwood, A., ed. see Cooper, C. P.

Lockwood, A, jt. ed. see Cooper, C. P.

Lockwood, Alan L. & Harris, David E. Reasoning with Democratic Values: Ethical Problems in United States History, 2 vols. (gr. 9-12). 1985. pap., teacher ed. 11.95 (*0-8077-6101-X*) Tchrs Coll.

— Reasoning with Democratic Values: Ethical Problems in United States History, 2 vols., Vol. I: 1607-1876. (gr. 9-12). 1985. pap. 9.95 (*0-8077-6094-3*) Tchrs Coll.

— Reasoning with Democratic Values: Ethical Problems in United States History, 2 vols., Vol. II: 1877 to Present. (gr. 9-12). 1985. pap. 12.95 (*0-8077-6095-1*) Tchrs Coll.

Lockwood, Albert. Notes on the Literature of the Piano. LC 67-30400. (Music Ser.). 1968. reprint ed. lib. bdg. 32.50 (*0-306-70983-X*) Da Capo.

Lockwood, Alisa, tr. see Bekhterev, V. M.

Lockwood, Allison. Passionate Pilgrims. LC 78-66808. (Illus.). 551p. 1981. 37.50 (*0-8453-4725-X*, Cornwall Bks) Assoc Univ Prs.

— Passionate Pilgrims: The American Traveler in Great Britain, 1800-1914. LC 78-66808. 650p. 1981. 37.50 (*0-8386-2272-0*) Fairleigh Dickinson.

Lockwood, Allison M. Children of Paradise: A Northampton Memoir. (Illus.). 166p. (Orig.). 1986. pap. 9.95 (*0-9618052-0-X*) Daily Hampshire.

— No Ordinary Man: Judge Forbes & His Library. (Illus.). 136p. (Orig.). 1994. pap. 12.95 (*0-9618052-4-2*) Daily Hampshire.

— Touched with Fire: An American Community in WWII. (Illus.). 216p. (Orig.). 1993. pap. 19.95 (*0-9618052-3-4*) Daily Hampshire.

Lockwood, Andrew, et al. Food & Beverage Management: A Selection of Readings. 3rd ed. LC 95-127281. 250p. 1995. pap. 47.95 (*0-7506-1950-3*) Buttrwrth-Heinemann.

Lockwood, Ann T. Tracking: Conflicts & Resolutions. LC 96-28060. (CIE Ser.). 80p. 1996. 35.95 (*0-8039-6480-3*); pap. 14.95 (*0-8039-6268-1*) Corwin Pr.

Lockwood, Anne. The Essential Wedding Planner. 168p. 1997. 15.95 (*0-446-91169-0*, Pub. by Warner Bks) Little.

Lockwood, Anne T. Character Education: Controversy & Consensus. LC 97-4904. (CIE Ser.). 80p. 1997. 35.95 (*0-8039-6616-4*); pap. 14.95 (*0-8039-6584-2*) Corwin Pr.

— Conversations with Educational Leaders: Contemporary Viewpoints on Education in America. LC 96-17472. (SUNY Series, Frontiers in Education). 254p. (C). 1997. text 65.50 (*0-7914-3287-4*); pap. text 21.95 (*0-7914-3288-2*) State U NY Pr.

— Standards: From Policy to Practice. LC 98-25309. (Critical Issues in Education Ser.). 72p. 1998. 35.95 (*0-8039-6622-9*); pap. 14.95 (*0-8039-6270-3*) Corwin Pr.

Lockwood, Antony P. Animal Body Fluids & Their Regulation. LC 64-9913. (Illus.). 184p. 1963. 25.50 (*0-674-03700-6*) HUP.

Lockwood, Barbara & McAuley, Marilyn M. God Made Little & Big. LC 87-62019. (Peek & Find Ser.). 18p. (J). (ps). 1988. bds. 4.29 (*1-55513-517-X*, Chariot Bks) Chariot Victor.

Lockwood, Brocton & Mendenhall, Harlan H. Operation Greylord: The Brocton Lockwood Story. LC 89-6022. (Illus.). 224p. (C). 1989. 21.95 (*0-8093-1545-9*) S Ill U Pr.

Lockwood, C. C. Around the Bend: A Mississippi River Adventure. LC 98-20245. (Illus.). 169p. 1998. 39.95 (*0-8071-2312-9*) La State U Pr.

— Atchafalaya. 1984. 35.00 (*0-87511-695-7*) Claitors.

— Beneath the Rim: A Photographic Journey Through the Grand Canyon. LC 96-4964. (Illus.). 144p. (C). 1996. 39.95 (*0-8071-2063-4*) La State U Pr.

— C. C. Lockwood's Louisiana Nature Guide for Kids. LC 94-38613. (Illus.). 94p. (J). 1995. 19.95 (*0-8071-1989-X*) La State U Pr.

***Lockwood, C. C., photos by.** Still Waters: Images, 1971-1999. LC 99-56961. (Illus.). 216p. 2000. 39.95 (*0-8071-2570-9*) La State U Pr.

Lockwood, C. C., photos by. Discovering Louisiana. LC 83-25614. (Illus.). vii, 150p. 1986. 39.95 (*0-8071-1335-2*) La State U Pr.

— Gulf Coast: Where Land Meets Sea. LC 83-25614. (Illus.). xvii, 150p. 1984. 39.95 (*0-8071-1170-8*) La State U Pr.

— The Yucatan Peninsula. LC 88-27260. (Illus.). xiv, 160p. 1989. 34.95 (*0-8071-1524-X*) La State U Pr.

Lockwood, Carol E. & American Bar Association Staff. The International Human Rights of Women: Instruments of Change. LC 98-220210. xvi, 607 p. 1998. write for info. (*1-57073-610-3*) Amer Bar Assn.

Lockwood, Charles. The Breakers: A Century of Grand Traditions. 96p. 1996. text 18.96 (*0-9649743-0-4*) Breakrs Palm.

Lockwood, D. The Physics of Semiconductors: Proceedings of the 22nd International Conference, 3 vols. 2852p. 1995. text 446.00 (*981-02-2021-9*) World Scientific Pub.

Lockwood, D. J., et al, eds. Advanced Luminescent Materials. LC 95-61598. (Proceedings Ser.: Vol. 95-25). (Illus.). 495p. 1996. 77.00 (*1-56677-120-X*) Electrochem Soc.

Lockwood, D. J. & Young, J. F., eds. Light Scattering in Semiconductor Structures & Superlattices. (NATO ASI Ser.: Vol. 273). (Illus.). 616p. (C). 1991. text 186.00 (*0-306-44036-9*, Kluwer Plenum) Kluwer Academic.

Lockwood, David. The Blackcoated Worker: A Study in Class Consciousness. 2nd ed. 272p. 1989. pap. 19.95 (*0-19-878022-2*) OUP.

***Lockwood, David.** The Destruction of the Soviet Union: A Study in Globalization. LC 99-49117. 2000. text 65.00 (*0-312-23015-X*) St Martin.

Lockwood, David. Francis Kilvert. 160p. 1990. 27.00 (*1-85411-032-2*, Pub. by Seren Bks) Dufour.

— Marked Paper. 62p. 1995. pap. 13.95 (*0-8464-4786-X*) Beekman Pubs.

— Solidarity & Schism: The Problem of Disorder in Durkheimian & Marxist Sociology. (Illus.). 450p. 1992. text 95.00 (*0-19-827717-2*) OUP.

— Winter Wheat. 61p. 1986. pap. 8.95 (*0-8464-4759-2*) Beekman Pubs.

Lockwood, David. Winter Wheat. 61p. (C). 1986. pap. 20.00 (*0-86383-229-6*, Pub. by Gomer Pr) St Mut.

Lockwood, David, ed. Kilvert, the Victorian: A New Selection from Kilvert's Diaries. (Illus.). 288p. 1992. 35.00 (*1-85411-077-2*, Pub. by Seren Bks) Dufour.

— Semiconductors & Semimetals Vol. 49: Light Emissions in Silicon. (Illus.). 351p. 1997. text 130.00 (*0-12-752157-7*) Morgan Kaufmann.

Lockwood, David G., et al, eds. Functional Approaches to Language, Culture & Cognition: Papers in Honor of Sydney M. Lamb. LC 98-46184. (Current Issues in Linguistic Theory Ser.: Vol. 163). xxxiv, 656p. 2000. 135.00 (*1-55619-879-5*) J Benjamins Pubng Co.

Lockwood, David G., jt. ed. see Makkai, Adam.

Lockwood, David J. & Pinczuk, Aron, eds. Optical Phenomena in Semiconductor Structures of Reduced Dimensions: Proceedings of the NATO Advanced Research Workshop on Frontiers of Optical Phenomena in Semiconductor Structures of Reduced Dimensions, Yountville, California, U. S. A. July 27-31, 1992. LC 93-31755. (NATO Advanced Study Institutes Series E, Applied Sciences: No. 248). 466p. (C). 1993. text 294.00 (*0-7923-2512-5*) Kluwer Academic.

Lockwood, David J., jt. auth. see Cottam, Michael G.

Lockwood, Dean H., jt. auth. see Streck, William F.

Lockwood, Dean P. Survey of Classical Roman Literature, 2 vols., Vol. 1. LC 34-40316. 1993. pap. text 14.95 (*0-226-48962-0*, Midway Reprint) U Ch Pr.

— Survey of Classical Roman Literature, 2 vols., Vol. 2. LC 34-40316. 1974. pap. text 16.00 (*0-226-48963-9*, Midway Reprint) U Ch Pr.

Lockwood, Deborah, compiled by. Library Instruction: A Bibliography. LC 78-20011. 166p. 1979. lib. bdg. 47.95 (*0-313-20720-8*, LLI/, Greenwood Pr) Greenwood.

Lockwood, DeLauna, ed. Cumulative Index to Nursing & Allied Health Literature, Vol. 31. LC 79-642922. 1986. 96.00 (*0-910478-23-6*) Cum Index Nursing.

— Cumulative Index to Nursing & Allied Health Literature, Vol. 32. LC 79-642922. 1987. 175.00 (*0-910478-24-4*) Cum Index Nursing.

— Cumulative Index to Nursing & Allied Health Literature, Vol. 33. LC 79-642922. 1988. 175.00 (*0-910478-25-2*) Cum Index Nursing.

— Cumulative Index to Nursing & Allied Health Literature, Vol. 34. LC 79-642922. 1989. 150.00 (*0-910478-26-0*) Cum Index Nursing.

An Asterisk (*) at the beginning of an entry indicates that the title is appearing for the first time.

— Cumulative Index to Nursing & Allied Health Literature, Vol. 35. LC 79-642922. 1990. 198.00 (*0-910478-30-9*) Cum Index Nursing.
— Cumulative Index to Nursing & Allied Health Literature, Vol. 36. LC 79-642922. 1991. write for info. (*0-910478-33-3*) Cum Index Nursing.
— Cumulative Index to Nursing & Allied Health Literature, Vol. 37. LC 79-642922. 1992. write for info. (*0-910478-39-2*) Cum Index Nursing.
— Cumulative Index to Nursing & Allied Health Literature, Vol. 38. LC 79-642922. 1993. write for info. (*0-910478-45-7*) Cum Index Nursing.
— Cumulative Index to Nursing & Allied Health Literature, Vol. 39. LC 79-642922. 1994. write for info. (*0-910478-48-1*) Cum Index Nursing.
Lockwood, E., jt. ed. see Strickland, L. H.
Lockwood, E. D., jt. auth. see Holden, F. A.
Lockwood, Edgar. South Africa's Moment of Truth. 196p. 1988. pap. 5.95 (*0-377-00180-5*) Friendship Pr.
Lockwood, Eugenia, tr. see Bekhterev, V. M.
Lockwood, Faith. The Angel in My Eye. rev. ed. (Illus.). 198p. 1998. pap. 12.00 (*0-9668442-0-3*) Lockwood & Marshall.
Lockwood, Frank. The Law & Lawyers of Pickwick. LC 72-1862. (Studies in Dickens: No. 52). 1972. reprint ed. lib. bdg. 75.00 (*0-8383-1445-7*) M S G Haskell Hse.
Lockwood, Frank C. The Apache Indians. LC 86-25103. (Illus.). xxxii, 388p. 1987. reprint ed. pap. 16.95 (*0-8032-7925-6*, Bison Books) U of Nebr Pr.
— Thumbnail Sketches of Famous Arizona Desert Riders, 1538-1946. LC 73-148224. (Biography Index Reprint Ser.). 1977. 16.95 (*0-8369-8071-9*) Ayer.
Lockwood, Frank C., ed. see Barnes, William C.
Lockwood, Fred. Activities in Self Instructional Texts. (Illus.). 160p. (C). 1992. pap. text 29.95 (*0-89397-379-3*) Nichols Pub.
— Data Collection in Distance Education Research: The Use of Self-Recorded Audiotape. (C). 1991. pap. 24.00 (*0-7300-1351-0*, IDE806, Pub. by Deakin Univ) St Mut.
— The Design & Production of Self-Instructional Materials. (Flexible Learning Staff Development Program Ser.). 160p. 1998. pap. 29.95 (*0-7494-1455-3*, Kogan Pg Educ) Stylus Pub VA.
Lockwood, Fred, ed. Open & Distance Learning Today. LC 95-8130. (Studies in Distance Education). 228p. (C). 1995. pap. 25.99 (*0-415-12759-9*) Routledge.
Lockwood, Fred, jt. auth. see Latchem, C. R.
Lockwood, G. The New Harmony Communities. 1972. 59.95 (*0-8490-0722-4*) Gordon Pr.
Lockwood, George B. The New Harmony Communities. LC 72-134410. reprint ed. 47.50 (*0-404-08456-7*) AMS Pr.
— The New Harmony Movement. LC 76-134411. reprint ed. 49.50 (*0-404-08457-5*) AMS Pr.
— The New Harmony Movement. LC 68-56245. (Illus.). vxi, 404p. 1970. reprint ed. 45.00 (*0-678-00667-9*) Kelley.
Lockwood, Georgene. The Complete Idiot's Guide to Organizing Your Life. LC 96-79348. (Illus.). 1996. 16.95 (*0-02-861090-3*) Macmillan Gen Ref.
***Lockwood, Georgene.** The Complete Idiot's Guide to Organizing Your Life. 2nd ed. (Complete Idiot's Guide Ser.). 384p. 1999. pap. 16.95 (*0-02-863382-2*, Pub. by Macmillan Gen Ref) S&S Trade.
Lockwood, Georgene & Korwin, Alan. The California Gun Owner's Guide Vol. 1: Who Can Bear Arms? Where Are Guns Forbidden? When Can You Shoot to Kill? 2nd ed. (Illus.). 168p. 1999. per. 14.95 (*0-9621958-9-8*) Bloomfield Pr.
Lockwood, Georgene M. The Complete Idiot's Guide to Crafts with Kids. LC 98-85129. 352p. 1998. pap. text 17.95 (*0-02-862406-8*) Macmillan Gen Ref.
***Lockwood, Gregory.** 1 Corinthians. LC 00-9327. (Commentary Ser.). 2000. pap. write for info. (*0-570-06314-0*) Concordia.
Lockwood, Helen D. Tools & the Man. LC 21-12534. reprint ed. 27.50 (*0-404-03999-5*) AMS Pr.
Lockwood, Ingersoll. Baron Trump's Marvellous Underground Journey. 235p. 1996. reprint ed. spiral bd. 17.50 (*0-7873-0567-7*) Hlth Research.
— Baron Trump's Marvellous Underground Journey (1893) 303p. 1996. reprint ed. pap. 16.50 (*1-56459-950-7*) Kessinger Pub.
Lockwood, James R., jt. auth. see Runion, Garth E.
Lockwood, Jill, jt. auth. see Martin, M.
Lockwood, Joanne. Basic Mathematics. (C). 1991. pap. text, teacher ed. 19.96 (*0-395-57741-1*) HM.
Lockwood, Joanne S., jt. auth. see Aufmann, Richard N.
Lockwood, John, jt. ed. see Smith, William, Jr.
Lockwood, John H. Westfield, Mass., & Its Historical Influences, 1669-1919: The Life of an Early Town, with a Survey of Events in New England & Bordering Regions to Which It Was Related in Colonial & Revolutionary Times, 2 vols., Set. 1996. reprint ed. lib. bdg. 119.00 (*0-8328-5209-0*) Higginson Bk Co.
Lockwood, John P., jt. ed. see Rhodes, J. Michael.
Lockwood, Jonathan S. The Soviet View of U. S. Strategic Doctrine: Implications for Decisionmaking. LC 82-14191. (Illus.). 202p. 1983. 39.95 (*0-87855-467-X*) Transaction Pubs.
Lockwood, Jonathan S. & Lockwood, Kathleen O. The Russian View of U. S. Strategy: Its Past - Its Future. 2nd ed. 233p. (C). 1992. 34.95 (*1-56000-031-7*) Transaction Pubs.
Lockwood, Karen. Lady's Choice. 288p. 1996. mass mkt. 5.99 (*0-515-11959-8*, Jove) Berkley Pub.
— Lilac Circle. 336p. (Orig.). 1995. mass mkt. 5.50 (*0-515-11769-2*, Jove) Berkley Pub.
— Stolen Kisses. (Orig.). 1994. pap. 4.99 (*0-515-11490-1*, Jove) Berkley Pub.
— Winter Song. 1993. mass mkt. 4.99 (*1-55773-958-7*, DiamondBks) Berkley Pub.
Lockwood, Katherine. Edwin & Johanna. (Illus.). 116p. (Orig.). 1989. pap. 9.99 (*0-925037-07-9*) Great Lks Poetry.
Lockwood, Kathleen O., jt. auth. see Lockwood, Jonathan S.
Lockwood, Lewis. Beethoven: Studies in the Creative Process. (Illus.). 320p. (C). 1992. 51.95 (*0-674-06362-7*) HUP.
Lockwood, Lewis, et al, eds. Beethoven Essays: Studies in Honor of Elliot Forbes. 288p. 1984. 28.00 (*0-674-06378-3*) HUP.
Lockwood, Lewis, ed. see Ruffo, Vincenzo.
Lockwood, Lewis C. & Forten, Charlotte L. Two Black Teachers During the Civil War: Mary S. Peake: The Colored Teacher at Fortress Monroa. 1970. 12.95 (*0-405-01931-9*, 16381) Ayer.
Lockwood, Lewis C., ed. see Palestrini, Giovanni P.
Lockwood, Lisa. The Woman's Study. 119p. 1994. spiral bd. 16.50 (*0-9643021-8-7*) Reality Living.
Lockwood, Lisa & Madden, Cindy. De Mujer a Mujer. 96p. 1997. 13.00 (*1-888220-04-X*) Reality Living.
— The Woman's Study. 128p. (C). 1996. text, student ed. 16.50 (*1-888220-00-7*) Reality Living.
Lockwood, Loni, tr. see Steiner, Rudolf.
Lockwood, Lucy A.D., jt. auth. see Constantine, Larry L.
Lockwood, Margo. Black Dog. LC 86-80007. 64p. 1986. 6.95 (*0-914086-60-X*); pap. 9.95 (*0-914086-61-8*) Alice James Bks.
— Left-Handed Happiness. (Illus.). 60p. (Orig.). 1987. pap. 12.00 (*0-9617521-0-6*) Dirty Dish Pr.
Lockwood, Margo, jt. auth. see Nyhart, Nina.
Lockwood, Mark W. Learn about... Texas Birds. Zappler, Georg, ed. LC 99-165913. (Learn About Ser.). (Illus.). 48p. (J). (gr. 1-6). 1997. pap. 7.95 (*1-885696-17-5*) TX Prks & Wldlife.
Lockwood, Matthew. Fertility & Household Labour in Tanzania: Demography, Economy & Society in Rufiji District, c.1870-1986. (Illus.). 216p. 1998. text 65.00 (*0-19-828754-2*) OUP.
Lockwood, Michael & Bhat, A. Vishnu. Metatheater & Sanskrit Drama. 174p. (C). 1995. 29.50 (*81-215-0679-4*, Pub. by M Manoharial) Coronet Bks.
Lockwood, Michael, ed. see Lawrence, D. H.
Lockwood, Michael B. & Ghillyer, Andrew. Quality Management in Hospitality: Best Practice in Action. (Illus.). 224p. 1997. pap. 31.95 (*0-304-33485-5*); text 80.00 (*0-304-33486-3*) Continuum.
Lockwood, Peter. Virginia's Civil War Battlefields. (Virginia Heritage Ser.). 72p. 1995. pap. 7.95 (*1-885937-01-6*) Casco Commns.
Lockwood, Randall & Ascione, Frank R. Cruelty to Animals & Interpersonal Violence: Readings in Research & Application. LC 97-41462. 452p. 1997. 56.95 (*1-55753-105-6*) Purdue U Pr.
Lockwood, Robert E., jt. auth. see McLean, James E.
***Lockwood, Robert P., ed.** Anti-Catholicism in American Culture. LC 99-75027. 256p. 2000. 19.95 (*0-87973-342-X*) Our Sunday Visitor.
Lockwood, Russ. Fish Cookery. 256p. 1993. 22.95 (*1-55821-246-9*) Lyons Pr.
Lockwood, Samuel, tr. see Easton, Stewart C. & Steiner, Rudolf.
Lockwood, Samuel, tr. see Steiner, Rudolf.
Lockwood, Sarah. New Lyrics. LC 72-77822. (Living Poets' Library). pap. 2.50 (*0-686-02576-8*) Dragons Teeth.
Lockwood, Shelley, ed. Sir John Fortescue: On the Laws & Governance of England. (Cambridge Texts in the History of Political Thought Ser.). 210p. (C). 1997. text 59.95 (*0-521-43445-9*); pap. text 19.95 (*0-521-58996-7*) Cambridge U Pr.
Lockwood, Stephen C. Augustine Heard & Company, 1858-1862: American Merchants in China. LC 78-120318. (East Asian Monographs: No. 37). (Illus.). 171p. 1971. pap. 20.00 (*0-674-05270-6*) HUP.
Lockwood, Theodore. Dreams & Promises: The Story of the Armand Hammer United World College. LC 97-2020. (Illus.). 196p. 1997. 26.95 (*0-86534-260-1*) Sunstone Pr.
Lockwood, Thomas. Post-Augustan Satire: Charles Churchill & Satirical Poetry, 1750-1800. LC 78-4366. 208p. 1979. 30.00 (*0-295-95612-7*) U of Wash Pr.
***Lockwood, Trevor.** Writer's Guide to the Internet. (Illus.). 2000. pap. 12.95 (*0-7490-0444-4*) Allison & Busby.
Lockwood, Victoria S. Tahitian Transformation: Gender & Capitalist Development in a Rural Society. LC 92-24045. (Women & Change in the Developing World Ser.). 180p. (C). 1993. pap. text 17.50 (*1-55587-391-X*) L Rienner.
Lockwood, Victoria S., et al. Contemporary Pacific Societies: Studies in Development & Change. 384p. (C). 1992. pap. text 27.60 (*0-13-174723-1*) P-H.
Lockwood, W. B. The Oxford Book of British Bird Names. 184p. 1984. 18.95 (*0-19-214155-4*) OUP.
— The Oxford Dictionary of British Bird Names. rev. ed. (OxfordPaperback Reference Ser.). 192p. 1993. pap. 16.95 (*0-19-866196-7*) OUP.
Lockwood, W. M. Continuity of Life a Cosmic Truth (1902) 234p. 1998. reprint ed. pap. 17.95 (*0-7661-0683-7*) Kessinger Pub.
Lockwood, William G. & Salo, Sheila. Gypsies & Travelers in North America: An Annotated bibliography. LC 94-18876. (Publications: No. 6). (Orig.). 1994. pap. 20.00 (*0-9617107-5-6*) Gypsy Lore Soc.
Lockwood, William W. The Economic Development of Japan: Growth & Structural Change. enl. ed. LC 68-56833. 702p. reprint ed. pap. 200.00 (*0-608-13046-X*, 201487600094) Bks Demand.
— The Economic Development of Japan: Growth & Structural Change, 1868-1938. LC 93-5709. (Michigan Classics in Japanese Studies: No. 10). xv, 603p. 1993. reprint ed. pap. 18.95 (*0-939512-62-9*) U MI Japan.
Lockwood, William W., ed. State & Economic Enterprise in Japan. LC 65-15386. (Studies in the Modernization of Japan). 763p. reprint ed. pap. 200.00 (*0-8357-9514-4*, 201522500098) Bks Demand.
Lockwood, Yvonne, ed. see Reuss, Richard A.
Lockwood, Yvonne R. Text & Context Folksong in a Bosnian Muslim Village. (Illus.). 220p. (Orig.). 1983. pap. 21.95 (*0-89357-120-2*) Slavica.
— Yugoslav Folklore: An Annotated Bibliography of Contributions in English. LC 75-38305. 1976. per. 10.00 (*0-88247-401-4*) Ragusan Pr.
Lockwood, Yvonne R., jt. ed. see Dewhurst, C. Kurt.
***Lockyear, W. H.** The Old Testament Names of God. 499p. 1999. pap. 38.00 (*1-57910-281-6*) Wipf & Stock.
***Lockyer.** The Early Stuarts: A Political History of England, 1603-1642. 2nd ed. LC 98-52958. 408p. (C). 1998. pap. 33.53 (*0-582-27768-X*) Longman.
Lockyer, Allan. Clamdiggers & Downeast Country Stores: Eastern Maine's Vanishing Culture. LC 93-84637. (Illus.). 12p. (Orig.). 1993. pap. 14.95 (*1-880811-12-X*) North Lights.
Lockyer, Andrew & Stone, Frederick H. Juvenile Justice in Scotland: Twenty-five Years of the Welfare Approach. LC 98-183441. xiii, 289 p. 1998. write for info. (*0-567-00528-3*) T & T Clark.
***Lockyer, Bill.** Attorney General's Summary of Results of Charitable Solicitation by Commercial Fundraisers in California. (Illus.). 88p. (C). 2000. pap. text 20.00 (*0-7881-8509-8*) DIANE Pub.
Lockyer, Daphne. Julio Iglesias: The Unsung Story. LC 96-50934. 304p. 1997. 21.95 (*1-55972-394-7*, Birch Ln Pr) Carol Pub Group.
Lockyer, H. Apocalipsis: El Drama de los Siglos.Tr. of Revelation: Drama of the Ages. (SPA.). 276p. 1982. pap. 8.99 (*0-8297-1292-5*) Vida Pubs.
Lockyer, Herbert. All about God in Christ. 160p. 1995. pap. 14.95 (*1-56563-199-4*) Hendrickson MA.
— All about the Holy Spirit. 256p. 1995. pap. 14.95 (*1-56563-200-1*) Hendrickson MA.
Lockyer, Herbert, Jr. All about the Second Coming. 242p. 1998. pap. 14.95 (*1-56563-334-2*) Hendrickson MA.
Lockyer, Herbert. All Series, 5 vols. 1991. pap. 94.95 (*0-310-28088-5*) Zondervan.
— The All Series, Bks. 1-14. Incl. Bk. 1. All the Apostles of the Bible. 288p. 1972. 17.95 (*0-310-28010-9*, 10052P); Bk. 3. All the Doctrines. 1966. 17.95 (*0-310-28050-8*, 10082); Bk. 4. All the Children of the Bible. 1986. 17.20 (*0-310-28030-3*, 10051); Bk. 7. All the Men of the Bible. 1958. 17.95 (*0-310-28080-X*, 10054); Bk. 8. All the Women of the Bible. 1967. 17.95 (*0-310-28150-4*, 10038); Bk. 9. All the Miracles of the Bible. 1988. 17.95 (*0-310-28100-8*, 10066); Bk. 10. All the Parables. 1964. 17.95 (*0-310-28110-5*, 10075); Bk. 11. All the Prayers of the Bible. 1959. 17.95 (*0-310-28120-2*, 10041); Bk. 12. All the Promises of the Bible. 1962. 17.95 (*0-310-28130-X*, 10074); Bk. 13. All the Trades & Occupations of the Bible. 1986. 17.20 (*0-310-28140-7*); Bk. 14. All the Messianic Prophecies. 1973. 19.95 (*0-310-28090-7*, 10076); 1988. write for info. (*0-318-56538-2*) Zondervan.
Lockyer, Herbert, Jr. All the Angels in the Bible. 176p. 1995. pap. 14.95 (*1-56563-198-6*) Hendrickson MA.
Lockyer, Herbert. All the Apostles of the Bible. (All Ser.). 288p. 1988. pap. 19.99 (*0-310-28011-7*, 10052P) Zondervan.
— All the Divine Names & Titles in the Bible. 308p. 1975. 17.95 (*0-310-28040-0*, 10077) Zondervan.
— All the Divine Names & Titles in the Bible. (All Ser.). 368p. 1988. pap. 19.99 (*0-310-28041-9*, 10077P) Zondervan.
— All the Doctrines of the Bible. 320p. 1988. pap. 19.99 (*0-310-28051-6*, 10082P) Zondervan.
— All the Kings & Queens of the Bible. 256p. 1988. pap. 14.95 (*0-310-28071-0*) Zondervan.
— All the Men of the Bible. (All Ser.). 384p. 1988. pap. 19.99 (*0-310-28081-8*, 10054P) Zondervan.
— All the Messianic Prophecies of the Bible. 528p. 1988. pap. 19.99 (*0-310-28091-5*, 10076P) Zondervan.
— All the Miracles of the Bible. (All Ser.). 320p. 1988. pap. 19.99 (*0-310-28101-6*, 10066P) Zondervan.
— All the Parables of the Bible. (All Ser.). 384p. 1988. pap. 19.99 (*0-310-28111-3*, 10075P) Zondervan.
— All the Prayers of the Bible. (All Ser.). 288p. 1990. pap. 19.99 (*0-310-28121-0*) Zondervan.
— All the Promises of the Bible. 352p. 1990. pap. 19.99 (*0-310-28131-8*) Zondervan.
— All the Teachings of Jesus. 320p. 1997. 9.98 (*0-7858-0812-4*) Bk Sales Inc.
— All the Teachings of Jesus. 310p. 1999. pap. 14.95 (*1-56563-109-9*) Hendrickson MA.
— All the Trades & Occupations of the Bible. 336p. 1988. pap. 14.95 (*0-310-28141-5*) Zondervan.
— All the Women of the Bible. 320p. 1988. pap. 19.99 (*0-310-28151-2*, 10038P) Zondervan.
— Daily Promises. 384p. 1996. 16.95 (*1-56563-259-1*) Hendrickson MA.
— Last Words of Saints & Sinners. LC 78-85429. 240p. 1975. pap. 11.99 (*0-8254-3111-5*) Kregel.
— Love Is Better Than Wine. LC 80-84903. 128p. 1981. pap. 3.95 (*0-89221-083-4*) New Leaf.
— The Mystery & Ministry of Angels. 111p. (YA). 1994. text 9.95 (*0-942516-13-3*) Plymouth Rock Found.
Lockyer, Herbert, Sr. The Psalms: A Devotional Commentary. LC 92-15243. 800p. 1993. pap. 27.99 (*0-8254-3137-9*) Kregel.
Lockyer, Herbert, ed. Light to Live By (Wedding Edition) 384p. 1980. 10.95 (*0-310-28230-6*, 10145) Zondervan.
Lockyer, J. Norman. The Dawn of Astronomy. 432p. (Orig.). 1992. reprint ed. pap. 45.00 (*1-56459-112-3*) Kessinger Pub.
Lockyer, Judith. Ordered by Words: Language & Narration in the Novels of William Faulkner. LC 90-39842. 224p. (C). 1991. 29.95 (*0-8093-1702-8*) S Ill U Pr.
Lockyer, Keith. Critical Path Analysis. pap. 34.95 (*0-8464-4376-7*) Beekman Pubs.
Lockyer, Keith & Gordon, James. Critical Path Analysis & Other Project Network Techniques. 5th ed. 272p. (Orig.). 1991. pap. text 47.50 (*0-273-03416-2*, Pub. by Pitman Pub) Trans-Atl Phila.
— Critical Path Analysis & Other Project Network Techniques: Solutions Manual. 5th ed. 272p. 1991. teacher ed. 47.50 (*0-273-03442-1*, Pub. by Pitman Pub) Trans-Atl Phila.
— Project Management & Project Network Techniques. 6th ed. 288p. (Orig.). 1995. pap. 57.50 (*0-273-61454-1*, Pub. by Pitman Pub) Trans-Atl Phila.
Lockyer, L., et al. Production & Operations Management. 576p. (C). 1988. 185.00 (*0-7855-5728-8*, Pub. by Inst Pur & Supply) St Mut.
— Production & Operations Management. 576p. (C). 1989. 147.00 (*0-7855-4641-3*, Pub. by Inst Pur & Supply) St Mut.
Lockyer, Norman J. Elements of Astronomy (1871) 320p. 1998. reprint ed. pap. 24.95 (*0-7661-0178-9*) Kessinger Pub.
***Lockyer, Robert K.** The Cur Song: An Alien's Quest for Meaning on the Strangest Planet in the Universe. LC 99-60373. 192p. 1999. pap. write for info. (*1-57921-212-3*) WinePress Pub.
Lockyer, Roger. Early Stuarts: 1603-1642. 1989. text 43.25 (*0-582-03294-6*, Pub. by Addison-Wesley) Longman.
— James 6 & I. LC 98-5726. (Profiles in Power Ser.). 248p. (C). 1998. pap. 22.26 (*0-582-27961-5*) Longman.
— Tudor & Stuart Britain, 1471-1714. 2nd ed. LC 84-10085. 494p. reprint ed. pap. 153.20 (*0-7837-1587-0*, 204187900024) Bks Demand.
Lockyer, Roger & O'Sullivan, Dan. Tudor England. LC 93-23514. (Sources & Opinions Ser.). 1994. pap. text 11.99 (*0-582-02202-9*, Pub. by Addison-Wesley) Longman.
Lockyer, Roger, jt. ed. see Pinciss, Gerald M.
***Lockyer, Thomas N.** Vector Particle & Nuclear Models: Mathematically Consistent Models for the Structures of Energy, Subatomic Particles & Nuclei. LC 00-90292. (Illus.). 160p. 2000. pap. 17.95 (*0-9631546-9-9*) TNL Pr.
— Vector Particle & Nuclear Models: Mathematically Consistent Models for the Structures of Energy, Subatomic Particles & Nuclei. LC 00-90292. (Illus.). 160p. (C). 2000. 24.95 (*0-9631546-8-0*) TNL Pr.
Lockyer, Thomas N. Vector Particle Physics: Mathematically Consistent Models for the Structures of Subatomic Particles. LC 91-90733. 112p. (C). 1992. 12.95 (*0-9631546-0-5*); pap. 6.95 (*0-9631546-1-3*) TNL Pr.
Locock, F. A. Biographical Guide to the Divina Commedia of Dante. 1972. 59.95 (*0-87968-750-9*) Gordon Pr.
Locock, Frances. Biographical Guide to the Divinnia Commedia. LC 74-6466. (Studies in Dante: No. 9). 1974. lib. bdg. 75.00 (*0-8383-1986-6*) M S G Haskell Hse.
Locock, K. B., ed. see De Deguileville, Guillaume.
Locock, Martin, ed. Meaningful Architecture: Social Interpretations of Buildings. (Worldwide Architecture Ser.: Vol. 9). 320p. 1994. 87.95 (*1-85628-708-4*, Pub. by Avebry) Ashgate Pub Co.
Loconte, Joe. Seducing the Samaritan: How Government Contracts Are Reshaping Social Services. LC 97-21676. (Pioneer Paper Ser.). 140p. 1997. 15.00 (*0-929930-18-5*) Pioneer Inst.
Locoste, Nathalie, jt. auth. see Cannat, Guillaume.
Locraft, Jim. Inspectors General: Veterans Affairs Special Inquiry Report Was Misleading. 48p. 1999. pap. text 20.00 (*0-7881-8027-4*) DIANE Pub.
Locsin, Raul L., ed. see Rizal, Jose.
Locurto, Charles. Sense & Nonsense about IQ: The Case for Uniqueness. LC 90-23133. 224p. 1991. 57.95 (*0-275-93803-4*, C3803, Praeger Pubs); pap. 22.95 (*0-275-93911-1*, B3911, Praeger Pubs) Greenwood.
Loczy, D. Land Evaluation Studies in Hungary. (Studies in Geography in Hungary: No. 23). 95p. (C). 1988. 50.00 (*963-05-5231-0*, Pub. by Akade Kiado) St Mut.
Loczy, Denes, jt. ed. see Bremer, Hanna.
Loda, Charles J., jt. auth. see Winder, Alan A.
Loda, G. Atlas of Finger & Thumb Reconstruction. LC 99-12945. (Illus.). 240p. 1998. 179.00 (*0-86577-585-0*) Thieme Med Pubs.
Lodahl, Michael. The Story of God: Wesleyan Theology & Biblical Narrative. 256p. (C). 1994. kivar 21.99 (*0-8341-1479-8*) Beacon Hill.
Lodahl, Michael, jt. ed. see Powell, Samuel.
Lodahl, Michael E. Shekhinah - Spirit: Divine Presence in Jewish & Christian Religion. LC 92-5525. (Stimulus Bks.). 272p. 1992. pap. 11.95 (*0-8091-3311-3*) Paulist Pr.
***Lodari, Carola.** Villa Taranto. LC 99-232643. 96p. 1999. 45.00 (*88-422-0865-5*) U Allemandi.
Lodato, Francis J., jt. auth. see Ryan, John B.
Loday, Jean-Louis. Cyclic Homology. LC 92-34146. (Grundlehren der Mathematischen Wissenschaften Ser.: Vol. 301). 1992. 163.95 (*0-387-53339-7*) Spr-Verlag.
— Cyclic Homology, Vol. 301. 2nd ed. LC 97-22418. (Grundlehren der Mathematischen Wissenschaften Ser.). 1997. write for info. (*3-540-63074-0*) Spr-Verlag.
Loday, Jean-Louis, et al. Operads: Proceedings of Renaissance Conferences, Vol. 202. LC 96-37049. (Contemporary Mathematics Ser.). 443p. 1996. pap. 85.00 (*0-8218-0513-4*, CONM/202) Am Math.
Lodder, Carol. Making Dolls' House Interiors in 1/12 Scale. (Illus.). 192p. 1997. pap. 19.95 (*0-7153-0615-4*) Sterling.

L

Lodder, Christina. Russian Constructivism. LC 83-40002. (Illus.). 328p. 1983. pap. 30.00 (*0-300-03406-7*, Y-516) Yale U Pr.

Lodder, V. Russian Avantgarde: Art & Russian Constructivism. (C). 1990. 450.00 (*0-7855-4449-6*, Pub. by Collets); pap. 190.00 (*0-7855-4450-X*, Pub. by Collets) St Mut.

Lodders, A. Catecismo Ilustrado. (SPA., Illus.). 1983. 1.50 (*0-89942-068-0*, 68/S) Catholic Bk Pub.

— St. Joseph Pocket Catechism. 1975. 1.25 (*0-89942-047-8*, 46-00) Catholic Bk Pub.

— San Jose Historia Biblica Condensada. (SPA.). 1989. 3.95 (*0-89942-771-5*, 771/S) Catholic Bk Pub.

Lodders, Katharina & Fegley, Bruce, Jr. The Planetary Scientist's Companion. (Illus.). 400p. 1998. pap. 24.95 (*0-19-511694-1*) OUP.

Lodding, William, ed. Gas Effluent Analysis. LC 67-19950. (Thermal Analysis Ser.: Vol. 13). (Illus.). 231p. reprint ed. pap. 71.70 (*0-608-30545-6*, 205500600007) Bks Demand.

Lodemel, Ivar. The Welfare Paradox: Income Maintenance & Personal Social Services in Norway & Britain, 1946-1966. 287p. 1997. 37.00 (*82-00-21242-4*) Scandnvan Univ Pr.

Loden, D. John. Megabrands: How to Build Them; How to Beat Them. 200p. 1991. 32.50 (*1-55623-469-4*, Irwn Prfssnl) McGraw-Hill Prof.

Loden, James M., ed. & tr. see Robeson, Bonnie & Mienville, Lisa.

***Loden, Marie & Maibach, Howard I.** Dry Skin & Moisturizers. LC 99-38984. (Series in Dermatology). 447p. 1999. write for info. (*0-8493-7520-7*) CRC Pr.

Loden, Marilyn. Implementing Diversity: Best Practices for Making Diversity Work in Your Organization. 200p. 1995. 22.95 (*0-7863-0460-X*, Irwn Prfssnl) McGraw-Hill Prof.

Loden, Marilyn & Rosener, Judy B. Workforce America! Managing Employee Diversity As a Vital Resource. 192p. 1990. 35.00 (*1-55623-386-8*, Irwn Prfssnl) McGraw-Hill Prof.

***Loden, Rachel.** Hotel Imperium. LC 99-32053. (Contemporary Poetry Ser.). 80p. 1999. pap. 15.95 (*0-8203-2169-9*) U of Ga Pr.

— The Last Campaign LC 99-198664. 32p. 1998. write for info. (*0-9624178-8-2*) Slapering Hol.

Loder, Ann. The Wet Hat: And Other Stories from Beyond the Black Stump. 2nd ed. (Illus.). 100p. (J). (gr. 4-8). 1993. pap. 6.95 (*0-9636643-0-1*) A L Loder.

Loder, Dorothy. The Land & People of Belgium. rev. ed. LC 72-13301. (Portraits of the Nations Ser.). (Illus.). (J). (gr. 5-9). 1973. lib. bdg. 12.89 (*0-397-31462-0*) HarpC Child Bks.

Loder, Eileen P., ed. Bibliography of the History & Organisation of Horse Racing & Thoroughbred Breeding in Great Britain & Ireland. 352p. 1990. 110.00 (*0-85131-297-7*, Pub. by J A Allen) St Mut.

Loder, Gale, jt. auth. see Loder, Steve.

Loder, James E. The Logic of the Spirit: Human Development in Theological Perspective. LC 98-29681. (Religion in Practice Ser.). 362p. 1998. pap. 27.95 (*0-7879-0919-X*) Jossey-Bass.

— The Transforming Moment. 2nd ed. 256p. 1989. reprint ed. pap. text 18.95 (*0-939443-17-1*) Helmers Howard Pub.

Loder, James E. & Neidhardt, W. Jim. The Knight's Move: The Relational Logic of the Spirit in Theology & Science. LC 92-17033. 1992. pap. 29.95 (*0-939443-25-2*) Helmers Howard Pub.

Loder, Kurt, jt. auth. see Turner, Tina.

***Loder, Phil.** Assessment of California's Largest Hazardous Waste Generators' Source Reduction Planning Efforts. Ingham, Alan & Wilhelm, Kim, eds. (Illus.). 65p. (C). 2000. reprint ed. pap. text 20.00 (*0-7881-8474-1*) DIANE Pub.

Loder, Steve & Loder, Gale. Quality Venison: Homemade Recipes & Homespun Deer Tales. LC 98-140318. (Illus.). 176p. 1998. 14.95 (*0-9662284-0-5*) Loders Game.

***Loder, Steve & Loder, Gale.** Quality Venison Vol. II: All New Recipes & Deer Tales Too. (Illus.). 192p. 1999. 14.95 (*0-9662284-1-3*) Loders Game.

Loder, Ted. Guerrillas of Grace: Prayers for the Battle. LC 84-26096. (Illus.). 136p. (Orig.). 1984. pap. 14.95 (*0-931055-04-0*) Innisfree Pr.

***Loder, Ted.** My Heart in My Mouth: Prayers for Soul-Searching Worship. 160p. 2000. pap. 14.95 (*1-880913-49-6*) Innisfree Pr.

Loder, Ted. Tracks in the Straw: Tales Spun from the Manger. 2nd rev. ed. LC 97-33610. 176p. (Orig.). 1997. pap. 12.95 (*1-880913-29-1*) Innisfree Pr.

— Wrestling the Light: Ache & Awe in the Human-Divine Struggle. LC 91-37123. (Illus.). 176p. (Orig.). 1991. pap. 14.95 (*0-931055-79-2*) Innisfree Pr.

Loderhose, Gary. Far Far from Home: The Ninth Florida Regiment in the Confederate Army. LC 99-71528. (Illus.). 126p. 1999. 22.95 (*1-57860-072-3*) Guild Pr IN.

Lodewick, Peter, et al. The Diabetic Man: A Guide to Health & Success in All Areas of Your Life. rev. ed. 352p. 1996. pap. 16.00 (*1-56565-439-0*) Lowell Hse.

Lodewick, Peter A. A Diabetic Doctor Looks at Diabetes: His & Yours. 1997. pap. text 14.95 (*1-890203-00-9*) DiaBetes Care Ctr.

— A Diabetic Doctor Looks at Diabetes: His & Yours. LC 98-4119. 336p. 1998. pap. 16.00 (*1-56565-940-6*, 09406W, Pub. by Lowell Hse) NTC Contemp Pub Co.

— A Diabetic Doctor Looks at Diabetes: His & Yours. (Illus.). 204p. 1984. pap. 7.95 (*0-910117-00-4*) RMI.

Lodewick, Peter A., et al. The Diabetic Man. 3rd rev. ed. LC 99-21681. 368p. 1999. pap. 17.95 (*0-7373-0085-X*, 0085XW) NTC Contemp Pub Co.

— The Diabetic Man: A Guide to Health & Success in All Areas of Your Life. 336p. 1992. pap. 15.00 (*0-929923-78-2*) Lowell Hse.

Lodewijckx, Marc, ed. Archeological & Historical Aspects of West-European Societies. (Acta Archaeologica Lovaniensia Monographiae Ser.: No. 8). (ENG & FRE., Illus.). 516p. (Orig.). 1996. pap. 157.50 (*90-6186-722-3*, Pub. by Leuven Univ) Coronet Bks.

Lodewyk, Christian P. Love in a Hate Situation. 156p. 1987. pap. 5.95 (*0-88144-107-4*) Christian Pub.

Lodgaard, Sverre, ed. Naval Arms Control. (International Peace Research Institute Ser.). (Illus.). 288p. (C). 1990. text 49.95 (*0-8039-8387-5*) Sage.

Lodgaard, Sverre & Thee, Marek, eds. Nuclear Disengagement in Europe. 272p. 1983. 63.00 (*0-85066-244-3*) Taylor & Francis.

Lodgaard, Sverre, ed. see Stockholm International Peace Research Institute S.

Lodge. Institutions & Policies of the European Community. (C). 1983. pap. text. write for info. (*0-86187-239-8*) St Martin.

— Perestroika for America. 225p. 1990. 25.00 (*0-07-103250-9*) McGraw.

Lodge & Lide. Introduction to Literature-Based Composition: Teacher's Manual. 1999. teacher ed. 12.99 (*0-02-654092-4*) Glencoe.

Lodge, A. E., ed. see Institute of Petroleum, London Staff.

Lodge, Arthur. Opportunities in Accounting Careers. LC 76-42889. (Illus.). (YA). (gr. 8 up). 1985. 13.95 (*0-8442-6341-9*, VGM Career) NTC Contemp Pub Co.

— Opportunities in Accounting Careers. LC 76-42889. (Illus.). (YA). (gr. 8 up). 1988. pap. 10.95 (*0-8442-6342-7*, VGM Career) NTC Contemp Pub Co.

Lodge, Barton, ed. see Palladius, Rutilius T.

***Lodge, Bernard.** Cloud Cuckoo Land. LC 99-18698. (Illus.). 32p. (J). (ps-3). 1999. 15.00 (*0-395-96318-4*, W Lorraine) HM.

Lodge, Bernard. Door to Door. LC 93-22203. (Illus.). 32p. (J). (ps-3). 1993. 14.95 (*1-879085-80-1*, Whispering Coyote) Charlesbridge Pub.

— The Grand Old Duke of York. rev. ed. LC 92-21339. (Illus.). 32p. (J). (ps-2). 1993. 13.95 (*1-879085-79-8*, Whispering Coyote) Charlesbridge Pub.

— The Half-Mile Hat. LC 94-724. (Illus.). 32p. (J). (gr. 1-5). 1995. 14.95 (*1-879085-89-5*, Whispering Coyote) Charlesbridge Pub.

— Mouldylocks. LC 97-51183. 32p. (J). (ps-2). 1998. 15.00 (*0-395-90945-7*) HM.

— Prince Ivan & the Firebird. (Illus.). 32p. (J). (gr. k-5). 1996. pap. 6.95 (*1-879085-63-1*, Whispering Coyote) Charlesbridge Pub.

Lodge, Bernard. Prince Ivan & the Firebird: A Russian Folk Tale. 1996. 12.15 (*0-606-08848-2*, Pub. by Turtleback) Demco.

— Shoe Shoe Baby. (Illus.). 32p. (J). (ps-3). 2000. 14.95 (*0-375-81084-6*) Random.

Lodge, Bernard. Tanglebird. LC 96-31030. (Illus.). 32p. (J). 1997. 14.95 (*0-395-84543-2*) HM.

— There Was an Old Woman Who Lived in a Glove: A Picture Book. LC 92-12967. (Illus.). 32p. (J). 1992. lib. bdg. 14.95 (*1-879085-55-0*, Whispering Coyote) Charlesbridge Pub.

— There Was an Old Woman Who Lived in a Glove: A Picture Book, 1. (J). (ps-2). 1999. pap. 6.95 (*1-58089-018-0*, Whispering Coyote) Charlesbridge Pub.

Lodge, Bernard, jt. auth. see Roffey, Maureen.

Lodge, Carlton, ed. see Saevick, C. W., et al.

Lodge, Caroline, ed. see Best, Ron, et al.

Lodge, David. The Art of Fiction. 256p. 1994. pap. 12.95 (*0-14-017492-3*, Penguin Bks) Viking Penguin.

— The British Museum Is Falling Down. 192p. 1989. pap. 12.95 (*0-14-012419-5*, Penguin Bks) Viking Penguin.

— Changing Places. 256p. 1979. pap. 12.95 (*0-14-017098-7*, Penguin Bks) Viking Penguin.

***Lodge, David.** Home Truths: A Novella. 128p. 2000. pap. 11.95 (*0-14-029180-6*) Viking Penguin.

Lodge, David. Modern Criticism & Theory. 480p. (C). 1988. pap. text 39.38 (*0-582-49460-5*, 73622) Longman.

— The Modes of Modern Writing: Metaphor, Metonymy, & the Typology of Modern Literature. xvi, 280p. 1988. pap. text 13.95 (*0-226-48978-7*) U Ch Pr.

— Nice Work. 288p. 1990. pap. 12.95 (*0-14-013396-8*, Penguin Bks) Viking Penguin.

— Out of the Shelter. 272p. 1989. pap. 12.95 (*0-14-012279-6*, Penguin Bks) Viking Penguin.

— Paradise News. 304p. 1993. pap. 12.95 (*0-14-016521-5*, Penguin Bks) Viking Penguin.

— Paradise News. large type ed. LC 92-11067. 509p. 1992. reprint ed. 20.95 (*1-56054-450-3*) Thorndike Pr.

— The Practice of Writing. 1997. pap. 13.95 (*0-14-026106-0*) Viking Penguin.

— Small World. 400p. 1995. pap. 12.95 (*0-14-024486-7*, Penguin Bks) Viking Penguin.

— Small World. 1989. mass mkt. 5.95 (*0-446-35999-8*, Pub. by Warner Bks) Little.

— Small World: An Academic Romance. 385p. 1991. mass mkt. 12.99 (*0-446-39327-4*, Pub. by Warner Bks) Little.

— Souls & Bodies. 256p. 1990. pap. 12.95 (*0-14-013018-7*, Penguin Bks) Viking Penguin.

— Therapy. 336p. 1996. pap. 12.95 (*0-14-024900-1*, Penguin Bks) Viking Penguin.

***Lodge, David, ed.** Modern Criticism & Theory: A Reader. 2nd ed. LC 99-21398. 500p. (C). 1999. pap. 32.80 (*0-582-31287-6*) Addison-Wesley.

Lodge, David, ed. & intro. see James, Henry.

Lodge, E. C., ed. The Account Book of a Kentish Estate, 1616-1704. (British Academy, London, Records of the Social & Economic History of England & Wales Ser.: Vol. 6). 1972. reprint ed. pap. 90.00 (*0-8115-1246-0*) Periodicals Srv.

Lodge, Eleanor C. The Estates of the Archbishop & Chapter of Saint-Andre of Bordeaux under English Rule. LC 73-22285. v, 206, 190p. 1974. write for info. (*0-374-96161-1*) FS&G.

Lodge, G., jt. auth. see Gildersleeve, B.

Lodge, G. A., ed. see Easter School in Agricultural Science (14th 1967,.

Lodge, George C. The American Disease. LC 86-8668. 354p. (C). 1986. pap. text 20.00 (*0-8147-5028-1*) NYU Pr.

— Managing Globalization in the Age of Interdependence. LC 95-17969. (Warren Bennis Executive Briefing Ser.). (Illus.). 128p. 1995. 22.50 (*0-89384-271-0*, Pfffr & Co) Jossey-Bass.

— The New American Ideology. 344p. (C). 1986. pap. text 19.00 (*0-8147-5027-3*) NYU Pr.

— Perestroika for America: Restructuring Business-Government Relations for World Competitiveness. 235p. 1990. 22.95 (*0-87584-234-8*) Harvard Busn.

— The Song of the Wave & Other Poems. LC 70-104517. 135p. reprint ed. lib. bdg. 22.00 (*0-8398-1168-3*) Irvington.

— The Song of the Wave & Other Poems. 135p. (C). 1986. reprint ed. pap. text 5.95 (*0-8290-2030-6*) Irvington.

Lodge, Gonzalex, jt. auth. see Gildersleeve, B. L.

Lodge, Gonzalez. The Vocabulary of High School Latin. LC 73-177003. (Columbia University. Teachers College. Contributions to Education Ser.: No. 9). (LAT.). reprint ed. 37.50 (*0-404-55009-6*) AMS Pr.

Lodge, Gonzalez, jt. auth. see Gildersleeve, Basil L.

Lodge, Helen C., jt. ed. see Cook, Lenora L.

Lodge, Henry C. Alexander Hamilton. Schlesinger, Arthur Meier, Jr., ed. LC 96-51449. (American Statesmen Ser.). 500p. 1997. lib. bdg. 34.95 (*0-7910-4542-0*, Chelsea Juniors) Chelsea Hse.

— Alexander Hamilton. Morse, John T., Jr., ed. LC 72-128971. (American Statesmen Ser.: No. 7). reprint ed. 45.00 (*0-404-50857-X*) AMS Pr.

— Alexander Hamilton. (BCL1 - U. S. History Ser.). 317p. 1991. reprint ed. lib. bdg. 89.00 (*0-7812-6125-2*) Rprt Serv.

— Alexander Hamilton. (Notable American Authors Ser.). 1999. reprint ed. lib. bdg. 125.00 (*0-7812-3809-9*) Rprt Serv.

— Certain Accepted Heroes. LC 79-37119. (Essay Index Reprint Ser.). 1977. reprint ed. 23.95 (*0-8369-2514-9*) Ayer.

— Certain Accepted Heroes & Other Essays. (Notable American Authors Ser.). 1999. reprint ed. lib. bdg. 125.00 (*0-7812-3814-5*) Rprt Serv.

— Daniel Webster. Morse, John T., Jr., ed. LC 71-128960. (American Statesmen Ser.: No. 21). reprint ed. 49.50 (*0-404-50871-5*) AMS Pr.

— Daniel Webster. (Notable American Authors Ser.). 1999. reprint ed. lib. bdg. 125.00 (*0-7812-3810-2*) Rprt Serv.

— Democracy of the Constitution, & Other Addresses & Essays. LC 67-22101. (Essay Index Reprint Ser.). 1977. 20.95 (*0-8369-0623-3*) Ayer.

— The Democracy of the Constitution & Other Addresses & Essays. (Essay Index Reprint Ser.). 297p. 1972. reprint ed. lib. bdg. 17.00 (*0-8290-0512-9*) Irvington.

— The Democracy of the Constitution & Other Essays. (Notable American Authors Ser.). 1999. reprint ed. lib. bdg. 125.00 (*0-7812-3819-6*) Rprt Serv.

— Early Memories. LC 75-1853. (Leisure Class in America Ser.). 1975. reprint ed. 26.95 (*0-405-06919-7*) Ayer.

— Early Memories. (Notable American Authors Ser.). 1999. reprint ed. lib. bdg. 125.00 (*0-7812-3818-8*) Rprt Serv.

— Essays in Anglo-Saxon Law. (Notable American Authors Ser.). 1999. reprint ed. lib. bdg. 125.00 (*0-7812-3806-4*) Rprt Serv.

— Fighting Frigate & Other Essays & Addresses. LC 79-90655. (Essay Index Reprint Ser.). 1977. 23.95 (*0-8369-1222-5*) Ayer.

— Frontier Town & Other Essays. LC 67-30220. (Essay Index Reprint Ser.). 1977. 21.95 (*0-8369-1975-0*) Ayer.

— A Frontier Town & Other Essays. (Notable American Authors Ser.). 1999. reprint ed. lib. bdg. 125.00 (*0-7812-3817-X*) Rprt Serv.

— George Washington, 2 vols. Morse, John T., Jr., ed. LC 74-128969. (American Statesmen Ser.: Nos. 4-5). reprint ed. 95.00 (*0-404-50890-1*) AMS Pr.

— George Washington. (Notable American Authors Ser.). 1999. reprint ed. lib. bdg. 125.00 (*0-7812-3812-9*) Rprt Serv.

— Historical & Political Essays. LC 72-282. (Essay Index Reprint Ser.). 1977. reprint ed. pap. 19.95 (*0-8369-2801-6*) Ayer.

— Historical & Political Essays. (Notable American Authors Ser.). 1999. reprint ed. lib. bdg. 125.00 (*0-7812-3813-7*) Rprt Serv.

— Life & Letters of George Cabot. (Notable American Authors Ser.). 1999. reprint ed. lib. bdg. 125.00 (*0-7812-3807-2*) Rprt Serv.

— The Senate of the United States. (Notable American Authors Ser.). 1999. reprint ed. lib. bdg. 125.00 (*0-7812-3820-X*) Rprt Serv.

— A Short History of the English Colonies in America. 560p. (Orig.). 1995. pap. text 35.00 (*0-7884-0189-0*) Heritage Bk.

— A Short History of the English Colonies in America. (Notable American Authors Ser.). (Orig.). 1999. reprint ed. lib. bdg. 125.00 (*0-7812-3808-0*) Rprt Serv.

— The Story of the Revolution. (Notable American Authors Ser.). 1999. reprint ed. lib. bdg. 125.00 (*0-7812-3815-3*) Rprt Serv.

— Story of the Spanish War. (Notable American Authors Ser.). 1999. reprint ed. lib. bdg. 125.00 (*0-7812-3816-1*) Rprt Serv.

— Studies in History. LC 70-39132. (Essay Index Reprint Ser.). 1977. reprint ed. 28.95 (*0-8369-2698-6*) Ayer.

— Studies in History. (Notable American Authors Ser.). 1999. reprint ed. lib. bdg. 125.00 (*0-7812-3811-0*) Rprt Serv.

— War with Spain. LC 70-111702. (American Imperialism: Viewpoints of United States Foreign Policy, 1898-1941 Ser.). 1970. reprint ed. 24.95 (*0-405-02035-X*) Ayer.

Lodge, Henry C. & Redmond, C. F., eds. Selections from the Correspondence of Theodore Roosevelt & Henry Cabot Lodge, 1884-1918, 2 vols. LC 72-146156. (American Public Figures Ser.). 1971. reprint ed. lib. bdg. 125.00 (*0-306-70129-4*) Da Capo.

Lodge, Henry C., ed. see Hamilton, Alexander.

Lodge, Henry Cabot. Daniel Webster. (American Statesmen Ser.). 1997. 39.95 (*0-7910-4546-3*) Chelsea Hse.

Lodge, Henry Cabot, jt. auth. see Roosevelt, Theodore.

Lodge, Jack. Hollywood: Fifty Great Years. 1989. 29.88 (*0-88365-743-0*) Galahad Bks.

Lodge, Jane. Computerized Litigation Support. 105p. 1990. pap. 37.50 (*1-86287-029-2*, Pub. by Federation Pr) Gaunt.

Lodge, Jeff. Where This Lake Is. LC 97-197265. (New American Voices Ser.: Vol. 1). 250p. (Orig.). 1997. pap. 14.00 (*1-877727-68-7*) White Pine.

Lodge, Jo. The Busy Farm: A Counting Book with Pull-Out Tabs. Fogelman, Phyllis, ed. LC 98-36809. (Illus.). 8p. (J). (ps-k). 1999. 9.99 (*0-8037-2416-0*, Dial Yng Read) Peng Put Young Read.

— Can You Do What Dog Can Do? In the Morning. (Illus.). 12p. (J). (ps-k). 1997. 5.95 (*0-7641-5069-3*) Barron.

— Can You Do What Rabbit Can Do? In the Evening. (Illus.). 12p. (J). 1997. 5.95 (*0-7641-5070-7*) Barron.

***Lodge, Jo.** Happy Birthday, Moo Moo! 16p. (J). 2001. 13.95 (*0-316-66644-0*) Little.

Lodge, Jo. If You're Happy & You Know It. LC 95-83379. (Illus.). 12p. (J). (ps). 1996. 5.95 (*0-8120-6608-1*) Barron.

— Patch Goes to the Park. LC 96-76302. (J). 1997. pap. 5.95 (*0-15-201379-2*) Harcourt.

— Patch's House. LC 96-80014. (J). 1997. pap. 11.95 (*0-15-201665-1*) Harcourt.

— Pull-Tab & Pop-Up Fun: If You're Happy & You Know It; This Is the Way We Make a Face, 2 bks. (Illus.). 12p. (J). 1996. boxed set 11.95 (*0-8120-8496-9*) Barron.

— This Is the Way We Make a Face. LC 95-83378. (Illus.). 12p. (J). (ps). 1996. 5.95 (*0-8120-6607-3*) Barron.

Lodge, John. I Remember Detroit. (American Autobiography Ser.). 208p. 1995. reprint ed. lib. bdg. 79.00 (*0-7812-8581-X*) Rprt Serv.

— Peerage of Ireland, or a Genealogical History of the Present Nobility of That Kingdom, 7 vols. Archdall, Mervyn, ed. LC 77-172749. reprint ed. 150.00 (*0-404-07970-9*) AMS Pr.

Lodge, John, ed. Computer Data Handling in the Primary School. (Roehampton Teaching Studies). 128p. 1991. pap. 27.00 (*1-85346-178-4*, Pub. by David Fulton) Taylor & Francis.

Lodge, Joseph H. Drug & Alcohol Abuse in the Workplace: An Assessment of Economic & Productivity Losses. LC 87-627. 107p. reprint ed. pap. 33.20 (*0-7837-0683-9*, 204101600019) Bks Demand.

Lodge, Josephine. Hide & Seek with Duck. (Illus.). 12p. (J). 1998. 5.95 (*0-7641-5075-8*) Barron.

— Pass the Parcel with Pig. (Illus.). 12p. (J). 1998. 5.95 (*0-7641-5076-6*) Barron.

Lodge, Juliet, ed. Euro-Elections, 1994. LC 95-31171. 256p. 1995. pap. 23.95 (*1-85567-281-2*) Bks Intl VA.

— The European Community & the Challenge of the Future. 2nd ed. LC 93-17954. 1993. pap. 19.95 (*0-312-09978-9*) St Martin.

— The 1994 Elections to the European Parliament. LC 95-31171. 242p. 1996. 99.00 (*1-85567-280-4*) Bks Intl VA.

Lodge, Karen & Barnes, Lisa T. Steve Tobin - Reconstructions. (Illus.). 80p. 1995. 20.00 (*0-9624021-9-2*) Ursinus College.

Lodge, Marc. Within the Bounds. 336p. 1994. mass mkt. 5.99 (*0-425-14457-7*) Berkley Pub.

Lodge, Milton. Magnitude Scaling. (Quantitative Applications in the Social Sciences Ser.: Vol. 25). 88p. 1981. pap. 10.95 (*0-8039-1747-3*) Sage.

Lodge, Milton & McGraw, Kathleen M., eds. Political Judgment: Structure & Process. 320p. (C). 1995. text 47.50 (*0-472-10541-8*, 10541) U of Mich Pr.

Lodge, O. R. The Recapture of Guam. (Elite Unit Ser.: No. 28). (Illus.). 248p. 1991. reprint ed. 39.95 (*0-89839-160-1*) Battery Pr.

— The Recapture of Guam: U.S. Marine Corps Monograph. (Illus.). 212p. 1994. reprint ed. pap. 15.00 (*0-915266-16-4*) Awani Pr.

Lodge, Olive. Peasant Life in Yugoslavia. LC 77-87722. (Illus.). 352p. reprint ed. 57.50 (*0-404-16582-6*) AMS Pr.

Lodge, Oliver. The Ether of Space. 1991. lib. bdg. 69.95 (*0-8490-4931-8*) Gordon Pr.

— Man & the Universe (1908) 306p. 1998. reprint ed. pap. 24.95 (*0-7661-0560-1*) Kessinger Pub.

— Raymond: or Life & Death: With Examples of the Evidence for Survival of Memory & Affection after Death. 415p. 1996. reprint ed. pap. 29.95 (*1-56459-632-X*) Kessinger Pub.

— Reason & Belief (1910) 166p. 1998. reprint ed. pap. 19.95 (*0-7661-0325-0*) Kessinger Pub.

— Spiritual Works, 4 vols. 1972. 400.00 (*0-8490-1114-0*) Gordon Pr.

Lodge, Oliver J. Signalling Through Space Without Wires: Being a Description of the Work of Hertz & His Successors. 3rd ed. LC 74-9688. (Telecommunications Ser.). (Illus.). 138p. 1974. 17.95 (*0-405-06051-3*) Ayer.

Lodge, Oliver J., tr. see Richet, Charles.

An Asterisk (*) at the beginning of an entry indicates that the title is appearing for the first time.

Lodge, R. Anthony. French: From Dialect to Standard. (Illus.). 272p. (C). 1993. pap. 22.99 (*0-415-08071-1*, 46869) Routledge.

Lodge, R. Anthony, et al. Exploring the French Language. LC 97-16561. 208p. 1997. pap. text 16.95 (*0-340-67662-0*, Pub. by E A) OUP.

— Exploring the French Language. (An Arnold Publication). (Illus.). 224p. 1997. text 65.00 (*0-340-67661-2*) OUP.

Lodge, Ray & Shanks, Susan. All Weather Surfaces for Horses. 80p. 1994. pap. 29.00 (*0-85131-598-4*, Pub. by J A Allen) Trafalgar.

***Lodge, Ray & Shanks, Susan.** All Weather Surfaces for Horses. 96p. 1999. 60.00 (*0-85131-756-1*, Pub. by J A Allen) St Mut.

Lodge, Richard. History of England from the Restoration to the Death of William Third. LC 70-5629. (Political History of England Ser.: No. 8). reprint ed. 45.00 (*0-404-50778-6*) AMS Pr.

— Studies in Eighteenth-Century Diplomacy, 1740-1748. LC 73-109771. 421p. 1970. reprint ed. lib. bdg. 75.00 (*0-8371-4261-X*, LODI, Greenwood Pr) Greenwood.

Lodge, Sally. The Cheyenne. (Native American People Ser.: Set II). (Illus.). 32p. (J). (gr. 4-8). 1990. lib. bdg. 22.60 (*0-86625-387-4*) Rourke Pubns.

— The Comanche. (Native American People Ser.: Set III). 32p. (J). (gr. 4-8). 1992. lib. bdg. 15.95 (*0-86625-390-4*) Rourke Pubns.

Lodge, Stuart. The Model Rocketry Handbook. (Illus.). 125p. (Orig.). 1990. pap. 19.95 (*1-85486-047-X*) Nexus Special Interests.

Lodge, Thomas. Rosalind. Beecher, Donald A., ed. (Publications of the Barnabe Riche Society : No. 7). 225p. 1997. 28.00 (*1-895537-27-4*, Pub. by Dovehouse) Sterling.

— Rosalynd. Nellist, Brian, ed. LC 96-143320. 128p. 1998. pap. 18.50 (*1-85331-106-5*, Pub. by Edinburgh U Pr) Col U Pr.

— Rosalynde, Being the Original of Shakespeare's As You Like It. Greg, W. W., ed. LC 75-128890. (Select Bibliographies Reprint Ser.). 1977. reprint ed. 18.95 (*0-8369-5510-2*) Ayer.

— A Treatise of the Plague: Containing the Nature, Signes & Accidents of the Same. LC 79-84119. (English Experience Ser.: No. 938). 92p. 1979. reprint ed. lib. bdg. 20.00 (*90-221-0938-0*) Walter J Johnson.

— Wits Miserie & the Worlds Madnesse. LC 70-25896. (English Experience Ser.: No. 198). 112p. 1969. reprint ed. 20.00 (*90-221-0198-3*) Walter J Johnson.

— The Wounds of Civil War. Houppert, Joseph W., ed. LC 68-63050. (Regents Renaissance Drama Ser.). 137p. 1969. reprint ed. pap. 42.50 (*0-608-02672-7*, 206332500004) Bks Demand.

Lodge, Thomas & Greene, Robert. Looking-Glass for London & England. LC 71-133697. (Tudor Facsimile Texts. Old English Plays Ser.: No. 67). reprint ed. 59.50 (*0-404-53367-1*) AMS Pr.

Lodge, Thomas E. The Everglades Handbook: Understanding the Ecosystem. LC 93-48083. (Illus.). 248p. (C). 1994. per. 41.95 (*1-884015-06-9*) St Lucie Pr.

— The Everglades Handbook: Understanding the Ecosystem. LC 93-48083. 247p. 1995. pap. 39.95 (*1-57003-061-8*) U of SC Pr.

Lodha, R. M. & Jain, P. S. Medieval Jainism: Culture & Environment. 1990. 22.50 (*81-7024-272-X*, Pub. by Ashish Pub Hse) S Asia.

Lodhi, A., jt. auth. see Otterbrandt, T.

Lodhi, Abdulaziz Y. Jifunze Kusema Kiswahill: A Compendium for Teachers & Course Participants. 166p. 1990. 16.95 (*91-7106-310-2*, Pub. by Nordic Africa) Transaction Pubs.

Lodhi, Abdulaziz Y. & Otterbrandt, Tommy. Kortfattad Svensk-Swahili Ordbok. 114p. 1978. write for info. (*91-7106-139-8*, Pub. by Nordic Africa) Transaction Pubs.

— Kortfattad Swahili-Svensk - Svensk-Swahili Ordbok. 319p. 1987. write for info. (*91-7106-260-2*, Pub. by Nordic Africa) Transaction Pubs.

Lodhi, Abdulaziz Y., jt. auth. see Otterbrandt, Tommy.

Lodhi, Abdulaztz Y. The Institutions of Slavery in Zanzibar & Pemba. (Research Report Ser.: No. 16). 40p. 1973. write for info. (*91-7106-066-9*, Pub. by Nordic Africa) Transaction Pubs.

Lodhi, Abdulaztz Y., jt. auth. see Kaluglia, Leonard.

Lodhi, M. A. & International Institute of Islamic Thought Staff, eds. The Islamization of Attitudes & Practices in Science & Technology: Proceedings of a Workshop on Islamization of Attitudes & Practices in Science & Technology. LC 89-15332. (Illus.). 150p. (C). 1989. pap. text 8.95 (*0-912463-42-2*) IIIT VA.

Lodi, Ed, jt. auth. see Ellis, Wade, Jr.

***Lodi, Edward.** Cranberry Chronicles: A Book about a Bog. 140p. 2000. pap. 12.95 (*0-9674204-2-3*) Rock Village.

— Shapes That Haunt New England: The Collected Ghost Stories of Edward Lodi. 140p. 2000. pap. 13.95 (*0-9674204-1-5*) Rock Village.

Lodi, Enzo & Auman, Jordan, trs. Saints of the Roman Calender: Including Feasts Proper to the English-Speaking World. LC 92-20261. 444p. 1992. pap. 9.95 (*0-8189-0652-9*) Alba.

Loding, Darlene. Economic Texts from the Third Dynasty. (Ur Excavations Ser.: No. 9). (Illus.). 84p. 1976. 25.00 (*0-934718-37-7*) U Museum Pubns.

Lodish. Experimental Biology, Prgm. 4. 1997. 132.00 (*0-12-454494-0*) Acad Pr.

— Experimental Biology, Prgm. 5. 1997. 132.00 (*0-12-454495-9*) Acad Pr.

— Experimental Biology, Prgm. 6. 1997. 132.00 (*0-12-454496-7*) Acad Pr.

— Knowledge Now in Experimental Biology: Model Organisms Series, 6 vols.; set. 1997. 750.00 incl. VHS (*0-12-454490-8*) Acad Pr.

— Molecular Cell Biology. 3rd ed. 2000. 73.00 (*0-7167-3053-7*) W H Freeman.

***Lodish.** Molecular Cell Biology. 4th ed. 1999. pap. 29.95 (*0-7167-3604-7*) W H Freeman.

— Molecular Cell Biology Art Notebook. 4th ed. 1999. pap. text. write for info. (*0-7167-4078-8*, Pub. by W H Freeman) VHPS.

— Molecular Cell Biology Preview Book. 4th ed. 1999. pap. text 2.95 (*0-7167-3888-0*, Pub. by W H Freeman) VHPS.

Lodish, H. Molecular Cell Biology: Mini Transparency Set. 3rd ed. (C). 2000. 160.00 (*0-7167-2673-4*) W H Freeman.

— Selected Topics from Molecular Cell Biology. 3rd ed. (C). 1995. pap. text 19.95 (*0-7167-2949-0*) W H Freeman.

Lodish, H. & Darnell, J. E. Molecular Cell Biology. 3rd ed. (C). 1995. pap. text, teacher ed., suppl. ed. 11.95 (*0-7167-2703-X*) W H Freeman.

— Molecular Cell Biology. 3rd ed. (C). 1995. pap. text, student ed. 27.95 (*0-7167-2672-6*) W H Freeman.

Lodish, H., jt. auth. see Darnell, J. E.

Lodish, Harvey. Molecular Cell Biology, Vol. 1. 1995. 75.95 (*0-7167-3686-1*) W H Freeman.

***Lodish, Harvey, et al.** Molecular Cell Biology. 4th ed. (C). 1999. 69.00 (*0-7167-3706-X*, Pub. by W H Freeman) VHPS.

***Lodish, Leonard M.** Entrepreneurial Marketing. 240p. 2000. text 29.95 (*0-471-38244-2*) Wiley.

Lodish, Richard. A Child in the Principal's Office: Laughing & Learning in the Schoolhouse. LC 95-21432. (Illus.). 152p. 1995. pap. 21.95 (*0-8039-6382-3*) Corwin Pr.

— A Child in the Principal's Office: Laughing & Learning in the Schoolhouse. LC 92-21432. (Illus.). 152p. 1995. 49.95 (*0-8039-6381-5*) Corwin Pr.

Lodl, Ann & Longguan, Zhang, eds. Enterprise Crime: Asian & Global Perspectives. LC 92-28793. 190p. 1992. pap. 14.95 (*0-942511-60-3*) OICJ.

Lodo, Venerable L. Bardo Teachings: The Way of Death & Rebirth. 2nd ed. Clark, Nancy & Parke, Caroline, eds. LC 87-20663. 93p. (C). 1987. reprint ed. pap. 8.95 (*0-937938-60-2*) Snow Lion Pubns.

— The Quintessence of the Animate & Inanimate: A Discourse on the Holy Dharma. Clark, Nancy & Parke, Caroline, eds. LC 85-2290. (Illus.). 238p. 1985. pap. 11.95 (*0-910165-01-7*) KDK Pubns.

Lodoiska, Emmanuel R. & Plummer, Susan E., eds. Introduction to Mental Health Nursing: A Workbook. 144p. (Orig.). 1997. pap. text, wbk. ed. 24.95 (*1-56593-763-5*, 1484) Singular Publishing.

Lodro, Geshe G. Calm Abiding & Special Insight: Achieving Spiritual Transformation Through Meditation. Hopkins, Jeffrey, ed. LC 98-34493. Orig. Title: Walking Through Walls: A Presentation of Tibetan Meditation. 334p. 1998. pap. 19.95 (*1-55939-110-3*) Snow Lion Pubns.

— Walking Through Walls: A Presentation of Tibetan Meditation. Hopkins, Jeffrey et al, eds. LC 92-16321. 448p. 1992. 35.00 (*1-55939-008-5*); pap. 19.95 (*1-55939-004-2*) Snow Lion Pubns.

Lods, Adolphe. Israel, from Its Beginning to the Middle of the Eighth Century. Hooke, Samuel H., tr. LC 75-41180. 1948. 45.00 (*0-404-14569-8*) AMS Pr.

— Prophets & the Rise of Judaism. Hooke, Samuel H., tr. LC 77-109772. (Illus.). 378p. (C). 1971. reprint ed. lib. bdg. 69.50 (*0-8371-4262-8*, LOPR, Greenwood Pr) Greenwood.

Lodwick, David, jt. auth. see Norman, Robert I.

Lodwick, John. Raiders from the Sea. (Illus.). 256p. 1990. 24.95 (*1-55750-525-X*) Naval Inst Pr.

Lodwick, Kathleen L. Crusaders Against Opium: Protestant Missionaries in China, 1847-1917. LC 95-11136. (Illus.). 232p. 1996. 32.50 (*0-8131-1924-3*) U Pr of Ky.

— Educating the Women of Hainan: The Career of Margaret Moninger in China, 1915-1942. LC 94-29319. (Illus.). 272p. 1994. 35.00 (*0-8131-1882-4*) U Pr of Ky.

Lodwick, Kathleen L., ed. The Chinese Recorder Index: A Guide to Christian Missions in Asia, 1867-1941, 2 vols. LC 85-26125. 1200p. 1986. 150.00 (*0-8420-2250-3*) Scholarly Res Inc.

Lodwick, Robert C., ed. Remembering the Future: The Challenge of the Churches in Europe. LC 94-39489. (Illus.). 128p. (Orig.). 1995. pap. 8.95 (*0-377-00290-9*) Friendship Pr.

Lody, M. E., ed. see White, Betty W.

Lodz, J., jt. ed. see Lawrynowicz, Julian.

Lodziak, Conrad. Manipulating Needs. (C). 49.95 (*0-7453-0853-8*, Pub. by Pluto GBR); pap. 15.95 (*0-7453-0854-6*, Pub. by Pluto GBR) Stylus Pub VA.

Lodziak, Conrad & Tatman, Jeremy. Andre Gorz: A Critical Reader. LC 96-51821. (Modern European Thinkers Ser.). 168p. (C). 1997. 45.00 (*0-7453-0786-8*, Pub. by Pluto GBR); pap. 17.95 (*0-7453-0787-6*, Pub. by Pluto GBR) Stylus Pub VA.

Loe, Gerald M. The Energy Wheel: How to Move Things with Your Mind. 1995. pap. text 7.95 (*1-56087-008-7*) Top Mtn Pub.

— The Gift of Healing: How to Receive & Use Your Natural Healing Powers. LC 90-41304. (Illus.). 256p. 1996. reprint ed. pap. 16.95 (*0-9648123-0-4*) Oakwood Pubng.

Loe, H. & Kleinman, D. V., eds. Dental Plaque Control Measures & Oral Hygiene Practices. 344p. 1986. pap. 60.00 (*0-947946-48-9*) OUP.

Loe, K. F. & Goto, E. DC Flux Parametron. (Series in Computer Science: Vol. 6). 216p. 1986. text 47.00 (*9971-5-0113-9*) World Scientific Pub.

Loe, K. F., jt. auth. see Wang, P. Z.

Loe, K. F., jt. ed. see Goto, E.

Loe, Kelley, jt. auth. see Neuberger, Richard L.

Loe, Mary, jt. ed. see Brottman, May.

Loe, Theresa. The Herbal Home Companion. LC 96-213928. 256p. 1996. pap. 14.00 (*1-57566-085-7*, Knsington) Kensgtn Pub Corp.

— The Herbal Home Companion. LC 99-47732. 2000. 7.99 (*0-517-20554-8*) Random Hse Value.

Loeb. Royalty Only: Do Not Use. 1986. pap. write for info. (*0-316-53057-3*) Little.

Loeb, Arthur L. Color & Symmetry. LC 78-13084. 196p. 1979. reprint ed. 26.50 (*0-88275-745-8*) Krieger.

— Concepts & Images: Visual Mathematics. (Design Science Collections). (Illus.). xi, 228p. 1992. 58.50 (*0-8176-3620-X*) Birkhauser.

— Space Structures: Their Harmony & Counterpoint. 192p. 1976. pap. text 35.50 (*0-201-04651-2*) Addison-Wesley.

— Space Structures: Their Harmony & Counterpoint. 5th rev. ed. (Design Science Collections). (Illus.). xviii, 169p. 1991. 29.50 (*0-8176-3588-2*) Birkhauser.

Loeb, Ben F., Jr. Animal Control Law for North Carolina Local Governments. 3rd ed. LC 97-139783. (Illus.). 208p. 1997. pap. text 24.00 (*1-56011-300-6*) Institute Government.

— Eminent Domain Procedure for North Carolina Local Governments. 2nd ed. 121p. 1998. pap. text 23.00 (*1-56011-311-1*) Institute Government.

— Fire Protection Law in North Carolina. 5th ed. 216p. (C). 1993. pap. text 9.50 (*1-56011-251-4*, 93.04) Institute Government.

— Wildlife & Boating Regulation: Local Legislation. LC 98-226186. 62p. (C). 1998. ring bd. 38.00 (*1-56011-328-6*) Institute Government.

***Loeb, Ben F., Jr. & Drennan, James C.** Motor Vehicle Law & the Law of Impaired Driving in North Carolina. (C). 2000. pap. 16.50 (*1-56011-360-X*) Institute Government.

— Motor Vehicle Law & the Law of Impaired Driving in North Carolina. (C). 2000. cd-rom. write for info. (*1-56011-383-9*) Institute Government.

Loeb, Ben F., Jr., jt. auth. see Rubin, John.

Loeb, Benjamin S., jt. auth. see Seaborg, Glenn Theodore.

Loeb, C. W., jt. ed. see Fieschi, C.

Loeb, Carl. The Black Art of Cooking. 127p. 1993. reprint ed. spiral bd. 12.00 (*0-7873-0568-5*) Hlth Research.

— The Black Art of Cooking: How Cooked Food Produces Disease, an Introduction to the Unfired Diet. 1991. lib. bdg. 79.95 (*0-8490-4547-9*) Gordon Pr.

Loeb, Carol. On My Own: Fix-It! Clean-It! large type ed. (Illus.). 63p. (Orig.). (YA). (gr. 9 up). 1996. pap. text 9.95 (*1-890524-02-6*) On My Own.

— On My Own: Getting (& Keeping) a Job. large type ed. (Illus.). (Orig.). (YA). (gr. 9 up). 1996. pap. text 9.95 (*1-890524-01-8*) On My Own.

— On My Own: How-To Moving Out - Moving On. large type ed. (Illus.). (Orig.). (YA). (gr. 9 up). 1996. pap. text 9.95 (*1-890524-03-4*) On My Own.

— On My Own: In the Kitchen. large type ed. (Illus.). 70p. (Orig.). (YA). (gr. 9 up). 1996. pap. text 9.95 (*1-890524-04-2*) On My Own.

— On My Own: Living Well on Not Much Money. large type ed. (Illus.). 69p. (Orig.). (YA). (gr. 9 up). 1996. pap. text 9.95 (*1-890524-00-X*) On My Own.

— On My Own: Setting up a Small Business. large type ed. (Illus.). 83p. (Orig.). (YA). (gr. 9 up). 1996. pap. text 9.95 (*1-890524-05-0*) On My Own.

Loeb, David. Fantasias for 8, 9, 10, 11 & 12 Viols. (Contemporary Consort Ser.: Vol. 31). 37p. (Orig.). 1997. pap. 21.00 (*1-56571-148-3*) PRB Prods.

— Nine Fantasias for the Japanese Consort (Three to Six Viols) (Contemporary Consort Ser.: No. 13). ii, 45p. 1991. 12.00 (*1-56571-015-0*) PRB Prods.

— Six Fantasias on Sephardic Themes for Solo Bass Viol. (Contemporary Instrumental Ser.: No. 6). 12p. 1992. pap. text 9.00 (*1-56571-058-4*, CI006) PRB Prods.

Loeb, David & Brown, David W. How to Change Your Name in California 6.2. (Illus.). 144p. 1995. pap. 24.95 (*0-87337-258-1*) Nolo com.

Loeb, David V. How to Change Your Name in California. 8th ed. LC 99-21567. 144p. 1999. pap. 34.95 (*0-87337-523-8*) Nolo com.

***Loeb, David V. & Brown, David Wayne.** How to Change Your Name in California. 9th ed. LC 00-39430. 2000. pap. write for info. (*0-87337-598-X*) Nolo com.

Loeb, Donald & Wightman, Kimberly J., contrib. by. A Harvest of Memories from Dunkirk. 1998. pap. 9.99 (*1-888911-06-9*) Benson Smythe.

Loeb, E. M. The Eastern Kuksu Cult. fac. ed. (University of California Publications in American Archaeology & Ethnology: Vol. 33: 2). 99p. (C). 1933. reprint ed. pap. text 11.25 (*1-55567-289-2*) Coyote Press.

— History & Traditions of Niue. (BMB Ser.). 1969. reprint ed. 35.00 (*0-527-02135-0*) Periodicals Srv.

— The Western Kuksu Cult. fac. ed. (University of California Publications in American Archaeology & Ethnology: Vol. 33: 1). 143p. (C). 1932. reprint ed. pap. text 15.63 (*1-55567-288-4*) Coyote Press.

Loeb, Edwin. Pomo Folkways. fac. ed. (University of California Publications in American Archaeology & Ethnology: Vol. 19: 2). 265p. (C). 1926. reprint ed. pap. text 28.13 (*1-55567-236-1*) Coyote Press.

Loeb, Edwin M. Blood Sacrifice Complex. LC 24-4020. (American Anthropological Association Memoirs Ser.: No. 30). 1924. pap. 25.00 (*0-527-00529-0*) Periodicals Srv.

Loeb, Evelyn. Dreidelcat. LC 98-140893. (Charming Petites Ser.). (Illus.). 64p. 1997. 4.95 (*0-88088-819-9*) Peter Pauper.

***Loeb, Evelyn.** Reflections: A Gold Guided Journal. (Guided Journals). (Illus.). 128p. 2000. 14.99 (*0-88088-228-X*) Peter Pauper.

***Loeb, Evelyn & Kaufman, Lois L.** Yule Always Be My Friend. gif. ed. (Illus.). 64p. 1999. 4.95 (*0-88088-105-4*) Peter Pauper.

Loeb, Evelyn, jt. auth. see Darling, Wendy.

Loeb, Frances L., jt. auth. see Loeb, John L.

Loeb, G. I., jt. auth. see Schrader, M. E.

Loeb, Gerald E. & Gans, Carl. Electromyography for Experimentalists. LC 85-28934. (Illus.). xx, 394p. 1986. pap. text 28.00 (*0-226-49015-7*) U Ch Pr.

— Electromyography for Experimentalists. LC 85-28934. (Illus.). xx, 394p. 1999. lib. bdg. 72.00 (*0-226-49014-9*) U Ch Pr.

Loeb, Gerald M. The Battle for Investment Survival. LC 95-52632. 320p. 1996. 24.95 (*0-471-13297-7*) Wiley.

— The Battle for Investment Survival. LC 88-81705. 320p. 1988. reprint ed. pap. 18.00 (*0-87034-084-0*) Fraser Pub Co.

— Battle for Stock Market Profits. LC 70-130483. 1974. 7.95 (*0-671-20751-2*) S&S Trade.

Loeb, Harold. Life in a Technocracy: What It Might Be Like. (Utopianism & Communitarianism Ser.). 230p. (C). 1996. pap. 17.95 (*0-8156-0380-0*, LOLTP) Syracuse U Pr.

Loeb, Helen M., jt. auth. see Woolever, Kristin R.

Loeb, Isidor. Legal Property Relations of Married Parties: A Study in Comparative Legislation. LC 68-56668. (Columbia University Studies in the Social Sciences Ser.: No. 34). reprint ed. 29.50 (*0-404-51034-5*) AMS Pr.

Loeb, J., jt. auth. see Bertin, J.

Loeb, J. David. Jack Rabbit Jack. (Illus.). 24p. (Orig.). (J). (ps-5). 1994. pap. 4.95 (*1-885744-01-3*) Otter Creek.

— Mandy's Backyard. LC 97-162667. (Illus.). 32p. (Orig.). (J). (gr. k-4). 1997. pap. 5.95 (*1-885744-04-8*) Otter Creek.

— The Pool on Otter Creek. (Illus.). 28p. (Orig.). (J). (ps-5). 1994. pap. 5.95 (*1-885744-00-5*) Otter Creek.

— The Rocking Horse. (Illus.). 32p. (J). (gr. k-4). 1997. pap. 5.95 (*1-885744-08-0*) Otter Creek.

— The Train Ride. (Illus.). 24p. (Orig.). (J). (ps-3). 1994. pap. 3.95 (*1-885744-02-1*) Otter Creek.

Loeb, Jacques. Comparative Physiology of the Brain & Comparative Psychology. LC 73-2973. (Classics in Psychology Ser.). 1978. reprint ed. 26.95 (*0-405-05146-8*) Ayer.

— Forced Movements, Tropisms & Animal Conduct. (Illus.). 1990. 12.50 (*0-8446-4776-4*) Peter Smith.

Loeb, James, tr. see Couat, A.

Loeb, James, tr. see Croiset, Maurice.

Loeb, James E. City Risk Kit. 500p. 1991. 335.00 (*0-9628164-4-2*) Indep Risk Insur Mgmt.

Loeb, Jane W., jt. auth. see Ferber, Marianne A.

Loeb, Jeph. Batman: Haunted Knight. Kahan, Bob, ed. LC 97-141361. (Illus.). 192p. 1996. pap. 12.95 (*1-56389-273-1*, Pub. by DC Comics) Time Warner.

— Batman: Long Halloween. LC 99-218572. (Illus.). 368p. 1998. 29.95 (*1-56389-427-0*, Pub. by DC Comics) Time Warner.

***Loeb, Jeph.** Batman: The Long Halloween. LC 99-218572. (Illus.). 368p. 1999. pap. text 19.95 (*1-56389-469-6*, Pub. by DC Comics) Time Warner.

Loeb, Jeph. Superman for All Seasons. (Illus.). 208p. 1999. 24.95 (*1-56389-528-5*, Pub. by DC Comics) Time Warner.

***Loeb, Jeph.** Superman for All Seasons. (Illus.). 208p. 2000. pap. 14.95 (*1-56389-529-3*) DC Comics.

Loeb, Jeph. The Ultimate X-Man. (Illus.). 96p. 1995. pap. 8.95 (*0-7851-0133-0*) Marvel Entrprs.

— Wolverine - Gambit: Victims. 96p. 1997. pap. text 12.95 (*0-7851-0258-2*) Marvel Entrprs.

— X-Men: Dawn of the Age Apocalypse. (Illus.). 96p. 1996. pap. 8.95 (*0-7851-0180-2*) Marvel Entrprs.

Loeb, Jo. Cathletics. 1990. 4.98 (*0-89009-728-3*) Bk Sales Inc.

Loeb, John L. & Loeb, Frances L. All in a Lifetime: A Personal Memoir. LC 96-94451. (Illus.). 312p. 1997. 39.95 (*0-9652569-0-1*) J L Loeb.

Loeb, Judy, ed. Feminist Collage: Educating Women in the Visual Arts. LC 79-15468. 335p. reprint ed. pap. 103.90 (*0-7837-1196-4*, 204172600023) Bks Demand.

Loeb, Julian. Return from Las Vegas. 302p. (Orig.). 1996. pap. write for info. (*1-57502-269-9*, PO712) Morris Pubng.

Loeb, Karen. Jump Rope Queen: And Other Stories. LC 92-64073. (Minnesota Voices Project Ser.: Vol. 58). 139p. (Orig.). 1993. pap. 5.00 (*0-89823-145-0*) New Rivers Pr.

Loeb, L., ed. Outcaste: Jewish Life in Southern Iran. (Library of Anthropology). xxvi, 328p. 1977. text 117.00 (*0-677-04530-1*) Gordon & Breach.

Loeb, Larry. Secure Electronic Transactions: Introduction & Technical Reference. LC 97-34127. 313p. 1998. 75.00 incl. cd-rom (*0-89006-992-1*) Artech Hse.

Loeb, Lawrence A., jt. auth. see Fry, Michael.

Loeb, Leonard L., et al. System Book for Family Law: A Forms & Procedures Handbook, 2 vols. 4th ed. 900p. 1993. ring bd. 165.00 incl. disk (*0-945574-00-2*) State Bar WI.

Loeb, Leonore A., et al, eds. Violence & the Prevention of Violence. LC 94-28007. (Illus.). 248p. 1995. 62.95 (*0-275-94873-0*, Praeger Pubs) Greenwood.

Loeb, Lisa & Nine Stories. Tails. 88p. 1996. otabind 16.95 (*0-7935-6077-2*) H Leonard.

Loeb, Lori A. Consuming Angels: Advertising & Victorian Women. LC 93-46094. (Illus.). 240p. 1994. text 45.00 (*0-19-508596-5*) OUP.

Loeb, M. Vonnegut's Duty Dance with Death: Theme & Structure in Slaughterhouse Five. (Umea Studies in the Humanities: No. 26). 138p. (Orig.). 1979. pap. 32.50 (*91-7174-031-7*, Pub. by Umea U Bibl) Coronet Bks.

Loeb, Marcia. Art Deco Designs & Motifs. (Pictorial Archive Ser.). (Illus.). 75p. (Orig.). 1972. pap. 6.95 (*0-486-22826-6*) Dover.

L

An Asterisk (*) at the beginning of an entry indicates that the title is appearing for the first time.

L

— New Art Deco Alphabets. LC 74-29015. (Pictorial Archive Ser.). (Illus.). 75p. (Orig.). 1975. pap. 5.95 (*0-486-23149-6*) Dover.

Loeb, Marshall. 52 Weeks to Financial Security: The First Edition. 288p. 2000. write for info. (*0-316-55699-8*) Little.

— Loeb's Money Guide 1991. 1990. pap. 14.95 (*0-316-53071-9*) Little.

***Loeb, Marshall.** Marshall Loeb's 52 Weeks to Financial Fitness. 2000. 25.00 (*0-8129-3337-0*, Times Business) Crown Pub Group.

Loeb, Marshall. Marshall Loeb's Lifetime Financial Strategies: The Ultimate Guide to Future Wealth & Security. LC 95-17011. (Illus.). 880p. 1996. 27.95 (*0-316-53075-1*, Pub. by Bulfinch Pr) Little.

— Marshall Loeb's Lifetime Financial Strategies: Your Ultimate Guide to Future Wealth & Security. 1996. 27.95 (*0-614-15440-5*) Little.

— Marshall Loeb's Money Guide, 1989. rev. ed. 512p. 1988. pap. 12.95 (*0-316-53067-0*) Little.

— Marshall Loeb's Money Guide, 1990, Vol. 1. 1989. pap. 13.95 (*0-316-53064-6*) Little.

— Money Guide '92. 1991. pap. 14.95 (*0-316-53072-7*) Little.

***Loeb, Marshall & Kindel, Stephen.** Leadership for Dummies. (For Dummies (Lifestyles) Ser.). 1999. audio 12.00 (*0-694-52221-X*) HarperAudio.

Loeb, Marshall & Kindel, Stephen. Leadership for Dummies. (For Dummies Ser.). 384p. 1999. pap. 19.99 (*0-7645-5176-0*, Dummies Trade Pr) IDG Bks.

Loeb, Michel. Noise & Human Efficiency. LC 85-16781. (Wiley Series on Studies in Human Performance). (Illus.). 283p. reprint ed. pap. 87.80 (*0-7837-4409-9*, 204415200012) Bks Demand.

Loeb, Nackey S. New Hampshire Life. (Illus.). 112p. Date not set. write for info. (*0-9648921-0-3*) Union Leader.

Loeb, P. A., jt. auth. see Hurd, A. E.

Loeb, Paul. Smarter Than You Think: A Revolutionary Approach to Teaching & Understanding Your Dog in Just a Few Hours. LC 96-49829. 272p. 1997. 22.00 (*0-671-00172-8*, PB Hardcover) PB.

— Supertraining Your Dog. 1990. mass mkt. 6.50 (*0-671-73209-9*) S&S Trade.

— You Can Train Your Cat. 1990. mass mkt. 5.50 (*0-671-73906-9*) PB.

Loeb, Paul & Hlavacek, Suzanne. The Heart of the Matter: Making Connections Between You, Your Dog & Your Cat. LC 99-26926. 224p. 1999. 23.00 (*0-671-02790-5*, PB Hardcover) PB.

Loeb, Paul & Hvlacek, Suzanne. Smarter Than You Think. 272p. 1998. per. 14.00 (*0-671-02328-4*, PB Trade Paper) PB.

Loeb, Paul R. Generation at the Crossroads: Apathy & Action on the American Campus. 460p. (C). 1995. pap. 17.95 (*0-8135-2256-0*) Rutgers U Pr.

— Generation at the Crossroads: Apathy & Action on the American Campus. LC 94-16186. 420p. (C). 1995. reprint ed. 24.95 (*0-8135-2144-0*) Rutgers U Pr.

***Loeb, Paul R.** Soul of a Citizen: Living with Conviction in a Cynical Time. 2nd ed. LC 99-14058. 368p. 1999. pap. 15.95 (*0-312-20435-3*, St Martin Griffin) St Martin.

***Loeb, Peter A. & Wolff, Manfred P. H.** Nonstandard Analysis for the Working Mathematician. LC 00-30655. (Mathematics & Its Applications Ser.). 2000. write for info. (*0-7923-6340-X*) Kluwer Academic.

Loeb, Peter D., et al. Causes & Deterrents of Transportation Accidents: An Analysis by Mode. LC 94-8541. 240p. 1994. 65.00 (*0-89930-806-6*, Quorum Bks) Greenwood.

***Loeb, Richard H., Jr.** Wolf in Chef's Clothing, 50th Anniversary. 4th ed. (Illus.). 150p. 2000. pap. 16.95 (*1-57284-035-8*) Surrey Bks.

Loeb, Sal, ed. The Garden Book. (Illus.). 136p. (Orig.). write for info. (*0-318-61323-9*) Corpus Christi Area.

Loeb, Sorel Goldberg & Kadden, Barbara Binder. Teaching Torah: A Treasury of Insights & Activities. LC 97-71132. 1997. pap. 29.95 (*0-86705-041-1*) A R E Pub.

Loeb, Walter F. & Quimby, Fred W. The Clinical Chemistry of Laboratory Animals. 2nd ed. LC 98-32441. 753p. 1999. 175.00 (*1-56032-717-0*) Hemisp Pub.

Loebbecke, jt. auth. see Arens.

Loebbecke, James K. The Auditor: An Instructional Novella. LC 98-5808. 120p. (C). 1998. pap. text 23.00 (*0-13-079976-9*) P-H.

Loebbecke, James K., jt. auth. see Arens, Alvin A.

Loebel & Mueller, Peter. Lexikon der Datenverarbeitung. (GER.). 704p. 1975. 165.00 (*0-8288-5918-3*, M7264) Fr & Eur.

Loebel, Arnold B. Chemical Problem-Solving by Dimensional Analysis, 3 vols. 3rd ed. LC 86-8913. 448p. (C). 1986. pap. 47.96 (*0-395-35678-4*) HM.

Loebel, Arnold B. Chemistry: Concepts & Calculations. LC 77-26720. 576p. reprint ed. pap. 178.60 (*0-608-10835-9*, 202250800027) Bks Demand.

Loebell, E., ed. International Association of Logopedics & Phoniatrics, Abstracts: 22nd World Congress, Hannover, August, 1992. (Journal: Folia Phoniatrica: Vol. 44, No. 1-2, 1992). 100p. 1992. pap. 63.50 (*3-8055-5652-7*) S Karger.

— International Association of Logopedics & Phoniatrics, Main Reports: 22nd World Congress, Hannover, August, 1992. (Journal: Folia Phoniatrica: Vol. 44, No. 3-4, 1992). (Illus.). 84p. 1992. pap. 63.50 (*3-8055-5653-5*) S Karger.

Loebell, E., ed. see International Association of Logopedics & Phoniatr.

Loebell, E., ed. see International Congress of Logopedics & Phoniatrics.

Loebelson, Andrew. How to Profit in Contract Design. (Interior Design Bks.). 192p. 1983. text 32.50 (*0-685-06953-2*) Inter Design.

Loebenstein, Gad, et al, eds. Virus & Virus-Like Diseases of Bulb & Flower Crops. LC 95-18716. 556p. 1996. 265.00 (*0-471-95293-1*) Wiley.

Loeber, D. A., ed. Ruling Communist Parties & Their Status under Law. 1986. lib. bdg. 232.50 (*90-247-3209-3*) Kluwer Academic.

Loeber, Dietrich A., et al, eds. Regional Identity under Soviet Rule: The Case of the Baltic States. (Illus.). xx, 469p. 1989. 50.00 (*0-685-29788-8*) Assn Advan Baltic Studies.

Loeber, Dietrich A., et al. Regional Identity under Soviet Rule: The Case of the Baltic States. LC 89-81415. (Publications of the Association for the Advancement of Baltic Studies). xxii, 470 p. 1990. write for info. (*0-9624906-0-1*) Assn Advan Baltic Studies.

Loeber, Rolf & Farrington, David P. Serious & Violent Juvenile Offenders: Risk Factors & Successful Interventions. LC 97-33930. 1998. 32.50 (*0-7619-1275-4*) Sage.

Loeber, Rolf, et al. Antisocial Behavior & Mental Health Problems: Explanatory Factors in Childhood & Adolescence. LC 97-38123. 350p. 1998. write for info. (*0-8058-2956-3*) L Erlbaum Assocs.

Loebl, Suzanne. At the Mercy of Strangers: Growing up on the Edge of the Holocaust. LC 97-5154. (Illus.). 182p. 1997. 24.95 (*0-935553-23-1*) Pacifica Military.

— The Wish Ring. LC 96-69776. (Illus.). 32p. (J). (gr. k-3). 1997. 14.95 (*1-887734-14-7*) Star Brght Bks.

Loebl, Suzanne & Spratto, George R. The Nurse's Drug Handbook. 6th ed. 1991. pap. 33.95 (*0-8273-4527-5*) Delmar.

Loeblein, John M. Memoirs of Kelly Field, 1917-1918. 61p. 1974. pap. text 23.95 (*0-89126-010-2*) MA-AH Pub.

Loeblich, A. B., et al. Studies in Foraminifera. 1970. 42.00 (*0-934454-75-2*) Lubrecht & Cramer.

Loeblich, Alfred R., Jr. & Tappan, Helen. Treatise on Invertebrate Paleontology Pt. C: Protista 2: Sarcodina, Chiefly "Thecamoebians" & Foraminiferida, 2 vols. Moore, Raymond C., ed. LC 53-12913. 936p. 1964. 43.00 (*0-8137-3003-1*) Geol Soc.

Loebs, William, jt. auth. see Kieth, Sam.

Loecher, Barbara, jt. auth. see Bascom, Lionel C.

Loecher, Joanne. Taking Time Together: Faith Experiences for Teens & Parents. (Illus.). 56p. 1996. pap. 12.95 (*0-88489-386-3*) St Marys.

***Loeck, Joyce, et al.** Living My Life with God. (Illus.). 2000. pap. write for info. (*0-9679793-0-7*) Jesus Cares.

Loeckx, Jacques & Sieber, Kurt. Foundations of Program Verific. 2nd ed. LC 86-19008. (Computer Science Ser.). 240p. 1987. 180.00 (*0-471-91282-4*) Wiley.

Loeckx, Jacques, et al. Specification of Abstract Data Types. LC 96-32367. 272p. 1996. 100.00 (*0-471-95067-X*) Wiley.

***Loedel, Peter H.** Deutsche Mark Politics: Germany in the European Monetary System. LC 98-47375. 264p. 1999. lib. bdg. 55.00 (*1-55587-835-0*) L Rienner.

Loedel, Peter H., jt. ed. see McKenzie, Mary M.

Loeding, Wilfried. The ABCs of Cockatiels. (Illus.). 96p. 1986. 9.95 (*0-86622-836-5*, KW-150) TFH Pubns.

Loedolff, Jeanette, jt. auth. see Argent, Sally.

Loef, Hans-Edi, ed. see Fisher, Irving.

Loeffelbein, Bob. Offbeat Golf: A Swingin' Guide to a Worldwide Obsession. LC 98-11158. (Illus.). 192p. 1998. pap. 17.95 (*1-891661-02-7*, 1-02-7) Snta Monica.

Loeffelbein, Robert L. Knight Life: Jousting in the United States. LC 78-53984. (Illus.). (J). 1978. pap. 4.95 (*0-9601258-1-7*) Golden Owl Pub.

— The Recreation Handbook: 342 Games & Other Activities for Teams & Individuals. LC 92-50310. (Illus.). 255p. (J). 1992. pap. 30.00 (*0-89950-744-1*) McFarland & Co.

Loeffelbein, Robert L. The United States Flagbook: Everything about Old Glory. LC 96-20026. (Illus.). 247p. 1996. pap. 35.00 (*0-7864-0156-7*) McFarland & Co.

Loeffelbein, Robert L., ed. Script Tease: The Treasury of Surprise Endings. (Illus.). 192p. (Orig.). 1979. pap. 4.95 (*0-9601258-2-5*) Golden Owl Pub.

***Loeffelholz, John.** Woodworking Plans for a Hillside Table Lamp: Inspired by the Work of Frank Lloyd Wright. Calvert, Stephen, ed. 45p. 2000. spiral bd. 22.00 (*0-9622783-3-5*) Cottonwood Hill Pub.

Loeffelholz, M. Experimental Lives: Women & Literature, 1900-1945. (Women & Literature Ser.). 250p. (Orig.). 1992. pap. 13.95 (*0-8057-8977-4*); text 22.95 (*0-8057-8976-6*) Macmillan.

Loeffelholz, Mary. Dickinson & the Boundaries of Feminist Theory. 192p. 1991. pap. text 13.95 (*0-252-06175-6*) U of Ill Pr.

— Experimental Lives: Women & Literature, 1900-1945. 1995. pap. 12.95 (*0-8057-8574-4*, Twyne) Mac Lib Ref.

***Loeffke, Bernard.** From Warrior to Healer: 99 True Stories from a General to His Children. 1998. 12.95 (*1-930622-00-7*) Pacific Institute Inc.

Loeffler, Carl & Tong, Darlene, eds. Performance Anthology: Source Book of California Performance Art. (Illus.). 532p. 1990. pap. 24.95 (*0-86719-366-2*) Last Gasp.

Loeffler, Carl E. & Tong, Darlene, eds. Performance Anthology: Source Book for a Decade of California Performance Art. LC 79-55054. (Contemporary Documents Ser.: Vol. 1). (Illus.). 500p. 1980. pap. 15.95 (*0-931818-01-X*) Contemporary Arts.

Loeffler, Charles M. Charles Martin Loeffler: Selected Songs with Chamber Accompaniment. Knight, Ellen, ed. (Recent Researches in American Music Ser.: No. RRAM16). (Illus.). 99, xxip. 1988. pap. 40.00 (*0-89579-223-0*) A-R Eds.

Loeffler, Chris, jt. auth. see Hunsberger, Eydie M.

Loeffler, Donald L. An Analysis of the Treatment of the Homosexual Character in Dramas Produced in the New York Theater from 1950-1968. LC 75-14262. (Homosexuality Ser.). 1975. reprint ed. 19.95 (*0-405-07398-4*) Ayer.

Loeffler, F. J., ed. see Materials Handling Conference Staff.

Loeffler, H., ed. Neue Therapeutische Strategien in der Haematologischen Onkologie. (Beitraege Zur Onkologie, Contributions to Oncology Ser.: Vol. 36). (Illus.). vi, 115p. 1989. 47.00 (*3-8055-5046-4*) S Karger.

***Loeffler, H. & Rastetter, J. W.** Atlas of Clinical Hematology. 5th ed. Telger, T., tr. (Illus.). 350p. 1999. 199.00 (*3-540-65085-7*) Spr-Verlag.

Loeffler, Jack. Headed Upstream: Interviews with Iconoclasts. LC 89-35707. (Illus.). 216p. (Orig.). 1989. pap. 10.95 (*0-943173-21-3*, Pub. by Western Edge Pr) Mountain Pr.

— Poem & Revolution Before Breakfast: The Life of Edward Abbey. 1993. 25.00 (*0-517-58632-0*, Crown) Crown Pub Group.

Loeffler, Jack, et al. La Musica de los Viejitos. (SPA., Illus.). 192p. 1999. 49.95 (*0-8263-2168-2*) U of NM Pr.

***Loeffler, Jack, et al.** La Musica de los Viejitos: Hispano Folk Music of the Rio Grande del Norte. 192p. 1999. pap. 19.95 (*0-8263-1884-3*) U of NM Pr.

Loeffler, Jane C. The Architecture of Diplomacy: Building America's Embassies. LC 97-45032. (Illus.). 306p. 1998. 27.50 (*1-56898-138-4*) Princeton Arch.

Loeffler, Jay, jt. ed. see Mauch, Peter.

Loeffler, Jay S., jt. auth. see Black, Peter M.

Loeffler, L. L. A Schema Theory Based Analysis of Voter Intent in 1980: Use of a Schema-Model in a Qualitative Choice Estimation. Nelson, M. E., ed. (Illus.). 617p. 1996. 995.00 (*1-56471-004-1*) Annenberg.

Loeffler, L. L., ed. see Nelson, Mark E.

Loeffler, Linda, ed. see Schwartz, Linda.

Loeffler, M., jt. ed. see Wichmann, H. E.

Loeffler, M. P. Oskar Waelterlin: Ein Profil. (GER.). 256p. 1979. 16.95 (*0-8176-1133-9*) Birkhauser.

Loeffler, Margaret, ed. Montessori in Contemporary American Culture. LC 92-523. 298p. (C). 1992. pap. text 26.00 (*0-435-08709-6*, 08709) Heinemann.

***Loeffler, Martha.** Boats in the Night: Knud Dyby's Involvement in the Rescue of the Danish Jews. Nielsen, John Mark, ed. (Illus.). xviii, 140p. 1999. pap. 14.95 (*0-930697-06-5*) Lur Pubns.

Loeffler, Reinhold. Islam in Practice: Religious Beliefs in a Persian Village. LC 87-12175. 312p. (C). 1988. text 67.50 (*0-88706-678-X*); pap. text 23.95 (*0-88706-679-8*) State U NY Pr.

Loeffler, Robert F. Step-by-Step Compo & Mold Making. LC 92-7144. (Illus.). 112p. 1992. 24.95 (*0-9632387-5-2*) LVI Pubns.

— Step by Step Inlay Banding Production. large type ed. LC 97-74306. (Illus.). 110p. 1997. spiral bd. 14.95 (*0-9632387-2-8*) LVI Pubns.

Loeffler, Robert H. A Guide to Preparing Cost-Effective Press Releases. LC 91-36042. (Illus.). 124p. 1993. lib. bdg. 39.95 (*1-56024-141-1*) Haworth Pr.

— A Guide to Preparing Cost-Effective Press Releases. 116p. 1993. pap. 12.95 (*1-56024-882-3*) Haworth Pr.

Loeffler, W., ed. see Sartor, K.

Loehe, Wilhelm. Liturgy for Christian Congregations of the Lutheran Faith. 3rd ed. 157p. 1997. reprint ed. 25.00 (*1-893118-01-0*) J Gerhard Inst.

— Questions & Answers to the Six Parts of Luther's Small Catechism. 2nd ed. Horn, Edward T., tr. from GER. 198p. (YA). 1998. reprint ed. 25.00 (*1-891469-14-2*) Repristination.

Loehe, Wilhelm, et al. Liturgy for Christian Congregations of the Lutheran Faith. Longaker, F. C., tr. from GER. 171p. 1997. reprint ed. 25.00 (*1-891469-12-6*) Repristination.

***Loeher, James.** Stress for Success. 1999. pap. (*0-8129-9059-5*) Random.

Loehle, Craig. On the Shoulders of Giants. 201p. (Orig.). 1994. pap. 9.95 (*0-85398-362-3*) G Ronald Pub.

— Thinking Strategically: For Innovation, Discovery & Problem Solving. LC 96-795. (Illus.). 195p. (C). 1996. pap. 17.95 (*0-521-56841-2*); text 54.95 (*0-521-56058-6*) Cambridge U Pr.

Loehlein, D., jt. ed. see Doelp, R.

Loehlein, Patricia. Management Information Systems: An Information Sourcebook. LC 87-38194. (Sourcebook Series in Business & Management). 232p. 1988. 57.50 (*0-89774-375-X*) Oryx Pr.

Loehlin, James N. Henry V. LC 96-31545. (Shakespeare in Performance Ser.). (Illus.). 192p. 1997. text 79.95 (*0-7190-4623-8*, Pub. by Manchester Univ Pr) St Martin.

Loehlin, Jennifer. From Rugs to Riches: Housework, Consumption & Modernity in Germany. (Illus.). 224p. 1999. 68.00 (*1-85973-284-4*, Pub. by Berg Pubs) NYU Pr.

Loehlin, John C. Genes & Environment in Personality Development. (Individual Differences & Development Ser.: Vol. 2). (Illus.). 160p. (C). 1992. 48.00 (*0-8039-4450-0*); pap. 21.50 (*0-8039-4451-9*) Sage.

— Latent Variable Models: An Introduction to Factor, Path, & Structural Analysis. 2nd ed. 304p. 1992. pap. 27.00 (*0-8058-1084-6*); text 59.95 (*0-8058-1083-8*) L Erlbaum Assocs.

— Latent Variable Models: An Introduction to Factor, Path, & Structural Analysis. 3rd ed. LC 97-48378. 325p. 1998. write for info. (*0-8058-2830-3*); pap. write for info. (*0-8058-2831-1*) L Erlbaum Assocs.

Loehlin, John C. & Nichols, Robert C. Heredity, Environment & Personality: A Study of 850 Sets of Twins. LC 75-33794. 214p. (C). 1976. 17.50 (*0-292-73003-9*) U of Tex Pr.

Loehman, Edna, jt. ed. see Conner, J. Richard.

Loehman, Edna T. & Kilgour, D. Marc, eds. Designing Institutions for Environmental & Resource Management. LC 98-9825. (New Horizons in Environmental Economics Ser.). 392p. 1998. 95.00 (*1-85898-537-4*) E Elgar.

Loehman, Edna T., jt. ed. see Dinar, Ariel.

Loehr, A. Mind over Tennis-Canc. 1982. 13.50 (*0-671-45026-3*) S&S Trade.

Loehr, A., jt. auth. see Jakobi, Gunter.

***Loehr, David & Bills, Joe.** The James Dean Collectors Guide. (Illus.). 384p. 1999. 49.95 (*0-89538-102-8*) L-W Inc.

Loehr, Franklin. The Development of Religion As a Science. LC 83-81796. 92p. (Orig.). 1983. pap. 3.95 (*0-915151-05-7*) Religious Res Pr.

— Diary after Death. rev. ed. LC 83-82486. 148p. 1992. reprint ed. pap. 7.95 (*0-915151-04-9*) Religious Res Pr.

Loehr, Franklin, ed. see Amidon, Horton W.

Loehr, Franklin, ed. see Hussey, Helen & Sherrod, Sandra.

Loehr, Franklin, ed. see Roberts, Helen.

***Loehr, George C.** Evolution of Electrical Power Transmission under Deregulation: Selected Readings. 400p. 1999. pap. 69.95 (*0-7803-4807-9*) Inst Electrical.

Loehr, Hermut. Umkehr und Suende im Hebraeerbrief. (Beiheft zur Zeitschrift fuer die Neuetestamentliche Wissenschaft Ser.: Bd. 73). (GER.). 375p. (C). 1994. lib. bdg. 129.25 (*3-11-014202-3*) De Gruyter.

***Loehr, James & Migdow, Jeffery.** Breathe in, Breathe Out: Inhale Energy & Exhale Stress by Guiding & Controlling Your Breathing. LC 99-38896. 208p. 1999. pap. 14.95 (*0-7370-1611-6*) T-L Custom Pub.

Loehr, James E. The Mental Game. 1990. pap. 11.95 (*0-452-26666-1*, Plume) Dutton Plume.

— The New Toughness Training for Sports. (Illus.). 224p. 1995. pap. 12.95 (*0-452-26998-9*, Plume) Dutton Plume.

— Stress for Success: The Proven Program for Turning Stress into Positive Energy at Work. 288p. 1998. pap. 14.00 (*0-8129-3009-6*, Times Bks) Crown Pub Group.

— Toughness Training for Life: A Revolutionary Program for Maximizing Health, Happiness, & Productivity. 320p. 1994. pap. 12.95 (*0-452-27243-2*, Plume) Dutton Plume.

Loehr, John P. Physics of Strained Quantum Well Lasers. LC 97-38984. 272p. 1998. text 121.00 (*0-7923-8098-3*) Kluwer Academic.

Loehr, Louise M. Willow Pattern China Price Guide. 1992. 4.00 (*0-685-56581-5*) H S Worth.

Loehr, Louise M., jt. auth. see Worth, Veryl M.

Loehr, Mallory. Babe: A Little Pig Goes a Long Way. LC 98-30342. (J). 1999. 7.99 (*0-375-80110-3*) Random.

— Earth Magic. LC 99-43276. 128p. (J). 1999. lib. bdg. 11.99 (*0-679-99218-9*) Random.

— Earth Magic, 3. LC 99-43276. (J). 1999. pap. 3.99 (*0-679-89218-4*) Random.

— Earth Wishes, 4. (J). 2001. pap. 3.99 (*0-679-89219-2*) Random.

— Little Red Barn. (Illus.). (J). 1995. 4.50 (*0-679-86006-1*) Random.

— Trucks. LC 91-75344. (Chunky Shape Bks.). (Illus.). 22p. (J). (ps). 1992. 3.99 (*0-679-83061-8*, Pub. by Random Bks Yng Read) Random.

— Water Wishes. LC 98-49558. (J). 1999. lib. bdg. 11.99 (*0-679-99216-2*, Pub. by Random Bks Yng Read) Random.

— Water Wishes, No. 1. LC 98-49558. 128p. (J). 1999. pap. 3.99 (*0-679-89216-8*, Pub. by Random Bks Yng Read) Random.

— Wind Spell. (Magic Elements Quartet Ser.: No. 3). (Illus.). 128p. (J). (gr. 3-5). 2000. pap. 3.99 (*0-679-89217-6*, Pub. by Random Bks Yng Read); lib. bdg. 11.99 (*0-679-99217-0*, Pub. by Random Bks Yng Read) Random.

Loehr, Raymond, et al. Innovative Site Remediation Technology Vol. 1: Bioremediation. Anderson, William C., ed. LC 93-20786. (Illus.). 288p. 1995. 79.95 (*1-883767-01-6*) Am Acad Environ.

Loehr, Raymond C. Pollution Control for Agriculture. 2nd ed. 1984. text 83.00 (*0-12-455270-6*) Acad Pr.

Loehr, Raymond C., et al, eds. Environmental Availability of Chlorinated Organics, Explosives, & Heavy Metals in Soils. LC 99-10502. (Illus.). 206p. 1999. 47.95 (*1-883767-28-8*) Am Acad Environ.

Loehr, Thomas M., ed. Iron Carriers & Iron Proteins, Vol. 5. LC 89-5667. (Physical Bioinorganic Chemistry Ser.). 533p. 1989. lib. bdg. 180.00 (*0-89573-298-X*, Wiley-VCH) Wiley.

Loehr, William & Sandler, Todd, eds. Public Goods & Public Policy. LC 77-17865. (Comparative Political Economy & Public Policy Ser.: Vol. 3). 240p. reprint ed. pap. 74.40 (*0-608-10136-2*, 202192300026) Bks Demand.

Loehr, Winrich A., ed. see Schaeferdiek, Knut.

Loehrer, Michael C. How to Change a Rotten Attitude: A Manual for Building Virtue & Character in Middle & High School Students. LC 97-21059. (Illus.). 192p. 1997. 69.95 (*0-8039-6649-0*); pap. 32.95 (*0-8039-6650-4*) Corwin Pr.

***Loehrer, Patrick, Sr., ed.** 2001 Year Book of Oncology. (Illus.). 420p. 2001. write for info. (*0-323-01509-3*) Mosby Inc.

— 2002 Year Book of Oncology. (Illus.). 420p. 2002. write for info. (*0-323-01510-7*) Mosby Inc.

— 2000 Year Book of Oncology. (Illus.). 395p. 2000. 89.00 (*0-323-01505-0*) Mosby Inc.

Loehry, H. The Oral Method of Latin Teaching. (C). 1982. pap. text 55.00 (*0-900269-10-3*, Pub. by Old Vicarage) St Mut.

Loeillet, Jean-Baptiste. Werken voor Clavecimbel. (Illus.). 1973. pap. 20.00 (*0-8450-0106-X*) Broude.

An Asterisk (*) at the beginning of an entry indicates that the title is appearing for the first time.

Loellgen, H., ed. Oberrheinisches Kardiologen-Symposium, Freiburg, May, 1982: Journal: Cardiology, Vol. 70, Suppl. 1, 1983. (Illus.). iv, 140p. 1983. pap. 41.75 (*3-8055-3688-7*) S Karger.

Loellgen, H. & Mellerowicz, H., eds. Progress in Ergometry: Quality Control & Test Criteria, Fifth International Seminar on Ergometry. (Illus.). 260p. 1984. 54.95 (*0-387-13570-7*) Spr-Verlag.

Loemker, Leroy E., ed. Gottfried Wilhelm Leibniz: Philosophical Papers & Letters. (Synthese Historical Library: No. 2). 1975. pap. text 72.00 (*90-277-0693-X*); lib. bdg. 141.50 (*90-277-0008-7*, Pub. by Kluwer Academic) Kluwer Academic.

Loen, Johann M. Von, see Von Loen, Johann M.

Loen, Raymond O. Superior Supervision: The Ten Percent Solution. 171p. 1994. 20.95 (*0-02-919091-6*) Jossey-Bass.

***Loenen, T. & Rodrigues, P. R.** Non-Discrimination Law: Comparative Perspectives. LC 99-29148. 464p. 1999. 111.00 (*90-411-1063-1*) Kluwer Law Intl.

Loengard, John. Georgia O'Keefe at Ghost Ranch. (Illus.). 80p. 1995. 35.00 (*1-55670-423-2*) Stewart Tabori & Chang.

— Life Classic Photographs: A Personal Interpretation Expanded Edition with New Photographs. (Illus.). 200p. 1996. pap. 19.95 (*0-8212-2263-5*, Pub. by Bulfinch Pr) Little.

— Life Photographers: What They Saw. LC 98-14442. (Illus.). 456p. (gr. 8). 1998. 35.00 (*0-8212-2518-9*) Little.

— Speaking for the Negative. LC 94-14301. (Illus.). 96p. 1994. 29.45 (*1-55970-282-6*, Pub. by Arcade Pub Inc) Time Warner.

Loengard, John, photos by. Georgia O'Keeffe at Ghost Ranch. (Illus.). 80p. 1999. 14.95 (*3-8238-9965-1*) te Neues.

Loening, Kurt L., jt. ed. see Sonneveld, Helmi B.

Loening, Stefan A., jt. ed. see Culp, David A.

Loening, Thomas C. The Reconciliation Agreement of 403/402 B. C. in Athens: Its Content & Application. LC 88-155333. (Hermes Ser.). 166 p. 1987. write for info. (*3-515-04832-4*) F Steiner Ver.

Loenneoken, S. Spansk-Norsk Ordbok: Spanish-Norwegian Dictionary. 2nd ed. (NOR & SPA.). 411p. 1980. 39.95 (*0-8288-1033-8*, S37620) Fr & Eur.

Loennroth, Erik, et al, eds. Conceptions of National History: Proceedings of Nobel Symposium 78. LC 93-33859. viii, 315p. (C). 1994. lib. bdg. 124.65 (*3-11-013504-3*, 3-94) De Gruyter.

Loeper, John J. Going to School in 1776. LC 72-86940. (Illus.). 112p. (J). (gr. 4-7). 1973. 16.00 (*0-689-30089-1*) Aladdin.

***Loeper, John J.** Meet the Allens in Whaling Days. LC 97-27963. (Early American Family Ser.). (Illus.). 64p. (J). (gr. 2-4). 1998. lib. bdg. 25.64 (*0-7614-0842-8*, Benchmark NY) Marshall Cavendish.

Loeper, John J. Meet the Drakes on the Kentucky Frontier. LC 97-42198. (Early American Family Ser.). (Illus.). (J). (gr. 2-4). 1998. lib. bdg. 25.64 (*0-7614-0845-2*, Benchmark NY) Marshall Cavendish.

— Meet the Dudleys in Colonial Times. LC 97-27962. (Early American Family Ser.). (J). 1998. lib. bdg. 25.64 (*0-7614-0841-X*, Benchmark NY) Marshall Cavendish.

— Meet the Wards on the Oregon Trail. LC 97-42199. (American Family Ser.). (J). (gr. 2-4). 1998. lib. bdg. 25.64 (*0-7614-0844-4*, Benchmark NY) Marshall Cavendish.

***Loeper, John J.** Meet the Webbers of Philadelphia. LC 97-42200. (Early American Family Ser.). (Illus.). 64p. (J). (gr. 2-4). 1998. lib. bdg. 25.64 (*0-7614-0843-6*, Benchmark NY) Marshall Cavendish.

Loeper, Nathalie De, see De Loeper, Nathalie.

Loepke, Mary A. Listen, Listen - Do You Hear . . . Vol. 1: Voices of the Seasons. Stevens, Shirley S., ed. LC 96-95354. (Illus.). 40p. (Orig.). 1996. pap. 6.00 (*0-9654487-0-3*, 96-625) M A Koepke.

***Loepp, Daniel.** Sharing the Balance of Power: An Examination of Shared Power in the Michigan House of Representatives. LC 99-6651. 216p. (C). 1999. text 34.50 (*0-472-09702-4*, 09702) U of Mich Pr.

— Sharing the Balance of Power: An Examination of Shared Power in the Michigan House of Representatives 1993-1994. (Illus.). 210p. (C). pap. text. write for info. (*0-472-06702-8*) U of Mich Pr.

Loeppky, Richard N. & Michejda, Christopher J., eds. Nitrosamines & Related N-Nitroso Compounds: Chemistry & Biochemistry. LC 94-2014. (Symposium Ser.: Vol. 553). 381p. 1994. text 98.00 (*0-8412-2856-6*, Pub. by Am Chemical) OUP.

Loepur. Going to School in the Old West. (J). 1995. 13.95 (*0-689-31897-9*) Atheneum Yung Read.

Loer, Barbara. Das Absolute & die Wirklichkeit in Schellings Philosophie: Mit der Erstedition einer Handschrift aus dem Berliner Schelling-Nachlass. LC 73-93164. (Quellen und Studien zur Philosophie: Vol. 7). (Illus.). viii, 288p. (C). 1974. 134.65 (*3-11-004329-7*) De Gruyter.

Loera, Gabriel, ed. see Colle, Marie-Pierre.

Loera, Julie. Quien Dice Que la Comida Mejicana Engorda? Quite el Miedo y la Grasa de la Comida Mejicana. Johnson, Robby, ed.Tr. of Who Said That Mexican Food Is Fattening? Take the Fear & Fat Out of Mexican Food. (ENG & SPA.). 100p. 1996. pap. 9.95 (*0-9655256-1-9*) RJL Bks.

— Who Said That Mexican Food Is Fattening? Take the Fear & Fat Out of Mexican Food. Johnson, Robby, ed.Tr. of Quien Dice Que la Comida Mejicana Engorda? Quite el Miedo y la Grasa de la Comida Mejicana. 100p. 1996. pap. 9.95 (*0-9655256-0-0*) RJL Bks.

Loerke, Jean P., jt. ed. see Langill, Ellen D.

Loers, Veit, jt. auth. see Lucan, Jacques.

Loertscher, David V. Biographical Index to Children's & Young Adult Authors & Illustrators: 1993 Edition. 400p. 1993. ring bd. 55.00 (*0-931510-47-3*) Hi Willow.

— Collection Mapping in the LMC: Building Library Media Center Collections in the Age of Technology. 120p. 1996. pap. 20.00 (*0-931510-58-9*) Hi Willow.

— Reinvent Your School's Library in the Age of Technology: A Handbook for Principals & Superintendents. 1998. pap. 15.00 (*0-931510-69-4*) Hi Willow.

— Taxonomies of the School Library Media Program. (Illus.). xvi, 336p. 1988. pap. text 26.50 (*0-87287-662-4*) Libs Unl.

***Loertscher, David V.** Taxonomies of the School Library Media Program. 2nd ed. 255p. 2000. pap. 30.00 (*0-931510-75-9*) Hi Willow.

Loertscher, David V., jt. ed. see Woolls, E. Blanche.

***Loes, Augustine.** The First de la Salle Brothers, 1681-1719. LC 99-71583. (Lasallian Resources Ser.: Vol. 2). (Illus.). xiv, 281p. 1999. pap. 20.00 (*0-944808-24-7*) Lasallian Pubns.

Loes, Augustine, ed. see De La Salle, John B.

Loes, Augustine, tr. see Hermans, Maurice-Auguste, et al.

Loes, Augustine, tr. see Wurth, Othmar.

Loes, Michael. Aspirin Alternative. 1985. pap. 13.95 (*1-893910-04-0*, Pub. by Freedom Pr Inc) BookWorld.

— Insulin: The Antibiotic Companion. 96p. 2000. pap. 4.95 (*1-893910-09-1*, 904-011, Pub. by Freedom Pr Inc) BookWorld.

— Non-Drug European Secret. 1999. pap. 5.95 (*1-893910-03-2*) Freedom Pr Inc.

Loes, Michael, et al. The Doctor's Cure. LC 98-4273. 224p. 1998. pap. 12.95 (*0-87983-929-5*, 39295K, Keats Publng) NTC Contemp Pub Co.

Loesberg, John. Folksongs & Ballads Popular in Ireland, Vol. 1. 66p. Date not set. 6.95 (*0-946005-00-1*, OS 10009, Pub. by Ossian) Music Sales.

— Folksongs & Ballads Popular in Ireland, Vol. 2. 73p. Date not set. 6.95 (*0-946005-01-X*, OS 10017, Pub. by Ossian) Music Sales.

— Folksongs & Ballads Popular in Ireland, Vol. 3. 66p. Date not set. 6.95 (*0-946005-02-8*, OS 10025, Pub. by Ossian) Music Sales.

— Folksongs & Ballads Popular in Ireland, Vol. 4. 73p. Date not set. 6.95 (*0-946005-33-8*, OS 10411, Pub. by Ossian) Music Sales.

— More Musical Reflections of Scotland. 1994. 10.95 (*0-946005-83-4*, OS00098) Omnibus NY.

— Musical Reflections of Scotland. 1994. 10.95 (*0-946005-82-6*, OS00097) Omnibus NY.

— Traditional Folksongs - Ballads of Scotland. 1994. 7.95 (*0-946005-80-X*) Omnibus NY.

Loesberg, John, ed. More Songs & Ballads of Ireland. pap. 7.95 (*0-946005-54-0*, OS 00077, Pub. by Ossian) Music Sales.

— Songs & Ballads of Ireland. 56p. 1997. pap. 8.95 (*0-946005-53-2*, OS 00076) Music Sales.

Loesberg, Jonathan. Aestheticism & Deconstruction: Pater, Derrida, & De Man. 276p. 1991. text 35.00 (*0-691-06884-4*, Pub. by Princeton U Pr) Cal Prin Full Svc.

— Fictions of Consciousness: Mill, Newman & the Reading of Victorian Prose. 280p. (C). 1986. pap. text 20.00 (*0-8135-1204-2*) Rutgers U Pr.

Loesburg, John. More Musical Reflections of Ireland. 1997. pap. text 10.95 (*0-946005-37-0*) Dufour.

— Musical Reflections or Ireland. 1997. pap. text 10.95 (*0-946005-36-2*) Dufour.

Loesburg, John, ed. Music from Ireland. 56p. pap. 7.95 (*0-946005-55-9*, Pub. by Ossian) Music Sales.

Loesburg, John, ed. Traditional Folksongs - Ballads of Scotland 1. 1994. 7.95 (*0-946005-78-8*, OS00093) Omnibus NY.

Loesch, Anne. Lutefisk on the Lens. 19.95 (*0-9642763-0-5*) Pilot Pubng.

Loesch, Ivan L. Unisonia. 272p. 1999. pap. 24.95 (*0-7392-0179-4*, PO3138) Morris Pubng.

***Loesch, Joe.** The Abraham Lincoln Logues. unabridged ed. Hutchinson, Cheryl, ed. (Backyard Adventure Ser.). (Illus.). (Orig.). (J). (gr. k-6). Date not set. pap. 16.95 incl. audio compact disk (*1-887729-77-1*); pap. 14.95 incl. audio (*1-887729-76-3*) Toy Box Prods.

Loesch, Joe. All about Adam's Apple. unabridged ed. Hutchinson, Cheryl J., ed. (Bible Stories for Kids Ser.: Vol. 3). (Illus.). 52p. (J). (gr. 1-5). 1996. pap. 14.95 incl. audio (*1-887729-10-0*); pap. 16.95 incl. audio compact disk (*1-887729-11-9*) Toy Box Prods.

— The Buffalo Horns Adventure: With Buffalo Biff & Farley's Raiders. unabridged ed. Hutchinson, Cheryl J., ed. (Backyard Adventure Ser.: Vol. 1). (Illus.). 56p. (J). (gr. 1-5). 1995. pap. 16.95 incl. audio compact disk (*1-887729-01-1*) Toy Box Prods.

— The Buffalo Horns Adventure: With Buffalo Biff & Farley's Raiders. unabridged ed. Hutchinson, Cheryl J., ed. (Backyard Adventure Ser.: Vol. 1). (Illus.). 56p. (J). (gr. 1-5). 1995. pap. 14.95 incl. audio (*1-887729-00-3*) Toy Box Prods.

— A Coat, a Pharaoh & a Family Reunion: "The Story of Joseph" unabridged ed. Hutchinson, Cheryl J., ed. (Bible Stories for Kids Ser.). (Illus.). 56p. (J). (gr. k-6). 1997. pap. 14.95 incl. audio (*1-887729-19-4*) Toy Box Prods.

— A Coat, a Pharaoh & a Family Reunion: "The Story of Joseph" unabridged ed. Hutchinson, Cheryl J., ed. (Bible Stories for Kids Ser.). (Illus.). 56p. (J). (gr. 1-5). 1997. pap. 16.95 incl. audio compact disk (*1-887729-20-8*) Toy Box Prods.

***Loesch, Joe.** David Faces Goliath: Showdown in the Desert. unabridged ed. Hutchinson, Cheryl, ed. (Bible Stories for Kids Ser.). (J). (gr. k-6). 1999. pap. 16.95 incl. audio compact disk (*1-887729-22-4*) Toy Box Prods.

— David Faces Goliath: Showdown in the Desert. unabridged ed. Hutchinson, Cheryl, ed. (Bible Stories for Kids Ser.). (Illus.). (J). (gr. k-6). 1999. pap. 14.95 incl. audio (*1-887729-21-6*) Toy Box Prods.

— He Is Risen: The True Meaning of Easter. Hutchinson, Cheryl, ed. (Bible Stories for Kids Ser.). (Illus.). (J). (gr. k-6). 2000. pap. 16.95 incl. audio compact disk (*1-887729-75-5*) Toy Box Prods.

Loesch, Joe. The Magnificent Recycling Machine Adventure: With Buffalo Biff & Farley's Raiders. unabridged ed. Hutchinson, Cheryl J., ed. (Backyard Adventure Ser.: Vol. 3). (Illus.). 56p. (J). (gr. 1-5). 1996. pap. 14.95 incl. audio (*1-887729-04-6*) Toy Box Prods.

— The Magnificent Recycling Machine Adventure: With Buffalo Biff & Farley's Raiders. unabridged ed. Hutchinson, Cheryl J., ed. (Backyard Adventure Ser.: Vol. 3). (Illus.). 56p. (J). (gr. 1-5). 1996. pap. 16.95 incl. audio compact disk (*1-887729-05-4*) Toy Box Prods.

— Noah's Journey. unabridged ed. Hutchinson, Cheryl J., ed. (Bible Stories for Kids Ser.). (Illus.). 50p. (J). (gr. 1 up). 1995. pap. 14.95 incl. audio (*1-887729-06-2*); pap. 16.95 incl. audio compact disk (*1-887729-07-0*) Toy Box Prods.

— Professor Patulli Sing-a-Long. abr. ed. Hutchinson, Cheryl J., ed. (Bible Stories for Kids Ser.). (Illus.). 16p. (J). (gr. 1-6). 1997. 7.95 incl. audio (*1-887729-16-X*) Toy Box Prods.

— Saving the Badlands Adventure: With Buffalo Biff & Farley's Raiders. unabridged ed. Hutchinson, Cheryl J., ed. (Backyard Adventure Ser.: Vol. 2). (Illus.). 56p. (J). (gr. 1-5). 1995. pap. 14.95 incl. audio (*1-887729-02-X*); pap. 16.95 incl. audio compact disk (*1-887729-03-8*) Toy Box Prods.

Loesch, Joe. The Star of Bethlehem. abr. ed. Hutchinson, Cheryl J., ed. (Bible Stories for Kids Ser.: Vol. 4). (Illus.). 52p. (J). (gr. 1-5). 1996. pap. 16.95 incl. audio compact disk (*1-887729-13-5*) Toy Box Prods.

— The Star of Bethlehem. unabridged ed. Hutchinson, Cheryl J., ed. (Bible Stories for Kids Ser.: Vol. 4). (Illus.). 52p. (J). (gr. 1-5). 1996. pap. 14.95 incl. audio (*1-887729-12-7*) Toy Box Prods.

Loesch, Joe. The Time Travelers' First Adventure: "The Wild West" with Buffalo Biff. large type unabridged ed. Hutchinson, Cheryl, ed. (Backyard Adventure Ser.: Vol. 4). (Illus.). 60p. (J). (gr. k-6). 1996. pap. 14.95 incl. audio (*1-887729-14-3*); pap. 16.95 incl. audio compact disk (*1-887729-15-1*) Toy Box Prods.

***Loesch, Joe.** The Underground Railroad: Featuring Harriet Tubman. unabridged ed. (Backyard Adventure Ser.: Vol. 5). (J). (gr. 1-6). 1999. pap. 16.95 incl. audio compact disk (*1-887729-18-6*) Toy Box Prods.

— The Underground Railroad: Featuring Harriet Tubman. unabridged ed. (Backyard Adventure Ser.: Vol. 5). (Illus.). (J). (gr. 1-6). 1999. pap. 14.95 incl. audio (*1-887729-17-8*) Toy Box Prods.

Loesch, Joe. A Whale of a Tale. unabridged ed. Hutchinson, Cheryl J., ed. (Bible Stories for Kids Ser.: Vol. 2). (Illus.). 54p. (J). (gr. 1 up). 1996. 14.95 incl. audio (*1-887729-08-9*); 16.95 incl. audio compact disk (*1-887729-09-7*) Toy Box Prods.

Loesch, Larry C. & Vacc, Nicholas A., eds. Research in Counseling & Therapy. 149p. (C). 1997. pap. text 18.95 (*1-56109-075-1*, EC215) CAPS Inc.

Loeschcke, V., et al, eds. Conservation Genetics. LC 93-49017. (Experientia Supplementa Ser.: No. 68). 1994. write for info. (*0-8176-2939-4*) Birkhauser.

Loeschcke, V., jt. auth. see Bijlsma, R.

Loesche-Scheller, Brigitta. Reparations to Poverty: Domestic Policy in America Ten Years after the Great Society. (European University Studies, Series 31: Vol. 289). 476p. 1995. pap. 68.95 (*3-906755-53-3*, Pub. by P Lang) P Lang Pubng.

Loesche, Walter J. Dental Caries: A Treatable Infection. rev. ed. (Illus.). 550p. (C). 1994. pap. 39.95 (*0-9639689-0-4*) Automat Diag.

Loeschen, John R. The Divine Community: Trinity, Church, & Ethics in Reformation Theologies. (Sixteenth Century Essays & Studies: Vol. I). 238p. 1981. 40.00 (*0-940474-01-8*) Truman St Univ.

Loeschen, R., jt. auth. see Bauer, Raymond A.

Loeschen, Sharon. Systematic Training in the Skills of Virginia Satir. LC 97-10297. (Counseling Ser.). 200p. 1997. mass mkt. 26.95 (*0-534-23172-1*) Brooks-Cole.

Loescher, Ann D., jt. auth. see Loescher, Gilburt D.

Loescher, Elizabeth. The Conflict Center's Conflict Management Middle School Curriculum. 64p. (J). (gr. 6-8). 1990. teacher ed. 20.00 (*1-887249-01-X*) Conflict Ctr.

— Haciendo la Paz En Lo Practico: Un Programa De Estudios Para la Resolucion De Problemas Para la Escuela Primaria. (SPA.). 84p. (J). (gr. 1-5). 1991. teacher ed. 25.00 (*1-887249-02-8*) Conflict Ctr.

— Peacemaking Made Practical: A Conflict Management Curriculum for the Elementary School. 86p. (J). (gr. 1-5). 1991. teacher ed. 25.00 (*1-887249-03-6*) Conflict Ctr.

Loescher, Elizabeth & Vobejda, Virginia. How to Avoid World War III at Home: Conflict Management for the Family. 126p. 1994. pap. 9.00 (*1-887249-00-1*) Conflict Ctr.

Loescher, Gilburt D. Beyond Charity: International Cooperation & the Global Refugee Crisis: A Twentieth Century Fund Book. (Illus.). 272p. 1996. reprint ed. pap. 22.00 (*0-19-510294-0*) OUP.

Loescher, Gilburt D., ed. Refugees & the Asylum Dilemma in the West. 184p. 1992. pap. 16.95 (*0-271-00856-3*) Pa St U Pr.

Loescher, Gilburt D. & Loescher, Ann D. The Global Refugee Crisis: A Reference Handbook. LC 94-25097. (Contemporary World Issues Ser.). 270p. (YA). (gr. 7 up). 1994. lib. bdg. 45.00 (*0-87436-753-0*) ABC-CLIO.

Loescher, Gilburt D. & Monahan, Laila, eds. Refugees & International Relations. 442p. 1990. reprint ed. pap. text 29.95 (*0-19-827858-6*) OUP.

Loescher, Gilburt D., jt. ed. see Nichols, Bruce.

Loeschke, Maravene S. Mime: Techniques & Class Formats: A Movement Program for the Visually Handicapped. LC PN2071.G4.L6. (American Foundation for the Blind Practice Ser.). 79p. reprint ed. pap. 30.00 (*0-7837-0132-2*, 204042000016) Bks Demand.

— The Path Between: An Historical Novel of the Dickinson Family of Amherst. LC 88-63314. (Illus.). 300p. (Orig.). (C). 1988. pap. 15.95 (*0-935132-11-2*) C H Fairfax.

Loeschnig, Louis. Simple Flight & Space Experiments. LC 98-4277. (Illus.). 128p. (J). (gr. 3-6). 1998. 14.95 (*0-8069-4246-0*) Sterling.

Loeschnig, Louis V. Simple Chemistry Experiments with Everyday Materials. (Illus.). 128p. (Orig.). (J). 1995. pap. 5.95 (*0-8069-0689-8*) Sterling.

— Simple Earth Science Experiments with Everyday Materials. LC 95-53977. (Illus.). 128p. (J). (gr. 3). 1996. 14.95 (*0-8069-0898-X*) Sterling.

— Simple Earth Science Experiments with Everyday Materials. (Illus.). 128p. (J). 1997. pap. 5.95 (*0-8069-0365-1*) Sterling.

— Simple Space & Flight Experiments With Everyday Materials. 1999. pap. text 5.95 (*0-8069-3932-X*) Sterling.

Loeser, Angela, et al. Chemotherapie - Kompendium fuer das Pflegepersonal. (Illus.). viii, 48p. 1990. pap. 14.00 (*3-8055-5295-5*) S Karger.

Loeser, Francois. Faisceaux Pervers, Transformation de Mellin et de Terminants. (Illus.). 105p. 1998. pap. 28.00 (*2-85629-053-1*) Am Math.

Loeser, Harrison T. Sonar Engineering Handbook. LC 92-63044. 216p. 1993. reprint ed. 41.95 (*0-932146-59-7*) Peninsula CA.

Loeser, John D. Bonica's Management of Pain, 2 vols. 3rd ed. 1,975p. text 259.00 (*0-683-30462-3*) Lppncott W & W.

Loeser, John D., jt. ed. see Chapman, Richard.

Loesser, Arthur. Men, Women & Pianos: A Social History. 672p. 1991. pap. 13.95 (*0-486-26543-9*) Dover.

Loesser, Frank. Bushel & a Peck. 32p. (J). (ps-1). pap. 7.95 (*0-06-443602-0*) HarpC Child Bks.

— A Bushel & a Peck. 32p. (J). (ps-1). Date not set. 14.95 (*0-06-028549-4*); lib. bdg. 14.89 (*0-06-028550-8*) HarpC Child Bks.

Loesser, Frank. Guys & Dolls for Easy Piano. (Easy Play Ser.). 48p. 1994. pap. 10.95 (*0-7935-2872-0*, 00222568) H Leonard.

— Sing the Songs of Frank Loesser: High Voice. 80p. 1995. pap. 19.95 incl. audio compact disk (*0-7935-3501-8*) H Leonard.

— Where's Charley? Vocal Selections. 32p. 1983. pap. 7.95 (*0-7935-4290-1*, 00447285) H Leonard.

***Loesser, Susan.** Most Remarkable Fella: Frank Loesser & the Guys & Dolls in His Life. (Illus.). 2000. pap. 14.95 (*0-634-00927-3*, Berklee Pr) H Leonard.

Loessin, Bruce A., jt. auth. see Duronio, Margaret A.

Loessin, Suzanne, jt. auth. see Patteson, Nelda.

Loethen, Mark L., ed. Water Management in Urban Areas. (Technical Publications: No. 95-4). (Illus.). 354p. (Orig.). 1995. pap. 40.00 (*1-882132-35-1*) Am Water Resources.

Loethen, Mark L., ed. see American Water Resources Association, Conference (.

***Loether, Herman J.** The Social Impacts of Infectious Disease in England 1600 to 1900. LC 00-35121. (Studies in Sociology: Vol. 24). 376p. 2000. pap. 99.95 (*0-7734-7764-0*) E Mellen.

Loether, Herman J. & McTavish, Donald G. Descriptive & Inferential Statistics: An Introduction. rev. ed. 512p. (C). 1988. write for info. (*0-318-62200-9*, H11877) P-H.

— Descriptive & Inferential Statistics: An Introduction. 3rd rev. ed. 512p. (C). 1988. text 46.00 (*0-205-11186-6*, H11869) Allyn.

Loetscher, Andreas. Semantische Strukturen im Bereich der alt und mittelhochdeutschen Schallwoerter. (Quellen und Forschungen zur Sprach und Kulturgeschichte der Germanischen Voelker: NF 53). (C). 1973. 86.15 (*3-11-003870-6*) De Gruyter.

Loetscher, H., et al. Friedrich Durrenmatt, 1921-1990. Evans, Tamara, ed. Agee, Joel, tr. (Illus.). 96p. (Orig.). (C). 1997. pap. 20.00 (*1-884692-05-2*) Swiss Inst.

Loetscher, Ken. The Happiest Man on Earth. 32p. 1999. pap. 8.00 (*0-8059-4638-1*) Dorrance.

Loetscher, Lefferts A. Facing the Enlightenment & Pietism: Archibald Alexander & the Founding of Princeton Theological Seminary, 8. LC 82-11995. (Contributions to the Study of Religion Ser.: No. 8). 303p. 1983. 65.00 (*0-313-23677-1*, LOE/) Greenwood.

Loev, Irv. Conflict Means I Love You. 3rd ed. 96p. (Orig.). 1985. pap. 9.95 (*0-9615931-7-2*) D & J Pr TX.

Loeve, M. Probability Theory I. 4th ed. LC 76-28332. (Graduate Texts in Mathematics Ser.: Vol. 45). 1977. 49.00 (*3-540-90210-4*) Spr-Verlag.

— Probability Theory II. (Graduate Texts in Mathematics Ser.: Vol. 46). 1994. 59.95 (*0-387-90262-7*) Spr-Verlag.

Loevgren, Sven. The Genesis of Modernism. LC 81-81720. (Illus.). xvi, 184p. 1983. reprint ed. lib. bdg. 50.00 (*0-87817-280-7*) Hacker.

Loevinger, J., ed. Scientific Ways in the Study of Ego Development. (Heinz Werner Lectures: No. 12). 1978. pap. 6.00 (*0-914206-14-1*) Clark U Pr.

Loevinger, Jane. Paradigms of Personality. (Psychology Ser.). (Illus.). 269p. (C). 1987. pap. text 24.95 (*0-7167-1840-5*) W H Freeman.

Loevinger, Jane, ed. Technical Foundations for Measuring Ego Development. LC 97-43778. (Personality & Clinical Psychology Ser.). 250p. 1998. pap. write for info. (*0-8058-2059-0*) L Erlbaum Assocs.

Loevinger, Jane, et al. Measuring Ego Development, Vol. 1. LC 71-92891. (Jossey-Bass Behavioral Science Ser.). 265p. pap. 82.20 (*0-7837-0179-9*, 204047600001) Bks Demand.

— Measuring Ego Development, Vol. 2. LC 71-92891. (Jossey-Bass Behavioral Science Ser.). 477p. pap. 147.90 (*0-7837-0180-2*, 204047600002) Bks Demand.

Loevinger, Jane, jt. auth. see Hy, Le-Xuan.

Loevinger, Robert, et al, eds. MIRD Primer for Absorbed Dose Calculations. rev. ed. LC 91-4858. (Illus.). 128p. 1991. text 49.00 (*0-932004-38-5*) Soc Nuclear Med.

***Loevner, Laurie A.** Brain Imaging: Case Review. LC 99-10768. (Illus.). 224p. (C). 1999. text. write for info. (*0-323-00430-X*) Mosby Inc.

Loevy, Hannelore T., tr. see Strassburg, Manfred & Knolle, Gerdt.

***Loevy, Robert D.** Colorado College: A Place of Learning, 1874-1999. LC 99-171549. viii, 501 p. 1999. write for info. (*0-935052-32-1*) Colorado College.

Loevy, Robert D. The Flawed Path to the Governorship, 1994: The Nationalization of a Colorado Statewide Election. LC 96-22958. (Illus.). 396p. 1996. pap. text 38.00 (*0-7618-0430-7*); lib. bdg. 58.00 (*0-7618-0429-3*) U Pr of Amer.

— The Flawed Path to the Presidency, 1992: Unfairness & Inequality in the Presidential Selection Process. LC 93-48105. 319p. (C). 1994. pap. text 21.95 (*0-7914-2188-0*) State U NY Pr.

— The Flawed Path to the Presidency, 1992: Unfairness & Inequality in the Presidential Selection Process. LC 93-48105. (SUNY Series on the Presidency: Contemporary Issues). 319p. (C). 1994. text 59.50 (*0-7914-2187-2*) State U NY Pr.

— The Manipulated Path to the White House - 1996: Maximizing Advantage in the Presidential Selection Process. LC 97-49697. 400p. (C). 1998. 64.00 (*0-7618-1023-4*); pap. 37.50 (*0-7618-1024-2*) U Pr of Amer.

— To End All Segregation: The Politics of the Passage of the Civil Rights Act of 1964. 382p. (Orig.). (C). 1990. pap. text 28.50 (*0-8191-7689-3*); lib. bdg. 58.00 (*0-8191-7688-5*) U Pr of Amer.

Loevy, Robert D., ed. The Civil Rights Act of 1964: The Passage of the Law That Ended Racial Segregation. LC 97-687. (SUNY Series in Afro-American Studies). 380p. (C). 1997. text 59.50 (*0-7914-3361-7*); pap. text 19.95 (*0-7914-3362-5*) State U NY Pr.

Loevy, Robert D., jt. auth. see Cronin, Thomas E.

Loevy, Steven R. William Carlos Williams's a Dream of Love. LC 83-4909. (Studies in Modern Literature: No. 22). 94p. reprint ed. pap. 30.00 (*0-8357-1450-0*, 207055900001) Bks Demand.

Loew, F., jt. ed. see Auer, L. M.

Loew, John. Wiring. Toht, David W., ed. (Easy-Step Ser.). (Illus.). 64p. (Orig.). 1997. pap. 6.95 (*0-614-18308-1*, Ortho Bks) Meredith Bks.

Loew, Leslie M., ed. Spectroscopic Membrane Probes, Vol. I. 240p. 1988. 137.00 (*0-8493-4535-9*, CRC Reprint) Franklin.

— Spectroscopic Membrane Probes, Vol. II. 208p. 1988. 126.00 (*0-8493-4536-7*, CRC Reprint) Franklin.

— Spectroscopic Membrane Probes, Vol. III. 240p. 1988. 137.00 (*0-8493-4537-5*, CRC Reprint) Franklin.

***Loew, Mike.** Tough Call: Hard-Hitting Phone Pranks. LC 00-29683. 224p. 2000. pap. 12.95 (*0-312-26400-3*, St Martin Griffin) St Martin.

Loew, Sebastian. Modern Architecture in Historic Cities: Policy, Planning, & Building in Contemporary France. LC 97-26097. (Illus.). 280p. (C). 1998. 85.00 (*0-415-15492-8*) Routledge.

***Loew, Sebastian.** The Promotion of Architecture Some Lessons from France. LC 99-236613. 40p. (Orig.). 1998. pap. text 12.00 (*1-901092-02-X*) Andreas Papadakis.

Loewe, jt. auth. see Lerner.

Loewe, Busso. Ancient Greek Theophoric Toponyms. 128p. 1980. pap. 15.00 (*0-89005-333-2*) Ares.

Loewe, Heinz. Von Cassiodor zu Dante: Ausgewaehlte Aufsaetze Zur Geschichtsschreibung und Politischen Ideenwelt des Mittelalters. LC 73-75491. 342p. (C). 1973. 142.30 (*3-11-003739-4*) De Gruyter.

Loewe, Johann C. Dr. Carl Loewes Selbstbiographie. xxiii, 458p. 1976. reprint ed. write for info. (*3-487-05988-6*) G Olms Pubs.

Loewe, Johann H. Die Philosophie Fichte's Nach Dem Gesammtergebnisse Ihrer Entwicklung und in Ihrem Verhaeltnisse Zu Kant und Spinoza. (Fichteana Ser.). (GER.). 340p. 1976. reprint ed. write for info. (*3-487-05974-6*) G Olms Pubs.

Loewe, Michael. Crisis & Conflict in Han China: Fourteen B. C. to A. D. Nine. LC 75-308728. 342p. reprint ed. pap. 106.10 (*0-608-11814-1*, 201216200080) Bks Demand.

— Divination, Mythology & Monarchy in Han China. LC 93-28327. (University of Cambridge Oriental Publications: No. 48). (Illus.). 375p. (C). 1994. text 80.00 (*0-521-45466-2*) Cambridge U Pr.

Loewe, Michael, ed. Early Chinese Texts: A Bibliographical Guide. LC 93-40281. (Early China Special Monographs: No. 2). 560p. 1994. 35.00 (*1-55729-043-1*) IEAS.

Loewe, Michael & Shaughnessy, Edward L., eds. The Cambridge History of Ancient China: From the Origins of Civilization to 221 B. C. LC 97-33203. (Illus.). 750p. (C). 1999. text 130.00 (*0-521-47030-7*) Cambridge U Pr.

Loewe, Michael, jt. ed. see Twitchett, Denis C.

Loewe, Raphael, jt. auth. see Sahula, Isaac I.

Loewe, Raymond D. Selecting a College & Financing College Costs. LC 99-165817. 102 p. 1995. write for info. (*0-15-601926-4*) Harcourt Legal.

Loewe, Robert, jt. ed. see Kulp, Karel.

Loewe, William P. The College Student's Introduction to Christology. LC 96-26127. 264p. (C). 1996. pap. text 19.95 (*0-8146-5018-X*, M Glazier) Liturgical Pr.

Loewen, Don, ed. Committed to World Missions: A Focus on International Strategy. 129p. 1990. pap. 4.95 (*0-921788-00-2*) Kindred Prods.

Loewen, E. G. & Popov, Evgeny. Diffraction Gratings & Applications. LC 97-2659. (Optical Engineering Ser.: Vol. 58). (Illus.). 632p. 1997. text 150.00 (*0-8247-9923-2*) Dekker.

Loewen, Eleanor, jt. auth. see Toews, John.

Loewen, Eleanor M. Make My Joy Complete: Philippians. Shelly, Maynard, ed. LC 87-83120. (Bible Studies). 80p. 1988. pap. 1.95 (*0-87303-123-7*) Faith & Life.

***Loewen, Grant & Sonntag, Patti, eds.** Moosemilk. (Moosehead Anthology Ser.: No. 7). 114p. 1999. 14.95 (*0-919688-52-7*, Pub. by DC Books) Genl Dist Srvs.

Loewen, Harry. No Permanent City: Stories from Mennonite History & Life. LC 92-73439. 224p. (Orig.). 1993. pap. 12.99 (*0-8361-3612-8*) Herald Pr.

Loewen, Howard J., ed. One Lord, One Church, One Hope, & One God: Mennonite Confessions of Faith. (Text-Reader Ser.: No. 2). 369p. 1985. pap. text 12.00 (*0-936273-08-9*) Inst Mennonite.

Loewen, Jacob A. The Bible in Cross-Cultural Perspective. LC 96-3432. Date not set. pap. text 11.95 (*0-87808-266-2*) William Carey Lib.

— The Practice of Translating: Drills for Training Translators. (Helps for Translators Ser.). xiv, 260p. 1981. pap. 19.99 (*0-8267-0028-4*, 102703) Untd Bible Soc.

Loewen, Jacob A. & Prieb, Wesley J. Only the Sword of the Spirit. (Perspectives on Mennonite Life & Thought Ser.: No. 11). 390p. (Orig.). 1997. pap. 15.95 (*0-921788-44-4*) Kindred Prods.

Loewen, James W. Lies Across America: What Our Historic Sites Get Wrong. LC 99-14212. 416p. 1999. 26.95 (*1-56584-344-4*, Pub. by New Press NY) Norton.

***Loewen, James W.** Lies Across America: What Our Historic Sites Get Wrong. 2000. pap. 15.00 (*0-684-87067-3*, Touchstone) S&S Trade Pap.

Loewen, James W. Lies My Teacher Told Me: Everything Your American History Textbook Got Wrong. (Illus.). 384p. 1995. 24.95 (*1-56584-100-X*, Pub. by New Press NY) Norton.

— Lies My Teacher Told Me: Everything Your American History Textbook Got Wrong. LC 96-20050. (Illus.). 384p. 1996. pap. 14.00 (*0-684-81886-8*) S&S Trade.

— The Mississippi Chinese: Between Black & White. 2nd ed. 240p. (C). 1988. reprint ed. pap. text 12.50 (*0-88133-312-3*) Waveland Pr.

— Truth about Columbus: A Subversively True Poster Book for a Dubiously Celebration Occasion. 48p. 1992. pap. 14.95 (*1-56584-008-9*, Pub. by New Press NY) Norton.

Loewen, Melvin J. The Descendants of Cornelius W. Loewen & Helena Bartel. 2nd ed. viii, 339p. pap. 22.00 (*0-9640876-2-6*) Heritageclassics.

Loewen, Melvin J., compiled by. The Believer's Way of Life Vol. 2: Selections of Bible Readings for Daily Devotions. xviii, 365p. 1994. pap. 9.95 (*0-9640876-1-8*) Heritageclassics.

— God's Way of Salvation Vol. 1: Selections of Bible Readings for Daily Devotions. xviii, 365p. 1994. pap. 9.95 (*0-9640876-0-X*) Heritageclassics.

Loewen, Nancy. Athena. LC 98-35117. (Greek & Roman Mythology Ser.). (J). 1999. write for info. (*0-7368-0048-4*, Rivr Front Bks) Capstone Pr.

— Athena. LC 98-35117. (Greek & Roman Mythology Ser.). 1998. 19.00 (*0-531-11612-3*) Watts.

— Atlanta. (Great Cities of the U. S. A. Ser.). (Illus.). 48p. (YA). (gr. 5 up). 1989. lib. bdg. 23.93 (*0-86592-543-7*) Rourke Enter.

— Beethoven. (Profiles in Music Ser.). (Illus.). 112p. (J). (gr. 5 up). 1989. lib. bdg. 25.26 (*0-86592-609-3*) Rourke Enter.

— Bicycle Safety. LC 95-45042. (Safety Sense Ser.). (Illus.). 24p. (J). (gr. k-4). 1996. lib. bdg. 18.50 (*1-56766-260-9*) Childs World.

— Emergencies. LC 95-25884. (Safety Sense Ser.). (Illus.). 24p. (J). (gr. k-4). 1996. lib. bdg. 18.50 (*1-56766-259-5*) Childs World.

— Fire Safety. LC 95-25896. (Safety Sense Ser.). (Illus.). 24p. (J). (gr. k-4). 1996. lib. bdg. 18.50 (*1-56766-258-7*) Childs World.

— Food in France. (International Food Library: Set II). 32p. (J). (gr. 3-6). 1989. lib. bdg. 21.27 (*0-86625-344-0*) Rourke Pubns.

— Food in Germany. (International Food Library: Set II). 32p. (J). (gr. 3-6). 1989. lib. bdg. 21.27 (*0-86625-347-5*) Rourke Pubns.

— Food in Greece. (International Food Library: Set II). 32p. (J). (gr. 3-6). 1989. lib. bdg. 21.27 (*0-86625-348-3*) Rourke Pubns.

— Food in Israel. (International Food Library: Set II). 32p. (J). (gr. 3-6). 1989. lib. bdg. 21.27 (*0-86625-349-1*) Rourke Pubns.

— Food in Korea. (International Food Library: Set II). 32p. (J). (gr. 3-6). 1989. lib. bdg. 21.27 (*0-86625-345-9*) Rourke Pubns.

— Food in Spain. LC 90-43595. (International Food Library: Set II). 32p. (J). (gr. 3-6). 1989. lib. bdg. 21.27 (*0-86625-346-7*) Rourke Pubns.

Loewen, Nancy. Greek & Roman Mythology. (Illus.). 48p. 63.80 (*0-7368-0464-1*, Capstone Bks) Capstone Pr.

Loewen, Nancy. Hercules. LC 98-35118. (Greek & Roman Mythology Ser.). (J). 1999. write for info. (*0-7368-0049-2*, Rivr Front Bks) Capstone Pr.

— Hercules. (Greek & Roman Mythology Ser.). 1998. 19.00 (*0-531-11613-1*) Watts.

— Home Safety. (Safety Sense Ser.). (Illus.). 24p. (J). (gr. k-4). 1996. lib. bdg. 18.50 (*1-56766-257-9*) Childs World.

— International Food Library, 6 bks., Set II. (J). 1991. 71.70 (*0-86625-324-6*) Rourke Pubns.

***Loewen, Nancy.** Jack London. LC 92-3739. (Notebooks Ser.). (J). 1998. spiral bd. 23.95 (*1-56846-157-7*, Creat Educ) Creative Co.

Loewen, Nancy. James Brown. (Profiles in Music Ser.). (Illus.). 112p. (J). (gr. 5 up). 1989. lib. bdg. 25.27 (*0-86592-607-7*) Rourke Enter.

— John Steinbeck. LC 93-1176. (Notebooks Ser.). (YA). (gr. 6 up). 2001. lib. bdg. 17.95 (*0-88682-511-3*, Creat Educ) Creative Co.

— Johnny Cash. (Profiles in Music Ser.). (Illus.). 112p. (J). (gr. 5 up). 1989. lib. bdg. 25.27 (*0-86592-608-5*) Rourke Enter.

— Mozart. (Profiles in Music Ser.). (Illus.). 112p. (J). (gr. 5 up). 1989. lib. bdg. 25.27 (*0-86592-605-0*) Rourke Enter.

— Outdoor Safety. LC 95-25905. (Safety Sense Ser.). (Illus.). 24p. (J). (gr. k-4). 1996. lib. bdg. 18.50 (*1-56766-256-0*) Childs World.

— Philadelphia. (Great Cities of the U. S. A. Ser.). (Illus.). 48p. (YA). (gr. 5 up). 1989. lib. bdg. 23.93 (*0-86592-542-9*) Rourke Enter.

Loewen, Nancy. Poe. (Illus.). 64p. (YA). (gr. 6-12). 1993. 22.60 (*1-56846-084-8*, Creat Educ) Creative Co.

Loewen, Nancy. Profiles in Music, 6 bks., Reading Level 6. (Illus.). 602p. (J). (gr. 5 up). 1989. 83.70 (*0-685-58764-9*) Rourke Corp.

— Profiles in Music, 4 bks., Set, Reading Level 6. (Illus.). 602p. (YA). (gr. 5 up). 1989. lib. bdg. 101.07 (*0-86592-604-2*) Rourke Enter.

— School Safety. LC 95-25898. (Safety Sense Ser.). (Illus.). 24p. (J). (gr. k-4). 1996. lib. bdg. 18.50 (*1-56766-255-2*) Childs World.

— Seattle. (Great Cities of the U. S. A. Ser.). (Illus.). 48p. (YA). (gr. 5 up). 1989. lib. bdg. 23.93 (*0-86592-545-3*) Rourke Enter.

— Traffic Safety. LC 95-25897. (Safety Sense Ser.). (Illus.). 24p. (J). (gr. k-4). 1996. lib. bdg. 18.50 (*1-56766-254-4*) Childs World.

— Venus. LC 98-35113. (Greek & Roman Mythology Ser.). (J). 1999. write for info. (*0-7368-0050-6*, Rivr Front Bks) Capstone Pr.

— Venus. LC 98-35117. (Greek & Roman Mythology Ser.). 1998. 19.00 (*0-531-11614-X*) Watts.

— Washington, D. C. (Great Cities of the U. S. A. Ser.). (Illus.). (YA). (gr. 5 up). 1989. lib. bdg. 11.95 (*0-685-58590-5*) Rourke Corp.

— Washington, D. C. (Great Cities of the U. S. A. Ser.). (Illus.). (YA). (gr. 5 up). 1989. lib. bdg. 23.93 (*0-86592-544-5*) Rourke Enter.

— Water Safety. LC 95-44769. (Safety Sense Ser.). (Illus.). 24p. (J). (gr. k-4). 1996. lib. bdg. 18.50 (*1-56766-261-7*) Childs World.

— Zeus. LC 98-35112. (Greek & Roman Mythology Ser.). (J). 1999. write for info. (*0-7368-0051-4*, Rivr Front Bks) Capstone Pr.

— Zeus. LC 98-35112. (Greek & Roman Mythology Ser.). 1998. 19.00 (*0-531-11615-8*) Watts.

***Loewen, Nancy & Bancroft, Ann.** Four to the Pole: The American Women's Expedition to Antarctica, 1992-93. (Illus.). 128p. (YA). (gr. 6 up). 2000. 22.50 (*0-208-02518-9*, Linnet Bks) Shoe String.

Loewen, Nancy & Stewart, Gail. Great Cities of the U. S., 7 bks., Set, Reading Level 6. (Illus.). 384p. (YA). (gr. 5 up). 1989. lib. bdg. 167.30 (*0-86592-537-2*) Rourke Enter.

Loewen, Philip D. Optimal Control Via Nonsmooth Analysis. LC 93-4143. (CRM Proceedings & Lecture Notes Ser.: Vol. 2). 153p. 1993. pap. 45.00 (*0-8218-6996-5*, CRMP/2) Am Math.

Loewen, Roland. Small Scale Refining of Jewelers Wastes. 1995. 39.95 (*0-931913-19-5*) Met-Chem Rsch.

Loewen, Royden. Family, Church & Market: A Mennonite Community in the Old & New Worlds 1850-1930. LC 92-34007. 370p. 1993. pap. text 25.95 (*0-8020-7766-8*) U of Toronto Pr.

Loewen, Royden K. Family, Church & Market: A Mennonite Community in the Old & New Worlds, 1850-1930. LC 92-34007. (Statue of Liberty-Ellis Island Centennial Ser.). (Illus.). 400p. (C). 1993. text 42.50 (*0-252-01980-6*); pap. text 17.95 (*0-252-06325-2*) U of Ill Pr.

— Family, Church & Market: A Mennonite Community in the Old & New Worlds 1850-1930. LC 92-34007. 370p. 1993. text 55.00 (*0-8020-2937-X*) U of Toronto Pr.

Loewenberg, Alfred. Annals of Opera, Fifteen Ninety-Seven to Nineteen Forty, 2 vols., Set. 1988. reprint ed. lib. bdg. 149.00 (*0-7812-0999-4*) Rprt Serv.

— Early Dutch Librettos & Plays with Music in the British Museum: In the Journal of Documentation. 60p. 1993. reprint ed. lib. bdg. 69.00 (*0-7812-9700-1*) Rprt Serv.

Loewenberg, Bert J. & Bogin, Ruth, eds. Black Women in Nineteenth-Century American Life: Their Words, Their Thoughts, Their Feelings. LC 75-27175. 350p. (C). 1976. 30.00 (*0-271-01207-2*); pap. 18.95 (*0-271-00507-6*) Pa St U Pr.

Loewenberg, Frank M. Fundamentals of Social Intervention. 2nd ed. LC 82-22025. 448p. 1983. text 46.00 (*0-231-05722-9*) Col U Pr.

— Religion & Social Work Practice in Contemporary American Society. 184p. 1988. text 34.50 (*0-231-06452-7*) Col U Pr.

Loewenberg, Frank M. & Dolgoff, Ralph. Ethical Decisions for Social Work Practice. 5th ed. LC 95-71666. 286p. (C). 1996. pap. text 35.00 (*0-87581-399-2*, ED5) F E Peacock Pubs.

Loewenberg, Gerhard. Handbook of Legislative Research. Patterson, Samuel C. & Jewell, Malcolm E., eds. LC 84-29059. (Illus.). 864p. 1985. 52.95 (*0-674-37075-9*) HUP.

Loewenberg, Gerhard & Patterson, Samuel C. Comparing Legislatures. (Illus.). 362p. (C). 1988. reprint ed. pap. text 31.00 (*0-8191-7050-X*) U Pr of Amer.

Loewenberg, Jacob. Dialogues from Delphi. LC 77-121485. (Essay Index Reprint Ser.). 1977. 21.95 (*0-8369-1886-X*) Ayer.

Loewenberg, Peter. Decoding the Past: The Psychohistorical Approach. 310p. (C). 1996. pap. text 24.95 (*1-56000-846-6*) Transaction Pubs.

— Fantasy & Reality in History. (Illus.). 248p. 1995. 45.00 (*0-19-506763-0*) OUP.

Loewenberg, Robert J. An American Idol: Emerson & the "Jewish Idea" LC 84-7206. 148p. (Orig.). (C). 1984. pap. text 19.50 (*0-8191-3956-4*); lib. bdg. 40.00 (*0-8191-3955-6*) U Pr of Amer.

Loewenberg, Robert J. & Alexander, Edward, eds. The Israeli Fate of Jewish Liberalism: Proceedings of a Conference in Jerusalem, at the Institute for Advanced Strategic & Political Studies, 1985. LC 88-20517. 158p. (Orig.). (C). 1988. pap. text 22.50 (*0-8191-7063-1*); lib. bdg. 47.00 (*0-8191-7062-3*) U Pr of Amer.

Loewenfeld, Irene E. & Lowenstein, Otto. The Pupil: Anatomy, Physiology & Clinical Applications. LC 98-53982. 2312p. 1999. text 250.00 (*0-7506-7143-2*) Buttrwrth-Heinemann.

Loewenfeld-Russ, Hans. Die Regelung der Volks-Ernahrung Im Kriege. (Wirtschafts-Und Sozialgeschichte des Weltkrieges (Osterreichische Und Ungarische Serie)). (GER.). 1926. 150.00 (*0-317-27542-9*) Elliots Bks.

Loewenheim, Francis, et al. Roosevelt & Churchill: Their Secret Wartime Correspondence. (Quality Paperbacks Ser.). (Illus.). 840p. 1990. reprint ed. pap. 17.95 (*0-306-80390-9*) Da Capo.

Loewenson, Rene. Modern Plantation Agriculture: Corporate Wealth & Labour Squalor. 208p. (C). 1992. text 62.50 (*0-86232-996-5*, Pub. by St Martin); text 22.50 (*0-86232-997-3*, Pub. by St Martin) St Martin.

Loewenstamm, Samuel E. The Evolution of the Exodus Tradition. xvii, 495p. 1992. 37.00 (*965-223-784-1*, Pub. by Magnes Pr) Eisenbrauns.

Loewenstein, Andrea F. Loathsome Jews & Engulfing Women: Metaphors of Projection in the Works of Wyndham Lewis, Charles Williams & Graham Greene. LC 93-16362. (Literature & Psychoanalysis Ser.: Vol. 2). 412p. (C). 1993. text 47.50 (*0-8147-5063-X*) NYU Pr.

— Loathsome Jews & Engulfing Women: Metaphors of Projection in the Works of Wyndham Lewis, Charles Williams & Graham Greene. LC 93-16362. 412p. (C). 1995. pap. text 19.50 (*0-8147-5096-6*) NYU Pr.

— The Worry Girl: Stories from a Childhood. LC 92-8021. 160p. (Orig.). 1992. pap. 8.95 (*1-56341-016-8*); lib. bdg. 18.95 (*1-56341-017-6*) Firebrand Bks.

Loewenstein, C. Jared. A Descriptive Catalogue of the Jorge Luis Borges Collection at the University of Virginia Library. 150p. 1993. text 35.00 (*0-8139-1333-0*) U Pr of Va.

Loewenstein, David. Milton & the Drama of History: Historical Vision, Iconoclasm & the Literary Imagination. (Illus.). 207p. (C). 1990. text 69.95 (*0-521-37253-4*) Cambridge U Pr.

Loewenstein, David & Turner, James G., eds. Politics, Poetics & Hermeneutics in Milton's Prose. (Illus.). 296p. (C). 1990. text 69.95 (*0-521-34458-1*) Cambridge U Pr.

Loewenstein, David, jt. ed. see Corns, Thomas N.

Loewenstein, Hubertus Z. Germans in History. LC 78-95395. reprint ed. 34.50 (*0-404-04008-X*) AMS Pr.

Loewenstein, Karl. Hitler's Germany. LC 72-7104. (Select Bibliographies Reprint Ser.). 1977. reprint ed. 21.95 (*0-8369-6947-2*) Ayer.

Loewenstein, Louis. Streets of San Francisco. 3rd ed. LC 96-3537. 1996. pap. 10.95 (*0-89997-192-X*) Wilderness Pr.

Loewenstein, Prince H. & Von Zuhlsdorff, Volkmar. NATO & the Defense of the West. Fitzgerald, Edward, tr. from GER. LC 74-20276. 383p. 1975. reprint ed. lib. bdg. 69.50 (*0-8371-7855-X*, LONA, Greenwood Pr) Greenwood.

Loewenstein, Rudolph M., ed. Drives, Affects, Behavior, 2 vols., Vol. 1. LC 53-11056. 399p. 1960. 60.00 (*0-8236-1480-8*) Intl Univs Pr.

— Drives, Affects, Behavior, 2 vols., Vol. 2. LC 53-11056. 502p. 1960. 75.00 (*0-8236-1500-6*) Intl Univs Pr.

***Loewenstein, Sandra.** FTCE Guidance Counseling. (Praxis Ser.). (C). 2000. per. 22.50 (*1-58197-075-7*) XAM.

— PRAXIS Guidance Counceling. (Praxis Ser.). (C). 2000. per. 22.50 (*1-58197-052-8*) XAM.

Loewenstein, Werner R. The Touchstone of Life: Molecular Information, Cell Communication & the Foundations of Life. LC 97-43408. (Illus.). 384p. 1999. 30.00 (*0-19-511828-6*) OUP.

***Loewenstein, Werner R.** The Touchstone of Life: Molecular Information, Cell Communication, & The Foundations of Life. (Illus.). 384p. 2000. pap. 17.95 (*0-19-514057-5*) OUP.

Loewenthal. Introduction Psychology Tests & Scales. 144p. 1996. pap. 19.95 (*1-85728-405-4*, Pub. by UCL Pr Ltd) Taylor & Francis.

— Mental Health & Religion. 256p. 1994. pap. 41.50 (*1-56593-356-7*, 0680) Singular Publishing.

***Loewenthal, Kate M.** Psychology of Religion: A Short Introduction. 2000. pap. 15.95 (*1-85168-212-0*, Pub. by Onewrld Pubns) Penguin Putnam.

An Asterisk (*) at the beginning of an entry indicates that the title is appearing for the first time.

An Asterisk (*) at the beginning of an entry indicates that the title is appearing for the first time.

— A World of Strangers: Order & Action in Urban Public Space. 223p. (C). 1985. reprint ed. pap. text 14.50 (*0-88133-136-8*) Waveland Pr.

Lofland, Lyn H., jt. auth. see Lofland, John.

Loflin, Andrea, ed. Keyboard Kinetics: Techniques for Building Speed & Efficiency on the Keyboard, Vol. 1. 4th rev. ed. 87p. (Orig.). 1999. pap. 19.95 (*1-893418-00-6*, 10095, CogniCom Pubg) Career Step.

Loflin, Christine. African Horizons: The Landscapes of African Fiction, 184. LC 97-9382. (Contributions in Afro-American & African Studies: Vol. 184). 136p. 1998. 49.95 (*0-313-29733-9*, Greenwood Pr) Greenwood.

Loflin, Marvin D. & Silverberg, James, eds. Discourse & Inference in Cognitive Anthropology: An Approach to Psychic Unity & Enculturation. (World Anthropology Ser.). xiv, 314p. 1978. 50.80 (*3-10-800185-X*) Mouton.

Loflin, Murrey E., jt. auth. see Kipp, Jonathan D.

Loflin, W. Jones. Prime Rib or Potted Meat? Thoughts on Getting More Out of Life. 239p. 1998. pap. 12.95 (*0-9662361-0-6*) HOPE Inc.

Lofman, Ron. Celebrity Vocals. LC 93-80695. (Illus.). 448p. 1994. pap. 16.95 (*0-87341-292-3*, CB01) Krause Pubns.

Lofmark, C., tr. see Pohlenz, M.

Lofmark, Carl. What Is the Bible? LC 92-34811. 118p. (C). 1992. 23.95 (*0-87975-781-7*) Prometheus Bks.

Lofmark, Carl, tr. see Soderberg, Hjalmar.

Lofmarker, R. & Pioud, G. Swedish-French Dictionary: Svensk-Fransk Fackordbok. (FRE & SWE.). 320p. 1984. 125.00 (*0-8288-0831-7*, F63000) Fr & Eur.

Lofquist, Lloyd H. & Dawis, Rene V. Essentials of Person-Environment-Correspondence Counseling. (Illus.). 192p. 1991. pap. 16.95 (*0-8166-2066-0*); text 42.95 (*0-8166-1889-5*) U of Minn Pr.

Lofquist, Lloyd H., jt. auth. see Dawis, Rene V.

Lofquist, Thelma J. Frail Elders & the Wounded Caregiver. LC 90-82851. 85p. (Orig.). 1990. pap. 8.00 (*0-8323-0483-2*) Binford Mort.

Lofquist, William, et al, eds. Debating Corporate Crime. LC 97-70136. (ACJS/Anderson Monograph Ser.). (C). 1997. pap. 25.95 (*0-87084-185-8*) Anderson Pub Co.

Lofquist, William A. Discovering the Meaning of Prevention: A Practical Approach to Positive Change. LC 83-72268. (Illus.). 151p. (C). 1983. pap. text 12.00 (*0-913951-00-5*) Develop Pubns.

Lofstedt, Bengt, ed. Vier Juvenal-Kommentare Aus Dem 12. JH. (GER.). xx, 492p. 1995. lib. bdg. 107.00 (*90-5063-306-4*, Pub. by Gieben) J Benjamins Pubng Co.

Lofstedt, Ragnar. Dilemma of Swedish Energy Policy: Implications for International Policymakers. LC 93-24407. (Avebury Studies in Green Research). 256p. 1993. 72.95 (*1-85628-217-1*, Pub. by Avebry) Ashgate Pub Co.

Lofstedt, Ragnar & Sjostedt, G., eds. Environmental Aid Programmes to Eastern Europe. (Avebury Studies in Green Research). 240p. 1996. 78.95 (*1-85972-201-6*, Pub. by Avebry) Ashgate Pub Co.

Lofstrom, Jan, ed. Scandinavian Homosexualities: Essays on Gay & Lesbian Studies. LC 98-6624. 257p. 1998. 59.95 (*0-7890-0508-5*, Harrington Park); pap. 24.95 (*1-56023-111-4*, Harrington Park) Haworth Pr.

Lofstrom, Mark D., jt. ed. see Wedemeyer, Dan J.

Lofstrom, William L. Paita - Outpost of Empire: The Impact of the New England Whaling Fleet on the Socioeconomic Development of Northern Peru, 1932-1865. (Illus.). 232p. 1996. pap. 24.95 (*0-913372-74-9*) Mystic Seaport.

***Loft & Publications Staff.** Waterfront Homes. 2000. 35.00 (*0-688-17978-9*) Morrow Avon.

Loft, Abram. Ensemble! A Rehearsal Guide to Thirty Great Works of Chamber Music. LC 91-26180. (Illus.). 360p. 1992. 34.95 (*0-931340-45-4*, Amadeus Pr) Timber.

— Violin & Keyboard, Vol. 1. LC 90-20922. 364p. 1991. reprint ed. 34.00 (*0-931340-36-5*, Amadeus Pr) Timber.

— Violin & Keyboard, Vol. 2. LC 90-20922. 436p. 1991. reprint ed. 34.00 (*0-931340-37-3*, Amadeus Pr) Timber.

Loft, Andrew, jt. auth. see Shepard, Tristram.

Loft, Randi, ed. see Aries, Ruby.

Loft, Randi, ed. see Pasquini, Katie.

Loftager, Jorn, jt. ed. see Eriksen, Erik O.

Lofthouse, Brenda, compiled by. The Study of Primary Education: A Source Book: The Curriculum, Vol. 2. 285p. 1990. 99.95 (*1-85000-718-7*, Falmer Pr); pap. 32.95 (*1-85000-719-5*, Falmer Pr) Taylor & Francis.

Lofthouse, Brenda, ed. The Study of Primary Education: A Source Book: Classroom & Teaching Studies, Vol. 4. 285p. 1990. 85.00 (*1-85000-737-3*, Falmer Pr); pap. 34.95 (*1-85000-738-1*, Falmer Pr) Taylor & Francis.

Lofthouse, Brenda, jt. compiled by see Southworth, Geoff.

***Lofthouse, Jacqui.** Bluethroat Morning. 304p. 2000. 23.95 (*1-58234-086-2*) Bloomsbury Pubg.

Lofthouse, Mary. The Gypsy Lady. 141p. 1987. 45.00 (*0-7223-2136-8*, Pub. by A H S Ltd) St Mut.

Lofthouse, Nigel. Pocket Guide to Wood Finishes. (Illus.). 64p. 1993. spiral bd. 16.95 (*1-55870-272-5*, Betrwy Bks) F & W Pubns Inc.

Lofthouse, Stephen. Equity Investment Management: How to Select Stocks & Markets. LC 93-29957. 1994. pap. text 42.00 (*0-471-94170-0*) Wiley.

— Personal Financial Planning: How to Fix Your Finances. LC 96-3434. 1996. pap. text 33.50 (*0-471-96702-5*) Wiley.

Lofthouse, Stephen, ed. Readings in Investments. LC 93-29957. 512p. 1995. pap. 105.00 (*0-471-95208-7*) Wiley.

Lofthouse, William F. Israel after the Exile: Sixth & Fifth Centuries B. C. LC 78-10629. (Illus.). 1979. reprint ed. lib. bdg. 69.50 (*0-313-21008-X*, LOIS, Greenwood Pr) Greenwood.

Lofthus, Myrna. A Spiritual Approach to Astrology: A Complete Textbook of Astrology. LC 78-62936. (Illus.). 444p. 1983. 15.95 (*0-916360-10-5*) CRCS Pubns CA.

Lofti, Vahid & Pegels, C. Carl. Decision Support Systems for Operations Management & Management Science. 3rd ed. LC 95-238003. 496p. (C). 1995. text 31.50 incl. 3.5 hd (*0-256-11559-1*, Irwn McGrw-H) McGrw-H Hghr Educ.

Loftie, W. J. Inns of Court & Chancery. (Illus.). xii, 302p. 1994. reprint ed. 42.50 (*0-8377-2416-3*, Rothman) W S Hein.

Loftin, Charlie F. How I Lost Fifty Pounds & Got Off Hypertension Medication. LC 96-123280. (Illus.). 74p. 1995. pap. 5.95 (*0-9647579-0-7*) CFL Enter.

Loftin, Glenda. Grits for Brains. Bledsoe, Jerry, ed. LC 94-71654. (Illus.). 89p. 1994. pap. 7.95 (*1-878086-29-4*, Pub. by Down Home NC) Blair.

***Loftin, John D.** The Big Picture: A Short World History of Religions. LC 99-44357. 270p. 1999. boxed set 35.00 (*0-7864-0635-6*) McFarland & Co.

Loftin, John D. Religion & Hopi Life in the Twentieth Century. LC 90-37968. (Religion in North America Ser.). 192p. 1991. 24.50 (*0-253-33517-5*) Ind U Pr.

— Religion & Hopi Life in the Twentieth Century. LC 90-37968. (Religion in North America Ser.). 192p. 1994. pap. 10.95 (*0-253-20857-2*) Ind U Pr.

Loftin, R. Bowen, jt. ed. see Bloom, Charles P.

Loftin, T. L. Contest for a Capital: George Washington, Robert Morris & Congress, 1783-1791 Contenders. (Illus.). 352p. (YA). 1989. pap. 19.95 (*0-934812-04-7*) Tee Loftin.

***Loftin, T. L.** Westward Go! Fremont, Randy & Kit Carson open Wide the Oregon Trail. (Illus.). 502p. 2000. pap. 29.95 (*0-934812-05-5*) Tee Loftin.

Lofting, Christopher. Story of Mrs. Tubbs. (J). 1998. pap. 14.00 (*0-671-79694-1*) Litle Simon.

Lofting, Hugh. Doctor Dolittle. (Doctor Dolittle Ser.). (J). (gr. 4-6). 1976. 5.50 (*0-87129-390-0*, D18) Dramatic Pub.

— Doctor Dolittle. LC 98-190468. (Illus.). 128p. (J). (gr. 3-7). 1998. pap. 4.99 (*0-440-41546-2*) Dell.

— Doctor Dolittle: A Treasury. (Doctor Dolittle Ser.). (J). (gr. 4-7). 1990. reprint ed. lib. bdg. 37.95 (*0-89966-674-4*) Buccaneer Bks.

— Gub-Gub's Book, an Encyclopedia of Food. LC 91-4672. (Doctor Dolittle Ser.). (J). (gr. 4-6). 1992. pap. 15.00 (*0-671-78355-6*) S&S Bks Yung.

— The Story of Doctor Dolittle. (Doctor Dolittle Ser.). (Illus.), 176p. (J). (gr. 4-7). 1968. pap. 4.99 (*0-440-48307-7*) Dell.

— The Story of Doctor Dolittle. LC 96-51193. (Doctor Dolittle Ser.). (Illus.). 176p. (J). (gr. 4-7). 1997. 20.00 (*0-688-14001-7*, Wm Morrow) Morrow Avon.

— The Story of Doctor Dolittle. (Doctor Dolittle Ser.). 128p. (J). (gr. 4-7). 1998. mass mkt. 3.99 (*0-8125-8006-0*, Pub. by Tor Bks) St Martin.

— The Story of Doctor Dolittle. (Doctor Dolittle Ser.). (J). (gr. 4-6). 1988. 9.60 (*0-606-03929-5*, Pub. by Turtleback) Demco.

— The Story of Doctor Dolittle. adapted ed. (Illus.). 128p. (J). (gr. 2-5). 1997. pap. 3.99 (*0-440-41233-1*, YB BDD) BDD Bks Young Read.

— The Story of Doctor Dolittle. unabridged ed. LC 96-51564. (Doctor Dolittle Ser.). (Illus.). 96p. (J). (gr. 4-6). 1997. reprint ed. pap. text 1.00 (*0-486-29350-5*) Dover.

— The Twilight of Magic. LC 67-17092. (J). (gr. 4-6). 1967. 11.95 (*0-397-30989-9*) HarpC Child Bks.

— The Twilight of Magic. LC 92-15766. (Illus.). (J). 1993. pap. 15.00 (*0-671-78358-0*) S&S Bks Yung.

***Lofting, Hugh.** Viages de Doctor Dolittle. (Doctor Dolittle Ser.: Vol. 94).Tr. of Voyages of Doctor Dolittle. (SPA., Illus.). (J). (gr. 4-7). 1999. pap. 11.95 (*84-239-7060-4*) Espasa Calpe.

Lofting, Hugh. The Voyages of Doctor Dolittle. LC 87-33067. (Doctor Dolittle Ser.). (Illus.). 316p. (J). (gr. 4-7). 1988. pap. 5.50 (*0-440-40002-3*, YB BDD) BDD Bks Young Read.

***Lofting, Hugh.** The Voyages of Doctor Dolittle. (Signet Classics Ser.). (J). (gr. 4-6). 2000. mass mkt. 4.95 (*0-451-52769-0*, Sig) NAL.

Lofting, Hugh. The Voyages of Doctor Dolittle. LC 98-14262. (Doctor Dolittle Ser.). (Illus.). 288p. (J). (gr. 4-7). 1998. 13.99 (*0-448-41863-0*, G & D) Peng Put Young Read.

Lofting, Hugh. The Voyages of Doctor Dolittle. (Doctor Dolittle Ser.). (J). (gr. 4-6). 1994. 10.09 (*0-606-03947-3*, Pub. by Turtleback) Demco.

Lofting, Hugh. The Voyages of Doctor Dolittle. abr. ed. (Doctor Dolittle Ser.). (Illus.). 240p. (J). (gr. 2-5). 1997. pap. 4.50 (*0-440-41240-4*, YB BDD) BDD Bks Young Read.

Lofting, Hugh, jt. auth. see Kleinbaum, N. H.

Loftis, Anne. Witnesses to the Struggle: Imaging the 1930s California Labor Movement. LC 97-22379. 240p. 1998. 29.95 (*0-87417-305-1*) U of Nev Pr.

Loftis, Chris. The Boy Who Sat by the Window: Helping Children Cope with Violence. (Illus.). 54p. (J). (gr. k-3). 1997. pap. 12.95 (*0-88282-147-4*) New Horizon NJ.

— The Words Hurt. LC 94-66754. (Illus.). 40p. (J). (ps-4). 1994. pap. 9.95 (*0-88282-132-6*) New Horizon NJ.

Loftis, David L., jt. ed. see Stringer, Jeffrey W.

Loftis, James R., jt. auth. see American Bar Association, Section of Antitrust Law.

Loftis, John. Comedy & Society from Congreve to Fielding. LC 76-51940. (Stanford University. Stanford Studies in Language & Literature: 19). reprint ed. 29.50 (*0-404-51829-X*) AMS Pr.

— Renaissance Drama in England & Spain: Topical Allusion & History Plays. (Illus.). 296p. 1987. text 45.00 (*0-691-06706-6*, Pub. by Princeton U Pr) Cal Prin Full Svc.

Loftis, John, et al, eds. The Works of John Dryden Vol. I, Pt. I: Plays: The Conquest of Granada. 1978. 80.00 (*0-520-02125-8*, Pub. by U CA Pr) Cal Prin Full Svc.

Loftis, John & Dearing, Vinton A., eds. The Works of John Dryden Vol. IX: Plays: The Indian Emperour, Secret Love, Sir Martin Mar-All. 1967. 80.00 (*0-520-00360-8*, Pub. by U CA Pr) Cal Prin Full Svc.

Loftis, John, ed. see Addison, Joseph.

Loftis, John, ed. see Halkett, Anne & Fanshawe, Ann.

Loftis, John, ed. see Lee, Nathaniel.

Loftis, John, ed. see Sheridan, Richard Brinsley.

Loftis, John C. Renaissance Drama in England & Spain: Topical Allusion & History Plays. LC 86-25431. (Illus.). 298p. 1987. reprint ed. pap. 92.40 (*0-608-07134-X*, 206736000009) Bks Demand.

— Sheridan & the Drama of Georgian England. 186p. 1976. 26.95 (*0-674-80632-8*) HUP.

— The Spanish Plays of Neoclassical England. LC 87-8685. 276p. 1987. reprint ed. lib. bdg. 69.50 (*0-313-25133-9*, LSPA, Greenwood Pr) Greenwood.

Loftis, John C. & Hardacre, Paul H., eds. Colonel Joseph Bampfield's Apology: "Written by Himself & Printed at His Desire," 1865. LC 91-58963. (Illus.). 312p. 1993. 48.50 (*0-8387-5231-4*) Bucknell U Pr.

Loftis, N. J. Black Anima. (New Writers Ser.). 1973. 4.95 (*0-87140-562-8*, Pub. by Liveright) Norton.

Loftis, Norman. Condition Zero. LC 91-17805. (American University Studies: Philosophy: Ser. V, Vol. 123). 148p. (C). 1994. text 34.95 (*0-8204-1698-3*) P Lang Pubng.

Loftis, Paula A. Decision Making in Gerontologic Nursing. 352p. (C). (gr. 13). 1993. pap. text 37.00 (*1-55664-186-9*) Mosby Inc.

Loftiss, Carolyn, ed. see Loftiss, Gary.

Loftiss, Gary. Model Makers. Loftiss, Carolyn, ed. (Illus.). 460p. 1995. pap. text 19.95 (*0-9642120-9-9*) Chiffon Pubs.

Loftiss, Gary, ed. see Allen, David.

Loftiss, Gary, ed. see Jones, William K.

Loftiss, Gary, ed. see Lee, Barbie.

Loftness, John & Mahaney, C. J. Disciplined for Life: Steps to Spiritual Strength. Somerville, Greg, ed. 112p. 1992. pap. 6.99 (*1-881039-00-5*) PDI Ministries.

Loftness, Marvin O. AC Power Interference Manual: New Insights into the Causes, Effects, Locating, & Correction of Power-Line Interference. unabridged ed. LC 96-94586. (Illus.). 260p. (Orig.). 1996. pap. 24.95 (*0-9653760-2-8*) Percival Pub.

— Power Line Interference: A Practical Handbook. LC 92-27686. 1992. write for info. (*0-917599-07-1*) Natl Rural.

Lofton, C. A. African-American Guide to Prosperity. 48p. 1999. pap. 14.95 (*0-9659321-3-3*); lib. bdg. 17.50 (*0-9659321-4-1*) Lofton Publ.

— Prosperity Plan: Starter Kit: A Metaphysical Catalyst to Health, Wealth & Happiness. 2nd rev. ed. (Illus.). 84p. 1997. 25.95 (*0-9659321-2-5*); pap. 14.00 (*0-9659321-0-9*); lib. bdg. 16.00 (*0-9659321-1-7*) Lofton Publ.

***Lofton, F. Douglas & Lofton, Mellanese S.** The Medi-Cal Advantage (How to Save the Family Home from the Cost of Nursing Home Care) large type ed. Lofton-Koponen, Robin M., ed. (Illus.). 116p. 1998. pap. 49.95 (*0-9667737-0-5*) Lailabela Pr.

Lofton, Fred C. A Crying Shepherd: A Therapy of Tears. 214p. (Orig.). 1993. pap. 9.95 (*0-9625423-7-7*) Four-G Pubs.

— Teach Us to Pray: The Disciples Request Cast Anew. 96p. 1983. pap. 4.00 (*0-89191-751-9*) Prog Bapt Pub.

Lofton, Fred C., jt. ed. see Pleasure, Mose, Jr.

Lofton, J. Mack, Jr. Healing Hands: An Alabama Medical Mosaic. LC 94-23119. (Illus.). 312p. (Orig.). 1995. pap. 29.95 (*0-8173-0779-6*) U of Ala Pr.

— Voices from Alabama: A Twentieth-Century Mosaic. LC 92-36110. (Illus.). 368p. (Orig.). 1993. pap. 24.95 (*0-8173-0684-6*) U of Ala Pr.

Lofton, John. Denmark Vesey's Revolt: The Slave Plot That Lit a Fuse to Fort Sumter. LC 83-11267. 316p. reprint ed. pap. 98.00 (*0-7837-4054-9*, 204388500011) Bks Demand.

Lofton-Koponen, Robin M., ed. see Lofton, F. Douglas & Lofton, Mellanese S.

Lofton, Marie C., jt. auth. see Norris, Donald M.

Lofton, Mellanese S., jt. auth. see Lofton, F. Douglas.

***Lofton, Ruth.** They Said I Wouldn't Make It. 52p. 2000. pap. 9.95 (*0-9679999-1-X*) Useful.

— You're Not Crazy & You're Not Dreaming: A Testimony of Spiritual Warfare. 88p. 2000. pap. 9.95 (*0-9679999-0-1*) Useful.

Lofton, Saab. A. D. 320p. (Orig.). 1995. pap. 12.00 (*0-9622937-8-4*) III Pub.

Lofton, Todd. Futures. 3rd ed. LC 96-40008. (Getting Started in Ser.). (Illus.). 278p. 1997. pap. 18.95 (*0-471-17759-8*) Wiley.

Lofts, Norah. Bless This House. reprint ed. lib. bdg. 23.95 (*0-89190-225-2*, Rivercity Pr) Amereon Ltd.

— Bless This House. 1977. reprint ed. lib. bdg. 26.95 (*0-89244-048-1*) Queens Hse-Focus Serv.

— House at Old Vine. 408p. 1990. reprint ed. lib. bdg. 26.95 (*0-89244-049-X*) Queens Hse-Focus Serv.

— The House at Old Vine. reprint ed. lib. bdg. 27.95 (*0-89190-226-0*, Rivercity Pr) Amereon Ltd.

— The House at Sunset. reprint ed. lib. bdg. 26.95 (*0-89190-227-9*, Rivercity Pr) Amereon Ltd.

— How Far to Bethlehem? 1976. 24.95 (*0-8488-1417-7*) Amereon Ltd.

— How Far to Bethlehem? 300p. 1991. reprint ed. lib. bdg. 29.95 (*0-89966-787-2*) Buccaneer Bks.

— Scent of Cloves. reprint ed. lib. bdg. 24.95 (*0-89190-228-7*, Rivercity Pr) Amereon Ltd.

— The Silver Nutmeg. reprint ed. lib. bdg. 26.95 (*0-89190-229-5*, Rivercity Pr) Amereon Ltd.

— The Town House. reprint ed. lib. bdg. 27.95 (*0-89190-230-9*, Rivercity Pr) Amereon Ltd.

— A Wayside Tavern. large type ed. 1982. 15.95 (*0-7089-0838-1*) Ulverscroft.

Lofts, Pamela, jt. auth. see Vaughan, Marcia K.

Lofts, S. G. Ernst Cassirer: A "Repetition" of Modernity. LC 99-39699. (C). 2000. text 73.50 (*0-7914-4495-3*); pap. text 24.95 (*0-7914-4496-1*) State U NY Pr.

Lofts, S. G., tr. & intro. see Cassirer, Ernst.

Lofts, Steve G., jt. auth. see Cassirer, Ernst.

Loftsgaarden, Don, et al. Statistical Abstract of Undergraduate Programs in the Mathematical Sciences in the United States: Fall 1995 CBMS Survey. (MAA Reports Ser.). 198p. 1997. pap. 29.95 (*0-88385-154-7*) Math Assn.

Loftus. Textbook of Carotid Artery Surgery. LC 99-30338. (Illus.). 379p. 1999. 159.00 (*0-86577-769-1*) Thieme Med Pubs.

Loftus & Doyle. Eyewitness Testimony, 1997. 3rd ed. LC 97-76678. 438p. 1997. text 100.00 (*1-55834-714-3*, 64394-11, MICHIE) LEXIS Pub.

Loftus, Bill. Idaho State Parks Guidebook. (Illus.). 130p. 1991. pap. 9.95 (*0-9607506-5-7*) News Rev Pub.

Loftus, Brendan G. Pathways in Pediatrics. 288p. 1995. 24.95 (*0-340-59036-X*, Pub. by E A) OUP.

Loftus, C. ADA Yearbook, 1994. LC 94-75423. (Studies in Computer & Communications Ser.). 460p. 1994. 94.00 (*90-5199-155-X*) IOS Press.

Loftus, C., ed. ADA Yearbook 1993. LC 92-63411. (Studies in Computer & Communications Systems: Vol. 5). 450p. 1993. 94.00 (*90-5199-124-X*, Pub. by IOS Pr) IOS Press.

Loftus, Christopher M. Carotid Endarterectomy: Principles & Techniques. 242p. 1995. text 130.00 (*0-942219-69-4*) Quality Med Pub.

— Clinical Neurosurgery Vol. 43: Proceedings of the Congress of Neurological Surgeons, Vol. 43. (Illus.). 458p. 1997. write for info. (*0-683-18300-1*) Lppncott W & W.

Loftus, Christopher M., jt. ed. see Grossman, Robert G.

Loftus, Diana S., jt. auth. see Thompson, Kimberly B.

***Loftus, Elizabeth & Ketcham, Katherine.** The Myth of Repressed Memory: False Memories & Allegations of Sexual Abuse. 290p. 2000. reprint ed. 23.00 (*0-7881-9282-5*) DIANE Pub.

Loftus, Elizabeth F. Eyewitness Testimony. LC 79-13195. (Illus.). 268p. 1980. 26.00 (*0-674-28775-4*) HUP.

— Eyewitness Testimony. LC 79-13195. (Illus.). 268p. 1981. pap. 15.95 (*0-674-28776-2*) HUP.

— Eyewitness Testimony. 272p. 1996. pap. text 17.95 (*0-674-28777-0*) HUP.

— Memory. (Illus.). 207p. 1980. pap. text 20.95 (*0-912675-28-4*) Ardsley.

Loftus, Elizabeth F. & Doyle, James M. Eyewitness Testimony: Civil & Criminal. 2nd ed. 475p. 1992. write for info. (*0-318-69710-6*, MICHIE); write for info. (*0-318-69712-2*, MICHIE); 100.00 (*0-87473-983-7*, MICHIE) LEXIS Pub.

— Eyewitness Testimony: Civil & Criminal, 1998 Supplement. 30p. 1998. pap. 35.00 (*0-327-00573-4*, 6439314) LEXIS Pub.

Loftus, Elizabeth F. & Ketcham, Katherine. The Myth of Repressed Memory: False Memories & Allegations of Sexual Abuse. 304p. 1996. pap. 13.95 (*0-312-14123-8*) St Martin.

Loftus, Elizabeth F., jt. auth. see Loftus, Geoffrey R.

Loftus, Elizabeth F., jt. auth. see Wortman, Camille B.

Loftus, Geoffrey, jt. auth. see Savageau, David.

Loftus, Geoffrey R. & Loftus, Elizabeth F. Human Memory: The Processing of Information. 192p. 1976. pap. text 27.50 (*0-89859-135-X*) L Erlbaum Assocs.

Loftus, Jean M. Smart Woman's Guide to Plastic Surgery: Essential Information from a Female Plastic Surgeon. LC 99-36975. 224p. 1999. pap. 17.95 (*0-8092-2583-2*, 258320, Contemporary Bks) NTC Contemp Pub Co.

Loftus, John. John Loftus at Seventy: Work from the Fifties to the Present. (Illus.). 52p. (Orig.). 1991. pap. 20.00 (*0-910969-01-9*) Hobart & Wm Smith.

— The Secret War Against the Jews. 1994. text 26.95 (*0-312-11057-X*) St Martin.

— The Secret War Against the Jews. 1997. pap. 16.95 (*0-312-15648-0*) St Martin.

Loftus, John A. Investment Management: An Analysis of the Experience of American Management Investment Trusts. LC 78-64181. (Johns Hopkins University. Studies in the Social Sciences. Thirtieth Ser. 1912: 1). 136p. 1983. reprint ed. 37.50 (*0-404-61289-X*) AMS Pr.

— Understanding Sexual Misconduct by Clergy: A Handbook for Ministers. 1994. pap. text 9.95 (*1-56929-024-5*, Pastoral Press) OR Catholic.

Loftus, John H., tr. see Nayatani, Yoshinobu, et al.

Loftus, Joseph & Walfish, Beatrice, eds. Breakthroughs in Union-Management Cooperation. LC 77-24837. 49p. 1977. pap. text 7.00 (*0-89361-002-X*) Work in Amer.

Loftus, Joseph P., Jr., ed. Orbital Debris from Upper-Stage Breakup. (PAAS Ser.: Vol. 121). 227p. 1989. 65.95 (*0-930403-58-4*, V-121) AIAA.

Loftus, Simon. Puligny-Montrachet. 1995. pap. write for info. (*0-8050-3175-8*) H Holt & Co.

Loftus, Tom. The Art of Legislative Politics. LC 94-19620. 150p. 1994. pap. 20.95 (*0-87187-980-8*) Congr Quarterly.

Lofty, J. R., jt. auth. see Edwards, C. A.

Lofvenberg, M. T. On the Syncope of the Old English Present Endings. (Essays & Studies on English Language & Literature: Vol. 1). 1974. reprint ed. pap. 25.00 (*0-8115-0199-X*) Periodicals Srv.

An Asterisk (*) at the beginning of an entry indicates that the title is appearing for the first time.

— Studies on Middle English Local Surnames. (Lund Studies in English: Vol. 11). 1974. reprint ed. pap. 45.00 (*0-8115-0554-5*) Periodicals Srv.

Lofy, Chuck. A Grain of Wheat: Giving Voice to the Spirit of Change. 127p. 1993. pap. 11.95 (*0-933173-56-3*) Chging Church Forum.

Logan. Art of Enjoying College Life. 432p. 1998. pap. text 26.20 (*0-536-01343-8*) Pearson Custom.

***Logan.** Black Family. 2nd ed. 250p. 2000. pap. 26.00 (*0-8133-6797-2*, Pub. by Westview) HarpC.

Logan. Environmental Geology. 122p. 1998. pap. text 22.00 (*0-536-01487-6*) Pearson Custom.

Logan. Oaks. Date not set. write for info. (*0-393-04773-3*) Norton.

Logan. Principle of Practice for the Acute Care Nurse Practioner. LC 98-26249. 1999. pap. text 115.00 (*0-8385-8125-0*, Medical Exam) Appleton & Lange.

***Logan.** Strengths & Common Heritages. 2000. pap. 55.00 (*0-8133-6779-4*, Pub. by Westview) HarpC.

Logan, et al. Louisiana Hayride Years. 1999. pap. 14.95 (*0-312-20661-5*, St Martin's Paperbacks) St Martin.

Logan, jt. auth. see Barrett.

Logan, jt. auth. see Leach.

Logan, A. Bulletins of American Paleontology Vol. 93: Neogene Paleontology in the Northern Dominican Republic: 6. The Phylum Brachiopoda, Issue 328. 74p. 1987. 30.00 (*0-614-17838-X*) Paleo Res.

Logan, A. H. & Wedderburn, A. J., eds. New Testament & Gnosis. 272p. 1983. 47.95 (*0-567-09344-1*, Pub. by T & T Clark) Bks Intl VA.

Logan, A. L. The Foot & Ankle: Clinical Application. 194p. 1994. 51.00 (*0-8342-0605-6*) Aspen Pub.

— The Knee: Clinical Applications. LC 93-39114. 192p. 1994. 51.00 (*0-8342-0522-X*, 20522) Aspen Pub.

Logan, A. M. The Cabinet of the Brothers Gerard & Jan Reynst. (Verhandelingen der Koninklijke Nederlandse Akademie van Wetenschappen, Afd. Letterkunde, Nieuwe Reeks Ser.: No. 99). 294p. 1979. text 62.00 (*0-7204-8342-5*) Elsevier.

Logan, Adelphena. Memories of Sweet Grass. LC 79-65401. (Illus.). 79p. 1979. 6.95 (*0-89488-006-3*) Inst Amer Indian.

Logan, Alan. Holocene Reefs of Bermuda. (Sedimenta Ser.: Vol. XI). (Illus.). 63p. 1988. 9.00 (*0-932981-10-0*) Univ Miami CSL.

Logan, Alastair, tr. see Westermann, Claus.

Logan, Alastair H. Gnostic Truth & Christian Heresy: A Study in the History of Gnosticism. 374p. 1996. 29.95 (*1-56563-243-5*) Hendrickson MA.

Logan, Albert B. & Cheney, William R. Strategy to Revitalize the American Dream: Justice in Jeopardy. (Illus.). 260p. 1973. 8.95 (*0-317-01152-9*); pap. 5.95 (*0-317-01153-7*) NIJD Colorado.

Logan, Alyssa. The Magic of Love. LC 96-45316. (Janet Dailey's Love Scenes Ser.). 1997. pap. 3.50 (*1-56853-031-5*, Signal Hill) New Readers.

Logan, Ann. Dial D for Destiny. (Superromance Ser.). 1994. per. 3.50 (*0-373-70585-9*, 1-70585-4) Harlequin Bks.

Logan, Ann, jt. auth. see Berry, M.

Logan, Anna & Koehler, Ed. The Jesus Tree Activity Book. (Illus.). 48p. (Orig.). (J). (ps-2). 1991. pap. 4.99 (*0-570-04197-X*, 56-1656) Concordia.

Logan, Anne. Finding Kendall. 1997. per. 4.50 (*0-373-82563-3*) Harlequin Bks.

— School's Out! (Illus.). 80p. 1987. 22.95 (*0-919783-72-4*, Pub. by Boston Mills) Genl Dist Srvs.

— That Old Devil Moon (Whem Old Devil Moon Dare) (Superromance Ser.). 1996. per. 3.99 (*0-373-70688-X*, 1-70688-6) Harlequin Bks.

— Twin Oaks. (Superromance Ser.). 1993. mass mkt. 3.50 (*0-373-70550-6*, 1-70550-8) Harlequin Bks.

Logan, Anne-Marie. British Artists Authority List. 1987. 20.00 (*0-685-54075-8*) Visual Resources Assn.

— Flemish Drawings in the Age of Rubens. (Illus.). 273p. 1993. text 30.00 (*1-881894-01-0*) WC Davis Mus & Cult.

Logan, Arnold. Building the Chorus. pap. 22.50 (*1-889511-02-1*, 1893, WindRose Pub) Rose Harmony.

— Building the Chorus: Folksong Arrangements. 15.00 (*1-889511-03-X*, 1894) Rose Harmony.

— Johnny Hears the Call. pap. 10.00 (*1-889511-01-3*, 1919, WindRose Pub) Rose Harmony.

— One-Two-Three for Rose Lyre. pap. 20.00 (*1-889511-04-8*, 1918, WindRose Pub) Rose Harmony.

Logan, Barbara & Dawkins, Cecilia. Family-Centered Nursing in the Community. 809p. (C). 1986. text 45.25 (*0-201-12684-2*, Health Sci) Addison-Wesley.

Logan, Beatrice & Blumenthal, Caroline. Electronic Connections. 2nd ed. 52p. (C). 1996. pap. text 14.95 (*0-7872-2879-6*, 41287901) Kendall-Hunt.

Logan, Ben. Christmas Remembered. LC 97-9616. (Illus.). 160p. (Orig.). 1997. 16.95 (*1-55971-636-3*, NorthWord Pr) Creat Pub Intl.

— The Empty Meadow. 2nd ed. LC 91-7977. 228p. 1991. pap. 12.95 (*1-879483-03-3*) Prairie Oak Pr.

— The Land Remembers: The Story of a Farm & Its People - 25th Anniversary Edition. anniversary ed. LC 99-14993. 277p. 1999. pap. 14.95 (*1-55971-718-1*, NorthWord Pr) Creat Pub Intl.

Logan, Beryl. A Religion Without Talking No. 7: Religious Beliefs & Natural Belief in Hume's Philosophy of Religion Studies in European Thought. LC 93-16910. XII, 184p. (C). 1993. text 42.95 (*0-8204-2201-0*) P Lang Pubng.

Logan, Beryl, ed. Immanuel Kant's Prolegomena to Any Future Metaphysics: In Focus. (Philosophers in Focus Ser.). 272p. (C). 1996. 85.00 (*0-415-11575-2*); pap. 27.99 (*0-415-11576-0*) Routledge.

Logan, Bey. Hong Kong Action Cinema. (Illus.). 191p. 1996. pap. 23.95 (*0-87951-663-1*, Pub. by Overlook Pr) Penguin Putnam.

Logan, Brian, jt. ed. see Baxter, Jeremy.

Logan, Brian W. The MacLeod Evaporite Basin, Western Australia: Holocene Environments, Seidments & Geological Evolution. LC 87-33455. (AAPG Memoir Ser.: Vol. 44). 152p. 1987. reprint ed. pap. 47.20 (*0-608-02775-8*, 206384100007) Bks Demand.

***Logan, Bruce E.** Environmental Transport Processes. LC 98-8018. 672p. 1998. 89.95 (*0-471-18871-9*) Wiley.

Logan, Cait. Delilah. 336p. (Orig.). 1995. mass mkt. 4.99 (*0-515-11565-7*, Jove) Berkley Pub.

Logan, Carole, jt. auth. see Stewart, John R.

Logan, Carolyn, ed. Counterbalance: Gendered Perspectives on Writing & Language. 400p. 1997. pap. 32.95 (*1-55111-127-6*) Broadview Pr.

Logan, Carolyn J. Winning the Land Use Game: A Guide for Developers & Citizen Protesters. LC 81-15710. 199p. 1982. 49.95 (*0-275-90849-6*, C0849, Praeger Pubs) Greenwood.

Logan, Charles H., jt. auth. see Sacks, Howard R.

Logan, Chris, jt. auth. see Thomas, Henk.

Logan, Chuck. The Big Law. LC 98-29852. 368p. 1998. 24.00 (*0-06-019133-3*) HarpC.

— The Big Law. 448p. 1999. mass mkt. 6.99 (*0-06-109687-3*) HarpC.

— Hunter's Moon: Hunter's Moon. 416p. 1996. mass mkt. 5.99 (*0-06-109384-X*, Harp PBks) HarpC.

— The Price of Blood. 496p. 1998. mass mkt. 6.99 (*0-06-109622-9*, Harp PBks) HarpC.

Logan, Cordell E. Medicine at the Crossroads: A Global View from Agriculture to Complementary Medicine. (Illus.). 444p. (Orig.). (C). 1993. pap. 19.95 (*0-9636519-0-0*) C E Logan.

Logan, Dan. Computer Resource Guide: San Luis Obispo & Santa Maria. (Illus.). xv, 129p. (Orig.). 1997. pap. 12.95 (*1-890077-00-3*) Runaway Press.

Logan, Dan, jt. auth. see Sheldon, Tom.

Logan, Dan P. Tilling the Good Earth. LC 89-83521. 185p. 1989. pap. 7.95 (*0-944419-08-9*) Everett Inc.

***Logan, Daniel.** Your Eastern Star. LC 00-102976. 248p. 2000. pap. 16.00 (*1-58776-046-0*, Mystic Oracle Bks) Vivisphere.

Logan, Daryl. First Course in Finite Element Methods Using Algorithms. LC 96-27704. (General Engineering Ser.). (C). 1997. mass mkt. 94.95 (*0-534-94692-5*) PWS Pubs.

Logan, Daryl L. A First Course in the Finite Element Method. 2nd ed. 640p. 1992. mass mkt. 82.95 (*0-534-92964-8*) PWS Pubs.

***Logan, Daryl L.** A First Course In the Finite Element Method Using Algor. LC 00-31281. 2000. write for info. (*0-534-38068-9*) Brooks-Cole.

Logan, David & Conference Board Staff. Community Involvement of Foreign-Owned Companies. LC 96-116339. (Report Ser.). 34 p. 1994. write for info. (*0-8237-0536-6*) Conference Bd.

Logan, David A. & Logan, Wayne A. North Carolina Tort Law. LC 94-73844. 662p. (C). 1996. lib. bdg. 100.00 (*0-89089-844-8*) Carolina Acad Pr.

Logan, David J. Applied Mathematics. 2nd ed. LC 96-31997. 496p. 1996. 89.95 (*0-471-16513-1*) Wiley.

Logan, Deborah, ed. see Penn, William.

Logan, Deborah A. Fallenness in Victorian Women's Writing: Marry, Stitch, Die, or Do Worse. LC 98-6618. 248p. 1998. 34.95 (*0-8262-1175-5*) U of Mo Pr.

***Logan, Debra Kay.** Information Skills Toolkit: Collaborative Integrated Instruction for the Middle Grades. LC 99-58998. (Professional Growth Ser.). (Illus.). 300p. 2000. pap. 39.95 (*0-938865-91-9*) Linworth Pub.

Logan, Don. ACC Bomber Triad: The B-52s, B-1s, & B-2s of Air Combat Command. LC 98-88033. (Illus.). 256p. 1999. 59.95 (*0-7643-0680-4*) Schiffer.

— The Boeing C-135 Series: Stratotanker, Stratolifter & Other Variants. LC 97-80210. 256p. 1998. 49.95 (*0-7643-0286-8*) Schiffer.

— General Dynamics F-111 Aardvark. LC 98-84262. 320p. 1998. 59.95 (*0-7643-0587-5*) Schiffer.

— Northrop's T-38 Talon: A Pictorial History. LC 95-68024. (Illus.). 152p. (Orig.). 1995. pap. 24.95 (*0-88740-800-1*) Schiffer.

— Northrop's YF-17 Cobra: A Pictorial History. LC 95-71769. (Illus.). 64p. (YA). (gr. 12). 1996. pap. 19.95 (*0-88740-910-5*) Schiffer.

— Republic's A-10 Thunderbolt II: A Pictorial History. LC 96-70468. (Illus.). 240p. 1997. 49.95 (*0-7643-0147-0*) Schiffer.

— The 388th Tactical Fighter Wing at Korat Royal Thai Air Force Base 1972. LC 95-67627. (Illus.). 128p. 1995. 29.95 (*0-88740-798-6*) Schiffer.

***Logan, Don.** USAF F-15 Eagles; Units, Colors & markings. (Illus.). 304p. 2000. 59.95 (*0-7643-1060-7*) Schiffer.

Logan, Donn, jt. auth. see Attoe, Wayne.

Logan, Donna, ed. see Sterett, Betty.

Logan, E. M. & Winterton, J. R., eds. Information Sources in Law. 2nd ed. LC 97-1205. 500p. 1997. 95.00 (*1-85739-041-5*) Bowker-Saur.

Logan, Earl, Jr. Handbook of Turbomachinery. LC 94-22880. (Mechanical Engineering Ser.: Vol. 93). (Illus.). 488p. 1994. text 185.00 (*0-8247-9263-7*) Dekker.

Logan, Earl. Thermodynamics: Processes & Applications. LC 99-15460. (Mechanical Engineering Ser.). (Illus.). 427p. 1999. text 150.00 (*0-8247-9959-3*) Dekker.

— Turbomachinery: Basic Theory & Applications. 2nd rev. ed. (Mechanical Engineering Ser.: Vol. 85). (Illus.). 280p. 1993. text 85.00 (*0-8247-9138-X*) Dekker.

Logan, Elisabeth & Gluck, Myke, eds. Electronic Publishing: Applications & Implications. LC 96-43638. 160p. 1997. 34.95 (*1-57387-036-6*) Info Today Inc.

Logan, Eunice S., et al. Charleston Receipts Repeats. 7th ed. (Illus.). 376p. 1986. 16.95 (*0-9607854-5-0*) Jun League Charl SC.

Logan, F. Donald. Runaway Religious in Medieval England, c. 1240-1540. (Cambridge Studies in Medieval Life & Thought: No. 32). 320p. (C). 1996. text 59.95 (*0-521-47502-3*) Cambridge U Pr.

— Vikings in History. 1991. pap. 19.95 (*0-04-446040-6*) Routledge.

— Vikings in History. 2nd ed. 224p. (C). 1995. pap. 21.99 (*0-415-08396-6*, Pub. by Tavistock) Routldge.

Logan, Frank. A Cave House Ranch in Arizona. 1987. 5.95 (*0-685-38470-5*) Intl Univ Pr.

— Westward to a Cave-House Ranch. write for info. (*0-89697-382-4*) Intl Univ Pr.

Logan, Gary W., jt. auth. see Young, Leonard M.

***Logan, George M.** The Indiana University School of Music: A History. LC 00-39630. 2000. 27.95 (*0-253-33820-4*) Ind U Pr.

Logan, George M. & Teskey, Gordon, eds. Unfolded Tales: Essays on Renaissance Romance. LC 88-47920. (Illus.). 368p. 1989. 45.00 (*0-8014-2268-X*) Cornell U Pr.

— Unfolded Tales: Essays on Renaissance Romance. LC 88-47920. (Illus.). 343p. reprint ed. pap. 106.40 (*0-608-20919-8*, 207201800003) Bks Demand.

Logan, George M., ed. see More, Thomas.

Logan, Gordon D., jt. ed. see Dulany, Donelson E.

Logan, Greg. This Universe of Men. (Illus.). 150p. 1992. pap. 10.95 (*0-943383-04-8*) FirstHand Ltd.

Logan, Heather. Exploration into World Cultures: An Oral History Biography of Hap Gilliland. 112p. 1995. pap. 9.95 (*0-89992-514-6*) Coun India Ed.

Logan, Horace & Slogan, Bill. Elvis Hank & Me. LC 98-9795. 256p. 1998. text 23.95 (*0-312-18573-1*) St Martin.

Logan, Ikubolajeh, jt. ed. see Mengisteab, Kidane.

Logan, J. David. Applied Partial Differential Equations. Gehring, F. W. & Halmos, P. R., eds. LC 97-48861. (Undergraduate Texts in Mathematics Ser.). (Illus.). 208p. 1998. 59.95 (*0-387-98441-0*); pap. 29.95 (*0-387-98439-9*) Spr-Verlag.

— An Introduction to Nonlinear Partial Differential Equations: Pure & Applied Mathematics. (Pure & Applied Mathematics: A Wiley-Interscience Series of Texts, Monographs & Tracts). 416p. 1994. 94.95 (*0-471-59916-6*) Wiley.

Logan, J. S., jt. auth. see Clarke, Richard.

Logan, Jake. Arizona Strip War, Vol. 214. (Jake Logan Ser.). 192p. 1997. mass mkt. 4.99 (*0-515-11997-0*, Jove) Berkley Pub.

— Blood in Kansas: John Slocum. (Slocum Ser.: Vol. 231). 1998. mass mkt. 4.99 (*0-515-12291-2*, Jove) Berkley Pub.

— Blood on the Brazos: John Slocum. (Slocum Ser.: Vol. 227). 192p. 1998. mass mkt. 5.99 (*0-515-12229-7*, Jove) Berkley Pub.

— Blood on the Rio Grande. (Slocum Ser.: No. 207). 1996. mass mkt. 4.50 (*0-515-11860-5*, Jove) Berkley Pub.

— Louisiana Lovely: John Slocum. (Slocum Ser.: Vol. 224). 192p. 1997. mass mkt. 4.99 (*0-515-12176-2*, Jove) Berkley Pub.

— Prairie Fires: John Slocum. (Slocum Ser.: Vol. 225). 192p. 1997. mass mkt. 4.99 (*0-515-12190-8*, Jove) Berkley Pub.

— Renegade Trail. (Slocum Ser.: No. 201). 192p. (Orig.). 1995. mass mkt. 4.50 (*0-515-11739-0*, Jove) Berkley Pub.

***Logan, Jake.** Sheriff Slocum. (Slocum Ser.). 272p. 2000. mass mkt. 5.99 (*0-515-12841-4*) Berkley Pub.

Logan, Jake. Showdown at Drowning Creek: John Slocum. (Slocum Ser.: Vol. 203). 192p. (Orig.). 1996. mass mkt. 4.50 (*0-515-11782-X*, Jove) Berkley Pub.

***Logan, Jake.** Showdown at Shiloh. (Slocum Ser.: Vol. 248). 1999. mass mkt. 4.99 (*0-515-12659-4*, Jove) Berkley Pub.

Logan, Jake. The Silver Stallion: John Slocum. (Slocum Ser.: Vol. 197). 192p. (Orig.). 1995. mass mkt. 3.99 (*0-515-11654-8*, Jove) Berkley Pub.

— Slocum & Doc Holliday. (Slocum Ser.: Vol. 221). 192p. 1997. mass mkt. 4.99 (*0-515-12131-2*, Jove) Berkley Pub.

— Slocum & the Apache Ransom. (Slocum Ser.: Vol. 209). 192p. 1996. mass mkt. 4.99 (*0-515-11894-X*, Jove) Berkley Pub.

— Slocum & the Aztec Priestess, No. 222. (Slocum Ser.). 192p. 1997. mass mkt. 4.99 (*0-515-12143-6*, Jove) Berkley Pub.

— Slocum & the Baroness. (Slocum Ser.: Vol. 238). 181p. 1999. mass mkt. 4.99 (*0-515-12436-2*, Jove) Berkley Pub.

— Slocum & the Big Three. (Slocum Ser.: Vol. 241). 192p. 1999. 4.99 (*0-515-12484-2*, Jove) Berkley Pub.

— Slocum & the Buffalo Hunter. (Slocum Ser.: Vol. 243). 1999. mass mkt. 4.99 (*0-515-12518-0*, Jove) Berkley Pub.

— Slocum & the Cattle King, 1 vol., (Slocum Ser.: Vol. 246). 185p. 1999. mass mkt. 4.99 (*0-515-12571-7*, Jove) Berkley Pub.

— Slocum & the Colorado Riverboat. (Slocum Ser.: Vol. 219). 192p. 1997. mass mkt. 4.99 (*0-515-12081-2*, Jove) Berkley Pub.

— Slocum & the Comanche Princess. (Slocum Ser.: Vol. 239). 1999. mass mkt. 4.99 (*0-515-12449-4*, Jove) Berkley Pub.

— Slocum & the Comanche Rescue. (Slocum Ser.: Vol. 223). 192p. 1997. mass mkt. 4.99 (*0-515-12161-4*, Jove) Berkley Pub.

— Slocum & the Comely Corpse. (Slocum Ser.: Vol. 230). 1998. mass mkt. 4.99 (*0-515-12277-7*, Jove) Berkley Pub.

— Slocum & the Dead Man's Spurs, Vol. 247. (Slocum Ser.: Vol. 247). 1999. mass mkt. 4.99 (*0-515-12613-6*, Jove) Berkley Pub.

— Slocum & the Dirty Game. (Slocum Ser.: Vol. 202). 192p. (Orig.). 1995. pap. text 4.50 (*0-515-11764-1*, Jove) Berkley Pub.

— Slocum & the Frisco Killers. (Slocum Ser.: Vol. 212). 192p. 1996. mass mkt. 4.99 (*0-515-11967-9*, Jove) Berkley Pub.

***Logan, Jake.** Slocum & the Gambler's Woman. (Slocum Ser.: Vol. 251). 2000. mass mkt. 4.99 (*0-515-12733-7*, Jove) Berkley Pub.

— Slocum & the Gila Rangers. (Jake Logan Paperback Ser.: Vol. 260). 2000. mass mkt. 4.99 (*0-515-12931-3*, Jove) Berkley Pub.

Logan, Jake. Slocum & the Great Diamond Hoax. (Slocum Ser.: Vol. 232). 1998. mass mkt. 4.99 (*0-515-12301-3*, Jove) Berkley Pub.

— Slocum & the Great Southern Hunt. (Slocum Ser.: Vol. 213). 192p. 1996. mass mkt. 4.99 (*0-515-11983-0*, Jove) Berkley Pub.

***Logan, Jake.** Slocum & the Gunrunners. (Slocum Ser.: Vol. 252). 2000. mass mkt. 4.99 (*0-515-12754-X*, Jove) Berkley Pub.

Logan, Jake. Slocum & the Irish Lass. (Slocum Ser.). 256p. 1997. mass mkt. 5.99 (*0-515-12155-X*, Jove) Berkley Pub.

***Logan, Jake.** Slocum & the Jersey Lily. (Slocum Ser.: Vol. 250). 1999. mass mkt. 4.99 (*0-515-12706-X*, Jove) Berkley Pub.

— Slocum & the Ketchem Gang. (Slocum Ser.: Vol. 249). 1999. mass mkt. 4.99 (*0-515-12686-1*, Jove) Berkley Pub.

Logan, Jake. Slocum & the Lady from Abilene. (Slocum Ser.: Vol. 245). 181p. 1999. mass mkt. 4.99 (*0-515-12555-5*, Jove) Berkley Pub.

— Slocum & the Lady in Blue. (Slocum Ser.: Vol. 217). 192p. 1997. mass mkt. 4.99 (*0-515-12049-9*, Jove) Berkley Pub.

— Slocum & the Last Gasp. (Slocum Ser.: Vol. 234). 182p. 1998. mass mkt. 4.99 (*0-515-12355-2*, Jove) Berkley Pub.

— Slocum & the Live Oak Boys. (Slocum Ser.: Vol. 240). 192p. 1999. mass mkt. 4.99 (*0-515-12467-2*, Jove) Berkley Pub.

— Slocum & the Lone Star Feud. (Slocum Ser.: Vol. 233). 1998. mass mkt. 4.99 (*0-515-12339-0*, Jove) Berkley Pub.

— Slocum & the Miner's Justice. (Slocum Ser.). 192p. 1998. pap. 4.99 (*0-515-12371-4*, Jove) Berkley Pub.

***Logan, Jake.** Slocum & the Mountain Spirit. (Jake Logan Western Ser.: Vol. 257). 2000. mass mkt. 4.99 (*0-515-12871-6*, Jove) Berkley Pub.

— Slocum & the Nebraska Storm. (Slocum Ser.: Vol. 253). 2000. mass mkt. 4.99 (*0-515-12769-8*, Jove) Berkley Pub.

— Slocum & the Pomo Chief. (Slocum Ser.: Vol. 256). 192p. 2000. mass mkt. 4.99 (*0-515-12838-4*, Jove) Berkley Pub.

Logan, Jake. Slocum & the Powder River Gamble. (Slocum Ser.: Vol. 218). 192p. 1997. mass mkt. 4.99 (*0-515-12070-7*, Jove) Berkley Pub.

— Slocum & the Real McCoy. (Slocum Ser.: Vol. 226). 192p. 1998. mass mkt. 4.99 (*0-515-12208-4*, Jove) Berkley Pub.

— Slocum & the Scalplock Trail. (Slocum Ser.: Vol. 228). 1998. mass mkt. 4.99 (*0-515-12243-2*, Jove) Berkley Pub.

— Slocum & the Spotted Horse. (Slocum Ser.: Vol. 198). 192p. (Orig.). 1995. mass mkt. 3.99 (*0-515-11679-3*, Jove) Berkley Pub.

— Slocum & the Texas Rose. (Slocum Ser.: Vol. 229). 1998. mass mkt. 4.99 (*0-515-12264-5*, Jove) Berkley Pub.

— Slocum & the Three Wives. (Slocum Ser.: Vol. 18). 281p. (Orig.). 1999. mass mkt. 5.99 (*0-515-12569-5*, Jove) Berkley Pub.

— Slocum & the Town Boss. (Slocum Ser.: Vol. 216). 192p. 1997. mass mkt. 4.99 (*0-515-12030-8*, Jove) Berkley Pub.

***Logan, Jake.** Slocum & the Undertaker. (Jake Logan Ser.: Vol. 255). 192p. 2000. mass mkt. 4.99 (*0-515-12807-4*) Berkley Pub.

Logan, Jake. Slocum & the Walapai War. (Slocum Ser.: Vol. 210). 1996. mass mkt. 4.99 (*0-515-11924-5*, Jove) Berkley Pub.

— Slocum & the Wolf Hunt. (Slocum Ser.: Vol. 237). 1998. mass mkt. 4.99 (*0-515-12413-3*, Jove) Berkley Pub.

— Slocum & the Yellow Rose of Texas. (Slocum Ser.: Vol. 244). 185p. 1999. mass mkt. 4.99 (*0-515-12532-6*, Jove) Berkley Pub.

***Logan, Jake.** Slocum & Wild Bill's Lady. (Jake Logan Ser.: Vol. 259). 192p. 2000. mass mkt. 4.99 (*0-515-12909-7*, Jove) Berkley Pub.

Logan, Jake. Slocum at Dead Dog. (Slocum Ser.: Vol. 215). 192p. 1997. mass mkt. 4.99 (*0-515-12015-4*, Jove) Berkley Pub.

— Slocum at Dog Leg Creek. (Slocum Ser.: Vol. 199). 192p. (Orig.). 1995. mass mkt. 3.99 (*0-515-11701-3*, Jove) Berkley Pub.

— Slocum at Hell's Acre. (Slocum Ser.: Vol. 236). 192p. 1998. pap. 4.99 (*0-515-12391-9*, Jove) Berkley Pub.

***Logan, Jake.** Slocum at Scorpion Bend, 1 vol. (Slocum Ser.: Vol. 242). 1999. mass mkt. 4.99 (*0-515-12510-5*, Jove) Berkley Pub.

Logan, Jake. Slocum in Paradise, No. 206. (Slocum Ser.: Vol. 206). 192p. (Orig.). 1996. mass mkt. 4.50 (*0-515-11841-9*, Jove) Berkley Pub.

***Logan, Jake.** Slocum's Close Call. (Slocum Ser.: Vol. 254). 2000. mass mkt. 4.99 (*0-515-12789-2*, Jove) Berkley Pub.

Logan, Jake. Slocum's Folly. (Slocum Ser.: Vol. 211). 1996. mass mkt. 4.99 (*0-515-11940-7*, Jove) Berkley Pub.

— Slocum's Grubstake. (Slocum Ser.: Vol. 212). 1996. mass mkt. 5.50 (*0-515-11955-5*, Jove) Berkley Pub.

— Slocum's Inheritence. (Slocum Ser.: Vol. 220). 192p. 1997. mass mkt. 4.99 (*0-515-12103-7*, Jove) Berkley Pub.

***Logan, Jake.** Slocum's Partner. (Jake Logan Ser.: No. 258). 2000. mass mkt. 4.99 (*0-515-12889-9*) Berkley Pub.

Logan, Jake. Slocum's Silver. (Slocum Ser.: No. 200). 192p. (Orig.). 1995. mass mkt. 3.99 (*0-515-11729-3*, Jove) Berkley Pub.

Logan, James. Correspondence Between William Penn & James Logan, 2 vols., Set. 1993. reprint ed. lib. bdg. 150.00 (*0-7812-5484-1*) Rprt Serv.

— The Scottish Gael: Or, Celtic Manners As Preserved among the Highlanders, 2 vols., Set. LC 77-87679. reprint ed. 59.50 (*0-404-16560-5*) AMS Pr.

Logan, James C. Christ for the World: United Methodist Bishops Speak on Evangelism. 176p. 1996. pap. 15.95 (*0-687-02206-1*) Abingdon.

Logan, James C., ed. Theology & Evangelism in the Wesleyan Heritage: Essays in the Theology of Evangelism. LC 93-6428. (Kingswood Ser.). 224p. (Orig.). 1994. pap. 14.95 (*0-687-41395-8*) Abingdon.

Logan, James C., jt. auth. see Rockway, John W.

Logan, James K., jt. auth. see Leach, W. Barton.

Logan, James V. Wordsworthian Criticism. LC 74-7025. 304p. 1974. reprint ed. 50.00 (*0-87752-171-9*) Gordian.

Logan, Janette. Confronting Prejudice. 307p. (Orig.). 1996. text 64.95 (*1-85742-359-3*, Pub. by Arena) Ashgate Pub Co.

Logan, Janice L. Breaking the Language Barrier with Spanish. 1977. pap. text 11.95 (*0-89420-035-6*, 176040); audio 237.60 (*0-89420-127-1*, 176000) Natl Book.

Logan, Jeanne. Your Gift . . . Should You Decide to Accept: Communications from Aristotle. 243p. (Orig.). 1987. pap. 10.00 (*0-9619742-0-6*) Harmony Haus.

Logan, Jennifer C. Winning Websites for Medical Personnel & Patients. (Illus.). 111p. 1998. pap. 18.00 (*0-9664575-0-1*) La Vida Bks.

Logan, Jesse A. & Hain, Fred P., eds. Chaos & Insect Ecology: Does Chaos Exist in Ecological Systems? (Illus.). 109p. (Orig.). (C). 1993. pap. text 40.00 (*0-7881-0092-0*) DIANE Pub.

Logan, Jim. Reclaiming Surrendered Ground: Protecting Your Family from Spiritual Attacks. pap. 10.99 (*0-8024-3948-9*, 267) Moody.

— Recuperemos el Terreno Perdido. 208p. 1997. pap. 8.99 (*0-8254-1442-3*) Kregel.

Logan, Joanna. Summer Sun, Winter Dreams. large type ed. (Linford Romance Large Print Ser.). 256p. 1997. pap. 16.99 (*0-7089-5175-9*) Ulverscroft.

— Winter Harvest. large type ed. 1991. pap. 16.99 (*0-7089-6980-1*) Ulverscroft.

Logan, John. The Anonymous Lover. 1973. 5.95 (*0-87140-564-4*, Pub. by Liveright) Norton.

— A Ballet for the Ear: Interviews, Essays, & Reviews. Poulin, A., Jr., ed. (Poets on Poetry Ser.). 328p. 1983. pap. 13.95 (*0-472-06336-7*, 06336) U of Mich Pr.

— The Bridge of Change: Poems 1974-1980. (American Poets Continuum Ser.: No. 7). 75p. 1981. pap. 8.00 (*0-918526-35-3*) BOA Edns.

— Christianity. (World Religions Ser.). (Illus.). 48p. (J). (gr. 4-7). 1995. lib. bdg. 24.26 (*1-56847-374-5*) Raintree Steck-V.

— John Logan: The Collected Fiction. (American Poets Continuum Ser.: No. 21). 204p. 1991. 25.00 (*0-918526-78-7*) BOA Edns.

— John Logan: The Collected Fiction. (American Poets Continuum Ser.: No. 21). 204p. 1991. pap. 12.50 (*0-918526-79-5*) BOA Edns.

— John Logan: The Collected Poems. 499p. 1989. 30.00 (*0-918526-64-7*) BOA Edns.

— John Logan: The Collected Poems. 499p. 1989. pap. 15.00 (*0-918526-65-5*) BOA Edns.

— Never the Sinner: The Leopold & Leob Story. LC 98-47733. 142p. 1999. pap. 12.95 (*0-87951-930-4*, Pub. by Overlook Pr) Penguin Putnam.

— The Poem As Relic. (Poetry/Rare Books Collection). 1989. pap. 6.00 (*0-922668-03-5*) SUNYB Poetry Rare Bks.

— The Transformation: Poems January to March, 1981. 22p. (Orig.). 1983. pap. 6.95 (*0-942908-06-6*) Pancake Pr.

***Logan, John A., Jr.** Academy of Broadcasting. 1999. 19.95 (*0-9676500-3-8*) Logan Comm.

Logan, John A., Jr. Dowered with Gifts: The Second Quarter of the Second Century of Christ Church Cathedral, Houston. (Illus.). 306p. (C). 1989. 20.00 (*0-317-01834-5*) Christ Church.

Logan, John A. The Great Conspiracy. LC 76-37311. (Black Heritage Library Collection). 1977. reprint ed. 71.95 (*0-8369-8948-1*) Ayer.

— No Transfer: An American Security Principle. 1961. 79.50 (*0-685-69838-6*) Elliots Bks.

***Logan, John A., Jr.** Rap, Ritual & Reality. 1999. 19.95 (*0-9676500-2-X*) Logan Comm.

— Reality of a Fantasy. 1999. 19.95 (*0-9676500-0-3*) Logan Comm.

Logan, John A. Reminiscences of a Soldier's Wife: An Autobiography. 2nd ed. Simon, John Y., ed. LC 97-17322. (Shawnee Classic Ser.). (Illus.). 486p. 1997. reprint ed. pap. 19.95 (*0-8093-2157-2*) S Ill U Pr.

— The Volunteer Soldier of America, with Memoir of the Author & Military Reminiscences from General Logan's Private Journal. Kohn, Richard H., ed. LC 78-22385. (American Military Experience Ser.). (Illus.). 1980. reprint ed. lib. bdg. 55.95 (*0-405-11861-9*) Ayer.

Logan, John H. A History of the Upper Country of S.C., Part. 2. 118p. 1980. reprint ed. 17.50 (*0-89308-195-7*) Southern Hist Pr.

Logan, John L. & Marks, Patricia H., eds. The Leonard L. Milberg Collection of Irish Poetry. (Illus.). 338p. 1998. 40.00 (*0-87811-043-7*, Pub. by Princeton Lib) Oak Knoll.

Logan, John M. Briefcase on Tort Law. (Cavendish Briefcase Ser.). 200p. 1995. pap. 20.00 (*1-85941-245-9*, Pub. by Cavendish Pubng) Gaunt.

Logan, John R. & Molotch, Harvey L., eds. Urban Fortunes: The Political Economy of Place. (C). 1987. pap. 18.95 (*0-520-06341-4*, Pub. by U CA Pr) Cal Prin Full Svc.

Logan, John R. & Spitze, Glenna D. Family Ties: Enduring Relations Between Parents & Their Grown Children. LC 96-13008. 288p. (C). 1996. 69.95 (*1-56639-471-6*) Temple U Pr.

— Family Ties: Enduring Relations Between Parents & Their Grown Children. LC 96-13008. 288p. (C). 1997. pap. 19.95 (*1-56639-472-4*) Temple U Pr.

Logan, John R. & Swanstrom, Todd, eds. Beyond the City Limits: Urban Policy & Economic Restructuring in Comparative Perspective. (Conflicts in Urban & Regional Development Ser.). 288p. 1991. pap. 24.95 (*0-87722-944-9*) Temple U Pr.

Logan, John W. Ten-Shun: The Making of a Soldier. Bird, Linda A., ed. 216p. (Orig.). 1995. pap. 16.95 (*1-878151-04-5*) J & J Bks NY.

Logan, Joshua & Heggen, Thomas. Mister Roberts. 1951. pap. 5.25 (*0-8222-0765-6*) Dramatists Play.

Logan, Judy. Teaching Stories. LC 93-91529. 110p. 1993. pap. text 11.95 (*0-9636822-0-2*) J Logan.

— Teaching Stories. LC 97-25761. 176p. 1997. 19.00 (*1-56836-195-5*) Kodansha.

— Teaching Stories. 1999. pap. 11.00 (*1-56836-276-5*) Kodansha.

Logan, Karen. Clean House, Clean Planet: Clean Your House for Pennies a Day -The Safe Nontoxic Way. 320p. 1997. pap. 12.00 (*0-671-53595-1*, PB Trade Paper) PB.

***Logan, Karen S.** A Compendium of Research-Based Information on the Education of Gifted & Talented Students. 93p. 2000. reprint ed. pap. text 20.00 (*0-7881-8520-9*) DIANE Pub.

Logan, Kate V. My Confederate Girlhood. Baxter, Annette K., ed. LC 79-8803. (Signal Lives Ser.). (Illus.). 1980. reprint ed. lib. bdg. 26.95 (*0-405-12849-5*) Ayer.

Logan, Kathleen. Haciendo Pueblo: The Development of a Guadalajaran Suburb. LC 83-3650. (Illus.). 157p. 1984. pap. 48.70 (*0-7837-8391-4*, 205920200009) Bks Demand.

Logan, Kathryn V., ed. Advanced Synthesis & Processing of Composites & Advanced Ceramics: Proceedings: International Symposium on Advanced Synthesis & Processing (1995: Cocoa Beach, FL) LC 95-24463. (Ceramic Transactions Ser.: No. 56). 379p. 1995. 88.00 (*1-57498-000-9*, CT056) Am Ceramic.

Logan, Kathryn V., et al, eds. Advanced Synthesis & Processing of Composites & Advanced Ceramics II. (Ceramic Transactions Ser.: No. 79). (Illus.). 1996. 95.00 (*1-57498-017-3*, CT056) Am Ceramic.

Logan, Kimberly M. Getting the Schools You Want: A Step-by-Step Guide to Conducting Your Own Curriculum Management Audit. LC 97-4767. (Illus.). 160p. 1997. 65.95 (*0-8039-6543-5*) Corwin Pr.

— Getting the Schools You Want: A Step-by-Step Guide to Conducting Your Own Curriculum Management Audit. LC 97-4767. (Illus.). 160p. 1997. pap. 29.95 (*0-8039-6544-3*) Corwin Pr.

Logan, Kristina. The Man Behind the Magic. (Romance Ser.). 1993. per. 2.75 (*0-373-08950-3*, 5-08950-3) Silhouette.

— A Man Like Jake. (Romance Ser.). 1994. per. 2.75 (*0-373-08998-8*, 5-08998-2) Silhouette.

— The Right Man for Loving. (Romance Ser.: No. 870). 1992. per. 2.69 (*0-373-08870-1*, 5-08870-3) Silhouette.

— The Right Man for Loving. large type ed. 251p. 1992. reprint ed. lib. bdg. 13.95 (*1-56054-538-0*) Thorndike Pr.

— To the Rescue. (Romance Ser.). 1993. per. 2.69 (*0-373-08918-X*, 5-08918-0) Silhouette.

— To the Rescue. large type ed. LC 93-20049. 226p. 1993. reprint ed. 13.95 (*1-56054-682-4*) Thorndike Pr.

— Two to Tango. (Romance Ser.: No. 852). 1992. per. 2.69 (*0-373-08852-3*, 5-08852-1) Silhouette.

— Two to Tango. large type ed. 240p. 1992. reprint ed. lib. bdg. 13.95 (*1-56054-461-9*) Thorndike Pr.

Logan, Lanny. Power Supply Troubleshooting & Repair. (Illus.). 195p. 1998. pap. 24.95 (*0-7906-1138-4*) Prompt Publns.

Logan, Laura, jt. auth. see Kahn, Louis.

Logan, Laurel O. Gillian. (Springsong Bks.). 192p. (Orig.). (YA). (gr. 9-12). 1995. mass mkt. 4.99 (*1-55661-681-3*) Bethany Hse.

— Impasse. LC 97-33834. (Portraits Ser.). 256p. 1997. pap. 8.99 (*1-55661-976-6*) Bethany Hse.

— In the Quiet of This Moment: A Women's Prayer Journal with Selected Quotes from Inspirational Writers. 192p. 1995. pap. 9.99 (*1-55661-611-2*) Bethany Hse.

— Janette Oke: A Heart for the Prairie; the Untold Story of the Most Beloved Novelist of Our Time. LC 96-754. (Illus.). 256p. 1993. text 16.99 (*1-55661-326-1*) Bethany Hse.

Logan, Leandra. Angel Baby. LC 95-22364. 217p. 1995. per. 3.25 (*0-373-25664-7*) Harlequin Bks.

— Bargain Basement Baby. LC 95-6880. (Temptation Ser.). 219p. 1995. mass mkt. 3.25 (*0-373-25635-3*, 1-25635-3) Harlequin Bks.

— A Bride for Daddy. (Weddings by DeWilde Ser.). 1996. per. 4.50 (*0-373-82541-2*, 1-82541-3) Silhouette.

— Cupid Connection. (Family Continuity Program Ser.: No. 14). 1999. mass mkt. 4.50 (*0-373-82162-X*, 1-82162-8) Harlequin Bks.

— Dillon after Dark. (Temptation Ser.: No. 362). 1991. mass mkt. 2.99 (*0-373-25462-8*) Harlequin Bks.

— Dillon after Dark. (Men at Work Ser.: Vol. 40). 1998. mass mkt. 4.50 (*0-373-81052-0*, 1-81052-2) Harlequin Bks.

— The Education of Jake Flynn. (Yours Truly Ser.). 1996. per. 3.50 (*0-373-52027-1*, 1-52027-9) Silhouette.

— Father Figure. (American Romance Ser.). 1998. per. 3.99 (*0-373-16732-6*, 1-16732-9) Harlequin Bks.

— Happy Birthday, Baby. (Temptation Ser.). 1994. per. 2.99 (*0-373-25619-1*, 1-25619-7) Harlequin Bks.

— Heaven-Sent Husband. (Temptation Ser.: No. 611). 1996. per. 3.50 (*0-373-25711-2*, 1-25711-2) Harlequin Bks.

— Her Favorite Husband. 1994. per. 2.99 (*0-373-25591-8*) Harlequin Bks.

— Hold That Groom! 1997. per. 3.50 (*0-373-25750-3*, 1-25750-0) Harlequin Bks.

— Joyride. (Temptation Ser.). 1993. per. 2.99 (*0-373-25572-1*, 1-25572-8) Harlequin Bks.

***Logan, Leandra.** Just for the Night: Bachelor Auction. 1999. per. 3.75 (*0-373-25825-9*, 1-25825-0, Harlequin) Harlequin Bks.

Logan, Leandra. The Last Bridesmaid. LC 96-434. 249p. 1995. per. 3.50 (*0-373-16601-X*, 1-16601-6) Harlequin Bks.

— The Last Honest Man. (Temptation Ser.: No. 393). 1992. per. 2.99 (*0-373-25493-8*, 1-25493-7) Harlequin Bks.

— Un Marie en Cavale. (Rouge Passion Ser.: No. 487). (FRE.). 1998. mass mkt. 3.50 (*0-373-37487-9*, 1-37487-5) Harlequin Bks.

— My Jingle Bell Baby. (Temptation Ser.: No. 663). 1997. per. 3.50 (*0-373-25763-5*, 1-25763-3) Harlequin Bks.

***Logan, Leandra.** Oh, Baby! Bachelors & Babies. (Temptation Ser.: No. 753). 1999. per. 3.75 (*0-373-25853-4*, 1-25853-2) Harlequin Bks.

Logan, Leandra. Santa & Son ⊞. 1996. per. 3.50 (*0-373-44010-3*, 1-44010-6) Harlequin Bks.

— Still Hitched, Cowboy: (Mail Order Men) (Temptation Ser.: Vol. 703). 1998. per. 3.75 (*0-373-25803-8*, 1-25803-7) Harlequin Bks.

***Logan, Leanne & Cole, Geert.** Brussels, Bruges & Antwerp. (Illus.). 224p. 1999. pap. 14.95 (*1-86450-070-0*) Lonely Planet.

Logan, Leanne & Cole, Geert. Lonely Planet New Caledonia. 3rd ed. (Illus.). 256p. 1997. pap. 14.95 (*0-86442-533-3*) Lonely Planet.

Logan, Leanne & Cole, Geert, contrib. by. Lonely Planet Egypt Travel Atlas. (Illus.). 72p. 1996. pap. 14.95 (*0-86442-376-4*) Lonely Planet.

Logan, Linda L., jt. auth. see Potter, Robert E.

Logan, Lloyd & Sachs, Judyth. Meeting the Challenges of Primary Schooling. LC 96-51866. (Educational Management Ser.). 280p. (C). 1997. pap. 27.99 (*0-415-14655-0*) Routledge.

Logan, M. Montana Is.... 1995. 24.95 (*1-56044-355-3*) Falcon Pub Inc.

Logan, Margaret. Deathampton Summer. 1988. 16.95 (*0-8027-5699-9*) Walker & Co.

Logan, Margaret. Happy Endings: The True Story of a Mother, a Daughter & Their Journey of Discovery. (Illus.). 164p. 1999. reprint ed. pap. 16.95 (*0-933855-19-2*) Anacus Pr.

Logan, Margaret. A Killing in Venture Capital. 224p. 1989. 19.95 (*0-8027-5734-0*) Walker & Co.

Logan, Marie. Mississippi-Louisiana Border Country: History of Rodney Mississippi & Environs. 1974. 35.00 (*0-87511-072-X*) Claitors.

Logan, Marie-Rose & Rudnytsky, Peter L., eds. Contending Kingdoms: Historical, Psychological, & Feminist Approaches to the Literature of Sixteenth-Century England & France. LC 90-12798. 373p. reprint ed. pap. 115.70 (*0-608-10545-7*, 207116500009) Bks Demand.

***Logan, Mary.** The Buck Stops Here: Legal & Ethical Responsibilities for UM Organizations. 48p. 2000. pap. text 9.95 (*0-88177-306-9*, DR306) Discipleship Res.

Logan, Mary S. The Part Taken by Women in American History. LC 72-2613. (American Women Ser.: Images & Realities). (Illus.). 956p. 1978. reprint ed. 59.95 (*0-405-04467-4*) Ayer.

Logan, Matt. Coffin Creek. large type ed. (Western Library). 272p. 1995. pap. 16.99 (*0-7089-7686-7*, Linford) Ulverscroft.

— Ride the High Lines. large type ed. (Linford Western Large Print Ser.). 288p. 1998. pap. 17.99 (*0-7089-5278-X*, Linford) Ulverscroft.

— Storm in the Saddle. large type ed. (Dales Western Ser.). 256p. 1998. pap. 19.99 (*1-85389-788-4*, Dales) Ulverscroft.

***Logan, Mawuena Kossi.** Narrating Africa: George Henty & the Fiction of Empire. LC 99-11196. (Children's Literature & Culture Ser.: Vol. 9). 224p. 1999. 55.00 (*0-8153-3275-0*) Garland.

Logan, Michael F. Fighting Sprawl & City Hall: Resistance to Urban Growth in the Southwest. LC 95-5590. 223p. 1995. 42.00 (*0-8165-1512-3*); pap. 18.95 (*0-8165-1553-0*) U of Ariz Pr.

Logan, Michael H. & Schmittou, Douglas A. With Pride They Made These: Tribal Styles in Plains Indian Art. LC 96-134274. (Illus.). 60p. (Orig.). (C). 1995. pap. 18.50 (*1-880174-03-0*) U TN F H McClung.

Logan, Mike. Bronc to Breakfast. LC 88-91264. (Illus.). 80p. (Orig.). 1988. pap. 9.95 (*0-937959-53-7*) Falcon Pub Inc.

— How to Kill Collections! Business Edition. Bethancourt, Charles, ed. 160p. 1998. mass mkt. 24.95 (*0-9665868-1-6*) Wisdom Pub Inc.

— Laugh Kills Lonesome & Other Poems. LC 90-84126. (Illus.). 80p. (Orig.). 1990. pap. 9.95 (*1-56044-056-2*) Falcon Pub Inc.

— Little Friends: In Verse & Photography. LC 92-70042. (Illus.). 30p. (J). (ps-3). 1992. pap. 9.95 (*1-56044-139-9*) Falcon Pub Inc.

— Men of the Open Range & Other Poems. LC 93-72958. (Illus.). 80p. (Orig.). 1993. pap. 9.95 (*1-56044-247-6*) Falcon Pub Inc.

— Montana Is . . . Montana in Verse & Photography. rev. ed. LC 89-91009. (Illus.). 96p. 1989. pap. 13.95 (*0-937959-82-0*) Falcon Pub Inc.

— Yellowstone Is . . . (Illus.). 94p. 1987. pap. 13.95 (*0-937959-20-0*) Falcon Pub Inc.

***Logan-Montgomery, Daty.** Self Help for the Grammatically Challenged. 112p. (C). 1999. pap. text 6.95 (*1-889668-14-1*) S & D.

Logan, Nancy R. Children of a Lost Spirit. 396p. (Orig.). 1993. pap. 10.00 (*1-883763-02-9*) Kideko Hse.

Logan, Niall A. Bacterial Systematics. LC 93-26811. (Illus.). 256p. 1994. pap. 44.95 (*0-632-03775-X*) Blackwell Sci.

Logan, Oliver. The Venetian Upper Clergy in the 16th & Early 17th Centuries: A Study in Religious Culture. LC 96-31329. (Texts & Studies in Religion: Vol. 68). 624p. 1997. text 129.95 (*0-7734-8927-4*) E Mellen.

Logan, Owen & Bowles, Paul. Al Maghrib: Photographs from Morocco. (Illus.). 1989. pap. 24.95 (*0-7486-6013-5*, Pub. by Edinburgh U Pr) Col U Pr.

Logan, P. J. Perverse Christianity: A Ministry of Death. 170p. 1995. pap. 10.95 (*0-9649074-0-2*) Uniquely Christian.

Logan, Pamela. Among Warriors. LC 97-43978. 1998. pap. 13.00 (*0-375-70076-5*) Vin Bks.

— Among Warriors: A Martial Artist in Tibet. LC 95-31758. 288p. 1996. 23.95 (*0-87951-643-7*, Pub. by Overlook Pr) Penguin Putnam.

— Jack Hylton Presents. 1996. pap. text 21.95 (*0-85170-551-0*, Pub. by British Film Inst) Ind U Pr.

Logan, Patrick. The Holy Wells of Ireland. (Illus.). 170p. 1980. 24.95 (*0-86140-026-7*, Pub. by Smyth); pap. 14.95 (*0-86140-046-1*, Pub. by Smyth) Dufour.

— Irish Country Cures. LC 93-43393. (Illus.). 160p. (Orig.). 1994. pap. 6.95 (*0-8069-0718-5*) Sterling.

***Logan, Patrick.** Irish Folk Medicine. rev. ed. Orig. Title: Irish Country Cures. 180p. 1999. pap. 17.95 (*0-86281-767-6*, Pub. by Appletree Pr) Irish Bks Media.

Logan, Peter M. Nerves & Narratives: A Cultural History of Hysteria in 19th-Century British Prose. 241p. 1997. pap. 17.95 (*0-520-20775-0*, Pub. by U CA Pr) Cal Prin Full Svc.

Logan, Ralph. Chemistry 2425. 1998. text 24.59 (*1-56870-316-3*) RonJon Pub.

— Chemistry 2423. 1998. text 21.12 (*1-56870-317-1*) RonJon Pub.

***Logan, Ralph.** Organic Chemistry 2425: Take Home Quizzes. 1999. pap. text 9.28 (*1-56870-351-1*) RonJon Pub.

— Organic Chemistry 2423: Take Home Quizzes. 1999. pap. text 9.28 (*1-56870-350-3*) RonJon Pub.

Logan, Rayford W. The Betrayal of the Negro from Rutherford B. Hayes to Woodrow Wilson: From Rutherford B. Hayes to Woodrow Wilson. LC 96-44577. Orig. Title: The Negro in American Life & Thought. 459p. (Orig.). 1997. reprint ed. pap. 15.95 (*0-306-80758-0*) Da Capo.

— The Senate & the Versailles Mandate System. LC 74-14357. 112p. 1975. reprint ed. lib. bdg. 55.00 (*0-8371-7798-7*, LOVM, Greenwood Pr) Greenwood.

***Logan, Rayford W.** What the Negro Wants. rev. ed. Janken, Kenneth R., ed. (African American Intellectual Heritage Ser.). 400p. 2001. pap. 22.95 (*0-268-01964-9*, Pub. by U of Notre Dame Pr); lib. bdg. 36.95 (*0-268-01966-5*, Pub. by U of Notre Dame Pr) Chicago Distribution Ctr.

Logan, Rayford W. & Winston, Michael R., eds. Dictionary of American Negro Biography. LC 81-9629. 1983. 65.00 (*0-393-01513-0*) Norton.

Logan, Regina L. & Fromberg, Robert M. Peers in the Classroom: Case Studies in Adult Higher Education. 172p. (C). 1999. pap. 18.95 (*1-58107-013-6*, Pub. by New Forums) Booksource.

Logan, Renne A. Shanghai Times: China as I Saw It! large type ed. Cary, Anna Marie, ed. LC 98-71698. (Illus.). 110p. 1998. pap. 14.95 (*0-9664126-0-5*) AMC Pubns.

Logan, Richard K. Logan: A Directory of the Descendants of Andrew & Lydia Logan of Albany, NY & Abbeville, SC. 329p. (Orig.). 1994. pap. text 25.00 (*1-55613-993-4*) Heritage Bk.

Logan, Robert. The Fifth Language: Learning a Living in the Computer Age. 320p. 1997. pap. 15.95 (*0-7737-5876-3*, Pub. by Hse of Anansi Pr) Genl Dist Srvs.

— The Fifth Language: Learning a Living in the Computer Age. 320p. 1995. 26.95 (*0-7737-2907-0*) Stoddart Publ.

***Logan, Robert.** The Sixth Language: Learning a Living in the Internet Age. 336p. 2000. pap. 18.95 (*0-7737-6104-7*) Stoddart Publ.

Logan, Robert, jt. auth. see George, Carl.

Logan, Robert A. Environmental Issues for the Nineties: A Handbook for Journalists 1995. 3rd ed. 340p. 1994. 44.95 (*0-937790-50-8*, 4440) Media Institute.

Logan, Robert A., et al. Social Responsibility & Science News: Four Case Studies. LC 97-70474. 248p. 1997. 24.95 (*0-937790-53-2*, 4490) Media Institute.

Logan, Robert E. Beyond Church Growth. LC 89-30490. 226p. 1989. pap. 10.99 (*0-8007-5332-1*) Revell.

Logan, Robert E. & Cole, Neil. Raising Leaders for the Harvest. (Illus.). 194p. (Orig.). 1996. pap. 75.00 incl. audio (*1-889638-11-0*) ChurchSmart.

Logan, Robert E. & Ogne, Steve. Caja de Herramientas. (SPA.). ring bd. 61.45 incl. audio (*1-55883-110-X*, 1930-0042C) Libros Desafio.

Logan, Robert E. & Ogne, Steven L. The Church Planter's Toolkit. (Illus.). 210p. (Orig.). 1996. pap. 95.00 incl. audio (*1-889638-08-0*) ChurchSmart.

— Churches Planting Churches. (Illus.). 172p. (Orig.). 1996. pap. 189.00 incl. audio, VHS (*1-889638-09-9*) ChurchSmart.

Logan, Robert E., et al. Releasing Your Church's Potential. 250p. (Orig.). 1998. pap. 95.00 incl. audio (*1-889638-12-9*) ChurchSmart.

An Asterisk (*) at the beginning of an entry indicates that the title is appearing for the first time.

L

L

Logsdon, Bette. Physical Education for Children: A Focus on the Teaching Process. 2nd ed. LC 83-11964. (Illus.). 476p. reprint ed. pap. 147.60 (0-8357-7648-4, 205697400096) Bks Demand.

Logsdon, Bette, et al. Physical Education Unit Plans for Grades 1-2. 2nd ed. LC 96-38313. (Illus.). 184p. (Orig.). 1997. pap. text 18.00 (0-87322-782-4, BLOG0782) Human Kinetics.

— Physical Education Unit Plans for Grades 3-4. 2nd ed. LC 96-35915. (Illus.). 184p. (Orig.). 1997. pap. text 18.00 (0-87322-783-2, BLOG0783) Human Kinetics.

— Physical Education Unit Plans for Grades 5-6. 2nd ed. LC 96-43908. (Illus.). 184p. (Orig.). 1997. pap. text 18.00 (0-87322-784-0, BLOG0784) Human Kinetics.

— Physical Education Unit Plans for Preschool-Kindergarten. LC 96-38312. (Illus.). 184p. (Orig.). 1997. pap. text 18.00 (0-87322-781-6, BLOG0781) Human Kinetics.

Logsdon, Bette J., et al. Physical Education Unit Plans for Preschool-Kindergarten, for Grades 1-2, for Grades 3-4, for Grades 5-6, 4 vols. LC 96-38312. (Illus.). 649p. 1997. pap. text 59.00 (0-88011-697-8, BLOG0697) Human Kinetics.

Logsdon, David R. Tennessee Antebellum Trail Guidebook. (Illus.). 128p. (Orig.). 1995. pap. text 8.95 (0-9626018-8-8) Kettle Mills Pr.

Logsdon, David R., ed. Eyewitnesses at the Battle of Fort Donelson, Vol. 4. (Illus.). 128p. 1998. pap. 9.95 (0-9626018-4-5) Kettle Mills Pr.

— Eyewitnesses at the Battle of Franklin, No. 1. 4th rev. ed. (Illus.). 96p. (Orig.). 1991. pap. text 9.95 (0-9626018-0-2) Kettle Mills Pr.

— Eyewitnesses at the Battle of Shiloh, No. 3. (Illus.). 112p. (Orig.). 1994. pap. text 9.95 (0-9626018-2-9) Kettle Mills Pr.

— Eyewitnesses at the Battle of Stones River, No. 2. (Illus.). 82p. (Orig.). 1990. pap. text 9.95 (0-9626018-1-0) Kettle Mills Pr.

Logsdon, Gary S., ed. Controlling Waterborne Giardiasis. 118p. 1988. 5.00 (0-87262-633-4) Am Soc Civil Eng.

— Slow Sand Filtration. LC 91-28171. 240p. 1991. pap. text 23.00 (0-87262-847-7) Am Soc Civil Eng.

Logsdon, Gene. The Contrary Farmer. 288p. 1995. pap. 16.95 (0-930031-74-1) Chelsea Green Pub.

— The Contrary Farmer's Invitation to Gardening. LC 97-5790. 242p. 1994. pap. 16.95 (0-930031-96-2) Chelsea Green Pub.

Logsdon, Gene. Good Spirits: A New Look at Ol' Demon Alcohol. (Illus.). 240p. pap. 14.95 (1-890132-66-7) Chelsea Green Pub.

Logsdon, Gene. Good Spirits: A New Look at Ol' Demon Alcohol. LC 99-38559. (Illus.). 240p. 1999. 24.95 (1-890132-43-8) Chelsea Green Pub.

***Logsdon, Gene.** Living at Nature's Pace: Farming & the American Dream. LC 99-57305. 224p. 2000. pap. 16.95 (1-890132-56-X) Chelsea Green Pub.

Logsdon, Gene. Wildlife in the Garden: How to Live in Harmony with Deer, Raccoons, Rabbits, Crows, & other Pesky Creatures. exp. ed. LC 99-10784. 1999. 35.00 (0-253-33562-0) Ind U Pr.

— Wildlife in the Garden: How to Live in Harmony with Deer, Raccoons, Rabbits, Crows & Other Pesky Creatures. expanded ed. LC 99-10784. 1999. pap. 14.95 (0-253-21284-7) Ind U Pr.

— You Can Go Home Again: Adventures of a Contrary Life. LC 98-17125. 224p. 1998. 22.95 (0-253-33419-5) Ind U Pr.

— You Can Go Home Again: Adventures of a Contrary Life. LC 98-17125. 1998. pap. write for info. (0-253-21218-9) Ind U Pr.

Logsdon, Gene & Zender, Steve. The Big Things in Life Are the Little Things. unabridged ed. LC 97-91150. (Illus.). 200p. 1998. 17.00 (0-9661483-0-4) Slowlane Pub.

Logsdon, Guy. The Whorehouse Bells Were Ringing & Other Songs Cowboys Sing. (Illus.). 416p. 1995. 15.95 (0-252-06488-7) U of Ill Pr.

Logsdon, Guy, ed. The Whorehouse Bells Were Ringing & Other Songs Cowboys Sing. LC 88-19931. (Music in American Life Ser.). (Illus.). 416p. 1989. text 24.95 (0-252-01583-5) U of Ill Pr.

Logsdon, Guy, jt. compiled by see Thorp, Nathan H.

Logsdon, Guy W., jt. auth. see Kroeker, Marvin E.

***Logsdon, John M.** Exploring the Unknown: Selected Documents in the History of the United States Civil Space Program, Vol. 4. 716p. 1999. boxed set 50.00 (0-16-050170-9) USGPO.

— Exploring the Unknown: Selected Documents in the History of the United States Civil Space Program, Organizing for Exploration, Vol. 1. 821p. 1996. boxed set 49.00 (0-16-061849-5) USGPO.

Logsdon, John M. Legislative Origins of the National Aeroneutics & Space Act of 1958: Proceedings of an Oral History Workshop Conducted April 3, 1992. (Monographs in Aerospace History: No. 8). (Illus.). 84p. 1998. pap. 7.00 (0-16-049641-1) USGPO.

Logsdon, John M., et al, eds. Exploring the Unknown - Selected Documents in the History of the United States Civilian Space Program Vol. 3: Using Space. (NASA History Ser.). 633p. 1998. per. 41.00 (0-16-049546-6) USGPO.

Logsdon, Joseph. Horace White, Nineteenth Century Liberal, 10. LC 77-105982. (Contributions in American History Ser.: No. 10). (Illus.). 418p. 1971. 69.50 (0-8371-3309-2, LHW/, Greenwood Pr) Greenwood.

Logsdon, Joseph, jt. ed. see Hirsch, Arnold R.

Logsdon, Joseph, ed. see Northup, Solomon.

Logsdon, Linda. Establishing a Psychiatric Private Practice. LC 85-7422. (Private Practice Monograph Ser.). 99p. reprint ed. pap. 30.70 (0-8357-7842-8, 203621700002) Bks Demand.

Logsdon, Loren & Mayer, Charles W., eds. Since Flannery O'Connor: Essays on the Contemporary American Short Story. LC 87-61274. (Essays in Literature Bks.: No. 7). (Illus.). 152p. (Orig.). (C). 1987. pap. 8.00 (0-934312-06-0) WIU Essays Lit.

Logsdon, Phyllis, jt. auth. see Lamb, Beth.

Logsdon, Rebecca G., jt. auth. see Albert, Steven M.

Logsdon, Richard. Alex the Wolf-God & Other Grim & Disturbing Tales. 161p. 1998. pap. 15.95 (1-892896-17-6) Buy Books.

Logsdon, Roslyn. People & Places: Roslyn Logsdon's Imagery in Fiber. (Illus.). 56p. 1999. pap. 14.95 (1-881982-14-9) Stackpole.

Logsdon, Tom. Mobile Communication Satellites: Theory & Applications. (Illus.). 277p. 1995. 55.00 (0-07-038476-2) McGraw.

— Orbital Mechanics: Theory & Applications. LC 97-6507. 288p. 1997. 80.00 (0-471-14636-6) Wiley.

Logsdon, Wendy & Rapoport, Roger. Walking Easy in the San Francisco Bay Area: A Hiking Guide for Active Adults. (Walking Easy Ser.). (Illus.). 184p. (Orig.). 1995. pap. 11.95 (0-933469-20-9) Globe Pequot.

Logston, Anne. Dagger's Edge. 240p. (Orig.). 1994. mass mkt. 4.99 (0-441-00036-3) Ace Bks.

— Dagger's Point. 272p. (Orig.). 1995. mass mkt. 4.99 (0-441-00134-3) Ace Bks.

***Logston, Anne.** Exile. 263p. 1999. mass mkt. 6.50 (0-441-00669-8) Ace Bks.

Logston, Anne. Firewalk. 352p. 1997. mass mkt. 6.50 (0-441-00427-X) Ace Bks.

— Guardian's Key. 320p. 1996. mass mkt. 5.99 (0-441-00327-3) Ace Bks.

— Shadow Hunt. 1992. mass mkt. 4.50 (0-441-76007-4) Ace Bks.

— Waterdance. 272p. (Orig.). 1999. mass mkt. 6.50 (0-441-00613-2) Ace Bks.

— Wild Blood. 240p. (Orig.). 1995. mass mkt. 4.99 (0-441-00243-9) Ace Bks.

Logstrup, Knud. Metaphysics, Vol. 1. Dees, Russell, ed. (Studies in Philosophy). (Orig.). 1995. pap. text 40.00 (0-87462-603-X) Marquette.

— Metaphysics, Vol. 2. Dees, Russell, ed. (Studies in Philosophy). (Orig.). 1995. pap. text 40.00 (0-87462-607-2) Marquette.

Logstrup, Knud E. The Ethical Demand. LC 96-26430. Orig. Title: Den Etiske Fordring. 344p. (C). 1997. pap. text 22.95 (0-268-00934-1) U of Notre Dame Pr.

Logue. Dancing with an Alien. LC 99-42906. 144p. (gr. 12 up). Date not set. pap. 4.95 (0-06-447209-4) HarpC Child Bks.

— Last Rights: Death Control & the Elderly in America. LC 92-39452. (Lexington Book Series on Social Issues). 372p. 1993. 25.95 (0-669-27370-8) Lxngtn Bks.

Logue, Alexandra W. The Psychology of Eating & Drinking. 2nd ed. (Illus.). 352p. (C). 1991. pap. 22.95 (0-7167-2197-X) W H Freeman.

— Self-Control: Waiting Until Tomorrow for What You Want Today. LC 94-5478. 224p. (C). 1994. pap. text 16.40 (0-13-803750-7) P-H.

***Logue, Alexandra W.** Why We Eat What We Eat? 2001. pap. text. write for info. (0-7167-3876-7) W H Freeman.

Logue, Antonia. Shadow-Box. LC 99-22553. 308p. 1999. 24.00 (0-8021-1647-7, Grove) Grove-Atltic.

***Logue, Antonia.** Shadow-Box. 320p. 2000. reprint ed. pap. 13.00 (0-8021-3722-9, Grove) Grove-Atltic.

Logue, Barbara, jt. auth. see Rosenwaike, Ira.

Logue, Cal M., ed. No Place to Hide: The South & Human Rights, 2 vols., Vol. 1 & 2. LC 84-1044. 766p. 1984. 40.00 (0-86554-108-6, MUP-H101) Mercer Univ Pr.

Logue, Calvin M., ed. Representative American Speeches, 1937-1997. LC 97-34361. 778p. 1998. 55.00 (0-8242-0931-1) Wilson.

Logue, Calvin M. & Dorgan, Howard, eds. New Diversity in Contemporary Southern Rhetoric. LC 86-21152. 272p. 1987. text 40.00 (0-8071-1312-3) La State U Pr.

Logue, Calvin M. & Freshley, Dwight L., eds. Richard B. Russell: Voice of Georgia. LC 97-37100. 1997. 35.00 (0-86554-586-3, MUP/H438) Mercer Univ Pr.

Logue, Calvin M. & Talmadge, Eugene. Rhetoric & Response: Great American Orators: Critical Studies, Speeches, & Sources, 3. LC 88-24748. 325p. 1989. lib. bdg. 65.00 (0-313-25855-4, LUE, Greenwood Pr) Greenwood.

Logue, Calvin M., ed. see McGill, Ralph.

Logue, Christopher. The Husbands: An Account of Books III & IV of Homer's Iliad. LC 95-13117. 56p. 1995. text 19.00 (0-374-17391-5) FS&G.

— Lucky Dust. Date not set. pap. 11.95 (0-85646-157-1, Pub. by Anvil Press) Dufour.

— Lucky Dust. 8p. 1985. pap. 7.95 (0-85646-158-X, Pub. by Anvil Press) Dufour.

— Songs. 1960. 10.95 (0-8392-1106-6) Astor-Honor.

— War Music: A Version of Books 1-4 & 16-19 of Homer's "Iliad" LC 96-48168. 256p. 1996. pap. 14.00 (0-374-52494-7, Noonday) FS&G.

Logue, Dennis E. Handbook of Modern Finance. 1989. 150.00 (0-7913-0311-X) Warren Gorham & Lamont.

— Handbook of Modern Finance. 1991. suppl. ed. 53.75 (0-685-56109-7) Warren Gorham & Lamont.

— Managing Corporate Pension Plans. 289p. 1991. text 39.95 (0-88730-341-2, HarpBusn) HarpInfo.

Logue, Dennis E., ed. Handbook of Modern Finance. 3rd ed. LC 93-60975. 1994. 150.00 (0-7913-1762-5) Warren Gorham & Lamont.

Logue, Dennis E., ed. The WG&L Handbook of Financial Markets. LC 94-20612. (C). 1994. pap. 31.95 (0-538-84250-4) S-W Pub.

— The WG&L Handbook of Financial Strategy & Policy. LC 94-20887. (C). 1994. pap. 31.95 (0-538-84252-0) S-W Pub.

Logue, Dennis E., ed. The WG&L Handbook of International Finance. LC 94-20613. (C). 1994. mass mkt. 20.50 (0-538-84253-9) S-W Pub.

Logue, Dennis E., ed. The WG&L Handbook of Securities & Investment Management. LC 94-20685. (C). 1994. pap. 31.95 (0-538-84249-0) S-W Pub.

Logue, Dennis E., ed. The WG&L Handbook of Short-Time & Long-Term Financial Management. LC 94-20686. (C). 1994. mass mkt. 31.95 (0-538-84251-2) S-W Pub.

Logue, Dennis E. & Rader, Jack S. Managing Pension Plans: A Comprehensive Guide to Improving Plan Performance. LC 97-25803. (Financial Management Association Survey & Synthesis Ser.). 432p. 1997. 45.00 (0-87584-791-9, HBS Pr) Harvard Busn.

Logue, Dennis E. & Rogalski, Richard J. Managing Corporation Pension Plans: The Impacts of Inflation. LC 83-25786. (AEI Studies: No. 355). 78p. reprint ed. pap. 30.00 (0-7837-1083-6, 204161400021) Bks Demand.

Logue, Frank & Logue, Victoria. Appalachian Trail Fun Book. (Illus.). 70p. (J). (ps-3). 1993. pap. 6.95 (0-917953-60-6) Appalachian Trail.

— Best of the Appalachian Trail: Overnight Hikes. (Illus.). 224p. 1994. pap. 14.95 (0-89732-139-1) Menasha Ridge.

— Best of the Appalachian Trail, Day Hikes. (Illus.). 198p. 1994. pap. 14.95 (0-89732-138-3) Menasha Ridge.

— Cooking for Campers & Backpackers. (Nuts-N-Bolts Guides Ser.). 32p. 1995. pap. 4.95 (0-89732-175-8) Menasha Ridge.

— Georgia Outdoors. LC 95-471. (Illus.). 318p. (Orig.). 1995. pap. 14.95 (0-89587-131-9) Blair.

— Knots for Hikers & Backpackers. LC 96-105126. (Illus.). 32p. 1997. pap. 4.95 (0-89732-146-4) Menasha Ridge.

Logue, Frank, jt. auth. see Logue, Victoria.

Logue, James. Projective Probability. (Oxford Philosophical Monographs). (Illus.). 184p. 1995. text 45.00 (0-19-823959-9) OUP.

Logue, Jeanne N. Beyond the Germ Theory: The Story of Dr. Cooper Curice. LC 95-21982. (Illus.). 168p. 1996. 29.95 (0-89096-673-7) Tex A&M Univ Pr.

Logue, John. On a Par with Murder. (Morris & Sullivan Mystery Ser.: Vol. 5). 288p. 1999. mass mkt. 5.99 (0-440-22400-4) Dell.

— Toward a Theory of Trade Union Internationalism. LC 80-153679. (University of Gothenberg (Sweden), Research Section Post-War History Publications Ser.: No. 7). 66p. (Orig.). 1980. pap. 2.95 (0-933522-02-9) Kent Popular.

Logue, John, et al, eds. Transforming Russian Enterprises: From State Control to Employee Ownership, 168. LC 95-6666. (Contributions in Economics & Economic History Ser.: No. 168). 304p. 1995. 69.50 (0-313-28748-1, Greenwood Pr) Greenwood.

***Logue, John & McCalla, Gary.** Life at Southern Living: A Sort of Memoir. LC 00-37066. (Illus.). 328p. 2000. 24.95 (0-8071-2561-X) La State U Pr.

Logue, John, et al. Buyout! Employee Ownership as an Alternative to Plant Shutdowns: The Ohio Experience. LC 86-623028. (Illus.). 104p. (Orig.). 1986. pap. text 9.95 (0-933522-15-0) Kent Popular.

— Participatory Employee Ownership: How It Works. (Illus.). 192p. 1998. pap. text 14.95 (0-933522-24-X); lib. bdg. 24.95 (0-933522-23-1) Kent Popular.

Logue, John, jt. see Hancock, M. Donald.

Logue, John, jt. auth. see Callesen, Gerd.

Logue, John, jt. auth. see Einhorn, Eric S.

Logue, John, jt. auth. see Keremetsky, Jacob.

Logue, John, ed. see Belton, Beth.

Logue, John, ed. see Einhorn, Eric S.

Logue, John J. The Great Debate on Charter Reform: A Proposal for a Stronger United Nations. LC 67-47309. (Publications in the Social Sciences: No. 2). 39p. reprint ed. pap. 30.00 (0-7837-5571-6, 204534900005) Bks Demand.

Logue, Judy. Forgiving the People You Love to Hate. LC 96-78939. 80p. (Orig.). 1997. pap. 4.95 (0-7648-0063-9) Liguori Pubns.

Logue, Larry M. To Appomattox & Beyond: The Civil War Soldier in War & Peace. (American Ways Ser.). 170p. 1995. 22.50 (1-56663-093-2, Pub. by I R Dee) Natl Bk Netwk.

— To Appomattox & Beyond: The Civil War Soldier in War & Peace. LC 95-30217. (American Ways Ser.). 168p. 1995. pap. text 9.95 (1-56663-094-0, Pub. by I R Dee) Natl Bk Netwk.

Logue, Mary. Blood Country. LC 99-22175. (Clare Watkins Mystery Ser.). 324p. 1999. 23.95 (0-8027-3339-5) Walker & Co.

— Dancing with an Alien. LC 99-42906. (Illus.). 144p. (YA). (gr. 7 up). 2000. 14.95 (0-06-028318-1) HarpC Child Bks.

***Logue, Mary.** Dancing with an Alien. LC 99-42906. (Illus.). 144p. (YA). (gr. 7 up). 2000. lib. bdg. 14.89 (0-06-028319-X) HarpC Child Bks.

— Dark Coulee. (Claire Watkins Mystery Ser.). 2000. 23.95 (0-8027-3351-4) Walker & Co.

Logue, Mary. Discriminating Evidence. LC 90-39386. (First Poetry Ser.). 70p. 1990. pap. 8.95 (0-922811-09-1) Mid-List.

— Forgiveness: The Story of Mahatma Gandhi. LC 95-43783. (Value Biographies Ser.). (Illus.). 32p. (J). (gr. 2-6). 1997. lib. bdg. 21.36 (1-56766-224-2) Childs World.

— Halfway Home: A Granddaughter's Biography. LC 96-2641. (Midwest Reflections Ser.). x, 201p. 1996. 22.95 (0-87351-331-2); pap. 14.95 (0-87351-332-0) Minn Hist.

— Imagination: The Story of Walt Disney. LC 98-34726. (Illus.). 32p. (J). 1999. lib. bdg. 21.36 (1-56766-608-6) Childs World.

— Love: The Story of Elizabeth Barrett Browning. LC 95-44422. (Value Biographies Ser.). (Illus.). 32p. (J). 1997. lib. bdg. 21.36 (1-56766-225-0, 62250) Childs World.

— Settling: Poems. LC 97-34119. 72p. 1997. pap. 11.00 (0-922811-33-4) Mid-List.

— Trust: The Story of Helen Keller. LC 98-30472. (Illus.). 32p. (J). 1999. lib. bdg. 21.36 (1-56766-605-1) Childs World.

Logue, Mary, ed. see Green, Kate, et al.

***Logue, Michael J.** The Do-It Yourself Living Will. large type ed. Slater, Liz A., ed. 20p. 1999. pap. 8.99 (0-9674502-0-9) Appeals.

***Logue, Paddy, ed.** The Border: Personal Reflections from Ireland, North & South. 198p. 2000. pap. 19.95 (1-86076-156-9, Pub. by Oak Tr) Midpt Trade.

Logue, Patricia H. One Child at a Time: A Parent's Guide to Rebuilding American Mindpower. (Illus.). 96p. (Orig.). 1992. pap. 10.00 (0-9630488-0-5) Mindbuilder.

Logue, Tom J. God, Could You Talk a Little Louder? The Father of a Dying Son Struggles with His Faith. 102p. (Orig.). 1990. pap. 6.95 (0-933522-21-5) Kent Popular.

***Logue, Victoria.** Backpacking: Essential Skills to Advanced Techniques. (Illus.). 320p. 2000. pap. 15.95 (0-89732-323-8) Menasha Ridge.

Logue, Victoria. Backpacking in the Nineties: Tips, Techniques & Secrets. LC 92-43314. (Illus.). 332p. 1992. pap. 14.95 (0-89732-163-4) Menasha Ridge.

— Camping in the 90's: Tips, Techniques & Secrets. (Illus.). 224p. 1995. pap. 15.95 (0-89732-181-2) Menasha Ridge.

Logue, Victoria & Logue, Frank. Appalachian Trail Backpacker: Trail-Proven Advice for Hikes of Any Length. LC 95-151020. 200p. (Orig.). 1990. pap. 10.95 (0-89732-161-8) Menasha Ridge.

— Touring the Backroads of North & South Georgia. LC 97-19095. (Touring the Backroads Ser.). (Illus.). (Orig.). 1997. pap. 20.95 (0-89587-171-8) Blair.

Logue, Victoria, et al. Kids Outdoors: The Totally Nonboring Backcountry Skills Guide. (Illus.). 139p. (J). (gr. 6-10). 1996. pap. 14.95 (0-07-038477-0) McGraw.

Logue, Victoria, jt. auth. see Logue, Frank.

Logue, William. Charles Renouvier, Philosopher of Liberty. LC 92-15585. 224p. (C). 1993. text 35.00 (0-8071-1788-9) La State U Pr.

— From Philosophy to Sociology: The Evolution of French Liberalism, 1870-1914. LC 82-22263. 278p. 1983. 32.00 (0-87580-088-2) N Ill U Pr.

— Leon Blum, 1872-1914: The Formative Years. LC 72-7515. 345p. 1973. 32.00 (0-87580-030-0) N Ill U Pr.

Logunov, A., ed. Current Problems of Mathematics: Differential Equations, Mathematical Analysis & Their Applications. LC 86-10929. (Proceedings of the Steklov Institute of Mathematics Ser.: Vol. 166). 271p. 1986. pap. 128.00 (0-8218-3093-7, STEKLO/166) Am Math.

— Current Problems of Mathematics: Mathematical Analysis, Algebra, Topology. LC 86-20640. (Proceedings of the Steklov Institute of Mathematics Ser.: Vol. 167). 304p. 1986. pap. 137.00 (0-8218-3095-3, STEKLO/167) Am Math.

Logunov, A. A. Lectures in Relativity & Gravitation: A Modern Look. Repyev, Alexander, tr. (Illus.). 256p. 1991. 92.00 (0-08-037939-7, Pergamon Pr) Elsevier.

Logunov, A. A., Jr., et al. Selected Topics in Statistical Mechanics. 556p. (C). 1990. text 130.00 (981-02-0118-4) World Scientific Pub.

Logunov, Anatolifi A. Relativistic Theory of Gravity. LC 98-48792. (Horizons in World Physics Ser.). 1998. 145.00 (1-56072-635-0) Nova Sci Pubs.

Logusz, Michael O. Galicia Division: The Waffen-SS 14th Grenadier Division, 1943-1945. LC 96-67287. (Illus.). 352p. 1996. 35.00 (0-7643-0081-4) Schiffer.

Loguz, C. H. Limiting Spur Gear Design. (Technical Papers: Vol. P59). (Illus.). 20p. 1925. pap. text 30.00 (1-55589-263-9) AGMA.

Logy, Nancy N. De, see De Bernardo, Mark A. & De Logy, Nancy N.

Loh, Eudora & Medford, Roberta, compiled by. Statistical Sources on the California Hispanic Population: Update. pap. 25.00 (0-915745-06-2) Floricanto Pr.

Loh, Eudora, jt. auth. see Medford, Roberta.

Loh, Grace, et al. Beyond Silken Robes: Profiles of Selected Chinese Entrepreneurs in Singapore. LC 98-945691. 97p. 1998. 25.00 (981-210-104-7, Pub. by Times Academic) Intl Spec Bk.

Loh, Horace H. & Ross, David H., eds. Neurochemical Mechanisms of Opiates & Endorphins. LC 78-24623. (Advances in Biochemical Psychopharmacology Ser.: No. 20). (Illus.). 575p. reprint ed. pap. 178.30 (0-7837-7129-0, 204695800004) Bks Demand.

Loh, I-Jin & Hatton, Howard. A Handbook on the Letter from James. LC 97-702. (UBS Handbook Ser.). 240p. 1997. pap. 10.99 (0-8267-0170-1, 105889) Untd Bible Soc.

Loh, I-Jin & Nida, Eugene A. A Handbook on Paul's Letters to the Philippians. LC 94-34753. (UBS Handbook Ser.). Orig. Title: Translator's Handbook on Paul's Letter to the Philippians. viii, 167p. 1977. pap. 16.99 (0-8267-0165-5, 102691) Untd Bible Soc.

Loh, Johannes. Paradies im Widerspiel der Machte: Mythenlogik - eine Herausforderung fur die Theologie. 338p. 1998. 55.95 (3-631-32173-2) P Lang Pubng.

Loh, Lily. Lily Loh's Chinese Seafood & Vegetables. Addison-Licameli, Amy, ed. (Illus.). 222p. 1991. 22.95 (0-9630299-0-8) Solana Pub.

Loh, Michael. Re-Engineering at Work. 2nd ed. 256p. 1997. pap. 33.95 (0-566-07941-0, Pub. by Gower) Ashgate Pub Co.

Loh, Morag. Tucking Mommy In. LC 87-16740. (Illus.). 40p. (J). (ps-2). 1991. pap. 5.95 (0-531-07025-5) Orchard Bks Watts.

Loh, Morag Jeanette. Tucking Mommy In. (J). 1991. 11.15 (0-606-09998-0, Pub. by Turtleback) Demco.

An Asterisk (*) at the beginning of an entry indicates that the title is appearing for the first time.

Loh, Muriel Van, see Van Loh, Muriel.

Loh, Pichon P. The Early Chiang Kai-Shek: A Study of His Personality & Politics, 1887-1924. LC 70-158461. (Columbia University East Asian Institute Occasional Papers). 230p. reprint ed. pap. 71.30 (*0-608-11065-5*, 200686900060) Bks Demand.

***Loh, Pit Fong, et al.** The Forbidden Realm. (Choreography & Dance Archives Ser.: Vol. 1). (Illus.). 28p. 1999. pap. text 46.00 incl. VHS (*90-5755-048-2*, Harwood Acad Pubs); pap. text 46.00 incl. VHS (*90-5755-049-0*, Harwood Acad Pubs) Gordon & Breach.

Loh, Sandra T. Aliens in America. LC 96-54622. 96p. 1997. pap. 10.95 (*1-57322-627-0*) Berkley Pub.

— Depth Takes a Holiday: Essays from Lesser Los Angeles. 240p. 1997. reprint ed. pap. 13.00 (*1-57322-611-4*, Riverhd Trade) Berkley Pub.

— If You Lived Here, You'd Be Home by Now: A Novel. LC 97-10056. 224p. 1997. 23.95 (*1-57322-068-X*, Riverhead Books) Putnam Pub Group.

Loh, Sandra Tsing. If You Lived Here, You'd Be Home by Now. 240p. 1998. pap. 13.00 (*1-57322-695-5*, Riverhd Trade) Berkley Pub.

***Loh, Stephan H.** The General Theory of Economic Efficiency. 246p. (C). 1999. pap. 85.00 (*0-9673668-0-1*) SHL Resources.

Loh, Y. Peng, ed. Mechanisms of Intracellular Trafficking & Processing of Proteins. 320p. 1992. lib. bdg. 155.00 (*0-8493-6870-7*, QH450) CRC Pr.

***Loha-Unchit, Kasma.** Dancing Shrimp: Favorite Thai Recipes for Seafood. LC 00-41268. (Illus.). 2000. write for info. (*0-684-86272-7*) Simon & Schuster.

Loha-Unchit, Kasma. It Rains Fishes: Legends, Traditions & the Joys of Thai Cooking. LC 94-49451. (Illus.). 224p. (Orig.). 1995. pap. 29.95 (*0-87654-356-5*) Pomegranate Calif.

Lohafer, Susan & Clarey, JoEllen, eds. Short Story Theory at a Crossroads. LC 89-30723. (Illus.). 280p. 1989. pap. 18.95 (*0-8071-1586-X*); text 40.00 (*0-8071-1546-0*) La State U Pr.

Lohan, Frank. Drawing Florida Wildlife. LC 95-42719. (Illus.). 96p. (Orig.). 1996. pap. 12.95 (*1-56164-090-5*) Pineapple Pr.

Lohan, Frank. The Inward Journey We Open Up Like Petals On a Rose, When We Discover Who We Really Are. LC 92-94216. 154p. 1995. pap. 10.95 (*0-9608960-7-4*) Single Vision.

Lohan, Frank J. The Drawing Handbook. 224p. 1993. pap. 16.95 (*0-8092-3786-5*, 378650, Contemporary Bks) NTC Contemp Pub Co.

— Pen & Ink Techniques. (Illus.). 96p. 1978. pap. 16.95 (*0-8092-7438-8*, 74388) NTC Contemp Pub Co.

Lohan, Kevin, jt. auth. see Rylatt, Alastair.

Lohani, Bindu N. Environmental Quality Management. Varshney, C. K., ed. (C). 1984. 28.50 (*0-8364-2409-3*, Pub. by S Asia Pubs) S Asia.

Lohani, Mohan P. Nepal & the United Nations, 1956-1996. 1996. pap. 27.00 (*0-7855-7449-2*, Pub. by Ratna Pustak Bhandar) St Mut.

Lohans, Alison. Foghorn Passage. 224p. (YA). (gr. 7-11). 1992. pap. 7.95 (*0-7737-5496-2*) Stoddart Publ.

— Foghorn Passage. unabridged ed. LC 99-159424. 224p. (YA). (gr. 7 up). 1997. pap. 5.99 (*0-7736-7451-9*) Stoddart Publ.

— Mystery of the Lunchbox Criminal. (Shooting Star: Vol. 3). (J). 1990. pap. 4.50 (*0-590-73367-2*) Scholastic Inc.

— Nathaniel's Violin. (Illus.). 32p. (J). (ps-3). 1996. pap. 6.95 (*1-55143-064-9*) Orca Bk Pubs.

Lohans, Alison. No Place for Kids. 98p. (J). (gr. 3-5). pap. 4.95 (*1-896184-50-2*) Roussan Pubs.

— Skateboard Kids. (Early Chapter Book Ser.). 76p. (J). 1999. pap. 4.95 (*1-896184-64-2*) Roussan Pubs.

Lohans, Alison. Sundog Rescue. (Illus.). 24p. (J). (ps-2). 1999. pap. 5.95 (*1-55037-570-9*, Pub. by Annick Pr); lib. bdg. 15.95 (*1-55037-571-7*, Pub. by Annick Pr) Firefly Bks Ltd.

Lohaus, Arnold, jt. auth. see Thomas, Hoben.

Lohaus, Sara & White, Jan, eds. A Colorado Christmas Anthology. (State Anthologies Ser.: No. 3). (Illus.). 1990. pap. 10.95 (*0-9621085-9-6*) Partridge Pr.

Lohbeck, Dave. CE Marketing Handbook. LC 98-21463. 144p. 1998. text 49.95 (*0-7506-9819-5*, Newnes) Buttrwrth-Heinemann.

Lohbeck, Kurt. Holy War, Unholy Victory: Eyewitness to the CIA's Secret War in Afghanistan. LC 93-24344. (Illus.). 320p. 1993. 24.00 (*0-89526-499-4*) Regnery Pub.

Lohberg, Rolf. Diccionario Basico del Ordenador. 2nd ed. (SPA.). 48p. 1987. pap. 8.95 (*0-7859-6449-5*) Fr & Eur.

Loheed, M. J. Finger: The Comprehensive Guide to Flipping Off. (Illus.). 112p. 1998. pap. text 16.95 (*1-888358-12-2*) Acid Test Prodns.

***Loher, Ann & Loker, Alech.** Oyster Recipes of St. Mary's County, Maryland. (Illus.). 97p. 1999. mass mkt. 8.00 (*1-928874-00-2*) Solitude Pr.

Loher, Elisabeth C. Out of the Luminous Silence: Spirit in Dreams. (Illus.). 80p. 1994. 12.95 (*0-9641910-1-6*) Blue Gate Pub.

Lohf, Kenneth A. & Ellenbogen, Rudolph, eds. The Rare Book & Manuscript Library of Columbia University: Collections & Treasures. 138p. 1985. pap. 25.00 (*0-9607862-1-X*) Columbia U Libs.

Lohf, Sabine. Things I Can Make. LC 93-40881. (Illus.). 128p. (J). (ps-3). 1994. pap. 13.95 (*0-8118-0667-7*) Chronicle Bks.

Lohfert, Walter, jt. auth. see Scherling, Theo.

Lohff, David C. The Dream Directory: A Comprehensive A-to-Z Guide to Analysis & Interpretation, with Explanations for More Than 350 Symbols & Theories. (Illus.). 320p. 1998. 9.98 (*0-7624-0301-2*, Courage) Running Pr.

***Lohff, David C.** Dreams: More Than 350 Symbols & Interpretations. (Illus.). 624p. 2000. pap. text 9.95 (*0-7624-0692-5*) Running Pr.

Lohfink, Gerhard. Does God Need the Church? Toward a Theology of the People of God. Maloney, Linda M., tr. from GER. LC 98-32331. 341p. (C). 1999. pap. 39.95 (*0-8146-5928-4*) Liturgical Pr.

— The Gospels: God's Word in Human Words. Poehlmann, William R., tr. (Herald Biblical Bklts.). 80p. 1972. pap. 1.00 (*0-8199-0212-8*, Frncscn Herld) Franciscan Pr.

— Jesus & Community: The Social Dimension of Christian Faith. Galvin, John P., tr. LC 84-47928. 224p. 1984. pap. 20.00 (*0-8006-1802-5*, 1-1802, Fortress Pr) Augsburg Fortress.

***Lohfink, Norbert.** Church Dreams: Talking Against the Trend. LC 00-8250. 2000. write for info. (*0-941037-91-6*, BIBAL Press) D & F Scott.

Lohfink, Norbert. The Covenant Never Revoked: Biblical Reflections on Christian-Jewish Dialogue. LC 90-261098. 1991. pap. 7.95 (*0-8091-3228-1*) Paulist Pr.

— Option for the Poor: The Basic Principle of Liberation Theoloy in the Light of the Bible. 2nd ed. Christensen, Duane L., ed. Maloney, Linda M., tr. LC 95-25305. (Berkeley Lectures: Vol. 1). 1996. 8.95 (*0-941037-38-X*, BIBAL Press) D & F Scott.

— Die Vater Israels Im Deuteronomium: Mit Einer Stellungnahme von Thomas Romer. (Orbis Biblicus et Orientalis Ser.: Vol. 111). (GER.). 133p. 1991. text 29.50 (*3-7278-0778-4*, Pub. by Presses Univ Fribourg) Eisenbrauns.

***Lohfink, Norbert & Zenger, Erich.** The God of Israel & the Nations: Studies in Isaiah & the Psalms. Kalin, Everett R., tr. 2000. pap. 39.95 (*0-8146-5925-X*) Liturgical Pr.

Lohfink, Norbert F. The Inerrancy of Scripture & Other Essays. Wilson, R. A., tr. LC 91-2720. 183p. 1992. pap. 13.95 (*0-941037-20-7*, BIBAL Press) D & F Scott.

Lohia, Sushama. Lalitavajra's Manual of Buddhist Iconography. (C). 1994. text 88.00 (*81-85689-97-0*, Pub. by Popular Prakashan) S Asia.

Lohkamp, Nicholas. Jesus at the Heart of Life: The Spirituality of Being Human. 90p. 1994. pap. 6.95 (*0-86716-225-2*) St Anthony Mess Pr.

Lohman, Anne A. Clay Lifting. Thompson, Bill, ed. LC 85-90939. 60p. (Orig.). 1985. pap. text 7.95 (*0-685-71262-1*) Scott Pubns MI.

Lohman, Helene, jt. auth. see Coppard, Brenda M.

Lohman, Jack & Kirkpatrick, Arnold. Successful Thoroughbred Investment in a Changing Market. (Illus.). 253p. 1984. 25.00 (*0-929346-10-6*) R Meerdink Co Ltd.

Lohman, Timothy G. Advances in Body Composition Assessment. LC 92-1476. (Current Issues in Exercise Science Ser.: Monograph No. 3). (Illus.). 160p. 1992. pap. text 17.00 (*0-87322-327-6*, BLOH0327) Human Kinetics.

Lohman, Timothy G., et al, eds. Anthropometric Standardization Reference Manual. abr. ed. LC 90-29003. (Illus.). 96p. 1991. reprint ed. pap. 30.00 (*0-608-06440-8*, 206727800009) Bks Demand.

— Anthropometric Standardization Reference Manual. LC 87-8623. (Illus.). 183p. 1988. reprint ed. pap. 56.80 (*0-608-07070-X*, 206727600009) Bks Demand.

Lohmann, Christoph, tr. see Rehmann, Ruth.

Lohmann, Christoph K., ed. Discovering Difference: Contemporary Essays in American Culture. LC 92-41566. 224p. 1993. 29.95 (*0-253-33607-4*); pap. 16.95 (*0-253-20815-7*) Ind U Pr.

Lohmann, Christopher, tr. see Assing, Ottilie.

Lohmann, Dieter. Die Andromache-Szenen in der Ilias. (Spudasmata Ser.: Bd. 42). (GER.). iv, 82p. 1988. write for info. (*3-487-09009-0*) G Olms Pubs.

Lohmann, G. P., jt. auth. see Tjalsma, R. C.

Lohmann, Hans. Drohung und Verheissung: Exegetische Untersuchungen zur Eschatologie bei den Apostolischen Vaetern. (Beiheft zur Zeitschrift fuer die Neuetestamentliche Wissenschaft Ser.: No. 55). (GER.). ix, 266p. (C). 1989. lib. bdg. 79.25 (*3-11-012018-6*) De Gruyter.

Lohmann, Hans-Martin, ed. Psychoanalyse und Nationalsozialismus: Beitraege zur Bearbeitung eines unbewaeltigten Traaumas. (GER.). 288p. 1994. pap. 18.00 (*3-596-12231-7*, Pub. by Fischer Tasch) Intl Bk Import.

Lohmann, Jeanne. Between Silence & Answer: New & Selected Poems. LC 94-21462. (Illus.). 98p. 1995. pap. 10.00 (*0-87574-919-4*, 6309) Pendle Hill.

***Lohmann, Jeanne.** Flying Horses: Poems. 96p. 2001. pap. 12.00 (*1-56474-351-9*) Fithian Pr.

Lohmann, Jeanne. Gathering a Life. LC 89-32034. 72p. (Orig.). 1989. pap. 7.50 (*0-936784-77-6*) J Daniel.

— Granite under Water: Poems. 80p. (Orig.). 1996. pap. 8.95 (*1-56474-180-X*) Fithian Pr.

Lohmann, Johann F. Karl Barth und der Neukantianismus: Die Rezeption des Neukantianismus im "Roemerbrief" und Ihre Bedetung Fuer die Weitere Ausarbeitung der Theologie Karl Barths. (Theologische Bibliothek Toepelmann Ser.: Bd. 72). (GER.). x, 421p. (C). 1995. lib. bdg. 167.70 (*3-11-014883-8*) De Gruyter.

Lohmann, Larry, jt. auth. see Carrere, Ricardo.

Lohmann, Larry, jt. ed. see Colchester, Marcus.

Lohmann, Martina, jt. ed. see Lieth, Helmut.

Lohmann, Melane, ed. Recherche Recipes from Sound Food Restaurant & Bakery. (Illus.). 51p. (Orig.). 1984. pap. 6.95 (*0-9615672-0-1*) Sound Food Co.

Lohmann, Michael & Haarmann, Knut. Vogelparadiese. Biotope Zwischen Wattenmeer und Bodensee. Bird Paradise of Germany from Wattan Sea (Soals & Shallows) to the Bodensee (Lake Constance), Bands 1-3. (Illus.). 1991. pap. 60.00 (*3-8263-8149-1*, Pub. by Blckwell Wissenschafts) Balogh.

Lohmann, Pamela, tr. see Rehmann, Ruth.

Lohmann, Roger A. Breaking Even: Financial Management in Human Service Organizations. LC 79-23692. 336p. 1981. pap. text 27.95 (*0-87722-247-9*) Temple U Pr.

Lohmann, U., tr. see Jungel, Eberhard.

Lohmann, W. J., Jr. The Cultural Shocks of Rudyard Kipling. LC 89-13330. (American University Studies: English Language & Literature: Ser. IV, Vol. 73). 309p. (C). 1991. text 46.95 (*0-8204-0649-X*) P Lang Pubng.

Lohmar, Dieter. Erfahrung Und Kategoriales Denken: Hume, Kant Und Husserl Uber Vorpradikative Erfahrung Und Pradikative Erkenntnis. 320p. 1998. 98.00 (*0-7923-5117-7*) Kluwer Academic.

— Phanomenologie der Mathematik: Elemente Einer Phanomenologischen Aufklarung der Mathematischen Erkenntnis Nach Husserl. (Phaenomenologica Ser.: No. 114). 252p. 1989. lib. bdg. 171.00 (*0-7923-0187-0*, Pub. by Kluwer Academic) Kluwer Academic.

Lohmus, J., et al. Nonassociative Algebras in Physics. LC 94-42052. (Monographs in Mathematics). 280p. 1994. pap. text 75.00 (*0-911767-71-1*) Hadronic Pr Inc.

Lohne, Raymond, jt. auth. see Holli.

***Lohnert, Beate, ed.** Coping with Changing Environments: Social Dimensions of Endangered Ecosystems in the Developing World. 330p. 1999. text 74.95 (*1-84014-958-2*, Pub. by Inst Materials) Ashgate Pub Co.

Lohnes, Marilyn. Finger Folk. LC 98-47639. 102p. 1999. pap. 16.95 (*1-57950-026-9*, Alleyside) Highsmith Pr.

Lohnes, Paul R., jt. auth. see Cooley, William W.

Lohnes, Walter F. & Nollendorfs, Valters, eds. German Studies in the United States: Assessment & Outlook. LC 76-13346. (Monatshefte Occasional Volume Ser.: Vol. 1). 272p. 1976. reprint ed. pap. 84.40 (*0-608-01963-1*, 206261800003) Bks Demand.

Lohnes, Walter F., et al. German: A Structural Approach. 4th ed. LC 93-230012. 33p. (C). 1988. text 67.50 (*0-393-95464-1*) Norton.

— German Instructor's Manual: A Structural Approach. (C). 1989. pap., teacher ed. 4.95 (*0-393-95470-6*) Norton.

— German Study Guide: A Structural Approach. 4th ed. (C). 1988. pap. text, student ed. 29.25 (*0-393-95467-6*) Norton.

Lohneysen, Georg E. Della Cavalleria. vi, 768p. 1977. write for info. (*3-487-08088-5*) G Olms Pubs.

Lohninger, H. Inspect: A Program System for Scientific & Engineering Data. 200p. 1996. 450.00 incl. disk (*3-540-14530-3*) Spr-Verlag.

— Teach/Me - Data Analysis: Single User Edition. 100p. 1999. 42.00 incl. cd-rom (*3-540-14743-8*) Spr-Verlag.

Lohof, Bruce A. American Commonplace: Essays on the Popular Culture of the United States. LC 82-73977. 1983. 16.95 (*0-87972-221-5*) Bowling Green Univ Popular Press.

Lohr. Survey Sampling. 494p. 1998. pap. 75.95 (*0-534-35361-4*) Brooks-Cole.

Lohr, Albrecht, jt. auth. see Jakobi, Gunter.

Lohr, Albrecht, jt. ed. see Jakobi, Gunter.

Lohr, Andrew. Born of Water & Spirit: Teachings in Mystic Christianity. LC 90-82118. 256p. (Orig.). 1990. pap. 11.95 (*0-9626563-4-8*) Folsom Lee.

— Talks on Mystic Christianity. Challgren, Crafer, ed. LC 84-90346. (Illus.). 143p. (Orig.). 1984. pap. text 6.50 (*0-9613401-0-X*) Fiery Water.

Lohr, Clark B. The Three Bad Sheep. (Illus.). 32p. (J). (gr. 1-5). 1997. 14.00 (*0-9661135-0-0*, 1) What the Hay.

Lohr, Dirk & Jenetzky, Johannes. Neutrale Liquiditat: Zur Theorie & Praktischen Umsetzung. (GER., Illus.). 204p. 1996. 42.95 (*3-631-30786-1*) P Lang Pubng.

Lohr, Eberhard, et al, eds. Clinical Neuroradiology: A Textbook. LC 94-35189. (Illus.). 336p. 1995. text 135.00 (*0-88937-132-6*) Hogrefe & Huber Pubs.

Lohr, Eberhard & Sievers, Klaus, eds. Urological Radiology: Radiological Diagnosis of Urological Diseases: Plain Film, Sonography, Angiography, CT, & MRI. LC 94-34633. (Illus.). 256p. 1995. text 89.00 (*0-88937-131-8*) Hogrefe & Huber Pubs.

Lohr-Heinemann, Brigitte. Die Haltungskongruenz Als Erkenntnis- und Handlungsleitender Indikator in Einem Familientherapeutischen Proze: Analyse von Videogestutzter Datenkonstitution und Hypothesenbildung in der Systemischen Therapie. (Psychologie Ser.: Bd. 614). (GER., Illus.). 346p. 1998. 51.95 (*3-631-33482-6*) P Lang Pubng.

Lohr, J. & Luce, T. Electron Cyclotron Emission & Electron Cyclotron Resonance Heating: Proceedings of the Joint Workshop. 600p. 1995. text 128.00 (*981-02-2338-2*) World Scientific Pub.

Lohr, J. E. Your First Cockatiel. (YF Ser.). (Illus.). 32p. (Orig.). (YA). 1991. pap. 2.29 (*0-86622-060-7*, YF-104) TFH Pubns.

— Your First Parakeet. (YF Ser.). (Illus.). 36p. (Orig.). (YA). 1991. pap. 2.29 (*0-7938-0015-3*, YF-102) TFH Pubns.

***Lohr, J. Matthias & New York Academy of Sciences Staff.** Cell & Molecular Biology of Pancreatic Carcinoma: Recent Developments in Research & Experimental Therapy LC 99-34747. (Annals of the New York Academy of Science Ser.). 1999. write for info. (*1-57331-220-7*) NY Acad Sci.

Lohr, Jacob A. Pediatric Outpatient Procedures. (Illus.). 400p. 1991. text 53.00 (*0-397-50897-2*) Lppncott W & W.

Lohr, Jacob A., et al, eds. Pediatric Outpatient Procedures. LC 90-13405. (Illus.). 399p. reprint ed. pap. 123.70 (*0-608-09743-8*, 206991200007) Bks Demand.

Lohr, James B. & Wisniewski, Alexander A. Movement Disorders: A Neuropsychiatric Approach. LC 86-27163. (Guilford Foundations of Modern Psychiatry Ser.). 387p. 1987. lib. bdg. 63.00 (*0-89862-176-3*) Guilford Pubns.

Lohr, Kathleen N., ed. Breast Cancer: Setting Priorities for Effectiveness Research: Report of a Study by a Committee of the Institute of Medicine, Division of Health Care Services. LC 89-64426. 72p. reprint ed. pap. 30.00 (*0-8357-2694-0*, 204023100015) Bks Demand.

Lohr, Kathleen N., ed. see Committee of the Institute of Medicine Division of.

Lohr, Kathleen N., jt. ed. see Heithoff, Kim A.

Lohr, Kathleen N., ed. see Institute of Medicine (U. S.) Staff.

Lohr, Kathleen N., ed. see Institute of Medicine, Committee on Pediatric Emer.

Lohr, Kathleen N., ed. see Institute of Medicine Committee on Regional Health.

Lohr, Kathleen N., ed. see Institute of Medicine, Committee to Advise the Pub.

Lohr, Kathleen N., ed. see Institute of Medicine Staff.

***Lohr, Lila.** Peterson's Game Plan for Getting into Private School. LC 99-89009. 200p. 2000. 14.95 (*0-7689-0387-4*) Petersons.

Lohr, Nancy. Pelts & Promises. LC 96-43861. 103p. (J). 1997. pap. 6.49 (*0-89084-899-8*, 102731) Bob Jones Univ.

Lohr, Neah J. Wisconsin Educational Technology Plan PK-12. 130p. (Orig.). 1996. pap. text 21.00 (*1-57337-038-X*) WI Dept Pub Instruct.

Lohr, R. & Steen, M., eds. Ultra High Temperature Mechanical Testing. 240p. 1995. 162.00 (*1-85573-155-X*, 73155X, Pub. by Woodhead Pubng) Am Educ Systs.

***Lohr, Sheri L.** Island Life: A Heart Apart. 24p. 1999. pap. 6.95 (*0-9673704-0-X*) Seastory.

Lohraff, Kevin. Hiking Missouri. LC 98-46240. (America's Best Day Hiking Ser.). (Illus.). 216p. 1999. pap. 19.95 (*0-88011-893-8*, PLOH0893) Human Kinetics.

Lohren, Carl. Getting Set for Golf. 176p. 1999. pap. 11.95 (*0-14-023757-7*) Viking Penguin.

Lohrentz, Kenneth P., jt. auth. see Easterbrook, David L.

Lohrenz, Mary & Stamper, Anita A. Mississippi Homespun: Nineteenth Century Textiles & the Women Who Made Them. (Illus.). 79p. 1989. pap. 15.00 (*0-938896-56-3*) Mississippi Archives.

Lohrey, Andrew. The Meaning of Consciousness. LC 97-4581. 320p. (C). 1997. text 42.50 (*0-472-10821-2*, 10821) U of Mich Pr.

Lohrey, Andrew, jt. auth. see Carey, Alex.

Lohrke, E. W. Armageddon: The World War in Literature. 1971. 69.95 (*0-87968-660-X*) Gordon Pr.

Lohrmann, Charles J., jt. auth. see Kapoun, Robert W.

Lohrmann, Dietrich, jt. ed. see Butzer, Paul L.

Lohrmann, H. P. & Schreml, W., eds. Cytotoxic Drugs & the Granulopoietic System. (Recent Results in Cancer Research Ser.: Vol. 81). (Illus.). 235p. 1981. 74.00 (*0-387-10962-5*) Spr-Verlag.

Lohrum, Frances M. And Again We Were Two. 172p. 1997. pap. 14.00 (*0-931541-46-8*) Mancorp Pub.

Lohs, Karlheinz, jt. ed. see Stock, Thomas.

Lohse, Bernhard. Martin Luther: An Introduction to His Life & Work. Schultz, Robert C., tr. from GER. LC 85-45496. 304p. 1986. pap. 23.00 (*0-8006-1964-1*, 1-1964, Fortress Pr) Augsburg Fortress.

— Martin Luther's Theology: Its Historical & Systematic Development. Harrisville, Roy, tr. from GER. LC 99-22239. 1999. 43.00 (*0-8006-3091-2*, Fortress Pr) Augsburg Fortress.

— A Short History of Christian Doctrine: From the First Century to the Present. rev. ed. Stoeffer, F. Ernest, tr. from GER. LC 66-21732. 320p. 1978. pap. 20.00 (*0-8006-1341-4*, 1-1341, Fortress Pr) Augsburg Fortress.

***Lohse, David J., et al, eds.** Interfacial Aspects of Multicomponent Polymer Materials: Proceedings of an American Chemical Society Symposium Held in Orlando, Florida, August 25-30, 1996. LC 97-35356. (Illus.). 312p. (C). 1998. 95.00 (*0-306-45718-0*, Plenum Trade) Perseus Pubng.

Lohse, David J., jt. auth. see Datta, Sudhin.

Lohse, Edward. Colossians & Philemon. Koester, Helmut, ed. Poehlman, William R. & Karris, Robert J., trs. from GER. LC 76-157550. (Hermeneia: A Critical & Historical Commentary on the Bible Ser.). 240p. 1971. 43.00 (*0-8006-6001-3*, 1-6001, Fortress Pr) Augsburg Fortress.

— The New Testament Environment. Steely, John E., tr. from GER. LC 75-43618. 320p. 1976. pap. 14.95 (*0-687-27944-5*) Abingdon.

Lohse, Friedrich, jt. auth. see Batzer, Hans.

Lohse, G. A. & Lucht, W. H., eds. Die Kaefer Mitteleuropas (The Beetles of Central Europe), Vol. 4. (Ergaenzungen und Berichtigungen zu Den Ser.: Band 15:4). (Illus.). 398p. 1998. 130.00 (*3-437-35398-5*) Gustav Fischer.

Lohse, Joyce B. A Yellowstone Savage: Life in Nature's Wonderland. LC 87-34212. (Illus.). 144p. (Orig.). 1988. pap. 7.95 (*0-944915-00-0*) J D Charles.

Lohser, Beate & Newton, Peter M. Unorthodox Freud: The View from the Couch. LC 96-12554. 241p. 1996. lib. bdg. 35.00 (*1-57230-128-7*, 1128) Guilford Pubns.

Lohtia, R. P., jt. auth. see Joshi, R. C.

Lohuizen, C. W. Van, see Schut, W. F. & Van Lohuizen, C. W., eds.

Lohwag, Heinrich. Anatomie der Asco- und Basidiomyceten. (Handbuch der Pflanzenanatomie Encyclopedia of Plant Anatomy - Traite d' Anatomie Vegetale Ser.: Band VI, Teil 8). (GER., Illus.). xii, 572p. 1965. 95.00 (*3-443-39009-9*, Pub. by Gebruder Borntraeger) Balogh.

Lohwater, A. J. Russian-English Dictionary of the Mathematical Sciences. LC 90-270. (ENG & RUS.). 343p. 1990. reprint ed. pap. 38.00 (*0-8218-0133-3*, REDS) Am Educ Systs.

Lohwater, A. J., jt. auth. see Collingwood, Edward F.

An Asterisk (*) at the beginning of an entry indicates that the title is appearing for the first time.

L

Lohwater, A. J., tr. see Ladyzhenskaya, Olga A.
Loi, Lee A. Randori No Kata. (Illus.). 74p. 1997. pap. 24.95 (*1-874250-20-0*, Pub. by P H Crompton) Midpt Trade.
Loi Lei Lai. Intelligent System Applications in Power Engineering: Evolutionary Programming & Neural Networks. LC 98-6560. 286p. 1998. 125.00 (*0-471-98095-1*) Wiley.
***Loibl, Bernard J., ed.** Naked Verses. 2000. 29.95 (*0-9636805-3-6*) Events Unltd.
Loibl, Bernard J., ed. see Broekstra, Robbert.
Loike, John D., jt. auth. see Ayres, David C.
Loimeier, Roman. Islamic Reform & Political Change in Northern Nigeria. 480p. 1997. 69.95 (*0-8101-1346-5*) Northwestern U Pr.
Loimer, N., et al, eds. Drug Addiction & AIDS. (Illus.). x, 431p. 1991. 76.95 (*0-387-82298-4*) Spr-Verlag.
Loiperdinger, Martin, ed. see Elsaesser, Thomas.
Loiperdinger, Martin, jt. ed. see Elsaesser, Thomas.
Loire, Rene. The Design Way: An Essay. 456p. 1990. 14.95 (*0-9611614-5-0*) A Ghosh.
— Place au Dessineur! Essai sur la Conception Technique. (FRE., Illus.). 630p. (Orig.). 1991. pap. 25.00 (*0-9611614-7-7*) A Ghosh.
Loiry, William S., ed. The U. S. - Eastern European Trade Sourcebook. 250p. 1991. 59.95 (*1-55862-156-3*) St James Pr.
— The U. S. - Soviet Trade Sourcebook. 283p. 1990. 59.95 (*1-55862-142-3*) St James Pr.
Lois, George. Covering the '60s: George Lois, the Esquire Era. (Illus.). 212p. (Orig.). 1996. pap. 35.00 (*1-885254-24-5*, Pub. by Monacelli Pr) Penguin Putnam.
Loiseau, Pascale. Amsterdam: The Travel Notebook. 104p. 1997. 14.95 (*2-911141-11-3*, Pub. by Les Edtns Pascale) Assoc Pubs Grp.
— Bahamas: The Travel Notebook. 104p. 1997. 14.95 (*2-911141-18-0*, Pub. by Les Edtns Pascale) Assoc Pubs Grp.
— California: The Travel Notebook. 104p. 1997. 14.95 (*2-911141-16-4*, Pub. by Les Edtns Pascale) Assoc Pubs Grp.
— Canaries: The Travel Notebook. 104p. 1997. 14.95 (*2-911141-05-9*, Pub. by Les Edtns Pascale) Assoc Pubs Grp.
— Florence: The Travel Notebook. 104p. 1997. 14.95 (*2-911141-10-5*, Pub. by Les Edtns Pascale) Assoc Pubs Grp.
— Florida: The Travel Notebook. 104p. 1997. 14.95 (*2-911141-15-6*, Pub. by Les Edtns Pascale) Assoc Pubs Grp.
— Greece: The Travel Notebook. 104p. 1997. 14.95 (*2-911141-04-0*, Pub. by Les Edtns Pascale) Assoc Pubs Grp.
— Hawaii: The Travel Notebook. 104p. 1997. 14.95 (*2-911141-17-2*, Pub. by Les Edtns Pascale) Assoc Pubs Grp.
— London: The Travel Notebook. 104p. 1997. 14.95 (*2-911141-01-6*, Pub. by Les Edtns Pascale) Assoc Pubs Grp.
— Morocco: The Travel Notebook. 104p. 1997. 14.95 (*2-911141-07-5*, Pub. by Les Edtns Pascale) Assoc Pubs Grp.
— New York: The Travel Notebook. 104p. 1997. 14.95 (*2-911141-00-8*, Pub. by Les Edtns Pascale) Assoc Pubs Grp.
— Paris: The Travel Notebook. 104p. 1997. 14.95 (*2-911141-03-2*, Pub. by Les Edtns Pascale) Assoc Pubs Grp.
— Prague: The Travel Notebook. 104p. 1997. 14.95 (*2-911141-13-X*, Pub. by Les Edtns Pascale) Assoc Pubs Grp.
— Quebec: The Travel Notebook. 104p. 1997. 14.95 (*2-911141-20-2*, Pub. by Les Edtns Pascale) Assoc Pubs Grp.
— Rome: The Travel Notebook. 104p. 1997. 14.95 (*2-911141-02-4*, Pub. by Les Edtns Pascale) Assoc Pubs Grp.
— Venice: The Travel Notebook. 104p. 1997. 14.95 (*2-911141-08-3*, Pub. by Les Edtns Pascale) Assoc Pubs Grp.
Loiseaux, Pierre R., jt. auth. see Fessler, Daniel W.
Loisel, Regis. Peter Pan: Neverland, Bk. 2. Baisden, Greg, ed. Irwin, Mary, tr. from FRE. (Illus.). 1992. 14.95 (*1-56862-000-4*) Kitchen Sink.
— Peter Pan Bk. 1: London. Baisden, Greg S., ed. Irwin, Mary, tr. from FRE. (Illus.). (C). reprint ed. 14.95 (*1-879450-42-9*) Kitchen Sink.
Loiselle, Andre & McIlroy, Brian, eds. Auteur - Provocateur: The Films of Denys Arcand. LC 95-3998. 208p. 1995. pap. 22.95 (*0-275-95297-5*, Praeger Pubs) Greenwood.
— Auteur - Provocateur: The Films of Denys Arcand, 45. LC 95-3998. (Contributions to the Study of Popular Culture Ser.: Vol. 45). 1995. 65.00 (*0-313-29672-3*, Greenwood Pr) Greenwood.
Loiselle, Beth. The Healing Power of Whole Foods. LC 93-91693. (Illus.). 384p. (Orig.). 1993. pap. 19.95 (*0-9637478-0-0*) Hlthways Nutrit.
Loiselle, Emery J. Doctor Your Own Compound Bow. (Illus.). 148p. 1976. pap. 9.95 (*0-9613281-0-X*) E J Loiselle.
— Sensabout Bow Tuning. (Illus.). 20p. (Orig.). 1971. pap. 3.00 (*0-9613281-1-8*) E J Loiselle.
Loiselle, Mindy B. & Wright, Leslie B. Back on Track: Boys Dealing with Sexual Abuse. Bear, Euan, ed. (Orig.). (J). (gr. 5-11). 1997. pap. 14.00 (*1-884444-43-1*) Safer Soc.
— Shining Through: Pulling It Together after Sexual Abuse. 2nd rev. ed. Bear, Euan, ed. LC 99-218577. 128p. (Orig.). (J). (gr. 5-11). 1997. pap. 14.00 (*1-884444-39-3*) Safer Soc.
Loiselle, Paul V. Catfish & Loaches. (Illus.). 1988. pap. 4.95 (*3-923880-88-X*, 16847) Tetra Pr.
— Cichlid Aquarium. 1994. 44.95 (*1-56465-146-0*, 16077) Tetra Pr.
— Fishkeeper's Guide to African Cichlids. (Illus.). 116p. 1995. 10.95 (*1-56465-144-4*, 16037) Tetra Pr.
Loiselle, Paul V. & Pool, David. Hobbyist Guide to Catfish & Loaches. (Illus.). 144p. 1994. 12.95 (*3-89356-138-2*, 16580) Tetra Pr.
Loiselle, Paul V., et al. Tetra's Popular Guide to Tropical Cichlids. LC 94-23254. 1994. 21.95 (*1-56465-147-9*, 16004) Tetra Pr.
Loiselle, Paul V., jt. auth. see Baensch, Hans.
Loiselle, Paul V., jt. auth. see Weiser, K. H.
Loiskandl, Helmut, tr. see Simmel, Georg.
Loisy, Alfred F. My Duel with the Vatican: The Autobiography of a Catholic Modernist. Boynton, Richard W., tr. LC 68-19290. 357p. 1968. reprint ed. lib. bdg. 65.00 (*0-8371-0148-4*, LODV, Greenwood Pr) Greenwood.
Loisy, Alfred F. & Hoffman, R. Joseph. The Gospel & the Church. LC 87-3262. (Classics of Biblical Criticism Ser.). 268p. 1988. 32.95 (*0-87975-441-9*) Prometheus Bks.
Loit, Aleksander, ed. The Baltic Countries, 1900-1914: Essays, 2 vols., Set. (Studia Baltica Stockholmiensia: No. 5, Vols. 1-2). (ENG & GER.). 787p. (Orig.). 1990. pap. 115.00 (*91-22-01389-X*) Coronet Bks.
— National Movements in the Baltic Countries During the 19th Century. (Studia Baltica Stockholmiensia). 572p. (Orig.). 1985. pap. 53.00 (*91-22-00776-8*) Coronet Bks.
Loit, Aleksander, jt. ed. see Hiden, John.
Loit, Alexander, ed. Emancipation & Interdependence: The Baltic States As New Entities in the International Economy, 1918-1940. LC 95-184862. (Studia Baltica Stockholmiensia: No. 13). 385p. 1994. pap. 57.50 (*91-22-01643-0*) Coronet Bks.
Loitsyanskii, L. G. Mechanics of Liquids & Gases. 6th ed. 984p. 1996. 130.00 (*1-56700-042-8*) Begell Hse.
— Mechanics of Liquids & Solids. 1993. write for info. (*0-8493-9912-2*) CRC Pr.
Loizeaux. The Numerical Bible: Hebrews to Revelation (1932) 520p. 1998. reprint ed. pap. 35.00 (*0-7661-0123-1*) Kessinger Pub.
Loizeaux, Elizabeth B. Yeats & the Visual Arts. (Illus.). 264p. (C). 1986. text 40.00 (*0-8135-1175-5*) Rutgers U Pr.
Loizeaux, J. D. Classic Houses of the Twenties. unabridged ed. LC 92-30766. Orig. Title: Loizeaux's Plan Book. (Illus.). 192p. 1993. reprint ed. pap. text 12.95 (*0-486-27388-1*) Dover.
Loizeaux, William. Anna: A Daughter's Life. 240p. 1993. 19.45 (*1-55970-197-8*, Pub. by Arcade Pub Inc) Time Warner.
— Anna: A Daughter's Life. 213p. 1993. pap. 9.70 (*1-55970-231-1*, Pub. by Arcade Pub Inc) Time Warner.
— The Shooting of Rabbit Wells: An American Tragedy. LC 97-29707. 272p. 1997. 24.45 (*1-55970-380-6*, Pub. by Arcade Pub Inc) Time Warner.
Loizes, Peter. Innovation in Ethnographic Film: From Innocence to Self-Consciousness, 1955-1985. LC 93-6877. 240p. 1993. pap. text 16.95 (*0-226-49227-3*); lib. bdg. 42.50 (*0-226-49226-5*) U Ch Pr.
***Loizos, Peter & Heady, Patrick, eds.** Conceiving Persons. LC 99-14803. (London School of Economics Monographs on Social Anthropology: Vol. 68). 240p. 1999. 90.00 (*0-485-19568-2*, Pub. by Athlone Pr) Humanities.
Loizos, Peter & Papataxiarchis, Evthymios, eds. Contested Identities: Gender & Kinship in Modern Greece. (Modern Greek Studies). (Illus.). 264p. 1991. pap. text 18.95 (*0-691-02859-1*, Pub. by Princeton U Pr) Cal Prin Full Svc.
Loizos, Peter, jt. auth. see Pratt, Brian.
Loizos, Tom. The Equation of One: A Logical Trip to a Metaphysical Crossroad. unabridged ed. LC 97-93815. 208p. 1997. pap. 14.95 (*0-9658557-0-8*) T Loizos.
— Metaphysically Yours: A Scrutiny of the "Core Concepts" Housed in Our Awareness. Date not set. pap. write for info. (*0-9658557-1-6*) T Loizos.
***Loizou.** Time Embodiment & the Self. 122p. 2000. 59.95 (*1-85972-182-6*) Ashgate Pub Co.
***Loizou, Andreas, ed.** Fitzroy Dearborn Guide to Financial Instruments. 350p. 1999. lib. bdg. 55.00 (*1-57958-061-0*) Fitzroy Dearborn.
Loizou, Andreas, jt. ed. see Sheimo, Michael.
Loizou, Andros & Lesser, Harry. Polis & Politics: Essays in Greek Moral & Political Philosophy. (Avebury Series in Philosophy). 166p. 1990. text 72.95 (*1-85628-052-7*, Pub. by Avebury) Ashgate Pub Co.
Lojac, Anthony. Transformation Mother: Looking East Seeing West with the Perfect Buddha's Head. LC 98-83110. 365p. 1999. 25.00 (*0-7388-0347-2*); pap. 15.00 (*0-7388-0348-0*) Xlibris Corp.
Lojasiewicz, Stanislaw. Introduction to Complex Analytic Geometry. Klimek, Maciej, tr. from POL. 540p. 1991. 175.00 (*0-8176-1935-6*) Birkhauser.
Lojek, Bohumil, jt. ed. see Fair, Richard B.
Lojek, Michael A. & Bement, Patricia. Cardiac Rehabilitation. Grin, Oliver D. & Bouwman, Dorothy L., eds. (Patient Education Ser.). (Illus.). 26p. (Orig.). 1992. pap. text 4.00 (*0-929689-48-8*) Ludann Co.
Lok, Ivan. Pro Audio Spectrum: The Official Book. 512p. 1993. pap. 34.95 (*0-07-881979-2*) McGraw.
Lok, Mary, tr. see Li, Kwok-sing.
Lokaj, Stanley, jt. ed. see Galloway, Rodney G.
Lokan, Jan. Describing Learning. 420p. 1997. pap. 35.00 (*0-86431-224-5*, Pub. by Aust Council Educ Res) Stylus Pub VA.
***Lokan, Jan & Doig, Brian.** Learning from Children. 162p. 1998. pap. 29.95 (*0-86431-255-5*, Pub. by Aust Council Educ Res) Stylus Pub VA.
Lokan, Jan & McKenzie, Phillip. Teacher Appraisal. (C). 1990. 90.00 (*0-86431-045-5*, Pub. by Aust Council Educ Res) St Mut.
Loke, Jacob, ed. Pathophysiology & Treatment of Inhalation Injuries. (Lung Biology in Health & Disease Ser.: Vol. 34). (Illus.). 576p. 1987. text 250.00 (*0-8247-7795-6*) Dekker.
Loke, Wing H. A Guide to Journals in Psychology & Education. LC 90-33603. 415p. 1990. 44.00 (*0-8108-2327-6*) Scarecrow.
Loke, Wing H., ed. Perspectives on Judgement & Decision Making. 324p. 1996. 37.00 (*0-8108-2642-9*) Scarecrow.
Loke, Y. W. & King, Ashley. Human Implantation: Cell Biology & Immunology. 313p. (C). 1996. text 95.00 (*0-521-44193-5*) Cambridge U Pr.
Loken, Joan K. The HACCP Food Safety Manual. LC 94-17915. 352p. 1995. pap. 69.95 (*0-471-05685-5*) Wiley.
Loken, Michael R., jt. auth. see Owens, Marilyn A.
Loken, S., ed. High Energy Physics - Twenty-Third International Conference on High Physics: Proceedings of the International Conference, Berkeley, California, U. S. A., July 16-23, 1986, 2 vols. 1636p. 1987. pap. 102.00 (*9971-5-0184-8*); text 290.00 (*9971-5-0183-X*) World Scientific Pub.
Lokensgard, Erik, jt. auth. see Richardson, Terry L.
Lokensgard, Ole. The Nantucket Collection. LC 89-50229. (Illus.). 128p. (Orig.). 1989. pap. 8.95 (*0-9622429-0-X*) Big Mtn.
Loker, Alech, jt. auth. see Loher, Ann.
Loker, Donald E. Lewis Leffman: Ordnance Sergeant United States Army. 64p. (Orig.). 1974. pap. 3.50 (*0-685-29131-6*) Niagara Cnty Hist Soc.
Loker, Donald E., ed. News of the Day . . . Yesterday. (Illus.). 94p. (Orig.). 1971. pap. 3.00 (*0-685-29126-X*) Niagara Cnty Hist Soc.
Loker, William M., ed. Globalization & the Rural Poor in Latin America. LC 98-7511. (Applied Anthropology Ser.). 232p. 1998. lib. bdg. 53.00 (*1-55587-809-1*) L Rienner.
Lokesh, M. B. Prout & the End of Capitalism & Communism. 126p. (Orig.). (C). 1990. pap. 6.95 (*0-685-35763-5*) Proutist Universal.
Lokeswarananda, Swami. The Way to God As Taught by Sri Ramakrishna. 457p. (Orig.). 1993. pap. 20.00 (*0-87481-572-X*, Pub. by Ramakrishna Math) Vedanta Pr.
***Lokh, Kron.** Blade of Vengeance: Chronicles of Garm. 321p. 2000. pap. 12.95 (*0-942407-49-0*) Father & Son.
Lokhorst, Gijsbert M. Comparative Taxonomic Studies on the Genus Klebsormidium (Charophyceate) in Europe. (Cryptogamic Studies: Vol. 5). (Illus.). vi, 136p. 1996. 105.00 (*3-437-30823-8*, Wiley-VCH) Wiley.
— Taxonomic Studies in the Genus Heterococcus (Tribophyceae, Tribonematales, Heteropediaceae) A Combined Cultural & Electron Microscopy Study. (Cryptogamic Studies: Vol. 3). (Illus.). 256p. 1992. pap. 112.00 (*1-56081-346-6*, Pub. by Gustav Fischer) Balogh.
Lokich, Jacob J., ed. Cancer Chemotherapy by Infusion. 2nd ed. LC 90-61367. 659p. 1990. 129.00 (*0-944496-14-8*) Precept Pr.
Lokich, Jacob J. & Byfield, John E., eds. Combined Modality Cancer Therapy: Radiation & Infusional Chemotherapy. LC 91-61357. 264p. 1991. 99.00 (*0-944496-22-9*) Precept Pr.
Lokin, J. H. & Stolte, B. H., eds. Subseciva Groningana IV: Studies in Roman & Byzantine Law. (ENG, GER & ITA.). x, 274p. (Orig.). 1990. pap. 39.50 (*90-6980-040-3*, Pub. by Egbert Forsten) Hod1der & Stoughton.
Lokin, J. H., jt. ed. see Wal, N.
Lokke, Bill, ed. Industrial Ecology: A Collection of Articles from "Science & Technology Review" (Illus.). 53p. (C). 1998. pap. text 20.00 (*0-7881-7384-7*) DIANE Pub.
Lokke, Hans, jt. ed. see Van Straalen, Nico M.
Lokke, Kari. Gerard de Nerval: The Poet As Social Visionary. LC 86-82649. (French Forum Monographs: No. 66). 165p. (Orig.). 1987. pap. 13.95 (*0-917058-67-4*) French Forum.
Lokke, Kari E., jt. ed. see Craciun, Adriana.
Lokke, Virgil L., jt. ed. see Koelb, Clayton.
Lokke, Virgil L., jt. ed. see Thompson, G. R.
Lokken, Lawrence, jt. auth. see Bittker, Boris I.
Lokken, Roscoe L. Iowa: Public Land Disposal. LC 72-2854. (Use & Abuse of America's Natural Resources Ser.). 320p. 1972. reprint ed. 25.95 (*0-405-04518-2*) Ayer.
Lokos, Ellen D. The Solitary Journey: Cervantes' Voyage to Parnassus. LC 90-2224. (Studies on Cervantes & His Times: Vol. 1). (Illus.). XIV, 230p. (C). 1991. text 48.95 (*0-8204-1452-2*) P Lang Pubng.
Lokotsch, Karl. Etymologisches Woerterbuch der Europaeischen Woerter Orientalischen Ursprungs. 2nd ed. (GER.). 1975. pap. 89.95 (*0-8288-5886-1*, M7369) Fr & Eur.
Lokshin, A. A. & Sagomonyan, E. A. Nonlinear Waves in Inhomogeneous & Hereditary Media. (Research Reports in Physics). (Illus.). x, 121p. 1992. 79.95 (*0-387-54536-0*) Spr-Verlag.
Lokshin, V. A., et al, eds. Standard Methods of Hydraulic Design for Power Boilers. Bronstein, Henri A., tr. from RUS. 345p. 1988. 320.00 (*0-89116-359-X*) Hemisp Pub.
Loktev, V. M., jt. ed. see Davydov, A. S.
Lokuge, Chandani, jt. see Satthianadhan, Krupabai.
Lokuge, Chandani, ed. see Satthianadhan, Krupabai.
Lokvam, Marian, et al. Sonja. Lovas, Emily & Pollack, Rhoda-Gale, eds. LC 81-82156. (Illus.). 100p. 1981. 12.95 (*0-940316-00-5*) E J Hill & Co Inc.
Lokvig, Tor, jt. auth. see de Brunhoff, Jean.
Lolande, Peter. Apocalypse. 270p. 1998. 19.95 (*0-9600758-2-7*) Prophecy Partners.
***Lolax, Paul.** Guitar Solos in Open & Altered Tuning. 56p. 1998. pap. 0.95 incl. cd-rom (*0-7866-2545-7*, 96326BCD) Mel Bay.
Lolis, Nicholas B., tr. from GRE. Greek Penal Code. (American Series of Foreign Penal Codes: Vol. 18). xii, 205p. 1973. 22.50 (*0-8377-0038-8*, Rothman) W S Hein.
Lolkkeborg, Svein, jt. auth. see Bjordal, Asmund.
Loll, Leo M., jt. auth. see Buckley, Julian G., Jr.
Lollar, Amanda. The Bat in My Pocket: A Memorable Friendship, 0.00 0.00 0.00. expanded rev. ed. LC 91-37907. (Illus.). 102p. (Orig.). 1996. pap. 10.95 (*0-88496-409-4*) Capra Pr.
Lollar, Amanda & Schmidt-French, Barbara. Captive Care & Medical Reference for the Rehabilitation of Insectivorous Bats. (Illus.). 1999. 45.00 (*0-9638248-3-X*) Bat Conserv.
Lollar, Jason D. For the Guitar Enthusiast, Basic Pickup Winding & Complete Guide to Making Your Own Pickup Winder. 2nd ed. (Illus.). 62p. 1999. pap. 18.95 (*0-9662599-1-2*) Lollar Enter.
Lollar, Phil. The Complete Guide to Adventures in Odyssey. LC 97-6691. 1997. pap. 19.99 (*1-56179-466-X*) Focus Family.
***Lollar, Phil.** Welcome to Odyssey: The Start of Something Big! LC 99-42762. (Odyssey Ser.). (Illus.). 32p. (J). (ps-3). 1999. 14.99 (*1-56179-104-0*) Tommy Nelson.
— Yippee Ti-Yay Happy Birthday. (Illus.). (J). 2000. 9.99 (*0-8499-7648-0*) Tommy Nelson.
Lollar, Xia L. China's Transition Toward a Market Economy, Civil Society & Democracy. LC 97-61376. 110p. (C). 1998. pap. text 16.00 (*1-55605-275-8*) Wyndham Hall.
Lolley, W. Randall, et al. Servant Songs: Reflections on the History & Mission of Southeastern Baptist Theological Seminary, 1950-1988. Bland, Thomas A., Jr., ed. LC 94-4441. 262p. 1994. pap. 17.00 (*1-880837-94-3*) Smyth & Helwys.
Lolli, Elizabeth M., jt. auth. see Kasten, Wendy C.
Lolli, Giorgio, et al. Alcohol in Italian Culture: Food & Wine in Relation to Sobriety Among Italians & Italian Americans. LC 58-9167. (Monographs: No. 3). 1958. 7.50 (*0-911290-27-3*) Rutgers Ctr Alcohol.
Lolling, Atsuko G. Aki & the Banner of Names: And Other Stories from Japan. (Orig.). (J). (gr. 1-6). pap. 4.95 (*0-377-00218-6*) Friendship Pr.
Lollis, Nicholas J. De, see De Lollis, Nicholas J.
Lollo, Robert, ed. see Edmunds, Arthur.
Lollo, Robert, ed. see Frankel, Michael L.
Lollo, Robert, ed. see Kaufman, John.
Lollo, Robert, ed. see Kaufman, John P.
Lolme, Jean L. De, see De Lolme, Jean L.
Lolo, Eduardo. Mar de Espuma: Marti y la Literatura Infantil. (SPA.). 1995. pap. 18.00 (*0-89729-771-7*) Ediciones.
***Lolo Woman's Club Staff.** Lolo Creek Reflections. (Illus.). 115p. 1999. reprint ed. pap. 13.95 (*0-912299-82-7*) Stoneydale Pr Pub.
Loloi, Parvin, ed. Robert Baron, Mirza: Two 17th Century Plays, No. 2. 210p. 1999. pap. 18.95 (*3-7052-0146-8*, Pub. by Poetry Salzburg) Intl Spec Bk.
— Sir John Denham, the Sophy: Two 17th Century Plays, No. 1. 92p. 1999. pap. 15.95 (*3-7052-0145-X*, Pub. by Poetry Salzburg) Intl Spec Bk.
Loloo, Kxao, jt. auth. see Biesele, Megan.
Lolos, Yannos B. The Late Helladic I Pottery of the Southwestern Peloponnesos & Its Local Characteristics, 2 vols. (Studies in Mediterranean Archaeology & Literature: No. 50). (Illus.). 1085p. (Orig.). 1985. pap. 177.50 (*91-86098-53-5*, Pub. by P Astroms) Coronet Bks.
Lom, Jiri & Dykova, Iva. Protozoan Parasites of Fishes. LC 92-15825. (Developments in Aquaculture & Fisheries Science Ser.: No. 24). 1992. 190.75 (*0-04-448943-9*) Elsevier.
Lom, Jiri, jt. auth. see Canning, Elizabeth U.
Lom, Jiri, jt. auth. see Dykova, Iva.
Lom, W. L., jt. auth. see Williams, A. F.
Lomack, Mary A. Atsiyalriit. large type ed.Tr. of People Who Are Going to Pick Berries. (ESK., Illus.). 12p. (J). (gr. 3-5). 1999. pap. text 6.00 (*1-58084-174-0*) Lower Kuskokwim.
Lomahaftewa, Gloria A. Glass Tapestry: Plateau Beaded Bags from the Elaine Horwitch Collection. LC 93-41282. (Illus.). 56p. (Orig.). 1993. pap. 15.00 (*0-934351-42-2*) Heard Mus.
***Lomakin, S. M. & Zaikov, G. E.** Ecological Aspects of Polymer Flame Retardancy. (New Concepts in Polymer Science Ser.). 174p. 1999. 170.00 (*90-6764-298-3*, Pub. by VSP) Coronet Bks.
Lomami-Tshibamba, Paul, et al. Ngando, Victoire de l'Amour, Le Mystere de l'Enfant Disparu. (B. E. Ser.: No. 28). (FRE.). 1962. 35.00 (*0-8115-2979-7*) Periodicals Srv.
Loman. Culture & Common Law. 1992. pap. text 64.50 (*90-6544-638-9*) Kluwer Academic.
Loman, Jim & Loman, Laurie. Family Ski Adventures: In Colorado. LC 93-90789. 170p. (Orig.). 1993. pap. 12.95 (*0-9638271-0-3*) Diversif Pubns.
Loman, Laurie, jt. auth. see Loman, Jim.
Loman, Roberta K. Lots of Bugs! 1999. pap. text 2.49 (*0-7847-0888-6*) Standard Pub.
Loman, Susan & Brandt, Rose. The Body Mind Connection in Human Movement Analysis. LC 92-70393. 235p. (C). 1992. pap. text 12.00 (*1-881245-00-4*) Antioch New Eng.
Loman, Susan, jt. auth. see Lewis, Penny.

An Asterisk (*) at the beginning of an entry indicates that the title is appearing for the first time.

Lomand, Turner C., ed. Social Science Research: A Cross Section of Journal Articles for Discussion & Evaluation. 2nd rev. ed. LC 99-229047. (Illus.). 193p. (C). 1999. pap. text 23.95 (*1-884585-14-0*) Pyrczak Pub.

Lomando, A. J., et al, eds. Lacustrine Reservoir & Depositional Systems. LC 95-103472. (Core Workshop Notes Ser.: No. 19). (Illus.). 388p. 1994. pap. 62.00 (*1-56576-011-5*) SEPM.

Lomando, A. J. & Harris, P. M. Mixed Carbonate-Siliciclastic Sequences. (Core Workshop Notes Ser.: Vol. 15). 568p. 1991. pap. 71.00 (*0-918985-87-0*) SEPM.

Lomanscanlon. Food Service Management. (Food & Hospitality Ser.). 1992. text 32.95 (*0-538-60692-4*) S-W Pub.

— Food Service Management. (Food & Hospitality Ser.). 1992. pap., student ed., suppl. ed. 9.00 (*0-538-60693-2*) S-W Pub.

Lomanto, Valeria & Marinone, Nino, eds. Index Grammaticus: An Index to Latin Grammartexts, 3 vols., Set. (Alpha-Omega, Reihe A Ser.: Vol. LXXXI). (GER.). x, 2568p. 1990. 637.00 (*3-487-09271-9*) G Olms Pubs.

— Index Grammaticus: An Index to the Latin Grammarians, 3 vols., Set. (Alpha-Omega, Reihe A Ser.: Vol. LXXXI). 2578p. 1990. 625.00 (*3-487-09178-X*) G Olms Pubs.

Lomanto, Valeria, ed. see Symmachus, Quintus A.

Lomas, jt. auth. see Knight, C.

Lomas, Clara, ed. see De Magnon, Leonor V.

Lomas, David. First Ypres, 1914. (Campaign Ser.). (Illus.). 96p. 1999. pap. 16.95 (*1-85532-573-X*, Pub. by Ospry) Stackpole.

***Lomas, David.** The Haunted Self: Surrealism, Psychoanalysis, Subjectivity. LC 00-40835. 2000. write for info. (*0-300-08800-0*) Yale U Pr.

Lomas, David. Mons, 1914. (Campaign Ser.: No. 46). (Illus.). 96p. 1996. pap. 15.95 (*1-85532-551-9*, Pub. by Ospry) Stackpole.

Lomas-Francis, Christine, jt. ed. see Reid, Marion E.

Lomas Garza, Carmen. Family Pictures (Cuadros de Familia) LC 89-27845. (ENG & SPA., Illus.). 32p. (YA). (gr. 1-7). 1990. 15.95 (*0-89239-050-6*) Childrens Book Pr.

— Family Pictures (Cuadros de Familia) (ENG & SPA., Illus.). 32p. (YA). (gr. 1). 1993. pap. 7.95 (*0-89239-108-1*) Childrens Book Pr.

— Family Pictures (Cuadros de Familia) (ENG & SPA., Illus.). 32p. (YA). (ps-3). 1998. pap. text 19.95 (*0-89239-152-9*) Childrens Book Pr.

— Family Pictures (Cuadros de Familia) (ENG & SPA., Illus.). (J). 1990. 12.15 (*0-606-05275-5*, Pub. by Turtleback) Demco.

Lomas, Graham. Five Little Kittens. 1994. 7.95 (*0-533-11017-3*) Vantage.

Lomas, Graham M. & Wood, Peter A. Employment Location in Regional Economic Planning. 186p. 1970. 26.00 (*0-7146-1587-0*, Pub. by F Cass Pubs) Intl Spec Bk.

Lomas, Herbert. Public Footpath. Date not set. pap. 14.95 (*0-85646-062-1*, Pub. by Anvil Press) Dufour.

Lomas, Herbert, ed. from FIN. Contemporary Finnish Poetry. 256p. (Orig.). 1990. pap. 19.95 (*1-85224-147-0*, Pub. by Bloodaxe Bks) Dufour.

Lomas, Herbert, tr. see Paasilinna, Arto.

Lomas, Herbert, tr. see Stenberg, Eira.

Lomas, Jeanette, jt. auth. see Lacey, Penny.

Lomas, Jonathan. First & Foremost in Community Health Centres: The Community Health Centre at Sault Ste. Marie & the CHC Alternatives. 215p. 1985. pap. 13.95 (*0-8020-6532-5*); text 30.00 (*0-8020-5635-0*) U of Toronto Pr.

Lomas, K., ed. see University College, London Staff.

Lomas, Mark C. Cryptographic Protocols, International Workshops: Proceedings: Cambridge, United Kingdom, April 10-12, 1996, Vol. 118. LC 96-53986. (Lecture Notes in Computer Science Ser.). 1997. pap. 43.00 (*3-540-62494-5*) Spr-Verlag.

Lomas, Pauline A. Bridges a Memoir of Love: From Hollywood to Madison County. (Illus.). 152p. (Orig.). 1995. pap. 14.95 (*0-9636864-1-0*) Veracity Pr.

Lomas, Peter. Cultivating Intuition: An Introduction to Psychotherapy. LC 93-9517. 232p. 1993. 40.00 (*0-87668-528-9*) Aronson.

— Doing Good? Psychotherapy Out of Its Depth. LC 99-34797. 160p. 2000. text 27.50 (*0-19-262868-2*) OUP.

— The Limits of Interpretation. LC 90-282. 168p. 1990. 25.00 (*0-87668-797-4*) Aronson.

— Personal Disorder & the Family. LC 97-31564. 227p. 1997. text 32.95 (*1-56000-341-3*) Transaction Pubs.

— The Psychotherapy of Everyday Life. LC 92-456. 168p. (C). 1992. pap. 21.95 (*1-56000-629-3*) Transaction Pubs.

— True & False Experience: The Human Element in Psychotherapy. 170p. (C). 1994. pap. 24.95 (*1-56000-733-8*) Transaction Pubs.

Lomas, R. A. North East England in the Middle Ages. 200p. (C). 1989. text 66.00 (*0-7855-6986-3*, Pub. by J Donald) St Mut.

Lomas, Richard A. North East England in the Middle Ages. 200p. (C). 1996. 66.00 (*0-85976-361-7*, Pub. by J Donald) St Mut.

Lomas, Robert, jt. auth. see Knight, Christopher.

Lomas, Thomas. Forty Days to Freedom. LC 94-79778. (Illus.). 176p. (Orig.). 1995. pap. 8.95 (*1-883928-11-7*) Longwood.

Lomas, Tim, jt. auth. see Griffin, James.

Lomask, Milton. Cure of Ars Priest Who Out Talked the Devil. LC 97-76848. 1997. pap. text 9.95 (*0-89870-600-9*) Ignatius Pr.

— Great Lives: Exploration. LC 88-15744. (Great Lives Ser.). (Illus.). 256p. (J). (gr. 4-6). 1988. 23.00 (*0-684-18511-3*) Scribner.

— Great Lives: Invention & Technology. LC 90-27619. (Illus.). 288p. (J). (gr. 4-6). 1991. 23.00 (*0-684-19106-7*) Scribner.

— St. Isaac & the Indians. 2nd rev. ed. LC 90-85767. (Vision Bks.). (Illus.). 170p. (J). (gr. 4-9). 1991. reprint ed. pap. 9.95 (*0-89870-355-7*) Ignatius Pr.

Lomasky, Brian & Kreines, David. Oracle Scripts. (Illus.). 208p. 1998. pap. 29.95 incl. cd-rom (*1-56592-438-X*) OReilly & Assocs.

Lomasky, Loren E. Persons, Rights & the Moral Community. (Illus.). 296p. 1990. reprint ed. pap. text 21.00 (*0-19-506474-7*) OUP.

Lomasky, Loren E., jt. ed. see Brennan, H. G.

Lomasky, Loren E., jt. ed. see Brennan, Harold G.

Lomasney, Eileen. Light from Another Room: New & Selected Poems, 1940-1994. Dempsey, Francine, ed. 98p. (Orig.). 1994. pap. 10.00 (*0-9641725-1-8*) Canticle Press.

— Two Children Who Knew Jesus: The Apple of Her Father's Eye & The Boy with the Picnic Lunch. (Illus.). 32p. (Orig.). (J). (gr. k-4). 1994. pap. 6.95 (*0-9641725-0-X*) Canticle Press.

Lomasney, Maureen. From Here to There & Back Again: A Travel Journal. 187p. (Orig.). 1995. pap. 24.95 (*1-889451-01-0*) Tannery Creek.

— My Life - Truths, Tales, Memories & Dreams: A Way to Write Your Life Story. 2nd ed. 224p. 1994. reprint ed. pap. 24.95 (*1-889451-00-2*) Tannery Creek.

Lomatewama, Ramson. Ascending the Reed: Poems. 63p. (Orig.). 1987. pap. 5.00 (*0-935825-01-0*) Heard Mus.

— Silent Winds: Poetry of One Hopi. 3rd ed. LC 83-61654. 64p. 1983. reprint ed. pap. 5.00 (*0-935825-00-2*) Badger Claw Pr.

— Silent Winds: Poetry of One Hopi. 4th ed. 1987. pap. 5.00 (*0-934351-32-5*) Heard Mus.

Lomatuway'ma, Michael, et al. Hopi Ruin Legends: Kiqotutuwutsi. Malotki, Ekkehart, ed. & tr. by. LC 93-358. xiv, 510p. 1993. text 70.00 (*0-8032-2905-4*) U of Nebr Pr.

Lomatuway'ma, Michael, jt. auth. see Geertz, Armin W.

Lomatuway'ma, Michael, jt. auth. see Malotki, Ekkehart.

Lomawaima, K. Tsianina. They Called It Prairie Light: The Story of Chilocco Indian School. LC 93-30255. (North American Indian Prose Award Ser.). (Illus.). xx, 215p. (C). 1994. pap. 12.00 (*0-8032-7957-4*, Bison Books) U of Nebr Pr.

Lomax. Telephone Triage & Advice Protocol Manual. 1998. 135.00 (*0-8342-0779-6*) Aspen Pub.

Lomax, ed. God & Man in Medieval Spain: Essays in Honour of J. R. L. Highfield. 1989. pap. 28.00 (*0-85668-486-4*, Pub. by Aris & Phillips) David Brown.

Lomax, ed. see Lopes, Ferano.

Lomax, A., jt. auth. see Lomax, J.

Lomax, Alan, compiled by. Hard Hitting Songs for Hard-Hit People. LC 00-265422. (Illus.). 376p. 1999. pap. 19.95 (*0-8032-7991-4*, Bison Books) U of Nebr Pr.

Lomax, Alan, ed. Folk Song Style & Culture. LC 68-21545. 384p. 1994. reprint ed. pap. 24.95 (*0-87855-640-0*) Transaction Pubs.

Lomax, Alan & Crowell, Sidney R. American Folksong & Folklore: A Regional Bibliography. LC 70-181204. 59p. 1942. reprint ed. 49.00 (*0-403-03504-X*) Scholarly.

Lomax, Alan & Lomax, Crowe. American Folksong & Folklore: A Regional Bibliography. 1988. reprint ed. lib. bdg. 59.00 (*0-7812-0767-3*) Rprt Serv.

Lomax, Alan, et al. Brown Girl in the Ring: An Anthology of Song Games from the Eastern Caribbean. (Illus.). 256p. 1997. 29.95 (*0-679-40453-8*) Pantheon.

Lomax, Alan, jt. auth. see Asch, Moses.

Lomax, Alan, jt. auth. see Lomax, John A.

Lomax, Bill, ed. Eyewitness in Hungary: The Soviet Invasion of 1956. 183p. 1981. pap. 22.50 (*0-85124-327-4*, Pub. by Spksman) Coronet Bks.

— The Hungarians Workers' Councils in 1956. 1990. text 79.50 (*0-88033-191-7*, Pub. by East Eur Monographs) Col U Pr.

Lomax, Crowe, jt. auth. see Lomax, Alan.

Lomax, Dana, ed. see Adamson, Bruce Campbell.

Lomax, Derek W., ed. God & Man in Medieval Spain: Essays in Honour of J. R. L. Highfield. 1989. 59.95 (*0-85668-443-0*, Pub. by Aris & Phillips) David Brown.

Lomax, Don. Vietnam Journal: Delta to Dak To. (Vietnam Journal Graphic Story Collection Ser.: Vol. 3). (Illus.). 144p. (Orig.). 1991. pap. 13.95 (*0-927203-07-3*) Apple Pr PA.

— Vietnam Journal: Indian Country. (Vietnam Journal Graphic Story Collection Ser.: Vol. 1). (Illus.). 144p. (Orig.). 1990. pap. 12.95 (*0-927203-02-2*) Apple Pr PA.

— Vietnam Journal: The Iron Triangle. (Vietnam Journal Graphic Story Collection Ser.: Vol. 2). (Illus.). 144p. (Orig.). 1991. pap. 12.95 (*0-927203-06-5*) Apple Pr PA.

Lomax, Eric G., ed. Amphoteric Surfactants. 2nd ed. (Surfactant Science Ser.: Vol. 59). (Illus.). 440p. 1996. text 190.00 (*0-8247-9392-7*) Dekker.

Lomax, Ian, jt. auth. see Reynolds, Steven.

Lomax, Ian S. & Reynolds, Steven. Enforcement in the Magistrates Courts: A Guide to Enforcing Money Payments. 178p. (C). 1988. 90.00 (*1-85190-045-4*, Pub. by Fourmat Pub) St Mut.

Lomax, Ian S., jt. ed. see Bazell, Chris.

***Lomax, J. & Lomax, A.** Our Singing Country: Folk Songs & Ballads. (J). 2000. pap. 14.95 (*0-486-41089-7*) Dover.

Lomax, J. Harvey, tr. see Lowith, Karl.

Lomax, J. Harvey, tr. see Meier, Heinrich.

Lomax, James & Perkins, Anne T. I Know Lots of Things. (Big Books - Mini Bks.). 16p. (J). (gr. k). 1994. 12.00 (*0-614-04636-X*) Teach Nxt Door.

Lomax, James D. & Johanning, Eckhardt. Occupational Medicine: Quick Reference Guides for Family Physicians. (The Academy Collection Ser.). 208p. pap. text 29.95 (*0-7817-2053-2*) Lppncott W & W.

Lomax, John. American Ballads & Folk Songs. 1993. reprint ed. lib. bdg. 75.00 (*0-7812-5942-8*) Rprt Serv.

— Cowboy Songs & Other Frontier Ballads. 1993. reprint ed. lib. bdg. 75.00 (*0-7812-5890-1*) Rprt Serv.

— Sezz Who? LC 73-83916. 1974. 21.95 (*0-87949-021-7*) Ashley Bks.

Lomax, John, jt. auth. see Pooley, Michael.

Lomax, John A. & Lomax, Alan. American Ballads & Folk Songs. unabridged ed. (Illus.). 672p. 1998. pap. text 13.95 (*0-486-28276-7*) Dover.

Lomax, John A., jt. auth. see Ledbetter, H.

Lomax, John B. John Lomax & His Descendants. LC 97-74183. (Illus.). 448p. 1997. 71.00 (*1-892660-03-2*) John B Lomax.

— Samuel Lomax & His Descendants. LC 91-76191. (Illus.). 334p. 1991. 31.00 (*1-892660-00-8*) John B Lomax.

— Thomas Lomax & His Descendants. LC 95-78698. (Illus.). 194p. 1995. 43.00 (*1-892660-01-6*) John B Lomax.

Lomax, John B. & White, Mary H. William Lomax & His Descendants. LC 95-78699. (Illus.). 468p. 1995. 78.00 (*1-892660-02-4*) John B Lomax.

Lomax, Joseph F., ed. see McGee, M. W.

Lomax, Joseph F., ed. see Miller, Vassar.

Lomax, Joseph J., ed. see Miller, Vassar.

Lomax, Judy. Walking in the Clouds. large type ed. 352p. 1983. 27.99 (*0-7089-0960-4*) Ulverscroft.

Lomax, Kenneth, jt. auth. see Harrington, H. James.

Lomax, Louis. To Kill a Black Man: M. L. K. Jr. & Malcolm X Examined. 256p. 1998. mass mkt. 5.99 (*0-87067-982-1*) Holloway.

Lomax, Louis E. When the Word Is Given . . . A Report on Elijah Muhammad, Malcolm X, & the Black Muslim World. LC 78-14002. (Illus.). 192p. 1979. reprint ed. lib. bdg. 59.50 (*0-313-21002-0*, LOWW, Greenwood Pr) Greenwood.

Lomax, Marion. Peep-Show Girl. 1989. pap. 11.95 (*1-85224-072-5*, Pub. by Bloodaxe Bks) Dufour.

— Raiding the Borders. 66p. 1996. pap. 15.95 (*1-85224-352-X*, Pub. by Bloodaxe Bks) Dufour.

Lomax, Marion, ed. see Ford, John.

Lomax, Marion, ed. & intro. see Ford, John.

***Lomax, Michael L.** A Light Warrior's Guide to High Level Energy Healing: Medical Qigong & a Shaman's Healing Vision. (Illus.). 180p. 2000. pap. 24.95 (*0-9674742-5-6*) Spirit Way.

Lomax, Nancy, tr. see McKnight, E. P.

Lomax, P. & Schoenbaum, E. Environment, Drugs & Thermoregulation: International Symposium on the Pharmacology of Thermoregulation, 5th, Saint-Paul-de-Vence, November 1982. (Illus.). xvi, 224p. 1983. 68.75 (*3-8055-3654-2*) S Karger.

Lomax, P. & Schoenbaum, E., eds. Thermoregulation: The Pathophysiological Basis of Clinical Disorders: Eighth International Symposium on the Pharmacology of Thermoregulation, Kananaskis, Alberta, August 1991. (Illus.). xiv, 200p. 1992. 135.75 (*3-8055-5513-X*) S Karger.

Lomax, P. & Schonbaum, Edward. Thermoregulation: Pathology, Pharmacology & Therapy. (International Encyclopedia of Pharmacology & Therapeutics Ser.). (Illus.). 692p. 1991. 206.25 (*0-08-036853-0*, Pub. by PPI) Elsevier.

Lomax, P., jt. auth. see Schonbaum, Edward.

Lomax, P., ed. see International Congress on Pharmacology Staff.

Lomax, P., ed. see Schonbaum, Edward & Zeisberger, E.

Lomax, P., jt. ed. see Schonbaum, Edward.

Lomax, Pamela. Managing Staff Development in Schools: An Action Research Approach. 110p. 1990. 59.00 (*1-85359-108-4*, Pub. by Multilingual Matters); pap. 19.95 (*1-85359-107-6*, Pub. by Multilingual Matters) Taylor & Francis.

Lomax, Pamela, ed. The Management of Change: Increasing School Effectiveness & Facilitating Staff Development Through Action Research. (BERA Dialogues Ser.: No. 1). 200p. 1989. 69.00 (*1-85359-061-4*, Pub. by Multilingual Matters); pap. 24.95 (*1-85359-060-6*, Pub. by Multilingual Matters) Taylor & Francis.

— Managing Better Schools & Colleges: The Action Research Way. (BERA Dialogues Ser.: No. 5). 134p. 1991. 69.00 (*1-85359-145-9*, Pub. by Multilingual Matters); pap. 24.95 (*1-85359-144-0*, Pub. by Multilingual Matters) Taylor & Francis.

— Quality Management in Education: Sustaining the Vision Through Action Research. 176p. (C). 1996. pap. 22.99 (*0-415-15253-4*) Routledge.

Lomax, Paul. Developing Microsoft Transaction Server Applications with Visual Basic. Petrusha, Ron, ed. (Illus.). 250p. 1999. pap. 29.95 (*1-56592-561-0*) OReilly & Assocs.

***Lomax, Paul.** Fingerpicking Scales. 32p. 2000. pap. 5.95 (*0-7866-5241-1*, 98651BCD) Mel Bay.

Lomax, Paul. Learning VB Script. Petrusha, Ronald, ed. (Illus.). 598p. (Orig.). 1997. pap. 39.95 (*1-56592-247-6*) Thomson Learn.

— Microsoft Visual Interdev Wizardry. 1997. pap. 39.99 (*1-57610-136-3*) Coriolis Grp.

***Lomax, Paul.** VBScript in a Nutshell. Petrusha, Ronald, ed. (Illus.). 350p. 2000. pap. 24.95 (*1-56592-720-6*) OReilly & Assocs.

Lomax, Paul. VB/VBA in a Nutshell: The Language. Petrusha, Ron, ed. 656p. (Orig.). 1998. pap. 24.95 (*1-56592-358-8*) OReilly & Assocs.

Lomax, Peter & Schonbaum, Eduard, eds. Body Temperature: Regulation, Drug Effects, & Therapeutic Implications. LC 79-879. (Modern Pharmacology-Toxicology Ser.: No. 16). (Illus.). 680p. reprint ed. pap. 200.00 (*0-7837-0809-2*, 204112400019) Bks Demand.

Lomax, Richard G. Statistical Concepts: A Second Course for Education & the Behavioral Sciences. LC 97-46865. 376p. 1998. pap. 55.00 (*0-8058-3051-0*) L Erlbaum Assocs.

***Lomax, Richard G.** Statistical Concepts for Education & the Behavioral Sciences. LC 99-55432. 2000. write for info. (*0-8058-2749-8*) L Erlbaum Assocs.

Lomax, Richard G., jt. auth. see Schumacker, Randall E.

Lomax, Ronald J. & Mazumder, Pinaki, eds. Great Lakes Symposium on VLSI: Proceedings, Great Lakes Symposium on VLSI (9th: 1999: Ypsilanti, MI) 400p. 1999. pap. 125.00 (*0-7695-0104-4*) IEEE Comp Soc.

***Lomax, Rosalyn.** Here You Are at Wayne Community College: Success Ahead. 2nd ed. 128p. (C). 1999. per. 20.95 (*0-7872-6328-1*, 41632801) Kendall-Hunt.

Lomax, Rosalyn. Wayne Community College. 112p. (C). 1995. pap., per. 15.95 (*0-7872-1553-8*) Kendall-Hunt.

Lomax, Ted L. Structural Loads Analysis for Commercial Transport Aircraft: Theory & Practice. LC 95-22159. (AIAA Education Ser.). 1995. 99.95 (*1-56347-114-0*, 14-0) AIAA.

***Lomax, Yve.** Writing the Image. (Illus.). 232p. 1999. text 22.50 (*1-86064-474-0*, Pub. by I B T) St Martin.

Lomazzi, Brad S. Railroad Timetables, Travel Brochures & Posters: A History & Guide for Collectors. LC 94-76651. (Illus.). 196p. 1995. 49.95 (*0-9614876-8-2*) Golden Hl Pr NY.

Lomazzo, Giovanni P. Idea Del Tempio Della Pittura. 700p. 1968. reprint ed. write for info. (*0-318-71587-2*) G Olms Pubs.

Lombana, Judy H. Guidance for Students with Disabilities. 2nd ed. 198p. 1992. pap. 34.95 (*0-398-06245-5*) C C Thomas.

— Guidance for Students with Disabilities. 2nd ed. 198p. (C). 1992. text 50.95 (*0-398-05804-0*) C C Thomas.

Lombard, Bill. Blueprint for Geometry. (Illus.). 88p. 1997. pap. text 16.95 (*1-57232-278-0*) Seymour Pubns.

Lombard, Carl. Mortal Beings. 224p. 1994. pap. 17.95 (*1-85702-103-7*) Fourth Estate.

Lombard, Charles M. Joseph de Maistre. LC 76-13846. (Twayne's World Authors Ser.). (C). 1976. text 17.95 (*0-8057-6247-7*) Irvington.

— Lamartine. (Twayne's World Authors Ser.). (C). 1973. lib. bdg. 20.95 (*0-8057-2510-5*) Irvington.

— Xavier De Maistre. LC 76-58855. (Twayne's World Authors Ser.). 155p. (C). 1977. 20.95 (*0-8057-6284-1*) Irvington.

Lombard, Charles M., jt. auth. see Chivers, Thomas Holley.

Lombard, Charles M., ed. see De Lamartine, Alphorse.

Lombard, Dawn A. Photo Pag. 1994. ring bd. 249.00 (*0-929321-22-7*) WEKA Pub.

— Photo ROM. 1994. ring bd. 249.00 (*0-929321-09-X*) WEKA Pub.

Lombard, Dawn A., ed. see Bender, Hy.

Lombard, Denys. Asian Merchants & Businessmen in the Indian Ocean & the China Sea. (Illus.). 390p. 2000. text 35.00 (*0-19-564109-4*) OUP.

Lombard, Emmett N. International Management of the Environment: Pollution Control in North America. LC 98-46793. 216p. 1999. 59.95 (*0-275-96004-8*) Greenwood.

Lombard, Frank A. Outline History of Japanese Drama. LC 68-717. (Studies in Drama: No. 39). 1969. reprint ed. lib. bdg. 75.00 (*0-8383-0585-7*) M S G Haskell Hse.

— An Outline History of the Japanese Drama. (Illus.). 356p. (C). 1996. reprint ed. text 65.00 (*0-7007-0265-2*, Pub. by Curzon Pr Ltd) UH Pr.

Lombard, Frederica K. Readings in Family Law. Divorce & Its Consequences. 182p. 1989. pap. text 10.50 (*0-88277-787-4*) Foundation Pr.

Lombard, G. L., jt. auth. see Lawrence, M. L.

Lombard Historical Society Staff, jt. auth. see Watts, Gerry R.

Lombard, Jay & Germano, Carl. The Brain Wellness Plan: Breakthrough Medical, Nutritional & Immune-Boosting Therapies to Prevent. LC 97-72050. 240p. 1997. 20.00 (*1-57566-230-2*) Kensgtn Pub Corp.

— The Brain Wellness Plan: Breakthrough Medical, Nutritional & Immune-Boosting Therapies to Prevent. rev. ed. LC 97-72050. 304p. 1998. pap. 14.00 (*1-57566-293-0*, Knsington) Kensgtn Pub Corp.

Lombard, Jenny. How to Stay Single Forever. LC 96-16775. 128p. (Orig.). 1997. mass mkt. 6.99 (*0-446-67194-0*, Pub. by Warner Bks) Little.

***Lombard, Joanna & Dunlop, Beth.** DPZ: The Architecture of Andres Duany & Elizabeth Plater-Zyberk. LC 99-37594. (Illus.). 256p. 2000. 60.00 (*1-56898-206-2*) Princeton Arch.

— DPZ: The Architecture of Andres Duany & Elizabeth Plater-Zyberk. LC 99-37594. (Illus.). 256p. 2000. pap. 40.00 (*1-56898-213-5*) Princeton Arch.

Lombard, John A., Jr. Speaking for God. LC 94-68387. 110p. 1995. pap. 8.99 (*0-87148-962-7*) Pathway Pr.

***Lombard, Kameron B.** Young People the Time Is Now. iv, 42p. 2000. pap. 5.00 (*0-9701005-0-7*) Immortal Word.

Lombard, Kathy. Rock Riffs for Keyboard. (Illus.). 40p. 1988. pap. 11.95 (*0-8256-1191-1*, AM63926) Music Sales.

Lombard, Lawrence B. Events: A Metaphysical Study. (International Library of Philosophy). 268p. (C). 1986. text 35.00 (*0-7102-0354-3*, Routledge Thoemms) Routledge.

Lombard, R. E. Comparative Morphology of the Inner Ear in Salamanders: Caudata-Amphibia. (Contributions to Vertebrate Evolution Ser.: Vol. 2). 1977. 65.25 (*3-8055-2408-0*) S Karger.

L

Lombard, Sylvia J. Yao-English Dictionary. Purnell, Herbert C., Jr., ed. LC 76-29799. (Cornell University, Southeast Asia Program, Data Paper Ser.: No. 69). 392p. reprint ed. pap. 121.60 (*0-608-18592-2*, 201047400068) Bks Demand.

Lombardero, Oscar J. Los Nombres Cientificos de los Parasitos y Su Significado. 2nd ed. (SPA.). 90p. 1978. 12.95 (*0-8288-5257-X*, S33068) Fr & Eur.

Lombardi. Weight Training. 1999. pap. text 15.50 (*0-697-10737-X*) McGraw.

Lombardi, Carlo. Giovanni Rutini: Father of Classic Sonata Procedures. Together with Translations of His Letters & Other Writings. (Dowling Studies in the Humanities & the Social Sciences). 394p. 1997. pap. 17.00 (*1-883058-18-X*, Dowling College) Global Pubns.

Lombardi, Cathryn & Lombardi, John V. Latin American History: A Teaching Atlas. LC 83-675775. (Illus.). 136p. 1983. pap. text 17.95 (*0-299-09714-5*) U of Wis Pr.

Lombardi, Donald N. Handbook for the New Health Care Manager: Practical Strategies for Challenging Times. LC 93-26300. 484p. 1993. pap. 52.00 (*1-55648-109-8*, 001121) AHPI.

— Reorganization & Renewal: Strategies for Healthcare Leaders. LC 97-18702. 1997. pap. 44.00 (*1-56793-062-X*) Health Admin Pr.

— Thriving in an Age of Change: Practical Strategies for Health Care Leaders. LC 96-6417. (Management Ser.). (Illus.). 1996. 44.00 (*1-56793-043-3*, 0978) Health Admin Pr.

Lombardi, Donald P. Chitin Sourcebook: A Guide to the Research Literature. LC 88-28082. 688p. 1989. 395.00 (*0-471-62423-3*) Wiley.

Lombardi, Emilia L., ed. see Russell, Lao.

Lombardi, Emilia L., ed. see Russell, Walter.

Lombardi, Fabrizio & Sami, Mariagiovanna, eds. Testing & Diagnosis of VLSI & ULSI. (C). 1988. text 201.00 (*90-247-3794-X*) Kluwer Academic.

Lombardi, Frances G., jt. auth. see Lombardi, Gerald S.

Lombardi, Gerald S. & Lombardi, Frances G. The Circle Without End: A Sourcebook of American Indian Ethics, Vol. 1. LC 82-12481. 208p. 1982. pap. 8.95 (*0-87961-115-4*) Naturegraph.

Lombardi, Jan, jt. auth. see Alexander, Roberta.

Lombardi, Joan, jt. auth. see Goffin, Stacie G.

Lombardi, Joan, jt. auth. see Shores, Elizabeth F.

Lombardi, John. Black Studies in the Community College. LC 72-186575. (ERIC Clearinghouse for Junior Colleges, American Association of Junior Colleges, Monograph Ser.: No. 13). 74p. reprint ed. pap. 30.00 (*0-8357-7298-5*, 202055100018) Bks Demand.

— Labor's Voice in the Cabinet. LC 68-58604. (Columbia University. Studies in the Social Sciences: No. 496). reprint ed. 32.50 (*0-404-51496-0*) AMS Pr.

Lombardi, John H., jt. auth. see Fennelly, Lawrence J.

Lombardi, John R., jt. ed. see Garetz, Bruce A.

Lombardi, John V. Decline & Abolition of Negro Slavery in Venezuela, 1820-1854, 7. LC 74-105976. (Contributions in Afro-American & African Studies: No. 1). (Illus.). 217p. 1971. 55.00 (*0-8371-3303-3*, LOD/, Greenwood Pr) Greenwood.

— People & Places in Colonial Venezuela. LC 75-25433. 500p. reprint ed. pap. 155.00 (*0-608-13199-7*, 205604300044) Bks Demand.

Lombardi, John V., jt. auth. see Lombardi, Cathryn.

Lombardi, Karen, jt. auth. see Rucker, Naomi.

Lombardi, Louis G. Moral Analysis: Foundations, Guides, & Applications. LC 87-12469. (SUNY Series in Philosophy). 185p. (C). 1988. pap. text 21.95 (*0-88706-666-6*) State U NY Pr.

Lombardi, M. & Zanetti, C. Serra. Pruning Made Easy. LC 98-121205. (Illus.). 160p. 1998. pap. 14.95 (*0-7063-7680-3*, Pub. by WrLock) Sterling.

Lombardi, Margherita. Topiary Basics. LC 99-14016. (Illus.). 144p. 1998. 27.95 (*0-8069-3899-4*) Sterling.

Lombardi, Marilyn M. The Body & the Song: Elizabeth Bishop's Poetics. LC 94-10653. 267p. (C). 1995. 29.95 (*0-8093-1885-7*) S Ill U Pr.

Lombardi, Marilyn M., ed. Elizabeth Bishop: The Geography of Gender. LC 93-908. 288p. (C). 1993. text 39.50 (*0-8139-1444-2*); pap. text 18.50 (*0-8139-1445-0*) U Pr of Va.

Lombardi, Mark O., jt. ed. see Denham, Mark E.

Lombardi, Mary. Brazilian Serial Documents: A Selective & Annotated Guide. LC 73-16533. (Indiana University Latin American Studies Program). 485p. reprint ed. pap. 150.40 (*0-8357-7387-6*, 201582800097) Bks Demand.

Lombardi, Max H. Radiation Safety in Nuclear Medicine. LC 98-25760. 216p. 1998. boxed set 84.95 (*0-8493-1897-1*) CRC Pr.

Lombardi-Nash, Michael A., tr. see Borneman, Ernest.

Lombardi-Nash, Michael A., tr. see Hirschfeld, Magnus.

Lombardi-Nash, Michael A., tr. see Hirschfeld, Magnus.

Lombardi-Nash, Michael A., tr. see Ulrichs, Karl H.

Lombardi, R., ed. see Riley, R.

***Lombardi, Ralph A.** California Automobile Insurance Law Guide: February 2000 Update. Piatt, Norma, ed. LC 72-619669. 232p. 2000. 52.00i (*0-7626-0403-4*, TO-30752) Cont Ed Bar-CA.

— California Automobile Insurance Law Guide - 2/99 Update. Waxman, Robert, ed. LC 72-619669. 230p. 1999. ring bd. 51.00 (*0-7626-0295-3*, TO-30751) Cont Ed Bar-CA.

Lombardi, Richard W. Debt Trap: Rethinking the Logic of Development. LC 84-18303. 217p. 1985. 57.95 (*0-275-90137-8*, C0137, Praeger Pubs) Greenwood.

Lombardi, Tarky & Hoffman, Gerald N. Medical Malpractice Insurance: A Legislator's View. LC 78-6409. 232p. reprint ed. pap. 72.00 (*0-8357-3985-6*, 203668300005) Bks Demand.

Lombardi, Thomas F. Portfolio of the Earth. LC 94-32367. 64p. 1995. pap. 14.95 (*0-7734-0003-6*, Mellen Poetry Pr) E Mellen.

— Wallace Stevens & the Pennsylvania Keystone: The Influence of Origins on His Life & Poetry. LC 95-19124. (Illus.). 296p. 1996. 43.50 (*0-945636-79-2*) Susquehanna U Pr.

***Lombardi, Thomas P., ed.** Inclusion: Policy & Practice. LC 99-67842. 105p. 1999. pap. 13.00 (*0-87367-820-6*) Phi Delta Kappa.

Lombardi, Vince. Coaching for Teamwork: Winning Concepts for Business in the Twenty-First Century. rev. ed. LC 95-71467. (Illus.). 168p. 1995. 14.95 (*0-9647810-0-X*) Reinforcemnt Pr.

Lombardi, Vince, Jr. & Baucom, John Q. Baby Steps to Success. LC 96-72370. 256p. 1997. pap. 12.95 (*0-914984-95-0*) Starburst.

— Little Baby Steps to Success. LC 96-72371. 160p. 1997. pap. 6.95 (*0-914984-96-9*) Starburst.

Lombardi, Vincent L. Matricide: The Tragedy on Prospect Hill. 345p. 1998. pap. 20.94 (*0-07-154153-5*) McGraw.

***Lombardi, Vincent L.** Matricide: The Tragedy on Prospect Hill. 287p. 2000. pap. 15.95 (*1-892590-31-X*, Fifth Way Pr) Out Your Bk.

Lombardi, Vincent P. Beginning Weight Training. 256p. (C). 1989. text. write for info. (*0-697-05496-9*) Brown & Benchmark.

***Lombardi, William D., Jr.** Business Marketing: Yesterday, Today & Tomorrow. LC 99-94963. 2000. 18.00 (*0-533-13242-8*) Vantage.

Lombardini, J. B., et al. Taurine Vol. 1: Nutritional Value & Mechanisms of Action. (Advances in Experimental Medicine & Biology Ser.: Vol. 315). (Illus.). 480p. (C). 1992. 135.00 (*0-306-44224-8*, Kluwer Plenum) Kluwer Academic.

Lombardini, Siro. Growth & Economic Development. LC 95-42285. 264p. 1996. 95.00 (*1-85898-394-0*) E Elgar.

Lombardini, Siro & Padoan, Pier C., eds. Europe Between East & South. LC 94-23316. 272p. (C). 1994. lib. bdg. 148.50 (*0-7923-3122-2*) Kluwer Academic.

Lombardino, Joseph G., ed. Nonsteroidal Anti-Inflammatory Drugs. LC 85-12018. (Chemistry & Pharmacology of Drugs Ser.: Vol. 5). 464p. reprint ed. pap. 143.90 (*0-7837-2399-7*, 204008400006) Bks Demand.

Lombardino, Linda J., jt. ed. see Langley, M. Beth.

Lombardo, Agostino, jt. ed. see Tuttleton, James.

Lombardo, Bruce. Chew Toy of the Gnat Gods: Reflections on the Wildlife of the Southeast Coast. large type ed. Selph, Alexa, ed. LC 97-34195. (Illus.). 224p. (Orig.). 1997. pap. 14.95 (*0-87797-273-7*) Cherokee.

Lombardo, Carole A., ed. see Youngson, Jeanne.

Lombardo, Chris, jt. auth. see Douglass, Don.

Lombardo, Daniel. Amherst & Hadley. LC 97-158202. (Images of America Ser.). 1997. pap. 16.99 (*0-7524-0483-0*) Arcadia Publng.

— Amherst & Hadley: Through the Seasons. LC 98-86003. (Images of America Ser.). (Illus.). 128p. 1999. pap. 16.99 (*0-7524-1203-5*) Arcadia Publng.

— A Hedge Away: The Other Side of Emily Dickinson's Amherst. LC 97-168275. 392p. 1997. pap. 15.95 (*0-9618052-6-9*) Daily Hampshire.

— Tales of Amherst: A Look Back. LC 85-23791. 140p. 1986. pap. 7.95 (*0-9616559-0-9*) Jones Lib.

***Lombardo, Daniel.** Wellfleet: Massachusetts. LC 00-101077. (Images of America Ser.). (Illus.). 128p. 2000. pap. 18.99 (*0-7385-0402-5*) Arcadia Publng.

***Lombardo, Dave.** Power Grooves. 48p. 1999. pap. 14.95 incl. audio compact disk (*0-7935-8849-9*) H Leonard.

Lombardo, David A. Advanced Aircraft Systems. (Practical Flying Ser.). 368p. 1993. pap. 24.95 (*0-07-038603-X*) McGraw.

— Advanced Aircraft Systems: Understanding Your Airplane. (Illus.). 304p. 1993. text 29.95 (*0-8306-3997-7*, 4170); pap. text 18.95 (*0-8306-3998-5*, 4170) McGraw-Hill Prof.

— Aircraft Systems. 2nd ed. LC 98-31966. (Illus.). 288p. 1998. pap. 34.95 (*0-07-038605-6*) McGraw.

— Aircraft Systems. 2nd ed. LC 98-31966. (Illus.). 288p. 1999. 39.95 (*0-07-038606-4*) McGraw.

— Aircraft Systems: Understanding Your Airplane. (Illus.). 304p. 1988. pap. 21.95 (*0-07-155265-0*) McGraw.

— Aircraft Systems: Understanding Your Airplane. (Practical Flying Ser.). (Illus.). 304p. 1988. pap. 19.95 (*0-8306-0823-0*, 2423) McGraw-Hill Prof.

— Aircraft Systems: Understanding Your Airplane. (Practical Flying Ser.). (Illus.). 208p. 1988. 27.95 (*0-8306-9426-9*, 2423H); pap. 16.95 (*0-8306-2426-0*, 2423P) McGraw-Hill Prof.

Lombardo de Ruiz, Sonia. El Pasado Prehispanico en la Cultura Nacional, 2 vols. Incl. Vol. 1. El Monitor Republicano (1877-1896) (SPA.). 312p. 1994. pap. 12.50 (*968-29-5146-1*, IN067); (Memoria Hemerografica, 1877-1911 Ser.). 1994. pap. write for info. (*968-29-5145-3*) UPLAAP.

Lombardo, Frank A. & Schroeder, Donald J. How to Prepare for the Court Officer Examination. LC 97-43517. 500p. 1998. pap. 14.95 (*0-7641-0287-7*) Barron.

Lombardo, Frank A., et al. Management & Supervision of Law Enforcement Personnel. 500p. 1995. pap. 34.95 (*0-87526-428-X*) Gould.

Lombardo, Frank A., jt. auth. see Schroeder, Donald J.

Lombardo, Frank J. Buffalo Breath. (Illus.). 130p. (Orig.). 1988. 6.95 (*0-945702-01-9*) Vertizon Bks.

— S. O. S. 320p. 1991. pap. write for info. (*0-945702-02-7*) Vertizon Bks.

— A Squiggley Line & Other Oddities: Investigations into the Corners of the World. (Illus.). 130p. (Orig.). 1988. pap. 6.95 (*0-945702-00-0*) Vertizon Bks.

Lombardo, Gian. Sky Open Again. LC 97-156050. 72p. (Orig.). 1997. pap. 10.00 (*0-940475-92-8*) Dolphin-Moon.

Lombardo, Glen, tr. see Bertrand, Aloysius.

Lombardo, Gregory J., tr. see Augustine, Saint.

***Lombardo, John.** Raiders Forever: Stars of the NFL's Most Colorful Team Recall Their Glory Days. 288p. 1999. pap. 15.95 (*0-658-00063-2*) NTC Contemp Pub Co.

Lombardo, John, jt. ed. see Johnson, Robert J.

Lombardo, Leigh A. One Woman's Experience: A Collection of Poems. LC 96-24859. 118p. 1997. pap. 19.95 (*0-7734-2702-3*, Mellen Poetry Pr) E Mellen.

Lombardo, Mario. Serenade for Violin & Piano. Proctor, Thom, ed. 20p. (Orig.). 1997. pap. text 14.95 (*0-7692-0091-5*) Wrner Bros.

***Lombardo, Michael M. & Eichinger, Robert W.** Eighty-Eight Assignments for Development in Place. 29p. 1998. pap. 15.00 (*1-882197-20-8*) Ctr Creat Leader.

Lombardo, Michael M. & Eichinger, Robert W. Preventing Derailment: What to Do Before It's Too Late. (Technical Reports: No. 138G). 62p. 1989. pap. 25.00 (*0-912879-36-X*) Ctr Creat Leader.

Lombardo, Michelle. The OrganWise Guys Vol. 2: Basic Training for Better Health, 2 vols. (Illus.). 35p. (J). (gr. 2-5). 1998. write for info. (*0-9648438-3-8*) Wellness GA.

Lombardo, Michelle & McNamara, Karen. The Low-Fat Kroger Cookbook. LC 95-91064. (Illus.). 176p. (Orig.). 1996. pap. 4.95 (*0-9648438-1-1*) Wellness GA.

Lombardo, Paul. 50 Cases in Health Care Law. 1999. write for info. (*0-89089-843-X*) Carolina Acad Pr.

***Lombardo, Samuel.** O'er the Land of the Free. 189p. 2000. pap. text 14.95 (*0-9677051-0-X*, Pub. by Lombardo Bks) White Mane Pub.

Lombardo, Skip. Real Estate on the Brink: Making Money in Distressed Properties. 225p. 1993. per. 24.95 (*1-55738-469-X*, Irwn Prfssnl) McGraw-Hill Prof.

Lombardo, Stan & Duermeier, Dennis, eds. Ten Gates: The Kong-An Teaching of Zen Master Seung Sahn. (Illus.). 96p. (Orig.). 1987. pap. 11.95 (*0-942795-01-6*) Primary Point Pr.

Lombardo, Stanley, pref. Parmenides & Empedocles. LC 81-7212. 76p. (Orig.). 1982. pap. 4.95 (*0-912516-66-6*) Grey Fox.

Lombardo, Stanley & Rayor, Diane, trs. Callimachus: Hymns, Epigrams, Select Fragments. LC 87-45479. 144p. 1987. pap. text 13.95 (*0-8018-3281-0*) Johns Hopkins.

Lombardo, Stanley, jt. auth. see Homer.

Lombardo, Stanley, jt. ed. see Addiss, Stephen.

Lombardo, Stanley, ed. see Homer.

Lombardo, Stanley, tr. see Hesiod.

Lombardo, Stanley, tr. see Homer.

Lombardo, Stanley, tr. see Lao-Tzu.

Lombardo, Stanley, tr. see Plato.

Lombardo, Stanley, tr. & contrib. by see Homer.

Lombardo, Stanley, tr. & intro. see Aratus.

Lombardo, Vincenzo, jt. auth. see De Vincenzi, Marica.

Lombardy, Anthony. Severe. LC 94-18349. (Illus.). 67p. 1995. 4.00 (*0-9624631-7-5*) Bennett & Kitchel.

Lombardy, William & Marshall, Bette. Chess for Children Step by Step: A New, Easy Way to Learn the Game. (Illus.). (J). 1977. 18.95i (*0-316-53091-3*); pap. 18.95i (*0-316-53090-5*) Little.

Lombeida, Ernesto, tr. see Rojas, Mary H.

***Lombino, Mary-Kay.** Seth Kaufman - Centric 59. Glenn, Constance W., ed. (Illus.). 32p. 2000. pap. 15.00 (*0-936270-41-1*) CA St U LB Art.

Lomboldt, O. The Sphecidae (Hymenoptera) of Fennoscandia & Denmark. (Fauna Entomologica Scandinavica Ser.: No. 4). (Illus.). 452p. 1984. text 67.50 (*87-87491-06-0*) Lubrecht & Cramer.

Lomborg, Bjorn. The Structure of Solutions in the Iterated Prisoner's Dilemma. (CIR Working PaperS: No. 4). 25p. (Orig.). (C). 1993. pap. 15.00 (*0-86682-095-7*) Ctr Intl Relations.

Lombra, Raymond E. & Witte, Willard E., eds. The Political Economy of International & Domestic Monetary Relations. LC 82-15320. (Illus.). 374p. 1982. reprint ed. pap. 116.00 (*0-608-00166-X*, 206094800006) Bks Demand.

Lombra, Raymond E., jt. auth. see Burton, Maureen.

Lombreglia, Ralph. Make Me Work. LC 93-26485. 1994. 20.00 (*0-374-20004-1*) FS&G.

— Men under Water. Rosenman, Jane, ed. 224p. 1991. reprint ed. pap. 7.95 (*0-671-73260-9*, WSP) PB.

Lombroso, Cesar & Ferrero, William. The Female Offender. (Illus.). xxvi, 313p. 1980. reprint ed. lib. bdg. 55.00 (*0-8377-0807-9*, Rothman) W S Hein.

Lombroso, Cesare. Gli Anarchi. (History of Political Violence Ser.). (ITA.). 1985. reprint ed. lib. bdg. 40.00 (*0-527-41196-5*) Periodicals Srv.

— Crime, Its Causes & Remedies. Horton, Henry P., tr. LC 68-55776. (Criminology, Law Enforcement, & Social Problems Ser.: No. 14). 1968. reprint ed. 40.00 (*0-87585-014-6*) Patterson Smith.

Lombroso-Ferrero, Gina & Savitz, Leonard D. Criminal Man: According to the Classification of Cesare Lombroso. LC 70-129338. (Criminology, Law Enforcement, & Social Problems Ser.: No. 134). (Illus.). 395p. (C). 1972. reprint ed. lib. bdg. 35.00 (*0-87585-134-7*) Patterson Smith.

Lome, Louis S., jt. ed. see Chen, Ray T.

Lomeli, Francisco, ed. The Handbook of Hispanic Cultures in the United States: Literature & Art. LC 93-13348. 413p. 1994. 60.00 (*1-55885-074-0*) Arte Publico.

Lomeli, Francisco, tr. see Morales, Alejandro.

***Lomeli, Francisco A. & Shirley, Carl R.** Chicano Writers. LC 99-27671. (Dictionary of Literary Biography Ser.). 400p. 1999. text 155.00 (*0-7876-3103-5*) Gale.

Lomeli, Francisco A., jt. auth. see Anaya, Rudolfo A.

Lomeli, Francisco A., jt. ed. see Martinez, Julio A.

Lomeli, Francisco A., jt. ed. see Shirley, Carl R.

Lomellini, C. A. De, see De Lomellini, C. A.

Lomen. Differential Equations. 177p. (C). 1998. pap., student ed. 40.95 (*0-471-32759-X*) Wiley.

Lomen. Exploring Differential Equations Via Graphics & Data. 118p. 1996. pap. text, student ed. 27.95 (*0-471-15645-0*) Wiley.

***Lomen, David & Lovelock, David.** Differential Equations: Graphics, Models, Data. LC 98-14494. 704p. 1998. text 102.95 (*0-471-07648-1*) Wiley.

***Lomen, David, et al.** Differential Equations: Graphics, Models, Data & ODE Architect Companion. 992p. 1998. text 156.90 (*0-471-34414-1*) Wiley.

Lomen, G. J. Lomen: Genealogies of the Lomen (Ringstad), Brandt & Joys Families. (Illus.). 361p. 1992. reprint ed. pap. 55.50 (*0-8328-2322-8*); reprint ed. lib. bdg. 65.50 (*0-8328-2321-X*) Higginson Bk Co.

Lomen, Mary. The Original American Wheat Dolly. (Illus.). 224p. (Orig.). 1992. pap. 19.95 (*0-942323-15-7*) N Amer Heritage Pr.

Lomeo, Angelo, jt. photos by see Bullaty, Sonja.

Lomer, C. J., jt. ed. see Prior, C.

Lomer, Cecile, jt. ed. see Zell, Hans M.

Lomer, Georg. Seven Hermetic Letters. Hanswille, Gerhard, tr. from GER. 192p. (Orig.). 1997. pap. text 16.95 (*1-885928-09-2*) Merkur Pubng.

Lomer, Mary. Robert of Normandy. large type ed. 490p. 1992. 11.50 (*0-7505-0308-4*) Ulverscroft.

Lomer, W. & Gardner, W. Electronic Structure of Pure Metals, Pts. A & B. LC 49-50107. (Progress in Materials Science Ser.: Vol. 1413). 1969. 41.00 (*0-08-006419-1*, Pub. by Pergamon Repr) Franklin.

Lomerson, Edwin O., Jr. Fundamentals of Nondestructive Testing: A Home-Study Course. Huber, Oren J., ed. (Illus.). 375p. (Orig.). 1977. pap. 221.50 (*0-931403-51-0*, 1945) Am Soc Nondestructive.

Lomet, David B., ed. Foundations of Data Organization & Algorithms: Fourth International Conference, FODO '93, Chicago, Illinois, U. S. A., October 13-15, 1993, Proceedings. LC 93-32226. (Lecture Notes in Computer Science Ser.: Vol. 730). 1993. 61.95 (*0-387-57301-1*) Spr-Verlag.

Lomheim, Terrence S., jt. ed. see Pain, Bedabrata.

Lomio, Margaret M. I Promise You. LC 94-61386. pap. 12.95 (*0-9638103-0-8*) M M Lomio.

Lommasson, Robert C. Nebraska Wild Flowers. LC 70-188343. (Illus.). 243p. reprint ed. pap. 75.40 (*0-8357-6597-0*, 203599500001) Bks Demand.

Lommatzsch, Ernst, jt. auth. see Segebade, Johannes.

Lommax, P., ed. see Pharmacology of Thermoregulation symposium Staff.

Lommel, Cookie. Cuba Gooding Jr. LC 00-22770. (Black Americans of Achievement Ser.). (Illus.). 144p. (gr. 5-9). 1999. pap. 9.95 (*0-7910-5276-1*) Chelsea Hse.

***Lommel, Cookie.** The History of Rap Music. LC 00-22274. (African-American Achievers Ser.). 2000. pap. 9.95 (*0-7910-5821-2*) Chelsea Hse.

— History of Rap Music. (African-American Achievers Ser.). 2000. 19.95 (*0-7910-5820-4*) Chelsea Hse.

— James Oglethorpe. LC 00-38382. (Colonial Leaders Ser.). 2000. 18.95 (*0-7910-5963-4*) Chelsea Hse.

— James Oglethorpe. (Colonial Leaders Ser.). (Illus.). 2000. pap. 8.95 (*0-7910-6120-5*) Chelsea Hse.

Lommel, Cookie. Johnnie Cochran: Lawyer. LC 99-31424. (Black Americans of Achievement Ser.). (Illus.). 144p. 1999. pap. 9.95 (*0-7910-5280-X*) Chelsea Hse.

— Johnnie Cochran: Lawyer. LC 99-31424. (Black Americans of Achievement Ser.). (Illus.). 144p. (gr. 4-7). 1999. 19.95 (*0-7910-5279-6*) Chelsea Hse.

— Madame C. J. Walker: Entrepreneur. (Black American Ser.). (Illus.). 192p. (YA). 1993. mass mkt. 3.95 (*0-87067-597-4*, Melrose Sq) Holloway.

— Robert Church: Entrepreneur. (Black American Ser.). (Illus.). 208p. (YA). 1995. mass mkt. 4.95 (*0-87067-789-6*) Holloway.

***Lommel, Cookie & Edeison, Paula.** Cuba Gooding Jr. LC 00-22770. (Black Americans of Achievement Ser.). (Illus.). 144p. (gr. 4-7). 2000. 19.95 (*0-7910-5275-3*) Chelsea Hse.

Lommel, Herman, tr. see De Saussure, Ferdinand.

Lommel, Lisa L. & Jackson, Patricia L. Assessing & Managing Common Signs & Symptoms: A Decision-Making Approach for Health Care Providers. 450p. (Orig.). 1997. pap. text 54.95 (*0-614-30641-8*) UCSF Schl Nursing.

Lomner, Nathan, ed. Gemaros with Linear Translation: Perek "Eilu Metzios" 1997. pap. 4.75 (*0-915537-00-1*, A246) Sayfer Publishing Co.

— Gemaros with Linear Translation: Perek "Hamafkid" 1997. pap. 4.75 (*0-915537-02-8*, A245) Sayfer Publishing Co.

— Gemaros with Linear Translation: Perek "Hamainiach" 1997. pap. 4.75 (*0-915537-01-X*, A247) Sayfer Publishing Co.

Lomnicka, Eva, jt. auth. see Ellinger, E. P.

Lomnicki, A. J. Law of Town & Country Planning: Including Compulsory Purchase & Compensation. 200p. (C). 1991. pap. 75.00 (*1-85352-901-X*, Pub. by HLT Pubns) St Mut.

Lomnicki, Adam. Population Ecology of Individuals. LC 87-3439. (Monographs in Population Biology: No. 25). (Illus.). 236p. 1988. reprint ed. pap. 73.20 (*0-608-07127-7*, 206735300009) Bks Demand.

Lomnitz-Adler, Claudio. Exits from the Labyrinth: Culture & Ideology in the Mexican National Space. LC 92-20242. 1992. 48.00 (*0-520-07788-1*, Pub. by U CA Pr) Cal Prin Full Svc.

Lomnitz, Cinna. Fundamentals of Earthquake Prediction. 344p. 1994. 140.00 (*0-471-57419-8*) Wiley.

An Asterisk (*) at the beginning of an entry indicates that the title is appearing for the first time.

— The Road to Total Earthquake Safety: The 7th Mallet-Milne Lecture. (Illus.). 100p. (C). 1999. text 33.00 (*90-5410-481-3*, Pub. by A A Balkema) Ashgate Pub Co.

Lomnitz, Larissa & Melnick, Ana. Chile's Middle Class: A Struggle for Survival in the Face of Neoliberalism. LC 91-19118. (LACC Studies on Latin America & the Caribbean). 180p. 1991. lib. bdg. 35.00 (*1-55587-258-1*) L Rienner.

Lomnitz, Larissa A. & Perez-Lizaur, Marisol. A Mexican Elite Family, 1820-1980: Kinship, Class, & Culture. (Illus.). 300p. 1988. pap. text 24.95 (*0-691-02284-4*, Pub. by Princeton U Pr) Cal Prin Full Svc.

Lomnitz, Larissa A., jt. auth. see Fortes, Jacqueline.

***Lomnitz, Larissa Adler & Melnick, Ana.** Chile's Political Culture & Parties: An Anthropological Explanation. (From the Helen Kellogg Institute for International Ser.). 168p. 2000. pap. 14.00 (*0-268-02262-3*, Pub. by U of Notre Dame Pr); lib. bdg. 26.00 (*0-268-00840-X*, Pub. by U of Notre Dame Pr) Chicago Distribution Ctr.

Lomolino, Mark V., jt. auth. see Brown, James H.

Lomonaco. Watch the Day Move. LC 89-26635. (J). 1990. 14.95 (*0-399-22162-X*) Putnam Pub Group.

LoMonaco, Martha S. Every Week, A Broadway Revue: The Tamiment Playhouse, 1921-1960, 45. LC 91-34159. (Contributions in Drama & Theatre Studies: No. 45). 208p. 1992. 52.95 (*0-313-27996-9*, LBY/, Greenwood Pr) Greenwood.

Lomonaco, Michael & Forsman, Donna. The Twenty-One Cookbook: Recipes & Lore from New York's Fabled Restaurant. LC 95-5983. (Illus.). 400p. 1995. 35.00 (*0-385-47570-5*) Doubleday.

Lomonaco, Samuel J., Jr., ed. Low Dimensional Topology. LC 83-10022. (Contemporary Mathematics Ser.: Vol. 20). 346p. 1983. pap. 38.00 (*0-8218-5016-4*, CONM/20) Am Math.

Lomonosov, Mikhail. Kratkoi Rossiiskoi Letopisets s Rodosloviem. (RUS.). xii, 75p. (C). 1993. reprint ed. pap. 12.00 (*0-933884-89-3*) Berkeley Slavic.

Lomonosov, Mikhail V. Mikhail Vasil'evich Lomonosov on the Corpuscular Theory. Leicester, Henry M., tr. LC 73-95927. (Illus.). 297p. 1970. 30.00 (*0-674-57420-6*) HUP.

Lomont, J. S. Applications of Finite Groups. unabridged ed. LC 92-34875. (Illus.). xi, 346p. 1992. reprint ed. pap. text 9.95 (*0-486-67376-6*) Dover.

Lomotey, Kofi. African-American Principals: School Leadership & Success, 124. LC 89-1881. (Contributions in Afro-American & African Studies: No. 124). 188p. 1989. 49.95 (*0-313-26375-2*, LBP, Greenwood Pr) Greenwood.

Lomotey, Kofi, ed. Going to School: The African-American Experience. LC 89-38816. (SUNY Series, Frontiers in Education). 242p. (C). 1990. text 21.50 (*0-7914-0317-3*) State U NY Pr.

— Sailing Against the Wind: African Americans & Women in U. S. Education. LC 96-8703. (SUNY Series, Frontiers in Education). 186p. (C). 1997. text 49.50 (*0-7914-3191-6*); pap. text 16.95 (*0-7914-3192-4*) State U NY Pr.

Lomotey, Kofi & Teddlie, Charles, eds. Readings on Equal Education: Forty Years after the Brown Decision: Implications of School Desegregation for U. S. Education, Vol. 13. 229p. 1996. 62.50 (*0-404-10113-5*) AMS Pr.

Lomotey, Kofi, jt. ed. see Altbach, Philip G.

Lomotey, Kofi, jt. ed. see Teddlie, Charles.

Lomov, S. A. Introduction to the General Theory of Singular Perturbations. Ivanov, Simeon, ed. Schulenberger, J. R., tr. from RUS. LC 92-26927. (Translations of Mathematical Monographs: Vol. 112). 375p. 1992. text 201.00 (*0-8218-4569-1*, MMONO/112) Am Math.

Lomperis, Linda & Stanbury, Sarah, eds. Feminist Approaches to the Body in Medieval Literature. LC 92 33033. (New Cultural Studies). 272p. (Orig.). (C). 1993. text 38.95 (*0-8122-3117-1*); pap. text 17.95 (*0-8122-1364-5*) U of Pa Pr.

Lomperis, Timothy J. From People's War to People's Rule: Insurgency, Intervention, & the Lessons of Vietnam. LC 95-36667. (Illus.). 456p. (C). 1996. pap. 19.95 (*0-8078-4577-9*) U of NC Pr.

— From People's War to People's Rule: Insurgency, Intervention, & the Lessons of Vietnam. LC 95-36667. (Illus.). 456p. (C). (gr. 13). 1996. lib. bdg. 55.00 (*0-8078-2273-6*) U of NC Pr.

— Reading the Wind: The Literature of the Vietnam War. LC 86-23982. xii, 174p. 1986. pap. text 18.95 (*0-8223-0749-9*) Duke.

— The War Everyone Lost - & Won: America's Intervention in Viet Nam's Twin Struggles. rev. ed. LC 92-36594. 203p. 1992. text 22.95 (*0-87187-825-9*) Congr Quarterly.

Lompscher, Joachim, jt. ed. see Hedegaard, Mariane.

Lomranz, J. Handbook of Aging & Mental Health: An Integrative Approach. LC 98-29824. (Series in Adult Development & Aging). (Illus.). 502p. 1998. 85.00 (*0-306-45750-4*, Kluwer Plenum) Kluwer Academic.

Lomranz, Jacob, jt. ed. see Mostofsky, David I.

Lomsky-Feder, Edna & Ben-Ari, Eyal, eds. The Military & Militarism in Israeli Society. LC 99-10884. (SUNY Series in Israeli Studies). (Illus.). 320p. (C). 2000. pap. text 23.95 (*0-7914-4352-3*) State U NY Pr.

— The Military & Militarism in Israeli Society. LC 99-10884. (SUNY Series in Israeli Studies). (Illus.). 320p. (C). 2000. text 71.50 (*0-7914-4351-5*) State U NY Pr.

Lomsky, Gerry. The Beanstalk Bandit: The Giant's Version of "Jack & the Beanstalk" (J). (gr. 2-7). 1993. audio 6.95 (*1-883499-01-1*) Princess NJ.

— The Beanstalk Bandit: The Giant's Version of "Jack & the Beanstalk" (Illus.). 30p. (J). (gr. 2-7). 1993. pap. 4.95 (*1-883499-00-3*) Princess NJ.

Lona, Horacio E. Ueber die Auferstehung des Fleisches: Studien zur Fruenchristlichen Eschatologie. (Beiheft zur Zeitschrift fuer die Neuetestamentliche Wissenschaft Ser.: Bd. 66). (GER.). xiv, 304p. (C). 1993. lib. bdg. 98.50 (*3-11-013828-X*) De Gruyter.

Lonabocker, Louise, jt. ed. see Gwinn, Donald.

Lonai, Peter, ed. Mammalian Development. 432p. 1996. text 114.00 (*3-7186-5862-3*, Harwood Acad Pubs); pap. text 39.00 (*3-7186-5920-4*, Harwood Acad Pubs) Gordon & Breach.

Lonard, Robert I. Guide to Grasses of the Lower Rio Grande Valley, Texas. (Illus.). 400p. (Orig.). (C). 1993. pap. text 18.95 (*0-938738-08-9*) U TX Pan Am Pr.

***Lonardo, Paul.** Apostate. 2000. pap. text. write for info. (*1-928781-38-1*) Hollis Bks.

Lonas, Barbara. Dear Kristen: Stepping from Darkness into Light. 144p. 1998. pap. 8.00 (*1-57502-880-8*, PO2397) Morris Pubng.

Lonay, David. Financial Services Representative. 3rd ed. Ketter, Varn, ed. (Illus.). 260p. (Orig.). 1996. pap. text 49.95 (*0-9651668-0-5*) Tech Txtbks.

Lonbardi, Raymond. Aspirin Alternatives: The Top Natural Pain Relieving Analgesics. Jacobs, Beth L., ed. LC 99-32411. 160p. 1999. pap. 8.95 (*1-890766-02-X*) B L Pubns.

Lonbay, Jules. Single European Market. 1995. pap. text. write for info. (*0-406-60940-3*, UK, MICHIE) LEXIS Pub.

Lonbay, Julian, ed. Enhancing the Legal Position of the European Consumer. 241p. 1996. pap. 75.00 (*0-903067-65-X*, Pub. by Brit Inst ICL) St Mut.

Lonbay, Julian & Biondi, Andrea. Remedies for Breach of EC Law. LC 96-38722. (Wiley Series in European Law). 1997. text 144.50 (*0-471-97109-X*) Wiley.

Lonberg-Holm, K. & Philipson, L. Early Interaction Between Animal Viruses & Cells. Melnick, Joseph L., ed. (Monographs in Virology: Vol. 9). (Illus.). 160p. 1974. 77.50 (*3-8055-1764-5*) S Karger.

Lonberg-Holm, Karl, ed. see American Society for Microbiology Staff.

Lonberger, William. Tips on How to Stay Safe & Survive Almost Anything! A Watchdog Resource for Students in Grades K Through 12 & Their Parents. 1994. 14.00 (*0-910609-28-4*) Gifted Educ Pr.

Lonborg, Rosemary. Helpin' Bugs. LC 95-77748. (Illus.). 32p. (J). (ps-3). 1995. 14.95 (*0-9641285-2-7*) Little Frnd.

— Helpin' Bugs. (Illus.). 32p. (J). (ps-3). 1997. pap. 6.95 (*1-890453-04-8*) Little Frnd.

— The Quiet Hero - A Baseball Story. (Illus.). 32p. (J). (gr. 2-6). 1993. per. 7.95 (*0-8283-1958-8*) Branden Bks.

Lonc, William. Radio Astronomy Projects. (Illus.). 224p. (Orig.). 1996. pap. 20.00 (*1-889076-00-7*) Radio-Sky.

Loncar, M. 66 Galaxie: Poems. LC 98-17474. (Bakeless Literary Publication Prize for Poetry, Bread Loaf Writer's Conference Ser.). 72p. 1998. pap. 12.95 (*0-87451-878-4*); text 25.00 (*0-87451-877-6*) U Pr of New Eng.

Lonchamp, F. C. L' Estampe a Gravure: Un Siecle D'Art Suisse, 1730-1830. (FRE.). 1998. reprint ed. 85.00 (*1-57898-073-9*) Martino Pubng.

Lonchamp, Frederic C. Bibliographie Generale des Ouvrages Publies ou Illustres en Suisse et a l'Etranger de 1475 a 1914. (FRE.). 500p. 1996. reprint ed. 125.00 (*1-888262-52-4*) Martino Pubng.

Lonchamp, Jean P. Science & Belief. 160p. (C). 1996. pap. 39.95 (*0-85439-434-6*, Pub. by St Paul Pubns) St Mut.

Loncke, F., et al, eds. Recent Research on European Sign Languages. vi, 166p. 1984. pap. 40.75 (*90-265-0465-9*) Swets.

***Londa, Jeffrey C., ed.** O'Connor's Annotated Texas Employment Codes Plus 2000. annot. ed. (Texas Annotated Codes Plus Ser.). 2000. pap. 49.95 (*1-884554-38-5*) J McClure Pubng.

Londei, Marco. T-Cell Autoimmunity & Multiple Sclerosis. LC 99-27041. 200p. 1998. 99.00 (*1-57059-567-4*) Landes Bioscience.

Londeix, Bernard. Cost Estimation for Software Development. 209p. (C). 1987. text 29.25 (*0-201-17451-0*) Addison-Wesley.

Londeix, Jean-Marie. One Hundred Fifty Years of Music for Saxophone: Bibliographical Index of Music & Educational Literature for the Saxophone: 1844-1994. Ronkin, Bruce, ed. LC 94-67611. (ENG & FRE.). 448p. 1994. 54.95 (*0-939103-04-4*) Roncorp.

Londen, S. O., et al. Volterra Integral & Functional Equations. (Encyclopedia of Mathematics & Its Applications Ser.: No. 34). 723p. (C). 1990. text 140.00 (*0-521-37289-5*) Cambridge U Pr.

Londeno, Joyce, ed. see Kaufman, John P.

Londergan. The Lotus Domino Server. 2nd ed. 1997. 39.95 (*0-8055-1574-7*, M&T Bks) IDG Bks.

***Londergan, J. Timothy, et al.** Binding & Scattering in Two-Dimensional Systems: Applications to Quantum Wires, Waveguides & Photonic Crystals. LC 99-51450. (Lecture Notes in Physics Ser.: No. 60). (Illus.). x, 222p. 2000. 52.80 (*3-540-66684-2*) Spr-Verlag.

Londergan, Stephen. Lotus Notes 4.5 for Dummies. LC 97-73622. 224p. 1997. spiral bd. 12.99 (*0-7645-0311-1*) IDG Bks.

Londergan, Stephen & Freeland, P. Lotus Notes 4.5 for Dummies. LC 97-70731. (Illus.). 384p. 1997. pap. 19.99 (*0-7645-0185-2*) IDG Bks.

Londergan, Stephen & Freeland, Pat. Lotus Notes 5 for Dummies. LC 99-61892. (For Dummies Ser.). (Illus.). 384p. 1999. pap. 19.99 (*0-7645-0320-0*) IDG Bks.

— Lotus Notes 5 for Dummies Quick Reference. LC 99-62475. (For Dummies). 224p. 1999. spiral bd. 12.99 (*0-7645-0319-7*) IDG Bks.

Londergan, Steve. The Lotus Domino Server. 2nd ed. 640p. 1997. pap. 39.95 incl. cd-rom (*1-55851-511-9*, M&T Bks) IDG Bks.

— The Lotus Notes Domino Server. 2nd ed. LC 97-30959. 672p. 1997. pap. 39.95 (*1-55851-574-7*, M&T Bks) IDG Bks.

Londero, Eleanor. Diccionario Collins Gem Espanol-Italiano, Italiano-Spagnolo. 5th ed. (ITA & SPA.). 640p. 1990. pap. 14.95 (*0-7859-5805-3*) Fr & Eur.

— Diccionario Collins Italiano-Espanol, Espanol-Italiano "Pocket" 6th ed. (ITA & SPA.). 416p. 1990. 24.95 (*0-7859-5804-5*) Fr & Eur.

Londero, Elio. Beneficios y Beneficiarios: Una Introduccion a la Estimacion de Efectos Distributivos en el Analisis Costo-Beneficio. 2nd ed. 324p. 1998. 19.95 (*0-940602-24-5*) IADB.

— Benefits & Beneficiaries: An Introduction to Estimating Distributional Effects in Cost-Benefit Analysis. rev. ed. LC 96-77939. (Inter-American Development Bank Ser.). 316p. 1997. text 19.95 (*0-940602-23-7*, Pub. by IADB) Johns Hopkins.

Londero, Elio, ed. Precios de Cuenta: Principios, Metodologia y Estudios de Casa. 438p. 1992. 21.50 (*0-940602-53-9*) IADB.

Londero, Elio & Teitel, Simon. Resources, Industrialization & Exports in Latin America: The Primary Input Content of Sustained Exports of Manufactures from Argentina, Colombia & Venezuela. LC 97-49939. 288p. 1998. text 79.95 (*0-312-21154-6*) St Martin.

Londgraf, R. W., jt. ed. see Mindlin, H.

London. Affordable Space Launch. (Orbit Ser.). Date not set. write for info. (*0-89464-057-7*) Krieger.

— The Gourmet Garage Cookbook. Date not set. pap. 15.95 (*0-8050-5412-X*) H Holt & Co.

— Imaging Drug Action in the Brain. 432p. 1992. lib. bdg. 195.00 (*0-8493-8843-0*, RM301) CRC Pr.

— New Fish Lover's Cookbook. 1991. 24.95 (*0-13-613423-8*) S&S Trade.

London & Jones Staff. Magic Wand: Short Course in Photography. (C). 1997. text 9.00 (*0-673-97304-2*) Addson-Wesley Educ.

London & Rosenblatt, eds. Transference & Transference Neurosis. (Psychoanalytic Inquiry Ser.: Vol. 7, No. 4). 1987. 20.00 (*0-88163-964-8*) Analytic Pr.

London & Senior. Principles of Caribbean Geography. 1992. pap. text. write for info. (*0-582-03989-4*, Pub. by Addison-Wesley) Longman.

London, A. L., jt. auth. see Kays, William M.

London, Abraham, tr. see Adler, Jacob.

London, Andrew. Jeremy Pickle Goes to Prague. 104p. 1996. pap. 8.95 (*1-56097-251-3*) Fantagraph Bks.

London, Anne. American-International Encyclopedic Cookbook. (J). 1972. 24.45i (*0-690-07236-8*) HarpC Child Bks.

London, Anne, et al. Diversity Supplement: Contemporary. 7th ed. 34p. (C). 1993. pap. text 15.00 (*0-03-097685-5*) Dryden Pr.

London, April. Women & Property in the Eighteenth-Century English Novel. LC 98-11651. 240p. (C). 1999. 59.95 (*0-521-65013-5*) Cambridge U Pr.

London, Barbara. A Short Course in Photography. 4th ed. (C). 2000. pap. text. write for info. (*0-321-04750-8*) Addson-Wesley Educ.

***London, Barbara.** A Short Course in Photography. 4th ed. 224p. (C). 2000. pap. 33.33 (*0-321-03439-2*) Addson-Wesley Educ.

London, Barbara. A Short Course in Photography & Digital Imaging. (C). 1999. pap. text. write for info. (*0-321-03419-8*); pap. text. write for info. (*0-321-03442-2*); pap. text. write for info. (*0-321-04752-4*) Addson-Wesley Educ.

— A Short Course in Photography & Digital Imaging. (C). 2000. pap. text. write for info. (*0-321-03441-4*) Addson-Wesley Educ.

— Video Spaces: Eight Installations. (Illus.). 80p. 1995. pap. 22.50 (*0-87070-646-2*, 0-8109-6146-6, Pub. by Mus of Modern Art) Abrams.

London, Barbara, ed. Photography. 6th ed. LC 97-20714. 408p. (C). 1997. pap. 69.00 (*0-321-01108-2*, Prentice Hall) P-H.

London, Barbara & Stone, Jim. A Short Course in Photography: An Introduction to Black-&-White Photographic Technique. 3rd ed. LC 95-31003. (Illus.). 186p. (C). 1997. 38.67 (*0-673-52439-6*) Addson-Wesley Educ.

***London, Barbara & Stone, Jim.** Short Course in Photography, Technique: An Introduction to Black & White Photography Technique. 4th ed. 224p. 2000. pap. 33.33 (*0-13-028317-7*) P-H.

London, Barbara, jt. auth. see Baker, Robert.

London, Barry, jt. auth. see Ritholz, Jules.

London, Bette. The Appropriated Voice: Narrative Authority in Conrad, Forster & Woolf. LC 89-48925. 212p. 1990. text 44.50 (*0-472-10160-9*, 10160) U of Mich Pr.

***London, Bette Lynn.** Writing Double: Women's Literary Partnerships. LC 99-37635. (Illus.). 256p. 1999. pap. 18.95 (*0-8014-8555-X*) Cornell U Pr.

— Writing Double: Women's Literary Partnerships. LC 99-37635. (Illus.). 256p. 2000. 45.00 (*0-8014-3563-3*) Cornell U Pr.

London, Bette M., ed. Edward Christiana: Retrospective Exhibition. (Illus.). 24p. (Orig.). 1989. pap. 7.50 (*0-915895-09-9*) Munson Williams.

London, Bill. Country Roads of Idaho. (Country Roads of... Ser.). (Illus.). 184p. (Orig.). 1995. pap. 9.95 (*1-56626-069-8*, 60698, Cntry Rds Pr) NTC Contemp Pub Co.

London, Bill, ed. The Role of Information Officers in Schools of Education. 1997. 15.00 (*0-89333-160-0*) AACTE.

London, Bill & Powell, Charles. Natural Wonders of Idaho. LC 93-44679. (Natural Wonders of... Ser.). (Illus.). 144p. (Orig.). 1994. pap. 9.95 (*1-56626-059-0*, 60590, Cntry Rds Pr) NTC Contemp Pub Co.

***London, Blue.** Uh Brota's Love, Vol. 1. 1999. pap. 20.00 (*1-884978-34-7*) Black Boys Dream.

London, Bonnie. A History of Georgia. Sims, Sarah E. & Andress, Faye, eds. (Illus.). 139p. 1992. 4.95 (*0-9623319-5-3*); teacher ed. 15.95 (*0-9623319-7-X*); teacher ed. 29.95 (*0-9623319-8-8*); text 26.95 (*0-9623319-4-5*); 3.95 (*0-9623319-6-1*) Clairmont Pr.

London, Brooks. Science Fiction after 1900. LC 96-44851. 1997. 33.00 (*0-8057-0962-2*, Twyne) Mac Lib Ref.

London, Bruce. Metropolis & Nation in Thailand: The Political Economy of Uneven Development. LC 79-3287. (Replica Edition Ser.). 1979. pap. text 37.50 (*0-89158-592-3*) Westview.

London, Bruce, jt. ed. see Palen, J. John.

London Business School Staff. London Business School Sourceguide to Central & East European Company Information. Scott, Julie, ed. (London Business School Sourceguide Ser.). 1994. 108.00 (*1-873477-70-8*) Gale.

London, Cait. Angel vs. McLean. rev. ed. (Men at Work Ser.: Vol. 17). 1998. mass mkt. 4.50 (*0-373-81029-6*, 1-81029-0) Harlequin Bks.

— Blaylock's Bride. 1999. per. 3.75 (*0-373-76207-0*, 1-76207-9) Silhouette.

— The Bride Says No. 1994. per. 2.99 (*0-373-05891-8*, 1-05891-6) Harlequin Bks.

— The Cowboy & the Cradle: The Tallchiefs. (Desire Ser.). 1996. per. 3.50 (*0-373-76006-X*, 1-76006-5) Silhouette.

— Every Girl's Guide to... 1995. per. 3.50 (*0-373-52005-0*, 1-52005-5) Silhouette.

— Every Groom's Guide To... (Yours Truly Ser.). 1996. per. 3.50 (*0-373-52017-4*, 1-52017-0) Silhouette.

— The Groom Candidate. 1997. per. 3.50 (*0-373-76093-0*, 1-76093-3) Silhouette.

***London, Cait.** Un Hombre y Sus Secretos. (Deseo Ser.).Tr. of Man & His Secrets. (SPA.). 1999. per. 3.50 (*0-373-35307-3*, 1-35307-7) Harlequin Bks.

— It Happened at Midnight. 384p. 2000. mass mkt. 5.99 (*0-380-81550-8*, Avon Bks) Morrow Avon.

— Last Dance: Man of the Month, Freedom Valley. 2000. per. 3.99 (*0-373-76285-2*) Silhouette.

London, Cait. La Leyenda del Anillo: Tallchief's Bride. (Deseo Ser.: Vol. 119).Tr. of Ring's Legend. (SPA.). 1998. per. 3.50 (*0-373-35249-2*, 1-35249-1) Harlequin Bks.

— Maybe No, Maybe Yes. (Desire Ser.). 1993. pap. 2.89 (*0-373-05782-2*, 5-05782-3) Silhouette.

— Miracles & Mistletoe. 1995. per. 3.25 (*0-373-05968-X*, 1-05968-2) Silhouette.

— Mr. Easy: Man of the Month, Hawk's Way. (Desire Ser.). 1995. mass mkt. 3.25 (*0-373-05919-1*, 1-05919-5) Silhouette.

— The Perfect Fit: Man of the Month/The Tallchiefs. (Desire Ser.: No. 1183). 1998. per. 3.75 (*0-373-76183-X*, 1-76183-2) Harlequin Bks.

— Rafe Palladin: Man of Secrets. (Desire Ser.). 1998. per. 3.75 (*0-373-76160-0*, 1-76160-0) Silhouette.

— Rio: Man of Destiny, (The Blaylocks) (Desire Ser.: No. 1233). 1999. per. 3.75 (*0-373-76233-X*, 1-76233-5) Silhouette.

— The Seduction of Fiona Tallchief. 1998. per. 3.75 (*0-373-76135-X*, 1-76135-2) Silhouette.

— The Seduction of Jake Tallman: Man of the Month. (Desire Ser.). 1993. per. 2.99 (*0-373-05811-X*, 5-05811-0) Silhouette.

***London, Cait.** Sleepless in Montana. 384p. 1999. mass mkt. 5.99 (*0-380-80038-1*, Avon Bks) Morrow Avon.

— Slow Fever. 2001. mass mkt. 3.99 (*0-373-76334-4*, 1 76334 1) Silhouette.

— Tallchief: The Homecoming. (Desire Ser.). 2000. mass mkt. 3.99 (*0-373-76310-7*, 1-76310-1) Silhouette.

London, Cait. Tallchief for Keeps. (Silhouette Promo Ser.). 304p. 1997. per. 5.99 (*0-373-48337-6*, 1-48337-9) Harlequin Bks.

— Tallchief's Bride. (Desire Ser.). 1996. per. 3.50 (*0-373-76021-3*, 1-76021-4) Silhouette.

***London, Cait.** Three Kisses. 384p. 1999. mass mkt. 5.99 (*0-380-80037-3*, Avon Bks) Morrow Avon.

— Tipicamente Masculino (Typically Male) (Deseo Ser.). (SPA.). 2000. mass mkt. 3.50 (*0-373-35344-8*, 1-35344-0) Harlequin Bks.

— Typical Male: Man of the Month, the Blaylocks, anniversary ed. (Desire Ser.: No. 125). 1999. per. 3.75 (*0-373-76255-0*) Harlequin Bks.

London, Carole. Earthwalk: A Compilation: Inspiring a Deeper Respect & Passion for Our Planet. (Illus.). 80p. 1998. pap. 4.95 (*0-9663998-0-3*) Earth-Cntrd Pubng.

London, Charmian. The Book of Jack London, 2 vols. 1992. reprint ed. lib. bdg. 150.00 (*0-7812-5061-7*) Rprt Serv.

London, Charmian & London, Jack. Book of Jack London, 2 vols. 894p. 1976. 62.95 (*0-8488-0886-X*) Amereon Ltd.

London, Charmian K. The Log of the Snack. 440p. 1998. pap. 16.95 (*1-885031-03-3*, Capstan Pr) Merritt Communs.

***London, Charmian Kittredge.** Jack London in Aloha-Land: The Hawaiian Journal of Mrs. Jack London. 230p. 2000. pap. text 35.00 (*0-7103-0688-1*) Col U Pr.

London, Christopher W., ed. Architecture in Victorian & Edwardian India. LC 94-901412. (C). 1994. 94.00 (*81-85026-26-2*, Pub. by Marg Publns) Art Media Resources.

London Cigarette Card Company Staff. Complete Catalog of British Cigarette Cards. 1999. 24.95 (*0-906671-48-5*) Viking Penguin.

L

— Complete Catalog of British Cigarette Cards. 2nd ed. 24.95 (*0-906671-85-X*) Viking Penguin.

London City Literary Institute Staff. Tradition & Experiment in Present-Day Literature. LC 68-761. (Studies in Comparative Literature: No. 35). (C). 1972. reprint ed. lib. bdg. 75.00 (*0-8383-0544-X*) M S G Haskell Hse.

London, Clement B. On Wings of Change: Self-Portrait of a Developing Country, Trinidad-Tobago. 201p. (Orig.). 1991. pap. 13.95 (*0-685-59146-8*) Calaloux Pubns.

— Through Caribbean Eyes: Reflections on an Era of Independence. LC 89-84287. 491p. pap. 12.95 (*0-938818-18-X*) ECA Assoc.

London, Clement B., jt. auth. see Carrasquillo, Angela L.

London, Colleen, tr. see Hukanovic, Rezak.

London College of Physicians Staff. Certain Necessary Directions As well for the Cure of the Plague As for Preventing the Infection: Also Certaine Select Statutes. LC 79-84120. (English Experience Ser.: No. 939). 148p. 1979. reprint ed. lib. bdg. 14.00 (*90-221-0939-9*) Walter J Johnson.

London County Council Staff. Bankside: The Parishes of St. Saviour & Christchurch, Southwark. LC 78-138274. (London County Council. Survey of London Ser.: No. 22). reprint ed. 84.50 (*0-404-51672-6*) AMS Pr.

London County Council Staff & Parish of St. Mary Labeth Staff. The Parish of St. Mary Lambeth Pt. 2: Southern Area. LC 74-6546. (London County Council Survey of London Ser.: No. 26). 1995. reprint ed. 84.50 (*0-404-51676-9*, NA995) AMS Pr.

London, David, contrib. by. Sun Dancer. LC 98-15487. 320p. 1998. pap. 14.95 (*0-8032-7978-7*, Bison Books) U of Nebr Pr.

London, David T. Twain's Tales. 38p. (Orig.). (J). 1994. pap. 4.00 (*1-57514-125-6*, 1165) Encore Perform Pub.

London Dialectical Society Staff. Report on Spiritualism: Together with the Evidence, Oral & Written. LC 75-36849. (Occult Ser.). 1976. reprint ed. 35.95 (*0-405-07965-6*) Ayer.

London, Dick. Survival Models & Their Estimation. 3rd rev. ed. (C). 1997. pap. text 52.50 (*1-56698-268-5*) Actex Pubns.

London, Fran, ed. Whinorrhea & Other Nursing Diagnoses: Best of Journal of Nursing Jocularity 1991-1993. (Illus.). 244p. 1995. pap. 18.95 (*0-9649276-0-8*) JNJ Pubng.

London, G. W., ed. Photon-Photon Interactions: Proceedings of the International Colloquium, 4th, Paris, France, April 6-9, 1981. 538p. 1981. text 76.00 (*9971-83-091-4*) World Scientific Pub.

***London Gallery Staff.** Renaissance. LC 93-21264. (Eyewitness Books). (Illus.). 64p. (J). (gr. 4-7). 2000. 15.95 (*0-7894-5582-X*, D K Ink) DK Pub Inc.

London, Gerard, jt. ed. see Loscalzo, Joseph.

London, H. B., Jr., ed. Refresh - Renew - Revive. (Pastor to Pastor Resource Ser.). 1996. 14.99 (*1-56179-467-8*) Focus Family.

London, H. B., Jr. & Wiseman, Neil B. Married to a Pastor: How to Stay Happily Married in the Ministry. Simon, Wil, ed. LC 99-28718. 264p. 1999. pap. 12.99 (*0-8307-2505-9*) Gospel Lght.

***London, H. B. & Wiseman, Neil B.** They Call Me Pastor. LC 00-32339. 2000. write for info. (*0-8307-2390-0*, Regal Bks) Gospel Lght.

London, H. B. & Wiseman, Neil B. Your Pastor Is an Endangered Species. LC 96-15082. 200p. 1996. 16.99 (*1-56476-585-7*) Chariot Victor.

London, H. B., Jr., jt. auth. see Toler, Stan.

London, Herbert. The Broken Apple: New York City in the 1980's. 256p. 1989. 39.95 (*0-88738-296-7*) Transaction Pubs.

London, Herbert & Rubenstein, Edwin S. From the Empire State to the Vampire State: New York in a Downward Transition. LC 94-20687. 210p. (Orig.). (C). 1994. reprint ed. pap. text 24.95 (*0-8191-9605-3*) U Pr of Amer.

London, Herbert I. Armageddon in the Classroom: An Examination of Nuclear Education. 146p. (Orig.). 1987. pap. text 18.50 (*0-8191-6548-4*); lib. bdg. 40.50 (*0-8191-6547-6*) U Pr of Amer.

— Military Doctrine & the American Character: Reflections on Air-Land Battle. LC 84-62054. (Agenda Paper Ser.: No. 14). 79p. reprint ed. pap. 30.00 (*0-7837-2122-6*, 204240400004) Bks Demand.

— Social Science Theory: Structure & Application. 375p. 1989. pap. text 24.95 (*0-88738-774-8*) Transaction Pubs.

London, Herbert I., ed. A Strategy for Victory Without War. LC 89-5731. 126p. (Orig.). (C). 1989. lib. bdg. 35.50 (*0-8191-7437-8*, Pub. by Hudson Instit IN) U Pr of Amer.

— A Strategy for Victory Without War. LC 89-5731. 126p. (Orig.). (C). 1989. pap. text 17.50 (*0-8191-7438-6*) U Pr of Amer.

London, Hilary. Scent of Gold. large type ed. (General Ser.). 416p. 1993. 27.99 (*0-7089-2845-5*) Ulverscroft.

London, Howard B., jt. ed. see Zwerling, L. Steven.

London Institute of World Affairs Staff, jt. auth. see Kelsen, Hans.

***London, Jack.** The Abysmal Brute. 176p. 2000. pap. 10.00 (*0-8032-7994-9*, Bison Books) U of Nebr Pr.

— The Abysmal Brute. (Collected Works of Jack London). 300p. 1998. reprint ed. lib. bdg. 88.00 (*1-58201-700-X*) Classic Bks.

— The Acorn-Planter: A California Forest Play. (Collected Works of Jack London). 84p. 1998. reprint ed. lib. bdg. 88.00 (*1-58201-701-8*) Classic Bks.

— Adventure. (Collected Works of Jack London). 376p. 1998. reprint ed. lib. bdg. 98.00 (*1-58201-702-6*) Classic Bks.

London, Jack. Adventure Stories. LC 97-49981. 475p. 1998. text 24.95 (*1-56000-523-8*) Transaction Pubs.

— The Assassination Bureau, Ltd. large type ed. LC 98-34563. 234p. 1998. 30.00 (*0-7838-0349-4*, G K Hall Lrg Type) Mac Lib Ref.

— The Assassination Bureau, Ltd. reprint ed. lib. bdg. 20.95 (*0-89190-655-X*, Rivercity Pr) Amereon Ltd.

***London, Jack.** Before Adam. LC 99-54898. (Bison Frontiers of Imagination Ser.). (Illus.). 249p. 2000. pap. 12.00 (*0-8032-7993-0*, Bison Books) U of Nebr Pr.

London, Jack. Before Adam. reprint ed. lib. bdg. 20.95 (*0-89190-651-7*, Rivercity Pr) Amereon Ltd.

***London, Jack.** Before Adam. (Collected Works of Jack London). 228p. 1998. reprint ed. lib. bdg. 88.00 (*1-58201-703-4*) Classic Bks.

London, Jack. The Best Short Stories of Jack London. 1986. mass mkt. 5.99 (*0-449-30053-6*) Fawcett.

— The Best Short Stories of Jack London. reprint ed. lib. bdg. 20.95 (*0-89190-656-8*, Rivercity Pr) Amereon Ltd.

— Brown Wolf. lib. bdg. 20.95 (*0-8488-1993-4*) Amereon Ltd.

— Burning Daylight. lib. bdg. 23.95 (*0-8488-1995-0*) Amereon Ltd.

— Burning Daylight. 1997. pap. text 12.95 (*0-9659544-0-4*) J London Mus.

***London, Jack.** Burning Daylight. (Collected Works of Jack London). 361p. 1998. reprint ed. lib. bdg. 98.00 (*1-58201-704-2*) Classic Bks.

London, Jack. Call of the Wild. 102p. pap. 7.95 (*0-88839-259-1*) Hancock House.

— Call of the Wild. (Illustrated Classics Ser.). (J). 1992. pap. 33.50 (*1-56156-094-4*) Kidsbks.

— Call of the Wild. (Enriched Classics Ser.). (Illus.). 102p. 1989. per. 4.50 (*0-671-70494-X*) PB.

— Call of the Wild. 128p. (YA). (gr. 9-12). 1990. pap. 2.50 (*0-8125-0432-1*, Pub. by Tor Bks) St Martin.

— Call of the Wild. LC 89-33890. (Illustrated Classics Ser.). (Illus.). 48p. (J). (gr. 3-6). 1990. lib. bdg. 12.89 (*0-8167-1863-6*) Troll Communs.

— Call of the Wild. LC 89-33890. (Illustrated Classics Ser.). (Illus.). 48p. (J). (gr. 3-6). 1997. pap. 5.95 (*0-8167-1864-4*) Troll Communs.

— Call of the Wild. (Airmont Classics Ser.). (J). 1964. 8.05 (*0-606-02504-9*, Pub. by Turtleback) Demco.

— The Call of the Wild. (Classics Illustrated Study Guides Ser.). (Illus.). 1997. mass mkt. 4.99 (*1-57840-042-2*, Pub. by Acclaim Bks) Penguin Putnam.

— The Call of the Wild. (Illustrated Classics Collection 1). 64p. (YA). (gr. 6-12). 1994. pap. 4.95 (*0-7854-0663-8*, 40334) Am Guidance.

— The Call of the Wild. 16.95 (*0-8488-0106-7*) Amereon Ltd.

— The Call of the Wild. LC 97-45019. (Scribner Classic Ser.). (Illus.). 128p. (YA). (gr. 7 up). 1999. per. 25.00 (*0-689-81836-X*) Atheneum Yung Read.

— The Call of the Wild. 64p. 1990. pap. 1.00 (*0-486-26472-6*) Dover.

— The Call of the Wild. LC 98-49244. (Illus.). 64p. 1999. pap. 1.00 (*0-486-40551-6*) Dover.

— The Call of the Wild. 1997. text 8.25 (*0-03-051498-3*) Holt R&W.

— The Call of the Wild. LC 93-18409. (Illus.). 144p. (J). (gr. 4 up). 1994. mass mkt. 19.95 (*0-02-759455-6*) Macmillan.

— The Call of the Wild. 1997. pap. 3.95 (*0-89375-344-0*) NAL.

— The Call of the Wild. Platt, Kin, ed. LC 73-75461. (Now Age Illustrated Ser.). (Illus.). 64p. (J). (gr. 5-10). 1973. pap. 2.95 (*0-88301-095-X*) Pendulum Pr.

— The Call of the Wild. (Puffin Classics Ser.). (Illus.). 134p. (J). (gr. 1-4). 1994. pap. 3.99 (*0-14-036669-5*, PuffinBks) Peng Put Young Read.

— The Call of the Wild. Vogel, Malvina, ed. (Great Illustrated Classics Ser.: Vol. 3). (Illus.). 240p. (J). (gr. 3-6). 1989. 9.95 (*0-86611-954-X*) Playmore Inc.

— The Call of the Wild. LC 87-20874. (Apple Classics Ser.). 172p. (YA). (gr. 4-7). 1987. pap. 3.99 (*0-590-44001-2*) Scholastic Inc.

— The Call of the Wild. 1997. pap. 4.95 (*0-8167-2881-X*) Troll Communs.

— The Call of the Wild. Dyer, Daniel, ed. & notes by. LC 95-15717. (Illus.). 320p. 1995. 37.95 (*0-8061-2757-0*) U of Okla Pr.

— The Call of the Wild. Bassett, Jennifer, ed. (Illus.). 64p. 1995. pap. text 5.95 (*0-19-422750-2*) OUP.

— The Call of the Wild. DeKoster, Katie, ed. LC 98-48970. (Literary Companion Ser.). (YA). (gr. 9-12). 1998. lib. bdg. 27.95 (*1-56510-831-0*) Greenhaven.

— The Call of the Wild. deluxe ed. (Whole Story Ser.). (Illus.). 128p. (J). (gr. 4-7). 1996. 14.99 (*0-670-86796-9*, Viking Child) Peng Put Young Read.

— The Call of the Wild. deluxe limited ed. (J). 1999. mass mkt. 75.00 (*0-689-81837-8*) S&S Childrens.

— Call of the Wild. large type ed. 1992. pap. 33.50 (*0-614-09865-3*, L-44972-00) Am Printing Hse.

— The Call of the Wild. large type ed. (Large Print Heritage Ser.). 139p. 1997. lib. bdg. 24.95 (*1-58118-012-8*, 21484) LRS.

— The Call of the Wild. 271p. 1983. reprint ed. lib. bdg. 19.95 (*0-89966-473-3*) Buccaneer Bks.

***London, Jack.** The Call of the Wild. (Collected Works of Jack London). 231p. 1998. reprint ed. lib. bdg. 88.00 (*1-58201-705-0*) Classic Bks.

London, Jack. The Call of the Wild: And Other Stories. deluxe ed. (Illustrated Junior Library). (Illus.). 192p. (J). (gr. 3-12). 1965. 14.95 (*0-448-06027-2*, G & D) Peng Put Young Read.

— The Call of the Wild: And Selected Stories. rev. ed. (Signet Classics Ser.). 179p. 1998. mass mkt. 3.95 (*0-451-52703-8*, Sig) NAL.

— The Call of the Wild: Annotated & Illustrated. annot. ed. Dyer, Daniel, ed. LC 96-42010. (Illus.). 134p. (YA). 1997. pap. 12.95 (*0-8061-2920-4*) U of Okla Pr.

London, Jack. Call of the Wild: Begley,&Ed. abr. ed. 1992. audio 12.00 (*1-55994-613-X*, DCN 1219) HarperAudio.

— Call of the Wild & Selected Stories. 1960. 9.05 (*0-606-01829-8*, Pub. by Turtleback) Demco.

London, Jack. The Call of the Wild & White Fang. 240p. 1997. pap. 3.95 (*1-85326-571-3*, Pub. by Wrdsworth Edits) NTC Contemp Pub Co.

— Call of the Wild & White Fang. (Bantam Classics Ser.). 1984. 9.05 (*0-606-00168-9*, Pub. by Turtleback) Demco.

— Call of the Wild & White Fang. (Classics Library). 1997. pap. 3.95 (*1-85326-026-6*, 0266WW, Pub. by Wrdsworth Edits) NTC Contemp Pub Co.

— Call of the Wild & White Fang. large type ed. 502p. 1995. lib. bdg. 24.00 (*0-939495-87-2*) North Bks.

— The Call of the Wild Readalong. (Illustrated Classics Collection 1). 64p. 1994. pap. 14.95 incl. audio (*0-7854-0704-9*, 40336) Am Guidance.

— The Call of the Wild; White Fang. (Classics Ser.). 304p. (gr. 7-12). 1991. mass mkt. 3.95 (*0-553-21233-8*) Bantam.

— The Call of the Wild; White Fang. 310p. 1998. reprint ed. lib. bdg. 24.00 (*1-58287-020-9*) North Bks.

— The Call of the Wild; White Fang. unabridged ed. 1997. reprint ed. pap. 14.95 (*1-57002-040-X*) Univ Publng Hse.

— The Call of the Wild, White Fang, & Other Stories. Labor, Earle & Leitz, Robert C., III, eds. (Oxford World's Classics Ser.). (Illus.). 392p. (Orig.). 1998. pap. 7.95 (*0-19-283514-9*) OUP.

— The Call of the Wild, White Fang, & Other Stories. Sinclair, Andrew, ed. 416p. (Orig.). 1993. pap. 7.95 (*0-14-018651-4*, Penguin Classics) Viking Penguin.

— Call of the Wild, White Fang, & Other Stories. (Penguin Twentieth-Century Classics). 1993. 13.05 (*0-606-00170-0*, Pub. by Turtleback) Demco.

— The Call of the Wild, White Fang & To Build a Fire. 98th ed. LC 98-19545. (Modern Library Ser.). 1998. pap. 7.95 (*0-375-75251-X*) Modern Lib NY.

***London, Jack.** Children of the Frost. (Collected Works of Jack London). 160p. 1998. reprint ed. lib. bdg. 88.00 (*1-58201-706-9*) Classic Bks.

— The Collected Stories Of Jack London. large type ed. 272p. 2000. pap. 22.00 (*0-06-095573-2*) HarpC.

London, Jack. The Complete Short Stories of Jack London, 3 vols., Set. Labor, Earle G. et al, eds. LC 92-44856. (Illus.). 2700p. (C). 1993. 180.00 (*0-8047-2058-4*) Stanford U Pr.

— Cruise of the Dazzler. reprint ed. lib. bdg. 17.95 (*0-89190-652-5*, Rivercity Pr) Amereon Ltd.

***London, Jack.** The Cruise of the Dazzler. (Collected Works of Jack London). 250p. 1998. reprint ed. lib. bdg. 88.00 (*1-58201-707-7*) Classic Bks.

— The Cruise of the Snark. LC 00-31842. 2000. pap. write for info. (*0-486-41248-2*) Dover.

— The Cruise of the Snark. (Collected Works of Jack London). 300p. 1998. reprint ed. lib. bdg. 88.00 (*1-58201-708-5*) Classic Bks.

London, Jack. The Cruise of the Snark. (Illus.). 340p. 1993. reprint ed. pap. 14.95 (*0-924486-46-5*) Sheridan.

— The Cruise of the Snark. unabridged ed. 1995. reprint ed. pap. 15.95 (*1-885031-02-5*, Capstan Pr) Merritt Communs.

— The Cruise of the Snark: A Pacific Voyage. 300p. 1986. 14.95 (*0-7103-0139-1*) Routledge.

***London, Jack.** A Daughter of the Snows. (Collected Works of Jack London). 334p. 1998. reprint ed. lib. bdg. 98.00 (*1-58201-709-3*) Classic Bks.

London, Jack. Daughters of the Rich: A Play. 1971. 5.00 (*0-910740-18-6*) Holmes.

— Diable, a Dog. (Jamestown Classics Ser.). 1995. pap., teacher ed. 7.32 (*0-89061-047-9*, Jamestwn Pub) NTC Contemp Pub Co.

— Diable, a Dog. (Jamestown Classics Ser.). (J). 1995. pap., student ed. 5.99 (*0-89061-046-0*, Jamestwn Pub) NTC Contemp Pub Co.

***London, Jack.** Dutch Courage & Other Stories. (Collected Works of Jack London). 180p. 1998. reprint ed. lib. bdg. 88.00 (*1-58201-710-7*) Classic Bks.

London, Jack. La Expedicion del Pirata. 3rd ed. (Punto Juvenil Ser.). (SPA.). (J). 1988. 10.05 (*0-606-05401-4*, Pub. by Turtleback) Demco.

— The Faith of Men & Other Stories. LC 73-122729. (Short Story Index Reprint Ser.). 1980. 18.95 (*0-8369-3562-4*) Ayer.

***London, Jack.** The Faith of Men & Other Stories. (Collected Works of Jack London). 243p. 1998. reprint ed. lib. bdg. 88.00 (*1-58201-711-5*) Classic Bks.

London, Jack. Fantastic Tales. Walker, Dale L., ed. LC 98-15487. 233p. 1999. pap. 11.00 (*0-8032-7979-5*, Bison Books) U of Nebr Pr.

— Favorite Novels & Stories: Three Somplete Books, 3 vols., Set. 320p. 1993. pap., boxed set 3.00 (*0-486-27424-1*) Dover.

— Five Great Short Stories. (Thrift Editions Ser.). 96p. 1992. reprint ed. pap. 1.00 (*0-486-27063-7*) Dover.

— Frontier Stories. 1991. pap. 12.95 incl. audio (*1-882071-30-1*) B&B Audio.

***London, Jack.** The Game. (Collected Works of Jack London). 182p. 1998. reprint ed. lib. bdg. 88.00 (*1-58201-712-3*) Classic Bks.

London, Jack. The God of His Fathers & Other Stories. LC 72-103523. (Short Story Index Reprint Ser.). 1977. 21.95 (*0-8369-3265-X*) Ayer.

***London, Jack.** The God of His Fathers & Other Stories. (Collected Works of Jack London). 299p. 1998. reprint ed. lib. bdg. 88.00 (*1-58201-713-1*) Classic Bks.

London, Jack. Gold-Hunters of the North. (Shorey Historical Ser.). 12p. reprint ed. pap. 10.00 (*0-8466-0176-1*, S176) Shoreys Bkstore.

— Hearts of Three. Reginald, R. & Melville, Douglas, eds. LC 77-84251. (Lost Race & Adult Fantasy Ser.). 1978. reprint ed. lib. bdg. 35.95 (*0-405-10997-0*) Ayer.

***London, Jack.** Hearts of Three. (Collected Works of Jack London). 292p. 1998. reprint ed. lib. bdg. 88.00 (*1-58201-714-X*) Classic Bks.

London, Jack. The Hobo & the Fairy. reprint ed. lib. bdg. 18.95 (*0-89190-653-3*, Rivercity Pr) Amereon Ltd.

***London, Jack.** The House of Pride. 232p. 2001. pap. text 35.00 (*0-7103-0694-6*) Col U Pr.

— The House of Pride & Other Tales of Hawaii. (Collected Works of Jack London). 232p. 1998. reprint ed. lib. bdg. 88.00 (*1-58201-715-8*) Classic Bks.

— The Human Drift. (Collected Works of Jack London). 190p. 1998. reprint ed. lib. bdg. 88.00 (*1-58201-716-6*) Classic Bks.

— In Hawaii with Jack London: A Polynesian Sojourn. 230p. 2000. pap. text 35.00 (*0-7103-0687-3*) Col U Pr.

London, Jack. The Iron Heel. 1976. 26.95 (*0-8488-0566-6*) Amereon Ltd.

***London, Jack.** The Iron Heel. 2000. pap. 12.95 (*0-86241-899-2*, Pub. by Canongate Books) Interlink Pub.

London, Jack. The Iron Heel. large type ed. 417p. 1995. lib. bdg. 24.00 (*0-939495-77-5*) North Bks.

***London, Jack.** The Iron Heel. (Collected Works of Jack London). 354p. 1998. reprint ed. lib. bdg. 98.00 (*1-58201-717-4*) Classic Bks.

London, Jack. The Iron Heel. 245p. 1998. reprint ed. lib. bdg. 24.00 (*1-58287-041-1*) North Bks.

— The Iron Heel. LC 80-81804. 224p. (C). reprint ed. pap. 11.95 (*0-904526-01-1*, Pub. by Pluto GBR) Stylus Pub VA.

— The Iron Heel. unabridged ed. (Classic Reprint Ser.). 354p. 1997. reprint ed. 35.00 (*0-936128-57-7*) De Young Pr.

— The Iron Heel. rev. ed. LC 80-81804. 240p. 1980. pap. 11.95 (*1-55652-071-9*, Lawrence Hill) Chicago Review.

***London, Jack.** Island Tales. (Collected Works of Jack London). 248p. 1998. reprint ed. lib. bdg. 88.00 (*1-58201-718-2*) Classic Bks.

London, Jack. Jack London: Author Kit. (Jamestown Classics). (J). (gr. 1-7). 1976. pap. 353.33 (*0-89061-607-8*) NTC Contemp Pub Co.

— Jack London Novels. 1987. 6.98 (*0-671-08621-9*) S&S Trade.

— Jack London on the Road: The Tramp Diary & Other Hobo Writings. Etulain, Richard W., ed. LC 78-17039. (Illus.). 227p. reprint ed. pap. 70.40 (*0-7837-7067-7*, 204687900004) Bks Demand.

***London, Jack.** The Jack London Reader. 1999. 5.98 (*0-7624-0546-5*) Running Pr.

London, Jack. Jack London's Golden State: Selected California Writings. Haslam, Gerald, ed. LC 99-20437. 304p. 1999. pap. 15.95 (*1-890771-02-3*) Heyday Bks.

— Jack London's Stories of the North. 256p. (J). (gr. 4 up). 1989. pap. 4.50 (*0-590-44229-5*) Scholastic Inc.

— Jack London's Tales of Hawaii. LC 81-23492. 80p. 1984. pap. 4.95 (*0-916630-25-0*) Pr Pacifica.

***London, Jack.** The Jacket. (Collected Works of Jack London). 300p. 1998. reprint ed. lib. bdg. 88.00 (*1-58201-719-0*) Classic Bks.

— Jerry of the Islands. (Collected Works of Jack London). 310p. 1998. reprint ed. lib. bdg. 98.00 (*1-58201-720-4*) Classic Bks.

London, Jack. John Barleycorn. 1976. 22.95 (*0-8488-1080-5*) Amereon Ltd.

***London, Jack.** John Barleycorn. (Collected Works of Jack London). 319p. 1998. reprint ed. lib. bdg. 98.00 (*1-58201-721-2*) Classic Bks.

— John Barleycorn: Alcoholic Memoirs. Sutherland, John, ed. (Oxford World's Classics Ser.). 286p. 1998. pap. 10.95 (*0-19-283717-6*) OUP.

London, Jack. John Barleycorn: Alcoholic Memoirs. LC 78-55743. 1978. reprint ed. lib. bdg. 16.00 (*0-8376-0423-0*) Bentley Pubs.

— John Barleycorn: Alcoholic Memoirs. 180p. 1997. reprint ed. pap. 9.95 (*0-938530-61-5*) Lexikos.

— John Barleycorn: Alcoholic Memoirs. (American Biography Ser.). 210p. 1991. reprint ed. lib. bdg. 69.00 (*0-7812-8249-7*) Rprt Serv.

***London, Jack.** The Kempton-Wace Letters. (Collected Works of Jack London). 154p. 1998. reprint ed. lib. bdg. 88.00 (*1-58201-722-0*) Classic Bks.

London, Jack. The Law of Life. Date not set. pap., teacher ed. 7.32 incl. audio (*0-89070-041-9*, Jamestwn Pub) NTC Contemp Pub Co.

— The Law of Life. (Jamestown Classics Ser.). (J). 1995. pap., student ed. 5.99 (*0-89061-040-1*, Jamestwn Pub) NTC Contemp Pub Co.

— The Letters of Jack London, 3 vols., Set. Labor, Earle G. et al, eds. LC 83-45346. (Illus.). 1768p. 1988. 149.50 (*0-8047-1227-1*); 199.50 (*0-8047-1507-6*) Stanford U Pr.

— Little Lady of the Big House. lib. bdg. 27.95 (*0-8488-1997-7*) Amereon Ltd.

***London, Jack.** The Little Lady of the Big House. (Collected Works of Jack London). 392p. 1998. reprint ed. lib. bdg. 98.00 (*1-58201-723-9*) Classic Bks.

— La Llamada de Lo Salvaje. 1992. 12.05 (*0-606-10477-1*, Pub. by Turtleback) Demco.

London, Jack. London, Jack, Short Stories Of. (Airmont Classics Ser.). (YA). (gr. 9 up). 1969. mass mkt. 2.50 (*0-8049-0198-8*, CL-198) Airmont.

***London, Jack.** Lost Face. (Collected Works of Jack London). 240p. 1998. reprint ed. lib. bdg. 88.00 (*1-58201-724-7*) Classic Bks.

London, Jack. Love of Life. lib. bdg. 20.95 (*0-8488-2000-2*) Amereon Ltd.

— Love of Life. rev. ed. (Read-along Radio Dramas Ser.). (YA). (gr. 6-12). 1986. ring bd. 38.00 (*1-878298-21-6*) Balance Pub.

An Asterisk (*) at the beginning of an entry indicates that the title is appearing for the first time.

***London, Jack.** Love of Life & Other Stories. (Collected Works of Jack London). 240p. 1998. reprint ed. lib. bdg. 88.00 (*1-58201-725-5*) Classic Bks.

London, Jack. The Marriage of Lit-lit. (Jamestown Classics Ser.). 1995. pap., teacher ed. 7.32 (*0-89061-045-2*, Jamestwn Pub) NTC Contemp Pub Co.

— The Marriage of Lit-lit. (Jamestown Classics Ser.). (J). 1995. pap., student ed. 5.99 (*0-89061-044-4*, Jamestwn Pub) NTC Contemp Pub Co.

— Martin Eden. (Airmont Classics Ser.). (J). (gr. 9 up). 1969. mass mkt. 3.50 (*0-8049-0209-7*, CL-209) Airmont.

— Martin Eden. lib. bdg. 27.95 (*0-8488-1992-6*) Amereon Ltd.

— Martin Eden. 480p. 1994. pap. 12.95 (*0-14-018772-3*, Penguin Classics) Viking Penguin.

***London, Jack.** Martin Eden. (Collected Works of Jack London). 411p. 1998. reprint ed. lib. bdg. 108.00 (*1-58201-726-3*) Classic Bks.

— Michael Brother of Jerry. (Collected Works of Jack London). 344p. 1998. reprint ed. lib. bdg. 98.00 (*1-58201-727-1*) Classic Bks.

London, Jack. Moon-Face, & Other Stories. LC 71-140334. (Short Story Index Reprint Ser.). 1977. 15.95 (*0-8369-3726-0*) Ayer.

***London, Jack.** Moon-Face & Other Stories. (Collected Works of Jack London). 273p. 1998. reprint ed. lib. bdg. 88.00 (*1-58201-728-X*) Classic Bks.

— The Mutiny of the Elsinore. (Collected Works of Jack London). 365p. 1998. reprint ed. lib. bdg. 98.00 (*1-58201-729-8*) Classic Bks.

London, Jack. Mutiny on the Elsinore: A Novel of Seagoing Gangsters. 378p. 1987. mass mkt. 5.95 (*0-935180-40-0*) Mutual Pub HI.

— Nam-Bok, the Liar. (Jamestown Classics Ser.). 1995. pap., teacher ed. 7.32 (*0-89061-043-6*, Jamestwn Pub) NTC Contemp Pub Co.

— Nam-Bok, the Liar. (Jamestown Classics Ser.). (J). 1995. pap., student ed. 5.99 (*0-89061-042-8*, Jamestwn Pub) NTC Contemp Pub Co.

***London, Jack.** The Night-Born. (Collected Works of Jack London). 290p. 1998. reprint ed. lib. bdg. 88.00 (*1-58201-730-1*) Classic Bks.

London, Jack. Northland Stories. Auerbach, Jonathan, ed. LC 96-21720. 1997. pap. 10.95 (*0-14-018996-3*) Viking Penguin.

— Novels & Social Writings: The People of the Abyss; The Road; The Iron Heel; Martin Eden; John Barleycorn; Essays. Pizer, Donald, ed. LC 82-6940. 1192p. 1982. 40.00 (*0-940450-06-2*, Pub. by Library of America) Penguin Putnam.

— Novels & Stories: The Call of the Wild; White Fang; The Sea-Wolf; Klondike Stories. Pizer, Donald, ed. LC 82-249. 1021p. 1982. 30.00 (*0-940450-05-4*, Pub. by Library of America) Penguin Putnam.

***London, Jack.** On the Makaloa Mat. (Collected Works of Jack London). 229p. 1998. reprint ed. lib. bdg. 88.00 (*1-58201-731-X*) Classic Bks.

London, Jack. The People of the Abyss. LC 93-2947. (Illus.). 388p. 1995. pap. 14.95 (*1-55652-167-7*, Lawrence Hill) Chicago Review.

— The People of the Abyss. (C). pap. 8.95 (*0-904526-17-8*, Pub. by Pluto GBR) LPC InBook.

— The People of the Abyss. (Pluto Classic Ser.). 1998. pap. 14.95 (*0-7453-1415-5*, Pub. by Pluto GBR) Stylus Pub VA.

***London, Jack.** The People of the Abyss. (Collected Works of Jack London). 1998. reprint ed. lib. bdg. 98.00 (*1-58201-732-8*) Classic Bks.

–The Plays of Jack London. (Ironweed American Classics Ser.). 395p. (Orig.). 2000. pap. 24.95 (0-9655309-7-3) Ironweed Pr.

The Plays of Jack London is a comprehensive collection of Jack London's plays, which are collected here for the first time. With an Introduction by the noted scholar & novelist Clay Reynolds of the University of Texas at Dallas. Available to trade via Baker & Taylor, Ingram, Brodart & Follet Library Resources. Ironweed American Classics books are printed on acid-free paper. *Publisher Paid Annotation.*

London, Jack. The Portable Jack London. Labor, Earle G., ed. LC 93-38740. 672p. 1994. pap. 15.95 (*0-14-017969-0*, Penguin Bks) Viking Penguin.

***London, Jack.** The Red One. (Collected Works of Jack London). 193p. 1998. reprint ed. lib. bdg. 88.00 (*1-58201-733-6*) Classic Bks.

— Revolution & Other Essays. (Collected Works of Jack London). 309p. 1998. reprint ed. lib. bdg. 98.00 (*1-58201-734-4*) Classic Bks.

London, Jack. Road. 150p. 1998. lib. bdg. 20.95 (*1-56723-073-3*) Yestermorrow.

***London, Jack.** The Road. (Collected Works of Jack London). 164p. 1998. reprint ed. lib. bdg. 88.00 (*1-58201-735-2*) Classic Bks.

London, Jack. The Road. (American Biography Ser.). 224p. 1991. reprint ed. lib. bdg. 69.00 (*0-7812-8250-0*) Rprt Serv.

— The Scarlet Plague. LC 74-16506. (Science Fiction Ser.). (Illus.). 181p. 1978. reprint ed. 20.95 (*0-405-06304-0*) Ayer.

***London, Jack.** The Scarlet Plague. (Collected Works of Jack London). 224p. 1998. reprint ed. lib. bdg. 88.00 (*1-58201-736-0*) Classic Bks.

— Science Fiction of Jack London. 1998. lib. bdg. 23.95 (*1-56723-074-1*) Yestermorrow.

London, Jack. Science Fiction Stories. 1976. 23.95 (*0-8488-1081-3*) Amereon Ltd.

— The Science Fiction Stories of Jack London. LC 92-39510. 1993. 11.95 (*0-8065-1407-8*, Citadel Pr) Carol Pub Group.

— The Science Fiction Stories of Jack London. 1994. reprint ed. lib. bdg. 27.95 (*1-56849-303-7*) Buccaneer Bks.

***London, Jack.** Scorn of Women. (Collected Works of Jack London). 181p. 1998. reprint ed. lib. bdg. 88.00 (*1-58201-737-9*) Classic Bks.

London, Jack. Sea Wolf. (Airmont Classics Ser.). (J). (gr. 6 up). 1965. mass mkt. 2.50 (*0-8049-0064-7*, CL-64) Airmont.

— Sea Wolf. 1985. 15.95 (*0-02-574630-8*) Macmillan.

***London, Jack.** Sea Wolf. Sutherland, John, ed. (Oxford World Classics Ser.). 418p. 2000. pap. 8.95 (*0-19-283825-3*) OUP.

London, Jack. The Sea Wolf. (Illustrated Classics Collection 4). 64p. 1994. pap. 4.95 (*0-7854-0756-1*, 40521) Am Guidance.

— The Sea Wolf. (Bantam Classics Ser.). 256p. (gr. 7 up). 1984. mass mkt. 4.95 (*0-553-21225-7*) Bantam.

— The Sea Wolf. Fago, John C., ed. (Now Age Illustrated IV Ser.). (Illus.). (gr. 4-12). 1978. student ed. 1.25 (*0-88301-346-0*); pap. text 2.95 (*0-88301-322-3*) Pendulum Pr.

— The Sea Wolf. 320p. 1993. pap. 2.50 (*0-8125-2276-1*, Pub. by Tor Bks) St Martin.

— The Sea Wolf. 368p. (YA). (gr. 5 up). 1998. pap. 4.99 (*0-14-038279-8*) Viking Penguin.

***London, Jack.** The Sea-Wolf. LC 99-45090. (Thrift Editions Ser.). 2000. pap. 2.00 (*0-486-41108-7*) Dover.

London, Jack. The Sea-Wolf. Sutherland, John, ed. (World's Classics Ser.). 418p. 1993. pap. 6.95 (*0-19-282931-9*) OUP.

— Sea-Wolf. 1960. 9.05 (*0-606-01336-9*, Pub. by Turtleback) Demco.

London, Jack. The Sea Wolf. abr. ed. Kay, Marilyn, ed. 1986. 15.95 incl. audio (*1-882071-08-5*, 010) B&B Audio.

London, Jack. The Sea-Wolf. large type ed. 504p. 1997. reprint ed. lib. bdg. 24.00 (*0-939495-19-8*) North Bks.

— The Sea Wolf. 351p. reprint ed. lib. bdg. 23.95 (*0-89190-657-6*, Rivercity Pr) Amereon Ltd.

***London, Jack.** The Sea-Wolf. (Collected Works of Jack London). 366p. 1998. reprint ed. lib. bdg. 98.00 (*1-58201-738-7*) Classic Bks.

London, Jack. The Sea-Wolf. 322p. 1998. reprint ed. lib. bdg. 24.00 (*1-58287-068-3*) North Bks.

London, Jack. Sea Wolf, Ch. 17-19. abr. ed. LC 81-740016. 1988. audio 14.00 (*0-694-50952-3*, SWC 1689, Caedmon) HarperAudio.

London, Jack. The Sea-Wolf & Other Selected Stories. 320p. 1989. pap. 9.95 (*0-14-018357-4*, Penguin Classics) Viking Penguin.

— The Sea-Wolf & Other Selected Stories. 1990. reprint ed. lib. bdg. 24.95 (*0-89968-539-0*) Buccaneer Bks.

— The Sea Wolf & Selected Stories. 352p. (J). (gr. 8). 1964. mass mkt. 4.95 (*0-451-52356-3*, Sig Classics) NAL.

— Sea-Wolf & Selected Stories. 1964. 10.05 (*0-606-01949-9*, Pub. by Turtleback) Demco.

— The Sea Wolf Readalong. (Illustrated Classics Collection 4). 64p. 1994. pap. 14.95 incl. audio (*0-7854-0772-3*, 40523) Am Guidance.

— Short Stories of Jack London: Authorized one-volume Edition. Leitz, Robert C., III et al, eds. 784p. 1992. pap. 16.00 (*0-02-022371-4*) Macmillan.

— Smoke Bellew. lib. bdg. 27.95 (*0-8488-1996-9*) Amereon Ltd.

— Smoke Bellew. 1992. reprint ed. lib. bdg. 19.95 (*0-89966-952-2*) Buccaneer Bks.

***London, Jack.** Smoke Bellew. (Collected Works of Jack London). 385p. 1998. reprint ed. lib. bdg. 99.00 (*1-58201-739-5*) Classic Bks.

London, Jack. Smoke Bellew. unabridged ed. LC 92-16275. (Illus.). 240p. 1992. reprint ed. pap. text 7.95 (*0-486-27364-4*) Dover.

***London, Jack.** A Son of the Sun. (Collected Works of Jack London). 284p. 1998. reprint ed. lib. bdg. 88.00 (*1-58201-740-9*) Classic Bks.

London, Jack. The Son of the Wolf. 1992. 39.00 (*0-403-08613-2*) Somerset Pub.

— Son of the Wolf. reprint ed. lib. bdg. 18.95 (*0-89190-654-1*, Rivercity Pr) Amereon Ltd.

— The Son of the Wolf. 1992. reprint ed. lib. bdg. 18.95 (*0-89966-953-0*) Buccaneer Bks.

— The Son of the Wolf: Tales of the Far North. Watson, Charles N., Jr., ed. (Oxford World's Classics Ser.). (Illus.). 368p. 1999. pap. 7.95 (*0-19-283486-X*) OUP.

***London, Jack.** Son of the Wolf: The Tales of the Far North. (Collected Works of Jack London). 251p. 1998. reprint ed. lib. bdg. 88.00 (*1-58201-741-7*) Classic Bks.

London, Jack. Son of Wolf. reprint ed. lib. bdg. 75.00 (*0-7812-0202-7*) Rprt Serv.

— South Sea Tales. lib. bdg. 24.95 (*0-8488-2001-0*) Amereon Ltd.

***London, Jack.** South Sea Tales. (Collected Works of Jack London). 327p. 1998. reprint ed. lib. bdg. 98.00 (*1-58201-742-5*) Classic Bks.

London, Jack. South Sea Tales. 352p. 1985. reprint ed. mass mkt. 6.95 (*0-935180-14-1*) Mutual Pub HI.

— The Star Rover. LC 98-76189. 352p. 1999. write for info. (*1-893766-01-2*) Aeon Pub Co.

— The Star Rover. 1976. 23.95 (*0-8488-1082-1*) Amereon Ltd.

***London, Jack.** The Star Rover. 2000. pap. 12.95 (*0-86241-887-9*, Pub. by Canongate Books) Interlink Pub.

London, Jack. The Star Rover. LC 99-18206. (Literary Classics Ser.). 335p. 1999. pap. 9.95 (*1-57392-695-7*) Prometheus Bks.

— The Star Rover. 348p. 1983. pap. 8.95 (*0-911842-31-4*, B914) Valley Sun.

— The Star Rover. (Collected Works of Jack London). 329p. 1998. reprint ed. lib. bdg. 98.00 (*1-58201-743-3*) Classic Bks.

— The Star Rover. 320p. (C). reprint ed. pap. 12.95 (*0-904526-10-0*, Pub. by Pluto GBR) LPC InBook.

— Stories of Hawaii. Day, A. Grove, ed. LC 65-11682. 282p. 1985. reprint ed. mass mkt. 6.95 (*0-935180-08-7*) Mutual Pub HI.

— Strength of the Strong. 1976. 21.95 (*0-8488-1083-X*) Amereon Ltd.

***London, Jack.** The Strength of the Strong. (Collected Works of Jack London). 257p. 1998. reprint ed. lib. bdg. 88.00 (*1-58201-744-1*) Classic Bks.

London, Jack. Surfing, a Royal Sport. Newborn, Sasha, ed. 19p. (C). 1994. pap. 2.00 (*0-942208-12-9*) Bandanna Bks.

— Tales of the Fish Patrol. LC 72-4454. (Short Story Index Reprint Ser.). 1977. reprint ed. 24.95 (*0-8369-4181-0*) Ayer.

***London, Jack.** Tales of the Fish Patrol. (Collected Works of Jack London). 243p. 1998. reprint ed. lib. bdg. 88.00 (*1-58201-745-X*) Classic Bks.

London, Jack. Tales of the North. 490p. 1989. 7.98 (*0-89009-439-X*) Bk Sales Inc.

— Tales of the Pacific. 240p. 1989. pap. 10.95 (*0-14-018358-2*, Penguin Classics) Viking Penguin.

***London, Jack.** Theft: A Play in Four Acts. (Collected Works of Jack London). 1999. reprint ed. 88.00 (*1-58201-746-8*) Classic Bks.

London, Jack. Thirteen Tales of Terror. 23.95 (*0-8488-0096-6*) Amereon Ltd.

— To Build a Fire & Other Stories. (Bantam Classics Ser.). 400p. 1986. mass mkt. 5.50 (*0-553-21335-0*) Bantam.

— To Build a Fire & Other Stories. 320p. 1999. mass mkt. 3.99 (*0-8125-6516-9*, Pub. by Tor Bks) St Martin.

London, Jack. To Build a Fire & Other Stories. (Bantam Classics Ser.). 1986. 10.60 (*0-606-01760-7*, Pub. by Turtleback) Demco.

— The Turtles of Tasman. (Collected Works of Jack London). 286p. 1998. reprint ed. lib. bdg. 88.00 (*1-58201-747-6*) Classic Bks.

— Two Jack London Favorites. unabridged ed. 1987. pap. 5.95 incl. audio (*1-882071-17-4*, 019) B&B Audio.

London, Jack. The Unabridged Jack London. abr. ed. Nicholls, Richard E. & Teacher, Lawrence, eds. LC 81-4383. (Illus.). 1152p. (Orig.). 1981. pap. 16.95 (*0-89471-124-5*) Running Pr.

— The Unabridged Jack London. unabridged ed. (Unabridged Classics Ser.). 1152p. (Orig.). 1997. 18.98 (*0-7624-0179-6*, Courage) Running Pr.

— The Valley of the Moon. lib. bdg. 32.95 (*0-614-30398-2*) Amereon Ltd.

— The Valley of the Moon. LC 98-36181. 400p. 1999. pap. 14.95 (*0-520-21820-5*, Pub. by U CA Pr) Cal Prin Full Svc.

***London, Jack.** The Valley of the Moon. (Collected Works of Jack London). 530p. 1998. reprint ed. lib. bdg. 118.00 (*1-58201-748-4*) Classic Bks.

— War of the Classes. (Collected Works of Jack London). 278p. 1998. reprint ed. lib. bdg. 88.00 (*1-58201-749-2*) Classic Bks.

London, Jack. When God Laughs. lib. bdg. 24.95 (*0-8488-1999-3*) Amereon Ltd.

***London, Jack.** When God Laughs & Other Stories. (Collected Works of Jack London). 152p. 1998. reprint ed. lib. bdg. 88.00 (*1-58201-750-6*) Classic Bks.

London, Jack. White Fang. (Airmont Classics Ser.). (YA). (gr. 6 up). 1964. mass mkt. 2.95 (*0-8049-0036-1*, CL-36) Airmont.

— White Fang. (Illustrated Classics Collection 3). 64p. 1994. pap. 4.95 (*0-7854-0728-6*, 40471) Am Guidance.

— White Fang. 1976. 22.95 (*0-8488-0567-4*) Amereon Ltd.

— White Fang. LC 98-19241. (Illus.). (J). 2000. 25.00 (*0-689-82431-9*) Atheneum Yung Read.

— White Fang. (J). 9.95 (*1-56156-306-4*) Kidsbks.

— White Fang. 1996. pap. 3.95 (*0-89375-346-7*) NAL.

— White Fang. LC 85-42971. (Classics for Young Readers Ser.). (Illus.). 272p. (YA). (gr. 4-7). 1994. pap. 3.99 (*0-14-036667-9*, PuffinBks) Peng Put Young Read.

— White Fang. Hanft, Joshua, ed. (Great Illustrated Classics Ser.: Vol. 34). (Illus.). 240p. (J). (gr. 3-6). 1994. 9.95 (*0-86611-985-X*) Playmore Inc.

— White Fang. LC 85-42971. (Illus.). 256p. (YA). (gr. 4-7). 1986. pap. 4.50 (*0-590-42591-9*, Apple Classics) Scholastic Inc.

— White Fang. 224p. (J). 1989. pap. 2.50 (*0-8125-0512-3*, Pub. by Tor Bks) St Martin.

— White Fang. (J). 1997. pap. 4.95 (*0-8167-2893-3*) Troll Communs.

— White Fang. 1964. 6.24 (*0-606-10363-5*) Turtleback.

— White Fang. abr. ed. Farr, Naunerle C., ed. (Now Age Illustrated III Ser.). (Illus.). (J). (gr. 4-12). 1977. pap. text 2.95 (*0-88301-271-5*) Pendulum Pr.

— White Fang. large type ed. (Large Print Heritage Ser.). 326p. 1998. lib. bdg. 32.95 (*1-58118-026-8*, 22021) LRS.

— White Fang. large type ed. LC 93-32332. 294p. 1993. lib. bdg. 20.95 (*0-8161-5889-4*, G K Hall Lrg Type) Mac Lib Ref.

— White Fang. large type ed. LC 93-32332. 294p. 1994. pap. 15.95 (*0-8161-5892-4*, G K Hall Lrg Type) Mac Lib Ref.

***London, Jack.** White Fang. (Collected Works of Jack London). 152p. 1998. reprint ed. lib. bdg. 98.00 (*1-58201-751-4*) Classic Bks.

London, Jack. White Fang. (Thrift Editions Ser.). 160p. 1991. reprint ed. pap. 1.00 (*0-486-26968-X*) Dover.

— White Fang. 160p. 1999. reprint ed. pap. 6.95 (*1-57002-095-7*) Univ Publng Hse.

— White Fang: Illustrated Classics. Arneson, D. J., ed. (Illus.). 128p. (Orig.). (J). 1990. pap. 2.95 (*0-942025-84-9*) Kidsbks.

— White Fang & The Call of the Wild. 288p. 1991. mass mkt. 4.95 (*0-451-52558-2*, Sig Classics) NAL.

— White Fang Readalong. (Illustrated Classics Collection 3). (Illus.). 64p. 1994. pap. 14.95 incl. audio (*0-7854-0744-8*, 40473) Am Guidance.

— The Whole Story: White Fang. 248p. (gr. 7 up). 1999. 25.99 (*0-670-88479-0*, Viking); pap. 17.99 (*0-670-88480-4*, Viking) Viking Penguin.

London, Jack, ed. Martin Eden. (Twelve-Point Ser.). 365p. 1999. lib. bdg. 24.00 (*1-58287-101-9*) North Bks.

London, Jack & Heron, Herbert. Gold: A Play. limited ed. 1972. 14.95 (*0-910740-19-4*) Holmes.

London, Jack & Heron, Herbert. Gold, a Play in Three Acts. 108p. 16.95 (*0-8488-2614-0*) Amereon Ltd.

London, Jack & Strunsky, Anna B. The Kempton-Wace Letters. Robillard, Douglas, ed. (Masterworks of Literature Ser.). 1991. 11.95 (*0-8084-0436-9*) NCUP.

— The Kempton-Wace Letters. LC 67-30817. (American Biography Ser.: No. 32). 1969. reprint ed. lib. bdg. 75.00 (*0-8383-0719-1*) M S G Haskell Hse.

London, Jack, et al. The Assassination Bureau, Ltd. LC 94-9213. 208p. 1994. pap. 10.00 (*0-14-018677-8*, Penguin Classics) Viking Penguin.

— The Call of the Wild. (Classics Illustrated Ser.). (Illus.). 52p. (YA). 1990. pap. 4.95 (*1-57209-010-3*) First Classics.

— World Premiere Performance of "Gold" 32p. 1973. pap. 3.00 (*0-918466-03-2*) Quintessence.

— World Premiere Performance of "Scorn of Women" 1979. pap. 3.00 (*0-918466-04-0*) Quintessence.

London, Jack, jt. auth. see Center for Learning Network Staff.

London, Jack, jt. auth. see Ewing, Jeanne B.

London, Jack, jt. auth. see London, Charmian.

London, Jack, jt. auth. see Monarch Notes Staff.

***London, John.** Modern Catalan Plays. 2000. pap. 14.95 (*0-413-74440-X*) Methn.

London, John, jt. ed. see George, David.

London, Jonathan. Ali, Child of the Desert. LC 92-44164. (Illus.). 32p. (J). (gr. 1 up). 1997. 16.00 (*0-688-12560-3*); lib. bdg. 15.93 (*0-688-12561-1*) Lothrop.

— At the Edge of the Forest. LC 97-23034. (Illus.). 32p. (J). (gr. k-3). 1998. 15.99 (*0-7636-0014-8*) Candlewick Pr.

— Baby Whale's Journey. LC 99-13020. (Endangered Species Ser.). (Illus.). 40p. (J). (gr. k-3). 1999. 14.95 (*0-8118-2496-9*) Chronicle Bks.

— Condor's Egg. (Illus.). 32p. (J). (ps-3). 1999. pap. 6.95 (*0-8118-2312-1*) Chronicle Bks.

— Dream Weaver. LC 95-22799. (Illus.). 32p. (J). (ps-4). 1998. 16.00 (*0-15-200944-2*) Harcourt.

— The Eyes of Gray Wolf. LC 92-35987. (Illus.). 32p. (J). (gr. 4 up). 1993. 14.95 (*0-8118-0285-X*) Chronicle Bks.

— Fire Race: A Karuk Coyote Tale about How Fire Came to the People. LC 92-32352. (Illus.). 40p. (J). (ps-3). 1993. 13.95 (*0-8118-0241-8*) Chronicle Bks.

— Fire Race: A Karuk Coyote Tale of How Fire Come to the People. (Illus.). 40p. (J). (ps-3). 1997. pap. 6.95 (*0-8118-1488-2*) Chronicle Bks.

— Fireflies, Fireflies, Light My Way. (Picture Puffin Ser.). (Illus.). 32p. (J). 1998. pap. 5.99 (*0-14-056188-9*, PuffinBks) Peng Put Young Read.

— Fireflies, Fireflies, Light My Way. (Picture Puffin Ser.). 1998. 11.19 (*0-606-13386-0*, Pub. by Turtleback) Demco.

***London, Jonathan.** Froggy Bakes a Cake. LC 99-51677. (Reading Railroad Bks.). (Illus.). 32p. (J). 2000. pap. 3.49 (*0-448-42153-4*, G & D) Peng Put Young Read.

London, Jonathan. Froggy Gets Dressed. LC 91-45805. (Illus.). 32p. (J). (ps-1). 1992. 15.99 (*0-670-84249-4*, Viking Child) Peng Put Young Read.

— Froggy Gets Dressed. (Illus.). 32p. (J). (ps-3). 1994. pap. 5.99 (*0-14-054457-7*, PuffinBks) Peng Put Young Read.

— Froggy Gets Dressed. (Illus.). 32p. (J). 1995. pap. 19.99 (*0-14-055378-9*, PuffinBks) Peng Put Young Read.

— Froggy Gets Dressed. 32p. (J). (ps-1). 1997. 5.99 (*0-670-87616-X*, Viking Child) Peng Put Young Read.

— Froggy Gets Dressed. (J). 1995. 10.19 (*0-606-07550-X*, Pub. by Turtleback) Demco.

— Froggy Gets Dressed. (J). (ps-1). 1997. pap. 7.99 incl. audio (*0-14-095409-0*) Viking Penguin.

— Froggy Gets Dressed: Book & Toy. (Illus.). 32p. (J). 1997. text 19.99 (*0-670-89600-4*, Viking Child) Peng Put Young Read.

***London, Jonathan.** Froggy Goes to Bed. LC 99-55401. (Illus.). 32p. (J). (ps-1). 2000. 15.99 (*0-670-88860-5*, Viking Child) Peng Put Young Read.

London, Jonathan. Froggy Goes to School. (Illus.). 32p. (J). (ps-1). 1996. 15.99 (*0-670-86726-8*, Viking Child) Peng Put Young Read.

— Froggy Goes to School. LC 95-53751. (Illus.). 32p. (J). (ps-1). 1998. pap. 5.99 (*0-14-056247-8*, PuffinBks) Peng Put Young Read.

— Froggy Learns to Swim. LC 94-43077. (Illus.). 32p. (J). (ps-3). 1995. 15.99 (*0-670-85551-0*, Viking) Viking Penguin.

— Froggy Learns to Swim. LC 94-43077. (Illus.). 32p. (J). (ps-1). 1997. pap. 5.99 (*0-14-055312-6*) Viking Penguin.

— Froggy Plays Soccer. LC 98-35725. (Illus.). 32p. (J). (ps-1). 1999. 15.99 (*0-670-88257-7*) Viking Penguin.

— Froggy Se Viste-Froggy Gets Dressed. LC 96-42281. (SPA & ACE). 32p. (J). (ps-1). 1997. 15.99 (*0-670-87414-0*) Viking Penguin.

***London, Jonathan.** Froggy Takes a Bath. (Illus.). 10p. (J). (ps-k). 2000. pap. 6.99 (*0-448-42294-8*, Planet Dexter) Peng Put Young Read.

L

L

— Froggy's First Christmas. LC 99-89442. (Illus.). 32p. (J). (ps-1). 2000. 15.99 (*0-670-89220-3*, Viking Child) Peng Put Young Read.
— Froggy's First Kiss. (Viking Easy-to-Read Ser.). (Illus.). 32p. (J). (ps-1). 1999. pap. 5.99 (*0-14-056570-1*, PuffinBks) Peng Put Young Read.
— Froggy's First Kiss. (Illus.). (J). 1999. 11.44 (*0-606-18404-X*) Turtleback.
London, Jonathan. Froggy's First Kiss. LC 97-18772. (Illus.). 32p. (J). (ps-1). 1998. 14.99 (*0-670-87064-1*) Viking Penguin.
***London, Jonathan.** Froggy's Playtime Activity Book. (Illus.). 16p. (J). (ps-3). 2000. pap. 7.99 (*0-670-89219-X*, Viking Child) Peng Put Young Read.
London, Jonathan. Gray Fox. 1995. 10.19 (*0-606-07599-2*, Pub. by Turtleback) Demco.
— Hip Cat. LC 93-1179. (Illus.). 40p. (J). (gr. k-4). 1993. 14.95 (*0-8118-0315-5*) Chronicle Bks.
— Hip Cat. (Illus.). 40p. (J). (gr. k-4). 1996. pap. 6.95 (*0-8118-1489-0*) Chronicle Bks.
— Honey Paw & Lightfoot. (Illus.). 40p. (J). (ps-3). 1995. 14.95 (*0-8118-0533-6*) Chronicle Bks.
— Honey Paw & Lightfoot. (Illus.). 40p. (J). (ps-3). 1998. pap. 6.95 (*0-8118-2037-8*) Chronicle Bks.
— I See Moon & Moon. (Illus.). 32p. (ps-1). 1998. pap. 5.99 (*0-14-055487-4*) Viking Penguin.
— I See the Moon & the Moon Sees Me. 1998. 11.19 (*0-606-13509-X*, Pub. by Turtleback) Demco.
***London, Jonathan.** Ice Bear & Little Fox. LC 98-10033. (Illus.). (J). (gr. k-4). 1998. 15.99 (*0-525-45907-3*, Dutton Child) Peng Put Young Read.
London, Jonathan. In a Season of Birds. (Rockbook Ser.: No. 7). 24p. (Orig.). 1978. pap. 3.00 (*0-685-20119-8*) J Mudfoot.
— A Koala for Katie: An Adoption Story. LC 93-16085. (Illus.). (J). (ps-1). 1993. lib. bdg. 13.95 (*0-8075-4209-1*) A Whitman.
— A Koala for Katie: An Adoption Story. (Illus.). 24p. (J). (ps-1). 1997. reprint ed. pap. 4.95 (*0-8075-4210-5*) A Whitman.
— Let the Lynx Come In. LC 95-34548. (Illus.). 32p. (J). (gr. k-3). 1996. 15.99 (*1-56402-531-4*) Candlewick Pr.
— Let's Go Froggy! (Illus.). 32p. (J). (ps-1). 1996. pap. 5.99 (*0-14-054991-9*, PuffinBks) Peng Put Young Read.
— Let's Go, Froggy! LC 93-24059. (Illus.). 32p. (J). (ps-1). 1994. 15.99 (*0-670-85055-1*, Viking Child) Peng Put Young Read.
— Let's Go, Froggy! LC 93-24059. 1996. 10.19 (*0-606-09543-8*, Pub. by Turtleback) Demco.
— Like Butter on Pan. 32p. 1998. pap. 5.99 (*0-14-055261-8*) Viking Penguin.
— Like Butter on Pancakes. 1998. 11.19 (*0-606-13571-5*, Pub. by Turtleback) Demco.
— The Lion Who Had Asthma. Levine, Abby, ed. LC 91-16553. (Albert Whitman Concept Bks.). (Illus.). 32p. (J). (ps-2). 1992. lib. bdg. 14.95 (*0-8075-4559-7*) A Whitman.
— The Lion Who Had Asthma. (Illus.). 32p. (J). (ps-1). 1997. reprint ed. pap. 5.95 (*0-8075-4560-0*) A Whitman.
— Liplap's Wish. LC 93-31007. (Illus.). 32p. (J). (ps-3). 1994. 13.95 (*0-8118-0505-0*) Chronicle Bks.
— Liplap's Wish. (Illus.). 32p. (J). (ps-3). 1997. pap. 6.95 (*0-8118-1810-1*) Chronicle Bks.
— Moshi Moshi. LC 97-10612. (Illus.). 32p. (J). (gr. 1-3). 1998. lib. bdg. 21.40 (*0-7613-0110-0*) Millbrook Pr.
— Old Salt, Young Salt. LC 94-14593. (Illus.). 32p. (J). (gr. 1 up). 1996. 16.00 (*0-688-12975-7*) Lothrop.
London, Jonathan. The Owl Who Became the Moon. LC 92-14699. (J). 1996. 11.19 (*0-606-11717-2*, Pub. by Turtleback) Demco.
— Panther: Shadow of the Swamp. LC 99-86437. (Illus.). 2000. 15.99 (*1-56402-623-X*) Candlewick Pr.
London, Jonathan. Puddles. (Illus.). (J). (ps-1). 1999. 5.99 (*0-14-056175-7*, PuffinBks) Peng Put Young Read.
— Puddles. LC 96-52794. (Illus.). 32p. (J). (ps-1). 1997. 15.99 (*0-670-87218-0*) Viking Penguin.
— Red Wolf Country. LC 95-10384. (Illus.). 32p. (J). (ps-4). 1996. 15.99 (*0-525-45191-9*, Dutton Child) Peng Put Young Read.
— Red Wolf Country. 32p. (YA). (ps-3). 1999. pap. 5.99 (*0-14-056450-0*, PuffinBks) Peng Put Young Read.
***London, Jonathan.** Shawn & Keeper: Show & Tell. LC 99-23500. (Illus.). (J). 2000. 13.99 (*0-525-46114-0*, Dutton Child) Peng Put Young Read.
— Shawn & Keeper: Show & Tell. (Puffin Easy-to-Read Program Ser.). (Illus.). 32p. (J). (ps-2). 2000. pap. 3.99 (*0-14-130367-0*, PuffinBks) Peng Put Young Read.
London, Jonathan. Shawn & Keeper & the Birthday Party, Vol. 1. (Illus.). 32p. 1999. pap. 3.99 (*0-14-130407-3*, PuffinBks) Peng Put Young Read.
— Smokey the Bear. LC 98-47409. (J). 1999. 15.99 (*0-525-45596-5*) NAL.
***London, Jonathan.** Snuggle Wuggle. LC 98-41769. (Illus.). 32p. (J). 2000. 13.00 (*0-15-202159-0*) Harcourt.
London, Jonathan. Sugaring off Party. (J). 1999. pap. 5.99 (*0-14-056360-1*) Viking Penguin.
— Sundance. 1999. 14.99 (*0-525-45404-7*) NAL.
— Tell Me a Story. LC 98-9374. (Meet the Author Ser.). (Illus.). 32p. (J). (gr. 2-5). 1998. 14.95 (*1-57274-194-5*, 720) R Owen Pubs.
— Walkin' Rap. LC 94-33713. (Illus.). (J). 2000. 14.95 (*0-688-13994-9*, Wm Morrow); lib. bdg. write for info. (*0-688-13995-7*, Wm Morrow) Morrow Avon.
— The Waterfall. LC 98-7828. (Illus.). 32p. (J). (ps-3). 1999. 15.99 (*0-670-87617-8*) Viking Penguin.
— What Do You Love? LC 97-49517. (Illus.). 32p. (J). (ps-k). 2000. 14.00 (*0-15-201919-7*, Harcourt Child Bks) Harcourt.
— What Newt Could Do for Turtle. LC 95-52361. (Illus.). 40p. (J). (ps-3). 1996. 16.99 (*1-56402-259-5*) Candlewick Pr.
— What Newt Could Do for Turtle. LC 95-10580. (Illus.). 40p. (J). (ps-2). 1998. pap. 6.99 (*0-7636-0580-8*) Candlewick Pr.
***London, Jonathan.** What Newt Could Do for Turtle. (J). 1998. 13.19 (*0-606-13902-8*, Pub. by Turtleback) Demco.
— Where's Home? (J). 1997. 9.19 (*0-606-12087-4*, Pub. by Turtleback) Demco.
London, Jonathan. Who Bop. LC 98-26110. (Illus.). 32p. (J). (ps-1). 2000. lib. bdg. 14.89 (*0-06-027918-4*) HarpC.
***London, Jonathan.** Who Bop. LC 98-26110. (Illus.). 32p. (J). (ps-1). 2000. 14.95 (*0-06-027917-6*) HarpC.
London, Jonathan. Wiggle Waggle. LC 98-10773. (Illus.). 32p. (J). 1999. 13.00 (*0-15-201940-5*) Harcourt.
London, Jonathan, ed. Thirteen Moons on Turtle's Back: A Native American Year of Moons. LC 91-3961. (Illus.). 32p. (J). (ps-8). 1992. 15.95 (*0-399-22141-7*, Philomel) Peng Put Young Read.
***London, Jonathan & Ford, Susan.** Loon Lake. LC 00-8935. (J). 2001. pap. write for info. (*0-8118-2003-3*) Chronicle Bks.
***London, Jonathan & Morin, Paul.** Crocodile: Disappearing Dragon. LC 00-37962. (Illus.). 2001. write for info. (*1-56402-634-5*) Candlewick Pr.
***London, Jonathan & Rex, Michael.** Crunch Munch. LC 00-9144. (Illus.). 2001. write for info. (*0-15-202603-7*, Si2lver Whistle) Harcourt Chldrns Bks.
***London, Jonathan, et al.** The Raft. LC 00-25919. (Illus.). (J). 2001. pap. write for info. (*0-7636-0922-6*) Candlewick Pr.
London, Jonathan, jt. auth. see Bruchac, Joseph.
London, Jonathon. The Candystore Man. LC 96-1047. (Illus.). 24p. (J). (gr. k-3). 1998. 16.00 (*0-688-13241-3*, Wm Morrow) Morrow Avon.
***London, Jonathon.** The Candystore Man. LC 96-1047. (Illus.). 24p. (J). (ps-2). 1998. 15.93 (*0-688-13242-1*, Wm Morrow) Morrow Avon.
London, Jonathon. Hurricane! LC 94-14518. (Illus.). 32p. (J). (gr. k-3). 1998. 16.00 (*0-688-12977-3*, Wm Morrow) Morrow Avon.
***London, Jonathon.** Hurricane! LC 94-14518. (Illus.). 32p. (J). (gr. k up). 1998. 15.89 (*0-688-12978-1*, Wm Morrow) Morrow Avon.
***London, Julia.** The Dangerous Gentleman. Vol. 1. 384p. 2000. mass mkt. 5.99 (*0-440-23561-8*) Bantam Dell.
London, Julia. The Devil's Love. 1998. mass mkt. 5.99 (*0-440-22631-7*) Dell.
***London, Julia.** The Ruthless Charmer. 31p. 2000. mass mkt. 5.99 (*0-440-23562-6*) Dell.
London, Julia. Wicked Angel. 384p. 1999. mass mkt. 5.99 (*0-440-22632-5*) Dell.
***London, Julie.** Garden Projects in a Weekend: Simple Step-by-Step Projects for Maximum Effect with Minimum Effort. LC 99-50240. 2000. pap. 14.95 (*1-58290-017-5*, Pub. by Jrny Editions) Tuttle Pubng.
— Pots & Planters in a Weekend: Simple Step-by-Step Projects for Maximum Effect with Minimum Effort. LC 99-50255. 2000. pap. 14.95 (*1-58290-028-0*) Jrny Editions.
London, Keith, jt. auth. see Wooldridge, Susan.
***London, Kip.** His Kentucky Smile & an Ireland Dream. LC 99-63660. 136p. 1999. pap. text 9.95 (*1-884778-71-2*) Old Mountain.
London, Kurt. Film Music. LC 70-124016. (Literature of Cinema Ser.). 1974. reprint ed. 31.95 (*0-405-01622-0*) Ayer.
London, Kurt, ed. The Soviet Union, a Half-Century of Communism: International Conference on World Politics, 6th, Berlin, 1967. LC 68-28874. 509p. 1968. reprint ed. pap. 157.80 (*0-608-04041-X*, 206477700011) Bks Demand.
— The Soviet Union in World Politics. LC 79-19503. 380p. 1980. text 50.00 (*0-89158-263-0*) Westview.
London, Kurt, ed. see International Conference on World Politics Staff.
***London, L. E.** Revelation Unsealed: A Prophetic Message for Our Age. LC 99-63464. (Illus.). 288p. 1999. pap. 12.99 (*0-9674425-4-0*) Praise Pubg.
— Shadow of the Shroud: The Story of Christ's Burial Cloth. 224p. 2000. pap. 11.99 (*0-9674425-5-9*) Praise Pubg.
London, Larry. The Passion Novena: A Scriptural Rosary. LC 95-73145. 136p. (Orig.). 1996. pap. 5.95 (*0-87973-733-6*) Our Sunday Visitor.
— Salvation Novena. LC 97-66784. 136p. 1997. pap. text 6.95 (*0-87973-917-7*) Our Sunday Visitor.
— The Seven-Day Scriptural Rosary. LC 88-63552. 128p. (Orig.). 1989. pap. 5.95 (*0-87973-524-4*, 524) Our Sunday Visitor.
***London, Louise.** Whitehall & the Jews, 1933-1948: British Immigration Policy & the Holocaust. (Illus.). 327p. (C). 2000. text 59.95 (*0-521-63187-4*) Cambridge U Pr.
London, M. D., ed. see ASTM Committee D-19 on Water.
London Magazine Editors. Coming to London. Lehmann, John, ed. LC 73-152189. (Essay Index Reprint Ser.). 1977. reprint ed. 19.95 (*0-8369-2409-6*) Ayer.
London, Manual. Interpersonal Insight: How People Gain Understanding of Themselves & Others in Organizations. (Industrial-Organizational Psychology Ser.). (Illus.). 352p. 1995. text 50.00 (*0-19-509077-2*) OUP.
London, Manuel. Achieving Performance Excellence in University Administration: A Team Approach to Organizational Change & Employee Development. LC 95-14427. 272p. 1995. 65.00 (*0-275-95246-0*, Praeger Pubs) Greenwood.
— Change Agents: New Roles & Innovation Strategies for Human Resource Professionals. LC 88-42793. (Management Ser.). 408p. 1988. text 38.95 (*1-55542-107-5*) Jossey-Bass.
— Developing Managers: A Guide to Motivating & Preparing People for Successful Managerial Careers. LC 84-43030. (Management Ser.). 276p. 1985. text 37.95 (*0-87589-646-4*) Jossey-Bass.
— Job Feedback: Giving, Seeking, & Using Feedback for Performance Inprovement. LC 96-35237. (Applied Psychology Ser.). 284p. 1997. 49.95 (*0-8058-2474-X*); pap. 27.50 (*0-8058-2475-8*) L Erlbaum Assocs.
— Overcoming Career Barriers: Cognitive & Emotional Reactions & Effective Coping Strategies. LC 97-22282. (Management Ser.). 300p. 1997. write for info. (*0-8058-2579-7*); pap. write for info. (*0-8058-2580-0*) L Erlbaum Assocs.
— Principled Leadership & Business Diplomacy: Values-Based Strategies for Management Development. LC 99-27821. 192p. 1999. 59.95 (*1-56720-347-7*, Quorum Bks) Greenwood.
London, Manuel, ed. Employees, Careers, & Job Creation: Developing Growth-Oriented Human Resource Strategies & Programs. (Management, Social & Behavioral Studies). 344p. 1995. 32.95 (*0-7879-0125-3*) Jossey-Bass.
London, Manuel, et al, eds. Human Resource Forecasting & Strategy Development: Guidelines for Analyzing & Fulfilling Organizational Needs. LC 89-24365. 280p. 1990. 55.00 (*0-89930-436-2*, LHS/, Greenwood Pr) Greenwood.
London, Manuel & Mone, Edward M., eds. Career Growth & Human Resource Strategies: The Role of the Human Resource Professional. LC 87-32281. 357p. 1988. 69.50 (*0-89930-229-7*, LHR/, Quorum Bks) Greenwood.
London, Manuel & Stempf, Stephen A. Managing Careers. (Management Ser.). (Illus.). 324p. 1982. pap. text 17.56 (*0-201-04559-1*) Addison-Wesley.
London, Manuel & Wueste, Richard A. Human Resource Development in Changing Organizations. LC 92-16208. 292p. 1992. 65.00 (*0-89930-741-8*, LCC, Quorum Bks) Greenwood.
London, Manuel, jt. auth. see Mone, Edward M.
London, Manuel, jt. auth. see Sessa, Valerie I.
London, Manuel, jt. auth. see Tornow, Walter W.
London, Marcus. Six Ladders of Learning: 1867: About How Things Are Made, Country, City & Rural. 250p. 1996. reprint ed. pap. 25.00 (*0-87556-835-1*) Saifer.
London, Marilyn R., jt. ed. see Selig, Ruth O.
London, Martin, jt. auth. see Dill, Barbara.
London, Mary. Look Fatter in Jeans: An Adventure in Growing Older & Wiser. LC 97-155546. (Illus.). vi, 306p. (Orig.). 1997. pap. 12.95 (*0-9656648-0-5*) Boomer Pubns.
London Mathematical Society Committee, ed. see Hardy, Godfrey H.
London, Mel & London, Sheryl. The Gourmet Garage Cookbook: 185 Recipes Using Fresh & Exciting Ingredients from Around the World. LC 99-15022. (Illus.). 494p. 2000. 30.00 (*0-8050-5411-1*) H Holt & Co.
London, Mel, jt. auth. see London, Sheryl.
London Mercury Staff. Second Mercury Story Book. LC 79-37553. (Short Story Index Reprint Ser.). 1977. reprint ed. 25.95 (*0-8369-4112-8*) Ayer.
***London, Michael E.** Landslide & Subsidence Liability: 9/99 Update. Briggs, Donald R., ed. LC 73-620016. 282p. 1999. ring bd. 59.00 (*0-7626-0361-5*, RE-31037) Cont Ed Bar-CA.
London, Ministry of Defense, Naval Library Staff. Author & Subject Catalogues of the Naval Library, Ministry of Defence, 5 vols., Set. 1970. 570.00 (*0-8161-0755-6*, G K Hall & Co) Mac Lib Ref.
***London Missionary Society Staff.** The London Missionary Society in Southern Africa, 1799-1999: Historical Essays in Celebration of the Bicentenary of the LMS in Southern Africa. rev. ed. De Gruchy, John W., ed. LC 00-36683. 240p. (C). 2000. pap. text 24.95 (*0-8214-1349-X*) Ohio U Pr.
London Missionary Society Staff. London Missionary Society's Report of the Proceedings Against the Late Rev. J. Smith of Demerara, Who Was Tried Under Martial Law & Condemned to Death, on a Charge of Aiding & Assisting in a Rebellion of Negro Slaves. LC 78-79809. 204p. 1970. reprint ed. lib. bdg. 49.50 (*0-8371-1506-X*, LMS&) Greenwood.
London, Nancy R. Japanese Corporate Philanthropy. 160p. 1990. text 55.00 (*0-19-506424-0*) OUP.
London News Staff. Marching to War. 192p. 1989. 24.95 (*0-385-25217-X*) Doubleday.
London, Oscar. Dr. Generic Will See You Now: 33 Ways You Can Survive Managed Care. LC 95-26085. 160p. (Orig.). 1996. pap. 11.95 (*0-89815-816-8*) Ten Speed Pr.
— Dr. Sunshine: A Novel. LC 92-34863. 224p. 1993. pap. 9.95 (*0-89815-526-6*) Ten Speed Pr.
London, Perry. The Modes & Morals of Psychotherapy. 2nd ed. LC 84-29769. (Clinical & Community Psychology Ser.). 350p. (C). 1986. pap. 27.95 (*0-89116-350-6*); text 79.95 (*0-89116-290-9*) Hemisp Pub.
London, Peter. No More Secondhand Art: Awakening the Artist Within. LC 89-42618. 208p. (Orig.). 1989. pap. 14.95 (*0-87773-482-8*, Pub. by Shambhala Pubns) Random.
— Step Outside: Community-Based Art Education. LC 93-11569. (Illus.). 138p. (C). 1994. pap. text 25.00 (*0-435-08794-0*, 08794) Heinemann.
***London Rape Crisis Centre Staff.** Sexual Violence: The Reality for Women. 1999. pap. 17.95 (*0-7043-4436-X*, Pub. by Womens Press) Trafalgar.
London, Rick. Dreaming Close By. LC 86-70316. 64p. 1986. 5.00 (*0-917588-14-2*) O Bks.
— The Motion Is a Fall. 1985. pap. 5.00 (*0-917588-11-8*) Trike.
— The Prone Body Under. 1982. pap. 3.00 (*0-917588-05-3*) Trike.
London, Robert. Nonroutine Problems: Doing Mathematics. (Illus.). 60p. (Orig.). (YA). (gr. 10 up). 1989. pap. text 19.95 (*0-939765-30-6*, G117) Janson Pubns.
London, Roy. The Amazing Activity of Charley Contrare & the Ninety-Eighth Street Gang. 1975. pap. 5.25 (*0-8222-0023-6*) Dramatists Play.
— Disneyland on Parade: Three Related Short Plays. 1985. pap. 5.25 (*0-8222-0315-4*) Dramatists Play.
— Mrs. Murray's Farm. 1977. pap. 5.25 (*0-8222-0788-5*) Dramatists Play.
London, Sara. Firehorse Max. LC 96-70885. (Michael di Capua Bks.). (Illus.). 32p. (J). (ps up). 1997. 14.95 (*0-06-205094-X*) HarpC Child Bks.
— Firehorse Max. LC 96-70885. (Michael di Capua Bks.). (Illus.). 32p. (J). (ps up). 1997. lib. bdg. 14.89 (*0-06-205095-8*) HarpC Child Bks.
***London, Sara.** Good Luck Glasses. LC 99-29207. (Hello Reader! Ser.). (Illus.). (J). 2000. pap. 3.99 (*0-590-97212-X*) Scholastic Inc.
London School of Economics & Political Science Dep. Annual Survey of English Law, 1928-1940, 13 vols. LC 87-83497. 5000p. 1988. reprint ed. lib. bdg. 1170.00 (*0-912004-63-0*) Gaunt.
London School of Economics & Political Science Dep, jt. auth. see Desai, Meghnad.
***London Science Museum Staff.** Electricity. (Eyewitness Books). 64p. (J). (gr. 4-7). 2000. 15.95 (*0-7894-5577-3*, D K Ink) DK Pub Inc.
London, Sheldon I. How to Comply with Federal Employee Laws. 1991. pap. 19.95 (*0-9613262-2-0*) London Pub.
— How to Comply with Federal Employee Laws: A Complete Guide for Employers Written in Plain English. 3rd rev. ed. LC 97-61981. (Illus.). 200p. 1998. pap. 39.95 (*0-9661129-0-3*) VIZIA.
— How to Comply with Federal Employee Laws: A Complete Guide for Employers Written in Plain English. 4th rev. ed. LC 98-61981. 200p. 1998. pap. 39.95 (*0-9661129-1-1*) VIZIA.
***London, Sheldon I.** How to Comply with Federal Employee Laws: A Complete Guide for Employers Written in Plain English. 5th rev. ed. LC 97-61981. 240p. (C). 1999. pap. 39.95 (*0-9661129-2-X*) VIZIA.
London, Sheldon I. How to Comply with Federal Employee Laws: Practical Advice for Employers. 160p. 1990. pap. 19.95 (*0-9613262-1-2*) London Pub.
***London, Sherry.** FrontPage 2000 Professional Results. (Illus.). 2000. pap. 29.99 (*0-07-212269-2*) McGrw-H Intl.
— Illustrator X F/X & Design. (Illus.). 480p. 2000. pap. 49.99 (*1-57610-750-7*) Coriolis Grp.
London, Sherry. Illustrator 8 F/X & Design. LC 99-11321. 1999. 49.99 (*1-57610-408-7*) Coriolis Grp.
***London, Sherry.** Painter 6 F/X & Design. LC 00-21571. (Illus.). 335p. 2000. pap. text. write for info. (*1-57610-611-X*) Coriolis Grp.
London, Sherry. Painter 6 in Depth, 1. 1999. pap. text 49.99 (*1-57610-381-1*) Coriolis Grp.
***London, Sherry.** Photoshop 5 Interactive Course. LC 98-66765. 1998. 49.99 (*1-57169-158-8*) Sams.
London, Sherry. Photoshop 4 Interactive Course. LC 96-37574. 884p. 1997. 49.99 (*1-57169-036-0*) Sams.
— Photoshop Textures Magic. 288p. 1997. 39.99 (*1-56830-368-8*) Hayden.
London, Sherry & Reinfeld, Eric. Real World after Effects. LC 98-161690. (Illus.). 504p. 1997. pap. 44.95 incl. cd-rom (*0-201-68839-5*) Peachpit Pr.
London, Sherry, jt. auth. see Reinfeld, Eric.
London, Sheryl. Seafood Celebration. 1998. 10.99 (*0-7858-0927-9*) Bk Sales Inc.
London, Sheryl & London, Mel. A Seafood Celebration: Healthful, Festive, Easy-to-Prepare Recipes for the Casual Cook or the Connoisseur. LC 93-19727. (Illus.). 1993. 30.00 (*0-671-76813-1*) S&S Trade.
London, Sheryl, jt. auth. see London, Mel.
London, Sondra, jt. auth. see Rolling, Danny.
London, Steve, jt. auth. see Chihal, H. Jane.
London, Steven H., et al, eds. The Re-Education of the American Working Class, 31. LC 90-36778. (Contributions in Labor Studies: No. 31). 312p. 1990. 65.00 (*0-313-26785-5*, LRB, Greenwood Pr) Greenwood.
London Times Staff. American Writing Today. Angoff, Allan, ed. LC 74-134144. (Essay Index Reprint Ser.). 1977. 30.95 (*0-8369-2030-9*) Ayer.
— Fifty Years: Memories & Contrasts. LC 71-843431. (Essay Index Reprint Ser.). 1977. reprint ed. 30.95 (*0-8369-1935-1*) Ayer.
— Modern Essays. LC 73-86788. (Essay Index Reprint Ser.). 1977. 23.95 (*0-8369-1630-1*) Ayer.
— Third Leaders, Reprinted from The Times. LC 68-16980. (Essay Index Reprint Ser.). 1977. 19.95 (*0-8369-0946-1*) Ayer.
London, Todd. The Artistic Home. LC 87-33600. 112p. (Orig.). (C). 1988. pap. 3.95 (*0-930452-76-3*) Theatre Comm.
London, Todd, ed. Contemporary American Monologues for Men. LC 97-5738. 160p. (Orig.). 1997. pap. 10.95 (*1-55936-134-4*) Theatre Comm.
London University, Board of Studies in History Sta. Tudor Studies Presented to Albert Frederick Pollard. Seton-Watson, Robert W., ed. LC 69-17582. (Essay Index Reprint Ser.). 1977. 20.95 (*0-8369-0083-9*) Ayer.
London University College Staff, ed. see Rady, Martyn C.
London-Vargas, Nasha. Faces of Diversity. LC 98-90375. 1999. pap. 10.95 (*0-533-12777-7*) Vantage.
London, W. T., ed. see International Symposium on Basic Progress in Blood.
Londonbridge Staff. Spice Girls: The Hottest Band Around. 1997. pap. text 9.99 (*0-7535-0126-0*) London Brdge.

An Asterisk (*) at the beginning of an entry indicates that the title is appearing for the first time.

Londong, W., et al, eds. Long-Term Intragastric pH Measurement in Man: Basic & Methodological Aspects - Journal: Digestive Diseases, Vol. 8, Suppl. 1, 1990. (Illus.). vi, 98p. 1990. pap. 29.75 (*3-8055-5274-2*) S Karger.

***Londono, Carmina.** Free Trade Area of the Americas (FTAA) Conformity Assessment Infrastructure. 94p. 1999. per. 9.00 (*0-16-058875-8*) USGPO.

Londono, Juan L. Pobreza, Desigualdad y Formacion del Capital Humano en America Latina, 1950-2025. (World Bank Latin American & Caribbean Studies).Tr. of Poverty, Inequality, & Human Capital Development in Latin America, 1950-2025. (SPA.). 48p. 1996. pap. 22.00 (*0-8213-3692-4*, 13692) World Bank.

— Poverty, Inequality, & Human Capital Development in Latin America, 1950-2025. LC 96-16979. (World Bank Latin American & Caribbean Studies). 48p. 1996. pap. 22.00 (*0-8213-3630-4*, 13630) World Bank.

Londono, Margarita. Tortuguita Se Perdio.Tr. of Little Turtle Got Lost. (SPA., Illus.). 52p. (J). (ps-2). 1997. 5.95 (*958-04-3456-5*, Pub. by SM Ediciones) IBD Ltd.

Londraville, Janis. On Poetry, Painting, & Politics: The Letters of May Morris & John Quinn. LC 96-20004. (Illus.). 232p. 1997. 38.50 (*0-945636-96-2*) Susquehanna U Pr.

Londraville, Janis & Londraville, Richard, eds. Too Long a Sacrifice: The Letters of Maud Gonne & John Quinn. LC 98-27786. (Illus.). 320p. 1999. 45.00 (*1-57591-024-1*) Susquehanna U Pr.

Londraville, Richard, jt. ed. see Londraville, Janis.

Londre, Felicia H. The History of World Theater: From the English Restoration to the Present. LC 75-1959. (Illus.). 656p. 1999. pap. 39.95 (*0-8264-1167-3*) Continuum.

Londre, Felicia H., ed. Love's Labour's Lost: Critical Essays. LC 97-526. (Shakespeare Criticism Ser.: Vol. 13). (Illus.). 496p. 1997. text 110.00 (*0-8153-0984-8*, H1643) Garland.

Londre, Felicia H. & Watermeier, Daniel J. The History of North American Theater: The United States, Canada, & Mexico: From Pre-Columbian Times to the Present. LC 66-28138. (Illus.). 600p. 1998. 95.00 (*0-8264-1079-0*) Continuum.

***Londre, Felicia H. & Watermeier, Daniel J.** History of North American Theater: The United States, Canada & Mexico; from Pre-Columbian Times to the Present. (Illus.). 544p. 2000. pap. 39.95 (*0-8264-1233-5*) Continuum.

Londre, Felicia H., tr. see Chedid, Andree.

***Londregan, John B.** Legislative Institutions & Ideology in Chile. (Political Economy of Institutions & Decisions Ser.). (Illus.). 328p. (C). 2000. 59.95 (*0-521-77084-X*) Cambridge U Pr.

Londregan, R. P. Life Safety in Underground Rail Systems, TR 833: The Australian Effort. 1983. 4.35 (*0-685-07672-5*, TR83-3) Society Fire Protect.

Londres, Albert. The Road to Buenos Aires. 260p. 1974. lib. bdg. 59.95 (*0-8490-0959-6*) Gordon Pr.

Lone & McGormack. Korea since 1850. 1994. pap. text. write for info. (*0-582-80138-9*, Pub. by Addison-Wesley) Longman.

Lone Dog, Louise. Strange Journey: The Vision Life of a Psychic Indian Woman. Powell, Patricia, ed. LC 89-13484. (Illus.). 105p. 1990. reprint ed. pap. 8.95 (*0-87961-207-X*) Naturegraph.

Lone, E. Miriam, jt. auth. see Harper, Lathrop C.

Lone Eagle Publishing Staff. Special Effects & Stunts Directory, 1998-1999. 3rd ed. 500p. 1998. pap. 60.00 (*1-58065-008-2*, Pub. by Lone Eagle Pub) Natl Bk Netwk.

***Lone Eagle Publishing Staff, ed.** Cinematographers, Production Designers, Costume Designers & Film Editors Directory. 7th ed. 650p. 1999. pap. 75.00 (*1-58065-017-1*, Pub. by Lone Eagle Pub) Natl Bk Netwk.

Lone Eagle Publishing Staff, ed. Film Producers, Studios, Agents & Casting Directors Guide 1999. 7th ed. 650p. 2000. pap. 75.00 (*1-58065-007-4*, Pub. by Lone Eagle Pub) Natl Bk Netwk.

Lone, Farooq A. Palaeoethnobotany: Plants & Ancient Man in Kashmir. (C). 1993. text 42.00 (*81-204-0717-2*, Pub. by Oxford IBH) S Asia.

Lone, Farooq A., et al. Palaeoethnobotany: Plants & Ancient Man in Kashmir. (Illus.). 288p. (C). 1993. text 82.00 (*90-6191-944-4*, Pub. by A A Balkema) Ashgate Pub Co.

***Lone, Stewart.** Army, Empire & Politics in Meiji Japan: The Three Careers of General Katsura Tareo. LC 99-88718. 2000. text 65.00 (*0-312-23289-6*) St Martin.

Lone, Susan T. De, see De Lone, Susan T.

Lonegren, Sig. The Pendulum Kit. 128p. 1990. per. 19.95 (*0-671-69140-6*) S&S Trade.

Lonegren, Sig, compiled by. The Dowsing Rod Kit. (Illus.). 160p. 1995. boxed set 27.95 (*0-8048-3049-5*) Tuttle Pubng.

***Lonely Planet Publications Staff.** Lonely Planet Australia Travel Atlas. (Travel Atlases Ser.). (Illus.). 128p. 2000. pap. 14.95 (*1-86450-065-4*) Lonely Planet.

— Lonely Planet CitySync. 2000. pap. 49.95 (*1-86450-228-2*) Lonely Planet.

— Lonely Planet Southern Africa Travel Atlas. (Travel Atlases Ser.). (Illus.). 128p. 2000. pap. 14.95 (*1-86450-101-4*) Lonely Planet.

— Lonely Planet Thailand, Vietnam, Laos & Cambodia Travel Atlas. (Travel Atlases Ser.). (Illus.). 112p. 2000. pap. 14.95 (*1-86450-102-2*) Lonely Planet.

***Lonely Planet Publications Staff, ed.** Lonely Planet Australia. 10th ed. (Travel Guides Ser.). (Illus.). 1082p. 2000. pap. text 24.95 (*1-86450-068-9*) Lonely Planet.

— Lonely Planet Chile & Easter Island. 5th ed. (Travel Guides Ser.). (Illus.). 2000. pap. text 19.95 (*1-86450-088-3*) Lonely Planet.

— Lonely Planet Hawaii. 5th ed. (Travel Guides Ser.). (Illus.). 2000. pap. text 19.95 (*1-86450-047-6*) Lonely Planet.

— Lonely Planet O'ahu. (Travel Guides Ser.). (Illus.). 288p. 2000. pap. text 14.95 (*1-86450-048-4*) Lonely Planet.

— Munich. (Travel Guides Ser.). (Illus.). 232p. 2000. pap. 14.95 (*1-86450-055-7*) Lonely Planet.

***Lonely Planet Publications Staff & Schulte Peevers, Andrea.** Berlin: Lonely Planet. 2nd ed. (Travel Guides Ser.). (Illus.). 296p. 2000. pap. 15.95 (*0-86442-790-5*) Lonely Planet.

***Lonely Planet Publications Staff, et al.** Amsterdam: Lonely Planet. 2nd ed. (Travel Guides Ser.). (Illus.). 224p. 2000. pap. 14.99 (*0-86442-789-1*) Lonely Planet.

— South-West France. (Travel Guides Ser.). (Illus.). 384p. 2000. pap. text 16.95 (*0-86442-794-8*) Lonely Planet.

Lonely Planet Publications Staff, ed. see Callan, Lou.

Lonely Planet Publications Staff, ed. see Fallon, Steve.

Lonely Planet Publications Staff, ed. see Flynn, Rob.

Lonely Planet Publications Staff, ed. see Geirlich, Marisa.

Lonely Planet Publications Staff, ed. see Hall, Nikki & Valent, Dani.

Lonely Planet Publications Staff, ed. see Hellander, Paul.

Lonely Planet Publications Staff, ed. see Oliver, Jeanne.

Lonely Planet Publications Staff, ed. see Valent, Dani.

Lonely Planet Publications Staff, ed. see Webb, Sally.

Lonely Planet Publications Staff, ed. see Willett, David.

Lonely Planet Publications Staff, ed. see Williams, Nicola.

***Lonely Planet Staff.** Amsterdam. 1999. pap. 5.95 (*1-86450-081-6*) Lonely Planet.

Lonely Planet Staff. Budapest. 1999. pap. 5.95 (*1-86450-077-8*) Lonely Planet.

— Cape Town. 1999. pap. 5.95 (*1-86450-076-X*) Lonely Planet.

— Istanbul. 1999. pap. 5.95 (*1-86450-080-8*) Lonely Planet.

***Lonely Planet Staff.** Jerusalem. 1999. pap. 5.95 (*1-86450-096-4*) Lonely Planet.

Lonely Planet Staff. Lonely Planet Afrique Du Sud. 3rd ed. 1998. pap. 29.95 (*2-84070-078-6*) Lonely Planet.

— Lonely Planet Andalousie. (Lonely Planet Travel Guides Ser.). 1999. pap. text 19.95 (*2-84070-083-2*) Lonely Planet.

— Lonely Planet Australie. 3rd ed. (Lonely Planet Travel Guides Ser.). 1999. pap. text 33.95 (*2-84070-085-9*) Lonely Planet.

— Lonely Planet Iles Grecques. 4th ed. (Lonely Planet Travel Guides Ser.). 1999. pap. text 22.95 (*2-84070-084-0*) Lonely Planet.

— Lonely Planet Laos. 3rd ed. (Lonely Planet Travel Guides Ser.). 1999. pap. text 22.95 (*2-84070-088-3*) Lonely Planet.

— Sacred India. (Illus.). 176p. 1999. pap. 39.95 (*1-86450-063-8*) Lonely Planet.

— Washington, D.C. 1999. pap. 5.95 (*1-86450-078-6*) Lonely Planet.

***Lonely Planet Staff & Hunt, Errol.** South Pacific. (Travel Guides Ser.). (Illus.). 864p. 2000. pap. 24.95 (*0-86442-717-4*) Lonely Planet.

***Lonely Planet Staff & Simonis, Damien.** Florence. (Travel Guides Ser.). (Illus.). 224p. 2000. pap. 14.95 (*0-86442-785-9*) Lonely Planet.

— Venice. (Travel Guides Ser.). (Illus.). 288p. 2000. pap. 14.95 (*0-86442-786-7*) Lonely Planet.

***Lonely Planet Staff & Ver Berkmoes, Ryan.** Russia, Ukraine & Belarus: Lonely Planet. 2nd ed. (Travel Guides Ser.). (Illus.). 1000 p. 2000. pap. 27.95 (*0-86442-713-1*) Lonely Planet.

***Lonely Planet Staff, et al.** Central Asia: Lonely Planet. 2nd ed. (Travel Guides Ser.). (Illus.). 576p. 2000. pap. 24.95 (*0-86442-673-9*) Lonely Planet.

— East Africa: Lonely Planet. 5th ed. (Travel Guides Ser.). (Illus.). 750p. 2000. pap. 24.95 (*0-86442-676-3*) Lonely Planet.

— Fiji: Lonely Planet. 5th ed. (Travel Guides Ser.). (Illus.). 312p. 2000. pap. 15.99 (*0-86442-679-8*) Lonely Planet.

— Germany: Lonely Planet. 2nd ed. (Travel Guides Ser.). (Illus.). 880p. 2000. pap. 21.95 (*0-86442-788-3*) Lonely Planet.

— Ireland: Lonely Planet. 4th ed. (Travel Guides Ser.). (Illus.). 768p. 2000. pap. 19.95 (*0-86442-753-0*) Lonely Planet.

— Jordan: Lonely Planet. 4th ed. (Travel Guides Ser.). (Illus.). 304p. 2000. pap. 17.95 (*0-86442-694-1*) Lonely Planet.

— Kenya: Lonely Planet. 4th ed. (Travel Guides Ser.). (Illus.). 448p. 2000. pap. 19.95 (*0-86442-695-X*) Lonely Planet.

— Tahiti & French Polynesia: Lonely Planet. 5th ed. (Travel Guides Ser.). (Illus.). 400p. 2000. pap. 17.99 (*0-86442-725-5*) Lonely Planet.

Loneragan, J. F. Copper in Soils & Plants. 1981. text 104.00 (*0-12-455520-9*) Acad Pr.

***Lonergan.** Car Games. 24p. 2000. pap. 7.99 (*0-307-30478-7*) Gldn Bks Pub Co.

— Dog Tricks. (Golden Bks.). 24p. 2000. pap. 7.99 (*0-307-30480-9*) Gldn Bks Pub Co.

— Statistics for Business & Economics. 552p. (C). 1998. pap. text 46.96 (*0-536-01720-4*) Pearson Custom.

Lonergan, Anne & Richards, Caroline, eds. Thomas Berry & the New Cosmology: In Dialogue with Gregory Baum, Margaret Brennan, Stephen Dunn, James Farris, Caroline Richards, Donald Senior, & Brian Swimme. LC 87-40528. 120p. (Orig.). (C). 1987. pap. 7.95 (*0-89622-337-X*) Twenty-Third.

Lonergan, Bernard. Doctrinal Pluralism. LC 70-155364. (Pere Marquette Lectures). 1971. 15.00 (*0-87462-503-3*) Marquette.

— For a New Political Economy, Vol. 21. McShane, Philip J., ed. (Collected Works of Bernard Lonergan: Vol. 21). 336p. 1999. text 60.00 (*0-8020-4385-2*); pap. text 21.95 (*0-8020-8222-X*) U of Toronto Pr.

— Insight. Crowe, Frederick E. & Doran, Robert M., eds. (Collected Works of Bernard Lonergan: No. 3). 900p. 1992. text 95.00 (*0-8020-3454-3*); pap. text 35.00 (*0-8020-3455-1*) U of Toronto Pr.

— Macroeconomic Dynamics: An Essay in Circulation Analysis. Lawrence, Frederick G. et al, eds. 368p. 1999. text 60.00 (*0-8020-4384-4*) U of Toronto Pr.

— Macroeconomic Dynamics: An Essay in Circulation Analysis. Lawrence, Frederick G. et al, eds. 368p. 1999. pap. text 21.95 (*0-8020-8195-9*) U of Toronto Pr.

— Method in Theology. LC 78-181008. 1984. 14.95 (*0-8164-2204-4*) Harper SF.

— Method in Theology. 403p. 1990. pap. text 19.95 (*0-8020-6809-X*) U of Toronto Pr.

— Philosophical & Theological Papers, 1958-1964. Croken, Robert C. et al, eds. 304p. 1996. text 60.00 (*0-8020-3473-X*) U of Toronto Pr.

— Philosophical & Theological Papers, 1958-1964. Croken, Robert C. et al, eds. (Collected Works of Bernard Lonergan: Vol. 6). 304p. 1996. pap. text 19.95 (*0-8020-3474-8*) U of Toronto Pr.

— Subject. LC 68-22238. (Aquinas Lectures). (C). 1968. 15.00 (*0-87462-133-X*) Marquette.

— Topics in Education: Lectures on the Philosophy of Education. Doran, Robert M. & Crowe, Frederick E., eds. (Collected Works of Bernard Lonergan: No. 10). 304p. 1993. text 60.00 (*0-8020-3440-3*); pap. text 24.95 (*0-8020-3441-1*) U of Toronto Pr.

— Understanding & Being. Crowe, Frederick E. & Doran, Robert M., eds. (Collected Works of Bernard Lonergan: Vol. 5). 476p. 1990. text 60.00 (*0-8020-3987-1*); pap. text 19.95 (*0-8020-3989-8*) U of Toronto Pr.

— Verbum: Word & Idea in Aquinas. (Collected Works of Bernard Lonergan: Vol. 2). 320p. 1997. pap. text 24.95 (*0-8020-7988-1*) U of Toronto Pr.

Lonergan, Bernard J. Collected Works of Bernard J. Lonergan. Crowe, Frederick E. & Doran, Robert M., eds. 349p. 1988. text 37.50 (*0-8020-3438-1*) U of Toronto Pr.

Lonergan, Bernard J., jt. auth. see Stewart, W. A.

Lonergan, Bernard J. F. Understanding & Being: An Introduction & Companion to Insight. Morelli, Elizabeth A. & Morelli, Mark D., eds. (Toronto Studies in Theology: Vol. 5). xii, 368p. 1980. lib. bdg. 99.95 (*0-88946-909-1*) E Mellen.

Lonergan, Carroll V. Brave Boys of Old Fort Ticonderoga. LC 87-22144. 144p. (YA). (gr. 6 up). 1987. pap. 7.95 (*1-55787-018-7*, NY16028, Empire State Bks) Hrt of the Lakes.

Lonergan, D. F., jt. auth. see Studwell, William E.

Lonergan, E. Peru: The Next Step. 2nd ed. (Illus.). 200p. 1994. 170.00 (*1-85564-455-X*, Pub. by Euromoney) Am Educ Systs.

Lonergan, Edmund. Clinical Manual of Geriatric Medicine. 632p. (Orig.). (C). 1996. pap. text 34.95 (*0-8385-1094-9*, A1094-0, Apple Lange Med) McGraw.

***Lonergan, Elaine.** Detective Kit. (Booktivity Ser.). (Illus.). 24p. (J). (ps-3). 2000. 7.99 (*0-307-30479-5*, 30479, Goldn Books) Gldn Bks Pub Co.

Lonergan, Elaine. The Sea's Many Color. LC 93-61820. (Shamu's Little Library). (Illus.). 12p. (J). (ps). 1994. 5.95 (*1-884506-01-1*) Third Story.

— Sir Winston Walrus & the Great Rescue. (Shamu & His Crew Adventure Ser.). (Illus.). 32p. (J). (gr. k-3). 1994. 5.95 (*1-884506-06-2*) Third Story.

Lonergan, Jean N., et al. Homecare Management of the Bone Marrow Transplant Patient. 2nd ed. 160p. 1995. pap. 33.75 (*0-86720-744-2*) Jones & Bartlett.

Lonergan, Joan P. Unlocking Your Potential: A Handbook for Personal Growth. (Illus.). 72p. 1993. student ed. 9.95 (*1-884168-00-0*) Chameleon Pub.

***Lonergan, Kenneth.** This Is Our Youth. 1999. pap. 5.25 (*0-8222-1703-1*) Dramatists Play.

— This Is Our Youth. LC 99-56899. 96p. 2000. pap. 11.95 (*1-58567-018-9*, Pub. by Overlook Pr) Penguin Putnam.

— The Waverly Gallery. 2000. pap. 13.00 (*0-8021-3756-3*, Grove) Grove-Atltic.

Lonergan, Leonard. The Iron Road. LC 81-51173. 68p. 1981. pap. 10.00 (*0-912292-66-0*) Smith.

Lonergan, Mark. Blues-Rock Guitar Handbook: Rock Lines. 56p. 1997. 9.95 incl. audio compact disk (*0-7866-2704-2*, 94172BCD) Mel Bay.

— Rock Guitar Handbook. 40p. 1997. 9.95 incl. audio compact disk (*0-7866-2705-0*, 94173BCD) Mel Bay.

Lonergan, Mark, jt. auth. see Bay, William.

Lonergan, Mary, jt. auth. see Hodge, Alice.

Lonergan, Stephen & Brooks, David. Watershed: The Role of Fresh Water in Israeli-Palestinian Conflict. 220p. 1994. pap. write for info. (*0-88936-719-1*) IDRC Bks.

Lonergan, Thomas A. BioTools: High School Biology Laboratory Manual. rev. ed. (Illus.). 290p. (Orig.). 1997. pap. text 19.95 (*1-890264-03-2*) Health-Science.

— BioWeb Search: Internet Biology Lessons. (Illus.). 168p. 1998. pap. text 29.95 (*1-890264-07-5*) Health-Science.

— Cellular Physiology: A Laboratory Manual. (Illus.). 102p. (Orig.). (C). 1995. pap. text, lab manual ed. write for info. (*1-890264-02-4*) Health-Science.

— Investigations of Form & Function. 2nd ed. (Illus.). 118p. (C). 1996. pap. text, lab manual ed. write for info. (*1-890264-00-8*) Health-Science.

— Laboratory Skills for Biology Teachers. (Illus.). 49p. (Orig.). 1993. pap. text, lab manual ed. write for info. (*1-890264-04-0*) Health-Science.

— Understanding Cancer & Its Treatments. (Illus.). 20p. 1992. pap. text 19.95 (*1-890264-08-3*) Health-Science.

Lonergan, Thomas A., et al. Cell & Molecular Biology: A Laboratory Manual. (Illus.). 150p. (Orig.). (C). 1996. pap. text, lab manual ed. write for info. (*1-890264-01-6*) Health-Science.

Lones, T. East, ed. see Wright, A. R.

Lonetree, G. L. Follow-Up on the Effectiveness of Tribally Operated Vocational Rehabilitation Projects. 70p. 1991. pap. text. write for info. (*1-888557-27-3*, 100100) No Ariz Univ.

— Results of a Survey of the American Indian Vocational Rehabilitation (Section 130) Projects Regarding Training & Technical Assistance Needs. 175p. 1989. pap. text. write for info. (*1-888557-34-6*, 100101) No Ariz Univ.

— Third-Year Follow-Up of the Section 130 Tribally Operated Vocational Rehabilitation Projects. 55p. 1992. pap. text. write for info. (*1-888557-18-4*, 100099) No Ariz Univ.

Lonetto, Richard. Children's Conceptions of Death. LC 79-24334. (Death & Suicide Ser.: Vol. 3). (Illus.). 238p. 1980. 34.95 (*0-8261-2550-6*) Springer Pub.

— Rhythm. 1988. 19.95 (*0-385-25105-X*) Doubleday.

Loney, Alan. Sidetracks: Notebooks, 1976-1991. LC 98-216930. 80p. 1998. pap. 14.95 (*1-86940-194-8*, Pub. by Auckland Univ) Paul & Co Pubs.

Loney, Glenn, ed. California Gold-Rush Plays. LC 83-61191. Orig. Title: American Pioneer Drama. 1983. 34.00 (*0-933826-34-6*); pap. 12.95 (*0-933826-35-4*) PAJ Pubns.

Loney, Glenn, jt. ed. see Helfer, Richard.

Loney, Glenn M., ed. Musical Theatre in America: Papers & Proceedings of the Conference on the Musical Theatre in America, 8. LC 83-8913. (Contributions in Drama & Theatre Studies: No. 8). (Illus.). 441p. 1984. 59.95 (*0-313-23524-4*, LMT/) Greenwood.

Loney, Glenn M., ed. see Wharton, Edith & Fitch, Clyde.

Loney, James R. A Dream of the Tattered Man & Other Meditations on Death & Love in Georgia. 264p. Date not set. pap. 17.00 (*0-8028-4280-1*) Eerdmans.

Loney, Jan, ed. The Young Hyperactive Child: Answers to Questions about Diagnosis, Prognosis & Treatment. LC 87-178. (Journal of Children in Contemporary Society: Vol. 19, Nos. 1-2). 178p. (Orig.). 1987. text 49.95 (*0-86656-670-8*) Haworth Pr.

Loney, Kevin. Oracle DBA Handbook. (Oracle Press Ser.). 608p. 1994. pap. text 34.95 (*0-07-881182-1*) McGraw.

— Oracle DBA Handbook: 7.3 Edition. 2nd ed. LC 97-132496. 1996. pap. text 39.99 (*0-07-882289-0*) Osborne-McGraw.

— Oracle 8 DBA Handbook. (Illus.). 822p. (Orig.). 1997. pap. text 44.99 (*0-07-882406-0*, Oracle Press) Osborne-McGraw.

Loney, Kevin & Carmichael, Rachel. Oracle SQL & PL/SQL Annotated Archives. LC 99-158016. 585p. 1998. pap. text 49.95 (*0-07-882536-9*) Osborne-McGraw.

***Loney, Kevin & Theriault, Marlene.** Oracle 8i DBA Handbook. 979p. 1999. pap. text 49.99 incl. cd-rom (*0-07-212188-2*, Oracle Press) Osborne-McGraw.

Loney, Kevin, et al. Advanced Oracle Tuning & Administration: Advanced Tools for Managing & Tuning Your Database. LC 97-122824. 560p. 1996. pap. 39.99 incl. cd-rom (*0-07-882241-6*) Osborne-McGraw.

— Oracle8 Advanced Tuning & Administration. 660p. 1998. pap. text 49.99 (*0-07-882534-2*) Osborne-McGraw.

Loney, Kevin, jt. auth. see Koch, George B.

Loney, Kevin, jt. auth. see Koch, George K.

***Loney, Koch.** Oracle 8I: Complete Reference. (Illus.). 1392p. 2000. pap. text 69.99 (*0-07-212364-8*, Oracle Press) Osborne-McGraw.

Loney, Martin. The Pursuit of Division: Race, Gender & Preferential Hiring in Canada. 360p. 1998. pap. 22.95 (*0-7735-1769-3*, Pub. by McG-Queens Univ Pr); text 65.00 (*0-7735-1744-8*, Pub. by McG-Queens Univ Pr) CUP Services.

Loney, Martin, et al, eds. Social Policy & Social Welfare. 352p. 1983. pap. 39.95 (*0-335-10408-8*) OpUniv Pr.

— The State or the Market: Politics & Welfare in Contemporary Britain. 288p. (C). 1987. text 35.00 (*0-8039-8104-X*); pap. text 16.50 (*0-8039-8105-8*) Sage.

Loney, Steve. 101 Offensive Line Drills. (Illus.). 120p. 1999. pap. 16.95 (*1-57167-391-1*) Coaches Choice.

Long. ADA Yearbook 1992. (ITCP-UK Computer Science Ser.). (C). 1992. mass mkt. 125.95 (*0-412-45630-3*) Chapman & Hall.

— Atlas of Historical County Boundaries: Missouri. 2000. 100.00 (*0-13-366428-7*) S&S Trade.

— Atlas of Operative Neurosurgical Technique, Vol. 1. (Illus.). 390p. 1988. 240.00 (*0-683-05148-2*) Lppncott W & W.

— Between Public Culture. 1994. pap. text 14.95 (*0-226-49262-1*) U Ch Pr.

— Between Public Culture. 1997. 32.00 (*0-226-49261-3*) U Ch Pr.

— Calculus. (C). 1997. pap. text, teacher ed. write for info. (*0-321-40727-X*) Addison-Wesley.

— Chemistry 111. (C). 1998. pap. text, lab manual ed. 9.75 (*0-471-32292-X*) Wiley.

— Chess Crymz & Other Business. Date not set. write for info. (*0-938650-90-4*) Thinkers Pr.

***Long.** Computer Aided Legal Research. (Paralegal Ser.). (C). 2002. pap. 34.75 (*0-7668-1333-9*) Delmar.

Long. Computer Chronicles. 4th ed. (C). 1995. 115.00 (*0-13-366758-8*, Macmillan Coll) P-H.

— Computers: Brief Edition. 6th abr. ed. 269p. 1998. pap. text 34.67 (*0-13-096254-6*) P-H.

— Conflict in the Classroom. 3rd ed. (Education Ser.). 1976. pap. 9.75 (*0-534-00400-8*) Wadsworth Pub.

— Edwardian House: The Middle-class Home in Britain 1880-1914. LC 93-14634. (Studies in Design & Material Culture). 1993. pap. write for info. (*0-7190-3729-8*, Pub. by Manchester Univ Pr) St Martin.

L

— Essentials of WordPerfect 6.0 for dBASE IV. 4th ed. LC 94-236382. (C). 1994. pap. text 11.00 (0-13-498148-0) P-H.
*Long. Exito. (C). 2001. pap. 45.00 (0-8384-1132-0) Heinle & Heinle.
Long. Finite Math: Instructor's Solutions Manual. (C). 1997. pap. text 24.00 (0-06-500392-6) Addison-Wesley.
— Finite Math & Calculus. (C). 1997. pap. text, teacher ed. write for info. (0-321-40729-6) Addison-Wesley.
*Long. Geology. 9th ed. 600p. 1999. pap. text 55.00 (0-536-02544-4) Pearson Custom.
Long. Human Sexuality. 1994. pap., wbk. ed. 18.50 (0-07-038694-3) McGraw.
*Long. It Works Cd-rom, Version 2.0 & Brief Office Professional 97 & Ess Computing Concepts Pkg. 5th ed. (C). 1998. 37.33 (0-13-010360-8) P-H.
Long. Lakeland CC Special Essentials. 148p. 1995. pap. text 5.00 (0-13-226671-7) P-H.
— Law Office Procedures. LC 96-22549. 350p. (C). 1996. mass mkt. 69.95 (0-314-09238-2) West Pub.
*Long. Legal Research Using the Internet. LC 99-38664. (C). 1999. pap. 24.95 (0-7668-1335-5) Delmar.
— Linear Raman Spectroscopy. text. write for info. (0-471-49028-8) Wiley.
Long. Mathematical Reasoning 2nd ed. 192p. (C). 1999. pap. text 26.40 (0-321-04325-1) Addison-Wesley.
— Mathematical Reasoning. 4th ed. (C). 2000. pap., lab manual ed. 27.40 (0-321-04328-6) Addson-Wesley Educ.
Long. New GED Interpretin. (Illus.). pap. 9.15 (0-8428-8704-0) Cambridge Bk.
— New GED Sciences. (Illus.). pap. 9.15 (0-8428-8703-2) Cambridge Bk.
— New GED Social Sciences. (Illus.). pap. 9.15 (0-8428-8702-4) Cambridge Bk.
Long. Perspectives in Culture. 1998. pap. text 27.00 (0-205-27478-1, Longwood Div) Allyn.
— The Physics Around You. (Physics Ser.). 1980. pap., teacher ed. write for info. (0-534-01974-9) Wadsworth Pub.
— Test Bank: General Chemistry. (C). 1989. pap. text 12.00 (0-7167-2059-0) W H Freeman.
— Vulcans the Way of Kolinahr. 1999. pap. 15.00 (0-671-04008-1, Pocket Books) PB.
— When Papa Snores. LC 98-24121. (J). (gr. 3). 2000. per. 16.00 (0-689-81943-9) S&S Childrens.
Long, ed. Calculus: An Applied Approach. (C). 1997. text. write for info. (0-673-99292-6) Addison-Wesley.
— Finite Mathematics & Calculus. (C). 1997. text. write for info. (0-673-99824-X) Addison-Wesley.
Long & Detemple. Math Reasoning for Elementary Teachers. (C). 1997. pap. text 66.00 (0-201-30472-4) Addison-Wesley.
Long & Graening. Finite Math Selectd Chap. 2nd ed. (C). 1998. pap. 59.00 (0-201-43468-7) Addison-Wesley.
Long & Grauer. Brief Office Windows 97 & Essentials 3.0. (C). 1998. pap. text 42.66 (0-13-082619-7) S&S Trade.
— Exploring Windows 95. 1997. pap. text 37.33 (0-13-095413-6) P-H.
— Issues in Computers: '98 Lectures. 5th ed. 1998. pap. text 9.33 (0-13-011362-X, Pub. by P-H) S&S Trade.
— Mini Core Concepts 98. 5th ed. 1997. pap. text 5.40 (0-13-095389-X) P-H.
Long & Morse. Conflict in the Classroom. 2nd ed. (Education Ser.). 1968. pap. 6.50 (0-534-00082-7) Wadsworth Pub.
Long, jt. auth. see Harding.
Long, jt. auth. see Hopkins.
Long, jt. auth. see James.
Long, A. Master It. (C). 1997. 128.00 (0-06-501599-1) Addison-Wesley.
Long, A., ed. see Taylor, R. E. & KPMG Peat Marwick Staff.
Long, A. A. Hellenistic Philosophy: Stoics, Epicureans, Sceptics. 2nd ed. 1986. pap. 18.95 (0-520-05808-9, Pub. by U CA Pr) Cal Prin Full Svc.
— Stoic Studies. 325p. (C). 1996. text 64.95 (0-521-48263-1) Cambridge U Pr.
*Long, A. A., ed. The Cambridge Companion to Early Greek Philosophy. LC 98-38077. (Companions to Philosophy Ser.). (Illus.). 448p. 1999. 54.95 (0-521-44122-6); pap. 19.95 (0-521-44667-8) Cambridge U Pr.
Long, A. A., ed. Problems in Stoicism. LC 96-39649. 272p. 1996. pap. 35.00 (0-485-12128-X, Pub. by Athlone Pr) Humanities.
Long, A. A. & Sedley, D. N. The Hellenistic Philosophers, Vol. 1: Translations of the Principal Sources, with Philosophical Commentary. (Illus.). 528p. 1987. pap. text 34.95 (0-521-27556-3) Cambridge U Pr.
— The Hellenistic Philosophers, Vol. 2: Greek & Latin Texts with Notes & Bibliography. 528p. (C). 1989. pap. text 36.95 (0-521-27557-1) Cambridge U Pr.
Long, A. A., jt. ed. see Dillon, J. M.
Long, A. J., jt. auth. see Wege, D. C.
Long, A. R., jt. ed. see Davies, J. H.
Long, Alice M., ed. Marriage Records of Hancock County, Maine Prior to 1892. LC 91-67682. 576p. 1992. 45.00 (0-929539-55-9, 1330) Picton Pr.
— Marriage Returns of Washington County, Maine, Prior to 1892. 128p. 1993. 24.50 (0-89725-140-7, 1454) Picton Pr.
Long, Alice M., jt. ed. see Gray, Ruth.
Long, Andrew, ed. see Dobson, Austin.
Long, Andrew, tr. see Del Conde, Teresa, ed.
Long, Andrew F., et al, eds. Health Manpower: Planning, Production & Management. 300p. 1987. lib. bdg. 49.50 (0-7099-4172-2, Pub. by C Helm) Routldge.
Long, Anne. Listening. pap. write for info. (0-232-51834-3) S Asia.
— The Windwalker: A Happening in the Smokies. 192p. (Orig.). 1991. pap. 7.95 (0-925591-19-X) Covenant Hse Bks.
Long, Anthony, et al, eds. Governments in Conflict? Provinces & Indian Nations in Canada. 304p. (C). 1988. pap. 19.95 (0-8020-6690-9); text 40.00 (0-8020-5779-9) U of Toronto Pr.
Long, Asphodel P. In a Chariot Drawn by Lions: The Search for the Female Deity. pap. 17.95 (0-7043-4295-2, Pub. by Womens Press) Trafalgar.
Long, Augustus W., jt. auth. see Parrott, Thomas M.
Long, B. Lancia Beta: Collector's Guide. (Illus.). 128p. 1996. 27.95 (0-947981-62-4, Pub. by Motor Racing) Motorbooks Intl.
Long, B. J. Naval Fighters No. 23: Convair XF24-1 & YF24-1 Seadart. (Illus.). 74p. 1993. pap. 14.95 (0-942612-23-X) Naval Fighters.
Long, B. O., ed. Images of Man & God: Old Testament Short Stories in Literary Focus. (Bible & Literature Ser.: No. 1). 128p. 1981. 46.50 (0-907459-00-5, Pub. by Sheffield Acad); pap. 17.95 (0-907459-01-3, Pub. by Sheffield Acad) CUP Services.
Long, Barbara. Jim Thorpe: Legendary Athlete. LC 96-9226. (Native American Biographies Ser.). (Illus.). 128p. (YA). (gr. 6 up). 1997. lib. bdg. 20.95 (0-89490-865-0) Enslow Pubs.
*Long, Barbara. United States v. Virginia: Virginia Military Institute Accepts Women. LC 99-50671. (Landmark Supreme Court Cases Ser.). (Illus.). 128p. (YA). (gr. 6 up). 2000. lib. bdg. 20.95 (0-7660-1342-1) Enslow Pubs.
Long, Barbara B. Des Moines & Polk County: Flag on the Prairie. 136p. 1988. 29.95 (0-89781-273-5, 5175) Am Historical Pr.
Long, Barbara C. Medical-Surgical Nursing. 3rd ed. 1992. 78.00 (0-8016-7416-6) Mosby Inc.
— Medical-Surgical Nursing No. 3: Student Learning Guide. 3rd ed. 193p. 1992. pap. text, student ed. 14.95 (0-8016-7417-4) Mosby Inc.
Long, Barbara C., et al. Medical-Surgical Nursing: A Nursing Process Approach. 3rd ed. (Illus.). 1728p. (C). (gr. 13). 1992. text 72.00 (0-8016-6672-4, 06672) Mosby Inc.
Long, Barbara C., et al. Medical-Surgical Nursing: A Nursing Process Approach. 3rd ed. (Illus.). 1728p. 1993. teacher ed. write for info. (0-8151-4282-X) Mosby Inc.
Long, Barry. Knowing Yourself: The True in the False. 2nd rev. ed. 186p. 1996. pap. 12.95 (1-899324-03-8) B Long Bks.
— Making Love: Sexual Love the Divine Way. Tempest, Clive, ed. LC 98-91353. 128p. 1999. pap. 12.95 (1-899324-14-3) B Long Bks.
— Meditation, a Foundation Course: A Book of Ten Lessons. 2nd rev. ed. LC 96-96014. 160p. 1995. pap. 10.95 (1-899324-00-3) B Long Bks.
— Only Fear Dies: A Book of Liberation. 2nd rev. ed. Tempest, Clive, ed. LC 96-96013. Orig. Title: Ridding Yourself of Unhappiness. 160p. 1994. pap. 12.95 (0-9508050-7-6) B Long Bks.
— Origins of Man & the Universe: The Myth That Came to Life. 2nd rev. ed. Tempest, Clive & Bell, Jade, eds. LC 97-93601. (Illus.). 381p. 1998. pap. 19.95 (1-899324-12-7) B Long Bks.
— Raising Children in Love, Justice & Truth. Tempest, Clive, ed. LC 97-92756. 400p. 1998. pap. 19.95 (1-899324-13-5) B Long Bks.
— Stillness Is the Way: An Intensive Meditation Course. Tempest, Clive, ed. LC 96-96015. 288p. 1995. pap. 14.95 (0-9508050-4-1) B Long Bks.
— To Man in Truth: Enlightening Letters. Bell, Jade, ed. LC 98-92188. 282p. 1999. pap. 11.95 (1-899324-15-1) B Long Bks.
— To Woman in Love: A Book of Letters. Bell, Jade, ed. LC 96-96019. 272p. 1995. pap. 12.95 (0-9508050-8-4) B Long Bks.
*Long, Barry. The Way In: A Book of Self-Discovery. Tempest, Clive, ed. LC 99-73760. 336p. 2000. pap. 16.95 (0-9508050-5-X, Pub. by B Long Bks) Assoc Pubs Grp.
Long, Barry. Wisdom: & Where to Find It: A Book of Truth. LC 96-96020. 128p. 1996. pap. 11.95 (1-899324-01-1) B Long Bks.
Long, Barry, jt. auth. see Dannen, Frederic.
*Long, Becky. The Best Bachelorette Party Book. LC 00-25100. (Illus.). 128p. 2000. pap. write for info. (0-88166-368-9) Meadowbrook.
— Best Bachelorette Party Book: A Complete Guide for Party Planners. (Illus.). 128p. 2000. per. 7.95 (0-671-31819-5) S&S Trade.
Long, Becky. Something Old, Something New: A Bride's Guide: Creative Ways to Personalize Your Wedding. LC 97-42114. 1998. pap. 9.95 (0-88166-306-9) Meadowbrook.
*Long, Ben & Schenk, Sonja. Digital Filmmaking Handbook. (Illus.). 550p. 2000. pap. write for info. (1-58450-017-4) Chrles River Media.
Long, Ben, jt. auth. see Lyn, Craig.
*Long, Benjamin. Backtracking: By Foot, Canoe & Subaru on the Lewis & Clark Trail. 256p. 2000. pap. 23.95 (1-57061-246-3) Sasquatch Bks.
Long, Betty. Something Old Something New. LC 97-42114. 160p. 1998. pap. 9.95 (0-671-58126-0) S&S Trade.
*Long, Bill. Brief Encounters: Meetings with Remarkable People. 190p. 2000. pap. 15.95 (1-874597-84-7, Pub. by New Island Books) Dufour.
Long, Bill. Bright Lights, White Water: The Lighthouses of Ireland. (Illus.). 224p. 1997. reprint ed. pap. 29.95 (1-874597-64-2, Pub. by New Island Books) Irish Bks Media.
— A Change of Heart: Journal of a Heart Transplant. 96p. (Orig.). 1995. pap. 11.95 (1-874597-21-9, Pub. by New Island Books) Irish Bks Media.
Long, Bill, jt. auth. see Carney, Glandion.
*Long, Bill L. International Environmental Issues & the OECD, 1950-2000: An Historical Perspective. (OECD Historical Ser.). 156p. 2000. pap. 24.00 (92-64-17171-1, 97 2000 01 1 P, Pub. by Org for Econ) OECD.
Long, Bob. Fishing the Queen Charlotte Islands. (Illus.). 127p. (Orig.). 1989. pap. 8.95 (0-9693727-0-1) Gordon Soules Bk.
Long, Bob, ed. see Gordon, Stephen W.
Long, Bob, ed. see Sawyer, Tim.
Long, Bonita C. & Kahn, Sharon E., eds. Women, Work & Coping: A Multidisciplinary Approach to Workplace Stress. 368p. 1993. 65.00 (0-7735-1128-8, Pub. by McG-Queens Univ Pr); pap. 22.95 (0-7735-1129-6, Pub. by McG-Queens Univ Pr) CUP Services.
Long-Bostrom, Kathleen. What Is God Like? LC 97-42349. (Questions from Little Hearts Ser.). (Illus.). (J). 1998. 9.99 (0-8423-5118-3) Tyndale Hse.
Long, Brian. Borland Pascal Solver. 400p. 1994. pap. 34.95 incl. disk (0-201-59383-1) Addison-Wesley.
— Datsun Z: From Fairlady to 280Z. (Illus.). 160p. 1998. 39.95 (1-901295-02-8, Pub. by Vloce Pub) Motorbooks Intl.
— Datsun/Nissan 280ZX & 300ZX. (Illus.). 160p. 1998. 39.95 (1-901295-06-0, Pub. by Vloce Pub) Motorbooks Intl.
— Jaguar XJS. (Illus.). 192p. 2000. 49.95 (1-901295-43-5, 128178AE, Pub. by Vloce Pub) Motorbooks Intl.
— Lancia: From Alpha to Zeta & Beyond. 2000. 34.95 (0-7509-2080-7) Sutton Pub Ltd.
*Long, Brian. The Lexus Story. (Illus.). 192p. 2000. 49.95 (1-901295-81-8, 130696AE, Pub. by Vloce Pub) Motorbooks Intl.
Long, Brian. Porsche 914 & 914/6. (Speed Pro Ser.). (Illus.). 160p. 1997. 39.95 (1-874105-84-7, Pub. by Vloce Pub) Motorbooks Intl.
*Long, Brian. Porsche 924. (Illus.). 192p. 2000. 49.95 (1-901295-85-0, 130692AE, Pub. by Vloce Pub) Motorbooks Intl.
Long, Brian. Porsche 356. (Illus.). 160p. 1996. 39.95 (1-874105-63-4, Pub. by Vloce Pub) Motorbooks Intl.
Long, Brian, et al. The Revolutionary Guide to Delphi 2. LC 95-61786. 800p. 1996. pap. 49.95 incl. cd-rom (1-874416-67-2) Wrox Pr Inc.
Long, Brian, jt. auth. see Reck, Ross R.
Long, Bruce. William Desmond Taylor: A Dossier. LC 91-32607. (Filmmakers Ser.: No. 28). (Illus.). 471p. 1991. 50.00 (0-8108-2490-6) Scarecrow.
Long, Bruce W. & Rafert, John A. Orthopaedic Radiography. LC 94-14941. (Illus.). 560p. 1994. text 75.00 (0-7216-6649-3, W B Saunders Co) Harcrt Hlth Sci Grp.
Long, Bryan K. & Long, Vivian R. Skin of the Oak. large type ed. LC 98-96039. (Illus.). 64p. 1998. pap. 12.99 (0-9663342-2-1) Artworks CO.
Long, Burke O. Planting & Reaping Albright: Politics, Ideology, & Interpreting the Bible. LC 95-42065. 1996. 32.50 (0-271-01576-4) Pa St U Pr.
— The Problem of Etiological Narrative in the Old Testament. (Beiheft zur Zeitschrift fuer die Alttestamentliche Wissenschaft Ser.: No. 108). (C). 1968. 33.85 (3-11-005590-2) De Gruyter.
Long, C. J., et al, eds. Handbook of Head Trauma: Acute Care to Recovery. (Critical Issues in Neuropsychology Ser.). (Illus.). 466p. (C). 1992. text 85.00 (0-306-43947-6, Kluwer Plenum) Kluwer Academic.
Long, C. J., et al. Behind Bars: Bar Coding Principles & Applications. LC 89-3167. (Illus.). 280p. 1989. 19.95 (0-945456-03-4) PT Pubns.
Long, C. J., jt. ed. see Williams, J. Mark.
Long, C. Michael. Understanding Census Data: A Quick & Simplified Reference. 71p. reprint ed. 25.00 (0-685-44383-3) West Econ Rsch.
Long, C. Thomas & Vartanian, Thomas P. Thrift Financing Devices. 246p. write for info. (0-318-60936-3) Harcourt.
Long, Calvin T. Elementary Introduction to Number Theory. 3rd ed. (Illus.). 292p. (C). 1995. text 42.95 (0-88133-836-2) Waveland Pr.
Long, Calvin T. & Detemple. Mathematical Reasoning for Elementary Teachers. 1124p. (C). 1997. text 86.00 (0-321-01330-1) Addison-Wesley.
*Long, Calvin T. & DeTemple, Duane. Mathematical Reasoning for Elementary School Teachers. 2nd ed. LC 99-22166. 962p. (C). 1999. 92.00 (0-321-04333-2) Addison-Wesley.
Long, Calvin T. & DeTemple, Duane W. Mathematical Reasoning for Elementary Teachers: Student's Solutions Manual. (C). 1997. pap. text, student ed. 25.00 (0-673-99391-4) Addson-Wesley Educ.
Long, Calvin T., jt. ed. see Kallaher, Michael J.
Long, Caroline B. Church Bells of Antigua (Campanas de las Iglesias de Antigua) And Surrounding Villages - Sacatepequez, Guatemala. deluxe ed. Becker, Dianne, ed. Mejia-Niconchuk, Marta, tr. (Illus.). 229p. 1999. pap. 10.00 (0-9672658-0-0) Caroline B Long.
Long, Caroline C. Church Bells of Antigua (Campanas de las Iglesias de Antigua) And Surrounding Villages - Sacatepequez, Guatemala. 2nd ed. Becker, Dianne G., ed. Mejia-Niconchuk, Marta, tr. (Illus.). 229p. 1999. pap. 10.00 (0-9672658-1-9) Caroline B Long.
*Long, Carolyn N. Religious Freedom & Indian Rights: The Case of Oregon vs. Smith. (Landmark Law Cases & American Society Ser.). 2000. 35.00 (0-7006-1063-4); pap. 14.95 (0-7006-1064-2) U Pr of KS.
Long, Catherine T., ed. State Antidiscrimination Laws: Protected Classes Disability Discrimination Family & Medical Leave. LC 98-207643. (Employment & Human Resources Professional Ser.). 2012p. 1997. pap. 125.00 (0-8080-0201-5) CCH INC.
Long, Cathryn. American History to 1900. (Crossword America Ser.). (Illus.). 64p. (J). (gr. 3-7). 1998. pap. 5.95 (1-56565-934-1, 09341W, Pub. by Lowell Hse Juvenile) NTC Contemp Pub Co.
*Long, Cathryn. The Presidents. (Crossword America Ser.). (Illus.). 64p. (J). (gr. 3-6). 2000. pap. 5.95 (0-7373-0364-6, 03646W, Pub. by Lowell Hse Juvenile) NTC Contemp Pub Co.
*Long, Cathryn & Nolte, Larry. Crossword America: American History 1900 to 2000. (Illus.). 64p. (J). (gr. 3-6). 2000. pap. 5.95 (0-7373-0366-2, 03662W, Pub. by Lowell Hse Juvenile) NTC Contemp Pub Co.
*Long, Cathryn J. The Cherokee (North America) LC 99-43152. (Indigenous Peoples Ser.). (Illus.). 144p. (YA). (gr. 8-12). 2000. lib. bdg. 23.70 (1-56006-617-2) Lucent Bks.
Long, Cathryn J. The 50 States. (Illus.). 64p. (J). (gr. 2-6). 1999. pap. 5.95 (0-7373-0173-2, 01732W) NTC Contemp Pub Co.
— The Middle East in Search of Peace. rev. ed. (Headliners Ser.). (Illus.). 64p. (J). (gr. 5-8). 1996. lib. bdg. 23.40 (0-7613-0105-4) Millbrook Pr.
— Ohio Studies Program: State Studies Program. (Illus.). 1996. teacher ed. 125.00 (0-87746-577-0) Graphic Learning.
Long, Charlene & Zottoli, Robert. Bahamian Polychaetes (Phylum Annelida Class Polychaeta) Annotated List & Bibliography. 57p. (C). 1997. pap. text 10.00 (0-935909-62-1) Bahamian.
Long, Charles. Cottage Projects. (Cottage Country Ser.). (Illus.). 160p. 1997. pap. 17.95 (1-895629-76-4); pap. text 17.95 (1-895629-75-6) Warwick Publ.
— How to Survive Without a Salary. (Orig.). 1996. pap. text 12.95 (0-07-038788-5) McGraw.
— How to Survive Without a Salary: Learning to Live the Conserver Lifestyle. rev. ed. 208p. 1996. pap. 14.95 (1-895629-68-3) Warwick Publ.
— The Stonebuilder's Primer: A Step-by-Step Guide for Owner-Builders. rev. ed. (Illus.). 128p. 1998. pap. 17.95 (1-55209-298-4) Firefly Bks Ltd.
— Undefended Borders. 256p. 1995. pap. 14.95 (1-895629-46-2) Warwick Publ.
Long, Charles, jt. ed. see Sbordone, Robert J.
Long, Charles A. Matinicus Isle, Maine, Its Story & Its People, in Two Parts. (Illus.). 245p. 1996. reprint ed. lib. bdg. 35.00 (0-8328-5202-3) Higginson Bk Co.
Long, Charles E., ed. see Symonds, Richard.
Long, Charles H. Coon Tales & Cockleburs. LC 95-77770. (Illus.). 227p. (Orig.). 1995. pap. 14.95 (1-878044-19-2, Wld Rose) Mayhaven Pub.
*Long, Charles H. Significations: Signs, Symbols & Images in the Interpretation of Religion. LC 98-89387. (Philosophical & Cultural Studies in Religion). 224 p. 1999. write for info. (1-888570-51-2) Davies Grp.
Long, Charles H., ed. Remembering John Krumm: A Biography Based on Tributes by His Friends. 142p. 1998. pap. 7.95 (0-88028-197-9, 1472) Forward Movement.
Long, Charles H., ed. see Allen, Roland.
Long, Charles J., jt. ed. see Williams, J. Michael.
Long, Charles M. The Little French Notebook: A Breakthrough in Early Speaking. LC 98-68584. (ENG & FRE., Illus.). v, 75p. 2000. 24.95 (0-9667172-2-8) Reflective Bks.
— The Little Spanish Notebook: A Breakthrough in Early Speaking. LC 98-68585. (ENG & SPA., Illus.). v, 75p. 1999. 24.95 (0-9667172-1-X) Reflective Bks.

Long, Charles Merlin. The Little German Notebook: A Breakthrough in Early Speaking. LC 98-92112. (GER & ENG., Illus.). 75p. 1999. 24.95 (0-9667172-0-1) Reflective Bks.
This highly innovative notebook introduces a revolutionary new learning technique that enables speaking of a European language in 12 weeks. Using the technique, a novice can mentally identify English cognate words & mentally transform them (in this case) into correct German words - instantly - without the aid of a dictionary! National think tank consultant & author, Charles Long, uses his recent linguistic discoveries, a patent-pending invention, & the well-proven knowledge transfer technique to forge this early speaking breakthrough. Chapters include "Prerequisites of Early Speaking," "Transfer English Words, Alphabet, Spelling & Pronunciation," "Learn Key Native German Words & Simplified German Grammar," "Multiply German Words with Simple Techniques," "Learn Self- Conceived Sentence Speaking" & "Appendix of 3,000 Transferable English Words." The Notebook has varied applications. It can be an opening 12-week language program for Middle School students, or a study aid for accelerating speaking at higher academic levels, or a self-learning book for international travelers & individuals for seeking career advancement. The Notebook's hardback, coffee-table quality, color-coded text learning aids, 40 colorful German photos, & 75-page brevity make the learning easy, pleasant & permanent. This is the first of "Little (foreign language) Notebooks." ***Publisher Paid Annotation.***

Long, Charlie. To Vietnam with Love: The Story of Charlie & E. G. Long. LC 94-80026. (Jaffray Collection of Missionary Portraits: Bk. 12). 204p. 1995. pap. 9.99 (0-87509-582-8) Chr Pubns.

An Asterisk (*) at the beginning of an entry indicates that the title is appearing for the first time.

Long, Charlotte J. Until Tomorrow. 48p. (Orig.). 1983. pap. 3.95 (*0-88100-036-1*) Marsh Creek.

Long, Charlotte R. The Ayia Triadha Sarcophagus: A Study of Late Minoan & Mycenaean Funerary Practices & Beliefs. (Studies in Mediterranean Archaeology: Vol. XLI). (Illus.). 124p. (Orig.). 1974. pap. 43.50 (*91-85058-59-9*, Pub. by P Astroms) Coronet Bks.

Long, Cheryl, ed. The Best of Scanfest: An Authentic Treasury of Scandinavian Recipes & Proverbs. rev. ed. 192p. 1995. per. 14.95 (*0-914667-13-0*) Culinary Arts Ltd.

Long, Cheryl & Kibbey, Heather. Classic Liqueurs: The Art of Making & Cooking with Liqueurs. rev. ed. LC 90-37387. 128p. (Orig.). 1996. per. 9.95 (*0-914667-11-4*) Culinary Arts Ltd.

***Long, Cheryl & Organic Gardening Staff.** Rodale Organic Gardening Solutions: Over 500 Gardening Answers to Real-Life Questions from Backyard Gardens. 256p. 2000. pap. 16.95 (*0-87596-852-X*, Pub. by Rodale Pr Inc) St Martin.

Long, Cheryl, jt. auth. see Fischborn, Cynthia.

Long, Chris. The Actuary in Practice, Tolley's. (C). 1989. 150.00 (*0-7855-4327-9*, Pub. by Witherby & Co) St Mut.

— Essential Heat Transfer. (C). 1999. pap. text. write for info. (*0-582-29279-4*) Addison-Wesley.

***Long, Chris, & Associates Staff, ed.** Gun Trader's Guide. 23rd ed. (Illus.). 592p. 2000. pap. 23.95 (*0-88317-219-4*) Stoeger Pub Co.

Long, Christopher & Gilbert, Jennifer. The Artist's Guide to Pricing Art. (Illus.). 28p. (Orig.). 1995. reprint ed. pap. 12.95 (*1-887724-01-X*) Fremantle Pr.

Long, Christopher, jt. auth. see Gilbert, Jennifer.

Long, Christpher, ed. see Gilbert, Jennifer.

Long, Cindy, jt. auth. see Long, Steve.

Long, Clarence D. The Labor Force in War & Transition: 4 Countries. (Occasional Papers: No. 36). 70p. 1952. reprint ed. 20.00 (*0-87014-351-4*) Natl Bur Econ Res.

— The Labor Force in Wartime America. (Occasional Papers: No. 14). 76p. 1944. reprint ed. 20.00 (*0-87014-329-8*) Natl Bur Econ Res.

— The Labor Force under Changing Income & Employment. (General Ser.: No. 65). 464p. 1958. reprint ed. 120.70 (*0-87014-064-7*) Natl Bur Econ Res.

— Wages & Earnings in the United States, 1860-1890. LC 75-19725. (National Bureau of Economic Research Ser.). (Illus.). 1975. reprint ed. 18.95 (*0-405-07603-7*) Ayer.

— Wages & Earnings in the United States, 1860-1890. (General Ser.: No. 67). 186p. 1960. reprint ed. 48.90 (*0-87014-066-3*) Natl Bur Econ Res.

Long, Clarence D., jt. auth. see Mills, Frederick C.

***Long, Clarisa.** Intellectual Property Rights in Emerging Markets. 150p. 2000. pap. 16.95 (*0-8447-4126-4*, Pub. by Am Enterprise) Pub Resources Inc.

***Long, Clarisa, ed.** Genetic Testing & the Use of Information. LC 99-30858. 150p. 1999. 34.95 (*0-8447-4109-4*, Pub. by Am Enterprise); pap. 16.95 (*0-8447-4110-8*, Pub. by Am Enterprise) Pub Resources Inc.

— Intellectual Property Rights in Emerging Markets. 150p. 2000. 29.95 (*0-8447-4125-6*, Pub. by Am Enterprise) Pub Resources Inc.

Long, Clarisa, jt. auth. see Buscaglia, Edgardo.

Long, Cleta M. History of Tucker County. (Illus.). 475p. 1996. 45.00 (*0-9619468-3-0*) C M Long.

Long, Cloyd D. School-Leaving Youth & Employment: Some Factors Associated with the Duration of Early Employment of Youth Whose Formal Education Ended at High School Graduation or Earlier. LC 74-177006. (Columbia University. Teachers College. Contributions to Education Ser.: No. 845). reprint ed. 37.50 (*0-404-55845-3*) AMS Pr.

Long, Connie. Easy Guide to Sewing Blouses. LC 96-27691. (Sewing Companion Library). (Illus.). 112p. 1997. pap. 17.95 (*1-56158-108-9*, 070224) Taunton.

— Easy Guide to Sewing Linings. LC 97-47113. (Sewing Companion Library). (Illus.). 144p. (Orig.). 1998. pap. 19.95 (*1-56158-225-5*, 070360) Taunton.

***Long, Connie.** Sewing with Knits: Classic, Stylish Garments from Swimsuits to Eveningwear. LC 99-42160. (Illus.). 160p. 2000. pap. 21.95 (*1-56158-311-1*) Taunton.

***Long, Cormac.** Cisco Internetworking & Troubleshooting. (Technical Expert Ser.). 1999. pap. 55.00 (*0-07-135598-7*) McGraw-Hill Prof.

Long, D. The Cross: Its True Meaning. 1996. pap. 4.99 (*0-946351-45-7*, Pub. by John Ritchie) Loizeaux.

— Law & Its Limitations in the GATT Multilateral Trade System. 1985. lib. bdg. 87.50 (*90-247-3189-5*) Kluwer Academic.

Long, D. A., ed. Anterior Segment & Strabismus Surgery: Proceedings of the 44th Annual Symposium, New Orleans, LA, U. S. A., February 9-12, 1995. LC 96-1883. 1996. 86.00 (*90-6299-134-3*) Kugler Pubns.

Long, D. A., jt. ed. see Clark, R. J.

Long, D. B. Revival: A Study in Biblical Patterns. 1996. pap. 9.99 (*0-946351-38-4*, Pub. by John Ritchie) Loizeaux.

Long, D. G., jt. auth. see Grierson, A. J.

Long, D. M., jt. ed. see Gildenberg, Philip L.

***Long, D. Stephen.** Divine Economy: Theology & the Market. (Radical Orthodoxy Ser.). 240p. 2000. 85.00 (*0-415-22672-4*); pap. 25.99 (*0-415-22673-2*) Routledge.

Long, Dana A., jt. auth. see Prufer, Olaf H.

Long, Dani L., jt. auth. see Bellange', Deborah.

Long, Dani L., jt. auth. see Jones, Harriet E.

***Long, Daniel & Preston, Dennis, eds.** Handbook of Perceptual Dialectology, Vol. 2. 2000. write for info. (*1-55619-757-8*) J Benjamins Pubng.

Long, Daniel a., ed. Cornea & Refractive Surgery. (Illus.). ix, 307p. 1998. 111.50 (*90-6299-140-8*) Kugler Pubns.

Long, Daryl. Jazz for Beginners. (Illus.). 156p. 1994. pap. 11.00 (*0-86316-165-0*) Writers & Readers.

— Miles Davis for Beginners. (Illus.). 100p. (Orig.). 1992. 18.00 (*0-86316-154-5*); pap. 9.00 (*0-86316-153-7*) Writers & Readers.

Long, David. Blue Spruce: Stories. 1995. 20.00 (*0-684-80033-0*) S&S Trade.

— Blue Spruce: Stories. 256p. 1996. per. 11.00 (*0-684-81589-3*, Scribner Pap Fic) S&S Trade Pap.

***Long, David.** The Daughters of Simon Lamoreaux. 272p. 2000. 23.50 (*0-684-85414-7*, Scb1) S&S Trade.

Long, David. The Falling Boy. LC 98-9231. 256p. 1998. pap. 12.95 (*0-452-27997-6*, Plume) Dutton Plume.

— Gold Braid & Foreign Relations: Diplomatic Activities of U. S. Naval Officers, 1798-1883. LC 87-34879. (Illus.). 448p. 1988. 46.95 (*0-87021-228-1*) Naval Inst Pr.

— The Hajj Today: A Survey of the Contemporary Pilgrimage to Makkah. LC 78-7473. (Illus.). 180p. (C). 1979. text 29.50 (*0-87395-382-7*) State U NY Pr.

— Home Fires. Stories. LC 82-4927. (Illinois Short Fiction Ser.). 136p. 1982. 9.95 (*0-252-00992-4*); text 14.95 (*0-252-00991-6*) U of Ill Pr.

— Towards a New Liberal Internationalism: The International Theory of J. A. Hobson. LC 97-671. (London School of Economics Monographs in International Studies). 286p. (C). 1996. text 59.95 (*0-521-45497-2*) Cambridge U Pr.

Long, David, ed. Oil Trading Manual: Updated Semi-Annually. (Illus.). 825p. 1999. 1250.00 (*1-85573-074-X*, Pub. by Woodhead Pubng) Am Educ Systs.

Long, David. Hold My Hand - Divorce Is Scary, Vol. 1. large type ed. 37p. (Orig.). (J). (ps-3). 1997. pap. text. write for info. (*0-9641630-1-6*) C B Louis.

Long, David & Mansor, Scott. Wyoming's Finest Mule Deer, Vol. 1. LC 97-97206. (Illus.). 320p. 1997. 24.95 (*0-9662746-0-1*) WFMD.

Long, David & Moore, Geoff, eds. Gas Trading Manual. 825p. 2000. ring bd. 1250.00 (*1-85573-446-X*) Am Educ Systs.

Long, David & Noice, Marshall. Glacier: Images from the Crown of the Continent. (Illus.). 52p. (Orig.). 1995. pap. 24.95 (*0-9645477-5-9*) Whitefish Ed.

Long, David & Wilson, Peter C. Thinkers of the Twenty Years' Crisis: Inter-War Idealism Reassessed. 360p. 1996. text 74.00 (*0-19-827855-1*) OUP.

Long, David, et al. Cross Country for Coaches & Runners. 90p. (Orig.). 1981. pap. 9.95 (*0-932741-97-5*) Championship Bks & Vid Prodns.

Long, David De, see De Long, David, ed.

Long, David E. Anatomy of Terrorism. 1990. text 27.95 (*0-02-919345-1*) Free Pr.

— The Jewel of Liberty: Abraham Lincoln's Re-Election & the End of Slavery. (Illus.). 416p. 1994. 24.95 (*0-8117-0217-0*) Stackpole.

— The Jewel of Liberty: Abraham Lincoln's Re-Election & the End of Slavery. LC 97-15672. (Illus.). 410p. 1997. reprint ed. pap. 15.95 (*0-306-80788-2*) Da Capo.

— The Kingdom of Saudi Arabia. LC 96-45618. 192p. 1997. pap. 19.95 (*0-8130-1473-5*) U Press Fla.

— The Kingdom of Saudi Arabia. LC 96-45618. (Illus.). 192p. 1997. 39.95 (*0-8130-1471-9*) U Press Fla.

— Lincoln & Liberty: The Emergence of a President. (Illus.). 400p. 1998. 29.95 (*0-8117-0971-X*) Stackpole.

— Saudi Arabia. (Profiles of the Middle East Ser.). 1996. text 49.95 (*0-8133-2402-5*) Westview.

— Saudi Arabia. (Profiles of the Middle East Ser.). (C). 1996. pap. text 18.95 (*0-8133-2403-3*) Westview.

Long, David E. & Rawls, Lucia. The People & Politics of the Gulf: A Region in Transition. 225p. 1994. text. write for info. (*0-8133-7668-8*) Westview.

Long, David E. & Reich, Bernard, eds. The Government & Politics of the Middle East & North Africa. 3rd ed. LC 95-5652. 502p. (C). 1995. pap. 35.00 (*0-8133-2126-3*, Pub. by Westview) HarpC.

— International Relations of the Middle East. 230p. (C). 1992. text. write for info. (*0-8133-7584-3*); pap. text. write for info. (*0-8133-7585-1*) Westview.

Long, David E., jt. auth. see Shaw, John A.

Long, David F. A Documentary History of U. S. Foreign Relations: From Seventeen Sixty to the Mid-Eighteen Nineties, Selections from Ruhl J. Bartlett's "The Record of American Diplomacy", Vol. I. LC 79-5349. 132p. 1980. pap. text 19.50 (*0-8191-1038-8*) U Pr of Amer.

— Mad Jack: The Biography of Captain John Percival, USN, 1779-1862, 136. LC 92-31763. (Contributions in Military Studies Ser.: No. 136). 288p. 1993. 62.95 (*0-313-28567-5*, LMJ, Greenwood Pr) Greenwood.

— Ready to Hazard: A Biography of Commodore William Bainbridge, 1774-1833. LC 80-29146. 359p. reprint ed. pap. 111.30 (*0-608-14449-5*, 202502100040) Bks Demand.

Long, David G. de, see De Long, David G., ed.

Long, David M. How to Tell the Future. Mortimer, Pamela, ed. (Illus.). 26p. (Orig.). 1993. pap. text. write for info. (*0-9632399-1-0*) Premier PA.

Long, Deborah. Posh Parties: Theme Party Interpretation. LC 96-96859. iv, 180p. 1996. pap. 15.95 (*0-9653705-1-8*) Delong Pub.

Long, Deborah H. Doing the Right Thing. 2nd ed. LC 97-14976. 138p. (C). 1997. pap. 15.00 (*0-13-780149-1*) P-H.

***Long, Deborah H.** Doing the Right Thing: Real Estate Practitioner's Guide to Ethical Decision Making. 3rd ed. 144p. 2000. pap. 16.00 (*0-13-085958-3*, Prentice Hall) P-H.

— Ethics & the Real Estate Professional. 64p. (C). 1997. pap. text 8.20 (*0-13-899576-1*) P-H.

— Ethics for the Real Estate Professional. 2nd ed. 64p. 2000. pap. 8.00 (*0-13-085953-2*, Prentice Hall) P-H.

Long, Delbert & Long, Roberta. Teacher Education Reform in Russia: Hope & Reality. Beauchamp, Edward R., ed. (Reference Books on International Education). Date not set. text 52.50 (*0-8153-1604-6*) Garland.

Long, Delbert H. & Long, Roberta A. Education of Teachers in Russia, 75. LC 98-51636. (Contributions to the Study of Education Ser.: No. 75). 240p. 1999. 65.00 (*0-313-31048-3*, GM1048, Greenwood Pr) Greenwood.

Long, Dennis. ESOP Answer Book. annuals 400p. 1996. 106.00 (*1-56706-071-4*) Panel Pubs.

Long, Dennis D. & Holle, Martha C. Macro Systems in the Social Environment. LC 96-71591. 200p. (C). 1997. pap. text 25.00 (*0-87581-409-3*, MSSE) F E Peacock Pubs.

Long, Diana E. & Golden, Janet, eds. The American General Hospital: Communities & Social Contexts. LC 89-7264. (Illus.). 216p. 1989. pap. text 16.95 (*0-8014-9604-7*) Cornell U Pr.

***Long, Dianne.** He's Just My Dad! 192p. 2000. 35.00 (*0-06-105148-9*, HarpEntertain) Morrow Avon.

Long, Dixon, jt. auth. see Long, Ruthanne.

Long, DJ. I Wish I Was the Baby. LC 94-40664. (Illus.). 32p. (J). (ps-2). 1995. 11.95 (*1-57102-035-7*, Ideals Child) Hambleton-Hill.

Long, Don L., et al. Introduction to Agribusiness Management. Lee, Jasper S., ed. (Career Preparation for Agriculture-Agribusiness Ser.). 1979. text 15.96 (*0-07-038665-X*) McGraw.

Long, Don M. Contemporary Diagnosis & Management of Pain. (Illus.). 206p. (Orig.). 1997. pap. 29.95 (*1-884065-13-9*) Assocs in Med.

Long, Doni L., jt. auth. see Jones, Harriett E.

Long, Donlin M. & McAfee, Paul C. Atlas of Spinal Surgery. (Illus.). 464p. 1992. 180.00 (*0-683-05149-0*) Lppncott W & W.

Long, Donlin M., jt. ed. see Hopkins, L. N.

Long, Donna, jt. auth. see Lucia, Al.

Long, Donna J., et al, eds. Isle of Flowers: Poems by Florida's Individual Artist Fellows. 240p. (Orig.). 1995. pap. 14.00 (*0-938078-41-0*) Anhinga Pr.

— Isle of Flowers: Poems by Florida's Individual Artist Fellows. 240p. (Orig.). (C). 1995. 21.95 (*0-938078-39-9*) Anhinga Pr.

Long, Donna J., ed. see Holmes, Janet.

***Long, Donna Lee.** A Guide for Using Boxcar Children: Surprise Island in the Classroom. (Illus.). 48p. 2000. pap., teacher ed. 7.95 (*1-57690-338-9*, TCM 2338) Tchr Create Mat.

Long, Donna Reseigh & MacIan, Janice Lynn. A Concernos. annot. ed. (College Spanish Ser.). (SPA.). (C). 1992. pap., teacher ed. 47.75 (*0-8384-5529-8*) Heinle & Heinle.

— A Concernos. 2nd ed. (College Spanish Ser.). (SPA.). (C). 1996. mass mkt., wbk. ed. 0.95 (*0-8384-6531-5*) Heinle & Heinle.

— A Concernos. 2nd ed. (College Spanish Ser.). (SPA.). (C). 1996. student ed., suppl. ed. 13.95 incl. cd-rom (*0-8384-6430-0*) Heinle & Heinle.

— A Concernos. 2nd ed. (College Spanish Ser.). (SPA.). (C). 1996. mass mkt. 15.95 (*0-8384-6428-9*) Heinle & Heinle.

— A Conocernos. (College Spanish Ser.). (C). Date not set. pap. 52.00 (*0-8384-2107-5*) Heinle & Heinle.

— A Conocernos. 1992. audio. write for info. (*0-318-69351-8*) Heinle & Heinle.

— A Conocernos. (C). 1992. pap., student ed. 31.75 (*0-8384-2344-2*) Heinle & Heinle.

— A Conocernos. (College Spanish Ser.). (C). 1992. pap., suppl. ed. 55.75 (*0-8384-2374-4*) Heinle & Heinle.

— A Conocernos. (College Spanish Ser.). (C). 1992. pap., teacher ed. 16.75 (*0-8384-2370-1*); pap., suppl. ed. 27.75 (*0-8384-2341-8*); pap., suppl. ed. 16.75 (*0-8384-2371-X*); pap., suppl. ed. 16.75 (*0-8384-2375-2*); suppl. ed. 30.95 incl. audio (*0-8384-3893-8*) Heinle & Heinle.

— A Conocernos. (College Spanish Ser.). (C). 1992. pap., suppl. ed. 38.75 (*0-8384-2555-0*) Heinle & Heinle.

— A Conocernos. 2nd ed. (College Spanish Ser.). (C). 1996. text, teacher ed. 58.95 (*0-8384-6529-3*); text, student ed. 58.95 (*0-8384-6528-5*) Heinle & Heinle.

— A Conocernos. 2nd ed. (College Spanish Ser.). (C). 1996. mass mkt., wbk. ed. 33.95 (*0-8384-6539-0*) Heinle & Heinle.

— A Conocernos. 2nd ed. 1996. text, student ed. 78.95 incl. audio (*0-8384-6821-7*) Heinle & Heinle.

— A Conocernos. 2nd ed. (College Spanish Ser.). (C). 1996. text, teacher ed. 13.95 (*0-8384-6530-7*) Heinle & Heinle.

— De Paseo. (C). 1994. text, teacher ed. 38.95 (*0-8384-2584-4*) Heinle & Heinle.

— De Paseo. (College Spanish Ser.). (C). 1994. mass mkt. 145.95 (*0-8384-2583-6*); mass mkt., suppl. ed. 0.95 (*0-8384-5482-8*) Heinle & Heinle.

— De Paseo. 2nd ed. (College Spanish Ser.). (C). 1999. pap., teacher ed. 24.00 (*0-8384-8116-7*) Heinle & Heinle.

***Long, Donna Reseigh & MacIan, Janice Lynn.** De Paseo. 2nd ed. 2000. pap. 42.75 (*0-8384-1192-4*) Heinle & Heinle.

Long, Donna Reseigh & MacIan, Janice Lynn. De Paseo. (C). 1994. mass mkt., student ed. 38.95 (*0-8384-2585-2*); mass mkt., wbk. ed., lab manual ed. 31.95 (*0-8384-2582-8*) Heinle & Heinle.

Long, Donnie. Forever & a Day. 116p. 1998. pap. 10.00 (*1-57502-950-2*, PO2613) Morris Pubng.

Long, Doris E. Unfair Competition & Section 43(a) of the Lanham Act. LC 93-3995. 540p. 1993. 95.00 (*0-87179-785-2*) BNA Books.

Long, Doris E., jt. ed. see D'Amato, Anthony.

Long, Dorothy R., jt. auth. see Long, Ralph B.

Long, Doucet. Dictionnaire Juridique et Economique: Russian - French, French - Russian. (FRE & RUS.). 1984. lib. bdg. 175.00 (*0-8288-2492-4*) Fr & Eur.

Long Doucet. Russian-French, French-Russian Legal & Economic Dictionary: Dictionnaire Juridique et Economique Russe-Francais-Russe. (FRE & RUS.). 844p. 1984. 175.00 (*0-8288-0402-8*, F800) Fr & Eur.

Long, Douglas E., jt. auth. see Young, Carol D.

Long, Duncan. AK47: The Complete Kalashnikov Family of Assault Rifles. (Illus.). 192p. 1988. pap. 20.00 (*0-87364-477-8*) Paladin Pr.

— Antigrav Unlimited. 176p. 1988. pap. 2.95 (*0-380-75357-X*, Avon Bks) Morrow Avon.

— AR-15 - M16 Super Systems. (Illus.). 144p. 1989. pap. 19.95 (*0-87364-511-1*) Paladin Pr.

— The AR-15-M16: A Practical Guide. LC 85-160984. (Illus.). 168p. 1985. pap. 22.00 (*0-87364-321-6*) Paladin Pr.

— AR-7 Super Systems. (Illus.). 144p. 1990. pap. 17.00 (*0-87364-573-1*) Paladin Pr.

— Assault Pistols, Rifles & Submachine Guns. 1987. pap. 12.95 (*0-8065-1042-0*, Citadel Pr) Carol Pub Group.

— Assault Pistols, Rifles & Submachine Guns. (Illus.). 152p. 1986. pap. 21.95 (*0-87364-353-4*) Paladin Pr.

— Automatics: Fast Firepower, Tactical Superiority. (Illus.). 144p. 1986. pap. 18.00 (*0-87364-397-6*) Paladin Pr.

— The Complete AR-15 - M16 Sourcebook. (Illus.). 1992. pap. 35.00 (*0-87364-687-8*) Paladin Pr.

— Defeating Industrial Spies. LC 91-61944. (Illus.). 144p. 1991. pap. 16.95 (*1-55950-073-5*, 55086) Loompanics.

— Hand Cannons: The World's Most Powerful Handguns. (Illus.). 208p. 1994. pap. 20.00 (*0-87364-809-9*) Paladin Pr.

— Homemade Ammo: How to Make It, How to Reload It, How to Cache It. (Illus.). 104p. 1995. pap. 16.00 (*0-87364-816-1*) Paladin Pr.

— How to Survive a Nuclear Accident. LC 87-81612. (Illus.). 160p. (Orig.). 1987. pap. 10.95 (*0-915179-67-9*, 11095) Loompanics.

— Making Your AR-15 into a Legal Pistol. (Illus.). 88p. 1991. 14.00 (*0-87364-622-3*) Paladin Pr.

— The Mini-14: The Plinker, Hunter, Assault, & Everything Else Rifle. (Illus.). 120p. 1987. pap. 17.00 (*0-87364-407-7*) Paladin Pr.

— Mini-14 Super Systems. (Illus.). 200p. 1991. pap. 16.95 (*0-87364-589-8*) Paladin Pr.

— Modern Ballistic Armor: Clothing, Bomb Blankets, Shields, Vehicle Protection... Everything You Need to Know. (Illus.). 104p. 1986. pap. 20.00 (*0-87364-391-7*) Paladin Pr.

— Modern Camouflage. 2nd rev. ed. LC 91-73266. (Illus.). 80p. 1992. pap. text 10.00 (*0-939427-65-6*) Alpha Pubns OH.

— Modern Combat Ammo. (Illus.). 216p. 1991. 30.00 (*0-87364-628-2*) Paladin Pr.

— Modern Sniper Rifles. (Illus.). 120p. 1988. pap. 20.00 (*0-87364-470-0*) Paladin Pr.

— The Poor Man's Fort Knox: Home Security with Inexpensive Safes. (Illus.). 48p. 1991. pap. 10.00 (*0-87364-645-2*) Paladin Pr.

— The Ruger .22 Automatic Pistol: Standard-Mark I-Mark II Series. (Illus.). 168p. 1988. pap. 16.00 (*0-87364-488-3*) Paladin Pr.

— Streetsweepers: The Complete Book of Combat Shotguns. (Illus.). 160p. 1987. pap. 24.95 (*0-87364-424-7*) Paladin Pr.

— The Sturm, Ruger 10-22 Rifle & .44 Magnum Carbine. (Illus.). 108p. 1988. pap. 15.00 (*0-87364-449-2*) Paladin Pr.

— Super Shotguns. (Illus.). 96p. 1992. pap. 18.00 (*0-87364-691-6*) Paladin Pr.

— Survival Bartering. 1998. pap. text 8.00 (*0-9666932-4-8*) Breakout Prods Inc.

L

L

— The Terrifying Three: Uzi, Ingram, & Intratec Weapons Families. (Illus.). 136p. 1989. pap. 20.00 (0-87364-523-5) Paladin Pr.
— To Break a Tyrant's Chains: Neo-Guerrilla Techniques for Combat. LC 91-70479. (Illus.). 152p. (Orig.). 1991. pap. 15.00 (0-939427-91-5, 09053) Alpha Pubns OH.
Long, E., jt. auth. see Kuklick, Henrika.
Long, E. B. The Civil War Day by Day: An Almanac 1861-1865. (Quality Paperbacks Ser.). (Illus.). xiv, 1135p. 1985. reprint ed. pap. 19.95 (0-306-80255-4) Da Capo.
— The Saints & the Union: Utah Territory During the Civil War. LC 80-16775. (Illus.). 326p. 1981. text 27.50 (0-252-00821-9) U of Ill Pr.
Long, E. B., jt. auth. see Grant, Ulysses S.
Long, E. Croft, ed. see Arbona, Guillermo, et al.
Long, Earl. Consolation. (Longman Critical Writers Ser.). 156p. (C). 1995. pap. 15.73 (0-582-23913-3) Addison-Wesley.
— Voices from a Drum. (Longman Caribbean Writers Ser.). 152p. (C). 1996. pap. 16.80 (0-582-28709-X) Addison-Wesley.
Long, Earlene R. Gone Fishing. LC 83-22558. (Illus.). 32p. (J). (ps-3). 1987. pap. 5.95 (0-395-44236-2) HM.
Long, Earnest A., jt. auth. see Long, Ernest A.
Long, Earnest A., ed. see Davidson, Al.
Long, Earnest A., jt. ed. see Long, Ida.
Long, Eddie. Taking Over. LC 98-28750. 1998. 12.99 (0-88419-484-1) Creation House.
Long, Eddie L. I Dont Want Delilah, I Need You! What a Woman Needs to Know, What a Man Needs to Understand. 256p. 1998. pap. 11.99 (1-57778-068-X, Pub. by Albury Pub) Appalach Bk Dist.
— Thy Kingdom Come. 64p. 1998. pap. 0.99 (1-57778-070-1, Pub. by Albury Pub) Appalach Bk Dist.
Long, Edward. The History of Jamaica, 3 vols. (Illus.). 1972. 145.95 (0-405-03293-5) Arno Press.
— History of Jamaica, 3 vols., Set. (Illus.). 1631p. 1970. reprint ed. 295.00 (0-7146-1942-6, Pub. by F Cass Pubs) Intl Spec Bk.
Long, Edward L., Jr. Higher Education As a Moral Enterprise. LC 92-13886. 224p. (Orig.). (C). 1992. pap. text 25.00 (0-87840-531-3) Georgetown U Pr.
Long, Edward L. Peace Thinking in a Warring World. LC 83-14675. 118p. reprint ed. pap. 36.60 (0-7837-2634-1, 204298400006) Bks Demand.
Long, Edward L., Jr. A Survey of Christian Ethics. 352p. 1982. pap. text 23.95 (0-19-503242-X) OUP.
— A Survey of Recent Christian Ethics. 230p. 1982. pap. text 21.95 (0-19-503160-1) OUP.
— To Liberate & Redeem: Moral Reflections on the Biblical Narrative. LC 97-5601. 280p. (Orig.). 1997. pap. 18.95 (0-8298-1176-1) Pilgrim OH.
Long, Edward S. Two Nativity Dramas. 1984. 5.00 (0-89536-697-5, 4874) CSS OH.
Long, Elaine. Bittersweet Country. large type ed. LC 99-18678. 589p. 1999. 27.95 (0-7838-8565-2, G K Hall & Co) Mac Lib Ref.
— Jenny's Mountain. large type ed. LC 97-48568. 1998. 25.95 (0-7838-8393-5, G K Hall & Co) Mac Lib Ref.
Long, Elaine, ed. see Pettem, Silvia.
Long, Eleanor R. Wilderness to Washington: An 1811 Journey by Horseback. LC 81-51895. 166p. 1981. reprint ed. pap. 7.95 (0-89917-324-1) Guild Pr IN.
***Long, Elgen M.** Amelia Earhart. 2001. pap. 14.00 (0-684-86006-6, Fireside) S&S Trade Pap.
Long, Elgen M. & Long, Marie K. Amelia Earhart: The Mystery Solved. LC 99-35861. (Illus.). 320p. 1999. 25.00 (0-684-86005-8) S&S Trade.
Long, Elizabeth. The American Dream & the Popular Novel. 224p. 1985. 32.50 (0-7100-9934-7, Routledge Thoemms) Routledge.
— Songs Unsung. LC 96-27223. (Illus.). 224p. 1996. pap. 16.95 (1-880090-37-6) Galde Pr.
— Ysabella de Trastamara - First Lady of the Renaissance: The Epic Reign of Queen Isabella of Spain. Douglas, Auriole, ed. (Illus.). 414p. 1992. 26.95 (0-9631244-5-5); pap. 16.95 (0-9631244-6-3) Alhamar Pub.
Long, Elizabeth, ed. From Sociology to Cultural Studies: New Perspectives. LC 97-556. 592p. (C). 1997. text 73.95 (1-57718-012-7); pap. text 31.95 (1-57718-013-5) Blackwell Pubs.
Long, Elizabeth T., jt. compiled by see Clark, Jewell T.
Long, Elliot. Death on High Mesa. large type ed. (Linford Western Library). 224p. 1994. pap. 16.99 (0-7089-7492-9, Linford) Ulverscroft.
— Death Trail. large type ed. (Dales Large Print Ser.). 211p. 1997. pap. 18.99 (1-85389-698-5) Ulverscroft.
***Long, Elliot.** Ethanol Programs (In Minnesota) A Program Evaluation Report. (Illus.). 101p. 1999. reprint ed. pap. text 25.00 (0-7881-8284-6) DIANE Pub.
Long, Elliot. The Hanging Man. large type ed. (Dales Large Print Ser.). 200p. 1997. pap. 18.99 (1-85389-750-7, Dales) Ulverscroft.
— A Killing at Tonto Springs. large type ed. (Linford Western Library). 224p. 1995. pap. 16.99 (0-7089-7765-0, Linford) Ulverscroft.
— Last Texas Gun. large type ed. 240p. 1998. pap. 19.99 (1-85389-846-5) Ulverscroft.
— Lawless Range. large type ed. 184p. 1996. pap. 18.99 (1-85389-581-4, Dales) Ulverscroft.
— Mankiller. large type ed. (Linford Western Library). 256p. 1996. pap. 16.99 (0-7089-7949-1, Linford) Ulverscroft.
***Long, Elliot.** Retribution Day. 272p. 2000. 18.99 (0-7089-5690-4) Ulverscroft.
— Scallon's Law. large type ed. 224p. 2000. pap. 20.99 (1-84137-007-X, Pub. by Mgna Lrg Print) Ulverscroft.
Long, Elliot. Showdown at Crazy Man Creek. large type ed. (Linford Western Library). 208p. 1996. pap. 16.99 (0-7089-7879-7, Linford) Ulverscroft.
— Sixgun Predator. large type ed. (Dales Western Ser.). 224p. 1998. pap. 19.99 (1-85389-789-2, Dales) Ulverscroft.
— Trail to Nemesis. large type ed. (Linford Western Large Print Ser.). 1994. pap. 16.99 (0-7089-7642-5) Ulverscroft.
— Warpath. large type ed. 224p. 1996. pap. 18.99 (1-85389-598-9, Dales) Ulverscroft.
— Wassala Valley Shootout. large type ed. (Linford Western Library). 224p. 1993. pap. 16.99 (0-7089-7444-9, Linford) Ulverscroft.
***Long, Elliot.** Welcome to Hell. large type ed. 272p. 1999. pap. 20.99 (1-85389-912-7, Dales) Ulverscroft.
Long, Ernest A. & Long, Earnest A. Dictionary of Toys Sold in America, Vol. I. (Illus.). 83p. (Orig.). 1987. reprint ed. pap. 17.50 (0-9604406-3-1) Deborah Davidson.
Long, Eugene T. Jaspers & Bultmann: A Dialogue Between Philosophy & Theology in the Existentialist Tradition. LC 68-31725. 165p. reprint ed. pap. 51.20 (0-608-15066-5, 202620800048) Bks Demand.
Long, Eugene T., ed. Experience, Reason & God. LC 80-11334. (Studies in Philosophy & the History of Philosophy: No. 8). 186p. reprint ed. pap. 57.70 (0-608-18720-8, 202949900061) Bks Demand.
— God, Reason & Religions: New Essays in the Philosophy of Religion. (Studies in Philosophy & Religion: Vol. 18). 220p. (C). 1995. text 100.50 (0-7923-3810-3) Kluwer Academic.
— Prospects for a Natural Theology. LC 91-41756. (Studies in Philosophy & the History of Philosophy: Vol. 25). 242p. 1992. text 51.95 (0-8132-0755-X) Cath U Pr.
Long, Eugene T., jt. ed. see Clarke, Bowman L.
***Long, Eugene Thomas.** Twentieth-Century Western Philosophny of Religion, 1900-2000. LC 00-38633. 2000. write for info. (0-7923-6285-3, Kluwer Plenum) Kluwer Academic.
Long, Eula F. My Country Home. 1998. pap. write for info. (1-57553-761-3) Watermrk Pr.
Long, F., ed. ADA Yearbook, 1992. 336p. 1992. 69.95 (0-442-31581-3) Chapman & Hall.
Long, F. A. & Schweitzer, Glenn E., eds. Risk Assessment at Hazardous Waste Sites. LC 82-16376. (Symposium Ser.: No. 204). 129p. 1982. lib. bdg. 38.95 (0-8412-0747-X) Am Chemical.
Long, F. Leslie & Long, Lucy B. The Henry Ford Era at Richmond Hill, Georgia. LC 98-74051. (Illus.). viii, 328p. 1998. write for info. (0-9667610-0-6) F Long.
Long, F. W., ed. Software Engineering Environments: Proceedings of the International Workshop in Environments Chinon, France, September 18-20, 1989. (Lecture Notes in Computer Science Ser.: Vol. 467). vi, 313p. 1990. 38.00 (0-387-53452-0) Spr-Verlag.
Long, Frank. Desirable Physical Facilities for an Activity Program. LC 78-177007. (Columbia University. Teachers College. Contributions to Education Ser.: No. 593). reprint ed. 37.50 (0-404-55593-4) AMS Pr.
— Restrictive Business Practices, Transnational Corporations & Development. (Dimensions of International Business Ser.). 192p. 1981. lib. bdg. 73.50 (0-89838-057-X) Kluwer Academic.
Long, Frank, ed. Ragnar Frisch: Economic Planning Studies. LC 75-44219. (International Studies in Economics & Econometrics: No. 8). 1975. lib. bdg. 88.00 (90-277-0245-4) Kluwer Academic.
Long, Frank B. The Darkling Tide: Previously Uncollected Poetry. Grayson, Perry M., ed. & notes by. (Illus.). 40p. (Orig.). Date not set. pap. 6.00 (1-887968-01-6) Tsathoggua Pr.
— The Eye above the Mantel & other Stories: 4 Previously Uncollected Weird Tales. Grayson, Perry M., ed. & intro. by. 28p. (Orig.). 1995. pap. 5.00 (1-887968-00-8) Tsathoggua Pr.
Long, Frank B., et al. The First World Fantasy Convention: The Interviews. Murray, Will & Grayson, Perry M., eds. 23p. (Orig.). 1995. pap. 6.00 (1-887968-02-4) Tsathoggua Pr.
Long, Frank W. Confessions of a Depression Muralist. LC 96-51958. (Illus.). 179p. 1997. 24.95 (0-8262-0994-7) U of Mo Pr.
Long, Franklin A. & Schweitzer, Glenn E., eds. Risk Assessment at Hazardous Waste Sites. LC 82-16376. (ACS Symposium Ser.: No. 204). (Illus.). 139p. 1982. reprint ed. pap. 43.10 (0-608-03217-4, 206373600007) Bks Demand.
Long, Freda M. The Dressmaker. large type ed. 1990. 27.99 (0-7089-2125-6) Ulverscroft.
***Long, Freda M.** The Gilded Cage. large type ed. 384p. 1999. pap. 18.99 (0-7089-5549-5, Linford) Ulverscroft.
Long, Freda M. The Heir of Frinton Park. large type ed. LC 97-30902. 278p. 1998. lib. bdg. 18.95 (0-7838-8290-4, G K Hall Lrg Type) Mac Lib Ref.
— The Master of Frinton Park. large type ed. (Dales Large Print Ser.). 321p. 1997. pap. 18.99 (1-85389-672-1) Ulverscroft.
***Long, Freda M.** Mischief at Frinton Park. large type ed. 384p. 2000. pap. 18.99 (0-7089-5635-1, Linford) Ulverscroft.
— The Soldier's Woman. large type ed. 368p. 1999. pap. 18.99 (0-7089-5487-1, Linford) Ulverscroft.
Long, G. Gilbert & Hentz, Forrest C. Problem Exercises for General Chemistry. 3rd ed. 460p. 1986. pap. 39.95 (0-471-82840-8) Wiley.
Long, G. J. Mossbauer Spectroscopy Applied to Inorganic Chemistry, Vol. 2. LC 84-13417. (Modern Inorganic Chemistry Ser.). (Illus.). 642p. (C). 1987. text 145.00 (0-306-42507-6, Kluwer Plenum) Kluwer Academic.
Long, G. J. & Grandjean, F. Mossbauer Spectroscopy Applied to Inorganic Chemistry, Vol. 3. (Modern Inorganic Chemistry Ser.). (Illus.). 660p. (C). 1989. text 145.00 (0-306-43073-8, Kluwer Plenum) Kluwer Academic.
— Mossbauer Spectroscopy Applied to Magnetism & Materials Science, Vol. 1. LC 93-14059. (Modern Inorganic Chemistry Ser.). (Illus.). 496p. (C). 1993. text 110.00 (0-306-44447-X, Kluwer Plenum) Kluwer Academic.
Long, Gabrielle M. World's Wonder & Other Essays. (Essay Index Reprint Ser.). 1977. 23.95 (0-8369-1223-3) Ayer.
Long, Gary J., ed. Industrial Applications of the Mossbauer Effect. LC 86-22669. 806p. 1987. 135.00 (0-306-42463-0, Plenum Trade) Perseus Pubng.
— Mossbauer Spectroscopy Applied to Inorganic Chemistry, Vol. 1. LC 84-13417. (Modern Inorganic Chemistry Ser.). (Illus.). 686p. (C). 1984. text 174.00 (0-306-41647-6, Kluwer Plenum) Kluwer Academic.
Long, Gary J. & Grandjean, Fernande, eds. Mossbauer Spectroscopy Applied to Magnetism & Materials Science, Vol. 2. (Modern Organic Chemistry Ser.). (Illus.). 330p. (C). 1996. text 107.00 (0-306-45398-3, Kluwer Plenum) Kluwer Academic.
— Supermagnets, Hard Magnetic Materials. (C). 1991. text 332.00 (0-7923-1092-6) Kluwer Academic.
— The Time Domain in Surface & Structural Dynamics. (C). 1988. text 299.00 (90-277-2688-4) Kluwer Academic.
Long, Gavin. MacArthur. (Military Commanders Ser.). 1998. pap. 18.95 (0-938289-14-4, 289144) Combined Pub.
Long, Gene. Reality & the Soul No. 100: The Key to Understanding the Soul. unabridged ed. 225p. 1997. pap. 8.95 (0-9665168-0-X) GDL Pubns.
Long, George. The Folklore Calendar. LC 89-63255. (Illus.). 240p. 1990. reprint ed. lib. bdg. 38.00 (1-55888-875-6) Omnigraphics Inc.
— The Thoughts of the Emperor: Marcus Aurelius Antoninus. 195p. 1995. pap. 25.00 (0-87556-785-1) Saifer.
— Treatise on the Law Relative to Sales of Personal Property. xvi, 288, xxiiip. 1982. reprint ed. 30.00 (0-8377-2403-1, Rothman) W S Hein.
Long, George, tr. see Aurelius, Marcus.
Long, George, tr. see Epictetus.
Long, George F., III, jt. auth. see McKenney, Charles E.
Long, Gerald P., jt. auth. see Patrick, John J.
Long, Greg. Examining the Earthlight Theory: The Yakima UFO Microcosm. (Illus.). 185p. (C). 1990. pap. text 17.95 (0-929343-57-3) J A Hynek Ctr UFO.
Long, H. W. Sane Sex Life. 14.95 (0-685-22094-X) Wehman.
Long, Haniel. Cabeza de Vaca: His Relation of the Journey Florida to the Pacific 1528-1536. (Illus.). 40p. 1988. reprint ed. 60.00 (0-942067-00-2) Okeanos Pr.
— The Marvelous Adventure of Cabeza de Vaca. (Basket of Tolerance Ser.). (Illus.). 64p. (Orig.). 1992. 11.95 (0-918801-46-X) Dawn Horse Pr.
— My Seasons. 2nd ed. Maguire, James H., ed. LC 77-72389. (Ahsahta Press Modern & Contemporary Poets of the West Ser.). 68p. 1977. pap. 6.95 (0-916272-06-0) Ahsahta Pr.
— Pittsburgh Memoranda. LC 90-33956. 88p. 1990. reprint ed. text 14.95 (0-8229-3657-7) U of Pittsburgh Pr.
Long, Haniel, ed. & tr. see De Vaca, Cabeza.
Long, Hanna. Huckleberry Horse. 76p. 1993. pap. 10.50 (1-56770-269-4) S Scheewe Pubns.
Long, Harold & Little, Phil. Okinawan Weapons: Sai & Tonfa Fighting Techniques. (Illus.). 127p. 1997. pap. 17.95 (0-9658459-1-5) Isshin-Ryu.
— Okinawan Weapons Bo Fighting Techniques. (Illus.). 112p. (Orig.). 1987. pap. 9.95 (0-89826-022-1) Natl Paperback.
Long, Harold & Wheeler, Allen. Counter-Attack: Isshinryu Self Defense for Men & Women. Condry, Steve, ed. (Illus.). 96p. 1983. pap. 7.95 (0-89826-010-8) Natl Paperback.
— Dynamics of Isshinryu Karate Black & Brown Belt, Bk. 3. Condry, Steve, ed. (Isshinryu Karate Ser.). (Illus.). 146p. (Orig.). 1980. pap. 6.95 (0-89826-006-X) Natl Paperback.
— Dynamics of Isshinryu Karate Blue & Green Belt, Bk. 2. Condry, Steve, ed. (Illus.). (Orig.). 1979. pap. 5.95 (0-89826-004-3) Natl Paperback.
— Dynamics of Isshinryu Karate Orange Belt, Bk. 1. Condry, Steve, ed. (Isshinryu Karate Ser.). (Illus.). 1978. pap. 6.95 (0-89826-002-7) Natl Paperback.
Long, Harold S. How to Collect Illegal Debts. LC 90-62065. 80p. (Orig.). 1990. pap. 10.00 (1-55950-041-7, 40067) Loompanics.
— Making Crime Pay. LC 88-81589. 88p. (Orig.). 1988. pap. text 9.95 (0-915179-83-0) Loompanics.
— Successful Armed Robbery. LC 89-63706. 56p. (Orig.). 1990. pap. 8.95 (1-55950-023-9, 40065) Loompanics.
Long, Harry. In the Beginning. (Orig.). 1993. pap. 10.95 (0-943383-07-2) FirstHand Ltd.
Long, Harry, ed. see Johnson, et al.
Long, Hei. Da Qiang Ji: Power Striking. (Illus.). 176p. 1994. pap. 15.00 (0-87364-803-X) Paladin Pr.
— Da Zhimingde: Striking Deadly Blows to Vital Organs. (Illus.). 200p. 1993. pap. 15.00 (0-87364-700-9) Paladin Pr.
— Dragons Touch: Weaknesses of the Human Anatomy. (Illus.). 184p. 1983. pap. 14.00 (0-87364-271-6) Paladin Pr.
— Iron Hand of the Dragon's Touch: Secrets of Breaking Power. (Illus.). 112p. 1987. pap. 14.00 (0-87364-434-4) Paladin Pr.
— Master's Guide to Basic Self-Defense: Progressive Retraining of the Reflexive Response. (Illus.). 124p. 1990. pap. 18.00 (0-87364-574-X) Paladin Pr.
— Neng Da: Super Punches. 151p. 1997. pap. 14.95 (1-880336-13-8) Turtle CT.
***Long, Helen.** Victorian Houses & Their Details. 144p. 2001. pap. 56.95 (0-7506-4848-1, Architectural Pr) Buttrwrth-Heinemann.
Long, Howard. Kingsport: A Romance of Industry. (Illus.). 218p. 1993. reprint ed. 21.95 (0-932807-89-5) Overmountain Pr.
Long, Howard R., jt. auth. see Lawhorne, Clifton O.
Long, Howie & Czarnecki, John. Football for Dummies. LC GV951.L744 1998. (For Dummies Ser.). 432p. 1998. pap. 19.99 (0-7645-5054-3) IDG Bks.
Long, Hua. The Moon Maiden & Other Asian Folktales. (Illus.). 32p. (J). 1993. 12.95 (0-8351-2494-0); pap. 8.95 (0-8351-2493-2) China Bks.
Long, Huey. My First Days in the White House. 1992. lib. bdg. 88.95 (0-8490-5514-8) Gordon Pr.
Long, Huey B. Adult Education in Church & Synagogue. LC 73-13292. (Occasional Papers: No. 37). 1973. pap. 2.50 (0-87060-061-3, OCP 37) Syracuse U Cont Ed.
— Adult Learning. 367p. 1988. text 25.00 (0-8428-2202-X) Cambridge Bk.
— Continuing Education of Adults in Colonial America. LC 75-38925. (Occasional Papers: No. 45). 75p. 1976. pap. text 2.75 (0-87060-070-2, OCP 45) Syracuse U Cont Ed.
Long, Huey B. & Confessore, Gary J. Abstracts of Literature in Self-Directed Learning. 168p. (Orig.). 1992. pap. text 24.95 (0-9622488-6-X) U OK PMC.
Long, Huey B. & Reddy, Terrence R. Self-Directed Learning Dissertation Abstracts, 1966-1991. 1991. pap. 24.95 (0-9622488-4-3) U OK PMC.
Long, Huey B., et al. Advances in Research & Practice in Self-Directed Learning. 295p. (Orig.). (C). 1990. pap. 25.95 (0-9622488-2-7) U OK PMC.
— Changing Approaches to Studying Adult Education. LC 78-62579. (Jossey-Bass Series in Higher Education). 174p. reprint ed. pap. 54.00 (0-7837-2520-5, 204267900006) Bks Demand.
— Self-Directed Learning: Consensus & Conflict. 300p. (Orig.). (C). 1991. pap. 25.95 (0-9622488-3-5) U OK PMC.
Long, Huey B., jt. auth. see Confessore, Gary J.
Long, Huey B., & Assoc. Staff. Current Developments in Self-Directed Learning. 257p. (Orig.). 1996. pap. text 26.95 (1-885584-01-6) U OK PMC.
— Emerging Perspectives of Self-Directed Learning. 281p. (Orig.). 1993. pap. text 25.95 (0-9622488-8-6) U OK PMC.
— New Dimensions in Self-Directed Learning. 419p. (Orig.). 1995. pap. text 26.95 (1-885584-00-8) U OK PMC.
— New Ideas about Self-Directed Learning. 246p. (Orig.). 1994. pap. text 26.95 (0-9622488-9-4) U OK PMC.
— Self-Directed Learning: Application & Research. 400p. (Orig.). 1992. pap. text 25.95 (0-9622488-7-8) U OK PMC.
Long, Huey B., & Associates Staff. Expanding Horizons in Self-Directed Learning. LC 96-92787. 325p. (Orig.). (C). 1997. pap. 27.95 (1-885584-02-4) U OK PMC.
— Self-Directed Learning: Emerging Theory & Practice. LC 89-611107. 144p. (Orig.). (C). 1989. pap. text 24.95 (0-9622488-0-0) U OK PMC.
Long, Huey P. Every Man a King: The Autobiography of Huey P. Long. LC 95-42402. (Illus.). 410p. 1996. reprint ed. pap. 15.95 (0-306-80695-9) Da Capo.
Long, Hugh W., ed. Confronting the Budget & Trade Deficits. LC 86-8077. (ITT Key Issues Lecture). 99p. 1986. pap. 15.00 (0-86569-144-4, R144, Auburn Hse) Greenwood.
Long, Ida & Long, Earnest A., eds. Dictionary of Toys Sold in America, Vol. II. (Illus.). 72p. 1987. reprint ed. pap. 17.50 (0-9604406-4-X) Deborah Davidson.
Long, Ida, ed. see Davidson, Al.
Long, Inez. Faces among the Faithful. LC 62-5029. 194p. reprint ed. pap. 60.20 (0-608-13562-3, 202241400026) Bks Demand.
Long Island Library Resources Council Committee on. A Directory of Government Documents Collections in Nassau & Suffolk Counties, New York. 3rd ed. 1992. pap. 16.50 (0-938435-33-7) LI Lib Resources.
Long, J., ed. Consumer Know-How. 64p. (Orig.). 1988. pap. text. write for info. (0-8428-7408-9) Cambridge Bk.
— Job Success Know-How. 64p. (Orig.). 1988. pap. text 2.70 (0-8428-7407-0) Cambridge Bk.
— Money Know-How. 64p. (Orig.). 1988. pap. text. write for info. (0-8428-7411-9) Cambridge Bk.
***Long, J. & Paul, K.** The Wonky Donkey. 1999. 11.95 (0-370-32466-8, Pub. by Bodley Head) Trafalgar.
Long, J. & Whitefield, A., eds. Cognitive Ergonomics & Human Computer Interaction. (Cambridge Series on Human-Computer Interaction: No. 1). 272p. (C). 1989. text 80.00 (0-521-37179-1) Cambridge U Pr.
Long, J. Anthony, jt. ed. see Boldt, Menno.
Long, J. L., jt. auth. see Oberst, B. B.
Long, J. P., jt. ed. see Gerald, M. C.
Long, J. S., jt. ed. see Myers, Raymond R.
Long, J. Scott. Common Problems - Proper Solutions: Avoiding Error in Quantitative Research. (Focus Editions Ser.: Vol. 94). 360p. 1988. 59.95 (0-8039-2806-8); pap. 26.00 (0-8039-2807-6) Sage.
— Confirmatory Factor Analysis. (Quantitative Applications in the Social Sciences Ser.: Vol. 33). 88p. 1983. pap. text 10.95 (0-8039-2044-X) Sage.
— Covariance Structure Models. LC 83-50602. (University Papers: Vol. 34). 95p. 1983. pap. text 10.95 (0-8039-2045-8) Sage.
— Regression Models for Categorical & Limited Dependent Variables: Analysis & Interpretation. (Advanced Quantitative Techniques in the Social Sciences Ser.: Vol. 7). 416p. 1997. 45.00 (0-8039-7374-8) Sage.
Long, J. Scott, ed. Common Problems/Proper Solutions: Avoiding Error in Quantitative Research. LC 87-20625. (Sage Focus Editions Ser.: Vol. 94). (Illus.). 355p. 1988. reprint ed. pap. 110.10 (0-608-01620-9, 205959900003) Bks Demand.
Long, J. Scott, jt. auth. see Fox, John.
Long, J. Scott, jt. ed. see Bollen, Kenneth A.

An Asterisk (*) at the beginning of an entry indicates that the title is appearing for the first time.

Long, J. Scott, jt. ed. see Fox, John.
Long, J. Scott, ed. see Panel to Study Gender Differences in Career Outcom.
Long, J. William. Cathedral: or Diary of a Dead Metaphysician. LC 96-35068. 96p. 1997. 15.95 (0-944957-89-7) Rivercross Pub.
Long, Jack. 12-Bar Blues Piano. 64p. 1997. pap. 14.95 (0-7119-4521-7, AM92445) Omnibus NY.
***Long, Jack, comment.** All the Blues Chords You'll Ever Need. (Illus.). 46p. 1999. pap. text 5.95 (0-7119-7770-4, AM955372) Music Sales.
— All the Jazz Chords you'll Ever Need. (Illus.). 46p. 1999. pap. text 5.95 (0-7119-7769-0, AM955361) Music Sales.
Long, Jack, ed. The Encyclopedia of Blues Chords. (Illus.). 101p. 1998. pap. 14.95 (0-7119-4669-8, AM92592) Music Sales.
— The Encyclopedia of Jazz Chords: Essential for Piano & Keyboard Players. (Illus.). 104p. 1997. pap. text 14.95 (0-7119-4668-X, AM92591) Music Sales.
— The Encyclopedia of Rock Chords: Essential for All Piano & Keyboard Players. 104p. 1997. pap. text 14.95 (0-7119-4670-1, AM92593) Music Sales.
Long, Jacqueline. Claudian's in Eutropium: Or, How, When, & Why to Slander a Eunuch. LC 95-23507. 320p. (C). 1996. text 55.00 (0-8078-2263-9) U of NC Pr.
Long, Jacqueline, jt. auth. see Cameron, Alan.
Long, James. Ferney. LC 99-11758. 352p. 1999. 23.95 (0-553-10844-1) Bantam.
***Long, James.** Ferney. 2000. mass mkt. 6.50 (0-553-58141-4) Bantam.
Long, James. It's Who You Are That Counts. LC 96-46095. (Deeper Devotions Ser.). 208p. (Orig.). (YA). (gr. 9-12). 1997. pap. 9.99 (0-310-20601-4) Zondervan.
— What Is Man? Leader's Guide. Chao, Lorna Y., tr. (Basic Doctrine Ser.). 1986. pap. write for info. (0-941598-36-5) Living Spring Pubns.
— When Things Get Tough: True Faith Keeps You Going. LC 97-24968. (Deeper Devotions Ser.). 192p. 1997. pap. 9.99 (0-310-20598-0) Zondervan.
Long, James, jt. auth. see Harding, Steven.
Long, James, jt. auth. see Williams, Robert.
Long, James A. Expanding Horizons. LC 65-24093. 254p. 1990. pap. 11.95 (0-911500-75-8) Theos U Pr.
— Expanding Horizons. LC 65-24093. 254p. 1990. reprint ed. 17.95 (0-911500-87-1) Theos U Pr.
— Expansion de Horizontes. LC 95-9183. (SPA.). 258p. (Orig.). 1995. pap. 11.95 (1-55700-024-7) Theos U Pr.
— Marching Forward Vol. 3: Women's First in the Northwest, 1444 Role Models. (Illus.). 202p. 1999. pap. 29.95 (1-882635-01-9) Pumpkin Ridge.
— Oregon Firsts: Oregon's Trailblazing Past & Present. (Illus.). 224p. (Orig.). (YA). 1993. pap. 24.95 (1-882635-00-0) Pumpkin Ridge.
Long, James D. Dream Chipper. (Shadowrun Ser.). (Illus.). 1990. pap. 8.00 (1-55560-120-0, 7303) FASA Corp.
Long, James D. & Williams, Robert L., eds. Classroom Management with Adolescents. LC 73-3077. 164p. 1973. pap. text 15.95 (0-8422-0288-9) Irvington.
Long, James E., jt. auth. see Long, Laura J.
Long, James P. & Warmbrod, Catharine P. Preparing for High Technology Bk. III: A Guide for Community Colleges. 15p. 1982. 2.75 (0-318-22174-8, RD231) Ctr Educ Trng Employ.
Long, James P., et al. How to Phase Out a Program. 47p. 1983. 4.95 (0-318-22127-6, SN42) Ctr Educ Trng Employ.
***Long, James W.** The Essential Guide to Chronic Illness: The Active Patient's Handbook. 625p. 2000. pap. text 20.00 (0-7881-6903-3) DIANE Pub.
Long, James W. The Essential Guide to Chronic Illness: The Active Patient's Handbook for:(see reading line) LC 96-47743. (Illus.). 640p. 1997. pap. 20.00 (0-06-273137-8, Perennial) HarperTrade.
— From Privileged to Dispossessed: The Volga Germans, 1860-1917. LC 88-1144. (Illus.). xvi, 337p. 1988. text 45.00 (0-8032-2881-3) U of Nebr Pr.
Long, James W., jt. auth. see Rybacki, James J.
***Long, Jane.** Conversations in Cold Rooms: Women, Work & Poverty in 19th-Century Northumberland. LC 98-45076. (Royal Historical Society Ser.). (Illus.). 256p. 1999. 75.00 (0-86193-240-4, Royal Historical Soc) Boydell & Brewer.
Long, Jane, et al, eds. Forging Identities: Bodies, Gender & Feminist History. LC 97-162314. 272p. 1997. pap. 24.95 (1-875560-86-6, Pub. by Univ of West Aust Pr) Intl Spec Bk.
***Long, Jane M.** Of Heartache Humor & Hope: A Collection of Poetry & Song. LC 98-91074. 2000. 14.95 (0-533-13032-8) Vantage.
***Long, Jane S. & Long, Richard W.** Caring for Your Family Treasures: Heritage Preservation. (Illus.). 162p. 2000. pap. 24.95 (0-8109-2909-0, Pub. by Abrams) Time Warner.
Long, Janet, ed. see Ervin, T. D.
***Long, Jay D.** Kookaburros Never Cry. (Illus.). 145p. 1999. pap. 12.95 (0-9669179-2-8) Fifth Wrld.
Long, Jean, ed. see Brown, Bernita J.
Long, Jean M. Beneath a Lakeland Moon. (Rainbow Romances Ser.). 160p. 1994. 14.95 (0-7090-5397-5, 916) Parkwest Pubns.
— Beneath a Lakeland Moon. large type ed. (Linford Romance Library). 272p. 1995. pap. 16.99 (0-7089-7775-8, Linford) Ulverscroft.
Long, Jean M. Island of Flowers. large type ed. 320p. 31.99 (0-7089-4026-9) Ulverscroft.
Long, Jean M. Island Serenade. large type ed. (Linford Romance Library). 1990. pap. 16.99 (0-7089-6822-8) Ulverscroft.
— To Dream of Gold Apples. large type ed. (Linford Romance Library). 320p. 1989. pap. 16.99 (0-7089-6664-0, Linford) Ulverscroft.
Long, Jeanne. Kaleidoscope. (Pathways to Poetry Ser.). 115p. 1984. pap. 17.95 (0-86617-031-6) Multi Media TX.
Long, Jeanne, et al. Pathways to Poetry Series: Kaleidoscope, Mosaics, Visions. Miller, Jo, ed. (J). (gr. 1-12). 1984. pap. text 44.74 (0-86617-033-2) Multi Media TX.
Long, Jeannie, jt. auth. see Alexander, Michele.
Long, Jeff. The Descent. LC 98-46829. 450p. 1999. 24.00 (0-609-60293-4, Crown) Crown Pub Group.
— Duel of Eagles: The Mexican & U. S. Fight for the Alamo. (Illus.). 432p. 1991. pap. 13.95 (0-688-10967-5, Quil) HarperTrade.
Long, Jeffrey E., jt. ed. see Finn, Marie T.
Long, Jennifer & Albert, Greg, eds. The Best of Decorative Painting. LC 98-12190. (Illus.). 144p. 1998. 28.99 (0-89134-905-7, North Lght Bks) F & W Pubns Inc.
Long, Jennifer, jt. ed. see Kipp, Kathryn.
Long, Jerry & Tenzer, Jeff. The Cambridge Program for the High School Equivalency Examination. Schenk, Brian, ed. (GED Preparation Ser.). (Illus.). 816p. (Orig.). 1988. pap. text 6.00 (0-8428-9385-7) Cambridge Bk.
Long, Jim. At the Breaking Point: Faith in the Face of Tragedy. 128p. 1991. pap. 6.99 (0-310-71201-7) Zondervan.
***Long, Jim.** Herbal Body Care Just for Men: Naturally Health Tips & Herbal Formulas for Skin Protection, Sore Muscle Relief, Aftershaves, Tonic & More. LC 99-23381. 144p. 1999. pap. 14.95 (1-58017-183-4) Storey Bks.
Long, Jim. Making Bentwood Trellises, Arbors, Gates & Fences. LC 98-11781. (Rustic Home Ser.). (Illus.). 156p. 1998. pap. 19.95 (1-58017-051-X) Storey Bks.
— Making Herbal Dream Pillows. LC 98-14498. (Spirit of Aromatherapy Ser.). (Illus.). 64p. 1998. 14.95 (1-58017-075-7) Storey Bks.
Long, Jimmy. Generating Hope: A Strategy for Reaching the Postmodern Generation. LC 97-8457. 235p. 1997. pap. 14.99 (0-8308-1680-1, 1680) InterVarsity.
***Long, Jo.** Council of Angels. LC 99-74545. 234p. 1999. pap. 12.95 (1-87844-74-5) Mayhaven Pub.
Long, Joanna O. Come Life Eternal. LC 95-71502. 184p. 1995. pap. 16.95 (1-881576-59-0) Providence Hse.
— The Cost. 64p. (Orig.). 1996. pap. 9.95 (1-881576-90-6) Providence Hse.
— Spirit Quickening: Thomas a Kempis - The Imitation of Christ in Verse. LC 98-66186. 128p. 1998. pap. 12.95 (1-57736-099-0) Providence Hse.
Long, Joel. Winged Insects. LC 99-19084. (Poetry Prize Ser.: Vol. 4). (Illus.). 112p. 1999. pap. 13.00 (1-877727-98-9, Pub. by White Pine) Consort Bk Sales.
Long, Joel M., jt. ed. see Cortez, Clifton J., Jr.
Long, John. Attacked! By Beasts of Prey & Other Deadly Creatures, True Stories of Survivors. LC 97-34529. xi, 206 p. 1998. pap. 13.95 (0-07-038699-4) Intl Marine.
***Long, John.** The Big Drop! Classic Big Wave Surfing Stories. LC 99-33815. (Adventure Ser.). 265p. 1999. pap. 14.95 (1-56044-917-9) Falcon Pub Inc.
Long, John. Climbing Anchors. (How to Rock Climb Ser.). (Illus.). 112p. (Orig.). 1993. pap. 12.95 (0-934641-37-4) Falcon Pub Inc.
— Close Calls. LC 99-25925. (Illus.). 182p. 1999. pap. 12.95 (1-56044-762-1) Falcon Pub Inc.
— Gorilla Monsoon. 192p. (Orig.). 1989. pap. 12.95 (0-934641-03-X) Falcon Pub Inc.
— Gym Climb. LC 96-162917. (How to Rock Climb Ser.). (Illus.). 58p. (Orig.). 1994. pap. 5.95 (0-934641-75-7) Falcon Pub Inc.
***Long, John.** The High Lonesome: Epic Solo Climbing Stories. LC 99-28159. (Adventure Ser.). 166p. 1999. pap. 14.95 (1-56044-858-X) Falcon Pub Inc.
Long, John. How to Rock Climb. 2nd ed. (How to Rock Climb Ser.). (Illus.). 186p. (Orig.). 1993. pap. 13.95 (0-934641-64-1) Falcon Pub Inc.
— How to Rock Climb. 3rd ed. LC 99-18639. (Illus.). (Orig.). 1998. pap. 13.95 (1-57540-114-2) Falcon Pub Inc.
— The Law of Illinois: Lincoln's Cases Before the Illinois Supreme Court, from His Entry into the Practice of Law until His Entry into Congress, Vol. 1. (Illus.). 301p. (Orig.). (C). 1993. pap. text 20.00 (0-9635192-0-4) Illinois Co.
***Long, John.** The Liquid Locomotive: Legendary Whitewater River Stories. LC 99-36761. (Adventure Ser.). 250p. 1999. pap. 14.95 (1-56044-856-3) Falcon Pub Inc.
— Mountains of Madness: A Scientist's Odyssey in Antartica. 2000. 24.95 (0-309-07077-5, Joseph Henry Pr) Natl Acad Pr.
Long, John. Rock Jocks, Wall Rats, & Hang Dogs: Rock Climbing on the Edge of Reality. LC 94-6416. 174p. 1994. pap. 11.00 (0-671-88466-2, Fireside) S&S Trade Pap.
— Rock Junction. LC 96-164666. 180p. (Orig.). 1994. pap. 12.95 (0-934641-68-4) Falcon Pub Inc.
— Three Ages Cave. (YA). 1997. pap. 9.95 (1-86368-164-7, Pub. by Fremantle Arts) Intl Spec Bk.
— Welcome to Lumpy Gravy. 1997. pap. 55.60 (0-7611-0858-0) Workman Pub.
— Welcome to Lumpy Gravy. LC 97-9722. (Illus.). 160p. 1997. pap. 8.95 (0-7611-0735-5, 10735) Workman Pub.
— Writer's Little Book of Wisdom. (Little Books of Wisdom Ser.: Vol. 8). 160p. (Orig.). 1996. pap. 5.95 (1-57034-037-4) Globe Pequot.
Long, John, ed. Campfire Howlers. LC 94-12380. 160p. 1994. pap. 11.99 (1-57034-000-5) Globe Pequot.
— Campfire Legends. LC 93-26008. 192p. (Orig.). 1993. pap. 14.95 (0-934802-16-5) Globe Pequot.
Long, John & Baddeley, Alan D., eds. Attention & Performance IX. (Attention & Performance Ser.). 672p. 1981. 135.00 (0-89859-156-2) L Erlbaum Assocs.
Long, John & Franklin, Gia P. Sport Climbing. LC 99-18640. (How to Rock Climb Ser.). (Illus.). 160p. (Orig.). 1997. pap. 12.95 (1-57540-078-2) Falcon Pub Inc.
Long, John & Gaines, Bob. More Climbing Anchors. (How to Rock Climb Ser.). (Illus.). 84p. (Orig.). 1996. pap. 9.95 (1-57540-000-6) Falcon Pub Inc.
Long, John & Hidgson, Michael. The Dayhiker's Handbook: An All-Terrain, All-Season Guide. 1996. pap. 14.95 (0-614-97898-X) McGraw.
Long, John & Hodgson, Michael. The Dayhiker's Handbook: An All-Terrain, All-Season Guide. (Illus.). 256p. 1996. pap. 14.95 (0-07-029146-2) McGraw.
Long, John & McCord, Grace D. McCord of Alaska. LC 74-28612. (Illus.). 150p. 1975. 7.95 (0-913228-15-X) Dillon-Liederbach.
Long, John & Middendorf, John. Big Walls. LC 96-165051. (How to Rock Climb Ser.). (Illus.). 146p. (Orig.). 1994. pap. 12.95 (0-934641-63-3) Falcon Pub Inc.
Long, John & Raleigh, Duane. Clip & Go. LC 96-163542. (How to Rock Climb Ser.). (Illus.). 56p. (Orig.). 1994. pap. 5.95 (0-934641-84-6) Falcon Pub Inc.
Long, John & Webber, Craig. Advanced Rock Climbing. LC 99-17330. (How to Rock Climb Ser.). (Illus.). 300p. (Orig.). 1997. pap. 14.95 (1-57540-075-8) Falcon Pub Inc.
Long, John, et al. Rock Prints: A Collection of Rock Climbing Photography. unabridged ed. LC 98-96607. (Illus.). 96p. 1998. 35.00 (0-9667271-0-X) G Epperson.
Long, John, jt. auth. see Lim, Kee Y.
Long, John, ed. see Craig, David, et al.
Long, John A. Dinosaurs of Australia & New Zealand & Other Animals of the Mesozoic Era. LC 97-41371. (Illus.). 245p. 1998. 39.95 (0-674-20767-X) HUP.
— Eve of Regression. 320p. 1988. mass mkt. 3.95 (0-373-97055-2) Harlequin Bks.
— The Rise of Fishes: 500 Million Years of Evolution. (Illus.). 224p. 1996. reprint ed. pap. text 34.95 (0-8018-5438-5) Johns Hopkins.
Long, John A., ed. Palaeozoic Vertebrate Biostratigraphy & Biogeography. LC 93-11551. 383p. 1994. reprint ed. pap. text 42.50 (0-8018-4779-6) Johns Hopkins.
Long, John A., jt. auth. see McNamara, Ken.
***Long, John Arthur.** The Applicant. 422p. 2000. pap. 14.95 (0-9700492-7-7) Steel Pr Pubng.
Long, John D. After Dinner & Other Speeches. LC 72-4550. (Essay Index Reprint Ser.). 1977. reprint ed. 20.95 (0-8369-2958-6) Ayer.
— The Bible in English: John Wycliffe & William Tyndale. LC 98-3529. 216p. (C). 1998. 49.00 (0-7618-1115-X); pap. 29.50 (0-7618-1116-8) U Pr of Amer.
— Ethics, Morality, & Insurance: A Long-Range Outlook. LC 71-633786. (Sesquicentennial Insurance Ser.). 1971. 8.50 (0-685-00047-8) Ind U Busn Res.
— The New American Navy, 2 vols. Kohn, Richard H., ed. LC 78-22386. (American Military Experience Ser.). (Illus.). 1980. reprint ed. lib. bdg. 61.95 (0-405-11862-7) Ayer.
— What Think Ye of Christ. LC 98-91751. 518p. 1998. pap. write for info. (1-57502-912-X, P02518) Morris Pubng.
Long, John H. Atlas of Historical County Boundaries: Maine, Massachusetts, Connecticut, & Rhode Island. (Illus.). 144p. 1995. 130.00 (0-13-051947-2) S&S Trade.
— Atlas of Historical County Boundaries: Mississippi. (Illus.). 192p. 1992. 130.00 (0-13-051970-7) S&S Trade.
— Atlas of Historical County Boundaries: New Hampshire & Vermont. (Illus.). 112p. 1995. 130.00 (0-13-051954-5) S&S Trade.
— Atlas of Historical County Boundaries: New York. (Illus.). 192p. 1992. 130.00 (0-13-051962-6) S&S Trade.
— Music in English Renaissance Drama. LC 68-12969. 200p. reprint ed. pap. 62.00 (0-608-10978-9, 200160900080) Bks Demand.
— Shakespeare's Use of Music: A Study of the Music & Its Performance in the Original Production of Seven Comedies. LC 77-4643. (Music Reprint Ser.). 1977. reprint ed. lib. bdg. 32.50 (0-306-77423-2) Da Capo.
— Shakespeare's Use of Music: The Final Comedies. LC 77-5644. (Music Reprint Ser.). 1977. reprint ed. lib. bdg. 29.50 (0-306-77424-0) Da Capo.
— Shakespeare's Use of Music Vol. 3: The Histories & Tragedies. LC 61-17588. 306p. 1971. 49.95 (0-8130-0311-3) U Press Fla.
Long, John H., ed. Atlas of Historical County Boundaries: Alabama. LC 94-15023. 1996. 130.00 (0-13-309568-1) S&S Trade.
— Atlas of Historical County Boundaries: Indiana. LC 94-15021. 1996. 130.00 (0-13-309550-9) S&S Trade.
— Atlas of Historical County Boundaries: Pennsylvania. LC 94-15024. 1996. 130.00 (0-13-315532-3) S&S Trade.
Long, John H. & DenBoer, Gordon, eds. Atlas of Historical County Boundaries: Kentucky. LC 94-15022. 1995. 130.00 (0-13-309543-6) S&S Trade.
Long, John H., jt. auth. see Smith Center for the History of Cartography Staff.
Long, John L. Madame Butterfly. 1997. pap. 14.95 (0-9666591-0-4) Seconda Donna.
— Madame Butterfly. 1972. reprint ed. lib. bdg. 27.00 (0-8422-8092-8) Irvington.
— Sixty Jane. LC 76-103524. (Short Story Index Reprint Ser.). 1977. 19.95 (0-8369-3266-8) Ayer.
Long, John V., jt. auth. see Green, Samuel.
Long, Jonathan & Paul, Korky. The Dog That Dug. LC 92-15093. (Illus.). 32p. (J). (ps-3). 1993. 13.95 (0-916291-44-8) Kane-Miller Bk.
Long, Josefina, tr. see Finn, Ken R. & Finn, Marie.
Long, Joseph. Theatre des Varietes. (Theatre in Focus Ser.). (Illus.). 120p. 1980. pap. text. write for info. incl. sl. (0-85964-063-9) Chadwyck-Healey.
***Long, Joseph, ed.** Armand Gatti: Three Plays. 192p. 2000. 29.95 (1-84127-120-9, Pub. by Sheffield Acad) CUP Services.
Long, Joseph C. Blue Sky Law, 2 vols. LC 85-11377. (Securities Law Ser.). 1985. ring bd. 250.00 (0-87632-468-5) West Group.
Long, Joseph K., ed. Extrasensory Ecology: Parapsychology & Anthropology. LC 77-6367. 437p. 1977. 37.00 (0-8108-1036-0) Scarecrow.
Long, Josephine A. Youth Leadership: A Guide to Understanding Leadership Development in Adolescents. LC 98-9020. 1998. 25.00 (0-7879-4059-3) Jossey-Bass.
Long, Judith. The Last Mass of the Knights Templars. LC 98-91410. 1998. pap. 13.95 (0-533-12656-8) Vantage.
— Minister's of Grace: Women in the Early Church. 151p. (C). 1996. pap. 39.95 (0-85439-298-X, Pub. by St Paul Pubns) St Mut.
Long, Judith R. Gene Stratton-Porter: Novelist & Naturalist. (Illus.). xvii, 286p. 1990. 24.95 (0-87195-052-9) Ind Hist Soc.
Long, Judy. Telling Women's Lives. LC 99-6297. (Feminist Crosscurrents Ser.). 185p. 1999. pap. text 19.50 (0-8147-5075-3) NYU Pr.
— Telling Women's Lives: Subject/Narrator/Reader/Text. LC 99-6297. 200p. 1999. text 55.00 (0-8147-5074-5) NYU Pr.
***Long, Judy, ed.** Literary New Orleans. 288p. 1999. pap. 16.95 (1-892514-05-2) Hill St Pr.
— Writing Home: Reflections of Southern Writers. (Illus.). 160p. 2000. 29.95 (1-892514-12-5) Hill St Pr.
Long, Judy & Allen, Patrick, eds. Southerners in NYC. 320p. 2000. 16.95 (1-892514-10-9) Hill St Pr.
***Long, Judy & Payton, Thomas, eds.** Southern Christmas: Literary Classics for the Holidays. 1998. pap. 15.95 (1-892514-08-7) Hill St Pr.
Long, Judy A. California Legal Directory. LC 99-49822. 298p. (C). 2000. pap. text 42.95 (0-7668-1339-8) Thomson Learn.
Long, Judy A., jt. auth. see Hemphill, Charles F., Jr.
Long, Justin T. Engineering for Nuclear Fuel Reprocessing. LC 78-50886. 1036p. 1978. 90.00 (0-89448-012-X, 300012) Am Nuclear Soc.
***Long, Katherine, ed.** The Seattle Times School Guide: Elementary & K-8 Schools. (Illus.). 246p. 1999. pap. write for info. (0-944912-06-0) Seattle Times.
Long, Kathi, jt. auth. see Curtis, Susan.
Long, Kathryn T. The Revival of 1857-58: Interpreting an American Religious Awakening. LC 96-48264. (Religion in America Ser.). (Illus.). 272p. 1998. text 45.00 (0-19-511293-8) OUP.
Long, Kathy. Fix It, Grandma, Fix It. LC 95-75579. (Ready, Set, Read Ser.). (Illus.). 32p. (J). (ps-2). 1995. pap. 5.99 (0-8066-2815-4, 9-2815) Augsburg Fortress.
— God Is Near. LC 92-72746. (Ready, Set, Read Ser.). 32p. (J). 1992. pap. 5.99 (0-8066-2634-8, 9-2634) Augsburg Fortress.
— No! No! No! (Illus.). 144p. (Orig.). 1994. pap. 10.95 (0-399-51845-2, Perigee Bks) Berkley Pub.
Long, Kathy A. Living in Harmony. (Illus.). 32p. (Orig.). (J). (gr. k-4). 1995. pap. text 5.00 (0-9642063-1-5) Best Frnds.
— Taylor Twinkle Finds a Home: A Christmas Story for All Seasons. (Illus.). 32p. (J). (gr. k-4). 1994. pap. 5.00 (0-9642063-0-7) Best Frnds.
Long, Katie, jt. auth. see Carroll, Mary.
***Long, Keith.** Room to Grow: Daily Thoughts for Men. 314p. 1999. 17.95 (1-56563-096-3) Hendrickson MA.
Long, Ken. Personal Finance: An American Experience. 256p. 1997. pap. text 26.50 (1-56226-359-5) CAT Pub.
— Personal Finance: An American Experience. 406p. 1998. pap. text 25.48 (1-56226-407-9) CAT Pub.
Long, Kenneth R. The Music of the English Church. (Illus.). 480p. 1991. lib. bdg. 87.50 (0-340-14962-0, Pub. by Hodder & Stought Ltd) Lubrecht & Cramer.
Long, Kevin, jt. auth. see Siembieda, Kevin.
Long, Kim. Almanac of Anniversaries. LC 92-28945. 1992. lib. bdg. 40.00 (0-87436-675-5) ABC-CLIO.
— The American Forecaster Almanac, 1998. 288p. 1997. pap. text 23.95 (0-9644540-6-8) Am Forecaster.
— The American Forecaster Almanac, 1999. 288p. 1998. pap. 23.95 (0-9644540-7-6) Am Forecaster.
— The American Forecaster Almanac, 1994: Business Edition. (Illus.). 279p. 1993. pap. 27.50 (0-936889-25-X) American Demo.
***Long, Kim.** American Forecaster Almanac, 2000, Vol. 17. 288p. 1999. pap. 23.95 (0-9644540-8-4) Am Forecaster.
Long, Kim. The American Forecaster Almanac 1995. 288p. (Orig.). 1994. pap. 14.95 (0-9644540-0-9); disk 14.95 (0-9644540-1-7) Am Forecaster.
— The American Forecaster Almanac 1996. 224p. (Orig.). 1995. pap. 18.95 (0-9644540-2-5); disk 18.95 (0-9644540-3-3) Am Forecaster.
— The American Forecaster Almanac 1997. 224p. (Orig.). 1996. pap. text 18.95 (0-9644540-4-1); disk 18.95 (0-9644540-5-X) Am Forecaster.
***Long, Kim.** Beavers: A Wildlife Handbook. (Illus.). 192p. 2000. pap. 15.95 (1-55566-251-X) Johnson Bks.
Long, Kim. Directory of Educational Contests for Students K-12. LC 91-25043. 300p. 1991. lib. bdg. 40.00 (0-87436-586-4) ABC-CLIO.
— Encyclopedia of Field Trips & Educational Destinations. LC 91-632. 200p. 1991. lib. bdg. 45.00 (0-87436-585-6) ABC-CLIO.
— Frogs: A Wildlife Handbook. LC 98-55481. 192p. 1999. pap. 15.95 (1-55566-226-9) Johnson Bks.
— Hummingbirds: A Wildlife Handbook. LC 96-49302. (Nature Ser.: Vol. 3). (Illus.). 192p. (Orig.). 1997. pap. 15.95 (1-55566-188-2) Johnson Bks.
— The Moon Book: Fascinating Facts about the Magnificent, Mysterious Moon. 2nd rev. ed. LC 98-26266. (Illus.). 160p. 1998. pap. 12.50 (1-55566-230-7) Johnson Bks.

L

— Owls: A Wildlife Handbook. LC 98-2578. (Nature Ser.: Vol. 4). (Illus.). 192p. 1998. pap. 15.95 (*1-55566-200-5*) Johnson Bks.
— Squirrels. LC 95-43163. (Nature Ser.). (Illus.). 192p. (Orig.). 1995. pap. 15.95 (*1-55566-152-1*) Johnson Bks.
Long, Kristi S. We All Fought for Freedom: Women in Poland's Solidarity Movement. (Studies in Ethnographic Imagination). 192p. (C). 1996. pap. 75.00 (*0-8133-2968-X*, Pub. by Westview) HarpC.
Long, Kristi S. & Nadelhaft, Matthew, eds. America under Construction: Boundaries & Identities in Popular Culture. LC 96-53692. (Studies in American Popular History & Culture). (Illus.). 216p. 1997. text 50.00 (*0-8153-2841-9*) Garland.
Long, L. Kristi. Empowering Employees. LC 95-32042. (Business Skills Express Ser.). 96p. 1995. 10.95 (*0-7863-0314-X*, Irwn Prfssnl) McGraw-Hill Prof.
Long, Larry. Basic Introductory to Computer. 96p. 1990. pap. text 10.80 (*0-13-170606-3*) P-H.
***Long, Larry.** Computers. 7th ed. LC 99-32131. 496p. (C). 1999. pap. text 48.00 (*0-13-083190-5*) P-H.
Long, Larry. Turnaround Time: The Best of Computerworld's Q & A's. 192p. 1987. 17.50 (*0-13-933029-1*) P-H.
Long, Larry & Kreutzer, Nathan. Introduction to Computers & Information Processing: Study Guide. 256p. (C). 1984. pap. text, teacher ed. write for info. (*0-318-57545-0*) P-H.
Long, Larry & Long, Nancy. Computers. 4th ed. 1996. 45.00 (*0-614-09430-5*) P-H.
— Computers. 5th abr. ed. 1997. pap. text 29.33 (*0-13-755604-7*) P-H.
***Long, Larry & Long, Nancy.** Computers. 8th ed. 528p. 2000. pap. 48.00 (*0-13-088236-4*) P-H.
Long, Larry & Long, Nancy. Microcomputer: Concepts & Software. 1992. write for info. (*0-318-68776-3*) P-H.
Long, Larry E. Computers. 6th ed. LC 98-19193. 524p. 1998. pap. text 48.00 (*0-13-096253-8*) P-H.
— Migration & Residential Mobility in the United States. LC 88-15758. (Population of the United States in the 1980s: A Census Monograph Ser.). 400p. 1988. 49.95 (*0-87154-555-1*) Russell Sage.
Long, Larry E. & Long, Nancy. Computers. 7th ed. LC 99-32128. 352p. 1999. pap. 34.67 (*0-13-084797-6*) P-H.
Long, Laura J. & Long, James E. Douglas' Forms, 5 vols. 3rd ed. 1983. 375.00 (*0-87215-716-4*, MICHIE) LEXIS Pub.
***Long, Laurie.** Valuable Bible Characters - New Testament Math Puzzle Grade 1-2. large type ed. (Illus.). 20p. (J). (gr. 1-2). 1999. pap. 4.50 (*1-878669-75-3*, 3513) Crea Tea Assocs.
— Valuable Bible Characters - New Testament Math Puzzles Grade 3-4. large type ed. (Illus.). 20p. (J). (gr. 3-4). 1999. pap. 4.50 (*1-878669-76-1*, 3514) Crea Tea Assocs.
— Valuable Bible Characters - Old Testament Math Puzzles Grades 3-4. large type ed. (Illus.). 20p. (J). (gr. 3-4). 1999. pap. 4.50 (*1-878669-73-7*, 3511) Crea Tea Assocs.
Long, Laurie. Valuable Bible Characters Math Puzzle Book. large type ed. (Illus.). 20p. (J). (gr. 1-2). 1998. 4.50 (*1-878669-72-9*, CRE3510) Crea Tea Assocs.
Long, Laurie S. The Doll's Tea Party. (Sticker Stories Ser.). (Illus.). 16p. (Orig.). (J). (ps-1). 1996. pap. 4.99 (*0-448-41309-4*, G & D) Peng Put Young Read.
Long, Leon E. Geology. 6th ed. (Illus.). 536p. 1994. pap. text 36.95 (*0-89641-265-2*) American Pr.
Long, Lilian P. Wine of the Spirit: Prayer. LC 87-91322. 208p. (Orig.). 1988. pap. 9.95 (*0-9619722-1-1*) L P Long Pub.
Long, Liu J. Longmen Grotto: The National Museums & Monuments of Ancient China. (National Museums & Monuments of Ancient China Ser.). (Illus.). 128p. 1997. 30.00 (*0-85667-456-7*) M T Train.
Long, Lois, jt. auth. see Cage, John M.
Long, Loretta. Courtney's Birthday Party. (Illus.). 32p. 1998. pap. 6.95 (*0-940975-83-1*) Just Us Bks.
***Long, Loretta M.** The Life of Selina Campbell: A Fellow Soldier in the Cause of Restoration. 2000. 34.95 (*0-8173-1059-2*) U of Ala Pr.
Long, Lorraine. Down at the Pond. (Illus.). 32p. (J). (ps-1). 1998. pap. 3.99 (*1-893919-05-6*, 006, Sing Read Ad) Peri Pk Ed Prodn.
— In the Deep Blue Sea. (Illus.). 32p. (J). (ps-1). 1998. pap. 3.99 (*1-893919-06-4*, 007, Sing Read Ad) Peri Pk Ed Prodn.
— The Sing to Read Adventure Teacher's Professional Book. (Illus.). 115p. 1998. pap., teacher ed. 29.95 (*1-893919-07-2*, Sing Read Ad) Peri Pk Ed Prodn.
Long, Lorraine & Roberts, Mary Lou. Here Kitty, Kitty! (Illus.). 32p. (J). (ps-1). 1998. pap. 3.99 (*1-893919-00-5*, 001, Sing Read Ad) Peri Pk Ed Prodn.
— The Indian's Week. (Illus.). 32p. (J). (ps-1). 1998. pap. 3.99 (*1-893919-01-3*, 002, Sing Read Ad) Peri Pk Ed Prodn.
— Jelly Beans & Gummy Things. (Illus.). 32p. (J). (ps-1). 1998. pap. 3.99 (*1-893919-04-8*, 005, Sing Read Ad) Peri Pk Ed Prodn.
— Packing for a Picnic. (Illus.). 32p. (J). (ps-1). 1998. pap. 3.99 (*1-893919-03-X*, 004, Sing Read Ad) Peri Pk Ed Prodn.
***Long, Lorraine & Roberts, Mary Lou.** The Sing to Read Adventure, 7 bks. (J). (ps-1). 1998. pap. 16.95 incl. audio compact disk (*1-893919-08-0*, 009, Sing Read Ad) Peri Pk Ed Prodn.
Long, Lorraine & Roberts, Mary Lou. What's All the Fuss? (Illus.). 32p. (J). (ps-1). 1998. pap. 3.99 (*1-893919-02-1*, 003, Sing Read Ad) Peri Pk Ed Prodn.
Long, Lucy B., jt. auth. see Long, F. Leslie.
Long, Lynellen D. Women's Experiences with HIV/AIDS: An International Perspective. Ankrah, E. Maxine, ed. LC 96-31322. 1997. pap. 18.50 (*0-231-10605-X*) Col U Pr.
Long, Lynellyn D. Ban Vinai: The Refugee Camp. (Illus.). 288p. 1992. pap. text 20.00 (*0-231-07863-3*) Col U Pr.
Long, Lynellyn D. & Ankrah, E. Maxine. Women's Experiences with HIV/AIDS: An International Perspective. LC 96-31322. 426p. 1996. 52.00 (*0-231-10604-1*) Col U Pr.
***Long, Lynette.** Dazzling Division: Games & Activities That Make Math Easy & Fun. (Illus.). 128p. (J). 2000. pap. 12.95 (*0-471-36983-7*) Wiley.
Long, Lynette. Dealing with Addition. LC 97-14075. (Illus.). 32p. (J). (ps-3). 1998. 15.95 (*0-88106-269-3*); pap. 6.95 (*0-88106-270-7*) Charlesbridge Pub.
— Dealing with Addition. 1998. 12.15 (*0-606-13322-4*, Pub. by Turtleback) Demco.
— Domino Addition. LC 95-20083. (Illus.). 32p. (J). (ps-3). 1996. 15.95 (*0-88106-878-0*); pap. 6.95 (*0-88106-877-2*) Charlesbridge Pub.
— Domino Addition. LC 95-20083. 1996. 12.15 (*0-606-09201-3*, Pub. by Turtleback) Demco.
— Domino Addition Book & Game Set. (Illus.). 32p. (J). 1997. pap. 14.95 (*0-88106-352-5*) Charlesbridge Pub.
***Long, Lynette.** Fun with Fractions: Games, Puzzles & Activities That Make Math Easy & Fun. 128p. (J). 2001. pap. 12.95 (*0-471-36981-0*) Wiley.
— Marvelous Multiplication: Games & Activities That Make Math Easy & Fun. LC 00-20473. (Illus.). 128p. 2000. 12.95 (*0-471-36982-9*) Wiley.
— Measurement Mania: Games & Activities That Make Math Easy & Fun. 128p. 2001. pap. 12.95 (*0-471-36980-2*) Wiley.
Long, Lynette. One Dollar: My First Book About Money. LC 97-42946. (Illus.). 32p. (J). (ps-2). 1998. bds. 8.95 (*0-7641-0319-9*); bds. 13.95 (*0-7641-7132-1*) Barron.
— Painless Algebra. LC 98-18911. (Illus.). 224p. (J). 1998. pap. 8.95 (*0-7641-0676-7*) Barron.
— Sumemos con el Domino (Domino Addition) LC 96-53687. (SPA., Illus.). 32p. (Orig.). (J). (ps-3). 1997. pap. 6.95 (*0-88106-909-4*) Charlesbridge Pub.
Long, Lynette. Sumemos con el Domino (Domino Addition) (SPA.). (Orig.). 1997. 12.15 (*0-606-13824-2*, Pub. by Turtleback) Demco.
Long, Lynette & Hershberger, Eileen. One Year to a College Degree. LC 91-72905. 208p. (Orig.). 1992. pap. 10.99 (*1-56384-001-4*) Huntington Hse.
Long, Lynette & Prophit, Penny. Understanding - Responding. 2nd ed. (Nursing Ser.). 1991. pap. 38.75 (*0-86720-433-8*) Jones & Bartlett.
— Understanding-Responding: A Communication Manual for Nurses. LC 80-17977. (C). 1981. pap. text 30.00 (*0-87872-284-X*) Jones & Bartlett.
Long, Lynn, jt. auth. see Young, Mark E.
Long, M. Right to Choose? 9.99 (*1-85792-054-6*, Pub. by Christian Focus) Spring Arbor Dist.
Long, Maria, jt. auth. see Metcalfe, Fray.
Long, Marie K., jt. auth. see Long, Elgen M.
Long, Marjorie, tr. see Levi-Civita, Tullio.
***Long, Mark.** Financing the New Venture: A Complete Guide to Raising Capital from Venture Capitalists, Investment Bankers, Private Investors & Other Sources. LC 99-53196. 408p. 1999. pap. 17.95 (*1-58062-207-0*) Adams Media.
Long, Mark. Raising Capital: In the New Economy. (Illus.). 410p. 1998. pap. 21.95 (*1-57901-034-2*) Intl Promotions.
— Unlimited Capital: For the New Century Entrepreneur. (Illus.). 297p. 1998. pap. 19.95 (*1-57901-033-4*) Intl Promotions.
— The World of Home Video Entertainment. (Illus.). 202p. 1991. pap. 15.95 (*0-929548-01-9*) MLE Inc.
— The World of Satellite TV. 9th rev. ed. LC 98-38140. (Illus.). 256p. 1998. reprint ed. pap. 24.95 (*1-57067-069-2*) Book Pub Co.
Long, Mark & Keating, Jeffrey. The World of Satellite TV: International Edition for Asia, the Middle East, & the Pacific Rim. (Illus.). 220p. (Orig.). 1992. pap. 19.95 (*0-929548-08-6*) MLE Inc.
— The World of Satellite TV: International Edition for Europe & Africa. (Illus.). 1993. pap. 24.95 (*0-929548-10-8*) MLE Inc.
— The World of Satellite TV: North & South America. 6th ed. LC 92-81289. (Illus.). 308p. (Orig.). (C). 1992. pap. text 24.95 (*0-929548-07-8*) MLE Inc.
Long, Mark, et al. The World of CB Radio. rev. ed. LC 87-70878. (Illus.). 240p. 1987. pap. 12.95 (*0-913990-53-1*) Book Pub Co.
***Long, Mark E.** Digital Satellite TV Handbook. LC 99-13017. 207p. 1999. pap. 59.95 (*0-7506-7171-8*, Newnes) Buttrwrth-Heinemann.
Long, Martin. The Dark Gateway. large type ed. 1989. 27.99 (*0-7089-2076-4*) Ulverscroft.
***Long, Martyn.** The Psychology of Education. LC 00-42466. 2000. write for info. (*0-415-23906-0*) Routledge.
***Long, Mary.** Complete Guide to Conducting Seminars at Sea. (Illus.). 1999. pap. 29.95 (*0-9666733-0-1*) Trav Resource.
Long, Mary. Stretchercize: Is Your Limber Lost? (Illus.). 75p. (Orig.). 1985. pap. 3.95 (*0-916005-03-8*) Silver Sea.
Long, Mary C. Fair Were Their Dreams: A History of the Family of John Boone of Boone Hall Plantation. (Illus.). 300p. 1990. write for info. (*0-9617517-1-1*) Bear Hllow TX.
— The Farrow Family: Memories, Tales & Laughter from South Carolina to Texas. LC 95-77108. (Illus.). 684p. 1996. 75.00 (*0-9617517-3-8*) Bear Hllow TX.
— Stranger in a Strange Land: From Beaufort, South Carolina to Galveston Island, Republic of Texas - A Biography of Judge James Pope Cole (1814-1886) (Illus.). 162p. (YA). 1986. text 45.00 (*0-9617517-0-3*) Bear Hllow TX.
— William Long, Huntsman to William Long, Family Physician: A History of the Long Family from Badminton, Gloucestershire to Belton, Texas. (Illus.). 168p. 1992. text 75.00 (*0-9617517-2-X*) Bear Hllow TX.
Long, Mary C., jt. ed. see Long, Willum B.
Long, Mary F. Alma. (Illus.). (Orig.). 1997. pap. 15.00 (*0-9614192-6-1*) Frazier-Long.
Long, Maurice W. Radar Reflectivity of Land & Sea. 2nd ed. LC 75-13435. (Illus.). 421p. reprint ed. pap. 130.60 (*0-8357-3937-6*, 203667200004) Bks Demand.
Long, Max F. Growing into Light. 177p. 1955. pap. 9.95 (*0-87516-043-3*) DeVorss.
— Huna Code in Religions. 1965. pap. 17.95 (*0-87516-495-1*) DeVorss.
— Mana: or Vital Force. 5th ed. 125p. 1976. pap. 4.00 (*0-910764-04-2*) Huna Res Inc.
— Recovering the Ancient Magic. (Illus.). 125p. 1978. reprint ed. pap. 6.95 (*0-910764-01-8*) Huna Res Inc.
— Secret Science at Work. 1953. pap. 15.95 (*0-87516-046-8*) DeVorss.
— Secret Science Behind Miracles. 416p. 1948. pap. 15.95 (*0-87516-047-6*) DeVorss.
— Short Talks on Huna. 2nd rev. ed. 1978. pap. 5.00 (*0-910764-02-6*) Huna Res Inc.
— Tarot Card Symbology. 3rd rev. ed. Wingo, E. Otha, ed. (Illus.). 1983. pap. 10.00 (*0-910764-07-7*) Huna Res Inc.
— What Jesus Taught in Secret. (Illus.). 137p. 1983. pap. 9.95 (*0-87516-510-9*) DeVorss.
Long, Mayapriya, ed. see Vira, Soma.
***Long, Melinda.** Hiccup Snickup. LC 99-462277. (Illus.). (J). 2000. write for info. (*0-689-82245-6*) S&S Childrens.
Long, Michael. Marvell, Nabokov: Childhood & Arcadia. 270p. (C). 1984. 55.00 (*0-19-812815-0*) OUP.
— The Medical Care System: A Conceptual Model. LC 94-34492. (Illus.). 176p. 1994. pap. 17.50 (*1-56793-016-6*, 0946) Health Admin Pr.
Long, Michael & Rosier, Malcolm E. The Science Achievement of Year 12 Students in Australia. (C). 1991. pap. text 65.00 (*0-86431-089-7*, Pub. by Aust Council Educ Res) St Mut.
Long, Michael H. & Richards, Jack C. Methodology in TESOL. 421p. (J). 1987. mass mkt. 28.95 (*0-8384-2695-6*, Newbury) Heinle & Heinle.
Long, Michael J. Health & Healthcare in the United States. LC 98-12438. 175p. 1988. 42.00 (*1-56793-086-7*) Health Admin Pr.
***Long, Michael L.** Answering the Call: Stories of WWII, Korea & Vietnam. LC 99-65738. 213p. 1999. 24.00 (*1-892298-16-3*) Abique.
***Long, Michael S.** If Your Dreams Are Big Enough, the Facts Don't Count! Taylor, Sandy, ed. LC 97-75680. 144p. 1999. per. 12.95 (*0-9650514-5-5*, Learn CA) Massey-Reyner.
Long, Michael W. & Gillis, Rick. Check This Out! A Collection of Naughty Little Thoughts on...Memos, Awards, Notices, Letters, Stories, Office Flyers, Applications, Recipes, Writings. (Illus.). 138p. (Orig.). 1995. pap. 14.95 (*0-9648646-0-6*) PTDB.
Long, Michael W. & Wicha, Max S., eds. The Hematopoietic Microenvironment: The Functional & Structural Basis of Blood Cell Development. LC 92-49721. (Johns Hopkins Series in Hematology - Oncology). 336p. 1993. text 140.00 (*0-8018-4566-1*) Johns Hopkins.
Long, Mike. Understanding Census Data. 71p. 1990. reprint ed. 25.00 (*0-923172-02-5*) West Econ Rsch.
Long, Mike, et al. Labor Market & Income Consequences of Participation in TAFE. pap. 35.00 (*0-86431-225-3*, Pub. by Aust Council Educ Res) Stylus Pub VA.
Long, Milbra. Fostoria Stemware: The Crystal for America. (Illus.). 288p. 1994. 24.95 (*0-89145-586-8*, 3883) Collector Bks.
***Long, Milbra.** Fostoria Useful & Ornamental The Crystal for America. (Illus.). 272p. 2000. 29.95 (*1-57432-166-8*) Collector Bks.
Long, Milbra & Seate, Emily. Fostoria Tableware 1924-1943. LC 99-212496. 336p. 1999. 24.95 (*1-57432-109-9*) Collector Bks.
— Fostoria Tableware the Crystal for America: 1944-1986. LC 99-462550. 304p. 1999. pap. 24.95 (*1-57432-143-9*) Collector Bks.
Long, Morrow, jt. auth. see Feit, Sidnie.
Long-Murdock, B., tr. see Gwynn, J. Wallace.
Long, Nancy, jt. auth. see Long, Larry.
Long, Nancy, jt. auth. see Long, Larry E.
Long, Neville. Lights of East Anglia. 182p. (C). 1988. 50.00 (*0-86138-028-2*, Pub. by T Dalton) St Mut.
— Lights of East Anglia. 182p. (C). 1990. pap. 35.00 (*0-86138-029-0*, Pub. by T Dalton) St Mut.
Long, Ngo V. Before the Revolution. 1991. text 69.50 (*0-231-07678-9*) Col U Pr.
Long, Ngo V., jt. auth. see Leonard, Daniel.
Long, Ngo Van, see Herberg, Horst & Van Long, Ngo, eds.
Long, Ngo Vinh. Before the Revolution. 320p. 1991. pap. text 19.00 (*0-231-07679-7*) Col U Pr.
Long, Nguyen & Kendall, Harry H. After Saigon Fell: Daily Life under the Vietnamese Communists. LC 81-85304. (Research Papers & Policy: No. 4). (Illus.). (Orig.). 1981. pap. 8.00 (*0-912966-46-7*) IEAS.
Long, Nguyen, et al. Spoken Vietnamese for Beginners. (VIE., Illus.). 401p. 1994. pap. text 33.95 (*1-877979-48-1*) SE Asia.
— Spoken Vietnamese for Beginners, with 3 Audio Tapes. (Southeast Asian Language Text Ser.). (Illus.). 401p. (C). 1994. pap. text 42.95 incl. audio (*1-877979-45-7*) SE Asia.
Long, Nicholas, jt. auth. see Forehand, Rex.
Long, Nicholas J. Metallocenes: An Introduction to Sandwich Complexes. LC 97-23272. (Illus.). 288p. 1998. pap. 58.95 (*0-632-04162-5*) Blackwell Sci.
Long, Nicholas J., et al. Conflict in the Classroom: The Education of At-Risk & Troubled Students. 5th rev. ed. 576p. (C). 1996. pap. text 39.00 (*0-89079-682-3*, 7814) PRO-ED.
Long, Nicholas J., jt. auth. see Wood, Mary M.
***Long, Nicholas Trott & Weeks, Kent M.** Legal Audit Assessment. 46p. (C). 1998. 25.00 (*1-881434-16-8*) Coll Legal Info.
— Strategic Legal Planning: The College & University Legal Audit. 288p. (C). 1998. 85.00 (*1-881434-14-1*) Coll Legal Info.
Long, Norton E. Aristotle & the Study of Local Government. (Reprint Series in Social Sciences). (C). 1993. reprint ed. pap. text 5.00 (*0-8290-3492-7*, PS-173) Irvington.
— The Polity. (Reprint Series in Sociology). reprint ed. pap. 9.95 (*0-685-70259-6*); reprint ed. lib. bdg. 27.50 (*0-685-70258-8*) Irvington.
Long, Oliver. Law & Its Limitations in the GATT Multilateral Trade System. 172p. (C). 1987. pap. text 64.50 (*0-86010-959-3*) Kluwer Academic.
Long, Olivia. Billy Bumble Is Missing! (Kaleidoscope Ser.). (Illus.). 32p. (J). (ps-4). Date not set. write for info. (*1-880042-02-9*) Shelf-Life Bks.
— The Boy & the Dog. (Pets & Their People Ser.). (Illus.). 32p. (J). (gr. k-5). Date not set. write for info. (*1-880042-07-X*) Shelf-Life Bks.
— The Dandelion Queen. (Our Precious Planet Ser.). (Illus.). 32p. (J). (ps-4). Date not set. 9.95 (*1-880042-08-8*, SL12461) Shelf-Life Bks.
— Diary of a Dog. (Pets & Their People Ser.). (Illus.). 32p. (J). (ps-4). Date not set. 9.95 (*1-880042-06-1*, SL12456) Shelf-Life Bks.
— The Elephant Who Forgot. (Kaleidoscope Ser.). (Illus.). 32p. (J). (ps-4). Date not set. write for info. (*1-880042-05-3*) Shelf-Life Bks.
— A Horse of a Different Color. (Kaleidoscope Ser.). (Illus.). 32p. (J). (ps-4). Date not set. 9.95 (*1-880042-01-0*, SL12451) Shelf-Life Bks.
— Hortense, the Happy Hippo. (Kaleidoscope Ser.). (Illus.). 32p. (J). (ps-4). Date not set. write for info. (*1-880042-03-7*) Shelf-Life Bks.
— The Impossible Peacock. (Kaleidoscope Ser.). (Illus.). 32p. (J). (ps-4). Date not set. write for info. (*1-880042-04-5*) Shelf-Life Bks.
— There's a Dinosaur in My Bathtub! (World of Dinosaurs Ser.). (Illus.). 32p. (J). (ps-4). Date not set. write for info. (*1-880042-11-8*) Shelf-Life Bks.
— Thunderbirds & Thunderbeings. (Our Precious Planet Ser.). (Illus.). 32p. (J). (ps-4). Date not set. write for info. (*1-880042-10-X*) Shelf-Life Bks.
— Too Many Kittens. (Pets & Their People Ser.). (Illus.). 32p. (J). (ps-4). Date not set. write for info. (*1-880042-09-6*) Shelf-Life Bks.
— Why Don't Cats Lay Eggs? (Our Precious Planet Ser.). (Illus.). 32p. (J). (ps-4). Date not set. write for info. (*1-880042-12-6*) Shelf-Life Bks.
Long, Olivier. Public Scrutiny of Protection. 114p. 1989. text 22.95 (*0-566-05780-8*, Pub. by Avebry) Ashgate Pub Co.
Long, Orie W. Literary Pioneers. 1975. 250.00 (*0-87968-301-5*) Gordon Pr.
— Literary Pioneers: Early American Explorers of European Culture. (BCL1-PS American Literature Ser.). 267p. 1993. reprint ed. lib. bdg. 79.00 (*0-7812-6576-2*) Rprt Serv.
***Long, Pamela O.** Technology, Society & Culture in Late Medieval & Renaissance Europe, 1300-1600. (Historical Perspectives on Technology, Society & Culture Ser.). (Illus.). (C). 2000. pap. 8.00 (*0-87229-120-0*) Am Hist Assn.
***Long, Patricia.** The Barbie Closet: Price Guide for Barbie & Friends Fashions & Accessories: 1959-1970. LC 99-61451. (Illus.). 352p. 2000. 34.95 (*0-87341-695-3*) Krause Pubns.
Long, Patrick D. & Ricard, Laura. The Dream Shattered: Vietnamese Gangs in America. 256p. 1995. pap. text 16.95 (*1-55553-314-0*) NE U Pr.
Long, Patrick D., et al. The Dream Shattered: Vietnamese Gangs in America. LC 95-20446. 256p. (C). 1995. text 42.50 (*1-55553-232-2*) NE U Pr.
Long, Patrick D. De, see De Long, Patrick D.
Long, Paul. Training Pointing Dogs. (Illus.). 128p. 1985. pap. 12.95 (*0-941130-08-8*) Lyons Pr.
Long, Paul E. Finite Math: An Applied Approach Student Solutions Manual. 2nd ed. 352p. (C). 1997. pap. text 25.00 (*0-321-00463-9*) Addson-Wesley Educ.
Long, Paul E. & Graening, Jay. Finite Mathematics: An Applied Approach. 2nd ed. LC 96-23302. 592p. (C). 1997. 96.00 (*0-673-99600-X*) Addison-Wesley.
Long, Paul E. & Graening, Jay. Finite Mathematics: Applied Approach. 320p. (C). 1997. pap., student ed. 30.00 (*0-06-500623-2*) Addson-Wesley Educ.
— Finite Mathematics Applied Approach: An Applied Approach. LC 92-26647. (Illus.). 560p. (C). 1997. pap. 95.00 (*0-06-500391-8*) Addson-Wesley Educ.
Long, Paul V. Big Eyes: The Southwestern Photographs of Simeon Schwemberger, 1902-1908. LC 91-24923. (Illus.). 221p. 1992. reprint ed. pap. 68.60 (*0-608-04113-0*, 206484500011) Bks Demand.
Long, Paula & Robillard, Linda. Long's Preschool & Daycare Directory: Massachusetts Edition. 254p. (Orig.). 1996. pap. 14.95 (*0-9651881-0-8*) ABC Pubng Assn.
Long, Pert. Alibis, Lies & the Truth. LC 98-14112. 200p. 1998. 16.95 (*0-944957-97-8*) Rivercross Pub.
***Long, Peter.** L'Amour des Lettre. 189p. 1999. 38.95 (*3-906762-50-5*, Pub. by P Lang) P Lang Pubng.
Long, Peter L., ed. Coccidiosis of Man & Domestic Animals. 352p. 1990. 205.00 (*0-8493-6269-5*, QR201) CRC Pr.
Long, Peter L., ed. see McDougald, Larry R.

An Asterisk (*) at the beginning of an entry indicates that the title is appearing for the first time.

Long, Phil. Performance Appraisal Revisited. 200p. (C). 1986. 105.00 (*0-85292-367-8*, Pub. by IPM Hse) St Mut.
— Retirement: Planned Liberation? 116p. (C). 1981. 102.00 (*0-85292-294-9*, Pub. by IPM Hse) St Mut.
Long, Phil & Hill, Margaret. Special Leave. 84p. (C). 1988. 90.00 (*0-85292-400-3*, Pub. by IPM Hse) St Mut.
Long, Phil, jt. auth. see Armstrong, Michael.
Long, Philip D. & Siefert, Beth L. Basic Bible for Real People: Six Key Books of the Bible in One Year of Daily Devotional Readings. 384p. 1991. pap. text 9.95 (*0-9631735-0-2*) E Lib Luth Church.
***Long, Philomene.** American Zen Bones: Maezumi Roshi Stories. (Illus.). 109p. 1999. pap. 10.00 (*1-892184-02-8*, Pub. by Beyond Baroque) SPD-Small Pr Dist.
Long, Priscilla, ed. The New Left: A Collection of Essays. LC 69-15528. (Extending Horizons Ser.). (Illus.). 500p. (C). 1969. 6.00 (*0-87558-042-4*); pap. 3.00 (*0-87558-043-2*) Porter Sargent.
Long, Quincy. The Johnstown Vindicator. 1988. pap. 5.25 (*0-8222-0599-8*) Dramatists Play.
— The Joy of Going Somewhere Definite. 1998. pap. 5.25 (*0-8222-1673-6*) Dramatists Play.
Long, R. A., jt. auth. see Jackman, E. R.
Long, R. E., tr. see Chekhov, Anton.
***Long, R. William.** Extreme Twisties - Southeastern U. S. A. (Illus.). 141p. 1999. pap. 14.95 (*0-9671257-0-7*) L & A Pubg.
Long, Ralph B. The Sentence & Its Parts: A Grammar of Contemporary English. LC 61-11895. (Midway Reprint Ser.). 1980. pap. text 16.00 (*0-226-49260-5*) U Ch Pr.
— The Sentence & Its Parts: A Grammar of Contemporary English. LC 61-11895. (Midway Reprint Ser.). 534p. reprint ed. pap. 165.60 (*0-608-09467-6*, 205426700005) Bks Demand.
— Structure Worksheets for Contemporary English. LC PE1114.L65. 253p. reprint ed. pap. 78.50 (*0-608-12564-4*, 202405600035) Bks Demand.
Long, Ralph B. & Long, Dorothy R. The System of English Grammar. LC 75-159449. 531p. (C). 1980. reprint ed. text 12.00 (*0-8477-3325-4*); reprint ed. pap. text 9.60 (*0-8477-3326-2*) U of PR Pr.
Long, Richard. From Time to Time. (Illus.). 104p. 1997. 50.00 (*3-89322-898-5*, Pub. by Edition Cantz) Dist Art Pubs.
— Richard Long: Mountains & Waters. LC 92-54548. 65p. 1993. 35.00 (*0-8076-1293-6*) Braziller.
— Studying Western Civilization: Reading Maps, Interpreting Documents, Preparing for Exams, a Student's Guide. (C). 1995. pap. text, teacher ed. 2.66 (*0-669-12169-X*) HM Trade Div.
— Studying Western Civilization: Reading Maps, Interpreting Documents, Preparing for Exams, a Student's Guide: Since 1320, Vol. 2. (C). text 21.56 (*0-669-35366-3*) HM Trade Div.
— Studying Western Civilization: Reading Maps, Interpreting Documents, Preparing for Exams, a Student's Guide: To 1787, Vol. 1. (C). text 21.56 (*0-669-12168-1*) HM Trade Div.
— A Walk Across England. LC 97-60275. (Illus.). 192p. (Orig.). 1997. pap. 29.95 (*0-500-27976-4*, Pub. by Thames Hudson) Norton.
Long, Richard, jt. auth. see Gelburd, Gail.
Long, Richard A. Grown Deep: Essays on the Harlem Renaissance. 160p. 1998. pap. text 12.00 (*1-885066-43-0*) Four-G Pubs.
Long, Richard A. & Collier, Eugenia W., eds. Afro-American Writing: An Anthology of Prose & Poetry. 2nd enl. ed. 784p. 1990. 16.95 (*0-271-00376-6*) Pa St U Pr.
Long, Richard J. & Skinner, Stephen C. Closed Loop Electrohydraulic Systems Manual. (Illus.). (C). 1992. text 55.00 (*0-9634162-1-9*) Vickers Inc Trng Ctr.
Long, Richard W., jt. auth. see Long, Jane S.
Long, Rob. Conversations with My Agent. 184p. 1998. pap. 11.95 (*0-452-27713-2*, Plume) Dutton Plume.
— Supporting Pupils with Emotional Difficulties: Creating a Caring Environment for All, Vol. 1. (Resource Materials for Teachers Ser.). 1999. pap. 26.95 (*1-85346-595-X*) David Fulton.
***Long, Robert.** Blue. 90p. 1999. pap. 15.00 (*1-886435-09-X*) Canios Edit.
Long, Robert. What Happens? LC 88-9423. 68p. (Orig.). 1988. pap. 9.95 (*0-913123-19-6*) Galileo.
Long, Robert, ed. For David Ignatow: An Anthology: Forty-Seven Poets Celebrate His 80th Birthday. 69p. (Orig.). 1994. pap. 10.00 (*0-9630164-6-6*) Canios Edit.
— The Last of the Dinosaurs. (Illus.). 1978. pap. 3.95 (*0-88388-054-7*) Bellerophon Bks.
Long, Robert & Long, Sharon. Watercolor for Real. (Illus.). 64p. 1997. pap. 10.50 (*1-56770-409-3*) S Scheewe Pubns.
Long, Robert, jt. auth. see Balague, Lin.
Long, Robert, ed. see Roberts, J. S., pseud.
Long, Robert A. Score! Specification System for Herd Improvement: A Field Guide for Sorting Cattle by Composition & Structure LC 98-88368. 60 p. 1998. write for info. (*0-9665486-0-4*) Breakthru Bus Soln.
Long, Robert A. & Houk, Rose. Dawn of the Dinosaurs: The Triassic of Petrified Forest. (Illus.). (Orig.). (C). 1988. pap. 14.95 (*0-945695-02-0*) Petrified Forest Mus Assn.
Long, Robert A. & Welles, Samuel P. All New Dinosaurs. (J). (gr. 7 up). 1975. pap. 4.95 (*0-88388-031-8*) Bellerophon Bks.
Long, Robert B. Separation Processes in Waste Minimization. LC 95-2944. (Environmental Science & Pollution Control Ser.: Vol. 16). (Illus.). 480p. 1995. text 190.00 (*0-8247-9634-9*) Dekker.
Long, Robert B., jt. auth. see Gerzadowicz, Stephan.
Long, Robert B., ed. see Christiansen, Larry, et al.
Long, Robert B., ed. see Curry, Ronald H.
Long, Robert B., ed. see Dunne, Alex.
Long, Robert B., ed. see Parr, Larry.
Long, Robert B., ed. see Raingruber, Bob & Maser, Lou.
Long, Robert B., ed. see Unger, Tom.
Long, Robert B., ed. see Wetzell, Rolf.
Long, Robert C. The Achieving of the Great Gatsby: F. Scott Fitzgerald, 1920-1925. LC 77-92572. 224p. 1979. 32.50 (*0-8387-2192-3*) Bucknell U Pr.
— The Achieving of the Great Gatsby: F. Scott Fitzgerald, 1920-1925. LC 77-92572. 224p. 1981. pap. 17.95 (*0-8387-5026-5*) Bucknell U Pr.
— The Politicians. rev. ed. 210p. (Orig.). 1997. pap. 18.00 (*0-9653792-1-3*) C Long.
Long, Robert Emmet. The Films of Merchant Ivory. LC 96-49188. (Illus.). 208p. 1991. 49.50 (*0-8109-3618-6*, Pub. by Abrams) Time Warner.
— Films of Merchant Ivory. (Illus.). 208p. 1993. pap. 19.95 (*0-8065-1470-1*, Citadel Pr) Carol Pub Group.
— The Great Succession: Henry James & the Legacy of Hawthorne. LC 79-922. (Critical Essays in Modern Literature Ser.). 215p. reprint ed. pap. 66.70 (*0-7837-2146-3*, 204243200004) Bks Demand.
— Multiculturalism. LC 97-29037. (Reference Shelf Ser.: Vol. 69, No. 5). 1997. pap. 25.00 (*0-8242-0918-4*) Wilson.
Long, Robert Emmet, ed. Affirmative Action. LC 96-16236. (Reference Shelf Ser.: Vol. 68, No. 3). 1996. pap. 25.00 (*0-8242-0888-9*) Wilson.
— Banking Scandals: The S&L's & BCCI. LC 93-16882. (Reference Shelf Ser.: Vol. 65, No. 3). 1993. pap. 25.00 (*0-8242-0842-0*) Wilson.
— Censorship. (Reference Shelf Ser.: Vol. 62, No. 3). 161p. 1990. pap. 25.00 (*0-8242-0792-0*) Wilson.
— Criminal Sentencing. LC 95-2365. (Reference Shelf Ser.: Vol. 67 No. 1). 1995. pap. 25.00 (*0-8242-0868-4*) Wilson.
— The Crisis in Health Care, Vol. 63, No. 1. 1991. pap. 25.00 (*0-8242-0811-0*) Wilson.
— Drugs in America. LC 93-16881. (Reference Shelf Ser.: Vol. 65, No. 4). 1993. pap. 25.00 (*0-8242-0843-9*) Wilson.
— Energy & Conservation, Vol. 61, No. 4. (Reference Shelf Ser.). 180p. 1989. pap. text 25.00 (*0-8242-0783-1*) Wilson.
— Immigration. LC 95-52085. (Reference Shelf Ser.: Vol. 68, No. 1). 1996. pap. 25.00 (*0-8242-0886-2*) Wilson.
— Immigration to the U.S. LC 92-28399. (Reference Shelf Ser.: Vol. 64, No. 4). 1992. pap. 25.00 (*0-8242-0828-5*) Wilson.
— Japan & the U. S. (Reference Shelf Ser.: Vol. 62, No. 2). 176p. 1990. pap. 25.00 (*0-8242-0791-2*) Wilson.
— Religious Cults in America. LC 94-16329. (Reference Shelf Ser.: Vol. 66, No. 4). 1994. pap. 25.00 (*0-8242-0855-2*) Wilson.
— The Reunification of Germany. LC 91-43545. (Reference Shelf Ser.: Vol. 64, No. 1). 132p. 1992. pap. 25.00 (*0-8242-0825-0*, DD262) Wilson.
— The State of U.S. Education. LC 91-20484. 197p. 1991. pap. 25.00 (*0-8242-0816-1*, LA217) Wilson.
— Suicide. LC 95-11850. (Reference Shelf Ser.: Vol. 67, No. 2). 1995. pap. 25.00 (*0-8242-0869-2*) Wilson.
Long, Robert F., ed. Youth Development Professionals: Connecting Competencies & Curriculum. (Youth Development Professionals Monographs: No. 1). 64p. (C). 1992. pap. text 10.00 (*1-881516-00-8*) U of NI Inst Youth Lead.
— Youth Develpment Professionals: Common Ground for Professional Development. (Youth Development Professionals Monographs: No. 2). 62p. (C). 1992. pap. text 10.00 (*1-881516-01-6*) U of NI Inst Youth Lead.
Long, Robert F. & Martinez, Cathy L., eds. Youth Development Professionals: Building Practice on Knowledge. (Youth Development Professionals Monographs: No. 3). 162p. (C). 1993. pap. text 10.00 (*1-881516-02-4*) U of NI Inst Youth Lead.
Long, Robert H. The Effigies. LC 97-65103. 96p. 1998. 24.00 (*1-887628-04-5*); pap. 12.00 (*1-887628-05-3*) Plinth Bks.
— The Power to Die. (CSU Poetry Ser.: Vol. XXIV). 108p. (Orig.). 1987. pap. 6.00 (*0-914946-63-3*) Cleveland St Univ Poetry Ctr.
— The Work of the Bow. (CSU Poetry Ser.: Vol. 40). 80p. 1996. pap. 10.00 (*1-880834-23-5*) Cleveland St Univ Poetry Ctr.
— The Work of the Bow. (CSU Poetry Ser.: Vol. L). 80p. 1996. 17.50 (*1-880834-22-7*) Cleveland St Univ Poetry Ctr.
Long, Robert H., jt. auth. see Gushee, David P.
Long, Robert L. Algebraic Number Theory. LC 76-40364. (Monographs & Textbooks in Pure & Applied Mathematics: Vol. 41). 208p. reprint ed. pap. 64.50 (*0-608-08951-6*, 206958600005) Bks Demand.
***Long, Robert L.** Long Way from Home: A Memoir. (Illus.). 80p. (Orig.). 1999. pap. 10.00 (*0-9674100-0-2*) New Sthrn Writers.
Long, Robert L. & O'Brien, Paul, eds. Fast Burst Reactors: Proceedings. LC 73-603552. (AEC Symposium Ser.). 646p. 1969. pap. 24.25 (*0-87079-208-3*, CONF-690102); fiche 9.00 (*0-87079-209-1*, CONF-690102) DOE.
Long, Roberta, jt. auth. see Long, Delbert.
Long, Roberta A., jt. auth. see Long, Delbert H.
Long, Rod & Dallal, Tamalyn. Belly Laughs: Adventures with Celebrities & Other Unusual Characters. Harris, Bev & Harris, Carl, eds. (Illus.). 224p. 1999. pap. 14.95 (*1-890916-50-1*) Talion Pub.
Long, Roger. Final Commitment: A Third Anthology of Murders in Old Berkshire. (Illus.). 128p. 1994. pap. 12.95 (*0-7509-0495-X*, Pub. by Sutton Pub Ltd) Intl Pubs Mktg.
— Javanese Shadow Theatre: Movement & Characterization in Ngayogyakarta Wayang Kulit. LC 81-16164. (Theater & Dramatic Studies: No. 11). (Illus.). 207p. 1982. reprint ed. pap. 64.20 (*0-8357-1283-4*, 207027400065) Bks Demand.
Long, Roger D. The Founding of Pakistan: An Annotated Bibliography. LC 98-30089. (Magill Bibliographies Ser.). 336p. 1998. 45.00 (*0-8108-3557-6*) Scarecrow.
— The Man on the Spot: Essays on British Empire History, 31. LC 95-9667. (Contributions in Comparative Colonial Studies: Vol. 31). 256p. 1995. 59.95 (*0-313-29524-7*, Greenwood Pr) Greenwood.
Long, Roland H. The Law of Liability Insurance, 5 vols., Set. 1976. ring bd. 1230.00 (*0-8205-1354-7*) Bender.
Long, Ron & Barrett, Joanne. Hark! the Herald Angels: Singers Activity Bk. 1996. pap. 3.99 (*0-8341-9455-4*, MC-94A) Nazarene.
Long, Ron & Curran, Peter A. Enforcing the Common Fisheries Policy. LC 98-35425. 1998. 165.00 (*0-85238-261-8*) Blackwell Sci.
Long, Rose-Carol W., ed. German Expressionism: Documents from the End of the Wilhelmine Empire to the Rise of National Socialism. LC 95-30730. (Documents of Twentieth Century Art Ser.). (Illus.). 370p. 1995. pap. 17.95 (*0-520-20264-3*, Pub. by U CA Pr) Cal Prin Full Svc.
Long, Roy C. The Long Family History. (Illus.). 304p. 1989. write for info. (*0-318-65517-9*) R C Long.
— The Long Family History. McClain Printing Co., Staff, ed. (Illus.). 304p. 1989. 30.00 (*0-9623739-0-7*) R C Long.
Long, Russ. Mekong Drillship. LC 98-90805. 1999. 25.00 (*0-533-12920-6*) Vantage.
Long, Ruth Y. Crackdown on Cancer with Good Nutrition. 2nd rev. ed. 172p. 1991. reprint ed. pap. 10.00 (*0-916243-15-X*) Nutrit Educ.
Long, Ruthanne & Long, Dixon. The Markets of Provence. (Illus.). 1996. 19.95 (*0-614-95771-0*) Harper SF.
— Markets of Provence: A Culinary Tour of Southern France. LC 95-42042. (Illus.). 144p. 1996. 22.00 (*0-00-225061-6*) Collins SF.
Long, S. Six Group Therapies. LC 87-7187. (Illus.). 358p. (C). 1987. 80.00 (*0-306-42642-0*, Plenum Trade) Perseus Pubng.
Long, Sabine. Men As Women, Women As Men: Changing Gender in Native American Cultures. Vantine, John L., tr. from GER. LC 97-34759. 432p. (C). 1998. 50.00 (*0-292-74700-4*, LANMEN) U of Tex Pr.
Long, Samuel, ed. Annual Review of Political Science, Vol. 1. 256p. (C). 1986. text 73.25 (*0-89391-393-6*) Ablx Pub.
— Annual Review of Political Science, Vol. 2. (Annual Review of Political Science Ser.). 288p. 1987. text 73.25 (*0-89391-401-0*) Ablx Pub.
— Annual Review of Political Science, Vol. 3. 256p. (C). 1990. text 73.25 (*0-89391-501-7*) Ablx Pub.
Long, Samuel L., ed. The Handbook of Political Behavior, 5 vols., Vol. 1. 388p. 1981. 110.00 (*0-306-40601-2*, Plenum Trade) Perseus Pubng.
— The Handbook of Political Behavior, 5 vols., Vol. 2. 380p. 1981. 110.00 (*0-306-40602-0*, Plenum Trade) Perseus Pubng.
— The Handbook of Political Behavior, 5 vols., Vol. 3. 422p. 1981. 110.00 (*0-306-40603-9*, Plenum Trade) Perseus Pubng.
— The Handbook of Political Behavior, 5 vols., Vol. 4. 386p. 1981. 110.00 (*0-306-40604-7*, Plenum Trade) Perseus Pubng.
— The Handbook of Political Behavior, 5 vols., Vol. 5. 392p. 1981. 110.00 (*0-306-40605-5*, Plenum Trade) Perseus Pubng.
Long, Sandra, jt. auth. see Phillips, Marcus.
Long, Sarah S, et al. Principles & Practice of Pediatric Infectious Diseases. LC 96-19019. 1996. text 225.00 (*0-443-08943-4*) Church.
Long, Scott M., jt. auth. see Bernard, Barbara.
Long, Sharon, jt. auth. see Long, Robert.
Long, Sharon K., et al. The Evaluation of the Washington State Family Independence Program. LC 94-818. (Urban Institute Report: No. 94-1). 174p. 1994. pap. 23.00 (*0-87766-622-9*) Urban Inst.
Long, Sheila M. Never Drink Coffee from Your Saucer . . . And Other Tips on Socially Correct Dining. 96p. (Orig.). 1996. pap. 7.95 (*0-8362-2169-9*) Andrews & McMeel.
***Long, Sheri S., et al.** Hacia la Literarura. LC 97-27137. (SPA.). 256p. 1998. pap. 42.95 (*0-471-16173-X*) Wiley.
Long, Sheri S., jt. auth. see Gerrard, Lisa.
Long, Sheron. The Goat in the Chile Patch. (ESL Theme Links Ser.). (Illus.). (Orig.). 1993. 35.00 (*1-56334-310-X*); audio 10.50 (*1-56334-309-6*) Hampton-Brown.
— The Goat in the Chile Patch, Set. (ESL Theme Links Ser.). (Illus.). (Orig.). 1993. 99.50 (*1-56334-311-8*) Hampton-Brown.
— The Goat in the Chile Patch: Big Book. (Illus.). 16p. (Orig.). (J). (gr. k-3). 1992. pap. text 29.95 (*1-56334-181-6*) Hampton-Brown.
— The Goat in the Chile Patch: Small Book. (ESL Theme Links Ser.). (Illus.). 16p. (Orig.). 1992. pap. text 6.00 (*1-56334-184-0*) Hampton-Brown.
Long, Sherry, jt. auth. see Tripp, Valerie.
Long, Sidney. Masterpieces of Americana: The Mr. & Mrs. Adolph Henry Meyer Collection. 1995. 39.00 (*0-614-15405-7*) Antique Collect.
Long, Sonny. A Long Look at Life: Prose & Poetry. 84p. 1999. pap. 7.95 (*0-9671441-0-8*) Pine Country.
***Long, Sonny.** A Long Look at Life Vol. 2: The Collected Columns. 140p. 1999. pap. 9.95 (*0-9671441-1-6*) Pine Country.
Long Standing Bear Chief. Ni-Kso-Ko-Wa: Blackfoot Spirituality, Traditions, Values & Beliefs. 1995. 9.95 (*0-614-06313-2*) Spirit Talk Pr.
***Long, Stephen.** Good News Foretold: Messianic Prophecies & the Life of Christ. 208p. 2000. pap. 10.99 (*0-9629550-4-3*) Word in Action.
— Karmic Ties: A Novel Of Modern Asia. 1999. pap. text 16.95 (*0-9651546-1-0*) Med Bear.
— Polycarp & the Second Century Church. 112p. 2000. pap. 8.99 (*0-9629550-3-5*) Word in Action.
— Song of Jesus, The Son of David. 40p. (YA). 2000. 3.95 (*0-9629550-6-X*) Word in Action.
Long, Stephen. The Song of the Spirit & the Bride: Finding Jesus in the Song of Songs. 76p. (Orig.). 1991. pap. 4.95 (*0-9629550-0-0*) Word in Action.
***Long, Stephen.** The Way to Everlasting Happiness & Purpose: Selections from the New Testament Books of John & Romans. 44p. (YA). 2000. 2.50 (*0-9629550-5-1*) Word in Action.
Long, Stephen. The Word Personalized Vol. 1: Names of God. 44p. 1993. pap. 10.97 incl. audio (*0-9629550-2-7*) Word in Action.
Long, Stephen, jt. auth. see Fishci, Amelia G.
Long, Stephen G. Meeting Places with Jesus. (Illus.). 60p. (Orig.). 1992. pap. 4.95 (*0-9629550-1-9*) Word in Action.
Long, Steve & Burghardt, Rita. Rehabilitation & the Law: Liability & the OT Practitioner. 60p. (Orig.). 1996. pap. text 21.00 (*1-56900-040-9*, 1145) Am Occup Therapy.
Long, Steve & Long, Cindy. Marketing Your Arts & Crafts. (Illus.). 192p. (Orig.). (C). 1987. pap. text 14.95 (*0-9618894-0-3*) Idahome Pubns.
— You Can Make Money from Your Arts & Crafts: The Arts & Crafts Marketing Book. rev. ed. Strickland, Al, ed. (Be Your Own Boss Ser.). (Illus.). 224p. 1988. pap. 17.95 (*0-937769-04-5*) Mark Inc CA.
Long, Steve, jt. auth. see Moore, Christian.
Long, Steven, et al. Heroic Adventures, Vol. 2. Arsenault, Mark, ed. (Illus.). 96p. (Orig.). 1996. pap. 16.00 (*1-890305-01-4*) Gold Rush.
Long, Stewart L. The Development of the Television Network Oligopoly. Sterling, Christopher H., ed. LC 78-21725. (Dissertations in Broadcasting Ser.). (Illus.). 1980. lib. bdg. 17.95 (*0-405-11764-7*) Ayer.
***Long, Susan O.** Caring for the Elderly in Japan & the U. S. Practices & Policies. LC 99-38453. 384p. 2000. 100.00 (*0-415-22352-0*) Routledge.
Long, Susan O. Family Change & the Life Course in Japan. LC 87-401842. (Cornell East Asia Ser.: No. 44). 140p. (Orig.). 1987. pap. 8.50 (*0-939657-44-9*) Cornell East Asia Pgm.
Long, Sylvester. Long Lance. LC 95-18985. 320p. 1995. pap. 16.95 (*0-87805-830-3*) U Pr of Miss.
Long, Sylvester, jt. auth. see Chief Buffalo Child.
***Long, Sylvia.** Deck the Hall: A Traditional Carol. LC 00-8934. (J). 2000. pap. write for info. (*0-8118-2821-2*) Chronicle Bks.
Long, Sylvia. Hush Little Baby. LC 96-28724. (Illus.). 32p. (J). 1997. 12.95 (*0-8118-1416-5*) Chronicle Bks.
***Long, Sylvia.** Hush Little Baby. 28p. 2000. bds. 16.95 (*0-8118-2265-6*) Chronicle Bks.
— Hush Little Baby Doll. 14.95 (*0-8118-1792-X*) Chronicle Bks.
— My Baby Journal. (Illus.). 64p. 1998. 16.95 (*0-8118-1890-X*) Chronicle Bks.
— Rain, Rain, Go Away Mouse Doll. (Illus.). (J). 2000. 10.95 (*0-8118-2839-5*) Chronicle Bks.
— Ring Around the Rosies Bunny Doll. (Illus.). (J). 2000. 10.95 (*0-8118-2840-9*) Chronicle Bks.
Long, Sylvia. Sylvia Long's Mother Goose. LC 98-52311. 109p. (J). (ps). 1999. 19.95 (*0-8118-2088-2*) Chronicle Bks.
Long, Sylvia, jt. auth. see Ervin, Gary W.
Long, Teddy C. Make Your Own Performing Puppets. LC 94-35536. (Illus.). 96p. (J). (gr. 4-7). 1995. 19.95 (*1-895569-32-X*, Pub. by Tamos Bks) Sterling.
— Super Masks & Fun Face Painting. LC 96-35803. (Illus.). 80p. (J). 1997. 19.95 (*1-895569-09-5*) Sterling.
Long, Teddy C., jt. auth. see Walter, F. Virginia.
Long, Thomas. Whispering the Lyrics: Sermons for Lent, Easter: Cycle A Gospel Texts. 1995. pap. 12.95 (*0-7880-0492-1*) CSS OH.
Long, Thomas E. Basic Mathematics Skills & Vocational Education. 28p. 1980. 2.80 (*0-318-22041-5*, IN199) Ctr Educ Trng Employ.
Long, Thomas G. Hebrews. (Interpretation Ser.). 176p. 1997. 22.00 (*0-8042-3133-8*) Westminster John Knox.
— Matthew. LC 97-16942. (Bible Companion Ser.). 1997. pap. 20.00 (*0-664-25257-5*) Westminster John Knox.
— Preaching & the Literary Forms of the Bible. LC 88-45243. 144p. 1988. pap. text 15.00 (*0-8006-2313-4*, 1-2313, Fortress Pr) Augsburg Fortress.
— Something Is about to Happen: Sermons for Advent & Christmas. LC 96-30408. 1996. 7.25 (*0-7880-0866-8*) CSS OH.
— The Witness of Preaching. 216p. 1989. pap. 19.00 (*0-8042-1571-5*) Westminster John Knox.
Long, Thomas G. & Plantinga, Cornelius, Jr., eds. A Chorus of Witnesses: Model Sermons for Today's Preacher. 320p. 1994. pap. 20.00 (*0-8028-0132-3*) Eerdmans.
Long, Thomas G., ed. see Buttrick, David G.
Long, Thomas G., jt. ed. see O'Day, Gail R.
Long, Thomas J. Safe at Home, Safe Alone. (Illus.). 64p. (Orig.). (J). (gr. 3-5). 1985. pap. 4.95 (*0-917917-01-4*) Miles River.
Long, Thomas J., et al. Completing Dissertations in the Behavioral Sciences & Education: A Systematic Guide for Graduate Students. LC 85-45063. (Higher & Adult Education Ser.). 238p. 1985. text 32.95 (*0-87589-658-8*) Jossey-Bass.
***Long, Tim.** Cleveland Sports Trivia Quiz. LC 99-6710. (Illus.). 224p. 1999. pap. 6.95 (*1-886228-29-9*) Gray & Co Pubs.

L

Long, Tim & Fox, Don. Indians Memories: Heroes, Heartaches, & Highlights from the Past 50 Years of Cleveland Indians. (Illus.). 144p. 1997. pap. 5.95 (1-886228-16-7) Gray & Co Pubs.

Long, Timothy. Barbarians in Greek Comedy. LC 85-18363. 328p. (C). 1986. text 31.95 (0-8093-1248-4) S Ill U Pr.

Long, Timothy E. & Hunt, Michael O., eds. Solvent-free Polymerizations & Processes: Minimization of Conventional Organic Solvents. LC 98-34535. (ACS Symmposium Ser.: Vol. 713). (Illus.). 17p. 1998. text 110.00 (0-8412-3591-0, Pub. by Am Chemical) OUP.

Long, Timothy J. Browns Memories: The 338 Most Memorable Heroes, Heartaches, & Highlights from 50 Seasons of Cleveland Browns Football. LC 96-45792. (Illus.). 176p. (Orig.). 1996. pap. 5.95 (1-886228-11-6) Gray & Co Pubs.

Long, Toby M. & Cintas, Holly M. Handbook of Pediatric Physical Therapy. LC 94-38122. (Illus.). 304p. 1995. pap. 28.00 (0-683-05155-5) Lppncott W & W.

Long, Trevor, jt. auth. see Harding, Sue.

Long-Turner, Sue, jt. auth. see Turner, Russ.

Long, V. Philips. The Art of Biblical History. (Foundations of Contemporary Interpretation Ser.: Vol. 5). 160p. 1994. 18.99 (0-310-43180-8) Zondervan.

Long, V. Philips, et al. Foundations of Contemporary Interpretation. (Expositor's Bible Commentary Ser.). 656p. 1996. boxed set 29.99 (0-310-20828-9) Zondervan.

Long, V. Phillips, ed. Israel's Past in Present Research: Essays on Ancient Israelite Historiography. LC 99-44925. (Sources for Biblical & Theological Study Ser.: Vol. 7). xx, 612p. 1999. 37.95 (1-57506-028-0) Eisenbrauns.

Long, Valentine. Upon This Rock. 255p. 1983. 12.00 (0-8199-0834-7, Frncscn Herld) Franciscan Pr.

Long, Virginia Love, jt. auth. see Holt, Rochelle L.

Long, Vivian R., jt. auth. see Long, Bryan K.

Long, Vonda. Experiential Counseling. (Adaptable Courseware Ser.). 1997. 26.00 (0-534-49867-1) Brooks-Cole.

Long, Vonda O. Communication Skills in Helping Relationships: A Framework for Facilitating Personal Growth. LC 95-23584. 290p. 1995. student ed., wbk. ed. 23.07 (0-534-33870-4) Brooks-Cole.

— Companion Workbook for Communication Skills in Helping Relationships: A Framework for Facilitating Personal Growth. LC 95-8350. 257p. 1995. 52.95 (0 534 33869-0) Brooks-Cole.

Long, W. G. Long: History of the Long Family of Pennsylvania. 365p. 1993. reprint ed. pap. 56.00 (0-8328-3706-7); reprint ed. lib. bdg. 66.00 (0-8328-3705-9) Higginson Bk Co.

Long, Wallace & Lake, David A. The History of Lothrop, Montana & Petty Creek. 200p. 1996. 17.95 (0-9644848-2-X) Meerkat Graph.

Long, Walter. Fingertip Chinese: Get to Know the Real China. 192p. 1996. pap. 9.95 (0-8348-0362-3) Weatherhill.

— Fingertip Japanese. (JPN.). 192p. 1994. pap. 9.95 (0-8348-0270-8) Weatherhill.

— Gift of Chinese Cooking. 1996. pap. text 9.95 (0-8348-0377-1) Weatherhill.

Long, Walter S. Brushwork Diary: Watercolors of Early Nevada. LC 91-12179. 136p. 1991. 24.95 (0-87417-174-1) U of Nev Pr.

Long, William, jt. auth. see Carney, Glandion.

Long, William B., jt. ed. see Elton, William R.

***Long, William E.** Advanced Technology Program Performance Of Completed Projects: Status Report No. 1. 144p. 1999. per. 16.00 (0-16-056926-5) USGPO.

Long, William J. Economic Incentives & Bilateral Cooperation. 168p. (C). 1996. text 42.50 (0-472-10747-X, 10747) U of Mich Pr.

— Northern Trails: Some Studies of Animal Life in the Far North. (Illus.). xxv, 390p. 1989. reprint ed. pap. 14.95 (0-936041-05-6) Barbary Coast Bks.

Long, Willum B. & Long, Mary C., eds. The Nose Brotherhood Knows: A Collection of Nothings & Non-Happenings 1926-1965. LC 96-95419. (Illus.). 200p. (Orig.). 1997. pap. text 25.00 (0-9617517-5-4) Bear Hllow TX.

Long, Zeb Bradford. Passage through the Wilderness: A Journey of the Soul. LC 98-7584. 192p. 1998. pap. 11.99 (0-8007-9262-9) Chosen Bks.

Long, Zeb Bradford & McMurry, Douglas. Receiving the Power: Preparing the Way for the Holy Spirit. LC 96-8075. 256p. (YA). (gr. 10). 1996. pap. 14.99 (0-8007-9246-7) Chosen Bks.

Long, Zhang, ed. Chinese Modern Folk Paintings. (CHI & ENG., Illus.). 151p. 1994. 74.50 (1-880132-05-2) Sci Pr NY.

Longabaugh, Karen, jt. auth. see Longabaugh, Rick.

Longabaugh, Rick & Longabaugh, Karen. Collapsible Basket Patterns: Over 100 Designs for the Bandsaw or Scrollsaw. (Illus.). 126p. 1997. pap. 12.95 (1-56523-087-6) Fox Chapel Pub.

— 400 Full-Size Mini-Clock Patterns. 128p. 1994. 14.95 (0-9633112-6-3) Berry Basket.

***Longabaugh, Rick & Longabaugh, Karen.** Holiday Scrollsaw Music Boxes. (Illus.). 128p. 1999. 14.95 (0-9633112-9-8) Berry Basket.

Longabaugh, Rick & Longabaugh, Karen. Multi-Use Collapsible Basket Patterns: Over 100 Designs for the Scrollsaw. (Illus.). 118p. 1997. pap. 12.95 (1-56523-088-4) Fox Chapel Pub.

***Longabaugh, Rick & Longabaugh, Karen.** North American Wildlife Realistic 3-D Scrollsaw Art. (Illus.). 128p. 1999. pap. 14.95 (0-9633112-8-X) Berry Basket.

— Wildlife Scrollsaw Collector Plates. (Illus.). 128p. 1999. pap. 14.95 (0-9633112-7-1) Berry Basket.

Longabaugh, Rick, jt. auth. see Spielman, Patrick.

Longaberger, Dave, jt. auth. see Williford, Steve.

Longacre, Celeste. Star Mates for Aquarius. Lewis, Lesle, ed. (Illus.). 44p. (Orig.). 1996. pap. 6.95 (0-930043-11-1) Sweet Fern.

— Star Mates for Aries. Lewis, Lesle, ed. (Illus.). (Orig.). 1994. pap. 6.95 (0-930043-01-4) Sweet Fern.

— Star Mates for Cancer. Lewis, Lesle, ed. (Illus.). (Orig.). 1994. pap. 6.95 (0-930043-04-9) Sweet Fern.

— Star Mates for Capricorn. Lewis, Lesle, ed. (Illus.). (Orig.). 1995. pap. 6.95 (0-930043-10-3) Sweet Fern.

— Star Mates for Gemini. Lewis, Lesle, ed. (Illus.). (Orig.). 1994. pap. 6.95 (0-930043-03-0) Sweet Fern.

— Star Mates for Leo. Lewis, Lesle, ed. (Illus.). (Orig.). 1994. pap. 6.95 (0-930043-05-7) Sweet Fern.

— Star Mates for Libra. Lewis, Lesle, ed. (Illus.). (Orig.). 1994. pap. 6.95 (0-930043-07-3) Sweet Fern.

— Star Mates for Pisces. Lewis, Lesle, ed. (Illus.). 44p. 1996. pap. 6.95 (0-930043-12-X) Sweet Fern.

— Star Mates for Sagittarius. Lewis, Lesle, ed. (Illus.). (Orig.). 1995. pap. 6.95 (0-930043-09-X) Sweet Fern.

— Star Mates for Scorpio. Lewis, Lesle, ed. (Illus.). (Orig.). 1994. pap. 6.95 (0-930043-08-1) Sweet Fern.

— Star Mates for Taurus. Lewis, Lesle, ed. (Illus.). (Orig.). 1994. pap. 6.95 (0-930043-02-2) Sweet Fern.

— Star Mates for Virgo. Lewis, Lesle, ed. (Illus.). (Orig.). 1994. pap. 6.95 (0-930043-06-5) Sweet Fern.

— Visitor's Guide to Planet Earth: An Astrological Primer. (Orig.). 1984. pap. 6.95 (0-930043-00-6) Sweet Fern.

Longacre, Doris. Living More with Less. LC 80-15461. 304p. 1980. pap. 12.99 (0-8361-1930-4) Herald Pr.

— More-with-Less Cookbook. LC 75-23563. 320p. 1976. spiral bd. 17.99 (0-8361-1786-7) Herald Pr.

***Longacre, Doris Janzen.** More-with-Less Cookbook. 25th anniversary rev. ed. 332p. 2000. spiral bd. 20.99 (0-8361-9103-X) Herald Pr.

Longacre, Edward G. Army of Amateurs. (Illus.). 416p. 1997. 34.95 (0-8117-0136-0) Stackpole.

— The Cavalry at Gettysburg: A Tactical Study of Mounted Operations During the Civil War's Pivotal Campaign, 9 June-14 July 1863. LC 92-37790. (Illus.). 338p. (C). 1993. pap. 14.95 (0-8032-7941-8, Bison Books) U of Nebr Pr.

— Grant's Cavalryman: The Life & Wars of General James H. Wilson. (Illus.). 320p. 1996. 24.95 (0-8117-0712-1) Stackpole.

— Jersey Cavaliers: A History of the First New Jersey Cavalry, 1861-1865. (Illus.). 423p. 1992. 35.00 (0-944413-19-6) Longstreet Hse.

— Joshua Chamberlain: The Man & the Soldier. LC 99-42720. 1999. 29.95 (1-58097-021-4, 970214) Combined Pub.

— Leader of the Charge: A Biography of General E. Pickett, C. S. A. LC 95-40941. 242p. 1998. pap. 14.95 (1-57249-126-4) White Mane Pub.

— Lincoln's Cavalrymen: A History of the Mounted Forces of the Army of the Potomac. LC 99-86635. 2000. 34.95 (0-8117-1049-1) Kitch Keepsakes.

— The Man Behind the Gun. 294p. 1977. 20.00 (0-942211-99-5) Olde Soldier Bks.

— To Gettysburg & Beyond: The Twelfth New Jersey Volunteer Infantry, II Corps, Army of the Potomac, 1862-1865. LC 87-82809. (Illus.). 467p. (C). 1988. 36.00 (0-944413-06-4) Longstreet Hse.

***Longacre, Edward G.** William Dorsey Pender. 2000. 29.95 (1-58097-034-6, 970346) Combined Pub.

Longacre, Edward G., ed. From Antietam to Fort Fisher: The Civil War Letters of Edward King Wightman, 1862-1865. LC 83-49343. (Illus.). 296p. 1985. 39.50 (0-8386-3210-6) Fairleigh Dickinson.

— Leader of the Charge: A Biography of George E. Pickett. LC 95-40941. 341p. 1995. 29.95 (1-57249-006-3) White Mane Pub.

Longacre, James B., jt. auth. see Herring, James.

Longacre, Judith E. The History of Wilson College 1868 to 1970. LC 96-37535. (Studies in Education: Vol. 28). 300p. 1997. text 89.95 (0-7734-8696-8) E Mellen.

Longacre, Paul, jt. auth. see Heisey, Nancy.

Longacre, R. D. Visualization & Guided Imagery in Complementary Medicine. 2nd ed. LC 98-66043. 216p. 1998. per. 8.46 (0-7872-4907-6) Kendall-Hunt.

Longacre, R. E. An Anatomy of Speech Notions. v, 394p. (Orig.). (C). 1986. pap. text 88.50 (3-11-013322-9) Mouton.

Longacre, R. E. The Grammar of Discourse. 2nd ed. LC 96-18969. (Topics in Language & Linguistics Ser.). (Illus.). 347p. (C). 1996. 54.00 (0-306-45235-9, Plenum Trade) Perseus Pubng.

Longacre, Robert E. Grammar Discovery Procedures: A Field Manual. (Janua Linguarum, Series Minor: No. 33). (Orig.). 1964. pap. text 26.15 (90-279-2431-7) Mouton.

— The Grammar of Discourse. LC 83-3993. (Topics in Language & Linguistics Ser.). 446p. 1983. 69.50 (0-306-41273-X, Plenum Trade) Perseus Pubng.

Longacre, Sean. Client-Centered Hypnotherapy. 176p. 1994. pap. text 20.95 (0-7872-0074-3) Kendall-Hunt.

— Prin.-Clin. Applications. 176p. 1994. pap. text, per. 20.95 (0-7872-0073-5) Kendall-Hunt.

Longacre, W. C. & DeWitt, Dave. Great Salsas by the Boss of Sauce: From the Southwest & Points Beyond. LC 97-11513. (Illus.). 128p. 1997. pap. 12.95 (0-89594-817-6) Crossing Pr.

Longacre, W. C., jt. auth. see DeWitt, Dave.

Longacre, William A. Archaeology As Anthropology: A Case Study. LC 79-113089. (Anthropological Papers: No. 17). 57p. 1970. pap. 7.95 (0-8165-0219-6) U of Ariz Pr.

Longacre, William A., et al, eds. Multidisciplinary Research at Grasshopper Pueblo, Arizona. LC 82-13715. (Anthropological Papers: No. 40). 138p. 1982. pap. 17.95 (0-8165-0425-3) U of Ariz Pr.

Longacre, William A. & Skibo, James M. Kalinga Ethnoarchaeology: Expanding Archaeological Method & Theory. (Series in Archaeological Inquiry). (Illus.). 256p. (C). 1994. text 55.00 (1-56098-272-1) Smithsonian.

***Longacve, Celeste B.** Love Signs. 360p. 2000. 24.00 (0-930043-13-8) Sweet Fern.

Longair, M. S. Galaxy Formation. LC 98-29744. (Astronomy & Astrophysics Library). (Illus.). 528p. 1998. 64.95 (3-540-63785-0) Spr-Verlag.

— High Energy Astrophysics Vol. 2: Stars, the Galaxy & Interstellar Medium. (Illus.). 411p. (C). 1994. text 85.00 (0-521-43439-4); pap. text 39.95 (0-521-43584-6) Cambridge U Pr.

— Theoretical Concepts in Physics: An Alternative View of Theoretical Reasoning in Physics. 384p. 1984. pap. text 37.95 (0-521-27553-9) Cambridge U Pr.

Longair, Malcolm. Alice & the Space Telescope. LC 85-23924. (Illus.). 208p. 1989. 36.00 (0-8018-2831-7) Johns Hopkins.

Longair, Malcolm, ed. see Penrose, Roger.

Longair, Malcolm S. High Energy Astrophysics, Vol. 1: Particles, Photons & Their Detection. 2nd ed. (Illus.). 436p. (C). 1992. text 85.00 (0-521-38374-9) Cambridge U Pr.

Longair, Malcolm S. High Energy Astrophysics, Vol. 1: Particles, Photons & Their Detection. 2nd ed. (Illus.). 436p. (C). 1992. pap. text 39.95 (0-521-38773-6) Cambridge U Pr.

Longair, Malcolm S. Our Evolving Universe. (Illus.). 197p. (C). 1996. text 39.95 (0-521-55091-2) Cambridge U Pr.

— Our Evolving Universe. (Illus.). 224p. 1997. pap. 20.95 (0-521-62975-6) Cambridge U Pr.

Longair, Malcolm S., jt. ed. see Einasto, Jaan.

Longair, Malcolm S., ed. see Penrose, Roger.

Longaker, ed. Art, Style & History Custom. 16p. (C). 1997. pap. text 39.00 (0-673-99656-5) Addison-Wesley.

Longaker, Christine. Facing Death. 288p. 1998. pap. 13.95 (0-385-48332-5) Doubleday.

Longaker, F. C., tr. see Loehe, Wilhelm, et al.

Longaker, Richard P., ed. see Rossiter, Clinton.

Longan, Kandis. It's Great to Be Short . . . Not. 28p. (J). 1992. pap. 5.00 (1-886210-07-1) Tyketoon Yng Author.

Longanecker, Diane. Foal-Leading Success: Comprehensive Approach to Teaching Foals to Lead. (Illus.). Date not set. write for info. (0-9635320-3-0) Roustabout Pr.

— Halter-Tying Success: A Step-by-Step Guide for Making Hand-Tied Rope Halters for Horses. (Illus.). Date not set. 19.95 (0-9635320-6-5) Roustabout Pr.

Longanecker, Georgia. Howdy Out There! Phonics Fun. LC 76-62681. (Illus.). (J). (ps-3). 1977. pap. 6.95 (0-9601126-1-8) Longanecker.

Longas, A. Ferrandez, see Ferrandez Longas, A., ed.

Longboat, Dianne, ed. see Green, Richard G.

Longbotham, Katherine A., ed. The Seattle Times Guide to Schools: High School - Middle School Edition. 192p. 1998. pap. 1.30 (0-944912-05-2) Seattle Times.

Longbotham, Lori. Quick & Easy Recipes to Boost Your Immune System. 112p. (Orig.). 1991. mass mkt. 3.95 (0-380-76080-0, Avon Bks) Morrow Avon.

Longbotham, Lori & Sonberg, Lynn. Quick & Easy Recipes to Lower Your Cholesterol. 112p. 1989. pap. 3.50 (0-380-75871-7, Avon Bks) Morrow Avon.

Longbottom, Roy. Computer System Reliability. LC 79-40649. (Wiley Series in Computing). 345p. reprint ed. pap. 107.00 (0-608-18445-4, 203266100080) Bks Demand.

***Longbow, Curt.** The Man from Socorro. large type ed. 224p. 1999. pap. 18.99 (0-7089-5539-8, Linford) Ulverscroft.

— Warbuck. 224p. 2000. 18.99 (0-7089-5691-2) Ulverscroft.

Longchamp, Ferdinand. Asmodeus in New York. LC 75-1854. (Leisure Class in America Ser.). 1975. reprint ed. 26.95 (0-405-06920-0) Ayer.

Longchamps, Joanne De, see De Longchamps, Joanne.

***Longchenpa.** You Are the Eyes of the World. Lippman, Kennard & Peterson, Merrill, trs. 114p. (Orig.). 2000. pap. 18.95 (1-55939-140-5) Snow Lion Pubns.

***Longden, Deric.** Cat Who Came in from the Cold. (J). 2000. pap. 8.95 (0-552-13822-3, Pub. by Transworld Publishers Ltd) Trafalgar.

— Diana's Story. 2000. pap. 8.95 (0-552-13944-0, Pub. by Transworld Publishers Ltd) Trafalgar.

— Enough to Make a Cat Laugh. 2000. 22.95 (0-593-03828-2, Pub. by Transworld Publishers Ltd) Trafalgar.

— Enough to Make a Cat Laugh. (J). 2000. pap. 10.95 (0-552-14301-4, Pub. by Transworld Publishers Ltd) Trafalgar.

— Lost for Words. 2000. pap. 8.95 (0-552-13943-2, Pub. by Transworld Publishers Ltd) Trafalgar.

Longden, Jennifer, ed. see Lewis, T. D.

Longden, Leicester R., jt. ed. see Oden, Thomas C.

Longden, Sanna & Weikart, Phyllis S. Cultures & Styling in Folk Dance. LC 97-52345. 1998. 37.95 (1-57379-016-8) High-Scope.

Longdom, Danny G., ed. see Mentzer, Richard C.

Longdon, Jean, jt. auth. see Meiss, Millard.

Longe. Card Tricks Galore. LC 99-22533. 1998. pap. 5.95 (0-8069-2060-2) Sterling.

— The Little Giant Encyclopedia of Magic. LC 99-30553. (Little Giant Ser.). 1999. pap. 9.95 (0-8069-2058-0) Sterling.

— Magical Math Book. (Illus.). 96p. (J). (gr. 3-7). 1998. pap. 5.95 (0-8069-9990-X) Sterling.

Longe, Bob. Easy Card Tricks. LC 94-25142. (Illus.). 128p. 1995. pap. 4.95 (0-8069-0950-1) Sterling.

— Easy Magic Tricks. (Illus.). 128p. (Orig.). (J). 1995. pap. 5.95 (0-8069-1265-0) Sterling.

— Great Card Tricks. LC 95-12702. (Illus.). 128p. 1995. pap. 4.95 (0-8069-3894-3) Sterling.

***Longe, Bob.** The Little Giant Book of Card Tricks. LC 99-87963. 2000. 6.95 (0-8069-4471-4) Sterling.

Longe, Bob. The Magical Math Book. LC 97-33100. (Illus.). 96p. (J). (gr. 3-7). 1997. 14.95 (0-8069-9989-6) Sterling.

Longe, Bob. Mejores Trucos de Cartas del Mundo, 1. 1997. pap. text 10.98 (968-855-229-1) Suromex.

— Los Mejores Trucos de Magia del Mundo. (SPA., Illus.). 147p. 1997. pap. 12.98 (968-855-230-5) J H Surovek.

Longe, Bob. Mind Reading Magic Tricks. LC 95-26204. (Illus.). 96p. 1996. 4.95 (0-8069-3896-X) Sterling.

— Mystifying Card Tricks. LC 96-35887. (Illus.). 128p. 1997. 5.95 (0-8069-9454-1) Sterling.

— Nutty Challenges & Zany Dares. LC 93-32391. (Illus.). 128p. (J). 1994. pap. 4.95 (0-8069-0454-2) Sterling.

— One Hundred One Amazing Card Tricks. LC 93-23861. (Illus.). 128p. 1993. pap. 4.95 (0-8069-0342-2) Sterling.

— World's Best Card Tricks. LC 90-46641. (Illus.). 128p. (YA). 1992. pap. 4.95 (0-8069-8233-0) Sterling.

— World's Best Coin Tricks. LC 92-11370. (Illus.). 128p. (J). (gr. 5-10). 1993. pap. 4.95 (0-8069-8661-1) Sterling.

— World's Greatest Card Tricks. LC 95-46815. (Illus.). 128p. 1996. pap. 4.95 (0-8069-5991-6) Sterling.

Longe, G., ed. Multi-User Communication Systems. (CISM International Centre for Mechanical Sciences Ser.: Vol. 265). (Illus.). 259p. 1981. 43.95 (0-387-81612-7) Spr-Verlag.

Longe, Karen. UPN Bar Code Labeling: A Guide for Implementation in Healthcare. (Illus.). 120p. (C). 1998. pap. 39.95 (0-941668-07-X) Tower Hill Pr.

Longe, Mary E. & Thomas, Karen. Consumer Health Resource Centers: A Guide to Successful Planning & Implementation. LC 97-53188. 180p. 1998. 25.00 (1-55648-231-0) AHPI.

Longe, R. Leon & Calvert, John C. Physical Assessment: A Guide for Evaluating Drug Therapy. Young, Lloyd Y., ed. LC 94-76859. 486p. (Orig.). (C). 1994. pap. text 44.50 (0-915486-20-2) Applied Therapeutics.

Longe, Robert. The Files of a Counterfeit Sex Therapist. LC 76-56729. 1977. 22.95 (0-87949-061-6) Ashley Bks.

Longenbach, James. Modern Poetry after Modernism. LC 96-45288. 224p. 1997. text 49.95 (0-19-510177-4); pap. text 19.95 (0-19-510178-2) OUP.

— Modernist Poetics of History: Pound, Eliot, & the Sense of the Past. LC 86-25189. 298p. reprint ed. pap. 92.40 (0-608-06350-9, 206671100008) Bks Demand.

— Threshold. LC 98-11462. 73p. 1998. pap. 12.00 (0-226-89935-7); lib. bdg. 26.00 (0-226-89934-9) U Ch Pr.

— Wallace Stevens: The Plain Sense of Things. 352p. 1991. pap. text 29.95 (0-19-507022-4) OUP.

***Longenecker, et al.** Web Tutor on Webct to Accompany Small Business Management. 11th ed. 1999. pap. 19.00 (0-534-76548-3) Wadsworth Pub.

Longenecker, Bruce W. Eschatology & the Covenant: A Comparison of 4 Ezra & Romans 1-11. (JSNT Supplement Ser.: Vol. 57). 318p. 1991. 85.00 (1-85075-305-9, Pub. by Sheffield Acad) CUP Services.

— 2 Esdras. (Guides to the Apocrypha & Pseudepigrapha Ser.: No. 1). 128p. 1995. pap. 14.95 (1-85075-726-7, Pub. by Sheffield Acad) CUP Services.

— The Triumph of Abraham's God: The Transformation of Identity in Galatians. LC 98-18437. 256p. 1998. 25.00 (0-687-03537-6) Abingdon.

Longenecker, Clarence E. How to Recover from a Stroke & Make a Successful Comeback. LC 77-79690. 1977. 18.95 (0-87949-105-1) Ashley Bks.

Longenecker, Gesina L. How Drugs Work. LC 95-109267. (How It Works Ser.). (Illus.). 256p. (Orig.). 1994. pap. 19.95 (1-56276-241-9, Ziff-Davis Pr) Que.

Longenecker, Harold L. Growing Leaders by Design: How to Use Biblical Principles for Leadership Development. LC 95-8345. 160p. 1995. pap. 10.99 (0-8254-3131-X) Kregel.

Longenecker, J. B., et al. Nutrition & Biotechnology in Heart Disease & Cancer: Proceedings of a Conference Held in Research Triangle Park, North Carolina, December 5-7, 1993. LC 95-7574. (Advances in Experimental Medicine & Biology Ser.: Vol. 369). (Illus.). 278p. (C). 1995. 95.00 (0-306-44994-3, Kluwer Plenum) Kluwer Academic.

Longenecker, J. Craig. High-Yield Acid Base. LC 97-44427. 100p. 1998. write for info. (0-683-30393-7) Lppncott W & W.

***Longenecker, Justin G.** Small Business Management: An Entrepreneurial Emphasis. 11th ed. LC 99-29259. 701p. 1999. 87.95 (0-538-89015-0) Thomson Learn.

Longenecker, Justin G., et al. Small Business Management. 10th ed. LC 96-6330. (GG - Small Business Management Ser.). 1996. mass mkt. 62.95 (0-538-85077-9) S-W Pub.

Longenecker, Martha W., ed. American Expressions of Liberty: Art of the People, by the People, for the People. LC 96-77117. (Illus.). 168p. 1996. 45.00 (0-8109-6338-8, Pub. by Abrams) Time Warner.

***Longenecker, Martha W., ed.** Art That Soars: Kites & Tails by Jackie Matisse. (Illus.). 120p. 2000. 33.00 (0-914155-12-1) Mingei Intl Mus.

— Ceramics of Tatsuzo Shimaoka: A Retrospective of a National Living Treasure of Japan. (Illus.). 160p. 2000. 45.00 (0-914155-13-X) Mingei Intl Mus.

Longenecker, Martha W., ed. Niki de Saint Phalle: Insider-Outsider--World Inspired Art. (Illus.). 120p. 1998. 35.00 (0-914155-10-5) Mingei Intl Mus.

— A Transcultural Mosaic: Folk Art from the Collection of Mingei International Museum. (Illus.). 168p. 1993. 45.00 (0-914155-03-2) Mingei Intl Mus.

Longenecker, Martha W., et al. Dowry: Eastern European Painted Furniture, Textiles & Related Folk Art. (Illus.). 96p. Date not set. 29.95 (0-914155-11-3) Mingei Intl Mus.

An Asterisk (*) at the beginning of an entry indicates that the title is appearing for the first time.

Longenecker, Richard. Biblical Exegesis in the Apostolic Period. 246p. 1993. reprint ed. pap. 32.00 (*1-57383-074-7*) Regent College.

Longenecker, Richard. The Christology of Early Jewish Christianity. 178p. 1994. reprint ed. pap. 16.95 (*1-57383-029-1*) Regent College.

— Paul, Apostle of Liberty: The Origin & Nature of Paul's Christianity. 310p. 1992. reprint ed. pap. 23.95 (*1-57383-005-4*) Regent College.

Longenecker, Richard N. Biblical Exegesis in the Apostolic Period. (Biblical & Theological Classics Library: Vol. 5). 246p. 1995. reprint ed. pap. 9.99 (*0-85364-708-9*, Pub. by Paternoster Pub) OM Literature.

Longenecker, Richard N. Biblical Exegesis in the Apostolic Period. 2nd rev. ed. LC 99-19538. 238p. 1999. pap. 20.00 (*0-8028-4301-8*) Eerdmans.

— Life in the Face of Death: The Resurrection Message of the New Testament. LC 99-161356. (McMaster New Testament Studies: Vol. 3). 288p. 1998. pap. 22.00 (*0-8028-4474-X*) Eerdmans.

— New Wine into Fresh Wineskins: Contextualizing the Early Christian Confessions. LC 99-46070. 220p. 1999. pap. 14.95 (*1-56563-098-X*) Hendrickson MA.

— The Road from Damascus: The Impact of Paul's Conversion on His Life, Thought, & Ministry. LC 97-7870. (McMaster New Testament Studies). 268p. 1997. 25.00 (*0-8028-4191-0*) Eerdmans.

***Longenecker, Richard N., ed.** The Challenge of Jesus' Parables. (McMaster New Testament Studies). 304p. 2000. pap. 28.00 (*0-8028-4638-6*) Eerdmans.

Longenecker, Richard N., ed. Patterns of Discipleship in the New Testament. (McMaster New Testament Studies). 319p. (Orig.). 1996. pap. 25.00 (*0-8028-4169-4*) Eerdmans.

Longenecker, Richard N., jt. auth. see Tenney, Merrill C.

Longenecker, Rolla R. How to Prepare a Case for Trial: A Brief Treatise. LC 95-186764. 42p. 1994. reprint ed. 28.00 (*0-89941-912-7*, 308560) W S Hein.

— Some Hints on the Trial of a Lawsuit. LC 95-77927. xxix, 314p. 1995. reprint ed. 68.00 (*0-89941-976-3*, 308830) W S Hein.

Longenecker, Ruth R. Financial & Health Care Planning for the Elderly in Ohio. 3rd ed. LC 98-48415. (Ohio Practice Manual Ser.). 1999. 80.00 (*0-87084-379-6*) Anderson Pub Co.

Longenecker, Ruth R. & Taps, Richard T. Financial & Health Care Planning for the Elderly in Ohio. 2nd ed. LC 95-120323. 374p. 1994. pap. 80.00 (*0-87084-405-9*) Anderson Pub Co.

Longenecker, Sharon. Crushed but Not Destroyed. 232p. (Orig.). 1984. pap. 7.95 (*0-9614244-0-0*) Sun Ray Pub.

Longenecker, Stephen. The Christopher Sauers. 160p. (Orig.). 1981. pap. 7.95 (*0-87178-141-7*, 8417) Brethren.

Longenecker, Stephen L. Piety & Tolerance: Pennsylvania German Religion, 1700-1850. LC 93-49988. (Pietist & Wesleyan Studies: No. 6). 216p. 1994. 32.00 (*0-8108-2771-9*) Scarecrow.

Longenecker, Stephen L. & Arnett, Ronald C. The Dilemma of Anabaptist Piety: Strengthening Or Straining the Bonds of Community? LC 97-66206. 1997. write for info. (*0-89725-302-7*, Penobscot Pr) Picton Pr.

Longere, Jean. Les Sermons Latins de Maurice de Sully, Eveque de Paris (1196) Contribution a l'Histoire de la Tradition Manuscrite. (C). 1989. pap. text 282.00 (*0-7923-0282-6*) Kluwer Academic.

***Longest.** Health Professionals in Management. 2nd ed. (C). 1999. pap. text 29.95 (*0-8385-3682-4*) Appleton & Lange.

Longest, Beaufort B. Health Policymaking in the United States. 2nd ed. LC 97-34809. 1998. 52.00 (*1-56793-072-7*) Health Admin Pr.

Longest, Beaufort B., Jr. Health Professionals in Management. LC 94-43677. 318p. (C). 1995. pap. text 31.95 (*0-8385-3679-4*, A3679-6, Apple Lange Med) McGraw.

— Seeking Strategic Advantage Through Health Policy Analysis. LC 96-26898. (Orig.). 1996. pap. 40.00 (*1-56793-047-6*) Health Admin Pr.

Longest, Beaufort B., et al, eds. Cases in Health Services Management. 2nd ed. LC 87-71839. 500p. 1987. teacher ed. 6.95 (*0-317-57997-5*); pap. text 36.00 (*0-317-57996-7*) AUPHA Pr.

***Longest, Beaufort B., et al.** Instructor's Manual for Managing Health Services Organizations & Systems. 4th rev. ed. 192p. 2000. pap. text, teacher ed. write for info. (*1-878812-58-0*) Hlth Prof Pr.

Longest, Beaufort B., Jr., et al. Managing Health Services Organizations. 2nd ed. (Illus.). 550p. 1985. 42.50 (*0-7216-2045-0*, W B Saunders Co) Harcrt Hlth Sci Grp.

***Longest, Beaufort B., et al.** Managing Health Services Organizations & Systems. 4th ed. 2000. text 78.00 (*1-878812-57-2*, 2572) Hlth Prof Pr.

Longest, David. Cartoon Toys & Collectibles: Identification & Values. LC 98-235169. 224p. 1998. pap. 19.95 (*1-57432-075-0*) Collector Bks.

— Toys Antique & Collectible. 1995. pap. 14.95 (*0-89145-402-0*, 2028) Collector Bks.

Longest, David, jt. auth. see Alcott, Louisa May.

Longest, George C. Genius in the Garden: Charles F. Gillette & Landscape Architecture in Virginia. LC 92-12464. 1992. 39.95 (*0-88490-172-6*) Library of VA.

Longest, Pauline. Going Places. LC 96-71763. (Illus.). 250p. 1997. 14.95 (*1-57197-047-9*) Pentland Pr.

Longfellow. The Song of Hiawatha: Piano - Vocal Score. (Illus.). 44p. (J). (gr. 2 up). 1988. 15.00 (*0-88680-303-9*) I E Clark.

Longfellow, Charles A. Charles Appleton Longfellow: Twenty Months in Japan, 1871-1873. Laidlaw, Christine W., ed. LC 98-96249. (Illus.). 208p. 1998. pap. 19.95 (*0-9662200-0-5*) Frnds Lngfellow Hse.

Longfellow, Henry Wadsworth. Aftermath. (Notable American Authors Ser.). 1999. reprint ed. lib. bdg. 125.00 (*0-7812-3841-2*) Rprt Serv.

— Ballads & Other Poems. (Notable American Authors Ser.). 1999. reprint ed. lib. bdg. 125.00 (*0-7812-3824-2*) Rprt Serv.

— The Bellfry of Bruges & Other Poems. (Notable American Authors Ser.). 1999. reprint ed. lib. bdg. 125.00 (*0-7812-3828-5*) Rprt Serv.

— La Cabalgata de Paul Revere: Paul Revere's Ride. 1996. 10.19 (*0-606-08792-3*, Pub. by Turtleback) Demco.

— The Children's Hour. (Illus.). 32p. 1993. 17.95 (*0-87923-971-9*) Godine.

— Children's Own Longfellow, 001. (Illus.). 109p. (J). (gr. 2 up). 1987. 20.00 (*0-395-06889-4*) HM.

— Complete Poems. 1992. reprint ed. lib. bdg. 45.95 (*0-89968-291-X*, Lghtyr Pr) Buccaneer Bks.

— Complete Writings, 11 vols., Set. (BCL1-PS American Literature Ser.). 1992. reprint ed. lib. bdg. 900.00 (*0-7812-6779-X*) Rprt Serv.

— The Courtship of Miles Standish & Other Poems. (Notable American Authors Ser.). 1999. reprint ed. lib. bdg. 125.00 (*0-7812-3836-6*) Rprt Serv.

— The Divine Comedy of Miles Standish & Other Poems. (Notable American Authors Ser.). 1999. reprint ed. lib. bdg. 125.00 (*0-7812-3839-0*) Rprt Serv.

— Evangeline. (FRE., Illus.). 200p. 1999. pap. 7.95 (*1-56554-475-7*) Pelican.

— Evangeline. Semple, Lewis B., ed. LC 98-50342. (Illus.). 176p. 1999. pap. 6.95 (*1-56554-474-9*) Pelican.

— Evangeline. (Notable American Authors Ser.). 1999. reprint ed. lib. bdg. 125.00 (*0-7812-3830-7*) Rprt Serv.

— Evangeline: A Tale of Acadie. 109p. 1991. pap. 5.95 (*0-920852-13-0*) Nimbus Publ.

— Evangeline: A Tale of Acadie. rev. ed. LC 95-195429. (Illus.). 144p. 1995. text 14.95 (*1-55109-116-X*) Nimbus Publ.

— Evangeline & Other Poems. 64p. 1995. pap. text 1.00 (*0-486-28255-4*) Dover.

— Evangeline & Selected Tales & Poems. Gregory, Horace, ed. 1964. mass mkt. 5.95 (*0-451-52003-3*, CE1724, Sig Classics) NAL.

— Favorite Poems. Orig. Title: The Complete Poetical Works of Henry Wadsworth Longfellow. 96p. 1992. reprint ed. pap. text 1.00 (*0-486-27273-7*) Dover.

— The Golden Legend. (Notable American Authors Ser.). 1999. reprint ed. lib. bdg. 125.00 (*0-7812-3833-1*) Rprt Serv.

— The Hanging of the Crane. (Notable American Authors Ser.). 1999. reprint ed. lib. bdg. 125.00 (*0-7812-3842-0*) Rprt Serv.

***Longfellow, Henry Wadsworth.** Henry Wadsworth Longfellow: Poems & Other Writings. McClatchy, J. D., ed. LC 00-26678. 875p. 2000. 35.00 (*1-883011-85-X*, Pub. by Library of America) Penguin Putnam.

Longfellow, Henry Wadsworth. Hiawatha. LC 83-7225. 1996. 11.19 (*0-606-10212-4*, Pub. by Turtleback) Demco.

— Hiawatha. (Illus.). 32p. (J). (gr. k up). 1996. pap. 5.99 (*0-14-055882-9*) Viking Penguin.

— Hiawatha, with Its Original Indian Legends. (BCL1-PS American Literature Ser.). 255p. 1993. reprint ed. lib. bdg. 79.00 (*0-7812-6984-9*) Rprt Serv.

— Hiawatha's Childhood. LC 84-47969. (Illus.). 32p. (J). (ps-3). 1984. 15.00 (*0-374-33065-4*) FS&G.

— Hiawatha's Childhood. LC 84-46969. (Illus.). 32p. (J). (gr. k-3). 1994. pap. 5.95 (*0-374-42997-9*) FS&G.

Longfellow, Henry Wadsworth. Hiawatha's Childhood. (Picture Puffin Ser.). (Illus.). (J). 1986. 9.19 (*0-606-02130-2*, Pub. by Turtleback) Demco.

Longfellow, Henry Wadsworth. Hyperion: A Romance. (Notable American Authors Ser.). 1999. reprint ed. lib. bdg. 125.00 (*0-7812-3822-6*) Rprt Serv.

— In the Harbor Pt. II: Ultima Thule. (Notable American Authors Ser.). 1999. reprint ed. lib. bdg. 125.00 (*0-7812-3846-3*) Rprt Serv.

— Kavanagh: A Tale. Downey, Jean, ed. (Masterworks of Literature Ser.). 1965. 15.95 (*0-8084-0198-X*); pap. 13.95 (*0-8084-0199-8*) NCUP.

— Kavanagh: A Tale. (Notable American Authors Ser.). 1999. reprint ed. lib. bdg. 125.00 (*0-7812-3831-5*) Rprt Serv.

— Keramos & Other Poems. (Notable American Authors Ser.). 1999. reprint ed. lib. bdg. 125.00 (*0-7812-3844-7*) Rprt Serv.

— The Letters of Henry Wadsworth Longfellow, 6 vols. Hilen, Andrew R., ed. Incl. Set. Longfellows Letters Vols. 1-2: 1814-1836 & 1837-1843., 2 vols. LC 66-18248. 1164p. 1967. 95.00 (*0-674-52725-9*); Set. Longfellows Letters Vols. 3-4: 1844-1856 & 1857-1865., 2 vols. LC 66-18248. 1126p. 1972. 95.00 (*0-674-52728-3*); Set. 1866-1875 & 1876-1882., 2 vols. LC 66-18248. 1792p. 1983. 127.50 (*0-674-52729-1*); LC 66-18248. write for info. (*0-318-53094-5*) Belknap Pr.

— Life of Henry Wadsworth Longfellow, with Extracts from His Journals & Correspondence, 3 vols., Set. Longfellow, Samuel, ed. LC 04-17165. 1968. reprint ed. 55.00 (*0-403-00078-5*) Scholarly.

Longfellow, Henry Wadsworth. LONGFELLOW EVANGELINE CAS. abr. ed. LC 66-1705. 1972. audio 14.00 (*0-694-50133-6*, SWC 1179, Caedmon) HarperAudio.

Longfellow, Henry Wadsworth. The Masque of Pandora & Other Poems. (Notable American Authors Ser.). 1999. reprint ed. lib. bdg. 125.00 (*0-7812-3843-9*) Rprt Serv.

***Longfellow, Henry Wadsworth.** The Midnight Ride of Paul Revere. LC 99-54540. (Illus.). 32p. (J). (gr. 1-4). 2000. 16.95 (*0-7922-7674-4*, Pub. by Natl Geog) S&S Trade.

Longfellow, Henry Wadsworth. The New England Tragedy. (Notable American Authors Ser.). 1999. reprint ed. lib. bdg. 125.00 (*0-7812-3837-4*) Rprt Serv.

— Outre-Mer: Essays. (Notable American Authors Ser.). 1999. reprint ed. lib. bdg. 125.00 (*0-7812-3821-8*) Rprt Serv.

— Paul Revere's Ride. LC 89-25630. (Illus.). 40p. (J). (gr. k-4). 1990. 16.99 (*0-525-44610-9*, Dutton Child) Peng Put Young Read.

— Paul Revere's Ride. (Illus.). 40p. (J). (gr. k up). 1996. pap. 6.99 (*0-14-055612-5*, PuffinBks) Peng Put Young Read.

— Paul Revere's Ride. 1996. 10.19 (*0-606-08842-3*, Pub. by Turtleback) Demco.

— Paul Revere's Ride. LC 92-23319. (Illus.). 48p. (J). (gr. 1 up). 1993. reprint ed. mass mkt. 4.95 (*0-688-12387-2*, Wm Morrow) Morrow Avon.

— Poems. (Notable American Authors Ser.). 1999. reprint ed. lib. bdg. 125.00 (*0-7812-3827-7*) Rprt Serv.

— Poems of Longfellow. 23.95 (*0-8488-2652-3*) Amereon Ltd.

— Poems on Slavery. (Notable American Authors Ser.). 1999. reprint ed. lib. bdg. 125.00 (*0-7812-3825-0*) Rprt Serv.

— The Poets & Poetry of Europe. (Notable American Authors Ser.). 1999. reprint ed. lib. bdg. 125.00 (*0-7812-3829-3*) Rprt Serv.

— Prose Works. (Notable American Authors Ser.). 1999. reprint ed. lib. bdg. 125.00 (*0-7812-3835-8*) Rprt Serv.

— The Seaside & the Fireside. (Notable American Authors Ser.). 1999. lib. bdg. 125.00 (*0-7812-3832-3*) Rprt Serv.

— Selected Poems. 224p. 1992. 7.99 (*0-517-08246-2*) Random Hse Value.

— Selected Poems. Thwaite, Anthony, ed. 384p. 1993. pap. 12.95 (*0-460-87229-X*, Everyman's Classic Lib) Tuttle Pubng.

— Selected Poems. Buell, Lawrence, ed. & intro. by. 240p. 1988. pap. 12.95 (*0-14-039064-2*, Penguin Classics) Viking Penguin.

— The Song of Hiawatha. Aaron, Daniel, ed. 176p. 1993. pap. 2.95 (*0-460-87268-0*, Everyman's Classic Lib) Tuttle Pubng.

— The Song of Hiawatha. (Notable American Authors Ser.). 1999. reprint ed. lib. bdg. 125.00 (*0-7812-3834-X*) Rprt Serv.

— The Song of Hiawatha: A 2-Act Musical Based on the Poem by Henry Wadsworth Longfellow. (Illus.). 44p. (J). (gr. 2 up). 1988. pap. 4.50 (*0-88680-302-0*) I E Clark.

— The Spanish Student: A Play in Three Acts. (Notable American Authors Ser.). 1999. reprint ed. lib. bdg. 125.00 (*0-7812-3826-9*) Rprt Serv.

— Tales of a Wayside Inn. (Notable American Authors Ser.). 1999. reprint ed. lib. bdg. 125.00 (*0-7812-3838-2*) Rprt Serv.

— Three Books of Song. (Notable American Authors Ser.). 1999. reprint ed. lib. bdg. 125.00 (*0-7812-3840-4*) Rprt Serv.

— Ultima Thule. (Notable American Authors Ser.). 1999. reprint ed. lib. bdg. 125.00 (*0-7812-3845-5*) Rprt Serv.

— Voices of the Night. (Notable American Authors Ser.). 1999. reprint ed. lib. bdg. 125.00 (*0-7812-3823-4*) Rprt Serv.

— Works, 14 vols., Set. reprint ed. write for info. (*0-404-04040-3*) AMS Pr.

— The Works of Henry Wadsworth Longfellow. (Poetry Library). 912p. 1998. pap. 7.95 (*1-85326-422-9*, 4229WW, Pub. by Wrdsworth Edits) NTC Contemp Pub Co.

— Your Life Depends on It!, 2 vol. set. Molina, Tarea, ed. & intro. by. (Illus.). 1994. student ed. write for info. (*0-9642779-2-1*) T Molina Ent.

Longfellow, Henry Wadsworth, jt. auth. see Fox, Finis.

Longfellow, Henry Wadsworth, jt. auth. see Schoonmaker, Frances.

Longfellow, Henry Wadsworth, tr. see Alighieri, Dante.

Longfellow, S., ed. see Johnson, Samuel.

Longfellow, Samuel. A Book of Hymns & Tunes. (Notable American Authors Ser.). 1999. reprint ed. lib. bdg. 125.00 (*0-7812-3849-8*) Rprt Serv.

— Final Memorials of Henry Wadsworth Longfellow. (Notable American Authors Ser.). 1999. reprint ed. lib. bdg. 125.00 (*0-7812-3852-8*) Rprt Serv.

— Hymns of the Spirit. (Notable American Authors Ser.). 1999. reprint ed. lib. bdg. 125.00 (*0-7812-3850-1*) Rprt Serv.

— Life of Henry Wadsworth Longfellow. (Notable American Authors Ser.). 1999. reprint ed. lib. bdg. 125.00 (*0-7812-3851-X*) Rprt Serv.

— Life of Henry Wadsworth Longfellow, with Extracts from His Journals & Correspondence, 3 vols., Set. (BCL1-PS American Literature Ser.). 1992. reprint ed. lib. bdg. 225.00 (*0-7812-6781-1*) Rprt Serv.

— Thalatta: A Book for the Seaside. 1999. reprint ed. lib. bdg. 125.00 (*0-7812-3848-X*) Rprt Serv.

Longfellow, Samuel, ed. see Longfellow, Henry Wadsworth.

Longfellow, Sandra P., jt. ed. see Nelson, James B.

Longfield, Bradley J. The Presbyterian Controversy: Fundamentalists, Modernists & Moderates. (Religion in America Ser.). (Illus.). 352p. 1993. reprint ed. pap. text 19.95 (*0-19-508674-0*) OUP.

Longfield, Bradley J. & McMurry, Doug. Prayer That Shapes the Future. LC 99-18212. 1999. pap. 12.99 (*0-310-22540-X*) HarpC.

Longfield, Diane M. Passage to ESL Literacy. (Illus.). 422p. (Orig.). 1981. pap., teacher ed. 22.95 (*0-937354-03-1*); pap. text, student ed. 10.50 (*0-937354-01-5*) Delta Systems.

— Passage to ESL Literacy Visuals. (Illus.). 182p. (Orig.). 1981. pap., teacher ed. 23.95 (*0-937354-11-2*) Delta Systems.

Longfield, Mountford. Lectures on Political Economy: London School of Economics. (LSE Scarce Tracts in Economics Ser.). 280p. (C). 1997. 90.00 (*0-415-14385-3*) Routledge.

— Three Lectures on Commerce & One on Absenteeism: London School of Economics. (LSE Scarce Tracts in Economics Ser.). 117p. (C). 1997. 60.00 (*0-415-14386-1*) Routledge.

Longfield, Mountiford. The Economic Writings of Mountiford Longfield. Black, R. D., ed. LC 73-144801. (Reprints of Economic Classics Ser.). 673p. 1971. 57.50 (*0-678-00836-1*) Kelley.

L

Longfish, George C., jt. auth. see Penney, David W.

Longfoot, Stephanie. Animales de la Granja. (Juega y Aprende Ser.).Tr. of Farm Animals. (ENG & SPA.). 12p. (J). (ps). 1995. bds. 3.98 (*1-85854-333-9*) Brimax Bks.

— Can You See Duckling? (Interactive Push-Pull Ser.). 14p. (J). (ps up). 1997. bds. 4.98 (*1-85854-702-4*) Brimax Bks.

— De Que Color Es? (Juega y Aprende Ser.).Tr. of What Color Is It?. (ENG & SPA.). 12p. (J). (ps). 1995. bds. 3.98 (*1-85854-334-7*) Brimax Bks.

— I Can Say These Words. (Now I Am Big Ser.). 24p. (J). (ps-1). 1997. 4.98 (*1-85854-712-1*) Brimax Bks.

— Mis Juguetes. (Juega y Aprende Ser.).Tr. of My Playthings. (ENG & SPA.). 12p. (J). (ps). 1995. bds. 3.98 (*1-85854-335-5*) Brimax Bks.

— My Christmas Counting Book. 20p. (J). (ps). 1996. bds. 5.98 (*0-86112-758-7*) Brimax Bks.

— Where's My Teddy? (Interactive Push-Pull Ser.). 14p. (J). (ps up). 1997. bds. 4.98 (*1-85854-701-6*) Brimax Bks.

— Yo Puedo Contar. (Juega y Aprende Ser.).Tr. of I Can Count. (ENG & SPA.). 12p. (J). (ps). 1995. bds. 3.98 (*1-85854-332-0*) Brimax Bks.

Longfoot, Stephanie & Davies, Gill. Our New Baby. (Now I Am Big Ser.). (Illus.). 24p. (J). (ps-1). 1996. 3.49 (*1-85854-367-3*) Brimax Bks.

Longfoot, Stephanie, jt. auth. see Davies, Gill.

Longford. Mishka & Plishka. LC 95-14692. (J). 1996. 16.00 (*0-689-80244-7*) Aladdin.

Longford, Frank P. & O'Neill, Thomas P. Eamon de Valera. LC 77-144076. xix, 499 p. 1971. write for info. (*0-395-12101-9*) HM.

— Eamon de Valera. LC 70-543347. 1970. write for info. (*0-09-104660-2*) Hutchnson.

Longford, Elizabeth. Queen Victoria. 2000. pap. text 9.95 (*0-7509-2143-9*) Sutton Pub Ltd.

— Royal Throne: The Future of the Monarchy. large type ed. (Isis Large Print Bks.). 195p. 1995. 21.95 (*1-85695-141-3*, Pub. by ISIS Lrg Prnt) Transaction Pubs.

Longford, Elizabeth, ed. The Oxford Book of Royal Anecdotes. (Illus.). 572p. 1989. 27.50 (*0-19-214153-8*) OUP.

Longford, Lindsay. Annie & the Wise Men: Under the Mistletoe. (Romance Ser.). 1993. per. 2.75 (*0-373-08977-5*, 5-08977-6) Silhouette.

— Baby, You're Mine: Bundles of Joy. (Romance Ser.: No. 1396). 1999. per. 3.50 (*0-373-19396-3*, 1-19396-0) Silhouette.

— The Cowboy & the Princess. 1995. per. 2.99 (*0-373-19115-4*, 1-19115-4) Silhouette.

— The Cowboy, the Baby & the: (Bundles of Joy) (Romance Ser.). 1995. per. 2.99 (*0-373-19073-5*, 1-19073-5) Silhouette.

— Daddy by Decision. (Romance Ser.). 1997. per. 3.25 (*0-373-19204-5*, 1-19204-6) Silhouette.

— Dark Moon. (Shadows Ser.). 1995. mass mkt. 3.50 (*0-373-27053-4*, 1-27053-7) Silhouette.

— A Kiss, a Kid & a Mistletoe Bride: Virgin Brides. (Romance Ser.: No. 1336). 1998. per. 3.50 (*0-373-19336-X*, 1-19336-6) Silhouette.

— Lover in the Shadows. (Shadows Ser.). 1994. per. 3.50 (*0-373-27029-1*, 5-27029-3) Silhouette.

— No Surrender: Expectantly Yours. (Intimate Moments Ser.: No. 947). 1999. per. 4.25 (*0-373-07947-8*, 1-07947-4) Silhouette.

— Pete's Dragon. (Romance Ser.: No. 854). 1992. per. 2.69 (*0-373-08854-X*, 5-08854-7) Silhouette.

— Renegade's Redemption. (Intimate Moments Ser.). 1997. per. 3.99 (*0-373-07769-6*, 1-07769-2) Silhouette.

— Sullivan's Miracle. (Intimate Moments Ser.). 1993. per. 3.50 (*0-373-07526-X*, 5-07526-2) Silhouette.

— Undercover Daddy. (Romance Ser.). 1996. per. 3.25 (*0-373-19168-5*, 1-19168-3) Silhouette.

Longford, Lord. History of the House of Lords. LC 99-209081. 1999. pap. text 23.95 (*0-7509-2191-9*) A Sutton.

Longford, Nicholas T. Random Coefficient Models. LC 93-35629. (Oxford Statistical Science Ser.: No. 11). (Illus.). 284p. (C). 1994. text 70.00 (*0-19-852264-9*, Clarendon Pr) OUP.

Longgood, William. The Queen Must Die & Other Affairs of Bees & Men. (Illus.). 1988. pap. 13.95 (*0-393-30528-7*) Norton.

Longguan, Zhang, jt. ed. see Lodl, Ann.

Longhauser, Elsa. Dorothea Hofmann: Drawings & Etchings. (Illus.). 16p. 1986. pap. 10.00 (*1-58442-022-7*) Galleries at Moore.

— Jackie Ferrara: Benches, Thrones, & a Table. (Illus.). 8p. 1987. pap. 10.00 (*1-58442-015-4*) Galleries at Moore.

Longhauser, Elsa & Rickman, Rebecca. History for Sale: 2000 Paintings by Stephen Keene. LC 97-77056. (Illus.). 12p. 1997. pap. 7.00 (*1-58442-021-9*) Galleries at Moore.

Longhauser, Elsa, et al. Femmes Fatales: An Installation by Lady Pink. (Illus.). 6p. 1984. pap. 10.00 (*1-58442-028-6*) Galleries at Moore.

— Tom Chimes: A Compendium: 1961-1986. LC 85-81570. (Illus.). 28p. 1986. pap. 20.00 (*1-58442-005-7*) Galleries at Moore.

An Asterisk (*) at the beginning of an entry indicates that the title is appearing for the first time.

L

Longhauser, Elsa, ed. see Bacon, Edmund N., et al.

Longhauser, Elsa, ed. see Cotter, Holland.

Longhauser, Elsa, ed. see De la Motte, Helga & Steiner, Wendy.

Longhauser, Elsa, ed. see Edelstein, Teri.

Longhauser, Elsa, ed. see Edwards, Robert, et al.

Longhauser, Elsa, ed. see Fleck, Robert, et al.

Longhauser, Elsa, ed. see Flood, Richard.

Longhauser, Elsa, ed. see Fraser, Andrea.

Longhauser, Elsa, ed. see Graham, Dan, et al.

Longhauser, Elsa, ed. see Grundberg, Andy.

Longhauser, Elsa, ed. see Haase, Amine, et al.

Longhauser, Elsa, ed. see Indiana, Gary.

Longhauser, Elsa, ed. see Jones, Kellie & Roth, Moria.

Longhauser, Elsa, ed. see Lewallen, Constance, et al.

Longhauser, Elsa, ed. see McEvilley, Thomas.

Longhauser, Elsa, ed. see Neugroschel, Joachim & Zucker, Barbara.

Longhauser, Elsa, ed. see Phillpot, Clive.

Longhauser, Elsa, ed. see Rand, Paul, et al.

Longhauser, Elsa, ed. see Ross, David A. & Lewallen, Constance.

Longhauser, Elsa, ed. see Rychlik, Otmar & Paoletti, John T.

Longhauser, Elsa, ed. see Saunders, Wade.

Longhauser, Elsa, ed. see Schwartzman, Allan & Harshav, Benjamin.

Longhauser, Elsa, ed. see Sekler, Eduard F., et al.

Longhauser, Elsa, ed. see Sims, Patterson & Clark, Garth.

Longhauser, Elsa, ed. see Tureck, Rosalyn.

Longhauser, Elsa, ed. see Van Leeuwen, Jolie.

Longhauser, Elsa, ed. see Vergne, Philippe & Ninio, Moshe.

Longhauser, Elsa, ed. see Wechsler, Max, et al.

Longhauser, Elsa, et al, eds. Mexican Journeys: Myth, Magic & Mummies. LC 90-262265. (Illus.). 32p. 1990. pap. write for info. (*1-58442-034-0*) Galleries at Moore.

Longhauser, Elsa, ed. see Bonk, Ecke, et al.

Longheed, L. Business Communication: Ten Steps to Success. (Business for Career Success Ser.). 144p. (C). 1993. pap. text 16.17 (*0-201-51676-4*) Addison-Wesley.

— Business Correspondence: Letters, Faxes & Memos. (English for Business Success Ser.). (Illus.). 144p. 1992. pap. text 16.17 (*0-201-55537-9*) Addison-Wesley.

— Business Small Talk: Five Steps to Success. (Business for Career Success Ser.). (YA). 1995. pap. text 12.00 (*0-201-54261-7*) Longman.

— Business Small Talk: Five Steps to Success. 5th ed. (Business for Career Success Ser.). (YA). 1997. pap. text. write for info. (*0-201-54262-5*) Longman.

— Words More Words & Ways to Use Them. 144p. (YA). (gr. 7 up). 1993. pap. text 14.33 (*0-201-53961-6*) Addison-Wesley.

Longhena, Maria. Ancient Mexico: The History & Culture of the Maya, Aztec & Other Pre-Columbian Peoples. LC 98-84847. (Illus.). 292p. 1998. 60.00 (*1-55670-826-2*) Stewart Tabori & Chang.

***Longhena, Maria.** Mayan Script: A Civilization Revealed Through the Signs. LC 00-22495. (Illus.). 2000. 35.00 (*0-7892-0653-6*) Abbeville Pr.

***Longhena, Maria & Alva, Walter.** The Incas & Other Andean Civilizations. LC 99-38224. 1999. write for info. (*1-57145-220-6*, Thunder Bay) Advantage Pubs.

Longhi, Bob. Longhi's: Recipes & Romance from Maui's Most Famous Restaurant. LC 97-45488. (Illus.). 172p. 1998. 29.95 (*0-89815-950-4*) Ten Speed Pr.

Longhi, Christian, jt. ed. see Arena, R.

Longhi, G. & Lusanna, L., eds. Constraint's Theory & Relativistic Dynamics: Proceedings of the International Workshop, Firenze, Italy May 28-30, 1986. 368p. 1987. text 100.00 (*9971-5-0182-1*) World Scientific Pub.

Longhi, Jim. Woody, Cisco, & Me: Seamen Three in the Merchant Marine. LC 96-25185. (Music In American Life Ser.). 304p. 1997. 24.95 (*0-252-02276-9*) U of Ill Pr.

— Woody, Cisco & Me: Seamen Three in the Merchant Marine. 304p. 1998. 16.95 (*0-252-06700-2*) U of Ill Pr.

Longhi, Jon. Bricks & Anchors. 128p. (Orig.). 1991. pap. 8.95 (*0-916397-12-2*) Manic D Pr.

— Flashbacks & Premonitions. LC 98-40166. 160p. 1998. pap. text 11.95 (*0-916397-54-8*) Manic D Pr.

— The Rise & Fall of Third Leg. 160p. (Orig.). 1994. pap. 9.95 (*0-916397-27-0*) Manic D Pr.

— Zucchini & Other Stories. (Illus.). 20p. 1990. 3.00 (*0-916397-07-6*) Manic D Pr.

Longhi, R. Caravaggio. 3rd ed. (Illus.). 168p. 1993. text 28.00 (*3-364-00227-4*) Gordon & Breach.

Longhi, Robert. Three Studies: Masolino & Masaccio, Caravaggio & His Forerunners, Carlo Braccessco. abr. ed. Tabbat, David & Jacobson, David, trs. from ITA. LC 96-16974.Tr. of Opere Complete di Roberto Longhi. (Illus.). 279p. 1996. text 28.95 (*1-878818-51-1*, Pub. by Sheep Meadow) U Pr of New Eng.

***Longhi, Roberto.** Piero della Francesca. Tabbat, David, tr. from ITA. & pref. by. LC 00-26564. (Illus.). 256p. 2000. write for info. (*1-878818-77-5*, Pub. by Sheep Meadow) U Pr of New Eng.

Longhurst, A. H. The Story of the Stupa. (C). 1995. 18.00 (*81-206-0160-2*, Pub. by Asian Educ Servs) S Asia.

Longhurst, Alan R. Ecological Geography of the Sea. LC 98-84363. (Illus.). 398p. 1998. boxed set 79.95 (*0-12-455558-6*) Acad Pr.

Longhurst, Alan R. & Pauly, Daniel, eds. Ecology of Tropical Oceans. 407p. 1987. text 79.00 (*0-12-455562-4*) Acad Pr.

Longhurst, Brian. Popular Music & Society. 278p. (C). 1995. text 61.95 (*0-7456-1437-X*); pap. text 28.95 (*0-7456-1464-7*) Blackwell Pubs.

Longhurst, Brian, jt. auth. see Abercrombie, Nicholas.

Longhurst, C. A., ed. see Unamuno, Miguel de.

Longhurst, Derek, ed. Gender, Genre & Narrative Pleasure. 176p. 1989. text 49.95 (*0-318-41096-6*) Routledge.

Longhurst, J. W. S., ed. Acid Deposition: Origins, Impacts & Abatement Strategies. (Illus.). 364p. 1991. 239.95 (*0-387-53741-4*) Spr-Verlag.

Longhurst, Jean, jt. auth. see Singelmann, Jay.

Longhurst, Jean, jt. auth. see Singlemann, Jay.

Longhurst, John E. The Age of Torquemada. 146p. 1964. 15.00 (*0-87291-052-0*) Coronado Pr.

— Will the Faculty Please Come to Order. 68p. 1969. pap. 5.00 (*0-87291-003-2*) Coronado Pr.

Longhurst, John E., intro. The Spartan Rhetra. 76p. 1970. pap. 7.50 (*0-87291-008-3*) Coronado Pr.

Longhurst, Nancy A. The Self-Advocacy Movement by People with Developmental Disabilities: A Demographic Study & Directory of Self-Advocacy Groups in the United States. LC 93-48121. 1994. 21.95 (*0-940898-32-2*) Am Assn Mental.

Longhurst, Peter, jt. auth. see Roberts, Graham.

Longhurst, Richard, jt. auth. see Lipton, Michael.

***Longhurst, Robyn.** Geography & the Body: Exploring Fluid Boundaries. LC 00-28077. (Critical Geographies Ser.). 2000. pap. write for info. (*0-415-18967-5*) Routledge.

Longhurst, Thomas, jt. auth. see Horton, Ann.

Longhurst, Thomas M., ed. Linguistic Analysis of Children's Speech: Readings. 1974. 32.00 (*0-8422-5173-1*); pap. text 12.95 (*0-8422-0404-0*) Irvington.

Longino, Charles & Murphy, John. The Old Age Challenge to the Biomedical Model: Paradigm Strain & Health Policy. LC 94-30642. (Society & Aging Ser.). 169p. (C). 1995. 28.95 (*0-89503-165-5*) Baywood Pub.

Longino, Charles F. Retirement Migration in America: An Analysis of the Size, Trends & Economic Impact of the Country's Newest Growth Industry. Fox, R. Alan, ed. & frwd. by. LC 94-62150. (Illus.). 185p. (Orig.). 1995. pap. 39.95 (*0-9644216-1-5*) Vacation Pubns.

Longino, Helen E. Science As Social Knowledge: Value & Objectivity in Scientific Inquiry. 252p. (Orig.). 1990. pap. text 16.95 (*0-691-02051-5*, Pub. by Princeton U Pr) Cal Prin Full Svc.

Longino, Helen E. & Miner, Valerie, eds. The Competition: A Feminist Taboo? LC 87-8515. 208p. 1987. pap. 12.95 (*0-935312-74-9*); text 35.00 (*0-935312-75-7*) Feminist Pr.

Longino, Helen E., jt. ed. see Keller, Evelyn F.

Longinotti-Buitoni, Gian Luigi. Selling Dreams: How to Make Any Product Irresistible. LC 99-21735. 336p. 1999. 24.50 (*0-684-85019-2*) S&S Trade.

Longinotto, Kim & Rosenthal, Joanna, eds. Cheatin' Heart: Women's Secret Stories. 1999. pap. 13.99 (*1-85242-555-5*) Serpents Tail.

Longinovic, Tomaslav. Moment of Silence: Stories. 1990. 10.00 (*0-936050-08-X*) Burning Bks.

Longinovic, Tomislav Z. Borderline Culture: The Politics of Identity in Four Twentieth-Century Slavic Novels. LC 92-20696. 216p. 1993. text 28.00 (*1-55728-262-5*) U of Ark Pr.

Longinus. Libellus de Sublimitate. 4th ed. Russell, Donald A., ed. (Oxford Classical Texts Ser.). 1968. reprint ed. text 12.95 (*0-19-814566-7*) OUP.

— Longinus - Longini de Sublimitate Lexicon. Neuberger, Ruth, ed. (Alpha-Reihe A Ser.). (GER.). viii, 118p. 1987. write for info. (*3-487-07896-1*) G Olms Pubs.

— Longinus on the Sublime. LC 78-41181. reprint ed. 32.50 (*0-404-14743-7*) AMS Pr.

— Longinus on the Sublime: The Peri Hupsous in Translations by Nicolas Boileau-Despreaux (1674) & William Smith (1739) LC 75-8892. 390p. 1975. lib. bdg. 60.00 (*0-8201-1153-8*) Schol Facsimiles.

— On Great Writing on the Sublime. Grube, G. M., tr. LC 57-14628. 1957. pap. 2.40 (*0-672-60261-X*, LLA79, Bobbs) Macmillan.

— On Great Writing (On the Sublime) Grube, G. M., tr. from GRE. & intro. by. LC 90-49700. 88p. (C). 1991. reprint ed. pap. text 6.95 (*0-87220-080-9*); reprint ed. lib. bdg. 24.95 (*0-87220-081-7*) Hackett Pub.

— On the Sublime. (Loeb Classical Library). write for info. (*0-318-53145-3*) HUP.

Longley. Data & Security. 1989. 49.00 (*0-8493-7110-4*) CRC Pr.

— Geocomputation. LC 98-27225. 290p. 1998. pap. 54.95 (*0-471-98576-7*) Wiley.

— Geographical Information System. 1998. text. write for info. (*0-471-33132-5*) Wiley.

— Geographical Information System. (C). 1998. text. write for info. (*0-471-33133-3*) Wiley.

Longley, A. J. What You Don't Know Can Hurt You: A Guide to the Medical Literature. (Orig.). (C). 1981. pap. 3.00 (*0-937038-00-8*) Star Pr.

Longley, Alcander. What Is Communism? 2nd enl. rev. ed. LC 73-8710. (Communal Societies in America Ser.). reprint ed. 55.00 (*0-404-10727-3*) AMS Pr.

***Longley, Clifford.** The Worlock Archive. LC 99-48961. 2000. 29.95 (*0-225-66857-2*) G Chapman.

***Longley, David.** Longman Companion to Imperial Russia, 1689 - 1917. LC 99-57966. 496p. (C). 2000. write for info. (*0-582-31989-7*); pap. text 24.00 (*0-582-31990-0*) Longman.

Longley, Dennis. Parat Lexikon Information und Kommunilation. (GER.). 637p. 1993. 195.00 (*0-7859-8683-9*, 352726843x) Fr & Eur.

Longley, Diane. Health Care Constitutions. Harpwood, Vivienne, ed. LC 96-157186. (Medico-Legal Practitioner Ser.). 193p. 1995. pap. 40.00 (*1-85941-020-0*, Pub. by Cavendish Pubng) Gaunt.

— Public Law & Health Service Accountability. LC 92-13011. (State of Health Ser.). 1993. 123.00 (*0-335-09686-7*); pap. 35.95 (*0-335-09685-9*) OpUniv Pr.

Longley, Diane & Jameson, Rhonda S. Administrative Justice: Central Issues in U. K. & European Administrative Law. 272p. 1999. pap. 54.00 (*1-85941-342-0*, Pub. by Cavendish Pubng) Gaunt.

Longley, Edna. Alice in Wormland: Selected Poems. 128p. 1990. pap. 15.95 (*1-85224-125-X*, Pub. by Bloodaxe Bks) Dufour.

— Essays. 1998. 55.00 (*1-85224-434-8*, Pub. by Bloodaxe Bks); pap. 24.95 (*1-85224-435-6*, Pub. by Bloodaxe Bks) Dufour.

— The Living Stream: Literature & Revisionism in Ireland. 302p. 1994. pap. 25.00 (*1-85224-217-5*, Pub. by Bloodaxe Bks) Dufour.

— The Living Stream: Literature & Revisionism in Ireland. 302p. 1995. 55.00 (*1-85224-216-7*, Pub. by Bloodaxe Bks) Dufour.

— Poetry in the Wars. LC 86-25069. 264p. 1987. 38.50 (*0-87413-322-X*) U Delaware Pr.

— Poetry in Waters. 270p. 1996. pap. 22.95 (*0-906427-99-1*, Pub. by Bloodaxe Bks) Dufour.

Longley, Edna, ed. see Hewett, Dorothy.

Longley, Enda, ed. From Cathleen to Anorexia: The Breakdown of Irelands. (C). 1989. 35.00 (*0-946211-99-X*) St Mut.

Longley, James W. Least Squares Computations Using Orthogonalization Methods. LC 84-14939. (Lecture Notes in Pure & Applied Mathematics Ser.). xi, 308p. 1984. write for info. (*0-8247-7232-6*) Dekker.

— Least Squares Computations Using Orthogonalization Methods. LC 84-14939. (Lecture Notes in Pure & Applied Mathematics Ser.: No. 93). 328p. reprint ed. pap. 101.70 (*0-8357-2529-4*, 205240800014) Bks Demand.

Longley, John L. The Tragic Mask: A Study of Faulkner's Heroes. LC 63-22806. 254p. reprint ed. pap. 78.80 (*0-8357-4414-0*, 203723400008) Bks Demand.

Longley, John L., ed. Robert Penn Warren: A Collection of Critical Essays. LC 78-25757. 259p. 1979. reprint ed. lib. bdg. 35.00 (*0-313-20807-7*, LORW, Greenwood Pr) Greenwood.

Longley, Judy. Parallel Lives: Judy Longley. 32p. 1990. pap. 7.00 (*0-937669-37-7*) Owl Creek Pr.

Longley, Kateryna, jt. auth. see Gunew, Sneja.

Longley, Katharine. Saint Margaret Clitherow. 3rd ed. 203p. 1998. reprint ed. pap. 11.95 (*0-85650-073-9*, Pub. by A Clarke Bks) Source Bks CA.

Longley, Kyle. The Sparrow & the Hawk: Costa Rica & the United States During the Rise of Jose Figueres. LC 96-19042. 208p. 1997. pap. text 29.95 (*0-8173-0831-8*) U of Ala Pr.

Longley, Lawrence D. Electoral College Primer. LC 96-61002. 240p. 1996. pap. 16.00 (*0-300-07010-1*) Yale U Pr.

***Longley, Lawrence D.** The Electoral College Primer 2000. LC 99-29115. 224p. 1999. 25.00 (*0-300-08035-2*) Yale U Pr.

— The Electoral College Primer 2000. LC 99-29115. (Illus.). 224p. 1999. 16.00 (*0-300-08036-0*) Yale U Pr.

***Longley, Lawrence D., et al, eds.** The Uneasy Relationships Between Parliamentary Members & Leaders. (Library of Legislative Studies). 300p. 2000. 59.50 (*0-7146-5059-5*, Pub. by F Cass Pubs); pap. 26.50 (*0-7146-8110-5*, Pub. by F Cass Pubs) Intl Spec Bk.

Longley, Lawrence D. & Braun, Alan G. The Politics of Electoral College Reform. 2nd ed. LC 72-75202. 238p. reprint ed. pap. 73.80 (*0-8357-8277-8*, 203380500087) Bks Demand.

Longley, Lawrence D. & Davidson, Roger H., eds. The New Roles of Parliamentary Committees. LC 98-13228. (Library of Legislative Studies). 264p. 1998. 52.50 (*0-7146-4891-4*, Pub. by F Cass Pubs); pap. 22.50 (*0-7146-4442-0*, Pub. by F Cass Pubs) Intl Spec Bk.

Longley, Mark. Analysis for Well Completion. Leecraft, Jodie, ed. (Oil & Gas Production Ser.). (Illus.). 108p. (Orig.). (C). 1984. pap. text 15.00 (*0-88698-084-4*, 3.31110) PETEX.

Longley, Mark, ed. Testing & Completing. 2nd ed. (Rotary Drilling Ser.: Unit II, Lesson 5). (Illus.). 72p. (C). 1983. pap. text 16.00 (*0-88698-120-4*, 2.20520) PETEX.

Longley, Michael. The Ghost Orchid. LC 95-62042. 62p. 1996. 15.95 (*0-916390-73-X*); pap. 9.95 (*0-916390-72-1*) Wake Forest.

— Gorse Fires. LC 91-72021. 52p. 1991. pap. 6.95 (*0-916390-48-9*) Wake Forest.

— No Continuing City - Poems, 1963-1968. LC 72-84906. 56p. 1969. 15.95 (*0-8023-1248-9*) Dufour.

***Longley, Michael.** Selected Poems. 1999. pap. text. write for info. (*0-916390-89-6*) Wake Forest.

Longley, Michael, intro. The Selected Poems of Louis MacNeice. LC 89-51504. 160p. 1990. 16.95 (*0-916390-39-X*); pap. 10.95 (*0-916390-38-1*) Wake Forest.

Longley, Michael, jt. auth. see Rodgers, W. R.

Longley, Paul. Geocomputation: A Primer. LC 98-27225. 290p. 1998. 125.00 (*0-471-98575-9*) Wiley.

Longley, Paul & Batty, Michael, eds. Spatial Analysis: Modelling in a GIS Environemt. LC 96-219734. 392p. 1997. text 71.50 (*0-470-23615-9*) Halsted Pr.

Longley, Paul & Clark, Graham. GIS for Business & Service Planning. LC 95-8670. 336p. 1996. pap. 69.95 (*0-470-23510-1*) Wiley.

Longley, Paul, et al. Geographical Information Systems: Principles & Applications, 2 vols. 2nd ed. 1296p. 1999. 345.00 (*0-471-32182-6*) Wiley.

Longley, Paul, jt. auth. see Batty, Michael.

Longley, Peter. Two Thousand Years Later. 1998. pap. 14.95 (*0-9666770-0-5*) Hovenden Pr.

— Two Thousand Years Later: A Novel. 1997. 25.00 (*0-8087-7550-2*) Pearson Custom.

Longley, Ronald S. Sir Francis Hincks: A Study of Canadian Politics, Railways, & Finance in the Nineteenth Century. Bruchey, Stuart, ed. LC 80-1326. (Railroads Ser.). 1981. reprint ed. lib. bdg. 44.95 (*0-405-13800-8*) Ayer.

Longley, Susanna. Weekend Gardener: Simple Ways to Create A Great Garden In A Limited Amount of Time. LC 97-38729. 1998. 24.95 (*0-7621-0018-4*, Pub. by RD Assn) Penguin Putnam.

Longley, William R., et al. Analytic Geometry & Calculus. LC 60-3940. 616p. reprint ed. pap. 191.00 (*0-8357-5446-4*, 205526700011) Bks Demand.

Longman. Active Critical Thinking. (Developmental Study/Stdy Skill). 1999. mass mkt. write for info. (*0-314-06807-4*) West Pub.

— China Investment Guide. 4th ed. Date not set. pap. text. write for info. (*0-582-99971-5*, Pub. by Addison-Wesley) Longman.

***Longman.** Dictionary American English Idioms. 1999. 23.33 (*0-582-30575-6*) Addison-Wesley.

— Dictionary of American English Idioms. 2000. 34.67 (*0-582-30576-4*) Addison-Wesley.

Longman. Dream & Other Stories. 1997. pap. text 5.90 (*0-582-27526-1*) Addison-Wesley.

— Effective Teaching of Mathematics. 1993. pap. text. write for info. (*0-582-01633-9*, Pub. by Addison-Wesley) Longman.

— Gender. Date not set. pap. text. write for info. (*0-582-38964-X*, Pub. by Addison-Wesley) Longman.

— Longman Dictionary Of Contemporary English. 3rd ed. 1995. 46.31 (*0-582-23751-3*, Pub. by Addison-Wesley) Longman.

— Physics Reference Guide. Date not set. pap. text. write for info. (*0-582-05794-9*, Pub. by Addison-Wesley) Longman.

— Science Dictionary. 136p. 1983. 39.95 (*0-8288-2096-1*, F34210) Fr & Eur.

— Study Methods. Date not set. pap. text, teacher ed. write for info. (*0-314-03382-3*) West Pub.

— Writer's Toolkit User's Manual. (C). 2000. pap. text. write for info. (*0-321-06520-4*) Addison-Wesley Educ.

***Longman.** Zaks Adventure Dictionary: Wordgames American. 1999. 16.80 (*0-582-32793-8*) Addison-Wesley.

Longman, ed. Dicionario Inicial Ilustrado Ingles-Espanol. (ENG & SPA.). 320p. 1994. 39.95 (*0-7859-9383-5*) Fr & Eur.

***Longman & Atkinson.** Class: College Learning & Study Skills. 6th ed. 2001. pap. 32.00 (*0-534-56962-5*) Wadsworth Pub.

Longman, jt. auth. see Atkinson.

Longman, A. Dictionary of Environmental Science. 1998. text 18.95 (*0-582-25356-X*) Addson-Wesley Educ.

Longman, A. Earl & Mulac, Pamela. Confessions of a Straight A Student: How to Dramatically Raise Your Grade Point Average in Less Formal Study Time. unabridged ed. (Illus.). 250p. 1999. pap. 23.95 (*0-9665547-0-1*) Arbie Publ.

Longman Business English Staff. Diana Life Long Original. 1998. pap. text 7.35 (*0-582-33552-3*) Addison-Wesley.

Longman, Cliff, jt. auth. see Hickman, Linda.

Longman Community Info Guide Staff. Social Services Year Book 1990-1991. 1990. pap. text. write for info. (*0-582-06040-0*, Pub. by Addison-Wesley) Longman.

Longman, David. The Instant Guide to Successful Houseplants. (Illus.). 1980. 17.95 (*0-686-65926-0*, Times Bks) Crown Pub Group.

Longman, Debbie G., jt. auth. see Atkinson, Rhonda H.

Longman, Donald R. Distribution Cost Analysis. Assael, Henry, ed. LC 78-235. (Century of Marketing Ser.). 1979. reprint ed. lib. bdg. 25.95 (*0-405-11167-3*) Ayer.

Longman, Ernest & Longman, Marion. Shared Love: A Sunrise of Hope for Personal Relationships. 145p. 1998. mass mkt. 10.00 (*0-9666651-0-4*, 1000) E R Longman Pubns.

Longman, George F. The Analysis of Detergents & Detergent Products. LC 74-4649. (Illus.). 649p. reprint ed. pap. 200.00 (*0-8357-8797-4*, 203361900086) Bks Demand.

Longman Hong Kong Staff. Active Study Chinese Dictionary. Date not set. pap. text. write for info. (*962-359-367-8*) Addison-Wesley.

Longman Imprint Bks Staff. Meetings & Partings. Date not set. pap. text. write for info. (*0-582-22311-3*, Pub. by Addison-Wesley) Longman.

Longman Imprint Bks. Staff. Pressures of Life. Date not set. pap. text. write for info. (*0-582-23329-1*, Pub. by Addison-Wesley) Longman.

Longman, Inc. Staff. Longman Dictionary of American English: A Dictionary for Learners of English. 792p. (Orig.). (C). 1983. pap. text 28.67 (*0-582-90611-3*, 75187) Longman.

Longman, Inc. Staff. New Blueprint Intermediate Student Book. 1995. pap. write for info. (*0-582-25830-8*) Addison-Wesley.

***Longman, Jere.** Girls of Summer. 2000. pap. 14.00 (*0-06-095651-8*) HarpC.

— The Girls Of Summer: The U.S. Women's Soccer Team & How It Changed The World. 336p. 2000. 24.00 (*0-06-019657-2*, HarpCollins) HarperTrade.

Longman, K. A. Tropical Forest Its Environment. 2nd ed. (C). 1996. text 82.75 (*0-582-44678-3*) Addison-Wesley.

— Vegetative Propagation of Trees in the 1980s. 1980. 75.00 (*0-85074-055-X*) St Mut.

Longman, Kenneth A. & Jenik, I. J. Longman Tropical Forest. LC 73-85681. (Illus.). 160p. 1974. pap. text 11.95 (*0-582-44045-9*) Longman.

Longman, Marion, jt. auth. see Longman, Ernest.

An Asterisk (*) at the beginning of an entry indicates that the title is appearing for the first time.

Longman, Mark W. Carbonate Diagenesis As a Control on Stratigraphic Traps: With Examples from the Williston Basin. LC QE0471.15.C3. (Education Course Note Ser.: No. 21). 166p. reprint ed. pap. 51.50 (*0-7837-3974-5*, 204380300011) Bks Demand.
Longman, Mark W., et al, eds. Rocky Mountain Carbonate Reservoirs. (Core Workshop Notes Ser.: No. 7). 482p. 1985. pap. 42.00 (*0-918985-55-2*) SEPM.
Longman, Mark W., jt. ed. see Goldman, Lawrence J.
Longman, Mark W., jt. ed. see Goolsby, Steven M.
***Longman Movieworld Staff.** A View to a Kill. 1998. pap. write for info. (*0-582-05762-0*) Addison-Wesley.
Longman Publishing Group Staff. Longman Idioms Dictionary. 1998. pap. text 32.89 (*0-582-30577-2*) Addison-Wesley.
Longman Publishing Group, Staff. More Tales from Shakespeare. 1997. pap. write for info. (*0-582-27510-5*) Addison-Wesley.
— Religious Studies. 2nd ed. 1995. pap. write for info. (*0-582-27687-X*) Addison-Wesley.
Longman Publishing Staff. The Arts 5-16: Practice & Innovation. 1993. pap. text. write for info. (*0-05-004580-6*) Addison-Wesley.
— Beyond the Wendy House. 1983. pap. text. write for info. (*0-582-38893-7*, Pub. by Addison-Wesley) Longman.
— Communication Personnel Management. Date not set. text. write for info. (*0-582-09341-4*, Pub. by Addison-Wesley) Longman.
— Directory of Dental Services. 1993. pap. text. write for info. (*0-582-09756-8*, Pub. by Addison-Wesley) Longman.
— Directory of Hospitals 1991. 1991. text. write for info. (*0-582-08277-3*, Pub. by Addison-Wesley) Longman.
— Directory of Mental Health Services 1994. 1993. pap. text. write for info. (*0-582-21758-X*, Pub. by Addison-Wesley) Longman.
— Directory of Youth Services & Childcare U. K. 1992. pap. text. write for info. (*0-582-08786-4*, Pub. by Addison-Wesley) Longman.
— Education Yearbook 1992. 1991. pap. text. write for info. (*0-582-07871-7*, Pub. by Addison-Wesley) Longman.
— Education Yearbook, 1995. 1995. text. write for info. (*0-582-09199-3*, Pub. by Addison-Wesley) Longman.
— Electronic Systems. (Science at Work Ser.). 1994. pap. text. write for info. (*0-582-21589-7*, Pub. by Addison-Wesley) Longman.
— European Research Centres 6. Date not set. pap. text. write for info. (*0-582-90027-1*, Pub. by Addison-Wesley) Longman.
— Family Circles. Date not set. pap. text. write for info. (*0-582-22111-0*, Pub. by Addison-Wesley) Longman.
— Growing up Christianity. 1990. pap. text. write for info. (*0-582-00283-4*, Pub. by Addison-Wesley) Longman.
— Growing up Hinduism. 1990. pap. text. write for info. (*0-582-00285-0*, Pub. by Addison-Wesley) Longman.
— Growing up Islam. 1990. pap. text. write for info. (*0-582-00287-7*, Pub. by Addison-Wesley) Longman.
— Growing up Judaism. 1990. pap. text. write for info. (*0-582-00284-2*, Pub. by Addison-Wesley) Longman.
— Growing up Sikhism. 1990. pap. text. write for info. (*0-582-00286-9*, Pub. by Addison-Wesley) Longman.
— Housing Yearbook 1986-1987. Date not set. pap. text. write for info. (*0-582-90413-7*, Pub. by Addison-Wesley) Longman.
— Language Issues. 1993. pap. text, student ed. write for info. (*0-582-07775-3*, Pub. by Addison-Wesley) Longman.
— Language Issues Workbook. 1993. pap. text. write for info. (*0-582-07776-1*, Pub. by Addison-Wesley) Longman.
— Longman A-Level Reference Guide: Geography. Date not set. pap. text. write for info. (*0-582-06388-4*) Addison-Wesley.
— Longman Dictionary of American English. 2nd ed. 1997. text. write for info. (*0-201-49120-6*) Addison-Wesley.
— Longman English & Chinese Dictionary. Date not set. text. write for info. (*0-582-04944-X*, Pub. by Addison-Wesley) Longman.
— Longman New Junior English Dictionary. 1993. pap. text. write for info. (*0-582-09485-2*, Pub. by Addison-Wesley) Longman.
— Longman New Pocket English Dictionary. 2nd ed. 1994. pap. text. write for info. (*0-582-09484-4*, Pub. by Addison-Wesley) Longman.
— Longman-Pitman Office Dictionary. 1990. pap. text. write for info. (*0-582-06623-9*, Pub. by Addison-Wesley) Longman.
— Longman Top Pocket Roget's Thesaurus. Date not set. pap. text. write for info. (*0-582-04793-5*, Pub. by Addison-Wesley) Longman.
— Michael Jackson - Who's Bad? Date not set. pap. text. write for info. (*0-17-556583-X*) Addison-Wesley.
— Mini-Concordancer 5.25. Date not set. pap. text. write for info. (*0-582-03816-2*, Pub. by Addison-Wesley) Longman.
— Mini-Concordancer 3.5. Date not set. pap. text. write for info. (*0-582-06343-4*, Pub. by Addison-Wesley) Longman.
— Mining International Yearbook, 1988. 1988. pap. text. write for info. (*0-582-00431-4*, Pub. by Addison-Wesley) Longman.
— My First Handwriting. (J). Date not set. pap. text. write for info. (*0-582-51112-7*, Pub. by Addison-Wesley) Longman.
— My Second Handwriting. (J). Date not set. pap. text. write for info. (*0-582-51113-5*, Pub. by Addison-Wesley) Longman.
— The Mystery of Dr. Fu Manchu. Date not set. pap. text. write for info. (*0-17-556692-5*) Addison-Wesley.
— Passatempo. Date not set. pap. text. write for info. (*0-85896-339-6*) Addison-Wesley.
— The People Who Came, Bk. 1. Date not set. pap. text. write for info. (*0-582-76648-6*, Pub. by Addison-Wesley) Longman.
— Plain English 1. Date not set. pap. text. write for info. (*0-582-75641-3*, Pub. by Addison-Wesley) Longman.
— Ring of Bright Water. Date not set. pap. text. write for info. (*0-582-34591-X*, Pub. by Addison-Wesley) Longman.
— Search Out Science, Bk. 2. 1990. pap. text. write for info. (*0-582-06247-0*, Pub. by Addison-Wesley) Longman.
— Social Services Year Book, 1994. 1994. pap. text. write for info. (*0-582-21682-6*, Pub. by Addison-Wesley) Longman.
— Starting Electronic Keyboard Bk. 1. Date not set. pap. text. write for info. (*0-582-03795-6*, Pub. by Addison-Wesley) Longman.
— Starting Electronic Keyboard Bk. 2. Date not set. pap. text. write for info. (*0-582-03796-4*, Pub. by Addison-Wesley) Longman.
— Teach Primary Drama. 2nd ed. Date not set. pap. text. write for info. (*0-582-87491-2*, Pub. by Addison-Wesley) Longman.
Longman Staff. Longman Dictionary of English Language & Culture. (Illus.). 1995. pap. text 34.59 (*0-582-08676-0*, 70796) Longman.
— Longman Handy Learner's Dictionary. (YA). (gr. 9-12). 1988. pap. text 11.95 (*0-582-96413-X*, 78324) Longman.
— Longman Handy Learner's Dictionary of American English. 1p. 1995. pap. 15.44 (*0-582-09483-6*) Addison-Wesley.
— Longman Junior American Dictionary. 1p. 1999. pap. text 12.67 (*0-582-33251-6*) Addison-Wesley.
— Western European Political Parties: A Comprehensive Guide. 550p. 1989. 180.00 (*0-582-00113-7*) Longman.
***Longman Staff, ed.** Elementary Middle School Mathematics. 4th ed. 576p. (C). 2000. pap. 72.67 (*0-8013-3253-2*) Longman.
— Foundations in Dual Language Instruction. 3rd ed. 208p. (C). 1999. pap. text 0.00 (*0-8013-3072-6*) Longman.
— Literature for Children. 4th ed. 288p. (C). 2000. pap. 42.00 (*0-8013-3086-6*); pap. 0.00 (*0-8013-3087-4*) Longman.
— Understanding the Political World: Comparative Introduction. 5th ed. (C). 2000. pap. text 0.00 (*0-8013-3296-6*) Longman.
Longman, Stanley V. Drama As Rhetoric Rhetoric As Drama: An Exploration of Dramatic & Rhetorical Criticism. 143p. 1998. pap. text 20.00 (*0-8173-0887-3*) U of Ala Pr.
— Remus Tales: Playscript. 40p. (J). 1991. pap. 6.00 (*0-87602-293-X*) Anchorage.
Longman, Stanley Vincent. Crosscurrents in the Drama: East & West. (Theatre Symposium Ser.). 139p. 1998. pap. text 20.00 (*0-8173-0926-8*) U of Ala Pr.
Longman, Tremper. The Book of Ecclesiastes. LC 97-24217. (New International Commentary on the Old Testament Ser.). 320p. 1997. 35.00 (*0-8028-2366-1*) Eerdmans.
Longman, Tremper, 3rd. Daniel. LC 98-46640. 1999. 21.99 (*0-310-20608-1*) Zondervan.
Longman, Tremper, III. Fictional Akkadian Autobiography: A Generic & Comparative Study. LC 90-20204. xi, 274p. 1991. text 37.50 (*0-931464-41-2*) Eisenbrauns.
— How to Read the Psalms. LC 88-8835. 166p. (Orig.). 1988. pap. 12.99 (*0-87784-941-2*, 941) InterVarsity.
— Making Sense of the Old Testament: 3 Crucial Questions. LC 98-30481. (3 Crucial Questions Ser.). 160p. (C). (gr. 13). 1998. pap. 11.99 (*0-8010-5828-7*) Baker Bks.
— Old Testament Commentary Survey. 2nd ed. LC 95-12250. 192p. 1995. pap. 12.99 (*0-8010-2024-7*) Baker Bks.
— Reading the Bible with Heart & Mind. LC 96-27858. Orig. Title: The Fiery Word of Life. 234p. (Orig.). 1997. pap. 14.00 (*0-89109-984-0*, 99840) NavPress.
Longman, Tremper, jt. auth. see Allender, Dan.
Longman, Tremper, jt. auth. see Allender, Dan B.
Longman, Tremper, III, jt. auth. see Dillard, Raymond B.
Longman, Tremper, III, jt. ed. see Ryken, Leland.
Longman U. K. Addison Wesley Staff. Longman Dictionary of American English. 2nd ed. 80p. 1997. pap. text, wbk. ed. 11.75 (*0-8013-2027-5*) Addison-Wesley.
— Longman Dictionary of American English Teacher's Companion. 2nd ed. 24p. 1997. pap. text, teacher ed. 10.28 (*0-8013-2028-3*) Addison-Wesley.
Longman U. K. Staff. Tale Myst & Imag. 2nd rev. ed. (Longman Fiction Ser.). 1996. pap. text 7.86 (*0-582-27498-2*, Pub. by Addison-Wesley) Longman.
Longman, W. Tokens of the Eighteenth Century, Connected with Booksellers & Bookmaker: Authors, Printers, Publishers, Engravers & Paper Makers. (Illus.). 1970. reprint ed. 35.00 (*1-55888-237-5*) Omnigraphics Inc.
Longmeyer, Carole M. An American Mystery: Script. (Lost Colony Collection). (Orig.). (J). (gr. 3-12). 1994. pap. 19.95 (*0-935326-50-2*) Gallopade Intl.
— Clemson Football Mystery. (Sportsmystery Ser.). (Illus.). (Orig.). (J). (gr. 3 up). 1994. pap. 19.95 (*0-935326-28-6*); lib. bdg. 29.95 (*1-55609-164-8*) Gallopade Intl.
— Deadly Duke Football Mystery. (Sportsmystery Ser.). (Illus.). (Orig.). (J). (gr. 3 up). 1994. pap. 19.95 (*0-935326-31-6*) Gallopade Intl.
— Georgia Tech Football Mystery. (Sportsmystery Ser.). (Illus.). (Orig.). (J). (gr. 3 up). 1994. pap. 19.95 (*0-935326-30-8*) Gallopade Intl.
— The Lost Colony Activity Book. (Lost Colony Collection). (Illus.). (Orig.). (J). (gr. 3 up). 1994. pap. 19.95 (*0-935326-41-3*) Gallopade Intl.
— The Lost Colony Storybook. (Lost Colony Collection). (Illus.). (J). (gr. 4 up). 1994. pap. 19.95 (*0-935326-38-3*) Gallopade Intl.
— Maryland Football Mystery. (Sportsmystery Ser.). (Illus.). 80p. (Orig.). (J). (gr. 3 up). 1994. pap. 19.95 (*0-935326-32-4*) Gallopade Intl.
— NC State Football Mystery. (Sportsmystery Ser.). (Illus.). (Orig.). (J). (gr. 3 up). 1994. pap. 19.95 (*0-935326-33-2*) Gallopade Intl.
— Next Time Say Where You're Going. (Lost Colony Collection). (Illus.). (Orig.). (J). (gr. 4-9). 1994. pap. 19.95 (*0-935326-42-1*) Gallopade Intl.
— North Carolina Football Mystery. (Sportsmystery Ser.). (Illus.). (Orig.). (J). (gr. 3 up). 1994. pap. 19.95 (*0-935326-29-4*) Gallopade Intl.
— Virginia Football Mystery. (Sportsmystery Ser.). (Illus.). 80p. (Orig.). (J). (gr. 3 up). 1994. pap. 19.95 (*0-935326-35-9*) Gallopade Intl.
— Wake Forest Football Mystery. (Sportsmystery Ser.). (Illus.). (Orig.). (J). (gr. 3 up). 1994. pap. 19.95 (*0-935326-34-0*) Gallopade Intl.
— What Did You Sayeth? (Lost Colony Collection). (Illus.). (Orig.). (J). (gr. 4 up). 1994. pap. 19.95 (*0-935326-45-6*) Gallopade Intl.
Longmeyer, Carole M., ed. Croatoan. (Lost Colony Collection). (Illus.). 76p. (gr. 4-12). 1994. pap. 19.95 (*0-935326-36-7*) Gallopade Intl.
Longmire, David. Sensory Development Self-Study Course. 2nd ed. (CIL Publications & Audiobooks). 1997. 22.00 incl. audio (*1-890786-00-4*) Visions-Srvs.
Longmire, Dennis R., jt. ed. see Flanagan, Timothy J.
Longmire, Linda & Merrill, Lisa, eds. Untying the Tongue: Gender, Power & the Word, 164. LC 97-44837. (Contributions in Women's Studies: Vol. 164). 328p. 1998. 69.50 (*0-313-30686-9*, Greenwood Pr) Greenwood.
Longmire, Linda, jt. ed. see Cernic, David.
Longmire, Linda A., jt. auth. see Hickey, James E., Jr.
Longmire, R. A. Soviet Relations in South East Asia. 280p. 1989. 65.00 (*0-7103-0343-2*, A3918) Routledge.
Longmire, W. P., Jr. & Tompkins, R. K. Manual of Liver Surgery. (Comprehensive Manuals of Surgical Specialties Ser.). (Illus.). 267p. 1981. 185.00 (*0-387-90212-0*) Spr-Verlag.
Longmore, D. B., jt. auth. see Mohiaddin, R. H.
Longmore, J., et al. The Thermal Environment. (Technical Guide Ser.: No. 8). 84p. (C). 1992. 180.00 (*0-905927-38-9*, Pub. by H&H Sci Cnslts) St Mut.
Longmore, Monica A., et al. Survey Research Project Manual. LC 96-109340. 192p. (C). 1995. 28.95 (*0-314-06110-X*) West Pub.
Longmore, Paul K. The Invention of George Washington. LC 98-44079. 352p. 1999. pap. 16.95 (*0-8139-1872-3*) U Pr of Va.
Longmuir, Ian S., ed. Oxygen Transport to Tissue, No. VIII. LC 86-15125. (Advances in Experimental Medicine & Biology Ser.: Vol. 200). 670p. 1986. 125.00 (*0-306-42379-0*, Plenum Trade) Perseus Pubng.
Longmuir, John, ed. see Jamieson, John.
***Longmuir, Marilyn.** The Money Trail: Burmese Currencies in Crisis, 1942-1947. (Illus.). 2000. pap. 16.95 (*1-891134-05-1*) SE Asia.
Longnecker. Business Plan - Small Business Management. 9th ed. (GC - Principles of Management Ser.). (C). 1994. pap. 12.95 (*0-538-84475-2*) S-W Pub.
— Small Business Management. 9th ed. (GC - Principles of Management Ser.). (C). 1993. pap., student ed. 18.50 (*0-538-83047-6*) S-W Pub.
Longnecker & Intelecom Staff. Something Ventured Telecourse Small Business: Small Business. 10th ed. (GG - Small Business Management Ser.). 1996. VHS 25.95 (*0-538-85079-5*) S-W Pub.
Longnecker & Sirica, Alphonse E., eds. Biliary & Pancreatic Ductal Epithelia. (Gastroenterology Ser.: Vol. 3). (Illus.). 592p. 1996. text 210.00 (*0-8247-9414-1*) Dekker.
Longnecker, et al. Small Business Management. 9th ed. (C). 1993. mass mkt. 54.50 (*0-538-83045-X*, GG70IA) S-W Pub.
Longnecker, Brian L. Medical Reports of the U. S. Office of Research Integrity: Index of New Information & Bibliography. 150p. 1996. 47.50 (*0-7883-0996-X*); pap. 44.50 (*0-7883-0997-8*) ABBE Pubs Assn.
Longnecker, David E. & Murphy, Frank L. Dripps-Eckenhoff-Vandam Introduction to Anesthesia. 9th ed. Day, Lesley, ed. 480p. 1996. text 49.95 (*0-7216-6279-X*, W B Saunders Co) Harcrt Hlth Sci Grp.
Longnecker, David E., ed. see Tinker, John H.
***Longnecker, Dwight.** Listen, My Son: St. Benedict for Fathers. LC 99-86446. 320p. 2000. pap. 17.95 (*0-8192-1856-1*) Morehouse Pub.
Longnecker, Nancy. Passion for Pulses: A Feast of Beans, Peas & Lentils from Around the World. (Illus.). 1998. pap. 24.95 (*1-876268-20-4*, Pub. by Univ of West Aust Pr) Intl Spec Bk.
Longnecker, Ott. Introduction to Statistical Methods & Data Analysis. 5th ed. LC 99-40068. 2000. pap. text 83.95 (*0-534-25122-6*) Wadsworth Pub.
Longnecker, Richard. Galatians. (Biblical Commentary Ser.: Vol. 41). 1990. 29.99 (*0-8499-0240-1*) Word Pub.
Longnon, Auguste. Polytyque de l'Abbaye de Saint-Germain-des-Pres, 2 vols. 852p. reprint ed. write for info. (*0-318-71374-8*) G Olms Pubs.
Longnon, Jean, jt. auth. see Meiss, Millard.
Longnus, Pierre. Vancouver. 2nd ed. Ulysses Travel Guide Staff, ed. (Ulysses Travel Guide Ser.). (Illus.). 200p. 1998. pap. 12.95 (*2-89464-120-6*) Ulysses Travel.
Longo, Aurora & Sanchez, Almudena. Talk Spanish. LC 98-33764. (Talk Short Language Courses Ser.). (ENG & SPA.). 1999. write for info. (*0-8442-1359-4*, Passprt Bks) NTC Contemp Pub Co.
Longo, Aurora & Sanchez, Almundena. Talk Spanish. LC 98-33764. (Talk Short Language Courses Ser.). (SPA.). 128p. 1999. pap. 18.95 incl. audio (*0-8442-1358-6*, 13586, Passprt Bks) NTC Contemp Pub Co.
***Longo, Bernadette.** Spurious Coin: A History of Science, Management & Technical Writing. LC 99-38253. (C). 2000. text 59.50 (*0-7914-4555-0*); pap. text 19.95 (*0-7914-4556-9*) State U NY Pr.
Longo, Cranni, jt. auth. see Brambilla, Roberto.
Longo, Dan L., jt. ed. see Chabner, Bruce A.
Longo, Daniel R. & Bohr, Deborah, eds. Quantitative Methods in Quality Management: A Guide for Practitioners. LC 90-14398. 150p. 1991. pap. 46.95 (*1-55648-060-1*, 169102) AHPI.
Longo, Frank J. Fertilization. (Outline Studies in Biology). (Illus.). 183p. (gr. 13). 1987. pap. text 36.95 (*0-412-26410-2*, A1196) Chapman & Hall.
Longo, G., ed. Information Theory: New Trends & Open Problems. (International Centre for Mechanical Sciences Ser.: No. 219). (Illus.). 1976. pap. 35.00 (*3-211-81378-0*) Spr-Verlag.
— Secure Digital Communications. (CISM International Centre for Mechanical Sciences Ser.: No. 279). (Illus.). v, 332p. 1984. 54.95 (*0-387-81784-0*) Spr-Verlag.
Longo, G., et al, eds. Geometries, Codes & Cryptography. (CISM International Centre for Mechanical Sciences Ser.: Vol. 313). (Illus.). v, 227p. 1990. 58.95 (*0-387-82205-4*) Spr-Verlag.
Longo, G. & Hartmenn, C. R., eds. Algebraic Coding Theory & Application. (CISM Courses & Lectures: Vol. 258). (Illus.). 529p. 1980. 96.95 (*0-387-81544-9*) Spr-Verlag.
Longo, G. & Picinbono, Bernard, eds. Time & Frequency Representation of Signals & Systems. (CISM Courses & Lectures: Vol. 309). (Illus.). vii, 175p. 1989. 50.95 (*0-387-82143-0*) Spr-Verlag.
Longo, G., jt. ed. see Davisson, L. D.
Longo, Gianni. A Guide to Great American Public Places: A Journey of Discovery, Learning & Delight in the Public Realm. (Illus.). 200p. (Orig.). 1996. pap. 15.00 (*0-936020-00-8*) Urban Initiat.
Longo, Gianni, jt. auth. see Brambilla, Roberto.
Longo, Giuseppe & De Vaucouleurs, Antoinette. A General Catalogue of Photoelectric Magnitudes & Colors in the UBV System of 3,578 Galaxies Brighter than the 16th V-Magnitude 1936-1982. LC 83-50257. (Monographs in Astronomy: No. 3). 214p. (Orig.). 1983. pap. 12.00 (*0-9603796-2-2*) U of Tex Dept Astron.
— Supplement to the General Catalogue of Photoelectric Magnitudes & Colors of Galaxies in the U, B, V System. LC 85-51711. (Monographs in Astronomy: No. 3A). 126p. (Orig.). 1985. pap. write for info. (*0-9603796-4-9*) U of Tex Dept Astron.
Longo, Giuseppe, jt. auth. see De Vaucouleurs, Antoinette.
Longo, Louise. Let Me Survive: A True Story. LC 96-8897. 160p. 1996. 17.95 (*1-57409-006-2*) Sheridan.
***Longo, Louise.** One Day as a Private Eye. LC 99-97059. 2000. 18.75 (*0-533-13382-3*) Vantage.
Longo, Michael J. Physics Laboratory Experiments, 1990. (Illus.). 244p. 1990. student ed. 7.50 (*0-9621002-2-6*) ML Pub MI.
Longo, Nancy. Predominantly Fish: New Interpretations for Cooking Fish & Shellfish. LC 87-82252. (Illus.). 128p. 1987. pap. 9.95 (*0-9619112-0-4*) Fissurelle.
Longo, Paul, jt. auth. see Trubowitz, Sidney.
Longo, Perie. The Privacy of Wind: Poems. LC 97-521. 80p. (Orig.). 1997. pap. 10.00 (*1-880284-23-5*) J Daniel.
Longo, Peter J., jt. auth. see Miewald, Robert D.
Longo, Susanna & Boutegege, Regine. Un Billet pour le Commissaire. (FRE.). 128p. (C). pap., student ed. 11.25 (*0-8442-1104-4*, VF1104-4) NTC Contemp Pub Co.
— La Fugue de Bach. (FRE.). 128p. (C). pap., student ed. 11.25 (*0-8442-1103-6*, VF1103-6) NTC Contemp Pub Co.
***Longo, Tracey.** Investing for the First Time. (Cliffs Consumer Extension Ser.). (Illus.). 128p. 1999. 8.99 (*0-7645-8539-8*) IDG Bks.
Longo, Tracey. Personal Finance in Your 20's & 30's. (Complete Idiot's Guides (Lifestyle) Ser.). (Illus.). 379p. 1999. pap. 16.95 (*0-02-862415-7*) Macmillan Gen Ref.
Longo, Vincent. Victory in Jesus: Living Answers for a Dying World. LC 96-84794. (Orig.). 1996. pap. 8.99 (*0-88270-694-2*) Bridge-Logos.
Longo, Walter E., et al. Intestinal Ischemia Disorders: Pathophysiology & Surgical Management. LC 98-29291. 329p. 1998. 85.00 (*1-57626-084-4*) Quality Med Pub.
Longo, William. Hazlet Township. LC 98-85883. (Images of America Ser.). (Illus.). 128p. 1998. pap. 16.99 (*0-7524-0536-5*) Arcadia Publng.
Longobardi, Cesare. Land Reclamation in Italy. 1976. lib. bdg. 34.95 (*0-8490-2127-8*) Gordon Pr.
— Land-Reclamation in Italy: Rural Revival in the Building of a Nation. LC 78-180410. (Illus.). reprint ed. 45.00 (*0-404-56134-9*) AMS Pr.
Longobardi, Giuseppe, jt. auth. see Giorgi, Alessandra.
Longon, Auguste, ed. see Villon, Francois.
Longoni, Robert. Woodpiles: Poems. LC 97-177085. 1997. write for info. (*0-934910-04-9*) Moon Pony.
Longoria, Arturo. Adios to the Brushlands. LC 97-14541. (Wardlaw Book Ser.). 144p. 1997. 19.95 (*0-89096-769-5*) Tex A&M Univ Pr.
***Longoria, Arturo.** Keepers of the Wilderness. LC 99-53326. 128p. 2000. 27.95 (*0-89096-929-9*); pap. 14.95 (*0-89096-942-6*) Tex A&M Univ Pr.
Longoria, Mario. Athletes Remembered: Mexicano/Latino Professional Football Players, 1929-1970. LC 96-43251. (Illus.). 232p. (Orig.). 1996. pap. 24.00 (*0-927534-63-0*) Biling Rev-Pr.
Longree, Karla, et al. Quantity Food Sanitation. 5th ed. LC 95-36504. (Illus.). 480p. 1996. 69.95 (*0-471-59660-4*) Wiley.

An Asterisk (*) at the beginning of an entry indicates that the title is appearing for the first time.

Longres, John F. Human Behavior in the Social Environment. 2nd ed. LC 93-84980. 566p. (C). 1995. boxed set 52.50 (0-87581-379-8, HBSE2) F E Peacock Pubs.

Longres, John F., ed. Men of Color: A Context for Service to Homosexually Active Men. LC 96-35141. (Journal of Gay & Lesbian Social Services: Vol. 5, Nos. 2/3). 174p. (C). 1996. 39.95 (1-56024-803-3, Haworth Pastrl) Haworth Pr.

— Men of Color: A Context for Service to Homosexually Active Men. LC 96-35141. (Journal of Gay & Lesbian Social Services Ser.: Vol. 5, Nos. 2/3). 174p. (C). 1996. pap. 19.95 (1-56023-083-5, Harrington Park) Haworth Pr.

Longridge, C. Nepean. The Anatomy of Nelson's Ships. LC 80-84981. (Illus.). 283p. 1980. 49.95 (0-87021-077-7) Naval Inst Pr.

***Longridge, C. Nepean.** The Anatomy of Nelson's Ships. 283p. 1999. 0.00 (1-85486-122-0) Nexus Pubng.

Longridge, Lyn. Managing & Communicating: Your Questions & Answers. LC 98-15830. (Practice Manager Library). 1998. write for info. (1-85775-233-3, Radcliffe Med Pr) Scovill Paterson.

Longrigg, James. Greek Rational Medicine: Philosophy & Medicine from Alcmaeon to the Alexandrians. LC 92-28865. (Illus.). 296p. (C). 1993. 75.00 (0-415-02594-X, B0350) Routledge.

Longrigg, James, ed. Greek Medicine: From the Heroic to the Hellenistic Age: A Source Book. LC 98-15593. 272p. (C). 1998. pap. 25.99 (0-415-92087-6, D5784) Routledge.

Longs, Robert, et al. Cosmic Circle: The Unification of Mind, Matter & Energy. LC 96-226157. (Illus.). 224p. 1996. 22.00 (1-887110-04-6) Allian Pubng.

Longsdorf, George F., jt. auth. see Shumaker, Walter A.

Longshaw, Robin, tr. see Selden, George.

Longshore, David. Encyclopedia of Hurricanes, Typhoons, & Cyclones. LC 97-20860. (Illus.). 372p. 1998. 45.00 (0-8160-3398-6, Checkmark) Facts on File.

***Longshore, David.** Encyclopedia of Hurricanes, Typhoons, & Cyclones. (Illus.). 372p. 2000. pap. 19.95 (0-8160-4291-8, Checkmark) Facts on File.

— Encyclopedia of Hurricanes, Typhoons, & Cyclones. (Illus.). 400p. 1999. lib. bdg. 50.00 (1-57958-150-1) Fitzroy Dearborn.

***Longshore, George F.** Top Docs: Managing the Search for Physician Leaders. 2nd ed. LC 99-62337. 125p. 1999. pap. 42.00 (0-924674-71-7) Am Coll Phys Execs.

Longshore, Randolph E. & Baars, Jan W., eds. Infrared Detectors for Remote Sensing Vol. 2816: Physics, Materials & Devices. 178p. 1996. 56.00 (0-8194-2204-5) SPIE.

Longshore, Shirley. Tx/td,office:careers W/o Coll Series. LC 94-1860. (Tech Prep). 95p. 1994. pap. 7.95 (1-56079-353-8) Petersons.

Longsoldier, Tilda, jt. auth. see St. Pierre, Mark.

***Longson, Sally.** Women Returning to Work: How to Work Out What You Want & Then Go Out & Get It. (Pathways Ser.: No. 7). 198p. 2000. pap. 15.95 (1-85703-479-1, Pub. by How To Bks) Midpt Trade.

***Longstaff, A.** Instant Notes in Neuroscience. (Instant Notes Ser.). 320p. 1999. pap. text 24.95 (0-387-91582-6) Spr-Verlag.

Longstaff, A., jt. auth. see Revest, P.

Longstaff, Alan & Revest, Patricia, eds. Protocols in Molecular Neurobiology, No. 13. LC 92-30701. (Methods in Molecular Biology Ser.: Vol. 13). (Illus.). 394p. 1992. spiral bd. 89.50 (0-89603-199-3) Humana.

Longstaff, P. H. Information Theory As a Basis for Rationalizing Regulation of the Communications Industry. (Illus.). 44p. (Orig.). 1994. pap. text. write for info. (1-879716-08-9, P-94-4) Ctr Info Policy.

— Telecommunications Competition & Universal Service: The Essential Tradeoffs. unabridged ed. 45p. (Orig.). 1996. pap. text. write for info. (1-879716-32-1, P-96-2) Ctr Info Policy.

Longstaff, Patricia H. & Finnegan, John R., Sr. Mass Communication Law in Minnesota. (State Law Ser.). 86p. (C). 1992. text 10.95 (0-913507-23-7) New Forums.

Longstaff, Thomas R. Evidence of Conflation Mark? A Study in the Synoptic Problem. LC 76-40001. (Society of Biblical Literature. Dissertation Ser.: No. 28). 255p. reprint ed. pap. 79.10 (0-7837-5430-2, 204519500005) Bks Demand.

Longstaff, W., jt. auth. see Argyros, S.

***Longstaffe, Moya.** Metamorphoses of Passion & the Heroic in French Literature - Corneille, Stendhal, Claudel. LC 99-29493. (Studies in French Literature: Vol. 35). 500p. 1999. text 109.95 (0-7734-7989-9) E Mellen.

Longstreet, Augustus Baldwin. Georgia Scenes. LC 91-67519. (Southern Classics Ser.). 330p. 1992. reprint ed. pap. 13.95 (1-879941-06-6) J S Sanders.

— Georgia Scenes. (Notable American Authors Ser.). 1999. reprint ed. lib. bdg. 125.00 (0-7812-3853-6) Rprt Serv.

— Georgia Scenes: Characters, Incidents, Etc. in the First Half Century of the Republic. 1990. 16.50 (0-8446-0777-0) Peter Smith.

— Georgia Scenes: Characters, Incidents, Etc., in the First Half Century of the Republic. (Illus.). 252p. 1992. 25.00 (0-88322-004-0) Beehive GA.

— Letters from President Longstreet to the Know-Nothing Preachers of the Methodist Church South. (Notable American Authors Ser.). 1999. reprint ed. lib. bdg. 125.00 (0-7812-3856-0) Rprt Serv.

— Letters on the Epistle of Paul to Philemon or, The Connection of Apostolic Christianity with Slavery. (Notable American Authors Ser.). 1999. reprint ed. lib. bdg. 125.00 (0-7812-3854-4) Rprt Serv.

— A Voice from the South. (Notable American Authors Ser.). 1999. reprint ed. lib. bdg. 125.00 (0-7812-3855-2) Rprt Serv.

Longstreet, E., jt. auth. see Longstreet, S.

Longstreet, Hazel. Communication & Parenting Skills for African-American Families. LC 96-90962. 60p. (Orig.). 1998. pap. 8.95 (0-533-12229-5) Vantage.

Longstreet, Helen D. Lee & Longstreet at High Tide: Gettysburg in the Light of the Official Records. (Illus.). 360p. 1989. reprint ed. 35.00 (0-916107-92-2) Broadfoot.

Longstreet, J. R. Turret Lathe Methods Applied to Small Lot Gear Production. (Technical Papers: Vol. P191). (Illus.). 14p. 1939. pap. text 30.00 (1-55589-447-X) AGMA.

Longstreet, James. From Manassas to Appomattox. (Illus.). 760p. 1992. reprint ed. pap. 15.95 (0-306-80464-6) Da Capo.

— From Manassus to Appomattox. (Great Commanders Ser.). 470p. 1994. reprint ed. 30.00 (1-56515-003-1) Collect Reprints.

Longstreet, Robert L. Arty II. LC 98-900247. 1998. pap. 11.95 (0-533-12683-5) Vantage.

Longstreet, Roxanne. Cold Kiss. 256p. 1995. mass mkt. 4.50 (0-8217-4812-2, Pinncle Kensgtn) Kensgtn Pub Corp.

— Slow Burn. 320p. 1996. pap. 5.50 (0-7860-0241-7, Pinncle Kensgtn) Kensgtn Pub Corp.

— The Undead. 320p. 1993. mass mkt. 4.50 (0-8217-4068-7, Zebra Kensgtn) Kensgtn Pub Corp.

Longstreet, Roy W. Viewpoints of a Commodity Trader. 160p. 1986. reprint ed. pap. 14.95 (0-934380-14-7, 4) Traders Pr.

Longstreet, S. & Longstreet, E. Yoshiwara: Pleasure Quarters of Japan. 1989. pap. 12.95 (0-8048-1599-2) Tuttle Pubng.

Longstreet, Stephen. The Canvas Falcons: The Men & the Planes of World War I. (Illus.). 365p. 1995. 39.50 (0-85052-441-1, Pub. by Leo Cooper) Trans-Atl Phila.

— A Century on Wheels, the Story of Studebaker: A History, 1852-1952. LC 70-100238. (Illus.). 121p. 1970. reprint ed. lib. bdg. 35.00 (0-8371-3978-3, LOCW, Greenwood Pr) Greenwood.

— Dance in Art. (Master Draughtsman Ser.). 1968. 10.95 (0-87505-042-5); pap. 4.95 (0-87505-195-2) Borden.

— How to Save Taxes on Your Lump Sum Distribution. 44p. 1982. 2.40 (0-685-07416-1) P-H.

— More Drawings of Delacroix. (Master Draughtsman Ser.). (Illus.). 48p. (Orig.). 1970. pap. 4.95 (0-87505-208-8) Borden.

— More Drawings of Rembrandt. (Master Draughtsman Ser.). 48p. 1970. pap. 4.95 (0-87505-207-X) Borden.

— Storyville to Harlem: Fifty Years in the Jazz Scene. 211p. (C). 1986. 29.95 (0-8135-1174-7) Rutgers U Pr.

— War Cries on Horseback. reprint ed. lib. bdg. 26.95 (0-89190-143-4, Rivercity Pr) Amereon Ltd.

Longstreet, Stephen, comment. Jazz - The Chicago Scene: The Art of Stephen Longstreet. LC 89-40611. (Illus.). 30p. (Orig.). 1989. pap. 3.50 (0-943056-11-X) Univ Chi Lib.

Longstreet, Stephen, ed. Animal in Art. (Master Draughtsman Ser.). (Illus.). (Orig.). 1966. 10.95 (0-87505-040-9); pap. 4.95 (0-87505-193-6) Borden.

— Child in Art. (Master Draughtsman Ser.). (Illus.). (Orig.). 1966. 10.95 (0-87505-041-7); pap. 4.95 (0-87505-194-4) Borden.

— Drawings of Augustus John. (Master Draughtsman Ser.). 1967. 10.95 (0-87505-014-X); pap. 4.95 (0-87505-167-7) Borden.

— Drawings of Dali. (Master Draughtsman Ser.). (Illus.). 1964. pap. 4.95 (0-87505-155-3) Borden.

— The Drawings of Matisse. 48p. 1973. pap. 4.95 (0-87505-174-X) Borden.

— Drawings of Pontormo. (Master Draughtsman Ser.). 1966. pap. 4.95 (0-87505-203-7) Borden.

— Drawings of Toulouse-Lautrec. (Master Draughtsman Ser.). (Illus.). 1966. pap. 4.95 (0-87505-172-3) Borden.

— Drawings of Winslow Homer. (Master Draughtsman Ser.). (Illus.). 1970. pap. 4.95 (0-87505-165-0) Borden.

— Figure in Art. (Master Draughtsman Ser.). (Illus.). (Orig.). 1968. 10.95 (0-87505-043-3); pap. 4.95 (0-87505-196-0) Borden.

— Horse in Art. (Master Draughtsman Ser.). (Illus.). (Orig.). (J). (ps). 1965. pap. 4.95 (0-87505-198-7) Borden.

— Portrait in Art. (Master Draughtsman Ser.). (Illus.). (Orig.). 1965. pap. 4.95 (0-87505-199-5) Borden.

— Self Portraits of Great Artists. (Master Draughtsman Ser.). (Illus.). 1973. pap. 4.95 (0-87505-201-0) Borden.

— Tree in Art. (Master Draughtsman Ser.). (Illus.). 1966. pap. 4.95 (0-87505-200-2) Borden.

Longstreet, Stephen, ed. see Cezanne, Paul.

Longstreet, Stephen, ed. see Daumier, Honore.

Longstreet, Stephen, ed. see Degas, Hilaire.

Longstreet, Stephen, ed. see Durer, Albrecht.

Longstreet, Stephen, ed. see Gauguin, Paul.

Longstreet, Stephen, ed. see Ingres, Jean A.

Longstreet, Stephen, ed. see Kollwitz.

Longstreet, Stephen, ed. see Modigliani.

Longstreet, Stephen, ed. see Picasso, Pablo.

Longstreet, Stephen, ed. see Poussin, Nicolas.

Longstreet, Stephen, ed. see Raphael.

Longstreet, Stephen, ed. see Rodin, Auguste.

Longstreet, Stephen, ed. see Romney, George.

Longstreet, Stephen, ed. see Rubens, Peter Paul.

Longstreet, Stephen, ed. see Stern, Jossi.

Longstreet, Stephen, ed. see Van Gogh, Vincent.

Longstreet, Stephen, ed. see Van Rijn, Rembrandt Harmensz.

Longstreet, Stephen, ed. see Von Menzel, Adolph F.

Longstreet, Wilma S. & Shane, Harold G. Curriculum for a New Millennium. LC 92-31356. 480p. 1992. 79.00 (0-205-13966-3) Allyn.

— Curriculum for a New Millennium. (C). 1993. pap., teacher ed. write for info. (0-205-14440-3, H4440-7) Allyn.

Longstreth, Billie J., et al. Tangled Emotions. 357p. 1989. 12.95 (0-317-99837-4); pap. 4.95 (0-317-99838-2) Shamrock Pubns.

***Longstreth, Richard.** The Buildings of Main Street: A Guide to American Commercial Architecture. (Illus.). 152p. 2000. pap. 22.95 (0-7425-0279-1) AltaMira Pr.

— Charnley House. 1998. 45.00 (0-226-49274-5) U Ch Pr.

Longstreth, Richard. City Center to Regional Mall: Architecture the Automobile & Retailing in Los Angeles, 1920-1950. (Illus.). 536p. 1998. pap. text 30.00 (0-262-62125-8) MIT Pr.

— The Drive-In, the Supermarket & the Transformation of Commercial Space in Los Angeles, 1914-1941. LC 98-39140. (Illus.). 304p. 1999. 55.00 (0-262-12214-6) MIT Pr.

***Longstreth, Richard.** The Drive-In, the Supermarket & the Transformation of Commercial Space in Los Angeles, 1914-1941. (Illus.). 272p. (C). 2000. pap. 34.95 (0-262-62142-8) MIT Pr.

Longstreth, Richard. History on the Line: Testimony in the Cause of Preservation. Tomlan, Michael A., ed. LC 98-70644. (Illus.). 114p. 1998. pap. 20.00 (0-9662723-0-7) Historic Urban.

— The Mixed Blessings of Success: The Hecht Company & Department Store Branch Development after World War II. (Occasional Papers: No. 014). (Illus.). 15p. (Orig.). 1995. pap. 7.50 (1-888028-26-2) GWU Ctr WAS.

Longstreth, Richard W. City Center to Regional Mall: Architecture, the Automobile, & Retailing in Los Angeles, 1920-1950. LC 96-25115. (Illus.). 536p. 1997. 65.00 (0-262-12200-6) MIT Pr.

— On the Edge of the World: Four Architects in San Francisco at the Turn of the Century. LC 97-36898. 455p. 1998. 24.95 (0-520-21415-3, Pub. by U CA Pr) Cal Prin Full Svc.

Longstreth, W. Thacher. Main Line Wasp. 1990. 21.95 (0-393-02780-5) Norton.

Longsworth, Basil N. Memorandum of Thoughts, Reflections & Transactions As Transcribed by Basil Nelson Tongsworth on His Journey from Washington Township, Guernsey County, Ohio, to Oregon in the Summer of 1853. 44p. 1972. reprint ed. pap. 7.95 (0-87770-664-6) Ye Galleon.

Longsworth, Elizabeth K., ed. Anatomy of a Start-Up: Why Some New Businesses Succeed & Others Fail. 456p. (Orig.). 1991. pap. 17.95 (0-9626146-6-1) Inc Pub MA.

Longsworth, Polly. Austin & Mabel: The Amherst Affair & Love Letters of Austin Dickinson & Mabel Loomis Todd. LC 99-33439. (Illus.). 480p. 1999. reprint ed. pap. 19.95 (1-55849-215-1) U of Mass Pr.

— The World of Emily Dickinson. (Illus.). 144p. (C). 1997. pap. 17.95 (0-393-31656-4) Norton.

Longsworth, Robert M. The Cornish Ordinalia: Religion & Dramaturgy. LC 67-22869. 185p. reprint ed. pap. 57.40 (0-7837-5935-5, 204573400007) Bks Demand.

Longtime, Sonny & Chappell, Laverne. Marquette: Then & Now. (Illus.). 280p. 1999. pap. 24.95 (0-9670793-0-6) North Shore Pubns.

Longton, R. E. The South Sandwich Islands Vol. IV: Botany. (British Antarctic Survey Report Ser.: No. 94). 56p. 1979. 25.00 (0-85665-048-X, Pub. by Brit Antarctic Surv) Balogh.

Longton, Royce E., ed. Population Studies. (Advances in Bryology Ser.: Vol. 6). (GER., Illus.). viii, 302p. 1997. 106.00 (3-443-52004-9, Pub. by Gebruder Borntraeger) Balogh.

Longton, Thomas & Sykes, Barbara. Training the Sheep Dog. (Illus.). 160p. 1997. 35.00 (1-86126-031-8, Pub. by Cro1wood) Trafalgar.

Longton, William, jt. ed. see Lora, Ronald Henry.

Longton, William Henry, jt. ed. see Lora, Ronald Henry.

Longuenesse, Beatrice. Kant & the Capacity to Judge: Sensibility & Discursivity in the Transcendental Analytic of the Critique of Pure Reason. LC 97-15848. 480p. 1998. text 59.50 (0-691-04348-5, Pub. by Princeton U Pr) Cal Prin Full Svc.

Longuet-Higgins, H. & Christopher, H. Mental Processes: Studies in Cognitive Science. (Explorations in Cognitive Science Ser.). 508p. 1987. 55.00 (0-262-12119-0) MIT Pr.

Longus. Daphnis & Chloe. Moore, George, tr. from GRE. (Illus.). 225p. 1977. boxed set 135.00 (0-8076-0880-7) Braziller.

— Daphnis & Chloe. (Loeb Classical Library: No. 69). 15.50 (0-674-99076-5) HUP.

— Daphnis & Chloe. LC 53-10378. write for info. Macmillan.

— Daphnis et Chloe Suivi d'Histoire Veritable de Lucien. (FRE.). 1991. pap. 8.95 (0-7859-4010-3) Fr & Eur.

— Longus: Daphnis & Chloe. Morgan, ed. 1994. write for info. (0-85668-562-3, Pub. by Aris & Phillips); pap. write for info. (0-85668-563-1, Pub. by Aris & Phillips) David Brown.

***Longus.** Marc Chagall: Daphnis & Chloe. (Illus.). 2000. pap. 9.95 (3-7913-2336-9) Prestel Pub NY.

Longus. The Story of Daphnis & Chloe. Connor, W. R., ed. LC 78-18586. (Greek Texts & Commentaries Ser.). (Illus.). 1979. reprint ed. lib. bdg. 21.95 (0-405-11428-1) Ayer.

Longval, Raymonde, jt. auth. see Morgan, Allen.

Longville, Tim, jt. auth. see Crozier, Andrew.

Longville, Tim, jt. tr. see Riley, John.

Longwell, Alicia G., jt. auth. see Pisano, Ronald G.

Longwell, Dennis, jt. auth. see Meisner, Sanford.

Longwell-Smiley, Jan. The Master of Disaster: A Tale of Manifestation, Mayhem, & Magic. LC 98-71587. 328p. 1998. pap. 13.95 (1-57174-105-4) Hampton Roads Pub Co.

***Longwith, John.** Light upon a Hill: The University at Chattanooga, 1886-1996. unabridged ed. (Illus.). 298p. 2000. 24.95 (0-944897-04-5) Magic Chef.

Longwith, John C. Castle on a Cliff: A History of Baylor School. (Illus.). 216p. 1994. 24.95 (0-944897-03-7) Magic Chef.

— Since Before the Yellow Fever: A History of Union Planters Bank. LC 94-60749. (Illus.). 224p. 1994. 19.95 (0-944897-02-9) Magic Chef.

— Spark of Enterprise: A History of Dixie Foundry - Magic Chef. Inc. LC 87-91291. (Illus.). 192p. 1988. 16.95 (0-944897-00-2) Magic Chef.

— Spark of Enterprise: A History of Dixie Foundry - Magic Chef, Inc. deluxe ed. LC 87-91291. (Illus.). 192p. 1988. lthr. 29.95 (0-944897-01-0) Magic Chef.

Longworth, Alice R. Crowded Hours. Baxter, Annette K., ed. LC 79-8799. (Signal Lives Ser.). (Illus.). 1980. reprint ed. lib. bdg. 41.95 (0-405-12846-0) Ayer.

Longworth, David L., jt. auth. see Stoller, James K.

Longworth, J. W., ed. Economic Aspects of Raw Wool Production & Marketing in China. 62p. (Orig.). 1992. pap. 75.00 (1-86320-082-7) St Mut.

Longworth, J. W. & Brown, C. G. Agribusiness Reforms in China: The Case of Wool. (Illus.). 288p. 1995. text 90.00 (0-85198-951-9) OUP.

Longworth, J. W. & Williamson, G. J. China's Pastoral Region: Sheep & Wool, Minority Nationalities, Rangeland Degradation & Sustainable Development. (Illus.). 368p. 1993. text 100.00 (0-85198-890-3) OUP.

***Longworth, James L.** TV Creators: Conversations with America's Top Producers of Television Drama. LC 00-39476. (Television Ser.). 296p. 2000. pap. 19.95 (0-8156-0652-4) Syracuse U Pr.

***Longworth, James L., Jr.** TV Creators: Conversations with America's Top Producers of Television Drama. (Illus.). 296p. 2000. 45.00 (0-8156-2874-9) Syracuse U Pr.

Longworth, James W., et al, eds. International Congress on Photobiology, 9th: Proceedings. LC 85-3379. 298p. 1985. 75.00 (0-275-91318-X, C1318, Praeger Pubs) Greenwood.

— Photobiology, 1984. LC 85-604. 202p. 1985. 59.95 (0-275-90189-0, C0189, Praeger Pubs) Greenwood.

Longworth, John W. Beef in Japan: Politics, Production, Marketing & Trade. LC 83-14792. (Illus.). 327p. 1984. 49.95 (0-7022-1965-7, Pub. by Univ Queensland Pr) Intl Spec Bk.

Longworth, John W., ed. China's Rural Development Miracle. 1989. pap. 34.95 (0-7022-2264-X, Pub. by Univ Queensland Pr) Intl Spec Bk.

Longworth, L. H., jt. auth. see Wainwright, G. J.

Longworth, Maria T. Teresina in America, 2 vols. LC 73-13158. (Foreign Travelers in America, 1810-1935 Ser.). 734p. 1974. reprint ed. 57.95 (0-405-05478-5) Ayer.

Longworth, Norman. Making Lifelong Learning Work: Learning Cities for a Learning Century. LC 99-235662. 240p. pap. 29.95 (0-7494-2727-2, Kogan Pg Educ) Stylus Pub VA.

Longworth, Norman & Davies, W. Keith. Lifelong Learning. 192p. 1997. pap. 29.95 (0-7494-1972-5, Kogan Pg Educ) Stylus Pub VA.

Longworth, Philip. The Making of Eastern Europe. 2nd ed. LC 97-1346. 320p. 1997. pap. 19.95 (0-312-17445-4) St Martin.

— The Making of Eastern Europe: From Prehistory to Postcommunism. 2nd ed. LC 97-1346. 320p. 1997. text 55.00 (0-312-17444-6) St Martin.

Longworth, Richard C. Global Squeeze. (Illus.). 320p. 1999. pap. 15.95 (0-8092-2975-7, 297570, Contemporary Bks) NTC Contemp Pub Co.

— Global Squeeze: The Coming Crisis for First-World Nations. LC 97-46457. 272p. 1998. 24.95 (0-8092-2974-9) NTC Contemp Pub Co.

Longyard, William H. Who's Who in Aviation History: 500 Biographies. (Illus.). 203p. 1999. reprint ed. text 30.00 (0-7881-6108-3) DIANE Pub.

Longyear, Barry B. The Change. Ryan, Kevin, ed. (Alien Nation Ser.: No. 4). 320p. (Orig.). 1994. mass mkt. 5.50 (0-671-73602-7) PB.

— The Enemy Papers. 1998. pap. 14.99 (1-56504-859-8, 11042, Borealis) White Wolf.

— Naked Came the Robot. 224p. (Orig.). 1988. mass mkt. 3.95 (0-445-20755-8, Pub. by Warner Bks) Little.

— Science Fiction Writer's Workshop I: An Introduction to Fiction Mechanics. 168p. 1980. pap. 9.50 (0-913896-18-7) Owlswick Pr.

— Sea of Glass. 384p. 1988. pap. 3.50 (0-380-70055-7, Avon Bks) Morrow Avon.

— Slag Like Me. Ryan, Kevin, ed. (Alien Nation Ser.: No. 5). 320p. (Orig.). 1994. mass mkt. 5.50 (0-671-79514-7) PB.

Longyear, Edmund J. Longyear: The Descendants of Jacob Longyear of Ulster County, New York. 622p. 1992. reprint ed. pap. 89.00 (0-8328-2393-7); reprint ed. lib. bdg. 99.00 (0-8328-2392-9) Higginson Bk Co.

Longyear, J. M., 3rd. Archaeological Investigations in El Salvador. (HU PMM Ser.: Vol. 9, No. 2). 1972. reprint ed. 25.00 (0-527-01173-8) Periodicals Srv.

Longyear, John M. Landlooker in the Upper Peninsula of Michigan. LC 60-53288. 80p. 1983. reprint ed. 8.95 (0-938746-06-5) Marquette Cnty.

Longyear, Rey M., ed. see Pavesi, Stepano.

Lonidier, Fred. Blueprint for a Strike: A Fragmentary Capsule History of the Ironworkers & Other Unions at NASSCO. (Illus.). 32p. (Orig.). 1992. pap. 8.00 (0-930495-16-0) San Fran Art Inst.

Lonidier, Lynn. Clitoris Lost. 1989. pap. 11.95 (0-317-04319-6) Man-Root.

Lonidier, Lynn & Mayers, Keith. The Rhyme of the Aged Mariness. 112p. 2000. pap. text 14.95 (1-58177-052-9, Pub. by Barrytown Ltd) Consort Bk Sales.

An Asterisk (*) at the beginning of an entry indicates that the title is appearing for the first time.

Lonie, John. Acts of Love. 1997. pap. text 12.95 (*1-875243-23-2*, Pub. by Blackwattle) LPC InBook.

Lonier, Terri. Frugal Entrepreneur: Creative Ways to Save Time, Energy & Money in Your Business. 192p. 1996. pap. text 12.95 (*1-883282-70-5*) Portico Pr.

— The Small Business Money Guide: How to Get It, Use It, Keep It. LC 98-24355. 204p. 1998. pap. 16.95 (*0-471-24799-5*) Wiley.

— Smart Strategies for Growing Your Business. LC 98-42280. (Working Solo Ser.). 320p. 1999. pap. 16.95 (*0-471-24800-2*) Wiley.

— Working Solo. 2nd ed. LC 98-10660. 354p. 1998. pap. 14.95 (*0-471-24713-8*) Wiley.

***Lonier, Terri.** Working Solo Sourcebook, 1. LC 98-9948. 315p. 1998. pap. 14.95 (*0-471-24714-6*) Wiley.

Lonigan, Christopher J. & Elbert, Jean C., eds. Empirically Supported Psychosocial Interventions for Children: A Special Issue of "Journal of Clinical Child Psychology" 100p. 1998. pap. 20.00 (*0-8058-9829-8*) L Erlbaum Assocs.

Lonigan, Paul R. The Druids: Priests of the Ancient Celts, 45. LC 95-46895. (Contributions to the Study of Religion Ser.: Vol. 45). 160p. 1996. 55.00 (*0-313-29955-2*, Greenwood Pr) Greenwood.

— The Early Irish Church. rev. ed. (Illus.). 90p. (C). 1988. pap. 7.95 (*0-9614753-2-3*) Celt Heritage Bks.

Lonik, Larry. Basically Morels: Mushroom Hunting, Cooking, Lore & Advice. Reed, Stephanie & Utley, James, eds. (Illus.). 132p. 1999. pap. 11.95 (*0-931715-01-6*) R K T Pub.

— Morels: True or False: The Essential Field Guide & More. Reed, Stephanie & Utley, James, eds. (Illus.). 80p. 1999. pap. 11.95 (*0-931715-04-0*) R K T Pub.

— Morels & More: Wild Mushrooms & Gourmet Recipes, Tales & Tips. Reed, Stephanie, ed. (Illus.). 160p. 1999. pap. 14.95 (*0-931715-02-4*) R K T Pub.

Lonik, Larry T. The Curious Morel: Mushroom Hunters' Recipes, Lore & Advice. 3rd ed. (Illus.). 144p. 1998. pap. 10.95 (*0-931715-00-8*) R K T Pub.

— The Healthy Taste of Honey: Bee People's Recipes, Anecdotes & Lore. (Illus.). 180p. 1984. pap. 11.95 (*0-931715-08-3*) R K T Pub.

Lonitz, Henri, ed. see Adorno, Theodor W. & Benjamin, Walter.

Lonkhurst, Bob. Man of Courage: The Life & Career of Tommy Farr. (Illus.). 367p. 1998. pap. 27.50 (*1-85776-373-4*, Pub. by Book Guild Ltd) Trans-Atl Phila.

Lonn, Ella. Desertion during the Civil War. LC 97-44252. (Illus.). 251p. 1998. pap. 12.00 (*0-8032-7975-2*, Bison Books) U of Nebr Pr.

— Desertion During the Civil War. (History - United States Ser.). 251p. 1992. reprint ed. lib. bdg. 79.00 (*0-7812-6180-5*) Rprt Serv.

— Foreigners in the Union Army & Navy. LC 74-90548. 725p. 1970. reprint ed. lib. bdg. 35.00 (*0-8371-2248-1*, LOFU, Greenwood Pr) Greenwood.

Lonnberg, Allan. Self & Savagery on the California Frontier: A Study of the Digger Stereotype. (Illus.). 98p. 1980. reprint ed. pap. text 10.94 (*1-55567-048-2*) Coyote Press.

Lonnborg, Barbara A., ed. Boys Town: A Photographic History. LC 92-18878. 144p. 1992. 19.95 (*0-938510-37-1*, 19-001); pap. 12.95 (*0-938510-31-2*, 19-002) Boys Town Pr.

Lonnborg, Barbara A., ed. see Reilly, Hugh J. & Hyland, Terry L.

Lonnderdal, Bo, jt. ed. see Hutchens, T. William.

***Lonnecke, Annette.** Anglo-Kanadische Autobiographien der Postmoderne: Radikale Formen der Selbstportratierung von John Glassco Bis Kristjana Gunnars. (Neue Studien zur Anglistik und Amerikanistik). 262p. 1999. 42.95 (*3-631-34732-4*) P Lang Pubng.

Lonner, Walter J. & Berry, John W., eds. Field Methods in Cross-Cultural Research. LC 85-18360. (Cross-Cultural Research & Methodology Ser.: No. 8). 368p. (Orig.). reprint ed. pap. 114.10 (*0-7837-6587-8*, 204615200011) Bks Demand.

Lonner, Walter J. & Malpass, Roy S., eds. Readings in Psychology & Culture. LC 93-14050. 400p. 1993. pap. text 33.00 (*0-205-14899-9*, H4899-4) Allyn.

Lonner, Walter J., ed. see International Association for Cross-Cultural Psych.

Lonnerdal, Bo, ed. Iron Metabolism in Infants. 176p. 1989. lib. bdg. 141.00 (*0-8493-5433-1*, RJ128) CRC Pr.

Lonnerdal, Bo, jt. auth. see Picciano, Mary F.

***Lonnerstrand, Sture.** I Have Lived Before: The True Story of the Reincarnation of Shanti Devi. Kippen, Leslie, tr. from SWE. LC 98-65383. Orig. Title: Shanti Devi en Berattelse Om Reinkarnation. (Illus.). 160p. 1998. pap. 21.95 (*1-886940-03-7*) Ozark Mountn.

Lonngren, Karl E. Electromagnetics with Matlab. 470p. 1997. pap. 60.00 (*1-898326-51-7*, Pub. by CISP) Balogh.

Lonngren, Karl E. Introduction to Physical Electronics. 350p. (C). 1988. write for info. (*0-318-62208-4*, H11422) P-H.

Lonngren, Karl E., jt. auth. see Hirose, Akira.

***Lonning, Kari.** The Art of Basketry. LC 99-87095. (Illus.). 2000. 24.95 (*0-8069-2041-6*) Sterling.

Lonnrot, Elias, ed. The Kalevala: Poems of the Kaleva District. Magoun, Francis P., Jr., tr. 448p. 1990. pap. 18.95 (*0-674-50010-5*) HUP.

Lonnroth, Mans, et al. Energy in Transition: A Report on Energy Policy & Future Options. LC 78-68827. (Illus.). 197p. reprint ed. pap. 61.10 (*0-608-18288-5*, 203153800075) Bks Demand.

Lono, Luz P., ed. see Ozaeta, Pablo.

Lonoff de Cuevas, Sue. The College Reader: Linking Reading to Writing. LC 92-15837. 656p. (C). 1997. 48.00 (*0-673-18726-8*) Addson-Wesley Educ.

Lonoff, Jon, jt. auth. see Keating, Barry.

Lonoff, Sue. Wilkie Collins & His Victorian Readers: A Study in the Rhetoric of Authorship. LC 79-8835. (Studies in the Nineteenth Century: No. 2). (Illus.). 1982. 34.50 (*0-404-18044-2*) AMS Pr.

Lonoff, Sue, ed. & tr. see Bronte, Charlotte & Bronte, Emily Jane.

Lonon, James L. Tall Tales of the Rails: On the Carolina, Clinchfield & Ohio Railway. Mintz, James W., ed. (Illus.). 216p. 1989. 19.95 (*0-932807-50-X*) Overmountain Pr.

Lons. Mummelmann. unabridged ed. (World Classic Literature Ser.). (GER.). pap. 5.95 (*3-89507-031-9*, Pub. by Bookking Intl) Distribks Inc.

Lonsberry, Daniel. Mr. Tall Cactus & His Shorter, Prickly Neighbors. LC 96-78886. (Illus.). 32p. (J). (ps-4). 1997. pap. write for info. (*0-9658255-1-5*) Magic Carpet Rides.

Lonsbury-Martin, Brenda L. Otoacoustic Emissions: A Manual for Clinical Applications. 100p. 2000. pap. 49.95 (*1-56593-952-2*, 1882) Thomson Learn.

Lonsbury-Martin, Brenda L. & Martin, Glen K. An Introduction to the Practical Applications of Otoacoustic Emissions. 264p. 2000. pap. 49.95 (*1-56593-709-0*, 1394) Singular Publishing.

Lonsdale, Alan, jt. auth. see Abbott, Jacqui.

***Lonsdale, Allison B., et al.** Investigating Translation: Selected Papers from the 4th International Congress on Translation, Barcelona, 1998. International Congress on Translation Staff, ed. LC 00-39824. (Translation Library). 2000. pap. write for info. (*1-55619-791-8*) J Benjamins Pubng Co.

Lonsdale, Chris. The U. K. Equity Gap: The Failure of Government Policy since 1945. LC 97-23058. (Illus.). 256p. 1997. text 78.95 (*1-85521-865-8*, HC256.5L63, Pub. by Dartmth Pub) Ashgate Pub Co.

Lonsdale, D., ed. see Butin, Heinz.

Lonsdale, David. Eyes to See, Ears to Hear: A Companion to the Spiritual Exercises of Saint Ignatius. LC 91-13247. 184p. 1991. reprint ed. pap. 10.95 (*0-8294-0721-9*, Jesuit Way) Loyola Pr.

***Lonsdale, David.** Eyes to See, Ears to Hear: An Introduction to Ignatian Spirituality. rev. ed. 196p. 2000. reprint ed. pap. 16.00 (*1-57075-336-9*) Orbis Bks.

Lonsdale, Derrick. Why I Left Orthodox Medicine: Healing for the 21st Century. LC 94-214685. 256p. 1994. pap. 10.95 (*1-878901-98-2*) Hampton Roads Pub Co.

Lonsdale, Ellias. Inside Degrees: Developing Your Soul Biography Using the Chandra Symbols. LC 96-49738. 225p. 1997. pap. 16.95 (*1-55643-241-0*) North Atlantic.

— Inside Star Vision: Planetary Awakening & Self-Transformtion. 200p. 2000. pap. 16.95 (*1-55643-324-7*, Pub. by North Atlantic) Publishers Group.

Lonsdale, Ellias & Lonsdale, Theanna. The Book of Theanna: In the Lands That Follow Death. LC 95-11220. 400p. 1995. pap. 16.95 (*1-883319-37-4*) Frog Ltd CA.

***Lonsdale, Frederick.** Lonsdale: Plays One. (Oberon Bks.). 2000. pap. 20.95 (*1-84002-073-3*) Theatre Comm.

Lonsdale, H. K. & Podall, H. E., eds. Reverse Osmosis Membrane Research. LC 72-87518. (Illus.). 515p. 1972. reprint ed. pap. 159.70 (*0-608-05501-8*, 206597000006) Bks Demand.

***Lonsdale, Harry P.** Smoking out a Killer. LC 99-96771. (Illus.). 256p. 2000. mass mkt. 5.99 (*0-380-80299-6*, Avon Bks) Morrow Avon.

Lonsdale, Harry P. & Jeffers, H. Paul. Where There's Smoke, There's Murder: A Nicholas Chase Cigar Mystery. LC 98-91014, (Nicholas Chase Mystery Ser.). (Illus.). 224p. 1999. mass mkt. 5.99 (*0-380-80298-8*, Avon Bks) Morrow Avon.

Lonsdale, John, jt. auth. see Berman, Bruce.

Lonsdale, Kathleen, jt. ed. see Kasper, John S.

Lonsdale, Mark. Alpine Operations Vol. 8: A Guide to Cold Weather & Mountain Operations. (Illus.). 300p. 1999. pap. 24.00 (*0-939235-07-2*) Spec Trning Unit.

Lonsdale, P. Public Water Supply: Models, Data & Operational Management. LC 98-231834. (Illus.). 480p. (C). 1998. 110.00 (*0-419-23220-6*, E & FN Spon) Routledge.

Lonsdale, Ray, jt. auth. see Elkin, Judith.

Lonsdale, Richard, ed. & intro. see Beckford, William.

Lonsdale, Roberta, jt. auth. see Gaiter, Lew.

Lonsdale, Roberta E. & Gaiter, Lew. Entrepreneur's Handbook. 200p. 1998. pap. 17.95 (*1-56315-113-8*) SterlingHse.

Lonsdale, Roger. Dr. Charles Burney: A Literary Biography. (Illus.). 544p. 1986. pap. text 19.95 (*0-19-812885-1*) OUP.

Lonsdale, Roger, ed. Eighteenth-Century Women Poets: An Oxford Anthology. 602p. 1990. reprint ed. pap. text 14.95 (*0-19-282775-8*) OUP.

— The New Oxford Book of Eighteenth-Century Verse. 912p. 1989. pap. 17.95 (*0-19-282054-0*) OUP.

Lonsdale, Steven H. Dance & Ritual Play in Greek Religion. LC 93-2787. (Ancient Society & History Ser.). (Illus.). 368p. (C). 1993. text 39.95 (*0-8018-4594-7*) Johns Hopkins.

Lonsdale, Susan. Work & Inequality. 1985. pap. text. write for info. (*0-582-29629-3*, Pub. by Addison-Wesley) Longman.

— Work & Inequality. LC 84-12235. (Social Policy in Modern Britain Ser.). 263p. reprint ed. pap. 81.60 (*0-7837-1603-6*, 204189500024) Bks Demand.

Lonsdale, Susan, et al. Long-Term Psychiatric Patients: A Study in Community Care. 1980. 15.00 (*0-7855-0572-5*, Pub. by Natl Inst Soc Work) St Mut.

Lonsdale, Theanna, jt. auth. see Lonsdale, Ellias.

Lonsdale, William, ed. Star Rhythms. 2nd ed. (Io Ser.: No. 27). (Illus.). 180p. 1982. pap. 8.95 (*0-938190-00-8*) North Atlantic.

Lonsdorf, Nancy, et al. A Woman's Best Medicine: Health, Happiness, & Long Life Through Ayur-Veda. LC 94-8619. 384p. 1995. pap. 15.95 (*0-87477-785-2*, Tarcher Putnam) Putnam Pub Group.

Lonse, Kris, ed. see Nielson, Norm.

Lonsinger, Nancy L. Around the Stove in Roscoe's General Store - 1866. (Illus.). 48p. (Orig.). 1976. pap. 2.00 (*1-880443-00-7*) Roscoe Village.

Lonstein, Albert I. & Marino, Vito R. The Revised Compleat Sinatra. rev. ed. LC 79-88307. (Illus.). 702p. 1980. 49.95 (*0-87990-000-8*) Lonstein Pubns.

Lont, Cynthia & Decker, Warren. Senior Seminar in Theories of Communicative Interaction. 404p. (C). 1993. per. 39.95 (*0-8403-8609-5*) Kendall-Hunt.

Lont, Cynthia M. Women & Media: Content, Careers, & Criticism. LC 94-36309. 415p. 1995. 50.95 (*0-534-24732-6*) Wadsworth Pub.

Lontai, Endre. Unification of Law in the Field of International Industrial Property. LC 95-201854. 230p. 1994. pap. 125.00 (*963-05-6741-5*, Pub. by Akade Kiado) St Mut.

Lontano, M., et al, eds. Superstrong Fields in Plasmas: First International Conference. LC 98-70235. (AIP Conference Proceedings Ser.: Vol. 426). (Illus.). xvii, 574p. 1998. 150.00 (*1-56396-748-0*) Am Inst Physics.

Lontie, Rene, ed. Copper Proteins & Copper Enzymes, Vol. 1. LC 82-24366. 256p. 1984. 135.00 (*0-8493-6470-1*, QP552, CRC Reprint) Franklin.

— Copper Proteins & Copper Enzymes, Vol. 2. LC 82-24366. 304p. 1984. 150.00 (*0-8493-6471-X*, QP552, CRC Reprint) Franklin.

— Copper Proteins & Copper Enzymes, Vol. III. 272p. 1984. 144.00 (*0-8493-6472-8*, QP552, CRC Reprint) Franklin.

Lonto, Jeff R. Fiasco at 1280 Vol. 1: The Rise & Hard Fall of a Twin Cities Radio Station. (Illus.). 234p. 1998. pap. 10.95 (*0-9660213-4-7*) Studio Z-Seven.

— Legend of the Brewery Vol. 1: A Brief History of the Minneapolis Brewing Heritage. (Illus.). 52p. 1998. pap. 9.95 (*0-9660213-3-9*) Studio Z-Seven.

Lonx, Michael J., tr. & intro. see William of Ockham.

Loo. Chinese Medicine. 320p. write for info. (*0-471-35603-4*) Wiley.

Loo, Andre. Pictorial Chinese Sayings: 1 to 10,000, 8 vols., Vol. 1. Dent-Young, Esther, tr. LC 97-61702. (Illus.). vi, 95p. 1997. pap. 8.95 (*1-890807-00-1*, L001) Silk Rd Pr.

— Pictorial Chinese Sayings Vol. 2: The Animal World. Dent-Young, Esther, tr. LC 97-61702. (Illus.). viii, 95p. 1997. pap. 8.95 (*1-890807-01-X*, L002) Silk Rd Pr.

— Pictorial Chinese Sayings Vol. 3: The Plant World. Lam, Adrienne, tr. LC 97-61702. (Illus.). viii, 102p. 1997. pap. 8.95 (*1-890807-02-8*, L003) Silk Rd Pr.

— Pictorial Chinese Sayings Vol. 4: Towards Nature. Lam, Adrienne, tr. LC 97-61702. (Illus.). vi, 104p. 1997. pap. 8.95 (*1-890807-03-6*, L004) Silk Rd Pr.

— Pictorial Chinese Sayings Vol. 5: The Physical Self. Lam, Adrienne, tr. LC 97-61702. (Illus.). v, 104p. 1997. pap. 8.95 (*1-890807-04-4*, L005) Silk Rd Pr.

— Pictorial Chinese Sayings Vol. 6, Pt. I: A Tale to Tell. Dent-Young, Esther, tr. LC 97-61702. (Illus.). viii, 104p. 1997. pap. 8.95 (*1-890807-05-2*, L006) Silk Rd Pr.

— Pictorial Chinese Sayings Vol. 7, Pt. II: A Tale to Tell. Lam, Adrienne, tr. LC 97-61702. (Illus.). viii, 95p. 1997. pap. 8.95 (*1-890807-06-0*, L007) Silk Rd Pr.

— Pictorial Chinese Sayings Vol. 8, Pt. III: A Tale to Tell. Lam, Adrienne, tr. LC 97-61702. (Illus.). viii, 95p. (Orig.). 1997. pap. 8.95 (*1-890807-07-9*, L008) Silk Rd Pr.

Loo, Chalsa. Chinatown: Most Time, Hard Time. LC 91-27984. 384p. 1991. 67.95 (*0-275-93893-X*, C3893, Praeger Pubs) Greenwood.

Loo, Chalsa M. Chinese America: Mental Health & Quality of Life in the Inner City. LC 98-9076. (Racial & Ethnic Minority Psychology Ser.). 328p. 1998. pap. 16.99 (*0-7619-1255-X*) Sage.

— Crowding & Behavior. LC 74-8362. 246p. 1974. 29.50 (*0-8422-5180-4*); pap. text 9.95 (*0-8422-0415-6*) Irvington.

Loo, Dolly D., ed. see Kwiatkowski, Philibert F.

Loo, Francis T., ed. see Failure Prevention & Reliability Conference Staff.

Loo, Humphrey Van, see Van Loo, Humphrey, ed.

Loo, J. Van de, see Van de Loo, J.

Loo, Marcus H. & Betancourt, Marian. The Prostate Cancer Sourcebook: How to Make Informed Treatment Choices. LC 97-33001. 256p. 1998. pap. 14.95 (*0-471-15927-1*) Wiley.

Loo, Oliver, ed. Contemporary Architectural Art Glass Studios: Glass by Fischer. LC 94-76586. (Illus.). 60p. (Orig.). 1994. pap. 14.95 (*0-9641371-0-0*) C&R Loo.

Loo, P. D. Van, see Huijser, A. P. & Van Loo, P. D.

Loo, P. D. Van, see Korteweg, Pieter & Van Loo, P. D., eds.

Loo, Ronald J. He Kalana Kakau Ki Hoalu Helu Ekahi: A Slack Key Notebook, No. 1. 57p. 1984. pap. 31.00 (*1-885332-01-7*) P Nahenahe.

— He Kalana Kakau Ki Hoalu Helu Elua: A Slack Key Notebook, No. 2. 76p. 1992. pap. 31.00 (*1-885332-02-5*) P Nahenahe.

— He Kalana Kakua Ki Ho'alu Helu 'Ekolu: A Slack Key Notebook, No. 3. 80p. 1995. pap. 31.50 incl. audio (*1-885332-04-1*) P Nahenahe.

— Logic - the Worksheet: A Study Guide for Chapters 1, 3, 8, 9 of Copi's Introduction to Logic (7th) 2nd ed. 114p. (C). 1986. student ed. 11.00 (*1-885332-03-3*) P Nahenahe.

Loo, Tina. Making Law, Order, & Authority in British Columbia, 1821-1871. (Social History of Canada Ser.). (Illus.). 352p. (C). 1994. text 45.00 (*0-8020-2961-2*); pap. text 18.95 (*0-8020-7784-6*) U of Toronto Pr.

Loo, Tina, jt. auth. see Strange, Carolyn.

Looby, Christopher. Benjamin Franklin. (World Leaders Past & Present Ser.). (Illus.). 120p. (J). (gr. 5 up). 1990. lib. bdg. 19.95 (*1-55546-808-X*) Chelsea Hse.

— Voicing America: Language, Literary Form, & the Origins of the United States. xii, 288p. 1997. pap. text 13.95 (*0-226-49283-4*) U Ch Pr.

— Voicing America: Language, Literary Form, & the Origins of the United States. LC 95-29993. (Illus.). 280p. (gr. 2). 1998. 29.95 (*0-226-49282-6*) U Ch Pr.

Looby, Christopher, ed. see Higginson, Thomas W.

Looby, P. Wimbledon. (Best of Britain in Old Photographs Ser.). (Illus.). 1998. pap. 14.50 (*0-7509-0729-0*, Pub. by Sutton Pub Ltd) Intl Pubs Mktg.

***Loock, Joan W.** Wisconsin's Model Academic Standards for Business. 26p. 1998. pap. text 9.00 (*1-57337-068-1*, 9004) WI Dept Pub Instruct.

Loock, Ulrich. Luc Tuymans. (Contemporary Artists Ser.). (Illus.). 160p. 1996. pap. 29.95 (*0-7148-3551-X*, Pub. by Phaidon Press) Phaidon Pr.

Loocke, Philip R. Van, see Van Loocke, Philip R.

Loocke, Philip Van, see Van Loocke, Philip, ed.

Loocke, R. J., ed. California Forest Soils: A Guide for Professional Foresters & Resource Managers & Planners. LC 79-62985. (Illus.). 184p. (Orig.). 1979. pap. text 5.00 (*0-931876-32-X*, 4094) ANR Pubns CA.

Loofbourow, John. Thackeray & the Form of Fiction. LC 75-42172. 224p. 1976. reprint ed. 50.00 (*0-87752-177-8*) Gordian.

Looff, Carolyn. Business & Economics Funding Guide. Bitting, Christina, ed. 134p. (Orig.). (C). 1987. pap. text 19.50 (*0-88044-088-0*); lib. bdg. 35.50 (*0-88044-087-2*) AASCU Press.

Loofs-Wissowa, H. H., et al. Vietnamese-English Archaeological Glossary. (ENG & VIE.). 116p. 1997. pap. text 25.00 (*0-7315-0665-0*, Pub. by Aust Nat Univ) UH Pr.

Looft, Mrcus. Nieder-Sachsisches Koch-Buch. (GER.). 557p. 1988. reprint ed. write for info. (*3-487-08218-7*) G Olms Pubs.

***Looijen, Rick C.** Holism & Reductionism in Biology & Ecology: The Mutual Dependence of Higher & Lower Level Research Programmes. LC 99-52308. (Episteme Ser.). 372p. 1999. 175.00 (*0-7923-6076-1*) Kluwer Academic.

Look, Burt. Spreadsheet Geomechanics: An Introduction. (Illus.). 256p. (C). 1994. pap. text 36.00 (*90-5410-152-0*, Pub. by A A Balkema) Ashgate Pub Co.

— Spreadsheet Geomechanics: An Introduction. (Illus.). 256p. (C). 1994. text 71.00 (*90-5410-151-2*) Ashgate Pub Co.

Look, David W. Seismic Retrofit of Historic Buildings: Keeping Preservation in the Forefront. 16p. 1997. pap. 2.00 (*0-16-061684-0*) USGPO.

Look, Lenore. Arthur's First-Moon Birthday Album. LC 98-21626. (J). 1920. 16.00 (*0-689-82294-4*) Atheneum Yung Read.

— Love As Strong As Ginger. LC 96-43459. (Illus.). 40p. (J). (gr. k-4). 1999. 15.00 (*0-689-81248-5*) S&S Childrens.

Look Magazine Staff, ed. Movie Lot to Beachhead: The Motion Picture Goes to War & Prepares for the Future. LC 79-6696. 1980. reprint ed. lib. bdg. 22.95 (*0-405-12935-1*) Ayer.

Look, Margaret K. At Home in Pittsburgh. LC 88-72337. (Illus.). 123p. (Orig.). 1989. pap. 4.95 (*0-916383-75-X*) M K Look.

— At Home on The Workhouse Farm. (Illus.). 132p. (Orig.). 1986. pap. 6.95 (*0-9616922-0-0*) M K Look.

— Courtney: Master Oarsman, Champion Coach. (Illus.). 168p. 1989. 9.95 (*1-55787-044-6*, NY55032) M K Look.

Look, P. F. Van, see Van Look, P. F., ed.

Look, P. F. Van, see Khanna, J.

Look, P. F. Van, see Puri, C. P. & Van Look, P. F.

Looker, Dan. Farmers for the Future. LC 95-37275. 192p. 1995. pap. 21.95 (*0-8138-2383-8*) Iowa St U Pr.

Looker, Earle. The White House Gang. 22.95 (*0-89190-546-4*) Amereon Ltd.

Looker, James M., jt. auth. see Painter, Mark P.

***Looker, Janet.** Disaster Canada. 200p. 1999. text 24.95 (*1-894073-13-4*) Lynx Images.

Looker, Lori, ed. see Chewning, Ronald J. & Chewning, Phyllis J.

Looker, Mark. Atlantic Passages: History, Community, & Language in the Fiction of Sam Selvon. (Studies of World Literature in English: Vol. 7). X, 244p. (C). 1996. 52.95 (*0-8204-2836-1*) P Lang Pubng.

***Looker, Thomas.** The Sound & the Story: NPR & the Art of Radio. 421p. 1999. reprint ed. text 25.00 (*0-7881-6330-2*) DIANE Pub.

Lookianova, N. A. English for Business: The Businessman's Companion. 3rd ed. 570p. 1993. 49.95 (*0-7859-9080-1*) Fr & Eur.

Lookingbill, Colleen. Incognita. 1992. pap. 8.00 (*0-9623806-2-8*) SINK Pr.

Lookingbill, Donald P. & Marks, James G., Jr. Principles of Dermatology. 2nd ed. LC 92-48750. (Illus.). 384p. 1993. pap. text 55.00 (*0-7216-4290-X*, W B Saunders Co) Harcrt Hlth Sci Grp.

Lookingbill, Donald P. & Marks, James G. Principles of Dermatology. 3rd ed. 335p. Date not set. pap. text. write for info. (*0-7216-7971-4*, W B Saunders Co) Harcrt Hlth Sci Grp.

Lookingbill, Len. From the Horse's Mouth Vol. 1: The Horseman's Guide to Equine Dental Health & Aging. 139p. text 18.95 (*0-9644682-0-4*) Diamond L Pub.

L

Lookofsky, Joseph. Understanding the CISG in the U. S. A. A Compact Guide to the 1980 United Nations Convention on Contracts for the International Sale of Goods. LC 95-36819. 1995. 35.50 (*90-411-0956-0*) Kluwer Law Intl.

Lookofsky, Joseph M. Transnational Litigation & Commercial Arbitration. A Comparative Analysis of American, European & International Law. 792p. (Orig.). 1992. pap. 280.00 (*87-574-5990-8*) Coronet Bks.

— Transnational Litigation & Commercial Arbitration under American, European & International Law. 800p. 1991. 65.00 (*0-929179-66-8*) Juris Pubng.

Lookofsky, Joseph M., jt. auth. see Bernstein, Herbert.

Looman, Janice E., jt. auth. see Herz, David A.

Loomans, Diane. The Lovables. (Illus.). 10p. (J). (ps). 1996. bds. 4.95 (*0-915811-71-5*, Starseed) H J Kramer Inc.

— The Lovables in the Kingdom of Self-Esteem. Carleton, Nancy, ed. LC 90-52633. (Illus.). 32p. (J). (ps-5). 1991. 15.95 (*0-915811-25-1*, Starseed) H J Kramer Inc.

— Today I Am Lovable: 365 Positive Activities for Kids. Carleton, Nancy, ed. (Illus.). 372p. (Orig.). (J). (gr. 2-6). 1996. pap. 14.00 (*0-915811-68-5*) H J Kramer Inc.

Loomans, Diane & Kolberg, Karen J. The Laughing Classroom: Everyone's Guide to Teaching with Humor & Play. LC 92-23351. (Illus.). 228p. 1993. pap. 14.95 (*0-915811-44-8*) H J Kramer Inc.

Loomans, Diane & Loomans, Julia. Full Esteem Ahead: One Hundred Ways to Teach Values & Build Self-Esteem for All Ages. Carleton, Nancy, ed. 360p. (Orig.). 1994. pap. 14.95 (*0-915811-57-X*) H J Kramer Inc.

Loomans, Diane, et al. Positively Mother Goose. Kramer, Linda, ed. LC 90-52634. (Illus.). 32p. (J). (ps-2). 1991. 14.95 (*0-915811-24-3*, Starseed) H J Kramer Inc.

Loomans, Julia, jt. auth. see Loomans, Diane.

Loomba, Ania. Colonialism - Postcolonialism. LC 97-46665. (New Critical Idiom Ser.). 320p. (C). 1998. 50.00 (*0-415-12808-0*); pap. 14.99 (*0-415-12809-9*) Routledge.

— Gender, Race, Renaissance Drama. (Oxford India Paperbacks Ser.). 188p. 1992. pap. 7.95 (*0-19-563004-1*) OUP.

Loomba, Ania & Orkin, Martin, eds. Post-Colonial Shakespeare. LC 98-235188. (New Accents Ser.). (Illus.). 288p. (C). (gr. 13). 1998. 60.00 (*0-415-17386-8*, D6270); pap. 17.99 (*0-415-17387-6*, D6274) Routledge.

Loomer, Bradley M. & Strege, Maxine G. Useful Spelling, Levels 2-8. (J). (gr. 2-8). 1990. write for info. (*1-878712-03-9*) Useful Lrn.

Loomer, Lisa. Accelerando. 1998. pap. 5.25 (*0-8222-1595-0*) Dramatists Play.

— Bocon! 44p. 1998. pap. 5.50 (*0-87129-870-8*, B36) Dramatic Pub.

— The Waiting Room. LC 98-228483. 1998. pap. 5.25 (*0-8222-1594-2*) Dramatists Play.

Loomes, Brian. Antique British Clocks: A Buyer's Guide. (Illus.). 224p. 1991. 35.00 (*0-7090-4611-1*, Pub. by R Hale Ltd) Antique Collect.

— Brass Dial Clocks. (Illus.). 464p. 1997. 79.50 (*1-85149-221-6*) Antique Collect.

— The Concise Guide to British Clocks. (Illus.). 192p. 1992. pap. 22.95 (*0-7126-5187-X*, Pub. by Barrie & Jenkins) Trafalgar.

— The Concise Guide to Tracing Your Ancestry. 192p. 1993. 22.95 (*0-7126-9877-9*, Pub. by Barrie & Jenkins) Trafalgar.

— Early Clockmakers of Great Britain. 589p. 1981. 59.50 (*0-7198-0200-8*, Pub. by NAG Press) Antique Collect.

— Painted Dial Clocks. (Illus.). 350p. 1995. 59.50 (*1-85149-183-X*) Antique Collect.

Loomes, Graham, jt. ed. see Hey, John D.

Loomes, Martin J., jt. ed. see Johnson, J. H.

Loomie, Albert J. Spain & the Early Stuarts, 1585-1655. (Variorum Collected Studies: Vol. CS522). 304p. 1996. 97.95 (*0-86078-576-9*, Pub. by Variorum) Ashgate Pub Co.

— The Spanish Elizabethans: The English Exiles at the Court of Philip II. LC 63-14407. 293p. reprint ed. pap. 90.90 (*0-7837-0453-4*, 204077600018) Bks Demand.

Loomie, Albert J., ed. English Polemics at the Spanish Court: Joseph Creswell's "Letter to the Ambassador from England": The English & Spanish Texts of 1606. LC 93-22673. xi, 210p. (C). 1993. 25.00 (*0-8232-1446-X*) Fordham.

Loomie, Albert J., ed. see Finet, John.

Loomis. Contemporary Congress. 2nd ed. LC 97-65174. 212p. 1997. pap. text 21.95 (*0-312-15395-3*) St Martin.

— Contemporary Congress. 2nd ed. LC 97-65174. 1997. text 45.00 (*0-312-17636-8*) St Martin.

***Loomis.** Contemporary Congress. 3rd ed. 1999. pap. text 21.95 (*0-312-20861-8*) St Martin.

***Loomis, Alan, et al.** Offramp 7: Detours & Dialogues. (Illus.). 112p. 2000. pap. 24.95 (*1-56898-222-4*) Princeton Arch.

Loomis, Albertine. Grapes of Canaan: Hawaii, 1820. LC 97-48692. xvi, 334p. 1999. reprint ed. pap. 19.95 (*1-881987-12-4*) Ox Bow.

Loomis, Andrew. Drawing the Head, Vol. 2. (How to Draw & Paint Ser.). (Illus.). 32p. (Orig.). 1989. pap. 6.95 (*1-56010-010-9*, HT197) W Foster Pub.

— Figures in Action. (How to Draw & Paint Ser.). (Illus.). 32p. (Orig.). 1989. pap. 6.95 (*1-56010-009-5*, HT191) W Foster Pub.

Loomis, Ann B. Write from the Start: Discover Your Writing Potential Through the Power of Psychological Type. LC 99-35262. 170p. 1999. pap. 19.95 (*0-935652-49-3*) Ctr Applications Psych.

Loomis, Arthur K. The Techniques of Estimating School Equipment Costs. LC 70-177010. (Columbia University. Teachers College. Contributions to Education Ser.: No. 208). reprint ed. 37.50 (*0-404-55208-0*) AMS Pr.

Loomis, Bardett A., jt. auth. see Cigler, Allan J.

Loomis, Bob & Kadash, Kathy. Reining: The Art of Performance in Horses. (Illus.). 240p. 1990. write for info. (*0-9625898-8-8*) EquiMedia.

Loomis, Burdett A. Time, Politics, & Policies: A Legislative Year. LC 93-29050. (Studies in Government & Public Policy). 200p. 1994. 29.95 (*0-7006-0621-1*); pap. 14.95 (*0-7006-0622-X*) U Pr of KS.

Loomis, Burdett A., jt. auth. see Cigler, Allan J.

Loomis, Charles B. Cheerful Americans. LC 73-86150. (Short Story Index Reprint Ser.). 1977. 21.95 (*0-8369-3054-1*) Ayer.

— Four-Masted Cat-Boat & Other Truthful Tales. LC 73-110206. (Short Story Index Reprint Ser.). 1977. 19.95 (*0-8369-3357-5*) Ayer.

— More Cheerful Americans. LC 72-101817. (Short Story Index Reprint Ser.). 1977. 20.95 (*0-8369-3205-6*) Ayer.

Loomis, Chauncey C. Weird & Tragic Shores: The Story of Charles Francis Hall, Explorer. LC 90-21280. (Illus.). xii, 403p. 1991. reprint ed. pap. 12.95 (*0-8032-7937-X*, Bison Books) U of Nebr Pr.

***Loomis, Chauncey C.** Weird & Tragic Shores: The Story of Charles Francis Hall, Explorer, Vol. 1. Krakauer, Jon, ed. LC 99-41614. (Modern Library Exploration Ser.). 2000. pap. 14.95 (*0-375-75525-X*) Modern Lib NY.

Loomis, Christine. Across America, I Love You. LC 99-39075. (Illus.). 32p. (J). 2000. lib. bdg. 16.49 (*0-7868-2314-3*, Pub. by Hyprn Child) Time Warner.

— Across America, I Love You. LC 99-39075. Vol. 1. (Illus.). 32p. (J). (ps-3). 2000. 15.99 (*0-7868-0366-5*, Pub. by Hyprn Child) Time Warner.

— Astro Bunnies. LC 97-6893. (Illus.). (J). 1998. 15.99 (*0-399-23175-7*, G P Putnam) Peng Put Young Read.

— At the Laundromat. LC 93-10884. (Illus.). (J). 1993. 14.95 (*0-590-72830-X*); pap. 4.95 (*0-590-49488-0*) Scholastic Inc.

— At the Library. LC 93-10882. (Illus.). (J). 1994. 14.95 (*0-590-72831-8*); pap. 4.95 (*0-590-49489-9*) Scholastic Inc.

— At the Mall. (Illus.). (J). 1994. 14.95 (*0-590-72832-6*); pap. 4.95 (*0-590-49490-2*) Scholastic Inc.

— Cowboy Bunnies. LC 96-43057. (Illus.). 32p. (J). (ps-2). 1997. 15.95 (*0-399-22625-7*, G P Putnam) Peng Put Young Read.

***Loomis, Christine.** Cowboy Bunnies. (Illus.). 32p. (J). (ps-3). 2000. pap. 5.99 (*0-698-11831-6*, PuffinBks) Peng Put Young Read.

— Cowboy Bunnies. (Illus.). (J). 2000. 11.44 (*0-606-18397-3*) Turtleback.

Loomis, Christine. The Hippo Hop. LC 94-31308. (Illus.). 32p. (J). (ps-3). 1995. 14.95 (*0-395-69702-6*) HM.

— In the Diner. (Illus.). 32p. (J). (ps-2). 1994. 14.95 (*0-590-46716-6*, Scholastic Hardcover) Scholastic Inc.

— One Cow Coughs: A Counting Book for the Sick & Miserable. LC 93-1836. (Illus.). 32p. (J). (ps-2). 1994. 14.95 (*0-395-67899-4*) Ticknor & Flds Bks Yng Read.

— Rush Hour. LC 94-47192. (Illus.). 32p. (J). (ps-3). 1996. 15.95 (*0-395-69129-X*) HM.

— Simplify Family Travel: Less-Stress Solutions for Trouble-Free Travel. LC 97-53242. (Simpler Life Ser.). (Illus.). 144p. 1998. 17.95 (*0-7621-0065-6*, Pub. by RD Assn) Penguin Putnam.

Loomis, Courtland, jt. auth. see Fink, Kathleen M.

Loomis, David. Combat Zoning: Military Land Use Planning in Nevada. LC 92-2838. (Illus.). 168p. (C). 1993. 24.95 (*0-87417-187-3*) U of Nev Pr.

***Loomis, David G. & Taylor, Lester D.** The Future of the Telecommunications Industry: Forecasting & Demand Analysis. LC 99-46057. (Topics in Regulatory Economics & Policy Ser.). 1999. write for info. (*0-7923-8667-1*) Kluwer Academic.

Loomis, Debbie. Best of Friends. Hood, W. Edmund, ed. (Illus.). (J). 1996. pap. 3.00 (*0-9647539-4-4*) QDP Pubng.

Loomis, E. The Descendants (by the Female Branches) of Joseph Loomis, Who Came from Braintree, England in 1638, & Settled in Windsor, Connecticut, in 1639, 2 vols. in 1, Vol. 1. 1132p. 1989. reprint ed. pap. 149.00 (*0-8328-0786-9*); reprint ed. lib. bdg. 159.00 (*0-8328-0785-0*) Higginson Bk Co.

Loomis, Edward. Superstrings: Poems. LC 94-5848. (Orig.). 1994. pap. 8.95 (*0-9639443-0-4*) Grafx Bks.

Loomis, Elias. The Recent Progress of Astronomy: Especially in the United States. Cohen, I. Bernard, ed. LC 79-7972. (Three Centuries of Science in America Ser.). 1980. reprint ed. lib. bdg. 23.95 (*0-405-12554-2*) Ayer.

Loomis, Ernest. Practical Occultism. 73p. 1996. reprint ed. spiral bd. 10.00 (*0-7873-0569-3*) Hlth Research.

Loomis, Evarts G. Amy: A Search for the Treasure Within. LC 85-73540. (Illus.). 144p. (Orig.). 1986. pap. 5.50 (*0-87516-564-8*) DeVorss.

Loomis, Evarts G., compiled by. To Self Be True: The Search Within. 144p. (Orig.). 1991. pap. 8.00 (*0-9630266-0-7*) Friendly Hills.

Loomis, F. A., jt. auth. see Rowland, Mary C.

Loomis, Farnsworth W. God Within. (Illus.). 1968. 7.95 (*0-8079-0122-9*) October.

Loomis, Frank F., 3rd. How to Improve Your Relationships, Dramatically: Methods That Really Work! (Illus.). 168p. 2000. pap. 17.95 (*0-9672089-0-4*) Glenn Pubg.

Loomis, Frank F. Is It Antique Yet? LC 97-33985. 286p. 1997. pap. text 16.95 (*1-57090-034-5*) Alexander Dist.

***Loomis, Frederic M.** Miner, Preacher, Doctor, Teacher: A Turn-of-the-19th-Century Odyssey from Ann Arbor, Michigan to Ketchikan, Alaska, to a Pioneering Medical Career in Oakland, California. (Illus.). 128p. 2000. pap. 19.50 (*0-9625429-9-7*, Pub. by Hardscratch Pr) Partners-West.

Loomis, George A., Jr., jt. auth. see Caswell, Lucy S.

Loomis, Harvey, ed. see Chambers, Nancy K., et al.

Loomis, Howard F. Enzymes: The Key to Health. LC 99-17910. 1999. pap. 24.95 (*0-9663436-2-X*) Grote Publ.

Loomis, J. Paul. Campfires in the Rain. 202p. 1979. 15.00 (*0-317-59458-3*) G K Westgard.

— Up Saskatchewan Way: An Anthology of Short Stories. (Illus.). 152p. 1985. 15.00 (*0-317-59459-1*) G K Westgard.

Loomis, James P., ed. High Speed Commercial Flight: From Inquiry to Action. LC 88-35013. (Proceedings of the Second High Speed Commercial Flight Symposium Ser.). 224p. 1989. 37.50 (*0-935470-49-2*) Battelle.

— High Speed Commercial Flight - the Coming Era: Proceedings of the First High Speed Commercial Flight Symposium, Oct. 1986. LC 86-32153. (Illus.). 288p. 1987. 27.50 (*0-935470-37-9*) Battelle.

Loomis, Jeffrey B. Dayspring in Darkness: Sacrament in Hopkins. LC 87-47819. 224p. 1988. 36.50 (*0-8387-5138-5*) Bucknell U Pr.

Loomis, Jennifer A. A Duck in a Tree. (Illus.). 40p. (J). (gr. 1-5). 1996. 18.95 (*0-88045-136-X*) Stemmer Hse.

Loomis, Jim. All Aboard: The Complete North American Train Travel Guide. 2nd rev. ed. LC 97-37108. 432p. 1998. per. 16.00 (*0-7615-1087-7*) Prima Pub.

Loomis, John A. Revolution of Forms: Cuba's Forgotten Art Schools. LC 98-25831. (Illus.). 200p. 1999. pap. 27.50 (*1-56898-157-0*) Princeton Arch.

Loomis, John B. Integrated Public Lands Management: Principles & Applications to National Forests, Parks, Wildlife Refuges, & BLM Lands. LC 93-17218. 474p. 1993. 60.00 (*0-231-08006-9*) Col U Pr.

Loomis, John B. & Walsh, Richard G. Recreation Economic Decisions: Comparing Benefits & Costs. 2nd rev. ed. LC 97-60788. 462p. 1997. text 41.95 (*0-910251-89-4*, ECO93) Venture Pub PA.

Loomis, Jon. Vanitas Motel. LC 97-75694. (Field Poetry Ser.: Vol. 6). 66p. 1998. pap. 12.95 (*0-932440-81-9*) Oberlin Coll Pr.

Loomis, Julia. Monarch Notes on Virgil's Aeneid & Other Works. (Orig.). (C). 4.95 (*0-671-00509-X*, Arco) Macmillan Gen Ref.

Loomis, Laura H. & Loomis, Roger S., eds. Medieval Romances. LC 57-11169. (Modern Library College Editions). 426p. (C). 1965. pap. 8.44 (*0-07-553650-1*, 30970) McGraw.

Loomis, Linda, tr. see Mullican, Judy.

Loomis, Linda, tr. see Smith, Beth Esh.

Loomis, Linn. Here & Now - Ohio's Canals: The Background of Ohio's Canal System. 5th ed. (Illus.). 73p. 1991. reprint ed. pap. 12.95 (*0-9673613-0-3*) L Loomis.

— Here & Now - Ohio's Canals: The Sandy & Beaver Canal. (Illus.). 135p. 1994. pap. 22.95 (*0-9673613-1-1*) L Loomis.

Loomis, Louise Ropes, jt. auth. see Shotwell, James T.

Loomis, Lynn H. Calculus. LC 81-14937. (Mathematics Ser.). (Illus.). 1000p. 1982. student ed. write for info. (*0-201-05046-3*) Addison-Wesley.

— The Lattice Theoretic Background of the Dimension Theory of Operator Algebras. LC 52-42839. (Memoirs Ser.: No. 1/18). 36p. 1972. pap. 17.00 (*0-8218-1218-1*, MEMO/1/18) Am Math.

— The Lattice Theoretic Background of the Dimension Theory of Operator Algebras. LC QA0003.A57. (Memoirs of the American Mathematical Society Ser.: No. 18). 42p. reprint ed. pap. 30.00 (*0-7837-5925-8*, 204572400007) Bks Demand.

Loomis, Lynn H. & Sternberg, Shlomo. Advanced Calculus. 2nd rev. ed. (Math Ser.). 592p. 1989. 62.50 (*0-86720-122-3*) Jones & Bartlett.

Loomis, Lynne, jt. auth. see Malmuth, Mason.

Loomis, Lynne, ed. see Malmuth, Mason.

Loomis, Lynne, ed. see Zee, Ray.

Loomis, M. Clarifying the Economics of War & Peace: Why the United States Must Fight in Iraq & the Middle East. 1991. lib. bdg. 75.00 (*0-8490-4060-4*) Gordon Pr.

Loomis, Mary. Object Databases in Practice. LC 97-40480. 336p. (C). 1997. 53.00 (*0-13-899725-X*) P-H.

Loomis, Mary E. Dancing the Wheel of Psychological Types. LC 90-25469. (Illus.). 128p. (Orig.). 1991. pap. 17.95 (*0-933029-49-7*) Chiron Pubns.

Loomis, Mary E. Her Father's Daughter: When Women Succeed in a Man's World. LC 94-40574. 112p. (Orig.). 1995. pap. 14.95 (*0-933029-88-8*) Chiron Pubns.

Loomis, Mary P. God's Pencil: Survival Poetry for Today's World. LC 98-67169. x, 70p. 1998. pap. 9.95 (*0-9665608-4-1*, 6340) Mustard Seed MD.

Loomis, Mildred. Clarifying the Economics of Peace. 1971. 250.00 (*0-87700-142-1*) Revisionist Pr.

Loomis, Mildred J. Alternative Americas. LC 81-19775. 175p. 1982. 12.50 (*0-87663-375-0*, Pub. by Universe) St Martin.

— Alternative Americas. LC 81-19775. 175p. 1982. pap. 7.95 (*0-87663-567-2*, Pub. by Universe) St Martin.

Loomis, Noel M. Heading West: Western Stories. Pronzini, Bill, ed. LC 99-41706. 1999. 19.95 (*0-7862-1844-4*) Mac Lib Ref.

***Loomis, Noel M.** Rim of the Caprock. 2000. 19.95 (*1-57490-273-3*, Sagebrush LP West) T T Beeler.

***Loomis, Noel M. & Pronzini, Bill.** Heading West: Western Stories. LC 00-40787. 2000. write for info. (*0-7838-9133-4*, G K Hall & Co) Mac Lib Ref.

Loomis, Patricia. Signposts. Muller, Kathleen, ed. (Illus.). 97p. 1982. 19.95 (*0-914139-06-1*) Hist San Jose.

— Signposts II. (Illus.). 104p. 1985. 19.95 (*0-914139-02-9*) Hist San Jose.

Loomis, R. S. & Connor, D. J. Crop Ecology: Productivity & Management in Agricultural Systems. (Illus.). 552p. (C). 1992. pap. text 47.95 (*0-521-38776-0*) Cambridge U Pr.

Loomis, Rich. Starweb Rulebook. 1988. 2.00 (*0-940244-76-4*) Flying Buffalo.

Loomis, Richard M., tr. Dafydd ap Gwilym: The Poems. LC 81-16968. (Medieval & Renaissance Texts & Studies: Vol. 9). (Illus.). 352p. 1982. 24.00 (*0-86698-015-6*, MR9) MRTS.

Loomis, Richard M. & Johnston, Dafydd, trs. Medieval Welsh Poems: An Anthology. 240p. 1992. pap. 9.95 (*0-86698-102-0*, P8) Pegasus Pr.

Loomis, Rick. Buffalo Castle. (Illus.). 1982. 3.00 (*0-940244-01-2*) Flying Buffalo.

— Heroic Fantasy Rulebook. 1982. 2.00 (*0-940244-77-2*) Flying Buffalo.

— Starweb - Heroic Fantasy Set. 1988. 5.00 (*0-940244-79-9*) Flying Buffalo.

Loomis, Rick, ed. see Arneson, Dave.

Loomis, Rick, ed. see O'Connor, Paul.

Loomis, Rick, ed. see Wykle, Debora & Stackpole, Michael A.

Loomis, Roger S. Celtic Myth & Arthurian Romance. 371p. 1997. pap. 16.95 (*0-89733-436-1*) Academy Chi Pubs.

— Celtic Myth & Arthurian Romance. LC 67-31638. (Arthurian Legend & Literature Ser.: No. 1). 1969. reprint ed. lib. bdg. 75.00 (*0-8383-0586-5*) M S G Haskell Hse.

— The Grail: From Celtic Myth to Christian Symbol. (Illus.). 304p. 1991. pap. text 12.95 (*0-691-02075-2*, Pub. by Princeton U Pr) Cal Prin Full Svc.

Loomis, Roger S. & Wells, Henry W., eds. Representative Medieval & Tudor Plays. LC 77-111109. (Play Anthology Reprint Ser.). 1977. 24.95 (*0-8369-8202-9*) Ayer.

Loomis, Roger S., jt. ed. see Loomis, Laura H.

Loomis, Sabra. Rosetree. LC 88-31561. 72p. (Orig.). 1989. pap. 9.95 (*0-914086-85-5*) Alice James Bks.

Loomis, Samuel L. Modern Cities & Their Religious Problems. LC 73-112558. (Rise of Urban America Ser.). 1976. reprint ed. 25.95 (*0-405-02464-9*) Ayer.

Loomis, Scott B., jt. auth. see Nash, Marcus.

***Loomis, Stacey, et al.** Artists & Writers Colonies. 2nd rev. ed. 2000. pap. 16.95 (*0-936085-62-2*) Blue Heron OR.

Loomis, Susan H. Clambakes & Fish Fries. LC 94-2420. (Illus.). 320p. 1994. pap. 10.95 (*1-56305-295-4*, 3295) Workman Pub.

— Farmhouse Cookbook. LC 91-50390. (Illus.). 528p. (Orig.). 1991. 22.95 (*1-56305-125-7*, 3125); pap. 14.95 (*0-89480-772-2*, 1772) Workman Pub.

— French Farmhouse Cookbook. LC 91-50390. (Illus.). 528p. 1996. 25.95 (*0-7611-0624-3*, 10624); pap. 15.95 (*1-56305-488-4*, 3488) Workman Pub.

— The Great American Seafood Cookbook. LC 87-40644. (Illus.). 320p. 1988. pap. 13.95 (*0-89480-578-9*, 1578) Workman Pub.

***Loomis, Susan H.** Italian Farmhouse Cookbook. LC 99-53776. (Farmhouse Cookbook Ser.). 560p. 1999. 28.95 (*0-7611-1791-1*); pap. 16.95 (*0-7611-0527-1*) Workman Pub.

Loomis, Susan Herrmann, jt. auth. see La\Maveleine Chefs.

Loomis, Ted A. & Hayes, A. Wallace. Essentials of Toxicology. 4th ed. LC 78-9005. (Illus.). 282p. 1996. text 35.00 (*0-12-455625-6*) Acad Pr.

Loomis, William T. Wages, Welfare Costs & Inflation in Classical Athens. LC 98-11372. 424p. 1999. text 42.50 (*0-472-10803-4*, 10803) U of Mich Pr.

Looms, J. S. Insulators for High Voltages. (Power Ser.: No. 7). 288p. 1988. 119.00 (*0-86341-116-9*, PO007) INSPEC Inc.

Loon, A. J. Van, see Brodzikowski, K. & Van Loon, A. J.

Loon, Bert. When We Meet . . . We Eat: When We Eat . . . We Plan the Next Meal. (Illus.). 238p. 1998. ring bd. 22.00 (*0-9663300-0-5*) Assoc Cnsltants.

Loon, Bert, jt. auth. see Lawrence, E.

Loon, Borin van, see Van Loon, Borin.

Loon, Boris Van, see Miller, Jonathan & Van Loon, Boris.

Loon, Dirk Van, see Van Loon, Dirk.

Loon, James van & Bontolotti, Paola. Echoes from the Edge. 226p. 1997. pap. 10.00 (*91-970984-5-0*, Pub. by Oxford Publng) Oxford Pub TX.

Loon, James Van, see Van Loon, James.

Loon, Joan Van, see Van Loon, Joan.

Loon, John Van, see Van Loon, Joan & Van Loon, John.

Loon, Jon C. Van, see Van Loon, Jon C.

Loon, Lesley, jt. auth. see Rosen, Myrna.

Loon, M. Van, see Liebowitz, Harold.

Loon, Maurits Van, see Matthiae, Paolo.

Loon, Michelle Van, see Van Loon, Michelle.

Loon, Paul J. Van, see Van Loon, Paul J.

Loon, Paul Van, see Van Loon, Paul.

Loon, Piet Van der, see Van der Loon, Piet.

Loon, Robin. Outbreak. 400p. (Orig.). 1996. pap. text 6.99 (*0-425-15396-7*) Berkley Pub.

Loonan, Elizabeth. Love Your Cat. 93p. 1994. write for info. (*1-57215-006-8*) World Pubns.

Looney. Agricultural Law: Principles & Cases. 2nd ed. 1993. pap. text, teacher ed. 18.75 (*0-07-038721-4*) McGraw.

Looney, Ben E. Beau Sejour: Watercolors of Louisiana Plantation Country. 1972. 19.95 (*0-87511-073-8*) Claitors.

— Drawings of the Vieux Carre: New Orleans French Quarter. 1976. 9.95 (*0-87511-074-6*) Claitors.

— Watercolors of Dixie. 1974. 20.00 (*0-87511-075-4*) Claitors.

***Looney, Brian B. & Falta, Ronald W.** Vadose Zone Science & Technology Solutions. LC 00-23080. 1500p. 2000. 95.00 incl. cd-rom (*1-57477-085-3*) Battelle.

An Asterisk (*) at the beginning of an entry indicates that the title is appearing for the first time.

Looney, C. & Castaing, J., eds. Intelligent Systems (ICIS-98), ISCA 7th International Conference, July 1-2, 1998, Melun, France: ICIS-98, July 1-2, 1998, Melun, FR. 246p. 1998. write for info. (*1-880843-24-2*) Int Soc Comp App.

Looney, Carl G. Pattern Recognition Using Neural Networks: Theory & Algorithms for Engineers & Scientists. LC 96-29042. (Illus.). 480p. (C). 1997. text 84.00 (*0-19-507920-5*) OUP.

Looney, Cornelia. All for the Love of a Child: A Memoir. Looney, Douglas S., ed. LC 97-1683. 96p. 1997. 5.95 (*1-57587-051-7*) Crane Hill AL.

Looney, Dennis. Compromising the Classics: Romance Epic Narrative in the Italian Renaissance. 244p. 1996. 39.95 (*0-8143-2600-5*) Wayne St U Pr.

Looney, Douglas S., ed. see Looney, Cornelia.

Looney, Dwight. Chinese Style, Vol. 1. (Cooking Together Ser.). 175p. 1995. ring bd. 19.50 (*0-9650310-0-4*) Rose & Rose.

Looney, George. Animals Housed in the Pleasure of Flesh: Poems. 1995. 24.00 (*1-878325-15-9*); pap. 10.00 (*1-878325-14-0*) Bluestem Press.

Looney, J. Anna, jt. auth. see Scheps, Walter.

Looney, J. Jefferson & Woodward, Ruth L. Princetonians, 1791-1794: A Biographical Dictionary. (Illus.). 586p. 1991. text 75.00 (*0-691-04772-3*, Pub. by Princeton U Pr) Cal Prin Full Svc.

Looney, J. Jefferson, ed. see Henry, James B. & Scharff, Christian H.

Looney, J. W. Business Management for Farmers. LC 80-67888. (Illus.). 739p. 1983. 42.00 (*0-932250-11-4*) Red Wing Busn.

Looney, J. W. & Uchtman, Donald L. Agricultural Law: Principles & Cases. 2nd ed. LC 93-1644. 1993. text. write for info. (*0-07-038720-6*) McGraw.

Looney, John. Alternative to Violence Workbook. deluxe ed. Bender, Danene M., ed. (Illus.). 372p. (C). 1995. wbk. ed. 25.00 (*0-9619819-4-6*) Peace Grows.

Looney, John & Bender, Danene M. The Media's Social Responsibility. (Illus.). 92p. (Orig.). 1986. pap. 4.00 (*0-9619819-0-3*) Peace Grows.

Looney, John G., ed. Chronic Mental Illness in Children & Adolescents. LC 87-1472. 267p. 1988. text 14.95 (*0-88048-236-2*, 8236) Am Psychiatric.

Looney, Kim, jt. auth. see Looney, Michael D.

Looney, Louisa P. Tennessee Sketches. (Short Story Index Reprint Ser.). 1977. reprint ed. 23.95 (*0-8369-4020-2*) Ayer.

Looney, Michael. General Chemistry. (C). 1995. pap. 21.28 (*1-56870-182-9*) RonJon Pub.

Looney, Michael D. & Looney, Kim. Southern Tailgating: Game Day Recipes & Traditions. LC 94-23210. (Illus.). 168p. (Orig.). 1994. pap. 12.95 (*0-9630700-9-6*, 641.5'78...dc20) Vision AL.

Looney, N. E., jt. ed. see Jackson, David.

Looney, N. E., jt. ed. see Webster, A. D.

Looney, Ralph. Haunted Highways: The Ghost Towns of New Mexico. LC 68-65623. (Illus.). 129p. 1979. reprint ed. pap. 17.95 (*0-8263-0506-7*) U of NM Pr.

— O'Keeffe & Me: A Treasured Friendship. (Illus.). 144p. 1995. 27.50 (*0-87081-406-0*) Univ Pr Colo.

— O'Keeffe & Me: A Treasured Friendship. (Illus.). 134p. 1997. pap. 18.95 (*0-87081-450-8*) Univ Pr Colo.

Looney, Robert. Economic Development in Saudi Arabia: Consequences of the Oil Price Decline. (Contemporary Studies in Economic & Financial Analysis: Vol. 66). 289p. 1990. 78.50 (*1-55938-153-1*) Jai Pr.

Looney, Robert E. Development Alternatives of Mexico: Beyond the 1980's. LC 82-11288. 268p. 1982. 49.95 (*0-275-90850-X*, C0850, Praeger Pubs) Greenwood.

— Economic Origins of the Iranian Revolution. LC 82-384. (Policy Studies on International Development). (Illus.). 320p. 1982. 80.00 (*0-08-025950-2*, L115, Pergamon Pr) Elsevier.

— Economic Policy-Making in Mexico: Factors Underlying the 1982 Crisis. LC 84-28739. (Duke Press Policy Studies). xviii, 309p. (C). 1985. text 54.95 (*0-8223-0557-7*) Duke.

— The Economics of Third World Defense Expenditures. LC 95-1539. (Contemporary Studies in Economic & Financial Analysis: Vol. 72). 1995. 78.50 (*1-55938-386-0*) Jai Pr.

— Industrial Development & Diversification of the Arabian Gulf Economies. LC 94-824. (Contemporary Studies in Economic & Financial Analysis: Vol. 70). 1994. 78.50 (*1-55938-384-4*) Jai Pr.

— Manpower Policies & Development in the Persian Gulf Region. LC 93-14137. 216p. 1994. 62.95 (*0-275-94217-1*, C4217, Praeger Pubs) Greenwood.

— The Pakistani Economy: Economic Growth & Structural Reform. LC 96-37731. 216p. 1997. 65.00 (*0-275-94737-8*, Praeger Pubs) Greenwood.

Looney, Robert F. Old Philadelphia in Early Photographs, 1839-1914: 215 Prints from the Collection of the Free Library of Philadelphia. LC 75-41688. (Illus.). 230p. 1976. pap. 14.95 (*0-486-23345-6*) Dover.

Looney, Sandra, et al, eds. The Prairie Frontier. (Illus.). 166p. (Orig.). 1984. pap. text 6.00 (*0-9604816-1-3*) Nordland Her Found.

Looney, Sandra, jt. ed. see Iluseboe, Arthur R.

Looney Tune Books Staff. Bugs & Daffy Play Wheel of Really, Really Good Luck: With Puppets. 1999. text 14.99 (*0-8289-1025-1*) Viking Penguin.

— Mission: Improbable. (Looney Tunes Ser.). 1999. text 12.99 (*0-8289-1026-X*) Viking Penguin.

Looney Tunes Books Staff. Hip! Hip! Hooray! With Puzzle Blocks. (Books & Puzzle Blocks Ser.). (J). 1999. text 10.99 (*0-8289-1027-8*) Viking Penguin.

— Looney Xylo-Tunes: Make Your Own Merry Melody Music. (Illus.). (J). 1999. 17.99 (*0-8289-1019-7*) Penguin Putnam.

Looney Tunes Staff. Baby Bugs' Bright Idea: Story Light Book. (J). 1999. text 10.99 (*0-8289-1022-7*) Viking Penguin.

— Baby Bugs Runs the Toy Factory. (J). 1999. text 6.99 (*0-8289-1023-5*) Viking Penguin.

— Baby Bugs's Wacky Dress-up. (Illus.). (J). 1997. pap. 7.99 (*0-8289-1001-4*, Pub. by Kensgtn Pub Corp) Penguin Putnam.

— Baby Daffy & the Hidden Treasure. (J). 1999. text 6.99 (*0-8289-1024-3*) Viking Penguin.

— Baby Tweety's Twinkling Rhymes: Story Bright Book. (J). (ps). 1999. text 10.99 (*0-8289-1021-9*) Viking Penguin.

— Bad Ol' Puddy-Tat. (Illus.). 24p. (J). (gr. k-5). 1999. text 9.99 (*0-8289-0998-9*) Viking Penguin.

— Coconut Cream Pie. 1999. text 12.99 (*0-8289-0996-2*) Viking Penguin.

— Fast & Furry-ous. 1999. text 9.99 (*0-8289-0997-0*) Viking Penguin.

***Loong, C-K, et al, eds.** Materials Research Using Cold Neutrons at Pulsed Neutron Sources: Argonne National Laboratory, USA 25 - 26 August 1997. 250p. 1999. 56.00 (*981-02-3748-0*) World Scientific Pub.

Loonin, Deanne, et al. Surviving Debt: A Guide for Consumers. 3rd rev. ed. LC 99-61226. 408p. 1999. pap. 17.00 (*1-881793-76-1*) Nat Consumer Law.

Loop, James, jt. auth. see Zaloga, Steven J.

Loop, Theo Van Der, see Van Der Loop, Theo.

Loope, Lloyd L., jt. auth. see Medeiros, Arthur C.

Looper. Bankers Guide to Personnel ADM. 1983. text 49.00 (*0-07-413135-4*) McGraw.

Looper, Don. Lament of the Cracker Cowboy: Rhymes & Reflections from the Florida Cattle Country. LC 98-94085. 168 p. 1998. write for info. (*0-7392-0004-6*) Morris Pubng.

Looper, Sandra, jt. auth. see Wyatt, Robert L., III.

Looper, Travis & Byron, George Gordon. Byron & the Bible: A Compendium of Biblical Usage in the Poetry of Lord Byron. LC 78-1518. 330p. 1978. 31.00 (*0-8108-1123-5*) Scarecrow.

Loor, F. & Roelants, G. E., eds. B & T Cells in Immune Recognition. LC 76-26913. (Illus.). 538p. reprint ed. pap. 166.80 (*0-8357-5935-0*, 203051100069) Bks Demand.

Loor, G. P. De, see De Loor, G. P., ed.

Loore, Camiel W. De, see De Loore, Camiel W.

Loore, Camiel W. De, see Conti, Peter S. & De Loore, Camiel W., eds.

Loore, Camiel W. De, see De Loore, Camiel W.

Loore, Camiel W. De, see Lamers, Henny G. & De Loore, Camiel W., eds.

Loori, John D. The Heart of Being: Moral & Ethical Teachings of Zen. Treace, Bonnie M. & Marchaj, Konrad R., eds. 208p. 1996. pap. 16.95 (*0-8048-3078-9*) Tuttle Pubng.

— Two Arrows Meeting in Mid-Air: The Zen Koan. LC 94-7737. (Library of Enlightenment). 288p. (Orig.). 1994. pap. 16.95 (*0-8048-3012-6*) Tuttle Pubng.

Loori, John D., jt. auth. see Maezumi, Hakuyu T.

***Loori, John Daido & Zen Mountain Monastery Staff.** Cave of Tigers. LC 00-22561. 1999. write for info. (*0-8348-0433-6*) Weatherhill.

Loos. Invasion & Resistance. (Australian National University Press Ser.). 1982. text 58.00 (*0-08-032922-5*, Pergamon Pr) Elsevier.

Loos, Adolf. Ornament & Crime: Selected Essays. Mitchell, Michael, tr. (Studies in Austrian Literature, Culture, & Thought). 204p. 1998. pap. 19.95 (*1-57241-046-9*) Ariadne CA.

Loos, Alfred C., jt. auth. see Dave, Raju S.

Loos, Amandus W., ed. Nature of Man. LC 69-18930. (Essay Index Reprint Ser.). 1977. 17.95 (*0-8369-1042-7*) Ayer.

— Religious Faith & World Culture. LC 71-128270. (Essay Index Reprint Ser.). 1977. 23.95 (*0-8369-1976-9*) Ayer.

Loos, Anita. "But Gentlemen Marry Brunettes" (Illus.). 248p. Date not set. reprint ed. pap. text 25.00 (*0-87556-857-2*) Saifer.

— Gentlemen Prefer Blondes. 1994. lib. bdg. 21.95 (*1-56849-512-9*) Buccaneer Bks.

— Gentlemen Prefer Blondes. 1958. 5.50 (*0-87129-412-5*, G13) Dramatic Pub.

— Gentlemen Prefer Blondes. LC 98-34385. (Illus.). 216p. 1998. pap. 10.95 (*0-87140-170-3*, Pub. by Liveright) Norton.

— Gentlemen Prefer Blondes: The Illuminating Diary of a Professional Lady; And, But Gentlemen Marry Brunettes. LC 98-15422. 352p. 1998. pap. 12.95 (*0-14-118069-2*) Penguin Putnam.

— Les Hommes Prefer les Blondes. (FRE.). 1982. pap. 10.95 (*0-7859-4171-1*) Fr & Eur.

— Mais Ils Epousent les Brunes. (FRE.). 192p. 1982. pap. 8.95 (*0-7859-4172-X*, 2070373967) Fr & Eur.

***Loos, Anita.** No Mother to Guide Her. (Humour Classics Ser.). (Illus.). 224p. 2000. 13.95 (*1-85375-366-1*, Pub. by Prion) Trafalgar.

Loos, Dorothy S., tr. Alfonsina Storni: Anthology of Poems. (SPA., Illus.). 200p. (Orig.). 1986. pap. 5.95 (*0-915597-31-4*) Amana Bks.

Loos, Dorothy S., tr. see De Queiroz, Rachel.

Loos, Eileen A. Schrottke, see Schrottke Loos, Eileen A.

Loos, Frank M. Research Foundations for Psychology & Behavior Sciences. (C). 1995. text 63.50 (*0-673-99481-3*) Addson-Wesley Educ.

Loos, Gregory P. Field Guide for International Health Project Planners & Managers. 80p. 1995. pap. 14.95 (*1-85756-159-7*) Paul & Co Pubs.

Loos, Jan-Baptist W. Modeling of Adsorption & Diffusion of Vapors in Zeolites. (Illus.). 211p. 1997. pap. 52.50 (*90-407-1533-5*, Pub. by Delft U Pr) Coronet Bks.

Loos, John, 3rd. Universal Love Tribe: Phase One. 1998. pap. write for info. (*1-57553-852-0*) Watermrk Pr.

***Loos, Pamela.** Elizabeth Cady Stanton: Woman Suffragist. (Illus.). 112p. 2000. 19.95 (*0-7910-5293-1*); pap. text 9.95 (*0-7910-5294-X*) Chelsea Hse.

Loos, Pamela. Maya Angelou: Author. LC 99-19890. (Overcoming Adversity Ser.). (Illus.). 128p. (YA). (gr. 4-7). 1999. pap. 9.95 (*0-7910-4947-7*) Chelsea Hse.

— Maya Angelou: Author. LC 99-19890. (Overcoming Adversity Ser.). (Illus.). 128p. (YA). (gr. 5 up). 1999. lib. bdg. 19.95 (*0-7910-4946-9*) Chelsea Hse.

Loos, Sigrun, jt. auth. see Breicha, Otto.

Loos, Victor, jt. auth. see Summerlin, Mary Lue.

Loos, W. S. De, see De Loos, W. S., ed.

Loos, Wiepke. On Country Roads & Fields: The Depiction of the 18th & 19th Century Landscape. LC 98-182980. 1998. pap. 50.00 (*90-6611-921-7*, Pub. by Lund Humphries) Antique Collect.

Loosdrecht, M. C. Van, see Van Loosdrecht, M. C., ed.

Loose, jt. auth. see Daws.

***Loose, Duane.** 3D Studio Max 3.0 Workshop. 512p. 2000. 34.99 (*0-7897-2343-3*) Hayden.

Loose, Frances F. Decimals & Percentages. (Illus.). 100p. (gr. 4-6). 1977. 12.00 (*0-87879-803-X*, Ann Arbor Div) Acad Therapy.

— Fractions: Teacher's Guide. 56p. 1973. 5.00 (*0-87879-797-1*, Ann Arbor Div) Acad Therapy.

— Fractions Bk. 2: Reusable Edition. (J). (gr. 4). 1973. student ed. 10.00 (*0-87879-795-5*, Ann Arbor Div) Acad Therapy.

— Fractions Bk. 2: Reusable Edition. (J). (gr. 4-6). 1973. student ed. 10.00 (*0-87879-796-3*, Ann Arbor Div) Acad Therapy.

— Metrics. (Illus.). 1975. teacher ed. 1.00 (*0-87879-802-1*, Ann Arbor Div) Acad Therapy.

— Metrics: Reusable Edition. (gr. 9-12). 1975. student ed. 6.50 (*0-87879-801-3*, Ann Arbor Div) Acad Therapy.

Loose, Gerhard. Ernst Junger. LC 74-4150. (Twayne's World Authors Ser.). 143p. (C). 1974. lib. bdg. 20.95 (*0-8057-2479-6*) Irvington.

Loose, Katherine R. House of Yost. 1993. reprint ed. lib. bdg. 89.00 (*0-7812-5485-X*) Rprt Serv.

Loose, Kenneth. Problem Solving Using Miranda. 224p. (C). 1995. spiral bd. 27.95 (*0-7872-1258-X*) Kendall-Hunt.

Loose Leaf Reference Services Staff. Clinical Dentistry, 5 vols. Hardin, ed. 1988. ring bd. 395.00 (*0-06-148003-7*) Lppncott W & W.

— Clinical Dentistry, 5 vols. rev. ed. Hardin, ed. 1988. 60.00 (*0-686-86014-4*) Lppncott W & W.

— Clinical Dermatology, 4 vols. Demis, D. Joseph et al, eds. ring bd. 450.00 (*0-06-148004-5*) Lppncott W & W.

— Clinical Dermatology, 4 vols. rev. ed. Demis, D. Joseph et al, eds. 75.00 (*0-686-86015-2*) Lppncott W & W.

— Duane's Clinical Ophthalmology, 5 vols. & index. Tasman, William S. et al, eds. (Illus.). ring bd. 495.00 (*0-06-148007-X*); 80.00 (*0-685-71848-4*) Lppncott W & W.

— Otolaryngology, 5 vols. English, Gerald M., ed. ring bd. 525.00 (*0-06-148010-X*) Lppncott W & W.

— Otolaryngology, 5 vols. rev. ed. English, Gerald M., ed. 85.00 (*0-686-86019-5*) Lppncott W & W.

Loose Leaf Reference Services Staff, et al. Gynecology & Obstetrics: Loose Leaf: New Page Service, 6 vols. Buchsbaum, Herbert J. et al, eds. 80.00 (*0-686-86017-9*) Lppncott W & W.

— Gynecology & Obstetrics: Loose Leaf: New Page Service, 6 vols., Set. Buchsbaum, Herbert J. et al, eds. ring bd. 495.00 (*0-06-148008-8*) Lppncott W & W.

Loose-Mitchell, David S., jt. auth. see Rosenfeld, Gary C.

Loose, Peter. Loose on Liquidators: The Role of a Liquidator in a Voluntary Winding-Up. xxiii, 216p. 1972. 18.95 (*0-85308-023-2*) W S Hein.

Loose-Schrantz, Sandy. Bongo Is a Happy Dog. LC 97-90923. (Illus.). 24p. (J). (ps-2). 1997. 14.95 (*0-9660244-0-0*) Flying Dog Prodns.

Loose, Warren. Bodie Bonanza. (Illus.). 246p. 1971. pap. 12.95 (*0-913814-32-6*) Nevada Pubns.

Looseleaf, Victoria. Leonardo. LC 98-38013. 1998. pap. 8.95 (*0-345-43222-3*) Ballantine Pub Grp.

Looseley, David L. The Politics of Fun: Cultural Policy & Debate in Contemporary France. 256p. 1995. 49.50 (*1-85973-013-2*); pap. 19.50 (*1-85973-153-8*, Pub. by Berg Pubs) MBIPubg.

***Loosemore, Sandra, et al.** The GNU C Library Reference Manual: For Version 2, 2 vols., Set. 1166p. 1999. per. 60.00 (*1-882114-54-X*) Free Software.

Loosen, Peter T., jt. ed. see Nemeroff, Charles B.

***Looser, Devoney.** British Women Writers & the Writing of History, 1670-1820. LC 00-8475. 320p. 2000. 45.00 (*0-8018-6448-8*) Johns Hopkins.

Looser, Devoney & Kaplan, E. Ann. Generations: Academic Feminists in Dialogue. LC 97-20528. 1997. pap. 19.95 (*0-8166-2899-8*) U of Minn Pr.

***Looser, Ueli & Schlapfer, Bruna.** New Venture Adventure: Succeed with Professional Business Planning. 240p. 2001. 29.95 (*1-58799-003-2*) Texere.

Loosley, Chris & Douglas, Frank. High-Performance Client-Server. LC 97-21747. 784p. 1997. pap. 44.99 (*0-471-16269-8*) Wiley.

Loosley, Ernest. When the Church Was Young. LC 88-63264. 92p. (Orig.). 1989. pap. 14.95 (*0-940232-32-4*) Seedsowers.

Loosmore, Judy. Reflections on Relaxation. (Life Line Ser.). (Illus.). 158p. (Orig.). 1994. pap. 16.95 (*1-55059-081-2*) Temeron Bks.

***Looss, Charlotte B.** Libanesische Immigranten in Ghana: Selbstwahrnehmungen und Rollenzuschreibungen in Autobiographischen Schriften. (Illus.). 193p. 1999. 39.95 (*3-631-34437-6*) P Lang Pubng.

Lootens, Douglas J., ed. see Symposium on Environmental Management for the 1990.

Lootens, Tricia. Lost Saints: Gender & Victorian Literary Canonization. (Victorian Literature & Culture Ser.). 288p. (C). 1996. text 35.00 (*0-8139-1652-6*) U Pr of Va.

Loots, Cheryl, jt. auth. see De Villiers Van Wisen, Louis.

***Loots, Johan.** Sea Kayaking. LC 00-39490. (Illus.). 2000. pap. 16.95 (*0-8117-2921-4*) Stackpole.

Loots, Philip C. Construction Law & Related Issues. 1213p. 1995. 194.00 (*0-7021-2924-0*, Pub. by Juta & Co) Gaunt.

— Engineering & Construction. 466p. 1985. 78.00 (*0-7021-1563-0*, Pub. by Juta & Co) Gaunt.

***Lootsma, Bart.** Dutch Architecture: The New Wave. (Illus.). 160p. 1999. 24.95 (*2-7450-0081-0*) Telleri Edit.

— SuperDutch: New Architecture in the Netherlands. (Illus.). 256p. 2000. 45.00 (*1-56898-239-9*) Princeton Arch.

Lootsma, Freerk A. Fuzzy Logic for Planning & Decision Making. LC 97-23864. (Applied Optimization Ser.: No. 8). 195p. 1997. text 124.00 (*0-7923-4681-5*) Kluwer Academic.

— Multi-criteria Decision Analysis Via Ratio & Difference Judgement. LC 99-14204. (Applied Optimization Ser.). 1999. write for info. (*0-7923-5669-1*) Kluwer Academic.

Loovis, E. Michael & Ersing, Walter F. Assessing & Programming Gross Motor Development for Children. 2nd ed. 1979. pap. text 12.95 (*0-89917-495-7*) Tichenor Pub.

Looy, Anne De, see Beck, Mervyn.

Looy, Anne De, see Corless, Barrie.

Looy, Mark, jt. auth. see Sterling, Robert M.

Looy, Van, see Van Looy, ed.

Looye, Johanna & Uphoff, Norman. Local Institutional Development for Non-Agricultural Enterprise. (Special Series on Local Institutional Development: No. 6). 46p. (Orig.). (C). 1985. pap. text 7.50 (*0-86731-113-4*) Cornell CIS RDC.

Looze, D. P., jt. auth. see Freudenberg, J. S.

Lopach, James J., et al. Tribal Government Today: Politics on Montana Indian Reservations. rev. ed. LC 97-49886. 286p. 1998. 32.50 (*0-87081-477-X*) Univ Pr Colo.

Lopata, Cynthia, jt. auth. see McClure, Charles R.

Lopata, Edwin L. Local Aid to Railroads in Missouri. Bruchey, Stuart, ed. LC 80-1327. (Railroads Ser.). (Illus.). 1981. reprint ed. lib. bdg. 18.95 (*0-405-13801-6*) Ayer.

Lopata, Helen Z. Circles & Settings: Role Changes of American Women. LC 93-14927. (SUNY Series in Gender & Society). 325p. (C). 1994. text 64.50 (*0-7914-1767-0*); pap. text 21.95 (*0-7914-1768-9*) State U NY Pr.

Lopata, Helena Z. City Women, Vol. 2. LC 84-15933. 576p. 1985. 75.00 (*0-275-90190-4*, C01902, Praeger Pubs) Greenwood.

— Current Widowhood: Myths & Realities. LC 95-35750. (Understanding Families Ser.: Vol. 4). 264p. 1995. 48.00 (*0-8039-7395-0*); pap. 22.95 (*0-8039-7396-9*) Sage.

— Occupation: Housewife. LC 80-23658. (Illus.). 387p. 1980. reprint ed. lib. bdg. 69.50 (*0-313-22697-0*, LOOH, Greenwood Pr) Greenwood.

— Widowhood in an American City. 369p. 1973. pap. text 24.95 (*0-87073-091-6*) Transaction Pubs.

Lopata, Helena Z., ed. Current Research on Occupations & Professions, Vol. 4. 282p. 1987. 73.25 (*0-89232-561-5*) Jai Pr.

— Current Research on Occupations & Professions, Vol. 5. (Current Research on Occupations & Professions Ser.). 187p. 1990. 73.25 (*0-89232-904-1*) Jai Pr.

— Current Research on Occupations & Professions, Vol. 6. 300p. 1991. 73.25 (*1-55938-236-8*) Jai Pr.

— Current Research on Occupations & Professions, Vol. 7. 252p. 1992. 73.25 (*1-55938-528-6*) Jai Pr.

— Current Research on Occupations & Professions, Vol. 9. 1996. 73.25 (*1-55938-877-3*) Jai Pr.

— Current Research on Occupations & Professions, Vol. 10. 1998. 73.25 (*0-7623-0034-5*) Jai Pr.

— Current Research on Occupations & Professions: Occupations & Professions in Culture Industries, Vol. 8. (Current Research on Occupations & Professions Ser.). 307p. 1994. 73.25 (*1-55938-588-X*) Jai Pr.

— Widows, Vol. I: The Middle East, Asia, & the Pacific. LC 87-5410. xiii, 258p. (C). 1987. pap. text 22.95 (*0-8223-0768-5*) Duke.

— Widows, Vol. II: North America. LC 87-5410. xii, 313p. (C). 1987. text 59.95 (*0-8223-0724-3*); pap. text 22.95 (*0-8223-0770-7*) Duke.

Lopata, Helena Z. & Erdmans, Mary. Polish Americans. LC 92-41516. 376p. (C). 1993. text 39.95 (*1-56000-100-3*) Transaction Pubs.

Lopata, Helena Z. & Maines, David R., eds. Friendship: In Context. LC 90-23155. 288p. 1991. pap. 25.75 (*1-55938-325-9*) Jai Pr.

Lopata, Helena Z., et al. City Women in America: Work, Jobs, Occupations, Careers. LC 84-15933. 316p. 1984. 33.95 (*0-275-91218-3*, C12181, Praeger Pubs) Greenwood.

Lopate, Carol. Women in Medicine. LC 68-19526. (Josiah Macy Foundation Ser.). (Illus.). 204p. 1968. 32.50 (*0-8018-0391-8*) Johns Hopkins.

Lopate, Phillip. Anchor Essay Annual, 1998. annuals 448p. 1998. pap. 11.95 (*0-385-48414-3*, Anchor NY) Doubleday.

— The Anchor Essay Annual, 1997: The Best of 1997. 432p. 1997. pap. 11.00 (*0-385-48413-5*, Anchor NY) Doubleday.

— Bridge of Dreams: The Rebirth of the Brooklyn Bridge. LC 99-16548. (Illus.). 120p. 1999. 45.00 (*1-55595-172-4*, Pub. by Hudson Hills); pap. 25.00 (*1-55595-173-2*, Pub. by Hudson Hills) Natl Bk Netwk.

— Lopate Essays. 1999. pap. 18.25 (*0-670-81435-0*) Viking Penguin.

L

An Asterisk (*) at the beginning of an entry indicates that the title is appearing for the first time.

— The Ordering Mirror: Readers & Contexts. LC 93-2065. (Ben Belitt Lectureships Ser.). xxiii, 304p. 1993. 30.00 (*0-8232-1515-6*) Fordham.
— Portrait of My Body. 240p. 1997. pap. 12.95 (*0-385-48377-5*, Anchor NY) Doubleday.
— Totally, Tenderly, Tragically: Essays & Criticism from a Lifelong Love Affair with the Movies. 1998. write for info. (*0-385-49249-9*) Doubleday.
— Totally, Tenderly, Tragically: Essays & Criticism from a Lifelong Love Affair with the Movies. LC 98-6829. 400p. 1998. pap. 12.95 (*0-385-49250-2*) Doubleday.
***Lopate, Phillip.** Writing New York: A Literary Anthology. 1088p. 2000. reprint ed. per. 22.95 (*0-671-04235-1*, WSP) PB.
Lopate, Phillip, ed. Journal of a Living Experiment. LC 79-19199. 239p. (Orig.). 1979. pap. 14.95 (*0-915924-09-9*) Tchrs & Writers Coll.
— Writing New York: A Literary Anthology. LC 98-19332. 1998. 40.00 (*1-883011-62-0*, Pub. by Library of America) Penguin Putnam.
Lopate, Phillip, intro. The Art of the Essay 1999. LC 99-28844. 416p. 1999. pap. 11.95 (*0-385-48415-1*, Anchor NY) Doubleday.
— The Art of the Personal Essay: An Anthology from the Classical Era to the Present. 832p. 1997. pap. 17.95 (*0-385-42339-X*, Anchor NY) Doubleday.
Lopategui, Edgar. El Ser Humano y la Salud. (SPA.). 430p. 1995. pap. write for info. (*0-929441-20-6*) Pubns Puertorriquenas.
Lopategui, Miren, text. Presents: A Gift Record Book. (Illus.). 142p. 1991. 14.95 (*0-948751-03-7*) Interlink Pub.
Lopater, Sanford, jt. auth. see Hahn, John F.
Lopatin. Political Unions Popular Politics of the Great Reform Act of 1832. LC 98-20136. 256p. 1999. text 65.00 (*0-312-21564-9*) St Martin.
Lopatin, A. K., jt. auth. see Mitropolaky, Yu. A.
Lopatin, Judy. Modern Romances. LC 86-7711. 256p. 1986. 15.95 (*0-932511-02-3*); pap. 7.95 (*0-932511-03-1*) Fiction Coll.
Lopatin, Lev, jt. auth. see Florenskij, Pavel.
Lopatin, Robert, jt. auth. see Kusnet, Jack.
***Lopatka, Angeline.** Moods Reflected in Poetry & Stories. 112p. 1999. (*1-58244-050-6*) Rutledge Bks.
Lopato, Marina, jt. auth. see Von Habsburg, Geza K.
Lopatto, Paul. Religion & the Presidential Election. LC 84-26281. (American Political Parties & Elections Ser.). 177p. 1985. 49.95 (*0-275-90138-6*, C0138, Praeger Pubs) Greenwood.
Lope, Hans-Joachim & Neuschafer, Anne, eds. Rene Kalisky (1936-1981) Et la Hantise de L'Histoire Actes du Colloque International Organise a L'Universite D'Osnabruck du 28 au 30 Octobre, 1996. (Studien und Dokumente zur Geschichte der Romanischen Literaturen: Bd. 32). (GER.). VII, 98p. 1998. 26.95 (*3-631-31601-1*) P Lang Pubng.
Lope, Julia I. Diccionario Juridico. 4th ed. (SPA.). 320p. 1990. pap. 45.00 (*0-7859-5899-1*, 8431500549) Fr & Eur.
Loper. Manufacturing Processes. (C). 1987. pap. text 47.50 (*0-03-071643-8*) Harcourt Coll Pubs.
Loper & Tedsen. Direct Current Fundamentals. 6th ed. LC 99-23624. 1999. mass mkt. 70.95 (*0-7668-0959-5*) Delmar.
Loper, David E., ed. Structure & Dynamics of Partially Solidified Systems. (C). 1987. text 278.50 (*90-247-3500-9*) Kluwer Academic.
Loper, Edward A. Building an Intergenerational Church. (Older Adult Issues Ser.). 50p. 1999. pap. 4.50 (*0-664-50088-9*) Geneva Press.
***Loper, G. Evan.** The Accountant's Desk Reference & Calendar 1999. 1998. ring bd. 49.00i (*0-7646-0531-3*) Prctnrs Pub Co.
Loper, G. Evan. The Accountant's Desk Reference & Calendar 1998. 1997. ring bd. 49.00 (*0-7646-0255-1*) Prctnrs Pub Co.
Loper, G. Evan, et al. Guide to Expense Reduction, 2 vols. Incl. Vol. 1. 1997. ring bd. 170.00 (*0-7646-0276-4*); Vol. 2. 1997. ring bd. 170.00 (*0-7646-0277-2*); 140.00 (*0-7646-0037-0*); 170.00 (*0-7646-0275-6*) Prctnrs Pub Co.
— Guide to Expense Reduction, 2 vols., Set. 1995. ring bd. 125.00 (*1-56433-797-9*) Prctnrs Pub Co.
— Guide to Expense Reduction, Vol. 1. 1995. ring bd. write for info. (*1-56433-798-7*) Prctnrs Pub Co.
— Guide to Expense Reduction, Vol. 2. 1995. ring bd. write for info. (*1-56433-799-5*) Prctnrs Pub Co.
***Loper, G. Evan, et al.** PPC'S Business Compliance Guide, Vol. 1. 1998. ring bd. 195.00 (*0-7646-0386-8*) Prctnrs Pub Co.
Loper, L., ed. see AIDS Foundation Dayton Staff & Volunteers.
Loper, Mark S. 101 Stupid Things Salespeople Do to Sabotage Success. LC 97-66240. (One Hundred One Stupid Things . . . Ser.). (Illus.). 130p. 1998. pap. 9.95 (*1-883553-95-4*, KGS-103) R Chang Assocs.
Loper, Mark S. & Garber, Peter R. 101 Stupid Things Supervisors Do to Sabotage Success. LC 97-65523. (Illus.). (Orig.). 1997. pap. 9.95 (*1-883553-94-6*, KGS-102) R Chang Assocs.
Loper, Neal, jt. intro. see Todd, Arnold R., III.
Loper, Orla E. & Tedsen, Edgar. Direct Current Fundamentals. 3rd ed. 386p. 1986. pap. 23.95 (*0-8273-2234-8*) Delmar.
— Direct Current Fundamentals. 4th ed. 516p. 1991. pap., teacher ed. 15.00 (*0-8273-4148-2*) Delmar.
Loper, Orla E. & Tedson, Edgar. Direct Current Fundamentals. 5th ed. LC 94-10135. 512p. 1995. mass mkt. 64.95 (*0-8273-6572-1*) Delmar.
— Direct Current Fundamentals. 5th ed. LC 94-10135. 88p. 1995. text, teacher ed. 15.50 (*0-8273-6573-X*) Delmar.

Loperfido, Allison, ed. see Silverstein, Lee M.
Lopes, Albert R. Bom Dia! One-Minute Dialogues in Portugese. (C). 1980. reprint ed. pap. text 4.95 (*0-89197-520-9*) Irvington.
Lopes, Albert R. & Yarbro, J. D. Bonjour: One Minute Dialogues in French. (FRE.). (C). 1947. reprint ed. pap. text 2.95 (*0-89197-521-7*) Irvington.
***Lopes, Ann & Roth, Gary.** Men's Feminism: August Bebel & the German Socialist Movement. 260p. 2000. 49.95 (*1-57392-868-2*) Prometheus Bks.
Lopes Cardozo, Nathan T. Between Silence & Speech: Essays on Jewish Thought. LC 94-37611. 264p. 1995. pap. 30.00 (*1-56821-336-0*) Aronson.
— The Written & Oral Torah: A Comprehensive Introduction. LC 97-1252. 304p. 1998. 30.00 (*0-7657-5989-6*) Aronson.
Lopes, Carlos. Enough Is Enough! For an Alternative Diagnosis of the African Crisis. LC 96-178416. (Discussion Papers: Vol. 5). 38p. 1994. pap. text 12.95 (*91-7106-347-1*) Transaction Pubs.
Lopes, Carlos, ed. Balancing Rocks: Environment & Development in Zimbabwe. 208p. (Orig.). 1996. pap. 46.50 (*91-7106-394-3*, Pub. by Almqvist Wiksell) Coronet Bks.
Lopes, Carlos & Rudebeck, Lars. The Socialist Ideal in Africa: A Debate. (Research Report Ser.: No. 81). 25p. 1988. 6.95 (*91-7106-280-7*, Pub. by Nordic Africa) Transaction Pubs.
Lopes Da Silva, F. H., jt. ed. see Pfurtscheller, G.
Lopes+aßilva, Fernando, jt. auth. see Niedermeyer, Ernst.
Lopes Da Silva, Jose, ed. Ajustamento e Crescimento na Actual Conjuntura Economica Mundial. xii, 200p. 1985. pap. 10.00 (*0-939934-47-7*) Intl Monetary.
Lopes, Damian. Towards the Quiet. LC 98-227446. 120p. 1997. pap. 12.00 (*1-55022-345-3*, Pub. by ECW) LPC InBook.
— Transentence. 28p. (Orig.). 1994. pap. 3.00 (*1-57141-005-8*) Runaway Spoon.
— Unclear Family. 24p. (Orig.). 1992. pap. 3.00 (*0-926935-65-8*) Runaway Spoon.
Lopes, Dominic. Understanding Pictures. (Oxford Philosophical Monographs). (Illus.). 248p. 1996. text 55.00 (*0-19-824097-X*) OUP.
Lopes, Duarte. A Report of the Kingdome of Congo, Gathered by P. Pigafetta. Hartwell, A., tr. LC 75-25675. (English Experience Ser.: No. 260). 1970. reprint ed. 65.00 (*90-221-0260-2*) Walter J Johnson.
Lopes, Emilia. O Encontro: Poemas. unabridged ed. Peregrinacao Publications Staff, ed. (POR.). 96p. 1998. boxed set 12.00 (*1-889358-10-X*, 08) Peregrinacao.
— Os Meus Amores: Poemas. unabridged ed. (Poetry/ Poesia Ser.: No. 6). (POR & ENG.). 96p. 1996. boxed set 12.95 (*1-889358-02-9*, 18) Peregrinacao.
— Remarkable Influence. LC 96-60786. 96p. (YA). (ps-12). 1996. per. 7.95 (*1-57258-119-0*) Teach Servs.
Lopes, Ferano. The English in Portugal, 1367-1387. Lomax, ed. (Hispanic Classics Ser.). 1988. 59.95 (*0-85668-341-8*, Pub. by Aris & Phillips); pap. 28.00 (*0-85668-342-6*, Pub. by Aris & Phillips) David Brown.
Lopes, Fernando. Flag Book: Interaction Towards a Better World. (Illus.). 1996. pap., boxed set 15.00 (*0-932526-56-X*) Nexus Pr.
— Flag Book: Interaction Towards a Better World. deluxe limited ed. (Illus.). 1996. pap., boxed set 400.00 (*0-932526-57-8*) Nexus Pr.
Lopes, Henri. Laughing Cry: An African Cock & Bull Story. Moore, Gerald, tr. from FRE. (Readers International Ser.). 260p. (C). 1987. 16.95 (*0-930523-32-6*); pap. 8.95 (*0-930523-33-4*) Readers Intl.
Lopes, Henri. Tribaliks: Contemporary Congolese Stories. Leskes, Andrea, tr. from FRE. (African Writers Ser.). Orig. Title: Tribaliques. 112p. (Orig.). (C). 1987. pap. 8.95 (*0-435-90762-X*, 90762) Heinemann.
Lopes, J. Leite. Gauge Field Theories: An Introduction. (Illus.). 450p. 1983. text 222.00 (*0-08-026501-4*, Pub. by Pergamon Repr) Franklin.
Lopes, Jose L. & Paty, Michel, eds. Quantum Mechanics, a Half Century Later. (Episteme Ser.: No. 5). 320p. 1977. text 155.50 (*90-277-0784-7*, D Reidel) Kluwer Academic.
Lopes, Marlene, jt. auth. see Lobban, Richard A.
Lopes, Michael. Mr. & Mrs. Mephistopheles & Son. 44p. 1975. pap. 2.50 (*0-913218-42-1*) Dustbooks.
Lopes, P. & Killick, S. R., eds. The New Option in Low-Dose Oral Contraception: Expanding the Gestadene Choice. LC 96-33683. (Illus.). 96p. 1996. text 25.00 (*1-85070-739-1*) Prthnon Pub.
Lopes, Sal. Living with AIDS: A Photographic Journal. (Illus.). 133p. 1997. reprint ed. text 15.00 (*0-7881-5077-4*) DIANE Pub.
Lopeshinskaya, Elena. Martyr Bishop Confessors under Communism. (RUS.). pap. 10.00 (*0-89981-055-1*) Eastern Orthodox.
Lopez. Asset & Risk Management. text. write for info. (*0-471-49144-6*) Wiley.
Lopez. Crow & Weasel. 11.50 (*0-394-22377-2*) Beginner.
— Guia Rapida Windows - Spanish Guide to Microsoft Windows. (FRE.). 1990. 12.95 (*0-7859-3717-X*, 842831781X) Fr & Eur.
— The Third Industrial Revolution. 1995. pap. text 24.95 (*0-07-031796-8*) McGraw.
Lopez- Davalos, Arturo & Zanette, Damian. Fundamentals of Electromagnetism: Vacuum Electrodynamics, Media & Relativity. LC 98-52461. (Illus.). 300p. 1999. 87.00 (*3-540-65448-8*) Spr-Verlag.
Lopez, Palacious. Divorcio y Segundos Matrimonios. (SPA.). 219p. 1997. pap. text 15.98 (*968-13-3086-2*) Edit Diana.

Lopez, A. Noether-Lefschetz Theory & the Picard Group of Projective Surfaces. LC 90-19299. (Memoirs Ser.: No. 89/438). 100p. 1991. pap. 20.00 (*0-8218-2500-3*, MEMO/89/438) Am Math.
Lopez, A. & Cliquet, R. Demographic Trends in the European Region Health & Social Implications. (WHO Regional Publications European Ser.: No. 17). 188p. 1984. pap. text 22.00 (*92-890-1108-4*) World Health.
Lopez, A. D., jt. ed. see Murray, C. J.
Lopez, Adalberto. The Revolt of the Communeros, 1721-1735: A Study in the Colonial History of Paraguay. 214p. 1976. 39.95 (*0-87073-124-6*) Transaction Pubs.
Lopez, Adalberto, ed. The Puerto Ricans: Their History, Culture & Society. 490p. 1981. pap. text 24.95 (*0-87073-845-3*) Schenkman Bks Inc.
Lopez-Adorno, Pedro. Concierto para Desobedientes. (SPA.). 104p. 1996. pap. 7.95 (*1-56328-110-4*) Edit Plaza Mayor.
Lopez, Adriana F., tr. see Pepper, Margot.
Lopez, Alan. Reality Construction in an Eastern Mystical Cult. LC 92-16320. (Cults & Nonconventional Religious Groups Ser.). 280p. 1992. text 25.00 (*0-8153-0772-1*) Garland.
Lopez, Alan D., et al, eds. Adult Mortality in Developed Countries: From Description to Explanation. (International Studies in Demography). (Illus.). 378p. 1995. text 69.00 (*0-19-823329-9*) OUP.
Lopez, Alan D., jt. auth. see Murray, Christopher J.
Lopez, Alan D., jt. ed. see Caselli, Graziella.
Lopez, Alan D., jt. ed. see Murray, Christopher J.
Lopez, Alfredo. Dova Licha's Island: Modern Colonialism in Puerto Rico. LC 87-15646. 178p. 1987. 30.00 (*0-89608-258-X*) South End Pr.
— Turn Around Once, & Keep Running. 180p. (Orig.). 1990. pap. 8.00 (*0-685-26446-7*) Atabex Collection.
Lopez, Alfredo R. & Garcia, Francisco M., contrib. by. Popularia Carmina: Index Popularium Carminum. (Alpha-Omega Ser.: Reihe B, Bd. XI). (GER.). viii, 199p. 1997. 95.00 (*3-487-10301-X*) G Olms Pubs.
Lopez, Alfredo R., jt. contrib. by see Garcia, Francisco M.
Lopez, Alfredo R., ed. see Aesop.
Lopez, Alfredo R., jt. ed. see Garcia, Francisco M.
Lopez, Alfredo R., jt. ed. see Garcia, Francisco.
Lopez, Alma G. The Triumph of the Holy Cross of Jesus. 112p. 1998. pap. 15.95 (*1-56167-449-4*) Am Literary Pr.
Lopez, Alonzo. Celebration. (J). (gr. k-2). 1993. pap. 8.95 incl. audio (*0-7608-0484-2*); pap. 4.95 (*0-88741-878-3*) Sundance Pub.
— Celebration: Big Book. (J). (gr. k-2). 1993. pap. 17.95 (*0-88741-897-X*) Sundance Pub.
Lopez-Alves, Fernando, jt. auth. see Centeno, Miguel Angel.
Lopez, Ana, tr. see Parangua, Paulo A., ed.
Lopez, Ana M., jt. ed. see Noriega, Chon A.
Lopez, Andrew. Natural Pest Control: Alternatives to Chemicals for the Home & Garden. 2nd rev. ed. (Illus.). 158p. Date not set. pap. 19.95 (*0-9629768-4-9*) Harmonious Tech.
Lopez, Andy & Kirkgard, John. Coaching Baseball Successfully. LC 95-52858. 216p. (Orig.). 1996. pap. 18.95 (*0-87322-609-7*, PLOP0609) Human Kinetics.
Lopez, Antoinette S., ed. Historical Themes & Identity: Mestizaje & Labels. LC 94-24661. (Latinos in the United States Ser.: Vol. 1). (Illus.). 568p. 1995. text 99.00 (*0-8153-1769-7*) Garland.
— Latina Issues: Fragments of Historia(elle) (Her story) LC 99-29040. (Paperback Ser.). 442p. 1999. reprint ed. pap. 24.95 (*0-8153-3406-0*) Garland.
— Latina Issues: Fragments of Historia(elle) (Herstory) LC 94-34157. (Latinos in the United States Ser.: Vol. 2). (Illus.). 456p. 1995. text 88.00 (*0-8153-1771-9*) Garland.
— Latino Employment, Labor Organizations, & Immigration. LC 94-33597. (Latinos in the United States Ser.: Vol. 4). 416p. 1994. text 88.00 (*0-8153-1773-5*) Garland.
— Latino Language & Education: Communication & the Dream Deferred. LC 94-36776. (Latinos in the United States Ser.: Vol. 5). (Illus.). 440p. 1995. reprint ed. text 88.00 (*0-8153-1774-3*) Garland.
Lopez, Antoinette S., ed. Criminal Justice & Latino Communities. LC 94-36051. (Latinos in the United States Ser.: Vol. 3). 312p. 1994. text 77.00 (*0-8153-1772-7*) Garland.
Lopez, Antonio C. & Macarro, Luis N.; eds. Algebraic Geometry & Singularities. LC 95-51222. (Progress in Mathematics Ser.: Vol. 134). 1995. write for info. (*0-8176-5334-1*) Birkhauser.
— Algebraic Geometry & Singularities. LC 95-51222. (Progress in Mathematics Ser.: Vol. 134). 432p. 1996. 99.50 (*3-7643-5334-1*) Birkhauser.
Lopez-Antuiano & Schmunis, G. Diagnosis of Malaria. (Scientific Publications: No. 512). 148p. 1999. text 16.00 (*92-75-11512-5*) PAHO.
Lopez, Arcadia. Barrio Teacher. LC 92-6876. 96p. (Orig.). (YA). (gr. 6-12). 1992. pap. text 9.50 (*1-55885-051-1*) Arte Publico.
Lopez, Arcadia H. Barrio Teacher. 1992. 14.60 (*0-606-01312-1*, Pub. by Turtleback) Demco.
Lopez-Arias, Julio. Peculiaridades Estilisticas de Fernao Lopes. LC 93-23087. (Iberica Ser.: Vol. 10). 210p. (C). 1994. text 47.95 (*0-8204-2251-7*) P Lang Pubng.
***Lopez, Aurora.** Estudios Sobre Comedia Romana. (Studien zur Klassischen Philologie: Vol. 119). (SPA.). 408p. 2000. pap. 63.95 (*3-631-35888-1*) P Lang Pubng.
Lopez Austin, Alfredo. The Human Body & Ideology: Concepts of the Ancient Nahuas, 2 vols. Ortiz De Montellano, Thelma & Ortiz De Montellano, Bernard R., trs. LC 87-10591. (SPA., Illus.). 832p. 1988. text 65.00 (*0-87480-260-1*) U of Utah Pr.
— The Myths of the Opossum: Pathways of Mesoamerican Mythology. Ortiz de Montellano, Bernard R. & Ortiz de Montellano, Thelma, trs. LC 92-27258. (Illus.). 434p. 1993. reprint ed. pap. 134.60 (*0-608-04129-7*, 206486200011) Bks Demand.
Lopez-Baison. Guia Rapida Serie Assistant de IBM. 2nd ed.Tr. of Spanish Guide to IBM Computers. (SPA.). 1991. write for info. (*0-7859-3691-2*, 8428317275) Fr & Eur.
— Guia Rapida Symphony, Hoya de Calculo. 2nd ed.Tr. of Spanish Guide to "Lotus Symphony". (SPA.). 1991. 59.95 (*0-7859-3696-3*, 8428317623) Fr & Eur.
— Guia Rapida Symphony, Utilidades, Tratamiento de Textos. 2nd ed.Tr. of Spanish Guide To "Lotus Symhony Utilities & Text Processing". (SPA.). 1991. 10.95 (*0-7859-3695-5*, 8428317615) Fr & Eur.
Lopez-Baralt, Jose. The Policy of the United States Towards Its Territories with Special Reference to Puerto Rico. LC 98-5820. 1998. write for info. (*0-8477-0341-X*) U of PR Pr.
Lopez-Baralt, Luce. Islam in Spanish Literature: From the Middle Ages to the Present. Hurley, Andrew, tr. LC 91-34243. xxii, 324p. 1992. 116.00 (*90-04-09460-1*) Brill Academic Pubs.
Lopez-Baralt, Mercedes. La Gestacion de Fortunata y Jacinta: Galdos y la Novela Como Re-Escritura. (SPA.). 225p. (Orig.). (C). 1992. pap. text 10.50 (*0-929157-17-6*) Ediciones Huracan.
Lopez-Baralt, Mercedes, jt. auth. see Pales Matos, Luis.
Lopez-Barneo, Jose & Weir, E. Kenneth, eds. Oxygen Regulation of Ion Channels & Gene Expression. LC 97-50337. (Illus.). 288p. 1998. 120.00 (*0-87993-694-0*) Futura Pub.
Lopez, Barry. About This Life. aut. ed. 1998. 24.00 (*0-676-54937-3*) Random.
— About This Life: Journeys on the Threshold of Memory. LC 98-14257. 273p. 1998. 24.00 (*0-679-43454-2*) Knopf.
— About This Life: Journeys on the Threshold of Memory. 288p. 1999. pap. 13.00 (*0-679-75447-4*) Knopf.
— Apologia. LC 97-43117. (Illus.). 24p. 1998. 19.95 (*0-8203-2004-8*) U of Ga Pr.
— Apologia. aut. limited num. ed. (Illus.). 24p. 1998. text 100.00 (*0-8203-2084-6*) U of Ga Pr.
***Lopez, Barry.** Crossing Open Ground. 2000. 25.25 (*0-8446-7127-4*) Peter Smith.
Lopez, Barry. Crow & Weasel. 64p. (J). (gr. 4-7). 1998. pap. 7.95 (*0-374-41613-3*) FS&G.
— Crow & Weasel. LC 90-31500. (Illus.). 64p. 1990. 16.95 (*0-86547-439-7*) N Point Pr.
— Field Notes: The Grace Note of the Canyon Wren. 176p. 1995. reprint ed. pap. 12.00 (*0-380-72482-0*, Avon Bks) Morrow Avon.
— Giv Bir Thunder Sleeping. 192p. 1990. pap. 9.00 (*0-380-71111-7*, Avon Bks) Morrow Avon.
***Lopez, Barry.** Light Action in the Caribbean: Stories. 176p. 2000. 22.00 (*0-679-43455-0*) Knopf.
Lopez, Barry. Northwest Passage. (Illus.). 96p. 1996. 68.00 (*0-89381-676-0*) Aperture.
Lopez, Barry. The Rediscovery of North America. LC 92-50087. 1992. pap. 8.00 (*0-679-74099-6*, Vin) Random.
Lopez, Barry. The Rediscovery of North America. LC 90-24487. 64p. 1991. 16.00 (*0-8131-1742-9*) U Pr of Ky.
— Winter Count. LC 99-21325. 1999. pap. 11.00 (*0-679-78141-2*) Vin Bks.
Lopez, Barry, jt. auth. see Beath, Mary.
Lopez, Barry H. Arctic Dreams: Imagination & Desire in a Northern Landscape. 496p. 1988. reprint ed. pap. 13.95 (*0-553-34664-4*) Bantam.
— Crossing Open Ground. 1988. write for info. (*0-333-46943-7*, Scribners Ref) Mac Lib Ref.
— Crossing Open Ground. 208p. 1989. pap. 12.00 (*0-679-72183-5*) Vin Bks.
— Desert Notes: Reflection. 144p. 1990. pap. 12.00 (*0-380-71110-9*, Avon Bks) Morrow Avon.
— Desert Notes: Reflections in the Eye of a Raven. LC 76-6099. (Illus.). 104p. 1976. 6.95 (*0-8362-0661-4*) Andrews & McMeel.
— Desert Notes: Reflections in the Eye of the Raven. 96p. 1981. pap. 7.95 (*0-380-53819-9*, Avon Bks) Morrow Avon.
— Giving Birth to Thunder, Sleeping with His Daughter: Coyote Builds North America. LC 77-17395. 206p. 1978. 8.95 (*0-8362-0726-2*) Andrews & McMeel.
— Lessons from the Wolverine. LC 96-54705. (Illus.). 1997. 15.95 (*0-8203-1927-9*) U of Ga Pr.
— Of Wolves & Men. LC 78-6070. (Illus.). 320p. 1979. pap. 18.00 (*0-684-16322-5*, Scribners Ref) Mac Lib Ref.
— Of Wolves & Men. 1994. 27.00 (*0-8446-6727-7*) Peter Smith.
— River Notes: The Dance of the Herons. LC 79-17192. 104p. 1979. 6.95 (*0-8362-6106-2*) Andrews & McMeel.
— River Notes: The Dance of the Herons. 96p. 1990. pap. 9.00 (*0-380-52514-3*, Avon Bks) Morrow Avon.
— Winter Count. 128p. 1982. mass mkt. 4.95 (*0-380-58107-8*, Avon Bks) Morrow Avon.
Lopez, Beatriz, ed. see Gonzalez, Lorenzo.
Lopez, Benito M., Jr., intro. Catholic Education: New Partnerships in the Service of the Church. (Current Issues in Catholic Higher Education Ser.: Vol. 14, No. 1). 46p. (Orig.). 1993. pap. text 6.00 (*1-55833-127-1*) Natl Cath Educ.
Lopez, Benjamin, tr. see Gonzalez, Lorenzo.
Lopez-Berestein, Gabriel & Klostergaard, Jim, eds. Mononuclear Phagocytes in Cell Biology. 256p. 1992. lib. bdg. 189.00 (*0-8493-4706-8*, QR185) CRC Pr.
Lopez, Billie A., jt. auth. see Hirsch, Peter.
***Lopez, Boris.** Just Bloomed. 64p. 2000. pap. 11.95 (*1-56163-257-0*, Amerotica) NBM.
Lopez-Bustos, Francisco, tr. see Jackins, Harvey.
Lopez, C., jt. auth. see Gonzalez-Arroyo, A.

An Asterisk (*) at the beginning of an entry indicates that the title is appearing for the first time.

Lopez, C., jt. ed. see Ades, Edwin W.
Lopez C., Carlos, jt. auth. see Cabrero C., Maria T.
Lopez, C. M., jt. auth. see McGowen, M. K.
Lopez, C. R. Un Analisis del Rock.Tr. of Analysis of Rock. (SPA.). 6.99 (*1-56063-906-7*, 498261) Editorial Unilit.
***Lopez Cabrales, Maria del Mar.** La Pluma y la Represion: Escritoras Argentinas Contemporaneas. (Wor(l)ds of Change: Vol. 44). (SPA.). 200p. (C). 2000. text 46.95 (*0-8204-4286-0*) P Lang Pubng.
Lopez-Cajun, C. S., jt. auth. see Angeles, J.
Lopez-Capestany, Pablo. Cuentos Sencillos. LC 98-85503. (Coleccion Caniqui). (SPA.). 128p. 1998. pap. 12.00 (*0-89729-872-1*) Ediciones.
— La Vina del Senor. LC 97-60681. (Coleccion Caniqui). (SPA.). 137p. 1997. pap. 13.00 (*0-89729-839-X*) Ediciones.
Lopez, Carl & Skip Barber Racing School Staff. Going Faster! Mastering the Art of Race Driving. LC 96-48026. 1997. 29.95 (*0-8376-0227-0*) Bentley Pubs.
Lopez, Carlos, ed. Immunobiology & Pathogenesis of Persistent Virus Infections. (Illus.). 318p. 1988. text 59.00 (*1-55581-000-4*) ASM Pr.
Lopez, Carlos, et al, eds. Immunobiology & Prophylaxis of Human Herpesvirus Infections. (Advances in Experimental Medicine & Biology Ser.: Vol. 278). (Illus.). 306p. (C). 1990. text 114.00 (*0-306-43696-5*, Kluwer Plenum) Kluwer Academic.
Lopez, Carlos & Roizman, Bernard, eds. Human Herpesvirus Infections: Pathogenesis, Diagnosis, & Treatment. LC 86-17908. 318p. 1986. reprint ed. pap. 98.60 (*0-608-03428-2*, 206412700008) Bks Demand.
Lopez, Carlos, jt. ed. see Roizman, Bernard.
Lopez, Carlos, jt. ed. see Rouse, Barry T.
Lopez, Carlos E. Investigaciones Arqueologicas en el Magdalena Medio, Cuenca del Rio Carare (Departamento de Santander) (SPA., Illus.). 126p. 1991. pap. 8.50 (*1-877812-27-7*, BR025) UPLAAP.
Lopez-Casasnovas, G. & Van Eimeren, W., eds. Incentives in Health Systems: Health Systems Research. (Illus.). 224p. 1991. 103.00 (*0-387-53933-6*) Spr-Verlag.
Lopez-Casero Olmedo, Francisco & Hierneis, Otto. Spanisch fur Kaufleute: Spanish Business Correspondence Guide. 10th ed. (GER & SPA.). 455p. 1981. reprint ed. 49.95 (*0-7859-5673-5*, 3468403402) Fr & Eur.
Lopez Castellon, Enrique, ed. & tr. see Plato.
Lopez, Cecilia L. Alexander Pope: An Annotated Bibliography, 1945-1967. LC 78-99213. 164p. reprint ed. pap. 50.90 (*0-8357-5302-6*, 200758500065) Bks Demand.
Lopez, Celia Maldonado. Ciudad de Mexico, 1800-1860: Epidemias y Poblacion. LC 96-136453. (Coleccibon Divulgacibon Historia Ser.). 149 p. 1995. write for info. (*968-29-5204-2*) Dir Gen Pubicaiones.
Lopez-Cepero, Heidi, ed. see Goto, Kunio & Gibson, David V.
Lopez, Charlotte & Dworkin, Susan. Lost in the System: Miss Tenn U. S. A.'s Triumphant Fight to Claim a Family of Her Own. (Illus.). 192p. 1996. pap. 11.00 (*0-684-81199-5*, Fireside) S&S Trade Pap.
Lopez-Chiclana, Margarita, tr. see Ramirez, Rafael E.
Lopez, Chris. The "Guitar Book"- For Those Who Have Just Landed on the Planet Earth!- Learn How to Play Guitar! 64p. 1999. spiral bd. 16.95 (*0-9667719-4-X*) C Winkle Prods.
— The "Guitar Stage" Guitar Book- Scale & Tab Worksheet Book- Learn How to Record Your Own Scale Patterns & Tabs Easily & Quickly! 1999. spiral bd. 18.50 (*0-9667719-3-1*) C Winkle Prods.
— The Next Stage Guitar Book: Learn How to Play Scale Patterns & Tabs Easily & Quickly! 1999. spiral bd. 18.95 (*0-9667719-2-3*) C Winkle Prods.
— The "Pre-Stage" Guitar Book- Learn How to Get a Grip on Your First Guitar!- Learn How to Play Guitar!! 1999. spiral bd. 14.95 (*0-9667719-5-8*) C Winkle Prods.
Lopez, Cira Martinez, see Martinez Lopez, Cira.
Lopez-Claros, Augusto. The Search for Efficiency in the Adjustment Process: Spain in the 1980s. (Occasional Paper Ser.: No. 57). 43p. 1988. pap. 7.50 (*1-55775-009-2*) Intl Monetary.
Lopez, Claude A. Mon Cher Papa: Franklin & the Ladies of Paris. LC 66-12507. 418p. reprint ed. pap. 129.60 (*0-8357-8230-1*, 203380600087) Bks Demand.
Lopez, Claude-Anne. Benjamin Franklin's "Good House" LC 81-607929. (Official National Park Handbook Ser.: No. 114). 1981. pap. 7.50 (*0-912627-11-5*) Natl Park Serv.
— Benjamin Franklin's "Good House" (National Park Service Handbook Ser.: No. 114). (Illus.). 65p. 1985. pap. 7.00 (*0-16-003491-4*, 024-005-00907-8) USGPO.
— Mon Cher Papa: Franklin & the Ladies of Paris. 424p. (C). 1990. reprint ed. 50.00 (*0-300-04800-9*); reprint ed. pap. 20.00 (*0-300-04758-4*) Yale U Pr.
***Lopez, Claude Anne.** My Life with Benjamin Franklin. LC 99-46231. 288p. 2000. 25.00 (*0-300-08192-8*) Yale U Pr.
Lopez, Claude-Anne & Herbert, Eugenia W. The Private Franklin: The Man & His Family. (Illus.). 400p. 1985. reprint ed. pap. 9.95 (*0-393-30227-X*) Norton.
Lopez-Corvo, Rafael E. God Is a Woman. LC 96-15630. 1996. 40.00 (*1-56821-862-1*) Aronson.
— Self-Envy: Therapy & the Divided Internal World. LC 94-7733. 248p. 1995. 40.00 (*1-56821-252-6*) Aronson.
Lopez, Cruz, jt. auth. see Tejera, Gomez.
Lopez, Daniel. Films by Genre: 775 Categories, Styles, Trends & Movements Defined, with a Filmography for Each. LC 92-56661. 519p. 1993. lib. bdg. 55.00 (*0-89950-780-8*) McFarland & Co.
Lopez, Daniel S., Jr. Religions of India in Practice. LC 94-34695. (Princeton Readings in Religion Ser.). 648p. 1995. pap. text 19.95 (*0-691-04324-8*, Pub. by Princeton U Pr) Cal Prin Full Svc.
Lopez, Danilo. 18 Poems. 32p. 1998. pap. 5.00 (*1-892820-02-1*) Stylus Pubns.
— 11 Nicaraguan Poets in the U. S. A. 103p. 1998. per. 10.00 (*1-892820-00-5*) Stylus Pubns.
Lopez, Danilo, jt. auth. see Juarez, Karla.
Lopez, David L., jt. auth. see Kozak, David L.
Lopez de Ayala, Pero. Coronica de Enrique III. Wilkins, Constance L. & Wilkins, Heanon M., eds. (Spanish Ser.: No. 74). xxvi, 136p. 1992. 20.00 (*0-940639-77-7*) Hispanic Seminary.
Lopez de la Vieja, M. Teresa. Figuras de Logos (Figures of Logos) Entre la Filosofia y la Literatura (Between Philosophy & Literature) (SPA.). 300p. 1994. pap. 13.99 (*84-375-0408-2*, Pub. by Fondo) Continental Bk.
***Lopez de Mantaras, Ramon & Plaza, Enric.** Machine Learning: ECML 2000: 11th European Conference on Machine Learning, Barcelona, Catalonia, Spain, May 31-June 2, 2000. LC 00-40012. (Lecture Notes in Computer Science Ser.). 2000. pap. write for info. (*3-540-67602-3*) Spr-Verlag.
Lopez de Mariscal, Blanca. The Harvest Birds (Los Pajaros de la Cosecha) LC 94-40016. (ENG & SPA., Illus.). 32p. (J). (ps-3). 1995. 14.95 (*0-89239-131-6*) Childrens Book Pr.
Lopez de Martinez, Adelaida, compiled by. Discurso Femenino Actual. (Mujeres de Palabra Ser.). (SPA.). 400p. 1995. pap. 17.95 (*0-8477-0234-0*) U of PR Pr.
Lopez de Martinez, Adelaida, ed. A Ricardo Gullon: Sus Discipulos. (Homenajes de Aldeeu Ser.). (SPA., Illus.). 320p. (C). 1995. pap. 35.00 (*0-9626630-3-4*) Spanish Profs Amer.
Lopez De Thorgood, Lucy, tr. see Robson, Ernest M.
Lopez de Ubeda, Francisco, see Perez, Andrea, pseud.
Lopez de Zuazo Algar, Antonio. Dictionary of Journalism: Diccionario del Periodismo. 5th ed. (ENG & SPA.). 256p. 1990. pap. 35.00 (*0-7859-4921-6*) Fr & Eur.
Lopez, Diana C. Graduate Education at Tennessee: An Historical Perspective. LC 90-37520. (Illus.). 325p. 1990. 19.95 (*0-9625933-0-3*) Univ TN Grad Schl.
Lopez, Diane. Teaching Children: A Curriculum Guide to What Children Need to Know at Each Grade Level Through Sixth Grade. LC 87-71895. 299p. 1988. pap. 12.99 (*0-89107-489-9*) Crossway Bks.
Lopez, Dolores R. Una Relectura del Fin de Siglo en el Marco de la Literatura Comparada: Teoria y Praxis. (Perspectivas Hispanicas Ser.: Tomo 9). (SPA.). 204p. 1998. 32.95 (*3-906759-74-1*) P Lang Pubng.
Lopez, Don S. Aviation. (Illus.). 256p. 1995. 18.00 (*0-02-860041-X*); 24.95 (*0-02-860006-1*) Macmillan.
Lopez, Donald, ed. see Time-Life Books Editors.
Lopez, Donald S. Asian Religions in Practice: An Introduction. LC 98-47112. (Princeton Readings in Religion Ser.). 1999. pap. text 15.95 (*0-691-00513-3*, Pub. by Princeton U Pr) Cal Prin Full Svc.
***Lopez, Donald S.** Buddhism & Science. 1999. 32.00 (*0-226-49312-1*) U Ch Pr.
— Critical Terms Buddhist Studies. 1999. pap. text 18.00 (*0-226-49315-6*); lib. bdg. 55.00 (*0-226-49314-8*) U Ch Pr.
Lopez, Donald S. Elaborations on Emptiness: Uses of the Heart Sutra. LC 95-44449. 277p. 1996. text 39.50 (*0-691-02732-3*, Pub. by Princeton U Pr) Cal Prin Full Svc.
— Fighter Pilot's Heaven: Flight Testing the Early Jets. LC 94-21061. (Illus.). 228p. 1995. 24.95 (*1-56098-457-0*) Smithsonian.
Lopez, Donald S., Jr. The Heart Sutra Explained: Indian & Tibetan Commentaries. LC 87-6479. (SUNY Series in Buddhist Studies). 230p. (C). 1987. pap. text 24.95 (*0-88706-590-2*) State U NY Pr.
Lopez, Donald S. Into the Teeth of the Tiger. LC 96-51012. (Smithsonian History of Aviation Ser.). 1997. pap. 17.95 (*1 56098-752-9*) Smithsonian.
— National Air & Space Museum: A Visit in Pictures. (Illus.). 64p. 1990. 6.99 (*0-517-69514-6*) Random Hse Value.
— National Air & Space Museum: A Visit in Pictures. LC 88-36586. (Illus.). 64p. 1989. 6.98 (*0-87474-710-4*) Smithsonian.
Lopez, Donald S., Jr. Prisoners of Shangri-La: Tibetan Buddhism & the West. LC 97-41202. 272p. 1998. 25.00 (*0-226-49310-5*) U Ch Pr.
— Prisoners of Shangri-La: Tibetan Buddhism & the West. LC 98-11679. 284p. 1999. pap. 14.00 (*0-226-49311-3*) U Ch Pr.
Lopez, Donald S. Religions of Tibet in Practice. LC 96-31592. (Princeton Readings in Religion Ser.). 560p. 1997. text 60.00 (*0-691-01184-2*, Pub. by Princeton U Pr); pap. text 19.95 (*0-691-01183-4*, Pub. by Princeton U Pr) Cal Prin Full Svc.
Lopez, Donald S., Jr. A Study of Svatantrika. LC 86-14636. 450p. (Orig.). (C). 1987. pap. 19.95 (*0-937938-19-X*); lib. bdg. 35.00 (*0-937938-20-3*) Snow Lion Pubns.
Lopez, Donald S., Jr., ed. Buddhism in Practice. LC 94-48201. (Princeton Readings in Religion Ser.). 640p. 1995. text 65.00 (*0-691-04442-2*, Pub. by Princeton U Pr); pap. text 19.95 (*0-691-04441-4*, Pub. by Princeton U Pr) Cal Prin Full Svc.
— Buddhist Hermeneutics. (Studies in East Asian Buddhism: No. 6). 320p. (C). 1988. reprint ed. pap. text 19.00 (*0-8248-1447-9*) UH Pr.
Lopez, Donald S., ed. Curators of the Buddha: The Study of Buddhism under Colonialism. 304p. 1995. pap. text 18.00 (*0-226-49309-1*); lib. bdg. 45.95 (*0-226-49308-3*) U Ch Pr.
Lopez, Donald S., Jr., ed. Religions of China in Practice. LC 95-41332. (Readings in Religions Ser.). 472p. 1996. text 65.00 (*0-691-02144-9*, Pub. by Princeton U Pr); pap. text 19.95 (*0-691-02143-0*, Pub. by Princeton U Pr) Cal Prin Full Svc.
— Religions of India in Practice. LC 94-34695. (Princeton Readings in Religion Ser.). 648p. 1995. text 65.00 (*0-691-04325-6*, Pub. by Princeton U Pr) Cal Prin Full Svc.
Lopez, Donald S., Jr., jt. auth. see Dalai Lama XIV.
Lopez, Donald S., Jr., ed. see Dalai Lama XIV.
Lopez, Eduardo. A Silent Thunder. 1995. pap. 6.95 (*0-88145-116-9*) Broadway Play.
Lopez Eire, Antonio, ed. see Homer.
Lopez, Elias. The California Central Valley Versus Other States? 8p. 1996. pap. write for info. (*1-58703-053-5*) CA St Libry.
— Fraud & Abuse in the Health Care Market of California. 20p. 1997. pap. write for info. (*1-58703-076-4*, CRB-97-013) CA St Libry.
— Major Demographic Shifts Occurring in California, Vol. 5. 11p. 1999. pap. write for info. (*1-58703-114-0*, CRB Note 6) CA St Libry.
— Vehicle License Fee: A Comparison among the Most Populous Cities of Each State. 13p. 1998. pap. write for info. (*1-58703-086-1*, CRB-98-008) CA St Libry.
— Who Is Least Likely to Attend Pre-School?, Vol. 6. 5p. 1999. pap. write for info. (*1-58703-116-7*, CRB Note 6) CA St Libry.
***Lopez, Elias, et al, eds.** A Coordinated Approach to Raising the Socio-Economic Status of Latinos in California. 63p. 2000. pap. write for info. (*1-58703-120-5*, CRB-00-003) CA St Libry.
***Lopez, Elias & Figueroa, Richard A.** Options for Expanding the Health Families Program: Estimates. 12p. 1999. pap. write for info. (*1-58703-101-9*, CRB-99-004) CA St Libry.
***Lopez, Elias, et al.** Latinos & Economic Development in California. 54p. 1999. pap. write for info. (*1-58703-107-8*, CRB-99-008) CA St Libry.
Lopez, Elias, jt. auth. see Bugarin, Alicia.
Lopez, Ellen R. Through Different Colored Glasses: The World as Seen Through the Left & Right Hemispheres of the Brain. (Illus.). 60p. 1989. pap. write for info. (*0-318-64915-2*) McDonald & Hezlep.
Lopez, Erica. Flaming Iguanas: An Illustrated All-Girl Road Novel Thing. LC 97-3125. (Illus.). 257p. 1997. 18.00 (*0-684-83722-6*) S&S Trade.
Lopez, Erika. Flaming Iguanas: An Illustrated All-Girl Road Novel Thing. 288p. 1998. pap. 11.00 (*0-684-85368-X*, S&S Edns) Simon & Schuster.
— Lap Dancing for Mommy. LC 97-7304. (Illus.). 192p. (Orig.). 1997. pap. 14.00 (*1-878067-96-6*) Seal Pr WA.
***Lopez, Erika.** They Call Me Mad Dog: A Novel for Bitter, Lonely People. 2001. pap. 13.00 (*0-684-84942-9*, Fireside) S&S Trade Pap.
Lopez, Erika. They Call Me Mad Dog: A Story for Bitter, Lonely People. LC 98-43002. (Illus.). 272p. 1998. 20.00 (*0-684-84941-0*, S&S Edns) Simon & Schuster.
Lopez-Escobar, Edgar G. K., jt. ed. see Kueker, David W.
Lopez, Estela R. El Teatro de Max Aub. LC 76-46372. (UPREX, Teatro y Cine Ser.: No. 52). 200p. (Orig.). 1976. pap. text 1.50 (*0-8477-0052-6*) U of PR Pr.
Lopez, Estrada F., ed. Historia Etiopica de Los Amores de Teagenes y Cariclea. Mena, Fernando de, tr. (SPA.). 430p. 1968. 100.00 (*0-614-00216-8*) Elliots Bks.
Lopez, Estrada F. & Keller, John E. Antonio de Villegas' "El Abencerraje" (Studies in Comparative Literature: No. 33). (C). 1964. pap. 5.95 (*0-8078-7033-1*) U of NC Pr.
Lopez, Estrada F., ed. see Bequer, Gustavo A.
Lopez, F. Solano & Lopez, Gabriel S. Ana. Thompson, Kim, tr. (Illus.). 120p. 1991. 12.95 (*1-56097-066-9*) Fantagraph Bks.
Lopez, F. Solano, jt. auth. see Barreiro.
Lopez, Felipe H., jt. auth. see Munro, Pamela.
Lopez, Frances B. Psychology of Anxiety, Worry & Troublesome Problems: Index of New Information with Authors & Subjects. rev. ed. LC 94-24769. 157p. 1994. 47.50 (*0-7883-0370-8*); pap. 44.50 (*0-7883-0371-6*) ABBE Pubs Assn.
Lopez, Francisco C. De Diis Gentium: Tradicion Clasica y Cultura Medieval, Vol. 30. (Iberica Ser.). 202p. (C). 1998. text 44.95 (*0-8204-3874-X*) P Lang Pubng.
***Lopez, G.** Partial Differential Equations of First Order & Their Applications to Physics. 250p. 1999. 58.00 (*981-02-3746-4*) World Scientific Pub.
Lopez, Gabriel S., jt. auth. see Lopez, F. Solano.
Lopez Galan, S. Guia Farmacologica en Psiquiatria. 2nd ed. (SPA.). 412p. 1995. pap. 25.50 (*84-7978-162-9*, Pub. by Ediciones Diaz) IBD Ltd.
***Lopez, Gary.** Sharks. LC 99-39014. (Nature Books Ser.). (Illus.). 32p. (J). (gr. 2-6). 1999. lib. bdg. 22.79 (*1-56766-614-0*) Childs World.
Lopez-Gaston, Jose R., tr. see Caponnetto, Antonio.
Lopez-Gaston, Rosa M., tr. see Caponnetto, Antonio.
Lopez, George A., ed. Morals & Might: Ethics & the Use of Force in Modern International Affairs. 288p. (C). 1997. pap. 55.00 (*0-8133-8726-4*) Westview.
Lopez, George A. & Myers, Nancy J., eds. Peace & Security: The Next Generation. (Illus.). 294p. 1997. 68.50 (*0-8476-8594-2*); pap. 17.95 (*0-8476-8595-0*) Rowman.
Lopez, George A. & Stohl, Michael, eds. Dependence, Development, & State Repression, 209. LC 87-32258. (Contributions in Political Science Ser.: No. 209). 286p. 1989. 65.00 (*0-313-25298-X*, LDV/, Greenwood Pr) Greenwood.
— Liberalization & Redemocratization in Latin America, 178. LC 87-272. (Contributions in Political Science Ser.: No. 178). 287p. 1987. 65.00 (*0-313-25299-8*, LLB/, Greenwood Pr) Greenwood.
Lopez, George A., et al. Testing Theories of State Violence, State Terror & Repression. (Series on State Violence, Terrorism & Human Rights). 265p. (C). 2000. pap. 31.00 (*0-8133-7525-8*) Westview.
Lopez, George A., jt. auth. see Cortright, David.
Lopez, George A., ed. see Mingst, Karen A. & Karns, Margaret P.
Lopez, George A., jt. ed. see Stohl, Michael.
Lopez, Gilbert T., ed. Technical Book Buyer's Guide. 2nd ed. (Illus.). 400p. (Orig.). 1991. pap. text 14.95 (*1-880072-00-9*) Utd Techbook.
Lopez, Gilbert T. & Cloney, Tom. Technical Book Buyer's Guide. 2nd ed. (Illus.). 370p. (Orig.). 1994. pap. text 19.95 (*1-880072-01-7*) Utd Techbook.
Lopez-Ginitsky, Claude. A Dictionary of Intercessions: A Guide to Orthodox Saints Invoked for Various Needs. 96p. 1997. pap. 6.00 (*0-912927-80-1*, X051) St John Kronstadt.
Lopez, Gloria, tr. see Stray-Gundersen, Karen.
Lopez, Gloribell. Constant Reminder. LC 98-65614. 1998. pap. 10.00 (*0-9662222-0-2*) Pequenas Ligas.
Lopez Gonzalez, Julio. El Ensayo y Su Ensenanza: Dos Ejemplos Puertorriquenos. LC 80-17712. (Coleccion Mente y Palabra). 153p. 1980. 6.00 (*0-8477-0568-4*); pap. 5.00 (*0-8477-0569-2*) U of PR Pr.
Lopez, Greg. What's Going On? Stories of Life. (Illus.). 352p. 1996. pap. 17.95 (*0-9654695-0-6*) Bohland Pub.
Lopez, Haudee V. Caballero Templario: El Homereave Capturo al Che Guevara. De Fana, Angel, ed. (Illus.). 468p. 1996. pap. 24.95 (*1-890829-01-3*) DFana Editions.
Lopez Hernandez, M., ed. Textos y Concordancias del Libro de los Olios, MS2262: Salamanca, Universitaria. (Medieval Spanish Medical Texts Ser.: No. 28). (SPA.). 8p. 1989. 10.00 incl. fiche (*0-940639-38-6*) Hispanic Seminary.
Lopez-Higuera. Handbook of Optical Fibre Sensing. text. write for info. (*0-471-82053-9*) Wiley.
Lopez, Hugo L., tr. see Bate, Barbara.
Lopez, Humberto. The New Professionalism: Connecting Science & Spirit to Empower Professional (& Other) Relationships. 152p. 1998. pap. 16.95 (*0-9661864-0-0*) Harmony-Quest.
Lopez, Ian F. White by Law. 1997. pap. text 18.50 (*0-8147-5137-7*) NYU Pr.
— White by Law: The Legal Construction of Race. (Critical America Ser.). 296p. (C). 1996. text 45.00 (*0-8147-5099-0*) NYU Pr.
Lopez-Ibor, J., ed. International College of Psychosomatic Medicine Madrid, October 1989, Selected Papers from the 10th World Congress: Journal: Psychotherapy & Psychosomatics, Vol. 52, No. 1-3, 1989. (Illus.). 172p. 1990. pap. 108.00 (*3-8055-5273-4*) S Karger.
Lopez-Ibor, Juan J., ed. see World Congress of Psychiatry Staff.
Lopez, Irma M. Historia, Escritura e Identidad: La Novelistica de Maria Luisa Puga. (Wor(l)ds of Change Ser.: Vol. 23). (SPA.). X, 140p. (C). 1996. text 37.95 (*0-8204-3052-8*) P Lang Pubng.
Lopez, Ivette & Garcia, Dwight. Cantos y Rimas. (Lecturas Faciles). (SPA.). 68p. 1983. pap. text 3.75 (*0-88345-524-2*, 21282) Prentice ESL.
— Cantos y Rimas. 1987. pap. text 7.00 (*0-13-113507-4*) Prentice ESL.
Lopez, J. A. La Tecnica. (SPA.). 7.95 (*84-241-5628-5*) E ' Torres & Sons.
Lopez, J. L. & Nanopoulos, D. V. Recent Advances in the Superworld: Proceedings of the International Workshop. 396p. 1994. text 106.00 (*981-02-1730-7*) World Scientific Pub.
Lopez, Jack. Cholos & Surfers: A Latino Family Album. LC 97-48564. 270p. 1998. pap. 15.95 (*0-88496-429-9*) Capra Pr.
***Lopez, Jack.** Snapping Lines: Stories. LC 00-9379. (Camino Del Sol Ser.). 2001. write for info. (*0-8165-2076-3*) U of Ariz Pr.
Lopez, James L. Here's the Pitch. LC 98-90578. xvi, 190p. 1998. pap. 19.95 (*0-9666093-0-1*) Twi-Night.
Lopez, Jesus M. Antonio Paoli: El Leon de Ponce. (SPA., Illus.). 921p. 1997. 70.00 (*0-9653433-0-8*) Ediciones Liricas.
***Lopez, Jorge A.** Lectures on Phase & Transformations in Nuclear Matter A Practictioner's Guide. 2000. 55.00 (*981-02-4007-4*) World Scientific Pub.
Lopez, Jorge M. & Ross, Kenneth A. Sidon Sets. LC 75-193. (Lecture Notes in Pure & Applied Mathematics Ser.: Vol. 13). 205p. reprint ed. pap. 63.60 (*0-608-08952-4*, 206958700005) Bks Demand.
Lopez, Jorge M., tr. see Stenmark, Jean K., et al.
***Lopez, Jose & Scott, John.** Social Structure. LC 00-35624. (Concepts in the Social Sciences Ser.). 2000. pap. write for info. (*0-335-20496-1*, Pub. by OpUniv Pr) Taylor & Francis.
***Lopez, Jose Escoriza.** Multiplication Objects in Monoidal Categories. 181p. 2000. lib. bdg. 79.00 (*1-56072-823-X*) Nova Sci Pubs.
Lopez, Josefina. Confessions. LC 97-212357. 48p. 1996. pap. 3.50 (*0-87129-727-2*, CA2) Dramatic Pub.
— Confessions of Women from East L.A. 62p. 1997. pap. 5.60 (*0-87129-728-0*, CA1) Dramatic Pub.
— Food for the Dead/La Pinta. LC 97-212359. 53p. 1996. pap. 5.60 (*0-87129-726-4*, F59 L85) Dramatic Pub.
— Real Women Have Curves. 80p. 1996. pap. 5.60 (*0-87129-725-6*, R60) Dramatic Pub.
— Simply Maria: or The American Dream. LC 97-212358. 51p. 1996. pap. 3.50 (*0-87129-723-X*, SB4) Dramatic Pub.
— Unconquered Spirits. 80p. 1997. pap. 5.60 (*0-87129-724-8*, U22) Dramatic Pub.
Lopez, Juan C., et al. Advanced Techniques for Embedded Systems Design & Test. LC 98-11763. 1998. 125.00 (*0-7923-8128-9*) Kluwer Academic.
Lopez, Julio C. Estaciones de la Vigilia. (SPA.). 324p. 1991. pap. 14.00 (*0-8477-3239-8*) U of PR Pr.
Lopez, Julio C., ed. see De Hostos, Eugenio M.
Lopez, Kathleen, jt. auth. see Jones, Patricia.

L

An Asterisk (*) at the beginning of an entry indicates that the title is appearing for the first time.

L

Lopez, Ken & Chaney, Bev. Robert Stone: A Bibliography, 1960-1992. LC 92-25363. (Illus.). 120p. 1992. 40.00 (*0-9632898-0-2*) Numinous Pr.

— Robert Stone: A Bibliography, 1960-1992. limited ed. LC 92-25363. (Illus.). 120p. 1992. 125.00 (*0-9632898-1-0*) Numinous Pr.

Lopez, Kimbell. Connecting with Traditional Literature: Using Folktales, Fables & Legends to Strengthen Students' Reading. LC 98-39351. 165p. (C). 1999. pap. text 28.50 (*0-205-27531-1*, Longwood Div) Allyn.

***Lopez, L. Luis.** Musings of a Barrio Sack Boy. LC 00-132264. x, 81p. 2000. pap. 10.00 (*0-9679844-0-8*) Farolito Pr.

— A Painting of Sand. LC 00-132305. vi, 56p. 2000. pap. 8.00 (*0-9679844-1-6*) Farolito Pr.

Lopez-Larrea, Carlos. HLA-B27 in the Development of Spondyloarthropathies. LC 96-8778. (Medical Intelligence Unit Ser.). 261p. 1996. 99.00 (*1-57059-375-2*) Landes Bioscience.

Lopez, Leonardo. Las Ofrendas del Templo Mayor de Tenochtitlan. 432p. 1993. pap. 30.00 (*968-29-4530-5*, IN001) UPLAAP.

Lopez, Leonardo, jt. ed. see Manzanilla, Linda.

Lopez, Loretta. The Birthday Swap. LC 96-24136. (Illus.). 32p. (J). (ps up). 1997. 15.95 (*1-880000-47-4*) Lee & Low Bks.

***Lopez, Loretta.** The Birthday Swap. (Illus.). 32p. (J). (gr. k-3). 1999. pap. 6.95 (*1-880000-89-X*, Pub. by Lee & Low Bks) Publishers Group.

Lopez, Loretta. Que Sorpresa de Cumpleanos. LC 97-6668.Tr. of Birthday Swap. (SPA., Illus.). 32p. (J). (gr. k-5). 1997. pap. 6.95 (*1-880000-56-3*) Lee & Low Bks.

— Que Sorpresa de Cumpleanos. LC 97-6668.Tr. of Birthday Swap. (SPA., Illus.). 32p. (J). (ps-3). 1997. 15.95 (*1-880000-55-5*) Lee & Low Bks.

— Que Sorpresa de Cumpleanos.Tr. of Birthday Swap. 1997. 12.15 (*0-606-12795-X*, Pub. by Turtleback) Demco.

Lopez, Louisa, jt. ed. see Jackson, Vivian H.

Lopez, Luce B. San Juan de la Cruz & el Islam: Estudio Sobre las Filiaciones Semiticas de su Literatura. 1986. 13.00 (*968-12-0294-5*) U of PR Pr.

Lopez, Luis, tr. see Pasquale, Jennifer.

Lopez, Luis, tr. see Stray-Gundersen, Karen.

Lopez, Luis I., tr. see Vieira, Waldo.

Lopez, Luisita. Manila Fugue. Date not set. write for info. (*0-393-03374-0*) Norton.

Lopez, M. Elena, et al. Paths to School Readiness: An In-Depth Look at 3 Early Childhood Programs. LC 93-79081. 126p. (Orig.). 1993. pap. text 10.95 (*0-9630627-2-7*) Harvard Fam.

Lopez, Manuel, tr. see Pirolo, Neal.

Lopez, Manuel D. Chinese Drama: An Annotated Bibliography of Commentary, Criticism, & Plays in English Translation. annot. ed. LC 91-15902. 535p. 1991. 65.00 (*0-8108-2347-0*) Scarecrow.

— New York: A Guide to Information & Reference Sources, 1979-1986. LC 87-16531. 384p. 1987. 39.50 (*0-8108-2018-8*) Scarecrow.

Lopez, Marcela, ed. Text & Concordance of Biblioteca Universitaria, Salamanca, MS2262: Doctor Gomez de Salamanca, Propiedades del Romero. (Medieval Spanish Medical Texts Ser.: No. 21). (SPA.). 6p. 1987. 10.00 incl. fiche (*0-940639-17-3*) Hispanic Seminary.

Lopez, Maria J., jt. auth. see Miranda, Julia.

Lopez, Maria M. & Zuniga Burmester, Ricardo. Perspectivas Criticas de la Psicologia Social. LC 85-1053. viii, 450p. 1988. pap. 16.00 (*0-8477-2909-5*) U of PR Pr.

***Lopez, Marianne Exum.** When Discourses Collide: An Ethnography of Migrant Children at Home & in School. LC 98-26797. (Rethinking Childhood Ser.: Vol. 11). 224p. (C). 1999. pap. text 29.95 (*0-8204-4165-1*) P Lang Pubng.

Lopez-Marron, Jose M. Unamuno y Su Camino a la "Individualizacion", Vol. 26. (Wor(l)ds of Change Ser.). XVI, 139p. (C). 1998. text 38.95 (*0-8204-3335-7*) P Lang Pubng.

Lopez-Medina, Sylvia. NECKLACE OF PEARLS. 320p. 2000. 23.00 (*0-06-017272-X*) HarpC.

Lopez Mendizabal, I. Diccionario Vasco-Castellano. 6th ed. (SPA.). 452p. 1976. 49.95 (*0-8288-5624-9*, S50439) Fr & Eur.

Lopez, Michael. Emerson & Power. LC 94-10716. 290p. 1996. lib. bdg. 32.00 (*0-87580-196-X*) N Ill U Pr.

Lopez, Michael J. Retail Store Planning & Design Manual. LC 94-42640. (NRF Publishing Program Ser.). 800p. 1995. 190.00 (*0-471-07629-5*) Wiley.

Lopez, Miguel, jt. auth. see Wong, Sau-Ling C.

***Lopez, Miguel R.** Chicano Timespace: The Poetry & Politics of Ricardo Sanchez. (Rio Grande/Rio Bravo Ser.: Vol. 3). (Illus.). 224p. (C). 2001. 37.95 (*0-89096-962-0*) Tex A&M Univ Pr.

Lopez Mondejar, Publio. Spain under Franco. (Illus.). 264p. 1999. 29.95 (*3-8290-2223-9*, 520980) Konemann.

Lopez Mora. Literatura Francofona. (SPA.). 16.99 (*968-16-4607-X*, Pub. by Fondo) Continental Bk.

Lopez-Morales, Humberto, ed. Corrientes Actuales en la Dialectologia del Caribe Hispanico: Actas de un Simposio. LC 77-12823. 247p. 1978. pap. 6.00 (*0-8477-3186-3*) U of PR Pr.

Lopez-Morillas, Consuelo. Qu'ran in Sixteenth-Century Spain: Six Morisco Versions of Sura. (Monagrafias A Ser.: Vol. LXXXII). (Illus.). 102p. (C). 1982. 69.00 (*0-7293-0121-4*, Pub. by Tamesis Bks Ltd) Boydell & Brewer.

Lopez-Morillas, Frances, tr. see Bello, Andres.

Lopez-Morillas, Frances M., tr. see Cela, Camilo Jose.

Lopez-Morillas, Frances M., tr. see Delibes, Miguel.

Lopez-Morillas, Frances M., tr. see Gaite, Carmen M.

Lopez-Morillas, Frances M., tr. see Marias, Julian.

Lopez-Morillas, Frances M., tr. see Pupo-Walker, Enrique, ed.

Lopez-Morillas, Frances M., tr. see Savater, Fernando.

Lopez-Morillas, Frances M., tr. see Weckmann, Luis.

Lopez, N. C. King Pancho & the First Clock. LC 63-16396. (Illus.). 32p. (J). (gr. 2-7). 1967. lib. bdg. 9.95 (*0-87783-020-7*) Oddo.

— King Pancho & the First Clock. deluxe ed. LC 63-16396. (Illus.). 32p. (J). (gr. 2-7). 1967. pap. 3.94 (*0-87783-098-3*) Oddo.

***Lopez, Nancy.** Complete Golfer. 2000. 12.99 (*1-57866-086-6*) Galahad Bks.

Lopez, Nancy & Wade, Don. Nancy Lopez's the Complete Golfer. (Illus.). 240p. 1989. reprint ed. pap. 15.95 (*0-8092-4711-9*, 471190, Contemporary Bks) NTC Contemp Pub Co.

Lopez, Nancy, tr. see Torruellas, Luz M. & Vazquez, Jose L.

Lopez, Nicoline. Art of Living in Singapore. 1996. 69.95 (*981-00-5490-4*, Pub. by Select Bks) Weatherhill.

Lopez, Nola. Health: A Woman's Record-Keeping Journal. 160p. 1996. spiral bd. 17.95 (*1-55670-473-9*) Stewart Tabori & Chang.

Lopez, Nora L., tr. see Mikatavage, Raimonda.

Lopez, Norbert. Cuento Del Rey Pancho y el Primer Reloj. LC 70-108730. (Illus.). 32p. (J). (gr. 2-7). 1970. lib. bdg. 9.95 (*0-87783-010-X*); audio 7.94 (*0-685-03700-2*) Oddo.

— Cuento Del Rey Pancho y el Primer Reloj. deluxe ed. LC 70-108730. (Illus.). 32p. (J). (gr. 2-7). 1970. pap. 3.94 (*0-87783-104-1*) Oddo.

Lopez, Nuria, jt. compiled by see Dominguez, Francesc.

Lopez Oliva, Manuel. Nelson Dominguez. (Illus.). 168p. 1998. text 35.00 (*90-5703-961-3*) Gordon & Breach.

Lopez, Orlando R. El Penon de las Animas. (Romance Real Ser.). 192p. (Orig.). pap. 1.50 (*0-88025-007-0*) Roca Pub.

Lopez, P. Fernando. Mami! Cuanto te Quiero! LC 83-80417. (Coleccion Espejo de Paciencia). (SPA., Illus.). 91p. (Orig.). 1983. pap. 6.00 (*0-89729-329-0*) Ediciones.

Lopez-Pacheco, Jesus. Poetic Asylum: Poems Written in Canada, 1968-1990. 80p. 1991. pap. 9.95 (*0-919626-54-8*, Pub. by Brick Bks) Genl Dist Srvs.

***Lopez, Paulino.** In God We Must Trust as the Year 2000 Comes! Our Only Hope for Glory. (Illus.). 120p. 2000. pap. 13.00 (*0-8059-4698-5*) Dorrance.

Lopez-Pedraza, Rafael. Anselm Kiefer: The Psychology of "After the Catastrophe" LC 96-9026. (Illus.). 95p. 1997. text 27.50 (*0-8076-1415-7*) Braziller.

— Hermes: And His Children. Hinshaw, Robert, ed. LC 97-52980. (Illus.). 201p. (C). 1993. reprint ed. pap. 17.95 (*3-85630-518-1*) Continuum.

***Lopez-Pedraza, Raphael.** Dionysus in Exile: On the Repression of the Body & Emotion. 96p. 2000. pap. write for info. (*1-888602-10-4*, Pub. by Chiron Pubns) Continuum.

Lopez-Pena, R., et al. Complex Systems & Binary Networks: Guanajuato Lectures Held at Guanajuato, Mexico, 16-22 January 1995. LC 95-44950. (Lecture Notes in Physics Ser.: Vol. 461). 223p. 1995. 77.95 (*3-540-60339-5*) Spr-Verlag.

Lopez-Pereira. New Carbohydrate Diet Counter. 1985. pap. 2.00 (*0-87980-107-7*) Wilshire.

Lopez, Pilar C. Teach Yourself Spanish Vocabulary. (Teach Yourself Ser.). (SPA., Illus.). 256p. 1996. pap. 7.95 (*0-8442-3986-0*, Teach Yrslf) NTC Contemp Pub Co.

Lopez-Quintela, M. A., jt. ed. see Rivas, J.

Lopez, R. J., ed. Maple V: Mathematics & Its Application. LC 94-29119. 234p. 1994. 42.50 (*0-8176-3791-5*) Birkhauser.

Lopez, R. M., jt. ed. see Ossowski, Liliana.

Lopez, Ralph, jt. auth. see Gee, Derek H.

***Lopez, Rambon & Valdes, Alberto.** Rural Poverty in Latin America. LC 00-42071. (Illus.). 2000. write for info. (*0-312-23728-6*) St Martin.

Lopez, Ramon E., jt. auth. see Carlowicz, Michael J.

Lopez, Ramon L., jt. auth. see Santos, Diana.

Lopez, Raul A., jt. auth. see Curl, Alan.

Lopez, Raymond & Aguilar, Miriam E. The Business Tool: A Business Start-up & Reference Guide. (Illus.). 221p. (Orig.). 1994. pap. 42.00 (*0-9643887-3-1*) West Comm Tech.

— The Business Tool: A Business Start-up & Reference Guide. (Illus.). 246p. (Orig.). 1994. pap. 21.00 (*0-9643887-1-5*) West Comm Tech.

— La Herramienta de Negocios: Una Guia de Referencia para Comenzar Su Negocio. (SPA., Illus.). 270p. (Orig.). 1994. pap. 21.00 (*0-9643887-0-7*) West Comm Tech.

— La Herramienta de Negocios: Una Guia de Referencia Para Comenzar Su Negocio. (SPA., Illus.). 246p. (Orig.). 1994. pap. 42.00 (*0-9643887-2-3*) West Comm Tech.

***Lopez-Rey, Jose.** Velazquez. 1998. pap. 24.99 (*3-8228-7561-9*) Benedikt Taschen.

Lopez-Rey, Jose. Velazquez. (Big Ser.). 1997. pap. 19.99 (*3-8228-8277-1*) Taschen Amer.

— Velazquez: Catalogue Raisonne, 2 vols. (Illus.). 620p. 1996. boxed set 79.95 (*3-8228-8657-2*) Taschen Amer.

***Lopez-Rey, Jose.** Velazquez: Catalogue Raisonne' (Jumbo Ser.). 1999. 49.99 (*3-8228-6533-8*) Benedikt Taschen.

Lopez-Rey, Jose. Velazquez: The Complete Paintings. limited ed. (Illus.). 536p. 1988. 175.00 (*1-55660-013-5*) A Wofsy Fine Arts.

Lopez-Rey, Manuel, et al. Extension, Carateristicas y Tendencias de la Criminalidad en Puerto Rico, 1964-1970. 2nd ed. (Centro de Investigaciones Sociales Ser.). 322p. 1975. reprint ed. pap. text 5.00 (*0-8477-2480-8*) U of PR Pr.

Lopez, Rigoberto A. & Polopolus, Leo C., eds. Vegetable Markets in the Western Hemisphere. LC 90-21777. (Illus.). 266p. 1992. text 39.95 (*0-8138-1052-3*) Iowa St U Pr.

Lopez-Rios. Enfermedades Ano-Rectales: Dia. (SPA.). (C). 1998. text 95.82 (*84-8174-327-5*) Harcourt.

Lopez, Robert, ed. see Sokei-an.

Lopez, Robert J. Maple via Calculus: Tutorial Approach. LC 94-28246. xiii, 166p. 1994. 18.50 (*0-8176-3771-0*) Birkhauser.

Lopez, Robert S. The Birth of Europe. 440p. 1998. 35.00 (*0-87131-863-6*) M Evans.

— Byzantium & the World Around It: Economic & Institutional Relations. (Collected Studies: No. CS85). (Illus.). 318p. (C). 1978. reprint ed. lib. bdg. 111.95 (*0-86078-030-9*, Pub. by Variorum) Ashgate Pub Co.

— The Commercial Revolution of the Middle Ages, 950-1350. LC 75-35453. (Illus.). 204p. 1976. pap. text 19.95 (*0-521-29046-5*) Cambridge U Pr.

— The Shape of Medieval Monetary History. (Collected Studies: No. CS247). (Illus.). 330p. (C). 1986. reprint ed. lib. bdg. 115.95 (*0-86078-195-X*, Pub. by Variorum) Ashgate Pub Co.

— Three Ages of the Italian Renaissance. LC 75-94759. 137p. reprint ed. 42.50 (*0-8357-9819-4*, 201146500078) Bks Demand.

***Lopez, Roberto E. & Piccaluga, Andrea.** Knowledge Flows in National Systems of Innovation: A Comparative Analysis of Sociotechnical Constituencies in Europe & Latin America. LC 00-34791. (New Horizons in the Economics of Innovation Ser.). 2001. write for info. (*1-84064-295-5*) E Elgar.

***Lopez-Rodriguez, Juana D.** American Job Resume: Your Employment Connection. (Illus.). 34p. 1998. pap. 19.95 (*0-9676792-0-6*) American Job.

Lopez-Roman, Juan E. La Obra Literaria de Vicente Pales Matos. LC 83-17123. (Coleccion Mente y Palabra). (SPA.). 293p. (Orig.). 1984. pap. 8.00 (*0-8477-0587-0*) U of PR Pr.

Lopez-Rubio, Jose. La Otra Orilla: Comedia en Tres Actos. Pasquariello, Anthony M. & Falconieri, John V., eds. LC 58-12829. (SPA.). 1977. reprint ed. pap. text 7.95 (*0-89197-324-9*) Irvington.

— Venda en los Ojos. Holt, Marion P., ed. LC 66-21587. (SPA.). (Orig.). 1966. pap. text 14.95 (*0-89197-464-4*) Irvington.

Lopez, Ruth, tr. see Pirolo, Neal.

Lopez, Ruth K. A Child's Garden Diary: Coloring & Activity Book. (Illus.). 56p. (Orig.). (J). (gr. k-6). 1992. pap. 5.95 (*0-9627463-4-7*) Gardens Growing People.

Lopez, Sandra. Clearcut. limited ed. Trusky, Tom, ed. (Hemingway Western Studies). (Illus.). 3p. (Orig.). 1994. 14.95 (*0-932129-23-4*) Heming W Studies.

Lopez-Santamaria, Maya. Musica de la Raza: Mexican & Chicano Music in Minnesota. LC 98-43709. (Minnesota Musical Traditions Ser.). (Illus.). 76p. 1999. pap. 16.95 incl. audio compact disk (*0-87351-366-5*, 366-5, Borealis Book) Minn Hist.

Lopez Sastre, Gerardo, ed. & tr. see Hume, David.

Lopez, Silvia L., et al, eds. Critical Practices in Post-Franco Spain. LC 94-1236. (Hispanic Issues Ser.: Vol. 11). 1994. pap. 18.95 (*0-8166-2474-7*); text 47.95 (*0-8166-2473-9*) U of Minn Pr.

Lopez, Silvia L., jt. auth. see Canclini, Nestor G.

Lopez-Solar, Joyce. Ace's Exambuster Spanish Study. Burchard, Elizabeth R., ed. (Exambusters Ser.). 384p. (YA). (gr. 7 up). 2000. reprint ed. pap. 10.95 (*1-881374-97-1*, Exambusters) Ace Acad.

Lopez-Soto, Edwin. Trying to Cope with Continuing Disability Review Regulations. 30p. 1986. pap. 3.25 (*0-685-44379-5*, 40,963) NCLS Inc.

Lopez Soto, V. Dictionary of Authors, Works & Personalities of Greek Literature: Diccionario de Autores, Obras y Personajes de la Literatura Griega. (ENG & SPA.). 316p. 1984. pap. 12.50 (*0-8288-1577-1*, S60272) Fr & Eur.

Lopez-Springfield, Consuelo. Daughters of Caliban: Caribbean Women in the Twentieth Century. LC 96-41477. 1997. 39.95 (*0-253-33249-4*) Ind U Pr.

Lopez-Springfield, Consuelo, ed. Daughters of Caliban: Caribbean Women in the Twentieth Century. LC 96-41477. 1997. pap. 17.95 (*0-253-21092-5*) Ind U Pr.

Lopez-Stafford, Gloria. A Place in El Paso: A Mexican-American Childhood. 222p. (C). 1996. pap. 16.95 (*0-8263-1709-X*) U of NM Pr.

Lopez, Steve. Land of Giants: Where No Good Deed Goes Unpunished. LC 95-9628. 230p. (Orig.). 1995. pap. 11.95 (*0-940159-30-9*) Camino Bks.

***Lopez, Steve.** The Sunday Macaroni Club. LC 99-42889. 1999. pap. 12.95 (*0-452-28138-5*, Plume) Dutton Plume.

Lopez, Steve. The Sunday Macaroni Club. LC 96-44062. 384p. 1997. 24.00 (*0-15-100264-9*) Harcourt.

— The Sunday Macaroni Club. 1998. mass mkt. 6.99 (*0-451-19723-2*, Sig) NAL.

— The Sunday Macaroni Club. 1999. pap. 23.95 (*0-670-86311-4*) Viking Penguin.

— Third & Indiana. 320p. 1995. pap. 12.95 (*0-14-023945-6*, Penguin Bks) Viking Penguin.

Lopez, Sue. Women on the Ball: A Guide to Women's Soccer. (Illus.). 210p. 1996. 39.95 (*1-85727-026-6*, Pub. by Scarlet Pr) LPC InBook.

— Women on the Ball: A Guide to Women's Soccer. 210p. 1996. pap. text 17.95 (*1-85727-016-9*, Pub. by Scarlet Pr) LPC InBook.

Lopez Suria, Violeta. Antologia Poetica. 262p. (C). 1970. 3.50 (*0-8477-3207-X*) U of PR Pr.

***Lopez, Suzanne.** Get Smart with Your Heart: The Intelligent Woman's Guide to Love, Lust & Lasting Relationships. LC 98-33358. 2000. reprint ed. pap. 13.95 (*0-399-52579-3*, Perigee Bks) Berkley Pub.

Lopez, Suzanne. Get Smart with Your Heart: The Intelligent Woman's Guide to Love, Lust & Lasting Relationships. LC 98-33358. 379p. 1999. 24.95 (*0-399-14462-5*, G P Putnam) Peng Put Young Read.

Lopez, Tessy. El Mundo Magico del Vidrio. (Ciencia Para Todos Ser.). (SPA.). pap. 6.99 (*968-16-4695-9*, Pub. by Fondo) Continental Bk.

Lopez, Tiffany A., ed. Growing Up Chicana O. 272p. 1995. pap. 12.50 (*0-380-72419-7*, Avon Bks) Morrow Avon.

Lopez, Tiffany Ana. Growing Up Chicana/o. LC 93-28195. 1993. 17.85 (*0-606-06431-1*) Turtleback.

***Lopez Tijerina, Reies & Gutierrez, Jose Angel.** They Called Me "King Tiger" My Struggle for the Land & Our Rights. 224p. 2000. pap. 14.95 (*1-55885-302-2*) Arte Publico.

Lopez, Tom. Exploring Idaho's Mountains: A Guide for Climbers, Hiking & Scramblers. LC 90-6679. (Illus.). 288p. (Orig.). 1990. pap. 17.95 (*0-89886-235-3*) Mountaineers.

***Lopez, Tom.** Idaho, A Climber's Guide: Climbs, Scrambles & Hikes. 2nd ed. (Illus.). 400p. 2000. pap. 35.00 (*0-89886-608-1*) Mountaineers.

***Lopez, Tony.** Devolution. 75p. 2000. pap. 10.00 (*0-935724-28-1*, Pub. by Figures) SPD-Small Pr Dist.

Lopez, Tony. The Poetry of W. S. Graham. 240p. 1989. 45.00 (*0-85224-587-4*, Pub. by Edinburgh U Pr) Col U Pr.

— The Poetry of W. S. Graham. 176p. 1990. pap. text 25.00 (*0-85224-588-2*, Pub. by Edinburgh U Pr) Col U Pr.

Lopez-Tushar, Olibama. The People of El Valle: A History of the Spanish Colonials in the San Luis Valley. 3rd ed. Simms, Charlene G. & Simms, Edward T., eds. (Illus.). 276p. 1997. pap. 16.95 (*0-9628974-4-2*) El Escrito.

Lopez-Valdez, Jeanne, ed. see Friedenberg, Joan E., et al.

Lopez Varela, Alejandra, tr. see Bourgeois, Paulette.

Lopez-Varela, Alejandra, tr. see Bourgeois, Paulette, et al.

Lopez Varela, Alejandra, tr. see Sykes, Julie.

Lopez-Vasquez, Alfredo R., ed. see De Claramonte, Andres.

***Lopez, Victor D.** Free & Low Cost Software for the PC. (Illus.). 216p. 2000. per. 32.00 (*0-7864-0847-2*) McFarland & Co.

Lopez, Victor D. The Legal Environment of Business. LC 95-53338. 480p. (C). 1996. 67.00 (*0-13-125386-7*) P-H.

Lopez-Vidriero, M. L., jt. ed. see Revenga, Luis.

Lopez-Vidriero, M. T., ed. Host Defense & the Role of Surfactant in the Lung, Amsterdam, September 1987. Lung Defensive System: Damages & Treatment, Milan, September, 1987: Journal: Respiration, Vol. 55, Supplement 1. (Illus.). 100p. 1989. pap. 30.50 (*3-8055-5071-5*) S Karger.

Lopez-Vigil, Jose I. Rebel Radio: The Story of El Salvador's Radio Venceremos. Fried, Mark, tr. from SPA. 240p. 1994. 19.95 (*1-880684-21-7*) Curbstone.

Lopez Vigil, Maria. Don Lito of El Salvador. Palumbo, Eugene, tr. LC 89-48225.Tr. of Don Lito del Salvador: Processo de una fe Martirial. 1990. pap. 13.00 (*0-88344-669-3*) Orbis Bks.

***Lopez Vigil, Maria.** Oscar Romero: Memories in Mosaic. LC 99-462256. (Illus.). 2000. write for info. (*0-918346-24-X*) EPICA.

Lopez Vigil, Maria, jt. auth. see Ignacio, Jose.

Lopez y Fuentes, Gregorio. El Indio. Brenner, Anita, tr. LC 61-17563. (Illus.). 256p. 1961. pap. text 11.95 (*0-8044-6429-4*) F Ungar Bks.

Lopez y Rivas, Gilberto. The Chicanos: Life & Struggles of the Mexican Minority in the United States, with Readings. Martinez, Elizabeth, ed. & tr. by. LC 73-8056. 192p. reprint ed. pap. 59.60 (*0-8357-6053-7*, 203434000089) Bks Demand.

Lopez Yustos, Alfonso. Compendio Historia de la Educacion. (SPA.). 168p. 1992. pap. write for info. (*0-929441-36-2*) Pubns Puertorriquenas.

— Compendio Historia Documental de la Educacion. (SPA.). 308p. 1991. pap. write for info. (*0-929441-12-5*) Pubns Puertorriquenas.

— Introduccion a la Educacion. (SPA.). 196p. 1994. pap. write for info. (*0-929441-63-X*) Pubns Puertorriquenas.

Lopiano-Misdom, Janine & De Luca, Joanne. Street Trends: How Today's Alternative Youth Cultures Are Creating Tomorrow's Mainstream Markets. LC 97-22786. (Illus.). 224p. 1998. pap. 13.50 (*0-88730-929-1*) HarpC.

— Street Trends: How Today's Alternative Youth Cultures Are Creating Tomorrow's Mainstream Markets. LC 97-22786. (Illus.). 224p. 1997. 25.00 (*0-88730-875-9*, HarpBusn) HarpInfo.

***Lopiano-Misdom, Janine & DeLuca, Joanne.** Street Trends: How Today's Alternative Youth Cultures Are Creating Tomorrow's Mainstream Markets. (Illus.). 206p. 2000. reprint ed. text 25.00 (*0-7881-6900-9*) DIANE Pub.

Lopiansky, Aaron. Time Pieces: Reflections on the Jewish Year. 295p. 1995. 18.95 (*1-56871-091-7*) Targum Pr.

LoPiccolo, J. & LoPiccolo, L. Handbook of Sex Therapy. LC 77-18818. (Perspectives in Sexuality Ser.). (Illus.). 552p. (C). 1978. 65.00 (*0-306-31074-0*, Plenum Trade) Perseus Pubng.

LoPiccolo Jennett, V. & Hagen, Paula. A Prayer Companion for MOMS. LC 93-19670. (Illus.). 104p. (C). 1993. pap. 7.95 (*0-89390-265-9*) Resource Pubns.

LoPiccolo, Joseph, jt. auth. see Heiman, Julia.

LoPiccolo, L., jt. auth. see LoPiccolo, J.

Lopina, Stephanie T. Chemical Discipline - Specific Review for the FE/EIT Exam. LC 97-25609. 100p. (Orig.). 1997. pap. 29.95 (*1-888577-21-5*, DSCH) Prof Pubns CA.

Lopinot, Alvin C., jt. auth. see Winterringer, Glen S.

Lopinski, Maciej, et al. Konspira: Solidarity Underground. Cave, Jane, tr. (Illus.). 261p. 1990. 38.00 (*0-520-06131-4*, Pub. by U CA Pr) Cal Prin Full Svc.

An Asterisk (*) at the beginning of an entry indicates that the title is appearing for the first time.

LoPinto, Charles, jt. auth. see LoPinto, Lidia.

***LoPinto, Lidia & LoPinto, Charles.** The Case of the Toxic Cruiseline: Agents Fight Pollution. (Environmental Mystery Ser.). 200p. 2000. 16.95 (*0-9677441-1-3*) EnviroCrime.

— The Case of the Toxic Cruiseline: Agents Fight Pollution. (Environmental Mystery Ser.: Vol. 1). 200p. 2000. pap. 16.95 (*0-9677441-0-5*) EnviroCrime.

LoPinto, Roslyn. A Guide to Centering: The Harmonious Response to Life. (Illus.). 72p. (Orig.). 1986. pap. 6.95 (*0-9619018-0-2*) Artistech.

— A Spiritual Concept: The Real Nature of Things. (Illus.). 86p. (Orig.). 1988. pap. 6.95 (*0-9619018-1-0*) Artistech.

Lopman, Charles S. The Activist Advocate: Policy Making in State Supreme Courts. LC 99-21597. 144p. 1999. 55.00 (*0-275-96455-8*, C6455, Praeger Pubs) Greenwood.

Lopo, Dan, ed. see Hossain, Akram & Suyut, Suzali.

***LoPopolo, Carlos.** History of the Western Horse Coloring Book, Vol. 1. LoPopolo, Cindy Rodger, ed. (Illus.). 35p. (J). (gr. 1-8). 2000. spiral bd. 14.95 (*1-58707-003-0*) C LoPopolo.

LoPopolo, Cindy Rodger, ed. see LoPopolo, Carlos.

Loporto, Marc. Fantasy Land: Venice Beach, California. Tsabar, Carmel, ed. LC 98-92217. (Illus.). ix, 100p. 1999. pap. 22.95 (*0-9668927-0-4*) M L Pubg.

Lopos, George J., et al, eds. Certificate Programs at American Colleges & Universities. LC 88-43018. 351p. (Orig.). 1988. pap. 35.95 (*0-87866-741-5*) Petersons.

Lopos, George J., jt. ed. see Holt, Margaret E.

Lopreato, Joseph. Human Nature & Biocultural Evolution. LC 84-402. (Illus.). 350p. 1984. text 34.95 (*0-04-573017-2*) Routledge.

Lopreato, Joseph & Crippen, Timothy. The Crisis in Sociology: The Need for Darwin. LC 98-50335. 378p. 1999. 34.95 (*1-56000-398-7*) Transaction Pubs.

LoPreato, Joseph, jt. auth. see Jackson, Eugene.

***Lopresti, Daniel P. & Zhou, Jiangying, eds.** Document Recognition & Retrieval VI. 208p. 1999. pap. text 62.00 (*0-8194-3122-2*) SPIE.

Lopresti, Daniel P. & Zhou, Jiangying, eds. Document Recognition V, Vol. 3305. LC 99-211182. 286p. 1998. 69.00 (*0-8194-2745-4*) SPIE.

Lopresti, Robert, ed. see Benchley, Robert.

Lopresti, Robert, ed. see Thurber, James.

LoPresti, Vincent & Boily, Chad. Sometimes It Takes Three Hearts. 214p. 1999. pap. 7.50 (*1-892614-18-9*, BWP-3H) Briarwood VA.

LoPresto, James C. Space-Time: Fabric of the Universe. LC 94-78959. (Illus.). 258p. 1995. pap. 29.95 (*0-910042-72-1*) Allegheny.

Loprete, Carlos A. Iberoamerica: Historia de su Civilizacion y Cultural. 3rd ed. (Illus.). 464p. (C). 1994. 54.67 (*0-13-323445-2*) P-H.

Loprieno, Antonio. Ancient Egyptian: A Linguistic Introduction. 338p. (C). 1995. text 59.95 (*0-521-44384-9*); pap. text 21.95 (*0-521-44849-2*) Cambridge U Pr.

— Ancient Egyptian Literature: History & Forms. 726p. 1996. 193.00 (*90-04-09925-5*) Brill Academic Pubs.

Loprieno, Nicola. Alternative Methodologies for the Safety Evaluation of Chemicals in the Cosmetic Industry. Hollinger, Mannfred A., ed. LC 95-2335. (Basic & Clinical Aspects Ser.). 272p. 1995. boxed set 179.95 (*0-8493-8546-6*, 8546) CRC Pr.

Lopshire, Robert. I Want to Be Somebody New. LC 85-43098. (Illus.). 48p. (J). (gr. k-3). 1986. 7.99 (*0-394-87616-4*) Beginner.

— I Want to Be Somebody New. LC 85-43098. (Illus.). 48p. (J). (gr. k-3). 1986. lib. bdg. 11.99 (*0-394-97616-9*) Beginner.

— New Tricks I Can Do! LC 95-36104. (Illus.). (J). 1996. lib. bdg. 11.99 (*0-679-97715-5*) Beginner.

— New Tricks I Can Do! (Illus.). (J). (ps-2). 1996. 7.99 (*0-679-87715-0*, Pub. by Random Bks Yng Read) Random.

— Put Me in the Zoo. LC 60-13494. (Beginner Books Ser.). (Illus.). 61p. (J). (ps-3). 1960. 7.99 (*0-394-80017-6*) Beginner.

— Put Me in the Zoo. LC 60-13494. (Illus.). 72p. (J). (gr. 1-2). 1966. lib. bdg. 11.99 (*0-394-90017-0*) Beginner.

***Lopshire, Robert.** Put Me in Zoo Puzzle Book. 1999. 7.99 (*0-375-80254-1*, Pub. by Random Bks Yng Read) Random.

Lopshire, Roger. I Want to Count Something New! (Beginner Workbooks Ser.). (J). (ps-1). 1997. pap. 3.99 (*0-614-28929-7*) Random Bks Yng Read.

Lopsinger, Lutz W. & Michler, Ralf, eds. Salvador Dali: The Catalogue Raisonne of Etchings & Mixed-Media Prints, 1924-1980. LC 94-157225. (Illus.). 262p. 1997. 130.00 (*3-7913-1279-0*, Pub. by Prestel) te Neues.

Lopsinger, Lutz W., jt. ed. see Michler, Ralf.

Loptson, Peter. Theories of Human Nature. 220p. 1995. pap. 16.95 (*1-55111-061-X*) Broadview Pr.

Loptson, Peter, ed. Readings on Human Nature. 800p. (C). 1998. pap. 35.95 (*1-55111-156-X*) Broadview Pr.

Loptson, Peter, jt. auth. see Conway, Anne.

Lopuck, Lisa. Kid's Web Kit. 64p. 1997. pap. 22.95 incl. cd-rom (*0-201-88675-8*) Peachpit Pr.

Lopuck, Lisa & Hampton, Sheryl. Adobe Seminars: Web Page Design. LC 97-73666. 241p. 1997. 40.00 (*1-56830-426-9*) Adobe Pr.

LoPucki, Lynn M. Bankruptcy: 1994 Supplement. 1994. 75.00 (*0-316-53170-7*, Aspen Law & Bus) Aspen Pub.

Lopucki, Lynn M. Commercial Transactions: A Systems Approach. LC 97-32983. 1998. 62.00 (*1-56706-643-7*) Panel Pubs.

Lopucki, Lynn M. 1995 Supplement to Bankruptcy. 1995. suppl. ed. 75.00 (*0-316-53101-4*, Aspen Law & Bus) Aspen Pub.

— Player's Manual for the Debtor Creditor Game. (Legal Exercise Ser.). 123p. (C). 1984. pap. text 17.50 (*0-314-89510-8*) West Pub.

— Secured Credit. 848p. 1995. 52.00 (*0-316-53219-3*) Little.

— Strategies for Creditors in Bankruptcy Proceedings. annuals 2nd ed. 1107p. boxed set 155.00 (*0-316-53221-5*, 32215) Aspen Law.

— Strategies for Creditors in Bankruptcy Proceedings. 2nd ed. 1991. 155.00 (*0-316-53228-2*, Aspen Law & Bus) Aspen Pub.

— Strategies for Creditors in Bankruptcy Proceedings. 3rd ed. LC 97-26000. 1998. boxed set 175.00 (*1-56706-614-3*) Aspen Law.

LoPucki, Lynn M. & Reilly, Ann T., eds. Law & Business Directory of Bankruptcy Attorneys, 1988. 1988. 125.00 (*0-318-36198-1*) P-H.

LoPucki, Lynn M. & Warren, Elizabeth. Secured Credit: A Systems Approach. 848p. 1995. teacher ed. write for info. (*0-316-53212-6*, 32126) Aspen Law.

Lopucki, Lynn M. & Warren, Elizabeth. Secured Credit: A Systems Approach. 2nd ed. LC 97-36520. 1998. 58.00 (*1-56706-692-5*) Aspen Law.

***LoPucki, Lynn M. & Warren, Elizabeth.** Secured Credit: A Systems Approach. 3rd ed. LC 00-35555. 2000. write for info. (*0-7355-1409-7*) Panel Pubs.

Lopukhin, Y. M. Physicochemical Aspects of Medicine Reviews Vol. 3, Pt. 4: The Skin & Atherosclerosis, a Three-Drop Test, Vol. 3. (Soviet Medical Reviews Ser.: Section B). 124p. 1992. pap. text 147.00 (*3-7186-5291-9*, Harwood Acad Pubs) Gordon & Breach.

Lopukhin, Yu. M. Physiochemical Aspects of Medicine Reviews, Vol. 1. xiii, 426p. 1987. text 500.00 (*3-7186-0316-0*) Gordon & Breach.

Lopukhin, Yu M., et al, eds. Cholesterosis - Membrane Cholesterol: Theoretical & Clinical Aspects, Vol. 4. (Physicochemical Biology Reviews Supplement Ser.: Soviet Scientific Reviews, Sect. D). xxii, 382p. 1984. text 515.00 (*3-7186-0159-1*) Gordon & Breach.

Lopushinsky, Cochran W. & McColley, P. D. Effect of Operational Fertilization on Foliar Nutrient Content & Growth of Young Douglas-Fir & Pacific Silver Fir. 16p. 1997. reprint ed. pap. 2.60 (*0-89904-925-7*, Ecosytems Resrch) Crumb Elbow Pub.

Lopushinsky, W. Effect of Jellyrolling & Acclimatization on Survival & Height Growth of Conifer Seedlings. (Illus.). 18p. 1997. reprint ed. pap. 2.80 (*0-89904-922-2*, Ecosytems Resrch) Crumb Elbow Pub.

Lopuszanzki, J. Introduction to Symmetry & Supersymmetry in Quantum Field Theory. 388p. (C). 1990. text 86.00 (*9971-5-0160-0*); pap. text 40.00 (*9971-5-0161-9*) World Scientific Pub.

Loqinov, V. & Obuchov, V. Helenie. (RUS., Illus.). 46p. (Orig.). 1990. 9.00 (*1-878445-50-2*) Antiquary CT.

Loque, Rufino E. The Fragrance of Tina & Other Stories. v, 82p. (Orig.). (C). 1992. pap. 7.50 (*971-10-0439-9*, Pub. by New Day Pub) Cellar.

Lora, Doris, ed. see Kay, James.

Lora, Doris, ed. see Linden, Ruth W.

Lora, Doris, ed. see Lund, Robert D.

Lora, Eduardo, jt. auth. see Fleischer, Lowell.

Lora, Guillermo. A History of the Bolivian Labour Movement, 1848-1971. LC 76-22988. (Cambridge Latin American Studies: no. 27). 418p. reprint ed. pap. 119.20 (*0-608-13577-1*, 2022458) Bks Demand.

Lora, Ronald. Conservative Minds in America. Van Tassel, David D., ed. LC 79-14219. 274p. 1980. reprint ed. lib. bdg. 35.00 (*0-313-21468-9*, LOCM, Greenwood Pr) Greenwood.

Lora, Ronald Henry & Longton, William, eds. The Conservative Press in Twentieth-Century America. LC 98-51891. (Historical Guides to the World's Periodicals & Newspapers Ser.). 744p. 1999. lib. bdg. 125.00 (*0-313-21390-9*, Greenwood Pr) Greenwood.

Lora, Ronald Henry & Longton, William Henry, eds. The Conservative Press in Eighteenth & Nineteenth-Century America. LC 98-51934. (Historical Guides to the World's Periodicals & Newspapers). 416p. 1999. lib. bdg. 85.00 (*0-313-31043-2*, GR1043, Greenwood Pr) Greenwood.

***Lorah, Deb, et al.** Christmas Through Our Eyes: Three Plays for Youth. 36p. 1999. pap. 6.50 (*0-7880-1516-8*) CSS OH.

Lorah, Priscilla A., ed. Chronicle of Professional Articles for Junior & Senior High School Counselors. 1996. 152.70 (*1-55631-263-6*) Chron Guide.

— Professional Articles for Elementary Counselors. 1996. 126.55 (*1-55631-265-2*) Chron Guide.

***Lorain, Douglas.** Backpacking Washington. (Illus.). 2000. pap. 16.95 (*0-89997-272-1*) Wilderness Pr.

Lorain, Douglas A. Backpacking Oregon. LC 99-40260. (Illus.). 276p. 1999. pap. 16.95 (*0-89997-252-7*) Wilderness Pr.

Loraine, John A. Sex & the Population Crisis. LC 85-24774. 213p. 1986. reprint ed. lib. bdg. 59.50 (*0-313-22505-2*, LOSP, Greenwood Pr) Greenwood.

Loraine, Philip. Ugly Money. large type ed. (Linford Mystery Large Print Ser.). 368p. 1997. pap. 16.99 (*0-7089-5168-6*) Ulverscroft.

Loram, Charlie. Leh & Trekking in Ladakh. 1996. pap. text 14.95 (*1-873756-09-7*, Pub. by Trailblazer) Seven Hills Bk.

— Trekking In Ladakh. 2nd ed. 1999. pap. text 16.95 (*1-873756-30-5*, Pub. by Trailblazer) Seven Hills Bk.

Loram, Ian C. & Phelps, Leland R., eds. Aus Unserer Zeit. 4th ed. (GER.). (C). 1988. pap. 32.00 (*0-393-95614-8*) Norton.

Loran, Donald F. & MacEwen, Caroline J., eds. Sports Vision. (Illus.). 256p. 1997. pap. text 58.50 (*0-7506-3616-5*, 85901) Buttrwrth-Heinemann.

Loran, Erle. Cezanne's Composition: Analysis of His Form with Diagrams & Photographs of His Motifs. 3rd ed. (Illus.). 1963. 55.00 (*0-520-00768-9*, Pub. by U CA Pr); pap. 24.95 (*0-520-05459-8*, Pub. by U CA Pr) Cal Prin Full Svc.

Lorand, Laszlo, et al, eds. Proteolytic Enzymes in Coagulation, Fibrinolysis, & Complement Activation Pt. A: Mammalian Blood Coagulation Factors & Inhibitors. (Methods in Enzymology Ser.: Vol. 222). (Illus.). 613p. 1993. text 104.00 (*0-12-182123-4*) Acad Pr.

— Proteolytic Enzymes in Coagulation, Fibrinolysis, & Complement Activation Pt. B: Complement Activation, Fibrinolysis, & Nonmammalian Blood Coagulation Factors & Inhibitors. (Methods in Enzymology Ser.: Vol. 223). (Illus.). 433p. 1993. text 94.00 (*0-12-182124-2*) Acad Pr.

Lorand, Laszlo, jt. ed. see Colowick, Sidney P.

Lorand, Laszlo, jt. ed. see Najjar, Victor A.

Lorand Olazagasti, Adelaida. El Indio en la Narrativa Guatemalteca. 280p. (C). 1968. pap. 3.25 (*0-8477-3138-3*) U of PR Pr.

***Lorand, Ruth.** Aesthetic Theory: A Philosophy of Beauty & Art. LC 00-25491. (Studies in Twentieth-Century Philosophy Ser.). 2000. write for info. (*0-415-23602-9*) Routledge.

Lorand, Sandor, ed. Psychoanalysis Today. LC BF0175.L6. (Medical War Bks.). 420p. 1944. reprint ed. pap. 130.20 (*0-608-09998-8*, 201068800070) Bks Demand.

Lorang, Dianne, ed. see Ripple, Wilhelminia.

L'Orange, Darlena. Herbal Healing Secrets of the Orient. LC 97-41799. (Illus.). 352p. (C). 1998. text 26.95 (*0-13-849324-3*); pap. text 14.95 (*0-13-849316-2*) P-H.

L'Orange, H. P. Apotheosis in Ancient Portraiture. (Illus.). 156p. 1982. reprint ed. lib. bdg. 55.00 (*0-89241-149-X*) Caratzas.

— Art Forms & Civic Life in the Late Roman Empire. (Illus.). 131p. 1965. pap. text 14.95 (*0-691-00305-X*, Pub. by Princeton U Pr) Cal Prin Full Svc.

— Likeness & Icon: Selected Studies in Classical & Early Medieval Art. 344p. (Orig.). 1973. pap. 67.50 (*87-7492-062-6*, Pub. by Odense Universitets Forlag) Coronet Bks.

— Studies on the Iconography of Cosmic Kingship in the Ancient World. (Illus.). 206p. 1982. reprint ed. lib. bdg. 55.00 (*0-89241-150-3*) Caratzas.

L'Orange, Hans P. & Von Gerkan, Arnim. Der Spaetantike Bildschmuck des Konstantinsbogen: Text Volume & Volume with Plates. (Studien zur Spaetantiken Kunstgeschichte: Vol. 10). (Illus.). 238p. (C). 1978. reprint ed. 542.35 (*3-11-002249-4*) De Gruyter.

Lorange, Peter, ed. Strategic Planning & Control: Issues in the Strategy Process. (Corporate Strategy, Organization, & Change Ser.). 256p. 1993. 44.95 (*1-55786-103-X*) Blackwell Pubs.

— Strategic Planning Process. (International Library Management). 400p. 1994. 199.95 (*1-85521-350-8*, Pub. by Dartmth Pub) Ashgate Pub Co.

Lorange, Peter, et al. Strategic Control. 1986p. (C). 1986. pap. text 38.25 (*0-314-85258-1*) West Pub.

Loranger, Alexina, jt. tr. see Notovitch, Nicolas.

Loranger, Armand W., et al, eds. Assessment & Diagnosis of Personality Disorders: The International Personality Disorder Examination (IPDE) LC 96-45992. (Illus.). 239p. (C). 1997. text 59.95 (*0-521-58043-9*) Cambridge U Pr.

Lorant, Emma. Baby Roulette. 408p. 1996. pap. 10.95 (*0-7472-5062-6*, Pub. by Headline Bk Pub) Trafalgar.

Lorant, John H. The Role of Capital: Improving Innovations in American Manufacturing During the 1920's. LC 75-2588. (Dissertations in American Economic History Ser.). (Illus.). 1975. 34.95 (*0-405-07207-4*) Ayer.

Lorant, Stefan. The Glorious Burden: The American Presidency. LC 76-48760. (Illus.). 1976. 19.95 (*0-918058-00-7*) Authors Edn MA.

— Pittsburgh: The Story of an American City. enl. ed. LC 75-24970. (Illus.). 736p. 1988. 24.95 (*0-685-92012-7*) Authors Edn MA.

***Lorant, Stefan, et al.** Pittsburgh, the Story of an American City: The Millennium Edition. 5th ed. (Illus.). 776p. 1999. 39.95 (*0-9674103-0-4*) Esselmont Bks.

Loras College Sesquicentennial Committee Staff. Look at Loras One Hundred & Fiftieth Celebration. Farrington, Anthony, ed. (Illus.). 100p. 1989. 39.95 (*0-936875-04-6*) Loras Coll Pr.

***Loraux, Nicole.** Born of the Earth: Myth & Politics in Athens. LC 00-21218. (Myth & Poetics Ser.). 2000. pap. write for info. (*0-8014-8443-X*) Cornell U Pr.

— Born of the Earth: Myth & Politics in Athens. (Myth & Poetics Ser.). 2000. 39.95 (*0-8014-3419-X*) Cornell U Pr.

Loraux, Nicole. Children of Athena: Anthenian Ideas about Citizenship & the Division Between the Sexes. 296p. 1993. pap. text 17.95 (*0-691-03762-0*, Pub. by Princeton U Pr) Cal Prin Full Svc.

— The Children of Athena: Athenian Ideas about Citizenship & the Division Between the Sexes. Levine, Caroline, tr. (Illus.). 320p. 1993. text 45.00 (*0-691-03272-6*, Pub. by Princeton U Pr) Cal Prin Full Svc.

***Loraux, Nicole.** The Divided City: Forgetting in the Memory of Athens. LC 00-28985. 2001. write for info. (*1-890951-09-9*) Zone Bks.

Loraux, Nicole. Experience of Tiresias: The Feminine & the Greek Man. 356p. 1995. pap. text 16.95 (*0-691-01717-4*, Pub. by Princeton U Pr) Cal Prin Full Svc.

— The Experiences of Tiresias: The Feminine & the Greek Man. Wissing, Paula, tr. LC 94-36789. 336p. 1995. text 45.00 (*0-691-02985-7*, Pub. by Princeton U Pr) Cal Prin Full Svc.

— Mothers in Mourning: With the Essay of Amnesty & Its Opposite. Pache, Corinne, tr. LC 97-29264. (Myth & Poetics Ser.). 136p. 1998. pap. 11.95 (*0-8014-8242-9*); text 29.95 (*0-8014-3090-9*) Cornell U Pr.

— Tragic Ways of Killing a Woman. Forster, Anthony, tr. LC 87-390. 120p. 1987. 25.95 (*0-674-90225-4*) HUP.

— Tragic Ways of Killing a Woman. 120p. (C). 1991. pap. 14.50 (*0-674-90226-2*) HUP.

Loraux, Nicole, et al, eds. Antiquities, 3 vols. Goldhammer, Arthur, tr. (Postwar French Thought Ser.: Vol. II). 496p. 2000. 40.00 (*1-56584-376-2*, Pub. by New Press NY) Norton.

***Lorayne, Harry.** Fell's Beginner's Guide to Magic. 2nd ed. (Illus.). 2000. pap. 16.95 (*0-88391-050-0*) F Fell Pubs Inc.

Lorayne, Harry. The Memory Book. LC 96-96797. 1996. pap. 10.00 (*0-345-41002-5*) Ballantine Pub Grp.

— Memory Makes Money. 256p. 1988. 16.95 (*0-316-53267-3*) Little.

***Lorayne, Harry.** The Official Know-It-All Guide to Secrets of Mind Power. LC 99-16290. 224p. 1999. pap. 16.95 (*0-88391-008-X*) F Fell Pubs Inc.

Lorayne, Harry. Page a Minute Memory Book. LC 96-223854. 1996. pap. 10.00 (*0-345-41014-9*) Ballantine Pub Grp.

— Remembering People: The Key to Success. 1996. pap. 14.95 (*0-8128-8557-0*, Scrbrough Hse) Madison Bks UPA.

— Secrets of Mind Power. rev. ed. 240p. 1995. 17.95 (*0-8119-0756-2*) F Fell Pubs Inc.

— Super Memory Super Student, Vol. 1. 180p. 1990. pap. 13.95 (*0-316-53268-1*) Little.

Lorayne, Harry, jt. auth. see Lucas, Jerry.

Lorbeer & Nelson. Science Activities for Children, Vols. 1 & 2. 10th ed. 1996. 65.50 (*0-697-38308-3*, WCB McGr Hill) McGrw-H Hghr Educ.

Lorbeer, Floyd I. Philosophy of Light: An Introductory Treatise. 259p. 1981. pap. 20.00 (*0-89540-102-9*, SB-102) Sun Pub.

Lorbeer, George C. Science Activities for Children, Vol. II. 416p. (C). 1992. text. write for info. (*0-697-14691-X*) Brown & Benchmark.

***Lorbeer, George C.** Science Activities for Elementary Students. 11th ed. LC 99-30368. 2000. write for info. (*0-697-37789-X*, WCB McGr Hill) McGrw-H Hghr Educ.

— Science Activities for Middle School Students. 2nd ed. LC 99-35891. 448p. (J). 1999. pap. 46.86 (*0-07-229916-9*) McGraw.

Lorbeer, George C. & Nelson, Leslie W. Science Activities for Children. 10th ed. 416p. (J). 1997. spiral bd. 4.87 (*0-07-114996-1*) McGraw.

— Science Activities for Children, Vol. 1. 10th ed. 416p. (C). 1995. text 30.05 (*0-697-24150-5*) Brown & Benchmark.

Lorber, Miriam, et al. Gateway to Torah. LC 98-182774. 2 Vp. 1991. 8.95 (*0-88125-397-9*) Ktav.

Lorber, Bennett, jt. ed. see Mandell, Gerald L.

Lorber, Brendan. Address Book. Date not set. pap. 8.00 (*0-9669430-1-5*, Pub. by Owl Pr CA) SPD-Small Pr Dist.

Lorber, Catharine C. Treasures of Ancient Coinage: From the Private Collections of American Numismatic Society Members. (Illus.). 128p. (Orig.). 1996. pap. 19.95 (*0-9636738-3-1*) Classical Numismatic Grp.

Lorber, Helene, ed. see Ager, Susan.

Lorber, Jakob. Earth & Moon. Hanswille, Gerhard, tr. from GER. 244p. (Orig.). 1997. pap. text 19.95 (*1-885928-01-7*) Merkur Pubng.

— The Healing Power of Sunlight. Hanswille, Gerhard & Gallo, Franca, trs. from GER. 60p. 1997. pap. text 6.95 (*1-885928-10-6*) Merkur Pubng.

— The Lord's Book of Life & Health. Hanswille, Gerhard, tr. from GER. 265p. (Orig.). 1994. per. 17.95 (*1-885928-00-9*) Merkur Pubng.

— The Lord's Sermons. Ozols, Violet & Von Koerber, Hildegard, trs. from GER. LC 80-50280. (Jakob Lorber Ser.). 256p. 1981. 12.95 (*0-934616-06-X*) Valkyrie Pub Hse.

— Saturn. Hanswille, Gerhard & Gallo, Franca, trs. from GER. 281p. 1998. per. 20.95 (*1-885928-07-6*) Merkur Pubng.

Lorber, Jakob & Mayerhofer, Gottfried. The Advent of Christ. 2nd ed. LC 97-1379. 92p. 1993. pap. 6.95 (*0-9693820-6-5*) Merkur Pubng.

Lorber, Judith. Gender & the Social Construction of Illness. LC 97-4588. (Gender Lens Ser.). 204p. 1997. pap. 14.95 (*0-8039-5814-5*) Sage.

— Gender & the Social Construction of Illness. LC 97-4588. (Gender Lens Ser.: Vol. 4). 148p. 1997. 45.00 (*0-8039-5813-7*) Sage.

— Gender Inequality: Feminist Theories & Politics. LC 97-26297. 210p. (C). 1998. pap. text. write for info. (*1-891487-02-7*) Roxbury Pub Co.

***Lorber, Judith.** Gender Inequality: Theories & Politics. 2nd ed. 202p. (C). 2001. pap. text. write for info. (*1-891487-60-4*) Roxbury Pub Co.

Lorber, Judith. Paradoxes of Gender. 1995. pap. 17.00 (*0-300-06497-7*) Yale U Pr.

— Women Physicians: Careers, Status & Power. 250p. 1985. 25.00 (*0-422-79040-0*, NO. 9071); pap. 12.95 (*0-422-79050-8*, NO. 9103) Routledge.

Lorber, Judith & Farrell, Susan A., eds. The Social Construction of Gender. (Illus.). 400p. (C). 1990. text 52.00 (*0-8039-3956-6*); pap. text 24.00 (*0-8039-3957-4*) Sage.

Lorber, Michael A. Objectives, Methods, & Evaluation for Secondary Teaching. 4th ed. LC 95-33143. 304p. (C). 1995. pap. text 58.00 (*0-205-19392-7*) Allyn.

Lorber, Robert, jt. auth. see Khadem, Riaz.

Lorberg, A. Otahki, Trail of Tears Princess. 1967. pap. 1.00 (*0-911208-13-5*) Ramfre.

Lorbiecki, Marybeth. Aldo Leopold: A Fierce Green Fire. LC 96-25723. (Illus.). 224p. 1996. 19.95 (*1-56044-478-9*) Falcon Pub Inc.

L

An Asterisk (*) at the beginning of an entry indicates that the title is appearing for the first time.

L

— Aldo Leopold: A Fierce Green Fire. LC QH31.L618L68 1999. (Illus.). 224p. 1999. pap. 13.95 (*0-19-512966-0*) OUP.

— The Children of Vietnam. LC 96-13899. (World's Children Ser.). (Illus.). (J). (gr. 4-7). 1996. lib. bdg. 21.27 (*1-57505-034-X*, Carolrhoda) Lerner Pub.

— Of Things Natural, Wild, & Free: A Story about Aldo Leopold. LC 92-44049. (Creative Minds Ser.). (Illus.). (J). (gr. 3-6). 1993. lib. bdg. 19.95 (*0-87614-797-X*, Carolrhoda) Lerner Pub.

Lorbiecki, Marybeth. Sister Anne's Hands. LC 97-26671. (Illus.). 40p. (J). (gr. 1-3). 1998. 15.99 (*0-8037-2038-6*, Dial Yng Read) Peng Put Young Read.

***Lorbiecki, Marybeth.** Sister Anne's Hands. LC 99-50872. (Illus.). 32p. (J). (ps-3). 2000. pap. 6.99 (*0-14-056534-5*, PuffinBks) Peng Put Young Read.

***Lorbiecki, Marybeth & Eastman, Seth.** Painting the Dakota: Seth Eastman at Fort Snelling. LC 00-40161. 2000. write for info. (*1-890434-32-9*) Afton Hist Soc.

Lorbiecki, Marybeth & Lowery, Linda. Earthwise at Play: A Guide to the Care & Feeding of Your Planet. LC 92-9870. (Illus.). (J). (gr. 1-4). 1993. lib. bdg. 19.93 (*0-87614-729-5*, Carolrhoda) Lerner Pub.

Lorbiecki, Marybeth, jt. auth. see Lowery, Linda.

Lorblanchet, Michel, ed. Rock Art in the Old World. (C). 1992. 78.00 (*0-685-66244-6*, Pub. by UBS Pubs Dist) S Asia.

Lorblanchet, Michel & Bahn, Paul, eds. Rock Art Studies: The Post-Stylistic Era: or Where Do We Go from Here? (Oxbow Monographs in Archaeology: No. 35). (Illus.). 220p. 1994. pap. 35.00 (*0-946897-63-8*, Pub. by Oxbow Bks) David Brown.

LORC Staff. Your New Life in the United States. (CAM, CHI, LAO, SPA & VIE.). 215p. 1984. pap. 5.00 (*0-685-16936-7*) Ctr Appl Ling.

Lorca, Federico Garcia, see Garcia Lorca, Federico.

Lorca, Federico Garcia, see Campo, Rafael & Garcia Lorca, Federico.

Lorca, Federico Garcia, see Garcia Lorca, Federico.

Lorch. Morte Accidentale Di un Anarchico. 192p. 1997. pap. 19.95 (*0-7190-3848-0*) St Martin.

Lorch, Carlos. Jungle Warriors: Defenders of the Amazon. (Illus.). 144p. 1992. 34.95 (*0-943231-48-5*) Howell Pr VA.

Lorch, Carlos & Lorch, Netalel. Shielf of Zion: The Israel Defense Forces. 144p. 1997. 80.00 (*1-86227-010-4*, Pub. by Spellmnt Pubs) St Mut.

Lorch, Carlos, jt. auth. see Ziegelmeyer, Wagner.

Lorch, Carol. Jungle Warriors: Defenders of the Amazon. 144p. 1997. 80.00 (*1-86227-009-0*, Pub. by Spellmnt Pubs) St Mut.

Lorch, Edgar R. Spectral Theory. LC 62-9824. (University Texts in the Mathematical Sciences Ser.). 170p. reprint ed. pap. 48.50 (*0-608-30436-0*, 2051947) Bks Demand.

Lorch, Frederick W. The Trouble Begins at Eight: Mark Twain's Lecture Tours. LC 68-17493. (Illus.). 391p. reprint ed. pap. 121.30 (*0-608-18796-8*, 203031800068) Bks Demand.

Lorch, Ingomar. Die Kirchenfassade in Italien von 1450 bis 1527: Die Grundlagen Durch Leon Battista Alberti und die Weiterentwicklung des Basilikalen Fassadenspiegels bis zum Sacco di Roma. (Studien zur Kunstgeschichte Ser.: Bd. 130). (GER.). 242p. 1999. 65.00 (*3-487-10872-0*, Pub. by G Olms Verlag) Lubrecht & Cramer.

Lorch, Janet. From Foal to Full-Grown. (Illus.). 192p. 1998. pap. 19.95 (*0-7153-0722-3*, Pub. by D & C Pub) Sterling.

Lorch, Jennifer, jt. ed. see Bassnett, Susan.

Lorch, Jennifer, tr. & intro. see Machiavelli, Niccolo, et al.

Lorch, Maristella, jt. auth. see Grassi, Ernesto.

Lorch, Maristella, tr. see Valla, Lorenzo.

Lorch, Natanel, ed. Major Knesset Debates, 1948-1981 Vol. 2: The Constituent Assembly - First Knesset (1949-1951) 360p. (C). 1991. lib. bdg. 69.50 (*0-8191-8343-1*) U Pr of Amer.

Lorch, Netalel, jt. auth. see Lorch, Carlos.

Lorch, Netanel. One Long War. 1976. 8.00 (*0-685-82597-3*) Herzl Pr.

— Shield of Zion: The Israel Defense Forces. (Illus.). 144p. 1992. 34.95 (*0-943231-47-7*) Howell Pr VA.

Lorch, Netanel, ed. Major Knesset Debates, 1948-1981 Vol. 1: Peoples Council & Provisional Council of State, 1948-1949. 364p. (C). 1992. lib. bdg. 69.50 (*0-8191-8342-3*) U Pr of Amer.

— Major Knesset Debates, 1948-1981 Vol. 3: Second Knesset (1951-1955), Third Knesset (1955-1959) 432p. (C). 1992. lib. bdg. 69.50 (*0-8191-8344-X*) U Pr of Amer.

— Major Knesset Debates, 1948-1981 Vol. 4: Fourth Knesset (1949-1961), Fifth Knesset (1961-1965), Sixth Knesset (1965-1969) 574p. (C). 1992. lib. bdg. 89.50 (*0-8191-8345-8*) U Pr of Amer.

— Major Knesset Debates, 1948-1981 Vol. 5: Seventh Knesset (1969-1973), Eighth Knesset (1974-1977) 405p. (C). 1991. lib. bdg. 69.50 (*0-8191-8346-6*) U Pr of Amer.

— Major Knesset Debates, 1948-1981 Vol. 6: Ninth Knesset (1977-1981) 445p. (C). 1992. lib. bdg. 69.50 (*0-8191-8347-4*) U Pr of Amer.

Lorch, Richard. Arabic Mathematical Science: Instruments, Texts, Transmission. (Collected Studies: Vol. CS517). 368p. 1995. 115.95 (*0-86078-555-6*, Pub. by Variorum) Ashgate Pub Co.

Lorch, Robert F. & O'Brien, Edward J., eds. Sources of Coherence in Reading. 416p. 1995. pap. 39.95 (*0-8058-1637-2*); text 89.95 (*0-8058-1339-X*) L Erlbaum Assocs.

Lorch, Robert S. Administrative Law: Cases & Materials. 2nd ed. 90p. (C). 1985. pap. 9.95 (*0-941436-01-2*) Stuart & Day Pub.

— Colorado's Government: Structure, Politics, Administration, & Policy. 6th rev. ed. LC 97-20417. (Illus.). 352p. 1997. pap. 24.95 (*0-87081-461-3*) Univ Pr Colo.

— Democratic Process & Administrative Law. LC 80-12461. (Waynebook Ser.: Vol. 39). 279p. reprint ed. pap. 86.50 (*0-608-10546-5*, 207116600009) Bks Demand.

— State & Local Politics: The Great Entanglement. 5th ed. LC 94-17182. 448p. 1994. 55.00 (*0-13-109117-4*) P-H.

***Lorch, Robert S.** State & Local Politics: The Great Entanglement. 6th ed. LC 00-27544. 456p. 2000. pap. 45.33 (*0-13-026006-1*) P-H.

Lorch, Walter. Competition Vehicles Choice Construction Maintenance. 74p. 1990. 66.00 (*0-85131-529-1*, Pub. by J A Allen) Trafalgar.

— Handbook of Water Purification. 2nd ed. LC 87-9093. (Water & Waste Water Technology Ser.). 777p. 1987. text 116.00 (*0-470-20899-6*) P-H.

Lorch, Wink, jt. ed. see Walker, Larry.

Lorcher, Adolf. Das Fremde und das Eigene in Ciceros Buchern De Finibus Bonorum et Malorum und der Academica. vii, 327p. 1975. reprint ed. write for info. (*3-487-05609-7*) G Olms Pubs.

Lorcin. Imperial Identities: Sterotyping, Prejudice & Race in Colonial Algeria. 323p. 2000. pap. 19.95 (*1-86064-376-0*, Pub. by I B T) St Martin.

Lord. Garbage! The Trashiest Book. 112p. (J). (gr. 3-7). 1993. pap. 2.75 (*0-590-46024-2*) Scholastic Inc.

— Social Psychology. (C). 1997. pap. text 33.50 (*0-03-019104-1*) Harcourt.

Lord, A. R., ed. A Stratigraphical Index of Calcareous Nannofossils. (British Micropalaeontological Society Ser.). 192p. 1982. text 114.00 (*0-470-27338-0*) P-H.

Lord, A. Roberts. Holbrook & Allied Families. McMaster, Annette C., ed. (Illus.). 177p. 1997. reprint ed. pap. 28.00 (*0-8328-9174-6*); reprint ed. lib. bdg. 38.00 (*0-8328-9173-8*) Higginson Bk Co.

Lord, Albert B. Epic Singers & Oral Tradition. LC 90-55888. (Myth & Poetics Ser.). 280p. 1991. text 45.00 (*0-8014-2472-0*); pap. text 17.95 (*0-8014-9717-5*) Cornell U Pr.

— The Singer of Tales. (Studies in Comparative Literature: No. 24). 319p. (C). 1981. pap. 17.95 (*0-674-80881-9*) HUP.

***Lord, Albert B.** Singer of Tales. 2nd ed. (Harvard Studies in Comparative Literature: Vol. 24). 2000. pap. text 18.95 (*0-674-00283-0*) HUP.

Lord, Albert B. The Singer Resumes the Tale. Lord, Mary L., ed. (Myth & Poetics Ser.). 336p. 1995. text 42.50 (*0-8014-3103-4*) Cornell U Pr.

Lord, Albert B., ed. Harvard Dissertations in Folklore & Oral Tradition, 16 vols., Set. 1991. 1205.00 (*0-8153-0206-1*) Garland.

Lord, Albert B. & Bynum, David E., eds. Serbo-Croatian Heroic Songs: Bijelo Polje: Three Texts from Avdo Mededovic, Vol. 3. (Milman Parry Collection, Texts & Translation Ser.: No. 4). (Illus.). 383p. 1980. 25.00 (*0-674-80166-0*) HUP.

Lord, Albert B., et al. The Multinational Literature of Yugoslavia, 21 vols. LC 77-126039. (Review of National Literatures Ser.: Vol. 5, No. 1). 128p. 1974. pap. 4.95 (*0-918680-64-6*) Griffon House.

Lord, Albert B., ed. see Afshar, Mahasti.

Lord, Albert B., ed. see Fisher, Laura G.

Lord, Albert B., ed. see Luethans, Tod N.

Lord, Albert B., ed. & tr. see Parry, Millman.

Lord, Allyn, et al. Steal This Handbook! A Template for Creating a Museum's Emergency Preparedness Plan. LC 94-92256. 240p. (Orig.). 1994. pap. 25.00 (*0-9621348-1-3*) SERA LA.

Lord, Allyn, jt. ed. see O'Reilly, Priscilla.

Lord, Arthur E., Jr. & Koerner, Robert M. Detection of Subsurface Hazardous Waste Containers by Nondestructive Techniques. LC 89-22800. (Pollution Technology Review Ser.: No. 172). (Illus.). 83p. 1990. 39.00 (*0-8155-1224-4*) Noyes.

Lord, Arthur R. The Principles of Politics. LC 70-179637. (Select Bibliographies Reprint Ser.). 1977. reprint ed. 23.95 (*0-8369-6658-9*) Ayer.

Lord, Athena V. A Spirit to Ride the Whirlwind LC 81-3775. 205p. 1981. write for info. (*0-02-761410-7*) Glencoe.

Lord Baden-Powell. Lessons from the Varsity of Life. (Illus.). 320p. 1992. pap. 17.95 (*0-9632054-7-1*) Stevens Pub.

— Rovering to Success: A Guide for Young Manhood. (Illus.). 247p. (Orig.). (YA). 1992. pap. 16.95 (*0-9632054-3-9*) Stevens Pub.

— Scouting Round the World. (Illus.). 200p. 1992. pap. 16.95 (*0-9632054-6-3*) Stevens Pub.

Lord, Barry & Lord, Gail D. The Manual of Museum Management. 261p. 1997. pap. 49.00 (*0-11-290518-8*, HM05188, Pub. by Statnry Office) Balogh.

Lord, Barry, jt. ed. see Lord, Gail D.

Lord, Benjamin. America's Wealthiest People: Their Philanthropic & Nonprofit Affiliations. 78p. 1984. pap. 57.50 (*0-914756-57-5*) Taft Group.

***Lord Berners.** The Chateau de Resenlieu. 96p. 2000. pap. 13.95 (*1-885586-15-9*, Pub. by Turtle Point Pr) Dist Art Pubs.

Lord Berners. A Distant Prospect. 128p. 1998. pap. 13.95 (*1-885983-32-8*) Turtle Point Pr.

Lord, Bette Bao. In the Year of the Boar & Jackie Robinson. LC 83-48440. (Illus.). 176p. (J). (gr. 2-5). 1984. lib. bdg. 15.89 (*0-06-024004-0*) HarpC Child Bks.

— In the Year of the Boar & Jackie Robinson. LC 83-48440. (Trophy Bk.). (Illus.). 176p. (J). (gr. 4-7). 1986. pap. 4.95 (*0-06-440175-8*, HarpTrophy) HarpC Child Bks.

— In the Year of the Boar & Jackie Robinson. 1986. 10.05 (*0-606-02475-1*, Pub. by Turtleback) Demco.

Lord, Bette Bao. In the Year of the Boar & Jackie Robinson, Homework Set. unabridged ed. (J). 1997. 40.20 incl. audio (*0-7887-1837-1*, 40617) Recorded Bks.

Lord, Bette Bao. Legacies: A Chinese Mosaic. 256p. 1991. pap. 10.00 (*0-449-90620-5*) Fawcett.

— Legacies: A Chinese Mosaic. large type ed. (General Ser.). 375p. 1991. lib. bdg. 20.95 (*0-8161-5065-6*, G K Hall Lrg Type) Mac Lib Ref.

Lord, Bette Bao. Legacies: A Chinese Mosaic. 245p. 1997. reprint ed. text 20.00 (*0-7881-5039-1*) DIANE Pub.

Lord, Bette Bao. The Middle Heart. 1997. mass mkt. 6.99 (*0-449-28808-0*); mass mkt. 6.99 (*0-449-22564-X*, Crest) Fawcett.

— The Middle Heart. 1997. pap. 12.00 (*0-449-91232-9*, Columbine) Fawcett.

— The Middle Heart. LC 95-36165. 352p. 1996. 25.00 (*0-394-53432-8*) Knopf.

— Spring Moon: A Novel of China. 592p. 1990. mass mkt. 6.99 (*0-06-100105-8*, Harp PBks) HarpC.

— Spring Moon: A Novel of China. 1982. mass mkt. 4.95 (*0-380-59923-6*, Avon Bks) Morrow Avon.

Lord Blake. The Office of Prime Minister. (Thank-Offering to Britain Fund Lectures). 1976. 7.98 (*0-19-725724-0*) David Brown.

Lord, Bob & Lord, Penny. Beyond Sodom & Gomorrah: Prophecies & Promises. (Illus.). 320p. 1999. pap. 14.95 (*1-58002-136-0*, BSG) Journeys Faith.

— Defenders of the Faith: Saints of the Counter Reformation. (Super Saints Ser.: Bk. III). (Illus.). 224p. 1998. pap. 10.95 (*1-58002-134-4*, BDF) Journeys Faith.

— Este ES Mi Cuerpo, Esta Es Mi Sangre: Milagros de la Eucaristia. Valls, Aminta et al, trs. from ENG. (SPA., Illus.). 205p. (Orig.). 1987. pap. 9.95 (*0-926143-03-4*) Journeys Faith.

— Holy Innocence. (Super Saints Ser.: Bk. II). (Illus.). 224p. 1998. pap. 10.95 (*1-58002-133-6*, BHI) Journeys Faith.

— Journey to Sainthood. (Super Saints Ser.: Bk. I). (Illus.). 224p. 1998. pap. 10.95 (*1-58002-132-8*, BJS) Journeys Faith.

— The Many Faces of Mary: A Love Story. (Illus.). 242p. (Orig.). 1987. 13.95 (*0-926143-06-9*); pap. 9.95 (*0-926143-07-7*) Journeys Faith.

— Martyrs - They Died for Christ. 320p. (Orig.). 1993. pap. 13.95 (*0-926143-14-X*) Journeys Faith.

— Los Muchos Rostros de Maria: Una Storia di Amor. Valls, Aminta & Sandoval, Luz E., trs.Tr. of Many Faces of Mary: A Love Story. (SPA., Illus.). 272p. 1994. pap. 9.95 (*0-926143-19-0*, BLOS) Journeys Faith.

— The Rosary: The Life of Jesus & Mary. 192p. 1993. 13.95 (*0-926143-12-3*) Journeys Faith.

— Saints & Other Powerful Men in the Church. (Illus.). 528p. 1990. pap. 14.95 (*0-926143-09-3*) Journeys Faith.

— Saints & Other Powerful Women in the Church. (Illus.). 400p. (Orig.). 1989. pap. 13.95 (*0-926143-08-5*) Journeys Faith.

— Scandal of the Cross & Its Triumph: Heresies Through the History of the Church. rev. ed. 320p. 1992. reprint ed. pap. 13.95 (*0-926143-15-8*) Journeys Faith.

— Super Saints Trilogy, 3 vols. 224p. 1998. pap. 25.00 (*1-58002-135-2*, BSS3) Journeys Faith.

— This is My Body, This is My Blood: Miracles of the Eucharist. (Illus.). 192p. (Orig.). 1986. pap. 9.95 (*0-926143-02-6*) Journeys Faith.

— This Is My Body, This Is My Blood: Miracles of the Eucharist, Vol. 2. (Illus.). 272p. 1994. pap. 13.95 (*0-926143-33-6*, BT-2) Journeys Faith.

— Trilogy of the Church, 3 vols. Incl. Cults: Battle of the Angels. (Illus.). 208p. 1997. pap. 9.95 (*1-58002-007-0*, BCUL); Tragedy of the Reformation. (Illus.). 208p. 1997. pap. 9.95 (*1-58002-006-2*, BTRA); Treasures of the Church: That Which Makes Us Catholic. (Illus.). 208p. 1997. pap. 9.95 (*1-58002-005-4*, BTRE); 1997. 25.00 (*1-58002-008-9*) Journeys Faith.

— Visionaries, Mystics & Stigmatists. (Illus.). 448p. 1995. pap. 13.95 (*0-926143-57-3*, BVMS) Journeys Faith.

— Visions of Heaven, Hell & Purgatory. (Illus.). 336p. (Orig.). 1996. pap. 13.95 (*0-926143-84-0*, BHHP) Journeys Faith.

Lord, Bob, jt. auth. see Lord, Penny.

Lord Bramall, jt. auth. see Gilbert, Adrian.

Lord, Brian I., et al, eds. Stem Cells & Tissue Homeostasis. LC 77-80844. (Symposium of the British Society for Cell Biology Ser.: No. 2). 376p. reprint ed. pap. 107.20 (*0-608-16526-3*, 2027336) Bks Demand.

Lord, Brian I., jt. auth. see Hendry, Jolyon H.

Lord, C. C. Lord: History of the Descendants of Nathan Lord of Ancient Kittery, Maine. Lord, G. E., ed. (Illus.). 218p. 1993. reprint ed. pap. 33.00 (*0-8328-3708-3*); reprint ed. lib. bdg. 43.00 (*0-8328-3707-5*) Higginson Bk Co.

Lord, C. E. Lord. (Illus.). 263p. 1991. reprint ed. pap. 42.00 (*0-8328-2026-1*); reprint ed. lib. bdg. 52.00 (*0-8328-2025-3*) Higginson Bk Co.

Lord, Carnes. Strategy & Governmental Organization. (Special Issue of Comparative Strategy Ser.: Vol. 6, No. 3). 127p. 1987. pap. 18.00 (*0-8448-1532-2*) Taylor & Francis.

Lord, Carnes & Barnett, Frank R., eds. Political Warfare & Psychological Operations: Rethinking the U. S. Approach. 242p. (Orig.). (C). 1996. reprint ed. pap. text 35.00 (*0-7881-3051-X*) DIANE Pub.

Lord, Carnes, tr. see Aristotle.

Lord, Carnes, tr. see Strauss, Leo.

Lord, Carol. Historical Change in Serial Verb Construction. LC 93-12679. (Typological Studies in Language (TSL): No. 26). x, 273p. 1993. 71.00 (*1-55619-416-1*); pap. 24.95 (*1-55619-417-X*) J Benjamins Pubng Co.

Lord, Catherine. Pervert. (Illus.). 48p. (Orig.). 1995. pap. 16.50 (*1-884355-01-3*) U CA Fine Arts.

Lord Chalmers. Further Dialogues of the Buddha, 2 vols., Set. (C). 1988. reprint ed. text 68.00 (*81-7030-139-4*) S Asia.

***Lord Chancellor's Department Staff.** Civil Procedure Rules, 3 bks., Set. 1500p. 2000. ring bd. 625.00 incl. cd-rom (*0-11-781818-6*, Pub. by Statnry Office) Balogh.

Lord, Charles G. Social Psychology. LC 96-76308. 738p. (C). 1996. text 75.00 (*0-03-055133-1*); pap. text, student ed. 25.00 (*0-03-019108-4*, Pub. by Harcourt Coll Pubs) Harcourt.

***Lord, Charles R.** Guide to Information Sources in Engineering & Technology. (Reference Sources in Science & Technology Ser.). (Illus.). 350p. 2000. 75.00 (*1-56308-699-9*) Libs Unl.

Lord, Christine, ed. see Eighth Grade Writers.

Lord, Christopher. Absent at the Creation: Britain & the Formation of the European Community 1950-2. LC 95-25910. 192p. 1996. 77.95 (*1-85521-520-9*, Pub. by Dartmth Pub) Ashgate Pub Co.

— British Entry to the European Community under the Heath Government of 1970-74. 194p. 1993. 72.95 (*1-85521-336-2*, Pub. by Dartmth Pub) Ashgate Pub Co.

— Democracy in the European Union. (Contemporary European Studies: Vol. 4). 148p. 1998. pap. 15.00 (*1-85075-868-9*, Pub. by Sheffield Acad) CUP Services.

***Lord, Christopher, ed.** Central Europe: Core or Periphery? 254p. 1999. 34.00 (*87-16-13447-8*, Pub. by Copenhagen Busn Schl) Bks Intl VA.

Lord, Christopher, jt. auth. see Bell, David S.

Lord, Christopher, jt. auth. see Hix, Simon.

Lord, Christopher, jt. auth. see Levitt, Malcolm.

Lord, Clayton A., Jr. The Church Newsletter Handbook. LC 97-17431. (Illus.). 96p. (Orig.). 1997. pap. 15.00 (*0-8170-1264-8*) Judson.

Lord, Clifford L., jt. auth. see Turnbull, Archibald D.

Lord Cooper. The Scottish Legal Tradition. 4th ed. Meston, Michael C., ed. 36p. 1986. 22.00 (*0-85411-023-2*, Pub. by Saltire Soc) St Mut.

Lord, David. Bach Flower Remedies. (Little Big Book Ser.). 72p. 1998. pap. 4.95 (*965-494-041-8*) Astrolog Pub.

***Lord, David.** Bach Flower Remedies A Practical Guide. (Healing Ser.). 1999. pap. 8.95 (*965-494-058-2*) Astrolog Pub.

Lord David Cecil. The English Poets. (Illus.). 96p. 1997. 11.95 (*1-85375-229-0*) Prion.

Lord, Del. Gem of a Jam. LC 92-11183. 1992. lib. bdg. 12.95 (*1-56239-167-4*) ABDO Pub Co.

Lord, Del & Ullman, Elwood. Busy Buddies. LC 92-11185. 1992. lib. bdg. 12.94 (*1-56239-164-X*) ABDO Pub Co.

Lord, Diana. The Silver Dolphin. 448p. 1995. mass mkt. 4.99 (*0-8217-5040-2*, Zebra Kensgtn) Kensgtn Pub Corp.

Lord Dunsany. The King of Elfland's Daughter. LC 99-90089. 1999. reprint ed. pap. 12.00 (*0-345-43191-X*, Del Rey) Ballantine Pub Grp.

Lord, E. Manual of Cotton Spinning: The Characteristics of Raw Cotton, Vol. 2, Pt. 1. 333p. 1971. 60.00 (*0-7855-7204-X*) St Mut.

Lord, E. & Bernicer, G. Plant Reproduction: From Floral Induction to Pollination. (C). 1991. text 165.00 (*81-7233-006-5*, Pub. by Scientific Pubs) St Mut.

Lord, E. A. & Wilson, C. B. The Mathematical Description of Shape & Form. LC 83-26685. (Mathematics & Its Applications Ser.: 1-176). 323p. 1986. pap. text 37.95 (*0-470-20254-8*) P-H.

Lord, Ed, jt. auth. see Hanners, LaVerne.

Lord, Edward O., ed. History of the Ninth Regiment New Hampshire Volunteers in the War of the Rebellion. unabridged ed. LC 96-44054. (Illus.). xii, 923p. (C). 1996. reprint ed. 49.95 (*1-889881-03-1*) Old Bks Pub.

Lord, Eliot, et al. The Italian in America. LC 71-130557. (Select Bibliographies Reprint Ser.). 1977. reprint ed. 20.95 (*0-8369-5530-7*) Ayer.

Lord, Elizabeth. The Angry Heart. large type ed. (Magna Large Print Ser.). 512p. 1998. 29.99 (*0-7505-1221-0*, Pub. by Mgna Lrg Print) Ulverscroft.

— A Better Life, 1. large type ed. 496p. 1998. 29.99 (*0-7505-1222-9*) Mgna Lrg Print.

***Lord, Elizabeth.** For All the Bright Promise. large type ed. 528p. 2000. 31.99 (*0-7505-1493-0*, Pub. by Mgna Lrg Print) Ulverscroft.

Lord, Elizabeth. Stolen Years. large type ed. (Magna Large Print Ser.). 594p. 1998. 29.99 (*0-7505-1220-2*, Pub. by Mgna Lrg Print) Ulverscroft.

***Lord, Elizabeth.** The Turning Tides. large type ed. 560p. 1999. 31.99 (*0-7505-1416-7*, Pub. by Mgna Lrg Print) Ulverscroft.

Lord, Elizabeth M. & Bernier, Georges, eds. Plant Reproduction: From Floral Induction to Pollination. LC 89-80454. 250p. 1989. pap. text 25.00 (*0-943088-14-3*) Am Soc of Plan.

Lord, Elliot. Comstock Mining & Miners. (Illus.). 451p. 1995. 39.95 (*0-913814-07-5*) Nevada Pubns.

***Lord, Evelyn.** Investigating the 20th Century. (Illus.). 176p. 1999. 32.50 (*0-7524-1426-7*, Pub. by Tempus Pubng) Arcadia Publng.

Lord, F. Townley. Acts of the Apostles: Missionary Message of the New Testament. 119p. 1946. 4.50 (*0-87921-003-6*) Attic Pr.

Lord, Frances. Christian Science Healing: Its Principles & Practice with Full Explanations for Home Students (1888) 485p. 1996. reprint ed. pap. 24.50 (*1-56459-669-9*) Kessinger Pub.

— Christian Science Healing, Its Principles & Practice. 471p. 1996. reprint ed. spiral bd. 25.50 (*0-7873-0570-7*) Hlth Research.

Lord, Francis A. Civil War Collector's Encyclopedia, Bk. 1. (Illus.). 600p. 1995. 30.00 (*0-7858-0467-6*) North South Trader.

— Civil War Collector's Encyclopedia, Bk. 2. (Illus.). 688p. 1995. 30.00 (*0-7858-0468-4*) North South Trader.

An Asterisk (*) at the beginning of an entry indicates that the title is appearing for the first time.

— They Fought for the Union. LC 81-6579. (Illus.). 375p. 1981. reprint ed. lib. bdg. 89.50 (*0-313-22740-3*, LOTF, Greenwood Pr) Greenwood.

Lord, Francis A., jt. auth. see Wise, Arthur.

Lord, Frederic M. Applications of Item Response Theory to Practical Testing Problems. LC 79-24186. (Illus.). 288p. 1980. text 69.95 (*0-89859-006-X*) L Erlbaum Assocs.

Lord, G. E., ed. see Lord, C. C.

***Lord, Gail D. & Lord, Barry, eds.** Manual of Museum Planning. 2nd ed. 480p. 2000. pap. 49.95 (*0-7425-0406-9*) AltaMira Pr.

Lord, Gail D., jt. auth. see Lord, Barry.

Lord, Gardner. Systems Analysis of Imagery. (C). 1992. text 21.00 (*0-913412-64-3*) Brandon Hse.

***Lord, Garman. The Way of the Heathen: A Handbook of Greater Theodism. (Illus.). 229p. 1999. pap. 21.00 (*1-929340-01-X*) Theod.**

Millennial alternative religion, almost defies category, truly a book like no other. Practical handbook of revised pre-Christian pan-Germanic folk religion "Theodish Belief". We are only too accustomed to Wicca, Neopaganism, New Age systems, to take one more pop-occultnik handbook all that seriously, but be warned Way of the Heathen is not that. This "revival" is not only real & radical, but often takes the whole belief system of the Western world to talk like an Old Testament prophet, weighing our modern ways & finding them wanting! Psychologically & sociologically sophisticated, Way of has a lot to say about social dynamics of alternative religious groups, how to organize & run them, author Gasman Lord has obviously been there, done that. Occasionally, scholarly, though footnote-free, goes in-depth on topics like morals & ethics, oaths, boasts, animal sacrifice, sacral kingship, leadership, followership, poetry, law & custom, non-Augustmian metaphysics, roles of women, true natures of the gods, true role of autochtonous religion in family & community. Gasman Lord rightly calls Theodism a "Wisdom Tradition," it's all of that ! Ordering Info: Order directly from THEOD, PO Box 8062, Watertown, NY 13601, *Publisher Paid Annotation.*

Lord, Gary. Great Paint Finishes for a Gorgeous Home. LC 98-18154. (Illus.). 128p. 1998. 27.99 (*0-89134-822-0*, North Lght Bks) F & W Pubns Inc.

***Lord, Gary & Schmidt, David.** Marvelous Murals You Can Paint. LC 00-37236. (Illus.). 128p. 2000. 27.99 (*0-89134-969-3*, North Lght Bks) F & W Pubns Inc.

Lord, George D. Heroic Mockery: Variations on Epic Themes from Homer to Joyce. LC 76-13930. 162p. 1977. 27.50 (*0-87413-117-0*) U Delaware Pr.

— Poems on Affairs of State: Augustan Satirical Verse, 1660-1714, Vol. 7, 1704-1714. Ellis, Frank H., ed. LC 63-7938. 830p. reprint ed. pap. 200.00 (*0-7837-2363-6*, 202202000023) Bks Demand.

— Trials of the Self: Heroic Ordeals in the Epic Tradition. LC 83-11727. x, 249p. (C). 1983. lib. bdg. 35.00 (*0-208-02013-6*, Archon Bks) Shoe String.

Lord, George D., ed. Poems on Affairs of State: Augustan Satirical Verse, 1660-1714, Vol. 1, 1669-1678. Vol. 1. (Illus.). 1963. 70.00 (*0-300-00726-4*) Yale U Pr.

Lord, George D., jt. ed. see Mack, Maynard.

Lord, Glenn, ed. see Howard, Robert E.

Lord, Gordon, jt. ed. see Harvey, John.

Lord, Graham. James Herriot: The Life of a Country Vet. 1998. pap. 12.95 (*0-7867-0581-7*) Carroll & Graf.

— James Herriot: The Life of a Country Vet. large type ed. LC 97-50374. (Basic Ser.). 1998. 25.95 (*0-7862-1387-6*) Thorndike Pr.

Lord, Guy. The French Budgetary Process. LC 70-186113. (Illus.). 233p. reprint ed. pap. 72.30 (*0-608-18289-3*, 203153900075) Bks Demand.

Lord, H. D. Memorial of the Family of Morse. (Illus.). 556p. 1989. reprint ed. pap. 85.00 (*0-8328-0887-3*); reprint ed. lib. bdg. 93.00 (*0-8328-0886-5*) Higginson Bk Co.

Lord Hailsham of St. Marylebone & Bowman, James, eds. Halsbury's Laws of England, 2 vols. ring bd. write for info. (*0-406-04776-6*, HL4ASET, MICHIE) LEXIS Pub.

Lord, Harold W., et al. Noise Control for Engineers. LC 87-22611. 448p. (C). 1987. reprint ed. lib. bdg. 53.50 (*0-89464-255-3*) Krieger.

***Lord, Henry & Sweetman, Will.** A Discovery of the Banian Religion & the Religion of the Persees: A Critical Edition of Two Early English Works on Indian Religions. LC 99-32873. (Critical Editions & Translations Ser.: Vol. 3). 212p. 1999. 89.95 (*0-7734-7928-7*) E Mellen.

Lord, Hunter & Masters, Ariel. Evermore. 160p. (Orig.). 1997. pap. 6.99 (*1-890096-01-6*) Padwolf Pub.

— Wombers & Innuendoes. 224p. 1998. pap. 9.99 (*1-890096-03-2*) Padwolf Pub.

Lord Irwin. Indian Problems: Speeches of Lord Irwin. 396p. 1987. 20.00 (*81-212-0068-7*, Pub. by Gian Publng Hse) S Asia.

Lord, Israel S. At the Extremity of Civilization: A Meticulously Descriptive Diary of an Illinois Physician's Journey in 1849 along the Oregon Trail to the Goldmines & Cholera of California, Thence in Two Years to Return by Boat Via Panama. Liles, Necia D., ed. (Illus.). 451p. 1995. lib. bdg. 45.00 (*0-7864-0000-5*) McFarland & Co.

— A Doctor's Gold Rush Journey to California. Liles, Necia D., ed. LC 99-38773. (Illus.). 452p. 1999. pap. 17.95 (*0-8032-7990-6*, Bison Books) U of Nebr Pr.

Lord, J. The Jews in India & the Far East. 1976. lib. bdg. 39.95 (*0-8490-2104-9*) Gordon Pr.

Lord, J. A., et al. Guide to Parenteral Administration of Drugs. 2nd ed. 314p. 1996. pap. 85.00 (*0-8036-0375-4*) Davis Co.

Lord, Jack. The Designated Driver: A Collection of Short Stories from the Life of a Designated Driver. LC 98-90521. 1999. pap. 13.95 (*0-533-12823-4*) Vantage.

Lord, James. Giacometti. (Illus.). 576p. 1997. pap. text 20.00 (*0-374-52525-0*) FS&G.

— A Giacometti Portrait. (Illus.). 117p. 1980. pap. 11.00 (*0-374-51573-5*) FS&G.

— Gift for Admiration: Further Memoirs. LC 97-50205. (Illus.). 192p. 1998. 22.00 (*0-374-28192-0*) FS&G.

— Making Memoirs. (Illus.). 19p. 1995. 145.00 (*0-9640399-4-X*); pap. 45.00 (*0-9640399-3-1*) Elysium Pr.

— Picasso & Dora: A Memoir. 1993. 35.00 (*0-374-23208-3*) FS&G.

— Picasso & Dora: A Personal Memoir. LC 94-23057. (Illus.). 352p. 1994. pap. 16.95 (*0-88064-162-2*) Fromm Intl Pub.

— Sam Szafran: Recent Works. (Illus.). 1987. 10.00 (*0-936827-05-X*) C Bernard Gallery Ltd.

— Six Exceptional Women. LC 93-42384. 384p. 1994. 27.50 (*0-374-26553-4*) FS&G.

— Some Remarkable Men: Further Memoirs. (Illus.). 360p. 1996. 27.50 (*0-374-26655-7*) FS&G.

Lord, James G. Building Your Case: The Step-by-Step System that Shows How the Most Successful Volunteers Raise Money. 1984. student ed. 295.00 incl. audio, sl. (*0-939120-04-6*) Third Sector.

— Philanthropy & Marketing: New Strategies for Fund Raising. LC 81-50197. 203p. (C). 1981. lib. bdg. write for info. (*0-939120-00-3*); ring bd. 65.00 (*0-939120-01-1*) Third Sector.

— The Raising of Money: Thirty-Five Essentials (Accompanied by a Guide for the Professional) LC 84-50377. 128p. 1984. 34.50 (*0-939120-02-X*) Third Sector.

Lord, James H. The Jews in India & the Far East. LC 70-97292. 120p. 1977. reprint ed. lib. bdg. 35.00 (*0-8371-2615-0*, LOJI, Greenwood Pr) Greenwood.

Lord, Janice H. Beyond Sympathy: What to Say & Do for Someone Suffering an Injury, Illness or Loss. 2nd ed. Wheeler, Eugene D., ed. LC 88-61044. 192p. 1989. pap. 11.95 (*0-934793-21-2*) Pathfinder CA.

***Lord, Janice Harris.** No Time for Goodbyes: Coping with Sorrow, Anger & Injustice After a Tragic Death. 5th ed. 1999. pap. 12.95 (*0-934793-68-9*) Pathfinder CA.

Lord, Jerome E. Adult Literacy Programs: Guidelines for Effectiveness. 28p. (Orig.). (C). 1995. pap. text 15.00 (*0-7881-2009-3*) DIANE Pub.

Lord, Jerome E., jt. ed. see Benjamin, L. Ann.

Lord, Jim. A Survival Guide for the Year 2000 Problem: How to Save Yourself from the Most Deadly Screw-Up in History. (Illus.). vi, 196p. 1997. pap. 29.97 (*0-9660200-0-6*) J Marion Publ.

Lord, John. Capital & Steam Power: 1750-1800. 2nd ed. 253p. 1966. 32.00 (*0-7146-1339-8*, Pub. by F Cass Pubs) Intl Spec Bk.

— Energy Eighty-Seven. rev. ed. 56p. 1986. pap. 1.50 (*0-934653-08-9*) Enterprise Educ.

— Energy in the United States. rev. ed. (Teaching about Energy Ser.: Pt. 6). 120p. 1986. pap. 6.50 (*0-934653-14-3*) Enterprise Educ.

— Hazardous Wastes from Homes. 36p. (Orig.). 1986. pap. 2.75 (*0-934653-07-0*) Enterprise Educ.

— Infection, the Immune System, & AIDS. (Illus.). 56p. (Orig.). (YA). (gr. 11-12). 1989. pap. 4.95 (*0-934653-18-6*) Enterprise Educ.

***Lord, John.** Sizes: The Illustrated Encyclopedia. (Illus.). 374p. 1999. reprint ed. pap. text 15.00 (*0-7881-6700-6*) DIANE Pub.

Lord, John & Braaten, Glenn. Energy Flows in Nature. rev. ed. (Teaching about Energy Ser.: Pt. 2). (Illus.). 136p. 1986. pap. 6.70 (*0-934653-12-7*) Enterprise Educ.

— Energy Fundamentals. rev. ed. (Teaching about Energy Ser.: Pt. 1). 200p. 1986. pap. 11.90 (*0-934653-11-9*) Enterprise Educ.

Lord, John & Wilson, Darlene. Energy Economics. rev. ed. (Teaching about Energy Ser.: Pt. 7). 136p. 1986. pap. 6.60 (*0-934653-15-1*) Enterprise Educ.

Lord, John, et al. Teaching about Energy: Nineteen Eighty-Four to Nineteen Eighty-Five Supplement. (Energy Eighty Ser.). 280p. 1985. pap. 10.00 (*0-934653-05-4*) Enterprise Educ.

Lord, John, jt. auth. see Wilson, George.

Lord, John B., jt. ed. see Brody, Aaron L.

Lord, John M. Genealogy of the Lord Family: Which Removed from Colchester, CT to Hanover, NH & Then to Norwich, VT. LC 99-475191. 116p. 1999. pap. 14.50 (*0-7884-1186-1*, L561) Heritage Bk.

Lord, John V. Mr. Mead & His Garden. LC 74-20766. (Illus.). (J). (gr. k-3). 1975. lib. bdg. 6.95 (*0-395-20278-7*) HM.

Lord, John V. & Burroway, Janet. The Giant Jam Sandwich. 001. LC 72-13578. (Illus.). 32p. (J). (gr. k-3). 1975. 17.00 (*0-395-16033-2*) HM.

— The Giant Jam Sandwich. LC 72-13578. (Illus.). 32p. (J). (gr. k-3). 1987. pap. 5.95 (*0-395-44237-0*) HM.

— The Giant Jam Sandwich. (Carry-Along Book & Cassette Favorites Ser.). (Illus.). 1p. (J). 1990. pap. 9.95 incl. audio (*0-395-53966-8*, 490026) HM.

Lord, John Vernon. Giant Jam Sandwich. 1972. 11.15 (*0-606-00874-8*, Pub. by Turtleback) Demco.

Lord, Jonathan T., ed. The Physician Leader's Guide. 200p. 1992. pap. text 20.00 (*0-915963-10-8*, TPLG) Capitol Publns.

Lord, Joni. The Bachelorette Party Book. (Illus.). 80p. (Orig.). 1986. pap. 6.95 (*0-916799-13-1*) Hollow Glen.

Lord, Kenneth. Lord: Certain Members of the Lord Family Who Settled in New York City in the Early 1800's, Descendants of Thomas Lord of Hartford, Connecticut. 92p. 1995. reprint ed. pap. 18.00 (*0-8328-4924-3*); reprint ed. lib. bdg. 28.00 (*0-8328-4923-5*) Higginson Bk Co.

Lord, Kenniston W. The Data Center Disaster Consultant. 2nd ed. LC 81-52826. 223p. reprint ed. pap. 69.20 (*0-8357-6085-5*, 203433000089) Bks Demand.

Lord, Lesli. The Cincinnati Police Division's Response to Anti-Abortion Demonstrations. LC 94-61299. (Case Studies in Police Decision-Making: Vol. 3). 70p. (Orig.). 1994. pap. 7.50 (*1-878734-35-0*) Police Exec Res.

— Response to Anti-Abortion Demonstrations: Cincinnati Police Division. 70p. 1996. reprint ed. pap. text 35.00 (*0-7881-3421-3*) DIANE Pub.

Lord, Lilia. Exotic Vegetable Cuisine of LA: Nutritional Content of Exotic Vegetables. (Illus.). 654p. (Orig.). 1992. pap. 24.99 (*0-9633575-0-6*) L Lord.

Lord, Linda A. & Ramsdell, Marcia. Guide to Florida Environmental Issues & Information. rev. ed. LC 92-75965. 366p. 1993. pap. 29.95 (*0-913207-06-3*) FL Conser Fnd.

Lord, Lindsay. Nautical Etiquette & Customs. 2nd rev. ed. LC 86-47716. (Illus.). 128p. 1987. pap. 8.95 (*0-87033-356-9*) Cornell Maritime.

Lord, Lisa. Success in Reading & Writing: Grade 3. 2nd ed. (Illus.). 288p. 1991. 27.95 (*0-673-36003-2*, GoodYrBooks) Addson-Wesley Educ.

— Success in Reading & Writing: Grade 6. 2nd ed. (Illus.). 288p. 1991. 27.95 (*0-673-36006-7*, GoodYrBooks) Addson-Wesley Educ.

Lord, Lorraine, jt. compiled by see Stanford, Judith A.

Lord, Lothian. Lord Lothian vs. Lord Lothian. 1991. lib. bdg. 76.00 (*0-8490-4420-0*) Gordon Pr.

Lord, Lynwood, ed. see Dahl, Mark V.

Lord, M. G. Prig Tales. 192p. (Orig.). 1990. mass mkt. 6.95 (*0-380-76004-5*, Avon Bks) Morrow Avon.

Lord, M. P., jt. auth. see James, Arthur M.

***Lord, Macauley.** L. L. Bean Fly-Casting Handbook. LC 99-51997. (Illus.). 1999. pap. 18.95 (*1-55821-964-1*) Lyons Pr.

Lord MacDermott. Protection from Power under English Law. (Legal Reprint Ser.). viii, 196p. 1986. reprint ed. 35.00 (*0-421-37590-6*) W S Hein.

Lord MacDermott. Protection from Power under English Law. (Legal Reprint Ser.). viii, 196p. 1986. reprint ed. 25.00 (*0-8377-2430-9*, Rothman) W S Hein.

Lord Mackenzie-Stuart of Dean. A French King at Holyrood. 200p. 1996. pap. 30.00 (*0-85976-413-3*, Pub. by J Donald) St Mut.

Lord, Marc, et al. Experiments in General Organic & Biological Chemistry. Mayer, Larry, ed. (Illus.). 240p. (C). 1997. pap. text, lab manual ed. 13.25 (*1-889766-07-0*) Columbus State Bks.

Lord, Marjorie F. Civil War Collector's Encyclopedia, Vol. V. 230p. 1989. lib. bdg. 35.00 (*0-916492-05-2*) Lord Americana.

Lord, Mary. The Penguin Best Australian Short Stories LC 92-103134. 335p. 1991. write for info. (*0-14-013916-8*) Pnguin Bks Ltd.

Lord, Mary, ed. see Porter, Hal.

Lord, Mary E., jt. ed. see Seymore, Bruce, 2nd.

Lord, Mary L., ed. see Lord, Albert B.

Lord Montague. The Blue Plaque Guide. (Illus.). 132p. (Orig.). (C). pap. 11.95 (*1-85172-005-7*, Pub. by Pluto GBR) Stylus Pub VA.

Lord, Montague J. Imperfect Competition & International Commodity Trade: Theory, Dynamics & Policy Modelling. (Illus.). 488p. 1991. text 95.00 (*0-19-828347-4*) OUP.

Lord, Montague J., ed. The Handbook of Latin American Trade in Manufactures. LC 97-29283. 352p. 1998. 215.00 (*1-85898-715-6*) E Elgar.

Lord Montague of Beaulieu. The Brighton Run. (Album Ser.: No. 251). (Illus.). 32p. (C). 1989. pap. 6.25 (*0-7478-0099-5*, Pub. by Shire Pubns) Parkwest Pubns.

Lord, Nancy. The Compass Inside Ourselves: Short Stories. 1984. pap. 5.95 (*0-914221-01-9*) Fireweed Pr AK.

— Darkened Waters: A Review of the History, Science, & Technology Associated with the Exxon Valdez Oil Spill & Cleanup. (Illus.). 61p. (Orig.). (C). 1992. pap. 5.00 (*0-9619026-0-4*) Homer Soc.

***Lord, Nancy.** Fishcamp: Life on an Alaskan Shore. LC 99-58244. 288p. 2000. pap. text 14.00 (*1-58243-070-5*, Pub. by Counterpt DC) HarpC.

Lord, Nancy. Fishcamp: Life on an Alaskan Shore. LC 96-52052. (Illus.). 224p. 1997. 22.95 (*1-55963-525-8*, Shearwater Bks) Island Pr.

— Fishcamp: Life on an Alaskan Shore. 1997. pap. write for info. (*1-55963-477-4*) Island Pr.

***Lord, Nancy.** Green Alaska: Dreams from the Far Coast. LC F910.5.L67 1999. (Illus.). 192p. 1999. text 23.00 (*1-58243-002-0*, Pub. by Counterpt DC) HarpC.

— Green Alaska: Dreams from the Far Coast. 192p. 2000. pap. text 13.00 (*1-58243-078-0*, Pub. by Counterpt DC) HarpC.

Lord, Nancy. Survival. LC 90-27025. 176p. 1991. pap. 10.95 (*0-918273-84-6*) Coffee Hse.

Lord, Nogah. Raise Your Vibration with Nutrition & Fasting. LC 91-27781. (Illus.). 80p. (Orig.). 1991. pap. 8.95 (*0-931892-68-6*) B Dolphin Pub.

Lord of Host Books Staff, ed. see Sartin, Michael K.

Lord of Ronaldshay. Lands of the Thunderbolt: Sikhim, Chumbi & Bhutsi. 3rd ed. LC 87-16628. (Illus.). 352p. 1987. reprint ed. 19.95 (*0-9617066-7-8*) Snow Lion-SLG Bks.

Lord of Ronaldshay, Zetland. Lands of the Thunderbolt: Sikhim, Chumbi & Bhutan. 3rd ed. LC 87-16628. (Illus.). 352p. 1987. reprint ed. pap. 12.95 (*0-9617066-6-X*) Snow Lion-SLG Bks.

Lord, P. Detailing for Acoustics. 3rd ed. (Illus.). 200p. (C). 1995. pap. 80.00 (*0-419-20210-2*, E & FN Spon) Routledge.

Lord, P. R. & Mohamed, M. H. Weaving: Conversion of Yarn to Fabric. 2nd ed. (Merrow Technical Library: Vol. 12). 1982. pap. 35.00 (*0-904095-38-X*, Pub. by Textile Inst) St Mut.

Lord, P. R. & Mohamed, M. H. Weaving: Conversion of Yarn to Fabric. 2nd ed. 408p. 1982. pap. text 50.00 (*1-85573-483-4*, Pub. by Woodhead Pubng) Am Educ Systs.

Lord, Patsy & Sebern, Margaret. Prepping Your Preschooler: A Sourcebook for Helping Your Child Succeed in School. (Illus.). 1987. 16.95 (*0-07-038755-9*) McGraw.

Lord, Penny & Lord, Bob. Heavenly Army of Angels. (Illus.). 256p. (Orig.). 1991. pap. 13.95 (*0-926143-10-7*) Journeys Faith.

Lord, Penny, jt. auth. see Lord, Bob.

Lord, Peter. The Aesthetics of Relevance. Stephens, Meic, ed. (Changing Wales Ser.). 55p. 1992. pap. 11.25 (*0-8464-4742-8*) Beekman Pubs.

— The Aesthetics of Relevance. 55p. 1998. pap. 11.95 (*0-8464-4682-0*) Beekman Pubs.

— Changing Wales Vol. II: The Aesthetics of Relevance. 1992. pap. 30.00 (*0-86383-897-9*, Pub. by Gomer Pr) St Mut.

— Gwenllian: Essays on Visual Culture. 192p. 1994. 38.95 (*0-8464-4681-2*) Beekman Pubs.

— Hearing God. 248p. (gr. 11). 1988. pap. 12.99 (*0-8010-5650-0*) Baker Bks.

***Lord, Peter.** Imaging the Nation. (Illus.). 380p. 2000. 55.00 (*0-7083-1587-9*, Pub. by U Wales Pr) Paul & Co Pubs.

Lord, Peter. Turkeys & Eagles. 104p. 1987. pap. 8.95 (*0-940232-40-5*) Seedsowers.

***Lord, Peter.** The Visual Culture of Wales Industrial Society. (Illus.). 272p. 1999. (*0-7083-1496-1*, Pub. by Univ Wales Pr) Paul & Co Pubs.

Lord, Peter. When Your Child Wanders from God. 176p. 1998. mass mkt. 5.99 (*0-8007-8656-4*) Revell.

Lord, Philip L., Jr. War over Walloomscolck: Land Use & Settlement Pattern on the Bennington Battlefield-1777. (Bulletin Ser.: No. 473). (Illus.). 190p. (Orig.). (C). 1989. pap. text 15.00 (*1-55557-186-7*) NYS Museum.

***Lord, Philippa.** Breaking Trust. large type ed. 192p. 1999. pap. 18.99 (*0-7089-5530-4*, Linford) Ulverscroft.

— Buried Desire. large type ed. 216p. 1999. pap. 18.99 (*0-7089-5615-7*, Linford) Ulverscroft.

Lord, Priscilla Sawyer & Foley, Daniel J. Easter Garland. LC 99-29132. 1999. lib. bdg. 38.00 (*0-7808-0316-7*) Omnigraphics Inc.

Lord, R. Ronstadt's Financials Professional Planning & Budgeting Software & Documentation. 50p. (Orig.). 1989. pap. 399.95 (*0-930204-20-4*) Lord Pub.

Lord, R. S. Surgery of Occlusive Cerebrovascular Disease. (Illus.). 300p. 1998. write for info. (*0-443-04951-3*) Church.

Lord Raglan. Jocasta's Crime: An Anthropological Study. LC 90-40113. xiv, 215p. 1991. reprint ed. lib. bdg. 29.50 (*0-86527-401-0*) Fertig.

Lord Reay, jt. auth. see Archer, Peter.

Lord, Richard. Culture Shock! Germany. LC 96-75618. (Illus.). 1996. pap. text 12.95 (*1-55868-251-1*) Gr Arts Ctr Pub.

— The Nonprofit Problem Solver: A Management Guide. LC 88-32188. 165p. 1989. 49.95 (*0-275-93125-0*, C3125, Praeger Pubs) Greenwood.

Lord, Richard & Salzedo, Simon. Guide to the Arbitration Act 1996. 1996. pap. 40.00 (*1-85941-310-2*, Pub. by Cavendish Pubng) Gaunt.

Lord, Richard A. Williston on Contracts, 28 vols., Vol. 1. 4th ed. LC 90-63284. 1990. 507.00 (*0-686-14488-0*) West Group.

Lord, Richard A. & Lewis, Charles C. North Carolina Security Interests. 450p. 1985. 40.00 (*0-614-05931-3*, MICHIE) LEXIS Pub.

Lord, Robert. Country Cops. 1988. pap. 6.95 (*0-88145-064-2*) Broadway Play.

— Words: A Hermeneutical Approach to the Study of Language. 358p. (C). 1995. lib. bdg. 47.50 (*0-7618-0138-3*) U Pr of Amer.

— The Words We Use. 128p. 1994. 16.95 (*1-871082-44-7*) Paul & Co Pubs.

Lord, Robert, ed. Hong Kong Language Papers. LC 79-106833. 256p. reprint ed. pap. 79.40 (*0-8357-2743-2*, 203985200013) Bks Demand.

Lord, Robert, tr. see Dianin, Sergei A.

Lord, Robert F. Country Depots in the Connecticut Hills. LC 96-94118. (Illus.). 168p. (Orig.). 1996. pap. 23.95 (*0-9617353-1-7*) Highland CT.

Lord, Robert G. & Maher, Karen J. Leadership & Information Processing: Linking Perceptions & Performance. LC 93-13076. (People & Organizations Ser.). 352p. (C). 1994. reprint ed. pap. 29.99 (*0-415-09901-3*, B2571) Routledge.

Lord, Robert H. Second Partition of Poland. LC 73-101268. 1970. reprint ed. 38.45 (*0-404-04009-8*) AMS Pr.

Lord, Robert H., jt. auth. see Coolidge, Harold J.

Lord, Robert W. Running Conventions, Conferences, & Meetings. LC 80-69704. 104p. reprint ed. pap. 32.30 (*0-608-11962-8*, 202350300033) Bks Demand.

Lord, Roberta, ed. see Orosz, Istvan.

L

An Asterisk (*) at the beginning of an entry indicates that the title is appearing for the first time.

Lord, Russell. Behold Our Land. LC 74-2395. (FDR & the Era of the New Deal Ser.). 309p. 1974. reprint ed. lib. bdg. 39.50 (*0-306-70593-1*) Da Capo.

— The Henry Wallaces of Iowa. LC 76-167843. (FDR & the Era of the New Deal Ser.). (Illus.). 615p. 1971. reprint ed. lib. bdg. 69.50 (*0-306-70325-4*) Da Capo.

— Men of Earth. McCurry, Dan C. & Rubenstein, Richard E., eds. LC 74-30642. (American Farmers & the Rise of Agribusiness Ser.). 1975. reprint ed. 33.95 (*0-405-06812-3*) Ayer.

— To Hold This Soil. LC 78-171385. (FDR & the Era of the New Deal Ser.). (Illus.). 124p. 1972. reprint ed. lib. bdg. 22.50 (*0-306-70384-X*) Da Capo.

Lord, Russell, ed. Voices from the Fields. LC 78-76945. (Granger Index Reprint Ser.). 1977. 18.95 (*0-8369-6026-2*) Ayer.

Lord, Russell, ed. see Wallace, Henry A.

Lord, Ruth. Henry F. Du Pont & Winterthur: A Daughter's Portrait. LC 98-35419. (Illus.). 287p. 1999. 27.50 (*0-300-07074-8*) Yale U Pr.

Lord, Sherrie. Air Waves. LC 98-5409. 260p. 1998. 9.99 (*1-56476-706-X*, Victor Bks) Chariot Victor.

— Only His Kiss. LC 99-18696. 360p. 1999. pap. 10.99 (*1-56476-707-8*, Victor Bks) Chariot Victor.

Lord, Shirley. The Crasher. 464p. 1999. mass mkt. 6.99 (*0-446-60663-4*, Pub. by Warner Bks) Little.

Lord, Shirley A. Social Welfare & the Feminization of Poverty. LC 92-33245. (Children of Poverty Ser.). 112p. 1993. text 15.00 (*0-8153-1119-2*) Garland.

Lord-Smith, Peter J. Avoiding Claims in Building Contracts. LC 94-166147. (Butterworth Architecture Legal Ser.). (Illus.). 199p. 1994. reprint ed. pap. 61.70 (*0-608-04416-4*, 206519700001) Bks Demand.

Lord-Smith, Peter J. & Dobson, John. Avoiding Claims in Building Contracts. (Architecture Legal Ser.). (Illus.). 181p. 1994. pap. 59.95 (*0-7506-1728-4*, Butterwrth Archit) Buttrwrth-Heinemann.

***Lord, Stephen, et al.** Falls in Older People: Risk Factors & Strategies for Prevention. (Illus.). 240p. (C). 2000. pap. text Price not set. (*0-521-58964-9*) Cambridge U Pr.

***Lord, Stuart C.** Common Good--Common Ground. 1999. pap. 7.99 (*0-88088-107-0*) Peter Pauper.

Lord, Suzanne. Animaniacs Get Dezanitized! (J). (gr. 4-7). 1996. pap. text 3.99 (*0-590-53529-3*) Scholastic Inc.

— Garbage! The Trashiest Book You'll Ever Read. (J). 1993. 7.95 (*0-606-05303-4*, Pub. by Turtleback) Demco.

— Heathcliff's Halloween. 1989. pap. 1.95 (*0-8167-1560-2*) Troll Communs.

— Sand Art Craft Kit. (Illus.). (gr. 4-7). 1996. 9.95 (*0-590-20252-9*) Scholastic Inc.

Lord, Thomas F. Decent Housing: A Promise to Keep. 176p. 1976. boxed set 29.95 (*0-87073-491-1*) Transaction Pubs.

Lord, Thomas R. More Stories of Lake George: Fact & Fancy. 218p. 1994. pap. 21.75 (*0-9640267-0-8*) Pinelands Pr.

— Poems of Lake George: Proses & Posey. 198p. 1995. pap. 21.75 (*0-9640267-2-4*) Pinelands Pr.

— Still More Stories of Lake George: Fact & Fancy, Vol. 4. 200p. 1999. pap. 21.75 (*0-9640267-3-2*) Pinelands Pr.

— Stories of Lake George: Fact & Fancy. 204p. 1986. pap. 21.75 (*0-9640267-1-6*) Pinelands Pr.

Lord, Todd, 3rd, ed. The Designment Review. LC 85-63787. (Residential Design & Market Trends Ser.). (Illus.). 40p. (Orig.). pap. 8.00 (*0-936909-00-5*) Northwest Home.

Lord, Todd, ed. Designment Review 1989. LC 86-657614. (Pacific Rim Edition Ser.). (JPN., Illus.). 40p. (Orig.). (C). 1988. pap. 8.00 (*0-936909-06-4*) Northwest Home.

Lord, Todd, ed. see Northwest Home Designing, Inc. Staff.

Lord, Todd, ed. see Northwest Home Designing Inc. Staff.

Lord, Tom. The Jazz Discography. (Discography Ser.: Vol. 18). 608p. 1998. pap. 60.00 (*1-881993-17-5*) Cadence Jazz.

— The Jazz Discography. 608p. 1998. pap. 60.00 (*1-881993-18-3*) Cadence Jazz.

— The Jazz Discography, Vol. 1: A-Bank. 608p. 1992. 70.00 (*1-881993-00-0*) Cadence Jazz.

— The Jazz Discography, Vol. 2: Ban-Bou. 608p. 1992. 70.00 (*1-881993-01-9*) Cadence Jazz.

— The Jazz Discography, Vol. 3: Bou-Cath. 608p. 1992. 70.00 (*1-881993-02-7*) Cadence Jazz.

— The Jazz Discography, Vol. 4: Cath-Da. 608p. 1993. 70.00 (*1-881993-03-5*) Cadence Jazz.

— The Jazz Discography, Vol. 5: Da-Dz. 608p. 1993. 70.00 (*1-881993-04-3*) Cadence Jazz.

— The Jazz Discography, Vol. 6: Dz-Fis. 608p. 1993. 70.00 (*1-881993-05-1*) Cadence Jazz.

— The Jazz Discography, Vol. 7: Fis-Go. 608p. 1993. 70.00 (*1-881993-06-X*) Cadence Jazz.

— The Jazz Discography, Vol. 8: Go-Ha. 608p. 1994. 70.00 (*1-881993-07-8*) Cadence Jazz.

— The Jazz Discography, Vol. 9: Har-Ho. 608p. 1994. 60.00 (*1-881993-08-6*) Cadence Jazz.

— The Jazz Discography, Vol. 10: Ho-Je. 608p. 1994. 60.00 (*1-881993-09-4*) Cadence Jazz.

— The Jazz Discography, Vol. 11. 608p. 1995. 60.00 (*1-881993-10-8*) Cadence Jazz.

— The Jazz Discography, Vol. 12. 608p. 1995. 70.00 (*1-881993-11-6*) Cadence Jazz.

— The Jazz Discography, Vol. 13. 608p. 1995. pap. 60.00 (*1-881993-12-4*) Cadence Jazz.

— The Jazz Discography, Vol. 15. 608p. 1996. pap. 70.00 (*1-881993-14-0*) Cadence Jazz.

— The Jazz Discography, 25 vols., Vol. 15. (Jazz Discography Ser.: Vol. 14). 608p. 1996. pap. 70.00 (*1-881993-13-2*) Cadence Jazz.

— The Jazz Discography, Vol. 16. 608p. 1997. pap. 60.00 (*1-881993-15-9*) Cadence Jazz.

— The Jazz Discography, Vol. 17. 600p. 1997. pap. 60.00 (*1-881993-16-7*) Cadence Jazz.

***Lord, Tom.** The Jazz Discography, 25 vols., Vol. 21. 608p. 1999. pap. 60.00 (*1-881993-20-5*, Pub. by Cadence Jazz) NorthCountry Distributors.

— The Jazz Discography, 25 vols., Vol. 22. 608p. 1999. pap. 60.00 (*1-881993-21-3*, Pub. by Cadence Jazz) NorthCountry Distributors.

— The Jazz Discography, Vol. 23. 608p. 2000. pap. 70.00 (*1-881993-22-1*, Pub. by Cadence Jazz) NorthCountry Distributors.

Lord, Tony. Beat Borders. rev. ed. LC 96-119369. (Illus.). 144p. 1996. pap. 21.95 (*0-14-023513-2*, Viking) Viking Penguin.

— Designing with Roses. 1999. 35.00 (*1-57076-148-5*, Trafalgar Sq Pub) Trafalgar.

***Lord, Tony.** Gardening at Sissinghurst. (Illus.). 160p. 1999. 45.00 (*0-7112-0991-X*, Pub. by F Lincoln) Antique Collect.

Lord, Tony. Gardening at Sissinghurst. (Illus.). 168p. 1996. 40.00 (*0-02-860389-3*) Macmillan.

— The New Wines of Spain. (Illus.). 160p. 24.95 (*0-932664-59-8*, 6517) Wine Appreciation.

Lord, Trevor. Amazing Bikes. LC 92-911. (Eyewitness Juniors Ser.: No. 22). (Illus.). 32p. (J). (ps-3). 1992. pap. 7.99 (*0-679-82772-2*, Pub. by Knopf Bks Yng Read) Random.

— Amazing Bikes. (Eyewitness Juniors Ser.: No. 22). (J). (ps-3). 1992. 13.19 (*0-606-01541-8*, Pub. by Turtleback) Demco.

***Lord, Trevor.** Big Book of Cars. LC 99-25463. 32p. (J). (gr. k-4). 1999. 14.95 (*0-7894-4738-X*) DK Pub Inc.

Lord, Ursula. Solitude Versus Solidarity in the Novels of Joseph Conrad: Political & Epistemological Implications of Narrative Innovation. LC 00-503333. 368p. 1998. text 60.00 (*0-7735-1670-0*, Pub. by McG-Queens Univ Pr) CUP Services.

Lord, Vicki. Fun with Alkyds & Oils. 72p. (Orig.). 1990. pap. 14.95 (*0-943295-14-9*) Graphics Plus FL.

— Painting Acrylics. LC 96-241. (First Steps Ser.). (Illus.). 128p. 1996. pap. 18.99 (*0-89134-668-6*, North Lght Bks) F & W Pubns Inc.

Lord, Walter. The Dawn's Early Light. LC 93-43700. (Maryland Paperback Bookshelf Ser.). 400p. 1994. pap. 14.95 (*0-8018-4864-4*) Johns Hopkins.

— Day of Infamy. 1998. pap. 12.99 (*1-85326-670-1*) NTC Contemp Pub Co.

— Day of Infamy. large type ed. (Niagara Large Print Ser.). (Illus.). 336p. 1997. 29.50 (*0-7089-5881-8*) Ulverscroft.

— Day of Infamy. (Illus.). (J). (gr. 9 up). 1991. reprint ed. 15.00 (*0-03-027620-9*) Adm Nimitz Foun.

— History of the Five Hundred Eighth Parachute Infantry. (Airborne Ser.: No. 2). (Illus.). 120p. 1990. reprint ed. 39.95 (*0-89839-002-8*) Battery Pr.

— Incredible Victory: The Battle of Midway. LC 98-10992. (Illus.). 331p. 1998. pap. 16.95 (*1-58080-059-9*) Burford Bks.

***Lord, Walter.** Midway: The Incredible Battle. (Illus.). 2000. pap. 12.99 (*1-84022-236-0*, Pub. by Wrdsworth Edits) Combined Pub.

Lord, Walter. Miracle of Dunkirk. (Wordsworth Collection). 452p. 1997. pap. 11.95 (*1-85326-685-X*, Pub. by Wrdsworth Edits) Combined Pub.

— Night Lives On. 1976. 22.95 (*0-8488-0568-2*) Amereon Ltd.

***Lord, Walter.** The Night Lives On: Keating & Charles, Set. 1998. audio 18.00 (*0-694-52107-8*) HarperAudio.

— The Night Lives On: The Untold Stories & Secrets Behind the Sinking of the "Unsinkable" Ship - Titanic! large type ed. 272p. 1999. 31.99 (*0-7089-9096-7*, Linford) Ulverscroft.

— The Night Lives On: The Untold Stories & Secrets Behind the Sinking of the Unsinkable Ship-Titanic. 1998. mass mkt. 5.99 (*0-380-73203-3*, Avon Bks) Morrow Avon.

Lord, Walter. A Night to Remember. 1987. 23.95 (*0-8488-0065-6*) Amereon Ltd.

— A Night to Remember. 224p. 1997. mass mkt. 6.50 (*0-553-27827-4*) Bantam.

— A Night to Remember. (Henry Holt Classics Library). 224p. 1995. 30.00 (*0-8050-1733-X*) H Holt & Co.

— A Night to Remember. 1991. 11.09 (*0-606-01137-4*, Pub. by Turtleback) Demco.

— A Night to Remember. large type ed. 1976. 12.00 (*0-85456-444-6*) Ulverscroft.

— A Night to Remember. large type ed. (Niagara Large Print Ser.). 240p. 1997. 29.50 (*0-7089-5874-5*) Ulverscroft.

— A Night to Remember. 300p. 1991. reprint ed. 25.95 (*0-89966-794-5*) Buccaneer Bks.

— A Time to Stand. LC 78-8708. (Illus.). 271p. 1978. reprint ed. pap. 10.95 (*0-8032-7902-7*, Bison Books) U of Nebr Pr.

Lord, Walter, ed. see Ungermann, Kenneth A.

Lord, Walton J. Chinese Paintings & Mounted Rocks: Exhibition Catalogue. (Illus.). 28p. 1979. pap. 2.00 (*0-911209-14-X*) Palmer Mus Art.

Lord, Wayne, Sr. Our Dhammapada. 112p. (Orig.). 1993. pap. 8.95 (*0-9636577-0-4*) Trego-Hill.

Lord Wedderburn, et al, eds. Labour Law in the Post-Industrial Era: Essays in Honour of Hugo Sinzheimer. 160p. 1994. text 57.95 (*1-85521-644-2*, Pub. by Dartmth Pub) Ashgate Pub Co.

Lord, Wendy. Big Mouth. Reck, Sue, ed. LC 94-1799. (Tabitha Sarah Bigbee Book). 112p. (J). (gr. 3-6). 1994. pap. 4.99 (*0-7814-0084-8*, Chariot Bks) Chariot Victor.

— Gorilla on the Midway. LC 93-1051. (Tabitha Sarah Bigbee Book). 96p. (J). 1994. pap. 4.99 (*0-7814-0892-X*, Chariot Bks) Chariot Victor.

— Pickle Stew. LC 93-19018. (Tabitha Sarah Bigbee Book). 96p. (J). 1994. pap. 4.99 (*0-7814-0886-5*, Chariot Bks) Chariot Victor.

Lord, Wendy, et al. Shepherds & Shoppers: Four Plays for the Christmas Season. Johns, Helen, ed. LC 92-72129. (Illus.). 55p. 1992. pap. 6.95 (*0-916035-49-2*) Evangel Indiana.

Lord Wharncliffe, ed. see Montagu, Lady Mary Wortley & Wharncliffe, Jame A.

Lord, William, ed. Electromagnetic Methods of Nondestructive Testing, Vol. 3. (Nondestructive Testing Monographs & Tracts). xii, 380p. 1985. pap. text 376.00 (*2-88124-020-8*) Gordon & Breach.

Lord, William B., ed. see Symposium on Indian Water Rights & Water Resources.

Lord, William G. Blue Ridge Parkway Guide Vol. 1: Rockfish Gap to Grandfather Mountain. LC 92-28237. (Illus.). 160p. 1992. reprint ed. pap. 8.95 (*0-89732-118-9*) Menasha Ridge.

— Blue Ridge Parkway Guide Vol. 2: Grandfather Mountain to Great Smoky Mountain National Park. LC 92-28238. (Illus.). 160p. 1992. reprint ed. pap. 8.95 (*0-89732-119-7*) Menasha Ridge.

Lord, William G., et al. Barker. Story with Genealogy of Some of the Descendants of Nathan Barker of Sandisfield, Massachusetts. 101p. 1995. reprint ed. pap. 19.50 (*0-8328-4742-9*); reprint ed. lib. bdg. 29.50 (*0-8328-4741-0*) Higginson Bk Co.

Lord, William H. Stagecraft 1: A Complete Guide to Backstage Work. 2nd ed. (Illus.). 67p. (C). 1991. pap., student ed. 6.00 (*0-9606320-4-2*); teacher ed., ring bd. 20.00 (*0-9606320-5-0*); per. 17.95 (*0-9606320-3-4*) W H Lord.

— Stagecraft 1: A Complete Guide to Backstage Work. 2nd ed. Zapel, Arthur L., ed. LC 90-26462. (Illus.). 160p. (C). 1991. reprint ed. pap. 17.95 (*0-916260-76-3*, B116) Meriwether Pub.

***Lord, William H.** Stagecraft 1: A Complete Guide to Backstage Work. 3rd rev. ed. LC 00-22998. (Illus.). 2000. pap. write for info. (*1-56608-062-2*) Meriwether Pub.

Lord, William H. Stagecraft I: Teacher's Guide to Student Workbook. 2nd ed. Zapel, Arthur L., ed. (Illus.). 80p. 1991. reprint ed. pap., teacher ed. 19.95 (*1-56608-018-5*, B199) Meriwether Pub.

Lord, William S., compiled by. Best Short Poems of the Nineteenth Century: Being the Twenty-Five Best Short Poems As Selected by Ballot by Competent Critics. LC 76-152152. (Granger Index Reprint Ser.). 1977. reprint ed. 13.95 (*0-8369-6261-3*) Ayer.

— This Is for You. LC 78-121926. (Granger Index Reprint Ser.). 1977. 19.95 (*0-8369-6167-6*) Ayer.

***Lord-Wolff, Peter.** The Silence in Heaven. LC 99-51783. 384p. 2000. 24.95 (*0-312-86675-5*, Pub. by Forge NYC) St Martin.

Lord Woolf of Barnes & Jowell, Jeffrey. De Smith, Woolf & Jowell: Judicial Review of Administrative Action. 5th ed. LC 96-204571. 1994. 176.00 (*0-420-46620-7*, Pub. by Sweet & Maxwll) Gaunt.

Lordahl, Jo A. 100 Motivators for Educators: Affirmations for Good Health & Good Living. LC 97-4903. 112p. 1997. 39.95 (*0-8039-6625-3*); pap. 16.95 (*0-8039-6626-1*) Sage.

Lordahl, Jo Ann. 100 Affirmations for Creative People. LC 99-174899. 100 p. 1998. pap. write for info. (*0-9664528-0-1*) Target Pubng.

Lordahl, JoAnn. Reflections for Busy Educators: 180 Affirmations to Help You Through the School Year. LC 95-21433. 112p. 1995. pap. 18.95 (*0-8039-6320-3*) Corwin Pr.

Lordan, Beth. And Both Shall Row. LC 98-15745. 176p. 1998. text 21.00 (*0-312-18682-7*, Picador USA) St Martin.

— Both Shall Row. 192p. 1999. pap. 12.00 (*0-312-20633-X*, Picador USA) St Martin.

Lorde, Audre Geraldine. The Black Unicorn: Poems. 136p. 1995. pap. 11.95 (*0-393-31237-2*) Norton.

— A Burst of Light. LC 88-3924. 134p. 1988. pap. 9.95 (*0-932379-39-7*); lib. bdg. 20.95 (*0-932379-40-0*) Firebrand Bks.

— A Burst of Light. 134p. pap. write for info. (*0-88961-174-2*, Pub. by Womens Pr) LPC InBook.

— The Cancer Journals. 2nd ed. LC 80-53110. 77p. 1980. pap. 7.00 (*1-879960-26-5*) Aunt Lute Bks.

— The Cancer Journals: Special Edition. LC 97-10954. 112p. 1997. 12.95 (*1-879960-51-6*) Aunt Lute Bks.

— Coal. rev. ed. 70p. 1996. pap. 10.00 (*0-393-31486-3*, Norton Paperbks) Norton.

— The Collected Poems of Audre Lorde. LC 97-10878. 500p. (C). 1997. 35.00 (*0-393-04090-9*) Norton.

— The Collected Poems of Audre Lorde. LC 97-10878. 512p. 2000. pap. 17.95 (*0-393-31972-5*, Norton Paperbks) Norton.

— From a Land Where Other People Live. LC 73-82075. (YA). (gr. 12 up). 1973. pap. 5.00 (*0-910296-97-9*) Broadside Pr.

— I Am Your Sister: Black Women Organizing Across Sexualities. (Freedom Organizing Pamphlet Ser.). 12p. (Orig.). (C). 1986. pap. 3.95 (*0-913175-07-2*) Kitchen Table.

— The Marvelous Arithmetics of Distance: Poems, 1987-1992. LC 92-40859. 96p. 1993. 18.95 (*0-393-03513-1*) Norton.

— The Marvelous Arithmetics of Distance: Poems, 1987-1992. 1994. pap. 8.95 (*0-393-31170-8*) Norton.

— Need: A Chorale for Black Woman Voices. (Freedom Organizing Pamphlet Ser.). 20p. 1991. pap. 3.95 (*0-913175-22-6*) Kitchen Table.

— Our Dead Behind Us: Poems. 88p. 1994. pap. 9.00 (*0-393-31238-0*) Norton.

— Sister Outsider: Essays & Speeches. LC 84-1844. (Feminist Ser.). (Illus.). 192p. 1984. pap. 14.95 (*0-89594-141-4*) Crossing Pr.

— Undersong: Chosen Poems Old & New. rev. ed. 224p. 1992. pap. 11.95 (*0-393-30975-4*) Norton.

— Zami: A New Spelling of My Name. LC 82-15086. (Feminist Ser.). (Illus.). 256p. 1983. pap. 16.95 (*0-89594-122-8*) Crossing Pr.

Lorde, Audre Geraldine & Woo, Merle. Apartheid U. S. A. & Our Common Enemy, Our Common Cause: Freedom Organizing in the Eighties. (Freedom Organizing Pamphlet Ser.). 28p. (Orig.). (C). 1986. pap. 3.95 (*0-913175-06-4*) Kitchen Table.

Lorden, G., ed. Jack Carl Kiefer: Introduction to Statistical Inference. (Texts in Statistics Ser.). (Illus.). xii, 360p. 1987. 74.95 (*0-387-96420-7*) Spr-Verlag.

Lordi, Robert J., ed. see Chapman, George.

Lordon. Crown Law. 784p. 1991. 113.00 (*0-409-89386-2*, MICHIE) LEXIS Pub.

— Crown Law-Tort. 94p. 1991. pap. 13.00 (*0-409-90628-X*, MICHIE) LEXIS Pub.

— Crown Property. 76p. 1991. pap. 12.00 (*0-409-90626-3*, MICHIE) LEXIS Pub.

Lordon, Randye. Brotherly Love. 272p. 1994. pap. 9.95 (*0-312-10947-4*, Stonewall Inn) St Martin.

— Father Forgive Me. 304p. (Orig.). 1997. mass mkt. 5.99 (*0-380-79165-X*, Avon Bks) Morrow Avon.

— Mother May I: A Sydney Sloane Mystery. 320p. 1998. mass mkt. 5.99 (*0-380-79166-8*, Avon Bks) Morrow Avon.

— Say Uncle. (Sydney Sloane Mystery Ser.). 320p. 1999. mass mkt. 5.99 (*0-380-79167-6*, Avon Bks) Morrow Avon.

— Sisters Keeper. 320p. 1996. pap. 10.95 (*0-312-14134-3*) St Martin.

Lords, Bill. Wonder Woman: The Contest. Kahan, Bob, ed. (Illus.). 120p. 1995. mass mkt. 9.95 (*1-56389-194-8*, Pub. by DC Comics) Time Warner.

Lore. An Atlas of Head & Neck Surgery. 4th ed. 1900. text. write for info. (*0-7216-7319-8*, W B Saunders Co) Harcrt Hlth Sci Grp.

***Lore & Borodovsky.** Corporate Financial Risk Practice & Applications. 2001. 74.95 (*0-7506-5019-2*) Buttrwrth-Heinemann.

— Credit Derivatives Risk Practice & Applications. 2001. 74.95 (*0-7506-5020-6*) Buttrwrth-Heinemann.

— Credit Risk Practice & Applications. 2001. 74.95 (*0-7506-5023-0*) Buttrwrth-Heinemann.

— Liquidity Risk Practice & Applications. 2001. 74.95 (*0-7506-5024-9*) Buttrwrth-Heinemann.

— Market Risk Practice & Applications. 2001. 74.95 (*0-7506-5022-2*) Buttrwrth-Heinemann.

— Operational Risk Practice & Applications. 2001. 74.95 (*0-7506-5021-4*) Buttrwrth-Heinemann.

Lore, John M. An Atlas of Head & Neck Surgery. 3rd ed. (Illus.). 1219p. 1988. text 199.00 (*0-7216-5816-4*, W B Saunders Co) Harcrt Hlth Sci Grp.

Lore, Lily, tr. see Kollontai, Aleksandra M.

Lore, Marc, jt. ed. see Borodovsky, Lev.

Lore, Mark, jt. auth. see Lore, Matthew.

Lore, Marvin D. De, see De Lore, Marvin D.

***Lore, Matthew & Lore, Mark.** Rubberneckers: Everyone's Favorite Travel Game. (Illus.). 1999. 12.95 (*0-8118-2217-6*) Chronicle Bks.

Lore, Nicholas. The Pathfinder: How to Choose or Change Your Career for a Lifetime of Satisfaction & Success. LC 97-36944. 400p. 1998. per. 14.00 (*0-684-82399-3*, Fireside) S&S Trade Pap.

Loredano, Giovanni. Life of Adam. LC 67-26617. 108p. 1967. reprint ed. 50.00 (*0-8201-1031-0*) Schol Facsimiles.

Loredo, Betsy. Faraway Families. LC 94-22978. (Family Ties Ser.). (Illus.). 64p. (J). (gr. 4-7). 1995. lib. bdg. 14.95 (*1-881889-61-0*) Silver Moon.

Loredo, Betsy, ed. see Albee, Sarah.

Loredo, Elizabeth. Boogie Bones. LC 95-42573. (Illus.). 32p. (J). (gr. k-3). 1997. 15.95 (*0-399-22763-6*, G P Putnam) Peng Put Young Read.

— The Jump Rope Book & the Jump Rope. LC 96-4471. (Illus.). 288p. (J). (ps-7). 1996. pap. 9.95 (*0-7611-0448-8*, 10448) Workman Pub.

Loredo, Elizabeth E., jt. auth. see Thase, Michael E.

Loredo, Miguel A. De la Necesidad y Del Amor: (Poesia, 1967-1979) LC 88-80054. (Coleccion Espejo de Paciencia). (SPA., Illus.). 160p. (Orig.). 1990. pap. 15.00 (*0-89729-475-0*) Ediciones.

— Despues del Silencio: Entrevistas al Padre Franciscano Fray Miguel Angel Loredo, O.F.M. por Nicolas Perez Diez-Arguelles. 2nd ed. LC 89-84404. (Coleccion Cuba y sus Jueces). (SPA., Illus.). 215p. 1989. reprint ed. pap. 15.00 (*0-89729-537-4*) Ediciones.

Loreen, Wendy. Easy Games for Early Learners. Milliken, Linda, ed. (Illus.). 64p. 1993. pap., teacher ed. 6.95 (*1-56472-013-6*) Edupress Inc.

Lorele, Reyna Thera. The Archer King. LC 99-71840. 454p. 2000. pap. 21.95 (*0-9625803-3-3*) Blue Arrow Bks.

***Lorelei, Mistress.** The Mistress Manual: A Good Girl's Guide to Female Dominance. 220p. 2000. 15.95 (*1-890159-19-0*) Greenery Pr.

Lorell, Beverly H., jt. ed. see Grossman, William.

Lorell, K. R., ed. see IFAC Symposium on Automatic Control in Aerospace S.

Lorell, Mark. Troubled Partnership: A History of U. S. - Japan Collaboration on the FS-X Fighter. LC 95-50670. 468p. 1996. pap. text 24.95 (*1-56000-891-1*) Transaction Pubs.

Lorell, Mark & Lowell, Julie. Pros & Cons of International Weapons Procurement Collaboration. LC 95-16550. 54p. 1995. pap. text 7.50 (*0-8330-1655-5*, MR-565-OSD) Rand Corp.

***Lorell, Mark, et al.** Cheaper, Faster, Better? Commercial Approaches to Weapons Acquisition. LC 99-58412. xxix, 215p. 2000. pap. 20.00 (*0-8330-2796-4*, MR-1147-AF) Rand Corp.

An Asterisk (*) at the beginning of an entry indicates that the title is appearing for the first time.

Lorell, Mark, et al. The Gray Threat: Assessing the Next-Generation European Fighters. LC 95-36511. xvi, 66p. 1995. pap. text 15.00 (*0-8330-2307-1*, MR-611-AF) Rand Corp.

Lorell, Mark A. Bomber R & D Since 1945: The Role of Experience. LC 95-47564. 88p. (Orig.). 1995. pap. 15.00 (*0-8330-2341-1*, MR-670-AF) Rand Corp.

Lorell, Mark A. & Levaux, Hugh P. The Cutting Edge: A Half Century of U. S. Fighter Aircraft R & D. (Illus.). 240p. 1998. 35.00 (*0-8330-2607-0*); pap. 16.50 (*0-8330-2595-3*, MR-939-AF, Pub. by Rand Corp) Natl Bk Netwk.

Lorelli, John. To Foreign Shores: U. S. Amphibious Operations in World War II. LC 94-32014. (Illus.). 392p. 1995. 41.95 (*1-55750-520-9*) Naval Inst Pr.

Lorelli, Michael K. Traveling Again, Dad? Struzan, Dylan, ed. LC 95-60604. (Illus.). 32p. (J). (ps-7). 1995. 17.95 (*0-9646302-0-6*) Awesome Bks.

Loren & MacLean Marine & Offshore Publications Sta. Inert Gas Systems Maintenance. (C). 1987. 70.00 (*0-7855-4369-4*, Pub. by Lorne & MacLean Marine) St Mut.

Loren, Jo An. Breast Cancer? Let Me Check My Schedule! Ten Remarkable Women Meet the Challenge of Fitting Breast Cancer into Their Very Busy Lives. McCarthy, Peggy, ed. LC 97-30632. (C). 1997. pap. 16.00 (*0-8133-3393-8*, Pub. by Westview) HarpC.

Loren, John, jt. auth. see McCarthy, Peggy.

Loren, Julia. The Note on the Mirror: Pregnant Teenagers Tell Their Stories. 160p. 1990. pap. 6.99 (*0-310-53531-X*) Zondervan.

Loren, Karl. Four Roads to Ruin: Your Health in the Twenty-First Century. (Illus.). 400p. (Orig.). 1995. 19.95 (*1-882537-06-8*) Bigelow Charter.

— Life Flow One: The Solution for Heart Disease. (Illus.). 300p. 1994. write for info. (*1-882537-02-5*) Bigelow Charter.

— Life Flow One: The Solution for Heart Disease. rev. ed. (Illus.). 400p. 1995. pap. 19.95 (*1-882537-05-X*) Bigelow Charter.

— Trust, Taxes & Freedom. 475p. 1991. 195.00 (*1-882537-00-9*) Bigelow Charter.

***Lorena, Jeanne Marie & Levy, Paula, eds.** Breaking Ritual Silence: An Anthology of Ritual Abuse Survivors' Stories. LC 98-60109. 256p. 1998. pap. 14.95 (*0-9664174-0-2*) Trout & Sons.

***Lorence, David H.** A Nomenclator of Mexican & Central American Rubiaceae. 177p. 1999. pap. 20.00 (*0-915279-62-2*) Miss Botan.

Lorence, David H. & Vaughan, Reginald E. Annotated Bibliography of Mascarene Plant Life: Including the Useful & Ornamental Plants of the Region, Covering the Period 1609-1990. (Illus.). 280p. (C). 1992. 29.95 (*0-915809-15-X*) Natl Trop Bot.

Lorence, James J. Enduring Voices: Document Sets to Accompany "The Enduring Vision", Vol. 1. 3rd ed. (C). pap. text 13.56 (*0-669-39920-5*) HM Trade Div.

— Gerald J. Boileau & the Progressive-Farmer-Labor Alliance: Politics of the New Deal. (Illus.). 344p. 1994. text 44.95 (*0-8262-0918-1*) U of Mo Pr.

— Organizing the Unemployed: Community & Union Activists in the Industrial Heartland. LC 95-33412. (SUNY Series in American Labor History). 407p. (C). 1996. text 68.50 (*0-7914-2987-3*); pap. text 22.95 (*0-7914-2988-1*) State U NY Pr.

***Lorence, James J.** The Suppression of Salt of the Earth: How Hollywood, Big Labor & Politicians Blacklisted a Movie in Cold War America. LC 98-58036. (Illus.). 256p. 1999. 45.00 (*0-8263-2027-9*) U of NM Pr.

— The Suppression of Salt of the Earth: How Hollywood, Big Labor, & Politicians Blacklisted a Movie in Cold War America. LC 98-58036. 1999. pap. 19.95 (*0-8263-2028-7*) U of NM Pr.

Lorence-Kot, Bogna. Child Rearing & Reform: A Study of the Nobility in Eighteenth-Century Poland, 9. LC 84-25203. (Contributions in Family Studies: No. 9). (Illus.). 170p. 1985. 49.95 (*0-313-24500-2*, LCR/, Greenwood Pr) Greenwood.

Lorendo, Leah C., ed. see Frattali, Carol M.

Lorene, Kristi. Florence Nightingale. (Young Reader's Christian Library). (Illus.). 224p. (J). (gr. 3-7). 1997. pap. 1.39 (*1-57748-104-6*) Barbour Pub.

— Thunder in the Valley. (Young Reader's Christian Library). 224p. (J). (gr. 3-7). 1994. pap. text 1.39 (*1-55748-551-8*) Barbour Pub.

Lorensen, Leonard. Accounting for Liabilities. fac. ed. LC 91-41025. (Accounting Research Monograph: No. 4). 189p. 1992. pap. 58.60 (*0-7837-8235-7*, 204799900009) Bks Demand.

— Illustrations of Pro Forma Financial Statements That Reflect Subsequent Events. fac. ed. LC 91-16949. (Financial Report Survey Ser.: No. 44). 92p. 1991. reprint ed. pap. 30.00 (*0-7837-8226-8*, 204798600009) Bks Demand.

— Illustrations of Reporting the Results of Operations: A Survey of the Recent Application of APB Opinion 30. fac. ed. LC 92-11043. (Financial Report Survey Ser.: No. 47). 118p. 1992. reprint ed. pap. 36.60 (*0-7837-8219-5*, 204797900009) Bks Demand.

— Illustrations of the Disclosure by Financial Institutions of Certain Information about Debt Securities Held As Assets: A Survey of the Application of SOP 90-11. fac. ed. LC 92-21816. (Financial Report Survey Ser.: No. 48). 117p. 1992. reprint ed. pap. 36.30 (*0-7837-8225-X*, 204798500009) Bks Demand.

— Illustrations of the Disclosure of Information about Financial Instruments with Off-Balance-Sheet Risk & Financial Instruments with Concentrations of Credit Risk: A Survey of the Application of FASB Statement No. 105. fac. ed. LC 92-12974. (Financial Report Survey Ser.: No. 46). 121p. 1992. reprint ed. pap. 37.60 (*0-7837-8227-6*, 204798700009) Bks Demand.

Lorensen, Leonard, jt. auth. see Clark, Hal G.

Lorensen, Leonard, ed. see American Institute of Certified Public Accountants.

Lorent, Kristin. Expression of the Alpha-2-Macroglobulin Receptor System & the Amyloid Precursor Protein Family in Embryos & in Adult Brain of Wild Type & Transgenic Mice. (Acta Biomedica Lovaniensia Ser.: Vol. 148). (Illus.). 151p. 1997. pap. 52.50 (*90-6186-810-6*, Pub. by Leuven Univ) Coronet Bks.

Lorente De No, Rafael. The Primary Acoustic Nuclei. LC 81-968. 189p. 1981. reprint ed. pap. 58.60 (*0-608-00388-3*, 206110200007) Bks Demand.

Lorente, J. Pedro. Cathedrals of Modernity: The Creation of the First Museums of Contemporary Art. LC 97-31675. (Historical Urban Studies). 322p. 1998. text 83.95 (*1-85928-383-7*, Pub. by Ashgate Pub) Ashgate Pub Co.

Lorente, Maria A. Palynology und Palynofacies of the Upper Tertiary in Venezuela. (Dissertationes Botanicae Ser.: Band 99). (Illus.). ix, 225p. 1986. pap. 71.00 (*3-443-64011-7*, Pub. by Gebruder Borntraeger) Balogh.

Lorente, Mariano J., jt. auth. see Blasco-Ibanez, Vincenti.

Lorentowicz, Irena. Old Warsaw Cookbook. 300p. pap. 12.95 (*0-87052-932-3*) Hippocrene Bks.

Lorents. Database Systems: Concepts, Management & Application. LC 97-65944. (C). 1997. text 69.50 (*0-15-500029-2*) Harcourt Coll Pubs.

Lorentz, jt. auth. see Dietl.

Lorentz, Elizabeth, jt. auth. see Sarason, Seymour B.

Lorentz, Elizabeth M., jt. auth. see Sarason, Seymour B.

Lorentz, Friedrich, et al. The Cassubian Civilization. LC 77-87520. 456p. 1983. reprint ed. 62.50 (*0-404-16603-2*) AMS Pr.

Lorentz, G. G. Bernstein Polynomials. LC 55-527. (Mathematical Expositions Ser.: No. 8). 140p. reprint ed. pap. 43.40 (*0-8357-7144-X*, 205196600018) Bks Demand.

Lorentz, G. G. & Lorentz, Rudolph A. Mathematics from Leningrad to Austin: George G. Lorentz's Selected Works in Real, Functional & Numerical Analysis. LC 96-16946. (Contemporary Mathematicians Ser.). 1996. write for info. (*3-7643-3710-9*); write for info. (*3-7643-3922-5*, Pub. by Birkhauser); write for info. (*3-7643-3923-3*) Birkhauser.

Lorentz, George G. Approximation of Functions. 2nd ed. LC 66-13296. ix, 184p. (C). 1985. text 16.95 (*0-8284-0322-8*) Chelsea Pub.

— Bernstein Polynomials. 2nd ed. x, 132p. 1985. text 14.95 (*0-8284-0323-6*) Chelsea Pub.

Lorentz, George G., et al. Birkhoff Interpolation. (Encyclopedia of Mathematics & Its Applications Ser.: No. 19). 237p. 1984. text 85.00 (*0-521-30239-0*) Cambridge U Pr.

— Constructive Approximation: Advanced Problems. (Grundlehren der Mathematischen Wissenschaflen Ser.: Vol. 304). 601p. 1996. 140.00 (*0-387-57028-4*) Spr-Verlag.

Lorentz, George G., jt. auth. see DeVore, Ronald A.

Lorentz, John H. Historical Dictionary of Iran. LC 94-45843. (Asian Historical Dictionaries Ser.: No. 16). (Illus.). 352p. 1995. 55.00 (*0-8108-2994-0*) Scarecrow.

Lorentz, Moses L. How to Prepare for the National Teacher Examination (NTE) Common Examinations. 1980. pap. text 5.95 (*0-07-038745-1*) McGraw.

Lorentz, Pare. FDR's Moviemaker: Memoirs & Scripts. LC 91-38493. (Illus.). 256p. 1992. 29.95 (*0-87417-186-5*) U of Nev Pr.

Lorentz, Rudolph A. Multivariate Birkhoff Interpolation. LC 92-27388. ix, 192p. 1992. 48.95 (*0-387-55870-5*); pap. 35.00 (*3-540-55870-5*) Spr-Verlag.

Lorentz, Rudolph A., ed. Mathematics from Leningrad to Austin: George G. Lorentz's Selected Works in Real, Functional, & Numerical Analysis, 2 vols., Set. LC 96-16946. (Contemporary Mathematicians Ser.). 1167p. 1996. 189.00 (*0-8176-3923-3*) Birkhauser.

— Mathematics from Leningrad to Austin: George G. Lorentz's Selected Works in Real, Functional, & Numerical Analysis, Vol. 1. LC 96-16946. (Contemporary Mathematicians Ser.). 538p. 1997. 110.00 (*0-8176-3710-9*) Birkhauser.

— Mathematics from Leningrad to Austin: George G. Lorentz's Selected Works in Real, Functional, & Numerical Analysis, Vol. 2. LC 96-16946. (Contemporary Mathematicians Ser.). 629p. 1996. 120.00 (*0-8176-3922-5*) Birkhauser.

Lorentz, Rudolph A., jt. auth. see Lorentz, G. G.

***Lorentzen, Anne, ed.** Institutional Change & Industrial Development in Central & Eastern Europe. 320p. 1999. text 74.95 (*0-7546-1014-4*, Pub. by Ashgate Pub) Ashgate Pub Co.

Lorentzen, Anne & Rostgaard, Marianne, eds. The Aftermath of 'Real Existing Socialism' in Eastern Europe Vol. 2: People & Technology in the Process of Transition. LC 96-25600. (International Political Economy Ser.). 309p. 1997. text 79.95 (*0-312-17490-X*) St Martin.

Lorentzen, Bob. The Hiker's Hip Pocket Guide to Sonoma County. 2nd ed. LC 90-44136. (Hiker's Hip Pocket Guide Ser.). (Illus.). 224p. (Orig.). 1995. pap. 15.00 (*0-939431-21-1*) Bored Feet Pubns.

— The Hiker's Hip Pocket Guide to the Humboldt Coast: Including Redwood National Park, King Range - Lost Coast, Del Norte Coast, Lake Earl State Park, Humboldt Bay, Redwood State Parks, Patrick's Point & Other Natural Areas. 2nd ed. LC 88-22293. (Hiker's Hip Pocket Guide Ser.). (Illus.). 224p. 1996. pap. 14.00 (*0-939431-13-0*) Bored Feet Pubns.

— The Hiker's Hip Pocket Guide to the Mendocino Coast. 3rd rev. ed. Edelman, Joshua, ed. (Hiker's Hip Pocket Guide Ser.). 240p. (Orig.). 1999. pap. 14.00 (*0-939431-17-3*) Bored Feet Pubns.

— The Hiker's Hip Pocket Guide to the Mendocino Highlands: Including Yolla-Bolly-Middle Eel Wilderness, Snow Mountain Wilderness, Mendocino National Forest, Clear Lake State Parks, Cow Mountain Recreation Area & Other Natural Areas. LC 92-23637. (Hiker's Hip Pocket Guide Ser.). (Illus.). 240p. (Orig.). 1992. pap. 13.95 (*0-939431-05-X*) Bored Feet Pubns.

— Hiker's Hip Pocket Guides: Boxed Gift Set. (Illus.). 1990. 42.00 (*0-939431-04-1*) Bored Feet Pubns.

— Mendocino Coast Bike Rides: Road & Trail Rides from Easy to Advanced. LC 97-128632. 168p. (Orig.). 1996. pap. 12.00 (*0-939431-11-4*) Bored Feet Pubns.

— The Mendocino Coast Glove Box Guide: Lodging, Eateries, Sights, History, Activities, & More. 2nd ed. LC 94-44204. (Glove Box Guides Ser.). (Illus.). 237p. 1997. pap. 13.00 (*0-939431-16-5*) Bored Feet Pubns.

Lorentzen, Bob & Nichols, Richard. Hiking the California Coastal Trail Vol. 1: Oregon to Monterey, the Guide to Walking the Golden State's Beaches & Bluffs from Border to Border. LC 98-22518. (Illus.). 320p. (Orig.). 1998. pap. 18.00 (*0-939431-18-1*) Bored Feet Pubns.

***Lorentzen, Bob & Nichols, Richard.** Hiking the California Coastal Trail Vol. 2: Monterey to Mexico: A Guide to Walking the Golden State's Beaches & Bluffs Border to Border. (Illus.). 352p. 2000. pap. 19.00 (*0-939431-19-X*) Bored Feet Pubns.

Lorentzen, Karen M. & Neal, Robert D., eds. Health Education, Principles, Preparation & Practice. (Illus.). 124p. 1990. pap. 18.75 (*0-87527-473-0*) Green.

Lorentzen, Karen M. & Roemer, Linda. Health Services Administration Handbook: Education & Practice. 128p. 1988. pap. 19.50 (*0-87527-353-X*) Green.

Lorentzen, Lisa & Waadeland, Haakon. Continued Fractions with Applications. LC 92-8592. (Studies in Computational Mathematics: Vol. 3). 606p. 1992. 207.50 (*0-444-89265-6*, North Holland) Elsevier.

Lorentzen, Lois A. & Turpin, Jennifer, eds. The Women & War Reader. LC 98-18165. 415p. 1998. text 65.00 (*0-8147-5144-X*); pap. text 22.50 (*0-8147-5145-8*) NYU Pr.

Lorentzen, Lois A., jt. ed. see Turpin, Jennifer.

Lorentzen, R. J., jt. ed. see Flamm, W. G.

Lorentzen, Robin. Women in the Sanctuary Movement. (Women in the Political Economy Ser.). 240p. 1991. 44.95 (*0-87722-768-3*) Temple U Pr.

Lorentzen, Sandra, jt. ed. see Breisacher, E. H.

Lorentzi, Jakob & Nilsson, Magnus. Spin-Off, Dual-Use & Conversion: Fashion or Reality? 44p. (Orig.). (C). 1994. pap. text 25.00 (*0-7881-1381-X*) DIANE Pub.

Lorentzon, Betsy. Life on the Edge of the Slashings. LC 93-85761. 128p. pap. write for info. (*0-9637996-0-6*) Shinglemill.

Lorentzon, Leif. An African Focus: A Study of Ayi Kwei Armah's Narrative Africanization. LC 98-138624. (Stockholm Studies in History of Literature: Vol. 37). 221p. 1998. pap. 42.50 (*91-22-01768-2*) Coronet Bks.

Lorenz. All About Nature: Point & Say. 1999. 9.98 (*1-84038-214-7*) Random.

— Amazing Book of Clever Crafts. 1999. 9.98 (*1-84038-353-4*) Random.

— Amazing Braids, Beads & Pretty. 1999. 9.98 (*1-84038-354-2*) Random.

— Amazing Clever Tricks. 1999. 9.98 (*1-84038-355-0*) Random.

— Amazing Faces & Disguises. (Illus.). 96p. (gr. 3-7). 1999. 9.98 (*1-84038-356-9*) Random.

— Amazing Things to Learn & Do. 1999. 9.98 (*1-84038-357-7*) Random.

— Annuals. 1999. pap. 12.95 (*0-7548-0168-3*) Random.

Lorenz. Around the World Cookbook. (Illus.). 19.98 (*0-7548-0256-6*, Pub. by Anness Pub) Random.

Lorenz. Book of Loving Sex. 1999. 14.98 (*1-84038-197-3*) Hermes Hse.

— Butterflies: Nature Watch. 1999. 12.95 (*1-85967-612-X*, Lorenz Bks) Anness Pub.

Lorenz. Cakes & Cake Decorating. 19.98 (*0-7548-0082-2*, Pub. by Anness Pub) Random.

— Cars. (Illus.). 19.98 (*0-7548-0170-5*, Pub. by Anness Pub) Random.

— Chinese Cooking. 19.98 (*0-7548-0291-4*, Pub. by Anness Pub) Random.

— Complete Home Decorator. (Illus.). 19.98 (*0-7548-0292-2*, Pub. by Anness Pub) Random.

— Complete Practical Gardening. (Illus.). 19.98 (*0-7548-0163-2*, Pub. by Anness Pub) Random.

— Container Gardening. (Illus.). 19.98 (*0-7548-0083-0*, Pub. by Anness Pub) Random.

— Diggers & Dumpers. (Illus.). (J). (ps). 2000. bds. 4.95 (*0-7548-0063-6*) Anness Pub.

— Elephants: Nature Watch. 1999. 12.95 (*1-85967-639-1*, Pub. by Anness Pub) Random.

Lorenz. Fantasy Cars. 1999. 15.98 (*1-84038-200-7*, Pub. by Hermes Hse) Random.

— The Floral Address & Day Book: An Exquisite Address Book & Dateless Diary in an Enchanting Floral Theme. (Illus.). 64p. 1998. 16.95 (*1-85967-331-7*) Anness Pub.

Lorenz. Fresh & Dried Flowers. (Illus.). 19.98 (*0-7548-0084-9*, Pub. by Anness Pub) Random.

Lorenz. Gifts from the Garden. 2000. 9.95 (*1-85967-881-5*) Anness Pub.

— High Vitality Healthy Eating. pap. 12.95 (*1-85967-884-X*, Lorenz Bks) Anness Pub.

Lorenz. Italian Cooking. (Illus.). 19.98 (*0-7548-0241-8*, Pub. by Anness Pub) Random.

Lorenz. Ivies: New Plant Library. 1999. 9.95 (*1-85967-902-1*) Anness Pub.

— Massage & Aromatherapy. 1999. 15.98 (*1-84038-204-X*, Pub. by Hermes Hse) Random.

Lorenz. 1,000 Classic Recipes. (Illus.). 19.98 (*0-7548-0255-8*, Pub. by Anness Pub) Random.

— Papercraft. (Illus.). 19.98 (*0-7548-0332-5*, Pub. by Anness Pub) Random.

Lorenz. Play School Fun: Point & Say. 1999. 9.98 (*1-84038-213-9*, Pub. by Hermes Hse) Random.

— Pressed Flowercraft. 1999. 12.95 (*1-85967-904-8*, Lorenz Bks) Anness Pub.

***Lorenz.** Rhododendrons: New Plant. 1999. 9.95 (*1-85967-903-X*) Anness Pub.

Lorenz. Rice & Noodles. 1999. 16.95 (*0-7548-0158-6*, Lorenz Bks) Anness Pub.

— Shrubs & Climbers. 1999. 15.98 (*1-84038-207-4*, Pub. by Hermes Hse) Random.

Lorenz. Steam & Rail. (Illus.). 19.98 (*0-7548-0295-7*, Pub. by Anness Pub) Random.

— Ultimate Cooking Course. (Illus.). 19.98 (*0-7548-0169-1*, Pub. by Anness Pub) Random.

— Vegetables. (Illus.). 19.98 (*0-7548-0294-9*, Pub. by Anness Pub) Random.

— Victorian Flowers: Photo Album. 1999. 9.95 (*1-85967-918-8*, Lorenz Bks) Anness Pub.

Lorenz. Webster's Desk Spanish/English, English/Spanish Dictionary. LC 99-18193. (ENG & SPA.). 1999. 5.99 (*0-517-16136-2*) Random Hse Value.

— Wedding Inspirations. 1999. 7.98 (*1-84038-275-9*) Random.

Lorenz. Wine & Beer. (Illus.). 19.98 (*0-7548-0334-1*, Pub. by Anness Pub) Random.

Lorenz. World of Motorcycling. 1999. 9.98 (*1-84038-202-3*, Pub. by Hermes Hse) Random.

Lorenz & Vivian. Workbook News. 1995. pap. text 27.00 (*0-205-15849-8*) P-H.

***Lorenz, Albert & Schleh, Joy.** Buried Blueprints: Maps & Sketches of Lost Worlds & Mysterious Places. LC 99-23417. (Illus.). 56p. (J). (gr. 3-7). 1999. 19.95 (*0-8109-4110-4*, Pub. by Abrams) Time Warner.

Lorenz, Albert & Schleh, Joy. House: Showing How People Have Lived Throughout History with Examples Drawn from the Lives. LC 98-26412. (Illus.). 48p. (J). (gr. 4 up). 1998. 17.95 (*0-8109-1196-5*, Pub. by Abrams) Time Warner.

— Metropolis: Ten Cities & Ten Centuries. LC 96-83709. (Illus.). 42p. 1996. 17.95 (*0-8109-4284-4*, Pub. by Abrams) Time Warner.

Lorenz, Alfred, jt. auth. see Vivian, John H.

Lorenz, Arness. Fast & Healthy Recipes: Over 100 Delicious Good-For-You Recipes in No Time at All. 1998. pap. text 16.95 (*1-85967-666-9*, Lorenz Bks) Anness Pub.

Lorenz, August F., contrib. by. Platus, Ausgewahlte Komodien Band 2: Mostellaria, Vol. 2. 239p. 1981. write for info. (*3-296-15001-3*) G Olms Pubs.

— Platus, Ausgewahlte Komodien Band 3: Miles Gloriosus, Vol. 3. (GER.). viii, 294p. 1981. write for info. (*3-296-15002-1*) G Olms Pubs.

— Platus, Ausgewahlte Komodien Band 4: Pseudolus, Vol. 4. viii, 289p. 1981. write for info. (*3-296-15003-X*) G Olms Pubs.

Lorenz, August O., ed. see Plautus.

Lorenz, Books. Assorted Car/Motorcycle. 1998. pap. 12.95 (*1-85967-812-2*) Anness Pub.

— The Language of Flowers: An Anthology of Poetry & Prose. (Illus.). 64p. 1997. 9.95 (*1-85967-334-1*, Lorenz Bks) Anness Pub.

— Numbers: With Over 50 Reusable Stickers. 1998. pap. text 5.95 (*1-85967-772-X*, Lorenz Bks) Anness Pub.

— The Romance of Roses: An Anthology of Verse & Prose. (Illus.). 64p. 1997. 9.95 (*1-85967-333-3*, Lorenz Bks) Anness Pub.

— Teddies. 1998. 12.95 (*1-85967-571-9*, Lorenz Bks) Anness Pub.

***Lorenz Books Staff.** Amazing Activities: All Kinds of Fun Projects to Keep You Busy! (Illus.). (J). 2000. pap. 9.95 (*0-7548-0358-9*, Lorenz Bks) Anness Pub.

— Amazing Clever Crafts: Lots of Really Crafty Things to Make! (Illus.). 2000. pap. 9.95 (*0-7548-0237-X*, Lorenz Bks) Anness Pub.

— Amazing Clever Tricks: Magic & More to Astound Your Friends! (Illus.). 2000. pap. 9.95 (*0-7548-0238-8*, Lorenz Bks) Anness Pub.

Lorenz Books Staff. Animals. (Fun to Learn Ser.). 1999. 7.95 (*0-7548-0033-4*, Lorenz Bks) Anness Pub.

***Lorenz Books Staff.** Animals. (Illus.). (J). 2000. 4.95 (*0-7548-0376-7*, Lorenz Bks) Anness Pub.

— Animals. (Illus.). (J). 2000. 7.95 (*0-7548-0227-2*, Lorenz Bks) Anness Pub.

Lorenz Books Staff. Annuals; A Complete Guide to Cultivation & Care. 1999. pap. text 12.95 (*1-85967-878-5*) Anness Pub.

— Assorted World Encyclopedia, 1. 1998. 35.83 (*1-85967-813-0*) Anness Pub.

***Lorenz Books Staff.** Baby Animals. (My Very First Picture Book Ser.). (Illus.). (J). 2000. 4.95 (*0-7548-0061-X*, Lorenz Bks) Anness Pub.

— Bodies. (Illus.). (J). 2000. 4.95 (*0-7548-0377-5*, Lorenz Bks) Anness Pub.

— Cameras. (Investigations Ser.). (Illus.). 64p. (J). (gr. 3-7). 2000. 12.95 (*0-7548-0455-0*, Lorenz Bks) Anness Pub.

— Chinese. 2000. pap. 9.95 (*0-7548-0349-X*, Lorenz Bks) Anness Pub.

— Christmas Scenes. (Illus.). 1998. pap. 12.95 (*1-85967-849-1*, Lorenz Bks) Anness Pub.

— Clothes. (Illus.). (J). 2000. 4.95 (*0-7548-0375-9*, Lorenz Bks) Anness Pub.

— Colours: With over 50 Reusable Stickers. (Sticker Fun Book Ser.). (Illus.). (J). 1998. pap. 4.95 (*1-85967-770-3*, Lorenz Bks) Anness Pub.

Lorenz Books Staff. Complete Guide to Cooking Techniques: Practical Handbook. 1999. pap. text 12.95 (*0-7548-0003-2*, Lorenz Bks) Anness Pub.

— Cook's Record Book & Tips Gift Set. (Illus.). 64p. 1997. 14.95 (*1-85967-427-5*, Lorenz Bks) Anness Pub.

— Essential Home Reference Manual: Practical Handbook. 1999. 12.95 (*0-7548-0009-1*, Lorenz Bks) Anness Pub.

L

L

***Lorenz Books Staff.** Exploration & Discovery: Charts Extraordinary Journeys into the Unknown. (Exploring History Ser.). (Illus.). 64p. (J). (gr. 3-7). 2000. 12.95 (*0-7548-0443-7*, Lorenz Bks) Anness Pub.

— Facts. (J). 2000. 7.95 (*0-7548-0228-0*, Lorenz Bks) Anness Pub.

— Farm Animals. (My Very First Picture Book Ser.). (Illus.). (J). 2000. 4.95 (*0-7548-0062-8*, Lorenz Bks) Anness Pub.

Lorenz Books Staff. Flash in the Pan. 1997. pap. text 16.95 (*1-85967-368-6*, Lorenz Bks) Anness Pub.

— Gardender's Hints & Tips & Record Book. 1998. 14.95 (*1-85967-349-X*, Lorenz Bks) Anness Pub.

— The Great Big Cookie Book: A Collection of the World's Best Cookie Recipes. (Illus.). 256p. 1998. 24.95 (*1-85967-570-0*, Lorenz Bks) Anness Pub.

— Gummi Bear Counting Board Book. (Illus.). 12p. (ps-2). 1999. 4.95 (*0-7548-0074-1*, Lorenz Bks) Anness Pub.

***Lorenz Books Staff.** Hop, Skip, Jump. (My Very First Picture Book Ser.). (Illus.). (J). 2000. 4.95 (*0-7548-0383-X*, Lorenz Bks) Anness Pub.

Lorenz Books Staff. Horse Breeds of the World: Practical Handbook. 1999. pap. 10.95 (*0-7548-0013-X*, Lorenz Bks) Anness Pub.

— Instant Gardens. 1999. pap. text 12.95 (*1-85967-888-2*) Anness Pub.

— Kittens. (First Picture Bks.). (Illus.). 24p. (J). 1996. 4.95 (*1-85967-246-9*, Lorenz Bks) Anness Pub.

***Lorenz Books Staff.** Kittens & Cats: Stickers. 1999. 4.95 (*1-85967-999-4*, Lorenz Bks) Anness Pub.

Lorenz Books Staff. Learn about Astronomy. 64p. (J). 1996. 7.95 (*1-85967-159-4*, Lorenz Bks) Anness Pub.

— Learn about Insects. 1998. 8.95 (*1-85967-644-8*, Lorenz Bks) Anness Pub.

— Learn about Pyramids. 1998. 8.95 (*1-85967-643-X*, Lorenz Bks) Anness Pub.

— Learn about the Body. (Illus.). 64p. (J). 1996. 7.95 (*1-85967-134-9*, Lorenz Bks) Anness Pub.

— Let's Look at Animals: Preschool Picture & First Word Books. (Illus.). 24p. (J). 1996. 4.95 (*1-85967-265-5*, Lorenz Bks) Anness Pub.

— Let's Look at Colors: Preschool Picture & First Word Books. (Illus.). 24p. (J). 1996. 3.95 (*1-85967-270-1*, Lorenz Bks) Anness Pub.

— Let's Look at Flowers: Preschool Picture & First Word Books. (Illus.). 24p. (J). 1996. 3.95 (*1-85967-314-7*, Lorenz Bks) Anness Pub.

— Let's Look at Fruit: Preschool Picture & First Word Books. (Illus.). 24p. (J). 1996. 3.95 (*1-85967-275-2*, Lorenz Bks) Anness Pub.

— Let's Look at Numbers: Preschool Picture & First Word Books. (Illus.). 24p. (J). 1996. 4.95 (*1-85967-280-9*, Lorenz Bks) Anness Pub.

— Let's Look at Opposites. (Illus.). 24p. (J). 1996. 3.95 (*1-85967-315-5*, Lorenz Bks) Anness Pub.

— Let's Look at Our Bodies: Preschool Picture & First Word Books. (Illus.). 24p. (J). 1998. 4.95 (*1-85967-316-3*, Lorenz Bks) Anness Pub.

— Let's Look at Shapes: Preschool Picture & First Word Books. (Illus.). 24p. (J). 1998. 4.95 (*1-85967-317-1*, Lorenz Bks) Anness Pub.

— Mix & Match. (Let's Look Ser.). (Illus.). 96p. (J). 1998. pap. 4.95 (*1-85967-520-4*, Lorenz Bks) Anness Pub.

***Lorenz Books Staff.** Mix & Match. (Illus.). (J). 2000. 16.95 (*0-7548-0379-1*, Lorenz Bks) Anness Pub.

— Modern Weapons & Warfare: The Technology of War from 1700 to the Present Day. (Exploring History Ser.). (Illus.). 64p. (J). (gr. 3-7). 2000. 12.95 (*0-7548-0453-4*, Lorenz Bks) Anness Pub.

— Opposites: With over 50 Reusable Stickers. (Sticker Fun Book Ser.). (J). 1998. pap. text 4.95 (*1-85967-773-8*, Lorenz Bks) Anness Pub.

Lorenz Books Staff. Painting with Watercolors, Oils, & Acrylics: Practical Handbook. 1999. pap. text 9.95 (*0-7548-0004-0*, Lorenz Bks) Anness Pub.

— The Pasta Bible, 1. 1999. 24.95 (*1-85967-905-6*) Anness Pub.

***Lorenz Books Staff.** Prehistoric Peoples: Discover the Long-Ago World of the First Humans. (Exploring History Ser.). (Illus.). 64p. (J). (gr. 3-7). 2000. 12.95 (*0-7548-0442-9*, Lorenz Bks) Anness Pub.

Lorenz Books Staff. Puppies. (First Picture Bks.). (Illus.). 24p. (J). 1996. 4.95 (*1-85967-124-1*, Lorenz Bks) Anness Pub.

***Lorenz Books Staff.** Puppies. (My Very First Picture Book Ser.). (Illus.). (J). 2000. 4.95 (*0-7548-0384-8*, Lorenz Bks) Anness Pub.

— Puppies & Dogs: Stickers. 1999. 4.95 (*1-85967-987-0*, Lorenz Bks) Anness Pub.

— Rocks & Minerals. (Investigations Ser.). (Illus.). (J). 2000. 12.95 (*0-7548-0457-7*, Lorenz Bks) Anness Pub.

— Science & Technology: Humanity's Quest for Knowledge & Explanations. (Exploring History Ser.). (Illus.). 64p. (J). (gr. 3-7). 2000. 12.95 (*0-7548-0454-2*, Lorenz Bks) Anness Pub.

Lorenz Books Staff. Shapes. (Let's Look at ... Ser.). 1999. 4.95 (*0-7548-0302-3*, Lorenz Bks) Anness Pub.

***Lorenz Books Staff.** Sizes: With over 50 Reusable Stickers. (Sticker Fun Book Ser.). (Illus.). (J). 1998. pap. text 4.95 (*1-85967-771-1*, Lorenz Bks) Anness Pub.

— Small Garden: A Guide to Gardening Successfully in Small Spaces. (Illus.). 2000. pap. 12.95 (*0-7548-0119-5*, Lorenz Bks) Anness Pub.

— Spanish. (Classics (Lorenz Books)). 2000. pap. 9.95 (*0-7548-0391-0*, Lorenz Bks) Anness Pub.

— Splish, Splash. (My Very First Picture Book Ser.). (Illus.). (J). 2000. 4.95 (*0-7548-0385-6*, Lorenz Bks) Anness Pub.

— Sticker School. 2000. pap. 9.95 (*0-7548-0372-4*, Lorenz Bks) Anness Pub.

— Teddy Bears. (My Very First Picture Book Ser.). (Illus.). (J). 2000. 4.95 (*0-7548-0065-2*, Lorenz Bks) Anness Pub.

— Things That Go. (Illus.). (J). 2000. 4.95 (*0-7548-0381-3*, Lorenz Bks) Anness Pub.

Lorenz Books Staff. Toys. (First Picture Bks.). (Illus.). 24p. (J). 1996. 4.95 (*1-85967-129-2*, Lorenz Bks) Anness Pub.

— Ultimate Barbeque. (Illus.). 256p. 1998. 24.95 (*1-85967-576-X*, Lorenz Bks) Anness Pub.

— The Ultimate Fat-Free Dessert Cookbook: The Best Ever Step-By-Step Collection of No-Fat & Low-Fat Recipes for Exciting , Satisfying & Healthy Eating. (Illus.). 256p. 1999. 24.95 (*1-85967-909-9*, Lorenz Bks) Anness Pub.

— The Ultimate Hot & Spicy Cookbook: 200 of the Most Fiery, Mouth-Searing & Palate-Pleasing Recipes Ever. (Illus.). 256p. 1997. 24.95 (*1-85967-367-8*, Lorenz Bks) Anness Pub.

***Lorenz Books Staff.** Vegetarian. (Classics (Lorenz Books)). (Illus.). 2000. pap. 9.95 (*0-7548-0252-3*, Lorenz Bks) Anness Pub.

— Wild Animals. (My Very First Picture Book Ser.). (Illus.). (J). 2000. 4.95 (*0-7548-0382-1*, Lorenz Bks) Anness Pub.

— Words. 1999. 7.95 (*0-7548-0032-6*, Lorenz Bks) Anness Pub.

***Lorenz Books Staff.** Words. (Illus.). (J). 2000. 7.95 (*0-7548-0226-4*, Lorenz Bks) Anness Pub.

***Lorenz Books Staff, ed.** African: Heartwarming Flavours from a Traditional Cuisine. (Illus.). 2000. pap. 9.95 (*0-7548-0042-3*, Lorenz Bks) Anness Pub.

— All about Me: A First Word & Picture Book. (Illus.). (J). 2000. 9.95 (*1-85967-799-1*, Lorenz Bks) Anness Pub.

— Animal Friends: A First Word & Picture Book. (Illus.). (J). 2000. 9.95 (*1-85967-800-9*, Lorenz Bks) Anness Pub.

— Beans: Wholesome Recipes from a Country Larder. (Illus.). 2000. 11.95 (*0-7548-0094-6*, Lorenz Bks) Anness Pub.

— Cajun: The Authentic Taste of Spicy Louisiana Cooking. (Illus.). 2000. pap. 9.95 (*0-7548-0164-0*, Lorenz Bks) Anness Pub.

— Caribbean: Irresistible Tropical Flavours from the Islands of the Sun. (Illus.). 2000. pap. 9.95 (*0-7548-0105-5*, Lorenz Bks) Anness Pub.

— Complete Guide to Hairstyling & Haircare. (Illus.). 2000. pap. 10.95 (*0-7548-0561-1*, Lorenz Bks) Anness Pub.

— Complete Guide to Microwave Cooking. (Illus.). 2000. pap. 11.95 (*0-7548-0559-X*, Lorenz Bks) Anness Pub.

— Complete Guide to Spirits & Liqueurs. (Illus.). 2000. pap. 10.95 (*0-7548-0449-6*, Lorenz Bks) Anness Pub.

— Complete Sex Manual. (Illus.). 2000. pap. 14.95 (*0-7548-0495-X*, Lorenz Bks) Anness Pub.

— Cook's Encyclopedia of Fish. (Illus.). 2000. pap. 14.95 (*0-7548-0468-2*, Lorenz Bks) Anness Pub.

— Cook's Encyclopedia of Spices. (Illus.). 2000. pap. 14.95 (*0-7548-0509-3*, Lorenz Bks) Anness Pub.

— Country Flowers: A Photograph Album. (Victorian Photograph Album Ser.). (Illus.). 22p. 1999. 19.95 (*0-7548-0299-X*, Lorenz Bks) Anness Pub.

— Craft Works: 100 Innovative Craft Projects. (Illus.). 2000. wbk. ed. 40.00 (*0-7548-0296-5*, Lorenz Bks) Anness Pub.

— Furniture Makeovers: Over 30 Instant Furniture Transformations. (Illus.). 2000. pap. 12.95 (*0-7548-0311-2*, Lorenz Bks) Anness Pub.

— Herbs. (Illus.). 2000. 11.95 (*0-7548-0095-4*, Lorenz Bks) Anness Pub.

— Irish: The Taste of Ireland in Traditional Home Cooking. (Illus.). 2000. pap. 9.95 (*0-7548-0392-9*, Lorenz Bks) Anness Pub.

— Italian: Easy, Delicious Dishes for Family & Friends. (Illus.). 2000. pap. 9.95 (*0-7548-0393-7*, Lorenz Bks) Anness Pub.

— Japanese. (Illus.). 2000. pap. 9.95 (*0-7548-0106-3*, Lorenz Bks) Anness Pub.

— Joy of Wine. (Illus.). 2000. pap. 11.95 (*0-7548-0345-7*, Lorenz Bks) Anness Pub.

— Learning Fun: A First Word & Picture Book. (Point & Say Bks.). (Illus.). (J). 2000. 9.95 (*1-85967-802-5*, Lorenz Bks) Anness Pub.

— Magic of Asia. (Illus.). 2000. pap. 24.95 (*0-7548-0239-6*, Lorenz Bks) Anness Pub.

— Mexican. (Illus.). 2000. pap. 9.95 (*0-7548-0107-1*, Lorenz Bks) Anness Pub.

— Middle Eastern. 2000. pap. 9.95 (*0-7548-0165-9*, Lorenz Bks) Anness Pub.

— Mind, Body, Spirit: A Practical Guide to Natural Therapies for Health & Well-Being. (Illus.). 2000. 35.00 (*0-7548-0447-X*, Lorenz Bks) Anness Pub.

— Moroccan. 2000. pap. 9.95 (*0-7548-0044-X*, Lorenz Bks) Anness Pub.

— Paper: Practical Papercraft in 30 Creative Projects. (Illus.). 2000. 11.95 (*0-7548-0353-8*, Lorenz Bks) Anness Pub.

— Papier-Mache: Fantastic Step-by-Step Creations from Papier-Mache. (Illus.). 2000. 11.95 (*0-7548-0100-4*, Lorenz Bks) Anness Pub.

— Perfect Barbecue. (Illus.). 2000. pap. 11.95 (*0-7548-0593-X*, Lorenz Bks) Anness Pub.

— Perfect Picnic Book. (Illus.). 2000. 11.95 (*0-7548-0545-X*, Lorenz Bks) Anness Pub.

— Thai. (Illus.). 2000. pap. 9.95 (*0-7548-0108-X*, Lorenz Bks) Anness Pub.

Lorenz Books Staff & Wall, Pam. The Gummi Bear Counting Book. (Illus.). 24p. (J). 1997. pap. 4.95 (*1-85967-601-4*, Lorenz Bks) Anness Pub.

Lorenz, Charlotte, jt. auth. see Umbreit, Paul.

Lorenz, Christoph, ed. see De La Motte Fouque, Friedrich.

Lorenz, Dagmar C. Keepers of the Motherland: German Texts by Jewish Women Writers. LC 96-30057. (Texts & Contexts Ser.: No. 21). xxiv, 404p. 1997. text 60.00 (*0-8032-2917-8*) U of Nebr Pr.

— Verfolgung bis zum Massenmord: Holocaust-Diskurse in Deutscher Sprache Aus der Sicht der Verfolgten. LC 91-37352. (German Life & Civilization Ser.: Vol. 11). (GER.). 451p. (C). 1992. text 66.95 (*0-8204-1751-3*) P Lang Pubng.

Lorenz, Dagmar C., ed. Contemporary Jewish Writing in Austria. LC 99-13472. 1999. pap. 25.00 (*0-8032-7983-3*) U of Nebr Pr.

— Contemporary Jewish Writing in Austria: An Anthology. LC 99-13472. (Jewish Writing in the Contemporary World Ser.). 1999. text 60.00 (*0-8032-2923-2*) U of Nebr Pr.

Lorenz, Dagmar C. & Posthofen, Renate S., eds. Transforming the Center, Eroding the Margins: Essays on Ethnic & Cultural Boundaries in German-Speaking Countries. LC 98-3144. (Studies in German Literature, Linguistics, & Culture). 350p. 1998. 75.00 (*1-57113-171-X*) Camden Hse.

Lorenz, Dagmar C. & Weinberger, Gabriele, eds. Insiders & Outsiders: Jewish & Gentile Culture in Germany & Austria. LC 93-46000. 378p. 1994. text 44.95 (*0-8143-2497-5*) Wayne St U Pr.

Lorenz, David. A New Industry Emerges: Making Construction Materials from Cellulosic Waste. 14p. 1995. 15.00 (*0-614-18033-3*) Inst Local Self Re.

Lorenz, Delores R., jt. auth. see Breitenfeldt, Dorvan H.

Lorenz, E. St. Anthony's Reimbursement Guide to Radiology Services, 1992. 340p. (C). 1992. ring bd. 177.00 (*1-56329-093-6*, SRA) St Anthony Pub.

Lorenz, E., jt. auth. see Dietl, C. E.

Lorenz, Edward. Economic Decline in Britain: The Shipbuilding Industry, 1890-1970. (Illus.). 176p. 1992. 46.00 (*0-19-828502-7*) OUP.

Lorenz, Edward, jt. ed. see Lazaric, Nathalie.

Lorenz, Edward N. The Essence of Chaos. LC 93-1835. (Jessie & John Danz Lectures). (Illus.). 240p. 1996. pap. 14.95 (*0-295-97514-8*) U of Wash Pr.

Lorenz, F. M. Euphrates Triangle: Security Implications of the Southeast Anatolia Project. LC 98-54666. 1999. write for info. (*1-57906-021-8*) Natl Defense.

Lorenz-Fife, Iris. Financing Your Business. 1996. pap. text 16.95 (*0-89384-303-2*) P-H.

— Financing Your Business. LC 96-39730. 192p. (C). 1997. pap. text 13.95 (*0-13-603382-2*) P-H.

***Lorenz, Frederick M.** Euphrates Triangle: Security Implications of the Southeastern Anatolia Project. 67p. 1999. per. 7.00 (*0-16-059054-X*) USGPO.

Lorenz, George G., et al. Constructive Approximation. 1996. write for info. (*3-540-57028-4*) Spr-Verlag.

Lorenz, H. W. Nonlinear Dynamical Economics & Chaotic Motion. 2nd enl. rev. ed. (Lecture Notes in Economics & Mathematical Systems Ser.: Vol. 334). (Illus.). 19p. 1995. reprint ed. 98.00 (*3-87568-816-3*) Spr-Verlag.

Lorenz, Hans-Walter. Nonlinear Dynamical Economics & Chaotic Motion. (Lecture Notes in Economics & Mathematical Systems Ser.: Vol. 334). xii, 248p. 1989. pap. 28.60 (*0-387-51413-9*) Spr-Verlag.

— Nonlinear Dynamical Economics & Chaotic Motion. 2nd enl. rev. ed. 1993. write for info. (*3-540-56881-6*) Spr-Verlag.

— Nonlinear Dynamical Economics & Chaotic Motion. 2nd enl. rev. ed. LC 93-5233. 1997. 98.00 (*0-387-56881-6*) Spr-Verlag.

Lorenz, Hans-Walter, jt. auth. see Gabisch, G.

Lorenz, Ilene L., jt. auth. see Martin, Janet L.

Lorenz, J., ed. 3-Dimensional Process Simulation. 200p. 1995. 70.95 (*3-211-82741-2*) Spr-Verlag.

Lorenz, Jinye. Change. LC 95-81446. (Illus.). 64p. (Orig.). (J). 1996. pap. 9.95 (*1-888350-01-6*) Lighted Lamp.

— God's Mountain Not the Mountain God. large type ed. Lorenz, Virginia O., ed. (Illus.). 120p. (YA). (gr. 6 up). 1998. pap. 12.95 (*1-888350-09-1*) Lighted Lamp.

***Lorenz, Joanna, ed.** Angels. 1999. 11.95 (*1-85967-105-5*, Lorenz Bks) Anness Pub.

Lorenz, Joanna, ed. Book of Love: An Anthology of Verse & Prose. (Illus.). 64p. 1998. 9.95 (*1-85967-172-1*, Lorenz Bks) Anness Pub.

Lorenz, Joseph P. Peace, Power & the United Nations: A Security System for the Twenty-First Century. LC 98-42242. 185p. (C). 1998. 65.00 (*0-8133-8061-8*, Pub. by Westview) HarpC.

Lorenz, Juliane, ed. Chaos As Usual: Conversations about Rainer Werner Fassbinder. Armstrong, Christa & Pelikan, Maria, trs. LC 96-37914. 270p. 1997. 25.95 (*1-55783-262-5*) Applause Theatre Bk Pubs.

— Chaos As Usual: Conversations about Rainer Werner Fassbinder. 320p. 1999. pap. 14.95 (*1-55783-359-1*) Applause Theatre Bk Pubs.

Lorenz, Juliane, jt. ed. see Kardish, Laurence.

Lorenz, K., ed. Konstruktionen Versus Positionen. Beitraege zur wissenschaftstheoretischen Diskussion zum 60: Geburtstag von Paul Lorensen, 2 vols., Set. (C). 1978. 288.50 (*3-11-006655-6*) De Gruyter.

Lorenz, Kim. A History of the Vienna Boys' Choir. (Illus.). 186p. 1998. 29.50 (*1-85776-351-3*, Pub. by Book Guild Ltd) Trans-Atl Phila.

Lorenz, Klaus & Kulp, Karel, eds. Handbook of Cereal Science & Technology. (Food Science & Technology Ser.: Vol. 41). (Illus.). 896p. 1990. text 275.00 (*0-8247-8358-1*) Dekker.

Lorenz, Konrad. Behind the Mirror: A Search for a Natural History of Human Knowledge. Taylor, Ronald, tr. LC 78-6031. (Helen & Kurt Wolff Bk.). (Illus.). 261p. 1978. pap. 7.95 (*0-15-611776-2*, Harvest Bks) Harcourt.

— Evolution & Modification Behavior. 1997. pap. text 8.00 (*0-226-49333-4*) U Ch Pr.

— Evolution & Modification of Behavior. LC 65-24436. vi, 128p. 1997. reprint ed. pap. text 12.00 (*0-226-49334-2*, Midway Reprint) U Ch Pr.

— The Foundations of Ethology. (Illus.). 380p. 1981. 86.95 (*0-387-81623-2*) Spr-Verlag.

— Here Am I - Where Are You? The Behavior of the Greylag Goose. Martin, Robert D., tr. (Illus.). 270p. 1991. 26.95 (*0-15-140056-3*) Harcourt.

— King Solomon's Ring. 1997. pap. 11.95 (*0-452-01175-2*, Mer) NAL.

— Man Meets Dog. Wilson, Marjorie K., tr. from GER. Orig. Title: So Kam der Mensch auf den Hund. (Illus.). 211p. (C). 1998. reprint ed. pap. text 15.00 (*0-7881-5861-9*) DIANE Pub.

— Man Meets Dog. Wilson, Marjorie K., tr. LC 94-33112. Orig. Title: So Kam der Mensch auf den Hund. (Illus.). 240p. 1994. reprint ed. pap. 12.00 (*1-56836-051-7*) Kodansha.

— The Natural Science of the Human Species: An Introduction to Comparative Behavioral Research: the "Russian Manuscript", 1944-1948. Von Cranach, Agnes, ed. Martin, Robert D., tr. LC 94-48788.Tr. of Naturwissenschaft vom Menschen. (ENG & GER., Illus.). 384p. 1995. 37.50 (*0-262-12190-5*) MIT Pr.

— The Natural Science of the Human Species: An Introduction to Comparative Behavioral Research the Russian Manuscript 1944-1948. (Illus.). 384p. 1997. reprint ed. pap. text 18.00 (*0-262-62120-7*) MIT Pr.

— On Aggression. 306p. 1996. 7.98 (*1-56731-107-5*, MJF Bks) Fine Comms.

— On Aggression. Wilson, Marjorie K., tr. from GER. LC 74-5306. (Helen & Kurt Wolff Bk.). (Illus.). 320p. 1974. reprint ed. pap. 13.00 (*0-15-668741-0*, Harvest Bks) Harcourt.

— The Waning of Humaneness. 1987. 17.95 (*0-316-53291-6*) Little.

Lorenz, Lee. The Art of the New Yorker, 1925-1995. 208p. 1996. pap. 25.00 (*0-679-76595-6*) Knopf.

***Lorenz, Lee.** Pig & Duck Buy a Truck: A Book of Colors. (Illus.). (ps-3). 2000. pap. text 10.95 (*0-689-83780-1*) Litle Simon.

Lorenz, Lee. A Weekend in the City. (Illus.). 32p. (J). (gr. k-3). 1991. 15.95 (*0-945912-15-3*) Pippin Pr.

Lorenz, Lee, ed. Real Dogs Don't Eat Leftovers: A Guide to All That Is Truly Canine. (Illus.). 1983. 3.95 (*0-671-47757-9*) S&S Trade.

***Lorenz, Lee, ed.** The Essential Charles Barsotti. LC 98-51797. (Essential Cartoonists Library). (Illus.). 149p. 1998. pap. 10.95 (*0-7611-0952-8*) Workman Pub.

— The Essential Ziegler. (Essential Cartoonist Library: No. 3). (Illus.). 144p. 2000. pap. 10.95 (*0-7611-1758-X*) Workman Pub.

Lorenz, Lee. Driving Me Crazy: Fun on Wheels Jokes. 40p. (J). (gr. 2-5). 1989. 13.95 (*0-945912-05-6*) Pippin Pr.

Lorenz, Lee, ed. see Steig, William.

Lorenz, Mark. Java As an Object-Oriented Language. (Java Report Professional Ser.: Vol. 1). (Orig.). 1996. pap. 85.00 (*1-884842-40-2*) SIGS Bks & Multimedia.

— Object-Oriented Software Development: A Practical Guide. LC 92-18566. 250p. 1992. text 41.20 (*0-13-726928-5*) Brady Pub.

— Object-Oriented Software Metrics. 146p. 1994. 55.00 (*0-13-179292-X*) P-H.

— Rapid Software Development with SmallTalk. (Advances in Object Technology: No. 7). 240p. 1995. pap. 32.95 (*0-13-449737-6*) Cambridge U Pr.

Lorenz, Melinda. Contemporary Collage: Extensions. (Illus.). 32p. 1983. 4.00 (*0-915478-47-1*) Montgomery Gallery.

— The Denver Boulder Show. (Illus.). 20p. 1984. 4.00 (*0-915478-50-1*) Williamson Gallery.

Lorenz, Michael D. & Cornelius, Larry M., eds. Small Animal Diagnosis. 2nd ed. LC 92-46032. 651p. 1993. pap. text 49.50 (*0-397-51200-7*) Lppncott W & W.

Lorenz, Michael D., et al. Small Animal Medical Therapeutics. (Illus.). 656p. 1991. pap. text 49.50 (*0-397-50994-4*) Lppncott W & W.

Lorenz, Mitzi, jt. auth. see Morgan, Jamie.

Lorenz Pub. Christmas Companion. 1998. 30.00 (*1-85967-775-4*) Anness Pub.

— Mosiacs: Inspirations. (Illus.). 96p. 1998. 12.95 (*1-85967-751-7*) Anness Pub.

— New Papercrafts. 1998. 24.95 (*1-85967-752-5*) Anness Pub.

— Wrap it Up. 1998. pap. 12.95 (*1-85967-741-X*) Anness Pub.

Lorenz, R., et al, eds. Advances in Neurosurgery: Intracerebral Hemorrhages Hydrocephalus Malresorptivus Peripheral Nerves, Vol. 21. (Illus.). 360p. 1993. 79.00 (*0-387-56304-0*) Spr-Verlag.

Lorenz, Richard. Imogen Cunningham: Ideas Without End: A Life in Photographs. LC 93-67. (Illus.). 160p. 1993. 35.00 (*0-8118-0390-2*); pap. 22.95 (*0-8118-0357-0*) Chronicle Bks.

— Imogen Cunningham: On the Body, 3. LC 97-73599. (Illus.). 168p. (gr. 8). 1998. 50.00 (*0-8212-2438-7*) Little.

— Landscape Images: Recent Photographs by Linda Connor, Judy Fiskin & Ruth Thorne-Thomsen. (Illus.). 40p. 1980. pap. 4.50 (*0-934418-08-X*) Mus Contemp Art.

Lorenz, Richard, jt. ed. see Rule, Amy.

Lorenz, Richardo, et al, eds. Scores & Recordings at the Indiana University Latin American Music Center. LC 94-945. 1995. 75.00 (*0-253-33273-7*) Ind U Pr.

Lorenz, Rita, jt. auth. see Adolph, A. L.

Lorenz, Rita, jt. auth. see Adolph, L.

Lorenz Staff. Ancient China. (Step into Ser.). 1998. 12.95 (*1-85967-762-2*) Anness Pub.

— Asian Kitchen. 1998. 30.00 (*1-85967-774-6*) Anness Pub.

— Aztec World. (Step into Ser.). 1998. 12.95 (*1-85967-763-0*) Anness Pub.

An Asterisk (*) at the beginning of an entry indicates that the title is appearing for the first time.

— Basket-Making: New Crafts. (Illus.). 96p. 1998. 15.95 (1-85967-617-0) Anness Pub.
— Best Christmas Ever. 1998. 17.95 (1-85967-106-3) Anness Pub.
— Big Cats: New Nature. 1998. 12.95 (1-85967-638-3) Anness Pub.
— Card Games: Pocket Entertainment. (Illus.). 96p. 1998. 7.95 (1-85967-768-1) Anness Pub.
— Clothes: Let's Look. 1998. 4.95 (1-85967-760-6) Anness Pub.
— Coddle Your Cat. 1998. pap. 11.95 (1-85967-745-2) Anness Pub.
— Complete Cake Decorator. 1998. 27.50 (1-85967-037-7) Anness Pub.
— Conjuring Tricks: Pocket Entertainment. (Illus.). 96p. 1998. 7.95 (1-85967-767-3) Anness Pub.
— Decorating with Beads: Inspiration. (Illus.). 96p. 1998. 12.95 (1-85967-749-5) Anness Pub.
— Drawing: Art School. 1998. 9.95 (1-85967-826-2) Anness Pub.
— Enamelling: New Crafts. (Illus.). 96p. 1998. 15.95 (1-85967-618-9) Anness Pub.
— Fortune Telling: Pocket Entertainment. (Illus.). 96p. 1998. 7.95 (1-85967-766-5) Anness Pub.
— French Recipe Cookbook. 1998. 30.00 (1-85967-082-2) Anness Pub.
— Gluten Free, Healthy Eating. (Illus.). 96p. 1998. 12.95 (1-85967-672-3, Lorenz Bks) Anness Pub.
— Golden Age of Steam. 1998. 17.95 (1-85967-737-1) Anness Pub.
— Grasses: New Plant Library. (Illus.). 64p. 1998. 9.95 (1-85967-635-9) Anness Pub.
— Homeopathy: New Life Library. (Illus.). 64p. Date not set. 9.95 (1-85967-626-X) Anness Pub.
— Instant Calm: New Life Library. (Illus.). 64p. 1998. 9.95 (1-85967-625-1) Anness Pub.
— Italian Kitchen. 1998. 30.00 (1-85967-776-2) Anness Pub.
— Juggling: Pocket Entertainment. (Illus.). 96p. 1998. 7.95 (1-85967-764-9) Anness Pub.
— Lilies: New Plant Library. (Illus.). 64p. 1998. 9.95 (1-85967-634-0) Anness Pub.
— Love, Sex & Intimacy. 1998. 30.00 (1-85967-088-1) Anness Pub.
— Low Cholesterol, Healthy Eating. 1998. 12.95 (1-85967-671-5) Anness Pub.
— Massage. 1998. 12.95 (1-85967-753-3) Anness Pub.
— New Guide to Herbs. Date not set. 14.95 (1-85967-736-3) Anness Pub.
— New Guide to Horses. 1998. 27.50 (1-85967-777-0) Anness Pub.
— New Guide to Mushrooms. 1998. 14.95 (1-85967-735-5) Anness Pub.
— New Guide to Spirits & Liqueur. 1998. 14.95 (1-85967-734-7) Anness Pub.
— Oil Painting: Art School. 1998. 9.95 (1-85967-824-6) Anness Pub.
— Pamper Your Pooch. 1998. 11.95 (1-85967-674-X) Anness Pub.
— Parlour Games: Pocket Entertainment. (Illus.). 96p. 1998. 7.95 (1-85967-765-7) Anness Pub.
— Pastels: Art School. 1998. 9.95 (1-85967-825-4) Anness Pub.
— Pets. (Let's Look Ser.). 1998. 4.95 (1-85967-761-4) Anness Pub.
— Practical Jokes: Pocket Entertainment. (Illus.). 96p. 1998. 7.95 (1-85967-769-X) Anness Pub.
— Rainforest: Learn About. 1998. 8.95 (1-85967-759-2) Anness Pub.
— Rocks & Minerals. (Learn about Ser.). 1998. 8.95 (1-85967-758-4) Anness Pub.
— Spiders: New Nature Watch. 1998. 12.95 (1-85967-610-3) Anness Pub.
— Stained Glass: Inspirations. 1998. 12.95 (1-85967-651-5) Anness Pub.
— Succulents: New Plant Library. (Illus.). 64p. 1998. 9.95 (1-85967-637-5) Anness Pub.
— Summer Bulbs: New Plant Library. (Illus.). 64p. 1998. 9.95 (1-85967-636-7) Anness Pub.
— Ultimate Aquarium. 1998. 35.00 (1-85967-081-4) Anness Pub.
— Ultimate Cacti & Succulents. (Illus.). 256p. 1998. 35.00 (1-85967-460-7) Anness Pub.
— Ultimate Cigar Book. (Illus.). 256p. 1998. 35.00 (1-85967-755-X) Anness Pub.
— Ultimate Martial Arts. (Illus.). 256p. 1998. 30.00 (1-85967-778-9) Anness Pub.
— Watercolors: Art School. 1998. 9.95 (1-85967-827-0) Anness Pub.
— Winter Wildcrafts. (Illus.). 128p. 1998. 21.95 (1-85967-756-8) Anness Pub.
— World Encyclopedia of Fruit. 1998. 35.00 (1-85967-757-6) Anness Pub.
— World of Wine. 1998. 40.00 (1-85967-254-X) Anness Pub.

Lorenz, Stephanie. Children with Down's Syndrome: A Guide for Teachers & Learning Support Assistants in Mainstream Society. LC 99-200425. 1998. pap. 22.95 (1-85346-506-2, Pub. by David Fulton) Taylor & Francis.
— Effective In Class Support: The Management of Support Staff in Mainstream & Special Schools. 1998. pap. text 21.95 (1-85346-505-4) Taylor & Francis.

Lorenz, Theodore, tr. see Paulsen, Friedrich.

Lorenz, Virginia O., ed. see Lorenz, Jinye.

Lorenz, W. J., ed. see Plieth, Waldfried.

Lorenz, William. Contemporary Industrial Relations. Date not set. pap. text. write for info. (1-56226-377-3) CAT Pub.

Lorenza, Olga. Vida y Obra de Una Maestra. LC 90-84146. (Coleccion Caniqui). (SPA.). 93p. (Orig.). 1990. pap. 9.95 (0-89729-574-9) Ediciones.

Lorenzana, Ronald, tr. see Dale, Ralph A.

Lorenzana, Ronald E. Cure Su Casa con Feng Shui: Feng Shui. LC 97-93606. 224p. 1997. lib. bdg. 18.95 (0-9646334-3-4) R E Lorenzana.

Lorenzana, Violetta. Pilipino (Tagalog) Language Survival Kit. 2nd ed. LC 99-168067. (Illus.). 200p. 1998. pap. 5.95 (0-86442-432-9) Lonely Planet.

Lorenzani, Shirley. Candida: A Twentieth Century Disease. LC 85-81549. (Pivot Original Health Bks.). 176p. (Orig.). 1986. pap. 4.95 (0-87983-375-0, Keats Publng) NTC Contemp Pub Co.

Lorenzani, Shirley S. Dietary Fiber. (Good Health Guide Ser.). 32p. (Orig.). 1988. pap. 3.95 (0-87983-479-X, 3479XX, Keats Publng) NTC Contemp Pub Co.

Lorenzatos, Zissimos. The Lost Center & Other Essays in Greek Poetry. Cicellis, Kay, tr. LC 79-3221. (Princeton Essays in Literature Ser.). 211p. reprint ed. pap. 65.50 (0-8357-4283-0, 203708200007) Bks Demand.

Lorenzen, Anna L. Tiger. (Illus.). 22p. (Orig.). (J). (gr. 1-2). 1989. pap. text 2.95 (0-9626133-0-4) ALL Ventura Pub.

Lorenzen, Betty. Dental Assistant Techniques. LC 74-18674. (Allied Health Ser.). 1976. pap. write for info. (0-672-61395-6) Macmillan.

Lorenzen, David. The Kapalikas & Kalamukhas: Two Lost Saivite Sects. (C). 1991. reprint ed. 17.50 (81-208-0708-1, Pub. by Motilal Bnarsidass) S Asia.

Lorenzen, David, ed. Bhakti Religion in North Africa: Community Identity & Political Action. (C). 1995. 40.00 (81-7304-171-7, Pub. by Manohar) S Asia.

Lorenzen, David N. Kabir Legends & Ananta-Das's Kabir Parachai: With a Translation of the Kabir Parachai Prepared in Collaboration with Jagdish Kumar & Uma Thukral & with an Edition of the Niranjani Revision of This Work. LC 90-30135. (SUNY Series in Hindu Studies). 282p. (C). 1991. pap. text 21.95 (0-7914-0462-5) State U NY Pr.
— The Kapalikas & Kalamukhas: Two Lost Saivite Sects. LC 70-138509. 228p. reprint ed. pap. 70.70 (0-608-18290-7, 203154000075) Bks Demand.
— Praises to a Formless God: Nirguni Texts from North India. LC 95-20931. (SUNY Series in Religious Studies). 303p. (C). 1996. text 49.50 (0-7914-2805-2); pap. text 16.95 (0-7914-2806-0) State U NY Pr.

Lorenzen, David N., ed. Bhakti Religion in North India: Community Identity & Political Action. LC 93-41538. (SUNY Series in Religious Studies). 331p. (C). 1994. pap. text 19.95 (0-7914-2026-4) State U NY Pr.
— Bhakti Religion in North India: Community Identity & Political Action. LC 93-41538. (SUNY Series in Religious Studies). 331p. (C). 1994. text 59.50 (0-7914-2025-6) State U NY Pr.

Lorenzen, Elizabeth A., ed. Career Planning & Job Searching in the Information Age. LC 96-20566. (Reference Librarian Ser.: No. 55). 120p. 1996. 39.95 (1-56024-838-6) Haworth Pr.

Lorenzen, Emme I. Momentous Days: An Account in Poetry & Prose of a Family in Early Walnut Creek, California. LC 90-62998. (Illus.). 64p. (Orig.). 1990. pap. text 12.00 (0-9627282-0-9) TYIL Pr.

Lorenzen, H. & Weissner, W. Intracellular & Intercellular Regulation & in Algae & Symbionts. (Illus.). 320p. 1981. pap. text 56.00 (3-437-30368-6) Lubrecht & Cramer.

Lorenzen, H., jt. ed. see Eschrich, W.

Lorenzen, Lynne F. The College Student's Introduction to the Trinity. LC 98-25617. 1998. 11.95 (0-8146-5518-1) Liturgical Pr.

Lorenzen, Paul. Constructive Philosophy. Pavlovic, Karl R., tr. from GER. LC 86-25003. 304p. 1987. lib. bdg. 35.00 (0-87023-564-8) U of Mass Pr.
— Formal Logic. Crosson, Frederick J., tr. from GER. (Synthese Library: Vol. 9). 131p. 1964. text 68.50 (90-277-0080-X, D Reidel) Kluwer Academic.

Lorenzen, Paul, jt. auth. see Kamlah, Wilhelm.

Lorenzen, Thomas J. & Anderson, Virgil L. Design of Experiments: A No-Name Approach. LC 93-2095. (Statistics: Textbooks & Monographs: Vol. 139). (Illus.). 432p. 1993. text 69.75 (0-8247-9077-4) Dekker.

Lorenzen, Thorwald. Resurrection & Discipleship: Interpretive Models, Biblical Reflections, Theological Consequences. LC 95-31252. 225p. (Orig.). 1995. pap. 22.00 (1-57075-042-4) Orbis Bks.

***Lorenzetti, Daniel, photos by.** The Birth of Coffee. LC 00-20334. (Illus.). 192p. 2000. 45.00 (0-609-60678-6) C Potter.

***Lorenzetti, Luigi.** Economie et Migrations au XIXe Siecle: Les Strategies de la Reproduction Familiale au Tessin. (Publications Universitaires Europeennes: Vol. 845). xxx, 612p. 1999. 64.95 (3-906763-08-0, Pub. by P Lang) P Lang Pubng.

Lorenzetti, Maureen S. Alternative Motor Fuels: A Nontechnical Guide. 175p. 1995. 64.95 (0-87814-448-X) PennWell Bks.

Lorenzetti, Michael, jt. ed. see Preas, Bryan.

Lorenzetti, R., jt. auth. see Lancini, G.

Lorenzi, A., jt. auth. see Kabanikhin, S. I.

Lorenzi, Harri. Arvores Brasileiras (Brazilian Trees), Vol. 2. (POR., Illus.). 384p. 1998. 125.00 (85-86714-07-0) Inst Plantarum.
— Arvores Brasilieras: Manual de Identificacao e Cultivo de Plantas Arboreas Nativas do Brasil. rev. ed. (POR., Illus.). 384p. 1998. 125.00 (85-86714-06-2) Inst Plantarum.
— Manual de Identificacao e Controle de Plantas Daninhas (Manual for the Identification & Control of Weeds. 4th ed. (POR., Illus.). 300p. 1994. 65.00 (85-86714-04-6, Pub. by Inst Plantarum) Balogh.
— Plantas Ornamentais no Brasil: Arbustivas, Herbaceas e Trepadeiras. (POR., Illus.). 730p. 1997. 129.95 (85-86714-01-1, Pub. by Inst Plantarum) Balogh.
— Plantas Ornamentais no Brasil: Arbustivas, Herbaceas e Trepadeiras. 2nd rev. ed. (POR., Illus.). 730p. 1999. 110.00 (85-86714-08-9, Pub. by Inst Plantarum) Balogh.

Lorenzi, Harri, et al. Palmeiras no Brasil: Nativas e Exoticas. (POR., Illus.). 320p. 1997. 90.00 (85-86714-03-8, Pub. by Inst Plantarum) Balogh.

Lorenzi, Lorenzo. Devils in Art: Florence from the Middle Ages to the Renaissance. Roberts, Mark, tr. from ITA. LC 97-164561. (Illus.). 200p. 1997. 34.95 (88-7038-298-2, Pub. by Art Bks Intl) Partners Pubs Grp.

Lorenzi, Nancy M., et al, eds. Transforming Health Care Through Information: Case Studies. LC 95-17731. (Computers in Health Care Ser.). (Illus.). 431p. 1995. 54.00 (0-387-94455-9) Spr-Verlag.

Lorenzi, Nancy M. & Riley, Robert T. Organizational Aspects of Health Informatics: Managing Technological Change. LC 94-19977. (Computers in Health Care Ser.). (Illus.). 312p. 1994. 54.00 (0-387-94226-2) Spr-Verlag.

Lorenzi, Peter, jt. auth. see Ivancevich, John M.

Lorenzi, Peter, jt. auth. see Sims, Henry P., Jr.

Lorenzin, Tom & Sechler, Tim. One Thousand Plus: The Amateur Astronomer's Field Guide to Deep Sky Observing. (Illus.). 168p. 1987. write for info. (0-912081-06-6) Delmar Co.

Lorenzini, Dino. An Invitation to Arithmetic Geometry. LC 95-24459. (Graduate Studies in Mathematics: Vol. 9). 397p. 1996. text 59.00 (0-8218-0267-4, GSM/9) Am Math.

Lorenzini, Jean A. & Lorenzini-Ley, Laura. Medical Phrase Index: A One-Step Reference to the Terminology of Medicine. 3rd ed. Rogers, Gregg & Swanson, Kathryn, eds. LC 93-42123. 1300p. 1994. 49.95 (1-878487-58-2, ME052) Practice Mgmt Info.

Lorenzini, Kathryn, jt. auth. see Brandt, Gloria.

Lorenzini-Ley, Laura, jt. auth. see Lorenzini, Jean A.

Lorenzo. The Relaxation Sensation: The Number One Success Factor in Life. (Illus.). 128p. (Orig.). 1981. pap. 9.95 (0-941122-00-X) Lorenzo Prema.

Lorenzo, Alejandro, ed. see Ariza, Rene.

Lorenzo, Carol L. Nervous Dancer. LC 94-13062. (Flannery O'Connor Award for Short Fiction Ser.). 184p. 1995. 22.95 (0-8203-1704-7) U of Ga Pr.

***Lorenzo, David J.** Tradition & the Rhetoric of Right: Popular Political Argument in the Aurobindo Movement. LC 98-44575. (Illus.). 344p. 1999. 49.50 (0-8386-3815-5) Fairleigh Dickinson.

Lorenzo, Enrico Di, see Di Lorenzo, Enrico, contrib. by.

***Lorenzo, George.** Sams Teach Yourself E-College Today: Applying for College, Taking Classes & Financing Your Ed. 300p. 2000. pap. 17.99 (0-672-31978-0) Sams.

Lorenzo, Jack M. The Leaves of Life & How to Change Your Mind about Growth, Love, Life, & Living. 90p. 1993. pap. write for info. (0-9636299-0-5) INCOM Pub Div.

Lorenzo, Jake. Cold Surveillance: The Jake Lorenzo Wine Columns. (Orig.). 1993. pap. 9.95 (0-9637438-4-8) Wine Patrol Pr.

Lorenzo, Jose L. Prehistoria y Arqueologia. 436p. 1991. pap. 8.00 (968-6487-43-3, IN050) UPLAAP.

Lorenzo, Leonardo De, see De Lorenzo, Leonardo.

Lorenzo, Lois De, see De Lorenzo, Lois.

Lorenzo, Luciano G. & Varey, J. E., eds. Teatros y Vida Teatral del Siglo de Oro a Traves las Fuentes Documentales. (Monagrafias A Ser.: No. 145). (C). 1992. pap. 53.00 (1-85566-007-5, Pub. by Tamesis Bks Ltd) Boydell & Brewer.

Lorenzo, Marjorie A. Di, see Strasinger, Susan K. & Di Lorenzo, Marjorie A.

Lorenzo, Marjorie Di, see Strasinger, Susan K. & Di Lorenzo, Marjorie.

Lorenzo-Rivero, Luis, ed. see De Larra, Mariano J.

Lorenzo, Robert & Clark, Nate, Jr. Bessemer & Lake Erie RR in Color. (Illus.). 128p. 1994. 49.95 (1-878887-34-3) Morning NJ.

Lorenzo, Vincent M. Di, see Di Lorenzo, Vincent M.

Lorenzoni, A. B., jt. auth. see Clark, Forrest D.

***Loret, John & Tanacredi, John T.** Experiment Central: Understanding Scientific Principles Through Projects, 4 vols. LC 99-54142. (Illus.). 830p. (J). (gr. 4-7). 1999. text 99.95 (0-7876-2892-1, GML00299-112457, UXL) Gale.

Loret, John, jt. ed. see Tanacredi, John T.

Loret, Victor. La Flore Pharaonique. 2nd ed. 145p. 1975. reprint ed. write for info. (3-487-05576-7) G Olms Pubs.

Loretan, Joseph O. Teaching the Disadvantaged: New Curriculum Approaches. LC 66-15325. (Illus.). 256p. reprint ed. 79.40 (0-8357-9610-8, 201693900005) Bks Demand.

Loretelli, Rosamaria & De Romanis, Roberto, eds. Narrating Transgression Vol. II: Representations of the Criminal in Early Modern England. (Anglo-American Studies). 172p. (C). 1999. pap. text 37.95 (0-8204-3599-6) P Lang Pubng.

Loreto, Luigi. Un Epoca di Buon Senso: Decisione, Consenso e Stato a Roma Tra il 264 A.C. (ITA.). 268p. 1993. pap. 64.00 (90-256-1059-5, Pub. by AM Hakkert) BookLink Distributors.

Loreto-Perez, Mariela, ed. see Detzler, Robert E.

Loreto, Remo A. The TI 99-4A in Bits & Bytes. Wartman, Robert, ed. (Illus.). (Orig.). 1983. pap. 14.99 (0-914209-01-9) R A Loreto.

Lorette, Lineaus H. Communitarianism: A Prospectus for Revolution. Scales, Nancy, ed. 65p. (Orig.). 1990. pap. 10.00 (0-932225-01-2) Comm Pr.
— Medicine Ball Exercise Cycles. (Illus.). 99p. 1984. 16.95 (0-932225-00-4) Comm Pr.

Lorette, Richard J. & Walton, Howard C. Cases in the Management of Information Systems & Information Technology. (C). 1994. text 40.95 (0-256-18454-2, Irwn McGrw-H) McGrw-H Hghr Educ.
— Cases in the Management of Information Systems & Information Technology: Select Cases. (C). 1994. 14.95 (0-256-18448-8, Irwn McGrw-H) McGrw-H Hghr Educ.

Lorette, Richard J., et al. Management Information Systems. 2nd ed. (C). 1994. text 74.90 (0-256-18450-X, Irwn McGrw-H) McGrw-H Hghr Educ.

Loretto, Jean. Reality Always Win. 1996. pap. write for info. (1-86106-001-7, Pub. by Minerva Pr) Unity Dist.

Loretto, M. H., ed. Dislocations & Properties of Real Materials. 382p. 1985. 62.00 (0-904357-74-0, Pub. by Inst Materials) Ashgate Pub Co.

Loretz, Oswald. Die Konigspsalmen: Die Altorientalisch-Kanaanaische Konigstradition in Judischer Sicht, Teil 1: Psalm 20, 21, 72, 101, 144. (Ugaritisch-Biblische Literatur Ser.: Vol. 6). (GER.). vii, 261p. 1988. text 58.00 (3-927120-01-4, Pub. by UGARIT) Eisenbrauns.
— Leberschau, Sundenbock, Asasel in Ugarit und Israel: Leberschau und Jahwestatue in Psalm 27, Psalm 74. (Ugaritisch-Biblische Literatur Ser.: Vol. 3). 138p. 1985. pap. text 34.00 (3-88733-061-7, Pub. by UGARIT) Eisenbrauns.
— Regenritual und Jahwetag im Joelbuch: Kanaanaischer Hintergrund, Kolometrie, Aufbau und Symbolik Eines Prophetenbuches. (Ugaritisch-Biblische Literatur Ser.: Vol. 4). (GER.). 189p. 1986. text 45.00 (3-88733-068-4, Pub. by UGARIT) Eisenbrauns.
— Ugarit-Texte und Thronbesteigungspsalmen: Die Metamorphose des Regenspenders Baal-Jahwe (Ps. 24: 7-10; 29; 47; 93; 95-100; Sowie Ps. 77: 17-20; 114) (Ugaritisch-Biblische Literatur Ser.: Vol. 7). (GER.). xiv, 550p. 1988. text 63.00 (3-927120-04-9, Pub. by UGARIT) Eisenbrauns.

Loretz, Oswald & Kottseiper, Ingo. Colometry in Ugaritic & Biblical Poetry: Introduction, Illustrations & Topical Bibliography. (Ugaritisch-Biblische Literatur Ser.: Vol. 5). 166p. 1987. pap. text 37.00 (3-88733-074-9, Pub. by UGARIT) Eisenbrauns.

Loretz, Oswald & Mayer, Werner R. Su-Ila - Gebete: Supplement zu L. W. King, Babylonian Magic & Sorcery. (Alter Orient und Altes Testament Ser.: Vol. 34). (GER.). xix, 30p. 1978. text 12.00 (3-7887-0573-6) NeukirchenerV.

Loretz, Oswald, jt. auth. see Dietrich, Manfried.

Loretz, Oswald, jt. ed. see Dietrich, Manfried.

Lorey, Christoph & Plews, John, eds. Queering the Canon: Defying Sights in German Literature & Culture. LC 97-32471. (Studies in German Literature & Culture). 300p. 1998. 60.00 (1-57113-178-7) Camden Hse.

Lorey, David E. The Rise of the Professions in Twentieth-Century Mexico: University Graduates & Occupational Change since 1929. LC 92-15245. (Cycles & Trends Research Ser.: Vol. 2). 1992. pap. 17.95 (0-87903-254-5) UCLA Lat Am Ctr.
— The Rise of the Professions in Twentieth-Century Mexico: University Graduates & Occupational Change Since 1929. 2nd ed. (Cycles & Trends Research Ser.: Vol. 2). 1994. pap. 21.95 (0-87903-257-X) UCLA Lat Am Ctr.

***Lorey, David E.** The U. S. Mexican Border in the Twentieth Century. LC 99-12906. (Latin American Silhouettes Ser.). (Illus.). 195p. 1999. pap. 17.95 (0-8420-2756-4) Scholarly Res Inc.
— The U. S.-Mexican Border in the Twentieth Century. LC 99-12906. (Latin American Silhouettes Ser.). (Illus.). 195p. 1999. 55.00 (0-8420-2755-6) Scholarly Res Inc.

Lorey, David E. The University System & Economic Development in Mexico since 1929. LC 93-20289. 288p. (C). 1993. 39.50 (0-8047-2124-6) Stanford U Pr.

Lorey, David E., ed. United States - Mexico Border Statistics since 1900. 512p. 1993. pap. 35.00 (0-87903-251-0) UCLA Lat Am Ctr.
— United States-Mexico Border Statistics since 1900: 1990 Update. LC 93-24225. (Statistical Abstract of Latin America Supplement Ser.: Vol. 13). 1993. pap. 32.50 (0-87903-256-1) UCLA Lat Am Ctr.

Lorey, David E., jt. ed. see Beezley, William H.

Lorf, Ira & Sander, Gabriele. Internationales Alfred-Doblin-Kolloquium Leipzig, 1997. 230p. 1999. 67.95 (3-906759-26-1) P Lang.

Lorge, Irving. Influence of Regularly Interpolated Time Intervals Upon Subsequent Learning. LC 73-177011. (Columbia University. Teachers College. Contributions to Education Ser.: No. 438). reprint ed. 37.50 (0-404-55438-5) AMS Pr.

Lorge, Irving, jt. auth. see Brunner, Edmund D.

***Lorgen, Eve F.** The Love Bite: Alien Interference in Human Love Relationships. (Illus.). 224p. 1999. 24.95 (0-918501-97-0, Archives Pr); pap. 19.95 (0-918501-98-9, Archives Pr) Media Assocs.

Lorho, Bernard, ed. Methods & Tools for Compiler Construction: An Advanced Course. LC 84-45239. 406p. reprint ed. pap. 115.80 (0-608-15261-7, 2029221) Bks Demand.

Lori Zeigler, jt. ed. see Zeigler, Tom.

Loria, Achille. The Economic Foundations of Society. 1972. 250.00 (0-87968-305-8) Gordon Pr.
— Karl Marx. 1976. 300.00 (0-87968-304-X) Gordon Pr.

Loria, Ana. Get Paid for Sex! The Big Bad Book of Sex Opportunities for Men & Women. 64p. 1999. pap. 24.95 (0-9651190-1-7) InfoNet Pubns.

***Loria, Ana.** 1-2-3 Be a Phone Sex Operator: A Step-by-Step Guide to the Adult Audiotext Industry for Men. 120p. 2000. pap. 21.95 (0-9651190-3-3) InfoNet Pubns.
— 1-2-3 Be a Porn Star! A Step-by-Step Guide to the Adult Sex Industry for Men & Women. 168p. 2000. pap. 24.95 (0-9651190-2-5) InfoNet Pubns.

***Loria, Catherine M.** Plan & Operation of the NHANES 2 Mortality Study, 1992. 22p. 1999. pap. 2.50 (0-16-050053-2) USGPO.

L

L

Loria, Edward A., ed. Superalloys, 718, 625, 706 & Various Derivatives: International Symposium on Superalloys 718, 625, 706 & Various Derivatives, 4th, 1997. LC 97-71554. (Illus.). 843p. 1997. 194.00 (*0-87339-376-7*, 3767) Minerals Metals.

Loria, Edward A., ed. see International Symposium on the Metallurgy & Applic.

Loria, Stefano. Picasso. LC 95-31830. (Masters of Art Ser.). (Illus.). 64p. (J). (gr. 4-7). 1995. lib. bdg. 22.50 (*0-87226-318-5*, 63185B, P Bedrick Books) NTC Contemp Pub Co.

***Loria, Wilson.** Strange Perfume. 2000. 24.95 (*1-902587-06-5*, Pub. by Opal Books) Brit Bk Co Inc.

Loria, Wilson, tr. see Coutinho, Edilberto.

Lorian, Nicole. A Birthday Present for Mama. LC 83-26849. (Step into Reading Ser.: A Step 2 Book). (Illus.). 48p. (J). (ps-3). 1984. pap. 3.99 (*0-394-86755-6*, Pub. by Random Bks Yng Read) Random.

Lorian, Victor. Antibiotics in Laboratory Medicine. 3rd ed. (Illus.). 1268p. 1991. 190.00 (*0-683-05168-7*) Lppncott W & W.

— Antibiotics in Laboratory Medicine. 4th ed. (Illus.). 1238p. 1996. 189.00 (*0-683-05169-5*) Lppncott W & W.

Lorian, Victor, ed. Antibiotics in Laboratory Medicine. 4th ed. LC 95-25829. Date not set. write for info. (*0-614-10236-7*) Lppncott W & W.

Lorian, Victor, jt. auth. see Silletti, Roger.

Loriaux, Michael. France after Hegemony: International Change & Financial Reform. LC 90-55721. (Cornell Studies in Political Economy). (Illus.). 304p. 1991. text 39.95 (*0-8014-2483-6*) Cornell U Pr.

Loriaux, Michael, et al. Liberalizing Finance in Interventionist States. LC 96-23238. (Illus.). 256p. 1996. text 39.95 (*0-8014-3176-X*); pap. text 15.95 (*0-8014-8281-X*) Cornell U Pr.

Loriaux, Michael, jt. ed. see Lynch, Cecelia.

Lorich, Sonja. The Unwomanly Woman in Bernard Shaw's Drama & Her Social & Political Background. 166p. (Orig.). 1973. pap. text 37.50 (*91-554-0081-7*) Coronet Bks.

***Lorie, Jonathan.** Traveler's Handbook: The Insider's Guide to World Travel. 8th ed. (Illus.). 2000. pap. 19.95 (*0-7627-0727-5*) Globe Pequot.

Lorie, Peter. Buddhist Directory: The Total Buddhist Resource Guide. LC 97-15876. 320p. 1997. pap. text 24.95 (*0-8048-3118-1*) Tuttle Pubng.

***Lorie, Peter.** Nostradamus: History of the Future: Year by Year, 2000-2025. 2000. 22.95 (*1-86204-790-1*, Pub. by Element MA) Penguin Putnam.

Lorie, Peter. Nostradamus: Prophecies for Women. (Illus.). 221p. 1998. text 23.00 (*0-7881-5904-6*) DIANE Pub.

***Lorie, Peter.** Quotable Spirit: A Treasury Religious & Spiritual Quotations, from Ancient Times for the 20th Century. 2000. 9.99 (*0-7858-1167-2*) Bk Sales Inc.

Lorie, Peter. Revelation: The Prophecies-Apocalypse, & Beyond. LC 93-49383. 224p. 1995. 22.50 (*0-671-88872-2*) S&S Trade.

— Superstitions. (Illus.). 256p. 1992. 22.50 (*0-671-78183-9*) S&S Trade.

***Lorie, Peter & Masceti, Manuela Dunn, eds.** The Quotable Spirit: A Treasury of Religious & Spiritual Quotations from Ancient Times to the 20th Century. 367p. 1999. reprint ed. text 25.00 (*0-7881-6737-5*) DIANE Pub.

Lorie, Peter & Mascetti, Manuela D. Nostradamus for Women: Prophecies for Women. 224p. 1995. 22.50 (*0-684-81178-2*) Simon & Schuster.

Lorie, Peter & Mascetti, Manuela D., compiled by. The Quotable Spirit: A Treasury of Religious & Spiritual Quotations from Ancient Times to the Twentieth Century. 448p. 1996. 25.00 (*0-02-861206-X*) Macmillan Info.

Lorie, Peter & Mascetti, Manuela Dunn. Prayer: Language of the Soul. LC 97-13472. (Illus.). 320p. 1997. 24.95 (*0-87596-428-1*) Rodale Pr Inc.

Loriedo, Camillo & Vella, Gaspare. Paradox & the Family System. LC 91-29684. 240p. 1992. text 35.95 (*0-87630-635-0*) Brunner-Mazel.

***Loriega, James.** The Scourge of the Dark Continent: The Martial Use of the African Sjambok. LC 99-65767. (Illus.). 143p. 1999. pap. 16.95 (*1-55950-198-7*, 19216) Loompanics.

— Sevillian Steel: The Traditional Knife-Fighting Arts of Spain. 184p. 1999. pap. 20.00 (*1-58160-039-9*) Paladin Pr.

Lorient, D., jt. auth. see Linden, G.

Lorient, D., jt. ed. see Dickinson, E.

Lorient, Denis, jt. auth. see Linden, G.

Loriferne, Bernard. Analog-Digital & Digital-Analog Conversion. fac. ed. LC TK7887.6.L67. 206p. 1983. reprint ed. pap. 63.90 (*0-7837-8287-X*, 204906900009) Bks Demand.

Lorig, Kate. Arthritis Helpbook. 3rd ed. 1990. pap. 12.95 (*0-201-52403-1*) Addison-Wesley.

— A Practical Approach. 2nd ed. LC 95-36414. 256p. 1995. pap. 26.95 (*0-7619-0074-8*) Sage.

— A Practical Approach: Patient Education. 2nd ed. LC 95-36414. 1995. 58.00 (*0-7619-0073-X*) Sage.

***Lorig, Kate & Fries, James F.** The Arthritis Helpbook: A Tested Self-Management Program for Coping with Arthritis & Fibromyalgia. 5th ed. (Illus.). 384p. 2000. pap. text 18.00 (*0-7382-0224-X*, Pub. by Perseus Pubng) HarpC.

Lorig, Kate & Fries, James F. The Arthritis Helpbook: A Tested Self-Management Program for Coping with Your Arthritis & Fibromyalgia. 4th ed. 288p. 1995. pap. 14.00 (*0-201-40963-1*) Addison-Wesley.

***Lorig, Kate, et al.** Living a Healthy Life with Chronic Conditions: Self-Management of Heart Disease, Arthritis, Diabetes, Asthma, Bronchitis, Emphysema & Others. 2nd rev. ed. (Illus.). 320p. 2000. pap. 18.95 (*0-923521-53-4*, Pub. by Bull Pub) Publishers Group.

Lorig, Kate, et al. Living a Healthy Life with Chronic Conditions: Self-Management of Heart Disease, Arthritis, Strokes, Diabetes, Asthma, Bronchitis, Emphysema & Others. 280p. 1994. pap. 18.95 (*0-923521-28-3*) Bull Pub.

Loriga, Ray. My Brother's Gun: A Novel of Disposable Lives, Immediate Fame, & a Big Black Automatic. Cordero, Kristina, tr. LC 97-16233. 128p. 1997. text 18.95 (*0-312-16947-7*) St Martin.

Loriggio, Francesco, ed. Social Pluralism & Literary History: The Literature of Italian Immigration. LC 95-75021. (Essay Ser.: No. 22). 330p. 1996. pap. 18.00 (*1-55071-018-4*) Guernica Editions.

Loriggio, Francesco, jt. ed. see Sbrocchi, Leonard G.

Loriggio, Francesco, tr. see Campanile, Achille.

LoriJean. Recovering from Life: Discovering Joy Through Inspiration & Encouragement. LC 97-62352. 256p. 1998. pap. 14.95 (*1-890394-14-9*, Sage Creek) Rhodes & Easton.

Lorilee, A. Sadler. Select: Internet Brief (Projects 1-4) 112p. (C). 1997. pap. text 19.00 (*0-201-31565-3*, Prentice Hall) P-H.

***Lorimer.** English & Irish Settlement on the River Amazon. 1998. 52.95 (*0-904180-27-1*) Ashgate Pub Co.

Lorimer, A. R. & Hillis, W. S. Cardiovascular Disease. (Treatment in Clinical Medicine Ser.). (Illus.). 300p. 1985. 47.95 (*0-387-15426-4*) Spr-Verlag.

Lorimer, D. L. R. & Lorimer, E. D. Persian Tales. LC 78-63210. (Illus.). reprint ed. 30.00 (*0-614-18074-0*) AMS Pr.

Lorimer, D. L. R. & Lorimer, Emily Overend, trs. Persian Tales: Fifty-Eight Traditional & Folk Tales from Iran. LC 98-42590. (Classics of Persian Literature Ser.: vol. 6). (Illus.). 366p. 2000. reprint ed. pap. 28.00 (*0-936347-91-0*) IBEX.

Lorimer, David. Spirit of Science: From Experiment to Experience. 1998. pap. text 26.95 (*0-86315-268-6*, Pub. by Floris Bks) Gryphon Hse.

— The Spirit of Science: From Experiment to Experience LC 98-32282. 366p. 1999. pap. 24.95 (*0-8264-1174-6*) Continuum.

Lorimer, David, ed. Prophet for Our Times: The Life & Teachings of Peter Deunov. 208p. 1993. pap. 14.95 (*1-85230-211-9*, Pub. by Element MA) Penguin Putnam.

Lorimer, Donald L., et al. Neal's Common Foot Disorders: Diagnosis & Management. 6th ed. LC 96-37052. 1997. pap. text 54.95 (*0-443-05258-1*) Church.

Lorimer, E. D., jt. auth. see Lorimer, D. L. R.

Lorimer, E. O., tr. see Carcopino, Jerome.

Lorimer, Emily Overend, jt. tr. see Lorimer, D. L. R.

Lorimer, Eric R. The First Deposit Guide to Starting a New Business: How & Where to Begin. (Illus.). (Orig.). 1992. pap., student ed. 15.00 (*0-9635134-0-0*) Frst Deposit NCCB.

Lorimer, Frank. Culture & Human Fertility: A Study of the Relation of Cultural Conditions to Fertility in Non-Industrial & Transitional Societies. LC 78-90549. 510p. 1970. reprint ed. lib. bdg. 79.50 (*0-8371-2152-3*, LOHF, Greenwood Pr) Greenwood.

— The Population of the Soviet Union: History & Prospects. LC 76-29424. reprint ed. 55.00 (*0-404-15339-9*) AMS Pr.

Lorimer, G. W. Proceedings of the 3rd International Magnesium Conference. (Illus.). 760p. 1997. 200.00 (*1-86125-013-4*, Pub. by Inst Materials) Ashgate Pub Co.

Lorimer, G. W., jt. ed. see Bennett, M. J.

Lorimer, Graeme & Lorimer, Sarah. Men Are Like Street Cars. LC 78-122730. (Short Story Index Reprint Ser.). (Illus.). 1977. 18.95 (*0-8369-3563-2*) Ayer.

Lorimer, Iris, jt. auth. see Walker, Gladys.

Lorimer, J. G., ed. Gazetteer of the Persian Gulf, Oman & Central Arabia, 9 vols. (Illus.). 5000p. (C). 1986. reprint ed. lib. bdg. 1295.00 (*1-85207-030-7*, Pub. by Archive Editions) N Ross.

Lorimer, James. The Developers. 307p. 1978. 29.95 (*0-88862-219-8*, Pub. by J Lorimer); pap. 14.95 (*0-88862-218-X*, Pub. by J Lorimer) Formac Dist Ltd.

Lorimer, James. The Institutes of Law: A Treatise of the Principles of Jurisprudence, As Determined by Nature. LC 94-75657. 468p. (C). 1994. reprint ed. 120.00 (*1-56169-086-4*) Gaunt.

Lorimer, James & Phillips, Myfawny. Working People: Life in A Downtown City Neighbourhood. LC 75-155770. 273 p. 1971. write for info. (*0-88862-011-X*) J Lorimer.

Lorimer, James J., et al. The Legal Environment of Insurance, 2 vols., Vol. 1. 4th ed. LC 93-71085. 342p. (C). 1993. text 41.00 (*0-89463-064-4*) Am Inst FCPCU.

Lorimer, Janet. A Cut of the Action. LC 95-76736. (Ten-Minute Thrillers Ser.). 32p. (YA). (gr. 6-12). 1995. pap. 2.95 (*0-7854-1063-5*, 40799) Am Guidance.

— A Cut of the Action Readalong. (Ten-Minute Thrillers Ser.). 32p. (YA). (gr. 6-12). 1995. pap. 12.95 incl. audio (*0-7854-1074-0*, 40801) Am Guidance.

— The Man Who Played with Fire. (Ten-Minute Thrillers Ser.). 32p. (YA). (gr. 6-12). 1995. pap. 2.95 (*0-7854-1067-8*, 40811) Am Guidance.

— The Man Who Played with Fire Readalong. (Ten-Minute Thrillers Ser.). 32p. (YA). (gr. 6-12). 1995. pap. 12.95 incl. audio (*0-7854-1078-3*, 40813) Am Guidance.

— The Middle of Nowhere. LC 95-76742. (Ten-Minute Thrillers Ser.). 32p. (YA). (gr. 6-12). 1995. pap. 2.95 (*0-7854-1068-6*, 40814) Am Guidance.

— The Middle of Nowhere Readalong. (Ten-Minute Thrillers Ser.). 32p. (YA). (gr. 6-12). 1995. pap. 12.95 incl. audio (*0-7854-1079-1*, 40816) Am Guidance.

— Skeleton Crew. LC 95-76741. (Ten-Minute Thrillers Ser.). 32p. (YA). (gr. 6-12). 1995. pap. 2.95 (*0-7854-1069-4*, 40817) Am Guidance.

— Skeleton Crew Readalong. (Ten-Minute Thrillers Ser.). 32p. (J). 1995. pap. 12.95 incl. audio (*0-7854-1080-5*, 40819) Am Guidance.

Lorimer, Jmaes & Phillips, Myfawny. Working People: Life in a Downtown City Neighborhood. 273p. 1971. pap. 14.95 (*0-88862-012-8*, Pub. by J Lorimer) Formac Dist Ltd.

Lorimer, John G. Gazetteer of the Persian Gulf, Oman & Central Arabia, 2 vols., Set. Birdwood, L., ed. 4,968p. Date not set. reprint ed. 995.00 (*0-7165-2380-9*, Pub. by Irish Acad Pr) Intl Spec Bk.

— Gazetteer of the Persian Gulf, Oman & Central Arabia, 8 vols., Set. Birdwood, L., ed. (Illus.). 4968p. 1990. reprint ed. 995.00 (*0-7165-2350-7*, Pub. by Irish Acad Pr) Intl Spec Bk.

***Lorimer, Joyce, ed.** Settlement Patterns in Early Modern Colonization: 16th-18th Centuries. LC JV105.S37 1998. 408p. 1998. 135.95 (*0-86078-517-3*, Pub. by Ashgate Pub) Ashgate Pub Co.

Lorimer, Kenneth. Education, Knowledge & the Computer. LC 95-78502. 224p. 1996. pap. 29.95 (*0-9647688-0-1*) Link-Frame.

Lorimer, Lawrence T. The Human Body: A Fascinating See-Through View of How Bodies Work. rev. ed. LC 98-73112. (Windows on Science Ser.: Vol. 6). (Illus.). 16p. (J). (gr. 4-6). 1999. 12.99 (*1-57584-248-3*, Pub. by Rdrs Digest) Random.

Lorimer, Michael. J. S. Bach Cello Suite. 48p. 1977. pap. 9.95 (*0-7866-0947-8*, 93910) Mel Bay.

— J. S. Bach Cello Suite 4. 24p. 1976. pap. 9.95 (*0-7866-0946-X*, 93909) Mel Bay.

— J. S. Bach Cello Suite 1 (Lorimer) 16p. 1989. pap. 9.95 (*1-56222-043-8*, 93906) Mel Bay.

— J. S. Bach Cello Suite 6. 28p. 1976. pap. 9.95 (*0-7866-0948-6*, 93911) Mel Bay.

— J. S. Bach Cello Suite 3 (Lorimer) 20p. 1977. pap. write for info. (*1-56222-059-4*, 93908) Mel Bay.

Lorimer, P. The Special Theory of Relativity for Mathematics Students. 112p. 1990. text 28.00 (*981-02-0254-7*) World Scientific Pub.

Lorimer, Phillip J., jt. auth. see Mason, Timothy J.

Lorimer, Robert, jt. auth. see Ackroyd, Neil.

***Lorimer, Rowland & Gasher, Michael.** Mass Communication in Canada. 4th ed. (Illus.). 400p. 2000. pap. text 35.00 (*0-19-541528-0*) OUP.

Lorimer, Rowland & McNulty, Jean. Mass Communication in Canada. 3rd ed. 376p. 1996. pap. text 49.95 (*0-19-541208-7*) OUP.

Lorimer, Rowland & Scanell, Paddy. Mass Communications: A Comparative Introduction. LC 94-19057. 1994. text 24.95 (*0-7190-3947-9*, Pub. by Manchester Univ Pr) St Martin.

Lorimer, Rowland M. The Nation in the Schools: Wanted, a Canadian Education. LC 84-215816. (Research in Education Ser.: No. 11). (Illus.). 131p. reprint ed. pap. 40.70 (*0-7837-0555-7*, 204089600019) Bks Demand.

Lorimer, Sarah, jt. auth. see Lorimer, Graeme.

Lorimer, William A., ed. History of Mercer County Illinois, with Biographical Sketches. (Illus.). 168p. 1998. reprint ed. lib. bdg. 27.50 (*0-8328-7085-4*) Higginson Bk Co.

Lorin, Amii, pseud. Breeze off the Ocean - Morgan Wade's Woman, 2 vols. in 1. 384p. 1994. mass mkt. 4.99 (*0-505-51977-1*, Love Spell) Dorchester Pub Co.

***Lorin, Amii, pseud.** Come Home to Love. 320p. 2000. pap. 5.50 (*0-505-52426-0*, Love Spell) Dorchester Pub Co.

Lorin, Amii, pseud. The Game Is Played. 192p. 1994. pap. text, mass mkt. 3.99 (*0-8439-3562-6*) Dorchester Pub Co.

— Night Striker. 288p. 1991. reprint ed. pap. text, mass mkt. 3.99 (*0-8439-3187-6*) Dorchester Pub Co.

— Power & Seduction. 192p. 1995. pap. text, mass mkt. 3.99 (*0-8439-3736-X*) Dorchester Pub Co.

Lorin, Elisabeth, jt. auth. see King-Hammond, Leslie.

Lorin, Harold. Doing It Right. 350p. (C). 1995. pap. 43.00 (*0-13-396425-6*) P-H.

— Introduction to Computer Architecture & Organization. 2nd ed. LC 88-27897. 384p. 1989. 117.95 (*0-471-61404-1*) Wiley.

— Sorting & Sort Systems. (Illus.). 480p. 1975. write for info. (*0-201-14453-0*) Addison-Wesley.

Lorin, Harold & Deitel, Harvey M. Operating Systems. LC 80-10625. (Computer Science: Systems Programming (IBM) Ser.). (Illus.). 480p. (C). 1981. text 41.95 (*0-201-14464-6*) Addison-Wesley.

Lorin, Martin I. Appleton & Lange's Review of Pediatrics. 5th ed. 222p. (C). 1996. pap. 34.95 (*0-8385-0057-9*, A0057-8, Apple Lange Med) McGraw.

— Appleton & Lange's Review of Pediatrics. 6th ed. (Illus.). 222p. (C). 1999. pap. 26.95 (*0-8385-0303-9*, A-0303-6) Appleton & Lange.

Lorinc, John M., ed. see Galova-Lorinc, Sylvia & Hoferka, Stephen R., Jr.

Lorinco, Sylvia & Lorino, John. Best of Slovak Cooking. LC 99-55469. 160p. 1999. 22.50 (*0-7818-0765-4*) Hippocrene Bks.

Lorinczy, A. Crystal Growth. 932p. 1992. text 320.00 (*0-87849-545-2*, Pub. by Trans T Pub) Enfield Pubs NH.

Loring. Love with Honor. LC 98-29031. 1998. 24.95 (*0-7862-1628-X*) Thorndike Pr.

Loring, Amasa. History of Piscataquis County: From Its Earliest Settlement to 1880. (Illus.). 304p. 1997. reprint ed. lib. bdg. 39.50 (*0-8328-5895-1*) Higginson Bk Co.

Loring, D. W., et al. Amobarbital Effects & Lateralized Brain Function: The Wada Test. King, D. W., ed. xiii, 138p. 1991. 81.00 (*0-387-97738-4*) Spr-Verlag.

Loring, David W., ed. INS Dictionary of Neuropsychology. LC 98-23696. 192p. 1998. text 55.00 (*0-19-506977-3*) OUP.

Loring, Denis W., ed. Monographs on Varieties of United States Large Cents, 1795-1803. LC 75-39497. (Illus.). 248p. 1976. 40.00 (*0-88000-075-9*) Quarterman.

Loring, Emilie. As Long As I Live. 1976. 21.95 (*0-88411-366-3*) Amereon Ltd.

— Beckoning Trails. 1976. reprint ed. lib. bdg. 21.95 (*0-88411-351-5*) Amereon Ltd.

— Behind the Cloud. reprint ed. lib. bdg. 19.95 (*0-88411-367-1*) Amereon Ltd.

— Beyond the Sound of Guns. reprint ed. lib. bdg. 23.95 (*0-88411-361-2*) Amereon Ltd.

— Bright Skies. 1976. reprint ed. lib. bdg. 22.95 (*0-88411-352-3*) Amereon Ltd.

— A Candle in Her Heart. 1976. reprint ed. lib. bdg. 22.95 (*0-88411-353-1*) Amereon Ltd.

— A Certain Crossroad. reprint ed. lib. bdg. 22.95 (*0-88411-375-2*) Amereon Ltd.

— Fair Tomorrow. reprint ed. 21.95 (*0-88411-368-X*) Amereon Ltd.

— Follow Your Heart. 1976. reprint ed. lib. bdg. 23.95 (*0-88411-354-X*) Amereon Ltd.

— For All Your Life. 1976. reprint ed. lib. bdg. 22.95 (*0-88411-355-8*) Amereon Ltd.

— Forsaking All Others. 276p. reprint ed. lib. bdg. 20.95 (*0-88411-382-5*) Amereon Ltd.

— Gay Courage. reprint ed. lib. bdg. 22.95 (*0-88411-369-8*) Amereon Ltd.

— Here Comes the Sun. reprint ed. lib. bdg. 23.95 (*0-88411-376-0*) Amereon Ltd.

— Hilltops Clear. reprint ed. lib. bdg. 24.95 (*0-88411-377-9*) Amereon Ltd.

— I Take This Man. reprint ed. lib. bdg. 18.95 (*0-88411-370-1*) Amereon Ltd.

— In Times Like This. 1976. reprint ed. lib. bdg. 22.95 (*0-88411-356-6*) Amereon Ltd.

— It's a Great World. 308p. reprint ed. lib. bdg. 24.95 (*0-88411-383-3*) Amereon Ltd.

— Keepers of the Faith. 1976. reprint ed. lib. bdg. 22.95 (*0-88411-357-4*) Amereon Ltd.

— A Key to Many Doors. 1976. reprint ed. lib. bdg. 22.95 (*0-88411-358-2*) Amereon Ltd.

— Lighted Windows. large type ed. 1998. 30.00 (*0-7838-0342-7*, G K Hall Lrg Type) Mac Lib Ref.

— Lighted Windows. reprint ed. lib. bdg. 24.95 (*0-88411-378-7*) Amereon Ltd.

— Look to the Stars. reprint ed. lib. bdg. 21.95 (*0-88411-371-X*) Amereon Ltd.

— Love Came Laughing By. 20.95 (*0-89190-128-0*) Amereon Ltd.

— My Dearest Love. 1976. reprint ed. lib. bdg. 21.95 (*0-88411-359-0*) Amereon Ltd.

— Rainbow at Dusk. 1976. reprint ed. lib. bdg. 24.95 (*0-88411-360-4*) Amereon Ltd.

— The Solitary Horseman. reprint ed. lib. bdg. 23.95 (*0-88411-379-5*) Amereon Ltd.

***Loring, Emilie.** Stars in Your Eyes. LC 99-55482. 2000. 30.00 (*0-7862-2299-9*) Mac Lib Ref.

Loring, Emilie. Stars in Your Eyes. 1976. reprint ed. lib. bdg. 22.95 (*0-88411-362-0*, 362) Amereon Ltd.

— Swift Water. reprint ed. lib. bdg. 25.95 (*0-88411-380-9*) Amereon Ltd.

— There Is Always Love. 1976. reprint ed. lib. bdg. 22.95 (*0-88411-363-9*) Amereon Ltd.

— Throw Wide the Door. reprint ed. lib. bdg. 21.95 (*0-88411-372-8*) Amereon Ltd.

— The Trail of Conflict. reprint ed. lib. bdg. 21.95 (*0-88411-381-7*) Amereon Ltd.

— Uncharted Seas. reprint ed. lib. bdg. 24.95 (*0-88411-373-6*) Amereon Ltd.

— We Ride the Gale. reprint ed. lib. bdg. 24.95 (*0-88411-374-4*) Amereon Ltd.

— When Hearts Are Light Again. 1976. reprint ed. lib. bdg. 23.95 (*0-88411-365-5*) Amereon Ltd.

— Where Beauty Dwells. 1976. reprint ed. lib. bdg. 24.95 (*0-88411-364-7*) Amereon Ltd.

Loring, Emilie B. Give Me One Summer. large type ed. LC 98-35580. 1998. 19.95 (*0-7862-1629-8*) Thorndike Pr.

***Loring, Emilie Baker.** As Long as I Live. large type ed. (Candlelight Romance Ser.). 2000. 22.95 (*0-7862-2459-2*) Thorndike Pr.

— High of Heart. LC 00-37695. 2000. write for info. (*0-7862-2658-7*) Thorndike Pr.

Loring, Emilie Baker. I Hear Adventure Calling. LC 99-14894. 1999. 23.95 (*0-7862-1978-5*) Mac Lib Ref.

***Loring, Emilie Baker.** Uncharted Seas. large type ed. LC 00-36459. 428p. 2000. 26.95 (*0-7862-2663-3*) Thorndike Pr.

— With Banners. large type ed. LC 99-41717. (Thorndike Candlelight Romance Ser.). 1999. 21.95 (*0-7862-2195-X*) Thorndike Pr.

Loring, Gloria. Gloria Lorings Guide to Health & Beauty. (Illus.). 128p. (Orig.). 1985. pap. write for info. (*0-932565-00-X*) Camex.

— Parenting a Child with Diabetes. 2nd ed. LC 99-41048. 224p. 1999. pap. 14.95 (*0-7373-0301-8*, 03018W, Pub. by Lowell Hse) NTC Contemp Pub Co.

— Parenting a Diabetic Child: A Practical, Empathetic Guide to Help You & Your Child Live with Diabetes. 240p. 1991. 19.95 (*0-929923-33-2*) Lowell Hse.

Loring, H. H., ed. see Cannon, Thomas H.

Loring, Honey & Birch, Jeremy. You're On . . . Teaching Assertiveness & Communication Skills. (Illus.). 85p. (Orig.). 1984. pap. 10.95 (*0-9613102-0-0*) StressPress.

Loring, J. Malcolm & Loring, Louise. Pictographs & Petroglyphs of the Oregon Country, Set, Pts. 1 & 2. 2nd ed. LC 96-3832. (UCLA Institute of Archaeology Publications: Nos. 21/23). (Illus.). 292p. 1996. pap. 48.00 (*0-917956-86-9*) UCLA Arch.

An Asterisk (*) at the beginning of an entry indicates that the title is appearing for the first time.

Loring, Jewell. Indialantic by the Sea: Then, Now, & Tomorrow. Coburn, Alan, ed. 96p. (Orig.). 1998. pap. 18.95 (*0-9636857-0-8*) Twn Indialantic.

Loring, John. Tiffany Jewels. LC 99-11057. (Illus.). 240p. 1999. 60.00 (*0-8109-3897-9*, Pub. by Abrams) Time Warner.

— Tiffany's 20th Century: A Portrait of American Style. LC 97-8128. (Illus.). 224p. 1997. 60.00 (*0-8109-3887-1*, Pub. by Abrams) Time Warner.

***Loring, John & Farnham, Paulding.** Paulding Farnham: Tiffany's Lost Genius. LC 00-22807. 160p. 2000. 49.50 (*0-8109-3511-2*, Pub. by Abrams) Time Warner.

***Loring, Jorge.** Motivos Para Creer. 1999. 17.95 (*84-08-02021-8*) Planeta Edit.

Loring, Louise, jt. auth. see Loring, J. Malcolm.

Loring, M. T., ed. Stories from the Heart: Case Studies of Emotional Abuse. 200p. 1997. 45.00 (*3-7186-0585-6*) Gordon & Breach.

Loring, Maggie. Skiing: A Woman's Guide. LC 99-32853. (Orig.). 1999. pap. 14.95 (*0-07-038867-9*, Ragged Mntain) McGraw-Hill Prof.

Loring, Marti T. Emotional Abuse. LC 94-10293. 140p. 1994. 29.95 (*0-02-919343-5*) Jossey-Bass.

— Emotional Abuse: The Trauma & the Treatment. LC 98-20964. (Psychology Ser.). 144p. 1998. reprint ed. pap. 19.95 (*0-7879-4377-0*) Jossey-Bass.

Loring, Marti T., ed. Stories from the Heart: Case Studies of Emotional Abuse. (New Directions in Therapeutic Intervention Ser.). 200p. 1997. text 30.00 (*90-5702-553-1*, Harwood Acad Pubs); pap. text 12.00 (*90-5702-554-X*, Harwood Acad Pubs) Gordon & Breach.

Loring, Murray, jt. auth. see Favre, David S.

Loring, Patricia. Spiritual Discernment & the Use of Clearness Committees among Friends. LC 92-62676. 32p. (Orig.). 1992. pap. 4.00 (*0-87574-305-6*) Pendle Hill.

Loring, Tamara, ed. Ricercar a 6 for Two Keyboards: From the Musical Offering. 2nd rev. ed. ii, 28p. 1995. pap. text 12.00 (*1-56571-126-2*) PRB Prods.

Loring, Tamara, ed. see Bach, Johann Sebastian.

Loring, Terry A. Lifting Solutions to Perturbing Problems in C*-Algebras. LC 96-43189. (Fields Institute Monographs Ser.: Vol. 8). 165p. 1996. text 44.00 (*0-8218-0602-5*, FIM/8) Am Math.

Loring, William C. An American Romantic-Realist Abroad: Templeton Strong & His Music. LC 94-19028. (Composers of North America Ser.: No. 4). 460p. 1995. 52.00 (*0-8108-2766-2*) Scarecrow.

Lorini, Alessandra. Rituals of Race: American Public Culture & the Search for Racial Democracy. LC 98-33171. (Carter G. Woodson Institute Series in Black Studies). 320p. 1999. pap. 19.50 (*0-8139-1871-5*); text 60.00 (*0-8139-1870-7*) U Pr of Va.

Lorino, John, jt. auth. see Lorinco, Sylvia.

Lorino, Sylvia. Slovak-English, English-Slovak Dictionary & Phrasebook. (ENG & SLO.). 180p. 1998. pap. 11.95 (*0-7818-0663-1*) Hippocrene Bks.

***Lorins, Cassandra.** Tantric Sex: Making Love Last. 2000. pap. 15.95 (*0-7225-3886-3*) Thorsons PA.

Lorio, Penny S. Expenses. Hines, Brenda K., ed. LC 90-64052. 192p. (Orig.). 1991. pap. 8.95 (*0-9628595-0-8*) Paradigm San Diego.

Lorion, Raymond P., ed. Protecting the Children: Strategies for Optimizing Emotional & Behavioral Development. LC 89-28933. (Prevention in Human Services Ser.: Vol. 7, No. 1). (Illus.). 275p. 1990. text 49.95 (*0-86656-970-7*) Haworth Pr.

Lorion, Raymond P., et al, eds. Psychology & Public Policy: Balancing Public Service & Professional Need. LC 95-26810. 417p. 1996. pap. text 19.95 (*1-55798-347-X*, 431-6700) Am Psychol.

Loriot-Raymer, Gisele & Vialet, Michele E. A Vous d'Ecrire: Atelier de Francais. 288p. (C). 1996. pap. text 23.50 (*0-07-044242-8*) McGraw.

— A Vous d'Ecrire: Atelier de Francais. (C). 1996. pap., wbk. ed. 32.19 (*0-07-044243-6*) McGraw.

Loris, Michelle, jt. ed. see Felton, Sharon C.

Loris, Michelle C. Innocence, Loss, & Recovery in the Art of Joan Didion. (American University Studies: English Language & Literature: Ser. IV, Vol. 74). VIII, 164p. (C). 1989. text 22.95 (*0-8204-0661-9*) P Lang Pubng.

Lorist, Monicque, jt. ed. see Snel, Jan.

Loriston-Clarke, Jennie. Lungeing & Long Reining. (Illus.). 95p. 1994. 34.95 (*1-872082-14-9*, Pub. by Kenilworth Pr) Half Halt Pr.

Lorit, Sergius C. Francoise Cabrini. (FRE.). 1989. reprint ed. pap. 7.00 (*0-9619397-1-0*) MSSH.

***Loritts, Crawford W.** Make It Home Before Dark: God's Call to Holiness in Our Walk with Him. 224p. 2000. 16.99 (*0-8024-5437-2*) Moody.

Loritts, Crawford W. Never Walk Away: Lessons on Integrity from a Father Who Lived It. 1998. pap. 9.95 (*0-8024-2742-1*) Moody.

Loritts, Crawford W., Jr. A Passionate Commitment: Recapturing Your Sense of Purpose. pap. 9.99 (*0-8024-5246-9*, 244) Moody.

Loritz, Donald. How the Brain Evolved Language. LC 98-29414. (Illus.). 240p. 1999. text 45.00 (*0-19-511874-X*) OUP.

Loriuar, Audrea. Horoscopo De Pasion. Creative Publishing Concepts Staff, ed. (SPA.). (Orig.). 1990. pap. write for info. (*0-944499-83-X*) Editorial Amer.

Lorkovic, Tanja, tr. see Pecujlit, Miroslav.

Lorkral. The Lady & the Fly. (I Love to Read Collection). (Illus.). 46p. (J). (ps-3). 1992. lib. bdg. 12.79 (*0-89565-812-7*) Childs World.

Lorler, Marie L. Shamanic Healing Within the Medicine Wheel. LC 89-7393. 272p. 1989. pap. 15.95 (*0-914732-23-4*) Bro Life Inc.

Lorman, Alba, tr. see Neumann, Eckhard.

Lorme, Anna. A Traitor's Daughter. Bononno, Robert, tr. from FRE. LC 91-39756. (French Expressions Ser.). 208p. 1993. 18.95 (*0-8419-1294-7*) Holmes & Meier.

Lorme, De. Of Man, Time & a River: The Skagit River, How Should It Be Used. (Occasional Papers: No. 10). 1986. pap. 4.00 (*0-318-23329-0*) WWU CPNS.

Lorme, Roland L. De, see Scott, James W. & De Lorme, Roland L.

Lormer, George H. Letters of a Self-Made Merchant to His Son: An American Father Gives Timeless Advice to His Son on How to Succeed in Life. 260p. 16.95 (*0-89526-475-7*) Regnery Pub.

Lormier, E. O., tr. see Beljame, Alexandre.

Lormor, Becky, ed. see King, Janie M.

Lorne & MacLean Marine & Offshore Productions Staf, ed. Peabody Holmes Inert Gas System. 1985. 95.00 (*0-7855-1042-7*, Pub. by Lorne & MacLean Marine) St Mut.

Lorne & MacLean Marine & Offshore Publications Sta. Chemical Tankers. (C). 1987. 75.00 (*0-7855-4388-0*, Pub. by Lorne & MacLean Marine) St Mut.

— COW - IGS Conference Papers & Proceedings. (C). 1987. 150.00 (*0-7855-4380-5*, Pub. by Lorne & MacLean Marine) St Mut.

— COW - IGS Manual. (C). 1987. 250.00 (*0-7855-4376-7*, Pub. by Lorne & MacLean Marine) St Mut.

— Dry Dock Planning Manual. (C). 1987. 495.00 (*0-7855-4372-4*, Pub. by Lorne & MacLean Marine) St Mut.

— English-Portuguese Marine Engineering Glossary. (C). 1987. 220.00 (*0-7855-4377-5*, Pub. by Lorne & MacLean Marine) St Mut.

— Gas Tankers. (C). 1987. 120.00 (*0-7855-4390-2*, Pub. by Lorne & MacLean Marine) St Mut.

— Guia de Operacoes Helicoptero Navio-Tanque.Tr. of Guide to Helicopter-Ship Operation. (POR.). (C). 1987. 150.00 (*0-7855-4384-8*, Pub. by Lorne & MacLean Marine) St Mut.

— Inert Gas Systems Manual. (C). 1987. 200.00 (*0-7855-4379-1*, Pub. by Lorne & MacLean Marine) St Mut.

— L & M Maritime Correspondence Course Guide. (C). 1987. 150.00 (*0-7855-4386-4*, Pub. by Lorne & MacLean Marine) St Mut.

— L & M Training Resources Manual. (C). 1987. 150.00 (*0-7855-4385-6*, Pub. by Lorne & MacLean Marine) St Mut.

— Manual de Controle de Incendio de Buques. (SPA.). (C). 1987. 165.00 (*0-7855-4383-X*, Pub. by Lorne & MacLean Marine) St Mut.

— Manual de Instrucciones - Sistema de Gas Inerte. (SPA.). (C). 1987. 600.00 (*0-7855-4370-8*, Pub. by Lorne & MacLean Marine) St Mut.

— Manual Internacional de Seguranca Maritima. (POR.). (C). 1987. 250.00 (*0-7855-4375-9*, Pub. by Lorne & MacLean Marine) St Mut.

— Offshore Fire-Fighting Manual. (C). 1987. 400.00 (*0-7855-4373-2*, Pub. by Lorne & MacLean Marine) St Mut.

— Oil Tankers. (C). 1987. 100.00 (*0-7855-4389-9*, Pub. by Lorne & MacLean Marine) St Mut.

— Operacion y Seguridad en Burques Tanqueros: Tanker Safety Manual. (SPA.). (C). 1987. 395.00 (*0-7855-4382-1*, Pub. by Lorne & MacLean Marine) St Mut.

— Peabody Holmes Inert Gas System Manual. (C). 1987. 140.00 (*0-7855-4381-3*, Pub. by Lorne & MacLean Marine) St Mut.

— S. O. S. (Ships Operational Safety) Manual. (C). 1987. 300.00 (*0-7855-4374-0*, Pub. by Lorne & MacLean Marine) St Mut.

— Ship Squat Manual. (C). 1987. 300.00 (*0-7855-4371-6*, Pub. by Lorne & MacLean Marine) St Mut.

— Shipowners Guide to Yard Repairs. (C). 1987. 195.00 (*0-7855-4378-3*, Pub. by Lorne & MacLean Marine) St Mut.

— Steering Gear Systems. (C). 1987. 75.00 (*0-7855-4387-2*, Pub. by Lorne & MacLean Marine) St Mut.

— Survival Techniques. (C). 1985. 75.00 (*0-7855-4391-0*, Pub. by Lorne & MacLean Marine) St Mut.

Lorne & MacLean Marine & Offshore Publications Sta, ed. Coal Fired Ships, 3 vols. 1987. 210.00 (*0-7855-1044-3*, Pub. by Lorne & MacLean Marine) St Mut.

— Guia de Operacoes Helicoptero Navio-Tanque.Tr. of Guide to Helicopter-Ship Operation. (POR.). 1985. 90.00 (*0-7855-1051-6*, Pub. by Lorne & MacLean Marine) St Mut.

— Marginal Oilfield & Tanker Conversion '85. 1985. 500.00 (*0-7855-1048-6*, Pub. by Lorne & MacLean Marine) St Mut.

— Offshore Safety Procedures Manual. 1987. 600.00 (*0-7855-1039-7*, Pub. by Lorne & MacLean Marine) St Mut.

— Ships Fire-Fighting Manual. 1987. 235.00 (*0-7855-1038-9*, Pub. by Lorne & MacLean Marine) St Mut.

Lorne, David. The Last Prisoner. 288p. (Orig.). 1991. mass mkt. 4.50 (*0-380-76287-0*, Avon Bks) Morrow Avon.

Lorne, Simon M. Acquisitions & Mergers: Negotiated & Contested Transactions, 4 vols. LC 85-4103. (Securities Law Ser.). 1985. ring bd. 445.00 (*0-87632-462-6*) West Group.

— Securities Law Considerations Affecting Employee Benefits Plans. 2nd ed. (Corporate Practice Ser.: No. 44). 1995. 92.00 (*1-55871-299-2*) BNA.

Lornell & Rasmussen, Anne K. New Perspectives in American Music. LC 97-19860. 1997. 35.00 (*0-02-864585-5*) Macmillan.

Lornell, Christopher. Introducing American Folk Music. 272p. (C). 1992. text. write for info. (*0-697-13383-4*) Brown & Benchmark.

— Introducing American Folk Music. (C). 1992. audio. write for info. (*0-697-16553-1*) Brown & Benchmark.

Lornell, Kip. Happy in the Service of the Lord: African-American Sacred Vocal Harmony Quartets in Memphis. 2nd ed. LC 94-18735. (Illus.). 272p. (C). 1995. pap. 19.95 (*0-87049-877-0*) U of Tenn Pr.

— Virginia's Blues, Gospel, & Country Records, 1902-1943: An Annotated Discography. LC 89-5613. 248p. 1989. 29.95 (*0-8131-1658-9*) U Pr of Ky.

Lornell, Kip, jt. auth. see Wolfe, Charles.

Lornier, Marcene. From the Inside: Poetic Philosophy & Contemplation. LC 95-61014. 96p. (Orig.). 1995. pap. 9.95 (*0-9646294-2-9*) Eleven Eleven Pub.

Lorning, Patrick & Johnson, Joy. Lucy Lettuce: A Story about Grief. (Illus.). 16p. 1994. pap. 4.95 (*1-56123-072-3*) Centering Corp.

Loroch, Kim J. Vessel Voyage Data Analysis: A Comparative Study. LC 65-20766. (Illus.). 160p. reprint ed. 49.60 (*0-8357-9075-4*, 201660100004) Bks Demand.

Lorona, Lionel V. Bibliography of Latin American & Caribbean Bibliographies, 1989-1990. (Bibliography & Reference Ser.: No. 27). viii, 48p. (Orig.). 1990. pap. 15.00 (*0-917617-27-4*) SALALM.

— Bibliography of Latin American & Caribbean Bibliographies, 1990-1991. (Bibliography & Reference Ser.: No. 30). 125p. 1992. pap. 19.00 (*0-917617-29-0*) SALALM.

Lorona, Lionel V., compiled by. Bibliography of Latin American & Caribbean Bibliographies, Annual Report, 1991-1992. (Bibliography & Reference Ser.: No. 31). 59p. (Orig.). 1992. pap. 17.50 (*0-917617-34-7*) SALALM.

Lorona, Lionel V., ed. A Bibliography of Latin American & Caribbean Bibliographies, 1985-1989, Supplement No. 5: Social Sciences & Humanities. 330p. 1993. 45.00 (*0-8108-2702-6*) Scarecrow.

— Bibliography of Latin American & Caribbean Bibliographies, 1987-1988. (Bibliography & Reference Ser.: No. 23). (Orig.). 1988. pap. 15.00 (*0-917617-20-7*) SALALM.

— Bibliography of Latin American & Caribbean Bibliographies, 1988-1989. (Bibliography & Reference Ser.: No. 25). 1989. 15.00 (*0-917617-23-1*) SALALM.

— A Bibliography of Latin American Bibliographies, 1980-1984: Social Sciences & Humanities, Supplement to Arthur E. Gropp's a Bibliography of Latin American Bibliographies, No. 4. LC 86-22093. 239p. 1987. 35.00 (*0-8108-1941-4*) Scarecrow.

Lorot, Pascal. Los Paises Balticos. (Breviarios Ser.). (SPA.). pap. 6.99 (*968-16-4957-5*, Pub. by Fondo) Continental Bk.

Lorquin, Bertrand. Maillol. LC 94-61693. (Illus.). 200p. 1995. 40.00 (*0-500-97417-9*, Pub. by Thames Hudson) Norton.

Lorr, David & Garshnek, Victoria, eds. Working in Orbit & Beyond: The Challenges for Space Medicine, Jul 20-21, 1987, Washington, D.C. LC 57-43769. (Science & Technology Ser.: Vol. 72). (Illus.). 188p. 1989. 45.00 (*0-87703-295-5*, Am Astronaut Soc); pap. 35.00 (*0-87703-296-3*, Am Astronaut Soc) Univelt Inc.

Lorr, Maurice. Cluster Analysis for Social Scientists. LC 82-49283. (Jossey-Bass Social & Behavioral Science Ser.). (Illus.). 251p. reprint ed. pap. 77.90 (*0-8357-4905-3*, 203783500009) Bks Demand.

Lorr, Maurice, jt. ed. see Strack, Stephen.

Lorr, Regina E. Miracles in the Kitchen: Delicious & Nutritious Replacements for Junk Foods. LC 91-60773. 304p. (Orig.). 1992. pap. 12.95 (*0-914711-09-1*) Rishis Inst.

Lorr, Regina E. & Crary, Robert W. The Path of Light. LC 83-71354. 192p. (Orig.). 1983. pap. 10.95 (*0-87516-520-6*) DeVorss.

Lorr, Ruth, ed. Where Have All the Beanies' Gone!?! 2nd rev. ed. Orig. Title: The Hunt. 183p. 1998. pap. 29.95 (*0-9662760-0-0*) BBear Pubns.

Lorrabee, Wayne. Roslyn: A Town's Portrait. (Illus.). 60p. 1995. pap. write for info. (*0-9673235-0-9*) Digital Design.

Lorrah, Jean. The Idic Epidemic, No. 38. (Star Trek Ser.: Vol. 38). 1990. mass mkt. 4.50 (*0-671-70768-X*) PB.

— Metamorphosis. (Star Trek: The Next Generation Ser.). 416p. 1990. per. 5.99 (*0-671-68402-7*) PB.

— Survivors. Stern, Dave, ed. (Star Trek: The Next Generation Ser.: No. 4). 1991. mass mkt. 5.50 (*0-671-74290-6*) PB.

— The Vulcan Academy Murders. (Star Trek Ser.: No. 20). (Orig.). 1991. mass mkt. 4.95 (*0-671-74283-3*) PB.

Lorrain. Electromagnetic Fields. 2000. text. write for info. (*0-7167-3568-7*) W H Freeman.

— Electromagnetic Fields & Waves. 4th ed. 2000. pap. text. write for info. (*0-7167-3569-5*) W H Freeman.

— Lushai Grammar & Dictionary. (ENG.). 346p. 1984. 24.95 (*0-7859-7514-4*) Fr & Eur.

— Solutions Manual: Electromagnetism. 2nd ed. (C). 1990. pap. text. write for info. (*0-7167-2139-2*) W H Freeman.

Lorrain, Jacques, et al, eds. Comprehensive Management of the Menopause. LC 93-3255. (Clinical Perspectives in Obstetrics & Gynecology Ser.). (Illus.). 455p. 1994. 96.00 (*0-387-97972-7*) Spr-Verlag.

Lorrain, Jean. Une Femme Par Jour. Desbrueres, Michel, ed. (FRE., Illus.). 346p. 1995. pap. 69.95 (*2-86808-002-2*) Intl Scholars.

— Histoires De Masques. (FRE., Illus.). 260p. 1987. pap. 69.95 (*2-86808-024-3*) Intl Scholars.

— La Maison Philibert. Desbrueres, Michel, ed. (FRE., Illus.). 368p. 1995. pap. 74.95 (*2-86808-067-7*) Intl Scholars.

— Monsieur de Phocas. 2nd ed. Amery, Francis, ed. & tr. by. LC 94-100376. (Decadence Ser.). 272p. 1999. reprint ed. pap. 14.95 (*1-873982-15-1*, Pub. by Dedalus) Hippocrene Bks.

Lorrain, Paul. Electromagnetism. 2nd ed. LC 89-23822. (Illus.). 472p. (C). 1990. pap. text 56.95 (*0-7167-2096-5*) W H Freeman.

Lorrain, Paul, et al. Electromagnetic Fields & Waves. 3rd ed. LC 86-31803. (Physics Ser.). (Illus.). 754p. (C). 1987. pap. text 73.95 (*0-7167-1823-5*) W H Freeman.

Lorrain, R. D., jt. auth. see Douglas, Ian.

Lorrain-Smith, R. An Economic Analysis of Silvicultural Options for Broadleaved Woodlands, Vol. II. 1982. 60.00 (*0-85074-042-8*) St Mut.

Lorraine, Miranda, jt. auth. see Kursinski, Anne.

Lorraine, Tamsin E. Irigaray & Deleuze: Experiments in Visceral Philosophy. LC 99-18218. 272p. 1999. pap. 19.95 (*0-8014-8586-X*) Cornell U Pr.

Lorrance, Arleen. Born of Love. (Illus.). 200p. 1981. pap. 14.95 (*0-916192-16-4*) L P Pubns.

— Images. LC 85-23118. 83p. 1995. pap. 8.95 (*0-916192-39-3*) L P Pubns.

— India Through Eyes of Love. (Illus.). (Orig.). 1982. pap. 7.95 (*0-916192-18-0*) L P Pubns.

— The Love Project. rev. ed. LC 78-15162. (Illus.). 103p. 1978. pap. 6.95 (*0-916192-14-8*) L P Pubns.

— Musings for Meditation. LC 76-14783. (Illus.). 180p. (Orig.). 1976. pap. 7.95 (*0-916192-03-2*) L P Pubns.

— Why Me? How to Heal What's Hurting You. LC 77-88151. 186p. 1982. 11.95 (*0-916192-19-9*) L P Pubns.

Lorrance, Arleen & Pike, Diane K. The Love Project Way. 216p. (Orig.). 1980. pap. 10.95 (*0-916192-15-6*) L P Pubns.

Lorre, C. De, see De Lorre, C., ed.

Lorre, E. N. Residential Steel Faming Construction Guide, Vol. 1. (Illus.). 234p. (Orig.). 1993. pap. 39.95 (*0-9651302-0-7*) Technical Pub.

Lorren, McGee, jt. auth. see Hicks, Larry K.

Lorriman, J. Continuing Professional Development: A Practical Approach. (Management of Technology Ser.: No. 19). 241p. 1997. pap. 35.00 (*0-85296-903-1*, MT019Z); boxed set 69.00 (*0-85296-915-5*, MT019) INSPEC Inc.

Lorriman, John & Kenjo, Takashi. Japan's Winning Margins: Management, Training, & Education. (Illus.). 264p. 1996. pap. text 19.95 (*0-19-856373-6*) OUP.

Lorriman, John, et al. Upside down Management: The Only Way to Win. LC 95-16851. 1995. pap. write for info. (*0-07-709067-5*) McGraw.

Lorrimer, Claire. Beneath the Sun. 224p. 1996. 22.00 (*0-7278-4975-1*) Severn Hse.

— Chantal. large type ed. (Charnwood Large Print Ser.). 704p. 1996. 27.99 (*0-7089-8907-1*) Ulverscroft.

— Connie's Daughter. large type ed. (Ulverscroft Large Print Ser.). 400p. 1997. 27.99 (*0-7089-3777-2*) Ulverscroft.

— Forbidden Love. 256p. 1999. 25.00 (*0-7278-5426-7*, Pub. by Severn Hse) Chivers N Amer.

— Frost in the Sun. large type ed. 848p. 1996. 27.99 (*0-7089-8867-9*, Charnwood) Ulverscroft.

— House of Tomorrow. large type ed. (Ulverscroft Large Print Ser.). (Illus.). 496p. 1998. 29.99 (*0-7089-3906-6*) Ulverscroft.

— Mavreen. large type ed. (Charnwood Large Print Ser.). 832p. 1996. 27.99 (*0-7089-8895-4*) Ulverscroft.

Lorrimer, Claire. Never Say Goodbye. 224p. 26.00 (*0-7278-5535-2*) Severn Hse.

Lorrimer, Claire. The Reckoning. 192p. 1998. 22.00 (*0-7278-5333-3*) Severn Hse.

***Lorrimer, Claire.** The Reckoning. 336p. 2000. 31.99 (*0-7505-1476-0*) Ulverscroft.

— Relentless Storm. large type ed. LC 99-89825. (General Ser.). 2000. pap. 22.95 (*0-7862-2457-6*) Thorndike Pr.

Lorrimer, Claire. The Reunion. 256p. 1997. 24.00 (*0-7278-5168-3*) Severn Hse.

***Lorrimer, Claire.** The Reunion. large type ed. 2000. 31.99 (*0-7505-1477-9*, Pub. by Mgna Lrg Print) Ulverscroft.

Lorrimer, Claire. Second Chance. 192p. 1999. 25.00 (*0-7278-2213-6*, Pub. by Severn Hse) Chivers N Amer.

***Lorrimer, Claire.** Second Chance. large type ed. 240p. 2000. 31.99 (*0-7089-4184-2*) Ulverscroft.

Lorrimer, Claire. The Secret of Quarry House. large type ed. 1991. 27.99 (*0-7089-2539-1*) Ulverscroft.

— The Secret of Quarry House. 1994. reprint ed. lib. bdg. 19.00 (*0-7278-4649-3*) Severn Hse.

— The Shadow Falls. large type ed. (Ulverscroft Large Print Ser.). 336p. 1998. 29.99 (*0-7089-3941-4*) Ulverscroft.

— The Shadow Falls. 224p. 1995. reprint ed. 22.00 (*0-7278-4796-1*) Severn Hse.

— The Silver Link. large type ed. (Charnwood Large Print Ser.). 736p. 1995. 27.99 (*0-7089-8815-6*, Charnwood) Ulverscroft.

— Tamarisk. large type ed. (Charnwood Large Print Ser.). 688p. 1996. 27.99 (*0-7089-8903-9*) Ulverscroft.

— Variations: Collected Short Stories. large type ed. (General Ser.). 368p. 1993. 27.99 (*0-7089-2880-3*) Ulverscroft.

— A Voice in the Dark. large type ed. 1991. 11.50 (*0-7089-2410-7*) Ulverscroft.

— The Woven Thread. 192p. 1998. 25.00 (*0-7278-5243-4*) Severn Hse.

Lorrimer, Clarie. Relentless Storm. 1994. 19.00 (*0-7278-4580-2*) Severn Hse.

Lorrin, Marc, jt. auth. see Lorrin, Shona.

***Lorrin, Shona & Lorrin, Marc.** The Half-Doll with Related Items, Maker & Values, Vol. 1. LC 99-94025. (Illus.). 224p. 1999. 64.95 (*0-9676167-0-0*) M & S Lorrin.

Lorring, David W. INS Dictionary of Neuropsychology. LC 98-23696. 192p. 1998. pap. text 24.95 (*0-19-506978-1*) OUP.

An Asterisk (*) at the beginning of an entry indicates that the title is appearing for the first time.

L

Lorris & Strubel, eds. Roman de la Rose. 1272p. 1992. write for info. (0-7859-9331-2) Fr & Eur.

Lorsch. Pawns or Potentates. 200p. 1989. 29.95 (0-07-103252-5) McGraw.

*__Lorsch, Martin.__ Systemische Gemeindeentwicklung: Ein Beitrag Zur Erneuerung der Gemeinde im Geist des Zweiten Vatikanischen Konzils. (Pastoralpsychologie und Spiritualitat Ser.). 254p. 1999. 42.95 (3-631-35299-9) P Lang Pubng.

Lorsch, Susan E. Where Nature Ends: The Designation of Landscape in Arnold, Swinburne, Hardy, Conrad & Woolf. LC 81-72056. 240p. 1983. 26.50 (0-8386-3162-2) Fairleigh Dickinson.

Lorsch, Susan E., jt. ed. see Keener, Frederick M.

Lorseyedi, jt. auth. see Norris.

Lorseyedi, Barb, ed. see Milliken, Linda.

*__Lorson, John C.__ Send Help! Delights, Dilemmas & Delusions of a Modern Midwestern Man. (Illus.). 158p. 1999. pap. 11.00 (0-9675615-0-7) PebbleTree.

Lort, Don. Coming of Age: A Pictorial Movie & Video Guide. (Illus.). 216p. (Orig.). 1997. pap. 18.95 (1-889138-02-9) Companion Press.

Lortat-Jacob, Bernard. Sardinian Chronicles. Fagan, Teresa L., tr. LC 94-10766. (Chicago Studies in Ethnomusicology). 128p. 1994. pap. text 19.95 (0-226-49341-5) U Ch Pr.

— Sardinian Chronicles. Fagan, Teresa L., tr. LC 94-10766. (Chicago Studies in Ethnomusicology). 128p. 1995. lib. bdg. 47.50 (0-226-49340-7) U Ch Pr.

Lorten, R. Body Sculpting for Women. 128p. 1996. 12.98 (0-7858-0563-X) Bk Sales Inc.

Lortie, Dan C. Schoolteacher: A Sociological Study. LC 74-11428. 296p. 1977. reprint ed. pap. text 13.00 (0-226-49354-7, P748) U Ch Pr.

Lorton, David. The Juridical Terminology for International Relations in Egyptian Texts through Dyn. XVIII. LC 73-8114. (Johns Hopkins Near Eastern Studies). 208p. reprint ed. pap. 64.50 (0-608-16399-6, 202632700049) Bks Demand.

Lorton, David, jt. auth. see Sauneron, Serge.

Lorton, David, tr. see Andreu, Guillemette.

Lorton, David, tr. see Chauveau, Michel.

Lorton, David, tr. see Hornung, Erik.

Lorton, David, tr. see Mysliwiec, Karol.

Lorton, Elizabeth, ed. see Blanc, Iris.

Lorton, Mary B. Workjobs II: Number Activities for Early Childhood. 1978. spiral bd. 17.50 (0-201-04302-5) Addison-Wesley.

Lorton, Paul, Jr., jt. auth. see Muscat, Eugene J.

*__Lorton, Roger.__ A-Z of Policing Law. LC 98-128646. 1998. write for info. (0-11-702200-4) Statnry Office.

Lorton, Sherry. Merchant's Edge: A Guide to Grain Marketing. 2nd ed. 330p. 1994. pap. 22.00 (0-87563-487-7) Stipes.

— Merchant's Edge: A Guide to Grain Marketing. 3rd ed. 428p. 1998. pap. 29.95 (0-87563-777-9) Stipes.

Lorton, Sherry & White, Don. The Art of Grain Merchandising. 75p. (Orig.). 1997. pap. text 14.95 (0-87563-716-7) Stipes.

— Profit on the Farm: A Marketing Guide to Help the Farmer Sell Better. 132p. (Orig.). (C). 1994. pap. text 14.95 (0-87563-501-6) Stipes.

— Profit on the Farm II: The One Habit of Top-Third Sellers. 138p. (Orig.). (C). 1994. pap. text 14.95 (0-87563-625-X) Stipes.

*__Lorton, Sherry, et al.__ The Farmer's Edge. 51p. 1999. pap. text 9.95 (0-87563-940-2) Stipes.

Lortz, Joseph. Francis, the Incomparable Saint. (Franciscan Pathways Ser.). 127p. 1986. pap. 6.00 (1-57659-067-4) Franciscan Inst.

Lortz, Richard. Bereavements. 215p. 1979. 22.00 (0-932966-08-X) Permanent Pr.

— Dracula's Children. 208p. 1982. 22.00 (0-932966-15-2) Permanent Pr.

— Lovers Living, Lovers Dead. 224p. 1980. 22.00 (0-933256-28-0) Second Chance.

— The Valdepenas. LC 79-66114. 224p. 1984. 22.00 (0-933256-06-X) Second Chance.

Lortzing, F., ed. see Zeller, Eduard.

Lorusso. Robert McAlmon. 1997. 23.95 (0-8057-4527-0, Twyne) Mac Lib Ref.

Lorusso, Edward N., ed. & intro. see McAlmon, Robert.

Lorusso, Julia & Glick, Joel. Healing Stoned: The Therapeutic Use of Gems & Minerals. 2nd ed. 113p. 1985. reprint ed. pap. 12.95 (0-914732-05-6) Bro Life Inc.

— Stratagems. 108p. (Orig.). 1985. pap. 10.95 (0-914732-15-3) Bro Life Inc.

Lorwin, Lewis L. The American Federation of Labor. LC 70-174559. (Library of American Labor History). xix, 573p. 1972. reprint ed. 30.00 (0-678-00880-9) Kelley.

— Labor & Internationalism. (Brookings Institution Reprint Ser.). reprint ed. lib. bdg. 32.50 (0-697-00164-4) Irvington.

— Youth Work Programs: Problems & Policies, Vol. 3. LC 74-1694. (Children & Youth Ser.). 212p. 1974. reprint ed. 23.95 (0-405-05970-1) Ayer.

Lorwin, Lewis L. & Flexner, Jean A. American Federation of Labor. LC 70-126699. 1970. reprint ed. 32.50 (0-404-04027-6) AMS Pr.

— Syndicalism in France, by Louis Levine. LC 76-127443. (Columbia University. Studies in the Social Sciences: No. 116). reprint ed. 39.50 (0-404-51116-3) AMS Pr.

Lorwin, Louis, see Levine, Louis, pseud.

Lorwin, Louis, ed. see Levine, Louis, pseud.

Lorwin, Val R. French Labor Movement. LC 54-7062. (Wertheim Publications in Industrial Relations). (Illus.). 365p. 1954. 22.50 (0-674-32200-2) HUP.

Lory, Eva M. Crosby. Crosbys of Henry County, Illinois, 1851-1936. (Illus.). 230p. 1997. reprint ed. pap. 35.00 (0-8328-8152-X); reprint ed. lib. bdg. 45.00 (0-8328-8151-1) Higginson Bk Co.

Lory, Hillis. Japan's Military Masters: The Army in Japanese Life. LC 72-9367. 256p. 1973. reprint ed. lib. bdg. 35.00 (0-8371-6581-4, LOMM, Greenwood Pr) Greenwood.

Los Alamos Historical Society Staff, jt. auth. see Martin, Craig.

Los Alamos Scientific Laboratory Public Relations Staff. Los Alamos: Beginning of an Era, 1943-1945. 5th ed. LC 92-8820. (Illus.). 64p. 1986. reprint ed. pap. 6.00 (0-941232-07-7) Los Alamos Hist Soc.

Los Alamos Young Writers Club. Life in Los Alamos, New Mexico: A Kid's View. LC 97-75730. (Illus.). 110p. (J). (gr. 4-12). 1997. pap. text 11.98 (0-9645703-5-1) Otowi Crossing Pr.

Los Angeles Commission on Assaults Against Women S, jt. auth. see Levy, Barrie.

Los Angeles County Bar Association, jt. see Fields, Michael S.

Los Angeles County Bar Association Staff, jt. auth. see Fields, Michael S.

Los Angeles County Museum of Art Staff. Masterpieces from the Shin-Enkan Collection: Japanese Painting of the Edo Period LC 85-45953. 139 p. 1986. write for info. (0-87587-128-3) LA Co Art Mus.

Los Angeles County Schools Staff. Audio Worksheets, 4 vol. set. (Auditory Skills Instructional Planning System Ser.: 3rd Component). (Illus.). 356p. 1980. ring bd. 380.00 (0-943292-13-1) Foreworks.

— Audio Worksheets, Vol. 1. (Illus.). 1980. 95.00 (0-943292-09-3) Foreworks.

— Audio Worksheets, Vol. 2. (Illus.). 1980. 95.00 (0-943292-10-7) Foreworks.

— Audio Worksheets, Vol. 3. (Illus.). 1980. 95.00 (0-943292-11-5) Foreworks.

— Audio Worksheets, Vol. 4. (Illus.). 1980. 95.00 (0-943292-12-3) Foreworks.

— Auditory Skills Curriculum. LC 79-52375. (Auditory Skills Instructional Planning System Ser.: 1st Component). 329p. 1979. ring bd. 50.00 (0-943292-07-7) Foreworks.

— Auditory Skills Instructional Planning System, 4 Components. (Illus.). 1979. ring bd. 555.00 (0-943292-06-9) Foreworks.

Los Angeles County Schools Staff. Test of Auditory Comprehension. (Auditory Skills Instructional Planning System Ser.: Vol. 2). (Illus.). 208p. 1979. 90.00 (0-943292-08-5) Foreworks.

Los Angeles Museum of Arts Staff, et al. Hirado Porcelain of Japan: From the Kurtzman Family Collection. LC 98-177065. 55p. 1997. write for info. (0-87587-182-8) LA Co Art Mus.

Los Angeles Police Department Staff. Law Enforcement in Los Angeles: Los Angeles Police Department Annual Report, 1924. LC 74-3831. (Criminal Justice in America Ser.). 1974. reprint ed. 24.95 (0-405-06151-X) Ayer.

Los Angeles Public Library Staff. Catalog of the Police Library of the Los Angeles Public Library, First Supplement. (Library Reference Ser.). 1980. 295.00 (0-8161-0328-3, G K Hall & Co) Mac Lib Ref.

Los Angeles Times Editors. Nominating a President: The Process & the Press. LC 80-13824. 168p. 1980. 38.50 (0-275-90509-8, Praeger Pubs); pap. 14.95 (0-03-057858-2, Praeger Pubs) Greenwood.

Los Angeles Times Food Section Staff. The Seasonal Kitchen. (Illus.). 144p. 1997. pap. 19.95 (1-883792-18-5) LA Times.

Los Angeles Times Staff. Best of Laugh Lines. 1996. pap. text 13.95 (1-883792-16-9) LA Times.

*__Los Angeles Times Staff.__ Imagining Los Angeles: Photographs of a 20th Century City. (Illus.). 2000. 29.95 (1-883792-52-5) LA Times.

Los Angeles Unified School District Staff. Drafting. LC 77-73291. 64p. (gr. 7-9). 1978. pap. text 5.76 (0-02-820320-8) Glencoe.

— Electricity. LC 77-73243. 96p. (gr. 7-9). 1978. pap. text 6.48 (0-02-820300-3) Glencoe.

— Getting a Job. (Project Get That Job Ser.). (Illus.). 48p. (Orig.). (YA). (gr. 7-12). 1990. teacher ed. 1.95 (1-56119-094-2); student ed. 5.95 (1-56119-093-4) Educ Pr MD.

— Getting a Job, Set. (Project Get That Job Ser.). (Illus.). 48p. (Orig.). (YA). (gr. 7-12). 1990. teacher ed., student ed. 59.95 (1-56119-095-0) Educ Pr MD.

— Graphic Arts. LC 77-73302. 128p. (gr. 7-9). 1978. pap. text 5.32 (0-02-820340-2) Glencoe.

— Metalworking. LC 77-73297. 96p. (gr. 7-9). 1978. pap. text 7.04 (0-02-820290-2) Glencoe.

— Starting Your New Job. (Project Get That Job Ser.). (Illus.). 48p. (Orig.). (YA). (gr. 7-12). 1990. teacher ed. 1.95 (1-56119-097-7); student ed. 5.95 (1-56119-096-9) Educ Pr MD.

— Starting Your New Job, Set. (Project Get That Job Ser.). (Illus.). 48p. (Orig.). (YA). (gr. 7-12). 1990. teacher ed., student ed. 59.95 (1-56119-098-5) Educ Pr MD.

— Working with Others. (Project Get That Job Ser.). (Illus.). 48p. (Orig.). (YA). (gr. 7-12). 1990. teacher ed. 1.95 (1-56119-091-8); teacher ed., wbk. ed. 59.95 (1-56119-092-6); student ed. 5.95 (1-56119-090-X) Educ Pr MD.

— You & Your Attitude. (Project Get That Job Ser.). (Illus.). 48p. (Orig.). (YA). (gr. 7-12). 1990. teacher ed. 1.95 (1-56119-088-8); student ed. 5.95 (1-56119-087-X) Educ Pr MD.

— You & Your Attitude, Set. (Project Get That Job Ser.). (Illus.). 48p. (Orig.). (YA). (gr. 7-12). 1990. 59.95 (1-56119-089-6) Educ Pr MD.

Los Angeles Unified School District Staff, et al. FORE Language. Bagai, Eric & Bagai, Judith, eds. (System FORE Ser.: Vol. 2). (Illus.). 452p. 1977. student ed. 25.00 (0-943292-02-6) Foreworks.

— FORE Mathematics. rev. ed. Bagai, Eric & Bagai, Judith, eds. (System FORE Ser.: Vol. 4). (Illus.). 232p. 1977. 15.00 (0-943292-04-2) Foreworks.

— FORE Reading. Bagai, Eric & Bagai, Judith, eds. (System FORE Ser.: Vol. 3). (Illus.). 305p. 1977. student ed. 28.00 (0-943292-03-4) Foreworks.

Los Condes, Santob De Carrion De, see De Carrion De Los Condes, Santob.

Los, D. Thou Holdest My Right Hand: On Pastoral Care of the Dying. Plantinga, Theodore, tr. from DUT. LC 93-39279. (Pastoral Perspectives Ser.: No. 2). 141p. 1993. pap. 8.90 (0-921100-45-0) Inhtce Pubns.

Los, L. I., jt. auth. see Worst, J. G.

Los Mar, Richard De, see De los Mar, Richard.

*__Los, Maria, et al.__ Privatizing the Police State. LC 99-88982. 272p. 2000. text 69.95 (0-312-23150-4) St Martin.

*__Los, Martin.__ Caroling with the Capitol Brass. 8p. 1998. pap. 14.95 incl. audio compact disk (0-7866-4411-7, 97850BCD) Mel Bay.

Los Montero, Patricia Espinosa De, see Espinosa De Los Montero, Patricia.

Los Reyes, Isabelo De, see De Los Reyes, Isabelo.

Los Rios, Emilio De, see De Los Rios, Emilio.

Los Rios, Francisco Giner De, see Giner de Los Rios, Francisco.

los Santos, Marisa De, see De los Santos, Marisa.

Los, Sergio. Carlo Scarpa: An Architectural Guide. 1996. pap. 17.95 (88-7743-145-8, Pub. by Arsenale Editrice) Antique Collect.

*__Los, Sergio.__ Carlo Scarpa: An Architectural Guide. 1999. 29.99 (3-8228-6730-6) Benedikt Taschen.

Los, Sergio. Scarpa. 1994. pap. 24.99 (3-8228-9441-9) Taschen Amer.

— Scarpa. (SPA.). 1996. pap. 24.99 (3-8228-0756-7) Taschen Amer.

*__Los, Sietse Oene.__ Linkages Between Global Vegetation & Climate: An Analysis Based on NOAA Advanced Very High Resolution Radiometer Data. 204p. 1998. pap. text 29.00 (0-16-049527-X) USGPO.

Losa, G. A., et al, eds. Fractals in Biology & Medicine, Vol. II. (Illus.). 350p. 1998. text 69.50 (3-7643-5715-0) Birkhauser.

Losack, Marcus, jt. auth. see Rogers, Michael.

*__Losada, I. J., ed.__ Coastal Structures '99: Proceedings of an International Conference, Santander, Spain, 7-10 June 1999, 2 vols. 1200p. 2000. text 165.00 (90-5809-092-2, Pub. by A A Balkema) Ashgate Pub Co.

*__Losada, Isabel.__ New Habits: Today's Women Who Choose to Become Nuns. 195p. 1999. pap. 14.95 (0-340-72238-X, Pub. by Hodder & Stought Ltd) Trafalgar.

Losada, Jose M., ed. Bibliography of the Myth of Don Juan in Literary History. LC 97-39651. (ENG & MUL.). 236p. 1997. text 89.95 (0-7734-8450-7) E Mellen.

Losada, Miguel A. Design & Construction of Maritime Structures for Protection Against Waves. (Advanced Series in Ocean Engineering). 400p. 1998. text 106.00 (981-02-2163-0); pap. text 58.00 (981-02-2414-1) World Scientific Pub.

Losano, Wayne, jt. auth. see Gould, Jay.

LoSapio, Carol, ed. see Guenter, Kim.

Loscalzo & Sasahara, Arthur A., eds. New Therapeutic Agents in Thrombosis & Thrombolysis. LC 97-12542. (Illus.). 700p. 1997. text 195.00 (0-8247-9866-X) Dekker.

Loscalzo, Anthony L., ed. see Werth, Jacques, et al.

*__Loscalzo, Craig A.__ Apologetic Preaching: Proclaiming Christ to a Postmodern World. LC 99-86868. 2000. pap. 11.99 (0-8308-1575-9) InterVarsity.

Loscalzo, Craig A. Evangelistic Preaching That Connects: Guidance in Shaping Fresh & Appealing Sermons. LC 95-40445. 180p. (Orig.). 1995. pap. 11.99 (0-8308-1863-4, 1863) InterVarsity.

Loscalzo, J. & Schafer, A. Thrombosis & Hemorrhage. (Illus.). 1360p. 1993. 265.00 (0-86542-263-X) Blackwell Sci.

Loscalzo, Joseph, et al, eds. Vascular Medicine: A Textbook of Vascular Biology & Diseases. 2nd ed. LC 95-39262. 1216p. 1996. text 210.00 (0-316-53400-5, Little Brwn Med Div) Lppncott W & W.

*__Loscalzo, Joseph & London, Gerard, eds.__ Cardiovascular Disease in End-Stage Renal Disease. (Oxford Clinical Nephrology Ser.). (Illus.). 512p. 2000. text 139.50 (0-19-262987-5) OUP.

Loscalzo, Joseph & Schafer, Andrew I. Thrombosis & Hemorrage. 2nd ed. LC 97-48547. (Illus.). 1449p. 1998. 195.00 (0-683-30114-4) Lppncott W & W.

*__Loscalzo, Joseph & Vita, Joseph A., eds.__ Nitric Oxide & the Cardiovascular System. (Contemporary Cardiology Ser.). 616p. 2000. 175.00 (0-89603-620-0) Humana.

Loscalzo, Joseph, jt. auth. see Jenkins, Jon L.

Loscalzo, William A. Cash Flow Forecasting. (Illus.). 192p. 1982. text 40.00 (0-07-038746-X) McGraw.

Loscerbo, J. Being in Technology: A Study of the Philosophy of Martin Heidegger. (Phaenomenologica Ser.: No. 82). 296p. 1981. lib. bdg. 171.00 (90-247-2411-2, Pub. by M Nijhoff) Kluwer Academic.

Losch, August. The Economics of Location. 2nd rev. ed. Woglom, William H. & Stolpher, Wolfgang F., trs. LC 52-9268. 548p. reprint ed. pap. 169.90 (0-8357-8110-0, 203380700087) Bks Demand.

Losch, Harald J., jt. auth. see Stosberg, Krista.

Losch, Naomi N., tr. see Casil, Kathleen L.

Losch, Rainer. Funktionelle Voraussetzungen der Adaptiven Nischenbesetzung in der Evolution der Makaronesischen Semperviven. (Dissertationes Botanicae Ser.: Band 146). (GER., Illus.). viii, 482p. 1990. pap. 100.00 (3-443-64058-3, Pub. by Gebruder Borntraeger) Balogh.

Loschcke, Eberhard, jt. auth. see Aragon, Rafael.

Loschcke, V., jt. ed. see Woehrmann, K.

Losche, Diane, jt. ed. see Thomas, Nicholas.

Losche, Norbert. Cosmic Tarot. 1988. pap. 18.50 (0-88079-395-3, CS78) US Games Syst.

Loscher, W., ed. Valproate: A Drug for Epilepsy, Psychiatry & Beyond. LC 99-18269. (Milestones in Drug Therapy Ser.). 250p. 1999. 150.00 (3-7643-5836-X) Birkhauser.

Loschmann, Mariane, jt. auth. see Loschmann, Martin.

Loschmann, Martin & Loschmann, Mariane. Einander Verstehen: Ein Deutsches Literarisches Lesebuch. LC 95-20012. (Studies in Modern German Literature: No. 67). (GER., Illus.). XVII, 323p. (C). 1997. pap. text 29.95 (0-8204-2399-8) P Lang Pubng.

*__Losco, Joseph & Fife, Brian L.__ Higher Education in Transition: The Challenges of the New Millennium LC 99-33210. 232p. 1999. 59.95 (0-89789-637-8, Bergin & Garvey) Greenwood.

Loscutoff, Lynn L. Art-to-Go: A Traveler's Guide to Painting in Watercolors. (Illus.). 76p. 1996. 18.99 (1-56496-248-2, Quarry Bks) Rockport Pubs.

— Painter's Wild Workshop: Expand Your Creativity: Inspiration from 4 Master Artists. (Illus.). 144p. 1998. 29.99 (1-56496-434-5, Quarry Bks) Rockport Pubs.

Loscutoff, Lynn L., jt. auth. see Duca, Alfred M.

Lose, John, ed. see Davis, Ken.

Lose, M. Phyllis. Blessed Are the Brood Mares. 2nd ed. (Illus.). 271p. 1991. 27.50 (87605-848-9) Howell Bks.

— Blessed Are the Foals. 2nd ed. LC 98-12642. 304p. 1998. 29.95 (0-87605-286-3) Howell Bks.

Lose, Patrick. At Home with Patrick Lose: Colorful Quilted Projects. Nelson, Annie & Lanzarotti, Sally, eds. LC 98-38375. (Illus.). 104p. 1999. pap. 24.95 (1-57120-061-4, 10184) C & T Pub.

— Country Woodcrafts to Make & Paint. (Illus.). 144p. 1998. 14.95 (0-8069-4228-2, Chapelle) Sterling.

— Fun & Fancy Jackets & Vests: Folk Art Using No-Sew Applique. LC 95-6. (Illus.). 144p. 1995. 24.95 (0-8069-1298-7, Chapelle) Sterling.

— Making Nosew Jackets & Vests. (Illus.). 144p. 1998. 14.95 (0-8069-1299-5, Chapelle) Sterling.

— Patrick Lose's Whimsical Cross-Stitch. LC 94-42099. (Illus.). 144p. 1995. 24.95 (0-8069-1292-8, Chapelle) Sterling.

— Patrick Lose's Whimsical Sweatshirts. LC 95-16328. (Illus.). 144p. (Orig.). 1995. 27.95 (0-8069-3179-5, Chapelle) Sterling.

— Patrick Lose's Whimsical Sweatshirts. (Illus.). 144p. (Orig.). 1996. pap. 14.95 (0-8069-3180-9, Chapelle) Sterling.

*__Lose, Patrick.__ Special Delivery Quilts. Lytle, Joyce & Kuhn, Barb, eds. LC 99-50515. (Illus.). 112p. 2000. pap. 24.95 (1-57120-088-6) C & T Pub.

Loseby, Paul H. Employment Security: Balancing Human & Economic Considerations. LC 92-1132. 192p. 1992. 49.95 (0-89930-692-6, LYT/, Quorum Bks) Greenwood.

Loseby, S. T., jt. ed. see Christie, Neil.

Losee, Ferril. RF Systems, Components, & Circuits Handbook. LC 97-13330. (Microwave Engineering Ser.). 599p. 1997. 93.00 (0-89006-933-6) Artech Hse.

Losee, John. A Historical Introduction to the Philosophy of Science. 3rd enl. rev. ed. LC 93-22328. (Illus.). 332p. 1993. pap. text 18.95 (0-19-289247-9) OUP.

— Philosophy of Science & Historical Enquiry. LC 86-23550. (Illus.). 160p. 1987. text 45.00 (0-19-824946-2) OUP.

— Religious Language & Complementarity. 280p. (C). 1991. lib. bdg. 49.50 (0-8191-8371-7) U Pr of Amer.

Losee, R. E. Doc: Then & Now With a Montana Physician. 1996. mass mkt. 5.99 (0-8041-1415-3) Ivy Books.

— Doc: Then & Now with a Montana Physician. 1996. pap. 5.99 (0-614-98047-X) Ivy Books.

— Doc: Then & Now with a Montana Physician. LC 94-28555. (Illus.). 232p. 1994. 22.95 (1-55821-323-6) Lyons Pr.

Losee, Rex, jt. auth. see McIntyre, Robert L.

Losee, Rita. The Waist Management Playbook. 160p. 1994. pap. text, per. 19.97 (0-8403-9917-0) Kendall-Hunt.

Losee, Rita H. Unlock Your Possibilities: How to Stop Shooting Yourself down & Selling Yourself Short. Neil, Winter C., ed. 192p. 1998. 19.95 (1-891643-00-2, Summer Bks) Pontalba Pr.

Losee, Robert M. Text Retrieval & Filtering: Analytic Models of Performance. LC 98-23431. (Series on Information Retrieval). 1998. 115.00 (0-7923-8177-7) Kluwer Academic.

Losee, Stephanie, jt. auth. see Lavington, Camille.

Loseff, Lev & Scherr, Barry P., eds. A Sense of Place Tsarskoe Selo & Its Poets: Papers from the Dartmouth Conference Dedicated to the Centennial of Anna Akhmatova, 1989. (Illus.). 368p. (Orig.). 1993. pap. 22.95 (0-89357-239-X) Slavica.

Loseke, Donileen R. The Battered Woman & Shelters: The Social Construction of Wife Abuse. LC 90-26166. (SUNY Series in Deviance & Social Control). 216p. (C). 1992. text 59.50 (0-7914-0831-0); pap. text 19.95 (0-7914-0832-9) State U NY Pr.

— Thinking about Social Problems: An Introduction to Constructionist Perspectives. LC 98-51926. (Social Problems & Social Issues Ser.). 238p. 1999. pap. text 18.95 (0-202-30620-8); lib. bdg. 37.95 (0-202-30619-4) Aldine de Gruyter.

Loseke, Donileen R., jt. ed. see Gelles, Richard J.

Losel, Friedrich, et al, eds. Psychology & Law: International Perspectives. LC 92-30454. xxviii, 557p. 1992. lib. bdg. 144.65 (3-11-013725-9) De Gruyter.

An Asterisk (*) at the beginning of an entry indicates that the title is appearing for the first time.

Losel, Friedrich, jt. ed. see Hurrelmann, Klaus.

Loselle, Andrea. History's Double 20th Century. LC 97-8426. 242p. 1997. text 39.95 (*0-312-17425-X*) St Martin.

Loselle, Andrea, tr. see Restany, Pierre.

Losensky, Paul E. Welcoming Fighani: Imitation & Poetic Individuality in the Safavid-Mughal Ghazal. LC 98-18794. (Bibliotheca Iranica Ser.: Vol. 5). (Illus.). xiv, 398p. 1998. lib. bdg. 45.00 (*1-56859-070-9*) Mazda Pubs.

Loser. Shaping Actors, Shaping Factors in Russia's Future. LC 98-17418. 120p. 1998. text 39.95 (*0-312-21603-3*) St Martin.

Loser, Eva, jt. auth. see Fauriol, Georges A.

Loser, Eva, jt. ed. see Fauriol, Georges A.

Loser, Paul. Shaping Actors, Shaping Factors in Russia. 1998. pap. text 25.00 (*0-7494-2714-0*) Kogan Page Ltd.

Loser, Werner, ed. see Von Balthasar, Hans U.

Loserth, Johann. Wiclif & Hus. Evans, M. J., tr. LC 78-63198. (Heresies of the Early Christian & Medieval Era Ser.: Second Ser.). 1979. reprint ed. 61.50 (*0-404-16236-3*) AMS Pr.

Losev, Lev, ed. & afterword by see Eremin, Mikhail.

Losev, S. A. Gasdynamic Laser. (Chemical Physics Ser.: Vol. 12). (Illus.). 300p. 1981. 62.95 (*0-387-10503-4*) Spr-Verlag.

Losey, Elizabeth B. Let Them Be Remembered. LC 97-91114. 761p. 2000. 29.95 (*0-533-12572-3*) Vantage.

***Losey, Jay & Brewer, William D.** Mapping Male Sexuality: Nineteenth-Century England. LC 99-53165. 2000. write for info. (*0-8386-3828-7*) Fairleigh Dickinson.

Losey, Kay M. Listen to the Silences: Mexican American Interaction in the Composition Classroom & the Community. LC 96-13155. (Second Language Learning Ser.). 238p. 1996. pap. 39.50 (*1-56750-269-5*); text 73.25 (*1-56750-268-7*) Ablx Pub.

Losey, Ralph, jt. auth. see Keyserling, Arnold.

Losh, John B. Who's Who in Luxury Real Estate. Burns, Emily E., ed. 400p. 1997. 19.95 (*1-886020-05-1*) Whos Who Lux Real Est.

— Who's Who in Luxury Real Estate, No. IX. 9th rev. ed. Burns, Emily, ed. 365p. 1996. 19.95 (*1-886020-04-3*) Whos Who Lux Real Est.

— Who's Who in Luxury Real Estate, Vol. VIII. 8th rev. ed. Burns, Emily E., ed. 344p. 1995. 19.95 (*1-886020-00-0*) Whos Who Lux Real Est.

— Who's Who in Luxury Real Estate, Vol. XI. rev. ed. Burns, Emily E., ed. 450p. 1998. 19.95 (*1-886020-06-X*) Whos Who Lux Real Est.

— Who's Who in Luxury Real Estate Vol. rev. ed. Burns, Emily E., ed. 279p. 1992. 19.95 (*1-886020-03-5*) Whos Who Lux Real Est.

— Who's Who in Luxury Real Estate Vol. rev. ed. Burns, Emily E., ed. 311p. 1993. 19.95 (*1-886020-02-7*) Whos Who Lux Real Est.

— Who's Who in Luxury Real Estate Vol. rev. ed. Burns, Emily E., ed. 336p. 1994. 19.95 (*1-886020-01-9*) Whos Who Lux Real Est.

Loshak, David. Munch. (Illus.). 112p. 1999. pap. 19.95 (*1-57715-070-8*) Knckerbocker.

***Loshin, David.** Efficient Memory Programming. LC 98-31719. 256p. 1998. 50.00 (*0-07-038868-7*) McGraw.

— Enterprise Knowledge Management: The Data Quality Approach. 350p. 2000. pap. 49.95 (*0-12-455840-2*) Acad Pr.

Loshin, David. Programming for Memory Efficiency. LC 97-12176. 304p. (C). 1997. pap. text. write for info. (*0-201-44212-4*) Addison-Wesley.

Loshin, David S. The Geometrical Optics Workbook. 224p. 1991. pap. text 35.00 (*0-7506-9052-6*) Buttrwrth-Heinemann.

***Loshin, Pete.** Big Book of Best Current Practices RFCs. 400p. 2000. 34.95 (*0-12-455847-X*) Morgan Kaufmann.

— Big Book of Border Gateway Protocol (BGP) RFCs. (Illus.). 300p. 2000. pap. 34.95 (*0-12-455846-1*) Morgan Kaufmann.

— Big Book of Internet File Transfer RFCs. (Big Book Ser.). (Illus.). 310p. 2000. pap. 34.95 (*0-12-455845-3*) Acad Pr.

— Big Book of Internet Host Standards. LC 99-69876. (Big Book Ser.). (Illus.). 423p. 2000. pap. 34.95 (*0-12-455844-5*) Acad Pr.

— Big Book of Lightweight Directory Access Protocol (LDAP) RFCs. LC 99-69872. (Big Book Ser.). (Illus.). 550p. 2000. pap. 34.95 (*0-12-455843-7*) Acad Pr.

— Big Book of Terminal Emulation RFCs. (Big Book Ser.). (Illus.). 500p. 2000. pap. 34.95 (*0-12-455842-9*) Acad Pr.

— Big Book of World Wide Web RFCs. (Big Book Ser.). (Illus.). 630p. 2000. pap. 34.95 (*0-12-455841-0*) Acad Pr.

— Essential ATM Standards: RFCs & Protocols Made Practical. LC 99-42976. 222p. 1999. 44.99 (*0-471-34598-9*) Wiley.

— Essential E-Mail Standards: RFCs & Protocol Made Practical. LC 99-38265. 339p. 1999. 49.99 (*0-471-34597-0*) Wiley.

— Essential Ethernet Standards: RFCs & Protocols Made Practical. LC 99-42975. 179p. 1999. 44.99 (*0-471-34596-2*) Wiley.

— IPV6 Clearly Explained. LC 98-38741. (Clearly Explained Ser.). 352p. (C). 1999. pap. 44.95 (*0-12-455838-0*) Morgan Kaufmann.

Loshin, Pete. Personal Encryption Clearly Explained. LC 98-19661. (Clearly Explained Ser.). (Illus.). 545p. (C). 1998. boxed set 39.95 (*0-12-455837-2*) Morgan Kaufmann.

— Selling Online with First Virtual. (Illus.). 400p. (Orig.). 1996. pap. 32.95 (*1-886801-41-X*) Thomson Learn.

— TCP/IP Clearly Explained. 3rd ed. (Clearly Explained Ser.). 450p. (C). 1999. pap. 44.95 (*0-12-455826-7*) Morgan Kaufmann.

***Loshin, Pete, compiled by.** Big Book of IPsec RFCs: IP Security Architecture. 1999. 34.95 (*0-12-455839-9*) Morgan Kaufmann.

Loshin, Pete, et al. Electronic Commerce: On-Line Ordering & Digital Money. 2nd ed. (Illus.). 300p. 1996. pap. 39.95 (*1-886801-67-3*) Thomson Learn.

Loshin, Peter. Extranet Design & Implementation. LC 97-66378. 464p. 1997. pap. text 49.99 (*0-7821-2091-1*) Sybex.

— TCP/IP Clearly Explained. 2nd ed. LC 96-48637. (Illus.). 419p. 1997. pap. text 34.95 (*0-12-455835-6*) Morgan Kaufmann.

Loshitzky, Yosefa. The Radical Faces of Godard & Bertolucci. LC 94-30602. (Contemporary Film & Television Ser.). (Illus.). 288p. 1994. text 44.95 (*0-8143-2446-0*) Wayne St U Pr.

Loshitzky, Yosefa, ed. Spielberg's Holocaust: Critical Perspectives on Schindler's List. LC 96-35930. 1997. 39.95 (*0-253-33232-X*); pap. 17.95 (*0-253-21098-4*) Ind U Pr.

Losi, Carol A. 512 Ants on Sullivan Street. 1997. 9.19 (*0-606-11013-5*, Pub. by Turtleback) Demco.

Losick, R. & Chamberlin, M., eds. RNA Polymerase. LC 76-17182. (Cold Spring Harbor Monographs). 909p. reprint ed. pap. 200.00 (*0-7837-6443-X*, 204644300012) Bks Demand.

Losick, Richard & Shapiro, Lucy, eds. Microbial Development. LC 84-9599. (Monographs: Vol. 16). 303p. 1984. 60.00 (*0-87969-172-7*); pap. 35.00 (*0-87969-173-5*) Cold Spring Harbor.

Losick, Richard, ed. see Levine, Arnold J., et al.

Losik, Len. Parent's Guide to Children's Martial Arts: What's the Right Style for Your Child? Losik, Sandra, ed. (Illus.). 110p. 1997. pap. 19.95 (*0-9661179-6-4*) SanLen Ent.

Losik, Sandra, ed. see Losik, Len.

***Losinger, Anton.** The Anthropological Turn: The Human Orientation of the Theology of Karl Rahner. LC 00-44227. (Moral Philosophy & Moral Theology Ser.). 2000. write for info. (*0-8232-2067-2*) Fordham.

— The Anthropological Turn: The Human Orientation of the Thology of Karl Rahner. (Modern Philosophy & Theology Ser.). 2000. 39.95 (*0-8232-2091-5*); pap. 19.95 (*0-8232-2092-3*) Fordham.

Losinger, Anton. Relative Autonomy: The Key to Understanding Vatican II. xii, 281p. 1997. pap. 54.95 (*3-631-31495-7*) P Lang Pubng.

— Relative Autonomy: The Key to Understanding Vatican II. XII, 281p. 1997. pap. 54.95 (*0-8204-3260-1*) P Lang Pubng.

Losique, Serge. Dictionnaire Etymologique des Noms de Pays et de Peuples.Tr. of Etymological Dictionary of People's & Place Names. (FRE.). 243p. 1971. pap. 35.00 (*0-8288-6453-5*, F-135990) Fr & Eur.

Losito, et al. Encyclopedia Animal World, 11 Vol., Set. (J). 1990. 157.95 (*0-8160-1957-6*) Facts on File.

Losito, Linda, et al. Birds: The Aerial Hunters. (Encyclopedia of the Animal World Ser.). (Illus.). 96p. (YA). 1989. 19.95 (*0-8160-1963-0*) Facts on File.

— Birds: The Plant- & Seed-Eaters. (Encyclopedia of the Animal World Ser.). (Illus.). 96p. (YA). 1989. 19.95 (*0-8160-1964-9*) Facts on File.

— Fish. (Encyclopedia of the Animal World Ser.). (Illus.). 96p. (J). (gr. 4-9). 1990. 19.95 (*0-8160-1966-5*) Facts on File.

— Insects & Spiders. (Encyclopedia of the Animal World Ser.). (Illus.). 96p. (J). (gr. 4-9). 1990. 19.95 (*0-8160-1967-3*) Facts on File.

— Mammals: The Small Plant-Eaters. (Encyclopedia of the Animal World Ser.). (Illus.). 96p. (J). (gr. 4-9). 1989. 19.95 (*0-8160-1958-4*) Facts on File.

— Pets & Farm Animals. (Encyclopedia of the Animal World Ser.). (Illus.). 96p. (J). (gr. 4-9). 1990. 19.95 (*0-8160-1969-X*) Facts on File.

— Simple Animals. (Encyclopedia of the Animal World Ser.). (Illus.). 96p. (J). (gr. 4-9). 1989. 19.95 (*0-8160-1968-1*) Facts on File.

Loske, Reinhard & Sachs, Wolfgang. Industrial Societies & Sustainability: Proposals for Managing the Transition. LC 99-168110. 247p. (C). 1997. text 65.00 (*1-85649-507-8*, Pub. by Zed Books) St Martin.

— Industrial Societies & Sustainability: Proposals for Managing the Transition. LC 99-168110. (C). 1998. text 25.00 (*1-85649-508-6*, Pub. by Zed Books) St Martin.

Loski, Diana. The Boy on the Bus. (Illus.). 30p. (Orig.). (J). (gr. k-5). 1994. pap. 6.99 (*1-885101-02-3*) Writers Pr ID.

— 1864: A Year in the Life of a Civil War Soldier. Bryninckx, John, ed. (Illus.). 152p. (Orig.). pap. 5.95 (*1-885101-18-X*) Writers Pr ID.

— I Am a Union Soldier. (Illus.). 30p. (J). (gr. 1-4). 1997. pap. 3.95 (*1-57747-022-2*) Thomas Publications.

— Zack Attacks. Kolsen, Wendy S., ed. (Illus.). 108p. (Orig.). (J). (gr. 3-8). 1995. pap. 3.50 (*1-885101-10-4*) Writers Pr ID.

Loski, Diana & Sniffen, Linda M. Dinosaur Hill. (Illus.). (Orig.). (J). (gr. 3-8). 1995. pap. 3.75 (*1-885101-16-3*) Writers Pr ID.

Loski, Diana H. The Chamberlains of Brewer. LC 98-85175. (Illus.). 128p. 1998. pap. 12.00 (*1-57747-039-7*) Thomas Publications.

Loskutov, A. Yu, jt. auth. see Mikhailov, A. S.

Losleben, Paul, ed. Advanced Research in VLSI: Proceedings of the Stanford Conference, 1987. 350p. 1987. 52.00 (*0-262-12121-2*) MIT Pr.

Losman, Donald L. & Liang, Shu-Jan. The Promise of American Industry: An Alternative Assessment of Problems & Prospects. LC 89-24329. 296p. 1990. 59.95 (*0-89930-508-3*, LAB/, Quorum Bks) Greenwood.

Losndale, Ellias. Inside Planets, Vol. I. LC 95-19457. (Inside Astrology Ser.: Vol. 1). 311p. (Orig.). 1995. pap. 16.95 (*1-55643-212-7*) North Atlantic.

Losoncy. Inner Self, Outer Self. 1996. pap. 9.95 (*1-57444-055-1*, L1552) St Lucie Pr.

Losoncy, Diane G., jt. auth. see Losoncy, Lewis E.

Losoncy, Lewis E. Best Team Skills: 50 Key Skills for Unlimited Team Achievement. 160p. (Orig.). 1996. per. 29.95 (*1-57444-085-3*) St Lucie Pr.

— The Motivating Team Leader. LC 94-46380. 256p. 1995. per. 29.95 (*1-884015-82-4*) St Lucie Pr.

— Salon Psychology: How to Succeed with People & Be a Positive Person. LC 87-63500. (Illus.). 242p. (Orig.). 1988. pap. text 12.95 (*0-9619951-0-6*) Matrix Univ Pr.

— Today! Grab It: 7 Vital Attitude Nutrients to Build the New You. LC 97-43529. 160p. 1997. per. 19.95 (*1-57444-213-9*) St Lucie Pr.

***Losoncy, Lewis E.** Turning People On: How to Be an Encouraging Person. 1999. pap. 21.95 (*0-9673439-4-1*, Pub. by InSync Commn) ACCESS Pubs Network.

Losoncy, Lewis E. & Losoncy, Diane G. What Is, Is? Encouraging Yourself to Accept What You Won't Change & Change What You Won't Accept. 168p. (Orig.). 1996. per. 29.95 (*1-57444-040-3*) St Lucie Pr.

Losoncy, Lewis E., jt. auth. see Dinkmeyer, Don.

Losoncy, Lewis E., jt. auth. see Scoleri, Donald W.

Losoncy, Renata, jt. auth. see Lipton, Gladys C.

Losonsky, Frank S. & Losonsky, Terry M. Flying Tiger: A Crew Chief's Story - The War Diary of an AVG Crew Chief. LC 95-72354. (Illus.). 112p. (C). (gr. 13). 1996. 35.00 (*0-7643-0045-8*) Schiffer.

Losonsky, Joyce & Losonsky, Terry. Collectibles 101: Fast Food Toys. (Illus.). 160p. 1999. pap. 16.95 (*0-7643-0965-X*) Schiffer.

— Collectibles 101: McDonald's Happy Meal Toys. (Illus.). 144p. 1999. pap. 16.95 (*0-7643-0966-8*) Schiffer.

— The Encyclopedia of Fast Food Toys: Arby's to IHOP. LC 98-88751. (Illus.). 160p. (Orig.). 1999. pap. 24.95 (*0-7643-0761-4*) Schiffer.

— The Encyclopedia of Fast Food Toys: Jack In The Box To White Castle. LC 98-88908. (Illus.). 160p. (Orig.). 1999. pap. 24.95 (*0-7643-0784-3*) Schiffer.

— McDonald's Glassware. (Illus.). 192p. 1999. pap. 16.95 (*0-7643-0879-3*) Schiffer.

— McDonald's Happy Meal Toys Around the World, 1996-Present. (Illus.). 192p. 1999. pap. 24.95 (*0-7643-0960-9*) Schiffer.

— McDonald's Happy Meal Toys from the Eighties. LC 98-21473. 192p. 1998. pap. 24.95 (*0-7643-0322-8*) Schiffer.

— McDonald's Happy Meal Toys from the Nineties. LC 98-24944. 240p. 1998. pap. 24.95 (*0-7643-0673-1*) Schiffer.

— McDonald's Pre-Happy Meal Toys from the Fifties, Sixties & Seventies. LC 98-17409. 224p. 1998. pap. 24.95 (*0-7643-0599-9*) Schiffer.

— The Unauthorized Guide to Smurfs Around the World. (Illus.). 176p. 1999. pap. 29.95 (*0-7643-0959-5*) Schiffer.

Losonsky, Joyce, jt. auth. see Clee, Ken.

Losonsky, Joyce, jt. auth. see Losonsky, Terry M.

Losonsky, Michael, jt. auth. see Geirsson, Heimer.

Losonsky, Michael, jt. ed. see Geirsson, Heimir.

Losonsky, Michael, ed. see von Humboldt, Wilhelm.

Losonsky, Michael, tr. see Reich, Klaus.

Losonsky, Terry, jt. auth. see Losonsky, Joyce.

Losonsky, Terry M. & Losonsky, Joyce. McDonald's Happy Meal Toys: Around the World. LC 95-37442. (Illus.). 270p. (Orig.). 1995. pap. 24.95 (*0-88740-835-4*) Schiffer.

Losonsky, Terry M., jt. auth. see Losonsky, Frank S.

Losordo, Stephen. Cow Moo Me. LC 98-213303. (Growing Tree Ser.). (Illus.). 16p. (J). (ps up). 1998. 5.95 (*0-694-01108-8*, HarpFestival) HarpC Child Bks.

Losordo, Thomas M., jt. ed. see Timmons, Michael B.

Losq, Christine. Understanding Division. (Whole Math Project Ser.). (Illus.). 188p. 1993. teacher ed., spiral bd. 29.95 (*1-56892-000-8*) CSL Assocs.

Loss. Anecdotes. 1995. 29.95 (*0-316-53282-7*, Aspen Law & Bus) Aspen Pub.

— Popular Culture in America: 1960. LC 98-72416. (C). 1998. pap. text 23.50 (*0-15-504146-0*, Pub. by Harcourt Coll Pubs) Harcourt.

— SEC Register, Vol. 8. 3rd ed. 1991. 147.50 (*0-316-53380-7*, Aspen Law & Bus) Aspen Pub.

— SEC Register, Vol. 10. 1993. 147.50 (*0-316-53407-2*, Aspen Law & Bus) Aspen Pub.

— SEC Register, Vol. 11. 1993. 147.50 (*0-316-53408-0*, Aspen Law & Bus) Aspen Pub.

— Supplement to Securities Regulations, 1995. 1995. 385.00 (*0-316-53447-1*, Aspen Law & Bus) Aspen Pub.

— Supplement to Securities Regulations, 1994. 1994. suppl. ed. 350.00 (*0-316-53283-5*, Aspen Law & Bus) Aspen Pub.

Loss, Archie K. Joyce's Visible Art: The Work of Joyce & the Visual Arts. LC 84-2657. (Studies in Modern Literature: No. 38). (Illus.). 140p. reprint ed. pap. 43.40 (*0-8357-1576-0*, 207059500004) Bks Demand.

— Of Human Bondage: Coming of Age in the Novel. (Masterwork Studies: No. 40). 128p. 1989. 23.95 (*0-8057-8067-X*, Twyne); pap. 13.95 (*0-8057-8112-9*, Twyne) Mac Lib Ref.

Loss, Barbara Rosenberg. Say the Word! A Guide to Improving Word Recognition Skills. 1993. teacher ed. 7.95 (*0-88336-154-X*); text, student ed. 14.00 (*0-88336-152-3*); 29.95 (*0-88336-153-1*) New Readers.

Loss, F. J., jt. ed. see Newman, J. C., Jr.

Loss, F. J., jt. ed. see Wessel, E. T.

***Loss, Joyce L.** Trabajos Cerebrales: De Nacimiento a Pre-Kinder (Tutorial) Orig. Title: Brainworks: Birth to Kindergarten. (SPA., Illus.). 26p. 2000. pap. 9.95 (*1-879774-28-3*) ICA Pub Co.

Loss, Louis. Commentary on the Uniform Securities Act. 1977. 45.00 (*0-316-53326-2*, Aspen Law & Bus) Aspen Pub.

— Federal Securities Code: Official Draft, 2 vols., Set. 1160p. 1980. 90.00 (*0-8318-5069-8*, 5069) Am Law Inst.

— Fundamental Set. 2nd ed. 1988. 145.00 (*0-316-53346-7*, Aspen Law & Bus) Aspen Pub.

— Fundamentals of Securities Regulation. 1302p. 1983. student ed. 52.00 (*0-316-53328-9*, Aspen Law & Bus); suppl. ed. 75.00 (*0-316-53332-7*, Aspen Law & Bus) Aspen Pub.

— Fundamentals of Securities Regulation. 2nd ed. 1400p. 1987. 145.00 (*0-316-53335-1*, Aspen Law & Bus) Aspen Pub.

— Fundamentals of Securities Regulation: 1984 Supplement. 100p. (C). 1984. pap., student ed. 12.50 (*0-316-53330-0*, Aspen Law & Bus) Aspen Pub.

— SEC Register, Vol. 9. 3rd ed. 1992. 147.50 (*0-316-53401-3*, Aspen Law & Bus) Aspen Pub.

— Securities Register, Vol. 2. 3rd ed. 1988. 147.50 (*0-316-53338-6*, Aspen Law & Bus) Aspen Pub.

— Securities Register, Vol. 4. 3rd ed. 1989. 147.50 (*0-316-53347-5*, Aspen Law & Bus) Aspen Pub.

— Securities Register, Vol. 5. 3rd ed. 1990. 147.50 (*0-316-53348-3*, Aspen Law & Bus) Aspen Pub.

— Securities Register, Vol. 6. 3rd ed. 1990. 147.50 (*0-316-53360-2*, Aspen Law & Bus) Aspen Pub.

— Securities Register, Vol. 7. 3rd ed. 1991. 147.50 (*0-316-53375-0*, Aspen Law & Bus) Aspen Pub.

— Securities Regulation, 6 vols. 2nd ed. Incl. 1969 Supplement., 3 vols. 2053p. 1969. 325.00 (*0-316-53320-3*, Aspen Law & Bus); 2199p. 1961. write for info. (*0-318-54101-7*) Little.

— Securities Regulation, Vol. 1. 3rd ed. 1988. 147.50 (*0-316-53337-8*, Aspen Law & Bus) Aspen Pub.

— Securities Regulation, Vol. 3. 3rd ed. 1988. 147.50 (*0-316-53339-4*, Aspen Law & Bus) Aspen Pub.

— Securities Regulation Complete Set. 3rd ed. 5740p. 1998. boxed set 1500.00 (*0-316-53343-2*, Aspen Law & Bus) Aspen Pub.

Loss, Louis & Seligman, Joel. Securities Regulation, 3 vols., Set. 3rd ed. 1800p. 1988. 240.00 (*0-318-36123-X*, Aspen Law & Bus) Aspen Pub.

Loss, Louis, et al. Fundamentals of Securities Regulation. 3rd ed. 1408p. 1998. boxed set 179.00 (*0-316-53437-4*, 34374) Aspen Law.

Loss, M. Choque Transcultural.Tr. of Culture Shock. (SPA.). 138p. 1996. 5.99 (*0-7899-0235-4*, 498685) Editorial Unilit.

Loss, Michael, jt. auth. see Lieb, Elliott H.

Loss Prevention Committee of AICHE Safety & Health, ed. Loss Prevention, 1992 Conference Proceedings, Vol. 16. (Technical Manual - Loss Prevention Ser.). 1992. ring bd. 35.00 (*0-8169-0571-1*, T-87) Am Inst Chem Eng.

Loss Prevention Committee of AIChE Safety & Health, et al, eds. LPS, 1997: Proceedings of the 31st Annual Loss Prevention Symposium. (Technical Manual - Loss Prevention Ser.). 744p. 1997. 120.00 (*0-8169-0726-9*, T-102) Am Inst Chem Eng.

Loss Prevention Committee of AIChE'S Safety & Heal & Griffin, M. L., contrib. by. LPS 1998 - Proceedings of the 32nd Annual Loss Prevention Symposium. 618p. 1998. pap. 125.00 (*0-8169-0765-X*, T-105) Am Inst Chem Eng.

Loss, Richard. The Modern Theory of Presidential Power: Alexander Hamilton & the Corwin Thesis, 253. LC 89-27372. (Contributions in Political Science Ser.: No. 253). 192p. 1990. 52.95 (*0-313-26751-0*, LPW/, Greenwood Pr) Greenwood.

Loss, Richard, ed. see Corwin, Edward S.

Loss, Richard, ed. see Von Gentz, Friedrich.

Losse, Bobb. Reading Company Freight Cars Vol. I: Covered Hopper Cars. 56p. (Orig.). 1995. pap. 24.95 (*1-882559-01-0*) C David Pubns.

Losse, Debra N. Sampling the Book: Renaissance Prologues & the French Conteurs. LC 92-55052. 1994. 29.50 (*0-8387-5244-6*) Bucknell U Pr.

Losse, Peter & Griffiths, Michael, eds. Loose on Liquidators: The Role of a Liquidator in a Voluntary Winding-Up. 400p. (C). 1989. 200.00 (*0-7855-6040-8*) St Mut.

Lossef, Steven V. The Interventional Radiology Advisor. 1998. write for info. (*0-683-30221-3*) Lppncott W & W.

Lossiah, Lynn King. Cherokee Little People: The Secrets & Mysteries of the Yunwi Tsunsdi. LC 99-28618. (Illus.). 151p. (YA). (gr. 10 up). 1998. pap. 19.95 (*0-935741-22-4*, Pub. by Cherokee Pubns) Book Pub Co.

Lossing, Benjamin J., ed. Diary of George Washington from 1789-1791. 246p. 1978. reprint ed. 24.95 (*0-87928-102-2*) Corner Hse.

Lossing, Benson J. Biography of James A. Garfield. (Notable American Authors Ser.). 1999. reprint ed. lib. bdg. 125.00 (*0-7812-3863-3*) Rprt Serv.

— Empire State: A Compendious History of the Commonwealth of New York. LC 68-57492. (Illus.). 1968. reprint ed. 25.00 (*0-87152-050-8*) Reprint.

***Lossing, Benson J.** The Hudson: From the Wilderness to the Sea. (Illus.). 472p. 2000. pap. 19.95 (*1-883789-26-5*) Blk Dome Pr.

Lossing, Benson J. The Hudson: From the Wilderness to the Sea. (Illus.). 484p. 1972. 39.50 (*0-912274-22-0*, 1267) Picton Pr.

— Lives of the Signers of the Declaration of Independence. (Illus.). 392p. (YA). (gr. 7-12). 1995. reprint ed. pap. 9.95 (*0-925279-45-5*) Wallbuilders.

L

— A Memorial of Alexander Anderson M. D. (Notable American Authors Ser.). 1999. reprint ed. lib. bdg. 125.00 (*0-7812-3862-5*) Rprt Serv.

— Our Countrymen. . . (Notable American Authors Ser.). 1999. reprint ed. lib. bdg. 125.00 (*0-7812-3859-5*) Rprt Serv.

— Outline History of the Fine Arts. (Notable American Authors Ser.). 1999. reprint ed. lib. bdg. 125.00 (*0-7812-3857-9*) Rprt Serv.

— Pictorial Field-Book of the Civil War, Vol. 1. LC 97-12445. Vol. 1. (Illus.). 722p. 1997. reprint ed. pap. 24.95 (*0-8018-5669-8*) Johns Hopkins.

— Pictorial Field-Book of the Civil War, Vol. 2. LC 97-12445. Vol. 2. (Illus.). 712p. 1997. reprint ed. pap. 24.95 (*0-8018-5671-X*) Johns Hopkins.

— Pictorial Field-Book of the Civil War, Vol. 3. LC 97-12445. Vol. 3. (Illus.). 730p. 1997. reprint ed. pap. 24.95 (*0-8018-5672-8*) Johns Hopkins.

— Pictorial Field Book of the Revolution, 2 vols. 1993. reprint ed. lib. bdg. 150.00 (*0-7812-5112-5*) Rprt Serv.

— Pictorial Field-Book of the Revolution: or Illustrations, by Pen & Pencil, of the History, Biography, Scenery, Relics & Traditions of the War for Independence, 2 Vols. LC 72-85457. (Select Bibliographies Reprint Ser.). 1977. 90.95 (*0-8369-5029-1*) Ayer.

— Pictorial Field Book of the War of 1812. 108p. 1993. reprint ed. lib. bdg. 119.00 (*0-7812-5113-3*) Rprt Serv.

— Pictorial History of the Civil War. (Notable American Authors Ser.). 1999. reprint ed. lib. bdg. 125.00 (*0-7812-3861-7*) Rprt Serv.

— The Romance of the Hudson. (Illus.). 42p. 1997. pap. 10.00 (*0-935796-11-8*) Purple Mnt Pr.

Lossing, Benson J., ed. see Washington, George.

Lossing, Thomas S. My Heart Goes Home: A Hudson Valley Memoir. Hannaford, Peter D., ed. LC 97-14258. (Illus.). 190p. 1997. pap. 17.50 (*0-935796-87-8*) Purple Mnt Pr.

Losskaia, Veronique. Marina Tsvetaeva V Zhizni: Neizdannye Vospominaniia Sovremennikov. LC 88-32032. (Russian Ser.). (Illus.). 332p. 1989. pap. 15.00 (*1-55779-011-6*) Hermitage Pubs.

Lossky, Andrew. Louis XIV & the French Monarchy. LC 93-39313. 312p. (C). 1994. text 59.00 (*0-8135-2081-9*) Rutgers U Pr.

Lossky, Andrew, ed. Seventeenth Century. LC 67-10426. (Orig.). 1967. pap. 14.95 (*0-02-919400-8*) Free Pr.

Lossky, Nicholas O. History of Russian Philosophy. 416p. (Orig.). 1969. reprint ed. 62.50 (*0-8236-2340-8*); reprint ed. pap. 24.95 (*0-8236-8074-6*, 22340) Intl Univs Pr.

Lossky, Vladimir. In the Image & Likeness of God. LC 76-383878. 232p. 1974. pap. 13.95 (*0-913836-13-3*) St Vladimirs.

— The Mystical Theology of the Eastern Church. LC 76-25448. Orig. Title: Essai sur la Theologie Mystique de l'Eglise d'Orient. 252p. 1976. reprint ed. pap. 13.95 (*0-913836-31-1*) St Vladimirs.

— Orthodox Theology: An Introduction. LC 78-1853. 137p. 1978. pap. 9.95 (*0-913836-43-5*) St Vladimirs.

— The Vision of God. 139p. 1963. 9.95 (*0-913836-19-2*) St Vladimirs.

Lossky, Vladimir & Ouspensky, Leonid. The Meaning of Icons. rev. ed. Palmer, G. E. & Kadloubovsky, E., trs. from RUS. LC 82-22979. (Illus.). 224p. (C). 1982. reprint ed. pap. 39.95 (*0-913836-99-0*); reprint ed. text 49.95 (*0-913836-77-X*) St Vladimirs.

Lossl, Josef. Intellectus Gratiae: Die Erkenntnistheoretische und Hermeneutische Dimension der Gnadenlehre, Augustions von Hippo. (Vigiliae Christianae, Supplements Ser.: Vol. 38). 520p. 1997. 171.50 (*90-04-10849-1*) Brill Academic Pubs.

Losson, Christopher. Tennessee's Forgotten Warriors: Frank Cheatham & His Confederate Division. LC 89-33944. (Illus.). 368p. 1990. 32.00 (*0-87049-615-8*) U of Tenn Pr.

Lossy, Rella. Time Pieces. (Illus.). 160p. (Orig.). 1996. 24.95 (*1-57143-059-8*) RDR Bks.

Lostracco, Felix, jt. auth. see Schick, Allen.

Lostracco-Wilkerson. Analyzing Short Stories. 4th ed. LC 98-67719. 304p. (C). 1998. per. 31.95 (*0-7872-4844-4*, 41484401) Kendall-Hunt.

Lostritto, Donald. Jai Alai Wagering to Win: The Complete Book for Jai Alai Wagering. LC 84-73514. (Illus.). 197p. 1985. pap. 14.95 (*0-932227-00-7*) Fair Haven Pr.

Lostutter, Robert. Robert Lostutter: The Watercolors. (Illus.). 38p. 1984. pap. 15.00 (*0-941548-06-6*) Ren Soc U Chi.

Losure, Bob. Five Seconds to Air: Behind the Scenes at CNN. LC 98-66552. (Illus.). 148p. 1998. 24.95 (*1-57736-107-5*) Providence Hse.

Losvacio, jt. auth. see Kile.

Losyk, Bob. Managing a Changing Workforce: Achieving Outstanding Service with Today's Employees. 210p. 1996. 24.95 (*0-9647393-4-8*) Workplace Trends Pub.

Lotan, Rachel A., jt. ed. see Cohen, Elizabeth G.

Lotan, Reuben, jt. ed. see Hong, Waun Ki.

Lotan, Yael, tr. see Rabinyan, Dorit.

Lotan, Yael, tr. see Shaked, Gershon.

Lotasch, H. K., ed. Cryptography & Coding: Proceedings, 5th IMA Conference, Cirencester, UK, December 18-20, 1995. LC 95-47128. (Lecture Notes in Computer Science Ser.: Vol. 1025). 291p. 1995. pap. 49.00 (*3-540-60693-9*) Spr-Verlag.

Lotasch, H. K., ed. see Boyd, Colin.

***Lotchin, Roger W.** Way We Really Were: The Golden State in the Second Great War. LC 99-6190. 264p. 1999. 44.95 (*0-252-02505-9*); pap. text 16.95 (*0-252-06819-X*) U of Ill Pr.

Lotchin, Roger W., ed. The Martial Metropolis: U. S. Cities in War & Peace, 1900-1970. LC 83-21250. 242p. 1984. 59.95 (*0-275-91219-1*, C1219, Praeger Pubs) Greenwood.

***Lote, Christopher J.** Principles of Renal Physiology. 4th ed. LC 99-52097. 1999. write for info. (*0-7923-6074-5*) Kluwer Academic.

Lotfi, Nasser. The Sword in the Sand: A Treatise on the Muslim Tradition & Its Challenge to the Christian World. Kearns, Marsha, ed. 104p. (Orig.). 1991. pap. write for info. (*1-878353-14-4*) Silent Partners.

Loth. Walter Hallstein. Ruppert, Bryan, tr. from GER. LC 97-38846. 260p. 1998. text 69.95 (*0-312-21293-3*) St Martin.

Loth & Wadsworth. Orthopedic Rehabilitation Review. (Illus.). 440p. (C). (gr. 13). 1997. pap. text 46.95 (*0-8151-2526-7*, 31050) Mosby Inc.

Loth, Bernard & Michel, Albert. Dictionnaire de Theologie Catholique, Tables Generales: De Raison a Stolz, 3 vols., Set.Tr. of Dictionary of Catholic Theology. (FRE.). 1970. 995.00 (*0-8288-6519-1*, M-6379) Fr & Eur.

Loth, Calder. Virginia Landmarks of Black History: Sites on the Virginia Landmarks Register & the National Register of Historic Places. LC 94-32817. (Carter G. Woodson Institute Series in Black Studies). (Illus.). 224p. (C). 1995. text 40.00 (*0-8139-1600-3*) U Pr of Va.

Loth, Calder, ed. The Virginia Landmarks Register. 4th ed. LC 98-41522. (Illus.). 601p. 1999. 59.95 (*0-8139-1862-6*) U Pr of Va.

Loth, Clader, ed. Virginia Landmarks of Black History: Sites on the Virginia Landmarks Register & the National Register of Historic Places. LC 94-32817. (Carter G. Woodson Institute Series in Black Studies). (Illus.). 224p. (C). 1995. pap. 18.95 (*0-8139-1601-1*) U Pr of Va.

Loth, David. Swope of G. E. The Story of Gerard Swope & General Electric in American Business. LC 75-41769. (Companies & Men: Business Enterprises in America Ser.). 1976. reprint ed. 33.95 (*0-405-08084-0*) Ayer.

Loth, David G. Chief Justice: John Marshall & the Growth of the Republic. LC 77-94588. (Illus.). 395p. 1970. reprint ed. lib. bdg. 79.50 (*0-8371-2450-6*, LOJM, Greenwood Pr) Greenwood.

Loth, Joshua, ed. Institute on Religion & Psychiatry, Congregation Adath Israel, Boston, 1947. 202p. 1977. 18.95 (*0-8369-2658-7*) Ayer.

Loth, Lipgens, ed. Documents on the History of European Integration Vol. 4: Transnational Organizations of the Political Parties & Pressure Groups in the Struggle for European Union, 1945-1950. (European University Institute Ser.: No. 1-4). xx, 650p. (C). 1990. lib. bdg. 229.25 incl. fiche (*3-11-011965-X*) De Gruyter.

Loth, P. Classifications of Abelian Groups & Pontrjagin Duality. 180p. 1998. text 30.00 (*90-5699-169-8*, ECU38) Gordon & Breach.

Loth, Paul. God Takes Care of Me: 75 Devotions for Families with Young Children. 162p. (J). (gr. k-4). 1995. 7.99 (*0-7852-7988-1*) Tommy Nelson.

— Just Like Jesus. (Illus.). 162p. (J). (gr. 1-4). 1995. 7.99 (*0-7852-7987-3*) Tommy Nelson.

— My First Study Bible: Exploring God's Word on My Own. 528p. (J). (gr. 1-5). 1994. 14.99 (*0-7852-8274-2*) Tommy Nelson.

Loth, Paul E. Teaching Adults with Confidence. 25p. 1984. ring bd. 4.25 (*0-910566-43-7*) Evang Trg Assn.

Loth, Paul J. First Steps: 75 Devotions for Families with Young Children. LC 92-11389. 162p. (J). (gr. 1-4). 1992. 12.99 (*0-8407-9167-4*) Tommy Nelson.

Loth, Richard. How To Profit from Reading Annual Reports. 176p. (Orig.). 1992. pap. 19.95 (*0-7931-0240-5*, 56084801) Dearborn.

Loth, Richard B. The Annual Report Glossary: An Easy-to-Understand Guidebook for Shareholders. LC 89-155320. 174p. 1988. ring bd. 26.00 (*0-924399-00-7*) FIPS Partners Inc.

Loth, Timothy S., ed. Orthopaedic Board Review. LC 92-22708. (Illus.). 648p. (C). (gr. 13). 1992. pap. text 62.00 (*0-8016-2740-0*, 02740) Mosby Inc.

— Orthopedic Boards Review No. II: A Case Study Approach. (Illus.). 480p. (C). (gr. 13). 1995. pap. text 80.00 (*0-8151-5322-8*, 24693) Mosby Inc.

Loth, Wilfried, jt. ed. see Lipgens, Walter.

Lothaire, M., ed. Combinatorics on Words. LC QA164.L67 1983b. (Cambridge Mathematical Library). (Illus.). 255p. (C). 1997. pap. text 29.95 (*0-521-59924-5*) Cambridge U Pr.

Lothane, Zvi. In Defense of Schreber: Soul Murder & Psychiatry. 568p. 1992. text 65.00 (*0-88163-103-5*) Analytic Pr.

Lothario. The Forbidden Apple. 30p. 1994. 7.95 (*0-9636309-1-1*) Lothario.

— A Simplified Existence. Pitts, Teresa A., ed. 17p. (Orig.). 1992. 7.95 (*0-9636309-0-3*, TXU514949) Lothario.

Lotharius, Alana. Numerology: Enrich Your Life Through Numbers: Numerology Can Guide You in Your Search for the Answers, Vol. I. 120p. 1992. text 24.95 (*0-9629732-9-7*) Quintile.

— Numerology Cards: Expand Your Knowledge of Yesterday, Today & Tomorrow. (Illus.). 106p. (Orig.). 1991. 7.95 (*0-9629732-0-3*) Quintile.

— Numerology Cards & Guide. (Illus.). 106p. 1991. 23.95 (*0-9629732-2-X*) Quintile.

Lothe, Jakob. Conrad's Narrative Method. (Illus.). 328p. 1991. pap. 29.95 (*0-19-812255-1*) OUP.

***Lothe, Jakob.** Narrative in Fiction & Film: An Introduction. LC 99-58885. 250p. 2000. write for info. (*0-19-875232-6*) OUP.

Lothe, Jakob, ed. Conrad in Scandinavia. (Social Science Monographs). 271p. 1995. 28.00 (*0-88033-972-1*, Pub. by East Eur Monographs) Col U Pr.

Lothe, Jens, jt. auth. see Hirth, John P.

Lother, H., et al, eds. Vectors As Tools for the Study of Normal & Abnormal Growth & Differentiation. (NATO ASI Series H: Vol. 34). viii, 475p. 1989. 206.95 (*0-387-50419-2*) Spr-Verlag.

Lothers, John E. Design in Structural Steel. 3rd ed. LC 71-160254. (Civil Engineering & Engineering Mechanics Ser.). (Illus.). 1972. 38.95 (*0-685-03824-6*) P-H.

Lothert, Gunter & Burian, Peter K. Canon 540 EZ Flash System. Ohlig, Hayley, tr. from GER. (Magic Lantern Guides Ser.). (Illus.). 176p. (C). 1998. pap. 19.95 (*1-883403-30-8*, H 102, Silver Pixel Pr) Saunders Photo.

Lothian, Andrew. Lothian: Petronius - the Book. 102p. 1988. pap. 24.00 (*0-406-10396-8*, MICHIE) LEXIS Pub.

Lothian, J. M., ed. see Shakespeare, William.

Lothman, Paul E. Biblical Studies Now Confirm It: Ten Errors in the King James New Testament Bible. 250p. 1997. pap. 28.95 (*0-9659907-0-2*) PAL Pub Hse.

Lothner, Susan C. Reflections: Book. (Illus.). 80p. (J). 1995. pap. text 11.95 (*1-887343-60-1*) Angel Works.

— Reflections: Card/Book Set. (Illus.). 80p. (J). 1995. boxed set 29.95 (*1-887343-61-X*) Angel Works.

Lothridge, Kevin L., et al. Instrumental Data for Drug Analysis, 7 Vols., Vol. VI. 2nd ed. (Forensics & Police Science Ser.). 624p. 1996. boxed set 169.95 (*0-8493-8114-2*, 8114) CRC Pr.

Lothrop, A. J., jt. auth. see Fuoco, Joe.

Lothrop, Eaton S., Jr. A Century of Cameras. rev. ed. LC 73-88444. (Illus.). 196p. 1982. pap. 24.00 (*0-87100-163-2*, 2163) Morgan.

Lothrop, Eleanor B. Throw Me a Bone: What Happens When You Marry an Archaeologist. (American Biography Ser.). 234p. 1991. reprint ed. lib. bdg. 69.00 (*0-7812-8251-9*) Rprt Serv.

Lothrop, Gloria R. A Guide to Historical Outings in Southern California. LC 91-73513. 144p. (Orig.). 1991. pap. 9.95 (*0-914421-03-4*) Hist Soc So CA.

Lothrop, Gloria R., jt. auth. see Jensen, Joan M.

Lothrop, Gloria R., jt. ed. see Nunis, Doyce B., Jr.

Lothrop, Hannah. Breastfeeding Naturally: A New Approach for Today's Mother. LC 98-43386.Tr. of Stillbuch. (Illus.). 288p. 1998. pap. 12.95 (*1-55561-131-1*) Fisher Bks.

— Help, Comfort & Hope after Losing Your Baby in Pregnancy. LC 96-48501.Tr. of Gute Hoffnung-Jahes Ende. 228p. 1997. pap. 12.95 (*1-55561-120-6*) Fisher Bks.

Lothrop, S. K. Inca Treasure As Depicted by Spanish Historians. (Frederick Webb Hodge Publications: No. 2). (Illus.). 1964. reprint ed. pap. 5.00 (*0-916561-24-0*) Southwest Mus.

— Metals from the Cenote of Sacrifice. (Harvard University Peabody Museum of Archaeology & Ethnology Papers: Vol. 10, No. 2). 1974. reprint ed. 30.00 (*0-527-01177-0*) Periodicals Srv.

Lothrop, S. K., et al. Indian Notes. fac. ed. (Museum of the American Indian, Heye Foundation Ser.: Vol. 3:3). (Illus.). 76p. (C). 1926. reprint ed. pap. text 8.75 (*1-55567-786-X*) Coyote Press.

Lothrop, Samuel K. Atitlan: An Archaeological Study of Ancient Remains on the Borders of Lake Atitlan, Guatemala. LC 77-11509. (Carnegie Institution of Washington. Publications: No. 444). reprint ed. 39.50 (*0-404-16268-1*) AMS Pr.

— Indians of the Parana Delta, Argentina. LC 76-44751. (Anthropology Ser.). (Illus.). reprint ed. 55.00 (*0-404-15867-6*) AMS Pr.

— The Indians of Tierra Del Fuego. LC 76-44752. reprint ed. 55.00 (*0-404-15868-4*) AMS Pr.

— Pre-Columbian Designs from Panama: 591 Illustrations of Cocle Pottery. LC 75-17177. (Pictorial Archive Ser.). (Illus.). 108p. 1976. pap. 7.95 (*0-486-23232-8*) Dover.

— Tulum: An Archaeological Study of the East Coast of Yucaton. 1976. lib. bdg. 69.95 (*0-8490-2779-9*) Gordon Pr.

— Zacualpa: A Study of Ancient Quiche Artifacts. LC 77-11508. (Carnegie Institution of Washington. Publications: No. 472). 1977. reprint ed. 37.50 (*0-404-16269-X*) AMS Pr.

Lothrop, Samuel K., et al. Essays in Pre-Columbian Art & Archaeology. LC 61-18531. 507p. reprint ed. pap. 157.20 (*0-7837-4116-2*, 205793900011) Bks Demand.

Lothrop, T. J. The Nicholas White Family, 1643-1900. (Illus.). 493p. 1989. reprint ed. pap. 74.00 (*0-8328-1253-6*); reprint ed. lib. bdg. 82.00 (*0-8328-1252-8*) Higginson Bk Co.

Lothrop, Thorton K. William Henry Seward. Morse, John T., Jr., ed. LC 77-128959. (American Statesmen Ser.: No. 27). reprint ed. 45.00 (*0-404-50877-4*) AMS Pr.

Loti. Vers Ispahan. Aelly & Cameron, eds. (Exeter French Texts Ser.: No. 72). (FRE.). 182p. Date not set. pap. text 19.95 (*0-85989-302-2*, Pub. by Univ Exeter Pr) Northwestern U Pr.

Loti, Pierre. Au Maroc. 2nd ed. Voti-Viaud, Pierre P. & Desbrueres, Michel, eds. (Around 1900 Collection). (FRE., Illus.). 304p. 1995. pap. 69.95 (*2-86808-039-1*) Intl Scholars.

— Aziyade. 182p. 1988. pap. 12.95 (*0-7103-0316-5*) Routledge.

— Aziyade. (Folio Ser.: No. 2058). (FRE.). 1990. pap. 12.95 (*2-07-038147-1*) Schoenhof.

— Japan: Madam Chrysanthemum. Ensor, Laura, tr. (Pacific Basin Bks.). (Illus.). 336p. (Orig.). 1985. pap. 19.95 (*0-7103-0138-3*) Routledge.

Loti-Viaud. Pecheur d'Islande. unabridged ed. (FRE.). pap. 5.95 (*2-87714-208-6*, Pub. by Bookking Intl) Distribks Inc.

Loti-Viaud, Pierre P. Le Desert, Vol. 1. 2nd ed. (FRE.). 234p. 1995. pap. 69.95 (*2-86808-023-5*) Intl Scholars.

— Pecheur d'Islande. Desbrueres, Michel, ed. (FRE., Illus.). 1995. pap. 69.95 (*2-86808-071-5*) Intl Scholars.

— Pecheur d'Islande. (Folio Ser.: No. 1982). (FRE.). 338p. 1988. pap. 9.95 (*2-07-038070-X*) Schoenhof.

— Ramuntcho. (Folio Ser.: No. 2120). (FRE.). pap. 9.95 (*2-07-038214-1*) Schoenhof.

— Roman d'Un Spahi. (Folio Ser.: No. 2393). (FRE.). pap. 10.95 (*2-07-038531-0*) Schoenhof.

— Tahiti: The Marriage of Loti. Bell, Clara, tr. 217p. 1987. pap. 19.95 (*0-7103-0231-2*, 02312) Routledge.

Loti-Viaud, Pierre P. & Desbrueres, Michel, eds. La Galilee, Vol. 3. (Around 1900 Collection). (FRE., Illus.). 248p. 1995. pap. 69.95 (*2-86808-037-5*) Intl Scholars.

— L' Inde (Sans les Anglais) 2nd ed. (Around 1900 Collection). (FRE., Illus.). 432p. 1995. pap. 69.95 (*2-86808-033-2*) Intl Scholars.

— Jerusalem. (Around 1900 Collection). (FRE., Illus.). 244p. 1995. pap. 69.95 (*2-86808-036-7*) Intl Scholars.

— Le Livre De la Pitie et De la Mort. (Around 1900 Collection). (FRE., Illus.). 248p. 1995. pap. 69.95 (*0-614-14013-7*) Intl Scholars.

— Mon Frere Yves. (FRE.). 320p. 1995. pap. 69.95 (*2-86808-046-4*) Intl Scholars.

— Vers Ispahan. 2nd ed. (Around 1900 Collection). (FRE., Illus.). 320p. 1995. pap. 69.95 (*2-86808-089-8*) Intl Scholars.

Lotito, Barbara, tr. see Alba, Victor.

Lotito, Michael, jt. auth. see Outwater, Lynn.

Lotka, Alfred J., ed. Analytical Theory of Biological Populations. Smith, David P. & Rossert, Helene, trs. from FRE. (Demographic Methods & Population Analysis Ser.). 200p. (C). 1998. text 49.50 (*0-306-45927-2*, Kluwer Plenum) Kluwer Academic.

Lotka, Alfred J., jt. auth. see Dublin, Louis I.

Lotke, Paul A., ed. Knee Arthroplasty. LC 93-42856. (Master Techniques in Orthopaedic Surgery Ser.). (Illus.). 400p. 1994. text 189.00 (*0-7817-0032-9*) Lppncott W & W.

— Postoperative Infections in Orthopedic Surgery: Prevention & Treatment. 73p. 1992. pap. 35.00 (*0-89203-099-2*) Amer Acad Ortho Surg.

Lotke, Paul A. & Garino, Jonathan P. Revision Total Knee Arthroplasty. rev. ed. LC 98-6927. 400p. 1998. text 189.00 (*0-7817-1024-3*) Lppncott W & W.

Lotman, Iu M. Lektsii Po Struktural'noe Poetike: Vvedenie, Teoriia Stikha. LC 68-10643. (Brown University Slavic Reprint Ser.: 5). 203p. reprint ed. pap. 63.00 (*0-608-16795-9*, 200897900055) Bks Demand.

Lotman, Jeff. Animation Art: The Later Years, 1954-1993. LC 95-68660. (Illus.). 420p. 1995. 125.00 (*0-88740-763-3*) Schiffer.

— Animation Art at Auction: Recent Years. LC 98-11598. (Illus.). 1998. 49.95 (*0-7643-0411-9*) Schiffer.

Lotman, Jeff & Smith, Jonathan. Animation Art: The Later Years, 1954-1993. LC 96-27005. (Illus.). 420p. 1996. 125.00 (*0-88740-979-2*) Schiffer.

Lotman, Ju M. & Uspenskij, B. A. Semiotics of Russian Culture. Shukman, Ann, ed. (Michigan Slavic Contributions Ser.: No. 11). 356p. 1984. pap. 15.00 (*0-930042-56-5*) Mich Slavic Pubns.

Lotman, Yuri. Universe of the Mind: A Semiotic Theory of Culture. Shukman, Ann, tr. LC 90-39870. (Second World Ser.). 300p. 1991. 45.00 (*0-253-33608-2*) Ind U Pr.

***Lotney, Karlyn.** The Ultimate Guide to Strap-On Sex: A Complete Resource for Women & Men. (Illus.). 160p. 1999. pap. 14.95 (*1-57344-085-X*) Cleis Pr.

Lotnik, Waledman. Nine Lives: Ethnic Conflict in the Polish-ukrainian Borderlands. 1999. pap. text 14.95 (*1-897959-40-0*) Serif.

Lotocki, Borys. Borys' Odyssey. Chang, M., ed. (Illus.). 1993. 23.95 (*0-938103-03-2*) ZZYZX Pub.

Lotosky, V. A. Evaluation of Adaptive Control Strategies in Industrial Applications. (IFAC Workshop Ser.: Vol. 9007). 392p. 1990. 197.75 (*0-08-037868-4*, Pergamon Pr) Elsevier.

***Lotowycz, Randall J.** In the Meanwhile. LC 99-91012. (Illus.). 280p. (YA). 2000. pap. 9.00 (*0-9674521-0-4*) Third Opt.

Lotring, Alfred H. Reason & Nature: A Taxonomy of the Abstract & Natural Sciences. McKinney, Aubrey R., ed. (Adventures in Science Ser.). (Illus.). 208p. 1989. 24.95 (*0-914587-06-4*) Helix Pr.

***Lotringer, Sylvere.** French Theory in America. 2000. 80.00 (*0-415-92536-3*); pap. text. write for info. (*0-415-92537-1*) Routledge.

***Lotringer, Sylvere, ed.** More & Less. 261p. 1999. pap. 14.00 (*1-57027-091-0*, Pub. by Autonomedia) SPD-Small Pr Dist.

Lotringer, Sylvere, jt. auth. see Virilio, Paul.

Lotringer, Sylvere, ed. see Burroughs, William.

Lotringer, Sylvere, ed. see Foucault, Michel.

Lotringer, Sylvere, ed. see Guattari, Felix.

Lotringer, Sylvere, ed. see Mueller, Heiner.

Lotschert, W. Palmen (Palms) 2nd rev. ed. (GER., Illus.). 159p. 1995. 58.00 (*3-8001-6532-5*, Pub. by Eugen Ulmer) Balogh.

Lotschert, Wilhelm & Beese, Gerhard. Tropical Plants. (Illus.). 256p. (J). 1984. 27.50 (*0-00-219112-1*, Pub. by HarpC) Trafalgar.

Lotschert, William & Beese, Gerhard. The Collins Guide to Tropical Plants. (Illus.). 256p. 1989. 24.95 (*0-685-44551-8*) Viking Penguin.

Lotspeich, Henry C. Classical Mythology in the Poetry of Edmund Spenser. LC 65-28856. (Princeton Studies in English: No. 9). 126p. 1965. reprint ed. 50.00 (*0-87752-064-X*) Gordian.

Lotspeich-Steininger, Cheryl A., et al. Clinical Hematology: Principles, Procedures & Correlations. LC 65-9558. (Illus.). 720p. 1991. 49.95 (*0-397-50790-9*, Lippnctt) Lppncott W & W.

Lott. Applied Econometrics. 2nd ed. (C). 1995. pap. text, teacher ed. 7.75 (*0-03-010091-7*) Harcourt Coll Pubs.

— Pediatric Pharmacopoeia. 1999. pap. text 15.00 (*0-7020-1833-3*) Harcourt.

Lott, Arnold S. Brave Ship, Brave Men. (Bluejacket Paperback Ser.). 288p. 1994. pap. 17.95 (*1-55750-523-3*) Naval Inst Pr.

An Asterisk (*) at the beginning of an entry indicates that the title is appearing for the first time.

L

Lott, Arnold S. & Sumrall, Robert F. Pearl Harbor Attack. (Illus.). 32p. 1992. reprint ed. pap. 2.95 (*0-9631388-1-2*) AZ Mem Mus.
Lott, Arnold S. & Sumrall, Robert F., eds. Ships Data 1. (Illus.). 32p. 1982. 3.00 (*0-915268-07-8*) USS North Car.
Lott, Bernard, ed. see Shakespeare, William.
Lott, Bernice. Women's Lives: Themes & Variations in Gender Learning. LC 86-26886. 367p. (C). 1987. mass mkt. 26.75 (*0-534-07440-5*) Brooks-Cole.
Lott, Bernice & Maluso, Diane, eds. The Social Psychology of Interpersonal Discrimination. LC 95-2851. 232p. 1995. lib. bdg. 32.00 (*1-57230-021-3*) Guilford Pubns.
Lott, Bernice & Reilly, Mary A., eds. Combating Sexual Harassment in Higher Education. (Excellence in the Academy Ser.). 1995. 21.95 (*0-8106-2678-0*) NEA.
Lott, Bob. Don't Be Afraid to Ask!! How to Date a Beautiful Woman. Colletti, Al, ed. 90p. 1998. mass mkt. 9.95 (*0-9663635-1-5*) DoveCo Pubns.
— Don't Be Afraid to Ask!! How to Date a Beautiful Woman. rev. ed. Colletti, Al, ed. 90p. 1998. reprint ed. 19.95 (*0-9663635-0-7*) DoveCo Pubns.
***Lott, Bret.** A Dream of Old Leaves. LC PS3562.O784D74. 138p. 1999. pap. 10.00 (*0-671-03821-4*, WSP) PB.
Lott, Bret. A Dream of Old Leaves. Rosenman, Jane, ed. LC 90-12620. 144p. 1991. reprint ed. pap. 6.95 (*0-671-69344-1*, WSP) PB.
— Fathers, Sons & Brothers: The Men in My Family. LC 96-45497. 208p. (C). 1997. 22.00 (*0-15-100262-2*) Harcourt.
***Lott, Bret.** Fathers, Sons & Brothers: The Men in My Family. (Illus.). 208p. 2000. reprint ed. per. 12.95 (*0-671-04176-2*, WSP) PB.
Lott, Bret. The Hunt Club. LC PS3562.O784H8 . 351p. 1999. mass mkt. 5.99 (*0-06-101390-0*) HarpC.
— Jewel. LC PS3562.O784J49. 1999. 23.00 (*0-671-03823-0*, WSP); per. 14.00 (*0-671-03818-4*, WSP) PB.
— Jewel. 1999. reprint ed. per. 7.99 (*0-671-04257-2*) PB.
— Jewel: A Novel LC 99-10947. 1950. 30.00 (*0-7838-8591-1*, G K Hall & Co) Mac Lib Ref.
— The Man Who Owned Vermont. LC PS3562.O784M3. 224p. 1988. mass mkt. 5.95 (*0-671-64587-0*, WSP) PB.
— The Man Who Owned Vermont. LC PS3562.O784M3. 231p. 1999. pap. 12.00 (*0-671-03820-6*) PB.
***Lott, Bret.** My Story, My Song: A Novel. 2001. 24.00 (*0-375-50377-3*) Random.
— Reed's Beach. LC PS3562.O784R43 . 1999. pap. 14.00 (*0-671-03819-2*) PB.
Lott, Bret. Reed's Beach. Rosenman, Jane, ed. LC PS3562.O784R43 . 352p. 1994. reprint ed. pap. 10.00 (*0-671-79239-3*, WSP) PB.
— A Stranger's House. LC PS3562.O784S77. 272p. 1990. pap. 7.95 (*0-671-68328-4*, WSP) PB.
— A Stranger's House. LC PS3562.O784S77. 256p. 1999. pap. 12.00 (*0-671-03822-2*) PB.
Lott, Bret, abr. The Hunt Club. 256p. 1999. pap. 13.00 (*0-06-097770-1*) HarpC.
Lott, Catherine S. How To Land a Better Job. 1993. pap. 7.95 (*0-8442-6675-2*, VGM Career) NTC Contemp Pub Co.
Lott, Catherine S. & Lott, Oscar C. How to Land a Better Job. 3rd ed. LC 93-46211. (Illus.). 144p. 1994. pap. 8.95 (*0-8442-4174-1*, VGM Career) NTC Contemp Pub Co.
Lott, Clarinda H. Domestic Animals. (Fanfare Ser.). 1982. pap. 2.00 (*0-932616-10-0*) Brick Hse Bks.
Lott, Clarinda H., jt. auth. see De Ford, Sara.
Lott, Clarinda H., jt. auth. see DeFord, Sara.
Lott, Clarinda H., ed. see Dove, Jennifer.
Lott, Clarinda H., ed. see Dowell, Lynne.
Lott, Clarinda H., ed. see Menaker, Donald.
Lott, Clarinda H., ed. see Sherrill, Jan M.
Lott, Clarinda H., ed. see Wallace, Laura.
Lott, Connerly. Forrest General Medical Center. 2nd ed. 208p. 1997. text, teacher ed. 18.00 (*0-8273-8181-6*) Delmar.
— Forrest General Medical Center: Advanced Medical Term & Transcript Course. 2nd ed. 240p. (C). 1997. pap. 50.95 (*0-8273-8179-4*) Delmar.
Lott, D. J., et al, eds. Studies in Osteoarthrosis: Pathogensis, Intervention, Assessment. LC 86-23428. 136p. 1987. 452.50 (*0-471-91336-7*) Wiley.
Lott, Darren. Street Luge Survival Guide. LC 97-95372. (Illus.). 224p. 1998. pap. 14.95 (*0-9662563-7-9*) Gravity Pub CA.
Lott, Davis N. Presidents Speak: The Inaugural Addresses of the American Presidents, from Washinton to Clinton. 434p. 1995. 35.00 (*0-8050-3305-X*) H Holt & Co.
***Lott, Deborah A.** In Session: The Bond Between Women & Their Therapists. Cohen, Marie, ed. 288p. 2000. pap. text 14.95 (*0-7167-4025-7*) W H Freeman.
Lott, Deborah A. & Cohen, Marie, eds. In Session: The Bond Between Women & Their Therapists. LC 98-52301. 288p. 1999. text 23.95 (*0-7167-3562-8*) W H Freeman.
Lott, Deborah A., jt. ed. see Hadorn, David C.
Lott, Donna T., et al. There's Someplace Like Home: Developing an Adult Day Care Center in Your Church. (Older Adult Issues Ser.). 50p. 1999. pap. 4.50 (*0-664-50086-2*) Geneva Press.
Lott, Eric. Love & Theft: Blackface Minstrelsy & the American Working Class. (Race & American Culture Ser.). (Illus.). 328p. 1995. pap. text 18.95 (*0-19-509641-X*) OUP.
Lott, James E. Practical Protocol: A Guide to International Courtesies. LC 73-75393. (Illus.). 208p. reprint ed. pap. 64.50 (*0-608-18169-2*, 203287500081) Bks Demand.
***Lott, John.** Diffeomorphisms & Noncommutative Analytic Torsion LC 99-27217. (Memoirs Ser.). 1999. write for info. (*0-8218-1189-4*) Am Math.
— Individual Reputations. 1996. 26.95 (*0-226-49357-1*) U Ch Pr.
Lott, John A., ed. Clinical Pathology of Pancreatic Disorders. LC 97-14956. (Pathology & Laboratory Medicine Ser.: Vol. 2). (Illus.). 232p. 1997. 125.00 (*0-89603-475-5*) Humana.
Lott, John L. Uncertainty & Economic Evolution: Essays in Honour of Armen Alchian. LC 97-17351. 224p. (C). 1997. 80.00 (*0-415-15166-X*) Routledge.
Lott, John R., Jr. Are Predatory Commitments Credible? Who Should the Courts Believe? LC 98-32261. 173p. 1999. 29.00 (*0-226-49355-5*) U Ch Pr.
— More Guns, Less Crime: Understanding Crime & Gun Control Laws. LC 97-51481. (Illus.). 232p. 1998. 23.00 (*0-226-49363-6*) U Ch Pr.
***Lott, John R., Jr.** More Guns, Less Crime: Understanding Crime & Gun Control Laws. 2nd ed. LC 00-20724. (Studies in Law & Economics). (Illus.). 280p. 1999. pap. 12.00 (*0-226-49364-4*) U Ch Pr.
Lott, Johnny W., jt. auth. see Billstein, Richard.
Lott, Joyce. A Teacher's Stories: Reflections on High School Writers. LC 93-43816. 168p. (J). 1994. pap. text 20.00 (*0-86709-331-5*, 0331, Pub. by Boynton Cook Pubs) Heinemann.
Lott, Juanita T. Asian Americans: From Racial Category to Multiple Identities. LC 98-8882. (Critical Perspectives on Asian Pacific Americans Ser.). 115p. 1998. 49.00 (*0-7619-9172-7*); pap. 17.95 (*0-7619-9173-5*) AltaMira Pr.
Lott, Lynn. Chores Without Wars. LC 97-35409. 208p. 1997. per. 12.00 (*0-7615-1252-7*) Prima Pub.
Lott, Lynn & Intner, Riki. The Family That Works Together: Turning Family Chores from Drudgery to Fun. LC 93-48112. (Illus.). 208p. 1994. pap. 9.95 (*1-55958-523-4*) Prima Pub.
***Lott, Lynn, et al.** Do-It-Yourself Therapy: How to Think, Feel & Act Like a New Person in Just 8 Weeks. LC 99-25215. 192p. 1999. pap. 14.99 (*1-56414-409-7*) Career Pr Inc.
Lott, Lynn, et al. Positive Discipline A-Z: From Toddlers to Teens - 1001 Solutions to Everyday Parenting Problems. 2nd expanded rev. ed. LC 98-51638. 384p. 1999. pap. 16.95 (*0-7615-1470-8*) Prima Pub.
Lott, Lynn, jt. auth. see Nelsen, Jane.
Lott, Lynn, jt. auth. see Nelson, Jane.
Lott, Oscar C., jt. auth. see Lott, Catherine S.
***Lott, Petra.** Gesture & Aphasia. LC 99-50313. vii, 200p. (C). 1999. pap. text 36.95 (*0-8204-4616-5*) P Lang Pubng.
Lott, Richard W. Auditing the Data Processing Function. LC 79-54841. 222p. reprint ed. pap. 68.90 (*0-8357-5874-5*, 202358800033) Bks Demand.
Lott, Rick. The Apple Pickers' Children. (Texas Review Southern & Southwestern Poets Breakthrough Ser.). 64p. 1993. pap. 8.00 (*1-881515-02-8*) TX Review Pr.
Lott, Robert E. Siglo de Oro Tradition & Modern Adolescent Psychology in Pepita Jimenez. LC 75-172751. (Catholic University of America. Studies in Romance Languages & Literatures: No. 58). reprint ed. 42.50 (*0-404-50358-6*) AMS Pr.
***Lott, Roland D., contrib. by.** The Castle in the Attic. 2000. 19.95 (*0-533-13428-5*) Vantage.
Lott, Ronnie. The Official Book of Super Bowl XXIX: The Golden State of Football. Hyman, Laurence J. & Rochmis, Jon, eds. LC 95-60136. (Official Books of the Super Bowl: No. 1). (Illus.). 144p. (Orig.). 1995. pap. 19.95 (*0-942627-25-3*) Woodford Pubng.
Lott, Sonia, jt. auth. see Linardakis, Nikos M.
Lott, Tommy, ed. Subjugation & Bondage: Critical Essays on Slavery & Social Philosophy. LC 97-35950. 288p. 1998. 68.00 (*0-8476-8777-5*); pap. 19.95 (*0-8476-8778-3*) Rowman.
Lott, Tommy L. The Invention of Race: Black Culture & the Politics of Representation. LC 98-26086. 288p. 1999. 49.95 (*0-631-21018-0*); pap. 19.95 (*0-631-21019-9*) Blackwell Pubs.
Lott, Tommy Lee, jt. ed. see Bernasconi, Robert.
Lott, Wanda, jt. auth. see Conerly, Donna.
Lott, William F. & Ray, Subhash C. Applied Econometrics. 450p. (C). 1992. pap. text 85.00 (*0-15-502907-X*) Dryden Pr.
***Lotta, Chuck.** Fast & Fun Mental Math: 250 Quick Quizzes to Sharpen Math Skills Every Day of the School Year. (Illus.). 80p. (J). 2000. pap. 11.95 (*0-439-13848-5*) Scholastic Inc.
Lotta, Raymond, afterword by. Maoist Economics & the Revolutionary Road to Communism: The Shanghai Textbook. LC 94-94131. 346p. (Orig.). (C). 1994. pap. text 15.00 (*0-916650-41-3*) Banner Pr Intl.
Lotta, Raymond, ed. And Mao Makes Five: Mao Tsetung's Last Great Battle. LC 78-70431. (Illus.). 1978. 15.00 (*0-916650-09-X*); pap. 5.95 (*0-916650-08-1*) Banner Pr Intl.
Lotta, Raymond & Shannon, Frank. America in Decline: An Analysis of the Developments Toward War & Revolution, in the U. S. & Worldwide in the 1980's, Vol 1. LC 83-22294. (Illus.). 278p. (Orig.). (C). 1984. 21.95 (*0-916650-12-X*); pap. 11.95 (*0-916650-13-8*) Banner Pr Intl.
Lotta, Raymond & Szymanski, Albert. The Soviet Union Pt. I: Socialist or Social-Imperialist? LC 83-17746. 90p. (Orig.). 1983. pap. 4.95 (*0-89851-067-8*) RCP Pubns.
Lotte, Fernand. Dictionnaire Biographique des Personnages Fictifs de la Comedie Humaine: Dictionnaire des Personnages Fictifs Anonymes. (FRE.). 96p. 1952. 18.95 (*0-7859-5129-6*) Fr & Eur.
Lotter, Andre. Palaeoekologische und Palaeolimnologische Studie des Rotsees Bei Luzern: Pollen-, Grossrest-, Diatomeen- und Sedimentanalytische Untersuchungen. (Dissertationes Botanicae Ser.: Band 124). (GER., Illus.). 187p. 1988. 65.00 (*3-443-64036-2*, Pub. by Gebruder Borntraeger) Balogh.
Lotter, Donald W. Earthscore: Your Personal Environmental Audit & Guide. (Illus.). 48p. (Orig.). (YA). (gr. 10 up). 1996. pap. 4.50 (*0-9629069-6-4*) Morn Sun Pr.
Lotter, Maria-Sibylla. Die Metaphysische Kritik des Subjekts Bei A. N. Whitehead. (Studien und Materialien Zur Geschichte der Philosophie: Band 43). (GER.). viii, 270p. 1996. write for info. (*3-487-10155-6*) G Olms Pubs.
Lotterhand, Jason C. Thursday Night Tarot. 379p. 1989. pap. 14.95 (*0-87877-147-6*) Newcastle Pub.
Lotterman, Andrew. Specific Techniques for the Psychotherapy of Schizophrenic Patients. 172p. 1996. 35.00 (*0-8236-6130-X*) Intl Univs Pr.
Lotters, Stefan. The Neotropical Toad Genus Atelopus: Checklist - Biology - Distribution. (Illus.). 143p. (Orig.). 1996. pap. 39.95 (*3-929449-02-1*) Serpents Tale.
Lottery Player's Magazine Staff, ed. Almanac & Traveler's Guide to Lotteries. (LOMAP Ser.: Vol. 2). (Illus.). 250p. 1987. 14.95 (*0-936918-05-5*) Intergalactic NJ.
— It Couldn't Happen to a Nicer Fella' Lottery & Casino Winners We Have Known. 96p. 1988. pap. 9.95 (*0-936918-11-X*) Intergalactic NJ.
Lotti, Antonio. Antonio Lotti: Duetti, Terzetti, e Madrigali a Plu Vocl. Day, Thomas, ed. (Recent Researches in Music of the Baroque Era Ser.: Vol. RRB44-45). (Illus.). xix, 200p. 1985. pap. 65.00 (*0-89579-191-9*, RRB44-45) A-R Eds.
Lotti, Sandra, jt. auth. see Bianchi, Anne.
Lotti, T. M., et al, eds. Oral Diseases: Textbook & Atlas. LC 98-26502. (Illus.). 400p. 1998. 219.00 (*3-540-62416-3*) Spr-Verlag.
Lotti, T. M., jt. auth. see Katsambast, A. D.
Lottich, Kenneth, jt. auth. see Roucek, Joseph S.
Lottinville, Savoie. The Rhetoric of History. LC 75-19418. 272p. 1976. pap. 14.95 (*0-8061-2190-4*) U of Okla Pr.
Lottinville, Savoie, jt. auth. see Nuttall, Thomas.
Lottinville, Savoie, ed. see Hyde, George E.
Lottman, Herbert. Albert Camus - A Biography. (Illus.). 848p. 1996. reprint ed. pap. 24.95 (*3-927258-06-7*) Gingko Press.
— Albert Camus in New York. 60p. (Orig.). (C). 1997. pap. 4.95 (*3-927258-40-7*) Gingko Press.
— Left Bank: Writers, Artists, & Politics from the Popular Front to the Cold War. LC 98-8786. 1998. pap. 17.00 (*0-226-49368-7*) U Ch Pr.
Lottman, Herbert R. Flaubert: A Biography. 1989. 24.95 (*0-316-53342-4*) Little.
Lottmann, Herbert, ed. see De l'Ecotais, Emmanuelle.
Lotto, Edward E., jt. auth. see Jenseth, Richard.
Lotto, Jill C., jt. auth. see Rosaw, Jerome M.
Lotto, Linda S. Building Basic Skills: Results from Vocational Education. 41p. 1983. 4.25 (*0-318-22048-2*, RD237) Ctr Educ Trng Employ.
Lotto, Lorenzo, jt. auth. see Humfrey, Peter.
Lottridge, Celia Barker. Music for the Tsar of the Sea. (Illus.). (J). (gr. 1-4). 1998. 16.95 (*0-88899-328-5*, Pub. by Gro1undwood-Douglas) Publishers Group.
— One Watermelon Seed. (J). 1986. 13.15 (*0-606-04765-4*, Pub. by Turtleback) Demco.
— One Watermelon Seed. (Illus.). 24p. (J). (ps up). 1990. reprint ed. pap. 8.95 (*0-19-540735-0*) OUP.
— Something Might Be Hiding. (Illus.). 24p. (J). (ps-2). 1996. text 14.95 (*0-88899-176-2*) Publishers Group.
— Ten Small Tales. LC 92-2878. (Illus.). 64p. (J). (gr. k-4). 1994. mass mkt. 15.95 (*0-689-50568-X*) McElderry Bks.
— Ticket to Canada. LC 95-10697. (Illus.). 144p. (J). (gr. 1-4). 1995. 11.95 (*0-382-39144-6*) Silver Burdett Pr.
— Ticket to Canada. LC 95-10697. (Illus.). 144p. (YA). (gr. 5 up). 1995. pap. 7.95 (*0-382-39146-2*); lib. bdg. 13.95 (*0-382-39145-4*) Silver Burdett Pr.
— The Wind Wagon. LC 94-39398. (Illus.). (J). (gr. 4-6). 1994. 10.95 (*0-382-24928-3*); pap. 4.95 (*0-382-24929-1*); lib. bdg. 12.95 (*0-382-24927-5*) Silver Burdett Pr.
— Wings to Fly. 216p. (J). (gr. 3-7). 1999. pap. 5.95 (*0-88899-346-3*, Pub. by Gro1undwood-Douglas) Publishers Group.
Lottridge, Celia Barker, frwd. Mother Goose: A Sampler. 64p. (J). (gr. k-1). 1996. 18.95 (*0-88899-260-2*) Publishers Group.
— Nursery Rhymes, North of the Border. (Illus.). 63p. (J). (ps-1). 1996. 18.95 (*0-88899-213-0*) Publishers Group.
Lottridge, Mike. Teach Yourself Word 6 for Windows. 1995. pap. 24.95 incl. disk (*1-55828-324-2*, MIS Pr) IDG Bks.
Lotts, Scott J. & Barnes-Rothmeier, Vicki. Golf for Beginners: The Official Survival Guide. 100p. 1994. pap. 10.99 (*0-9645700-0-9*) Mulligans Pr.
Lottspeich, F., et al, eds. High Performance Liquid Chromatography in Protein & Peptide Chemistry. (Illus.). 1982. 123.10 (*3-11-008542-9*) De Gruyter.
Lotu, Denize. Father & Son. LC 91-29413. 1996. 11.15 (*0-606-09261-7*, Pub. by Turtleback) Demco.
Lotus, Amber. Meditation Journal. 112p. 1998. spiral bd. 8.95 (*0-945798-27-X*) Amber Lotus.
— Nature Journal. 112p. 1990. pap. 11.95 (*0-945798-30-X*) Amber Lotus.
Lotus Books Staff. The Lotus Guide to 1-2-3 Advanced MACRO Commands: Programming Techniques. LC 86-32213. 1987. pap. 23.95 (*0-201-16822-7*) Addison-Wesley.
Lotus Development Corporation Staff. LOTUS GD LRNG 123 REL2.2. 1989. pap. 22.95 (*0-201-52320-5*) Addison-Wesley.
— The Lotus Guide to Learning 1-2-3 Macros. 1986. pap. text 19.18 (*0-201-16821-9*) Addison-Wesley.
— Lotus Guide to Learning Symphony: Revised for Release 2.0. 3rd rev. ed. (Lotus Bks.). 1988. pap. 22.95 (*0-201-16699-2*) Addison-Wesley.
— Lotus Worksheet File Formats: Essential Data File Facts about 1-2-3-, Symphony, & Jazz. write for info. (*0-318-60208-3*) Addison-Wesley.
Lotus Staff. Passport, Lotus Approach. (NO - Novell/Wordperfect Ser.). 1995. 26.95 (*0-538-65269-1*) S-W Pub.
— Passport Lotus Approach Maintenance. (NO - Novell/Wordperfect Ser.). 1995. 15.95 (*0-538-65270-5*) S-W Pub.
— Passport Lotus Notes Client Maintenance. (NO - Novell/Wordperfect Ser.). 1995. 31.95 (*0-538-65268-3*) S-W Pub.
— Worksheet File Formats. 1986. pap. 19.95 (*0-201-16824-3*) Addison-Wesley.
Lotz, Anne G. Daily Light Devotional. 1998. 19.97 (*0-8499-5462-2*); 19.97 (*0-8499-5464-9*); 19.97 (*0-8499-5465-7*) Word Pub.
***Lotz, Anne G.** Daily Light Devotional. 1998. 19.97 (*0-8499-5463-0*) Word Pub.
Lotz, Anne G. The Glorious Dawn of God's Story. LC 97-28113. 1997. 17.99 (*0-8499-1531-7*) Word Pub.
— The Glorious Dawn of God's Story: Finding Meaning for Your Life in Genesis. 1997. 15.99 incl. audio (*0-8499-6280-3*) Word Pub.
— The Vision of His Glory. LC 98-114001. 304p. 1997. pap. 12.99 (*0-8499-4016-8*) Word Pub.
— Vision of His Glory. 1996. audio 15.99 (*0-8499-6209-9*) Word Pub.
Lotz, Anne G., jt. auth. see Bagster, Samuel.
Lotz, Anne Graham. Daily Light Devotional. 1998. 24.99 (*0-8499-5448-7*) Word Pub.
— Daily Light Devotional. 1998. 24.99 (*0-8499-5407-X*) Word Pub.
***Lotz, Anne Graham.** Daily Light Devotional Saddlebrown. 1998. 24.99 (*0-8499-5446-0*) Word Pub.
Lotz, Anne Graham. Daily Light Journal. 384p. 1999. 27.99 (*0-8499-5565-3*) Word Pub.
***Lotz, Anne Graham.** Daily Light Journal: Morning Edition. (Illus.). 1999. 27.99 (*0-8499-5562-9*); 27.99 (*0-8499-5563-7*) J Countryman.
— Daily Light Journal: Morning Edition. 1999. 27.99 (*0-8499-5564-5*) Tommy Nelson.
Lotz, Anne Graham. God's Story, 1. 1999. pap. text 12.99 (*0-8499-3758-2*) Word Pub.
***Lotz, Anne Graham.** Just Give Me Jesus, 1. 300p. 2000. 19.99 (*0-8499-1646-1*) J Countryman.
— La Vision de su Gloria: Encontrando Esperanza Mediante la Revelacion de Jesucristo. (SPA.). 360p. 2000. pap. text 11.99 (*0-8254-1402-4*) Kregel.
— The Vision of His Glory. 128p. 1999. pap. text, wbk. ed. 9.95 (*0-7673-9116-0*, LifeWy Press) LifeWay Christian.
Lotz, Arthur. Das Feuerwerk. 178p. write for info. (*3-283-00010-7*) G Olms Pubs.
Lotz, Jan, jt. auth. see Hawthorne, Luanda.
Lotz, John. Script, Grammar, & the Hungarian Writing System. LC 74-167265. (Hungarian-English Contrastive Linguistics Project, Working Papers: No. 2). 61p. reprint ed. pap. 30.00 (*0-8357-3344-0*, 203957400013) Bks Demand.
— Uralic & Altaic Program of the American Council of Learned Societies 1959-1965. LC 66-64408. (Uralic & Altaic Ser.: Vol. 63). (Orig.). 1966. pap. text. write for info. (*0-87750-088-6*) Curzon Pr Ltd.
Lotz, Karen E. Can't Sit Still. 40p. (J). 1998. pap. 5.99 (*0-14-056361-X*) Viking Penguin.
— Snowsong Whistling. 1997. 10.19 (*0-606-13782-3*, Pub. by Turtleback) Demco.
Lotz, Philip H., ed. Distinguished American Jews. LC 78-111842. (Essay Index Reprint Ser.). 1977. 17.95 (*0-8369-1671-9*) Ayer.
— Founders of Christian Movements. LC 71-111843. (Essay Index Reprint Ser.). 1977. 19.95 (*0-8369-1672-7*) Ayer.
— Rising above Color. LC 78-152190. (Essay Index Reprints - Creative Personalities Ser.: Vol. 5). 1977. reprint ed. 15.95 (*0-8369-2605-6*) Ayer.
— Unused Alibis, Creative Personalities, Vol. 7. LC 79-126322. (Biography Index Reprint Ser.). 1977. 17.95 (*0-8369-8028-X*) Ayer.
Lotz, Rainer E., jt. auth. see Bergmeier, H. J. P.
Lotz, Ranier E., jt. ed. see Heier, Uli.
Lotz, Robert, ed. Inter-Noise '86: Proceedings of the International Conference on Noise Control, Massachusetts Institute of Technology, Cambridge, MA, July 21-23, 1986, 2 vols., Vols. 1 & 2. (Inter-Noise Ser.). 1986. 75.00 (*0-931784-15-8*) Noise Control.
— Noise-Con, '83: Proceedings - National Conference on Noise Control Engineering 1983. 512p. 1983. 42.00 (*0-931784-08-5*) Noise Control.
Lotz, Roy, et al. Juvenile Delinquency & Juvenile Justice. (C). 1985. pap. text, teacher ed. 13.50 (*0-07-554754-6*) McGraw.
Lotz, Roy E. Crime & the American Press. LC 91-4623. (Praeger Series in Political Communication). 192p. 1991. 49.95 (*0-275-94012-8*, C4012, Praeger Pubs) Greenwood.
Lotz, Walther. Die Deutsche Staatsfinanz-Wirtschaft im Kriege. (Wirtschafts-Und Sozialgeschichte des Weltkrieges (Osterreichische Und Ungarische Serie)). (GER.). 1927. 100.00 (*0-317-27438-4*) Elliots Bks.
Lotz, Wolfgang. Architecture in Italy, 1500-1600. LC 95-9124. (Pelican History of Art Ser.). 1995. pap. 30.00 (*0-300-06469-1*) Yale U Pr.
— Architecture in Italy, 1500-1600. LC 95-9124. (Pelican History of Art Ser.). (Illus.). 1995. 50.00 (*0-300-06468-3*) Yale U Pr.
Lotze, Barbara, ed. Making Contributions: An Historical Overview of Women's Roles in Physics. (Occasional Publications). 132p. 1984. per. 12.50 (*0-917853-09-1*, OP-52) Am Assn Physics.
Lotze, Detlef & Hample, Franz. Metary Eleutheron Kai Doulon & Die Lakesdaemonischen Perickon, 2 vols. Vlastos, Gregory, ed. LC 78-14616. (Morals & Law in Ancient Greece Ser.). 1979. reprint ed. lib. bdg. 17.95 (*0-405-11591-1*) Ayer.

An Asterisk (*) at the beginning of an entry indicates that the title is appearing for the first time.

Lotze, F. Allgemein-Geologischer, Band I. (Steinsalz und Kalisalze Ser.). x, 466p. 1957. 39.00 (*3-443-39052-8*, Pub. by Gebruder Borntraeger) Balogh.

Lotze, Michael T. Surgical Treatment of Metastatic Cancer. LC 97-5524. 650p. 1997. text 146.00 (*0-397-51474-3*) Lppncott W & W.

Lotze, Michael T. & Thomson, Angus, eds. Denddritic Cells: Biology & Clinical Applications. LC 98-86759. (Illus.). 700p. 1998. boxed set 149.95 (*0-12-455860-7*) Acad Pr.

Lotze, Rudolf Hermann. Microcosmus: An Essay Concerning Man & His Relation to the World, 2 vols, Set. Hamilton, Elizabeth & Jones, E. E., trs. LC 76-169769. (Select Bibliographies Reprint Ser.). 1977. reprint ed. 84.95 (*0-8369-5989-2*) Ayer.

— Outlines of Aesthetics. 1973. 59.95 (*0-8490-0790-9*) Gordon Pr.

Lotze, Rudolf Hermann. Outlines of Psychology. 173p. 55.00 (*1-85506-668-8*) Thoemmes Pr.

Lotze, Rudolf Hermann. Outlines of Psychology. LC 73-2974. (Classics in Psychology Ser.). 1978. reprint ed. 16.95 (*0-405-05147-6*) Ayer.

— Outlines of Psychology, 6. Ladd, George T., tr. from GER. LC 77-72191. (Contributions to the History of Psychology Ser.: Vol. 6, Pt. A, Orientations). 454p. 1977. reprint ed. lib. bdg. 79.50 (*0-313-26930-0*, U6930, Greenwood Pr) Greenwood.

Lotze, Wilhelm, tr. see Busch, Wilhelm, et al.

Lotzova, Eva. NK Cell Medicated Cytotoxicology: Receptors, Signaling & Mechanics. 512p. 1992. lib. bdg. 239.00 (*0-8493-6267-9*, QR188) CRC Pr.

Lotzova, Eva, ed. Natural Immunity & Biological Response International Symposium, Honolulu, Nov. 1985. (Journal: Natural Immunity & Cell Growth Regulation: Vol. 4, No. 5, 1985). 64p. 1985. pap. 28.00 (*3-8055-4243-7*) S Karger.

— Natural Immunity, Cancer & Biological Response Modification. (Illus.). xii, 324p. 1986. 191.50 (*3-8055-4412-X*) S Karger.

— Natural Killer Cells: Their Definition, Functions, Lineage & Regulation. (Journal: Natural Immunity: Vol. 12, Nos. 4-5, 1993). (Illus.). 128p. 1993. pap. 40.00 (*3-8055-5875-9*) S Karger.

— Potential of Gene Therapy in Cancer: Journal: Natural Immunity, Vol. 13, Nos. 2-3, 1994. (Illus.). 104p. 1994. pap. 41.00 (*3-8055-5956-9*) S Karger.

Lotzova, Eva, et al, eds. International Natural Killer Cell Workshop, 8th, & First Meeting of the Society for Natural Immunity, St. Petersburg Beach, October 1992: Abstracts. (Journal: Natural Immunity: Vol. 11, No. 5, 1992). 80p. 1992. pap. 41.00 (*3-8055-5690-X*) S Karger.

— International Symposium on AIDS & Cancer, Sao Paulo, Brazil, August 1988: Natural Immunity & Cell Growth Regulation Journal, Vol. 9, No. 3, 1990. (Illus.). 108p. 1990. pap. 68.00 (*3-8055-5225-4*) S Karger.

— International Workshop on Natural Killer Cells: 7th, Stockholm (Lidingo), June 1991 - Journal: Natural Immunity & Cell Growth Regulation, Vol. 10, No. 3, 1991. 68p. 1991. pap. 38.50 (*3-8055-5447-8*) S Karger.

Lotzova, Eva & Herberman, Ronald B., eds. Immunobiology of Natural Killer Cells, Vol. II. 272p. 1986. 138.00 (*0-8493-6543-0*, QR185, CRC Reprint) Franklin.

— Immunobiology of Natural Killer Cells: Assays for NK Cell Cytotoxicity; Their Values & Pitfalls, Vol. I. 256p. 1986. 170.00 (*0-8493-6542-2*, QR185) CRC Pr.

— Interleukin-2 & Killer Cells in Cancer. (Illus.). 384p. 1989. boxed set 254.00 (*0-8493-5388-2*, RC271) CRC Pr.

Lotzova, Eva & Sredni, B., eds. Future Trends in Research on AIDS, Cancer & Therapies. (Journal: Natural Immunity & Cell Growth Regulation: Vol. 7, No. 3, 1988). (Illus.). 68p. 1988. pap. 34.00 (*3-8055-4859-1*) S Karger.

Lotzsch, Ronald. Duden Taschenbucher: Jiddisches Woerterbuch. 2nd ed. (GER & YID.). 204p. 1992. 29.95 (*0-7859-8676-6*, 341106241x) Fr & Eur.

Lou. College Physics. 3rd ed. 1997. pap. text, student ed. 32.00 (*0-13-505116-9*) P-H.

Lou, Hans C. Developmental Neurology: With Neuropathologic Illustrations & Legends by Edith Reske-Nielsen. LC 80-6283. (Illus.). 301p. 1982. reprint ed. pap. 93.40 (*0-608-00297-6*, 205932700009) Bks Demand.

Lou, Herbert H. Juvenile Courts in the United States. LC 77-169394. (Family in America Ser.). 297p. 1977. reprint ed. 20.95 (*0-405-03871-2*) Ayer.

Lou, Jea-Hong, jt. auth. see Kuo, James B.

Lou, Kerry. Red Planet Blues: A Tale of Interstellar Love & the End of the World As We Know It. 288p. 1998. pap. 12.95 (*0-9662604-0-6*) Mothership Pr.

Lou, Nils. The Art of Firing. 120p. 1995. pap. text 30.00 (*0-9638064-0-8*) Clay Pacific.

Lou, Sue, et al. Get Ready! Get Set! Worship! LC 97-27904. 125p. 1998. pap. 20.95 (*0-664-50006-4*) Geneva Press.

— Get Ready! Get Set! Worship! (Illus.). 125p. 1992. ring bd. 25.00 (*0-9632053-0-7*) Sharing Tree.

— Get Ready! Get Set! Worship! Adapted for Use by United Methodist Church by Donna Strieb. (Illus.). 124p. 1994. ring bd. 25.00 (*0-9632053-1-5*) Sharing Tree.

Lou, Y. K., ed. see American Society of Mechanical Engineers Staff.

Louapre, Albert C., jt. ed. see Campion, Donald R.

Loubat, Joseph F. Gustavus Fox's Mission to Russia in 1866. LC 70-115559. (Russia Observed, Series I). 1970. reprint ed. 26.95 (*0-405-03045-2*) Ayer.

Loubere, Leo A. Louis Blanc: His Life & His Contribution to the Rise of French Jacobin-Socialism, Number 1. LC 80-23424. (Northwestern University Studies in History: No.1). 256p. 1980. reprint ed. lib. bdg. 65.00 (*0-313-22690-3*, LOBL) Greenwood.

— Nineteenth-Century Europe: The Revolution of Life. LC 93-4487. 367p. (C). 1993. pap. text 54.00 (*0-13-221086-X*) P-H.

— The Red & the White: The History of Wine in France & Italy in the Nineteenth Century. LC 78-2304. (Illus.). 401p. (C). 1978. text 19.50 (*0-87395-370-3*) State U NY Pr.

Louberge, Henri, ed. Financial Risk & Derivatives. 148p. (C). 1996. lib. bdg. 139.00 (*0-7923-9801-7*) Kluwer Academic.

— Risk, Information & Insurance. (C). 1990. lib. bdg. 95.50 (*0-7923-9041-5*, Pub. by Graham & Trotman) Kluwer Academic.

Loubet, Beth, et al. Privateer Playtesters' Guide. (Illus.). 96p. (Orig.). 1994. pap. 14.95 (*0-929373-16-2*) Origin Syst.

Loubet, Bruno. Bistro Bruno: Cooking from l'Odeon. (Illus.). 224p. 1995. 52.50 (*0-333-61140-3*, Pub. by Pan) Trans-Atl Phila.

***Loubet, Denis.** Cardboard Heroes: 436 Full-Color Fantasy Miniatures. 24p. 1999. pap. 19.95 (*1-55634-370-1*, Pub. by S Jackson Games) BookWorld.

— Cardboard Heros: Dungeon Floors. 16p. 2000. pap. 19.95 (*1-55634-425-2*, 925-119, Pub. by S Jackson Games) BookWorld.

Loubier, Christiane. English - French Vocabulary of Editing & Binding. (ENG & FRE.). 56p. 1987. pap. 29.95 (*0-8288-9401-9*) Fr & Eur.

Loubriel, Estela C. De, see De Loubriel, Estela C.

Loubser, Anneli. Case Book on the Law of Partnership, Company Law & Insolvency Law. 251p. 1992. pap. 30.00 (*0-7021-2782-5*, Pub. by Juta & Co) Gaunt.

Loubser, J. A. A Critical Review of Racial Theology in South Africa. LC 90-19168. (Texts & Studies in Religion: Vol. 53). (Illus.). 224p. 1990. reprint ed. lib. bdg. 89.95 (*0-7734-9794-3*) E Mellen.

— A Critical Review of Racial Theology in South Africa: The Apartheid Bible. (Texts & Studies in Religion: No. 53). 224p. 1990. write for info. (*0-88946-976-8*) E Mellen.

Loubser, M. Extinctive Prescription. LC 97-162762. 239p. 1996. 66.00 (*0-7021-3717-0*, Pub. by Juta & Co) Gaunt.

Louca, Francisco. Turbulence in Economics: An Evolutionary Appraisal of Cycles & Complexity in Historical Processes. LC 97-13455. 400p. 1997. 95.00 (*1-85898-563-3*) E Elgar.

***Louca, Francisco & Perlman, Mark, eds.** Is Economics an Evolutionary Science? The Legacy of Thorstein Veblen. LC 99-89246. 240p. 2000. 90.00 (*1-84064-195-9*) E Elgar.

***Louca, Francisco & Reijnders, Jan, eds.** The Foundations of Long Wave Theory: Models & Methodology, 2 vols. LC 98-31841. (International Library of Critical Writers in Economics). 1104p. 1999. 395.00 (*1-85898-842-X*) E Elgar.

Louch, Mary, tr. see Claparede, Edouard.

Louchheim, Katie, ed. The Making of the New Deal: The Insiders Speak. (Illus.). 392p. 1983. pap. text 10.95 (*0-674-54346-7*) HUP.

Louck, J. D. & Metropolis, N. Symbolic Dynamics of Trapezoidal Maps. (Mathematics & Its Applications Main Ser.). 1986. text 169.50 (*90-277-2197-1*) Kluwer Academic.

***Loucks, Cynthia.** But This Is My Mother! The Plight of Our Elders in American Nursing Homes. 184p. 2000. 21.95 (*1-889242-13-6*); pap. 14.95 (*1-889242-12-8*) VanderWyk & Burnham.

Loucks, Daniel P., ed. Restoration of Degraded Rivers: Challenges, Issues & Experiences; Proceedings of the NATO Advanced Research Workshop on Environmental Rehabilitation of Large Scale Water Resource Systems, Yaroslavl, Russia, October 1 to 7, 1995. 12p. 1998. write for info. (*0-7923-4942-3*) Kluwer Academic.

Loucks, Daniel P. & Da Costa, J. R., eds. Decision Support Systems: Water Resources Planning. (NATO ASI Series G: Ecological Sciences: Vol. 26). xvi, 600p. 1991. 277.95 (*0-387-53097-5*) Spr-Verlag.

Loucks, Daniel P. & Gladwell, John S., eds. Sustainability Criteria for Water Resource Systems. LC 98-29507. (International Hydrology Ser.). (Illus.). 256p. (C). 1999. text 85.00 (*0-521-56044-6*) Cambridge U Pr.

Loucks, E. P., jt. auth. see Ghosh, B.

Loucks, Eric D., et al. Water Resources & the Urban Environment: Proceedings of the 25th Annual Conference on Water Resources Planning & Management. LC 98-16639. 832p. 1998. 85.00 (*0-7844-0343-0*) Am Soc Civil Eng.

Loucks, Hazel E. & Waggoner, Jan E. Keys to Reengaging Families in the Education of Young Adolescents. LC 98-9944. 1998. pap. 24.00 (*1-56090-124-1*) Natl Middle Schl.

Loucks, Henry L. The Great Conspiracy of the House of Morgan & How to Defeat It. McCurry, Dan C. & Rubenstein, Richard E., eds. LC 74-30643. (American Farmers & the Rise of Agribusiness Ser.). 1975. reprint ed. 29.95 (*0-405-06813-1*) Ayer.

Loucks-Horsley, Susan, et al. Designing Professional Development for Teachers of Science & Mathematics. LC 97-33794. (Illus.). 352p. 1997. 69.95 (*0-8039-6661-X*); pap. 32.95 (*0-8039-6662-8*) Corwin Pr.

Loucks-Horsley, Susan, jt. auth. see Olson, Steve.

Loucks, James M., ed. see Browning, Robert.

Loucks, Kenneth. Training Entrepreneurs for Small Business Creation: Lessons from Experience. (Management Development Ser.: No. 26). xi, 137p. (Orig.). 1990. pap. 20.25 (*92-2-106343-7*) Intl Labour Office.

Loucks, Ori L. Sustainability Perspectives for Resources & Business. LC 98-38870. 6p. 1994. lib. bdg. 44.95 (*1-57444-058-6*, SL0586) St Lucie Pr.

Loucks, R. G., jt. ed. see Bebout, Don G.

Loucks, Robert G. & Sarg, J. Frederick, eds. Carbonate Sequence Stratigraphy Recent Developments & Applications. (AAPG Memoir Ser.: No. 57). (Illus.). vi, 545p. 1993. 59.00 (*0-89181-336-5*, 585) AAPG.

Loucks, Robert G., ed. see SEPM Core Workshop Staff.

Loucks, Sandra, jt. auth. see Burstein, Alvin G.

Loucks, Terry, jt. auth. see Loucks, Ursula.

Loucks, Ursula & Loucks, Terry. Burning Words. LC 97-94293. 266p. 1998. pap. 14.95 (*0-9656929-3-0*) InfoNovels.

Loucks, Wayne & Preiss, Bruno, eds. 10th Workshop on Parallel & Distributed Simulation (PADS '96) PADS 96. 212p. 1996. pap. 80.00 (*0-8186-7539-X*, PADS-96) Soc Computer Sim.

***Loucky, James & Moors, Marilyn M., eds.** The Maya Diaspora: Guatemalan Roots, New American Lives. (Illus.). 248p. 2000. 64.50 (*1-56639-794-4*); pap. 22.95 (*1-56639-795-2*) Temple U Pr.

Loucopoulos, P. & Karakostas, Vassilios. Advanced Requirements Analysis & Specifications. 200p. 1995. 40.00 (*0-07-707464-5*) McGraw.

Loucopoulos, P., ed. see International Conference on Entity-Relationship Ap.

Loucopoulos, Peri, et al, eds. Advanced Information Systems Engineering: Proceedings of the Fourth International Conference, CAiSE 1992, Manchester, U. K., May 12-15, 1992. LC 92-16718. (Lecture Notes in Computer Science Ser.: Vol. 593). xi, 650p. 1992. 96.95 (*0-387-55481-5*) Spr-Verlag.

Loud, G. A. Church & Society in the Norman Principality of Capua, 1058-1197. (Oxford Historical Monographs). (Illus.). 1985. 55.00 (*0-19-822931-3*) OUP.

Loud, G. A. & Wiedemann, T. E., eds. A History of the Tyrants of Sicily by 'Hugo Falcandus', 1153-69. LC 98-222089. (Medieval Sources Ser.). 272p. 1998. text 79.95 (*0-7190-4894-X*, Pub. by Manchester Univ Pr) St Martin.

— A History of the Tyrants of Sicily by 'Hugo Falcandus', 1153-69. LC 98-222089. (Medieval Sources Ser.). 272p. 1998. pap. 29.95 (*0-7190-5435-4*, Pub. by Manchester Univ Pr) St Martin.

Loud, G. H., jt. ed. see Wood, Ian.

Loud, Gordon. Megiddo: Text F, Vol. 2. 1997. lib. bdg. 10.00 (*0-226-49386-5*) U Ch Pr.

— Megiddo Plate F, Vol. 2. 1994. lib. bdg. 12.00 (*0-226-49385-7*) U Ch Pr.

Loud, Graham. Conquerors & Churchmen in Norman Italy. (Variorum Collected Studies Ser.: Vol. CS658). 350p. 1999. text 101.95 (*0-86078-803-2*, Pub. by Ashgate Pub) Ashgate Pub Co.

Loud, Grover C. Evangelized America. LC 70-169770. (Select Bibliographies Reprint Ser.). 1977. reprint ed. 30.95 (*0-8369-5990-6*) Ayer.

Loud, John F., ed. & tr. see Andric, Ivo.

Loud, Llewellyn L. Ethnogeography & Archaeology of the Wiyot Territory. fac. ed. (University of California Publications in American Archaeology & Ethnology: Vol. 14: 3). 224p. (C). 1918. reprint ed. pap. text 23.75 (*1-55567-218-3*) Coyote Press.

— The Stege Mounds at Richmond, California. fac. ed. (University of California Publications in American Archaeology & Ethnology: Vol. 17: 6). 22p. (C). 1924. reprint ed. pap. text 2.81 (*1-55567-231-0*) Coyote Press.

Loud, Llewellyn L. & Harrington, M. R. Lovelock Cave. fac. ed. (University of California Publications in American Archaeology & Ethnology: Vol. 25: 1). (Illus.). 259p. (C). 1929. reprint ed. pap. text 27.50 (*1-55567-026-1*) Coyote Press.

Loud, Patricia C. The Art Museums of Louis I. Kahn. LC 89-51072. (Illus.). 304p. (Orig.). (C). 1990. pap. 34.95 (*0-8223-0998-X*) Duke.

Loud, Pattricia C. The Art Museums of Louis I. Kahn. LC 89-51072. (Illus.). 304p. (Orig.). (C). 1990. 64.95 (*0-8223-0989-0*) Duke.

Loud, Warren S. Periodic Solutions of Perturbed Second-Order Autonomous Equations. LC QA0003.A57. (Memoirs of the American Mathematical Society Ser.: No. 47). 141p. reprint ed. pap. 43.80 (*0-7837-1632-X*, 204192500024) Bks Demand.

— Periodic Solutions of X Double Prime Plus C Times X Plus G of (X) Equals F of T. LC 52-42839. (Memoirs Ser.: No. 1/31). 58p. 1978. reprint ed. pap. 16.00 (*0-8218-1231-9*, MEMO/1/31) Am Math.

— Periodic Solutions of X" Plus CX' Plus G(X) Equals EF(T) fac. ed. LC QA0371.A57. (Memoirs of the American Mathematical Society Ser.: No. 31). 60p. 1959. pap. 30.00 (*0-7837-7552-0*, 204730500007) Bks Demand.

Loudder, jt. auth. see Lawrence.

Louden. Compiler Design. LC 96-49664. (Computer Science Ser.). (C). 1997. mass mkt. 79.95 (*0-534-93972-4*) PWS Pubs.

Louden-Brown, P. The White Star Line. 1990. 59.00 (*0-9516038-2-5*, Pub. by Ship Pictorial Pubng) St Mut.

***Louden, Bruce.** The Odyssey: Structure, Narration, & Meaning. LC 98-41521. 200p. 1999. 35.95 (*0-8018-6058-X*) Johns Hopkins.

Louden, D. NLN Guide to Undergraduate RN Education. 5th ed. 200p. 1997. 19.95 (*0-88737-737-8*, 19-7378, NLN Pr) Natl League Nurse.

Louden, Delroy & Jones, Dawnette. Nurse Educators, 1997: Findings from the RN & LPN Faculty Census. 150p. 1997. 26.95 (*0-88737-755-6*, 19-7556, NLN Pr) Natl League Nurse.

Louden, Delroy, et al. Profiles of the Newly Licensed Nurse. 120p. 1997. 29.95 (*0-88737-756-4*, 19-7564, NLN Pr) Natl League Nurse.

Louden, Jane. The Lady's Country Companion. (Illus.). 448p. 1998. reprint ed. pap. 75.00 (*0-948285-02-8*) St Mut.

***Louden, Jennifer.** The Comfort Queen's Guide to Life: Create All That You Need with Just What You've Got. LC 99-58209. (Illus.). 224p. 2000. 19.95 (*0-609-60527-5*) Harmony Bks.

Louden, Jennifer. The Couple's Comfort Book: A Creative Guide for Renewing Passion, Pleasure & Commitment. LC 93-20733. 336p. 1994. pap. 17.00 (*0-06-250853-9*, Pub. by Harper SF) HarpC.

— El Arte de Cuidar de Ti Misma. 1998. pap. text 9.95 (*84-08-02727-1*) Planeta Edit.

— A Little Book of Sensual Comfort. LC 93-46348. (Little Book of Wisdom Ser.). 96p. 1994. pap. 8.00 (*0-06-251112-2*, Pub. by Harper SF) HarpC.

— The Pregnant Woman's Comfort Book: A Self-Nurturing Guide to Your Emotional Well-Being During Pregnancy & Early Motherhood. LC 94-47638. 240p. 1995. pap. 16.00 (*0-06-251165-3*, Pub. by Harper SF) HarpC.

Louden, Jennifer. The Woman's Comfort Book: A Self-Nurturing Guide for Restoring Balance in Your Life. LC 91-55316. 224p. 1992. pap. 17.00 (*0-06-250531-9*, Pub. by Harper SF) HarpC.

Louden, Jennifer. The Women's Retreat Book: A Guide to Restoring, Rediscovering, & Reawakening Your True Self - in a Moment, an Hour, a Day, or a Week. 1997. pap. 17.00 (*0-614-27682-9*) Harper SF.

Louden, Keith E., jt. ed. see Wright, James A.

Louden, Kenneth C. Programming Languages: Principles & Practice. 641p. 1993. mass mkt. 69.95 (*0-534-93277-0*) PWS Pubs.

— Programming Languages: Principles & Practice. 2nd ed. (Computer Science Ser.). (C). 2000. 55.75 (*0-534-95341-7*) PWS Pubs.

Louden, Robert B. Kant's Impure Ethics: From Rational Beings to Human Beings. LC 99-13606. 272p. 2000. text 45.00 (*0-19-513041-3*) OUP.

— Morality & Moral Theory: A Reappraisal & Reaffirmation. 256p. 1992. text 70.00 (*0-19-507145-X*); pap. text 26.00 (*0-19-507292-8*) OUP.

Louden, Robert B. & Schollmeier, Paul, eds. The Greeks & Us: Essays in Honor of Arthur W. H. Adkins. LC 96-16375. 272p. 1996. pap. text 18.95 (*0-226-49395-4*) U Ch Pr.

— The Greeks & Us: Essays in Honor of Arthur W. H. Adkins. LC 96-16375. (Illus.). 272p. 1996. lib. bdg. 48.00 (*0-226-49394-6*) U Ch Pr.

Louden, Sandra M. Write Well & Sell: Greeting Cards. (Blueprint Ser.). 96p. 1998. pap. 9.95 (*1-892356-00-7*) Jam-Packed.

Louden, William. Understanding Teaching: Continuity & Change in Teachers' Knowledge. 224p. (C). 1991. pap. text 18.95 (*0-8077-3101-3*) Tchrs Coll.

Louden, William, jt. auth. see Wallace, John.

Louder, Dean R., ed. The Heart of French Canada: Quebec & Ontario. LC 92-11924. (Touring North America Ser.). (Illus.). 150p. 1992. 25.00 (*0-8135-1888-1*); pap. 9.95 (*0-8135-1889-X*) Rutgers U Pr.

Louder, Dean R. & Waddell, Eric, eds. French America: Mobility, Identity, & Minority Experience Across the Continent. Philip, Franklin, tr. LC 92-7982. (Illus.). 344p. (C). 1992. text 50.00 (*0-8071-1669-6*); pap. text 19.95 (*0-8071-1776-5*) La State U Pr.

Louderback, jt. auth. see Dominiak.

Louderback, Joseph G. Survey Accounting. Date not set. pap. text, teacher ed. write for info. (*0-314-01400-4*) West Pub.

Louderback, Joseph G., III, jt. auth. see Dominiak, Geraldine F.

Louderback, Joseph G., jt. auth. see Dominiak, Geraldine J.

Loudermilk, Arvin. Vigil: Desertion. (Illus.). 24p. (C). 1998. pap. 2.95 (*1-892579-02-2*) Duality Pr.

Loudermilk, Arvin, III. Vigil: Dirt. (Illus.). 24p. 1998. 2.95 (*1-892579-01-4*) Duality Pr.

Loudermilk, Arvin S., III. Vigil One. (Illus.). 250p. 1998. reprint ed. pap. 19.95 (*1-892579-00-6*) Duality Pr.

Loudin, Frank & Spees, Marcia. Capture the Charm of Your Hometown in Watercolor. LC 97-31260. (Illus.). 144p. 1998. 28.99 (*0-89134-792-5*, North Lght Bks) F & W Pubns Inc.

Loudin, Jan. The Witch & the Roo of Wicky Roo. (J). (gr. k-4). 1996. pap. 8.95 (*1-888345-02-0*) Paper Jam.

Loudiyi, Dounia & Meares, Alison. Women in Conservation: Tools for Analysis & a Framework for Action. 153p. (C). 1993. pap. text 27.00 (*2-8317-0196-1*, Pub. by IUCN) Island Pr.

Loudne, Jennifer. The Woman's Retreat Book: A Guide to Restoring, Rediscovering & Reawakening Your True Self. LC 97-4954. 336p. 1997. pap. 17.00 (*0-06-251466-0*, Pub. by Harper SF) HarpC.

Loudon. Consumer Behavior. 4th ed. 1993. text, teacher ed. 50.00 (*0-07-038768-0*) McGraw.

***Loudon.** Geoscience. (Computer Methods in the Geosciences Ser.: Vol. 17). 2000. pap. 35.00 (*0-08-043672-2*, Pergamon Pr) Elsevier.

Loudon, A. Loudon's Indian Narratives: A Selection of Some of the Most Interesting Narratives of Outrages Committed by the Indians in Their Wars with the White People. LC 96-78507. (The Great Pennsylvania Frontier Ser.: Vol. 8). (Illus.). 658p. 1996. reprint ed. 49.95 (*1-889037-07-9*, 8) Wennawoods.

Loudon, A. G., ed. see Hill, Hilson C.

Loudon, A. S. & Racey, P. A., eds. Reproductive Energetic in Mammals. (Symposia of the Zoological Society of London Ser.: No. 57). (Illus.). 394p. 1987. text 95.00 (*0-19-854005-1*) OUP.

Loudon, Archibald. Narratives of Outrages, Committed by the Indians in Their Wars with the White People, 2 vols. Van Every, Dale, ed. LC 76-106124. (First American Frontier Ser.). 658p. 1971. reprint ed. 85.54 (*0-405-02866-0*) Ayer.

 An Asterisk (*) at the beginning of an entry indicates that the title is appearing for the first time.

Loudon, Archibald & Lyman, Phineas. General Orders of 1757 Issued by the Earl of Loudoun & Phineas Lyman in the Campaign Against the French. LC 71-126241. (Select Bibliographies Reprint Ser.). 1977. reprint ed. 17.95 (*0-8369-5468-8*) Ayer.

Loudon, David L. & Della Britta, Albert J. Consumer Behavior: Concepts & Applications. 4th ed. LC 92-27875. (C). 1992. text 68.00 (*0-07-038767-2*) McGraw.

Loudon, David L., jt. auth. see Stevens, Robert E.

Loudon, G. Marc. Organic Chemistry. LC 83-7075. (Chemistry Ser.). 1150p. 1984. text. write for info. (*0-201-14438-7*); student ed. write for info. (*0-201-14436-0*) Addison-Wesley.

— Organic Chemistry. 3rd ed. 1994. 94.25 (*0-8053-6550-8*) Benjamin-Cummings.

Loudon, Irvine. Childbed Fever: A Documentary History. LC 94-33390. (Disease, Epidemics & Medicine Ser.: Vol. 2). (Illus.). 288p. 1995. text 61.00 (*0-8153-1079-X*, SS868) Garland.

Loudon, Irvine. Death in Childbirth: An International Study of Maternal Care & Maternal Mortality, 1800-1950. LC 92-20160. (Illus.). 646p. 1993. text 110.00 (*0-19-822997-6*, Clarendon Pr) OUP.

— Medical Care & the General Practitioner, 1750-1850. LC 86-14172. (Illus.). 368p. (C). 1987. text 75.00 (*0-19-822793-0*) OUP.

— The Tragedy of Childbed Fever. LC 99-33268. (Illus.). 256p. 2000. text 65.00 (*0-19-820499-X*) OUP.

Loudon, Irvine, ed. Western Medicine: An Illustrated History. LC 97-218848. (Illus.). 364p. (C). 1997. 49.95 (*0-19-820509-0*) OUP.

Loudon, Irvine, et al, eds. General Practice under the National Health Service, 1948-1997. LC 98-209963. (Illus.). 360p. 1998. text 85.00 (*0-19-820675-5*) OUP.

Loudon, J. C. Encyclopedia of Plants, Vols. 1 & 2. (C). 1988. text 200.00 (*0-7855-6006-8*, Pub. by Scientific) St Mut.

Loudon, J. H. James Scott & William Scott, Bookbinders. (Illus.). 1980. 65.00 (*0-19679-003-7*) Moretus Pr.

Loudon, J. W. Victorian Flower Postcards: 24 Ready-to-Mail. (Illus.). 1995. pap. 4.95 (*0-486-28458-1*) Dover.

Loudon, Jame W., jt. auth. see Loudon, Jane W.

Loudon, Jane W. The Mummy! A Tale of the Twenty-Second Century. LC 87-60458. 500p. 1988. reprint ed. 30.00 (*0-915431-03-3*); reprint ed. pap. 19.95 (*0-915431-04-1*) N American Archives.

Loudon, Jane W. & Loudon, Jame W. The Mummy!: or A Tale of the Twenty-Second Century. abr. ed. LC 94-12992. 344p. 1994. text 44.50 (*0-472-09574-9*, 09574, Ann Arbor Bks); pap. text 18.95 (*0-472-06574-2*, 06574) U of Mich Pr.

***Loudon, Janice, et al.** The Clinical Orthopedic Assessment Guide. LC 97-49234. (Illus.). 248p. 1998. pap. text 32.00 (*0-88011-507-6*, BLOU0507) Human Kinetics.

Loudon, Jim. The Oneonta Roundhouse. 100p. 1993. pap. 17.95 (*0-9641119-0-X*) LRHS.

Loudon, John, jt. auth. see Roth, Gabrielle.

Loudon, Kyle. Mastering Algorithms with C. Oram, Andy, ed. (Illus.). 540p. 1999. pap. 34.95 (*1-56592-453-3*) OReilly & Assocs.

Loudon, Marc. Organic Chemistry. 2nd ed. (Illus.). 1300p. (C). 1988. trans. 100.00 (*0-8053-6645-8*) Benjamin-Cummings.

— Organic Chemistry. 3rd ed. 1390p. (C). 1994. 115.00 (*0-8053-6650-4*) Benjamin-Cummings.

— Organic Chemistry. 3rd ed. (C). 1996. text 135.00 (*0-8053-6667-9*) Benjamin-Cummings.

— S/G&STUD/S/M V2 ORGANIC. 3rd ed. 352p. (C). 1996. pap. text 13.00 (*0-8053-6664-4*) Addison-Wesley.

Loudon, Mary. Unveiled: Nuns Talking. 290p. 1993. pap. 14.95 (*0-87243-201-7*) Templegate.

Loudon, Nancy, et al, eds. Handbook of Family Planning & Reproductive Health Care. 3rd ed. (Illus.). 462p. (C). 1995. pap. write for info. (*0-443-05157-7*) Church.

Loudon, Penny, jt. auth. see Wilkins, Robert.

Loudon, Rodney. The Quantum Theory of Light. 2nd ed. (Illus.). 410p. 1983. pap. text 44.95 (*0-19-851155-8*) OUP.

Loudon, Rodney & Knight, P. L., eds. Squeezed Light: Special Issue of Journal of Modern Optics, Vol 34: 6/7. 310p. 1987. 51.00 (*0-85066-922-7*) Taylor & Francis.

Loudy, Adlai. God's Eonian Purpose. 1978. 12.00 (*0-910424-56-X*); pap. 9.00 (*0-685-42097-3*) Concordant.

Loudy, Aldai. The Gospel of Our Salvation. 122p. 1973. text 4.50 (*0-910424-60-8*) Concordant.

Loue, S., ed. Handbook of Immigrant Health. LC 98-34164. (Illus.). 668p. 1998. 115.00 (*0-306-45959-0*, Kluwer Plenum) Kluwer Academic.

Loue, Sana. Forensic Epidemiology. LC 98-3783. (Medical Humanities Ser.). (Illus.). 254p. 1998. 39.95 (*0-8093-2222-6*) S Ill U Pr.

***Loue, Sana.** Gender, Ethnicity & Health Research. LC 99-33678. (C). 1999. text. write for info. (*0-306-46172-2*, Kluwer Plenum) Kluwer Academic.

Loue, Sana. Immigration Law & Health: Patients & Providers. LC 93-11171. (Immigration Law Ser.). 1993. ring bd. 125.00 (*0-87632-920-2*) West Group.

— Legal & Ethical Aspects of HIV-Related Research. LC 95-34011. (Illus.). 214p. 1995. 47.00 (*0-306-45055-0*, Plenum Trade) Perseus Pubng.

***Loue, Sana, et al.** The Assessment of Immigration Status in Health Research. LC 99-40419. (Vital Ser.). 1999. write for info. (*0-8406-0558-7*) Natl Ctr Health Stats.

Louf, Andre. The Cistercian Way. (Cistercian Studies: No. 76). 1983. pap. 12.95 (*0-87907-976-2*) Cistercian Pubns.

— Teach Us to Pray: A Cowley Classic. LC 92-5949. 115p. 1992. pap. 8.95 (*1-56101-058-8*) Cowley Pubns.

— Tuning in to Grace the Quest for God. Vriend, John, tr. (Cistercian Studies). 300p. 1992. pap. 15.95 (*0-87907-929-0*) Cistercian Pubns.

Loufek, Betty McMillen, jt. auth. see Walters, Claire L.

Louflas, Ted. Filthy. 1999. pap. 9.95 (*1-56097-315-3*) Fantagraph Bks.

Louganis, Greg & Marcus, Eric. Breaking the Surface. LC 95-26491. (Illus.). 304p. 1996. pap. 12.95 (*0-452-27590-3*, Plume) Dutton Plume.

Louganis, Greg & Siino, Betsy Sikora. For the Life of Your Dog: A Complete Guide to Having a Dog in Your Life, from Adoption & Birth Through Sickness & Health. LC 99-17170. (Illus.). 266p. 1999. 24.00 (*0-671-02450-7*, PB Hardcover) PB.

***Louganis, Greg & Siino, Betsy Sikora.** For the Life of Your Dog: A Complete Guide to Having a Dog in Your Life, from Adoption & Birth Through Sickness & Health. 272p. 1999. per. 14.00 (*0-671-02451-5*, PB Trade Paper) PB.

Lough, Annette R. Decorating with Collectibles. LC 96-76693. 160p. 1997. 24.95 (*0-87341-458-6*, LDC) Krause Pubns.

Lough, David A. & Howe, Christopher J. Business Basics for Compensation: Linking Pay to Financial Performance. (Building Blocks Ser.: Vol. 34). (Illus.). 20p. (Orig.). 1996. pap. 24.95 (*1-57963-035-9*, A0234) Am Compensation.

Lough, Francis. Politics & Philosophy in the Early Novels of Ramon J. Sender, 1930-1936. LC 95-19531. (Hispanic Literature Ser.: Vol. 28). 228p. 1996. text 89.95 (*0-7734-8897-9*) E Mellen.

Lough, George, jt. auth. see Sanford, John A.

Lough, Glenn D. Now & Long Ago. (Illus.). 720p. (C). 1969. reprint ed. 40.00 (*0-87012-513-3*) McClain. NOW & LONG AGO is a collection of colorful & informative stories of the pioneers of the Monogahela Valley & those men & women in whom the spirit of the Old Defenders ("the spirit of fire") continued, & continues to exist, even now. Explorers, traders, settlers, & citizens relate the thrilling, informative & authentic story of the discovery & settlement of the Monogahela country in this masterwork of researched regional history. Reprinted, 1991. ***Publisher Paid Annotation.***

Lough, John. An Introduction to Eighteenth Century France. LC 60-2946. 397p. reprint ed. pap. 123.10 (*0-608-30084-5*, 200367000038) Bks Demand.

Lough, John & Lough, Muriel. An Introduction to Nineteenth Century France. LC 79-305880. 360p. reprint ed. pap. 111.60 (*0-7837-4029-8*, 204385800011) Bks Demand.

Lough, John, ed. see Diderot, Denis.

***Lough, Laura, ed.** Federal Payroll Tax Laws & Regulations: 2000 Edition. 6th rev. ed. 1100p. 2000. 76.95 (*1-930471-11-4*, 0800) American Payroll.

Lough, Loree. Dream Seekers: Roger William's Stand for Freedom. LC 98-19953. (American Adventure Ser.: No. 3). (Illus.). 144p. (J). (gr. 4-7). 1999. lib. bdg. 15.95 (*0-7910-5043-2*) Chelsea Hse.

***Lough, Loree.** Dream Seekers: Roger William's Stand for Freedom. 3rd ed. (American Adventure Ser.: No. 3). (Illus.). (J). (gr. 3-7). 1998. pap. 3.97 (*1-57748-073-2*) Barbour Pub.

— Fire by Night: The Great Fire Devastates Boston. (American Adventure Ser.: No. 4). (J). (gr. 3-6). 1998. pap. 3.97 (*1-57748-074-0*) Barbour Pub.

Lough, Loree. Fire by Night: The Great Fire Devastates Boston. LC 98-19951. (American Adventure Ser.: No. 4). 144p. (J). (gr. 3-6). 1999. lib. bdg. 15.95 (*0-7910-5044-0*) Chelsea Hse.

***Lough, Loree.** Jake Walker's Wife. (Harlequin Historical Ser.). 1999. mass mkt. 4.99 (*0-373-29089-6*, Harlequin) Harlequin Bks.

Lough, Loree. Lord Baltimore. (Colonial Leaders Ser.). (Illus.). 80p. (J). (gr. 3 up). 1999. pap. 8.95 (*0-7910-5692-9*) Chelsea Hse.

— Nathan Hale. (Revolutionary War Leaders Ser.). (Illus.). 80p. (J). (gr. 3 up). 1999. pap. 8.95 (*0-7910-5704-6*) Chelsea Hse.

— Suddenly Daddy. (Love Inspired Ser.). 1998. per. 4.50 (*0-373-87028-0*, 1-87028-6) Harlequin Bks.

— Suddenly Married. Vol. 52. 1999. mass mkt. 4.50 (*0-373-87052-3*) Harlequin Bks.

— Suddenly Mommy. (Love Inspired Ser.). 1998. mass mkt. 4.50 (*0-373-87034-5*, Harlequin) Harlequin Bks.

***Lough, Loree.** Suddenly Reunited. (Love Inspired Ser.: Bk. 107). 2000. mass mkt. 4.50 (*0-373-87113-9*, 1-87113-6, Steeple Hill) Harlequin Bks.

— Wedding Wishes. 1998. mass mkt. 1.66 (*1-57748-337-5*) Barbour Pub.

Lough, Loree, et al. Season of Love: Four New Inspirational Love Stories from Christmas Present. 352p. 1998. pap. 4.97 (*1-57748-350-2*) Barbour Pub.

Lough, Lori. Lord Baltimore. LC 99-33136. (Colonial Leaders Ser.). (Illus.). 80p. (YA). (gr. 3 up). 1999. 16.95 (*0-7910-5349-0*) Chelsea Hse.

— Nathan Hale. LC 99-32043. (J). 1999. 16.95 (*0-7910-5361-X*) Chelsea Hse.

Lough, Mark, ed. see Perkins Coie Product Liability Practice Group Staf & Gerrard, Keith.

Lough, Mary E., ed. see Urden, Linda D., et al.

Lough, Muriel, jt. auth. see Lough, John.

Lough, Tom, ed. see Barrowman, Tom, et al.

Lough, W. J., ed. Chiral Liquid Chromatography. (Illus.). 256p. 1989. 112.00 (*0-412-01741-5*, A2081, Chap & Hall NY) Chapman & Hall.

Lough, W. John, ed. see Riley, Christopher M.

Lough, William H. High-Level Consumption: Its Behavior; Its Consequences. LC 75-39258. (Getting & Spending: the Consumer's Dilemma Ser.). (Illus.). 1976. reprint ed. 29.95 (*0-405-08031-X*) Ayer.

Loughan, Susan, jt. auth. see Blum, Ralph H.

Loughary, Jack & Ripley, Theresa M. Working It Out Together: A Guide for Dual Career Couples. 167p. 1987. pap. 12.95 (*0-685-19247-4*) United Learn.

Loughary, John W. Uncle Jack among the English. (Illus.). 60p. (Orig.). 1984. pap. 3.95 (*0-915671-00-X*) United Learn.

Loughary, John W. & Ripley, Theresa M. Helping Others Help Themselves: A Guide to Counseling Skills. (Illus.). 218p. (C). 1979. pap. text 41.87 (*0-07-038756-7*) McGraw.

Loughborough, J. N. The Great Second Advent Movement: Its Rise & Progress. LC 71-38453. (Religion in America, Ser. 2). 502p. 1977. reprint ed. 35.95 (*0-405-04073-3*) Ayer.

Loughborough, Jas. M. My Cave Life in Vicksburg with Letters of Trial & Travel. LC 75-46574. 196p. 1988. reprint ed. 25.00 (*0-87152-217-9*) Reprint.

Loughborough, John N. The Great Second Advent Movement. 1992. pap. 9.95 (*0-9633711-1-8*) Advent Pioneer Lib.

Loughborough, Mary A. My Cave Life in Vicksburg. 212p. 1989. reprint ed. 25.00 (*0-916107-65-5*) Broadfoot.

Lougheed, A. L., jt. auth. see Kenwood, A. G.

Lougheed, A. L., jt. ed. see Kenwood, A. G.

Lougheed, Lin. English International Language Text: Answer Key to 14182. (C). 1986. pap. text 3.58 (*0-201-14187-6*) Addison-Wesley.

***Lougheed, Lin.** How to Prepare for the Computer-Based TOEFL Essay. LC 99-55699. (Illus.). 240p. 2000. pap. write for info. (*0-7641-1479-4*) Barron.

— How to Prepare for the TOEIC: Test of English for International Communication. 2nd rev. ed. LC 98-39883. (Illus.). 672p. 1999. pap. 16.95 (*0-7641-0877-8*) Barron.

— How to Prepare for the TOEIC - Test of English for International Communication. 2nd rev. ed. LC 98-39883. (Illus.). 688p. 1999. pap. 29.95 incl. audio compact disk (*0-7641-7266-2*) Barron.

Lougheed, Lin. On Target for the Toeic. (C). 1994. pap. text. write for info. (*0-201-59496-X*) Addison-Wesley.

— Prentice Hall Regent Prep Series for the Toefl Test. (Regents Prep Series for the TOEFL Test). (Illus.). 80p. 1995. pap. text 15.80 (*0-13-100645-2*) P-H.

— Prentice Hall Regents Preparation TOEFL: Grammar. (Regents Prep Series for the TOEFL Test). (Illus.). 192p. 1994. pap. text 15.80 (*0-13-100637-1*, PH Regents) P-H.

***Lougheed, Lin.** 600 Essential Words for the TOEIC: Test of English for International Communication. LC 98-51863. 272p. 1999. pap. 8.95 (*0-7641-0879-4*) Barron.

Lougheed, Lin. TOEIC Preparation Workbook. 1991. pap. text, wbk. ed. 15.65 (*0-201-56236-7*) Addison-Wesley.

Lougheed, Linford. English for Business Success: Introductory Course. 2nd ed. (Longman Preparation Series for the TOEIC). 1996. pap. text 24.26 (*0-201-87789-9*) Longman.

— Four Practice Tests for the TOEFL. 192p. (C). 1995. pap. text 19.00 (*0-13-870015-X*) P-H.

— How to Prepare for the TOEIC: Test of English for International Communication. 1995. pap., student ed. 14.95 (*0-8120-1057-4*) Barron.

— Longman Preparation Series for the TOEIC Test: Advanced Course. 2nd rev. ed. LC 96-4683. (English for Business Success Ser.). Orig. Title: English the International Language. 1996. pap. text 23.10 (*0-201-87791-0*, Pub. by Addison-Wesley) Longman.

— Longman Preparation Series for the TOEIC Test: Basic Course. 2nd rev. ed. LC 96-2499. (English for Business Success Ser.). 1996. write for info. (*0-614-98002-X*) Longman.

— Prentice Hall Prep Series for the Toefl Test: Listening Skills Builder. (C). 1994. pap., student ed. 48.00 (*0-13-187790-9*) P-H.

— Prentice Hall Regents Prep Series for the Toefl Test: Vocabulary Reading Skills Builder. (Regents Prep Series for the TOEFL Test). (Illus.). 80p. 1994. pap. text 15.80 (*0-13-100660-6*) P-H.

— Prentice Hall Regents Prep Series for the TOEFL Test: 4 Practice Tests. (C). 1994. pap. 50.25 (*0-13-187717-8*) P-H.

— Regents Prentice Hall TOEFL Prep Book. 2nd ed. 1993. pap. 25.27 (*0-13-782632-X*) P-H.

Lougheed, Peter & Shernofsky, Sari. Calgary: Harnessing the Future. LC 97-40315. (Urban Tapestry Ser.). (Illus.). 320p. 1997. 49.95 (*1-881096-49-1*) Towery Pub.

Lougheed, Victor. Vehicles of the Air: A Popular Exposition of Modern Aeronautics with Working Drawings. LC 75-169427. (Literature & History of Aviation Ser.). 1972. reprint ed. 48.95 (*0-405-03770-8*) Ayer.

Lougheed, Vivien. Central America by Chickenbus. 3rd rev. ed. LC 96-1461. (Illus.). 504p. 1993. pap. 17.95 (*0-920104-22-3*, Pub. by Repository Pr) Genl Dist Srvs.

— The Kluane National Park Hiking Guide. 2nd rev. ed. (Illus.). 242p. 1997. pap. 16.00 (*0-921586-60-4*, Pub. by New Star Bks) Genl Dist Srvs.

Loughery, John. Alias S. S. Van Dine. 320p. 1992. text 24.00 (*0-684-19358-2*, Scribners Ref) Mac Lib Ref.

— John Sloan: Painter & Rebel, Vol. 1. 464p. 1997. pap. 15.95 (*0-8050-5221-6*) H Holt & Co.

— The Other Side of Silence: Men's Lives & Gay Identities - A Twentieth-Century History. (Illus.). 544p. 1999. pap. 16.95 (*0-8050-6124-X*, Pub. by H Holt & Co) VHPS.

— The Other Side of Silence: Men's Lives & Gay Identities - A Twentieth-Century History. LC 97-42575. 507p. 1998. text 35.00 (*0-8050-3896-5*) St Martin.

Loughery, John, ed. The Eloquent Essay: An Anthology of Classic & Creative Nonfiction from the Twentieth Century. LC 99-13309. 210p. 2000. pap. 12.95 (*0-89255-241-7*, Pub. by Persea Bks) Norton.

Loughery, John, ed. Into the Widening World: International Coming-of-Age Stories. 288p. (Orig.). 1995. pap. 11.95 (*0-89255-204-2*) Persea Bks.

Loughery, John, intro. First Sightings: Contemporary Stories of American Youth. 320p. 1993. 29.95 (*0-89255-186-0*); pap. 11.95 (*0-89255-187-9*) Persea Bks.

Loughlin. Ulster Question since 1945. LC 98-5558. 168p. 1998. text 45.00 (*0-312-21446-4*) St Martin.

Loughlin, A. J. Alienation & Value-Neutrality. LC 98-47213. (Avebury Series in Philosophy). 1p. (C). 1999. text 63.95 (*1-84014-190-5*, Pub. by Ashgate Pub) Ashgate Pub Co.

Loughlin, Ambrose. The Art of Balance: San-Datchi Kata. LC 96-43352. (Illus.). 112p. (Orig.). 1997. pap. 14.95 (*1-880090-34-1*) Galde Pr.

Loughlin, C. Sensors for Industrial Inspection. 1992. text 307.50 (*0-7923-2046-8*) Kluwer Academic.

Loughlin, Caroline & Anderson, Catherine. Forest Park. 304p. 1994. pap. 19.95 (*0-9638298-0-7*) Jr Leag St Louis.

Loughlin, Catherine E. & Suina, Joseph H. The Learning Environment: An Instructional Strategy. LC 81-23353. (Illus.). 249p. (C). 1982. pap. text 18.95 (*0-8077-2714-8*) Tchrs Coll.

Loughlin, Gerald M. & Eigen, Howard. Pediatric Lung Disease: Diagnosis & Management. LC 93-1902. (Illus.). 862p. 1994. reprint ed. 125.00 (*0-683-05190-3*) Lppncott W & W.

Loughlin, Gerard. Telling God's Story: Bible, Church & Narrative Theology. (Illus.). 282p. (C). 1996. text 59.95 (*0-521-43285-5*) Cambridge U Pr.

— Telling God's Story: Bible, Church & Narrative Theology. 282p. 1999. pap. 22.95 (*0-521-66515-9*) Cambridge U Pr.

Loughlin, Gerard, jt. ed. see Davies, Jon.

Loughlin, James. The Ulster Question since 1945 LC 96-162449. (Studies in Contemporary History). xvi, 151p. 1998. write for info. (*0-333-69351-5*) Macmillan.

— Ulster Unionism & British National Identity since 1885. LC 95-3881. 257p. 1995. 99.00 (*0-86187-845-0*) Bks Intl VA.

Loughlin, John & Mazey, Sonia, eds. The End of the French Unitary State: 10 Years of Regionalization, 1982-1992. LC 95-179207. (Regional Politics & Policy Journals). 164p. 1995. 47.50 (*0-7146-4643-1*, Pub. by F Cass Pubs); pap. 22.50 (*0-7146-4164-2*, Pub. by F Cass Pubs) Intl Spec Bk.

Loughlin, John, jt. ed. see Keating, Michael.

Loughlin, Julia, jt. auth. see Glassner, Barry.

Loughlin, Kathleen A. Women's Perceptions of Transformative Learning Experiences Within Consciousness-Raising. LC 93-32039. 426p. 1993. text 109.95 (*0-7734-2252-8*) E Mellen.

Loughlin, Kevin R., et al. Principles of Endosurgery. (Illus.). 352p. 1995. pap. 59.95 (*0-86542-264-8*) Blackwell Sci.

Loughlin, Laurie. Catmas Carols. LC 92-34649. (Illus.). 48p. 1993. 6.95 (*0-8118-0237-X*) Chronicle Bks.

— Catmas Carols. (Illus.). 48p. 1994. 12.95 incl. audio (*0-8118-0755-X*) Chronicle Bks.

— Hanukcats: Cat Parodies of Traditional Jewish Songs. LC 94-1393. (Illus.). 48p. 1994. 6.95 (*0-8118-0798-3*) Chronicle Bks.

— Holiday Hounds: Traditional Songs for Festive Dogs. LC 96-1838. (Illus.). 48p. 1996. 7.95 (*0-8118-1432-7*) Chronicle Bks.

Loughlin, Marie H. Hymeneutics: Interpreting Virginity on the Early Modern Stage. LC 96-31110. (Illus.). 224p. 1997. 36.50 (*0-8387-5339-6*) Bucknell U Pr.

Loughlin, Martin. Legality & Locality: The Role of the Law in Central-Local Government Relations. LC 96-13511. 460p. (C). 1996. text 99.00 (*0-19-826015-6*, Clarendon Pr) OUP.

— Public Law & Political Theory. LC 92-5647. 304p. 1992. pap. text 27.00 (*0-19-876268-2*) OUP.

***Loughlin, Martin.** Sword & Scales: An Introduction to Law & Politics. 160p. 2000. 45.00 (*1-901362-51-5*, Pub. by Hart Pub); pap. 20.00 (*1-901362-52-3*, Pub. by Hart Pub) Intl Spec Bk.

***Loughlin, Martin F.** Memories of World War II. LC 99-98158. 2000. pap. 8.95 (*0-533-13455-2*) Vantage.

Loughlin, Mike A. Muscle Biopsy: Techniques. (Illus.). 242p. 1993. text 97.50 (*0-7506-1406-4*) Buttrwrth-Heinemann.

Loughlin, Nancy, jt. auth. see Gelb, Eric.

Loughlin, Patrick, jt. auth. see Cohen, Leon.

Loughlin, Peter. New Hampshire Local Government Law. 2nd ed. LC 95-81570. 531p. 1995. text 65.00 (*1-55834-297-4*, 82056-11, MICHIE) LEXIS Pub.

Loughlin, Peter J. Land Use Planning & Zoning. LC 93-11259. (New Hampshire Practice Ser.: Vol. 15). 600p. 1993. 70.00 (*1-56257-361-6*, MICHIE) LEXIS Pub.

— Land Use Planning & Zoning, 2 vols., Set. (NH Practice Ser.: Vols. 1 & 1A). 920p. 1991. ring bd. 140.00 (*0-88063-703-X*, MICHIE) LEXIS Pub.

— Local Government Law, Set. (New Hampshire Practice Ser.: Vols. 13 & 14). 1500p. 1994. boxed set 140.00 (*0-614-05922-4*, MICHIE) LEXIS Pub.

— Municipal Finance & Taxation. (New Hampshire Municipal Practice Ser.: Vol. 2). 880p. 1991. ring bd. 70.00 (*0-88063-704-8*, MICHIE) LEXIS Pub.

— Municipal Finance & Taxation. LC 93-33897. (New Hampshire Practice Ser.: Vol. 16). 860p. 1993. 70.00 (*1-56257-362-4*, MICHIE) LEXIS Pub.

L

An Asterisk (*) at the beginning of an entry indicates that the title is appearing for the first time.

L

— New Hampshire Local Government Law, 1990-93. 24p. 1993. ring bd., suppl. ed. 34.50 (*0-614-03165-6*, MICHIE) LEXIS Pub.

— New Hampshire Local Government Law, 1990-93, Vols. 13 & 14. (NH Practice Ser.). 1500p. 1990. 130.00 (*0-88063-654-8*, MICHIE) LEXIS Pub.

— New Hampshire Municipal Practice Series, 4 vols., Set. ring bd. 225.00 (*0-88063-780-3*, MICHIE) LEXIS Pub.

— New Hampshire Practice: Land Use Planning & Zoning, 1998 Cumulative Supplement. 90p. 1998. pap. write for info. (*0-327-00583-1*, 8441714) LEXIS Pub.

— New Hampshire Practice Vol. 13: Local Government Law, 1998 Cumulative Supplement. 100p. 1998. pap., suppl. ed. write for info. (*0-327-00679-X*, 8441514) LEXIS Pub.

— New Hampshire Practice Vol. 14: Local Government Law, 1998 Cumulative Supplement. 100p. 1998. pap., suppl. ed. write for info. (*0-327-00680-3*, 8441614) LEXIS Pub.

— New Hampshire Practice Vol. 14A: Local Government Law, 1998 Cumulative Supplement. 100p. 1998. pap., suppl. ed. write for info. (*0-327-00681-1*, 8442514) LEXIS Pub.

— New Hampshire Practice Vol. 16: Municipal Finance & Taxation, 1998 Cumulative Supplement. 70p. 1998. pap., suppl. ed. write for info. (*0-327-00702-8*, 8441814) LEXIS Pub.

Loughlin, Peter J. New Hampshire Practice Series: Local Government Law, 3 vols., Vols. 13, 14, 14A. 2nd ed. 195.00 (*0-327-01018-5*) LEXIS Pub.

Loughlin, Peter J. Public Health, Safety & Highways. (New Hampshire Municipal Practice Ser.: Vol. 3). 590p. 1991. ring bd. 70.00 (*0-88063-705-6*, MICHIE) LEXIS Pub.

Loughlin, Richard L. Verses Vice Verses. LC 80-81692. 120p. 1981. 15.95 (*0-911906-18-5*); pap. 9.95 (*0-911906-19-3*) Harian Creative Bks.

Loughlin, Sandra E. & Fallon, James H., eds. Neurotrophic Factors. (Illus.). 607p. 1992. text 104.00 (*0-12-455830-5*) Acad Pr.

Loughlin, Thomas R., ed. Marine Mammals & the "Exxon Valdez" (Illus.). 395p. 1994. text 53.00 (*0-12-456160-8*) Acad Pr.

***Loughlin, Thomas R. & Ohtani, Kiyotaka, eds.** Dynamics of the Bering Sea. (Illus.). 836p. 1999. 40.00 (*1-56612-062-4*) AK Sea Grant CP.

Loughman, B. C., et al. Structural & Functional Aspects of Transport in Roots. (Developments in Plant & Soil Sciences Ser.). (C). 1900. pap. text 79.00 (*0-7923-0061-0*) Kluwer Academic.

Loughman, B. C., jt. ed. see Gabelman, W. H.

Loughman, Michael. Learning to Rock Climb. LC 80-28639. (Outdoor Activities Guides Ser.). (Illus.). 192p. 1982. pap. 14.00 (*0-87156-281-2*, Pub. by Sierra) Random.

Loughmiller, Campbell & Loughmiller, Lynn, eds. Big Thicket Legacy. fac. ed. LC 76-46329. (Illus.). 254p. 1994. pap. 72.40 (*0-7837-7641-1*, 2047394) Bks Demand.

Loughmiller, Campbell & Sherrod, Lynn. Texas Wildflowers: A Field Guide. (Illus.). 287p. 1984. pap. 14.95 (*0-292-78060-5*) U of Tex Pr.

Loughmiller, Campbell, jt. auth. see Loughmiller, Lynne.

Loughmiller, Lynn, jt. ed. see Loughmiller, Campbell.

Loughmiller, Lynne & Loughmiller, Campbell. Texas Wildflowers: A Field Guide. (Illus.). 287p. 1984. 29.95 (*0-292-78059-1*) U of Tex Pr.

Loughna, P. T. & Pell, J. M., eds. Molecular Physiology of Growth. (Society for Experimental Biology Seminar Ser.: No. 60). (Illus.). 170p. (C). 1997. text 59.95 (*0-521-47110-9*) Cambridge U Pr.

Loughney, Katherine. Film, Television, & Video Periodicals: A Comprehensive Annotated List. LC 90-14071. 448p. 1991. text 25.00 (*0-8240-0647-X*) Garland.

Loughran, Charles S. How to Prepare & Present a Labor Arbitration Case: Strategy & Tactics for Advocates. 1996. 65.00 (*0-87179-887-5*) BNA Books.

— Negotiating a Labor Contract: A Management Handbook. 2nd ed. LC 92-280. 590p. 1992. trans. 58.00 (*0-87179-745-3*, HD6483) BNA Books.

Loughran, David, jt. auth. see Knight, Lynn.

Loughran, Edward J., jt. auth. see Guarino-Ghezzi, Susan.

Loughran, Elizabeth L., jt. ed. see Reed, Horace B.

Loughran, J. John. Developing Reflective Practice: Learning about Teaching & Learning Through Modelling. LC 95-47194. 224p. 1996. 79.95 (*0-7507-0515-9*, Falmer Pr); pap. 27.95 (*0-7507-0516-7*, Falmer Pr) Taylor & Francis.

— Teaching about Teaching: Purpose, Passion & Pedagogy in Teacher Education. LC 97-170596. 1997. pap. text 27.95 (*0-7507-0622-8*, Falmer Pr) Taylor & Francis.

Loughran, J. John & Northfield, Jeffrey. Opening the Classroom Door: Teacher, Researcher, Learner. 192p. 1996. pap. 27.95 (*0-7507-0591-4*, Falmer Pr) Taylor & Francis.

Loughran, John L. Researching Teaching: Methodologies & Practices for Understanding Pedagogy. LC 99-218180. 224p. 1999. 95.00 (*0-7507-0948-0*, Falmer Pr) Taylor & Francis.

***Loughran, John L.** Researching Teaching: Methodologies & Practices for Understanding Pedagogy. LC 99-218180. 224p. 1999. pap. text 28.95 (*0-7507-0947-2*, Falmer Pr) Taylor & Francis.

Loughran, Joni. Natural Skin Care: Alternative & Traditional Techniques. 2nd ed. LC 95-18914. (Illus.). 250p. (C). 1996. reprint ed. pap. 16.95 (*1-883319-75-7*) Frog Ltd CA.

***Loughran, Joni & Bull, Ruah.** Aromatherapy & Subtle Energy Techniques: Compassionate Healing with Essential Oils. (Illus.). 150p. 2000. pap. write for info. (*1-58394-015-4*, Pub. by Frog Ltd CA) Publishers Group.

Loughran, Joni, ed. see Spiers, Katy.

Loughran, Katheryne S., et al, eds. Somalia in Word & Image. LC 85-45470. (Illus.). 176p. 1986. pap. 27.50 (*0-253-20376-7*, MB-376) Ind U Pr.

Loughran, Thomas J., jt. auth. see Friend, Michael A.

Loughrey & Cookson, eds. Julius Caesar. (Longman Critical Essays Ser.). 1992. pap. text. write for info. (*0-582-07579-3*, Pub. by Addison-Wesley) Longman.

Loughrey, Bryan, ed. see Bradford, Richard.

Loughrey, Bryan, ed. see Bronfen, Elisabeth.

Loughrey, Bryan, ed. see Bygrave, Stephen.

Loughrey, Bryan, ed. see Conradi, Peter J.

Loughrey, Bryan, ed. see Davies, Stevie.

Loughrey, Bryan, ed. see Gay, John.

Loughrey, Bryan, jt. ed. see Holderness, Graham.

Loughrey, Bryan, ed. see Holt, Michael.

Loughrey, Bryan, ed. see Larrissy, Edward.

Loughrey, Bryan, ed. see McDonagh, Josephine.

Loughrey, Bryan, ed. see Middleton, Thomas.

Loughrey, Bryan, ed. see Msiska, Mpalive.

Loughrey, Bryan, ed. see Parker, Kenneth.

Loughrey, Bryan, ed. see Priestman, Martin.

Loughrey, Bryan, ed. see Ridgman, Jeremy.

Loughrey, Bryan, ed. see Rigney, Jim.

Loughrey, Bryan, ed. see Shakespeare, William.

Loughrey, Leo C., jt. auth. see Hegler, Jean.

Loughrey, Patrick, ed. The People of Ireland. (Illus.). 208p. (C). 1989. 25.00 (*0-941533-55-7*, NAB) I R Dee.

Loughridge, Brendan. Which Dictionary? A Consumer's Guide to Selected English-Language Dictionaries, Thesauri & Language Guides. LC 90-32395. 185p. 1990. reprint ed. pap. 57.40 (*0-608-08871-4*, 206951000004) Bks Demand.

Loughrin, Judy. The Taste of Time, 1842-1992: One Hundred Fifty Years of Good Cooking Made Easy for Today's Kitchens. Patterson, Ce C., ed. LC 92-81893. (Illus.). 224p. (Orig.). 1992. pap. text 12.00 (*0-9632981-2-7*) Lucky Canyon.

Loughrin-Sacco, Steven J. & Abrate, Jayne, eds. Making Business French Work: Models, Materials, Methodologies. LC 97-62140. 250p. 1997. pap. text 25.00 (*1-891611-00-3*) SDSU Ciber Pr.

Loughrin-Sacco, Steven J. & Gagnon, Robert A. Quebec Inc. Un Manuel de Francais des Affaires. (FRE.). (C). 1998. pap. text 29.95 (*1-891611-01-1*) SDSU Ciber Pr.

Loughrin, Susan, et al. Math Combo Story Problems: Grade 4. (Math Combo Bks.: No. 02204). (Illus.). 64p. (Orig.). (J). (gr. 4-4). 1997. pap., wbk. ed. 3.25 (*0-88743-140-2*, 02204) Sch Zone Pub Co.

***Loughry, Marcia.** MCSE Windows 2000 Directory Services for Dummies. (For Dummies Ser.). (Illus.). 504p. 2000. pap. 29.99 incl. cd-rom (*0-7645-0710-9*) IDG Bks.

— Microsoft Active Directory for Dummies. (For Dummies Ser.). 408p. 1999. pap. 24.99 incl. cd-rom (*0-7645-0659-5*) IDG Bks.

Lougy, Cameran, jt. auth. see Aaron, Henry J.

Lougy, Robert. Martin Chuzzlewit: An Annotated Bibliography. LC 89-23263. (Dickens Bibliographies Ser.: Vol. 10). 320p. 1990. text 20.00 (*0-8240-4608-0*, H01083) Garland.

Lougy, Robert E. Charles Robert Maturin. 89p. 1975. 8.50 (*0-8387-7941-7*); pap. 1.95 (*0-8387-7986-7*) Bucknell U Pr.

***Louhenjoki-Schulman, Pirkko-Liisa.** Finland, a Cultural Guide. Hoyle, Russ, ed. (Scandinavian Cultural Guides Ser.: No. 1). (Illus.). 256p. 2000. pap. 24.95 (*0-9672846-0-0*, Pub. by M-K Prodns) IPG Chicago.

Louhija, A., ed. see International Congress on Internal Medicine Staff.

Louhija, A., ed. see Paavo Nurmi Symposium Staff.

Loui, Shirley M. Murasaki's Genji & Proust's Recherche: A Comparative Study. LC 90-33212. (Studies in Comparative Literature: Vol. 8). 248p. 1991. lib. bdg. 89.95 (*0-88946-424-3*) E Mellen.

Louie, Ai-Ling. Yeh Shen: A Cinderella Story from China. LC 80-11745. (Illus.). 32p. (J). (ps-2). 1982. 15.95 (*0-399-20900-X*, Philomel) Peng Put Young Read.

— Yeh-Shen: A Cinderella Story from China. (Illus.). 32p. (J). (ps-3). 1996. pap. 5.99 (*0-698-11388-8*, PapStar) Peng Put Young Read.

Louie, Ai-Ling. Yeh-Shen: A Cinderella Story from China. (J). 1996. 11.15 (*0-606-03967-8*, Pub. by Turtleback) Demco.

Louie, Andrea. Moon Cakes. LC 94-48115. 1995. 341.10 (*0-345-39622-7*) Ballantine Pub Grp.

Louie, Barbara G. Novi. LC 98-87869. (Images of America Ser.). 1998. write for info. (*0-7385-0012-7*) Arcadia Publng.

***Louie, David Wong.** The Barbarians Are Coming. LC 99-36902. 384p. 2000. 23.95 (*0-399-14603-2*, Marion Wood) Putnam Pub Group.

***Louie, Elaine.** Living in New England. (Illus.). 192p. 2000. 34.50 (*0-7432-0375-5*) S&S Trade.

Louie, Elaine. New York City Man. 240p. (Orig.). 1989. mass mkt. 8.95 (*0-446-38708-8*, Pub. by Warner Bks) Little.

— New York City Woman. 240p. (Orig.). 1989. mass mkt. 8.95 (*0-446-38706-1*, Pub. by Warner Bks) Little.

— Premier Beer: A Guide to America's Best Bottled Microbrews. LC 96-21554. 192p. 1996. per. 14.00 (*0-671-53676-1*) PB.

Louie, Emma W. Chinese American Names: Tradition & Transition. LC 97-41692. (Illus.). 240p. 1998. lib. bdg. 32.50 (*0-7864-0418-3*) McFarland & Co.

Louie, Kam. Inheriting Tradition: Interpretations of the Classical Chinese Philosophers in Communist China, 1949-1966. 286p. (C). 1987. text 39.95 (*0-19-584046-1*) OUP.

Louie, Kam, intro. Strange Tales from Strange Lands: Stories by Zheng Wanlong. (Cornell East Asia Ser.: No. 66). 147p. (C). 1993. 18.70 (*0-939657-85-6*); pap. 11.90 (*0-939657-66-X*) Cornell East Asia Pgm.

Louie, Kam & Edwards, Louise, eds. Censored by Confucius: Ghost Stories. LC 95-34203. (New Studies in Asian Culture). (Illus.). 259p. (C). (gr. 13). 1996. pap. text 24.95 (*1-56324-681-3*, East Gate Bk) M E Sharpe.

Louie, Kam & Edwards, Louise, eds. Censored by Confucius: Ghost Stories by Yuan Mei. LC 95-34203. (New Studies in Asian Culture). (Illus.). 259p. (C). 1996. text 79.95 (*1-56324-680-5*, East Gate Bk) M E Sharpe.

Louie, Kam & McDougall, Bonnie S. Literature of China in the 20th Century. LC 97-2533. 352p. 1997. 37.00 (*0-231-11084-7*) Col U Pr.

— The Literature of China in the Twentieth Century. 320p. 1999. pap. 17.50 (*0-231-11085-5*) Col U Pr.

Louie, Kam, jt. auth. see Hodge, Bob.

Louie, R. L. The Cultural Connection of Californian & Plateau Shoshonean Tribes. fac. ed. (University of California Publications in American Archaeology & Ethnology: Vol. 20: 9). 12p. (C). 1923. reprint ed. pap. text 1.56 (*1-55567-245-0*) Coyote Press.

Louie, Rachel, jt. auth. see Kilburn, Rebecca M.

Louie, Robert H. The Matrilineal Complex. fac. ed. (University of California Publications in American Archaeology & Ethnology: Vol. 16: 2). 16p. (C). 1919. reprint ed. pap. text 2.19 (*1-55567-222-1*) Coyote Press.

Louie, Stan G., jt. ed. see Shen, Wei-Chiang.

Louie, Steven G., jt. ed. see Chelikowsky, James R.

Louis, jt. auth. see Livingstone.

Louis, A. K., et al. Wavelets: Theory & Applications. LC 97-212472. 342p. 1997. 110.00 (*0-471-96792-0*) Wiley.

Louis, Adrian C. Among the Dog Eaters. 91p. (Orig.). 1992. pap. 9.95 (*0-931122-69-4*) West End.

***Louis, Adrian C.** Ancient Acid Flashes Back: Poems. LC 00-8552. (Western Literature Ser.). 88p. 2000. pap. 11.00 (*0-87417-352-3*) U of Nev Pr.

Louis, Adrian C. Blood Thirsty Savages. LC 94-7444. 109p. 1994. 18.95 (*1-56809-010-2*); pap. 12.50 (*1-56809-011-0*) Time Being Bks.

— Ceremonies of the Damned: Poems. LC 97-15208. (Western Literature Ser.). 80p. 1997. pap. 10.00 (*0-87417-302-7*) U of Nev Pr.

— Vortex of Indian Fevers. LC 94-45837. 62p. 1995. 29.95 (*0-8101-5017-4*, TriQuart); pap. 11.95 (*0-8101-5042-5*, TriQuart) Northwestern U Pr.

— Wild Indians & Other Creatures. LC 95-47239. (Western Literature Ser.). 200p. 1997. reprint ed. 20.00 (*0-87417-279-9*) U of Nev Pr.

— Wild Indians & Other Creatures. LC 95-47239. (Western Literature Ser.). 200p. 1997. reprint ed. pap. 17.00 (*0-87417-303-5*) U of Nev Pr.

Louis, Adrian C., et al. Days of Obsidian, Days of Grace: Selected Poetry & Prose by Four Native American Writers. 152p. 1994. pap. 13.95 (*0-9641986-0-6*) Poetry Harbor.

Louis, Anthony. Aprenda Como Leet el Tarot: Una Gui Practica. LC 99-48193. (SPA., Illus.). 264p. 1999. pap. 12.95 (*1-56718-402-2*) Llewellyn Pubns.

— Horary Astrology Plain & Simple. LC 97-52798. (Illus.). 288p. 1999. pap. 19.95 (*1-56718-401-4*) Llewellyn Pubns.

— Tarot Plain & Simple. LC 96-30422. (Illus.). 336p. (Orig.). 1999. pap. 14.95 (*1-56718-400-6*, K-400-6) Llewellyn Pubns.

Louis, Cynthia B. Jailhouse Key: Prevention vs. Conviction. Hodges, Jim & Williams, Larry, eds. (Juvenile Law Ser.). (Illus.). 113p. (Orig.). 1994. pap. text 9.95 (*0-9644630-0-8*) C B Louis.

Louis, Daphne R., jt. auth. see Johnson, Terry D.

Louis, David. Two Thousand Two Hundred & One Fascinating Facts, 2 vols. in 1. (Illus.). 384p. 1988. 11.99 (*0-517-39574-6*) Random Hse Value.

Louis, Diana F. & Marinos, June. Prospero's Kitchen: Mediterranean Cooking of the Ionian Islands from Corfu to Kythera. LC 94-49418. (Illus.). 256p. 1995. 21.95 (*0-87131-782-6*) M Evans.

Louis, Dorothy. How Lilacs Came to Rochester. 1982. pap. 20.00 incl. lp (*0-9609624-4-1*) Bookworm Rochester NY.

— How Lilacs Came to Rochester, Set. 1982. pap. write for info. (*0-9609624-3-3*) Bookworm Rochester NY.

Louis, Dorothy. My Father, the Chef. 148p. (Orig.). 1978. pap. 15.00 (*0-9609624-0-9*) Bookworm Rochester NY.

Louis, Frances. Swift's Anatomy of Misunderstanding: A Study of Swift's Epistemological Imagination in "A Tale of a Tub" & "Gulliver's Travels" 220p. 1981. 52.50 (*0-389-20074-3*, 06804) B&N Imports.

Louis Harris & Associates, compiled by. Hostile Hallways: The AAUW Survey on Sexual Harassment in America's School. LC 94-21180. 28p. 1994. pap. 11.95 (*1-879922-01-0*) Am Assoc U Women.

Louis, Harry, et al. The Classic Motorcycles. LC 76-8038. 125 p. 1976. write for info. (*0-525-08203-4*, Dutton Child) Peng Put Young Read.

Louis, Herbert. Zur Reliefentwicklung der Oberpfalz. (Relief, Boden, Palaeoklima Ser.: Band 3). (GER., Illus.). vii, 1500p. 1984. pap. 53.00 (*3-443-09003-6*, Pub. by Gebruder Borntraeger) Balogh.

Louis, J. Nonperturbative Aspects of Strings, Branes & Supersymmetry. LC 99-27206. 500p. 1999. 166.00 (*981-02-3785-5*) World Scientific Pub.

Louis, J., jt. auth. see Louis, V.

Louis-Jacques, Lyonette, ed. see American Association of Law Libraries Staff.

***Louis, Jean-Victor & Bronkhorst, Hajo, eds.** The Euro & European Integration. LC 99-89231. (European Policy Ser.: Vol. 21). 365p. 2000. pap. 35.95 (*0-8204-4652-1*) P Lang Pubng.

Louis, Jeanne H., ed. Separation from the World: For American Peace Churches: Asset or Handicap? 76p. 1997. pap. 23.00 (*0-7855-2848-2*, Pub. by W Sessions) St Mut.

***Louis, Jeanne Henriette, ed.** Separation from the World for American Peace Churches - Asset or Handicap? 1999. pap. 21.00 (*1-85072-189-0*, Pub. by W Sessions) St Mut.

Louis, Jennifer M., jt. auth. see Louis, Victor E.

Louis Joos, Rascal. Oregon's Journey. LC 93-11796. 40p. (J). (gr. k-4). 1997. 15.95 (*0-8167-3305-8*) BrdgeWater.

Louis, Joseph. Madelaine. 1987. pap. 2.95 (*0-317-54101-3*) Bantam.

Louis, K. S., jt. auth. see Rosenblum, S.

Louis, Karen S. & Kruse, Sharon D. Professionalism & Community: Perspectives on Reforming Urban Schools. LC 94-46409. (Illus.). 272p. 1995. 65.95 (*0-8039-6252-5*); pap. 29.95 (*0-8039-6253-3*) Corwin Pr.

Louis, Karen S. & Miles, Matthew B. Improving the Urban High School: What Works & Why. 360p. (C). 1990. text 45.00 (*0-8077-3022-X*); pap. text 23.95 (*0-8077-3021-1*) Tchrs Coll.

Louis, Karen S. & Sieber, Sam D., eds. Bureaucracy & the Dispersed Organization: The Educational Extension Agent Experiment. LC 78-31623. (Modern Sociology Ser.). 256p. 1979. text 73.25 (*0-89391-018-X*) Ablx Pub.

Louis, Karen S., jt. auth. see Leithwood, Kenneth.

Louis, Karen S., jt. ed. see Murphy, Joseph.

***Louis, Kenneth W.** Mass of Saint Cyprian, 1. 1999. 15.95 (*5-550-73196-7*); pap. 10.95 (*5-550-73197-5*) Nairi.

Louis, Liliane N. & Hay, Frederick J. When Night Falls--Kric, Krac! Haitian Folktales. LC 98-35608. (World Folkore Ser.). (Illus.). 200p. 1999. 26.50 (*1-56308-579-8*) Libs Unl.

Louis, Lisa. Butterflies of the Night: Mama-sans, Geisha, Strippers, & the Japanese Men They Serve. 224p. (C). 1992. 19.95 (*0-8348-0249-X*, Tengu Bks) Weatherhill.

Louis, Margot K. Swinburne & His Gods: The Roots & Growth of an Agnostic Poetry. 256p. (C). 1990. text 65.00 (*0-7735-0715-9*, Pub. by McG-Queens Univ Pr) CUP Services.

Louis, Mary-Ben. Sing Me to Sleep. 288p. 1993. mass mkt. 4.50 (*0-8217-4405-4*, Zebra Kensgtn) Kensgtn Pub Corp.

Louis, Melinda J. St., see St. Louis, Melinda J.

Louis, Meryl R., jt. auth. see Bartunek, Jean M.

Louis-Napoleon, Geoffroy-Chateau & Geoffroy-Chateau, Louis-Napoleon. Napoleon & the Conquest of the World: A Fictional Account of Napoleon's Escape from Russia, Invasion of England, & Conquest of Asia & America. LC 94-72170. (Illus.). 440p. 1994. reprint ed. lib. bdg. 39.95 (*0-9642115-3-X*) Campaign Press.

Louis, Natalie. Life in Your Backyard Theme Pack. (Ranger Rick Science Spectacular Ser.). (Illus.). 16p. (J). (gr. 2-5). 1996. pap. 36.90 (*1-56784-284-4*) Newbridge Educ.

Louis of Granada. Pathways to Holiness. Aumann, Jordan, tr. from ENG. & adapted by by. LC 97-36682. 144p. 1998. pap. 7.95 (*0-8189-0805-X*) Alba.

— Summa of the Christian Life, 3 vols., 1. Aumann, Jordan, tr. from SPA. LC 79-65716. 1979. reprint ed. pap. write for info. (*0-89555-118-7*) TAN Bks Pubs.

— Summa of the Christian Life, 3 vols., 2. Aumann, Jordan, tr. from SPA. LC 79-65716. 1979. reprint ed. pap. write for info. (*0-89555-119-5*) TAN Bks Pubs.

— Summa of the Christian Life, 3 vols., 3. Aumann, Jordan, tr. from SPA. LC 79-65716. 1979. reprint ed. pap. write for info. (*0-89555-120-9*) TAN Bks Pubs.

— Summa of the Christian Life, 3 vols., Set. Aumann, Jordan, tr. from SPA. LC 79-65716. 1979. reprint ed. pap. 36.00 (*0-89555-121-7*) TAN Bks Pubs.

Louis, P. J. Across the Networks: Network Interconnection & Convergence. (Illus.). 352p. 1998. 69.00 (*0-9650658-5-5*) APDG.

***Louis, P. J.** Telecommunications Internetworking: Delivering Services Across the Networks. (Telecommunications Ser.). 450p. 2000. pap. 60.00 (*0-07-135654-1*) McGraw-Hill Prof.

Louis, R. Sexpectations: Women Talk Candidly on Sex & Dating. LC 97-186697. (Illus.). 180p. (Orig.). 1997. pap. 10.95 (*0-9613177-4-4*) MPC Pr.

— Surgery of the Spine: Surgical Anatomy & Operative Approaches. (Illus.). 328p. 1983. 288.00 (*0-387-11412-2*) Spr-Verlag.

Louis, R. & Weidner, A., eds. Cervical Spine, No. II. (Illus.). 304p. 1990. 112.00 (*0-387-82151-1*, 3624) Spr-Verlag.

Louis, Raymond. Labour Co-Operatives: Retrospect & Prospects. vi, 162p. 1983. 31.50 (*92-2-103011-3*); pap. 22.50 (*92-2-103012-1*) Intl Labour Office.

Louis, Raymond J. Integrating Kanban with MRPII: Automating a Pull System for Enhanced JIT Inventory Management. LC 97-28312. (Illus.). 200p. 1997. 45.00 (*1-56327-182-6*) Productivity Inc.

Louis, Rene, jt. auth. see De Troyes, Chretien.

Louis, Rita, tr. see Shaw, Luci.

Louis, Roger, jt. ed. see Brown, Judith M.

Louis, Roger, jt. ed. see Winks, Robin.

Louis, Roger W., jt. ed. see Gifford, Prosser.

***Louis, Ron.** How to Succeed with Men. LC 99-51498. 2000. 34.00 (*0-13-014509-2*) P-H.

Louis, Ron & Copeland, David. How to Succeed with Men. LC 99-51498. 2000. pap. 14.00 (*0-7352-0140-4*) PH Pr.

— How to Succeed with Women. LC 98-27038. 320p. (C). 1998. text 24.95 (*0-13-095091-2*) P-H.

— How to Succeed with Women. LC 98-27038. 320p. 1998. pap. 14.00 (*0-7352-0030-0*) PH Pr.

An Asterisk (*) at the beginning of an entry indicates that the title is appearing for the first time.

***Louis, Ron & Copeland, David.** The Sex Lovers Book of Lists. 2001. pap. 12.00 (*0-7352-0216-8*) PH Pr.

Louis, S., ed. Golden West Conference on Intelligent Systems (GWICS), 4th International Conference, June 12-14, 1995, San Francisco, California, U.S.A: June 12-14, 1995, San Francisco, CA. (Conference Proceedings Ser.). (C). 1995. write for info. (*1-880843-12-9*) Int Soc Comp App.

Louis, Sang B. Anyabwile. (Illus.). 374p. 1995. pap. 14.95 (*0-9645582-0-3*) R L Jackson.

Louis, Thomas A., jt. auth. see Carlin, Bradley P.

Louis, V. Information Moscow. 178p. (C). 1991. 75.00 (*0-89771-897-6*, Pub. by Collets) St Mut.

Louis, V. & Louis, J. Complete Guide to the Soviet Union: New York St. Martin's Press, 1980. (Illus.). 378p. (C). 1980. 115.00 (*0-7855-4031-8*) St Mut.

Louis, Victor E. & Louis, Jennifer M. Louis Motorists' Guide to the Soviet Union. 2nd ed. LC 85-21830. (Illus.). 625p. 1987. pap. 69.00 (*0-08-031816-9*, Pergamon Pr) Elsevier.

Louis, W. Roger. The Oxford History of the Twentieth Century. Howard, Michael, ed. LC 98-12861. (Illus.). 540p. 1998. 39.95 (*0-19-820428-0*) OUP.

Louis, W. Roger, jt. ed. see Howard, Michael.

Louis, W. Roger, jt. ed. see Livingston, William S.

Louis, William R. The British Empire in the Middle East, 1945-1951: Arab Nationalism, the United States, & Postwar Imperialism. (Illus.). 820p. 1986. pap. text 38.00 (*0-19-822960-7*) OUP.

Louis, William R. Imperialism at Bay: The United States & the Decolonization of the British Empire, 1941-1945. 610p. 1987. reprint ed. pap. text 35.00 (*0-19-822972-0*) OUP.

***Louis, William R.** More Adventures with Britannia. LC 98-61464. x, 388 p. 1998. write for info. (*1-86064-293-4*) I B T.

Louis, William R., ed. More Adventures with Britannia: Personalities, Politics, & Culture in Britain. LC 98-61464. (Illus.). 384p. 1999. 40.00 (*0-292-74708-X*); pap. 19.95 (*0-292-74709-8*) U of Tex Pr.

Louis, William R. & Bull, Hedley, eds. The Special Relationship: Anglo-American Relations since 1945. 428p. 1987. reprint ed. text 75.00 (*0-19-822925-9*) OUP.

— The Special Relationship: Anglo-American Relations since 1945. 432p. 1989. reprint ed. pap. text 29.95 (*0-19-820183-4*) OUP.

Louis, William R. & Stookey, Robert W., eds. The End of the Palestine Mandate. (Center for Middle Eastern Studies, Modern Middle East Ser.: No. 12). (Illus.). 197p. (C). 1986. reprint ed. pap. 10.95 (*0-292-72063-7*) U of Tex Pr.

Louis, William R., jt. auth. see Gifford, Prosser.

Louis, William R., jt. ed. see Blake, Robert.

Louis, William R., jt. ed. see Fernea, Robert A.

***Louise, Ann.** Birthday Boy. (Illus.). (J). 1999. pap. 9.95 (*0-9661451-0-0*) Chadko Pub.

Louise, Chandra B. Jump Start Your Career in Bio Science. LC 97-75974. (Illus.). 220p. (Orig.). (C). 1998. pap. 19.95 (*0-9661790-0-5*) Peer Prods.

Louise-Diana. Seeds of Consciousness: Affirmations for Daily Living. (Illus.). 96p. 1999. pap. 7.95 (*0-87516-724-1*) DeVorss.

Louise Hsi, jt. auth. see Yuan Hsi Kuo.

Louise, Jay D. How to Have an Affair' & Never Get Caught! LC 94-74957. (Illus.). 128p. 1995. 17.95 (*0-9644789-0-0*, Roxan Bks) DeBergerac Pub.

Louise, M. & Pupolin, S., eds. Broadband Wireless Communications: Transmission, Access, & Services. LC 97-47334. vii, 432p. 1998. pap. 79.95 (*3-540-76237-X*) Spr-Verlag.

Louise, Mary, see Mary Louise, ed.

Louise, T., ed. see Sprague, Ruth M.

Louise, Virginia, jt. auth. see Draper, Linda.

Louisell, David W. Evidence: Adaptable to Courses Utilizing Materials by Louisell. 5th ed. 273p. write for info. (*0-318-62084-7*) Harcourt.

— Evidence & Proof. Date not set. pap. text, teacher ed. write for info. (*0-88277-516-2*) Foundation Pr.

Louisell, David W. & Louisell, Williams H. Medical Malpractice, 4 vols. 1960. ring bd. 900.00 (*0-8205-1370-9*) Bender.

Louisell, David W. & Mueller, Christopher B. Federal Evidence, 5 vols. 2nd ed. LC 94-75978. 1994. 455.00 (*0-686-22901-0*) West Group.

Louisell, David W., et al. Principles of Evidence & Proof. 3rd ed. 1977. text 35.00 (*0-88277-424-7*) Foundation Pr.

Louisell, Robert D. & Descamps, Jorge. Developing a Teaching Style: Methods for Elementary School Teachers. (Illus.). 320p. (C). 1996. reprint ed. pap. text 31.95 (*0-88133-931-8*) Waveland Pr.

Louisell, William H. Quantum Statistical Properties of Radiation. (Classics Library). 544p. 1990. pap. 84.95 (*0-471-52365-8*) Wiley.

Louisell, Williams H., jt. auth. see Louisell, David W.

Louisi, Gary. Dashiell Hammett & Raymond Chandler: A Bibliography of Their Paperback Appearances. LC 96-134119. 100p. 1994. pap. 15.00 (*0-936071-36-2*) Gryphon Pubns.

— Instant Expert: Science Fiction. (Illus.). 130p. (Orig.). 1997. pap. 14.00 (*0-614-24069-7*) Allian Pubng.

Louisiana. Louisiana Related Laws to the Insurance Laws. LC 97-65766. 1997. write for info. (*0-89246-470-4*) NILS Pub.

Louisiana Appellate Court Handbook Committee. Louisiana Appellate Practice Handbook. LC 86-81536. 1986. 115.00 (*0-318-21801-1*) West Group.

— Louisiana Appellate Practice Handbook: Supplement, 1992. LC 86-81536. 1992. suppl. ed. 52.50 (*0-317-04348-X*) West Group.

Louisiana Commission des Avoyelles. Avoyelles: Crossroads of Louisiana Where All Cultures Meet. Woolfolk, Doug, ed. (Illus.). 228p. 1981. 29.95 (*0-86518-021-0*) Moran Pub Corp.

Louisiana Crawfish-Man. The Adventures of Crawfish-Man. (Louisiana Crawfish-Man's Tales from the Atchafalaya Ser.). (Illus.). 40p. (J). (gr. k-8). 1979. spiral bd. 8.00 (*0-931108-04-7*) Little Cajun Bks.

— Coocan: Boy of the Swamp. (Louisiana Crawfish-Man's Tales from the Atchafalaya Ser.). (Illus.). 40p. (J). (gr. k-8). 1983. spiral bd. 8.00 (*0-931108-09-8*) Little Cajun Bks.

— Crawfish-Man Rescues Ron Guidry. deluxe ed. (Louisiana Crawfish-Man's Tales from the Atchafalaya Ser.). (Illus.). (J). (gr. k-8). 1980. spiral bd. 8.00 (*0-931108-05-5*) Little Cajun Bks.

— Crawfish-Man Rescues the Ol' Beachcomber. deluxe ed. (Louisiana Crawfish-Man's Tales from the Atchafalaya Ser.). (Illus.). 32p. (J). (gr. k-8). 1985. spiral bd. 8.00 (*0-931108-13-6*) Little Cajun Bks.

— Crawfish-Man's Fifty Ways to Keep Kids from Using Drugs. (Louisiana Crawfish-Man's Tales from the Atchafalaya Ser.). (Illus.). 52p. (J). (gr. k-8). 1982. spiral bd. 8.00 (*0-931108-08-X*) Little Cajun Bks.

— Crawfish-Man's Night Befo' Christmas. (Illus.). 40p. (J). (gr. k-8). 1984. spiral bd. 8.00 (*0-931108-12-8*) Little Cajun Bks.

— Dark Gator. (Louisiana Crawfish Man New Swamp Wars Ser.). (Illus.). 48p. (J). (gr. k-8). 1980. spiral bd. 8.00 (*0-931108-06-3*) Little Cajun Bks.

— Maurice the Snake & Gaston the Near-Sighted Turtle: Louisiana Crawfish Man's Tales from the Atchafalaya. (Louisiana Crawfish-Man's Tales from the Atchafalaya Ser.). (Illus.). 36p. (J). (gr. k-8). 1977. spiral bd. 8.00 (*0-931108-00-4*) Little Cajun Bks.

— Real Cajun School of Cooking Cookbook. (Illus.). 64p. 1990. spiral bd. 8.00 (*0-931108-15-2*) Little Cajun Bks.

— Rhombus: The Cajun Unicorn. (Louisiana Crawfish-Man's Tales from the Atchafalaya Ser.). (Illus.). 40p. (J). (gr. k up). 1984. spiral bd. 8.00 (*0-931108-10-1*) Little Cajun Bks.

— Santa's Cajun Christmas Adventure. (Louisiana Crawfish-Man's Tales from the Atchafalaya Ser.). (Illus.). 48p. (J). (gr. k-8). 1981. spiral bd. 8.00 (*0-931108-07-1*) Little Cajun Bks.

— T-Boy & the Trial for Life. (Louisiana Crawfish-Man's Tales from the Atchafalaya Ser.). (Illus.). 36p. (J). (gr. k-8). 1978. spiral bd. 8.00 (*0-931108-02-0*) Little Cajun Bks.

— T-Boy in Mossland. (Louisiana Crawfish-Man's Tales from the Atchafalaya Ser.). (Illus.). 48p. (J). (gr. k-8). 1978. spiral bd. 8.00 (*0-931108-03-9*) Little Cajun Bks.

— T-Boy the Little Cajun. (Louisiana Crawfish-Man's Tales from the Atchafalaya Ser.). (Illus.). 36p. (J). (gr. k-8). 1978. spiral bd. 8.00 (*0-931108-01-2*) Little Cajun Bks.

— World Famous New Iberia, La. Cooking. (Illus.). 40p. 1997. spiral bd. 8.00 (*0-931108-16-0*) Little Cajun Bks.

Louisiana District Judges Staff. Judges of Louisiana. 1972. 6.00 (*0-685-27203-6*) Claitors.

Louisiana Farm Bureau Federation Staff. Louisiana Temptations. LC 96-84999. 1996. 16.95 (*0-9652035-0-6*) LA Farm Bureau.

Louisiana Historical Quarterly Staff. Louisiana Historical Quarterly, 37 vols., Set. 1995. reprint ed. 3439.50 (*0-614-07691-9*) AMS Pr.

Louisiana Historical Society Staff & Parish of St. Mary Labeth Staff. Louisiana Historical Society Publications, 10 vols., Set. 1995. reprint ed. 700.00 (*0-404-19531-8*) AMS Pr.

Louisiana Law Staff. Louisiana Insurance Laws. LC 98-66269. 1998. write for info. (*0-89246-498-4*) NILS Pub.

Louisiana Pen Women Staff. Louisiana Leaders. 1970. 20.00 (*0-87511-067-3*) Claitors.

— Vignettes of Louisiana History. 1967. 20.00 (*0-87511-068-1*) Claitors.

Louisiana Restaurant Association Staff. Chef's Secrets from Great Restaurants in Louisiana. (Illus.). 228p. 1989. 16.95 (*0-88289-639-3*); pap. 16.95 (*1-56554-621-0*) Pelican.

Louisiana School Students Staff. Ascending. (Illus.). 302p. (Orig.). (J). (gr. 1-12). 1989. pap. 25.00 (*1-882913-00-0*) Thornton LA.

Louisiana State Staff. Civil Code of the State of Louisiana: By Authority. LC 74-19620. reprint ed. 94.50 (*0-404-12456-9*) AMS Pr.

Louisiana Tech University Staff, jt. auth. see Martin, F. Lestar.

Louismet, Dom S. The Burning Bush: Being a Treatise on the Ecstatic Contemplation of the Blessed Trinity. 261p. 1996. reprint ed. pap. 18.95 (*1-56459-566-8*) Kessinger Pub.

— Mystical Initiation. 233p. 1996. reprint ed. pap. 18.95 (*1-56459-544-7*) Kessinger Pub.

— The Mystical Knowledge of God: An Essay in the Art of Knowing & Loving the Divine Majesty. 159p. 1996. reprint ed. pap. 17.95 (*1-56459-565-X*) Kessinger Pub.

— Mysticism True & False. 178p. 1996. reprint ed. pap. 17.95 (*1-56459-548-X*) Kessinger Pub.

Louisville Courier Journal Staff. Legacy of Champions: The Story of the Men Who Built Kentucky Basketball. 1997. 99.95 (*1-57028-179-3*, Mstrs Pr) NTC Contemp Pub Co.

Louisville Division of Fire Staff. Louisville Fire Department, Vol. II. LC 88-51134. (Illus.). 144p. 1988. 39.95 (*1-56311-337-6*) Turner Pub KY.

Louisville's Young Playwrights Staff. Insight. 1986. 5.50 (*0-87129-578-4*, I42) Dramatic Pub.

Louizos, Dianna. The Greater Northern California Road Map, Eatery Guide, & Cookbook. Paxton, Vicki, ed. (Illus.). 52p. (Orig.). 1994. pap. 10.00 (*0-9643901-0-8*) J Levy Ctr.

Louka, Elli. Overcoming National Barriers to International Waste Trade: A New Perspective on the Transnational Movement of Hazardous & Radioactive Wastes. (International Environmental Law & Policy Ser.). 240p. (C). 1994. lib. bdg. 92.00 (*0-7923-2850-7*) Kluwer Academic.

Loukaides, Loukes G. Essays on the Developing Law of Human Rights. LC 94-23941. (International Studies in Human Rights: Vol. 39). 1995. lib. bdg. 90.50 (*0-7923-3276-8*, Pub. by M Nijhoff) Kluwer Academic.

Loukaitou-Sideris, Anastasia & Banerjee, Tridib. Urban Design Downtown: Poetics & Politics of Form. LC 97-10758. 348p. 1998. 40.00 (*0-520-20930-3*, Pub. by U CA Pr) Cal Prin Full Svc.

Loukakis, Angelo. For the Patriarch. 191p. 1982. pap. 14.95 (*0-7022-1600-3*, Pub. by Univ Queensland Pr) Intl Spec Bk.

— Vernacular Dreams. LC 85-14088. 228p. 1986. pap. 14.95 (*0-7022-2025-6*, Pub. by Univ Queensland Pr) Intl Spec Bk.

Loukashevitch, Claudia. Sejatel.Tr. of Sower. (Illus.). 462p. 1966. 20.00 (*0-317-30416-X*); pap. 15.00 (*0-317-30417-8*) Holy Trinity.

Loukes, Harold. Readiness for Religion. LC 63-11818. (Orig.). 1963. pap. 4.00 (*0-87574-126-6*) Pendle Hill.

Loukianoff, Gregoire. Poeme Heroique sur le Bataille de Qadech (1288 Av. J. C.) (FRE.). 24p. (Orig.). (C). 1988. reprint ed. pap. 10.00 (*0-933175-18-3*) Van Siclen Bks.

Loukides, Michael, ed. see Ballew, Scott.

Loukides, Mike. System Performance Tuning. (Computer Science). 336p. (Orig.). 1990. pap. 29.95 (*0-937175-60-9*) Thomson Learn.

Loukides, Mike & Oram, Andy. Programming with GNU Software: Tools from Cygnus Support. LC 97-115579. 260p. 1996. pap. 39.95 (*1-56592-112-7*) Thomson Learn.

Loukides, Mike, ed. see Bolinger, Don & Bronson, Tan.

Loukides, Mike, ed. see Dowd, Kevin.

Loukides, Mike, ed. see DuBois, Paul.

Loukides, Mike, ed. see Electronic Frontier Foundation Staff.

Loukides, Mike, ed. see Englander, Rob.

Loukides, Mike, ed. see Farley, Jim.

Loukides, Mike, ed. see Gilly, Daniel.

Loukides, Mike, ed. see Hall, Eric.

Loukides, Mike, ed. see Harold, Elliotte Rusty.

Loukides, Mike, ed. see Hunt, Craig.

Loukides, Mike, ed. see Knudsen, Jonathan B.

Loukides, Mike, ed. see Lewis, Kevin.

Loukides, Mike, ed. see Liu, Cricket & Albitz, Paul.

Loukides, Mike, ed. see Liu, Cricket, et al.

Loukides, Mike, ed. see Monson-Haefel, Richard.

Loukides, Mike, ed. see Musciano, Chuck.

Loukides, Mike, ed. see Musciano, Chuck & Kennedy, Bill.

Loukides, Mike, ed. see Niemeyer, Patrick & Knudsen, Jonathan.

Loukides, Mike, ed. see Niemeyer, Pat & Peck, Jash.

Loukides, Mike, ed. see Niemeyer, Pat & Peck, Josh.

Loukides, Mike, ed. see Oaks, Scott & Wong, Henry.

Loukides, Mike, ed. see O'Reilly & Associates Staff, et al.

Loukides, Mike, ed. see Radin, Dave.

Loukides, Mike, ed. see Rosenblatt, Bill.

Loukides, Mike, ed. see Sun, Andrew.

Loukides, Mike, ed. see Zukowski, John.

Loukides, Paul, et al, eds. Beyond the Stars 5: Themes & Ideologies in American Popular Film, Vol. 5. 301p. 1996. 39.95 (*0-87972-701-2*) Bowling Green Univ Popular Press.

Loukides, Paul & Fuller, Linda K. Beyond the Stars 2: Plot Conventions in American Popular Film. LC 89-82334. 225p. (C). 1991. 39.95 (*0-87972-517-6*) Bowling Green Univ Popular Press.

Loukides, Paul & Fuller, Linda K., eds. Beyond the Stars 1: Stock Characters in American Popular Film. LC 89-82334. (Illus.). 245p. (C). 1990. 40.95 (*0-87972-479-X*) Bowling Green Univ Popular Press.

— Beyond the Stars 3: The Material World in American Popular Film. LC 89-82334. 245p. 1993. 35.95 (*0-87972-622-9*) Bowling Green Univ Popular Press.

— Beyond the Stars 3: The Material World in American Popular Film. LC 89-82334. 245p. 1993. pap. 13.95 (*0-87972-623-7*) Bowling Green Univ Popular Press.

— Beyond the Stars 4: Locales in American Popular Film. LC 89-82334. 280p. (C). 1993. 39.95 (*0-87972-588-5*); pap. 18.95 (*0-87972-589-3*) Bowling Green Univ Popular Press.

Loukides, Paul, jt. auth. see Boswell, Parley A.

Loukom, John A., ed. see Luther, Martin & Sverdrup, H. U.

Loukomsky. Memoirs of the Russian Revolution. 1976. lib. bdg. 59.95 (*0-8490-2225-8*) Gordon Pr.

Loukopoulos, Dimitris, ed. Prenatal Diagnosis of Thalassemia & the Hemoglobinopathies. 272p. 1988. 151.00 (*0-8493-5972-4*, RJ416, CRC Reprint) Franklin.

Loukopoulos, Dimitris, jt. ed. see Bartsocas, Christos S.

Loukopoulos, Louisa D., ed. see Andronicos, Manolis, et al.

Loulakis, Michael C., et al. Construction Management: Law & Practice, 1. LC 95-35624. 600p. 1995. boxed set 150.00 (*0-471-00659-9*) Wiley.

Loulan, Jo Ann. The Lesbian Erotic Dance: Butch, Femme, Androgyny, & Other Rhythms. LC 90-10177. 304p. (Orig.). 1990. pap. 12.95 (*0-933216-76-9*) Spinsters Ink.

— Lesbian Passion: Loving Ourselves & Each Other. LC 87-60781. 325p. (Orig.). 1987. pap. 12.95 (*0-933216-29-7*) Spinsters Ink.

— Lesbian Sex. LC 84-52008. (Illus.). 320p. (Orig.). 1984. pap. 12.95 (*0-933216-13-0*) Spinsters Ink.

***Loulan, Joann & Worthen, Bonnie.** Period. rev. ed. 100p. 2000. pap. 9.99 (*0-916773-96-5*) Book Peddlers.

Loulides, Mike, ed. see Harrison, Mark.

Loulie. Elements or Principles of Music. Cohen, Albert, ed. (Musical Theorists in Translation Ser.: Vol. 6). 1966. lib. bdg. 34.00 (*0-912024-26-7*) Inst Mediaeval Mus.

Loulis, John K. Greece under Papandreou: NATO's Ambivalent Partner. (C). 1985. 35.00 (*0-907967-50-7*, Pub. by Inst Euro Def & Strat) St Mut.

Loumaye, Jacqueline. The Tale of the Kite. (Child's World Library). (Illus.). 32p. (J). (gr. k-5). 1992. lib. bdg. 18.50 (*0-89565-759-7*) Childs World.

Loumidis, K., jt. ed. see Kroese, Biza.

Loumiet, James R. & Jungbauer, William G. Train Accident Reconstruction & FELA & Railroad Litigation. 3rd ed. LC 98-17389. (Illus.). 921p. 1998. 119.00 (*0-913875-53-8*) Lawyers & Judges.

Loumiet, Robin & Levack, Nancy. Independent Living: A Curriculum with Adaptations for Students with Visual Impairments. 2nd ed. 600p. 1993. pap. 55.00 (*1-880366-00-2*) TSBVI.

— Independent Living: A Curriculum with Adaptations for Students with Visual Impairments, 1. 2nd ed. LC 93-6746. 1993. pap. write for info. (*1-880366-07-X*) TSBVI.

— Independent Living: A Curriculum with Adaptations for Students with Visual Impairments, 2. 2nd ed. LC 93-6746. 1993. pap. write for info. (*1-880366-08-8*) TSBVI.

— Independent Living: A Curriculum with Adaptations for Students with Visual Impairments, 3. 2nd ed. LC 93-6746. 1993. pap. write for info. (*1-880366-09-6*) TSBVI.

Lound, Karen. In the Family. LC 99-38096. (Girl Power Ser.). 98p. (YA). (gr. 6-9). 1999. 25.26 (*0-8225-2692-1*, Lerner Publctns) Lerner Pub.

Lound, Karen, jt. auth. see Flynn, Tom.

Loundagin, Choeleen. The Inner Champion: A Mental Toughness Training Manual for Figure Skaters. LC 97-93376. 136p. 1997. pap., wbk. ed. 29.95 (*0-9663949-8-4*) InnerChamp.

Lounesto, Pertti, jt. ed. see Ablamowicz, Rafal.

Lounesto, Pertti, ed. see Riesz, Marcel.

Loungo, Tracy. The 10 Minute Guide to Household Budgeting. 144p. 1997. 10.95 (*0-02-861442-9*) Macmillan.

Lounibos, L. Phil, et al, eds. Ecology of Mosquitoes: Proceedings of a Workshop. LC 85-80456. (Illus.). 580p. 1985. 15.00 (*0-9615224-0-2*) Fla Med Entom.

Lounibus, L. P., jt. ed. see Frank, J. H.

Lounsberry, Barbar C., et al, eds. The Tales We Tell: Perspectives on the Short Story, 88. LC 97-13712. (Contributions to the Study of World Literature Ser.: Vol. 88). 248p. 1998. 55.00 (*0-313-30396-7*, Greenwood Pr) Greenwood.

Lounsberry, Barbara. The Art of Fact: Contemporary Artists of Nonfiction, 35. LC 89-17222. (Contributions to the Study of World Literature Ser.: No. 53). 232p. 1990. 62.95 (*0-313-26893-2*, LCB/, Greenwood Pr) Greenwood.

Lounsbury, Carl. The Architecture of Southport. (Illus.). ii, 62p. 1996. reprint ed. pap. 15.00 (*1-892444-00-3*) Southport Hist.

***Lounsbury, Carl R.** From Statehouse to Courthouse: An Architectural History of South Carolina's Colonial Capitol & Charleston Courthouse. (Illus.). 128p. 2001. 19.95 (*1-57003-378-1*) U of SC Pr.

Lounsbury, Carl R. An Illustrated Glossary of Early Southern Architecture & Landscape. LC 99-30063. (Illus.). 1999. pap. 30.00 (*0-8139-1923-1*) U Pr of Va.

Lounsbury, Charles. Pictures in the Fire. (Illus.). 48p. 1993. 18.95 (*0-9621131-9-0*) Laughing Elephant.

Lounsbury, Floyd G. Oneida Verb Morphology. LC 76-49736. (Yale University Publications in Anthropology Reprints Ser.: No. 48). 111p. 1976. pap. 20.00 (*0-87536-528-0*) HRAFP.

Lounsbury, Floyd G., ed. see Antone, Harvey & Elm, Demus.

***Lounsbury, John & Nesin, Gert.** Curriculum Integration: Twenty Questions - With Answers. Sheppard, Ronnie, ed. 68p. 1999. pap. 14.00 (*0-9675081-0-X*) Georgia Middle Sch.

Lounsbury, John F., et al, eds. Land Use: A Spatial Approach. LC 81-81132. (National Council for Geographic Education, Pacesetter Ser.). (Illus.). 236p. 1981. reprint ed. pap. 73.20 (*0-7837-9720-6*, 206045100005) Bks Demand.

Lounsbury, John F. & Aldrich, Frank T. Introduction to Geographic Field Methods & Techniques. 2nd ed. 224p. (C). 1990. pap. text 34.60 (*0-675-20509-3*, Merrill Coll) P-H.

Lounsbury, John F. & Ogden, Lawrence. Earth Science. 3rd ed. LC 78-21130. 523p. reprint ed. pap. 162.20 (*0-608-13394-9*, 202250500027) Bks Demand.

Lounsbury, John H. As I See It. 102p. (Orig.). 1991. pap. text 14.00 (*1-56090-058-X*) Natl Middle Schl.

Lounsbury, John H., ed. Connecting the Curriculum Through Interdisciplinary Instruction. 168p. (Orig.). 1992. pap. text 22.00 (*1-56090-071-7*) Natl Middle Schl.

Lounsbury, John H. & Johnston, J. Howard. Life in the Three Sixth Grades. 144p. (Orig.). 1988. pap. text 11.00 (*0-88210-212-5*) Natl Assn Principals.

Lounsbury, John H., ed. see Hoff, Joseph W.

***Lounsbury, Keith.** Beaver Fever: The Story of a Teenage Mountain Man. LC 00-190315. (Illus.). 64p. 2000. write for info. (*1-57579-184-6*) Pine Hill Pr.

Lounsbury, Myron, ed. & comment see Lindsay, Vachel.

Lounsbury, Myron O. The Origins of American Film Criticisms, 1909-1939. LC 72-556. (Dissertations on Film Ser.). 560p. 1974. reprint ed. 36.95 (*0-405-04099-7*) Ayer.

L

Lounsbury, Richard C., ed. Louisa S. McCord: Poems, Drama, Biography, Letters. (Southern Texts Society Ser.). 480p. (C). 1996. text 37.50 (0-8139-1653-4) U Pr of Va.

— Louisa S. McCord: Political & Social Essays. (Southern Texts Society Ser.). (Illus.). 608p. (C). 1995. text 45.00 (0-8139-1570-8) U Pr of Va.

— Louisa S. McCord: Selected Writings. LC 97-8829. (Southern Texts Society Ser.). 288p. 1997. pap. text 14.50 (0-8139-1760-3) U Pr of Va.

Lounsbury, Thomas R. Early Literary Career of Robert Browning. LC 68-760. (Studies in Browning: No. 4). 1969. reprint ed. lib. bdg. 75.00 (0-8383-0587-3) M S G Haskell Hse.

— The Early Literary Career of Robert Browning. (Notable American Authors Ser.). 1999. reprint ed. lib. bdg. 125.00 (0-7812-3871-4) Rprt Serv.

— English Spelling & Spelling Reform. (Notable American Authors Ser.). 1999. reprint ed. lib. bdg. 125.00 (0-7812-3870-6) Rprt Serv.

— History of the English Language. (Notable American Authors Ser.). 1999. reprint ed. lib. bdg. 125.00 (0-7812-3864-1) Rprt Serv.

— James Fenimore Cooper. (BCL1-PS American Literature Ser.). 306p. 1992. reprint ed. lib. bdg. 89.00 (0-7812-6694-7) Rprt Serv.

— The Life & Times of Tennyson from 1809 to 1850. (Notable American Authors Ser.). 1999. reprint ed. lib. bdg. 125.00 (0-7812-3872-2) Rprt Serv.

— Pro-Slavery Overthrown & the True Principles of Abolitionism Declared. 1977. 16.95 (0-8369-9169-9, 9044) Ayer.

— Shakespeare & Voltaire. LC 72-172753. reprint ed. 37.50 (0-404-04029-2) AMS Pr.

— Shakespeare & Voltaire. LC 68-20237. 1972. reprint ed. 24.95 (0-405-08754-3, Pub. by Blom Pubns) Ayer.

— Shakespeare & Voltaire. (Notable American Authors Ser.). 1999. reprint ed. lib. bdg. 125.00 (0-7812-3868-4) Rprt Serv.

— Shakespeare as a Dramatic Artist. (Notable American Authors Ser.). 1999. reprint ed. lib. bdg. 125.00 (0-7812-3867-6) Rprt Serv.

— The Standard of Usage in English. (Notable American Authors Ser.). 1999. reprint ed. lib. bdg. 125.00 (0-7812-3869-2) Rprt Serv.

— Studies in Chaucer, 3 vols. (Notable American Authors Ser.). 1999. reprint ed. lib. bdg. 375.00 (0-7812-3866-8) Rprt Serv.

— Text of Shakespeare. LC 74-130240. reprint ed. 62.50 (0-404-04035-7) AMS Pr.

Lounsbury, Warren C. & Boulanger, Norman C. Theatre Backstage from A to Z. 4th rev. expanded ed. LC 98-4854. (Illus.). 262p. 1998. 27.50 (0-295-97717-5) U of Wash Pr.

Loup Garou Press Staff, ed. My Life Story: The LGP Autobiography System. 250p. 1988. student ed., ring bd. 35.00 (0-9621860-1-5) Loup Garou Pr.

Loup, Jacques. Can the Third World Survive? LC 82-9945. 261p. reprint ed. pap. 81.00 (0-608-06409-2, 206662300008) Bks Demand.

Loupy, Andre & Tchoubar, Bianca. Salt Effects in Organic & Organometallic Chemistry. 316p. 1992. 195.00 (3-527-28025-1, Wiley-VCH) Wiley.

Lourandos, Harry. Continent of Hunter-Gatherers: New Perspectives in Australian Prehistory. LC 96-28528. (Illus.). 408p. (C). 1997. text 74.95 (0-521-35106-5); pap. text 26.95 (0-521-35946-5) Cambridge U Pr.

Lourdaux, W. & Verhelst, D., eds. Benedictine Culture, 750-1050. No. 11. 247p. (Orig.). 1983. pap. 57.50 (90-6186-144-6, Pub. by Leuven Univ) Coronet Bks.

— The Bible & Medieval Culture. No. 7. 294p. (Orig.). 1979. pap. 42.50 (90-6186-089-X, Pub. by Leuven Univ) Coronet Bks.

— The Concepts of Heresy in the Middle Ages (11th-13th c.) No. 4. 240p. 1976. pap. 67.50 (90-6186-043-1, Pub. by Leuven Univ) Coronet Bks.

Lourdeaux, Lee. Italian & Irish Filmmakers in America: Ford, Capra, Coppola & Scorsese. (Illus.). 288p. 1990. 39.95 (0-87722-697-0) Temple U Pr.

— Italian & Irish Filmmakers in America: Ford, Capra, Coppola & Scorsese. (Illus.). 288p. 1993. pap. 22.95 (1-56639-087-7) Temple U Pr.

Lourdes Cabrera, Yvette De, see De Lourdes Cabrera, Yvette.

Lourdes Martinez, Maria De, see Glasser, Ruth.

Lourdes Rodriguez Schettino. The Iguanid Lizards of Cuba. LC 99-10011. 1999. 85.00 (0-8130-1647-9) U Press Fla.

Loureiro, A. P., ed. Surface Engineering with High Energy Beams. 610p. (C). 1990. text 183.00 (0-87849-607-6, Pub. by Trans T Pub) Enfield Pubs NH.

***Loureiro, Angel G.** The Ethics of Autobiography: Replacing the Subject in Spain. LC 99-50475. 288p. 1999. 39.95 (0-8265-1349-2); pap. text 19.95 (0-8265-1350-6) Vanderbilt U Pr.

Loureiro, Joao. Monetary Policy in the European Monetary System: A Critical Appraisal. LC 96-1959. (European & Transatlantic Studies). (Illus.). 147p. 1996. text 79.00 (3-540-60784-6) Spr-Verlag.

Lourekas, Peter, jt. auth. see Weinmann, Elaine.

Lourenco, P. B. Computational Strategies for Masonry Structures. (Illus.). 210p. (Orig.). 1996. pap. 87.50 (90-407-1221-2, Pub. by Delft U Pr) Coronet Bks.

Lourenco, W. Biogeographie de Madagascar (Biogeography of Madagascar) (ENG & FRE., Illus.). 588p. 1996. pap. 50.00 (2-7099-1324-0, Pub. by LInstitut Francais) Balogh.

Louri, Peter. In the Path of Lewis & Clark: Traveling the Missouri. LC 96-3496. (Illus.). 128p. (J). (gr. 5-9). 1996. 14.95 (0-382-39306-6) Silver Burdett Pr.

— In the Path of Lewis & Clark: Traveling the Missouri. LC 96-3496. (J). 1996. lib. bdg. 19.95 (0-382-39307-4) Silver Burdett Pr.

— In the Path of Lewis & Clark: Traveling the Missouri. LC 96-3496. (Illus.). 128p. (J). (gr. 5-9). 1996. pap. 14.95 (0-382-39308-2) Silver Burdett Pr.

***Louria, Margot.** Triumph & Downfall: America's Pursuit of Peace & Prosperity, 1921-1933, 75. LC 99-462051. (Contributions to the Study of World History Ser.: Vol. 75). 272p. 2000. 62.00 (0-313-31272-9, GM1272, Greenwood Pr) Greenwood.

Lourie, Arthur. Sergei Koussevitsky & His Epoch. LC 78-121287. reprint ed. 27.50 (0-404-04036-5) AMS Pr.

— Sergei Koussevitzky & His Epoch. Pring, S. W., tr. LC 78-94276. (Select Bibliographies Reprint Ser.). 1977. 26.95 (0-8369-5050-X) Ayer.

Lourie, Dick. Anima. 1977. pap. 5.00 (0-914610-09-0) Hanging Loose.

— Ghost Radio. LC 97-46107. 1997. 20.00 (1-882413-49-0) Hanging Loose.

— Ghost Radio. LC 97-46107. 120p. 1998. pap. 12.00 (1-882413-48-2) Hanging Loose.

Lourie, Dick & Pawlak, Mark, eds. Smart Like Me: High School Age Writers from the Sixties to Now. 200p. 1988. pap. 10.00 (0-914610-58-9) Hanging Loose.

— Smart Like Me: High School Age Writing From the Sixties to Now. 1988. 20.00 (0-914610-59-7) Hanging Loose.

Lourie, Donold K. Dark Rainbow. LC 98-89528. 375p. 1998. text 25.00 (0-7388-0243-3); pap. text 15.00 (0-7388-0244-1) Xlibris Corp.

Lourie, Elena. Crusade & Colonisation: Muslims, Christians & Jews under the Crown of Aragon. (Collected Studies: No. 317). 350p. 1990. text 115.95 (0-86078-266-2, Pub. by Variorum) Ashgate Pub Co.

Lourie, Eugene. My Work in Films. (Illus.). 384p. 1985. pap. 16.95 (0-15-662342-0, Harvest Bks) Harcourt.

Lourie, Iven, jt. auth. see Gold, E. J.

Lourie, Iven, ed. see Kirk, Margaret.

Lourie, Iven, ed. see Sams, Margaret, et al.

Lourie, J. A., jt. auth. see Weiner, J. S.

Lourie, John, et al. Essentials of Accident & Emergency Care. (Illus.). 132p. 1987. pap. 22.00 (0-443-03903-8) Church.

Lourie, Margaret & Conklin, Nancy. A Host of Tongues: Language Communities in the United States. 272p. (C). 1983. pap. 17.95 (0-02-906500-3) Free Pr.

***Lourie, Michelle, ed.** The Countryside: An Illustrated Treasury. 48p. 2000. reprint ed. text 17.00 (0-7881-6813-4) DIANE Pub.

Lourie, Peter. Amazon: A Young Reader's Look at the Last Frontier. LC 90-85720. (River Ser.). (Illus.). 48p. (J). 1998. pap. text 9.95 (1-56397-712-5) Boyds Mills Pr.

— Erie Canal: Canoeing America's Great Waterway. LC 96-80393. (Illus.). 48p. (J). (gr. 2). 1997. 17.95 (1-56397-669-2) Boyds Mills Pr.

— Erie Canal: Canoeing America's Great Waterway. LC 96-80393. (Illus.). 48p. (J). (gr. 2-5). 1999. pap. 9.95 (1-56397-764-8) Boyds Mills Pr.

— Everglades: Buffalo Tiger & the River of Grass. LC 92-73989. (River Ser.). (Illus.). 48p. (J). 1998. pap. 9.95 (1-56397-702-8) Boyds Mills Pr.

— Hudson River: An Adventure from the Mountains to the Seas. LC 91-72870. (River Ser.). (Illus.). 48p. (J). 1998. pap. 9.95 (1-56397-703-6) Boyds Mills Pr.

***Lourie, Peter.** The Lost Treasure of Captain Kidd. (Illus.). 96p. (Orig.). (J). (gr. 4-7). 2000. pap. 8.95 (1-56397-851-2) Boyds Mills Pr.

Lourie, Peter. The Lost Treasure of Captain Kidd. LC 95-40852. (Illus.). 157p. (Orig.). (J). (gr. 3 up). 1996. pap. 10.95 (1-885482-03-5) Shawangunk Pr.

— Lost Treasure of the Inca. (Illus.). 48p. (YA). (gr. 5-8). 1999. 18.95 (1-56397-743-5) Boyds Mills Pr.

***Lourie, Peter.** Mississippi River: From the Northern Pines to the Tropical Mangroves. LC 98-88235. (Illus.). 48p. (YA). (gr. 2-5). 2000. 17.95 (1-56397-756-7) Boyds Mills Pr.

Lourie, Peter. Rio Grande: From the Rocky Mountains to the Gulf of Mexico. LC 97-77907. (Illus.). 48p. (J). (gr. 2 up). 1999. 17.95 (1-56397-706-0) Boyds Mills Pr.

***Lourie, Peter.** Rio Grande: From the Rocky Mountains to the Gulf of Mexico. LC 97-77907. (Illus.). 48p. (YA). (gr. 3-7). 2000. pap. 9.95 (1-56397-896-2) Boyds Mills Pr.

Lourie, Peter. River of Mountains: A Canoe Journey down the Hudson. (Illus.). 342p. 1995. 29.95 (0-8156-0315-0) Syracuse U Pr.

— River of Mountains: A Canoe Journey down the Hudson. (Illus.). 344p. 1998. pap. 19.95 (0-8156-0316-9) Syracuse U Pr.

— Sweat of the Sun, Tears of the Moon: A Chronicle of an Incan Treasure. 320p. 1991. text 19.95 (0-689-12111-3) Atheneum Yung Read.

— Yukon River: An Adventure to the Gold Fields of the Klondike. LC 91-77600. (Illus.). 48p. (J). (gr. 3-7). 1992. lib. bdg. 15.95 (1-878093-90-8) Boyds Mills Pr.

***Lourie, Peter.** Yukon River: An Adventure to the Gold Fields of the Klondike. LC 91-77600. (Illus.). 48p. (J). 2000. pap. 9.95 (1-56397-878-4) Boyds Mills Pr.

Lourie, Peter, contrib. by. Sweat of the Sun, Tears of the Moon: A Chronicle of an Incan Treasure. LC 98-16170. 307p. 1998. pap. 14.00 (0-8032-7980-9, Bison Books) U of Nebr Pr.

Lourie, Richard. The Autobiography of Joseph Stalin. LC PS3562.0833A95 1999. 272p. 1999. text 25.00 (1-58243-004-7, Pub. by Counterpt DC) HarpC.

***Lourie, Richard.** The Autobiography of Joseph Stalin: A Novel. 2000. pap. 15.00 (0-306-80997-4, Pub. by Da Capo) HarpC.

Lourie, Richard. First Loyalty. LC 84-25169. 448p. 1985. 17.95 (0-15-131287-7) Harcourt.

— Zero Gravity. 1987. 16.95 (0-15-199984-8) Harcourt.

Lourie, Richard, tr. see Czarnecka, Ewa & Fiut, Aleksander.

Lourie, Richard, tr. see Grynberg, Henry K.

Lourie, Richard, tr. see Grynberg, Henryk.

Lourie, Richard, tr. see Hertz, Aleksander.

Lourie, Richard, tr. see Konwicki, Tadeusz.

Lourie, Richard, tr. see Likhanov, Albert.

Lourie, Richard, tr. see Milosz, Czeslaw.

Lourie, Richard, tr. see Sakharov, Andrei D.

Lourie, Richard, tr. see Shulevitz, Uri.

Lourie, Richard, tr. see Voinovich, Vladimir.

Lourie, Richard, tr. & intro. see Konwicki, Tadeusz.

Lourie, Sylvain. Education & Development. 202p. 1989. pap. 20.00 (0-948080-14-0, Trentham Bks) Stylus Pub VA.

Lourik, Nina. 1234 5th Avenue. LC 98-67432. 304p. 1999. pap. 17.95 (1-57197-138-6) Pentland Pr.

Lourteig, A. Flora of Ecuador No. 135: Lythraceae. (Opera Botanica Series B). 46p. 1989. pap. 25.00 (87-88702-34-0, Pub. by Coun Nordic Pubs) Balogh.

Lourtie, Isabel M., jt. ed. see Moura, Jose M.

Lourtioz, J.-M., et al. Group IV Heterostructures, Physics & Devices: Proceedings of Symposium D on Group IV Heterostructures, Physics & Devices (Si, Ge, C, Sn) LC 98-149215. (European Materials Research Society Symposia Proceedings Ser.: Vol. 60). 380p. 1997. 224.00 (0-444-20502-0) Elsevier.

Loury, Glenn, et al. Are Black & Hispanic Priorities Due for a Change? 13p. 1989. pap. text 8.00 (1-57655-124-5) Independ Inst.

Loury, Glenn C. One by One from the Inside Out: Essays & Reviews on Race & Responsibility in America. LC 94-46593. 332p. 1995. 25.00 (0-02-919441-5) Free Pr.

Lousada, Patricia. Game Cookery. (Illus.). 224p. 1991. pap. 22.95 (0-7195-4774-1, Pub. by John Murray) Trafalgar.

***Lousada, Patricia.** Great Big Baking Book: Great American Baking. 1998. 19.98 (1-84038-138-8) Anness Pub.

Lousada, Patricia. Ultimate Chocolate. LC 97-13144. 144p. 1997. 24.95 (0-7894-2084-8) DK Pub Inc.

Lousada, Sandra, et al. Choosing Colors. 14p. 1995. 5.99 (0-525-45475-6, Dutton Child) Peng Put Young Read.

Lousberg, Arlene L. You & Me - Me & You: A Kid's Own Life Story. (Illus.). 40p. (Orig.). (J). (gr. 3-9). 1990. pap. 9.95 (0-9625397-1-6) Memories In Print.

Louscher, David J., jt. ed. see Kennedy, Charles H.

Loushine, Robert, jt. auth. see Bellizzi, Ralph.

Lousin, Ann & Klein, Carter H. Law of Sales under the U. C. C. write for info. (0-318-59314-9, Aspen Law & Bus) Aspen Pub.

***Loussier, Jean & Sommer, Robin Langley, eds.** Lost Europe: Images of a Vanished World. (Illus.). 160p. 2000. reprint ed. text 30.00 (0-7881-9008-3) DIANE Pub.

Loustau, John & Dillon, Meighan. Linear Geometry with Computer Graphics. (Pure & Applied Mathematics Ser.: Vol. 170). (Illus.). 458p. 1992. text 69.75 incl. disk (0-8247-8898-2) Dekker.

Loustaunau, Martha O. & Lobo, Elisa J. The Cultural Context of Health, Illness & Medicine. LC 97-16136. 232p. 1997. pap. 22.95 (0-89789-548-7, Bergin & Garvey) Greenwood.

Loustaunau, Martha O. & Sobo, Elisa J. The Cultural Context of Health, Illness & Medicine. LC 97-16136. 232p. 1997. 59.95 (0-89789-487-1, Bergin & Garvey) Greenwood.

Loustaunau, Martha Oehmke & Sanchez-Bane, Mary, eds. Life, Death & In-Between on the U. S./Mexico Border: Asi es la Vida. LC 99-14380. 256p. 1999. 65.00 (0-89789-568-1, Bergin & Garvey); pap. 22.95 (0-89789-569-X, Bergin & Garvey) Greenwood.

Loustaunau, Philippe, jt. auth. see Adams, William W.

Loutfi, Martha F. Rural Women: Unequal Partners in Development. (WEP Study). (Illus.). 80p. 1987. pap. 13.50 (92-2-102389-3) Intl Labour Office.

Louth, Andrew. Denys the Areopagite. (Outstanding Christian Thinkers Ser.). 144p. 1989. pap. 10.95 (0-8192-1485-X) Morehouse Pub.

— Discerning the Mystery: An Essay on the Nature of Theology. 164p. 1990. reprint ed. pap. text 24.95 (0-19-826196-9) OUP.

— Maximus the Confessor. LC 95-20531. (Early Church Fathers Ser.). 240p. (C). 1996. 75.00 (0-415-11845-X); pap. 22.99 (0-415-11846-8) Routledge.

— The Origins of the Christian Mystical Tradition: From Plato to Denys. 232p. (C). 1983. pap. text 22.00 (0-19-826668-5) OUP.

— The Wilderness of God. 176p. 1996. pap. 14.96 (0-687-05770-1) Abingdon.

***Louth, Andrew, ed.** The Wisdom of the Greek Fathers. (Wisdom of Ser.). (Illus.). 48p. 2000. 6.95 (0-664-22213-7, Pub. by Westminster John Knox) Presbyterian Pub.

Louth, Andrew, tr. see Von Balthasar, Hans U.

Louth, Charlie, jt. auth. see Marlow, Mandy.

Louth, Janet, ed. William Law (1686-1761) Selected Writings. pap. write for info. (0-85635-862-2, Pub. by Carcanet Pr) Paul & Co Pubs.

Louth, Janet, tr. see Bove, Emmanuel.

Louthan, Andrea S. & Louthan, Howard. Staying Faithful. (Christian Character Bible Studies). 64p. (Orig.). 1992. pap., wbk. ed. 4.99 (0-8308-1146-X, 1146) InterVarsity.

Louthan, Doniphan. The Poetry of John Donne: A Study in Explication. LC 75-40927. 193p. 1976. reprint ed. lib. bdg. 49.75 (0-8371-8693-5, LOPJ, Greenwood Pr) Greenwood.

Louthan, Howard. The Quest for Compromise: Peacemakers in Counter-Reformation Vienna. (Studies in Early Modern History). (Illus.). 204p. (C). 1997. text 59.95 (0-521-58082-X) Cambridge U Pr.

Louthan, Howard & Sterk, Andrea, trs. from CZE. John Comenius: The Labyrinth of the World & the Paradise of the Heart. LC 97-16711. (Classics of Western Spirituality: Vol. 90). 272p. 1997. 24.95 (0-8091-0489-X, 0489-X); pap. 16.95 (0-8091-3739-9, 3739-9) Paulist Pr.

Louthan, Howard, jt. auth. see Louthan, Andrea S.

Louthan, Robert. Shrunken Planets. LC 79-54883. 64p. 1980. pap. 3.95 (0-914086-28-6) Alice James Bks.

Louthan, William C., jt. ed. see Pinkele, Carl F.

Loutner, Darrell, ed. see Gage, Terry.

Louv, Richard. FatherLove: What We Need, What We Seek, What We Must Create. 276p. 1999. reprint ed. text 21.00 (0-7881-6267-5) DIANE Pub.

***Louv, Richard.** Fly Fishing for Sharks: An American Journey. 496p. 2000. 25.00 (0-684-83698-X) S&S Trade.

Louv, Richard. One Hundred Things You Can Do for Our Children's Future. LC 93-3774. 384p. 1993. pap. 10.00 (0-385-46878-4, Anchor NY) Doubleday.

— The Web of Life: Weaving the Values That Sustain Us. (Illus.). 256p. 1996. 14.95 (1-57324-036-2) Conari Press.

— The Web of Life: Weaving the Values That Sustain Us. (Illus.). 250p. 1998. reprint ed. pap. 13.95 (1-57324-140-7) Conari Press.

Louvar, Joseph F., jt. auth. see Crowl, Daniel A.

Louveau, jt. auth. see Hallum.

Louveau, Alain, jt. auth. see Kechris, Alexander S.

Louveaux, Francois, jt. auth. see Birge, John R.

Louver Gallery New York Staff & Cameron, Dan. Inconsolable: An Exhibition about Painting. (Illus.). 40p. 1990. 15.00 (0-9624271-3-6) Louver Gallery.

— Tony Bevan. (Illus.). 80p. 1991. pap. write for info. (0-9624271-4-4) Louver Gallery.

L'Ouverture, Toussaint. Toussaint L'Ouverture: A Biography & Autobiography. LC 77-152924. (Black Heritage Library Collection). 1977. 35.00 (0-8369-8768-3) Ayer.

***Louviere, Jordan J., et al.** Stated Choice Methods: Analysis & Application. (Illus.). 464p. 2001. write for info. (0-521-78275-9); pap. write for info. (0-521-78830-7) Cambridge U Pr.

Louviere, Jordon J. Analyzing Decision-Making: Metric Conjoint Analysis, No. 67. (Quantitative Applications in the Social Sciences Ser.: Vol. 67). 96p. (C). 1988. pap. text 10.95 (0-8039-2757-6) Sage.

Louviere, Pat. Louisiana Backroads & Bayous. (Illus.). 128p. 1992. vinyl bd. 60.00 (0-9620814-2-6) Louviere Fine Arts.

— Louisiana Backroads & Bayous. deluxe ed. (Illus.). 128p. 1992. lthr. 200.00 (0-9620814-1-8) Louviere Fine Arts.

Louvish, David, ed. see Orevkov, V. P.

Louvish, David, tr. see Fraisse, R.

Louvish, Misha, tr. see Lipshitz, Arye.

Louvish, Simon. The Days of Miracles & Wonders. LC 97-221614. 440p. 1997. write for info. (0-86241-666-3) Canongate Books.

Louvish, Simon. The Days of Miracles & Wonders. 560p. 34.95 (1-895897-75-0) Somerville Hse.

Louvish, Simon. The Days of Miracles & Wonders: An Epic of the New World Disorder. LC 99-10143. 1999. pap. 16.00 (1-56656-316-X) Interlink Pub.

— It's a Gift. (BFI Film Classics Ser.). 75p. 1994. pap. 10.95 (0-85170-472-7) Ind U Pr.

— Man on the Flying Trapeze: The Life & Times of W. C. Fields. LC 97-23731. 576p. 1997. 29.95 (0-393-04127-1) Norton.

— Man on the Flying Trapeze: The Life & Times of W. C. Fields. (Illus.). 574p. 1999. pap. 18.00 (0-393-31840-0, Norton Paperbks) Norton.

***Louvish, Simon.** Monkey Business: The Lives & Legends of the Marx Brothers. (Illus.). 480p. 2000. 25.95 (0-312-25292-7) St Martin.

Louvish, Simon. The Resurrections. LC 94-10509. 215p. 1994. 18.95 (1-56858-014-2) FWEW.

— The Silencer. LC 92-24536. (Emerging Voices: New International Fiction Ser.). 264p. (Orig.). 1993. 29.95 (1-56656-116-7); pap. 10.95 (1-56656-108-6) Interlink Pub.

Louw, D. J. A Mature Faith: Spiritual Direction & Anthropology in a Theology of Pastoral Care & Counseling. (Louvain Theological & Pastoral Monographs). 323p. 1999. pap. 30.00 (0-8028-4670-X) Eerdmans.

Louw, Eric & Duffy, Neil. Managing Computer Viruses. (Illus.). 184p. 1992. pap. text 24.95 (0-19-853974-6) OUP.

Louw, Gideon. Why Elephants & Fleas Don't Sweat: A Zoological Miscellany. (Illus.). 224p. (Orig.). (YA). (gr. 7 up). 1996. pap. write for info. (1-55059-125-8) Detselig Ents.

Louw, Gideon N. Physiolgcl Animal Ecolgy. 288p. (C). 1992. pap. text 54.50 (0-582-05922-4, Pub. by Addison-Wesley) Longman.

Louw, J. & Steeb, W. H., eds. Chaos & Quantum Chaos: Proceedings of the 1986 Winter School Chaos & Quantum Chaos, Johannesburg, South Africa, July 7-12, 1986. 146p. 1986. text 60.00 (9971-5-0172-4) World Scientific Pub.

Louw, Lente-Louise, jt. ed. see Griggs, Lewis B.

Louw, Leon, jt. auth. see Kendall, Frances.

Louw-Potgieter, J. Afrikaner Dissidents: A Social Psychological Study of Identity & Dissent. 148p. 1988. 79.00 (1-85359-012-6, Pub. by Multilingual Matters); pap. 29.00 (1-85359-011-8, Pub. by Multilingual Matters) Taylor & Francis.

Louwaars, Niels, jt. auth. see Almekinders, Conny.

Louwagie, A., jt. ed. see Kazatchkine, M. D.

Louwers, Timothy J. Athletronics, Inc: A Practice Set for Intermediate Accounting. 24p. (C). 1995. text 28.35 (0-256-18872-6, Irwn McGrw-H) McGrw-H Hghr Educ.

An Asterisk (*) at the beginning of an entry indicates that the title is appearing for the first time.

— Shoe Business, Inc: Practice Set for Understanding Annual Reports. 76p. (C). 1995. text 28.35 (*0-256-19077-1*, Irwn McGrw-H) McGrw-H Hghr Educ.

Louwers, Timothy J., jt. auth. see Robertson, Jack.

Louwers, Timothy J., jt. auth. see Robertson, Jack C.

***Louwhoff, S. H.** Parmotrema & Allied Lichen Genera in Papua New Guinea. (Bibliotheca Lichenologica Ser.: Band 73). (Illus.). 152p. 1999. 56.00 (*3-443-58052-1*, Pub. by Gebruder Borntraeger) Balogh.

Louwrier, K., et al, eds. European Geothermal Update. (C). 1989. text 355.00 (*0-7923-0198-6*) Kluwer Academic.

***Loux, Andrea & Finnie, Wilson, eds.** Human Rights & Scots Law: Comparative Perspectives on the Incorporation of the ECHR. 272p. 2000. 54.00 (*1-84113-044-3*, Pub. by Hart Pub) Intl Spec Bk.

Loux, Ann K. The Limits of Hope: An Adoptive Mother's Story. LC 96-46372. 280p. 1997. 24.95 (*0-8139-1710-7*) U Pr of Va.

Loux, Lynn. Crow Girl. 32p. write for info. (*0-7868-2196-5*, Pub. by Hyperion) Little.

Loux, Michael J. Metaphysics: A Contemporary Introduction. LC 97-11036. (Routledge Contemporary Introduction to Philosophy Ser.). 256p. (C). 1997. 65.00 (*0-415-14033-1*); pap. 20.99 (*0-415-14034-X*) Routledge.

— Primary Ousia: An Essay on Aristotle's Metaphysics Z & H. LC 90-25775. 288p. 1991. text 49.95 (*0-8014-2598-0*) Cornell U Pr.

— Substance & Attribute: A Study in Ontology. (Philosophical Studies: No. 14). 198p. 1978. pap. text 51.50 (*90-277-0955-6*) Kluwer Academic.

Loux, Michael J., intro. The Possible & the Actual: Readings in the Metaphysics of Modality. LC 79-7618. 336p. 1979. pap. text 16.95 (*0-8014-9178-9*) Cornell U Pr.

Loux, Robert R., ed. High-Level Nuclear Waste Shipping Route Maps to Yucca Mountain & Shipment Number Estimates: Multi-Purpose Canister Base Case. (Illus.). 91p. (C). 1998. pap. text 30.00 (*0-7881-7532-7*) DIANE Pub.

Louys, Pierre. Aphrodite. (Illus.). 56p. 1999. 21.95 (*0-9672401-0-7*) Humanoids.

***Louys, Pierre.** Aphrodite. deluxe ed. (Illus.). 56p. 1999. 21.95 (*0-9672401-3-1*) Humanoids.

Louys, Pierre. Aphrodite, Moeurs Antiques. LC 75-41182. (FRE.). reprint ed. 57.50 (*0-404-14795-X*) AMS Pr.

— The Collected Tales. LC 70-160941. (Short Story Index Reprint Ser.). (Illus.). 1977. reprint ed. 22.95 (*0-8369-3920-4*) Ayer.

— The She-Devils. (Velvet Ser.: Vol. 2). 192p. (Orig.). 1996. pap. 12.95 (*1-871592-51-8*) Creation Books.

***Louys, Pierre.** The She-Devils. rev. ed. 224p. (Orig.). 2000. pap. 13.95 (*1-84068-013-X*, Pub. by Creation Bks) Subterranean Co.

Louys, Pierre. The Songs of Bilitis. (Illus.). 192p. 1988. reprint ed. pap. 5.95 (*0-486-25670-7*) Dover.

— Two Erotic Tales by Pierre Louys: Aphrodite & The Songs of Bilitis. Kavka, Dorothy, ed. Harrison, Mary H., tr. from FRE. LC 94-70836. 320p. (Orig.). 1994. pap. 18.00 (*1-879260-24-7*) Evanston Pub.

— The Woman & the Puppet. Moore, Jeremy, tr. from FRE. (European Classics).Tr. of Femme et le Pantin. 124p. 1999. pap. 11.99 (*1-873982-29-1*, Pub. by Dedalus) Subterranean Co.

Louza, Marcy, jt. auth. see Seabrook, Charles.

Louzecky, D. & Flannery, R. The Good Life: Personal & Public Choices. xiv, 258p. (Orig.). (C). 1989. pap. text 12.00 (*0-917930-55-X*); lib. bdg. 35.00 (*0-917930-95-9*) Ridgeview.

Lovaas, O. Ivar. The Autistic Child: Language Development Through Behavior Modification. LC 76-5890. (Illus.). 256p. 1984. pap. text 16.95 (*0-8290-1003-3*) Irvington.

— The Autistic Child: Language Development Through Behavior Modification. LC 76-5890. (Illus.). 256p. (C). 1986. reprint ed. text 29.95 (*0-8290-0253-7*) Irvington.

— Teaching Developmentally Disabled Children: The Me Book. LC 80-26047. 250p. 1981. pap. 34.00 (*0-936104-78-3*, 1213) PRO-ED.

Lovaas, O. Ivar, et al. Problems of Autistic Behavior: Experimental Analysis of Autism, Vol. 1. 300p. text. write for info. (*0-8290-0740-7*) Irvington.

Lovag, Z. & Kovacs, D. The Hungarian Crown & Other Regalia. 98p. 1980. 50.00 (*0-7855-1518-6*) St Mut.

***Lovaglia, Michael J.** Knowing People: The Personal Use of Social Psychology LC 99-33206. 256p. 1999. pap. 32.19 (*0-07-303996-9*) McGraw.

Lovall, L., jt. auth. see Sanders, Dennis.

Lovallo, Lee T. Anton Bruckner: A Discography. LC 86-46229. (Reference Books in Music: No. 6). xviii, 200p. 1991. 33.00 (*0-914913-05-0*, Fallen Lef Pr) Scarecrow.

Lovallo, William R. Stress & Health: Biological & Psychological Interactions. (Behavioral Medicine & Health Psychology Ser.: Vol. 1). 224p. 1997. 29.00 (*0-8039-7000-5*); pap. 13.99 (*0-8039-7001-3*) Sage.

Lovas, Emily, ed. see Lokvam, Marian, et al.

Lovas, John C. Experiences: Reader for Developing Writers. Date not set. pap., teacher ed. write for info. (*0-673-46879-8*) Addson-Wesley Educ.

Lovas, John C. Experiences: The Reader for Developing Writers. LC 95-17059. 456p. (C). 1997. pap. text 43.00 (*0-673-46878-X*) Addson-Wesley Educ.

Lovas, Michael, jt. auth. see Hollon, J. R.

Lovas, Paula M., jt. ed. see Abramson, Marcia.

Lovasik. Bible En Images. (SPA., Illus.). 116p. (J). 1996. 9.50 (*0-89942-437-6*) Catholic Bk Pub.

Lovasik. Book of Saints, Bk. 10. (Saint Joseph Picture Bks.). 1997. pap. 1.25 (*0-89942-506-2*) Catholic Bk Pub.

— Book of Saints, Pt. 11. (Saint Joseph Picture Bks.). 1997. pap. 1.25 (*0-89942-507-0*) Catholic Bk Pub.

Lovasik. Book of Saints XII, Vol. XII. Catholic Book Publishing Staff, ed. (St. Joseph Picture Bks.). (Illus.). 32p. (J). (gr. 3-4). 1998. 1.25 (*0-89942-515-1*, 512) Catholic Bk Pub.

— Livre des Saints. (SPA., Illus.). 124p. (J). 1996. 8.95 (*0-89942-237-3*, 237/5) Catholic Bk Pub.

Lovasik, Lawrence. Our Father/Hail Mary. (St. Joseph Beginner Ser.). (Illus.). 32p. (J). (gr. k-3). 1996. 3.50 (*0-89942-228-4*, 228/22) Catholic Bk Pub.

— Our Heavenly Mother. LC 97-221214. (St. Joseph Board Bks.). (Illus.). 32p. (J). (ps-1). 1997. bds. 5.95 (*0-89942-272-1*, 272/22) Catholic Bk Pub.

— Pocket Book of Catholic Devotions. (Pocket Book Ser.). (Illus.). 96p. 1997. pap. 3.95 (*0-89942-034-6*, 34/04) Catholic Bk Pub.

Lovasik, Lawrence G. The Angels: God's Messengers & Our Helpers. (Saint Joseph Picture Bks.). (Illus.). 1978. pap. 1.25 (*0-89942-281-0*, 281-00) Catholic Bk Pub.

— The Apostles of Jesus. (Saint Joseph Picture Bks.). (Illus.). 1978. pap. 1.25 (*0-89942-285-3*, 285-00) Catholic Bk Pub.

***Lovasik, Lawrence G.** The Basic Book of Catholic Prayer: How to Pray & Why. abr. ed. LC 99-57341. Orig. Title: Prayer in Catholic Life. 240p. 1999. pap. 16.95 (*1-928832-04-0*) Sophia Inst Pr.

Lovasik, Lawrence G. Best-Loved Saints. (Illus.). 1996. pap. 5.95 (*0-89942-160-1*, 160/04) Catholic Bk Pub.

— Blessed Kateri Tekakwitha: The Lily of the Mohawks. (Saint Joseph Picture Bks.). (Illus.). 1996. pap. 1.25 (*0-89942-298-5*, 298-00) Catholic Bk Pub.

— Book of Saints I. (Saint Joseph Picture Bks.). (Illus.). 1987. pap. text 1.25 (*0-89942-295-0*, 295-00) Catholic Bk Pub.

— Book of Saints II. (Saint Joseph Picture Bks.). (Illus.). 1991. pap. 1.25 (*0-89942-296-9*, 296-00) Catholic Bk Pub.

— Book of Saints III. (Saint Joseph Picture Bks.). (Illus.). 1991. pap. 1.25 (*0-89942-307-8*, 307-00) Catholic Bk Pub.

— Book of Saints IV. (Saint Joseph Picture Bks.). (Illus.). 1991. pap. 1.25 (*0-89942-308-6*, 308-00) Catholic Bk Pub.

— Book of Saints IX. (Saint Joseph Picture Bks.). (Illus.). 1996. pap. 1.25 (*0-89942-504-6*, 504-00) Catholic Bk Pub.

— Book of Saints V. (Saint Joseph Picture Bks.). (Illus.). 1993. pap. 1.25 (*0-89942-393-0*, 393-00) Catholic Bk Pub.

— Book of Saints VI. (Saint Joseph Picture Bks.). (Illus.). 1993. pap. 1.25 (*0-89942-394-9*, 394-00) Catholic Bk Pub.

— Book of Saints VII. (Saint Joseph Picture Bks.). (Illus.). 1995. pap. 1.25 (*0-89942-500-3*, 500-00) Catholic Bk Pub.

— Book of Saints VIII. (Saint Joseph Picture Bks.). (Illus.). 1995. pap. 1.25 (*0-89942-501-1*, 501-00) Catholic Bk Pub.

— Children Prayers: All Occasion. (Saint Joseph Picture Bks.). (Illus.). 1991. pap. text 1.25 (*0-89942-493-7*, 493-00) Catholic Bk Pub.

— Clean Love in Courtship. 1992. reprint ed. pap. 2.50 (*0-89555-095-4*) TAN Bks Pubs.

— Creo en Dios. (San Jose de Libros en Laminas Ser.). (SPA., Illus.). (J). 1985. pap. 1.50 (*0-89942-461-9*, 461/S) Catholic Bk Pub.

— The Eight Beatitudes. (Saint Joseph Picture Bks.). (Illus.). 1982. pap. 1.25 (*0-89942-384-1*, 384-00) Catholic Bk Pub.

— Las Estaciones de la Cruz. (San Jose de Libros en Laminas Ser.). (SPA., Illus.). (J). 1987. pap. 1.50 (*0-89942-472-4*, 472/S) Catholic Bk Pub.

— Favorite Novenas to Jesus. 64p. 1995. pap. text 1.95 (*0-89942-060-5*, 60/04) Catholic Bk Pub.

— Favorite Novenas to Mary. (Illus.). 64p. 1994. pap. text 1.95 (*0-89942-059-1*, 59/04) Catholic Bk Pub.

— Favorite Novenas to the Holy Spirit. (St. Joseph Prayerbook Ser.). (Illus.). 64p. 1997. pap. 1.95 (*0-89942-062-1*, 61/04) Catholic Bk Pub.

— Favorite Novenas to the Saints. (Illus.). 64p. 1993. pap. text 1.95 (*0-89942-058-3*, 58/04) Catholic Bk Pub.

— The Feasts of Jesus. (Saint Joseph Picture Bks.). (Illus.). 1981. pap. 1.25 (*0-89942-301-9*, 301-00) Catholic Bk Pub.

— Following Jesus. (Saint Joseph Picture Bks.). (Illus.). 1983. 1.25 (*0-89942-292-6*, 292-00) Catholic Bk Pub.

— The Gifts of the Holy Spirit. (St. Joseph Picture Bks.). (Illus.). 32p. (J). (gr. 1-4). 1997. pap. 1.25 (*0-89942-508-9*, 508) Catholic Bk Pub.

— God Loves Us All. (Saint Joseph Picture Bks.). (Illus.). 1978. pap. 1.25 (*0-89942-282-9*, 282-00) Catholic Bk Pub.

— Going to Confession. (Saint Joseph Picture Bks.). (Illus.). 1990. pap. 1.25 (*0-89942-392-2*, 392-00) Catholic Bk Pub.

— Going to Confession. (Saint Joseph Beginner Ser.). (Illus.). (J). 1992. 3.50 (*0-89942-220-9*, 220/22) Catholic Bk Pub.

— Good St. Joseph. (Saint Joseph Picture Bks.). (Illus.). 1978. pap. 1.25 (*0-89942-283-7*, 283-00) Catholic Bk Pub.

***Lovasik, Lawrence G.** The Hidden Power of Kindness: A Practical Handbook for Souls Who Dare to Transform the World. abr. ed. LC 99-43436. 256p. 1999. 17.95 (*1-928832-00-8*) Sophia Inst Pr.

Lovasik, Lawrence G. The Holy Eucharist. (Saint Joseph Picture Bks.). (Illus.). 1987. pap. text 1.25 (*0-89942-397-3*, 397-00) Catholic Bk Pub.

— The Holy Rosary. (Saint Joseph Picture Bks.). (Illus.). 1978. pap. 1.25 (*0-89942-284-5*, 284-00) Catholic Bk Pub.

— The Holy Spirit. (Saint Joseph Picture Bks.). (Illus.). 1987. pap. text 1.25 (*0-89942-310-8*, 310-00) Catholic Bk Pub.

— I Believe in God: The Apostles' Creed. (Saint Joseph Picture Bks.). (Illus.). 1984. pap. 1.25 (*0-89942-276-4*, 276-00) Catholic Bk Pub.

— I Love My Pets. (Saint Joseph Picture Bks.). (Illus.). 1996. pap. 1.25 (*0-89942-505-4*, 505-00) Catholic Bk Pub.

— Lives of the Saints Boxed Set. large type ed. (Illus.). 1992. boxed set 16.95 (*0-89942-876-2*, 876/GS) Catholic Bk Pub.

— Maria, Mi Madre. (San Jose de Libros en Laminas Ser.). (SPA., Illus.). (J). 1990. pap. 1.50 (*0-89942-463-5*, 463/S) Catholic Bk Pub.

— Mary My Hope. large type ed. (Illus.). 1977. 7.75 (*0-89942-364-7*, 365/00) Catholic Bk Pub.

— Mary, My Mother. rev. ed. (Saint Joseph Picture Bks.). (Illus.). 1978. pap. 1.25 (*0-89942-280-2*, 280-00) Catholic Bk Pub.

— Mass for Children. (Saint Joseph Picture Bks.). (Illus.). 1990. pap. text 1.25 (*0-89942-489-9*, 489-00) Catholic Bk Pub.

— Meditations on the Rosary. LC 82-72204. (Living Meditation & Prayerbook Ser.). (Illus.). 270p. (Orig.). 1985. pap. text 5.00 (*0-932406-09-2*) AFC.

— Mi Primer Catecismo, 10 vols. (San Jose de Libros en Laminas Ser.). (SPA., Illus.). (J). 1989. pap. 1.50 (*0-89942-470-8*, 470/S) Catholic Bk Pub.

— Mi Primer Libro de Oraciones. (San Jose de Libros en Laminas Ser.). (SPA., Illus.). (J). 1989. pap. 1.50 (*0-89942-460-0*, 460/S) Catholic Bk Pub.

— The Miracles of Jesus. (Saint Joseph Picture Bks.). 1978. pap. 1.25 (*0-89942-279-9*, 279-00) Catholic Bk Pub.

— My Day with Jesus. (Saint Joseph Picture Bks.). (Illus.). 1987. pap. text 1.25 (*0-89942-294-2*, 294-00) Catholic Bk Pub.

— My First Catechism. (Saint Joseph Picture Bks.). (Illus.). 1985. pap. 1.25 (*0-89942-382-5*, 382-00) Catholic Bk Pub.

— My First Catholic Picture Dictionary. (Saint Joseph Picture Bks.). (Illus.). 1984. pap. 1.25 (*0-89942-306-X*, 306-00) Catholic Bk Pub.

— My First Prayer Book. (Saint Joseph Picture Bks.). (Illus.). 1987. pap. text 1.25 (*0-89942-288-8*, 288-00) Catholic Bk Pub.

— My First Prayerbook. (Saint Joseph Beginner Ser.). (Illus.). (J). 1991. 3.50 (*0-89942-205-5*, 205/22) Catholic Bk Pub.

— My Friend Jesus. (Saint Joseph Picture Bks.). (Illus.). 1989. pap. 1.25 (*0-89942-293-4*, 293-00) Catholic Bk Pub.

— My Friends the Saints. (J). 1992. 5.75 (*0-89942-271-3*, 270/22) Catholic Bk Pub.

— My Picture Missal. (Saint Joseph Picture Bks.). (Illus.). (J). (ps-3). 1978. pap. 1.25 (*0-89942-275-6*, 275-00) Catholic Bk Pub.

— My Picture Prayer Book. (Illus.). (J). (ps-3). 1987. 5.75 (*0-89942-134-2*, 134/22) Catholic Bk Pub.

— First Book of Saints. (Illus.). 96p. (J). 1987. 5.75 (*0-89942-133-4*, 133/22) Catholic Bk Pub.

— A Novena of Holy Communions. 51p. 1995. pap. 2.00 (*0-89555-519-0*) TAN Bks Pubs.

— Novenas Favoritas A los Santos. (SPA., Illus.). 64p. 1995. pap. 2.50 (*0-89942-658-1*, 658/S) Catholic Bk Pub.

— Novenas Favoritas a Maria. (SPA.). 1993. pap. 2.50 (*0-89942-061-3*, 159/04S) Catholic Bk Pub.

— Our Baby. (Illus.). 1995. 10.95 (*0-89942-266-7*, 266/97) Catholic Bk Pub.

— Our Father. LC 98-170511. 1993. 7.95 (*0-89942-375-2*, 375/09) Catholic Bk Pub.

— Our Father & Hail Mary. (Saint Joseph Picture Bks.). (Illus.). 1987. pap. 1.25 (*0-89942-389-2*, 389-00) Catholic Bk Pub.

— Our Lady of Fatima. (Saint Joseph Picture Bks.). (Illus.). 1985. pap. 1.25 (*0-89942-387-6*, 387-00) Catholic Bk Pub.

— Our Lady of Guadalupe. (Saint Joseph Picture Bks.). (Illus.). 1985. pap. 1.25 (*0-89942-390-6*, 390-00) Catholic Bk Pub.

— Our Lady of Lourdes. (Saint Joseph Picture Bks.). (Illus.). (J). 1985. pap. 1.25 (*0-89942-391-4*, 391-00) Catholic Bk Pub.

— Picture Book of Prayers. LC 97-221272. (Illus.). (J). 1994. 5.95 (*0-89942-265-9*, 265/22) Catholic Bk Pub.

— Picture Book of Saints. (Illus.). (J). 1988. 7.95 (*0-89942-235-7*, 235/22) Catholic Bk Pub.

— Pocket Book of Catholic Novenas. (Pocket Book Ser.). (Illus.). 96p. 1997. pap. 3.95 (*0-89942-037-0*, 36/04) Catholic Bk Pub.

— Pocket Book of Catholic Prayers. (Pocket Book Ser.). (Illus.). 96p. 1997. pap. 3.95 (*0-89942-032-X*, 32/04) Catholic Bk Pub.

— Pray Always. (Saint Joseph Picture Bks.). (Illus.). 1987. pap. 1.25 (*0-89942-309-4*, 309-00) Catholic Bk Pub.

— Prayers for Everyday. (Saint Joseph Picture Bks.). (Illus.). (J). 1987. pap. 1.25 (*0-89942-381-7*, 381-00) Catholic Bk Pub.

— Prayers to the Boy Jesus. (Saint Joseph Picture Bks.). (Illus.). 1987. pap. text 1.25 (*0-89942-388-4*, 388-00) Catholic Bk Pub.

— Prayers to the Saints. (Saint Joseph Beginner Ser.). (J). 1993. 3.50 (*0-89942-216-0*, 216/22) Catholic Bk Pub.

— The Promises of the Sacred Heart. (Saint Joseph Picture Bks.). (Illus.). 1976. pap. 1.25 (*0-89942-303-5*, 303-00) Catholic Bk Pub.

— The Psalms. (Saint Joseph Picture Bks.). (Illus.). 1987. pap. 1.25 (*0-89942-398-1*, 398-00) Catholic Bk Pub.

— Receiving Holy Communion. (Saint Joseph Picture Bks.). (Illus.). 1991. pap. text 1.25 (*0-89942-491-0*, 491-00) Catholic Bk Pub.

— Receiving Holy Communion. (Saint Joseph Beginner Ser.). (Illus.). (J). 1992. 3.50 (*0-89942-221-7*, 221/22) Catholic Bk Pub.

— The Sacrament of Reconciliation. (St. Joseph Picture Bks.). (Illus.). 32p. (J). (gr. 1-4). 1997. pap. 1.25 (*0-89942-509-7*, 509) Catholic Bk Pub.

— St. Elizabeth Ann Seton. (Saint Joseph Picture Bks.). (Illus.). 1980. pap. 1.25 (*0-89942-297-7*, 297-00) Catholic Bk Pub.

— St. Joseph Beginner's Book of Saints. LC 97-222001. (J). 1996. 5.50 (*0-89942-152-0*) Catholic Bk Pub.

— St. Joseph Book of Prayers for Children. (Pocket-Size Ser.). (Illus.). 64p. (J). (ps-3). 1999. pap. 5.95 (*0-89942-148-2*, 148/22) Catholic Bk Pub.

— St. Joseph Church History. large type ed. (Illus.). (Orig.). 1989. pap. 6.50 (*0-89942-262-4*, 262/04) Catholic Bk Pub.

— St. Joseph Confirmation Book. large type ed. (Illus.). (J). 1978. 7.25 (*0-89942-249-7*, 249/04) Catholic Bk Pub.

— St. Joseph New American Catechism. large type ed. (New American Catechism Ser.: No. 3). (Illus.). (J). (gr. 9-12). 1978. student ed. 3.95 (*0-89942-253-5*, 253/05) Catholic Bk Pub.

— St. Joseph New American Catechism. large type ed. (New American Catechism Ser.: No. 1). (Illus.). (J). (gr. 3-5). 1989. student ed. 3.25 (*0-89942-251-9*, 251/05) Catholic Bk Pub.

— St. Joseph New American Catechism. large type ed. (New American Catechism Ser.: No. 2). (Illus.). (J). (gr. 6 up). 1989. pap., student ed. 3.75 (*0-89942-252-7*, 252/05) Catholic Bk Pub.

— St. Joseph New American Catechism: First Communion. large type ed. (New American Catechism Ser.: Vol. 0). (Illus.). (J). (gr. 1-2). 1989. pap., student ed. 2.50 (*0-89942-250-0*, 250/05) Catholic Bk Pub.

— Saint Patrick. (Saint Joseph Picture Bks.). (Illus.). 1987. pap. 1.25 (*0-89942-385-X*, 385-00) Catholic Bk Pub.

— St. Paul the Apostle. (Saint Joseph Picture Bks.). (Illus.). 1977. pap. 1.25 (*0-89942-289-6*, 289-00) Catholic Bk Pub.

— Saint Peter the Apostle. (Saint Joseph Picture Bks.). (Illus.). 1987. pap. text 1.25 (*0-89942-290-X*, 290-00) Catholic Bk Pub.

— La Santa Misa: Mi Misal en Laminas, 10 vols. (San Jose de Libros en Laminas Ser.). (SPA., Illus.). (J). 1988. pap. 1.50 (*0-89942-467-8*, 467/S) Catholic Bk Pub.

— El Santo Rosario. (San Jose de Libros en Laminas Ser.). (SPA., Illus.). (J). 1989. pap. 1.50 (*0-89942-466-X*, 466/S) Catholic Bk Pub.

— The Seven Sacraments. (Saint Joseph Picture Bks.). (Illus.). (J). (gr. 1-6). 1978. pap. 1.25 (*0-89942-278-0*, 278-00) Catholic Bk Pub.

— Los Siete Sacramentos. (San Jose de Libros en Laminas Ser.). (SPA., Illus.). (J). 1985. pap. 1.50 (*0-89942-462-7*, 462/S) Catholic Bk Pub.

— Stations of the Cross. (Saint Joseph Picture Bks.). (Illus.). 1978. pap. 1.25 (*0-89942-299-3*, 299-00) Catholic Bk Pub.

— The Story of Jesus. (Illus.). (J). 1978. 5.50 (*0-89942-535-6*, 535/22) Catholic Bk Pub.

— The Teaching of Jesus. (Saint Joseph Picture Bks.). (Illus.). 1978. pap. 1.25 (*0-89942-302-7*, 302-00) Catholic Bk Pub.

— The Ten Commandments. (Saint Joseph Picture Bks.). (Illus.). (J). (gr. 1-6). 1978. pap. 1.25 (*0-89942-287-X*, 287-00) Catholic Bk Pub.

— Ten Commandments. (Saint Joseph Beginner Ser.). (Illus.). (J). 1993. 3.50 (*0-89942-222-5*, 222/22) Catholic Bk Pub.

— Tesoro de Novenas. (SPA.). 1988. vinyl bd. 8.50 (*0-89942-346-9*, 346/22S) Catholic Bk Pub.

— Treasury of Novenas. 352p. 1986. vinyl bd. 7.75 (*0-89942-345-0*, 345/22) Catholic Bk Pub.

— What Catholics Believe. (Illus.). 1977. pap. 5.00 (*0-89555-027-X*) TAN Bks Pubs.

Lovasy, Ernst. Dictionnaire des Termes d'Anatomie, d'Embryologie et d'Histologie. (FRE.). 624p. 1954. 65.00 (*0-8288-6871-9*, M-6380) Fr & Eur.

Lovasz, Laszio. Combinatorial Problems & Exercises. 2nd ed. 636p. 1993. 183.00 (*0-444-81504-X*, North Holland) Elsevier.

Lovasz, Laszlo. An Algorithmic Theory of Numbers, Graphs, & Convexity. LC 86-61532. (CBMS-NSF Regional Conference Ser.: No. 50). v, 91p. 1986. pap. 23.00 (*0-89871-203-3*) Soc Indus-Appl Math.

Lovasz, Laszlo & Plummer, M. D. Matching Theory. 544p. 1986. 161.50 (*0-444-87916-1*, North Holland) Elsevier.

Lovat, Simon. Disorder & Choas. 249p. 1996. pap. text 12.95 (*1-873741-26-X*) Millvres Bks.

Lovato, Charles. Life Under the Sun: The Art of Charles Lovato. Hausman, Gerald, ed. LC 81-23189. (Illus.). 48p. 1982. 35.00 (*0-86534-010-2*) Sunstone Pr.

Lovatt, Edwin A., jt. auth. see Herail, Rene J.

***Lovatt, Marie, ed.** English Episcopal Acta. (English Episcopal Acta Ser.). (Illus.). 280p. 2000. text 72.00 (*0-19-726210-4*) OUP.

Lovatt-Smith, Lisa. The Fashion House: Inside the Homes of Leading Designers. (Illus.). 208p. 50.00 (*1-85029-898-X*, Pub. by Conran Octopus) Antique Collect.

— Fashion Images de Mode, No. 3. (Illus.). 176p. 1998. 34.95 (*3-88243-543-7*) Steidl.

— Fashion Images De Mode #04. 1999. 34.95 (*3-88243-644-1*) Steidlmayer Sftware.

***Lovatt-Smith, Lisa.** Interiores de Marrveccos. 1998. 49.99 (*3-8228-7656-9*) Benedikt Taschen.

Lovatt-Smith, Lisa. London Living. LC 97-61390. 216p. 1998. 35.00 (*0-8230-2836-4*) Watsn-Guptill.

— Mediterranean Living. LC 98-2702. 1998. 35.00 (*0-8230-2837-2*) Watsn-Guptill.

L

— Moroccan Interiors. (Jumbo Ser.). 1998. 39.99 (*3-8228-8177-5*) Taschen Amer.

— New York Living. LC 99-62116. (Illus.). 216p. 1999. 35.00 (*0-8230-3182-9*) Watsn-Guptill.

— Paris Interiors. 1995. 39.99 (*3-8228-8932-6*) Taschen Amer.

— Provence Interiors. (Jumbo Ser.). (Illus.). 1996. 39.99 (*3-8228-8176-7*) Taschen Amer.

Lovatt-Smith, Lisa & Remy, Patrick, eds. Fashion Images de Mode, No. 2. (Illus.). 208p. 1997. 29.95 (*3-88243-480-5*, 720202) Dist Art Pubs.

Lovberg, Ralph H., jt. auth. see Glasstone, Samuel.

Lovboll, Odd S., ed. see Mauk, David C.

Love. Love. 100p. 1982. pap. 4.75 (*0-9608692-0-4*) Love.

— Making Most of Outdoor Spaces. LC 98-65892. 80p. 1999. 19.95 (*0-8478-2135-8*, Pub. by Rizzoli Intl) St Martin.

***Love.** Mallinford. 2000. pap. 12.95 (*0-552-99771-4*, Pub. by Transworld Publishers Ltd) Trafalgar.

— So You Want to Be a Star, Bk. 2. (gr. 5 up). 1993. 18.95 (*0-694-00560-6*, HarpFestival) HarpC Child Bks.

— The Truth about Love: The Highs, the Lows & How You Can Make It Last. 2001. pap. write for info. (*0-684-87188-2*, Fireside) S&S Trade Pap.

Love. Who Loves Brian? 1999. text 19.95 (*0-312-08335-1*) St Martin.

Love & Reilly. A Sound Way. 1994. pap. text. write for info. (*0-582-80414-0*, Pub. by Addison-Wesley) Longman.

Love, A. Cytotaxonomical Atlas of the Pteridophyta. (Cytotaxonomical Atlases Ser.: Vol. 3). 1977. 98.00 (*3-7682-1103-7*) Lubrecht & Cramer.

Love, A. & Love, D. Cytotaxonomical Atlas of the Arctic Flora. (Cytotaxonimical Atlases Ser.: Vol. 2). (Illus.). 598p. 1975. lib. bdg. 130.00 (*3-7682-0976-8*) Lubrecht & Cramer.

— Cytotaxonomical Atlas of the Slovenian Flora. (Cytotaxonimical Atlases Ser.: Vol. 1). (Illus.). 1242p. 1974. lib. bdg. 130.00 (*3-7682-0932-6*) Lubrecht & Cramer.

— Plant Chromosomes. 1975. 25.00 (*3-7682-0966-0*) Lubrecht & Cramer.

Love, A., jt. auth. see Bailin, D.

Love, Alease. Daily Personal Prayer Journal. (Illus.). 43p. Date not set. wbk. ed. 10.00 (*0-9613093-0-X*) Alease Love MBA.

Love, Anami & Bradford, Anita J. Field Trips & Assemblies: A Guide to Exciting Education in Northern California. (Orig.). 1992. pap. 19.95 (*0-9627649-3-0*) Trumpetvine.

Love, Andrea. Secret Sex Lives of the Rich & Famous. 1999. pap. 12.95 (*1-85868-296-7*, Pub. by Carlton Bks Ltd) Natl Bk Netwk.

Love, Angelica. Expressions from the Heart & Spirit: A Collection of Poems & Songs. Stancil, Mary H., ed. & illus. by. 110p. 1998. pap. 7.95 (*1-892212-04-8*) Love Pubg Co.

— Words Can Break a Heart. Stancil, Mary H., ed. & illus. by. 20p. (J). (gr. k-2). 1998. pap. 4.95 (*1-892212-07-2*) Love Pubg Co.

***Love, Ann.** Fishing. (America at Work Ser.). 32p. 1999. 12.95 (*1-55074-457-7*, Pub. by Kids Can Pr) Genl Dist Srvs.

Love, Ann. Ice Cream at the Castle. LC 98-51975. 32p. 1999. 13.99 (*0-85953-677-7*); pap. 6.99 (*0-85953-678-5*) Childs Play.

— A Present for Prince Paul. (Illus.). (J). 1995. 13.99 (*0-85953-943-1*) Childs Play.

— The Prince Who Wrote a Letter. LC 92-27587. (Illus.). 32p. (J). 1992. 13.99 (*0-85953-398-0*, Pub. by Childs Play); pap. 6.99 (*0-85953-399-9*, Pub. by Childs Play) Random House.

— The Prince Who Wrote a Letter. (J). 1996. lib. bdg. 15.95 (*0-85953-888-5*) Childs Play.

— The Prince Who Wrote a Letter. (FRE., Illus.). 32p. (J). (gr. k-3). 1996. pap. 6.99 (*0-85953-459-6*) Childs Play.

— The Prince Who Wrote a Letter. (Children's Stories Published in Other Lands Ser.). (Illus.). 32p. (J). (gr. k-3). 1996. lib. bdg. 16.95 (*1-56674-212-9*) Forest Hse.

Love, Ann. Taking Control: Historical Adventure. rev. ed. 1996. reprint ed. pap. 5.00 (*0-88092-998-7*) Royal Fireworks.

Love, Ann & Drake, Jane. Explorations In Science Take Action. LC 92-30412. (Illus.). 96p. (J). 1993. pap. 7.95 (*0-688-12465-8*) Morrow Avon.

Love, Ann & Drake, Jane. Fishing. (Canada at Work Ser.). (Illus.). 32p. (J). (gr. 2-4). 1997. 14.99 (*1-55074-339-2*) Kids Can Pr.

— Kids & Grandparents: An Activity Book. unabridged ed. (Illus.). 160p. (YA). (gr. 1). 2000. 21.95 (*1-55074-784-3*, Pub. by Kids Can Pr); pap. 14.95 (*1-55074-492-5*, Pub. by Kids Can Pr) Genl Dist Srvs.

Love, Ann & Drake, Jane. The Kids Guide to the Millennium. unabridged ed. (Illus.). 64p. (J). (gr. 3-6). 1998. pap. 9.95 (*1-55074-436-4*, Pub. by Kids Can Pr) Genl Dist Srvs.

— The Kid's Guide to the Millennium. unabridged ed. (Illus.). 64p. (J). (gr. 3-6). 1998. 16.95 (*1-55074-556-5*, Pub. by Kids Can Pr) Genl Dist Srvs.

***Love, Ann & Drake, Jane.** Mining. (America at Work Ser.). (Illus.). 31p. (J). (gr. 2). 1999. 12.95 (*1-55074-508-5*, Pub. by Kids Can Pr) Genl Dist Srvs.

***Love, Ann, et al.** Kids Book of the Far North. (Illus.). 48p. (J). (gr. 3-7). 2000. 15.95 (*1-55074-563-8*, Pub. by Kids Can Press) Genl Dist Srvs.

Love, Ann, jt. auth. see Drake, Jane.

Love, Anne D. Bess's Log Cabin. (Illus.). (J). 1996. pap. 4.99 (*0-440-91154-0*) BDD Bks Young Read.

— Bess's Log Cabin Quilt. 1996. 9.09 (*0-606-11115-8*, Pub. by Turtleback) Demco.

Love, Anne G. & Love, Patrick G. Enhancing Student Learning: Intellectual, Social & Emotional Integration. Fife, Jonathan D., ed. LC 96-77446. (ASHE-ERIC Higher Education Reports: Vol. 95-4). (Illus.). 100p. (Orig.). 1996. pap. 24.00 (*1-878380-68-0*) GWU Grad Schl E&HD.

Love, Arnold J. Internal Evaluation: Building Organizations from Within. (Applied Social Research Methods Ser.: Vol. 24). (Illus.). 160p. 1991. 42.00 (*0-8039-3200-6*); pap. 18.95 (*0-8039-3201-4*) Sage.

Love, Augustus E. Treatise on the Mathematical Theory of Elasticity. 4th ed. (Illus.). 643p. 1944. pap. text 15.95 (*0-486-60174-9*) Dover.

Love, Barbara. Re-Evaluation Counseling: A Component in Higher Education. 1987. pap. 2.00 (*0-913937-28-2*) Rational Isl.

Love, Barbara & Froidevaux, Frances L., eds. Lady's Choice: Ethel Waxham. 394p. 1997. pap. 16.95 (*0-8263-1786-3*) U of NM Pr.

Love, Barbara, jt. ed. see Abbott, Sidney.

Love, Benjamin T. The Bendcrypt Methodology for Developing "Uncrackable" Batch Encryption Algorithms. 320p. (Orig.). (C). 1995. pap. 200.00 (*0-9649302-0-X*) gamma pubng.

Love, Berna. Arkansas Indians: Learning & Activity Book. 1996. pap. 4.95 (*0-87483-490-2*) August Hse.

Love, Bert & Gamble, Jim. The Meccano System. (Hornby Companion Ser.: Vol. 6). 432p. 1992. 60.00 (*0-904568-36-9*) Pincushion Pr.

Love, Bertha, jt. auth. see Peterson, Christina.

***Love, Beth L.** Fairfield & Southport. (Postcard History Ser.). (Illus.). 128p. 2000. pap. 18.99 (*0-7385-0437-8*) Arcadia Publng.

Love, Betty R., et al, eds. Mixed Waste III: Proceedings of the Third International Symposium, Baltimore MD, August 7-10. (Illus.). 800p. 1995. pap. text 75.00 (*1-882345-04-5*) Cognizant Comm.

Love, Bill. Corn Snake Manual. 1999. pap. text 8.95 (*1-882770-54-4*, Pub. by Adv Vivarium) IPG Chicago.

***Love, Bill.** Corn Snake Manual. (Herpetocultural Library). (Illus.). 2000. pap. 8.95 (*1-882770-47-1*) Adv Vivarium.

***Love, Bob & Watkins, Mel.** The Bob Love Story. LC 99-46672. 288p. 1999. 24.95 (*0-8092-2597-2*, 259720, Contemporary Bks) NTC Contemp Pub Co.

Love, Bob, jt. auth. see Page, Terry.

Love, Bobby, II. The Penguin. (Illus.). (Orig.). 1991. write for info. (*1-879460-50-5*) A Love Memorial.

Love, Brenda. The Encyclopedia of Unusual Sex Practices. LC 92-16420. 336p. 1992. 29.95 (*0-942637-64-X*) Barricade Bks.

— Encyclopedia of Unusual Sex Practices. 336p. 1994. pap. 22.00 (*1-56980-011-1*) Barricade Bks.

Love, Bruce. The Paris Codex: Handbook for a Maya Priest. LC 93-13028. (Illus.). 176p. (C). 1994. text 37.50 (*0-292-74674-1*) U of Tex Pr.

Love, C. & Scott, V. D. Quantitative Electron-Probe Microanalysis. 2nd ed. 384p. (C). 1995. pap. text 77.00 (*0-13-104050-2*) P-H.

Love, C. & Tinervia, Joseph. Commercial Correspondence: For Students of English As a Second Language. 2nd ed. 1980. text 8.97 (*0-07-038785-0*) McGraw.

Love, C. E. & Clari, M. Collins Italian Dictionary College Edition. (ENG & ITA.). 745p. (C). 1990. write for info. (*0-7859-7406-7*, 0062755064) Fr & Eur.

Love, Carla, jt. ed. see Jankowsky, Karen.

Love, Carolyn. Leisure & Aging: A Practical & Theoretical Guide. 2nd ed. 96p. (C). 1997. pap. text, per. 35.95 (*0-7872-3324-2*, 41332401) Kendall-Hunt.

Love, Catherine E. Collins-Mondadori Gem Italian Dictionary. (ENG & ITA.). 629p. 1992. write for info. (*0-7859-7415-6*, 0004700473) Fr & Eur.

— Larousse Dictionnaire Compact Francais-Anglais, Anglias-Francais. (ENG & FRE.). 1184p. 1993. vinyl bd. 49.95 (*0-7859-7123-8*, 2034016319) Fr & Eur.

Love, Cathleen, et al. Career Exploration in the Middle School. 57p. (C). 1997. pap. 8.00 (*0-911365-38-9*) Family & Consumer Sci Educ.

Love, Cathleen T., et al. Teaching Strategies to Facilitate Learning. 1995. 8.00 (*0-911365-36-2*, A261-08486) Family & Consumer Sci Educ.

Love, Charles. Designing to Help People Get Where They're Going. 238p. 1992. 49.95 (*0-685-60212-5*) McGraw.

Love, Charles J. Cardiac Pacing. LC 98-26333. 145p. 1998. spiral bd. 45.00 (*1-57059-496-1*) Landes Bioscience.

— Cardiac Pacing. LC 98-26333. (Vademecum Ser.). (Illus.). 145p. 1998. spiral bd. 45.00 (*1-57059-492-9*) Landes Bioscience.

Love, Christopher. Grace: The Truth, Growth & Different Degrees. Kistler, Don, ed. LC 97-190938. 173p. 1997. 22.95 (*1-57358-034-1*) Soli Deo Gloria.

— The Mortified Christian. rev. ed. Kistler, Don, ed. 150p. 1998. 16.95 (*1-57358-078-3*) Soli Deo Gloria.

— Treatise of Effectual Calling & Election. Kistler, Don, ed. 300p. 1998. 24.95 (*1-57358-064-3*) Soli Deo Gloria.

— The Works of Christopher Love, Vol. 1. LC 97-104419. 676p. 1995. 40.00 (*1-57358-007-4*) Soli Deo Gloria.

Love, Clyde E. Bridge Squeezes Complete: or Winning End Play Strategy. LC 68-25410. (Illus.). 260p. 1968. pap. 6.95 (*0-486-21968-2*) Dover.

***Love, Crystal.** The Mystic Mind. (Illus.). 224p. 2000. pap. 14.95 (*1-58394-023-5*, Pub. by Frog Ltd CA) Publishers Group.

Love, Cynthia B. Genetic Testing for Cystic Fibrosis, January 1989 Through February 1997, CBM 97-2. 78p. 1997. pap. 7.50 (*0-16-061584-4*) USGPO.

Love, Cynthia B. & Jahrling, Peter B. Viral Hemorrhagic Fever: Current Bibliographies in Medicine (January 1990-June 1996) 65p. (Orig.). (C). 1996. pap. text 30.00 (*0-7881-3508-2*) DIANE Pub.

Love, D., jt. auth. see Love, A.

Love, D. Anne. Bess's Log Cabin Quilt. LC 94-24435. (Illus.). 128p. (J). (gr. 4-7). 1996. pap. 4.50 (*0-440-41197-1*) Dell.

— Bess's Log Cabin Quilt. (Illus.). 123p. (J). (gr. 2-6). 1995. 15.95 (*0-8234-1178-8*) Holiday.

— Dakota Spring. (Illus.). 96p. (J). (gr. 3-7). 1997. pap. 3.99 (*0-440-41290-0*, YB BDD) BDD Bks Young Read.

— Dakota Spring. (J). 1997. pap. 3.99 (*0-440-91306-3*) BDD Bks Young Read.

— Dakota Spring. (J). 1997. 9.09 (*0-606-11234-0*, Pub. by Turtleback) Demco.

— I Remember the Alamo. LC 98-43331. 156p. (J). (gr. 4-7). 1999. 15.95 (*0-8234-1426-4*) Holiday.

— My Lone Star Summer. 192p. (J). (gr. 7-12). 1996. 15.95 (*0-8234-1235-0*) Holiday.

***Love, D. Anne.** My Lone Star Summer. 1998. 9.09 (*0-606-13636-3*, Pub. by Turtleback) Demco.

Love, D. Anne. My Lone Star Summer. 192p. (J). (gr. 4-7). 1998. reprint ed. pap. 3.99 (*0-440-41375-3*, YB BDD) BDD Bks Young Read.

***Love, D. Anne.** Three Against the Tide. (Illus.). 176p. (J). (gr. 4-7). 2000. pap. 4.50 (*0-440-41634-5*, Yearling) BDD Bks Young Read.

Love, D. Anne. Three Against the Tide. LC 98-11461. 162p. (J). (gr. 5-7). 1998. 15.95 (*0-8234-1400-0*) Holiday.

***Love, D. Anne.** A Year Without Rain. LC 99-35825. 96p. (J). (gr. 3-7). 2000. 15.95 (*0-8234-1488-4*) Holiday.

Love, D. W., et al, eds. Carlsbad Region. (Guidebook Ser.: No. 44). (Illus.). 357p. 1993. pap. 55.00 (*1-58546-079-6*) NMex Geol Soc.

Love, D. W., Jr., jt. auth. see Toski, B.

Love, Dane. Pictorial History of Ayr. 1980. pap. 40.00 (*0-907526-58-6*, Pub. by Alloway Publ) St Mut.

— Pictorial History of Cumnock. 1980. pap. 30.00 (*0-907526-54-3*, Pub. by Alloway Publ) St Mut.

***Love, Dane.** Scottish Covenanter Stories: Tales from the Killing Times. (Illus.). 2000. pap. 15.00 (*1-897784-98-8*, Pub. by N Wilson Pubng) Interlink Pub.

Love, Darlene, et al. My Name Is Love: Darlene Love. LC 98-19242. (Illus.). 320p. 1998. 24.00 (*0-688-15657-6*, Wm Morrow) Morrow Avon.

Love, David. Buns Travels Across America. (Illus.). 48p. (J). (gr. k-5). 1992. pap. 7.95 (*1-881274-01-2*) Cotton Tale.

Love, David, jt. auth. see Buckle, Keith.

Love, David, jt. auth. see Freedman, David.

Love, Davis, III. Every Shot I Take: Lessons Learned about Golf, Life, & a Father's Love. LC 97-9321. 192p. 1997. 19.50 (*0-684-83400-6*) S&S Trade.

***Love, Diane.** Yes/No Design: Discover Your Decorating Style with Taste-Revealing Exercises & Examples. (Illus.). 168p. 2000. text 35.00 (*0-8478-2300-8*) Rizzoli Intl.

Love, Doris, tr. see Andre, Edouard F.

Love, Doris, tr. see Duval, Leon.

***Love, Dorothy.** And Then Came You. 2000. pap. 8.95 (*1-58571-024-5*, 909-101, Pub. by Genesis Press) BookWorld.

Love, Dorothy. Whispers in the Night. 293p. (Orig.). 1999. pap. 8.95 (*1-885478-98-4*, Pub. by Genesis Press) BookWorld.

Love, Douglas. The Backyard Camp-Out Book. LC 96-41806. (Illus.). 80p. (J). (gr. 2 up). 1997. mass mkt. 6.95 (*0-688-15258-9*, Wm Morrow) Morrow Avon.

— Disney's Face Painting & Costume Kit. LC 97-65679. (Illus.). 64p. (J). 1997. 17.95 (*0-7868-4180-X*, Pub. by Disney Pr) Time Warner.

— Great American Kids Backyard Camp-Out Book. (Illus.). (J). (gr. 2 up). 1997. pap. 7.95 (*0-614-28869-X*, Wm Morrow) Morrow Avon.

— Great American Kids Slumber Party Book. (Illus.). (J). (gr. 2 up). 1997. pap. 7.95 (*0-614-28868-1*, Wm Morrow) Morrow Avon.

***Love, Douglas.** 102 Dalmatians: Numbers. 64p. (J). 2000. 14.99 (*0-7364-0192-X*, Pub. by Mouse Works) Time Warner.

Love, Douglas. The Slumber Party Book. LC 96-41807. (Illus.). 80p. (J). 1997. mass mkt. 6.95 (*0-688-15259-7*, Wm Morrow) Morrow Avon.

— So You Want to Be a Star. (Illus.). 32p. (YA). (gr. 5 up). 1993. 18.95 (*0-694-00428-6*, HarpFestival) HarpC Child Bks.

Love, Douglas E. Martyr. LC 90-90401. (Illus.). (Orig.). 1990. pap. 5.00 (*0-9628240-0-3*) D E Love.

Love, Douglas O. & Deichert, Jerome A. Locating Financial Branch Facilities: A Guide to Techniques & Literature. (Nebraska Economic & Business Reports: No. 34). 1983. 10.00 (*0-318-02060-2*) Bur Busn Res U Nebr.

Love, Douglas O. Minimum Cost of Living in Nebraska, Vol. I-II. 1986. 20.00 (*0-317-46859-6*) Bur Busn Res U Nebr.

Love, E. L. World Textile Trade: An International Perspective. 52p. 1978. 39.00 (*0-7855-7235-X*) St Mut.

***Love-Eastham, Judith A. & Carrie, Sean A.** Accommodating Asia... Hong Kong/Macau. (Illus.). 124p. 2000. pap. 11.95 (*962-85435-1-2*, Pub. by Accom Asia) SCB Distributors.

Love, Edgar J., jt. ed. see Miller, Max J.

Love, Edmund G. Hanging On: Or How to Get Through a Depression & Enjoy Life. LC 87-18897. (Great Lakes Bks.). 286p. 1987. reprint ed. 28.50 (*0-8143-1931-9*); reprint ed. pap. 16.95 (*0-8143-1932-7*) Wayne St U Pr.

— The Hourglass: A History of the 7th Infantry Division in World War II. (Divisional Ser.). (Illus.). 496p. 1988. reprint ed. 49.95 (*0-89839-118-0*) Battery Pr.

— The Situation in Flushing. LC 87-17769. (Great Lakes Bks.). 272p. 1987. reprint ed. 29.95 (*0-8143-1916-5*); reprint ed. pap. 17.95 (*0-8143-1917-3*) Wayne St U Pr.

— Small Bequest. LC 87-16202. (Great Lakes Bks.). 238p. 1987. 29.95 (*0-8143-1925-4*); pap. 15.95 (*0-8143-1926-2*) Wayne St U Pr.

Love, Florene, jt. auth. see Schreiner-Yantis, Netti.

Love, Frank. Hell's Outpost: A History of Old Fort Yuma. LC 92-60166. (Publication Ser.). (Illus.). 63p. (Orig.). 1992. pap. 6.95 (*0-9632228-0-5*) Yuma Crossing.

— Mining Camps & Ghost Towns: Along the Lower Colorado in Arizona & California. LC 73-86960. (Great West & Indian Ser.: Vol. 42). (Illus.). 240p. 24.95 (*0-87026-031-6*) Westernlore.

***Love, Frank, et al.** Ministry to Muslim Women: Longing to Call Them Sisters. LC 00-31228. 2000. pap. write for info. (*0-87808-338-3*) William Carey Lib.

Love, Frederick R. Nietzsche's St. Peter: Genesis & Cultivation of an Illusion. (Monographien und Texte zur Nietzscge-Forschung Ser.: Vol. 5). xvi, 296p. (C). 1981. 80.00 (*3-11-007875-9*) De Gruyter.

— Young Nietzsche & the Wagnerian Experience. LC 63-63585. (North Carolina. University. Studies in the Germanic Languages & Literatures: No. 39). reprint ed. 27.00 (*0-404-50939-8*) AMS Pr.

***Love, G., et al, eds.** Modern Developments & Applications in Microbeam Analysis. (Mikrochimica Acta Supplementa Ser.: Suppl. 15). (Illus.). 400p. 1998. pap. 120.00 (*3-211-83106-1*) Spr-Verlag.

Love, G., jt. ed. see Scott, V. D.

***Love, George.** Ear Reflexology: Magnet Acupressure Therapy. 2nd large type rev. ed. LC 00-90602. (Illus.). 100p. 2000. pap. text 24.95 (*1-878944-00-2*) Shield Soc.

Love, Gilly. Food Combining Cookbook. 1998. pap. text 12.95 (*1-85967-668-5*, Lorenz Bks) Anness Pub.

— Fresh Flowers: Over 20 Imaginative Arrangements for the Home. (Inspirations Ser.). 1998. 12.95 (*1-85967-607-3*, Lorenz Bks) Anness Pub.

***Love, Gilly.** Garden Decorator. (Illus.). 2000. 24.95 (*1-57145-667-8*, Laurel Glen Pub) Advantage Pubs.

Love, Gilly. Gardening in Your Apartment: Creating an Interior Oasis. (Illus.). 144p. 1996. 27.50 (*1-85967-104-7*, Lorenz Bks) Anness Pub.

***Love, Gilly.** Inspirations: Flowerwork. 96p. 2000. pap. 12.95 (*1-84215-164-9*) Anness Pub.

Love, Gilly. Making Most of Kitchens. LC 97-65577. (Illus.). 80p. 1997. 19.95 (*0-8478-2031-9*, Pub. by Rizzoli Intl) St Martin.

— Roses: Inspirations for Natural Gifts, Country Crafts & Decorative Displays. (Illus.). 128p. 1996. 19.95 (*1-85967-211-6*, Lorenz Bks) Anness Pub.

Love, Glen A. Babbitt: An American Life. LC 92-27096. (Masterwork Studies: No. 105). 105p. 1993. 23.95 (*0-8057-9440-9*, Twyne); pap. 13.95 (*0-8057-8562-0*, Twyne) Mac Lib Ref.

— Don Berry. LC 78-52564. (Western Writers Ser.: No. 35). 46p. 1978. pap. 4.95 (*0-88430-059-5*) Boise St U W Writ Ser.

***Love, Glen A.** Fishing the Northwest: An Angler's Reader. LC 00-8388. (Northwest Readers Ser.). (Illus.). 240p. 2000. 28.95 (*0-87071-481-3*) Oreg St U Pr.

Love, Glen A. New Americans: The Westerner & the Modern Experience in the American Novel. LC 80-65717. 288p. 1982. 36.50 (*0-8387-5011-7*) Bucknell U Pr.

Love, Glen A., ed. The World Begins Here: An Anthology of Oregon Short Fiction. LC 92-43642. (Oregon Literature Ser.: Vol. 1). (Illus.). 320p. (Orig.). (YA). 1993. pap. 21.95 (*0-87071-370-1*); pap. text 35.95 (*0-87071-369-8*) Oreg St U Pr.

Love, Glen A., ed. see Anderson, Sherwood.

Love, Glen A., jt. ed. see Bingham, Edwin R.

***Love, Gordon D., ed.** Adaptive Optics for Industry & Medicine: Proceedings of the 2nd International Workshop. 320p. 1999. 78.00 (*981-02-4115-1*) World Scientific Pub.

Love, Harold. The Culture & Commerce of Texts: Scribal Publication in Seventeenth-Century England. LC 97-40966. 400p. 1998. pap. 19.95 (*1-55849-134-1*) U of Mass Pr.

— The Golden Age of Australian Opera: W. S. Lyster & His Companies, 1861-1880. (C). 1981. 35.00 (*0-86819-051-9*, Pub. by Currency Pr) Accents Pubns.

— Restoration Verse. LC 97-221845. 352p. 1997. pap. 14.95 (*0-14-042407-5*) Viking Penguin.

— The Royal Belfast Hospital for Sick Children: A History, 1948-1998. LC 98-181194. (Illus.). 304p. 1998. 39.95 (*0-85640-621-X*, Pub. by Blackstaff Pr) Dufour.

— Scribal Publication in Seventeenth-Century England. (Illus.). 390p. 1993. text 69.00 (*0-19-811219-X*) OUP.

Love, Harold, intro. Poeta de Tristibus: or The Poet's Complaint: A Poem in Four Canto's. LC 92-24287. (Augustan Reprints Ser.: No. 149). 1971. reprint ed. 14.50 (*0-404-70149-3*, PR3291) AMS Pr.

Love, Harold, ed. see Southerne, Thomas.

Love, Harold, ed. see Wilmot, John.

Love, Harold D. Assessment of Intelligence & Development of Infants & Young Children: With Specialized Measures. 138p. 1990. pap. 23.95 (*0-398-06246-3*) C C Thomas.

— Assessment of Intelligence & Development of Infants & Young Children: With Specialized Measures. 138p. (C). 1990. text 36.95 (*0-398-05676-5*) C C Thomas.

— Characteristics of the Mildly Handicapped: Assisting Teachers, Counselors, Psychologists, & Families to Prepare for Their Roles in Meeting the Needs of the Mildly Handicapped in a Changing Society. LC 96-28214. (Illus.). 210p. 1996. text 44.95 (*0-398-06713-9*); pap. text 29.95 (*0-398-06714-7*) C C Thomas.

— Psychological Evaluation of Exceptional Children. (Illus.). 132p. 1985. 31.95 (*0-398-05045-7*); pap. 20.95 (*0-398-06247-1*) C C Thomas.

Love, Harold D. & Litton, Freddie W. Teaching Reading to Disabled & Handicapped Learners. LC 94-3917. (Illus.). 260p. 1994. pap. 37.95 (*0-398-06248-X*) C C Thomas.

An Asterisk (*) at the beginning of an entry indicates that the title is appearing for the first time.

— Teaching Reading to Disabled & Handicapped Learners. LC 94-3917. (Illus.). 260p. (C). 1994. text 54.95 (*0-398-05909-8*) C C Thomas.

Love, Henry Davison. Vestiges of Old Madras, 4 vols. in 3. reprint ed. 310.00 (*0-404-04060-8*) AMS Pr.

— Vestiges of Old Madras, 1640-1800: Traced from the East India Company's Records Preserved at Fort St. George & the India Office & From Other Sources. LC 98-904954. (Indian Records Ser.). 1996. write for info. (*81-206-0320-6*) Asian Educ Servs.

Love, J. Barry. The Colonial Surveyor in Pennsylvania. (Illus.). 171p. Date not set. 50.00 (*0-9701352-0-3*) Penn Lnd Srvyrs.

Love, J. D., ed. Yellowstone & Grand Teton National Parks & the Middle Rocky Mountains. (IGC Field Trip Guidebooks Ser.). 104p. 1989. 21.00 (*0-87590-668-0*, T328) Am Geophysical.

Love, J. D., jt. auth. see Reed, John C.

Love, J. Richard. Liberating Leaders from the Superman Syndrome. 254p. (C). 1994. lib. bdg. 37.50 (*0-8191-9241-4*) U Pr of Amer.

Love-Jackson, Marcia. Waitressing: Inside Tips for Better Tips. rev. ed. (Illus.). 44p. 1994. pap. 4.95 (*0-9614315-0-4*) Love-Jackson.

Love, Jacob W. Samoan Variations: Essays on the Nature of Traditional Oral Arts. LC 91-6778. (Illus.). 310p. 1991. text 25.00 (*0-8240-2985-2*) Garland.

Love, Jacob W. & Kaeppler, Adrienne L., eds. Australia & the Pacific Islands. LC 97-9671. (Encyclopedia of World Music Ser.: Vol. 9). (Illus.). 832p. 1998. text 150.00 incl. cd-rom (*0-8240-6038-5*, H1171) Garland.

Love, James H., jt. auth. see Ashcroft, Brian.

Love, James K. Deafmutism. 1976. 250.00 (*0-87968-303-1*) Gordon Pr.

***Love, Janice.** Hardanger - Basic & Beyond. (Illus.). 1999. pap. 15.00 (*1-888417-26-9*, LoveN Stitches) Dimefast.

— Hardanger - Fundamentals Made Fancy. (Illus.). 1999. pap. 20.00 (*1-888417-27-7*, LoveN Stitches) Dimefast.

Love, Janice. The United States Anti-Apartheid Movement: Local Activism in Global Politics. LC 85-3564. 316p. 1985. 59.95 (*0-275-90139-4*, C0139, Praeger Pubs) Greenwood.

Love, Jason. Snapshots: The Big Picture. (Illus.). Date not set. pap. 9.95 (*0-9662241-0-8*) Snapshots Cartoon.

Love, Jean, jt. auth. see Cox, Wendell.

Love, Jean C., et al. Equitable Remedies, Restitution & Damages: Cases & Materials. 5th ed. (American Casebook Ser.). 1228p. (C). 1994. 65.00 (*0-314-03719-5*) West Pub.

Love, Jeffrey. Swamp Cats. 176p. (Orig.). 1996. pap. 11.95 (*0-9653524-0-4*) Russn Hill Pr.

Love, Joe, jt. auth. see LMP, Inc. Staff.

Love, John. Geodaesia: or the Art of Surveying & Measuring Land Made Easy. Clark, Samuel, ed. (Illus.). 288p. 1997. reprint ed. 18.50 (*0-9633659-5-9*) US Hist Res Srv.

— Penguins. LC 96-48510. (WorldLife Library). (Illus.). 72p. (J). (gr. 5 up). 1997. pap. 16.95 (*0-89658-339-2*) Voyageur Pr.

Love, John & Watson, Jeff. The Golden Eagle. (Natural History Ser.: No. 56). (Illus.). 24p. 1989. pap. 5.25 (*0-7478-0091-X*, Pub. by Shire Pubns) Parkwest Pubns.

Love, John A. Eagles. (Illus.). 128p. text 19.95 (*0-905483-79-0*, Pub. by Whittet Bks) Diamond Farm Bk.

— Penguins. (Illus.). 128p. pap. text 19.95 (*1-873580-16-9*, Pub. by Whittet Bks) Diamond Farm Bk.

Love, John F. McDonald's: Behind the Arches. rev. ed. LC 95-11540. 496p. 1995. pap. 14.95 (*0-553-34759-4*) Bantam.

Love, Joseph L. Crafting the Third World: Theorizing Underdevelopment in Rumania & Brazil. LC 95-22991. 426p. 1996. 60.00 (*0-8047-2546-2*) Stanford U Pr.

Love, Joseph L. Crafting the Third World: Theorizing Underdevelopment in Rumania & Brazil. LC 95-22991. (Comparative Studies in History, Institutions, & Public Policy Ser.). 426p. (Orig.). 1996. pap. 24.95 (*0-8047-2705-8*) Stanford U Pr.

Love, Joseph L. Sao Paulo in the Brazilian Federation, 1889-1937. LC 78-66177. (Illus.). xvii, 398p. 1980. 52.50 (*0-8047-0991-2*) Stanford U Pr.

Love, Joseph L. & Jacobsen, Nils, eds. Guiding the Invisible Hand: Economic Liberalism & the State in Latin American History. LC 88-11985. (Illus.). 232p. 1988. 55.00 (*0-275-92945-0*, C2945, Praeger Pubs) Greenwood.

Love, Joseph L., jt. ed. see Byars, Robert S.

Love, Joseph LeRoy, jt. auth. see Baer, Werner.

Love, Karen, ed. see Rose, Tui.

Love, Karl F. Sudden Death Vol. 1: Your Guide to Reversing Heart Disease with Vitamins, Minerals, & Herbs. 200p. 1998. pap. text 14.95 (*0-9663652-1-6*) Promot Edge Pub.

Love, Katherine. Eating with America's Elite: Favorite Recipes of U. S. A. Athletes. Johnson, Marie, ed. 136p. 1995. 14.95 (*0-9648516-0-1*) Quinlan Press.

Love, Katherine & Johnson, Cindy. Blessings: A Century's Collection of Treasured Recipes. 2nd ed. 244p. 1996. reprint ed. 16.95 (*0-9659080-1-1*) First Presby.

Love, Kenna & Woodring, Kip. 101 Harley-Davidson Evolution Weekend Projects. LC 98-37893. (Illus.). 256p. 1998. pap. 24.95 (*0-7603-0370-3*) Motorbooks Intl.

Love, Kenny. Millennium Eve. unabridged ed. LC 98-91378. 320p. 1998. 24.95 (*0-9663064-0-6*, MT-01) Mys-Tech.

Love, Laurie M. Using ClarisWorks 2.0 for the Macintosh. 2nd ed. 512p. (C). 1993. pap. text 24.95 (*0-201-62629-2*) Addison-Wesley.

Love, Leo, ed. see Light, Joanna R.

Love, Lo'Retta. The Redneck Cookbook: 134 Down Home Recipes Complete with All the Trimmin's. LC 97-20705. 1997. write for info. (*1-889372-57-9*) Sweetwater Pr.

— The Redneck Cookbook: 165 Mighty Fine Down Home Recipes - Complete with All the Trimmin's. LC 96-53240. (Illus.). 128p. 1997. pap. 7.98 (*1-884822-69-X*) Blck Dog & Leventhal.

Love, Louise. The Complete Book of Pizza. (Illus.). 100p. (Orig.). 1983. pap. 8.00 (*0-930528-03-4*) Sassafras Pr.

Love, Lucille T., et al, eds. Remembering Margaret Mitchell: Author of Gone with the Wind. (Illus.). 212p. 1992. 29.95 (*0-9634245-0-5*) E Ross Pubs.

Love, Mabel R. The Love Clan: The Family of Daniel Love & Sarah McColl. (Illus.). 192p. (Orig.). 1992. pap. 20.00 (*0-9632429-0-3*) Love Pubs.

— Mc Carroll: The Family of Simon Mc Carroll & Ann Cosky Glenn of County Derry, Ulster, Ireland to America 1775-1993. (Illus.). 278p. (Orig.). 1993. 38.00 (*0-9632429-1-1*) Love Pubs.

Love, Marianne. Pocket Girdles: And Other Confessions of a Northwest Farmgirl. Sullivan, Noelle, ed. LC 94-76285. (Illus.). 213p. (Orig.). 1994. pap. 9.95 (*1-56044-293-X*) Falcon Pub Inc.

— This Ol' Sack of Spuds Ain't No Netted Gem & Other Postcards from Potato Land. (Illus.). 184p. 1997. pap. 11.95 (*1-56044-538-6*, Skyhse) Falcon Pub Inc.

Love, Mark. Love: Animals & the Law. 1997. pap. write for info. (*0-406-04967-X*, LAL, MICHIE) LEXIS Pub.

***Love, Mark Cameron.** The Evasive Text: Zechariah 1-8 & the Frustrated Reader. (Journal for the Study of the Old Testament Supplement Ser.: No. 296). 272p. 1999. 82.00 (*1-84127-020-2*, Pub. by Sheffield Acad) CUP Services.

Love, Marla. Twenty Decoding Games. (J). (gr. 2-6). 1982. pap. 13.99 (*0-8224-5801-2*) Fearon Teacher Aids.

— Twenty Reading Comprehension Games. (Makemaster Bk.). (J). (gr. 4-6). 1977. pap. 9.99 (*0-8224-5800-4*) Fearon Teacher Aids.

— Twenty Word Structure Games. (J). (gr. 2-6). 1983. pap. 13.99 (*0-8224-5802-0*) Fearon Teacher Aids.

Love, Mary. Angela. 2nd ed. 1997. reprint ed. mass mkt. 6.95 (*1-56333-545-X*) Masquerade.

— Mastering Mary Sue. 2nd ed. (Orig.). 1998. reprint ed. mass mkt. 6.95 (*1-56333-660-X*) Masquerade.

***Love, Mary A.** The ABC's & Symbols. (Illus.). 32p. (J). 1998. pap. 4.50 (*1-929548-01-X*) Loves Creat Res.

— Learning Through Symbolism & Celebrations. LC 97-92797. (Illus.). x, 150p. (J). 1998. pap. 18.00 (*1-929548-00-1*) Loves Creat Res.

Love-Meeh, Amy J. Who's Minding Your Minerals? A Comprehensive Guide to Understanding Mineral Ownership. 84p. 1996. 14.95 (*1-57502-223-0*, P0884) Morris Pubng.

Love, Mervyn. Peace Building Through Reconciliation in Northern Ireland. LC 95-78515. 336p. 1995. 77.95 (*1-85972-136-2*, Pub. by Avebry) Ashgate Pub Co.

Love, Michael C. Better Takeoffs & Landings. LC 95-13583. 1995. 29.95 (*0-07-038805-9*) McGraw-Hill Prof.

— Better Takeoffs & Landings. LC 95-13583. (Illus.). 240p. 1995. 21.95 (*0-07-038806-7*) McGraw-Hill Prof.

— Flight Maneuvers. (Practical Flying Ser.). (Illus.). 242p. 1998. 39.95 (*0-07-038866-0*) McGraw.

— Flight Maneuvers. (Practical Flying Ser.). (Illus.). 224p. 1998. pap. 34.95 (*0-07-038865-2*) McGraw.

— Spin Management & Recovery. (Illus.). 237p. 1997. 36.95 (*0-07-038809-1*); pap. 24.95 (*0-07-038810-5*) McGraw.

Love, Milton. Probably More Than You Want to Know about the Fishes of the Pacific Coast. 2nd rev. ed. LC 91-90108. (Illus.). 386p. 1996. pap. 19.95 (*0-9628725-5-5*) Really Big Pr.

Love, Monifa A. Freedom in The Dismal. LC 97-47583. 191p. 1998. 20.00 (*0-917635-26-4*); pap. 10.00 (*0-917635-27-2*) Plover Pr.

— My Magic Pours Secret Libations. (Illus.). 80p. (Orig.). 1997. pap. 19.95 (*1-889282-01-4*) FSU Mus Fine Arts.

Love, Mother. Forgive Or Forget. 2001. pap. 12.95 (*0-06-093252-X*, Quil) HarperTrade.

***Love, Mother & Bolden, Tonya.** Forgive or Forget: Never Underestimate the Power of ForgivenessLove,&Mother, Set. 1999. audio 18.00 (*0-694-52244-9*) HarperAudio.

***Love, Mother & Church, Connie.** Listen up, Girlfriends! Lessons on Life from the Queen of Advice. (Illus.). 185p. 2000. reprint ed. text. write for info. (*0-7881-9047-4*) DIANE Pub.

Love, Myra N. Christa Wolf: Literature & the Conscience of History. LC 91-17401. (DDR-Studien - East German Studies: Vol. 6). 202p. (C). 1992. text 42.95 (*0-8204-1651-7*) P Lang Pubng.

Love, Nancy S. Marx, Nietzsche, & Modernity. 224p. 1986. text 57.50 (*0-231-06238-9*) Col U Pr.

— Marx, Nietzsche, & Modernity. 264p. 1996. pap. 18.50 (*0-231-06239-7*) Col U Pr.

— Understanding Dogmas & Dreams: A Text. LC 97-4916. (Studies in Political Thinking). 224p. 1997. pap. text 22.95 (*1-56643-044-5*, Chatham House Pub) Seven Bridges.

Love, Nancy S., ed. Dogmas & Dreams: A Reader in Modern Political Ideologies. 2nd ed. LC 97-17502. (Studies in Political Thinking). 640p. (C). 1998. pap. text 37.95 (*1-56643-043-7*, Chatham House Pub) Seven Bridges.

Love, Nat. The Life & Adventures of Nat Love. LC 95-23385. (Blacks in the American West Ser.). (Illus.). xviii, 162p. 1995. pap. 9.00 (*0-8032-7955-8*, Bison Books) U of Nebr Pr.

— The Life & Adventures of Nat Love. (Illus.). 162p. 1988. reprint ed. pap. 11.95 (*0-933121-17-2*) Black Classic.

— The Life & Adventures of Nat Love, Better Known in the Cattle Country As Deadwood Dick. LC 68-29007. (American Negro: His History & Literature. Series 1). 1968. reprint ed. 25.95 (*0-405-01827-4*) Ayer.

— The Life & Adventures of Nat Love, Better Known in the Cattle Country As Deadwood Dick, by Himself. (American Biography Ser.). 162p. 1991. reprint ed. lib. bdg. 59.00 (*0-7812-8252-7*) Rprt Serv.

***Love, Neil A. & Brant-Love, Joan.** The Project Sponsor Guide. LC 00-23371. 2000. write for info. (*1-880410-15-X*) Proj Mgmt Inst.

Love, Nigel. Generative Phonology: A Case Study from French. (Lingvisticae Investigationes Supplementa Ser.: Vol. 4). viii, 241p. 1981. 62.00 (*90-272-3113-3*) J Benjamins Pubng Co.

Love, Nigel, ed. The Foundations of Linguistic Theory: Selected Writing by Roy Harris. 273p. 1989. 65.00 (*0-415-03613-5*, A3469) Routledge.

Love, Nigel, ed. see Harris, Roy.

Love, Patricia. Emotional Incest Syndrome: What to Do When a Parent's Love Rules Your Life. 304p. 1991. pap. 14.95 (*0-553-35275-X*) Bantam.

Love, Patricia & Robinson, Jo. Hot Monogamy: Essential Steps to More Passionate, Intimate Lovemaking. 320p. 1995. pap. 13.95 (*0-452-27366-8*, Plume) Dutton Plume.

Love, Patricia, ed. see Santiago, J. K.

Love, Patrick G., jt. auth. see Love, Anne G.

Love, Paul. Modern Dance Terminology. (Illus.). 96p. 1997. pap. 16.95 (*0-87127-206-7*) Princeton Bk Co.

Love, Paul, ed. Michigan State University Art Collection. (Illus.). 45p. (Orig.). 1966. pap. 4.00 (*1-879147-00-9*) Kresge Art Mus.

Love, Paula M. Will Rogers Book. 1972. 11.95 (*0-87244-030-3*) Texian.

Love, Presley. The Classic Rock Quiz Book: From the Animals to Frank Zappa. 264p. 1995. pap. 10.95 (*0-8065-1689-5*, Citadel Pr) Carol Pub Group.

— The Classic Rock Quiz Book: From the Animals to Frank Zappa. rev. ed. LC 98-45825. 324p. 1999. pap. 12.95 (*0-8065-2080-9*, Citadel Pr) Carol Pub Group.

— Rock Lyrics Quiz Book. LC 93-46589. 1994. 10.95 (*0-8065-1527-9*, Citadel Pr) Carol Pub Group.

Love, Presley. Rock Lyrics Trivia: Quiz Book. 1992. pap. 5.95 (*1-56391-004-7*) Hi-Lite Pub.

Love, Preston. A Thousand Honey Creeks Later: My Life in Music from Basie to Motown - & Beyond. LC 97-14684. (Music/Culture Ser.). (Illus.). 296p. 1997. text 45.00 (*0-8195-6318-8*, Wesleyan Univ Pr) U Pr of New Eng.

Love, Preston. A Thousand Honey Creeks Later: My Life in Music from Basie to Motown - & Beyond. LC 97-14684. (Music/Culture Ser.). (Illus.). 296p. 1997. pap. 19.95 (*0-8195-6320-X*, Wesleyan Univ Pr) U Pr of New Eng.

Love, R. Johnny Can Read, So Can Jane. 1982. text 11.20 (*0-201-04439-0*) Addison-Wesley.

Love, R. R., et al, eds. Manual of Clinical Oncology: UICC International Union Against Cancer. 6th ed. LC 94-37384. 802p. 1994. 49.00 (*0-387-58193-6*) Spr-Verlag.

Love, Ralph N., jt. ed. see Goodman, Louis J.

Love, Reeve & Sosa, Alicia S. Sex Stereotyping & Bias Training Module IV: Their Origin & Effects. rev. ed. 40p. 1995. pap. text 8.50 (*1-878550-57-8*) Inter Dev Res Assn.

Love, Richard H. Carl W. Peters: American Scene Painter from Rochester to Rockport. LC 98-42873. (Illus.). xv, 927p. 1999. 99.00 (*1-58046-024-0*) Univ Rochester Pr.

Love, Robert. Chic Simple Tools. 104p. 1994. 12.50 (*0-679-43223-X*) Knopf.

— How to Start Your Own School. LC 72-90275. 176p. 1975. reprint ed. pap. 1.95 (*0-916054-01-2*) Jameson Bks.

Love, Robert A. Federal Financing. LC 68-58605. (Columbia University. Studies in the Social Sciences: No. 337). reprint ed. 29.50 (*0-404-51337-9*) AMS Pr.

Love, Robert W., Jr. History of the U. S. Navy. 1775-1941. LC 91-27510. (Illus.). 752p. 1992. 39.95 (*0-8117-1862-X*) Stackpole.

— History of the U. S. Navy, 1942-1991, Vol. 2. LC 91-27510. (Illus.). 912p. 1992. 39.95 (*0-8117-1863-8*) Stackpole.

Love, Robert W., Jr. & Major, John, eds. The Year of D-Day: The Nineteen Forty-Four Diary of Admiral Sir Bertram Ramsay, RN. (Illus.). 208p. 1994. 25.00 (*0-85958-622-7*, Pub. by Univ of Hull Pr) Paul & Co Pubs.

Love, Robertus. The Rise & Fall of Jesse James. LC 89-24965. xxiv, 446p. (YA). 1990. reprint ed. pap. 15.00 (*0-8032-7932-9*, Bison Books) U of Nebr Pr.

Love, Roger & Frazier, Donna. Set Your Voice Free. LC 99-10081. (Illus.). 240p. 1999. 24.95 (*0-316-44179-1*) Little.

Love, Rosaleen, ed. Darwin & Social Darwinism. 69p. (C). 1982. 38.00 (*0-86828-132-8*, Pub. by Deakin Univ) St Mut.

Love, Rosalind C., ed. Three Eleventh-Century Anglo-Latin Saints' Lives: Vita S. Birini, Vita et Miracula S. Kenelmi, & Vita S. Rummoldi. (Oxford Medieval Texts Ser.). 340p. 1996. text 89.00 (*0-19-820524-4*) OUP.

***Love, Russell & Webb, Rhonda G.** Neurology for the Speech-Language Pathologist. 4th ed. (Illus.). 384p. 2000. pap. 35.00 (*0-7506-7252-8*) Buttrwrth-Heinemann.

***Love, Russell J.** Childhood Motor Speech Disability. 2nd ed. LC 99-16113. 202p. (C). 1999. pap. text 36.00 (*0-205-29781-1*, Longwood Div) Allyn.

Love, Russell J. & Webb, Wanda G. Neurology for the Speech-Language Pathologist. 3rd ed. LC 96-20156. 337p. 1996. pap. text 35.00 (*0-7506-9686-9*) Buttrwrth-Heinemann.

Love, Shirley. God Is My Collaborator. Woodbury, Tina, ed. (Orig.). 1997. pap. 5.00 (*1-889732-06-0*) Word-For-Word.

Love Spell Staff. Night Before Christmas, 1 vol. 400p. 1998. mass mkt. 5.99 (*0-505-52318-3*) Dorchester Pub Co.

Love, Spencie. One Blood: The Death & Resurrection of Charles R. Drew. 400p. 1997. pap. 17.95 (*0-8078-4682-1*) U of NC Pr.

Love, Steve. Florida Facts & Fiction. (Illus.). (Orig.). 1984. pap. 4.95 (*0-9613239-0-6*) S F Love.

Love, Steve & Griffels, David. Wheels of Fortune: The Story of Rubber in Akron. Van Tassell, Debbie & Kirkman, Susan, eds. LC 98-36729. (Ohio History & Culture Ser.). (Illus.). 359p. 1998. pap. 22.95 (*1-884836-38-0*) U Akron Pr.

Love, Steve, et al. Wheels of Fortune: The Story of Rubber in Akron. Van Tassell, Debbie & Kirkman, Susan, eds. LC 98-36729. (Ohio History & Culture Ser.). (Illus.). 359p. 1998. 49.95 (*1-884836-37-2*) U Akron Pr.

Love, Steve, jt. auth. see Faust, Gerry.

Love, Susan M. Dr. Susan Love's Breast Book. 1991. pap. 16.00 (*0-201-57097-1*) Addison-Wesley.

— Dr. Susan Love's Breast Book. 2nd ed. 1995. pap. 17.00 (*0-201-31599-8*) Addison-Wesley.

Love, Susan M. & Lindsey, Karen. Dr. Susan Love's Breast Book. 1990. 18.95 (*0-201-09665-X*) Addison-Wesley.

— Dr. Susan Love's Breast Book. 2nd rev. ed. (Illus.). 608p. 1995. pap. 18.00 (*0-201-40835-X*) Addison-Wesley.

***Love, Susan M. & Lindsey, Karen.** Dr. Susan Love's Breast Book. 3rd ed. 632p. 2000. pap. text 19.95 (*0-7382-0235-5*, Pub. by Perseus Pubng) HarpC.

— Dr. Susan Love's Hormone Book: Making Informed Choices about Menopause. (Illus.). 375p. 1998. pap. 15.00 (*0-8129-6392-X*, Times Bks) Crown Pub Group.

Love, Susan M., et al. Atlas of Techniques in Breast Surgery. (Illus.). 176p. 1995. text 107.00 (*0-397-50946-4*) Lppncott W & W.

Love, Sydney F. Mastery & Management of Time. (Illus.). 1978. 14.95 (*0-13-559971-7*, Busn) P-H.

Love, Sydney S. Planning & Creating Successful Engineered Designs. rev. ed. (Illus.). 292p. 1986. 40.00 (*0-912907-00-2*) Adv Prof Dev.

Love, T. W. Construction Manual: Concrete & Formwork. (Illus.). 176p. 1973. pap. 17.75 (*0-910460-03-5*) Craftsman.

— Construction Manual: Finish Carpentry. LC 74-12339. (Illus.). 1974. pap. 15.25 (*0-910460-08-6*) Craftsman.

— Stair Builders Handbook. LC 74-4298. (Illus.). 1974. pap. 19.50 (*0-910460-07-8*) Craftsman.

Love, Terrence L. The Guide to Appraisal Office Policies & Procedures. 96p. 1991. pap. 12.00 (*0-922154-03-1*, 0618M) Appraisal Inst.

Love, Terry. A-RA-5 "Mini" in Action. (Mini in Action Ser.). (Illus.). 50p. 1995. pap. 5.95 (*0-89747-334-5*) Squad Sig Pubns.

— Wings of Air America: A Photo History. LC 98-85008. 104p. 1998. pap. 19.95 (*0-7643-0619-7*) Schiffer.

Love, Thomas A. Bar Chart Scheduling for Residential Construction. LC 96-48634. (Illus.). 64p. (Orig.). 1997. pap. 30.00 (*0-86718-424-8*) Home Builder.

— Scheduling Residential Construction for Builders & Remodelers. LC 94-41539. (Illus.). 128p. (Orig.). 1995. pap. 29.00 (*0-86718-401-9*) Home Builder.

Love, Tom. Object Lessons: Lessons Learned in Object-Oriented Development Projects. (Advances in Object Technology Ser.: No. 1). 281p. (Orig.). 1993. pap. 32.95 (*0-13-472432-1*) Cambridge U Pr.

Love, Val. Backpacks: To Crochet. (Illus.). 8p. 1998. pap. 7.00 (*1-886828-09-1*) Dovetail Desgn.

— Cat Sweaters & Cushions: To Knit by Hand or Machine. (Illus.). 20p. (Orig.). 1994. pap. 10.00 (*1-886828-01-6*) Dovetail Desgn.

— Christmas Tree Decorations: To Knit by Hand or Machine. rev. ed. (Illus.). 24p. (Orig.). 1997. pap. 8.00 (*1-886828-08-3*) Dovetail Desgn.

— Holiday Decorations: To Knit by Hand or Machine. (Illus.). 24p. 1992. pap. 9.50 (*1-886828-02-4*) Dovetail Desgn.

— Pocket Pals: To Knit by Hand or Machine. (Illus.). 32p. 1995. pap. 10.00 (*1-886828-00-8*) Dovetail Desgn.

— Shoulder Bags: To Crochet. rev. ed. (Illus.). 8p. 1997. pap. 7.00 (*1-886828-07-5*) Dovetail Desgn.

— Story Book Afghans & Toys: To Crochet. (Illus.). 20p. (Orig.). 1990. pap. 8.00 (*1-886828-05-9*) Dovetail Desgn.

— Story Book Sweaters: To Knit by Hand or Machine. (Illus.). 16p. (Orig.). 1988. pap. 8.00 (*1-886828-04-0*) Dovetail Desgn.

Love, Valerie L., jt. auth. see Copeland, Edna D.

Love, Vincent J. & Ernst & Young Staff. Understanding & Using Financial Data: An Ernst & Young Guide for Attorneys. 2nd ed. LC 96-19756. 544p. 1996. 125.00 (*0-471-16213-2*) Wiley.

Love, Vincent J., et al. Figuring Out the Deal: Using Financial Information to Your Clients' Advantage. LC 97-144345. 424p. 1997. write for info. (*0-87224-310-9*) PLI.

Love, W. D. Houghton. Descendants of Captain William Houghton, 1774-1863, & Marilla Clay, 1780-1858, with Data of Collateral Relatives of William Houghton & Direct Line of Houghton Ancestry. (Illus.). 67p. 1997. reprint ed. pap. 14.00 (*0-8328-9215-7*); reprint ed. lib bdg. 24.00 (*0-8328-9214-9*) Higginson Bk Co.

Love, W. D., jt. ed. see Freeman, C. E.

Love, Warner & Lattman, Eaton, eds. Biophysical Applications of Crystallographic Techniques. (Transactions of the American Crystallographic Association Ser.: Vol. 9). 140p. 1973. pap. 25.00 (*0-686-60380-X*) Polycrystal Bk Serv.

Love, William D. Colonial History of Hartford (Conn.) (Illus.). 368p. 1993. reprint ed. lib. bdg. 42.00 (*0-8328-3130-1*) Higginson Bk Co.

— Wisconsin in the War of the Rebellion: History of All Regiments & Batteries. (Illus.). 1144p. 1997. reprint ed. lib. bdg. 105.00 (*0-8328-6961-9*) Higginson Bk Co.

An Asterisk (*) at the beginning of an entry indicates that the title is appearing for the first time.

L

Love, William D. & Honig, Lucille J. Options & Perspectives: A Sourcebook of Innovative Foreign Language Programs in Action, K-12. LC 73-78994. 381p. reprint ed. pap. 118.20 (*0-608-16280-9*, 202655300053) Bks Demand.

Loveall, Jaquelyn. Phila Campbell: A Story of 1909. 120p. 1994. 14.95 (*1-878208-39-X*) Guild Pr IN.

Lovece, Frank. The X-Files Declassified: The Unauthorized Guide. LC 95-26390. (Illus.). 288p. 1996. pap. 17.95 (*0-8065-1745-X*) Carol Pub Group.

Lovechild. Gag. (Orig.). 1995. mass mkt. 6.95 (*1-56333-369-4*, Rosebud) Masquerade.

Lovecraft, H. P. The Annotated H. P. Lovecraft. LC 96-53689. 368p. 1997. pap. 13.95 (*0-440-50660-3*) Dell.

***Lovecraft, H. P.** The Annotated Supernatural Horror in Literature. annot. ed. Joshi, S. T., ed. 175p. 2000. pap. 15.00 (*0-9673215-0-6*) Hippocampus Pr.

Lovecraft, H. P. At the Mountains of Madness. (Illus.). 1990. 120.00 (*0-937986-69-0*) D M Grant.

— At the Mountains of Madness & Other Novels. rev. ed. Joshi, S. T., ed. LC 85-1254. (Collected Lovecraft Fiction Ser.: Vol. 2). (Illus.). 458p. 1985. reprint ed. 25.95 (*0-87054-038-6*) Arkham.

— At the Mountains of Madness & Other Tales of Terror. 192p. 1985. mass mkt. 5.99 (*0-345-32945-7*, Del Rey) Ballantine Pub Grp.

— Blood Curdling Tales of Horror. (I). 384p. 1987. pap. 10.00 (*0-345-35080-4*, Del Rey) Ballantine Pub Grp.

***Lovecraft, H. P.** The Call of Cthulhu & Other Stories. Joshi, S. T., ed. LC 99-19100. 304p. 1999. pap. 12.95 (*0-14-118234-2*, Penguin Classics) Viking Penguin.

Lovecraft, H. P. The Case of Charles Dexter Ward. 128p. (Orig.). 1987. mass mkt. 0.05 (*0-345-35490-7*) Ballantine Pub Grp.

— Crawling Chaos. rev. ed. 256p. 1998. pap. 19.95 (*1-871592-72-0*) Creation Books.

— Dagon & Other Macabre Tales. rev. ed. Joshi, S. T., ed. LC 86-14105. (Collected Lovecraft Fiction Ser.: Vol. 3). (Illus.). 475p. 1987. 25.95 (*0-87054-039-4*) Arkham.

— The Doom That Came to Samath. 1997. pap. write for info. (*0-345-41952-9*, Del Rey) Ballantine Pub Grp.

— The Doom That Came to Sarnath. 224p. 1985. mass mkt. 5.99 (*0-345-33105-2*, Del Rey) Ballantine Pub Grp.

— The Dream Cycle of H. P. Lovecraft: Dreams of Terror & Death. LC 95-15061. 400p. 1995. pap. 10.00 (*0-345-38421-0*) Ballantine Pub Grp.

— The Dream-Quest of Unknown Kadath. 256p. 1986. mass mkt. 5.99 (*0-345-33779-4*, Del Rey) Ballantine Pub Grp.

— The Dream-Quest of Unknown Kadath. 1997. pap. write for info. (*0-345-41953-7*, Del Rey) Ballantine Pub Grp.

— The Dunwich Horror & Others. rev. ed. Joshi, S. T., ed. LC 84-14478. (Collected Lovecraft Fiction Ser.: Vol. 1). (Illus.). 433p. 1985. reprint ed. 25.95 (*0-87054-037-8*) Arkham.

— An Epicure in the Terrible: A Centennial Anthology of Essays in Honor of H. P. Lovecraft. Schultz, David E. & Joshi, S. T., eds. LC 90-55007. 1991. 48.50 (*0-8386-3415-X*) Fairleigh Dickinson.

— Four Prose Poems. (Illus.). (Orig.). 1987. pap. 2.50 (*0-940884-10-0*) Necronomicon.

— The Fungi from Yuggoth. 2.50 (*0-686-31236-8*) Necronomicon.

— The H. P. Lovecraft Christmas Book. Michaud, Susan, ed. (Illus.). 12p. (Orig.). 1984. pap. 1.95 (*0-940884-22-4*) Necronomicon.

— Herbert West Reanimator. 35p. (Orig.). 1985. pap. 3.50 (*0-318-04714-4*) Necronomicon.

— History of the Necronomicon. 12p. (Orig.). 1984. pap. 1.50 (*0-318-04715-2*) Necronomicon.

— The Horror in the Museum. 248p. 1996. mass mkt. 4.95 (*0-7867-0387-3*) Carroll & Graf.

— The Horror in the Museum & Other Revisions. enl. rev. ed. Joshi, S. T., ed. LC 88-7921. (Collected Lovecraft Fiction Ser.: Vol. 4). 464p. 1989. reprint ed. 25.95 (*0-87054-040-8*) Arkham.

***Lovecraft, H. P.** Lord of a Visible World: An Autobiography in Letters. Joshi, S. T. & Schultz, David E., eds. 424p. 2000. 49.95 (*0-8214-1332-5*, Ohio U Ctr Intl); pap. 24.95 (*0-8214-1333-3*, Ohio U Ctr Intl) Ohio U Pr.

Lovecraft, H. P. The Loved Dead. 224p. 1997. mass mkt. 4.95 (*0-7867-0445-4*) Carroll & Graf.

— The Lurking Fear & Other Stories. 192p. 1985. mass mkt. 5.99 (*0-345-32604-0*) Ballantine Pub Grp.

— Miscellaneous Writings. Joshi, S. T., ed. & intro. by. LC 94-27323. (Illus.). xiv, 570p. 1995. 32.95 (*0-87054-168-4*) Arkham.

— More Annotated H. P. Lovecraft. Joshi, S. T. & Cannon, Peter, eds. LC 99-23457. (Illus.). 320p. 1999. pap. 13.95 (*0-440-50875-4*, Dell Trade Pbks) Dell.

— The Night Ocean. (Illus.). (Orig.). 1986. pap. 2.50 (*0-940884-16-X*) Necronomicon.

— The Road to Madness: The Transition of H. P. Lovecraft. LC 96-294. 384p. 1996. pap. 10.00 (*0-345-38422-9*) Ballantine Pub Grp.

— Selected Letters Five. Derleth, August & Turner, James, eds. LC 75-44847. (Illus.). 400p. 1976. 22.95 (*0-87054-036-X*) Arkham.

— Selected Letters Four. Derleth, August & Turner, James, eds. LC 75-44847. (Illus.). 424p. 1976. 22.95 (*0-87054-035-1*) Arkham.

— Selected Letters, 1929-1931, Vol. I. 1998. 22.95 (*0-87054-032-7*, Arkham Hse) Arkham.

— Something about Cats & Other Pieces. Derleth, August W., ed. LC 79-156681. (Essay Index Reprint Ser.). 1977. reprint ed. 24.95 (*0-8369-2410-X*) Ayer.

— Supernatural Horror in Literature. Bleiler, Everett F., ed. 111p. 1973. reprint ed. pap. 5.95 (*0-486-20105-8*) Dover.

— Tales Of Lovecraft. Oates, Joyce Carol, ed. LC 96-47196. 384p. 1997. 23.00 (*0-88001-541-1*) HarpC.

— The Tomb & Other Tales. 192p. 1986. mass mkt. 5.99 (*0-345-33661-5*) Ballantine Pub Grp.

— The Tomb & Other Tales. 1997. pap. write for info. (*0-345-41955-3*, Del Rey) Ballantine Pub Grp.

— A Winter Wish. Collins, Tom, ed. & intro. by. LC 76-58618. (Illus.). 1977. 15.00 (*0-918372-00-3*) Whispers.

Lovecraft, H. P. & Derleth, August. The Lurker at the Threshold. 192p. 1988. mass mkt. 4.50 (*0-88184-408-X*) Carroll & Graf.

— The Watchers Out of Time. 272p. 1991. mass mkt. 4.95 (*0-88184-769-0*) Carroll & Graf.

Lovecraft, H. P., et al. Cthulhu Cycle. Price, Robert M., ed. (Call of Cthulhu Fiction Ser.). (Illus.). 270p. 1996. pap. 10.95 (*1-56882-038-0*) Chaosium.

— The Hastur Cycle: 13 Tales of Horror Defining Hastur, the King in Yellow, Yuggoth, & the Dread City of Carcosa. 2nd rev. ed. Price, Robert, ed. (Call of Cthulhu Fiction Ser.). 336p. (Orig.). 1997. pap. 10.95 (*1-56882-094-1*, 6020) Chaosium.

— Innsmouth Cycle. Price, Robert M., ed. (Call of Cthulhu Fiction Ser.). 1998. pap. 12.95 (*1-56882-113-1*) Chaosium.

Lovecraft, H. P., et al. Tales of the Cthulhu Mythos. LC 87-17503. (Illus.). 525p. 1990. 26.95 (*0-87054-159-5*) Arkham.

Lovecraft, H. P., et al. Tales of the Cthulhu Mythos. LC PS648.H6T35 1998. 480p. 1998. pap. 12.00 (*0-345-42204-X*, Del Rey) Ballantine Pub Grp.

— Tales of the Unnatural. abr. ed. Baxter, Beth, ed. 1987. pap. 7.95 incl. audio (*1-882071-18-2*, 020) B&B Audio.

Lovecraft, H. P., jt. auth. see Eckhardt, Jason C.

Lovecy, Ian. Automating Library Procedures: A Survivor's Handbook. LC 84-221628. (Illus.). 255p. reprint ed. pap. 79.10 (*0-7837-7014-6*, 204682800004) Bks Demand.

Loveday. Electronic Fault. 2nd ed. 1982. pap. text. write for info. (*0-582-98852-7*, Pub. by Addison-Wesley) Longman.

Loveday & Cannon. The Footbook for Thinker's 3-7. 1993. text. write for info. (*0-582-87630-3*, Pub. by Addison-Wesley) Longman.

Loveday, jt. auth. see Frost.

Loveday, A. Britain & World Trade. LC 76-37894. (Select Bibliographies Reprint Ser.). 1977. reprint ed. 19.95 (*0-8369-6731-3*) Ayer.

— History & Economics of Indian Famines. 1986. reprint ed. 18.50 (*0-8364-1611-2*, Pub. by Usha) S Asia.

Loveday, Alexander. Acts. (New Testament Readings Ser.). 160p. (C). 1998. 65.00 (*0-415-09687-1*) Routledge.

— Reflections on International Administration. LC 74-9168. 334p. 1974. reprint ed. lib. bdg. 75.00 (*0-8371-7618-2*, LOIA, Greenwood Pr) Greenwood.

Loveday, Amos J., Jr. The Rise & Decline of the American Cut Nail Industry: A Study of the Interrelationships of Technology, Business Organization, & Management Techniques, 53. LC 83-5542. (Contributions in Economics & Economic History Ser.: No. 53). (Illus.). 160p. 1983. 49.95 (*0-313-23918-5*, LAC/) Greenwood.

Loveday, Bronwen. The Teacher's Footbook. 1988. pap. text. write for info. (*0-582-65992-2*, Pub. by Addison-Wesley) Longman.

Loveday, Chrissie. Lovers Don't Lie. (Scarlet Ser.). 1998. mass mkt. 3.99 (*1-85487-565-5*, Pub. by Scarlet Bks) London Brdge.

— The Path to Love. 400p. (Orig.). 1997. mass mkt. 3.99 (*1-85487-924-3*, Pub. by Scarlet Bks) London Brdge.

Loveday, G. C. Designing Electronic Hardware. (Illus.). 336p. (Orig.). (C). 1992. pap. text (*0-582-08612-4*) Addison-Wesley.

— Electronic Fault Diagnosis. 4th ed. (Illus.). 176p. 1994. pap. 36.50 (*0-582-22911-1*, Pub. by Addison-Wesley) Trans-Atl Phila.

— Electronic Testing & Diagnosis Fault. 3rd ed. (Illus.). 320p. (C). 1996. pap. 45.95 (*0-582-25242-3*, Pub. by Addison-Wesley) Trans-Atl Phila.

Loveday, Helen. Chinese Bronzes. (Illus.). 48p. 1990. pap. 6.95 (*1-85444-003-9*, 003-9, Pub. by Ashmolean Mus) A Schwartz & Co.

***Loveday, Helen.** Iran. 2nd ed. 1999. pap. 19.95 (*962-217-609-7*) Norton.

Loveday, John. Goodbye, Buffalo Sky. LC 96-45402. 176p. (J). (gr. 7 up). 1997. 16.00 (*0-689-81370-8*) McElderry Bks.

— Halo. LC 93-35930. 1994. 19.95 (*0-15-100070-0*) Harcourt.

— Halo. 286p. 1994. pap. 9.95 (*0-15-600113-6*) Harcourt.

Loveday, Leo. Explorations in Japanese Sociolinguistics. LC 86-26369. (Pragmatics & Beyond Ser.: Vol. VII:1). xi, 153p. 1986. text 53.00 (*1-55619-000-X*) J Benjamins Pubng Co.

Loveday, Peter & Cooke, P. Aboriginal Arts & Crafts & the Market. LC 84-108002. (Monograph Ser.). xvi, 88 p. 1983. write for info. (*0-86784-278-4*) ANU Res Sch.

Loveday, Peter, et al. Australia's 7th State. LC 88-189440. xxiii, 322 p. 1988. write for info. (*0-7315-0161-6*, Pub. by Aust Nat Univ) UH Pr.

Lovegren, Sylvia. Fashionable Food. LC 94-5371. (Illus.). 1995. 25.00 (*0-02-575059-3*) Macmillan.

Lovegrove, A. Judicial Decision Making, Sentencing Policy & Numerical Guidance. (Research in Criminology Ser.). (Illus.). 310p. 1988. 167.00 (*0-387-96764-8*) Spr-Verlag.

Lovegrove, Austin. The Framework of Judicial Sentencing: A Study in Legal Decision Making. (Cambridge Criminology Ser.). 293p. (C). 1997. text 59.95 (*0-521-58427-2*) Cambridge U Pr.

Lovegrove, G., et al, eds. Women into Computing: Selected Papers, 1988-1990. (Workshops in Computing Ser.). (Illus.). 448p. 1991. 59.00 (*0-387-19648-X*) Spr-Verlag.

***Lovegrove, J. M. H.** Guardians: Berserker. LC 99-43358. 352p. 1999. pap. 9.95 (*1-57500-048-2*, Pub. by TV Bks) HarpC.

Lovegrove, J. M. H. Guardians: The Krilov Continuum. 1999. 9.95 (*1-57500-033-4*, Pub. by TV Bks) HarpC.

Lovegrove, James, jt. auth. see Crowther, Peter.

***Lovegrove, Keith.** Airline: Identity, Design & Culture. (Illus.). 144p. 2000. pap. 24.95 (*3-8238-5460-7*) te Neues.

Lovegrove, Roger. Collins Field Notebook of British Birds. 1987. 21.95 (*0-317-54060-2*) Viking Penguin.

***Lovegrove, William, et al.** The Cheque Books of the Royal: With Additional Material from the Manuscripts of William Lovegrove & Marmaduke Alford. LC 00-23896. 2000. write for info. (*1-84014-664-8*, Pub. by Ashgate Pub) Ashgate Pub Co.

Lovei, Laszlo. Energy in Europe & Central Asia: A Sector Strategy for the World Bank Group. LC 98-46453. (Discussion Paper Ser.: No. 393). 49p. 1998. pap. 22.00 (*0-8213-4392-0*, 14392) World Bank.

Lovei, Magda. Phasing Out Lead from Gasoline: Worldwide Experience & Policy Implications. LC 97-32833. (Technical Paper Ser.: No. 397). 36p. 1998. pap. 22.00 (*0-8213-4157-X*, 14157) World Bank.

Lovei, Magda, ed. Phasing Out Lead from Gasoline in Central & Eastern Europe: Health Issues, Feasibility, & Policies. LC 97-12022. 94p. 1997. pap. 22.00 (*0-8213-3915-X*, 13915) World Bank.

Lovei, Magda & Weiss, Charles, Jr. Environmental Management & Institutions in OECD Countries: Lessons from Experience. LC 98-14304. (Technical Paper Ser.: No. 391). 76p. 1999. pap. 22.00 (*0-8213-4204-5*, 14204) World Bank.

Lovei, Magda, jt. auth. see Hughes, Gordon.

Lovejoy. Getting Results. 192p. 1994. pap. 26.95 (*0-566-07541-5*) Ashgate Pub Co.

Lovejoy, Addison. The Baseball Song Book. 24p. (YA). (gr. 8 up). 1971. 1.95 (*0-87884-015-X*) Unicorn Ent.

Lovejoy, Ann. The American Mixed Border: Gardens for All Seasons. LC 92-27309. 240p. 1993. 35.00 (*0-02-575580-3*) Macmillan.

***Lovejoy, Ann.** Ann Lovejoy's Organic Garden Design School. (Illus.). 2000. 35.00 (*0-87596-836-8*, Rodale Org Garden) Rodale Pr Inc.

Lovejoy, Ann. The Border in Bloom: A Northwest Garden Through the Seasons. LC 90-32901. (Illus.). 264p. (Orig.). 1990. pap. 14.95 (*0-912365-26-9*) Sasquatch Bks.

— Cascadia: Inspired Gardening in the Pacific Northwest. LC 96-42378. (Illus.). 96p. 1997. pap. 16.95 (*1-57061-099-1*) Sasquatch Bks.

— Eight Items or Less Cookbook: Fine Food in a Hurry. LC 88-4513. (Illus.). 264p. 1993. pap. 11.95 (*0-912365-43-9*) Sasquatch Bks.

— Fragrance in Bloom: Cultivating the Scented Garden Throughout the Year. (Illus.). 160p. (Orig.). 1996. pap. 14.95 (*1-57061-026-6*) Sasquatch Bks.

— Further Along the Garden Path. LC 95-11939. (Illus.). 256p. 1995. 40.00 (*0-02-575585-4*) Macmillan.

— The Garden in Bloom: Plants & Wisdom for the Year-Round Gardener in the Pacific Northwest. 256p. 1998. pap. 15.95 (*1-57061-139-4*) Sasquatch Bks.

— Gardening from Scratch. LC 98-19919. 160p. 1998. 14.95 (*0-02-861589-1*) Mac Lib Ref.

— Naturalistic Gardening: Reflecting the Planting Patterns of Nature. LC 98-6130. (Illus.). 144p. 1998. pap. 21.95 (*1-57061-120-3*) Sasquatch Bks.

— Seasonal Bulbs. (Cascadia Gardening Ser.). (Illus.). 96p. (Orig.). 1995. pap. 10.95 (*1-57061-027-4*) Sasquatch Bks.

— Tea Gardens: Places to Make & Take Tea. LC 97-49826. (Illus.). 120p. 1998. 17.95 (*0-8118-1905-1*) Chronicle Bks.

— The Year in Bloom: Gardening for All Seasons in the Pacific Northwest. LC 87-60480. (Illus.). 288p. 1987. pap. 11.95 (*0-912365-11-0*) Sasquatch Bks.

Lovejoy, Ann, ed. Herbs & Cooking. (Plants & Gardens Ser.). (Illus.). 1990. per. 7.95 (*0-945352-55-7*) Bklyn Botanic.

— Perennials: Toward Continuous Bloom. (New Voices from American Gardens Ser.). 304p. 1991. pap. 17.95 (*0-913643-06-8*) Capabilities.

Lovejoy, Ann & Openshaw, Leona Holdworth. All about Annuals. LC 98-66922. (Ortho's All about Ser.). (Illus.). 96p. 1998. pap. 11.95 (*0-89721-430-7*, Ortho Bks) Meredith Bks.

Lovejoy, Ann & Riggenbach, Jan. All about Perennials. LC 98-66915. (Ortho's All about Ser.). (Illus.). 96p. 1998. pap. 11.95 (*0-89721-423-4*, Ortho Bks) Meredith Bks.

Lovejoy, Arthur Oncken. Essays in the History of Ideas. LC 78-17473. 359p. 1978. reprint ed. lib. bdg. 35.00 (*0-313-20504-3*, LOEH, Greenwood Pr) Greenwood.

— Great Chain of Being: A Study of the History of an Idea. LC 36-14264. (William James Lectures). 382p. 1936. pap. text 17.50 (*0-674-36153-9*) HUP.

— The Reason, the Understanding, & Time. LC 61-8177. 224p. reprint ed. pap. 69.50 (*0-608-12097-9*, 202413500035) Bks Demand.

— Reflections on Human Nature. LC 61-15700. 285p. reprint ed. pap. 88.40 (*0-608-07396-2*, 206762300009) Bks Demand.

— The Revolt Against Dualism: An Inquiry Concerning the Existence of Ideas. 424p. (C). 1996. pap. text 29.96 (*1-56000-847-4*) Transaction Pubs.

— Three Studies in Current Philosophical Questions. LC 75-3249. reprint ed. write for info. (*0-404-59237-6*) AMS Pr.

Lovejoy, Arthur Oncken, et al. Primitivism & Related Ideas in Antiquity. LC 96-47993. 496p. 1997. reprint ed. pap. text 19.95 (*0-8018-5611-6*) Johns Hopkins.

Lovejoy, B. S., jt. auth. see Straughton, C. T.

Lovejoy, Bahija, jt. auth. see Cohen, Barbara.

Lovejoy, Carol. Living in Two Worlds. Oakes, Sandy, ed. 180p. (Orig.). 1992. pap. 12.95 (*0-9633137-6-2*) Golden Globe.

Lovejoy, David S. The Glorious Revolution in America. LC 86-22482. 423p. 1987. reprint ed. pap. 25.00 (*0-8195-6177-0*, Wesleyan Univ Pr) U Pr of New Eng.

— Religious Enthusiasm in the New World: Heresy to Revolution. 304p. 1985. 43.00 (*0-674-75864-1*) HUP.

— Rhode Island Politics & the American Revolution, 1760-1776. LC 58-10478. (Brown University Studies: Vol. 23). 266p. reprint ed. pap. 82.50 (*0-608-18418-7*, 203002500067) Bks Demand.

Lovejoy, Denise. Making the Transition to Home Health Nursing: A Practical Guide. LC 97-16428. 200p. 1997. 32.95 (*0-8261-9740-X*) Springer Pub.

Lovejoy Derek & Patrners Staff & Davis Langdon & Everest Staff, eds. Spon's Landscape & External Works Price Book, 1992. 11th ed. 240p. 1991. write for info. (*0-419-17390-0*, E & FN Spon) Routledge.

Lovejoy, Eddie. Better Born Lucky Than Rich. (C). 1989. 39.00 (*0-86303-322-9*) St Mut.

***Lovejoy, Elijah P.** Essential Asp for Web Professionals. 2000. pap. 29.99 (*0-13-030499-9*) P-H.

Lovejoy, Elizabeth, jt. auth. see Dawson, David B.

Lovejoy, Eunice G. Library Service to People with Disabilities: Ten Case Studies. (Professional Librarian Ser.). 176p. 1989. 35.00 (*0-8161-1922-8*, Hall Reference); 25.00 (*0-8161-1923-6*, Hall Reference) Macmillan.

Lovejoy, Evelyn M. History of Royalton, Vermont with Family Genealogies, 1769-1911. (Illus.). 1146p. 1992. reprint ed. lib. bdg. 100.00 (*0-8328-2257-4*) Higginson Bk Co.

Lovejoy, I. Psyche-Therapy: How to Master Your Mind(s) & Emotions. 250p. (Orig.). 1991. pap. 19.95 (*0-9601978-7-7*) Health Res Las Vegas.

Lovejoy, Jennifer C., jt. ed. see Bergman, Richard N.

Lovejoy, Joseph C. & Lovejoy, Owen. Memoir of the Rev. Elijah P. Lovejoy. LC 72-117882. (Select Bibliographies Reprint Ser.). 1977. reprint ed. 34.95 (*0-8369-5335-5*) Ayer.

— Memoir of the Reverend Elijah P. Lovejoy. LC 72-90183. (Mass Violence in America Ser.). 1969. reprint ed. 32.95 (*0-405-01323-X*) Ayer.

Lovejoy, Kim B., jt. auth. see Davis, Kenneth W.

Lovejoy, Margot. The Book of Plagues: Panic, Blame, Indifference. 48p. 1993. pap. 30.00 (*0-9637531-0-X*) M Lovejoy.

— Paradoxic Mutations. 28p. 1993. pap. 28.00 (*0-9637531-1-8*) M Lovejoy.

— Postmodern Currents: Art & Artists in the Age of Electronic Media. 2nd ed. 319p. (C). 1996. pap. text 48.00 (*0-13-158759-5*) P-H.

Lovejoy, Margot, et al. Off the Shelf & On-Line: Computers Move the Book Arts into Twenty-First Century Design. (Illus.). 56p. 1992. pap. 10.00 (*1-879832-04-6*) MN Ctr Book Arts.

Lovejoy, Mary I., compiled by. Poetry of the Seasons. LC 71-98083. (Granger Index Reprint Ser.). 1977. 23.95 (*0-8369-6082-3*) Ayer.

Lovejoy, Mona. Listening to Muzac: Trapped in the Great Elevator of Life or Rising above Self-Esteem. 1997. pap. text 5.95 (*0-9650821-2-1*, Halfway Hse) Lazarus Trust.

Lovejoy, Mona & Knight, Sunny. Overcoming Co-Dependency Through the Elimination of Human Relations: The Mildly Depressed Person's Guide to Daily Living. (Illus.). xx, 96p. 1995. pap. 5.95 (*0-9650821-0-5*, Halfway Hse) Lazarus Trust.

***Lovejoy, N. L.** The DWEEBZ: JaneLee & Some DWEEBZ, Bk. 1. (Illus.). 48p. (J). (ps-3). 2000. 8.95 (*0-9700943-0-2*) Small Secrets.

Lovejoy, Owen, jt. auth. see Lovejoy, Joseph C.

Lovejoy, Pamela. Fish On a Dish. (Illus.). 11p. (Orig.). (J). (ps-2). 1994. pap. write for info. (*1-880038-17-X*) Learn-Abouts.

— If I Were An Astronaut. (Illus.). 14p. (Orig.). (J). (ps-2). 1994. pap. write for info. (*1-880038-18-8*) Learn-Abouts.

— Rainbow Children. (Illus.). 7p. (Orig.). (J). 1994. pap. text. write for info. (*1-880038-19-6*) Learn-Abouts.

***Lovejoy, Paul E.** The Biography of Muhomnah J. Bagnagua: A Native of Zoogoo in the Interior of Africa. enl. ed. Law, Robin, ed. 120p. 2000. reprint ed. pap. 12.95 (*1-55876-248-5*) Wiener Pubs Inc.

Lovejoy, Paul E. Transformations in Slavery: A History of Slavery in Africa. LC 82-1284. (African Studies: No. 36). (Illus.). 368p. 1983. pap. text 25.95 (*0-521-28646-8*) Cambridge U Pr.

***Lovejoy, Paul E.** Transformations in Slavery: A History of Slavery in Africa. 2nd ed. LC 99-59862. (African Studies Ser.: Vol. 36). (Illus.). 349p. (C). 2000. text 54.95 (*0-521-78012-8*); pap. text 19.95 (*0-521-78430-1*) Cambridge U Pr.

Lovejoy, Paul E., ed. Africans in Bondage: Studies in Slavery & the Slave Trade: Essays in Honor of Philip D. Curtin on the Occasion of the Twenty-Fifth Anniversary of African Studies at the University of Wisconsin. LC 86-24611. (Illus.). 390p. reprint ed. pap. 120.90 (*0-7837-7025-1*, 204684000004) Bks Demand.

***Lovejoy, Paul E., ed.** Identity in the Shadow of Slavery. LC 99-86059. 256p. 2000. 74.95 (*0-8264-4724-4*); pap. 27.95 (*0-8264-4725-2*) Continuum.

Lovejoy, Paul E., ed. The Ideology of Slavery in Africa. LC 81-9240. (Sage Series on African Modernization & Development: No. 6). 311p. reprint ed. pap. 96.50 (*0-8357-8492-4*, 203476600091) Bks Demand.

***Lovejoy, Paul E., ed.** Slavery & the Muslim Diaspora: African Slaves in Dar es-Salam. 180p. 2000. pap. text 18.95 (*1-55876-246-9*) Wiener Pubs Inc.

An Asterisk (*) at the beginning of an entry indicates that the title is appearing for the first time.

Lovejoy, Paul E. & Falola, Toyin. Africa: The Legacy of Slavery & Colonialism in the Modern World. (C). 1999. pap. 35.00 (*0-8133-0441-5*); pap. 16.95 (*0-8133-0442-3*) Westview.

***Lovejoy, Paul E. & Law, Robin, eds.** The Biography of Muhomnah J. Bagnagua: A Native of Zoogoo in the Interior of Africa. enl. ed. 120p. 2000. reprint ed. 28.95 (*1-55876-247-7*) Wiener Pubs Inc.

Lovejoy, Paul E. & Rogers, Nicholas, eds. Unfree Labour in the Development of the Atlantic World. LC 94-31528. (Studies in Slave & Post-Slave Societies & Cultures). (Illus.). 272p. 1995. 49.50 (*0-7146-4579-6*, Pub. by F Cass Pubs); pap. 22.50 (*0-7146-4152-9*, Pub. by F Cass Pubs) Intl Spec Bk.

Lovejoy, Paul E. & Williams, Pat A. Displacement & the Politics of Violence in Nigeria. LC 97-16208. (International Studies in Sociology & Social Anthropology Ser.). viii, 146p. 1997. pap. 42.50 (*90-04-10876-9*) Brill Academic Pubs.

Lovejoy, Paul E., jt. ed. see Coquery-Vidrovitch, Catherine.

Lovejoy, S., jt. auth. see Schertzer, D.

Lovejoy, S., jt. ed. see Schertzer, D.

Lovejoy, Sharon. Hollyhock Days: Garden Adventures for the Young at Heart. Ligon, Lindon, ed. LC 94-19071. (Illus.). 96p. 1994. pap. 16.95 (*0-934026-90-4*) Interweave.

— Hollyhock Days: Garden Adventures for the Young at Heart. Ligon, Lindon, ed. LC 94-19071. (Illus.). 1994. 24.95 (*1-883010-01-2*) Interweave.

***Lovejoy, Sharon.** Roots, Shoots, Buckets & Boots: Gardening Together with Children. (Illus.). 159p. (J). (gr. 1-4). 1999. 24.95 (*0-7611-1765-2*) Workman Pub.

Lovejoy, Sharon. Sunflower Houses. 144p. 1995. pap. 16.95 (*1-883010-00-4*) Interweave.

— Sunflower Houses: Garden Discoveries for Children of All Ages. LC 91-29880. (Illus.). 144p. 1991. 24.95 (*0-934026-70-X*) Interweave.

Lovejoy, Sharon, jt. auth. see Blose, Nora.

Lovejoy, Stephen B. & Napier, Ted L., eds. Conserving Soil: Insights from Socioeconomic Research. LC 86-1752. 155p. 1986. text 9.00 (*0-935734-12-0*) Soil & Water Conserv.

Lovejoy, Stephen B., jt. ed. see Braden, John B.

Lovejoy, Surya. Getting Results: A Systematic Approach. 300p. 1993. 61.95 (*0-566-07326-9*, Pub. by Gower) Ashgate Pub Co.

Lovejoy, Surya, jt. auth. see De Haas, Paul.

Lovejoy, T. E., 3rd, et al. Nearctic Avian Migrants in the Neotropics: Maps, Appendices, & Bibliography. 2nd ed. Leathery, Sharon, ed. (Illus.). 325p. 1995. pap. text 12.00 (*0-9638408-5-1*) C & RC Nat Zool.

Lovejoy, Thomas. Exploring Our World: Twenty-Eight Gatefolds of the World's Ecological Zones. Hare, Tony, ed. LC 98-75010. Orig. Title: Nature Worlds. (Illus.). 144p. 1999. 12.98 (*0-7651-1027-X*) Smithmark.

Lovejoy, Thomas E., jt. auth. see Peters, Robert L.

Lovejoy, Thomas E., jt. ed. see Primack, Richard B.

Lovejoy, W., jt. auth. see Garfield, Paul.

Lovejoy, Wallace F. Methods of Estimating Reserves of Crude Oil, Natural Gas, & Natural Gas Liquids. LC 65-24790. 182p. reprint ed. pap. 56.50 (*0-608-12540-7*, 202380500034) Bks Demand.

Lovejoy, Wallace F. & Homan, Paul T. Economic Aspects of Oil Conservation Regulation. (Resources for the Future Ser.). 295p. 1967. 22.50 (*0-8018-0397-7*) Resources Future.

Lovejoy, William H. Back Slash. LC 96-76493. 400p. 1996. 21.95 (*1-57566-081-4*, Kensington) Kensgtn Pub Corp.

— Backslash. 480p. 1997. mass mkt. 5.99 (*0-7860-0437-1*, Pinncle Kensgtn) Kensgtn Pub Corp.

— China Dome. 544p. 1995. mass mkt. 5.99 (*0-8217-0111-8*, Zebra Kensgtn); mass mkt. 5.99 (*0-7860-0111-9*, Pinncle Kensgtn) Kensgtn Pub Corp.

— Dark Morning. 448p. 1998. pap. 5.99 (*0-7860-0492-4*, Pinncle Kensgtn) Kensgtn Pub Corp.

— Delta Blue. 1991. mass mkt. 4.50 (*0-8217-3540-3*, Zebra Kensgtn) Kensgtn Pub Corp.

— Delta Green. 384p. 1993. mass mkt. 4.50 (*0-8217-4131-4*, Zebra Kensgtn) Kensgtn Pub Corp.

— Red Rain. 512p. 1996. mass mkt. 5.99 (*0-7860-0230-1*, Pinncle Kensgtn) Kensgtn Pub Corp.

— Rip Cord. 288p. (Orig.). 1992. mass mkt. 3.99 (*0-380-76447-4*, Avon Bks) Morrow Avon.

— Seaghost. 256p. (Orig.). 1991. mass mkt. 3.99 (*0-380-76577-2*, Avon Bks) Morrow Avon.

— Shanghai Star. 496p. 1996. mass mkt. 5.99 (*0-7860-0329-4*, Pinncle Kensgtn) Kensgtn Pub Corp.

— Ultra Deep. 1992. mass mkt. 4.50 (*0-8217-3694-9*, Zebra Kensgtn) Kensgtn Pub Corp.

Lovejoy, William J. Flash Factor. pap. 5.99 (*0-7860-0615-3*) Kensgtn Pub Corp.

Lovekin, David. Technique, Discourse, & Consciousness: An Introduction to the Philosophy of Jacques Ellul. LC 89-85467. 256p. 1991. 42.50 (*0-934223-01-7*) Lehigh Univ Pr.

Lovel, T. W. I. & Hassan, W. U. The Clinicians' Guide to Pain. (Clinicians' Guide Ser.). (Illus.). 224p. 1999. pap. text 49.95 (*0-340-74097-3*, Pub. by E A) OUP.

Lovelace, jt. auth. see Cryer.

Lovelace, Austin C. A Musical Gift: Organ Preludes on Fourteen Familiar Hymn Tunes by Austin C. Lovelace. 32p. 1994. pap., student ed. 8.00 (*1-889079-07-3*) Darcey Pr.

Lovelace, Austin C. Welcome Easter Morning. 1.25 (*0-687-07155-0*) Abingdon.

Lovelace, Austin C. & Rice, William C. Music & Worship in the Church: The Complete Resource for Musician, Minister, & Layperson. enl. rev. ed. 1983. pap. 16.95 (*0-687-27357-9*) Abingdon.

Lovelace, Barry, jt. auth. see Hazeltine, Cheryl.

Lovelace, Carey, tr. see Bernadac, Marie-Laure & Du Bouchet, Paule.

Lovelace, Cyndi, jt. ed. see Kotz, Sam.

Lovelace, Daniel D. China & People's War in Thailand, 1964-1969. LC 72-184630. (China Research Monographs: No. 8). 101p. reprint ed. pap. 31.40 (*0-608-30345-3*, 200458600044) Bks Demand.

Lovelace, Delos, jt. auth. see Lovelace, Maud Hart.

Lovelace, E. A., ed. Aging & Cognition: Mental Processes, Self-Awareness & Interventions. (Advances in Psychology Ser.: No. 72). 452p. 1991. 185.25 (*0-444-88367-3*, North Holland) Elsevier.

Lovelace, Earl. A Brief Conversion & Other Stories. (Caribbean Writers Ser.). 141p. (Orig.). (C). 1988. pap. 7.50 (*0-435-98882-4*, 98882) Heinemann.

— The Dragon Can't Dance. LC 98-11237. 240p. 1998. 24.00 (*0-89255-234-4*) Persea Bks.

— Salt. LC 96-50266. 260p. 1997. 23.00 (*0-89255-226-3*) Persea Bks.

— Salt. 266p. 1998. pap. 15.00 (*0-89255-235-2*) Persea Bks.

Lovelace, Earl. The Schoolmaster. (Caribbean Writers Ser.). 171p. (C). 1983. reprint ed. pap. 7.95 (*0-435-98550-7*, 98550) Heinemann.

Lovelace, Earl & Thorpe, Marjorie. The Wine of Astonishment. (Caribbean Writers Ser.). 146p. (C). 1986. reprint ed. pap. 9.95 (*0-435-98880-8*, 98880) Heinemann.

Lovelace, Jayne P., jt. auth. see Roberts, George M.

Lovelace, Jeff. Mount Mitchell: Its Railroad & Toll Road. (Illus.). 96p. 1994. pap. 9.95 (*0-932807-84-4*) Overmountain Pr.

Lovelace, Linda & McGrady, Mike. Ordeal. 1980. 10.00 (*0-8065-0687-3*, Citadel Pr) Carol Pub Group.

— Out of Bondage. 1986. 14.95 (*0-8184-0386-1*) Carol Pub Group.

Lovelace, Maud Hart. Betsy & Joe. LC 48-8096. (Illus.). 256p. (YA). (gr. 5 up). 1948. 14.95 (*0-690-13378-2*) HarpC Child Bks.

Lovelace, Maud Hart. Betsy & Joe. LC 48-8096. (Trophy Bk.). (Illus.). 336p. (J). (gr. 3 up). 1995. pap. 5.95 (*0-06-440546-X*, HarpTrophy) HarpC Child Bks.

Lovelace, Maud Hart. Betsy & Tacy Go Downtown. LC 43-51264. (Illus.). 240p. (YA). (gr. 4-7). 2000. pap. 5.95 (*0-06-440098-0*, HarpTrophy) HarpC Child Bks.

— Betsy & Tacy Go Over the Big Hill (pb repkg) LC 42-23557. (Illus.). 192p. (YA). (gr. 4-7). 2000. pap. 5.95 (*0-06-440099-9*, HarpTrophy) HarpC Child Bks.

— Betsy & the Great World. LC 52-8657. (Illus.). 305p. (J). (gr. 5 up). 1952. 14.95 (*0-690-13591-2*) HarpC Child Bks.

***Lovelace, Maud Hart.** Betsy & the Great World. LC 52-8657. (Illus.). 336p. (J). (gr. 3 up). 2000. pap. 5.95 (*0-06-440545-1*, HarpTrophy) HarpC Child Bks.

Lovelace, Maud Hart. Betsy in Spite of Herself. LC 46-11995. (Illus.). 272p. (J). (gr. 5 up). 1946. 14.95 (*0-690-13662-5*) HarpC Child Bks.

Lovelace, Maud Hart. Betsy in Spite of Herself. LC 46-11995. (Trophy Bk.). (Illus.). 304p. (J). (gr. 3 up). 1980. pap. 5.95 (*0-06-440111-1*, HarpTrophy) HarpC Child Bks.

Lovelace, Maud Hart. Betsy-Tacy. LC 40-30965. (Illus.). 128p. (J). (gr. 2-5). 1994. 12.95 (*0-06-024415-1*) HarpC Child Bks.

— Betsy-Tacy. LC 40-30965. (Illus.). 144p. (YA). (gr. 4-7). 2000. pap. 5.95 (*0-06-440096-4*, HarpTrophy) HarpC Child Bks.

Lovelace, Maud Hart. Betsy-Tacy. (Betsy Bks.). (J). 1979. 10.05 (*0-606-01999-5*, Pub. by Turtleback) Demco.

Lovelace, Maud Hart. Betsy Tacy. write for info. (*0-690-13804-0*) HarpC Child Bks.

— Betsy-Tacy & Tib. LC 40-18714. (Illus.). 128p. (J). (gr. 2-5). 1994. 13.95 (*0-06-024416-X*) HarpC Child Bks.

— Betsy-Tacy & Tib. LC 41-18714. (Illus.). 160p. (YA). (gr. 4-7). 2000. pap. 5.95 (*0-06-440097-2*, HarpTrophy) HarpC Child Bks.

***Lovelace, Maud Hart.** Betsy-Tacy Mother-Daughter Reading Group Guide. (J). 2000. pap. write for info. (*0-06-449207-9*, HarpTrophy) HarpC Child Bks.

Lovelace, Maud Hart. Betsy Was a Jr. LC 46-11995. (Illus.). 248p. (YA). (gr. 5 up). 1947. 14.95 (*0-690-13946-2*) HarpC Child Bks.

Lovelace, Maud Hart. Betsy Was a Junior: A Betsy - Tacy High School Story. LC 46-11995. (Trophy Bk.). (Illus.). 304p. (J). (gr. 3 up). 1995. pap. 5.95 (*0-06-440547-8*, HarpTrophy) HarpC Child Bks.

Lovelace, Maud Hart. Betsy's Wedding. LC 55-11108. (Illus.). 241p. (J). (gr. 5 up). 1955. 14.95 (*0-690-13733-8*) HarpC Child Bks.

***Lovelace, Maud Hart.** Betsy's Wedding. LC 55-11108. (Illus.). 272p. (J). (gr. 3 up). 2000. pap. 5.95 (*0-06-440544-3*, HarpTrophy) HarpC Child Bks.

Lovelace, Maud Hart. Carney's House Party. (J). (gr. 3). 1976. 22.95 (*0-8488-1084-8*) Amereon Ltd.

***Lovelace, Maud Hart.** Carney's House Party: A Deep Valley Book. (Illus.). 288p. (YA). (gr. 3 up). 2000. lib. bdg. 16.89 (*0-06-028874-4*); mass mkt. 6.95 (*0-06-440859-0*, HarpTrophy) HarpC Child Bks.

Lovelace, Maud Hart. Early Candlelight. LC 91-38314. xix, 322p. 1992. reprint ed. pap. 12.95 (*0-87351-269-3*, Borealis Book) Minn Hist.

— Emily of Deep Valley. 1976. 24.95 (*0-8488-1085-6*) Amereon Ltd.

***Lovelace, Maud Hart.** Emily of Deep Valley. (Illus.). 272p. (J). (gr. 3 up). 2000. mass mkt. 6.95 (*0-06-440858-2*, HarpTrophy) HarpC Child Bks.

— Emily of Deep Valley. (Illus.). 272p. (YA). (gr. 3 up). 2000. lib. bdg. 16.89 (*0-06-028873-6*) HarpC Child Bks.

— Heaven to Betsy. LC 45-9806. (Trophy Bk.). (Illus.). 368p. (J). (gr. 3 up). 1945. pap. 5.95 (*0-06-440110-3*, HarpTrophy) HarpC Child Bks.

Lovelace, Maud Hart. Heaven to Betsy. LC 45-9806. (Illus.). 268p. (J). (gr. 5-11). 1945. 14.95 (*0-690-37449-6*) HarpC Child Bks.

— The Trees Kneel at Christmas. LC 94-10512. (Illus.). 110p. (J). (gr. 3-8). 1994. lib. bdg. 16.98 (*1-56239-999-3*) ABDO Pub Co.

— Winona's Pony Cart. 1976. 18.95 (*0-8488-1420-7*) Amereon Ltd.

***Lovelace, Maud Hart.** Winona's Pony Cart. (Illus.). 128p. (J). (gr. 3-7). 2000. lib. bdg. 15.89 (*0-06-028875-2*); mass mkt. 5.95 (*0-06-440860-4*, HarpTrophy) HarpC Child Bks.

Lovelace, Maud Hart & Lovelace, Delos. Gentlemen from England. LC 93-9412. xv, 361p. 1993. reprint ed. pap. 12.95 (*0-87351-287-1*, Borealis Book) Minn Hist.

Lovelace, Merline. Beauty & the Bodyguard. (Fortune's Children Ser.). 1996. per. 4.50 (*0-373-50179-X*, 1-50179-0) Harlequin Bks.

— Call of Duty. 1998. mass mkt. 6.99 (*0-451-40673-7*, Onyx) NAL.

— Countess in Buckskin. (Historical Ser.: No. 396). 1998. per. 4.99 (*0-373-28996-0*, 1-28996-6) Harlequin Bks.

— The Cowboy & the Cossack. (Intimate Moments Ser.). 1995. per. 3.75 (*0-373-07657-6*, 1-07657-9) Silhouette.

— The Cowboy & the Cossack. large type ed. 1998. 21.95 (*0-373-59920-X*, G K Hall & Co) Mac Lib Ref.

— Un Crucero Inolvidable: Halloween Honeymoon. (Deseo Ser.).Tr. of An Unforgettable Cruise. (SPA.). 1997. per. 3.50 (*0-373-35211-5*, 1-35211-1) Harlequin Bks.

— Duty & Dishonor. 1997. mass mkt. 5.99 (*0-451-40672-9*, Onyx) NAL.

— The 14th & Forever. (Intimate Moments Ser.). 1997. per. 3.99 (*0-373-07764-5*, 1-07764-3) Silhouette.

— Halloween Honeymoon. (Desire Ser.). 1996. per. 3.50 (*0-373-76030-2*, 1-76030-5) Silhouette.

— His Lady's Ransom. LC 96-563. (Historical Ser.). 352p. 1995. per. 4.50 (*0-373-28875-1*, 1-28875-2) Harlequin Bks.

***Lovelace, Merline.** The Horse Soldier. 2001. mass mkt. 5.99 (*1-55166-784-3*, Mira Bks) Harlequin Bks.

Lovelace, Merline. If a Man Answers. (Intimate Moments Ser.). 1998. per. 4.25 (*0-373-07878-1*, 1-07878-1) Silhouette.

— Lady of the Upper Kingdom. (Historical Ser.). 1996. per. 4.99 (*0-373-28920-0*, 1-28920-6) Harlequin Bks.

— Line of Duty. 416p. 1996. mass mkt. 5.99 (*0-451-40671-0*, Onyx) NAL.

— Line of Duty. 1999. pap. 21.95 (*0-525-94176-2*) NAL.

— Maggie & Her Colonel. (Great Escapes Ser.). 1994. pap. 1.99 (*0-373-83273-7*, 1-83273-2) Harlequin Bks.

— A Man of His Word: Home on the Ranch. (Intimate Moments Ser.: Bk. 938). 1999. per. 4.25 (*0-373-07938-9*, 1-07938-3) Silhouette.

— The Mercenary & the New Mom: Follow That Baby. 1999. per. 4.25 (*0-373-07908-7*, Harlequin) Harlequin Bks.

***Lovelace, Merline.** Mistaken Identity. (Intimate Moments Ser.: Vol. 987). 2000. mass mkt. 4.50 (*0-373-07987-7*) Silhouette.

Lovelace, Merline. The Night of the Jaguar. large type ed. (Silhouette Ser.). 1998. 20.95 (*0-373-59862-9*, Harlequin) Harlequin Bks.

— Night of the Jaguar: IM Extra, Code Name - Danger. (Intimate Moments Ser.). 1995. per. 3.75 (*0-373-07637-1*, 1-07637-1) Silhouette.

— No Habra Mas Adioses (No More Good-Byes) (SPA.). 1997. per. 3.50 (*0-373-35198-4*, 1-35198-0) Harlequin Bks.

— Perfect Double. 1998. 21.95 (*0-373-59932-3*) Harlequin Bks.

— Perfect Double. (Intimate Moments Ser.). 1996. per. 3.99 (*0-373-07692-4*, 1-07692-6) Silhouette.

***Lovelace, Merline.** Un Plan Perfecto. (Deseo Ser.: Bk. 206).Tr. of Perfect Plan. (SPA.). 156p. 2000. per. 3.50 (*0-373-35336-7*, 1-35336-6) Harlequin Bks.

Lovelace, Merline. Return to Sender. (Intimate Moments Ser.). 1998. per. 4.25 (*0-373-07866-8*, 1-07866-6) Silhouette.

— River Rising. 306p. 1999. mass mkt. 5.99 (*0-451-40850-0*, Onyx) NAL.

— Sweet Song of Love. (Historical Ser.). 1994. mass mkt. 3.99 (*0-373-28830-1*, 1-28830-7) Harlequin Bks.

— The Tiger's Bride: 10th Anniversary Promotion. anniversary ed. (Historical Ser.: Vol. 423). 304p. 1998. per. 4.99 (*0-373-29023-3*, 1-29023-8) Harlequin Bks.

— Undercover Groom: Fortune's Children: The Brides. (Desire Ser.: No. 1220). 1999. per. 3.75 (*0-373-76220-8*, 1-76220-2) Silhouette.

— Undercover Man. 1995. per. 3.75 (*0-373-07669-X*, 1-07669-4) Silhouette.

— Undercover Man. large type ed. 1998. 21.95 (*0-373-59926-9*) Silhouette.

— Wrong Bride, Right Groom. 1996. per. 3.50 (*0-373-76037-X*, 1-76037-0) Silhouette.

Lovelace, Merline & Buck, Carole. Holiday Honeymoons: Two Tickets to Paradise. 1999. pap. 5.99 (*0-373-48392-9*, 1-48392-4, Harlequin) Harlequin Bks.

***Lovelace, Merline, et al.** Special Report. 2001. mass mkt. 4.50 (*0-373-27115-8*, 1-27115-4) Silhouette.

Lovelace, Richard. Poems, 2 vols., Set. Wilkinson, C. H., ed. (BCL1-PR English Literature Ser.). 1992. reprint ed. lib. bdg. 150.00 (*0-7812-7369-2*) Rprt Serv.

— Richard Lovelace (1618-1658) Selected Poems. Hammond, Gerald, ed. 1987. pap. 9.50 (*0-85635-673-5*) Carcanet Pr.

Lovelace, Richard F. Dynamics of Spiritual Life. LC 78-24757. 456p. 1979. pap. 21.99 (*0-87784-626-X*, 626) InterVarsity.

Lovelace, Richard H. Mr. Taft's School: The First Century. (Illus.). 208p. 1989. 20.00 (*0-9624435-0-6*) Taft Schl.

Lovelace, Robert E., et al, eds. Charcot - Marie - Tooth Disorders. LC 99-43216. 550p. 1999. lib. bdg. 150.00 (*1-57331-182-0*) NY Acad Sci.

***Lovelace, Ruth A.** It's Not My Fault: A Sensitive, Realistic & Candid Journey into Alzheimer's Disease. (Illus.). 92p. 1999. 9.50 (*0-9679191-0-X*) R A Lovelace.

Lovelace, Terry W., et al. Guide to Real Estate Taxation. 1997. ring bd. 150.00 (*0-7646-0140-7*) Prctnrs Pub Co.

— Guide to Real Estate Taxation. 1998. ring bd. 150.00 (*0-7646-0503-8*) Prctnrs Pub Co.

Lovelace, Terry W., jt. auth. see Blanco-Best, Mimi.

Lovelace, Terry W., jt. auth. see Saunders-Aguirre, Kim L.

***Lovelace, Tommy & Streett, Betty.** Murder at Rainbow Falls. (Illus.). 144p. (J). (gr. 5-7). 1999. pap. 7.95 (*0-88028-208-8*, 1505) Forward Movement.

Lovelady, Janet. Annie & the Old One Literature Mini-Unit. (Illus.). 32p. (J). (gr. 3-5). 1990. student ed. 4.95 (*1-56096-018-3*) Mari.

— Big Bad Bruce Literature Mini-Unit. (Illus.). 32p. (J). (gr. 2-4). 1989. student ed. 4.95 (*1-56096-001-9*) Mari.

— Bread & Jam for Frances Literature Mini-Unit. (Illus.). 32p. (J). (gr. 2-4). 1989. student ed. 4.95 (*1-56096-002-7*) Mari.

— The Drinking Gourd Literature Mini-Unit. (Illus.). 32p. (J). (gr. 3-5). 1990. student ed. 4.95 (*1-56096-019-1*) Mari.

— Hill of Fire Literature Mini Unit. (Illus.). 32p. (J). (gr. 2-4). 1989. student ed. 4.95 (*1-56096-005-1*) Mari.

— The Hundred Dresses Literature Mini-Unit. (Illus.). 32p. (J). (gr. 3-5). 1990. student ed. 4.95 (*1-56096-014-0*) Mari.

— The Little House Literature Mini-Unit. (Illus.). 32p. (J). (gr. 2-4). 1989. student ed. 4.95 (*1-56096-000-0*) Mari.

— Long Way to a New Land Literature Mini-Unit. (Illus.). 32p. (J). (gr. 3-5). 1990. student ed. 4.95 (*1-56096-013-2*) Mari.

— Make Way for Ducklings Literature Mini-Unit. (Illus.). 32p. (J). (gr. 2-4). 1989. student ed. 4.95 (*1-56096-006-X*) Mari.

— Miss Rumphius Literature Mini-Unit. (Illus.). 32p. (J). (gr. 2-4). 1989. student ed. 4.95 (*1-56096-003-5*) Mari.

— Sam, Bangs & Moonshine Literature Mini-Unit. (Illus.). 32p. (J). (gr. 3-5). 1990. student ed. 4.95 (*1-56096-012-4*) Mari.

— Shoeshine Girl Literature Mini-Unit. (Illus.). 32p. (J). (gr. 3-5). 1990. student ed. 4.95 (*1-56096-017-5*) Mari.

— Song of the Swallows Literature Mini-Unit. (Illus.). 32p. (J). (gr. 2-4). 1989. student ed. 4.95 (*1-56096-007-8*) Mari.

— Stone Soup Literature Mini-Unit. (Illus.). 32p. (J). (gr. 2-4). 1989. student ed. 4.95 (*1-56096-008-6*) Mari.

— Strega Nona Literature Mini-Unit. (Illus.). 32p. (J). (gr. 2-4). 1989. student ed. 4.95 (*1-56096-009-4*) Mari.

— The Ugly Duckling Literature Mini-Unit. (Illus.). 32p. (J). (gr. 3-5). 1990. student ed. 4.95 (*1-56096-015-9*) Mari.

— Velveteen Rabbit Literature Mini-Unit. (Illus.). 32p. (J). (gr. 3-5). 1990. student ed. 4.95 (*1-56096-011-6*) Mari.

— Wagon Wheels Literature Mini-Unit. (Illus.). 32p. (J). (gr. 3-5). 1990. student ed. 4.95 (*1-56096-010-8*) Mari.

Lovelady, Janet, ed. see Gimbel, Cheryl F.

Lovelady, Janet, ed. see Kehayan, V. Alex.

Lovelady, Janet, ed. see McDaniel, Sandy & Bielen, Peggy.

Lovelady, Janet, ed. see Schriner, Christian.

Lovelady, Janet, ed. see Sevaly, Karen & Truax, Harry.

Lovelady, Richard, jt. auth. see Johnson, Hans.

Loveland, Anne C. American Evangelicals & the U. S. Military, 1942-1993. LC 96-26309. 376p. 1997. text 55.00 (*0-8071-2091-X*) La State U Pr.

— Lillian Smith, a Southerner Confronting the South. LC 86-10641. (Southern Biography Ser.). xii, 298p. 1986. text 42.50 (*0-8071-1343-3*) La State U Pr.

— Southern Evangelicals & the Social Order, 1800-1860. LC 80-11200. xiv, 354p. 1980. pap. text 19.95 (*0-8071-0783-2*) La State U Pr.

Loveland, Cherylon, jt. auth. see Rutherford, Clarice.

Loveland, Christine A. & Loveland, Franklin O., eds. Sex Roles & Social Change in Native Lower Central American Societies. LC 80-27814. (Illus.). 232p. 1982. text 24.95 (*0-252-00858-8*) U of Ill Pr.

Loveland-Coen, Victoria. Manifesting Your Desires: How to Apply Timeless Spiritual Truths to Achieve Fulfillment. 2nd expanded rev. ed. (Illus.). 200p. (Orig.). 1998. pap. 19.95 (*0-9644765-0-9*) Self-Mastery Pr.

Loveland, D. W., ed. see Kruse, Robert, et al.

Loveland, D. W., ed. see Marek, Wiktor & Trusczynski, M.

Loveland, D. W., ed. see Michalewicz, Zbigniew.

Loveland, D. W., ed. see Navinchandra, D.

Loveland, D. W., ed. see Peng, Y. & Reggia, J. A.

Loveland, Donald, jt. ed. see Bledsoe, W. W.

Loveland, Franklin O., jt. ed. see Loveland, Christine A.

Loveland, G., jt. auth. see Loveland, J. B.

Loveland, Geneva K., jt. auth. see Loveland, J. B.

Loveland, Ian. By Due Process of Law: Racial Discrimination & the Right to Vote in South Africa, 1855-1960. 420p. 1999. 63.00 (*1-84113-049-4*, Pub. by Hart Pub) Intl Spec Bk.

— Housing the Homeless: Administrative Law & the Administrative Process. (Oxford Socio-Legal Studies). (Illus.). 388p. 1995. text 69.00 (*0-19-825876-3*) OUP.

— Loveland: Constitutional Law - a Critical Introduction. 1996. pap. write for info. (*0-406-04968-8*, LCLC, MICHIE) LEXIS Pub.

***Loveland, Ian.** Political Libels: A Comparative Style. 224p. 2000. 45.00 (*1-84113-115-6*, Pub. by Hart Pub) Intl Spec Bk.

L

An Asterisk (*) at the beginning of an entry indicates that the title is appearing for the first time.

Loveland, Ian, ed. Importing the First Amendment: Freedom of Speech & Expression in Britain, Europe & the U. S. A. LC 98-198131. 256p. 1998. pap. 60.00 (*1-901362-28-0*, Pub. by Hart Pub) Northwestern U Pr.

— A Special Relationship? American Influences on Public Law in the UK. 332p. 1996. text 75.00 (*0-19-826014-8*) OUP.

***Loveland, Ian D., ed.** Constitutional Law. LC 99-55547. (International Library of Essays in Law & Legal Theory). 460p. 2000. text 185.95 (*0-7546-2066-2*, Pub. by Ashgate Pub) Ashgate Pub Co.

Loveland, J. B. & Loveland, G. Genealogy of the Loveland Family in the United States, 1635 to 1892, Containing the Descendants of Thomas Loveland of Wethersfield, Now Glastonbury, Connecticut. (Illus.). 838p. 1989. reprint ed. pap. 125.50 (*0-8328-0788-5*) Higginson Bk Co.

Loveland, J. B. & Loveland, Geneva K. Genealogy of the Loveland Family in the United States, 1635 to 1892, Containing the Descendants of Thomas Loveland of Wethersfield, Now Glastonbury, Connecticut. (Illus.). 838p. 1989. reprint ed. lib. bdg. 133.50 (*0-8328-0787-7*) Higginson Bk Co.

Loveland, Jim A. Dinner Is Served: Fine Dining Aboard the Southern Pacific. LC 96-46979. (Illus.). 242p. 1996. 39.95 (*0-87095-112-2*) Gldn West Bks.

Loveland, Karen, jt. auth. see Adey, Walter H.

Loveland, Nicole. Boogins Gets a Basket. (Illus.). 32p. (J). (ps-2). 1984. lib. bdg. 4.95 (*0-917107-00-4*) Cat-Tales Pr.

— Boogins' Rainy Day. (Illus.). (J). (ps-3). 1985. lib. bdg. 5.95 (*0-917107-02-0*) Cat-Tales Pr.

Loveland, Peter J., jt. ed. see Rounsevell, Mark D.

Loveland, Roger P. Photomicrography: A Comprehensive Treatise, 2 vols. LC 80-12428. 1070p. 1981. reprint ed. lib. bdg. 119.50 (*0-89874-392-3*) Krieger.

Loveland, Walter D., jt. auth. see Seaborg, Glenn Theodore.

Loveless, Avril. The Role of It: Practical Issues for the Primary Teacher. LC 97-127566. (Children, Teachers & Learning Ser.). (Illus.). 160p. 1996. 95.00 (*0-304-33214-3*); pap. 33.95 (*0-304-33217-8*) Continuum.

***Loveless, Belmo.** Jimi Hendrix: Experience the Music. (Illus.). 1998. pap. 15.95 (*1-896522-45-9*) CN06.

Loveless, Caron. Hugs from Heaven Embraced by the Savior: Sayings, Scriptures, & Stories from the Bible Revealing God's Love. LC 98-38160. (Illus.). 128p. 1998. 10.99 (*1-878990-91-8*) Howard Pub LA.

***Loveless, Caron.** The Words That Inspired the Dreams: True Stories about the Power of a Few Choice Words. xvi, 230p. 2000. pap. 12.99 (*1-58229-124-1*) Howard Pub LA.

Loveless, Ganelle, jt. auth. see Bullock, Waneta B.

Loveless, James M., ed. see State Bar of Texas Family Law Practice Committee.

Loveless, Joan, jt. auth. see Erikson, Joan M.

Loveless, Joan P. The Century Book: A Family Record. 224p. 1993. pap. 19.95 (*0-9637654-0-X*) Century Pr NM.

Loveless, Liz. One, Two, Buckle My Shoe. LC 92-40947. 32p. (J). (ps). 1993. 13.95 (*1-56282-477-5*, Pub. by Hyprn Child) Little.

Loveless, Richard L., ed. see University of South Florida, Computer Revolution &.

Loveless, Robert W., jt. auth. see Barney, Richard W.

Loveless, Stephen C., et al. Immigration & Its Impact on American Cities. LC 95-40580. 200p. 1996. 59.95 (*0-275-94500-6*, Praeger Pubs) Greenwood.

Loveless, Thomas L. Selling Your Own Real Estate: Secrets from a Realtor. LC 92-81723. 194p. (Orig.). 1992. pap. 28.95 (*0-9633103-0-5*) TRuth Pub.

Loveless, Tom. The Tracking Wars: State Reform Meets School Policy. LC 99-6372. 1999. 39.95 (*0-8157-5306-3*); pap. 16.95 (*0-8157-5305-5*) Brookings.

***Loveless, Tom, ed.** Conflicting Missions: Teachers Unions & Educational Reform. 288p. 2000. 44.95 (*0-8157-5304-7*); pap. 18.95 (*0-8157-5303-9*) Brookings.

Loveless, W. & Barlow, R. J. Some Applications of Advanced Instrumentation Techniques to Double Enveloping Worm Gear Testing. (Technical Papers: Vol. P109.40). (Illus.). 10p. 1978. pap. text 30.00 (*1-55589-422-4*) AGMA.

Lovelich, Henry. The History of the Holy Grail, Pts. 1 & 5. Furnivall, F. J., ed. (EETS, ES Ser.: Nos. 20, 24,). 1969. reprint ed. 55.00 (*0-527-00234-8*) Periodicals Srv.

— Merlin, Pt. 1. Kock, Ernst A., ed. (EETS, ES Ser.: Nos. 93, 112). 1974. reprint ed. 45.00 (*0-527-00184-8*) Periodicals Srv.

— Merlin, Pt. 2. Kock, Ernst A., ed. (EETS, ES Ser.: Nos. 93, 112). 1974. reprint ed. 30.00 (*0-527-00185-6*) Periodicals Srv.

— Merlin, a Middle-English Metrical Version of a French Romance, Pt. III. (EETS. OS Ser.: No. 185). 1974. reprint ed. 55.00 (*0-527-00183-X*) Periodicals Srv.

Lovell. Complete Video Production Book. (Graphic Communications Ser.). 1995. pap. 32.95 (*0-8273-6123-8*) Delmar.

— The Handbook of Photography. 3rd ed. 1993. teacher ed. 16.00 (*0-8273-5597-1*) Delmar.

— Russian Reading Revolution LC 99-48631. 1999. text 65.00 (*0-312-22601-2*) St Martin.

Lovell, jt. auth. see Pope.

Lovell, jt. auth. see Stojkovic.

Lovell, A. Anarchist Cinema. 1974. 250.00 (*0-87968-189-6*) Gordon Pr.

***Lovell, Alan & Kramer, Peter, eds.** Screen Acting. LC 99-24317. 208p. (C). 1999. text 75.00 (*0-415-18293-X*) Routledge.

Lovell, Alan & Krhamer, Peter. Screen Acting. LC 99-24317. 208p. 1999. pap. 22.99 (*0-415-18294-8*) Routledge.

Lovell, Alred C. Man's Relation to the Universe. LC 84-1443. 266p. reprint ed. pap. 82.50 (*0-608-08666-5*, 206918900003) Bks Demand.

Lovell, Ann. Flying Time. large type ed. 1990. 27.99 (*0-7089-2213-9*) Ulverscroft.

Lovell, Anne, jt. auth. see Chu, Tony.

Lovell, Arnold, ed. Evangelism in the Reformed Tradition. 160p. (Orig.). 1990. pap. 10.00 (*1-885121-02-4*) CTS Press.

Lovell, Bernard. Adult Learning. 1979. pap. text 15.95 (*0-415-03693-3*) Routledge.

— Echoes of War: The Story of H2S Radar. (Illus.). 312p. 1991. 47.00 (*0-85274-317-3*) IOP Pub.

— The Jodrell Bank Telescopes. (Illus.). 308p. 1985. text 21.00 (*0-19-858178-5*) OUP.

— Voice of the Universe: Building the Jodrell Bank Telescope. rev. ed. LC 87-9322. 331p. 1987. 59.95 (*0-275-92678-8*, C2678, Praeger Pubs); pap. 17.95 (*0-275-92679-6*, B2679, Praeger Pubs) Greenwood.

Lovell, Bernard & Bank, Jodrell. Emerging Cosmology. Anshen, Ruth N., ed. LC 84-17954. (Convergence Ser.). 224p. 1984. pap. 17.95 (*0-275-91790-8*, B1790, Praeger Pubs) Greenwood.

Lovell, Bernard & Smith, F. Graham. Pathways to the Universe. (Illus.). 242p. 1989. text 38.95 (*0-521-32004-6*) Cambridge U Pr.

Lovell, C. A., jt. auth. see Fried, Harold.

Lovell, C. A., jt. auth. see Fried, Harold O.

Lovell, C. A., jt. ed. see Gulledge, Thomas R., Jr.

Lovell, C. A. Knox, jt. auth. see Kumbhaker, Subal C.

Lovell, C. R. Plants & the Skin. (Illus.). 280p. 1993. 99.95 (*0-632-02562-X*) Blackwell Sci.

Lovell, C. W. & Wiltshire, Richard L., eds. Engineering Aspects of Soil Erosion, Dispersive Clays & Loess. 176p. 1987. 21.00 (*0-87262-590-7*) Am Soc Civil Eng.

Lovell, C. W., jt. ed. see Khera, Raj P.

Lovell, Caroline C. The Light of Other Days. LC 95-20858. 183p. 1995. 25.00 (*0-86554-465-4*, MUP/H366) Mercer Univ Pr.

Lovell, Catherine H. Breaking the Cycle of Poverty: The BRAC Strategy. LC 92-5270. (Kumarian Press Library of Management for Development Ser.). 216p. Date not set. reprint ed. pap. 67.00 (*0-608-20746-2*, 207179400003) Bks Demand.

Lovell, Charles M. & Hester, Erwin, eds. Minnie Evans: Artist. (Illus.). 72p. (Orig.). 1993. pap. 24.50 (*0-9636759-0-7*) East Carolin Mus.

Lovell, Charles M., ed. & intro. see Gaston, Diana.

***Lovell, Chris.** Productive Water Points in Dryland Areas: Guidelines on Integrated Planning for Rural Water Supply. 208p. 2000. pap. 22.00 (*1-85339-516-1*, Pub. by Intermed Tech) Stylus Pub VA.

Lovell, D. J., ed. Optical Anecdotes, Vol. X40. 148p. 1981. 15.00 (*0-89252-353-0*) SPIE.

Lovell, David W. Marx's Proletariat: The Making of a Myth. 320p. (C). 1988. lib. bdg. 52.50 (*0-415-00116-1*) Routledge.

***Love'll, Dorothy.** God's Annointing Has Set Me Free. 182p. 2000. pap. 15.95 (*0-9676386-0-7*) D Lovell.

Lovell, Douglas D. & Martin, Robert S. Subdivision Analysis. 120p. 1993. 25.00 (*0-922154-11-2*) Appraisal Inst.

Lovell, George. Analysis & Design: A Handbook for Practitioners & Consultants in Church & Community Work. 304p. 1994. pap. 45.00 (*0-86012-234-4*, Pub. by Srch Pr) St Mut.

Lovell, George & Widdicombe, Catherine. Churches & Communities. 222p. 1994. pap. 24.00 (*0-85532-387-6*, Pub. by Srch Pr) St Mut.

***Lovell, George W.** A Beauty That Hurts: Life & Death in Guatemala, Revised Edition. rev. ed. (Illus.). 220p. 2001. pap. 19.95 (*0-292-74717-9*) U of Tex Pr.

Lovell, Glenville. Fire in the Canes. 272p. 1997. mass mkt. 6.99 (*0-425-16040-8*) Berkley Pub.

— Fire in the Canes. LC 95-10704. 272p. 1995. 22.00 (*1-56947-044-8*) Soho Press.

— Song of Night. LC 97-53058. 256p. 1998. 23.00 (*1-56947-122-3*) Soho Press.

Lovell, James B. Anastasia: The Lost Princess. LC 91-7807. (Illus.). 528p. 1991. 24.95 (*0-89526-536-2*) Regnery Pub.

— Anastasia: The Lost Princess. (Illus.). 528p. 1995. pap. 15.95 (*0-312-11133-9*) St Martin.

— Royal Russia. 1997. text 25.00 (*0-312-17936-7*) St Martin.

***Lovell, Jim.** Apollo 13. (Illus.). 400p. 2000. 26.00 (*0-618-05665-3*) HM.

Lovell, Jim & Kluger, Jeffrey. Apollo 13: Lost Moon - Movie Tie-In. 1995. mass mkt. 6.99 (*0-671-53464-5*) PB.

— Lost Moon: The Perilous Voyage of Apollo 13. LC 99-89647. (Illus.). 384p. 1994. 25.00 (*0-395-67029-2*) HM.

Lovell, John. Trade Unions in Twentieth-Century Britain. 112p. 1996. pap. 12.50 (*1-85728-250-7*, Pub. by UCL Pr Ltd) Taylor & Francis.

Lovell, John P., ed. Insights from Film into Violence & Oppression: Shattered Dreams of the Good Life. LC 97-23878. 184p. 1998. 55.00 (*0-275-95972-4*, Praeger Pubs) Greenwood.

Lovell, John P. & Albright, David E. To Sheathe the Sword: Civil-Military Relations in the Quest for Democracy, 379. LC 96-28068. (Contributions in Political Science Ser.). 248p. 1997. 59.95 (*0-313-30037-2*) Greenwood.

Lovell, John P. & Kronenberg, Philip S., eds. New Civil Military Relations. LC 72-94547. (Social Policy Ser.). 352p. 1974. 44.95 (*0-87855-075-5*); pap. 24.95 (*0-87855-571-4*) Transaction Pubs.

Lovell, M. A., et al, eds. Borehole Images: Applications & Case Histories. 235p. 1999. 108.00 (*1-86239-043-6*) Geol Soc Pub Hse.

Lovell, M. A. & Harvey, P. K., eds. Developments in Petrophysics. (Geological Society Special Publication Ser.: No. 122). (Illus.). 408p. 1997. 125.00 (*1-897799-81-0*, Pub. by Geol Soc Pub Hse) AAPG.

Lovell, M. A., jt. ed. see Harvey, P. K.

Lovell, Margaret. Fateful Journey. large type ed. (Linford Romance Library). 272p. 1992. pap. 16.99 (*0-7089-7283-7*) Ulverscroft.

— Fateful Journey. large type ed. (Linford Romance Library). 304p. 1992. pap. 16.99 (*0-7089-7293-4*) Ulverscroft.

— Stranger in the Village. large type ed. (Linford Romance Library). 272p. 1994. pap. 16.99 (*0-7089-7526-7*, Linford) Ulverscroft.

— Teacher on the Wards. large type ed. (Linford Romance Library). 272p. 1993. pap. 16.99 (*0-7089-7471-6*) Ulverscroft.

Lovell, Margaretta M. Venice: The American View, 1860-1920. LC 84-81857. (Illus.). 174p. 1984. pap. 19.95 (*0-88401-044-9*) Fine Arts Mus.

— A Visitable Past: Views of Venice by American Artists, 1860-1915. (Illus.). 152p. 1988. 47.95 (*0-226-49412-8*) U Ch Pr.

Lovell, Margaretta M., jt. auth. see Cartwright, Derrick R.

Lovell, Mark R. & Franzen, Michael D. Study Guide & Self-Assessment for the American Psychiatric Press Textbook of Psychiatry. LC RC0341.A44. 406p. 1988. reprint ed. pap. 125.90 (*0-608-02025-7*, 206268100003) Bks Demand.

Lovell, Mark R., jt. auth. see Franzen, Michael D.

Lovell, Mary. Pay Pack & Follow. Date not set. write for info. (*0-393-04551-X*) Norton.

— A Rage To Live: A Biography of Richard & Isabel Burton. LC 98-29886. (Illus.). 736p. 1998. 39.95 (*0-393-04672-9*) Norton.

***Lovell, Mary.** Rage to Live: A Biography of Richard & Isabel Burton. 944p. 2000. pap. 19.95 (*0-393-32039-1*) Norton.

Lovell, Mary S. The Sound of Wings: The Life of Amelia Earhart. (Illus.). 448p. 1991. pap. 18.95 (*0-312-05160-3*) St Martin.

Lovell, Nadia, ed. Locality & Belonging. LC 98-24886. (European Association of Social Anthropologists Ser.). 240p. (C). (gr. 13). 1998. 85.00 (*0-415-18281-6*, D6213) Routledge.

— Locality & Belonging. LC 98-24886. (European Association of Social Anthropologists Ser.). 240p. (C). (gr. 13). 1998. pap. 25.99 (*0-415-18282-4*, D6217) Routledge.

Lovell, Nadine. Art Activities (Creative Corners) (Illus.). 56p. pap. 8.95 (*1-56861-016-5*) Swift Lrn Res.

— Children Around the World: Passport to Adventure. (Illus.). 89p. (J). (gr. 1-6). pap. 9.95 (*1-56861-058-0*) Swift Lrn Res.

— Creative Corners - Wild Animals, Bk. 1. (Illus.). 84p. 1992. pap. 8.95 (*1-56861-002-5*) Swift Lrn Res.

Lovell, Nancy C. Patterns of Injury & Illness in Great Apes: A Skeletal Analysis. LC 89-600389. (Illus.). 288p. 1990. 45.00 (*0-87474-678-7*) Smithsonian.

Lovell, P. A. & El-Aasser, Mohamed S. Emulsion Polymerization & Emulsion Polymers. LC 96-30344. 826p. 1997. 570.00 (*0-471-96746-7*) Wiley.

Lovell, Percy & Marcham, William, eds. Parish of St. Pancras Pt. 1: The Village of Highgate. LC 70-37855. (London County Council. Survey of London Ser.: No. 17). reprint ed. 84.50 (*0-404-51667-X*) AMS Pr.

— Parish of St. Pancras Pt. 2: Old St. Pancras & Kentish Town. LC 70-37855. (London County Council. Survey of London Ser.: No. 19). reprint ed. 84.50 (*0-404-51669-6*) AMS Pr.

Lovell, Richard. Churchill's Doctor: A Biography of Lord Moran. (Illus.). 457p. 1993. 49.00 (*1-85070-485-6*) Prthnon Pub.

***Lovell, Rick.** Muslims, Magic & the Kingdom of God. LC 00-31222. 2000. pap. write for info. (*0-87808-443-6*) William Carey Lib.

Lovell, Rick, jt. auth. see Stojkovic, Stan.

Lovell, Robert. Probability Activities. 308p. (YA). (gr. 9-12). 1993. pap. 19.50 (*1-55953-067-7*) Key Curr Pr.

Lovell, Ronald. Free-Lancing: A Guide to Writing for Magazines & Other Markets. LC 94-222132. 356p. (C). 1994. pap. text 21.95 (*0-88133-752-8*) Waveland Pr.

Lovell, Ronald P. Reporting Public Affairs: Problems & Solutions. 2nd ed. (Illus.). 506p. 1993. pap. text 28.95 (*0-88133-696-3*) Waveland Pr.

Lovell, Ronald P., et al. Handbook of Photography. 3rd ed. 337p. 1993. pap. 31.50 (*0-8273-5279-4*) Delmar.

Lovell, Ronald P., et al. Handbook of Photography. 4th ed. LC 96-29942. (Illus.). 448p. (C). 1997. mass mkt. 53.95 (*0-8273-7913-7*) Delmar.

***Lovell, Russell A., Jr. & American Bar Association Staff.** Court-Awarded Attorney's Fees. LC 99-16997. 1999. write for info. (*1-57073-692-8*) Amer Bar Assn.

Lovell, Russell A., Jr., jt. compiled by see Kardell, Caroline L.

Lovell, Sandra, jt. auth. see Lister, Marcie.

Lovell, Sarah, ed. see Trotsky, Leon.

Lovell, Scarlett & Snowball, Diane. Esto Es Un Monstruo?, 1. Gonzalez-Prats, Martha, tr. (SPA., Illus.). 24p. (J). (ps-3). 1998. pap. 4.95 (*1-57255-494-0*) Mondo Pubng.

— Is This a Monster? LC 95-4740. 24p. (J). (gr. k-4). 1995. pap. 4.95 (*1-57255-018-X*) Mondo Pubng.

Lovell, Scarlett, et al. Exploring Mountain Habitats. LC 97-20290. (Mondo's Exploring Ser.). (Illus.). 24p. (J). (gr. 1-5). 1999. pap. 4.95 (*1-57255-164-X*) Mondo Pubng.

Lovell, Sherry, jt. auth. see Hickman, Mina.

***Lovell, Stephen, et al.** Bribery & Blat in Russia: Negotiating Reciprocity from the Middle Ages to the 1990s. LC 99-54893. 2000. 69.95 (*0-312-23127-X*) St Martin.

Lovell, Stephen, jt. ed. see Kelly, Catriona.

Lovell, T. Nutrition & Feeding of Fish. (Illus.). 224p. (C). (gr. 13). 1988. text 72.95 (*0-412-12291-X*) Chapman & Hall.

Lovell, Terry. British Feminist Thought: A Reader. 256p. (C). 1990. pap. text 29.95 (*0-631-16915-6*) Blackwell Pubs.

Lovell, Terry, ed. Feminist Cultural Studies, 2 vols., Set. LC 95-11856. (International Library of Studies in Media & Culture: Vol. 1). 1216p. 1995. 450.00 (*1-85278-767-8*) E Elgar.

***Lovell, Thoreau.** Amnesia's Diary. 73p. 1999. pap. 10.00 (*0-9663224-4-4*, Pub. by Ex Hihilo) SPD-Small Pr Dist.

Lovell, Tom. Nutrition & Feeding of Fish. 1998. 150.00 (*0-7923-8311-7*) Kluwer Academic.

***Lovell, Tom.** Nutrition & Feeding of Fish. 2nd ed. LC 98-44242. 280p. 1999. 150.00 (*0-412-07701-9*) Kluwer Academic.

Lovell-Troy, Larry, jt. auth. see Eickmann, Paul E.

Lovell-Troy, Lawrence A., ed. The Social Basis Ethnic Enterprise: Greeks in the Pizza Business. LC 90-42045. (European Immigrants & American Society Ser.). 264p. 1990. reprint ed. text 20.00 (*0-8240-7426-2*) Garland.

Lovell, W. George. Conquest & Survival in Colonial Guatemala: A Historical Geography of the Cuchumat[00a0]n Highlands, 1500-1821. rev. ed. (Illus.). 312p. 1992. pap. 22.95 (*0-7735-0903-8*, Pub. by McG-Queens Univ Pr) CUP Services.

— Conquista y Cambio Cultural: La Sierra de Los Cuchumatanes de Guatemala, 1500-1821. LC 90-82409. (Serie Monografica: No. 6). (SPA., Illus.). 288p. 1990. pap. 16.50 (*0-910443-08-4*) Plumsock Meso Studies.

Lovell, W. George, jt. ed. see Cook, Noble D.

Lovelock, Christopher H. Principles of Services Marketing & Management. LC 98-49946. 414p. (C). 1999. 93.00 (*0-13-676875-X*, Macmillan Coll) P-H.

— Service Marketing. 3rd ed. 660p. 1996. 96.00 (*0-13-455841-3*) P-H.

***Lovelock, Christopher H.** Services Marketing: People, Technology, Strategy. 4th ed. 720p. 2000. 84.00 (*0-13-017392-4*, Prentice Hall) P-H.

Lovelock, Christopher H. & Weinberg, Charles B. Public & Nonprofit Marketing: Readings & Cases. 380p. (C). 1990. pap. text 37.50 (*0-89426-148-7*) Course Tech.

Lovelock, Christopher H. & Weinberg, Charles B., eds. Marketing Challenges: Cases & Exercises. 3rd ed. LC 92-38991. (Marketing Ser.). 1993. write for info. (*0-07-911577-2*) McGraw.

Lovelock, Christopher H., et al. Marketing Public Transit: A Strategic Approach. LC 87-11583. (Public & Nonprofit Sector Marketing Ser.). 238p. 1987. 52.95 (*0-275-92499-8*, C2499, Praeger Pubs) Greenwood.

Lovelock, D. W., jt. ed. see Board, R. G.

Lovelock, David. Tensors Differential Forms. 384p. 1989. pap. 10.95 (*0-486-65840-6*) Dover.

Lovelock, David, jt. auth. see Lomen, David.

Lovelock, Harold J., jt. auth. see Ambrose, Paul V.

Lovelock, Harry, jt. auth. see Ambrose, Paul V.

***Lovelock, James.** Gaia: A New Look at Life on Earth. (Illus.). 176p. 2000. pap. 13.95 (*0-19-286218-9*) OUP.

Lovelock, James. Gaia: The Practical Science of Planetary Medicine. (Illus.). 192p. 1991. 32.50 (*1-85675-040-X*) Gaia Bks.

***Lovelock, James.** Gaia: The Practical Science of Planetary Medicine. (Illus.). 192p. 2000. pap. 18.95 (*0-19-521674-1*) OUP.

— Healing Gaia: Practical Medicine for the Planet. (Illus.). 192p. 1999. reprint ed. text 25.00 (*0-7881-6732-4*) DIANE Pub.

Lovelock, James E. The Ages of Gaia: A Biography of Our Living Earth. 272p. 1995. pap. 13.00 (*0-393-31239-9*) Norton.

— Gaia: A New Look at Life on Earth. (Illus.). 176p. 1987. pap. 11.95 (*0-19-286030-5*) OUP.

Lovelock, Julian. Donne Songs & Sonets. LC 73-169733. (Casebook Ser.). 256p. 1973. write for info. (*0-333-11661-5*) Macmillan.

Lovelock, Robin. Visual Impairment: Social Support: Recent Research in Context. 309p. 1995. 87.95 (*1-85628-391-7*, Pub. by Avebry) Ashgate Pub Co.

Lovelock, Robin & Powell, Jackie. Disability - Britain in Europe: An Evaluation of U. K. Participation in the HELIOS Programme (1988-1991) LC 94-19937. 272p. 1994. 72.95 (*1-85628-646-0*, Pub. by Avebry) Ashgate Pub Co.

Lovelock, Robin, jt. ed. see Brier, Alan.

Lovelock, Yann. Landscapes with Voices: Poems 1980-95. 126p. pap. write for info. (*3-7052-0433-5*, Pub. by Poetry Salzburg) Intl Spec Bk.

Lovelock, Yann, ed. Building Jerusalem. (C). 1988. 25.00 (*0-904524-48-5*, Pub. by Rivelin Grapheme Pr) St Mut.

Lovelock, Yann, ed. Physic Meet & Metaphysic. 157p. pap. write for info. (*3-7052-0636-2*, Pub. by Poetry Salzburg) Intl Spec Bk.

Lovely, Mary E. Thinking Locally, Acting Globally: Congressman Jim Walsh & the NAFTA Vote. (Pew Case Studies in International Affairs). 50p. (C). 1994. pap. text 3.50 (*1-56927-160-7*, GU Schl Foreign) Geo U Inst Dplmcy.

Loveman, Amy, et al, eds. Varied Harvest. LC 73-134109. (Essay Index Reprint Ser.). 1977. 23.95 (*0-8369-1981-5*) Ayer.

Loveman, Aurelia. Lace. Brenner, Carla, ed. (Illus.). 24p. (Orig.). 1988. pap. text 4.00 (*0-911886-36-2*) Walters Art.

Loveman, Brian. Chile: The Legacy of Hispanic Capitalism. 2nd ed. (Latin American Histories Ser.). (Illus.). 464p. 1988. pap. text 23.95 (*0-19-505219-6*) OUP.

***Loveman, Brian.** Chile: The Legacy of Hispanic Capitalism. 3rd ed. (Latin American Histories Ser.). (Illus.). 480p. (C). 2001. pap. 24.50 (*0-19-512020-5*); text 49.95 (*0-19-512019-1*) OUP.

Loveman, Brian. The Constitution of Tyranny: Regimes of Exception in Spanish America. (Latin American Ser.). 496p. 1994. pap. 19.95 (*0-8229-5536-9*) U of Pittsburgh Pr.

— The Constitution of Tyranny: Regimes of Exception in Spanish America. (Latin American Ser.). 496p. (C). 1994. text 49.95 (*0-8229-3766-2*) U of Pittsburgh Pr.

Loveman, Brian. For la Patria: Politics & the Armed Forces in Latin America. LC 98-7793. (Latin American Silhouettes Ser.). (Illus.). 333p. 1999. pap. 23.95 (*0-8420-2773-4*) Scholarly Res Inc.

***Loveman, Brian.** For la Patria: Politics & the Armed Forces in Latin America. LC 98-7793. (Latin American Silhouettes Ser.). (Illus.). 333p. 1999. 60.00 (*0-8420-2772-6*) Scholarly Res Inc.

Loveman, Brian, et al, eds. The Politics of Antipolitics: The Military in Latin America. 3rd rev. ed. LC 96-9466. (Latin American Silhouettes Ser.). 438p. (C). 1996. 55.00 (*0-8420-2609-6*); pap. 23.95 (*0-8420-2611-8*) Scholarly Res Inc.

Loveman, Jason. Building COM Applications with Internet Explorer. LC 98-34251. 400p. 1998. pap. text 49.99 (*0-13-081909-3*) P-H.

***Loveman, Laurie.** The Farm Fires. LC 99-91000. (Firehouse Family Ser.: Bk. 3). 1999. 25.00 (*0-7388-0568-8*); pap. 18.00 (*0-7388-0569-6*) Xlibris Corp.

Loveman, Laurie. Memories. LC 98-88466. (Firehouse Family Ser.). 325p. 1998. 25.00 (*0-7388-0155-0*); pap. 15.00 (*0-7388-0156-9*) Xlibris Corp.

***Loveman, Laurie.** The Quarry. LC 99-91220. (Firehouse Family Ser.: Bk. 2). 476p. 1998. 25.00 (*0-7388-0676-5*); pap. 18.00 (*0-7388-0677-3*) Xlibris Corp.

Loven, Galen D. Succession Planning for Closely Held Businesses. 123p. 1993. pap. 19.95 (*1-883480-00-0*) Brkthgh Pubns.

— Winning Without Selling: Practice Building Handbook for Accountants. 3rd ed. 96p. 1993. 34.50 (*1-883480-01-9*) Brkthgh Pubns.

Loven, Juanita. Dvorak in Spillville: 100 Days 100 Years Ago 1893-1993. 1993. pap. 8.95 (*1-57216-057-8*) Penfield.

Loven, Sven. Origins of the Tainan Culture, West Indies. LC 76-44753. (Taino Indians of Hispaniola & Eastern Cuba Ser.). (Illus.). reprint ed. 95.00 (*0-404-15948-6*) AMS Pr.

Lovendahl, Shari, ed. see Schilling, Vivian.

Lovendale, Mark. Quality Longevity, Vol. 10. rev. ed. LC 94-73781. (Illus.). 260p. (Orig.). 1998. pap. 28.00 (*0-945196-22-9*) Advanced CA.

Lovendale, Mark, ed. see Meinig, George E.

Lovenduski, Joni. Women & European Politics: Contemporary Feminism & Public Policy. LC 85-16501. 336p. 1986. lib. bdg. 19.95 (*0-87023-507-9*) U of Mass Pr.

Lovenduski, Joni, ed. Feminism & Politics, Vols. I & II. LC 99-28315. (International Library of Politics & Comparative Government). 1250p. 1999. text 148.95 (*1-85521-903-4*, Pub. by Ashgate Pub) Ashgate Pub Co.

Lovenduski, Joni & Norris, Pippa, eds. Gender & Party Politics. (Illus.). 288p. (C). 1994. text 62.00 (*0-8039-8659-9*); pap. text 22.95 (*0-8039-8660-2*) Sage.

Lovenduski, Joni, jt. auth. see Norris, Pippa.

Lovenheim, Barbara, et al. A Family among Families. unabridged ed. LC 97-73986. (Illus.). vii, 140 p. 1997. 24.95 (*0-9651374-1-4*) Jewish Home Aux.

Lovenheim, Peter. How to Mediate Your Dispute: Find a Solution Quickly & Cheaply Outside the Courtroom. (Illus.). 464p. 1996. pap. 18.95 (*0-87337-329-4*) Nolo com.

— Mediate, Don't Litigate. 290p. 1990. 19.95 (*0-07-038832-6*) McGraw.

Lovenheim, Peter, jt. ed. see Katz, David A.

Loventhal, Milton & McDowell, Jennifer. Ronnie Goose Rhymes for Grown-Ups. LC 84-60716. (Mother Goose Rhymes for Grown-ups Ser.). 1984. 10.95 (*0-930142-07-1*) Merlin Pr.

***Lover, Linda.** Season Sampler. (Illus.). 46p. 1999. pap. 9.95 (*1-57377-070-1*, 019884) Easl Pubns.

— Season Sampler, Vol. 2. (Illus.). 52p. 2000. 10.95 (*1-57377-104-X*, 0-19884-02346-3) Easl Pubns.

Lover, Myron J. The Pharmaceutical Aerosol: A Drug Delivery System in Transition. 215p. 1994. ring bd. 99.95 (*1-56676-200-6*) Technomic.

Lover of Philalethes, tr. see Von Rosenroth, Knorr.

***Lover, Stanley.** Soccer Laws Illustrated. (Orig.). 1999. pap. 10.95 (*0-7207-1999-2*, Pelham Bks) Viking Penguin.

Lover, Stanley. Soccer Rules Explained. LC 97-51734. 192p. 1998. pap. 12.95 (*1-55821-722-3*) Lyons Pr.

— Soccer Rules Illustrated, Vol. 1. 1998. pap. 12.95 (*1-57243-330-2*) Triumph Bks.

Loverance, Rowena. The Anglo-Saxons: A BBC Fact Finders Book. (Fact Finders Ser.). (Illus.). 48p. (YA). (gr. 7 up). 1993. pap. 8.95 (*0-563-35001-6*, BBC-Parkwest) Parkwest Pubns.

— Byzantium. LC 88-539. (Illus.). 72p. (Orig.). 1988. pap. 14.00 (*0-674-08972-3*) HUP.

Loverancer, Rowena. Ancient Greece. (J). 1993. 19.99 (*0-670-84754-2*) Viking Penguin.

Loverde, Joy. The Complete Eldercare Planner: Where to Start, Questions to Ask & How to Find Help. LC 96-43370. 288p. (J). 1997. pap. 14.45 (*0-7868-8229-8*, Pub. by Hyperion) Little.

— Complete Eldercare Planner Where to Start, Which Questions to Ask & How to Find Help. 2nd ed. LC 99-48602. 272p. 2000. pap. 19.95 (*0-8129-3278-1*, Times Bks) Crown Pub Group.

LoVerde, Mary. Stop Screaming at the Microwave: How to Connect Your Disconnected Life. LC 98-22592. (Illus.). 238p. 1998. pap. 12.00 (*0-684-85397-3*, Fireside) S&S Trade Pap.

Loveren, Harry R. Van, see Tew, John M., Jr.

Loveren, Harry R. Van, see Tew, John M., Jr. & Van Loveren, Harry R.

Loveren, Harry R. Van, see Tew, John M., Jr.

Loveren, Harry R. Van, see Tew, John M., Jr. & Van Loveren, Harry R.

Loveren, Harry R. Van, see Tew, John M., Jr.

Loveren, Harry R. Van, see Tew, John M., Jr. & Van Loveren, Harry R.

Loveridge. Cardio Assessement for Physical Therapy. 1998. text. write for info. (*0-7216-3276-9*, W B Saunders Co) Harcrt Hlth Sci Grp.

Loveridge, Catherine E. & Cummings, Susan H. Nursing Management in the New Paradigm. 350p. 1997. 49.00 (*0-8342-0620-X*, 20620) Aspen Pub.

Loveridge, Emma W. Egypt. LC 96-33473. (Country Fact Files Ser.). (Illus.). 48p. (J). (gr. 4-8). 1997. lib. bdg. 24.26 (*0-8172-4626-6*) Raintree Steck-V.

Loveridge, J. W., jt. auth. see Hughes, H. G.

Loveridge, John W., jt. auth. see McArthur, Alfred G.

Loveridge, Mark. A History of Augustan Fable. LC 97-32207. (Illus.). 322p. (C). 1999. 59.95 (*0-521-63062-2*) Cambridge U Pr.

Loveridge, Peter. A Cruising Guide to Nova Scotia: Digby to Cape Breton Island, Including the Bras d'Or Lakes. LC 96-43313. (Illus.). 252p. 1996. 29.95 (*0-07-038808-3*) McGraw.

Loveridge, Raymond. Collective Bargaining by National Employees in the United Kingdom. LC 78-634399. (Comparative Studies in Public Employment Labor Relations Ser.). 1971. 10.00 (*0-87736-015-4*); pap. 5.00 (*0-87736-016-2*) U of Mich Inst Labor.

Loveridge, Raymond & Starkey, Ken, eds. Continuity & Crisis in the NHS. 224p. 1992. 123.00 (*0-335-15620-7*); pap. 42.95 (*0-335-15599-5*) OpUniv Pr.

Loveridge, Scott, jt. see Schaeffer, Peter V.

Lovering, D. G., jt. auth. see Gale, R. J.

Lovering, David G. Molten Salt Techniques, Vol. 1. Gale, Robert J., ed. LC 83-9582. (Illus.). 290p. (C). 1983. text 132.00 (*0-306-41307-8*, Kluwer Plenum) Kluwer Academic.

Lovering, David G., ed. Molten Salt Technology. LC 82-14982. 550p. 1982. 125.00 (*0-306-41076-1*, Plenum Trade) Perseus Pubng.

Lovering, David G. & Gale, Robert J., eds. Molten Salt Techniques, Vol. 2. LC 83-9582. (Illus.). 276p. (C). 1984. text 132.00 (*0-306-41549-6*, Kluwer Plenum) Kluwer Academic.

— Molten Salt Techniques, Vol. 3. LC 83-9582. (Illus.). 368p. (C). 1987. text 132.00 (*0-306-42504-1*, Kluwer Plenum) Kluwer Academic.

Lovering, David G., jt. ed. see Inman, Douglas.

Lovering, Eugene H., Jr. & Sumney, Jerry L., eds. Theology & Ethics in Paul & His Interpreters: Essays in Honor of Victor Paul Furnish. LC 96-31336. 288p. 1996. pap. 19.95 (*0-687-00767-4*) Abingdon.

***Lovering, John.** Global Arms Economy. 256p. 2000. 69.95 (*0-7453-1445-7*, Pub. by Pluto GBR); pap. 24.95 (*0-7453-1440-6*, Pub. by Pluto GBR) Stylus Pub VA.

Lovering, Joseph P. S. Weir Mitchell. LC 76-125256. (Twayne's United States Authors Ser.). 1971. pap. text 9.95 (*0-8290-0002-X*); lib. bdg. 20.95 (*0-89197-984-0*) Irvington.

Lovering, Martin. History of the Town of Holland, Mass. (Illus.). 745p. 1989. reprint ed. lib. bdg. 75.00 (*0-8328-0832-6*, MA0058) Higginson Bk Co.

Lovering, Robert. Out of the Darkness: Coping with Disability. 148p. (Orig.). 1993. pap. 7.95 (*0-614-05342-0*) ARCS Inc.

— Out of the Ordinary: A Digest on Disability. LC 85-71798. 260148p. (Orig.). 1985. 14.95 (*0-9615213-0-9*) ARCS Inc.

Lovering, Thomas S. & Stoll, W. M. Rock Alteration As a Guide to Ore East Tintic District, Utah. LC 50-6493. (Economic Geology, Monograph: No. 1). 102p. reprint ed. pap. 31.70 (*0-608-13060-5*, 201476400093) Bks Demand.

Lovern. Business Skills Improvement Exercises. (Office Procedures Ser.). 1987. 12.00 (*0-538-11441-X*) S-W Pub.

— Calculator Applications for Business. 2nd ed. (KH - Office Machines Ser.). 1990. mass mkt. 11.00 (*0-538-60318-6*) S-W Pub.

— Paula's Plantscape - A Clerical Skills Simulation. 2nd ed. (KM - Office Procedures Ser.). 1990. mass mkt. 11.50 (*0-538-60316-X*) S-W Pub.

— Plants Galore - The General Clerk Simulation. (KM - Office Procedures Ser.). 1984. pap. 15.95 (*0-538-25510-2*) S-W Pub.

Lovern, Anna, jt. auth. see Lovern, Wayne.

Lovern, John D. Pathways to Reality: Erickson-Inspired Treatment Approaches to Chemical Dependency. LC 91-13541. 240p. 1991. text 34.95 (*0-87630-633-4*) Brunner-Mazel.

Lovern, Wayne & Lovern, Anna. Navigating the Marketplace: Growth Strategies for Your Business. LC 98-29049. 300p. 1998. pap. 21.95 (*1-55571-458-7*, NVMPP, Oasis Pr) PSI Resch.

Lovero, Joan D. Hudson County, the Left Bank. (Illus.). 188p. 1999. 29.95 (*1-892724-01-4*) Am Historical Pr.

***Loverro, Thom.** Cammi Granato: Hockey Pioneer. (Sports Achievers Biographies Ser.). (Illus.). 64p. (YA). (gr. 4-7). 2000. pap. 5.95 (*0-8225-9862-0*, LernerSports) Lerner Pub.

— Cammi Granato: Hockey Pioneer. (Sports Achievers Biographies Ser.). (Illus.). 64p. (YA). (gr. 4-7). 2000. 22.60 (*0-8225-3682-X*, LernerSports) Lerner Pub.

Loverro, Thom. Home of the Game: The Story of Camden Yards. LC 99-12020. 1999. 24.95 (*0-87833-222-7*) Taylor Pub.

— The Washington Redskins. LC 96-41452. 1996. 39.95 (*0-87833-136-0*); 75.00 (*0-87833-137-9*) Taylor Pub.

Loverseed, Helga. Guide to Eastern Canada. 6th ed. LC 97-51430. (Illus.). 416p. 1998. pap. 17.95 (*0-7627-0179-X*) Globe Pequot.

Loverseed, Helga V. Brampton: An Illustrated History. LC 87-6254. 304p. 1987. 29.95 (*0-89781-207-7*) Am Historical Pr.

Loversky, Doug. Discover Baseball Basics. (Illus.). (J). (ps-6). 1998. pap. 5.95 (*1-893690-75-X*) Home Team.

***Loves, June.** Grandparents Handbook: Up to Date...Safety...Games...Activities for Grandchildren of All Ages. (Illus.). 248p. 2001. pap. 14.95 (*0-7322-6602-5*) HarpC.

Loves, June. The Grasshopper. LC 92-34263. (Voyages Ser.). (Illus.). (J). 1993. 4.25 (*0-383-03626-7*) SRA McGraw.

— I Know That. LC 92-34262. (Voyages Ser.). (Illus.). (J). 1993. 4.25 (*0-383-03633-X*) SRA McGraw.

— This Is the Book That I Borrowed. LC 92-31955. (Voyages Ser.). (Illus.). (J). 1993. 4.25 (*0-383-03598-8*) SRA McGraw.

Lovesey. Butcher's Stories. 1988. mass mkt. write for info. (*0-445-40546-5*) Little.

Lovesey, E. J., ed. Contemporary Ergonomics, 1991: Ergonomics-Design for Performance. 503p. 1991. pap. 85.00 (*0-7484-0007-9*, Pub. by Tay Francis Ltd) Taylor & Francis.

— Contemporary Ergonomics, 1992: Ergonomics for Industry. 576p. 1992. 90.00 (*0-7484-0030-3*, Pub. by Tay Francis Ltd) Taylor & Francis.

— Contemporary Ergonomics, 1993: Ergonomics for Industry. 511p. 1993. pap. 116.00 (*0-7484-0070-2*) Taylor & Francis.

Lovesey, Peter. Bertie & the Seven Bodies. 1991. mass mkt. 4.95 (*0-445-40858-8*, Pub. by Warner Bks) Little.

— Bertie & the Tinman. 1989. mass mkt. 3.95 (*0-445-40592-9*, Pub. by Warner Bks) Little.

— Bloodhounds. 368p. 1997. mass mkt. 5.99 (*0-446-40535-3*, Pub. by Warner Bks) Little.

— Butchers & Other Stories of Crime. LC 87-42706. 208p. 1987. 15.95 (*0-89296-195-3*, Pub. by Mysterious Pr) Little.

— Butchers & Other Stories of Crime. LC 87-7718. 208p. 1988. 9.95 (*0-89296-960-1*) Mysterious Pr.

***Lovesey, Peter.** The Detective Wore Silk Drawers: A Sergeant Cribb Mystery. large type ed. LC 99-87702. (General Ser.). 294p. 2000. pap. 23.95 (*0-7862-2426-6*) Thorndike Pr.

Lovesey, Peter. Diamond Solitaire. large type ed. LC 93-35504. 544p. 1993. lib. bdg. 21.95 (*0-7862-0076-6*) Thorndike Pr.

— Do Not Exceed the Stated Dose. LC 98-154514. 212p. 1998. pap. 16.00 (*1-885941-21-8*) Crippen & Landru.

***Lovesey, Peter.** Keystone. 256p. 1999. 21.95 (*0-7540-8551-1*, Black Dagger) Chivers N Amer.

— The Last Detective. 336p. 2000. pap. 13.00 (*1-56947-209-2*) Soho Press.

Lovesey, Peter. On the Edge. 1990. mass mkt. 4.50 (*0-445-40863-4*, Pub. by Warner Bks) Little.

— Rough Cider. 224p. 1987. 15.45 (*0-89296-194-5*, Pub. by Mysterious Pr) Little.

— Rough Cider. 1988. mass mkt. 3.95 (*0-445-40545-7*, Pub. by Warner Bks) Little.

Lovesey, Peter. The Summons. LC 95-2915. 368p. 1995. 21.45 (*0-89296-551-7*, Pub. by Mysterious Pr) Little.

Lovesey, Peter. The Summons. large type ed. (Cloak & Dagger Ser.). 562p. 1995. 24.95 (*0-7862-0560-1*) Thorndike Pr.

— Swing, Swing Together. 1976. 21.95 (*0-89190-093-4*) Amereon Ltd.

— Upon a Dark Night. large type ed. LC 98-21233. 2595p. 1998. 30.00 (*0-7862-1530-5*) Thorndike Pr.

***Lovesey, Peter.** The Vault. 304p. 2000. 23.00 (*1-56947-208-4*) Soho Press.

Lovesey, Peter. Wobble to Death. large type ed. LC 99-11734. 270p. 1999. 22.95 (*0-7862-1868-1*) Thorndike Pr.

Lovesey, Stephen W. Theory of Neutron Scattering from Condensed Matter, Vol. 2. (International Series of Monographs on Physics). (Illus.). 310p. 1986. pap. 35.00 (*0-19-852029-8*) OUP.

Lovesey, Stephen W., et al, eds. Magnetic Excitations & Fluctuations. (Solid-State Sciences Ser.: Vol. 54). (Illus.). 240p. 1984. 69.95 (*0-387-13789-0*) Spr-Verlag.

Lovesey, Stephen W., jt. auth. see Balcar, Ewald.

Lovesey, Steven W. & Collins, S. P. X-Ray Scattering & Absorption by Magnetic Materials. (Oxford Series on Synchrotron Radiation: No. 1). (Illus.). 390p. 1996. text 135.00 (*0-19-851737-8*) OUP.

***Lovesick, James R.** Fundamentals of Scientific Charge-Coupled Devices. LC 00-36616. 2000. write for info. (*0-8194-3698-4*) SPIE.

Lovesick Lake Native Women's Association Staff. Native Indian Wild Game, Fish & Wild Foods Cookbook: 340 Mouthwatering Recipes from Native Cooks. Hunt, David, ed. 222p. 1992. 24.95 (*1-56523-008-6*) Fox Chapel Pub.

— Native Indian Wild Game, Fish & Wild Foods Cookbook: 340 Mouthwatering Recipes from Native Cooks. 2nd rev. ed. Hunt, David, ed. (Illus.). 222p. 1996. pap. 14.95 (*1-56523-077-9*) Fox Chapel Pub.

Lovestam, Evald. Jesus & "This Generation" A New Testament Study. (Coniectanea Biblica New Testament Ser.: No. 25). 130p. 1995. pap. 37.50 (*91-22-01668-6*) Coronet Bks.

Lovett & Scott. Pasture Production & Management. 1998. 69.95 (*0-909605-85-8*) Buttrwrth-Heinemann.

Lovett, K., jt. auth. see Lever, E.

Lovett, A. W. Early Habsburg Spain, Fifteen Seventeen to Fifteen Ninety-Eight. (Illus.). 300p. 1986. 59.00 (*0-19-822139-8*); pap. 24.95 (*0-19-822138-X*) OUP.

Lovett, Ann. Palimpsest. LC 90-70210. (Illus.). 48p. (Orig.). 1990. pap. 16.95 (*0-89822-064-5*) Visual Studies.

— Relation. (Illus.). 14p. 1999. write for info. (*1-893125-02-5*) Womens Studio Wrkshop.

Lovett, Anthony, jt. auth. see Maranian, Matt.

Lovett, Barbara M. & Lovett, Charles S. Day Care What It's Really Like. (Illus.). 128p. 1997. pap. 6.95 (*0-9661273-0-7*) North Bay Learn.

***Lovett, Bobby L.** The African-American History of Nashville, Tennessee, 1780-1930: Elites & Dilemmas. LC 98-53915. (Black Community Studies). 320p. 1999. 36.00 (*1-55728-555-1*); pap. 18.00 (*1-55728-556-X*) U of Ark Pr.

Lovett, Brian, ed. Wisconsin Hunting: A Comprehensive Guide to Wisconsin's Public Hunting Lands. LC 93-77542. (Illus.). 208p. (Orig.). 1993. pap. 16.95 (*0-87341-249-4*, HW02) Krause Pubns.

Lovett, C. Academics & Career Change. Date not set. write for info. (*0-275-90016-9*, C0016, Praeger Pubs) Greenwood.

Lovett, C. S. C. S. Lovett: Maranatha Man. (Illus.). 1978. pap. 2.95 (*0-938148-02-8*) Prsnl Christianity.

— Census Manual. 1961. pap. 2.95 (*0-938148-18-4*) Prsnl Christianity.

— The Compassionate Side of Divorce. 1975. pap. 7.45 (*0-938148-08-7*) Prsnl Christianity.

— Dealing with the Devil. 1967. pap. 7.45 (*0-938148-05-2*) Prsnl Christianity.

— Death: Graduation to Glory. 1974. pap. 6.25 (*0-938148-20-6*) Prsnl Christianity.

— Dynamic Truths for the Spirit-Filled Life. 1973. pap. 7.95 (*0-938148-13-3*) Prsnl Christianity.

— Help Lord-The Devil Wants Me Fat! (Illus.). (Orig.). 1977. pap. 8.45 (*0-938148-33-8*) Prsnl Christianity.

— It's Your Turn to Be Blessed. (Illus.). 128p. (Orig.). 1985. pap. 6.95 (*0-938148-39-7*) Prsnl Christianity.

— Jesus Is Coming-Get Ready Christian. 1969. pap. 6.95 (*0-938148-04-4*) Prsnl Christianity.

— Jesus Wants You Well. 1973. pap. 8.45 (*0-938148-29-X*) Prsnl Christianity.

— Jogging with Jesus. (Illus.). 1978. pap. 5.45 (*0-938148-34-6*) Prsnl Christianity.

— Latest Word on the Last Days. (Illus.). (Orig.). 1980. pap. 8.95 (*0-938148-00-1*) Prsnl Christianity.

— Let Your Spirit Soar (365 Inspirational Flights) (Illus.). 560p. 1994. pap. 19.95 (*0-938148-47-8*) Prsnl Christianity.

— Longing to Be Loved. 1982. pap. 7.95 (*0-938148-36-2*) Prsnl Christianity.

— Lovett's Lights on Acts. 1972. pap. 8.95 (*0-938148-28-1*) Prsnl Christianity.

— Lovett's Lights on I Corinthians with Gems from II Corinthian. (Illus.). 392p. (Orig.). (C). 1996. pap. 14.95 (*0-938148-48-6*) Prsnl Christianity.

— Lovett's Lights on Galatians, Ephesians, Philippians, Colossians, 1 & 2 Thessalonians. 1970. pap. 7.95 (*0-938148-25-7*) Prsnl Christianity.

— Lovett's Lights on Hebrews. 1976. pap. 8.45 (*0-938148-32-X*) Prsnl Christianity.

— Lovett's Lights on John. 1970. pap. 8.45 (*0-938148-24-9*) Prsnl Christianity.

— Lovett's Lights on Revelation. (Illus.). 352p. 1992. pap. 12.95 (*0-938148-44-3*) Prsnl Christianity.

— Lovett's Lights on Romans. 1975. pap. 8.95 (*0-938148-30-3*) Prsnl Christianity.

— Lovett's Lights on the Sermon on the Mount. 176p. (Orig.). 1985. pap. 7.45 (*0-938148-40-0*) Prsnl Christianity.

— Now Anyone Can . . . Teach Revelation. (Illus.). 128p. 1993. pap., teacher ed. 5.95 (*0-938148-46-X*) Prsnl Christianity.

— The One Hundred Percent Christian. 1970. pap. 6.95 (*0-938148-07-9*) Prsnl Christianity.

— Operation Manhunt Made Easy. 1961. pap. 4.95 (*0-938148-17-6*) Prsnl Christianity.

— Soul-Winning Made Easy. 1978. pap. 6.25 (*0-938148-10-9*) Prsnl Christianity.

— Teach Dynamic Truths. 1973. pap., teacher ed. 7.95 (*0-938148-14-1*) Prsnl Christianity.

— Teach Soul-Winning. 1962. pap., teacher ed. 4.95 (*0-938148-12-5*) Prsnl Christianity.

— Teach Them about Satan. 1970. pap., teacher ed. 7.45 (*0-938148-26-5*) Prsnl Christianity.

— Teach Witnessing. 1966. pap., teacher ed. 7.95 (*0-938148-09-5*) Prsnl Christianity.

— The Thrill of Faith. 1960. pap. 4.95 (*0-938148-21-4*) Prsnl Christianity.

— Unequally Yoked Wives. 1968. pap. 7.45 (*0-938148-22-2*) Prsnl Christianity.

— Visitation Made Easy. 1959. pap. 4.95 (*0-938148-15-X*) Prsnl Christianity.

— What to Do When Your Friends Reject Christ. 1966. pap. 6.25 (*0-938148-06-0*) Prsnl Christianity.

— What's a Parent to Do? 1971. pap. 8.45 (*0-938148-27-3*) Prsnl Christianity.

— Witnessing Made Easy. 1964. pap. 7.95 (*0-938148-01-X*) Prsnl Christianity.

Lovett, Charles. Lewis Carroll & the Press. LC 98-52495. (Illus.). 135p. 1999. text 35.00 (*1-884718-87-6*, R53904) Oak Knoll.

— Olympic Marathon: A Centennial History of the Games' Most Storied Race. LC 96-47618. 192p. 1997. 37.95 (*0-275-95771-3*, Praeger Pubs) Greenwood.

Lovett, Charles, ed. Proceedings of the 2nd International Lewis Carroll Conference. LC 94-73512. (Illus.). 191p. 1994. 25.00 (0-930326-10-5) L Carroll Soc.

Lovett, Charles C. Alice on Stage: A History of the Early Theatrical Productions of Alice in Wonderland. 356p. 1989. lib. bdg. 72.95 (0-313-27681-1, LVS/, Greenwood Pr) Greenwood.

— Alice on Stage: History of the Early Theatrical Productions of Alice in Wonderland, Together with a Checklist of Dramatic Adaptations of Charles Dodgson's Works. LC 89-9248. 239 p. 1990. write for info. (0-88736-390-3) Mecklermedia.

***Lovett, Charles C.** Lewis Carroll & the Press: An Annotated Bibliography of Charles Dodgson's Contributions to Periodicals LC 98-52495. vi, 1117p. 1999. write for info. (0-7123-4627-9, Pub. by B23tish Library) S Asia.

— Love, Ruth: A Son's Memoir. (Illus.). 240p. 1999. pap. 17.00 (0-9672040-4-6) Callanwolde.

Lovett, Charles C. & Lovett, Stephanie B. Lewis Carroll's Alice: An Annotated Checklist of the Lovett Collection, 1965-1986. 565p. 1989. lib. bdg. 89.50 (0-313-27682-X, LLR/) Greenwood.

Lovett, Charles C., et al. Lewis Carroll's Alice: An Annotated Checklist of the Lovett Collection, 1965-1986. LC 89-13494. xvii, 548p. 1990. write for info. (0-88736-166-8) Mecklermedia.

Lovett, Charles C., jt. auth. see Imholtz, August A.

Lovett, Charles C., jt. auth. see Lovett, Robert W.

Lovett, Charles S., jt. auth. see Lovett, Barbara M.

Lovett, Clara M. The Democratic Movement In Italy, Eighteen Thirty to Eighteen Seventy-Six. LC 81-6403. 295p. 1982. 46.50 (0-674-19645-7) HUP.

Lovett, Clara M., jt. ed. see Berkin, Carol R.

Lovett, D. Demonstrating Science with Soap Films. (Illus.). 216p. 1994. 110.00 (0-7503-0270-4); pap. 39.00 (0-7503-0269-0) IOP Pub.

— Tensor Properties of Crystals. 2nd ed. LC 99-51356. 160p. 1999. 34.00 (0-7503-0626-2) IOP Pub.

Lovett, D. R. Tensor Properties of Crystals. LC 88-34757. (Illus.). 152p. reprint ed. pap. 47.20 (0-7837-3927-3, 205791700010) Bks Demand.

Lovett-Doust, Jon & Lovett-Doust, Lesley, eds. Plant Reproductive Ecology: Patterns & Strategies. (Illus.). 360p. (C). 1990. pap. text 33.95 (0-19-506394-5) OUP.

Lovett-Doust, Lesley, jt. ed. see Lovett-Doust, Jon.

Lovett, Etheridge G. Pookies ABC's Coloring Book. (Illus.). 32p. (J). (ps-6). 1998. pap. 3.00 (0-9671805-0-3) Lovett & Brown.

Lovett, Etheridge G. & Pereira, Anthony. The Arrival of the Zumebatuu Year 2050. (Illus.). 350p. (YA). (gr. 6-12). 1998. pap. 20.00 (0-9671805-2-X) Lovett & Brown.

Lovett, Francis N. National Parks & the Common Good: A Communitarian Perspective. LC 97-39380. (Rights & Responsibilities Ser.). 144p. 1998. 53.00 (0-8476-8977-8); pap. 21.95 (0-8476-8978-6) Rowman.

Lovett, Gabriel. The Duke of Rivas. LC 77-5136. (Twayne's World Authors Ser.). 191p. (C). 1977. lib. bdg. 20.95 (0-8057-6289-2) Irvington.

Lovett, Gabriel H. Romantic Spain: Voices from Within, Views from Without. (American University Studies: Romance Languages & Literature: Ser. II, Vol. 74). IX, 247p. (C). 1990. text 43.95 (0-8204-0605-8) P Lang Pubng.

Lovett, Gabriel H., jt. auth. see Martin, Michael R.

Lovett, H. A. Canada & the Grand Trunk, 1829-1924. Bruchey, Stuart, ed. LC 80-1328. (Railroads Ser.). 1981. reprint ed. lib. bdg. 24.95 (0-405-13802-4) Ayer.

Lovett, H. Verney. History of the Indian Nationalist Movement. 303p. 1968. 32.00 (0-7146-2016-5, Pub. by F Cass Pubs) Intl Spec Bk.

— A History of the Indian Nationalist Movement. 3rd ed. LC 79-94540. 303p. 1969. reprint ed. lib. bdg. 39.50 (0-678-05100-3) Kelley.

Lovett, Herbert. Cognitive Counseling & Persons with Special Needs: Adapting Behavioral Approaches to the Social Context. LC 85-3495. 160p. 1985. pap. 19.95 (0-275-91651-0, B1651, Praeger Pubs) Greenwood.

— Learning to Listen: Positive Approaches & People Who Are Difficult to Serve. 224p. 1996. pap. 29.95 (1-85302-374-4) Taylor & Francis.

— Learning to Listen: Positive Approaches & People with Difficult Behavior. 224p. 1996. pap. 27.00 (1-55766-164-2) P H Brookes.

Lovett, James E. Nuclear Materials: Accountability Management Safeguards. LC 74-78611. (ANS Monographs). 310p. 1974. 32.00 (0-89448-001-4, 300007) Am Nuclear Soc.

Lovett, Jennifer G. A Romance with Realism: The Art of Jean-Baptiste Carpeaux. LC 89-60886. (Illus.). 48p. 1989. pap. 12.95 (0-931102-26-X) S & F Clark Art.

Lovett, Jim D., jt. auth. see Branton, James L.

Lovett, Jim D., jt. ed. see Branton, James L.

Lovett, Joan. Small Wonders: Healing Childhood Trauma with EMDR. LC 98-30742. 256p. 1999. 27.95 (0-684-84446-X) S&S Trade.

Lovett, John R., Jr. & DeWitt, Donald L. Guide to Native American Ledger Drawings & Pictographs in United States Museums, Libraries & Archives, 39. LC 98-41033. (Bibliographies & Indexes in American History Ser.: Vol. 39). 160p. 1998. lib. bdg. 55.00 (0-313-30693-1, Greenwood Pr) Greenwood.

Lovett, Keith. Hooked on Ebonics. 1997. pap. text 5.99 (0-9647867-9-6) St Simons Pr.

Lovett, Leonard. Close Your Back Door as You Widen the Front Door of Your Church. LC 98-91607. 168p. 1998. pap. text 11.99 (1-57502-874-3, PO2379) Morris Pubng.

Lovett, Lisetta, jt. auth. see Seedhouse, David.

Lovett, Lois, tr. see Brunel, Philippe.

Lovett, Marc, jt. auth. see Munk, Robert J.

Lovett, Margaret, jt. auth. see Faye, Christine.

Lovett, Martha. Social Studies Teacher's Survival Kit: Ready-to-Use Activities for Teaching Specific Skills. 304p. 1988. pap. text 29.95 (0-87628-782-8) Ctr Appl Res.

Lovett, Maurice. Brewing & Breweries. (Album Ser.: No. 72). (Illus.). 32p. pap. 4.75 (0-7478-0314-5, Pub. by Shire Pubns) Parkwest Pubns.

— Brewing & Breweries. (C). 1989. pap. 30.00 (0-85263-568-0, Pub. by Shire Pubns) St Mut.

Lovett Parent Association, the Lovett School Staff & Lovett School Staff. Cook & Love It. (Illus.). 287p. 1996. spiral bd. 16.95 (0-9610846-3-4) Lovett Sch.

***Lovett, Patricia.** Calligraphy & Illumination: A History & Practical Guide. LC 00-31318. (Illus.). 320p. 2000. 39.95 (0-8109-4119-8, Pub. by Abrams) Time Warner.

Lovett, Patricia. Teach Yourself Calligraphy. (Illus.). 256p. 1994. pap. 11.95 incl. audio (0-8442-3638-1, Teach Yrslf) NTC Contemp Pub Co.

Lovett, Patricia & Watt, Fiona M. Starting Lettering. (First Skills Ser.). (Illus.). 32p. (J). (gr. k-3). 1997. pap. 4.95 (0-7460-2379-0, Usborne); lib. bdg. 12.95 (0-88110-893-6, Usborne) EDC.

Lovett, Patricia, jt. auth. see Watt, Fiona.

Lovett, Richard. The Essential Touring Cyclist: A Complete Course for the Bicycle Traveler. (Illus.). 176p. 1994. pap. 15.95 (0-07-038849-0, Ragged Mntain) McGraw-Hill Prof.

***Lovett, Richard.** Obedience of a Christian Man. 320p. 1999. pap. 60.00 (1-57074-377-0) Greyden Pr.

***Lovett, Richard A.** Essential Touring Cyclist. 2nd ed. (Illus.). 2001. pap. 14.95 (0-07-136019-0) McGraw.

Lovett, Robert M. History of the Novel in England. 1988. reprint.ed. lib. bdg. 59.00 (0-7812-0768-1) Rprt Serv.

— Preface to Fiction: A Discussion of Great Modern Novels. LC 68-16948. (Essay Index Reprint Ser.). 1977. 17.95 (0-8369-0625-X) Ayer.

Lovett, Robert M. & Hughes, Helen S. History of the Novel in England. (Illus.). 1971. reprint ed. 69.00 (0-403-00752-6) Scholarly.

Lovett, Robert W. & Lovett, Charles C. Robinson Crusoe: A Bibliographical Checklist of English Language Editions (1719-1979), 30. LC 87-28952. (Bibliographies & Indexes in World Literature Ser.: No. 30). 328p. 1991. lib. bdg. 65.00 (0-313-27695-1, LRS/, Greenwood Pr) Greenwood.

Lovett, Sarah. Acquired Motives. 1997. mass mkt. 6.99 (0-614-27756-6) Ivy Books.

— Dantes' Inferno. (Dr. Sylvia Strange Novel Ser.: No. 4). 288p. 1999. 23.50 (0-684-85598-4) Simon & Schuster.

— A Desperate Silence: A Novel. 1999. mass mkt. 5.99 (0-8041-1299-1) Ivy Books.

— A Desperate Silence: A Novel. LC 98-21428. 1998. 24.95 (1-57490-152-4) T T Beeler.

— Extremely Weird Animal Defenses. LC 96-40014. (Extremely Weird Ser.). (Illus.). 32p. (J). (gr. 1-6). 1997. pap. 5.95 (1-56261-358-8, J Muir) Avalon Travel.

— Extremely Weird Animal Defenses. (Extremely Weird Ser.). (Illus.). 32p. (J). (gr. 1-5). 1997. lib. bdg. 21.27 (1-884756-32-8) Davidson Titles.

— Extremely Weird Animal Disguises. LC 96-49546. (Extremely Weird Ser.). (Illus.). 32p. (J). (gr. 3-7). 1997. pap. 5.95 (1-56261-357-X, J Muir) Avalon Travel.

— Extremely Weird Animal Disguises. (Extremely Weird Ser.). (Illus.). 32p. (J). (gr. 1-5). 1997. lib. bdg. 21.27 (1-884756-33-6) Davidson Titles.

— Extremely Weird Animal Hunters. LC 96-29847. (Extremely Weird Ser.). (Illus.). 32p. (J). (gr. 3-7). 1997. pap. 5.95 (1-56261-359-6, J Muir) Avalon Travel.

— Extremely Weird Animal Hunters. (Extremely Weird Ser.). (Illus.). 32p. (J). (gr. 1-5). 1997. lib. bdg. 21.27 (1-884756-34-4) Davidson Titles.

— Extremely Weird Bats. (Extremely Weird Ser.). (Illus.). 32p. (J). (gr. 1-5). 1997. lib. bdg. 21.27 (1-884756-25-5) Davidson Titles.

— Extremely Weird Bats. 2nd ed. (Extremely Weird Ser.). (Illus.). 32p. (J). (gr. 4-7). 1996. pap. 5.95 (1-56261-278-6, J Muir) Avalon Travel.

— Extremely Weird Birds. (Extremely Weird Ser.). (Illus.). 32p. (J). (gr. 1-5). 1997. lib. bdg. 21.27 (1-884756-17-4) Davidson Titles.

— Extremely Weird Birds. 2nd ed. LC 96-14769. (Extremely Weird Ser.). (Illus.). 32p. (J). (gr. 1-7). 1996. pap. 5.95 (1-56261-279-4, J Muir) Avalon Travel.

— Extremely Weird Endangered Species. (Extremely Weird Ser.). (Illus.). 32p. (J). (gr. 1-5). 1997. lib. bdg. 21.27 (1-884756-26-3) Davidson Titles.

— Extremely Weird Endangered Species. 2nd ed. LC 95-50827. (Extremely Weird Ser.). (Illus.). 32p. (J). (gr. 1-6). 1995. pap. 5.95 (1-56261-280-8, J Muir) Avalon Travel.

— Extremely Weird Fishes. (Extremely Weird Ser.). (Illus.). 32p. (J). (gr. 1-5). 1997. lib. bdg. 21.27 (1-884756-27-1) Davidson Titles.

— Extremely Weird Fishes. 2nd ed. LC 95-50829. (Extremely Weird Ser.). (Illus.). 32p. (J). (gr. 4-7). 1995. pap. 5.95 (1-56261-281-6, J Muir) Avalon Travel.

— Extremely Weird Frogs. (Extremely Weird Ser.). (Illus.). 32p. (J). (gr. 1-5). 1997. lib. bdg. 21.27 (1-884756-28-X) Davidson Titles.

— Extremely Weird Frogs. 2nd ed. LC 95-50830. (Extremely Weird Ser.). (Illus.). 32p. (J). (gr. 4-7). 1996. pap. 6.95 (1-56261-282-4, J Muir) Avalon Travel.

— Extremely Weird Insects. (Extremely Weird Ser.). (Illus.). 32p. (J). (gr. 1-5). 1997. lib. bdg. 21.27 (1-884756-18-2) Davidson Titles.

— Extremely Weird Insects. 2nd ed. LC 96-14770. (Extremely Weird Ser.). (Illus.). 32p. (YA). (gr. 4-7). 1996. pap. 6.95 (1-56261-283-2, J Muir) Avalon Travel.

— Extremely Weird Mammals. (Extremely Weird Ser.). (Illus.). 32p. (J). (gr. 1-5). 1997. lib. bdg. 21.27 (1-884756-19-0) Davidson Titles.

— Extremely Weird Micro Monsters. (Extremely Weird Ser.). (Illus.). 32p. (J). (gr. 1-5). 1997. lib. bdg. 21.27 (1-884756-20-4) Davidson Titles.

— Extremely Weird Micro Monsters. 2nd ed. LC 96-14766. (Extremely Weird Ser.). (Illus.). 32p. (J). 1996. pap. 5.95 (1-56261-293-X, J Muir) Avalon Travel.

— Extremely Weird Primates. (Extremely Weird Ser.). (Illus.). 32p. (J). (gr. 1-5). 1997. lib. bdg. 21.27 (1-884756-21-2) Davidson Titles.

— Extremely Weird Primates. 2nd rev. ed. LC 96-14772. (Extremely Weird Ser.). (Illus.). 32p. (J). (gr. 4-7). 1995. pap. 5.95 (1-56261-285-9, J Muir) Avalon Travel.

— Extremely Weird Reptiles. (Extremely Weird Ser.). (Illus.). 32p. (J). (gr. 1-5). 1997. lib. bdg. 21.27 (1-884756-29-8) Davidson Titles.

— Extremely Weird Reptiles. 2nd rev. ed. LC 95-50828. (Extremely Weird Ser.). (Illus.). 32p. (J). (gr. 1-7). 1995. pap. 5.95 (1-56261-286-7, J Muir) Avalon Travel.

— Extremely Weird Sea Creatures. (Extremely Weird Ser.). (Illus.). 32p. (J). (gr. 1-5). 1997. lib. bdg. 21.27 (1-884756-22-0) Davidson Titles.

— Extremely Weird Sea Creatures. 2nd rev. ed. LC 96-14767. (Extremely Weird Ser.). (Illus.). 32p. (J). (gr. 4-7). 1996. pap. 5.95 (1-56261-287-5, J Muir) Avalon Travel.

— Extremely Weird Snakes. (Extremely Weird Ser.). (Illus.). 32p. (J). (gr. 1-5). 1997. lib. bdg. 21.27 (1-884756-23-9) Davidson Titles.

— Extremely Weird Snakes. 2nd ed. LC 96-14768. (Extremely Weird Ser.). (Illus.). 32p. (J). (gr. 4-7). 1995. pap. 6.95 (1-56261-288-3, J Muir) Avalon Travel.

— Extremely Weird Spiders. (Extremely Weird Ser.). (Illus.). 32p. (J). (gr. 1-5). 1997. lib. bdg. 21.27 (1-884756-30-1) Davidson Titles.

— Extremely Weird Spiders. 2nd ed. LC 95-50831. (Extremely Weird Ser.). (Illus.). 32p. (J). (gr. 1-6). 1995. pap. 5.95 (1-56261-289-1, J Muir) Avalon Travel.

— Unique Colorado: A Guide to the State's Quirks, Charisma & Character. LC 93-13452. (Unique Travel Ser.). (Illus.). 112p. 1993. pap. 10.95 (1-56261-103-8) Avalon Travel.

— Unique Florida: A Guide to the State's Quirks, Charisma & Character. LC 93-3232. (Unique Travel Ser.). (Illus.). 112p. 1993. pap. 10.95 (1-56261-104-6) Avalon Travel.

— Unique New England: A Guide to the Region's Quirks, Charisma, & Character. LC 93-32352. (Unique Travel Ser.). (Illus.). 112p. 1994. pap. 10.95 (1-56261-146-1) Avalon Travel.

— Unique New Mexico: A Guide to the State's Quirks, Charisma & Character. LC 93-3003. (Unique Travel Ser.). (Illus.). 112p. 1993. pap. 10.95 (1-56261-102-X) Avalon Travel.

— Unique Texas: A Guide to the State's Quirks, Charisma, & Character. LC 93-30384. (Unique Travel Ser.). (Illus.). 112p. 1994. pap. 10.95 (1-56261-145-3) Avalon Travel.

Lovett, Sarah, text. Extremely Weird Mammals. 2nd ed. LC 96-14771. (Extremely Weird Ser.). (Illus.). 32p. (J). (gr. 4-7). 1996. pap. 5.95 (1-56261-284-0, J Muir) Avalon Travel.

Lovett School Staff, jt. auth. see Lovett Parent Association, the Lovett School Staff.

Lovett, Sean-Patrick, ed. see Mother Teresa of Calcutta.

Lovett Staff. Cook & Love It More. 1989. pap. 14.95 (0-9610846-2-6) Lovett Sch.

Lovett, Stephanie B., jt. auth. see Lovett, Charles C.

Lovett, Steven R. California Partnership Handbook, 2 vols. 2nd rev. ed. 520p. 1984. pap. text 51.50 (0-89074-090-9) Lega Bks.

Lovett, Steven R., jt. auth. see Faber, Stuart J.

Lovett, T. Adult Education, Community Development & the Working Class. 176p. (C). 1982. text 60.00 (0-7855-6020-3, Pub. by Univ Nottingham) St Mut.

Lovett, Terrin, ed. IT Cost Management Sorucebook: The Up-to-Date Financial Guide to IT Equipment Acquisiton & Control of IT Expenses. 1500p. Date not set. ring bd. 2500.00 (0-945052-29-4) Computer Econ.

Lovett, Tom, ed. Adult Education, Community Development & the Working Class. (C). 1982. 35.00 (0-902031-84-8, Pub. by Univ Nottingham) St Mut.

Lovett, William A. Banking & Financial Institutions Law in a Nutshell. 3rd ed. LC 92-18870. (Nutshell Ser.). 470p. (C). 1992. pap. text 18.00 (0-314-00929-9) West Pub.

— Banking & Financial Institutions Law in a Nutshell. 4th ed. LC 96-46013. (Nutshell Ser.). 461p. (C). 1996. pap. 22.95 (0-314-20590-X) West Pub.

Lovett, William A., ed. United States Shipping Policies & the World Market. LC 95-37483. 344p. 1996. 80.00 (0-89930-945-3, Quorum Bks) Greenwood.

Lovett, William A., et al. U. S. Trade Policy: History, Theory & the WTO. LC 98-26369. (Illus.). 240p. (gr. 13). 1999. text 62.95 (0-7656-0323-3); pap. text 26.95 (0-7656-0324-1) M E Sharpe.

***Lovette, Ed & Spaulding, Dave.** Defensive Living: Attitudes, Tactics & Proper Handgun Use to Secure Your Personal Well-Being. LC 99-88411. (Illus.). 100p. 2000. pap. 11.95 (1-889031-26-7) Looseleaf Law.

***Lovette, Kay.** Caring for an Alzheimer's Patient at Home. LC 99-36202. (Illus.). 200p. 1999. pap. 14.95 (1-885987-16-1, ME092, Health Info Pr) Practice Mgmt Info.

Lovette, Lance, jt. auth. see Brain, Marshall.

Lovey, Jane. Supporting Special Educational Needs in Secondary School Classrooms. (Roehampton Teaching Studies). 160p. 1995. pap. 24.95 (1-85346-339-6, Pub. by David Fulton) Taylor & Francis.

— Teaching Troubled & Troublesome Adolescents. 128p. 1992. pap. 24.95 (1-85346-194-6, Pub. by David Fulton) Taylor & Francis.

***Lovgren, Gosta H.** The Ponder's Bible: All You Need to Know to Build Your Own Pond. (Illus.). 177p. 2000. pap. 14.95 (1-929741-08-1) Carolelle.

Lovgren, Hakan, ed. Eisenstein's Labyrinth: Aspects of a Cinematic Synthesis of the Arts. LC 96-223540. (Stockholm Studies in Russian Literature: No. 31). (Illus.). 139p. 1996. pap. 39.50 (91-22-01729-1) Coronet Bks.

Lovgren, Hakan, jt. ed. see Kleberg, Lars.

Lovgren, Torbjorn, jt. auth. see Falck-Ytter, Harald.

Lovi, jt. auth. see Tirion, Wil.

Lovi, George. Sky & Telescope Monthly Star Charts: 24 All-Sky Charts for Star Watchers Worldwide. (Illus.). 56p. 1994. spiral bd. 24.95 (0-933346-69-7) Sky Pub.

***Lovibond, Sabina & Williams, S. G., eds.** Identity, Truth & Value: Essays for David Wiggins. (Aristotelian Society Monographs: Vol. 16). 304p. 1999. pap. text 27.95 (0-631-22068-2, Pub. by Blackwell Pubs) Blackwell Pubs.

Lovie, A. D. & Mosteller, Frederick, eds. New Developments in Statistics for Psychology & the Social Sciences. 200p. 1986. 57.50 (0-901715-46-8, 1020, Pub. by Brit Psychol Soc) Routledge.

Lovie, A. D., et al. New Developments in Statistics for Psychology & the Social Sciences. 2nd ed. 256p. (C). 1992. text 70.00 (1-85433-017-9, A5028, Pub. by Brit Psychol Soc) Routledge.

Lovie-Kitchin, Jan E. & Bowman, Ken. Age-Related Macular Degeneration: Management & Rehabilitation. 1996. 50.00 (0-7506-9684-2) Buttrwrth-Heinemann.

Lovik, Thomas, et al. Vorsprung: An Introduction to German Language & Culture for Communication. (GER.). 576p. (C). 1996. text 61.16 (0-395-74557-8) HM.

— Vorsprung: An Introduction to German Language & Culture for Communication. (GER.). (C). 1996. pap. text, wbk. ed., lab manual ed. 30.36 (0-395-74560-8) HM.

— Vorsprung: An Introduction to German Language & Culture for Communication. annot. ed. (GER.). (C). 1996. text, teacher ed. 62.36 (0-395-74559-4) HM.

Lovil, Thomas M., jt. auth. see Young, Michael B.

Lovill, J. E., jt. ed. see McCormick, Patrick M.

Lovin-Boyd, Stacy, jt. auth. see Jackson, Janet.

Lovin, Clifford R. A School for Diplomats: The Paris Peace Conference of 1919. LC 97-9796. 182p. 1997. 32.50 (0-7618-0755-1) U Pr of Amer.

Lovin, Hugh T. Labor in the West. (Illus.). 88p. 1986. pap. text 15.00 (0-89745-090-6) Sunflower U Pr.

Lovin, Robin W. Reinhold Niebuhr & Christian Realism. 265p. (C). 1995. pap. text 22.95 (0-521-47932-0) Cambridge U Pr.

Lovin, Robin W. & Reynolds, Frank E., eds. Cosmogony & Ethical Order: New Studies in Comparative Ethics. LC 85-1159. viii, 448p. 1993. pap. text 19.95 (0-226-49417-9) U Ch Pr.

— Cosmogony & Ethical Order: New Studies in Comparative Ethics. LC 85-1159. viii, 448p. 1996. lib. bdg. 66.00 (0-226-49416-0) U Ch Pr.

Loving, Aretta H. Slices of Life: From the Plate of a Bible Translator. LC 98-60322. (Illus.). 240p. 1998. pap. 9.95 (1-57921-108-9) WinePress Pub.

***Loving, Aretta H.** Slices of Life: Stories & Devotions from a Bible Translator. Orig. Title: Slices of Life from the Plate of a Bible Translator. 208p. 2000. pap. 9.99 (1-57658-200-0) YWAM Pub.

Loving, Bill. JMC 2033 Lab Manual. 120p. (C). 1996. pap. text, spiral bd. 14.95 (0-7872-2664-5) Kendall-Hunt.

***Loving, Bill.** JMC 2033 Lab Manual. 2nd ed. 90p. (C). 1999. 24.95 (0-7872-6000-2, 41600001) Kendall-Hunt.

Loving, Carol. My Son, My Sorrow: The Tragic Tale of Dr. Kevorkian's Youngest Patient. LC 97-66563. (Illus.). 300p. 1998. 22.95 (0-88282-161-X) New Horizon NJ.

Loving, David W. & University Publications of America (Firm). Civil Rights During the Nixon Administration, 1969-1974. LC 91-15726. (Black Studies Research Sources). 1989. write for info. (1-55655-133-9) U Pubns Amer.

Loving, Jean. Massage Therapy: Theory & Practice. LC 98-3419. 300p. 1998. pap. text 42.95 (0-8385-6161-6) Appleton & Lange.

Loving, Jerome. Lost in the Customhouse: Authorship in the American Renaissance. LC 92-33051. 268p. 1993. text 36.95 (0-87745-404-3) U of Iowa Pr.

Loving, Jerome. Walt Whitman: The Song of Himself. LC 98-29647. 595p. 1999. 35.00 (0-520-21427-7, Pub. by U CA Pr) Cal Prin Full Svc.

***Loving, Jerome.** Walt Whitman: The Song of Himself. (Illus.). 582p. 2000. pap. 18.95 (0-520-22687-9) U CA Pr.

Loving, Jerome, ed. see Norris, Frank.

Loving, Jerome, ed. & intro. see Norris, Frank.

Loving, Jerome, ed. & intro. see Whitman, Walt.

Loving, Jerome M., ed. see Whitman, George.

Loving, Laura, jt. auth. see Payden, Deborah A.

Loving, Nancy J. Along the Rim: A Road Guide to the South Rim of Grand Canyon. (Illus.). 52p. 1981. pap. 4.95 (0-938216-13-9) GCA.

Loving, Nancy S. Conformation & Performance: A Guide for Buyers & Trainers. 1997. spiral bd. 39.95 (0-914327-75-5) Breakthrgh NY.

— Go the Distance: The Complete Resource for Endurance Horses. LC 97-17545. (Illus.). 264p. 1998. 26.00 (1-57076-044-6, Trafalgar Sq Pub) Trafalgar.

— Veterinary Manual for the Performance Horse. Wagoner, Don M., ed. (Illus.). 608p. (C). 1993. text 75.00 (0-935842-06-3) Equine Res.

Loving, Neal V. Loving's Love: A Black American's Experience in Aviation. LC 93-24418. (History of Aviation Ser.). (Illus.). 304p. 1994. 29.95 (1-56098-342-6) Smithsonian.

Lovinger, David M., jt. ed. see Dunwiddie, Thomas V.

***Lovinger, Paul W.** The Penguin Dictionary of American English Usage & Style: A Readable Reference Book, Illuminating Thousands of Traps That Snare Writers & Speakers. LC 99-53704. 2000. 40.00 (*0-670-89166-5*) Penguin Putnam.

Lovinger, Robert J. Working with Religious Issues in Therapy. LC 84-6198. 328p. 1984. 50.00 (*0-87668-727-3*) Aronson.

Lovinger, Robert L., jt. auth. see Lovinger, Sophie L.

Lovinger, Sophie L. & Lovinger, Robert L. Child Psychotherapy: From Initial Therapeutic Contact to Termination. LC 97-10296. 232p. 1998. 45.00 (*0-7657-0084-0*) Aronson.

Lovinggood, Penman. Famous Modern Negro Musicians. LC 77-22215. (Music Reprint Ser.). (Illus.). 1978. reprint ed. lib. bdg. 19.50 (*0-306-77523-9*) Da Capo.

Lovingood, Paul & Reiman, Robert. Emerging Patterns in the Southern Highlands: A Reference Atlas: Introduction, Vol. I. (Emerging Patterns in the Southern Highlands Ser.). (Illus.). 163p. (Orig.). (C). 1985. reprint ed. pap. text 6.95 (*0-913239-36-4*) Appalach Consortium.

— Emerging Patterns in the Southern Highlands: Agriculture, Vol. II. Crutchfield, Malinda, ed. (Emerging Patterns in the Southern Highlands Ser.). (Illus.). 163p. (Orig.). (C). 1987. pap. text 6.95 (*0-913239-46-1*) Appalach Consortium.

— Emerging Patterns in the Southern Highlands: Health Care, Vol. III. Buxton, Barry, ed. (Emerging Patterns in the Southern Highlands Ser.). (Illus.). 270p. (Orig.). (C). 1987. pap. text 6.95 (*0-614-06599-2*) Appalach Consortium.

Lovingood, Paul, et al. Emerging Patterns in the Southern Highlands: Business Patterns, Vol. IV. (Illus.). 326p. (Orig.). pap. 11.95 (*0-913239-54-2*) Appalach Consortium.

Lovingood, Sut, ed. see Lifshin, Lyn, et al.

Lovink, H. J. & Pine, L. A., eds. The Hydrocarbon Chemistry of FCC Naphtha Formation: Proceedings, Symposium of the Division of Petroleum Chemistry, Inc., American Chemical Society, Miami, 1989. (Illus.). 256p. (C). 1990. 540.00 (*2-7108-0588-X*, Pub. by Edits Technip) Enfield Pubs NH.

***Lovins, Amory & Lovins, Hunter.** Beyond Backyard Environmentalism. 2000. pap. 13.00 (*0-8070-0445-6*) Beacon Pr.

Lovins, Amory B. Openpit Mining. (Earth Island Ser.). 1973. pap. 1.75 (*0-85644-020-5*) Friends of Earth.

Lovins, Hunter, jt. auth. see Lovins, Amory.

Loviny, Christophe. Che: A Photobiography of Che Guevara. LC 98-2882. (Illus.). 128p. 1998. pap. 15.95 (*1-56025-187-5*, Thunders Mouth) Avalon NY.

Lovis, F. B. & Tagg, E. D., eds. Informatics Education for All Students at University Level. 226p. 1984. 54.50 (*0-444-86807-0*, North Holland) Elsevier.

Lovis, William A., ed. see Anderson, Margaret U., et al.

Lovis, William A., ed. see Cleland, Nancy N., et al.

Loviscek, Anthony L., et al. West Virginia Input-Output Study, 1975: Modeling a Regional Economy. 37p. 1979. pap. 5.95 (*0-930284-01-1*) West Va U Pr.

***Lovisi, Gary.** Blood in Brooklyn. 188p. (Orig.). 1999. pap. 15.95 (*1-899344-48-9*, Pub. by Do-Not Pr) Dufour.

Lovisi, Gary. Extreme Measures: Stories of Murder, Mystery, Mayhem & Madness. 161p. 1995. pap. 15.00 (*0-936071-61-3*) Gryphon Pubns.

— The Gargoyle. (Illus.). 56p. (Orig.). 1988. 5.00 (*0-936071-12-5*) Gryphon Pubns.

— Hellbent on Homicide. LC 97-210549. (Bloodlines Ser.). 140p. 1997. pap. 14.95 (*1-899344-18-7*, Pub. by Do-Not Pr) Dufour.

— The Nemesis. (Illus.). 56p. (Orig.). 1988. 4.00 (*0-936071-10-9*) Gryphon Pubns.

— Relics of Sherlock Holmes. 2nd ed. (Illus.). 52p. (Orig.). 1989. reprint ed. 4.00 (*0-936071-16-8*) Gryphon Pubns.

— The Saga of Filster Stein. (Illus.). 52p. (Orig.). 1988. 4.00 (*0-936071-07-9*) Gryphon Pubns.

— Sarasha: A Novel of the Future. LC 98-139855. (Illus.). 208p. 1997. pap. 15.00 (*0-936071-82-6*) Gryphon Pubns.

— Science Fiction Detective Tales: A Brief Overview of Futuristic Detective Fiction in Paperback. (Illus.). 107p. (Orig.). 1986. pap. 7.95 (*0-936071-01-X*) Gryphon Pubns.

Lovisi, Gary & Arnone, Terry. The Woman in the Dugout: The Story of the Brooklyn Kings. 100p. 1992. pap. 9.95 (*0-936071-29-X*) Gryphon Pubns.

Lovisi, Gary & Corrick, James A. Double Your Pleasure: The Ace Science Fiction Double. 2nd ed. (Illus.). 88p. 1991. pap. text 6.95 (*0-936071-21-4*) Gryphon Pubns.

Lovisi, Gary & Reasoner, James. Minesweeper & Terran Girls Make Wonderful Wives. (Gryphon Double Novel Ser.: No. 8). 1995. per. 12.00 (*0-936071-40-0*) Gryphon Pubns.

Lovisi, Gary, jt. auth. see Black, Mike.

Lovisi, Gary, jt. auth. see Smith, P.

Lovisi, Gary, ed. see Dolphin, Jack & Fitzgerald, Ted.

Lovisi, Gary, ed. see Kuttner, Henry.

Lovisi, Gary, ed. see Vaughan, Ralph E.

***Lovisolo, Carlo & Pesando, Paolo.** The Implantable Contact Lens & Other Phakic IOLs. 386p. 1999. text. write for info. (*88-87333-12-2*, Pub. by Fabiano) SLACK Inc.

Lovitt. Math's Problem Solving & Modelling. (UM - International Math Ser.). 1991. text 47.95 (*0-538-62776-X*) S-W Pub.

— Maths Problem Solving & Modelling. (Um - International Math Ser.). 1991. text 38.95 (*0-538-62777-8*) S-W Pub.

***Lovitt & Jones.** Chemical Engineering, Vol.5. 4th ed. 2000. pap. text 56.95 (*0-7506-4141-X*) Buttrwrth-Heinemann.

Lovitt & Lowe. Change & Data Investigations, Vol. 2. 212p. 1994. pap. text 35.00 (*1-86366-162-X*, 00779) Heinemann.

Lovitt, Carl R. & Goswami, Dixie, eds. Exploring the Rhetoric of International Professional Communication: An Agenda for Teachers & Researchers. LC 98-44883. (Technical Communications Ser.). 336p. 1999. text 49.95 (*0-89503-191-4*) Baywood Pub.

Lovitt, Charles & Lowe, Ian. Chance & Data Investigations, Vol. 1. 218p. 1994. pap. text 35.00 (*1-86366-137-9*, 00777) Heinemann.

Lovitt, Chip. American Gymnasts: Gold Medal Dreams. (J). mass mkt. 4.99 (*0-671-78545-1*, Archway) PB.

Lovitt, Chip. The Flamingos Are Tickled Pink: A Book of Idioms. (Illus.). 32p. (J). (ps-2). 1995. 12.95 (*0-7868-3036-0*, Pub. by Disney Pr) Time Warner.

— Michael Jordan. (Scholastic Biography Ser.). 1996. 9.09 (*0-606-09610-8*, Pub. by Turtleback) Demco.

— Michael Jordan. 2nd rev. ed. LC 99-160139. (Scholastic Biography Ser.). (Illus.). 213p. (YA). (gr. 4-9). 1998. pap. 4.50 (*0-590-59644-6*) Scholastic Inc.

***Lovitt, Chip.** Michael Jordan. 3rd ed. 1999. mass mkt. 4.50 (*0-439-12961-3*) Scholastic Inc.

Lovitt, Chip. Michael Jordon. rev. ed. 128p. (J). (gr. 3-9). 1995. pap. 3.50 (*0-590-65174-9*) Scholastic Inc.

— Rock On! The Great Rock & Roll Activity Book. (J). (gr. 5-7). 1990. pap. 2.50 (*0-590-42973-6*) Scholastic Inc.

— Sharing. LC 98-48387. (Doing the Right Thing Ser.). 32p. 1999. lib. bdg. write for info. (*1-55916-236-8*) Rourke Bk Co.

— Skating for the Gold: Michelle Kwan & Tara Lipinski. (J). (gr. 5 up). 1997. per. 3.99 (*0-671-01679-2*) PB.

— Skating for the Gold, Tara Lipinski & Michelle Kwan. 1997. 9.09 (*0-606-12811-5*, Pub. by Turtleback) Demco.

— The Ultimate Disney Joke Book. LC 94-71693. (Illus.). 64p. (J). (gr. 4-7). 1995. pap. 3.50 (*0-7868-4022-6*, Pub. by Disney Pr) Little.

Lovitt, Harriet B., jt. auth. see Lovitt, William.

Lovitt, Joe. Body Language. 1995. pap. 8.99 (*0-8341-9435-X*, MP-765) Nazarene.

Lovitt, Thomas C. Preventing School Dropouts: Tactics for At-Risk, Remedial, & Mildly Handicapped Adolescents. LC 90-27493. 509p. 1991. pap. text 38.00 (*0-89079-454-5*, 1998) PRO-ED.

Lovitt, Thomas C. Tactics for Teaching. 2nd ed. (Illus.). 352p. (C). 1994. pap. text 60.00 (*0-02-371813-7*, Macmillan Coll) P-H.

Lovitt, Thomas C., jt. auth. see Goodlad, John I.

Lovitt, William & Lovitt, Harriet B. Modern Technology in the Heideggerian Perspective. LC 95-1886. (Problems in Contemporary Philosophy Ser.: Vol. 17a). 1995. write for info. (*0-88946-345-X*) E Mellen.

— Modern Technology in the Heideggerian Perspective. LC 95-1886. (Problems in Contemporary Philosophy Ser.: Vol. 17b). 1995. write for info. (*0-88946-269-0*) E Mellen.

Lovitt, William, tr. see Heidegger, Martin.

Lovka, Bob. Cats Rule: All the Rules, Laws, Wisdom & Witticism That Go Along with Being a Cat. LC 98-39296. (Illus.). 128p. 2000. pap. 12.95 (*1-889540-31-5*) Bowtie Press.

— Dogs Rule! The Rules, Wisdom, & Witticisms That Go along with Being a Dog. LC 98-39297. (Illus.). 128p. 2000. pap. 12.95 (*1-889540-32-3*) Bowtie Press.

— The Splendid Little Book of All Things Cat. LC 97-32165. (Illus.). 112p. 1998. pap. 12.95 (*1-889540-28-5*) Bowtie Press.

— The Splendid Little book of All Things Dog. LC 97-32161. (Illus.). 112p. 1998. pap. 12.95 (*1-889540-27-7*) Bowtie Press.

***Lovka, Robert.** Twins 2001 Desk Calendar. 640p. 2000. pap. 10.99 (*0-8431-7579-6*) Peng Put Young Read.

***Lovley, Derek, ed.** Environmental Microbe-Metal Interactions. (Illus.). 380p. 2000. 105.95 (*1-55581-195-7*) ASM Pr.

Lovoi, Joseph W. Listen - My Children: (So It Can't Happen Again) unabridged ed. LC 96-94410. (Illus.). 200p. 1996. 9.50 (*0-9652646-0-2*) J W Lovoi.

***Lovoi, Joseph W.** Listen, My Children -- So It Can't Happen Again. 2000. 17.95 (*0-533-13225-8*) Vantage.

Lovold, Lars & Kuspit, Donald. Xingu Chronicles: Per Fronth. (Illus.). 1998. 20.00 (*0-9648340-6-5*) Dillon Gallery.

Lovold, S. & Mullin, B., eds. Narrow Gap Semiconductors: Proceedings of the NATO Workshop, 25-27 June 1991, Oslo, Norway. (Illus.). 144p. 1992. 218.00 (*0-7503-0158-9*) IOP Pub.

Lovoll, Odd S., ed. see Shaw, Joseph M.

Lovoll, Odd Sverre. A Century of Urban Life: The Norwegians in Chicago Before 1930. (Illus.). 384p. 1988. 30.00 (*0-87732-075-6*) Norwegian-Am Hist Assn.

— A Folk Epic: The Bygdelag in America. LC 74-18430. (Illus.). 342p. reprint ed. pap. 106.10 (*0-608-15593-4*, 202966500062) Bks Demand.

— The Promise of America: A History of the Norwegian-American People. LC 83-27350. (Illus.). 248p. 1984. pap. 17.95 (*0-8166-1334-6*) U of Minn Pr.

***Lovoll, Odd Sverre.** The Promise of America: A History of the Norwegian-American People. LC 99-10492. 1999. pap. write for info. (*0-8166-3350-9*) U of Minn Pr.

Lovoll, Odd Sverre, ed. Cultural Pluralism versus Assimilation: The Views of Waldemar Ager. (Topical Studies: Vol. 2). 236p. 1977. 15.00 (*0-87732-059-4*) Norwegian-Am Hist Assn.

***Lovoll, Odd Sverre, ed.** Norwegian-American Studies. (Illus.). 404p. 2000. 20.00 (*0-87732-089-6*) Norwegian-Am Hist Assn.

Lovoll, Odd Sverre, ed. Norwegian-American Studies, Vol. 29. 402p. 1983. 15.00 (*0-87732-068-3*) Norwegian-Am Hist Assn.

— Norwegian-American Studies, Vol. 31. (Illus.). 346p. 1986. 18.00 (*0-87732-072-1*) Norwegian-Am Hist Assn.

— Norwegian-American Studies, Vol. 32. (Illus.). 297p. 1989. 18.00 (*0-87732-076-4*) Norwegian-Am Hist Assn.

— Norwegian-American Studies, Vol. 33. (Studies & Records). 370p. 1992. 18.00 (*0-87732-080-2*) Norwegian-Am Hist Assn.

— Norwegian-American Studies, Vol. 34. (Illus.). 360p. 1995. 20.00 (*0-87732-084-5*) Norwegian-Am Hist Assn.

Lovoll, Odd Sverre, intro. Nordics in America: The Future of Their Past. (Special Publications). (Illus.). 228p. 1993. 20.00 (*0-87732-081-0*) Norwegian-Am Hist Assn.

Lovoll, Odd Sverre & Bjork, Kenneth O. The Norwegian-American Historical Association. LC 75-15444. 80p. 1975. pap. 30.00 (*0-608-04840-2*, 206549700004) Bks Demand.

Lovoll, Odd Sverre & Norwegian-American Historical Association. The Promise Fulfilled: A Portrait of Norwegian Americans Today. LC 98-4000. 352p. 1998. 29.95 (*0-8166-2832-7*); pap. write for info. (*0-8166-2833-5*) U of Minn Pr.

Lovoll, Odd Sverre, jt. auth. see Clausen, C. A.

Lovoll, Odd Sverre, jt. auth. see Leiren, Terje I.

Lovoll, Odd Sverre, jt. auth. see Soike, Lowell J.

Lovoll, Odd Sverre, ed. see Chrislock, Carl.

Lovoll, Odd Sverre, ed. see Naess, Harald S. & Stafford, Kate.

Lovoll, Odd Sverre, ed. see Overland, Orm.

Lovoll, Odd Sverre, ed. see Rolvaag, Ole Edvart.

Lovoll, Odd Sverre, ed. & frwd. see Gieske, Millard & Keillor, Steven.

Lovoos, Janice & McClelland, Gordon. Phil Dike. (Illus.). 64p. 1989. 27.50 (*0-914589-03-2*) Hillcrest Pr.

Lovorn, Tom. How to Build a Praying Church. Spear, Cindy G. & Johnson, Tamara, eds. 63p. (Orig.). 1992. pap. 2.19 (*0-941005-85-2*); ring bd. 89.95 (*0-941005-49-6*) Chrch Grwth VA.

Lovret, Fredrick J. The Way & the Power: Secrets of Japanese Strategy. (Illus.). 328p. 1987. pap. 30.00 (*0-87364-409-3*) Paladin Pr.

***Lovric, Michelle.** How to Write Love Letters. (Illus.). 96p. 2000. reprint ed. 15.00 (*0-7881-9327-9*) DIANE Pub.

Lovric, Michelle. Victorian Card Kit. 1996. pap. text 9.95 (*1-55670-477-1*) Stewart Tabori & Chang.

— Woman to Woman: Letters to Mothers, Sisters, Daughters & Friends: An Anthology. LC 98-84697. (Illus.). 48p. 1998. 22.95 (*0-8362-6836-9*) Andrews & McMeel.

Lovric, Michelle, compiled by. Bleeding Hearts: Love Poems for the Nervous & Highly Strung. LC 98-51961. 128p. 1998. text 14.95 (*0-312-19168-5*) St Martin.

***Lovric, Michelle & Balia, Mimma.** Ruskin's Rose: A Venetian Love Story. LC 98-46997. (Illus.). 96p. 2000. 20.00 (*1-57965-137-2*) Artisan.

Lovric, Michelle & Mardas, Nikiforos D. The Sweetness of Honey & the Sting of Bees: A Book of Love. 96p. 1997. 14.95 (*1-55670-680-4*) Stewart Tabori & Chang.

Lovric, Michelle, jt. auth. see Philo, Maggie.

Lovric, Miroslav, ed. see Besson, Gerard, et al.

Lovrich, Frank M. The Social System of a Rural Yugoslav-American Community-Oysterville. LC 79-155329. 1963. pap. 10.00 (*0-88247-119-8*) Ragusan Pr.

Lovrich, Nicholas P. Yugoslavs & Italians in San Pedro: Political Culture & Civic Involvement. LC 77-75809. 173p. 1977. pap. 10.00 (*0-918660-01-7*) Ragusan Pr.

Lovrick, Peter. Chinese Opera: Images & Stories. LC 96-39595. (CHI., Illus.). 160p. 1997. reprint ed. 50.00 (*0-295-97610-1*) U of Wash Pr.

***Lovrien, Peggy.** The Liturgical Music Answer Book. LC 99-27873. (101 Most-Asked Questions Ser.). 160p. 1999. 14.95 (*0-89390-454-6*) Resource Pubns.

Lovrinic, Jean H., jt. auth. see Durrant, John D.

Lovtrup, Soren. Darwinism: The Refutation of a Myth. 480p. 1987. lib. bdg. 85.00 (*0-7099-4153-6*, Pub. by C Helm) Routldge.

Lovullo, Sam & Eliot, Marc. Life in the Kornfield: My 25 Years at Hee Haw. LC 97-117524. (Illus.). 288p. (Orig.). 1996. pap. 15.00 (*1-57297-028-6*) Blvd Books.

Lovy, Charles W., see Diez, Klemens, pseud.

Low. Atlas Testing Program. (Global ESL/ELT Ser.). (J). 1996. mass mkt. 36.00 (*0-8384-5684-7*) Heinle & Heinle.

— Criminal Law. 2nd ed. Date not set. pap. text, teacher ed. write for info. (*0-88277-353-4*) West Pub.

— Pop This a Behind the Scenes Look at the Best of Pop Up Video. 1999. pap. 18.00 (*0-671-02724-7*) S&S Trade.

Low, Adrian A. Introductory Computer Vision & Image Processing. 1991. pap. 29.95 (*0-07-707403-3*) McGraw-Hill Prof.

Low, A. M., jt. auth. see Haugum, J.

Low, Abraham A. Manage Your Fears, Manage Your Anger: A Psychiatrist Speaks. LC 95-60989. 472p. 1995. 20.00 (*0-915005-05-0*) Willett Pub Co.

— Mental Health Through Will-Training: A System of Self Help in Psychotherapy As Practiced by Recovery, Incorporated. 3rd ed. LC 97-60039. 448p. (C). 1997. reprint ed. text 20.00 (*0-915005-06-9*) Willett Pub Co.

— Mental Illness, Stigma & Self-Help: The Founding of Recovery, Inc. 174p. 1991. reprint ed. 20.00 (*0-915005-04-2*) Willett Pub Co.

— Peace Versus Power in the Family: Domestic Discord & Emotional Distress. LC 84-51729. 197p. 1984. reprint ed. 20.00 (*0-915005-03-4*) Willett Pub Co.

Low, Aik M., jt. auth. see Tan, Teck M.

Low, Alaine. A Bibliographical Survey of Rotating Savings & Credit Associations. (Oxfam Research Discussion Papers). (C). 1995. pap. 15.95 (*0-85598-298-5*, Pub. by Oxfam Pub) Stylus Pub VA.

Low, Alaine, jt. ed. see Marshall, P. J.

Low, Albert. Butterfly's Dream: In Search of the Spiritual Roots of Zen. 160p. 1993. pap. 14.95 (*0-8048-1822-3*) Tuttle Pubng.

— An Invitation to Practice Zen. (Illus.). 152p. 1989. pap. 9.95 (*0-8048-1598-4*) Tuttle Pubng.

— The Iron Cow of Zen. LC 85-40413. 226p. 1985. pap. 6.50 (*0-8356-0598-1*, Quest) Theos Pub Hse.

— The Iron Cow of Zen. 240p. 1991. pap. 9.95 (*0-8048-1669-7*) Tuttle Pubng.

— To Know Yourself: To Know Zen. 1997. pap. text 16.95 (*0-8048-3119-X*) Tuttle Pubng.

— The World: A Gateway: Koan Commentaries for Self Study. LC 94-46614. 320p. (Orig.). 1995. pap. 16.95 (*0-8048-3046-0*) Tuttle Pubng.

— Zen & Creative Management. 256p. 1993. pap. 12.95 (*0-8048-1883-5*) Tuttle Pubng.

***Low, Albert.** Zen & the Sutras. LC 98-53965. (Tuttle Library of Enlightenment Ser.). 176p. 2000. pap. 16.95 (*0-8048-3201-3*) Tuttle Pubng.

— Zen Meditation Plain & Simple: Invitation to Zen Meditation. (Illus.). 152p. 2000. pap. 12.95 (*0-8048-3211-0*) Tuttle Pubng.

Low, Alfred D. The Anschluss Movement, 1931-1938. 507p. 1985. 77.50 (*0-88033-078-3*, Pub. by East Eur Monographs) Col U Pr.

— Men Around Hitler: The Nazi Elite & Its Collaborators. 250p. 1996. 45.00 (*0-88033-348-0*, 451, Pub. by East Eur Monographs) Col U Pr.

— The Sino-Soviet Confrontation since Mao Zedong: Dispute, Detente, or Conflict. (Social Science Monographs). 322p. 1987. text 72.00 (*0-88033-958-6*, Pub. by East Eur Monographs) Col U Pr.

— The Sino-Soviet Dispute: An Analysis of the Polemics. LC 74-2949. 364p. 1976. 39.50 (*0-8386-1479-5*) Fairleigh Dickinson.

— Soviet Jewry & Soviet Policy. (East European Monographs). 272p. 1990. text 46.50 (*0-88033-178-X*, Pub. by East Eur Monographs) Col U Pr.

Low, Alfred M. America at Home. LC 73-13142. (Foreign Travelers in America, 1810-1935 Ser.). (Illus.). 278p. 1974. reprint ed. 21.95 (*0-405-05465-3*) Ayer.

Low, Alice. The Macmillan Book of Greek Gods & Heroes. LC 85-7170. (Illus.). 192p. (J). (gr. 2-6). 1985. lib. bdg. 17.00 (*0-02-761390-9*, Mac Bks Young Read) S&S Childrens.

— The Popcorn Shop. LC 92-21423. (Hello Reader! Ser.). (Illus.). 32p. (J). (ps-3). 1994. 2.95 (*0-590-47121-X*) Scholastic Inc.

— Spooky. 1994. 15.15 (*0-606-09888-7*, Pub. by Turtleback) Demco.

— Stories to Tell a Five-Year-Old. (Illus.). 160p. (J). (gr. k-3). 1996. pap. 8.95 (*0-316-53416-1*) Little.

— The Witch Who Was Afraid of Witches. LC 98-36631. (I Can Read Chapter Bks.). (Illus.). 48p. (J). (gr. 3-4). 1999. 14.95 (*0-06-028305-X*) HarpC Child Bks.

— The Witch Who Was Afraid of Witches. LC 98-36631. (I Can Read Chapter Bks.). (Illus.). 48p. (J). (gr. 3-5). 1999. lib. bdg. 14.89 (*0-06-028306-8*) HarpC Child Bks.

— The Witch Who Was Afraid of Witches. LC 98-36631. (I Can Read Chapter Bks.). (Illus.). 48p. (J). (gr. 3 up). 2000. pap. 3.95 (*0-06-444255-1*, HarpTrophy) HarpC Child Bks.

— Witches' Holiday. LC 49-255980. 32p. (J). (gr. k-3). 1997. pap. text 2.99 (*0-590-46891-X*) Scholastic Inc.

— Witches' Holiday. (J). 1997. 8.19 (*0-606-12107-2*, Pub. by Turtleback) Demco.

Low, Alice, ed. Spooky Stories for a Dark & Stormy Night. LC 93-33638. (Illus.). 128p. (J). (gr. 3 up). 1994. 19.95 (*0-7868-0012-7*, Pub. by Hypm Child) Little.

— Stories to Tell a Six-Year-Old. LC 96-5387. (Illus.). 192p. (J). (gr. k-3). 1997. pap. 8.95 (*0-316-53418-8*) Little.

Low, Alice, jt. auth. see Zheng Zhensun.

Low, Allan. Agricultural Development in Southern Africa: Farm Household-Economics & the Food Crisis. 218p. (C). 1989. pap. text 22.50 (*0-435-08027-X*, 08027) Heinemann.

Low-Altitude Wind Shear & Its Hazard to Aviation C & National Research Council Staff. Low-Altitude Wind Shear & Its Hazard to Aviation. 112p. 1983. pap. text 14.95 (*0-309-03432-9*) Natl Acad Pr.

Low, Andrew R. & Hayward, Brent J., eds. Applied Aviation Psychology: Achievement Change & Challenge. LC 96-86206. 490p. 1996. 93.95 (*0-291-39840-5*) Ashgate Pub Co.

Low, Angus, jt. auth. see Durant, Stuart.

Low, Ann M. Dust Bowl Diary. LC 84-3672. (Illus.). x, 188p. 1984. pap. 9.95 (*0-8032-7913-2*, Bison Books) U of Nebr Pr.

Low, Annabel, jt. auth. see Blonder, Ellen.

Low, Anne G., ed. see Kuspit, Donald, et al.

Low, Anthony. Augustine Baker. LC 74-99527. (Twayne's English Authors Ser.). 170p. (C). 1970. lib. bdg. 17.95 (*0-8290-1759-3*) Irvington.

— The Georgic Revolution. LC 84-26520. (Illus.). 382p. 1985. reprint ed. pap. 118.50 (*0-608-02545-3*, 206318900004) Bks Demand.

— The Reinvention of Love: Poetry, Politics, & Culture from Sidney to Milton. LC 93-18184. 272p. (C). 1993. text 59.95 (*0-521-45030-6*) Cambridge U Pr.

Low, Archibald R. Normal Elliptic Functions: A Normalized Form of Weierstrass's Elliptic Functions. LC 55-37289. 32p. reprint ed. pap. 30.00 (*0-608-15660-4*, 203192700077) Bks Demand.

Low, Barbara, tr. see Freud, Anna.

Low, Barbara B., contrib. by. Leasing Sourcebook, 1994: The Directory of the U. S. Capital Equipment Leasing Industry, No. 1045-2508. 352p. 1994. pap. 135.00 (*0-936857-05-6*) Bibliotec Systems & Pub.

Low, Barbara B., ed. Leasing Sourcebook, 1997-1998: The Directory of the U. S. Capital Equipment Leasing Industry. 360p. (Orig.). 1997. pap. 135.00 (*0-936857-07-2*) Bibliotec Systems & Pub.

Low, Barbara B., intro. Leasing Sourcebook, 1992-1993: The Directory of the U. S. Capital Equipment Leasing Industry. 340p. 1992. pap. text 135.00 (*0-936857-04-8*) Bibliotec Systems & Pub.

L

L

Low-Beer, F. H. Questions of Judgment: Determining What's Right. LC 95-8726. 217p. 1995. 30.95 (*0-87975-960-7*) Prometheus Bks.
— Why Is Snow So White? 64p. 1992. pap. 12.95 (*1-55082-057-5*, Pub. by Quarry Pr) LPC InBook.
Low, Benjamin R. Seth Low. LC 70-137256. reprint ed. 20.00 (*0-404-04037-3*) AMS Pr.
— Seth Low. (BCL1 - United States Local History Ser.). 92p. 1991. reprint ed. lib. bdg. 59.00 (*0-7812-6276-3*) Rprt Serv.
Low, Betty-Bright P. France Views America, 1765-1815: An Exhibition to Commemorate the Bicentenary of French Assistance in the American War of Independence. (Illus.). 90p. 1978. pap. 4.95 (*0-914650-16-5*) Hagley Museum.
— France Views America, 1765-1815: An Exhibition to Commemorate the Bicentenary of French Assistance in the American War of Independence. LC 78-104642. (Illus.). 80p. reprint ed. pap. 30.00 (*0-8357-3127-8*, 203938800012) Bks Demand.
Low, Bill. Pughis Total Design: Integrated Methods for Successful Product. 2nd ed. 320p. (C). 2000. pap. 59.95 (*0-201-17783-8*) Addison-Wesley.
*****Low, Bobbi S.** Why Sex Matters: A Darwinian Look at Human Behavior. LC 99-24612. 1999. 26.95 (*0-691-02895-8*, Pub. by Princeton U Pr) Cal Prin Full Svc.
Low, Brian & Withers, Graeme, eds. Developments in School & Public Assessment. (C). 1990. pap. 55.00 (*0-86431-070-6*, Pub. by Aust Council Educ Res) St Mut.
Low, C. M., jt. auth. see Ley, S. V.
Low, C. R., ed. History of the Indian Navy, 1613-1863, 2 vols. 1160p. 1992. reprint ed. lib. bdg. 195.00 (*1-85207-336-5*, Pub. by Archive Editions) N Ross.
Low, Chan-Kee. Actuarial & Insurance Practices in Singapore. LC 95-35299. 1995. write for info. (*0-201-88905-6*) Addison-Wesley.
*****Low, Chee Keong.** Financial Markets in Hong Kong. LC 00-22906. 2000. write for info. (*981-4021-73-3*, Pub. by Spr-Verlag) Spr-Verlag.
Low Cheng Hock, ed. Biochemical Modulation: Its Pharmacological Basis & Clinical Applications Symposium, Singapore, October 1995. (Journal Ser.: Vol. 54, Supplement 1, 1997). (Illus.). iv, 40p. 1996. pap. 24.50 (*3-8055-6450-3*) S Karger.
Low, Colin, et al. Participation in Services for the Handicapped: Two Contrasting Models-Discussion Paper. 1979. 30.00 (*0-7855-0569-5*, Pub. by Natl Inst Soc Work) St Mut.
Low, D. A. Britain & Indian Nationalism: The Imprint of Ambiguity, 1929-1942. LC 96-49356. 374p. (C). 1997. text 74.95 (*0-521-55017-3*) Cambridge U Pr.
— Eclipse of Empire. 391p. (C). 1993. pap. text 19.95 (*0-521-45754-8*) Cambridge U Pr.
— The Egalitarian Moment: Asia & Africa, 1950-1980. 145p. (C). 1995. text 49.95 (*0-521-49665-9*); pap. text 16.95 (*0-521-56765-3*) Cambridge U Pr.
Low, D. A., ed. The Indian National Congress: Centenary Hindsights. 284p. 1989. 26.00 (*0-19-562142-5*) OUP.
Low, D. A. & Brasted, Howard. Freedom, Trauma, Continuities: Northern India & Independence. LC 97-32071. (Studies in Contemporary South Asia Ser.). 1997. pap. write for info. (*0-7619-9226-X*) Sage.
Low, D. A. & Brasted, Howard, eds. Freedom, Trauma, Continuities: Northern India & Independence. LC 97-32071. (Studies on Contemporary South Asia Ser.: Vol. 2). 220p. (C). 1998. 45.00 (*0-7619-9225-1*) Sage.
Low, D. M., tr. see Ginzburg, Natalia.
Low, David H., tr. Ballads of Marco Kraljevic. LC 69-10123. (Illus.). 196p. 1968. reprint ed. lib. bdg. 38.50 (*0-8371-0151-4*, LOMK, Greenwood Pr) Greenwood.
Low, Denise. Spring Geese & Other Poems. Collins, Joseph T., ed. (Illus.). 84p. 1984. pap. 4.00 (*0-89338-024-5*) U KS Nat Hist Mus.
— Touching the Sky. 132p. 1994. pap. 16.50 (*0-9632475-8-1*) Penthe Pub.
— Tulip Elegies: An Alchemy of Writing. LC 92-85531. 70p. 1993. pap. 10.00 (*0-9632475-0-6*) Penthe Pub.
Low, Denise, ed. see Poage, Michael.
Low, Denise, ed. & intro. see Mirriam-Goldberg, Caryn.
Low, Donald, ed. Robert Burns. (Everyman's Poetry Ser.). 116p. 1997. pap. 1.95 (*0-460-87814-X*, Everyman's Classic Lib) Tuttle Pubng.
Low, Donald A. Lion Rampant: Essays in the Study of British Imperialism. (Studies in Commonwealth Politics & History: No. 1). 232p. 1973. 35.00 (*0-7146-2986-3*, Pub. by F Cass Pubs) Intl Spec Bk.
*****Low, Donald A.** The Regency Underworld. LC 99-206115. 192p. 1999. 34.95 (*0-7509-2121-8*, Pub. by A Sutton) Motorbooks Intl.
— The Regency Underworld. 2000. reprint ed. pap. 21.95 (*0-7509-2470-5*, Pub. by Sutton Publng) Intl Pubs Mktg.
Low, Donald A., ed. see Byron, George Gordon.
Low, Douglas, jt. auth. see Bray, David K.
Low, Francis. Struggle for Asia. LC 79-167379. (Essay Index Reprint Ser.). 1977. reprint ed. 20.95 (*0-8369-2699-4*) Ayer.
Low, Francis E. Classical Field Theory: Electromagnetism & Gravitation. LC 96-25448. 440p. 1997. 69.95 (*0-471-59551-9*) Wiley.
Low, Gail C. White Skins/Black Masks: Representation, Colonialism & Cultural Cross-Dressing. LC 95-8889. 312p. (C). (gr. 13). 1995. 90.00 (*0-415-08147-5*) Routledge.
Low, George & Barkow, Al. The Master of Putting. LC 96-39940. (Illus.). 96p. 1997. reprint ed. pap. 12.95 (*1-55821-524-7*) Lyons Pr.
Low, George, jt. auth. see Barkow, Al.
Low, Graham, jt. auth. see Cameron, Lynne.
Low, Hugh. Sarawak: Its Inhabitants & Productions. (Asian Folk Tales Ser.). (Illus.). 440p. 1995. pap. 17.00 (*967-67-1009-1*, Pub. by Delta Edits) Weatherhill.
— Sarawak: Its Inhabitants & Productions. (Illus.). 416p. 1968. reprint ed. 35.00 (*0-7146-2017-3*, Pub. by F Cass Pubs) Intl Spec Bk.
Low, I. M. & Li, X. S., eds. Advanced Ceramic Tools for Machining Application II. (Key Engineering Materials Ser.: Vol. 114). (Illus.). 284p. 1996. text 116.00 (*0-87849-703-X*, Pub. by Trans T Pub) Enfield Pubs NH.
Low, Immanuel. Aramaische Pflanzennamen. (GER.). 1997. 128.00 (*3-487-04989-9*) G Olms Pubs.
— Studien Zur Judischen Folklore. (Collectanea Ser.: No. XVI). (GER.). x, 150p. 1975. write for info. (*3-487-04327-0*) G Olms Pubs.
Low, It-Meng, jt. ed. see Shi, Xing Sheng.
Low, J. O., jt. auth. see Warner, W. Lloyd.
*****Low, Jackson Mac.** Two Plays Vol. 64: Verdurous Sanguinaria & the Marrying Maiden. 2000. pap. 10.95 (*1-892295-63-6*) Green Integer.
*****Low, Jaye.** Spirit of Life. LC 99-63540. 164p. 1999. 16.95 (*1-56167-529-6*) Noble Hse MD.
Low, Jeanie W. Chooey, see Chooey Low, Jeanie W.
Low, Jennie. Jennie Low's Chopsticks, Cleaver & Wok: Homestyle Chinese Cooking. LC 96-51125. 1997. pap. 12.95 (*0-8118-1666-4*) Chronicle Bks.
Low, John & Reed, Ann. Basic Biomechanics Explained. (Illus.). 288p. 1996. pap. text 42.00 (*0-7506-2103-6*) Buttrwrth-Heinemann.
*****Low, John & Reed, Ann.** Electrotherapy Explained: Principles & Practice. 3rd ed. LC 99-49791. 431p. 2000. pap. text 47.50 (*0-7506-4149-5*) Buttrwrth-Heinemann.
Low, John, jt. auth. see MacDonald, Ian.
Low, John L. F. G. Tait - A Record. rev. ed. (Illus.). 250p. 1989. text 28.00 (*0-940889-21-8*) Classics Golf.
Low, Joseph. Mice Twice. 1983. 11.19 (*0-606-00922-1*, Pub. by Turtleback) Demco.
— Mice Twice. LC 85-26768. (Illus.). 32p. (J). (ps-3). 1986. reprint ed. mass mkt. 5.99 (*0-689-71060-7*) Aladdin.
Low, Kathleen. Legislative Reference Services & Sources. LC 93-39408. 100p. 1994. lib. bdg. 39.95 (*1-56024-891-2*) Haworth Pr.
— Recruiting Library Staff. LC 99-31281. (How-to-Do-It Manuals for Librarians Ser.: Vol. 94). 120p. 1999. pap. 45.00 (*1-55570-355-0*) Neal-Schuman.
— The Roles of Reference Librarians: Today & Tomorrow. LC 96-12748. (Reference Librarian Ser.: No. 54). 173p. (C). 1996. 39.95 (*1-56024-798-3*) Haworth Pr.
Low, Linda. Economics of Information Technology & the Media. 300p. 1999. pap. 26.00 (*981-02-3844-4*) World Scientific Pub.
*****Low, Linda.** The Economics of Information Technology & the Media. 300p. 1999. 58.00 (*981-02-3843-6*) World Scientific Pub.
Low, Linda & Aw, T. C. Housing a Healthy Educated & Wealthy Nation Through the CPF. LC 97-945611. 133p. 1997. pap. 12.00 (*981-210-101-2*, Pub. by Times Academic) Intl Spec Bk.
Low, Linda & Heng, Toh M., eds. Public Policies in Singapore: Changes in the 1980s & Future Signposts. 392p. 1992. pap. 25.00 (*981-210-022-9*, Pub. by Times Academic) Intl Spec Bk.
Low, Linda & Toh, Mun-Heng. Principles of Economics. LC 95-32430. 1995. write for info. (*0-201-42080-5*) Addison-Wesley.
Low, Linda & Toh Mun Heng. Principles of Economics. LC 96-25486. 1997. write for info. (*0-201-42089-9*) Addison-Wesley.
Low, Linda, jt. auth. see Heng, Toh M.
Low, Linda, jt. auth. see Yuan, Lee T.
Low, Linda, jt. ed. see Heng, Toh M.
Low, Lyman H. Hard Times Tokens. (Illus.). 1994. reprint ed. pap. 20.00 (*0-915262-16-9*) S J Durst.
— Observations on the Practice of Counterfeiting Coins & Medals. 1979. reprint ed. pap. 2.00 (*0-915262-25-8*) S J Durst.
Low, Mary. Celtic Christianity & Nature: The Early Irish & Hebridean Traditions. LC 96-159507. (Illus.). 240p. 1996. pap. 23.00 (*0-7486-0772-2*, Pub. by Edinburgh U Pr) Col U Pr.
— A Voice in Three Mirrors: Poems. 48p. 1983. pap. 12.00 (*0-941194-21-3*) Black Swan Pr.
— Where the Wolf Sings. (Illus.). 64p. (Orig.). 1994. pap. 12.00 (*0-941194-31-0*) Black Swan Pr.
Low, Morris, et al. Science, Technology & Society in Contemporary Japan. LC 99-35364. (Contemporary Japanese Society Ser.). (Illus.). 272p. (C). 1999. 59.95 (*0-521-65282-0*); pap. 19.95 (*0-521-65425-4*) Cambridge U Pr.
Low, N. P. & Power, J. M. Policy Systems in An Australian Metropolitan Region: Political & Economic Determinants of Change in Victoria, Vols. 22 & 23. (Illus.). 70p. 1984. pap. 22.00 (*0-08-032329-4*, Pergamon Pr) Elsevier.
*****Low, Nicholas, ed.** Global Ethics & Environment. (Illus.). 304p. (C). 2000. pap. 29.99 (*0-415-19736-8*); text 90.00 (*0-415-19735-X*) Routledge.
*****Low, Nicholas, et al, eds.** Consuming Cities: Urban Environment in Global Economy. LC 99-18549. 256p. (C). 1999. text. write for info. (*0-415-18768-0*) Routledge.
Low, Nicholas & Gleeson, Brendan. Justice, Society, & Nature: An Exploration of Political Ecology. LC 97-20418. 272p. (C). 1998. 80.00 (*0-415-14516-3*); pap. 25.99 (*0-415-14517-1*) Routledge.
Low, Nicholas, jt. auth. see Gleeson, Brendan.
Low, Niels L., jt. auth. see Downey, John A.
Low, Patrick. Preshipment Inspection Services. LC 94-49060. (World Bank Discussion Papers: No. 278). 176p. 1995. pap. 22.00 (*0-8213-3185-X*, 13185) World Bank.
— Trading Free: The GATT & U. S. Trade Policy. LC 93-12630. 310p. (C). 1993. pap. 14.95 (*0-87078-351-3*) Century Foundation.
Low, Peter W. Criminal Law. 2nd rev. ed. (Black Letter Ser.). 443p. (C). 1990. reprint ed. pap. text 24.50 (*0-314-73494-5*) West Pub.
Low, Peter W. & Hoffman, Joseph L. Federal Criminal Law. LC 96-33057. (University Casebook Ser.). 1997. text 38.25 (*1-56662-346-4*) Foundation Pr.
Low, Peter W. & Jefferies, John C., Jr. Federal Courts & the Law of Federal-State Relations. 4th ed. LC 98-21334. (University Casebook Ser.). 1281p. (C). 1998. text. write for info. (*1-56662-618-8*) Foundation Pr.
Low, Peter W. & Jeffries, John C., Jr. Civil Rights Actions: Section 1983 & Related Statutes. 2nd ed. LC 94-7715. (University Casebook Ser.). 953p. 1994. text 42.50 (*1-56662-149-6*) Foundation Pr.
— Civil Rights Actions: Selection 1983 & Related Statutes, 1997 Supplement. 2nd ed. (University Casebook Ser.). 159p. (C). 1997. pap. text. write for info. (*1-56662-497-5*) Foundation Pr.
— Federal Courts & the Law of Federal-State Relations. 3rd ed. (University Casebook Ser.). 1341p. (C). 1994. text 47.50 (*1-56662-160-7*) Foundation Pr.
— Federal Courts & the Law of Federal-State Relations, 1997 Supplement To. 3rd ed. (University Casebook Ser.). 307p. (C). 1997. pap. text. write for info. (*1-56662-518-1*) West Pub.
Low, Peter W. & Jeffries, John C. 1998 Supplement to Civil Rights Actions: Section 1983 & Related Statutes. 2nd ed. (University Casebook Ser.). 160p. 1998. pap. text, suppl. ed. write for info. (*1-56662-654-4*) Foundation Pr.
Low, Peter W. & Jeffries, John C., Jr. 1998 Supplement to Federal Courts & the Law of Federal-State Relations. 4th ed. (University Casebook Ser.). 50p. 1998. pap. text, suppl. ed. 4.95 (*1-56662-721-4*) Foundation Pr.
— 1995 Supplement to Civil Rights Actions: Section 1983 & Related Statutes. 2nd ed. (University Casebook Ser.). 59p. 1995. pap. text 4.95 (*1-56662-299-9*) Foundation Pr.
— 1995 Supplement to Federal Courts & the Law of Federal-State Relations. 3rd ed. (University Casebook Ser.). 93p. 1995. pap. text 5.95 (*1-56662-300-6*) Foundation Pr.
— 1996 Supplement to Civil Rights Actions: Section 1983 & Related Statutes. 2nd ed. (University Casebook Ser.). 90p. 1996. pap. text, suppl. ed. write for info. (*1-56662-386-3*) Foundation Pr.
— 1996 Supplement to Federal Courts & the Law of Federal-State Relations. 3rd ed. (University Casebook Ser.). 125p. 1996. pap. text, suppl. ed. write for info. (*1-56662-388-X*) Foundation Pr.
Low, Peter W., et al. Criminal Law: Cases & Materials. 2nd ed. (University Casebook Ser.). 1089p. 1990. reprint ed. text 41.95 (*0-88277-325-9*) Foundation Pr.
— Trial of John W. Hinckley, Jr. A Case Study in the Insanity Defense. (University Casebook Ser.). 137p. 1986. pap. text 10.50 (*0-88277-333-X*) Foundation Pr.
Low, Philip A., ed. Clinical Autonomic Disorders. 2nd ed. LC 97-11278. (Illus.). 849p. 1997. text 179.00 (*0-316-53281-9*) Lppncott W & W.
Low, Poh-Gek. China Market Intelligence Report. 25p. 1995. 75.00 (*1-882866-31-2*) Pac Asia Trvl.
— India Market Intelligence Report. 24p. 1995. 75.00 (*1-882866-32-0*) Pac Asia Trvl.
Low, Rachael. Film Making in Nineteen Thirties Britain. (Illus.). 384p. 1985. 39.95 (*0-04-791042-9*) Routledge.
Low, Rachael & Richards, Jeffrey. Rachael Low's History of British Film. LC 96-51734. 2444p. (C). 1997. 700.00 (*0-415-15451-0*) Routledge.
Low, Robert. La Pasionaria: The Spanish Firebrand. (Illus.). 224p. 1993. 39.95 (*0-09-174572-1*, Pub. by Hutchnson) Trafalgar.
— Peoples of the Desert, 6 vols., Set. LC 96-7753. (Peoples & Their Environments Ser.). (Illus.). 24p. (J). (gr. k-4). 1996. lib. bdg. 15.93 (*0-8239-2296-0*, PowerKids) Rosen Group.
— Peoples of the Mountains, 6 vols., Set. LC 96-14814. (Peoples & Their Environments Ser.). (Illus.). 24p. (J). (gr. k-4). 1996. lib. bdg. 15.93 (*0-8239-2298-7*, PowerKids) Rosen Group.
— Peoples of the Rain Forest, 6 vols., Set. LC 96-5551. (Peoples & Their Environments Ser.). (Illus.). 24p. (J). (gr. k-4). 1996. lib. bdg. 15.93 (*0-8239-2297-9*, PowerKids) Rosen Group.
— Peoples of the River Valley, 6 vols., Set. LC 96-1532. (Peoples & Their Environments Ser.). (Illus.). 24p. (J). (gr. k-4). 1996. lib. bdg. 15.93 (*0-8239-2295-2*, PowerKids) Rosen Group.
— Peoples of the Savanna, 6 vols. LC 96-14279. (Peoples & their Environments Ser.). (Illus.). 24p. (J). (gr. k-4). 1996. lib. bdg. 15.93 (*0-8239-2299-5*, PowerKids) Rosen Group.
Low, Robert, et al. Peoples of the Arctic, 6 vols., Set. LC 96-294. (Peoples & Their Environments Ser.). (Illus.). 24p. (J). (gr. k-4). 1996. lib. bdg. 15.93 (*0-8239-2294-4*, PowerKids) Rosen Group.
Low, Robert J. Bottom Line Basics: Understand & Control Business Finances. Pinkham, Linda, ed. LC 94-24774. (Successful Business Library). (Illus.). 280p. 1995. pap. 19.95 (*1-55571-330-0*, Oasis Pr) PSI Resch.
Low, Rodolfo. Victory over Migraine: The Breakthrough Study That Explains What Causes It & How It Can Be Completely Prevented Through Diet. LC 86-7708. 208p. 1995. pap. 7.95 (*0-8050-0927-2*, Owl) H Holt & Co.
Low, Rosemary. Encyclopedia of Lories. (Illus.). 432p. 1998. 70.00 (*0-88839-413-6*) Hancock House.
— The Loving Care of Pet Parrots. (Illus.). 160p. 1999. pap. 12.95 (*0-88839-439-X*) Hancock House.
— Parrot in Aviculture. (Illus.). 1992. 39.95 (*1-56465-179-7*, 16116) Tetra Pr.
*****Low, Rosemary.** Why Does My Parrot... ? 224p. 2000. 24.95 (*0-285-63569-7*, Pub. by Souvenir Pr Ltd) IPG Chicago.
— Why Does My Parrot... ? (Illus.). 224p. 2000. 24.95 (*0-285-63570-0*) Souvenir Pr Ltd.
Low, Ruth H. & Valls, Lito, eds. St. John Backtime. LC 80-68089. (Illus.). 96p. (Orig.). 1985. pap. 14.95 (*0-9614355-0-X*) Eden Hill Pr.
Low, S. M., jt. auth. see Altman, I.
*****Low, Setha M.** On the Plaza: The Politics of Public Space & Culture. LC 99-50899. (Illus.). 288p. 2000. 40.00 (*0-292-74713-6*); pap. 18.95 (*0-292-74714-4*) U of Tex Pr.
Low, Setha M. Theorizing the City: The New Urban Anthropology Reader. LC 99-17712. 432p. 1999. pap. 27.00 (*0-8135-2720-1*) Rutgers U Pr.
Low, Setha M., jt. ed. see Davis, Dona L.
Low, Sethna M., ed. Theorizing the City: The New Urban Anthropology Reader. LC 99-17712. (Illus.). 432p. 1999. text 59.00 (*0-8135-2719-8*) Rutgers U Pr.
Low, Shirley P., jt. auth. see Alderson, William T.
Low, Sidney & Sanders, Lloyd C. History of England During the Reign of Victoria, 1837-1907. LC 68-25247. (British History Ser.: No. 30). (Illus.). 1969. reprint ed. lib. bdg. 75.00 (*0-8383-0267-X*) M S G Haskell Hse.
Low, Sidney J. & Sanders, Lloyd C. History of England During the Reign of Victoria, 1837-1901. LC 74-5630. (Political History of England Ser.: No. 12). reprint ed. 45.00 (*0-404-50782-4*) AMS Pr.
*****Low, Su-Lin.** CDMA Internetworking: Deploying the Open A-Interface. (Illus.). 550p. 2000. 75.00 (*0-13-088922-9*) P-H.
Low Sui Pheng & Yue Meng Chan. Managing Productivity in Construction: JIT Operations & Measurements. LC 97-70343. 256p. 1997. text 69.95 (*1-85972-607-0*, Pub. by Ashgate Pub) Ashgate Pub Co.
*****Low, Tad.** Truth About, No. 2. 2000. pap. 16.00 (*0-06-107354-7*) HarpC.
Low, Tom A., ed. Botey: The Autobiography of Elinor Boterweg Low. (Illus.). 167p. 1999. 25.00 (*1-887301-06-2*) Palmetto Bookworks.
— One Furrow at a Time: The Autobiography of Dave Low. (Illus.). 160p. 1995. 25.00 (*1-887301-00-3*) Palmetto Bookworks.
Low, Trevor. Gymnastics: Floor, Vault, Beam & Bar. (Skills of the Game Ser.). (Illus.). 128p. pap. 19.95 (*1-85223-752-X*, Pub. by Crolwood) Trafalgar.
Low, Ulrike. Figurlich Verzierte Metallgefabe aus Nord-und Nordwestiran: Eine Stilkritische Untersuchung. (Altertumskunde Des Vorderen Orients Ser.: No. 6). 1998. text 160.00 (*3-927120-34-0*) UGARIT.
Low, Victor N. Three Nigerian Emirates: A Study in Oral History. LC 74-176163. 328p. reprint ed. pap. 101.70 (*0-608-13155-5*, 201542400093) Bks Demand.
Low, W. Augustus & Clift, Virgil A. Encyclopedia of Black America. (Quality Paperbacks Ser.). (Illus.). 941p. (C). 1984. reprint ed. pap. 39.50 (*0-306-80221-X*) Da Capo.
Low, Werner. Acerbic Amusings. (WEP Poetry Ser.: No. 1). 1978. pap. 1.00 (*0-917976-03-7*, White Ewe Pr) Thunder Baas Pr.
— Low Wit. LC 81-69718. 79p. (Orig.). 1982. pap. 3.95 (*0-917976-15-0*, White Ewe Pr) Thunder Baas Pr.
— Rime & Punishment. (Poetry Ser.: No. 2). (Illus.). (Orig.). 1989. pap. 3.00 (*0-938823-02-7*) Pogment Pr.
Low, William. Chinatown. LC 96-44211. (Illus.). 32p. (J). (ps-2). 1997. pap. 15.95 (*0-8050-4214-8*, Bks Young Read) H Holt & Co.
*****Lowance, Mason I.** Against Slavery: An Abolitionist Reader. LC 99-16211. 2000. pap. 13.95 (*0-14-043758-4*) Penguin Putnam.
Lowance, Mason I., Jr. The Language of Canaan: Metaphor & Symbol in New England from the Puritans to the Transcendentalists. LC 79-21179. 345p. 1980. 37.95 (*0-674-50949-8*) HUP.
Lowance, Mason I., et al, eds. The Stowe Debate: Rhetorical Strategies in "Uncle Tom's Cabin" LC 94-12254. 328p. (C). 1994. pap. 17.95 (*0-87023-952-X*) U of Mass Pr.
Lowance, Mason I., Jr. & Watters, David, eds. Increase Mather's "New Jerusalem" Millenialism in Late Eighteenth-Century New England. 66p. 1977. pap. 5.00 (*0-944026-62-6*) Am Antiquarian.
Lowbury, E. J. L., et al, eds. Control of Hospital Infection. 3rd ed. (Illus.). 400p. 1992. text 75.00 (*0-412-28440-5*, Pub. by E A) OUP.
Lowbury, Edward. Collected Poems, 1934-1992. 300p. pap. write for info. (*3-7052-0616-8*, Pub. by Poetry Salzburg) Intl Spec Bk.
— Hallmarks of Poetry: Reflections on a Theme. 158p. pap. write for info. (*3-7052-0811-X*, Pub. by Poetry Salzburg) Intl Spec Bk.
Lowbury, Edward & Young, Alison. To Shirk No Idleness: A Critical Biography of the Poet Andrew Young. 311p. 1998. pap. 23.95 (*3-7052-0125-5*, Pub. by Poetry Salzburg) Intl Spec Bk.
Lowden, Eric. Practical Transformer Design Handbook. LC 80-50057. 1980. pap. 23.95 (*0-672-21657-4*) Sams.
Lowden, J. Alexander, jt. ed. see Callahan, John W.
Lowden, John. Early Christian & Byzantine Art. (Art & Ideas Ser.). (Illus.). 448p. 1997. pap. 22.95 (*0-7148-3168-9*, Pub. by Phaidon Press) Phaidon Pr.
— Illuminated Prophet Books: A Study of Byzantine Manuscripts of the Major & Minor Prophets. LC 86-43164. (Illus.). 176p. 1989. 58.50 (*0-271-00604-8*) Pa St U Pr.
*****Lowden, John.** Making of the Bibles Moralisees, 2 vols. Incl. Book of Ruth. LC 98-46494. (Illus.). 320p. 2000. 85.00 (*0-271-01919-0*); Vol. 1. Making of the Bibles Moralisees. LC 98-46494. (Illus.). 352p. 2000. 85.00 (*0-271-01909-3*); (Illus.). 2000. 160.00 Pa St U Pr.

An Asterisk (*) at the beginning of an entry indicates that the title is appearing for the first time.

L

Lowden, John. The Octateuchs: A Study of Illustrated Byzantine Manuscripts. (Illus.). 246p. 1992. text 55.00 (*0-271-00771-0*) Pa St U Pr.

Lowden, M. Dancing to Learn, Learning to Dance. 1989. 79.95 (*1-85000-618-0*); pap. 34.95 (*1-85000-619-9*) Taylor & Francis.

Lowden, Pamela. Moral Opposition to Authoritarian Rule in Chile, 1973-1990. LC 95-36938. (St. Antony's Ser.). 224p. 1996. text 65.00 (*0-312-15870-X*) St Martin.

Lowden, Pamela, jt. ed. see Fiszbein, Ariel.

Lowden, R. A., et al, eds. Ceramic Matrix Composites - Advanced High-Temperature Structural Materials, Vol. 365. (MRS Symposium Proceedings Ser.). 478p. 1995. 72.00 (*1-55899-266-9*) Materials Res.

Lowden, Stephanie G. Emily's Sadhappy Season: The Story of a Young Girl's Feelings after the Death of Her Father. Johnson, Joy, ed. (Illus.). 24p. (J). (gr. 1-7). 1993. pap. 4.95 (*1-56123-066-9*, ESHC) Centering Corp.

Lowder, Eleanor. Nonprofit Guide to 403(b) Plans. 300p. 1996. 62.00 (*0-8342-0616-1*) Aspen Pub.

***Lowder, Eleanor A.** 403(B) Plans. LC 99-28018. 137p. 1999. pap. 37.00 (*0-7931-3354-8*) Dearborn.

Lowder, Eleanor A. & Cook, Kristi. The 403(b) Primer. 270p. 1998. ring bd. 75.00 (*1-891942-00-X*) N T S S A.

Lowder, Hughston E. The Silent Service: U. S. Submarines in World War II. LC 87-90657. 504p. (C). 1987. 24.95 (*0-9619189-0-X*) Silent Serv Bks.

Lowder, James. Forgotten Realms: Prince of Lies. (Finder's Stone Trilogy Ser.). 388p. (Orig.). 1993. pap. 5.95 (*1-56076-626-3*, Pub. by TSR Inc) Random.

***Lowder, James.** GURPS Villains. Pace, Richard et al, eds. (GURPS Ser.). (Illus.). 128p. 2000. pap. 19.95 (*1-55634-414-7*, 925-123, Pub. by S Jackson Games) BookWorld.

Lowder, James. Ravenloft: Knight of the Black Rose. LC 90-71507. 320p. (Orig.). 1991. pap. 5.99 (*1-56076-156-3*, Pub. by TSR Inc) Random.

— Realms of Infamy. (Forgotten Realms Ser.). 1995. pap. 4.95 (*1-56076-911-4*, Pub. by TSR Inc) Random.

***Lowder, James, ed.** The Doom of Camelot. 320p. 2000. pap. 14.95 (*1-928999-09-3*) Green Knight.

Lowder, James, et al. Realms of Valor: Anthology. 320p. (Orig.). 1993. pap. 5.99 (*1-56076-557-7*, Pub. by TSR Inc) Random.

Lowder, Josef G. The Time Investment Register. (What in the World Are You Doing with Your Life Ser.: No. 2). 32p. 1986. pap. 1.50 (*0-935597-02-6*, 8507-02); disk 29.95 (*0-935597-03-4*) Comm Architects.

— The Ultimate Purpose & Fundamental Principles of Life. LC 85-701. (What in the World Are You Doing with Your Life Ser.: No. 1). 72p. 9.95 (*0-935597-00-X*); pap. 3.95 (*0-935597-01-8*); disk 9.95 (*0-935597-04-2*) Comm Architects.

Lowder, Stella. The Geography of Third World Cities. LC 86-17366. 304p. 1986. 58.00 (*0-389-20671-7*, N8228) B&N Imports.

Lowder, Stella, jt. ed. see Morris, Arthur S.

Lowder, Wayne M., ed. The Natural Radiation Environment: International Symposium on the Natural Radiation Environment, 1963 Houston, Texas. LC 64-12256. (Rice University Semicentennial Publications). 1083p. pap. 200.00 (*0-8357-8963-2*, 205676500085) Bks Demand.

***LOWDERMILK.** Maternity & Woman's Health. 7th ed. 2000. pap. text. write for info. (*0-323-01180-2*) Mosby Inc.

Lowdermilk, Deitra L. Maternity Nursing: Quick Reference. 4th ed. (Illus.). 64p. (C). (gr. 13). 1994. pap. text 8.95 (*0-8151-0612-2*, 24708) Mosby Inc.

Lowdermilk, Deitra L. & Bobak, Irene M. Maternity & Women's Health Care. 6th ed. (Illus.). 328p. (C). (gr. 13). 1996. pap. text, student ed. 19.95 (*0-8151-5579-4*, 28012) Mosby Inc.

Lowdermilk, Deitra L., et al. Maternity & Women's Health Care. 6th ed. (Illus.). 1997. teacher ed. write for info. (*0-8151-5578-6*) Mosby Inc.

***Lowdermilk, Deitra L., et al.** Maternity Nursing. 5th ed. (Illus.). 1998. teacher ed. write for info. (*0-323-00217-X*) Mosby Inc.

Lowdermilk, Deitra Leonard, see Leonard Lowdermilk, Deitra.

Lowdermilk, Deitra Leonard, et al. High Risk Antepartal Home Care. LC 98-50868. (March of Dimes Nursing Modules Ser.). 1998. write for info. (*0-86525-073-1*) March of Dimes.

***Lowdermilk, W. H., ed.** Solid State Lasers for Application to Inertial Confinement Fusion. 1090p. 1999. pap. text 163.00 (*0-8194-2951-1*) SPIE.

Lowdermilk, Will H. History of Cumberland from the Time of the Indian Town Cafuctucue in 1728, up to the Present Day (1878) (Illus.). 554p. 1997. reprint ed. lib. bdg. 57.50 (*0-8328-5951-6*) Higginson Bk Co.

— History of Cumberland, (Maryland) LC 79-173260. (Illus.). 556p. 1997. reprint ed. 42.00 (*0-8063-7983-9*, Pub. by Clearfield Co) ACCESS Pubs Network.

Lowdernilk, Janet. Dimensions: A Youth Focus on Churches in Solidarity with Women. (Illus.). 32p. (Orig.). (YA). 1992. pap. 7.95 (*0-377-00244-5*) Friendship Pr.

***Lowdin.** Advances in Quantum Chemistry. 400p. (C). 1999. 125.00 (*0-12-034834-9*) Acad Pr.

— Advances in Quantum Chemistry. 500p. (C). 1999. text 145.00 (*0-12-034836-5*) Acad Pr.

***Lowdin, Per-Olov.** Linear Algebra for Quantum Theory. LC 97-22362. 458p. 1998. 94.95 (*0-471-19958-3*, Wiley-Interscience) Wiley.

Lowdin, Per-Olov, ed. Quantum Biology & Quantum Pharmacology - Quantum Biology Symposium Proceedings, 17. 17th ed. 248p. 1991. pap. 183.95 (*0-471-54598-8*) Wiley.

Lowdin, Per-Olov, et al, eds. Advances in Quantum Chemistry, Vol. 27. (Illus.). 407p. 1996. text 80.00 (*0-12-034827-6*) Acad Pr.

— Advances in Quantum Chemistry, Vol. 28. (Illus.). 370p. 1997. text 105.00 (*0-12-034828-4*) Morgan Kaufmann.

— Advances in Quantum Chemistry Vol. 29: Direct Variational X-I Method. (Illus.). 487p. 1998. text 110.00 (*0-12-034829-2*) Morgan Kaufmann.

— Advances in Quantum Chemistry Vol. 30: Modern Trends in Atomic Physics, Vol. 30. (Illus.). 506p. (C). 1998. text 125.00 (*0-12-034830-6*) Acad Pr.

— Advances in Quantum Chemistry Vol. 31, Pt. I: Quantum Systems in Chemistry & Physics. (Illus.). 345p. (C). 1998. boxed set 99.95 (*0-12-034831-4*) Acad Pr.

— Advances in Quantum Chemistry Vol. 32, Pt. II: Quantum Systems in Chemistry & Physics. (Illus.). 338p. (C). 1998. boxed set 99.95 (*0-12-034833-0*) Acad Pr.

***Lowdin, Per-Olov, et al, eds.** Advances in Quantum Chemistry Vol. 35. 368p. 1999. 130.00 (*0-12-034835-7*) Acad Pr.

Lowdin, Per-Olov, et al, eds. International Journal of Quantum Chemistry, 1993: Proceedings of the International Symposium on Quantum Chemistry - Atomic, Molecular & Condensed Matter Theory & Computational Methods. (Quantum Chemistry Symposium Ser.: Vol. 27). 864p. 1993. pap. 285.00 (*0-471-02505-4*) Wiley.

Lowdin, Per-Olov & Pullman, Bernard, eds. New Horizons of Quantum Chemistry. 1982. text 220.00 (*90-277-1526-2*) Kluwer Academic.

Lowdin, Per-Olov, ed. see Zerner, Michael C.

Lowdon. Practical Transfer Handbook. 2nd ed. 1996. text 59.50 (*0-07-038860-1*) McGraw.

Lowdon, Brian, et al. Wellness. 1995. pap. 56.00 (*0-949823-49-X*, Pub. by Deakin Univ) St Mut.

Lowe. Chemicals, Industry & Environment. 1993. pap. text, teacher ed. 86.87 (*0-697-17088-8*) McGraw.

— Consumer Educations & Economics. 3rd ed. 1989. 38.47 (*0-02-820240-6*) Glencoe.

— Containing Cold War East Asia. LC 97-165203. 1997. text 69.95 (*0-7190-2508-7*) St Martin.

— Hypermedia & the Web. LC 98-28199. 626p. 1999. pap. 69.99 (*0-471-98312-8*) Wiley.

***Lowe.** Judging Fences for Cross Country. 2000. pap. 14.95 (*0-85131-592-5*, Pub. by J A Allen) Trafalgar.

— MSN.com for Dummies. (For Dummies Ser.). 384p. 2000. pap. 19.99 (*0-7645-0649-8*) IDG Bks.

Lowe. Reconstruct Quat Environ. 2nd ed. (C). 1996. pap. text 51.95 (*0-582-10266-9*, Pub. by Addison-Wesley) Longman.

— Teach Interactive Science Technology. Date not set. pap. text. write for info. (*0-582-87310-X*, Pub. by Addison-Wesley) Longman.

— Vietnam War. LC 98-21141. 272p. 1998. text 59.95 (*0-312-21693-9*) St Martin.

Lowe. Warren Buffett Speaks: Wit & Wisdom from the World's Greatest Investor & Jack Welch Speaks: Wisdom from the World's Greatest Business Leader. 464p. 29.95 (*0-471-29952-9*) Wiley.

Lowe. Wildland Firefighting Practices. (C). 2000. pap. 39.95 (*0-7668-0147-0*) Delmar.

***Lowe.** Wildland Firefighting Practices. (C). 2000. 12.95 (*0-7668-0148-9*) Delmar.

Lowe, ed. Pre-GED Critical Reading Skills Exercises. 1992. pap., wbk. ed. 7.65 (*0-8092-3885-3*) NTC Contemp Pub Co.

Lowe, jt. auth. see Amitrano.

Lowe, jt. auth. see Ashton.

Lowe, jt. auth. see Gould, Jeanni.

Lowe, jt. auth. see Krahn.

Lowe, jt. auth. see Lovitt.

Lowe, A. L. & Perry, G. W., eds. Zirconium in the Nuclear Industry: 3rd Conference - STP 633. 690p. 1977. 55.50 (*0-8031-0756-0*, STP633) ASTM.

Lowe, A. V., jt. auth. see Churchill, R. R.

Lowe, Adolph. Has Freedom a Future? LC 87-29943. (Convergence Ser.). 184p. 1988. 49.95 (*0-275-92937-X*, C2937, Praeger Pubs); pap. 17.95 (*0-275-92938-8*, B2938, Praeger Pubs) Greenwood.

— On Economic Knowledge: Toward a Science of Political Economics. enl. ed. LC 83-649. 365p. 1983. reprint ed. pap. 113.20 (*0-7837-9947-0*, 206067400006) Bks Demand.

Lowe, Albert G., jt. auth. see Stewart, Martha A.

Lowe, Alex, jt. auth. see Boga, Steven.

***Lowe, Alfonso.** The Companion Guide to the South of Spain. 320p. 2000. pap. 24.95 (*1-900639-33-5*) Boydell & Brewer.

Lowe, Allen. American Pop: From Minstrel to Mojo: On Record, 1893-1956. 282p. 1998. pap. 18.00 (*1-881993-33-7*) Cadence Jazz.

Lowe, Andrew. Porting UNIX Applications to Windows NT. LC 96-78993. 544p. 1997. 49.99 (*1-57870-004-3*) Macmillan Tech.

***Lowe, Anne.** Raven's Flight. LC 99-64039. (Illus.). 88p. (J). (gr. 3-9). 1999. pap. 8.95 (*0-89716-932-8*, Peanut Btr Pubng) Elton-Wolf Pub.

Lowe, Anthony M. 300 Years in Eastern Virginia: Descendants of Arthur Jones (1630-1692) LC 95-1161. 1995. write for info. (*0-89865-934-5*) Donning Co.

Lowe Art Museum Staff. Lowe Art Museum Selected Works: Handbook of the Permanent Collection. 176p. 1996. pap. 19.95 (*0-9648614-0-2*) Lowe Art Mus.

Lowe, Barry. Media Mythologies. LC 95-142112. 196p. 1995. pap. 19.95 (*0-86840-006-8*, Pub. by New South Wales Univ Pr) Intl Spec Bk.

Lowe, Ben. Imagining Peace: A History of Early English Pacifist Ideas. LC 96-50136. 1997. 60.00 (*0-271-01688-4*); pap. 19.95 (*0-271-01689-2*) Pa St U Pr.

Lowe Besteman, Catherine. Unraveling Somalia: Race, Violence & the Legacy of Slavery. LC 98-33372. (Ethnography of Political Violence Ser.). 1999. 19.95 (*0-8122-1688-1*) U of Pa Pr.

***Lowe, Betty B.** The Ladies Who Sing with the Band. LC 99-49460. (Studies in Jazz: Vol. 36). 160p. 2000. 35.00 (*0-8108-3714-5*) Scarecrow.

Lowe, Bia. Wild Ride: Earthquakes, Sneezes, & Other Thrills. 192p. 1996. pap. 11.00 (*0-06-092695-3*) HarpC.

***Lowe, Brian.** Fundamentals of Mixed Signal Testing. Perry, Guy, ed. (Illus.). (C). 1999. pap. text 100.00 (*0-9658797-2-0*) Soft Test.

Lowe, Brian, ed. & illus. see Perry, Guy A., et al.

Lowe, C. Fergus, et al, eds. Behavior Analysis & Contemporary Psychology. 288p. 1986. text 59.95 (*0-86377-025-8*) L Erlbaum Assocs.

Lowe, C. J. Salisbury & the Mediterranean, 1886-1896. 1965. 20.00 (*0-89979-072-0*) British Am Bks.

Lowe, C. Marshall. Value Orientations in Counseling & Psychotherapy: The Meanings of Mental Health. 2nd ed. LC 76-25957. 1976. pap. text 19.50 (*0-910328-09-9*) Sulzburger & Graham Pub.

Lowe, C. V., jt. auth. see Goodwin, Astly J.

Lowe, C. W. Industrial Statistics, Vol. 2. 1970. pap. 32.00 (*0-8464-0512-1*) Beekman Pubs.

Lowe, Carl. The Civil War Remembered. LC 94-8757. (Illus.). 120p. 1994. 12.95 (*1-56799-107-6*, Friedman-Fairfax) M Friedman Pub Grp Inc.

— The Complete Vitamin Book. 320p. (Orig.). 1994. mass mkt. 5.99 (*0-425-14365-1*) Berkley Pub.

— Complete Vitamin Book. 1994. pap. 5.99 (*0-425-14377-5*) Berkley Pub.

Lowe, Carl & Philip Lief Group Inc. Staff. Toxic Food: What You Need to Know to Feed Your Family Safely. 128p. 1990. mass mkt. 3.95 (*0-380-76001-0*, Avon Bks) Morrow Avon.

Lowe, Carl, jt. auth. see Fuentes, Robert.

Lowe, Carol, jt. ed. see Lugo, Ariel E.

Lowe, Celia, jt. auth. see Ottmann, Klaus.

Lowe, Charles. Alexander the Third of Russia. LC 72-4219. (Select Bibliographies Reprint Ser.). 1977. reprint ed. 23.95 (*0-8369-6889-1*) Ayer.

Lowe, Charles H., ed. see Cockrun, E. Lendell, et al.

Lowe, Cheng Y. Pharmaceutical Applications in the European Union: A Guide Through the Registration Maze. LC 97-43310. (Illus.). 278p. 1998. 179.00 (*1-57491-064-7*) Interpharm.

Lowe, Christopher. St. Boniface Church, Orkney: Coastal Erosion & Archaeological Assessment. LC 99-170743. (Illus.). 215p. 1998. 69.95 (*0-7509-1755-5*, Pub. by Sutton Pub Ltd) Intl Pubs Mktg.

Lowe, Christopher R. & Dean, P. D. Affinity Chromatography. LC 73-17598. 284p. reprint ed. pap. 88.10 (*0-8357-5219-4*, 202399700035) Bks Demand.

Lowe, Chuan-Hua. Facing Labor Issues in China. LC 75-32322. (Studies in Chinese History & Civilization). 202p. 1977. reprint ed. lib. bdg. 59.95 (*0-313-26972-6*, U6972, Greenwood Pr) Greenwood.

Lowe, Claudia J. Guide to Reference & Bibliography for Theatre Research. 2nd ed. 149p. 1980. pap. 20.00 (*0-88215-049-9*) Friends Ohio St U Lib.

Lowe, Cylvia A. Words of Wisdom from the Masters. 2nd ed. 120p. 1981. reprint ed. pap. 9.00 (*0-9606080-0-1*) Book Dept.

Lowe, D. The Transport & Distribution Manager's Guide to 1992. 206p. (C). 1989. 180.00 (*0-7855-5725-3*, Pub. by Inst Pur & Supply) St Mut.

Lowe, D. & Fox, H., eds. Advances in Gynaecological Pathology. (Illus.). 384p. 1992. text 131.00 (*0-443-04377-9*) Church.

Lowe, D. & Stiles, A. Pesticides Nomenclature, Specifications, Analysis, Use & Residues in Food. (Progress in Standardization Ser.: No. 1). 40p. 1973. pap. text 6.00 (*92-4-154101-6*, 1260001) World Health.

***Lowe, D. & Underwood, J.** Recent Advances in Histopathology - 18. (Illus.). 280p. 1998. write for info. (*0-443-06036-3*) Church.

Lowe, D. Armstrong. Guide to International Recommendations on Names & Symbols for Quantities & on Units of Measurement. (Progress in Standardization: No. 2). 1975. pap. text 36.00 (*92-4-068521-9*, 1260002) World Health.

Lowe, D. G., ed. Reporting Histopathology Sections. (Illus.). 208p. 1997. pap. text 55.00 (*0-412-43040-1*, Pub. by E A) OUP.

Lowe, Dave. Horses & Ponies. (Super Tough Hidden Pictures Ser.). (Illus.). 48p. (J). (gr. k-2). 1993. pap. 3.99 (*0-8431-3538-7*, Price Stern) Peng Put Young Read.

Lowe, Dave. Snakes & Lizards. (Super Tough Hidden Pictures Ser.). (Illus.). 48p. (J). (gr. k-2). 1993. pap. 3.99 (*0-8431-3539-5*, Price Stern) Peng Put Young Read.

***Lowe, Dave C. & Guianan, Eve.** Grade Boosters First Grade Language. 320p. (J). (gr. 1-2). 1999. pap. 18.95 (*0-7373-0149-X*, 0149XW) NTC Contemp Pub Co.

Lowe, David. An Insiders Guide to Dealing with the Yellow Pages. 95p. (Orig.). 1997. pap. 14.95 (*0-9653794-1-8*) Persona Corp.

***Lowe, David.** Menzies & the 'Great World Struggle' Australia's Cold War, 1948-1954. 242p. 1999. pap. 35.00 (*0-86840-553-1*, Pub. by NSW U Pr) Intl Spec Bk.

Lowe, David. Perceptual Organization & Visual Recognition. 176p. (C). 1985. reprint ed. text 122.00 (*0-89838-172-X*) Kluwer Academic.

Lowe, David, ed. The Great Chicago Fire in Eyewitness Accounts & Sixty-Three Contemporary Photographs & Illustrations. LC 78-73518. (Illus.). 87p. 1979. reprint ed. pap. 7.95 (*0-486-23771-0*) Dover.

Lowe, David & Richards, Jack. The Lace Heritage: A Guide to Nottingham Lace. (C). 1988. 60.00 (*0-7855-3794-5*, Pub. by Lace Centre) St Mut.

Lowe, David & Shimmen, Andrea. Australia. (Modern Industrial World Ser.). (J). (gr. 6-7). 1996. lib. bdg. 24.26 (*0-8172-4553-7*) Raintree Steck-V.

— Australia. (Modern Industrial World Ser.). (Illus.). 48p. (J). (gr. 6-8). 1996. lib. bdg. 24.26 (*1-56847-433-4*) Raintree Steck-V.

Lowe, David, jt. auth. see Darian-Smith, Kate.

Lowe, David, jt. auth. see Richard, Jack.

Lowe, David, jt. ed. see Beacham, Walton.

Lowe, David A., ed. Critical Essays on Ivan Turgenev. (Critical Essays Ser.). 176p. 1988. 49.00 (*0-8161-8842-4*, G K Hall & Co) Mac Lib Ref.

Lowe, David A., ed. & tr. see Dostoyevsky, Fyodor.

Lowe, David A., tr. see Dostoyevsky, Fyodor.

Lowe, David A., tr. see Trifonov, Yury V.

Lowe, David G. Beaux Arts New York: The City in the Gilded Years. LC 98-3935. 128p. 1998. pap. 19.95 (*0-8230-0481-3*) Watsn-Guptill.

— Stanford White's New York. LC 98-51408. (Illus.). 352p. 1999. pap. text 24.95 (*0-8230-4914-0*) Watsn-Guptill.

***Lowe, David Garrard.** Lost Chicago. (Illus.). 272p. 2000. pap. 29.95 (*0-8230-2871-2*) Watsn-Guptill.

Lowe, David J. ENDOR & EPR of Metalloproteins. LC 95-18866. (Molecular Biology Intelligence Unit Ser.). 167p. 1995. 69.00 (*1-57059-198-9*) Landes Bioscience.

Lowe, Deborah, et al. Product Tampering: A Worldwide Problem: A Crisis Communications Tool for Newsrooms & Corporations. Ramsey, Doug & Warner, John, eds. (Illus.). 28p. 1993. pap. 7.95 (*0-910755-00-0*) Foun Am Comm.

***Lowe, Denise.** Women & American Television: An Encyclopedia. LC 99-50178. 325p. 1999. lib. bdg. 75.00 (*0-87436-970-3*) ABC-CLIO.

***Lowe, Donald & Lowe, Roberta.** Columbia River Gorge Hiking Guide. (Illus.). 80p. 2000. pap. 24.95 (*1-57188-203-0*) F Amato Pubns.

Lowe, Donald M. The Body in Late-Capitalist U. S. A. LC 95-9237. (Post-Contemporary Interventions Ser.). 224p. 1995. text 49.95 (*0-8223-1660-9*); pap. text 16.95 (*0-8223-1672-2*) Duke.

— History of Bourgeois Perception. LC 81-7529. (Illus.). x, 226p. 1997. pap. text 9.00 (*0-226-49429-2*) U Ch Pr.

Lowe, Donald M., jt. auth. see Balrow, Tani E.

Lowe, Donald M., jt. auth. see Barlow, Tani E.

Lowe, Donald R. Geologic Evolution of the Barberton Greenstone Belt, South Africa, Vol. 329. LC 98-53073. (Special Papers-Geological Society of America Ser.). 1999. write for info. (*0-8137-2329-9*) Geol Soc.

Lowe, Donald R., jt. ed. see Graham, Stephan A.

Lowe, Doug. Approach 3 for Windows for Dummies. LC 94-79314. (For Dummies Ser.). 384p. 1994. pap. 19.99 (*1-56884-233-3*) IDG Bks.

Lowe, Doug. At Home with Microsoft Works: 101 Easy & Practical Projects. LC 96-79059. 400p. 1996. pap. 19.99 (*0-7645-3026-7*) IDG Bks.

— CICS for the COBOL Programmer Pt. 1: An Introductory Course. 2nd ed. LC 92-17814. 409p. 1992. pap. 42.50 (*0-911625-60-7*) M Murach & Assoc.

— CICS for the COBOL Programmer Pt. 2: An Advanced Course. 2nd ed. LC 92-17814. 352p. 1992. pap. 42.50 (*0-911625-67-4*) M Murach & Assoc.

— The CICS Programmer's Desk Reference. 2nd ed. LC 92-38014. 507p. 1992. pap. 49.50 (*0-911625-68-2*) M Murach & Assoc.

— Client/Server Computing for Dummies. (For Dummies Ser.). 432p. 1995. pap. 19.99 (*1-56884-329-1*) IDG Bks.

***Lowe, Doug.** Client/Server Computing for Dummies. 3rd ed. LC 99-60182. (For Dummies Ser.). 432p. 1999. pap. 24.99 (*0-7645-0476-2*) IDG Bks.

— Creating Web Pages for Dummies: Quick Reference Guide. 2nd ed. LC 99-60191. (For Dummies Ser.). 224p. 1999. spiral bd. 12.99 (*0-7645-0505-X*) IDG Bks.

Lowe, Doug. Internet Explorer 4 for Windows for Dummies. 2nd ed. LC 97-80309. (Illus.). 384p. 1997. pap. 19.99 (*0-7645-0121-6*) IDG Bks.

***Lowe, Doug.** Internet Explorer "X" for Windows for Dummies. (For Dummies Ser.). (Illus.). 384p. 2000. pap. 19.99 (*0-7645-0738-9*) IDG Bks.

— Internet Explorer 5 for Windows for Dummies. LC 98-88738. (For Dummies Ser.). (Illus.). 384p. 1999. pap. 19.99 (*0-7645-0455-X*) IDG Bks.

— Memory Management for Dummies Quick Reference. 2nd ed. LC 96-75758. 384p. 1996. pap. 19.99 (*1-56884-987-7*) IDG Bks.

Lowe, Doug. Microsoft Office 97 for Windows. LC 96-79261. (For Dummies). (Illus.). 224p. 1997. spiral bd. 12.99 (*0-7645-0062-7*) IDG Bks.

***Lowe, Doug.** Microsoft Office 2000 for Windows. LC 98-88795. (Windows for Dummies Ser.). (Illus.). 240p. 1999. spiral bd. 12.99 (*0-7645-0453-3*) IDG Bks.

Lowe, Doug. More Word for Windows 97 for Dummies. LC 97-70744. 416p. 1997. pap. 22.99 (*0-7645-0137-2*) IDG Bks.

— MVS JCL. 2nd ed. LC 94-37779. 496p. 1994. pap. 49.50 (*0-911625-85-2*) M Murach & Assoc.

— MVS TSO Pt. 1: Concepts & ISPF. 2nd ed. LC 90-19907. 467p. 1990. pap. 42.50 (*0-911625-56-9*) M Murach & Assoc.

— MVS TSO Pt. 2: Commands & Procedures. 2nd ed. LC 90-19907. 450p. 1991. pap. 42.50 (*0-911625-57-7*) M Murach & Assoc.

— Networking for Dummies. (For Dummies Ser.). (Illus.). 350p. 1994. pap. 19.95 (*1-56884-079-9*) IDG Bks.

***Lowe, Doug.** Networking for Dummies. 4th ed. (For Dummies Ser.). 384p. 1999. pap. 19.99 (*0-7645-0498-3*) IDG Bks.

Lowe, Doug. The Only DOS Book You'll Ever Need 6.0. 2nd ed. LC 93-859. (Illus.). 610p. 1993. pap. 27.50 (*0-911625-71-2*) M Murach & Assoc.

— OS Utilities. LC 80-84103. (Illus.). 185p. 1981. pap. 22.50 (*0-911625-11-9*) M Murach & Assoc.

— PowerPoint for Windows 95 for Dummies. 368p. 1996. pap. 19.99 (*1-56884-931-1*) IDG Bks.

L

— PowerPoint 97 for Windows for Dummies. LC 96-79270. (For Dummies Ser.). (Illus.). 384p. 1997. pap. 19.99 (*0-7645-0051-1*) IDG Bks.

*Lowe, Doug. Powerpoint 2000 for Dummies. LC T385.L6923 1999. (Windows for Dummies Ser.). (Illus.). 384p. 1999. pap. 19.99 (*0-7645-0450-9*) IDG Bks.

Lowe, Doug. QR/Memory Management for Dummies: Quick Reference. 240p. 1995. spiral bd. 9.99 (*1-56884-362-3*) IDG Bks.

— VSAM: Access Method Services & Application Programming. LC 86-60204. 260p. 1986. pap. 32.50 (*0-911625-33-X*) M Murach & Assoc.

— VSAM for the COBOL Programmer. 2nd ed. LC 88-60035. 187p. 1989. pap. 27.50 (*0-911625-45-3*) M Murach & Assoc.

Lowe, E. A. Paleographical Papers, 1907-1965, 2 vols. Bieler, Ludwig, ed. 1972. 69.00 (*0-19-818220-1*) OUP.

Lowe, E. A., ed. Codices Latini Antiquiores - Supplement. (Illus.). 1972. 72.00 (*0-19-818218-X*) OUP.

***Lowe, E. J.** An Introduction to the Philosophy of Mind. LC 99-21498. 342p. (C). 2000. 54.95 (*0-521-65285-5*); pap. 19.95 (*0-521-65428-9*) Cambridge U Pr.

Lowe, E. J. Locke on Human Understanding. LC 94-43131. (Philosophical Guidebooks Ser.). 224p. (C). (gr. 13). 1995. pap. 12.99 (*0-415-10091-7*, B7020) Routledge.

— The Possibility of Metaphysics: Substance, Identity & Time. LC 98-27587. 286p. 1998. text 65.00 (*0-19-823683-2*) OUP.

— Subjects of Experience. LC 95-15748. (Studies in Philosophy). 211p. (C). 1996. text 54.95 (*0-521-47503-1*) Cambridge U Pr.

***Lowe, E. Joseph D., ed.** Chiang Kai-Shek of China: His Rise & Fall, 20 vols. large type ed. (CHI., Illus.). 3700p. 1999. pap. 285.00 (*0-930325-40-0*) Lowe Pub.

Lowe, Ed. Not As I Do: A Father's Report. 208p. 1995. pap. 9.95 (*0-8362-7045-2*) Andrews & McMeel.

Lowe, Ed, jt. auth. see Siegel, Stanley.

Lowe, Edwin N. Bear Tales: Humorous Stories of Bears, Bunnies, Bulls & Fun. LC 97-97016. (Illus.). 140p. (Orig.). 1998. pap. 12.95 (*0-9660314-0-7*) Bitterroot Publ.

Lowe, Elizabeth. The City in Brazilian Literature. LC 80-66823. 360p. 1982. 34.50 (*0-8386-3009-X*) Fairleigh Dickinson.

Lowe, Elizabeth, tr. see Lispector, Clarice.

Lowe, Elizabeth, tr. see Machado de Assis, Joaquim Maria.

Lowe, Emola, jt. auth. see Stone, Connie.

Lowe, Ernest. Diabetes: A Guide to Living Well: A Program of Individualized Self-Care. 3rd ed. 384p. 1997. pap. 14.95 (*0-471-34677-2*) Wiley.

Lowe, Ernest & Arsham, Gary. Diabetes: A Guide to Living Well. 3rd ed. LC 99-159057. 384p. (Orig.). 1997. pap. 14.95 (*1-56561-112-8*) Wiley.

Lowe, Ernest A., et al. Discovering Industrial Ecology: An Executive Briefing & Sourcebook. LC 97-20763. 202p. 1997. pap. 19.95 (*1-57477-034-9*) Battelle.

***Lowe, Eugene Y.** Promise & Dilemma: Perspectives on Racial Diversity & Higher Education. LC 98-45778. 1999. 29.95 (*0-691-00489-7*, Pub. by Princeton U Pr) Cal Prin Full Svc.

Lowe-Evans, Mary. Crimes Against Fecundity: Joyce & Population Control. (Irish Studies). 160p. 1989. text 39.95 (*0-8156-2460-3*) Syracuse U Pr.

— Critical Essays on Mary Wollstonecraft Shelley. LC 97-40297. 1998. 49.00 (*0-7838-0057-6*) Mac Lib Ref.

— Frankenstein: Mary Shelley's Wedding Guest. LC 92-41553. (Masterwork Studies: No. 126). 112p. 1993. 29.00 (*0-8057-8376-8*); pap. 14.95 (*0-8057-8597-3*) Macmillan.

Lowe, Fonda, jt. ed. see Schopmeyer, Betty B.

***Lowe, Frances Noland.** Anna, a Civil War Story. 204p. 1999. pap. 12.95 (*1-929264-00-3*) Blue Grey.

Lowe, G. The Cysteine Proteinases. 1976. pap. 15.50 (*0-08-020471-6*, Pergamon Pr) Elsevier.

***Lowe, Gary R. & Reid, P. Nelson, eds.** The Professionalization of Poverty: Social Work & the Poor in the Twentieth Century. LC 99-45674. (Modern Applications of Social Work Ser.). 272p. 1999. pap. text 18.95 (*0-202-36112-8*); lib. bdg. 37.95 (*0-202-36111-X*) Aldine de Gruyter.

Lowe, Geoff, et al. Adolescent Drinking & Family Life. LC 93-19119. 216p. 1993. text 51.00 (*3-7186-5413-X*); pap. text 29.00 (*3-7186-5414-8*) Gordon & Breach.

Lowe, George L. B. G. Vol. 1: The Little Drummer Girl Who Drums for the Sun. (Illus.). 21p. (Orig.). (J). (ps). 1988. lib. bdg. 5.00 (*0-685-22681-6*) G L Lowe.

— Ninety Thousand Ninety-Nine: Environs of Infinity. LC 81-90003. 105p. (Orig.). 1981. pap. 4.95 (*0-686-30362-8*) G L Lowe.

Lowe, Gordon D., jt. ed. see Rizza, Charles R.

Lowe, Gordon D. O., ed. Clinical Blood Rheology, Vol. I. 224p. 1988. 137.00 (*0-8493-4598-7*, RB45, CRC Reprint) Franklin.

— Clinical Blood Rheology, Vol. II. 240p. 1988. 146.00 (*0-8493-4599-5*, RB45, CRC Reprint) Franklin.

Lowe, Gordon D. O., jt. auth. see Tooke, John.

Lowe, Gordon R. Growth of Personality from Infancy to Old Age. 1994. pap. 16.95 (*0-14-013677-0*, Pub. by Pnguin Bks Ltd) Trafalgar.

Lowe, Graeme J., intro. Institution of Engineers National Conference, 1990: Government, Engineering & the Nation. (Illus.). 233p. (Orig.). 1990. pap. 57.75 (*0-85825-497-2*, Pub. by Inst Engrs Aust-EA Bks) Accents Pubns.

***Lowe, Graham S.** The Quality Work: A People-Centered Agenda. (Illus.). 200p. 2000. pap. text 19.95 (*0-19-541479-9*) OUP.

Lowe, Graham S. Women in the Administrative Revolution: The Feminization of Clerical Work. 1987. pap. 18.95 (*0-8020-6686-0*); text 37.50 (*0-8020-2657-5*) U of Toronto Pr.

Lowe, Graham S., jt. ed. see Ashton, David.

Lowe, H. Y. The Adventures of Wu: The Life Cycle of a Peking Man, Vols. 1 & 2. LC 82-48568. 274p. 1983. reprint ed. pap. 85.00 (*0-608-06412-2*, 206662500008) Bks Demand.

Lowe, Harry J. & Ernst, Edward A. The Quantitative Practice of Anesthesia: Use of Closed Circuit. LC 80-21803. (Illus.). 249p. reprint ed. pap. 77.20 (*0-608-15558-6*, 205638600063) Bks Demand.

Lowe, Heinz-Dietrich. The Tsars & the Jews: Reform, Reaction, & Antisemitism in Imperial Russia, 1772-1917 (Antisemitismus und Reaktion Are Utopie. LC 92-25147. (ENG & GER.). 456p. 1993. text 92.00 (*3-7186-5289-7*) Gordon & Breach.

Lowe, I. M., ed. Advanced Cermaic Tools for Machining Application, No. 3. (Key Engineering Materials Ser.: Vol. 138-140). (Illus.). 696p. (C). 1998. text 220.00 (*0-87849-768-4*, Pub. by Trans T Pub) Enfield Pubs NH.

Lowe, Iain Macfarlane, jt. auth. see Joy, David.

Lowe, Ian. Etchings of Wilfred Fairclough: A Catalogue Raisonne. 112p. 1990. text 69.95 (*0-85967-846-6*, Pub. by Scolar Pr) Ashgate Pub Co.

— Our Universities Are Turning Us into the Ignorant Country. 1995. pap. 9.95 (*0-86840-126-9*, Pub. by New South Wales Univ Pr) Intl Spec Bk.

Lowe, Ian, jt. auth. see Lovitt, Charles.

***Lowe, J.** Kontextuale Theorie der Volkswirtschaft: Der Ansatz Von Karl Knies Als Ansatz Zukunftiger Wirtschaftspolitik. 270p. 1998. text 58.00 (*90-5708-041-9*, Harwood Acad Pubs); pap. text 28.00 (*90-5708-042-7*, Harwood Acad Pubs) Gordon & Breach.

Lowe, J. Wendell. Conflict Management & Reconciliation. (Equipped to Serve Ser.). (Illus.). 56p. 1997. pap. text 4.95 (*1-889505-09-9*) White Wing Pub.

— Help When the Family Is in Trouble. (Equipped to Serve Ser.). 52p. (Orig.). 1996. pap. text 4.95 (*0-934942-98-6*) White Wing Pub.

Lowe, J. Wendell. Manejo de Conflictos y Reconciliacion (Conflict Management & Reconciliation) (Equipped to Serve Ser.: No. 4). (SPA.). Date not set. pap. text. write for info. (*1-889505-32-3*) White Wing Pub.

Lowe, Jacqueline, et al, eds. Coping with Disaster: Voices from the 1955 Flood, Sutter County, California. (Illus.). 138p. (Orig.). 1995. pap. 18.00 (*0-9625659-1-1*) Comm Mem Mus Sutter Cnty.

Lowe, Jacqueline, et al. Worth Keeping: An Architectural History of Sutter & Yuba Counties, California. (Illus.). 168p. (Orig.). (C). 1990. pap. 18.00 (*0-9625659-0-3*) Comm Mem Mus Sutter Cnty.

Lowe, Jacques. Camelot: The Kennedy Years. LC 96-83989. 1996. 4.95 (*0-8362-2195-8*, Arie Bks) Andrews & McMeel.

— Jacqueline Kennedy Onassis: A Tribute. (Illus.). 128p. (Orig.). 1995. pap. 25.00 (*1-887767-00-2*) J Lowe Vis Arts.

— JFK Remembered. LC 97-52741. 192p. 1998. 19.99 (*0-517-20308-1*) Random Hse Value.

— What Kids Do... 1998. 8.95 (*0-8362-5212-8*) Andrews & McMeel.

Lowe, James. Creative Process of James Agee. LC 93-44684. (Southern Literary Studies). (Illus.). 200p. 1994. text 27.50 (*0-8071-1896-6*) La State U Pr.

Lowe, James, jt. auth. see Delbridge, Rick.

Lowe, James A. The Bridger Trail: A Viable Alternative Route to the Gold Fields of Montana Territory. LC 98-48923. (American Trails Ser.: Vol. 19). (Illus.). 1999. 37.50 (*0-87062-285-4*) A H Clark.

— Insiders Guide to Government Benefits. rev. ed. 402p. 1996. pap. 24.95 (*1-884350-55-0*) Alpha Pubng.

Lowe, James E., jt. ed. see Abdel-Aleem, Salah.

Lowe, James L. Lincoln Postcard Catalog. LC 73-83549. (Illus.). 144p. 1973. reprint ed. pap. 5.95 (*0-913782-05-X*) Deltiologists Am.

— Washington Postcard Catalog. LC 74-30734. (Illus.). 128p. 1986. pap. 5.95 (*0-913782-06-8*) Deltiologists Am.

Lowe, James L. & Papell, Ben, eds. Detroit Publishing Company Collector's Guide. LC 75-4127. (Illus.). 288p. 1975. pap. 12.95 (*0-913782-07-6*) Deltiologists Am.

Lowe, James N. Chemistry, Industry & the Environment. 352p. (C). 1993. text 41.00 (*0-697-17087-X*, WCB McGr Hill) McGrw-H Hghr Educ.

Lowe, James S., jt. auth. see Stevens, Alan.

Lowe, James T. The Philosophy of Air Power. LC 84-5254. 474p. (Orig.). (C). 1984. pap. text 34.00 (*0-8191-3954-8*); lib. bdg. 62.00 (*0-8191-3953-X*) U Pr of Amer.

Lowe, Janet. Benjamin Graham on Value Investing: Lessons from the Dean of Wall Street. 272p. 1996. pap. 14.95 (*0-14-025534-6*) Viking Penguin.

— Bill Gates Speaks: Wisdom from the World's Greatest Entrepreneur. LC 98-25931. 272p. 1998. 16.95 (*0-471-29353-9*) Wiley.

— Billy Graham Speaks: Insight from the World's Greatest Preacher. 219p. (C). 1999. 17.95 (*0-471-34535-0*) Wiley.

***Lowe, Janet.** Damn Right: Behind the Scenes with Berkshire Billionaire Charlie Munger. 256p. 2000. 27.95 (*0-471-24473-2*) Wiley.

Lowe, Janet. George Soros Speaks: Insight from the World's Greatest Financier. LC 99-11235. (Janet Lowe's Speaks Ser.). 208p. 1999. 17.95 (*0-471-34883-X*) Wiley.

***Lowe, Janet.** Jack Welch Speaks; Wisdom from the World's Greatest Business Leader. LC 97-42942. 256p. 1998. 17.95 (*0-471-24272-1*) Wiley.

Lowe, Janet. Michael Jordan Speaks: Insight from the World's Greatest Champion. LC 99-30533. 240p. 1999. 17.95 (*0-471-34564-4*) Wiley.

— Ted Turner Speaks: Insights from the World's Greatest Maverick. LC 99-42193. 230p. 1999. 17.95 (*0-471-34563-6*) Wiley.

— Value Investing Made Easy: Benjamin Graham's Classic Investment Strategy Explained For Everyone. (Illus.). 205p. 1996. 22.95 (*0-07-038859-8*) McGraw.

— Value Investing Made Easy: Benjamin Graham's Classic Investment Strategy Explained for Everyone. (Illus.). 224p. 1997. pap. 14.95 (*0-07-038864-4*) McGraw.

Lowe, Janet C. Keys to Investing in International Stocks. 1992. pap. 4.95 (*0-8120-4759-1*) Barron.

— Warren Buffett Speaks: Wit & Wisdom from the World's Greatest Investor. LC 96-38904. 208p. 1997. 17.95 (*0-471-16996-X*) Wiley.

***Lowe, Janet C. & Graham, Benjamin.** The Rediscovered Benjamin Graham: Selected Writings of the Wall Street Legend. 304p. (C). 1999. 29.95 (*0-471-24472-4*) Wiley.

Lowe, Janet C. & Winfrey, Oprah. Oprah Winfrey Speaks: Insights from the World's Most Influential Voice. LC 98-36572. 512p. 1998. 16.95 (*0-471-29864-6*) Wiley.

***Lowe, Jayne J.** Time Navigation. 176p. 2000. pap. text 11.95 (*1-57558-054-3*) Hearthstone OK.

Lowe, Jeff. Ice World: Techniques & Experiences of Modern Ice Climbing. 256p. 1996. 39.95 (*0-89886-471-2*) Mountaineers.

— Ice World: Techniques & Experiences of Modern Ice Climbing. expanded rev. ed. 256p. 1996. pap. 29.95 (*0-89886-446-1*) Mountaineers.

Lowe, Jeffrey C. & Hodges, Sam, eds. Letters to Amanda: The Civil War Letters of Marion Hill Fitzpatrick, Army of North Virginia. LC 98-38817. (Civil War Georgia Ser.). 256p. 1998. text 29.95 (*0-86554-591-X*, H444) Mercer Univ Pr.

Lowe, Jim. Mountain Boys Are Free: Portrait of Ned Guthrie, the Musicians' Abraham Lincoln. (Illus.). 160p. (Orig.). 1993. pap. write for info. (*0-9635197-0-0*) J G Lowe.

Lowe, Jim, jt. auth. see Stevens, Alan.

Lowe, Jimmy. Jesse Stuart - The Boy from the Dark Hills: A Boyography. Herndon, Jerry A. & Charles, Chuck D., eds. LC 90-62199. (Jesse Stuart Foundation Juvenile Ser.). (Illus.). 79p. (J). (gr. 4-12). 1990. pap. text 15.00 (*0-945084-19-6*) J Stuart Found.

Lowe, John. Britain & Foreign Affairs, 1815-1885: Europe & Overseas. LC 97-27212. (Lancaster Pamphlets Ser.). (Illus.). 120p. (C). 1998. pap. 11.99 (*0-415-13617-2*) Routledge.

— The Great Powers, Imperialism, & the German Problem, 1865-1925. LC 93-36394. (Illus.). 240p. (C). 1994. pap. 20.99 (*0-415-10444-0*, B3741) Routledge.

— Jump at the Sun: Zora Neale Hurston's Cosmic Comedy. 392p. 19.95 (*0-252-06637-5*) U of Ill Pr.

— Jump at the Sun: Zora Neale Hurston's Cosmic Comedy. LC 94-10586. 392p. 1994. text 34.95 (*0-252-02110-X*) U of Ill Pr.

***Lowe, John.** Old Kyoto. (Images of Asia Ser.). (Illus.). 96p. 2000. 16.95 (*0-19-590940-2*) OUP.

— Warden: A Life of John Sparrow. 1998. 40.00 (*0-00-215392-0*, Pub. by HarpC) Trafalgar.

Lowe, John, contrib. by. Wiring. LC 99-182108. (Easy-Step Ser.). (Illus.). 64p. 1998. pap. 4.95 (*0-8069-7053-7*) Sterling.

Lowe, John, ed. Conversations with Ernest Gaines. LC 95-13838. (Literary Conversations Ser.). xix, 335 p. 1995. pap. 15.95 (*0-87805-783-8*); text 39.50 (*0-87805-782-X*) U Pr of Miss.

Lowe, John, jt. ed. see Humphries, Jefferson.

Lowe, John B., jt. auth. see LaPolla, Randy J.

Lowe, John C. The Metabolic Treatment of Fibromyalgia. unabridged ed. Yellin, Jackie G., ed. (Illus.). 850p. 1998. boxed set 99.95 (*0-914609-02-5*) McDowell Pub Co.

— Speeding up to Normal: Metabolic Solutions to Fibromyalgia. Yellin, Jackie G., ed. (Illus.). 550p. 1998. 29.95 (*0-914609-03-3*) McDowell Pub Co.

Lowe, John J. Radiocarbon Dating No. 1: Recent Applications & Future Potential, 1991. 96p. 1997. pap. 75.00 (*0-471-95699-6*) Wiley.

— Reconstructing Quarternary Environments. 2nd ed. 400p. (C). 1997. pap. 49.00 (*0-582-10166-2*) Addison-Wesley.

Lowe, John P. Quantum Chemistry. 2nd ed. (Illus.). 711p. 1993. text 71.00 (*0-12-457555-2*) Acad Pr.

Lowe, John S. Oil & Gas Law in a Nutshell. 2nd ed. (Nutshell Ser.). 465p. (C). 1993. reprint ed. pap. text 18.50 (*0-314-39781-7*) West Pub.

— Oil & Gas Law in a Nutshell. 3rd ed. LC 95-30469. (Nutshell Ser.). 474p. (C). 1995. pap. 22.95 (*0-314-06415-X*) West Pub.

Lowe, Jonathan. Postmarked for Death. 312p. 1996. 22.95 (*1-885173-13-X*) Write Way.

Lowe, Joseph. A New Most Excellent Dancing Master: The Journal of Joseph Lowe's Visits to Balmoral & Windsor (1852-1860) to Teach Dance to the Family of Queen Victoria. Thomas, Allan, ed. LC 92-13521. (Dance & Music Ser.: No. 5). 150p. 1992. lib. bdg. 36.00 (*0-945193-30-0*) Pendragon NY.

— The Present State of England in Regard to Agriculture, Trade & Finance. 2nd ed. LC 66-21682. (Reprints of Economic Classics Ser.). xxviii, 524p. 1967. reprint ed. 65.00 (*0-678-00320-3*) Kelley.

Lowe, Joseph D. A Catalog of the Official Gazeteers of China in the University of Washington (Seattle) expanded rev. ed. (Illus.). xiv, 121p. 1994. pap. 38.00 (*0-930325-31-1*) Lowe Pub.

— The Changing Scenes of the United States Defense: Essays on National Security. LC 90-91734. (Illus.). xiv, 186p. 1982. reprint ed. pap. 54.00 (*0-9605506-5-8*) Lowe Pub.

— China's Cultural Development: From the Earliest Dynasties to the Present Day. LC 90-91679. (Illus.). xxiv, 565p. 1994. text 80.00 (*0-930325-15-X*) Lowe Pub.

— China's Foreign Relations Conducted by the Warlords: 1916-1928. LC 88-91012. (Illus.). xii, 52p. 1991. 30.00 (*0-930325-05-2*) Lowe Pub.

— Chinese Language for Beginners with Exercises in Writing & Speaking. LC 90-91682. (Illus.). xxviii, 660p. 1994. text 162.00 (*0-930325-01-X*) Lowe Pub.

— The Concept & Practice of International Law During the Period of the Warring States: 403-221 B.C. LC 88-91011. (Illus.). xi, 42p. 1994. 24.00 (*0-930325-04-4*) Lowe Pub.

— Dictionary of Diplomatic, International Law, International Relations Terms. limited ed. LC 92-90084. (CHI & ENG., Illus.). 800p. 1994. pap. 195.00 (*0-930325-22-2*) Lowe Pub.

— Dictionary of Military Law: Chinese & English. (CHI & ENG.). 750p. 1987. 175.00 (*0-8288-0973-9*, M8721) Fr & Eur.

— Dictionary of Military Law: Chinese & English. LC 83-83213. (CHI & ENG., Illus.). xiv, 775p. 1994. 195.00 (*0-9605506-6-6*) Lowe Pub.

— Dictionary of Military Terms & Military Intelligence Phrases: Chinese-English & English-Chinese. limited ed. LC 88-91316. (CHI & ENG., Illus.). 725p. 1994. 195.00 (*0-930325-11-7*) Lowe Pub.

— Dictionary of Political Terms: Chinese-English, English-Chinese. LC 80-85163. (CHI & ENG., Illus.). 1250p. 1994. 240.00 (*0-9605506-0-7*) Lowe Pub.

— How the Two Chinas (PRC & ROC) Have Been Governed? (Illus.). xxiii, 225p. 1994. pap. 58.00 (*0-930325-32-X*) Lowe Pub.

— International Relations in Ancient China. LC 88-91010. (Illus.). xii, 168p. 1994. pap. 16.00 (*0-930325-03-6*) Lowe Pub.

— International System of the Warring States in Ancient China: 403-221 B.C. (Illus.). xxviii, 540p. 1994. pap. 68.00 (*0-930325-29-X*) Lowe Pub.

— Li Ssu's Contributions to the Founding of China's First Empire. LC 88-91009. (Illus.). xii, 80p. 1994. pap. 48.00 (*0-930325-02-8*) Lowe Pub.

— Major Problems in China's Foreign Relations since 1840. (Illus.). xxxii, 180p. 1994. pap. 52.00 (*0-930325-30-3*) Lowe Pub.

— The North Atlantic Treaty Organization vs. the Warsaw Pact Military Alliance - a Geopolitical Struggle: Essays on National Security. LC 89-91186. (Illus.). 325p. 1994. 100.00 (*0-930325-13-3*) Lowe Pub.

— The Role Played by the American Political Scientists in the Supreme Command for the Allied Powers: The Purge Program: Why & How Japan Invaded China & the United States, & Why & How Japan Was Defeated & Occupied. LC 90-91738. (Illus.). xii, 201p. 1982. reprint ed. pap. 54.00 (*0-9605506-9-0*) Lowe Pub.

— The Role Played by the Ch'in Army: With Emphasis on Political & Legal Aspects. LC 90-91739. (Illus.). iii, 24p. 1976. reprint ed. pap. 24.00 (*0-9605506-7-4*) Lowe Pub.

— The Sino-American Foreign Policy & Relations since World War II. LC 88-91014. (Illus.). xii, 125p. 1994. pap. 45.00 (*0-930325-07-9*) Lowe Pub.

— Sino-Japanese Relations since 1894. LC 89-91187. (Illus.). xxxii, 375p. 1994. 80.00 (*0-930325-14-1*) Lowe Pub.

— The Sino-Soviet Relations, 1917-1949. LC 88-91013. (Illus.). xiv, 55p. 1994. pap. 30.00 (*0-930325-06-0*) Lowe Pub.

— Spy System of Soviet Russia: From Their Very Beginning to the Present Day. LC 90-91681. (Illus.). xxvi, 560p. 1994. text 90.00 (*0-930325-16-8*) Lowe Pub.

— A Study on the Library Resources at the Military Institutions in Japan, the United States, England, France, Belgium, the Netherlands, Germany, & Switzerland. LC 90-91743. iii, 28p. 1973. reprint ed. pap. 10.00 (*0-9605506-1-5*) Lowe Pub.

— The Superpower Triumvirs - The United States Faces China & Russia since World War II: Their Geopolitical Intentions & Military Capabilities: Essays on National Security. LC 89-91185. (Illus.). xxv, 325p. 1994. 75.00 (*0-930325-12-5*) Lowe Pub.

— The Traditional Chinese Legal Thought: The Pre-Ch'in Period. LC 84-80994. (Illus.). 101p. 1984. pap. 30.00 (*0-9605506-8-2*) Lowe Pub.

— Translation & Interpretation in Principle & Practice: From English into Chinese & from Chinese into English. LC 88-90988. (Illus.). xviii, 475p. 1994. 90.00 (*0-930325-00-1*) Lowe Pub.

— The Yellow River Valley: A Geopolitical Appraisal. LC 90-91744. (Illus.). vii, 46p. 1982. reprint ed. pap. 20.00 (*0-9605506-4-X*) Lowe Pub.

Lowe, Judy. All about Pruning. LC 98-66914. (Ortho's All about Ser.). (Illus.). 96p. 1998. pap. 11.95 (*0-89721-429-3*, Ortho Bks) Meredith Bks.

Lowe, Jurgen. Der Unersattliche Mensch. 258p. 1995. text 75.00 (*3-7186-5774-0*, Harwood Acad Pubs); pap. text 33.00 (*3-7186-5700-7*, Harwood Acad Pubs) Gordon & Breach.

Lowe, K. J. Church & Politics in Renaissance Italy: The Life & Career of Cardinal Francesco Soderini, 1453-1524. LC 92-33576. (Studies in Italian History & Culture). (Illus.). 328p. (C). 1993. text 64.95 (*0-521-42103-9*) Cambridge U Pr.

Lowe, K. J., jt. ed. see Dean, Trevor.

Lowe, K. J., ed. see Musacchio, Jacqueline & Van Boxel, Piet.

***Lowe, K. J. P., ed.** Cultural Links Between Portugal & Italy in the Renaissance. LC 99-16103. (Illus.). 352p. 2000. text 105.00 (*0-19-817428-4*) OUP.

Lowe, Kris. Girls to the Rescue. (Girls R. U. L. E. Ser.: No. 1). 160p. (J). 1998. pap. 3.99 (*0-425-16609-0*, JAM) Berkley Pub.

— Seal Island Scam. (Girls R. U. L. E. Ser.: No. 3). 160p. (J). 1998. pap. 3.99 (*0-425-16520-5*, JAM) Berkley Pub.

An Asterisk (*) at the beginning of an entry indicates that the title is appearing for the first time.

— Trail of Terror. (Girls R. U. L. E. Ser.: No. 2). 160p. (J). 1998. pap. 3.99 (*0-425-16620-1*, JAM) Berkley Pub.

Lowe, L. & Woodroffe, W. Consumer Law & Practice. 425p. (C). 1985. 180.00 (*0-7855-5674-5*, Pub. by Inst Pur & Supply) St Mut.

Lowe, L. F. & De Montreuil, Gerbert. Gerard de Nevers, a Study of the Prose Version of the Roman de la Violette ou, Gerat de Nevers. (Elliot Monographs: Vol. 22). 1928. 25.00 (*0-527-02616-6*) Periodicals Srv.

Lowe, Lisa. Critical Terrains: French & British Orientalisms. LC 91-55058. 232p. 1991. 37.50 (*0-8014-2579-4*) Cornell U Pr.

— Immigrant Acts: On Asian American Cultural Politics. LC 96-20952. 264p. 1996. text 49.95 (*0-8223-1858-X*); pap. text 16.95 (*0-8223-1864-4*) Duke.

Lowe, Lisa, jt. ed. see Kim, Elaine H.

Lowe, Lisa, jt. ed. see Lloyd, David.

Lowe, M. J., et al. Elliott - The South African Notary. 6th ed. 411p. 1987. 72.00 (*0-7021-1980-6*, Pub. by Juta & Co) Gaunt.

Lowe, Madelaine. A Prairie Waltz: Poetry, Art, & "Receipts"...from the Heart of a West Texan. (Illus.). 32p. (Orig.). 1995. pap. 7.95 (*0-9641166-1-8*) Flatland Pubng.

Lowe, Malcolm G. The Mulready Advertisements. (Illus.). lib. bdg. 45.00 (*0-911451-00-5*) Mulready Res.

Lowe, Marcia D. Alternatives to the Automobile. 70p. (Orig.). 1990. pap. 5.00 (*0-916468-99-2*) Worldwatch Inst.

— The Bicycle: Vehicle for a Small Planet. (Orig.). (C). 1989. pap. write for info. (*0-916468-91-7*) Worldwatch Inst.

— Shaping Cities: The Environmental & Human Dimensions. 70p. (Orig.). 1991. pap. 5.00 (*1-878071-06-8*) Worldwatch Inst.

Lowe, Marian & Hubbard, Ruth. Woman's Nature: Rationalizations of Inequality. (Athene Ser.). 140p. 1983. text 50.00 (*0-08-030143-6*, Pergamon Pr); pap. text 19.95 (*0-08-030142-8*, Pergamon Pr) Elsevier.

— Woman's Nature: Rationalizations of Inequality. LC 83-4066. (Athene Ser.). (Illus.). 169p. 1983. reprint ed. pap. 52.40 (*0-7837-6797-8*, 204662900003) Bks Demand.

Lowe, Marie R. Women of Steel: Female Bodybuilders & the Struggle for Self-Definition. LC 97-21216. 1998. text 45.00 (*0-8147-5093-1*); pap. text 18.00 (*0-8147-5094-X*) NYU Pr.

Lowe, Marjorie. Jess. large type ed. 464p. 1985. 27.99 (*0-7089-1380-6*) Ulverscroft.

Lowe, Mark, jt. auth. see Franklin, Denise.

Lowe, Mark, ed. see Buttram, Nora.

Lowe, Martin D., et al. Cardiology. 2nd ed. LC 97-22076. (Colour Guide Ser.). (C). 1998. pap. text 16.95 (*0-443-05912-8*) Harcrt Hlth Sci Grp.

Lowe, Maurice. The Sculpture of Maurice Lowe: Selected Works, 1956-1990. LC 91-60772. (Illus.). 110p. (Orig.). 1991. pap. text 24.95 (*0-9629150-0-9*) M Lowe.

Lowe-McConnell, R. H. Ecological Studies in Tropical Fish Communities. (Cambridge Tropical Biology Ser.). 390p. 1987. pap. text 32.95 (*0-521-28064-8*) Cambridge U Pr.

Lowe-McConnell, R. H., et al, eds. Symposium on Resource Use & Conservation of the African Great Lakes, Bujumbura, 1989. (International Association of Theoretical & Applied Limnology, Communications Ser.: No. 23). (Illus.). 132p. 1989. pap. 38.00 (*3-510-52023-8*, Pub. by E Schweizerbartsche) Balogh.

Lowe, Melissa, ed. see Buechel, Jenifer.

Lowe, Melissa, ed. see Buffington, Adriene.

Lowe, Melissa, ed. see Dunnewold, Jane.

Lowe, Melissa, ed. see Hussain, Donna.

Lowe, Melissa, ed. see Milne, Hollie A.

Lowe, Melissa, ed. see Murrah, Judy.

Lowe, Melissa, ed. see Noble, Elin.

Lowe, Melissa, ed. see Rolfe, Margaret.

Lowe, Melissa, ed. see Weidman, Mary L.

Lowe, Melissa, ed. see White, Saundra.

Lowe, Michael, et al. Early Childhood Teacher's Activities Handbook: A Resource Recipe for Early Childhood Learning Programs. 160p. 1981. pap. 9.95 (*0-685-03848-3*) P-H.

Lowe, Michael A. The Paper Trip. (Illus.). 78p. 1999. pap. 12.99 (*0-9669687-1-9*) M A Lowe.

Lowe, Michelle & Graham, Ben. English Language for Beginners. (For Beginners Ser.). (Illus.). 176p. 1998. pap. 11.00 (*0-86316-263-0*) Writers & Readers.

Lowe, Michelle, jt. auth. see Gregson, Nicky.

Lowe, Mick. A Conspiracy of Brothers. 464p. 1989. pap. 8.99 (*0-7704-2304-3*) Bantam.

Lowe, Mike, jt. auth. see Eisinger, Chris.

Lowe, Mike, jt. auth. see Hylland, Michael D.

Lowe, Morgan. Risque Rhymes Naughty Poetry. 1994. pap. 20.00 (*0-685-72626-6*) Moonlite Pubng.

***Lowe, N. J.** The Classical Plot & the Invention of Western Narrative. (Illus.). 307p. (C). 2000. 59.95 (*0-521-77176-5*) Cambridge U Pr.

Lowe, N. J. & Hensby, C., eds. Nonsteroidal Anti-Inflammatory Drugs. (Pharmacology & the Skin Ser.: Vol. 2). (Illus.). x, 158p. 1989. 129.75 (*3-8055-4898-2*) S Karger.

Lowe, N. J., jt. ed. see Maibach, Howard I.

Lowe, Nicholas. Consuming Cities: Urban Environment in the Global Economy after the Rio Declaration. LC 99-18549. 1999. pap. write for info. (*0-415-18769-9*) Routledge.

— Physician's Guide to Sunscreens. (Illus.). 232p. 1990. text 110.00 (*0-8247-8496-0*) Dekker.

***Lowe, Nicholas.** Psoriasis: A Patient's Guide. 91p. 1999. 14.95 (*1-85317-599-4*, Pub. by Martin Dunitz) Blackwell Sci.

Lowe, Nicholas & Marks, Ronald. Retinoids: A Clinician's Guide. 1995. 75.00 (*0-614-07390-1*) Scovill Paterson.

Lowe, Nicholas & McMillan, M. Living Proof: Views of a World Living with HIV & AIDs. 167p. 1992. pap. 21.00 (*0-9509797-2-4*, Pub. by Bloodaxe Bks) Dufour.

Lowe, Nicholas & Sellar, Polly. Skin Secrets: The Medical Facts vs. the Beauty Fiction. (Illus.). 144p. 1999. pap. 19.95 (*1-85585-665-4*, Pub. by Collins & Br) Sterling.

Lowe, Nicholas J., et al, eds. Sunscreens: Development, Evaluation, & Regulatory Aspects. 2nd ed. LC 96-43444. (Cosmetic Science & Technology Ser.: Vol. 15). (Illus.). 744p. 1996. text 225.00 (*0-8247-9306-4*) Dekker.

Lowe, Nicholas J. & Marks, Ronald. Retinoids. 184p. 1998. write for info. (*1-85317-427-0*) Martin Dunitz.

Lowe, Nicholas J., jt. auth. see Lask, Gary P.

Lowe, Nicholas J., ed. see Leppard, Barbara & Ashton, Richard.

Lowe, Nigel V. & Douglas, Gillian, eds. Families Across Frontiers. LC 96-7887. 1996. lib. bdg. 228.00 (*90-411-0239-6*, Pub. by M Nijhoff) Kluwer Academic.

***Lowe-Norris, Alistair G.** Windows 2000 Active Directory. Denn, Robert, ed. (Illus.). 400p. 2000. pap. 39.95 (*1-56592-638-2*) OReilly & Assocs.

Lowe, P., jt. ed. see Brouwer, F. J.

Lowe, Pamela M., ed. see Contreras, Francisco.

***Lowe, Paul.** In Each Moment: A New Way to Live. abr. ed. Ronner, Devon, ed. 200p. 1998. pap. 14.95 (*0-9684109-0-1*, Pub. by Look Glass Pr) Bookpeople.

Lowe, Paul G. The Experiment Is Over. 272p. (Orig.). 1989. pap. 11.95 (*0-924239-00-X*) Roximillion Pubns.

Lowe, Paula C. CarePooling: How to Get the Help You Need to Care for the Ones You Love. LC 93-26746. 300p. (Orig.). 1993. pap. 14.95 (*1-881052-16-8*) Berrett-Koehler.

Lowe, Paula C. & Ferraro, Richard F. Dolphin KidKit, Set. 30p. (J). (ps-3). 1994. pap. 16.00 incl. audio (*1-886476-00-4*) BigEye.

— Dolphin KidKit: Discovery Edition, Set. 50p. (J). (gr. 2-7). 1994. pap. 10.00 incl. audio (*1-886476-01-2*) BigEye.

Lowe, Percival G. Five Years a Dragoon ('49-'54) And Other Adventures on the Great Plains. LC 65-11223. (Illus.). 384p. 1991. pap. 15.95 (*0-8061-1089-9*) U of Okla Pr.

Lowe, Peter. Amazon Colonists: Family Photographs from the Ecuadorian Amazon. (Illus.). 48p. 1999. pap. write for info. (*0-9670569-0-X*) P Lowe.

Lowe, Peter. Britain in the Far East: A Survey from 1819 to the Present. 1981. 25.00 (*0-582-48730-7*) Longman.

Lowe, Peter. Britain in the Far East: A Survey from 1819 to the Present. LC 79-42619. 272p. reprint ed. pap. 84.40 (*0-8357-6044-8*, 203448600090) Bks Demand.

Lowe, Peter. The Korean War. pap. 15.95 (*0-312-23304-3*); text 59.95 (*0-312-23303-5*) St Martin.

Lowe, Peter. Success Spirituality. 2000. write for info. (*0-684-85055-9*) S&S Trade.

***Lowe, Peter, ed.** Quito. (SPA & ENG., Illus.). 56p. 2000. write for info. (*0-9670569-1-8*) P Lowe.

Lowe, Peter & Moeshart, Herman, eds. Western Interactions with Japan: Expansions, the Armed Forces & Readjustment, 1859-1956. 118p. (C). 1996. pap. text 18.00 (*0-904404-84-6*, Pub. by Curzon Pr Ltd) UH Pr.

Lowe, Phil. Coaching & Counseling: The McGraw-Hill One-Day Workshop. 128p. 1995. 110.00 (*0-07-912092-X*) McGraw.

— Creativity & Problem Solving: The McGraw-Hill One-Day Workshop. 128p. 1995. 110.00 (*0-07-912091-1*) McGraw.

— Empowerment: The McGraw-Hill One-Day Workshop. 128p. 1995. 110.00 (*0-07-912093-8*) McGraw.

Lowe, Phil. Health & Safety Awareness Extra Participant's Guide. 62p. 1993. ring bd. 59.95 (*0-7494-0925-8*, Kogan Pg Educ) Stylus Pub VA.

— Leadership Skills. 120p. 1995. ring bd. 299.00 (*0-7494-1150-3*, Kogan Pg Educ); ring bd. 59.95 (*0-7494-1151-1*, Kogan Pg Educ) Stylus Pub VA.

Lowe, Phil. Presentation Skills: Trainer's Guide. LC 94-13299. (McGraw-Hill One-Day Workshop Ser.). 156p. 1994. 110.00 (*0-07-038852-0*) McGraw.

Lowe, Phil & Kennedy, Kim. Health & Safety Awareness. 157p. 1993. ring bd. 299.00 (*0-7494-0924-X*, Kogan Pg Educ) Stylus Pub VA.

Lowe, Phil & Lewis, Ralph. Management Development Beyond the Fringe: A Practical Guide to Alternative Approaches. LC 93-42469. 192p. 1994. pap. text 19.95 (*0-89397-397-1*) Nichols Pub.

Lowe, Philip, et al, eds. Regulating Agriculture. 198p. 1995. 145.00 (*0-471-95932-4*) Wiley.

— Technological Change & the Rural Enviornment. (Critical Perspectives on Rural Change Ser.). 208p. 1995. text 130.00 (*0-471-95928-6*, GE11) Wiley.

Lowe, Philip & Ward, Stephen. British Environmental Policy & Europe. LC 97-15808. (Global Environmental Change Ser.). 352p. (C). 1998. 85.00 (*0-415-15500-2*); pap. 27.99 (*0-415-15501-0*) Routledge.

Lowe, Philip, et al. Moralizing the Environment: Countryside Change, Farming & Pollution. 224p. 1998. 69.95 (*1-85728-839-4*, Pub. by UCL Pr Ltd); pap. 22.95 (*1-85728-840-8*, Pub. by UCL Pr Ltd) Taylor & Francis.

Lowe, Philip D., et al, eds. European Integration & Environmental Policy. LC 93-14599. 256p. 1994. 125.00 (*0-471-94811-X*) Wiley.

Lowe-Porter, H. T., tr. see Mann, Thomas.

Lowe-Porter, Helen T., tr. see Frank, Bruno.

Lowe-Porter, Helen T., tr. see Mann, Thomas.

Lowe, R., jt. auth. see Brigden, Paul.

Lowe, R. W. A Bibliographical Account of English Theatrical Literature from Earliest Times to the Present Day. 1972. 59.95 (*0-87968-735-5*) Gordon Pr.

Lowe, R. W., ed. see Cibber, Colley.

Lowe, R. W., ed. see Doran, John.

Lowe, Richard, ed. Texas Cavalry Officer's Civil War: The Diary & Letters of James C. Bates. LC 99-14901. (Illus.). 328p. 1999. 34.95 (*0-8071-2372-2*) La State U Pr.

Lowe, Richard C. & Bearup, George F. Michigan Revocable Grantor Trusts. LC 90-85064. 1991. ring bd., suppl. ed. 95.00 incl. disk (*0-685-47729-0*) U MI Law CLE.

— Michigan Revocable Grantor Trusts. LC 90-85064. 1992. suppl. ed. 40.00 (*0-685-58921-8*, 92-010) U MI Law CLE.

— Michigan Revocable Grantor Trusts. LC 90-85064. 1993. suppl. ed. 55.00 incl. disk (*0-685-58922-6*, 93-012) U MI Law CLE.

Lowe, Richard G. Republicans & Reconstruction in Virginia, 1856-70. LC 90-44920. 271p. reprint ed. pap. 84.10 (*0-608-08547-2*, 206907000002) Bks Demand.

Lowe, Richard G. & Campbell, Randolph B. Planters & Plain Folk: Agriculture in Antebellum Texas. LC 85-27844. 240p. 1987. 22.50 (*0-87074-212-4*) SMU Press.

***Lowe, Robert.** Improvisation, Inc. Harnessing Spontaneity to Engage People & Groups. 2000. pap. 19.95 (*0-7879-5142-0*) Jossey-Bass.

Lowe, Robert & Miner, Barbara. Selling Out Our Schools: Vouchers, Markets, & the Future of Public Education. (Illus.). 88p. 1996. pap. 5.00 (*0-942961-19-6*) Rethinking Schls.

Lowe, Robert, jt. ed. see Southwell, Ian.

Lowe, Robert C. Louisiana Divorce. LC 83-82099. (Louisiana Practice Systems Library). 1984. ring bd. 120.00 (*0-317-00651-7*) West Group.

— Louisiana Divorce. LC 83-82099. (Louisiana Practice Systems Library). 1993. suppl. ed. 70.00 (*0-317-03231-3*) West Group.

— State Public Welfare Legislation. LC 75-165602. (Research Monographs: Vol. 20). 1971. reprint ed. lib. bdg. 49.50 (*0-306-70352-1*) Da Capo.

Lowe, Robert E. West of the Scioto. LC 90-92260. (Illus.). 210p. (Orig.). 1993. pap. text. write for info. (*1-878455-05-2*) Markas Pub.

Lowe, Robert G. My Own Two Feet. Hill, Thelma L., ed. LC 94-77361. 110p. (Orig.). 1994. pap. text 10.00 (*1-878455-10-9*) Markas Pub.

Lowe, Robert H. A Crow Text, with Grammatical Notes. fac. ed. (University of California Publications in American Archaeology & Ethnology: Vol. 29:2). 25p. (C). 1930. reprint ed. pap. text 2.81 (*1-55567-781-9*) Coyote Press.

Lowe, Robert J. Phonology: Applications to Assessment & Intervention. (Illus.). 272p. 1994. 33.00 (*0-683-05205-5*) Lppncott W & W.

— Workbook for the Identification of Phonological Processes. 2nd ed. 107p. (C). 1996. pap. text 16.00 (*0-89079-646-7*, 7805) PRO-ED.

Lowe, Robert J. & Weitz, Julia M. Picture Resources for the Remediation of Articulation & Phonological Disorders. (Illus.). 111p. (Orig.). 1992. pap. 19.95 (*0-9626939-5-2*) Janelle Pubns.

Lowe, Robert L. & Weitz, Julia M. Activities for the Remediation of Phonological Disorders. (Illus.). 125p. 1992. pap. 17.95 (*0-9626939-6-0*) Janelle Pubns.

Lowe, Robert W. Play Ball: Home Runs for Life. LC 96-44095. 1996. write for info. (*0-87197-451-7*) Favorite Recipes.

— Thomas Betterton. LC 77-144652. reprint ed. 37.50 (*0-404-04038-1*) AMS Pr.

Lowe, Roberta, jt. auth. see Lowe, Donald.

Lowe, Robin, jt. auth. see Gilligan, Colin.

Lowe, Rodney. Adjusting to Democracy: The Role of the Ministry of Labour in British Politics, 1916-1939. LC 86-733. 300p. 1986. text 65.00 (*0-19-820094-3*) OUP.

— The Welfare State in Britain since 1945. 2nd ed. LC 98-18577. 424p. 1998. text 55.00 (*0-312-21633-5*) St Martin.

Lowe, Rodney, jt. auth. see Fawcett, Helen.

Lowe, Romana N. The Fictional Female: Sacrificial Rituals & Spectacles of Writing in Baudelaire, Zola & Cocteau. LC 96-44619. (Currents in Comparative Romance Languages & Literatures Ser.: Vol. 54). XII, 239p. (C). 1997. text 47.95 (*0-8204-3694-1*) P Lang Pubng.

Lowe, Ronnie W. Man's Greatest Questions. 1992. pap. 7.15 (*0-89137-132-X*) Quality Pubns.

Lowe, Rose M. Thoughts That Stem from the Rose. LC 98-92135. 104p. 1999. pap. 12.00 (*0-9666862-0-9*) Ray Rose Pubs.

Lowe, Ross E., et al. Consumer Education & Economics. 1997. teacher ed. write for info. (*0-02-637224-X*) Glencoe.

Lowe, Roy. Education in the Post-War Years: A Social History, 1945-1964. 224p. (C). 1988. lib. bdg. 55.00 (*0-415-00592-2*) Routledge.

***Lowe, Roy.** History of Education. LC 99-48736. 1976p. 2000. 750.00 (*0-415-14046-3*) Routledge.

Lowe, Roy. Schooling & Social Change, 1964-1990. LC 96-51714. (Illus.). 208p. (C). 1997. 85.00 (*0-415-02397-1*) Routledge.

— Schooling & Social Change, 1964-1990. LC 96-51714. (Illus.). 208p. (C). 1997. pap. 24.99 (*0-415-16689-6*) Routledge.

— A Western Acropolis of Learning: The University of California in 1897. LC 96-33926. (Chapters in the History of the University of California Ser.: Vol. 5). (Illus.). 47p. 1996. pap. 10.00 (*0-87772-368-0*) UCB IGS.

Lowe, Roy, ed. Education & the Second World War: Studies in Schooling & Social Change. 224p. 1992. 89.95 (*0-7507-0054-8*, Falmer Pr); pap. 34.95 (*0-7507-0055-6*, Falmer Pr) Taylor & Francis.

Lowe, Roy W., jt. auth. see Bayer, Range D.

Lowe, Ruby H. David Kalakaua. (Kamehameha Schools Intermediate Reading Program Ser.). (Illus.). 126p. (J). (gr. 3-7). 1998. pap. 9.95 (*0-87336-041-9*) Kamehameha Schools.

— Kamehameha IV: Alexander Liholiho. LC 96-196206. (Kamehameha Schools Intermediate Reading Program Ser.). (Illus.). 128p. (Orig.). (J). (gr. 3-7). 1996. pap. 7.95 (*0-87336-045-1*) Kamehameha Schools.

— Lili'uokalani. (Kamehameha Schools Intermediate Reading Program Ser.). (Illus.). 111p. (Orig.). (J). (gr. 3-7). 1993. pap. 7.95 (*0-87336-018-4*) Kamehameha Schools.

— O Lili'uokalani. Pau, Hannah H., ed. Walk, Kamoa'elehua, tr. (HAW., Illus.). 111p. (Orig.). (YA). (gr. 7-12). 1994. pap. 7.95 (*0-87336-027-3*) Kamehameha Schools.

Lowe, Rupert, tr. see Fo, Dario.

Lowe, S. & Ince, A. Taking Over. large type ed. 1990. 27.99 (*0-7089-2307-0*) Ulverscroft.

Lowe, Sarah M. Tina Modotti: Photographs. LC 95-889. (Illus.). 160p. 1995. 49.50 (*0-8109-4280-1*, Pub. by Abrams) Time Warner.

— Tina Modotti: Photographs. (Illus.). 160p. 1998. pap. 19.95 (*0-8109-2763-2*, Pub. by Abrams) Time Warner.

— Tina Modotti: Photographs. (Illus.). 160p. 1995. pap. 30.00 (*0-87633-095-2*, 30084) Phila Mus Art.

Lowe, Sarah M., suppl. Elena Climent: Re-Encounters. (Illus.). 24p. 1995. pap. 15.00 (*1-930191-06-5*) M Martin Fine Art.

Lowe, Scott. Mo Tzu's Religious Blueprint for a Chinese Utopia: The Will & the Way. LC 92-4366. 200p. 1992. lib. bdg. 79.95 (*0-7734-9490-1*) E Mellen.

Lowe, Scott & Lane, David. DA: The Strange Case of Franklin Jones. (Understanding Cults & Spiritual Movements Ser.). 115p. 1999. pap. 9.95 (*1-56543-054-9*) Mt SA Coll Philos.

Lowe, Scott & Trauner, Theodore J. Construction on Contaminated Sites. LC 96-33169. (Illus.). 254p. 1996. 54.95 (*0-07-038878-4*) McGraw.

***Lowe, Sheila.** The Complete Idiot's Guide to Handwriting Analysis. (Complete Idiot's Guides (Lifestyle) Ser.). (Illus.). 456p. 1999. pap. 16.95 (*0-02-863202-8*, Pub. by Macmillan Gen Ref) S&S Trade.

Lowe, Shirley. Microscopic Procedures for Primary Care Providers. LC 98-22966. 1998. write for info. (*0-7817-1432-X*) Lppncott W & W.

Lowe, Shirley & Ince, Angela. Shaping Up. 256p. 1992. 24.95 (*0-340-52830-3*, Pub. by Hodder & Stought Ltd) Trafalgar.

— Swapping. 240p. 1988. 17.95 (*0-316-53381-5*) Little.

Lowe, Shirley A. Born & Raised a Mormon: A Journey Through the Maze. LC 99-94250. 76p. 1999. pap. 5.95 (*0-7392-0156-5*, PO3103) Morris Pubng.

Lowe, Sigmund. Seventy Steps Toward Wisdom. 2nd ed. 95p. 1981. pap. 3.50 (*0-87516-050-6*) DeVorss.

Lowe, Stephen. Arthur Lowe - A Life. (Illus.). 224p. 1996. 32.95 (*1-85459-279-3*, Pub. by N Hern Bks) Theatre Comm.

— Divine Gossip & Tibetan Inroads. (Methuen New Theatrescripts Ser.). 136p. (Orig.). (C). 1989. pap. write for info. (*0-413-61220-1*, A0371, Methuen Drama) Methn.

— Touched. (Methuen Modern Plays Ser.). 80p. (C). 1989. reprint ed. pap. write for info. (*0-413-61210-4*, A0372, Methuen Drama) Methn.

Lowe, Stephen, ed. see Mitchell, Adrian, et al.

Lowe, Stephen, ed. see Stayton, Richard, et al.

Lowe, Stephen R. The Kid on the Sandlot: Congress & Professional Sports, 1910-1992. LC 94-79195. 1995. 34.95 (*0-87972-675-X*); pap. 15.95 (*0-87972-676-8*) Bowling Green Univ Popular Press.

***Lowe, Stephen R.** Sir Walter & Mr. Jones: Walter Hagen, Bobby Jones & the Rise of American Golf. (Illus.). 350p. 2000. 35.00 (*1-58536-009-0*) Sleepng Bear.

Lowe, Stuart & Hughes, David, eds. A New Century of Social Housing. 1991. text 59.00 (*0-7185-1353-3*) St Martin.

Lowe, Sue D. Stieglitz: A Memoir-Biography. LC 82-18341. (Illus.). 419p. 1983. 25.50 (*0-374-26990-4*) FS&G.

Lowe, Sue D., et al. Ten Minutes Ahead of the Rest of the World. 2nd rev. ed. LC 81-81534. (Illus.). 308p. 1982. reprint ed. 30.00 (*0-9607742-0-3*) Milford Hist Soc.

Lowe, Sue J., jt. auth. see Graham, John.

Lowe, T. L. & Rounce, J. F. Calculations for A-Level Physics. 3rd ed. 424p. 1997. pap. 37.50 (*0-7487-2399-4*, Pub. by S Thornes Pubs) Trans-Atl Phila.

Lowe, Terry C. Business of Insurance: A Comprehensive Introduction to Insurance. 70p. 1998. pap. text 10.00 (*1-879143-44-5*) Health Ins Assn Am.

Lowe, Terry C. & Denning, Elizabeth. Disability Income Insurance: An Overview of Income Protection Insurance. 2nd ed. 41p. (Orig.). 1994. pap. text 10.00 (*1-879143-23-2*) Health Ins Assn Am.

Lowe, Terry C., ed. see Minerals, Metals & Materials Society Staff.

Lowe, Thomas. Adoptive Masonry. 6.00 (*0-911164-00-6*) Powner.

Lowe, Tom. Spin. LC 98-235596. 327p. 1998. 23.00 (*0-671-01923-6*, Pocket Books) PB.

— Spin: A Novel. 304p. 1999. per. 12.95 (*0-671-01924-4*, PB Trade Paper) PB.

— A Very Special Doctor. 32p. (J). Date not set. write for info. (*0-7868-3060-3*) Disney Pr.

Lowe, Truman. Streams: Catalogue for the Exhibition. (Illus.). 24p. (Orig.). 1991. pap. 5.00 (*0-9621886-1-1*) Univ WI Art Gal.

Lowe, Vaughan & Fitzmaurice, Malgosia, eds. Fifty Years of the International Court of Justice: Essays in Honour of Sir Robert Jennings. (Illus.). 680p. (C). 1996. text 125.00 (*0-521-55093-9*) Cambridge U Pr.

Lowe, Vaughan, jt. auth. see Collier, John.

L

An Asterisk (*) at the beginning of an entry indicates that the title is appearing for the first time.

L

Lowe, Vaughn, jt. ed. see Crawford, James.

Lowe, Vicki & Howell, Lou. How Do We Know They Know? Alternative Assessments in Home Economics. 1994. 8.00 (*0-911365-35-4*, A261-08484) Family & Consumer Sci Educ.

Lowe, Victor. Alfred North Whitehead Vol. 1: The Man & His Work: 1861-1910. LC 84-15467. 392p. 1985. 39.95 (*0-8018-2488-5*) Johns Hopkins.

— Understanding Whitehead. LC 62-15312. 416p. 1966. reprint ed. pap. 129.00 (*0-608-03723-0*, 206454800009) Bks Demand.

Lowe, Victor, et al. Whitehead & the Modern World: Science, Metaphysics, & Civilization. LC 72-5738. (Essay Index Reprint Ser.). 1977. reprint ed. 18.95 (*0-8369-7281-3*) Ayer.

Lowe, Vincent. Perl Programmer's Interactive Workbook. 656p. 1999. pap. text 39.99 (*0-13-020868-X*) P-H.

Lowe, Virginia, jt. auth. see Bliss, Pamela.

Lowe, W. D. Herodotus: The Wars of Greece & Persia. (Illus.). (C). 1984. reprint ed. pap. 13.00 (*0-86516-054-6*) Bolchazy-Carducci.

Lowe, W. D. & Freeman, C. E., eds. Rome & Her Kings: Extracts from Livy I. (Textbook Ser.). 110p. 1981. pap. text 11.00 (*0-86516-000-7*) Bolchazy-Carducci.

***Lowe, W. D. & Freeman, C. E., eds.** Rome & Her Kings Livy 1: Graded Selections. 110p. (C). 2000. pap. 12.00 (*0-86516-450-9*) Bolchazy-Carducci.

Lowe, W. J. The Irish in Mid-Victorian Lancashire: The Shaping of a Working-Class Community. (American University Studies: History: Ser. IX, Vol. 77). 235p. (C). 1989. text 46.50 (*0-8204-0999-5*) P Lang Pubng.

Lowe, Walter. Evil & the Unconscious. LC 82-19147. (American Academy of Religion, Studies in Religion). 142p. (C). 1983. 24.95 (*0-89130-600-5*, 01 00 30) OUP.

— Theology & Difference: The Wound of Reason. LC 92-26531. (Indiana Series in the Philosophy of Religion). 204p. 1993. 31.50 (*0-253-33611-2*) Ind U Pr.

Lowe, Warren, et al. Leroy's Zoo: Featuring the Folk Art Carvings of Leroy Ramon Archuleta. LC 97-7696. (Illus.). (J). 1997. 21.00 (*1-881320-87-1*, Black Belt) Black Belt Communs.

Lowe-Whitehead, Sally. The Truth Shall Set You Free: A Memoir: A Family's Passage from Fundamentalism to a New Understanding. LC 98-31596. 266p. 1999. pap. 15.00 (*0-664-25818-2*) Westminster John Knox.

Lowe, Whitney. Functional Assessment in Massage Therapy. 3rd rev. ed. (Illus.). 181p. 1995. pap. text 29.95 (*0-9661196-0-6*) OMERI.

Lowe, William C. Blessing of Liberty: Safeguarding Civil Rights. LC 92-9756. (Human Rights Ser.). 112p. (J). 1992. lib. bdg. 18.95 (*0-86593-173-9*) Rourke Corp.

Lowe, William T. After the Summer People Leave: 12 Baffling Adirondack Mystery Stories. LC 96-69805. 252p. (Orig.). 1996. pap. 12.95 (*0-9632476-4-6*) Pinto Pr.

Lowehndorf, Dan, jt. auth. see Larson, Dana.

Lowell, A. Lawrence. New England Aviators, 1914-1918: Their Portraits & Their Records, Vol. 1. LC 97-66730. (Illus.). 472p. 1997. 49.95 (*0-7643-0345-7*) Schiffer.

— New England Aviators, 1914-1918: Their Portraits & Their Records, Vol. 2. LC 97-66730. (Illus.). 480p. 1997. 49.95 (*0-7643-0346-5*) Schiffer.

Lowell, Abbott L. Public Opinion in War & Peace. LC 73-14167. (Perspectives in Social Inquiry Ser.). 320p. 1974. reprint ed. 21.95 (*0-405-05512-9*) Ayer.

— What a University President Has Learned. LC 77-93355. (Essay Index Reprint Ser.). 1977. 18.95 (*0-8369-1303-5*) Ayer.

Lowell, Amy. Can Grande's Castle. (Collected Works of Amy Lowell). 322p. 1999. reprint ed. lib. bdg. 98.00 (*1-58201-752-2*, c0752) Classic Bks.

— Can Grande's Castle. LC 71-131771. 232p. 1918. reprint ed. 29.00 (*0-403-00658-9*) Scholarly.

— A Critical Fable. LC 78-64043. (Des Imagistes: Literature of the Imagist Movement Ser.). 112p. reprint ed. 27.50 (*0-404-17126-5*) AMS Pr.

— A Critical Fable. (Collected Works of Amy Lowell). 99p. 1999. reprint ed. lib. bdg. 88.00 (*1-58201-753-0*) Classic Bks.

— A Dome of Many-Coloured Glass. LC 78-64044. (Des Imagistes: Literature of the Imagist Movement Ser.). 152p. reprint ed. 29.50 (*0-404-17127-3*) AMS Pr.

— A Dome of Many-Coloured Glass. (Collected Works of Amy Lowell). 139p. 1999. reprint ed. lib. bdg. 88.00 (*1-58201-755-7*, c0755) Classic Bks.

— Dream Drops: or Stories from Fairy Land by a Dreamer. (Collected Works of Amy Lowell). 118p. 1999. reprint ed. lib. bdg. 88.00 (*1-58201-756-5*, c0756) Classic Bks.

— John Keats, 2 vols., Set. (BCL1-PR English Literature Ser.). 1992. reprint ed. lib. bdg. 150.00 (*0-7812-7573-3*) Rprt Serv.

— Legends. (Collected Works of Amy Lowell). 259p. 1999. reprint ed. lib. bdg. 88.00 (*1-58201-757-3*, c0757) Classic Bks.

— Men, Women & Ghosts. (Collected Works of Amy Lowell). 363p. 1999. lib. bdg. 98.00 (*1-58201-758-1*, c0758) Classic Bks.

— Pictures of the Floating World. LC 78-64045. (Des Imagistes: Literature of the Imagist Movement Ser.). reprint ed. 42.50 (*0-404-17128-1*) AMS Pr.

— Pictures of the Floating World. (Collected Works of Amy Lowell). 257p. 1999. reprint ed. lib. bdg. 88.00 (*1-58201-759-X*, c0759) Classic Bks.

— Poetry & Poets. LC 77-162298. 1971. reprint ed. 30.00 (*0-8196-0274-4*) Biblo.

— Selected Poems. 1988. reprint ed. lib. bdg. 49.00 (*0-7812-0518-2*) Rprt Serv.

— Selected Poems. 1971. reprint ed. 49.00 (*0-403-00657-0*) Scholarly.

— Six French Poets: Studies in Contemporary Literature. LC 67-28737. (Essay Index Reprint Ser.). 1977. 22.95 (*0-8369-0626-8*) Ayer.

— Six French Poets: Studies in Contemporary Literature. (Collected Works of Amy Lowell). 488p. 1999. reprint ed. lib. bdg. 108.00 (*1-58201-760-3*, c0760) Classic Bks.

— Sword Blades & Poppy Seed. LC 78-64046. (Des Imagistes: Literature of the Imagist Movement Ser.). 256p. reprint ed. 39.50 (*0-404-17129-X*) AMS Pr.

— Sword Blades & Poppy Seed. (Collected Works of Amy Lowell). 256p. 1999. reprint ed. lib. bdg. 88.00 (*1-58201-761-1*, c0761) Classic Bks.

— Tendencies in American Poetry. LC 68-54171. (Studies in Poetry: No. 38). 1969. reprint ed. lib. bdg. 75.00 (*0-8383-0588-1*) M S G Haskell Hse.

— Tendencies in Modern American Poetry. (Collected Works of Amy Lowell). 349p. 1999. reprint ed. lib. bdg. 98.00 (*1-58201-762-X*, c0762) Classic Bks.

— Tendencies in Modern American Poetry. (BCL1-PS American Literature Ser.). 349p. 1992. reprint ed. lib. bdg. 89.00 (*0-7812-6629-7*) Rprt Serv.

Lowell, B. Lindsay. Foreign Temporary Workers in America: Policies That Benefit the U. S. Economy. LC 98-18500. 296p. 1999. 49.95 (*1-56720-227-6*, Quorum Bks) Greenwood.

Lowell, Bruce K. Dr. Bruce Lowell's Fat Percentage Finder: The New, Easy-to-Use System for Measuring the Fat in Your Diet. 192p. (Orig.). 1991. pap. 9.00 (*0-399-51653-0*, Perigee Bks) Berkley Pub.

— Mid-Life Body Signals: The Over-40 Guide to Health Symptoms & What They Mean. 464p. 1997. pap. 14.00 (*0-06-273477-6*, Harper Ref) HarpC.

***Lowell, Christopher.** Christopher Lowell's Seven Layers of Design: Fearless, Fabulous Decorating. (Illus.). 176p. 2000. 29.95 (*1-56331-922-5*, Pub. by Discovery) Random.

Lowell, Cym H., jt. auth. see Hammer, Richard M.

Lowell, Cym H., jt. auth. see Weistart, John C.

Lowell, D. R. The Historic Genealogy of the Lowells of America from 1639-1899. (Illus.). 878p. 1989. reprint ed. pap. 130.50 (*0-8328-0790-7*); reprint ed. lib. bdg. 138.50 (*0-8328-0789-3*) Higginson Bk Co.

Lowell, Edgar L. & Stoner, Marguerite. Play It by Ear! 1963. reprint ed. spiral bd. 9.00 (*0-9606312-0-8*) John Tracy Clinic.

Lowell, Edward J. Eve of the French Revolution. LC 72-1016. reprint ed. 42.50 (*0-404-07145-7*) AMS Pr.

— The Hessians: And Other German Auxiliaries of Great Britain in the Revolutionary War. 3rd unabridged ed. Andrews, Raymond J., ed. 360p. 1997. reprint ed. pap. 18.95 (*0-87928-116-2*) Corner Hse.

— The Hessians & the Other German Auxiliaries of Great Britain in the Revolutionary War. (Illus.). 328p. 1995. reprint ed. lib. bdg. 42.00 (*0-8328-4495-0*) Higginson Bk Co.

Lowell, Elizabeth. Amber Beach. LC 97-15119. 400p. 1997. mass mkt. 22.00 (*0-380-97317-0*, Avon Bks) Morrow Avon.

— Amber Beach. 1998. mass mkt. 6.99 (*0-380-77584-0*, Avon Bks) Morrow Avon.

— Amber Beach. large type ed. LC 98-24020. (Romance Ser.). 1998. 26.95 (*1-56895-577-4*) Wheeler Pub.

Lowell, Elizabeth. Autumn Lover. 416p. (Orig.). 1996. mass mkt. 6.99 (*0-380-76955-7*, Avon Bks) Morrow Avon.

— Beautiful Dreamer. 2000. 19.95 (*0-380-78993-0*) Morrow Avon.

Lowell, Elizabeth. Chain Lightning. 1993. per. 4.50 (*0-373-48278-7*) Harlequin Bks.

— Chain Lightning. (Mira Bks.). 1997. per. 5.50 (*1-55166-312-0*, 1-66312-9, Mira Bks) Harlequin Bks.

— Chain Lightning. 256p. 1999. per. 5.99 (*1-55166-538-7*, Mira Bks) Harlequin Bks.

— Dark Fire. 1996. per. 5.50 (*1-55166-310-4*, 1-66310-3, Mira Bks) Harlequin Bks.

— Dark Fire. 248p. 1998. mass mkt. 5.50 (*1-55166-453-4*, 1-66451-1, Mira Bks) Harlequin Bks.

— Desert Rain. LC 96-96071. 400p. 1996. mass mkt. 6.50 (*0-380-76762-7*, Avon Bks) Morrow Avon.

Lowell, Elizabeth. Desert Rain. large type ed. LC 97-9240. 1997. 25.95 (*1-56895-431-X*, Compass) Wheeler Pub.

Lowell, Elizabeth. Enchanted. 400p. 1994. mass mkt. 6.50 (*0-380-77257-4*, Avon Bks) Morrow Avon.

— Fever. (Mira Bks.). 1997. per. 5.50 (*1-55166-314-7*, 1-66314-5, Mira Bks) Harlequin Bks.

— Fever. 256p. 1999. per. 5.99 (*1-55166-488-7*, Mira Bks) Harlequin Bks.

— Fire & Rain. (Mira Bks.). 1997. per. 5.50 (*1-55166-313-9*, 1-66313-7, Mira Bks) Harlequin Bks.

— Fire & Rain. 1999. per. 5.99 (*0-373-48399-6*, 1-48399-9) Harlequin Bks.

Lowell, Elizabeth. Fires of Eden. Date not set. mass mkt. write for info. (*0-380-78995-7*) Morrow Avon.

Lowell, Elizabeth. Forbidden. LC 97-90321. 400p. 1993. mass mkt. 6.50 (*0-380-76954-9*, Avon Bks) Morrow Avon.

— Forbidden. large type ed. LC 93-42109. 571p. 1994. lib. bdg. 22.95 (*0-7862-0144-4*) Thorndike Pr.

— Forget Me Not. 368p. 1994. mass mkt. 6.99 (*0-380-76759-7*, Avon Bks) Morrow Avon.

— Forget Me Not. 384p. 1998. 25.00 (*0-7278-5347-3*) Severn Hse.

— Granite Man. 256p. 1995. per. 4.99 (*1-55166-015-6*, Mira Bks) Harlequin Bks.

***Lowell, Elizabeth.** Jade Island. LC 98-22742. 384p. 1998. mass mkt. 23.00 (*0-380-97403-7*, Avon Bks) Morrow Avon.

Lowell, Elizabeth. Jade Island. 372p. 1999. mass mkt. 7.50 (*0-380-78987-6*, Avon Bks) Morrow Avon.

— Jade Island. LC 98-44846. 1998. 26.95 (*1-56895-691-6*) Wheeler Pub.

— Love Song for a Raven. 1996. per. 5.50 (*1-55166-311-2*, 1-66311-1, Mira Bks) Harlequin Bks.

— Love Song for a Raven. (Mira Bks.). 1998. per. 5.50 (*1-55166-422-4*, 1-66422-6, Mira Bks) Harlequin Bks.

— Love Song for a Raven. 1993. mass mkt. 4.50 (*0-373-48276-0*, 5-48276-5) Silhouette.

— Lover in the Rough. 320p. 1994. mass mkt. 6.99 (*0-380-76760-0*, Avon Bks) Morrow Avon.

***Lowell, Elizabeth.** Midnight in Ruby Bayou. LC 00-29198. 400p. 2000. 24.00 (*0-380-97405-3*, Wm Morrow) Morrow Avon.

— Midnight in Ruby Bayou. large type ed. 592p. 2000. 24.00 (*0-06-019740-4*) HarpC.

Lowell, Elizabeth. Only His. 400p. (Orig.). 1991. mass mkt. 6.99 (*0-380-76338-9*, Avon Bks) Morrow Avon.

— Only His. large type ed. LC 95-49498. (Large Print Bks.). (Orig.). 1996. pap. 22.95 (*1-56895-292-9*) Wheeler Pub.

— Only Love. 416p. (Orig.). 1995. mass mkt. 6.99 (*0-380-77256-6*, Avon Bks) Morrow Avon.

— Only Love. large type ed. (Large Print Bks.). (Orig.). 1995. pap. 22.95 (*1-56895-260-0*, Compass) Wheeler Pub.

— Only Mine. 400p. 1992. mass mkt. 6.99 (*0-380-76339-7*, Avon Bks) Morrow Avon.

— Only Mine. large type ed. LC 96-11049. (Large Print Bks.). 1996. pap. 22.95 (*1-56895-322-4*) Wheeler Pub.

— Only You. 384p. 1992. mass mkt. 6.99 (*0-380-76340-0*, Avon Bks) Morrow Avon.

— Only You. large type ed. LC 96-31679. 1996. pap. 22.95 (*1-56895-363-1*, Compass) Wheeler Pub.

— Outlaw. 256p. 1994. per. 4.99 (*1-55166-006-7*, 1-66066-7, Mira Bks) Harlequin Bks.

— Outlaw. 1998. mass mkt. 5.99 (*1-55166-559-X*, Mira Bks) Harlequin Bks.

***Lowell, Elizabeth.** Outlaw. 2000. 6.99 (*1-55166-619-7*, 1-66573-6, Mira Bks) Harlequin Bks.

Lowell, Elizabeth. Outlaw. 1994. mass mkt. 4.50 (*0-373-48304-X*, 5-48304-5) Silhouette.

***Lowell, Elizabeth.** Pearl Cove. LC 99-21639. 376p. 1999. 24.00 (*0-380-97404-5*, Avon Bks) Morrow Avon.

— Pearl Cove. 432p. 2000. mass mkt. 7.50 (*0-380-78988-4*, Avon Bks) Morrow Avon.

— Pearl Cove. LC 99-31381. (Large Print Book Ser.). 1999. write for info. (*1-56895-746-7*, Wheeler) Wheeler Pub.

— Pearl Cove. large type ed. 2000. pap. 11.95 (*1-56895-964-8*) Wheeler Pub.

— Pearl Cove, Set. unabridged ed. 1999. audio 73.25 Highsmith Pr.

Lowell, Elizabeth. Reckless Love. LC 95-21591. 376p. 1995. mass mkt. 5.99 (*0-373-15308-2*, 1-15308-9) Harlequin Bks.

— Reckless Love. 1996. mass mkt. 5.99 (*0-373-83328-8*, 1-83328-4) Harlequin Bks.

***Lowell, Elizabeth.** Reckless Love. 2000. per. 5.99 (*1-55166-525-5*, 1-66525-6, Mira Bks) Harlequin Bks.

Lowell, Elizabeth. Remember Summer. 384p. 1999. mass mkt. 6.99 (*0-380-76761-9*, Avon Bks) Morrow Avon.

Lowell, Elizabeth. Sequel Valley of the Sun. Date not set. mass mkt. write for info. (*0-380-78994-9*) Morrow Avon.

Lowell, Elizabeth. Sweet Wind, Wild Wind. 1997. mass mkt. 5.50 (*1-55166-288-4*, 0-66288-2, Mira Bks) Harlequin Bks.

— Tell Me No Lies. 1996. per. 5.99 (*1-55166-096-2*, 1-66096-8, Mira Bks) Harlequin Bks.

— To the Ends of the Earth. LC 97-94417. 368p. 1998. mass mkt. 6.99 (*0-380-76758-9*, Avon Bks) Morrow Avon.

— Too Hot to Handle. 1992. mass mkt. 3.99 (*0-373-48249-3*, 5-48249-2) Harlequin Bks.

— Too Hot to Handle. 256p. 1997. per. 5.50 (*1-55166-267-1*, 1-66267-5, Mira Bks) Harlequin Bks.

— Untamed. 416p. 1993. mass mkt. 6.50 (*0-380-76953-0*, Avon Bks) Morrow Avon.

— Untamed. large type ed. LC 93-13230. 565 p. 1993. lib. bdg. 22.95 (*1-56054-757-X*) Thorndike Pr.

— Warrior. 249p. 1995. per. 4.99 (*1-55166-032-6*, 1-66032-3, Mira Bks) Harlequin Bks.

— Warrior. 1999. 5.99 (*1-55166-501-8*, 1-66501-7) Silhouette.

— Where the Heart Is. LC 96-95170. 376p. 1997. mass mkt. 6.50 (*0-380-76763-5*, Avon Bks) Morrow Avon.

— Winter Fire. LC 96-19220. 384p. 1997. mass mkt. 6.99 (*0-380-77583-2*, Avon Bks) Morrow Avon.

***Lowell, Elizabeth.** A Woman Without Lies. 352p. 1999. 26.00 (*0-7278-2218-7*, Pub. by Severn Hse) Chivers N Amer.

Lowell, Elizabeth. Woman without Lies. 384p. 1995. mass mkt. 6.99 (*0-380-76764-3*, Avon Bks) Morrow Avon.

Lowell, Francis C. Joan of Arc. 1977. 22.95 (*0-8369-7117-5*, 7951) Ayer.

***Lowell, Gloria Roth.** Elana's Ears: or How I Became the Best Big Sister in the World. (Illus.). 32p. (J). (ps-3). 2000. 14.95 (*1-55798-598-7*, 441-5987, Magination Press); pap. 8.95 (*1-55798-702-5*, 441-7025, Magination Press) Am Psychol.

Lowell, H. Bret & Rudnick, Lewis G. Investigate Before Investing: Guidance for Prospective Franchises. 32p. 1992. 6.00 (*0-317-66115-9*) Intl Franchise Assn.

Lowell House Juvenile Staff. Farm Animals in Art. (Animals in Art Ser.). 5p. (J). (ps). 1997. bds. 4.95 (*1-56565-826-4*, 08264W, Pub. by Lowell Hse) NTC Contemp Pub Co.

***Lowell House Juvenile Staff.** My Big Book of Animals. (My Big Board Books Ser.). (Illus.). 24p. (J). (ps-k). 2000. bds. 8.95 (*0-7373-0410-3*, 04103W, Pub. by Lowell Hse Juvenile) NTC Contemp Pub Co.

— My Big Book of Words. (My Big Board Books Ser.). (Illus.). 24p. (J). (ps-k). 2000. bds. 8.95 (*0-7373-0407-3*, 04073W, Pub. by Lowell Hse) NTC Contemp Pub Co.

Lowell House Juvenile Staff. Wild Animals in Art. (Animals in Art Ser.). 5p. (J). (ps). 1997. bds. 4.95 (*1-56565-825-6*, 08256W, Pub. by Lowell Hse) NTC Contemp Pub Co.

Lowell, James. How to Survive in the Real World: Financial Independence for the Recent Grad. LC 94-23396. (Illus.). 272p. (Orig.). 1995. pap. 10.95 (*0-14-023873-5*, Penguin Bks) Viking Penguin.

— Investing from Scratch: A Handbook for the Young Investor. LC 96-8966. 272p. 1997. pap. 12.95 (*0-14-025511-7*) Penguin Putnam.

***Lowell, James.** Smart Money Moves: Mutual Fund Investing from Scratch. 320p. 2000. pap. 13.95 (*0-14-028849-X*) Viking Penguin.

Lowell, James Russell. Among My Books. LC 75-126666. 1970. reprint ed. 20.00 (*0-404-04039-X*) AMS Pr.

— Among My Books. (BCL1-PS American Literature Ser.). 380p. 1992. reprint ed. lib. bdg. 89.00 (*0-7812-0053-9*) Rprt Serv.

— Among My Books. (Notable American Authors Ser.). 1999. reprint ed. lib. bdg. 125.00 (*0-7812-3894-3*) Rprt Serv.

— Among My Books. 1870. reprint ed. 9.00 (*0-403-00032-7*) Scholarly.

— The Biglow Papers. (Notable American Authors Ser.). 1999. reprint ed. lib. bdg. 125.00 (*0-7812-3880-3*) Rprt Serv.

— The Biglow Papers. LC 71-107179. 1970. reprint ed. 15.00 (*0-403-00235-4*) Scholarly.

— The Biglow Papers: First Series. (BCL1-PS American Literature Ser.). 198p. 1992. reprint ed. lib. bdg. 69.00 (*0-7812-6786-2*) Rprt Serv.

— The Biglow Papers: Second Series. (BCL1-PS American Literature Ser.). 564p. 1992. reprint ed. lib. bdg. 99.00 (*0-7812-6787-0*) Rprt Serv.

— The Biglow Papers 1st Series. Wilbur, Homer, ed. LC 75-93775. reprint ed. 45.00 (*0-404-04055-1*) AMS Pr.

— The Biglow Papers 2nd Series. Wilbur, Homer, ed. LC 76-37650. reprint ed. 45.00 (*0-404-04056-X*) AMS Pr.

— The Cathedral. (Notable American Authors Ser.). 1999. reprint ed. lib. bdg. 125.00 (*0-7812-3886-2*) Rprt Serv.

— The Complete Poetical Works. (BCL1-PS American Literature Ser.). 492p. 1992. reprint ed. lib. bdg. 99.00 (*0-7812-6784-6*) Rprt Serv.

— Complete Writings, 16 vols., Set. Norton, Charles E., ed. LC 74-181949. reprint ed. write for info. (*0-404-04070-5*) AMS Pr.

— Complete Writings, 16 vols., Set. (BCL1-PS American Literature Ser.). 1992. reprint ed. lib. bdg. 1440.00 (*0-7812-6783-8*) Rprt Serv.

— Conversations on Some of the Old Poets. 1977. 18.95 (*0-8369-7226-0*, 8025) Ayer.

— The Courtin. (Notable American Authors Ser.). 1999. reprint ed. lib. bdg. 125.00 (*0-7812-3887-0*) Rprt Serv.

— Democracy & Other Addresses. (Notable American Authors Ser.). 1999. reprint ed. lib. bdg. 125.00 (*0-7812-3896-X*) Rprt Serv.

— Essays, Poems & Letters. (BCL1-PS American Literature Ser.). 424p. 1993. reprint ed. lib. bdg. 99.00 (*0-7812-6985-7*) Rprt Serv.

— Fable for Critics. LC 72-6895. (Essay Index Reprint Ser.). 1977. reprint ed. 17.95 (*0-8369-7244-9*) Ayer.

— A Fable for Critics. (Notable American Authors Ser.). 1999. reprint ed. lib. bdg. 125.00 (*0-7812-3881-1*) Rprt Serv.

— Fireside Travels. (Notable American Authors Ser.). 1999. reprint ed. lib. bdg. 125.00 (*0-7812-3893-5*) Rprt Serv.

— Four Poems. (Notable American Authors Ser.). 1999. reprint ed. lib. bdg. 125.00 (*0-7812-3891-9*) Rprt Serv.

— Heartsease & Rue. (Notable American Authors Ser.). 1999. reprint ed. lib. bdg. 125.00 (*0-7812-3889-7*) Rprt Serv.

— James Russell Lowell: Representative Selections. (BCL1-PS American Literature Ser.). 498p. 1993. reprint ed. lib. bdg. 99.00 (*0-7812-6986-5*) Rprt Serv.

— Last Poems. (Notable American Authors Ser.). 1999. reprint ed. lib. bdg. 125.00 (*0-7812-3890-0*) Rprt Serv.

— Latest Literary Essays & Addresses. (Essay Index Reprint Ser.). 1977. reprint ed. 19.95 (*0-518-10184-3*) Ayer.

— Latest Literary Essays & Addresses. (Notable American Authors Ser.). 1999. reprint ed. lib. bdg. 125.00 (*0-7812-3898-6*) Rprt Serv.

— Lectures on English Poets. (Notable American Authors Ser.). 1999. reprint ed. lib. bdg. 125.00 (*0-7812-3901-X*) Rprt Serv.

— A Legend of Brittany & Other Miscellaneous Poems & Sonnets. (Notable American Authors Ser.). 1999. reprint ed. lib. bdg. 125.00 (*0-7812-3877-3*) Rprt Serv.

— Letters. (Notable American Authors Ser.). 1999. reprint ed. lib. bdg. 125.00 (*0-7812-3900-1*) Rprt Serv.

— Letters of James R. Lowell, 2 vols. Norton, Charles E., ed. LC 76-172754. 1894. 115.00 (*0-404-00080-0*) AMS Pr.

— Literary Criticism of James Russell Lowell. Smith, Herbert F., ed. LC 69-10408. 290p. reprint ed. pap. 89.90 (*0-7837-6016-7*, 204582800008) Bks Demand.

— Literary Essays, 2 vols, Set. LC 72-5803. (Essay Index Reprint Ser.). 1977. reprint ed. 49.95 (*0-8369-2998-5*) Ayer.

— My Study Windows. LC 70-126664. reprint ed. 31.50 (*0-404-04057-8*) AMS Pr.

— My Study Windows. (BCL1-PS American Literature Ser.). 433p. 1992. reprint ed. lib. bdg. 99.00 (*0-7812-6788-9*) Rprt Serv.

— My Study Windows. (Notable American Authors Ser.). 1999. reprint ed. lib. bdg. 125.00 (*0-7812-3895-1*) Rprt Serv.

— New Letters. (Notable American Authors Ser.). 1999. reprint ed. lib. bdg. 125.00 (*0-7812-3902-8*) Rprt Serv.

 An Asterisk (*) at the beginning of an entry indicates that the title is appearing for the first time.

— Ode: Recited at Commemoration of the Living & Dead Soldiers of Harvard University. (Notable American Authors Ser.). 1999. reprint ed. lib. bdg. 125.00 (0-7812-3884-6) Rprt Serv.

— The Old English Dramatists. 1977. text 12.95 (0-8369-8166-9, 8306) Ayer.

— The Old English Dramatists. (Notable American Authors Ser.). 1999. reprint ed. lib. bdg. 125.00 (0-7812-3899-4) Rprt Serv.

— Poems. (Notable American Authors Ser.). 1999. reprint ed. lib. bdg. 125.00 (0-7812-3875-7); reprint ed. lib. bdg. 125.00 (0-7812-3876-5); reprint ed. lib. bdg. 125.00 (0-7812-3882-X); reprint ed. lib. bdg. 125.00 (0-7812-3883-8) Rprt Serv.

— Poems: 2D Series. (Notable American Authors Ser.). 1999. reprint ed. lib. bdg. 125.00 (0-7812-3878-1) Rprt Serv.

— Poetry Class Poem. (Notable American Authors Ser.). 1999. reprint ed. lib. bdg. 125.00 (0-7812-3873-0) Rprt Serv.

— Political Essays. (Notable American Authors Ser.). 1999. reprint ed. lib. bdg. 125.00 (0-7812-3897-8) Rprt Serv.

— Prose-Conversations on Some of the Old Poets. (Notable American Authors Ser.). 1999. reprint ed. lib. bdg. 125.00 (0-7812-3892-7) Rprt Serv.

— Three Memorial Poems. (Notable American Authors Ser.). 1999. reprint ed. lib. bdg. 125.00 (0-7812-3888-9) Rprt Serv.

— Under the Willows & Other Poems. (Notable American Authors Ser.). 1999. reprint ed. lib. bdg. 125.00 (0-7812-3885-4) Rprt Serv.

— The Vision of Sir Launfal. (Notable American Authors Ser.). 1999. reprint ed. lib. bdg. 125.00 (0-7812-3879-X) Rprt Serv.

— A Years Life. (Notable American Authors Ser.). 1999. reprint ed. lib. bdg. 125.00 (0-7812-3874-9) Rprt Serv.

Lowell, James Russell, ed. The Pioneer. LC 47-30458. 200p. 1947. reprint ed. lib. bdg. 50.00 (0-8201-1215-1) Schol Facsimiles.

Lowell, Jax P. Against the Grain: The Slightly Eccentric Guide to Living Well Without Gluten or Wheat. LC 94-39985. 88p. 1995. 22.50 (0-8050-3624-5) H Holt & Co.

— Against the Grain: The Slightly Eccentric Guide to Living Well Without Gluten or Wheat. LC 94-39985. 294p. 1995. pap. 14.95 (0-8050-3625-3, Owl) H Holt & Co.

— Mothers. 336p. 1996. pap. 13.95 (0-312-14373-7) St Martin.

Lowell, John. Handbook Of Materials Management. (C). 1993. 69.95 (0-13-374141-9, Macmillan Coll) P-H.

Lowell, John, jt. auth. see Waynant, Ronald W.

Lowell, Josephine S. Public Relief & Private Charity. LC 76-137176. (Poverty U. S. A. Historical Record Ser.). 1975. reprint ed. 16.95 (0-405-03115-7) Ayer.

Lowell, Julia & Yager, Loren. Pricing & Markets: U. S. & Japanese Responses to Currency Fluctuations. LC 94-16352. 1994. pap. text 13.00 (0-8330-1540-0, MR-438-CAPP) Rand Corp.

Lowell, Julia, et al. Financial Crises & Contagion in Emerging Market Countries. LC 98-17566. 75p. 1998. pap. text 10.00 (0-8330-2611-9, MR-962) Rand Corp.

Lowell, Julie, jt. auth. see Lorell, Mark.

Lowell, Julie C. Prehistoric Households at Turkey Creek Pueblo, Arizona. LC 90-48539. (Anthropological Papers: No. 54). (Illus.). 95p. (Orig.). 1991. pap. 24.95 (0-8165-1238-8) U of Ariz Pr.

Lowell, L. M. Observations of a Skeptic: How to Prosper in a Hostile World. LC 97-60042. (Illus.). x, 396p. (Orig.). 1997. pap. 15.95 (0-9656292-4-4) Tableau Pub.

***Lowell, Laura & Willard, Carolyn.** Sifting Through Science. Bergman, Lincoln et al, eds. (Great Explorations in Math & Science (GEMS) Ser.). (Illus.). 104p. (J). (gr. k-2). 1999. pap., teacher ed. 13.50 (0-924886-46-3, GEMS) Lawrence Science.

Lowell, Lindsay & Papademetriou, Demetrios G., eds. Immigration & U. S. Integration Policy Reforms. (Orig.). 1992. pap. 15.00 (0-944285-29-5) Pol Studies.

Lowell, Mary C. Chandler - Parsons: Edmond Chaundeler, Geoffrey Parsons & Allied Families. (Illus.). 112p. 1997. lib. bdg. 27.50 (0-8328-7907-X) Higginson Bk Co.

— Chandler - Parsons: Edmond Chaundeler, Geoffrey Parsons & Allied Families. (Illus.). 112p. 1997. reprint ed. pap. 17.50 (0-8328-7908-8) Higginson Bk Co.

— Old Foxcroft Maine: Traditions & Memories, with Family Records. (Illus.). 262p. 1997. reprint ed. lib. bdg. 32.00 (0-8328-7104-4) Higginson Bk Co.

Lowell, Melissa. Chance of a Lifetime. (Gold Medal Dreams Ser.: No. 3). 176p. (J). (gr. 4-7). 1998. pap. 3.99 (0-553-48527-X, Skylark BDD) BDD Bks Young Read.

— Going for the Gold. (Silver Blades Ser.). 128p. (J). (gr. 4-7). 1994. pap. 3.50 (0-553-48137-1, Skylark BDD) BDD Bks Young Read.

— Ice. (Silver Blades Ser.: Vol. 7). (J). 1994. pap. 4.50 (0-553-54202-8) BDD Bks Young Read.

— More Than Friends. (J). 1996. pap. 4.75 (0-553-54277-X) BDD Bks Young Read.

— Now or Never. (Silver Blades Ser.: No. 2). 160p. (J). (gr. 4-7). 1997. pap. 3.50 (0-553-48519-9) BDD Bks Young Read.

— Rival Roommates. (Silver Blades Ser.: No. 21). 144p. (J). 1997. pap. 3.50 (0-553-48511-3) BDD Bks Young Read.

— Silver Blades. (Silver Blades Ser.: No. 22). 1998. pap. 3.50 (0-553-48531-8) Bantam.

— Silver Blades. (Silver Blades Ser.: No. 23). 1998. pap. 3.50 (0-553-48535-0) Bantam.

Lowell, Melissa. Silver Blades, 10 bks. large type ed. Incl. Breaking the Ice. large type ed. LC 97-39601. 144p. (J). 1998. lib. bdg. 21.27 (0-8368-2063-0); . Center Ice. large type ed. LC 97-40810. 144p. (J). (gr. 4 up). 1998. lib. bdg. 21.27 (0-8368-2099-1); Competition. large type ed. LC 97-39608. (J). 1998. lib. bdg. 21.27 (0-8368-2065-7); Going for the Gold. large type ed. LC 97-39607. 128p. (J). (gr. 4 up). 1998. lib. bdg. 21.27 (0-8368-2066-5); Ice Princess. large type ed. LC 97-40821. 144p. (J). (gr. 4 up). 1998. lib. bdg. 21.27 (0-8368-2096-7); In the Spotlight. large type ed. LC 97-39609. 128p. (J). 1998. lib. bdg. 21.27 (0-8368-2064-9); Perfect Pair. large type ed. LC 97-39605. 96p. (J). 1998. lib. bdg. 21.27 (0-8368-2067-3); Rumors at the Rink. large type ed. LC 97-40822. 144p. (J). (gr. 4 up). 1998. lib. bdg. 21.27 (0-8368-2097-5); Skating Camp. large type ed. LC 97-39604. 96p. (J). 1998. lib. bdg. 21.27 (0-8368-2068-1); Spring Break. large type ed. LC 97-40823. 144p. (J). (gr. 4 up). 1998. lib. bdg. 21.27 (0-8368-2098-3); (J). Set lib. bdg. 127.60 (0-8368-2062-2) Gareth Stevens Inc.

Lowell, Melissa. Silver Blades, 4 vols., Set. 1994. pap. 14.00 (0-553-63494-1) Bantam.

— Silver Blades: On the Edge. (Gold Medal Dreams Ser.: No. 1). 144p. (Orig.). (J). (gr. 4-7). 1997. pap. 3.50 (0-553-48515-6) BDD Bks Young Read.

— The Winning Spirit. (Silver Blades Ser.: Vol. 12). 128p. (J). (gr. 4-7). 1995. pap. 3.50 (0-553-48321-8, Skylark BDD) BDD Bks Young Read.

Lowell, Michele. Your Purebred Kitten. 1995. 27.50 (0-8050-3268-1); pap. 12.95 (0-8050-3269-X) H Holt & Co.

***Lowell, Michele.** Your Purebred Puppy. rev. ed. 2000. pap. text 16.00 (0-8050-6445-1) H Holt & Co.

Lowell, Michele. Your Purebred Puppy: A Buyer's Guide. 288p. 1995. pap. 10.95 (0-8050-1892-1, Owl) H Holt & Co.

Lowell, Michelle. Your Pet Bird: A Buyer's Guide. 224p. 1995. 27.50 (0-8050-2325-9); pap. 15.95 (0-8050-2326-7) H Holt & Co.

Lowell, Percival. Occult Japan. (Illus.). 400p. 1990. pap. 12.95 (0-89281-306-7) Inner Tradit.

Lowell, Robert. Collected Poems. LC 96-17254. 1997. write for info. (0-374-12553-8) FS&G.

***Lowell, Robert.** Collected Poems of Robert Lowell. Bidart, Frank & Gewanter, David, eds. 2000. text 40.00 (0-374-12617-8) FS&G.

Lowell, Robert. The Collected Prose. 350p. 1987. text 25.00 (0-374-12625-9) FS&G.

— Day by Day. LC 77-6799. 138p. 1978. pap. 9.00 (0-374-51471-2) FS&G.

— Imitations. enl. rev. ed. 149p. 1990. pap. 11.00 (0-374-50260-9) FS&G.

— Life Studies & for the Union Dead. 72p. 1967. pap. 12.00 (0-374-50628-0) FS&G.

— Notebook. 265p. 1995. pap. 12.00 (0-374-50947-6) FS&G.

***Lowell, Robert.** The Old Glory: Endecott & the Red Cross; My Kinsman, Major Molineux; & Benito Cereno. 208p. 2000. pap. 13.00 (0-374-52704-0) FS&G.

Lowell, Robert. Selected Poems. LC 76-2000. 320p. 1977. pap. 17.00 (0-374-51400-3) FS&G.

Lowell, Robert T. Antony Brade: A Story of a School. (Notable American Authors Ser.). 1999. reprint ed. lib. bdg. 125.00 (0-7812-3906-0) Rprt Serv.

— Fresh Hearts That Failed Three Thousand Years Ago: With Other Things. (Notable American Authors Ser.). 1999. reprint ed. lib. bdg. 125.00 (0-7812-3904-4) Rprt Serv.

— The New Priest in Conception Bay, 2 vols. reprint ed. write for info. (0-318-53718-4); reprint ed. write for info. (0-318-53719-2) Irvington.

— The New Priest in Conception Bay. (Notable American Authors Ser.). 1999. reprint ed. lib. bdg. 125.00 (0-7812-3903-6) Rprt Serv.

— The New Priest in Conception Bay, 2 vols., Set. LC 72-104520. reprint ed. lib. bdg. 40.00 (0-8398-1173-X) Irvington.

— Poems. (Notable American Authors Ser.). 1999. reprint ed. lib. bdg. 125.00 (0-7812-3905-2) Rprt Serv.

***Lowell, Ross.** Matters of Light & Depth. 1999. pap. 28.95 (0-9662504-0-0) Lowel-Light.

Lowell, S. & Shields, J. E. Powder Surface Area & Porosity. 3rd ed. (Powder Technology Ser.). (Illus.). 250p. (gr. 13). 1991. text 109.95 (0-412-39690-4, A5566) Chapman & Hall.

Lowell, Susan. The Bootmaker & the Elves. LC 96-53303. (Illus.). 32p. (J). (ps-3). 1997. 15.95 (0-531-30044-7); lib. bdg. 16.99 (0-531-33044-3) Orchard Bks Watts.

— The Bootmaker & the Elves. LC 96-53303. (Illus.). 32p. (J). (ps-3). 1999. pap. 6.95 (0-531-07138-3) Orchard Bks Watts.

— The Boy with Paper Wings. LC 95-12818. (Illus.). 200p. (J). (gr. 4-7). 1995. 14.95 (1-57131-605-1); pap. 6.95 (1-57131-604-3) Milkweed Ed.

— Cindy Ellen: A Wild Western Cinderella. LC 99-21194. (Joanna Cotler Bks.). (Illus.). 40p. (J). (ps-3). 2000. 15.95 (0-06-027446-8); lib. bdg. 15.89 (0-06-027447-6) HarpC Child Bks.

— Ganado Red: A Novella & Stories. LC 87-63531. (Illus.). 152p. (Orig.). 1988. pap. 9.95 (0-915943-26-3) Milkweed Ed.

— I Am Lavina Cumming. LC 93-24155. (Illus.). 200p. (J). (gr. 3-7). 1992. pap. 6.95 (0-915943-77-8) Milkweed Ed.

— I Am Lavina Cumming. LC 93-24155. (Illus.). 200p. (J). (gr. 3-7). 1993. 14.95 (0-915943-39-5) Milkweed Ed.

— I Am Lavina Cumming. 1993. 12.05 (0-606-07158-X, Pub. by Turtleback) Demco.

— Little Red Cowboy Hat. LC 96-31201. (Illus.). (J). 1995. 14.95 (0-8050-3508-7) H Holt & Co.

***Lowell, Susan.** Little Red Cowboy Hat. (Illus.). 32p. (J). (ps-3). 2000. pap. 6.95 (0-8050-6483-4) H Holt & Co.

Lowell, Susan. The Three Little Javelinas. LC 92-14232. (Illus.). 32p. (J). (ps-3). 1992. lib. bdg. 15.95 (0-87358-542-9, Rising Moon Bks) Northland AZ.

— The Tortoise & the Jackrabbit. LC 94-19461. (Illus.). 32p. (J). (ps-3). 1994. lib. bdg. 14.95 (0-87358-586-0, Rising Moon Bks) Northland AZ.

— Los Tres Pequenos Jabalies. (SPA., Illus.). 32p. (J). (gr. k-3). 1996. lib. bdg. 15.95 (0-87358-661-1, Rising Moon Bks) Northland AZ.

***Lowell, Susan, et al.** The Many Faces Mata Ortiz: The Postcard Book. (Illus.). 32p. 2000. pap. 9.95 (1-887896-19-8, Rio Nuevo) Treas Chest Bks.

Lowell, Susan, et al. The Many Faces of Mata Ortiz. (Illus.). 224p. 1999. 50.00 (1-887896-18-X, Rio Nuevo); pap. 29.95 (1-887896-08-2, Rio Nuevo) Treas Chest Bks.

Lowell, Waverly. Architecture Records in the San Francisco Bay Area: A Guide to Research. LC 89-16904. 370p. 1988. text 20.00 (0-8240-6614-6) Garland.

Lowen, Alexander. Bioenergetics. 352p. 1994. pap. 14.95 (0-14-019471-1) Penguin Putnam.

— Depression & the Body. 1993. pap. 14.95 (0-14-019465-7, Arkana) Viking Penguin.

— Fear of Life. 274p. 1981. pap. 6.95 (0-02-077330-7) Macmillan.

— Joy: The Surrender to the Body & to Life. 320p. 1995. pap. 13.95 (0-14-019493-2, Penguin Bks) Viking Penguin.

— Language of the Body. 416p. 1971. pap. 6.95 (0-02-077310-2) Macmillan.

— Love & Orgasm: A Revolutionary Guide to Sexual Fulfillment. (Illus.). 319p. 1975. pap. 7.00 (0-02-077320-X) Macmillan.

— Narcissism. 1997. per. 8.00 (0-684-84299-8) S&S Trade.

— Spirituality of the Body. 224p. 1990. 18.95 (0-02-575871-3) Macmillan.

Lowen, Allan A. Cobwebs on the Ocean Floor. LC 93-93521. 1999. 16.95 (0-533-10773-3) Vantage.

Lowen, Deborah, jt. contrib. by see Jenny, Carole.

Lowen, Irene. Empty Moon. LC 97-60009. 432p. (Orig.). 1997. 19.95 (1-57921-002-3); pap. 14.95 (0-614-29770-2) WinePress Pub.

Lowen, Jeannette, ed. see Engelbreit, Mary.

Lowen, R. Fuzzy Set Theory: Basic Concepts, Techniques & Bibliography. LC 96-15901. 408p. (C). 1996. text 217.50 (0-7923-4057-4) Kluwer Academic.

Lowen, R., ed. Fuzzy Logic: State of the Art. (Theory & Decision Library: No. D). 600p. (C). 1993. text 285.50 (0-7923-2324-6) Kluwer Academic.

Lowen, R., jt. ed. see Aull, Charles E.

Lowen, Rebecca S. Creating the Cold War University: The Transformation of Stanford. LC 96-5022. 300p. 1997. 45.00 (0-520-20541-3, Pub. by U CA Pr) Cal Prin Full Svc.

Lowen, Robert. Approach Spaces: The Missing Link in the Topology-Uniformity-Metric Triad. LC 97-13158. (Oxford Mathematical Monographs). (Illus.). 264p. 1997. text 110.00 (0-19-850030-0) OUP.

Lowen, Tirzah. Peter Hall Directs Antony & Cleopatra. LC 90-36644. (Illus.). 208p. 1991. pap. 16.95 (0-87910-147-4) Limelight Edns.

Lowenberg, jt. auth. see Conrad.

Lowenberg, Anton D. & Kaempfer, William H. The Origins & Demise of South African Apartheid: A Public Choice Analysis. (Illus.). 296p. (C). 1998. text 54.50 (0-472-10905-7, 10905) U of Mich Pr.

Lowenberg, B. & Hagenbeek, A., eds. Minimal Residual Disease in Acute Leukemia. (Developments in Oncology Ser.). 382p. 1984. text 211.50 (0-89838-630-6) Kluwer Academic.

Lowenberg, Carlton. Emily Dickinson's Textbooks. Lowenberg, Territa A. & Brown, Carla L., eds. (Illus.). 119p. (Orig.). 1986. 22.50 (0-9617374-1-7); pap. 12.75 (0-9617374-0-9) Carlton Lowenberg.

— Musicians Wrestle Everywhere: Emily Dickinson & Music. LC 92-9923. (Reference Books in Music: No. 19). xxviii, 210p. 1992. 39.50 (0-914913-20-4, Fallen Lef Pr) Scarecrow.

Lowenberg-DeBoer, James. The Microeconomic Roots of the Farm Crisis. LC 86-21202. 185p. 1986. 57.95 (0-275-92226-X, C2226, Praeger Pubs) Greenwood.

Lowenberg, Heather. Lady Bug's Ball. LC 97-10830. (J). 1998. lib. bdg. 9.99 (0-679-98539-5, Pub. by Random Bks Yng Read) Random.

— Ladybug's Ball. LC 97-10830. (J). 1998. 7.99 (0-679-88539-0, Pub. by Random Bks Yng Read) Random.

— Unicorns & Other Fabulous Creatures. (Tattoo Tales Ser.). (Illus.). 24p. (Orig.). (J). (ps-3). 1994. pap. 4.99 (0-679-86437-7, Pub. by Random Bks Yng Read) Random.

Lowenberg, June S. Caring & Responsibility: The Crossroads of Holistic Practice & Traditional Medicine. LC 88-15067. (Studies in Health, Illness, & Caregiving). (Illus.). 306p. (C). 1989. pap. 18.95 (0-8122-1408-0); text 42.50 (0-8122-8174-8) U of Pa Pr.

Lowenberg, Miriam E., et al. Food & Man. 2nd ed. LC 73-15800. (Illus.). 470p. reprint ed. pap. 145.70 (0-7837-3491-3, 205782400008) Bks Demand.

Lowenberg, Peter H., ed. see Georgetown University Round Table Meeting on Langu.

Lowenberg, Susan. C. S. Lewis: A Reference Guide, 1972-1988. LC 92-42316. (Reference Guide to Literature Ser.). 320p. 1993. 60.00 (0-8161-1846-9, G K Hall & Co) Mac Lib Ref.

Lowenberg, Territa A., ed. see Lowenberg, Carlton.

***Lowendahl, Bente.** Strategic Management of Professional Service Firms. LC 98-106328. 1999. 25.00 (87-16-13323-4) Mksgaard.

Lowenfeld, Andreas F. Conflict of Laws: Federal, State, & International Perspectives. 3rd ed. LC 97-53263. (Casebook Ser.). 1998. 58.00 (0-8205-3111-1) Bender.

— International Economic Law: Trade Controls for Political Ends, Pt. III. 2nd ed. 1983. 49.00 (0-8205-2989-3) Bender.

— International Litigation & Arbitration. (American Casebook Ser.). 869p. (C). 1992. 65.00 (0-314-01188-9) West Pub.

— International Litigation & Arbitration: Selected Treaties, Statutes & Rules. (American Casebook Ser.). 277p. (C). 1992. pap. 19.75 (0-314-01201-X) West Pub.

— International Litigation & Arbitration: Teacher's Manual & Supplemental Litigation & Arbitration. (American Casebook Ser.). 530p. 1993. pap. text. write for info. (0-314-02297-X) West Pub.

— International Litigation & the Quest for Reasonableness: Essays in Private International Law. LC 95-47048. 270p. (C). 1996. text 65.00 (0-19-826059-8) OUP.

— International Private Trade. 3rd ed. (International Economic Law Ser.: Vol. 1). 1995. write for info. (0-256-17951-4, Irwn McGrw-H) McGrw-H Hghr Educ.

— Revolutionary Days: The American Hostages & the Iranian Revolution: Record of a Conference Held at New York University School of Law on the Fifteenth Anniversary of the Algiers Accords, January 19-20, 1996. LC 98-41829. 1998. 70.00 (1-57823-063-2) Juris Pubng.

Lowenfeld, Andreas F. & Tillinghast. International Economic Law, Pt. I: International Private Trade. 2nd ed. 1988. write for info. (0-8205-0601-X, 554) Bender.

— International Economic Law, Pt. II: International Private Investment. 2nd ed. 1982. write for info. (0-8205-0606-0) Bender.

— International Economic Law, Pt. IV: The International Monetary System. 2nd ed. 1984. 49.00 (0-8205-0616-8) Bender.

— International Economic Law, Pt. V: Tax Aspects of International Transaction. 2nd ed. 1984. write for info. (0-8205-0621-4) Bender.

— International Economic Law, Pt. VI: Public Controls on International Trade. 2nd ed. 1983. write for info. (0-8205-0626-5) Bender.

Lowenfeld, Berthold. Our Blind Children: Growing & Learning with Them. 3rd ed. (Illus.). 260p. 1977. 39.95 (0-398-02200-3); pap. 27.95 (0-398-06249-8) C C Thomas.

Lowenfeld, Margaret. The Lowenfeld Mosaic Test. 2nd ed. 1994. reprint ed. pap. 55.00 (0-9521788-1-8, Pub. by M Lowenfeld) Intl Spec Bk.

— Play in Childhood. (Classics in Developmental Medicine Ser.: No. 6). (Illus.). 242p. (C). 1991. text 19.95 (0-521-41331-1, Pub. by Mc Keith Pr) Cambridge U Pr.

— Understanding Children's Sandplay Lowenfeld's World Technique. 1993. reprint ed. pap. 19.95 (0-9521788-0-X, Pub. by M Lowenfeld) Intl Spec Bk.

Lowenfeld, Viktor. The Nature of Creative Activity. 1988. reprint ed. lib. bdg. 69.00 (0-7812-0376-7) Rprt Serv.

— The Nature of Creative Activity. 2nd ed. LC 65-7654. 272p. 1959. reprint ed. 69.00 (0-686-01428-6) Somerset Pub.

— Viktor Lowenfeld Speaks on Art & Creativity. National Art Education Association Staff, ed. 64p. (C). 1968. pap. 10.00 (0-937652-26-1, 206) Natl Art Ed.

Lowenfeld, Viktor & Brittain, W. Lambert. Creative & Mental Growth. 8th ed. LC 86-8529. 510p. (C). 1987. 120.00 (0-02-372110-3, Macmillan Coll) P-H.

Lowenfels, Lewis D., jt. auth. see Bromberg, Alan R.

Lowenfels, Walter & Whitman, Walt. Walt Whitman's Civil War. (Quality Paperbacks Ser.). (Illus.). 368p. 1989. pap. 14.95 (0-306-80355-0) Da Capo.

Lowenfels, Walter, et al. The Life of Fraenkel's Death: A Biographical Inquest. LC 71-11331. (Illus.). 102p. reprint ed. pap. 31.70 (0-608-18349-0, 203303000083) Bks Demand.

Lowenfelt, Walter. Reality Prime: Selected Poems. Lewis, Joel, ed. LC 98-39219. 128p. 1998. 32.95 (1-883689-72-4); pap. 12.95 (1-883689-71-6) Talisman Hse.

Lowenfish, Lee, jt. auth. see Major League Baseball Training Staff.

Lowengert, M. & Yasgur, B. The Mystery of the Matching Lockets. Felder, Ilana, ed. (Bina Gold Mystery Ser.). (Illus.). (YA). Date not set. pap. 9.95 (0-911643-23-0) Aura Bklyn.

Lowengrub, M. & Sneddon, Ian N. Crack Problems in the Classical Theory of Elasticity. LC 75-84971. (Siam Series in Applied Mathematics). 231p. reprint ed. pap. 71.70 (0-608-30939-7, 200631200058) Bks Demand.

Lowenhardt, John. The Reincarnation of Russia: Struggling with the Legacy of Communism, 1990-1994. LC 94-38510. 256p. 1995. text 49.95 (0-8223-1606-4); pap. text 16.95 (0-8223-1623-4) Duke.

Lowenhardt, John, ed. Party Politics in Postcommunist Russia. LC 98-16306. (Illus.). 256p. (C). 1998. text 49.50 (0-7146-4892-2, Pub. by F Cass Pubs); pap. text 24.50 (0-7146-4443-9, Pub. by F Cass Pubs) Intl Spec Bk.

***Lowenhaupt, Mary A. & Stephanik, Corinne E.** Making Student Teaching Work: Creating a Partnership. (Fastback Ser.). 46p. 1999. pap. 3.00 (0-87367-647-5, FB447) Phi Delta Kappa.

Lowenheim, F., ed. Guide to the Selection & Use of Electroplated & Related Finishes- STP 785. 69p. 1982. pap. 18.00 (0-8031-0749-8, STP785) ASTM.

Lowenheim, Frederick A. Electroplating. 594p. 1997. pap. 220.00 (1-872422-03-9) St Mut.

Lowenheim, Frederick A., ed. Modern Electroplating. 3rd ed. (Electrochemical Society Ser.). (Illus.). 832p. 1974. 199.00 (0-471-54968-1) Wiley.

***Lowenherz, David H.** The Greatest Love Letters of All Time. 2001. 20.00 (0-8129-3277-3) Crown Pub Group.

Lowenkamp, William & McCall, Vicki B. The Country Poet: On the Road Again. (Illus.). 64p. (Orig.). 1984. pap. 6.00 (0-913667-00-5) Lowenkamp Pub.

Lowenkopf, Anne N., intro. Memories of Some of Anne's Friends. 125p. (Orig.). 1992. pap. 12.95 (0-9633753-2-6) Two Down Pr.

Lowenkopf, E. L., jt. auth. see Klebanow, S.

Lowens, Irving, pref. Lectures on the History & Art of Music: The Louis Charles Elson Memorial Lectures at the Library of Congress 1946-1965. LC 68-55319. (Music Ser.). 1968. reprint ed. lib. bdg. 32.50 (*0-306-71193-1*) Da Capo.

Lowens, Irving, et al. Bibliography of Songsters Printed in America Before 1821. LC 75-5021. 268p. 1976. 35.00 (*0-912296-05-4*) Oak Knoll.

Lowenstam, Heinz A. Biostratigraphic Studies of the Niagaran Inter-Reef Formations of Northeastern Illinois. (Scientific Papers: Vol. IV). (Illus.). 146p. 1948. 3.00 (*0-89792-093-7*); pap. 2.00 (*0-89792-005-8*) Ill St Museum.

Lowenstam, Heinz A. & Weiner, Stephen. On Biomineralization. (Illus.). 336p. 1989. text 75.00 (*0-19-504977-2*) OUP.

Lowenstam, Steven. The Scepter & the Spear: Studies on Forms of Repetition in the Homeric Poems. LC 93-19243. (Greek Studies: Interdisciplinary Approaches). 280p. (C). 1992. text 62.50 (*0-8476-7772-9*); pap. text 28.50 (*0-8476-7790-7*) Rowman.

Lowenstam, Steven, et al. The Extramural Sanctuary of Demeter & Persephone at Cyrene, Libya Vol. III: Scarabs, Inscribed Gems, & Engraved Finger Rings; Attic Black-Figured & Black-Glazed Pottery; Hellenistic & Roman Fine Ware; & Conservation of Objects. White, Donald, ed. (University Museum Monographs: No. 66). (Illus.). xliv, 131p. 1987. text 55.00 (*0-934718-77-6*) U Museum Pubns.

***Lowenstein.** Innovative Teaching Strategies in Nursing. 3rd ed. 2000. 49.00 (*0-8342-1668-X*) Aspen Pub.

Lowenstein, jt. auth. see Ross.

Lowenstein, Otto, jt. auth. see Loewenfeld, Irene E.

Lowenstein, Amy C., ed. Middle East: Abstracts & Index, 1978, Vol. 1. 1979. 250.00 (*0-318-50002-7*) Northumberland Pr.

— Middle East: Abstracts & Index, 1979, Vol. 2. 1979. 250.00 (*0-318-50003-5*) Northumberland Pr.

— Middle East: Abstracts & Index, 1980, Vol. 3. 1980. 250.00 (*0-318-50004-3*) Northumberland Pr.

— Middle East: Abstracts & Index, 1981, Vol. 4. 1981. pap. 250.00 (*0-934565-00-7*) Northumberland Pr.

— Middle East: Abstracts & Index, 1982, Vol. 5. 1986. 250.00 (*0-318-49998-3*) Northumberland Pr.

— Middle East: Abstracts & Index, 1983, Vol. 6. 1988. 250.00 (*0-318-49999-1*) Northumberland Pr.

— Middle East: Abstracts & Index, 1984, Vol. 7. 1989. 250.00 (*0-318-50000-0*) Northumberland Pr.

— Middle East: Abstracts & Index, 1985, Vol. 8. 1990. 250.00 (*0-318-50001-9*) Northumberland Pr.

Lowenstein Associates, et al. Black Health Library Guide to Diabetes, 1. 192p. 1999. mass mkt. 5.99 (*1-57566-452-6*) Kensgtn Pub Corp.

Lowenstein, Bill. Hunting in Michigan: The Early 80's. Arnold, David A., ed. 192p. 1981. pap. 6.95 (*0-941912-24-8*) Mich Nat Res.

Lowenstein, Daniel H. Election Law. 60p. (C). 1996. pap. text, suppl. ed. 15.00 (*0-89089-174-5*) Carolina Acad Pr.

— Election Law: Cases & Materials. LC 95-70417. (Illus.). 848p. (C). 1995. boxed set 75.00 (*0-89089-806-5*) Carolina Acad Pr.

Lowenstein, Eleanor. Bibliography of American Cookery Books 1742-1860. 132p. 1972. 35.00 (*0-912296-02-X*) Am Antiquarian.

Lowenstein, Felicia. The Abortion Battle: Looking at Both Sides. LC 95-42448. (Issues in Focus Ser.). (Illus.). 128p. (YA). (gr. 6 up). 1996. lib. bdg. 20.95 (*0-89490-724-7*) Enslow Pubs.

***Lowenstein, Frank W. & Lechner, Sheryl.** Bugs: Insects, Spiders, Centipedes, Millipedes & Other Closely Related Arthropods. LC 99-23723. (Illus.). 112p. 1999. 29.98 (*1-57912-068-7*) Blck Dog & Leventhal.

Lowenstein, Jerome. The Midnight Meal & Other Essays about Doctors, Patients, & Medicine. LC 96-26159. 144p. 1997. 18.00 (*0-300-06816-6*) Yale U Pr.

Lowenstein, John M., ed. Citric Acid Cycle: Control & Compartmentation. LC 77-82152. 386p. reprint ed. pap. 119.70 (*0-608-16782-7*, 202708100054) Bks Demand.

Lowenstein, K. L. The Manufacturing Technology of Continuous Glass Fibres. 3rd rev. ed. LC 92-39909. (Glass Science & Technology Ser.: Vol.6). 368p. 1993. 269.25 (*0-444-89346-6*) Elsevier.

Lowenstein, Karl. Political Power & the Governmental Process. LC 65-8901. (Chicago University Charles R. Walgreen Foundation for the Study of American Institutions, Lecture Ser.). 474p. reprint ed. pap. 147.00 (*0-608-10788-3*, 202010900016) Bks Demand.

Lowenstein, Leopold. Zur Geschichte der Juden in Furth. (GER.). 374p. 1974. reprint ed. write for info. (*3-487-05315-2*) G Olms Pubs.

Lowenstein, Liana. Creative Interventions for Troubled Children & Youth. 128p. (Orig.). 1999. pap. 19.95 (*0-9685199-0-3*) C2 Press.

Lowenstein, Liana, et al. Paper Dolls & Paper Airplanes: Therapeutic Exercises for Sexually Traumatized Children. (Illus.). 478p. 1997. 39.95 (*1-55864-048-7*) Kidsrights.

Lowenstein, Louis. Sense & Nonsense in Corporate Finance: An Antidote to Conventional Thinking about LOBs Capital Budgeting Divident Policy & Creating Shareholder Value. (Illus.). 272p. 1992. pap. 14.00 (*0-201-63223-3*) Addison-Wesley.

— What's Wrong with Wall Street? 1989. pap. 10.53 (*0-201-51796-5*) Addison-Wesley.

— What's Wrong with Wall Street? Short-Term Gain & the Absentee Shareholder. 1988. 17.26 (*0-201-17169-4*) Addison-Wesley.

Lowenstein, Michael W. The Customer Loyalty Pyramid. LC 97-5886. 280p. 1997. 59.95 (*1-56720-076-1*, Quorum Bks) Greenwood.

— Customer Retention: An Integrated Process for Keeping Your Best Customers. (Illus.). 179p. 1995. text 27.50 (*0-87389-257-7*, H0812) ASQ Qual Pr.

Lowenstein, Michael Z., jt. auth. see Easterly, James L.

Lowenstein, Nancy, jt. auth. see Halloran, Patricia.

Lowenstein, P. R. & Enquist, Lynn W., eds. Protocols for Gene Trans in Ne. LC 95-45487. 446p. 1996. pap. 229.95 (*0-471-95766-6*) Wiley.

Lowenstein, Ralph L. Pragmatic Fund-Raising for College Administrators & Development Officers. LC 97-15573. 128p. 1997. 24.95 (*0-8130-1525-1*) U Press Fla.

Lowenstein, Richard, ed. see Gassman, Conrad.

Lowenstein, Roger. Buffett: The Making of an American Capitalist. LC 96-18265. 496p. 1996. pap. 15.95 (*0-385-48491-7*) Doubleday.

***Lowenstein, Roger.** When Genius Failed: The Rise & Fall of Long-Term Capital Management. LC 00-28091. 288p. 2000. 26.95 (*0-375-50317-X*) Random.

Lowenstein, Sallie. Evan's Voice. LC 98-92071. (Illus.). 192p. (YA). (gr. 6-12). 1998. pap. 15.00 (*0-9658486-1-2*) Lion Stone.

— The Festival of Lights: A Family Hanukkah Service. (Illus.). 26p. 1999. pap. 25.00 (*0-9658486-2-0*) Lion Stone.

— The Mt. Olympus Zoo. LC 97-93862. (Illus.). 252p. (Orig.). (J). (gr. 3-8). 1997. pap. 14.99 (*0-9658486-0-4*) Lion Stone.

Lowenstein, Sandler, Kohl, Fisher & Boylan Staff. New Jersey Environmental Law Handbook. 5th ed. LC 98-119096. 420p. 1999. pap. text 95.00 (*0-86587-641-X*) Gov Insts.

Lowenstein, Sharyn, jt. auth. see Todd, Peaco.

***Lowenstein, Steve M.** The Jewish Cultural Tapestry: International Jewish Folk Traditions. LC 99-88194. 2000. 30.00 (*0-19-513425-7*) OUP.

Lowenstein, Steven. German-Jewish History in Modern Times: Integration in Dispute, 1871-1918, Vol. 3. (Illus.). 466p. 1998. 52.50 (*0-231-07476-X*) Col U Pr.

— The Jews of Oregon, 1850-1950. (Illus.). 236p. 1988. 29.95 (*0-9619786-0-0*); pap. 19.95 (*0-9619786-1-9*) OR Jewish Mus.

— The Jews of Oregon, 1850-1950. limited ed. (Illus.). 236p. 1988. 100.00 (*0-9619786-2-7*) OR Jewish Mus.

— Lawyers, Legal Education & Development: An Examination of the Process of Reform in Chile. x, 310p. 1970. pap. 25.00 (*0-8377-0803-6*, Rothman) W S Hein.

Lowenstein, Steven M. Frankfurt on the Hudson: The German Jewish Community of Washington Heights, 1933-1983, Its Structure & Culture. LC 88-20520. (Illus.). 348p. 1989. pap. 22.95 (*0-8143-2385-5*) Wayne St U Pr.

***Lowenstein, Tom.** Ancient Land, Sacred Whale: The Inuit Hunt, Its Rituals & Poetry. (Illus.). 196p. 2000. pap. 14.00 (*1-86046-575-7*, Pub. by Harvill Press) FS&G.

Lowenstein, Tom. The Death of Mrs. Owl. 92p. 1977. pap. 14.95 (*0-85646-031-1*, Pub. by Anvil Press) Dufour.

Lowenstein, Tom, jt. tr. see Omnik, Tukummiq C.

Lowenthal. Heritage. 1996. 23.00 (*0-02-919475-X*) Free Pr.

Lowenthal, A. Agar Gel Electrophoresis in Neurology. 1964. pap. 22.00 (*0-444-40377-9*) Elsevier.

Lowenthal, A. & Raus, J., eds. Cellular & Humoral Components of Cerebrospinal Fluid in Multiple Sclerosis. (NATO ASI Series A, Life Sciences: Vol. 129). (Illus.). 538p. 1987. 135.00 (*0-306-42578-5*, Plenum Trade) Perseus Pubng.

Lowenthal, Abraham F. Brazil & the United States. LC 86-81679. (Headline Ser.: No. 279). 64p. (Orig.). (C). 1986. pap. 5.95 (*0-87124-109-9*) Foreign Policy.

Lowenthal, Abraham F. The Dominican Intervention. LC 94-32274. 246p. (C). 1995. reprint ed. pap. text 14.95 (*0-8018-4755-9*) Johns Hopkins.

Lowenthal, Abraham F. Partners in Conflict: The United States & Latin America in the 1990s. rev. ed. 272p. 1990. text 41.00 (*0-8018-4061-9*) Johns Hopkins.

Lowenthal, Abraham F., ed. Exporting Democracy: Themes & Issues. LC 90-24061. 288p. 1991. pap. text 14.95 (*0-8018-4132-1*) Johns Hopkins.

— Latin America & Caribbean Contemporary Record, 1985-1986, Vol. V. (Latin America & Caribbean Contemporary Record Ser.). (Illus.). 1000p. (C). 1988. 380.00 (*0-8419-1123-1*) Holmes & Meier.

— Latin America & Caribbean Contemporary Record, 1986-1987, Vol. VI. (Latin American & Caribbean Contemporary Record Ser.). 1000p. 1989. 380.00 (*0-8419-1170-3*) Holmes & Meier.

— The Peruvian Experiment: Continuity & Change under Military Rule. LC 75-2998. 502p. reprint ed. pap. 155.70 (*0-8357-6254-8*, 203465600090) Bks Demand.

Lowenthal, Abraham F. & Burgess, Katrina, eds. The California-Mexico Connection. LC 92-45247. 392p. 1993. 47.50 (*0-8047-2188-2*); pap. 17.95 (*0-8047-2187-4*) Stanford U Pr.

Lowenthal, Abraham F. & Fitch, J. Samuel, eds. Armies & Politics in Latin America. 2nd ed. LC 86-14918. 300p. (C). 1986. pap. 24.50 (*0-8419-0916-4*) Holmes & Meier.

— Armies & Politics in Latin America. 2nd ed. LC 86-14918. 300p. (C). 1986. 45.00 (*0-8419-0913-X*) Holmes & Meier.

Lowenthal, Abraham F. & Starr, Pamela K. The United States & the Cuban Revolution, 1958-1960. (Pew Case Studies in International Affairs). 50p. (C). 1994. pap. text 3.50 (*1-56927-328-6*) Geo U Inst Dplmcy.

Lowenthal, Abraham F. & Treverton, Gregory F. America Latina en un Mundo Nuevo (Latin America in a New World) (SPA.). 314p. 1996. pap. 12.99 (*968-16-4740-8*, Pub. by Fondo) Continental Bk.

Lowenthal, Abraham F., jt. ed. see Dominguez, Jorge I.

Lowenthal, Abraham F., jt. ed. see McClintock, Cynthia.

Lowenthal, Anne W. Joachim Wtewael: Mars & Venus Surprised by Vulcan. LC 94-17632. (Getty Museum Studies on Art). 94p. 1995. pap. 17.50 (*0-89236-304-5*, Pub. by J P Getty Trust) OUP.

Lowenthal, Anne W., ed. The Object As Subject: Studies in the Interpretation of Still Life. LC 95-45798. 204p. 1996. 49.50 (*0-691-03354-4*, Pub. by Princeton U Pr) Cal Prin Full Svc.

Lowenthal, Cynthia. Lady Mary Wortley Montagu & the Eighteenth-Century Familiar Letter. LC 92-41757. 264p. 1994. 40.00 (*0-8203-1545-1*) U of Ga Pr.

Lowenthal, D., jt. ed. see Gathercole, P.

Lowenthal, D., jt. ed. see Penning-Roswell, Edmund C.

***Lowenthal, David.** George Perkins Marsh: Prophet of Conservation. (Illus.). 650p. 2000. 40.00 (*0-295-97942-9*) U of Wash Pr.

Lowenthal, David. The Heritage Crusade & the Spoils of History. LC 97-44370. 344p. (C). 1998. pap. 18.95 (*0-521-63562-4*) Cambridge U Pr.

— The Past Is a Foreign Country. LC 85-10990. (Illus.). 516p. 1988. pap. text 29.95 (*0-521-29480-0*) Cambridge U Pr.

— Shakespeare & the Good Life: Ethics & Politics in Dramatic Form. LC 97-33306. 288p. 1997. 71.50 (*0-8476-8844-5*) Rowman.

— The West Indies Federation, Research Series No. 23--23. LC 76-21682. (American Geographical Society; Research Ser.: No. 23). (Illus.). 142p. 1976. reprint ed. lib. bdg. 55.00 (*0-8371-9005-3*, LOWI, Greenwood Pr) Greenwood.

Lowenthal, David, ed. Environmental Perception & Behavior. LC 66-29233. (University of Chicago, Department of Geography, Research Paper Ser.: No. 109). 96p. reprint ed. pap. 30.00 (*0-7837-0391-0*, 204071200018) Bks Demand.

Lowenthal, David & Mansfield, Harvey C. No Liberty for License: The Forgotten Logic of the First Amendment. LC 97-30379. 344p. 1997. 27.95 (*0-9653208-4-7*) Spence Pub.

Lowenthal, David & Riel, Marquita. Environmental Structures: Semantic & Experiental Components. (Publications in Environmental Perception: Report 8). 48p. 1972. 8.00 (*0-318-12730-X*) Am Geographical.

Lowenthal, David, ed. see Marsh, George P.

Lowenthal, David, tr. see Montesquieu.

Lowenthal, F. & Vandamme, Fernand, eds. Pragmatics & Education. 352p. 1986. 75.00 (*0-306-42374-X*, Plenum Trade) Perseus Pubng.

Lowenthal, Jeffrey. The Last Chance . . . For the Church to Love the Jewish People. LC 98-60059. 128p. 1998. pap. 9.95 (*1-57921-099-6*, Pub. by WinePress Pub) BookWorld.

Lowenthal, Jeffrey N. Reengineering the Organization: A Step-by-Step Approach to Corporate Revitalization. LC 93-44774. (Illus.). 185p. 1994. text 30.00 (*0-87389-258-5*, H0813) ASQ Qual Pr.

Lowenthal, Jessica. As If in Turning: Poems. (Burning Deck Poetry Chapbooks Ser.). 30p. 1996. pap. 8.00 (*1-886224-17-X*) Burning Deck.

— As If in Turning: Poems. deluxe ed. (Burning Deck Poetry Chapbooks Ser.: No. 10). 30p. 1996. pap. 15.00 (*1-886224-18-8*) Burning Deck.

Lowenthal, Larry. From the Coalfields to the Hudson: A History of the Delaware & Hudson Canal. LC 97-16372. 298p. 1997. pap. 25.00 (*0-935796-85-1*) Purple Mnt Pr.

— Iron Mine Railroads of New Jersey. (Illus.). 145p. 1981. 17.95 (*0-686-36238-1*); pap. 12.95 (*0-686-99308-X*) Tri-State Rail.

***Lowenthal, Larry.** Marinus Willett: Defender of the Northern Frontier. LC 00-32352. (New Yorkers & the Revolution Ser.). 2000. pap. write for info. (*1-930098-07-3*) Purple Mnt Pr.

Lowenthal, Larry. Titanic Railroad: The Southern New England. (Illus.). 264p. 1998. 39.95 (*0-9662736-0-5*) Marker Pr.

Lowenthal, Leo. Critical Theory & Frankfurt Theorists: Correspondence, Speeches, & Origins. (Communication & Society Ser.: Vol. 4). 236p. 1989. 39.95 (*0-88738-224-X*) Transaction Pubs.

— False Prophets: Studies on Authoritarianism Communication in Society, Vol. 3. 400p. 1986. 44.95 (*0-88738-136-7*) Transaction Pubs.

— Literature & Mass Culture. (Communication & Society Ser.: Vol. 1). 338p. 1984. 44.95 (*0-87855-489-0*) Transaction Pubs.

— Literature & the Image of Man. LC 78-134110. (Essay Index Reprint Ser.). 1980. 21.95 (*0-8369-1982-3*) Ayer.

— Literature & the Image of Man, Vol. 2. (Communication & Society Ser.). 224p. (C). 1985. 44.95 (*0-88738-057-3*) Transaction Pubs.

— Literature, Popular Culture & Society. LC 61-13532. (Paperbounds Ser.: No. PB-4). xxiv, 169p. 1968. reprint ed. pap. 12.95 (*0-87015-166-5*) Pacific Bks.

— An Unmastered Past: The Autobiographical Reflections of Leo Lowenthal. LC 86-24942. (Illus.). 240p. 1987. 45.00 (*0-520-05638-8*, Pub. by U CA Pr) Cal Prin Full Svc.

Lowenthal, Leo & Guterman, Norbert. Prophets of Deceit: A Study of the Techniques of the American Agitator. 2nd ed. LC 68-31291. (Paperbounds Ser.: No. PB-8). (Illus.). xx, 164p. 1970. pap. 1.95 (*0-87015-182-7*) Pacific Bks.

Lowenthal, Marc, tr. see Picabia, Francis.

Lowenthal, Marc, tr. see Queneau, Raymond.

Lowenthal, Marjorie F. Lives in Distress: The Paths of the Elderly to the Psychiatric Ward. Stein, Leon, ed. LC 79-8675. (Growing Old Ser.). 1980. reprint ed. lib. bdg. 28.95 (*0-405-12791-X*) Ayer.

Lowenthal, Marjorie F., et al. Aging & Mental Disorder in San Francisco: A Social Psychiatric Study. LC 67-13168. (Langley Porter Institute Studies of Aging). (Illus.). 361p. reprint ed. pap. 112.00 (*0-8357-4906-1*, 203783600009) Bks Demand.

— Four Stages of Life. LC 74-27911. (Jossey-Bass Behavioral Science Ser.). 318p. reprint ed. pap. 98.60 (*0-608-17776-8*, 205656100072) Bks Demand.

***Lowenthal, Mark M.** Intelligence: From Secrets to Policy. LC 99-37035. 264p. 1999. pap. 28.95 (*1-56802-512-2*) Congr Quarterly.

Lowenthal, Mark M. U. S. Intelligence: Evolution & Anatomy, 157. 2nd ed. Laqueur, Walter & Spitler, Donna R., eds. LC 92-15913. (Washington Papers: No. 157). 200p. 1992. 47.95 (*0-275-94435-2*, C4435); pap. 20.95 (*0-275-94434-4*, B4434) Greenwood.

— The U. S. Intelligence Community: An Annotated Bibliography. LC 94-10298. (Organizations & Interest Groups Ser.: Vol. 11). 224p. 1994. text 15.00 (*0-8153-1423-X*, H1765) Garland.

Lowenthal, Martin & Short, Lar. Opening the Heart of Compassion: Transform Suffering Through Buddhist Psychology & Practice. (Illus.). 192p. 1993. pap. 12.95 (*0-8048-1985-8*) Tuttle Pubng.

Lowenthal, Marvin. A World Passed By: Great Cities in Jewish Diaspora History. LC 90-30824. (Illus.). 560p. (C). 1990. reprint ed. 34.50 (*0-934710-19-8*) Rachelle Simon.

Lowenthal, Marvin, jt. auth. see Monaghan, Frank.

Lowenthal, Marvin, ed. see Herzl, Theodor.

Lowenthal, Marvin, ed. & tr. see Montaigne, Michel de.

Lowenthal, Marvin, tr. see Gluckel of Hameln.

***Lowenthal, Michael.** Obsessed: A Flesh & the Word Collection of Gay Erotic Memoirs. LC 98-50411. 256p. 1999. pap. 12.95 (*0-452-27999-2*, Plume) Dutton Plume.

Lowenthal, Michael. The Same Embrace. LC 98-10171. 304p. 1998. 23.95 (*0-525-94416-8*, Dutt) Dutton Plume.

— The Same Embrace. 289p. 1999. pap. 12.95 (*0-452-27975-5*, Plume) Dutton Plume.

Lowenthal, Michael, ed. The Badboy Erotic Library, Vol. II. (Orig.). 1994. mass mkt. 4.95 (*1-56333-211-6*, Badboy) Masquerade.

— The Best of the Badboys. LC 96-226091. (Orig.). 1995. pap. 12.95 (*1-56333-233-7*, R Kasak Bks) Masquerade.

— Flesh & the Word No. 4: An Anthology of Gay Erotic Writing, Vol. 4. LC 96-48595. 320p. 1997. pap. 13.95 (*0-452-27760-4*, Plume) Dutton Plume.

— Gay Men at the Millennium: Sex, Spirit, Community. LC 97-21683. (New Consciousness Reader Ser.). 304p. 1997. pap. 15.95 (*0-87477-892-1*, Tarcher Putnam) Putnam Pub Group.

Lowenthal, Michael, jt. ed. see Preston, John.

Lowenthal, Michael, ed. & intro. see Preston, John.

Lowenthal, Richard, et al. An Overview of East-West Relations: A Report to the Trilateral Commission. (Triangle Papers: No. 15). 1978. 6.00 (*0-930503-42-2*) Trilateral Comm.

Lowenthal, Werner. Pharmaceutical Calculations: A Self-Instructional Text. rev. ed. LC 74-9564. 460p. 1978. reprint ed. pap. 27.50 (*0-88275-573-0*) Krieger.

Lowenthal, Wolfe. Gateway to the Miraculous: Further Explorations in the Tao of Cheng Man-ch'ing. LC 93-39498. (Illus.). 124p. (Orig.). (C). 1994. pap. 14.95 (*1-883319-13-7*) Frog Ltd CA.

— There Are No Secrets: Professor Cheng Man Ch'ing & His Ta Chi Chuan. 200p. 1991. pap. 14.95 (*1-55643-112-0*) North Atlantic.

Lower & Rajendra. A History of Asia. 2nd ed. 1992. pap. text. write for info. (*0-582-87642-7*, Pub. by Addison-Wesley) Longman.

Lower, Anne R. Centennial History of Sheltering Arms Hospital. (Illus.). 96p. 1989. pap. write for info. (*0-9623370-1-3*); lib. bdg. 20.00 (*0-9623370-0-5*) Sheltering Arms.

— Sheltering Arms Hospital: One Hundred Years of Caring. (Illus.). 100p. (Orig.). 1989. pap. write for info. (*0-318-65239-0*); lib. bdg. 20.00 (*0-685-26159-X*) Sheltering Arms.

Lower, Arthur R. Canada & the Far East, 1940. LC 73-3016. 152p. 1973. reprint ed. 65.00 (*0-8371-6831-7*, LOCF, Greenwood Pr) Greenwood.

Lower, Arthur R. Canadians in the Making: A Social History of Canada. LC 81-4142. (Illus.). 475p. 1981. reprint ed. lib. bdg. 89.50 (*0-313-23037-4*, LOCAN, Greenwood Pr) Greenwood.

Lower, Dorothy M., jt. ed. see Filby, P. William.

Lower Hudson Conference Staff. History Keepers' Companion: Guide to Sites & Sources of the Lower Hudson Valley & Western Connecticut. LC 98-40581. (Illus.). 264p. 1998. pap. 16.50 (*0-916346-63-3*) Purple Mnt Pr.

Lower, J. L. Lower: Some Account of the Lower Family in America, Principally of the Descendants of Adam Lower, Who Settled in Williamsport, PA in 1779. (Illus.). 144p. 1993. reprint ed. pap. 25.00 (*0-8328-3710-5*); reprint ed. lib. bdg. 35.00 (*0-8328-3709-1*) Higginson Bk Co.

Lower, Joyce Q. & Grix, Henry M. Michigan Estate Planning, Will Drafting & Estate Administration Forms, 2 vols. 1989. disk. write for info. (*0-318-71302-0*, MICHIE) LEXIS Pub.

— Michigan Estate Planning, Will Drafting & Estate Administration Forms, 2 vols. 1993. suppl. ed. 80.00 (*0-685-74622-4*, MICHIE) LEXIS Pub.

— Michigan Estate Planning, Will Drafting & Estate Administration Forms, 2 vols., Set. 970p. 1994. spiral bd. 294.00 (*0-8342-0087-2*, 81711-10, MICHIE) LEXIS Pub.

Lower Kuskokwim School District Staff. Yup'ik Alphabet Book Set, 18 vols. large type ed. (ESK., Illus.). (J). (gr. k-3). 1997. pap. 108.00 (*1-58084-013-2*) Lower Kuskokwim.

Lower, L., jt. auth. see Klosowski, J.

Lower, L., jt. auth. see Konsowski, J.

An Asterisk (*) at the beginning of an entry indicates that the title is appearing for the first time.

Lower, Mark A. Contributions to Literature: Historical, Antiquarian, & Metrical. LC 72-4578. (Essay Index Reprint Ser.). 1977. reprint ed. 23.95 (*0-8369-2959-4*) Ayer.

— Patronymica Britannica: A Dictionary of the Family Names of the United Kingdom. 443p. 1996. pap. 33.00 (*0-7884-0456-3*, L581) Heritage Bk.

Lower Merion Historical Society. The First 300: The Amazing & Rich History of Lower Merion. LC 99-57322. 284p. text 39.95 (*0-7881-8500-4*) DIANE Pub.

Lower, Richard C. A Bloc of One: The Political Career of Hiram W. Johnson. LC 93-6975. xiv, 442p. (C). 1993. 47.50 (*0-8047-2081-9*) Stanford U Pr.

***Lowerberg, Tara.** FYI Fashion Source: New York City 2000. Zalla, Christopher, ed. (Illus.). 200p. 2000. pap. 14.95 (*1-930404-00-X*) F Y I.

Loweree, James H., jt. auth. see Kimmons, Robert L.

Lowerre, George F. Critical Reading: Workbook B: Reusable Edition. 70p. (J). (gr. 3-8). 1973. student ed. 10.00 (*0-87879-720-3*, Ann Arbor Div) Acad Therapy.

— Critical Reading: Workbook C: Reusable Edition. 78p. (J). (gr. 3-8). 1973. student ed. 10.00 (*0-87879-721-1*, Ann Arbor Div) Acad Therapy.

Lowerre, George F. & Scandura, Alice M. Critical Reading: Workbook A: Reusable Edition. 28p. 1973. teacher ed. 5.00 (*0-87879-723-8*, Ann Arbor Div) Acad Therapy.

— Critical Reading: Workbook A: Reusable Edition. 54p. (J). (gr. 3-8). 1973. 10.00 (*0-87879-719-X*, Ann Arbor Div) Acad Therapy.

— Critical Reading: Workbook D: Reusable Edition. 68p. (J). (gr. 3-8). 1973. student ed. 10.00 (*0-87879-722-X*, Ann Arbor Div) Acad Therapy.

Lowerre, Susan. Under the Neem Tree. LC 90-53323. 256p. 1991. 22.00 (*1-877946-03-6*) Permanent Pr.

Lowers, James K. Candide Notes. (Cliffs Notes Ser.). 80p. 1965. pap. 4.95 (*0-8220-0283-3*, Cliff) IDG Bks.

— Hamlet Notes. (Cliffs Notes Ser.). 112p. 1959. pap. 4.95 (*0-8220-0018-0*, Cliff) IDG Bks.

— Henry IV, part 1 Notes. (Cliffs Notes Ser.). 80p. 1960. pap. 4.95 (*0-8220-0023-7*, Cliff) IDG Bks.

— Henry IV, part 2 Notes. (Cliffs Notes Ser.). Orig. Title: '. 72p. 1963. pap. 4.95 (*0-8220-0026-1*, Cliff) IDG Bks.

— King Lear: Notes. (Cliffs Notes Ser.). 96p. 1960. pap. 4.95 (*0-8220-0041-5*, Cliff) IDG Bks.

— Richard III Notes. (Cliffs Notes Ser.). 88p. 1961. pap. 4.95 (*0-8220-0071-7*, Cliff) IDG Bks.

— Shakespeare's Sonnets Notes. (Cliffs Notes Ser.). 64p. 1965. pap. 4.95 (*0-8220-0077-6*, Cliff) IDG Bks.

— Shaw's Pygmalion & Arms & the Man Notes. (Cliffs Notes Ser.). 80p. (Orig.). 1981. pap. 4.95 (*0-8220-1103-4*, Cliff) IDG Bks.

— Troilus & Cressida Notes. (Cliffs Notes Ser.). 88p. 1964. pap. 4.95 (*0-8220-0091-1*, Cliff) IDG Bks.

*** Lowers, Jane, ed.** Aspen's Health Care Quality Review. 248p. 1999. pap. 79.00 (*0-8342-1607-8*) Aspen Pub.

Lowerson, John. Sport & the English Middle Classes, 1870-1914. (International Studies in the History of Sport). 320p. 1996. text 27.95 (*0-7190-4651-3*, Pub. by Manchester Univ Pr) St Martin.

Lowery. Introduction to Social Work. 2000. pap. text 11.97 (*0-395-97310-4*) HM.

Lowery, jt. auth. see Cullison.

Lowery, A. J., jt. auth. see Turner, Capstan.

Lowery, Charles D. James Barbour: A Jeffersonian Republican. LC 83-3453. 334p. 1984. pap. 103.60 (*0-7837-8392-2*, 205920300009) Bks Demand.

Lowery, Charles D. & Marszalek, John F., eds. Encyclopedia of African-American Civil Rights: From Emancipation to the Present. LC 91-27814. 688p. 1992. 65.00 (*0-313-25011-1*, LDR/, Greenwood Pr) Greenwood.

Lowery, Charles D., jt. auth. see Scott, Roy V.

Lowery, Daniel L. Day by Day Through Lent: Reflections, Prayers, Practices. LC 83-82033. 142p. 1983. pap. 5.95 (*0-89243-194-6*) Liguori Pubns.

— Following Christ: Referenced to the Catechism of the Catholic Church. rev. ed. LC 95-23750. 196p. (Orig.). 1996. pap. 10.95 (*0-89243-850-9*) Liguori Pubns.

Lowery, David, jt. auth. see Berry, William.

Lowery, David, jt. auth. see Gray, Virginia.

Lowery, Deborah Garrison & Weight Watchers International Staff. Weight Watchers, Cook Quick, Cook Healthy. LC 97-68809. 192p. 1997. write for info. (*0-8487-1648-5*) Oxmoor Hse.

Lowery, Fred. Whistling in the Dark: The Story of Fred Lowery, the Blind Whistler. LC 83-4085. (Illus.). 304p. 1983. pap. 25.00 (*1-56554-582-6*) Pelican.

Lowery, Gail. Managing Projects with Microsoft Project '97. 3rd ed. LC 97-217904. (Business Technology Ser.). 400p. (Orig.). 1997. pap. 34.95 (*0-442-02552-1*, VNR) Wiley.

Lowery, George H., Jr. Mammals of Louisiana & Its Adjacent Waters. LC 73-89662. (Illus.). xxiv, 565p. 1974. 29.95 (*0-8071-0609-7*) La State U Pr.

Lowery, Glenda, ed. see Evans, Jimmy.

Lowery, Glenda, ed. see Evans, Jimmy D.

Lowery, Gwen. Managing Projects with Microsoft Project: Version 4.0 for Windows & the Macintosh. 3rd ed. 416p. 1994. pap. 34.95 (*0-442-01768-5*, VNR) Wiley.

Lowery, Gwen. Managing Projects with Microsoft Project 4.0: For Windows & Macintosh. 2nd ed. 432p. 1994. pap. 34.95 (*0-471-28611-7*, VNR) Wiley.

Lowery, Gwen. Managing Projects with Microsoft Project '97. 1997. pap. 34.95 (*0-614-28537-2*, VNR) Wiley.

Lowery, Gwen & Ferrara, Rob. Managing Projects with Microsoft Project 98 for Windows: For Windows & Macintosh. 2nd ed. 400p. 1997. pap. 34.95 (*0-471-29253-2*, VNR) Wiley.

Lowery, Janet. Thin Dimes. (New Texas Poetry Sampler Ser.). 20p. 1992. pap. 10.00 (*0-930324-19-6*) Wings Pr.

Lowery, Joan E., ed. Culture Shift: A Leader's Guide to Managing Change in Health Care. LC 97-25187. 1997. write for info. (*1-55648-208-6*) AHPI.

Lowery, Joanne. Coming to This. LC 90-2779. 80p. (Orig.). 1990. pap. 7.50 (*0-931832-50-0*) Fithian Pr.

Lowery, Joe. Teach Yourself Internet Explorer 4 in 10 Minutes. LC 98-84596. (Teach Yourself Ser.). 1998. pap. 12.99 (*0-672-31319-7*) Sams.

— 10 Minute Guide to the Internet Explorer 4. LC 97-80985. (10 Minute Guide Ser.). 206p. 1997. pap. text 14.99 (*0-7897-1585-6*) Que.

Lowery, John. Anatomy of a Spin: A Complete Study of the Stall-Spin Phenomena. (Illus.). 102p. 1998. pap. write for info. (*0-934754-05-5*) Airguide Pubns.

***Lowery, Joseph.** Dreamweaver 3 Bible: Gold Edition. LC 00-39569. 1518p. 2000. 59.99 (*0-7645-3479-3*) IDG Bks.

Lowery, Joseph. Netrepreneur: The Dimensions of Transferring Your Business Model to the Internet. 1998. pap. 29.99 (*0-7897-1725-5*) Que.

***Lowery, Joseph W.** Dreamweaver 3 Bible. 1128p. 2000. 39.99 (*0-7645-3458-0*) IDG Bks.

— Dreamweaver 2.0 Bible. LC 99-19199. (Bible Ser.). (Illus.). 1080p. 1999. pap. 39.99 incl. cd-rom (*0-7645-3322-3*) IDG Bks.

— Fireworks 3 Bible. 700p. 2000. pap. text 39.99 (*0-7645-3475-0*) IDG Bks.

— Fireworks 2 Bible. LC 99-36224. 800p. 1999. pap. 39.99 (*0-7645-3334-7*) IDG Bks.

Lowery, Lawrence. The Everyday Science Sourcebook: Ideas for Teaching in the Elementary & Middle School. 1997. text 19.95 (*0-86651-260-8*) Seymour Pubns.

Lowery, Lawrence & Verbeeck, Carol. Explorations in Earth Science. 1987. pap. 6.99 (*0-8224-2315-4*) Fearon Teacher Aids.

— Explorations in Life Science. 1987. pap. 6.99 (*0-8224-2314-6*) Fearon Teacher Aids.

— Explorations in Physical Science. 1987. pap. 6.99 (*0-8224-2316-2*) Fearon Teacher Aids.

— Explorations in Science Set, 3 bks., Set. (J). (gr. 1-3). 19.99 (*1-56417-730-0*, FE0006) Fearon Teacher Aids.

Lowery, Lawrence F. Thinking & Learning: Matching Developmental Stages with Curriculum & Instruction. 101p. (Orig.). 1996. reprint ed. pap. 12.95 (*0-9624475-6-0*) Bks Educators.

Lowery, Linda. Aunt Clara Brown. LC 98-24259. (Illus.). 48p. (J). (gr. 2-4). 1999. 19.93 (*1-57505-045-5*, Carolrhoda) Lerner Pub.

— Aunt Clara Brown. LC 98-24259. (J). 1999. pap. text 5.95 (*1-57505-416-7*) Lerner Pub.

— Earth Day. (Holiday on My Own Ser.). (Illus.). 48p. (J). (gr. k-3). 1991. lib. bdg. 18.60 (*0-87614-662-0*, Carolrhoda) Lerner Pub.

— Earth Day. (Illus.). 56p. (J). (gr. k-3). 1992. pap. 5.95 (*0-87614-560-8*, Carolrhoda) Lerner Pub.

— Earth Day. (Illus.). (J). (gr. 2-4). 1993. 22.95 incl. audio (*0-87499-303-2*) Live Oak Media.

Lowery, Linda. Earth Day. (Illus.). (J). 1992. 11.30 (*0-606-18818-5*) Turtleback.

Lowery, Linda. Earth Day. unabridged ed. (Illus.). (J). (gr. 2-4). 1993. pap. 15.95 incl. audio (*0-87499-302-4*) Live Oak Media.

— Earth Day, Set. unabridged ed. (Illus.). (J). (gr. 2-4). 1993. pap. 33.95 incl. audio (*0-87499-304-0*) Live Oak Media.

— Georgia O'Keeffe. LC 94-25413. (Illus.). (J). 1995. lib. bdg. 18.60 (*0-87614-860-7*, Carolrhoda) Lerner Pub.

— Georgia O'Keeffe. (Illus.). 48p. (J). (gr. k-3). 1996. pap. text 5.95 (*0-87614-898-4*) Lerner Pub.

— Laurie Tells. LC 93-9786. (Illus.). (J). (gr. 3-6). 1994. lib. bdg. 19.95 (*0-87614-790-2*, Carolrhoda) Lerner Pub.

— Laurie Tells. (Illus.). 40p. (J). (gr. 1-4). 1995. pap. 4.95 (*0-87614-961-1*) Lerner Pub.

— Martin Luther King Day. (Carolrhoda On My Own Bks.). (Illus.). 56p. (J). (gr. k-3). 1987. lib. bdg. 18.60 (*0-87614-299-4*, Carolrhoda) Lerner Pub.

— Martin Luther King Day. (Illus.). (J). (gr. 1-6). 1987. pap. 15.95 incl. audio (*0-87499-070-X*) Live Oak Media.

— Martin Luther King Day. (Holiday on My Own Bks.). (Illus.). 56p. (J). (gr. k-3). 1988. reprint ed. pap. 5.95 (*0-87614-468-7*, Carolrhoda) Lerner Pub.

— Martin Luther King Day. unabridged ed. (Illus.). (J). (gr. 1-6). 1987. 24.95 incl. audio (*0-87499-071-8*) Live Oak Media.

— Martin Luther King Day, 4 bks., Set. unabridged ed. (Illus.). (J). (gr. 1-6). 1987. teacher ed. 33.95 incl. audio (*0-87499-072-6*) Live Oak Media.

— Pablo Picasso. LC 99-21965. (On My Own Biographies Ser.). 48p. (J). (gr. 2-4). 1999. pap. 5.95 (*1-57505-370-5*, Carolrhoda) Lerner Pub.

— Pablo Picasso. LC 99-21965. (On My Own Bks.). (Illus.). 48p. (J). (gr. 1-3). 1999. 19.93 (*1-57505-331-4*) Lerner Pub.

— Somebody Somewhere Knows My Name. LC 94-49538. (First Person Ser.). (Illus.). 40p. (J). (gr. 2-4). 1995. lib. bdg. 14.95 (*0-87614-946-8*, Carolrhoda) Lerner Pub.

— Twist with a Burger, Jitter with a Bug. LC 93-38236. (Illus.). 32p. (J). (ps-2). 1995. 14.95 (*0-395-67022-5*, Pub. by Ticknor & Fields) HM.

— Wilma Mankiller. LC 95-12203. (On My Own Bks.). (Illus.). (J). 1996. lib. bdg. 13.95 (*0-87614-880-1*, Carolrhoda) Lerner Pub.

— Wilma Mankiller. LC 95-12203. (On My Own Bks.). (Illus.). 48p. (J). (gr. k-3). 1996. pap. 5.95 (*0-87614-953-0*, Carolrhoda) Lerner Pub.

Lowery, Linda & Botts, Betty. Earthwise Teaching Guide. (J). (gr. 1-4). 1994. pap. 19.93 (*0-87614-461-X*) Lerner Pub.

Lowery, Linda & Lorbiecki, Marybeth. Earthwise at Home: A Guide to the Care & Feeding of Your Planet. (Illus.). (J). (gr. 1-4). 1992. lib. bdg. 19.93 (*0-87614-730-9*, Carolrhoda) Lerner Pub.

— Earthwise at School: A Guide to the Care & Feeding of Your Planet. LC 92-11221. (Illus.). (J). (gr. 1-4). 1993. lib. bdg. 19.93 (*0-87614-731-7*, Carolrhoda) Lerner Pub.

Lowery, Linda, jt. auth. see Lorbiecki, Marybeth.

Lowery, Marilyn. Blue Ribbons for Juliet. (J). (gr. 5-7). 1997. pap. 9.99 (*0-88092-397-0*) Royal Fireworks.

***Lowery, Mike.** Dance & Rave Cultures, Vol. 1. 2000. pap. text 17.95 (*1-84126-020-7*) Meyer & Meyer.

Lowery, Missy. Not Just Another Day: Families, Grief & Special Days. 1992. pap. 2.95 (*1-56123-055-3*) Centering Corp.

Lowery, R. H. The Reforming Kings: Cult & Society in First Temple Judah. (Journal for the Study of the Old Testament Supplement Ser.: No. 120). 236p. (C). 1991. 70.00 (*1-85075-318-0*, Pub. by Sheffield Acad) CUP Services.

Lowery, Richard H. Revelation: Hope for the World in Troubled Times. LC 93-45777. (Covenant Bible Studies). 86p. 1994. pap. 5.95 (*0-87178-739-3*, 8350) Brethren.

***Lowery, Richard H.** Sabbath & Jubilee. LC 99-50534. (Understanding Biblical Themes Ser.). 168p. 2000. pap. 16.99 (*0-8272-3826-6*) Chalice Pr.

Lowery, Robert, ed. see Nathan, George J.

Lowery, Robert G. Sean O'Casey's Autobiographies: An Annotated Index. LC 83-826. 487p. 1983. lib. bdg. 69.50 (*0-313-23765-4*, LYS/, Greenwood Pr) Greenwood.

Lowery, Robert G., ed. A Whirlwind in Dublin: The Plough & the Stars Riots, 11. LC 83-22652. (Contributions to Drama & Theatre Studies: No. 11). 121p. 1984. 32.95 (*0-313-23764-6*, LOW/, Greenwood Pr) Greenwood.

Lowery, Robert G., ed. see O'Casey, Sean.

Lowery, Roger C. & Cody, Sue A. Political Science: Illustrated Search Strategy & Sources. (Library Research Guides Ser.: No. 12). 224p. 1993. pap. 25.00 (*0-87650-290-7*) Pierian.

Lowery, Shearon A. Milestones in Mass Communication Research. 4th ed. (C). 1999. pap. text. write for info. (*0-8013-1795-9*) Longman.

Lowery, Shearon A. & DeFleur, Melvin L. Milestones in Mass Communication Research: Media Effects. 3rd ed. LC 94-3707. 415p. (C). 1994. pap. text 56.00 (*0-8013-1437-2*) Longman.

Lowery, Skip. Listening, Thinking, Speaking: A College Course. 112p. (C). 1997. per. 16.95 (*0-7872-3733-7*) Kendall-Hunt.

— Listening, Thinking, Speaking: A College Course. 2nd ed. 110p. (C). 1998. per. 25.95 (*0-7872-5244-1*, 41524401) Kendall-Hunt.

Lowery, T. L. Gifted to Serve. 179p. 1997. pap. 9.99 (*0-87148-369-6*) Pathway Pr.

— Gifted to Serve. LC 98-17070. 182p. 1998. pap. 12.99 (*0-88368-525-6*) Whitaker Hse.

Lowery, T. L., ed. El Don del Espiritu Santo. (SPA.). 80p. 1978. pap. 3.95 (*0-87148-307-6*) Pathway Pr.

Lowery, William R., et al. College Admissions Counseling. LC 82-48086. (Jossey-Bass Series in Higher Education). 652p. reprint ed. pap. 200.00 (*0-7837-0181-0*, 204047700017) Bks Demand.

Lowes, Mark D. Inside the Sports Page: Work Routines, Professional Ideologies, & the Manufacture of Sports News. 150p. 1999. text 40.00 (*0-8020-4359-3*); pap. text 16.95 (*0-8020-8183-5*) U of Toronto Pr.

Lowes, Bryyan. Business & Microeconomics: An Introduction to the Market Environment. Edwards, John R., ed. LC 93-39826. (Elements of Business Ser.). (Illus.). 224p. (C). (gr. 13). 1994. pap. 64.95 (*0-415-06845-2*, B3534) Thomson Learn.

Lowes, Catherine D. A Seven-Step Program for Getting Through Menopause & Enjoying a Longer Healthier Life Without Drugs. 2nd rev. ed. (Illus.). 144p. 1998. pap. write for info. (*0-9681492-1-9*) Hl1th Issues.

***Lowes, James O.** The Outcasts. large type ed. 224p. 1999. pap. 18.99 (*0-7089-5540-1*, Linford) Ulverscroft.

Lowes, John L. Art of Geoffrey Chaucer. LC 70-114910. (Select Bibliographies Reprint Ser.). 1977. 6.00 (*0-8369-5315-0*) Ayer.

— Geoffrey Chaucer. LC 83-45446. reprint ed. 26.00 (*0-404-20161-X*) AMS Pr.

— The Road to Xanadu: A Study in the Ways of the Imagination. (BCL1-PR English Literature Ser.). 639p. 1992. reprint ed. lib. bdg. 109.00 (*0-7812-7501-6*) Rprt Serv.

Lowes, Peter D. The Genesis of International Narcotics Control. Grob, Gerald N., ed. LC 80-1267. (Additionn in America Ser.). 1981. reprint ed. lib. bdg. 23.95 (*0-405-13605-6*) Ayer.

***Lowes, Robin.** The Incompleat Angler: A Light Cast Over River & Loch. (Illus.). 160p. 1999. 42.50 (*0-9536969-0-1*, Pub. by Thrd Millennium) Trans-Atl Phila.

Lowesdale School Children Staff. Sarah Snail. LC 92-27084. (Voyages Ser.). (Illus.). (J). 1993. 3.75 (*0-383-03592-9*) SRA McGraw.

Loweth, Garth S., ed. see Davis, Robert E.

Lowett, Garth E., ed. see Berg, Charles M.

Lowett, Garth S., ed. see Karimi, A. M.

Lowett, Garth S., ed. see Pryluck, Calvin.

Lowett, Garth S., ed. see Shain, Russell E.

Lowett, Garth S., ed. see Stuart, Frederic.

Lowett, Garth S., ed. see Wead, George.

Lowey, Iklana & Inserm. The Polish School of Philosophy of Medicine: From Tytus Chalubinski (1820-1889) to Ludwick Fleck (1896-1961) (Philosophy & Medicine Ser.). 296p. 1990. lib. bdg. 135.00 (*0-7923-0958-8*, Pub. by Kluwer Academic) Kluwer Academic.

Lowey, Warren, ed. see Maskell, Charles F.

Lowhagen, Torsten, jt. auth. see Stanley, Michael W.

***Lowi.** American Government. 5th ed. 1998. pap. text. write for info. (*0-393-97311-5*) Norton.

Lowi & Ginsberg. American Government. 5th ed. 1998. pap. write for info. (*0-393-97258-5*) Norton.

Lowi, jt. auth. see Ginsberg, Benjamin.

Lowi, Miriam R. Water & Power: The Politics of a Scarce Resource in the Jordan River Basin. (Middle East Library: No. 31). (Illus.). 326p. (C). 1995. pap. text 22.95 (*0-521-55836-0*) Cambridge U Pr.

Lowi, Shaw, abr. Environment & Security. LC 99-33852. 1999. text 59.95 (*0-312-22485-0*) St Martin.

Lowi, Theodore. American Government. 2nd ed. 1998. pap. text. write for info. (*0-393-97249-6*); pap. text. write for info. (*0-393-97262-3*) Norton.

— American Government. 4th ed. 1997. pap. text. write for info. (*0-393-97264-X*) Norton.

— American Government. 5th ed. Date not set. pap. text. write for info. (*0-393-97255-0*) Norton.

— American Government. 5th ed. 1998. pap. text. write for info. (*0-393-97246-1*); pap. text. write for info. (*0-393-97253-4*) Norton.

— American Government. 5th ed. 1998. pap. text 34.00 (*0-393-97251-8*) Norton.

— American Government. 5th ed. 1998. pap. text 44.50 (*0-393-95877-9*) Norton.

— American Government. 5th ed. (C). 1998. pap. text. write for info. (*0-393-97184-8*) Norton.

***Lowi, Theodore.** American Government. 5th ed. (C). 1998. pap. text 73.00 (*0-393-98399-4*) Norton.

Lowi, Theodore. American Government. 5th ed. 1998. pap. text. write for info. (*0-393-95873-6*) Norton.

***Lowi, Theodore.** American Government. 5th ed. (C). 1999. pap. text. write for info. (*0-393-98859-7*) Norton.

— American Government. 6th ed. (C). 2000. pap. text 48.50 (*0-393-98296-3*) Norton.

— American Government. 6th ed. (C). 2000. pap. text 55.25 (*0-393-98298-X*) Norton.

— American Government: Brief Edition Freedom & Power. 6th ed. LC 99-37632. 2000. pap. 43.25 (*0-393-97495-2*, Norton Paperbks) Norton.

— American Government Study Guide: Freedom & Power. 6th ed. LC 99-37633. 2000. pap. text 53.00 (*0-393-97471-5*, Norton Paperbks) Norton.

***Lowi, Theodore, et al.** Electoral Deadlock: Politics & Policy in the Clinton Era. 1999. pap. write for info. (*0-393-97485-5*) Norton.

Lowi, Theodore J. The End of Liberalism: The Second Republic of the United States. 2nd ed. (Illus.). 331p. (C). 1979. pap. text 21.00 (*0-393-09000-0*) Norton.

— The End of the Republican Era. LC 94-31038. (Julia J. Rothbaum Distinguished Lectures: Vol. 5). (Illus.). 296p. 1995. 24.95 (*0-8061-2701-5*) U of Okla Pr.

— The End of the Republican Era. LC 94-31038. (Julian J. Rothbaum Distinguished Lectures: Vol. 5). 312p. 1996. pap. 13.95 (*0-8061-2887-9*, 2887) U of Okla Pr.

— The Intelligent Person's Guide to Political Corruption. 1981. 1.00 (*1-55614-053-3*) U of SD Gov Res Bur.

— The Personal President: Power Invested, Promise Unfulfilled. LC 84-45804. 240p. 1985. pap. text 14.95 (*0-8014-9426-5*) Cornell U Pr.

***Lowi, Theodore J.** Readings for American Government: Freedom & Power. 6th ed. LC 00-22045. 2000. pap. write for info. (*0-393-97603-3*) Norton.

Lowi, Theodore J. & Ginsberg, Benjamin. Embattled Democracy: Politics & Policy in the Clinton Era. LC 95-3403. (C). 1995. pap. text 10.00 (*0-393-96197-4*) Norton.

— Poliscide: Big Government, Big Science, Lilliputian Politics. LC 89-25001. 330p. (C). 1990. reprint ed. pap. text 24.50 (*0-8191-7654-0*) U Pr of Amer.

Lowi, Theodore J. & Romance, Joseph. Debating the Two Party System: A Republic of Parties?: Debating the Two-Party System. McWilliams, Wilson C., ed. LC 98-24980. (Enduring Questions in American Political Life Ser.). 200p. 1998. 49.00 (*0-8476-8608-6*); pap. 14.95 (*0-8476-8609-4*) Rowman.

Lowi, Theodore J. & Stone, Alan, eds. Nationalizing Government: Public Policies in America. LC 78-19848. (Illus.). 455p. reprint ed. pap. 141.10 (*0-8357-8493-2*, 203467600091) Bks Demand.

Lowic, Nicholas. Coinage & History of the Islamic World. Cribb, Joe, ed. (Collected Studies: No. CS311). 352p. 1990. text 109.95 (*0-86078-259-X*, Pub. by Variorum) Ashgate Pub Co.

Lowick, Nicholas. Islamic Coins & Trade in the Medieval World. Cribb, Joe, ed. (Collected Studies: No. 318). 300p. 1990. text 115.95 (*0-86078-267-0*, Pub. by Variorum) Ashgate Pub Co.

Lowie, P., jt. auth. see Nicholaus, B.

Lowie, Robert H. The Assiniboine. LC 74-7978. reprint ed. 29.50 (*0-404-11868-2*) AMS Pr.

— The Crow Indians. LC 35-9409. (Illus.). 350p. 1982. reprint ed. pap. 9.95 (*0-8290-0409-2*) Irvington.

— The Crow Indians. LC 82-20103. (Illus.). 350p. 1983. reprint ed. pap. 15.00 (*0-8032-7909-4*, Bison Books) U of Nebr Pr.

— Ethnographic Notes on the Washo. fac. ed. Kroeber, A. L. & Olson, Ronald L., eds. (University of California Publications in American Archaeology & Ethnology: Vol. 36: 5). 55p. (C). 1939. reprint ed. pap. text 6.56 (*1-55567-306-6*) Coyote Press.

— Hidatsa Texts. LC 74-7979. reprint ed. 27.50 (*0-404-11870-4*) AMS Pr.

— Indians of the Plains. LC 81-21813. xxvi, 223p. 1982. reprint ed. pap. 10.95 (*0-8032-7907-8*, Bison Books) U of Nebr Pr.

— The Material Culture of the Crow Indians. LC 74-7980. reprint ed. 27.50 (*0-404-11869-0*) AMS Pr.

L

L

— Myths & Traditions of the Crow Indians. LC 74-7981. reprint ed. 41.50 (*0-404-11872-0*) AMS Pr.

— The Northern Shoshone. LC 74-7983. reprint ed. 36.00 (*0-404-11871-2*) AMS Pr.

— Notes on Hopi Clans. LC 74-7984. (Anthropological Papers of the American Museum of Natural History: Vol. 30, Pts. 6-7). 34.50 (*0-404-11873-9*) AMS Pr.

— Notes on the Social Organizations & Customs of the Mandan, Hidatsa, & Crow Indians. LC 74-7985. 1976. reprint ed. 34.50 (*0-404-11874-7*) AMS Pr.

— The Religion of the Crow Indians. LC 74-7986. reprint ed. 39.50 (*0-404-11876-3*) AMS Pr.

— Robert H. Lowie, Ethnologist: A Personal Record. LC 59-8762. (Illus.). 226p. reprint ed. pap. 70.10 (*0-608-17471-8*, 202995500066) Bks Demand.

— Social Life of the Crow Indians. LC 74-7987. reprint ed. 32.50 (*0-404-11875-5*) AMS Pr.

— The Sun Dance of the Crow Indians. LC 76-43771. (AMNH. Anthropological Papers: Vol. 16, Pt. 1). 1977. reprint ed. 34.50 (*0-404-15624-X*) AMS Pr.

— The Tobacco Society of the Crow Indians. LC 74-7988. reprint ed. 35.00 (*0-404-11878-X*) AMS Pr.

Lowie, Robert H., ed. see Barnett, H. G.

Lowie, Robert H., ed. see Driver, Harold E.

Lowie, Robert H., ed. see Drucker, Philip.

Lowie, Robert H., ed. see DuBois, Cora.

Lowie, Robert H., ed. see Erikson, Erik H.

Lowie, Robert H., ed. see Gayton, A. H.

Lowie, Robert H., ed. see Gayton, A. H. & Newman, S. S.

Lowie, Robert H., ed. see Gifford, E. W. & Kroeber, A. L.

Lowie, Robert H., ed. see Gifford, E. W., et al.

Lowie, Robert H., ed. see Heizer, R. F. & Cook, S. F.

Lowie, Robert H., ed. see Holt, Catherine.

Lowie, Robert H., ed. see Kelly, Isabel J.

Lowie, Robert H., ed. see Kroeber, A. L.

Lowie, Robert H., ed. see Kroeber, A. L. & Richardson, J.

Lowie, Robert H., ed. see Nomland, Gladys A.

Lowie, Robert H., ed. see Olson, Ronald L.

Lowie, Robert H., ed. see Pettitt, George A.

Lowie, Robert H., ed. see Radin, Paul A.

Lowie, Robert H., ed. see Shimkin, D. B.

Lowie, Robert H., ed. see Stewart, Omer C.

Lowie, Robert H., ed. see Strong, William D.

Lowie, Robert H., ed. see Voegelin, Erminie W.

Lowie, Robert H., ed. & tr. see Nimuendaju, Curt.

Lowie, Robert H., tr. see Nimuendaju, Curt.

Lowig, Robert H. Always Putt in Two (with Little or No Practice) A Guide for the Weekend Golfer. LC 71-28834. (Illus.). 75p. (Orig.). 1994. pap. 16.95 (*0-9657551-0-X*) Loday Industries.

Lowin, Joseph. Cynthia Ozick. 208p. 1988. 32.00 (*0-8057-7526-9*, TUSAS 545, Twyne) Mac Lib Ref.

— Hebrewspeak: An Insider's Guide to the Way Jews Think. LC 94-46454. 240p. 1995. 30.00 (*1-56821-418-9*) Aronson.

Lowing, Ann. Yasmin. large type ed. 1995. 27.99 (*0-7089-3419-6*) Ulverscroft.

Lowinger, Thomas C. & Hinman, George W., eds. Nuclear Power at the Crossroads: Challenges & Prospects for the Twenty-First Century. LC 93-81259. (Illus.). 218p. 1994. 24.00 (*0-918714-42-7*) Intl Res Ctr Energy.

Lowings, John. At the Edge of the World. 1998. pap. 16.95 (*0-8050-5401-4*) H Holt & Co.

— At the Edge of the World. LC 97-39616. (Illus.). 192p. 1998. 29.95 (*0-8050-5400-6*) H Holt & Co.

Lowinsky, Edward E. Music in the Culture of the Renaissance & Other Essays, 2 vols. (Illus.). 1023p. 1989. lib. bdg. 300.00 (*0-226-49478-0*) U Ch Pr.

— Tonality & Atonality in Sixteenth-Century Music. (Music Reprint Ser.). 1989. 25.00 (*0-306-76299-4*) Da Capo.

Lowinsky, Edward E., ed. Medici Codex of 1518, Vol. 1: Historical Introduction & Commentary. LC 67-13810. (Monuments of Renaissance Music Ser.: Vols. 1, 2 & 3). 259p. 1968. lib. bdg. 120.00 (*0-226-49480-2*) U Ch Pr.

— Medici Codex of 1518, Vol. 2: Transcription. LC 67-13810. (Monuments of Renaissance Music Ser.: Vols. 1, 2 & 3). 415p. 1968. lib. bdg. 120.00 (*0-226-49481-0*) U Ch Pr.

— Medici Codex of 1518, Vol. 3: Facsimile Edition. LC 67-13810. (Monuments of Renaissance Music Ser.: Vols. 1, 2 & 3). 318p. 1968. lib. bdg. 120.00 (*0-226-49482-9*) U Ch Pr.

Lowinsky, Simon, jt. auth. see Curtis, Edward S.

Lowinson, Joyce H. & Stimmel, Barry, eds. Conceptual Issues in Alcoholism & Substance Abuse. LC 84-3762. (Advances in Alcohol & Substance Abuse Ser.: Vol. 3, No. 3). 102p. 1984. text 39.95 (*0-86656-316-4*) Haworth Pr.

Lowinson, Joyce H., et al. Substance Abuse: A Comprehensive Textbook. 2nd ed. (Illus.). 1136p. 1992. text 142.00 (*0-683-05211-X*) Lppncott W & W.

Lowinson, Joyce J., et al. Substance Abuse: A Comprehensive Textbook. 3rd ed. LC 96-43039. (Illus.). 1088p. 1997. 155.00 (*0-683-18179-3*) Lppncott W & W.

Lowis, George W., compiled by. Sociodemographic Factors in the Epidemiology of Multiple Sclerosis: An Annotated Bibliography, 5. LC 90-14016. (Bibliographies & Indexes in Medical Studies: No. 5). 256p. 1991. lib. bdg. 65.00 (*0-313-26838-X*, LSY/, Greenwood Pr) Greenwood.

Lowis, Peter. South Africa. LC 95-12096. (Topics in the News Ser.). (J). 1996. lib. bdg. 22.83 (*0-8172-4175-2*) Raintree Steck-V.

Lowit, Roxanne, photos by. Moments: Roxanne Lowit Photographs. LC 93-11115. (Illus.). 1993. text 45.00 (*0-86565-145-0*) Vendome.

Lowith, Karl. From Hegel to Nietzsche: The Revolution in Nineteenth Century Thought. 1991. pap. text 22.00 (*0-231-07499-9*) Col U Pr.

— Martin Heidegger & European Nihilism. Wolin, Richard, ed. Steiner, Gary, tr. from GER. LC 94-48411. (European Perspectives Ser.). 256p. 1995. 47.50 (*0-231-08406-4*) Col U Pr.

— Martin Heidegger & European Nihilism. 304p. 1998. pap. 17.50 (*0-231-08407-2*) Col U Pr.

— Max Weber & Karl Marx. LC 93-18705. (Classics in Sociology Ser.). 144p. (C). 1993. pap. 22.99 (*0-415-09381-3*) Routledge.

— Meaning in History: The Theological Implications of the Philosophy of History. LC 57-7900. 266p. 1957. pap. text 15.00 (*0-226-49555-8*, P16) U Ch Pr.

— My Life in Germany Before & after 1933: A Report. King, Elizabeth, tr. LC 93-43772. (Illus.). 192p. 1994. text 32.95 (*0-252-02121-5*); pap. text 14.95 (*0-252-06409-7*) U of Ill Pr.

— Nietzsche's Philosophy of the Eternal Recurrence of the Same. Lomax, J. Harvey, tr. from GER. LC 96-19802. 1997. 40.00 (*0-520-06519-0*, Pub. by U CA Pr) Cal Prin Full Svc.

Lowitt, Richard. Bronson M. Cutting: Progressive Politician. LC 92-15345. (Illus.). 432p. 1992. reprint ed. pap. 134.00 (*0-608-07279-6*, 206750700009) Bks Demand.

— George W. Norris: The Making of a Progressive, 1861 to 1912. LC 79-18826. (Illus.). 341p. 1980. reprint ed. lib. bdg. 69.50 (*0-313-22103-0*, LOGN, Greenwood Pr) Greenwood.

— George W. Norris: The Persistence of a Progressive, 1913-1933. LC 76-147923. (Illus.). 605p. 1971. text 44.95 (*0-252-00176-1*) U of Ill Pr.

— The New Deal & the West. LC 93-15538. 1993. 14.95 (*0-8061-2557-8*) U of Okla Pr.

Lowitt, Richard, ed. America in Depression & War. 7.95 (*0-88295-022-3*) Forum Pr IL.

Lowitt, Richard, ed. Politics in the Postwar American West. LC 94-43095. (Illus.). 400p. 1995. 49.50 (*0-8061-2711-2*) U of Okla Pr.

— Politics in the Postwar American West. LC 94-43095. (Illus.). 416p. 1995. pap. 21.95 (*0-8061-2741-4*) U of Okla Pr.

Lowitt, Richard, ed. see Garst, Roswell.

Lowitt, Richard, ed. see Hickok, Lorena.

Lowitt, Richard, ed. see Olsen, Nils A.

Lowitz, Barry B., jt. auth. see Casciato, Dennis A.

Lowitz, Barry B., jt. ed. see Casciato, Dennis A.

Lowitz, Leza. Beautiful Japan: A Souvenir. (Illus.). 100p. 1996. boxed set 16.95 (*0-8048-2054-6*) Tuttle Pubng.

Lowitz, Leza. Old Ways to Fold - New Paper. 98p. (Orig.). 1996. pap. 10.00 (*0-9653304-1-9*) Wandering Mind.

— Yoga Poems: Lines to Unfold. LC 00-25569. (Illus.). 126p. 2000. 14.95 (*1-880656-45-0*) Stone Bridge Pr.

Lowitz, Leza & Aoyama, Miyuki, eds. Other Side River: Free Verse. LC 95-14440. (Rock Spring Collection of Japanese Literature). (Illus.). 256p. (Orig.). 1995. pap. 14.00 (*1-880656-16-7*) Stone Bridge Pr.

Lowkie-Wanamaker, Tamanu. The Broken Chains: Bondage, Still Struggling, There Is Hope. 63p. 1997. pap. 10.00 (*0-9661959-0-6*) Nu-Nu & You.

— What Do You See in the Mirror: Love, Pain, Living & Learning. (Broken Chains Ser.: Vol. II). 36p. 1998. pap. 10.00 (*0-9661959-2-2*) Nu-Nu & You.

***Lowly, Jonathan.** Elvis & Nixon: A Novel. 2001. 22.95 (*0-609-60818-5*) Crown Pub Group.

Lowman. Super Shrink II: Jennifer. (C). 1990. pap. text, teacher ed. 7.00 (*0-15-584765-1*) Harcourt Coll Pubs.

Lowman, Al. Printing Arts in Texas. (Illus.). 109p. 1981. 25.00 (*0-686-73481-X*, PA2-16-7528) Jenkins.

***Lowman, David B.** Magic: The Untold Story of U. S. Intelligence & the Evacuation of... (Illus.). 2000. pap. 24.95 (*0-9602736-1-1*) Athena Pr.

Lowman, Dianne K. & Murphy, Suzanne M. The Educator's Guide to Feeding Children with Disabilities. LC 98-17858. 1998. pap. 34.95 (*1-55766-375-0*) P H Brookes.

Lowman, Evelyn. Arts & Crafts for the Elderly: A Resource Book for Activity Directors in Healthcare Facilities. LC 91-24182. (Illus.). 232p. 1992. 32.95 (*0-8261-7860-X*) Springer Pub.

Lowman, Guy S., Jr., jt. auth. see Kurath, Hans.

Lowman, Gwen, jt. ed. see Cater, Erlet.

Lowman, John & MacLean, Brian D., eds. Realist Criminology: Crime Control & Policing in the 1990s. LC 92-95006. 370p. 1992. pap. text 24.95 (*0-8020-7702-1*) U of Toronto Pr.

Lowman, Joseph. Mastering the Techniques of Teaching. LC 83-49265. (Jossey-Bass Higher Education Ser.). 267p. reprint ed. pap. 82.80 (*0-7837-2517-5*, 204267600006) Bks Demand.

— Mastering the Techniques of Teaching. 2nd ed. LC 95-12476. (Higher & Adult Education Ser.). 368p. 1995. text 34.45 (*0-7879-0127-X*) Jossey-Bass.

— Supershrink II: 3.5" 119p. (C). 1990. pap. text 41.50 (*0-15-584764-3*, Pub. by Harcourt Coll Pubs) Harcourt.

— Supershrink II: 5.25" 119p. (C). 1990. pap. text 51.50 (*0-15-584763-5*) Harcourt.

Lowman, Kathleen D., jt. ed. see Benjamin, Ludy T., Jr.

Lowman, Kaye. Of Cradles & Careers: A Guide to Reshaping Your Job to Include a Baby in Your Life. LC 84-80085. (Illus.). 300p. 1984. pap. 5.00 (*0-912500-14-X*) La Leche.

Lowman, Margaret D. Life in the Treetops: Adventures of a Woman in Field Biology. LC 98-48691. (Illus.). 240p. 1999. 30.00 (*0-300-07818-8*) Yale U Pr.

***Lowman, Margaret D.** Life in the Treetops: Adventures of a Woman in Field Biology. (Illus.). 240p. 1999. pap. 13.95 (*0-300-08464-1*) Yale U Pr.

Lowman, Margaret D. & Nadkarni, Nalini M., eds. Forest Canopies. (Physiological Ecology Ser.). (Illus.). 626p. 1995. text 74.00 (*0-12-457650-8*) Acad Pr.

— Forest Canopies. (Physiological Ecology Ser.). (Illus.). 626p. 1996. pap. text 39.95 (*0-12-457651-6*) Acad Pr.

Lowman, Michael, et al, eds. Sidney M. Jourard: Selected Writings. (Illus.). 371p. (Orig.). (C). 1994. pap. text 23.95 (*0-917982-49-5*) Capitol Enquiry.

Lowman, Robert G., et al. Experimental Introductory Chemistry: Organic & Biochemistry. (Illus.). 84p. 1983. pap. text 10.95 (*0-89641-125-7*) American Pr.

— Experimental Introductory Chemistry in 2 Pts. (Illus.). 274p. 1981. pap. text 14.95 (*0-89641-096-X*) American Pr.

Lowman, Rodney L. The Clinical Practice of Career Assessment: Interest, Abilities & Personality. (Illus.). 318p. (C). 1991. pap. 19.95 (*1-55798-119-1*) Am Psychol.

— Counseling & Psychotherapy of Work Dysfunctions. LC 93-852. (Illus.). 333p. 1993. text 29.95 (*1-55798-204-X*); pap. text 24.95 (*1-55798-205-8*) Am Psychol.

— Pre-Employment Screening for Psychopathology: A Guide to Professional Practice. Smith, Harold H., Jr., ed. LC 88-43546. (Practitioner's Resource Ser.). 86p. 1989. pap. 16.45 (*0-943158-34-6*, PESPB) Pro Resource.

Lowman, Rodney L., ed. The Ethical Practice of Psychology in Organizations. LC 97-47450. 299p. 1998. pap. 24.95 (*1-55798-486-7*, 431-2070) Am Psychol.

Lowman, Rodney L. & Resnick, Robert J., eds. The Mental Health Professional's Guide to Managed Care. LC 93-47570. 191p. 1994. pap. text 24.95 (*1-55798-232-5*) Am Psychol.

Lowman, Sarah, jt. auth. see Knox, Lucy.

Lowman, Zelvin D. A Voice in the Desert: A History of First Presbyterian Church, Las Vegas, Nevada. (Illus.). 168p. 1992. 19.95 (*1-881576-03-5*) Providence Hse.

Lowmiller, Cathie, jt. auth. see Mike, Jan M.

Lown, Bernard. Lost Art of Healing. LC R733.L684 1999. 344p. 1999. pap. 14.00 (*0-345-42597-9*) Ballantine Pub Grp.

— Lost Art of Healing. LC 96-18184. 288p. 1996. 24.95 (*0-395-82525-3*) HM.

Lown, David, jt. auth. see Lown, Patricia T.

Lown, David, jt. auth. see Twohill Lown, Patricia.

Lown, David A. & Twohill Lown, Patricia. All London: The Source Guide. LC 99-70290. 448p. 1999. 35.00 (*0-9643256-4-0*) Palancar.

Lown, David A., jt. auth. see Lown, Patricia T.

Lown, David A., jt. auth. see Twohill Lown, Patricia.

Lown, Patricia T. & Lown, David. Tout Paris: The Source Guide to the Art of French Decoration. (Illus.). 410p. 29.50 (*0-9643256-0-8*) Palancar.

— Treasures of France: A Tout Paris Guide. (Illus.). 540p. 1996. 29.00 (*0-9643256-2-4*) Palancar.

Lown, Patricia T. & Lown, David A. All Paris: The Source Guide. 400p. 1999. 35.00 (*0-9643256-6-7*, Pub. by Palancar) Antique Collect.

Lown, Patricia Twohill, see Twohill Lown, Patricia.

Lown, Patricia Twohill, see Lown, David A. & Twohill Lown, Patricia.

Lown, Patricia Twohill, see Twohill Lown, Patricia.

Lowndes. Electrophysiology in Neurotoxins, Vol. I. 128p. 1987. 81.00 (*0-8493-4694-0*, CRC Reprint) Franklin.

— Electrophysiology in Neurotoxins, Vol. II. 152p. 1987. 90.00 (*0-8493-4695-9*, CRC Reprint) Franklin.

Lowndes, Belloc. The Lodger. 1976. 24.95 (*0-8488-0180-6*) Amereon Ltd.

Lowndes, Florin. Enlivening the Chakra of the Heart: The Fundamental Spiritual Exercises of Rudolf Steiner. Barton, M., tr. from GER. 200p. 2000. reprint ed. pap. 19.95 (*1-85584-053-7*, 3048, Pub. by R Steiner Pr) Anthroposophic.

Lowndes, H. E. Electrophysiology in Neurotoxicology, 2 vols., Set. 1987. reprint ed. 170.00 (*0-8493-4693-2*, CRC Reprint) Franklin.

***Lowndes, H. E. & Reuhl, K. R.** Nervous System & Behavioral Toxicology, 13 vols. (Comprehensive Toxicology Ser.: Vol. 11). 564p. 1999. 165.00 (*0-08-042976-9*) Elsevier.

Lowndes, L. & Rudolf, R. Law of General Average. (C). 1975. 800.00 (*0-7855-4106-3*, Pub. by Witherby & Co) St Mut.

***Lowndes, Leil.** How to Be a People Magnet! To Attract Friends & Lovers. LC 00-34550. 256p. 2000. 22.95 (*0-8092-2434-8*, Contemporary Bks) NTC Contemp Pub Co.

Lowndes, Leil. How to Make Anyone Fall in Love with You. 336p. 1996. 21.95 (*0-8092-3211-1*, 321110, Contemporary Bks) NTC Contemp Pub Co.

— How to Make Anyone Fall in Love with You. 336p. 1997. pap. 14.95 (*0-8092-2989-7*, 298970, Contemporary Bks) NTC Contemp Pub Co.

Lowndes, Leil. How to Make Anyone Fall in Love with You. abr. ed. 1997. 16.95 incl. audio (*1-882071-93-X*) B&B Audio.

— How to Talk to Anybody about Anything: Breaking the Ice with Everyone from Accountants to Zen Buddhists. rev. ed. LC 96-26075. 272p. 1996. pap. 12.95 (*0-8065-1820-0*, Citadel Pr) Carol Pub Group.

Lowndes, Leil. How to Talk to Anybody about Anything: Breaking the Ice with Everyone from Accountants to Zen Buddhists. 3rd rev. ed. LC 98-49774. 312p. 1999. pap. 14.95 (*0-8065-2077-9*, Citadel Pr) Carol Pub Group.

— In the Business of Family: The NFO Story. (Illus.). 104p. 1996. write for info. (*0-944641-20-2*) Greenwich Pub Group.

— Talking the Winner's Way. LC 98-17924. 368p. 1999. 22.95 (*0-8092-2981-1*, 298110, Contemporary Bks) NTC Contemp Pub Co.

— Talking the Winner's Way: 92 Little Tricks for Big Success in Business & Personal Relationships. 368p. 1999. pap. 16.95 (*0-8092-2503-4*, 250340, Contemporary Bks) NTC Contemp Pub Co.

Lowndes, Marie A. The End of Her Honeymoon. LC 75-32763. (Literature of Mystery & Detection Ser.). 1976. reprint ed. 20.95 (*0-405-07884-6*) Ayer.

— Some Men & Women. LC 75-150549. (Short Story Index Reprint Ser.). 1977. reprint ed. 23.95 (*0-8369-3846-1*) Ayer.

— Studies in Love & in Terror. LC 74-167462. (Short Story Index Reprint Ser.). 1977. reprint ed. 21.95 (*0-8369-3988-3*) Ayer.

Lowndes, Marie B. The Lodger. 224p. 1986. reprint ed. pap. 5.95 (*0-89733-299-7*) Academy Chi Pubs.

Lowndes, Rosemary, jt. auth. see Kailer, Claude.

Lowndes, William. The Royal Crescent in Bath: A Fragment of English Life. 96p. 1988. 60.00 (*0-905459-34-2*, Pub. by Redcliffe Pr Ltd) St Mut.

— The Theatre Royal at Bath. 1988. 39.00 (*0-7855-0720-5*, Pub. by Redcliffe Pr Ltd) St Mut.

Lowndes, William, jt. auth. see Hardy, Paul.

***Lownds, Sue.** Fast Track to Change on the Heathrow Express. 160p. 2000. pap. 29.95 (*0-8464-5058-5*) Beekman Pubs.

Lownes, Millicent G. Entrepreneurially Yours: A Compilation of Articles about Starting & Managing a Small Business. Deming, Lynne, ed. 50p. (Orig.). 1990. pap. 5.95 (*0-943267-13-7*) Busn Your Own.

— The Purple Rose Within: A Woman's Basic Guide for Developing a Business Plan. Deming, Lynne, ed. 70p. (Orig.). 1989. pap. 9.95 (*0-943267-14-5*) Busn Your Own.

Lowney, Frank, ed. see Kujichagulia, Phavia.

Lowney, John. The American Avant-Garde Tradition: William Carlos Williams, Postmodern Poetry, & the Politics of Cultural Memory. LC 96-7249. 176p. 1997. 32.50 (*0-8387-5333-7*) Bucknell U Pr.

Lowney, Kathleen S. Baring Our Souls: TV Talk Shows & the Religion of Recovery. LC 99-36442. (Social Problems & Social Issues Ser.). 171p. 1999. pap. text 21.95 (*0-202-30594-5*) Aldine de Gruyter.

***Lowney, Kathleen S.** Baring Our Souls: TV Talk Shows & the Religion of Recovery. LC 99-36442. (Social Problems & Social Issues Ser.). 171p. 1999. lib. bdg. 42.95 (*0-202-30593-7*) Aldine de Gruyter.

Lowney, Kathleen S. Passport to Heaven: Gender Roles in the Unification Church. LC 92-20892. (Cults & Nonconventional Religious Groups Ser.). 248p. 1992. text 25.00 (*0-8153-0775-6*) Garland.

***Lowney, Paul B.** Little Lessons from Life: My Professors & My Jewish Mother. 1999. pap. 4.95 (*0-9609946-5-3*) C & L Pubs.

— Toads. 3rd expanded ed. 1998. pap. text 8.95 (*0-9609946-4-5*) C & L Pubs.

Lowneys, Paul B. Toads. 2nd ed. 1997. 8.95 (*0-9609946-3-7*) C & L Pubs.

Lownie, Andrew. John Buchan: A Presbyterian Cavalier. 1998. pap. 16.95 (*0-86241-667-1*, Pub. by Canongate Books) Interlink Pub.

Lownie, Andrew & Nilne, William. John Buchan's Collected Poems. 256p. 1990. pap. 39.00 (*1-898218-47-1*) St Mut.

Lownsbery, Eloise. Saints & Rebels. LC 72-156682. (Essay Index Reprint Ser.). 1977. reprint ed. 24.95 (*0-8369-2322-7*) Ayer.

Lownsborough, Roger. Electronic Aids to Navigation. (Electrical Engineering Ser.). 1994. pap. 46.50 (*0-340-59258-3*, VNR) Wiley.

Lowood, Henry. Patriotism, Profit & Promotion in the German Enlightenment: The Economic & Scientific Societies, 1760-1815. rev. ed. LC 91-27131. (Modern European History Ser.: No. 2). 464p. 1991. text 25.00 (*0-8153-0677-6*) Garland.

Lowood, Henry, compiled by. Ernest Rutherford: A Bibliography of His Non-Technical Writings. LC 77-94210. (Berkeley Papers in History of Science: No. 4). 61p. (Orig.). 1979. pap. 5.00 (*0-918102-02-2*) U Cal Hist Sci Tech.

— William Henry Bragg & William Lawrence Bragg: A Bibliography of Their Non-Technical Writings. LC 77-94209. (Berkeley Papers in History of Science: No. 2). 109p. 1978. pap. 5.00 (*0-918102-01-4*) U Cal Hist Sci Tech.

Lowood, Henry E., jt. compiled by see Rider, Robin E.

Lowrance, Judi M. Puppy Book, My Dog's Tail: A Complete Journal. (Illus.). 50p. 1995. 19.95 (*0-9651391-1-5*) SCT Retrievers.

Lowrance, Richard, et al, eds. Agricultural Ecosystems: Unifying Concepts. LC 83-23504. (Wiley-Interscience Publications). 245p. reprint ed. pap. 76.00 (*0-7837-2400-4*, 204008500006) Bks Demand.

Lowrekas, Peter, jt. auth. see Weinmann, Elaine.

Lowrey, Alvin L. Lowrey's International Trumpet Discography. LC 89-23960. 1200p. 1990. 180.00 (*0-938100-79-3*) Camden Hse.

***Lowrey, Carol.** Dan Ostermiller. (Illus.). 26p. 1999. pap. 10.00 (*0-945936-22-2*) Spanierman Gallery.

Lowrey, Carol. A Noble Tradition: American Painting from the National Arts Club. (Illus.). 31p. (Orig.). 1995. pap. 14.00 (*1-880897-04-0*) Lyme Hist.

Lowrey, Carol, et al. Dialogues with Nature: Works by Charles Salis Kaelin (1858-1929) LC 99-170484. 41 p. 1990. write for info. (*0-945936-09-5*) Spanierman Gallery.

Lowrey, Christy H. Hankins: Ancestors, Descendants & Relations. (Illus.). 120p. 1997. lib. bdg. 49.50 (*1-889137-05-7*) Genie Pubng.

Lowrey, Christy H., jt. auth. see Wood, Lucia P.

Lowrey, Ernest, jt. auth. see Echols, William.

Lowrey, Janette S. The Poky Little Puppy. (Little Golden Bks.). (Illus.). 24p. (J). (ps-2). 1992. bds. 2.29 (*0-307-02134-3*, 98100, Goldn Books) Gldn Bks Pub Co.

An Asterisk (*) at the beginning of an entry indicates that the title is appearing for the first time.

Lowrey, Jeanette S. The Poky Little Puppy. (Little Golden Storybks.). (J). 1998. 3.99 (*0-307-16026-2*, 16026, Goldn Books) Gldn Bks Pub Co.

Lowrey, Joseph W. Macromedia Dreamweaver Bible. LC TK5105.8885.D74L69. 816p. 1998. pap. 39.99 (*0-7645-3225-1*) IDG Bks.

Lowrey, Lawrence. Secrets of Winning at Casino Roulette. 32p. 1997. pap. 7.95 (*0-934650-15-2*) Sunnyside.

Lowrey, Nathan, jt. auth. see Boynton, Mia.

Lowrey, Robert. The Indonesian Armed Forces. 160p. 1996. pap. 24.95 (*0-522-84624-6*, Pub. by Melbourne Univ Pr) Paul & Co Pubs.

Lowrey, Wilson H. Radio in Rural Guatemala: Three Case Studies. (Illus.). 150p. (Orig.). (C). 1990. pap. text 9.95 (*0-943089-01-8*) U GA CFIMCTR.

Lowrie, Allen. Carnivorous Plants, Vol. 3. (Illus.). 1996. pap. write for info. (*1-875560-59-9*, Pub. by Univ of West Aust Pr) Intl Spec Bk.

— Carnivorous Plants of Australia, Vol. 2. (Illus.). 272p. 1989. 38.50 (*0-85564-299-8*, Pub. by Univ of West Aust Pr) Intl Spec Bk.

— Carnivorous Plants of Australia, Vol. 2. (Illus.). 272p. 1989. pap. 27.50 (*0-85564-300-5*, Pub. by Univ of West Aust Pr) Intl Spec Bk.

— Seismic Stratigraphy & Hydrocarbon Traps: Louisiana Offshore & Onshore. LC 94-35381. (Course Notes Ser.). 224p. 1994. 30.00 (*1-56080-025-9*, 255A) Soc Expl Geophys.

Lowrie, Douglas B. & Whalen, Robert, eds. DNA Vaccines: Methods & Protocols. LC 98-55325. (Methods in Molecular Medicine Ser.: No. 29). (Illus.). 550p. 1999. 99.50 (*0-89603-580-8*) Humana.

Lowrie, Ernest B. The Shape of the Puritan Mind: The Thought of Samuel Willard. LC 74-76650. 267p. reprint ed. pap. 82.80 (*0-8357-8319-7*, 203380800087) Bks Demand.

Lowrie, Jean, ed. Great Expectations: Standard, Innovative Programs, New Technology: Conference Proceedings of the 17th Annual Conference of the IASL. 331p. 1988. pap. 25.00 (*1-890861-09-X*) IASL.

Lowrie, Jean E. & Nagakura, Mieko, eds. School Libraries: International Developments. 2nd ed. LC 91-10920. (Illus.). 403p. 1991. 47.50 (*0-8108-2390-X*) Scarecrow.

Lowrie, Michele. Horace's Narrative Odes. LC 97-217752. 394p. 1997. text 90.00 (*0-19-815053-9*) OUP.

Lowrie Nason, Janet, jt. auth. see Lowrie, Roy W.

Lowrie, P., jt. auth. see Nicholaus, B.

Lowrie, Paul. Conversation Piece: Creative Questions to Tickle the Mind. expanded rev. ed. 1996. 9.95 (*0-345-40711-3*) Ballantine Pub Grp.

Lowrie, Paul & Nicholaus, Bret. The Christmas Conversation Piece: Creative Questions to Illuminate the Holidays. LC 96-97047. 144p. 1996. 10.00 (*0-345-40712-1*) Ballantine Pub Grp.

— Toe Tappin' Trivia. LC ML3524.N53 1999. 1999. mass mkt. 5.50 (*0-345-43370-X*) Ballantine Pub Grp.

***Lowrie, Paul & Nicholaus, Bret.** Who We Are: Questions to Celebrate Your Family. 208p. 2000. 15.00 (*1-57731-131-0*, Pub. by New Wrld Lib) Publishers Group.

Lowrie, Paul, jt. auth. see Nicholaus, Bret.

Lowrie, Roy W. & Lowrie Nason, Janet. To Those Who Teach in Christian Schools. 2nd rev. ed. 117p. 1998. pap. write for info. (*1-58331-001-0*) Assn Christ Sch.

Lowrie, Samuel H. Culture Conflict in Texas, 1821-1835. 1993. reprint ed. lib. bdg. 75.00 (*0-7812-5943-6*) Rprt Serv.

Lowrie, Walter. Kierkegaard, Vol. 1. 1990. 14.75 (*0-8446-0778-9*) Peter Smith.

— Land Claims in the Eastern District of the Orleans Territory: Communicated to the House of Representatives, Jan. 9, 1812. 160p. 1985. reprint ed. pap. 27.50 (*0-89308-582-0*) Southern Hist Pr.

— Short Life of Kierkegaard. 284p. 1942. pap. text 16.95 (*0-691-01957-6*, Pub. by Princeton U Pr) Cal Prin Full Svc.

Lowrie, Walter, tr. see Kierkegaard, Soren.

Lowrie, Walter, tr. & intro. see Kierkegaard, Soren.

Lowrie, William. Fundamentals of Geophysics. (Illus.). 369p. (C). 1997. text 85.00 (*0-521-46164-2*); pap. text 34.95 (*0-521-46728-4*) Cambridge U Pr.

Lowringer, Gene. Bluegrass Fiddle. LC 73-92395. (Illus.). 1974. pap. 14.95 (*0-8256-0150-9*, OK62794, Oak) Music Sales.

Lowrinson, G. C. Fertilizer Technology. (Applied Science Ser.). 1989. text 120.00 (*0-470-21505-4*) P-H.

Lowry, ed. Mechanics & Theory in Organic Chemistry: Answer Book. 4th ed. (C). 1999. pap. text. write for info. (*0-321-40081-X*) Addison-Wesley.

Lowry & Meyers. Conflict Resolution. (Resources for Christian Counseling Ser.: Vol. 28). 18.99 (*0-8499-0602-4*) Word Pub.

Lowry, Brigid. Guitar Highway Rose. LC 98-200376. (Little Ark Book Ser.). 205 p. (J). 1997. write for info. (*1-86448-442-X*) Allen & Unwin Pty.

Lowry, Bates. Building a National Image: Architectural Drawings for the American Democracy, 1789-1912. (Illus.). 228p. 1992. pap. text 45.00 (*0-226-49557-4*) U Ch Pr.

— Renaissance Architecture. LC 61-13691. (Great Ages of World Architecture Ser.). (Illus.). 127p. 1965. pap. 9.95 (*0-8076-0335-X*) Braziller.

Lowry, Betty. The Nantucket Book: A Complete Guide. LC 97-46095. (Great Destinations Ser.). (Illus.). 320p. 1998. pap. 17.95 (*0-936399-95-3*) Berkshire Hse.

Lowry, Beverly. Biography of Madame C. J. Walker. 1999. pap. write for info. (*0-679-76803-3*) Knopf.

***Lowry, Beverly.** Come Back, Lolly Ray. LC 99-86603. (Voices of the South Ser.). 248p. 2000. pap. 15.95 (*0-8071-2574-1*) La State U Pr.

Lowry, Beverly. Crossed Over. 1999. text 20.00 (*0-670-83637-0*) Viking Penguin.

— Crossed Over: The True Story of the Houston Pickax Murders. 304p. 1994. mass mkt. 5.99 (*0-446-36510-6*) Warner Bks.

Lowry, Brian. Trust No One: The Official Third Season Guide to the X-Files. (X-Files Ser.). 288p. 1996. mass mkt. 15.00 (*0-06-105353-8*, HarperPrism) HarpC.

Lowry, Brian. The Truth Is Out There: The Official Guide to the X-Files. LC 95-45337. 288p. 1995. 16.00 (*0-06-105330-9*, HarperPrism) HarpC.

Lowry, Bullitt. Armistice 1918. LC 96-7600. 344p. (C). 1997. text 16.00 (*0-87338-651-5*) Kent St U Pr.

Lowry, Charles W. To Pray or Not to Pray: A Handbook for Study of Recent Supreme Court Decisions & American Church-State Doctrine. enl. ed. LC 68-8899. 260p. 1969. 29.95 (*0-87419-013-4*) Cherokee.

— William Temple: An Archbishop for All Seasons. LC 81-43869. 170p. (Orig.). 1982. pap. text 17.00 (*0-8191-2356-0*) U Pr of Amer.

Lowry, Christopher, jt. ed. see Smith, Whitney.

Lowry, Christopher A. Mastering No-Load Mutual Funds: The Road Map to Investment Success. 304p. 1996. pap. 24.95 (*1-888164-04-2*) No-Load Fund.

Lowry, Clara, jt. auth. see Kendig, Bobbi.

Lowry, Dave. Autumn Lightning: The Education of An American Samurai. LC 84-23562. (Illus.). 179p. (Orig.). 1985. pap. 8.95 (*0-87773-305-8*, 73027-5, Pub. by Shambhala Pubns) Random.

— Autumn Lightning: The Education of an American Samurai. 1985. pap. 8.95 (*0-394-73027-5*, Pub. by Shambhala Pubns) Random.

— Bokken: Art of the Japanese Sword. Lee, Mike, ed. LC 85-63391. (Weapons Ser.). 192p. 1985. pap. 11.95 (*0-89750-104-7*, 443) Ohara Pubns.

***Lowry, Dave.** Moving Toward Stillness: Lessons in Daily Life from the Martial Ways of Japan. LC 99-29183. (Illus.). 176p. 2000. pap. 16.95 (*0-8048-3160-2*) Tuttle Pubng.

Lowry, Dave. Persimmon Wind: A Martial Artist's Journey in Japan. LC 97-45548. (Illus.). 272p. 1998. pap. 19.95 (*0-8048-3142-4*) Tuttle Pubng.

— Sword & Brush: The Spirit of the Martial Arts. LC 95-5653. (Illus.). 144p. (Orig.). 1995. pap. 14.95 (*1-57062-112-8*, Pub. by Shambhala Pubns) Random.

Lowry, Dave & Lee, Mike. Jo: Art of the Japanese Short Staff. LC 87-42877. (Weapons Ser.). 192p. 1987. pap. 14.95 (*0-89750-116-0*, 455) Ohara Pubns.

Lowry, David. Indoor Air Quality: A Marketing Manual. (Illus.). 52p. 1992. pap. 88.00 (*0-944352-38-3*) Cleaning Cons.

Lowry, David. The Prophetic Element in the Church: As Conceived in the Theology of Karl Rahner. 258p. (C). 1990. lib. bdg. 50.50 (*0-8191-7857-8*) U Pr of Amer.

Lowry, Don. Fly Your True Colors. 220p. Date not set. pap. 16.95 (*1-885221-93-2*) BookPartners.

***Lowry, Donal.** Aspects of the South African War. LC 99-45465. 256p. 2000. pap. 29.95 (*0-7190-5825-2*, Pub. by Manchester Univ Pr) St Martin.

— Aspects of the South African War 1899-1902. LC 99-45465. 256p. 2000. text 79.95 (*0-7190-5258-0*, Pub. by Manchester Univ Pr) St Martin.

Lowry, Donald, jt. auth. see Kalil, Carolyn.

Lowry, Ed, et al. Joe Frisco: Comic, Jazz Dancer, & Railbird. LC 98-34721. 1999. 22.40 (*0-8093-2240-4*) S Ill U Pr.

— Joe Frisco: Comic, Jazz Dancer, & Railbird. Levitt, Paul M., ed. LC 98-34721. 154p. 1999. pap. 14.95 (*0-8093-2241-2*) S Ill U Pr.

Lowry, Edward. The Filmology Movement & Film Study in France. Kirkpatrick, Diane, ed. LC 84-24099. (Studies in Cinema: No. 33). 225p. 1985. reprint ed. pap. 69.80 (*0-8357-1630-9*, 207045800093) Bks Demand.

Lowry, Edward G. Washington Close-Ups. LC 70-142656. (Essay Index Reprint Ser.). 1977. 23.95 (*0-8369-2057-0*) Ayer.

Lowry, Eugene L. The Homiletical Plot: The Sermon As Narrative Art Form. LC 79-92074. 100p. (Orig.). 1983. pap. 14.95 (*0-8042-1652-5*) Westminster John Knox.

— How to Preach a Parable: Designs for Narrative Sermons. LC 89-191. 176p. 1989. pap. 13.95 (*0-687-17924-6*) Abingdon.

— Living with the Lectionary: Preaching the Revised Common Lectionary. 128p. (Orig.). 1992. pap. 5.18 (*0-687-17921-1*) Abingdon.

— The Sermon: Dancing on the Edge of Mystery. LC 97-6707. 208p. 1997. 19.95 (*0-687-01543-X*) Abingdon.

Lowry, Eve. Great Low Fat Food, Nutrition & Recipes: Living Lean & Loving It. 2nd ed. 1993. 24.95 (*1-878060-08-2*) GW Medical.

Lowry, George, et al. Lab Experiments in General Chemistry. 1992. 30.65 (*0-88252-146-2*) Paladin Hse.

Lowry, George G., ed. Markov Chains & Monte Carlo Calculations in Polymer Science. LC 70-84777. (Monographs in Macromolecular Chemistry). 338p. reprint ed. pap. 104.80 (*0-608-30342-9*, 205504800008) Bks Demand.

Lowry, George G. & Lowry, Robert C. Handbook of Hazard Communication & OSHA Requirements. LC 85-6982. (Illus.). 300p. 1985. lib. bdg. 68.00 (*0-87371-022-3*, L022) Lewis Pubs.

— Lowrys' Handbook of Right-to-Know & Emergency Planning. (Illus.). 421p. 1988. lib. bdg. 119.00 (*0-87371-112-2*, L112) Lewis Pubs.

Lowry, Glenn R. Systems Development Through the AD - Cycle: Using the Techniques & Tools of the 90's. 592p. (C). 1995. write for info. (*0-697-20225-9*) Bus & Educ Tech.

— Systems Development Through the AD - Cycle: Using the Techniques & Tools of the 90's. 224p. (C). 1995. pap., student ed. write for info. (*0-697-20240-2*); pap., student ed. write for info. (*0-697-20241-0*) Bus & Educ Tech.

Lowry, Ira S. Development Regulation & Housing Affordability. LC 92-60666. 180p. 1992. pap. text 42.95 (*0-87420-729-0*, D82) Urban Land.

Lowry, J., et al, eds. Plants Fed to Village Ruminants in Indonesia: Notes on 136 Species, Their Composition & Significance in Village Farming Systems. 60p. 1992. pap. 45.00 (*1-86320-071-1*, Pub. by ACIAR) St Mut.

Lowry, James. Doc Source International. 1991. 95.00 (*0-316-53404-8*) Little.

Lowry, James K. Soft Bottom Macrobenthic Community of Arthur Harbor, Antarctica: Paper 1 in Biology of the Antarctic Seas V. Pawson, David L., ed. LC 75-22056. (Antarctic Research Ser.: Vol. 23). (Illus.). 20p. 1975. pap. 5.20 (*0-87590-123-9*) Am Geophysical.

***Lowry, James S.** Low-Back, Ladder-Back, Cane-Bottom Chair: Biblical Meditations. 128p. 1999. pap. 12.95 (*0-88489-566-1*) St Marys.

Lowry, James W. Haskins Genealogy: The Descendants of Jonas Haskins (1788-1837) LC 92-97185. (Illus.). 350p. 1992. text 26.95 (*1-883453-04-6*) Deutsche Buchhandlung.

— In the Whale's Belly & Other Martyr Stories. (Illus.). (YA). (gr. 7 up). 1981. pap. 6.95 (*0-87813-513-8*) Christian Light.

— North America Is the Lord's. (Christian Day School Ser.). (J). (gr. 5). 1980. 18.95 (*0-87813-916-8*) Christian Light.

Lowry, Jan M. The Worm Whistle. (Illus.). (J). (gr. 2). 1994. pap. text 12.95 (*1-881116-36-0*, Pub. by Black Forest Pr) Epic Bk Promo.

— The Worm Whistle. (Illus.). 39p. (J). (ps-4). 1995. pap. 12.95 (*0-9646183-0-3*) J M Lowry.

***Lowry, John & Edmunds, Rod, eds.** Environmental Protection & the Common Law. 28p. 2000. 40.00 (*1-901362-93-0*, Pub. by Hart Pub) Intl Spec Bk.

***Lowry, John & Rawlings, Philip.** Insurance Law: Doctrines & Principles. 454p. 1999. 54.00 (*1-84113-003-6*, Pub. by Hart Pub); pap. 35.00 (*1-84113-004-4*, Pub. by Hart Pub) Intl Spec Bk.

Lowry, John, jt. auth. see Oughton, David.

Lowry, John, jt. auth. see Oughton, David W.

***Lowry, John T.** Performance of Light Aircraft LC 99-34583. (Education Ser.). 1999. write for info. (*1-56347-330-5*) AIAA.

Lowry, Judith L. Gardening with a Wild Heart: Restoring California's Native Landscapes at Home. LC 98-16177. (Illus.). 280p. 1999. 35.00 (*0-520-21516-8*, Pub. by U CA Pr); pap. 17.95 (*0-520-21517-6*, Pub. by U CA Pr) Cal Prin Full Svc.

Lowry, Judith Larner. Maintain Your Yard the Lazy Way. 304p. 1999. pap. text. write for info. (*0-02-863012-2*) Macmillan.

Lowry, Kem. Final Report - Sri Lanka Coastal Resources Management Project. (Coastal Management Report Ser.: Vol. 2217). (Illus.). Date not set. pap. write for info. (*1-885454-19-8*) Coastal Res.

Lowry, L. Randolph, jt. auth. see Wiggins, Charles B.

Lowry, Lawrence F., ed. NSTA Pathways to the Science Standards: Guidelines for Moving the Vision into Practice, Elementary School Edition. (Illus.). 152p. 1997. pap. text 29.95 (*0-87355-161-3*, PB124X) Natl Sci Tchrs.

Lowry, Linda. Inside Colorado: An Artist's View of Colorado Interiors. Publishing Group Staff, ed. (Illus.). 64p. 1993. 24.50 (*0-9635461-0-4*) Trails End Edit.

Lowry, Lois. All about Sam. (Illus.). 144p. (J). (gr. 4-7). 1989. pap. 1.99 (*0-440-40221-2*, YB BDD) BDD Bks Young Read.

— All about Sam. LC 88-13231. (Illus.). 144p. (J). (gr. 4-7). 1988. 15.00 (*0-395-48662-9*) HM.

— All about Sam. (J). 1988. 9.09 (*0-606-00311-8*, Pub. by Turtleback) Demco.

— Anastasia. (J). write for info. (*0-318-60131-1*) HM.

— Anastasia, Absolutely. 128p. (J). (gr. 4-7). 1997. pap. 3.99 (*0-440-41222-6*, YB BDD) BDD Bks Young Read.

— Anastasia, Absolutely. LC 95-9710. 128p. (J). (gr. 3-6). 1995. 16.00 (*0-395-74521-7*) HM.

— Anastasia, Absolutely. 119p. (J). (gr. 3-7). 1996. 13.95 (*0-614-12880-3*) HM.

Lowry, Lois. Anastasia, Absolutely. 1997. 9.09 (*0-606-11041-0*, Pub. by Turtleback) Demco.

Lowry, Lois. Anastasia Again! 160p. (J). (gr. 4-7). 1982. pap. 3.99 (*0-440-40009-0*, YB BDD) BDD Bks Young Read.

— Anastasia Again!, 001. (Illus.). 160p. (J). (gr. 3-6). 1981. 16.00 (*0-395-31147-0*) HM.

— Anastasia Again! (J). 1981. 9.09 (*0-606-02808-0*, Pub. by Turtleback) Demco.

— Anastasia Answers. (J). 1995. pap. 4.99 (*0-440-91077-3*) BDD Bks Young Read.

— Anastasia, Ask Your Analyst. LC 83-26687. 128p. (J). (gr. 4-7). 1992. pap. 4.50 (*0-440-40289-1*, YB BDD) BDD Bks Young Read.

— Anastasia, Ask Your Analyst, 001. LC 83-26687. 128p. (J). (gr. 3-6). 1984. 16.00 (*0-395-36011-0*, 5-90388) HM.

— Anastasia, Ask Your Analyst. (J). 1985. 9.09 (*0-606-00251-0*, Pub. by Turtleback) Demco.

— Anastasia at This Address. 144p. (J). (gr. 4-7). 1992. pap. 4.50 (*0-440-40652-8*, YB BDD) BDD Bks Young Read.

— Anastasia at This Address. LC 90-48308. 112p. (J). (gr. 3-7). 1991. 16.00 (*0-395-56263-5*) HM.

— Anastasia at This Address. 1991. 9.09 (*0-606-00853-5*, Pub. by Turtleback) Demco.

— Anastasia at Your Service. 160p. (J). (gr. 3-6). 1983. pap. 4.50 (*0-440-40290-5*, YB BDD) BDD Bks Young Read.

— Anastasia at Your Service. LC 82-9231. (Illus.). 160p. (J). (gr. 3-6). 1982. 16.00 (*0-395-32865-9*) HM.

Lowry, Lois. Anastasia at Your Service. 149p. (J). (gr. 4-6). pap. 3.99 (*0-8072-1409-4*) Listening Lib.

Lowry, Lois. Anastasia at Your Service. (J). 1984. 9.09 (*0-606-02648-7*, Pub. by Turtleback) Demco.

***Lowry, Lois.** Anastasia de Nuevo. (Juvenil Ser.: Vol. 77).Tr. of Anastasia Again. (SPA., Illus.). (J). (gr. 5-7). 1999. pap. 9.95 (*84-239-9047-8*) Espasa Calpe.

Lowry, Lois. Anastasia de Nuevo.Tr. of Anastasia Again. (SPA.). (J). 1996. pap. text 9.75 (*84-239-2793-8*) Lectorum Pubns.

Lowry, Lois. Anastasia Elige Profession. 1996. pap. 9.95 (*84-239-7133-3*) Espasa Calpe.

Lowry, Lois. Anastasia Has the Answers. 128p. (J). (gr. k-6). 1987. pap. 4.50 (*0-440-40087-2*, YB BDD) BDD Bks Young Read.

— Anastasia Has the Answers. 128p. (J). (gr. 5 up). 1986. 16.00 (*0-395-41795-3*) HM.

— Anastasia Has the Answers. (J). 1986. 9.09 (*0-606-03544-3*, Pub. by Turtleback) Demco.

— Anastasia Krupnik. 144p. (J). (gr. 4-7). 1984. pap. 1.99 (*0-440-40852-0*) Dell.

— Anastasia Krupnik. 160p. (J). (gr. 3-6). 1979. 16.00 (*0-395-28629-8*) HM.

Lowry, Lois. Anastasia Krupnik. 1979. 9.60 (*0-606-05118-X*, Pub. by Turtleback) Demco.

Lowry, Lois. Anastasia on Her Own. 144p. (J). (gr. 2-6). 1986. pap. 4.50 (*0-440-40291-3*, YB BDD) BDD Bks Young Read.

— Anastasia on Her Own, 001. LC 84-22432. 131p. (J). (gr. 5-7). 1985. 16.00 (*0-395-38133-9*) HM.

Lowry, Lois. Anastasia on Her Own. (J). 1985. 9.09 (*0-606-02375-5*, Pub. by Turtleback) Demco.

— Anastasia Tiene Problemas. Vol. 48. (SPA., Illus.). (gr. 5-7). 1999. pap. 9.95 (*84-239-9026-5*) Espasa Calpe.

Lowry, Lois. Anastasia's Chosen Career. 160p. (J). (gr. 4-8). 1988. pap. 4.50 (*0-440-40100-3*, YB BDD) BDD Bks Young Read.

— Anastasia's Chosen Career. 192p. (J). (gr. 3-7). 1987. 16.00 (*0-395-42506-9*) HM.

— Anastasia's Chosen Career. (J). 1987. 9.09 (*0-606-04083-8*, Pub. by Turtleback) Demco.

— Attaboy, Sam! (Illus.). 128p. (J). (gr. 4-7). 1993. pap. 4.50 (*0-440-40816-4*) Dell.

— Attaboy, Sam! LC 91-31016. (Illus.). 128p. (J). (gr. 4-7). 1992. 16.00 (*0-395-61588-7*) HM.

— Attaboy, Sam! (J). 1992. 8.60 (*0-606-05129-5*, Pub. by Turtleback) Demco.

— Autumn Street. 192p. (J). (gr. 4-7). 1986. pap. 4.50 (*0-440-40344-8*, YB BDD) BDD Bks Young Read.

— Autumn Street, 001. 160p. (J). (gr. 5 up). 1980. 16.00 (*0-395-27812-0*) HM.

— Autumn Street. 1980. 9.60 (*0-606-02576-6*, Pub. by Turtleback) Demco.

— El Dador. (SPA.). (J). 1996. pap. text 12.50 (*84-241-5953-5*) Lectorum Pubns.

— El Dador. (J). 1996. 17.60 (*0-606-10406-2*, Pub. by Turtleback) Demco.

— Find a Stranger, Say Good-Bye. 192p. (YA). 1990. mass mkt. 4.99 (*0-440-20541-7*, LLL BDD) BDD Bks Young Read.

— Find a Stranger, Say Good-Bye, 001. LC 78-1024. 192p. (J). (gr. 5 up). 1978. 16.95 (*0-395-26459-6*) HM.

— Find a Stranger, Say Goodbye. 1978. 9.09 (*0-606-01070-X*, Pub. by Turtleback) Demco.

***Lowry, Lois.** Gathering Blue. (Illus.). (J). 2000. pap. 15.00 (*0-618-05581-9*) HM.

Lowry, Lois. The Giver. 192p. (J). (gr. 7-11). 1994. mass mkt. 6.50 (*0-440-21907-8*, LLL BDD) BDD Bks Young Read.

— The Giver. 192p. (YA). 1999. mass mkt. 6.99 (*0-553-57133-8*) BDD Bks Young Read.

— The Giver. (J). 1994. pap. write for info. (*0-614-22196-X*) Dell.

— The Giver. LC 92-15034. 208p. (J). (gr. 7-9). 1993. 14.95 (*0-395-64566-2*) HM.

***Lowry, Lois.** The Giver. (Cliffs Notes Ser.). (J). 1999. pap. 4.95 (*0-8220-0530-1*, Cliff) IDG Bks.

— The Giver. 180p. (YA). (gr. 5 up). pap. 5.99 (*0-8072-8314-2*) Listening Lib.

Lowry, Lois. The Giver. (J). 1994. 10.60 (*0-606-06990-9*, Pub. by Turtleback) Demco.

— The Giver. large type ed. LC 93-21002. (Teen Scene Ser.). (YA). (gr. 9-12). 1993. 16.95 (*0-7862-0055-3*) Thorndike Pr.

— Looking Back: A Book of Memories. LC 98-11376. (Illus.). 192p. (YA). (gr. 5 up). 1998. 16.00 (*0-395-89543-X*) HM.

***Lowry, Lois.** Looking Back: A Book of Memories. (Illus.). (J). 2000. 18.30 (*0-606-18106-7*) Turtleback.

Lowry, Lois. Number the Stars. 144p. (YA). (gr. 5 up). 1990. pap. 5.50 (*0-440-40327-8*, YB BDD) BDD Bks Young Read.

Lowry, Lois. Number the Stars. (J). 1992. pap. 3.50 (*0-440-80291-1*) BDD Bks Young Read.

Lowry, Lois. Number the Stars. 144p. (J). 1994. pap. 3.99 (*0-440-91002-1*) Dell.

— Number the Stars. LC 98-104337. (J). 1996. pap. 5.50 (*0-87129-711-6*, N45) Dramatic Pub.

— Number the Stars. LC 88-37134. 160p. (J). (gr. 4-7). 1989. 16.00 (*0-395-51060-0*) HM.

Lowry, Lois. Number the Stars. (Literature Experience 1993 Ser.). (J). (gr. 6). 1992. pap. 11.04 (*0-395-61834-7*) HM.

— Number the Stars. (J). (gr. 6). 1995. 9.28 (*0-395-73270-0*) HM.

Lowry, Lois. Number the Stars. (J). 1989. 10.09 (*0-606-04493-0*, Pub. by Turtleback) Demco.

— Number the Stars. (J). 1998. 10.09 (*0-606-13670-3*, Pub. by Turtleback) Demco.

— Number the Stars. large type ed. 172p. (J). (gr. 6). 43.00 (*0-614-20609-X*, L-38209-00 APHB) Am Printing Hse.

L

— Number the Stars. 144p. (J). (gr. 5-9). 1998. reprint ed. mass mkt. 5.50 (*0-440-22753-4*, LLL BDD) BDD Bks Young Read.

***Lowry, Lois.** Number the Stars - Musical. 33p. 1998. pap. 5.95 (*0-87129-834-1*, N03) Dramatic Pub.

Lowry, Lois. The One Hundredth Thing about Caroline. 160p. (J). (gr. k-6). 1985. pap. 4.50 (*0-440-46625-3*, YB BDD) BDD Bks Young Read.

— The One Hundredth Thing about Caroline, 001. 160p. (J). (gr. 3-6). 1983. 16.00 (*0-395-34829-3*) HM.

— The One Hundredth Thing about Caroline. 1985. 9.09 (*0-606-00972-8*, Pub. by Turtleback) Demco.

— Quien Cuenta las Estrellas? (SPA.). (J). 1998. pap. text 8.95 (*84-239-8867-8*, Pub. by Espasa Calpe) Continental Bk.

— Quien Cuenta las Estrellas? 1990. 14.05 (*0-606-10493-3*, Pub. by Turtleback) Demco.

***Lowry, Lois.** Quien Cuenta Las Estrellas?, Vol. 20. (SPA., Illus.). (gr. 7 up). 1999. pap. text 9.95 (*84-239-8887-2*) Espasa Calpe.

Lowry, Lois. Rabble Starkey. 208p. (J). (gr. k-6). 1988. pap. 4.99 (*0-440-40056-2*, YB BDD) BDD Bks Young Read.

— Rabble Starkey. 208p. (YA). (gr. 5 up). 1987. 16.00 (*0-395-43607-9*) HM.

Lowry, Lois. Rabble Starkey. 1988. 9.09 (*0-606-12493-4*, Pub. by Turtleback) Demco.

Lowry, Lois. Rabble Starkey. large type ed. 1989. lib. bdg. 14.95 (*0-8161-4776-0*, G K Hall Lrg Type) Mac Lib Ref.

— See You Around, Sam! LC 96-1213. (J). 1996. write for info. (*0-614-13120-0*) HM.

— See You Around, Sam! (Illus.). 144p. (J). (gr. 2-7). 1996. 15.00 (*0-395-81664-5*) HM.

***Lowry, Lois.** See You Around, Sam! (J). 1998. 9.09 (*0-606-13084-5*, Pub. by Turtleback) Demco.

Lowry, Lois. Stay! Keeper's Story. 128p. (J). (gr. 4-7). 1999. pap. 4.50 (*0-440-41524-1*) BDD Bks Young Read.

— Stay! Keeper's Story. LC 97-1569. (Illus.). 127p. (J). (gr. 2-7). 1997. 15.00 (*0-395-87048-8*) HM.

— A Summer to Die. 128p. (YA). (gr. 7-12). 1983. mass mkt. 4.99 (*0-440-21917-5*) Bantam.

— A Summer to Die, 001. (Illus.). 160p. (J). (gr. 3-7). 1977. 16.00 (*0-395-25338-1*) HM.

— Summer to Die. 1977. 9.60 (*0-606-01656-2*, Pub. by Turtleback) Demco.

— Switcharound. 128p. (J). (gr. k-6). 1991. pap. 4.50 (*0-440-48415-4*, YB BDD) BDD Bks Young Read.

— Switcharound, 001. 128p. 1985. 16.00 (*0-395-39536-4*) HM.

Lowry, Lois. Switcharound. 1991. 8.60 (*0-606-12530-2*, Pub. by Turtleback) Demco.

Lowry, Lois. Taking Care of Terrific. 176p. (J). (gr. 4-7). 1964. pap. 4.50 (*0-440-48494-4*, YB BDD) BDD Bks Young Read.

— Taking Care of Terrific, 001. LC 82-23331. 160p. (J). (gr. 5 up). 1983. 16.00 (*0-395-34070-5*) HM.

Lowry, Lois. Taking Care of Terrific. (J). 1983. 9.09 (*0-606-03177-4*, Pub. by Turtleback) Demco.

— Us & Uncle Fraud, 001. LC 84-12783. 192p. (gr. 5-9). 1984. 16.00 (*0-395-36633-X*) HM.

Lowry, Lois. Your Move, J. P. LC 89-24707. 128p. (J). (gr. 4-7). 1991. pap. 3.99 (*0-440-40497-5*) Dell.

— Your Move, J. P. 128p. (J). (gr. 3-7). 1990. 16.00 (*0-395-53639-1*) HM.

— Your Move, J. P. 1990. 9.09 (*0-606-05052-3*, Pub. by Turtleback) Demco.

***Lowry, Lois.** Zooman Sam. 2001. pap. 4.99 (*0-440-41676-0*) BDD Bks Young Read.

— Zooman Sam. LC 98-56006. (Illus.). 160p. (J). (gr. 2-7). 1999. 16.00 (*0-395-97393-7*, W Lorraine) HM.

***Lowry, Lois, ed.** The Neuman Systems Model & Nursing Education: Teaching Strategies & Evaluation Outcomes. (Monographs). 76p. 1998. pap. text 20.00 (*0-9656391-5-0*) Sigma Theta Tau.

Lowry, Lois, intro. Dear Author: Students Write about the Books That Changed Their Lives. 150p. (Orig.). (J). (gr. 5-12). 1995. pap. 9.95 (*1-57324-003-6*) Conari Press.

Lowry, Lois & De Groat, Diane. See You Around, Sam! (Illus.). 128p. (J). (gr. 3-7). 1998. reprint ed. pap. 3.99 (*0-440-41400-8*, YB BDD) BDD Bks Young Read.

Lowry, Lois, jt. auth. see Center for Learning Network Staff.

Lowry, Macia D. Preservation & Conservation in Small Libraries. (LAMA Small Libraries Publications: No. 5). 16p. 1989. pap. text 8.00 (*0-8389-5718-8*) ALA.

Lowry, Malcolm. Au-Dessous de Volcan. (FRE.). 1973. pap. 17.95 (*0-7859-4004-9*) Fr & Eur.

— Hear Us O'Lord from Heaven Thy Dwelling Place. 1986. pap. 9.95 (*0-88184-281-8*) Carroll & Graf.

— Selected Poems. (Pocket Poets Ser.: No. 17). (Orig.). 1962. pap. 6.95 (*0-87286-030-2*, PP17) City Lights.

— Sursum Corda! The Collected Letters of Malcolm Lowry, 1926-1946, Vol. I. Grace, Sherrill E., ed. (Illus.). 736p. (C). 1995. text 49.95 (*0-8020-0748-1*) U of Toronto Pr.

***Lowry, Malcolm.** Under the Volcano: A Novel. LC 99-56296. (Perennial Classics Ser.). 432p. 2000. pap. 14.00 (*0-06-095522-8*, Perennial) HarperTrade.

Lowry, Malcolm & Fitzgerald, F. Scott. The Cinema of Malcolm Lowry: A Scholarly Edition of Malcolm Lowry's Tender Is the Night. Mota, Miguel & Tiessen, Paul, eds. 276p. 1990. 65.00 (*0-7748-0345-2*) U of Wash Pr.

Lowry, Malcolm, jt. auth. see Aiken, Conrad.

Lowry, Mark. Good Ol Noah. 2000. 12.99 (*0-310-23198-1*) HarpC.

***Lowry, Mark.** Live Long & Die Laughing. 204p. 2000. pap. 12.99 (*0-8499-4204-7*) Word Pub.

Lowry, Mark. Mary, Did You Know? The Story of God's Great Plan. (Illus.). 32p. (J). (ps-2). 1998. 14.95 (*1-57856-179-5*) Waterbrook Pr.

***Lowry, Mark.** Nighttime Is Just Daytime with Your Eyes Closed. LC 99-40180. (The Adventures of Piper the Hyper Mouse Ser.). (Illus.). 32p. (gr. k-4). 1999. 14.99 (*1-58229-076-8*) Howard Pub LA.

Lowry, Mark. Out of Control. 208p. 1997. pap. 10.99 (*0-8499-4049-4*) Word Pub.

***Lowry, Mark & Bolton, Martha.** Piper Steals the Show! (Adventures of Piper the Hyper Mouse Ser.). (Illus.). 32p. (J). (ps-5). 2000. 14.99 (*1-58229-127-6*) Howard Pub LA.

Lowry, Mark & Bolton, Martha. Piper's Night Before Christmas. LC 98-42458. (The Adventures of Piper the Hyper Mouse Ser.). (Illus.). 24p. (J). (gr. k-3). 1998. 14.99 (*1-58229-000-8*) Howard Pub LA.

Lowry, Michael R. Major Depression: Prevention & Treatment. 136p. 1984. 15.00 (*0-87527-186-3*) Green.

Lowry, Miriam B. Living Through Florida History. Frost, Anne, ed. (Illus.). 150p. 1996. 12.95 (*0-9614624-9-3*) Frost Pub.

Lowry, Montecue J. The Forge of West German Rearmament: Theodor Blank & the Amt Blank. LC 89-12894. (American University Studies: History: Ser. IX, Vol. 83). XVI, 358p. 1989. text 56.50 (*0-8204-1157-4*) P Lang Pubng.

— Glasnost: Deception, Desperation, Dialectics. LC 90-48821. (American University Studies: History: Ser. IX, Vol. 103). (Illus.). XXIV, 263p. (C). 1991. text 46.95 (*0-8204-1522-7*) P Lang Pubng.

Lowry, Nick. Aikido: Principles of Kata & Randori. LC 98-60569. xii, 154p. 1998. write for info. (*0-9663911-0-1*) Twelve Winds Pub.

Lowry, Peter, compiled by. The Good Money Guide to the Social Investment Community, 1985. 33p. (Orig.). 1985. pap. 5.00 (*0-933609-02-7*) Good Money Pubns.

Lowry, Porter P., jt. auth. see Lowry, William P.

Lowry, Ralph L., jt. auth. see Kratzer, Edward.

Lowry, Ray. Ink. LC 99-209673. 1997. pap. 17.95 (*1-899344-21-7*, Pub. by Do-Not Pr) Dufour.

Lowry, Richard. The Architecture of Chance: An Introduction to the Logic & Arithmetic of Probability. (Illus.). 192p. (C). 1989. pap. text 21.95 (*0-19-505608-6*) OUP.

— The Evolution of Psychological Theory: A Critical History of Concepts & Presuppositions. 2nd ed. 256p. 1982. pap. text 23.95 (*0-202-25135-7*); lib. bdg. 51.95 (*0-202-25134-9*) Aldine de Gruyter.

Lowry, Richard S. "Littery Man" Mark Twain & Modern Authorship. (Commonwealth Center Studies in American Culture). 192p. (C). 1996. text 45.00 (*0-19-510212-6*) OUP.

Lowry, Ritchie P. Good Money: A Guide to Profitable Social Investing in the '90s. 224p. 1993. pap. 9.95 (*0-393-30951-7*) Norton.

— Is the Peaceful Atom a Good Investment? 52p. (Orig.). 1983. spiral bd. 1.75 (*0-933609-03-5*) Good Money Pubns.

— Socially Responsible Stock Guide (With Supplement Insert, "How to Screen Traditional Investments for Social Factors") 48p. (Orig.). 1985. spiral bd. 2.50 (*0-933609-01-9*) Good Money Pubns.

Lowry, Robert. The Armed Forces of Indonesia. LC 97-152925. 312p. 1997. pap. 29.95 (*1-86448-144-7*, Pub. by Allen & Unwin Pty) Paul & Co Pubs.

— The Violent Wedding. LC 76-110831. 255p. 1971. reprint ed. lib. bdg. 55.00 (*0-8371-2566-9*, LOVW, Greenwood Pr) Greenwood.

Lowry, Robert, ed. Nonprofit Organizations & Public Policy, Vol. 14:1/2. 140p. 1995. pap. 15.00 (*0-944285-43-0*) Pol Studies.

Lowry, Robert & McCardle, William H. History of Mississippi from the Discovery of the Great River by Hernando De Soto. LC 70-172755. reprint ed. 87.50 (*0-404-04610-X*) AMS Pr.

— A History of Mississippi from the Discovery of the Great River by Hernando Desoto Including the Earliest Settlement Made by the French under Iberville to the Death of Jefferson Davis. LC 78-2335. 1978. reprint ed. 35.00 (*0-87152-265-9*) Reprint.

Lowry, Robert & Ployhar, James. Tunes for Clarinet Technic: Level Three (Advanced-Intermediate) Proctor, Thom, ed. (Student Instrumental Course Ser.). 32p. (C). 1971. pap. text 5.95 (*0-7692-1750-8*, BIC00308) Wrner Bros.

Lowry, Robert C., jt. auth. see Lowry, George G.

Lowry, Robert W. & Dickman, David. Professional Pool & Spa Technicians' Guide to pH, Alkalinity, Water Testing, & Water Balance. 64p. 1988. pap. 6.95 (*0-685-29431-5*) Serv Industry Pubns.

Lowry, Robert W., ed. see Taylor, Charlie.

Lowry, Robin P. & Takeuchi, Takumi. The Th1-Th2 Paradigm & Transplantation Tolerance: Exploring the Microcosm of Transplantation-Of What Is Past, Passing & to Come. (Medical Intelligence Unit Ser.). 118p. 1994. 99.00 (*1-57059-108-3*, LN9108) Landes Bioscience.

Lowry, S. Todd. The Archaeology of Economic Ideas. LC 87-15507. (Illus.). xviii, 366p. (C). 1988. text 59.95 (*0-8223-0774-X*) Duke.

Lowry, S. Todd, ed. Perspectives on the History of Economic Thought: Contributions to the History of Economics. (Perspectives on the Hostory of Economic Thought Ser.: Vol. 8). 288p. 1992. 95.00 (*1-85278-448-2*) E Elgar.

— Perspectives on the History of Economic Thought: Perspectives on Administrative Tradition: from Antiquity to the 20th Century. (Perspectives on the History of Economic Thought Ser.: Vol. 7). 240p. 1992. 95.00 (*1-85278-447-4*) E Elgar.

Lowry, S. Todd & Gordon, Barry, eds. Ancient & Medieval Economic Ideas & Concepts of Social Justice. LC 97-40119. (Illus.). 600p. 1997. 141.50 (*90-04-09964-6*) Brill Academic Pubs.

Lowry, Scot. Magic of Moving Averages. 240p. 1998. pap. 29.95 (*0-934380-43-0*, 1287) Traders Pr.

Lowry, Shannon. Natives of the Far North: Alaska's Vanishing Culture in the Eye of Edward Sheriff Curtis. (Illus.). 160p. 1994. 29.95 (*0-8117-1102-1*) Stackpole.

Lowry, Shannon R. Flight of the Imagination. 1999. 12.95 (*0-533-12803-X*) Vantage.

***Lowry, Stuart.** Carousel to the Stars. 2000. 14.95 (*1-57860-081-2*) Guild Pr IN.

Lowry, Susan. Illustrated Encyclopedia of Mammals. 1993. 12.98 (*1-55521-880-6*) Bk Sales Inc.

Lowry, Terry. The Battle of Scary Creek: Military Operations in the Kanawha Valley, April-July 1861. 2nd rev. ed. LC 98-154780. (Illus.). 272p. 1998. pap. 15.95 (*0-9646197-7-6*) Quarrier Pr.

— Last Sleep: The Battle of Droop Mountain November 6, 1863. (Illus.). 320p. (Orig.). 1996. pap. 17.95 (*1-57510-024-X*) Pictorial Hist.

— Twenty-Sixth Battalion Virginia Infantry. (Virginia Regimental Histories Ser.). (Illus.). 167p. 1992. 19.95 (*1-56190-028-1*) H E Howard.

Lowry, Terry D. Twenty-Second Virginia Infantry. (Virginia Regimental Histories Ser.). (Illus.). 216p. 1988. 19.95 (*0-930919-55-6*) H E Howard.

Lowry, Thea S. Empty Shells. LC 99-62144. (Chicken Farm Chronicles Ser.). (Illus.). ix,256p. 1999. pap. 34.95 (*0-9610116-1-0*) Manifold Pr.

— Petaluma's Poultry Pioneers: Recall the Heyday of Chicken Ranching. (Illus.). 128p. (Orig.). 1993. pap. 10.95 (*0-9610116-0-2*) Manifold Pr.

Lowry, Thea S., jt. ed. see Petersen, Laura M.

Lowry, Thomas H. & Richardson, Kathleen S. Mechanism & Theory in Organic Chemistry. 3rd ed. 1090p. (C). 1997. 115.00 (*0-06-044084-8*) Addson-Wesley Educ.

Lowry, Thomas P. The Civil War Bawdy Houses of Washington, D. C. Including a Map of Their Former Location. LC 97-12519. (Illus.). 104p. 1997. 19.95 (*1-887901-14-0*) Sergeant Kirk.

— The Clitoris. LC 73-704. (Illus.). 304p. 1976. 22.50 (*0-87527-112-X*) Green.

— Don't Shoot That Boy! Abraham Lincoln & Military Justice. LC 99-71105. (Illus.). 288p. (C). 1999. 24.95 (*1-882810-38-4*) Savas Pub.

— The Story the Soldiers Wouldn't Tell: Sex in the Civil War. (Illus.). 240p. 1994. 19.95 (*0-8117-1515-9*) Stackpole.

— Tarnished Eagles: The Courts-Martial of 50 Union Colonels & Lieutenant Colonels. LC 97-39994. (Illus.). 272p. 1998. 24.95 (*0-8117-1597-3*) Stackpole.

***Lowry, Thomas P. & Welsh, Jack D.** Tarnished Scalpels: The Court-Martials of Fifty Union Surgeons. LC 99-87411. (Illus.). 288p. 2000. 24.95 (*0-8117-1603-1*) Stackpole.

Lowry, W. McNeil, ed. The Arts & Public Policy in the U. S. LC 84-17686. 1984. reprint ed. 7.95 (*0-13-047689-7*) Am Assembly.

— The Performing Arts in American Society. LC 78-1404. (American Assembly Guides Ser.). 1978. 10.95 (*0-13-657155-7*); pap. 4.95 (*0-13-657148-4*) Am Assembly.

Lowry, William B., jt. auth. see Bischof, Larry.

Lowry, William P. Atmospheric Ecology for Designers & Planners. LC 88-90598. (Illus.). 435p. (Orig.). 1988. 48.75 (*1-882002-08-3*) Peavine Pubns.

— Atmospheric Ecology for Designers & Planners. LC 88-90598. (Illus.). 435p. (Orig.). (C). 1988. pap. 35.25 (*1-882002-07-5*) Peavine Pubns.

Lowry, William P. & Lowry, Porter P. Fundamentals of Biometeorology: Interactions of Organisms & the Atmosphere, 2 vols., Vols. 1 & 2. (Illus.). 650p. pap. 66.00 (*1-882002-05-9*) Peavine Pubns.

— Fundamentals of Biometeorology - Interactions of Organisms & the Atmosphere Vol. 1: The Physical Environment, Vol. 1: The Physical Environment. LC 89-90922. (Illus.). 310p. (Orig.). (C). 1989. pap. 32.50 (*1-882002-03-2*) Peavine Pubns.

— Fundamentals of Biometeorology - Interactions of Organisms & the Atmosphere Vol. 2: The Biological Environment, Vol. 2: The Biological Environment. LC 95-67346. (Illus.). 340p. 1998. pap. 37.50 (*1-882002-04-0*) Peavine Pubns.

Lowry, William R. The Capacity for Wonder: Preserving National Parks. 280p. (C). 1994. 38.95 (*0-8157-5298-9*) Brookings.

— The Capacity for Wonder: Preserving National Parks. 280p. (C). 1995. reprint ed. pap. 18.95 (*0-8157-5297-0*) Brookings.

— Preserving Public Lands for the Future: The Politics of Intergenerational Goods. Rabe, Barry & Tierney, John, eds. LC 98-13259. (American Governance & Public Policy Ser.). 320p. 1998. 60.00 (*0-87840-701-4*); pap. 24.95 (*0-87840-702-2*) Georgetown U Pr.

Lowry, Wiilliam R. The Dimensions of Federalism: State Governments & Pollution Control Policies. LC 91-13582. 192p. 1999. pap. text 16.95 (*0-8223-1819-9*) Duke.

Lowski, Woytek. The Art of Teaching Classical Ballet. (Illus.). 78p. 1998. pap. 24.95 (*1-85273-045-5*, Dance Horizons) Princeton Bk Co.

Lowsley, B. A Glossary of Berkshire Words & Phrases. (English Dialect Society Publications: No. 56). 1969. reprint ed. pap. 25.00 (*0-8115-0477-8*) Periodicals Srv.

Lowstuter, Clyde, jt. auth. see Curns, Eileen.

Lowstuter, Clyde C. & Robertson, David P. In Search of the Perfect Job. 320p. 1992. 24.95 (*0-07-038880-6*); pap. 14.95 (*0-07-038881-4*) McGraw.

Lowth, Robert. Lectures on the Sacred Poetry of the Hebrews, 2 vols., Set. Gregory, G., tr. from LAT. (Anglistica & Americana Ser.: No. 43). 935p. 1969. reprint ed. 180.70 (*0-685-25147-0*, 05102488) G Olms Pubs.

— A Short Introduction to English Grammar. LC 79-4675. (American Linguistics Ser.). 160p. 1979. reprint ed. lib. bdg. 50.00 (*0-8201-1332-8*) Schol Facsimiles.

***Lowther, Christine, et al.** New Power. 72p. 1999. pap. 9.75 (*0-921411-94-4*) Genl Dist Srvs.

Lowther, David A. & Silvester, Peter P. Computer Aided Design in Magnetics. (Illus.). 324p. 1985. 184.95 (*0-387-15756-5*) Spr-Verlag.

Lowther, David A., jt. auth. see Silvester, Peter P.

Lowther, E. H., jt. auth. see Bates, R. S.

Lowther, George. The Adventures of Superman. LC 94-43029. (Illus.). 228p. (YA). (gr. 5 up). 1995. reprint ed. 17.95 (*1-55709-228-1*) Applewood.

Lowther, Gerald E. Dryness, Tears, & Contact Lens Wear. LC 96-39911. (New Contact Lens Update Ser.). 105p. 1997. pap. text 26.50 (*0-7506-9514-5*) Buttrwrth-Heinemann.

Lowther, Gerald E. & Snyder, Christopher. Contact Lenses: Procedures & Techniques. 2nd ed. 432p. 1992. text 77.50 (*0-7506-9187-5*) Buttrwrth-Heinemann.

Lowther, John. .1 (Point One) deluxe limited ed. 32p. 1997. 20.00 (*0-937013-72-2*) Potes Poets.

Lowther, John, jt. auth. see Hainsworth, D. R.

Lowther, Minnie K. History of Ritchie County: With Biographical Sketches of Its Pioneers & Their Ancestors, & Interesting Reminiscences of Revolutionary & Indian Times. (Illus.). 679p. 1997. reprint ed. lib. bdg. 69.50 (*0-8328-6953-8*) Higginson Bk Co.

Lowther, Minnie Kendall. History of Ritchie County. 700p. 1911. reprint ed. 40.00 (*0-87012-630-X*) McClain.

Much requested reprint of the history of Ritchie County, West Virginia. Reprinted 1999. ***Publisher Paid Annotation.***

Lowther, Richard. Decorative Paint Recipes: A Step-by-Step Guide to Finishing Touches for Your Home. LC 97-41013. 1997. pap. text 19.95 (*0-8118-1848-9*) Chronicle Bks.

***Lowther, Richard & Robinson, Lynne.** Recipes & Ideas: Windows: Simple Solutions for the Home. LC 99-37296. (Illus.). 104p. 2000. pap. 16.95 (*0-8118-2720-8*) Chronicle Bks.

Lowther, Richard, jt. auth. see Robinson, Lynne.

Lowy. Agents. 59.95 (*1-85521-225-0*) Ashgate Pub Co.

Lowy, Albert, jt. ed. see Society of Hebrew Literature Staff.

Lowy, Aranka I. The Story of Aranka Ickovic Lowy: The Ugly Duckling (Non-Fiction Autobiography with Reference to WW II in Europe) 2nd ed. LC 81-90799. (Illus.). 264p. (Orig.). 1988. pap. 8.25 (*0-317-99842-0*) Lowy Pub.

Lowy, David C. Pencil Drawings by David X: 101 Amusing, Artistic & Entertaining Drawings of Pencils. LC 79-88698. (Illus.). 1979. pap. 3.25 (*0-9602940-0-7*) Lowy Pub.

Lowy, Ilana. Between Bench & Bedside: Science, Healing, & Interleukin-2 in a Cancer Ward. LC 96-25407. (Illus.). 384p. 1996. 43.00 (*0-674-06809-2*) HUP.

Lowy, Lance. Handball Handbook: Strategies & Techniques. 3rd ed. (Illus.). 143p. 2000. pap. text 12.95 (*0-89641-207-5*) American Pr.

Lowy, Louis. Social Work with the Aging: The Challenge & Promise of the Later Years. 2nd ed. 435p. (C). 1991. reprint ed. pap. text 26.95 (*0-88133-614-9*) Waveland Pr.

Lowy, Martin. High Rollers: Inside the Savings & Loan Debacle. LC 91-8344. 336p. 1991. 55.00 (*0-275-93988-X*, C3988, Praeger Pubs) Greenwood.

— Practical Handbook for Bank Directors. LC 95-95284. 160p. 1995. pap. 19.95 (*0-9649801-0-X*) Finan Srvs Pr.

Lowy, Michael. Fatherland or Mother Earth? Essays on the National Question. LC 98-24904. 128p. 1998. 55.00 (*0-7453-1348-5*, Pub. by Pluto GBR) Stylus Pub VA.

***Lowy, Michael.** Fatherland or Mother Earth? Essays on the National Question. LC 98-24904. (IIRE Notebook for Study & Research Ser.: Nos. 27 & 28). 128p. 1998. pap. 17.95 (*0-7453-1343-4*, Pub. by Pluto GBR) Stylus Pub VA.

Lowy, Michael. Redemption & Utopia - Jewish Libertarian Thought in Central Europe: A Study in Elective Affinity. Heaney, Hope, tr. from FRE. LC 89-51763. 282p. (C). 1992. 37.50 (*0-8047-1776-1*) Stanford U Pr.

— The War of the Gods: Religion & Politics in Latin America. LC 96-12017. 192p. (C). 1996. pap. 18.00 (*1-85984-002-7*, Pub. by Verso) Norton.

Lowyck, J. & Clark, C., eds. Teacher Thinking & Professional Action. (Studia Paedagogica: No. 9). 418p. (Orig.). 1989. pap. 63.50 (*90-6186-349-X*, Pub. by Leuven Univ) Coronet Bks.

Lox, Curt, jt. auth. see Pellett, Tracy L.

Lox, Dennis, jt. auth. see Windsor, Robert E.

Loxdale, Hugh D. & Hollander, J. Den. Electrophoretic Studies on Agricultural Pests. (Systematics Association Special Volume Ser.: Vol. 39). (Illus.). 512p. 1990. 135.00 (*0-19-857710-9*) OUP.

Loxley, Andrew, jt. auth. see Thomas, Gary.

Loxley, Ann. Collaboration in Health & Welfare: Working with Difference. 120p. 1996. pap. 24.95 (*1-85302-394-9*, Pub. by Jessica Kingsley) Taylor & Francis.

Loxley, John. Interdependence, Disequilibrium & Growth: Reflections on the Political Economy of North-South Relations at the Turn of the Century. LC 97-40992. (International Political Economy Ser.). 192p. 1998. text 65.00 (*0-312-21242-9*) St Martin.

***Loxley, John & International Development Research Centre Staff.** Interdependence, Disequilibrium & Growth: Reflections on the Political Economy of

An Asterisk (*) at the beginning of an entry indicates that the title is appearing for the first time.

North-South Relations at the Turn of the Century. 200p. 1998. 65.00 (*0-88936-849-X*, Pub. by IDRC Bks); pap. 30.00 (*0-88936-826-0*, Pub. by IDRC Bks) Stylus Pub VA.

Loxterkamp, David. A Measure of My Days: The Journal of a Country Doctor. LC 96-54704. 333p. 1997. 35.00 (*0-87451-799-0*); pap. 15.95 (*0-87451-885-7*) U Pr of New Eng.

Loxton, Bruce & Coultard-Clark, Chris. The Shame of Savo: Anatomy of a Naval Disaster. (Bluejacket Bks.). (Illus.). 346p. 1997. pap. 19.95 (*1-55750-838-0*) Naval Inst Pr.

Loxton, Cathy, jt. auth. see Bartley, Paula.

Loxton, Howard. Christmas. 39.00 (*1-56696-141-6*) Jackdaw.

— The Golden Age of the Circus. (Illus.). 112p. 2000. reprint ed. text. write for info. (*0-7881-9011-3*) DIANE Pub.

Loxton, Howard. Guide to Cats of the World. 1991. 5.98 (*1-55521-603-X*) Bk Sales Inc.

— Illustrated Cat. (Illus.). 1994. 12.98 (*0-7858-0179-0*) Bk Sales Inc.

— Illustrated Dog. (Illus.). 1994. 12.98 (*0-7858-0178-2*) Bk Sales Inc.

— Illustrated Horse. (Illus.). 1994. 12.98 (*0-7858-0180-4*) Bk Sales Inc.

— 99 Lives: Cats in History, Legend, & Literature. LC 98-16444. (Illus.). 144p. 1998. pap. 17.95 (*0-8118-2161-7*) Chronicle Bks.

Loxton, Howard. Shakespeare's Theatre. 39.00 (*1-56696-007-X*) Jackdaw.

Loxton, Howard, jt. auth. see Sayer, Angela.

Loxton, J. H. & Van der Poorten, A. J., eds. Diophantine Analysis: Proceedings at the Number Theory Section of the 1985 Australian Mathematical Society Convention. (London Mathematical Society Lecture Note Ser.: No. 109). 170p. 1986. pap. text 44.95 (*0-521-33923-5*) Cambridge U Pr.

Loxton, Margaret. Provence. LC 93-5084. (Robert Stewart Bk.). 64p. 1993. 14.00 (*0-684-19664-6*) S&S Trade.

Loxton, R. & Pope, P., eds. Instrumentation: A Reader. 290p. (Orig.). 1986. 30.00 (*0-335-15097-7*) OpUniv Pr.

Loy, D. Gareth, jt. ed. see Todd, Peter.

Loy, David. Lack & Transcendence: The Problem of Death & Life in Psychotherapy, Existentialism, & Buddhism. LC 95-255. 224p. (C). 1996. text 49.95 (*0-391-03860-5*) Humanities.

— Nonduality: A Study in Comparative Philosophy. LC 97-2516. 356p. (Orig.). (C). 1997. pap. 22.50 (*0-391-04020-0*) Humanities.

— Nonduality: A Study in Comparative Philosophy. LC 99-10394. (Orig.). 1999. 18.95 (*1-57392-359-1*, Humanity Bks) Prometheus Bks.

Loy, David, ed. Healing Deconstruction: Postmodern Thought in Buddhism & Christianity. LC 96-6921. (AAR Reflection & Theory in the Study of Religion Ser.: No. 3). 135p. (C). 1996. 35.95 (*0-7885-0121-6*, 011003) OUP.

Loy, J. D., et al. The Behavior of Gonadectomized Rhesus Monkeys. (Contributions to Primatology Ser.: Vol. 20). (Illus.). viii, 144p. 1983. 57.50 (*3-8055-3795-6*) S Karger.

Loy, J. Robert, tr. see Brooks, Phyllis & Guy, Basil, eds.

***Loy, James.** Overture. 1999. pap. 39.95 (*1-892465-32-9*) G Gallery.

Loy, James & Peters, Calvin B., eds. Understanding Behavior: What Primate Studies Tell Us about Human Behavior. (Illus.). 280p. (C). 1991. text 55.00 (*0-19-506020-2*) OUP.

Loy, James D., jt. ed. see Campbell, Bernard G.

***Loy, Jessica.** Kids Outdoors. 2000. pap. text 18.95 (*0-8050-6195-9*) St Martin.

Loy, John W., et al. Sport, Culture & Society: A Reader on the Sociology of Sport. 2nd rev. ed. LC 81-3692. (Illus.). 385p. reprint ed. pap. 119.40 (*0-8357-7649-2*, 205697500096) Bks Demand.

Loy, John W., ed. see Association for the Anthropological Study of Play,.

Loy, John W., Jr., jt. ed. see Ingham, Alan G.

Loy, Joy A., ed. see Murdock, Michael D.

***Loy, Lawrence R.** The White House Beat: The U.S. Secret Service Uniformed Division Commemorates 75 Years of Presidential Protection. LC 98-61482. (Illus.). 88p. 1998. 25.00 (*0-943335-11-6*) Marblehead Pub.

Loy, Marc & Berry, Thomas. A Complete Java Database Training Course. 32p. (C). 1997. 99.95 incl. cd-rom (*0-13-759507-7*) P-H.

Loy, Marc, et al. Java Swing. (Illus.). 1252p. 1998. pap. 44.95 (*1-56592-455-X*) OReilly & Assocs.

Loy, Mina. The Lost Lunar Baedeker: Poems of Mina Loy. LC 95-7622. 184p. 1996. 20.00 (*0-374-25872-4*) FS&G.

— The Lost Lunar Baedeker: Poems of Mina Loy. 256p. 1997. pap. 13.00 (*0-374-52507-2*, Noonday) FS&G.

Loy, Nancy, ed. see Quinones, Sherri & Kirshstein, Rita.

Loy, Nicholas J. An Engineer's Guide to FIR Digital Filters. LC 87-1352. (Illus.). 256p. (C). 1987. text 40.60 (*0-13-278011-9*) P-H.

Loy, Patrick. TEC Course - Software Requirements Analysis & Specification Workshop. 1990. ring bd. write for info. (*0-201-41872-X*) Addison-Wesley.

— TEC Course - Structure Analysis & Design for Real-Time. 1990. ring bd. write for info. (*0-201-41873-8*) Addison-Wesley.

***Loy, Rosetta.** First Words: A Childhood Fantasy in Fascist Italy. Conti, Gregory, tr. from ITA. 224p. 2000. 23.00 (*0-8050-6258-0*, Metropol Bks) H Holt & Co.

***Loy, Spike.** Getting a Grip on Your Diabetes: A Guide for Kids. 2000. 14.95 (*1-58040-053-1*) Am Diabetes.

Loy, W. E. Hard Gear Processing with Azumi Skiving Hobs. (Technical Papers: Vol. P129.27). (Illus.). 8p. 1982. pap. text 30.00 (*1-55589-541-7*) AGMA.

Loya, Joseph A., et al. The Tao of Jesus: An Experiment in Inter-Traditional Understanding. LC 97-45162. 160p. 1998. pap. 14.95 (*0-8091-3764-X*) Paulist Pr.

Loya, Olga. Momentos Magicos: Latin American Folktales Told in English & Spanish. Lizardi-Rivera, Carmen, tr. LC 97-38582. 1997. pap. text 11.95 (*0-87483-497-X*) August Hse.

***Loya, Rami R.** Incentive Compensation Strategies for the New Millennium: How to Design & Implement Innovative Programs to Compete Successfully in the Tech. (Illus.). 196p. 2000. 99.00 (*0-9679891-0-8*) IncenSoft.

Loyacono, Laura L. Reinventing the Wheel: A Design for Student Achievement in the 21st Century. 96p. 1992. pap. 25.00 (*1-55516-220-7*, 2110) Natl Conf State Legis.

— Transforming Education Through the Arts. 38p. 1995. 15.00 (*1-55516-221-5*, 2111) Natl Conf State Legis.

Loyacono, Laura L., jt. auth. see Rafool, Amanda.

***Loyal, W. Gustve.** A Dangerous Game. LC 97-91365. 1999. pap. 12.95 (*0-533-12645-2*) Vantage.

Loyalka, Sudarshan K., jt. auth. see Williams, M. M.

Loyd. Electrical Raceways. 2nd ed. (Electrical Trades Ser.). 24p. 1996. text, teacher ed. 13.50 (*0-8273-6660-4*) Delmar.

— Electrician's Technical Reference: Hazardous Locations. LC 98-44676. 224p. 1999. text 26.95 (*0-8273-8380-0*) Delmar.

— Hazardous Locations. (Electrical Trades Ser.). 1997. pap., teacher ed. 13.50 (*0-8273-6983-2*, VNR) Wiley.

***Loyd.** Journeyman Electrician's Review. 3rd ed. LC 99-14460. (Electrical Trades Ser.). 320p. (C). 1999. pap. 46.95 (*0-7668-1277-4*) Delmar.

Loyd. Physics. 2nd ed. (C). 1997. pap. text, teacher ed., lab manual ed. 31.50 (*0-03-025106-0*) Harcourt Coll Pubs.

— PHYSICS LAB MANUAL 2/E. 2nd ed. LC 97-2566. 576p. (C). 1997. pap. text, lab manual ed. 54.50 (*0-03-024561-3*) SCP.

***Loyd, Anthony.** My War Gone by, I Miss It So. LC 99-43963. 336p. 2000. 25.00 (*0-87113-769-0*, Pub. by Grove-Atltic) Publishers Group.

— My War Gone By, I Miss It So. 2001. pap. 13.00 (*0-14-029854-1*) Penguin Putnam.

Loyd, Gerald. Preachers Are People Too! 266p. (Orig.). 1994. pap. 10.99 (*1-56043-817-7*, Treasure Hse) Destiny Image.

Loyd, J. H., jt. auth. see Paley, William.

Loyd, Mary, tr. see Merimee, Prosper.

Loyd, Richard. Electrical Raceways & Other Wiring Methods. 3rd ed. LC 98-30003. (Electrical Trades Ser.). 256p. (C). 1998. text 32.95 (*0-7668-0266-3*) Delmar.

— Hazardous Classified Locations. (Electrical Trades Ser.). 208p. 1996. mass mkt. 33.95 (*0-8273-6982-4*) Delmar.

— Master Electrician's Review. 2nd ed. (Electrical Trades Ser). 432p. 1996. pap. 61.95 (*0-8273-6678-7*) Thomson Learn.

Loyd, Richard E. Electrical Raceways & Other Wiring Methods. 2nd ed. 18p. 1993. teacher ed. 13.50 (*0-8273-5494-0*) Delmar.

— Electrical Raceways & Other Wiring Methods. 2nd ed. LC 95-17395. 240p. 1996. mass mkt. 23.25 (*0-8273-6659-0*) Delmar.

— Electrical Raceways & Other Wiring Methods Design Manual. 2nd ed. LC 92-40582. 223p. 1993. pap. 22.00 (*0-8273-5493-2*) Delmar.

***Loyd, Richard E.** Electrician's Technical Reference with Wiring Methods. LC 99-17191. 270p. 1999. 37.95 (*0-8273-8379-7*) Delmar.

Loyd, Richard E. Journeyman Electrician's Exam Preparation Book. 283p. 1993. pap. 26.00 (*0-8273-5725-7*) Delmar.

— Journeyman Electricians Review. 2nd ed. (Electrical Trades Ser.). 320p. 1996. pap. 46.95 (*0-8273-6680-9*) Delmar.

— Master Electrician's Exam Preparation. LC 94-174544. 305p. 1993. pap. 35.95 (*0-8273-5852-0*) Delmar.

***Loyd, Richard E.** Master Electrician's Review. 3rd ed. LC 99-24747. 352p. 1999. 61.95 (*0-7668-1276-6*) Delmar.

Loyd, Robert J. & Brolin, Donn E. Life Centered Career Education: Modified Curriculum for Individuals with Moderate Disabilities. LC 97-3896. 120p. 1997. pap. text 30.00 (*0-86586-293-1*, P5194) Coun Exc Child.

Loyd, Roger, ed. see Grimes, Lewis H.

***Loyd, S.** Cold Water Storage Tanks. 1998. pap. 80.00 (*0-86022-504-6*, Pub. by Build Servs Info Assn) St Mut.

— Software for Building Services. 1997. pap. 80.00 (*0-86022-472-4*, Pub. by Build Servs Info Assn) St Mut.

Loyd, S., jt. auth. see BSRIA Staff.

Loyd, S. R. Building Services for Swimming Pools: An Annotated Bibliography. 1992. 110.00 (*0-86022-325-6*, Pub. by Build Servs Info Assn) St Mut.

— Building Services Maintenance. (C). 1987. 135.00 (*0-86022-129-6*, Pub. by Build Servs Info Assn) St Mut.

— Building Services Maintenance. 1990. 65.00 (*0-86022-264-0*, Pub. by Build Servs Info Assn) St Mut.

— Combined Heat & Power: An Annotated Bibliography. 1990. 75.00 (*0-86022-247-0*, Pub. by Build Servs Info Assn) St Mut.

— Fire Dampers. (C). 1994. pap. 60.00 (*0-86022-368-X*, Pub. by Build Servs Info Assn) St Mut.

Loyd, S. R. Guidance & the Standard Specification for Ventilation Hygiene. 1997. pap. 100.00 (*0-86022-454-6*, Pub. by Build Servs Info Assn) St Mut.

Loyd, S. R. The Heat Pump. (C). 1981. 75.00 (*0-86022-099-0*, Pub. by Build Servs Info Assn) St Mut.

— Heat Recovery from Buildings. (C). 1984. 63.00 (*0-86022-151-2*, Pub. by Build Servs Info Assn) St Mut.

***Loyd, S. R.** Information Sources for Building Services Professionals. 70p. 1999. pap. 24.00 (*0-86022-521-6*, Pub. by Build Servs Info Assn) St Mut.

Loyd, S. R. Information Sources in Building Services. 1993. 40.00 (*0-86022-344-2*, Pub. by Build Servs Info Assn) St Mut.

— Software for Building Services: A Selection Guide. 1993. 120.00 (*0-86022-354-X*, Pub. by Build Servs Info Assn) St Mut.

— Ventilation System Hygiene. 6th ed. (C). 1993. 110.00 (*0-86022-377-9*, Pub. by Build Servs Info Assn) St Mut.

— Ventilation System Hygiene: A Review. 1993. 100.00 (*0-86022-356-6*, Pub. by Build Servs Info Assn) St Mut.

Loyd, S. R., ed. Commissioning Building Services: An Annotated Bibliography. (C). 1987. 110.00 (*0-86022-149-0*, Pub. by Build Servs Info Assn) St Mut.

— Smoke Control in Buildings: An Annotated Bibliography. (C). 1988. 120.00 (*0-86022-221-7*, Pub. by Build Servs Info Assn) St Mut.

Loyd, Sam. Best Mathematical Puzzles of Sam Loyd. Gardner, Martin, ed. 1959. pap. 5.95 (*0-486-20498-7*) Dover.

— More Mathematical Puzzles of Sam Loyd. 1960. pap. 5.95 (*0-486-20709-9*) Dover.

Loyd, S.R. & Jerdin, D. Coordination of Building Services. (C). 1983. 75.00 (*0-86022-156-3*, Pub. by Build Servs Info Assn) St Mut.

Loyd, William H. Early Courts of Pennsylvania. (University of Pennsylvania Law School Ser.: Vol. 2). vii, 287p. 1986. reprint ed. 45.00 (*0-8377-0875-3*, Rothman) W S Hein.

Loydell, Rupert. Distances. LC 93-13724. 24p. 1993. pap. 4.00 (*0-940895-12-9*) Cornerstone IL.

Loydell, Rupert. Timbers Across the Sun. 136p. pap. write for info. (*3-7052-0609-5*, Pub. by Poetry Salzburg) Intl Spec Bk.

Loydell, Rupert, ed. Ladder to the Next Floor. 200p. pap. write for info. (*3-7052-0246-4*, Pub. by Poetry Salzburg) Intl Spec Bk.

Loydell, Rupert, ed. My Kind of Angel: I. M. William Burroughs. LC 99-218805. 1998. 19.95 (*1-900152-42-8*, Pub. by Stride Pubns) SPD-Small Pr Dist.

Loydell, Rupert M. Frosted Light: Fourteen Sequences, 1978-1988. LC 97-171835. 114p. 1996. pap. 12.95 (*3-7052-0983-3*, Pub. by Poetry Salzburg) Intl Spec Bk.

***Loye, David.** An Arrow Through Chaos: How We See into the Future. LC 99-59964. (Illus.). 320p. 2000. pap. 16.95 (*0-89281-849-2*, Inner Trad Espanol) Inner Tradit.

Loye, David. Darwin's Lost Theory: A Vision for the 21st Century. LC 99-61547. 300p. (C). 1999. pap. write for info. (*1-58348-107-9*) iUniversecom.

— The Knowable Future: A Psychology of Forecasting & Prophecy. LC 77-26713. 218p. reprint ed. pap. 67.60 (*0-608-12434-6*, 202518000042) Bks Demand.

— The Leadership Passion: A Psychology of Ideology. LC 76-45481. (Jossey-Bass Behavioral Science Ser.). 269p. reprint ed. pap. 83.40 (*0-608-16953-6*, 202776100056) Bks Demand.

Loye, David, ed. The Evolutionary Outrider: The Impact of the Human Agent on Evolution Essays Honouring Ervin Laszlo. LC 98-18868. (Praeger Studies on the 21st Century). 304p. 1998. 65.00 (*0-275-96408-6*, Praeger Pubs); pap. 25.00 (*0-275-96409-4*, Praeger Pubs) Greenwood.

Loye, David, jt. auth. see Eisler, Riane.

Loye, J. F., Jr., et al. Lam Son 719: The South Vietnamese Incursion into Laos. 166p. 1993. reprint ed. pap. 20.00 (*0-923135-54-5*) Dalley Bk Service.

Loyn, H. R. Anglo-Saxon England & Norman. 2nd ed. (Social & Economic History of England Ser.). 432p. (C). 1991. text 62.50 (*0-582-07297-2*, 78873) Longman.

— Anglo-saxon England & the Norman Conquest. LC 72-190093. (A Longman Paperback Ser.). xii, 422p. 1970. write for info. (*0-582-48232-1*) Longman.

Loyn, H. R. Anglo-Saxon England & the Norman Conquest. 2nd ed. LC 90-48513. (Social & Economic History of England Ser.). 456p. (C). 1995. pap. 55.00 (*0-582-07296-4*, 78874) Longman.

Loyn, H. R. The Governance of Anglo-Saxon England, 500-1087. (Governance of England Ser.). xviii, 222p. 1984. 35.00 (*0-8047-1217-4*) Stanford U Pr.

Loyn, Henry. The Vikings in Britain. 1995. pap. 16.95 (*0-631-18712-X*) Blackwell Pubs.

Loyning, Yngve, jt. ed. see Mostofsky, David I.

Loyo, Ernestina, tr. see Impey, Rose.

Loyo, Ernestina, tr. see Jennings, Paul.

Loyo, Ernestina, tr. see Smith, Lane.

Loyo, Ernestina, tr. see Walsh, Ellen S.

Loyola, Fray A. De Avendano y, see De Avendano y Loyola, Fray A.

Loyola, Mary. The American Occupation of New Mexico, 1821-1852. Cortes, Carlos E., ed. LC 76-1281. (Chicano Heritage Ser.). 1977. reprint ed. 15.95 (*0-405-09512-0*) Ayer.

***Loyola Press Staff.** Mama Says: Inspiration, Prayers, Wit & Wisdom from the Mothers in Our Lives. LC 99-37630. 273p. 2000. pap. 10.95 (*0-8294-1342-1*) Loyola Pr.

Loyola, Rodolfo. Antologia Poetica. (SPA.). pap. 5.99 (*0-8297-1477-4*) Vida Pubs.

— Dejad Que el Amor Presida.Tr. of Let Love Preside. (SPA.). 1994. pap. 6.99 (*1-56063-437-5*, 498579) Editorial Unilit.

— Veinte Enemigos del Matrimonio. (Serie Guia de Bolsillo - Pocket Guides Ser.).Tr. of Twenty Enemies of Marriage. (SPA.). 93p. 1989. pap. 2.79 (*1-56063-106-6*, 498070) Editorial Unilit.

Loyrette, Henri. Degas: The Man & His Art. Paris, I. Mark, tr. (Discoveries Ser.). (Illus.). 192p. 1993. pap. 12.95 (*0-8109-2897-3*, Pub. by Abrams) Time Warner.

***Loyrette, Henri & Pantazzi, Michael.** Daumier, 1808,1879. (Illus.). 600p. 2000. 95.00 (*0-300-08359-9*) Yale U Pr.

Loyseau, Charles. A Treatise of Orders & Plain Dignities. Lloyd, Howell A., ed. (Cambridge Texts in the History of Political Thought Ser.). 305p. (C). 1994. text 69.95 (*0-521-40519-X*) Cambridge U Pr.

— A Treatise of Orders & Plain Dignities. Lloyd, Howell A., ed. (Cambridge Texts in the History of Political Thought Ser.). 305p. (C). 1994. pap. text 24.95 (*0-521-45624-X*) Cambridge U Pr.

Loyst, Ken, et al. Dive Computers: A Consumer's Guide to History, Theory & Performance. 191p. (Orig.). 1991. pap. text 12.95 (*0-922769-09-5*) Watersport Pub.

— Night Diving: A Consumer's Guide to the Specialty of Night Diving. 1992. pap. 12.95 (*0-922769-33-8*) Watersport Pub.

Loyst, Ken, ed. see McPeak, Ronald H., et al.

Loza, D. F. Fighting for the Soviet Motherland: Recollections from the Eastern Front. Gebhardt, James F., ed. & tr. by. from ENG. LC 98-11253. xii, 271p. 1998. text 49.50 (*0-8032-2929-1*) U of Nebr Pr.

Loza, Dmitriy. Commanding the Red Army's Sherman Tanks: The World War II Memoirs of Hero of the Soviet Union Dmitriy Loza. Gebhardt, James F., ed. & tr. by. LC 96-7366. (Illus.). xviii, 173p. 1996. text 35.00 (*0-8032-2920-8*) U of Nebr Pr.

Loza, Steven. Barrio Rhythm: Mexican American Music in Los Angeles. (Illus.). 392p. (C). 1993. 16.95 (*0-252-06288-4*); text 42.50 (*0-252-01902-4*) U of Ill Pr.

Loza, Steven J. Tito Puente & the Making of Latin Music. LC 98-25507. (Music in American Life Ser.). 352p. 1999. 59.95 (*0-252-02332-3*) U of Ill Pr.

— Tito Puente & the Making of Latin Music. LC 98-25507. (Music in American Life Ser.). 352p. 1999. pap. 26.95 (*0-252-06778-9*) U of Ill Pr.

Lozac'h, N., et al. Forty Years of Heterocyclic Sulfur Chemistry: The Chemistry of 1, 2-Dithiins, Vol. 9. Senning, Alexander, ed. (Sulfer Reports: Vol. 9, No. 3). 108p. 1989. pap. text 167.00 (*3-7186-4994-2*) Gordon & Breach.

***Lozada, Francisco.** A Literary Reading of John 5: Text as Construction. (Studies in Biblical Literature: Vol. 20). 152p. (C). 2000. text 40.95 (*0-8204-4533-9*) P Lang Pubng.

Lozada, Gabriel A., jt. auth. see Beard, T. Randolph.

Lozada, Hector R., jt. ed. see Mintu-Wimsatt, Alma T.

Lozada, Hector R., jt. ed. see Polonsky, Michael J.

Lozane, jt. auth. see Feng.

Lozano. Airborne. (C). 1995. pap., teacher ed. 33.96 (*0-395-74671-X*) HM.

— Airborne: Writer's Text. (C). 1995. pap. text 32.76 (*0-395-67692-4*) HM.

— Airborne Writers Text. (C). Date not set. write for info. (*0-395-77732-1*) HM.

***Lozano.** Fruit Products: Quality Changes During Processing & Storage. 2000. pap. write for info. (*0-412-15541-9*) Thomson Learn.

***Lozano, A. M., ed.** Movement Disorder Surgery: Progress & Challenges. (Progress in Neurological Surgery Ser.: Vol. 15). (Illus.). x, 404p. 2000. 243.50 (*3-8055-6990-4*) S Karger.

Lozano, Albert, jt. auth. see Petrovsky, John.

Lozano, Alberto H. & Petrovsky, John R. New Spanish for Travelers. 36p. 1998. pap. text 16.95 (*0-940935-01-5*) Vista Press.

Lozano, Anthony G. & Zayas-Bazan, Eduardo, eds. Del Amor a la Revolucion. 225p. (C). 1975. pap. text 15.50 (*0-393-09283-6*) Norton.

Lozano, Beverly. The Invisible Work Force: Transforming American Business with Outside & Home-Based Workers. 200p. 1989. 29.95 (*0-02-919442-3*) Free Pr.

Lozano, Carlos, tr. see Alegria, Fernando.

Lozano-Diaz, Nora O., jt. ed. see Baxter, Anne.

Lozano, Ed, ed. Bob Dylan Greatest Hits, Vol. 2. (Bob Dylan's Greatest Hits Ser.). (Illus.). 94p. 1999. pap. text 17.95 (*0-8256-1637-9*, AM945274, Amsco Music) Music Sales.

— The Gig Bag Book of Guitar Tab Chords. LC 97-217509. (Gig Bag Bks.). (Illus.). 268p. 1997. pap. text 12.95 (*0-8256-1619-0*, AM943250, Amsco Music) Music Sales.

— 300 Tips & Tricks for Guitar. LC 99-478471. (Illus.). 64p. 1998. pap. text 5.95 (*0-8256-1632-8*, AM945220) Music Sales.

Lozano, Eduardo E. Community Design & the Culture of Cities: The Crossroad & the Wall. (Illus.). 354p. (C). 1990. text 80.00 (*0-521-38067-7*); pap. text 32.95 (*0-521-38979-8*) Cambridge U Pr.

Lozano, Fernando. American Painting. (Illus.). 64p. 1991. 32.00 (*1-56721-008-2*) Twnty-Fifth Cent Pr.

— Contemporary Painting. (Illus.). 64p. 1991. 32.00 (*1-56721-007-4*) Twnty-Fifth Cent Pr.

— European Painting. (Illus.). 64p. 1991. 32.00 (*1-56721-006-6*) Twnty-Fifth Cent Pr.

— Latin American Painting. (Illus.). 64p. 1991. 32.00 (*1-56721-005-8*) Twnty-Fifth Cent Pr.

— Modern - Impressionist Painting, Vol. 1. (Illus.). 64p. 1991. 32.00 (*1-56721-009-0*) Twnty-Fifth Cent Pr.

— Modern - Impressionist Painting, Vol. 2. (Illus.). 64p. 1991. 32.00 (*1-56721-010-4*) Twnty-Fifth Cent Pr.

— Modern - Impressionist Painting, Vol. 3. (Illus.). 64p. 1991. 32.00 (*1-56721-011-2*) Twnty-Fifth Cent Pr.

— Modern - Impressionist Painting, Vol. 4. (Illus.). 64p. 1991. 32.00 (*1-56721-012-0*) Twnty-Fifth Cent Pr.

— World Travelogue. (Illus.). 64p. 1991. 32.00 (*1-56721-004-X*) Twnty-Fifth Cent Pr.

Lozano Irueste, Jose M. Bilingual Spanish-English, English-Spanish Economics & Business Dictionary. 128p. 1991. pap. write for info. (*0-7859-5981-5*, 8436806344); pap. write for info. (*0-7859-5988-2*, 8436806417); pap. write for info. (*0-7859-5989-0*, 8436806425) Fr & Eur.

An Asterisk (*) at the beginning of an entry indicates that the title is appearing for the first time.

— Bilingual Spanish-English, English-Spanish Economics & Business Dictionary, 10 vols., Set. 1991. pap. write for info. (*0-7859-5991-2*, 8436806441) Fr & Eur.

— Bilingual Spanish-English, English-Spanish Economics & Business Dictionary, Vol. 2. 128p. 1991. pap. write for info. (*0-7859-5982-3*, 8436806352) Fr & Eur.

— Bilingual Spanish-English, English-Spanish Economics & Business Dictionary, Vol. 3. 128p. 1991. pap. write for info. (*0-7859-5983-1*, 8436806360) Fr & Eur.

— Bilingual Spanish-English, English-Spanish Economics & Business Dictionary, Vol. 5. 128p. 1991. pap. write for info. (*0-7859-5985-8*, 8436806387) Fr & Eur.

— Bilingual Spanish-English, English-Spanish Economics & Business Dictionary, Vol. 6. 128p. 1991. pap. write for info. (*0-7859-5986-6*, 8436806395) Fr & Eur.

— Bilingual Spanish-English, English-Spanish Economics & Business Dictionary, Vol. 7. 128p. 1991. pap. write for info. (*0-7859-5987-4*, 8436806409) Fr & Eur.

— Bilingual Spanish-English, English-Spanish Economics & Business Dictionary, Vol. 10. 128p. 1991. pap. write for info. (*0-7859-5990-4*, 8436806433) Fr & Eur.

Lozano, Joaquin R. Una Poetica de la Oscuridad: La Recepcion Critica de las Soledades en el Siglo XVII. (Monagrafias A Ser.: No. 155). (SPA.). 234p. (C). 1994. 72.00 (*1-85566-026-1*, Pub. by Tamesis Bks Ltd) Boydell & Brewer.

***Lozano, Jorge E., et al, eds.** Trends in Food Engineering. LC 00-102585. 360p. 2000. text 124.95 (*1-56676-991-4*) Technomic.

***Lozano, Josep M.** Ethics & Organizations: Understanding Business Ethics as a Learning Process. LC 00-41589. (Issues in Business Ethics Ser.). 2000. write for info. (*0-7923-6463-5*) Kluwer Academic.

Lozano, Josep M., et al. Jesus Grows Up. (Illus.). 64p. (J). (gr. k-4). 1997. boxed set 15.95 (*0-86716-331-3*, B3313) St Anthony Mess Pr.

Lozano, Leopoldo. The Self-Help Guide to Successful Living. Botta, David A., tr. from SPA.Tr. of Etiqueta y Buenos Modales le Llevaran al Exito Economico y Social. (Illus.). 109p. (Orig.). 1996. pap. 14.99 (*0-9653530-0-1*) Intnl O Ctr.

Lozano, Leticia, ed. see Gibson, Edwin W.

Lozano, Lidia, tr. see Garcia Canclini, Nestor.

Lozano, Lidia, tr. see Semo, Enrique.

Lozano-Lopez, Gracia, ed. Texto y Concordancias de Libro de las Donas, Escorial MS. h.III.20. (Spanish Ser.: No. 67). 20p. 1992. 10.00 incl. fiche (*0-940639-63-7*) Hispanic Seminary.

Lozano, Louis-Martin, jt. auth. see Del Conde, Teresa.

Lozano, M., et al, eds. Nuclear Astrophysics. (Research Reports in Physics). (Illus.). 350p. 1989. pap. 66.00 (*0-387-50751-5*) Spr-Verlag.

Lozano, M. & Madurga, G., eds. Theory of Nuclear Structure & Reactions: Proceedings of the Second La Rabida International Summer School on Nuclear Physics, Huelva, Spain, June 23-July 6, 1985. 650p. 1986. text 146.00 (*9971-5-0074-4*) World Scientific Pub.

Lozano, M., jt. auth. see Madurga, G.

Lozano Marcos, Miguel A., ed. see Miro, Gabriel.

Lozano Marcos, Miguel A., ed. see Perez De Ayala, Ramon.

Lozano, Neal. The Older Brother Returns: Finding a Renewed Sense of God's Love & Mercy. LC 95-41024. 152p. (Orig.). 1995. pap. 10.00 (*1-883551-51-X*) Attic Studio Pub.

Lozano, Patti. Guide to Successful After-School Elementary Foreign-Language Programs. 1993. pap. 9.95 (*0-8442-9365-2*, Natl Textbk Co) NTC Contemp Pub Co.

Lozano-Perez, Tomas, et al. Handey: A Robot Task Planner. (Artificial Intelligence - Bobrow, Brady & Davis Ser.). (Illus.). 256p. 1992. 42.50 (*0-262-12172-7*) MIT Pr.

***Lozano, R.** Dissipative Systems Analysis & Control. LC 00-28464. 2000. write for info. (*1-85233-285-9*) Spr-Verlag.

Lozano, Robert, ed. see Andrei, Moscovit.

Lozano, Roberto, tr. see Schreuder, Sally A.

Lozano, Ruben R. Viva Tejas: The Story of the Tejanos, the Mexican-Born Patriots of the Texas Revolution. (Illus.). 82p. (Orig.). 1991. pap. 8.95 (*0-943260-02-7*) Alamo Pr TX.

Lozano, Salvador, tr. see LaRouche, Lyndon H., Jr.

Lozanov, G. & Gateva, E. The Foreign Language Teacher's Suggestopedic Manual. 1988. pap. 41.00 (*0-685-50152-3*) Gordon & Breach.

— The Foreign Language Teacher's Suggestopedic Manual. x, 372p. 1988. text 116.00 (*0-677-21660-2*); pap. text 53.00 (*0-677-21750-1*) Gordon & Breach.

Lozansky, E. & Rousseau, C. Winning Solutions. (Problem Books in Mathematics). 244p. 1996. pap. 34.95 (*0-387-94743-4*) Spr-Verlag.

Lozansky, Edward & Sakharov, Andrei D., eds. Andrei Sakharov & Peace. 325p. 1985. pap. 8.95 (*0-380-89819-5*, Avon Bks) Morrow Avon.

Lozansky, Riva, et al. If I Forget Thee... The Destruction of the Shtetl Butrimantz. LC 98-68604. (Illus.). 152p. 1999. pap. 14.95 (*0-9669349-0-3*) Remembrance Bks.

Lozarnick, George. Netsuke & Inro Artists, & How to Read Their Signatures. LC 81-51945. (Illus.). 1376p. 1982. 295.00 (*0-917064-02-X*) Reed Pubs.

Lozet, J. Dictionary de Science du Sol: French/English/ French. 3rd ed. (ENG & FRE.). 496p. 1997. 195.00 (*0-320-00033-8*) Fr & Eur.

Lozet, J. & Mathieu, Clement. French-English Dictionary of Earth Science with English-French Index. 2nd ed. (ENG & FRE.). 384p. 1990. pap. 145.00 (*2-85206-617-3*, Pub. by Technique et Documentation) IBD Ltd.

Lozet, Jean & Mathieu, Clement. Dictionary of Soil Science. 2nd enl. rev. ed. (FRE.). 358p. (C). 1991. text 123.00 (*90-5410-201-2*, Pub. by A A Balkema) Ashgate Pub Co.

— French & English Dictionary of Earth Science: Dictionnaire de Science du Sol. 2nd ed. (ENG & FRE.). 270p. 1990. pap. 225.00 (*0-8288-2290-5*, F12660) Fr & Eur.

Lozier, G. Gregory, jt. ed. see Teeter, Deborah J.

Lozina-Lozinskij, A. Trottuar: Tpottyar. 65p. (Orig.). 1990. reprint ed. 12.00 (*1-878445-54-5*) Antiquary CT.

Lozinskaya, Natalya, ed. see Usov, Vladimir.

Lozinskaya, Tatjana A. Supernovae & Stellar Wind. Damashek, Marc, tr. (Translation Ser.). (Illus.). 352p. 1990. 89.95 (*0-88318-659-4*) Spr-Verlag.

Lozinsky, Sergio. Enterprise-Wide Software Solutions: Integration Strategies & Practices. LC 97-44128. 224p. (C). 1998. pap. text 29.95 (*0-201-30971-8*) Addison-Wesley.

Lozoff, Bo. Deep & Simple: A Spiritual Path for Modern Times. LC 99-90204. Date not set. pap. 10.00 (*0-9614444-6-0*) Human Kind Found.

— Just Another Spiritual Book. (Illus.). 384p. (Orig.). 1991. pap. 12.00 (*0-9614444-5-2*) Human Kind Found.

— Lineage & Other Stories. 120p. (Orig.). 1989. pap. 7.00 (*0-9614444-1-X*) Human Kind Found.

— Todos Estamos Encarcelados. Dialogos International Staff, ed. Beas, Ricardo, tr. from ENG. (SPA., Illus.). 336p. (Orig.). 1989. pap. 10.00 (*0-9614444-3-6*) Human Kind Found.

— We're All Doing Time. LC 84-62787. (Illus.). 336p. (Orig.). (C). 1985. pap. 10.00 (*0-9614444-0-1*) Human Kind Found.

Lozoff, Bo & Braswell, Michael. Inner Corrections: Finding Peace & Peace Making. 210p. 1989. pap. 15.95 (*0-932930-85-9*) Anderson Pub Co.

***Lozoff, Bo & Lama, Dalai.** It's a Meaningful Life: It Just Takes Practice. 280p. 2000. 23.95 (*0-670-88910-5*, Viking) Viking Penguin.

Lozon. Emergency Pediatric Management. 1999. pap. text. write for info. (*0-7216-7651-0*, W B Saunders Co) Harcrt Hlth Sci Grp.

Lozovskaya, Elana, jt. auth. see Draper, Michael.

Lozovskaya, Elena. Essential Genetics Thru Problem Solving. (Life Science Ser.). 128p. 1996. pap. 21.25 (*0-7637-0364-8*) Jones & Bartlett.

***Lozovsky, Natalia.** The Earth is our Book: Geographical Knowledge in the Latin West Ca. 400-1000. LC 99-50981. (Recentiores: Later Latin Texts & Contexts Ser.). (Illus.). 216p. (C). 2000. text 42.50 (*0-472-11132-9*, 11132) U of Mich Pr.

Lozowick, Lee. Acting God. LC 80-85142. 64p. 1980. pap. 5.95 (*0-934252-05-X*) Hohm Pr.

— The Alchemy of Love & Sex. LC 95-77755. 312p. (C). 1995. pap. 16.95 (*0-934252-58-0*, Pub. by Hohm Pr) SCB Distributors.

— The Alchemy of Transformation. Ryan, Regina S., ed. LC 95-51641. (Illus.). 192p. (Orig.). 1996. pap. 14.95 (*0-934252-62-9*, Pub. by Hohm Pr) SCB Distributors.

— The Cheating Buddha. LC 80-80802. 144p. 1980. pap. 7.95 (*0-934252-03-3*, Pub. by Hohm Pr) SCB Distributors.

— Conscious Parenting. LC 97-23949. 384p. (Orig.). 1997. pap. 17.95 (*0-934252-67-X*, Pub. by Hohm Pr) SCB Distributors.

— In the Fire. LC 78-54139. 264p. 1978. pap. 9.95 (*0-89556-002-X*, Pub. by Hohm Pr) SCB Distributors.

— Laughter of the Stones. 140p. 1984. pap. 9.95 (*0-934252-00-9*, Pub. by Hohm Pr) SCB Distributors.

— Living God Blues. 168p. 1984. pap. 9.95 (*0-934252-09-2*, Pub. by Hohm Pr) SCB Distributors.

— The Only Grace Is Loving God. LC 82-81992. 106p. 1982. pap. 5.95 (*0-934252-07-6*, Pub. by Hohm Pr) SCB Distributors.

— Yoga of Enlightenment: Book of Unenlightenment. LC 80-85141. 240p. 1980. pap. 9.95 (*0-934252-06-8*) Hohm Pr.

Lozowick, Louis. William Gropper. (Illus.). 200p. 1983. 40.00 (*0-87982-033-0*) Art Alliance.

— William Gropper. LC 80-67118. (Illus.). 240p. 1983. 40.00 (*0-8453-4730-6*, Cornwall Bks) Assoc Univ Prs.

Lozowick, Toni L. Leftovers. LC 98-89521. 375p. 1998. text 25.00 (*0-7388-0207-6*); pap. text 15.00 (*0-7388-0208-5*) Xlibris Corp.

Lozoya, Jorge A., ed. Asia & the New International Economic Order. LC 80-25758. (Policy Studies on the New International Economic Order). 1981. 52.00 (*0-08-025116-1*, Pergamon Pr) Elsevier.

— International Trade, Industrialization & the New International Economic Order. (Policy Studies). 1981. 52.00 (*0-08-025120-X*, Pergamon Pr) Elsevier.

— The Social & Cultural Issues of the New International Economic Order. (Policy Studies). 1981. 52.00 (*0-08-025123-4*, Pergamon Pr) Elsevier.

Lozoya, Jorge A. & Estevez, Jaime, eds. Latin America & the New International Economic Order. LC 79-27384. (Policy Studies on the New International Economic Order). 112p. 1980. 44.00 (*0-08-025118-8*, Pergamon Pr) Elsevier.

Lozoya, Oscar. Fine Art Portrait Photography. LC 98-71932. (Illus.). 128p. 1999. pap. 29.95 (*0-936262-71-0*) Amherst Media.

Lozuk, Larry & Ketcham, Emily M. Understanding & Using Microsoft Word for Windows 2.0. Leyh, ed. LC 93-1658. (Microcomputing Ser.). 384p. (C). 1993. pap. text 28.75 (*0-314-02473-5*) West Pub.

Lozynsky, Artem. The Letters of Dr. Richard Maurice Bucke to Walt Whitman. LC 77-58. 317p. reprint ed. 98.30 (*0-8357-9829-1*, 201553900001) Bks Demand.

Lozzi, Larsen K. Medical Studies of Saliva: Index of Modern Authors & Subjects with Guide for Rapid Research. LC 90-56295. 160p. 1991. 47.50 (*1-55914-366-5*); pap. 44.50 (*1-55914-367-3*) ABBE Pubs Assn.

Lpanz, David L. Official Guide to U. S. Commemorative Coins: Current Information That All Collectors Want & Need. (Illus.). 320p. 1999. pap. 12.95 (*1-56625-124-9*) Bonus Books.

Lpoez-Pedraza, Rafael. Cultural Anxiety. 117p. 1995. pap. 15.00 (*3-85630-520-3*) Continuum.

L.R.A. Staff. Constitution of the Kingdom of Nepal: 2047 & Electoral Laws. (C). 1991. text 40.00 (*0-7855-0131-2*, Pub. by Ratna Pustak Bhandar) St Mut.

LRP Publications (Firm) Staff. Special Education Dictionary. LC 97-10261. 1997. write for info. (*1-57834-002-0*) LRP Pubns.

LRP Publications Staff. Illinois Public Employee Reporter. write for info. (*0-934753-02-4*) LRP Pubns.

— Indiana Public Employee Reporter. text. write for info. (*0-934753-05-9*) LRP Pubns.

— Labor Arbitration Information System. text 475.00 (*0-934753-12-1*) LRP Pubns.

— Labor Arbitration Information Systems: Indexes-Tables. write for info. (*0-934753-11-3*) LRP Pubns.

— National Public Employee Reporter. text. write for info. (*0-934753-10-5*) LRP Pubns.

— National Public Employment Reporter: Tables. text 475.00 (*0-934753-09-1*) LRP Pubns.

— New Jersey Public Employee Reporter. text 645.00 (*0-934753-07-5*) LRP Pubns.

— New Jersey Public Employee Reporter, Vol. 12. 1987. write for info. (*0-934753-15-6*) LRP Pubns.

— NLRB Advice Memorandum Reporter. text 510.00 (*0-934753-08-3*) LRP Pubns.

— Ohio Public Employee Reporter. text 480.00 (*0-934753-03-2*) LRP Pubns.

— Pennsylvania Public Employee Reporter. text 645.00 (*0-934753-04-0*) LRP Pubns.

— Public Employee Reporter for California. text. write for info. (*0-934753-01-6*) LRP Pubns.

LRP Publications Staff, ed. Federal Labor Relations Reporter: 1986. 1987. 685.00 (*0-934753-23-7*) LRP Pubns.

— Federal Merit Systems Reporter: 1986. 1987. 685.00 (*0-934753-24-5*) LRP Pubns.

— Federal Pay Benefits Reporter: 1986. 1987. 470.00 (*0-934753-25-3*) LRP Pubns.

— Florida Public Employee Reporter, Vol. 2. text 640.00 (*0-934753-06-7*) LRP Pubns.

— Florida Public Employee Reporter, Vol. 12. 1987. write for info. (*0-934753-16-4*) LRP Pubns.

— Illinois Public Employee Reporter, Vol. 2. 1987. write for info. (*0-934753-21-0*) LRP Pubns.

— Indiana Public Employee Reporter, Vol. II. 1987. write for info. (*0-934753-17-2*) LRP Pubns.

— Labor Arbitration Information System, Vol. 13. 1987. write for info. (*0-934753-27-X*) LRP Pubns.

— Labor Arbitration Index: 1987 Edition. text. write for info. (*0-934753-29-6*) LRP Pubns.

— New York Workers' Compensation Law Reporter, Vol. 1. 1987. text 605.00 (*0-934753-22-9*) LRP Pubns.

— NLRB Advice Memorandum Reporter, Vol. 14. 1987. text. write for info. (*0-934753-26-1*) LRP Pubns.

— Ohio Public Employee Reporter, Vol. 3. 1987. text. write for info. (*0-934753-20-2*) LRP Pubns.

— Pennsylvania Public Employee Reporter, Vol. 17. 1987. text. write for info. (*0-934753-14-8*) LRP Pubns.

— Public Employee Reporter for California, Vol. 10. 1987. text. write for info. (*0-934753-18-0*) LRP Pubns.

Lsm. Knowing & Experiencing Life Level 4: Lesson Book. 192p. 1990. per. 8.00 (*0-87083-524-6*, 16-021-001) Living Stream Ministry.

Lstiburek, Joseph & Carmody, John. Moisture Control Handbook: Principles & Practices for Residential & Small Commercial Buildings. 232p. 1996. 69.95 (*0-471-31863-9*) Wiley.

***Lstiburek, Joseph & Eng, P.** The Builder's Guide to Cold Climates: A Comprehensive Guide to the Best Cold-Climate Building Techniques. LC 99-59396. (Illus.). 335p. 2000. pap. text 40.00 (*1-56158-374-X*) Taunton.

— The Builder's Guide to Mixed Climates: A Comprehensive Guide to the Best Mixed-Climate Building Techniques. (Illus.). 328p. 2000. pap. text 40.00 (*1-56158-375-8*) Taunton.

Lstiburek, Joseph, jt. auth. see Carmody, John.

Lstiburek, Joseph W., jt. auth. see Bomberg, Mark T.

LTA Publishing Company Staff. Images of Los Angeles. LC 91-22804. (Illus.). 52p. (Orig.). 1991. pap. 6.95 (*1-55988-299-9*) Am Prods.

— Images of Portland. (Illus.). 52p. (Orig.). 1990. pap. 6.95 (*1-55988-220-4*) Am Prods.

— Images of San Diego. LC 91-20177. (Illus.). 52p. (Orig.). 1991. pap. 6.95 (*1-55988-304-9*) Am Prods.

LTA Staff. Images of Pennsylvania. 1990. pap. 6.95 (*1-55988-219-0*) Am Prods.

Ltaif, Nadine. Entre les Fleuves. (Collection Voix: No. 16). 52p. 1991. pap. write for info. (*2-89135-034-0*) Guernica Editions.

— Les Metamorphoses d'Ishtar. 2nd ed. (FRE.). 62p. 1989. pap. write for info. (*2-89135-025-1*) Guernica Editions.

***LTC Publishing Company Staff, ed.** The International Adventure & Extreme Sports Source Directory. unabridged ed. 742p. 2000. 24.95 (*0-9677512-0-9*) LTC Pub Co.

LTD Publications International Staff. Great-Tasting Wraps. LC 98-225016. 94 p. 1998. write for info. (*0-7853-2802-5*) Pubns Intl Ltd.

LTD Publications International Staff, jt. auth. see Mathieu, Kristen.

LTI-Research Group Staff, ed. Long-Term Integration of Renewable Energy Sources into the European Energy System. LC 98-3940. (Environmental & Resource Economics Ser.). (Illus.). x, 268p. 1998. pap. 67.00 (*3-7908-1104-1*) Spr-Verlag.

L'Trouve, Marianne, ed. Favorite Prayers & Novenas. 432p. (Orig.). 1997. 12.95 (*0-8198-2665-0*); pap. 9.95 (*0-8198-2664-2*) Pauline Bks.

L'Trouve, Marianne, tr. see Sotillos, Eugenio.

LTV Corporation Staff, jt. auth. see American Political Network, Inc. Staff.

Lu. Peptides Biology & Chemistry. 1995. text 166.00 (*90-72199-20-0*) Kluwer Academic.

***Lu, Aiguo.** China & the Global Economy Since 1840 LC 99-15427. 1999. text 75.00 (*0-312-22628-4*) St Martin.

Lu, Aiguo & World Institute for Development Economics Research. Welfare Changes in China During the Economic Reforms. LC 97-189434. (Research for Action Ser.). ix, 89p. 1996. write for info. (*952-9520-40-9*) UN.

Lu, Albert K., jt. auth. see Roberts, Gordon W.

***Lu, Alvin.** The Hell Screens: A Novel. 238p. 2000. pap. text 24.00 (*1-56858-167-X*, Pub. by FWEW) Publishers Group.

Lu, C. K., et al. Singularities & Complex Geometry: Seminar on Singularities & Complex Geometry, June 15-20, 1994, Beijing, People's Republic of China. LC 96-47630. (AMS-IP Studies in Advanced Mathematics: Vol. 5). 342p. 1997. text 49.00 (*0-8218-0662-9*, AMSIP/5) Am Math.

Lu, Cary. The Race for Bandwidth: Understanding Data Transmission. LC 97-4204. 250p. 1997. pap. text 19.99 (*1-57231-513-X*) Microsoft.

Lu Chi. The Art of Writing: Lu Chi's Wen Fu. Hamill, Sam, tr. from CHI. LC 90-25970. 64p. (Orig.). 1991. pap. 9.95 (*0-915943-62-X*) Milkweed Ed.

***Lu, Chi Fa & White, Becky C.** Double Luck. LC 99-48509. 2000. write for info. (*0-8234-1560-0*) Holiday.

Lu, Chih. The Sino-Indian Border Dispute: A Legal Study, 139. LC 85-12713. (Contributions in Political Science Ser.: No. 139). 153p. 1986. 45.00 (*0-313-25024-3*, LSI/, Greenwood Pr) Greenwood.

Lu, Chuanrong, jt. auth. see Lin, Cheng-Yen.

Lu Dadao, jt. auth. see Li Wenyan.

Lu, David J. Japan: A Documentary History, 2 vols., Vols. I & II. LC 96-24433. (Illus.). 686p. (C). 1996. text 47.95 (*1-56324-906-5*, East Gate Bk) M E Sharpe.

Lu, David J. Japan : A Documentary History: The Dawn of History to the Late Tokugawa Period Century, Vol. I. LC 96-24433. (Illus.). 330p. (C). (gr. 13). 1996. pap. text 24.95 (*1-56324-907-3*, East Gate Bk) M E Sharpe.

Lu, David J., tr. see Ishikawa, Kaoru.

Lu, David J., tr. see Japan Management Association Staff, ed.

Lu, Diane & Zung, Michael, eds. Access Asia: Guide to Specialists & Their Current Research. 100p. 1991. pap. text 50.00 (*0-9631625-0-0*) Nat Bur Asian.

— AccessAsia: A Guide to Specialists & Current Research. 1992nd ed. 180p. 1992. 75.00 (*0-9631625-1-9*) Nat Bur Asian.

Lu, Ding & Tang, Zhimin. State Intervention & Business in China: The Role of Preferential Policies. LC 97-33594. 168p. 1997. 80.00 (*1-85898-476-9*) E Elgar.

Lu, Donald & Weiss, Thomas G. International Negotiations on the Code of Conduct for Transnational Corporations. (Pew Case Studies in International Affairs). 50p. (C). 1994. pap. text 3.50 (*1-56927-117-8*) Geo U Inst Dplmcy.

Lu, Fei-Pai. T. S. Eliot: The Dialectical Structure of His Theory of Poetry. LC 66-13877. 182p. reprint ed. pap. 56.50 (*0-608-13417-1*, 202409800035) Bks Demand.

Lu, Frank C. Basic Toxicology: Fundamentals, Target Organs, & Risk Assessment. 3rd ed. 376p. 1996. 120.00 (*1-56032-379-5*); pap. 52.95 (*1-56032-380-9*) Taylor & Francis.

***Lu, G. Q.** Nanoporous Materials. (Illus.). 2000. pap. 48.00 (*1-86094-211-3*) Imperial College.

Lu, Guiying, tr. see Kong, Yaoqi, et al, eds.

Lu, Gulru Necipo, see Necipo Lu, Gulru, ed.

Lu, Guojun. Communication & Computing for Distributed Multimedia Systems. LC 96-46064. 416p. 1996. 83.00 (*0-89006-884-4*) Artech Hse.

— Multimedia Database Management Systems. LC 99-41773. 373p. 1999. 79.00 (*0-89006-342-7*) Artech Hse.

Lu, H., et al, eds. Query Processing in Parallel Relationship Database Systems. LC 93-45665. 392p. 1994. 62.00 (*0-8186-5452-X*, 5452) IEEE Comp Soc.

Lu, H. J. Knowledge Discovery & Data Mining: Techniques & Applications. Motoda, H. & Liu, H., eds. LC 97-160040. 376p. 1997. text 52.00 (*981-02-3072-9*) World Scientific Pub.

Lu, H. J. & Ooi, B. C. Geographic Information Systems: Technology & Application. 500p. 1993. text 121.00 (*981-02-1445-6*) World Scientific Pub.

***Lu, Han-Chao.** Beyond the Neon Lights: Everyday Shanghai in the Early Twentieth Century. LC 98-31298. 473p. 1999. 50.00 (*0-520-21564-8*, Pub. by U CA Pr) Cal Prin Full Svc.

Lu, Henry C. Chinese Herbal Cures. LC 93-43376. (Illus.). 160p. 1993. pap. 10.95 (*0-8069-0762-2*) Sterling.

— Chinese Herbs with Common Foods: Recipes for Health & Healing. LC 97-35459. 1997. pap. text 15.00 (*4-7700-2074-0*, Pub. by Kodansha Intl) OUP.

— The Chinese System of Food Cures: Prevention & Remedies. LC 86-5678. (Illus.). 192p. (Orig.). 1986. pap. 10.95 (*0-8069-6308-5*) Sterling.

***Lu, Henry C.** Chinese System of Foods for Health & Healing. (Illus.). 2000. pap. 11.95 (*0-8069-7065-0*) Sterling.

Lu, Henry C. Chinese System of Natural Cures. LC 94-13706. 160p. 1994. pap. 10.95 (*0-8069-0616-2*) Sterling.

— The Chinese System of Using Foods to Stay Young. 192p. 1996. pap. 10.95 (*0-8069-9460-6*) Sterling.

Lu, Hongjun, jt. auth. see Zhou, Aoying.

***Lu, Hsiao-Po.** Cadres & Corruption: The Organizational Involution of the Chinese Communist Party. LC 00-27396. (Studies of the East Asian Institute). 2000. write for info. (*0-8047-3958-7*) Stanford U Pr.

Lu Hsun, pseud. Ah Q, & Others: Selected Stories of Lu Xun. Wang, Chi-Chen, tr. LC 70-150542. (Short Story Index Reprint Ser.). 1977. reprint ed. 19.95 (*0-8369-3839-9*) Ayer.

— Ah Q, & Others: Selected Stories of Lu Xun. Wang, Chi-Chen, tr. from CHI. LC 75-143310. 1971. reprint ed. lib. bdg. 59.50 (*0-8371-5965-2*, CHAQ, Greenwood Pr) Greenwood.

— The Complete Stories of Lu Xun. Xianyi, Yang & Yang, Gladys, trs. LC 81-47585. 309p. 1981. reprint ed. pap. 95.80 (*0-608-18256-7*, 205670800081) Bks Demand.

— Diary of a Madman & Other Stories. Lyell, William A., tr. from CHI. LC 90-36785. (Illus.). 432p. 1990. text 42.00 (*0-8248-1278-6*) UH Pr.

Lu Hsun, pseud. Diary of a Madman & Other Stories. Lyell, William A., tr. from CHI. LC 90-36785. (Illus.). 432p. 1990. pap. 19.95 (*0-8248-1317-0*) UH Pr.

Lu Hsun, pseud. Lu Xun Xiao Shuo Ji: Vocabulary (Selected Short Stories of Lu Xun) (Illus.). 207p. 1979. reprint ed. pap. 14.95 (*0-917056-22-1*) Cheng & Tsui.

— Selected Stories of Lu Hsun. 3rd ed. 255p. 1994. pap. 11.95 (*0-8351-2272-7*) China Bks.

— Selected Stories of Lu Hsun. 3rd ed. Yang, Gladys & Hsien-Yi Yang, trs. from CHI. (Illus.). 255p. (C). 1989. pap. 11.95 (*0-917056-71-X*, Pub. by Foreign Lang Pr) Cheng & Tsui.

— Selected Writings of Lu Xun, 4 vols. (Studies in Chinese Literature). 1990. lib. bdg. 750.00 (*0-8490-4058-2*) Gordon Pr.

— The True Story of Ah-Q. 5th ed. Yang Hsien-Yi & Yang, Gladys, trs. from CHI. LC 89-81931. (C & T Asian Literature Ser.). 68p. (Orig.). (C). 1990. pap. 3.95 (*0-917056-93-0*) Cheng & Tsui.

Lu Huang, Jane & Wurmbrand, Michael, trs. from CHI. The Primordial Breath Vol. I: An Ancient Chinese Way of Prolonging Life Through Breath Control. 170p. (C). 1987. 22.50 (*0-944558-00-3*) Original Bks.

Lu, J. K. Boundary Value Problems for Analytic Functions. (Series in Pure Mathematics: No. 16). 480p. 1994. text 74.00 (*981-02-1020-5*) World Scientific Pub.

— Complex Variable Methods in Plane Elasticity. (Series in Pure Mathematics). 300p. 1995. text 61.00 (*981-02-2093-6*) World Scientific Pub.

Lu, J. L. The Missing Patient. 1978. pap. 2.75 (*0-9601768-0-2*) J L Lu.

Lu, Jian, ed. see Society for Experimental Mechanics, Inc. Staff.

***Lu, Jian-Ke & Wen, Guo Chun.** Boundary Value Problems, Integral Equations & Related Problems: Proceedings Of The Second International Conference: Beijing & Chengde, Hebei, China, 8-14 August 1999. LC 00-21465. 2000. write for info. (*981-02-4197-6*) World Scientific Pub.

Lu, John H. Mandarin Chinese, Vol. I. LC 89-183898. 119p. (C). 1989. pap. 29.95 incl. audio (*0-9626654-0-1*) East Oak Hse.

— Mandarin Chinese, Vol. II. LC 89-183898. 129p. 1994. pap. 35.95 incl. audio (*0-9626654-1-X*) East Oak Hse.

***Lu, Ju S.** Tobacco: The Growing Epidemic: Proceedings of the Tenth World Conference on Tobacco or Health, 24-28 August 1997, Bejing, China LC 99-15363. 1999. write for info. (*981-4021-49-0*) Spr-Verlag.

Lu, Ju-Shan, jt. auth. see World Conference on Tobacco & Health Staff.

Lu, Jyhren & Shen, Kuo-I. How Did We Help Our Children to Increase Their IQ. Lu, Steve, ed. (Illus.). 96p. (Orig.). 1996. pap. write for info. (*1-889838-18-7*) Mgmt Syst Input.

Lu, Ke Y. The Essence of Qi Gong. 1998. pap. 13.95 (*0-9649912-1-7*) Abode Eternal Tao.

Lu, L., jt. ed. see Gardner, G. H.

Lu, L. H. The Static Strength of I-Beam to Rectangular Hollow Section Column Connections. (Illus.). 205p. 1997. pap. 52.50 (*90-407-1603-X*, Pub. by Delft U Pr) Coronet Bks.

Lu, Li. Moving the Mountain: My Life in China. 1990. 21.95 (*0-399-13545-6*) Putnam Pub Group.

Lu, Li & Lai, Man O. Mechanical Alloying. LC 97-35207. xv, 276p. 1998. text 135.00 (*0-7923-8066-5*) Kluwer Academic.

Lu, Luisw & Fine, Howard I. Phacoemulsification in Difficult & Challenging Cases. LC 98-4055. 1998. write for info. (*3-13-114671-0*) Thieme Med Pubs.

— Phacoemulsification in Difficult & Challenging Cases. LC 98-4055. (Illus.). 200p. 1998. 99.00 (*0-86577-791-8*) Thieme Med Pubs.

Lu, Min-Zhan, jt. auth. see Haswell, Richard H.

Lu, Min-Zhan, jt. auth. see Horner, Bruce.

Lu, Ming-Wei, jt. ed. see Pham, Hoang.

***Lu, Nan.** TCM: A Woman's Guide to Trouble-Free Menopause. 384p. 2000. pap. 14.00 (*0-380-80904-4*) Morrow Avon.

— Traditional Chinese Medicine: A Natural Guide to Weight Loss That Lasts. 384p. 2000. pap. 14.00 (*0-380-80905-2*, HarpRes) HarpInfo.

Lu, Nan & Schaplowsky, Ellen. TCM: A Woman's Guide to Healing from Breast Cancer. LC 99-94877. 384p. 1999. pap. 14.00 (*0-380-80902-8*, Avon Bks) Morrow Avon.

Lu, Nancy. A Rainbow Childhood. (CHI., Illus.). 88p. (Orig.). 1997. pap. 14.95 (*1-889838-98-5*) Mgmt Syst Input.

Lu, Ning. Flashpoint Spratlys! LC 97-945723. 214 p. 1995. write for info. (*981-00-6617-1*) AgBe Pub.

— Fractal Imaging. LC 97-6616. (Illus.). 432p. 1997. text 49.95 (*0-12-458010-6*) Morgan Kaufmann.

Lu, Oliver, tr. Gustav Just: Witness in His Own Cause: The Fifties in the German Democratic Republic. 170p. (C). 1995. lib. bdg. 39.00 (*0-7618-0107-3*) U Pr of Amer.

Lu, P. & Opella, Stanley J., eds. NMR & Biochemistry: A Symposium Honoring Mildred Cohn. LC 79-19485. (Illus.). 448p. reprint ed. pap. 138.90 (*0-7837-0618-9*, 204096300019) Bks Demand.

Lu, Pamela. Pamela: A Novel. LC 99-230981. 98p. 1998. pap. 12.95 (*1-891190-04-0*, Pub. by Atelos) SPD-Small Pr Dist.

Lu, Pau-Chang. Fluid Mechanics: An Introductory Course. LC 78-15543. (Illus.). 494p. 1979. reprint ed. pap. 153.20 (*0-608-00098-1*, 206086300006) Bks Demand.

Lu, Phillip, jt. ed. see Davis Philip, A. G.

***Lu, Qiwen.** China's Leap into the Information Age: Innovation & Organization in the Computer Industry. LC 99-86804. (Illus.). 300p. 2000. text 72.00 (*0-19-829537-5*) OUP.

Lu, Quincey, jt. auth. see Wong, Vivien.

Lu, R. Q. New Approaches to Knowledge Acquisition. 360p. 1994. text 58.00 (*981-02-1316-6*) World Scientific Pub.

Lu, S. C., jt. auth. see Wilhelm, R.

Lu, S. Z. Four Lectures on Real HP Spaces. 228p. 1995. text 53.00 (*981-02-2158-4*) World Scientific Pub.

Lu, Sarah. Teach Yourself Living Mandarin Vol. 1: Beginner's Course, Set. 236p. 1988. pap. 69.95 incl. audio (*0-582-99910-3*) Cheng & Tsui.

— Teach Yourself Living Mandarin Vol. 2: Lower Intermediate Course, 2 cass., Set. 182p. 1994. pap. 69.95 incl. audio (*962-00-0071-4*) Cheng & Tsui.

Lu, Sheldon H. From Historicity to Fictionality: The Chinese Poetics of Narrative. LC 93-31744. xii, 213p. 1994. 39.50 (*0-8047-2319-2*) Stanford U Pr.

Lu, Sheldon H., ed. Transnational Chinese Cinemas: Identity, Nationhood, Gender. LC 97-11153. (Illus.). 432p. 1997. pap. text 28.00 (*0-8248-1845-8*) UH Pr.

Lu, Shen-Shin. Insider Trading & the Twenty-Four Hour Securities Market: A Case Study of Legal Regulation in the Emerging Global Economy. LC 95-70227. (Illus.). 264p. (C). 1999. 24.95 (*0-8158-0516-0*) Chris Mass.

Lu, Sheng-Yen. A Complete & Detailed Exposition on the True Buddha Dharma. Chow, Janny, tr. LC 95-22298. 1995. pap. 10.00 (*1-881493-04-0*) Purple Lotus Soc.

— Dharma Talks by a Living Buddha. Chow, Janny, tr. LC 94-36517. 1994. pap. 10.00 (*1-881493-05-9*) Purple Lotus Soc.

— Encounters with the World of Spirits. Chow, Janny, tr. from CHI. LC 95-8839.Tr. of Ling Chi Shen Suan Man Tan. 1995. write for info. (*1-881493-03-2*) Purple Lotus Soc.

— The Mystical Experiences of True Buddha Disciples. rev. ed. Ho, Siong-Chow et al, trs. from CHI. 192p. 1993. pap. 10.00 (*1-881493-01-6*) Purple Lotus Soc.

— New Realm of the Buddhaking. LC 98-52714. 1999. pap. write for info. (*1-881493-07-5*) Purple Lotus Soc.

— An Overview of the Buddhadharma. Chow, Janny, tr. from CHI. LC 97-11942. 1997. pap. write for info. (*1-881493-06-7*) Purple Lotus Soc.

***Lu, Shenghui.** Transformation et Reception Du Texte Par le Film. (Regards Sur l'Image: Vol. 3). 1999. 51.95 (*3-906759-88-1*, Pub. by P Lang) P Lang Pubng.

Lu, Steve, ed. see Lu, Jyhren & Shen, Kuo-I.

Lu, T. M., et al. Diffraction from Rough Surfaces & Growth Fronts. 240p. 1993. text 48.00 (*981-02-1536-3*) World Scientific Pub.

***Lu, Toh-Ming.** Turmoil & Opportunities in Higher Education: The Road of an Academic Department at the Dawn of the 21st Century. 218p. 2000. pap. 15.00 (*0-9675372-0-7*) TM Lu.

Lu, Tonglin, ed. Gender & Sexuality in Twentieth Century Chinese Literature & Society. LC 92-6365. (SUNY Series in Feminist Criticism & Theory). 204p. (C). 1993. pap. text 21.95 (*0-7914-1372-1*) State U NY Pr.

— Gender & Sexuality in Twentieth-Century Chinese Literature & Society. LC 92-6365. (SUNY Series in Feminist Criticism & Theory). 204p. (C). 1993. text 64.50 (*0-7914-1371-3*) State U NY Pr.

Lu Van Thanh. The Inviting Call of Wandering Souls: Memoir of an Arvn Liaison Officer to United States Forces in Vietnam Who Was Imprisoned in Communist Re-Education Camps & Then Escaped. LC 97-26162. (Illus.). 197p. 1997. pap. 26.50 (*0-7864-0374-8*) McFarland & Co.

Lu, Vivian H., et al. Pattern Sentence: For Elementary Chinese. (CHI.). 1994. pap. 14.95 (*0-88710-182-8*) Yale Far Eastern Pubns.

Lu, Wei, jt. ed. see Andrieu, Jean-Marie.

Lu, Wu-Sheng & Antoniou, Andreas. Two-Dimensional Digital Filters. LC 92-18745. (Electrical Engineering & Electronics Ser.: Vol. 80). (Illus.). 416p. 1992. text 155.00 (*0-8247-8434-0*) Dekker.

Lu, Xiaobo & Perry, Elizabeth J., eds. Danwei: The Changing Chinese Workplace in Historical & Comparative Perspective. LC 97-9979. (Socialism & Social Movements Ser.). 270p. (C). (gr. 13). 1997. text 80.95 (*0-7656-0075-7*, East Gate Bk); pap. text 34.95 (*0-7656-0076-5*, East Gate Bk) M E Sharpe.

Lu, Y. C., ed. Palaeontologia Cathayana, Vol. 5. 334p. 1990. 118.95 (*0-387-52145-3*) Spr-Verlag.

Lu, Y. P., jt. auth. see Sun, C. T.

Lu, Yingzhong. Fueling One Billion: An Insider's Story of Chinese Energy Policy Development. (Illus.). 266p. 1993. 24.95 (*0-88702-064-X*); pap. 19.95 (*0-88702-065-8*) Washington Inst Pr.

Lu, Yong-Zai, ed. Industrial Intelligent Control: Fundamentals & Applications. 346p. 1996. 149.95 (*0-471-95058-0*, EE20) Wiley.

Lu, Yong-Zai & Williams, Theodore J. Modelling, Estimation & Control of the Soaking Pit: An Example of the Development & Application of Some Modern Control Techniques to Industrial Processes. LC 83-101. (Illus.). 482p. reprint ed. pap. 149.50 (*0-8357-2998-2*, 203926600011) Bks Demand.

Lu, Youngling, jt. ed. see Hayoe, Ruth.

Lu, Yu, et al. Low-Dimensional Quantum Field Theories for Condensed Matter Physicists - Lecture Notes of ICTP. (Series on Modern Condensed Matter Physics: Vol. 6). 624p. 1995. text 109.00 (*981-02-2140-1*) World Scientific Pub.

Lu, Yu, jt. auth. see Randjbar-Daemi, S.

Lu, Yu, jt. ed. see Butcher, P. N.

Lu, Yuan. Management Decision Making in Chinese Enterprises. (Studies on the Chinese Economy). 230p. 1996. text 69.95 (*0-312-15850-5*) St Martin.

Lu, Yuan, jt. ed. see Child, John.

Lu, Z. W., ed. Mathematical Logic for Computer Science. (Series in Computer Science: Vol. 13). 260p. (C). 1989. text 60.00 (*9971-5-0251-8*) World Scientific Pub.

Lu, Zuyin. Scientific Qigong Exploration: The Wonders & Mysteries of Qi. Dao, Ming, ed. Lin, Hui, tr. LC 97-74377. (Illus.). 404p. 1997. 36.00 (*0-9657135-7-1*) Amber Leaf.

Luaces, Juan G., tr. see Bronte, Charlotte.

***Lualdi, Katharine Jackson & Thayer, Anne T.** Penitence in the Age of Reformations. LC 00-38981. (St. Andrews Studies in Reformation History). 2000. write for info. (*0-7546-0096-3*, Pub. by Ashgate Pub) Ashgate Pub Co.

***LuAllen, Matthew.** CCNP Support Exam Cram. LC 00-22734. (Exam Cram Ser.). (Illus.). 400p. 2000. pap. write for info. (*1-57610-681-0*) Coriolis Grp.

***Luan, Lee Seng, et al.** Wavelets, Splines & Applications for Engineers & Computer Scientists. 400p. 1999. 38.00 (*981-02-4065-1*) World Scientific Pub.

Luangpraseut, Khamchong. Cambodia & Cambodians. (CAM., Illus.). 96p. (Orig.). (J). (gr. 2-5). 1995. pap. 13.95 (*1-879600-40-4*) Pac Asia Pr.

— Laos & Laotians. (ENG & LAO., Illus.). 96p. (Orig.). (J). (gr. 2-5). 1995. pap. 14.95 (*1-879600-41-2*) Pac Asia Pr.

— Vietnam & Vietnamese. (VIE., Illus.). 96p. (Orig.). (J). (gr. 2-5). 1995. pap. 13.95 (*1-879600-43-9*) Pac Asia Pr.

***Luard.** Family Life. 2000. pap. 12.95 (*0-552-14544-0*, Pub. by Transworld Publishers Ltd) Trafalgar.

— Horse - Its Action & Anatomy. 2000. pap. 29.95 (*0-85131-645-X*, Pub. by J A Allen) Trafalgar.

Luard, Elisabeth. The Cooking of Spain. 96p. (Orig.). 1997. reprint ed. pap. text 15.00 (*0-7881-5032-4*) DIANE Pub.

***Luard, Elisabeth.** The Old World Kitchen: The Rich Tradition of European Peasant Cooking. (Common Reader Edition Ser.). 2000. reprint ed. pap. 24.95 (*1-888173-50-5*, Pub. by Akadine Pr) Trafalgar.

***Luard, Elizabeth.** Emerald. 2000. 16.95 (*0-593-02243-2*, Pub. by Transworld Publishers Ltd) Trafalgar.

Luard, Evan. The Balance of Power: The System of International Relations, 1648-1815. 340p. 1992. text 59.95 (*0-312-06208-7*) St Martin.

— The Blunted Sword: The Erosion of Military Power in Modern World Politics. 196p. (C). 1989. 25.00 (*0-941533-48-4*, NAB) I R Dee.

— Conflict & Peace in the Modern International System: A Study of the Principles of International Order. LC 87-27977. 318p. (C). 1988. text 64.50 (*0-88706-696-8*); pap. text 21.95 (*0-88706-697-6*) State U NY Pr.

— International Society. 273p. (C). 1990. 25.00 (*0-941533-80-8*, NAB) I R Dee.

Luard, Evan, intro. Basic Texts in International Relations: The Evolution of Ideas about International Society. LC 91-10832. 300p. (C). 1992. pap. 24.95 (*0-312-06511-6*); text 49.95 (*0-312-06506-X*) St Martin.

Luard, Henry R., ed. Annales Monastici: Index & Glossary, Vol. 5. (Rolls Ser.: No. 36). 1972. 70.00 (*0-8115-1088-3*) Periodicals Srv.

— Annales Monastici Vol. 1: De Margam, Vol. 1. (Rolls Ser.: No. 36). 1972. 70.00 (*0-8115-1084-0*) Periodicals Srv.

— Annales Monastici Vol. 2: De Wintonia. (Rolls Ser.: No. 36). 1972. 70.00 (*0-8115-1085-9*) Periodicals Srv.

— Annales Monastici Vol. 3: De Dunstaplia. (Rolls Ser.: No. 36). 1972. 70.00 (*0-8115-1086-7*) Periodicals Srv.

— Annales Monastici Vol. 4: De Osenia. (Rolls Ser.: No. 36). 1972. 70.00 (*0-8115-1087-5*) Periodicals Srv.

— Bartholomaeus de Cotton, Historia Anglicana (499-1298) Necnon Ejusdem Liber de Archiepiscopis et Episcopis Angliae. (Rolls Ser.: No. 16). 1972. reprint ed. 70.00 (*0-8115-1021-2*) Periodicals Srv.

— Flores Historiarum per Mattaeum Westmonasteriensem Collecti Vol. 1: Creation-1066. (Rolls Ser.: No. 95). 1972. write for info. (*0-8115-1172-3*) Periodicals Srv.

— Flores Historiarum per Matthaeum Westmonasteriensem Collecti Vol. 2: 1067-1264. (Rolls Ser.: No. 95). 1972. write for info. (*0-8115-1173-1*) Periodicals Srv.

— Flores Historiarum per Matthaeum Westmonasteriensum Collecti Vol. 3: 1265-1326. (Rolls Ser.: No. 95). 1972. write for info. (*0-8115-1174-X*) Periodicals Srv.

— Lives of Edward the Confessor. (Rolls Ser.: No. 3). 1969. reprint ed. 70.00 (*0-8115-1003-4*) Periodicals Srv.

— Matthaei Parisiensis, Monachi Sancti Albani: Chronica Majora, 7 vols., Set. Incl. Vol. 1. Creation-1066. 1969. (*0-8115-1119-7*); Vol. 2. 1067-1216. Luard, Henry R. 1969. (*0-8115-1120-0*); Vol. 6. Additamenta. 1969. (*0-8115-1124-3*); Vol. 7. Index Glossary. 1969. (*0-8115-1125-1*); Vol. 3. 1216-1239. 1969. (*0-8115-1121-9*); 1240-1247. 1969. (*0-8115-1122-7*); 1248-1259. 1969. (*0-8115-1123-5*); (Rolls Ser.: No. 57). 1969. reprint ed. 490.00 (*0-685-10006-5*) Periodicals Srv.

— Roberti Grosseteste Episcopi Quondam Lincolniensis Epistolae. (Rolls Ser.: No. 25). 1974. reprint ed. 70.00 (*0-8115-1041-7*) Periodicals Srv.

Luard, Nicholas. Himalaya. large type ed. 640p. 1994. 27.99 (*0-7089-8774-5*) Ulverscroft.

Luark, Patterson F. From the Old Northwest to the Pacific Northwest: The 1853 Oregon Trail Diaries of Patterson Fletcher Luark & Michael Fleenen Luark. LC 98-31797. 1998. 27.95 (*0-9635901-7-0*) OR-CA Trails.

Luark, Patterson F., et al. From the Old Northwest to the Pacific Northwest: The 1853 Oregon Trail Diaries of Patterson Fletcher Luark & Michael Fleenen Luark. LC 98-31797. (Emigrant Trails Historical Studies Ser.). 1998. pap. 14.95 (*0-9635901-8-9*) OR-CA Trails.

Luba, Thea, ed. see Bauer, Billy.

Lubac, Henri De, see De Lubac, Henri.

Lubach, Vanessa, jt. auth. see Pfeffer, Wendy.

Lubala, R. T., jt. ed. see Kampunzu, A. B.

Luban, David. Just War & Human Rights. 66p. 1980. 2.50 (*0-318-17326-3*) IPPP.

— Legal Modernism. (Law, Meaning, & Violence Ser.). 424p. (C). 1994. text 59.50 (*0-472-10380-6*, 10380) U of Mich Pr.

— Legal Modernism. 424p. (C). 1997. pap. text 25.95 (*0-472-08439-9*, 08439) U of Mich Pr.

— Paternalism & the Legal Profession. 1981. 2.50 (*0-318-33307-4*) IPPP.

Luban, David, ed. The Ethics of Lawyers. LC 94-30377. (The International Library of Essays in Law & Theory, Areas Ser.: Vol. 25). (C). 1993. lib. bdg. 150.00 (*0-8147-5066-4*) NYU Pr.

— The Good Lawyer: Lawyers' Roles & Lawyers' Ethics. LC 83-16125. (Maryland Studies in Public Philosophy). 376p. 1984. 60.00 (*0-8476-7276-X*) IPPP.

— The Good Lawyer: Lawyer's Roles & Lawyers' Ethics. 1984. 60.00 (*0-317-05528-3*); pap. 27.25 (*0-317-05225-X*) IPPP.

Luban, David & Rhode, Deborah L. Legal Ethics. 2nd ed. (University Casebook Ser.), 930p. 1995. text 43.00 (*1-56662-249-2*) Foundation Pr.

Luban, David J. & Rhode, Deborah L. Legal Ethics: Cases & Materials. (University Casebook Ser.). 1040p. (C). 1991. text 42.95 (*0-88277-939-7*) Foundation Pr.

Luban, David J., jt. auth. see Rhode, Deborah L.

Luban, Haim. Adam & Eve in the Garden of Eden: Exploring the Foundations of Jewish Thought. 1998. 30.00 (*0-7657-6014-2*) Aronson.

Luban, Marianne. The Samaritan Treasure. LC 90-2690. 226p. (Orig.). 1990. pap. 9.95 (*0-918273-79-X*) Coffee Hse.

Luban, Naomi L., ed. Transfusion Therapy in Infants & Children. LC 90-4280. (Johns Hopkins Series in Contemporary Medicine & Public Health). (Illus.). 248p. reprint ed. pap. 76.90 (*0-608-06165-4*, 206649800008) Bks Demand.

***Luban, Ruth.** Are You a Corporate Refugee? A Survival Guide for Downsized, Disillusioned & Displaced Workers. 2001. pap. 15.00 (*0-14-029632-8*) Penguin Putnam.

Luban, Ruth & Luban, Ruth J. Burnout: Keeping the Fire. 28p. 1996. pap. 19.95 incl. audio (*1-55678-058-3*, 3270) Learn Inc.

Luban, Ruth J. Keeping the Fire from Burnout to Balance. 125p. 1995. spiral bd. 15.00 (*0-9641741-0-3*) R Luban Audio & Bks.

Luban, Ruth J., jt. auth. see Luban, Ruth.

Lubar, David. The Accidental Vampire, Vol. 1. (Accidental Monsters Ser.). 144p. (J). (gr. 3-7). 1997. pap. text 3.99 (*0-590-90718-2*) Scholastic Inc.

— Gloomy Ghost. Vol. 4. (J). (gr. 3-7). 1998. pap. text 3.99 (*0-590-90721-2*) Scholastic Inc.

***Lubar, David.** Gloomy Ghost, 4. (Accidental Monsters Ser.). 1998. 9.09 (*0-606-13108-6*, Pub. by Turtleback) Demco.

Lubar, David. Hidden Talents. LC 99-24560. 224p. 1999. 16.95 (*0-312-86646-1*, Pub. by Tor Bks) St Martin.

***Lubar, David.** Hidden Talents. 2000. 4.99 (*0-8125-4170-7*) Tor Bks.

Lubar, David. It's Not a Bug, It's a Feature! Computer Wit & Wisdom. 208p. (C). 1995. pap. text 9.95 (*0-201-48304-1*) Addison-Wesley.

***Lubar, David.** Monster Road. (Illus.). 128p. (gr. 2-5). 1999. pap. 3.99 (*0-590-28168-2*) Scholastic Inc.

Lubar, David. Psychozone: Kidzilla & Other Stories. 1997. pap. 4.99 (*0-8125-5880-4*, Pub. by Tor Bks) St Martin.

— Psychozone: The Witches' Monkey & Other Stories. 1997. mass mkt. 4.99 (*0-8125-5881-2*, Pub. by Tor Bks) St Martin.

— Unwilling Witch. (Accidental Monsters Ser.). 1997. 9.09 (*0-606-11022-4*, Pub. by Turtleback) Demco.

— Unwilling Witch, Vol. 2. (The Accidental Monsters Ser.: Vol. 2). 144p. (J). (gr. 3-7). 1997. pap. text 3.99 (*0-590-90719-0*) Scholastic Inc.

— Vanishing Vampire. (Accidental Monsters Ser.). 1997. 9.09 (*0-606-11021-6*, Pub. by Turtleback) Demco.

— The Wavering Werewolf. (The Accidental Monsters Ser.: No. 3). (J). 1997. pap. 3.99 (*0-590-90720-4*, Little Apple) Scholastic Inc.

— The Wavering Werewolf, 3. (Accidental Monsters Ser.). 1997. 9.09 (*0-606-12867-0*, Pub. by Turtleback) Demco.

Lubar, Robert S. Antoni Tapies. LC 93-83249. (Illus.). 64p. (Orig.). 1993. pap. write for info. (*1-878283-28-6*) PaceWildenstein.

***Lubar, Robert S.** Dali: The Salvador Dali Museum Collection, St. Petersburg, Florida. LC 99-87333. (Illus.). 208p. 2000. 60.00 (*0-8212-2480-8*, Pub. by Bulfinch Pr) Little.

Lubar, Steven & Kingery, W. David, eds. History from Things: Essays on Material Culture. LC 92-20535. (Illus.). 352p. (C). 1996. reprint ed. pap. text 15.95 (*1-56098-613-1*) Smithsonian.

Lubar, Steven, jt. auth. see Hindle, Brooke.

An Asterisk (*) at the beginning of an entry indicates that the title is appearing for the first time.

Lubaroff, Martin I. & Altman, Paul M. Limited Partnerships: A Practitioner's Guide under Delaware Law, 2 vols. 1270p. 1992. ring bd. 225.00 (*0-13-110222-2*) Aspen Law.

— Lubaroff & Altman on Delaware Limited Partnerships. LC 95-43524. 1270p. 1998. ring bd. 185.00 (*1-56706-288-1*) Aspen Law.

Lubarsky, David A., jt. auth. see Gallagher, Christopher J.

Lubarsky, Jared. Noble Heritage: Five Centuries of Portraits from the Hosokawa Family. LC 92-12047. (Illus.). 112p. (Orig.). 1992. pap. 24.95 (*1-56098-209-8*) Smithsonian.

Lubarsky, Sandra B. Tolerance & Transformation: Jewish Approaches to Religious Pluralism. LC 90-4206. (Jewish Perspectives Ser.: Vol. 4). 159p. 1990. reprint ed. pap. 49.30 (*0-608-00734-X*, 206151000009) Bks Demand.

Lubarsky, Sandra B. & Griffin, David R., eds. Jewish Theology & Process Thought. LC 95-22274. (SUNY Series in Constructive Postmodern Thought). 328p. (C). 1996. text 64.50 (*0-7914-2809-5*); pap. text 21.95 (*0-7914-2810-9*) State U NY Pr.

Lubarsky, Steve, et al. How to Improve Your Racquetball. 1980. pap. 5.00 (*0-87980-374-6*) Wilshire.

***Lubasch, Lisa.** How Many More of Them Are You? 99p. 1999. pap. 14.00 (*1-880713-19-5*, Pub. by AVEC Bks) SPD-Small Pr Dist.

Lubatti, H. & Green, D., eds. Physics at Fermilab in the 1990's. 576p. (C). 1990. text 113.00 (*981-02-0103-6*) World Scientific Pub.

Lubavitch Women's Organization Staff. The Spice & Spirit of Kosher-Jewish Cooking. Blau, Esther, ed. LC 77-72116. (Illus.). 1977. 16.95 (*0-930178-01-7*) Lubavitch Women.

Lubbe, G. F. & Murray, C. Farlam & Hathaway: Contract - Cases, Commentary & Materials. 3rd ed. 825p. 1988. write for info. (*0-7021-2172-X*, Pub. by Juta & Co); pap. 53.00 (*0-7021-2173-8*, Pub. by Juta & Co) Gaunt.

Lubbe, Jan C. van der, see Van der Lubbe, Jan C.

Lubbe, Jan C. Van Der, see Van Der Lubbe, Jan C.

Lubbe, Klaus. Deutsche Seitengewehre und Bajonette, 1740-1945. (GER., Illus.). 279p. 1991. pap. 25.00 (*3-926598-48-4*) Johnson Ref Bks.

Lubbe, Sam. Information Technology in Developing Countries: An Assessment & Practical Guideline. LC 98-51687. 232p. 1999. pap. text 49.95 (*1-878289-55-1*) Idea Group Pub.

Lubbeke, Isolde. Early German Painting in the Thyssen-Bornemisza Collection, 1350-1530. (Illus.). 432p. 1991. 250.00 (*0-85667-376-5*) Sothebys Pubns.

Lubben, Twyla & Hunt, Linda L. Christina's World. 160p. (Orig.). 1985. pap. 3.95 (*0-310-36921-5*, 11650P) Zondervan.

Lubbers, Darcy, jt. ed. see Landgarten, Helen B.

***Lubbers, David.** Persistence of Vision. (Illus.). 96p. 2000. 48.00 (*0-8028-3884-7*) Eerdmans.

Lubbers, David & Rowe, Stephen C. Abiding: Landscape of the Soul. LC 98-34647. (Illus.). 64p. 1998. 35.00 (*0-8028-3859-6*) Eerdmans.

Lubbers, Frank. El Lissitzky, 1890-1941. 1991. pap. 55.00 (*0-500-97393-8*, Pub. by Thames Hudson) Norton.

Lubbers, Jeffrey S. A Guide to Federal Agency Rulemaking. 3rd ed. LC 98-15306. 1998. write for info. (*1-57073-568-9*) Amer Bar Assn.

Lubbers, Ruud. Europe, a Continent of Traditions. (William & Mary Lecture: No. 1). 28p. (C). 1994. pap. text 7.95 (*0-521-46708-X*) Cambridge U Pr.

Lubbers, Terry, jt. auth. see Cox, Lynn.

Lubbig, H., jt. ed. see Koch, H.

Lubbig, Heinz, jt. ed. see Hahlbohm, Hans-Dieter.

Lubbock, Basil. The Arctic Whalers. (C). 1987. 138.00 (*0-85174-107-X*) St Mut.

— The Blackwall Frigates. (C). 1987. 114.00 (*0-85174-108-8*) St Mut.

— The China Clippers. (C). 1987. 126.00 (*0-85174-109-6*) St Mut.

— The Colonial Clippers. (C). 1987. 126.00 (*0-85174-110-X*) St Mut.

— Coolie Ships & Oil Sailers. (C). 1987. 125.00 (*0-85174-111-8*) St Mut.

— The Down Easters. (C). 1987. 125.00 (*0-85174-112-6*) St Mut.

— The Last of the Windjammers, Vol. I. (C). 1987. 126.00 (*0-85174-113-4*) St Mut.

— The Last of the Windjammers, Vol. II. (C). 1987. 126.00 (*0-85174-114-2*) St Mut.

— The Log of the Cutty Sark. (C). 1987. 145.00 (*0-85174-115-0*) St Mut.

— The Nitrate Clippers. (C). 1987. 125.00 (*0-85174-116-9*) St Mut.

— The Nitrate Clippers: History of Sailing Ships & Trade Along the West Coast of South America. 1979. lib. bdg. 75.00 (*0-8490-2978-3*) Gordon Pr.

— The Opium Clippers. (C). 1987. 150.00 (*0-85174-241-6*) St Mut.

— Round the Horn Before the Mast. (C). 1987. 120.00 (*0-85174-506-7*) St Mut.

— The Western Ocean Packets. (C). 1987. 120.00 (*0-85174-118-5*) St Mut.

— The Western Ocean Packets. (Illus.). 192p. 1988. reprint ed. pap. 5.95 (*0-486-25684-7*) Dover.

Lubbock, John. Pre-Historic Times. LC 74-169771. (Select Bibliographies Reprint Ser.). 1977. reprint ed. 42.95 (*0-8369-5991-4*) Ayer.

— Scientific Lectures. LC 72-4522. (Essay Index Reprint Ser.). 1977. reprint ed. 20.95 (*0-8369-2960-8*) Ayer.

— The Uses of Life. LC 72-4585. (Essay Index Reprint Ser.). 1977. reprint ed. 23.95 (*0-8369-2961-6*) Ayer.

— Wild Flowering Plants Relation to Insects. 194p. 1989. 100.00 (*81-7041-178-5*, Pub. by Scientific Pubs) St Mut.

Lubbock, Jules. The Tyranny of Taste: A Study of British Public Policy on Design Architecture & Town Planning Since 1550. LC 94-26853. 1995. 60.00 (*0-300-05889-6*) Yale U Pr.

Lubbock, Jules, jt. auth. see Crinson, Mark.

***Lubbock, Mark & Krosch, Louise.** E-Commerce: Dong Business Electronically. (Legal Guidance Ser.). vi, 74p. 2000. 20.00 (*0-11-702392-2*, Pub. by Statnry Office) Balogh.

Lubbock, Percy. Earlham. LC 74-11936. (Illus.). 254p. 1974. reprint ed. lib. bdg. 65.00 (*0-8371-7722-7*, LUEA, Greenwood Pr) Greenwood.

— Elizabeth Barrett Browning in Her Letters. LC 75-148814. reprint ed. 52.50 (*0-404-08879-1*) AMS Pr.

Lubbock, Roger, jt. auth. see Keen, Alan.

Lube, E. L., jt. auth. see Bagdasarov, Kh S.

Lubec, G. Noninvasive Diagnosis of Kidney Disease. (Continuing Education Ser.: Vol. 3). (Illus.). xii, 368p. 1983. 85.25 (*3-8055-3051-X*) S Karger.

— Renal Immunology. (Contributions to Nephrology Ser.: Vol. 35). (Illus.). vi, 194p. 1983. pap. 29.75 (*3-8055-3587-2*) S Karger.

Lubec, G., ed. The Glomerular Basement Membrane. (Illus.). vii, 434p. 1981. 135.75 (*3-8055-2952-X*) S Karger.

***Lubec, G., ed.** The Molecular Biology of Down Syndrome. LC 99-59530. (Journal of Neural Transmission Ser.: Suppl. 57, 1999). (Illus.). 350p. 1999. 119.00 (*3-211-83378-1*) Spr-Verlag.

Lubec, Gert & Rosenthal, Gerald A., eds. Amino Acids Chemistry, Biology & Medicine. 1992. text 344.50 (*90-72199-04-9*) Kluwer Academic.

Lubeck, Maria-Garza & Salinas, Ana M. Mexican Celebrations. 54p. (J). (gr. k-12). 1987. pap. text 3.95 (*0-86728-019-0*) U TX Inst Lat Am Stud.

Lubeck, Sally, jt. ed. see Swadener, Beth B.

Lubeck, Walter. Complete Reiki Handbook. 191p. 1994. pap. 14.95 (*0-941524-87-6*) Lotus Pr.

— Healing Power of Pau D'Arco. LC 97-78481. 132p. 1998. pap. 12.95 (*0-914955-52-7*) Lotus Pr.

***Lubeck, Walter.** L-Carnitine: The Supernutrient for Fitness: The Safe & Stress-Free Way to Manage Weight, Increase Physical Performance & Mental. (Illus.). 2000. pap. 14.95 (*0-914955-59-4*) Lotus Pr.

Lubeck, Walter. Pendulum Healing Handbook. LC 97-76439. (Sangri-La Ser.). 208p. 1998. pap. 15.95 (*0-914955-54-3*) Lotus Pr.

— Reiki - for First Aid: Reiki Treatment As Accompanying Therapy for Over 40 Types of Illness. With a Supplement on Natural Healing. 160p. (Orig.). 1995. pap. 14.95 (*0-914955-26-8*) Lotus Pr.

— Reiki - Way of the Heart: The Reiki Path of Initiation. (Illus.). 191p. (Orig.). 1996. pap. 14.95 (*0-941524-91-4*) Lotus Pr.

Lubecki, John. The End of Cancer. 2nd ed. (Illus.). 198p. reprint ed. write for info. (*1-884030-00-9*) Better Hlth Bks.

Lubek, Ian, et al, eds. Trends & Issues in Theoretical Psychology. 412p. 1995. pap. 69.95 (*0-8261-8810-9*) Springer Pub.

Lubell. English for the Disenchanted. (EC - HS Communication/English Ser.). 1992. mass mkt. 18.95 (*0-538-60995-8*) S-W Pub.

— Language Works. (EC - HS Communication/English Ser.). 1991. mass mkt. 11.95 (*0-538-60947-8*) S-W Pub.

Lubell, David L. The Cath Lab: An Introduction. 2nd ed. LC 92-48998. (Illus.). 144p. 1993. pap. text 29.95 (*0-8121-1675-5*) Lppncott W & W.

Lubell, Ellen B., jt. auth. see Wynne, Mary E.

Lubell, Marcia, jt. auth. see Townsend, Ruth.

Lubell, Myron S. The Significance of Organizational Conflict on the Legislative Evolution of the Accounting Profession in the United States. Brief, Richard P., ed. LC 80-1515. (Dimensions of Accounting Theory & Practice Ser.). 1980. lib. bdg. 49.95 (*0-405-13494-0*) Ayer.

Lubell, Winifred M. The Metamorphosis of Baubo: Myths of Woman's Sexual Energy. (Illus.). 219p. (C). 1998. pap. text 16.00 (*0-7881-5588-1*) DIANE Pub.

Lubelska, Diana & Matthews, Margaret. Looking at Language Classrooms: Trainer's Guide. LC 97-222165. (Illus.). 1997. write for info. (*0-521-58873-1*) Cambridge U Pr.

Lubenenco, J., jt. ed. see Hobson, S.

Lubenow, Gerald C., ed. California Votes - The 1990 Governor's Race: An Inside Look at the Candidates & Their Campaigns by the People Who Managed Them. LC 91-29441. 240p. (Orig.). (C). 1991. pap. 15.95 (*0-87772-329-X*) UCB IGS.

— California Votes - The 1994 Governor's Race: An Inside Look at the Candidates & Their Campaigns by the People Who Managed Them. LC 95-51696. 296p. (Orig.). 1995. pap. 19.95 (*0-87772-367-2*) UCB IGS.

***Lubenow, Gerald C., ed.** The 1998 Governor's Race: An Inside Look at the Candidates & Their Campaign by the People Who Managed Them. LC 99-38459. 310p. 1999. pap. 21.95 (*0-87772-390-7*) UCB IGS.

Lubenow, Gerald C. & Cain, Bruce E., eds. Governing California: Politics, Government, & Public Policy in the Golden State. LC 97-36692. 373p. 1997. pap. 19.95 (*0-87772-376-1*) UCB IGS.

Lubenow, W. C. The Cambridge Apostles, 1820-1914: Liberalism, Imagination & Friendship in British Intellectual & Professional Life. LC 97-35252. (Illus.). 472p. (C). 1999. text 59.95 (*0-521-57213-4*) Cambridge U Pr.

— Parliamentary Politics & the Home Rule Crisis: The British House of Commons in 1886. 450p. 1988. 85.00 (*0-19-822966-6*) OUP.

Lubens, Herman & Kiley, John C. Perish the Thought: The Stress Connection. 129p. (Orig.). 1995. pap. 14.95 (*0-9633198-4-1*) Jason Pr.

Lubensky. Nachalo, Bk. 2. 1996. pap., student ed. 48.75 (*0-07-039040-1*) McGraw.

— Nachalo: When in Russia. 1995. audio 11.56 (*0-07-039038-X*) McGraw.

— Nachalo: When in Russia Stdt Ca. 1997. audio 11.56 (*0-07-039045-2*) McGraw.

Lubensky, S. Random House Russian-English Dictionary. (ENG & RUS.). 1997. pap. write for info. (*0-679-77374-6*) Random Ref & Info.

Lubensky, Sophia. Random House Russian-English Dictionary of Idioms. 1044p. 1995. 75.00 (*0-679-40580-1*) Random.

Lubensky, Sophia & Ervin, Gerald L. Nachalo: When in Russia, Vol. 1. (C). 1996. pap., wbk. ed., lab manual ed. 25.94 (*0-07-038918-7*) McGraw.

— Nachalo: When in Russia, Vol. 1, Bk. 1. 368p. (C). 1996. 53.75 (*0-07-912203-5*) McGraw.

— Nachalo: When in Russia, Vol. 2. (C). 1996. pap., wbk. ed. 24.69 (*0-07-039042-8*) McGraw.

— Nachalo: When in Russia, Vol. 2. 368p. (C). 1997. 53.75 (*0-07-912205-1*) McGraw.

Lubensky, Sophia, et al. Nachalo: When in Russia. LC 95-41041. 1996. 49.95 (*0-07-038917-9*) McGraw.

Lubensky, T. C., jt. auth. see Chaikin, P. M.

Luber. Joan Miro: A Retrospective. 1991. pap. 29.50 (*0-89207-062-5*) S R Guggenheim.

Luber, Alan D. Solving Business Problems with MRP II. 2nd ed. 332p. 1995. pap. 44.95 (*1-55558-132-3*, Digital DEC) Buttrwrth-Heinemann.

Luber, B. Abruestungsatlas. Chancen und Risiken Des Amerikanischen Truppenabzugs Aus Der BRD. (Anstoesse Zur Friedensarbeit Ser.). (GER.). 98p. 1990. pap. 17.50 (*3-487-09377-4*) Lubrecht & Cramer.

Luber, Burkhard. When Trees Become the Enemy (Wenn Baeume Die Gegner Sind), Military Use of Defoliants. (ENG & GER.). 128p. 1990. pap. text 13.50 (*3-487-09372-3*) G Olms Pubs.

— When Trees Become the Enemy (Wenn Baume die Gegner Sind) Military Use of Defoliants - Militarische Verwendung von Entlaubungsmitteln. (Anstoesse Zur Friedensarbeit Ser.: Vol. 2). 136p. 1990. 11.57 (*0-685-66491-0*) G Olms Pubs.

— The World at Your Keyboard: An Alternative Guide to Global Computer Networking. 1993. pap. 15.95 (*1-897766-00-9*, Pub. by Jon Carpenter) Paul & Co Pubs.

Luber, Katherine C. Albrecht Durer & the Venetian Renaissance. LC 97-18153. (Illus.). 304p. (C). 1999. text 60.00 (*0-521-56288-0*) Cambridge U Pr.

Luber, Philip. Deliver Us from Evil. LC 95-96174. 324p. 1997. mass mkt. write for info. (*0-449-14940-4*) Fawcett.

— Forgive Us Our Sins. (Boston Mysteries Ser.). 1994. mass mkt. 5.99 (*0-449-14849-1*) Fawcett.

— Have Mercy on Us. 304p. 1999. mass mkt. 5.99 (*0-449-18330-0*, GM) Fawcett.

— Pray for Us. LC 97-97040. (Orig.). 1998. mass mkt. 5.99 (*0-449-18329-7*, GM) Fawcett.

Luber, R. F., ed. Partial Hospitalization: A Current Perspective. LC 78-31915. (Illus.). 222p. 1979. 39.50 (*0-306-40201-7*, Plenum Trade) Perseus Pubng.

Luber, Walter J. The Circle Form: A Picture Essay. (Illus.). 147p. 1995. ring bd. 30.00 (*0-9657477-0-0*) Circle Concepts.

Lubertozzi, Alex, ed. see Dykstra, Art.

Lubeski, Lori. Dissuasion Crowds the Slow Worker. LC 88-90557. 56p. 1988. 6.50 (*0-929022-01-7*) O Bks.

Lubet, Steven. Developing Deposition Skills: Vending Operator Inc. Vs. Nita Department of Transportation/ Materials for the Advocates. 2nd ed. 140p. 1993. pap. 22.95 (*1-55681-370-8*) Natl Inst Trial Ad.

— Developing Deposition Skills: Vending Operator Inc. Vs. Nita Department of Transportation/Materials for the Barristers. 2nd ed. 138p. 1993. pap. 22.95 (*1-55681-371-6*) Natl Inst Trial Ad.

— Expert Testimony: A Guide for Expert Witnesses & the Lawyers Who Examine Them. LC 98-33936. 1998. pap. 32.95 (*1-55681-595-6*) Natl Inst Trial Ad.

— Modern Trial Advocacy: Analysis & Practice. 2nd ed. LC 97-44830. 486p. 1997. 45.95 (*1-55681-539-5*) Natl Inst Trial Ad.

— Vending Operator, Inc. v. Nita Department of Transportation: Breach of Contract. 3rd ed. 238p. 1993. pap. 22.95 (*1-55681-368-6*) Natl Inst Trial Ad.

Lubet, Steven & Burns, Robert P. Problems & Materials in Evidence & Trial Advocacy. 2nd ed. LC 99-169128. 1998. 26.95 (*1-55681-632-4*) Natl Inst Trial Ad.

Lubet, Steven & Rosenbaum, Judith. Financial Disclosure by Judges: Functional Analysis & Critique. LC 89-84613. 128p. (Orig.). 1989. pap. 12.95 (*0-938870-43-2*) Am Judicature.

Lubet, Steven, et al. Modern Trial Advocacy, Canadian Edition. 424p. 1995. 44.95 (*1-55681-481-X*) Natl Inst Trial Ad.

Lubet, Steven, jt. auth. see Burns, Robert P.

Lubet, Steven, jt. auth. see Cooley, John W.

Lubetkin, Daniel I. Basic Estate Administration (1992) (Illus.). 270p. pap. 35.00 (*0-685-09818-4*) NJ Inst CLE.

Lubetkin, Wendy. Deng Xiaoping. (World Leaders Past & Present Ser.). (Illus.), 120p. (YA). (gr. 5 up). 1988. lib. bdg. 19.95 (*1-55546-830-6*) Chelsea Hse.

Lubetski, Meir & Gottlieb, Claire, eds. Boundaries of the Ancient Near Eastern World: A Tribute to Cyrus H. Gordon. (JSOTS Ser.: Vol. 273). 576p. 1998. 90.00 (*1-85075-871-9*, Pub. by Sheffield Acad) CUP Services.

***Lubetzky, Seymour, et al.** The Future of Cataloging: The Lubetzky Symposium, April 18, 1998, University of California, Los Angeles. LC 99-87247. (Illus.). 192p. 2000. 65.00 (*0-8389-0778-4*) ALA.

Lubheid, Colm. John Climacus, The Ladder of Divine Ascent. (Classics of Western Spirituality Ser.). 224p. 1982. pap. 15.95 (*0-8091-2330-4*) Paulist Pr.

Lubiano, Wahneema, ed. The House That Race Built: Original Essays by Toni Morrison, Angela Y. Davis, Cornel West, & Others on Black Americans & Politics in America Today. 336p. 1998. reprint ed. pap. 14.00 (*0-679-76068-7*) Vin Bks.

Lubiano, Wahneema H. The House That Race Built: Black Americans, U. S. Terrain. LC 96-25159. 1997. 26.00 (*0-679-44090-9*) Vin Bks.

Lubich, Chiara. A Call to Love. 2nd ed. Hearne, Jerry, tr. from ITA. 177p. 1989. pap. 9.95 (*1-56548-077-5*) New City.

— Christian Living Today: Meditations. 7th ed. LC 97-8616. 168p. 1997. pap. 9.95 (*1-56548-094-5*) New City.

— Christmas Joy: Spiritual Insights. LC 98-36054. 64p. 1998. 9.95 (*1-56548-120-8*) New City.

— Diary,1964-65. 188p. 1987. pap. 6.95 (*0-911782-55-9*) New City.

***Lubich, Chiara.** Heaven on Earth: Meditations & Reflections. 176p. 2000. 18.95 (*1-56548-145-3*); pap. 12.95 (*1-56548-144-5*) New City.

— Here & Now: Meditations on Living in the Present. 2000. 9.95 (*1-56548-138-0*) New City.

Lubich, Chiara. Jesus - The Heart of His Message: Unity & Jesus Forsaken. 2nd rev. ed. (Spirituality of Unity Ser.).Tr. of L'Unita e Gesu Abbandonato. 112p. 1997. pap. 8.95 (*1-56548-090-2*) New City.

— The Love That Comes from God: Reflections on the Family. Stead, Julian, tr. from ITA. (Spirituality of Unity Ser.). 96p. 1995. pap. 6.95 (*1-56548-030-9*) New City.

— When Our Love Is Charity Vol. 2: Spiritual Writings. New City Press Editorial Staff, ed. 152p. 1991. pap. 9.95 (*0-911782-93-1*) New City.

Lubich, Frederick A., ed. Death in Venice, Tonio Kroger, & Other Writings. LC 98-53761. (German Library: Vol. 63). 324p. (C). 1999. pap. 19.95 (*0-8264-0971-7*) Continuum.

Lubich, Frederick A., ed. see Mann, Thomas.

Lubich, Hannes P. Towards a CSCW Framework for Scientific Cooperation in Europe. LC 94-46548. (Lecture Notes in Computer Science Ser.: Vol. 889). 1995. 45.00 (*3-540-58844-2*) Spr-Verlag.

Lubick, Diana C., jt. auth. see Wallace, Andrew.

Lubick, Donald C., ed. Report to the Congress on Joint Liability & Innocent Spouse Issues. 58p. (C). 1998. pap. text 20.00 (*0-7881-7536-X*) DIANE Pub.

Lubick, George M. Petrified Forest National Park: A Wilderness Bound in Time. LC 95-32549. (Illus.). 212p. 1996. 47.00 (*0-8165-1604-9*) U of Ariz Pr.

— Petrified Forest National Park: A Wilderness Bound in Time. LC 95-32549. 212p. 1996. pap. 16.95 (*0-8165-1629-4*) U of Ariz Pr.

Lubicz Milosz, Oscar V. De, see De Lubicz Milosz, Oscar V.

Lubicz, R. A. Schwaller De, see Schwaller De Lubicz, R. A.

Lubieniecki, Stanislas. The History of the Polish Reformation: Stanislaw Lubieniecki & Nine Related Documents. Williams, George H., ed. (Harvard Theological Studies Ser.). (Illus.). 1008p. 1992. text 150.00 (*0-8006-7085-X*, 1-7085, Fortress Pr) Augsburg Fortress.

Lubin, Albert J. Stranger on the Earth: A Psychological Biography of Vincent Van Gogh. LC 96-14082. (Illus.). 304p. 1996. reprint ed. pap. 14.95 (*0-306-80726-2*) Da Capo.

Lubin, Alice W., et al, eds. Family Therapy: A Bibliography, 4. LC 88-18682. 470p. 1988. lib. bdg. 85.00 (*0-313-26172-5*, LFT/, Greenwood Pr) Greenwood.

Lubin, Bernard. Comprehensive Index of Group Psychotherapy Writings. (American Group Psychotherapy Association Monographs: No. 2). (C). 1987. 85.00 (*0-8236-1045-4*) Intl Univs Pr.

Lubin, Bernard, ed. Pressure Vessel & Piping Codes & Standards, 1998: Proceedings, ASME/JSME Joint Pressure Vessels & Piping Conference (1998, San Diego, CA) LC 98-207927. 360. 536p. 1998. pap. 140.00 (*0-7918-1865-9*) ASME.

Lubin, Bernard, et al, eds. Organizational Change: Sourcebook I: Cases in Organizational Development. 1979. pap. text 19.95 (*0-88390-150-1*) L Erlbaum Assocs.

Lubin, Bernard & Wilson, C. Research on Group Treatment Methods: A Selectively Annotated Bibliography, 9. LC 96-23114. (Bibliographies & Indexes in Psychology Ser.: No. 9). 264p. 1996. lib. bdg. 75.00 (*0-313-28339-7*, Greenwood Pr) Greenwood.

Lubin, Bernard, jt. auth. see Gist, Richard.

Lubin, Bernard, jt. auth. see Hanson, Philip G.

Lubin, Bernard, jt. auth. see Wilson, C. Dwayne.

Lubin, Bernard, jt. compiled by see Van Whitlock, Rodney.

Lubin, Bernard, jt. ed. see Gist, Richard.

Lubin, Carl K. Language Disturbance & Intellectual Functioning: A Comparison of the Performance of Hemiplegic Patients with Aphasia & Hemiplegic Patients Without Aphasia in Non-Verbal Tasks of Intellectual Functioning. LC 68-17904. (Janua Linguarum, Series Minor: No. 48). (Orig.). 1969. pap. text 24.65 (*3-10-800093-4*) Mouton.

Lubin, Carol R. & Winslow, Anne. Social Justice for Women: The International Labor Organization & Women. LC 90-2003. (Duke Press Policy Studies). 348p. (C). 1990. text 54.95 (*0-8223-1062-7*) Duke.

Lubin, David M. Picturing a Nation: Art & Social Change in Nineteenth-Century America. LC 93-19392. (Illus.). 584p. 1994. 55.00 (*0-300-05732-6*) Yale U Pr.

— Picturing a Nation: Art & Social Change in Nineteenth-Century America. 1996. pap. 30.00 (*0-300-06637-6*) Yale U Pr.

***Lubin, David M.** Titanic. (BFI Modern Classics Ser.). 1999. pap. 13.95 (*0-85170-760-2*) Ind U Pr.

LuBin, Deanna R. Monster Mother. Fosten, Tom, tr. (Illus.). (J). (ps-9). 1991. lib. bdg. write for info. (*0-318-67146-8*); audio. write for info. (*0-318-67147-6*) Lubin Pr.

Lubin, Ernest. The Piano Duet. LC 76-10328. (Quality Paperbacks Ser.). (Illus.). 240p. 1976. pap. 5.95 (*0-306-80045-4*) Da Capo.

— Step One: Play Piano. (Step One Ser.). 40p. 1998. text 5.95 incl. cd-rom (*0-8256-1610-7*, AM943162) Music Sales.

Lubin, George. Handbook of Composites. 786p. (gr. 13). 1982. mass mkt. 153.95 (*0-442-24897-0*) Chapman & Hall.

Lubin, Georges, ed. see Sand, George.

Lubin, Gilbert. The Master Race: What Every Jewish Child Should Know about Inherited Jewish Blood. St. John, Charlotte, ed. LC 92-43704. 224p. 1998. 19.95 (*0-89896-492-X*) Larksdale.

Lubin, J., tr. see Merli, Giorgio.

Lubin, Jean. Train up a Child. 1994. pap. 14.99 (*1-56507-217-0*) Harvest Hse.

LuBin, L., ed. see Foster, Tom.

Lubin, Martin. Test Your IQ Skills: Exercise Your Brain with 100 Intellectual Work-Outs. (Illus.). 64p. 1996. pap. text 4.98 (*1-884822-71-1*) Blck Dog & Leventhal.

Lubin, Martin, ed. Public Policy, Canada, & the United States. 164p. (Orig.). 1986. pap. 15.00 (*0-918592-89-5*) Pol Studies.

Lubin, Martin & Foschia, Diana. How Smart Are You? Test Your Child's I. Q. (Illus.). 64p. (Orig.). 1996. spiral bd. 4.98 (*1-884822-74-6*) Blck Dog & Leventhal.

Lubin, Maurice A., jt. auth. see Saint-Louis, Carlos.

Lubin, Nancy, et al. Preventing Conflict in Central Asia: The Ferghana Valley. LC 99-30898. 120p. 1998. pap. 11.95 (*0-87078-414-5*) Century Foundation.

Lubin, Rose. Call It What You Will. 22p. 1987. pap. 5.95 (*0-943454-07-7*) Jotarian.

Lubin, Yevgeny. Drevo Shizni: Poems. 1984. 3.95 (*0-685-22659-X*) RWCPH.

— In the Core: Three Novels about Yakov Bolotov. (Illus.). 424p. 1989. 23.95 (*0-929924-00-2*); pap. 19.95 (*0-685-24999-9*) RWCPH.

— On Shel na Svijaz: A Novel. 1980. 5.00 (*0-685-44306-X*) RWCPH.

— The Russian Triptych. 2nd ed.Tr. of Pycckuii Tpuniux. 230p. 1989. write for info. (*0-929924-06-1*); pap. 7.95 (*0-929924-07-X*) RWCPH.

— Russkii Triptich: A Novel & Stories. 1982. 7.95 (*0-685-22656-5*) RWCPH.

Lubiner, Alan M., jt. auth. see Kimmel, Barbara Brooks.

Lubiner, Elaine D. Learning about Languages: Upper Elementary Through First Year High School. (SPA.). 91p. (YA). 1992. teacher ed. 22.60 (*0-8442-9371-7*, Natl Textbk Co) NTC Contemp Pub Co.

— Learning about Languages: Upper Elementary Through First Year High School. (SPA.). 120p. (YA). 1994. pap. text 11.95 (*0-8442-9370-9*, Natl Textbk Co) NTC Contemp Pub Co.

***Lubiner, Jean-Paul.** Tour Eiffel. (Illus.). 2000. pap. 35.00 (*2-84576-022-1*) Vilo Intl.

Lubini, A. La Vegetation de la Reserve de Biosphere de Luki au Mayombe, Zaire, Vol. 10. (Illus.). 155p. 1998. 42.00 (*90-72619-33-1*, Pub. by Natl Botanic Grdn Belgium) Balogh.

Lubiniecki, Anthony S. Large-Scale Mammalian Cell Culture Technology. (Bioprocess Technology Ser.: Vol. 10). (Illus.). 656p. 1990. text 235.00 (*0-8247-8327-1*) Dekker.

Lubiniecki, Anthony S. & Vargo, Susan A., eds. Regulatory Practice for Biopharmaceutical Production. 566p. 1994. 185.00 (*0-471-04900-X*) Wiley.

Lubiniecki, Anthony S., jt. ed. see Brown, Fred.

Lubinski. Professional Issues in Speech Language Pathology/Audiology. 2nd ed. 2000. pap. 57.95 (*0-7693-0002-2*) Singular Publishing.

Lubinski, Arthur. Developments in Petroleum Engineering: Collected Works of Arthur Lubinski. Miska, Stefan, ed. LC 87-169. (Stability of Tubulars: Vol. 1). (Illus.). 472p. pap. 146.40 (*0-608-05078-4*, 206563300001) Bks Demand.

— Developments in Petroleum Engineering: Collected Works of Arthur Lubinski. Miska, Stefan, ed. LC 87-169. (Stability of Tubulars: Vol. 2). (Illus.). 416p. pap. 129.00 (*0-608-05079-2*, 206563300002) Bks Demand.

Lubinski, David & Dawis, Rene V., eds. Assessing Individual Differences in Human Behavior: New Concepts, Methods, & Findings. LC 95-11398. 400p. (C). 1995. text 49.95 (*0-89106-072-3*, 7220, Davies-Black Pub) Consulting Psychol.

Lubinski, David, jt. auth. see Benbow, Camilla P.

***Lubinski, J.** Consolidated Guidance about Material Licenses: Applications for Sealed Source & Device Evaluations & Registration, Final Report. 153p. 1998. per. 13.00 (*0-16-062757-5*) USGPO.

Lubinski, Mary Lou, tr. see Johnson, Anne Walker & Johnson, Robert Eugene, eds.

Lubinski, Rosemary. Communication Technologies for the Elderly: Hearing, Speech, & Vision. Higginbotham, Jeffrey, ed. LC 96-46039. 350p. (Orig.). 1997. pap. 55.00 (*1-56593-634-5*, 1314) Thomson Learn.

Lubinski, Rosemary, ed. Dementia & Communication. (Illus.). 320p. (C). 1995. pap. text 49.95 (*1-56593-084-3*, 1138) Singular Publishing.

Lubinski, Rosemary & Shadden, Barbara B. Enhancing Communication Services of Older Persons in Extended Care Settings. 140p. 1997. pap. 110.00 incl. VHS (*1-58041-001-4*) Am Speech Lang Hearing.

Lubinski, Rosemary, ed. see Frattali, Carol.

Lubinsky, D. S. & Saff, Edward B. Strong Asymptotics for Extremal Polynomials Associated with Weights on IR. (Lecture Notes in Mathematics Ser.: Vol. 1305). vii, 153p. 1988. 35.95 (*0-387-18958-0*) Spr-Verlag.

Lubinsky, D. S., jt. auth. see Levin, A. L.

Lubis, Mochtar. Indonesia: Land under the Rainbow. (Illus.). 236p. 1991. pap. text 24.95 (*0-19-588977-0*) OUP.

Lubitz, Petra, jt. auth. see Lubitz, Wolfgang.

Lubitz, Rita. Marital Power in Dickens' Fiction, Vol. 3. (Dickens' Universe Ser.). XI, 146p. (C). 1996. text 39.95 (*0-8204-2729-2*) P Lang Pubng.

Lubitz, Wolfgang & Lubitz, Petra. Trotskyist Serials Bibliography: With Locations & Indices. 475p. 1993. 128.00 (*3-598-11157-6*) K G Saur Verlag.

Lubitz, Wolfgang, jt. auth. see Kriste, Burkhard.

Lubjuhn, T., jt. auth. see Epplen, Jhorg T.

Lubjuhn, Thomas, jt. auth. see Epplen, Jhorg T.

***Lubka, Willie & Holden, Nancy.** The Kiss Guide to the Internet. LC 00-8358. (Keep It Simple Ser.). (Illus.). 352p. 2000. 18.95 (*0-7894-5980-9*) DK Pub Inc.

Lubke, Martin & Teleman, Andrei. The Kobayashi-Hitchin Correspondence. LC 95-31015. 200p. 1995. 48.00 (*981-02-2168-1*) World Scientific Pub.

Lubke, Roy & De Moor, Irene, eds. Field Guide to the Eastern & Southern Cape Coasts. LC 98-163686. (Illus.). 604p. 1998. pap. 79.95 (*1-919713-03-4*, U Pr W Africa) Intl Scholars.

Lubkeman, Dan, ed. see Van Patten, George F. & Bust, Alyssa F.

Lubker, Detlev L. & Schroder, Hans. Lexikon der Schleswig-Holstein-Lauenburgischen und Eutinischen Schriftsteller Von 1796 Bis 1828, Vols. 1-2. xxxvii, 904p. 1983. write for info. (*0-318-71926-6*) G Olms Pubs.

Lubkin, Gregory. A Renaissance Court: Milan under Galeazzo Maria Sforza. LC 93-17529. 1994. 55.00 (*0-520-08146-3*, Pub. by U CA Pr) Cal Prin Full Svc.

Lubkin, Ilene & Larsen, Pamela. Chronic Illness. 4th ed. LC 98-14256. (Nursing Ser.). 571p. 1998. 52.50 (*0-7637-0549-7*) Jones & Bartlett.

Lubkin, Ilene M. Chronic Illness: Impact & Interventions. 3rd ed. LC 94-37265. (Series in Nursing). 592p. 1995. 49.95 (*0-86720-712-4*) Jones & Bartlett.

Lubkin, James L., ed. The Teaching of Elementary Problem Solving in Engineering & Related Fields. 198p. 1980. 10.00 (*0-318-13172-2*) Am Soc Eng Ed.

Lublin, David. The Paradox of Representation. 176p. 1999. pap. text 15.95 (*0-691-01010-2*, Pub. by Princeton U Pr) Cal Prin Full Svc.

— The Paradox of Representation: Racial Gerrymandering & Minority Interests in Congress. LC 96-45560. 174p. 1997. text 29.95 (*0-691-02669-6*, Pub. by Princeton U Pr) Cal Prin Full Svc.

Lublin, Mary. A Rare Elegance: The Paintings of Charles Sprague Pearce. LC 93-61440. (Illus.). 95p. 1993. 35.00 (*0-614-29363-4*) V Jordan Fine Art.

Lublin, Nancy. Pandora's Box: Feminism Confronts Reproductive Technology. LC 97-26354. (New Feminist Perspectives Ser.). 208p. 1998. 60.00 (*0-8476-8636-1*); pap. 14.95 (*0-8476-8637-X*) Rowman.

Lubliner, Jacob. Plasticity Theory. 500p. (C). 1990. text 75.00 (*0-02-372161-8*, Macmillan Coll) P-H.

***Lubliner, Jean-Paul.** Eiffel Tower 2000: The Last Year in Paris. (Illus.). 2000. pap. text 24.95 (*1-893263-09-6*) Ipso Facto.

Lubliner, Murray J. Global Corporate Identity: The Cross-Border Marketing Challenge. (Illus.). 176p. 1994. 39.99 (*1-56496-110-9*) Rockport Pubs.

Lubliner, Murray J., intro. International Brand Packaging Awards, No. 2. (Illus.). 192p. 1995. 39.99 (*1-56496-154-0*) Rockport Pubs.

Lubliner, Murray J., jt. auth. see Meyers, Herbert M.

Lubliner, Paul. New York Ontario & Western in Color. LC 96-78483. (Illus.). 128p. 1997. 49.95 (*1-878887-73-4*) Morning NJ.

Lubman, David & Wetherill, Ewart A., eds. Acoustics of Worship Spaces. LC 85-70273. 91p. 1985. pap. 26.00 (*0-88318-466-4*) Acoustical Soc Am.

Lubman, David M., ed. Lasers & Mass Spectrometry. (Oxford Series on Optical Sciences). (Illus.). 560p. 1990. text 105.00 (*0-19-505929-8*) OUP.

***Lubman, Stanley B.** Bird in A Cage: Legal Reform in China After Mao. LC 99-27415. 1999. 65.00 (*0-8047-3664-2*) Stanford U Pr.

Lubman, Stanley B., ed. China's Legal Reforms. LC 96-16981. (Studies on Comtemporary China). (Illus.). 226p. 1996. pap. text 26.00 (*0-19-823344-2*) OUP.

Lubochinsky, Catherine, jt. auth. see Cuny, Christopher.

Luboff, Ken. Live Well in Mexico: How to Relocate, Retire & Increase Your Standard of Living. LC 99-24014. (Illus.). 256p. 1999. pap. 15.95 (*1-56261-432-0*) Avalon Travel.

Luboff, Pat & Luboff, Pete. 88 Songwriting Wrongs & How to Right Them. 144p. 1992. pap. 17.99 (*0-89879-508-7*, Wrtrs Digest Bks) F & W Pubns Inc.

Luboff, Pete, jt. auth. see Luboff, Pat.

Lubonja, Fatos T. The Second Sentence: A Prison Memoir. 256p. 1999. 23.95 (*1-55970-446-2*, Pub. by Arcade Pub Inc) Time Warner.

Luborsky, Lester. Principles of Psychoanalytic Psychotherapy: A Manual for Supportive-Expressive Treatment. LC 83-54377. 292p. 1984. pap. 37.50 (*0-465-06328-4*, Pub. by Basic) HarpC.

Luborsky, Lester. The Symptom-Context Method: Symptoms As Opportunities in Psychotherapy. LC 96-4876. 422p. 1996. text 29.95 (*1-55798-354-2*, 431-6730) Am Psychol.

Luborsky, Lester & Crits-Christoph, Paul. Understanding Transference: The Core Conflictual Relationship Theme Method. 2nd rev. ed. LC 97-26192. 379p. 1997. text 39.95 (*1-55798-453-0*) Am Psychol.

Luborsky, Peter, tr. see Lindenberg, Christoph.

Luborsky, Ruth S. & Ingram, Elizabeth M. A Guide to English Illustrated Books, 1536-1603. LC 98-2632. (Medieval & Renaissance Texts & Studies: No. 166). (Illus.). 1168p. 1998. 75.00 (*0-86698-207-8*, MR166) MRTS.

Lubot, Eugene. Liberalism in an Illiberal Age: New Culture Liberals in Republican China, 1919-1937, 5. LC 81-13409. (Contributions in Intercultural & Comparative Studies: No. 5). 194p. 1982. 49.95 (*0-313-23256-3*, LUL/, Greenwood Pr) Greenwood.

Lubotsky, Alexander. A Rgvedic Word Concordance, 2 vols. LC 97-219365. 1997. 125.00 (*0-940490-12-9*); 125.00 (*0-940490-13-7*) Am Orient Soc.

Lubotsky, Alexander & Magid, Andy R. Varieties of Representations of Finitely Generated Groups. LC 85-21444. (Memoirs Ser.: No. 58/336). 117p. 1985. pap. 18.00 (*0-8218-2337-X*, MEMO/58/336) Am Math.

Lubotsky, Dana, jt. auth. see Park, Barbara.

Lubotzky, A., jt. auth. see Bass, Hyman.

Lubotzky, Alexander. Discrete Groups, Expanding Graphs & Invariant Measures. Rogawski, Jonathan D., ed. LC 94-21726. (Progress in Mathematics Ser.: Vol. 125). 208p. 1994. 49.50 (*0-8176-5075-X*) Birkhauser.

Lubov, Don. East End Illustrated. 3rd ed. 55p. 1988. pap. 11.95 (*0-939820-05-6*) Lindon Ent.

— The East End Illustrated, Vol. 3. (Illus.). 55p. 1988. pap. write for info. (*0-939820-06-4*) Lindon Ent.

Lubove, ed. Pittsburgh. LC 76-3119. (Documentary History of American Cities Ser.). (C). 1976. reprint ed. pap. 6.95 (*0-531-05590-6*) Wiener Pubs Inc.

Lubove, Roy. The Professional Altruist: The Emergence of Social Work As a Career, 1880-1930. LC 65-12786. (Publication of the Center for the Study of the History of Liberty in America, Harvard University Ser.). 299p. reprint ed. pap. 92.70 (*0-7837-4117-0*, 205794000011) Bks Demand.

— The Progressives & the Slums. LC 74-4843. (Illus.). 284p. 1974. reprint ed. lib. bdg. 59.75 (*0-8371-7487-2*, LUPS, Greenwood Pr) Greenwood.

— The Struggle for Social Security, 1900-1935. LC 85-40854. (Series in Policy & Institutional Studies). 304p. 1986. reprint ed. pap. 14.95 (*0-8229-5379-X*) U of Pittsburgh Pr.

— Twentieth Century Pittsburgh: Government, Business & Change. rev. ed. (Illus.). 208p. (C). 1996. pap. 19.95 (*0-8229-5551-2*) U of Pittsburgh Pr.

— Twentieth-Century Pittsburgh: The Post-Steel Era, Vol. 2. LC 85-40854. (Illus.). 426p. (C). 1996. pap. 19.95 (*0-8229-5566-0*); text 44.95 (*0-8229-3892-8*) U of Pittsburgh Pr.

— The Urban Community: Housing & Planning in the Progressive Era. LC 81-6328. (American Historical Sources: Research & Interpretation Ser.). 148p. 1981. reprint ed. lib. bdg. 55.00 (*0-313-22731-4*, LUUC, Greenwood Pr) Greenwood.

Lubow, Allen. Bar Code Pro. 72p. 1991. pap. text 149.95 (*1-880773-00-7*); disk 450.00 (*0-685-59076-3*) SNX.

— Bar Code Pro ersion 3.0. 88p. 1995. pap. text. write for info. (*1-880773-21-X*) SNX.

— Bar Code Pro Filemaster: User's Guide. Hunter, Stacy, ed. (Illus.). 222p. (Orig.). 1996. pap. write for info. (*1-880773-22-8*) SNX.

— Bar Code Pro Version 3.5. 88p. 1995. pap. text 19.95 (*1-880773-23-6*) SNX.

— Label Press: Label Printing Software Tamed. (Illus.). 188p. (Orig.). 1994. pap. text. write for info. (*1-880773-19-8*) SNX.

— MacEnvelop Professional: Reference Manual. 192p. 1992. pap. text 250.00 incl. disk (*1-880773-06-6*) SNX.

— MacEnvelope. 131p. 1990. pap. text. write for info. (*1-880773-05-8*) SNX.

Lubow, Arthur. The Reporter Who Would Be King: A Biography of Richard Harding Davis. (Illus.). 448p. 1992. text 25.00 (*0-684-19404-X*) S&S Trade.

Lubow, Joseph. Choose a College Town for Retirement. LC 99-11644. (Choose Retirement Ser.). (Illus.). 330p. 1999. pap. text 14.95 (*0-7627-0393-8*) Globe Pequot.

Lubow, Joseph, ed. see Mayall, Donald.

Lubow, Joseph M. Reaching for Answers: Bill Belton's Story. (Illus.). 240p. (Orig.). 2000. pap. 14.95 (*0-89407-093-2*) Strawberry Hill.

Lubow, R. E. Latent Inhibition & Conditioned Attention Theory. (Problems in the Behavioral Sciences Ser.). (Illus.). 336p. (C). 1989. text 69.95 (*0-521-36307-1*) Cambridge U Pr.

Lubrano, Annteresa. The Telegraph: How Technology Innovation Caused Social Change. rev. ed. Bruchey, Stuart, ed. LC 97-25292. (Studies on Industrial Productivity). (Illus.). 205p. 1997. text 54.00 (*0-8153-3001-4*) Garland.

Lubrecht, A. A., jt. auth. see Venner, C. H.

Lubro, Camille & Chayet, Stephanie. New York Confidential. 168p. 45.00 (*2-84323-173-6*, Pub. by Assouline) Rizzoli Intl.

Lubs, Herbert A. The Chemistry of Synthetic Dyes & Pigments. LC 64-7905. (ACS Monograph Ser.: Vol. 127). (Illus.). 750p. 1955. reprint ed. pap. 200.00 (*0-608-06936-1*, 206714400009) Bks Demand.

Lubs, Herbert A. & De La Cruz, Felix, eds. Genetic Counseling. LC 76-52601. (Monograph of the National Institute of Child Health & Human Development Ser.). (Illus.). 615p. 1977. reprint ed. pap. 190.70 (*0-608-05866-1*, 205983300007) Bks Demand.

Lubulwa, A. S. The Implications of Regulatory Failure for Rail & Road Industries. 157p. 1990. text 67.95 (*1-85628-128-0*, Pub. by Avebry) Ashgate Pub Co.

Luby, Barry J. & Finke, Wayne H., eds. Anthology of Contemporary Latin American Literature: 1960 to 1984. 320p. 1986. 48.50 (*0-8386-3255-6*) Fairleigh Dickinson.

Luby, James P. James Luby, Journalist. (American Newspapermen 1790-1933 Ser.). 135p. 1974. reprint ed. 29.95 (*0-8464-0014-6*) Beekman Pubs.

Luby, M., et al, eds. Randomization & Approximation Techniques in Computer Science: Second International Workshop, Random'98, Barcelona, Spain, October 8-10, 1998. (Lecture Notes in Computer Science Ser.: Vol. 1518). ix, 385p. 1998. pap. 59.00 (*3-540-65142-X*) Spr-Verlag.

Luby, Thia. Children's Book of Yoga: Games & Exercises Mimic Plants & Animals & Objects. LC 98-9712. (Illus.). 112p. (J). (ps-7). 1997. 14.95 (*1-57416-003-6*) Clear Light.

— Yoga for Teens: How to Improve Your Fitness, Confidence, Appearance & Health & Have Fun Doing It. LC 99-41214. (Illus.). 120p. (YA). (gr. 8-12). 1999. 14.95 (*1-57416-032-X*) Clear Light.

Luc, D. T. Theory of Vector Optimization. (Lecture Notes in Economics & Mathematical Systems Ser.: Vol. 319). viii, 173p. 1988. 30.70 (*0-387-50541-5*) Spr-Verlag.

Luc, Laura A. & Beattie, Michele. Long-Term Patient Care Policies & Procedures Manual. LC 92-48193. 174p. 1993. pap. 55.00 (*0-8342-0320-0*, 20320) Aspen Pub.

Luc, M., et al, eds. Plant Parasitic Nematodes in Subtropical & Tropical Agriculture. (Illus.). 648p. 1990. text 160.00 (*0-85198-630-7*) OUP.

Luc, Viviane. Aujourd'hui le Paradis: Comment Retrouver le Sens Spirituel de la Bature et des Choses de la Vie. 326p. 1992. 22.95 (*2-920083-64-3*) Edns Roseau.

***Luca.** Tradg In Globl Curr Mkts. 2nd ed. 384p. 2000. text 65.00 (*0-7352-0146-3*) PH Pr.

Luca & Cornelius. Technical Analysis Applications in the Global Currency Markets. 2nd ed. LC 00-20841. 2000. text 80.00 (*0-7352-0147-1*) PH Pr.

Luca, A. De, see De Luca, A.

Luca, Araldo De, see De Luca, Araldo, photos by.

Luca, Cornelius. Foreign Exchange Markets Handbook. 1995. text 59.95 (*0-13-293424-8*) P-H.

— Technical Analysis Applications in the Global Currency Markets. LC 97-11241. (Illus.). 512p. (C). 1997. 75.00 (*0-13-494055-5*) P-H.

Luca, Giuseppe De, see Moses, Julian M. & De Luca, Giuseppe.

Luca, J. De, see De Luca, J.

Luca, Johanne De, see De Luca, Johanne.

Luca, Susan. Of Mice. (Illus.). 1970. pap. 12.50 (*0-912020-16-4*) Turtles Quill.

Luca, Teresa De, see De Luca, Teresa.

Luca, Vincent A. De, see De Luca, Vincent A.

Lucadamo, Rhonda, jt. auth. see Dean, Theresa.

Lucadamo, Rhonda, jt. auth. see Dean, Theresa M.

Lucadano, Theresa A. Reclamation. Sherman, Alana, ed. (Chapbooks Fourth Ser.). 20p. 1991. pap. 4.95 (*0-939689-13-8*) Alms Hse Pr.

Lucado, M. Caminando con el Salvador. (Meditacion Diaria Ser.).Tr. of Walking with the Savior. 7.99 (*0-7899-0487-X*, 496628) Editorial Unilit.

— Dios Se Acerco.Tr. of God Came Near. (SPA.). 126p. 1992. pap. 7.99 (*0-8297-0339-X*) Vida Pubs.

Lucado, M. Sobre el Yunque.Tr. of On the Anvil. (SPA.). 1995. 8.99 (*1-56063-924-5*, 498420) Editorial Unilit.

Lucado, Max. Alabaster's Song. LC 96-14749. (Illus.). 32p. (J). (ps-2). 1996. 14.99 (*0-8499-1307-1*) Tommy Nelson.

— And the Angels Were Silent: The Final Week of Jesus. 264p. 1999. 19.99 (*1-57673-598-2*) Multnomah Pubs.

***Lucado, Max.** And the Angels Were Silent: The Final Week of Jesus. 264p. 1999. pap. 12.99 (*1-57673-599-0*) Multnomah Pubs.

Lucado, Max. Aplauso del Cielo.Tr. of Applause of Heaven. (SPA.). 212p. 1996. 9.99 (*0-88113-418-X*, B008-418X) Caribe Betania.

— Applause of Heaven. 1. 1999. pap. text 12.99 (*0-8499-3752-3*) Word Pub.

— The Applause of Heaven. deluxe rev. ed. 240p. 1996. 20.00 (*0-8499-1324-1*) Word Pub.

— Applause of Heaven. large type ed. pap. 14.99 (*0-8499-3693-4*, 2432) Word Pub.

— Because I Love You. LC 97-48306. (Illus.). 32p. (J). (gr. 1-3). 1999. 14.99 (*0-89107-992-0*) Crossway Bks.

— Book of Hebrews. (Life Lessons Ser.). 1997. pap. 6.99 (*0-8499-5301-4*) Word Pub.

— Book of James. LC 96-223510. (Life Lessons Ser.). 1996. pap. 6.99 (*0-8499-5248-4*) Word Pub.

— Book of John. LC 96-223497. (Life Lessons Ser.). 1996. pap. 6.99 (*0-8499-5247-6*) Word Pub.

— Book of Mark. (Life Lessons Ser.). 1997. pap. 6.99 (*0-8499-5299-9*) Word Pub.

— Book of Psalms. (Life Lessons Ser.). 1997. pap. 6.99 (*0-8499-5298-0*) Word Pub.

— Book of Romans. LC 96-223521. (Life Lessons Ser.). 1996. pap. 6.99 (*0-8499-5249-2*) Word Pub.

— Books of Ruth & Esther. LC 96-223522. (Life Lessons Ser.). 1996. pap. 6.99 (*0-8499-5246-8*) Word Pub.

— The Children of the King: Read along sing along. (J). 1995. audio 9.99 (*0-89107-895-9*, Crossway Audio) Crossway Bks.

— The Christmas Cross. LC 98-24180. (Illus.). 48p. 1998. 17.99 (*0-8499-1546-5*) Word Pub.

— The Christmas Cross: A Short Story for Christmas. LC 98-24180. 1998. 11.99 incl. audio (*0-8499-6287-0*) Word Pub.

***Lucado, Max.** Como Jesus. 1999. pap. write for info. (*0-88113-549-6*) Caribe Betania.

Lucado, Max. Con Razon Lo Llamen el Salvador.Tr. of No Wonder They Call Him Savior. (SPA.). 182p. 1995. pap. 7.99 (1-56063-879-6, 498395) Editorial Unilit.

***Lucado, Max.** El Corderito Tullido. (SPA.). 1999. pap. 8.99 (0-88113-569-0) Caribe Betania.

Lucado, Max. Cosmic Christmas. LC 97-26523. 128p. 1997. 12.99 (0-8499-1530-9) Word Pub.

— The Crippled Lamb. LC 94-19865. (Illus.). 32p. (J). (ps-2). 1994. 14.99 (0-8499-1005-6) Tommy Nelson.

***Lucado, Max.** The Crippled Lamb. (Illus.). 32p. (J). 1999. 5.99 (0-8499-7502-6) Tommy Nelson.

— The Crippled Lamb. anniversary ed. 32p. (J). 1999. 17.99 incl. audio compact disk (0-8499-5979-9) Tommy Nelson.

— Cuando Cristo Venga: El Principio de Lo Incomparablemente Bueno. (SPA.). 2000. pap. 9.99 (0-88113-557-7) Caribe Betania.

Lucado, Max. Cuando Dios Susurra Tu Nombre.Tr. of When God Whispers Your Name. (ENG & SPA.). 235p. 1995. 9.99 (0-88113-377-9, B008-3779) Caribe Betania.

***Lucado, Max.** Embraced by God, 1. (Life Lessons Ser.: Vol. 5). 128p. 2000. pap. text 7.99 (0-8499-5430-4) J Countryman.

Lucado, Max. En Manos de la Gracia: Nada Nos Puede Desprender de Su Amor.Tr. of In the Grip of Grace. 1997. pap. text 10.99 (0-88113-446-5) Caribe Betania.

— The Final Week of Jesus: Excerpts from & the Angels Were Silent. gif. ed. 128p. 1994. 19.99 (0-88070-630-9, Multnomah Bks) Multnomah Pubs.

— Finding Joy in the Journey. 32p. 1995. pap. 2.99 (0-8499-5213-1) Word Pub.

— Genesis. (Inspirational Bible Study; Life Lessons Ser.). 1997. pap. 6.99 (0-8499-5320-0) Word Pub.

— A Gentle Thunder: Hearing God Through the Storm. 224p. 1995. 19.99 (0-8499-1138-9) Word Pub.

— A Gentle Thunder: Hearing God Through the Storm. (Mini Bk.). 80p. 1996. 4.99 (0-8499-5142-9) Word Pub.

— The Gift for All People: Thoughts on God's Great Grace. LC 98-31656. 144p. 1999. 12.99 (1-57673-464-1) Multnomah Pubs.

***Lucado, Max.** Glimpse of Glory, Vol. 3. (Topical Bible Study Ser.). 120p. 1999. pap. text 7.99 (0-8499-5427-4) Word Pub.

Lucado, Max. God Came Near. large type ed. 256p. 1995. pap. 12.95 (0-8027-2693-3) Walker & Co.

— God Came Near: Chronicles of the Christ. 200p. 1998. 19.99 (1-57673-387-4); pap. 12.99 (1-57673-386-6) Multnomah Pubs.

***Lucado, Max.** God Came Near: Chronicles of the Christ. 2000. 12.99 (1-57673-723-3) Multnomah Pubs.

— God's Inspirational Promise Book. 1999. 14.99 (0-8499-5583-1) J Countryman.

Lucado, Max. Gods Open Arms: Studies on Grace, 1, 2. 1999. pap. 6.99 (0-8499-5425-8) Word Pub.

***Lucado, Max.** Grace for the Moment. (Illus.). 398p. 2000. 12.99 (0-8499-5624-2) J Countryman.

Lucado, Max. La Gran Casa de Dios.Tr. of Great House of God. 256p. 1998. pap. 9.99 (0-88113-498-8) Caribe Betania.

— The Great House of God. LC 97-22821. 240p. 1997. 19.99 (0-8499-1295-4) Word Pub.

— The Greatest Moments. (Illus.). 128p. 1995. 9.99 (0-8499-5226-3) Word Pub.

***Lucado, Max.** Greatest Moments in the Life of Christ. 2000. pap. 3.97 (0-8499-5751-6) J Countryman.

Lucado, Max. Greatest Moments in the Life of Christ. 1999. pap. text 5.99 (0-8499-5493-2) Word Pub.

***Lucado, Max.** He Chose the Nails. 240p. 2000. 21.99 (0-8499-1655-0) Word Pub.

— He Chose the Nails: What God Did to Win Your Heart. 144p. 2000. pap. 14.99 (0-8499-4245-4) Word Pub.

Lucado, Max. He Still Moves Stones. 1993. 19.99 (0-8499-0864-7) Word Pub.

— He Still Moves Stones, 1. 1999. pap. text 12.99 (0-8499-3753-1) Word Pub.

***Lucado, Max.** He Still Moves Stones. large type ed. LC 99-87509. 352p. 2000. reprint ed. pap. 16.95 (0-8027-2757-3) Walker & Co.

— Hear with Your Heart. Orig. Title: Song of the King. (Illus.). 32p. (YA). (ps-3). 2000. 15.99 (1-58134-210-1) Crossway Bks.

Lucado, Max. How Hurts Bring Hope. 32p. 1995. pap. 2.99 (0-8499-5126-7) Word Pub.

***Lucado, Max.** In His Presence, 1. (Life Lessons Ser.). 2000. pap. text 7.99 (0-8499-5432-0) J Countryman.

Lucado, Max. In the Eye of the Storm. 1991. 19.99 (0-8499-0890-6) Word Pub.

— In the Eye of the Storm. 1994. 4.99 (0-8499-5090-2) Word Pub.

***Lucado, Max.** In the Footsteps of Jesus. 2000. 15.99 (0-8423-3910-8) Tyndale Hse.

Lucado, Max. In the Grip of Grace. 272p. 1996. 19.99 (0-8499-1143-5) Word Pub.

***Lucado, Max.** In the Grip of Grace. 256p. 1999. pap. 14.99 (0-8499-3726-4) Word Pub.

Lucado, Max. Jacob's Gift. LC 98-6490. (Illus.). 32p. (J). (ps-3). 1998. 14.99 (0-8499-5830-X) Tommy Nelson.

***Lucado, Max.** Joy in the Morning: Studies on Peace. (Topical Bible Study Ser.). 2000. pap. 7.99 (0-8499-5646-3) Word Pub.

Lucado, Max. Just in Case You Ever Wonder. (Illus.). 30p. (J). (ps-3). 1992. 14.99 (0-8499-0978-3) Tommy Nelson.

***Lucado, Max.** Just in Case You Ever Wonder. (Illus.). 16p. (J). (ps). 2000. 5.99 (0-8499-7509-3) Tommy Nelson.

Lucado, Max. Just in Case You Ever Wonder. (Mini Bk.). 32p. (J). 1996. 14.99 (0-8499-5253-0) Word Pub.

***Lucado, Max.** Just Like Jesus. 2000. pap. 14.99 (0-8499-4252-7) Word Pub.

Lucado, Max. Just Like Jesus: Living in the Heart of the Savior. LC 98-22587. 240p. 1998. 19.99 (0-8499-1296-2) Word Pub.

— Just Like Jesus: Living in the Heart of the Savior. LC 98-22587. 1998. 16.99 incl. audio (0-8499-6285-4) Word Pub.

— Just the Way You Are. LC 99-16876. Orig. Title: Children of the King. (Illus.). 32p. (J). (ps-5). 1999. reprint ed. 15.99 (1-58134-114-8) Crossway Bks.

***Lucado, Max.** Let the Journey Begin: God's Roadmap for New Beginnings. LC 98-182743. (Illus.). 120p. 1998. 12.99 (0-8499-5342-1) Word Pub.

Lucado, Max. Life Lessons: Book of Acts. (Life Lessons Ser.). 1997. pap. 6.99 (0-8499-5300-6) Word Pub.

— Life Lessons: Book of Revelation. (Inspirational Bible Study Guides: Vol. 12). 1997. pap. 6.99 (0-8499-5323-5) Word Pub.

— Life Lessons: Book of 1 Corinthians. (Inspirational Bible Study; Life Lessons Ser.). 1997. pap. 6.99 (0-8499-5321-9) Word Pub.

— Life Lessons: Books of 1 & 2 Peter. (Inspirational Bible Study Guides: Vol. 11). 1997. pap. 6.99 (0-8499-5322-7) Word Pub.

— Lucado 3 in 1: In the Eye of the Storm, He Still Moves Stones, a Gentle Thunder. 1998. 16.99 (0-8499-1552-X) Word Pub.

***Lucado, Max.** Lucado 3 in 1: In the Grip of Grace/When God Whispers Your Name/Applause of Heaven. 2000. 16.99 (0-8499-1664-X) Tommy Nelson.

Lucado, Max. No Wonder They Call Him the Savior: Chronicles of the Cross. 216p. 1998. 19.99 (1-57673-389-0); pap. 12.99 (1-57673-388-2) Multnomah Pubs.

— No Wonder They Call Him the Savoir. large type ed. (Large Print Inspirational Ser.). 224p. 1987. pap. 12.95 (0-8027-2579-1) Walker & Co.

— On the Anvil. 140p. 1994. 14.99 (0-8423-4568-X) Tyndale Hse.

— On the Anvil: Stories on Being Shaped into God's Image. large type ed. 180p. 1996. pap. 13.95 (0-8027-2704-2) Walker & Co.

***Lucado, Max.** Path to Greatness: Studies on Trials. (Topical Bible Study Ser.). 2000. pap. 7.99 (0-8499-5431-2) Word Pub.

Lucado, Max. Peace That Defies Pain. 32p. 1995. pap. 2.99 (0-8499-5211-5) Word Pub.

Lucado, Max. Por Si Lo Querias Saber, 1vol. 1992. 8.99 (0-88113-566-6) Caribe Betania.

— Porque Te Amo. (SPA.). 2000. 10.99 (0-7899-0765-8) Editorial Unilit.

— El Regalo Para Todo el Mundo. 2000. pap. 9.99 (0-88113-554-2); pap. 4.99 (0-89922-600-0) Caribe Betania.

— Seis Horas de Un Viernes (Six Hours One Friday) (SPA.). 1999. pap. 7.99 (0-8297-1974-1) Vida Pubs.

Lucado, Max. Six Hours One Friday: Anchoring to the Power of the Cross. 238p. 1999. 19.99 (1-57673-600-8) Multnomah Pubs.

***Lucado, Max.** Six Hours One Friday: Anchoring to the Power of the Cross. 238p. 1999. pap. 12.99 (1-57673-601-6) Multnomah Pubs.

Lucado, Max. Six Hours One Friday: Anchoring to the Power of the Cross. large type ed. 280p. 1996. pap. 13.95 (0-8027-2696-8) Walker & Co.

***Lucado, Max.** Small Gifts in God's Hands. (Illus.). 32p. (J). (ps-2). 2000. 15.99 (0-8499-5842-3) Tommy Nelson.

Lucado, Max. The Song of the King: Read along sing along. (J). 1995. audio 9.99 (0-89107-894-0, Crossway Audio) Crossway Bks.

— Tell Me the Secrets. LC 93-25957. (Illus.). 48p. (J). 1993. 16.99 (0-89107-730-8) Crossway Bks.

— Tell Me the Story. LC 92-26963. (Illus.). 48p. 1992. 16.99 (0-89107-679-4) Crossway Bks.

***Lucado, Max.** A Thirst for God. (Topical Study Guide Ser.). 120p. 1999. pap. 7.99 (0-8499-5428-2) Word Pub.

Lucado, Max. Todavia Remueve Piedras.Tr. of He Still Moves Stones. (SPA.). 240p. 1993. pap. text 9.99 (0-88113-182-2) Caribe Betania.

— Tomorrow's Dream, Today's Courage. 32p. 1995. pap. 2.99 (0-8499-5212-3) Word Pub.

— Touch of the Masters Hand: Studies on Jesus, 1, 1. 1999. pap. text 6.99 (0-8499-5426-6) Word Pub.

— El Trueno Apacible.Tr. of Gentle Thunder. (SPA.). 288p. 1996. 9.99 (0-88113-348-5, B008-3485) Caribe Betania.

***Lucado, Max.** Tu Eres Especial. (SPA.). 2000. 10.99 (0-7899-0752-6) Editorial Unilit.

Lucado, Max. Walking with the Savior. 160p. 1996. 13.99 (0-8423-7930-4) Tyndale Hse.

***Lucado, Max.** When Christ Comes. LC 99-30283. 240p. 1999. 21.99 (0-8499-1298-9) Word Pub.

Lucado, Max. When God Whispers Your Name. LC 94-17302. 241p. 1994. 19.99 (0-8499-1099-4) Word Pub.

— When God Whispers Your Name. 1995. 4.99 (0-8499-5108-9) Word Pub.

— When God Whispers Your Name, 1. 1999. pap. text 12.99 (0-8499-3741-8) Word Pub.

— When God Whispers Your Name. large type ed. 272p. pap. 14.99 (0-8499-3945-3, 2437) Word Pub.

— When You Can't Hide Your Mistakes. 32p. 1995. pap. 2.99 (0-8499-5149-6) Word Pub.

— Where Do I Go for Strength? 32p. 1995. pap. 2.99 (0-8499-5151-8) Word Pub.

— The Woodcutter's Wisdom & Other Favorite Stories. 32p. 1995. pap. 2.99 (0-8499-5214-X) Word Pub.

— Y Los Angeles Guardaron Silencio: La Ultima Semana de Jesus.Tr. of And the Angels Were Silent. (SPA.). 264p. 1993. pap. 7.99 (1-56063-396-4, 498546) Editorial Unilit.

— You Are Special. LC 97-5387. (Illus.). 32p. (J). (gr. k-3). 1997. 15.99 (0-89107-931-9) Crossway Bks.

***Lucado, Max.** You Are Special. (Illus.). 28p. (YA). (ps-1). 2000. 5.99 (1-58134-219-5) Crossway Bks.

Lucado, Max. Your Place at God's Table. 32p. 1995. pap. 2.99 (0-8499-5150-X) Word Pub.

Lucado, Max, ed. Life Lessons: Books of 1 & 2 Timothy & Titus. (Inspirational Bible Study Guides Ser.). 120p. 1998. pap. 6.99 (0-8499-5327-8) Word Pub.

— Life Lessons: Book of Ephesians. (Inspirational Bible Study Guides Ser.). 120p. 1998. pap. 6.99 (0-8499-5326-X) Word Pub.

— Life Lessons: Book of Luke. (Inspirational Bible Study Guides Ser.). 120p. 1998. pap. 6.99 (0-8499-5325-1) Word Pub.

— Life Lessons: Books of Ezra & Nehemiah. (Inspirational Bible Study Guides Ser.). 120p. 1998. pap. 6.99 (0-8499-5324-3) Word Pub.

Lucado, Max, text. The Cross: Selected Writings & Images. LC 96-40126. (Images & Reflections Ser.). (Illus.). 60p. 1998. 21.99 (1-57673-093-X, Multnomah Gift Bks) Multnomah Pubs.

Lucado, Max & Countryman, J. God's Inspirational Promise Book. LC 96-232411. 201p. 1996. 12.99 (0-8499-5235-2) Word Pub.

***Lucado, Max & Klauba, Douglas.** All You Ever Need. LC 99-45155. (Illus.). 32p. (J). (ps-3). 2000. 15.99 (1-58134-134-2) Crossway Bks.

Lucado, Max & Wangerin, Walt. Christmas by the Hearth: A Treasury of Stories Celebrating the Mystery & Meaning of Christmas. 200p. (J). 1996. 25.00 (0-8423-0239-5) Tyndale Hse.

Lucado, Max, et al. The Heart of Christmas. LC 98-21491. (Illus.). 160p. 1998. 14.99 (0-7852-8213-0) Nelson.

***Lucado, Max, et al.** Opening Windows: Spiritual Refreshment for Your Walk with Christ. LC 99-16440. (Illus.). 269p. 1999. 15.99 (1-58229-072-5) Howard Pub LA.

Lucado, Max, et al. The Spirit of Christmas. LC 99-15322. 192p. 1999. 14.99 (0-7852-6949-5) Nelson.

Lucado, Max, jt. ed. see Gray, Alice.

Lucaire, Ed. Cat Lover's Book of Fascinating Facts. LC 96-34189. (Illus.). 224p. 1997. 7.99 (0-517-15051-4) Random Hse Value.

— Famous Names for Your Pampered Pet: A Fun-&-Fact Filled A-Z Guide to Finding the Perfect Name for Your Pet. 319p. 1998. pap. text 6.00 (0-7881-5400-1) DIANE Pub.

Lucaire, Luigi. Howard Stern A to Z. LC 96-44781. 208p. 1997. pap. 10.95 (0-312-15144-6) St Martin.

Lucaites, John L., et al, eds. Contemporary Rhetorical Theory: A Reader. LC 98-37101. (Revisioning Rhetoric Ser.). 627p. 1998. pap. text 45.00 (1-57230-401-4) Guilford Pubns.

Lucaites, John L. & Bernabo, Lawrance M., eds. Great Speakers & Speeches. 2nd ed. 384p. 1991. per. 28.95 (0-8403-7149-7) Kendall-Hunt.

Lucaites, John L., jt. auth. see Condit, Celeste M.

Lucaites, John L., jt. ed. see Calloway-Thomas, Carolyn.

Lucal, Jane B. Estate Planning - a View from the Bench: The Beginner's Guide to the Basics. LC 94-208433. 480p. 1994. pap. 22.95 (0-9640191-0-8) Pro Pubng.

Lucan. Civil War. (Oxford World's Classics Ser.). (Illus.). 400p. 2000. pap. 9.95 (0-19-283949-7) OUP.

— De Bello Civili: Bk. II. Fantham, Elaine, ed. (Cambridge Greek & Latin Classics Ser.). (Illus.). 256p. (C). 1992. text 65.00 (0-521-41010-X) Cambridge U Pr.

— Lucan No. VIII: Civil War. Mayer, R., ed. (Classical Texts Ser.). 1981. 59.99 (0-85668-155-5, Pub. by Aris & Phillips) David Brown.

— Lucan VIII: Civil War. Mayer, R., ed. (Classical Texts Ser.). 1981. pap. 28.00 (0-85668-176-8, Pub. by Aris & Phillips) David Brown.

Lucan, D. M. Annael Lucani de Bello Civili, Liber I. Connor, W. R. & Getty, R. J., eds. LC 78-67133. (Latin Texts & Commentaries Ser.). (ENG & LAT.). 1979. reprint ed. lib. bdg. 22.95 (0-405-11603-9) Ayer.

Lucan, Jacques & Loers, Veit. Herzog & De Meuron: Goetz Sammlung. (Illus.). 76p. 1997. pap. 24.95 (3-7757-0574-0) Dist Art Pubs.

Lucan, Medlar. The Decadent Gardener. Martin, Alex, ed. (Illus.). 252p. 1997. pap. 13.99 (1-873982-82-8, Pub. by Dedalus) Subterranean Co.

Lucan, Medlar & Gras, Durian. The Decadent Cookbook. Martin, Alex & Fletcher, Jerome, eds. (Bizarre Concept Bks.). (Illus.). 220p. 1997. pap. 13.99 (1-873982-22-4, Pub. by Dedalus) Subterranean Co.

Lucan, Medlar & Gray, Durian. The Decadent Traveller. Martin, Alex & Fletcher, Jerome, eds. (Bizarre Concept Book Ser.). 256p. 1999. pap. 15.99 (1-873982-09-7, Pub. by Dedalus) Subterranean Co.

Lucanio, Patrick. Them or Us: Archetypal Interpretations of Fifties Alien Invasion Films. LC 86-43049. (Illus.). 204p. reprint ed. pap. 63.30 (0-608-09348-3, 205409400002) Bks Demand.

Lucanio, Patrick & Coville, Gary. American Science Fiction Television Series of the 1950s: Episode Guides & Casts & Credits for 20 Shows. LC 97-45051. (Illus.). 261p. 1998. lib. bdg. 49.95 (0-7864-0434-5) McFarland & Co.

Lucanio, Patrick, jt. auth. see Coville, Gary.

Lucanus, Ocellus. Neue Philologische Untersuchungen, Heft 1. xxix, 161p. 1966. write for info. (3-296-14750-0) G Olms Pubs.

Lucardie, Paul, jt. ed. see Dobson, Andrew.

Lucarella, Dario, ed. Text for Scientific Documentation of the First European Conference Como, Italy. 224p. 1986. pap. write for info. (0-201-13399-7) Addison-Wesley.

***Lucarelli, Bill.** The Origins & Evolution of the Single Market in Europe. LC 99-72654. 206p. 1999. text 65.95 (0-7546-1108-6, Pub. by Ashgate Pub) Ashgate Pub Co.

Lucas. Art. 3rd ed. 1989. VHS 534.06 (0-07-909608-5) McGraw.

— The Art of Public Speaking. 6th ed. 136p. 1998. pap., student ed. 15.94 (0-07-043519-7) McGraw.

— The Art of Public Speaking. 7th ed. 2000. 35.50 (0-07-231569-5) McGraw.

— The Conflict Between Christianity & Judaism. 1992. pap. 22.00 (0-85668-572-0, Pub. by Aris & Phillips) David Brown.

— Conflict Between the Jews & Christians. 1992. 39.95 (0-85668-586-0, Pub. by Aris & Phillips) David Brown.

— Dinosaurs: The Textbook. 2nd ed. 1996. 16.87 (0-697-33965-3, WCB McGr Hill) McGrw-H Hghr Educ.

— The French Revolution, 3 vols., Vol. 2. 1988. 50.00 (0-08-036277-X, Pergamon Pr) Elsevier.

— Information Systems Concept Management. 5th ed. 1994. text, teacher ed. 25.00 (0-07-039012-6) McGraw.

— Introduction To Abstract Mathematics. (Math). 1986. 29.00 (0-534-06318-7) Brooks-Cole.

— Mastering Prolog. 224p. 1995. pap. 44.95 (1-85728-400-3, Pub. by UCL Pr Ltd) Taylor & Francis.

— Retailing. (C). 1994. pap. text, student ed. 20.76 (0-395-56793-9) HM.

— Retailing. (C). 1994. pap., teacher ed., suppl. ed. 5.96 (0-395-69237-7) HM.

— The Rhetoric of Campaigns & Revolts. 4th ed. 1998. 40.00 (0-07-229637-2) McGraw.

— A Road to Damascus: Mainly Diplomatic Memoirs from the Middle East. LC 97-177422. (Illus.). 256p. 1997. text 39.50 (1-86064-152-0, Pub. by I B T) St Martin.

— Speech Communication. 5th ed. 1994. 6.25 (0-07-039030-4) McGraw.

— Teacher Education in America 1999. pap. 19.95 (0-312-22454-0) St Martin.

Lucas, jt. auth. see Donovan.

Lucas, A. Bioenergetics of Aquatic Animals. 169p. 1996. 39.95 (0-7484-0564-X) Taylor & Francis.

Lucas, A. & Harris, J. Ancient Egyptian Materials & Industries. 4th unabridged ed. LC 98-43429. 540p. 1999. pap. 16.95 (0-486-40446-3) Dover.

Lucas, A. De, see De Lucas, A.

Lucas, A. E. Ozark Almanac. 1986. pap. 8.00 (0-8309-0443-3) Independence Pr.

Lucas, Alan. Australian Cruising Guide. (Illus.). 160p. 1994. pap. 125.00 (0-85288-246-7, Pub. by Laurie Norie & Wilson Ltd) St Mut.

— Cruising the Coral Coast. 330p. 1996. pap. 125.00 (0-646-27858-4, Pub. by Laurie Norie & Wilson Ltd) St Mut.

— Cruising the New South Wales Coast. 250p. 1995. pap. 125.00 (0-646-23979-1, Pub. by Laurie Norie & Wilson Ltd) St Mut.

— Illustrated Encyclopedia of Boating. LC 78-9809. (Illus.). 1980. 3.89 (0-684-15900-7, Scribners Ref) Mac Lib Ref.

— Red Sea & Indian Ocean Cruising Guide. 190p. (C). 1985. 160.00 (0-85288-096-0, Pub. by Laurie Norie & Wilson Ltd) St Mut.

Lucas, Alan K. Giving & Taking Help. rev. ed. 194p. 1994. pap. 18.00 (0-9623634-5-6) N American Assn.

Lucas, Alice. Cambodians in America: Courageous People from a Troubled Country. (New Faces of Liberty Background Essays Ser.). (Illus.). 25p. 1993. pap. text 5.00 (0-936434-70-8) SF Study Ctr.

— How the Farmer Tricked the Evil Demon. Tan, Samol, tr. from CAM. (Illus.). 32p. (J). (gr. 1-5). 1994. 14.95 (1-879600-20-X) Pac Asia Pr.

— How the Farmer Tricked the Evil Demon. Nguyen, Anh, tr. from CAM. (ENG & VIE., Illus.). 32p. (J). (gr. 1-5). 1994. 15.95 (1-879600-23-4) Pac Asia Pr.

— How the Farmer Tricked the Evil Demon. Sivongsay, Vandy, tr. from CAM. (ENG & LAO., Illus.). 32p. (J). (gr. 1-5). 1994. 15.95 (1-879600-24-2) Pac Asia Pr.

— How the Farmer Tricked the Evil Demon: (English/Hmong Edition) Xiong, Ia, tr. from CAM. (MUL., Illus.). 32p. (J). (gr. 1-5). 1994. 15.95 (1-879600-25-0) Pac Asia Pr.

— How the Farmer Tricked the Evil Demon: (Khmer/English Edition) Tan, Samol, tr. from CAM. (MUL., Illus.). 32p. (J). (gr. 1-5). 1994. 15.95 (1-879600-21-8) Pac Asia Pr.

— Twelve Years a Slave: Excerpts from the Narrative of Solomon Northup. Link, Geoffrey, ed. (Illus.). 43p. (Orig.). (J). (gr. 5-12). 1992. pap. text, teacher ed. 5.00 (0-936434-59-7, Pub. by Zellerbach Fam Fund) Intl Spec Bk.

— Voices of Liberty Storybooks Complete Package: Magic Crossbow (Vietnam), Four Champa Trees (Laos), Mountain of Men (Cambodia) (Illus.). 1990. pap. text 40.00 incl. audio (0-936434-49-X, Pub. by Zellerbach Fam Fund) Intl Spec Bk.

Lucas, Alice, ed. Folk Stories from the Philippines. Consul, Wilma, tr. LC 95-61432.Tr. of Mga Kuwentong Bayan. (ENG & TAG., Illus.). 64p. (YA). 1995. 18.95 (0-936434-85-6, Many Cultures Pubng); pap. 12.95 (0-936434-89-9, Many Cultures Pubng) SF Study Ctr.

Lucas, Alice, ed. see Northup, Solomon.

Lucas, Andrew. Desktop Publishing: Using Pagemaker on the Apple Macintosh. (Computers & Their Applications Ser.). 233p. 1987. pap. text 29.95 (0-470-20819-8) P-H.

Lucas, Andrew J. & Ranger, Jeff. Northwest Passage. (Cyberpunk Ser.). 64p. 1996. pap. 10.00 (1-887801-44-8, Atlas Games) Trident MN.

Lucas, Anelissa. Chinese Medical Modernization: Comparative Policy Continuities 1930's-1980's. LC 81-23361. 188p. 1982. 45.00 (0-275-90851-8, C0851, Praeger Pubs) Greenwood.

Lucas, Angela M., ed. Anglo-Irish Poems of the Middle Ages. LC 95-164261. 224p. 1997. pap. 49.95 (1-85607-142-1, Pub. by Columba Press) Intl Scholars.

— Anglo-Irish Poems of the Middle Ages. 224p. 1997. 69.95 (1-85607-216-9) Intl Scholars.

Lucas, Ann F. Strengthening Departmental Leadership: A Team-Building Guide for Chairs in Colleges & Universities. LC 94-21302. (Higher & Adult Education Ser.). 319p. 1994. text 34.45 (0-7879-0012-5) Jossey-Bass.

*Lucas, Ann F., et al. Leading Academic Change: Essential Roles for Department Chairs. LC 99-6977. (Higher Education Ser.). 320p. 2000. 32.95 (0-7879-4682-6, Pfffr & Co) Jossey-Bass.

Lucas, Ann L., tr. & intro. see Collodi, Carlo.

Lucas, Anthony J., jt. auth. see Marco, Gayle J.

Lucas, Anton. One Soul, One Struggle. (Illus.). 224p. 1991. pap. text 24.95 (0-04-442249-0, Pub. by Allen & Unwin Pty) Paul & Co Pubs.

Lucas, Arthur, jt. ed. see Black, Paul.

Lucas, Barbara, tr. see Lindgren, Astrid.

Lucas, Barbara A. & Freedman, Stephen, eds. Technology Choice & Change in Developing Countries: Internal & External Constraints. (Illus.). 155p. 1983. 70.00 (0-907567-32-0, Tycooly Pub); pap. 40.00 (0-907567-33-9, Tycooly Pub) Weidner & Sons.

*Lucas, Ben. Rifts Australia. Marciniszyn, Alex et al, eds. (Rifts Worldbook Ser.: Vol. 19). (Illus.). 224p. (YA). (gr. 8 up). 1999. pap. 20.95 (1-57457-018-8, 834) Palladium Bks.

Lucas, Berny. Brewster Rooster. unabridged ed. (Illus.). 32p. (J). (gr. k-2). 1993. 10.95 (1-55074-109-8, Pub. by Kids Can Pr) Genl Dist Srvs.

— Brewster Rooster. unabridged ed. (Illus.). 32p. (J). (gr. k-2). 1997. pap. 5.95 (1-55074-292-2, Pub. by Kids Can Pr) Genl Dist Srvs.

*Lucas Books. Star Wars Giant Coloring Fun. (Star Wars Ser.). 1999. pap. 8.99 (0-375-80234-7) Random.

Lucas Books, ed. Queen Amidala Paper Dolls, 1. 1999. pap. 3.99 (0-375-80020-4) Random.

Lucas Books & Random House Staff, creators. Mask Punch Out Book. 1999. pap. 4.99 (0-375-80019-0) Random.

*Lucas Books Staff, ed. Jedi Punch-Out Book. (Illus.). (J). 2000. pap. 3.99 (0-375-80565-6) Random.

— Podracer Punch-Out Book. (Illus.). (J). 2000. pap. 3.99 (0-375-80566-4) Random.

Lucas, Caroline. Writing for Women: The Example of Woman As Reader in Elizabethan Romance. (Gender in Writing Ser.). 160p. 1990. pap. 35.95 (0-335-09017-6) Taylor & Francis.

Lucas, Caroline, et al. Population/Family Planning Thesaurus: An Alphabetical & Hierarchical Display of Terms Drawn from Population-Related Literature in the Social Sciences LC 74-25288. xx, 286p. 1975. write for info. (0-89055-047-6) Carolina Pop Ctr.

Lucas, Carrie. Dinosaurs. 3rd ed. LC 99-18617. 304p. 1999. pap. 67.50 (0-07-303642-0) McGraw.

*Lucas, Cecil. Italia Contemporanea: Conversations with Native Speakers. LC 00-26889. 2000. pap. write for info. (0-300-08302-5) Yale U Pr.

Lucas, Cedric, jt. illus. see Stroud, Bettye.

Lucas, Ceil, ed. Multicultural Aspects of Sociolinguistics in Deaf Communities. (Sociolinguistics in Deaf Communities Ser.: Vol. 2). 246p. 1996. text 39.95 (1-56368-046-7) Gallaudet Univ Pr.

— Pinky Extensions & Eye Gaze: Language Use in Deaf Communities. (Sociolinguistics in Deaf Communities Ser.: Vol. 4). 224p. 1998. text 55.00 (1-56368-070-X) Gallaudet Univ Pr.

— Sign Language Research: Theoretical Issues. LC 89-28131. (Illus.). 398p. 1990. text 49.95 (0-930323-58-0) Gallaudet Univ Pr.

— Sociolinguistics in Deaf Communities. (Sociolinguistics in Deaf Communities Ser.: Vol. 1). 352p. 1995. text 39.95 (1-56368-036-X) Gallaudet Univ Pr.

— The Sociolinguistics of the Deaf Community. 307p. 1989. text 65.00 (0-12-458045-9) Acad Pr.

Lucas, Ceil & Borders, Denise G. Language Diversity & Classroom Discourse. LC 93-37619. (Language & Educational Processes Ser.). 1994. pap. 39.50 (1-56750-076-5) Ablx Pub.

Lucas, Ceil & Borders, Denise G., eds. Language Diversity & Classroom Discourse. LC 93-37619. (Language & Educational Processes Ser.). 1994. text 73.25 (0-89391-969-1) Ablx Pub.

Lucas, Ceil & Valli, Clayton. Language Contact in the American Deaf Community. LC 92-4929. (Illus.). 161p. 1992. text 39.95 (0-12-458040-8) Acad Pr.

Lucas, Ceil, jt. auth. see Valli, Clayton.

Lucas, Celia. Prisoners of Santo Tomas: A True Account of Women POWs under Japanese Control. 1996. pap. 16.95 (0-85052-541-1, 525411) Leo Cooper.

Lucas, Charles, ed. The Pitcairn Island Register Book. LC 75-3444. (Illus.). reprint ed. 32.50 (0-404-14447-0) AMS Pr.

Lucas, Charles, ed. see Lee, Douglas.

Lucas, Charles, ed. see Nitobe, Inazo O.

Lucas, Chester L., jt. auth. see Kangari, Roozbeh.

Lucas, Chris, ed. see deTagle, Lillian Lorca.

Lucas, Christine A., jt. auth. see Lucas, John F.

Lucas, Christopher, ed. see Ricalton, James.

Lucas, Christopher J. American Higher Education. 385p. 1996. pap. 17.95 (0-312-12945-9) St Martin.

— Crisis in the Academy: Rethinking Higher Education in America. 1998. pap. 17.95 (0-312-17686-4) St Martin.

— Teacher Education in America: Reform Agendas for the 21st Century. LC 96-35421. 320p. 1997. text 39.95 (0-312-16444-0) St Martin.

Lucas, Christopher J., ed. see Richalton, James.

Lucas, Claudia, tr. see Renirkens, Clement.

Lucas, Colin, ed. Rewriting the French Revolution: The Andrew Browning Lectures, 1989. 224p. 1991. 59.00 (0-19-821976-8) OUP.

Lucas, Colleen. The Bible-Sermon Companion. pap. text. write for info. (0-9634547-0-6) Lucas Assocs.

Lucas County Chapter of OGS Staff. Andreas & Bakins' Illustrated Atlas of Lucas County & Wood County, Ohio. (Illus.). 136p. 1999. pap. 60.00 (0-7884-1094-6, L810) Heritage Bk.

Lucas, Craig. Blue Window: A Comedy LC 85-158558. 78 p. 1985. write for info. (0-573-61954-9) French.

— Missing Persons. 1996. pap. 5.25 (0-8222-1474-1) Dramatists Play.

*Lucas, Craig. Prelude to a Kiss & Other Plays. 300p. 2000. pap. 16.95 (1-55936-193-X) Theatre Comm.

Lucas, Craig. Reckless. rev. ed. 1985. pap. 5.25 (0-8222-0937-3) Dramatists Play.

— Reckless & Blue Window: 2 Plays. LC 89-4413. 128p. 1989. reprint ed. pap. 11.95 (0-930452-95-X) Theatre Comm.

— What I Meant Was: New Plays & Selected One-Acts. LC 98-49478. 400p. 1999. pap. 17.50 (1-55936-159-X, Pub. by Theatre Comm) Consort Bk Sales.

Lucas, Craig & Carnelia, Craig. Three Postcards. rev. ed. 1995. pap. 6.00 (0-8222-1477-6) Dramatists Play.

Lucas, Craig, jt. auth. see Sussler, Betsy.

Lucas, D. Understanding the Church. 1996. pap. 15.99 (1-85792-257-3, Pub. by Christian Focus) Spring Arbor Dist.

Lucas, D. & Gorman, M. Dione Lucas Book of French Cooking. 1986. 14.98 (0-685-16789-5, 615347) Random Hse Value.

Lucas, D. A., et al. Near Miss Reporting As a Safety Tool. (Illus.). 160p. 1991. 84.95 (0-7506-1178-2) Buttrwrth-Heinemann.

Lucas, Daniel B. Nicaragua: War of the Filibusters . . . 2194p. 1986. reprint ed. 25.00 (0-913129-10-0) La Tienda.

Lucas, Daniel M., jt. ed. see Gall, Timothy L.

Lucas, Daryl & Veerman, David. 105 Questions Children Ask about Money Matters. LC 97-951. 249p. 1997. pap. 9.99 (0-8423-4526-4) Tyndale Hse.

— 107 Questions Children Ask about Prayer. LC 98-23034. 1998. pap. 10.99 (0-8423-4542-6) Tyndale Hse.

— 106 Questions Children Ask about Our World. LC 97-41761. (J). 1998. 8.99 (0-8423-4527-2) Tyndale Hse.

Lucas, Daryl, ed. see Smith, Carol & Weidemann, Valerie.

Lucas, Daryl J. God Is Great: An Eager Reader Devotional. (Illus.). 360p. (J). 1995. 14.99 (0-8423-1618-3) Tyndale Hse.

*Lucas, Daryl J. & Veerman, David R. 104 Preguntas Que los Ninos Haven Acerca del Cielo y los Angeles: Con Respuestas Biblicas Para Padre, Vol. 1.Tr. of 104 Questions Children Ask about Heaven & Angles. (SPA., Illus.). 240p. 1998. pap. text 9.99 (0-311-38653-9, Edit Mundo) Casa Bautista.

Lucas, Daryl J., jt. ed. see Kendrick, Michael.

Lucas, Daryl J., ed. see Veerman, David R., et al.

Lucas, David. First Science Dictionary: English with Arabic Glossary. 1986. 12.00 (0-86685-077-5) Intl Bk Ctr.

— Lucas vs. the Green Machine: Landmark Supreme Court Property Rights Decision by the Man Who Won It Against the Odds. Bolkey, Lorna et al, eds. LC 95-12090. (Illus.). 319p. (Orig.). 1995. pap. 16.95 (1-57090-011-6) Alexander Dist.

Lucas, David, jt. auth. see LeBeau, Charles.

*Lucas, David J. & Veerman, David R. 106 Preguntas Que los Ninos Hacen Acerca. Adkison, Sandra, tr. (SPA., Illus.). 256p. 2000. pap. text 9.99 (0-311-38655-5, Edit Mundo) Casa Bautista.

Lucas, David W., jt. auth. see LeBeau, Charles.

Lucas, Dennis. Rodeo Harpsicord. (Sundown Ser.). 22p. 1991. pap. 5.00 (1-879969-01-7) CRS Outloudbooks.

— Thirteen Ways of Looking at a Crow. 32p. (Orig.). 1992. pap. 9.00 (1-880516-05-5) Left Hand Bks.

Lucas, Dewitt. Handwriting & Character (1923) 364p. 1998. reprint ed. pap. 27.95 (0-7661-0542-3) Kessinger Pub.

Lucas, DeWitt B. Handwriting & Character Analysis. 64p. 1996. reprint ed. spiral bd. 11.00 (0-7873-0571-5) Hlth Research.

*Lucas, Dione. The Cordon Bleu Cookbook. LC 98-52467. (Illus.). 352p. 1999. reprint ed. pap. 16.95 (1-55821-807-6) Lyons Pr.

Lucas, Dione, jt. auth. see Klapthor, Margaret.

Lucas, Dolores D. Emily Dickinson & Riddle. LC 73-76428. 151p. 1969. 25.00 (0-87580-011-4) N Ill U Pr.

Lucas, Don. The Father of American Tattooing: Franklin Paul Rogers. (Illus.). 96p. 1990. lib. bdg. 35.00 (0-916638-78-2) Meyerbooks.

Lucas-Dubreton, Jean. Restoration & the July Monarchy. LC 29-16694. (National History of France Ser.: No. 8). reprint ed. 45.00 (0-404-50798-0) AMS Pr.

Lucas, E. V. The Life of Charles Lamb, 2 vols. in 1. 5th rev. ed. LC 68-59324. reprint ed. 124.50 (0-404-04059-4) AMS Pr.

Lucas, E. V., jt. auth. see Graves, Charles L.

Lucas, E. V., ed. see Lamb, Charles & Lamb, Mary.

Lucas, Edward V. Adventures & Misgivings. LC 78-105027. (Essay Index Reprint Ser.). 1977. 18.95 (0-8369-1523-2) Ayer.

— All of a Piece: New Essays. LC 68-22923. (Essay Index Reprint Ser.). 1977. reprint ed. 19.95 (0-8369-0627-6) Ayer.

— Another Book of Verses for Children. LC 73-37017. (Granger Index Reprint Ser.). (Illus.). 1977. reprint ed. 29.95 (0-8369-6316-4) Ayer.

— Boswell of Bagdad. LC 79-107722. (Essay Index Reprint Ser.). 1977. 20.95 (0-8369-1579-8) Ayer.

— Cloud & Silver. LC 73-156665. (Essay Index Reprint Ser.). 1977. reprint ed. 19.95 (0-8369-2411-8) Ayer.

— The Colvins & Their Friends. (BCL1-PR English Literature Ser.). 365p. 1992. reprint ed. lib. bdg. 89.00 (0-7812-7505-9) Rprt Serv.

— Encounters & Diversions. LC 70-156684. (Essay Index Reprint Ser.). 1977. reprint ed. 20.95 (0-8369-2560-2) Ayer.

— English Leaves. LC 73-99709. (Essay Index Reprint Ser.). 1977. 21.95 (0-8369-1361-2) Ayer.

— Fireside & Sunshine. LC 68-8480. (Essay Index Reprint Ser.). 1977. 19.95 (0-8369-0628-4) Ayer.

— The Friendly Town: A Little Book for the Urbane. LC 70-152153. (Granger Index Reprint Ser.). 1977. reprint ed. 24.95 (0-8369-6262-1) Ayer.

— Fronded Isle, & Other Essays. LC 68-29225. (Essay Index Reprint Ser.). 1977. reprint ed. 18.95 (0-8369-0629-2) Ayer.

— Giving & Receiving. LC 73-142657. (Essay Index Reprint Ser.). 1977. 19.95 (0-8369-2058-9) Ayer.

— Lemon Verbena & Other Essays. LC 76-84320. (Essay Index Reprint Ser.). 1977. 18.95 (0-8369-1090-7) Ayer.

— The Life of Charles Lamb, 2 vols., Set. (BCL1-PR English Literature Ser.). 1992. reprint ed. lib. bdg. 150.00 (0-7812-7586-5) Rprt Serv.

— Loiterer's Harvest. LC 77-142658. (Essay Index Reprint Ser.). 1977. 20.95 (0-8369-2059-7) Ayer.

— Luck of the Year. LC 76-90657. (Essay Index Reprint Ser.). 1977. 19.95 (0-8369-1224-1) Ayer.

— Only the Other Day: A Volume of Essays. LC 67-28756. (Essay Index Reprint Ser.). 1977. 19.95 (0-8369-0630-6) Ayer.

— Phantom Journal & Other Essays & Diversions. LC 75-111844. (Essay Index Reprint Ser.). 1977. 20.95 (0-8369-1615-8) Ayer.

— Pleasure Trove. LC 68-57329. (Essay Index Reprint Ser.). 1977. 19.95 (0-8369-0631-4) Ayer.

— Reading, Writing & Remembering: A Literary Record. (Illus.). 1971. reprint ed. 24.00 (0-403-01076-4) Scholarly.

— Saunterer's Rewards. LC 75-128271. (Essay Index Reprint Ser.). 1977. 19.95 (0-8369-1887-8) Ayer.

— Specially Selected. LC 77-117891. (Essay Index Reprint Ser.). 1977. 19.95 (0-8369-1673-5) Ayer.

— Turning Things Over. LC 72-107723. (Essay Index Reprint Ser.). 1977. 19.95 (0-8369-1524-0) Ayer.

— Urbanities. LC 79-128272. (Essay Index Reprint Ser.). 1977. 19.95 (0-8369-1888-6) Ayer.

— Vermeer the Magical. LC 79-37352. (Select Bibliographies Reprint Ser.). (Illus.). 1977. reprint ed. 16.95 (0-8369-6699-6) Ayer.

— Visibility Good. LC 68-54356. (Essay Index Reprint Ser.). 1977. 18.95 (0-8369-0632-2) Ayer.

Lucas, Edward V., compiled by. Book of Verses for Children. LC 71-121927. (Granger Index Reprint Ser.). 1977. 20.95 (0-8369-6168-4) Ayer.

— Open Road. 7th ed. LC 75-121928. (Granger Index Reprint Ser.). 1977. 19.95 (0-8369-6169-2) Ayer.

Lucas, Edward V., jt. auth. see Graves, C. L.

*Lucas, Eileen. Al Gore: Vice President. (Gateway Biography Ser.). 48p. (J). (gr. 2-7). 1999. pap. 8.95 (0-7613-1329-X, Copper Beech Bks) Millbrook Pr.

Lucas, Eileen. Aruba Stories Series, 4 bks. Incl. Abdu the Fisherman. (Illus.). 24p. (Orig.). (J). (ps). 1995. pap. Not sold separately (977-5325-45-5, Pub. by Hoopoe Bks); Belia's Ball. (Illus.). 24p. (J). (ps). 1995. pap. Not sold separately (977-5325-43-9, Pub. by Hoopoe Bks); New Baby. (Illus.). 24p. (Orig.). (J). (ps). 1995. pap. Not sold separately (977-5325-46-3, Pub. by Hoopoe Bks); Tofaha's Basket. (Illus.). 24p. (Orig.). (J). (ps). 1995. pap. Not sold separately (977-5325-44-7, Pub. by Hoopoe Bks); (J). (ps up). 11.95 (0-614-23174-4) AMIDEAST.

*Lucas, Eileen. Bill Bradley: A Shot at the Presidency. LC 99-28668. (Gateway Biography Ser.). 48p. (J). (gr. 2-7). 1999. pap. 8.95 (0-7613-1328-1, Copper Beech Bks) Millbrook Pr.

Lucas, Eileen. The Cherokees: People of the Southeast. LC 92-40874. (Native Americans Ser.). (Illus.). 64p. (J). (gr. 4-6). 1993. lib. bdg. 21.90 (1-56294-312-X) Millbrook Pr.

— Civil Rights: The Long Struggle. LC 96-12264. (Issues in Focus Ser.). (Illus.). 112p. (YA). (gr. 6 up). 1996. lib. bdg. 20.95 (0-89490-729-8) Enslow Pubs.

— Contemporary Human Rights Activists. LC 96-41253. (Global Profiles Ser.). (J). 1997. 19.95 (0-8160-3298-X) Facts on File.

— Cracking the Wall: The Story of the Little Rock Nine. LC 96-45003. (On My Own Bks.). (Illus.). 48p. (J). (gr. 1-3). 1997. 13.95 (0-87614-990-5, Carolrhoda); pap. 5.95 (1-57505-227-X, Carolrhoda) Lerner Pub.

Lucas, Eileen. Cracking the Wall: The Story of the Little Rock Nine. (Carolrhoda on My Own Bks.). (Illus.). (J). 1997. 11.30 (0-606-18248-9) Turtleback.

Lucas, Eileen. The Eighteenth & Twenty-First Amendments: Alcohol, Prohibition, & Repeal. LC 97-20073. (Constitution Ser.). (Illus.). 128p. (YA). (gr. 6 up). 1998. lib. bdg. 20.95 (0-89490-926-6) Enslow Pubs.

— Eisenhower, Kennedy, & Johnson. LC 95-43543. (Complete History of Our Presidents Ser.: Vol. 10). (J). 1996. write for info. (0-86593-411-8) Rourke Corp.

— Elizabeth Dole: A Leader in Washington. LC 97-6279. (Gateway Biographies Ser.). (Illus.). 48p. (J). (gr. 3-6). 1998. lib. bdg. 20.90 (0-7613-0203-4) Millbrook Pr.

*Lucas, Eileen. Elizabeth Dole: A Leader in Washington. (Gateway Biography Ser.). 48p. (J). (gr. 2-7). 1999. pap. 8.95 (0-7613-1327-3, Copper Beech Bks) Millbrook Pr.

— Elizabeth Dole: A Leader in Washington. (Illus.). (J). 1999. 14.40 (0-606-18288-8) Turtleback.

Lucas, Eileen. European Conquest. LC 95-5426. (Native Latin American Cultures Ser.). 64p. (J). (gr. 4-8). 1995. lib. bdg. 23.93 (0-86625-556-7) Rourke Pubns.

— Everglades. LC 94-26278. (Wonders of the World Ser.). (Illus.). 64p. (J). (gr. 4-7). 1995. lib. bdg. 25.64 (0-8114-6373-7) Raintree Steck-V.

— Jane Goodall: Friend of the Chimps. (J). (gr. 4-7). 1992. pap. 4.80 (0-395-63570-5) HM.

— Naturalists, Conservationists & Environmentalists. (American Profiles Ser.). (Illus.). 160p. (YA). (gr. 5-12). 1994. 19.95 (0-8160-2919-9) Facts on File.

— Nixon, Ford, & Carter. LC 95-43537. (Complete History of Our Presidents Ser.: Vol. 11). (J). 1996. write for info. (0-86593-412-6) Rourke Corp.

— Our Postal System. LC 98-23316. (I Know America Ser.). 48p. (J). (gr. 2-4). 1999. lib. bdg. 20.90 (0-7613-0966-7, Copper Beech Bks) Millbrook Pr.

— Reagan, Bush, & Clinton. LC 95-26666. (Complete History of Our Presidents Ser.: Vol. 12). (J). 1996. write for info. (0-86593-414-2) Rourke Corp.

— Trade. LC 95-7292. (Native Latin American Cultures Ser.). 64p. (J). (gr. 4-8). 1995. lib. bdg. 23.93 (0-86625-555-9) Rourke Pubns.

— Vincent Van Gogh. LC 96-27617. (On My Own Bks.). (Illus.). (J). 1997. lib. bdg. 13.13 (1-57505-038-2, Carolrhoda) Lerner Pub.

— Vincent Van Gogh. (Illus.). 48p. (J). 1997. pap. text 5.95 (1-57505-062-5, Carolrhoda) Lerner Pub.

Lucas, Elizabeth. Inspirations. Anderson, Mac, ed. 78p. (Orig.). 1990. pap. 7.95 (0-931089-94-8) Great Quotations.

— Thinking of You. Anderson, Mac, ed. 78p. (Orig.). 1990. pap. 7.95 (0-931089-87-5) Great Quotations.

Lucas, Elizabeth, ed. Nurses & Health Care. 1976. pap. 24.95 (0-8464-0679-9) Beekman Pubs.

*Lucas, Emmett & Sheffield, Ella. Washington Co., Tennessee, Settlements of Estates, 1790-1841. 200p. 1999. 30.00 (0-89308-528-6) Southern Hist Pr.

*Lucas, Eric. Hidden British Columbia. (Hidden Travel Ser.). (Illus.). 432p. 1999. pap. 17.95 (1-56975-174-9) Ulysses Pr.

Lucas, Eric. Hidden Pacific Northwest. 4th rev. ed. (Hidden Travel Ser.). (Illus.). 592p. 1998. pap. 17.95 (1-56975-131-5) Ulysses Pr.

*Lucas, Eric. Hidden Pacific Northwest. 5th rev. ed. (Hidden Travel Ser.). (Illus.). 592p. 2000. pap. 18.95 (1-56975-204-4, Pub. by Ulysses Pr) Publishers Group.

Lucas, Eric. Hidden Washington. 2nd ed. (Hidden Travel Ser.). (Illus.). 392p. 1998. reprint ed. pap. 14.95 (1-56975-164-1) Ulysses Pr.

*Lucas, Eric. The Sovereigns: Jewish Country Life During the Nazi Rise to Power. 2001. pap. 16.95 (0-8101-1167-5) Northwestern U Pr.

Lucas, F. L., ed. see Webster, John.

Lucas, Frances. If Looks Could Kill. LC 94-38405. 190p. (Orig.). 1995. pap. 9.95 (0-934678-63-4) New Victoria Pubs.

Lucas, Frank L. Authors Dead & Living. LC 68-29226. (Essay Index Reprint Ser.). 1977. reprint ed. 20.95 (0-8369-0633-0) Ayer.

— The Decline & Fall of the Romantic Ideal. LC 75-30007. 1976. reprint ed. 24.50 (0-404-14013-0) AMS Pr.

— Seneca & Elizabethan Tragedy. 1973. 250.00 (0-87968-047-4) Gordon Pr.

— Seneca & Elizabethan Tragedy. LC 68-1142. (Studies in Comparative Literature: No. 35). 1969. reprint ed. lib. bdg. 75.00 (0-8383-0668-3) M S G Haskell Hse.

— Studies French & English. LC 69-17583. (Essay Index Reprint Ser.). 1977. 21.95 (0-8369-0084-7) Ayer.

— Woman Clothed with the Sun, & Other Stories. LC 71-122731. (Short Story Index Reprint Ser.). 1977. 20.95 (0-8369-3564-0) Ayer.

Lucas, Franz D. & Heitmann, Margret. Stadt des Glaubens. (Wissenschaftliche Abhandlungen des Salomon Ludwig Steinheim-Instituts fur Deutsch-Judische Geschichte Ser.: Bd. 3). (GER.). viii, 583p. 1992. write for info. (3-487-09495-9) G Olms Pubs.

Lucas, G. B., jt. ed. see Shew, H. D.

Lucas, G. E., jt. ed. see Corwin, W. R.

Lucas, G. G. Road Vehicle Performance. (Transportation Studies: Vol. 7). xiv, 202p. 1986. text 156.00 (0-677-21400-6) Gordon & Breach.

Lucas, Gail E. Trevor, the Traveling Tree. large type ed. LC 96-2053. (Illus.). 32p. (J). (ps-3). 1997. 15.95 (1-887813-24-1) Cucumber Island.

*Lucas, Gavin. Encountering Archaeology: Fieldwork, Specialism & Practice. LC 00-32213. 2000. pap. write for info. (0-415-23534-0) Routledge.

Lucas, Gene A. Siamese Fighting Fish. (Illus.). 64p. 1997. 12.95 (0-7938-0120-6, WW-017) TFH Pubns.

Lucas, Geoffrey. Imagexercise Golf: The Complete Story. 1986. pap. write for info. (0-9692902-2-5) AZ Edge.

Lucas, George. The Empire Strikes Back. 1994. 8.98 (1-57042-172-2) Warner Bks.

*Lucas, George. Episode I: The Phantom Menace Movie Storybook. (Star Wars). (Illus.). 64p. (YA). (gr. k up). 1999. lib. bdg. 11.99 (0-375-90009-8, Pub. by Random Bks Yng Read) Random.

Lucas, George. From the Adventures of Luke Skywalker. LC 77-88169. 224p. 1986. mass mkt. 5.99 (0-345-34146-5, Del Rey) Ballantine Pub Grp.

— A New Hope. (Star Wars Ser.). 272p. 1995. 16.00 (0-345-40077-1, Del Rey) Ballantine Pub Grp.

— A New Hope. deluxe ed. LC PN1997.S65943 1998b. (Star Wars Ser.). (Illus.). 192p. 1998. pap. 18.95 (0-345-42080-2, Del Rey) Ballantine Pub Grp.

— The Phantom Menace, Vol.1. (Star Wars Ser.). (Illus.). 112p. 1999. pap. 12.95 (1-56971-359-6) Dark Horse Comics.

— Return of the Jedi. 1995. 8.98 (1-57042-208-7) Warner Bks.

*Lucas, George. Star Wars: Episode I: The Phantom Menace Facsimile Script. (Script Facsimile Ser.). (Illus.). 144p. 2000. pap. 18.95 (0-345-43123-5, Del Rey) Ballantine Pub Grp.

L

Lucas, George. Star Wars: Episode I: The Phantom Menace Illustrated Screenplay. LC 99-90053. (Star Wars Ser.). (Illus.). 150p. (Orig.). 1999. pap. 14.95 (*0-345-43110-3*, Del Rey) Ballantine Pub Grp.

— Star Wars Adventure. 1994. 8.98 (*1-57042-153-6*) Warner Bks.

— Star Wars: Empire Strikes Back: From the Adventures of Luke Skywalker. (Star Wars Ser.). 1997. mass mkt. 3.99 (*0-614-27736-1*, Del Rey) Ballantine Pub Grp.

— Star Wars Episode I - The Phantom Menace: A Storybook. (Star Wars). (Illus.). 64p. (J). (gr. k-3). 1999. pap. 7.99 (*0-375-80009-3*) Random.

— Star Wars: Return of the Jedi: From the Adventures of Luke Skywalker. (Star Wars Ser.). 1997. mass mkt. 3.99 (*0-614-27737-X*, Del Rey) Ballantine Pub Grp.

— Star Wars Trilogy. (Star Wars Ser.). 1987. 15.10 (*0-606-01231-1*, Pub. by Turtleback) Demco.

Lucas, George & Claremont, Chris. Shadow Dawn. 560p. 1998. reprint ed. mass mkt. 5.99 (*0-553-57289-X*) Bantam.

Lucas, George & Kasdan, Lawrence. Return of the Jedi. LC 97-97056. (Illus.). 208p. 1998. pap. 12.00 (*0-345-42079-9*, Del Rey) Ballantine Pub Grp.

— Return of the Jedi. deluxe ed. LC PN1997.R515 1998b. (Star Wars Ser.). (Illus.). 144p. 1998. pap. 18.95 (*0-345-42082-9*, Del Rey) Ballantine Pub Grp.

Lucas, George, et al. The Empire Strikes Back. deluxe ed. LC PN1997.E6243 1998b. (Star Wars Ser.). (Illus.). 160p. 1998. pap. 18.95 (*0-345-42081-0*, Del Rey) Ballantine Pub Grp.

— Star Wars Trilogy, 3 vols. LC 87-91126. (Star Wars Ser.). 480p. 1987. pap. 10.00 (*0-345-34806-0*, Del Rey) Ballantine Pub Grp.

— Star Wars Trilogy. (Star Wars Ser.). 1997. mass mkt. 6.99 (*0-345-91126-1*) Ballantine Pub Grp.

— Star Wars Trilogy: Star Wars; The Empire Strikes Back; Return of the Jedi, 3 vols. in 1. 1993. mass mkt. 0.05 (*0-345-38438-5*, Del Rey) Ballantine Pub Grp.

Lucas, George, jt. auth. see Claremont, Chris.

Lucas, George A. The Diary of George A. Lucas: An America Art Agent in Paris, 1857-1909, Vol. 1. LC 77-85561. (Illus.). 209p. 1979. reprint ed. pap. 64.80 (*0-7837-9415-0*, 206017100001) Bks Demand.

— The Diary of George A. Lucas: An America Art Agent in Paris, 1857-1909, Vol. 2. LC 77-85561. (Illus.). 979p. 1979. reprint ed. pap. 200.00 (*0-7837-9416-9*, 206017100002) Bks Demand.

Lucas, George B. Every Other Day: Letters from the Pacific. LC 95-8682. (Illus.). 312p. 1995. 32.95 (*1-55750-528-4*) Naval Inst Pr.

Lucas, George B., et al. Introduction to Plant Diseases: Identification & Management. 2nd ed. (Illus.). 368p. 1992. pap. 42.95 (*0-442-00578-4*) Chapman & Hall.

Lucas, George, Educational Foundation Staff. Learn & Live. LC 97-70481. (Illus.). 275p. (Orig.). (J). (gr. k-12). 1997. pap. 20.00 (*0-9656326-0-1*) George Lucas Educ Found.

Lucas, George F. American Drop Shippers Directory, Vol. 20. 15th ed. 40p. 1997. pap. text 15.00 (*0-911652-00-0*) Wrld Wide Trade.

— Importers Confidential Drop-Ship Directory. 16p. 1985. pap. text 5.00 (*0-911652-01-9*) Wrld Wide Trade.

Lucas, George L., et al. A Primer of Biomechanics. LC 97-48865. 240p. 1998. pap. 45.00 (*0-387-98456-9*) Spr-Verlag.

Lucas, George R., Jr. The Rehabilitation of Whitehead: An Analytic & Historical Assessment of Process Philosophy. LC 88-22607. (SUNY Series in Philosophy). 261p. (C). 1989. text 24.50 (*0-88706-988-6*) State U NY Pr.

Lucas, George R. Two Views of Freedom in Process & Thought. LC 79-12287. (American Academy of Religion. Dissertation Ser.: No. 28). 186p. reprint ed. pap. 57.70 (*0-7837-5415-9*, 204517900005) Bks Demand.

Lucas, George R., Jr., ed. Hegel & Whitehead: Contemporary Perspectives on Systematic Philosophy. LC 85-9745. (SUNY Series in Hegelian Studies). 325p. (C). 1986. text 19.50 (*0-88706-144-3*) State U NY Pr.

Lucas, George R., Jr. & Braeckman, Antoon, eds. Whitehead und der Deutsche Idealismus: Whitehead & German Idealism. 164p. 1990. pap. 27.00 (*3-261-04212-5*) P Lang Pubng.

Lucas, George T. & Stubbs, David A. Nontraditional Methods of Sensing Stress, Strain & Damage in Materials & Structure. LC 97-18165. (Illus.). 231p. 1997. pap. text 52.00 (*0-8031-2403-1*, STP1318) ASTM.

Lucas, H. J. Rock 'n Roll Is Here to Stay. 138p. 1983. 40.00 (*0-901976-82-2*, Pub. by United Writers Pubns) St Mut.

Lucas, H. M., tr. see Ehrenberg, Richard.

Lucas, H. M., tr. see Knapp, Georg F.

Lucas, Henry C., Jr. Implementation: The Key to Successful Information Systems. LC 80-27009. 224p. 1981. text 69.00 (*0-231-04434-8*) Col U Pr.

Lucas, Henry C. Information Technology & the Productivity Paradox: Assessing the Value of Investing in IT. LC 98-21470. (Illus.). 240p. 1999. 27.50 (*0-19-512159-7*) OUP.

— Information Technology for Management. 6th ed. LC 96-77621. 700p. (C). 1996. 83.75 (*0-07-039061-4*) McGraw.

***Lucas, Henry C.** Information Technology for Management. 7th ed. LC 99-14924. 2000. write for info. (*0-07-229763-8*) McGrw-H Hghr Educ.

Lucas, Henry C., Jr. The T-Form Organization: Using Technology to Design Organizations for the 21st Century. (Management Ser.). 272p. 1995. 32.95 (*0-7879-0167-9*) Jossey-Bass.

Lucas, Henry C. Why Information Systems Fail. LC 74-18395. (Illus.). 141p. reprint ed. pap. 43.80 (*0-608-11444-8*, 202197000024) Bks Demand.

Lucas, Henry S. The Renaissance & the Reformation. LC 83-45665. reprint ed. 67.50 (*0-404-19815-5*) AMS Pr.

Lucas, I., ed. see Comparative Pathology of the Heart Symposium Staff.

Lucas, Ian. Growing up Positive: Stories from a Generation of Young People Affected by AIDS. LC 96-207951. (AIDS Awareness Ser.). 192p. 1997. 69.95 (*0-304-33197-X*) Continuum.

— Growing up Positive: Stories from a Generation of Young People Affected by AIDS. LC 96-207951. (AIDS Awareness Ser.). 192p. 1997. pap. 19.95 (*0-304-33207-0*) Continuum.

— Impertinent Decorum: Gay Theatrical Maneuvers. LC 95-142633. (Sexual Politics Ser.). 224p. 1994. pap. 21.95 (*0-304-32797-2*, Pub. by Cassell) LPC InBook.

— Outrage! An Oral History. 256p. 1999. pap. text 21.50 (*0-304-33358-1*) Continuum.

— Outrage! An Oral History. 256p. 1999. 55.00 (*0-304-33357-3*) Continuum.

Lucas, J. & Moynihan, C. T., eds. Halide Glasses. (Material Science Forum Ser.: Vols. 5/6). 840p. (C). 1985. pap. text 233.00 (*0-87849-540-1*, Pub. by Trans T Pub) Enfield Pubs NH.

Lucas, J. A., et al, eds. Septoria on Cereals: A Study of Pathosystems. LC 98-44780. (CABI Publishing Ser.). (Illus.). 368p. 1999. text 100.00 (*0-85199-269-2*) OUP.

Lucas, J. D., et al, eds. Phytophthora. (British Mycological Society Symposium Ser.: No. 17). 461p. (C). 1991. text 125.00 (*0-521-40080-5*) Cambridge U Pr.

Lucas, J. Desha. Admiralty, Cases & Materials On. 4th ed. (University Casebook Ser.). 136p. 1996. pap. text, teacher ed. write for info. (*1-56662-445-2*) Foundation Pr.

Lucas, J. Olumide. The Religion of the Yorubas: Being an Account of the Religious Beliefs & Practices of the Yoruba Peoples of Southern Nigeria. 2nd unabridged ed. (Illus.). 414p. 1999. reprint ed. pap. 29.95 (*0-9638787-8-6*) Athelia-Henrietta.

Lucas, J. R. Conceptual Roots of Mathematics. LC 99-20193. 1999. text. write for info. (*0-415-20738-X*) Routledge.

***Lucas, J. R.** 1,001 Ways to Connect with Your Kids. LC 99-55351. 2000. pap. 10.99 (*0-8423-3154-9*) Tyndale Hse.

Lucas, J. R. Responsibility. (Illus.). 306p. 1995. pap. text 23.00 (*0-19-823578-X*) OUP.

Lucas, J. S., jt. auth. see Copland, J. W.

Lucas, James. Hitler's Enforcers: Leaders of the German War Machine, 1938-1945. (Illus.). 272p. 1997. pap. 16.95 (*1-85409-431-9*, Pub. by Arms & Armour) Sterling.

— Hitler's Enforcers: Leaders of the German War Machine 1939-45. (Illus.). 272p. 1996. 29.95 (*1-85409-273-1*, Pub. by Arms & Armour) Sterling.

***Lucas, James.** Hitler's Mountain Troops: Fighting at the Extremes. (Military Classics). (Illus.). 224p. 1999. pap. 9.95 (*0-304-35204-7*, Pub. by Cassell) Sterling.

Lucas, James. Kommando: German Special Forces of World War II. (Cassell Military Classics Ser.). 1999. pap. text. write for info. (*0-304-35127-X*) Continuum.

— The Last Year of the German Army: May 1944-May 1945. (Illus.). 240p. 1996. pap. 16.95 (*1-85409-334-7*, Pub. by Arms & Armour) Sterling.

***Lucas, James.** Das Reich: The Military Role of the 2nd SS Division. (Military Classics). (Illus.). 2000. pap. 9.95 (*0-304-35199-7*) Continuum.

Lucas, James. SS-Kampfgruppe Peiper: An Episode in the War in Russia, February 1943. 2nd ed. 210p. 1998. pap. 11.95 (*1-899765-89-1*) Intl Spec Bk.

Lucas, James & Von Habsburg, Otto. The Fighting Troops of the Austro-Hungarian Army 1868-1914. 256p. (C). 1991. 150.00 (*0-946771-04-9*, Pub. by Spellmnt Pubs) St Mut.

***Lucas, James A.** What's That Supposed to Mean? Using the Catechism in the 21st Century. LC 99-52801. 2000. pap. 21.95 (*0-7880-1564-8*) CSS OH.

Lucas, James R. Balance of Power: Authority or Empowerment? How You Can Get the Best of Both in the "Interdependent" Organization. LC 97-46428. 256p. 1998. 24.95 (*0-8144-0393-X*) AMACOM.

— Fatal Illusions: Shedding a Dozen Unrealities That Can Keep Your Organization from Success. LC 97-1324. 240p. 1997. 24.95 (*0-8144-0359-X*) AMACOM.

— The Passionate Organization: Igniting the Fire of Employee Commitment. LC 98-54184. 240p. 1999. 24.95 (*0-8144-0477-4*) AMACOM.

— Walking Through the Fire: Finding the Purpose of Pain in the Christian Life. 224p. 1996. pap. 12.99 (*0-8054-6194-9*, 4261-94) Broadman.

Lucas, James S. War on the Eastern Front: The German Soldier in Russia, 1941-1945. LC 97-38290. 1998. pap. 19.95 (*1-85367-311-0*) Greenhill Bks.

Lucas, James S. & Caesar, Kurt. Rommel's Year of Victory: The Wartime Illustrations of the Afrika Korps by Kurt Caesar. LC 97-38288. (Illus.). 1998. 39.95 (*1-85367-302-1*) Greenhill Bks.

***Lucas, James W. & Woodworth, Warner D.** Working Toward Zion: Principles of the United Order for the Modern World. 498p. 1999. pap. 15.95 (*1-56236-244-5*, Pub. by Aspen Bks) Origin Bk Sales.

Lucas, James W. & Woodworth, Warner P. Working Toward Zion: Principles of the United Order for the Modern World. 484p. 1996. 19.95 (*1-56236-228-3*, Pub. by Aspen Bks) Origin Bk Sales.

Lucas, Jane & Nicholson, James. Paediatric MCQ Revision for MRCP & MRCPCH. 192p. 1997. pap. text 32.00 (*0-7506-3014-0*, Newnes) Buttrwrth-Heinemann.

Lucas, Janice. Long Sun. LC 93-48028. 266p. 1994. 22.00 (*1-56947-013-8*) Soho Press.

Lucas, Jay H., jt. auth. see Woods, James D.

Lucas, Jeff. Elijah. LC 98-20913. (Victor Bible Character Ser.). 208p. 1998. 7.99 (*1-56476-714-0*, Victor Bks) Chariot Victor.

— Pass, Set, Crush: Volleyball Illustrated. 3rd rev. ed. (Illus.). 417p. (Orig.). 1993. pap. 24.95 (*0-9615088-6-8*) Euclid NW Pubns.

Lucas, Jerri M. Lessons from Esther. 1991. pap. 6.95 (*0-89137-459-0*) Quality Pubns.

Lucas, Jerri M., ed. Planning a Future. 1986. pap. 6.55 (*0-89137-816-2*) Quality Pubns.

***Lucas, Jerry.** Bible Basics: A Fun & Easy Way for Families to Learn Together. (Ready - Set - Believe Ser.). (Illus.). 52p. 2000. pap. 21.95 incl. audio (*1-930853-06-8*) Lucas Ed Systm.

— Grammar Graphics & Picture Perfect Punctuation: A Fun & Easy Way to Learn Through Pictures. LC 00-104328. (Ready - Set - Remember Ser.). (Illus.). 112p. (J). 2000. pap. 23.95 incl. audio (*1-930853-04-1*) Lucas Ed Systm.

— Learning How to Learn: A Total Breakthrough in Learning Techniques. LC 00-104326. (Illus.). 384p. 2000. 27.95 (*1-930853-02-5*) Lucas Ed Systm.

— Names & Faces Made Easy: The Fun & Easy Way to Remember People. LC 00-104325. (Illus.). 216p. 2000. pap. 17.95 (*1-930853-01-7*) Lucas Ed Systm.

— Picture Perfect Spanish: A Survival Guide to Speaking Spanish. LC 00-104324. (Illus.). 240p. 2000. pap. 21.95 (*1-930853-00-9*) Lucas Ed Systm.

— States & Capitals & the Presidents: A Fun & Easy Way to Learn Through Pictures. LC 00-104327. (Ready - Set - Remember Ser.). (Illus.). 96p. (J). 2000. pap. 21.95 (*1-930853-03-3*) Lucas Ed Systm.

— The Times Tables: A Fun & Easy Way to Learn Through Pictures. (Ready - Set - Remember Ser.). 104p. (J). 2000. pap. 23.95 incl. audio (*1-930853-05-X*) Lucas Ed Systm.

Lucas, Jerry & Lorayne, Harry. The Memory Book: Classic Guide to Improving Your Memory At Work, At School, & At Play. 224p. 1986. mass mkt. 5.99 (*0-345-33758-1*) Ballantine Pub Grp.

Lucas, Jim. Birth in a Chicken House: A Collection of Stories by James Lucas, D. V. M. (Illus.). 1999. 15.95 (*0-9671823-0-1*) Stone Tablets.

Lucas, Jo D. Admiralty: Cases & Materials On. 3rd ed. (University Casebook Ser.). 1146p. 1986. text 42.95 (*0-88277-352-6*) Foundation Pr.

— Admiralty: Cases & Materials On. 4th ed. LC 96-371. (University Casebook Ser.). 1097p. 1996. text. write for info. (*1-56662-337-5*) Foundation Pr.

— Admiralty, 1991 Statute: Rule & Case Supplement for Use with Cases & Materials On. 3rd ed. (University Casebook Ser.). 408p. (C). 1991. pap. text 14.95 (*0-88277-940-0*) Foundation Pr.

— Admiralty, 1996 Statute & Rule Supplement for Use with Cases & Materials On. 4th ed. (University Casebook Ser.). 250p. 1996. pap. text. write for info. (*1-56662-357-X*) Foundation Pr.

Lucas, Joe & Koppenhaver, Katherine M. Red Flags on Forged Checks: Detection & Defense. 63p. (Orig.). (C). 1995. pap. text 20.00 (*0-9632206-5-9*) Foren Pubs Joppa.

Lucas, John. John Clare. (Writers & Their Work Ser.). 95p. 1996. pap. text 15.00 (*0-7463-0729-2*, Pub. by Northcote House) U Pr of Miss.

Lucas, John. Katy Keene Swimsuit Illustrated Paper Dolls. (Illus.). 24p. 1995. pap. 5.95 (*0-87588-437-7*) Hobby Hse.

Lucas, John. Low-Water Gardening: Creating & Running the Ideal Garden with Less Water. (Illus.). 176p. 1993. pap. 16.95 (*0-460-86151-4*) Trafalgar.

— The Radical Twenties: Writings, Politics, & Culture. LC 98-52817. 272p. (C). 1999. text 50.00 (*0-8135-2681-7*); pap. text 20.00 (*0-8135-2682-5*) Rutgers U Pr.

— Romantic to Modern Literature: Essays & Ideas of Culture, 1750-1900. LC 82-6842. 240p. (C). 1982. text 58.50 (*0-389-20311-4*, N7148) B&N Imports.

— William Blake. LC 97-42999. (Critical Readers Ser.). 224p. (C). 1998. 65.00 (*0-582-23711-4*) Longman.

— Writing & Race. LC 97-1412. (Crossconcurrents Ser.). (C). 1997. 70.31 (*0-582-27374-9*) Longman.

— Writing & Race. LC 97-1412. (Crossconcurrents Ser.). 321p. (C). 1998. pap. text 26.25 (*0-582-27375-7*) Longman.

Lucas, John, ed. Writing Radicalism. (Crosscurrents Ser.). 320p. (C). 1996. text 57.00 (*0-582-21414-9*); pap. text 28.50 (*0-582-21415-7*) Addison-Wesley.

Lucas, John, jt. auth. see Oyewole, Anthony.

Lucas, John, jt. auth. see Woggins, Bill.

Lucas, John, jt. auth. see Woggon, Bill.

Lucas, John, ed. see Goldsmith, Oliver.

Lucas, John, tr. see Fell, Christine, ed.

Lucas, John A. Future of the Olympic Games. (Illus.). 248p. 1996. reprint ed. pap. text 24.00 (*0-88011-699-4*, BLUC0699) Human Kinetics.

***Lucas, John A. & Dickinson, C. H.** Plant Pathology & Plant Pathogens. 3rd ed. LC 97-48463. (Illus.). 274p. 1998. pap. 49.95 (*0-632-03046-1*) Blackwell Sci.

Lucas, John C. Conscious Marriage: From Chemistry to Communication. LC 98-5021. (Illus.). 168p. 1998. pap. 14.95 (*0-89594-915-6*) Crossing Pr.

Lucas, John F. Introduction to Abstract Mathematics. 2nd ed. (Illus.). 382p. 1990. text 48.95 (*0-912675-73-X*); pap. text, teacher ed. write for info. (*0-912675-74-8*) Ardsley.

Lucas, John F. & Lucas, Christine A. A Guided Tour of the TI-85 Graphics Programmable Calculator with Emphasis on Calculus. 117p. 1992. pap. text 20.95 (*1-880157-10-1*) Ardsley.

Lucas, John J. Wisdom from the Ages with Love & Truth Combined (1910) 474p. 1998. reprint ed. pap. 33.00 (*0-7661-0529-6*) Kessinger Pub.

Lucas, John R. Freedom of the Will. 190p. 1970. text 49.95 (*0-19-824343-X*) OUP.

Lucas, John T. & Gurman, Richard. Truth in Advertising: An AMA Research Report. LC 72-79980. (AMA Research Report Ser.). 40p. reprint ed. pap. 30.00 (*0-608-13617-4*, 205130900094) Bks Demand.

Lucas, John W., ed. Heat Transfer & Spacecraft Thermal Control. LC 70-147076. (PAAS Ser.: Vol. 24). (Illus.). 427p. 1971. 54.95 (*0-262-12042-9*, V-24) AIAA.

— Thermal Characteristics of the Moon. LC 79-39803. (PAAS Ser.: Vol. 28). (Illus.). 340p. 1972. 43.95 (*0-262-12058-5*, V-28) AIAA.

Lucas, Jonathan. Ace in the Hole. 190p. mass mkt. 4.99 (*1-55197-098-8*) Picasso Publ.

Lucas, Joy. It Started in the Mountains: The History of Pacific Northwest Ski Instructors. LC 95-73048. (Illus.). 153p. 1996. 35.00 (*0-9650523-0-3*) Pro Ski Inst Am.

Lucas, K. Applied Statistical Thermodynamics. (Illus.). xvii, 514p. 1991. 237.95 (*0-387-52007-4*) Spr-Verlag.

Lucas, Kenneth. Outwitting Your Alcoholic: Exploring & Escaping from the Strange World of Alcoholism. LC 98-17877. 1998. pap. 14.00 (*1-882883-38-1*) Idyll Arbor.

Lucas, Kenneth W., Sr. Federal Law Enforcement Badges. 391p. 1991. 65.00 (*0-9630225-0-4*); pap. 35.00 (*0-9630225-1-2*) K W Lucas.

Lucas, Laddie, ed. Thanks for the Memories: Unforgettable Characters in Air Warfare, 1939-1945. 468p. 1998. pap. 24.95 (*1-898697-85-X*, Pub. by Grub St) Seven Hills Bk.

Lucas, Lawrence E. & Wright, Bruce M. Black Priest, White Church: Catholics & Racism. LC 88-71876. 280p. (C). 1989. 29.95 (*0-86543-108-6*); pap. 9.95 (*0-86543-109-4*) Africa World.

Lucas, Leonard. Tell the Children the Truth. 46p. 1997. pap. 10.00 (*0-9654173-0-1*) Chi-Town Polyrhythm.

Lucas, Leopold. Zur Geschichte der Juden Im 4. Jahrhundert. (GER.). 134p. 1991. reprint ed. write for info. (*3-487-07627-6*) G Olms Pubs.

— Zur Geschichte der Juden Im Vierten Jahrhundert. (GER.). 1991. reprint ed. write for info. (*3-487-09428-2*) G Olms Pubs.

Lucas, Lois. Plants of Old Hawaii. LC 82-72199. (Illus.). 112p. (Orig.). 1982. pap. 7.95 (*0-935848-11-8*) Bess Pr.

Lucas, Luzanne. A Sweet Breath of Life: A Salute to Your Magnificent Being. LC 95-92000. 160p. 1995. 16.95 (*0-9645269-6-4*) Desirata Pr.

Lucas, Lynn, jt. auth. see Stokes, P. Burton.

***Lucas, Malcolm, et al.** Incontinence: A Pelvic Team Approach. LC 98-49186. (Illus.). 1999. 139.95 (*0-632-05003-9*) Blackwell Sci.

Lucas, Marc, tr. see Renirkens, Clement.

Lucas, Marc G. Strebbezogene Tatigkeitsanalysen des Nichtarztlichen Arbeitsplatzes Im Rettungsdienst. (Europaische Hochschulschriften Ser.: Reihe 6, Bd. 591). (GER., Illus.). 223p. 1997. 42.95 (*3-631-32237-2*) P Lang Pubng.

Lucas, Margaret B. The Conversion of Margaret Lucas (1701-1769) in Her Own Words. rev. ed. LC 96-71982. Orig. Title: An Account of the Convincement & Call to the Ministry of Margaret Lucas (18th c. Title). ix, 76p. 1997. reprint ed. pap. 10.95 (*1-889298-60-3*) Rhwymbooks.

Lucas, Margeaux. Mazes. (Home Workbooks Ser.). 64p. (Orig.). (J). (ps-1). 1997. pap., wbk. ed. 2.49 (*0-88724-369-X*, CD-6866) Carson-Dellos.

Lucas, Maria E. Forged under the Sun - Forjada bajo el Sol: The Life of Maria Elena Lucas. LC 92-46311. (Illus.). 336p. 1993. pap. 16.95 (*0-472-06432-0*, 06432) U of Mich Pr.

Lucas, Marilyn, jt. auth. see Jenkins, Jeanne B.

Lucas, Marion B. A History of Blacks in Kentucky, Vol. 1: From Slavery to Segregation, 1760-1891. LC 92-24574. 1992. 29.95 (*0-916968-20-0*) Kentucky Hist.

***Lucas, Marion B.** Sherman & the Burning of Columbia. 2000. pap. text 12.95 (*1-57003-358-7*) U of SC Pr.

Lucas, Marion B. & Wright, George C. A History of Blacks in Kentucky, Set. LC 92-24574. 1992. 50.00 (*0-916968-23-5*) Kentucky Hist.

Lucas, Mark. Southern Vision of Andrew Lytle. LC 86-21076. (Southern Literary Studies). 192p. 1987. text 30.00 (*0-8071-1338-7*) La State U Pr.

Lucas, Mark, ed. Home Voices: A Sampler of Southern Writing. LC 90-24521. (New Books for New Readers). 64p. 1991. pap. text 5.95 (*0-8131-0906-X*) U Pr of Ky.

Lucas, Mayo. Matters of the Heart. 368p. 1988. pap. 3.95 (*0-380-75537-8*, Avon Bks) Morrow Avon.

Lucas, Michael. Handbook of the Acoustic Characteristics of Turbomachinery Cavities. LC 97-36356. 1997. write for info. (*0-7918-0054-7*) Am Soc Civil Eng.

***Lucas, Michael A.** Aspects of Conrad's Literary Language. 240p. 2000. text 30.00 (*0-88033-984-5*) Col U Pr.

Lucas, Michael R. The Western Alliance after INF: Redefining U. S. Policy Toward Europe & the Soviet Union. LC 89-38359. 266p. 1989. lib. bdg. 35.00 (*1-55587-159-3*) L Rienner.

Lucas, Michael W. Believe It or Else! An Adventure Supplement of Fractured Folklore & Tabloid Reality for Use with the Gatecrasher Fantasy Game. (Illus.). 96p. 1993. pap. 12.95 (*1-887154-03-5*, GGG3002) Grey Ghost Press.

Lucas, Michel, jt. auth. see Gardan, Yvon.

Lucas, Mike. Antarctica. (Illus.). 160p. 1997. 40.00 (*0-7892-0257-3*) Abbeville Pr.

— Antarctica. (Illus.). 160p. 1999. 17.98 (*0-89660-108-0*, Artabras) Abbeville Pr.

Lucas, Miranda. Bouvier Des Flandres. (Book of the Breed). (Illus.). 160p. 1995. 24.95 (*0-948955-41-4*, Pub. by Ringpr Bks) Seven Hills Bk.

***Lucas, Monteen.** Aging as a Shared Journey: A Guide for Healthy Aging. 260p. 2000. pap. 22.95 (*0-9658690-1-6*) Hlth Positive.

Lucas, N. J. Local Energy Centres. (Illus.). 261p. 1978. 63.00 (*0-85334-782-4*) Elsevier.

Lucas, Noah, jt. ed. see Troen, S. Ilan.

An Asterisk (*) at the beginning of an entry indicates that the title is appearing for the first time.

Lucas, Oliver W. The Design of Forest Landscapes. (Illus.). 394p. 1991. text 185.00 (0-19-854280-1) OUP.

*Lucas, P. B. Flying Colours: The Epic Story of Douglas Bader. (Illus.). 2000. reprint ed. pap. 12.99 (1-84022-224-7, Pub. by Wrdsworth Edits) Combined Pub.

Lucas, P. G., tr. see Martin, Gottfried.

Lucas, Pam & Harrison, Hal, Jr. The Day I Was Baptized. 24p. 1998. 11.95 (0-8298-1279-2) Pilgrim OH.

Lucas, Pam & Harrison, Hal. The Day I Was Confirmed. 24p. 1998. 11.95 (0-8298-1280-6) Pilgrim OH.

Lucas, Patricia L. Desperada-Desperada: A Reading from the Book of Southwestern Saints. (Illus.). 154p. 1997. pap. 11.95 (0-9660094-1-X) Spider Woman.

*Lucas, Patricia Latourette. Bridging the Generations: The History of Manson Construction Co. LC 99-55082. 2000. write for info. (0-935503-32-3) Document Bk.

*Lucas, Patsye, ed. The Heritage of Pike County, Alabama. (Heritage of Alabama Ser.: Vol. 55). 400p. 2001. 60.00 (1-891647-62-8) Herit Pub Consult.

Lucas, Patty L. The Land of Tears Is a Secret Place. 88p. 1992. student ed. 12.95 (0-9632065-0-8) Agape Acad Pr.

Lucas, Paul D. Modern Construction Accounting Methods & Controls. LC 83-22897. 252p. 1984. 39.95 (0-13-590241-X, Busn) P-H.

Lucas, Paul J. The C++ Programmer's Handbook. 128p. (C). 1992. pap. 39.00 (0-13-118233-1) P-H.

Lucas, Paul R. Valley of Discord: Church & Society along the Connecticut River, 1636-1725. LC 75-22520. 291p. reprint ed. pap. 90.30 (0-7837-6205-4, 204592600009) Bks Demand.

Lucas, Peggy C. Mt. Bachelor, Bill Healy's Dream: History & Development of Mt. Bachelor Ski Resort. LC 99-70179. (Illus.). 208p. 1999. pap. 19.95 (0-89288-277-8) Maverick.

Lucas, Peter J. From Author to Audience: John Capgrave & Medieval Publication. LC 98-120978. 300p. 1998. 90.00 (1-900621-05-3) Dufour.

Lucas, Peter J., ed. Exodus. 200p. 1995. pap. text 19.95 (0-85989-383-9, Pub. by Univ Exeter Pr) Northwestern U Pr.

— John Capgrave's Abbreuiacion of Cronicles. (OS 285 Ser.: No. 285). (Illus.). 1983. 84.00 (0-19-722287-0) OUP.

Lucas, Philip C. The Odyssey of a New Religion: The Holy Order of MANS from New Age to Orthodoxy. LC 94-12587. (Religion in North America Ser.). 1995. 25.00 (0-253-33612-0) Ind U Pr.

Lucas, Phillip, et al, eds. Prime-Time Religion: An Encyclopedia of Religious Broadcasting. LC 96-39495. (Illus.). 432p. 1997. boxed set 64.95 (0-89774-902-2) Oryx Pr.

Lucas Powell, Mary. Nodena: An Account of 90 Years of Archeological Investigation in Southeast Mississippi County, Arkansas. Morse, Dan F., ed. (Illus.). 150p. 1989. pap. 10.00 (1-56349-057-9, RS30) AR Archaeol.

Lucas, Prosper. Prosper Lucas's "On the Heredity of Mental Illness" (1850) Mellon, Charles D., ed. Mellon, Linda F., tr. from FRE. LC 96-94516. (Illus.). 83p. 1996. 29.50 (0-9653362-1-2) Genetics Heritage.

Lucas, R. D. & Eveson, John W. Atlas of Oral Pathology. (Current Histopathology Ser.). 1985. text 355.00 (0-85200-328-5) Kluwer Academic.

Lucas, Randolph. Illustrated Encyclopedia of Minerals & Rocks. 1993. 12.98 (1-55521-877-6) Bk Sales Inc.

Lucas, Ray F., jt. auth. see Conrad, Glenn R.

Lucas, Rex A. Minetown, Milltown, Railtown: Life in Canadian Communities of Single Industry. LC 70-166934. 450p. reprint ed. pap. 139.50 (0-8357-4158-3, 203693200007) Bks Demand.

Lucas, Richard B. Charles August Lindberg Sr. A Case Study of Congressional Insurgency, 1906-1912. (Studia Historica Upsaliensia: No. 61). (Illus.). 194p. (Orig.). 1974. pap. 25.00 (91-554-0214-3, Pub. by Uppsala Univ Acta Univ Uppsaliensis) Coronet Bks.

Lucas, Richard E., compiled by. Index to the New Atlas & Directory of Grand Traverse County, Michigan, 1895. 110p. 1988. pap. 9.00 (0-940133-18-0) Kinseeker Pubns.

*Lucas, Richard H. & McCoy, K. Byron. The Winning Edge: Effective Communication & Persuasion Techniques for Lawyers. LC 99-27268. 220p. 1999. pap. 55.00 incl. audio (0-913875-38-4, 5384-N) Lawyers & Judges.

Lucas, Richard M. Herbal Health Secrets from Europe & Around the World. LC 83-556. 226p. 1983. pap. 5.95 (0-318-00000-8, Parker Publishing Co) P-H.

— Magic Herbs for Arthritis, Rheumatism & Related Ailments. LC 80-22346. 248p. 1981. 14.95 (0-13-543900-0, Parker Publishing Co); 4.95 (0-685-03916-1, Parker Publishing Co) P-H.

— Miracle Medicine Herbs. 224p. (C). 1991. text 24.95 (0-13-585142-4, Busn); pap. text 10.95 (0-13-585134-3, Busn) P-H.

— Secrets of the Chinese Herbalists. rev. ed. 252p. (C). 1986. reprint ed. text 26.95 (0-13-797879-0); reprint ed. pap. text 10.95 (0-13-798174-0) P-H.

Lucas, Richie L. Richie's Song. 1998. pap. 8.95 (0-533-12615-0) Vantage.

Lucas, Robert. Customer Service: Skills & Concepts for Business. 304p. (C). 1995. text 16.40 (0-256-18742-8, Irwn McGrw-H) McGrw-H Hghr Educ.

— Database Applications Using Prolog. 159p. 1988. text 39.95 (0-470-21166-0) P-H.

— Frieda Lawrence: The Story of Frieda von Richthofen & D. H. Lawrence. LC 73-179440. x, 307p. 1973. write for info. (0-436-26910-4) M Secker & Warburg.

Lucas, Robert A. The Grants World Inside Out. (Illus.). 192p. 1992. text 21.95 (0-252-01862-1) U of Ill Pr.

Lucas, Robert C., jt. auth. see Shechter, Mordechai.

*Lucas, Robert E. Restructuring the Malaysian Economy Development & Human Resources. LC 98-53725. 1999. text 55.00 (0-312-22252-1) St Martin.

Lucas, Robert E., Jr. Studies in Business-Cycle Theory. 312p. (C). 1983. pap. text 22.00 (0-262-62044-8) MIT Pr.

Lucas, Robert E., Jr. & Sargent, Thomas J., eds. Rational Expectations & Econometric Practice, 2 vols., 1. LC 80-24602. 776p. (C). 1981. pap. 19.95 (0-8166-0917-9) U of Minn Pr.

Lucas, Robert E., Jr., jt. auth. see Stokey, Nancy L.

*Lucas, Robert E B. Restructuring The Malaysian Economy: Development & Human Resources. LC 98-53722. 1999. text 75.00 (0-312-22264-5) St Martin.

Lucas, Robert W. The Big Book of Flip Charts: A Comprehensive Guide for Presenters, Trainers & Facilitators. LC 99-31728. (Illus.). 200p. 1999. pap. 24.95 (0-07-134311-3) McGraw.

— Coaching Skills: A Guide for Supervisors. LC 93-44766. (Business Skills Express Ser.). 112p. 1994. text 10.95 (0-7863-0220-8, Irwn Prfssnl) McGraw-Hill Prof.

— Customer Service: Skills & Concepts for Business. LC 95-39280. (C). 1995. text 16.00 (0-256-18712-6, Irwn Prfssnl) McGraw-Hill Prof.

— Customer Service: Skills & Concepts for Business. 1996. teacher ed. 23.54 (0-256-21426-3, Irwn McGrw-H) McGrw-H Hghr Educ.

— Effective Interpersonal Relationships. LC 93-48220. (Business Skills Express Ser.). 120p. 1994. text 10.95 (0-7863-0255-0, Irwn Prfssnl) McGraw-Hill Prof.

— Job Strategies for New Employees. LC 96-84913. (How-to Book Ser.). 80p. (Orig.). 1996. pap. 12.95 (1-884926-55-X, JOBST) Amer Media.

— Training Skills for Supervisors. LC 94-4999. (Business Skills Express Ser.). 112p. 1994. text 10.95 (0-7863-0313-1, Irwn Prfssnl) McGraw-Hill Prof.

Lucas, Robin. Stepmothers. 140p. 1996. pap. 16.95 (0-7022-2644-0, Pub. by Univ Queensland Pr) Intl Spec Bk.

Lucas, Robin & Forster, Clare, eds. Wilder Shores: Women's Travel Stories of Australia & Beyond. (Orig.). 1992. pap. 15.95 (0-7022-2477-4, Pub. by Univ Queensland Pr) Intl Spec Bk.

Lucas, Roger S. The Bellevue - Stratford Hotel. (Illus.). 66p. 1994. pap. 8.00 (1-887287-02-7) Res Rev Pubns.

— Boldt Castle - Heart Island. 8th rev. ed. (Illus.). 84p. 1999. pap. 10.00 (1-887287-00-0) Res Rev Pubns.

— Boldt's Boats: Alexandria Bay, New York & the Thousand Islands. 3rd ed. (Illus.). 62p. 1998. reprint ed. pap. 8.00 (1-887287-01-9) Res Rev Pubns.

— The Waldorf Hotel. (Illus.). 66p. 1997. pap. 8.00 (1-887287-03-5) Res Rev Pubns.

Lucas, Rosemary. Managing Employee Relations in the Hotel & Catering Industry. LC 95-2056. (Illus.). 256p. 1995. 110.00 (0-304-32910-X); pap. 29.95 (0-304-32897-9) Continuum.

Lucas, Rosemary & McCredden, Lyn. Bridgings: Readings in Australian Women's Poetry. LC 96-218824. 240p. 1997. 42.00 (0-19-553595-2) OUP.

Lucas, Rowland. The Voice of a Nation? 233p. (C). 1990. text 59.00 (0-85088-745-3, Pub. by Gomer Pr) St Mut.

Lucas, Russell H., ed. Outstanding American Statesmen: Lectures by William Henry Harbaugh, Arthur S. Link, Frank Freidel, Alfred I. Chandler, Jr. LC 70-118577. 92p. 1970. reprint ed. pap. 30.00 (0-608-05342-2, 206504700012) Bks Demand.

Lucas, Ruta. The Blushing Detectives. LC 95-77614. (Illus.). 1996. pap. 9.95 (0-916897-21-4) Andrew Mtn Pr.

Lucas, S. E., Jr. Dodson - Dotson, Lucas, Pyles, Rochester & Allied Families. (Illus.). 239p. 1993. reprint ed. pap. 37.50 (0-8328-3664-8); reprint ed. lib. bdg. 47.50 (0-8328-3663-X) Higginson Bk Co.

— Powell Family of Norfolk & Elizabeth City Cos. Virginia & Their Descendants, with Notes & Data on Collateral Families of Bush, Beckwith, Bowles, Cargill & Others. 305p. 1992. reprint ed. pap. 46.00 (0-8328-2461-5); reprint ed. lib. bdg. 56.00 (0-8328-2460-7) Higginson Bk Co.

Lucas, S. E., Jr., ed. Quakers in South Carolina, Wateree & Bush River, Cane Creek, Piney Grove & Charleston Meetings. (Illus.). 150p. 1991. reprint ed. pap. 25.00 (0-89308-450-6, SC 90) Southern Hist Pr.

Lucas, S. G., et al, eds. San Juan Basin, Vol. IV. (Guidebook Ser.: No. 43). (Illus.). 411p. 1992. 70.00 (1-58546-078-8) NMex Geol Soc.

Lucas, S. G. & Hunt, A. P., eds. Northeastern New Mexico. (Guidebook Ser.: No. 38). (Illus.). 354p. 1987. 20.00 (1-58546-073-7) NMex Geol Soc.

Lucas, S. G. & Zidek, J., eds. Santa Rosa - Tucumcari Region. (Guidebook Ser.: No. 36). (Illus.). 344p. 1985. 20.00 (1-58546-071-0) NMex Geol Soc.

Lucas, S. G., jt. ed. see Pazzaglia, F. J.

Lucas, Sally. Dancing Dinos. LC 98-12019. (Road to Reading Ser.). (Illus.). 32p. (J). 1998. pap. 3.99 (0-307-26200-6, 26200) Gldn Bks Pub Co.

Lucas, Samuel R. Tracking Inequality: Stratification & Mobility in American High Schools. LC 98-47094. (Sociology of Education Ser.). 240p. 1999. text 53.00 (0-8077-3799-2); pap. text 24.95 (0-8077-3798-4) Tchrs Coll.

Lucas, Scott. Britain & the Suez Crisis: The Lion's Last Roar. (Documents in Contemporary History Ser.). 172p. 1996. text 24.95 (0-7190-4580-0, Pub. by Manchester Univ Pr) St Martin.

— Freedom's War: The American Crusade Against the Soviet Union. LC 99-32211. 1999. text 45.00 (0-8147-5159-8) NYU Pr.

— The Not-So-Good Shepherd. LC 98-89473. 375p. 1998. text 25.00 (0-7388-0281-6); pap. text 15.00 (0-7388-0282-4) Xlibris Corp.

*Lucas, Scott. The Zakopane Dilemma. LC 99-64395. 1999. 25.00 (0-7388-0502-5); pap. 18.00 (0-7388-0503-3) Xlibris Corp.

Lucas, Scott & Kreinberg, Luke. The Book of Goals: Achievements, Plans, & Dreams of a Lifetime. 125p. 1994. pap. text 14.95 (0-9642856-0-6) First Step CA.

Lucas, Sidney. The Quaker Message. (C). 1948. pap. 4.00 (0-87574-040-5) Pendle Hill.

Lucas, Silas, Jr. & Holcomb, Brent. Marriage & Death Notices from Raleigh, N. C., Newspapers, 1796-1826. 168p. 1978. reprint ed. 20.00 (0-89308-046-2) Southern Hist Pr.

Lucas, Silas E., Jr. The Eighteen Thirty-Two Gold Lottery of Georgia. rev. ed. (Illus.). 568p. 1987. 42.50 (0-89308-638-X, GA 28) Southern Hist Pr.

— The Fourth or 1821 Land Lotteries of Georgia. rev. ed. 262p. 1986. 32.50 (0-89308-586-3, GA 66) Southern Hist Pr.

— History of the Powell Families of Virginia & the South: An Encyclopedia. 604p. 1982. reprint ed. 40.00 (0-89308-027-6) Southern Hist Pr.

— Marriages from Early Tennessee Newspapers, 1794-1851. 1981. reprint ed. 37.50 (0-89308-092-6) Southern Hist Pr.

— Some Georgia County Records, Vol. 3. 368p. 1990. reprint ed. 40.00 (0-89308-058-6, GA 33) Southern Hist Pr.

— Some Georgia County Records, Vol. 4. 430p. 1990. 40.00 (0-89308-685-1, GA 92) Southern Hist Pr.

— Some Georgia County Records, Vol. 5. 326p. 1990. 40.00 (0-89308-686-X, GA 93) Southern Hist Pr.

— The Third or 1820 Land Lotteries of Georgia. rev. ed. (Seven Land Lotteries of Georgia & Other Land Records Ser.). 382p. 1986. reprint ed. 35.00 (0-89308-585-5, GA 26) Southern Hist Pr.

Lucas, Silas E., Jr., ed. Thirty-Five Thousand Tennessee Marriage Records & Bonds, 3 vols. 1981. 135.00 (0-89308-226-0); write for info. (0-89308-223-6); write for info. (0-89308-224-4); write for info. (0-89308-225-2) Southern Hist Pr.

Lucas, Silas E., Jr. & Davis, Robert S., Jr., eds. The Georgia Land Lottery Papers, 1805-1914. 366p. 1979. 37.50 (0-89308-156-6, GA 30) Southern Hist Pr.

Lucas, Silas E., Jr. & Sheffield, Ella E., eds. The Hawkins County Minutes of the Court of Common Pleas, 1822-1825, & Fragment for the Period, November 1827-August 1828. 176p. 1983. pap. 21.50 (0-89308-347-X) Southern Hist Pr.

Lucas, Silas E., Jr. & Wilson, Caroline P. Records of Effingham County, Georgia. 410p. 1976. 30.00 (0-89308-019-5) Southern Hist Pr.

Lucas, Silas E., Jr., jt. auth. see Holcomb, Brent.

Lucas, Silas E., Jr., jt. auth. see Williams, Sherman.

Lucas, Silas E., Jr., jt. ed. see Sheffield, Ella L.

*Lucas, Silas Emmett. Anderson County, Tennessee, 1801-1831: Land Deed Genealogy of. 209p. 1999. 30.00 (0-89308-527-8) Southern Hist Pr.

*Lucas, Silas Emmett, Jr. Lawrence Co., Tennessee, Marriages, 1818-1870. 114p. 1999. 25.00 (0-89308-724-6) Southern Hist Pr.

Lucas, Spencer G. Dinosaurs: The Textbook. 320p. (C). 1993. text. write for info. (0-697-14429-1, WCB McGr Hill) McGrw-H Hghr Educ.

— Dinosaurs: The Textbook. 2nd ed. LC 96-84634. 336p. (C). 1996. text 62.50 (0-697-27995-2, WCB McGr Hill) McGrw-H Hghr Educ.

Lucas, Stephen. The Art of Public Speaking. 6th ed. LC 97-6719. (C). 1997. pap. text 35.50 (0-07-039064-9) McGraw.

*Lucas, Stephen. The Art of Public Speaking. 7th ed. LC 00-34858. 2001. write for info. (0-07-118003-6) McGraw.

Lucas, Stephen E. The Art of Public Speaking. 45p. (C). 1991. suppl. ed. 12.19 (0-07-041736-9) McGraw.

— The Art of Public Speaking. (C). 1991. text 5.62 (0-07-038987-X) McGraw.

— The Art of Public Speaking. (C). 1992. text 25.62 (0-07-038988-8) McGraw.

— The Art of Public Speaking. 1993. VHS. write for info. (0-07-038980-2) McGraw.

— The Art of Public Speaking. 2nd ed. 416p. (C). 1985. pap. text 13.00 (0-685-10323-4) Random.

— The Art of Public Speaking. 3rd ed. (Illus.). 432p. (C). 1989. pap. text. write for info. (0-318-63109-1) Random.

— The Art of Public Speaking. 4th ed. (C). 1992. text 61.87 (0-07-038991-8) McGraw.

— The Art of Public Speaking. 5th ed. LC 94-30496. (C). 1994. pap. text 37.74 (0-07-039015-0) McGraw.

— The Art of Public Speaking: Annotated Instructor's Edition. 6th ed. 1998. write for info. (0-07-039065-7) McGrw-H Hghr Educ.

— The Art of Public Speaking: Be Prepared to Speak Video. (C). 1988. pap. text 206.25 (0-07-540825-2) McGraw.

— The Art of Public Speaking: Instructor's Manual. 6th ed. 1998. write for info. (0-07-039066-5) McGrw-H Hghr Educ.

Lucas, Stephen E., ed. Quotable George Washington: The Wisdom Of An American Patriot. LC 99-27478. 128p. 1999. 17.95 (0-945612-66-4) Madison Hse.

Lucas, Suzanne. In Praise of Toadstools. 1996. 125.00 (0-9520456-0-5, Pub. by Lucas Art) Antique Collect.

Lucas, T. M. Chyrology for the Deaf: Reading, Spelling & Ciphering by the Fingers. 1972. 250.00 (0-87968-054-7) Gordon Pr.

Lucas, Tamara. Into, Through, & Beyond Secondary School: Critical Transitions for Immigrant Youths. LC 97-15333. (Topics in Immigrant Education Ser.). 1997. pap. write for info. (1-887744-03-7) Delta Systems.

Lucas, Teacia E. Solomon's Instruction of Things Hateful to God. LC 95-94287. 50p. (YA). write for info. (0-9646486-0-1) TDE Lucas.

Lucas, Thomas, et al. A Guide for Analysis Using Advanced Distributed Systems (ADS) LC 97-29216. (Illus.). 113p. 1997. pap. 13.00 (0-8330-2546-5, MR-879-AF) Rand Corp.

Lucas, Thomas, tr. see Martini, Carlo M.

Lucas, Thomas E. Elder Olson. LC 70-125817. (Twayne's United States Authors Ser.). 195p. (C). 1972. lib. bdg. 20.95 (0-8290-1705-4) Irvington.

Lucas, Thomas J. Zulus & the British Frontiers. LC 73-78579. 371p. 1969. reprint ed. lib. bdg. 38.50 (0-8371-1413-6, Greenwood Pr) Greenwood.

Lucas, Thomas M. Landmarking: City, Church & Jesuit Urban Strategy. LC 97-21981. (Illus.). 245p. 1997. 34.95 (0-8294-0973-4, Jesuit Way) Loyola Pr.

Lucas, Thomas M., ed. Saint, Site & Sacred Strategy: Ignatius, Rome, & Jesuit Urbanism. (Illus.). 232p. 1992. pap., per. 45.00 (88-210-0625-5, SSASS, Jesuit Way) Loyola Pr.

Lucas, Thomas W., et al. Improving the Analytic Contribution of Advanced Warfighting Experiments. LC 98-145115. (Illus.). 58p. 1998. pap. 6.00 (0-8330-2508-2, DB-207-A) Rand Corp.

Lucas, Tim. The Video Watchdog Book. (Illus.). 416p. 1992. pap. 19.95 (0-9633756-0-1) Video Watchdog.

*Lucas, Tony. Rufus at Ocean Beach. 229p. 1999. pap. 14.95 (1-900152-36-3, Pub. by Stride Pubns) SPD-Small Pr Dist.

Lucas Travel Staff. Selling & Planning Travel. (C). 1997. write for info. (0-13-805730-3, Macmillan Coll) P-H.

Lucas, Virginia H. & Barbe, Walter B. Resource Book for the Special Education Teacher. (Illus.). 1982. 34.95 (0-88309-117-8) Zaner-Bloser.

Lucas, W. TIG & Plasma Welding: Process Techniques, Recommended Practices & Applications. 112p. 1990. pap. 79.95 (1-85573-005-7, Pub. by Woodhead Pubng) Am Educ Systs.

Lucas, W., ed. Process Pipe & Tube Welding: A Guide to Welding Process Options, Techniques, Equipment, NDT & Codes of Practice. (Illus.). 160p. 1991. 135.00 (1-85573-012-X, Pub. by Woodhead Pubng) Am Educ Systs.

Lucas, W., jt. ed. see Gerull, Sally-Anne.

Lucas, W. F., ed. Modules in Applied Mathematics: Differential Equation Models, Vol. 1. (Illus.). 400p. 1991. 67.95 (0-387-90695-9) Spr-Verlag.

— Modules in Applied Mathematics Vol. 2: Political & Related Models. (Illus.). 396p. 1982. 67.95 (0-387-90696-7) Spr-Verlag.

— Modules in Applied Mathematics Vol. 4: Life Science Models. (Illus.). 366p. 1983. 65.95 (0-387-90739-4) Spr-Verlag.

Lucas, W. F., et al, eds. Modules in Applied Mathematics Vol. 3: Discrete & System Models. (Illus.). 353p. 1983. 49.00 (0-387-90724-6) Spr-Verlag.

Lucas, Weldon, jt. auth. see Thurman, Nita.

Lucas, William F. Fair Voting: Weighted Voting for Unequali Constituencies. (Hi Map Ser.: No. 19). (Illus.). 60p. pap. text 11.99 (0-614-05308-0, 5619) COMAP Inc.

Lucas, William F., ed. Game Theory & Its Applications. LC 81-12914. (Proceedings of Symposia in Applied Mathematics Ser.: Vol. 24). 136p. 1982. reprint ed. pap. 22.00 (0-8218-0025-6, PSAPM/24) Am Math.

Lucas, William H., jt. auth. see Darden, William R.

Lucas, William J. & Berry, Joseph A., eds. Inorganic Carbon Uptake by Aquatic Photosynthetic Organisms. 512p. 1985. pap. text 20.00 (0-943088-05-4) Am Soc of Plan.

Lucas, Winafred B. Regression Therapy: A Handbook for Professionals, 2 vols. 1175p. 1993. 49.50 (1-882530-00-4) Deep Forest Pr.

— Regression Therapy: A Handbook for Professionals, 2 vols., Vol. I. 1175p. 1993. write for info. (1-882530-01-2) Deep Forest Pr.

— Regression Therapy: A Handbook for Professionals, 2 vols., Vol. II. 1175p. 1993. write for info. (1-882530-02-0) Deep Forest Pr.

Lucas, Winafred B., ed. see Blake, Doron W.

Lucas, Winafred B., ed. see Cunningham, Janet.

Lucash, Frank S., ed. Justice & Equality Here & Now. LC 85-19465. 176p. 1986. 35.00 (0-8014-1807-0); pap. text 14.95 (0-8014-9350-1) Cornell U Pr.

Lucash, Peter D. Medical Practice Change Management: Strategies & Techniques for the Changing Business of Healthcare. LC 96-45342. 240p. 1996. text 45.00 (0-7863-0998-9, Irwn McGrw-H) McGrw-H Hghr Educ.

*Lucashenko, Melissa. Hard Yards. 1999. pap. 19.95 (0-7022-3080-4, Pub. by Univ Queensland Pr) Intl Spec Bk.

Lucashenko, Melissa. Killing Darcy. LC 98-217364. 230p. (YA). (gr. 8-12). 1998. pap. 12.95 (0-7022-3041-3, Pub. by Univ Queensland Pr) Intl Spec Bk.

— Steam Pigs. LC 98-105644. (Black Australian Writers Ser.). 200p. 1997. pap. 16.95 (0-7022-2935-0, Pub. by Univ Queensland Pr) Intl Spec Bk.

Lucassen, Anneke, jt. auth. see Rose, Peter W.

*Lucassen, Jan & Lucassen, Leo. Migration, Migration History, History: Old Paradigms & New Perspectives. 2nd ed. LC 99-210132. (International & Comparative Social History Ser.: Vol. 4). (Illus.). 454p. 1999. 53.95 (0-8204-4227-5) P Lang Pubng.

Lucassen, Jan & Lucassen, Leo, eds. Migration, Migration History, History: Old Paradigms & New Perspectives. (International & Comparative Social History Ser.: Vol. 4). 454p. 1997. 68.95 (3-906756-86-6, Pub. by P Lang) P Lang Pubng.

— Migration, Migration History, History: Old Paradigms & New Perspectives. LC 97-13081. (International & Comparative Social History Ser.: Vol. 4). 454p. (C). 1997. text 68.95 (0-8204-3405-1, Pub. by P Lang) P Lang Pubng.

Lucassen, Jan, jt. ed. see Davids, Karel.

Lucassen, Leo, jt. auth. see Lucassen, Jan.

Lucassen, Leo, jt. ed. see Lucassen, Jan.

L

Lucatelli, Adriano. Finance & World Order: Financial Fragility, Systematic Risk & Transnational Regimes, 186. LC 96-47432. (Contributions in Economics & Economic History Ser.: Vol. 186). 128p. 1997. 59.95 (0-313-30378-9, Greenwood Pr) Greenwood.

Lucatorto, Thomas, ed. see Wong, Po-Zen.

Lucatt, Edward. Rovings in the Pacific from 1837 to 1849, 2 vols. in 1. LC 75-35203. reprint ed. 110.00 (0-404-14280-X) AMS Pr.

Lucca, Carmen D. Brushstrokes & Landscapes (from My Pen) Pinceladas y Paisajes (de Mi Pluma) Ediciones Mairena Staff, ed. LC 89-92209. (ENG & SPA., Illus.). 130p. (Orig.). 1990. pap. 7.00 (0-9623968-0-X) Poets Refuge.

Lucca, Carmen D., ed. & tr. see De Burgos, Julia.

Lucca, Don A., ed. Proceedings from ASPE 1997 Annual Meeting. (Illus.). 536p. 1997. pap. write for info. (1-887706-18-6) Am Soc Prec Engr.

Lucca, Don A., jt. ed. see Wright, Roger N.

Luccarelli, Mark. Lewis Mumford & the Ecological Region: The Politics of Planning. LC 95-30860. (Critical Perspectives Ser.). 230p. 1995. lib. bdg. 35.00 (1-57230-001-9) Guilford Pubns.

— Lewis Mumford & the Ecological Region: The Politics of Planning. LC 95-30860. (Critical Perspectives Ser.). 230p. 1997. pap. text 18.95 (1-57230-228-3, 0228) Guilford Pubns.

Lucchesi, Benedict R., et al, eds. Clinical Pharmacology of Antiarrhythmic Therapy. LC 84-1931. (Perspectives in Cardiovascular Research Ser.: No. 10). (Illus.). 291p. 1984. reprint ed. pap. 90.30 (0-7837-9564-5, 206031300005) Bks Demand.

Lucchesi, Bruno. Modeling the Figure in Clay. (Illus.). 144p. 1996. pap. text 19.95 (0-8230-3096-2) Watsn-Guptill.

— Modeling the Head in Clay. (Illus.). 160p. 1996. pap. text 19.95 (0-8230-3099-7) Watsn-Guptill.

Lucchesi, C. L., et al, eds. Latin '98: Theoretical Informatics: Third Latin American Symposium, Campinas, Brazil, April 20-24, 1998. LC 98-3115. (Lecture Notes in Computer Science: Vol. 1380). xi, 391p. 1998. pap. 67.00 (3-540-64275-7) Spr-Verlag.

Lucchesi, D. C. The Secrets of the Flying Saucers from Khabaram Khoom. 75p. 1985. reprint ed. spiral bd. 18.00 (0-7873-0572-3) Hlth Research.

Lucchesi, M. Dizionario Medico Ragionato Inglese-Italiano: Regionato English-Italian Medical Dictionary. (ENG & ITA.). 1489p. 1978. 150.00 (0-8288-5206-5, M9353) Fr & Eur.

Lucchesi, Mario. Dizionario Medico: Inglese-Italiano/ Italiano-Inglese. (ENG & ITA.). 1460p. 1987. 160.00 (0-913298-52-2) S F Vanni.

Lucchesi, Serena. Bob Chinn's Crabhouse Cookbook. LC 97-48840. (Illus.). 160p. 1998. 29.95 (0-89815-964-4) Ten Speed Pr.

Lucchesi, Tony & Palombo, Fulvio. European Art to 1850. Turner, C. M., ed. LC 97-165192. (International Encyclopedia of Art Ser.). 64p. 1997. 19.95 (0-8160-3333-1) Facts on File.

Lucchetti, Roberto, ed. Recent Developments in Well-Posed Variational Problems. (Mathematics & Its Applications Ser.). 276p. (C). 1995. text 145.00 (0-7923-3576-7) Kluwer Academic.

Lucchi, Lorna De, see De Lucchi, Lorna, tr.

Lucchin, Francesco, jt. auth. see Coles, Peter.

Lucci, Franco R. Sedimentographica: Photographic Atlas of Sedimentary Structures. 2nd ed. LC 94-24952.Tr. of Sedimentografica. 280p. 1995. 50.00 (0-231-10018-3) Col U Pr.

***Lucciano, Anna M.** Jani Christou: The Works & Temperament of a Greek Composer. (Contemporary Music Studies: Vol. 17). (Illus.). 221p. 1999. text 70.00 (90-5702-158-7, Harwood Acad Pubs); pap. text 30.00 (90-5702-159-5, Harwood Acad Pubs) Gordon & Breach.

Luccio, A. U. & Weng, W. T., eds. Workshop on Space Charge Physics in High Intensity Hadron Rings. (Conference Proceedings Ser.: Vol. 448). 448p. 1998. 125.00 (1-56396-824-X) Am Inst Physics.

Luccio, L. V. Orbit Correction & Analysis in Circular Accelerators. Niederer, J. A. et al, eds. (AIP Conference Proceedings Ser.: No. 315). 200p. 1994. text 95.00 (1-56396-373-6) Am Inst Physics.

Luccioni, Jean. La Pensee Politique de Platon. Mayer, J. P., ed. LC 78-67365. (European Political Thought Ser.). (FRE.). 1980. reprint ed. lib. bdg. 28.95 (0-405-11715-9) Ayer.

Lucco. Giorgione: I Maestri. (ITA., Illus.). 156p. 1997. 57.95 (88-435-5189-2, Pub. by Art Bks Intl) Partners Pubs Grp.

Luccock, Halford E. American Mirror: Social, Ethical & Religious Aspects of American Literature, 1930-1940. LC 75-156806. 300p. 1971. reprint ed. lib. bdg. 60.50 (0-8154-0385-2) Cooper Sq.

— Contemporary American Literature & Religion. LC 73-111471. 1970. reprint ed. 39.50 (0-404-00607-8) AMS Pr.

Luccock, Robert E. Basic Bible Commentary Vol. 17: Matthew. Deming, Lynne M., ed. LC 94-10965. 160p. (Orig.). 1994. pap. 5.95 (0-687-02636-9) Abingdon.

Luce. Ancient Writers, Vol. 1. 1982. 110.00 (0-684-17814-1) Simon & Schuster.

— Ancient Writers, Vol. 2. 1983. 110.00 (0-684-17815-X) Simon & Schuster.

— Lit en Cont Text & Cassette. 1994. 50.50 (0-15-501561-3, Pub. by Harcourt Coll Pubs) Harcourt.

— Litteratures En Contexte: Le Monde Francophonr. (C). 1994. wbk. ed. 36.00 (0-15-501103-0) Harcourt Coll Pubs.

— Litteratures en Contexte Grammar. (C). 1994. pap. text 48.50 (0-15-501102-2) Harcourt Coll Pubs.

Luce, A. Evidencias Cristianas.Tr. of Christian Evidences. (SPA.). 96p. 1965. pap. 4.99 (0-8297-0554-6) Vida Pubs.

— Mensajero y Su Mensaji.Tr. of Messenger & His Message. (SPA.). 96p. 1964. pap. 3.99 (0-8297-0582-1) Vida Pubs.

Luce, A. A. Fishing & Thinking. (Illus.). 160p. 1996. pap. text 12.95 (0-07-039059-2) Intl Marine.

Luce, A. A., ed. see Berkeley, George.

Luce, Arthur A. The Life of George Berkeley Bishop of Cloyne: 1949 Edition. 302p. 1996. reprint ed. 58.00 (1-85506-128-7) Bks Intl VA.

Luce, B. Dictionary Gastronomic Terms, French to English. (ENG & FRE.). 512p. 1997. 79.95 (0-320-00419-8) Fr & Eur.

— French-English Dictionary of Gastronomic Terms. 500p. 1997. pap. 24.95 (0-7818-0555-4, 655) Hippocrene Bks.

Luce, Carol D. Night Game. 1996. mass mkt. 4.99 (0-8217-5287-1, Zebra Kensgtn) Kensgtn Pub Corp.

— Night Passage. 432p. 1995. mass mkt. 4.99 (0-8217-4966-8, Pinncle Kensgtn) Kensgtn Pub Corp.

— Night Prey. 1992. mass mkt. 4.99 (0-8217-3661-2, Zebra Kensgtn) Kensgtn Pub Corp.

— Night Stalker. 1990. mass mkt. 4.99 (0-8217-4245-0, Zebra Kensgtn) Kensgtn Pub Corp.

— Skin Deep. 1990. mass mkt. 4.50 (1-55817-398-6, Pinncle Kensgtn) Kensgtn Pub Corp.

Luce, Clare Boothe. Margin for Error: Manuscript Edition. 1940. pap. 13.00 (0-8222-1456-3) Dramatists Play.

— Slam the Door Softly. 1970. pap. 3.25 (0-8222-1039-8) Dramatists Play.

— Stuffed Shirts. LC 77-163043. (Short Story Index Reprint Ser.). 1977. reprint ed. 24.95 (0-8369-3957-3) Ayer.

— The Women. 1966. pap. 5.25 (0-8222-1270-6) Dramatists Play.

Luce, Clare Boothe, ed. Saints for Now. LC 93-78817. 300p. 1993. 12.95 (0-89870-476-6) Ignatius Pr.

Luce, Clare Boothe, et al. Plays by American Women, 1930-1960. Barlow, Judith E., ed. LC 94-7760. 416p. 1994. pap. 16.95 (1-55783-164-5) Applause Theatre Bk Pubs.

Luce, Dianne C., jt. ed. see Arnold, Edwin T.

Luce, Don, jt. ed. see Sun-ai, Lee.

Luce, Donald T. Francis Lee Jaques: Artist-Naturalist. (Illus.). (C). 1982. pap. 13.95 (0-8166-1146-7) U of Minn Pr.

Luce, Donald T., intro. Wildlife Art in America: February 26 - May 15, 1994. (Illus.). 104p. (Orig.). 1994. pap. 15.00 (1-884879-00-4) UMN J F B Mus.

Luce, G. H. Phases of Pre-Pagan Burma: Languages & History, 2 vols. (Illus.). 1986. 155.00 (0-19-713595-1) OUP.

Luce, Gay G. Longer Life, More Joy: Techniques for Enhancing Health, Happiness & Inner Vision. 1992. pap. 12.95 (0-87877-171-9) Newcastle Pub.

Luce, Gertrude E. Life is Not an Empty Dream: Or a Glass Half Full, 1. LC 98-86129. 1998. pap. text 12.00 (1-889131-34-2, Casananda Pub) Padaran Pubns.

Luce, Gordon H. Old Burma, Early Pagan, 3 Vols., Set. 1969. 380.00 (0-686-92654-4) J J Augustin.

Luce, J. V. Celebrating Homer's Landscapes: Troy & Ithaca Revisited. LC 98-3859. (Illus.). 224p. 1998. 40.00 (0-300-07411-5) Yale U Pr.

— Introduction to Greek Philosophy. LC 91-75043. 176p. 1992. pap. 16.95 (0-500-27655-2, Pub. by Thames Hudson) Norton.

Luce, James, Jr., ed. Roman History, 43 vols. 1975. 1787.00 (0-405-07177-9) Ayer.

Luce, Janet, et al, eds. Combining Service & Learning Vol. 3: An Annotated Bibliography for Community & Public Service. 81p. (C). 1998. pap. text 15.00 (0-536-01241-5) Pearson Custom.

Luce, John M., et al. Intensive Respiratory Care. 2nd ed. LC 92-48898. (Illus.). 400p. 1993. pap. text 29.00 (0-7216-4270-5, W B Saunders Co) Harcrt Hlth Sci Grp.

Luce, Judith de, see De Luce, Judith, ed.

Luce, Judith de, see Baldwin, A. Dwight, Jr.

Luce-Kapler, Rebecca, jt. auth. see Upitis, Rena Brigit.

Luce, Katie. The Pursuit of Beauty: Finding True Beauty That Will Last Forever. LC 97-75890. 160p. 1998. pap. 10.99 (0-89221-373-6) New Leaf.

Luce, Larry. The Single Cook's Book: One Hundred & Six Unusual Recipes for One-Person Servings. (Illus.). 1976. pap. 4.00 (0-686-16919-0) Other Bks.

Luce, Louise F. The Spanish-Speaking World: An Anthology of Cross-Cultural Perspectives. (SPA.). 400p. 1994. pap. 25.35 (0-8442-7161-6, Natl Textbk Co) NTC Contemp Pub Co.

Luce, Louise F. & Smith, Elise F., eds. Toward Internationalism: Readings in Cross-Cultural Communication. 2nd ed. 293p. (J). 1986. mass mkt. 27.95 (0-8384-2689-1, Newbury) Heinle & Heinle.

Luce, Morton. Handbook to the Works of William Shakespeare. 2nd rev. ed. LC 73-172756. reprint ed. 41.50 (0-404-04064-0) AMS Pr.

Luce, R. Duncan. Games & Decisions. 509p. 1989. pap. 13.95 (0-486-65943-7) Dover.

— Response Times: Their Role in Inferring Elementary Mental Organization. (Oxford Psychology Ser.: No. 8). (Illus.). 576p. 1986. text 100.00 (0-19-503642-5) OUP.

— Response Times: Their Role in Inferring Elementary Mental Organization. (Oxford Psychology Ser.: No. 8). (Illus.). 584p. 1991. reprint ed. pap. text 60.00 (0-19-507001-1) OUP.

— Sound & Hearing. 344p. 1993. pap. 32.50 (0-8058-1389-6); text 69.95 (0-8058-1251-2); cd-rom 49.95 (0-8058-1450-7); cd-rom 19.95 (1-56321-116-5) L Erlbaum Assocs.

***Luce, R. Duncan.** Utility of Gains & Losses: Measurement, Theoretical & Experimental Approaches. LC 99-55910. (Scientific Psychology Ser.). 336p. 2000. 59.95 (0-8058-3460-5) L Erlbaum Assocs.

Luce, R. Duncan, et al, eds. Foundations of Measurement, Vol. 2. 760p. 1989. text 129.95 (0-12-425402-0) Acad Pr.

— Leading Edges in Social & Behavioral Science. LC 89-24186. 720p. 1990. 59.95 (0-87154-560-8) Russell Sage.

Luce, Robert. Legislative Assemblies. LC 73-5617. (American Constitutional & Legal History Ser). 692p. 1974. reprint ed. lib. bdg. 75.00 (0-306-70583-4) Da Capo.

— Legislative Problems. LC 76-152834. (American Constitutional & Legal History Ser). 1971. reprint ed. lib. bdg. 75.00 (0-306-70153-7) Da Capo.

Luce, Robert B. Lifelines. (Illus.). 48p. 1994. 8.95 (0-8378-6948-X) Gibson.

— Marriage: A Treasury of Words to Live By. (Illus.). 1992. 8.95 (0-8378-2501-6) Gibson.

Luce, Robert D. Individual Choice Behavior: A Theoretical Analysis. LC 78-25881. (Illus.). 153p. 1979. reprint ed. lib. bdg. 35.00 (0-313-20778-X, LUIC, Greenwood Pr) Greenwood.

Luce, Robert D., ed. Developments in Mathematical Psychology: Information, Learning & Tracking. LC 80-14533. (Illus.). 294p. 1980. reprint ed. lib. bdg. 65.00 (0-313-22464-1, LUDM, Greenwood Pr) Greenwood.

***Luce, Ron.** Columbine Courage. 2000. pap. 9.99 (0-8499-5696-X) J Countryman.

— Columbine Courage: Totally Worth It! 1999. 12.99 (0-8499-5607-2) J Countryman.

Luce, Ron. Fifty-Six Days Ablaze. LC 94-68471. 1995. pap. 7.99 (0-88419-385-3) Creation House.

— Inspire the Fire: Giving Today's Youth Something Real to Believe In. 1994. pap. 10.99 (0-88419-370-5) Creation House.

— Mature Christians Are Boring People: And Other Myths about Maturity in Christ - A Daily Devotional for Teens. LC 98-208051. 208p. (YA). 1997. pap. 9.99 (1-57778-037-X, Pub. by Albury Pub) Appalach Bk Dist.

— Quit Playing with Fire. LC 94-69835. 192p. 1995. pap. 8.95 (0-89221-280-2) New Leaf.

— Rescue Manual for Parents: How to Successfully Survive the Teenage Years. LC 98-130881. 224p. 1997. pap. 9.99 (1-57778-011-6, Pub. by Albury Pub) Appalach Bk Dist.

— Spiritual Shock Treatment: Get Real with JesusTeen Devotional. 199p. (YA). (gr. 8-12). 1998. 11.99 (1-57778-100-7, Pub. by Albury Pub) Appalach Bk Dist.

— Spiritual Shock Treatment Devotional: Get Real with Jesus. 216p. 1998. pap. 9.99 (1-57778-097-3, Pub. by Albury Pub) Appalach Bk Dist.

Luce, S. Introduction to Composite Technology. 40p. 1988. pap. text 10.00 (0-87263-322-5) SME.

Luce, Simeon. Histoire de Bertrand Du Gueselin et de Son Epoque. LC 78-63505. reprint ed. 37.50 (0-404-17154-0) AMS Pr.

Luce, Stanford L. Celine & His Critics: Scandals & Paradox. (Stanford French & Italian Studies: Vol. 44). 224p. 1986. pap. 56.50 (0-915838-59-1) Anma Libri.

Luce, Stephanie, jt. auth. see Pollin, Robert.

Luce, Stephen B. Corpus Vasorum Antiquorum, Fasc. 1. (Illus.). 1933. 5.00 (0-911517-16-2) Mus of Art RI.

Luce, Stephen C. & Christian, Walter P. How to Reduce Autistic & Severely Maladaptive Behaviors. (Teaching the Autistic Ser.). 39p. 1981. pap. 8.00 (0-89079-053-1, 1032) PRO-ED.

Luce, Stephen C., jt. auth. see Dyer, Kathleen.

Luce, T., jt. auth. see Lohr, J.

Luce, T. James. The Greek Historians. LC 96-19960. 168p. (C). 1997. 60.00 (0-415-10592-7); pap. 17.99 (0-415-10593-5) Routledge.

Luce, T. James, ed. Ancient Writers: Greece & Rome, 2 vols., Vol. 2. LC 82-50612. 1184p. 1982. 200.00 (0-684-16595-3, Scribners Ref) Mac Lib Ref.

Luce, T. James, Jr., ed. & tr. see Livy.

Luce, Thom. Computer Hardware, Systems Software, & Architecture. (C). 1989. text 51.50 (0-07-557772-0) McGraw.

— Using VP-Expert in Business. 1992. pap. text. write for info. (0-07-038984-5) McGraw.

Luce, Thom, jt. auth. see Hawkins, Tom.

Luce, Thomas F., jt. auth. see Summers, Anita A.

Luce, Thomas G. Genetics with a Computer. pap. 16.95 (0-87567-076-8) Entelek.

Luce, Torrey J. Livy: The Composition of His History. LC 77-72126. 351p. reprint ed. pap. 108.90 (0-608-18438-1, 203263400080) Bks Demand.

Luce, Torrey J. & Woodman, A. J., eds. Tacitus & the Tacitean Tradition. LC 92-25050. (Magie Classical Publications). (Illus.). 224p. reprint ed. pap. 69.50 (0-608-09100-6, 206973400005) Bks Demand.

Luce, Warren. So You Want to Get to Heaven. LC 98-91452. 303p. 1998. pap. 17.95 (0-9663987-1-8) Probe Press.

Luce, William. Lillian. 1986. pap. 5.25 (0-8222-0666-8) Dramatists Play.

Luceigh, Betty. Chem TV: Faculty IBM II 2.0. (C). 1996. disk 247.50 (0-86720-922-4) Jones & Bartlett.

— Chem TV: Student Workbook II. 130p. (C). 1996. pap. text, wbk. ed. 18.74 (0-86720-501-6) Jones & Bartlett.

— Chem TV: Workbook Version. (Chemistry Ser.). 1994. pap. 17.50 (0-86720-906-2) Jones & Bartlett.

— Chem TV I: Student Mac I 2.0. 1996. student ed. 14.00 (0-7637-0032-0) Jones & Bartlett.

Luceno, Alberto, jt. auth. see Box, George E.

***Luceno, James.** Agents of Chaos I: Hero's Trial. (Star Wars: No. 4). 416p. (J). (gr. 3-7). 2000. mass mkt. 6.99 (0-345-42860-9, Del Rey) Ballantine Pub Grp.

— Jedi Eclipse. (Star Wars: Bk. 2). 2000. mass mkt. 6.99 (0-345-42859-5, Ballantine) Ballantine Pub Grp.

Luceno, James. Mask of Zorro. 1998. 9.09 (0-606-13600-2, Pub. by Turtleback) Demco.

— Mission Impossible: The Aztec Imperative. 1996. mass mkt. 5.99 (0-671-00232-5) PB.

— Zorro. 224p. 1998. per. 6.50 (0-671-51989-1) PB.

***Lucent Netcare Staff.** CCIE Routing & Switching Exam Guide 350-001. (Illus.). 600p. 2000. pap. 39.99 (0-7897-2359-X) Que.

Lucent Technologies Staff, jt. auth. see Sproat, Richard W.

Lucente, Carla E., pref. The French Revolution, Literature & the Arts: Proceedings of the Western Pennsylvania Symposium on World Literatures: 1989. LC 90-81724. (Humanities Ser.: No. 4). 72p. (Orig.). (C). 1991. pap. 10.95 (0-929914-07-4) Eadmer Pr.

— The Western Pennsylvania Symposium on World Literatures, 1974-1991: Selected Proceedings, a Retrospective. LC 92-54567. (Humanities Ser.: No. 6). (Illus.). 266p. (C). 1992. text 40.00 (0-929914-13-9) Eadmer Pr.

Lucente, Frank E. & Sobol, Steven M. Essentials of Otolaryngology. 4th ed. Gady, Har-Ed, ed. LC 99-21310. 1999. 36.00 (0-7817-1463-X) Lppncott W & W.

Lucente, Frank E. & Sobol, Steven M., eds. Essentials of Otolaryngology. 3rd ed. LC 92-48778. 608p. 1993. pap. text 38.00 (0-88167-996-8) Lppncott W & W.

Lucente, Gregory L. Beautiful Fables: Self-Consciousness in Italian Narrative from Manzoni to Calvino. LC 86-7373. 400p. reprint ed. pap. 124.00 (0-608-06166-2, 206649900008) Bks Demand.

— Crosspaths in Literary Theory & Criticism: Italy & the United States. LC 96-44321. 1997. 39.50 (0-8047-2829-1); pap. write for info. (0-8047-2830-5) Stanford U Pr.

— The Narrative of Realism & Myth: Verga, Lawrence, Faulkner, Pavese. LC 81-2084. 205p. 1981. reprint ed. pap. 63.60 (0-608-07330-X, 206755800009) Bks Demand.

— Over the Mountain. LC 97-145523. 229p. (Orig.). 1996. pap. 12.95 (0-9653968-0-0) G Lucente.

Lucente, Gregory L., ed. Italian Criticism: Literature & Culture. LC 81-50963. (Michigan Romance Studies: No 16). (Illus.). 241p. (Orig.). 1997. pap. 15.00 (0-939730-15-4) Mich Romance.

***Lucente, Paul.** Contractor's State License: Study Guide for the Law & Business Examination for the State of CA. 13th rev. ed. 445p. 2000. pap. 54.95 (1-889892-20-3) Builders Bk Inc.

Lucentini, Franco, jt. auth. see Fruttero, Carlo.

***Lucero, Al & Harrisson, John.** The Great Margarita Book. (Illus.). 160p. 1999. pap. 15.95 (1-58008-053-7) Ten Speed Pr.

***Lucero, Evelina Zuni.** Night Sky, Morning Star. LC 00-8119. (First Book Awards Ser.). 235p. 2000. pap. 16.95 (0-8165-2055-0) U of Ariz Pr.

Lucero, Faustina H. Little Indians' ABC. LC 73-87800. (Illus.). 32p. (J). (gr. k-2). 1974. lib. bdg. 9.95 (0-87783-129-7) Oddo.

— Little Indians' ABC. deluxe ed. LC 73-87800. (Illus.). 32p. (J). (gr. k-2). 1974. pap. 3.94 (0-87783-130-0) Oddo.

Lucero, Helen R. & Baizerman, Suzanne. Chimayo Weaving: The Transformation of a Tradition. LC 98-23210. (Illus.). 1998. 80.00 (0-8263-1975-0); pap. 39.95 (0-8263-1976-9) U of NM Pr.

Lucero, Joan & Guy, Janice. How to Survive Dying. LC 95-95057. 120p. 1995. pap., spiral bd. 13.00 (0-9648687-0-9) J J Books.

Lucero, Roberto A. Sangre del Monte. 192p. (Orig.). 1994. pap. 12.95 (0-9642480-3-4) Mrningstar Bks.

Lucero, Ruth, tr. see Winter, Gerald A.

Lucero-White, et al. Hispano Culture of New Mexico: An Original Anthology. Cortes, Carlos E., ed. & intro. by. LC 76-5929. (Chicano Heritage Ser.). (Illus.). 1977. 23.95 (0-405-09537-6) Ayer.

Lucey, Beryl. Twenty Centuries in Sedlescombe. 523p. 1984. 40.00 (0-7212-0548-8, Pub. by Regency Pr GBR) St Mut.

Lucey, Clare, jt. ed. see Reder, Peter.

***Lucey, Donna M.** Photographing Montana, 1894-1928: The Life & Work of Evelyn Cameron. (Illus.). 268p. 2000. reprint ed. 60.00 (0-87842-426-1); reprint ed. pap. 35.00 (0-87842-425-3) Mountain Pr.

Lucey, James V., jt. ed. see O'Mahony, Gerald.

Lucey, Jerold F., jt. auth. see Dickerman, Joseph D.

Lucey, Kenneth G., ed. On Knowing & the Known: Introductory Readings in Epistemology. LC 96-12549. 437p. 1998. pap. 23.95 (1-57392-050-9) Prometheus Bks.

— What Is God? The Selected Essays of Richard LaCroix. LC 93-20193. 200p. (C). 1993. 36.95 (0-87975-739-6) Prometheus Bks.

Lucey, M. N. A Sailor View of Live Yeshu. 759p. (C). 1989. text 75.00 (1-872795-55-2, Pub. by Pentland Pr) St Mut.

Lucey, M. R., et al, eds. Liver Transplantation & the Alcoholic Patient. (Illus.). 144p. (C). 1994. text 57.95 (0-521-43332-0) Cambridge U Pr.

Lucey, Michael. Gide's Bent: Writing, Sexuality & Politics. (Ideologies of Desire Ser.). (Illus.). 248p. 1995. text 50.00 (0-19-508086-6); pap. text 24.95 (0-19-508087-4) OUP.

Lucey, Michael, jt. ed. see Neuberger, James.

Lucey, Paul. Story Sense: Writing Story & Script for Feature Films & Television. 336p. (C). 1996. pap. 23.13 (0-07-038996-9) McGraw.

Lucey, T. Cost & Management Accounting. 304p. 1995. pap. 59.95 (1-85805-127-4, Pub. by DP Publns) St Mut.

— Management Information Systems. 336p. 1995. pap. 59.95 (1-85805-106-1, Pub. by DP Publns) St Mut.

— Management Information Systems. 8th ed. LC 98-130408. v, 282 p. 1997. write for info. (1-85805-303-X) Letts Educ.

Lucha-Burns, Carol. Musical Notes: A Practical Guide to Staffing & Staging Standards of the American Musical Theatre. LC 85-10017. 598p. 1986. lib. bdg. 85.00 (0-313-24648-3, BMN/, Greenwood Pr) Greenwood.

An Asterisk (*) at the beginning of an entry indicates that the title is appearing for the first time.

Luchaire, Achille. Social France at the Time of Philip Augustus. 1976. lib. bdg. 59.95 (*0-8490-2617-2*) Gordon Pr.

Luchawich, Alexandria, jt. auth. see Wynne, Sharon.

Luche, Jean-Louis. Synthetic Organic Sonochemistry. LC 98-20264. (Illus.). 456p. (C). 1998. text 115.00 (*0-306-45916-7*, Kluwer Plenum) Kluwer Academic.

Luchenbach, Dave & Martin, Bob. Grumman XF5F-1 & XP-50 Skyrocket, V. Ginter, Steve, ed. & photos by by. (Naval Fighters Ser.: Vol. 31). (Illus.). 33p. (Orig.). 1995. pap. 7.95 (*0-942612-31-0*) Naval Fighters.

Luchene, Stephen R. Van, see Van Luchene, Stephen R.

Luchessi, M. Italian-English - English-Italian Medical Dictionary. 1456p. 1987. 150.00 (*88-7078-037-6*) IBD Ltd.

Luchetta, Tracy, jt. auth. see Pardie, Lynn.

Luchetti, Cathy. Hot Flash Cookbook: Delicious Recipes for Health & Well-Being Through Menopause. LC 97-6982. 1997. pap. 16.95 (*0-8118-1540-4*) Chronicle Bks.

— Motherhood & Child. Date not set. pap. write for info. (*0-517-88450-X*, Crown) Crown Pub Group.

— Under God's Spell. 1989. 27.95 (*0-15-192799-5*) Harcourt.

Luchetti, Emily. Stars Desserts. LC 90-56386. (Illus.). 272p. 1993. reprint ed. pap. 22.50 (*0-06-092218-4*, Perennial) HarperTrade.

Luchinat, Christina A., ed. The Chapel of the Magi: The Frescoes of Benozzo Gozzoli. LC 94-60292. (Illus.). 388p. 1994. 100.00 (*0-500-23691-7*, Pub. by Thames Hudson) Norton.

Luchinat, Claudio, jt. auth. see Bertini, Ivano.

Luchinat, Cristina A. Benozzo Gozzoli. Evans, Christopher, tr. from ITA. (Library of Great Masters). (Illus.). 80p. (Orig.). 1995. pap. 14.99 (*1-878351-47-8*) Riverside NY.

Luchini, P. & Motz, H. Undulators & Free-Electron Lasers. (International Series of Monographs on Physics: No. 79). (Illus.). 334p. 1990. text 89.00 (*0-19-852019-0*) OUP.

Luchins, Abraham S. & Luchins, Edith H. Revisiting Wertheimer's Seminars, 2 vols. Incl. Vol. 1. Value, Social Influence, & Power. LC 72-3525. 1978. 85.00 (*0-8387-1227-4*); Vol. 2. Problems in Social Psychology. LC 72-3525. 1978. 85.00 (*0-8387-1570-2*); LC 72-3525. 1046p. 1978. write for info. (*0-686-96685-6*) Bucknell U Pr.

— Wertheimer's Seminars Revisited: Problem Solving & Thinking, 3 vols., Vol. 1. LC BF0441.L8. (Illus.). 439p. reprint ed. pap. 136.10 (*0-8357-4204-0*, 203698300001) Bks Demand.

— Wertheimer's Seminars Revisited: Problem Solving & Thinking, 3 vols., Vol. 2. LC BF0441.L8. (Illus.). 430p. reprint ed. pap. 133.30 (*0-8357-4205-9*, 203698300002) Bks Demand.

— Wertheimer's Seminars Revisited: Problem Solving & Thinking, 3 vols., Vol. 3. LC BF0441.L8. (Illus.). 445p. reprint ed. pap. 138.00 (*0-8357-4206-7*, 203698300003) Bks Demand.

Luchins, Edith H., jt. auth. see Luchins, Abraham S.

Luchinsky, Ellen, ed. see Enoch Pratt Free Library Staff.

Luchner, K., et al, eds. Teaching Modern Physics. 500p. (C). 1989. text 55.00 (*9971-5-0923-7*); pap. text 33.00 (*9971-5-0960-1*) World Scientific Pub.

Luchnig, L. J., jt. auth. see Luschnig, C. A.

Luchok, John, ed. see Brown, Clifford W. & Brown, Clifford W.

Luchs, Alison. Tullio Lombardo & Ideal Portait Sculpture in Renaissance Italy, 1490-1530. (Illus.). 320p. (C). 1995. text 80.00 (*0-521-47075-7*) Cambridge U Pr.

Luchs, Alison, tr. see Wackernagel, Martin.

Luchs, Alvin S. Torchbearers of the Middle Ages. LC 77-160924. (Biography Index Reprint Ser.). (Illus.). 1977. reprint ed. 18.95 (*0-8369-8087-5*) Ayer.

Luchs, Kathleen, jt. auth. see Campbell, Andrew.

Luchs, Kathleen, jt. ed. see Goold, Michael.

Luchsinger, Arlene E., jt. auth. see Jones, Samuel B.

Luchsinger, Frank. Love Is Your Disguise: Sermons for Lent/Easter. LC 98-13655. (Second Lessons Ser.). 110p. 1998. pap. 9.95 (*0-7880-1269-X*) CSS OH.

— Moving at the Speed of Light: Sermons for Advent/Christmas/Epiphany. (Second Lessons Ser.). 1998. pap. 9.50 (*0-7880-1268-1*) CSS OH.

— Moving at the Speed of Light: Sermons for Advent/Christmas/Epiphany. LC 98-5617. (Second Lessons Ser.). 102p. 1998. pap. 9.50 (*0-7880-1265-7*) CSS OH.

Luchsinger, Jack. The Politician. LC 96-69944. 499p. 1996. pap. 10.00 (*0-9648622-8-X*) Pine Grve Pr.

***Luchsinger, M. Lou.** Indulge Yourself with Aromatherapy. LC 00-33901. 2000. write for info. (*0-8069-2763-1*) Sterling.

Luchsinger, Vincent P., jt. auth. see Vroman, H. William.

Lucht, Irmgard. The Red Poppy. large type ed. Jacoby-Nelson, Frank, tr. LC 94-15057. (Illus.). 32p. (J). (ps-3). 1995. 13.95 (*0-7868-0055-0*, Pub. by Hyprn Child); lib. bdg. 13.89 (*0-7868-2043-8*, Pub. by Hyprn Child) Little.

Lucht, John. Executive Job-Changing Workbook. 640p. 1995. pap. 29.95 (*0-942785-22-3*) H Holt & Co.

***Lucht, John.** Rites of Passage at $100,000+ New Thinking: Your Insider's Lifetime Guide to Executive Job-Changing & Faster Career Progress in 21st Century. 2000. 29.95 (*0-942785-30-4*) Viceroy Pr.

Lucht, John, rev. The Rites of Passage at One Hundred Thousand Dollars Plus: The Insider's Lifetime Guide to Executive Job-Changing & Faster Career Progress. rev. ed. 625p. 1993. 29.95 (*0-942785-21-5*) Viceroy Pr.

Lucht, W. H., jt. ed. see Lohse, G. A.

***Luchtefeld, Henry T.** Take Control of Your Prescription Health: 14 Questions - 7 Minutes to Safeguard Your Health. 144p. 1999. pap. 10.95 (*0-9675265-4-X*, SAN 253-0058) J Consulting.

***Luchterband, Lyle L.** Man: Bible Study. (People's Bible Teachings Ser.). 1999. 37.99 (*0-8100-0878-5*) Northwest Pub.

Luchterhand, Charlene & Murphy, Nancy. Helping Adults with Mental Retardation Grieve a Death Loss. LC 97-38964. 132p. 1998. pap. 14.95 (*1-56032-768-5*) Hemisp Pub.

Luchterhand, Elmer & Sydiaha, Daniel. Choice in Human Affairs: An Application to Aging-Accident-Illness Problems. 1966. pap. 15.95 (*0-8084-0075-4*) NCUP.

Luchterhand, Kubet. Early Archaic Projectile Points & Hunting Patterns in the Lower Illinois Valley. (Reports of Investigations: No. 19). (Illus.). 67p. 1986. reprint ed. pap. 3.50 (*0-89792-043-0*) Ill St Museum.

Luci, Anna. Baby Jesus. (Illus.). 16p. (J). (ps-2). 1995. pap. 1.95 (*0-8198-1145-9*) Pauline Bks.

Lucia, Al & Long, Donna. Rock Your Way to Happiness: Harmogenize: a Fun New Way to a More Fulfilling Life. (Illus.). 220p. 1999. 29.95 (*0-9669099-3-3*) JukeBox Pubg.

Lucia, Alexander, jt. auth. see Harvey, Eric.

Lucia, Alexandria D., jt. auth. see Harvey, Eric L.

Lucia, Alfredo C., ed. Advances in Structural Reliability. 1987. text 154.00 (*90-277-2429-6*) Kluwer Academic.

Lucia, Anntoinette D., jt. auth. see Lepsinger, Richard.

Lucia, Ellis. Tillamook Burn Country: A Pictorial History. LC 83-18164. (Illus.). (Orig.). 1983. pap. 14.95 (*0-87004-296-3*) Caxton.

Lucia, Ellis, jt. auth. see Hanley, Mike.

Lucia, F. Jerry. Carbonate Reservoir Characterization. LC 98-29500. 216p. 1999. 99.00 (*3-540-63782-6*) Spr-Verlag.

Lucia, Salvatore P. Wine & Your Well Being. 160p. 1999. reprint ed. pap. 9.95 (*0-932664-08-3*) Wine Appreciation.

Lucia, Tina. Releasing: The Key to Physical Manifastion, No. 1. Craig, Linda, ed. (Releasing Ser.). (Illus.). 30p. 1988. pap. 6.95 (*0-317-91334-4*) T Ketch-Bennett.

— Releasing Through Numerology, No. 3. Craig, Linda, ed. (Releasing Ser.). (Illus.). 150p. 1988. 12.95 (*0-317-91330-1*); pap. 9.95 (*0-317-91331-X*) T Ketch-Bennett.

— Releasing Through Tarot, No. 2. Craig, Linda, ed. (Releasing Ser.). 150p. 1988. 19.95 (*0-317-91332-8*); pap. 9.95 (*0-317-91333-6*) T Ketch-Bennett.

Lucia, Victor O. Modern Gnathological Concepts-Updated. (Illus.). 440p. 1983. text 186.00 (*0-86715-105-6*) Quint Pub Co.

— Treatment of the Edentulous Patient. LC 85-30060. (Illus.). 248p. 1986. text 148.00 (*0-86715-122-6*, 1226) Quint Pub Co.

Luciak, Ilja A. The Sandinista Legacy: Lessons from a Political Economy in Transition. LC 95-6520. (Illus.). 248p. 1995. 49.95 (*0-8130-1369-0*) U Press Fla.

Lucian. Dialogues, 3. (Loeb Classical Library: No. 14, 54, 130, 162, 302, 430-432). 498p. 1921. text 19.95 (*0-674-99144-3*) HUP.

— Dialogues, 4. (Loeb Classical Library: No. 14, 54, 130, 162, 302, 430-432). 430p. 1925. text 19.95 (*0-674-99179-6*) HUP.

— Dialogues, 5. (Loeb Classical Library: No. 14, 54, 130, 162, 302, 430-432). 548p. 1936. text 19.95 (*0-674-99333-0*) HUP.

— Dialogues, 6. (Loeb Classical Library: No. 14, 54, 130, 162, 302, 430-432). 280p. 1959. text 19.95 (*0-674-99474-4*) HUP.

— Dialogues, 7. (Loeb Classical Library: No. 14, 54, 130, 162, 302, 430-432). 488p. 1961. text 19.95 (*0-674-99475-2*) HUP.

— Dialogues, 8. (Loeb Classical Library: No. 14, 54, 130, 162, 302, 430-432). 544p. 1967. text 19.95 (*0-674-99476-0*) HUP.

— Lucian: A Selection. McLeod, M. C., ed. (Classical Texts Ser.). 320p. (C). 1991. pap. 32.00 (*0-85668-416-3*, Pub. by Aris & Phillips) David Brown.

— Opera: Tomus IV: Libelli 69-86. MacLeod, M. D., ed. (Classical Texts Ser.). 538p. 1987. text 60.00 (*0-19-814596-9*) OUP.

— Opera Tomus III: Libelli 44-68. Macleod, M. D., ed. (Oxford Classical Texts Ser.). 406p. (C). 1980. text 55.00 (*0-19-814592-6*) OUP.

— Selected Works. Reardon, B. P., tr. LC 64-16706. (Orig.). 1965. pap. 5.65 (*0-672-60385-3*, LLA161, Bobbs) Macmillan.

Lucian, Justin. Systematic Desensitization: Student Guide. 1976. pap. text 6.95 (*0-89420-000-3*, 480011); audio 37.80 (*0-89420-186-7*, 480000) Natl Book.

Lucian, M. D. Lucian: A Selection. McLeod, M. C., ed. (Classical Texts Ser.). 320p. (C). 1991. 59.99 (*0-85668-415-5*, Pub. by Aris & Phillips) David Brown.

***Luciana, James & Watts, Judith.** The Art of Enhanced Photography: Beyond the Photographic Image. (Illus.). 144p. 1999. text. write for info. (*90-5703-462-X*, Pub. by Craftsman House) Gordon & Breach.

Luciana, James & Watts, Judith. The Art of Enhanced Photography: Extending the Photographic Image. (Illus.). 144p. 1999. 29.99 (*1-56496-379-9*) Rockport Pubs.

Luciani. More What Canadians Believe But Shouldn't about Their Economy. 1997. pap. text. write for info. (*0-201-89286-3*) Addison-Wesley.

***Luciani, James V.** Black-&-White Photography, Manifest Visions: An International Collection, (Illus.). 143p. 2000. 35.00 (*1-56496-647-X*) Rockport Pubs.

Luciani, A., jt. ed. see Kunii, T. L.

Luciani, Giacomo, ed. The Arab State. 1989. 55.00 (*0-520-06432-1*, Pub. by U CA Pr) Cal Prin Full Svc.

— Migration Policies in Europe & the United States. LC 93-23464. 172p. (C). 1993. lib. bdg. 134.50 (*0-7923-2537-0*) Kluwer Academic.

Luciani, Giacomo, et al, eds. Nation, State & Integration in the Arab World Vol. 4: The Politics of Arab Integration. 300p. (C). 1988. text 90.00 (*0-7099-4148-X*, Pub. by C Helm) Routldge.

Luciani, Giacomo & Salame, Ghassan, eds. Nation, State & Integration in the Arab World, 4 vols., Set. 300p. 1988. lib. bdg. 192.50 (*0-317-64358-4*, Pub. by C Helm) Routldge.

Luciani, Giacomo, jt. auth. see Bebuawu, Gazen.

Luciani, Giacomo, ed. see Salame, Ghassan.

Luciani, Lucio, et al, eds. Basic Research in Urological Oncology. viii, 182p. 1996. 172.25 (*3-8055-6120-2*) S Karger.

Luciani, Patrick. Economic Myths: Making Sense of Canadian Policy Issues. 3rd ed. 2000. pap. text. write for info. (*0-201-61436-7*) Addison-Wesley.

— What Canadians Believe, but Shouldn't about Their Economy. 1993. pap. write for info. (*0-201-60168-0*) Addison-Wesley.

Luciani, S., jt. auth. see Santi, R.

Luciani, Vincent. A Brief History of Italian Literature. (C). 1967. 15.00 (*0-913298-09-3*) S F Vanni.

— A Concise History of the Italian Theatre. (C). 1961. pap. 5.95 (*0-913298-10-7*) S F Vanni.

— Italian Idioms with Proverbs. (ENG & ITA.). (C). 1981. pap. 8.95 (*0-913298-15-8*) S F Vanni.

Luciani, Vincent & Colaneri, John. Italian Verbs. (Verbs Ser.). (ITA & ENG.). 350p. 1990. pap. 5.95 (*0-8120-4313-8*) Barron.

Luciani, Vincent, jt. auth. see Colaneri, John.

Luciani, Vincent, ed. see Betti, Ugo.

Luciani, Vincent, ed. see Bracco, Roberto.

Luciani, Vincent, ed. see Giacosa, Giuseppe.

Luciani, Vincent, ed. see Goldoni, Carlo.

Luciani, Vincent, ed. see Machiavelli, Niccolo.

Luciano, Danny. Jazz: Today & Tomorrow: An Encyclopedia of People, Places, Venues, & the Media Chronicling 100 Years of Jazz. (Illus.). 325p. (Orig.). (C). 1996. pap. text 30.00 (*0-7881-2711-X*) DIANE Pub.

— Jazz Crossword Puzzles. (Illus.). 56p. (Orig.). (C). 1996. pap. text 10.00 (*0-7881-2710-1*) DIANE Pub.

Luciano, Eleonora & Georgia Museum of Art Staff. Animals in Bronze: The Michael & Mary Erlanger Collection. Eiland, William U., ed. LC 96-46925. (Illus.). 96p. 1996. pap. 16.00 (*0-915977-30-3*) Georgia Museum of Art.

Luciano, Eugene W. Our Blood & His Guts. 212p. 1995. 22.00 (*1-57087-187-6*) Prof Pr NC.

Luciano, Lisa, jt. auth. see Altmann, Patricia.

***Luciano, Lynn.** Looking Good: Male Body Image in Modern America. (Illus.). 272p. 2001. 25.00 (*0-8090-6637-8*) Hill & Wang.

Luciano, Patrick. With Fire & Sword: Italian Spectacles on American Screens, 1958-1968. LC 93-43344. 1994. 75.00 (*0-8108-2816-2*) Scarecrow.

Luciano, Ralph, jt. auth. see Stevens, Rikki.

Luciano, Robert. How to Write Packaging Machinery Specifications. (Illus.). 86p. (C). 1995. pap. 50.00 (*1-930268-20-3*) Packaging Prof.

Lucic, Karen. Charles Sheeler & the Cult of the Machine. (Illus.). 167p. 1991. pap. 22.50 (*0-674-11111-7*) HUP.

— Charles Sheeler & the Cult of the Machine. (Illus.). 128p. (C). 1991. 41.50 (*0-674-11110-9*) HUP.

— Charles Sheeler in Doylestown: American Modernism & the Pennsylvania Tradition. LC 97-70845. (Illus.). 120p. 1997. pap. 30.00 (*0-295-97643-8*) U of Wash Pr.

Lucid, Daniel P., ed. Soviet Semiotics: An Anthology. LC 77-4543. (Illus.). 1978. text 35.00 (*0-8018-1980-6*) Johns Hopkins.

— Soviet Semiotics: An Anthology. LC 77-4543. 271p. reprint ed. pap. 84.10 (*0-608-06287-1*, 206661600008) Bks Demand.

Lucid, Joanne, ed. For Those We Love: A Spiritual Perspective on AIDS. 2nd enl. ed. (Illus.). 96p. (Orig.). 1990. pap. 7.50 (*1-879035-01-4*) AIDS Ministry.

Lucido, Jerome. Racing with the Hawk: The Man Behind Dale Earnhardt. LC 97-48349. (Illus.). 160p. 1998. pap. 11.99 (*0-8007-5657-6*) Revell.

Lucie C.Phillips, jt. auth. see Clark, Andrew F.

***Lucie, Doug.** Doug Lucie Plays I. 1998. pap. 14.95 (*0-413-71690-2*) Methn.

Lucie, Doug. Fashion, Progress, Hard Feelings & Doing the Business. (Methuen Modern Plays Ser.). 282p. (Orig.). (C). 1991. pap. write for info. (*0-413-65090-1*, AO557, Methuen Drama) Methn.

— Grace. 96p. 1993. pap. 11.95 (*1-85459-245-9*, G55, Pub. by N Hern Bks) Theatre Comm.

— Progress. 1985. pap. 5.25 (*0-8222-0920-9*) Dramatists Play.

— Progress & Hard Feelings. 86p. (Orig.). (C). 1988. pap. 8.95 (*0-413-57760-0*, A0229) Heinemann.

Lucie, Smith E. British Poetry since 1945. pap. 16.95 (*0-14-058564-8*, Pub. by Pnguin Bks Ltd) Trafalgar.

Lucie-Smith, Edward. Adam: The Male Figure in Art. LC 98-65445. (Illus.). 192p. 1998. 45.00 (*0-8478-2125-0*, Pub. by Rizzoli Intl) St Martin.

— Art & Civilization. LC 92-17099. (Illus.). 560p. 1993. 75.00 (*0-8109-1924-9*, Pub. by Abrams) Time Warner.

— Art Deco Painting. (Illus.). 160p. 1996. reprint ed. pap. 24.95 (*0-7148-3576-5*, Pub. by Phaidon Press) Phaidon Pr.

— Art in the Seventies. (Illus.). 128p. 1980. pap. text 21.95 (*0-8014-9194-0*) Cornell U Pr.

— The Art of Albert Paley: Iron, Bronze, Steel. LC 96-16604. (Illus.). 224p. 1996. 49.50 (*0-8109-3748-4*, Pub. by Abrams) Time Warner.

***Lucie-Smith, Edward.** Art Today. 512p. 1999. pap. 39.95 (*0-7148-3888-8*) Phaidon Pr.

Lucie-Smith, Edward. Art Today. (Illus.). 512p. (C). 1995. 69.95 (*0-7148-3201-4*, Pub. by Phaidon Press) Phaidon Pr.

— Dunbar: Mining the Surfaces. (Illus.). 48p. 1997. pap. 12.95 (*0-89494-061-9*) New Orleans Mus Art.

***Lucie-Smith, Edward.** Flesh & Stone. 2000. 44.95 (*1-893263-10-X*) Ipso Facto.

Lucie-Smith, Edward. Fletcher Benton. (Illus.). 358p. 1990. 49.50 (*0-8109-3110-9*, Pub. by Abrams) Time Warner.

— Furniture: A Concise History. (World of Art Ser.). (Illus.). 216p. 1985. pap. 14.95 (*0-500-20172-2*, Pub. by Thames Hudson) Norton.

— Furniture: A Concise History. (World of Art Ser.). (Illus.). 216p. 1985. 19.95 (*0-500-18173-X*, Pub. by Thames Hudson) Norton.

— Impressionist Women. (Illus.). 160p. 1993. 19.98 (*0-89660-039-4*, Artabras) Abbeville Pr.

— John Kirby: The Company of Strangers. (Illus.). 120p. 1995. 35.00 (*1-85158-625-3*, Pub. by Mainstream Pubng) Trafalgar.

— Latin American Art of the Twentieth Century. LC 92-70861. (World of Art Ser.). (Illus.). 216p. 1993. pap. 14.95 (*0-500-20260-5*, Pub. by Thames Hudson) Norton.

— Life Class: The Academic Male Nude, 1820-1920. 1995. per. 25.00 (*0-85449-103-1*, Pub. by Gay Mens Pr) LPC InBook.

— Lin Emery: Borrowing the Forces of Nature. (Illus.). 64p. 1996. pap. 19.95 (*0-89494-055-4*) New Orleans Mus Art.

— The Liverpool Scene. (Illus.). 1990. 15.50 (*0-8446-2495-0*) Peter Smith.

— Lives of Great 20th Century Artists. LC 98-75076. (Illus.). 352p. 1999. 45.00 (*0-500-23739-5*, Pub. by Thames Hudson) Norton.

— Masterpieces of Time: Long-Case Clocks & Fine Furniture by Wendell Castle. (Illus.). 20p. (Orig.). 1985. pap. 5.00 (*0-915577-07-0*) Taft Museum.

— Movements in Art since 1945: Issues & Concepts. 3rd rev. ed. LC 94-61061. (World of Art Ser.). (Illus.). 304p. 1995. pap. 14.95 (*0-500-20282-6*, Pub. by Thames Hudson) Norton.

— Race, Sex, & Gender in Contemporary Art: The Rise of Minority Culture. LC 93-29218. (Illus.). 224p. 1994. 49.50 (*0-8109-3767-0*, Pub. by Abrams) Time Warner.

— Sexuality in Western Art. rev. ed. LC 90-71871. (World of Art Ser.). (Illus.). 288p. 1991. pap. 14.95 (*0-500-20252-4*, Pub. by Thames Hudson) Norton.

— Symbolist Art. (World of Art Ser.). (Illus.). 216p. 1985. pap. 14.95 (*0-500-20125-0*, Pub. by Thames Hudson) Norton.

— The Thames & Hudson Dictionary Art Terms. LC 83-51331. (World of Art Ser.). (Illus.). 208p. 1988. pap. 14.95 (*0-500-20222-2*, Pub. by Thames Hudson) Norton.

— Thinking about Art. 237p. 1968. 15.95 (*0-7145-0552-8*) Dufour.

— Toulouse-Lautrec. (Color Library). (Illus.). 128p. (C). 1994. reprint ed. pap. 14.95 (*0-7148-2761-4*, Pub. by Phaidon Press) Phaidon Pr.

— Visual Arts in the Twentieth Century. LC 96-18460. (Illus.). 400p. 1997. 60.00 (*0-8109-3934-7*, Pub. by Abrams) Time Warner.

— Visual Arts in the 20th Century. LC 97-145249. (Illus.). 4002p. (C). 1996. pap. text 56.67 (*0-13-494436-4*) P-H.

— Zoo: Animals in Art. LC 98-85579. (Illus.). 400p. 1998. 19.95 (*0-8230-5981-2*) Watsn-Guptill.

***Lucie-Smith, Edward & Chicago, Judy.** Judy Chicago: An American Vision. LC 99-55367. (Illus.). 192p. 2000. write for info. (*0-8230-2585-3*) Watsn-Guptill.

Lucie-Smith, Edward, jt. auth. see Chicago, Judy.

Lucie-Smtih, Edward. Ars Erotica: An Arousing History of Erotic Art. LC 97-67799. (Illus.). 192p. 1997. 40.00 (*0-8478-2060-2*, Pub. by Rizzoli Intl) St Martin.

***Lucien, Dan.** Sandra & Julie. 72p. (J). (gr. 4-5). 1999. pap. 4.50 (*0-9686093-0-9*, Herald Pr Ltd) Dan Lucien.

Lucien, Michele. My World. 44p. (J). (gr. k-3). 1994. spiral bd. 10.95 (*0-9639678-0-0*) Write For You.

Lucier, A. A. & Haines, S. G., eds. Mechanisms of Forest Response to Acidic Deposition. 232p. 1990. 102.95 (*0-387-97205-6*) Spr-Verlag.

Lucier, Alvin. Chambers: Interviews with the Composer by Douglas Simon. fac. ed. LC 79-24870. 187p. 1980. reprint ed. pap. 58.00 (*0-7837-8197-0*, 204790200008) Bks Demand.

Lucier, Armand F. Boston, the Redcoats, & the Homespun Patriots, 1766-1775. LC 99-169809. 407p. 1998. pap. 36.50 (*0-7884-0999-9*, L811) Heritage Bk.

— French & Indian War Notices - Abstracts from Colonial Newspapers Vol. I: 1754-1755. LC 99-208043. 368p. 1999. pap. 30.50 (*0-7884-1085-7*, L818) Heritage Bk.

***Lucier, Armand F.** French & Indian War Notices Abstracted from Colonial Newspapers, 1756-1757, Vol. 2. 364p. 1999. (*0-7884-1219-1*, L819) Heritage Bk.

Lucier, Armand F. Jolly Old England. vi, 286p. 1996. pap. 27.00 (*0-7884-0384-2*, L814) Heritage Bk.

— Journal of Occurences: Patriot Propaganda on the British Occupation of Boston, 1768-1769. vi, 239p. (Orig.). 1996. pap. 21.00 (*0-7884-0569-1*, L815) Heritage Bk.

— New England Chronicle News of New England from January 1722-December 1731. LC 97-190837. vi, 213p. 1997. pap. 19.00 (*0-7884-0634-5*, L816) Heritage Bk.

— 1767 Chronicle. 174p. (Orig.). 1995. pap. 17.50 (*0-7884-0356-7*, L813) Heritage Bk.

***Lucier, Armand Francis.** French & Indian War Notices Abstracted from Colonial Newspapers Vol. 3: January 1, 1758 - September 17, 1759. (Illus.). 367p. 1999. pap. 31.00 (*0-7884-1303-1*, L820) Heritage Bk.

— French & Indian War Notices Abstracted from Colonial Newspapers Vol. 4: September 17, 1759-December 30, 1760. 316p. 2000. pap. 26.50 (*0-7884-1378-3*, 1378) Heritage Bk.

Lucier, Barbara V., ed. see Lucier, Thomas J.

***Lucier, Charles B.** Of My Flesh & This Wicked World. LC 99-60692. 288p. 1999. 21.95 (*1-56167-491-5*) Noble Hse MD.

L

Lucier, Charles E. Business Analysis: Mastering the Language of Strategy. 1999. 35.00 (0-7879-4003-8) Jossey-Bass.

Lucier, George W., jt. ed. see Hook, Gary E. R.

Lucier, George W., jt. ed. see Hook, Garye R.

Lucier, Richard L. The International Political Economy of Coffee: From Juan Valdez to Yank's Diner. LC 87-38477. (Illus.). 341p. 1988. 59.95 (0-275-92898-5, C2898, Praeger Pubs) Greenwood.

Lucier, Ronald D., ed. Selected Papers on Temperature Sensing--Optical Methods, Vol. MS 116. LC 95-32740. (Milestone Ser.). 1995. 110.00 (0-8194-2011-5) SPIE.

Lucier, Thomas J. How to Buy Used & Bruised Houses for Fast Profits (Diamonds in the Rough) 2nd rev. ed. Lucier, Barbara V., ed. 150p. (Orig.). 1988. per. 21.95 (0-945343-00-0) Home Eq.

— How to Make Money Buying Pre-Foreclosure Properties Before They Hit the County Courthouse Steps. 3rd rev. ed. 160p. 1993. ring bd. 39.95 (0-945343-06-X) Home Eq.

— How to Make Money with Real Estate Options. 230p. 1992. ring bd. 49.95 (0-945343-07-8) Home Eq.

— How to Master the Landlording Game: The Complete Guide to Running a Profitable Rental Housing Business. Reuter, Frank, ed. 200p. (C). 1989. per. 22.95 (0-945343-03-5) Home Eq.

— The National Real Estate Directory. 2nd rev. ed. Lucier, Barbara V., ed. 150p. 1992. per. 39.95 (0-945343-01-9) Home Eq.

— The Smart Investor's Guide to Distressed Property. Reuter, Frank, ed. 200p. (Orig.). 1990. per. 29.95 (0-945343-05-1) Home Eq.

Lucifora, Claudio, jt. auth. see Guillotin, Yves.

Lucignani, G. Clinical Pet. Bares, R., ed. LC 96-25021. (Developments in Nuclear Medicine Ser.). 152p. (C). 1996. text 70.50 (0-7923-4160-0) Kluwer Academic.

***Lucille, Francis.** Eternity Now: Dialogues on Happiness. 180p. 2000. pap. 20.00 (1-882874-00-5) Truespeech.

Lucille, Helene. Le Parle Express Basic French. 82p. 1993. 95.00 incl. audio (1-882874-25-0) Truespeech.

Lucina, Mary. Guardians of Air. 64p. 1997. pap. 8.50 (1-880286-27-0) Singular Speech Pr.

Lucio, J. L., et al, eds. Mexican School of Particles & Fields. LC 86-81187. (AIP Conference Proceedings Ser.: No. 143). 267p. 1986. lib. bdg. 60.00 (0-88318-342-0) Am Inst Physics.

Lucio, J. L. & Zepeda, A., eds. Particles & Fields: Third Mexican School. 3rd ed. 310p. (C). 1989. text 113.00 (9971-5-0967-9) World Scientific Pub.

— Particles & Fields - Fourth Mexican School. 500p. (C). 1992. text 130.00 (981-02-0666-6) World Scientific Pub.

Lucio, J. L., ed. see Zepeda, A.

Luciom, S. L. & Vargas, M., eds. Fifth Mexican School of Particles & Fields. (AIP Conference Proceedings Ser.: No. 317). 416p. 1994. text 135.00 (1-56396-378-7) Am Inst Physics.

***Lucioni, Luigi.** Luigi Lucioni in the Collection of the Elizabeth Dec. Wilson Museum on the Occasion of the Museum's Grand Opening, Southern Vermont Art Center, 22 July, 2000. LC 00-26276. (Illus.). 2000. pap. write for info. (0-9669382-3-2) Gallery Press.

***Lucire, Yolande.** Inventing RSI: The Social Construction of an Occupational Hazard. 368p. 2000. pap. 35.00 (0-86840-778-X, Pub. by NSW U Pr) Intl Spec Bk.

***Luciuk, Lubomyr.** Searching for a Place: Ukrainian Displaced Persons, Ottawa & the Migration of Memory. 2000. pap. text 29.95 (0-8020-8088-X) U of Toronto Pr.

Luciuk, Lubomyr Y. Ukrainians in the Making: Their Kingston Story. (Builders of Canada Ser.: No. 1). (Illus.). 1980. 16.50 (0-919642-91-8) Limestone Pr.

Luciuk, Lubomyr Y. & Kordan, Bohdan S. Anglo-American Perspectives on the Ukrainian Question, 1938 to 1958. Pierce, Richard A., ed. (Studies in East European Nationalisms: No. 1). 1987. 20.00 (0-919642-26-8) Limestone Pr.

— Creating a Landscape: A Geography of Ukrainians in Canada. (Illus.). 72p. 1989. text 40.00 (0-8020-5823-X) U of Toronto Pr.

Luciuk, Lubomyr Y., jt. auth. see Kordan, Bohdan S.

Lucius, Jim. Golf As It Should Be. Burgin, C. David, ed. LC 98-60856. (Illus.). 192p. 1998. 24.95 (0-942627-41-5) Woodford Pubng.

— Golf as It Should Be. 1998. 24.95 (0-942627-52-0) Woodford Pubng.

Luciw, Paul A. & Steimer, Kathelyn Sue. HIV Detection by Genetic Engineering Methods. 320p. 1989. text 155.00 (0-8247-7900-2) Dekker.

Luck, ed. Tibulli, Albii. (LAT.). 1988. 37.50 (3-519-01865-9, T1865, Pub. by B G Teubner) U of Mich Pr.

— Tibulli, Albii. (LAT.). 1998. pap. 27.95 (3-519-11864-5, T1864, Pub. by B G Teubner) U of Mich Pr.

Luck & Markus. McGraw-Hill Guide to Passing the CLAST: The Essay. 2nd ed. (C). 1993. pap. text 8.74 (0-07-040473-9) McGraw.

Luck, Anthony D. The Niltown Neighbors in "Don't Tell Stephen" (J). (gr. k). 1996. pap. 6.95 (0-533-11969-3) Vantage.

Luck, Barbara R. "Moving" with Mattie Lou O'Kelley. LC 95-11614. (Illus.). 51p. 1995. 9.99 (0-87935-156-X) Colonial Williamsburg.

Luck, C., ed. Babel' Red Cavalry (Konarmiia) (Bristol Russian Texts Ser.). (RUS.). 170p. 1994. pap. 18.95 (1-85399-403-0, Pub. by Brist Class Pr) Focus Pub-R Pullins.

Luck, Donald G. Why Study Theology? LC 99-40160. 1999. pap. 14.99 (0-8272-4242-5) Chalice Pr.

***Luck, Edward C.** Mixed Messages: American Politics & International Organization, 1919-1999. LC 99-6514. 1999. pap. 19.95 (0-8157-5307-1) Brookings.

— Mixed Messages: American Politics & International Organization 1919-1999. LC 99-6514. 1999. 49.95 (0-8157-5308-X) Brookings.

Luck, Erich. The Compact Dictionary of Food Technology. (ENG & GER.). 443p. 1985. 150.00 (0-8288-0843-0, M8221) Fr & Eur.

— Dictionary of Food, Nutrition & Cookery. (ENG & GER.). 392p. 1983. 175.00 (0-8288-0842-2, M15385) Fr & Eur.

— Food Technology Dictionary English-German-French-Spanish. (ENG, FRE & GER.). 680p. 1991. text 195.00 (3-86022-010-1) IBD Ltd.

— Viersprachiges Woerterbuch der Lebensmitteltechnologie: English-German-Spanish-French. (ENG, FRE & GER.). 655p. 1992. 295.00 (0-7859-7051-7) Fr & Eur.

Luck, Erich & Jager, Martin. Antimicrobial Food Additives: Characteristics, Uses, Effects. 2nd ed. Laichena, S. F., tr. from GER. LC 96-39964. 1997. pap. write for info. (0-387-61138-X) Spr-Verlag.

— Antimicrobial Food Additives: Characteristics, Uses, Effects. 2nd enl. rev. ed. Laichena, S. F., tr. from GER. LC 96-39964. (Illus.). 276p. 1997. 117.00 (3-540-61138-X) Spr-Verlag.

Luck, Georg. Ancient Pathways, Hidden Pursuits: Religion, Morals, & Magic in the Ancient World. LC 99-45162. 328p. 2000. text 54.50 (0-472-10790-9, 10790) U of Mich Pr.

— Arcana Mundi: Magic & the Occult in the Greek & Roman Worlds. LC 84-28852. 416p. 1985. pap. text 17.95 (0-8018-2548-2) Johns Hopkins.

Luck, H. D. Arkansas Higher Education 1971-1995. 152p. (Orig.). 1996. pap. 15.00 (0-934955-29-8) Watercress Pr.

Luck, Hans Von, see Von Luck, Hans.

Luck, J. M., et al, eds. Number Theory & Physics. (Proceedings in Physics Ser.: Vol. 47). (Illus.). xiii, 311p. 1990. 74.95 (0-387-52129-1) Spr-Verlag.

Luck, J. Murray. History of Switzerland: From Before the Beginnings to the Days of the Present. LC 85-50338. (Illus.). 887p. 1985. 36.00 (0-930664-06-X) SPOSS.

Luck, J. Murray, compiled by. The Excitement & Fascination of Science, Vol. 1. 1965. pap. 25.00 (0-8243-1602-9) Annual Reviews.

***Luck, James M.** Reminiscences. 260p. 1999. 40.00 (0-8243-1603-7) Annual Reviews.

Luck, James M., et al, eds. Annual Review of Biochemistry, Vol. 31. LC 32-25093. 1962. text 41.00 (0-8243-0831-X) Annual Reviews.

— Annual Review of Biochemistry, Vol. 32. LC 32-25093. 1963. text 41.00 (0-8243-0832-8) Annual Reviews.

— Annual Review of Biochemistry, Vol. 33. LC 32-25093. 1964. text 41.00 (0-8243-0833-6) Annual Reviews.

— Annual Review of Biochemistry, Vol. 34. LC 32-25093. 1965. text 41.00 (0-8243-0834-4) Annual Reviews.

Luck, Jeff, jt. auth. see Levine, Arnold S.

Luck, Joyce. Melissa Etheridge: Our Little Secret. LC 97-146279. (Illus.). 225p. 1997. pap. text 16.95 (1-55022-298-8) LPC InBook.

Luck, Kai von & Marburger, Heinz, eds. Management & Processing of Complex Data Structures: Third Workshop on Information Systems & Artificial Intelligence, Hamburg, Germany, February 28-March 2, 1994: Proceedings. LC 94-1559. (Lecture Notes in Computer Science Ser.: Vol. 777). v, 220p. 1994. 39.95 (0-387-57802-1) Spr-Verlag.

Luck, Kenneth. Drugs & Ships. 60p. 1992. 80.00 (1-85609-005-1, Pub. by Witherby & Co) St Mut.

Luck, Kenneth L. 52 Maneras de Cultivar las Habilidades Naturales de Su Hijo. (Fifty-Two Maneras de...Ser.). (SPA.). 150p. 1995. pap. 7.99 (0-88113-355-8) Caribe Betania.

— 52 Maneras de Estirar Su Dinero. (Serie "52 Maneras"). (SPA.). 153p. 7.99 (0-88113-227-6, B001-2276) Caribe Betania.

Luck-Lestrade, Brigite. Le Travail Interimaire en Republique Federale d'Allemagne (1697-1982) Analyse d'Un Echec Programme. (Contacts Ser.: Series IV, Vol. 5). (FRE.). xiii, 670p. 1995. 71.95 (3-906754-07-3, Pub. by P Lang) P Lang Pubng.

Luck, Martha S. Instant Secretary's Handbook: A Guide for the Professional Secretary. LC 72-76551. (Instant Ser.). 320p. 1992. 6.95 (0-911744-11-8) Career Pub IL.

Luck, Martin. Your Student Research Project. LC 99-11288. 1999. 22.95 (0-566-08213-6, Pub. by Gower) Ashgate Pub Co.

Luck, Philip, jt. auth. see Elifson, Kirk W.

***Luck, Richard.** Sam Peckinpah. 2000. pap. 5.95 (1-903047-20-X, Pub. by Pocket Essentials) Trafalgar.

— Steve McQueen. 2000. pap. 5.95 (1-903047-23-4, Pub. by Pocket Essentials) Trafalgar.

Luck, Steve, ed. The American Desk Encyclopedia. LC 98-233151. (Illus.). 912p. 1998. 21.95 (0-19-521465-X) OUP.

***Luck, Steve, ed.** The International Encyclopedia of Science & Technology. LC 99-222952. (Illus.). 560p. 1999. 49.95 (0-19-521531-1) OUP.

Luck, Vick. Globalization: How to Achieve Competitive Advantage in a Global Market. 1998. 30.00 (0-7494-2530-X) Kogan Page Ltd.

Luck, W. A. Transformation Groups & Algebraic K-Theory. (Lecture Notes in Mathematics Ser.: Vol. 1408). xii, 443p. 1989. 73.95 (0-387-51846-0) Spr-Verlag.

Luck, Wilbert H. Journey to Honey Hill: Civil War 55th Mass-Like 54th Mass-Movie: Glory. 99p. 1985. pap. text 3.50 (0-9626979-0-7) Wiluk Pr.

Lucka, Emil. Eros: The Development of the Sex Relation Through the Ages. Schleussner, Ellie, tr. & intro. by. LC 72-9661. reprint ed. 42.50 (0-404-57472-6) AMS Pr.

Luckas, Micheal R. Economic Activity. 1992. pap. text. write for info. (0-582-35584-2, Pub. by Addison-Wesley) Longman.

Luckasson, jt. auth. see Smith.

Luckasson, Ruth A., et al. Mental Retardation: Definition, Classification & Systems of Support. 9th ed. 189p. 1992. 79.00 (0-940898-30-6); pap., student ed. 22.95 (0-940898-35-7) Am Assn Mental.

Lucke, Bernd. Price Stabilization on World Agricultural Markets: An Application to the World Market for Sugar. LC 92-31169. (Lecture Notes in Economics & Mathematical Systems Ser.: Vol. 393). 1992. 58.95 (0-387-56099-8) Spr-Verlag.

Lucke, K. & Laqua, H. Silicone Oil in the Treatment of Complicated Retinal Detachments: Techniques, Results, & Complications. (Illus.). xix, 161p. 1990. 64.00 (0-387-53035-5) Spr-Verlag.

Lucke, Lewis W. Waiting for Rain: Life & Development in Mali, West Africa. LC 97-66245. 144p. 1998. pap. 16.95 (0-8158-0529-2) Chris Mass.

Lucke, Margaret. Writing Great Short Stories. LC 98-31510. (Schaum's Quick Guides). (Illus.). 144p. 1998. pap. 10.95 (0-07-039077-0) McGraw.

— Writing Mysteries. 280p. 1999. pap. 17.95 (1-55180-205-8) Self-Counsel Pr.

Lucke, Peggy, jt. auth. see Bergquist, Craig.

Lucken, Karol, jt. auth. see Blomberg, Thomas G.

Luckenbach, Al. Providence 1649: The History & Archaeology of Anne Arundel County, Maryland. LC 99-489351. (Studies in Local History). 1995. pap. 10.00 (0-942370-41-4) MD St Archives.

Luckenbach, R., ed. Beilstein: Centennial Index - Generalregister. 4th ed. (Handbook of Organic Chemistry Ser.: Vol. 28, Pts. 3-6). 1991. 642.00 (0-685-74382-9) Spr-Verlag.

— Beilstein: Centennial Index - Generalregister, Vol. 28, Pt. 3: Benzol-Bz. 4th ed. (Handbook of Organic Chemistry Ser.: Vol. 28, Pts. 3-6). iv, 1483p. 1991. 775.00 (0-387-54082-2) Spr-Verlag.

— Beilstein: Centennial Index - Generalregister, Vol. 28, Pt. 4: D-F. (Handbook of Organic Chemistry Ser.: Vol. 28, Pts. 3-6). 1600p. 1991. 775.00 (0-387-54085-7) Spr-Verlag.

— Beilstein: Centennial Index - Generalregister, Vol. 28, Pt. 6: G-I. 4th ed. (Handbook of Organic Chemistry Ser.: Vol. 28, Pts. 3-6). 1600p. 1991. 775.00 (0-387-54086-5) Spr-Verlag.

— Beilstein: Compound-Name Index for Vols. 20-22: E-Pq. 4th ed. (Handbook of Organic Chemistry, Supplementary Ser.). iv, 976p. 1992. 1295.00 (0-387-54625-1) Spr-Verlag.

— Beilstein: Compound-Name Index for Vols. 20-22: Pr-Z. 4th ed. (Handbook of Organic Chemistry, Supplementary Ser.). 1000p. 1992. 1295.00 (0-387-54626-X) Spr-Verlag.

— Beilstein Handbook of Organic Chemistry: Formula Index for Vols. 20-22. 4th ed. (Supplementary Series 5). iv, 859p. 1993. 1135.00 (0-387-56103-X) Spr-Verlag.

— Beilstein Handbook of Organic Chemistry: Heterocyclic Compounds. 4th ed. (Fifth Supplementary Ser.: Vol. 26, Pt. 1). lxxxvi, 772p. 1993. 2460.00 (0-387-56118-8) Spr-Verlag.

— Beilstein, Handbook of Organic Chemistry, Vol. 28, Pt. 1: Centennial Index - Generalregister, General Compound-Name Index - General-Sachregister. 4th ed. 1600p. 1991. 775.00 (0-387-54047-4) Spr-Verlag.

— Formula Index Vols. 20-22, Subvol. 2: Collective Indexes. (Beilstein Handbook of Organic Chemistry Ser.: 5th Suppl.). iv, 992p. 1993. 1300.00 (0-387-56101-3) Spr-Verlag.

— Formula Index to Supplementary Series Five to the Handbook of Organic Chemistry, Vols. 20-22. iv, 1050p. 1993. 1385.00 (0-387-56102-1) Spr-Verlag.

— Heterocyclic Compounds. (Beilstein Handbook of Organic Chemistry Ser.: 5th Suppl.: Vol. 24, Pt. 4). (Illus.). xxii, 824p. 1992. 2325.00 (0-387-55110-7) Spr-Verlag.

— Heterocyclic Compounds. (Beilstein Handbook of Organic Chemistry Ser.: 5th Suppl.: Vol. 24, Pt. 5). (Illus.). 785p. 1992. 1745.00 (0-387-55134-4) Spr-Verlag.

— Heterocyclic Compounds. (Handbook of Organic Chemistry, Supplementary Ser.: Vol. 25, Pt. 14). xxii, 815p. 1993. 2580.00 (0-387-56113-7) Spr-Verlag.

— Heterocyclic Compounds. 4th ed. (Beilstein Handbook of Organic Chemistry Ser.: 5th Suppl.: Vol. 22, Pt. 13). 960p. 1991. 2510.00 (0-387-53167-X) Spr-Verlag.

— Heterocyclic Compounds. 4th ed. (Beilstein Handbook of Organic Chemistry Ser.: 5th Suppl.: Vol. 23, Pt. 4). 745p. 1991. 1935.00 (0-387-53670-1) Spr-Verlag.

— Heterocyclic Compounds. 4th ed. (Beilstein Handbook of Organic Chemistry Ser.: 5th Suppl.: Vol. 23, Pt. 5). 675p. 1991. 1750.00 (0-387-53758-9) Spr-Verlag.

— Heterocyclic Compounds. 4th ed. (Beilstein Handbook of Organic Chemistry Ser.: 5th Suppl.: Vol. 25, Pt. 8). xxii, 785p. 1993. 2490.00 (0-387-56107-2) Spr-Verlag.

— Heterocyclic Compounds. 4th ed. (Beilstein Handbook of Organic Chemistry Ser.: 5th Suppl.: Vol. 25, Pt. 10). 760p. 1993. 2400.00 (0-387-56109-9) Spr-Verlag.

— Heterocyclic Compounds. 4th ed. (Beilstein Handbook of Organic Chemistry Ser.: 5th Suppl.: Vol. 25, Pt. 11). 800p. 1993. 2475.00 (0-387-56110-2) Spr-Verlag.

— Heterocyclic Compounds. 4th ed. (Beilstein Handbook of Organic Chemistry Ser.: 5th Suppl.: Vol. 25, Pt. 13). 700p. 1993. 2140.00 (0-387-56112-9) Spr-Verlag.

— Heterocyclic Compounds, 2 pts., Pt. 10. 4th ed. (Beilstein Handbook of Organic Chemistry Ser.: 5th Suppl.: Vol. 23). 770p. 1991. 2095.00 (0-387-54163-2) Spr-Verlag.

— Heterocyclic Compounds, 2 pts., Pt. 11. 4th ed. (Beilstein Handbook of Organic Chemistry Ser.: 5th Suppl.: Vol. 23). 980p. 1991. 1935.00 (0-387-54164-0) Spr-Verlag.

— Heterocyclic Compounds, 2 vols., Vol. 24, Pt. 7. 4th ed. (Beilstein Handbook of Organic Chemistry Ser.: 5th Suppl.). xxii, 774p. 1992. 2465.00 (0-387-55219-7) Spr-Verlag.

— Heterocyclic Compounds, 2 vols., Vol. 24, Pt. 8. 4th ed. (Beilstein Handbook of Organic Chemistry Ser.: 5th Suppl.). 720p. 1992. 2430.00 (0-387-55334-7) Spr-Verlag.

— Heterocyclic Compounds, Vol. 25, Pt. 1. xxxvi, 564p. 1992. 1920.00 (0-387-55575-7) Spr-Verlag.

— Heterocyclic Compounds, Vol. 25, Pt. 2. 770p. 1992. 1660.00 (0-387-55576-5) Spr-Verlag.

Luckenbach, R. & Beilstein Institut fur Literatur der Organischen Chemie, eds. Formula Index, Vols. 17-19, Pt. 3. 4th ed. (Beilstein Collective Indexes Ser.). 1005p. 1991. 1290.00 (0-387-52585-8) Spr-Verlag.

— Formula Index, Vols. 17-19, Pt. 4. 4th ed. (Beilstein Collective Indexes Ser.). 965p. 1991. 1235.95 (0-387-52586-6) Spr-Verlag.

— Formula Index, Vols. 17-19, Pts. 1-4. 4th ed. (Beilstein Collective Indexes Ser.). 3960p. 1991. 4740.00 (0-387-52587-4) Spr-Verlag.

Luckenbach, R., ed. see Beilstein Institut fur Literatur der Organischen Chemie.

Luckenbach, R., jt. ed. see Beilstein Institut fur Literatur der Organischen Chemie.

Luckenbach-Sawyers, Phyllis, jt. auth. see Henry, Frances L.

Luckenbill, Daniel D. The Annals of Sennacherib. 1996. lib. bdg. 7.50 (0-226-49644-9) U Ch Pr.

Luckenbill, Daniel D. The Annals of Sennacherib. LC 78-72760. (Ancient Mesopotamian Texts & Studies). reprint ed. 37.50 (0-404-18206-2) AMS Pr.

Luckenbill, David F., jt. auth. see Best, Joel.

Lucker, G. William, et al, eds. Psychological Aspects of Facial Form: Proceedings of a Sponsored Symposium Honoring Professor Robert E. Moyers, Held February 29 & March 1, 1980, in Ann Arbor, MI. LC 83-132873. (Craniofacial Growth Monographs: No. 11). (Illus.). 233p. reprint ed. pap. 72.30 (0-8357-7560-7, 205232400097) Bks Demand.

Lucker, Raymond A., et al, eds. The People's Catechism: Catholic Faith for Adults. 224p. (Orig.). 1995. pap. 14.95 (0-8245-1466-1) Crossroad NY.

Luckert, Karl W. Navajo Mountain & Rainbow Bridge Religion. Goossen, Irvy W. & Bilagody, Harry, Jr., trs. LC 77-153661. (American Tribal Religions Ser.: No. 1). 165p. reprint ed. pap. 51.20 (0-8357-7771-5, 203613100002) Bks Demand.

***Luckert, Karl W.** Planet Earth Expanding & the Eocene Tectonic Event: Paradigm Shift Toward Expansion Tectonics. (Illus.). 78p. 1999. pap. 9.50 (0-9675806-0-9) Lufa.

Luckert, Karl W., jt. auth. see Li, Shujiang.

Luckert, Karl W., ed. see Haile, Berard.

Luckert, Karl W., ed. see Haile, Berard & Goossen, Irvy W.

Luckert, Karl W., ed. & intro. see Haile, Berard.

Luckert, Yelena. Soviet Jewish History, 1917-1991: An Annotated Bibliography. LC 92-1682. 296p. 1992. text 15.00 (0-8240-2583-0, SS611) Garland.

Luckett, Michael. Kahluti. 325p. 1997. 14.95 (1-57532-016-9) Press-Tige Pub.

Luckett, Moya, jt. ed. see Radner, Hilary.

Luckett, P., ed. Reproductive Biology of the Primates. (Contributions to Primatology Ser.: Vol. 3). 284p. 1974. pap. 112.25 (3-8055-1671-1) S Karger.

Luckett, Perry D. Charles A. Lindbergh: A Bio-Bibliography. LC 86-3165. (Popular Culture Bio-Bibliographies Ser.). 159p. 1986. lib. bdg. 47.95 (0-313-23098-6, LCL/, Greenwood Pr) Greenwood.

Luckett, Pete, jt. auth. see Robinson, Kathleen.

Luckett, Richard. Handel's Messiah: A Celebration. LC 95-19716. 256p. 1995. pap. 13.00 (0-15-600138-1, Harvest Bks) Harcourt.

Luckett, Rosemary. Crosses & Prayers. LC 98-171954. (Illus.). 96p. 1998. pap. 10.95 (1-58051-020-5, LL2020) Sheed & Ward WI.

***Luckett, Victoria, et al.** The Menu Dictionary: Words & Ways of the International Restaurant World. deluxe ed. 150p. 1999. pap. 14.95 (0-9673014-0-8) Sweetwtr Pr.

Luckey, Carl F. Collecting Antique Bird Decoys & Duck Calls: An Identification & Value Guide. 2nd ed. 248p. 1992. pap. 22.95 (0-89689-078-3, Bks Amrcana) Krause Pubns.

— Luckey's Hummel Figurines & Plates: ID & Value Guide. 11th ed. LC 97-73775. (Illus.). 456p. 1997. pap. 24.95 (0-89689-119-4, HUM11) Krause Pubns.

— Old Fishing Lures & Tackle. 5th ed. LC 98-87368. (Illus.). 672p. 1999. per. 29.95 (0-87341-728-3) Krause Pubns.

Luckey, Carl F., jt. auth. see Tordia, K. J.

Luckey, E. Z., jt. auth. see Arnold, L. W.

Luckey, Hugh A. & Kubli, Fred, Jr., eds. Titanium Alloys in Surgical Implants - STP 796. LC 84-72888. 295p. 1983. text 37.50 (0-8031-0241-0, STP796) ASTM.

Luckey, Robert A. Designing & Implementing Computer Workgroups. LC 99-24936. (Illus.). 420p. (C). 1999. pap. 49.00 (0-13-082709-6) P-H.

— Lester Young Solos. unabridged ed. 39p. 1994. pap. 10.00 (0-9667047-0-3, 02) Olympia LA.

— Saxophone Altissimo: High Note Development for the Contemporary Player. 2nd rev. ed. (Illus.). vii, 200p. 1998. pap. text, spiral bd. 20.00 (0-9667047-2-X, 01) Olympia LA.

— West Coast Jazz Saxophone Solos. unabridged ed. 63p. 1996. pap. 12.00 (0-9667047-1-1, 03) Olympia LA.

Luckey, T. D. Hormesis with Ionizing Radiation. 232p. 1980. 134.00 (0-8493-5841-8, QP82, CRC Reprint) Franklin.

— Radiation Hormesis. (Illus.). 336p. 1991. lib. bdg. 195.00 (0-8493-6159-1, QC) CRC Pr.

Luckey, T. D., jt. auth. see Venugopal, B.

Luckham, Claire. The Choice. LC 95-145833. 1995. 5.50 (0-87129-482-6, C89) Dramatic Pub.

An Asterisk (*) at the beginning of an entry indicates that the title is appearing for the first time.

Luckham, Clare. Luckham: Plays. 220p. 1999. pap. 19.95 (*1-870259-68-8*, Pub. by Theatre Comm) Consort Bk Sales.

Luckham, David C. Programming with Specifications: An Introduction to ANNA: A Language for Specifying Ada Programs. (Texts & Monographs in Computer Science). (Illus.). 440p. 1990. text 55.00 (*0-387-97254-4*) Spr-Verlag.

Luckham, R., ed. Studies of Law in Social Change & Development: Law & Social Enquiry-Case Studies of Research. 1981. 20.00 (*91-7106-181-9*); pap. 12.00 (*91-7106-178-9*) Intl Ctr Law.

Luckham, Robin. The Nigerian Military: A Sociological Analysis of Authority & Revolt, 1960-67. LC 73-152643. (African Studies: No. 4). 390p. reprint ed. pap. 111.20 (*0-608-17521-8*, 2030607) Bks Demand.

Luckham, Robin & White, Gordin. Democratization in the South: The Jagged Wave. LC 96-18065. 320p. 1997. text 29.95 (*0-7190-4942-3*, Pub. by Manchester Univ Pr) St Martin.

Luckham, Robin & White, Gordon. Democratization in the South: The Jagged Wave. LC 96-18065. 320p. 1997. text 79.95 (*0-7190-4941-5*, Pub. by Manchester Univ Pr) St Martin.

Luckhardt, C. G., ed. Wittgenstein: Sources & Perspectives. (Wittgenstein Studies). 342p. 1996. pap. 27.00 (*1-85506-491-X*) Bks Intl VA.

Luckhardt, C. G., tr. see Wittgenstein, Ludwig Josef Johann.

Luckhardt, C. Grant & Bechtel, William. How to Do Things with Logic. 104p. 1994. student ed. 13.50 (*0-8058-0077-8*); pap. 22.50 (*0-8058-0076-X*); pap., student ed. 27.50 (*0-8058-1665-8*) L Erlbaum Assocs.

— How to Do Things with Logic. 272p. 1994. text 59.95 (*0-8058-0075-1*) L Erlbaum Assocs.

Luckhardt, C. J., tr. see Wittgenstein, Ludwig Josef Johann.

Luckhardt, Carol, ed. Intelligent Tutoring System Authoring Tools: Papers from the 1997 Fall Symposium. (Technical Reports). 92p. 1997. spiral bd. 25.00 (*1-57735-038-3*) AAAI Pr.

Luckhardt, H. Extensional Goedel Functional Interpretation: A Consistency Proof of Classical Analysis. LC 72-96046. (Lecture Notes in Mathematics Ser.: Vol. 306). 161p. 1973. 35.95 (*0-387-06119-3*) Spr-Verlag.

Luckhardt, Miriam. Organisationstransformation und Transformationsmanagement. (Wirtschaftspsychologie Ser.: Bd. 4). (GER., Illus.). 180p. 1996. pap. 42.95 (*3-631-30787-X*) P Lang Pubng.

Luckhardt, Ulrich. Lyonel Feininger. (Illus.). 188p. 1989. 65.00 (*3-7913-1022-4*, Pub. by Prestel) te Neues.

Luckhardt, Ulrich, jt. auth. see Melia, Paul.

Luckhaus, Linda. Pensions Law. (European Community Law Ser.). (C). 1997. text 90.00 (*0-485-70014-X*) Humanities.

Luckhurst, Charlotte T., compiled by. Deaths & Burials in Schoharie County. (Illus.). 200p. 1997. reprint ed. pap. 24.50 (*0-8328-6233-9*) Higginson Bk Co.

Luckhurst, G. R. & Veracini, C. A., eds. The Molecular Dynamics of Liquid Crystals: Proceedings of the NATO Advanced Study Institute, Il Ciocco, Barga, Italy, September 11-23, 1989. LC 94-7985. (NATO ASI Series C: Mathematical & Physical Sciences: Vol. 431). 624p. (C). 1994. text 332.00 (*0-7923-2809-4*) Kluwer Academic.

Luckhurst, Mary, jt. ed. see Giannachi, Gabriella.

***Luckhurst, Nicola.** Science & Structure in Proust's A La Recherche Du Temps Perdu. LC 99-48574. 272p. 2000. 74.00 (*0-19-816002-X*) OUP.

Luckhurst, Roger. Angle Between Two Walls. LC 97-5811. 213p. 1998. text 39.95 (*0-312-17439-X*) St Martin.

***Luckhurst, Roger & Marks, Peter.** Literature & the Contemporary. LC 98-37102. (Studies in Twentieth-Century Literature). (C). 1999. 65.95 (*0-582-31203-5*) Addison-Wesley.

— Literature & the Contemporary: Fictions & Theories of the Present. LC 98-37102. (Studies in Twentieth-Century Literature). 232p. 1999. pap. 29.73 (*0-582-31204-3*) Longman.

Luckhurst, Roger, jt. ed. see Ledger, Sally.

Luckie, Anita, ed. see Wynn, Mychal.

Luckie, William R. & Smethurst, Wood. Study Power: Study Skills to Improve Your Learning & Your Grades. LC 97-44338. 128p. 1997. pap. 15.95 (*1-57129-046-X*) Brookline Bks.

Luckiesh, M. Visual Illusions: Their Causes, Characteristics & Applications. (Illus.). 1990. 21.25 (*0-8446-0780-0*) Peter Smith.

Luckiesh, Matthew. Visual Illusions: Their Causes, Characteristics & Applications. (Illus.). 252p. 1998. pap. 6.95 (*0-486-21530-X*) Dover.

Luckiewicz, Edward T. & Sandler, Henry J. Practical Process Engineering: A Working Approach to Plant Design. rev. ed. (Illus.). 639p. 1993. reprint ed. pap. text 55.00 (*0-9650257-0-5*) XIMIX.

Luckin, Joyce. Making Teddy Bears. LC 95-45368. (Illus.). 128p. 1996. pap. 14.95 (*0-486-29209-6*) Dover.

Luckin, Richard W. Butterpat World. (Illus.). 256p. 1996. 42.95 (*0-9626362-2-3*) RK Pub.

— Dining on Rails: An Encyclopedia of Railroad China. 4th rev. ed. (Illus.). 488p. 1998. reprint ed. 69.95 (*0-9626362-0-7*) RK Pub.

— Syracuse China & the Railroads. (Illus.). 1999. 50.00 (*0-614-29636-6*) RK Pub.

— Teapot Treasury. (Illus.). 152p. 1987. 19.95 (*0-685-59604-4*) RK Pub.

Lucking, Richard C. Mathematics for Management. LC 80-40127. (Illus.). 340p. reprint ed. pap. 105.40 (*0-7837-6388-3*, 204610100010) Bks Demand.

Lucking, Robert. Additions & Corrections to the Knowledge of the Foliicolous Lichen Flora of Costa Rica: The Family Gomphillaceae. (Bibliotheca Lichenologica Ser.: Vol. 65). (Illus.). 109p. 1997. 41.30 (*3-443-58044-0*, Pub. by Gebruder Borntraeger) Balogh.

Lucking, Robert, ed. Foliicolous Lichens: A Contribution to the Knowledge of the Lichen Flora of the Costa Rica (C. A.) (Nova Hedwigia, Beihefte/Supplementary Issues Ser.: Beih 104). (Illus.). vi, 179p. 1992. pap. 100.00 (*3-443-51026-4*, Pub. by Gebruder Borntraeger) Balogh.

Lucking, Robert, et al, eds. Scripta Lichenologica Lichenological Papers Dedicated to Antonin Vezda: Nebentitel "Festschrift A. Vezda" (Bibliotheca Lichenologica: Vol. 58). (GER., Illus.). xvi, 502p. 1995. pap. 106.00 (*3-443-58037-8*, Pub. by Gebruder Borntraeger) Balogh.

Luckingham, Barbara, jt. auth. see Luckingham, Brad.

Luckingham, Brad & Luckingham, Barbara. Discovering Greater Phoenix: An Illustrated History. Parks, Lori, ed. LC 98-73494. (Illus.). 350p. 1998. 49.95 (*1-886483-25-6*) Heritge Media.

Luckingham, Bradford. Minorities in Phoenix: A Profile of Mexican American, Chinese American, & African American Communities, 1860-1992. LC 94-8103. 258p. 1994. 39.50 (*0-8165-1457-7*) U of Ariz Pr.

— Phoenix: The History of a Southwestern Metropolis. LC 88-24276. 316p. 1995. pap. 12.95 (*0-8165-1116-0*) U of Ariz Pr.

Luckman, A. Dick, ed. see Sloan, Tod S.

Luckman, Harriet & Kulzer, Linda, eds. Purity of Heart in Early Ascetic & Monastic Literature: Essays in Honor of Juana Raasch, O. S. B. LC 98-37386. 252p. 1999. pap. 21.95 (*0-8146-2485-5*) Liturgical Pr.

Luckman, Phyllis. Handbook for Cello Students: Music Theory & Other Facts. LC 98-94239. (Illus.). xii, 230p. (YA). (gr. 7 up). 1999. spiral bd. 33.00 (*0-9669810-0-6*) P Luckman.

Luckman, Sidney. Luckman at Quarterback. (American Autobiography Ser.). 233p. 1995. reprint ed. lib. bdg. 79.00 (*0-7812-8582-8*) Rprt Serv.

Luckmann. Transcultural Communication in Health Care. LC 99-40689. (Allied Health Ser.). 320p. (C). 1999. mass mkt. 22.95 (*0-7668-0593-X*) Delmar.

— Transcultural Communication in Nursing. LC 98-50682. 400p. 1998. text 26.95 (*0-7668-0256-6*) Delmar.

Luckmann, Joan, ed. see Saunders.

Luckmann, Thomas. The Sociology of Language. LC 74-19085. (Studies in Sociology). 79p. 1975. pap. 3.00 (*0-672-61262-3*, Bobbs) Macmillan.

Luckmann, Thomas, jt. auth. see Berger, Peter L.

Luckmann, Thomas, jt. auth. see Schutz, Alfred.

Luckmann, Thomas, jt. ed. see Beckford, James A.

Luckmann, William H., jt. ed. see Metcalf, Robert L.

Luckner, Carmen B. A Gift of Light. 33p. Date not set. 4.95 (*1-879934-23-X*) St Andrews NC.

Luckner, John, jt. auth. see Luetke-Stahlman, Barbara.

Luckner, John L. & Nadler, Reldan S. Processing the Experience: Enhancing & Generalizing Learning. 2nd ed. 464p. 1997. per. 36.95 (*0-7872-1000-5*, 41100001) Kendall-Hunt.

Luckner, Ludwig. Migration Processes in Soil & Groundwater Zone. 504p. 1991. lib. bdg. 110.00 (*0-87371-302-8*, L302) Lewis Pubs.

Luckner, M. Secondary Metabolism in Microorganisms, Plants & Animals. 400p. 1990. 129.00 (*0-387-50287-4*) Spr-Verlag.

— Secondary Metabolism in Microorganisms, Plants & Animals. 2nd rev. ed. (Illus.). 570p. 1984. 93.50 (*0-387-12771-2*) Spr-Verlag.

Lucko, Peter, jt. ed. see Carls, Uwe.

Luckovich, Mike. Lots of Luckovich. LC 96-221424. 96p. 1996. pap. 10.00 (*0-671-54519-1*) PB.

***Luckovich, Mike, et al.** Market Research in Health & Social Care. LC 99-87923. 200p. 2000. write for info. (*0-415-20754-1*); pap. write for info. (*0-415-20755-X*) Routledge.

— Men's Health: Perspectives, Diversity & Paradox LC 99-32983. 1999. write for info. (*0-632-05288-0*) Blackwell Sci.

Luckow, Melissa. Monograph of Desmanthus (Leguminosae-Mimosoideae) Anderson, Christiane, ed. (Systematic Botany Monographs: Vol. 38). (Illus.). 166p. 1993. pap. 20.00 (*0-912861-38-X*) Am Soc Plant.

Lucks, Naomi, ed. Fresh Start: Real Health, Real Results for Real People. (Illus.). 238p. 1999. reprint ed. pap. text 20.00 (*0-7881-6366-3*) DIANE Pub.

Luckstead, Eugene F. & Greydanus, Donald E. Medical Care of the Adolescent Athlete. (Illus.). 325p. 1993. pap. 45.95 (*1-878487-18-3*, 5847M) Practice Mgmt Info.

Luckstead, Ingrid, jt. auth. see Harris, Carolyn.

Luckstone, Harold, Jr. & Holliday, Richard W. Werbel Approved Course for Rental Vehicle Companies & Their Franchisees. 64p. 1991. pap. text 7.95 (*1-884803-14-8*) Werbel Pub.

Luckstone, Harold C. Life Insurance Multiple Choice Practice Questions. 100p. (Orig.). 1997. pap. text 14.95 (*1-884803-12-1*) Werbel Pub.

Lucktenberg, George, ed. Haydn - First Book for Pianists. (Alfred Masterwork Edition Ser.). 24p. 1978. 4.95 (*0-7390-0589-8*, 1718) Alfred Pub.

Lucktenberg, George, jt. auth. see Kottick, Edward L.

Lucktenberg, George, ed. see Haydn.

Luckterhand, Lyle L. Man: From Glory to Ashes & Back. LC 97-69964. (People's Bible Teachings Ser.). 181p. 1998. pap. text 9.99 (*0-8100-0799-1*, 15N0609) Northwest Pub.

Luckus, Vitas. Hard Way. (Illus.). 144p. 1994. 45.00 (*3-905514-13-3*, Pub. by Edit Stemmle) Dist Art Pubs.

***Lucky, Jerry.** Progressive. (20th Century Rock & Roll Ser.). 2000. pap. 13.95 (*1-896522-20-3*) CN06.

— Progressive Rock Files. 4th ed. 1998. pap. 26.95 (*1-896522-10-6*) CN06.

Lucky, Robert. Lucky Strikes... Again: Feats & Foibles of Engineers. LC 92-30769. (Illus.). 296p. (C). 1993. 34.95 (*0-7803-0433-0*, PC03301) Inst Electrical.

Lucky, Robert W. Lucky 6, 6 bks., Set. 1993. 164.75 (*0-7803-1018-7*) Inst Electrical.

Lucky, William A. High Line Rider. 1985. mass mkt. 2.50 (*0-8217-1615-8*, Zebra Kensgtn) Kensgtn Pub Corp.

Luckyj, Christine, ed. The White Devil. 2nd ed. (New Mermaids Ser.). pap. 8.00 (*0-393-90078-9*) Norton.

Luckyj, G., jt. auth. see Kulish, Pantelejmon.

Luckyj, George S. Between Gogol & Sevcenko: Polarity in the Literary Ukraine, 1798-1847. 439p. 1.65 (*3-7705-0388-0*) Adlers Foreign Bks.

— Discordant Voices: The Non-Russian Soviet Literatures, 1952-1973. 160p. 1986. pap. 9.95 (*0-88962-014-8*) Mosaic.

— Literary Politics in the Soviet Ukraine, 1917-1934. LC 75-165645. (Select Bibliographies Reprint Ser.). 1977. reprint ed. 24.95 (*0-8369-5954-X*) Ayer.

— Literary Politics in the Soviet Ukraine, 1917-1934. rev. ed. LC 90-3499. (Studies of the Harriman Institute). 367p. (C). 1990. reprint ed. text 49.95 (*0-8223-1081-3*); reprint ed. pap. text 24.95 (*0-8223-1099-6*) Duke.

— Panteleimon Kulish: A Sketch of His Life & Times. (East European Monographs: No. 127). 229p. 1983. text 55.50 (*0-88033-016-3*, Pub. by East Eur Monographs) Col U Pr.

— Ukrainian Literature in the Twentieth Century: A Reader's Guide. 136p. (Orig.). 1992. text 40.00 (*0-8020-5019-0*); pap. text 18.95 (*0-8020-6003-X*) U of Toronto Pr.

Luckyj, George S., ed. Modern Ukrainian Short Stories. rev. ed. 230p. 1995. lib. bdg. 27.50 (*1-56308-391-4*) Libs Unl.

— Shevchenko & the Critics, 1861-1980. 1981. pap. 11.95 (*0-8020-6377-2*) U of Toronto Pr.

— Shevchenko & the Critics, 1861-1980. Ferguson, Dolly & Yurkevich, Sophia, trs. LC 81-192007. 536p. reprint ed. pap. 166.20 (*0-8357-4731-X*, 203764700009) Bks Demand.

Luckyj, George S., jt. auth. see Cyzevs'kyj, Dmytro.

Luckyj, George S., jt. ed. see Lindheim, Ralph.

Luckyj, George S., tr. see Zaitsev, Pavlo.

Lucock, John & Peak, Robin, eds. Workouts in Modern Economics. 3rd ed. LC 94-42567. 1994. pap. text. write for info. (*0-582-25938-X*, Pub. by Addison-Wesley) Longman.

***Luconi, Stefano.** From Paesani to White Ethnics: The Italian Experience in Philadelphia. (C). 2001. pap. text 19.95 (*0-7914-4858-4*) State U NY Pr.

— From Paesani to White Ethnics: The Italian Experience in Philadelphia. (C). 2001. text 59.50 (*0-7914-4857-6*) State U NY Pr.

Lucotte, G. Genetique Moleculaire. 106p. pap. 39.00 (*2-905936-00-2*) Elsevier.

Lucotte, G. & Baneyx, Francois, eds. Introduction to Molecular Cloning Techniques. 298p. 1993. 84.95 (*0-471-18849-2*) Wiley.

Lucotte, Gerald & Baneyx, Francois. Introduction to Molecular Cloning Techniques. LC 93-22418. 298p. 1993. 49.00 (*1-56081-613-9*, Wiley-VCH) Wiley.

Lucotte, M., et al, eds. Mercury in the Biogeochemical Cycle: Natural Environment & Hydroelectric Reservoirs of Northern Quebec (Canada. LC 99-24587. (Environmental Science Ser.). (Illus.). xviii, 334p. 1999. 109.00 (*3-540-65755-X*) Spr-Verlag.

Lucovsky, G., et al, eds. Characterization of Plasma-Enhanced CVD Processes Vol. 165: Materials Research Society Symposium Proceedings. 251p. 1990. text 17.50 (*1-55899-053-4*) Materials Res.

Lucovsky, G., ed. see American Institute of Physics.

Lucovsky, G., jt. ed. see Joannopoulos, John D.

Lucovsky, Gerald, ed. see Brillson, L. J.

Lucovsky, Gerald, jt. ed. see Rubloff, Gary.

Lucques. Food & Sex: The Wicked Book of Erotic Appetizers. Carle, Cliff, ed. 1994. pap. 4.99 (*0-918259-74-6*) CCC Pubns.

Lucquin, B. & Pironneau, Olivier. Introduction to Scientific Computing. LC 97-22466. 380p. 1998. pap. 65.00 (*0-471-97266-5*) Wiley.

Lucretius. De Rerum Natura, 3 vols. Bailey, Cyril, ed. 1,840p. 1986. text 210.00 (*0-19-814405-9*) OUP.

— De Rerum Natura. 2nd ed. Bailey, Cyril, ed. (Oxford Classical Texts Ser.). 254p. 1922. text 24.95 (*0-19-814624-8*) OUP.

— De Rerum Natura, Bk. 3. Kenney, Edwin J., ed. (Cambridge Greek & Latin Classics Ser.). 256p. 1977. pap. text 22.95 (*0-521-29177-1*) Cambridge U Pr.

— De Rerum Natura: The Latin Text of Lucretius. Leonard, William E. & Smith, Stanley B., eds. (Illus.). 896p. 1942. text 49.95 (*0-299-00362-0*) U of Wis Pr.

— Lecretius No. IV: De Rerum Natura. Godwin, J., ed. (Classical Texts Ser.). 1987. pap. 22.00 (*0-85668-309-4*, Pub. by Aris & Phillips) David Brown.

— Lecretius No. VI: De Rerum Natura. Godwin, ed. 1991. 59.99 (*0-85668-499-6*, Pub. by Aris & Phillips) David Brown.

— Lecretius No. IV: De Rerum Natura. Godwin, J., ed. (Classical Texts Ser.). 1987. 59.99 (*0-85668-308-6*, Pub. by Aris & Phillips) David Brown.

— Lucretius: De Rerum Natura V. Costa, C. D., ed. (C). 1985. pap. 17.95 (*0-19-814457-1*) OUP.

— Lucretius: The Way Things Are: The De Rerum Natura of Titus Lucretius Carus. Humphries, Rolfe, tr. LC 68-27349. (Greek & Latin Classics Ser.). 256p. 1968. reprint ed. pap. 10.95 (*0-253-20125-X*, MB-125) Ind U Pr.

— Lucretius No. VI: De Rerum Natura. Godwin, ed. 1991. pap. 28.00 (*0-85668-500-3*, Pub. by Aris & Phillips) David Brown.

— On the Nature of the Universe. Fowler, Don, ed. Melville, Ronald, tr. LC 97-40071. 310p. 1998. text 86.00 (*0-19-815097-0*) OUP.

— On the Nature of the Universe. LC 98-35967. 314p. 1999. pap. 11.95 (*0-19-281761-2*) OUP.

— On the Nature of Things. 1976. 20.95 (*0-8488-0824-X*) Amereon Ltd.

— On the Nature of Things. Watson, John S., tr. from LAT. LC 97-34295. (Great Books in Philosophy). 310p. 1997. pap. text 7.95 (*1-57392-179-3*) Prometheus Bks.

— On the Nature of Things. rev. ed. (Loeb Classical Library: No. 181). 664p. 1975. text 18.95 (*0-674-99200-8*) HUP.

— On the Nature of Things-De Rerum Natura. Esolen, Anthony M., ed. LC 94-25165. 336p. 1995. text 38.00 (*0-8018-5054-1*) Johns Hopkins.

Lucretius, jt. auth. see Catto, Bonnie.

Lucuham, Robin, jt. ed. see Austin, Dennis.

Lucwig, Friedrich. Repertorium Organorum Recentioris et Motetorum Vetustissimi Stili, 4 vols. 1972. reprint ed. write for info. (*3-487-04197-9*) G Olms Pubs.

Lucy Brown Design Staff, des. The Gardens of Thomas Kinkade. 48p. 1997. pap. 62.00 (*0-9638635-5-X*) Lightpost Pubng.

— Reflections of Light by Thomas Kinkade. 48p. 1997. pap. 62.00 (*0-9638635-6-8*) Lightpost Pubng.

Lucy, Jack A., jt. ed. see Brown, Susan C.

Lucy, John A. Gramatical Categories & Cognition. 270p. 1996. pap. 17.95 (*0-521-56536-7*) Cambridge U Pr.

— Grammatical Categories & Cognition: A Case Study of the Linguistic Relativity Hypothesis. (Studies in the Social & Cultural Foundations of Language: No. 13). 227p. 1996. pap. text 20.95 (*0-521-56620-7*) Cambridge U Pr.

Lucy, John A., ed. Reflexive Language: Reported Speech & Metapragmatics. (Illus.). 424p. (C). 1993. text 85.00 (*0-521-35164-2*) Cambridge U Pr.

Lucy, Margaret. Shakespeare & the Supernatural. LC 70-144653. reprint ed. 24.50 (*0-404-04065-9*) AMS Pr.

Lucy, Niall. Debating Derrida. LC 96-139465. (Interpretations Ser.). 128p. pap. 14.95 (*0-522-84625-4*, Pub. by Melbourne Univ Pr) Paul & Co Pubs.

— Postmodern Literary Theory: An Introduction. LC 97-12841. 288p. (C). 1997. text 62.95 (*0-631-20000-2*); pap. text 26.95 (*0-631-20001-0*) Blackwell Pubs.

***Lucy, Niall, ed.** Postmodern Literary Theory: An Anthology. LC 99-31612. 480p. 1999. pap. text 29.95 (*0-631-21028-8*) Blackwell Pubs.

Lucy, Niall, ed. Postmodern Literary Theory: An Anthology. LC 99-31612. 480p. (C). 1999. text 62.95 (*0-631-21027-X*) Blackwell Pubs.

***Lucy, Pringle.** Crop Circles: The Greatest Mystery of Modern Times. 2000. 27.00 (*0-7225-3855-3*) Thorsons PA.

Lucy, Sean, ed. Irish Poets in English. 1972. pap. 7.95 (*0-85342-301-6*) Dufour.

Lucy, William. Understanding & Explaining Adjudication. LC 99-34492. 408p. 1999. text 70.00 (*0-19-826025-3*) OUP.

***Lucy, William H. & Phillips, David L.** Confronting Suburban Decline: Strategic Planning for Metropolitan Renewal. (Illus.). 384p. 2000. pap. 35.00 (*1-55963-770-6*) Island Pr.

Lucyk, Blaine. Advanced Topics in DB2. (Illus.). 528p. (C). 1993. pap. 56.95 (*0-201-57652-X*) Addison-Wesley.

Lucyszyn, Andrew, jt. ed. see Brohaugh, Bill.

Luczak, Holger, et al, eds. Work with Display Units, '92: Selected Proceedings of the 3rd International Scientific Conference on Work with Display Units, Berlin, Germany, September 1-4, 1992. LC 93-19702. 566p. 1993. 159.25 (*0-444-89759-3*, North Holland) Elsevier.

Luczak, James E. Rats. 1992. pap. 3.50 (*0-87129-169-X*, R52) Dramatic Pub.

Luczak, Raymond. St. Michael's Fall. LC 95-83673. 86p. 1995. pap. 12.95 (*0-9634016-8-8*, Deaf Life Pr) MSM Prods.

Luczak, Stefan. Sprecherausschusse fur Leitende Angestellte im Rahmen der Unternehmungsverfassung: Ergebnisse einer Empirischen Untersuchung aus Organisatorischer Sicht. (Europaische Hochschulschriften: Reihe 5: Bd. 2008). (GER., Illus.). 261p. 1996. pap. 51.95 (*3-631-30669-5*) P Lang Pubng.

Luczkiw, Stash, tr. see Brizzi, Enrico.

Luczkovich, Joseph J., et al, eds. Ecomorphology of Fishes. (Developments in Environmental Biology of Fishes Ser.: Vol. 16). 1995. text 202.50 (*0-7923-3744-1*) Kluwer Academic.

Luczyc-Wyhowska, J., jt. auth. see Hull, Alastair.

Luczyc-Wyhowska, Jose, jt. auth. see Hull, Alastair.

Luczynski, Miroslaw, et al, eds. Biology & Management of Coregonid Fishes - 1993: Proceedings of the 5th International Symposium on the Biology & Management of Coregonid Fishes Held in Olsztyn, Poland, August 22-27, 1993. (Advances in Limnology Ser.: Vol. 46). (GER., Illus.). viii, 485p. 1995. 103.00 (*3-510-47047-8*, Pub. by E Schweizerbartsche) Balogh.

***Luczywek, Mark.** Cisco Voice-Over IP Handbook. 400p. 2000. pap. 29.99 (*0-7645-4680-5*) IDG Bks.

Ludanyi, Andrew, jt. ed. see Joo, Rudolf.

Ludanyi, Julianna N. Advanced Hungarian 2: Student Manual. (HUN., Illus.). 292p. (C). 1988. pap. text, student ed. 23.50 (*0-87415-126-0*, 52) Foreign Lang.

— Advanced Hungarian 2: Instructor Manual. (HUN., Illus.). 123p. (Orig.). (C). 1988. pap., teacher ed. 13.00 (*0-87415-127-9*, 52A) Foreign Lang.

Ludanyi, Julianna N., jt. auth. see Pereszlenyi-Pinter, Martha.

Ludas, Joseph M. Fingerprint Discoveries: The Illustrated Textbook of Fingerprint Identification. 80p. (J). (gr. 6). 1996. pap. text 22.95 (*0-9650202-1-5*) Forensic Press.

— Fingerprint Discoveries Workbook: Assignments, Projects & Tests. 30p. 1996. 22.95 (*0-9650202-2-3*) Forensic Press.

L

L

— Fingerprint Discovery Kit: Discover the Science at Your Fingertips, 2 bks., Set. (Illus.). 92p. (YA). (gr. 6 up). 1996. pap. 28.95 (*0-9650202-0-7*) Forensic Press.

Ludat, Herbert. Bistum Lebus. (GER.). viii, 324p. 1993. reprint ed. 78.00 (*3-487-09656-0*) G Olms Pubs.

— Die Ostdeutschen Kietze. (GER.). viii, 220p. 1984. reprint ed. write for info. (*3-487-07573-3*) G Olms Pubs.

***Ludd, Deran.** No Aloha: The Friendly Happy Music of the Past. (Native Agents Ser.: No. 14). 197p. 1999. pap. 10.00 (*1-58435-008-3*, Pub. by Semiotexte); pap. 10.00 (*1-58435-000-8*, Native Agents) Semiotexte.

Ludd, Deran. Sick Burn Cut. 1992. pap. 7.00 (*0-936756-85-3*) Autonomedia.

Ludd, Deran, et al, eds. Good to Go: Short Stories West Coast Style. 1994. pap. 9.95 (*0-9638594-0-4*) Zero Hour.

Ludd, Steven O., jt. ed. see Reichert, William O.

Luddeke, Christof F. & Johnson, Andrew. A Guide to the Hamburg Rules: From Hague to Hamburg Via Visby. 5th ed. (Marine Engineers Review Ser.). 200p. 1995. 105.00 (*1-85044-884-1*) LLP.

***Ludden, David.** An Agrarian History of South Asia. LC 98-43856. (New Cambridge History of India Ser.: No. IV, Pt. 4). 298p. 1999. 64.95 (*0-521-36424-8*) Cambridge U Pr.

Ludden, David, ed. Agricultural Production & Indian History. LC 95-902016. (Oxford in India Readings Ser.: Themes in Indian History). (Illus.). 392p. 1995. text 24.95 (*0-19-563268-0*) OUP.

— Contesting the Nation: Religion, Community, & the Democracy in India. 320p. 1996. text 39.95 (*0-8122-3354-9*); pap. text 19.95 (*0-8122-1585-0*) U of Pa Pr.

Ludden, David E. Peasant History in South India. LC 85-42692. (Illus.). 332p. reprint ed. pap. 103.00 (*0-608-04521-7*, 206526600001) Bks Demand.

Ludden, LaVerne. Franchise Opportunity Handbook: A Complete Guide for People Who Want to Start Their Own Franchise. 2nd ed. 380p. 1995. pap. 16.95 (*1-57112-073-4*) Park Ave.

Ludden, LaVerne & Capazolli, Tom. Supervisor Savvy: How to Help New & Inexperienced Employees Succeed at Work. 220p. 1999. pap. 18.95 (*1-56370-669-5*) Park Ave.

Ludden, LaVerne, jt. auth. see Farr, J. Michael.

Ludden, LaVerne L. Back to School: A College Guide for Adults. 290p. (Orig.). 1995. pap. 14.95 (*1-57112-070-X*, P070X) Park Ave.

— Franchise Opportunities: A Complete Guide for People Who Want to Start Their Own Franchise. 2nd ed. LC 98-38529. 380p. 1998. pap. 19.95 (*1-57112-091-2*) Park Ave.

— Job Savvy: How to Be a Success at Work. Hall, Sara, ed. 169p. (Orig.). (J). 1992. pap. 10.95 (*0-942784-79-0*, JS) JIST Works.

— Job Savvy: How to Be a Success at Work. 2nd ed. LC 97-30762. (Illus.). 224p. (Orig.). 1997. pap. 10.95 (*1-56370-304-1*) Park Ave.

Ludden, LaVerne L. & Ludden, Marsha. Job Savvy Instructor's Guide: How to Be a Success at Work. 2nd ed. 320p. pap. 19.95 (*1-56370-435-8*) JIST Works.

Ludden, LaVerne L. & Ludden, Marsha J. Job Savvy Instructor's Guide: How to Be a Success at Work. Hall, Sara, ed. 112p. 1992. pap. 12.95 (*0-942784-80-4*, JSTM) JIST Works.

— Ludden's Adult Guide to Colleges & Universities. LC 96-34855. (Illus.). 576p. (Orig.). (C). 1996. pap. 19.95 (*1-57112-076-9*, P0769) Park Ave.

Ludden, LaVerne L. & Maitlen, Bonnie. Mind Your Own Business: Getting Started As an Entrepreneur. LC 93-6007. 212p. 1993. pap. 9.95 (*1-56370-083-2*, MYOB) JIST Works.

Ludden, LaVerne L., jt. auth. see Farr, J. Michael.

Ludden, Marsha. The Basics: Skills You Need to Keep Your Job. Ingraham, Lina, ed. (Illus.). 90p. 1998. pap. 10.95 (*1-891818-01-5*) Linx Educ Pubg.

— The Basics: Skills You Need to Keep Your Job - Instructor's Guide. Ingraham, Lina, ed. 47p. 1998. pap., teacher ed. 8.95 (*1-891818-02-3*, 01-TG02) Linx Educ Pubg.

Ludden, Marsha, jt. auth. see Ludden, LaVerne L.

Ludden, Marsha J. Checking & Saving: What They Are & How to Use Them. (Living Skills Ser.). (Illus.). 120p. (Orig.). (YA). (gr. 7 up). 1995. text, wbk. ed. 6.95 (*1-56370-158-8*, CSA) JIST Works.

— Effective Communication Skills: Essential Tools for Success in Work, Social & Personal Situations. Hall, Sara, ed. (Living Skills Ser.). (Illus.). 138p. 1992. pap. 8.95 (*1-56370-038-7*, ECS) JIST Works.

Ludden, Marsha J., jt. auth. see Ludden, LaVerne L.

Ludden, Mary C., tr. see Honore, Jean.

Luddington, John. Starting to Collect Silver. (Illus.). 228p. 1984. 49.50 (*0-907462-48-0*) Antique Collect.

Luddy, Jean A., jt. auth. see Abbott, S. Ardis.

Luddy, Maria. Women & Philanthropy in Nineteenth-Century Ireland. 265p. (C). 1995. text 69.95 (*0-521-47433-7*); pap. text 27.95 (*0-521-48361-1*) Cambridge U Pr.

— Women in Ireland, 1800-1918: A Documentary History. 1995. pap. 28.00 (*1-85918-038-8*, Pub. by Cork Univ) Intl Spec Bk.

— Women in Ireland, 1800-1918: A Documentary History. 1996. 65.00 (*1-85918-037-X*, Pub. by Cork Univ) Intl Spec Bk.

Luddy, Maria, ed. Irish Women's Writing, 1839-1888, 6 vols. fac. ed. 2000p. (C). (gr. 13). 1998. 745.00 (*0-415-19016-9*, D6191) Routledge.

Luddy, Maria & Murphy, Cliona. Women Surviving: Studies in Irish Women's History in 19th-20th Century. 224p. 1990. pap. 18.95 (*1-85371-064-4*, Pub. by Poolbeg Pr) Dufour.

Luddy, Maria, jt. auth. see Cullen, Mary.

Luddy, Maria, jt. ed. see Cullen, Mary.

Ludecke, Alison, ed. Consoliere Classics II. 1998. pap. 8.95 (*0-937690-45-7*, 3061) Wrld Lib Pubns.

Ludecke, Dieter K., et al, eds. ACTH, Cushing's Syndrome, & Other Hypercortisolemic States. LC 90-8801. (Progress in Endocrine Research & Therapy Ser.: No. 5). (Illus.). 336p. 1990. reprint ed. pap. 104.20 (*0-608-00597-5*, 206118400007) Bks Demand.

Ludecke, Dieter K. & Tolis, George, eds. Growth Hormone, Growth Factors, & Acromegaly. LC 87-4708. (Progress in Endocrine Research & Therapy Ser.: Vol. 3). 303p. 1987. reprint ed. pap. 94.00 (*0-608-00331-X*, 206104800007) Bks Demand.

Ludecke, Kristin B., jt. auth. see Drake, James A.

Ludecke, Kurt G. I Knew Hitler: The Story of a Nazi Who Escaped the Blood Purge. LC 78-63687. (Studies in Fascism: Ideology & Practice). (Illus.). 848p. reprint ed. 74.00 (*0-404-16904-X*) AMS Pr.

Ludeke, Kenneth L., jt. auth. see Day, Arden D.

Ludeke, Paul & Swebeck, Brad. Enterprise Bargaining: A Practical Approach. 160p. pap. 33.00 (*1-86287-079-9*, Pub. by Federation Pr) Gaunt.

Ludel, Leonard. How to Cut a Diamond. LC 86-223110. (Illus.). 250p. 1985. 47.50 (*0-9617615-0-4*) L Ludel.

— Recutting & Repairing Diamonds. Riggs, Michael, ed. LC 96-95231. (Illus.). 75p. (Orig.). 1996. pap. 33.20 (*0-9617615-1-2*) L Ludel.

Ludel, Moses. Ford-F Series Pickup Owner's Bible: A Hands-on Guide to Getting the Most from Your F-Series Pickup. LC 94-35251. (Ford F-Ser.). (Illus.). 370p. 1994. 29.95 (*0-8376-0152-5*) Bentley Pubs.

— Harley-Davidson Evolution V-Twin Owner's Bible. LC 97-41253. (Illus.). 286p. 1997. 29.95 (*0-8376-0146-0*) Bentley Pubs.

— Jeep Owners Bible. (Illus.). 356p. 1998. reprint ed. pap. 29.95 (*0-8376-0154-1*) Bentley Pubs.

— Toyota Truck & Land Cruiser Owner's Bible: A Hands-on Guide to Getting the Most from Your Toyota. LC 95-51695. (Illus.). 378p. 1995. pap. text 29.95 (*0-8376-0159-2*) Bentley Pubs.

Ludell, M. Chevrolet & GMC Light Truck Owner's Bible. (Illus.). 384p. 1995. 29.95 (*0-8376-0157-6*) Bentley Pubs.

Ludema, K. C., et al, eds. Wear of Materials. Incl. Wear of Materials. 1983. pap. text 85.00 Wear of Materials, 1979. 685p. 1979. 60.00 585p. 1977. Set pap. text 50.00 (*0-685-81976-0*, H00100) ASME.

Ludema, K. C., ed. see International Conference on Wear of Materials Staf.

Ludema, Kenneth C. Friction, Wear, Lubrication: A Textbook in Tribology. LC 96-12440. 272p. 1996. boxed set 84.95 (*0-8493-2685-0*, 2685) CRC Pr.

Ludema, Kenneth C., et al, eds. Wear of Materials: Proceedings of the 9th International Conference, San Francisco, U. S. A., 13-16 April, 1993, 2 vols. xxviii, 1164p. 1993. 390.75 (*0-444-81471-X*) Elsevier.

Ludema, Kenneth C. & Bayer, Raymond G., eds. Tribological Modeling for Mechanical Designers. LC 91-8238. (Special Technical Publication Ser.: No. STP 1105). (Illus.). 195p. 1991. text 76.00 (*0-8031-1412-5*, STP1105) ASTM.

Ludema, Kenneth C., jt. auth. see Dorinson, A.

Ludeman & Hazen. Introduction to Electronic Devices & Circuits. (C). 1990. pap. text, teacher ed., suppl. ed. 42.00 (*0-03-032013-5*) Harcourt Coll Pubs.

— Introduction to Electronic Devices & Circuits. (C). 1990. pap. text, lab manual ed. 39.00 (*0-03-032008-9*, Pub. by Harcourt Coll Pubs) Harcourt.

Ludeman, Kate, jt. auth. see Hendricks, Gay.

Ludeman, Lonnie C. Fundamentals of Digital Signal Processing. 352p. 1986. text 103.95 (*0-471-60363-5*) Wiley.

Ludeman, Robert A. Introduction to Electronic Devices & Circuits. 576p. (C). 1989. text 90.50 (*0-03-009538-7*, Pub. by SCP) Harcourt.

Ludemann. Child Development. 2000. pap. text 11.97 (*0-395-97201-9*) HM.

Ludemann, Gerd. Heretics: The Other Side of Early Christianity. LC 96-20250. 354p. 1996. 28.95 (*0-664-22085-1*) Westminster John Knox.

***Ludemann, Gerd.** Studien Zur Gnosis. (Arbeiten zur Religion und Geschichte des Urchristentums Ser.). 287p. 1999. 42.95 (*3-631-34331-0*) P Lang Pubng.

Ludemann, Gerd. The Unholy in Holy Scripture: The Dark Side of the Bible. LC 96-52254. (Orig.). 1997. pap. 17.95 (*0-664-25739-9*) Westminster John Knox.

***Ludemann, Gerd.** Virgin Birth? The Real Story of Mary & Her Son Jesus. LC 98-14994. 176p. 1998. pap. 20.00 (*1-56338-243-1*) TPI PA.

Ludemann, Gerd, ed. Die Religionsgeschichtliche Schule: Facetten Eines Theologischen Umbruchs. (Studien und Texte zur Religionsgeschichtlichen Schule Ser.: Bd. 1). (GER., Illus.). 298p. 1996. 44.95 (*3-631-30038-7*) P Lang Pubng.

***Ludemann, Gerd & Janssen, Martina.** Suppressed Prayers: Gnostic Spirituality in Early Christianity. 192p. 1998. pap. 18.00 (*1-56338-250-4*) TPI PA.

Ludemann, Gerd & Ozen, Alf. What Really Happened to Jesus: A Historical Approach to the Resurrection. Bowden, John, tr. from GER. LC 95-35036. 160p. (Orig.). 1996. pap. 15.95 (*0-664-25647-3*) Westminster John Knox.

Ludemann, Gerd, ed. see Hurd, John C.

Ludemann, Gerd, ed. see Hyldahl, Niels.

Ludemann, Uwe. Denken - Glauben - Predigen: Eine Kritische Auseinandersetzung mit Emil Brunners Lehre vom Menschen im Widerspruch. 682p. 1998. 56.95 (*3-631-33095-2*) P Lang Pubng.

Ludena, Eduardo V., jt. auth. see Kryachko, Eugene S.

Ludend, ed. Condensed Matter Theories. 540p. 1996. 195.00 (*1-56072-374-2*) Nova Sci Pubs.

Ludendorff, Eric Von, see Von Ludendorff, Eric.

Ludendorff, Erich Von. The General Staff & Its Problems, 2 Vols., Set. Holt, F. A., tr. LC 79-165646. (Select Bibliographies Reprint Ser.). 1977. reprint ed. 51.95 (*0-8369-5955-8*) Ayer.

— Ludendorff's Own Story, 2 Vols., Set. LC 72-165647. (Select Bibliographies Reprint Ser.). 1977. reprint ed. 60.95 (*0-8369-5956-6*) Ayer.

Luder, George. Daddy's Collection, Bk. 3. (Illus.). 50p. (J). 1999. write for info. (*1-884083-45-5*) Maval Pub.

— Epele: Evaluacion del Dominio del Espanol como Lenguaje Extranjero, Cuadernillo 1. (SPA., Illus.). 60p. 1997. pap. text 15.00 incl. audio (*1-884083-36-6*) Maval Pub.

— Epele: Evaluacion del Dominio del Espanol como Lenguaje Extranjero, Cuadernillo 2. 60p. 1997. pap. text 15.00 incl. audio (*1-884083-37-4*) Maval Pub.

— Epele: Evaluacion del Dominio del Espanol como Lenguaje Extranjero, Cuadernillo 3. 60p. 1997. pap. text 15.00 incl. audio (*1-884083-38-2*) Maval Pub.

— Preparation for the TOEFL: Test of English As a Foreign Language, Bklet. 2. 60p. (Orig.). 1996. pap. 15.00 incl. audio (*1-884083-33-1*) Maval Pub.

— Preparation for the TOEFL: Test of English As a Foreign Language, Bklet. 3. 60p. (Orig.). 1996. pap. 15.00 incl. audio (*1-884083-35-8*) Maval Pub.

Luder, George, ed. Daddy's Collection, Bk. 2. (Illus.). 50p. (J). 1999. write for info. (*1-884083-46-3*) Maval Pub.

— Daddy's Collection, Bk. 4. (Illus.). 50p. (J). 1999. write for info. (*1-884083-44-7*) Maval Pub.

— Daddy's Collection, Bk. 5. (Illus.). 50p. (J). 1999. write for info. (*1-884083-43-9*) Maval Pub.

— Daddy's Collection, Bk. 6. (Illus.). 50p. (J). 1999. write for info. (*1-884083-42-0*) Maval Pub.

— Daddy's Collection, Bk. 7. (Illus.). 50p. (J). 1999. write for info. (*1-884083-41-2*) Maval Pub.

— Daddy's Collection, Bk. 8. (Illus.). 50p. (J). 1999. write for info. (*1-884083-40-4*) Maval Pub.

— Daddy's Collection, Bk. 9. (Illus.). 50p. (J). 1999. write for info. (*1-884083-39-0*) Maval Pub.

— Daddy's Collection, Bk. 10. (Illus.). 50p. (J). 1999. write for info. (*1-884083-05-6*) Maval Pub.

Luder, George, ed. see Luder, Maria.

Luder, George, ed. see Waintrub, Mauricio, et al.

Luder, Hans U. Postnatal Development, Aging & Degeneration of the TMJ. (Craniofacial Growth Ser.: Vol. 32). (Illus.). 270p. 1996. 55.00 (*0-929921-28-3*) UM CHGD.

Luder, Hope E. Women & Quakerism. LC 74-82914. 36p. (Orig.). 1974. pap. 4.00 (*0-87574-196-7*) Pendle Hill.

Luder, Ian & Mock, Patricia. Tax & Remuneration Strategies. 275p. 1994. boxed set 154.00 (*0-406-02801-X*, UK, MICHIE) LEXIS Pub.

Luder, Maria. GED Preparation Test 1. Luder, George & Waintrub, Mauricio L., eds. (GED Ser.). 76p. 1999. pap. text 15.00 (*1-884083-87-0*) Maval Pub.

Luder, Maria, jt. auth. see Waintrub, Valentin.

Luder, Maria, ed. see Waintrub, Mauricio L., et al.

Luder, Maria, ed. see Waintrub, Valentin A. & Waintrub, Mauricio L.

Luder, Maria, ed. see Waintrub, Valentin, et al.

Luder, Maria, ed. & illus. see Walling, Hobart, et al.

Luderer, Albert A. & Weetall, Howard H., eds. The Human Oncogenic Viruses. LC 86-7518. (Oncogenes Ser.). (Illus.). 281p. 1986. 125.00 (*0-89603-088-1*) Humana.

Luderer, William, ed. Making Global Connections in the Middle School: Lessons on the Environment, Development & Equity. 87p. (Orig.). 1994. pap. text 12.00 (*0-928630-02-1*) Global Learning.

Luderitz, Berndt. History of the Disorders of Cardiac Rhythm. rev. ed. LC 94-26949.Tr. of Geschichte der Herzhythmusst Orungen. (GER., Illus.). 188p. 1997. 60.00 (*0-87993-606-1*) Futura Pub.

Luderitz, Berndt, jt. ed. see Saksena, Sanjeev.

Luderitz, P., jt. auth. see Elster, P.

Luders. Epileptic Seizures. LC RC372.5.E657 2000. 1999. text 85.00 (*0-443-08959-0*, W B Saunders Co) Harcrt Hlth Sci Grp.

Luders, H., jt. auth. see Balzer, D.

Luders, Hans, ed. Advanced Evoked Potentials. (Topics in Neurosurgery Ser.). (C). 1989. text 155.00 (*0-89838-963-1*) Kluwer Academic.

Luders, Hans O. Epilepsy Surgery. 880p. 1991. text 142.00 (*0-88167-821-X*) Lppncott W & W.

Luders, Hans O. & Noachtar, Soheyi. Atlas of Epileptic Seizures & Syndromes. (Illus.). 205p. 1998. text. write for info. (*0-7216-6946-8*, W B Saunders Co) Harcrt Hlth Sci Grp.

Luders, Hans O. & Noachtar, Soheyl. Atlas & Classification of Electroencephalography. Ross, Allan, ed. LC 98-32243. (Illus.). 205p. 1999. text 885.00 (*0-7216-6554-3*, W B Saunders Co) Harcrt Hlth Sci Grp.

Luders, Hans O., jt. ed. see Kotagal, Prakash.

Luders, Lesa. Lady God. LC 95-19139. 185p. (Orig.). 1995. pap. 9.95 (*0-934678-59-6*) New Victoria Pubs.

***Luders, Mary.** The Ants Go Marching. 20p. (J). (ps-2). 2000. 7.95 (*0-694-01447-8*, HarpFestival) HarpC Child Bks.

— The Twelve Days of Christmas. LC 99-69944. 24p. (J). (ps-3). 2000. 9.95 (*0-694-01446-X*, HarpFestival) HarpC Child Bks.

Luders, Rolf, jt. auth. see Hachette, Dominique.

Luders, Rolf, jt. ed. see De Brun, Julio.

Ludes, B., jt. auth. see Mangin, P.

Ludescher, Matt, jt. auth. see Marget, Richard.

Ludewig, Elke. Direkte und Indirekte Anthropogene Beeinflussung und Veraenderung der Ufervegetation der Saar. (Dissertationes Botanicae Ser.: Band 301). (GER., Illus.). 282p. 1999. 72.00 (*3-443-64213-6*, Pub. by Gebruder Borntraeger) Balogh.

Ludford, G., ed. Reacting Flows: Combustion & Chemical Reactors, 2 pts. LC 86-1088. (Lectures in Applied Mathematics: Vol. 24). 1048p. 1986. text 107.00 (*0-8218-1124-X*, LAM/24) Am Math.

— Reacting Flows: Combustion & Chemical Reactors, 2 pts., Pt. I. LC 86-1088. (Lectures in Applied Mathematics: Vol. 24). 512p. 1986. text 64.00 (*0-8218-1127-4*, LAM/24.1) Am Math.

— Reacting Flows: Combustion & Chemical Reactors, 2 pts., Pt. II. LC 86-1088. (Lectures in Applied Mathematics: Vol. 24). 536p. 1986. text 64.00 (*0-8218-1128-2*, LAM/24.2) Am Math.

Ludford, G. S., jt. auth. see Buckmaster, John D.

Ludgate, John, tr. see Boccaccio, Giovanni.

Ludgate, John W. Maximizing Psychotherapeutic Gains & Preventing Relapse in Emotionally Distressed Clients. LC 95-20029. (Practitioner's Resource Ser.). 81p. (Orig.). 1995. pap. 16.45 (*1-56887-014-0*, MPGBP, Prof Resc Pr) Pro Resource.

Ludgate, Katherine E. The Effect of Manual Guidance upon Maze Learning. (Psychology Monographs General & Applied: Vol. 33). 1972. reprint ed. 55.00 (*0-8115-1432-3*) Periodicals Srv.

Ludgate, Thomas B., ed. & intro. see Kitzler, Janice L.

***Ludi, Heidi & Ludi, Tony.** Movie Worlds: Production Design in Film. (ENG & GER., Illus.). 128p. 2000. 62.00 (*3-932565-13-4*) Edition A Menges.

***Ludi, Maria Alogna & Hull, Nancy.** Balance Your Act: A Book for Adults with Diabetes. large type ed. Hubbard, Karen, ed. (Illus.). 96p. 2000. pap. 8.95 (*0-939838-55-9*) Pritchett & Hull.

Ludi, Tony, jt. auth. see Ludi, Heidi.

Ludig, Sandra G. Between the Lines: Ladies & Letters at the Clark. (Illus.). 39p. 1982. pap. 2.00 (*0-931102-14-6*) S & F Clark Art.

Ludik, Jacques, jt. ed. see Stein, Dan J.

Ludin, H. P., ed. Electromyography, No. 5. LC 93-36498. (Handbook of Electroencephalography & Clinical Neurophysiology, Revised Ser.: Vol. 5). 732p. 1995. 298.25 (*0-444-81256-3*) Elsevier.

Ludin, Irwin S., jt. auth. see Kliem, Ralph L.

Ludington, Aileen. Dynamic Living. 208p. 1995. pap. 10.99 (*0-8280-0949-X*) Review & Herald.

— Feeling Fit. LC 97-29250. 238p. 1997. pap. 12.99 (*0-8280-1284-9*) Review & Herald.

Ludington, Aileen & Diehl, Hans. Dynamic Living Workbook. rev. ed. LC 95-7074. Orig. Title: Lifestyle Capsules. 112p. 1995. pap. 5.99 (*0-8280-0942-2*) Review & Herald.

Ludington, Townsend. John Dos Passos: A Twentieth-Century Odyssey. LC 98-16801. (Illus.). 568p. 1998. pap. 17.95 (*0-7867-0527-2*) Carroll & Graf.

— Marsden Hartley: The Biography of an American Artist. LC 98-29358. (Illus.). 325p. 1998. pap. text 21.00 (*0-8014-8580-0*) Cornell U Pr.

— Seeking the Spiritual: The Paintings of Marsden Hartley. LC 97-49813. (Illus.). 80p. 1998. text 25.00 (*0-8014-3553-6*) Cornell U Pr.

Ludington, Townsend, ed. The Fourteenth Chronicle: Letters & Diaries of John Dos Passos. LC 72-94006. (Illus.). 662p. 1973. 15.00 (*0-87645-073-7*) Harvard Common Pr.

***Ludington, Townsend, ed.** A Modern Mosaic: Art & Modernism in the United States. (Illus.). 480p. 2000. 59.95 (*0-8078-2578-6*); pap. 29.95 (*0-8078-4891-3*) U of NC Pr.

Ludington, Townsend, ed. see Dos Passos, John.

Ludington, Townsend, ed. & intro. see Benet, Stephen Vincent.

Ludins, George H. Seamanship for New Skippers. (Illus.). 1980. pap. 5.95 (*0-916224-54-6*) Banyan Bks.

Ludium, David. The American Weather Book. (Illus.). 296p. 1989. reprint ed. pap. 20.00 (*0-933876-97-1*) Am Meteorological.

Ludke, Jill B., jt. auth. see Cresanta, Judy.

Ludkovskyy, G., ed. see Metallurgical Society of AIME Staff.

Ludlam, jt. auth. see Wilson-Ludlum.

Ludlam, A. J. Horncastle & Woodhall Junction Railway. 56p. (C). 1985. 39.00 (*0-85361-326-5*) St Mut.

— Louth, Mablethorpe & Willoughby Loop. 64p. (C). 1985. 39.00 (*0-85361-354-0*) St Mut.

— Spilsby to Firsby Railway. 52p. (C). 1985. 39.00 (*0-85361-310-9*) St Mut.

Ludlam, A. J. & Herbert, W. B. Louth to Bardney Branch. 52p. (C). 1985. 39.00 (*0-85361-348-6*) St Mut.

Ludlam, Christopher A., ed. Clinical Haematology. (Illus.). 496p. 1990. pap. text 59.00 (*0-443-03834-1*) Church.

Ludlam, F. H. Clouds & Storms: The Behavior & Effect of Water in the Atmosphere. LC 77-22281. (Illus.). 1980. 65.00 (*0-271-00515-7*) Pa St U Pr.

***Ludlam, Harry.** My Quest for Bram Stoker. 110p. 2000. pap. 15.00 (*1-888893-02-8*) Dracula Pr.

Ludlam, Harry, jt. auth. see Lund, Paul.

Ludlam, James E. Health Policy--The Hard Way: An Anecdotal Personal History by One of the California Players. LC 98-14909. (Illus.). 300p. 1998. pap. 16.95 (*0-932727-94-8*) Hope Pub Hse.

Ludlam, Mae R., ed. see Goode, John H.

***Ludlam, Steve & Smith, Martin J.** New Labour in Government. LC 00-42245. 2000. write for info. (*0-312-23743-X*) St Martin.

Ludlow, Barbara L., et al. Distance Education & Tomorrow's Schools. (Fastback Ser.: No. 439). 55p. 1998. pap. 3.00 (*0-87367-639-4*, FB439) Phi Delta Kappa.

Ludlow, Charles. Brisbane's River. 64p. (C). 1990. 100.00 (*0-86439-016-5*, Pub. by Boolarong Pubns) St Mut.

Ludlow, Daniel H. A Companion to Your Study of the Book of Mormon. LC 76-27139. 396p. 1976. 23.95 (*0-87747-610-1*) Deseret Bk.

An Asterisk (*) at the beginning of an entry indicates that the title is appearing for the first time.

— A Companion to Your Study of the Doctrine & Covenants. LC 78-64752. 721p. 1978. pap. 24.95 (*1-57345-224-6*) Deseret Bk.
— Companion to Your Study of the New Testament: The Four Gospels. 454p. 1982. 19.95 (*0-87747-945-3*) Deseret Bk.
— A Companion to Your Study of the Old Testament. LC 80-28088. 437p. 1981. 15.95 (*0-87747-853-8*) Deseret Bk.
*Ludlow, Daniel H.** Selected Writing of Daniel H. Ludlow. LC 00-21966. (Gospel Scholars Ser.). 2000. write for info. (*1-57345-553-9*) Deseret Bk.
Ludlow, Daniel H., ed. The Church & Society: Selections from the Encyclopedia of Mormonism. LC 95-31445. (Orig.). 1995. pap. 18.95 (*0-87579-925-6*) Deseret Bk.
— Church History: Selections from the Encyclopedia of Mormonism. LC 94-44792. (Orig.). 1995. pap. 18.95 (*0-87579-924-8*) Deseret Bk.
— Jesus Christ & His Gospel: Selections from the Encyclopedia of Mormonism. LC 94-68130. xxxi, 525p. (Orig.). 1994. pap. 16.95 (*0-87579-922-1*) Deseret Bk.
— Priesthood & Church Organization: Selections from the Encyclopedia of Mormonism. LC 95-7691. (Orig.). 1995. pap. 18.95 (*0-87579-926-4*) Deseret Bk.
— Scriptures of the Church: Selections from the Encyclopedia of Mormonism. LC 94-24006. 768p. (Orig.). 1995. pap. 18.95 (*0-87579-923-X*) Deseret Bk.
*Ludlow, Daniel H., et al.** To All the World: The Book of Mormon Articles from the Encyclopedia of Mormonism. LC 99-58964. 2000. write for info. (*0-934893-47-0*) Res Press UT.
Ludlow, Edmund. The Memoirs of Edmund Ludlow, Lieutenant-General of the Horse in the Army of the Commonwealth of England, 1625-1672, 2 vols., Set. Firth, C. H., ed. LC 75-31098. (Illus.). reprint ed. 95.00 (*0-404-13520-X*) AMS Pr.
*Ludlow, Gaylon O.** Chahta Siah: Palpitations of a Choctaw Heart. 81p. 1999. pap. 12.95 (*0-9672133-3-9*) Akin Native Am.
Ludlow, Helen W., jt. auth. see Armstrong, Mary F.
Ludlow, James M. The Age of the Crusades. 1977. lib. bdg. 59.95 (*0-8490-1405-0*) Gordon Pr.
Ludlow, John M. Woman's Work in the Church. LC 75-33300. 1976. reprint ed. 30.00 (*0-89201-007-X*) Zenger Pub.
Ludlow, John W., ed. Protein Phosphatase Protocols. LC 98-15957. (Methods in Molecular Biology Ser.: Vol. 93). (Illus.). 336p. 1998. 79.50 (*0-89603-468-2*) Humana.
Ludlow, Larry H., et al. Objective Measurement: Theory into Practice, Vol. 3. Engelhard, George, Jr. & Wilson, Mark, eds. 471p. 1996. text 78.50 (*1-56750-182-6*) Ablx Pub.
Ludlow, Margaret. Temari: A Traditional Japanese Embroidery Technique. LC 99-215376. 132p. 1999. pap. 17.95 (*1-86108-080-8*, Pub. by Guild Master) Sterling.
*Ludlow, Morwenna.** Universal Salvation: Eschatology in the Thought of Gregory of Nyssa & Karl Rahner. (Oxford Theological Monographs). 280p. 2000. text 70.00 (*0-19-827022-4*) OUP.
Ludlow, N. Piers. Dealing with Britain: The Six & the First British Application to the EEC. (Studies in International Relations: Vol. 56). 300p. (C). 1997. text 64.95 (*0-521-59242-9*); pap. text 24.95 (*0-521-59536-3*) Cambridge U Pr.
Ludlow, Nicholas H. The Development Bank Business Market: What the MDBs Lend For, Why They Lend for It, & How Much They Lend, Including a Lending Scenario for the Year 2000. LC 93-71061. (Illus.). 460p. 1993. 383.00 (*0-943781-03-5*) Develop Bank.
— A Practical Guide to the Development Bank Business: How to Identify It, Market to It, & Win It; A Comprehensive Guide for Exporters of Goods & Services. LC 88-71941. (Illus.). 312p. 1988. pap. text 193.00 (*0-943781-00-0*) Develop Bank.
Ludlow, Nicholas H. & Pappas, Benjamin C. Trends in Development Bank Lending, 1995: A Professional Reference Guide, Including Projected Lending Figures to FY 1998. LC 94-71589. (Illus.). 358p. 1995. pap. 303.00 (*0-943781-08-6*) Develop Bank.
Ludlow, Nicholas H., et al. Financing Urban Transport - Sources & Techniques: North America, Vol. 1. (Illus.). 341p. (C). 1987. pap. 93.00 (*0-943781-04-3*) Develop Bank.
Ludlow, Nicholas H., jt. auth. see Kelleher, John J.
Ludlow, Noah M. Dramatic Life As I Found It. LC 66-16759. 1972. reprint ed. 30.95 (*0-405-08755-1*, Pub. by Blom Pubns) Ayer.
Ludlow, Patricia D. Dear Santa. LC 93-28618. (J). 1993. 13.99 (*0-85953-778-1*) Childs Play.
Ludlow, Peter. Europe & the Mediterranean. 272p. 1994. 56.00 (*1-85753-059-4*, Pub. by Brasseys) Brasseys.
— Semantics, Tense & Time: An Essay in The Metaphysics of Natural Language. LC 99-13958. (Illus.). 264p. 1999. 42.50 (*0-262-12219-7*, Bradford Bks) MIT Pr.
Ludlow, Peter, ed. High Noon on the Electronic Frontier: Conceptual Issues in Cyberspace. LC 96-3987. (Illus.). 558p. 1996. pap. text 32.50 (*0-262-62103-7*, Bradford Bks) MIT Pr.
— Readings in the Philosophy of Language. LC 96-39198. 1096p. 1997. 77.00 (*0-262-12205-7*, Bradford Bks); pap. text 38.50 (*0-262-62114-2*, Bradford Bks) MIT Pr.
Ludlow, Peter & Gros, Daniel. Setting European Community Priorities. 154p. 1994. 25.00 (*0-08-041314-5*) Elsevier.
Ludlow, Peter & Martin, Norah, eds. Externalism & Self-Knowledge. LC 98-14147. (Lecture Notes Ser.: Vol. 85). 500p. (C). 1998. text 64.95 (*1-57586-107-0*); pap. text 25.95 (*1-57586-106-2*) CSLI.
Ludlow, Peter, jt. ed. see Beakley, Brian.
Ludlow, Peter, ed. see Centre for European Policy Studies Staff.
Ludlow, Rose B. Total Health & Food Power: Famous Recipes & a Plan for Health. LC 85-29594. (Illus.). 240p. (Orig.). 1986. pap. 7.95 (*0-88007-158-3*) Woodbridge Pr.
*Ludlow, Susie Nickens.** Carry Me Back: A Family & National History of Slavery & Freedom. Tennant, Roberta, ed. 288p. 2000. pap. 17.95 (*0-9679879-0-3*) Honocan.
Ludlow, Victor L. Isaiah: Prophet, Seer, & Poet. LC 82-1444. (Illus.). 578p. 1982. 24.95 (*0-87747-884-8*) Deseret Bk.
— Principles & Practices of the Restored Gospel. LC 92-29955. ix, 656p. 1992. 21.95 (*0-87579-649-4*) Deseret Bk.
— Unlocking the Old Testament. LC 81-68266. (Illus.). 239p. 1981. 11.95 (*0-87747-873-2*) Deseret Bk.
Ludlow, W. James. The Road to Wealth: How to Improve Your Investing, Saving & Spending Skills for Worry-Free Living & Retirement. LC 93-90503. 144p. (Orig.). 1994. pap. 16.95 (*0-9635781-0-3*) Applewood Pub.
Ludlow, William L. The Enigma of the Revelation. LC 98-90131. 1998. 14.95 (*0-533-12711-4*) Vantage.
— What It Means to Be a Christian. LC 85-73080. 1988. pap. 8.95 (*0-8158-0434-2*) Chris Mass.
Ludlum, Anne. Kate & Isabel. 1995. 3.50 (*0-87129-591-1*, K24) Dramatic Pub.
— Shame the Devil! An Audience with Fanny Kemble. 76p. 1998. pap. 5.60 (*0-87129-852-X*, SC5) Dramatic Pub.
Ludlum, Charles. Mystery of Irma Vep & Other Plays. LC 99-44196. 300p. 1999. pap. 16.95 (*1-55936-173-5*, Pub. by Theatre Comm) Consort Bk Sales.
Ludlum, David. The Audubon Society Field Guide to North American Weather. LC 91-52707. (Audubon Field Guide Ser.). (Illus.). 640p. 1991. 19.00 (*0-679-40851-7*) Knopf.
— The Nantucket Weather Book. Farlow, Lesley, ed. (Illus.). 195p. (Orig.). 1986. pap. text 17.95 (*0-9607340-4-X*) Nantucket Hist Assn.
Ludlum, David M. Early American Tornados, 1586-1870. (History of American Weather-Historical Monograph Ser.). (Illus.). 219p. 1970. 20.00 (*0-933876-32-7*) Am Meteorological.
— Early American Winters, 1604-1820: The History of American Weather. (History of American Weather - Historical Monograph Ser.). (Illus.). 283p. 1966. 20.00 (*0-933876-23-8*) Am Meteorological.
— Early American Winters, 1821-1870, Vol. II. (History of American Weather - Historical Monograph Ser.). (Illus.). 255p. 1968. 20.00 (*0-933876-24-6*) Am Meteorological.
— The Vermont Weather Book. 2nd rev. ed. LC 85-6223. (Illus.). 320p. 1996. pap. 18.95 (*0-934720-30-4*) VT Hist Soc.
Ludlum, James S. Security Report Ten: A Comprehensive Guide for Preventing & Detecting the Sexual Abuse of Our Youth. Costillo, Roger & Belita, Christopher, eds. 285p. 1998. pap. 29.95 (*0-9665882-0-7*) United Youth Security.
Ludlum, Robert. La Agenda de Lcaro. 1998. pap. 12.95 (*84-08-00022-5*) Planeta.
— The Apocalypse Watch. 768p. 1996. mass mkt. 7.99 (*0-553-56957-0*) Bantam.
— The Apocalypse Watch. large type ed. LC 95-23558. 1995. 28.95 (*1-56895-238-4*) Wheeler Pub.
— The Aquitaine Progression. 704p. 1997. mass mkt. 7.99 (*0-553-26256-4*) Bantam.
— The Bourne Identity. 544p. 1981. mass mkt. 7.99 (*0-553-26011-1*) Bantam.
— The Bourne Identity, Set. abr. ed. 1987. audio 18.00 (*0-553-45053-0*) BDD Aud Pub.
— The Bourne Supremacy. 656p. 1989. mass mkt. 7.99 (*0-553-26322-6*) Bantam.
— The Bourne Ultimatum. 672p. 1991. mass mkt. 7.99 (*0-553-28773-7*) Bantam.
— Carretera de Gandolfo. (SPA.). 1996. pap. 13.19 (*84-01-49221-1*) Lectorum Pubns.
— El Caso Burne. 1999. 14.95 (*84-01-49926-7*) Plaza.
— The Chancellor Manuscript. 448p. 1984. mass mkt. 7.99 (*0-553-26094-4*) Bantam.
Ludlum, Robert. The Cry of the Halidon. 448p. 1996. mass mkt. 7.99 (*0-553-57614-3*) Bantam.
Ludlum, Robert. The Cry of the Halidon. large type ed. LC 97-16199. (Wheeler Large Print Book Ser.). 1997. write for info. (*1-56895-445-X*) Wheeler Pub.
— The Gemini Contenders. 416p. 1989. mass mkt. 7.99 (*0-553-28209-3*) Bantam.
— The Holcroft Covenant. 512p. 1984. mass mkt. 7.50 (*0-553-26019-7*) Bantam.
— The Icarus Agenda. 688p. 1989. mass mkt. 7.99 (*0-553-27800-2*) Bantam.
— The Matarese Circle. 544p. 1983. mass mkt. 7.99 (*0-553-25899-0*) Bantam.
— Matarese Countdown. 576p. 1998. mass mkt. 7.99 (*0-553-57983-5*) Bantam.
— The Matarese Countdown. large type ed. LC 97-32902. 1997. pap. 27.95 (*0-7838-8353-6*, G K Hall Lrg Type) Mac Lib Ref.
*Ludlum, Robert.** The Matarese Countdown. large type ed. LC 97-32902. (Core Ser.). 794p. 1998. 29.95 (*0-7838-8352-8*, G K Hall & Co) Mac Lib Ref.
Ludlum, Robert. The Matlock Paper. 384p. 1989. mass mkt. 7.99 (*0-553-27960-2*) Bantam.
— El Mito de Bourne. 1998. pap. 12.95 (*84-08-00021-7*) Planeta.
— The Osterman Weekend. 336p. 1984. mass mkt. 7.99 (*0-553-26430-3*) Bantam.
— El Pacto de Holcroft. Orig. Title: Holcroft Covenant. 1999. 11.95 (*84-01-49929-1*) Plaza.
— The Parsifal Mosaic. 704p. 1983. mass mkt. 7.99 (*0-553-25270-4*) Bantam.
— La Progresion de Aquitania. 1998. pap. 9.95 (*84-08-00023-3*) Planeta.
*Ludlum, Robert.** The Prometheus Deception. 384p. 2000. 27.95 (*0-312-25346-X*) St Martin.
Ludlum, Robert. The Rhinemann Exchange. 448p. 1989. mass mkt. 7.50 (*0-553-28063-5*) Bantam.
— The Rhinemann Exchange. 464p. 1991. reprint ed. lib. bdg. 31.95 (*0-89966-778-3*) Buccaneer Bks.
— The Road to Gandolfo. 320p. 1992. mass mkt. 7.99 (*0-553-27109-1*) Bantam.
— The Road to Omaha. 608p. 1993. mass mkt. 7.50 (*0-553-56044-1*) Bantam.
— The Scarlatti Inheritance. 368p. 1982. mass mkt. 7.99 (*0-553-27146-6*) Bantam.
— The Scorpio Illusion. 672p. 1994. mass mkt. 7.99 (*0-553-56603-2*); mass mkt. 8.99 (*0-553-56838-8*) Bantam.
*Ludlum, Robert.** Title to Come. 2000. mass mkt. write for info. (*0-312-97305-5*) St Martin.
Ludlum, Robert. Trece En Zurich. 1999. 11.95 (*84-01-49925-9*) Plaza.
— Trevayne. 480p. 1989. mass mkt. 7.99 (*0-553-28179-8*) Bantam.
*Ludlum, Robert & Lynds, Gayle.** The Hades Factor. LC 00-25685. 448p. 2000. pap. 15.95 (*0-312-26437-2*, St Martin Griffin) St Martin.
— Robert Ludlum's the Hades Factor. large type ed. LC 00-41182. 2000. write for info. (*0-7862-2683-8*) Thorndike Pr.
Ludlum, Stuart D. They Turned the War Around at Coral Sea & Midway. 3rd rev. ed. (World War II Monograph: Vol. 308). (Illus.). 105p. 1997. 29.95 (*1-57638-085-8*, M308H); pap. 19.95 (*1-57638-016-5*, M308S) Merriam Pr.
Ludman. Physical Geology. 1992. lab manual ed. 67.50 (*0-697-14708-8*, WCB McGr Hill) McGrw-H Hghr Educ.
— Physical Geology. 1993. teacher ed., lab manual ed. 20.00 (*0-697-14707-X*, WCB McGr Hill) McGrw-H Hghr Educ.
Ludman, Allan. Laboratory Exercises in Physical Geology. 240p. (C). 1992. text. write for info. (*0-697-14706-1*, WCB McGr Hill) McGrw-H Hghr Educ.
*Ludman, Allan & West, David P.** Norumbega Fault System of the Northern Appalachians LC 99-22075. (Special Paper Ser.). 1999. write for info. (*0-8137-2331-0*) Geol Soc.
Ludman, Dianne M. Hugh Stubbins & His Associates: The First Fifty Years. LC 86-61773. (Illus.). 152p. (Orig.). 1986. pap. 20.00 (*0-9617416-1-9*) Stubbins Assocs.
— Hugh Stubbins & His Associates: The First Fifty Years. deluxe ed. LC 86-61773. (Illus.). 152p. (Orig.). 1986. write for info. (*0-9617416-0-0*) Stubbins Assocs.
Ludman-Exley, Sharon, jt. auth. see Krantz, Les.
Ludman, Harold. ABC of Otolaryngology. 3rd ed. (Illus.). 68p. 1993. pap. text 22.00 (*0-7279-0765-4*, Pub. by BMJ Pub) Login Brothers Bk Co.
— ABC of Otolaryngology. 4th ed. (Illus.). 57p. 1997. pap. text 29.00 (*0-7279-1205-4*, Pub. by BMJ Pub) Login Brothers Bk Co.
— Mawson's Diseases of the Ear. 5th ed. 688p. pap. text. write for info. (*0-7131-4580-3*, Pub. by E A) Routldge.
Ludman, Harold & Wright, Tony, eds. Diseases of the Ear. 6th ed. LC 97-26916. (Arnold Publication). (Illus.). 608p. 1998. text 149.50 (*0-340-56441-5*, Pub. by E A) OUP.
Ludman, Joan. Prints by Fairfield Porter: From the Lauris & Daniel J. Mason Collection. (Illus.). 8p. 1982. 10.00 (*0-685-70930-2*) Gal Assn NY.
Ludman, Joan, jt. auth. see Mason, Lauris.
Ludman, Mark D., jt. auth. see Wynbrandt, James.
Ludmer, Joyce P. Carlo Pedretti: A Bibliography of His Work on Leonardo Da Vinci & the Renaissance, 1944-1984. In Celebration of His Twenty Five Years at the University of California, Los Angeles. (Illus.). 144p. (Orig.). 1987. pap. write for info. (*0-9617550-0-8*) E Belt Lib.
*Ludmer, Larry.** Arizona Guide. 2nd ed. 2000. pap. 16.95 (*1-892975-25-4*) Open Rd Pub.
Ludmer, Larry. Colorado Guide. 360p. 1998. pap. 16.95 (*1-883323-86-X*) Open Rd Pub.
*Ludmer, Larry.** New Mexico Guide. 2nd ed. (Illus.). 336p. 1999. pap. 16.95 (*1-892975-11-4*) Open Rd Pub.
Ludmer, Larry. Utah Guide. 360p. 1999. pap. text 16.95 (*1-892975-07-6*) Open Rd Pub.
Ludmer, Larry H. Cruisng Alaska. 4th ed. (Illus.). 144p. 1998. pap. 11.95 (*1-55650-849-2*) Hunter NJ.
— The Great American Wilderness: Touring America's National Parks. 3rd rev. ed. (Illus.). 320p. 1999. pap. 15.95 (*1-55650-877-8*) Hunter NJ.
Ludmerer, Kenneth M. American Medical Education in the 20th Century. 352p. 1997. 22.95 (*0-465-00167-X*) Basic.
Ludmerer, Kenneth M. Genetics & American Society: A Historical Appraisal. LC 72-4227. 238p. reprint ed. pap. 73.80 (*0-8357-8143-7*, 203415300088) Bks Demand.
— Learning to Heal: The Development of American Medical Education. 359p. 1996. reprint ed. pap. text 16.95 (*0-8018-5258-7*) Johns Hopkins.
— Time to Heal: American Medical Education from the Turn of the Century to the Era of Managed Care. LC 98-55496. (Illus.). 544p. 1999. text 29.95 (*0-19-511837-5*) OUP.
Ludmila, Shtern. Okhota K Peremene Mest: Rasskazy o Puteshestviiakh. LC 98-10776. (RUS., Illus.). 208p. 1998. pap. 12.00 (*1-55779-106-6*) Hermitage Pubs.
Ludovici, A. Nietzsche & Art. LC 72-148824. (Studies in German Literature: No. 13). 1971. reprint ed. lib. bdg. 75.00 (*0-8383-1229-2*) M S G Haskell Hse.
Ludovici, A. M. The Secret of Laughter. 1972. 79.95 (*0-8490-1011-X*) Gordon Pr.
— Specious Origins of Liberalism. 1972. 59.95 (*0-8490-1106-X*) Gordon Pr.
— Who Is to Be Master of the World? an Introduction to the Philosophy of Friedrich Nietzsche. 1972. 99.95 (*0-8490-1295-3*) Gordon Pr.
Ludovici, A. M., tr. see Lichtenberger, Henri.
Ludovici, A. N., tr. see Nietzsche, Friedrich Wilhelm.
Ludovici, Anthony. The Sanctity of Private Property. 1977. lib. bdg. 59.95 (*0-8490-2566-4*) Gordon Pr.
Ludovici, Anthony M., tr. see Nietzsche, Friedrich Wilhelm.
Ludovici, Carl G. Gesammelte Werke: Abteilung: Ergaenzungsreihe, Vol. 1. (GER.). 73p. 1977. write for info. (*3-487-06377-8*) G Olms Pubs.
— Gesammelte Werke: Abteilung: Ergaenzungsreihe, Vol. 2. (Materialien und Dokumente Ser.). (GER.). 24p. 1976. write for info. (*3-487-06026-4*) G Olms Pubs.
— Gesammelte Werke: Abteilung: Ergaenzungsreihe, Vol. 4. (Materialien und Dokumente Ser.). (GER.). 27p. 1973. write for info. (*3-487-04750-0*) G Olms Pubs.
— Gesammelte Werke: Abteilung: Ergaenzungsreihe, Vol. 5. 2nd ed. (Materialien und Dokumente Ser.). (GER.). 6p. 1983. write for info. (*3-487-04816-7*) G Olms Pubs.
— Gesammelte Werke: Abteilung: Ergaenzungsreihe, Vol. 7. (Materialien und Dokumente Ser.). (GER.). 558p. 1978. write for info. (*3-487-06034-5*) G Olms Pubs.
Ludovici, Carl G. Neueste Merckwurdigkeiten der Leibnitz-Wolffischen Weltweisheit. (GER.). 1973. reprint ed. write for info. (*3-487-04749-7*) G Olms Pubs.
Ludovici, Carl G., et al. Gesammelte Werke Bd. 6: Abteilung: Ergaenzungsreihe. (Materialien und Dokumente Ser.). (GER.). 236p. 1980. reprint ed. write for info. (*3-487-06969-5*) G Olms Pubs.
Ludowyk, E. F. The Story of Ceylon. 1986. reprint ed. 28.50 (*81-7013-020-4*, Pub. by Navarang) S Asia.
Ludowyk, Evelyn F. Understanding Shakespeare. LC 62-6756. 284p. reprint ed. pap. 81.00 (*0-608-12061-8*, 2024489) Bks Demand.
Luds, Peter, jt. auth. see Apel, Max.
Ludtka, John. The Tradition Lives: A 75 Year History of the Ellensburg Rodeo. (Illus.). 192p. 1997. write for info. (*0-9658735-0-1*) Ellensburg.
Ludtke & Horst. Ernst Marcus Als Kantinterpret. (Philosophische Texte und Studien: Vol. 23). (GER.). x, 206p. 1989. write for info. (*3-487-09225-5*) G Olms Pubs.
Ludtke, Alf, ed. The History of Everyday Life: Reconstructing Historical Experiences & Ways of Life. Templer, William, tr. from GER. LC 94-35512.Tr. of Alltagsgeschichte. 336p. 1995. text 49.50 (*0-691-05693-5*, Pub. by Princeton U Pr) Cal Prin Full Svc.
Ludtke, David A., jt. auth. see Kelley, Donald H.
*Ludtke, G., et al.** Geologie de la Region Haute Comoe du Nord (Geology of the Haute Comoe North Area (Ivory Coast) (FRE & ENG., Illus.). 178p. 1999. 45.00 (*3-510-95848-9*, Pub. by E Schweizerbartsche) Balogh.
Ludtke, Horst. Ernst Marcus Als Kantinterpret. (Philosophische Texte und Studien: Vol. 23). (GER.). x, 206p. 1989. write for info. (*0-614-22124-2*) G Olms Pubs.
Ludtke, Jean E. Atlantic Peeks: An Ethnographic Guide to the Portuguese-Speaking Islands. LC 87-70196. 1989. 24.95 (*0-8158-0441-5*) Chris Mass.
Ludtke, Melissa. On Our Own: Unmarried Motherhood in America. LC 96-52233. 496p. 1997. 25.95 (*0-679-42414-8*) Random.
— On Our Own: Unmarried Motherhood in America. LC 98-38033. 465p. 1999. pap. 16.95 (*0-520-21830-2*, Pub. by U CA Pr) Cal Prin Full Svc.
Luduena, Richard F. Learning. 344p. 1995. pap. 49.95 (*0-471-01887-2*) Wiley.
— Learning More Biochemistry: 100 Case-Oriented Problems. LC 96-46129. 303p. 1997. pap. 49.95 (*0-471-17054-2*) Wiley.
Ludviasen, Karl. Stirling Moss: A Pictorial Tribute. (Illus.). 192p. 1997. 49.95 (*1-85260-564-2*) Haynes Manuals.
*Ludvig, Johan Heiberg.** Danish Plays. 96p. 1999. pap. 13.95 (*1-84002-060-1*, Pub. by Theatre Comm) Consort Bk Sales.
Ludvigsen, Carol, jt. auth. see Roberts, Kathleen.
Ludvigsen, Carole & Roberts, Kathleen. Health Care Policies & Europe: The Implications for Practice. LC 96-13094. 288p. 1997. pap. text 42.00 (*0-7506-2485-X*) Buttrwrth-Heinemann.
*Ludvigsen, Karl.** Alberto Ascari. (Illus.). 208p. 2000. 49.95 (*1-85960-680-6*, 130755AE, Pub. by Haynes Manuals) Motorbooks Intl.
— Battle for the Beetle. LC 99-58859. (Illus.). 440p. 2000. 39.95 (*0-8376-0071-5*, GVBB) Bentley Pubs.
— Classic Grand Prix Cars. (Illus.). 224p. 2000. 29.95 (*0-7509-2189-7*) Sutton Publng.
— Corvette: The Experimental Cars. LC 99-76046. (Illus.). 128p. 2000. pap. 19.95 (*1-58388-017-8*, 129952AE, Pub. by Iconografix) Motorbooks Intl.
Ludvigsen, Karl. Creating the Customer-Driven Car Company. 208p. 1996. 50.00 (*0-412-73760-4*) Chapman & Hall.
— Creating the Customer Driven Car Company. 175p. 1996. 39.00 (*1-56091-851-9*, R-170) Soc Auto Engineers.
*Ludvigsen, Karl.** Dan Gurney: The Ultimate Motor Racer. (Illus.). 208p. 2000. 39.95 (*1-85960-655-5*, 130026AE, Pub. by Haynes Manuals) Motorbooks Intl.
— Indy Cars of the 1950s. LC 99-76047. (Illus.). 128p. 2000. pap. 19.95 (*1-58388-018-6*, 129953AE, Pub. by Iconografix) Motorbooks Intl.
— Juan Manuel Fangio: Motor Racing's Grand Master. (Illus.). 208p. 1999. 49.95 (*1-85960-625-3*, 129514AE, Pub. by Haynes Manuals) Motorbooks Intl.
Ludvigsen, Karl E. Jackie Stewart. LC 98-72321. 1998. 49.95 (*1-85960-436-6*) J H Haynes & Co.

L

L

Ludvigsen, Malcolm. General Relativity: A Geometric Approach. LC 98-37546. (Illus.). 256p. (C). 1999. text 74.95 (*0-521-63019-3*); pap. text 27.95 (*0-521-63976-X*) Cambridge U Pr.

Ludvigsen, Rolf. Fossils of Ontario: The Trilobites. (Illus.). 96p. 16.00 (*0-88854-221-6*) Brill Academic Pubs.

Ludvigsen, Rolf, ed. Life in Stone: A Natural History of British Columbia's Fossils. LC 97-121468. (Illus.). 320p. 1996. 65.00 (*0-7748-0577-3*) U of Wash Pr.

— Life in Stone: A Natural History of British Columbia's Fossils. (Illus.). 320p. 1997. pap. 27.95 (*0-7748-0578-1*) U of Wash Pr.

Ludvigson, Susan. Everything Winged Must Be Dreaming. Poems. LC 93-10738. 64p. 1993. pap. 11.95 (*0-8071-1837-0*) La State U Pr.

— Northern Lights: Poems. fac. ed. LC 81-6039. 79p. 1981. reprint ed. pap. 30.00 (*0-7837-7805-8*, 204756100007) Bks Demand.

***Ludvigson, Susan.** Sweet Confluence: New & Selected Poems. 200p. 2000. 34.95 (*0-8071-2619-5*); pap. 18.95 (*0-8071-2620-9*) La State U Pr.

Ludvigson, Susan. The Swimmer. Poems. LC 83-25593. 53p. 1984. 15.95 (*0-8071-1155-4*) La State U Pr.

— Trinity. LC 96-9573. 376p. 1996. pap. 9.95 (*0-8071-2116-9*); text 16.95 (*0-8071-2115-0*) La State U Pr.

Ludvik, Catherine. Hanuman: In the Ramayana of Valmiki & the Ramacaritamanasa of Tulasi Dasa. (C). 1994. text 14.00 (*81-208-1122-4*, Pub. by Motilal Bnarsidass) S Asia.

Ludvik, M. & Mohyla, O. Czechoslovakia-Prague Guide. (Illus.). 282p. (C). 1989. pap. 100.00 (*0-569-09232-9*, Pub. by Collets) St Mut.

Ludwich, A., ed. see Homer.

Ludwich, Arthur. Aristarchs Homerische Textkritik, 2 vols., Set. viii, 1409p. 1971. reprint ed. write for info. (*3-487-04082-4*) G Olms Pubs.

Ludwich, Arthur, ed. Scholia in Homeri Odysseae A 1-309. iv, 120p. 1966. reprint ed. write for info. (*0-318-71024-2*) G Olms Pubs.

Ludwickson, John, jt. auth. see O'Shea, John M.

Ludwig. Ultrasonics for Engineering NDE. (Engineering NDE Ser.). (C). (gr. 13). 1997. text. write for info. (*0-412-46310-5*) Chapman & Hall.

Ludwig, Allan I. Graven Images: New England Stonecarving & Its Symbols, 1650-1815. LC 66-14665. (Illus.). 514p. reprint ed. pap. 146.50 (*0-608-18769-0*, 2029783) Bks Demand.

— Graven Images: New England Stonecarving & Its Symbols, 1650-1815. 2nd ed. LC 99-43590. (Illus.). 514p. 1999. reprint ed. pap. 29.95 (*0-8195-6040-5*, Wesleyan Univ Pr) U Pr of New Eng.

Ludwig, Anke. Entwurf Eines Oekonomischokologischen Rechnungswesens: Integrierte Datenerfassung Und Datenverarbeitung Okonomisch Und Okologisch Relevanter Daten. (Illus.). XX, 232p. 1998. 48.95 (*3-631-34313-2*) P Lang Pubng.

Ludwig, Armin K., et al. Radial Freeways & the Growth of Office Space in Central Cities. 417p. (Orig.). 1977. pap. 25.00 (*1-55719-008-9*) U NE CPAR.

Ludwig, Arnold M. How Do We Know Who We Are? The Biography of the Self. LC 96-23944. (Illus.). 304p. 1997. 27.50 (*0-19-509573-1*) OUP.

— The Price of Greatness: Resolving the Creativity & Madness Controversy. LC 94-44905. 310p. 1995. lib. bdg. 38.95 (*0-89862-839-3*) Guilford Pubns.

— The Price of Greatness: Resolving the Creativity & Madness Controversy. LC 94-44905. 310p. 1996. pap. text 18.95 (*1-57230-117-1*) Guilford Pubns.

— Understanding the Alcoholic's Mind: The Nature of Craving & How to Control It. (Illus.). 208p. 1989. reprint ed. pap. 13.95 (*0-19-505918-2*) OUP.

Ludwig, Art. Builder's Greywater Guide: Installation of Greywater Systems in New Construction & Remodeling; a Supplement to the Book "Create an Oasis with Greywater" rev. ed. 49p. 1999. pap. 14.95 (*0-9643433-2-0*) Oasis Design.

— Create an Oasis with Greywater: Your Complete Guide to Choosing, Building & Using Graywater Systems. 4th rev. ed. (Illus.). 51p. 2000. pap. 14.95 (*0-9643433-0-4*) Oasis Design.

Ludwig, Arwin K., et al. The Impact of Rural Nebraska Industrial Development on the Migration of Rural Youth. 150p. (Orig.). 1978. pap. 9.00 (*1-55719-007-0*) U NE CPAR.

Ludwig, Barbara, jt. auth. see Mathew, Paul.

Ludwig-Becker, Marsha. Electronic Systems Quality Management Handbook. LC 97-20755. (Illus.). 736p. 1997. 89.50 (*0-07-039055-X*) McGraw.

Ludwig, Charles. At Pentecost. 1992. pap. 2.99 (*0-87162-603-9*, D8151) Warner Pr.

— At the Cross. 1991. pap. 2.99 (*0-87162-596-2*, D1379) Warner Pr.

— At the Tomb. 1991. per. 2.99 (*0-87162-514-8*, D8150) Warner Pr.

— A Foot in Two Cultures. 1992. 2.99 (*0-87162-620-9*, D8152) Warner Pr.

— George Frideric Handel: Composer of Messiah. (Sower Ser.). (Illus.). 186p. (J). (gr. 5-9). 1987. pap. 7.99 (*0-88062-048-X*) Mott Media.

— Jason Lee: Winner of the Northwest. (Sower Ser.). (Illus.). 170p. (YA). (gr. 5-9). 1992. pap. 7.99 (*0-88062-161-3*) Mott Media.

— Michael Faraday, Father of Electronics. LC 78-15028. 224p. (YA). (gr. 7-10). 1988. ring bd. 9.99 (*0-8361-3479-6*) Herald Pr.

— Queen of the Reformation. LC 86-11754. 224p. 1986. pap. 7.99 (*0-87123-652-4*) Bethany Hse.

***Ludwig, Charles.** Rogue Elephant & Man-Eaters Don't Laugh. 164p. (YA). (gr. 5-8). 2000. reprint ed. pap. 7.95 (*0-9673806-1-8*) Kings Bkshelf.

Ludwig, Charles. Spinning Shoes. 1989. pap. 2.99 (*0-87162-582-2*, D7225) Warner Pr.

— Stonewall Jackson: Loved in the South, Admired in the North. (Sower Ser.). (Illus.). 177p. (YA). (gr. 5-9). 1989. pap. 7.99 (*0-88062-157-5*) Mott Media.

— Susanna Wesley: Mother of John & Charles. LC 84-60314. (Sower Ser.). (Illus.). 195p. (J). (gr. 5-9). 1984. pap. 7.99 (*0-88062-110-9*) Mott Media.

— The Wright Brothers: They Gave Us Wings. (Sower Ser.). (Illus.). 192p. (J). (gr. 5-9). 1985. pap. 7.99 (*0-88062-141-9*) Mott Media.

Ludwig, Christa. In My Own Voice: Memoirs. Domeraski, Regina, tr. from GER. LC 99-43233. (Illus.). 306p. 1999. 30.00 (*0-87910-281-0*) Limelight Edns.

Ludwig, Christa & Csobadi, Peter. Christa Ludwig: And I So Wanted to Be a Prima Donna. Koch, John B., tr. from GER. (Great Voices Ser.: Vol. 8).Tr. of Christa Ludwig: Und Ich Ware So Gern Prima Donna. (Illus.). 360p. 1997. 38.00 incl. audio compact disk (*1-880909-59-6*) Baskerville.

Ludwig, Claudia. Sonderformen Byzantinischer Hagiographie und Ihr Literarisches Vorbild: Untersuchungen zu den Viten des Asop, des Philaretos, des Symeon Salos und des Andreas Salos. (Berliner Byzantinistische Studien: Bd. 3). (GER.). xxxii, 408p. 1997. 76.95 (*3-631-48528-X*) P Lang Pubng.

Ludwig, Cordula. Korruption und Nationalsozialismus in Berlin, 1924-1934. (Geschichtliche Grundlagen der Politik Ser.: Band 1). (GER., Illus.). XV, 417p. 1998. pap. 56.95 (*3-631-32961-X*) P Lang Pubng.

Ludwig, Coy. Maxfield Parrish. LC 73-5691. (Illus.). 224p. 1993. reprint ed. 39.95 (*0-88740-527-4*) Schiffer.

Ludwig, D. Stochastic Population Theories. (Lecture Notes in Biomathematics Ser.: Vol. 3). 1978. reprint ed. pap. 22.00 (*0-387-07010-9*) Spr-Verlag.

Ludwig, Dale. Blood Secrets. 304p. 1993. mass mkt. 4.50 (*1-55817-695-0*, Pinncle Kensgtn) Kensgtn Pub Corp.

Ludwig, David. Test Yourself College Algebra. LC 98-13196. (Test Yourself Ser.). (Illus.). 192p. 1997. pap. 12.95 (*0-8442-2385-9*, 23859) NTC Contemp Pub Co.

Ludwig, David J. Renewing the Family Spirit. 149p. 1989. pap. 7.99 (*0-570-04527-4*, 12-3134) Concordia.

***Ludwig, David J.** Social Work & the Family Unit. LC 00-40845. 2000. write for info. (*0-7890-1197-2*) Haworth Pr.

Ludwig, Dean C., ed. Business & Society in a Changing World Order. LC 93-18882. 312p. 1993. text 99.95 (*0-7734-9267-4*) E Mellen.

Ludwig, Dean C. & Paul, Karen, eds. Contemporary Issues in the Business Environment. LC 92-16202. 264p. 1992. lib. bdg. 89.95 (*0-7734-9543-6*) E Mellen.

Ludwig, Delton, ed. see Goff, Bruce.

Ludwig, Dorene. But It Was Just a Joke ... ! Theater Scenes & Monologues for Eliminating Sexual Harassment: A Performance Manual & Workshop Guide. 170p. 1991. student ed. 17.50 (*0-89215-170-6*) U Cal LA Indus Rel.

Ludwig, Emil. Cleopatra - Story of a Queen. (African Studies). 221p. reprint ed. 25.00 (*0-938818-92-9*) ECA Assoc.

— Defender of Democracy: Masaryk of Czechoslovakia. LC 70-135814. (Eastern Europe Collection). 1971. reprint ed. 20.95 (*0-405-02756-7*) Ayer.

— The Germans: Double History of a Nation. LC 78-63688. (Studies in Fascism: Ideology & Practice). (Illus.). 560p. reprint ed. 45.00 (*0-404-16951-1*) AMS Pr.

***Ludwig, Emil.** Napoleon. 2000. per. 69.90 (*0-671-78259-2*, Pocket Books) PB.

Ludwig, Emil. Nine Etched from Life. LC 70-90658. (Essay Index Reprint Ser.). 1977. 26.95 (*0-8369-1225-X*) Ayer.

— Of Life & Love. LC 72-128273. (Essay Index Reprint Ser.). 1977. 20.95 (*0-8369-1984-X*) Ayer.

— Three Portraits: Hitler, Mussolini, Stalin. LC 78-63689. (Studies in Fascism: Ideology & Practice). 128p. reprint ed. 37.50 (*0-404-16905-8*) AMS Pr.

— Wilhelm Hohenzollern: The Last of the Kaisers. LC 74-100815. (Illus.). reprint ed. 31.25 (*0-404-04067-5*) AMS Pr.

Ludwig, Ernest. The Visit of Teshoo Lama to Peking. LC 78-70096. reprint ed. 18.50 (*0-404-17345-4*) AMS Pr.

Ludwig, Ernest E. Applied Process Design for Chemical & Petrochemical Plants, Vol. 1. 3rd ed. 480p. 1995. 150.00 (*0-88415-025-9*, 5025) Gulf Pub.

— Applied Process Design for Chemical & Petrochemical Plants, Vol. 2. 2nd ed. LC 64-18181. (Illus.). 318p. 1983. reprint ed. pap. 98.60 (*0-608-07551-5*, 204914200002) Bks Demand.

— Applied Process Design for Chemical & Petrochemical Plants, Vol. 2. 3rd ed. 320p. 1997. 150.00 (*0-88415-101-8*, 5101) Gulf Pub.

— Applied Process Design for Chemical & Petrochemical Plants, 3 vols., Vol. 3. 2nd ed. LC 76-40867. 506p. 1983. 95.00 (*0-87201-754-0*, 1754) Gulf Pub.

— Applied Process Design for Chemical & Petrochemical Plants Vol. 1. 2nd ed. LC 76-40867. (Illus.). 379p. 1977. pap. 117.50 (*0-7837-8352-3*, 204914200001) Bks Demand.

— Applied Project Engineering & Management. 2nd ed. LC 87-38320. 582p. 1988. 89.00 (*0-87201-045-7*) Gulf Pub.

— Applied Project Management for the Process Industries. LC 72-93694. (Illus.). 381p. reprint ed. pap. 118.20 (*0-8357-5687-4*, 205187200013) Bks Demand.

Ludwig, Frank, jt. ed. see McHardy, John.

Ludwig, Fredrich. Repertorium Organorum Recentioris et Motetorum Vetustissimi Stili, Band I, 2: Handschiften in Mensuralnotation. (Wissenschaftliche Abhandlungen-Musicological Studies: Vol. 26). (GER.). 350p. 1979. lib. bdg. 134.00 (*0-912024-37-2*) Inst Mediaeval Mus.

***Ludwig, Frieder.** Church & State in Tanzania. (Studies of Religion in Africa). (Illus.). 224p. 1999. 84.00 (*90-04-11506-4*) Brill Academic Pubs.

Ludwig, Frieder. Kirche Im Kolonialen Kontext: Anglikanische Missionare und Afrikanische Propheten Im Sudostlichen Nigeria, 1879-1918. (Studien zur Interkulturellen Geschichte des Christentums, 0170-9240, Studies in the Intercultural History of Christianity: Bd. 80). (GER.). 405p. 1992. 60.80 (*3-631-44362-5*) P Lang Pubng.

Ludwig, Friedrich. Repertorium Organorum Recentioris et Motetorum Vetustissimi Stili, Katalog. Dittmer, Luther, ed. (Wissenschaftliche Abhandlungen-Musicological Studies: Vol. 17). (GER.). 128p. 1971. lib. bdg. 54.00 (*0-912024-87-9*) Inst Mediaeval Mus.

Ludwig, G. An Axiomatic Basis for Quantum Mechanics, Vol. 1. (Illus.). 240p. 1985. 99.95 (*0-387-13773-4*) Spr-Verlag.

— Foundations of Quantum Mechanics I. (Texts & Monographs in Physics). (Illus.). 426p. 1983. 99.95 (*0-387-11683-4*) Spr-Verlag.

— Foundations of Quantum Mechanics II. Hein, C., tr. from GER. (Texts & Monographs in Physics). (Illus.). 430p. 1985. 149.95 (*0-387-13009-8*) Spr-Verlag.

— Wave Mechanics. 1968. 106.00 (*0-08-012302-3*, Pub. by Pergamon Repr) Franklin.

Ludwig, G., jt. ed. see Weidner, W.

***Ludwig, Garth D.** Order Restored: A Biblical Interpretation of Health, Medicine & Healing. LC 99-21264. 272p. 1999. pap. 19.95 (*0-570-04272-0*) Concordia.

Ludwig, Gerd. Sit! Stay! Train Your Dog the Easy Way. Bye, Eric A., tr. from GER. LC 98-4267. (Barron's Complete Pet Owner's Manuals). (Illus.). 64p. 1998. pap. 6.95 (*0-7641-0663-5*) Barron.

Ludwig, Gerd & Rice, Dan. Fun & Games with Your Dog. LC 96-19484. (Illus.). 72p. 1996. pap. 6.95 (*0-8120-9721-1*) Barron.

Ludwig, Gerd & Steimer, Christine. Bernese & Other Mountain Dogs: Bernese, Greater Swiss, Appenzellers, & Entlebuchers: Everything about Purchase, Care, Nutrition, Breeding, Behavior, & Training. Crawford, Elizabeth D., tr. from GER. LC 94-49012. (Complete Pet Owner's Manual Ser.). (Illus.). 1995. pap. 6.95 (*0-8120-9135-3*) Barron.

***Ludwig, Glenn E.** Changing a Paradigm or Two: Gospel Sermons for Sundays after Pentecost (First Third), Cycle C. LC 00-35800. 70p. 2000. pap. 7.95 (*0-7880-1734-9*); disk 7.95 (*0-7880-1735-7*) CSS OH.

Ludwig, Glenn E. Walking to, Walking with, Walking Through: Sermons for Lent, Holy Week, & Easter - Gospel. LC 93-51081. (Orig.). 1994. pap. 10.95 (*0-7880-0005-5*) CSS OH.

Ludwig, Glenn E. & Smothers, Rodney T. Homiletic Meditations, Vol. 2: Lent Through Ascension of Our Lord, First Reading & Gospel, Cycle C, Pt. C. LC 94-207. (Orig.). 1994. pap. 17.25 (*0-7880-0055-1*) CSS OH.

***Ludwig, Gregory.** A Transient: A Novel. iv, 136p. 1999. spiral bd. 15.00 (*0-9674300-0-3*) Bootstrap Edit Ser.

***Ludwig, H., ed.** Advances in High Pressure Bioscience & Biotechnology: Proceedings of the International Conference on High Pressure Bioscience & Biotechnology, Heidelberg, August 30-September 3, 1998. LC 99-28992. 570p. 1999. 219.00 (*3-540-65869-6*) Spr-Verlag.

Ludwig, Herbert R., jt. auth. see Leitch, Jay A.

Ludwig, Irene, ed. see Weiss, Diane S., et al.

Ludwig, J. Liver Biopsy Diagnoses & Reports. (Illus.). x, 158p. 1984. 50.50 (*3-8055-3841-3*) S Karger.

Ludwig, J., et al. Gallium Arsenide & Related Compounds: Proceeding of the 3rd International Workshop. 300p. 1996. text 84.00 (*981-02-2393-5*) World Scientific Pub.

— Landscape Ecology, Function & Management: Principles from Australia's Rangelands. (Illus.). 162p. 1997. pap. 59.95 (*0-643-05797-8*, Pub. by CSIRO) Accents Pubns.

Ludwig, Jackie. Everything under the Moon. (Illus.). 60p. 1998. pap. 10.50 (*1-56770-421-2*) S Scheewe Pubns.

Ludwig, Jean, jt. auth. see Leptin, Horst.

Ludwig, Jeanne. My Little Angel Is Watching over Me. (Illus.). 24p. (J). (gr. 1-3). 1996. 9.95 (*1-56550-060-1*) Vis Bks Intl.

Ludwig, Jens, jt. auth. see Cook, Philip J.

***Ludwig, Jim, ed.** The Climax Mine: An Old Man Remembers the Way It Was. (Illus.). 146p. 2000. pap. 17.95 (*0-9679419-0-3*) Pleasant Ave.

Ludwig, Johann. Handbuch der Buecherkunde Fuer die Aeltere Medizin. fac. ed. (GER.). 456p. 1956. reprint ed. 30.00 (*3-201-00001-9*, Pub. by Akademische Druck-und) Balogh.

Ludwig, John A. & Reynolds, James F. Statistical Ecology: A Primer on Methods & Computing. LC 87-26348. 368p. 1988. 110.00 (*0-471-83235-9*) Wiley.

Ludwig, Jurgen. Practical Liver Biopsy Interpretation: A Manual of Diagnostic Tables. 248p. 1992. 75.00 (*0-89189-347-4*) Am Soc Clinical.

Ludwig, Jurgen & Batts, Kenneth P. Practical Liver Biopsy Interpretation: Diagnostic Algorithms. 2nd ed. LC 98-9870. 1998. 105.00 (*0-89189-431-4*) Am Soc Clinical.

Ludwig, Jurgen & Ishak, Kamal G., eds. Diseases of the Liver & Bile Ducts: Proceedings of the Fifty Fourth Annual Anatomic Pathology Slide Seminar of the ASCP. LC 89-17874. 133p. 1989. 35.00 (*0-89189-294-X*, D50-1-055-00) Am Soc Clinical.

Ludwig, K. S. & Hartels, H., eds. Progress in Comparative Placentology. (Illus.). 1973. 35.00 (*3-8055-1365-8*) S Karger.

Ludwig, Katherine, ed. see Andrews, Peter.

Ludwig, Ken. Lend Me a Tenor: A Comedy. LC 87-209454. ii, 81p. 1986. write for info. (*0-573-01640-2*) S French Trade.

Ludwig, Ken. Postmortem. LC 91-144218. 131p. 1989. write for info. (*0-573-69133-9*) S French Trade.

Ludwig, Knoll. Lexikon der Praktischen Psychologie. (GER.). 488p. 1993. 29.95 (*0-7859-8543-3*, 3893501657) Fr & Eur.

Ludwig, Larry L. Battle at K-H Butte: Apache Outbreak, 1881 Arizona Territory. 90p. 1993. 16.95 (*0-87026-085-5*) Westernlore.

Ludwig, Lother & Fietz, Hans-Werner. Poetry in the British Isles: Non-Metropolitan Perspectives. 288p. pap. 27.95 (*0-7083-1266-7*, Pub. by Univ Wales Pr) Paul & Co Pubs.

Ludwig, Luckii. Rites of Passage. 261p. 1997. pap. 14.95 (*0-9661139-0-X*) ForeReel Pubns.

Ludwig, Lyndell. The Little White Dragon. (Illus.). 23p. (YA). (gr. 5 up). 1989. pap. 4.95 (*0-9621782-0-9*) Star Dust Bks.

— The Shoemaker's Gift. LC 82-73196. (Illus.). 36p. (J). (ps-1). 1983. pap. 4.95 (*0-916870-53-7*) Star Dust Bks.

— Ts'ao Chung Weighs an Elephant. LC 82-73197. (Illus.). 48p. (Orig.). (J). (ps-1). 1983. pap. 4.95 (*0-916870-52-9*) Star Dust Bks.

Ludwig, M., jt. auth. see Kopp, H.

Ludwig, Mark. The Giant Black Book of Computer Viruses. 2nd ed. (Illus.). 464p. 1998. pap. 39.95 incl. disk (*0-929408-23-3*) Amer Eagle Pubns Inc.

Ludwig, Mark A. Computer Viruses, Artificial Life & Evolution. 384p. 1993. pap. 26.95 (*0-929408-07-1*) Amer Eagle Pubns Inc.

— The Third Paradigm: God & Government in the 21st Century. (Illus.). 304p. (Orig.). 1997. pap. 14.95 (*0-929408-18-7*) Amer Eagle Pubns Inc.

Ludwig, Martina. Wort Als Gesetz: Eine Untersuchung Zum Verstandnis von "Wort" und "Gesetz" in Israelitsch-Fruhjudischen und Neutestamenthlichen Schriften. (Europaische Hochschulschriften Ser.: Reihe 23, Bd. 502). (GER., Illus.). 217p. 1994. 37.95 (*3-631-46437-1*) P Lang Pubng.

Ludwig, Mary S. Accounts Payable: A Guide to Running an Efficient Department. LC 98-28232. 366p. 1998. 110.00 (*0-471-29857-3*) Wiley.

— Understanding Interest Rate Swaps. LC 92-39058. 320p. 1992. 49.95 (*0-07-039020-7*) McGraw.

Ludwig-Mayerhofer, Wolfgang, jt. ed. see Albrecht, Guenter.

Ludwig, Nancy. Vegetable Garden Journal. (Illus.). 1999. write for info. (*1-893296-19-9*) Meadowsweet Kit.

Ludwig, Nancy, ed. Adventures in Grilling: A Journal. (Illus.). 50p. 1998. write for info. (*1-893296-04-0*) Meadowsweet Kit.

— Coffee Journal. (Illus.). 50p. 1997. write for info. (*1-893296-02-4*) Meadowsweet Kit.

— Collected Recipes Cookbook: Abstract Cafe. (Illus.). 44p. 1995. write for info. (*1-893296-10-5*) Meadowsweet Kit.

— Collected Recipes Cookbook: Blue Ribbons. (Illus.). 44p. 1999. write for info. (*1-893296-20-2*) Meadowsweet Kit.

— Collected Recipes Cookbook: European Garden. (Illus.). 44p. 1996. write for info. (*1-893296-09-1*) Meadowsweet Kit.

— Collected Recipes Cookbook: Fruitful Impressions. (Illus.). 44p. 1997. write for info. (*1-893296-07-5*) Meadowsweet Kit.

— Collected Recipes Cookbook: Mediterranean Slice. (Illus.). 44p. 1997. write for info. (*1-893296-08-3*) Meadowsweet Kit.

— Collected Recipes Cookbook: Pinstripe Kitchen. (Illus.). 44p. 1995. write for info. (*1-893296-11-3*) Meadowsweet Kit.

— Flower Garden Journal. (Illus.). 50p. 1999. write for info. (*1-893296-18-0*) Meadowsweet Kit.

— Great Recipe! Tracking Guide. (Illus.). 100p. 1998. write for info. (*1-893296-23-7*) Meadowsweet Kit.

— My Favorite Holiday Recipes. (Illus.). 50p. 1998. write for info. (*1-893296-06-7*) Meadowsweet Kit.

— Receipe Card Cookbook: European Garden. (Illus.). 59p. 1996. write for info. (*1-893296-15-6*) Meadowsweet Kit.

— Recipe Card Cookbook: Abstract Cafe. (Illus.). 59p. 1995. write for info. (*1-893296-16-4*) Meadowsweet Kit.

— Recipe Card Cookbook: Blue Ribbon. (Illus.). 29p. 1999. write for info. (*1-893296-21-0*) Meadowsweet Kit.

— Recipe Card Cookbook: Country Market. (Illus.). 29p. 1998. write for info. (*1-893296-12-1*) Meadowsweet Kit.

— Recipe Card Cookbook: Fruitful Impressions. (Illus.). 59p. 1997. write for info. (*1-893296-13-X*) Meadowsweet Kit.

— Recipe Card Cookbook: Mediterranean Slice. (Illus.). 59p. 1997. write for info. (*1-893296-14-8*) Meadowsweet Kit.

— Restaurant Reviews. (Illus.). 50p. 1997. write for info. (*1-893296-01-6*) Meadowsweet Kit.

— Wine Journal. (Illus.). 50p. 1997. write for info. (*1-893296-00-8*) Meadowsweet Kit.

Ludwig, Nancy & Harte, Cheryl, eds. Beer Notes: A Journal. (Illus.). 50p. 1998. write for info. (*1-893296-03-2*) Meadowsweet Kit.

Ludwig, Nohl. Life of Haydn. 195p. 1990. reprint ed. lib. bdg. 59.00 (*0-685-35205-6*, 10,068) Rprt Serv.

Ludwig, Otto, jt. ed. see Guenther, Hartmut.

Ludwig, Otto, jt. ed. see Gunther, Hartmut.

Ludwig, R. A., jt. ed. see Taylor, Roy L.

Ludwig, Ray & Morrison, Ivy. The Pride & Joy of Working Cattle. Alward, Edgar C. & Bannish, Sally, eds. (Illus.). 68p. (Orig.). 1995. pap. 24.50 (*1-880836-09-2*) Pine Isl Pr.

Ludwig, Raymond H. Illustrated Handbook of Electronic Tables, Symbols, Measurements & Values. 2nd ed. LC 83-17620. 415p. 1986. 22.95 (*0-685-07964-3*, Busn) P-H.

Ludwig, Richard. A Manufacturing CEO's Secret Tips for Improving Profit. LC 95-22725. 237p. 1996. 34.95 (*0-471-12555-5*) Wiley.

Ludwig, Richard, ed. see McGuire, Bill & Wheeler, Leslie.

An Asterisk (*) at the beginning of an entry indicates that the title is appearing for the first time.

Ludwig, Richard M., ed. Dr. Panofsky & Mr. Tarkington: An Exchange of Letters, 1938-1946. LC 74-10252. (Illus.). 151p. 1974. 15.00 (0-87811-019-4) Princeton Lib.

Ludwig, Richard M., jt. auth. see Jones, H. Mumford.

Ludwig, Richard M., jt. auth. see Jones, Howard M.

Ludwig, Robert. Reconstructing Catholicism. 192p. (Orig.). 1995. pap. 17.95 (0-8245-1462-9) Crossroad NY.

***Ludwig, Robert A.** Reconstructing Catholicism. 252p. 2000. pap. 23.00 (1-57910-338-3) Wipf & Stock.

Ludwig, Ron, jt. auth. see Rosen, Corey.

Ludwig, Rosemarie. Thoughts in Solitude: A Guide to Your Inner Journey. 120p. (Orig.). 1993. pap. 17.95 (1-879046-01-6) Jacaranda AZ.

Ludwig, Ruth P., ed. Balloon Digest: A Publication of the Balloon Federation of America. rev. ed. (Illus.). 154p. 1995. pap. 30.00 (0-9646656-0-3) Balloon Fed Am.

Ludwig, Sally A. & Mentley, Kaye W. Quality Is the Key: Stories from Huntington Woods School. LC 97-92693. 200p. 1997. pap. 14.00 (0-9660916-0-4) KWM Educ.

Ludwig, Sami. Concrete Language: Intercultural Communication in Maxine Hong Kingston's "The Woman Warrior" & & Ishmael Reed's "Mumbo Jumbo" Hess-Luttich, Ernest W. & Watts, Richard, eds. (Cross Cultural Communication Ser.: Vol. 2). (Illus.). 493p. 1996. pap. 76.95 (3-631-49687-7) P Lang Pubng.

— Concrete Language: Intercultural Communication in Maxine Hong Kingston's "The Woman Warrior" & Ishmael Reed's "Mumbo Jumbo" Hess-Luttich, Ernest W. & Watts, Richard, eds. LC 96-24833. (Cross Cultural Communication Ser.: Vol. 2). (Illus.). 493p. 1996. pap. 76.95 (0-8204-2966-X) P Lang Pubng.

Ludwig, Stephen, ed. Pediatric Emergencies. (Clinics in Emergency Medicine Ser.: Vol. 7). (Illus.). 266p. 1985. text 48.00 (0-443-08303-7) Church.

Ludwig, Stephen & Kornberg, Allan E., eds. Child Abuse: A Medical Reference. 2nd ed. (Illus.). 563p. 1991. text 79.00 (0-443-08722-9) Church.

Ludwig, Stephen, jt. auth. see Fleisher, Gary R.

Ludwig, Stephen, jt. auth. see Reece, Robert M.

Ludwig, Stephen, jt. ed. see Altschuler, Steven.

Ludwig, Stephen, jt. ed. see Fleisher, Gary R.

Ludwig, Theodore M. The Sacred Paths: Understanding Religions of World. 3rd ed. (C). 2000. pap. write for info. (0-13-025848-2) P-H.

***Ludwig, Theodore M.** Sacred Paths: Understanding Religions of World. 3rd ed. LC 99-37756. 576p. (C). 2000. 49.33 (0-13-025682-X) P-H.

Ludwig, Theodore M. The Sacred Paths: Understanding the Religions of the World. 2nd ed. LC 95-40351. (Illus.). 574p. (C). 1995. 71.00 (0-02-372175-8, Macmillan Coll) P-H.

— The Sacred Paths of the East. (Illus.). 320p. (Orig.). (C). 1992. pap. text 53.00 (0-02-372163-4, Macmillan Coll) P-H.

— The Sacred Paths of the West. LC 93-5914. (Illus.). 336p. (Orig.). (C). 1994. pap. text 53.00 (0-02-372181-2, Macmillan Coll) P-H.

***Ludwig, Timothy D., et al.** Intervening to Improve the Safety of Occupational Driving: A Behavior-Change Model & Review of Empirical Evidence. LC 00-39602. (Illus.). 2000. write for info. (0-7890-1012-7) Haworth Pr.

Ludwig, Timothy G. The Flower & the Caterpillar: A Program about Accepting Differences for Students in Grades One Through Four. LC 94-77201. 16p. (J). (gr. 1-4). 1991. 5.95 (1-884063-22-5) Mar Co Prods.

— The Name-Game: A Program about Inappropriate Behavior. LC 94-77202. 32p. (J). (gr. 1-4). 1991. 6.95 (1-884063-21-7) Mar Co Prods.

— Terry's Temper: A Program about Anger for Students in Grades One Through Four. LC 94-77205. 316p. (J). (gr. 1-4). 1991. 5.95 (1-988406-32-3) Mar Co Prods.

Ludwig, Verle E. Archie Smallwood & the Marine Raiders: A Rifleman's Brief .30-Caliber History of the 20th Century. LC 97-12388. (Illus.). 272p. (Orig.). 1988. pap. 15.95 (1-56474-236-9) Fithian Pr.

Ludwig, W. D. Recent Developments in Lattice Theory. (Tracts in Modern Physics Ser.: Vol. 43). (Illus.). 1967. 86.95 (0-387-03982-1) Spr-Verlag.

Ludwig, W. D. & Falter, C. Symmetries in Physics. (Solid-State Sciences Ser.: Vol. 64). (Illus.). 470p. 1988. 66.00 (0-387-18021-4) Spr-Verlag.

— Symmetries in Physics: Group Theory Applied to Physical Problems. 2nd ed. LC 95-39620. (Springer Series in Solid-State Sciences: Vol. 64). 473p. 1996. pap., teacher ed., student ed. 69.00 (3-540-60284-4) Spr-Verlag.

Ludwig, W. D. & Thiel, E., eds. Recent Advances in Cell Biology of Acute Leukemia: Impact on Clinical Diagnosis & Therapy. LC 93-16157. (Recent Results in Cancer Research Ser.: Vol. 131). 1993. 150.00 (0-387-56417-9) Spr-Verlag.

Ludwig, Walter, jt. auth. see Felt, Thomas E.

Ludwig, Warren K. A German Heritage Remembered: An Illustrated History of Andreas & Charlotte (Reich) Ludwig (1826-1918) of the Koschmin & Krotoschin Districts, Province Posen, Prussia, Germany; Their Known German Ancestors & American Descendants, & the Related Families of Marth, Fabianke, & Knipstein. LC 92-81320. (Illus.). 512p. 1996. write for info. (0-9632935-0-8) Warren Ludwig.

Ludwig, William B. & Roach, Lee S. Studies on the Animal Ecology of the Hocking River Basin: The Bottom Invertebrates of the Hocking River & the Plankton of the Hocking River. (Bulletin Ser.: No. 26). 1932. pap. text 2.00 (0-86727-025-X) Ohio Bio Survey.

***Ludwigsen, J. S.** Posttest Analysis of the Steel Containment Vessel Model. 37p. 2000. pap. 4.00 (0-16-059113-9) USGPO.

Ludwigson, Susan. Ludwigson: Selected Poems. 160p. (Orig.). pap. 13.95 (0-7145-4187-7) Riverrun NY.

Ludwikowski, Rett R. Constitution-Making in the Region of Former Soviet Dominance. LC 96-3566. 568p. 1996. text 75.00 (0-8223-1802-4) Duke.

— Continuity & Change in Poland: Conservatism in Polish Political Thought. LC 90-25001. 313p. 1991. text 39.95 (0-8132-0743-6) Cath U Pr.

Ludwikowski, Rett R. & Fox, William F. The Beginning of the Constitutional Era. LC 92-34679. 331p. 1993. 49.95 (0-8132-0776-2) Cath U Pr.

Ludwikowski, Rett R., jt. ed. see Thompson, Kenneth W.

Ludwin, William G., jt. ed. see Worthley, John A.

Ludy, Andrew. Diet Diary: The Culinary Companion for a New You! (Illus.). 193p. (Orig.). 1984. pap. 4.95 (0-943912-01-6) Landing Pr.

Ludy, Claude E. The End of the Age: A Commentary on the Revelation. LC 89-92157. (Illus.). 125p. (Orig.). 1989. pap. 7.00 (0-9625164-1-4) C E Ludy.

— The Vile & the Holy: A Commentary on the Book of Daniel. LC 77-94874. (Illus.). 100p. (Orig.). (YA). 1978. pap. 5.00 (0-9625164-0-6) C E Ludy.

Ludy, Eric & Ludy, Leslie. Romance God's Way. Bagnull, Marlene, ed. (Illus.). 130p. (Orig.). 1997. pap. write for info. (0-9656251-0-9) Makarios.

***Ludy, Eric & Ludy, Leslie.** When God Writes Your Love Story: The Ultimate Guide to Guy-Girl Relationships. 224p. 1999. pap. 13.99 (1-929125-00-3, Pub. by Loyal Pubng) BookWorld.

— Whrn Dreams Come True: The True Story of a Love Worth Waiting For. 2000. pap. 13.99 (1-929125-17-8, Pub. by Loyal Pubng) BookWorld.

Ludy, Leslie, jt. auth. see Ludy, Eric.

Ludy, Mark S. The Farmer. 2 vols. Farabaugh, Sue-Kyung Y., ed. LC 98-73805. (Illus.). 64p. (J). (ps-6). 1999. 18.95 (0-9664276-0-2) Grn Pastures.

***Ludy, Perry J.** Profit Building: Cutting Costs Without Cutting People. 200p. 2000. 27.95 (1-57675-108-2, Pub. by Berrett-Koehler) Publishers Group.

Ludz, Peter C. The German Democratic Republic from the Sixties to the Seventies: A Socio-Political Analysis. (Harvard University. Center for International Affairs. Occasional Papers in International Affairs: No. 26). reprint ed. 27.50 (0-404-54626-9) AMS Pr.

Lue, Eugene. The Mysteries of Paris. 2nd ed. 423p. 1997. reprint ed. pap. 11.99 (0-946626-30-8, Pub. by Dedalus) Subterranean Co.

Lue, H. C., ed. Pediatric Cardiology Updates. (Illus.). 200p. 1997. 85.00 (4-431-70179-6) Spr-Verlag.

Lue-Hing, Cecil, et al, eds. Municipal Sewage Sludge Management: A Reference Text on Processing, Utilization & Disposal. 2nd ed. (Water Quality Management Library: Vol. 4). 816p. 1998. 104.95 (1-56676-621-4) Technomic.

— Municipal Sewage Sludge Management Vol. 4: Processing, Utilization & Disposal. LC 92-53520. (Water Quality Management Library). 830p. 1992. text 99.95 (0-87762-930-7) Technomic.

Lue, Tom F. Contemporary Diagnosis & Management of Erectile Dysfunction. LC 98-70695. 1999. pap. text 29.95 (1-884065-27-9) Assocs in Med.

***Lue, Tom F.** A Patient's Guide to Male Sexual Dysfunction. (Illus.). 120p. 2000. pap. write for info. (1-884065-82-1, Hndbks Hlth Care) Assocs in Med.

Lue, Tom F., jt. auth. see Goldstein, Marc.

Lue, Willard De, see De Lue, Willard.

Luebbe, Herrmann, ed. Wozu Philosophie? Stellungnahmen eines Arbeitskreises. (C). 1978. 29.25 (3-11-007513-X) De Gruyter.

Luebbe, Richard L., jt. auth. see Finch, Byron J.

Luebbe, Weyma, ed. Kausalitaet und Zurechnung: Ueber Verantwortung in Komplexen Kulturellen Prozessen. (Philosophie & Wissenschaft - Tranzdisziplinaere Studien: Bd. 5). (GER.). 320p. (C). 1994. pap. text 44.65 (3-11-014398-4) De Gruyter.

Luebben, Craig. How to Ice Climb. LC 99-10555. (How to Climb Ser.). (Illus.). 200p. 1999. pap. 13.95 (1-56044-760-5) Falcon Pub Inc.

***Luebben, Craig.** Rappelling. (How to Climb Ser.). (Illus.). 100p. 2000. pap. 9.95 (1-56044-759-1) Falcon Pub Inc.

Luebben, Tom. Historical Background of the Santa Ana Pueblo. (Treaty Manuscripts Ser.: No. 13). 25p. 8.50 (0-944253-35-0) Inst Dev Indian Law.

Luebbering, Ken, jt. auth. see Burnett, Robyn K.

Luebbermann, Mimi. Bread Baking with Herbs: Breads, Muffins, Foccacia & More. (Country Baker Ser.). (Illus.). 224p. 1996. 15.00 (0-7615-0245-9) Prima Pub.

— Cactus & Succulents: Simple Secrets for Glorious Gardens - Indoors & Out. LC 96-28041. 1997. pap. 14.95 (0-8118-1446-7) Chronicle Bks.

— Climbing Vines: Simple Secrets for Glorious Gardens, Indoors & Out. LC 94-13127. (Illus.). 108p. 1995. pap. 12.95 (0-8118-0723-1) Chronicle Bks.

— Coping with Miscarriage: A Simple, Reassuring Guide to Emotional & Physical Healing. LC 94-27377. 208p. 1994. 17.95 (1-55958-503-X) Prima Pub.

— Coping with Miscarriage: A Simple, Reassuring Guide to Emotional & Physical Healing. 240p. 1996. per. 14.00 (0-7615-0436-2) Prima Pub.

— Easy Orchids: Simple Secrets for Glorious Gardens-Indoors & Out: A Garden Style Book. LC 95-15159. (Garden Style Ser.). (Illus.). 108p. 1996. pap. 14.95 (0-8118-1033-X) Chronicle Bks.

— Heirloom Gardens: Simple Secrets for Old-Fashioned Flowers & Vegetables. LC 96-38866. 1997. pap. 14.95 (0-8118-1451-3) Chronicle Bks.

— Homegrown Fruit: Simple Secrets for Glorious Gardens, Indoors & Out. LC 97-30799. (Illus.). 108p. 1998. pap. text 14.95 (0-8118-1602-8) Chronicle Bks.

— Little Potted Gardens: Simple Secrets for Glorious Gardens, Indoors & Out. LC 97-30800. 1998. pap. text 14.95 (0-8118-1603-6) Chronicle Bks.

***Luebbermann, Mimi.** Money Making Backyard Gardening. 256p. 2000. pap. 16.95 (0-7615-2299-9) Prima Pub.

Luebbermann, Mimi. Pay Dirt: How to Raise & Sell Herbs & Produce for Serious Cash. 2nd rev. ed. LC 96-49878. 256p. 1997. per. 15.00 (0-7615-0844-9) Prima Pub.

— Pay Dirt: How to Raise & Sell Specialty Herbs & Vegetables for Serious Cash. LC 92-39923. 208p. (Orig.). 1993. pap. 12.95 (1-55958-287-1) Prima Pub.

— Salad Gardens: Simple Secrets for Glorious Gardens-Indoors & Out. LC 96-163553. (Garden Style Ser.). (Illus.). 108p. 1996. pap. 12.95 (0-8118-1062-3) Chronicle Bks.

Luebbermann, Mimi, jt. auth. see Brennan, Georgeanne.

Luebbermann, Mimi, jt. ed. see Bennett, Julienne.

Luebbers, Raymond J. The Electromagnetics Handbook. (Electrical Engineering Handbook Ser.). 2000. 129.95 (0-8493-8575-X) CRC Pr.

Luebbers, Raymond J., jt. auth. see Kunz, Karl S.

Luebbert, Gregory M. Liberalism, Fascism, or Social Democracy: Social Classes & the Political Origins of Regimes in Interwar Europe. 432p. 1991. text 75.00 (0-19-506610-3); pap. text 26.00 (0-19-506611-1) OUP.

Luebbert, M. C., jt. ed. see Rosen, D. H.

Luebbert, Peggy P. Laboratory Safety & Infection Control. (NLM Ser.: No. WA485). 1990. 50.00 incl. VHS (0-89189-303-2) Am Soc Clinical.

— OSHA's Bloodborne Pathogens Standard: Compliance in Clinical Laboratory. 1992. 50.00 incl. VHS (0-89189-349-0) Am Soc Clinical.

Luebbig, H., jt. ed. see Hahlbohm, H. D.

Luebeck, Walter. Rainbow Reiki: Expanding the Reiki System with Powerful Spiritual Abilities. LC 97-71446. (Illus.). 192p. (Orig.). 1997. pap. 14.95 (0-914955-28-4) Lotus Pr.

Luebering, Carol. A Retreat with Job & Julian of Norwich: Trusting That All Will Be Well. 144p. 1995. pap. 9.95 (0-86716-227-9) St Anthony Mess Pr.

— What Do You Ask for Your Child? 30p. (Orig.). 1980. pap. text 1.95 (0-912228-64-4) St Anthony Mess Pr.

— What Would Jesus Do to Finding Meaning in Suffering? LC 97-78270. 88p. 1998. pap. 4.95 (0-87029-314-1, 20136) Abbey.

— What Would Jesus Do to Live in Love Each Day? LC 97-78273. 88p. 1998. pap. 4.95 (0-87029-311-7, 20139) Abbey.

***Luebering, Carol.** Your Child's Baptism. 2nd ed. (Handing on the Faith Ser.). (Illus.). 40p. 2000. pap. 2.95 (0-86716-343-7) St Anthony Mess Pr.

— Your Child's Confirmation. 2nd ed. (Handing on the Faith Ser.). 40p. 2000. pap. 2.95 (0-86716-345-3) St Anthony Mess Pr.

Luebering, Carol. Your Child's Confirmation: Reflections for Parents on the Sacrament of Christian Identity. 32p. 1990. pap. text 1.95 (0-86716-076-4) St Anthony Mess Pr.

***Luebering, Carol.** Your Child's First Communion. 2nd ed. (Handing on the Faith Ser.). (Illus.). 40p. 2000. pap. 2.95 (0-86716-344-5) St Anthony Mess Pr.

Luebering, Carol. Your Child's First Communion: A Look at Your Dreams. 32p. (Orig.). 1984. pap. text 1.95 (0-86716-035-7) St Anthony Mess Pr.

***Luebering, Carol.** Your Child's First Penance. (Handing on the Faith Ser.). (Illus.). 40p. 2000. pap. 2.95 (0-86716-346-1) St Anthony Mess Pr.

Luebke, Barbara & Reilly, Mary E. Women's Studies Graduates: The First Generation. (Athene Ser.). 224p. (C). 1994. text 44.00 (0-8077-6275-X); pap. text 21.95 (0-8077-6274-1) Tchrs Coll.

Luebke, David M. His Majesty's Rebels: Communities, Factions, & Rural Revolt in the Black Forest, 1725-1745. LC 97-720. (Illus.). 296p. 1996. text 45.00 (0-8014-3346-0) Cornell U Pr.

Luebke, David M., ed. The Counter-Reformation: The Essential Readings. LC 99-19862. (Essential Readings in History Ser.). 272p. 1999. 62.95 (0-631-21103-9); pap. 27.95 (0-631-21104-7) Blackwell Pubs.

Luebke, Frederick C. Bonds of Loyalty: German Americans & World War I. LC 73-15097. xvii, 366p. 1974. pap. 16.00 (0-87580-514-0) N Ill U Pr.

— Germans in Brazil: A Comparative History of Cultural Conflict During World War I. LC 86-27371. (Illus.). 272p. 1987. text 37.50 (0-8071-1347-6) La State U Pr.

— Germans in the New World: Essays in the History of Immigration. (Statue of Liberty-Ellis Island Centennial Ser.). 224p. 1990. text 24.95 (0-252-01680-7) U of Ill Pr.

***Luebke, Frederick C.** Germans in the New World: Essays in the History of Immigration. LC 89-35122. (Statue of Liberty-Ellis Island Centennial Ser.). 198p. 1999. pap. 18.95 (0-252-06847-5) U of Ill Pr.

Luebke, Frederick C. Immigrants & Politics: The Germans of Nebraska, 1880-1900. LC 69-15924. (Illus.). 234p. reprint ed. pap. 72.60 (0-7837-6018-3, 204583000008) Bks Demand.

Luebke, Frederick C., ed. Ethnic Voters & the Election of Lincoln. LC 72-139370. 260p. reprint ed. pap. 80.60 (0-7837-6017-5, 204582900008) Bks Demand.

— Ethnicity on the Great Plains. LC 79-17743. (Illus.). 271p. reprint ed. pap. 84.10 (0-608 08693-2, 206921600003) Bks Demand.

— European Immigrants in the American West: Community Histories. LC 98-24613. (Historians of the Frontier & American West Ser.). (Illus.). 198p. 1998. lib. bdg. 45.00 (0-8263-1991-2) U of NM Pr.

— European Immigrants in the American West: Community Histories. LC 98-24613. (Historians of the Frontier & American West Ser.). (Illus.). 198p. 1998. pap. 19.95 (0-8263-1992-0) U of NM Pr.

— A Harmony of the Arts: The Nebraska State Capitol. LC 89-4773. (Great Plains Photography Ser.). (Illus.). x, 122p. 1990. text 50.00 (0-8032-2887-2) U of Nebr Pr.

— A Harmony of the Arts: The Nebraska State Capitol. LC 89-4773. (Great Plains Photography Ser.). (Illus.). x, 122p. (C). 1990. pap. 19.95 (0-8032-7931-0, Bison Books) U of Nebr Pr.

— Nebraska: An Illustrated History. LC 94-47569. (Great Plains Photography Ser.). (Illus.). xxiv, 407p. 1995. text 45.00 (0-8032-2902-X) U of Nebr Pr.

Luebke, Frederick C., ed. see Cultural Heritage of the Plains Symposium Staff.

Luebke, Frederick C., jt. ed. see Faulkner, Virginia.

Luebke, Paul. Tar Heel Politics, 2000. LC 98-16381. 288p. 1998. 34.95 (0-8078-2452-6); pap. 14.95 (0-8078-4756-9) U of NC Pr.

Luebke, William. Astronomy: A Student Study Guide. 2nd ed. 232p. (C). 1996. spiral bd. 29.95 (0-7872-2104-X, 41210401) Kendall-Hunt.

Luebking, Sandra H., jt. ed. see Szucs, Loretto D.

Luechak, Rebecca. Kuba. LC 97-25410. (Heritage Library of African Peoples: Set 3). (Illus.). 64p. (YA). (gr. 7-12). 1996. lib. bdg. 16.95 (0-8239-1996-X, D1996-X) Rosen Group.

Lueck, Beth L. American Writers & the Picturesque Tour: The Search for National Identity, 1790-1860. Fisher, Benjamin F., ed. LC 97-19947. (Studies in 19th Century American LIterature: Vol. 7). (Illus.). 232p. 1997. text 54.00 (0-8153-2285-2, H1967) Garland.

Lueck, E. Antimicrobial Food Additives: Characteristics, Uses, Effects. (Illus.). 280p. 1980. 68.95 (0-387-10056-3) Spr-Verlag.

Lueck, Karen, ed. see Scribner, Ronda.

Lueck, Therese L., jt. ed. see Endres, Kathleen L.

Luecke, Barbara K. Feeding the Frontier Army, 1775-1865. (Illus.). 141p. 1996. reprint ed. 12.00 (0-9621020-1-6) Grenadier Pubns.

Luecke, Barbara K. & Luecke, John C. The Snellings: Minnesota's First First Family. (Illus.). 298p. (Orig.). 1993. pap. 21.95 (0-9621020-3-2) Grenadier Pubns.

Luecke, David S. The Other Story of Lutherans at Worship: Reclaiming Our Heritage of Diversity. 126p. (Orig.). 1995. pap. 7.00 (0-9628303-7-2) Fellow Minist.

— Talking with God. 236p. 1997. pap. 8.00 (0-9628303-9-9) Fellow Minist.

Luecke, Editha L. Factors Related to Children's Participation in Certain Types of Home Activities. LC 70-177013. (Columbia University. Teachers College. Contributions to Education Ser.: No. 839). reprint ed. 37.50 (0-404-55839-9) AMS Pr.

Luecke, Gerald & Allen, James B. The Phone Book: Money-Saving Guide to Installing or Replacing Telephone Equipment in Your Home or Business. 2nd ed. (Illus.). 176p. 1997. pap. 24.95 (0-7906-1133-3) Prompt Publns.

Luecke, Gerald, ed. see Fulton, Stanley R. & Rawlins, John C.

Luecke, Gerald, ed. see West, Gordon.

Luecke, Gerald, ed. see West, Gordon & Maia, Fred.

Luecke, John C. Dreams, Disaster, Demise: The Milwaukee Road in Minnesota. (Illus.). 230p. (C). 1988. 39.95 (0-9621020-0-8) Grenadier Pubns.

— The Great Northern in Minnesota: The Foundations of an Empire. LC 95-75154. (Illus.). viii, 289p. 1997. 49.95 (0-9621020-4-0) Grenadier Pubns.

Luecke, John C., jt. auth. see Luecke, Barbara K.

Luecke, Richard, ed. A New Dawn in Guatemala: Toward a Worldwide Health Vision. (Illus.). 264p. (C). 1993. pap. text 14.95 (0-88133-734-X) Waveland Pr.

Luecke, Richard A. Scuttle Your Ships Before Advancing: And Other Lessons from History on Leadership & Change for Today's Managers. (Illus.). 208p. 1995. pap. 12.95 (0-19-509642-8) OUP.

Luecke, Richard A., jt. auth. see Bunnell, David.

Luecke, Richard W. Living Life Intentionally. (Illus.). xviii, 270p. 1996. 24.00 (1-889774-02-2) Lucky Lning.

Lueckenhoff, Laura. A Taste of Palm Beach: Rich Traditions in Fine Dining. (Illus.). 1996. pap. 9.95 (0-9662265-0-X) Tst Palm Bch.

Lueckenhoff, Mark. Neighbors of the U. S. A. (Illus.). 144p. (YA). (gr. 5-8). 1993. pap. text 12.95 (1-58037-046-2, Pub. by M Twain Media) Carson-Dellos.

Lueckenotte. Gerontologic Nursing. 2nd ed. 2000. text 58.00 (0-323-00757-0) Mosby Inc.

Lueckenotte, Annette. Gerontologic Nursing. teacher ed. write for info. (0-8151-5599-9) Mosby Inc.

— Pocket Guide to Gerontologic Assessment. 3rd ed. LC 97-34218. (Illus.). 432p. (C). (gr. 13). 1997. text 22.95 (0-8151-2799-5, 31133) Mosby Inc.

— Pocket Guide to Gerontologic Assessment, No. 2. 310p. 1994. write for info. (0-08-151778-5) Mosby Inc.

— Textbook of Gerontologic Nursing. (Illus.). 1024p. (C). (gr. 13). 1995. text 57.00 (0-8016-7414-X, 07414) Mosby Inc.

Luecking, D. H. & Rubel, Lee A. Complex Analysis: A Functional Analysis Approach. (Illus.). 180p. 1984. 31.95 (0-387-90993-1) Spr-Verlag.

Luecking, Dave. Hockey's Scorers & Goalies: The NHL's Biggest Stars. Gramling, Scott, ed. 32p. (J). (gr. 1-9). 1999. pap. 3.99 (1-886749-55-8) SI For Kids.

Luecking, Evelyn M., jt. auth. see Sumption, Merle R.

Luedde, Marie-Elisabeth. Die Rezeption, Interretation & Transformation Biblischer Motiv & Mythen in der DDR-Literatur & Ihre Bedeutung fuer die Theologie. (Arbeiten zur Praktischen Theologie Ser.: Bd 4). (GER.). vi, 178p. (C). 1993. lib. bdg. 90.80 (3-11-013773-9) De Gruyter.

***Luedde, Nick.** Pop Synthetics & Metropolis Film. (Illus.). 130p. 1999. pap. 12.00 (0-9652528-9-2, Pub. by Neshui Pubng) Booksource.

Luedecke, Alison, ed. Consoliere Classics, Vol. 1. 1997. pap. 8.95 (0-937690-38-4, WLP3060) Wrld Lib Pubns.

***Luedecke, Alison.** Consoliere Classics IV. 2000. pap. 8.95 (1-58459-065-3, 3063) Wrld Lib Pubns.

L

Luedeking, Leila & Edmonds, Michael. Leonard Woolf: A Bibliography. (Illus.). 310p. 1992. 78.00 (0-938768-41-7) Oak Knoll.

Luedeking, Sylvia, ed. see Lawrence, Jeannette.

Luedemann, Gerd. The Great Deception: And What Jesus Really Said & Did. LC 98-54609.Tr. of Dergrosse Betrug: Und Was Jesus Wirklich Sagte und Tat. 126p. 1999. pap. 16.95 (1-57392-688-4) Prometheus Bks.

— The Resurrection of Jesus: History, Experience, Theology. Bowden, John, tr. from GER. 224p. 1995. pap. 20.00 (0-8006-2792-X) Augsburg Fortress.

Lueder, Dianne & Webb, Sally. Administrator's Guide to Library Building Maintenance. LC 92-5566. 290p. (C). 1992. pap. text 45.00 (0-8389-3409-9) ALA.

Lueder, Donald C. Creating Partnerships with Parents: An Educator's Guide. LC 97-61844. 290p. 1997. text 44.95 (1-56676-583-8) Scarecrow.

Lueder, Rani, ed. The Ergonomics Payoff: Designing the Electronic Office. (Illus.). 388p. 1986. 35.00 (0-9629901-0-8) Humanics ErgoSysts.

Lueders, Bill. An Enemy of the State: The Life of Erwin Knoll. LC 96-14004. 300p. 1996. pap. 17.95 (1-56751-098-1); lib. bdg. 29.95 (1-56751-099-X) Common Courage.

Lueders, Edward. The Clam Lake Papers: A Winter in the North Woods. 148p. 1977. pap. write for info. (0-7734-1333-2) E Mellen.

— Clam Lake Papers: A Winter in the North Woods: Introducting the Metaphorical Imperative & Kindred Matters with a Prologue & Epilogue. LC 96-7743. xvi, 148p. 1996. reprint ed. 20.00 (0-940473-32-1); reprint ed. pap. 9.95 (0-940473-33-X) Wm Caxton.

Lueders, Edward & Koriyama, Naoshi, trs. from JPN. Like Underground Water: Poetry of Mid-20th Century Japan. LC 95-32541. 350p. (Orig.). 1995. 30.00 (1-55659-102-0); pap. 15.00 (1-55659-103-9) Copper Canyon.

Lueders, Edward G. The Wake of the General Bliss. LC 88-20687. 196p. reprint ed. pap. 60.80 (0-7837-5533-3, 204530600005) Bks Demand.

***Lueders, Jeffrey R.** Second Chances: Receiving the Gift of Life. (Illus.). 168p. 2000. pap. 9.95 (1-57249-219-8, Ragged Edge) White Mane Pub.

Lueders, Volker, jt. ed. see Moller, Peter.

Luedi, Marcus. Room 105: The Compelling True-Life Story of Victory over Suffering & Death. Roberts, Allen, ed. & illus. by. 204p. 1998. 19.95 (0-9643136-2-6) Meister Pr.

Luedke, John, et al, contrib. by. Remains to Be Seen. (Illus.). 72p. 1983. pap. 18.95 (0-932718-15-9) Kohler Arts.

Luedke, M. Jack, jt. ed. see Foley, Bill.

Luedtke, Barbara E. An Archaeologist's Guide to Chert & Flint. LC 92-46805. (UCLA Institute of Archaeology Publications: No. 7). (Illus.). 156p. (C). 1992. pap. 25.00 (0-917956-75-3) UCLA Arch.

Luedtke, Gerhard, ed. Kuerschners Deutscher Literatur-kalender Nekrolog, 1901-1935. 976p. (C). 1973. reprint ed. 119.25 (3-11-004432-3) De Gruyter.

Luedtke, Helmut, ed. Kommunikationstheoretische Grundlagen des Sprachwandels. (Grundlagen der Kommunikation Ser.). 280p. (C). 1979. text 84.60 (3-11-007271-8) De Gruyter.

Luedtke, Luther S. Nathaniel Hawthorne & the Romance of the Orient. LC 88-46018. (Illus.). 304p. 1989. 12.95 (0-253-33613-9) Ind U Pr.

Luedtke, Luther S., ed. Making America: The Society & Culture of the United States. LC 91-50786. (Illus.). xii, 570p. (C). 1992. pap. 19.95 (0-8078-4370-9) U of NC Pr.

Luedtke, Ralph D., jt. ed. see Kanenberg, Cyndee.

Luedtke, Robert, jt. auth. see Bodian, Nat G.

Lueger, Robert J. Assessing Quality in Outpatient Psychotherapy: Implications for Designing & Selecting Cost-Efficient Mental Health Care Benefits. LC 93-77662. 75p. (Orig.). 1993. pap. 15.00 (0-89154-463-1) Intl Found Employ.

Luehlfing, Michael S. The Development of the Second Partner Review in Audit Engagements. 20p. 1991. pap. text 19.50 (0-933179-05-7) Bus Account Pubns.

— Minimizing the Impact of Alternative Recording Methods on the Consolidation Process - "Conversion to Complete Equity" 21p. 1995. pap. text 19.50 (0-933179-09-X) Bus Account Pubns.

Luehrman, Timothy A., jt. ed. see Kester, W. Carl.

Luehrmann, A., ed. see Falicov, L. M.

Luehrmann, Arthur. Computer Literacy: A Hands-on-Approach, Apple Version. 248p. 1985. teacher ed. 32.00 (0-07-049246-8); student ed. 9.80 (0-07-049245-X) McGraw.

— Computer Literacy: A Hands-on-Approach, Apple Version. rev. ed. 400p. 1985. text 30.88 (0-07-049242-5) McGraw.

— Computer Literacy: A Hands-on-Approach, TRS-80 Version. Hague, Nola J., ed. 256p. 1985. teacher ed. 32.00 (0-07-049251-4); student ed. 9.80 (0-07-049250-6); text 30.88 (0-07-049247-6) McGraw.

— Introduction to Computer Applications: Apple Version. 104p. 1985. teacher ed. 26.88 (0-07-049244-1); text 15.56 (0-07-049243-3) McGraw.

— Introduction to Computer Applications: TRS-80. 160p. 1986. text 15.56 (0-07-049248-4) McGraw.

***Luehrmann, Arthur & Peckham, Herbert.** Hands-On Microsoft Office. 512p. 1999. spiral bd. 46.60 (1-57426-145-2) Computer Lit Pr.

— Microsoft Works 2000: A Hands-On Guide. 148p. 2000. spiral bd. 26.60 (1-57426-062-6) Computer Lit Pr.

Luehrmann, Arthur & Peckham, Herbert D. Computer Literacy: A Hands-on Approach. 1985. 32.52 (0-07-049186-0); 32.12 (0-07-049191-7); student ed. 11.04 (0-07-049187-9); student ed. 11.04 (0-07-049188-7) McGraw.

— Hands-On Clarisworks: Macintosh 4.0 & 5.0. 3rd ed. LC 97-40452. (Illus.). 512p. 1997. spiral bd. 46.60 (1-57426-070-7) Computer Lit Pr.

— Hands-on Pascal: For the IBM Personal Computer. (Personal Programmimg Ser.). 448p. (C). 1996. pap. text 11.00 (0-07-049176-3) McGraw.

Luehrs, John. Flexibility & Waiver Authority for Health Care Reform: A Primer for States. Glass, Karen, ed. 94p. (Orig.). 1992. pap. text 20.00 (1-55877-172-7) Natl Governor.

Luehrs, John, jt. auth. see McCloskey, Amanda H.

Luehrs, John, jt. auth. see Phillips, Stephen.

Luehrs, Kai, contrib. by. Excentrische Einsatze: Studien und Essay zum Werk Heimito von Doderers. 350p. 1998. 118.00 (3-11-015198-7) De Gruyter.

Lueke, Ada, jt. auth. see Musladin, Judith M.

Lueker, Erwin L., ed. Lutheran Cyclopedia: A Concise In-Home Reference for the Christian Family. 845p. 1975. 29.99 (0-570-03255-5, 15-2163) Concordia.

Luellen, Valentina. Hostage of Love. 1999. per. 4.99 (0-373-30341-6) Harlequin Bks.

Luellmann, Heinz, et al. Pocket Atlas of Pharmacology. LC 92-48531. (Flexibook Ser.).Tr. of Tashenatlas der Pharmakologie. (ENG & GER., Illus.). 374p. 1993. pap. text 29.90 (0-86577-455-2) Thieme Med Pubs.

Luelsdorff, P. Soviet Contributions to the Sociology of Language. 1977. pap. text 60.80 (90-279-7613-9) Mouton.

Luelsdorff, Philip A. Constraints on Error Variables in Grammar: Bilingual Misspelling Orthographies. LC 85-30823. vii, 442p. 1986. 118.00 (0-915027-73-9); pap. 27.95 (0-915027-74-7) J Benjamins Pubng Co.

— Developmental Orthography. LC 91-7333. xii, 258p. 1991. 89.00 (90-272-2065-4) J Benjamins Pubng Co.

Luelsdorff, Philip A., ed. The Prague School of Structural & Functional Linguistics: A Short Introduction. LC 94-31089. (Linguistic & Literary Studies in Eastern Europe: No. 41). vii, 385p. 1994. lib. bdg. 95.00 (1-55619-266-5) J Benjamins Pubng Co.

Luelsdorff, Philip A., et al, eds. Praguiana 1945-1990. LC 93-44739. (Linguistic & Literary Studies in Eastern Europe: No. 40). x, 250p. 1994. 75.00 (1-55619-265-7) J Benjamins Pubng Co.

Luelsdorff, Phillip A., ed. Orthography & Phonology. LC 87-9361. xi, 238p. (C). 1987. 74.00 (90-272-2039-5) J Benjamins Pubng Co.

Luenberger, David G. Introduction to Dynamic Systems: Theory, Models & Applications. LC 78-12366. 464p. 1979. text 100.95 (0-471-02594-1) Wiley.

— Investment Science. LC 96-41158. (Illus.). 512p. (C). 1997. text 76.95 (0-19-510809-4) OUP.

— Microeconomic Theory. 496p. (C). 1994. 65.31 (0-07-049313-8) McGraw.

— Optimization. 344p. 1997. pap. 80.00 (0-471-18117-X) Wiley.

— Solutions Manual for Investment Science. 108p. 1998. pap. write for info. (0-19-512517-7) OUP.

Lueneburg, H., ed. Translation Planes. 256p. 1980. 102.95 (0-387-09614-0) Spr-Verlag.

Luengo, Ernesto Mendez, see Mendez Luengo, Ernesto.

Luenn. Mother Earth. (J). 1998. pap. 4.95 (0-87628-942-1) Ctr Appl Res.

— Nessa's Fish. (J). 1998. pap. 5.99 (0-87628-954-5) Ctr Appl Res.

Luenn, Nancy. Celebrations of Light: A Year of Holidays Around the World. LC 96-2761. (Illus.). 32p. (J). (gr. 4-6). 1998. pap. 16.00 (0-689-31986-X) Atheneum Yung Read.

— The Dragon Kite. LC 81-11709. (Illus.). 32p. (J). (gr. 1-5). 1983. pap. 5.95 (0-15-224197-3, Voyager Bks) Harcourt.

— A Gift for Abuelita (Un Regalo para Abuelita) Celebrating the Day of the Dead (En Celebration del Dia de los Muertos) LC 98-22277. (ENG & SPA.). 32p. (J). (gr. 1-5). 1998. 15.95 (0-87358-688-3, Rising Moon Bks) Northland AZ.

— The Miser on the Mountain: A Nisqually Legend of Mount Rainier. LC 96-42392. (Illus.). 32p. (J). (gr. 1-12). 1997. 15.95 (1-57061-082-7) Sasquatch Bks.

— Mother Earth. (Illus.). 32p. (J). (ps-3). 1995. mass mkt. 5.99 (0-689-80164-5) Aladdin.

— Mother Earth. LC 90-19134. (Illus.). 32p. (J). (ps-3). 1992. 15.00 (0-689-31668-2) Atheneum Yung Read.

— Mother Earth. (J). 1995. 10.15 (0-606-07890-8) Turtleback.

— Mother Earth Spanish. (Illus.). (J). 1999. pap. 15.00 (0-689-80000-2) Atheneum Yung Read.

— Nessa's Fish. (J). (gr. k-3). 1997. per. 5.99 (0-689-81465-8) Aladdin.

— Nessa's Fish. LC 89-10548. (Illus.). 32p. (J). (gr. k-3). 1990. 15.00 (0-689-31477-9) Atheneum Yung Read.

— Nessa's Fish. (Aladdin Picture Bks.). 1997. 11.19 (0-606-12781-X, Pub. by Turtleback) Demco.

— Nessa's Story (El Cuento de Nessa) Ada, Alma F., tr. LC 93-34814. (ENG & SPA., Illus.). 32p. (J). (gr. k-3). 1994. 14.95 (0-689-31782-4); 14.95 (0-689-31919-3) Atheneum Yung Read.

— Otter Play. LC 96-34026. 32p. (ps-4). 1998. 16.00 (0-689-81126-8) S&S Childrens.

— La Pesca de Nessa. (J). 1997. per. 6.99 (0-689-81467-4) Aladdin.

— La Pesca de Nessa. (SPA., Illus.). 32p. (J). (gr. k-3). 1994. mass mkt. 15.95 (0-689-31977-0) Atheneum Yung Read.

— La Pesca de Nessa. 1997. 12.19 (0-606-12752-6, Pub. by Turtleback) Demco.

— La Pesca de Nessa Nessas. (SPA.). (J). 1996. pap. 4.95 (0-689-31978-9) S&S Bks Yung.

— Song for the Ancient Forest. LC 91-17187. (Illus.). 32p. (J). (gr. k-3). 1993. 14.95 (0-689-31719-0) Atheneum Yung Read.

— Squish! A Wetland Walk. LC 93-22628. (Illus.). 32p. (J). (ps-3). 1994. 16.00 (0-689-31842-1) Atheneum Yung Read.

Luenn, Nancy, ed. A Horse's Tale: Ten Adventures in One Hundred Years. LC 88-61152. (Illus.). 96p. (Orig.). (J). (gr. 2-6). 1988. pap. 9.95 (0-943990-50-5); lib. bdg. 16.95 (0-943990-51-3) Parenting Pr.

Luepke, Niels-Peter, ed. see International Workshop on Monitoring Environmental.

Luepnitz, Deborah A. The Family Interpreted: Feminist Theory in Clinical Practice. LC 88-47761. 352p. 1992. reprint ed. pap. 16.50 (0-465-02351-7, Pub. by Basic) HarpC.

— Schopenhauers Porcupines. 2000. 25.00 (0-465-04286-4, Pub. by Basic); pap. 15.00 (0-465-04287-2, Pub. by Basic) HarpC.

Lueptow, R. M., et al, eds. Vibration Control, Analysis, & Identification Vol. 19-230: Flow Noise Modeling, Measurement & Control, DE-Vol. 84-3. (Proceedings of the 1995 ASME Design Technical Engineering Conferences Ser.: Vol. 3, Pt. C). 1516p. 1995. 420.00 (0-7918-1720-2, H1000C) ASME.

***Lueptow, Richard M.** Graphics Concepts. LC 00-29824. (Engineering Source Ser.). (Illus.). 2000. write for info. (0-13-030687-8) P-H.

Luer, C. A. Icones Pleurothallidinarum Vol. XII: Systematics of Brachionidium, & Addenda to Dresslerella, Platystele & Porroglossum (Orchidaceae) (Illus.). 146p. 1995. 26.95 (0-915279-36-3, MSB-57) Miss Botan.

***Luer, Carlyle.** Icones Pleurothallidinarum XV: Systematics of Trichosalpinx, Including an Addenda to All Genus Names Dracula, Masdevallia, Myoxanthus & Scaphosepalum & Corrigenda to Lepanthes of Ecuador (Orchidaceae) (Illus.). 136p. 1998. pap. 42.00 (0-915279-51-7) Miss Botan.

— Icones Pleurothallidinarum XIX Pt. 1: Systematics of Masdevallia. (Illus.). 264p. 2000. pap. 45.00 (0-915279-80-0) Miss Botan.

— Icones Pleurothallidinarum XVII: Pleurothallis Subgenus Pleurothallis Sections Pleurothallis & Acroniae; Pleurothallis Subgenera Dracontia & Unciferia. (Illus.). 121p. 1998. pap. 25.00 (0-915279-63-0) Miss Botan.

— Icones Pleurothallidinarum XVI: Systematics of Pleurothallis Subgenera Crocodeilanthe, Rhynchopera & Talpinaria. (Illus.). 128p. 1998. pap. 22.00 (0-915279-54-1) Miss Botan.

— Icones Pleurothallidinarum XVIII: Pleurothallis - Subsections Antenniferae, Longiracemosae, Macrophyllae-Racemosae, & Questiones & Two Subgenera: Acuminatia & Schweinfurthia. (Illus.). 182p. 2000. pap. 35.00 (0-915279-79-7) Miss Botan.

Luer, Carlyle. Treasure of Masdevallia, Vol. 22. 1997. 60.00 (0-915279-50-9) Miss Botan.

***Luer, Carlyle.** Treasure of Masdevallia, Vol. 23. (Illus.). 68p. 1999. pap. 60.00 (0-915279-64-9) Miss Botan.

— Treasure of Masdevallia, Vol. 24. (Illus.). 68p. 1999. pap. 60.00 (0-915279-75-4) Miss Botan.

Luer, Carlyle A. Icones Pleurothallidinarum IX - Systematics of Myoxanthus: Addenda to Platystele, Pleurothallus Subgenus Scopula & Scaphosepalum (Orchidaceae) (Monographs in Systematic Botany from the Missouri Botanical Garden). (Illus.). 128p. 1992. pap. 19.95 (0-685-70548-X) Miss Botan.

Luer, Carlyle A. & Escobar, Rodrigo R. Thesaurus Dracularum V: Eine Monographie der Gattung Dracula - A Monograph of the Genus Dracula. Hamer, Fritz, tr. (Thesaurus Draculrum Ser.). (GER., Illus.). 62p. 1992. pap. 55.95 (0-614-04648-3) Miss Botan.

— Thesaurus Draculrum IV: Eine Monographie der Gattung Dracula - A Monograph of the Genus Dracula. Hamer, Fritz, tr. (Thesaurus Draculrum Ser.). (GER., Illus.). 62p. 1991. pap. 53.95 (0-614-04647-5) Miss Botan.

— Thesaurus Draculrum I: Eine Monographie der Gattung Dracula - A Monograph of the Genus Dracula. Hamer, Fritz, tr. (Thesaurus Draculrum Ser.). (GER., Illus.). 62p. 1988. pap. 49.95 (0-614-04644-0) Miss Botan.

— Thesaurus Draculrum VII: Eine Monographie der Gattung Dracula - A Monograph of the Genus Dracula. Hamer, Fritz, tr. (Thesaurus Draculrum Ser.). (GER., Illus.). v, 78p. 1994. pap. 57.00 (0-915279-28-2) Miss Botan.

— Thesaurus Draculrum VI: Eine Monographie der Gattung Dracula - A Monograph of the Genus Dracula. Hamer, Fritz, tr. (Thesaurus Draculrum Ser.). (GER., Illus.). 64p. 1993. pap. 55.95 (0-614-04649-1) Miss Botan.

— Thesaurus Draculrum III: Eine Monographie der Gattung Dracula - A Monograph of the Genus Dracula. Hamer, Fritz, tr. (Thesaurus Draculrum Ser.). (GER., Illus.). 66p. 1990. pap. text 49.95 (0-614-04646-7) Miss Botan.

— Thesaurus Draculrum II: Eine Monographie der Gattung Dracula - A Monograph of the Genus Dracula. Hamer, Fritz, tr. (Thesaurus Draculrum Ser.). (GER., Illus.). 62p. 1989. pap. 49.95 (0-614-04645-9) Miss Botan.

Luer, Carlyle A., ed. see Chase, Mark W.

Luer, Carlyle A., ed. see Stewart, Joyce.

Luer, Carlyle A., ed. see Wood, Jeffrey J.

Luer, Carlyle A., ed. see Wood, Jeffrey J., et al.

Luer, Carlyle A., ed. & frwd. see Cribb, Phillip J. & Bell, Sandra.

Luer, George M., jt. auth. see Almy, Marion A.

Lueras, Leonard. Bali: The Ultimate Island. (Illus.). 240p. 1987. text 45.00 (0-312-00863-5) St Martin.

Lueras, Leornard, ed. Kanyaku Imin: A Hundred Years of Japanese Life in Hawaii. (Illus.). 160p. 1986. pap. text 15.00 (0-9615045-0-1) Kanyaku Imin JV.

Luere, Jeane & Berger, Sidney, eds. Playwright vs. Director: Authorial Intentions & Performance Interpretations, 54. LC 93-44134. (Contributions in Drama & Theatre Studies: No. 54). 200p. 1994. 59.95 (0-313-28679-5, Greenwood Pr) Greenwood.

— The Theatre Team: Playwright, Producer, Director, Designers & Actors, 80. LC 97-15298. (Contributions in Drama & Theatre Studies: Vol. 80). 192p. 1998. 49.95 (0-313-30050-X, Greenwood Pr) Greenwood.

Luerkens, David W. Theory & Application of Morphological Analysis: Fine Particles & Surfaces. Beddow, John K., ed. (Fine Particle Science & Technology Ser.). 336p. 1991. lib. bdg. 125.00 (0-8493-6777-8, TA418) CRC Pr.

Luers, Marc, jt. auth. see Tonelli, Joe.

Luescher, T. F. Endothelial Vasoactive Substances & Cardiovascular Disease. (Illus.). xiv, 134p. 1988. 125.75 (3-8055-4675-0) S Karger.

***Luesley, David, ed.** Cancer & Pre-Cancer of the Vulva. LC 99-43210. (An Arnold Publication). 288p. 2000. text 98.50 (0-340-74210-0, Pub. by E A) OUP.

Luesley, David, ed. Common Conditions in Gynecology: A Problem Solving Approach. LC 97-66879. (Illus.). 224p. 1997. pap. 24.50 (0-412-72380-8, Pub. by E A) OUP.

Luesley, David, et al, eds. Handbook of Colposcopy. LC 96-86086. (Illus.). 176p. 1996. pap. text 26.00 (0-412-71550-3, Pub. by E A) OUP.

***Luesley, David & Barrasso, R., eds.** Cancer & Pre-Cancer of the Cervix. LC 98-70533. (Illus.). 472p. 1999. text 98.50 (0-412-56600-1, Pub. by E A) OUP.

Luessen, Lawrence H., jt. ed. see Kunhardt, Erich E.

Luessen, Lawrence H., jt. ed. see Proud, Joseph M.

Luessen, Lawrence H., jt. ed. see Thompson, James E.

Luest, R., ed. see International Astronomical Union Staff.

Lueth, Shirley. Bubble, Bubble, Toil & Trouble. 264p. 1993. reprint ed. pap. 7.95 (0-937911-03-8) Lueth Hse Pub.

— I Didn't Plan to Be a Witch. 238p. 1988. reprint ed. pap. 7.95 (0-937911-02-X) Lueth Hse Pub.

— Prayer & Peanut Butter. (Illus.). 147p. (Orig.). 1986. reprint ed. pap. 7.95 (0-937911-01-1) Lueth Hse Pub.

— Watch Out! I'm Peeking in Your Window! 140p. (Orig.). 1986. pap. 7.95 (0-937911-00-3) Lueth Hse Pub.

Luethans, Tod N. Gormont et Isembart: The Epic As Seen in the Light of the Oral Theory. Lord, Albert B., ed. LC 90-2973. (Harvard Dissertations in Folklore & Oral Literature Ser.). 249p. 1990. reprint ed. text 20.00 (0-8240-2787-6) Garland.

***Luethge, Irene I.** Potpourri from Kettle Land. 200p. 2000. pap. 9.95 (1-886028-46-X, Pub. by Savage Pr) Bookmen Inc.

Luethi, Molly, tr. see Hsueh, Regina & Wu, Wen-Bin.

Luethi, Molly, tr. see Ma, Qingsheng.

Luethi, Molly, tr. see Zhu, Jian.

Luethy, Rae A. Adolescents as Parents, Custom Pub. 1993. pap. text. write for info. (0-07-049311-1) McGraw.

Luetje, Carolyn & Marcrander, Meg. Face to Face with God in Your Home: Guiding Children & Youth in Prayer. LC 94-48475. 104p. 1995. pap. 19.99 (0-8066-2767-0, 10-27670, Augsburg) Augsburg Fortress.

Luetjen-Drecoll, E., ed. Perspectives in Glaucoma Research, Pt. I. (Journal: Ophthalmologica: Vol. 210, No. 5, 1996). (Illus.). 70p. 1996. pap. 69.75 (3-8055-6378-7) S Karger.

Luetjohann, Sylvia. Healing Power of Black Cumin. LC 97-76440. 160p. 1998. pap. 14.95 (0-914955-53-5) Lotus Pr.

Luetjohann, Sylvia, jt. auth. see Junemann, Monika.

Luetke, Frederick. Voyage Around the World, 1826-1829 Vol. 1: To Russian America & Siberia. Pierce, Richard A., ed. Marshall, Renee, tr. from FRE. (Alaska History Ser.: No. 29). (Illus.). 1986. 26.50 (0-919642-97-7) Limestone Pr.

Luetke-Stahlman, Barbara. Hannie. (Illus.). 192p. (Orig.). (J). 1996. pap. 9.95 (1-884362-15-X) Butte Pubns.

— Language Across the Curriculum When Students Are Deaf or Hard of Hearing. LC 99-213863. 464p. (C). 1999. pap. 44.00 (1-884362-27-3) Butte Pubns.

— Language Issues in Deaf Education. LC 99-165358. 376p. (Orig.). (C). 1998. pap., per. 44.00 (1-884362-26-5) Butte Pubns.

Luetke-Stahlman, Barbara & Luckner, John. Effectively Educating Students with Hearing Impairments. 384p. (Orig.). (C). 1991. pap. text 54.38 (0-8013-0317-6, 78085) Longman.

Luetke-Stahlman, Barbara, jt. auth. see Stewart, David A.

Luetkemeyer, Mary A., ed. Our Stuff - A Literary Sampler: An Approach to Creative Writing from the Classroom. (Illus.). 113p. 1998. 12.95 (1-882935-33-0) Westphalia.

Luetscher, George D. Early Political Machinery in the United States. LC 70-155356. (Studies in American History & Government). 1971. reprint ed. lib. bdg. 27.50 (0-306-70187-1) Da Capo.

Luetschg, J., ed. Neuropaediatrie III, III. (Paediatrische Fortbildungskurse fuer die Praxis Ser.: Vol. 60). (Illus.). xii, 92p. 1986. pap. 47.00 (3-8055-4232-1) S Karger.

Luettge, U. & Higinbotham, N. Transport in Plants. (Illus.). 1979. 107.95 (0-387-90383-6) Spr-Verlag.

Luettig, G. W. General Geology of the Federal Republic of Germany: With Two Excursions to Industrial Mineral Rocks & Environmental Research. Published for the 26th International Geological Congress, Paris 1980. 96p. 1980. pap. 27.00 (3-510-65102-2, Pub. by E Schweizerbartsche) Balogh.

Luettig, G. W., ed. Recent Technologies in the Use of Peat: Reports of the International Symposium of Deutsche Gesellschaft Fuer Moor- und Torfkunde e.V. (DGMT) & Section II of the International Peat Society (IPS), Bad Zwischenahn, FRG, Nov. 5-8, 1979. (Illus.). vi, 223p. 1983. pap. text 52.00 (3-510-65115-4, Pub. by E Schweizerbartsche) Balogh.

Luettig, G. W., jt. ed. see Arndt, P.

Luettig, Gerd W., ed. Peatlands Use--Present, Past & Future Vols. 1-4: 10th International Peat Congress 27 May--2 June, 1996, Bremen, Germany. 1043p. 1996. pap. 112.00 (3-510-65171-5, Pub. by E Schweizerbartsche) Balogh.

Luetzeler, Heinrich. Dictionary of Art: Bildwoerterbuch der Kunst. 3rd ed. (ENG & GER.). 448p. 1980. pap. 45.00 (0-8288-1422-8, M7310) Fr & Eur.

An Asterisk (*) at the beginning of an entry indicates that the title is appearing for the first time.

Luetzeler, Paul M., ed. Hoffnung Europa: Deutsche Essays von Novalis bis Enzensberger. (GER.). 512p. 1994. 61.25 (*3-10-045310-7*, Pub. by S Fischer) Intl Bk Import.

Luevano, Daniel. The Future Called Something O'Clock. 25p. 1998. pap. 6.00 (*0-9665754-0-7*) Firewheel Edit.

Luey, Beth. Handbook for Academic Authors. 3rd ed. (Illus.). 330p. (C). 1995. pap. 16.95 (*0-521-49892-9*) Cambridge U Pr.

Luey, Beth, jt. ed. see Kobrak, Fred.

Luey, Beth E. Editing Documents & Texts: An Annotated Bibliography. LC 89-14552. 304p. 1990. text 19.95 (*0-945612-13-3*) Madison Hse.

Lufburrow, Bill. The Most Honest People. LC 80-69253. (Illus.). (Orig.). 1980. pap. 4.95 (*0-918464-23-4*) D Armstrong.

Luff, Alan. Welsh Hymns & Their Tunes. LC 90-81524. 255p. (Orig.). (C). 1990. 18.95 (*0-916642-42-9*, 63) Hope Pub.

Luff, David. Bulldog: The Bristol Bulldog Fighter. LC 88-60697. (Illus.). 188p. 1988. text 32.50 (*0-87474-648-5*) Smithsonian.

— Mollison, the Flying Scotsman: The Life of Pioneer Aviator James Allan Mollison. (Illus.). 416p. 1996. 37.95 (*1-56098-621-2*) Smithsonian.

Luff, Martin L. The Carabidae, Coleoptera, Larvae of Fennoscandia & Denmark. LC 93-3419. (Fauna Entomologica Scandinavica Ser.: Vol. 27). (Illus.). 185p. 1993. lib. bdg. 91.00 (*90-04-09836-4*) Brill Academic Pubs.

Luff, Moe. United States Postal Slogan Cancel Catalog. rev. ed. LC 68-2266. 128p. 1977. pap. text 5.75 (*0-9600162-0-1*) M Luff.

Luff, Paul, et al, eds. Computers & Conversation. (Computers & People Ser.). 284p. 1990. text 73.00 (*0-12-459560-X*) Acad Pr.

***Luff, Paul, et al, eds.** Workplace Studies: Recovering Work Practice & Informing System Design. (Illus.). 272p. (C). 2000. text 64.95 (*0-521-59186-4*); pap. text 24.95 (*0-521-59821-4*) Cambridge U Pr.

Luff, Paul, jt. auth. see Heath, Christian.

Luff, R., jt. auth. see Browne, C. A.

Luff, Rosemary & Rowley-Conwy, Peter, eds. Whither Environmental Archaeology? (Oxbow Monographs in Archaeology: No. 38). (Illus.). 224p. 1994. pap. 50.00 (*0-946897-69-7*, Pub. by Oxbow Bks) David Brown.

Luff, Rosemary M. Animal Remains in Archaeology. 1989. pap. 25.00 (*0-85263-633-4*, Pub. by Shire Pubns) St Mut.

Luff, S. G. The Christian's Guide to Rome. rev. ed. 336p. 1994. pap. 25.00 (*0-86012-178-X*, Pub. by Srch Pr) St Mut.

***Luff, William G.** The Life & Times of Jesus. (Illus.). 1999. pap. 10.00 (*0-7880-1400-5*) CSS OH.

Luffe, Peter, jt. auth. see Camsong, Thidavadee.

Luffman, George A., jt. auth. see Newbould, Gerald D.

Lufford, Philip, jt. tr. see Bool, Hilary.

Luffy, Jake. Knitly Joined Together. (Orig.). 1997. pap. 6.95 (*0-9639416-4-X*) Pinecrest Bible.

Lufkens, Matthias, tr. see Belonogoff, Catherine.

***Lufkin.** Teaching Atlas of Head & Neck Imaging. 1999. 119.00 (*0-86577-691-1*) Thieme Med Pubs.

Lufkin, Alan, ed. California's Salmon & Steelhead: The Struggle to Restore an Imperiled Resource. (Illus.). 288p. 1991. 29.95 (*0-520-07029-1*, Pub. by U CA Pr) Cal Prin Full Svc.

Lufkin, Elise. Found Dogs. LC 97-229060. 144p. 1997. 17.95 (*0-87605-597-8*) Howell Bks.

Lufkin Historical Society Staff, ed. see Cline, Nell & Harold, Florence.

Lufkin, Peter S. & Silsbee, Robert M. The Whitestone Building Maintenance & Repair Cost Reference, 1999. 5th ed. (Illus.). 245p. 1999. pap. 210.00 (*0-9670629-0-X*) Whitestone Res Corp.

Lufkin, Robert B. Interventional MRI. LC 98-39428. (Illus.). 421p. (C). (gr. 13). 1998. text 129.00 (*0-8151-4545-4*, 30561) Mosby Inc.

— The MRI Manual. 2nd ed. LC 97-20148. (Illus.). 480p. (C). (gr. 13). 1997. pap. text 64.95 (*0-8151-5665-0*, 27077) Mosby Inc.

Lufkin, Robert B. MRI of the Head & Neck. 2nd ed. 256p. text 89.95 (*0-7817-2572-0*) Lppncott W & W.

Lufkin, Robert B., et al, eds. The Raven MRI Teaching File, 10 vols. 1991. text 495.00 (*0-7817-0204-6*, RA004) Lppncott W & W.

Lufkin, Robert B. & Hanafee, William N. MRI of the Head & Neck. (MRI Teaching File Ser.). 253p. 1991. text 76.00 (*0-88167-704-3*) Lppncott W & W.

— Pocket Atlas of Head & Neck MRI Anatomy. (Illus.). 83p. 1989. pap. text 16.95 (*0-88167-498-2*) Lppncott W & W.

Lufkin, Robert B., jt. auth. see De Salles, Antonio A.

Lufkin, Robert B., jt. auth. see Groenemeyer, Dietrich H.

Lufrano, Richard J. Honorable Merchants: Commerce & Self-Cultivation in Late Imperial China. LC 96-34019. 1996. text 39.00 (*0-8248-1740-0*) UH Pr.

Lufrano, Richard J., jt. auth. see De Bary, W. Theodore.

Luft & Tsuo, Y. Simon. Hydrogenated Amorphous Silicon Alloy Deposition Processes. LC 93-18931. (Applied Physics Ser.: Vol. 1). (Illus.). 344p. 1993. text 150.00 (*0-8247-9116-0*) Dekker.

Luft, jt. auth. see Wray, Ralph D.

Luft, C. P., jt. auth. see Fernandes, F.

Luft, Carl F. Understanding & Trading Futures: A Hands-On Study Guide for Investors & Traders. rev. ed. 250p. 1994. per. 22.95 (*1-55738-570-X*, Irwn Prfssnl) McGraw-Hill Prof.

Luft, Carl F. & Sheiner, Richard K. Listed Stock Options: The Hands-On Study Guide for Investors & Traders. rev. ed. 1993. per. 24.95 (*1-55738-520-3*, Irwn Prfssnl) McGraw-Hill Prof.

Luft, David S., ed. & tr. see Musil, Robert.

Luft, Edward D., jt. auth. see Ellmann-Kruger, Angelika.

Luft, Ella M. Dear Descendant. LC 95-95124. 280p. (Orig.). (YA). (gr. 7-12). 1995. per. 19.95 (*0-9648936-1-4*) Luft Pubng.

Luft, Eric, ed. Hegel, Hinrichs & Schleiermacher on Feeling & Reason in Religion: The Texts of Their 1821-1822 Debate. LC 87-5550. (Studies in German Thought & History: Volume 3). 544p. 1984. lib. bdg. 119.95 (*0-88946-352-2*) E Mellen.

Luft, Eric Von der, see Von der Luft, Eric, ed.

Luft, Hans. Blickpunkt Landwirtschaft. Eckart, Karl, ed. (Humangeographie. Sozialokonomische Strukturen in Europa Ser.: Vol. 1). (Illus.). 173p. 1998. pap. 34.95 (*3-631-31606-2*) P Lang Pubng.

Luft, Harold S. Health Maintenance Organizations: Dimensions of Performance. 468p. 1986. pap. 29.95 (*0-88738-681-4*) Transaction Pubs.

Luft, Herbert A., jt. auth. see Burnham, Robert, Jr.

Luft, Joseph. Group Processes: An Introduction to Group Dynamics. 3rd ed. LC 83-62828. xii, 237p. 1984. pap. text 31.95 (*0-87484-542-4*, 542) Mayfield Pub.

Luft, Kathleen, tr. see Barron's Educational Editors.

Luft, Kathleen, tr. see Hertle, Bernd, et al.

Luft, Kathleen, tr. see Lazaro, Olga J.

Luft, Kathleen, tr. see Von Rauch, Holger.

Luft, Klaus P. Erscheinungsformen des Androgynen bei Thomas Mann. (Studies on Themes & Motifs in Literature: Vol. 30). (GER.). VIII, 202p. (C). 1998. text 44.95 (*0-8204-3098-6*) P Lang Pubng.

Luft, Lorna. Me & My Shadows. large type ed. LC 98-35559. 1998. 26.95 (*0-7862-1623-9*) Thorndike Pr.

— Me & My Shadows. unabridged ed. 1998. pap. 25.00 incl. audio (*0-671-58243-7*, Audioworks) S&S Trade.

— Me & My Shadows: A Family Memoir - Living with the Legacy of Judy Garland. 352p. 1998. 25.00 (*0-671-01899-X*, PB Hardcover) PB.

— Me & My Shadows: A Family Memoir. rev. ed. (Illus.). 432p. 2000. pap. 14.00 (*0-671-01900-7*, PB Trade Paper) PB.

Luft, Lya. The Red House. Pontiero, Giovanni, tr. from POR. LC 94-202788. 182p. 1995. 27.95 (*1-85754-019-0*, Pub. by Carcanet Pr) Paul & Co Pubs.

Luft, Roger L. & Schoen, Janice L. Index to Doctoral Dissertations in Business Education, Supplement, 1980-1985. 3rd ed. 26p. (C). 1986. pap. text 8.00 (*1-881530-08-6*) Delta Pi Epsilon.

Luft, S., jt. auth. see Smith, M.

Luft, Werner, ed. Photovoltaic Safety. LC 88-42854. (AIP Conference Proceedings Ser.: No. 166). 264p. 1988. lib. bdg. 60.00 (*0-88318-366-8*) Am Inst Physics.

Luftensteiner, Horst W. Untersuchungen Zur Verbreitungsbiologie Von Pflanzengemeinschaften an Vier Standorten in Niederosterreich. (Bibliotheca Botanica: Vol. 135). (GER., Illus.). iv, 68p. 1982. 69.00 (*3-510-48006-6*, Pub. by E Schweizerbartsche) Balogh.

Luftglass, Manny. Gone Fishin' for Carp, Vol. 4. (Gone Fishin' Ser.). (Illus.). 104p. (Orig.). 1996. pap. 12.95 (*0-9650261-3-2*) Gone Fishin.

***Luftglass, Manny.** Gone Fishin' in Lake Hopatcong. (Gone Fishin' Ser.: Vol. 8). (Illus.). 112p. 1999. pap. 13.95 (*0-9650261-5-9*) Gone Fishin.

Luftglass, Manny. Gone Fishin' in Round Valley Reservoir, Vol. 2. (Illus.). 110p. (Orig.). 1997. reprint ed. pap. 13.95 (*0-9650261-1-6*) Gone Fishin.

— Gone Fishin' in Spruce Run Reservoir, Vol. 1. (Illus.). 90p. (Orig.). 1997. reprint ed. pap. 12.95 (*0-9650261-0-8*) Gone Fishin.

— Gone Fishin'in Round Valley Reservoir, Vol. 3. (Gone Fishin' Ser.). (Illus.). 110p. 1997. reprint ed. pap. 14.95 (*0-9650261-2-4*) Gone Fishin.

Luftglass, Manny & Bern, Ron. Gone Fishin' The 100 Best Spots in New Jersey. LC 98-22950. (Illus.). 176p. (Orig.). 1998. pap. 15.00 (*0-8135-2595-0*) Rutgers U Pr.

Luftglass, Manny, jt. auth. see Bern, Ron.

Luftglass, Manny, jt. auth. see Perrone, Joe, Jr.

Luftig. Microbiology. LC 97-50434. (Rypins' Intensive Reviews Ser.). 325p. 1998. pap. text 19.95 (*0-397-51547-2*) Lppncott W & W.

Luftig, Jeffrey T. & Jordan, Victoria S. Design of Experiments in Quality Engineering. LC 97-24465. (Illus.). 343p. 1997. 64.95 (*0-07-038807-5*) McGraw.

Luftig, Milton. Computer Programmer Analyst Trainee. 3rd ed. LC 73-150615. (Arco Professional Career Examination Ser.). 316 p. (Orig.). 1973. write for info. (*0-668-01344-3*, Arco) Macmillan Gen Ref.

Luftig, Richard L. Teaching the Mentally Retarded Student. 1986. text 46.00 (*0-205-10262-X*, H02629) Allyn.

Luftig, Victor. Seeing Together: Friendship Between the Sexes in English Writing from Mill to Woolf. 320p. 1995. pap. 15.95 (*0-8047-2591-8*) Stanford U Pr.

— Seeing Together: Friendship Between the Sexes in English Writing from Mill to Woolf. LC 92-44199. 320p. (C). 1995. 45.00 (*0-8047-2168-8*) Stanford U Pr.

Luftman, Jerry N., ed. Competing in the Information Age: Strategic Alignment in Practice. (Illus.). 432p. 1996. 35.00 (*0-19-509016-0*) OUP.

Lug, Sieglinde, tr. see Muller, Herta.

Lugalla, Joe. Crisis, Urbanization, & Urban Poverty in Tanzania: A Study of Urban Poverty & Survival Politics. (Illus.). 248p. (C). 1995. lib. bdg. 48.00 (*0-8191-9741-6*) U Pr of Amer.

Lugan, A. Fray Luis De Leon. 159p. 1924. 1.00 (*0-318-14268-6*) Hispanic Inst.

Lugani, R. S., et al. Learning Composite Mathematics, Bk. I. 168p. 1997. pap. 50.00 (*81-209-0362-5*, Pub. by Pitambar Pub) St Mut.

— Learning Composite Mathematics, Bk. II. 168p. 1997. pap. 50.00 (*81-209-0363-3*, Pub. by Pitambar Pub) St Mut.

— Learning Composite Mathematics, Bk. III. 208p. 1997. pap. 50.00 (*81-209-0364-1*, Pub. by Pitambar Pub) St Mut.

— Learning Composite Mathematics, Bk. IV. 192p. 1997. pap. 50.00 (*81-209-0365-X*, Pub. by Pitambar Pub) St Mut.

— Learning Composite Mathematics, Bk. V. 240p. 1997. pap. 60.00 (*81-209-0366-8*, Pub. by Pitambar Pub) St Mut.

— Learning Composite Mathematics, Bk. VI. 236p. 1997. pap. 60.00 (*81-209-0367-6*, Pub. by Pitambar Pub) St Mut.

— Learning Composite Mathematics, Bk. VII. 268p. 1997. pap. 60.00 (*81-209-0368-4*, Pub. by Pitambar Pub) St Mut.

— Learning Composite Mathematics, Bk. VIII. 232p. 1997. pap. 60.00 (*81-209-0369-2*, Pub. by Pitambar Pub) St Mut.

Lugar, Richard & Nuland, Victoria, contrib. by. Russia, Its Neighbors, & an Enlarging NATO. (Report of an Independent Task Force Ser.). 1997. pap. 5.00 (*0-87609-203-2*) Coun Foreign.

Lugar, Richard, et al. Foreign Policy into the 21st Century: The U. S. Leadership Challenge. Johnston, Douglas, ed. LC 96-34430. (CSIS Report Ser.). 176p. (C). 1996. pap. text 25.00 (*0-89206-292-4*) CSIS.

***Lugar, Richard G., ed.** Agricultural Transportation Problems: Congressional Hearing. (Illus.). 112p. 2000. pap. text 30.00 (*0-7567-0103-1*) DIANE Pub.

— Animal Waste Management Legislation: Congressional Hearing. (Illus.). 206p. 2000. reprint ed. pap. text 40.00 (*0-7567-0108-2*) DIANE Pub.

Lugar, Richard G., ed. Renewable Fuels & the Future Security of U. S. Energy Supplies: Hearing Before the Committee on Agriculture, Nutrition, & Forestry, U. S. Senate. (Illus.). 117p. (C). 1999. reprint ed. pap. text 25.00 (*0-7881-3572-4*) DIANE Pub.

***Lugar, Richard G., ed.** United States Agricultural Trade Policy: Congressional Hearing. (Illus.). 151p. (C). 2000. reprint ed. pap. text 30.00 (*0-7567-0112-0*) DIANE Pub.

Lugar, Richard G. & Raflo, Diane. Indianapolis: Crossroads of the American Dream. LC 96-4853. (Urban Tapestry Ser.). (Illus.). 352p. 1996. 39.50 (*1-881096-27-0*) Towery Pub.

Lugard, Flora S. A Tropical Dependency: An Outline of the Ancient History of the Western Sudan with an Account of the Modern Settlement of Northern Nigeria. 508p. 1997. reprint ed. 54.00 (*0-933121-72-5*) Black Classic.

Lugard, Flora S. A Tropical Dependency: An Outline of the Ancient History of the Western Sudan with an Account of the Modern Settlement of Northern Nigeria. LC 97-74312. 508p. 1997. reprint ed. pap. 24.95 (*0-933121-92-X*) Black Classic.

Lugard, Frederick J. Political Memoranda: Revision of Instructions to Political Officers on Subjects Chiefly Political & Administrative, 1913-1918. 3rd rev. ed. 480p. 1970. 59.50 (*0-7146-1693-1*, Pub. by F Cass Pubs) Intl Spec Bk.

Lugardon, B., jt. auth. see Tryon, Alice F.

Lugaresi, E. & Parmeggiani, P. L. Somatic & Autonomic Regulations in Sleep: Physiological & Clinical Aspects. LC 97-28727. 120p. 1997. 50.00 (*3-540-75046-0*) Spr-Verlag.

Lugbill, Ann, jt. auth. see Helmer, James B., Jr.

Lugbill, Ann, jt. auth. see Helmer, James B.

Lugenbuchl, Michael. Bed & Breakfast Book: Southern California. Miller, Kristine & Canfield, Andrea, eds. 1999. 5.95 (*1-56413-458-X*) Auto Club.

***Lugenbuehl, Michael & Brown, Sandy S.** Central Coast. Miller, Kristine, ed. 2000. pap. write for info. (*1-56413-480-6*) Auto Club.

Luger, George F. Artificial Intelligence. 3rd ed. LC 97-33235. 868p. (C). 1997. 76.00 (*0-8053-1196-3*) Addison-Wesley.

— Cognitive Science: The Science of Intelligent Systems. (Illus.). 666p. 1994. text 59.95 (*0-12-459570-7*) Acad Pr.

Luger, George F., ed. Artificial Intelligence & Manufacturing Research Planning Workshop. LC 99-179775. (Illus.). 225p. 1998. pap. text 30.00 (*1-57735-072-3*) AAAI Pr.

— Computation & Intelligence: Collected Readings. (AAAI Press Ser.). (Illus.). 749p. (C). 1995. pap. text 40.00 (*0-262-62101-0*) MIT Pr.

Luger, George F., jt. ed. see Interrante, Leslie.

Luger, H. J., jt. ed. see Vermeer, P. A.

Luger, Harriett. Bye, Bye, Bali Kai. 192p. (J). (gr. 3-7). 1996. pap. 5.00 (*0-15-200863-2*, Harcourt Child Bks) Harcourt.

— Bye, Bye, Bali Kai. LC 95-33452. 192p. (J). (gr. 4-6). 1996. 11.00 (*0-15-200862-4*, Harcourt Child Bks) Harcourt.

Luger, Harriett M. The Last Stronghold: A Story of the Modoc Indian, War, 1872-1873. LC 94-26615. (Illus.). x, 224p. (YA). (gr. 6-12). 1995. pap. text 16.50 (*0-208-02403-4*, Linnet Bks) Shoe String.

Luger, Jack. Ask Me No Questions, I'll Tell You No Lies: How to Survive Being Interviewed, Interrogated, Questioned, Quizzed, Sweated, Grilled... 1998. pap. text 16.95 (*0-9666932-6-4*) Breakout Prods Inc.

***Luger, Jack.** The Big Book of Secret Hiding Places. 1999. pap. text 14.95 (*1-893626-09-1*) Breakout Prods Inc.

Luger, Jack. Counterfeit I. D. Made Easy. LC 90-60515. (Illus.). 131p. 1990. pap. 15.95 (*0-915179-90-3*, 61111) Loompanics.

— How to Use Mail Drops: For Profit, Privacy & Self-Protection. 2nd ed. 1999. pap. text 16.95 (*1-893626-12-1*) Breakout Prods Inc.

Luger, Michael I. & Goldstein, Harvey A. Technology in the Garden: Research Parks & Regional Economic Development. LC 91-50255. (Illus.). xxii, 242p. (C). 1991. 55.00 (*0-8078-2000-8*); pap. 19.95 (*0-8078-4345-8*) U of NC Pr.

***Luger, Michael I. & Tempkin, Kenneth.** Red Tape & Housing Costs: How Regulation Affects New Residential Development. 185p. 2000. 24.95 (*0-88285-168-3*) Ctr Urban Pol Res.

Luger, Peter. Modern X-Ray Analysis on Single Crystals. 312p. 1980. 77.70 (*3-11-006830-3*) De Gruyter.

***Luger, Stan.** Corporate Power, American Democracy & the Automobile Industry. LC 99-21388. (Illus.). 200p. (C). 1999. 59.95 (*0-521-63173-4*) Cambridge U Pr.

***Luger, Thomas A.** Cutaneous Neuroimmunomodulation: The Proopiomelanocortin System. LC 99-46380. 1999. pap. write for info. incl. 5.25 hd (*1-57331-201-0*) NY Acad Sci.

Luger, Thomas A., et al, eds. Cutaneous Neuroimmunomodulation: The Proopiomelanocortin System. LC 99-46380. 1999. lib. bdg. 140.00 (*1-57331-200-2*) NY Acad Sci.

Luger, Thomas A. & Schwarz, Thomas, eds. Epidermal Growth Factors & Cytokines. LC 93-27742. (Basic & Clinical Dermatology Ser.: Vol. 10). (Illus.). 504p. 1993. text 215.00 (*0-8247-9102-9*) Dekker.

Luger, Von H. Routinen und Rituale in der Alltagskommunikation. (Fernstudieneinheit Ser.: No. 6). (GER.). 112p. 1997. pap. 11.25 (*3-468-49674-5*) Langenscheidt.

***Lugg, Andrew.** Wittgenstein's Investigations 1-133: A Guide & Interpretation. LC 99-89678. (Illus.). 2000. write for info. (*0-415-23245-7*) Routledge.

Lugg, Catherine A. For God & Country: Conservatism & American School Policy. (Counterpoints Ser.: Vol. 32). IX, 213p. (C). 1996. pap. text 29.95 (*0-8204-3088-9*) P Lang Pubng.

— Kitsch: From Education to Public Policy. (Pedagogy & Popular Culture Ser.: Vol. 3). 130p. 1999. 45.00 (*0-8153-2595-9*, SS1146) Garland.

Lugg, George W., ed. see Burroughs, John.

***Lugg, Sarah.** Book of Days. 1999. 9.95 (*0-7407-0158-4*) Andrews & McMeel.

— Objects of My Affection. 64p. 2000. 10.95 (*0-7407-1248-9*) Andrews & McMeel.

— A Week in France IV. (Illus.). 128p. 1999. spiral bd. 10.95 (*0-7407-0157-6*) Andrews & McMeel.

Luggen, Ann S., et al. NGNA Core Curriculum for Gerontological Advance Practice Nurses. LC 98-9043. 717p. 1998. 99.95 (*0-7619-1300-9*); pap. 55.00 (*0-7619-1301-7*) Sage.

***Luggen, Ann Schmidt & Meiner, Sue E., eds.** Handbook for the Care of the Older Adult with Cancer. 216p. 2000. pap. text 30.00 (*1-890504-16-5*) Oncology Nursing.

Luggen, William W. Computer Numerical Control: A First Look Primer. LC 96-2895. (Machine Tools Ser.). 416p. (C). 1996. pap. 64.95 (*0-8273-7245-0*) Delmar.

Luggen, William W. Computer Numerical Control: A First Look Primer. 96p. 1996. pap. text, teacher ed. 14.00 (*0-8273-7246-9*) Delmar.

— Fundamentals of Computer Numerical Control. (Machine Tools Ser.). 1994. teacher ed. 14.95 (*0-8273-6497-0*) Delmar.

— Fundamentals of Computer Numerical Control. 3rd ed. LC 93-30141. 336p. 1994. mass mkt. 64.95 (*0-8273-6496-2*) Delmar.

— Fundamentals of Numerical Control. 2nd ed. (Illus.). 256p. 1988. pap. 41.95 (*0-8273-3139-8*) Delmar.

— Fundamentals of Numerical Control. 2nd ed. (Illus.). 256p. 1988. pap., teacher ed. 14.95 (*0-8273-3140-1*) Delmar.

— Introduction to NC-CNC Operation. LC 85-20237. 296p. 1986. pap. text 18.50 (*0-471-81743-0*) P-H.

Lugger, Phyllis, ed. Asteroids to Quasars: A Symposium for the 60th Birthday of William Liller. 333p. (C). 1991. text 85.00 (*0-521-35231-2*) Cambridge U Pr.

Lugi, Lucia, jt. auth. see Berzins, Valdis.

Lugiato, L. A., jt. ed. see Pike, E. R.

Lugin, Alejandro Perez, see Perez Lugin, Alejandro, adapted by.

Luginbuhl, Christian B. & Skiff, Brian A. Observing Handbook & Catalogue of Deep Sky Objects. 2nd ed. (Illus.). 364p. (C). 1998. pap. 34.95 (*0-521-62556-4*) Cambridge U Pr.

Luginbuhl, Martha, jt. auth. see Emerson, Haven.

Luginbuhl, Martin. Gewalt Im Gesprach: Verbale Gewalt In Politischen Fernsehdiskussionen Am Beispiel der (Arena) 334p. 1999. 49.95 (*3-906762-20-3*) P Lang.

Luginskii, I. N., et al. English-Russian Dictionary of Electrical & Power Engineering. unabridged ed. (ENG & RUS.). 613p. (Orig.). (C). 1994. pap. 39.95 (*0-8285-5099-9*) Firebird NY.

Luginsky, Y. N., et al, eds. Dictionary of Electrical Engineering: English, German, French, Dutch & Russian. (DUT, ENG, FRE, GER & RUS.). (C). 1987. text 211.00 (*90-201-1910-9*) Kluwer Academic.

Lugira, Aloysius M. African Religion. LC 99-10254. (World Religions Ser.). (Illus.). 128p. (YA). (gr. 7 up). 1999. 26.95 (*0-8160-3876-7*) Facts on File.

Lugli, P., jt. auth. see Jacobini, C.

Lugli, Paolo, jt. auth. see Sabella, R.

Lugn, Alvin L. Sedimentation in the Mississippi River Between Davenport, Iowa, & Cairo, Illinois. LC 28-14418. (Augustana College Library Publications: No. 11). 104p. 1927. pap. 1.00 (*0-910182-08-6*) Augustana Coll.

***Lugo, Alejandro.** Gender Matters: Rereading Michelle Z. Rosaldo. LC 99-6290. 272p. (C). 2000. text 49.50 (*0-472-11046-2*, 11046); pap. text 22.95 (*0-472-08618-9*, 08618) U of Mich Pr.

Lugo, Ariel E., et al, eds. Ecological Development in the Humid Tropics: Guidelines for Planners. (Illus.). 362p. 1988. per. 19.50 (*0-933595-20-4*) Winrock Intl.

— Forested Wetlands No. 15: Ecosystems of the World. 504p. 1990. 284.00 (*0-444-42812-7*) Elsevier.

L

L

Lugo, Ariel E. & Lowe, Carol, eds. Tropical Forests: Management & Ecology. LC 94-23823. (Ecological Studies: Vol. 112). 1995. 118.00 (*0-387-94320-X*) Spr-Verlag.

Lugo, Ariel E., jt. ed. see Wisniewski, Joe.

Lugo, Carlos Rivera, see Garcia Passalacqua, Juan M. & Rivera Lugo, Carlos.

Lugo, Carlos Rivera, see Garcia Passalacqua, Juan & Rivera Lugo, Carlos.

Lugo de Kaplan, Sarah. Manual Ilustrado de Laboratorio Para Botanica. 2nd ed. 145p. (C). 1990. pap. text, student ed. 24.95 (*1-881375-10-2*) Libreria Univ.

— Manual Ilustrado de Laboratorio Para Curso Basico de Biologia. 124p. (C). 1980. pap. text, student ed. 24.95 (*1-881375-09-9*) Libreria Univ.

Lugo, Elena. Etica Medica. 173p. (C). 1984. pap. text 24.95 (*1-881375-13-7*) Libreria Univ.

— Etica Profesional Para la Ingenieria. 263p. (C). 1985. pap. text 24.95 (*1-881375-12-9*) Libreria Univ.

Lugo-Guernelli, A., et al. Manuel de Gramatica Comercial. (ENG & SPA.). 204p. 1976. pap. 14.95 (*0-8288-5741-5*, S50369) Fr & Eur.

Lugo-Guernelli, Adelaida. Hostos y la Literatura. 19p. 1988. pap. 3.00 (*0-685-51573-7*) U of PR Pr.

Lugo, Herminio L., intro. Primer Simposio sobre Ecologia Islena-First Symposium on Island Ecological Systems: Papers of the Symposium Held at Inter American University, Oct. 28, 1983. (ENG & SPA.). 160p. (Orig.). (C). 1984. pap. text 5.95 (*0-913480-62-2*) Inter Am U Pr.

Lugo, James. Living Psychology Handbook. 156p. (C). 1990. pap. text 15.78 (*0-929655-98-2*) CAT Pub.

— Living Psychology Instructor's Manual. 118p. (C). 1990. pap. text. write for info. (*1-56226-025-1*) CAT Pub.

Lugo, James, jt. auth. see Dixon, Lugenia.

Lugo, James, jt. auth. see Till, Robert.

Lugo, James O. Living Psychology: A Lifespan Approach. 4th ed. 628p. (C). 1991. pap. text 44.89 (*1-56226-039-1*) CAT Pub.

***Lugo, Jeanice.** What's a Mother to Do? The ABCs of Raising a Child. 2000. pap. write for info. (*1-928781-36-5*) Hollis Bks.

Lugo, Leanne F., jt. auth. see Lugo, Leland.

Lugo, Leland & Lugo, Leanne F. Jeremy & Grandpa's Magic Clock: A Musical Tale. LC 97-92506. (Illus.). 32p. (J). (ps-5). 1997. text 25.00 (*0-9661454-1-0*); pap. text 15.00 (*0-9661454-0-2*) CML Publng.

***Lugo, Luis E.** Religion, Pluralism & Public Life. LC 00-41731. 2000. pap. write for info. (*0-8028-4716-1*) Eerdmans.

Lugo, Luis E., ed. Sovereignty at the Crossroads? Morality & International Politics in the Post-Cold War Era. 208p. (C). 1996. pap. text 24.95 (*0-8476-8215-3*); lib. bdg. 60.50 (*0-8476-8214-5*) Rowman.

Lugo, Margarita. Fun, Sun & Mexico: The Spanish Phrasebook. (Illus.). 220p. (Orig.). 1994. pap., per. 9.95 (*0-9643536-4-4*) Type Team.

Lugo, Marta. Dominican Republic Guidebook. 1989. pap. 15.95 (*0-932030-29-7*) Eurasia Pr NY.

Lugo, Miguel. Competitive Dominoes: How to Play Like a Champion. LC 98-30849. (Illus.). 128p. 1998. pap. 6.95 (*0-8069-1793-8*) Sterling.

Lugo, Roberto, jt. ed. see Catala, Rafael.

Lugoe. From the Womb to War. 1998. 17.95 (*0-533-12674-6*) Vantage.

Lugones, Leopoldo. Strange Forces. Alter-Gilbert, Gilbert, tr. from SPA. 128p. 1999. pap. 13.95 (*1-891270-05-2*, Pub. by Lat Am Lit Rev Pr) Consort Bk Sales.

Lugones, Nestor, jt. ed. see Ramos-Garcia, Luis A.

Lugosi, L. & Hennessen, W., eds. BCG Vaccines & Tuberculins Part A & B. (Developments in Biological Standardization Ser.: Vol. 58). (Illus.). xviii, 782p. 1987. pap. 61.00 (*3-8055-4279-8*) S Karger.

Lugowshi, Marek & Ripin, Kathy M. Insider Strategies for Outsourcing Information Systems: How to Build Productive Partnerships & Avoid Seductive Traps. LC 99-13604. (Illus.). 288p. 1999. 30.00 (*0-19-512566-5*) OUP.

***Lugowski, Marek.** Agnieszka's Dowry (AD) Issue 10: For the Nonlinear & Color-Filled Experience. Craig, Katrina Grace, ed. (Agnieszka's Dowry (AgD)). 52p. 2000. pap. 3.00 (*1-888431-25-3*) ASGP.

Lugowski, Marek. Selamat Jalan, Mate: Poems from a Short Trip. LC 97-112707. (Illus.). 36p. (Orig.). 1996. pap. 3.00 (*1-888431-07-5*) ASGP.

— Utah Poems. LC 96-203588. (Illus.). 40p. (Orig.). 1995. pap. 3.00 (*1-888431-00-8*) ASGP.

Lugowski, Marek, ed. Agnieszka's Dowry (AgD) For the Non-Linear & Color-Filled Experience: http://www.enteract.com/~asgp/agnieszka.html, Issues 2 & 3. (Illus.). 60p. 1997. pap. 3.00 (*1-888431-13-X*) ASGP.

Lugowski, Marek, ed. Agnieszka's Dowry (AgD) For the Non-Linear & Color-Filled Experience: http://www.enteract.com/~asgp/agnieszka.html, Issue 1. 52p. 1996. pap. 3.00 (*1-888431-09-1*) ASGP.

Lugowski, Marek, et al, eds. Agnieszka's Dowry AgD: For the Non-Linear & Color Filled Experience: http://www.enteract.com/~asgp/agnieszka.html, Issue 8. 1998. pap. 3.00 (*1-888431-22-9*) ASGP.

Lugowski, Marek & Craig, Katrina G., eds. Agnieszka's Dowry (AgD) For the Non-Linear & Color-Filled Experience: http://www.enteract.com/~asgp/agnieszka.html, Issue 4. (Illus.). 52p. 1997. pap. 3.00 (*1-888431-15-6*) ASGP.

— Agnieszka's Dowry (AgD) For the Non-Linear & Color-Filled Experience: http://www.enteract.com/~asgp/agnieszka.html, Issue 5. (Illus.). 42p. 1997. pap. 3.00 (*1-888431-16-4*) ASGP.

— Agnieszka's Dowry (AgD) For the Non-Linear & Color-Filled Experience: http://www.enteract.com/~asgp/agnieszka.html, Issue 6. (Illus.). 52p. 1998. pap. 3.00 (*1-888431-19-9*) ASGP.

— Agnieszka's Dowry (AgD) For the Non-Linear & Color-Filled Experience: http://www.enteract.com/nasgp/agnieszka.html, Issue 7. (Illus.). 40p. 1998. pap. 3.00 (*1-888431-21-0*) ASGP.

***Lugowski, Marek & Craig, Katrina Grace, eds.** Agnieszka's Dowry (AgD) Issue 9: For the Nonlinear & Color-Filled Experience: Http://www.enteract.com/wasgp/agnieszka.html. (Illus.). 44p. 1999. 3.00 (*1-888431-24-5*) ASGP.

Lugowski, Marek, ed. see Andreyev, Alexey V.

Lugowski, Marek, ed. see Heringer, LeeAnn.

Lugt, Frits. Les Marques de Collections de Dessins & d'Estampes. LC 75-21068. (FRE., Illus.). 608p. 1975. reprint ed. 125.00 (*0-915346-08-7*) A Wofsy Fine Arts.

— Les Marques de Collections de Dessins et d'Estampes: Supplement. (FRE., Illus.). 476p. 1988. reprint ed. 125.00 (*1-55660-023-2*) A Wofsy Fine Arts.

Lugt, Hans J. Introduction to Vortex Theory. (Illus.). xviii, 627p. (C). 1997. text 65.00 (*0-9657689-0-2*) Vortex Flow.

— Vortex Flow in Nature & Technology. 316p. (C). 1994. lib. bdg. 64.50 (*0-89464-916-7*) Krieger.

Lugt, Robert D. Vander, see Lefever, Ernest W. & Vander Lugt, Robert D., eds.

Lugtenberg, B. J., ed. Signal Molecules in Plants & Plant-Microbe Interactions. (NATO ASI Series H: Vol. 36). (Illus.). 448p. 1990. 189.95 (*0-387-50381-1*) Spr-Verlag.

Lugton. Palliative Care: The Nurses's R. LC 98-48825. (C). 1999. pap. text 29.95 (*0-443-05513-0*) Church.

Lugton, Alan. The Making of Hibernian. 300p. 1996. 45.00 (*0-85976-424-9*, Pub. by J Donald) St Mut.

***Lugton, Alan.** The Making of Hibernian. 228p. 2000. pap. 25.95 (*0-85976-509-1*, Pub. by J Donald) Dufour.

Lugton, Alan. The Making of Hibernian, Vol. 3. 280p. 1998. pap. 47.85 (*0-85976-498-2*, Pub. by J Donald) St Mut.

Lugton, Robert C. American Topics. 2nd ed. (Illus.). 288p. (C). 1986. pap. text 33.00 (*0-13-029588-4*) P-H.

Luguy, Phillipe, jt. auth. see Leturgie, Jean.

Luh, Bor S., ed. Rice, 2 vols. 2nd enl. rev. ed. (Illus.). 1014p. (C). (gr. 13). 1991. pap. 255.00 (*0-442-00735-3*) Chapman & Hall.

Luh, Chih Wei. On Chinese Poetry. 1972. lib. bdg. 79.95 (*0-87968-540-9*) Krishna Pr.

Luh, Lan Luk, jt. auth. see Hou, Wee Chow.

Luhan, Mabel D. Lorenzo in Taos. 1988. reprint ed. lib. bdg. 79.00 (*0-7812-0464-X*) Rprt Serv.

— Winter in Taos. (Illus.). 264p. 1983. reprint ed. 18.95 (*0-911695-50-8*) Las Palomas.

Luhan, Mabel Dodge. Edge of Taos Desert: An Escape to Reality. LC 86-25283. 338p. 1987. reprint ed. pap. 16.95 (*0-8263-0971-2*) U of NM Pr.

Luhan, Mabel G. Lorenzo in Taos. LC 78-145147. 352p. 1932. reprint ed. 59.00 (*0-403-01077-2*) Scholarly.

Luhe, Barbara von der, see von der Luhe, Barbara.

Luhman. Race & Ethnicity in the U. S. (C). 1999. pap. text 62.00 (*0-15-503876-1*, Pub. by Harcourt Coll Pubs) Harcourt.

Luhman, John C. A Taxonomic Revision of Nearctic Endasys Foerster, 1868: Hymenoptera: Ichneumonidae, Gelinae. LC 89-20636. (Publications in Entomology: Vol. 109). (Illus.). 198p. 1991. pap. 30.00 (*0-520-09757-2*, Pub. by U CA Pr) Cal Prin Full Svc.

***Luhman, Reid.** The Sociological Outlook: A Text with Readings. 6th rev. ed. LC 94-72319. (Illus.). (C). 1999. pap. text 45.75 (*0-939693-50-X*) Collegiate Pr.

Luhmann, Frederick J. Millennium Pope: A Novel of Spiritual Journey. 288p. 1999. pap. write for info. (*0-7392-0135-2*, PO3057) Morris Pubng.

Luhmann, J. G., et al, eds. Venus & Mars: Atmospheres, Ionospheres, & Solar Wind Interactions. (Geophysical Monograph Ser.: Vol. 66). (Illus.). 448p. 1992. 59.00 (*0-87590-032-1*) Am Geophysical.

***Luhmann, Niklas.** Art as a Social System. (Illus.). 2000. 65.00 (*0-8047-3906-4*); pap. text 24.95 (*0-8047-3907-2*) Stanford U Pr.

Luhmann, Niklas. Ecological Communication. Bednarz, John, Jr., tr. LC 89-4843. 204p. 1989. 41.95 (*0-226-49651-1*) U Ch Pr.

— Essays in Self-Realization. 320p. 1990. text 57.50 (*0-231-06368-7*) Col U Pr.

— Love As Passion: The Codification of Intimacy. Gaines, Jeremy & Jones, Doris L., trs. from GER. LC 86-14929. 256p. 1987. 43.00 (*0-674-53923-0*) HUP.

— Observations on Modernity. Whobrey, William, tr. from GER. LC 97-40908. (Writing Science Ser.). 1998. write for info. (*0-8047-3234-5*); pap. write for info. (*0-8047-3235-3*) Stanford U Pr.

— Political Theory in the Welfare State. vi, 239p. (C). 1990. lib. bdg. 46.95 (*3-11-011932-3*) De Gruyter.

— Religious Dogmatics & the Evolution of Societies. Beyer, Peter F., tr. LC 84-8976. (Studies in Religion & Society: Vol. 9). 192p. 1984. lib. bdg. 79.95 (*0-88946-866-4*) E Mellen.

— Risk: A Sociological Theory. (Communication & Social Order Ser.). 249p. 1993. lib. bdg. 49.95 (*0-202-30443-4*) Aldine de Gruyter.

— Social Systems. Bednarz, John, Jr. & Baecker, Dirk, trs. from GER. LC 94-46175. (Writing Science Ser.).Tr. of Soziale Systeme. 570p. 1995. pap. 24.95 (*0-8047-2625-6*) Stanford U Pr.

— Social Systems. Bednarz, John, Jr. & Baecker, Dirk, trs. LC 94-46175. (Writing Science Ser.).Tr. of Soziale Systeme. (GER.). 570p. 1995. 69.50 (*0-8047-1993-4*) Stanford U Pr.

— A Sociological Theory of Law. King-Utz, Elizabeth & Albrow, Martin, trs. 448p. 1985. 59.95 (*0-7100-9747-6*, Routledge Thoemms) Routledge.

— Soziologie des Risikos. 252p. 1993. pap. 37.70 (*3-11-012939-6*) De Gruyter.

— Trust & Power: Two Works. Burns, Tom & Poggi, Gianfranco, eds. Davis, Howard et al, trs. LC 79-40579. 228p. reprint ed. pap. 70.70 (*0-608-18820-4*, 203052800069) Bks Demand.

Luhmann, Niklas & Schorr, Karl-Eberhard. Problems of Reflection in the System of Education, Vol. 3. Neuwirth, Rebecca A., tr. 480p. 1999. 85.00 (*1-57181-735-2*) Berghahn Bks.

Luhmann, Nuklas. Love As Passion: The Codification of Intimacy. Gaines, Jeremy & Jones, Doris L., trs. from ENG. LC 98-17103. (Cultural Memory in the Present Ser.). 248p. 1998. pap. 18.95 (*0-8047-3253-1*) Stanford U Pr.

Luhn, Rebecca. Buying Your First Franchise: Options for the New Entrepreneur. Shotwell, Nancy, ed. LC 92-54373. (Small Business & Entrepreneurship Ser.). 252p. (Orig.). 1994. pap. 15.95 (*1-56052-190-2*) Crisp Pubns.

— Employee Benefits with Cost Control: Delivering Maximum Benefits at Minimum Cost. Keppler, Kay, ed. LC 91-76244. (Fifty-Minute Ser.). 93p. (Orig.). 1992. pap. 10.95 (*1-56052-133-3*) Crisp Pubns.

— Managing Anger: Methods for a Happier & Healthier Life. Brett, Elaine, ed. LC 91-76242. (Fifty-Minute Ser.). (Illus.). 111p. (Orig.). 1992. pap. 10.95 (*1-56052-114-7*) Crisp Pubns.

***Luhnow, Glennda G.** An Examination of the Ethnographic Boundary Shared by Gumbatwas & Kokiwas Modoc Triblets, Northeastern California. fac. ed. (Illus.), 185p. (C). 1998. reprint ed. pap. text 20.00 (*1-55567-813-0*) Coyote Press.

Luhr, James F. & Simkin, Tom. Paricutin: The Volcano Born in a Mexican Cornfield. LC 93-77812. (Illus.). 456p. (Orig.). 1993. 50.00 (*0-945005-14-8*) Geoscience Pr.

Luhr, Overton. Physics Tells Why: An Explanation of Some Common Physical Phenomena. 2nd ed. LC 51-30387. (Illus.). 397p. reprint ed. pap. 123.10 (*0-608-10329-2*, 201236300081) Bks Demand.

Luhr, William. Raymond Chandler & Film. 2nd ed. 224p. (C). 1991. reprint ed. pap. 16.95 (*0-8130-1091-8*) U Press Fla.

Luhr, William & Lehman, Peter. Returning to the Scene: Blake Edwards, Vol. 2, Vol. 2. LC 80-28440. (Illus.). 284p. (C). 1989. 29.95 (*0-8214-0917-4*); pap. 14.95 (*0-8214-0918-2*) Ohio U Pr.

Luhr, William, jt. auth. see Lehman, Peter.

Luhr, William, ed. see Huston, John.

Luhrmann, Baz & Pearce, Craig. Strictly Ballroom. 86p. (C). 1993. pap. 17.95 (*0-86819-359-3*, Pub. by Currency Pr) Accents Pubns.

Luhrmann, Dieter. Galatians. 168p. 1992. 33.00 (*0-8006-9618-2*, 1-9618, Fortress Pr) Augsburg Fortress.

— An Itinerary for New Testament Study. LC 89-5024. 144p. 1989. pap. 10.00 (*0-334-02076-X*) TPI PA.

***Luhrmann, T. M.** Of Two Minds: The Growing Disorder in American Psychiatry. LC 99-40732. 400p. 2000. 26.95 (*0-679-42191-2*) Knopf.

Luhrmann, Tanya M. The Good Parsi: The Fate of a Colonial Elite in a Postcolonial Society. 352p. 1996. 54.00 (*0-674-35675-6*); pap. 22.95 (*0-674-35676-4*) HUP.

— Persuasions of the Witch's Craft: Ritual Magic in Contemporary England. LC 88-33382. (Illus.). 380p. 1989. 32.00 (*0-674-66323-3*) HUP.

— Persuasions of the Witch's Craft: Ritual Magic in Contemporary England. (Illus.). 416p. 1991. pap. text 16.95 (*0-674-66324-1*, LUHPEX) HUP.

Luhrs, Dietrich. Untersuchungen Zu Den Athetesen Aristarchs in der Ilias und Zu Ihrer Behandlung Im Corpus der Exegetischen Scholien. (Beitrage Zur Altertumswissenschaft Ser.: Bd. 11). (GER.). xviii, 286p. 1992. write for info. (*3-487-09629-3*) G Olms Pubs.

Luhrs, Janet. The Simple Living Guide: A Sourcebook for Less Stressful, More Joyful Living. LC 97-13486. (Illus.). 464p. 1997. pap. 20.00 (*0-553-06796-6*) Broadway BDD.

***Luhrs, Janet.** Simple Loving: A Path to Deeper, More Sustainable Relationships. LC 99-87441. 2000. pap. 15.95 (*0-14-019610-2*) Viking Penguin.

Luhrs, Jeannece Jackson, jt. auth. see Lester, Vivian.

Luhrs, Kathleen, ed. see Caldwell, John, pseud, et al.

Lui, A. T. Y., jt. ed. see Xu, R. L.

Lui, Adam. Two Rulers in One Reign: Dorgon & Shun-Chih, 1644-1660. (Faculty of Asian Studies Monographs: Vol. 13). (Illus.). 170p. 1997. pap. text 25.00 (*0-7315-0654-5*, Pub. by Aust Nat Univ) UH Pr.

Lui, Adam Yuen-Chung. The Hanlin Academy: Training Ground for the Ambitious, 1644-1850. LC 80-24259. (Illus.). xviii, 286p. (C). 1981. lib. bdg. 36.00 (*0-208-01833-6*, Archon Bks) Shoe String.

Lui, Anthony T., ed. Magnetotail Physics. LC 86-27614. (Johns Hopkins Studies in Earth & Planetary Sciences Ser.). (Illus.). 404p. 1987. text 70.00 (*0-8018-3496-1*) Johns Hopkins.

Lui, B. The Gasteromycetes of China. (Nova Hedwigia Beiheft Ser.: No. 76). (Illus.). 240p. 1984. lib. bdg. 78.00 (*3-7682-5476-3*) Lubrecht & Cramer.

Lui, Baoding & Esogbue, Augustine O. Decision Criteria & Optimal Inventory Processes. LC 99-12054. (International Series in Operations Research & Management Science). 1999. write for info. (*0-7923-8468-7*) Kluwer Academic.

Lui, C. W., jt. auth. see Besant, C. B.

Lui, E. M., jt. auth. see Chen, Wai-Fah.

Lui, E. M, ed. see Chen, W. F.

Lui, Elizabeth G. Closed Mondays. (Illus.). 136p. 50.00 (*3-923922-73-6*) Nazraeli Pr.

Lui, Elizabeth G., ed. Spirit & Flight Vol. 1: A Photographic Salute to the United States Air Force Academy. LC 96-84751. (Illus.). xxv, 135p. 1996. 60.00 (*0-9652585-0-5*) Assn Graduate USAF Academy.

Lui, Gillian. What's That Noise? (Early Words Ser.). (Illus.). 24p. (J). (gr. 1-3). 1996. write for info. (*0-237-51429-X*) EVN1 UK.

Lui, M. T. Chemistry of Diazirines, Vol. 2. LC 87-10276. 1987. reprint ed. 84.00 (*0-8493-5049-2*, CRC Reprint) Franklin.

Lui-Ma, Amy, ed. see Yun, Hsing.

Luibheid, Colm, ed. Pseudo Dionysius: The Complete Works. (Classics of Western Spirituality Ser.: Vol. 54). 336p. 1987. pap. 22.95 (*0-8091-2838-1*) Paulist Pr.

Luibheid, Colm, tr. see Cassian, John.

Luick, Bret R., ed. see Grohman, Joann S.

Luick, Toivo, jt. auth. see Guthrie, Owen.

Luidens, Donald A., et al, eds. Reformed Vitality: Continuity & Change in the Face of Modernity. LC 98-27765. 226p. 1998. 49.00 (*0-7618-1232-6*); pap. 29.50 (*0-7618-1233-4*) U Pr of Amer.

Luig, Ulrich. Conversion As a Social Process: A History of Missionary Christianity among the Valley Tonga, Zambia. 320p. 1997. pap. text 32.95 (*3-8258-3047-0*) Transaction Pubs.

Luig, Ute, jt. ed. see Behrend, Heike.

Luiggi, Alice H. Sixty-Five Valiants. LC 65-28692. (Illus.). 213p. reprint ed. pap. 66.10 (*0-7837-4930-9*, 204459600004) Bks Demand.

Luiggi, Sadi O. Introduccion a las Cooperativas de Ahorro y Credito. Bauza, Carmen M., ed. (Cooperatives Ser.). (SPA.). 268p. (Orig.). 1990. 12.00 (*0-934885-02-8*) Edit Nosotros.

Luigi, Giocchino Vincenzo Raffaele, see Leo XIII, pseud.

Luijpen, W. A. & Koren, H. J. First Introduction to Existential Phenomenology. LC 79-75975. 243p. 1969. pap. text 18.50 (*0-8207-0110-6*) Duquesne.

Luijten, Erik. Interaction Range, Universality & the Upper Critical Dimension. (Illus.). 212p. 1997. pap. 52.50 (*90-407-1552-1*, Pub. by Delft U Pr) Coronet Bks.

Luijten, Ger & Meij, A. W., eds. From the Pisanello to Cezanne: Master Drawings from the Museum Boymans-van Beuningen, Rotterdam. (Illus.). 276p. (C). 1990. text 130.00 (*0-521-40105-4*) Cambridge U Pr.

Luijten, Ger, jt. ed. see DePauw, Carl.

***Luiken, N. M.** Running on Instinct. 2000. text 23.95 (*0-312-87344-1*) St Martin.

Luine, Jerome. Science Mysteries. LC 94-5355. 80p. (J). 1994. pap. 5.95 (*1-56565-173-1*, 01731W, Pub. by Lowell Hse Juvenile) NTC Contemp Pub Co.

Luine, Victoria & Harding, Cheryl F., eds. Hormonal Restructuring of the Adult Brain: Basic & Clinical Perspectives, 743. LC 94-24685. (Annals Ser.: Vol. 743). 1994. pap. text 75.00 (*0-89766-920-7*) NY Acad Sci.

— Hormonal Restructuring of the Adult Brain: Basic & Clinical Perspectives, 743. LC 94-24685. (Annals Ser.: Vol. 743). (Illus.). 273p. 1994. 75.00 (*0-89766-919-3*) NY Acad Sci.

Luinenberg, Oline & Osborne, Stephen. The Little Green Book: Quotations on the Environment. 96p. 1995. per. 3.95 (*0-88978-225-3*, Pub. by Arsenal Pulp) LPC InBook.

Luinenburg, Oline & Osborne, Stephen. The Little Grey Flannel Book: Quotations on Men. 108p. 1995. per. 3.95 (*0-88978-239-3*, Pub. by Arsenal Pulp) LPC InBook.

— The Little Pink Book: Quotations on Women's Issues. 96p. 1995. per. 4.95 (*0-88978-226-1*, Pub. by Arsenal Pulp) LPC InBook.

***Luini, Luigi.** Uncertain Decisions: Bridging Theory & Experiments. LC 98-45359. 5p. 1999. 129.95 (*0-7923-8391-5*) Kluwer Academic.

Luis, Carlos M. El Oficio de la Mirada: Ensayos de Arte y Literatura Cubana. LC 98-87742. (Coleccion Arte). (SPA., Illus.). 231p. (Orig.). 1998. pap. 18.00 (*0-89729-884-5*) Ediciones.

— Transito de la Mirada. (Illus.). 266p. (Orig.). 1991. pap. 12.00 (*0-917049-56-X*) Saeta.

Luis de Leon, Fray. A Bilingual Edition of Fray Luis De Leon's La Perfecta Casada: The Role of Married Women in Sixteenth-Century Spain, Vol. 2. Jones, John A. & San Jose Lera, Javier, eds. LC 98-52445. (Spanish Studies: No. 2). 348p. 1999. text 99.95 (*0-7734-8178-8*) E Mellen.

Luis, Garfias M. Revolucion Mexicana. 1997. pap. text 11.98 (*968-38-0268-0*) Panorama Edit.

Luis, Jose, ed. see Cowman, Charles E.

Luis, Julio Garcia. Cuban Revolution Reader: A Documented History of 40 Years of the Cuban Revolution. 2000. pap. 21.95 (*1-876175-10-9*) Ocean Pr NJ.

Luis Vives, Juan. Dialogos, No. 128. (SPA.). 153p. 1959. write for info. (*0-8288-8580-X*) Fr & Eur.

***Luis, William.** Culture & Customs of Cuba. LC 00-35324. (Culture & Customs of Latin America & the Caribbean Ser.). 2000. write for info. (*0-313-30433-5*) Greenwood.

Luis, William. Dance Between Two Cultures: Latino Caribbean Literature Written in the United States. LC 97-21192. 376p. (C). 1997. 39.95 (*0-8265-1302-6*) Vanderbilt U Pr.

— Literary Bondage: Slavery in Cuban Narrative. LC 89-37603. (Texas Pan American Ser.). 326p. 1990. text 40.00 (*0-292-72463-2*) U of Tex Pr.

Luis, William, ed. Voices from Under: Black Narrative in Latin America & the Caribbean, 76. LC 83-22792. (Contributions in Afro-American & African Studies: No. 76). 263p. 1984. 62.95 (*0-313-23826-X*, LUV/, Greenwood Pr) Greenwood.

Luis, William, jt. auth. see Desnoes, Edmundo.

Luisada, Aldo A. Pulmonary Edema in Man & Animals. LC 71-96988. (Illus.). 168p. 1970. 15.00 (*0-87527-050-6*) Green.

An Asterisk (*) at the beginning of an entry indicates that the title is appearing for the first time.

— The Sounds of the Diseased Heart. LC 74-176171. (Illus.). 416p. 1973. text 32.50 (*0-87527-113-8*) Green.
— The Sounds of the Normal Heart. LC 78-176172. (Illus.). 280p. 1972. 32.50 (*0-87527-051-4*) Green.
Luisada, Aldo A. & Portaluppi, Francesco. The Heart Sounds: New Facts & Their Clinical Implications. LC 81-19240. 246p. 1982. 59.95 (*0-275-91372-4*, C1372, Praeger Pubs) Greenwood.
Luisada, Aldo A. & Sainani, Gurmukh S. A Primer of Cardiac Diagnosis: The Physical & Technical Study of the Cardiac Patient. LC 68-20943. (Illus.). 262p. 1968. 12.75 (*0-87527-049-2*) Green.
Luise, Fulvia De, see De Luise, Fulvia.
Luise, Marco, jt. ed. see Biglieri, Ezio.
Luise, Marco, jt. ed. see De Denzi, Riccardo.
***Luise, Marie.** Family Chronicle. LC 99-97055. 2000. pap. 18.95 (*0-533-13380-7*) Vantage.
Luise, Robert R. Applications of High Temperature Polymers. LC 96-8586. (Illus.). 272p. 1996. boxed set 149.95 (*0-8493-7672-6*) CRC Pr.
Luiselli, Cassio. The Route to Food Self-Sufficiency in Mexico: Interactions with the U. S. Food System. (Monographs: No. 17). 64p. (Orig.). (C). 1985. pap. 7.50 (*0-935391-68-1*, MN-17) UCSD Ctr US-Mex.
— The Sistema Alimentario Mexicano (SAM) Elements of a Program of Accelerated Production of Basic Foodstuffs in Mexico. (Research Reports: No. 22). 24p. (Orig.). (C). 1982. pap. 5.00 (*0-935391-21-5*, RR-22) UCSD Ctr US-Mex.
Luiselli, Cassio, jt. ed. see Glade, William P.
Luiselli, J. K., ed. Behavioral Medicine & Developmental Disabilities. (Disorders of Human Learning, Behavior, & Communication Ser.). (Illus.). 235p. 1989. 82.95 (*0-387-96875-X*) Spr-Verlag.
Luiselli, J. K., et al, eds. Self-Injurious Behavior: Analysis, Assessment & Treatment. (Disorders of Human Learning, Behavior, & Communication Ser.). (Illus.). x, 393p. 1991. 96.95 (*0-387-97580-2*) Spr-Verlag.
Luiselli, James K. & Cameron, Michael J., eds. Antecedent Control: Innovative Approaches to Behavioral Support. LC 98-19004. 416p. 1998. pap. 40.00 (*1-55766-334-3*, 3343) P H Brookes.
***Luisi, Pier L.** Giant Vesicles. LC 99-24961. (Perspectives in Supramolecular Chemistry Ser.). (Illus.). 426p. 2000. 205.00 (*0-471-97986-4*) Wiley.
Luisi, Pier L. & Straub, B. E., eds. Reverse Micelles: Biological & Technological Relevance of Amphiphilic Structures in Apolar Media. 364p. 1984. 85.00 (*0-306-41620-4*, Plenum Trade) Perseus Pubng.
Luisi, T., jt. ed. see Flamm, J.
Luisi, Vincent, jt. auth. see De Quesada, Alejandro M., Jr.
Luisi, Vincent, jt. auth. see DeQuesada, Alejandro M., Jr.
Luisigi, W. Planning Human Activities on Protected Natural Ecosystems. (Dissertationes Botanicae Ser.: No. 48). (Illus.). 1979. pap. 24.00 (*3-7682-1214-9*) Lubrecht & Cramer.
Luisotti, Theresa, ed. see Mahurin, Matt.
Luithlen, Lutz. Office Development & Capital Accumulation in the U. K. 320p. 1994. 72.95 (*1-85628-627-4*, Pub. by Avebry) Ashgate Pub Co.
Luithui, Luingam. Nagaland File: A Question of Human Rights. 1985. 21.00 (*0-8364-1358-X*, Pub. by Lancer India) S Asia.
Luitjters, Guus & Timmer, Gerard. Sexbomb: The Life & Death of Jane Mansfield. Pachter, Josh, tr. from DUT. (Illus.). 164p. 1988. pap. 12.95 (*0-8065-1049-8*, Citadel Pr) Carol Pub Group.
Luizzi, Vincent. A Case for Legal Ethics: Legal Ethics As a Source for a Universal Ethic. LC 91-46962. (SUNY Series in Ethical Theory). 176p. (C). 1993. text 64.50 (*0-7914-1271-7*); pap. text 21.95 (*0-7914-1272-5*) State U NY Pr.
Lujan, Jess. Directory of Native American Tribes of the United States. LC 95-95216. 81p. (Orig.). 1995. ring bd. 19.50 (*0-9649798-0-2*) Apache Arts.
Lujan, Luis, jt. auth. see Navarrete, Carlos.
Lujan, Manuel & Snyder, Harry M. Surface Coal Mining Reclamation Pt. 2: 15 Years of Progress, 1977-1992. Statistical Information. (Illus.). 78p. (C). 1997. reprint ed. pap. text 25.00 (*0-7881-4215-1*) DIANE Pub.
Lujan, Nestor. Diccionari Lujan de Gastronomie Catalana. 2nd ed. (CAT.). 192p. 1990. pap. 34.95 (*0-7859-6401-0*, 8486491347) Fr & Eur.
Lujan, Pedro, jt. auth. see Ingberman, Jeanette.
Lujan, Roger Patron. Un Regalo Excepcional. 184p. 1997. 18.98 (*968-409-618-6*) Edamex.
Lujan, Roger Patron. Un Regalo Excepcional. (SPA.). 1997. pap. 13.98 (*968-409-861-8*) Edit Diana.
— Un Regalo Excepcional III. (SPA.). 1997. pap. 13.98 (*968-409-985-1*) Edit Diana.
Luk, Bernard H., ed. Eastern Asia: History & Social Sciences. LC 92-39880. (Contacts Between Cultures Ser.: Vol. 4). 668p. 1993. text 129.95 (*0-7734-9206-2*) E Mellen.
Luk, Bernard H. & Steben, Barry D., eds. Eastern Asia: Humanities. LC 92-39880. (Contacts Between Cultures Ser.: Vol. 3). 640p. 1993. text 129.95 (*0-7734-9204-6*) E Mellen.
Luk, Charles. Secrets of Chinese Meditation. LC 99-52439. (Illus.). 240p. 1972. pap. 14.95 (*0-87728-066-5*) Weiser.
— Taoist Yoga. LC 83-60831. (Illus.). 224p. 1973. pap. 12.95 (*0-87728-067-3*) Weiser.
Luk, Franklin T. Advanced Signal Processing: Algorithms, Architectures & Implementations VII. 50p. 1997. pap. 89.00 (*0-8194-2584-2*) SPIE.
Luk, Franklin T., ed. Advanced Signal Processing Algorithms, Architectures & Implementations VI, Vol. 2846. 472p. 1996. 94.00 (*0-8194-2234-7*) SPIE.
— Advanced Signal Processing Algorithms, Architectures, & Implementations VIII, Vol. 3461. 1998. 99.00 (*0-8194-2916-3*) SPIE.
Luk, Helen, jt. auth. see Sang, Larry.
Luk, Henry. China Bride. LC 98-11925. 304p. 1998. text 22.95 (*0-312-86521-X*) St Martin.
***Luk, Henry.** China Bride. 304p. 1999. mass mkt. 6.99 (*0-8125-4018-2*, Pub. by Tor Bks) St Martin.
— The Heir. 2000. text 23.95 (*0-312-87192-9*) St Martin.
Luk, Ivan. Microsoft Windows Sound System Book. 1994. pap. 24.95 (*0-07-882015-4*) Osborne-McGraw.
Luk, Michael Y. The Origins of Chinese Bolshevism: An Ideology in the Making, 1921-1928. (South-East Asian Historical Monographs). (Illus.). 376p. (C). 1990. text 35.00 (*0-19-584209-X*) OUP.
Luk, Sherman, jt. auth. see Dardia, Michael.
Luk, Shiu-Hung & Whitney, Joseph, eds. Megaproject: A Case Study of China's Three Gorges Project. LC 91-22964. (Studies in Chinese Environment & Development). 248p. (C). (gr. 13). 1992. text 79.95 (*0-87332-733-0*) M E Sharpe.
***Luk, V. K.** Design, Instrumentation & Testing of a Steel Containment Vessel Model. 193p. 2000. per. 18.00 (*0-16-059112-0*) USGPO.
— Round Robin Pretest Analyses of a Steel Containment Vessel Model & Contact Structure Assembly Subject to Static Internal Pressurization. 672p. 1998. per. 57.00 (*0-16-062946-2*) USGPO.
Luk, V. K., jt. ed. see Chen, E. P.
Luk, Wayne, et al, eds. Field Programmable Logic & Applications: 7th International Workshop, FPL '97, London, U. K., September, 1-3, 1997, Proceedings. LC 97-30988. (Lecture Notes in Computer Science Ser.: Vol. 1304). xi, 503p. 1997. pap. 75.00 (*3-540-63465-7*) Spr-Verlag.
Luk, Y. F. Hong Kong's Economic & Financial Future. (Significant Issues Ser.). 91p. (C). 1995. pap. 9.95 (*0-89206-306-8*) CSIS.
Lukac, Jemi. Kaddish. (Artists' Books Ser.). (Illus.). 64p. (Orig.). 1995. pap. 15.00 (*0-89822-113-7*) Visual Studies.
Lukac, Louis, et al. Comparison of Twelve Technical Trading Systems. 72p. 1990. pap. text 25.00 (*0-934380-18-X*, 301) Traders Pr.
Lukac, P. Plasticity of Metals & Alloys: ISPMA-6. (Key Engineering Materials Ser.: Vols. 97-98). (Illus.). 526p. (C). 1995. text 207.00 (*0-87849-687-4*, Pub. by Trans T Pub) Enfield Pubs NH.
***Lukach, Justin.** Pickup Trucks: A Heavy-Duty History of the Great American Vehicle. (Illus.). 112p. (YA). (gr. 7 up). 1999. 24.98 (*1-57912-011-3*) Blck Dog & Leventhal.
Lukacher, Maryline. Maternal Fictions: Stendhal, Sand, Rachilde & Bataille. LC 93-38693. 192p. 1994. text 49.95 (*0-8223-1432-0*); pap. text 16.95 (*0-8223-1436-3*) Duke.
Lukacher, Ned. Daemonic Figures: Shakespeare & the Question of Conscience. (Illus.). 240p. 1994. text 42.50 (*0-8014-3052-6*); pap. text 16.95 (*0-8014-8223-2*) Cornell U Pr.
— Primal Scenes: Literature, Philosophy, Psychoanalysis. LC 85-25513. 368p. (C). 1986. 45.00 (*0-8014-1886-0*); pap. text 17.95 (*0-8014-9486-9*) Cornell U Pr.
— Time-Fetishes: The Secret History of Eternal Recurrence. LC 98-18862. (Post-Contemporary Interventions Ser.). 1999. 49.95 (*0-8223-2253-6*); pap. 17.95 (*0-8223-2273-0*) Duke.
Lukacher, Ned, tr. see Roustang, Francois.
Lukacs. The Meaning of Contemporary Realism. (C). 1979. text. write for info. (*0-85036-069-2*, Pub. by MRLN) Paul & Co Pubs.
Lukacs, B., jt. auth. see Diosi, L.
Lukacs, E. & Laha, R. G. Applications of Charateristics Functions. (J). 1964. 17.95 (*0-85264-086-2*) Lubrecht & Cramer.
Lukacs, Gabor. Le Roman Historique. (FRE.). 1977. pap. 28.95 (*0-7859-3036-1*) Fr & Eur.
Lukacs, Gabor, ed. Recent Progress in the Chemical Synthesis of Antibiotics & Related Microbial Products, Vol. 2. LC 93-2183. (Illus.). 980p. 1993. 307.95 (*0-387-56754-2*) Spr-Verlag.
Lukacs, Gabor & Ohno, M., eds. Recent Progress in the Chemical Synthesis of Antibiotics. 816p. 1990. 290.95 (*0-387-52444-4*) Spr-Verlag.
Lukacs, Georg. The Destruction of Reason. (C). 1952. text 49.95 (*0-85036-247-4*, Pub. by MRLN) Paul & Co Pubs.
— Essays on Thomas Mann. Mitchell, Stanley, tr. (C). 1995. pap. 18.50 (*0-85036-238-5*, Pub. by MRLN) Paul & Co Pubs.
— Georg Lukacs: Selected Correspondence, 1902-1920. Marcus, Judith & Tar, Zoltan, eds. & trs. by. LC 85-19027. (Illus.). 256p. 1986. text 57.50 (*0-231-05968-X*) Col U Pr.
***Lukacs, Georg.** German Realist in the Nineteenth Century. 396p. (C). 2000. pap. 24.95 (*0-262-62143-6*) MIT Pr.
Lukacs, Georg. German Realists in the Nineteenth Century. Gaines, Jeremy & Keast, Paul, trs. LC 92-5005. (Illus.). 350p. 1993. 37.50 (*0-262-12171-9*) MIT Pr.
— Goethe & His Age. Anchor, Robert, tr. from GER. 260p. (C). 1979. pap. 19.95 (*0-85036-071-4*, Pub. by MRLN) Paul & Co Pubs.
— Goethe & His Age. Anchor, Robert, tr. from GER. 1978. reprint ed. 15.00 (*0-86527-256-5*) Fertig.
— History & Class Consciousness. Livingstone, Rodney, tr. from GER. 1972. reprint ed. pap. text 18.50 (*0-262-62020-0*) MIT Pr.
— In Defense of History & Class Consciousness. Leslie, Esther, tr. 1999. 23.00 (*1-85984-747-1*, Pub. by Verso) Norton.
— Lenin: A Study in the Unity of His Thought. 1998. pap. 15.00 (*1-85984-174-0*, Pub. by Verso) Norton.
— The Lukacs Reader. Kadarky, Arpad, ed. 352p. (C). 1995. pap. 28.95 (*1-55786-571-X*) Blackwell Pubs.
— The Meaning of Contemporary Realism. 137p. (C). 1979. pap. write for info. (*0-85036-250-4*, Pub. by MRLN) Paul & Co Pubs.
— Ontology of Social Being Vol. 1: Hegel. (C). 1982. pap. write for info. (*0-85036-226-1*, Pub. by MRLN) Paul & Co Pubs.
— Ontology of Social Being Vol. 2: Marx, Vol. 2. (C). 1982. pap. write for info. (*0-85036-227-X*, Pub. by MRLN) Paul & Co Pubs.
— Ontology of Social Being Vol. 3: Labour, Vol. 3. (C). 1980. pap. write for info. (*0-85036-255-5*, Pub. by MRLN) Paul & Co Pubs.
— The Process of Democratization. Bernhardt, Susanne & Levine, Norman, trs. from GER. LC 90-47554. (SUNY Series in Contemporary Continental Philosophy). 189p. (C). 1991. pap. text 19.95 (*0-7914-0762-4*) State U NY Pr.
— Studies in European Realism. 267p. 2000. reprint ed. pap. text 12.00 (*0-86527-421-5*) Fertig.
— Studies in European Realism: A Sociological Survey of the Writings of Balzac, Stendhal, Tolstoy, Gorky, & Others. Bone, Edith, tr. from HUN. 267p. Date not set. reprint ed. lib. bdg. 35.00 (*0-86527-427-4*) Fertig.
— The Theory of the Novel. Bostock, Anna, tr. from GER. 1974. pap. text 12.50 (*0-262-62027-8*) MIT Pr.
Lukacs, Janos, jt. auth. see Burawoy, Michael.
Lukacs, John. Budapest, Nineteen Hundred: A Historical Portrait of a City & Its Culture. LC 88-15290. (Illus.). 304p. 1990. pap. 14.00 (*0-8021-3250-2*, Grove) Grove-Atltic.
***Lukacs, John.** Confessions of an Original Sinner. LC 00-29102. 344p. 2000. reprint ed. 30.00 (*1-890318-12-4*, Pub. by St Augustines Pr) U Ch Pr.
Lukacs, John. Destinations Past: Traveling Through History with John Lukacs. LC 93-45629. 240p. (C). 1994. 29.95 (*0-8262-0956-4*) U of Mo Pr.
***Lukacs, John.** Five Days in London: May 1940. LC 99-27583. (Illus.). 230p. 1999. 19.95 (*0-300-08030-1*) Yale U Pr.
Lukacs, John. Historical Consciousness: The Remembered Past. rev. ed. LC 93-48925. 420p. 1994. pap. 24.95 (*1-56000-732-X*) Transaction Pubs.
— Hitler of History. LC 98-26451. 279p. 1998. pap. 14.00 (*0-375-70113-3*) Vin Bks.
***Lukacs, John.** A Student's Guide to the Study of History. LC 00-66794. 2000. pap. 5.95 (*1-882926-41-2*) ISI Books.
Lukacs, John. A Thread of Years. LC 97-25045. 496p. 1998. 35.00 (*0-300-07188-4*) Yale U Pr.
— A Thread of Years. 496p. 1999. pap. 16.95 (*0-300-08075-1*) Yale U Pr.
Lukacs, John & Hearon, Shelby. Footprints. 320p. 1997. 26.00 (*0-679-44649-4*) Knopf.
Lukacs, John, jt. auth. see Kennan, George F.
Lukacs, John R., ed. The People of South East Asia: Biological Anthropology of India, Pakistan & Nepal. 458p. 1984. 110.00 (*0-306-41407-4*, Plenum Trade) Perseus Pubng.
Lukacs, K. Hungarian-Slovak Pocket Dictionary. 576p. 1988. 35.00 (*963-205-219-6*, Pub. by Akade Kiado) St Mut.
Lukacs, Lajos. Chapters on the Hungarian Political Emigration (1849-1867) Chapters on the Hungarian Political Emigration (1849-1867) LC 96-198397. (Studia Historica Academiae Scientarium Hungaricae Ser.: No. 196). 188p. 1996. pap. 75.00 (*963-05-6838-1*, Pub. by Akade Kiado) St Mut.
— The Vatican & Hungary 1846-1878: Reports & Correspondence on Hungary of the Apostolic Nuncios in Vienna. Kormos, Zsofia, tr. 796p. (C). 1981. 150.00 (*963-05-2446-5*, Pub. by Akade Kiado) St Mut.
***Lukacs, Paul.** American Vintage: The Rise of American Wine. (Illus.). 304p. 2000. 28.00 (*0-395-91478-7*) HM.
Lukacs, Yehuda. Israel, Jordan, & the Peace Process. LC 96-20089. (Syracuse Studies on Peace & Conflict Resolution). 360p. 1996. text 45.00 (*0-8156-2720-3*, LUIJ) Syracuse U Pr.
***Lukacs, Yehuda.** Israel, Jordan, & the Peace Process. 276p. 1999. pap. text 22.95 (*0-8156-2855-2*) Syracuse U Pr.
Lukan, Marianne. Documentation for Physical Therapist Assistants. (Illus.). 204p. (C). 1996. pap. text 23.95 (*0-8036-0187-5*) Davis Co.
Lukanen, Erland O., jt. auth. see Tayabji, Shiraz D.
***LuKanic, Steve, ed.** Film Actors Directory. 5th ed. 800p. 2000. pap. 85.00 (*1-58065-020-1*, Pub. by Lone Eagle Pub) Natl Bk Netwk.
Lukas, Carol. Consulting with Nonprofts: A Practioner's Guide. Hyman, Vincent, ed. LC 98-21983. (Illus.). 220p. 1998. per., wbk. ed. 35.00 (*0-940069-17-2*) A H Wilder.
***Lukas, Catherine.** Night Train: Little Lionel Book about Opposites. (Night Train : No. 4). (Illus.). 48p. (J). (gr. k-3). 2000. bds. 4.99 (*0-689-83366-0*) Litle Simon.
— Rosie the Riveter. (J). 2000. 4.99 (*0-689-83368-7*) Litle Simon.
— Time Traveling. (Lionel Trains Board Book Ser.). (J). 2000. bds. 4.99 (*0-689-83367-9*) Litle Simon.
— Train Song: Little Lionel Book about Sounds. (Train Song Ser.: No. 3). (Illus.). (J). (gr. k-3). 2000. bds. 4.99 (*0-689-83365-2*) Litle Simon.
Lukas, Christopher & Seiden, Henry M. Silent Grief: Living in the Wake of Suicide. LC 96-37735. (Master Works). 1997. pap. 40.00 (*0-7657-0056-5*) Aronson.
Lukas, Dale, jt. auth. see Burchinal, Lee.
Lukas, David. Watchable Birds of the Great Basin. LC 99-25750. (Watchable Birds Ser.: No. 3). (Illus.). 174p. 1999. pap. 16.00 (*0-87842-397-4*) Mountain Pr.
***Lukas, David.** Wild Birds of California. Schlenz, Mark A., ed. (Illus.). 136p. 2000. 34.95 (*0-944197-63-9*, Pub. by Companion CA) U of Nev Pr.
— Wild Birds of California. Schlenz, Mark A., ed. (Illus.). 136p. 2000. pap. 19.95 (*0-944197-62-0*, Pub. by Companion CA) U of Nev Pr.
Lukas, Elisabeth. Meaning in Suffering: Comfort in Crisis Through Logotherapy. Fabry, Joseph, tr. from GER.Tr. of Auch Dein Leiden hat Sinn. 160p. (Orig.). 1986. pap. 9.95 (*0-917867-05-X*) V Frankl Inst.
Lukas, George. Home Brewmastery. 112p. 1991. pap. text 7.95 (*0-9631242-1-8*) Yerba Buena.
Lukas, J. Anthony. Big Trouble: A Murder in a Small Western Town Sets off a Struggle for the Soul of America. LC 97-21359. (Illus.). 592p. 1997. 32.50 (*0-684-80858-7*) S&S Trade.
— Big Trouble: A Murder in a Small Western Town Sets off a Struggle for the Soul of America. (Illus.). 880p. 1998. pap. 17.00 (*0-684-84617-9*, Touchstone) S&S Trade Pap.
— Common Ground: A Turbulent Decade in the Lives of Three American Families. LC 86-40132. 784p. 1986. pap. 18.00 (*0-394-74616-3*) Vin Bks.
***Lukas, J. Anthony.** Nightmare: The Underside of the Nixon Years. 3rd ed. LC 75-30667. 626p. 1999. reprint ed. pap. 24.95 (*0-8214-1287-6*) Ohio U Pr.
Lukas, Johannes. A Study of the Kanuri Language, Grammar & Vocabulary. LC 38-24176. 272p. 1937. reprint ed. pap. 84.40 (*0-8357-3017-4*, 205710300010) Bks Demand.
Lukas, Josef, jt. ed. see Albert, Dietrich.
Lukas, Jurgen, jt. auth. see Eiden, Heribert.
Lukas, Karen. The Educational System of the Former German Democratic Republic. 80p. (Orig.). 1991. pap. 20.00 (*0-910054-94-0*) Am Assn Coll Registrars.
Lukas, Karen, jt. auth. see Dickey, Karlene N.
Lukas, Karen H. Austria: A Study of the Educational System of Austria & a Guide to the Academic Placement of Students in Educational Institutions of the United States. LC 87-980. (World Education Ser.). (Illus.). 178p. reprint ed. pap. 55.20 (*0-8357-3114-6*, 203937100012) Bks Demand.
Lukas, Larry. Childhood Memories. 20p. (Orig.). 1997. pap. text 6.95 (*1-889416-06-1*, LS40007) Lukasound.
— Little Book of Classics. 32p. (Orig.). 1997. pap. text 7.95 (*1-889416-07-X*, LS40008) Lukasound.
— Reflections in the Gardens. Rolando, Akika & Tani, Peggy, trs. (ENG & JPN., Illus.). 32p. 1997. per. 29.95 (*1-889416-09-6*, 40010) Lukasound.
Lukas, Larry, contrib. by. Cityscapes. 24p. (Orig.). 1996. pap. text 6.95 (*1-889416-03-7*, LS40004) Lukasound.
— Creatures. 16p. (Orig.). 1996. pap. text 6.95 (*1-889416-00-2*, LS40001) Lukasound.
— Diversions. 16p. (Orig.). 1996. pap. text 6.95 (*1-889416-02-9*, LS40003) Lukasound.
— Modern Ages. 12p. (Orig.). 1996. pap. text 6.95 (*1-889416-04-5*, LS40005) Lukasound.
— Potpourri. 24p. (Orig.). 1996. pap. text 6.95 (*1-889416-05-3*, LS40006) Lukasound.
— Under the Bigtop. 24p. (Orig.). 1996. pap. text 6.95 (*1-889416-01-0*, LS40002) Lukasound.
Lukas, P., jt. auth. see Klesnil, M.
Lukas, Richard. Forgotten Holocaust: The Poles under German Occupation, 1939-1945. 3rd rev. ed. LC 96-50368. (Illus.). 318p. 1997. 24.95 (*0-7818-0528-7*) Hippocrene Bks.
Lukas, Richard C. Bitter Legacy: Polish-American Relations in the Wake of World War II. LC 82-1972. (Illus.). 200p. 1982. 24.95 (*0-8131-1460-8*) U Pr of Ky.
— Eagles East: The Army Air Forces & the Soviet Union, 1941-1945. LC 78-126957. 266p. reprint ed. pap. 75.90 (*0-7837-4949-X*, 2044615) Bks Demand.
— The Strange Allies: The United States & Poland, 1941-1945. LC 77-8585. 240p. reprint ed. 74.40 (*0-608-16862-9*, 202756600055) Bks Demand.
Lukas, Richard C., ed. Out of the Inferno: Poles Remember the Holocaust. LC 89-5646. 224p. 1989. 27.50 (*0-8131-1692-9*) U Pr of Ky.
Lukas, Scott E. Amphetamines: Danger in the Fast Lane. (Encyclopedia of Psychoactive Drugs Ser.: No. 1). (Illus.). 124p. (YA). (gr. 7 up). 1992. lib. bdg. 19.95 (*0-87754-755-6*) Chelsea Hse.
— Steroids. LC 93-38524. (Drug Library Ser.). (Illus.). 128p. (YA). (gr. 6 up). 1994. lib. bdg. 20.95 (*0-89490-471-X*) Enslow Pubs.
Lukas, Susan. Where to Start & What to Ask: The Assessment Handbook. 220p. (C). 1993. pap. 14.95 (*0-393-70152-2*) Norton.
***Lukas, Verena Anna.** Der Dialog im Dialog: Das Inzitament bei Friedrich von Hardenberg. 2000. 18.95 (*3-906764-33-8*, Pub. by P Lang) P Lang Pubng.
Lukas, Victor, jt. auth. see Podolsky, M. Lawrence.
Lukas, Viktor. Guide to Organ Music. Wyburd, Anne, tr. from GER. LC 89-30795. (Illus.). 272p. 1989. 22.95 (*0-931340-10-1*, Amadeus Pr) Timber.
Lukasevich, Ann. Favorites, Friendships, Food & Fantasy: Literature-Based Thematic Units for Early Primary, Vol. 1. 1993. pap. 24.95 (*0-201-81844-2*) Addison-Wesley.
— Food & Fantasy Vol. 2: Literature-Based Thematic Units for Early Primary, Vol. 2. (J). (ps-3). 1994. pap. text 18.95 (*0-201-49037-4*) Addison-Wesley.
Lukashevich, Stephen. Ivan Aksakov, 1823-1886: A Study in Russian Thought & Politics. LC 65-22050. (Historical Monographs: No. 57). (Illus.). 203p. 1965. 15.00 (*0-674-46975-5*) HUP.
— N. F. Federov (1828 to 1903) A Study in Russian Eupsychian & Utopian Thought. LC 75-29731. 316p. 1977. 39.50 (*0-87413-113-8*) U Delaware Pr.
Lukasiewicz, J. Elements of Mathematical Logic. 2nd ed. (International Series on Pure & Applied Mathematics: Vol. 31). 1964. 60.00 (*0-08-010393-6*, Pub. by Pergamon Repr) Franklin.
Lukasiewicz, Jan. Uber den Satz des Widerspruchs Bei Aristoteles, Band V. (Zur Modernendeutung der Aristotelischen Logik Ser.). (GER.). 1910. 80.00 (*3-487-09761-3*) G Olms Pubs.

Lukasiewicz, Julius. The Ignorance Explosion: Understanding Industrial Civilization. (Illus.). 272p. 1994. 31.95 (*0-88629-234-4*, Pub. by McG-Queens Univ Pr); pap. 22.95 (*0-88629-237-9*, Pub. by McG-Queens Univ Pr) CUP Services.

Lukasiewicz, Michael A., ed. see Symposium on Industrial Combustion Technologies St.

Lukasz, Czeslaw. Evangelizzazione e Conflitto: Indagine Sulla Coerenza Letteraria e Tematica della Pericope di Cornelio (Atti 10, 1-11, 18) (Europaische Hochschulschriften Ser.: Reihe 23, Bd. 484). 300p. 1993. 55.80 (*3-631-46161-5*) P Lang Pubng.

Lukaszewicz, G. Micropolar Fluids: Theory & Application. LC 98-29998. (Modeling & Simulation in Science, Engineering & Technology Ser.). 256p. 1998. 59.95 (*0-8176-4008-8*) Spr-Verlag.

Lukaszewicz, Grzegorz. Micropolar Fluids: Theory & Applications. LC 98-29998. xv, 253p. 1999. write for info. (*3-7643-4008-8*) Birkhauser.

Lukaszewicz, Joseph. Girys I Biruta: Poemat Z Dawnych Czasow Litewskich. 1964. 2.75 (*0-685-09284-4*) Endurance.

Lukaszewics, Charles, jt. auth. see Buchanan, Robert W.

Lukaszewski, James. Influencing Public Attitudes: Strategies to Reduce the Media's Power. (Illus.). 64p. (Orig.). 1992. pap. 14.95 (*0-913869-03-1*) Issue Action Pubns.

Lukaszewski, James E. Becoming a Verbal Visionary: How to Have a Happy, Successful, & Important Life. 10p. 1997. pap. 15.00 (*1-883291-22-4*) Lukaszewski.

— Building Quality Community Relationships: A Planning Model to Gain & Maintain Public Consent. 59p. 1995. pap. 40.00 (*1-883291-11-9*) Lukaszewski.

— Communication Standards: The Principles & Protocols for Standard-Setting Individual & Corporate Communication. 10p. 1995. pap. 20.00 (*1-883291-12-7*) Lukaszewski.

— Coping with Activist Intrusions & Threats. 9p. 1995. pap. 20.00 (*1-883291-13-5*) Lukaszewski.

***Lukaszewski, James E.** Coping with Corporate Campaigns: Patterns of Activist Intrusion. 16p. (C). 2000. pap. 30.00 (*1-883291-33-X*) Lukaszewski.

Lukaszewski, James E. Crisis Communication Planning Strategies: A Crisis Communication Management Workbook. 3rd rev. ed. (Crisis Communication Management Ser.: No. 2). (Illus.). 170p. 2000. ring bd. write for info. (*1-883291-26-7*) Lukaszewski.

— Current Crisis Communication Issues: Getting Your Boss to Buy into Crisis Planning; Building a Crisis Response Plan That Works; When to Send Your Boss Out to Meet the Press; Managing the Lawyers; Managing the Violent Threat. 22p. 1996. pap. 30.00 (*1-883291-17-8*) Lukaszewski.

— Executive Action Crisis Management Workbook. 120p. 1993. VHS 40.00 (*1-883291-04-6*) Lukaszewski.

— Exxon Valdez: The Great Crisis Management Paradox. 26p. 1995. pap. 20.00 (*1-883291-14-3*) Lukaszewski.

— Finding & Keeping Clients: Critical Success Factors for Building Your Consulting Practice. 40p. 1999. pap. 30.00 (*1-883291-32-1*) Lukaszewski.

— First Response: Critical First Response Steps - A Management Model for Effective Response to Crisis; Scenario Response Checklist: A Work-Up Model; The Case Study: A Conclusions /Lessons Learners Framework, Pts. I, II & III. 28p. 1996. pap. 30.00 (*1-883291-20-8*) Lukaszewski.

— How to Establish a Professional Relationship with Reporters. 10p. 1996. pap. 20.00 (*1-883291-19-4*) Lukaszewski.

— Media Relations Strategies During Emergencies: A Crisis Communication Management Guide. 3rd rev. ed. (Crisis Communication Management Ser.: No. 4). 100p. 2000. ring bd. write for info. (*1-883291-27-5*) Lukaszewski.

— Moving Out of the Target Zone: What to Do When Activitists Attack. 5p. 1999. pap. 20.00 (*1-883291-28-3*) Lukaszewski.

— The Newest Discipline: Managing Legally Driven Issues: Providing Public Affairs Advice in the Lawyer-Dominated Problem Environment. 14p. 1996. pap. 20.00 (*1-883291-18-6*) Lukaszewski.

— The Peppermill Public Hearing: A Communication Skill-Building Simulation Exercise. 11p. 1995. pap. 30.00 (*1-883291-15-1*) Lukaszewski.

— Preparing Your Company for Terrorist Attack. 5p. 1998. pap. 20.00 (*1-883291-24-0*) Lukaszewski.

— Surviving "60 Minutes" & the Other News Magazine Shows. 16p. 1995. pap. 40.00 (*1-883291-16-X*) Lukaszewski.

— The Tactical Ingenuity Pyramid & Thinker's Manual. 12p. 1990. pap. 10.00 (*1-883291-00-3*) Lukaszewski.

— Ten Strategies for Successful Contract Negotiations. 5p. 1999. pap. 20.00 (*1-883291-23-2*) Lukaszewski.

— War Stories & Crisis Communication Strategies: A Crisis Communication Management Anthology. 2nd rev. ed. (Crisis Communication Management Ser.: No. 1). 208p. 2000. ring bd. write for info. (*1-883291-25-9*) Lukaszewski.

— Working Through Embarrassing Revelations: How to Manage the Operational Changes Required & the Enormous Visibility. 6p. 1996. pap. 20.00 (*1-883291-21-6*) Lukaszewski.

Lukaszewski, Leon. The Stone in the Road. 27p. 1956. pap. 3.50 (*0-87129-673-X*, S52) Dramatic Pub.

Lukauskas, Arvid J. Regulating Finance: The Political Economy of Spanish Financial Policy from Franco to Democracy. LC 97-4888. 344p. (C). 1997. text 54.50 (*0-472-10836-0*, 10836) U of Mich Pr.

Luke. Complete Luke Multi-Pesticide Residue Method. 1994. write for info. (*0-8493-7993-8*) CRC Pr.

Luke, Allan & Gilbert, Pamela, eds. Literacy in Contexts: Australian Perspectives & Issues. 144p. (Orig.). 1993. pap. text 14.95 (*1-86373-340-X*, Pub. by Allen & Unwin Pty) Paul & Co Pubs.

Luke, Allan, jt. ed. see Baker, Carolyn D.

Luke, Allan, jt. ed. see Baldauf, Richard B.

Luke, B. & Keith, Louis G. Principles & Practice of Maternal Nutrition. (Illus.). 161p. 1992. 39.00 (*1-85070-324-8*) Prthnon Pub.

Luke, Barbara. Every Pregnant Woman's Guide to Preventing Premature Birth. 1996. pap. write for info. (*0-8129-2830-X*, Times Bks) Crown Pub Group.

— Good Bones: The Complete Guide to Building & Maintaining the Healthiest Bones. LC 98-33849. (Illus.). 200p. 1998. pap. 14.95 (*0-923521-44-5*, 445) Bull Pub.

Luke, Barbara & Eberlein, Tamara. When You're Expecting Twins or More: A Complete Resource. LC 98-40780. (Illus.). 320p. 1999. pap. 12.95 (*0-06-095723-9*) HarpC.

Luke, Barbara, et al. Clinical Maternal-Fetal Nutrition. LC 92-48905. (Illus.). 368p. 1993. 79.95 (*0-316-53614-8*, Little Brwn Med Div) Lppncott W & W.

Luke, Carmen. Constructing the Child Viewer: A History of the American Discourse on Television & Children, 1950-1980. LC 90-7354. 344p. 1990. 65.00 (*0-275-93516-7*, C3516, Praeger Pubs) Greenwood.

— Pedagogy, Printing, & Protestantism: The Discourse on Childhood. LC 88-13924. (SUNY Series, the Philosophy of Education). 171p. (C). 1989. pap. text 21.95 (*0-7914-0003-4*) State U NY Pr.

Luke, Carmen, ed. Feminisms & Pedagogies of Everyday Life. LC 96-1356. 327p. (C). 1996. text 62.50 (*0-7914-2965-2*); pap. text 21.95 (*0-7914-2966-0*) State U NY Pr.

Luke, Carmen & Gore, Jennifer. Feminisms & Critical Pedagogy. 224p. (C). 1992. pap. 19.99 (*0-415-90534-6*, A6758) Routledge.

Luke, Carmen, jt. ed. see Manley-Casimir, Michael E.

Luke, Catriona. The She Magazine Names for Baby Book. 176p. 1995. pap. write for info. (*1-85479-752-2*, Pub. by M OMara) Assoc Pubs Grp.

Luke, Cheryl M. & Swafford, Ann J. Word Processing Communication Skills. 136p. (C). 1988. pap. text 25.00 (*0-15-596660-X*) Dryden Pr.

Luke, David, jt. auth. see Alexander, Liza.

Luke, David, ed. & tr. see Goethe, Johann Wolfgang Von.

Luke, David, tr. see Goethe, Johann Wolfgang Von.

Luke, David, tr. see Morike, Eduard.

Luke, David, tr. see Von Kleist, Heinrich.

Luke, David, tr. & intro. see Goethe, Johann Wolfgang Von.

Luke, David, tr. & intro. see Mann, Thomas.

Luke, David F. Labour & Parastatal Politics in Sierra Leone: A Study of African Working-Class Ambivalence. (Dalhousie African Studies). (Illus.). 306p. (Orig.). (C). 1984. pap. text 25.50 (*0-8191-3958-0*) U Pr of Amer.

***Luke, Deanna.** Chris Mouse & the Christmas House. LC 00-190709. (Illus.). 40p. (J). 2000. 14.95 (*1-928777-04-X*) Blessing Our Wrld.

— Marky & the Cat. LC 99-91778. (Marky Ser.: No. 2). (Illus.). 40p. (J). (gr. 2). 2000. 8.95 (*1-928777-06-6*) Blessing Our Wrld.

— Marky & the Mouse. LC 99-91777. (Marky Ser.: No. 1). (Illus.). 32p. (J). (gr. 2-7). 2000. 8.95 (*1-928777-05-8*) Blessing Our Wrld.

— Marky & the Rat. LC 99-91779. (Marky Ser.: No. 3). (Illus.). 40p. (J). (gr. 2-7). 2000. 8.95 (*1-928777-07-4*) Blessing Our Wrld.

— Truth & Tradition: The Story of Christmas. LC 99-90503. (Illus.). 128p. 2000. 15.95 (*1-928777-01-5*) Blessing Our Wrld.

Luke, Deanna. What Good Is... LC 99-90371. (Illus.). 32p. (J). (gr. k-2). 2000. 15.95 (*1-928777-00-7*) Blessing Our Wrld.

Luke, Elmer, ed. Monkey Brain Sushi: New Tastes in Japanese Fiction. (Japan's Modern Writers Ser.). (Illus.). 312p. 1993. pap. 10.00 (*4-7700-1688-3*) Kodansha.

Luke, Elmer, ed. see Kennedy, Rick.

Luke, Elmer, ed. see Murakami, Haruki.

Luke, Elmer, ed. see Shimada, Masahiko.

Luke, G. L. & Mishchenko, Aleksandra S. Vector Bundles & Their Applications. LC 98-26525. (Mathematics & Its Applications Ser.). 254p. 1998. write for info. (*0-7923-5154-1*) Kluwer Academic.

Luke, Harry C. In the Margin of History. LC 67-26755. (Essay Index Reprint Ser.). 1977. 23.95 (*0-8369-0634-9*) Ayer.

Luke, Heather. Design & Make Bedroom Furnishings. (Illus.). 80p. 1998. 14.95 (*1-85368-533-X*, Pub. by New5 Holland) Sterling.

— Design & Make Curtains & Drapes. (Illus.). 80p. 1996. 19.95 (*0-88266-850-1*, 850-1, Storey Pub) Storey Bks.

— Design & Make Cushions. LC 98-159779. (Illus.). 80p. 1998. 14.95 (*1-85368-531-3*, Pub. by New5 Holland) Sterling.

— Design & Make Decorative Details. LC 98-162677. (Illus.). 80p. 1998. 14.95 (*1-85368-943-2*, Pub. by New5 Holland) Sterling.

— Design & Make Fabric Window Shades. LC 95-42898. (Illus.). 80p. 1996. pap. 19.95 (*0-88266-895-1*, 895-1, Storey Pub) Storey Bks.

Luke, heather. Easy Upholstery: Step by Step. (Illus.). 192p. 1994. pap. 24.95 (*0-8019-8630-3*) Krause Pubns.

Luke, Heather. Slip Covers. LC 98-184237. (Illus.). 80p. 1998. 14.95 (*1-85368-467-8*, Pub. by New5 Holland) Sterling.

— Soft Furnishings. (Home Decorator Ser.). (Illus.). 96p. 1997. pap. 15.95 (*1-85368-617-4*, Pub. by New5 Holland) Sterling.

— Soft Furnishings. LC 98-168622. (Illus.). 96p. 1998. pap. 14.95 (*1-85238-539-1*) Sterling.

— Window Treatments. (Illus.). 1995. write for info. (*1-85391-487-8*, Pub. by Merehurst Ltd) Sterling.

Luke, Helen M. Dark Wood to White Rose: Journey & Transformation in Dante's Divine Comedy. 2nd ed. (Illus.). 206p. 1989. pap. 14.95 (*0-930407-28-8*) Parabola Bks.

— Kaleidoscope: The Way of Woman & Other Essays. Baker, E. Rob, ed. 341p. 1992. 17.95 (*0-930407-24-5*) Parabola Bks.

— Kaleidoscope: The Way of Woman & Other Essays. Baker, E. Rob, ed. 341p. 1993. pap. 14.95 (*0-930407-29-6*) Parabola Bks.

— Life of the Spirit in Women: A Jungian Approach. LC 79-91960. (C). 1980. pap. 4.00 (*0-87574-230-0*) Pendle Hill.

— Old Age: Journey into Simplicity. 4th ed. (Illus.). 112p. 1987. pap. 9.95 (*0-930407-05-9*) Parabola Bks.

***Luke, Helen M.** Such Stuff as Dreams Are Made On: The Autobiography & Journals of Helen M. Luke. Mowat, Barbara A., ed. (Illus.). 267p. 2000. 29.95 (*0-930407-47-4*, Pub. by Parabola Bks) IPG Chicago.

Luke, Helen M. The Way of Woman: Awakening the Perennial Feminine. 224p. 1996. pap. 10.95 (*0-385-48574-3*) Doubleday.

Luke, Howard. My Own Trail. 10.00 (*1-877962-32-5*) Todd Commns.

Luke, Hugh J., Jr., ed. see Shelley, Mary Wollstonecraft.

Luke, Hugh J., ed. see Swinburne, Algernon Charles.

Luke, Igumen, ed. see Anatoly, Elder.

Luke, Jeffery S. Catalytic Leadership: Strategies, Tactics & Skills for Pursuing the Public Interest. LC 97-21085. 1997. 25.95 (*0-7879-0917-3*) Jossey-Bass.

Luke, Jeffrey S. A Preliminary Study of the Homeless in Omaha-Douglas County. 43p. (Orig.). 1986. pap. 3.50 (*1-55719-020-8*) U NE CPAR.

Luke, Jeffrey S. & Webb, Vincent J., eds. Nebraska Policy Choices, 1986. (Illus.). 240p. (Orig.). 1986. pap. 9.95 (*1-55719-000-3*) U NE CPAR.

Luke, Joy T. To Die For: Art Materials & Health Hazards. Kittner, Craig, ed. (Art Calendar Guide Ser.). 35p. 1999. pap. 9.95 (*0-945388-15-2*) Art Calendar.

Luke, Kang Kwong. Utterance Particles in Cantonese Conversation. LC 90-31714. (Pragmatics & Beyond New Ser.: Vol. 9). xvi, 329p. 1990. 76.00 (*1-55619-275-4*) J Benjamins Pubng Co.

Luke, Mary. The Nine Days Queen. 448p. 1994. reprint ed. lib. bdg. 49.95 (*1-56849-526-9*) Buccaneer Bks.

***Luke, Melinda & Ramsey, Marcy Dunn.** Helping Paws: Dogs That Serve. LC 00-36540. (Hello Reader! Ser.). (Illus.). (J). 2001. pap. write for info. (*0-439-20542-5*) Scholastic Inc.

Luke, Melinda, ed. see Zallinger, Peter.

Luke, Michelle. Victoria Elizabeth's Magical Dream Paper Dolls. (Illus.). 32p. (J). (gr. 2-5). 1998. 7.99 (*0-9660672-2-3*) Its a Girl.

Luke, Michelle. In My Black Galoshes. 24p. (J). (ps-2). 1997. write for info. (*0-9660672-1-5*) Its a Girl.

— Victoria Elizabeth's Magical Dream. 24p. (J). (gr. 3-6). 1997. write for info. (*0-9660672-0-7*) Its a Girl.

Luke, Peter. Mad Pomegranate & the Praying Mantis: An Andalusian Adventure. 238p. 1984. 27.00 (*0-86140-200-6*, Pub. by Smyth) Dufour.

Luke, Peter, ed. Enter Certain Players: Edwards - MacLiammoir & the Gate, 1928-1978. (Illus.). 104p. 1978. pap. 9.95 (*0-318-40002-2*, Pub. by Smyth) Dufour.

Luke, Peter, tr. see Garcia Lorca, Federico.

Luke, Robert A., ed. see Ulmer, Curtis.

Luke, Susan. Awesome Family Nights. LC 95-117817. 1994. pap. 7.95 (*1-55503-689-9*, 01111639) Covenant Comms.

— Experiments upon the Word. LC 97-220958. 1998. pap. 7.95 (*1-57734-137-6*, 01112988) Covenant Comms.

— Fantastic Family Nights. LC 92-75978. 1991. pap. 7.95 (*1-55503-520-5*, 01111175) Covenant Comms.

— Little Talks for Little People. 1994. pap. 7.95 (*1-55503-654-6*, 01111507) Covenant Comms.

— Log Cabin Logic: Creating Success Where You Are with What You Have. 150p. 1995. pap. 12.50 (*0-9646034-0-3*) Luke Communs.

***Luke, Susan.** More Experiments upon the Word. LC 99-183453. 1998. pap. 7.95 (*1-57734-314-X*, 01113577) Covenant Comms.

Luke, Susan. More Little Talks for Little People. (J). 1996. pap. 7.95 (*1-55503-833-6*, 01112031) Covenant Comms.

— Positively Primary. 1996. pap. 7.95 (*1-55503-727-5*, 019412) Covenant Comms.

— Sharing Time: I Know the Scriptures Are True. 1997. pap. 1.17 (*1-57734-188-0*, 01113194) Covenant Comms.

***Luke, Susan.** Sharing Time: I Will Make & Keep My Baptismal Covenant. 1999. pap. 8.95 (*1-57734-513-4*, 01114123) Covenant Comms.

Luke, Susan. Super Sundays! 1996. pap. 8.95 (*1-55503-975-8*, 01112392) Covenant Comms.

Luke, Timothy W. Capitalism, Democracy & Ecology: Departing from Marx. LC 98-9100. 288p. 1998. text 49.95 (*0-252-02422-2*) U of Ill Pr.

— Capitalism, Democracy & Ecology: Departing from Marx. LC 98-9100. xii, 254 p. 1999. text 19.95 (*0-252-06729-0*) U of Ill Pr.

— Ecocritique: Contesting the Politics of Nature, Economy, & Culture. LC 97-12049. 272p. 1997. pap. 19.95 (*0-8166-2847-5*); text 49.95 (*0-8166-2846-7*) U of Minn Pr.

— Ideology & Soviet Industrialization, 120. LC 84-12812. (Contributions in Political Science Ser.: No. 120). 283p. 1985. 59.95 (*0-313-23831-6*, LIS/, Greenwood Pr) Greenwood.

— Screens of Power: Ideology, Domination, & Resistance in Informational Society. LC 88-37528. 280p. 1989. text 34.95 (*0-252-01629-7*); pap. text 14.95 (*0-252-06154-3*) U of Ill Pr.

— Shows of Force: Power, Politics, & Ideology in Art Exhibitions. LC 91-20018. 264p. 1992. pap. text 18.95 (*0-8223-1123-2*) Duke.

— Social Theory & Modernity: Critique, Dissent, & Revolution. 280p. (C). 1990. text 49.95 (*0-8039-3860-8*); pap. text 24.00 (*0-8039-3861-6*) Sage.

Luke, Timothy W., jt. auth. see Levine, Victor T.

Luke, Timothy W., jt. ed. see Toulouse, Chris.

Luke, Tony. Sin 7. LC 98-181006. (Illus.). 64p. 1997. pap. 9.95 (*1-56163-194-9*, Eurotica) NBM.

***Luke, William A.** Greyhound Buses: 1914-2000 Photo Archive. (Illus.). 128p. 2000. pap. 29.95 (*1-58388-027-5*, 130663AE, Pub. by Iconografix) Motorbooks Intl.

— Trailways Buses: 1936-2000 Photo Archive. (Illus.). 128p. 2000. pap. 29.95 (*1-58388-029-1*, 120664AE, Pub. by Iconografix) Motorbooks Intl.

Luke, Y. L., et al. Index to Mathematics of Computation, 1943-1969. 461p. 1972. pap. 47.00 (*0-8218-4000-2*, MCOMIN-1) Am Math.

Lukefahr, Oscar. The Catechism Handbook. LC 95-45290. 128p. (Orig.). 1996. pap. 5.95 (*0-89243-864-9*) Liguori Pubns.

— The Catechism Handbook Workbook. 64p. (Orig.). 1996. pap., wbk. ed. 2.95 (*0-89243-865-7*) Liguori Pubns.

— Catholic Guide to the Bible. LC 97-75918. 224p. 1998. pap. 7.95 (*0-7648-0201-1*) Liguori Pubns.

— Catholic Guide to the Bible Workbook. 64p. 1998. pap. text, wbk. ed. 2.95 (*0-7648-0202-X*) Liguori Pubns.

***Lukefahr, Oscar.** Christ's Mother & Ours: A Catholic Guide to Mary. LC 98-65699. 208p. 1998. pap. 7.95 (*0-7648-0214-3*) Liguori Pubns.

Lukefahr, Oscar. The Privilege of Being Catholic. LC 93-79725. 208p. 1993. pap. 7.95 (*0-89243-563-1*) Liguori Pubns.

— The Privilege of Being Catholic Workbook. 64p. (Orig.). 1993. pap., student ed. 2.95 (*0-89243-564-X*) Liguori Pubns.

— We Believe... A Survey of the Catholic Faith. rev. ed. LC 90-60495. 224p. (Orig.). 1995. pap. 7.95 (*0-89243-536-4*) Liguori Pubns.

— We Believe... A Survey of the Catholic Faith: Workbook. rev. ed. 64p. 1995. pap. text, student ed. 2.95 (*0-89243-539-9*) Liguori Pubns.

Lukehart, Peter M., ed. see National Gallery of Art Staff.

Lukehart, Peter M., jt. ed. see Smyth, Craig H.

***Lukeman, Alex.** Nightmares: Dreams from the Dark. LC 00-37134. 224p. 2000. 19.95 (*0-87131-917-9*) M Evans.

Lukeman, Alex. Sleep Well, Sleep Deep: How Sleeping Well Can Change Your Life. LC 99-47495. 224p. 1999. 19.95 (*0-87131-891-1*, Pub. by M Evans) Natl Bk Netwk.

— What Your Dreams Can Teach You. 2nd expanded rev. ed. LC 97-23110. 366p. 1999. pap., wbk. ed. 14.95 (*0-87542-475-9*) Llewellyn Pubns.

Lukeman, Alex & Lukeman, Gayle. Beyond Blame: Reclaiming the Power You Give to Others. LC 98-170497. 192p. 1996. pap. 14.95 (*1-880823-14-4*) N Star Pubns.

Lukeman, Chester M. Schools--Progress, Activities, & Trends: Index of New Information with Authors, Subjects, & References. 1995. write for info. (*0-7883-0464-X*); pap. write for info. (*0-7883-0465-8*) ABBE Pubs Assn.

Lukeman, Gayle, jt. auth. see Lukeman, Alex.

***Lukeman, Josh.** The Market Maker's Edge: Day Trading Tactics from a Wall Street Insider. LC 00-21162. (Illus.). 288p. 2000. 34.95 (*0-07-135975-3*) McGraw.

***Lukeman, Noah T.** First Five Pages: A Writer's Guide to Staying Out of the Rejection Pile. LC 99-47928. 208p. 2000. per. 11.00 (*0-684-85743-X*) S&S Trade.

Luken, Charlie & Neff, Jack. Cincinnati: Crowning Glory. LC 96-43945. (Urban Tapestry Ser.). (Illus.). 480p. 1996. 44.95 (*1-881096-35-1*) Towery Pub.

Luken, James O. & Thieret, John W. Assessment & Management of Plant Invasions. LC 96-19131. (Series in Environmental Management). 352p. 1997. 84.50 (*0-387-94809-0*) Spr-Verlag.

Luken, Paul. Bird Songs. viii, 20p. (Orig.). 1996. pap. 6.00 (*0-9651356-0-8*) Avian Press.

***Lukenbill, Grant.** Belvedere. 2000. 24.95 (*0-929435-36-2*) Damron Co.

Lukenbill, Grant. Smart Spending: The Gay & Lesbian Guide to Socially Responsible Shopping & Investing. LC 99-44829. 1999. pap. 15.95 (*1-55583-414-0*, Pub. by Alyson Pubns) Consort Bk Sales.

— Untold Millions: The Truth about Gay & Lesbian Consumers. LC 98-47911. (Illus.). 200p. 1999. pap. 29.95 (*1-56023-948-4*, Harrington Park) Haworth Pr.

Lukenbill, Stewart. Youth Literature: An Interdisciplinary, Annotated Guide to North American Dissertation Research, 1930-1985. LC 87-38077. 482p. 1988. text 94.00 (*0-8240-8498-5*) Garland.

Lukenbill, W. Bernard. AIDS & HIV Programs & Services for Libraries. xvi, 262p. 1994. lib. bdg. 32.00 (*1-56308-175-X*) Libs Unl.

***Lukens, Buz.** A Critical Handbook of Children's Literature. 6th ed. 2001. (*0-201-66672-3*) Longman.

Lukens, Joan E., ed. see Episcopal Society for Ministry on Aging Staff.

Lukens, Michael, jt. auth. see Guinup, Kenneth.

Lukens, Michael B. Conflict & Community: New Studies in Thomistic Thought. LC 89-34167. 204p. (C). 1992. text 39.95 (*0-8204-1204-X*) P Lang Pubng.

Lukens, Nancy & Rosenberg, Dorothy, eds. Daughters of Eve: Women's Writing from the German Democratic Republic. LC 92-31238. (European Women Writers Ser.). xi, 332p. 1993. text 50.00 (*0-8032-2892-9*); pap. text 20.00 (*0-8032-7942-6*) U of Nebr Pr.

Lukens, Nancy, tr. see Bonhoeffer, Dietrich.

Lukens, Nancy, tr. see Green, Clifford, ed.

An Asterisk (*) at the beginning of an entry indicates that the title is appearing for the first time.

***Lukens, Rebecca J.** A Critical Handbook of Children's Literature. 6th ed. 2001. write for info. (*0-201-66670-7*) Addison-Wesley.

Lukens, Rebecca J. Critical Handbook of Children's Literature. 6th ed. LC 98-19333. 400p. (C). 1999. pap. 42.00 (*0-321-00361-6*) Addson-Wesley Educ.

Lukens, Rebecca J. & Cline, Ruth K. J., eds. Critcal Handbook Of Life: Critical Handbook of Young Adult & Children's Literature. 160p. (C). 1997. 33.53 (*0-06-501108-2*) Addson-Wesley Educ.

Luker, Benjamin F. Use of the Infinitive Instead of a Finite Verb in French. LC 16-16932. (Columbia University. Studies in Romance Philology & Literature: No. 18). reprint ed. 27.50 (*0-404-50618-6*) AMS Pr.

Luker, Karen A. & Orr, Jean. Health Visiting: Towards Community Health Nursing. 2nd ed. (Illus.). 272p. 1992. pap. 34.95 (*0-632-03324-X*) Blackwell Sci.

Luker, Karen A. & Wolfson, David J., eds. Medicines Management for Clinical Nurses. LC 98-35983. 348p. 1998. pap. 39.95 (*0-632-04247-8*) Blackwell Sci.

Luker, Karen A., jt. ed. see Kenrick, Maria.

Luker, Kristin. Abortion & the Politics of Motherhood. LC 83-47849. (California Series on Social Choice & Political Economy: Vol. 3). 350p. (C). 1984. pap. 17.95 (*0-520-05597-7*, Pub. by U CA Pr) Cal Prin Full Svc.

***Luker, Kristin.** Abortion & the Politics of Motherhood. (California Series on Social Choice & Political Economy: Vol. 3). 324p. 2000. pap. 17.95 (*0-520-22477-9*, Pub. by U CA Pr) Cal Prin Full Svc.

Luker, Kristin. Dubious Conceptions: The Politics of Teenage Pregnancy. 256p. 1996. 24.95 (*0-674-21702-0*) HUP.

— Dubious Conceptions: The Politics of Teenage Pregnancy. (Illus.). 304p. 1997. reprint ed. pap. 14.95 (*0-674-21703-9*) HUP.

Luker, Mark. Preparing Your Campus for a Networked Future. LC 99-48099. 8p. 1999. pap. text 16.95 (*0-7879-4734-2*) Jossey-Bass.

Luker, Nicholas, ed. From Furmanov to Sholokhov: An Anthology of the Classics of Socialist Realism. (Illus.). (C). 1988. pap. text 17.95 (*0-87501-037-7*) Ardis Pubs.

Luker, Paul, ed. Proceedings, 1992 Summer Computer Simulation Conference. 1273p. 1992. 180.00 (*1-56555-014-5*, SCSC-92) Soc Computer Sim.

Luker, Ralph. Historical Dictionary of the Civil Rights Movement. LC 96-19853. (Historical Dictionaries of Religions, Philosophies & Movements Ser.: No. 11). 1996. 68.00 (*0-8108-3163-5*) Scarecrow.

— A Southern Tradition in Theology & Social Criticism, 1830-1930. LC 84-8954. (Studies in American Religion: Vol. 11). 468p. 1984. lib. bdg. 109.95 (*0-88946-655-6*) E Mellen.

Luker, Ralph E. The Social Gospel in Black & White: American Racial Reform, 1885-1912. LC 91-50257. (Studies in Religion). (Illus.). 464p. 1998. pap. 18.95 (*0-8078-4720-8*) U of NC Pr.

Luker, Ralph E., ed. see Ovington, Mary W.

Luker, Stan. The Simple Mental Secrets of Golf: How to Make Them Work for You. LC 96-85471. (Illus.). 125p. (Orig.). 1996. pap. 10.95 (*0-9653253-0-X*) Chubasco Pr.

Lukert, Barbara P., jt. auth. see Adams, John S.

Lukert, Barbara P., jt. auth. see Overton, Meredith H.

Lukes, Bonnie. The Dred Scott Decision. (Famous Trials Ser.). (Illus.). (YA). 1996. lib. bdg. 22.45 (*1-56006-270-3*) Lucent Bks.

— Henry Wadsworth Longfellow: America's Beloved Poet. LC 98-7934. (World Writers Ser.). 112p. (YA). (gr. 5 up). 1997. lib. bdg. 19.95 (*1-883846-31-5*) M Reynolds.

Lukes, Bonnie L. The American Revolution. LC 95-50721. (World History Ser.). 112p. (YA). (gr. 7 up). 1996. lib. bdg. 22.45 (*1-56006-287-8*) Lucent Bks.

— The Boston Massacre. LC 97-27445. (Famous Trials Ser.). (Illus.). (YA). (gr. 5 up). 1997. lib. bdg. 18.96 (*1-56006-467-6*) Lucent Bks.

— Colonial America. LC 99-40171. (World History Ser.). (Illus.). 128p. (YA). (gr. 6-9). 2000. lib. bdg. 23.70 (*1-56006-321-1*) Lucent Bks.

— How to Be a Reasonably Thin Teenage Girl (Without Starving, Losing Your Friends, or Running Away from Home) LC 86-3347. (Illus.). 96p. (YA). (gr. 6 up). 1986. text 15.00 (*0-689-31269-5*) Aladdin.

Lukes, Igor. Czechoslovakia Between Stalin & Hitler: The Diplomacy of Edward Benes in the 1930s. (Illus.). 352p. 1996. pap. 30.00 (*0-19-510267-3*); text 65.00 (*0-19-510266-5*) OUP.

Lukes, Igor & Goldstein, Erik, eds. The Munich Crisis, 1938: Prelude to World War II. LC 99-21340. (Diplomacy & Statecraft Ser.: Vol. 10). 374p. 1999. pap. 26.50 (*0-7146-8056-7*, Pub. by F Cass Pubs) Intl Spec Bk.

***Lukes, Igor & Goldstein, Erik, eds.** The Munich Crisis, 1938: Prelude to World War II. LC 99-21340. (Diplomacy & Statecraft Ser.: Vol. 10). 402p. 1999. 57.50 (*0-7146-4995-3*, Pub. by F Cass Pubs) Intl Spec Bk.

Lukes, J., et al. Fine Topology Methods in Real Analysis & Potential Theory. (Lecture Notes in Mathematics Ser.: Vol. 1189). x, 472p. 1986. 58.00 (*0-387-16474-X*) Spr-Verlag.

Lukes, Roy. Toft Point: A Legacy of People & Pines. unabridged ed. Fever, Dave et al, eds. (Illus.). 271p. 1998. pap. 17.95 (*0-9665181-0-1*) Nature-Wise.

Lukes, Steven. The Curious Enlightenment of Professor Caritat: A Novel. 1996. pap. 18.00 (*1-85984-073-6*, Pub. by Verso) Norton.

— Curious Enlightightenment of Professor Caritat: A Novel. 200p. 1995. 35.00 (*1-85984-948-2*, Pub. by Verso) Norton.

— Emile Durkheim: His Life & Work: A Historical & Critical Study. LC 85-50791. x, 676p. 1985. reprint ed. 67.50 (*0-8047-1282-4*) Stanford U Pr.

— Essays in Social Theory. LC 77-8505. 1977. text 52.50 (*0-231-04450-X*) Col U Pr.

— Essays in Social Theory. (Modern Revivals in Sociology Ser.). 240p. 1994. 61.95 (*0-7512-0315-7*, Pub. by Gregg Revivals) Ashgate Pub Co.

Lukes, Steven, ed. Power. LC 86-8511. (Readings in Social & Political Theory Ser.). 256p. (C). 1986. text 45.00 (*0-8147-5030-3*); pap. text 17.50 (*0-8147-5031-1*) NYU Pr.

Lukes, Steven, jt. ed. see Hollis, Martin.

Lukes, Steven, jt. ed. see Joppke, Christian.

Lukes, Timothy J. The Flight into Inwardness: Herbert Marcuse & Liberatory Aesthetics. LC 83-40508. 184p. 1985. 32.50 (*0-941664-04-X*) Susquehanna U Pr.

Lukes, Timothy J., jt. ed. see Bokina, John.

Lukesh, Jean, ed. see Brown, Marion M.

Lukesh, Jean, ed. see Smith, R. P.

Lukevics, E. & Ignatovich, L. M. Organosilicon & Organogermanium Derivatives of Furan, Vol. 12. (Chemistry Reviews Ser.: SSR Sec. B, Vol. 12, Pt. 3). 106p. 1988. pap. text 87.00 (*3-7186-4854-7*) Gordon & Breach.

Lukevics, E., et al. Molecular Structure of Organosilicon Compounds. (Organic Chemistry Ser.). 1989. text 149.00 (*0-470-21525-9*) P-H.

— Thiophene Derivatives of Group IV B Elements, Vol. 2. (Sulfur Reports: Vol. 2, No. 5). 38p. 1982. pap. text 123.00 (*3-7186-0133-8*) Gordon & Breach.

Lukey, Robert J. The Culture of Food. 304p. (C). 2001. pap. 34.00 (*0-13-761909-X*, Macmillan Coll) P-H.

Lukezic, Joyce & Schwarz, Ted. False Arrest: The Joyce Lukezic Story. LC 89-63990. 342p. 1990. 23.95 (*0-88282-050-8*) New Horizon NJ.

Lukezich, S. J. Sealed Source & Device Design Safety Testing: Technical Report on the Findings of Task 4, Investigation of a Failed Brachytherapy Needle Applicator. 77p. 1997. pap. 7.50 (*0-16-062842-3*) USGPO.

Lukhaup, D., jt. auth. see Junge, Hans-Dieter.

Lukhaup, Dieter. Dictionary of Environmental Protection: English-German, German-English. (FRE & GER.). 500p. 1993. 250.00 (*0-7859-8418-6*, 3527282432) Fr & Eur.

— Parat Dictionary of Environmental Protection: English-German, German-English. (ENG & GER.). 532p. 1992. 225.00 (*0-7859-6956-X*) Fr & Eur.

Lukianowicz, Andrew, tr. see Norbu, Chogyal N. & Clemente, Adriano.

Lukic, Marie. Pasquale's Gift. LC 93-29002. (Voyages Ser.). (Illus.). (J). 1994. 4.25 (*0-383-03768-9*) SRA McGraw.

Lukic, Miodrag L., et al, eds. Immunoregulation in Health & Disease: Experimental & Clinical Aspects. LC 97-6622. (Illus.). 480p. 1997. text 99.95 (*0-12-459460-3*) Morgan Kaufmann.

Lukic, Reneo. Les Relations Sovieto-Yougoslaves de 1935 a 1945: De la Dependance a l'Autonomie et a l'Alignement. (Publications Universitaires Europeennes Ser.: Series 3, Vol. 710). (FRE.). xx, 287p. 1996. 47.95 (*3-906754-57-X*, Pub. by P Lang) P Lang Pubng.

— Rethinking the International Conflict in Communist & Post-Communist States: Essays in Honour of Miklos Molnar. LC 98-19212. 228p. 1998. text 68.95 (*1-84014-476-9*, Pub. by Ashgate Pub) Ashgate Pub Co.

Lukic, Reneo & Lynch, Allen C. Europe from the Balkans to the Urals: The Disintegration of Yugoslavia & the U. S. S. R. & World Politics. (SIPRI Publication). (Illus.). 454p. 1996. text 65.00 (*0-19-829200-7*) OUP.

Lukic, Sveta. Contemporary Yugoslav Literature: Sociopolitical Approach. Robinson, Gertrude J., ed. Triandis, Pola, tr. LC 77-166116. 296p. reprint ed. pap. 91.80 (*0-608-10688-7*, 202086400020) Bks Demand.

Lukierski, J., jt. ed. see Jancewicz, B.

Lukiewicz, Stanislaw & Zweier, Jay L., eds. Nitric Oxide in Transplant Rejection & Anti-Tumor Defense. LC 98-45219. 376p. 1998. text 139.95 (*0-7923-8389-3*, QP535) Kluwer Academic.

***Lukin, Alexander.** The Political Culture of the Russian 'Democrats' LC 99-57191. 352p. 2000. write for info. (*0-19-829558-8*) OUP.

Lukin, Anne. The Big Carrot Vegetarian Cookbook: From the Kitchen of Big Carrot Natural Food Mart. (Illus.). 144p. 1991. pap. 14.95 (*0-929005-05-8*, Pub. by Sec Story Pr) LPC InBook.

— On the Road to Vegetarian Cooking: Easy Meals for Everyone. (Illus.). 255p. 1991. pap. 14.95 (*0-929005-28-7*, Pub. by Sec Story Pr) LPC InBook.

Lukin, James, ed. Turning Lathes: A Guide to Turning, Screw Cutting, Metal Spinning & Ornamental Turning. LC 94-70622. (Illus.). 432p. 1994. reprint ed. pap. 24.95 (*1-879335-49-2*) Astragal Pr.

Lukin, Konstantin A., jt. auth. see Harmuth, Henning F.

Lukin, Vladimir P. Atmospheric Adaptive Optics. Schippnick, Paul F., tr. from RUS. LC 95-12082.Tr. of Atmosfernaia Adaptivnaia Optika. 1996. 80.00 (*0-8194-1871-4*, PM23) SPIE.

Lukinich, Imre. History of Hungary in Biographical Sketches. LC 68-20314. (Essay Index Reprint Ser.). 1977. 19.95 (*0-8369-0635-7*) Ayer.

Lukins, Sheila. Sheila Lukins All Around the World Cookbook. LC 94-2421. (Illus.). 608p. 1994. 27.95 (*1-56305-636-4*, 3636); pap. 18.95 (*1-56305-237-7*, 3237) Workman Pub.

— U. S. A. Cookbook. LC 97-9411. (Illus.). 624p. 1997. pap. 19.95 (*1-56305-807-3*, 3807) Workman Pub.

— U. S. A. Cookbook. LC 97-9411. (Illus.). 624p. 1997. 29.95 (*0-7611-0775-4*, 10775) Workman Pub.

Lukins, Sheila, jt. auth. see Rosso, Julee.

Lukito, Daniel L. Making Christology Relevant to the Third World: Applying Christopraxis to Local Struggle. LC 98-20867. (European University Studies: Series 23, Vol. 630). 266p. (C). 1998. pap. 41.95 (*0-8204-3442-6*) P Lang Pubng.

— Making Christology Relevant to the Third World Vol. 630: Applying Christopraxis to Local Struggle, Vol. 630. (European University Studies: No. 23). 266p. 1998. 41.95 (*3-906760-27-8*) P Lang Pubng.

Lukitsh, Joanne. Julia Margaret Cameron: Her Work & Career. (Illus.). 103p. (Orig.). 1986. pap. 15.00 (*0-935398-13-9*) G Eastman Hse.

Lukitz, Liora. Iraq: The Search for National Indentity. 224p. 1995. 47.50 (*0-7146-4550-8*, Pub. by F Cass Pubs); pap. 26.50 (*0-7146-4128-6*, Pub. by F Cass Pubs) Intl Spec Bk.

Lukk, Tiiu. Movie Marketing: Opening the Picture & Giving It Legs. LC 97-31744. xxiv, 274p. (Orig.). 1998. pap. 19.95 (*1-879505-38-X*) Silman James Pr.

***Lukka, Kari & Groot, Tom.** Cases in Management Accounting: Practices in European Companies. LC 00-44273. 2000. write for info. (*0-273-64616-8*) F T P H.

Lukka, T. J. Tuomas J. Lukka's Object-Oriented Programming in Perl. 700p. 1999. pap. 39.95 (*1-893115-03-8*) APress L P.

Lukken, Miriam W. Read This Book Before Your Child Starts School. (Illus.). 240p. 1994. pap. 29.95 (*0-398-06093-2*) C C Thomas.

— Read This Book Before Your Child Starts School. (Illus.). 240p. (C). 1994. text 43.95 (*0-398-05916-0*) C C Thomas.

Lukken, Miriam W., ed. see Junior Service League of LaGrange Staff.

Lukman, Mphahlele K. The Critical Issues of Skin Colour: A Treatise on the Sociological, Economic & Political Reality of Blacks in a White Society. 300p. 1985. text 19.95 (*0-9602660-0-3*) M Lukman.

Lukner, R. F., tr. see Aitmatov, Chingiz.

Lukoff, David. Mental Health Internet Pocket Guide. 1998. pap. 10.00 (*0-9665126-0-X*) Internet Guides.

— Navigating the Mental Health Internet: An Internet Guided Course. (Internet Guided Courses Ser.). 1999. pap. 30.00 (*0-9665126-1-8*) Internet Guides.

Lukoff, Fred. English for Koreans. (Spoken English As a Foreign Language Ser.). (ENG & KOR.). xvi, 480p. 1980. student ed. 110.00 incl. audio (*0-87950-611-3*) Spoken Lang Serv.

Lukoff, Fred. English for Koreans. (English for Foreigners Ser.). (ENG & KOR.). xvi, 480p. 1980. reprint ed. pap. 20.00 (*0-87950-306-8*) Spoken Lang Serv.

Lukoff, Fred. English for Koreans. (Spoken English As a Foreign Language Ser.). (ENG & KOR.). xvi, 480p. 1980. reprint ed. audio 90.00 (*0-87950-610-5*) Spoken Lang Serv.

— Spoken Korean. LC 73-17223. (Spoken Language Ser.). 370p. (gr. 9-12). 1975. audio 75.00 (*0-87950-155-3*) Spoken Lang Serv.

Lukoff, Fred. Spoken Korean, Bk. 1. LC 73-17223. (Spoken Language Ser.). 370p. (gr. 9-12). 1975. pap. 90.00 incl. audio (*0-87950-156-1*) Spoken Lang Serv.

— Spoken Korean, Bk, 1, Units 1-12. LC 73-17223. (Spoken Language Ser.). 370p. (gr. 9-12). 1975. pap. 15.00 (*0-87950-150-2*) Spoken Lang Serv.

— Spoken Korean, Bk. 2, Units 13-30. LC 73-17223. (Spoken Language Ser.). 305p. (gr. 9-12). 1975. pap. 20.00 (*0-87950-151-0*) Spoken Lang Serv.

Lukoff, Irving F. & Whiteman, Martin. The Social Sources of Adjustment to Blindness. LC 73-84034. (American Foundation for the Blind Research Ser.: No. 21). 301p. reprint ed. pap. 93.40 (*0-7837-2759-3*, 204314200006) Bks Demand.

Lukoff, Irving F., et al. Attitudes Toward Blind Persons. LC 72 82239. 80p. reprint ed. pap. 30.00 (*0-7837-5187-7*, 204492100004) Bks Demand.

Lukomski-Borowiak-Dunkelberg. Zum Arabischen Pferd. (Documenta Hippologica Ser.). (Illus.). 78p. 1979. reprint ed. write for info. (*3-487-08192-X*) G Olms Pubs.

Lukoschus, Joachim. Gesetz Und Gluck: Untersuchungen Zum Naturalismus der Stoischen Ethik. 453p. 1998. 67.95 (*3-631-32613-0*) P Lang Pubng.

Lukose, Ani. Labour Movements & Agrarian Relations. (C). 1991. 23.00 (*81-7033-100-5*, Pub. by Rawat Pubns) S Asia.

Lukose, Dickson, et al, eds. Conceptual Structures - Fulfilling Peirce's Dream: Proceedings, Fifth International Conference on Conceptual Structures, ICCS'97, Seattle, Washington, August 3-8, 1997. LC 97-27287. (Lecture Notes in Artificial Intelligence Ser.: Vol. 1257). xii, 621p. pap. write for info. (*3-540-63308-1*) Spr-Verlag.

— Multi-Agent Systems - Theories, Languages & Applications: 4th Australian Workshop on Distributed Artificial Intelligence, Brisbane, QLD, Australia, July 13, 1998: Proceedings. LC 98-53825. (Lecture Notes in Computer Science Ser.: Vol. 1544). vii, 200p. 1999. pap. 40.00 (*3-540-65477-1*) Spr-Verlag.

Lukose, Dickson, jt. auth. see Zhang, Chengqi.

Lukoshkova, L. Cardiology Reviews Vol. 3, Pt. 2: Profiles & Pharmacological Aspects of Selected Cardiovascular Drugs, Vol. 3. (Soviet Medical Reviews Ser.: Section A). 196p. 1992. pap. text 143.00 (*3-7186-5312-5*, Harwood Acad Pubs) Gordon & Breach.

Lukovich, Istvan. Electric Foil Fencing: Advanced Competitive Training. Khinoy, Stephan, ed. Butykai, Istvan, tr. (Illus.). 304p. 1998. 30.00 (*0-9659468-2-7*) SKA.

— Fencing: The Modern International Style. Date not set. 30.00 (*0-9659468-1-9*) SKA.

Lukow, Gregory, jt. ed. see Davidson, Steven.

Lukowich, E., et al. Curling To Win. 160p. 1987. text 11.95 (*0-07-549442-6*) McGraw.

Lukowski, Jerzy. Partitions of Poland 1772 93 95. LC 98-8061. 248p. (C). 1998. pap. 30.13 (*0-582-29274-3*) Longman.

— Partitions Poland 1772. LC 98-8061. (C). 1998. 63.95 (*0-582-29275-1*) Longman.

Lukowski, Susan, jt. ed. see Grayson, Cary T., Jr.

Luks, Allan & Barbato, Joseph. You Are What You Drink: The Authoritative Report on What Alcohol Does to Your Mind, Body & Longevity. 1989. pap. 7.95 (*0-318-41620-4*) Villard Books.

Luksic, Mladen, et al. Differential Geometry: The Interface Between Pure & Applied Mathematics. LC 87-30648. (Contemporary Mathematics Ser.: Vol. 68). 273p. 1988. pap. 37.00 (*0-8218-5075-X*, CONM/68) Am Math.

Lukyanchikova, N. B. Noise Research in Semiconductor Physics. Jones, B. K., ed. 416p. 1997. text 98.00 (*90-5699-006-3*) Gordon & Breach.

Lukyanov, S. L. Physics Reviews Vol. 15, Pt. 2: Additional Symmetries & Exactly Solvable Models in Two Dimensional Conformal Field Theory, Vol. 15. (Soviet Scientific Reviews Ser.: Section A). 117p. 1991. text 121.00 (*3-7186-5047-9*, Harwood Acad Pubs) Gordon & Breach.

Lukyanov, V. K., ed. Dubna Deuteron-93: Proceedings of the International Symposium Dubna Deuteron-93, 1993, Dubna, Russia. 391p. (C). 1995. pap. 50.00 (*1-57485-003-2*) Hadronic Pr Inc.

Lula, R., ed. Materials Properties Handbook: Stainless Steels. 500p. 1996. 192.00 (*0-87170-588-5*, 6195) ASM.

— Toughness of Ferritic Stainless Steels, Vol. STP 706. 348p. 1980. 32.50 (*0-8031-0792-7*, STP706) ASTM.

Lula, R. A., ed. see American Society for Metals Staff.

Lula, R. A., ed. see ASM International Staff.

Lula, R. A., ed. see Conference on Manganese Containing Stainless Steel.

Lulat, Y. G. The Academic Impact of Foreign Graduate Students: Perceptions of Faculty. 205p. 1996. pap. text 29.90 (*0-944265-16-2*, Cerebrum Bks); lib. bdg. 39.90 (*0-944265-13-8*, Cerebrum Bks) Librosmondiale.

— Analyzing U. S. Relations with South Africa: Past, Present & Future. LC 90-38974. 1024p. (C). 1997. pap. text. write for info. (*0-944265-07-3*); lib. bdg. write for info. (*0-944265-08-1*) Librosmondiale.

— Librarians & the Selection of Publications from Small Presses: Implications for Intellectual Freedom. 176p. 1996. pap. text 29.90 (*0-944265-15-4*, Cerebrum Bks); lib. bdg. 39.90 (*0-944265-14-6*, Cerebrum Bks) Librosmondiale.

Lulat, Y. G. & Pappas, James G. Perspectives on Blacks in Cinema: An Introductory Text on Select Topics. LC 93-11628. 708p. 1993. lib. bdg. 55.50 (*0-944265-11-1*, Cerebrum Bks) Librosmondiale.

— Perspectives on Blacks in Cinema: An Introductory Text on Select Topics. LC 93-11628. 512p. 1997. pap. text 45.50 (*0-944265-12-X*, Cerebrum Bks) Librosmondiale.

Lulat, Y. G., et al. Governmental & Institutional Policies on Foreign Students: Analysis, Evaluation & Bibliography. LC 86-17559. (Special Studies in Comparative Education: No. 16). (Illus.). 114p. 1986. pap. text 10.00 (*0-937033-05-7*) Grad Schl of Educ.

Lulchak, L., jt. auth. see Kolesnikova, A.

***Lule, Jack.** Daily News, Eternal Stories: The Mythological Role of Journalism. 2001. 35.00 (*1-57230-608-4*); pap. 17.95 (*1-57230-606-8*) Guilford Pubns.

Lulek, T. Symmetry & Structural Properties of Condensed Matter: Proceedings of the 5th International School. 500p. 1999. 127.00 (*981-02-3931-9*) World Scientific Pub.

Lulek, T., et al, eds. Symmetry & Structural Properties of Condensed Matter. 440p. (C). 1991. text 137.00 (*981-02-0422-1*) World Scientific Pub.

Lulek, T., et al. Symmetry & Structural Properties of Condensed Matter: Proceedings of the 3rd International School on Theoretical Physics. 524p. 1995. text 109.00 (*981-02-2059-6*) World Scientific Pub.

Lulic, Margaret A. Who We Could Be at Work. LC 93-73454. 261p. 1994. 19.95 (*0-9638526-3-9*) Blue Edge Pub.

— Who We Could Be at Work. rev. ed. LC 95-46389. 256p. 1996. pap. text 17.95 (*0-7506-9739-3*) Buttrwrth-Heinemann.

— Working As If Life Mattered. 128p. (Orig.). 1995. pap. 7.95 (*0-9638526-1-2*) Blue Edge Pub.

Lulic, Margaret A., ed. Working As If Life Mattered. 120p. (Orig.). 1995. pap. write for info. (*0-614-29621-8*) Blue Edge Pub.

Luling, Virginia. Threatened Cultures, Set II. (World Issues Ser.). (Illus.). 48p. (J). (gr. 5 up). 1990. lib. bdg. 25.27 (*0-86592-096-6*) Rourke Enter.

Lull, David J. The Spirit in Galatia: Paul's Interpretation of Pneuma As Divine Power. LC 79-26094. (Society of Biblical Literature. Dissertation Ser.: No. 49). 254p. reprint ed. pap. 78.80 (*0-7837-5443-4*, 204520800005) Bks Demand.

Lull, H. & Sopper, William E. Forest Hydrology: Proceedings of the National Science Foundation Seminar, University Park, Aug. 1965. LC 66-27642. 1967. 360.00 (*0-08-012088-1*, Pub. by Pergamon Repr) Franklin.

Lull, Howard W., jt. auth. see Reifsynder, William E.

***Lull, James.** Culture in the Communication Age. LC 00-32320. 2000. pap. write for info. (*0-415-22117-X*) Routledge.

Lull, James. Media, Communication, Culture: A Global Approach. 200p. 1995. 46.00 (*0-231-10264-X*) Col U Pr.

— Media, Communication, Culture: A Global Approach. (Illus.). 200p. 1995. pap. 18.00 (*0-231-10265-8*) Col U Pr.

***Lull, James.** Media, Communication, Culture: A Global Approach. 2nd ed. LC 99-54090. 288p. 2000. 18.50 (*0-231-12073-7*) Col U Pr.

L

L

Lull, James. Media Scandals: Morality & Desire in the Popular Culture Marketplace. LC 97-22261. 270p. 1997. pap. 18.50 (*0-231-11165-7*) Col U Pr.

— Media Scandals: Morality & Desire in the Popular Culture Marketplace. LC 97-22261. 270p. 1998. 47.50 (*0-231-11164-9*) Col U Pr.

***Lull, James.** Why White Guys Play Golf! 135p. 1999. pap. 10.95 (*0-9666552-0-6*, Pub. by East Side Bks) ACCESS Pubs Network.

Lull, James, ed. Popular Music & Communication. LC 91-30886. (Sage Focus Editions Ser.: Vol. 89). (Illus.). 256p. 1992. reprint ed. pap. 79.40 (*0-608-07686-4*, 206777600010) Bks Demand.

— Popular Music & Communication. 2nd ed. (Focus Editions Ser.: Vol. 89). 334p. (C). 1991. text 59.95 (*0-8039-3916-7*); pap. text 26.00 (*0-8039-3917-5*) Sage.

— World Families Watch Television. LC 88-9658. (Communication & Human Values Ser.). (Illus.). 264p. 1988. pap. 81.90 (*0-7837-8965-3*, 204974600003) Bks Demand.

Lull, Janis. The Metaphysical Poets: A Chronology. LC 93-8212. (Reference Ser.). 240p. 1994. 50.00 (*0-8161-7251-X*, Hall Reference) Macmillan.

— The Poem in Time: Reading George Herbert's Revisions of The Church. LC 88-40586. (Illus.). 168p. 1990. 32.50 (*0-87413-357-2*) U Delaware Pr.

Lull, Janis, ed. see Shakespeare, William.

Lull, Ramon, pseud. The Art of Contemplation. Peers, Allison, tr. 1976. lib. bdg. 250.00 (*0-8490-1451-4*) Gordon Pr.

— Blanquerna. 2nd ed. Reeb, E. A., ed. & tr. by. from CAT. Irwin, Robert, ed. (European Classics). 530p. Date not set. reprint ed. pap. 14.95 (*0-946626-22-7*) Dedalus.

— The Order of Chivalry. Ellis, F. S., ed. Caxton, William, tr. from FRE. LC 79-8368. reprint ed. 45.00 (*0-404-18352-2*) AMS Pr.

— Romancing God: Contemplating the Beloved. Carrigan, Henry, ed. LC 99-11223. (Christian Classics Ser.). 122p. 1999. pap. 11.95 (*1-55725-216-5*, 930-019, Pub. by Paraclete MA) BookWorld.

Lull, Ramon, pseud & Caxton, William. The Book of the Order of Chivalry. 118p. 1991. 24.95 (*0-9633100-0-3*) START Grp.

Lull, Richard S. The Sauropod Dinosaur Barosaurus Marsh. (Connecticut Academy of Arts & Sciences Ser., Trans.: Vol. 6). 1919. pap. 150.00 (*0-685-22867-3*) Elliots Bks.

Lull, Timothy F. My Conversations with Martin Luther: In Which I Learn about God, Faith, Marriage, Sexuality, Family, Education, War, Spirituality, Church Life, the Future, Heaven & Hell & Other Things, Too. LC 99-28310. 128p. 1999. pap. 6.99 (*0-8066-3898-2*, 9-3898, Augsburg) Augsburg Fortress.

Lull, Timothy F., ed. Martin Luther's Basic Theological Writings. LC 89-34201. 752p. (Orig.). 1989. pap. 30.00 (*0-8006-2327-4*, 1-2327, Fortress Pr) Augsburg Fortress.

***Lulla, Kamlesh & Dessinov, Lev V.** Dynamic Earth Environments: Remote Sensing Observations from Shuttle-Mir Missions. LC 00-26818. 2000. write for info. (*0-471-39005-4*) Wiley.

***Lullmann, Heinz.** Color Atlas of Pharmacology. 2nd rev. expanded ed. LC 99-33662. (Illus.). 380p. 2000. pap. 32.00 (*0-86577-843-4*) Thieme Med Pubs.

Lully. Armide. (Fropse Ser.). Date not set. write for info. (*0-945193-47-5*) Pendragon NY.

Lully, Jean-Baptiste. Acis et Galatee. (Tragedies Lyriques in Facsimile Ser.: Vol. 14). 1998. lib. bdg. 200.00 (*0-89371-164-0*) Broude Intl Edns.

— Atys. (Tragedies Lyriques in Facsimile Ser.: Vol. 4). 1998. lib. bdg. 200.00 (*0-89371-154-3*) Broude Intl Edns.

— Bellerophon. (Tragedies Lyriques in Facsimile Ser.: Vol. 7). 1998. lib. bdg. 200.00 (*0-89371-157-8*) Broude Intl Edns.

— The Livrets of Jean-Baptiste Lully's Tragedies Lyriques: A Catalogue Raisonne. LC 95-203910. 1998. lib. bdg. 150.00 (*0-943930-50-2*) Performers Edit.

— Oeuvres Completes de Jean-Baptiste Lully, 11 vols. Prunieres, Henry et al, eds. Incl. Ballets, I, 1654-1657: Ballet du Temps; Ballet des Plaisirs; Ballet de l'Amour malade. (Illus.). 1966. reprint ed. pap. 95.00 (*0-8450-1261-4*); Ballets, II, 1658-1660 Tome 2: Ballet d'Alcidiane; Ballet des Gardes; Ballet de Xerxes. (Illus.). 1966. reprint ed. pap. 95.00 (*0-8450-1262-2*); Comedies-Ballets, I 1664-1665 Tome 1: Le Mariage force; L'Amour medecin. (Illus.). 1966. reprint ed. pap. 95.00 (*0-8450-1263-0*); Comedies-Ballets, III 1669-1670 Tome 3: Monsieur de Pourceaugnac; Le Bourgeois Gentilhomme; Les Amants magnifiques. (Illus.). 1966. reprint ed. pap. 95.00 (*0-8450-1265-7*); Comedies-Ballets, II 1666-1668 Tome 2: Les Plaisirs de l'Ile enchantee; La Pastorale comique; Le Sicilien; Le Grand Di. (Illus.). 1966. reprint ed. pap. 95.00 (*0-8450-1264-9*); Motets, I ,1664 Tome 1: Miserere Mei Deus. (Illus.). 1966. reprint ed. pap. 95.00 (*0-8450-1266-5*); Motets, 1668-1677 Tome 2: Plaude, Laetare, Gallia; Te Deum Laudamus; Dies Irae; Dies Illa. (Illus.). 1966. reprint ed. pap. 95.00 (*0-8450-1267-3*); Operas Tome 1: Cadmus et Hermione. (Illus.). 1966. reprint ed. pap. 135.00 (*0-8450-1269-X*); Operas II Tome 2: Alceste. (Illus.). 1966. reprint ed. pap. 135.00 (*0-8450-1270-3*); Operas, 1684 Tome 3: Amadis. (Illus.). 1966. reprint ed. pap. 135.00 (*0-8450-1271-1*); (Illus.). 1972. reprint ed. Set pap. 1165.00 (*0-8450-1260-6*) Broude.

— Persee. (Tragedies Lyriques in Facsimile Ser.: Vol. 9). 1998. lib. bdg. 200.00 (*0-89371-159-4*) Broude Intl Edns.

— Quare Fremuerunt Gentes, Notus in Judaea Deus, Exaudiat Te Dominus. (Collected Works: Vol. 4/5). 1997. lib. bdg. 200.00 (*0-8450-7851-8*) Broude.

Lully, Raymond. The Hermetic Mercuries of Raymond Lully. 1984. reprint ed. pap. 4.95 (*0-916411-36-2*) Holmes Pub.

Lully, Raymond, see Lull, Ramon, pseud.

Lulof, Patricia S. The Ridge-Pole Status from the Late Archaic Temple at Satricum. LC 99-228982. (Scrinium XI). (Illus.). 432p. 1996. 157.00 (*90-5170-355-4*, Pub. by Thesis Pubs) D Brown Bk Co.

***Lulof, Patricia S. & Moormann, Eric M., eds.** Deliciae Fictiles II. (Scrinium XII). (Illus.). 274p. 1998. 113.50 (*90-5170-441-0*, Pub. by Thesis Pubs) D Brown Bk Co.

Luloff, A. E. & Steahr, Thomas E. Rural Population Growth in New England. 92p. 1987. pap. 5.00 (*0-9609010-2-7*) NE Regional Ctr.

Luloff, A. E., jt. ed. see Steahr, Thomas E.

Lulofs. Persuasion Context People. 410p. 1997. pap. text 53.00 (*0-13-777905-4*) P-H.

Lulofs, H. J. Drossaart, ed. see Nicolaus of Damascus.

***Lulofs, Roxane S.** Conflict: From Theory, from Action. 2nd ed. LC 98-47878. 384p. (C). 1999. pap. text 44.00 (*0-205-29030-2*) Allyn.

Lulu Huang Chang. From Confucius to Kublai Khan: Music & Poetics Through the Centuries. (Wissenschaftliche Abhandlungen-Musicological Studies: Vol. 58). xxi, 184p. 1992. lib. bdg. 120.00 (*0-931902-75-4*) Inst Mediaeval Mus.

Lulushi & Stowe, Harriet Beecher. Oracle Developers Research Library. 1998. boxed set 119.99 (*0-13-010620-8*) P-H.

Lulushi, Albert. Developing Oracle Forms Applications. LC 96-16603. 752p. (C). 1996. pap. text 44.95 (*0-13-531229-9*) P-H.

— Oracle Designer - 2000. LC 97-44451. 992p. (C). 1997. pap. text 49.95 (*0-13-849753-2*, Pub. by P-H) S&S Trade.

— Oracle Developer/2000 Forms. LC 98-30448. 1000p. 1998. pap. text 49.99 (*0-13-949033-7*) P-H.

***Lum.** Social Work Practice & People of Color: A Process-Stage Approach. 4th ed. LC 99-28881. 350p. 1999. 49.95 (*0-534-35639-7*) Brooks-Cole.

Lum, Ada. Luke: Good News of Hope & Joy. (LifeGuide Bible Studies). 112p. (Orig.). 1992. pap., wbk. ed. 4.99 (*0-8308-1005-6*, 1005) InterVarsity.

Lum, Allen. Internet Business Security. (C). 1997. text. write for info. (*0-201-63482-1*) Addison-Wesley.

Lum, Arlene, ed. Sailing for the Sun: The Chinese in Hawaii, 1789-1989. (Illus.). 200p. 1989. 39.95 (*0-8248-1313-8*) Univ of HI Fnd.

Lum, Bernice. More Steps to Heaven. (Illus.). 28p. 1993. 6.00 (*1-872819-06-0*, Pub. by Tuppy Owens) AK Pr Dist.

— Twelve Steps to Heaven: My First Impression of Sex. (Illus.). 78p. (Orig.). 1995. 6.00 (*1-872819-00-1*, Pub. by Tuppy Owens) AK Pr Dist.

Lum, Bernice, jt. auth. see Johansen, K. V.

Lum, Cal, ed. see Kratz, Karl.

Lum, Casey M. In Search of a Voice: Karaoke & the Construction of Identity in Chinese America. LC 95-25506. (Everyday Communication Ser.). 136p. 1996. 29.95 (*0-8058-1911-8*) L Erlbaum Assocs.

— In Search of a Voice: Karaoke, Communication & the Construction of Identity. LC 95-25506. (Everyday Communication Ser.). 136p. 1996. pap. 14.50 (*0-8058-1912-6*) L Erlbaum Assocs.

Lum, Darrell. The Golden Slipper: A Vietnamese Legend. LC 93-33588. (Legends of the World Ser.). (Illus.). 32p. (J). (gr. 2-5). 1994. pap. 4.95 (*0-8167-3406-2*) Troll Communs.

— The Golden Slipper: A Vietnamese Legend. LC 93-33588. (Legends of the World Ser.). (Illus.). 32p. (J). (gr. 2-5). 1997. lib. bdg. 18.60 (*0-8167-3405-4*) Troll Communs.

Lum, Darrell, jt. ed. see Chock, Eric.

Lum, Darrell H. Sun: Short Stories & Drama. (Bamboo Ridge Ser.: No. 8). 77p. 1980. pap. 8.00 (*0-910043-02-7*) Bamboo Ridge Pr.

Lum, Darrell H., jt. ed. see Chock, Eric.

Lum, Darrell H. Y. Golden Slipper: A Vietnamese Legend. LC 93-33588. (Legends of the World Ser.). 1994. 10.15 (*0-606-06416-8*, Pub. by Turtleback) Demco.

— Pass on, No Pass Back! LC 90-85158. (Bamboo Ridge Ser.: Nos. 48-49). 128p. (Orig.). 1990. pap. 8.00 (*0-910043-19-1*) Bamboo Ridge Pr.

Lum, Darrell H. Y., jt. ed. see Chock, Eric.

***Lum, Dee, compiled by.** Everyone, Eat Slowly: The Chong Family Food Book. (Illus.). 128p. 1999. spiral bd. 18.00 (*0-9634186-1-0*) Chong Hee Bks.

Lum, Doman. Culturally Competent Practice: A Framework for Growth & Action. LC 98-17046. 1998. pap. 42.95 (*0-534-35686-9*) Brooks-Cole.

— Social Work Practice & People of Color: A Process-Stage Approach. LC 85-17047. (Social Work Ser.). 220p. (C). 1986. pap. 33.75 (*0-534-05586-9*) Brooks-Cole.

— Social Work Practice & People of Color: A Process-Stage Approach. 2nd ed. 336p. (C). 1992. pap. 25.75 (*0-534-17040-4*) Brooks-Cole.

— Social Work Practice & People of Color: A Process-Stage Approach. 3rd ed. LC 95-2871. 336p. 1995. pap. 30.50 (*0-534-33854-2*) Brooks-Cole.

Lum, Dyer D. Concise History of the Great Trial of the Chicago Anarchists in 1886. LC 75-90181. (Mass Violence in America Ser.). 1973. reprint ed. 24.95 (*0-405-01324-8*) Ayer.

— The Mormon Question in Its Economic Aspects. 1973. lib. bdg. 59.95 (*0-8490-0672-4*) Gordon Pr.

Lum, Edward H. Lum: Genealogy of the Lum Family. 270p. 1993. reprint ed. pap. 42.50 (*0-8328-3712-1*); reprint ed. lib. bdg. 52.50 (*0-8328-3711-3*) Higginson Bk Co.

Lum, Henry, jt. ed. see Heer, Ewald.

***Lum, Kate.** What! Cried Granny. Skwarek, Skip, ed. LC 98-19642. (Illus.). 32p. (J). (ps-2). 1999. 15.99 (*0-8037-2382-2*, Dial Yng Read) Peng Put Young Read.

***Lum, Kate & Johnson, Adrian.** What! Cried Granny. LC 99-488178. (Illus.). 32p. (J). 1999. write for info. (*0-7475-4178-7*) Blmsbury Pub.

***Lum, Kit-Wye, et al.** Contract Law. LC 98-182975. viii, 336 p. 1998. write for info. (*0-409-99904-0*) Buttrwrth-Heinemann.

Lum, Lewis. Proceedings of the Fifth Annual International Conference on Technology in Collegiate Mathematics. (C). 1993. pap. text 29.33 (*0-201-54304-4*) Addison-Wesley.

***Lum, Mary & Tauke, Beth.** Occupational Information. (Illus.). 48p. 1999. pap. 10.00 (*0-936739-25-8*) Hallwalls Inc.

Lum, Peter. Growth of Civilization. LC 73-77311. (Illus.). 258p. (J). (gr. 8 up). 1997. 38.95 (*0-87599-144-0*) S G Phillips.

— Six Centuries in East Asia: China, Japan & Korea from the 14th Century to 1912. LC 72-12582. (Illus.). 288p. 1973. 38.95 (*0-87599-183-1*) S G Phillips.

Lum, Ray J. The Rebus Escape. LC 91-76970. 64p. (Orig.). (J). (gr. 3-5). 1992. pap. 5.95 (*0-943864-63-1*) Davenport.

Lum, Raymond Mun Kong, jt. auth. see Lum, Yansheng Ma.

Lum, Roseline. Culture Shock! Mauritius. LC 97-225523. (Culture Shock Ser.). 1997. pap. 12.95 (*1-55868-305-4*) Gr Arts Ctr Pub.

Lum, Shelly. True & Tried Recipes. Herr, Ethel et al, eds. (Illus.). 200p. (Orig.). pap. 14.95 (*0-941201-06-6*) INNPRO.

Lum, Wing T. Expounding the Doubtful Points. LC 87-72145. (Bamboo Ridge Ser.: Nos. 34-35). 108p. (Orig.). (C). 1987. pap. 10.00 (*0-910043-14-0*) Bamboo Ridge Pr.

***Lum, Yansheng Ma & Lum, Raymond Mun Kong.** Sun Yat-Sen in Hawaii: Activities & Supporters. LC 99-20725. (Illus.). 128p. 1999. pap. 19.95 (*0-8248-2179-3*); text 29.00 (*0-8248-2254-4*) UH Pr.

Lumans, Valdis O. Himmler's Auxiliaries: The Volkdeutsche Mittelstelle & the German National Minorities of Europe, 1933-1945. LC 92-24080. xiv, 336p. (C). 1993. 55.00 (*0-8078-2066-0*) U of NC Pr.

***Lumari.** Alawashka Language of Creation. 2000. pap. 15.95 (*0-9679553-6-X*) Amethyst NM.

***Lumas, Susan.** Making Use of the Census. 2nd rev. ed. 117p. 1999. pap. 9.95 (*1-873162-43-X*) PRO Pubns.

***Lumatec Industries Staff.** Novelist Adventure Booklight & Flashlight. 1999. pap. 14.95 (*1-884595-28-6*) Lumatec Industries Inc.

***Lumb, Andrew & Nunn, J. F.** Nunn's Applied Respiratory Physiology. 5th ed. LC 99-40687. 687p. 1999. text 115.00 (*0-7506-3107-4*) Buttrwrth-Heinemann.

Lumb, Nick. Beginner's Guide to Golf. (Illus.). 112p. 1998. pap. 14.95 (*0-8069-3770-X*) Sterling.

— Golf Tips. 1996. 6.98 (*0-7858-0541-9*) Bk Sales Inc.

Lumb, R. D. Australian Constitutionalism. 1983. pap. 44.00 (*0-409-49300-7*, AT, MICHIE) LEXIS Pub.

— The Constitution of the Commonwealth of Australia Annotated. 4th ed. 1986. 85.00 (*0-409-49128-4*, AT, MICHIE); pap. 69.00 (*0-409-49129-2*, AT, MICHIE) LEXIS Pub.

— Constitutions of the Australian States. 5th rev. ed. 1991. pap. 29.95 (*0-7022-2218-6*, Pub. by Univ Queensland Pr) Intl Spec Bk.

Lumbala, Francois K., jt. ed. see Chauvet, Louis-Marie.

Lumbala, Kabasele & Power, David N., eds. The Specter of Mass Death. (Concilium Ser.). 1993. 15.00 (*0-88344-871-8*) Orbis Bks.

Lumbert, David E. & Bennett, Margo E. A. S. C. Tattoo Directory, 1994. (Illus.). 220p. 1994. pap. 15.95 (*1-887080-00-7*) Action Publ.

— A. S. C. Tattoo Directory, 1995. (Illus.). 250p. 1995. pap. 15.95 (*1-887080-01-5*) Action Publ.

Lumbert, David E., jt. auth. see Bennett, Margo E.

Lumbert, Lindy H. Dear Diary. 119p. (J). (gr. 4-10). 1981. pap. 8.50 (*0-943280-00-1*) Blossom Bks.

— The Two Minute Philosopher. 19.00 (*0-943280-01-X*); pap. 8.50 (*0-943280-02-8*) Blossom Bks.

Lumbley, Joe. The Informix Database Administrator's Survival Guide. 1994. pap. text 27.00 (*0-685-70700-8*) P-H.

— Informix DBA Survival Guide. 2nd ed. 512p. 1998. pap. text 44.99 incl. cd-rom (*0-13-079623-9*) P-H.

Lumbra, Elaine. More Hoosier Cooking. LC 82-47959. 256p. 1994. pap. 13.95 (*0-253-20917-X*) Ind U Pr.

Lumby. Investment Appraisal & Financial Decision Making, Vol. 1. 6th ed. (ITBP Textbooks Ser.). 1998. pap. 23.99 (*1-86152-257-6*) Thomson Learn.

Lumby, Catherine. Bad Girls: The Media, Sex & Feminism in the 90s. LC 97-146301. 196p. 1997. pap. 16.95 (*1-86448-076-9*, Pub. by Allen & Unwin Pty) Paul & Co Pubs.

Lumby, Dana, compiled by. Slavic Specialties. 158p. 1996. spiral bd. 6.95 (*1-57216-025-X*) Penfield.

Lumby, E. W., ed. Policy & Operations in the Mediterranean, 1912 to 1914. 1986. 80.00 (*0-7855-1151-2*) St Mut.

Lumby, Joseph R. Ratis Raving, & Other Moral & Religious Pieces. (EETS, OS Ser.: No. 43). 1974. reprint ed. 40.00 (*0-527-00038-8*) Periodicals Srv.

Lumby, Joseph R., ed. Be Domes Daege, de die Judicii: An Old English Version of the Latin Poem Ascribed to Bede. (EETS Original Ser.). 1964. reprint ed. 20.00 (*0-19-722065-7*, Pub. by EETS) Boydell & Brewer.

— Bernardus de Cura Rei Famuliaris with Some Early Scottish Prophecies. (EETS Original Ser.: Vol. 42). 1970. reprint ed. pap. 20.00 (*0-19-722042-8*, Pub. by EETS) Boydell & Brewer.

— Chronicon Henrici Knighton: Vel Cnitthon, Monachi Leycestrensis, 2 vols. (Rolls Ser.: No. 92). 1972. reprint ed. 140.00 (*0-8115-1169-3*) Periodicals Srv.

Lumby, Joseph R. & McKnight, G. H., eds. King Horn, Floritz & Blauncheflur, Etc. (EETS, OS Ser.: No. 14). 1969. reprint ed. 36.00 (*0-8115-3345-X*) Periodicals Srv.

Lumby, Joseph R., jt. ed. see Babington, Churchill.

Lumby, Judy. Nursing: Reflecting on an Evolving Practice. (C). 1991. pap. 65.00 (*0-7300-1263-8*, NPR300, Pub. by Deakin Univ) St Mut.

Lumby, Roy, jt. auth. see Van Daele, Patrick.

Lumby, S. P. Investment Appraisal & Financial Decisions. 5th ed. 688p. 1996. pap. 39.95 (*0-412-58840-4*) Chapman & Hall.

— Investment Appraisal & Financial Decisions. 5th ed. 152p. 1994. pap., teacher ed. 68.15 (*0-412-58850-1*) Thomson Learn.

— Investment Appraisal & Financing Decisions. 4th ed. (Accounting & Finance Ser.). 544p. (C). 1990. pap. 44.95 (*0-412-41070-2*) Chapman & Hall.

Lumby, Ted, jt. auth. see Leach, Andy.

Lumer, Gunter, et al, eds. Partial Differential Equations: Models in Physics & Biology. LC 94-40002. (Mathematical Research Ser.: Vol. 82). 418p. 1994. text 102.90 (*3-05-501657-2*, Pub. by Akademie Verlag) Wiley.

Lumer, Gunter, jt. auth. see Antoniou, Ioannis.

Lumer, Gunter, jt. ed. see Clement, Philippe.

Lumer, Hyman. Israel Today: War or Peace? 1970. pap. 0.45 (*0-87898-061-X*) New Outlook.

— Jewish Defense League: A New Face for Reaction. 1971. pap. 0.35 (*0-87898-072-5*) New Outlook.

— Middle East Crisis. 1967. pap. 0.25 (*0-87898-023-7*) New Outlook.

— What Happened in Poland? 1969. pap. 0.35 (*0-87898-035-0*) New Outlook.

— Which Way Israel? 1966. pap. 0.20 (*0-87898-010-5*) New Outlook.

Lumer, Wilfred. Small Business at the Crossroad. Bruchey, Stuart & Carosso, Vincent P., eds. LC 78-18967. (Small Business Enterprise in America Ser.). (Illus.). 1979. reprint ed. lib. bdg. 15.95 (*0-405-11471-0*) Ayer.

Lumet, L., jt. auth. see Keim, A.

Lumet, Sidney. Making Movies. 1996. pap. 12.00 (*0-679-75660-4*) Random.

***Lumetta, Gregg J., et al.** Calixarene Molecules for Separations. (ACS Symposium Ser.: No. 757). (Illus.). 448p. 2000. text 125.00 (*0-8412-3660-7*, Pub. by Am Chemical) OUP.

***Lumgair, Christopher.** Creative Design with Your Computer. (Teach Yourself Ser.). (Illus.). 192p. 1999. pap. 12.95 (*0-8442-0275-4*, 025754) NTC Contemp Pub Co.

Lumgair, Christopher. QuarkXPress, Version 4. (Teach Yourself Ser.). 208p. 1999. pap. 10.95 (*0-8442-2628-9*) NTC Contemp Pub Co.

***Lumgair, Christopher.** Teach Yourself Illustrator 8.0. (Teach Yourself Ser.). 192p. 2000. pap. 12.95 (*0-658-00083-7*, 000837) NTC Contemp Pub Co.

Lumgair, Irene. Wave Action. (How to Draw & Paint Ser.). (Illus.). 32p. (Orig.). 1995. pap. 6.95 (*1-56010-143-1*, HT244) W Foster Pub.

Lumholtz. Among Cannibals. (Australian National University Press Ser.). 1996. write for info. (*0-08-033014-2*, Pergamon Pr) Elsevier.

Lumholtz, Carl. New Trails in Mexico. LC 90-30449. (Southwest Center Ser.). 411p. 1990. reprint ed. pap. 20.95 (*0-8165-1175-6*) U of Ariz Pr.

— Unknown Mexico, 2 vols. 1973. 500.00 (*0-8490-1249-X*) Gordon Pr.

Lumholtz, Carl & De la Cruz, Pablo. Huichol Shamanic Emblems: Sacred Origins of the Yarn Paintings. large type unabridged ed. LC 95-83907. (Huichol Shamanic Library: Vol. 3). (Illus.). 95p. 1998. pap. 20.00 (*0-943907-20-9*) Bruce Finson.

Lumholtz, Carl, jt. auth. see De la Cruz, Pablo.

Lumholtz, Karl S. Through Central Borneo: An Account of Two Years' Travel in the Land of the Head-Hunters Between the Years 1913 & 1917, 2 vols., Set. LC 77-87504. (Illus.). reprint ed. 53.00 (*0-404-16760-8*) AMS Pr.

— Unknown Mexico: A Record of Five Years' Exploration among the Tribes of the Western Sierra Madre, in the Tierra Caliente of Tepic & Jalisco, & Among the Tarascos of Michoacan, 2 vols. LC 72-5010. (Antiquities of the New World Ser.: Vol. 15). (Illus.). reprint ed. 125.00 (*0-404-57315-0*) AMS Pr.

Lumholtz, Ludvig L. A Slice of Life. 220p. (C). 1989. text 65.00 (*1-872795-51-X*, Pub. by Pentland Pr) St Mut.

Lumiansky, R. M., tr. see Chaucer, Geoffrey.

Lumiansky, Robert M. Malory's Originality: A Critical Study of Le Morte D'Arthur. LC 78-19255. 1979. 28.95 (*0-405-10612-2*) Ayer.

Lumiansky, Robert M. & Mills, David. The Chester Mystery Cycle: Essays & Documents. LC 82-1838. 347p. reprint ed. pap. 107.60 (*0-7837-3769-6*, 204358600010) Bks Demand.

Lumiansky, Robert M. & Mills, David, eds. Chester Mystery Cycle Vol. II: Commentary & Glossary, Vol. II. (SS 9 Ser.: No. 8). 550p. 1986. 45.00 (*0-19-722408-3*) OUP.

Lumiere, Auguste & Lumiere, Louis. Letters: Inventing the Cinema. Hodgson, Pierre, tr. (Illus.). 336p. 1997. 33.95 (*0-571-17545-7*) Faber & Faber.

Lumiere, Louis, jt. auth. see Lumiere, Auguste.

Lumijarvi, Ismo & Salo, Sari. Steering & Auditing: Public Management Reform & the New Role of the Parliamentary Actors. 136p. (C). 1997. pap. text 26.95 (*0-8204-3422-1*) P Lang Pubng.

***Luminare-Rosen, Carista.** Parenting Begins Before Conception: A Guide to Preparing Body, Mind & Spirit for You & Your Future Child. LC 99-89235. (Illus.). 288p. 2000. pap. 16.95 (*0-89281-827-1*) Inner Tradit.

An Asterisk (*) at the beginning of an entry indicates that the title is appearing for the first time.

Luminescence Conference (1965 Hakone-machi, Japan). Bioluminescence in Progress: Proceedings of the Luminescence Conference. Johnson, Frank H. & Haneda, Yata, eds. LC 66-17702. 671p. 1966. reprint ed. pap. 200.00 (*0-608-02932-7*, 206399800008) Bks Demand.

Luminet, Jean-Pierre. Black Holes. (Illus.). 332p. (C). 1992. pap. 22.95 (*0-521-40906-3*); text 59.95 (*0-521-40029-5*) Cambridge U Pr.

Luminet, Jean-Pierre, jt. auth. see Brunier, Serge.

Lumiste, V. & Peetre, J. Edgar Krahn: A Centenary Volume (1894-1961) LC 94-76402. 196p. (gr. 12). 1994. pap. 53.00 (*90-5199-168-1*) IOS Press.

Lumley. Essential Anatomy. 4th ed. 1987. pap. text 39.00 (*0-443-03573-3*, W B Saunders Co) Harcrt Hlth Sci Grp.

— MCQ's in Anatomy. 2nd ed. 272p. 1988. pap. 26.00 (*0-443-03574-1*) Church.

Lumley, Benjamin. Reminiscences of the Opera. LC 76-15185. (Music Reprint Ser.). 448p. 1976. reprint ed. 55.00 (*0-306-70842-6*) Da Capo.

Lumley, Brian. Blood Brothers. 576p. 1993. mass mkt. 5.99 (*0-8125-2061-0*, Pub. by Tor Bks) St Martin.

— Bloodwars. 576p. 1995. mass mkt. 5.99 (*0-8125-3628-2*, Pub. by Tor Bks) St Martin.

— Brian Lumley. 1990. 13.85 (*0-8125-2858-1*, Pub. by Tor Bks) St Martin.

— The Burrowers Beneath. limited ed. (Illus.). 192p. 1988. reprint ed. 22.50 (*0-932445-30-6*) Ganley Pub.

— The Clock of Dreams. deluxe limited ed. LC 91-75683. (Illus.). 1994. reprint ed. boxed set 42.50 (*0-932445-52-7*) Ganley Pub.

— The Clock of Dreams. LC 91-75683. (Illus.). 1994. reprint ed. 26.50 (*0-932445-51-9*) Ganley Pub.

— The Compleat Crow. LC 86-81094. (Illus.). 192p. 1987. 21.00 (*0-932445-22-5*) Ganley Pub.

— The Compleat Khash Vol. II: Sorcery in Shad. LC 90-81729. (Illus.). 192p. 1994. 26.50 (*0-932445-53-5*) Ganley Pub.

— The Compleat Khash Vol. II: Sorcery in Shad. deluxe ed. LC 90-81729. (Illus.). 192p. 1994. 42.50 (*0-932445-54-3*) Ganley Pub.

— The Compleat Khash, Vol. I: Never a Backward Glance. LC 90-81729. (Illus.). 1991. 25.00 (*0-932445-43-8*); 40.00 (*0-932445-44-6*) Ganley Pub.

— A Coven of Vampires. 261p. 1998. 27.00 (*1-878252-37-2*) Fedogan & Bremer.

— Deadspawn. (Necroscope Ser.: No. V). (Orig.). 1991. mass mkt. 5.99 (*0-8125-0835-1*, Pub. by Tor Bks) St Martin.

— Deadspeak. (Necroscope Ser.: No. 4). 1992. mass mkt. 5.99 (*0-8125-3032-2*, Pub. by Tor Bks) St Martin.

— Demogorgon. 1992. mass mkt. 4.99 (*0-8125-1199-9*, Pub. by Tor Bks) St Martin.

— Elysia: The Coming of Cthulhu. LC 88-81853. (Illus.). 192p. 1989. 25.00 (*0-932445-33-0*); pap. 8.50 (*0-932445-32-2*) Ganley Pub.

— Fruiting Bodies & Other Fungi. 288p. 1996. pap. 12.95 (*0-312-86200-8*) St Martin.

— Fruiting Bodies & Other Fungi. 288p. 1993. 18.95 (*0-312-85458-7*, Pub. by Tor Bks) St Martin.

— Hero of Dreams. LC 85-80774. (Illus.). 192p. 1986. 21.00 (*0-932445-18-7*); pap. 7.50 (*0-932445-17-9*) Ganley Pub.

— Hero of Dreams. 256p. 1993. mass mkt. 4.99 (*0-8125-2419-5*, Pub. by Tor Bks) St Martin.

— House of Doors. 480p. 1990. mass mkt. 4.99 (*0-8125-0832-7*, Pub. by Tor Bks) St Martin.

— Iced on Aran. 256p. (Orig.). 1994. mass mkt. 4.99 (*0-8125-2422-5*, Pub. by Tor Bks) St Martin.

— Iced on Aran: And Other Dream Quests. limited ed. LC 91-75679. (Dream Quest Ser.: 4). (Illus.). 184p. 1992. reprint ed. boxed set 40.00 (*0-932445-48-9*) Ganley Pub.

— Iced on Aran: And Other Dream Quests. LC 91-75679. (Illus.). 184p. 1992. reprint ed. 25.00 (*0-932445-47-0*) Ganley Pub.

— In the Moons of Borea. LC 95-78451. (Illus.). 192p. 1995. 27.50 (*0-932445-61-6*) Ganley Pub.

— In the Moons of Borea. deluxe limited ed. LC 95-78451. (Illus.). 192p. 1995. reprint ed. boxed set 45.00 (*0-932445-62-4*) Ganley Pub.

***Lumley, Brian.** Invaders. (Necroscope Ser.). 608p. 2000. mass mkt. 6.99 (*0-8125-7552-0*) Tor Bks.

Lumley, Brian. The Last Aerie. 832p. 1994. mass mkt. 5.99 (*0-8125-2062-9*, Pub. by Tor Bks) St Martin.

— Mad Moon of Dreams. LC 87-82043. (Illus.). 192p. 1987. 21.00 (*0-932445-28-4*); pap. 7.50 (*0-932445-27-6*) Ganley Pub.

— Mad Moon of Dreams. 256p. 1994. mass mkt. 4.99 (*0-8125-2421-7*, Pub. by Tor Bks) St Martin.

— Maze of Worlds. LC 98-11451. 384p. 1998. 25.95 (*0-312-86604-6*, Pub. by Tor Bks) St Martin.

— Maze of Worlds. 512p. 1999. mass mkt. 6.99 (*0-8125-7780-9*, Pub. by Tor Bks) St Martin.

Lumley, Brian. Necroscope: Deadspawn, Vol. 5. 1991. mass mkt. 9.71 (*0-586-20905-0*) HAR3.

Lumley, Brian. Necroscope: Deadspeak, Vol. 4. 1990. mass mkt. 8.32 (*0-586-20904-2*) HAR3.

***Lumley, Brian.** Necroscope: Defilers. LC 00-23325. 448p. 2000. 25.95 (*0-312-87261-5*, Pub. by Tor Bks) St Martin.

Lumley, Brian. Necroscope: Invaders. 2nd ed. LC 99-24562. (Necroscope Ser.: 10). 384p. 1999. 25.95 (*0-312-86814-6*, Pub. by Tor Bks) St Martin.

— Necroscope: Resurgence. 1997. mass mkt. 6.99 (*0-8125-5364-0*, Pub. by Tor Bks) St Martin.

— Necroscope: The Lost Years. 1992. mass mkt. 5.99 (*0-8125-2137-4*, Pub. by Tor Bks) St Martin.

— Necroscope: The Lost Years. 384p. 1994. 23.95 (*0-312-85787-X*, Pub. by Tor Bks) St Martin.

— Necroscope: The Lost Years. 1996. mass mkt. 6.99 (*0-8125-5363-2*, Pub. by Tor Bks) St Martin.

— Psychamok. 512p. (Orig.). 1993. mass mkt. 5.99 (*0-8125-2032-7*, Pub. by Tor Bks) St Martin.

— Psychomech. 448p. (Orig.). 1992. mass mkt. 5.99 (*0-8125-2023-8*, Pub. by Tor Bks) St Martin.

— Psychosphere. 448p. (Orig.). 1992. mass mkt. 5.99 (*0-8125-2030-0*, Pub. by Tor Bks) St Martin.

— Ship of Dreams. LC 86-81017. (Illus.). 192p. 1986. 21.00 (*0-932445-25-X*); pap. 7.50 (*0-932445-24-1*) Ganley Pub.

— Ship of Dreams. 256p. 1994. mass mkt. 4.99 (*0-8125-2420-9*, Pub. by Tor Bks) St Martin.

Lumley, Brian. Short Story Collection 2. text. write for info. (*0-312-87694-7*) St Martin.

Lumley, Brian. Source. LC 98-42576. 1998. 26.95 (*0-312-86764-6*, Pub. by Tor Bks) St Martin.

— The Source: Necroscope III. 1989. mass mkt. 4.95 (*0-8125-2127-7*, Pub. by Tor Bks) St Martin.

— Spawn of the Winds. deluxe ed. LC 95-77334. (Illus.). 1995. boxed set 42.50 (*0-932445-60-8*) Ganley Pub.

— Spawn of the Winds. LC 95-77334. (Illus.). 1995. reprint ed. 26.50 (*0-932445-59-4*) Ganley Pub.

Lumley, Brian. Third Book in Invaders Trilogy. text. write for info. (*0-312-87716-1*) St Martin.

Lumley, Brian. Titus Crow. LC 96-33984. 1996. text 24.95 (*0-312-86299-7*) St Martin.

— Titus Crow, Vol. 2. 384p. 1997. text 24.95 (*0-312-86347-0*) St Martin.

— Titus Crow, Vol. 3. LC 96-33984. 384p. 1997. text 24.95 (*0-312-86365-9*) St Martin.

***Lumley, Brian.** Titus Crow, Vol. 3. 384p. 2000. pap. 15.95 (*0-312-86866-9*) St Martin.

Lumley, Brian. Titus Crow Vol. 2: The Clock of Dreams & Spawn of the Winds. (Necroscope Ser.). 318p. 1999. pap. 14.95 (*0-312-86868-5*, Pub. by Tor Bks) St Martin.

— Titus Crow Omnibus, Vol. 1. 2nd ed. LC 98-54972. 352p. 1999. pap. 14.95 (*0-312-86867-7*, Pub. by Tor Bks) St Martin.

— The Transition of Titus Crow. rev. ed. LC 88-81855. (Illus.). 192p. 1992. reprint ed. 25.00 (*0-932445-45-4*); reprint ed. 40.00 (*0-932445-46-2*) Ganley Pub.

— Vamphyri. LC 96-23842. 384p. 1996. text 24.95 (*0-312-86212-1*) St Martin.

— Vamphyri. 1989. mass mkt. 5.99 (*0-8125-2126-9*, Pub. by Tor Bks) St Martin.

***Lumley, Brian.** The Whisperer & Other Voices. 2001. text. write for info. (*0-312-87695-5*) St Martin.

Lumley, Brian, et al. Disciples of Cthulhu. Berglund, Edward P., ed. (Call of Cthulhu Fiction Ser.). (Illus.). 260p. 1996. pap. 10.95 (*1-56882-054-2*, 6011) Chaosium.

Lumley, Cyndy E., jt. ed. see Griffiths, Susan A.

Lumley, Dan & Bailey, Gerald. Planning for Technology: A Guidebook for Teachers, Technology Leaders & School Administrators. LC 98-160762. 171p. 1997. ring bd. 69.00 (*1-879639-54-8*) Natl Educ Serv.

Lumley, Dan, jt. auth. see Bailey, Gerald.

Lumley, Dan, jt. auth. see Bailey, Gerald D.

Lumley, Dan, jt. auth. see Fagan, Carol.

Lumley, Dan, jt. auth. see Fagen, Carol.

Lumley, Elizabeth. Canadian Who's Who 1998, Vol. XXXIII. 1350p. 1998. text 170.00 (*0-8020-4913-3*); 275.00 (*0-8020-4921-4*) U of Toronto Pr.

— Ontario Legal Directory 1998. 950p. 1998. pap. text 48.00 (*0-8020-4911-7*) U of Toronto Pr.

Lumley, Elizabeth, ed. Canadian Who's Who, 1999, 34 vols. annuals 1350p. 1999. 195.00 (*0-8020-4933-8*); 275.00 (*0-8020-4934-6*) U of Toronto Pr.

— Canadian Who's Who 1996, Vol. 31. rev. ed. 1300p. 1996. text 165.00 (*0-8020-4687-8*) U of Toronto Pr.

— Toronto Legal Directory. 71st rev. ed. 890p. 1997. text 48.00 (*0-8020-4985-0*) U of Toronto Pr.

Lumley, Frederick H. Measurement in Radio. LC 71-161164. (History of Broadcasting: Radio to Television Ser.). 1977. reprint ed. 28.95 (*0-405-03576-4*) Ayer.

Lumley, J. L., ed. Annual Review of Fluid Mechanics, Vol. 19. LC 74-80866. (Illus.). 1987. text 40.00 (*0-8243-0719-4*) Annual Reviews.

— Annual Review of Fluid Mechanics, Vol. 21. LC 74-80866. (Illus.). 1989. text 40.00 (*0-8243-0721-6*) Annual Reviews.

— Annual Review of Fluid Mechanics, Vol. 22. LC 74-80866. 1990. text 40.00 (*0-8243-0722-4*) Annual Reviews.

— Annual Review of Fluid Mechanics, Vol. 23. LC 74-80866. 1991. text 40.00 (*0-8243-0723-2*) Annual Reviews.

— Annual Review of Fluid Mechanics, Vol. 24. LC 74-80866. 1992. text 44.00 (*0-8243-0724-0*) Annual Reviews.

Lumley, J. S. & Benjimen, W. Research: Some Ground Rules. (Illus.). 260p. 1995. text 70.00 (*0-19-854823-0*); pap. text 35.00 (*0-19-854822-2*) OUP.

Lumley, J. S. & Bouloux, P. M. Clinical Examination of the Patient: A Pocket Atlas. LC 95-102576. (Illus.). 320p. 1994. pap. text 32.00 (*0-7506-1671-7*) Buttrwrth-Heinemann.

Lumley, J. S. & Clain, Allan. Hamilton Bailey's Demonstration of Physical Signs in Clinical Surgery 18th ed. (Illus.). 512p. 1997. pap. text 67.50 (*0-7506-1621-0*) Buttrwrth-Heinemann.

Lumley, J. S. & Craven, J. L. MCQ's in Anatomy: A Self-Testing Supplement to Essential Anatomy. 3rd ed. LC 95-40796. 1996. pap. text 17.95 (*0-443-04977-7*) Church.

Lumley, J. S., et al. Essential Anatomy & Some Clinical Applications. 5th ed. LC 94-18967. 1995. text 39.00 (*0-443-04808-8*) Church.

Lumley, J. S. P. Essentials of Experimental Surgery. 262p. 1997. text 199.00 (*0-407-01395-4*) Buttrwrth-Heinemann.

***Lumley, J. S. P.** Hamilton Bailey's Physical Signs Picture Tests. LC RD35.H334 1999. (Illus.). 208p. 2000. pap. 30.00 (*0-7506-4339-0*) Buttrwrth-Heinemann.

Lumley, J. S. P., jt. auth. see Visvanathan, R.

***Lumley, James.** Five Magic Paths to Making a Fortune in Real Estate. LC 99-15468. 294p. 1999. pap. 14.95 (*0-471-29786-0*) Wiley.

Lumley, James E. How to Get a Mortgage in Twenty-Four Hours. 3rd ed. 263p. 1994. pap. 16.95 (*0-471-59938-7*) Wiley.

— Real Estate Psychology: The Dynamics of Successful Selling. LC 81-10473. (Real Estate For Professional Practitioners Ser.). 248p. reprint ed. pap. 76.90 (*0-7837-3454-9*, 205778000008) Bks Demand.

Lumley, Jim. Challenge Your Taxes: Homeowner's Guide to Reducing Property Taxes. LC 98-141283. 257p. 1998. pap. 16.95 (*0-471-19065-9*) Wiley.

Lumley, Joanna. Girl Friday: The Co-Star of "Absolutely Fabulous" Spends 9 Days on a Desert. large type ed. 23.95 (*1-85695-206-1*, Pub. by ISIS Lrg Prnt) Transaction Pubs.

Lumley, John L. Annual Review of Fluid Mechanics, Vol. 26. LC 74-80866. (Illus.). 1994. text 47.00 (*0-8243-0726-7*) Annual Reviews.

— Engines: An Introduction. LC 99-11974. (Illus.). 272p. (C). 1999. 80.00 (*0-521-64277-9*); pap. 34.95 (*0-521-64489-5*) Cambridge U Pr.

— Research Trends in Fluid Dynamics: Report from the United States National Committee on Theoretical & Applied Mechanics. LC 95-25488. (Illus.). 328p. 1995. text 50.00 (*1-56396-459-7*) Spr-Verlag.

Lumley, John L., ed. Annual Review of Fluid Mechanics, Vol. 20. LC 74-80866. (Illus.). 1988. text 40.00 (*0-8243-0720-8*) Annual Reviews.

— Annual Review of Fluid Mechanics, Vol. 25. LC 74-80866. (Illus.). 1993. text 44.00 (*0-8243-0725-9*) Annual Reviews.

— Annual Review of Fluid Mechanics, Vol. 27. LC 74-80866. (Illus.). 550p. 1995. text 47.00 (*0-8243-0727-5*) Annual Reviews.

— Annual Review of Fluid Mechanics, Vol. 29. LC 74-80866. 1997. text 60.00 (*0-8243-0729-1*) Annual Reviews.

Lumley, John L., et al, eds. Annual Review of Fluid Mechanics, Vol. 28. 1996. text 52.00 (*0-8243-0728-3*) Annual Reviews.

— Annual Review of Fluid Mechanics 1999, Vol. 31. LC 74-80866. 646p. 1999. 120.00 (*0-8243-0731-3*) Annual Reviews.

— Wither Turbulence? Turbulence at the Crossroads: Proceedings of a Workshop Held at Cornell University, Ithaca, New York, March 22-24, 1989. (Lecture Notes in Physics Ser.: Vol. 357). iv, 525p. 1990. 82.95 (*0-387-52535-1*) Spr-Verlag.

Lumley, John L. & Van Dyke, Milton, eds. Annual Review of Fluid Mechanics, Vol. 30. LC 74-80866. 1998. text 60.00 (*0-8243-0730-5*) Annual Reviews.

Lumley, John L., jt. auth. see Tennekes, Hendrik.

Lumley, John S. Surface Anatomy: The Anatomical Basis of Clinical Examination. 2nd ed. LC 96-10352. (Illus.). 1996. pap. text 25.99 (*0-443-05302-2*) Church.

Lumley, Judith, jt. ed. see Chamberlain, Geoffrey V.P.

Lumley, K. W. Monkeys & Apes. LC 82-12779. (New True Books Ser.). (Illus.). 48p. (J). (gr. k-4). 1982. pap. 5.50 (*0-516-41633-2*) Childrens.

Lumley, Robert. Italian Journalism: A Critical Anthology. LC 95-25045. 224p. 1996. text 27.95 (*0-7190-3889-8*) Manchester Univ Pr.

Lumley, Robert & Morris, Jonathan, eds. The New History of the Italian South: The Mezzogiorno Revisited. (Illus.). 160p. 1998. pap. text 22.50 (*0-85989-506-8*, Pub. by Univ Exeter Pr) Northwestern U Pr.

Lumley, Robert, jt. ed. see Forgacs, David.

***Lumm, Thomas.** Problems of Democratization in China. LC 00-42692. (East Asia Ser.). 2000. write for info. (*0-8153-3871-6*) Garland.

***Lumma, Eike & Romano, Frank J.** QuarkXPress 4 Only. LC 98-37889. 1999. pap. 34.99 (*0-13-099770-6*) P-H.

Lumme, Annareetta, et al. Informal Venture Capital: Investors, Investments & Policy Issues in Finland. LC 97-50259. 1998. text 89.95 (*0-7923-8111-4*) Kluwer Academic.

Lumme, Helena & Manninen, Mika. Screenwriters: America's Storytellers in Portrait. LC 98-40163. (Illus.). 128p. 1999. 30.00 (*1-883318-18-1*) Angel City Pr.

Lummer, Scott L. & Riepe, Mark W. Pension Investment Handbook. 700p. boxed set 165.00 (*1-56706-432-9*, 64329) Panel Pubs.

— Pension Investment Handbook. annuals 614p. 1996. 165.00 (*1-56706-145-1*) Panel Pubs.

Lummis, Adair T., jt. auth. see Haddad, Yvonne Y.

Lummis, Adair T., jt. auth. see Walmsley, Roberta C.

Lummis, C. Douglas. Radical Democracy. 224p. 1996. text 29.95 (*0-8014-3169-7*) Cornell U Pr.

— Radical Democracy. 200p. 1997. pap. 13.95 (*0-8014-8451-0*) Cornell U Pr.

Lummis, Charles. Letters from the Southwest. Byrkit, James W., ed. LC 88 27793. 309p. 1989. 39.00 (*0-8165-1039-3*) U of Ariz Pr.

Lummis, Charles F. The Enchanted Burro: Stories of New Mexico & South America. (Illus.). 277p. 1977. 24.95 (*0-8369-4154-3*) Ayer.

— King of the Broncos, & Other Stories of New Mexico. LC 73-125231. (Short Story Index Reprint Ser.). 1977. 19.95 (*0-8369-3598-5*) Ayer.

— The Man Who Married the Moon & Other Pueblo Indian Folk Stories. LC 74-7989. (Illus.). reprint ed. 37.50 (*0-404-11877-1*) AMS Pr.

— My Friend Will. 1972. pap. 5.00 (*0-87516-161-8*) DeVorss.

— New Mexico David, & Other Stories, & Sketches of the South-West. LC 76-90586. (Short Story Index Reprint Ser.). 1977. 19.95 (*0-8369-3069-X*) Ayer.

— Pueblo Indian Folk-Stories. LC 91-40614. (Illus.). xxx, 257p. 1992. reprint ed. pap. 15.00 (*0-8032-7938-8*, Bison Books) U of Nebr Pr.

— Some Strange Corners of Our Country. LC 88-26703. 270p. 1989. reprint ed. pap. 16.95 (*0-8165-0852-6*) U of Ariz Pr.

— A Tramp Across the Continent. LC 81-16194. xxvi, 270p. 1982. reprint ed. pap. 8.95 (*0-8032-7908-6*, Bison Books) U of Nebr Pr.

Lummis, Dayton. Hawks Belong with Hawks: Journeys in the Changing American West. 340p. 1997. pap. 14.95 (*1-880047-54-3*) Creative Des.

— High Lonesome: The Vanishing American West. 1993. pap. 9.95 (*1-879395-24-X*) CA Classics Bks.

Lummis, Suzanne. Falling Short of Heaven. (Red Ser.). (Illus.). 32p. (Orig.). 1990. pap. 5.00 (*0-938631-12-8*) Pennywhistle Pr.

— In Danger. LC 99-25604. (California Poetry Ser.: Vol. 2). 72p. 1999. pap. 12.50 (*0-9666691-1-8*, Pub. by Heyday Bks) SPD-Small Pr Dist.

***Lummis, Suzanne, ed.** Matchbook: A Little Collection of Flammable Poems. 33p. 1999. pap. 12.00 (*1-889504-01-7*) Red Wind Bks.

Lummis, Suzanne, ed. Spreading the Word. 1993. 7.00 (*0-9622847-7-7*) Red Wind Bks.

Lummis, Trevor. The Labour Aristocracy, 1851-1914. LC 94-6771. 1994. 78.95 (*1-85928-049-8*, Pub. by Scolar Pr) Ashgate Pub Co.

— Listening to History: The Authenticity of Oral Evidence. 175p. 1988. 48.50 (*0-389-20779-9*, N8338) B&N Imports.

— Pitcairn Island: Life & Death in Eden. LC 97-18806. (Illus.). 184p. 1997. text 61.95 (*1-85928-431-0*, Pub. by Scolar Pr) Ashgate Pub Co.

Lummus, James L. & Azar, J. J. Drilling Fluids Optimization: A Practical Field Approach. 294p. (C). 1986. 25.00 (*0-87814-306-8*) PennWell Bks.

Lumpe, Lora. Running Guns: The Black Market in Small Arms. pap. 27.50 (*1-85649-873-5*, Pub. by Zed Books); text 69.95 (*1-85649-872-7*, Pub. by Zed Books) St Martin.

Lumpkin. Physical Education. 5th ed. 2001. pap. text 37.60 (*0-07-232901-7*) McGraw.

— Sport Ethics. 2nd ed. LC 98-38662. 240p. 1998. pap. 48.13 (*0-07-092117-2*) McGraw.

Lumpkin, Alex H. & Eyberger, Catherine, eds. Beam Instrumentation Workshop. (AIP Conference Proceedings Ser.: No. 390). (Illus.). 619p. 1997. 150.00 (*1-56396-612-3*, AIP Pr) Spr-Verlag.

Lumpkin, Alva M. The Life & Times of Thomas Waties, Patriot, Jurist, & Churchman (1760-1828) 128p. 1995. 24.50 (*0-9644928-0-6*) A M Lumpkin.

Lumpkin, Angela. A Guide to the Literature of Tennis. LC 85-9941. 235p. 1985. lib. bdg. 42.95 (*0-313-24492-8*, LUT/, Greenwood Pr) Greenwood.

— Physical Education: A Contemporary Introduction. 1993. write for info. (*0-8016-7821-8*) Mosby Inc.

Lumpkin, Angela. Women's Tennis: A Historical Documentary of the Players & Their Game. LC 79-57328. xiv, 193p. 1981. 45.00 (*0-87875-189-0*) Whitston Pub.

Lumpkin, Angela, ed. see Stoll, Sharon K. & Beller, Jennifer M.

***Lumpkin, Beatrice.** Always Bring a Crowd: The Story of Frank Lumpkin. LC 99-35042. 254p. 1999. pap. 12.95 (*0-7178-0725-8*) Intl Pubs Co.

Lumpkin, Beatrice. Senefer: A Young Genius in Old Egypt. LC 92-71026. (Young Reader's Ser.). (Illus.). 32p. (J). (gr. 2-5). 1992. 16.95 (*0-86543-244-9*); pap. 8.95 (*0-86543-245-7*) Africa World.

— Senefer & Hatshepsut. LC 91-75349. (Young Reader's Ser.). (Illus.). 64p. 1995. reprint ed. 24.95 (*0-86543-272-4*); reprint ed. pap. 9.95 (*0-86543-273-2*) Africa World.

Lumpkin, Beatrice, tr. see Gerdes, Paulus.

Lumpkin, Beryl, ed. The Kudzu Crypt, Dark Visions to Haunt & Entwine You. (Illus.). 1989. pap. 7.95 (*0-9622568-3-8*) Earthtide Pubns.

Lumpkin, Beryl, ed. see Thompson, Naomi J.

Lumpkin, Beryl O. From Vines to Vessels. 2nd ed. (Illus.). 124p. 1987. reprint ed. pap. 9.95 (*0-932807-25-9*) Overmountain Pr.

— Something Gentle: Quiet Words for Hurried Times. (Illus.). 60p. (Orig.). 1988. pap. text 3.95 (*0-9622568-0-3*) Earthtide Pubns.

Lumpkin, Beryl O., ed. see Sisson, Patricia H.

Lumpkin, Betty S., jt. auth. see Sorrow, Barbara H.

Lumpkin, Emily S. Get Paid to Shop: Be a Personal Shopper for Corporate America. LC 98-93443. (Illus.). 315p. 1999. pap. 29.95 (*0-9666351-0-8*) Forte Pubg.

Lumpkin, Grace. To Make My Bread. LC 95-3561. (Radical Novel Reconsidered Ser.). 424p. 1995. 15.95 (*0-252-06501-8*) U of Ill Pr.

Lumpkin, James R., et al. Direct Marketing, Direct Selling, & the Mature Consumer: A Research Study. LC 88-18519. 240p. 1989. 62.95 (*0-89930-298-X*, LDI/, Quorum Bks) Greenwood.

Lumpkin, Joan B., et al. Getting Started with the Internet. 104p. 1995. pap. 21.95 (*0-471-12418-4*) Wiley.

Lumpkin, Katharine D. The Making of a Southerner. LC 91-26583. (Brown Thrasher Bks.). 280p. 1991. reprint ed. pap. 15.95 (*0-8203-1385-8*) U of Ga Pr.

Lumpkin, Katharine D. Child Workers in America. xiv, 321 p. 1977. 21.95 (*0-8369-6860-3*) Ayer.

***Lumpkin, Libby.** Deep Design: Nine Little Art Histories. LC 99-71243. (Illus.). 126p. 1999. pap. 17.95 (*0-9637264-6-3*, Pub. by Fnd Adv Crit) Dist Art Pubs.

Lumpkin, Libby, ed. see Wynn, Stephen A.

An Asterisk (*) at the beginning of an entry indicates that the title is appearing for the first time.

Lumpkin, Libby O. & Wynn, Stephen A. Picasso at the Bellagio. Clewell, Kathleen M., ed. (Illus.). 42p. 1999. pap. 16.95 (*0-9666625-1-2*) Mirage Resorts.

Lumpkin, Libby O., ed. see Wynn, Stephen A.

Lumpkin, Linda L. Lilly's Pond: The Adventure of Silly Willy Caterpillie. (Illus.). 48p. (J). (ps-6). 1997. 17.95 (*1-891543-00-8*, Wide-Eyed Pub) MicroNova.

Lumpkin, Peggy. Remember When God Was a Woman: Feminine Secrets Unveiled. LC 99-42374. (Illus.). 224p. 2000. 19.95 (*1-58151-024-1*, Pub. by BookPartners) Midpt Trade.

— The Stepkin Stories: Helping Children Cope with Divorce & Adjust to Stepfamilies. LC 98-73478. (Illus.). 142p. 1999. pap. 16.95 (*1-58151-015-2*) BookPartners.

Lumpkin, Susan. Big Cats. LC 92-26838. (Great Creatures of the World Ser.). (Illus.). 72p. (YA). (gr. 6-9). 1993. 17.95 (*0-8160-2847-8*) Facts on File.

— Look at Me! large type ed. (HRL Cuddle Bks.). (Illus.). 7p. (J). (ps-k). 1999. pap. text 10.95 (*1-57332-145-1*) HighReach Lrning.

— Small Cats. LC 92-26837. (Great Creatures of the World Ser.). (Illus.). 72p. (J). (gr. 4-9). 1993. 17.95 (*0-8160-2848-6*) Facts on File.

Lumpkin, Susan & Weinberg, Susan. Animals of the National Zoological Park Coloring Book. (Illus.). 24p. (Orig.). (J). (ps-4). 1989. pap. 3.95 (*0-9622062-1-0*) Friends Natl Zoo.

Lumpkin, Susan, jt. auth. see Greenberg, Russell.

Lumpkin, Susan, ed. see Roberson, Mary-Russell.

Lumpkin, Susan, jt. ed. see Seidensticker, John.

Lumpkin, Susan, ed. see Time-Life Books Editors.

Lumpkin, T. A. & McClary, D. C. Azuki Bean: Botany, Production & Uses. LC 97-179021. (Illus.). 256p. 1994. text 80.00 (*0-85198-765-6*) OUP.

Lumpkin, William L. Baptist Confessions of Faith. (Illus.). 1959. 23.00 (*0-8170-0016-X*) Judson.

Lumpkin, William L. & Butterfield, Lyman. Colonial Baptists & Southern Revivals: An Original Anthology. Gaustad, Edwin S., ed. LC 79-52585. (Baptist Tradition Ser.). 1980. lib. bdg. 28.95 (*0-405-12452-X*) Ayer.

Lumpkin, Wilson. Removal of the Cherokee Indians from Georgia. LC 79-90182. (Mass Violence in America Ser.). 1977. reprint ed. 50.95 (*0-405-01325-6*) Ayer.

Lumpkins, William. La Casa Adobe. 2nd rev. ed. LC 86-71415. (SPA., Illus.). 64p. 1987. reprint ed. pap. 12.95 (*0-941270-34-3*) Ancient City Pr.

Lumpkins, William T., jt. auth. see Traugott, Joseph.

Lumpuy, Luis Bernal, tr. see Averill, Diane & Bajema, Edith.

Lumpuy, Luis Bernal, tr. see Rudie, Carol Veldman.

Lumpuy, Luis Bernal, tr. see Vander Griend, Donna.

Lumsdaine, David H. Moral Vision in International Politics: The Foreign Aid Regime, 1949-1989. LC 92-18508. (Illus.). 416p. (C). 1993. text 60.00 (*0-691-07887-4*, Pub. by Princeton U Pr); pap. text 19.95 (*0-691-02767-6*, Pub. by Princeton U Pr) Cal Prin Full Svc.

Lumsdaine, Edward & Lumsdaine, Monika. Creative Problem Solving: Thinking Skills for a Changing World. 472p. (C). 1994. pap. 48.75 (*0-07-039091-6*) McGraw.

Lumsdaine, Edward, ed. see Thomas, Lindon C.

Lumsdaine, Monika, jt. auth. see Lumsdaine, Edward.

***Lumsden.** Communicating in Groups & Teams: Sharing Leadership. 3rd ed. LC 99-19732. (Speech & Theater). 1999. pap. 50.95 (*0-534-56232-9*) Wadsworth Pub.

Lumsden, jt. auth. see Baker.

Lumsden, Alec, jt. auth. see Thetford, Owen.

Lumsden, Barry D., jt. auth. see Alexander-Mott, LeeAnn.

Lumsden, Charles J. & Wilson, Edward O. Genes, Mind, Culture: The Coevolutionary Process. LC 80-26543. (Illus.). 442p. 1981. 37.50 (*0-674-34475-8*) HUP.

— Promethean Fire: Reflections on the Origin of Mind. (Illus.). 224p. 1983. 30.00 (*0-674-71445-8*) HUP.

— Promethean Fire: Reflections on the Origin of Mind. (Illus.). 224p. 1983. pap. text 11.50 (*0-674-71446-6*) HUP.

Lumsden, Charles J., et al. Physical Theory in Biology: Foundations & Explorations. LC 97-7676. (Studies of Nonlinear Phenomena in Life Sciences). 1997. write for info. (*981-02-3082-6*); pap. write for info. (*981-02-3121-0*) World Scientific Pub.

Lumsden, D. Barry. Ph.D. Experience: Multidisciplinary Perspectives. 1997. pap. text 24.95 (*1-56032-538-0*) Hemisp Pub.

Lumsden, D. Barry, jt. auth. see Sherron, Ronald H.

Lumsden, Donald, jt. auth. see Lumsden, Gay.

Lumsden, Douglas W., jt. auth. see Russell, Jeffrey Burton.

Lumsden, E. S. Art of Etching. (Illus.). 376p. 1962. pap. 9.95 (*0-486-20049-3*) Dover.

— Art of Etching. (Illus.). 1990. 23.50 (*0-8446-2497-7*) Peter Smith.

Lumsden, Ennis, jt. auth. see Boylston & Associates Staff.

Lumsden, Gay & Lumsden, Donald. Communicating in Groups & Teams: Sharing Leadership. 410p. (C). 1992. mass mkt. 27.25 (*0-534-19068-5*) Wadsworth Pub.

— Communicating in Groups & Teams: Sharing Leadership. 2nd ed. LC 96-5076. (C). 1996. pap. 32.50 (*0-534-51258-5*) Wadsworth Pub.

— Communicating with Credibility & Confidence. LC 95-4931. (C). 1995. pap. 52.95 (*0-534-20736-7*) Wadsworth Pub.

Lumsden, George I., ed. Geology & the Environment in Western Europe: A Coordinated Statement by the Western European Geological Survey. (Illus.). 338p. 1994. reprint ed. pap. text 49.95 (*0-19-854870-2*) OUP.

Lumsden, George J. Getting up to Speed: 115 Quick Tips for the New or Future Manager. LC 92-23822. 192p. 1992. pap. 17.95 (*0-8144-7789-5*) AMACOM.

— How to Succeed in Middle Management. LC 82-71323. 256p. reprint ed. pap. 79.40 (*0-608-11913-X*, 202356500033) Bks Demand.

— Impact Management: Personal Power Strategies for Success. LC 79-11632. 158p. reprint ed. pap. 49.00 (*0-608-12856-2*, 202358600033) Bks Demand.

Lumsden, Ian. Machos, Maricones, & Gays: Cuba & Homosexuality. 288p. (Orig.). (C). 1996. pap. text 22.95 (*1-56639-371-X*); lib. bdg. 69.95 (*1-56639-370-1*) Temple U Pr.

Lumsden, Ian, ed. Close the Forty-Ninth Parallel Etc. The Americanization of Canada. LC 79-477171. 343p. reprint ed. pap. 106.40 (*0-8357-6385-4*, 202364500033) Bks Demand.

Lumsden, Ian G., jt. auth. see Shone, Richard.

Lumsden, Ken. Complete Book of Drills for Winning Basketball. LC 98-28756. (C). 1998. spiral bd. 29.95 (*0-13-082979-X*) P-H.

Lumsden, Ken & Jones, Sally. Ready-to-Use Secondary Physical Education Activities Program: Lessons, Tournaments & Assessments. 288p. (C). 1996. pap. text 29.95 (*0-13-470007-4*) P-H.

Lumsden, Linda J. Rampant Women: Suffragists & the Right of Assembly. LC 97-4627. (Illus.). 312p. (C). 1997. text 42.00 (*0-87049-986-6*) U of Tenn Pr.

Lumsden, Linda S. Student Motivation: Cultivating a Love of Learning. LC 99-20577. 1999. 9.50 (*0-86552-141-7*) U of Oreg ERIC.

Lumsden, M. S. Affirmations: Poems in Scots & English. (Illus.). 76p. 1990. text 19.00 (*0-08-040929-6*, Pub. by Aberdeen U Pr) Macmillan.

Lumsden, Marshall, ed. Beyond the Killing Fields. LC DS554.8H35 1992. (Illus.). 216p. 1992. pap. 44.95 (*0-89381-505-5*) Aperture.

Lumsden, Michael. Existential Sentences: Their Structure & Meaning. 208p. 1988. lib. bdg. 59.95 (*0-7099-4114-5*) Routledge.

Lumsden, P. & Thomas, B. Biological Rhythms & Photoperiodism in Plants. (Illus.). 300p. 1997. 157.50 (*1-85996-216-5*, Pub. by Bios Sci) Coronet Bks.

Lumsden, P. J., et al, eds. Physiology, Growth, & Development of Plants in Culture. LC 93-20900. 430p. (C). 1994. text 298.50 (*0-7923-2516-8*) Kluwer Academic.

Lumsden, Peter, ed. Plants & UV-B: Responses to Environmental Change. (Society for Experimental Biology Seminar Ser.: Vol. 64). (Illus.). 375p. (C). 1997. text 110.00 (*0-521-57222-3*) Cambridge U Pr.

Lumsden, R. D., jt. ed. see Whipps, J. M.

Lumsden, Robert D. & Vaughn, James L., eds. Pest Management: Biologically Based Technologies: Proceedings of the Beltsville Symposium XVIII, Agricultural Research Service, U. S. Department of Agriculture, Beltsville, Maryland, May 2-6, 1993. LC 93-26355. 436p. 1993. text 120.00 (*0-8412-2726-8*, Pub. by Am Chemical) OUP.

Lumsden, Robin. The Allegmeine SS. (Men-at-Arms Ser.). (Illus.). 48p. 1993. pap. 11.95 (*1-85532-358-3*, 9237, Pub. by Ospry) Stackpole.

— The Black Corps: A Collector's Guide to the History & Regalia of the SS. (Illus.). 160p. (Orig.). 1992. pap. 19.95 (*0-7818-0112-5*) Hippocrene Bks.

***Lumsden, Robin.** A Collector's Guide to Third Reich Militaria. (Illus.). 2000. pap. 22.95 (*0-7110-2669-6*, Pub. by Ian Allan) Combined Pub.

— Detecting the Fakes: A Collector's Guide to Third Reich Militaria. (Illus.). (Orig.). 2000. pap. 22.95 (*0-7110-2670-X*, Pub. by Ian Allan) Combined Pub.

Lumsden, Roddy. Yeah Yeah Yeah: Poems. LC 97-192002. 96p. 1997. pap. 17.95 (*1-85224-403-8*, Pub. by Bloodaxe Bks) Dufour.

Lumsden, Sharon L. Green Byways: Garden Discoveries In the Great Lakes States. LC 93-78515. (Illus.). 317p. 1993. pap. 19.95 (*0-9636467-0-2*) Lime Tree Pubns.

Lumsdon, Les. Tourism Marketing. 260p. 1997. pap. 22.99 (*1-86152-045-X*) Thomson Learn.

***Lumumba-Kasongo, Tukumbi.** Dynamics & Policy Implications of the Global Reforms at the End of the Second Millennium. LC 00-33682. (International Studies in Sociology & Social Anthropology). 2000. pap. write for info. (*90-04-11847-0*) Brill Academic Pubs.

Lumumba-Kasongo, Tukumbi. The Dynamics of Economic & Political Relations Between Africa & Foreign Powers: A Study in International Relations. LC 97-33708. 144p. 1999. 55.00 (*0-275-96086-2*, Praeger Pubs) Greenwood.

— Nationalistic Ideologies: Their Policy Implications & the Struggle for Democracy in African Politics. LC 91-27345. (African Studies: Vol. 23). 148p. 1991. lib. bdg. 69.95 (*0-7734-9696-3*) E Mellen.

— Political Re-Mapping of Africa: Transnational Ideology & the Redefinition of Africa in World Politics. LC 93-30867. 170p. (C). 1993. lib. bdg. 39.00 (*0-8191-9299-6*) U Pr of Amer.

— The Rise of Multipartyism & Democracy in the Context of Global Change: The Case of Africa. LC 97-34753. 168p. 1998. 55.00 (*0-275-96087-0*, Praeger Pubs) Greenwood.

Lumumba-Kasongo, Tukumbi, jt. ed. see Kennett, David.

Lun, Hrvoje. Revolucija I Sloboda. 1978. pap. 16.00 (*0-9602138-1-3*) Plamen Pub.

Lun, Joe. Memoirs of the Maelstrom: A Senegalese Oral History of the First World War. LC 99-29405. 280p. 1999. lib. bdg. 25.95 (*0-325-00138-3*); lib. bdg. 65.00 (*0-325-00139-1*) Greenwood.

Lun Xun. Causerie. (CHI.). pap. 12.95 (*7-5004-1699-7*, Pub. by China Intl Bk) Distribks Inc.

Luna, A. J. De, see De Luna, A. J., ed.

Luna, Antonio Baybes de, see Baybes de Luna, Antonio.

Luna, Antonio Bayes de, see Bayes de Luna, Antonio.

Luna, David. Ultimate Fitness. LC 88-61234. (Illus.). 152p. (Orig.). 1989. pap. 16.95 (*0-915677-38-5*) Roundtable Pub.

Luna, Elena, tr. see De La Pena, Jose E.

Luna, G. Cajetan. Youths Living with HIV: Self-Evident Truths. LC 96-51906. 206p. (C). 1997. pap. 14.95 (*1-56023-904-2*, Harrington Park) Haworth Pr.

Luna, G. Cajetan. Youths Living with HIV: Self-Evident Truths. LC 96-51906. 195p. (C). 1997. 39.95 (*0-7890-0176-4*, Harrington Park) Haworth Pr.

Luna, Gaye & Cullen, Deborah L. Empowering the Faculty: Mentoring Redirected & Renewed. Fife, Jonathan D., ed. LC 96-77447. (ASHE-ERIC Higher Education Reports: No. 95-3). (Illus.). 113p. (Orig.). 1996. pap. 24.00 (*1-878380-67-2*) GWU Grad Schl E&HD.

Luna, Guillermo A. Hacia una Administracion Eficaz.Tr. of Towards Effective Management. (SPA.). 144p. 1985. 7.99 (*0-88113-114-8*) Caribe Betania.

Luna Imaging Inc. Frank Lloyd Wright: Presentation & Conceptual Drawings. (Illus.). 1995. pap. 1500.00 incl. cd-rom, 3.5 ld (*0-19-509576-6*) OUP.

Luna, James G. Youth of the Eighties, Vol. 1. 152p. (Orig.). 1994. pap. text 10.95 (*0-9641606-0-9*) Easy Break.

Luna, Julie Y. Prose & Poetry of the Millennium. 1998. pap. 18.00 (*1-57553-934-9*) Watermrk Pr.

Luna, Lee G. Histopathologic Methods & Color Atlas of Special Stains & Tissue Artifacts. LC 92-70140. (Illus.). 767p. 1992. 80.00 (*0-9649737-0-7*) Am HistoLabs.

Luna, Luis E. & Amaringo, Pablo. Ayahuasca Visions: The Religious Iconography of a Peruvian Shaman. LC 91-53239. (Illus.). 180p. 1991. 120.00 (*1-55643-064-7*) North Atlantic.

***Luna, Luis Eduardo & White, Steven F., eds.** Ayahuasca Reader: Encounters with the Amazon's Sacred Vine. (Illus.). 288p. 2000. pap. 29.95 (*0-907791-32-8*, Pub. by Synergetic Press) Pubs Services.

Luna, Orpha. Personalidad Transformada. (Serie Actualidades - Actualities Ser.).Tr. of Transformed Personality. (SPA.). 65p. 1993. pap. 2.29 (*1-56063-454-5*, 498158) Editorial Unilit.

Luna, Phyllis K. De, see De Luna, Phyllis K.

Luna, R. K. Plantation Forestry in India. 509p. (C). 1989. 595.00 (*0-7855-6881-6*, Pub. by Intl Bk Distr); text 595.00 (*0-7855-6587-6*, Pub. by Intl Bk Distr) St Mut.

— Plantation Forestry in India. 519p. 1989. pap. 500.00 (*81-7089-141-8*, Pub. by Intl Bk Distr) St Mut.

— Plantation Trees. LC 96-900510. 974p. 1996. pap. 1250.00 (*81-7089-235-X*, Pub. by Intl Bk Distr) St Mut.

Luna, Rachel N. The Animals' Nutcracker Ballet. (Illus.). 28p. (J). (ps-3). pap. write for info. (*1-886551-03-0*) E Howard Bks.

— Central Park Activity & Coloring Book. (Illus.). 23p. (J). (ps-3). 1998. pap. 4.95 (*1-886551-02-2*) E Howard Bks.

— Darinka, the Little Artist Deer. LC 99-94093. (Illus.). 36p. (J). (gr. 3-4). 1999. 12.95 (*1-886551-06-5*, Pub. by E Howard Bks) North Country.

— Nutcracker Magic. (Illus.). 20p. (J). (ps-3). pap. write for info. (*1-886551-04-9*) E Howard Bks.

— The Thank You God Book. (Illus.). 10p. (J). (ps). 1994. pap. 7.95 (*1-886551-00-6*) E Howard Bks.

— Where Is Muffy Hiding? (Illus.). 10p. (J). (ps). 1994. pap. 7.95 (*1-886551-01-4*) E Howard Bks.

Luna, Rachel N., ed. Cape Cod Coloring Book. (Illus.). 16p. (J). (gr. k-3). 1998. pap. 4.95 (*1-886551-30-8*) E Howard Bks.

Luna, Roger M., tr. see Desramaut, Francis.

Luna, Rose Mary, tr. see Miller, Billie M.

***Lunan, Bert.** Legacy of Leadership. LC 99-47655. 1999. write for info. (*0-9675005-0-8*) S C Bus Hall of Fame.

Lunan-Ferguson, Ira. Don't Marry That Woman: Or, How to Get & Hold a Husband. LC 73-92689. 456p. 1973. 12.95 (*0-685-03126-8*) Lunan-Ferguson.

— G. Wash Carter, White. LC 74-81532. 1969. 7.95 (*0-685-03129-2*) Lunan-Ferguson.

— I Dug Graves at Night, to Attend College by Day, Vol. 1. LC 67-31239. (Illus.). 1968. 12.95 (*0-685-03130-6*) Lunan-Ferguson.

— I Dug Graves at Night, to Attend College by Day, Vol. 2. LC 67-31239. (Illus.). 1970. 12.95 (*0-911724-06-0*) Lunan-Ferguson.

— I Dug Graves at Night, to Attend College by Day, Vol. 3. LC 67-31239. 1970. 10.95 (*0-911724-07-9*) Lunan-Ferguson.

— Lectures in Black Studies. LC 72-83316. (C). 1972. text 10.95 (*0-911724-12-5*) Lunan-Ferguson.

— Our Two Ocean Voyages: The Orient & the Mediterranean. LC 68-31071. 319p. 1968. 9.95 (*0-685-03131-4*) Lunan-Ferguson.

— Twenty-Five Good Reasons Why Men Should Marry: With a Marriage Manual for Husbands on How to Treat a Wife. LC 76-2990. 1976. 9.95 (*0-685-03132-2*) Lunan-Ferguson.

— Which One of You Is Interracial? & Other Stories. LC 78-79431. 1969. 6.95 (*0-685-03133-0*) Lunan-Ferguson.

Lunar & Planetary Institute Staff. Proceedings of the Lunar & Planetary Science Conference, 10th, Houston, Texas, March 19-23, 1979, 3 vols. LC 79-22554. (Illus.). 3200p. 1980. 400.00 (*0-08-025128-5*, Pergamon Pr) Elsevier.

— Proceedings of the Lunar & Planetary Science Conference, 12th, Houston, Texas, March 16-20, 1981. (Geochimica & Cosmochimica Acta Ser.: No. 16). (Illus.). 2000p. 1982. 235.00 (*0-08-028074-9*, Pergamon Pr) Elsevier.

— Proceedings of the Lunar & Planetary Science Conference, 9th, Houston, Texas, 1978, 3 vols., Set. (Geochimica & Cosmochimica Acta Ser.: Suppl. 10). 1979. 450.00 (*0-08-022966-2*, Pergamon Pr) Elsevier.

Lunar & Planetary Institute Staff, compiled by. Proceedings: Eleventh Lunar & Planetary Science Conference, Houston, Texas, March 17-21, 1980, 3 vols. (Geochimica & Cosmochimica Acta Ser.: Suppl. 14). 3000p. 1981. 265.00 (*0-08-026314-3*, Pergamon Pr) Elsevier.

Lunar & Planetary Institute Staff, ed. Proceedings of the Conference on Multi-Ring Basins, Houston, Texas. 300p. 1981. 47.00 (*0-08-028045-5*, Pergamon Pr) Elsevier.

Lunar & Planetary Institute Staff & Criswell, D. Proceedings 3rd Lunar Science Conference, Houston 1-72: Physical Properties, Vol. 3. 1972. write for info. (*0-318-69664-9*, Pub. by Pergamon Repr) Franklin.

Lunar & Planetary Institute Staff & Levinson, A. A. Journal of Geochemical Society & Meteoritical Society, 3 vols., Suppl. 2. LC 78-165075. 1971. 1222.00 (*0-08-020602-6*, Pub. by Pergamon Repr) Franklin.

Lunar & Planetary Institute, 8th, Houston, 1977. Proceedings, 3 vols. (Lunar Science Ser.: No. 8). (Illus.). 1977. 1770.00 (*0-08-022052-5*, Pub. by Pergamon Repr) Franklin.

Lunardi, Alessandra. Analytic Semigroups & Optimal Regularity in Parabolic Problems. 424p. 1995. pap. text 98.00 (*3-7643-5172-1*, QA377) Birkhauser.

— Analytic Semigroups & Optimal Regularity in Parabolic Problems. LC 94-47600. (Progress in Nonlinear Differential Equations & Their Applications Ser.: Vol. 16). 1995. 98.00 (*0-8176-5172-1*) Birkhauser.

Lunardi, Egidio & Nugent, Robert, trs. from ITA. Giovanni Pascoli: Convivial Poems, Vol. VIII. (Lake Erie College Studies). 1979. pap. 12.50 (*0-935518-02-9*) Lake Erie Col Pr.

— Giovanni Pascoli Part II: Convivial Poems, Vol. IX. (Lake Erie College Studies). 1981. pap. 7.50 (*0-935518-03-7*) Lake Erie Col Pr.

Lunardi, Joe & Dortch, Chris, eds. Blue Ribbon College Basketball Yearbook, 97/98 Edition. 17th ed. (Illus.). 386p. 1997. pap. 19.95 (*0-9651550-1-3*) Blue Ribbon Bsktball.

Lunardi, Joe, jt. ed. see Dortch, Chris.

Lunardini, Christine. What Every American Should Know about Women's History: 200 Events That Shaped Our Destiny. LC 94-33212. 1994. 16.00 (*1-55850-417-6*) Adams Media.

— What Every American Should Know about Women's History: 200 Events That Shaped Our Destiny. LC 96-27818. 416p. (gr. 4-7). 1996. pap. text 11.95 (*1-55850-687-X*) Adams Media.

Lunardini, Christine A. American Peace Movement in the Twentieth Century. LC 94-10405. (Clio Companions Ser.). 269p. 1994. lib. bdg. 55.00 (*0-87436-714-X*) ABC-CLIO.

— Women's Rights. LC 95-21712. (Social Issues in American History Ser.). (Illus.). 232p. 1995. boxed set 29.95 (*0-89774-872-7*) Oryx Pr.

Lunardini, Christine A., jt. auth. see Clinton, Catherine.

Lunati, M., jt. ed. see Andrews, J.

Lunati, M. Teresa. Ethical Issues in Economics: From Altruism to Cooperation to Equity. LC 97-7118. 256p. 1997. text 69.95 (*0-312-17496-9*) St Martin.

Lunati, Montserrat, ed. Rainy Days: Dias de Lluvia: An Anthology of Spanish Women Writers. (Hispanic Classics Ser.). (Illus.). 250p. 1997. 59.95 (*0-85668-635-2*, Pub. by Aris & Phillips); pap. 25.00 (*0-85668-636-0*, Pub. by Aris & Phillips) David Brown.

Lunatic, Humphrey, jt. auth. see McDermot, Murtagh.

Lunau, F. W., jt. ed. see Leslie, G. B.

Lunbeck, C. J. Child Care in Omaha Pt. 1: Facilities. (Illus.). 33p. (Orig.). 1971. pap. 3.00 (*1-55719-073-9*) U NE CPAR.

— CUA Census Report No. 3: Indian Population in Douglas County. 23p. (Orig.). 1972. pap. 2.50 (*1-55719-054-2*) U NE CPAR.

Lunbeck, Elizabeth. The Psychiatric Persuasion: Knowledge, Gender, & Power in Modern America. LC 93-43818. 456p. (C). 1994. text 45.00 (*0-691-04804-5*, Pub. by Princeton U Pr) Cal Prin Full Svc.

Lunc, M. & Contensou, P. Proceedings of the Nineteenth International Astronautical Congress, New York, 1968, 4 vols., Set. LC 58-23647. 1970. 909.00 (*0-08-006933-9*, Pub. by Pergamon Repr) Franklin.

— Proceedings of the 18th International Astronautical Congress Belgrade 1967, 4 vols., Set. (Interntional Astronautical Congress Ser.). 1968. reprint ed. 735.00 (*0-08-013012-7*, Pub. by Pergamon Repr) Franklin.

Lunceford, Lloyd, ed. see Munson, Donna P.

***Lunch, Lydia.** Adulterer's Anomymous II. 120p. 1999. pap. 14.95 (*0-86719-439-1*) Last Gasp.

Lunch, Lydia. Adulterers Anonymous. 1996. pap. 12.95 (*0-86719-423-5*) Last Gasp.

— Incriminating Evidence: The Collected Writings of Lydia Lunch. 120p. 1992. pap. 12.95 (*0-86719-380-8*) Last Gasp.

— Toxic Gumbo. Berger, Karen, ed. LC 98-207761. (Illus.). 48p. 1998. pap. 5.95 (*1-56389-347-9*) DC Comics.

Lunch, Richard L., jt. ed. see Lynch, Richard L.

Lund. Environmental Pollution. 1978. text 135.00 (*90-277-0949-1*) Kluwer Academic.

— Food Microbiology. (Illus.). 1300p. (C). 1999. pap. 359.95 (*0-412-63300-0*, Chap & Hall NY) Chapman & Hall.

— Leech Lake, Yesterday & Today. 120p. 1998. pap. 9.95 (*1-885061-53-6*) Adventure Pubns.

— Making Sense of it All. LC 98-33536. 190p. 1998. pap. text 27.80 (*0-13-924002-0*) P-H.

— Understanding & Using Wordstar. 11th ed. (DF - Computer Applications Ser.). (C). 1988. pap., student ed. 31.00 (*0-314-40884-3*) West Pub.

— Understanding & Using Wordstar 4.0. (DF - Computer Applications Ser.). 1988. mass mkt. 25.50 (*0-314-34742-9*) West Pub.

Lund, jt. auth. see Sloan.

Lund, A. & Shiotani, M. Radical Ionic Systems Properties in Condensed Physics. (Topics in Molecular Organization & Engineering Ser.). 488p. 1991. text 248.50 (*0-7923-0988-X*) Kluwer Academic.

Lund, Adrienne F. An Amish Potpourri Cookbook. (Illus.). 170p. (Orig.). 1991. pap. 12.95 (*1-886645-02-7*) Jupiter Press.

— The Amish Recipe Sampler. 65p. (Orig.). 1982. pap. 4.95 (*1-886645-00-0*) Jupiter Press.

— The Amish Way Cookbook. rev. ed. (Illus.). 203p. 1979. pap. 12.95 (*0-938400-06-1*) Jupiter Press.

— Appletreats from Amish Country. (Illus.). 65p. (Orig.). 1996. pap. 6.95 (*1-886645-07-8*) Jupiter Press.

***Lund, Adrienne F.** The Harvest Table: Comfort Foods from Amish Kitchens & Country Gardens. (Illus.). 112p. 2000. pap. 8.95 (*1-886645-08-6*) Jupiter Press.

Lund, Adrienne F. Katie's Dream. (Illus.). 30p. (Orig.). (J). (gr. k-5). 1987. pap. 5.95 (*1-886645-03-5*) Jupiter Press.

— Plain & Fancy Amish Cookie Recipes. (Illus.). 69p. (Orig.). 1993. pap. 6.95 (*1-886645-01-9*) Jupiter Press.

Lund, Adrienne F. & Pitts, Walter C. Canning the Amish Way. (Illus.). 89p. (Orig.). 1994. reprint ed. pap. 6.95 (*1-886645-06-X*) Jupiter Press.

Lund, Anders & Rhodes, Christopher, eds. Radicals on Surfaces. LC 94-31444. (Topics in Molecular Organization & Engineering Ser.: 13). 260p. (C). 1995. text 176.50 (*0-7923-3108-7*) Kluwer Academic.

Lund, Ann. Dining in Style. 250p. 1992. spiral bd. write for info. (*0-9634750-0-2*) A Lund.

Lund, Annabel & Kelley, Mark. Juneau Portrait, Vol. II. LC 96-94897. (Illus.). 98p. 1997. 29.95 (*1-880865-08-4*); pap. 19.95 (*1-880865-09-2*) Mark Kelley.

Lund, Annabel M. & Sydeman, Michelle. Alaska Wildlife Viewing Guide. LC 96-1233. (Illus.). 96p. 1996. pap. 8.95 (*1-56044-066-X*) Falcon Pub Inc.

Lund, Barbara M., et al. The Microbiological Safety & Quality of Food, 2 vols. LC 99-14425. (Illus.). 2752p. 1999. 425.00 (*0-8342-1323-0*, 13230) Aspen Pub.

Lund, Bill. The Apache Indians. (Native Peoples Ser.). (Illus.). 24p. (J). (gr. k-3). 1997. lib. bdg. 14.00 (*0-516-20895-0*) Childrens.

— Getting Ready for a Career As a Computer Animator. (Getting Ready Ser.). (Illus.). 48p. (J). (gr. 3-7). 1997. lib. bdg. 19.00 (*0-516-20914-0*) Childrens.

— Getting Ready for a Career As a Computer Technician. (Getting Ready Ser.). (Illus.). 48p. (J). (gr. 3-7). 1997. lib. bdg. 19.00 (*0-516-20911-6*) Childrens.

— Getting Ready for a Career As a Video Game Designer. (Getting Ready Ser.). (Illus.). 48p. (J). (gr. 3-7). 1997. lib. bdg. 19.00 (*0-516-20912-4*) Childrens.

— Getting Ready for a Career As an Internet Designer. (Getting Ready Ser.). (Illus.). 48p. (J). (gr. 3-7). 1997. lib. bdg. 19.00 (*0-516-20913-2*) Childrens.

— Getting Ready for a Career in Computers. (Illus.). 48p. (J). (gr. 3-7). 1995. 19.00 (*0-516-35290-3*) Childrens.

— Getting Ready for a Career in Health Care. (Illus.). 48p. (J). (gr. 3-7). 1995. lib. bdg. 19.00 (*0-516-35292-X*) Childrens.

— Integrating PC & UNIX Network Operating Systems. 1996. 34.00 (*0-614-14490-6*) P-H.

— The Iroquois Indians. (Native Peoples Ser.). (Illus.). (J). 1997. 13.75 (*0-516-20523-4*) Childrens.

— Kayaking. (Extreme Sports Ser.). (Illus.). 48p. (J). (gr. 3-7). 1996. 19.00 (*0-516-20255-3*) Childrens.

— The Manatees of Florida. (Animals of the World Ser.). (Illus.). 24p. (J). (gr. k-3). 1997. lib. bdg. 14.00 (*0-531-11463-5*, Hlltop Bks) Capstone Pr.

— The Manatees of Florida. LC 97-12673. (Animals of the World Ser.). (J). 1998. lib. bdg. write for info. (*1-56065-579-8*) Capstone Pr.

— Native Peoples Series, 10 bks. Incl. Apache Indians. LC 97-6396. (Illus.). 24p. (J). (gr. 2-3). 1998. lib. bdg. 13.75 (*1-56065-561-5*, Bridgestone Bks); Cherokee Indians. LC 96-39767. (Illus.). 24p. (J). (gr. 2-3). 1997. lib. bdg. 13.75 (*1-56065-477-5*, Bridgestone Bks); Chumash Indians. LC 97-6395. (Illus.). 24p. (J). (gr. 2-3). 1998. lib. bdg. 13.75 (*1-56065-562-3*, Bridgestone Bks); Comanche Indians. LC 96-39766. (Illus.). 24p. (J). (gr. 2-3). 1997. lib. bdg. 13.75 (*1-56065-478-3*, Bridgestone Bks); Iroquois Indians. LC 96-51504. (Illus.). 24p. (J). (gr. 2-3). 1997. lib. bdg. 13.75 (*1-56065-480-5*); Ojibwa Indians. LC 96-39765. (Illus.). 24p. (J). (gr. 2-3). 1997. lib. bdg. 13.75 (*1-56065-481-3*, Bridgestone Bks); Pomo Indians. LC 96-39763. (Illus.). 24p. (J). (gr. 2-3). 1997. lib. bdg. 13.75 (*1-56065-479-1*, Bridgestone Bks); Seminole Indians. LC 96-39764. (Illus.). 24p. (J). (gr. 2-3). 1997. lib. bdg. 13.75 (*1-56065-482-1*, Bridgestone Bks); Sioux Indians. LC 97-6394. (Illus.). 24p. (J). (gr. 2-3). 1998. lib. bdg. 13.75 (*1-56065-563-1*, Bridgestone Bks); Wampanoag Indians. LC 97-6397. (Illus.). 24p. (J). (gr. 2-3). 1998. lib. bdg. 13.75 (*1-56065-564-X*, Bridgestone Bks); (J). Set lib. bdg. 137.50 (*1-56065-659-X*, Bridgestone Bks) Capstone Pr.

— The Ojibwa Indians. (Native Peoples Ser.). (Illus.). (J). 1997. lib. bdg. 14.00 (*0-516-20524-2*) Childrens.

— The Pomo Indians. (Native Peoples Ser.). (Illus.). (J). 1997. lib. bdg. 14.00 (*0-516-20525-0*) Childrens.

— Powhatan Indians. (Native Peoples Ser.). (J). 1998. 14.00 (*0-516-21356-3*) Childrens.

— Rock Climbing. (Extreme Sports Ser.). (Illus.). 48p. (J). (gr. 3-7). 1996. 19.00 (*0-516-20256-1*) Childrens.

— The Seminole Indians. (Native Peoples Ser.). (J). 1997. 14.00 (*0-516-20526-9*) Childrens.

— The Sioux Indians. (Native Peoples Ser.). (Illus.). 24p. (J). (gr. k-3). 1997. lib. bdg. 14.00 (*0-516-20897-7*) Childrens.

— Triathlon. (Extreme Sports Ser.). (Illus.). 48p. (J). (gr. 3-7). 1996. 19.00 (*0-516-20257-X*) Childrens.

— The Wampanoag Indians. (Native Peoples Ser.). (Illus.). 24p. (J). (gr. 1-3). 1997. lib. bdg. 14.00 (*0-516-20898-5*) Childrens.

— Weightlifting. (Extreme Sports Ser.). (Illus.). 48p. (J). (gr. 3-7). 1996. 19.00 (*0-516-20258-8*) Childrens.

Lund, Bill & Ryan, Pat. Extreme Skateboarding. (Extreme Sports Ser.). (Illus.). 48p. (J). (gr. 3-7). 1997. lib. bdg. 19.00 (*0-516-20907-8*) Childrens.

— Extreme Snowboarding. (Extreme Sports Ser.). (Illus.). 48p. (J). (gr. 3-7). 1997. lib. bdg. 19.00 (*0-516-20908-6*) Childrens.

— Sky Surfing. (Extreme Sports Ser.). (Illus.). 48p. (J). (gr. 3-7). 1997. lib. bdg. 19.00 (*0-516-20909-4*) Childrens.

— Street Luge Racing. (Extreme Sports Ser.). (Illus.). 48p. (J). (gr. 3-7). 1997. lib. bdg. 19.00 (*0-516-20910-8*) Childrens.

Lund, Birger, jt. ed. see Danneskiold-Samsoe, Bente.

Lund, Bonnie. Business Communication That Really Works! Technology for Business. Engel, Peter H., ed. (Office Depot's Small Business Solutions Ser.). (Illus.). 128p. (Orig.). 1995. pap. 13.95 (*1-886111-24-3*) Affinity CA.

Lund, C. A. Coastal & Deep Sea Navigation for Yachtsmen. (C). 1987. 40.00 (*0-85174-119-3*) St Mut.

— Compasses in Small Craft. (C). 1987. 40.00 (*0-85174-453-2*) St Mut.

— The Handling of Motor Craft. (C). 1987. 35.00 (*0-85174-121-5*) St Mut.

Lund, Charles. Dot Paper Geometry: With or Without a Geoboard. (Illus.). 84p. 1980. pap. text 10.95 (*0-914040-87-1*) Cuisenaire.

— Graphing Calculator Activities: Exploring Topics in Precalculus. 182p. (C). 1994. pap. text 28.00 (*0-201-54216-1*) Addison-Wesley.

— TI-82 Graphing Calculator Activities for Middle School Math. (Illus.). 200p. 1995. pap. text 18.95 (*0-9623629-6-4*) MathWare.

— Tricks of the Trade with Cards. Laycock, Mary, ed. (Illus.). 64p. (J). (gr. 2-9). 1978. pap. text 8.50 (*0-918932-57-2*, AE-1398) Activity Resources.

Lund, Charles & Andersen, Edwin. Graphing Calculator Activities: Exploring Topics in Algebra I & II. rev. ed. Zacny, Carol & Faust, Deborah D., eds. (Illus.). 132p. (YA). (gr. 9-12). 1997. pap. text 15.95 (*1-57232-852-5*, 21853) Seymour Pubns.

Lund, Charles & Andersen, Edwin D. Computer Graphing Experiments, 3 vols., Set. 1982. write for info. (*0-201-23480-7*) Addison-Wesley.

— Computer Graphing Experiments, 4 vols., Vol. 1. 1982. write for info. (*0-201-23465-3*) Addison-Wesley.

— Computer Graphing Experiments, 4 vols., Vol. 2. 1982. write for info. (*0-201-23470-X*) Addison-Wesley.

— Computer Graphing Experiments, 4 vols., Vol. 3. 1982. write for info. (*0-201-23475-0*) Addison-Wesley.

— Introduction to the TI-92: 37 Experiments in Precalculus & Calculus. (Illus.). 112p. (Orig.). 1996. pap. text, teacher ed. 14.95 (*0-9623629-7-2*) MathWare.

Lund, Charles & Smart, Margaret. Focus on Calculator Math. (Illus.). 64p. (YA). (gr. 5-12). 1979. pap. text 8.50 (*0-918932-66-1*, AE-1597) Activity Resources.

***Lund, Christian.** Law, Power & Politics in Niger: Land Struggles & the Rural Code. 268p. 1998. pap. 26.95 (*3-8258-3405-0*, Pub. by CE24) Transaction Pubs.

Lund, Christian, ed. see European Association of Development Research & Training Institutes Staff.

Lund, D., jt. ed. see Oksendal, Bernt K.

***Lund, Dale, ed.** Men Coping with Grief. LC 99-87525. (Death, Value & Meaning Ser.). 300p. 2000. 58.00 (*0-89503-211-2*) Baywood Pub.

***Lund, Dale A.** Men Coping with Grief. LC 99-87525. (Death, Value & Meaning Ser.). 300p. 2000. pap. 34.94 (*0-89503-212-0*) Baywood Pub.

Lund, Dale A., ed. Older Bereaved Spouses. 196p. 1989. pap. 30.95 (*1-56032-240-3*) Hemisp Pub.

Lund, Daryle B., jt. ed. see Heldman, Denise R.

Lund, David, jt. auth. see Lund, Lauren.

Lund, David H. Death & Consciousness. LC 84-43211. 204p. 1985. lib. bdg. 34.50 (*0-89950-140-0*) McFarland & Co.

— Perception, Mind & Personal Identity: A Critique of Materialism. LC 94-25527. 286p. (Orig.). (C). 1994. reprint ed. pap. text 29.50 (*0-8191-9616-9*); reprint ed. lib. bdg. 53.00 (*0-8191-9615-0*) U Pr of Amer.

Lund, Deborah S. Ambiguity As Narrative Strategy in the Prose of C. F. Meyer. (Studies in Nineteenth-Century German Literature: Vol. 6). 218p. (C). 1990. text 45.95 (*0-8204-1279-1*) P Lang Pubng.

Lund, Deborah S. Waiting for Me. (Illus.). 32p. (J). 15.89 (*0-06-028877-9*) HarpC.

— Waiting for Me. (Illus.). 32p. (J). (ps-1). 15.95 (*0-06-028876-0*); 5.95 (*0-06-443660-8*) HarpC.

Lund-Dillon, Karen. Finding Karen: The Journey Through Sadness. (Illus.). 164p. (Orig.). pap. 14.95 (*0-9642000-0-7*) K Lund-Dillon.

***Lund, Doris.** Eric. 352p. 2000. pap. 11.00 (*0-06-095637-2*, Perennial) HarperTrade.

Lund, Doris. Eric. LC 74-7061. 1974. 16.95 (*0-397-01046-X*, Lippnctt) Lppncott W & W.

— Eric. LC 88-45954. 352p. 1989. reprint ed. mass mkt. 6.50 (*0-06-080925-6*, P 925, Perennial) HarperTrade.

Lund, Duane. Indian Wars. 134p. 1995. pap. 8.95 (*1-885061-09-9*) Adventure Pubns.

***Lund, Duane.** 150 Ways to Enjoy Potatoes. (Illus.). 100p. 2000. 9.95 (*1-885061-85-4*) Adventure Pubns.

Lund, Duane R. Andrew the Youngest Lumberjack. 108p. 1990. pap. 8.95 (*0-934860-62-9*) Adventure Pubns.

— A Beginner's Guide to Hunting & Trapping Secrets. 99p. 1988. pap. 8.95 (*0-934860-52-1*) Adventure Pubns.

— Camp Cooking. 108p. 1991. pap. 8.95 (*0-934860-05-X*) Adventure Pubns.

— Early Native American Recipes. 84p. 1996. pap. 9.95 (*0-934860-57-2*) Adventure Pubns.

— Entertainment Helpers, Quick & Easy. 100p. 1997. pap. text 9.95 (*1-885061-21-8*) Adventure Pubns.

— Fishing & Hunting Stories. 101p. 1992. pap. 9.95 (*0-934860-95-5*) Adventure Pubns.

— Gourmet Freshwater Fish Recipes. 96p. 1994. pap. 9.95 (*0-934860-09-2*) Adventure Pubns.

***Lund, Duane R.** Gull Lake, Yesterday & Today. 1999. pap. 9.95 (*1-885061-65-X*) Adventure Pubns.

Lund, Duane R. A Kid's Guide to Fishing Secrets. 96p. 1984. pap. 8.95 (*0-934860-37-8*) Adventure Pubns.

— Lake of the Woods II. 1984. pap. 8.95 (*0-934860-36-X*) Adventure Pubns.

— Lake of the Woods, Yesterday & Today. 112p. 1976. pap. 8.95 (*0-934860-03-3*) Adventure Pubns.

— Nature's Bounty for Your Table. 1982. pap. 8.95 (*0-934860-20-3*) Adventure Pubns.

— The North Shore of Lake Superior Yesterday & Today. 112p. 1993. pap. 8.95 (*0-934860-01-7*) Adventure Pubns.

— One Hundred & One Favorite Wild Rice Recipes. 76p. 1983. pap. 8.95 (*0-934860-24-6*) Adventure Pubns.

— One Hundred One Favorite Freshwater Fish Recipes. 88p. 1979. pap. 8.95 (*0-934860-11-4*) Adventure Pubns.

— One Hundred One Ways to Add to Your Income. 100p. 1994. pap. 8.95 (*0-934860-10-6*) Adventure Pubns.

— Our Historic Boundary Waters. 1980. pap. 8.95 (*0-934860-13-0*) Adventure Pubns.

— Our Historic Upper Mississippi. 96p. 1991. pap. 8.95 (*0-934860-73-4*) Adventure Pubns.

— Sauces, Seasonings & Marinades for Fish & Wild Game. 95p. 1991. pap. 8.95 (*0-934860-74-2*) Adventure Pubns.

— Scandinavian Cookbook. 70p. 1992. pap. 9.95 (*0-934860-88-2*) Adventure Pubns.

***Lund, Duane R.** The Soup Cookbook: More Than 150 Soup, Stew & Chili Recipes! 112p. 1999. pap. 9.95 (*1-885061-57-9*) Adventure Pubns.

Lund, Duane R. Tales of Four Lakes. 120p. pap. 9.95 (*0-934860-04-1*) Adventure Pubns.

— Traditional Holiday Ethnic Recipes. (Illus.). 144p. 1996. pap. 9.95 (*1-885061-17-X*) Adventure Pubns.

— White Indian Boy. 1981. pap. 8.95 (*0-934860-17-3*) Adventure Pubns.

— The Youngest Voyageur. 1985. pap. 7.95 (*0-934860-41-6*) Adventure Pubns.

Lund, Duane R. & Finch, Lewis W. Lessons in Leadership: Mostly Learned the Hard Way. 96p. (Orig.). (C). 1987. pap. 8.95 (*0-934860-47-5*) Adventure Pubns.

Lund, E. Hermeneutica, Introduccion Biblica.Tr. of Hermeneutica & Introduction to the Bible. (SPA.). 224p. 1964. pap. 6.99 (*0-8297-0564-3*) Vida Pubs.

Lund, Eloise E., ed. see Lund, Harry C.

Lund, Eric. Alternatives to Lumber & Plywood in Home Construction. (Illus.). 61p. (Orig.). (C). 1994. pap. text 45.00 (*0-7881-0264-8*) DIANE Pub.

Lund, Erik A. War for the Every Day: Generals, Knowledge & Warfare in Early Modern Europe, 1680-1740, 181. LC 99-18593. 256p. 1999. 65.00 (*0-313-31041-6*, Greenwood Pr) Greenwood.

***Lund, Evelyn.** It Happened on Alphabet Street. LC 98-66590. (Illus.). 32p. (J). 1998. pap. 12.95 (*1-878044-50-8*, Wld Rose) Mayhaven Pub.

Lund, Francie & Madlala, Nozizwe. Caring for Elderly People: A Workbook in Tswana. (TSW., Illus.). 92p. 1993. pap. 7.00 (*0-86980-899-0*, Pub. by Univ Natal Pr) Intl Spec Bk.

— Caring for Elderly People: A Workbook in Xhosa. (XHO., Illus.). 92p. 1993. pap. 7.00 (*0-86980-900-8*, Pub. by Univ Natal Pr) Intl Spec Bk.

— Caring for Elderly People: A Workbook in Zulu. (ZUL., Illus.). 92p. 1993. pap. 7.00 (*0-86980-901-6*, Pub. by Univ Natal Pr) Intl Spec Bk.

Lund, Fred B. Greek Medicine. LC 75-23668. (Clio Medica Ser.: 18). (Illus.). reprint ed. 37.50 (*0-404-58918-9*) AMS Pr.

Lund, Gary. Life: Before, During & After. (Celebration of Discovery Ser.: Vol. II). 192p. (Orig.). 1988. pap. 12.95 (*0-938283-01-4*) Spirit Speaks.

Lund, Gene J., tr. see Fagerberg, Holsten.

Lund, Gene J., tr. see Hagglund, Bengt.

Lund, Gerald N. The Coming of the Lord. 1971. 15.95 (*0-88494-229-5*) Bookcraft Inc.

***Lund, Gerald N.** The Kingdom & the Crown Vol. 1: Fishers of Men. 2000. 25.95 (*1-57345-820-1*, Shadow Mount) Deseret Bk.

— The Selected Writings of Gerald N. Lund. LC 99-41730. (Gospel Scholars Ser.). 1999. write for info. (*1-57345-549-0*) Deseret Bk.

Lund, Gerald N. Some Clippings from a Writer's Handbook. 8p. (Orig.). 1995. pap. text 2.50 (*1-57636-003-2*) SunRise Pbl.

— The Work & Glory Vol. 8: So Great a Cause. 1997. 23.95 (*1-57008-358-4*) Bookcraft Inc.

— The Work & the Glory: No Unhallowed Hand, Vol. 7. 1996. 23.95 (*1-57008-277-4*) Bookcraft Inc.

— The Work & the Glory Vol. 1: Pillar of Light. 1990. 17.95 (*0-88494-770-X*) Bookcraft Inc.

— The Work & the Glory Vol. 2: Like a Fire Is Burning. 1991. 21.95 (*0-88494-801-3*) Bookcraft Inc.

— The Work & the Glory Vol. 3: Truth Will Prevail. 1992. 19.95 (*0-88494-853-6*) Bookcraft Inc.

— The Work & the Glory Vol. 4: Thy Gold to Refine. 1993. 19.95 (*0-88494-893-5*) Bookcraft Inc.

— The Work & the Glory Vol. 5: A Season of Joy. 1994. 21.95 (*0-88494-960-5*) Bookcraft Inc.

— The Work & the Glory Vol. 6: Praise to the Man. 1995. 21.95 (*0-88494-999-0*) Bookcraft Inc.

— The Work & the Glory Vol. 9: All Is Well, Vol. 9. 1998. 25.95 (*1-57008-563-3*) Bookcraft Inc.

— The Work & the Glory Collector's Set, 9 vols. 1998. 199.95 (*1-57008-586-2*) Bookcraft Inc.

Lund, Gerald N., jt. auth. see Lund, Lynn S.

Lund, Hans. Text As Picture: Studies in the Literary Transformation of Pictures. (Illus.). 228p. 1992. lib. bdg. 89.95 (*0-7734-9449-9*) E Mellen.

Lund, Harry C. Michigan Wildflowers in Color. Lund, Eloise E., ed. (Illus.). 120p. (Orig.). 1985. pap. 10.95 (*0-685-10417-6*) H C Lund.

— Michigan Wildflowers in Color: Revised Edition with Wildflower Walks. 3rd rev. ed. (Illus.). 144p. 1998. pap. 18.95 (*1-882376-56-0*) Thunder Bay Pr.

Lund, Helen S., jt. auth. see Jackson, Norman.

Lund, Henning & Baizer, Manuel M., eds. Organic Electrochemistry: An Introduction & a Guide. 3rd ed. (Illus.). 1576p. 1991. text 295.00 (*0-8247-8154-6*) Dekker.

Lund, Henning, jt. ed. see Bard, Allan J.

***Lund, Herbert F.** The McGraw-Hill Recycling Handbook. 2nd ed. LC 00-28382. (Illus.). 1152p. 2000. 99.95 (*0-07-039156-4*) McGraw.

Lund, Humphries. A Calendar of Art Exhibition, 1998-99: The Lund Humphries Calendar of Art Exhibition in U. K. Galleries & Museums, January 1998-July 1999. (Illus.). 96p. 1997. pap. 13.95 (*0-85331-750-X*, Pub. by Lund Humphries) Antique Collect.

— A Calendar of Art Exhibitions, 1995-6: Art Exhibitions in UK Galleries & Museums 1/95-7/96. 56p. 1995. pap. 9.95 (*0-85331-673-2*, Pub. by Lund Humphries) Antique Collect.

— Calendar of Art Exhibitions, 1996-7: The Lund Humphries Calendar of Art Exhibitions in U.K. Galleries & Museums 1996-1997. 56p. 1996. pap. 9.95 (*0-85331-671-6*, Pub. by Lund Humphries) Antique Collect.

***Lund Humphries Publishing Staff.** The Guide to Art Exhibitions 2000-2001. (Illus.). 144p. 1999. pap. 15.00 (*0-85331-788-7*, Pub. by Lund Humphries) Antique Collect.

Lund Humphries Publishing Staff. James Ensor: Visionary Landscapes Masqueraders, & a Taste for the Macabre. 1997. 50.00 (*0-85331-751-8*, Pub. by Lund Humphries) Antique Collect.

— Ralph Koltai: Designer for the Stage. (Illus.). 128p. 1997. 50.00 (*0-85331-770-4*, Pub. by Lund Humphries) Antique Collect.

Lund, Ingeborg, tr. see Behrend, William.

Lund, J., jt. ed. see Bowers, K. L.

Lund, J. A., jt. ed. see Chaklader, A. C.

Lund, J. W., jt. auth. see Canter-Lund, Hilda.

***Lund, Jack, ed.** Simulcast Strategy: Revised Guide to Winning at Horseraces. 96p. 2000. pap. 18.95 (*0-9700165-3-0*) Twin Rivers NC.

Lund, James R. & Heidkamp, Mary. Moving Faith into Action: A Facilitator's Guide for Creating Parish Social Ministry Organizations. 192p. 1990. pap. 9.95 (*0-8091-3157-9*) Paulist Pr.

Lund, Jennifer. Internet at a Glance. 1996. pap. write for info. (*0-201-63494-5*) Addison-Wesley.

Lund, Jens. Flatheads & Spooneys: Fishing for a Living in the Ohio River Valley. LC 95-23982. (Ohio River Valley Ser.). (Illus.). 216p. 1995. 27.50 (*0-8131-1927-8*) U Pr of Ky.

***Lund, Jillian.** Two Cool Coyotes. LC 98-50625. (Illus.). 32p. (J). (ps-2). 1999. 15.99 (*0-525-46151-5*) NAL.

Lund, Jillian. Way Out West Lives a Coyote Named Frank. LC 91-46011. (Illus.). 32p. (J). (ps-2). 1993. 15.99 (*0-525-44982-5*, Dutton Child) Peng Put Young Read.

— Way Out West Lives a Coyote Named Frank. (Illus.). 32p. (J). 1997. pap. 5.99 (*0-14-056232-X*) Viking Penguin.

***Lund, Joanna.** String of Pearls: Recipes for Living Well in the Real World. 192p. 2000. 19.95 (*0-399-14654-7*) Putnam Pub Group.

Lund, JoAnna M. The Arthritis Healthy Exchanges Cookbook. LC 97-32731. 320p. 1998. pap. 14.00 (*0-399-52377-4*, Perigee Bks) Berkley Pub.

— Best of Healthy Exchanges Food Newsletter. (Illus.). 180p. (Orig.). 1993. 11.50 (*0-9635632-1-1*) Hlthy Exchange.

— The Diabetic's Healthy Exchanges Cookbook. 256p. 1996. pap. 14.00 (*0-399-52235-2*, Perigee Bks) Berkley Pub.

— The Diabetic's Healthy Exchanges Cookbook. large type ed. LC 97-11521. (Spec-Hall Ser.). 270p. 1997. lib. bdg. 25.95 (*0-7838-8199-1*, G K Hall Lrg Type) Mac Lib Ref.

— Healthy Exchanges Cookbook. 1995. pap. 16.95 (*0-399-14065-4*, G P Putnam) Peng Put Young Read.

***Lund, JoAnna M.** Healthy Exchanges Cookbook. 1999. reprint ed. pap. 13.95 (*0-399-52554-8*, Perigee Bks) Berkley Pub.

Lund, JoAnna M. The Heart Smart Healthy Exchanges Cookbook. LC 98-33232. 304p. 1999. pap. 14.00 (*0-399-52474-6*, Perigee Bks) Berkley Pub.

Lund, Joanna M. Help: Healthy Exchanges Lifetime Plan. 272p. 1996. 21.95 (*0-399-14164-2*, G P Putnam) Peng Put Young Read.

Lund, Joanna M. & Alpert, Barbara. Cooking Healthy with a Man in Mind. LC 96-35509. (Illus.). 352p. 1997. 19.95 (*0-399-14265-7*, G P Putnam) Peng Put Young Read.

— Cooking Healthy with the Kids in Mind: A Healthy Exchanges Cookbook. LC 97-34162. 288p. 1998. 19.95 (*0-399-14358-0*, G P Putnam) Peng Put Young Read.

***Lund, Joanna M. & Alpert, Barbara.** Cooking Healthy with the Kids in Mind: A Healthy Exchanges Cookbook. (Illus.). 352p. 2000. reprint ed. pap. 13.95 (*0-399-52605-6*, Perigee Bks) Berkley Pub.

Lund, JoAnna M. & Alpert, Barbara. Dessert Every Night! A Healthy Exchanges Cookbook. LC 98-3427. 320p. 1998. 21.95 (*0-399-14422-6*, G P Putnam) Peng Put Young Read.

*Lund, JoAnna M. & Alpert, Barbara. String of Pearls: Recipes for Living in the Real World. LC 00-35639. (Illus.). (YA). 2000. write for info. (0-399-14595-8, G P Putnam) Peng Put Young Read.

Lund, JoAnna M., et al. Make a Joyful Table: A Healthy Exchanges Cookbook. LC 99-17055. (Illus.). 336p. 1999. 22.95 (0-399-14527-3, G P Putnam) Peng Put Young Read.

*Lund, JoAnne M. & Alpert, Barbara. The Cancer Recovery Healthy Exchanges Cookbook: More than 175 Recipes for Delicious, Easy-to-Prepare Dishes Designed to Promote Cancer Prevention & Recovery. LC 99-55709. 320p. 2000. pap. 14.00 (0-399-52576-9, Perigee Bks) Berkley Pub.

Lund, John. Auditing Local Union Financial Records: A Guide for Local Union Trustees. LC 92-27352. (ILR Bulletin Ser.: No. 67). 96p. 1992. pap. text 9.95 (0-87546-194-8, ILR Press) Cornell U Pr.

Lund, John & Bowers, Kenneth. Sinc Methods for Quadrature & Differential Equations. LC 92-12139. (Miscellaneous Bks.: No. 32). x, 304p. 1992. 56.00 (0-89871-298-X) Soc Indus-Appl Math.

Lund, John, et al. Project Air Force Analysis of the Air War in the Gulf: An Assessment of Strategic Airlift Operational Efficiency. LC 93-3532. 1993. pap. 10.00 (0-8330-1351-3, R-4269/4-AF) Rand Corp.

Lund, John, jt. auth. see Bowers, Kenneth L.

Lund, John, jt. ed. see Bowers, Kenneth L.

Lund, John L. The Art of Giving & Receiving Criticism. viii, 199p. (Orig.). 1997. pap. 14.95 (1-891114-30-1) Commun Co.

*Lund, John L. How to Hug a Porcupine: Dealing with Toxic & Difficult to Love Personalities. (Illus.). 320p. 1999. pap. 19.95 (1-891114-34-4) Commun Co.

Lund, John W. More Southern Oregon Cross Country Ski Trails. (Illus.). 138p. (Orig.). (C). 1990. pap. 8.95 (0-9619389-2-7) J W Lund.

— Southern Oregon Cross-Country Ski Trails. (Illus.). 222p. (Orig.). 1987. pap. 9.95 (0-9619389-1-9) J W Lund.

Lund, John W., et al. Geothermal Direct Use Engineering & Design Guidebook. 3rd ed. (Illus.). 470p. 1998. spiral bd. 49.00 (1-880228-00-9) OR Inst Tech.

Lund, John W., jt. auth. see Lecklider, G. Robert.

*Lund-Jones, Barbara & Nielsen, John W., eds. Embracing Two Worlds: The Thorvald Muller Family of Kimballton. LC 99-213842. (Illus.). xviii, 180 p. 1998. pap. 14.95 (0-930697-04-9) Lur Pubns.

Lund, Kevin, jt. auth. see Yorgason, Brenton G.

Lund, Kristin. Dogs in Marin: A Reference Guide for Marin County Dog Owners. 200p. 1994. pap. 9.95 (0-9643445-0-5) Lundehund Pr.

*Lund, Kristin. Inside the Worlds of Star Wars Episode I: The Complete Guide to the Incredible Locations from the Movie. (Illus.). 48p. (J). (gr. 4-7). 2000. 19.95 (0-7894-6692-9) DK Pub Inc.

Lund, Lauren. Bunny: A Storybook for Children Who Have a Parent with Multiple Personalities. (Illus.). 36p. (Orig.). (J). 1993. pap. text 5.95 (0-9637149-1-0) Soft Words.

Lund, Lauren & Lund, David. Many Minds: Information for People Who Have Multiple Personalities. (Illus.). 34p. (Orig.). 1993. pap. text 4.95 (0-9637149-0-2) Soft Words.

Lund, Linda O., jt. auth. see Hulme, Ashley.

Lund, Lynn S. Book of Mormon Songs. 1996. pap. 10.95 (1-57008-272-3); audio 9.95 (1-57008-274-X); cd-rom 14.95 (1-57008-273-1) Bookcraft Inc.

— Piano Hymn Favorites: Songs of Eternal Faith, Songs of Everlasting Joy, Songs of Inspiration, 3 bks., Set. 1994. pap. 29.98 (0-88290-492-2) Horizon Utah.

— Songs of Eternal Faith: Artistic Piano Arrangements of Best-Loved Hymns. LC 81-80954. 56p. (Orig.). 1982. pap. 9.98 (0-88290-184-2, 2901) Horizon Utah.

— Songs of Everlasting Joy: Artistic Piano Arrangements of Best-Loved Hymns. 1980. 9.98 (0-88290-155-9) Horizon Utah.

— Songs of Inspiration: Artistic Piano Arrangements of New Latter-Day Saint Hymns. 40p. 1986. pap. text 9.98 (0-88290-276-8) Horizon Utah.

Lund, Lynn S. & Lund, Gerald N. The Music of the Work & Glory Vol. 2: Songbook. 1997. pap. 10.95 (1-57008-349-5) Bookcraft Inc.

— The Music of the Work & the Glory, Vol. 1. 1995. pap. 10.95 (1-57008-188-3) Bookcraft Inc.

Lund, Marcia. Olympic Winners: Reading Activities for Schools & Libraries. LC 96-15624. 1996. pap. 14.95 (0-917846-81-8, Alleyside) Highsmith Pr.

Lund, Mark W., ed. see Openshaw, Eli C., et al.

*Lund-Meyer, Kristin, et al. Star Wars: Incredible Locations. LC 99-39927. (Star Wars Ser.). (Illus.). (J). 2000. 19.95 (0-7894-5310-X) DK Pub Inc.

Lund, Michael. America's Continuing Story: An Introduction to Serial Fiction, 1850-1900. LC 92-18953. 228p. (C). 1992. text 19.95 (0-8143-2401-0) Wayne St U Pr.

— Preventing Violent Conflicts: A Strategy for Preventive Diplomacy. LC 96-4786. 1996. pap. text 14.95 (1-878379-52-6) US Inst Peace.

— Reading Thackeray. LC 88-1295. 176p. 1988. 26.95 (0-8143-1987-4) Wayne St U Pr.

— Reading Thackeray. LC 88-1295. 176p. (C). 1992. pap. text 16.95 (0-8143-1988-2) Wayne St U Pr.

Lund, Michael & Austin, Kathi. Democratization & Violence in Burundi: The Failure of Preventive Action. 120p. 1997. pap. 11.95 (0-87078-413-7) Century Foundation.

Lund, Michael, jt. auth. see Hughes, Linda K.

Lund, Michael S., jt. ed. see Salamon, Lester M.

Lund, Nancy, jt. auth. see Gullard, Pamela.

Lund, Natalie. Enchanted Catnip Seeds & Silver Whisker Kisses. (Illus.). 40p. (Orig.). (J). (gr. k-3). 1997. pap. 5.95 (0-9655038-0-1) Tack Sa Mycket Pr.

Lund, Niels, jt. ed. see Wood, Ian.

*Lund, Orval. Casting Lines: Poems. LC 98-89718. (Minnesota Voices Project Ser.: Vol. 93). 96p. 1999. pap. 13.95 (0-89823-197-3, Pub. by New Rivers Pr) Consort Bk Sales.

Lund, Orval. Ordinary Days. 31p. 1996. 3.50 (0-941127-18-4) Dacotah Terr Pr.

Lund, Orval, Jr., et al, eds. Great River Review, No. 25. (Illus.). 90p. 1995. pap. 6.00 (1-884102-02-6) Grt Riv Review.

Lund, Patsy H. Understanding & Using Application Software, Vol. 4. Leyh, ed. 718p. (C). 1990. pap. text 49.25 (0-314-66777-6) West Pub.

Lund, Patsy H. & Hayden, Barbara A. Understanding & Using Displaywrite 3 & 4. 204p. (C). 1988. pap. text 28.75 (0-314-78996-0) West Pub.

Lund, Patsy H., et al. Understanding & Using WordPerfect. LC 86-26727. (Microcomputing Ser.). 227p. (C). 1987. pap. text 28.75 (0-314-30122-4); pap. text, teacher ed. write for info. (0-314-35883-8) West Pub.

Lund, Paul & Ludlam, Harry. Atlantic Jeopardy: PQ17 Convoy to Hell, Trawlers Go to War, & Night of the U-Boats, 3 vols. in 1. 720p. 1995. 29.95 (0-572-01577-1, Pub. by Foulsham UK) Assoc Pubs Grp.

Lund, Phillip R. Sales Reports, Records & Systems. (Illus.). 128p. 22.95 (0-8464-0812-0) Beekman Pubs.

Lund, Preben. Generation of Precision Artwork for Printed Circuit Boards. LC 77-12388. 371p. reprint ed. pap. 115.10 (0-608-14245-X, 202400700035) Bks Demand.

Lund, Ragnhild, jt. auth. see Lie, Merete.

Lund, Reinhard, jt. ed. see Pedersen, Peder J.

Lund, Robert. Pig Tale. 8p. 1994. pap. 5.00 (0-941543-07-2) Sun Dog Pr.

Lund, Robert A. Taming the HP 3000 Vol. 1: Over 101 Ways to Monitor, Manage, & Maximize System Performance on the Hewlett-Packard 3000. LC 87-92025. 142p. (Orig.). (C). 1990. pap. text 49.95 (0-945325-01-0) Perf Pr OR.

— Taming the HP 3000, Vol. 2: The Theory & Practice of Successful Performance Management for Hewlett-Packard HP 3000 Computer Systems. LC 87-92025. 282p. (C). 1992. text 99.95 (0-945325-02-9); pap. text 79.95 (0-945325-03-7) Perf Pr OR.

Lund, Robert A., contrib. by. Taming UNIX: An Introductory Guide to Performance Management for the HP-UX System Administrator. 180p. 1999. pap. text 12.50 (0-945325-04-5) Perf Pr OR.

*Lund, Robert D. It'll Just Take a Minute. Winters, Kate & Lora, Doris, eds. (Illus.). 115p. 2000. write for info. (1-888069-23-6) Biography For Everyone.

Lund, Roger D. Critical Essays on Daniel Defoe. LC 96-46819. 1997. 49.00 (0-7838-0007-X, G K Hall & Co) Mac Lib Ref.

— Restoration & Early Eighteenth-Century English Literature, 1660-1740: A Selected Bibliography of Resource Materials. LC 79-87585. (Selected Bibliographies in Language & Literature Ser.: No. 1). 42p. (Orig.). 1980. pap. text 10.00 (0-87352-950-2, SB001) Modern Lang.

Lund, Roger D., ed. The Margins of Orthodoxy: Heterodox Writing & Cultural Response, 1660-1750. 312p. (C). 1996. text 64.95 (0-521-47177-X) Cambridge U Pr.

Lund, Shirley & Foster, Julia A. Variant Versions of Targumic Traditions Within Codex Neofiti 1. LC 77-5389. (Society of Biblical Literature. Aramaic Studies: No. 2). 186p. reprint ed. pap. 57.70 (0-7837-5457-4, 204522200005) Bks Demand.

Lund, Sophie, tr. see Bunin, Ivan A.

*Lund, Susan A. Prayer Journal for Busy Women: Convenient Easy to Use Guide for Personal Growth & Practical Application. Schlagenhaft, Jenny, ed. 208p. 1999. pap. 14.95 (0-9676629-0-7) Learn By Design.

Lund, Thomas W., jt. auth. see Eron, Joseph B.

Lund, Tricia, jt. auth. see Pollard, Judy.

Lund, Valerie J. Let's Make Banners. (Illus.). 8p. (Orig.). 1995. pap. text 14.95 (0-9622405-2-4) V J Lund.

— Let's Make Seasonal Windsocks. (Illus.). 70p. (Orig.). 1992. pap. text 10.95 (0-9622405-1-6) V J Lund.

— Let's Make Windsocks. rev. ed. (Illus.). 70p. (C). 1995. pap. text 10.95 (0-9622405-0-8) V J Lund.

Lund, Valerie J., jt. ed. see Harrison, Donald.

Lund, William B. Integrating Unix & PC Network Operating Systems. LC 95-50770. (Hewlett-Packard Bks.). 192p. 1996. pap. 31.60 (0-13-207374-9) P-H.

Lund, William R. Guide for the Preparation of Reports for the Utah Geological Survey. LC QE169.A322. (Circular Ser.: Vol. 85). 74p. 1992. pap. 8.00 (1-55791-290-4, C-85) Utah Geological Survey.

Lund, William R., ed. Engineering Geology of the Salt Lake City Metropolitan Area, Utah. (Bulletin of the Utah Geological Survey Ser.: No. 126). (Illus.). 66p. (Orig.). 1990. pap. 8.00 (1-55791-093-6, B-126) Utah Geological Survey.

Lund, William R. & Black, Bill D. Paleoseismic Investigation at Rock Canyon, Provo Segment, Wasatch Fault Zone, Utah County, Utah. LC TN24.U8A315. (Special Study of the Utah Geological Survey Ser.: Vol. 93, No. 8). (Illus.). 21p. 1998. pap. 8.00 (1-55791-613-6, SS-93) Utah Geological Survey.

Lund, William R., et al. Fault Behavior & Earthquake Recurrence on the Provo Segment of the Wasatch Fault Zone at Mapleton, Utah County, Utah. LC TN24.U8 A322. (Special Study Ser.: Vol. 75). (Illus.). 41p. 1991. pap. 7.00 (1-55791-194-0, SS-75) Utah Geological Survey.

Lund, William R., jt. auth. see Mulvey, William E.

Lund, William R., ed. see Solomon, B. J., et al.

Lunda, Karen A., jt. auth. see Peate, Wayne F.

Lundahl, ed. Quantitative Analysis of Biospecific Interactions. (Illus.). 248p. 1998. text 120.00 (90-5702-378-4, Harwood Acad Pubs) Gordon & Breach.

Lundahl, Craig R. The Nature of Humanity & the State of America: A Unified Theory of the Social World. LC 98-49107. 208p. (C). 1998. 49.00 (0-7618-1304-7); pap. 29.50 (0-7618-1305-5) U Pr of Amer.

Lundahl, Craig R. & Widdison, Harold A. The Eternal Journey: How Near-Death Experiences Illuminate Our Earthly Lives. 294p. 1999. reprint ed. text 24.00 (0-7881-6358-2) DIANE Pub.

Lundahl, G. D. & Lundahl, Ruth C. Divorce: How You Can Survive & Thrive in Spite of It. Achziger, John, ed. 156p. (Orig.). 1989. pap. write for info. (0-318-64644-7) How Pub CA.

Lundahl, Mats. Growth or Stagnation? South Africa Heading for the Year 2000. LC 99-73115. (Making of Modern Africa Ser.). 160p. 1999. text 61.95 (0-7546-1018-7, Pub. by Ashgate Pub) Ashgate Pub Co.

— Themes in International Economics. LC 98-73751. 10p. 1998. text 72.95 (1-85972-437-X, Pub. by Avebry) Ashgate Pub Co.

Lundahl, Mats & Ndulu, Benno J., eds. New Directions in Development Economics: Growth, Environmental Concerns, & Government in the 1990s. LC 95-24256. (Studies in Development Economics: Vol. 3). 472p. (C). 1996. 95.00 (0-415-12121-3) Routledge.

Lundahl, Mats & World Institute for Development Economics Research Staff. Towards the Abyss? The Political Economy of Emergency in Haiti. LC 98-213899. (Research for Action Ser.). 45p. 1997. write for info. (952-9520-64-6) UN.

Lundahl, Mats, jt. auth. see Hedlund, Hans.

Lundahl, Mats, jt. auth. see Hedlund, Stefan.

Lundahl, Mats, jt. auth. see Lundius, Jan.

Lundahl, Max, ed. Themes in Development Economics: Essays on Method, Peasants & Governmental. 400p. 1995. 91.95 (1-85628-689-4, Pub. by Avebry) Ashgate Pub Co.

Lundahl, Ruth C., jt. auth. see Lundahl, G. D.

Lundbaek, Knud. Joseph de Premare, S. J., 1666-1736: Chinese Philology & Figurism. (Acta Jutlandica Ser.: No. 66, Pt. 2). (Illus.). 240p. (C). 1991. pap. text 27.00 (87-7288-344-8, Pub. by Aarhus Univ Pr) David Brown.

— T. S. Bayer, 1694-1738: A Study of a Pioneer Sinologist. (SIAS Monographs: No. 54). (Illus.). 256p. (C). 1996. pap. text 21.00 (0-7007-0189-3, Pub. by Curzon Pr Ltd) UH Pr.

— The Traditional History of the Chinese Script: From a Seventeenth Century Jesuit Manuscript. (Illus.). 64p. (C). 1988. 33.00 (87-7288-179-8, Pub. by Aarhus Univ Pr) David Brown.

Lundbeck, J., jt. auth. see Sahrhage, D.

Lundberg, Ante, ed. The Environment & Mental Health. LC 97-43761. 250p. 1998. write for info. (0-8058-2907-5) L Erlbaum Assocs.

Lundberg, Arne & Alatalo, Rauno V. The Pied Flycatcher. (Illus.). 267p. 1992. text 39.00 (0-85661-072-0, 784672) Acad Pr.

Lundberg, Carol W. The Secret Life. LC 93-33743. 68p. 1993. pap. 14.95 (0-7734-2801-1, Mellen Poetry Pr) E Mellen.

Lundberg, Craig, ed. Consultation Education: A Special Issue of Consultation: An International Journal. 66p. 1987. 14.95 (0-89885-368-0, Kluwer Acad Hman Sci) Kluwer Academic.

Lundberg, Craig C. Managing Organizational Transitions. (C). 1989. pap. text. write for info. (0-201-18253-X) Addison-Wesley.

Lundberg, Dag B., jt. auth. see Mueller, Robert A.

Lundberg, Dag B., jt. auth. see Mueller, Robery A.

Lundberg, David W. Government by the People: What You Can Do for America. LC 79-65905. 1979. 10.95 (0-934762-00-7); pap. 7.95 (0-934762-01-5) Voice of Liberty.

Lundberg, Donald, jt. auth. see Amendola, Joseph.

Lundberg, Donald E. The Hotel & Restaurant Business. 6th ed. (Hospitality, Travel & Tourism Ser.). 384p. 1994. pap. 54.95 (0-471-28508-0, VNR) Wiley.

— The Hotel & Restaurant Business. 6th ed. LC 92-28353. (Illus.). 416p. 1994. pap. 48.95 (0-442-01246-2, VNR) Wiley.

— International Travel & Tourism. 2nd ed. 480p. 1993. 59.95 (0-471-53146-4) Wiley.

Lundberg, Donald E. & Armatas, James P. The Management of People in Hotels & Restaurants. 5th ed. 288p. (C). 1992. text 36.50 (0-697-08416-7) Brown & Benchmark.

Lundberg, Donald E. & Walker, John. The Restaurant: From Concept to Operation. 2nd ed. 400p. 1994. pap. text, teacher ed. write for info. (0-471-30618-5) Wiley.

Lundberg, Donald E. & Walker, John R. The Restaurant: From Concept to Operation. 2nd ed. LC 92-39761. 384p. 1993. 59.95 (0-471-57883-5) Wiley.

Lundberg, Donald E., et al. Tourism Economics. 208p. 1995. 54.95 (0-471-57884-3) Wiley.

Lundberg, Elaine & Thurston, Cheryl M. If They're Laughing: Ideas for Using Humor Effectively in the Classroom - Even If You're Not Funny Yourself. 96p. 1992. pap. text 12.95 (1-877673-14-5, IF) Cottonwood Pr.

Lundberg, Elaine M. No More Bummers! 121 Ways to Add Levity to Your Life. (Illus.). 192p. 1999. pap. 6.95 (0-9670956-0-3) Sockboy Pubns.

Lundberg, Emma O. & Lenrott, Katherine F. Illegitimacy As a Child-Welfare Problem. LC 74-1713. (Children & Youth Ser.: Pts. 1 & 2). 1974. 41.95 (0-405-05972-8) Ayer.

Lundberg, Eric. The Development of Swedish & Keynesian Macroeconomic Policy & Its Impact on Policy. (Raffaele Mattioli Lectures on the History of Economic Thought). 225p. 1996. text 57.95 (0-521-57076-X) Cambridge U Pr.

Lundberg, Erik. Instability & Economic Growth. LC 68-13917. (Studies in Comparative Economics: No. 8). (Illus.). 449p. reprint ed. pap. 139.20 (0-608-10725-5, 202201600024) Bks Demand.

Lundberg, Ferdinand. Imperial Hearst. LC 73-125704. (American Journalists Ser.). 1971. reprint ed. 25.95 (0-405-01685-9) Ayer.

— The Myth of Democracy. 1989. 11.95 (0-8184-0500-7) Carol Pub Group.

— The Natural Depravity of Mankind: Observations on the Human Condition. LC 93-40407. 1994. 15.95 (1-56980-003-0) Barricade Bks.

— Politicians & Other Scoundrels. LC 92-17314. 1992. pap. 7.95 (0-942637-72-0) Barricade Bks.

— Politicians & Other Scoundrels. 160p. 1988. reprint ed. pap. 6.95 (0-8184-0483-3) Carol Pub Group.

— The Rich & Super-Rich. 820p. reprint ed. pap. 14.95 (0-8184-0486-8) Carol Pub Group.

— Rich & the Super-Rich. Brand, Eileen, ed. LC 67-10015. 1968. 15.00 (0-8184-0069-2) Carol Pub Group.

— The Rockefeller Syndrome. LC 75-23031. 1975. 12.50 (0-8184-0215-6) Carol Pub Group.

— The Treason of the People. LC 73-19114. 370p. 1974. reprint ed. lib. bdg. 75.00 (0-8371-7307-8, LUTP, Greenwood Pr) Greenwood.

*Lundberg, Gary B. I Dont Have to Make Everything All Better: Six Practical Principles to Empower Others to Solve. 304p. 2000. pap. 12.95 (0-14-028643-8, Penguin Bks) Viking Penguin.

Lundberg, Gary B. & Lundberg, Joy S. I Don't Have to Make Everything All Better: A Practical Approach to Walking Emotionally with Those You Care About While Empowering Them to Solve Their Own Problems. Christy, Howard A., ed. 344p. 1995. pap. 12.95 (0-915029-02-2) Riverpark Pub.

*Lundberg, Gary B. & Lundberg, Joy S. I Don't Have to Make Everything All Better: 6 Practical Principles That Empower Others to Solve Their Own Problems While Enriching Your Relationships. LC 98-42304. 304p. 1999. 21.95 (0-670-88485-5, Viking) Viking Penguin.

Lundberg, George A. Can Science Save Us? 2nd ed. LC 79-16792. 150p. 1979. reprint ed. lib. bdg. 55.00 (0-313-21299-6, LUCS, Greenwood Pr) Greenwood.

— Foundations of Sociology. LC 79-9742. (Illus.). 179p. 1979. reprint ed. lib. bdg. 38.50 (0-313-21264-3, LUFS, Greenwood Pr) Greenwood.

— Some Neglected Aspects of the 'Minorities' Problem. 1994. lib. bdg. 250.00 (0-8490-5666-7) Gordon Pr.

— Some Neglected Aspects of the 'Minorities' Problems. 1982. lib. bdg. 250.00 (0-87700-411-0) Revisionist Pr.

Lundberg, Gertrude W., compiled by. Cook County Illinois 1850 Federal Census: Not Including the City of Chicago. 1987. pap. 15.00 (1-881125-11-4) Chi Geneal Soc.

*Lundberg, Ingvar, et al, eds. Dyslexia: Advances in Theory & Practice. LC 99-34300. (Neuropsychology & Cognition Ser.). 300p. 1999. 145.00 (0-7923-5837-6) Kluwer Academic.

Lundberg, Joy S., jt. auth. see Lundberg, Gary B.

Lundberg, Kathryn T. Bats for Kids. LC 95-35665. (Wildlife for Kids Ser.). (Illus.). 48p. (Orig.). (J). (gr. 3-7). 1996. pap. 6.95 (1-55971-545-6, NorthWord Pr) Creat Pub Intl.

Lundberg, Lars, jt. ed. see Fagerberg, Jan.

Lundberg, Margaret J. The Incomplete Adult, 15. LC 74-67. (Illus.). 245p. 1974. 59.95 (0-8371-7362-0, LUA/, Greenwood Pr) Greenwood.

Lundberg, Mattias K., jt. auth. see Dorosh, Paul A.

Lundberg, Paul. The Book of Shiatsu. (Illus.). 192p. (Orig.). 1992. pap. 14.95 (0-671-74488-7, Fireside) S&S Trade Pap.

Lundberg, Steven W. & Durant, Stephen C. Electronic & Software Patent Law. 450p. 2000. 245.00 (1-57018-159-4, 1159) BNA Books.

Lundberg, Thomas & Tylczak, Lynn. Slash Your Workers' Comp Costs. LC 97-2281. 192p. 1997. 27.95 (0-8144-0347-6) AMACOM.

Lundberg, Todd, jt. auth. see Lardner, Ted.

Lundbergh, Holger, tr. see Donner, Jorn.

Lundblad, Jane. Nathaniel Hawthorne & European Literary Tradition. (BCL1-PS American Literature Ser.). 196p. 1993. reprint ed. lib. bdg. 69.00 (0-7812-6965-2) Rprt Serv.

— Nathaniel Hawthorne & the Tradition of Gothic Romance. LC 65-15898. (Studies in Hawthorne: No. 15). 1969. reprint ed. lib. bdg. 75.00 (0-8383-0589-X) M S G Haskell Hse.

Lundblad, Roger L. Chemical Reagents for Protein Modification. 2nd ed. LC 83-15076. (Illus.). 352p. 1991. boxed set 195.00 (0-8493-5097-2, QP551, CRC Reprint) Franklin.

— Techniques in Protein Modification. LC 94-11646. 296p. 1994. per. 73.95 (0-8493-2606-0, 2606) CRC Pr.

Lundblad, Roger L. & Noyes, Claudia M. Chemical Reagents for Protein Modification, Vol. 1. LC 83-15076. 192p. 1984. 112.00 (0-8493-5086-7, TP453, CRC Reprint) Franklin.

— Chemical Reagents for Protein Modification, Vol. 2. LC 83-15076. 184p. 1984. 111.00 (0-8493-5087-5, TP453, CRC Reprint) Franklin.

Lundbom, Jack R. The Early Career of the Prophet Jeremiah. LC 93-5511. (Biblical Press Ser.: Vol. 12). 128p. 1993. text 59.95 (0-7734-2372-9, Mellen Biblical Pr) E Mellen.

— Jeremiah: A Study in Ancient Hebrew Rhetoric. LC

75-15732. (Society of Biblical Literature. Dissertation Ser.: No. 18). 209p. reprint ed. 64.80 (*0-8357-9574-8*, 201752000007) Bks Demand.

— Jeremiah: A Study in Ancient Hebrew Rhetoric. 2nd ed. LC 96-53337. 220p. 1997. pap. text 19.50 (*1-57506-016-7*) Eisenbrauns.

— Jeremiah 1-20: A New Translation with Introduction & Commentary. LC 97-35473. (Anchor Bible Ser.). 1998. write for info. (*0-385-49007-0*) Doubleday.

— Master Painter: Warner E. Sollman. LC 99-18430. (Illus.). 260p. 1998. 29.95 (*0-86554-610-X*, H460) Mercer Univ Pr.

Lundborg, Goran. Nerve Injury & Repair. (Illus.). 256p. 1988. text 135.00 (*0-443-03528-8*) Church.

Lundborg, Per. The Economics of Export Embargoes. 128p. 1987. 55.00 (*0-7099-4151-X*, Pub. by C Helm) Routldge.

Lundborg, William. Wish You Were Here! Postcard Views of the Minneapolis Lakes District. (Illus.). 134p. 1996. spiral bd. 19.95 (*0-9655500-0-1*) West Forty-Fourth.

Lundborn, Jack R. Jeremiah 1-20: A New Translation with Introduction & Commentary. 960p. 1999. 49.00 (*0-385-41112-X*) Doubleday.

Lundby, Knut, jt. ed. see Hoover, Stewart M.

Lunde, Anders S. Easy-to-Make Whirligigs. 2nd unabridged ed. (Illus.). 113p. 1996. reprint ed. pap. 7.95 (*0-486-28965-6*) Dover.

— Making Animated Whirligigs. 2nd unabridged ed. LC 98-4576. Orig. Title: More Whirligigs. (Illus.). 160p. 1998. pap. 9.95 (*0-486-40049-2*) Dover.

***Lunde, Anders S.** Whimsical Whirligigs & How to Make Them. LC 00-31390. (Illus.). 2000. pap. 9.95 (*0-486-41233-4*) Dover.

***Lunde, Darrin, et al.** Rodents of Viet Nam. (Illus.). 75p. 2000. pap. write for info. (*1-930465-09-2*) Ctr Biodiv & Conserv.

Lunde, David. Blues for Port City. 24p. (Orig.). 1995. pap. 5.00 (*0-932412-07-6*) Mayapple Pr.

— Calibrations. LC 79-16512. 1980. 8.00 (*0-931588-07-3*); pap. 3.50 (*0-931588-08-1*) Allegany Mtn Pr.

— Heart Transplants & Other Misappropriations. LC 93-36484. 64p. 1996. pap. 14.95 (*0-7734-0008-7*, Mellen Poetry Pr) E Mellen.

Lunde, Erik S. & Noverr, Douglas A., eds. Film History. LC 88-17395. (Selected Course Outlines in Popular Culture Ser.). 300p. (Orig.). (C). 1989. pap. text 16.95 (*1-55876-002-4*) Wiener Pubs Inc.

***Lunde, Henrik O.** Rolfsnes, Ase & Related Families, 2 vols., Set. (Illus.). 912p. 2000. 110.00 (*1-885794-18-5*) E Haga Pub.

— Rolfsnes, Ase & Related Families, Vol. 2. (Illus.). 400p. 2000. 65.00 (*1-885794-21-5*) E Haga Pub.

— Rolfsnes, Ase & Related Families Vol. 1: Later Generations. (Illus.). 512p. 2000. 75.00 (*1-885794-20-7*) E Haga Pub.

— Rolfsnes, Ase og Inngifte Slekter, Bind 2. Kvarme, Alf, tr. (NOR., Illus.). 400p. 2000. 65.00 (*1-885794-23-1*) E Haga Pub.

— Rolfsnes, Ase og Inngifte Slekter, 2 vols., Set. Kvarme, Alf, tr. (NOR., Illus.). 902p. 2000. 110.00 (*1-885794-19-3*) E Haga Pub.

— Rolfsnes, Ase og Inngifte Slekter Bind 1: Seinare Generasjonar. Kvarme, Alf, tr. (NOR., Illus.). 502p. 2000. 75.00 (*1-885794-22-3*) E Haga Pub.

Lunde, Joyce P. Reshaping Curricula: Revitalization Programs at Three Land Grand Universities. Baker, Maurice et al, eds. 288p. (C). 1995. text 35.95 (*1-882982-09-6*) Anker Pub.

Lunde, Karl. John Day. (Illus.). 96p. 1985. 30.00 (*0-932169-00-7*) Tenth Ave Edit.

Lunde, Ken. CJKV Information Processing: Chinese, Japanese, Korean & Vietnamese Computing. 2nd ed. Estabrook, Gigi, ed. (Illus.). 1101p. 1997. pap. 64.95 (*1-56592-224-7*) Thomson Learn.

Lunde, Norman. You Unlimited. LC 65-23608. 1985. reprint ed. pap. 7.95 (*0-87516-249-5*) DeVorss.

Lunde, Paul & Wintle, Justin. A Dictionary of Arabic & Islamic Proverbs. (ARA & ENG.). 200p. 1984. 19.95 (*0-7102-0179-6*, Routledge Thoemms) Routledge.

Lunde, Paul, tr. see Masudi.

Lunde, Paul D. Great Restraint. LC 85-73100. 478p. (Orig.). 1986. 19.95 (*0-935689-07-9*); pap. 12.95 (*0-935689-16-8*) CRI Pubns.

Lundeberg, Mary A., et al, eds. Who Learns What from Cases & How? The Research Base for Teaching with Cases. LC 99-17946. 304p. 1999. 59.95 (*0-8058-2777-3*); pap. 29.95 (*0-8058-2778-1*) L Erlbaum Assocs.

Lundeberg, Philip K. Samuel Colt's Submarine Battery: The Secret & the Enigma. LC 74-7322. (Smithsonian Studies in History & Technology: No. 29). (Illus.). 96p. reprint ed. pap. 30.00 (*0-608-10516-3*, 200422700042) Bks Demand.

Lundeberg, Philip K. & Cohn, Arthur B. The Gunboat Philadelphia & the Defense of Lake Champlain in 1776. expanded rev. ed. LC 95-80935. (Illus.). 102p. 1995. reprint ed. pap. 14.95 (*0-9641856-1-X*) LCMM.

Lundeen, Connie R. Alpha-Pets: A to Z. LC 98-3152. (Illus.). 32p. (J). (gr. k-1). 1998. pap. 10.95 (*1-880090-72-4*, Weasel Bks) Galde Pr.

Lundeen, Gerald W., jt. auth. see Davis, Charles H.

Lundeen, Howard K., et al, eds. The Tenant Retention Solution: A Revolutionary Approach to Commercial Real Estate Management. 238p. 1995. 120.00 (*0-7855-2839-3*, Pub. by R-I-C-S Bks) St Mut.

Lundeen, Howard K., et al. The Tenant Retention Solution: A Revolutionary Approach to Commercial Real Estate Management. LC 95-11791. (Illus.). 238p. 1995. text 49.95 (*1-57203-008-9*, 742) Inst Real Estate.

Lundeen, Jan, jt. auth. see Wagner, Jon.

Lundeen, Joel W., ed. Luther's Works-Index, Vol. 55. LC 86-45197. 512p. 1986. 30.00 (*0-8006-0355-9*, 1-355, Fortress Pr) Augsburg Fortress.

Lundeen, Joyce, jt. auth. see Kapland, Harold M.

***Lundeen, Kathleen.** Knight of the Living Dead: William Blake & the Problem of Ontology. LC 99-87999. 2000. 38.50 (*1-57591-041-1*) Susquehanna U Pr.

Lundeen, Lyman T. Risk & Rhetoric in Religion: Whitehead's Theory of Language & the Discourse of Faith. LC 71-171501. 288p. reprint ed. pap. 89.30 (*0-608-16281-7*, 202686800053) Bks Demand.

Lundeen, Richard O. Manual of Ankle & Foot Arthroscopy. (Manuals in Podiatric Surgery Ser.). (Illus.). 121p. (Orig.). 1991. pap. text 49.00 (*0-443-08694-X*) Church.

Lundegradh, H. Environment & Plants Development. 1330p. 1981. reprint ed. 200.00 (*0-7855-3115-7*, Pub. by Intl Bk Distr) St Mut.

Lundegren, Herberta M., jt. auth. see Farrell, Patricia.

Lundell, Cyrus L. The Vegetation of Peten. LC 77-11507. (Carnegie Institution of Washington. Publications: No. 478). reprint ed. 35.00 (*0-404-16270-3*) AMS Pr.

Lundell, Dean. Sun Tzu's Art of War for Traders & Investors. LC 96-52325. 219p. 1997. 19.95 (*0-07-039141-6*) McGraw.

— Tricks of the Trade. 26p. 1995. text. write for info. (*0-9649955-2-2*); pap. text. write for info. (*0-9649955-3-0*) Osiris Trading.

Lundell, In-Gyeong K. Bridging the Gaps: Contextualization among Korean Churches in America. LC 94-20468. (Asian Thought & Culture Ser.: Vol. 18). XII, 156p. (C). 1995. text 38.95 (*0-8204-2541-9*) P Lang Pubng.

Lundell, Kerth, et al. Criterion Test of Basic Skills. 1974. pap. 65.00 (*0-87879-154-X*) Acad Therapy.

Lundell, Liz. Estates of Old Toronto. LC 98-151448. (Illus.). 176p. 1997. 28.00 (*1-55046-219-9*, Pub. by Boston Mills) Genl Dist Srvs.

— Summer Camp: Great Camps of Algonquin. LC 97-138001. (Illus.). 120p. 1995. 42.95 (*1-55046-092-7*, Pub. by Boston Mills) Genl Dist Srvs.

***Lundell, Liz & Standfield, Don.** Stories from the Bow Seat: The Wisdom & Waggery of Canoe Tripping. (Illus.). 156p. 1999. text 37.95 (*1-55046-188-5*) Boston Mills.

***Lundell, Liz & Stanfield, Donald.** Algonquin: The Park & Its People. (Illus.). 208p. 2001. pap. 24.95 (*0-7710-8233-9*) McCland & Stewart.

***Lundell, Margo.** Bad Puppy. (Lad a Dog Ser.). (J). 1998. 9.09 (*0-606-13561-8*, Pub. by Turtleback) Demco.

Lundell, Margo. Disney Babies A to Z. (Sturdy Shape Bks.). (Illus.). 14p. (J). (ps). 1989. bds. 3.99 (*0-307-12317-0*, 12317, Goldn Books) Gldn Bks Pub Co.

— Disney's 101 Dalmatians: Puppy Roundup. (Illus.). 24p. (J). 1996. pap. text 1.29 (*0-307-98754-X*, Goldn Books) Gldn Bks Pub Co.

— Dream Date. LC 97-67745. (Sabrina, the Teenage Witch Ser.: NO. 2). (Illus.). 32p. (J). (gr. 1-6). 1998. pap. 3.99 (*0-689-82124-7*, Simon Spot) Litle Simon.

— The Enchanted Christmas. LC 97-71691. (Look-Look Bks.). (Illus.). (J). 1997. pap. text 3.29 (*0-307-12974-8*, 12974, Goldn Books) Gldn Bks Pub Co.

— The Furry Bedtime Book: Lovey Bear's Story. LC 95-71772. (Furry Bedtime Bk.). (Illus.). 16p. (J). (ps-1). 1996. 11.95 (*0-590-86371-1*, Cartwheel) Scholastic Inc.

— A Girl Named Helen Keller. LC 94-38219. (Hello Reader! Ser.). (Illus.). 48p. (J). (gr. 2-4). 1995. pap. 3.99 (*0-590-47963-6*, Cartwheel) Scholastic Inc.

— Girl Named Helen Keller. (Hello, Reader! Ser.). 1995. 9.19 (*0-606-09328-1*, Pub. by Turtleback) Demco.

— Lad is Lost. (Lad a Dog Ser.). (J). 1998. 9.19 (*0-606-13560-X*, Pub. by Turtleback) Demco.

Lundell, Margo. Lad to the Rescue. (Hello, Reader! Ser.). (J). 1997. 9.19 (*0-606-11545-5*, Pub. by Turtleback) Demco.

Lundell, Margo. My Book of Funny Valentines. LC 93-178587. (Read with Me Paperback Ser.). (Illus.). 32p. (J). (ps-3). 1993. pap. 2.50 (*0-590-44187-6*) Scholastic Inc.

— What Does Baby See? (Poke & Look Bks.). (Illus.). 16p. (J). (ps-1). 1990. spiral bd., bds. 9.95 (*0-448-19098-2*, G & D) Peng Put Young Read.

— Woody, Be Good! A First Book of Manners. (Illus.). 24p. (J). (ps-2). 1988. 3.95 (*0-448-09288-3*, G & D) Peng Put Young Read.

Lundell, Margo & Driscoll, Laura. Horses: An Abridgment of Harold Roth's Big Book of Horses. LC 97-13765. (All Aboard Reading Ser.). (Illus.). 32p. (J). (ps-3). 1997. pap. 2.95 (*0-448-41735-9*, G & D) Peng Put Young Read.

Lundell, Margo & Terhune, Albert Pason. Lad, a Dog: Best Dog in the World. LC 96-20937. (Hello Reader! Ser.). (Illus.). (J). (gr. 4). 1997. write for info. (*0-590-92974-7*) Scholastic Inc.

— Lad, a Dog: Lad & the Bad Puppy. LC 96-27681. (Hello Reader! Ser.). (Illus.). (J). 1997. 3.99 (*0-590-92981-X*) Scholastic Inc.

— Lad, a Dog: Lad Is Lost. LC 96-27682. (Hello Reader! Ser.). (Illus.). 48p. (J). (gr. 2-4). 1997. 3.99 (*0-590-92978-X*) Scholastic Inc.

— Lad, a Dog: Lad to the Rescue. LC 96-20936. (Hello Reader! Ser.). (Illus.). (J). (gr. 4). 1997. pap. 3.99 (*0-590-92973-9*, Apple Classics) Scholastic Inc.

Lundell, Torborg. Fairy Tale Mothers. (American University Studies: Germanic Languages & Literature: Ser. I, Vol. 82). 304p. (C). 1990. text 53.95 (*0-8204-0980-4*) P Lang Pubng.

Lunden & Asch. Richard Rodgers. (Pop Song Writers Ser.). 2000. 25.00 (*0-02-864842-0*) S&S Trade.

***Lunden, Joan.** Wake-Up Calls: Making the Most Out of Every Day (Regardless or What Life Throws You) (Illus.). 240p. 2000. 21.95 (*0-07-136126-X*) McGraw.

***Lunden, Joan & Cagan, Andrea.** A Bend in the Road Is Not the End of the Road: Ten Positive Principles for Dealing with Change. Set. abr. ed. 1998. audio 18.00 (*0-694-52104-3*, 396214) HarperAudio.

Lunden, Joan & Cagan, Andrea. Joan Lunden's: Bend in the Road. LC 98-27579. (Illus.). 239p. 1998. 25.95 (*0-688-16083-2*, Wm Morrow) Morrow Avon.

Lunden, Joan & Morton, Laura. Joan Lunden's Healthy Cooking. 256p. (gr. 8). 1996. 24.95 (*0-316-53588-5*) Little.

— Joan Lunden's Healthy Cooking. (Illus.). 256p. 1997. pap. 13.95 (*0-316-55726-9*) Little.

Lunden, Richard. Risk-Needs Assessment & Parole Outcome in Massachusetts: An Evaluation Study. (Illus.). 65p. (Orig.). (C). 1993. pap. text 25.00 (*1-56806-902-2*) DIANE Pub.

Lunden, Rolf. Business & Religion in the American, 1920s, Vol. 91. LC 87-17597. (Contributions in American Studies: No. 91). (Illus.). 217p. 1988. 57.95 (*0-313-25151-7*, LBU/, Greenwood Pr) Greenwood.

Lunden, Rolf. The Inevitable Question: The Antithetic Pattern of Theodore Dreiser's Thought & Art. 186p. (Orig.). 1973. pap. text 21.50 (*91-554-0084-1*) Coronet Bks.

Lunden, Rolf & Asard, Erik, eds. Networks of Americanization: Aspects of the American Influence in Sweden. (Studia Anglistica Upsaliensia Ser.: No. 79). 182p. (Orig.). 1992. pap. 46.00 (*91-554-2981-5*) Coronet Bks.

Lunden, Walter A. Crimes & Criminals. LC 66-21643. 353p. reprint ed. pap. 109.50 (*0-608-13457-0*, 202276600029) Bks Demand.

Lundergardh, H., ed. Environment & Plant Development. (C). 1981. text 275.00 (*0-89771-580-2*, Pub. by Intl Bk Distr) St Mut.

Lundervold, Duane A. & Lewin, Lewis M. Behavior Analysis & Therapy in Nursing Homes. (Illus.). 178p. 1992. pap. 34.95 (*0-398-06250-1*) C C Thomas.

— Behavior Analysis & Therapy in Nursing Homes. (Illus.). 178p. (C). 1992. text 47.95 (*0-398-05807-5*) C C Thomas.

Lundestad, Geir. The American Empire: And Other Studies of U. S. Foreign Policy in a Comparative Perspective. 213p. 1991. pap. 35.00 (*82-00-21092-8*) Scandnvan Univ Pr.

***Lundestad, Geir.** East, West, North, South: Major Developments in International Politics since 1945. 4th ed. Kvam, Gail Adams, tr. LC D843.L8413 1999. (Illus.). 376p. (C). 1999. text 50.00 (*0-19-878237-3*); pap. text 25.95 (*0-19-878238-1*) OUP.

Lundestad, Geir. East, West, North, South: Major Developments in International Politics 1945-1990. 2nd ed. 335p. 1992. pap. 29.00 (*82-00-21319-6*) Scandnvan Univ Pr.

— East, West, North, South: Major Developments in International Politics 1945-1996. 3rd ed. LC 98-229478. 368p. 1998. pap. text 24.95 (*82-00-37674-5*) OUP.

— "Empire" by Integration: The United States & European Integration, 1945-1997. LC 97-22509. 210p. 1998. text 85.00 (*0-19-878212-8*) OUP.

— "Empire" by Integration: The United States & European Integration, 1945-1997. LC 97-22509. 210p. 1998. pap. text 19.95 (*0-19-878211-X*) OUP.

— No End to Alliance: The United States & Western Europe: Past, Present, & Future: Nobel Symposium 105. LC 98-23856. 268p. 1998. text 69.95 (*0-312-21761-7*) St Martin.

Lundestad, Geir, ed. The Fall of Great Powers: Peace, Stability & Legitimacy. LC 94-238374. 414p. 1994. 20.00 (*82-00-21922-4*) Scandnvan Univ Pr.

Lundestad, Geir & Westad, Odd A., eds. Beyond the Cold War: New Dimensions in International Relations. 257p. 1993. 34.00 (*82-00-21712-4*) Scandnvan Univ Pr.

Lundgaard, Kris. Enemy Within: Straight Talk about the Power & Defeat of Sin. 1998. pap. 8.99 (*0-87552-201-7*) P & R Pubng.

***Lundgaard, Kris.** Through the Looking Glass: Reflections on Christ that Change Us. 230p. 2000. pap. 9.99 (*0-87552-199-1*) P & R Pubng.

Lundgaard, Kris, jt. auth. see Bailey, T. E.

Lundgreen-Nielsen, Kay. The Polish Problem at the Paris Peace Conference: A Study of the Great Powers & the Poles, 1918-1919. (Odense Studies in History & Social Sciences: No. 59). 603p. (Orig.). 1979. pap. 42.50 (*87-7492-261-0*, Pub. by Odense Universitets Forlag) Coronet Bks.

Lundgren, Anders. Technological Innovation & Network Evolution. LC 94-10897. 304p. (C). 1994. pap. 81.95 (*0-415-08219-6*, B4764) Thomson Learn.

Lundgren, Anders & Bensande-Vincent, Bernadette, eds. Chemical Textbook, 1800-1930: Studies in Their Use & Functions. LC 99-52211. (European Studies in Science History & the Arts: No. 3). (Illus.). 465p. 2000. 56.00 (*0-88135-274-8*, Sci Hist) Watson Pub Intl.

Lundgren, Anna, ed. see Evans, David.

Lundgren, Anna, ed. see Wilson, Sarah.

Lundgren, Carol A., et al. Teaching Computer Applications. (Illus.). 66p. (Orig.). (C). 1996. pap. text 20.00 (*1-881530-01-9*) Delta Pi Epsilon.

Lundgren, Christopher. Electra. 330p. 1999. pap. 4.95 (*0-9672454-0-0*) C Lundgren.

Lundgren, Claes & Miller, John M., eds. The Lung at Depth. LC 99-22838. (Lung Biology in Health & Disease Ser.). (Illus.). 712p. 1999. text 225.00 (*0-8247-0158-5*) Dekker.

Lundgren, Dale A., et al. Airborne Pollutants: Characteristics & Detection. (Air Pollution Ser.: Vol. 7). 153p. (C). 1974. text 27.00 (*0-8422-7158-9*) Irvington.

Lundgren, Dale A., ed. see Aerosol Measurement Workshop Staff.

Lundgren, Eva. Feminist Theory & Violent Empiricism. 456p. 1995. 91.95 (*1-85628-541-3*, Pub. by Avebry) Ashgate Pub Co.

Lundgren, Jane. Acute Neuroscience Nursing: Concepts & Care. 400p. (C). 1986. 56.25 (*0-86720-355-2*) Jones & Bartlett.

Lundgren, Laura, tr. see Von Sacher-Masoch, Leopold.

Lundgren, Lawrence. Environmental Geology. 2nd ed. LC 98-45002. 511p. 1998. 76.67 (*0-13-792813-0*) P-H.

Lundgren, Linnea. The Best Places to Kiss in Northern California: A Romantic Travel Guide. 5th rev. ed. Fulsaas, Kris, ed. (Best Places to Kiss Ser.). 414p. 1999. pap. 16.95 (*1-877988-27-8*, Pub. by Beginning Pr) Publishers Group.

Lundgren, Linnea, jt. auth. see Kraemer, Laura.

Lundgren, Maja-Brita & Wendt, Leni. Acquarossa Vol. III: Zone A. (Acta Instituti Romani Regni Sueciae, Series in 4 Degrees: Vol. XXXVIII:III). (Illus.). 106p. 1982. pap. 49.50 (*91-7042-083-1*, Pub. by P Astroms) Coronet Bks.

Lundgren, Mary B. We Sing the City. LC 93-34860. (Illus.). 32p. (J). (gr. k-3). 1997. 14.95 (*0-395-68188-X*, Clarion Bks) HM.

Lundgren, Regina E. & McMakin, Andrea H. Risk Communication: A Handbook for Communicating Environmental, Safety, & Health Risks. 2nd ed. LC 98-23239. 342p. 1998. pap. 29.95 (*1-57477-055-1*) Battelle.

Lundgren, Regina E., jt. auth. see Gephart, R. E.

Lundgren, Shirley & Young, Woody. One Hundred Plus Desserts & Appetizers. (Illus.). 96p. 1992. pap. 9.95 (*0-939513-63-3*) Joy Pub SJC.

Lundgren, Stefan, jt. auth. see Carlsson, Olle.

Lundgren, Svante. Fight Against Idols: Erich Fromm on Religion, Judaism & the Bible. LC 98-9391. 193p. (C). 1998. pap. text 37.95 (*0-8204-3557-0*) P Lang Pubng.

— Fight Against Idols: Erich Fromm on Religion, Judaism & the Bible. 193p. 1998. pap. 37.95 (*3-631-32757-9*) P Lang Pubng.

Lundgren, Terry. Systems Analysis & Design. (C). 1996. 62.00 (*0-02-372671-7*, Macmillan Coll) P-H.

Lundgren, Ulf P. Between Education & Schooling: Outline of a Diachronic Curriculum Theory. 73p. (C). 1991. pap. 60.00 (*0-7300-1242-5*, ECS802, Pub. by Deakin Univ) St Mut.

— Frame Factors & the Teaching Process: A Contribution to Curriculum Theory & Theory on Teaching. (Goteborg Studies in Educational Sciences: No. 8). 378p. (Orig.). 1972. pap. 67.50 (*0-317-65794-1*) Coronet Bks.

***Lundgren, Wolf.** The Renos. 256p. 2000. 18.99 (*0-7089-5692-0*) Ulverscroft.

Lundgvist, Lars & Persson, Lars O. Visions & Strategies in European Integration: A Northern European Perspective. LC 93-1585. 1993. 111.95 (*0-387-56615-5*) Spr-Verlag.

Lundh, Christer, ed. Demography, Economy & Welfare. (Scandinavian Population Studies: Vol. 10). 493p. 1995. pap. 77.50 (*91-7966-321-4*) Coronet Bks.

Lundh, Dan, et al, eds. Biocomputing & Emergent Computation: Proceedings of BCEC97 Skovde, Sweden 1-2 September, 1997. 320p. 1997. 68.00 (*981-02-3262-4*) World Scientific Pub.

Lundh, Lennart. H-34 Choctaw in Action. (Aircraft in Action Ser.). (Illus.). 50p. 1994. pap. 9.95 (*0-89747-319-1*) Squad Sig Pubns.

— Sikorsy H-34: An Illustrated History. LC 97-80805. (Illus.). 160p. 1998. pap. 24.95 (*0-7643-0522-0*) Schiffer.

***Lundh, Lennart.** US Army Aviation Color Schemes & Markings,1942-present. (Illus.). 192p. 2000. 49.95 (*0-7643-1180-8*) Schiffer.

Lundholm, Andrew S. Ssri Circ Simulatn Optim. LC 92-23513. (Six Sigma Research Institute Ser.). 1993. pap. text 21.95 (*0-201-63427-9*) Addison-Wesley.

Lundie, Catherine A., ed. Restless Spirits: Ghost Stories by American Women, 1872-1926. LC PS648 G48R47 1996. 328p. 1996. 55.00 (*1-55849-055-8*) U of Mass Pr.

— Restless Spirits: Ghost Stories by American Women, 1872-1926. LC 96-19250. 328p. 1996. pap. 19.95 (*1-55849-056-6*) U of Mass Pr.

Lundin. Role of Gene Duplications in Metazoan Evolution. 256p. 1997. text. write for info. (*0-412-75520-3*, Chap & Hall NY) Chapman & Hall.

Lundin, Anne H. & Cubberley, Carol W. Teaching Children's Literature: A Resource Guide, with a Directory of Courses. LC 94-32679. 363p. 1994. lib. bdg. 45.00 (*0-89950-990-8*) McFarland & Co.

Lundin, Anne H., jt. ed. see Lundin, G. Edward.

Lundin, Brien F., ed. see Veneroso, Frank.

Lundin, C. E., jt. ed. see Nachman, Joseph F.

Lundin, Carl G., jt. auth. see Post, Jan.

Lundin, Carl G., jt. auth. see Zilinskas, Raymond A.

***Lundin, Deanne.** The Ginseng Hunter's Notebook. LC 98-67449. (Illus.). 1999. write for info. (*0-932826-71-7*) New Issues MI.

Lundin, Deanne. The Ginseng Hunter's Notebook: Poems. LC 98-67449. (Poetry Ser.). 64p. 1999. pap. 12.00 (*0-932826-72-5*) WMU Poetry & Prose.

Lundin, G. Edward & Lundin, Anne H., eds. Contemporary Religious Ideas: Bibliographic Essays. (Illus.). 650p. 1996. lib. bdg. 87.50 (*0-87287-679-9*) Libs Unl.

Lundin, Irwin, jt. auth. see Kleim, Ralph.

Lundin, Jon W. Rockford: An Illustrated History. LC 96-78830. (Illus.). 220p. 1996. 37.95 (*0-9654754-1-7*) Am Historical Pr.

Lundin, Kathleen, jt. auth. see Lundin, William.

Lundin, Keith M. Chapter 13 Bankruptcy, 1997-98 Cumulative Supplement. 2nd ed. 1168p. 1997. pap. 140.00 (*0-9661805-1-8*) Bankruptcy Pr.

Lundin, Lena. On Building-Related Causes of Sick Building Syndrome. (Illus.). 314p. (Orig.). 1992. pap. 52.50 (*91-22-01466-7*) Coronet Bks.

L

Lundin, Norman, et al. Drawing: At the Henry. LC 80-17746. (Illus.). 56p. 1980. pap. 5.95 (*0-935558-06-3*) Henry Art.

Lundin, Rickard, et al, eds. The Freja Mission. LC 94-46544. 1995. text 107.00 (*0-7923-3317-9*) Kluwer Academic.

Lundin, Robert. Agency Compensation: A Guidebook. 1995. pap. 39.50 (*1-56318-018-9*) Assn Natl Advertisers.

— Trends in Agency Compensation - 1998. 11th ed. (Orig.). 1998. pap. 44.95 (*1-56318-057-X*) Assn Natl Advertisers.

Lundin, Robert, ed. see Starr, Randy.

Lundin, Robert W. Theories & Systems of Psychology. 5th ed. 432p. (C). 1996. text 63.96 (*0-669-35446-5*) HM Trade Div.

Lundin, Roger. Disciplining Hermeneutics: Interpretation in Christian Perspective. LC 97-4925. 185p. 1997. pap. text 18.00 (*0-8028-0858-1*) Eerdmans.

— Emily Dickinson & the Art of Belief. 272p. 1998. 24.00 (*0-8028-3857-X*); pap. text 16.00 (*0-8028-0157-9*) Eerdmans.

Lundin, Roger & Gallagher, Susan. Literature Through the Eyes of Faith: Christian College Coalition Series. LC 88-45684. (Christian College Coalition Ser.). 192p. 1989. pap. 13.00 (*0-06-065318-3*, Pub. by Harper SF) HarpC.

Lundin, Roger & Noll, Mark A., eds. Voices from the Heart: Four Centuries of American Piety. LC 87-441. 414p. reprint ed. pap. 128.40 (*0-7837-3183-3*, 204278700006) Bks Demand.

***Lundin, Roger, et al.** The Promise of Hermeneutics. LC 99-12924. 272p. 1999. pap. 20.00 (*0-8028-4635-1*) Eerdmans.

***Lundin, Rolf A. & Hartman, Francis T.** Projects as Business Constituents & Guiding Motives. 280p. 2000. 120.00 (*0-7923-7834-2*) Kluwer Academic.

***Lundin, Rolf A. & Midler, Christopher.** Projects As Arenas for Renewal & Learning Processes. LC 98-26076. 29p. 1998. write for info. (*0-7923-8124-6*) Kluwer Academic.

Lundin, S. J., ed. Verification of Dual-Use Chemicals under the Chemical Weapons Convention: The Use of Thiodiglycol. (SIPRI Chemical & Biological Warfare Studies: No. 13). (Illus.). 156p. 1992. pap. text 39.95 (*0-19-829156-6*) OUP.

— Views on Possible Verification Measures for the Biological Weapons Convention. (SIPRI Chemical & Biological Warfare Studies: No. 12). 140p. 1991. pap. text 39.95 (*0-19-829142-6*, 12316) OUP.

Lundin, Stephen C. & Arnold, James K. Personal Accountability: Your Path to a Rewarding Work Life. (Illus.). 52p. 1997. pap. 7.95 (*0-9661944-0-3*) Charthouse Intl.

Lundin, Stephen C., et al. Fish! A Remarkable Way to Boost Morale & Improve Results. LC 99-49306. 112p. 2000. 19.95 (*0-7868-6602-0*, Pub. by Hyperion) Time Warner.

***Lundin, Steve.** Revolvo & Other Canadian Tales. LC 98-126183. 160p. 1998. pap. 12.95 (*0-920661-58-0*) TSAR Pubns.

***Lundin, Susanne & Akesson, Lynn, eds.** Amalgamations: Fusing Technology & Culture. 2000. pap. 32.50 (*91-89116-07-0*, Pub. by Nordic Acad Pr) Intl Spec Bk.

Lundin, Susanne & Ideland, Malin, eds. Gene Technology & the Public: An Interdisciplinary Perspective. 1997. pap. 25.95 (*91-89116-00-3*, Pub. by Nordic Acad Pr) Intl Spec Bk.

Lundin, Tom, Jr. Intro to Insurance Company Accounting. (Step One Ser.). 140p. spiral bd. 34.95 (*1-57974-056-1*, Pub. by Life Office) PBD Inc.

Lundin, Tom, Jr. Supplement to Canadian Life & Health Insurance Law. LC 99-70641. (FLMI Insurance Education Program Ser.). pap. text, suppl. ed. 19.95 (*1-57974-025-1*, Pub. by Life Office) PBD Inc.

Lundin, William & Lundin, Kathleen. The Healing Manager: How to Build Quality Relationships & Productive Cultures at Work. LC 93-2704. (Illus.). 312p. 1993. 27.95 (*1-881052-13-3*) Berrett-Koehler.

— When Smart People Work for Dumb Bosses: How to Survive in a Crazy & Dysfunctional Workplace. LC 98-17907. 240p. 1998. 21.95 (*0-07-039147-5*, BusinessWeek Bks) McGraw.

— When Smart People Work for Dumb Bosses: How to Survive in a Crazy & Dysfunctional Workplace. 1999. reprint ed. pap. 12.95 (*0-07-134808-5*) McGraw.

— Working with Difficult People. LC 95-24862. (WorkSmart Ser.). 128p. (Orig.). 1995. pap. 10.95 (*0-8144-7838-7*) AMACOM.

Lundius, Jan. The Great Power of God in the San Juan Valley: Syncretism & Messianism in the Dominican Republic. (Lund Studies in History of Religions: No. 4). 418p. (Orig.). 1995. pap. 67.50 (*91-22-01674-0*) Coronet Bks.

Lundius, Jan & Lundahl, Mats. Peasants & Religion: A Socioeconomic Study of Dios Olivorio & the Palma Sola Movement in the Dominican Republic LC 99-24619. 1999. write for info. (*0-415-17411-2*) Routledge.

Lundkvist, Artur. Journeys in Dream & Imagination. Weissmann, Ann B. & Planck, Annika, trs. 132p. 1991. 17.95 (*0-941423-67-0*) FWEW.

— The Talking Tree: Poems in Prose. Wormuth, Diana W. & Sondrup, Steven P., trs. from SPA. LC 82-14606. xviii, 201p. 1983. 9.95 (*0-8425-2099-6*, Friends of the Library) Brigham.

Lundkvist, Sven, jt. ed. see Alekseyev, Veniamin.

Lundman, Peter, jt. ed. see Erdman, David V.

Lundman, Richard J. Prevention & Control of Juvenile Delinquency. 2nd ed. (Illus.). 304p. (C). 1993. pap. text 21.95 (*0-19-506407-0*) OUP.

Lundman, Richard J., jt. auth. see Ermann, M. David.

***Lundon, Katie.** Orthopedic Rehabilitation Science: Principles for Clinical M. LC 99-39419. (Illus.). 224p. 1999. pap. text 52.50 (*0-7506-7155-6*) Buttrwrth-Heinemann.

Lundow, Merry. Discovering Country Walks in North London. (Handbook Ser.: No. 240). (Illus.). 88p. pap. 8.50 (*0-7478-0265-3*, Pub. by Shire Pubns) Parkwest Pubns.

Lundquist. Industrial Electrical Troubleshooting. LC 99-49721. (Electrical Trades Ser.). 1999. pap. 36.95 (*0-7668-0603-0*) Delmar.

Lundquist, Eric G. Salvage of Water Damaged Books, Documents, Micrographic & Magnetic Media. 144p. (Orig.). 1986. pap. 12.95 (*0-9616850-0-X*) Doc Reprocessors.

Lundquist, Gunar, jt. auth. see Spehr, Paul C.

***Lundquist, Joegil K.** English from the Roots Up: Help for Reading, Writing, Spelling & S. A. T. Scores. 1999. 37.95 (*1-885942-12-5*) Cune.

Lundquist, Joegil K. English from the Roots Up: Help for Reading, Writing, Spelling & S. A. T. Scores, Vol. I. 125p. 1989. pap. 27.95 (*0-9643210-3-3*) Lit Unltd.

Lundquist, John M. The Temple. LC 92-62138. (Art & Imagination Ser.). (Illus.). 96p. 1993. pap. 15.95 (*0-500-81040-0*, Pub. by Thames Hudson) Norton.

Lundquist, Karen, ed. & frwd. see Bamburak, Gary P.

Lundquist, Kathleen F. SuperWoman's Rite of Passage: From Midlife to Whole Life. LC 95-47533. 240p. 1996. pap. 14.95 (*1-56718-447-2*) Llewellyn Pubns.

Lundquist, Lennart. The Party & the Masses: Lenin's Model for the Bolshevik Revolution. LC 82-8505. 336p. 1982. lib. bdg. 40.00 (*0-941320-03-0*) Transnatl Pubs.

Lundquist, Leslie, jt. auth. see Lynch, Daniel C.

Lundquist, Leslie Heeter. Selling Online for Dummies: A Reference for the Rest of Us. LC 98-70129. (For Dummies Ser.). 384p. 1998. pap. 24.99 incl. cd-rom (*0-7645-0334-0*) IDG Bks.

***Lundquist, Lita & Jarvella, R. J.** Language, Text & Knowledge: Mental Models of Expert Communication. LC 00-35163. 2000. write for info. (*3-11-016724-7*) De Gruyter.

Lundquist, Lynn. On-Line Electrical Troubleshooting. 240p. 1989. text 47.00 (*0-07-039110-6*) McGraw.

— The Tetragrammaton & the Christian Greek Scriptures. 216p. 1996. pap. 9.95 (*1-883858-66-6*) Witness CA.

Lundquist, N., jt. auth. see Ahlberg, A. W.

***Lundquist, Richard.** What We Come in For: Stories. 192p. 2000. pap. 17.95 (*0-8262-1270-0*) U of Mo Pr.

Lundquist, Suzanne. The Trickster: A Transformation Archetype. LC 90-29311. 128p. 1991. lib. bdg. 59.95 (*0-7734-9958-X*) E Mellen.

Lundqvist, Jan. The Economic Structure of Morogoro Town: Some Sectoral & Regional Characteristics of a Medium-Sized African Town. (Research Report Ser.: No. 17). 70p. 1973. write for info. (*91-7106-068-5*, Pub. by Nordic Africa) Transaction Pubs.

Lundqvist, Jan, et al, eds. Strategies for River Basin Management: Environmental Integration of Land & Water in a River Basin. LC 85-18293. 1985. lib. bdg. 162.50 (*90-277-2111-4*) Kluwer Academic.

Lundqvist, Jan, jt. auth. see Lindskog, Per.

***Lundqvist, L., et al, eds.** Network Infrastructure & the Urban Environment: Advances in Spatial Systems Modelling. LC 98-28004. (Advances in Spatial Science Ser.). (Illus.). x, 414p. 1998. 99.00 (*3-540-64585-3*) Spr-Verlag.

Lundqvist, L. J. Dislodging the Welfare State? Housing a Privatisation in Four European Nations. 160p. (Orig.). 1992. pap. 42.50 (*90-6275-771-5*, Pub. by Delft U Pr) Coronet Bks.

Lundqvist, Nils & Moberg, Roland, eds. Hymenomycetes in the Perspective of 200 Years. LC 97-106146. (Symbolae Botanicae Upsalienisa Ser.: No. XXX:3). (Illus.). 212p. (Orig.). 1995. pap. 49.50 (*91-554-3571-8*) Coronet Bks.

Lundqvist, S. & March, N. H. Theory of the Inhomogeneous Electron Gas. (Physics of Solids & Liquids Ser.). (Illus.). 408p. (C). 1983. text 125.00 (*0-306-41207-1*, Kluwer Plenum) Kluwer Academic.

Lundqvist, S., et al. Order & Chaos in Nonlinear Physical Systems. LC 88-15113. (Physics of Solids & Liquids Ser.). (Illus.). 488p. (C). 1988. text 135.00 (*0-306-42847-4*, Kluwer Plenum) Kluwer Academic.

Lundqvist, S. O., ed. Nobel Lectures in Physics 1971-1980. 600p. (C). 1994. text 97.00 (*981-02-0726-3*) World Scientific Pub.

Lundqvist, S. O., ed. Nobel Lectures in Physics 1971-1980. 600p. (C). 1994. pap. text 48.00 (*981-02-0727-1*) World Scientific Pub.

Lundqvist, S. O., et al, eds. High Temperature Superconductivity: Proceedings of the Adriatic Research Conference. (Progress in High Temperature Superconductivity Ser.: Vol. 1). 532p. (C). 1987. pap. 58.00 (*9971-5-0400-6*); text 153.00 (*9971-5-0399-9*) World Scientific Pub.

— Path Summation: Achievements & Goals. 536p. (C). 1988. pap. 48.00 (*9971-5-0700-5*); text 117.00 (*9971-5-0597-5*) World Scientific Pub.

— Towards the Theoretical Understanding of High Temperature Superconductors: ICTP, Trieste, Italy, June 20-July 29, 1988. (Progress in High Temperature Superconductivity Ser.: Vol. XIV). 808p. 1988. pap. 53.00 (*9971-5-0640-8*); text 138.00 (*9971-5-0639-4*) World Scientific Pub.

Lundqvist, S. O. & Cerdeira, Hilda A., eds. Frontiers in Physics: High Technology & Mathematics. 328p. (C). 1990. pap. 36.00 (*981-02-0173-7*); text 130.00 (*981-02-0172-9*) World Scientific Pub.

Lundqvist, S. O. & Nilsson, N. R., eds. Nobel Symposium '73, Physics of Low-Dimensional Systems. 168p. (C). 1989. text 81.00 (*9971-5-0971-7*); pap. text 36.00 (*9971-5-0972-5*) World Scientific Pub.

Lundqvist, Thomas. Cognitive Dysfunctions in Chronic Cannabis Users Observed During Treatment: An Integrative Approach. (Studia Psychologica et Paedagogica). 282p. (Orig.). 1995. pap. 52.50 (*91-22-01699-6*) Coronet Bks.

Lundrigan, Margaret & Navarra, Tova. Levittown, Vol. II. (Images of America Ser.). (Illus.). 128p. 1998. pap. 16.99 (*0-7524-0982-4*) Arcadia Publng.

— Staten Island in the Twentieth Century. LC 98-85877. (Images of America Ser.). (Illus.). 128p. 1998. pap. 16.99 (*0-7524-1243-4*) Arcadia Publng.

Lundrigan, Margaret, et al. Staten Island. (Images of America Ser.). 1999. pap. 16.99 (*0-7524-0855-0*) Arcadia Publng.

Lundrigan, Margaret, jt. auth. see Navarra, Tova.

***Lundrigan, Paul S.** Treating Youth Who Sexually Abuse: An Integrated Multi-Component Approach. LC 00-33532. 2000. write for info. (*0-7890-0937-4*) Haworth Pr.

***Lundrigan, Robert F. & Borchert, James R.** The Challenge: Increasing Profits Through Focused Management. 196p. (Orig.). 2000. pap. 19.95 (*0-9678283-0-9*) R Lundrigan.

Lundrigan, Ted N. Hunting the Sun: A Passion for Grouse. DeLaurier, Art, Jr., ed. LC 97-21759. (Illus.). 248p. 1997. 30.00 (*0-924357-70-3*, 21500-A) Countrysport Pr.

— Hunting the Sun: A Passion for Grouse. limited ed. DeLaurier, Art, Jr., ed. (Illus.). 248p. 1997. lthr. 95.00 (*0-924357-71-1*, 21550-B) Countrysport Pr.

Lundrstrom, S. F. Defining the Global Information Infrastructure: Infrastructure, Systems, & Services. 554p. 1994. 30.00 (*0-8194-1680-0*) SPIE.

Lundsager, Soren, jt. auth. see Tuve, Merle A.

Lundsgaard-Hansen, P., ed. Surgical Hemotherapy. (Bibliotheca Haematologica Ser.: No. 46). (Illus.). viii, 252p. 1980. pap. 78.50 (*3-8055-0361-X*) S Karger.

Lundsgaard-Hansen, P. & Blauhut, B., eds. Albumin & Systematic Circulation. (Current Studies in Hematology & Blood Transfusion: No. 53). (Illus.). xiv, 234p. 1986. 154.00 (*3-8055-4367-0*) S Karger.

Lundskr-Nielsen, Tom, jt. auth. see Holmes, Philip.

Lundsted, Betty. Astrological Insights into Personality. 368p. (Orig.). 1982. pap. 16.95 (*0-917086-22-8*) ACS Pubns.

— Planetary Cycles: That Get You from Beginning to End Without a Guide. LC 84-51107. (Illus.). 194p. (Orig.). 1984. pap. 12.95 (*0-87728-630-2*) Weiser.

— Transits: The Time of Your Life. LC 83-159289. 176p. 1980. reprint ed. pap. 9.95 (*0-87728-503-9*) Weiser.

Lundstedt, Sven B. & Dervin, Brenda, eds. Telecommunications, Values & the Public Interest. LC 90-999. (Communication & Information Science Ser.). 320p. (C). 1990. pap. 39.50 (*0-89391-733-8*); text 73.25 (*0-89391-693-5*) Ablx Pub.

Lundsteen, C. & Piper, J., eds. Automation of Cytogenetics. (Illus.). 335p. 1989. 101.95 (*0-387-51105-9*, 2914) Spr-Verlag.

Lundstrohm, Torsten, jt. auth. see Aronsson, Bertil.

Lundstrom, Boyce. Advanced Fusing Techniques Glass Fusing Book Two. Lundstrom, Kathleen, ed. LC 83-50657. (Illus.). 144p. (Orig.). 1989. pap. 40.00 (*0-9612282-1-0*) Vitreous Pubns.

— Glass Casting & Moldmaking: Glass Fusing, Bk. III. Lundstrom, Kathleen, ed. LC 83-50657. 144p. (Orig.). 1989. pap. 40.00 (*0-9612282-2-9*) Vitreous Pubns.

Lundstrom, Boyce & Lundstrom, Kathleen. Kiln Firing Glass Bk. 1: Glass Fusing. 2nd ed. LC 94-60542. (Illus.). 137p. 1994. pap. text 30.00 (*0-9612282-3-7*) Vitreous Pubns.

Lundstrom, David E. A Few Good Men from Univac. LC 97-46740. 248p. 1997. reprint ed. lib. bdg. 34.95 (*0-7351-0010-1*) Replica Bks.

Lundstrom, Johan. The History of the Sodefors Anchorworks 1791. Hedin, Lars-Erik, tr. (Kress Library of Business & Economics Publication: No. 21). (Illus.). ix, 83p. 1970. pap. 9.95 (*0-678-09915-4*) Kelley.

Lundstrom, John B. The First Team: Pacific Naval Air Combat from Pearl Harbor to Midway. LC 84-9822. (Illus.). 576p. 1984. 49.95 (*0-87021-189-7*) Naval Inst Pr.

— The First Team & the Guadalcanal Campaign: Naval Fighter Combat from August to November 1942. LC 93-8184. (Illus.). 626p. 1993. 49.95 (*1-55750-526-8*) Naval Inst Pr.

Lundstrom, John B., jt. auth. see Ewing, Steve.

Lundstrom, Karl J. North-Eastern Ethiopia: Society in Famine. A Study of Three Social Institutions in a Period of Severe Strain. (Research Report Ser.: No. 34). 80p. 1976. write for info. (*91-7106-098-7*, Pub. by Nordic Africa) Transaction Pubs.

Lundstrom, Kathleen, jt. auth. see Lundstrom, Boyce.

Lundstrom, Kathleen, ed. see Lundstrom, Boyce.

Lundstrom, Lowell. Heaven's Answer for the Home. 143p. 1985. mass mkt. 5.99 (*0-938220-16-0*) Whitaker Hse.

— Oracion de Poder.Tr. of How You Can Pray with Power. (SPA.). 160p. 1983. pap. 5.99 (*0-8297-1361-1*) Vida Pubs.

— Praying with Power. Orig. Title: How You Can Pray with Power & Get Results. 263p. 1984. mass mkt. 5.99 (*0-88368-470-5*) Whitaker Hse.

— Que Va-T-Il Arriver? Cosson, Annie L., ed. Chardenal, Valerie, tr. from ENG.Tr. of What's Coming Next. (FRE.). 304p. 1985. mass mkt. 4.75 (*0-8297-0435-3*) Vida Pubs.

***Lundstrom, Mark.** Fundamentals of Carrier Transport. 2nd ed. LC 99-49980. (Illus.). 425p. (C). 2000. 54.95 (*0-521-63134-3*) Cambridge U Pr.

Lundstrom, Mark S. Fundamentals of Carrier Transport. Vol. IX. (Illus.). 288p. (C). 1990. text. write for info. (*0-318-66312-0*) Addison-Wesley.

Lundstrom, Meg, jt. auth. see Belitz, Charlene.

Lundstrom, Rinda F. William Poel's Hamlets: The Director As Critic. LC 84-22. (Theater & Dramatic Studies: No. 20). (Illus.). 204p. reprint ed. pap. 58.20 (*0-8357-1547-7*, 2070489) Bks Demand.

Lundstrom, Stephen F., ed. Defining the Global Information Infrastructure Vol. CR56: Infrastructure, Systems & Services. 554p. 1994. 100.00 (*0-8194-1681-9*) SPIE.

Lundstrom, Tommy & Wijkstrom, Filip. Defining the Nonprofit Sector: Sweden. Salamon, Lester M. & Anheier, Helmut K., eds. (Working Papers of the Johns Hopkins Comparative Nonprofit Sector Project: No. 16). (Illus.). 28p. 1995. pap. text 6.00 (*1-886333-06-8*) JH Univ Inst Pol Studies.

— The Nonprofit Sector in Sweden. LC 97-13575. (Johns Hopkins Nonprofit Sector Ser.). 1998. text. write for info. (*0-7190-5126-6*) Manchester Univ Pr.

— The Nonprofit Sector in Sweden. LC 97-13575. (Johns Hopkins Nonprofit Sector Ser.). 304p. 1998. 69.95 (*0-7190-5125-8*, Pub. by Manchester Univ Pr) St Martin.

Lundt, Henry, jt. auth. see Israel, John.

Lundvall, Bengt-Ake. National Systems of Innovation: Towards a Theory of Innovation & Interactive Learning. 1995. pap. 29.95 (*1-85567-338-X*) St Martin.

Lundvall, Bengt-Ake, jt. ed. see Freeman, Chris.

Lundwall, N. B. Lectures on Faith. pap. 5.95 (*0-88494-442-5*) Bookcraft Inc.

— Temples of the Most High. deluxe ed. 1993. 12.95 (*0-88494-875-7*) Bookcraft Inc.

Lundwall, Paul W. Lundwall. Lundwalls, Gustavsons, & Allied Swedish Families: Family History, Biography & More. Wright, Wm. E., ed. (Illus.). 71p. 1998. pap. 15.50 (*0-8328-9679-9*) Higginson Bk Co.

— Lundwall. Lundwalls, Gustavsons, & Allied Swedish Families: Family History, Biography & More. Wright, William E., ed. (Illus.). 71p. 1998. lib. bdg. 25.50 (*0-8328-9678-0*) Higginson Bk Co.

Lundy. Neuroscience. (C). 1998. text 49.95 (*0-7216-4717-0*, W B Saunders Co) Harcrt Hlth Sci Grp.

***Lundy & Cooling.** Strategic Human Resource Management. 2nd ed. 2001. pap. write for info. (*1-86152-584-2*) Thomson Learn.

Lundy, A. L. Feasibility of Underwater Welding of Highly Irradiated in-Vessel Components of Boiling-Water Reactors: A Literature Review. 48p. 1997. pap. 4.50 (*0-16-054783-0*) USGPO.

Lundy, Angela V. Uphill Journey: Between Two Worlds. 104p. 1998. pap. 12.00 (*1-888434-04-X*) Ecnerret Pub.

Lundy, Benjamin. The Life, Travels & Opinions of Benjamin Lundy. (American Biography Ser.). 316p. 1991. reprint ed. lib. bdg. 79.00 (*0-7812-8253-5*) Rprt Serv.

— The Life Travels & Opinions of Benjamin Lundy: Including His Journeys to Texas. Earle, Thomas, ed. LC 76-136302. 316p. 1971. reprint ed. lib. bdg. 49.50 (*0-678-00809-4*) Kelley.

Lundy, Bob. Relief Carving with Bob Lundy. LC 92-60641. (Illus.). 96p. 1992. pap. 14.95 (*0-88740-439-1*) Schiffer.

Lundy, Charles W. Robbing the One-Armed Bandits: Finding & Exploiting an Advantageous Slot. 1999. pap. 14.95 (*0-910575-10-X*) RGE Publishing.

***Lundy, Charlotte.** Thank You, Mary. Waldrep, Evelyn L., ed. LC 00-131764. (Illus.). 32p. (J). (ps-3). 2001. 15.95 (*0-9670280-6-X*) Bay Light.

Lundy, Charlotte. Thank You, Moses. Waldrep, Evelyn L., ed. LC 99-72124. (Illus.). 32p. (J). (gr. k-5). 2000. 15.95 (*0-9670280-3-5*) Bay Light.

— Thank You, Noah. Waldrep, Evelyn L., ed. LC 99-72123. (Illus.). 32p. (J). (gr. k-5). 2000. 15.95 (*0-9670280-2-7*) Bay Light.

***Lundy, Charlotte.** Thank You, Paul. Waldrep, Evelyn L., ed. LC 00-131765. (Illus.). 32p. (J). (ps-3). 2001. 15.95 (*0-9670280-7-8*) Bay Light.

Lundy, Daniel, ed. see Brown, Gene.

***Lundy, David.** We Are the World: Globalisation & the Changing Face of Missions. 174p. 1999. reprint ed. mass mkt. 9.99 (*1-85078-342-X*, Pub. by O M Pubng) OM Literature.

Lundy, Derek. Godforsaken Sea: Racing the World's Most Dangerous Waters. LC 98-56209. 304p. 1999. 22.95 (*1-56512-229-1*, 72229) Algonquin Bks.

***Lundy, Derek.** Godforsaken Sea: Racing the World's Most Dangerous Waters. large type ed. LC 99-40888. 1999. 26.95 (*1-57490-215-6*, Beeler LP Bks) T T Beeler.

— Godforsaken Sea: The True Story of a Race Through the World's Most Dangerous Waters. (Illus.). 304p. 2000. pap. 13.00 (*0-385-72000-9*, Anchor NY) Doubleday.

Lundy, Derek. Scott Turow: Meeting the Enemy. LC 95-196075. (Illus.). 160p. 1995. pap. 9.95 (*1-55022-234-1*) LPC InBook.

Lundy-Ekamn, Laurie. Neuroscience: Fundamentals for Rehabilitation. (Illus.). 475p. 1998. pap., teacher ed. write for info. (*0-7216-4718-9*, W B Saunders Co) Harcrt Hlth Sci Grp.

Lundy, Hunter. Let Us Prey: The Public Trial of Jimmy Swaggart. 1999. pap. 25.95 (*1-885478-70-4*, Pub. by Genesis Press) BookWorld.

Lundy, James. Teams: Together Each Achieves More Success. 222p. 1992. 24.95 (*0-85013-207-X*, TE7607) Dartnell Corp.

— Teams: Together Each Achieves More Success. 222p. 1994. pap. 24.95 (*0-85013-228-2*) Dartnell Corp.

Lundy, Jeremy. Fantasy Football Preview, 1993. 208p. (Orig.). 1993. pap. 14.95 (*0-917939-08-5*) SandFroid Pr.

Lundy, John P. Monumental Christianity: The Art & Symbolism of the Primitive Church. 1977. lib. bdg. 59.95 (*0-8490-2278-9*) Gordon Pr.

— Monumental Christianity, or The Art & Symbolism of the Primitive Church. (Illus.). 453p. 1998. reprint ed. pap. 39.95 (*1-55818-460-0*) Holmes Pub.

An Asterisk (*) at the beginning of an entry indicates that the title is appearing for the first time.

Lundy, Joseph E., ed. The Journal of Taxation of Exempt Organizations. 175.00 (0-685-69581-6, EOTJ) Warren Gorham & Lamont.

Lundy, Katherine C. Sidewalk Talk: A Naturalistic Study of Street Kids. rev. ed. LC 94-42201. (Children of Poverty Ser.). 248p. 1995. text 25.00 (0-8153-2014-0) Garland.

Lundy, Kathryn R. Women View Librarianship: Nine Perspectives. LC 80-23611. (ACRL Publications in Librarianship: No. 41). 108p. reprint ed. pap. 33.50 (0-7837-5951-7, 204575100007) Bks Demand.

*Lundy, Kay Saucier, et al. Nursing in the Community. (Illus.). 832p. (C). 2000. text 52.50 (0-7637-0706-6) Jones & Bartlett.

Lundy, Lewis. Managing Computer Networks: A Case-Based Reasoning Approach. LC 95-33933. 250p. 1995. 69.00 (0-89006-799-6) Artech Hse.

Lundy, Marta & Younger, Beverly, eds. Empowering Women in the Workplace: Perspectives, Innovations, & Techniques for Helping Professionals. LC 94-43715. (Employee Assistance Quarterly Ser.). (Illus.). 228p. 1995. pap. text 14.95 (1-56023-062-2, Harrington Park) Haworth Pr.

— Women in the Workplace & Employee Assistance Programs: Perspectives, Innovations, & Techniques for Helping Professionals. 144p. 1994. 39.95 (1-56024-674-X) Haworth Pr.

Lundy, Mike. Baby Farm. 256p. 1987. 15.95 (0-8184-0408-6) Carol Pub Group.

— Raven. 224p. 1985. 15.95 (0-8184-0377-2) Carol Pub Group.

Lundy, Olive & Cowling, Alan. Strategic Human Resource Management. 416p. 1995. pap. 69.95 (0-415-13603-2) Thomson Learn.

Lundy, Olive, jt. auth. see Cowling, Alan.

*Lundy, Patricia. Debt & Adjustment: Social & Environmental Consequences in Jamaica. LC 98-74639. (Studies in Green Research). 11p. 1999. text 56.95 (1-85972-114-1, Pub. by Ashgate Pub) Ashgate Pub Co.

*Lundy, Randy. Under the Night Sun. 96p. 1999. pap. 8.95 (1-55050-155-0, Pub. by Coteau) Genl Dist Srvs.

Lundy, Robert E. Carving the Historic Western Face. LC 87-73231. 112p. (Orig.). 1988. pap. 34.95 (0-9619094-0-4) BJ Enterprises.

— Carving the Historic Western Face. LC 87-73231. (Illus.). 160p. (Orig.). 1991. pap. 14.95 (0-88740-321-2) Schiffer.

Lundy, Ronni. Butter Beans to Blackberries: Recipes from the Southern Garden. LC 98-44304. (Illus.). 432p. 1999. 30.00 (0-86547-547-4) N Point Pr.

*Lundy, Ronni. Butterbeans to Blackberries. 2000. pap. write for info. (0-86547-588-1) N Point Pr.

Lundy, Ronni. Festive Table: Recipes & Stories for Your Own Celebrations. 356p. 1995. 27.50 (0-86547-492-3) N Point Pr.

— Shuck Beans, Stack Cakes & Honest Fried Chicken: The Heart & Soul of Southern Country Kitchens. LC 91-18142. (Illus.). 400p. 1994. pap. 16.50 (0-87113-600-7, Atlntc Mnthly) Grove-Atltic.

Lundy-Ruvolo, Francine, ed. see Simons, George & Zuckerman, Amy J.

*Lune, Alison. Fringist Epiphany. 1999. pap. 7.00 (1-893541-03-7, Pub. by Potes Poets) SPD-Small Pr Dist.

Lune, Denis. Cloud & Silver Lining: Ezekiel, the Christian & the Power of God. 1985. pap. 1.00 (9971-972-28-X) OMF Bks.

Luneau, Andre, ed. see Leskov, Saltykov-Chtchedrine & Leskov, Chtchedri.

Luneburg, H. Kombinatorik. (Elemente der Mathematik Vom Hoeheren Standpunkt Aus Ser.: Band 6). (GER.). 108p. 1980. 26.00 (0-8176-0548-7) Birkhauser.

Luneburg, William V. & American Bar Association Staff. The Lobbying Manual. 2nd ed. LC 98-14636. 1998. pap. 89.95 (1-57073-551-4) Amer Bar Assn.

Lunel, Armand. The Nicolo-Peccavi: ou L'Affaire Dreyfus a Carpentras. (FRE.). 1976. pap. 10.95 (0-7859-4064-2) Fr & Eur.

Lunel, Sjoerd M., jt. auth. see Hale, Jack K.

Lunelli, Aldo, ed. Curae Ennianae Ultimae in Editionem Alteram Impensae. (GER & ITA.). 84p. (Orig.). 1989. pap. 20.00 (90-256-0956-2, Pub. by AM Hakkert) BookLink Distributors.

Lunenburg, Fred C. & Irby, Beverly J. High Expectations: An Action Plan for Implementing Goals 2000. LC 98-25464. (1-Off Ser.). (Illus.). 216p. 1998. 61.95 (0-8039-6605-9); pap. 27.95 (0-8039-6606-7) Corwin Pr.

Lunenburg, Frederick C. & Ornstein, Allan C. Educational Administration: Concepts & Practices. 557p. (C). 1991. mass mkt. 44.25 (0-534-14850-6) Wadsworth Pub.

— Educational Administration: Concepts & Practices. 2nd ed. LC 95-34427. (C). 1995. 52.75 (0-534-25848-4) Wadsworth Pub.

*Lunenfeld, B. Textbook of Men's Health. 2001. 125.00 (1-84214-011-6) Prthnon Pub.

Lunenfeld, B. & Insler, V., eds. GnRH Analogues: The State of the Art, 1993. (Illus.). 156p. 1993. 55.00 (1-85070-526-7) Prthnon Pub.

*Lunenfeld, Bruno. GNRH Analogues: The State of the Art at the Millennium. LC 99-33960. (Illus.). 120p. 1999. 59.00 (1-85070-097-4) Prthnon Pub.

Lunenfeld, Bruno, ed. GnRH Analogues: The State of the Art 1996. (Illus.). 190p. 1996. 55.00 (1-85070-759-6) Prthnon Pub.

Lunenfeld, Bruno, et al. Diagnosis & Treatment of Functional Infertility. 3rd ed. (Illus.). 216p. 1993. pap. 85.00 (3-89412-129-7) Blackwell Sci.

Lunenfeld, Bruno, jt. auth. see Brosens, I. A.

Lunenfeld, Bruno, jt. ed. see Insler, Vaclav.

Lunenfeld, Bruno, jt. ed. see Vickers, B. H.

Lunenfeld, Bruno, jt. ed. see Vickery, B. H.

Lunenfeld, Marvin. College Basics: How to Start Right & Finish Strong. 144p. (C). 1993. pap. text, per. 16.95 (0-8403-8655-9) Kendall-Hunt.

Lunenfeld, Marvin, ed. Fourteen Ninety-Two: Discovery, Invasion, Encounter: Sources & Interpretations. LC 90-80531. (Sources in Modern History Ser.). 355p. (C). 1990. pap. text 25.96 (0-669-21115-X) HM Trade Div.

Lunenfeld, Marvin & Lunenfeld, Peter. College Basics: How to Start Right & Finish Strong. 2nd ed. LC 91-90353. (Illus.). 144p. 1992. pap. 12.95 (0-9629783-1-0) Semester Pr.

Lunenfeld, Marvin & Lunenfeld, Peter B. College Basics: How to Start Right & Finish Strong. LC 91-90353. (Illus.). 144p. 1991. pap. 11.95 (0-9629783-0-2) Semester Pr.

*Lunenfeld, Peter. Snap to Grid: A User's Guide to Digital Arts, Media & Cultures. LC 99-40216. (Illus.). 240p. 2000. 32.95 (0-262-12226-X) MIT Pr.

Lunenfeld, Peter, ed. The Digital Dialectic: New Essays on New Media. LC 98-25750. (Illus.). 320p. 1999. 35.00 (0-262-12213-8) MIT Pr.

*Lunenfeld, Peter, ed. The Digital Dialectic: New Essays on New Media. (Illus.). 320p. 2000. reprint ed. pap. 17.95 (0-262-62137-1) MIT Pr.

Lunenfeld, Peter, jt. auth. see Lunenfeld, Marvin.

Lunenfeld, Peter B., jt. auth. see Lunenfeld, Marvin.

Lunenschloss, J. & Albrecht, W., eds. Non-Woven Bonded Fabrics. Hock, Janet, tr. LC 84-25175. (Applied Science & Industrial Technology Ser.). 549p. 1985. text 173.00 (0-470-20150-9) P-H.

Luner, Philip, ed. Paper Preservation: Current Issues & Recent Developments. LC 90-46550. 160p. reprint ed. pap. 49.60 (0-8357-2957-5, 203921900011) Bks Demand.

*Luneski, Dori. Health Metamorphosis. 2nd ed. LC 99-61. 262p. 1999. per. 14.95 (0-7872-5934-9) Kendall-Hunt.

Lunet De Lajonquiere, Etienne E. Ethnographie du Tonkin Septentrional. LC 77-87043. reprint ed. 49.50 (0-404-16836-1) AMS Pr.

*Lunetta, Ross S. Remote Sensing Change Detection: Environmental Monitoring Methods & Applications. 2000. 89.95 (0-7484-0861-4, Pub. by Tay Francis Ltd) Taylor & Francis.

Lunetta, Ross S. & Elvidge, Christopher D., eds. Remote Sensing Change Detection: Environmental Monitoring Methods & Applications. LC 98-9658. (Illus.). 350p. 1998. 69.95 (1-57504-037-9) Sleepng Bear.

Lunetta, Steven, ed. see Primrose, David W.

Lunetta, Vincent N. & Novick, Shimshon. Inquiring & Problem Solving in the Physical Sciences: A Sourcebook. 224p. (C). 1982. per., boxed set 46.95 (0-8403-2631-9) Kendall-Hunt.

Lunev, Staanislov & Winkler, Ira. Through the Eyes of the Enemy. LC 98-7203. 304p. 1998. 24.95 (0-89526-390-4) Regnery Pub.

*Lunev, Vladimir V. High-Velocity Dynamics of Real Gases. 1999. 129.00 (0-8493-2869-1) CRC Pr.

Luney, Percy. Professional Responsibility. 2nd rev. ed. (Quick Review Ser.). 227p. (C). 1996. pap. text 18.95 (1-57793-008-8) Sum & Substance.

Luney, Percy R., Jr. & Yakahashi, Kazuyuki, eds. Japanese Constitutional Law. 330p. (C). 1994. text 67.50 (0-86008-497-3, Pub. by U of Tokyo) Col U Pr.

Lung. Water Quality Modeling for Wasteload Allocations. 400p. 2000. text 74.95 (0-471-15883-6) Wiley.

Lung & French. Water Quality Modeling Vol. 3: Applications to Estuaries. 208p. 1993. lib. bdg. 165.00 (0-8493-6973-8, TD370) CRC Pr.

Lung, E., jt. auth. see Johnson, C.

Lung, Haha. Knights of Darkness: Secrets of the World's Deadliest Night Fighters. LC 99-174318. (Illus.). 160p. 1998. pap. 16.00 (0-87364-971-0) Paladin Pr.

— Ninja Craft. LC 97-72942. (Illus.). 144p. (Orig.). 1997. pap. 16.00 (0-939427-84-2) Alpha Pubns OH.

*Lung, Haha & Prowant, Christopher B. Shadowhand: The History & Secrets of Ninja Taisavaki. (Illus.). 168p. 2000. pap. 20.00 (1-58160-071-2, 10011344) Paladin Pr.

Lung, Hoang N. Strategy & Tactics. 137p. 1994. pap. text 15.00 (0-923135-27-8) Dalley Bk Service.

Lung, James & Hinsdale, C. E. Oaths of Office for the Use of City, County & State Officials in North Carolina. 42p. 1975. 4.00 (1-56011-121-6) Institute Government.

*Lung, Yannick, et al, eds. Coping with Variety: Flexible Productive Systems for Product Variety in the Auto Industry. 434p. 1999. text 86.95 (0-7546-1115-9, Pub. by Ashgate Pub) Ashgate Pub Co.

Lungago. Santa Stories. rev. ed. 1989. write for info. (0-930061-26-8) Interspace Bks.

Lunge-Larsen, Lise & Preus, Margi. The Legend of the Lady Slipper. LC 97-47209. (Illus.). 32p. (ps-3). 1999. 15.00 (0-395-90512-5) HM.

Lunger, Max. Hemp Masters: Ancient Hippie Secrets for Knotting Hip Hemp Jewelry. Kright, Denise, ed. (Illus.). 100p. 1998. pap. 13.95 (0-943604-57-5, BOO/31) Eagles View.

Lunghi, Elvio. The Basilica of St. Francis in Assisi. (Illus.). 192p. (Orig.). 1996. pap. 24.99 (1-878351-51-6) Riverside NY.

Lungies, N. J., jt. auth. see Hayes, M.

*Lungley, Martin. Gardenware. (Illus.). 160p. 2000. 40.00 (1-86126-226-4, Pub. by Cro1wood) Trafalgar.

Lungness, Leah, jt. auth. see Engber, Andrea.

Lungstrum, Janet & Sauer, Elizabeth, eds. Agonistics: Arenas of Creative Contest. LC 97-1951. (SUNY Series, the Margins of Literature). 359p. (C). 1997. text 62.50 (0-7914-3411-7); pap. text 20.95 (0-7914-3412-5) State U NY Pr.

Lungu, Dov B. Romania & the Great Powers, 1933-1940. LC 89-1553. 294p. 1989. text 54.95 (0-8223-0915-7) Duke.

Lungu, Karen L. Children with Special Needs: A Resource Guide for Parents, Educators, Social Workers & Other Caregivers. LC 98-47290. 234p. 1999. text 49.95 (0-398-06933-6); pap. text 36.95 (0-398-06934-4) C C Thomas.

*Lungu, Radu. Dracula. (Temporis Ser.). (Illus.). 206p. 2000. 55.00 (1-85995-780-3, Pub. by Parkstone Pr) Bks Intl VA.

Lungu, Radu, jt. auth. see Roman, Radu Anton.

Lungwitz, Anton. A Textbook of Horseshoeing for Horseshoers & Veterinarians. Adams, John W., tr. LC 66-28443. (Illus.). 216p. 1995. reprint ed. pap. 19.95 (0-87071-026-5) Oreg St U Pr.

Lungwitz, Hans. Psychology & Cognitive Therapy of the Neuroses. rev. ed. Becker, Reinhold, ed. Maclean, Norman, tr. from GER. LC 93-17037.Tr. of Systematik der Neurosen. (Illus.). 200p. 1993. 48.50 (0-8176-2866-5) Birkhauser.

*Lunigan, Catherine & Blanco, Jodee. The Evolving Woman: Intimate Confessions of Surving Mr. Wrong. LC 00-36955. 250p. 2000. pap. 11.95 (1-55874-759-1) Health Comm.

Lunine, Jonathan I. Earth: Evolution of a Habitable World. LC 98-28902. (Illus.). 352p. (C). 1998. 74.95 (0-521-47287-3); pap. 29.95 (0-521-64423-2) Cambridge U Pr.

Lunine, Leo R. How to Research, Write & Package Administrative Manuals. LC 84-45785. 320p. 1985. 75.00 (0-8144-5805-X) AMACOM.

Luning, Klaus, et al. Seaweeds: Their Environment, Biogeography & Ecophysiology. LC 89-22633. 527p. 1990. 175.00 (0-471-62434-9) Wiley.

Luning Prak, Niels. The Language of Architecture: A Contribution to Architectural Theory. (Illus.). 1968. 44.65 (90-279-6394-0) Mouton.

Lunis, Natalie. Backyard Scientist. (Thinking Like a Scientist Ser.). (Illus.). 20p. (J). Date not set. pap. 16.95 (1-58273-107-1) Newbridge Educ.

— Bugs All Around. (Thinking Like a Scientist Ser.). (Illus.). 20p. (J). Date not set. pap. 16.95 (1-58273-091-1) Newbridge Educ.

— A Closer Look. (Thinking Like a Scientist Ser.). (Illus.). 20p. (J). Date not set. pap. 16.95 (1-58273-109-8) Newbridge Educ.

Lunis, Natalie. Discovering Electricity: Big Book. (Ranger Rick Science Spectacular Ser.). 16p. (J). (gr. 2-5). 1997. pap. 16.95 (1-56784-452-9) Newbridge Educ.

— Discovering Electricity: Student Book. (Ranger Rick Science Spectacular Ser.). 16p. (J). (gr. 2-5). 1997. pap. 19.95 (1-56784-477-4) Newbridge Educ.

— How We Use Electricity: Photo Card Set. Evento, Susan, ed. (Early Science Ser.). (J). (ps-1). 1997. pap. text 14.95 (1-56784-388-3) Newbridge Educ.

— Life in Your Backyard. (Ranger Rick Science Spectacular Ser.). 16p. (J). (gr. 2-4). 1996. pap. 16.95 (1-56784-223-2) Newbridge Educ.

— Life in Your Backyard: Student Book. (Ranger Rick Science Spectacular Ser.). (Illus.). 16p. (Orig.). (J). (gr. 2-4). 1996. pap. 3.95 (1-56784-248-8) Newbridge Educ.

— Rocks & Soil. Ellis, Linette, ed. (Early Science Big Bks.). (Illus.). 16p. (J). (ps-2). 1998. pap. 16.95 (1-56784-383-2) Newbridge Educ.

— Rocks & Soil: Student Book. Ellis, Linette, ed. (Early Science Ser.). 16p. (Orig.). (J). (ps-2). 1998. pap. text, student ed. 3.33 (1-56784-384-0) Newbridge Educ.

Lunis, Natalie. Watching the Night Sky. (Thinking Like a Scientist Ser.). (Illus.). 20p. (J). Date not set. pap. 16.95 (1-58273-079-2) Newbridge Educ.

Lunis, Natalie & White, Nancy. Being a Scientist. (Thinking Like a Scientist Ser.). (Illus.). 20p. (J). Date not set. pap. 16.95 (1-58273-085-7) Newbridge Educ.

— Exploring everyday Wonders. (Thinking Like a Scientist Ser.). (Illus.). 20p. (J). Date not set. pap. 16.95 (1-58273-368-6) Newbridge Educ.

— Investigating Rocks. (Thinking Like a Scientist Ser.). (Illus.). 20p. (J). Date not set. pap. 16.95 (1-58273-081-4) Newbridge Educ.

— Let's Experiment! (Thinking Like a Scientist Ser.). (Illus.). 20p. (J). Date not set. pap. 16.95 (1-58273-111-X) Newbridge Educ.

— Popcorn Science. (Thinking Like a Scientist Ser.). (Illus.). 20p. (J). Date not set. pap. 16.95 (1-58273-370-8) Newbridge Educ.

— A World of Change. (Thinking Like a Scientist Ser.). (Illus.). 20p. (J). Date not set. pap. 16.95 (1-58273-077-6) Newbridge Educ.

Lunis, Natalie, ed. see Berger, Melvin.

Lunis, Natalie, ed. see White, Nancy.

Lunman, Larry, jt. auth. see Stewart, Jim.

Lunn. HPLC Methods, 4 vols. 7009p. 2000. 995.00 (0-471-33192-9) Wiley.

— Industrial Organization. (C). 1998. text 52.00 (0-03-029914-4) Harcourt Coll Pubs.

Lunn. Race & Labour in Britain. 49.95 (1-85928-251-2) Ashgate Pub Co.

Lunn, jt. auth. see McEachern.

Lunn, Arnold. Within That City. 285p. 1999. reprint ed. 19.95 (0-912141-71-9) Roman Cath Bks.

Lunn, Arnold H. The Revolt Against Reason. LC 72-108396. 273p. 1971. reprint ed. lib. bdg. 49.75 (0-8371-3819-1, LURA, Greenwood Pr) Greenwood.

— Roman Converts. LC 67-22102. (Essay Index Reprint Ser.). 1977. 20.95 (0-8369-0636-5) Ayer.

— Roman Converts. (Essay Index Reprint Ser.). 275p. 1982. reprint ed. lib. bdg. 20.00 (0-8290-0482-3) Irvington.

Lunn, Carolyn. Bobby's Zoo. LC 88-36865. (Rookie Readers Ser.). (Illus.). 32p. (J). (ps-2). 1989. pap. 4.95 (0-516-42089-5); lib. bdg. 17.00 (0-516-02089-7) Childrens.

— A Buzz Is Part of a Bee. LC 89-25434. (Rookie Readers Ser.). (Illus.). 32p. (J). (ps-2). 1990. pap. 4.95 (0-516-42062-3); lib. bdg. 17.00 (0-516-02062-5) Childrens.

— Joy . . . Anyway! 192p. 1997. pap. 10.99 (0-8341-1441-0) Beacon Hill.

— Spiders & Webs. LC 89-34665. (Rookie Readers Ser.). (Illus.). 32p. (J). (gr. k-2). 1989. lib. bdg. 17.00 (0-516-02093-5) Childrens.

— A Whisper Is Quiet. LC 88-11968. (Rookie Readers Ser.). (Illus.). 32p. (J). (gr. k-2). 1988. pap. 4.95 (0-516-42087-9); lib. bdg. 17.00 (0-516-02087-0) Childrens.

Lunn, Colin. The Essence of Analog Electronics. LC 96-25456. (Essence of Engineering Ser.). 240p. (C). 1996. pap. text 24.95 (0-13-360223-0) P-H.

Lunn, David, ed. The English Benedictines, 1540-1688: From Reformation to Revolution. 296p. 1994. 41.00 (0-86012-095-3, Pub. by Srch Pr) St Mut.

Lunn, Eugene. Marxism & Modernism: An Historical Study of Lukacs, Brecht, Benjamin, & Adorno. LC 81-23169. 344p. 1982. pap. 17.95 (0-520-05330-3, Pub. by U CA Pr) Cal Prin Full Svc.

— Prophet of Community: The Romantic Socialism of Gustav Landauer. 434p. 1973. 35.00 (0-88286-136-0) C H Kerr.

Lunn, Geoff. The Venting of Weak Explosions & the Effect of Vent Ducts, Pt. 3. (Dust Explosion Prevention & Protection Guides Ser.). 190p. 1988. pap. 30.00 (0-85295-230-9, 9CH33) Gulf Pub.

Lunn, George. Capillary Electrophoresis Methods for Pharmaceutical Analysis. LC 98-48818. 1544p. 2000. 295.00 (0-471-33188-0) Wiley.

— HPLC Methods for Pharmaceutical Analysis, Vol. 2. 2327p. 1999. 295.00 (0-471-33189-9) Wiley.

— HPLC Methods for Pharmaceutical Analysis, Vol. 3. 1856p. 1999. 295.00 (0-471-33190-2) Wiley.

— HPLC Methods for Pharmaceutical Analysis, Vol. 4. 1818p. 2000. 295.00 (0-471-33191-0) Wiley.

*Lunn, George. HPLC Methods for Pharmaceutical Analysis, Vols. 2-4. 5400p. 2000. 750.00 (0-471-33296-8) Wiley.

— HPLC Methods for Pharmaceutical Analysis, Vols. 2-4. 5400p. 2000. 1995.00 incl. cd-rom (0-471-33295-X) Wiley.

Lunn, George & Hellwig, Louise C. Handbook of Derivatization Reactions for HPLC. LC 97-22137. 1795p. 1998. 275.00 (0-471-23888-0, Wiley-Interscience) Wiley.

— Handbook of Derivatization Reactions for HPLC. LC 97-22137. 1632p. 1998. text 495.00 incl. cd-rom (0-471-16458-5, Wiley-Interscience) Wiley.

Lunn, George & Sansone, Eric B. Destruction of Hazardous Chemicals in the Laboratory. 2nd ed. 520p. 1994. 94.95 (0-471-57399-X) Wiley.

Lunn, George & Schmuff, Norman R. HPLC Methods for Pharmaceutical Analysis. LC 96-29417. 1632p. 1997. 295.00 (0-471-18176-5) Wiley.

— HPLC Methods for Pharmaceutical Analysis. LC 96-29417. xxii, 1609p. 1997. cd-rom 325.00 (0-471-18198-6) Wiley.

— HPLC Methods for Pharmaceutical Analysis. LC 96-29417. 1632p. 1997. 495.00 (0-471-13078-8) Wiley.

Lunn, Harry H., Jr. Milton Avery Prints, 1933 to 1955. 99p. 1973. pap. 50.00 (1-55660-121-2) A Wofsy Fine Arts.

— Milton Avery Prints, 1933-1955: With an Original Etching. limited ed. (Illus.). 99p. 1973. boxed set 400.00 (1-55660-159-X) A Wofsy Fine Arts.

Lunn, Hugh. Head over Heels: Hugh Lunn's 60s Sequel to Over the Top with Jim. 312p. 1995. pap. 14.95 (0-7022-2530-4, Pub. by Univ Queensland Pr) Intl Spec Bk.

— Lunn Family Album. (Illus.). 200p. 1995. pap. 19.95 (0-7022-2563-0, Pub. by Univ Queensland Pr) Intl Spec Bk.

— More over the Top with Jim Stories. (Fred & Olive's Blessed Lino Collection). 184p. 1995. pap. 14.95 (0-7022-2863-X, Pub. by Univ Queensland Pr) Intl Spec Bk.

— Over the Top with Jim. 278p. 1998. reprint ed. pap. 16.95 (0-7022-2255-0, Pub. by Univ Queensland Pr) Intl Spec Bk.

*Lunn, Hugh. Over the Top with Jim. 2nd ed. 356p. 1999. pap. 16.95 (0-7022-3138-X, Pub. by Univ Queensland Pr) Intl Spec Bk.

Lunn, Hugh. Spies Like Us. 1995. pap. 16.95 (0-7022-2757-9, Pub. by Univ Queensland Pr) Intl Spec Bk.

— Vietnam: A Reporter's War. LC 85-40967. (Illus.). 272p. 1987. 18.95 (0-8128-3088-1, Scrbrough Hse) Madison Bks UPA.

— Vietnam: A Reporter's War. (Illus.). 283p. 1989. reprint ed. pap. 14.95 (0-7022-2018-3, Pub. by Univ Queensland Pr) Intl Spec Bk.

Lunn, Hugh, see Kingsmill, Hugh, pseud.

Lunn, Hugh K., ed. see Inge, William R.

Lunn, Janet. Allons a la Foire.Tr. of Come to the Fair. (FRE., Illus.). 24p. (J). (gr. 1-3). 1997. 17.95 (0-88776-422-3) Tundra Bks.

— Amos's Sweater. (Illus.). (J). (ps-3). 1997. text 15.95 (0-88899-074-X) Publishers Group.

— Charlotte. LC 96-61150. (Illus.). 32p. (J). (gr. 2-4). 1998. 15.95 (0-88776-383-9) Tundra Bks.

— Come to the Fair. LC 97-60509. (Illus.). 24p. (J). (gr. 1-4). 1997. 15.95 (0-88776-409-6) Tundra Bks.

*Lunn, Janet. Hollow Tree. 2000. 15.99 (0-670-88949-0, Viking) Viking Penguin.

Lunn, Janet. The Root Cellar. LC 96-102579. 240p. (J). (gr. 5-9). 1996. pap. 4.99 (0-14-038036-1, PuffinBks) Peng Put Young Read.

L

An Asterisk (*) at the beginning of an entry indicates that the title is appearing for the first time.

L

— The Root Cellar. LC 83-3246. 256p. (YA). (gr. 5 up). 1983. lib. bdg. 17.00 (0-684-17855-9) Scribner.
— The Root Cellar. (J). 1996. 10.09 (0-606-03439-0, Pub. by Turtleback) Demco.
— The Umbrella Party. LC 98-182915. (Illus.). 32p. 1998. 14.95 (0-88899-298-X) Publishers Group.
Lunn, Kenneth. A Social History of British Labour, 1870-1970. 224p. 1993. pap. 19.95 (0-7131-6478-6, A3400, Pub. by E A) Routldge.
Lunn, Kenneth, ed. Race & Labour in Twentieth-Century Britain. 192p. 1986. 32.00 (0-7146-3238-4, Pub. by F Cass Pubs); pap. 17.50 (0-7146-4052-2, Pub. by F Cass Pubs) Intl Spec Bk.
Lunn, Kenneth & Day, Ann. History of Work & Labour Relations in the Royal Dockyards. LC 97-33513. (Employment & Work Relations in Context Ser.). 1998. 85.00 (0-7201-2349-6) Continuum.
Lunn, Kenneth, ed. see Evans, Martin.
Lunn, Marti & Brownsey, Lois. Big Yellow School Bus. 1991. pap. 34.95 incl. audio (0-88284-838-0) Alfred Pub.
— Here Comes the New Year. 1993. pap. 34.95 incl. audio (0-88284-839-9) Alfred Pub.
Lunn, Martin. Earth & Space: A BBC Fact Finders Book. (Illus.). 48p. (J). 1996. pap. 8.95 (0-563-39739-X, Pub. by BBC) Parkwest Pubns.
Lunn, Martin, et al. Factfinders: Earth & Beyond. (Fact Finders Ser.). (J). 23.95 (0-563-37622-8, BBC-Parkwest) Parkwest Pubns.
Lunn, Mary. A First Course in Mechanics. (Illus.). 202p. 1991. pap. text 32.00 (0-19-853433-7) OUP.
Lunn, Patricia Vining & Decesaris, Janet A. Investigacion de Gramatica. (C). 1992. mass mkt. 40.95 (0-8384-2348-5) Heinle & Heinle.
Lunn, Richard. Feast of All Souls. LC 97-169386. (Illus.). 1997. write for info. (0-09-183453-8) Trafalgar.
Lunn, Terry & Neff, Susan A. Material Requirements Planning: Integrating Material Requirement Planning & Modern Business. (APICS Ser.). (Illus.). 275p. 1992. 47.50 (1-55623-656-5, Irwn Prfssnl) McGraw-Hill Prof.
Lunn, Wendy, jt. auth. see Mort, David.
Lunne, T. Cone Penetration Testing in Geotechnical Practice. 352p. (C). (gr. 13). 1997. text 140.00 (0-7514-0393-8, Pub. by B Acad & Prof) Routldge.
Lunne, T., et al. Cone Penetrating Testing: In Geotechnical Practice. (Illus.). 312p. 1997. 0.00 (0-419-23750-X) Routledge.
Lunneborg. Data Analysis by Resampling. LC 99-40284. 2000. pap. text 86.95 (0-534-22110-6) Thomson Learn.
Lunneborg, Clifford E. Modeling Experimental & Observational Data. 1994. teacher ed. write for info. incl. disk (0-534-21427-4) Brooks-Cole.
Lunneborg, Patricia. Chosen Lives of Childfree Men. LC 98-44208. 160p. 1999. 35.00 (0-89789-598-3, Bergin & Garvey) Greenwood.
— O U Women: Undoing Educational Obstacles. LC 98-119889. (Cassell Education Ser.). 160p. 1994. 79.50 (0-304-33161-9); pap. 24.95 (0-304-33163-5) Continuum.
— OU Men: Work Through Learning. 140p. 1998. pap. 24.95 (0-7188-2972-7, Lutterworth-Parkwest) Parkwest Pubns.
Lunneborg, Patricia W. Abortion: A Positive Decision. LC 91-27946. 232p. 1992. 29.95 (0-89789-243-7, H243, Bergin & Garvey) Greenwood.
— Women Changing Work. LC 90-48. (Contributions in Women's Studies: No. 112). 232p. 1990. pap. 17.95 (0-89789-214-3, G214, Bergin & Garvey) Greenwood.
— Women Changing Work, 112. LC 89-25673. (Contributions in Women's Studies: No. 112). 232p. 1990. 57.95 (0-313-26843-6, LWD/, Bergin & Garvey) Greenwood.
— Women Police Officers: Current Career Profile. 222p. 1989. pap. 31.95 (0-398-06251-X) C C Thomas.
— Women Police Officers: Current Career Profile. 222p. (C). 1989. text 48.95 (0-398-05623-4) C C Thomas.
Lunney, jt. auth. see Recher.
Lunney, Daniel & Grigg, Gordon, eds. Kangaroo Harvesting & the Conservation of Arid & Semi-Arid Lands. 72p. (C). 1988. text 39.00 (0-7855-0033-2, Pub. by Surrey Beatty & Sons) St Mut.
***Lunney, Mark & Oliphant, Ken.** Tort Law: Text, Cases & Materials. 800p. 2000. pap. text 45.00 (0-19-876401-4) OUP.
Lunniss, P., jt. ed. see Phillips, R.
Lunniss, Vivien. Celtic Calligraphy. (Illus.). 48p. 2000. pap. 16.95 (0-85532-770-7, Pub. by Srch Pr) St Mut.
Lunny, William J. The Jesus Option. LC 93-28023. 224p. (Orig.). 1994. pap. 12.95 (0-8091-3445-4) Paulist Pr.
Lunqvist, S., jt. ed. see Jaric, M. V.
***Lunsford, Alyce.** Everyday Writer: Comb Bound. 2nd ed. 2000. pap. text 32.95 (0-312-24349-9) St Martin.
***Lunsford, Alyce, et al.** Research & Documents. 1999. pap. text 7.95 (0-312-25601-9) St Martin.
Lunsford, Andrea. Easy Writer. 1997. pap. text 13.50 (0-312-19101-4) St Martin.
Lunsford, Andrea. Easy Writer. 2nd ed. pap. text. write for info. (0-312-24348-0) St Martin.
Lunsford, Andrea. Easy Writer: Dictionary. 1997. pap. text 20.00 (0-312-19099-9) St Martin.
***Lunsford, Andrea.** Everday Writer/Exercises for the Everyday Writer, 2 Vols. 2000. pap. 27.90 (0-312-25711-2) Forge NYC.
Lunsford, Andrea. Everyday Write Online-Windows, Vol. 1. 1997. pap. 32.95 (0-312-16728-8) St Martin.
***Lunsford, Andrea.** Everyday Writer Metal. 2nd ed. 2000. pap. text 31.95 (0-312-24347-2) St Martin.
Lunsford, Andrea. Everyday Writer Spiral/Grammar. 1997. pap. text 20.00 (0-312-17822-0) St Martin.
— Everyday Writer 1998. 1999. pap. text 32.95 (0-312-18793-9); pap. text 32.95 (0-312-18794-7) St Martin.
— Everyday Writer/Exercises. 1997. pap. text 22.05 (0-312-16756-3) St Martin.
— Everyday Writer/Online. 1997. pap. text 24.00 (0-312-17074-2) St Martin.
— Everyday Writting Signs of Life, Vol. 1. 1997. pap. text 38.70 (0-312-18004-7) St Martin.
— Everythings an Argument. LC 97-66541. 1998. pap. text 22.95 (0-312-17088-2) St Martin.
— Everything's an Argument. 1998. pap. text, teacher ed. 5.00 (0-312-19731-4) St Martin.
— New St. Martin's Handbook. 4th ed. LC 98-84406. 1998. pap. text 36.95 (0-312-16744-X) St Martin.
— New St Martins Handbook Answers Exercise, Vol. 1. 1998. pap. text 5.00 (0-312-18976-1) St Martin.
— New St Martins Handbook Online, Vol. 1. 1999. pap. text 31.95 (0-312-18973-7) St Martin.
***Lunsford, Andrea.** Presence of Others. 3rd ed. 1999. pap. text 35.95 (0-312-20172-9) St Martin.
Lunsford, Andrea & Bridges. Longwood to Writing. LC 99-52642. 700p. 1999. 46.00 (0-205-27206-1) Allyn.
— Longwood Writing Brief. LC 99-52643. 612p. 1999. pap. text 42.00 (0-205-27207-X) Allyn.
***Lunsford, Andrea & Connors.** New St. Martin's Handbook. 1999. pap. text 32.95 (0-312-25101-7) St Martin.
— New St Martin's Handbook. 4th ed. 1999. pap. text 36.95 (0-312-25117-3) St Martin.
Lunsford, Andrea & Connors, Robert. The St. Martin's Handbook. 3rd ed. 876p. 1995. pap. text 28.95 (0-312-13817-2) St Martin.
***Lunsford, Andrea & Murphy.** St Martins Source for Writing Tutors. 2nd ed. 2000. pap. text 11.95 (0-312-18850-1) St Martin.
Lunsford, Andrea & Qurik. St Martins Pocet Guide Research & Documents. 1995. pap. text 7.95 (0-312-11727-2) St Martin.
***Lunsford, Andrea & Ruskiewicz, John.** Everythings an Argument with Readings. 2000. pap. text. write for info. (0-312-25034-7) St Martin.
***Lunsford, Andrea & White.** New St Martins Handbook Assign Respond & Evaluate. 3rd ed. 1998. pap. text 19.95 (0-312-19732-2) St Martin.
Lunsford, Andrea, jt. auth. see Harnack.
Lunsford, Andrea A. Everyday Writer Exercise. 150p. 1997. pap. text 8.95 (0-312-14827-5) St Martin.
— Literacy, Intellectual Property, & the Status Quo. Bridwell-Bowles, Lillian & Donehower, Kim, eds. (Technical Reports: Vol. 6). 12p. (Orig.). 1996. pap. 2.00 (1-881221-12-1) U Minn Ctr Interdis.
— The Presence of Others. 1996. pap. text 21.00 (0-312-14830-5) St Martin.
— The Presence of Others. 2nd ed. LC 95-73172. 668p. 1996. pap. text 35.95 (0-312-13295-6) St Martin.
— St. Martin's Handbook. 3rd ed. 1995. pap. text, teacher ed. 22.50 (0-312-10213-5) St Martin.
— Z-Im Presence of Others. 1997. pap. text 5.00 (0-312-14831-3) St Martin.
Lunsford, Andrea A., ed. Reclaiming Rhetorica: Women in the Rhetorical Tradition. LC 95-3298. (Series in Composition, Literary, & Culture). (Illus.). 354p. 1995. text 59.95 (0-8229-3872-3) U of Pittsburgh Pr.
— Reclaiming Rhetorica: Women in the Rhetorical Tradition. LC 95-3298. (Pitt Series in Composition, Literacy, & Culture). 354p. 1995. pap. 22.95 (0-8229-5553-9) U of Pittsburgh Pr.
Lunsford, Andrea A., et al, eds. The Future of Doctoral Studies in English. LC 89-36166. xii, 179p. 1989. pap. 15.50 (0-87352-185-4, W420P); lib. bdg. 32.00 (0-87352-184-6, W420C) Modern Lang.
— The Right to Literacy. LC 90-33855. iv, 306p. 1990. pap. text 18.00 (0-87352-198-6, W430P); lib. bdg. 19.75 (0-87352-197-8, W430C) Modern Lang.
Lunsford, Andrea A. & Connors, Robert J. St. Martin's Handbook. 2nd annot. ed. 848p. (C). 1992. teacher ed. write for info. (0-312-06814-X) St Martin.
Lunsford, Andrea L. The Everyday Writer: A Brief Reference. LC 95-73167. 384p. 1997. pap. text 32.95 (0-312-09569-4) St Martin.
Lunsford, Angela A. The Presence of Others. 1994. pap. text, teacher ed. 45.00 (0-312-09571-6) St Martin.
Lunsford, Anne & Skrobise, Jan. Goldilocks & the Three Bears: Told in Signed English. (Awareness & Caring Ser.: Vol. 10). 48p. (J). (ps-3). 1996. lib. bdg. 17.95 (1-56674-207-2) Forest Hse.
Lunsford, Barbara, jt. auth. see Allen, Lew.
***Lunsford, David E., Jr.** We Haven't Been to Norway Yet. LC 99-93738. 1999. pap. 10.95 (0-533-13139-1) Vantage.
Lunsford, E. Michael. Classic 1-2-3 Macros. 3rd ed. LC 94-30064. 448p. 1995. pap. 29.99 (0-471-06398-3) Wiley.
Lunsford, John, ed. see Patton, Pamela.
Lunsford, L. D., et al, eds. Gamma Knife Brain Surgery. LC 98-12266. (Progress in Neurological Surgery Ser.: Vol. 14, 1998). (Illus.). viii, 228p. 1998. 188.00 (3-8055-6637-9) S Karger.
— Proceedings of the Meeting of the American Society for Stereotactic & Functional Neurosurgery, Pittsburgh, PA, June 1991, Pt. 1: Journal: Stereotactic & Functional Neurosurgery, Vol. 58, Nos. 1-4, 1992. (Illus.). vi, 214p. 1992. pap. 188.00 (3-8055-5684-5) S Karger.
— Proceedings of the Meeting of the American Society for Stereotactic & Functional Neurosurgery, Pittsburgh, PA, June 1991, Pt. 2: Journal: Stereotactic & Functional Neurosurgery, Vol. 59, Nos. 1-4, 1992. (Illus.). vi, 210p. 1992. pap. 188.00 (3-8055-5688-8) S Karger.
Lunsford, L. Dade, ed. Modern Stereotactic Neurosurgery. (C). 1988. text 309.50 (0-89838-950-X) Kluwer Academic.
Lunsford, Michael. PC Magazine Guide to 1-2-3 for Windows. (Guide to...Ser.). 643p. (Orig.). 1991. pap. 27.95 (1-56276-021-1, Ziff-Davis Pr) Que.
Lunsford, Ron & Straub, Richard O. Twelve Readers Reading: Responding to College Student Writing. Farr, Marcia, ed. LC 95-8716. (Written Language Ser.). 464p. 1995. pap. text 32.50 (1-881303-40-3) Hampton Pr NJ.
Lunsford, Ronald F., jt. auth. see Haley, Michael C.
Lunsford, Ronald F., jt. ed. see Moran, Michael G.
***Lunsford, Susan.** Literature-Based Mini-Lessons: 15 Engaging Lessons That Use Your Favorite Picture Books to Help Every Student Become a More Fluent Reader. (Illus.). 160p. (J). 2000. pap. 16.95 (0-439-08682-5) Scholastic Inc.
Lunsing, Wim. Beyond Common Sense: Negotiating Constructions of Gender & Sexuality in Contemporary Japan. LC 97-43992. 256p. 1997. 110.00 (0-7103-0593-1, Pub. by Kegan Paul Intl) Col U Pr.
Lunstedt, Sven B. & Moss, Thomas H., eds. Managing Innovation & Change. (C). 1989. lib. bdg. 154.50 (0-7923-0079-3) Kluwer Academic.
Lunstroth, Claudia, ed. Adobe Anthology. 78p. 1993. pap. 5.00 (0-9639737-0-3) Adobe Bkstore.
— Adobe Anthology, Vol. 2. (Illus.). 84p. 1994. pap. 7.50 (0-9639737-1-1) Adobe Bkstore.
Lunstrum, John P. & Taylor, Bob L. Teaching Reading in the Social Studies. LC 78-17205. 98p. reprint ed. pap. 30.40 (0-8357-2628-2, 204011600014) Bks Demand.
Lunt. Handbook of Psychology in Education. text. write for info. (0-471-49145-4) Wiley.
Lunt, Anthony. Apollo Versus the Echomaker: A Langian Approach to Psychotherapy Dreams & Shamanism. 1993. pap. 12.95 (1-85230-153-8, Pub. by Element MA) Penguin Putnam.
Lunt, Bob. The Man Without a Mate Cookbook: The Successful Lifestyle Cookbook for the Unmarried Man. LC 91-66424. (Successful Life Alone Cookbook Ser.). (Illus.). 135p. 1991. 10.95 (0-9630296-3-0) SKM Pub.
***Lunt, Dean Lawrence, ed.** Hauling by Hand: The Life & Times of a Maine Island. LC 99-90467. (Illus.). xvi, 479p. (YA). 1999. 35.00 (0-9671662-0-9) Islandport Pr.
Lunt, Dolly S. A Woman's Wartime Journal: An Account of Sherman's Devastation of a Southern Plantation. LC 88-20209. 64p. 1990. reprint ed. pap. 5.95 (0-87797-149-8) Cherokee.
Lunt, Dudley C. Road to the Law. (C). 1962. pap. 2.25 (0-393-00183-0) Norton.
— The Road to the Law. LC 97-74798. xiv, 281p. 1997. reprint ed. 88.00 (1-56169-335-9) Gaunt.
Lunt, Dudley C., ed. see Thoreau, Henry David.
Lunt, Edward C. Key to the Publications of the United States Census, 1790-1887. LC 75-38138. (Demography Ser.). 1976. reprint ed. 15.95 (0-405-07991-5) Ayer.
Lunt, George G. & Olsen, R. W., eds. Comparative Invertebrate Neurochemistry. LC 87-27446. (Illus.). 300p. 1988. text 59.95 (0-8014-2177-2) Cornell U Pr.
Lunt, Henry J., jt. auth. see Blake, John.
Lunt, Horace G. Old Church Slavonic Grammar. rev. ed. (Slavistic Printings & Reprintings Ser.: No. 3). 1974. text 66.15 (90-279-3362-6) Mouton.
Lunt, Horace G., et al, eds. Harvard Slavic Studies, Vol. 5. LC 52-12516. viii, 166p. 1970. text 21.50 (0-674-37804-0) HUP.
Lunt, Horace G., et al. The Slavonic Book of Esther: Text, Lexicon, Linguistic Analysis, Problems of Translation. LC 98-19993. (Harvard Series in Ukrainian Studies: \). (Illus.). 324p. (C). 1998. text 39.95 (0-916458-80-6, LUNSLA) Harvard Ukrainian.
Lunt, Horace G., jt. ed. see Altbauer, Moshe.
Lunt, Ingrid, ed. Psychology & Education for Special Needs. 264p. 1995. 69.95 (1-85742-306-2, Pub. by Arena) Ashgate Pub Co.
Lunt, Ingrid, et al. Working Together: Inter-School Collaboration for Special Needs. 144p. 1994. pap. 18.95 (1-85346-301-9, Pub. by David Fulton) Taylor & Francis.
***Lunt, Karl.** Build Your Own Robot! LC 99-45830. (Illus.). 560p. 2000. pap. 34.95 (1-56881-102-0) AK Peters.
Lunt, Lawrence K., frwd. Leave Me My Spirit: An American's Story of Fourteen Years in Castro's Prisons. (Illus.). 288p. 1990. 19.95 (0-918080-58-4) Affil Writers America.
Lunt, Neil & Coyle, Douglas, eds. Welfare & Policy: Agendas & Issues. 224p. 1996. 85.00 (0-7484-0401-5); pap. 29.95 (0-7484-0402-3) Taylor & Francis.
Lunt, Paul S., jt. auth. see Warner, William L.
Lunt, Peter & Furnham, Adrian, eds. Economic Socialization: The Economic Beliefs & Behaviours of Young People. LC 95-49730. (Illus.). 224p. (C). 1996. text 85.00 (1-85898-416-5) E Elgar.
Lunt, Peter, jt. auth. see Livingstone, Sonia M.
Lunt, Richard D. The High Ministry of Government: The Political Career of Frank Murphy. LC 65-10195. (Illus.). 264p. reprint ed. pap. 81.90 (0-7837-3603-7, 204346800009) Bks Demand.
— Law & Order vs. the Miners: West Virginia, 1906-1933. 182p. 1992. reprint ed. pap. 12.95 (0-9627486-2-5) Applchin Eds.
Lunt, S. S., jt. ed. see Wonnacott, S.
Lunt, Susie. Prague. LC 97-180598. (World Bibliographical Ser.). 204p. 1997. lib. bdg. 60.00 (1-85109-252-8) ABC-CLIO.
Lunt, Susie & Milenkovic, Zora. Slovakia. lib. bdg. 69.00 (1-85109-281-1) ABC-CLIO.
Lunt, T. F., ed. Research Directions in Database Security. (Illus.). 288p. 1992. 67.95 (0-387-97736-8) Spr-Verlag.
Lunt, T. S. A History of the Lunt Family in America. (Illus.). 306p. 1989. reprint ed. pap. 46.00 (0-8328-0792-3); reprint ed. lib. bdg. 54.00 (0-8328-0791-5) Higginson Bk Co.
Lunt, W. E. Financial Relations of the Papacy with England to 1327. (Medieval Academy Bks.: No. 33). 1967. reprint ed. 45.00 (0-910956-13-8) Medieval Acad.
— Financial Relations of the Papacy with England, 1327-1534. LC 62-19287. (Medieval Academy Bks.: No. 74). 1962. 45.00 (0-910956-48-0) Medieval Acad.
Lunt, William E. Accounts Rendered by Papal Collectors in England, 1317-1378. LC 67-19647. (American Philosophical Society, Memoirs Ser.: Vol. 70). 633p. reprint ed. pap. 180.00 (0-8357-5073-6, 2019712) Bks Demand.
Lunte, Susan M. & Radzik, Donna M. Pharmaceutical & Biomedical Applications of Capillary Electrophoresis. (Progress in Pharmaceutical & Biomedical Analysis Ser.: Vol. 2). 502p. 1996. text 133.50 (0-08-042014-1, Pergamon Pr) Elsevier.
Lunteren, Ton Van, see Sheridan, Thomas B. & Van Lunteren, Ton, eds.
Luntley, Michael. Contemporary Philosophy of Thought & Language: Truth, World, Content. LC 98-8525. (Contemporary Philosophy Ser.). 320p. (C). 1999. 59.95 (0-631-19076-7) Blackwell Pubs.
— Reason, Truth & Self: The Postmodern Reconditioned. LC 95-14748. 272p. (C). 1995. pap. 22.99 (0-415-11853-0) Routledge.
— Reason, Truth & Self: The Postmodern Reconditioned. LC 95-14748. 272p. (C). (gr. 13). 1995. 75.00 (0-415-11852-2) Routledge.
Luntley, Mihcael. Contemporary Philosophy of Thought & Language. (Contemporary Philosophy Ser.). 320p. (C). 1999. pap. 29.95 (0-631-19077-5) Blackwell Pubs.
Lunts, G. L., jt. auth. see Volkovskii, L.
Lunts, Lev. Things in Revolt. Kern, Gary, tr. from RUS. & intro. by. Date not set. 29.95 (0-88233-924-9) Ardis Pubs.
Lunts, Valery, jt. auth. see Bernstein, Joseph.
Luntta, Karl. Moon Handbooks: Caribbean Vacations: How to Create Your Own Tropical Adventure. (Illus.). 910p. 1998. pap. 18.95 (1-56691-125-7, Moon Handbks) Avalon Travel.
***Luntta, Karl.** Moon Handbooks: Jamaica. 4th rev. ed. Vol. 4. (Illus.). 340p. 2000. 15.95 (1-56691-161-3, Moon Handbks) Avalon Travel.
Luntta, Karl. Moon Handbooks: Virgin Islands. (Illus.). 220p. 1997. pap. 13.95 (1-56691-093-5, Moon Handbks) Avalon Travel.
Luntta, Karl, jt. auth. see Heseltine, Sasha.
Luntz, Elizabeth D., jt. auth. see McBride, Karen H.
Luntz, Frank I. The American Dream: Renewing the Promise. 1994. 2.50 (0-614-17716-2) Hudson Instit IN.
Luntz, H. & Hambly, D. Torts: Cases & Commentary. 4th ed. 1072p. 1995. pap. write for info. (0-409-30949-4, MICHIE) LEXIS Pub.
Luntz, Maurice H. & Harrison, R. Glaucoma Surgery. LC 95-122876. 228p. 1994. text 159.00 (981-02-1418-9) World Scientific Pub.
Luntzel, Jim. Leningrad Diary: One Surprise after Another in the U. S. S. R. LC 91-90331. (Illus.). 180p. (Orig.). 1991. pap. 8.00 (0-9629878-0-8, Samizdat Press) Luntzel Enterp.
Lunwerg Editing Staff. Development of a Genius, 1890-1904: Drawings in the Museu Picasso Barcelona. 1998. pap. text 45.00 (84-7782-478-9) Lunwerg Edit.
Lunz, Sharon. Menopause & Hormone Replacement Therapy: A Simple but Complete Guide for Today's Busy Woman. LC 99-94059. 70p. 1999. pap. 11.95 (0-9669985-0-2) SL Pubs.
Lunzer, E. A. Child Development at Primary School: A Report of the Educational Research Workshop Held in Madrid, 24-27 September 1985. 162p. 1987. pap. 15.00 (0-317-91053-1) Taylor & Francis.
Luo, Yiqi & Mooney, Harold A. Carbon Dioxide & Environmental Stress. (Physiological Ecology Ser.). (Illus.). 432p. (C). 1999. text 69.95 (0-12-460370-X) Acad Pr.
Luo, D. J. & Teng, L. B. Theory of Dynamical Systems. (Advanced Series in Dynamical Systems). 280p. 1993. text 61.00 (981-02-1268-2) World Scientific Pub.
Luo, D. J., et al. Bifurcation Theory & Methods of Dynamical Systems. LC 99-474922. (Advanced Series in Dynamical Systems). 400p. 1997. text 86.00 (981-02-2094-4) World Scientific Pub.
***Luo, Daisheng.** Pattern Recognition & Image Processing. 250p. 1999. pap. 45.00 (1-898563-52-7, Pub. by Horwood Pub) Paul & Co Pubs.
Luo, Damin. Telecommunications Market Review & Forecast. 279p. 1991. pap. 595.00 (0-940919-27-3, 200) MultiMedia Telecomm.
Luo, F., jt. auth. see Freedman, M.
Luo, Fa-Long & Unbehauen, Rolf. Applied Neural Networks for Signal Processing. (Illus.). 367p. (C). 1999. pap. 29.95 (0-521-64400-3) Cambridge U Pr.
Luo, Fang-Chen, et al, eds. Display Technologies II. LC 98-226761. (Proceedings of SPIE Ser.: Vol. 3421). 244p. 1998. 80.00 (0-8194-2875-2) SPIE.
Luo, Haibo, ed. see Guan, Zenyzhu.
Luo, Haibo, ed. see Lang, Hua.
Luo, Haibo, ed. see Tai, Shuangyuan.
Luo, Haibo, ed. see Wang, Fan.
Luo, Haibo, ed. see Zhang, Yaoning.
Luo, J., jt. auth. see Wu, Dan-Di.
Luo, J., jt. ed. see Reijns, G. L.
Luo, Jenn-Ching. LAIPE: Parallel Direct Solvers for Linear System Equations. LC 95-92416. (LAIPE-001 Ser.). 364p. (Orig.). (C). 1995. 23.50 (0-9644361-1-6) Paral Integ.
— Parallel Computations on Windows NT. LC 94-93901. 281p. (C). 1995. pap. 25.00 (0-9644361-0-8); pap. text 49.00 (0-614-03971-1) Paral Integ.
Luo, Jing. Let's Speak Chinese. LC 99-37502. (Illus.). 180p. 2000. pap. 27.50 (1-57524-082-3) Krieger.

An Asterisk (*) at the beginning of an entry indicates that the title is appearing for the first time.

L

***Luo, Qingming, et al, eds.** Biomedical Optics. 570p. 1999. pap. text 111.00 (*0-8194-3455-8*) SPIE.

Luo, Ronnier, jt. auth. see MacDonald, L. W.

***Luo, Wei.** The Contract Law of the People's Republic of China: With English Translation & Introduction. LC 99-46045. (Chinese Law Ser.: Vol. 2). x, 190p. 1999. 68.00 (*1-57588-490-9*, 322280) W S Hein.

Luo, Wei. New Chinese Criminal Code. LC 98-9889. Vol. 1. vii, 341p. 1998. 72.50 (*1-57588-398-8*, 311580) W S Hein.

— A Pathfinder to U. S. Export Control Laws & Regulations. LC 94-18558. (Legal Research Guides Ser.: Vol. 18). xiv, 109p. 1994. 42.50 (*0-89941-889-9*, 308320) W S Hein.

Luo, Yadong. Entry & Cooperative Strategies in International Business Expansion. LC 98-48946. 328p. 1999. 69.50 (*1-56720-161-X*, Quorum Bks) Greenwood.

***Luo, Yadong.** Guanxi & Business. 250p. 2000. 48.00 (*981-02-4114-3*) World Scientific Pub.

— How to Enter China: Choices & Lessons. (Illus.). 328p. (C). text 59.50 (*0-472-11188-4*, 11188) U of Mich Pr.

Luo, Yadong. International Investment Strategies in the People's Republic of China. LC 98-6529. (Illus.). 311p. 1998. text 76.95 (*1-84014-026-7*, Pub. by Ashgate Pub) Ashgate Pub Co.

***Luo, Yadong.** Multinational Corporations in China: Benefiting from Structural Transformation. 300p. 2000. 54.00 (*87-16-13490-7*, Pub. by Copenhagen Busn Schl) Bks Intl VA.

— Partnering with Chinese Firms: Lessons for International Managers. 360p. 2000. text 73.95 (*1-84014-763-6*, Pub. by Ashgate Pub) Ashgate Pub Co.

— Strategy, Structure, & Performance of MNCs in China. LC 00-32813. 2000. write for info. (*1-56720-385-X*, Quorum Bks) Greenwood.

Luo, Yadong, jt. auth. see Kelley, Nelson Lane.

Luo, Yadong, jt. auth. see Yan, Aimin.

Luo, Yanzhong & Zhang, Guiqing. Theory & Application of Spectral Induced Polarization. LC 97-34221. (Geophysical Monographs). (Illus.). 171p. 1997. pap. text 43.00 (*1-56080-048-8*, 148A) Soc Expl Geophys.

Luo, Zhaohui. Computation & Reasoning: A Type Theory for Computer Science. LC 93-46644. (International Series of Monographs on Computer Science: No. 11). (Illus.). 240p. 1994. text 55.00 (*0-19-853835-9*, Clarendon Pr) OUP.

Luo, Zheng-hua, et al. Stability & Stabilization of Infinite Dimensional Systems with Applications. Dickinson, B. W. et al, eds. LC 98-49594. (Communications & Control Engineering Ser.). (Illus.). xiv, 410p. 1999. 129.00 (*1-85233-124-0*) Spr-Verlag.

Luo Zhewen, jt. compiled by see Zhang Yuhuan.

Luo, Zhi Quan, et al. Mathematical Programs with Equilibrium Constraints. LC 96-19428. (Illus.). 425p. (C). 1996. text 59.95 (*0-521-57290-8*) Cambridge U Pr.

Luoma, Bill. My Trip to New York City. 1994. pap. 5.00 (*0-935724-65-6*) Figures.

— Swoon Rocket. 1996. pap. 6.00 (*0-935724-74-5*) Figures.

***Luoma, Jon R.** The Hidden Forest. 2000. pap. 15.00 (*0-8050-6448-6*) H Holt & Co.

Luoma, Jon R. The Hidden Forest: The Biography of an Ecosystem. LC 98-46559. 288p. 1999. 22.00 (*0-8050-1491-8*) H Holt & Co.

Luoma, Robert C. Music Mode & Words in Lasso's Last Works. LC 87-28228. (Studies in the History & Interpretation of Music: Vol. 11). 200p. 1988. lib. bdg. 79.95 (*0-88946-435-9*) E Mellen.

Luomala, K. Ethnobotany of the Gilbert Islands. (BMB Ser.: No. 213). 1972. reprint ed. 25.00 (*0-527-02321-3*) Periodicals Srv.

— Maui-of-a-Thousand-Tricks: His Oceanic & European Biographers. (BMB Ser.: No. 198). 1969. reprint ed. 45.00 (*0-527-02306-X*) Periodicals Srv.

— Oceanic, American Indian, & African Myths of Snaring the Sun. (BMB Ser.: No. 168). 1974. reprint ed. 25.00 (*0-527-02276-4*) Periodicals Srv.

Luomala, K., et al. Specialized Studies in Polynesian Anthropology. (BMB Ser.). 1974. reprint ed. 25.00 (*0-527-02301-9*) Periodicals Srv.

Luomala, Katharine. Voices on the Wind: Polynesian Myths & Chants. (Illus.). 209p. 1986. reprint ed. pap. 15.95 (*0-930897-83-8*) Bishop Mus.

Luong, Hy V. Discursive Practices & Linguistic Meanings: The Vietnamese System of Person Reference. LC 90-31711. (Pragmatics & Beyond New Ser.: Vol. 11). x, 213p. 1990. 59.00 (*1-55619-277-0*) J Benjamins Pubng Co.

Luong, Hy V., jt. auth. see Brook, Timothy.

Luong, Hy V., jt. auth. see Nguyen, Dac B.

Luong, Hy Van, see Brook, Timothy & Van Luong, Hy, eds.

Luong Si Hang. Baby Tam Talking to You, Vol. II. Vuong, Son T. & Messick, William, eds. Nguyen, Xuan-Mai, tr. from VIE. 96p. 1994. pap. 6.00 (*0-9633690-3-2*) VoVi LED.

— Practical Method of Vovi Esoteric Science. rev. ed. Nguyen, Mai et al, eds. Vinh, Hoang, tr. from VIE. (Illus.). 104p. 1994. pap. 5.00 (*0-9633690-4-0*) VoVi LED.

— Die Praktische Methode der Vovi Kontemplation. Nguyen, Mai et al, eds. Hua Bach Mai, tr. from ENG. (GER., Illus.). 76p. (Orig.). 1993. pap. 5.00 (*0-9633690-2-4*) VoVi LED.

Luong, Tuoc V., et al. Internationalization: Developing Software for Global Markets. LC 95-10551. 293p. 1995. pap. 29.95 (*0-471-07661-9*) Wiley.

***Luongo, Albert M.** Soccer Drills: Skill-Builders for Field Control. LC 99-47698. (Illus.). 192p. 1999. pap. 24.50 (*0-7864-0682-8*) McFarland & Co.

Luongo, Albert M. The Soccer Handbook for Players, Coaches & Parents. LC 96-27651. (Illus.). 212p. 1996. pap. 25.00 (*0-7864-0159-1*) McFarland & Co.

***Luongo, Andrew P.** It Was Fascination . . . 100p. 1998. 15.00 (*0-8059-4517-2*) Dorrance.

Luongo, John. The Adventure of Faith: When Religion Is Just the Beginning. LC 92-15128. 176p. 1992. pap. 5.95 (*0-8091-3313-X*) Paulist Pr.

Luongo, Kenneth N. & Wander, W. Thomas, eds. The Search for Security in Space. LC 88-47928. (Cornell Studies in Security Affairs). 304p. 1989. 42.50 (*0-8014-2145-4*); pap. 15.95 (*0-8014-9482-6*) Cornell U Pr.

Luongo, Kenneth N., jt. ed. see Wander, W. Thomas.

***Luongo, Pino.** Simply Tuscan: Recipes for a Well Lived Life. LC 99-33049. (Illus.). 304p. 2000. 35.00 (*0-385-49290-1*) Doubleday.

Luongo, Pino, et al. A Tuscan in the Kitchen: Recipes & Tales from My Home. (Illus.). 1988. 27.50 (*0-517-56916-7*) C Potter.

Luongo, Robert. The Gold Thread: Ezra Pound's Principles of Good Government & Sound Money. 136p. (Orig.). 1995. pap. text. write for info. (*0-9631722-4-7*) Hamilton Print.

Luonsi, A. A., jt. ed. see Rantala, P. K.

Luopa, Michael. A Spiritual Primer on Abortion: A Simple Handbook for the Spiritual Truth about Abortion. LC 95-117615. 32p. 1994. pap. 4.95 (*0-9640549-0-6*) Ruby Ray Pubng.

Luorie, Richard, tr. see Szczypiorski, Andrzej.

Luostari, Kenneth, jt. auth. see Pontti, John.

Luoto, Patricia K., jt. auth. see Lieux, Elizabeth M.

Luotola, M., jt. auth. see Munawar, M.

Luotonen, Ari. Web Proxy Servers. LC 97-40619. 448p. 1997. pap. 44.95 (*0-13-680612-0*) P-H.

Luotto, James, jt. auth. see Stoll, Edwina.

Luotto, James A. & Stoll, Edwina L. Speech Communication: A Collaborative Learning Workbook. 176p. (C). 1992. pap. text 13.95 (*0-8403-6966-2*) Kendall-Hunt.

***Luoy, Mark.** The Grump. Brunner, Pat, ed. LC 00-190056. (Illus.). 32p. (YA). (gr. 4 up). 2000. 16.95 (*0-9664276-1-0*, Pub. by Grn Pastures) IPG Chicago.

Lup, Dom. Fast Tips for Golf: The Easy Golf Guide. 10p. (Orig.). 1996. pap. 3.95 (*1-887562-19-2*) FastMark.

Lupack, Alan, ed. Lancelot of the Laik & Sir Tristrem. (Teams Middle English Text Ser.). 1997. pap. 12.00 (*1-879288-50-8*) Medieval Inst.

— Modern Arthurian Literature: An Anthology of English & American Arthuriana from the Renaissance to the Present. LC 91-46442. 502p. 1992. text 40.00 (*0-8153-0055-7*, H#1420) Garland.

— Modern Arthurian Literature: An Anthology of English & American Arthuriana from the Renaissance to the Present. LC 91-46442. 502p. 1992. pap. text 24.95 (*0-8153-0843-4*) Garland.

— Three Middle English Charlemagne Romances. (TEAMS Middle English Text Ser.). 1990. pap. 7.00 (*0-918720-44-3*) Medieval Inst.

Lupack, Alan & Lupack, Barbara T. Arthurian Literature by Women. LC 99-11197. (Reference Library of the Humanities: Vol. 2137). 400p. 1999. reprint ed. 60.00 (*0-8153-3305-6*) Garland.

— King Arthur in America. LC 98-51847. (Arthurian Studies: No. 0261-9814). (Illus.). 320p. 1999. 75.00 (*0-85991-543-3*) Boydell & Brewer.

Lupack, Alan & Lupack, Barbara T., eds. Arthurian Literature by Women. (Reference Library of the Humanities: Vol. 2137). 400p. 1999. reprint ed. pap. 19.95 (*0-8153-3483-4*) Garland.

Lupack, Alan, jt. ed. see Hahn, Tom.

Lupack, Barbara T. Insanity As Redemption in Contemporary American Fiction: Inmates Running the Asylum. LC 94-29265. 256p. (C). 1995. 49.95 (*0-8130-1331-3*) U Press Fla.

Lupack, Barbara T., ed. Take Two: Adating the Contemporary American Novel to Film. LC 93-72985. (Illus.). 198p. (C). 1994. 45.95 (*0-87972-641-5*); pap. 18.95 (*0-87972-642-3*) Bowling Green Univ Popular Press.

— Vision/Re-Vision: Adapting Contemporary American Fiction by Women to Film. LC 96-28222. (Illus.). 250p. 1996. 45.95 (*0-87972-713-6*); pap. 24.95 (*0-87972-714-4*) Bowling Green Univ Popular Press.

Lupack, Barbara T., jt. auth. see Lupack, Alan.

Lupack, Barbara T., jt. auth. see Lupack, Alan.

***Lupack, Barbara Tepa, ed.** Nineteenth-Century Women at the Movies: Adapting Classic Women's Fiction to Film. LC 99-38681. (Illus.). 331p. 1999. 59.95 (*0-87972-805-1*) Bowling Green Univ Popular Press.

— Nineteenth-Century Women at the Movies: Adapting Classic Women's Fiction to Film. LC 99-38681. (Illus.). 331p. 1999. pap. 29.95 (*0-87972-806-X*) Bowling Green Univ Popular Press.

Lupack, Tepa. Critical Essays on Jerzy Kosinski. LC 97-45948. 1998. 49.00 (*0-7838-0073-8*, G K Hall & Co) Mac Lib Ref.

Lupak, Mario J. Byron as a Poet of Nature: The Search for Paradise. LC 99-14243. (Salzburg Studies in English Literature). 11p. 1999. text 99.95 (*0-7734-8187-7*) E Mellen.

Lupandin, K. K., jt. auth. see Rabinowitch, Z. E.

Lupart, Judy L., jt. auth. see Fry, Prem S.

Lupart, Judy L., jt. ed. see McKeough, Anne.

Lupas, Liana. Phonologie du Grec Attique. (Janua Linguarum, Series Practica: No. 164). (FRE.). 186p. (Orig.). 1972. pap. 49.25 (*90-279-2325-6*) Mouton.

Lupe, Nathan S., jt. auth. see BlueWolf, James Don.

Luper, Albert T., jt. auth. see Gleason, Harold.

Luper, Albert T., jt. auth. see Helm, Eugene.

Luper-Foy, Steven, ed. The Possibility of Knowledge: Nozick & His Critics. 352p. 1987. 65.00 (*0-8476-7446-0*); pap. 26.50 (*0-8476-7447-9*) Rowman.

Luper-Foy, Steven & Brown, Curtis. The Moral Life. 480p. (C). 1992. pap. text 51.50 (*0-03-033969-3*) Harcourt Coll Pubs.

Luper-Foy, Steven & Brown, Curtis, eds. Drugs, Morality, & the Law. LC 93-48114. (Studies in Applied Ethics: Vol. 3). 392p. 1994. text 15.00 (*0-8153-0485-4*, SS666) Garland.

Luper, Gregory L. Teletheory: Grammatology in the Age of Video. 256p. 1989. 45.00 (*0-415-90120-0*, A3232); pap. 14.95 (*0-415-90121-9*, A3236) Routledge.

Luper, Steven. Existing: An Introduction to Existential Thought. LC 98-52827. viii, 456p. 1999. pap. text 44.95 (*0-7674-0587-0*) Mayfield Pub.

— Invulnerability: On Securing Happiness. 190p. 1996. pap. 19.95 (*0-8126-9322-1*) Open Court.

— Invulnerability: On Securing Happiness. LC 96-10746. (Illus.). 190p. 1996. 39.95 (*0-8126-9321-3*) Open Court.

***Luper, Steven.** Living Well: Introductory Readings in Ethics. LC 98-88277. 592p. (C). 1999. text 40.00 (*0-15-508459-3*) Harcourt Coll Pubs.

Luper, Steven. Social Ideals & Policies: Readings in Social & Political Philosophy. LC 97-50277. xi, 675p. 1998. pap. text 46.95 (*0-7674-0010-0*, 0010-0) Mayfield Pub.

Luper, Steven & Brown, Curtis. The Moral Life. 2nd ed. 168p. (C). 1998. pap. text 51.50 (*0-15-505547-X*, Pub. by Harcourt Coll Pubs) Harcourt.

Lupertz, Markus. Manner Ohne Fraune - Parsifal. 1994. pap. 30.00 (*1-881616-31-2*) Dist Art Pubs.

Lupfer, E. A. Ornate Pictorial Calligraphy: Instructions & over 150 Examples. (Lettering, Calligraphy, Typography Ser.). (Illus.). 80p. 1982. pap. 4.95 (*0-486-21957-7*) Dover.

***Lupia, Arthur, et al, eds.** Elements of Reason: Cognition, Choice & the Bounds of Rationality. LC 99-59174. (Cambridge Studies in Political Psychology & Public Opinion). (Illus.). 394p. (C). 2000. pap. text Price not set. (*0-521-65332-0*) Cambridge U Pr.

Lupia, Arthur & McCubbins, Mathew D. The Democratic Dilemma: Can Citizens Learn What They Need to Know? LC 97-18130. (Political Economy of Institutions & Decisions Ser.). (Illus.). 304p. (C). 1998. text 64.95 (*0-521-58448-5*); pap. text 19.95 (*0-521-58593-7*) Cambridge U Pr.

***Lupia, Arthur, et al.** Elements of Reason: Cognition, Choice & the Bounds of Rationality. LC 99-59174. (Cambridge Studies in Political Psychology & Public Opinion). (Illus.). 394p. (C). 2000. text Price not set. (*0-521-65329-0*) Cambridge U Pr.

Lupia, Charles. Two Times in the Stream. 100p. 1993. pap. 5.00 (*0-9637558-0-3*) Celnote Pr.

***Lupica, Mike.** Bump & Run. 320p. 2000. 24.95 (*0-399-14647-4*) Putnam Pub Group.

Lupica, Mike. Jump. 384p. 1996. pap. 5.99 (*0-7860-0303-0*); mass mkt. 5.99 (*1-57566-112-8*, Knsington) Kensgtn Pub Corp.

— Mad As Hell. LC 97-40087. 256p. 1997. pap. 14.95 (*0-8092-3008-9*, 300890, Contemporary Bks) NTC Contemp Pub Co.

***Lupica, Mike.** Summer of '98: When Homers Flew, Records Fell & Baseball Reclaimed America. 224p. 2000. pap. 14.95 (*0-8092-2444-5*, 244450, Contemporary Bks) NTC Contemp Pub Co.

Lupica, Mike. Summer of '98: When Homers Flew, Records Fell & Baseball Reclaimed America. LC 98-50425. 240p. 1999. 23.95 (*0-399-14514-1*, G P Putnam) Peng Put Young Read.

Lupin, M. S., et al. Briquetting: Alternative Process for Urea Supergranules. LC 83-18396. (Technical Bulletin Ser.: No. T-26). (Illus.). 20p. (Orig.). 1983. pap. 4.00 (*0-88090-046-6*) Intl Fertilizer.

Lupin, Mimi. New England Autumn. 1988. 9.95 (*0-07-039163-7*) McGraw.

Lupinacci, Alicia S. Women & Business Ownership: Entrepreneurs in Dallas. LC 98-28442. (Studies in Entrepreneurship). (Illus.). 186p. 1998. 46.00 (*0-8153-3195-9*) Garland.

Lupinacci, Romeo V. From Chef Romeo's Recipe Collection. Greene, Deborah, ed. (Illus.). 429p. (Orig.). Date not set. pap. 12.50 (*0-9634333-0-X*) Lundeberg MD.

Lupini, Valeri. There Goes the Neighbourhood. (Northern Lights Young Novels Ser.). 112p. (YA). (gr. 4-10). 1995. pap. 7.95 (*0-88995-128-4*, Pub. by Red Deer) Genl Dist Srvs.

Lupinski, John H. & Moore, Robert S., eds. Polymeric Materials for Electronics Packaging & Interconnection. (ACS Symposium Ser.: No. 407). 512p. 1989. text 110.00 (*0-8412-1679-7*, Pub. by Am Chemical) OUP.

Lupis, Claude H. Chemical Thermodynamics of Materials. 608p. 1983. pap. 60.00 (*0-444-00779-2*) P-H.

Lupis, Ivo F. Medu Nasim Narodom U Americi. LC 71-155327. 1971. reprint ed. 10.00 (*0-88247-053-1*) Ragusan Pr.

Lupiy, Bohdan. Ukraine & European Security: International Mechanisms As Non-Military Security Options for Ukraine. NATO Defense College Staff, ed. (Euro-Atlantic Security Studies: Vol. 3). (Illus.). 122p. 1996. pap. 32.95 (*3-631-30356-4*) P Lang Pubng.

— Ukraine & European Security: International Mechanisms As Non-Military Security Options for Ukraine. NATO Defense College Staff, ed. (Euro-Atlantic Security Studies: Vol. 3). (Illus.). 122p. 1996. pap. 32.95 (*0-8204-3193-1*) P Lang Pubng.

Lupke, Theodor Von, see Krischen, Fritz.

***Lupo, Alan.** The Messiah Comes Tomorrow: Tales from the American Shtetl. 2000. 19.95 (*1-55849-283-6*) U of Mass Pr.

Lupo, Ann. Being Me & Drug Free Kid-Pak. rev. ed. Fox, Greg, ed. (Life-Skill Builder Educational Ser.). (Illus.). 16p. (J). (gr. k-3). 1991. pap. text 3.95 (*1-56230-135-7*); pap. text 4.95 incl. audio (*1-56230-125-X*) Syndistar.

— Healthy Bodies Don't Need Drugs Kid-Pak. rev. ed. Fox, Greg, ed. (Life-Skill Builder Educational Ser.). (Illus.). 20p. (J). (gr. 3-5). 1991. pap. text 3.95 (*1-56230-138-1*); pap. text 4.95 (*1-56230-128-4*) Syndistar.

— Red the Firedog's How to Plan for a Safe Escape Kid-Pak. rev. ed. Fox, Greg, ed. (Life-Skill Builder Educational Ser.). (Illus.). 20p. (J). (ps-3). 1991. pap. text 3.95 (*1-56230-137-3*); pap. text 4.95 incl. audio (*1-56230-134-9*) Syndistar.

Lupo, Ann, ed. see Bosco, James.

Lupo, Jasper, et al, eds. DARPA Neural Network Study. LC 88-31655. (Illus.). 625p. (C). 1988. text 49.95 (*0-916159-17-5*) AFCEA Intl Pr.

Lupo, John. Chattahoochee Valley Sources & Resources Vol. II: The Georgia Counties: An Annotated Bibliography. 736p. 1994. 31.00 (*0-945477-07-4*) Hist Chattahoochee.

Lupo, John, compiled by. Chattahoochee Valley Sources & Resources--an Annotated Bibliography: The Alabama Counties, Vol. 1. 497p. 1988. lib. bdg. 19.95 (*0-945477-06-6*) Hist Chattahoochee.

***Lupo, Larry.** When the Mets Played Baseball on Staten Island. LC 99-96816. 2000. pap. 10.95 (*0-533-13357-2*) Vantage.

Lupo, Maxine Van Evera. How to Master a Great Golf Swing. 304p. 1992. pap. 16.95 (*0-8092-4032-7*, 403270, Contemporary Bks) NTC Contemp Pub Co.

Lupo, Nunzio, ed. see Henry Ford Heart & Vascular Institute of Henry Ford Hospital Staff.

Lupo, Raphael V. & Tanguay, Donna M. What Corporate & General Practitioners Should Know about Intellectual Property Litigation. LC 91-71727. 242p. 1991. text 34.00 (*0-8318-0576-5*, B576) Am Law Inst.

Lupoff, Dick & Thompson, Don, eds. All in Color for a Dime. LC 97-156447. 272p. 1997. pap. 14.95 (*0-87341-498-5*, ACD01) Krause Pubns.

Lupoff, Dick, jt. auth. see Thompson, Don.

Lupoff, Richard. The Outer Limits, Vol. 2. LC 96-67914. (Illus.). 224p. 1997. pap. 12.00 (*0-7615-0620-9*) Prima Pub.

— The Outer Limits, Vol. 3. LC 96-67914. 272p. 1997. pap. 12.00 (*0-7615-0621-7*) Prima Pub.

— Stroka Prospekt. Disch, Thomas M., ed. LC 82-19269. (Singularities Ser.). (Illus.). 45p. (Orig.). 1982. pap. 20.00 (*0-915124-73-4*) Coffee Hse.

Lupoff, Richard, jt. auth. see Kurland, Michael.

Lupoff, Richard A. Before...12:01...& After. (Illus.). 378p. 1996. 27.00 (*1-878252-23-2*); boxed set 95.00 (*1-878252-24-0*) Fedogan & Bremer.

— Gryphon Double: The Digital Wristwatch of Philip K. Dick & Hyperprism. No. 7. LC 96-133922. 1994. per. 12.00 (*0-936071-25-7*) Gryphon Pubns.

Lupoff, Richard A., ed. see Davidson, Avram.

Lupoi, Maurizio. The Origins of the European Legal Order. LC 98-8258. 656p. (C). 2000. text 125.00 (*0-521-62107-0*) Cambridge U Pr.

***Lupoi, Maurizio.** Trusts: A Comparative Study. LC 99-24171. 1999. write for info. (*0-521-62329-4*) Cambridge U Pr.

Lupold, Harry F. & Haddad, Gladys, eds. Ohio's Western Reserve: A Regional Reader. LC 88-691. 290p. 1988. pap. 15.00 (*0-87338-372-9*) Kent St U Pr.

Lupowski, Anne & Assouline, Susan. Jane & Johnny Love Math. 1992. pap. 14.99 (*0-89824-539-7*) Trillium Pr.

Lupp, Thomas. The Tuscarora Trail: A Guide to the North Half. LC 97-76060. 88p. 1997. 6.00 (*0-915746-80-8*) Potomac Appalach.

— The Tuscarora Trail: A Guide to the South Half. LC 97-76061. 96p. 1997. 6.00 (*0-915746-81-6*) Potomac Appalach.

Luppa, Annelies. Die Verbrechergestal Im Zeitalter des Realismus von Fontane Bis Mann. (Studies in European Thought: Vol. 10). (GER.). 164p. (C). 1995. text 37.95 (*0-8204-2545-1*) P Lang Pubng.

Luppens, Michel. What Do the Fairies Do with All Those Teeth. (Illus.). 24p. (J). (gr. k-3). 1996. 12.95 (*1-55209-001-9*) Firefly Bks Ltd.

— What Do the Fairies Do with All Those Teeth. (Illus.). 24p. (J). (ps-3). 1996. pap. 4.95 (*1-55209-002-7*) Firefly Bks Ltd.

Luppens, Michel & Beha, Phillipe. What Do the Fairies Do with All Those Teeth? (Illus.). (J). 15.95 (*0-590-74050-4*) Scholastic Inc.

— What Do the Fairies Do with All Those Teeth? (Illus.). (J). 1991. pap. 5.95 (*0-590-74075-X*) Scholastic Inc.

Luppert, Eve. Rules for the Road: Surviving Your First Job Out of School. LC 97-35106. 224p. 1998. 13.00 (*0-399-52411-8*) Berkley Pub.

Luppi, Diana, jt. auth. see Jho, Zoev.

Luppino. Family Law. 400p. (C). 2001. 50.67 (*0-13-901125-0*, Macmillan Coll) P-H.

***Luprecht, Mark.** Of Angels, Things & Death: Paul Klee's Last Painting in Context. LC 98-21962. (Hermeneutics of Art Ser.: Vol. 9). (Illus.). xii, 187p. (C). 1999. text 48.95 (*0-8204-4115-5*) P Lang Pubng.

Luprecht, Mark. What People Call Pessimism: Sigmund Freud, Arthur Schnitzler & Nineteenth-Century Controversy at the University of Vienna Medical School. (Studies in Austrian Literature, Culture, & Thought). 172p. 1990. pap. 23.00 (*0-929497-28-7*) Ariadne CA.

Lupsewicz, Veronica A. Misty the Manatee. Weinberger, Jane, ed. LC 93-61193. (Illus.). 46p. (J). (ps-4). 1996. pap. 9.95 (*0-932433-96-0*) Windswept Hse.

Lupson, Peter. Guide to German Idioms. (Guides to...Idioms Ser.). (GER., Illus.). 128p. 1994. pap. 7.95 (*0-8442-2501-0*, Passprt Bks) NTC Contemp Pub Co.

Lupson, Peter & Aufderstrasse, H. Los Geht's: Coursebook 2, Stage 2. 176p. (C). 1988. pap., student ed. 18.95 (0-85950-725-4) Dufour.

Lupson, Peter & Pelissier, Michel. Guide to French Idioms. LC 98-16234. (Guides to...Idioms Ser.). (FRE., Illus.). 128p. 1995. pap. 6.95 (0-8442-1502-3, 15023, Passprt Bks) NTC Contemp Pub Co.

Lupson, Peter, et al. Los Geht's: Coursebook 1, Stage 1. 177p. (C). 1986. pap., student ed. 18.95 (0-85950-508-1) Dufour.

— Working with German: Coursebook, Level 2. 160p. 1990. pap. 25.00 (0-7487-0147-8); pap. 35.00 (0-7487-0148-6) Dufour.

— Working with German Level 1: Coursebook. (Illus.). 201p. 1996. pap. 34.50 (0-7487-2450-8, Pub. by S Thornes Pubs) Trans-Atl Phila.

Lupton, et al. Managing Public Involvement. LC 97-44933. (Health Services Management Ser.). 192p. 1997. 95.00 (0-335-19633-0) OpUniv Pr.

— Managing Public Involvement. LC 97-44933. (Health Services Management Ser.). 192p. 1998. pap. 29.95 (0-335-19632-2) OpUniv Pr.

Lupton, Charles T. Oil & Gas in the Olympic Peninsula. (Shorey Prospecting Ser.). 60p. reprint ed. pap. 10.00 (0-8466-0055-2, S55) Shoreys Bkstore.

Lupton, Dan. People of Promise: Adventure Guidebook. Mains, Laurie, ed. (Nineteen Ninety-Nine 50-Day Spiritual Adventure Ser.). 160p. 1998. pap. 7.00 (1-57849-111-8) Mainstay Church.

Lupton, David W. & Lupton, Dorothy R. Lancaster Platt Lupton Vol. 1: The Legacy of a Fur Trader. (Road to Delhi). (Illus.). 124p. (Orig.). 1994. pap. 11.50 (0-9644165-1-4) S Platte Valley.

***Lupton, Deborah.** The Emotional Self: A Sociocultural Exploration LC 97-62538. 195 p. 1998. write for info. (0-7619-5602-6) Sage.

Lupton, Deborah. Food, Body & the Self. 192p. (C). 1996. 69.95 (0-8039-7647-X); pap. 24.95 (0-8039-7648-8) Sage.

— The Imperative of Health: Public Health & the Regulated Body. 192p. (C). 1995. 69.95 (0-8039-7935-5); pap. 24.00 (0-8039-7936-3) Sage.

— Medicine As Culture: Illness, Disease & the Body in Western Societies. 256p. (C). 1994. text 69.95 (0-8039-8924-5); pap. text 24.95 (0-8039-8925-3) Sage.

— Moral Threats & Dangerous Desires: AIDS in the News Media. (Social Aspects of AIDS Ser.). 208p. 1994. 75.00 (0-7484-0179-2, Pub. by Tay Francis Ltd); pap. 27.00 (0-7484-0180-6, Pub. by Tay Francis Ltd) Taylor & Francis.

— Risk. LC 98-37774. (Key Ideas Ser.). 1999. write for info. (0-415-18333-2) Routledge.

Lupton, Deborah. Risk. LC 98-37774. (Key Ideas Ser.). 1999. pap. text 17.99 (0-415-18334-0) Routledge.

***Lupton, Deborah, ed.** Risk & Sociocultural Theory: New Directions & Perspectives. 201p. (C). 2000. text 57.95 (0-521-64207-8); pap. text 21.95 (0-521-64554-9) Cambridge U Pr.

Lupton, Deborah & Barclay, Lesley. Constructing Fatherhood: Discourses & Experiences. LC 97-67292. 192p. 1997. 65.00 (0-7619-5340-X); pap. 23.95 (0-7619-5341-8) Sage.

Lupton, Deborah, jt. auth. see Petersen, Alan.

Lupton, Deborah, jt. auth. see Tulloch, John.

Lupton, Deborah, jt. ed. see Chapman, S.

Lupton, Deborah, tr. see Jacobus, Verheiden.

Lupton, Donald. London & the Countrey Carbonadoed & Quartered into Several Characters. LC 77-7413. (English Experience Ser.: No. 879). 1977. reprint ed. lib. bdg. 20.00 (90-221-0879-1) Walter J Johnson.

Lupton, Dorothy R., jt. auth. see Lupton, David W.

Lupton, E., jt. ed. see Schofield, Philip F.

Lupton, Ellen. Design Writing Research: Writing on Graphic Design. 1999. pap. text 24.95 (0-7148-3851-9) Phaidon Press.

— Mechanical Brides: Women & Machines from Home to Office. Aakre, Nancy, ed. LC 93-22169. (Illus.). 64p. (Orig.). 1993. pap. 17.95 (1-878271-97-0) Princeton Arch.

— Mixing Messages: Graphic Design in Contemporary American Culture. LC 96-18695. (Illus.). 176p. 1996. 55.00 (1-56898-098-1); pap. 35.00 (1-56898-099-X) Princeton Arch.

Lupton, Ellen & Cohen, Elaine L. Letters from the Avant-Garde: Modern Graphic Design. (Illus.). 128p. 1996. pap. 24.95 (1-56898-052-3) Princeton Arch.

Lupton, Ellen & Miller, J. Abbott. The Bathroom, the Kitchen, & the Aesthetics of Waste. 2nd ed. (Illus.). 80p. 1996. pap. 19.95 (1-56898-096-5) Princeton Arch.

— The Process of Elimination: The Bathroom, the Kitchen, & the Aesthetics of Waste. (Illus.). 80p. (Orig.). 1992. pap. 19.95 (0-938437-42-9) MIT List Visual Arts.

Lupton, F. G. Wheat Breeding & Its Scientific Basis. 580p. 1987. lib. bdg. 145.00 (0-412-24470-5) Chapman & Hall.

Lupton, Gillian, et al. Society & Gender: An Introduction to Sociology. 368p. 1994. 69.95 (0-7329-1303-9, Pub. by Macmill Educ) Paul & Co Pubs.

Lupton, Hugh. Freaky Tales from Far & Wide. (Illus.). 48p. (J). (ps-1). 1999. 15.95 (1-902283-16-3) Barefoot Bks NY.

— Tales of Wisdom & Wonder. (Illus.). 80p. (J). (gr. k-7). 1998. 18.95 (1-901223-09-4) Barefoot Bks NY.

Lupton, Hugh R. Whence? Where? Whither? & Occasional Verse. 120p. 1984. 40.00 (0-7212-0678-6, Pub. by Regency Pr GBR) St Mut.

Lupton, James F. My Mother, Your Mother: She Is for All God's Children. Bissex, Sandra & Tanner, Margaret, eds. (Illus.). 120p. (Orig.). 1996. pap. write for info. (0-614-25692-5) Jabbok Encounter.

Lupton, Julia R. Afterlives of the Saints: Hagiography, Typology, & Renaissance Literature. LC 95-50474. 1995. 39.50 (0-8047-2643-4) Stanford U Pr.

Lupton, Julia R. & Reinhard, Kenneth. After Oedipus: Shakespeare in Psychoanalysis. LC 92-54975. (Illus.). 288p. 1993. text 42.50 (0-8014-2407-0); pap. text 16.95 (0-8014-9687-X) Cornell U Pr.

Lupton, K., jt. auth. see Covell, W.

Lupton, Mary J. Menstruation & Psychoanalysis. LC 92-39667. 240p. 1993. text 34.95 (0-252-02012-X); pap. text 14.95 (0-252-06315-5) U of Ill Pr.

Lupton, Mary Jane. Maya Angelou: A Critical Companion. LC 98-17489. (Critical Companions to Popular Contemporary Writers Ser.). 200p. 1998. 29.95 (0-313-30325-8, Greenwood Pr) Greenwood.

Lupton, Robert. Statistics in Theory & Practice. LC 92-36396. (Illus.). 128p. (C). 1993. text 35.00 (0-691-07429-1, Pub. by Princeton U Pr) Cal Prin Full Svc.

Lupton, Robert D. Theirs Is the Kingdom. 1989. write for info. (0-318-65615-9) Harper SF.

— Theirs Is the Kingdom: Celebrating the Gospel in Urban America. LC 89-45252. 144p. 1989. pap. 13.00 (0-06-065307-8, Perennial) HarperTrade.

Lupton, Thomas. All for Money. LC 79-133700. (Tudor Facsimile Texts. Old English Plays Ser.: No. 51). reprint ed. 59.50 (0-404-53351-5) AMS Pr.

Lupton, Tom. Industrial Behaviour & Personnel Management. 96p. (C). 1978. 50.00 (0-85292-164-0) St Mut.

Lupton, Tom, ed. Human Factors in Manufacturing: Proceedings of the International Conference on Human Factors in Manufacturing, Stratford-upon-Avon, 3rd, November 4-6, 1986. (Illus.). ix, 409p. 1987. 142.95 (0-387-16333-6) Spr-Verlag.

Lupton, Tom & Tanner, Ian. Achieving Change: A Systematic Approach. 100p. 1987. text 56.95 (0-566-02526-4, Pub. by Gower) Ashgate Pub Co.

Lupul, Manoly R. The Roman Catholic Church & the North-West School Question: A Study in Church-State Relations in Western Canada, 1875-1905. LC 73-89844. 304p. reprint ed. pap. 94.30 (0-8357-3646-6, 203637300003) Bks Demand.

Lupulescu, Aurel. Hormones & Carcinogenesis. LC 82-15110. 357p. 1983. 80.00 (0-275-91402-X, C1402, Praeger Pubs) Greenwood.

— Hormones & Vitamins in Cancer Treatment. (Illus.). 336p. 1990. lib. bdg. 229.00 (0-8493-5973-2, 5973) CRC Pr.

Lupus, Bernhard. Der Sprachgebrauch des Cornelius Nepos. vii, 224p. 1972. reprint ed. write for info. (3-487-04508-7) G Olms Pubs.

Lupus, Peter, jt. auth. see Leebow, Ken.

Luque, Antonio. Photovoltaic Conversion of Sol. text. write for info. (0-471-49196-9) Wiley.

Luque, Antonio. Solar Cells & Optics for Photovoltaic Concentration. (Optics & Optoelectronics Ser.). (Illus.). 552p. 1989. 250.00 (0-85274-106-5) IOP Pub.

Luque, Antonio, et al, eds. Tenth E. C. Photovoltaic Solar Energy Conference. 1490p. (C). 1991. text 468.00 (0-7923-1389-5) Kluwer Academic.

Luque, Antonio & Araujo, G. L., eds. Physical Limitations to Photovoltaic Energy Conversion. (Illus.). 192p. 1990. 105.00 (0-7503-0030-2) IOP Pub.

Luque, Antonio & Palz, Wolfgang, eds. Photovoltaic Concentration: A Special Issue of International Journal of Solar Energy, Vol. 6, No. 6. 84p. 1988. pap. text 106.00 (3-7186-4861-X) Gordon & Breach.

Luque de Castro, M. D., jt. auth. see Valcarcel, M.

Luque De Sanchez, Maria D. Ocupacion Norteamericana y la Ley Foraker: Como Reaccionaron los Puertorriquenos. LC 77-10859. 197p. 1986. pap. 7.00 (0-8477-0851-9) U of PR Pr.

Luque, E., ed. Mini & Microcomputers & Their Applications - Mimi, 1985: Proceedings, ISMM Symposium, Sant Feliu de Guixols, Spain, June 25-28, 1985. LC 91-343. (Illus.). 518p. 1985. 108.00 (0-88986-121-8, 077) Acta Pr.

— Mini & Microcomputers & Their Applications - Mimi, 1988: Proceedings of the ISMM Symposium, Sant Feliu de Guixols, Spain, June 27-30, 1988. 680p. 1988. 125.00 (84-7488-121-8, 148) Acta Pr.

Luque, E., et al, eds. Parallel & Distributed Systems EURO-PDS '97. LC 97-18562. (Illus.). 348p. 1997. pap. 105.00 (0-88986-225-7) Acta Pr.

Luque, E., jt. ed. see Abdelrahman, K.

Luque Faxardo, Francisco de. Fiel Desengano Contra La Ociosidad y Los Juegos, 2 vols. Riquer, Martin de, ed. (SPA.). 529p. 1968. 200.00 (0-614-00215-X) Elliots Bks.

Luqueer, Frederick L. Hegel As Educator. LC 03-12359. reprint ed. 27.50 (0-404-04068-3) AMS Pr.

Luquet, F. M., jt. auth. see Boudier, J. F.

Luquet, Wade. Short-Term Couples Therapy Bk. 8027: The Imago Model in Action. LC 96-1961. 224p. 1996. pap. text 38.95 (0-87630-802-7) Brunner-Mazel.

Luquet, Wade & Hannah, Mo T., eds. Healing in the Relational Paradigm: The Image Relationship Therapy Casebook. LC 97-45130. 225p. 1997. 31.95 (0-87630-861-2) Brunner-Mazel.

Luquire, Wilson, ed. Coordinating Cooperative Collection Development: A National Perspective. LC 85-24847. (Resource Sharing & Information Networks Ser.: Vol. 2, Nos. 3-4). 253p. 1986. text 49.95 (0-86656-543-4) Haworth Pr.

— Experiences of Library Network Administrators: Paper Based on the Symposium "From Our Past: Toward 2000" LC 84-22428. (Resource Sharing & Information Networks Ser.: Vol. 2, Nos. 1-2). 131p. 1985. text 7.95 (0-86656-388-1) Haworth Pr.

— Library Networking: Current Problems & Future Prospects. LC 83-18474. (Resource Sharing & Information Networks Ser.: Vol. 1, Nos. 1-2). 140p. 1983. text 49.95 (0-86656-270-2) Haworth Pr.

Luraghi, Raimondo. A History of the Confederate Navy. LC 95-49315. (Illus.). 552p. 1996. 39.95 (1-55750-527-6) Naval Inst Pr.

***Luraschi, Susan.** French Hotels, Inns & Other Places. (Alastair Sawday's Special Places to Stay Ser.). (Illus.). 208p. 2000. pap. 19.95 (0-7627-0725-9) Globe Pequot.

Lurati, O. Parole Nuovo. 1991. 49.95 (0-8288-3918-2, F112072) Fr & Eur.

Luray, Stanley B. Physical Examinations--Infants to Old Age & Body Parts: Index of New Information. (Illus.). 163p. 1999. 47.50 (0-7883-1888-8); pap. 44.50 (0-7883-1889-6) ABBE Pubs Assn.

Lurdang, Laurence & Robbins, Ceila D. Every Bite a Delight & Other Slogans. (Illus.). 432p. 1992. 15.95 (0-8103-9423-5) Visible Ink Pr.

Luree Staff. Cyber Warrior: The Ultimate Manifesto for Adventure & Profit on the Internet. 327p. 1998. pap. text 19.95 (1-896912-10-9) Uphill Hse.

Luria. Kitvei Ari: Hebrew Text, 18 vols., Set. 1985. 260.00 (0-943688-16-7) Res Ctr Kabbalah.

Luria, A. R. Basic Problems of Neurolinguistics. Haigh, Basil, tr. from RUS. (Janua Linguarum, Series Major: No. 73). 1976. text 107.70 (90-279-3205-0) Mouton.

— Higher Cortical Functions in Man. 2nd ed. LC 77-20421. (Illus.). 656p. 1980. 54.50 (0-306-10966-2, Kluwer Plenum) Kluwer Academic.

— Traumatic Aphasia: Its Syndromes, Psychology & Treatment. Bowden, Douglas M., tr. LC 68-17903. (Janua Linguarum, Ser. Major: No. 5). 1970. text 101.55 (90-279-0717-X) Mouton.

Luria, A. R. & Tsvetkova, L. S. The Neuropsychological Analysis of Problem Solving. Tichinas Staff, tr. from RUS. LC 90-83131. (Classics in Soviet Psychology Ser.). 256p. 1990. boxed set 57.95 (1-878205-10-2) St Lucie Pr.

Luria, A. R. & Vygotsky, L. S. Ape, Primitive Man & Child: Essays in the History of Behavior. Rossiter, Evelyn, tr. from RUS. LC 91-73523. (Classics in Soviet Psychology Ser.). (Illus.). 192p. (C). 1992. per. 29.95 (1-878205-43-9) St Lucie Pr.

Luria, A. R., jt. auth. see Vygotsky, L. S.

Luria, Aleksandr R. Cognitive Development: Its Cultural & Social Foundations. (Illus.). 180p. 1976. pap. 14.95 (0-674-13732-9) HUP.

— The Making of Mind: A Personal Account of Soviet Psychology. Cole, Michael & Cole, Sheila, eds. (Illus.). 234p. 1979. pap. 17.50 (0-674-54327-0) HUP.

— The Making of Mind: A Personal Account of Soviet Psychology. Cole, Michael & Cole, Sheila, eds. (Illus.). 234p. (C). 1979. 30.00 (0-674-54326-2) HUP.

— The Man with a Shattered World: The History of a Brain Wound. LC 86-31866. 168p. 1987. pap. 14.95 (0-674-54625-3) HUP.

— The Mind of a Mnemonist: A Little Book about a Vast Memory. LC 86-33487. 160p. 1987. pap. text 7.95 (0-317-59999-2) HUP.

— The Mind of a Mnemonist: A Little Book about a Vast Memory. LC 86-31847. 160p. 1987. pap. 14.95 (0-674-57622-5) HUP.

— Neuropsychological Studies in Aphasia. (Neurolinguistics Ser.: Vol. 6). 184p. 1977. 52.00 (90-265-0244-3) Swets.

— The Working Brain. Haigh, B., tr. LC 72-95540. 408p. 1976. pap. 20.00 (0-465-09208-X, Pub. by Basic) HarpC.

Luria, Aleksandr R. & Haigh, B. Restoration of Function after Brain Injury. LC 63-10016. 1963. 127.00 (0-08-010130-5, Pub. by Pergamon Repr) Franklin.

Luria, Daniel D. Beyond Free Trade & Protectionism: The Public Interest in a U. S. Auto Policy. 30p. 1990. 10.00 (0-944826-08-3) Economic Policy Inst.

Luria, Daniel D. & Rogers, Joel. Metro Futures: Economic Solutions for Cities & Their Suburbs. LC 99-28328. 80p. 1999. pap. 11.00 (0-8070-0603-3) Beacon Pr.

Luria, Emile. Tornado Weather. LC 93-13597. 64p. 1993. pap. 14.95 (0-7734-2763-5, Mellen Poetry Pr) E Mellen.

Luria, Isaac. Gates of Reincarnation (Shaar Hagilgulim) (HEB.). 200p. 1985. pap. 10.00 (0-943688-49-3) Res Ctr Kabbalah.

— Tzadik Yesod Olam. 124p. 1960. 10.00 (0-943688-21-3) Res Ctr Kabbalah.

Luria, Joseph. God Is Your Neighbor: And the Stranger He Is, the More He's God. 128p. 2000. pap. 18.00 (0-9672802-0-6) Twelve OClock.

Luria, Keith P. Territories of Grace: Cultural Change in the Seventeenth-Century Diocese of Grenoble. LC 90-38259. (Studies on the History of Society & Culture: No. 11). (Illus.). 275p. 1991. 45.00 (0-520-06810-6, Pub. by U CA Pr) Cal Prin Full Svc.

Luria, Maxwell. A Reader's Guide to the Roman de la Rose. LC 81-22767. xii, 282p. (C). 1982. lib. bdg. 39.50 (0-208-01838-7, Archon Bks) Shoe String.

Luria, Maxwell, ed. Elijah Benamozegh: Israel & Humanity. LC 94-34906. (Classics of Western Spirituality Ser.).Tr. of Israel et l'Humanite. 1995. 29.95 (0-8091-0468-7) Paulist Pr.

Luria, Maxwell, tr. from FRE. Elijah Benamozegh: Israel & Humanity. LC 94-34906.Tr. of Israel et l'Humanite. 1995. pap. 22.95 (0-8091-3541-8) Paulist Pr.

Luria, Maxwell, ed. see Taub, Lawrence.

Luria, Maxwell S. Middle English Lyrics. 2nd ed. (Critical Editions Ser.). (C). Date not set. pap. write for info. (0-393-96649-6, Norton Paperbks) Norton.

Luria, Maxwell S. & Hoffman, Richard L., eds. Middle English Lyrics. (Critical Editions Ser.). (Illus.). 360p. (C). 1974. pap. text 12.50 (0-393-09338-7) Norton.

Luria, Paul. Magda Rose. large type ed. LC 98-74551. 150p. (J). (gr. 4-5). 1999. pap. 12.95 (0-943864-98-4) Davenport.

Luria, R. Issac. Bet Shaar Hakavanot. (HEB.). 1983. 11.00 (0-924457-48-1) Res Ctr Kabbalah.

Luria, S. E. The Multiplication of Viruses. (Protoplasmatologia Ser.: Vol. 4, Pts. 3, 4a, 4b, 5). (ENG & GER., Illus.). iv, 118p. 1958. 32.50 (0-387-80488-9) Spr-Verlag.

Luria, Salvador E., et al. Instructors Guide View of Life. 1981. teacher ed. 10.75 (0-8053-6649-0) Benjamin-Cummings.

— A View of Life. 1981. text, teacher ed. 10.75 (0-8053-6648-2) Benjamin-Cummings.

Luria, Salvador Edward. A Slot Machine, a Broken Test Tube: An Autobiography. 1985. pap. 6.95 (0-465-07831-1) Basic.

Luria-Sukenick, Lynn. Houdini Houdini. (CSU Poetry Ser.: No. X). 55p. 1982. pap. 4.50 (0-914946-29-3) Cleveland St Univ Poetry Ctr.

Luria-Svkemck, Lynn. Danger Wall May Fall. LC 96-37562. 192p. (Orig.). 1997. pap. 13.95 (0-944072-76-3) Zoland Bks.

Lurie, A. I. Non-Linear Theory of Elasticity. (Applied Mathematics & Mechanics Ser.: No. 36). 618p. 1990. 227.50 (0-444-87439-9, North Holland) Elsevier.

Lurie, Abraham, et al, eds. Social Work with Groups in Health Settings. LC 82-18151. 124p. 1982. pap. 7.95 (0-88202-137-0) Watson Pub Intl.

Lurie, Abraham & Rosenberg, Gary, eds. Social Work Administration in Health Care. LC 84-799. 310p. 1984. pap. 49.95 (0-86656-314-8); text 59.95 (0-917724-42-9) Haworth Pr.

Lurie, Alison. The Black Geese: A Baba Yaga Story from Russia. LC 98-3681. (Illus.). (J). (ps-3). 1999. 14.95 (0-7894-2558-0, D K Ink) DK Pub Inc.

— Don't Tell the Grown-Ups: The Subversive Power of Children's Literature. 256p. 1998. pap. 14.00 (0-316-24625-5) Little.

— Don't Tell the Grown-Ups: Why Kids Love the Books They Do. 256p. 1991. reprint ed. pap. 9.95 (0-380-71402-7, Avon Bks) Morrow Avon.

— Fabulous Beasts. (Illus.). 32p. (YA). (gr. 1 up). 1999. pap. 6.95 (0-374-42254-0, Sunburst Bks) FS&G.

— Foreign Affairs. 1990. pap. 12.50 (0-380-70990-2, Avon Bks) Morrow Avon.

— Heavenly Zoo: Legends & Tales of the Stars. LC 79-21263. (Illus.). 64p. (J). (ps-3). 1996. pap. 6.95 (0-374-42927-8) FS&G.

— Heavenly Zoo: Legends & Tales of the Stars. LC 79-21263. 1996. 12.15 (0-606-09400-8, Pub. by Turtleback) Demco.

— Imaginary Friends. LC 97-24563. 304p. 1998. pap. 13.00 (0-8050-5180-5) H Holt & Co.

— Imaginary Friends. 1991. pap. 8.95 (0-380-71136-2, Avon Bks) Morrow Avon.

***Lurie, Alison.** Language of Clothes. LC 99-41520. (Illus.). 272p. 2000. pap. 22.50 (0-8050-6244-0, Owl) H Holt & Co.

Lurie, Alison. The Last Resort. 336p. 1999. pap. 13.00 (0-8050-6174-6, Pub. by H Holt & Co) VHPS.

— The Last Resort. large type ed. LC 98-30791. 1998. 30.00 (0-7862-1642-5, G K Hall Lrg Type) Mac Lib Ref.

— The Last Resort: A Novel. LC 97-42985. 321p. 1998. 22.00 (0-8050-5866-4) H Holt & Co.

— Love & Friendship. LC 97-2226. 1997. pap. text 12.00 (0-8050-5178-3, Owl) H Holt & Co.

— Love & Friendship. 304p. 1993. pap. 9.00 (0-380-71945-2, Avon Bks) Morrow Avon.

— The Nowhere City. LC 97-796. 1997. pap. 12.00 (0-8050-5179-1, Owl) H Holt & Co.

— The Nowhere City. 336p. 1986. mass mkt. 4.50 (0-380-70070-0, Avon Bks) Morrow Avon.

— The Nowhere City. 336p. 1992. pap. 9.00 (0-380-71936-3, Avon Bks) Morrow Avon.

— Only Children. 272p. 1990. pap. 7.95 (0-380-70875-2, Avon Bks) Morrow Avon.

— Real People. LC 97-18192. 188p. 1998. pap. 12.00 (0-8050-5181-3) H Holt & Co.

— The War Between the Tates. 1991. pap. 8.95 (0-380-71135-4, Avon Bks) Morrow Avon.

Lurie, Alison, ed. The Oxford Book of Modern Fairy Tales. 480p. 1994. reprint ed. pap. 14.95 (0-19-282385-X) OUP.

Lurie, Alison, ed. & intro. see Burnett, Frances Hodgson.

Lurie, Ann T., et al. European Paintings of the Sixteenth, Seventeenth, & Eighteenth Centuries: The Cleveland Museum of Art Catalogue of Paintings, Pt. 3. LC 81-3961. (Illus.). 542p. 1982. 40.00 (0-910386-66-8) Cleveland Mus Art.

***Lurie, B. J. & Enright, Paul J.** Classical Feedback Control with Matlab. LC 99-87832. (Control Engineering Ser.). 2000. write for info. (0-8247-0370-7) Dekker.

Lurie, Elinore E., et al. Longitudinal Retirement History Study: Student Workbook. (Gerontology Research Toolkit Ser.). 168p. (Orig.). 1994. pap. text, student ed. 49.00 (0-8018-5045-2) Johns Hopkins.

— Longitudinal Study of Aging: Student Workbook. (Gerontology Research Toolkit Ser.). 182p. (Orig.). 1994. pap. text, student ed. 49.00 (0-8018-5043-6) Johns Hopkins.

— National Long Term Care Survey: Student Workbook. (Gerontology Research Toolkit Ser.). 206p. (Orig.). 1994. pap. text, student ed. 49.00 (0-8018-5041-X) Johns Hopkins.

Lurie, Hannah R. The Edge of an Era. Buckalew, Jean, ed. LC 73-76165. 82p. 1974. student ed. 3.00 (0-685-41240-7); pap. 3.00 (0-9600728-1-0) H R Lurie.

— The Edge of an Era. 3rd ed. Buckalew, Jean & Ferson, Jean, eds. 74p. 1983. pap. 3.00 (0-686-79368-4) H R Lurie.

Lurie, Hannah R., et al, eds. The Mystic Muse. LC 76-20284. 1976. pap. 3.00 (0-9600728-2-9) H R Lurie.

An Asterisk (*) at the beginning of an entry indicates that the title is appearing for the first time.

Lurie, Hugh J. Practical Management of Emotional Problems in Medicine. enl. rev. ed. LC 81-40019. 272p. 1982. pap. 84.40 (*0-7837-8357-4*, 204914700010) Bks Demand.

Lurie, Ian, jt. auth. see Murphy, Colin R.

Lurie, Ira S. & Wittwer. High-Performance Liquid Chromatography in Forensic Chemistry. (Chromatographic Science Ser.: Vol. 24). (Illus.). 456p. 1983. text 210.00 (*0-8247-1756-2*) Dekker.

Lurie, Jaon B. & Delaney, Thomas, eds. Multispectral Imaging for Terrestrial Applications II, Vol. 3119. LC 98-122075. 220p. 1997. 59.00 (*0-8194-2541-9*) SPIE.

Lurie, Joan B., jt. ed. see Fujisada, Hiroyuki.

Lurie, Joe & Miller, Jonathan. A Foreign Student's Selected Guide to Financial Assistance for Study & Research in the U. S. 1983. pap. 22.50 (*0-88461-010-1*) Adelphi Univ.

Lurie, Jon. Fundamental Snowboarding. LC 95-11721. (Illus.). 64p. (J). (gr. 4-8). 1996. lib. bdg. 21.27 (*0-8225-3457-6*, Lerner Publctns) Lerner Pub.

Lurie, Jonathan. Arming/Pursuing Military Justice, 2 vols. Incl. Arming Military Justice Vol. 1: The Origins of the United States Court of Military Appeals, 1775-1950. (Illus.). 280p. 1992. text 59.50 (*0-691-06944-1*, Pub. by Princeton U Pr); Pursuing Military Justice Vol. 2: The History of the United States Court of Appeals for the Armed Forces, 1951-1980. LC 97-19771. (Illus.). 312p. 1998. text 59.50 (*0-691-06945-X*, Pub. by Princeton U Pr); 99.00 (*0-691-00123-5*, Pub. by Princeton U Pr) Cal Prin Full Svc.

Lurie, Jonathan. The Chicago Board of Trade, 1859-1905: The Dynamics of Self-Regulation. LC 78-20881. (Illus.). 250p. 1979. text 24.95 (*0-252-00732-8*) U of Ill Pr.

— The Constitution & Economic Change. LC 88-71596. (Bicentennial Essays on the Constitution Ser.). 52p. 1988. pap. 7.00 (*0-87229-041-7*) Am Hist Assn.

Lurie, Joseph. Directory of Financial Aid for American Undergraduates Interested in Overseas Study & Travel. 1981. pap. 9.00 (*0-88461-007-1*) Adelphi Univ.

Lurie, K. A. Applied Optimal Control Theory of Distributed Systems. (Mathematical Concepts & Methods in Science & Engineering Ser.: Vol. 43). (Illus.). 512p. (C). 1993. text 125.00 (*0-306-43993-X*, Kluwer Plenum) Kluwer Academic.

Lurie, Karen. The Princeton Review: LSAT-GRE Analytic Workout. 1996. pap. 16.00 (*0-679-77358-4*) Villard Books.

— TV Chefs: The Dish on the Stars of Your Favorite Cooking Shows. LC 99-21725. (Illus.). 256p. 1999. pap. 16.95 (*1-58063-073-1*, Pub. by Renaissance) St Martin.

Lurie, Leonard. Senator Pothole: The Unauthorized Biography of Al D'Amato. LC 93-47232. 1994. 21.95 (*1-55972-227-4*, Birch Ln Pr) Carol Pub Group.

Lurie, Marc, jt. auth. see Busey, Andrew.

Lurie, Max B. Resistance to Tuberculosis: Experimental Studies in Native & Acquired Defense Mechanisms. LC 64-25055. (Commonwealth Fund Publications). (Illus.). 410p. 1965. 40.00 (*0-674-76516-8*) HUP.

Lurie, Maxine N., ed. A New Jersey Anthology. LC 94-2821. 502p. (Orig.). (C). 1994. pap. 18.95 (*0-911020-29-2*) NJ Hist Soc.

Lurie, Maxine N. & Walroth, Joanne R., eds. The Minutes of the Board of Proprietors of the Eastern Division of New Jersey from 1764 to 1794, Vol. IV. LC 84-42826. xlii, 522p. 1985. 30.00 (*0-911020-11-X*) NJ Hist Soc.

Lurie, Morris. Welcome to Tangier. LC 97-130129. 196p. 1997. pap. write for info. (*0-14-026068-4*, Penguin Bks) Viking Penguin.

Lurie, Morris, et al. Jewish Writing from down Under: Australia & New Zealand. Kalechofsky, Roberta & Kalechofsky, Robert, eds. LC 84-1098. (Echad: No. 4). 304p. (Orig.). 1984. pap. 15.00 (*0-916288-16-1*) Micah Pubns.

Lurie, Nancy O. Wisconsin Indians. LC 80-10758. (Illus.). 68p. 1980. pap. 2.00 (*0-87020-195-6*) State Hist Soc Wis.

— Wisconsin Indians. (Illus.). 66p. 1987. 3.00 (*0-87020-252-9*) State Hist Soc Wis.

— Women & the Invention of American Anthropology. 88p. (C). 1999. pap. 7.95 (*1-57766-056-0*) Waveland Pr.

Lurie, Nancy O., ed. Mountain Wolf Woman, Sister of Crashing Thunder: The Autobiography of a Winnebago Indian. rev. ed. (Ann Arbor Paperbacks Ser.). (Illus.). 176p. 1961. pap. 15.95 (*0-472-06109-7*, 06109, Ann Arbor Bks) U of Mich Pr.

Lurie, Nancy O., jt. ed. see Leacock, Eleanor B.

Lurie, Patty. Guide to Impressionist Paris. (Illus.). 180p. (Orig.). 1997. pap. 24.95 (*0-9654027-5-4*) Robson Pr.

Lurie, Rhoda. Discovering the Magic Pots of Mata Ortiz. (Illus.). 46p. 1997. pap. 9.95 (*0-9660324-0-3*) Rho Designs.

Lurie, S. A. & Vasiliev, V. V. The Biharmonic Problem of the Theory of Elasticity. 260p. 1995. text 99.00 (*2-88449-054-X*) Gordon & Breach.

Lurie, Susan. Unsettled Subjects: Restoring Feminist Politics to Poststructuralist Critique. LC 97-3845. 192p. 1997. pap. text 16.95 (*0-8223-1999-3*); lib. bdg. 49.95 (*0-8223-2003-7*) Duke.

Lurie, Toby. Cliff House Poems. (Orig.). 1992. pap. 6.50 (*0-945349-04-1*) Journeys Into Language.

— Duets. LC 95 11880. 72p. 1996. pap. 14.95 (*0-7734-2727-9*, Mellen Poetry Pr) E Mellen.

— The Haight Street Blues. (Orig.). 1988. pap. 6.95 (*0-945349-00-9*) Journeys Into Language.

— Hiroshima: A Symphonic Elegy for Spoken Voices. LC 97-39732. 104p. 1997. pap. 14.95 (*0-7734-2817-8*, Mellen Poetry Pr) E Mellen.

— New Forms New Spaces. (Illus.). 94p. (Orig.). 1971. reprint ed. pap. 5.95 (*0-945349-03-3*) Journeys Into Language.

— Quartets. LC 90-32741. (Poetry Ser.: Vol. 8). 84p. 1990. lib. bdg. 24.95 (*0-88946-883-4*) E Mellen.

— Quintets. LC 92-30599. (Poetry Ser.: Vol. 20). 76p. 1993. text 24.95 (*0-7734-9515-0*) E Mellen.

— Trios. 1988. 24.95 (*0-88946-002-7*) E Mellen.

***Lurie, Yuval.** Cultural Beings: Reading the Philosophers of Genesis. (Value Inquiry Book Ser.: Vol. 89). vii, 217p. 2000. pap. 38.50 (*90-420-0469-X*) Editions Rodopi.

Lurier, Harold. The Emergence of the Western World. 288p. (C). 1994. pap. text, per. 33.95 (*0-8403-9963-4*) Kendall-Hunt.

***Lurigio, Arthur J., ed.** Community Corrections in America: New Directions & Sounder Investments for Persons with Mental Illness & Codisorders. 171p. 1999. reprint ed. pap. text 30.00 (*0-7881-8183-1*) DIANE Pub.

Lurigio, Arthur J., et al, eds. Victims of Crime: Problems, Policies, & Programs. (Criminal Justice System Annuals Ser.). (Illus.). 320p. (C). 1990. text 58.00 (*0-8039-3369-X*); pap. text 26.00 (*0-8039-3370-3*) Sage.

Lurigio, Arthur J. & Bensinger, Gad J., eds. Domestic Violence: A Hidden Epidemic. 91p. 1995. pap. text 12.00 (*0-942852-09-5*) Loyola U Crim.

— Drugs & Community Corrections. 104p. (C). lib. bdg. 15.00 (*0-942854-19-5*) Loyola U Crim.

Lurigio, Arthur J., jt. auth. see Bensinger, Gad J.

Lurigio, Arthur J., jt. auth. see Davis, Robert C.

Lurigio, Arthur J., jt. auth. see Lewis, Dan A.

Lurigio, Arthur J., jt. auth. see Rosenbaum, Dennis P.

Lurigio, Arthur J., jt. ed. see Bensinger, Gad J.

Lurin, Ely. Copper, Fiber, & Wireless Telecommunications Test Equipment - World Markets. Competitors, & Opportunities: 1998-2002 Analysis & Forecasts. 100p. 1998. pap. text 2700.00 (*1-878218-88-3*) World Info Tech.

***Lurin, Ely.** Electric Utilities Opportunities in Telecommunications: New Revenue for Utilities in Selling Services; New Opportunities for Manufacturers in Selling Equipment: 1998-2003 Analysis & Forecasts. 100p. 1999. pap. text 2900.00 (*1-878218-97-2*) World Info Tech.

Lurin, Ely. On-Premises Wireless Telecommunications Equipment - World Markets & Opportunities: 1997-2002 Analysis & Forecasts. 93p. 1997. pap. text 2400.00 (*1-878218-81-6*) World Info Tech.

— Telecommunications Systems Integration EF&I Services - U. S. Markets, Competitors, & Opportunities: 1997-2002 Analysis & Forecasts. 100p. 1997. pap. text 2400.00 (*1-878218-83-2*) World Info Tech.

***Lurin, Ely.** Telecommunications Systems Integration Engineering, Furbishing & Installation Services: U. S. Markets, Competitors & Opportunities: 1999-2004 Analysis & Forecasts. 100p. 1999. pap. text 2900.00 (*1-929904-02-9*) World Info Tech.

— Telecommunications Test Equipment: World Markets, Competitors & Opportunities: 1999-2004 Analysis & Forecasts. 100p. 2000. pap. text 2900.00 (*1-929904-05-3*) World Info Tech.

Lurin, Ely S. Digital/Data Telecommunications Test Equipment, World Markets, Technologies, & Competitors: 1996-2000 Analysis & Forecasts. 219p. 1996. pap. text 2400.00 (*1-878218-67-0*) World Info Tech.

— Radio & Wireless Telecommunications Equipment & Services - U. S. Markets & Opportunities: 1992-1997 Analysis. (Illus.). 237p. 1993. pap. text 1900.00 (*1-878218-36-0*) World Info Tech.

— Telecommunications Test Equipment - U. S. Markets & Opportunities: 1991-1996 Analysis. (Illus.). 220p. 1992. pap. text 1900.00 (*1-878218-26-3*) World Info Tech.

— Telecommunications Test Equipment - U.S. Markets & Opportunities: 1993-1998 Analysis & Forecasts. 250p. 1994. pap. text 1900.00 (*1-878218-47-6*) World Info Tech.

Lurker, Manfred. Dictionary of Biblical Terms & Symbols: Woerterbuch Biblischer Bilder und Symbole. 4th ed. (ENG & GER.). 505p. 1990. 75.00 (*0-8288-2308-1*, M7046) Fr & Eur.

— Dictionary of Gods & Goddesses, Devils & Demons. 460p. 1987. 45.00 (*0-415-03943-6*, 08774, Routledge Thoemms) Routledge.

— Dictionary of Gods & Goddesses, Devils & Demons. LC 86-21911. 451p. (C). 1987. 45.00 (*0-7102-0877-4*, Routledge Thoemms); pap. 15.95 (*0-7102-1106-6*, Routledge Thoemms) Routledge.

— Dictionary of Gods & Goddesses, Devils & Demons. 352p. 1987. pap. 20.99 (*0-415-03944-4*, 11066, Routledge Thoemms) Routledge.

— Gods & Symbols of Ancient Egypt: An Illustrated Dictionary. (Illus.). 142p. 1984. pap. 15.95 (*0-500-27253-0*, Pub. by Thames Hudson) Norton.

— Woerterbuch der Symbolik. 5th ed. (GER.). 871p. 1991. 49.95 (*0-7859-8409-7*, 3520464055) Fr & Eur.

Lurkis, Alexander. The Power Brink: Con Edison, A Centennial of Electricity. (Illus.). 207p. (Orig.). (C). 1982. 13.95 (*0-9609492-1-6*); pap. 9.95 (*0-9609492-0-8*) ICARE Pr.

Lurkis, Alexander. A Serpent at Her Breast. 325p. mass mkt. 4.99 (*1-896329-61-6*) Picasso Publ.

Lurquin, Georges. Elsevier's Dictionary of Greek & Latin Word Constituents: Greek & Latin Affixes, Words, & Roots Used in English, German, French, Dutch, Italian, & Spanish. LC 97-39155. 1200p. 1997. 262.50 (*0-444-82890-7*) Elsevier.

Lurry-Wright, Jerome W. Custom & Conflict on a Bahamian Out-Island. LC 86-31785. (Orig.). (C). 1987. pap. text 21.00 (*0-8191-6098-9*) U Pr of Amer.

***L'Ursula, Betty.** Not Just a Romance: A Collection of Sensual Adventurous Novellas. 2000. pap. 18.00 (*0-7388-2150-0*) Xlibris Corp.

Lury, Cecilia. Prosthetic Culture. LC 98-120999. (International Library of Sociology Ser.). 256p. (C). 1998. 80.00 (*0-415-10293-6*); pap. 24.99 (*0-415-10294-4*) Routledge.

Lury, Celia. Consumer Culture. (Illus.). 290p. (C). 1996. text 50.00 (*0-8135-2328-1*); pap. text 18.95 (*0-8135-2329-X*) Rutgers U Pr.

— Cultural Rights: Technology, Legality, & Personality. LC 92-37656. (International Library of Sociology Ser.). 256p. (C). 1993. pap. 27.99 (*0-415-09578-6*) Routledge.

Lury, D. A., jt. auth. see Casley, D. J.

Luryi, et al. Future Trends in Microelectronics. LC 99-26481. 485p. (C). 1999. 94.95 (*0-471-32183-4*) Wiley.

Luryi, Serge, et al. Future Trends in Microelectronics Reflections on the Road to Nanotechnology: Proceedings of the NATO Advanced Research Workshop, Ile de Bendor, France, July 17-21 1995. LC 96-28440. (NATO Advanced Science Institutes Series C). 436p. (C). 1996. text 225.00 (*0-7923-4169-4*) Kluwer Academic.

Luryi, Yuri I. Soviet Family Law. LC 80-83797. vi, 93p. 1980. lib. bdg. 34.00 (*0-89941-062-6*, 300890) W S Hein.

Lusa, John M. The Network Manager's Handbook. LC 98-2700. 1998. lib. bdg. 175.00 (*0-8493-9958-0*) CRC Pr.

***Lusa, John M.** The Network Manager's Handbook. LC 98-46525. 25p. 1998. lib. bdg. 95.00 (*0-8493-9990-4*) CRC Pr.

— Network Manager's Handbook. 3rd ed. LC 99-43797. (Best Practices Ser.). 592p. 1999. boxed set 79.95 (*0-8493-9841-X*) CRC Pr.

Lusaka, Jane, jt. ed. see Willis, Deborah.

Lusane, Clarence. African Americans at the Crossroads: The Restructuring of Black Leadership & the 1992 Elections. 262p. 1994. 40.00 (*0-89608-469-8*); pap. text 16.00 (*0-89608-468-X*) South End Pr.

— No Easy Victories: Black Americans & the Vote. LC 96-21469. (African-American Experience Ser.). 160p. (YA). (gr. 9-12). 1996. lib. bdg. 24.00 (*0-531-11270-5*) Watts.

— Pipe Dream Blues: Racism & the War on Drugs. 293p. 1991. 30.00 (*0-89608-411-6*); pap. 14.00 (*0-89608-410-8*) South End Pr.

— Race in the Global Era: African Americans at the Millennium. LC 97-31302. 256p. 1997. 40.00 (*0-89608-574-0*); pap. 17.00 (*0-89608-573-2*) South End Pr.

— The Struggle for Equal Education. (African-American Experience Ser.). (Illus.). 144p. (YA). (gr. 7-12). 1992. lib. bdg. 24.00 (*0-531-11121-0*) Watts.

Lusanna, L., ed. Knots, Topology & Quantum Field Theory. 664p. (C). 1989. text 144.00 (*981-02-0126-5*) World Scientific Pub.

— New Trends in Particle Theory: Proceedings of the 9th Johns Hopkins Workshop on Current Problems in Particle Theory, Firenze, Italy, June 5-7, 1985. 184p. 1985. 46.00 (*9971-5-0044-2*) World Scientific Pub.

Lusanna, L., jt. ed. see Longhi, G.

Lusardi, Frank. Netbois Programming. 1990. pap. 45.00 (*5-550-35980-4*) Nairi.

Lusardi, James P. & Schlueter, June. Reading Shakespeare in Performance: King Lear. LC 89-46412. (Illus.). 248p. 1991. 37.50 (*0-8386-3394-3*) Fairleigh Dickinson.

Lusardi, Michelle M. & Nielsen, Caroline. Orthotics & Prosthetics in Rehabilitation. 600p. 2000. 99.00 (*0-7506-9807-1*) Buttrwrth-Heinemann.

Lusas, E. W., et al, eds. Food Uses of Whole Oil & Protein Seeds. 410p. 1989. 90.00 (*0-935315-23-3*) Am Oil Chemists.

Lusby, Keith S., jt. auth. see Neumann, A. L.

Lusby, Phil & Wright, Jenny. Scottish Wild Plants: Their History, Ecology & Conservation. (Illus.). 116p. 1996. 40.00 (*1-872291-17-1*, Pub. by Royal Botanic Edinburgh) Balogh.

Lusby, Philip & Wright, Jenny. Scottish Wild Plants: Their History, Ecology & Conservation. (Discovering Historic Scotland Ser.). (Illus.). 124p. 1996. pap. 26.00 (*0-11-495802-5*, Pub. by Statnry Office) Balogh.

Lusch & Wehinger. North American Endangered & Protected Species. Flint, Mark, ed. LC 94-77816. (Illus.). 180p. (C). 1995. 500.00 (*1-885743-00-9*) Internat Wildlife.

Lusch, Robert F. & Darden, William R., eds. Retail Patronage Theory Proceedings. 1981. 17.00 (*0-931880-02-5*) U OK Ctr Econ.

Lusch, Robert F. & Dunne, Patrick. Cases in Retailing. LC 95-16259. (C). 1995. mass mkt. 19.95 (*0-538-84791-3*) S-W Pub.

Lusch, Robert F. & Zinszer, Paul H., eds. Contemporary Issues in Marketing Channels. 187p. 1979. 12.00 (*0-931880-00-9*) U OK Ctr Econ.

Lusch, Robert F. & Zizzo, Deborah. Competing for Customers: How Wholesaler-Distributors Can Meet the Power Retailer Challenge. 123p. 1995. pap. 130.00 (*0-614-06918-1*) Natl Assn Wholesale Dists.

Lusch, Robert F., et al. Retail Management. 704p. (C). 1990. text. write for info. (*0-538-80294-4*, SF62AA) S-W Pub.

Lusch, Robert F., jt. auth. see Constantin, James A.

Lusch, Robert F., jt. auth. see Dunne.

Lusch, Robert F., jt. ed. see Harvey, Michael G.

Luschei, Glenna. Back into My Body & New Poems. LC 94-75462. (Illus.). 64p. (Orig.). 1994. pap. 8.95 (*0-9638843-2-8*) Mille Grazie.

— In Search of the Artist in Search of the Artist in Julio Cortazar. 1987. 10.00 (*0-318-22931-5*) Solo Pr.

— Matriarch: Selected Poems (1968-1992) LC 92-80450. 96p. (Orig.). 1992. pap. 10.95 (*0-912292-98-9*) Smith.

***Luschei, Glenna.** Pianos Around the Cape. 105p. 1999. pap. 10.00 (*0-9648562-2-0*) Aspermont.

Luschei, Glenna & Rogers. I Had Been Hungry All the Years: An Anthology of Women's Poetry. LC 75-5309. 1975. 9.25 (*0-941490-08-4*) Solo Pr.

Luschei, Glenna, et al. A Near Country: Poem of Loss. (Illus.). ix, 71p. 1999. pap. 13.00 (*0-941490-35-1*) Solo Pr.

— A Near Country: Poem of Loss. aut. limited ed. (Illus.). ix, 71p. 1999. 45.00 (*0-941490-34-3*) Solo Pr.

Luschen, Gunther & Sage, George H., eds. Handbook of Social Science of Sport. 700p. 1981. text 32.00 (*0-87563-191-6*) Stipes.

Luschen, Gunther, tr. see Schmalenbach, Herman.

Luscher, E., et al, eds. Amorphous & Liquid Materials. 1987. text 234.00 (*90-247-3411-8*) Kluwer Academic.

Luscher, E. & Coufal, H., eds. Liquid & Amorphous Metals: Mechanics of Plastic Solids. (NATO-Advanced Study Institute Ser.). 672p. 1980. text 247.50 (*90-286-0680-7*) Kluwer Academic.

Luscher, Evelyn, ed. see Swift, Stanley.

Luscher, Keith F. Advertise! An Assessment of Fundamentals for Small Business. LC 90-91596. (Illus.). 140p. (Orig.). 1991. pap. 14.95 (*0-9625977-9-1*) K & L Pubns.

— Don't Wait Until You Graduate: How to "Jumpstart" Your Career While Still in School. LC 97-76207. (Illus.). 280p. 1998. pap. 13.95 (*0-88282-175-X*) New Horizon NJ.

— Promotional Publishing: Turn Wary Prospects into Trusting Clients by Packaging Your Knowledge, Experience & Expertise. LC 94-78028. 40p. (Orig.). 1994. pap. 4.75 (*0-9625977-0-8*) K & L Pubns.

Luscher, Max. The Luscher Color Test. 224p. 1990. per. 6.99 (*0-671-73145-9*, PB Trade Paper) PB.

Luscher, N. Decubitus Ulcers of the Pelvic Region: Diagnostics & Surgical Therapy. (Illus.). 152p. 1992. text 113.00 (*0-88937-049-4*) Hogrefe & Huber Pubs.

Luscher, Robert M. John Updike: A Study of the Short Fiction. (Twayne's Studies in Short Fiction). 170p. 1993. 29.00 (*0-8057-0850-2*) Macmillan.

Luscher, Thomas F., ed. The Endothelium in Cardiovascular Disease: Pathophysiology, Clinical Presentation, & Pharmacology. 192p. 1995. 130.00 (*3-540-59352-7*) Spr-Verlag.

Luscher, Thomas F., et al, eds. Coronary Artery Graft Disease: Mechanism & Prevention. LC 94-16135. 1994. 135.00 (*0-387-57438-7*) Spr-Verlag.

Luscher, Thomas F. & Kaplan, N. M., eds. Renovascular & Renal Parenchymatous Hypertension. (Illus.). 560p. 1992. 187.00 (*0-387-53324-9*) Spr-Verlag.

Luscher, Thomas F., jt. ed. see Vanhoutte, Paul M.

Luschgy, Harald, jt. auth. see Graf, Siegfried.

Luschnig, C. A. The Gorgon's Severed Head: Studies in Alcestis, Electra & Phoenissae. (Mnemosyne Ser.: Suppl. 153). 280p. 1995. 82.00 (*90-04-10382-1*) Brill Academic Pubs.

— An Introduction to Ancient Greek. 1984. 19.95 (*0-684-14710-6*, Scribners Ref) Mac Lib Ref.

— An Introduction to Ancient Greek. LC 86-17427. 406p. (C). 1976. pap. text 39.00 (*0-13-033739-0*) P-H.

— Time Holds the Mirror: A Study of Knowledge in Euripides' Hippolytus. (Mnemosyne Ser.: Supplement 102). 1988. pap. 36.50 (*90-04-08601-3*) Brill Academic Pubs.

Luschnig, C. A. & Luchnig, L. J. Etymidion II: A Student's Workbook for Vocabulary Building. 2nd ed. 246p. (C). 1994. pap. text 39.50 (*0-8191-9387-9*) U Pr of Amer.

Luschnig, C. A. & Luschnig, L. J. Etyma: An Introduction to Vocabulary-Building from Latin & Greek. LC 82-45038. 346p. (Orig.). 1982. pap. text 26.00 (*0-8191-2571-7*) U Pr of Amer.

— Etymidion: A Students's Workbook for Vocabulary Building from Latin & Greek. 184p. (Orig.). 1985. student ed. 22.50 (*0-8191-4838-5*) U Pr of Amer.

Luschnig, L. J., jt. auth. see Luschnig, C. A.

Luscomb, Sally C. The Collector's Encyclopedia of Buttons. rev. ed. 256p. 1992. 24.95 (*0-7643-0254-X*) Schiffer.

— The Collector's Encyclopedia of Buttons. 3rd rev. ed. (Illus.). 256p. 1999. 24.95 (*0-7643-0889-0*) Schiffer.

Luscombe, Chris & McKee, Malcolm. The Shakespeare Revue. 128p. 1994. pap. 14.95 (*1-85459-252-1*, Pub. by N Hern Bks) Theatre Comm.

Luscombe, Christopher, jt. auth. see McKee, Malcolm.

Luscombe, D. E., ed. see Abelard, Peter.

Luscombe, D. E., ed. see Knowles, David.

Luscombe, D. K., et al, eds. Progress in Medicinal Chemistry, Vol. 34. 270p. 1998. 198.50 (*0-444-82632-7*) Elsevier.

Luscombe, D. K., jt. auth. see Ellis, G. P.

Luscombe, D. K., jt. ed. see Ellis, G. P.

Luscombe, David. Medieval Thought No. 2: History of Western Philosophy. LC 96-29604. (A History of Western Philosophy Ser.: No. 2). 256p. 1997. pap. 14.95 (*0-19-289179-0*) OUP.

Luscombe, David E. & Evans, Craig A., eds. Anselm: Aosta, Bec & Canterbury. 320p. 1996. write for info. (*1-85075-591-4*, Pub. by Sheffield Acad) CUP Services.

Luscott, Jeff. Jack Russell Terriers Today. (Illus.). 224p. 1995. 29.95 (*0-87605-194-8*) Howell Bks.

Luse. Applied Graphics Algorithms. 496p. 1995. pap. 44.95 incl. disk (*0-201-40845-7*) Addison-Wesley.

Luse, Marv. Bitmapped Graphics Programming in C++/Book & Disk. LC 92-38363. 720p. 1993. pap. text 39.95 (*0-201-63209-8*) Addison-Wesley.

Lusebrink, Amy L. Celtic Borders, Alphabets, & Motifs. LC 93-10729. (Pictorial Archive Ser.). 48p. 1993. pap. 5.95 (*0-486-27688-0*) Dover.

Lusebrink, Hans-Jurgen & Reichardt, Rolf. The Bastille: A History of a Symbol of Despotism & Freedom. Schurer, Norbert, tr. from GER. LC 96-51990. (Bicentennial Reflections on the French Revolution Ser.). (Illus.). 336p. 1997. pap. text 16.95 (*0-8223-1894-6*); lib. bdg. 49.95 (*0-8223-1902-0*) Duke.

L

Lusebrink, V. B. Imagery & Visual Expression in Therapy. LC 90-6901. (Emotions, Personality, & Psychotherapy Ser.). (Illus.). 300p. (C). 1990. 49.50 (*0-306-43453-9*, Plenum Trade) Perseus Pubng.

Luserke, Matthias. Tractatus Methodo-Logicus. (Philosophische Texte und Studien: Vol. 19). (GER.). x, 74p. 1988. write for info. (*3-487-09135-6*) G Olms Pubs.

Luserke, Matthias, ed. Jacob Michael Lenz Im Spiegel der Forschung. (Olms Studien: Vol. 42). (GER.). viii, 418p. 1995. write for info. (*3-487-10003-7*) G Olms Pubs.

Lush, Andrew P., jt. auth. see Miller, David M.

Lush, Dora. Understanding Your 9 Year Old. Osborne, Elsie, ed. (Understanding Your Child Ser.: Vol. 10). 96p. 1997. pap. text 8.95 (*1-894020-09-X*) Warwick Publ.

Lush, Jay L. Animal Breeding Plans. LC SF0105.L9. 451p. reprint ed. pap. 139.90 (*0-7837-1249-9*, 204138600020) Bks Demand.

Lush, Jean & Rushford, Patricia H. Emotional Phases of a Woman's Life. LC 86-33931. 226p. (gr. 10). 1990. pap. 9.99 (*0-8007-5377-1*) Revell.

Lush, Jean & Vredevelt, Pamela. Mothers & Sons: Raising Boys to Be Men. LC 88-18210. 230p. 1994. pap. 9.99 (*0-8007-5503-0*) Revell.

Lush, Minnie. California Real Estate Finance. 4th ed. LC 98-131162. 1998. pap. text 39.95 (*0-7931-2770-X*) Dearborn.

Lush, Minnie & Sirota, David. California Real Estate Finance. 3rd rev. ed. LC 95-46381. 512p. 1995. pap. 37.95 (*0-7931-1641-4*, 1523-133A, Real Estate Ed) Dearborn.

Lusha, Masiela. Inner Thoughts Poetry. 90p. 1998. pap. 10.00 (*0-9668409-0-9*) G & D Pubg Co.

Lusher, J. Las Mujeres y el Estres.Tr. of Women & Stress. (SPA.). pap. 9.99 (*1-56063-671-8*, 498435) Editorial Unilit.

Lusher, J., jt. auth. see Novozhilov, V.

Lusher, T. J., jt. ed. see Haricombe, Lorraine J.

Lushington, Laura, jt. photos by see Halliday, Sonia.

Lushington, Nolan, jt. auth. see Ferro, Frank.

Lusht, Kenneth M. CPS Real Estate Valuation Custom Edition. 750p. (C). 1995. 49.95 (*0-256-21378-X*, Irwn McGrw-H) McGrw-H Hghr Educ.

— Real Estate Mathematics: Fundamentals & Applications. 2nd ed. (SWC-Finance). 1986. pap. 21.75 (*0-538-19680-7*, S68) S-W Pub.

— Real Property Valuation: Principles & Applications. 608p. (C). 1996. text 64.00 (*0-256-19059-3*, Irwn McGrw-H) McGrw-H Hghr Educ.

Lusht, Kenneth M., jt. auth. see Palmer, Ralph A.

Lusi, Susan F. The Role of State Department of Education in Complex School Reform. LC 97-9743. (Series on School Reform). 396p. (C). 1997. text 54.00 (*0-8077-3629-5*); pap. text 24.95 (*0-8077-3628-7*) Tchrs Coll.

Lusin, Natalia. Russian. (Master the Basics Ser.). 290p. 1995. pap. 11.95 (*0-8120-9164-7*) Barron.

— Russian Grammar. (RUS.). 250p. 1992. pap., vinyl bd. 6.95 (*0-8120-4902-0*) Barron.

Lusis, A. J., jt. ed. see Sparkes, Robert S.

Lusis, A. S. Chess: An Annotated Bibliography, 1969-1988. 350p. 1991. text 130.00 (*0-7201-2079-9*) Continuum.

Lusk, Daniel. The Cow Wars. Zarucchi, Roy, ed. (Chapbook Ser.). (Illus.). 36p. (Orig.). 1995. pap. 7.95 (*1-879205-60-2*) Nightshade Pr.

— Kissing the Ground: New & Selected Poems. LC 99-70102. 1999. pap. 12.95 (*0-9657144-3-8*) Onion River Pr.

Lusk, Daniel, ed. Onion River, Six Vermont Poets. LC 97-66698. 99p. (Orig.). 1997. pap. 11.95 (*0-9657144-0-3*) Onion River Pr.

Lusk, David T. Within the Halls of Pilate. 1983. pap. 5.45 (*0-89137-538-4*) Quality Pubns.

Lusk, Dorothy. Oral Tragedy. 20p. 1988. pap. 4.00 (*0-921331-08-8*) SPD-Small Pr Dist.

Lusk, Dorothy T. Redactive. 64p. 1991. pap. 8.95 (*0-88922-279-7*) SPD-Small Pr Dist.

Lusk, Ewing L. & Overbeek, R., eds. Ninth International Conference on Automated Deduction. (Lecture Notes in Computer Science Ser.: Vol. 310). 775p. 1988. 79.00 (*0-387-19343-X*) Spr-Verlag.

Lusk, Harold F., jt. auth. see French, William.

Lusk, Julie T. Desktop Yoga: The Anytime, Anywhere Relaxation Program for Office Slaves & Internet Addicts. LC 98-19187. 176p. 1998. pap. 13.00 (*0-399-52446-0*, Perigee Bks) Berkley Pub.

— Thirty Scripts for Relaxation, Imagery & Inner Healing. 192p. 1992. pap. 24.95 (*0-938586-69-6*) Whole Person.

— Thirty Scripts for Relaxation, Imagery & Inner Healing, Vol. 2. LC 92-80231. 192p. 1993. pap. 24.95 (*0-938586-76-9*) Whole Person.

Lusk, Linda, jt. auth. see Gerou, Tom.

Lusk, Rodney P. Pediatric Sinusitis. 160p. 1992. text 131.50 (*0-88167-894-5*, 2386) Lppncott W & W.

Lusk, Vickey. I'm Special: Empowering Children/Building Self Esteem, 10, 1. (Keep the Dream Alive Ser.). (Illus.). 20p. (Orig.). (J). (gr. k-6). 1996. pap. 14.99 (*1-889004-00-6*) Storytellers Lit.

Lusk, Wilma J. Cat's Paws & Morning Glories. 61p. (Orig.). 1985. pap. 4.95 (*0-942424-00-X*) W Anglia Pubns.

Luske, Bruce. Mirrors of Madness: Patroling the Psychic Border. (Social Problems & Social Issues Ser.). 143p. 1990. pap. text 24.95 (*0-202-30423-X*); lib. bdg. 47.95 (*0-202-30422-1*) Aldine de Gruyter.

Luski, Sarah W. Cien Poesias de Sarah Wekselbaum Luski. LC 80-69466. (Coleccion Espejo de Paciencia). (SPA., Illus.). 267p. (Orig.). 1981. pap. 14.95 (*0-89729-272-3*) Ediciones.

Luskin, Allan T., ed. Management of Asthma During Pregnancy. (Illus.). 74p. (C). 1999. reprint ed. pap. text 20.00 (*0-7881-7683-8*) DIANE Pub.

Luskin, Donald L., ed. Portfolio Insurance: A Guide to Dynamic Hedging. LC 88-37151. 322p. 1988. 99.95 (*0-471-85849-8*) Wiley.

Luskin, M., jt. ed. see Bjorstad, P.

Lusky, Louis. Our Nine Tribunes. LC 92-28482. 232p. 1993. 55.00 (*0-275-94463-8*, C4463, Praeger Pubs) Greenwood.

Lusnikov, Aleksey. Soviet Thin Film Technology: From Research to Production. Nobel, Erika D., ed. (Illus.). 130p. (Orig.). 1987. pap. text 75.00 (*1-55831-002-9*) Delphic Associates.

Lusry, Anita B., tr. see Yerodhalmi, Shmuel.

Luss, Dan & Weekman, Vern W., Jr., eds. Chemical Reaction Engineering Reviews: Houston. LC 78-8477. (ACS Symposium Ser.: No. 72). 1978. 36.95 (*0-8412-0432-2*) Am Chemical.

Luss, Dan, ed. see International Symposium on Chemical Reaction Engin.

Luss, Dan, jt. ed. see Weekman, Vern W., Jr.

Lussert, Anneliese. The Christmas Visitor. LC 95-1642.Tr. of Simons Weihnacht. (Illus.). 32p. (J). (gr. k-3). 1998. pap. 6.95 (*0-7358-1006-0*, Pub. by North-South Bks NYC) Chronicle Bks.

Lusseyran, Jacques. Against the Pollution of the "I": Selected Writings of Jacques Lusseyran. LC 99-29783. 180p. 1999. 19.95 (*0-930407-46-6*) Parabola Bks.

— And There Was Light: The Autobiography of a Blind Hero in the French Resistance. 256p. 1990. pap. text 14.95 (*0-86315-507-3*, 1005, Pub. by Floris Bks) Anthroposophic.

— And There Was Light: The Autobiography of a Blind Hero of the French Resistance. Cameron, Elizabeth R., tr. from ENG. LC 98-3497. 328p. 1998. pap. 14.95 (*0-930407-40-7*) Parabola Bks.

— The Blind in Society & Blindness, a New Seeing of the World. Winkler, Dorothea, tr. from FRE. 32p. (gr. 7-12). 1978. pap. 1.50 (*0-913098-11-6*) Orion Society.

***Lusseyran, Jacques.** Conversation Amoureuse. 2nd ed. Querido, Rene, tr. from FRE. xxiii, 148p. 1998. pap. 22.50 (*0-945803-31-1*, 00172) R Steiner Col.

Lussiana, Bernard & Pininska, Mary. Poland's Gourmet Cuisine. (Illus.). 143p. 1999. 35.00 (*0-7818-0790-5*) Hippocrene Bks.

***Lussier.** Management Fundamentals. LC 99-28301. (SWC-Management Ser.). 606p. 1999. pap. 59.95 (*0-324-01337-X*) Thomson Learn.

Lussier. Romantic Dynamics. LC 99-16403. 1999. text 59.95 (*0-312-22671-3*) St Martin.

***Lussier, Achua.** Leadership: Theory, Application & Skill Developement. 2000. pap. 62.95 (*0-324-04166-7*) Thomson Learn.

Lussier, Donald E. How to Get the "L" Out of Learning: The Job Search Book That Shows You How to Turn Your Degree into Dollars. 148p. (C). 1991. pap. 12.95 (*0-9628723-0-X*) Premium Pr.

Lussier, Donald E., et al. Job Search Secrets: The Only Guide You'll Ever Need to Get the Job You Want. LC 97-15803. (Illus.). 192p. 1997. pap. 12.95 (*0-8442-4473-2*, 44732) NTC Contemp Pub Co.

***Lussier, Ellen & Vogel, Susan.** Private Schools of the San Francisco Peninsula/Silicon Valley: Elementary & Middle. (Illus.). 130p. 1999. pap. 16.95 (*0-9648757-6-4*, Pub. by Pince Nez Pr) Sunbelt Pubns.

Lussier, Ernest. Naturalists' Directory & Almanac (International) 47th ed. 400p. 1996. pap. 35.00 (*1-889130-00-1*) Naturalists Dir.

Lussier, Frances M. An Analysis of U. S. Army Helicopter Programs. (Illus.). 75p. (Orig.). (C). 1996. pap. text 30.00 (*0-7881-2756-X*) DIANE Pub.

***Lussier, Frances M.** Structuring the Active & Reserve Army for the 21st Century. (Illus.). 52p. 1999. reprint ed. pap. text 20.00 (*0-7881-7997-7*) DIANE Pub.

Lussier, Frances M., jt. auth. see Pinkston, Elizabeth.

***Lussier, Francis M.** Structuring the Active & Reserve Army for the 21st Century. LC 98-109975. 76p. 1998. pap. 7.00 (*0-16-049378-1*, Congress) USGPO.

Lussier, Kyle. Power 3D: High Speed Graphics in Windows 95-NT. LC 96-45698. 552p. 1997. 54.95 (*1-884777-33-3*) Manning Pubns.

Lussier, Mark & Heninger, S. K., eds. Perspective As a Problem in the Art, History & Literature of Early Modern England. LC 92-8707. (Illus.). 152p. 1992. lib. bdg. 69.95 (*0-7734-9620-3*) E Mellen.

***Lussier, Paul.** Last Refuge of Scoundrels. LC 99-86028. 320p. 2001. 26.95 (*0-446-52342-9*) Warner Bks.

Lussier, Robert N. Human Relations in Organizations: A Skill-Building Approach. 3rd ed. LC 95-4180. 576p. (C). 1995. text 57.75 (*0-256-16207-7*, Irwn McGrw-H) McGrw-H Hghr Educ.

— Human Relations in Organizations: Applications & Skill Building. 4th ed. LC 98-5444. 1998. 49.74 (*0-256-26145-8*, Irwn Prfssnl) McGraw-Hill Prof.

— Management: Applications & Skill Development. LC 96-15162. (GC - Principles of Management Ser.). 1996. mass mkt. 84.95 (*0-538-85126-0*) S-W Pub.

— Supervision: A Skill-Building Approach. 2nd ed. LC 93-10673. 624p. (C). 1993. text 54.50 (*0-256-09050-5*, Irwn McGrw-H) McGrw-H Hghr Educ.

Lussier, Robert N., jt. auth. see Corman, Joel.

Lussier, Virginia L., jt. ed. see Wheeler, Kenneth W.

Lusson, Michelle. Creative Wellness: A Holistic Guide to Total Health. 320p. (Orig.). 1987. mass mkt. 7.95 (*0-446-38225-6*, Pub. by Warner Bks) Little.

Lusson, Michelle, jt. auth. see Mella, Dorothee L.

Lussu, Emilio. An Autobiographical Account by a Leading Sardinian Republican Politician of Resistance to Fascism in Sardinia from 1918-1930: Marcia su Roma e Dintorni (The March on Rome & Thereabouts) Davis, Roy W., tr. from LAT. LC 92-15142. 224p. 1992. lib. bdg. 89.95 (*0-7734-9558-4*) E Mellen.

— Enter Mussolini: Observations & Adventures of an Anti-Fascist. Rawson, Marion, tr. from ITA. LC 78-63690. (Studies in Fascism: Ideology & Practice). reprint ed. 28.50 (*0-404-16952-X*) AMS Pr.

***Lussu, Emilio.** Sardinian Brigade. (Lost Treasures Ser.). 286p. 2000. pap. 14.95 (*1-85375-360-2*, Pub. by Prion) Trafalgar.

Lust, et al. New Mime in North America. (Mime Journal Ser.). (Illus.). 183p. (Orig.). 1982. pap. text 12.00 (*0-9611066-8-9*) Mime Jour.

Lust, Annette. From the Greek Mimes to Marcel Marceau & Beyond: Mimes, Actors, Pierrots & Clowns: A Chronicle of the Many Visages of Mime in the Theatre. LC 98-37892. (Illus.). 560p. 1999. 65.00 (*0-8108-3510-X*) Scarecrow.

***Lust, Barbara.** Lexical Anaphors & Pronouns in Selected South Asian Languages. LC 99-52518. (Empirical Approaches to Language Typology Ser.). 950p. 1999. write for info. (*3-11-014388-7*) Mouton.

Lust, Barbara, ed. Studies in the Acquisition of Anaphora. 1986. pap. text 62.50 (*90-277-2122-X*) Kluwer Academic.

— Studies in the Acquisition of Anaphora. (C). 1987. text 176.50 (*1-55608-022-0*) Kluwer Academic.

— Studies in the Acquisition of Anaphoria. 1986. lib. bdg. 154.50 (*90-277-2121-1*) Kluwer Academic.

Lust, Barbara, et al, eds. Syntactic Theory & First Language Acquisition Cross-Linguistic Perspectives, 2 vols., Set. 1994. text 140.00 (*0-8058-1575-9*) L Erlbaum Assocs.

— Syntactic Theory & First Language Acquisition Cross-Linguistic Perspectives Vol. 1: Heads, Projections & Learnability. 376p. 1994. text 79.95 (*0-8058-1351-9*) L Erlbaum Assocs.

— Syntactic Theory & First Language Acquisition Cross-Linguistic Perspectives Vol. 2: Binding, Dependences & Learnability. 568p. 1994. text 99.95 (*0-8058-1350-0*) L Erlbaum Assocs.

Lust, Barbara & Pentelodimos. Dictionary French to Greek Moderne. (FRE & GRE.). 1998. 95.00 (*0-320-00387-6*) Fr & Eur.

Lust, Barbara C., ed. & selected by see Gair, James W.

Lust, Benedict. About Herbs: Nature's Medicine. 1983. pap. 2.95 (*0-87904-045-9*) Lust.

— About Prostate Trouble. 1983. pap. 2.95 (*0-87904-042-4*) Lust.

— Kneipp Herbs: Regeneration Thru Herbal Juices. (Illus.). 1968. pap. 0.75 (*0-87904-009-2*) Lust.

— Only Nature Cures. 1983. pap. 5.95 (*0-87904-014-9*) Lust.

— Superbath: The Blood Washing Method. (Illus.). 1982. pap. 2.00 (*0-87904-027-0*) Lust.

— Zone Therapy: Regeneration Through Nerve Pressure. (Illus.). 140p. 1980. pap. 3.95 (*0-87904-038-6*) Lust.

Lust, D. & Theisen, S. Lectures on String Theory. (Lecture Notes in Physics Ser.: Vol. 346). vii, 346p. 1989. 17.95 (*0-387-51882-7*) Spr-Verlag.

Lust, Herbert. Violence & Defiance. LC 83-81847. 184p. 1984. write for info. (*0-930794-91-5*); pap. write for info. (*0-930794-90-7*) Station Hill Pr.

Lust, Herbert C. Giacometti (Alberto) The Complete Graphics. rev. ed. (Illus.). 240p. 1991. 150.00 (*1-55660-093-3*) A Wofsy Fine Arts.

***Lust, Herbert C. & Gallant, Aprile.** Alberto Giacometti. Skwire, Jessica, ed. LC 00-131667. (Illus.). 64p. 2000. pap. write for info. (*0-916857-20-4*) Port Mus Art.

Lust, J. & Hauspie, K. Greek to English Lexique of Septuagint Vol. 1: A-I. (ENG & GRE.). 217p. 1995. 69.95 (*0-320-00552-6*) Fr & Eur.

— Greek to English Lexique of Septuagint Vol. 2: K-Omega. (ENG & GRE.). 317p. 1996. 75.00 (*0-320-00523-2*) Fr & Eur.

Lust, John. Chinese Popular Prints. LC 95-46336. (Handbook of Oriental Studies: Vol. 4, No. 11). 1996. 151.00 (*90-04-10472-0*) Brill Academic Pubs.

— Western Books on China Published up to 1850. (Illus.). 352p. 1987. 67.50 (*1-870076-02-8*, Pub. by Bamboo Pub) Antique Collect.

Lust, John B. About Diabetes & the Diet. pap. 2.95 (*0-87904-046-7*) Lust.

— About Raw Juices. 1982. pap. 2.95 (*0-87904-047-5*) Lust.

— The Complete Massage Book. (Illus.). 1982. 15.95 (*0-87904-021-1*) Lust.

— Drink Your Troubles Away: Raw Juice Therapy. LC 66-28198. 182p. 1999. pap. 4.95 (*0-87904-006-8*) Lust.

— The Herb Book. LC 74-75368. (Illus.). 640p. 1974. 19.95 (*0-87904-007-6*); pap. 6.99 (*0-87904-055-6*) Lust.

— Kneipp's My Water Cure. 1978. 15.95 (*0-87904-022-X*) Lust.

— Lust for Living. 1982. 12.95 (*0-87904-036-X*) Lust.

— Raw Juice Therapy. 1982. 5.95 (*0-87904-026-2*) Lust.

— The Royal Jelly Miracle. 1998. pap. 1.95 (*0-87904-023-8*) Lust.

Lust, John B., ed. The Herb Book. 672p. 1979. mass mkt. 7.99 (*0-553-26770-1*) Bantam.

Lust, John B. & Tierra, Michael. The Natural Remedy Bible: Everyone's Guide to the Natural of Healing. McCarthy, Paul, ed. 384p. 1990. reprint ed. mass mkt. 6.99 (*0-671-66127-2*) PB.

Lust, John B., jt. auth. see Scott, Cyril.

Lust, Patricia, compiled by. American Vocal Chamber Music, 1945-1980: An Annotated Bibliography, 4. LC 84-25212. (Music Reference Collection: No. 4). (Illus.). 273p. 1985. lib. bdg. 57.95 (*0-313-24599-1*, LUC/, Greenwood Pr) Greenwood.

Lust, Peter. The Last Seal Pup: The Story of Canada's Seal Hunt. LC 67-21282. 152p. reprint ed. pap. 47.20 (*0-608-13593-3*, 202230900026) Bks Demand.

— Two Germanies. LC 66-23304. 237p. reprint ed. pap. 73.50 (*0-8357-6441-9*, 203581200097) Bks Demand.

***Lust, Teresa.** Pass the Polenta: And Other Writings from the Kitchen. (Illus.). 288p. 1999. pap. 11.95 (*0-345-43565-6*, Ballantine) Ballantine Pub Grp.

Lust, Teresa. Pass the Polenta: And Other Writings from the Kitchen. LC 98-25789. 269p. 1998. 24.00 (*1-883642-95-7*) Steerforth Pr.

***Lustachowski, John M.** Ryan's Tale: Isle in the Mists. 259p. 1998. 24.99 (*1-893202-00-3*) TGA.

Lustbader, Eric. Dark Homecoming. LC 96-48909. 368p. 1997. 23.00 (*0-671-00329-1*) PB.

— Dark Homecoming. 1998. per. 6.99 (*0-671-00330-5*, Pocket Books) PB.

— Dark Homecoming Export. 1998. per. 6.99 (*0-671-01742-X*) PB.

— The Kaisho. 1998. 3.99 (*0-671-02329-2*, Pocket Books) PB.

— The Kaisho. Zion, Claire, ed. 576p. 1994. reprint ed. mass mkt. 6.99 (*0-671-86807-1*, Pocket Star Bks) PB.

Lustbader, Joyce W., et al. Glycoprotein Hormone. LC 93-33014. 1994. 138.00 (*0-387-94165-7*) Spr-Verlag.

Lustbader, Michael & Rotenberg, Nancy. Close-Up Photography: Capturing Nature's Intimate Landscapes. (Illus.). 170p. 1997. pap. text 18.95 (*0-9656266-0-1*) Natural Tapestries.

Lustbader, Michael, jt. auth. see Rotenberg, Nancy.

Lustbader, Wendy. Counting on Kindness: The Dilemmas of Dependency. Arellano, Susan, ed. LC 90-44842. 206p. 1993. pap. 15.95 (*0-02-919516-0*) Free Pr.

***Lustbader, Wendy.** What's Worth Knowing. 2001. 18.95 (*1-58542-071-9*, Tarcher Putnam) Putnam Pub Group.

Lustbader, Wendy & Hooyman, Nancy R. Taking Care of Aging Family Members: A Practical Guide. enl. rev. ed. LC 93-24322. 322p. 1993. pap. 17.95 (*0-02-919518-7*) Free Pr.

— Taking Care of Aging Family Members: A Practical Guide. 2nd enl. rev. ed. LC 93-24322. 322p. 1993. 24.95 (*0-02-919517-9*) Free Pr.

Lustburg, Lynn, ed. see Morgan, Diane, et al.

Lusted, David, ed. The Media Studies Book: A Guide for Teachers. (Comedia Bk.). 242p. (C). 1991. pap. 22.99 (*0-415-01461-1*) Routledge.

Lusted, David, jt. ed. see Geraghty, Christine.

Lustenberger, Kurt. Adolf Loos. (Studio Paperback Ser.). (GER., Illus.). 192p. 1996. pap. 19.95 (*3-7643-5587-5*, Pub. by Birkhauser) Princeton Arch.

Luster, Bill, photos by. University of Kentucky - Then & Now. (Illus.). 112p. 1993. 39.95 (*1-56469-004-0*) Harmony Hse Pub.

Luster, Ivon. The Power in Sex. Lattiboudeaine, Michael & Peterson, Carlisle, eds. 140p. (Orig.). (YA). (gr. 10). 1998. pap. 12.95 (*1-889448-50-8*) NBN Publishers Group.

Luster, J. Scott, jt. auth. see Brill, Lynda D.

Luster, Michelle. God's Plan of Redemption: What Redemption Provides for the Believers. 84p. 1995. pap. 7.99 (*1-888246-00-6*) Covenant IL.

Luster, Robert E. The Amelioration of the Slaves in the British Empire, 1790-1833, Vol. 134. LC 92-27278. (American University Studies: Series IX). XI, 186p. (C). 1995. text 38.95 (*0-8204-2068-9*) P Lang Pubng.

Luster, Sharon. Summer Days. unabridged ed. (Illus.). 20p. (Orig.). 1996. pap. 5.00 (*1-929326-62-9*) Hal Bar Pubg.

Luster, Tom & Okagaki, Lynn, eds. Parenting: An Ecological Perspective. 272p. 1993. pap. 29.95 (*0-8058-0857-4*); text 59.95 (*0-8058-0792-6*) L Erlbaum Assocs.

Lusterman. Infidelity, a Survival Guide. 224p. 1999. 6.98 (*1-56731-333-7*, MJF Bks) Fine Comms.

Lusterman, Don-David. Infidelity: A Survival Guide. LC 97-75477. 196p. 1998. pap. 13.95 (*1-57224-087-3*) New Harbinger.

Lusterman, Seymour. The Organization & Staffing of Corporate Public Affairs. (Report: No. 894). (Illus.). v, 31p. (Orig.). 1987. pap. text 60.00 (*0-8237-0336-3*) Conference Bd.

Lusternik, L. A. & Sobolev, V. J. Elements of Functional Analysis. (Russian Monographs). (Illus.). xvi, 412p. 1962. text 262.00 (*0-677-20270-9*) Gordon & Breach.

Lustgarten, Laurence & Leigh, Ian. In from the Cold: National Security & Parliamentary Democracy. 576p. 1994. text 39.95 (*0-19-825234-X*) OUP.

Lustgarten, Laurence, jt. auth. see Barendt, Eric.

Lustgarten, Lionel S., jt. auth. see Winston, Milton W.

Lustgarten, Steven. Productivity & Prices: The Consequences of Industrial Concentration. LC 83-17133. (AEI Studies: No. 392). (Illus.). 62p. reprint ed. pap. 30.00 (*0-8357-4526-0*, 203739000008) Bks Demand.

***Lusthaus, Charles, et al.** Enhancing Organizational Performance: A Toolbox for Self-Assessment. 140p. 1999. pap. 16.95 (*0-88936-870-8*, Pub. by IDRC Bks) Stylus Pub VA.

— Evaluation Institutionelle: Cadre pour le Renforcement des Organisations Partenaires du CRDI. LC 97-701401. (FRE.). xiii, 81p. 1996. pap. 12.00 (*0-88936-798-1*, Pub. by IDRC Bks) Stylus Pub VA.

— Institutional Assessment: A Framework for Strengthening Organizational Capacity for IDRC'S Research Partners. LC 95-705213. 88p. 1995. pap. 12.00 (*0-88936-771-X*, Pub. by IDRC Bks) Stylus Pub VA.

Lusthaus, Dan. Buddhist Phenomenology: A Philosophical Investigation of Yogacara Buddhism & the Ch'eng Wei-shih Lun. (Critical Studies in Buddhism: Vol. 13). 288p. 1999. text 55.00 (*0-7007-1186-4*, Pub. by Curzon Pr Ltd) UH Pr.

Lustick, Ian, ed. The Conflict with the Arabs in Israeli Politics & Society. LC 93-51015. (Arab-Israeli Relations Ser.: Vol. 7). 384p. 1994. text 20.00 (*0-8153-1587-2*) Garland.

Lustick, Ian, intro. From War to War: Israel vs. the Arabs, 1948-1967. LC 93-50084. (Arab-Israeli Relations Ser.: Vol. 3). 336p. 1994. text 20.00 (*0-8153-1583-X*) Garland.

Lustick, Ian S. Unsettled States, Disputed Lands: Britain & Ireland, France & Algeria, Israel & the West Bank/Gaza. (Wilder House Series in Politics, History, & Culture). (Illus.). 592p. 1993. text 49.95 (*0-8014-2840-8*) Cornell U Pr.

— Unsettled States, Disputed Lands: Britain & Ireland, France & Algeria, Israel & the West Bank/Gaza. (Wilder House Ser.). (Illus.). 592p. 1995. pap. text 21.95 (*0-8014-8088-4*) Cornell U Pr.

Lustick, Ian S., ed. Arab-Israeli Relations: Historical Background & Origins of the Conflict. LC 93-50089. 424p. 1994. reprint ed. text 20.00 (*0-8153-1581-3*) Garland.

— Arab-Israeli Relations in World Politics, Vol. 10. LC 93-49876. 360p. 1994. reprint ed. text 20.00 (*0-8153-1590-2*) Garland.

— The Conflict with Israel in Arab Politics & Society. LC 93-50083. (Arab-Israeli Relations Ser.: Vol. 8). 408p. 1994. reprint ed. text 20.00 (*0-8153-1588-0*) Garland.

— Economic, Legal, & Demographic Dimensions of Arab-Israeli Relations. LC 93-49091. (Arab-Israeli Relations Ser.: Vol. 6). 368p. 1994. reprint ed. text 20.00 (*0-8153-1586-4*) Garland.

— From Wars Toward Peace in the Arab-Israeli Conflict, 1969-1993. LC 93-48175. (Arab-Israeli Relations Ser.: Vol. 4). (Illus.). 376p. 1994. reprint ed. text 20.00 (*0-8153-1584-8*) Garland.

— Palestinians under Israeli Rule. LC 93-51256. (Arab-Israeli Relations Ser.: Vol. 9). 352p. 1994. reprint ed. text 20.00 (*0-8153-1589-9*) Garland.

— Religion, Culture, & Psychology in Arab-Israeli Relations. LC 93-48221. (Arab-Israeli Relations Ser.: Vol. 5). (Illus.). 416p. 1994. reprint ed. text 20.00 (*0-8153-1585-6*) Garland.

— Triumph & Catastrophe: The War of 1948, Israeli Independence, & the Refugee Problem. LC 93-50088. (Arab-Israeli Relations Ser.: Vol. 2). (Illus.). 384p. 1994. reprint ed. text 20.00 (*0-8153-1582-1*) Garland.

Lustick, Ian S. & Rubin, Barry, eds. Critical Essays on Israeli Society, Politics, & Culture: Books on Israel, Vol. II. LC 90-10055. (SUNY Series in Israeli Studies). 229p. (C). 1991. text 54.50 (*0-7914-0646-6*); pap. text 18.95 (*0-7914-0647-4*) State U NY Pr.

Lustick, Sheldon I., jt. ed. see Aspey, Wayne P.

Lustig & Brown Staff. Errors & Omissions Loss Control Manual. Atwater, R. Scott & Paige, David H., eds. 165p. pap. write for info. (*0-9674787-1-5*) I A A C.

Lustig, Arnost. Children of the Holocaust. 1995. pap. 19.95 (*0-8101-1279-5*) Northwestern U Pr.

— Dita Saxova. 320p. 1994. pap. 17.95 (*0-8101-1132-2*) Northwestern U Pr.

— Dita Saxova. 320p. (J). 1994. 49.95 (*0-8101-1131-4*) Northwestern U Pr.

***Lustig, Arnost.** The House of Returned Echoes. 2001. pap. 17.95 (*0-8101-1859-9*) Northwestern U Pr.

Lustig, Arnost. Indecent Dreams. Urwin-Levit, Iris et al, trs. from CZE. 159p. 1990. pap. 12.95 (*0-8101-0909-3*) Northwestern U Pr.

— Night & Hope. Theiner, George, tr. from CZE. 219p. 1985. reprint ed. pap. 9.95 (*0-8101-0702-3*) Northwestern U Pr.

— Street of Lost Brothers. 207p. (Orig.). 1990. 39.95 (*0-8101-0959-X*); pap. 13.95 (*0-8101-0960-3*) Northwestern U Pr.

— The Unloved: From the Diary of Perla S. LC 96-25849. (Jewish Lives Ser.). 196p. 1996. pap. 14.95 (*0-8101-1347-3*) Northwestern U Pr.

Lustig, B. Andrew, ed. Bioethics Yearbook Vol. 1: Theological Developments in Bioethics, 1988-1990. 232p. (C). 1991. lib. bdg. 180.50 (*0-7923-1280-5*, Pub. by Kluwer Academic) Kluwer Academic.

— Bioethics Yearbook Vol. 4: Regional Developments in Bioethics: 1991-1993. (Bioethics Yearbook Ser.: No. 4). 440p. 1994. lib. bdg. 237.50 (*0-7923-3237-7*, Pub. by Kluwer Academic) Kluwer Academic.

— Bioethics Yearbook Vol. 5: Theological Developments in Bioethics: 1992-1994, Vol. 5. 312p. 1997. text 185.00 (*0-7923-4428-6*) Kluwer Academic.

Lustig, B. Andrew, et al, eds. Bioethics Yearbook Vol. 2: Regional Developments in Bioethics: 1989-1991. 448p. (C). 1992. lib. bdg. 265.50 (*0-7923-1893-5*, Pub. by Kluwer Academic) Kluwer Academic.

— Bioethics Yearbook Vol. 3: Theological Developments in Bioethics: 1990-1992. (Bioethics Yearbook Ser.: No. 3). 320p. 1993. lib. bdg. 178.50 (*0-7923-2555-9*, Pub. by Kluwer Academic) Kluwer Academic.

Lustig, B. Andrew, jt. ed. see Campbell, Courtney S.

Lustig, David A., jt. auth. see Silverman, Marvin.

Lustig, Gerhard. Automatische Indexierung Zwischen Forschung und Anwendung. (Sprache und Computer Ser.: Bd. 5). (GER.). xiii, 182p. 1986. write for info. (*3-487-07825-2*) G Olms Pubs.

Lustig, Harold L. 4 Steps to Financial Security for Lesbian & Gay Couples. LC 98-45371. 296p. (Orig.). 1999. pap. 14.00 (*0-449-00249-7*) Fawcett.

Lustig, Herbert S., jt. auth. see Allen, Carol.

Lustig, Irma S., ed. Boswell: Citizen of the World, Man of Letters. 296p. 1995. text 39.95 (*0-8131-1910-3*) U Pr of Ky.

Lustig, Jill & Warren, Jean. Sing a Song of Holidays. (Learn with Piggyback Songs Ser.). (Illus.). 48p. (J). (ps-k). 1998. pap. 3.95 (*1-57029-170-5*, 3308) Totline Pubns.

— Sing a Song of Me. (Learn with Piggyback Songs Ser.). (Illus.). 48p. (J). (ps-k). 1998. pap. 3.95 (*1-57029-186-1*, 3309) Totline Pubns.

— Sing a Song of Numbers. (Learn with Piggyback Songs Ser.). (Illus.). 48p. (J). (ps-k). 1998. pap. 3.95 (*1-57029-188-8*, 3311) Totline Pubns.

Lustig, Joel W., ed. The National Directory of Corporate Distress Specialists: A Comprehensive Guide to Firms & Professionals Providing Services in Bankruptcies, Workouts, Turnarounds & Distressed Securities Investing. 720p. 1992. 99.00 (*0-9630173-0-6*) Lustig Data Res.

Lustig, Judith, ed. Anthropology & Egyptology: Developing Dialogue. (MMA Ser.: Vol. 8). 147p. 1998. 60.00 (*1-85075-676-7*, Pub. by Sheffield Acad) CUP Services.

Lustig, Keith. Portfolio Assessment: A Handbook for Middle Level Teachers. LC 96-30253. 1996. pap. write for info. (*1-56090-111-X*) Natl Middle Schl.

Lustig, Laura J., et al. Scintilla's Journal, 12 vols., Vol. 1. 100p. 1996. pap. 40.00 (*1-889008-00-1*) Projects.

***Lustig, Laura Joy.** Oscar. (Illus.). 24p. 2000. pap. 3.95 (*0-9676660-3-1*, Pick Pocket Pr) Phony Lid Pubns.

Lustig, Loretta. The Three Billy Goats Gruff. (Children's Classics Ser.). 32p. (J). 1991. 6.95 (*0-8362-4913-5*) Andrews & McMeel.

Lustig, Mary L. Privilege & Prerogative: New York's Provincial Elite, 1710-1776. LC 93-51010. (C). 1995. 39.50 (*0-8386-3554-7*) Fairleigh Dickinson.

— Robert Hunter, 1666-1734: New York's Augustan Statesman. LC 83-4750. (New York State Study Ser.). (Illus.). 296p. reprint ed. pap. 91.80 (*0-608-06975-2*, 206718300009) Bks Demand.

Lustig, Mary L., et al, eds. The Papers of William Livingston: Guide to the Microfilm Edition. 205p. 1986. 20.00 (*0-8357-0723-7*) Univ Microfilms.

Lustig, Mary L., jt. ed. see Prince, Carl E.

Lustig, Michael M. Ukraine. LC 98-7988. (Illus.). 122p. (YA). (gr. 7-12). 1999. 19.95 (*0-8160-3757-4*) Facts on File.

Lustig, Myron W. Among Us. LC 99-31067. 266p. (C). 1999. pap. text 41.00 (*0-321-04920-9*) Addison-Wesley.

— Intercultural Competence: Intercultural Competence. 3rd ed. LC 98-14658. 400p. (C). 1998. pap. 48.00 (*0-321-00612-7*) Addson-Wesley Educ.

Lustig, Nora. Mexico: The Remaking of an Economy. 186p. (C). 1992. 14.95 (*0-8157-5314-4*) Brookings.

— Mexico: The Remaking of an Economy. LC 98-26072. 260p. 1998. pap. 18.95 (*0-8157-5319-5*); text 44.95 (*0-8157-5320-9*) Brookings.

***Lustig, Nora.** Shielding the Poor: Social Protection in the Developing World. 2000. pap. 26.95 (*0-8157-5321-7*) Brookings.

Lustig, Nora, ed. Coping with Austerity: Poverty & Inequality in Latin America. LC 94-28839. 460p. (C). 1995. 52.95 (*0-8157-5318-7*); pap. 24.95 (*0-8157-5317-9*) Brookings.

Lustig, Nora, et al, eds. North American Free Trade: Assessing the Impact. 288p. (C). 1992. 42.95 (*0-8157-5316-0*); pap. 18.95 (*0-8157-5315-2*) Brookings.

Lustig, Nora, jt. ed. see Edwards, Sebastian.

Lustig, Osnat & Albrizio, Ann. Classic Millinery Techniques: A Complete Guide to Making & Designing Hats. LC 97-45828. (Illus.). 176p. 1998. 29.95 (*1-57990-016-X*, Pub. by Lark Books) Random.

Lustig, Roger, tr. see Dahlhaus, Carl.

Lustig, Susan. The Magi. 16p. (Orig.). 1995. pap. 2.50 (*1-57514-178-7*, 3052) Encore Perform Pub.

Lustig, Theodore S., jt. auth. see Bledsoe, John D.

Lustig, Tim, ed. & intro. see James, Henry.

Lustiger, Arnold, contrib. by. Before Hashem You Shall Be Purified: Rabbi Joseph B. Soloveitchik on the Days of Awe. 187p. 1998. 21.95 (*0-9666232-0-7*) Ohr Publishing.

***Lustiger, Gila.** The Inventory. 2001. 24.95 (*1-55970-549-3*, Pub. by Arcade Pub Inc) Time Warner.

Lustiger, Jean-Marie C. Dare to Live. 164p. (C). 1990. 49.00 (*0-85439-276-9*, Pub. by St Paul Pubns) St Mut.

Lustiger-Thaler, Henri, ed. Political Arrangements: Power & the City. LC 92 72628. 224p. 1993. 48.99 (*1-895431-55-7*, Pub. by Black Rose); pap. 19.99 (*1-895431-54-9*, Pub. by Black Rose) Consort Bk Sales.

Lustiger-Thaler, Henri & Salee, Daniel, eds. Artful Practices: The Political Economy of Everday Life, Vol. 5. 188p. 1995. 48.99 (*1-895431-93-X*, Pub. by Black Rose); pap. 19.99 (*1-895431-92-1*, Pub. by Black Rose) Consort Bk Sales.

Lustigmann, Pascal. Das Heinz Erhardt Kochbuch. (GER., Illus.). 64p. (C). 1996. 15.00 (*3-8170-0029-4*, Pub. by Knstvrlag Weingrtn) Intl Bk Import.

Lustman, Francois. Managing Computer Projects. 400p. (C). 1987. text 33.33 (*0-317-60112-1*) P-H.

Lustrup, Karen. Pluto: Transforming the New You. LC 96-181131. 1995. pap. 13.00 (*0-86690-448-4*) Am Fed Astrologers.

Lusty, James R., ed. Handbook of Nucleobase Complexes, Vol. I. 192p. 1990. lib. bdg. 160.00 (*0-8493-3281-8*, QP625) CRC Pr.

Lusty, James R., et al. Handbook of Nucleobase Complexes: Transition Metal Complexes of the Naturally Occurring Nucleobases & Their Derivatives, Vol. II. (Illus.). 512p. 1991. lib. bdg. 240.00 (*0-8493-3282-6*, QP625) CRC Pr.

Lusty, Tim. Selective Feeding Programmes: Oxfam Practical Health Guide no. 1, No. 1. (Oxfam Practical Guide Ser.: 1). (Illus.). 96p. (C). 1984. pap. 9.95 (*0-85598-097-4*, Pub. by Oxfam Pub) Stylus Pub VA.

Lusty, Tim, jt. auth. see Shears, Paul.

Luszig, George. Introduction to Quantum Groups. LC 93-7800. (Progress in Mathematics Ser.: Vol. 110). xii, 346p. 1994. 54.50 (*0-8176-3712-5*) Birkhauser.

Luszki. Psych Yourself to Better Tennis. 1978. pap. 2.00 (*0-87980-246-4*) Wilshire.

Luszki, Walter A. A Rape of Justice: MacArthur & the New Guinea Hangings. 196p. (C). 1991. 24.95 (*0-8191-8348-2*) Madison Bks UPA.

Lusztig. Finance. 5th ed. 1993. text. write for info. (*0-471-64072-7*) Wiley.

— Finance. 5th ed. (C). 1993. pap. text, teacher ed. write for info. (*0-471-64097-2*) Wiley.

— Finance. 6th ed. (C). 1998. pap. text. write for info. (*0-471-64185-5*) Wiley.

Lusztig, George. The Discrete Series of GLn over a Finite Field. LC 74-11058. (Annals of Mathematics Studies: No. 81). (Illus.). 106p. 1974. reprint ed. pap. 32.90 (*0-608-06625-7*, 206682200009) Bks Demand.

— Introduction to Quantum Groups. LC 93-7800. (Progress in Mathematics Ser.: Vol. 110). 341p. 1993. 49.50 (*3-7643-3712-5*) Birkhauser.

— Representations of Finite Chevalley Groups. LC 78-24068. (CBMS Regional Conference Series in Mathematics: Vol. 39). 48p. 1979. reprint ed. pap. 19.00 (*0-8218-1689-6*, CBMS/39C) Am Math.

Lusztig, Michael. Risking Free Trade: The Politics of Free Trade in Britain, Canada, Mexico, & the United States. LC 96-25208. (Pitt Series in Political Science). 272p. 1996. pap. 22.95 (*0-8229-5589-X*); text 49.95 (*0-8229-3932-0*) U of Pittsburgh Pr.

Lutaud, O. Des Revolutions d'Angleterre a la Revolution Francaise: Le Tyrannicide & 'Killing No Murder' (Cromwell, Athalie, Bonaparte) (International Archives of the History of Ideas Ser.: No. 56). 479p. 1973. lib. bdg. 199.50 (*90-247-1509-1*) Kluwer Academic.

Lute, Gwen. Photo Retouching with Adobe Photoshop. (Illus.). 120p. 1999. pap. 29.95 (*0-936262-91-5*, Pub. by Amherst Media) IPG Chicago.

Lutejen-Drecoll, E. & Zrenner, E., eds. Hereditary Retinal Degeneration. (Acta Anatomica Ser.: Vol. 162, No. 2-3 (1998)). (Illus.). 124p. 1998. pap. 151.50 (*3-8055-6810-X*) S Karger.

Lutemaker, Einar, pseud, ed. Scientiae Draconis Project Book. (Illus.). (Orig.). 1989. pap. 2.00 (*1-877934-02-X*) Rose & Nefr Pr.

Luten, Joop B., et al, eds. Seafood from Producer to Consumer, Integrated Approach to Quality: Proceedings of an International Seafood Conference, held on the Occasion of the 25th Anniversary of the WEFTA, Noordwijkerhout, The Netherlands, 13-16 November 1995. LC 97-31933. (Developments in Food Science Ser.: Vol. 38). 722p. 1997. 244.00 (*0-444-82224-0*) Elsevier.

Luten, Robert C., ed. Problems in Pediatric Emergency Medicine. LC 88-4302. (Contemporary Issues in Emergency Medicine Ser.). (Illus.). 310p. reprint ed. pap. 96.10 (*0-7837-8708-1*, 204955600013) Bks Demand.

Luten, Robert C., jt. ed. see Harwood-Nuss, Ann.

Luten, Susan B. California Civil Litigation Study Gde 3e. 3rd ed. (Paralegal). (C). 1997. pap. 16.50 (*0-314-20684-1*) West Pub.

— California Civil Litigation 2e. 2nd ed. Hannan, ed. LC 92-24750. (Paralegal). 420p. (C). 1992. pap. 34.50 (*0-314-01031-9*) West Pub.

— California Civil Litigation 3e. 3rd ed. LC 96-41170. (Paralegal). (C). 1996. mass mkt. 49.95 (*0-314-20228-5*) West Pub.

Lutenegger, A. J., jt. auth. see Benoit, Jean.

Lutenegger, Alan J. In Situ Techniques in Geotechnical Engineering. 600p. 2000. text 90.00 (*0-471-12161-4*, EV25) Wiley.

Lutens, Serge. Serge Lutens. (Illus.). 180p. 2000. 125.00 (*2-84323-066-7*, Pub. by Assouline) Rizzoli Intl.

Luter, Boyd. The Wisdom of Jesus LC 97-75576. 320p. 1998. write for info. (*0-7853-2555-7*) Pubns Intl Ltd.

Luter, Boyd, jt. auth. see McReynolds, Kathy.

Luter, James G. Pronunciation of Standard American English. 131p. (Orig.). (C). 1988. pap. text 10.50 (*0-939085-00-3*) Garrett.

Luter, James G., Jr. Pronunciation of Standard American English. Beaufait, Kathleen B., ed. pap. text 14.50 (*0-939085-01-1*, GPC-002) Garrett Pub Co.

Luter, James G., Jr., jt. auth. see Modisett, Noah F.

Luterbacher, Urs, jt. ed. see Intriligator, Michael D.

Luterman, David. Counseling Parents of Hearing-Impaired Children. 1979. text 15.00 (*0-316-53750-0*, Little Brwn Med Div) Lppncott W & W.

— In the Shadows: Living & Coping with a Loved One's Chronic Illness. LC 95-94103. 1995. pap. 19.95 (*0-9644862-0-2*) Jade Pr.

— The Young Deaf Child. LC 99-11344. (C). 1999. pap. text 28.00 (*0-912752-46-7*) York Pr.

Luterman, David M. Counseling Persons with Communication Disorders & Their Families. 3rd ed. 196p. (C). 1996. pap. text 29.00 (*0-89079-680-7*, 7815) PRO-ED.

Luterman, David M. & Ross, Mark. When Your Child Is Deaf: A Guide for Parents. LC 91-3239. (Illus.). 182p. 1991. pap. text 20.25 (*0-912752-27-0*) York Pr.

Lutes, Chris. Lo Que Dicen de los Adolescentes de Drogas y el Alcohol.Tr. of What Teenagers Are Saying about Drugs & Alcohol. (SPA.). 250p. 1995. pap. 7.99 (*1-56063-088-4*, 490236) Editorial Unilit.

— What Teenagers Are Saying about Drugs & Alcohol. (YA). 1990. pap. 7.99 (*0-310-71051-0*) Zondervan.

Lutes, Chris, jt. auth. see Smarsnick, Willard A.

Lutes, Della T. The Country Kitchen. (American Biography Ser.). 264p. 1991. reprint ed. lib. bdg. 69.00 (*0-7812-8254-3*) Rprt Serv.

— The Country Kitchen. LC 92-26831. (Great Lakes Bks.). 292p. (C). 1992. reprint ed. pap. 17.95 (*0-8143-2438-X*, Great Lks Bks) Wayne St U Pr.

***Lutes, Jason.** City of Stones. (Berlin Ser.: Bk. 1). 2000. pap. text 15.95 (*1-896597-29-7*) Drawn & Quarterly.

***Lutes, Kenneth & Lutes, Lyndell.** Words of Christ: Restored for the Last Days. 356p. 1999. 21.95 (*1-890558-49-4*, 58494) Granite UT.

Lutes, Kenneth O. & Lutes, Lyndell Johnson, compiled by. The Bible Corrected by Joseph Smith. LC 99-186963. 350p. 1998. pap. 14.95 (*1-890558-28-1*, 58281) Granite UT.

Lutes, L. D. & Sarkani, Shahram. Stochastic Analysis of Structural & Mechanical Vibrations. LC 96-33323. 510p. 1996. student ed. 95.00 (*0-13-490533-4*) P-H.

***Lutes, Leasa Y.** Allende, Buitrago, Luiselli: Approximaciones Teoricas al Concepto del Bildungsroman Femenino. (Currents in Comparative Romance Languages & Literature Ser.: Vol. 87). (SPA.). 144p. 2000. 45.95 (*0-8204-4472-3*) P Lang Pubng.

Lutes, Loren D. & Niedzwecki, John M., eds. Engineering Mechanics: Proceedings of the Ninth Conference. LC 92-8712. 112p. 1992. pap. text 97.00 (*0-87262-867-1*) Am Soc Civil Eng.

Lutes, Lyndell, jt. auth. see Lutes, Kenneth.

Lutes, Lyndell Johnson, jt. compiled by see Lutes, Kenneth O.

Lutes, Margaret D., ed. see Dilworths.

Lutes, W. John. Cunningham Gambit. 236p. (Orig.). 1990. pap. 12.95 (*0-945470-00-2*) Chess Ent.

— Danish Gambit. 212p. (Orig.). 1992. pap. 14.95 (*0-945470-19-3*) Chess Ent.

— Petroff Defense Cochrance Gambit. 243p. (Orig.). 1994. pap. 14.95 (*0-945470-44-4*) Chess Ent.

— Scandinavian Defense, Anderssen Counter Attack. 148p. (Orig.). 1992. pap. 14.95 (*0-945470-21-5*) Chess Ent.

— Sicilian Defense O'Kelly Variation. (Orig.). 1993. pap. 14.95 (*0-945470-26-6*) Chess Ent.

— Tennison Gambit. (Orig.). 1995. pap. 12.95 (*0-945470-55-X*) Chess Ent.

Luteyn. Paramos: A Checklist of Plant Diversity, Geographical Distribution & Botanical Literature. LC 99-17171. (Memoirs of the New York Botanical Garden Ser.: Vol. 84). 14p. 1998. 64.00 (*0-89327-427-5*, MEM84) NY Botanical.

Luteyn, J., et al. Building on the Rock Bk. 3: A Collection of Christian Stories for Children. (Illus.). 165p. (J). (gr. 2-8). 1993. pap. 3.50 (*1-892777-07-X*) Reform Heritage Bks.

Luteyn, J. L. Flora of Ecuador No. 147: Ericaceae. (Opera Botanica Series B). 404p. 1996. pap. 99.00 (*87-88702-81-2*, Pub. by Coun Nordic Pubs) Balogh.

Luteyn, J. L., jt. auth. see Stahl, B.

Luteyn, James L. A Revision of the Mexican-Central American Species of Cavendishia (Vacciniaceae) LC 66-6394. (Memoirs Ser.: Vol. 28, No. 3). (Illus.). 138p. 1976. pap. 5.00 (*0-89327-011-3*) NY Botanical.

Luteyn, James L. & O'Brien, Mary E., eds. Contributions Toward a Classification of Rhododendron. LC 79-27378. (Illus.). 330p. 1980. pap. 30.00 (*0-89327-221-3*) NY Botanical.

Luteyn, James L., et al. Ericaceae, Pt. 2. (Flora Neotropica Monographs: No. 66). (Illus.). 560p. 1995. 85.00 (*0-89327-389-9*) NY Botanical.

Lutfiyya, Abdulla H. Readings in Arab Middle Eastern Societies & Cultures. Churchill, Charles W., ed. LC 69-19116. (Orig.). 1970. pap. text 38.50 (*90-279-1062-6*) Mouton.

Lutfiyya, M. Nawal. The Social Construction of Context Through Play. 238p. (Orig.). 1987. pap. text 23.00 (*0-8191-6135-7*) U Pr of Amer.

***Lutfy, Bob, et al.** KidneyHelper Cookbook Middle Eastern: Delicious New Recipes for Dialysis & Pre-Dialysis Patients. 210p. 1999. 24.95 (*1-891546-00-7*) Cons MedHelp.

Lutgendorf, Philip. The Life of a Text: Performing the "Ramcaritmanas of Tulsidas" (Illus.). 450p. 1990. 55.00 (*0-520-06690-1*, Pub. by U CA Pr) Cal Prin Full Svc.

Lutgendorf, Philip, jt. auth. see Wallewaert, Winand M.

Lutgens. Atmosphere. 7th ed. 1997. pap. text, lab manual ed 39.80 (*0-13-760844-6*) P-H.

***Lutgens & Tarbuck.** Essentials of Geology. 7th ed. 1999. suppl. ed. write for info. (*0-13-018831-X*) P-H.

Lutgens, et al. Foundations of Earth Science. 2nd ed. LC 98-44447. 454p. 1998. pap. text 70.67 (*0-13-914037-9*) P-H.

Lutgens, jt. auth. see Tarbuck.

Lutgens, Frederick K. & Tarbuck. Essentials of Geology. 7th ed. LC 99-32023. 449p. 1999. pap. text 68.00 (*0-13-014544-0*) P-H.

Lutgens, Frederick K. & Tarbuck, Edward. Atmosphere. 7th ed. LC 97-13878. 434p. 1997. 70.00 (*0-13-742974-6*) P-H.

***Lutgens, Frederick K. & Tarbuck, Edward J.** The Atmosphere. 8th ed. LC 00-25168. (Illus.). 480p. 2000. 66.67 (*0-13-087957-6*) P-H.

Lutgens, Frederick K. & Tarbuck, Edward J. Foundations of Earth Science. LC 95-32189. (Illus.). 482p. (C). 1995. pap. text 66.00 (*0-02-372821-3*, Macmillan Coll) P-H.

***Lutgens, Frederick K., et al.** Applications & Investigations in Earth Science. 3rd ed. 353p. 1999. spiral bd. 46.00 (*0-13-011288-7*) P-H.

Luth, Hans. Surfaces & Interfaces of Solids. LC 92-28267. (Surface Sciences Ser.: Vol. 15). 1993. 89.00 (*0-387-52681-1*) Spr-Verlag.

Surfaces & Interfaces of Solids. 3rd ed. LC 96-38355. (Illus.). 487p. 1997. 49.00 (*3-540-58576-1*) Spr-Verlag.

Luth, Hans & Ibach, Harald. Solid-State Physics: An Introduction to Principles of Materials Science. LC 96-3237. 1996. write for info. (*0-387-58573-7*) Spr-Verlag.

Luth, Hans, jt. auth. see Ibach, Harald.

Luth, Paul. Woerterbuch Zur Medizinischen Soziologie. (GER.). 408p. 1980. 79.95 (*0-8288-2362-6*, M15305) Fr & Eur.

Luth, Seth. Matter & Methods at Low Temperatures. 3rd ed. (Illus.). 352p. 1996. pap. text 69.95 (*3-540-58572-9*) Spr-Verlag.

L

An Asterisk (*) at the beginning of an entry indicates that the title is appearing for the first time.

L

Luth, Sophie A. The Special Princess. (Illus.). 36p. (J). 1990. 3.95 (*0-9626153-0-7*) Luth & Assocs.

Luthanen, Doug. Who Is This 'Cut-Off' Man & Why Do They All Want to Hit Him? The Parents Guide to Baseball. (Illus.). 88p. (Orig.). 1997. pap. 8.00 (*0-9656366-0-7*) Picadilly Pr.

Luthans. Organizational Behavior. 9th ed. 2001. 65.74 (*0-07-231288-2*) McGraw.

Luthans & Hodgetts. Introduction to Business Today: Functions & Challenges. 1995. student ed. 39.95 (*0-87393-313-3*) Dame Pubns.

— Introduction to Business Today: Functions & Challenges (Study Guide) 1995. pap., student ed. 21.95 (*0-87393-382-6*) Dame Pubns.

Luthans, Fred. Organizational Behavior. 7th ed. 1995. write for info. incl. VHS (*0-07-911790-2*) McGraw.

— Organizational Behavior. 8th ed. LC 97-15805. 704p. 1997. 84.06 (*0-07-039184-X*) McGraw.

Luthans, Fred & American Management Association Staff. The Competitive Advantage: Linking Human Resources Practices with Strategy. LC 96-52168. (Special Report from Organizational Dynamics Ser.). 1997. write for info. (*0-8144-6717-2*) AMACOM.

Luthans, Fred, jt. auth. see Hodgetts, Richard M.

Luthar, Suniya S. Poverty & Children's Adjustment. LC 98-51240. (Developmental Clinical Psychology & Psychiatry Ser.). 158p. 1999. 21.95 (*0-7619-0519-7*) Sage.

— Poverty & Children's Adjustment. LC 98-51240. (Developmental Clinical Psychology & Psychiatry Ser.: Vol. 41). 131p. 1999. 52.00 (*0-7619-0518-9*) Sage.

Luthar, Suniya S., et al, eds. Developmental Psychopathology: Perspectives on Adjustment, Risk, & Disorder. (Illus.). 639p. (C). 1997. text 69.95 (*0-521-47142-7*); pap. text 27.95 (*0-521-47715-8*) Cambridge U Pr.

***Luthardt, Constance M., et al.** Property & Liability Insurance Principles. 3rd ed. LC 99-73210. (Illus.). 312p. (C). 1999. pap. text 31.00 (*0-89462-132-7*) IIA.

Luthe, Rainer. Die Zweifelhafte Schuldfahigkeit: Einfuhrung in Theorie und Praxis der Begutachtung Fur Beteiligte an Gerichtsverfahren. (GER.). 636p. 1996. 108.95 (*3-631-49825-X*) P Lang Pubng.

Luther. Persons in Love. 1972. pap. text 65.00 (*90-247-1292-0*) Kluwer Academic.

— Table Talk. 1959. pap. 2.00 (*0-8358-0052-0*) Upper Room Bks.

Luther, Andreas. Die Syrische Chronik des Josua Stylites. (Untersuchungen Zur Antiken Literatur Und Geschichte Ser.: Vol. 49). (GER., Illus.). viii, 307p. (C). 1997. lib. bdg. 146.70 (*3-11-015470-6*) De Gruyter.

Luther, Arch. Principles of Digital Audio & Video. LC 97-12550. (Communications Engineering Ser.). 408p. 1997. 79.00 (*0-89006-892-5*) Artech Hse.

Luther, Arch, jt. auth. see Inglis, Andrew F.

Luther, Arch C. Video Camera Technology. LC 98-10936. 360p. 1998. 79.00 (*0-89006-556-X*) Artech Hse.

Luther, Arch C., jt. auth. see Inglis, Andrew F.

Luther, Bernard J., jt. auth. see Bois, Thomas J., II.

***Luther, Bil.** Beaches. (Pale Ale Poets Ser.). (Illus.). 46p. 1999. pap. 4.95 (*1-929250-03-7*) FarStarFire Pr.

— Beaches, Vol. 2. (Pale Ale Poets Ser.). (Illus.). 47p. 1999. pap. 4.95 (*1-929250-04-5*) FarStarFire Pr.

— Scream! 52p. 2000. 4.95 (*1-929250-14-2*) FarStarFire Pr.

***Luther, Bruce.** Elements of Creation. LC 00-9394. 64p. 2000. pap. 9.50 (*1-929882-02-5*) Biograph Pub.

***Luther, Carole.** The Blue Book Poems. (Pale Ale Poets Ser.). 43p. 1999. pap. 4.95 (*1-929250-01-0*) FarStarFire Pr.

Luther, Donald J., ed. Preparing for Marriage: A Guide for Christian Couples. 72p. 1992. pap. 8.99 (*0-8066-2569-4*, 9-2569) Augsburg Fortress.

Luther, Edward T. Our Restless Earth: The Geologic Regions of Tennessee. LC 77-21433. (Tennessee Three Star Ser.). (Illus.). 106p. 1977. pap. 7.00 (*0-87049-230-6*) U of Tenn Pr.

Luther, Ernest W. Ethiopia Today. LC 58-7842. 171p. reprint ed. pap. 53.10 (*0-608-11632-7*, 200057300031) Bks Demand.

Luther, Florence. Was Luther a Spiritualist? (1917) 132p. 1998. reprint ed. pap. 14.95 (*0-7661-0547-4*) Kessinger Pub.

Luther-Heyeckhaus, Frieda. Seven Songs - In Memoriam. 42p. 1995. spiral bd. 34.95 (*0-9615847-2-6*) Marwolf Pub.

Luther, Johannes. Die Titeleinfassungen der Reformationszeit, 3 pts. in 1. 20p. 1973. reprint ed. write for info. (*3-487-04662-8*) G Olms Pubs.

Luther, Kem. Cottonwood Roots. LC 92-44167. 164p. reprint ed. pap. 50.90 (*0-608-05995-1*, 206632300008) Bks Demand.

Luther, Kurt R. & Deschouwer, Kris. Party Elites in Divided Societies: Political Parties in Consociational Democracy. LC 98-43802. 1999. text. write for info. (*0-415-20127-6*) Routledge.

Luther, Kurt R. & Muller, Wolfgang C., eds. Politics in Austria: Still a Case for Consociationalism. 232p. 1992. text 32.00 (*0-7146-3461-1*, Pub. by F Cass Pubs) Intl Spec Bk.

Luther, Kurt R. & Pulzer, Peter. Austria, 1945-1995: Fifty Years of the Second Republic. LC 97-39130. (Illus.). 251p. 1998. text 68.95 (*1-84014-404-1*, Pub. by Ashgate Pub) Ashgate Pub Co.

Luther, Luana, ed. see Abney, Don.

Luther, Luana, ed. see Andersson, Dee Dee.

Luther, Luana, ed. see Bennett, William A.

Luther, Luana, ed. see Bruno, Emmy.

Luther, Luana, ed. see Bulanda, Susan.

Luther, Luana, ed. see Craige, Patricia V.

Luther, Luana, ed. see Cusick, William D.

Luther, Luana, ed. see Daniels, Julie.

Luther, Luana, ed. see Grossman, Alvin.

Luther, Luana, ed. see Grossman, Alvin & Grossman, Beverly.

Luther, Luana, ed. see Martin, Nancy A.

Luther, Luana, ed. see McDaniel, Jack & McDaniel, Colleen.

Luther, Luana, ed. see McLennan, Bardi.

Luther, Luana, ed. see Olejniczak, Denise & Olejniczak, Anne.

Luther, Luana, ed. see Ross, Nina P.

Luther, Luana, ed. see Smith, Sally A.

Luther, Luana, ed. see Starkweather, Patricia.

Luther, Luana, ed. see Van Goron Kline, David & Hoffman, Patricia B.

Luther, Martin. Away in a Manger. (Happy Day Bks.). (Illus.). 24p. (J). (ps). 1995. pap. 1.99 (*0-7847-0345-0*, 04225) Standard Pub.

— Away in a Manger: Sing & Color Book. (Coloring & Activity Bks.). (Illus.). 16p. (J). 1978. pap. 1.49 (*0-87403-859-6*, 02458) Standard Pub.

— Basic Luther. LC 95-60058. 1995. pap. 12.95 (*0-87243-213-0*) Templegate.

— The Bondage of the Will. LC 58-8660. 326p. (C). 1989. pap. 14.99 (*0-8007-5342-9*) Revell.

***Luther, Martin.** By Faith Alone. (Devotion Ser.). 370p. 1999. pap. 13.25 (*1-885216-27-0*) Evan Formosan.

Luther, Martin. Christian Liberty. Grimm, Harold J., ed. Lambert, W. A., tr. from GER. 40p. 1976. pap. 12.00 (*0-8006-0182-3*, 1-182, Fortress Pr) Augsburg Fortress.

— Commentary on Galatians. LC 78-59151. 416p. 1987. pap. 15.99 (*0-8254-3124-7*, Kregel Class) Kregel.

— Commentary on Galatians: Modern-English Edition. abr. rev. ed. 416p. 1998. pap. 14.99 (*0-8007-5648-7*) Revell.

— Commentary on Peter & Jude. LC 82-4652. 304p. 1990. pap. 13.99 (*0-8254-3147-6*, Kregel Class) Kregel.

— Commentary on Romans. Mueller, J. Theodore, tr. LC 76-12077. Orig. Title: Commentary on the Epistle to the Romans. 224p. 1976. pap. 12.99 (*0-8254-3119-0*, Kregel Class) Kregel.

— Daily Readings from Luther's Writings. Owen, Barbara, ed. LC 93-14902. 336p. 1993. kivar 21.99 (*0-8066-2639-9*, 9-2639) Augsburg Fortress.

— Daily Readings with Martin Luther. Atkinson, James, ed. 96p. 1987. pap. 4.95 (*0-87243-157-6*) Templegate.

— Day by Day We Magnify Thee: Daily Readings for the Entire Year. LC 82-2481. 448p. 1982. pap. 22.00 (*0-8006-1637-5*, 1-1637, Fortress Pr) Augsburg Fortress.

— Galatians. abr. ed. LC 97-51470. (Crossway Classic Commentaries Ser.). 320p. 1998. pap. 17.99 (*0-89107-994-7*) Crossway Bks.

Luther, Martin. Glory, Honor & Power. 52p. 1987. pap. 9.99 (*0-8341-9683-2*) Lillenas.

Luther, Martin. The Jews & Their Lies. 1982. lib. bdg. 250.00 (*0-87700-378-5*) Revisionist Pr.

Luther, Martin. The Jews & Their Lies. 64p. 1996. pap. 3.00 (*0-9600358-9-3*) CPA Bk Pub.

Luther, Martin. The Large Catechism of Martin Luther. 105p. 1963. text 14.00 (*0-8006-0885-2*, 1-885, Fortress Pr) Augsburg Fortress.

— Luther: Letters of Spiritual Counsel. Tappert, T. G., ed. & tr. by. 465p. (C). 1997. pap. 26.95 (*1-57383-092-5*) Regent College.

— Luther's Family Devotions for Every Day of the Church Year. Link, George, ed. Baseley, Joel, tr. from GER. Orig. Title: Luther's Taeglich Hausandacht auf Alle Tage des Kirchenjahres. 688p. 1996. 22.00 (*0-9652403-0-4*) M V Publns.

— Luther's Large Catechism: A Contemporary Translation with Study Questions. 1988. 5.65 (*0-570-03539-2*, 14-2021) Concordia.

— Luther's Ninety-Five Theses. Jacobs, C. M., tr. 18p. 1957. pap. 4.99 (*0-8006-1265-5*, 1-1265, Fortress Pr) Augsburg Fortress.

— Luther's Small Catechism. 32p. 1992. pap. text 0.95 (*1-58572-010-0*) Ambassador Pubns.

— Luthers Werke, 4 vols., Set. (GER.). 1920p. 1982. pap. 113.85 (*3-11-008942-4*) De Gruyter.

— Luthers Werke in Auswahl, 8 vols. Clemen, Otto & Leitzmann, Albert, eds. Incl. Vol. 1. Schriften von 1517 bis 1520. 6th rev. ed. (Illus.). xxxii, 512p. 1966. 28.00 (*3-11-003152-3*); Vol. 2. Schriften von 1520 bis 1524. 6th rev. ed. vi, 464p. 1967. 28.00 (*3-11-003153-1*); Vol. 3. Schriften von 1524 bis 1528. 6th rev. ed. vi, 516p. 1966. 28.00 (*3-11-003154-X*); Vol. 4. Schriften von 1529 bis 1545. 6th rev. ed. vi, 428p. 1967. 28.00 (*3-11-003151-5*); Vol. 5. Junge Luther. 3rd rev. ed. Vogelsang, Erich, ed. xi, 434p. 1963. 32.00 (*3-11-005609-7*); Vol. 6. Luthers Briefe. 3rd rev. ed. Rueckert, Hanns, ed. xv, 451p. 1966. 32.00 (*3-11-005610-0*); Vol. 7. Predigten. 3rd ed. Hirsch, Emanuel, ed. xii, 420p. 1962. 32.00 (*3-11-005611-9*); Vol. 8. Tischreden. 3rd ed. x, 387p. 1962. 32.00 (*3-11-005612-7*); write for info. (*0-318-51629-2*) De Gruyter.

— Luther's Works, Vol. 6. Pahl, Paul D., tr. LC 55-9893. 1969. 29.00 (*0-570-06406-6*, 15-1748) Concordia.

— Luther's Works, Vol. 7. Pahl, Paul D., tr. LC 55-9893. 1964. 29.00 (*0-570-06407-4*, 15-1749) Concordia.

— Luther's Works, Vol. 9. Pelikan, Jaroslav J., ed. LC 55-9893. 1960. 29.00 (*0-570-06409-0*, 15-1751) Concordia.

— Luther's Works, Vol. 12. LC 55-9893. 1955. 29.00 (*0-570-06412-0*, 15-1754) Concordia.

— Luther's Works, Vol. 14. LC 55-9893. 1958. 29.00 (*0-570-06414-7*, 15-1756) Concordia.

— Luther's Works, Vol. 15. Pelikan, Jaroslav J. et al, trs. from LAT. LC 55-9893. 1971. 29.00 (*0-570-06415-5*, 15-1757) Concordia.

— Luther's Works, Vol. 17. Bouman, Herbert J., tr. LC 55-9893. 1972. 29.00 (*0-570-06417-1*, 15-1759) Concordia.

— Luther's Works, Vol. 21. Pelikan, Jaroslav J. & Steinhaeu, A. T., trs. LC 55-9893. 1968. 29.00 (*0-570-06421-X*, 15-1763) Concordia.

— Luther's Works, Vol. 24. Pelikan, Jaroslav J., ed. Bertram, Martin H., tr. LC 55-9893. 1961. 29.00 (*0-570-06424-4*, 15-1766) Concordia.

— Luther's Works: Genesis Chapters 15-20, Vol. 3. Pelikan, Jaroslav J., ed. Schick, George V., tr. LC 55-9893. 1961. 29.00 (*0-570-06403-1*, 15-1745) Concordia.

— Luther's Works: Genesis Chapters 26-30, Vol. 5. Schick, George V., tr. LC 55-9893. 1967. 29.00 (*0-570-06405-8*, 15-1747) Concordia.

— Luther's Works: Genesis Chapters 45-50, Vol. 8. Pahl, Paul D., tr. LC 55-9893. 1965. 29.00 (*0-570-06408-2*, 15-1750) Concordia.

— Luther's Works: Genesis Chapters 6-11, Vol. 2. Pelikan, Jaroslav J., ed. Schick, George V., tr. LC 55-9893. 1960. 29.00 (*0-570-06402-3*, 15-1744) Concordia.

— Luther's Works: Lectures on Galatians, Vol. 27. Pelikan, Jaroslav J., ed. Jungkuntz, Richard, tr. LC 55-9893. 1963. 29.00 (*0-570-06427-9*, 15-1769) Concordia.

— Luther's Works: Lectures on Galatians (Chapters 1 - 4), Vol. 26. Pelikan, Jaroslav J., ed. LC 55-9893. 1968. 29.00 (*0-570-06426-0*, 15-1768) Concordia.

— Luther's Works: Lectures on Isaiah (Chs. 1-29), Vol. 16. Bouman, Herbert J., tr. 1968. 29.00 (*0-570-06416-3*, 15-1758) Concordia.

— Luther's Works: Lectures on Minor Prophets III, Vol. 20. Dinda, R. J. & Miller, W. B., trs. LC 55-9893. 300p. 1973. 29.00 (*0-570-06420-1*, 15-1762) Concordia.

— Luther's Works: Lectures on Romans Glosses & Scholia, Vol. 25. Preus, J. A. & Tillmanns, W. G., trs. LC 55-9893. (Luther's Works). 1972. 29.00 (*0-570-06425-2*, 15-1767) Concordia.

— Luther's Works: Lectures on the Psalms I, Vol. 10. Bouman, H. J., tr. 1981. 29.00 (*0-570-06410-4*, 15-1752) Concordia.

— Luther's Works: Lectures on the Psalms III, Vol. 11. Oswald, Hilton C., ed. Bowman, Herbert J., tr. from LAT. LC 55-9893. 560p. 1976. 29.00 (*0-570-06411-2*, 15-1753) Concordia.

— Luther's Works: Lectures on Titus, Philemon, Hebrews, Vol. 29. Pelikan, Jaroslav J. & Hansen, W. A., trs. 1968. 29.00 (*0-570-06429-5*, 15-1771) Concordia.

— Luther's Works: Selected Psalms 2, Vol. 13. Pelikan, Jaroslav J., ed. LC 55-9893. 1956. 29.00 (*0-570-06413-9*, 15-1755) Concordia.

— Luther's Works: Sermons on the Gospel of St. John, Vol. 23. Bertram, Martin H., tr. LC 55-9893. 1958. 29.00 (*0-570-06423-6*, 15-1765) Concordia.

— Martin Luther: Selections from His Writings. Dillenberger, John, ed. LC 61-9503. 560p. 1958. pap. 12.95 (*0-385-09876-6*, Anchor NY) Doubleday.

— Martin Luther - Faith in Christ & the Gospel: Selected Spiritual Writings. Gritsch, Eric W., ed. LC 95-34532. 192p. 1996. pap. 11.95 (*1-56548-041-4*) New City.

— The Schmalkald Articles. 64p. 1995. pap. 11.00 (*0-8006-2661-3*, 1-2661, Fortress Pr) Augsburg Fortress.

***Luther, Martin.** Simple Way to Pray. 2000. write for info. (*0-664-22273-0*) Westminster John Knox.

Luther, Martin. Theologia Germanica. 240p. 1992. reprint ed. pap. 13.95 (*1-56459-012-7*) Kessinger Pub.

— Three Treatises. rev. ed. LC 73-114753. 312p. 1970. pap. 16.00 (*0-8006-1639-1*, 1-1639, Fortress Pr) Augsburg Fortress.

Luther, Martin & Sandberg, Irving L. The 1529 Holy Week & Easter Sermons of Dr. Martin Luther. LC 98-43556. 1999. 20.00 (*0-570-04281-X*) Concordia.

Luther, Martin & Sverdrup, H. U. Luther's Small Catechism Explained. abr. rev. ed. Loukom, John A., ed. Urseth, H. A., tr. 128p. 1995. reprint ed. text 4.95 (*1-58572-015-1*) Ambassador Pubns.

Luther, Martin E. The Compasses of God: Science & Human Destiny. LC 91-90546. 144p. (Orig.). 1991. pap. 14.95 (*0-9615847-1-8*) Marwolf Pub.

— The Free Market - Your Stake in Its Future. LC 85-90462. 160p. (Orig.). (C). 1986. pap. 9.95 (*0-9615847-0-X*) Marwolf Pub.

— The Infinite Voyage: A Metaphysical Odyssey. LC 96-94062. (Illus.). 256p. (Orig.). 1996. pap. 19.95 (*0-9615847-3-4*) Marwolf Pub.

Luther, Martin H. Luther's Works, Vol. 22. Pelikan, Jaroslav J., ed. Bertram, Martin, tr. LC 55-9893. 1957. 29.00 (*0-570-06422-8*, 15-1764) Concordia.

— Luther's Works, Vol. 28. Sittler, E. et al, trs. LC 55-9893. 1973. 29.00 (*0-570-06428-7*, 15-1770) Concordia.

— Luther's Works: Catholic Epistles, Vol. 30. Pelikan, Jaroslav J., ed. Bertram, M. H. & Hansen, W. A., trs. LC 55-9893. 1967. 29.00 (*0-570-06430-9*, 15-1772) Concordia.

— Luther's Works: Lectures on the Minor Prophets, 2: Jonah & Habakkuk, Vol. 19. Oswald, Hilton C., ed. Bertram, M. & Froelich, C., trs. from GER. LC 55-9893. 1974. 29.00 (*0-570-06419-8*, 15-1761) Concordia.

Luther, Marv & Luther, Nona. Water-Mill Inns of France: A Gastronomic Guide to Romantic Country Inns. LC 95-71951. 232p. 1996. pap. 16.95 (*0-9649085-4-9*) Corinthian CA.

Luther, Nona, jt. auth. see Luther, Marv.

***Luther, Robert.** Skybolt. deluxe ed. LC 99-93459. (Aviation Ser.). 390p. 2000. 19.95 (*0-9673919-0-3*) Centurion Pubs.

Luther, Sara F. The United States & the Direct Broadcast Satellite: The Politics of International Broadcasting in Space. (Illus.). 238p. 1988. text 75.00 (*0-19-505138-6*) OUP.

Luther, Sara F., et al. Diverse Perspectives on Marxist Philosophy: East & West. 53. LC 94-25057. (Contributions in Philosophy Ser.: Vol. 53). 168p. 1995. 59.95 (*0-313-29396-1*, Greenwood Pr) Greenwood.

***Luther, Susan.** Breathing in the Dark: Poems. LC 00-190696. (Illus.). xiv, 124p. 2000. pap. 15.95 (*0-9673919-1-1*, Banyon Swamp Creek) Centurion Pubs.

***Luther, Tal, et al.** Studies In Frank Waters vol. 21: Contributions. 85p. 1999. pap. 10.00 (*1-878277-16-2*) Frank Waters Soc.

Luther, Tal, jt. auth. see Swinford, T. A.

Luther, Vicki & Wall, Milan. Clues to Rural Community Survival LC 98-87755. 157 p. 1998. write for info. (*0-9666699-0-8*) Heartland Ctr.

— A Practical Guide to Community Assessment. 120p. 1999. pap. 10.00 (*0-9666699-1-6*) Heartland Ctr.

Luther, Walter. Darlehen im Konkurs. (GER.). 144p. 1990. pap. 42.00 (*3-7890-1938-0*, Pub. by Nomos Verlags) Intl Bk Import.

Luther-Wilder, Judith. For the Working Artist No. 2: A Handbook for Anyone Who Chooses to Manage Their Own Career. rev. ed. Orig. Title: For the Working Artist. (Illus.). 300p. 1999. pap. 24.95 (*0-945941-34-X*) NNAP.

Luther, William M. How to Develop a Business Plan in Fifteen Days. LC 86-47854. 255p. reprint ed. pap. 79.10 (*0-7837-7062-6*, 204687400004) Bks Demand.

— The Marketing Plan: How to Prepare & Implement It. 2nd expanded ed. LC 92-17618. 208p. 1992. pap. 17.95 (*0-8144-7805-0*) AMACOM.

— The Start-Up Business Plan. 240p. 1991. pap. 15.95 (*0-13-842543-4*, Lasser) Macmillan Gen Ref.

Lutheran Church in America Task Group for Long-Ran. Theology: An Assessment of Current Trends Report. LC 68-55757. 174p. reprint ed. pap. 54.00 (*0-608-16328-7*, 202688000053) Bks Demand.

Lutheran Episcopal Dialogue III Staff. Implications of the Gospel. 128p. (Orig.). 1988. pap. 4.95 (*0-88028-089-1*, 967) Forward Movement.

Lutheran Research Society Staff. The Sedition Case of 1944. 1979. lib. bdg. 59.95 (*0-8490-3005-6*) Gordon Pr.

***Lutheran World Federation Staff & Catholic Church.** Joint Declaration on the Doctrine of Justification. LC 00-28845. 2000. write for info. (*0-8028-4774-9*) Eerdmans.

Lutherer, Lorenz O. & Simon, Margaret S. Targeted: The Anatomy of an Animal Rights Attack. LC 92-32505. 1993. 19.95 (*0-8061-2492-X*) U of Okla Pr.

Luthert, Joanna M. & Robinson, Lorraine. The Royal Marsden Hospital Manual of Multidisciplinary Standards of Care. (Illus.). 256p. 1993. pap. 26.95 (*0-632-03386-X*) Blackwell Sci.

***Luthi, Ambros & Sommaruga, Giovanni.** Die Entstehung von Planetensystemen Im Lichte Neuer Entdeckungen: Ein Rekursives Modell und Wissenschaftsphilosophische Betrachtungen. 178p. 1999. 30.95 (*3-906763-28-5*, Pub. by P Lang) P Lang Pubng.

Luthi, Ann L. Sentimental Jewellery. (Illus.). 40p. 1998. pap. 8.50 (*0-7478-0363-3*, Pub. by Shire Pubns) Parkwest Pubns.

Luthi, H. J., jt. ed. see Kall, P.

Luthi, J. J. Dictionnaire General de la Francophonie. (FRE.). 390p. 1986. 95.00 (*0-8288-1944-0*, F59710) Fr & Eur.

Luthi, Max. The European Folktale: Form & Nature. Niles, John D., tr. LC 85-45990. (Folklore Studies in Translation). 196p. 1986. pap. 11.95 (*0-253-20393-7*, MB-393) Ind U Pr.

— Once upon a Time: On the Nature of Fairy Tales. Chadeayne, Lee & Gottwald, Paul, trs. LC 76-6992. 192p. 1976. reprint ed. pap. 13.95 (*0-253-20203-5*, MB-203) Ind U Pr.

***Luthin, Herbert W.** Surviving Through the Days: Translations of Native California Stories & Songs. LC 00-31630. (Indian Reader Ser.). 2001. pap. write for info. (*0-520-22270-9*) U CA Pr.

Luthke, Martin F. Riding the Tide of Change: Preparing for Personal & Planetary Transformation. LC 97-90108. iv, 107p. (Orig.). 1997. pap. 9.95 (*0-9656927-2-8*) Expansion Pub.

***Luthke, Martin F. & Stein-Luthke, Linda.** Beyond Psychotherapy: Introduction to Psychoenergetic Healing. 2000. pap. 29.95 (*0-9656927-4-4*, Pub. by Expansion Pub) New Leaf Dist.

Luthke, Martin F., jt. auth. see Stein-Luthke, Linda.

Luthman, Shirley G. Collection, Nineteen Seventy-Nine. LC 79-92404. (Orig.). (C). 1980. pap. 8.95 (*0-936094-02-8*) Mehetabel & Co.

— Energy & Personal Power. (Orig.). (C). 1982. pap. 10.95 (*0-686-98386-6*) Mehetabel & Co.

— Intimacy: The Essence of Male & Female. LC 72-81832. (C). 1977. pap. 8.95 (*0-936094-01-X*) Mehetabel & Co.

Lutholtz, M. William. Grand Dragon: D. C. Stephenson & the Ku Klux Klan in Indiana. LC 90-20132. (Illus.). 384p. 1991. 29.95 (*1-55753-010-6*) Purdue U Pr.

— Grand Dragon: D. C. Stephenson & the Ku Klux Klan in Indiana. (Illus.). 384p. 1993. reprint ed. pap. 18.95 (*1-55753-046-7*) Purdue U Pr.

Luthra, H. L. Gautma the Buddha: Great Masters. 80p. 1996. 75.00 (*81-209-0974-7*, Pub. by Pitambar Pub) St Mut.

— The Little Clay Cart. 1998. pap. 20.00 (*81-209-0807-4*, Pub. by Pitambar Pub) St Mut.

— Tales from Kalidasa. 136p. (C). 1989. 60.00 (*81-209-0228-9*, Pub. by Pitambar Pub) St Mut.

— Tales from Kalidasa. 120p. (C). 1997. pap. 25.00 (*81-209-0037-5*, Pub. by Pitambar Pub) St Mut.

— Vision of Vasavadatta. 1996. pap. 20.00 (*81-209-0799-X*, Pub. by Pitambar Pub) St Mut.

Luthra, Mohan. Britain's Black Population. 3rd ed. 456p. 1997. pap. 35.95 (*1-85742-189-2*, Pub. by Arena); text 83.95 (*1-85742-041-1*, Pub. by Arena) Ashgate Pub Co.

Luthra, Nirupamja, jt. auth. see Mahajan, Amar J.

Luthy, Melvin J. Phonological & Lexical Aspects of Colloquial Finnish, Vol. 119. (Uralic & Altaic Ser.). x, 94p. 1973. pap. text 11.00 (*0-87750-173-4*) Res Inst Inner Asian Studies.

An Asterisk (*) at the beginning of an entry indicates that the title is appearing for the first time.

Luthy, W., jt. auth. see Weber, H. P.

***Lutjen-Drecoll, E.** Aging & Age Related Ocular Diseases. (Opthalmologica Ser.: Vol. 214, No. 1). (Illus.). 104p. 2000. pap. 34.00 (3-8055-7038-4) S Karger.

Lutjen-Drecoll, Elke, ed. Perspectives in Glaucoma Research, Pt. II. (Journal: Vol. 211, No. 3, 1997). (Illus.). 84p. 1997. pap. 60.00 (3-8055-6515-1) S Karger.

Lutjen-Drecoll, Elke & Rohen, Johannes W. Atlas of Anatomy: The Functional Systems of the Human Body. LC 98-23048. 152p. 1998. 19.95 (0-683-30641-3) Lppncott W & W.

Lutjens, Louette R. Callista Roy: An Adaptation Model. (Notes on Nursing Theories Ser.: Vol. 3). (Illus.). 68p. (C). 1991. 22.95 (0-8039-4577-9); pap. 9.95 (0-8039-4228-1) Sage.

— Martha Rogers: The Science of Unitary Human Beings. (Notes on Nursing Theories Ser.: Vol. 1). (Illus.). 40p. (C). 1991. 22.95 (0-8039-4578-7) Sage.

— Martha Rogers: The Science of Unitary Human Beings, No. 1. (Notes on Nursing Theories Ser.: Vol. 1). (Illus.). 40p. (C). 1991. pap. 9.95 (0-8039-4229-X) Sage.

Lutjering, G., jt. auth. see Nowack, H.

Lutkehaus, Nancy & Roscoe, Paul, eds. Gender Rituals: Female "Initiation" in Papua New Guinea. LC 94-39869. (Illus.). 288p. (C). 1995. pap. 21.99 (0-415-91107-9, B4824) Routledge.

Lutkehaus, Nancy, et al. Sepik Heritage: Tradition & Change in Papua New Guinea. LC 90-80282. (Illus.). 688p. 1990. lib. bdg. 75.00 (0-89089-322-5) Carolina Acad Pr.

Lutkehaus, Nancy, jt. auth. see Mead, Margaret.

Lutkehaus, Nancy C. Zaria's Fire: Engendered Moments in Manam Ethnography. LC 95-68695. (Illus.). 506p. 1995. boxed set 65.00 (0-89089-800-6) Carolina Acad Pr.

Lutkehaus, Nancy C., jt. ed. see Huber, Mary T.

Lutkenhof, Marlene, ed. Children with Spina Bifida: A Parents' Guide. LC 99-35403. 395p. 1999. pap. 16.95 (0-933149-60-3) Woodbine House.

Lutkenhoff, Marlene. Spinabilities: A Young Person's Guide to Spina Bifida. LC 96-42056. (Illus.). 250p. (YA). 1996. pap. text 16.95 (0-933149-86-7) Woodbine House.

Lutkenhuff, Steven D., jt. ed. see Mehlman, Myron A.

Lutkepohl, H., et al, eds. Money Demand in Europe. LC 99-11541. (Studies in Empirical Economics). (Illus.). x, 260p. 1999. 84.95 (3-7908-1182-3) Spr-Verlag.

Lutkepohl, Helmut. Forecasting Aggregated Vector ARMA Processes. (Lecture Notes in Economics & Mathematical Systems Ser.: Vol. 284). x, 323p. 1987. 44.80 (0-387-17208-4) Spr-Verlag.

— Handbook of Matrices. LC 96-222153. 320p. 1997. pap. 79.95 (0-471-97015-8) Wiley.

— Introduction to Multiple Time Series Analysis. 552p. 1991. pap. text 59.00 (0-387-53194-7) Spr-Verlag.

— Introduction to Multiple Time Series Analysis. 2nd ed. LC 93-28356. (Illus.). xxi, 545p. 1993. 59.95 (0-387-56940-5); pap. write for info. (3-540-56940-5) Spr-Verlag.

Lutkin, Peter C. Music in the Church. LC 72-135722. reprint ed. 42.50 (0-404-04069-1) AMS Pr.

Lutkus, Anthony D., jt. ed. see Baird, John C.

Lutman, Frank C. Rhodesian Ridgebacks. (Illus.). 192p. 1994. 9.95 (0-7938-1101-5, KW159) TFH Pubns.

Lutman, M. E. & Haggard, M. P., eds. Hearing Science & Hearing Disorders. 1983. text 99.95 (0-12-460440-4) Acad Pr.

Luton, Larry S. The Politics of Garbage: A Community Perspective on Solid Waste Policy Making. LC 96-10050. (Pitt Series in Policy & Institutional). (Illus.). 272p. 1997. pap. 22.95 (0-8229-5605-5); text 49.95 (0-8229-3946-0) U of Pittsburgh Pr.

***Luton, Mary K.** La Comtesse de Segur: A Marquise de Sade? LC 98-33747. (Currents in Comparative Romance Languages & Literatures Ser.: Vol. 83). 118p. (C). 1999. text 41.00 (0-8204-4254-2) P Lang Pubng.

Luton, Mildred. Christmas Time in the Mountains. (Illus.). 44p. (Orig.). (J). (gr. 1-6). 1981. pap. 6.95 (0-87516-434-X) DeVorss.

Lutoslawski, Wincenty. The Origin & Growth of Plato's Logic: With an Account of Plato's Style & of the Chronology of His Writings. xviii, 547p. 1983. reprint ed. 89.70 (3-487-07336-6) G Olms Pubs.

— The Origin & Growth of Plato's Logic: With an Account of Plato's Style & the Chronology of His Writings. (Classical Studies). reprint ed. lib. bdg. 62.00 (0-697-00041-9) Irvington.

***Lutovac, Miroslav D, et al.** Filter Design for Signal Processing Using Matlab & Mathematica. 785p. 2000. 100.00 (0-201-36130-2, Prentice Hall) P-H.

Lutovich, Diane & Chan, Janis F. How to Write Reports & Proposals: A Self-Paced Training Program. 180p. 1998. pap. 48.00 (0-9637455-5-7) Adv Comm Designs.

— Just Commas. 75p. 1999. pap. write for info. (0-9637455-6-5) Adv Comm Designs.

— Professional Writing Skills: A Self-Paced Training Program. 2nd rev. ed. 217p. (Orig.). 1997. pap. 45.00 (0-9637455-4-9) Adv Comm Designs.

Lutovich, Diane, jt. auth. see Chan, Janis F.

***Lutrin, Carl E. & Settle.** American Public Administration: Concepts & Cases. 5th ed. 2002. pap. text. write for info. (0-312-25845-3) St Martin.

Lutrin, Carl E. & Settle, Allen K. American Public Administration: Concepts & Cases. 4th ed. Jucha, ed. 522p. (C). 1992. 64.75 (0-314-91349-1) West Pub.

Lutschg-Emmenegger, Margrith. The Guide to Forfaiting. 1998. pap. 225.00 (1-85564-588-2, Pub. by Euromoney) Am Educ Systs.

Lutsenburg Maas, Jacob Van, see Karmokolias, Yannis & Van Lutsenburg Maas, Jacob.

Lutske, Harvey. The Book of Jewish Customs. 400p. 1995. pap. 30.00 (1-56821-608-4) Aronson.

— The Book of Jewish Customs. LC 86-22362. 400p. 1987. reprint ed. 40.00 (0-87668-916-0) Aronson.

— History in Their Hands: A Book of Jewish Autographs. LC 94-19626. 344p. 1996. 50.00 (1-56821-290-9) Aronson.

Lutskevich, Nelly. Museum of Western & Oriental Art: Odessa. (Illus.). 180p. (C). 1985. text 85.00 (0-7855-5850-0, Pub. by Collets) St Mut.

Lutsko, Ron & Menigoz, Robin S. Landscape Plans. Feller-Roth, Barbara, ed. (Illus.). 96p. Date not set. 14.95 (0-89721-360-2, Ortho Bks) Meredith Bks.

Luttbeg, Norman R. Comparing the States & Communities. (C). 1997. 58.00 (0-673-46184-X) Addson-Wesley Educ.

***Luttbeg, Norman R.** Comparing the States & Communities. 1998. pap. 34.95 (0-945483-99-6) E Bowers Pub.

— The Grassroots of Democracy: A Comparative Study of Competition & Its Impact in American Cities of the 1990s. LC 99-43467. 224p. 1999. 55.00 (0-7391-0047-5) Lxngtn Bks.

Luttbeg, Norman R. & Gant, Michael M. American Electoral Behavior, 1952-1992. 2nd ed. LC 94-66866. 234p. (C). 1994. pap. text 30.00 (0-87581-386-0, AEB2) F E Peacock Pubs.

Luttbeg, Norman R. & Zeigler, Harmon. Attitude Consensus & Conflict in an Interest Group: An Assessment of Cohesion. (Reprint Series in Social Sciences). (C). 1993. reprint ed. pap. text 5.00 (0-8290-3351-3, PS-395) Irvington.

Luttenberger, Gerard H. An Introduction to Christology. LC 98-60129. 392p. 1998. pap. 24.95 (0-89622-924-6) Twenty-Third.

Luttenton, Mark R. Aquatic Ecosystems of the Great Lakes Region. (Illus.). (C). text. write for info. (0-472-09669-9); pap. text. write for info. (0-472-06669-2) U of Mich Pr.

***Lutter, Horst.** Die Padagogische Ausbildung Von Berufsschullehrern im Studienseminar. (Beitrage zur Empirischen Erziehungswissenschaft und Fachdidaktik. Bd. 11 Ser.). 350p. 1999. 48.95 (3-631-35725-7) P Lang Pubng.

Lutter, Judy M. Of Heroes, Hopes & Level Playing Fields: A Collection of Insights & Observations on Physical Activity & Women. LC 96-94034. (Illus.). 104p. (Orig.). 1996. pap. 10.00 (0-9651137-0-1) Melpomene Inst.

Lutter, Judy M. & Jaffee, Lynn. The Bodywise Woman. 2nd rev. ed. LC 96-13088. (Illus.). 328p. 1996. reprint ed. pap. 16.95 (0-87322-606-2, PLUT0606) Human Kinetics.

Lutter, Lowell D. Atlas of Adult Foot & Ankle Surgery. (Illus.). 368p. (C). (gr. 13). 1996. text 159.00 (0-8016-6280-X, 06280) Mosby Inc.

Lutter, Marcus, ed. Die Grundung einer Tochtergesellschaft im Ausland. (GER.). 359p. 1983. 98.50 (3-11-008787-1) De Gruyter.

Lutter, Tiiu J., ed. see Gilkes, Lolita W.

Lutterbie, John. Hearing Voices: Modern Drama & the Problem of Subjectivity. LC 96-51215. 192p. (C). 1997. text 39.50 (0-472-10808-5, 10808) U of Mich Pr.

Lutterjohann, Martin. IQ Tests for Children. LC 77-1520. 192p. 1978. pap. 4.95 (0-8128-2271-4, Scrbrough Hse) Madison Bks UPA.

— IQ Tests for School Children: How to Test Your Child's Intelligence. (Illus.). 1980. pap. 5.95 (0-8128-6026-8, Scrbrough Hse) Madison Bks UPA.

Lutterman, Kenneth G., jt. auth. see Alvarez, Rodolfo.

Lutterman, LaVonne. How to Make & Repair Leather Doll Bodies. Shields, Kim, ed. 64p. (Orig.). 1995. pap. 14.95 (1-879825-17-1) Jones Publish.

Lutterodt, Sarah A. & Grafinger, Deborah J. Developing Objective Test Items I. (Self-paced Instructor Training Mod. Ser.). (Illus.). 56p. (Orig.). 1985. pap. text 16.50 (0-87683-687-2) GP Courseware.

— How to Write Learning Objectives. (Instructor Training Ser.). (Illus.). 40p. (Orig.). 1985. pap. text 16.50 (0-317-38598-4) GP Courseware.

— Measurement & Evaluation: Basic Concepts. (Instructor Training Ser.). (Illus.). 40p. (Orig.). 1985. pap. text 16.50 (0-87683-686-4) GP Courseware.

Luttery, Kevin. A Stranger in My Bed. Martin, Tonya, ed. LC 97-75168. 224p. 1997. 23.95 (1-889408-03-4) Bryant & Dillon.

Luttge, Dieter, et al. Aspekte der Sozialen Interaktion in Erziehung und Unterricht. (Hildesheimer Beitrage Zu Den Erziehungs und Sozial Wissenschaften Ser.: Bd. 9). (GER.). 190p. 1978. 20.00 (3-487-06631-9) G Olms Pubs.

Luttge, Ulrich. Physiological Ecology of Tropical Plants. LC 96-52359. 392p. 1997. 45.95 (3-540-61161-4) Spr-Verlag.

Luttge, Ulrich, ed. Vascular Plants As Epiphytes. (Ecological Studies: Vol. 76). (Illus.). 280p. 1989. 139.00 (0-387-50796-5) Spr-Verlag.

Luttgens. Kinesiology. 10th ed. 2001. pap. text 51.75 (0-07-232919-X) McGraw.

Luttgens, et al. Kinesiology. 9th ed. 1996. 15.50 (0-697-34113-5, WCB McGr Hill) McGrw-H Hghr Educ.

Luttgens, Gunter & Wilson, Norman. Electrostatic Hazards. LC 97-15502. (Illus.). 192p. 1997. text 65.00 (0-7506-2782-4) Buttrwrth-Heinemann.

Luttgens, Kathryn & Hamilton, Nancy. Kinesiology. 9th ed. LC 95-83190. 704p. (C). 1996. text, lab manual ed. write for info. (0-697-24655-8) Brown & Benchmark.

Luttgens, Kathryn, et al. Kinesiology: Scientific Basis of Human Motion. 8th ed. 704p. (C). 1992. text. write for info. (0-697-11632-8) Brown & Benchmark.

Luttger, Hans & Jeschek, Hans H., eds. Festschrift fuer Eduard Dreher zum 70. Geburtstag. (C). 1977. 253.85 (3-11-005988-6) De Gruyter.

Lutthans, R. V., jt. auth. see Drago, Raymond J.

Luttig, John C. Journal of a Fur Trading Expedition on the Upper Missouri, 1812-1813. (Illus.). 1964. reprint ed. 17.50 (0-87266-019-2) Argosy.

Luttikhuizen, Frances. The World of Science & Technology. (Illus.). 240p. (C). 1995. 25.00 (0-472-08339-2, 08339) U of Mich Pr.

Luttikhuizen, Frances. The World of Science & Technology: A Theme-Based, Study-Skills Approach. 240p. 1995. pap. text 16.95 (0-472-08269-8, 08269) U of Mich Pr.

Luttikhuizen, Frances. The World of Science & Technology: A Theme-based, Study-skills Approach. LC 93-61900. (Illus.). 240p. (C). 1995. audio 15.00 (0-472-00239-2, 00239) U of Mich Pr.

Luttikhuizen, Gerard, jt. ed. see Martinez, Florentino G.

***Luttikhuizen, Gerard P.** The Creation of Man & Woman: Jewish & Christian Interpretations of the Biblical Narratives in Genesis 1 & 2. LC 00-25992. (Themes in Biblical Narrative Ser.). 200p. 2000. 70.00 (90-04-11671-0) Brill Academic Pubs.

Luttikhuizen, Gerard P. Paradise Interpreted: Interpretations of Biblical Paradise in Judaism & Christianity. LC 99-13596. 208p. 1999. 87.50 (90-04-11331-2) Brill Academic Pubs.

— The Revelation of Elchasai: Investigations into the Evidence for a Mesopotamian Jewish Apocalypse of the Second Century & Its Reception by Judeo-Christian Propagandists. 263p. 1985. lib. bdg. 87.50 (3-16-144935-5, Pub. by JCB Mohr) Coronet Bks.

Luttikhuizen, Henry, jt. auth. see Zuidervaart, Lambert.

Luttinger, Nina, jt. auth. see Dicum, Gregory.

Luttmann, Gail. Raising Milk Goats Successfully. Griffith, Roger, ed. LC 86-26694. (Illus.). 176p. (Orig.). 1986. pap. 9.95 (0-913589-24-1) Williamson Pub Co.

Luttmann, Gail, jt. auth. see Luttmann, Rick.

Luttmann, Rick & Luttmann, Gail. Chickens in Your Backyard. LC 76-14357. 168p. 1976. pap. 11.95 (0-87857-125-6, 13-488-1) Rodale Pr Inc.

Lutton Staff. Big Picture, Small Screen. LC 97-152215. 1997. pap. 39.95 (1-86020-005-2, Pub. by U of Luton Pr) Bks Intl VA.

— BJR, Vol. 8, No. 3. 1997. pap. 19.95 (1-86020-027-3, Pub. by U of Luton Pr) Bks Intl VA.

— Broadcasting, Soc. & Policy. 1997. pap. 11.95 (1-86020-550-X, Pub. by U of Luton Pr) Bks Intl VA.

— Changing Channels. 1998. pap. 29.95 (1-86020-544-5, Pub. by U of Luton Pr) Bks Intl VA.

— Contours of Multimedia. 1997. pap. 29.95 (1-86020-511-9, Pub. by U of Luton Pr) Bks Intl VA.

— Convergence, Vol. 3, No. 3. 1997. pap. 19.95 (1-86020-023-0, Pub. by U of Luton Pr) Bks Intl VA.

— Copycat TV. LC 99-233952. 1998. pap. 29.95 (1-86020-537-2, Pub. by U of Luton Pr) Bks Intl VA.

— Cross Media Revolution. 1997. pap. 19.95 (0-86196-545-0, Pub. by J Libbey Med) Bks Intl VA.

— Decentralisation in Global Era. 1997. pap. 35.95 (0-86196-475-6, Pub. by J Libbey Med) Bks Intl VA.

— Devils & Angels. 1998. 24.95 (1-86020-545-3, Pub. by U of Luton Pr) Bks Intl VA.

— Dictionary of A-V Terms & New Media. 1997. pap. 49.95 (0-86196-482-9, Pub. by J Libbey Med) Bks Intl VA.

— Diverse Practices. 1997. pap. 34.95 (1-86020-500-3, Pub. by U of Luton Pr) Bks Intl VA.

— Dramatic Notes. 1998. pap. 33.95 (1-86020-548-8, Pub. by U of Luton Pr) Bks Intl VA.

— Euro TV: Immigration & Ethnic. LC 95-186642. Date not set. pap. 39.95 (0-86196-460-8, Pub. by J Libbey Med) Bks Intl VA.

— Global Newsroom, Local Audience. 1997. pap. 31.95 (0-86196-463-2, Pub. by J Libbey Med) Bks Intl VA. Global Newsrooms, Local Aud. 1997. 54.95 (0-86196-451-9, Pub. by J Libbey Med) Bks Intl VA.

— Global Spotlights on Lillehammer. LC 97-102213. 1997. pap. 49.95 (1-86020-520-8, Pub. by U of Luton Pr) Bks Intl VA.

— Measuring Bias on Television. LC 98-201470. 1997. 29.95 (1-86020-526-7, Pub. by U of Luton Pr) Bks Intl VA.

— Media Use As Social Action. 1997. pap. 49.95 (0-86196-485-3, Pub. by J Libbey Med) Bks Intl VA.

— Moving Experience. LC 96-133565. 1997. pap. 29.95 (0-86196-515-9, Pub. by J Libbey Med) Bks Intl VA.

— Night in at the Opera. LC 95-182149. 1997. pap. 34.95 (0-86196-466-7, Pub. by J Libbey Med) Bks Intl VA.

— Pioneering Television News. LC 95-219766. 1997. pap. 35.95 (0-86196-484-5, Pub. by J Libbey Med) Bks Intl VA.

— Political Marketing & Commun. 1997. pap. 39.95 (0-86196-377-6, Pub. by J Libbey Med) Bks Intl VA.

— Post-Broadcasting Age. 1997. pap. 31.95 (1-86020-502-X, Pub. by U of Luton Pr) Bks Intl VA.

— Press As Public Educator. 1997. pap. 29.95 (1-86020-536-4, Pub. by U of Luton Pr) Bks Intl VA.

— Public Broadcasting 21st Century. LC 96-206805. 1997. pap. 49.95 (1-86020-006-0, Pub. by U of Luton Pr) Bks Intl VA.

— Reseaux, Vol. 5, No. 1. 1997. pap. 19.95 (1-86020-029-X, Pub. by U of Luton Pr) Bks Intl VA.

— Satellite TV & Everyday Life. 1997. pap. 24.95 (1-86020-506-2, Pub. by U of Luton Pr) Bks Intl VA.

— Secret State, Silent Press. 1998. pap. 29.95 (1-86020-539-9, Pub. by U of Luton Pr) Bks Intl VA.

— TV & Gender Representation. 1997. pap. 35.95 (0-86196-478-0, Pub. by J Libbey Med) Bks Intl VA.

— TV & the Olympics. 1997. pap. 49.95 (0-86196-538-8, Pub. by J Libbey Med) Bks Intl VA.

— TV in Europe: Regulatory Bodies. 1997. pap. 59.95 (0-86196-546-9, Pub. by J Libbey Med) Bks Intl VA.

— TV in Scandinavia. 1997. pap. 49.95 (1-86020-509-7, Pub. by U of Luton Pr) Bks Intl VA.

— What Price Creativity? 1998. pap. 29.95 (1-86020-553-4, Pub. by U of Luton Pr) Bks Intl VA.

— Writing Long-Running TV Series, Vol. 2. 1998. 29.95 (1-86020-503-8, Pub. by U of Luton Pr) Bks Intl VA.

Lutton, Thomas, jt. auth. see Gordon, Patrice L.

Lutton, Wayne. The Myth of Open Borders. 47p. 1988. pap. 2.00 (0-936247-09-6) Amer Immigration.

Lutton, Wayne & Tanton, John. The Immigration Invasion. LC 94-212529. 192p. (Orig.). 1994. pap. 4.95 (1-881780-01-5) Social Contract.

Luttrell. Hospitallers in Cyprus Rhodes Greece. 1978. 119.95 (0-86078-022-8) Ashgate Pub Co.

Luttrell, Anthony. The Hospitaller State on Rhodes & Its Western Provinces, 1306-1462. LC 99-22717. (Collected Studies Ser.: No. 655). (Illus.). 352p. 1999. text 106.95 (0-86078-796-6, Pub. by Variorum) Ashgate Pub Co.

Luttrell, Anthony, jt. auth. see Jeppesen, Kristian.

Luttrell, Anthony T. Approaches to Medieval Malta. 70p. 1975. pap. 9.00 (0-614-21814-4, Pub. by British Schl Rome) David Brown.

— The Hospitallers of Rhodes & Their Mediterranean World. (Collected Studies: No. CS360). 352p. 1992. 113.95 (0-86078-307-3, Pub. by Variorum) Ashgate Pub Co.

Luttrell, Barbara. Mirabeau. LC 90-39621. 317p. (C). 1990. 36.95 (0-8093-1705-2) S Ill U Pr.

Luttrell, Chuck. Everything's Going Wrong. 74p. (Orig.). (J). (gr. 3-6). 1986. pap. 6.95 (0-9617609-0-7) Shade Tree NV.

Luttrell, Chuck & Luttrell, Jean. Heavy Weather Boating Emergencies: What to Do When Everything Goes Wrong. LC 98-7274. (Illus.). 288p. 1999. pap. 19.95 (0-943400-97-X) Marlor Pr.

Luttrell, Claude, ed. see De Troyes, Chretien.

Luttrell, Dan E., ed. Proceedings from ASPE 1998 Annual Meeting. (Illus.). 648p. 1998. pap. write for info. (1-887706-20-8) Am Soc Prec Engr.

Luttrell, Ida. The Bear Next Door. (I Can Read Bks.). (Illus.). 64p. (J). (gr. 1-3). 1991. 11.95 (0-06-024023-7) HarpC Child Bks.

— Milo's Toothache. (Illus.). 40p. (J). (gr. k-3). 1997. pap. 3.99 (0-14-038429-4) Viking Penguin.

— Tillie & Mert. LC 85-42641. (I Can Read Bks.). (Illus.). 64p. (J). (ps-3). 1985. 10.95 (0-06-024027-X) HarpC Child Bks.

Luttrell, Jean. Arizona Strip: Christmas on the Homestead & Other Stories. (Illus.). 40p. (Orig.). 1988. pap. 4.25 (0-9617609-1-5) Shade Tree NV.

— Winning Isn't Everything. (Dave Owens Adventures Ser.). (Illus.). 76p. (Orig.). (J). (gr. 3-5). 1990. pap. 6.95 (0-9617609-2-3) Shade Tree NV.

Luttrell, Jean, jt. auth. see Luttrell, Chuck.

Luttrell, Julia, jt. auth. see Radwanski, George.

Luttrell, M. Esther. Tools of the ScreenWriting Trade. unabridged ed. 308p. 1999. pap. 24.95 (0-9667485-1-4) Oak Shadow Pr.

Luttrell, Narcissus. A Brief Historical Relation of State Affairs from September 1678 to April 1714, 6 vols., Set. Straka, Gerald M., ed. LC 72-83165. (English Studies). 1972. reprint ed. lib. bdg. 324.00 (0-8420-1423-3) Scholarly Res Inc.

Luttrell, Steve. Home Movies: A Collection of Poems by Steve Luttrell. 61p. 1998. 9.95 (1-878471-05-8) Big Bridge Pr.

Luttrell, Steve, et al. Animus: Winter into Spring. Farnsworth, Anne, ed. & illus. by. 32p. 1999. pap. 6.00 (0-9672567-0-4) Sheltering Pines.

Luttrell, Susan E. Love Was Born at Christmas. (Orig.). (J). (gr. k-4). 1981. pap. 3.50 (0-89536-483-2, 1234) CSS OH.

Luttrell, Wanda. Hannah's Sojourn. LC 98-35693. (Immigrants Chronicles Ser.). (J). 1999. 5.99 (0-7814-3082-8) Chariot Victor.

— Home on Stoney Creek. LC 93-47084. 208p. (YA). (gr. 4 up). 1995. 12.99 (0-7814-0234-4) Chariot Victor.

— Reunion in Kentucky. LC 94-31114. (Illus.). 208p. (J). 1995. 12.99 (0-7814-0236-0, Chariot Bks) Chariot Victor.

— Reunion in Kentucky. LC 94-31114. (Sarah's Journey Ser.: Vol. 3). (Illus.). 208p. (J). (gr. 4-7). 1995. pap. 5.99 (0-7814-0907-1) Chariot Victor.

— Shadows on Stoney Creek. Vol. 5. 208p. (J). (gr. 3-7). 1997. write for info. (0-7814-3005-4, Chariot Bks) Chariot Victor.

— Stranger in Williamsburg. LC 94-20574. 196p. (YA). 1995. 12.99 (0-7814-0235-2, Chariot Bks) Chariot Victor.

— Stranger in Williamsburg. LC 94-20574. (Sarah's Journey Ser.: Vol. 2). 196p. (J). (gr. 4-7). 1995. pap. 5.99 (0-7814-0902-0, Chariot Bks) Chariot Victor.

— Whispers in Williamsburg. LC 98-156067. Vol. 4. (Illus.). 208p. (J). (gr. 3-7). 1997. pap. 5.99 (0-7814-3008-9, Chariot Bks) Chariot Victor.

Luttrell, Wendy. Schoolsmart & Motherwise: Working-Class Women's Identity & Schooling. LC 96-39655. (Perspectives on Gender Ser.). 184p. (C). 1997. pap. 17.99 (0-415-91012-9) Routledge.

— Schoolsmart & Motherwise: Working-Class Women's Identity & Schooling. LC 96-39655. (Perspectives on Gender Ser.). 184p. (C). 1997. 65.00 (0-415-91011-0) Routledge.

Luttrell, William L. Post-Capitalist Industrialization: Planning Economic Independence in Tanzania. LC 86-9452. (Illus.). 208p. 1986. 57.95 (0-275-92310-X, C2310, Praeger Pubs) Greenwood.

Luttropp, John C., jt. auth. see Greenwald.

Luttropp, John C., jt. auth. see Greenwald, Martin L.

Lutts, Ralph H. The Nature Fakers: Wildlife, Science & Sentiment. LC 89-29521. (Illus.). 272p. 1990. 22.95 (1-55591-054-8) Fulcrum Pub.

L

Lutts, Ralph H., ed. The Wild Animal Story. LC 97-23906. (Animals, Culture & Society Ser.). 328p. 1998. 34.95 (*1-56639-593-3*) Temple U Pr.

Luttwak, Edward. Turbo-Capitalism: Winners & Losers in the Global Economy. LC 99-177816. 304p. 1999. 26.00 (*0-06-019330-1*) HarpC.

— Turbo-Capitalism: Winners & Losers in the Global Economy. 1998. pap. 13.00 (*0-88730-991-7*, HarpBusn) HarpInfo.

***Luttwak, Edward.** Turbo-Capitalism: Winners & Losers in the Global Economy. 304p. 2000. pap. 15.00 (*0-06-093137-X*, Perennial) HarperTrade.

Luttwak, Edward & Koehl, S. Dictionary of Modern War. LC 97-48755. 688p. 1998. 12.99 (*0-517-18828-7*) Random Hse Value.

Luttwak, Edward N. Coup d'Etat: A Practical Handbook. (Illus.). 215p. 1979. pap. text 16.50 (*0-674-17547-6*) HUP.

Luttwak, Edward N. The Endangered American Dream. 368p. 1994. pap. 14.00 (*0-671-89667-9*, Touchstone) S&S Trade Pap.

— The Grand Strategy of the Roman Empire: From the First Century A. D. to the Third. LC 76-17232. (Illus.). 272p. 1977. pap. 15.95 (*0-8018-2158-4*) Johns Hopkins.

— The Political Uses of Sea Power. LC 74-8219. (Washington Center of Foreign Policy Research. Studies in International Affairs: No. 23). 90p. reprint ed. pap. 30.00 (*0-608-16366-X*, 202632400049) Bks Demand.

— Strategy: The Logic of War & Peace. 320p. 1987. pap. text 17.50 (*0-674-83996-X*) HUP.

— Strategy & History: Collected Essays. 225p. (C). 1985. 39.95 (*0-88738-065-4*) Transaction Pubs.

— Strategy & Politics: Collected Essays. LC 79-65224. 328p. 1980. pap. 24.95 (*0-87855-904-3*) Transaction Pubs.

Luttwak, Edward N. & Horowitz, Daniel. The Israeli Army, 1948 to 1973, Vol. 1. 408p. 1983. text 40.00 (*0-89011-585-0*) Abt Bks.

Lutwack, Leonard. Birds in Literature. LC 93-30647. 304p. (C). 1994. 39.95 (*0-8130-1254-6*) U Press Fla.

— The Role of Place in Literature. LC 83-24264. 304p. 1984. 39.95 (*0-8156-2305-4*) Syracuse U Pr.

Lutwak-Mann, C., jt. auth. see Mann, T.

Lutwick, Larry I., ed. Tuberculosis: A Clinical Handbook. (Illus.). 392p. 1994. pap. text 40.00 (*0-412-60740-9*, Pub. by E A) OUP.

Lutwiniak, W. & Mackaye, W. Washington Post Sunday Crossword Omnibus, 1. 2nd ed. 1998. pap. 11.00 (*0-8129-3068-1*, Times Business) Random.

Lutwiniak, William. Scrabble Crossword Puzzle Book, No. 4. 1988. pap. 4.95 (*0-02-688817-3*) Macmillan.

— The Washington Post Sunday Crossword Puzzles, Vol. 3. 3rd ed. 1992. pap. 9.00 (*0-8129-2109-7*, Times Bks) Crown Pub Group.

Lutwiniak, William, et al, eds. The Washington Post Sunday Crossword Puzzles, Vol. 1. Vol. 1. 64p. 1991. pap. 9.00 (*0-8129-1933-5*, Times Bks) Crown Pub Group.

Lutwiniak, William & Mackaye, William R., eds. The Washington Post Sunday Crossword Puzzles, Vol. 2. 2nd ed. 64p. 1991. pap. 9.00 (*0-8129-1934-3*, Times Bks) Crown Pub Group.

Luty, F., ed. Proceedings of the International Conference on Defects in Insulating Crystals: A Special Issue of Crystal Lattice Defects & Amorphous Materials, Vol. 1. xiv, 266p. 1979. text 218.00 (*3-7186-0009-9*) Gordon & Breach.

— Proceedings of the International Conference on Defects in Insulating Crystals: A Special Issue of Crystal Lattice Defects & Amorphous Materials, Vol. 2. x, 272p. 1980. text 279.00 (*3-7186-0035-8*) Gordon & Breach.

— Proceedings of the International Conference on Defects in Insulating Crystals: A Special Issue of Crystal Lattice Defects & Amorphous Materials, Vol. 3. vii, 256p. 1981. text 249.00 (*3-7186-0066-8*) Gordon & Breach.

— Proceedings of the International Conference on Defects in Insulating Crystals: A Special Issue of Crystal Lattice Defects & Amorphous Materials, Vol. 4. x, 232p. 1982. text 249.00 (*3-7186-0119-2*) Gordon & Breach.

Luty, J. & Harrison, P. Basic & Clinical Pharmacology Made Memorable. (Illus.). 116p. 1997. pap. write for info. (*0-443-05598-X*) Church.

Luty, Kathy & Philippart, David, eds. Clip Notes for Church Bulletins. LC 97-30052. (Illus.). 79p. 1997. pap. 30.00 (*1-56854-169-4*, NOTES1) Liturgy Tr Pubns.

Luty, P. A. Expedient Homemade Firearms: The 9mm Submachine Gun. LC 98-216674. (Illus.). 96p. 1998. pap. 20.00 (*0-87364-983-4*) Paladin Pr.

Lutyens, Edwin, jt. auth. see Edwards, Brian.

Lutyens, Elisabeth, et al. The Choral Music of Twentieth-Century Women Composers. LC 95-20903. (Contributions to the Study of Music & Dance Ser.: Vol. 39). 1997. text 53.00 (*0-313-27502-5*) Greenwood.

Lutyens, Elizabeth, jt. auth. see Levine, Robert.

***Lutyens, Mary.** Effie in Venice: Mrs. John Ruskin's Letters Home, 1849-52. 2000. pap. 18.95 (*1-873429-33-9*) Pallas Athene.

Lutyens, Mary. Krishnamurti: The Open Door. 1991. pap. 7.95 (*0-380-70971-6*, Avon Bks) Morrow Avon.

— Krishnamurti: The Years of Awakening. (Illus.). 355p. 1991. pap. 9.95 (*0-380-71113-3*, Avon Bks) Morrow Avon.

— Krishnamurti: The Years of Awakening. LC 96-25653. 384p. 1997. pap. 15.95 (*1-57062-288-4*, Pub. by Shambhala Pubns) Random.

— Krishnamurti: The Years of Fulfillment. 264p. 1991. pap. 8.95 (*0-380-71112-5*, Avon Bks) Morrow Avon.

— Krishnamurti & the Rajagopals. LC 96-75777. 129p. 1996. per. 6.00 (*1-888004-08-8*) Krishnamurti.

Lutyens, Sally. A Pocket Full of Wry. Weinberger, Jane, ed. LC 94-61887. (Illus.). 84p. (Orig.). 1995. pap. 6.00 (*1-883650-14-3*) Windswept Hse.

Lutyk, Carol B., ed. Discover America. (Illus.). 336p. (YA). 1989. 38.95 (*0-87044-805-6*); lib. bdg. 39.95 (*0-87044-806-4*) Natl Geog.

— Discover America. (Illus.). 336p. (YA). 1993. 35.00 (*0-87044-804-8*) Natl Geog.

— Our World's Heritage. LC 87-17174. 312p. 1987. 21.95 (*0-87044-696-7*); text 21.95 (*0-87044-698-3*); lib. bdg. 23.95 (*0-87044-697-5*) Natl Geog.

Lutz. En Route: Review Grammar. 1985. student ed. 37.25 (*0-15-381920-0*) Harcourt Schl Pubs.

— En Route - Review Grammar. 1985. pap. text, teacher ed. 18.00 (*0-15-381921-9*) Holt R&W.

— Import Propensities. 1999. text. write for info. (*0-312-22229-7*) St Martin.

— Surviving Hypoxia: Mechanisms of Control & Adaptation. 592p. 1993. boxed set 166.95 (*0-8493-4226-0*, RB150) CRC Pr.

— A Vous d'Ecrire for Advanced French.Tr. of Workbook for Advanced French. 1986. pap., student ed. 11.00 (*0-15-381925-1*) H Holt & Co.

Lutz, jt. auth. see Schmitt.

Lutz, A. M., jt. ed. see Nguyen-Khac, U.

Lutz, Alma. Emma Willard: Daughter of Democracy. LC 75-37635. 1976. reprint ed. 23.95 (*0-89201-018-5*) Zenger Pub.

— Emma Willard: Pioneer Educator of American Women. LC 83-18567. 143p. 1984. reprint ed. lib. bdg. 38.50 (*0-313-24254-2*, LUEW, Greenwood Pr) Greenwood.

— Susan B. Anthony: Rebel, Crusader, Humanitarian. LC 75-37764. 1976. reprint ed. 27.95 (*0-89201-017-7*) Zenger Pub.

Lutz-Bachmann, Matthias, jt. ed. see Bohman, James.

Lutz, Bruno V., jt. ed. see Gohrbandt, Detlev.

Lutz, Bruno Von, see Gohrbandt, Detlev, ed.

Lutz, Bruno Von, see Gohrbandt, Detlev & Von Lutz, Bruno, eds.

Lutz, Bruno Von, see Gohrbandt, Detlev, ed.

Lutz, Bruno Von, see Gohrbandt, Detlev & Von Lutz, Bruno, eds.

Lutz, Bruno Von, see Gohrbandt, Detlev, ed.

Lutz, Bruno Von, see Gohrbandt, Detlev & Von Lutz, Bruno, eds.

Lutz, C., ed. see Joannes, S. E.

***Lutz, Carl.** Dangerous Diplomacy: The Story of Carl Lutz, Rescuer of 62,000 Hungarian Jews. 2000. 25.00 (*0-8028-3905-3*) Eerdmans.

Lutz, Carl F. How to Develop, Conduct & Use Pay-Benefit Surveys. 211p. 1986. ring bd. 125.00 (*0-916506-22-3*) Abbott Langer Assocs.

Lutz, Carroll A. & Przytulski, Karen R. Nutrition & Diet Therapy. 2nd ed. LC 97-4030. (Illus.). 630p. 1997. pap. 39.95 (*0-8036-0231-6*) Davis Co.

Lutz, Catherine & Bartlett, Lesley. Making Soliders in the Public Schools: An Analysis of the Army JROTC Curriculum. (Illus.). 40p. (Orig.). (C). 1995. pap. text 20.00 (*0-7881-1895-1*) DIANE Pub.

Lutz, Catherine A. Unnatural Emotions: Every Day Sentiments on a Micronesian Atoll & Their Challenge to Western Theory. (Illus.). 286p. 1988. pap. text 17.00 (*0-226-49722-4*) U Ch Pr.

Lutz, Catherine A. & Collins, Jane L. Reading National Geographic. LC 92-40698. (Illus.). 328p. (C). 1993. pap. text 20.00 (*0-226-49724-0*) U Ch Pr.

— Reading National Geographic. LC 92-40698. (Illus.). 312p. (C). 1994. lib. bdg. 59.95 (*0-226-49723-2*) U Ch Pr.

Lutz, Charles P. Surprising Gift: The Story of Holden Village, Church Renewal Center. (Illus.). 144p. (Orig.). 1987. pap. 6.00 (*0-9618617-0-3*) Holden Village.

Lutz, Charles P., ed. A Reforming Church . . . Gift & Task: Essays from a Free Conference. LC 95-34890. 256p. 1995. pap. 13.95 (*1-886513-02-3*) Kirk Hse Pubs.

Lutz, Christopher. Endgame Secrets. 1998. pap. text 19.95 (*0-7134-8165-X*, Pub. by B T B) Branford.

Lutz, Christopher H. Historia Sociodemografica de Santiago de Guatemala, 1541-1773. LC 82-73081. (Monograph Ser.: No. 2). (SPA.). 499p. 1982. pap. 16.50 (*0-910443-02-5*) Plumsock Meso Studies.

— Santiago de Guatemala, 1541-1773: City, Caste, & the Colonial Experience. LC 93-46131. (Illus.). 368p. 1997. pap. 17.95 (*0-8061-2911-5*) U of Okla Pr.

Lutz, Cora E. Dunchad: Glossae in Martianum. (American Philological Association Philological Monographs). 68p. 1982. 15.95 (*0-89130-705-2*, 40-00-12) OUP.

Lutz, Dick. Hidden Amazon: The Greatest Voyage in Natural History. unabridged ed. LC 98-18054. (Illus.). 1998. pap. 16.95 (*0-931625-33-5*) DIMI Pr.

Lutz, Dick & Lutz, J. Marie. Komodo, the Living Dragon. rev. ed. LC 94-44423. (Illus.). 180p. 1996. pap. 16.95 (*0-931625-27-0*) DIMI Pr.

Lutz, Dick, ed. see Henderson, John L. & Henderson, Lilli I.

Lutz, Dieter S. Towards a Methodology of Military Force Comparison. 255p. 1986. pap. 45.00 (*3-7890-0915-6*, Pub. by Nomos Verlags) Intl Bk Import.

Lutz, Don. The Weaning of America: The Case Against Dairy Products. LC 97-70573. (Illus.). 115p. (Orig.). 1997. pap. 10.95 (*0-9630275-1-4*) Innerpeace.

Lutz, Donald S. Cautions for Constitution-Makers. (Issue Papers: No. 12-87). 11p. 1987. pap. text 8.00 (*1-57655-017-6*) Independ Inst.

— The Origins of American Constitutionalism. LC 88-6415. 178p. 1988. pap. text 14.95 (*0-8071-1506-1*) La State U Pr.

— A Preface to American Political Theory. LC 92-11700. (American Political Thought Ser.). xii, 188p. 1992. 27.50 (*0-7006-0545-2*); pap. 12.95 (*0-7006-0546-0*) U Pr of KS.

Lutz, Donald S., ed. Colonial Origins of the American Constitution: A Documentary History. LC 97-12481. 396p. 1998. 17.00 (*0-86597-156-0*); pap. 9.00 (*0-86597-157-9*) Liberty Fund.

Lutz, Donald S., jt. auth. see Hyneman, Charles S.

Lutz, E. A. Some Problems & Alternatives in Developing Federal Block Grants: To States for Public Welfare Purposes. LC 77-74945. (American Federalism-the Urban Dimension Ser.). (Illus.). 1978. lib. bdg. 33.95 (*0-405-10493-6*) Ayer.

Lutz, E. G. Animated Cartoons: How They Are Made; Their Origin & Development. LC 97-49496. (Illus.). 216p. 1998. reprint ed. pap. 14.95 (*1-55709-474-8*) Applewood.

Lutz, Edwin G. Motion-Picture Cameraman. LC 76-169332. (Literature of Cinema, Ser. 2). (Illus.). 264p. 1978. reprint ed. 18.95 (*0-405-03899-2*) Ayer.

Lutz, Ellen L., jt. auth. see Randall, Glenn R.

***Lutz, Erich, et al.** Satellite Systems for Personal & Broadband Communication. xiv, 433p. 2000. 92.00 (*3-540-66840-3*) Spr-Verlag.

Lutz, Ericka. Baby Maneuvers. LC 97-71185. 224p. 1997. 14.95 (*0-02-861732-0*) IDG Bks.

***Lutz, Ericka.** The Complete Idiot's Guide to Looking Great for Teens. 2000. pap. 12.95 (*0-02-863985-5*, Alpha Ref) Macmillan Gen Ref.

Lutz, Ericka. The Complete Idiot's Guide to Stepparenting. 352p. 1998. pap. text 16.95 (*0-02-862407-6*) Macmillan Gen Ref.

— The Complete Idiot's Guide to Well-Behaved Child. (Complete Idiot's Guides Ser.). (Illus.). 388p. 1999. pap. text 18.95 (*0-02-863107-2*, Pub. by Macmillan Gen Ref) S&S Trade.

Lutz, Ericka, jt. auth. see Poretta, Vicki.

Lutz, Ernst, ed. Toward Improved Accounting for the Environment. LC 93-13831. 344p. 1993. pap. 40.00 (*0-8213-2436-5*, 12436) World Bank.

Lutz, Ernst, et al, eds. Economic & Institutional Analyses of Soil Conservation Projects in Central America & the Caribbean. LC 93-45505. (Environment Papers: Vol. 8). 218p. 1994. pap. 22.00 (*0-8213-2741-0*, 12741) World Bank.

Lutz, Ernst & Caldecott, Julian, eds. Decentralization & Biodiversity Conservation: A World Bank Symposium. LC 96-30475. 184p. 1997. pap. 40.00 (*0-8213-3688-6*, 13688) World Bank.

Lutz, Ernst & World Bank Staff. Agriculture & the Environment: Perspectives on Sustainable Rural Development. LC 98-36512. (World Bank Symposium Ser.). 400p. 1998. pap. 35.00 (*0-8213-4249-5*) World Bank.

Lutz, F. A. The Theory of Interest. Witlich, Claus, tr. from GER. 336p. 1967. lib. bdg. 99.50 (*90-277-0099-0*) Kluwer Academic.

Lutz, Francis E. Richmond in World War II. 1951. 7.50 (*0-87517-026-9*) Dietz.

Lutz, Frank. Die Deutsche Gemeindeordnung in Bremen. (Historische Texte und Studien Ser.: Bd. 3). (GER.). vi, 139p. 1980. write for info. (*3-487-06963-6*) G Olms Pubs.

Lutz, Frank & Merz, Carol. The Politics of School-Community Relations. 224p. (C). 1992. text 19.95 (*0-8077-3162-5*); pap. text 19.95 (*0-8077-3161-7*) Tchrs Coll.

Lutz, Frank W. & Ferrante, Reynolds. Emergent Practices in the Continuing Education of School Administrators. 48p. (Orig.). (C). 1972. pap. text 1.25 (*1-55996-114-7*, W113) Univ Council Educ Admin.

Lutz, Friedrich A. Corporate Cash Balances, 1914-43: Manufacturing & Trade. (Financial Research Program III: Studies in Business Financing: No. 8). 148p. 1945. reprint ed. 38.50 (*0-87014-136-8*) Natl Bur Econ Res.

Lutz, Friedrich A. & Lutz, Vera C. Theory of Investment of the Firm. LC 69-13978. 253p. 1970. reprint ed. lib. bdg. 65.00 (*0-8371-1108-0*, LUTI, Greenwood Pr) Greenwood.

***Lutz, Gerhard.** Semiconductor Radiation Detectors: Device Physics. LC 99-14932. (Accelerator Physics Ser.). (Illus.). xii, 343p. 1999. 72.95 (*3-540-64859-3*) Spr-Verlag.

Lutz, Gotze Von, see von Lutz, Gotze.

Lutz, H. & Demling, L., eds. Diagnostic Imaging Methods in Hepatology. 1984. text 225.00 (*0-85200-807-4*) Kluwer Academic.

Lutz, H. & Meudt, R. Manual of Ultrasound. (Illus.). 160p. 1983. 73.95 (*0-387-12377-6*) Spr-Verlag.

Lutz, Helma. Crossfires: Nationalism, Racism & Gender in Europe. LC 95-24362. 1996. 70.00 (*0-7453-0994-1*) Pluto GBR.

Lutz, Helma, et al. Crossfires: Gender, Nationalism & Racism in Europe. 196p. 1995. pap. 21.95 (*0-7453-0995-X*, Pub. by Pluto GBR) Stylus Pub VA.

Lutz, Henry F. Early Babylonian Letters from Larsa. LC 78-63531. (Yale Oriental Series: Babylonian Texts: No. 2). (Illus.). reprint ed. 34.50 (*0-404-60252-5*) AMS Pr.

— The Intensifying Conjunction in Egyptian. LC 36-1182. (University of California Publications in Social Welfare: Vol. 10, No. 4). 8p. reprint ed. pap. 30.00 (*0-608-11098-1*, 202147500021) Bks Demand.

— Real Estate Transactions from Kish. LC 32-813. (University of California Publications in Social Welfare: Vol. 10, No. 3). 32p. reprint ed. pap. 30.00 (*0-608-11092-2*, 202147400021) Bks Demand.

— The Unidentified Sign. LC 72-995. (University of California Publications in Social Welfare: Vol. 10, No. 2). 4p. reprint ed. pap. 30.00 (*0-608-11089-2*, 202147300021) Bks Demand.

— An Uruk Document of the Time of Cambyses. LC PJ3874.. (University of California Publications in Social Welfare: Vol. 10, No. 8). 10p. reprint ed. pap. 30.00 (*0-608-11099-X*, 202147900021) Bks Demand.

Lutz, J. Marie, jt. auth. see Lutz, Dick.

Lutz, J. T. & Grossman, Richard F. Polymer Modifiers & Additives. (Plastics Engineering Ser.). Date not set. write for info. (*0-8247-9949-6*) Dekker.

Lutz, James M. Protectionism: An Annotated Bibliography with Analytical Introductions. LC 88-15273. (Resources on Contemporary Issues Ser.: No. 2). 215p. 1988. pap. 40.00 (*0-87650-249-4*) Pierian.

Lutz, James M. & Kihl, Young W. World Trade Issues: Regime, Structure & Policy. LC 84-15986. 273p. 1985. 55.00 (*0-275-90127-0*, C0127, Praeger Pubs) Greenwood.

Lutz, Jean A. & Storms, C. Gilbert. The Practice of Technical & Scientific Communication: Writing in Professional Contexts. LC 97-30772. (ATTW Studies in Technical Communication). 250p. 1998. 73.25 (*1-56750-361-6*); pap. 24.95 (*1-56750-362-4*) Ablx Pub.

Lutz, Jerre, ed. Complications of Interventional Procedures. LC 94-46842. (Topics in Clinical Cardiology Ser.). (Illus.). 264p. 1995. 73.95 (*0-89640-260-6*) Igaku-Shoin.

— Hurst's the Heart: Pre-Test Self-Assessment & Review. 9th ed. LC 98-2988. (Illus.). 275p. 1998. pap. text 45.00 (*0-07-039142-4*) McGraw-Hill HPD.

Lutz, Jerry. Pitchman's Melody: Shaw About Shakespeare. LC 72-3529. 175p. 1974. 18.00 (*0-8387-1247-9*) Bucknell U Pr.

Lutz, Jessie G. & Lutz, Rolland R. Hakka Chinese Confront Protestant Christianity, 1850-1900: With the Autobiographies of Eight Hakka Christians, & Commentary. LC 97-20828. (Studies on Modern China). (Illus.). 300p. (C). (gr. 13). 1998. 77.95 (*0-7656-0037-4*, East Gate Bk) M E Sharpe.

— Hakka Chinese Confront Protestant Christianity, 1850-1900: With the Autobiographies of Eight Hakka Christians, & Commentary. LC 97-20828. (Studies on Modern China). (Illus.). 300p. (YA). (gr. 13 up). 1998. pap. 32.95 (*0-7656-0038-2*, East Gate Bk) M E Sharpe.

Lutz, John. Blood Fire. (Fred Carver Mystery Ser.). 224p. 1992. reprint ed. mass mkt. 3.99 (*0-380-71446-9*, Avon Bks) Morrow Avon.

— Burn: A Fred Carver Mystery. LC 94-32187. (Henry Holt Mystery Ser.). 1995. 22.50 (*0-8050-3480-3*) H Holt & Co.

— Burning Evidence: A Mystery Jigsaw Puzzle. (BePuzzled Ser.). (Orig.). (C). 1993. 20.00 (*0-922242-53-4*) Bepuzzled.

— The Ex. LC 96-76018. 256p. 1996. 21.00 (*1-57566-078-4*, Knsington) Kensgtn Pub Corp.

— The Ex. 304p. 1997. mass mkt. 5.50 (*1-57566-178-0*, Knsington) Kensgtn Pub Corp.

— The Ex. 320p. 1999. mass mkt. 4.99 (*0-7860-0186-0*) Kensgtn Pub Corp.

— Final Seconds. 384p. 1998. mass mkt. 5.99 (*1-57566-364-3*) Kensgtn Pub Corp.

— Flame. 88p. 1996. pap. 5.95 (*0-8050-4567-8*) H Holt & Co.

— Flame. 272p. 1991. pap. 3.95 (*0-380-71070-6*, Avon Bks) Morrow Avon.

— Grounds for Murder: A Mystery Jigsaw Puzzle Thriller. (Bepuzzled Ser.). (Orig.). (YA). (gr. 7 up). 1995. 20.00 (*0-922242-74-7*) Bepuzzled.

— Hot: A Fred Carver Mystery. 256p. 1993. mass mkt. 4.99 (*0-380-71447-7*, Avon Bks) Morrow Avon.

***Lutz, John.** An Introduction to Learning & Memory. 366p. 2000. pap. 29.95 (*1-57766-132-X*) Waveland Pr.

Lutz, John. Kiss. (Fred Carver Mystery Ser.). 88p. 1995. pap. 5.95 (*0-8050-4566-X*, Owl) H Holt & Co.

— Kiss. 272p. 1990. pap. 3.95 (*0-380-70934-1*, Avon Bks) Morrow Avon.

— Lightning: A Fred Carver Mystery. 88p. 1995. 22.50 (*0-8050-4379-9*) H Holt & Co.

— Oops! large type ed. LC 98-29242. (Large Print Book Ser.). 1998. 22.95 (*1-56895-653-3*) Wheeler Pub.

— Oops! A Nudger Mystery. LC 97-36529. 304p. 1997. text 22.95 (*0-312-18152-3*) St Martin.

— Scorcher. 272p. 1995. pap. 5.95 (*0-8050-3829-9*, Owl) H Holt & Co.

— Scorcher. 256p. 1988. pap. 3.95 (*0-380-70526-5*, Avon Bks) Morrow Avon.

— Shadowtown. LC 88-40068. 256p. 1988. 16.45 (*0-89296-221-6*, Pub. by Mysterious Pr) Little.

— Single White Female. Rubenstein, Julie, ed. 288p. 1992. reprint ed. mass mkt. 4.99 (*0-671-74500-X*) PB.

— Taxed to Death: Mystery Jigsaw Puzzle Thriller. (Bepuzzled Ser.). (Orig.). 1996. pap. 21.00 (*1-57561-007-8*, 00517TTD) Bepuzzled.

— Torch. LC 93-28431. (Henry Holt Mystery Ser.). 1995. 22.00 (*0-8050-2610-X*) H Holt & Co.

— Tropical Heat. 252p. 1995. pap. 5.95 (*0-8050-3828-0*, Owl) H Holt & Co.

— Tropical Heat. 256p. 1987. pap. 3.95 (*0-380-70309-2*, Avon Bks) Morrow Avon.

— Until You Are Dead. LC 98-42586. 1998. 20.95 (*0-7862-1660-3*, Five Star MI) Mac Lib Ref.

Lutz, John & August, David. Final Seconds. LC 97-75929. 336p. 1998. 23.00 (*1-57566-259-0*, Knsington) Kensgtn Pub Corp.

Lutz, John, jt. auth. see Pronzini, Bill.

Lutz, John T. & Dunkelberger, David L. Impact Modifiers for PVC: The History & Practice. LC 90-49460. (Society of Plastics Engineers Monographs: No. 1262). 216p. 1991. 105.00 (*0-471-52764-5*) Wiley.

Lutz, Katia B. Finance & Accounting: Lectures & Vocabulary in French. 201p. (C). 1993. pap. 10.95 (*0-07-056810-3*) McGraw.

Lutz, Katia B. & Schmitt, Conrad J. Tourisme & Hotellerie: Tourism & Hotel Management, Lectures & Vocabulary. LC 92-20942. (FRE.). 224p. (C). 1993. pap. 10.95 (*0-07-056820-0*) McGraw.

Lutz, Katia B., jt. auth. see Schmitt, Conrad J.

An Asterisk (*) at the beginning of an entry indicates that the title is appearing for the first time.

***Lutz, Lorrie.** Child Welfare & Managed Care - Ready or Not: A Guide to Applying Managed Care Principles to the Child Welfare System. (Illus.). 101p. 1999. spiral bd. 129.00 (*1-878586-19-X*, HB-8) Open Minds PA.

Lutz, Lorry. Women As Risk-Takers for God. LC 97-38092. (World Evangelical Fellowship Ser.). 288p. (C). 1998. pap. 17.99 (*0-8010-5813-9*) Baker Bks.

Lutz, Lorry, jt. auth. see Foster, Robert L.

Lutz, Marcetta R., et al. Arvada, Just Between You & Me: 1904-1941. LC 82-71574. (Dual Ser.). (Illus.). 207p. 1985. 17.50 (*0-9615540-0-2*) Arvada Hist.

Lutz, Mark. Programming Python: Object-Oriented Scripting. LC 97-102075. (Illus.). 904p. (Orig.). 1996. pap. 44.95 (*1-56592-197-6*) Thomson Learn.

— Python Pocket Reference. Estabrook, Gigi, ed. (Illus.). 80p. 1998. reprint ed. pap. 8.95 (*1-56592-500-9*) OReilly & Assocs.

***Lutz, Mark & Ascher, David.** Learning Python. Willison, Frank, ed. (Illus.). 312p. 1999. pap. 29.95 (*1-56592-464-9*) OReilly & Assocs.

Lutz, Mark & Lux, Kenneth. Humanistic Economics: The New Challenge. LC 88-7324. 352p. (Orig.). 1988. 28.50 (*0-942850-10-6*); pap. 15.50 (*0-942850-06-8*) Bootstrap Pr.

Lutz, Mark, jt. ed. see Diwan, Romesh.

Lutz, Mark A. Economics for the Common Good: Two Centuries of Economic Thought in the Humanistic Tradition. LC 99-222946. 1999. pap. 29.99 (*0-415-14313-6*) Routledge.

***Lutz, Mark A.** Economics for the Common Good: Two Centuries of Social Economic Thought in the Humanistic Tradition. LC 99-222946. 1999. write for info. (*0-415-14312-8*) Routledge.

Lutz, Mark A., ed. Social Economics: Retrospect & Prospect. (C). 1989. lib. bdg. 110.00 (*0-7923-9004-0*) Kluwer Academic.

Lutz, Mark A. & Nudler, Oscar, eds. Economics, Culture & Society: Alternative Approaches: Dissenting Views from Economic Orthodoxy. LC 96-38310. 238p. (Orig.). 1996. 39.50 (*0-945257-73-2*, SAN 246-2664); pap. 18.50 (*0-945257-72-4*, SAN 246-2664) Apex Pr.

Lutz, Mark J. Socrates' Education to Virtue: Learning the Love of the Noble. LC 97-16696. 208p. (C). 1998. pap. text 19.95 (*0-7914-3654-3*) State U NY Pr.

— Socrates' Education to Virtue: Learning the Love of the Noble. LC 97-16696. 208p. (C). 1998. text 59.50 (*0-7914-3653-5*) State U NY Pr.

Lutz, Martha. Intimacy with God, Vol. 1. LC 96-85798. 80p. 1997. 12.95 (*0-8158-0523-3*) Chris Mass.

***Lutz, Michael W.** Quantitative Molecular Pharmacology & Informatics in Drug Discovery. LC 99-29628. (Illus.). 428p. 1999. 140.00 (*0-471-98861-8*) Wiley.

Lutz, Norma, ed. see Ellis, Neil C.

***Lutz, Norma Jean.** Battling the Klan. LC 99-192559. (American Adventure Ser.: No. 39). (J). (gr. 3-6). 1998. pap. 3.97 (*1-57748-453-3*) Barbour Pub.

Lutz, Norma Jean. Benedict Arnold: Traitor to the Cause. LC 99-20422. 1999. 16.95 (*0-7910-5358-X*) Chelsea Hse.

— Benedict Arnold: Traitor to the Cause. (Revolutionary War Leaders Ser.). (Illus.). 80p. (gr. 3 up). 1999. pap. 8.95 (*0-7910-5701-1*) Chelsea Hse.

***Lutz, Norma Jean.** Britney Spears. (Galaxy of Superstars Ser.). (Illus.). (J). 2000. 14.45 (*0-606-18033-8*) Turtleback.

Lutz, Norma Jean. Brittany Spears. LC 99-49831. (Galaxy of Superstars Ser.). 1999. 17.95 (*0-7910-5499-3*) Chelsea Hse.

***Lutz, Norma Jean.** Celine Dion. (Galaxy of Superstars Ser.). 2000. 17.95 (*0-7910-5777-1*) Chelsea Hse.

— Celine Dion. LC 99-462034. (Galaxy of Superstars Ser.). (Illus.). 2000. pap. 9.95 (*0-7910-5778-X*) Chelsea Hse.

— Clash with the Newsboys. 34th ed. (American Adventure Ser.: No. 34). (Illus.). (J). (gr. 3-7). 1998. pap. 3.97 (*1-57748-407-X*) Barbour Pub.

Lutz, Norma Jean. Cotton Mather. (Colonial Leaders Ser.). (Illus.). 80p. (J). (gr. 3 up). 1999. pap. 8.95 (*0-7910-5686-4*) Chelsea Hse.

***Lutz, Norma Jean.** Cotton Mather. LC 99-25344. (Colonial Leaders Ser.). (Illus.). 80p. (J). 1999. 16.95 (*0-7910-5343-1*) Chelsea Hse.

— Enemy or Friend? (American Adventure Ser.: No. 20). (J). (gr. 3-6). 1998. pap. 3.97 (*1-57748-258-1*) Barbour Pub.

— Escape from Slavery: A Family's Fight for Freedom. LC 98-140469. (American Adventure Ser.: No. 16). (J). (gr. 3-6). 1998. pap. 3.97 (*1-57748-233-6*) Barbour Pub.

— Escape from Slavery: A Family's Fight for Freedom, Vol. 16. LC 99-38687. (American Adventure Ser.: No. 16). 144p. (J). (gr. 3-6). 1999. lib. bdg. 15.95 (*0-7910-5590-6*) Chelsea Hse.

— Fight for Freedom. (American Adventure Ser.: No. 19). (J). (gr. 3-6). 1998. pap. 3.97 (*1-57748-257-3*) Barbour Pub.

— Frederick Douglass. (Illus.). (J). 2000. 18.95 (*0-7910-6003-9*) Chelsea Hse.

— Frederick Douglass. LC 00-38394. (Famous Figures of the Civil War Ser.). (Illus.). 2000. pap. 8.95 (*0-7910-6141-8*) Chelsea Hse.

— The Great War. LC 99-193162. (American Adventure Ser.: No. 36). (J). (gr. 3-6). 1998. pap. 3.97 (*1-57748-411-8*) Barbour Pub.

— Harriet Tubman. (Famous Figures of the Civil War Era Ser.). (Illus.). (J). 2000. 18.95 (*0-7910-6008-X*) Chelsea Hse.

— Harriet Tubman. LC 00-38389. (Famous Figures of the Civil War Ser.). (Illus.). (J). 2000. pap. 8.95 (*0-7910-6146-9*) Chelsea Hse.

— History of the Black Church. (African-American Achievers Ser.). 2000. 19.95 (*0-7910-5822-0*); pap. 9.95 (*0-7910-5823-9*) Chelsea Hse.

— Increase Mather. (Colonial Leaders Ser.). 2000. 18.95 (*0-7910-5962-6*) Chelsea Hse.

— Increase Mather. (Colonial Leaders Ser.). (Illus.). 2000. pap. 8.95 (*0-7910-6119-1*) Chelsea Hse.

Lutz, Norma Jean. J.C. Watts: Politician. (Black Americans of Achievement Ser.). (Illus.). 144p. 2000. 19.95 (*0-7910-5338-5*) Chelsea Hse.

— John Paul Jones. (Revolutionary War Leaders Ser.). (Illus.). 80p. (gr. 3 up). 1999. pap. 8.95 (*0-7910-5702-X*) Chelsea Hse.

— John Paul Jones. LC 99-25051. (Revolutionary War Leaders Ser.). (Illus.). 80p. (YA). (gr. 3 up). 1999. 16.95 (*0-7910-5359-8*) Chelsea Hse.

***Lutz, Norma Jean.** Jonathan Edwards. (Colonial Leaders Ser.). 2000. 18.95 (*0-7910-5961-8*) Chelsea Hse.

— Jonathan Edwards. (Colonial Leaders Ser.). (Illus.). 2000. pap. 8.95 (*0-7910-6118-3*) Chelsea Hse.

— Maggie's Choice: Jonathan Edwards & the Great Awakening. (American Adventure Ser.: No. 8). (J). (gr. 3-6). 1998. pap. 3.97 (*1-57748-145-3*) Barbour Pub.

Lutz, Norma Jean. Maggie's Choice: Jonathan Edwards & the Great Awakening. LC 98-17241. (American Adventure Ser.: No. 8). (Illus.). 144p. (J). (gr. 4-7). 1999. lib. bdg. 15.95 (*0-7910-5048-3*) Chelsea Hse.

***Lutz, Norma Jean.** Marching with Sousa. 33rd ed. (American Adventure Ser.: No. 33). (Illus.). (J). (gr. 3-7). 1998. pap. 3.97 (*1-57748-406-1*) Barbour Pub.

— Prelude to War. 35th ed. LC 99-207054. (American Adventure Ser.: No. 35). (Illus.). (J). (gr. 3-7). 1998. pap. 3.97 (*1-57748-410-X*) Barbour Pub.

— The Rebel Spy. LC 99-159243. (American Adventure Ser.: No. 23). (J). (gr. 3-6). 1998. pap. 3.97 (*1-57748-267-0*) Barbour Pub.

— Rumbling of War. (American Adventure Ser.: No. 45). 144p. (J). (gr. 3-6). 1999. pap. 3.97 (*1-57748-511-4*) Barbour Pub.

— Smallpox Strikes! Cotton Mather's Bold Experiment. (American Adventure Ser.: No. 7). (J). (gr. 3-6). 1998. pap. 3.97 (*1-57748-144-5*) Barbour Pub.

Lutz, Norma Jean. Smallpox Strikes! Cotton Mather's Bold Experiment. LC 98-19849. (American Adventure Ser.: No. 7). (Illus.). 144p. (J). (gr. 3-6). 1999. lib. bdg. 15.95 (*0-7910-5047-5*) Chelsea Hse.

***Lutz, Norma Jean.** Sojourner Truth. (Famous Figures of the Civil War Era Ser.). (Illus.). (J). 2000. 18.95 (*0-7910-6007-1*) Chelsea Hse.

— Sojourner Truth. LC 00-38403. (Famous Figures of the Civil War Era Ser.). (Illus.). (J). 2000. pap. write for info. (*0-7910-6145-0*) Chelsea Hse.

— Trouble on the Ohio River: Drought Shuts Down a City. 15th ed. LC 98-141999. (American Adventure Ser.: No. 15). (Illus.). (J). (gr. 3-7). 1998. pap. 3.97 (*1-57748-232-8*) Barbour Pub.

— Trouble on the Ohio River: Drought Shuts down a City, Vol. 15. LC 99-38686. (American Adventure Ser.: No. 15). 144p. (J). (gr. 3-6). 1999. lib. bdg. write for info. (*0-7910-5588-4*) Chelsea Hse.

— War Strikes. (American Adventure Ser.: No. 46). 144p. (J). (gr. 3-6). 1999. pap. 3.97 (*1-57748-512-2*) Barbour Pub.

— War's End. LC 99-159249. (American Adventure Ser.: No. 24). (J). (gr. 3-6). 1998. pap. 3.97 (*1-57748-268-9*) Barbour Pub.

Lutz, Norma Jean. William Penn. LC 99-25345. (Colonial Leaders Ser.). (Illus.). 80p. (J). 1999. 16.95 (*0-7910-5344-X*) Chelsea Hse.

— William Penn. (Colonial Leaders Ser.). (Illus.). 80p. (J). (gr. 3 up). 1999. pap. 8.95 (*0-7910-5687-2*) Chelsea Hse.

Lutz, Norma Jean, jt. auth. see Perris, P.Harold.

Lutz, Norma Jean, ed. see Holmes, Jean.

Lutz, Pamela B., jt. ed. see Holdzkom, David.

Lutz, Peter L. & Musick, John A., eds. The Biology of Sea Turtles. LC 96-36432. (CRC Marine Science Ser.). 448p. 1996. boxed set 94.95 (*0-8493-8422-2*) CRC Pr.

Lutz, Peter L. & Nilsson, Goran E. The Brain Without Oxygen: Causes of Failure & Mechanisms for Survival. 2nd ed. LC 97-20847. (Neuroscience Intelligence Unit Ser.). 1997. 99.00 (*1-57059-458-9*) Landes Bioscience.

Lutz, Peter L., jt. auth. see Dabrowski, Konrad.

Lutz, R., jt. ed. see Brinberg, D.

Lutz, Ralph H. The German Revolution, Nineteen Eighteen to Nineteen Nineteen. LC 68-54283. (Stanford University. Stanford Studies in Language & Literature: Vol. 1, Pt. 1). reprint ed. 27.50 (*0-404-50961-4*) AMS Pr.

Lutz, Richard A., jt. ed. see Kennish, Michael J.

Lutz, Richard A., jt. ed. see Rhoads, Donald C.

Lutz, Richard L. Feel Better! Live Longer! Relax. LC 88-10872. 144p. 1988. pap. 7.95 (*0-931625-18-1*) DIMI Pr.

Lutz, Robert A. Guts: The Seven Laws of Business That Made Chrysler the World's Hottest Car Company. LC 98-29124. 240p. 1998. 24.95 (*0-471-29561-2*) Wiley.

— Guts: The Seven Laws of Business That Made Chrysler the World's Hottest Car Company. 240p. 1999. pap. 16.95 (*0-471-35765-0*) Wiley.

Lutz, Robert A., jt. auth. see Johnson, Ramon E.

Lutz, Robert E., jt. ed. see Handl, Gunther.

Lutz, Robert R. & Taylor, Bruce T. Surviving in Ministry: Navigating the Pitfalls, Experiencing the Renewals. 1990. pap. 11.95 (*0-8091-3156-0*) Paulist Pr.

Lutz, Rolland R., jt. auth. see Lutz, Jessie G.

Lutz, Rudiger. The Secret of the Desert: The Rock Art of the Messak Sattafet & Messak Mellet, Libya. (Illus.). xxii, 177p. 1995. 60.00 (*3-900773-10-6*) Cities in Color.

Lutz, Sandy. MED Inc. How Consolidation Is Shaping Tomorrow's Health Care System. LC 97-40890. 192p. 1998. 26.95 (*0-7879-4040-2*) Jossey-Bass.

Lutz, Sandy & Gee, E. Preston. Columbia HCA: Healthcare on Overdrive. 232p. 1997. 21.95 (*0-07-024804-4*) McGraw.

Lutz, Sandy, jt. auth. see Gee, E. Preston.

Lutz, Susan & Haller, Janeen. Seniors & Children: Building Bridges Together: Intergenerational Projects Pairing Older Adults & Children at Risk. 64p. 1996. ring bd. 15.00 (*0-910883-85-8*) Natl Coun Aging.

Lutz, Susan, jt. auth. see Mott, Steve.

Lutz, Thomas. Crying: A Natural & Cultural History of Tears. LC 99-21295. 356p. 1999. text 25.95 (*0-393-04756-3*) Norton.

***Lutz, Thomas.** Crying: The Natural & Cultural History of Tears. 352p. 2000. reprint ed. pap. 14.95 (*0-393-32103-7*) Norton.

Lutz, Tim. Gem Hunter's Kit. (Discovery Kit Ser.). (Illus.). 64p. (Orig.). (J). (gr. 3 up). 1990. 18.95 (*0-89471-828-2*) Running Pr.

— The Gem Hunter's Kit: Discover the Earth's Mineral Treasures. (Illus.). 64p. (J). 1998. pap. 29.95 incl. cd-rom (*1-56138-781-9*) Running Pr.

Lutz, Tom. American Nervousness, 1903: An Anecdotal History. LC 90-55737. (Illus.). 344p. 1993. pap. text 16.95 (*0-8014-9901-1*) Cornell U Pr.

Lutz, Tom & Ashton, Susanna, eds. These "Colored" United States: African American Essays from the 1920s. LC 95-52258. (Illus.). 300p. (C). 1996. text 50.00 (*0-8135-2305-2*); pap. text 17.95 (*0-8135-2306-0*) Rutgers U Pr.

Lutz, Uli & Pafel, Jurgen, eds. On Extraction & Extraposition in German. LC 95-51022. (Linquistik Aktuell/Linguistics Today Ser.: No. 11). xii, 315p. 1996. lib. bdg. 74.00 (*1-55619-229-0*) J Benjamins Pubng Co.

***Lutz, Uli, et al.** WH-Scope Marking. LC 00-31283. (Linguistik Aktuell Ser.). 2000. write for info. (*1-55619-994-5*) J Benjamins Pubng Co.

Lutz, Vera C. Italy: A Study in Economic Development. LC 75-3738. (Illus.). 342p. 1975. reprint ed. lib. bdg. 75.00 (*0-8371-8055-4*, LUIT, Greenwood Pr) Greenwood.

Lutz, Vera C., jt. auth. see Lutz, Friedrich A.

Lutz, William. Doublespeak Defined: Cut Through the Bull**** and. LC 99-19253. (Illus.). 208p. 1999. pap. 12.95 (*0-06-273412-1*) HarpC.

— The New Doublespeak: Why No One Knows What Anyone's Saying Anymore. 256p. 1997. pap. 13.00 (*0-06-092839-5*, Perennial) HarperTrade.

Lutz, William & Brent, Harry. The Critical Reader: Responding Through Writing. LC 89-35628. (C). 1990. teacher ed. write for info. (*0-06-044114-3*) Addson-Wesley Educ.

Lutz, William, jt. auth. see Brent, Harry.

Lutz, William D. The Cambridge Thesaurus of American English. LC 93-31878. 525p. (C). 1994. 19.95 (*0-521-41427-X*) Cambridge U Pr.

— Double-Speak: Rom Revenue Enhancement to Terminal Living How Government, Business, Advertisers & Others Use the Language to Deceive You. 1990. 8.95 (*0-00-003850-4*, Perennial) HarperTrade.

***Lutz, Wolfgang.** Life Without Bread: How a Low-Carbohydrate Diet Can Save Your Life. 288p. 2000. pap. 16.95 (*0-658-00170-1*, 001701, Keats Publng) NTC Contemp Pub Co.

Lutz, Wolfgang, ed. Future Demographic Trends in Europe & North America: What Can We Assume Today? (Studies in Population). (Illus.). 585p. (C). 1991. text 149.00 (*0-12-460445-5*) Acad Pr.

— Population-Development-Environment: Understanding Their Interactions in Mauritius. LC 94-26937. 1994. 127.95 (*0-387-58301-7*); write for info. (*3-540-58301-7*) Spr-Verlag.

Lutz, Wolfgang, et al, eds. Demographic Trends & Patterns in the Soviet Union Before 1991. (Illus.). 544p. (C). (gr. 13). 1993. 160.00 (*0-415-10194-8*, B2448) Routledge.

Lutz, Wolfgang, et al. Frontiers of Population Forecasting. LC 99-21220. 199p. 1999. write for info. (*0-87834-096-3*) Population Coun.

Lutze, Beverly, ed. see Hollimon-Miller, Jereleen.

Lutze, L., ed. see Narain, Iqbal.

Lutze, Lothar. Hindi Writings in Post-Colonial India. 1985. 27.00 (*0-8364-1422-5*, Pub. by Manohar) S Asia.

Lutze, Peter C. Alexander Kluge: The Last Modernist. LC 97-37942. (Contemporary Film & Television Ser.). 1998. pap. 29.95 (*0-8143-2656-0*) Wayne St U Pr.

Lutze, W. & Ewing, R. C., eds. Radioactive Waste Forms for the Future. 778p. 1988. 398.25 (*0-444-87104-7*, North Holland) Elsevier.

Lutze, W. & Ewing, R. C., eds. Scientific Basis for Nuclear Waste Management XII, Vol. 127. (Materials Research Society Symposium Proceedings Ser.). 1989. text 17.50 (*0-931837-97-9*) Materials Res.

Lutzeier, Elizabeth, tr. see Nissen, Hans J.

Lutzeier, Peter, ed. see Railton, Nicholas.

Lutzeier, Peter R., ed. German Studies Vol. 1: Old & New Challenges: Undergraduate Programmes in the United Kingdom & the Republic of Ireland. LC 98-13294. (German Linguistic & Cultural Studies). 249p. (C). 1998. pap. text 45.95 (*0-8204-3411-6*, Pub. by P Lang) P Lang Pubng.

— German Studies Old & New Challenges: Undergraduate Programmes in the United Kingdom & the Republic of Ireland. LC 98-13294. (German Linguistic & Cultural Studies: Vol. 1). 249p. 1998. pap. 45.95 (*3-906757-59-5*, Pub. by P Lang) P Lang Pubng.

Lutzeler, Paul M. Europe after Maastricht: American & European Perspectives. LC 75-12340. 324p. 1994. 29.95 (*0-8264-0783-8*) Continuum.

Lutzeler, Paul M., ed. Europe after Maastricht: American & European Perspectives. LC 94-33658. 320p. (C). 1994. 29.95 (*1-57181-020-X*) Berghahn Bks.

Lutzen, Hanna. Vlad the Undead. 192p. (YA). (gr. 8 up). 1998. pap. 15.95 (*0-88899-342-0*, Pub. by Gro1undwood-Douglas) Publishers Group.

Lutzen, J. Joseph Liouville, 1809-1882. (Studies in the History of Mathematics & Physical Sciences: Vol. 15). (Illus.). 824p. 1990. 130.95 (*0-387-97180-7*) Spr-Verlag.

***Lutzen, Karl F.** A-186 Build Homebrew Equipment. LC 98-37259. 1998. pap. 3.95 (*1-58017-138-9*, Pub. by Storey Bks) Random.

Lutzen, Karl F. & Stevens, Mark. Brew Ware: How to Find, Adapt & Build Homebrewing Equipment. McHale, Elizabeth, ed. (Illus.). 304p. (Orig.). 1996. pap. 16.95 (*0-88266-926-5*, Storey Pub) Storey Bks.

— Homebrew Favorites: A Coast-to-Coast Collection of More Than 240 Beer & Ale Recipes. LC 93-33377. (Illus.). 256p. 1994. pap. 14.95 (*0-88266-613-4*, Storey Pub) Storey Bks.

— More Homebrew Favorites: More Than 260 New Brews! LC 97-6490. 1997. pap. 14.95 (*0-88266-968-0*) Storey Bks.

Lutzer, Erwin. Putting Your Past Behind You: Finding Hope for Life's Deepest Hurts. expanded rev. ed. 168p. 1997. pap. 11.99 (*0-8024-5644-8*, 12) Moody.

Lutzer, Erwin W. Chiseled by the Master's Hand. 144p. (Orig.). 1993. pap. 8.99 (*1-56476-059-6*, 6-3059, Victor Bks) Chariot Victor.

— Christ among Other Gods. 216p. 1997. pap. 10.99 (*0-8024-1649-7*, 109) Moody.

***Lutzer, Erwin W.** De Pastor a Pastor. (SPA.). 128p. 1999. pap. 8.99 (*0-8254-1408-3*, Edit Portavoz) Kregel.

Lutzer, Erwin W. The Doctrines That Divide: A Fresh Look at the Historic Doctrines That Separate Christians. LC 99-162015. 256p. 1998. pap. 12.99 (*0-8254-3165-4*) Kregel.

— Failure: The Back Door to Success. 138p. pap. 9.99 (*0-8024-2593-3*, 138) Moody.

***Lutzer, Erwin W.** Getting Closer to God: Erwin Lutzer. LC 00-23558. (Illus.). 233p. 2000. 10.99 (*1-56955-210-X*, Vine Bks) Servant.

Lutzer, Erwin W. Hitler's Cross: The Revealing Story of How the Cross of Christ Was Used As a Symbol of the Nazi Agenda. 222p. 1998. pap. 11.99 (*0-8024-3583-1*) Moody.

— How to Say No to a Stubborn Habit. LC 79-64039. 143p. 1979. pap. 7.99 (*0-88207-787-2*, Victor Bks) Chariot Victor.

— How to Say No to a Stubborn Habit. 2nd ed. LC 94-29507. 144p. 1994. pap. 9.99 (*1-56476-331-5*, 6-3331, Victor Bks) Chariot Victor.

Lutzer, Erwin W. How You Can Be Sure That You Will Spend Eternity With God, 2 bks. 1996. pap. 11.99 (*0-8024-2722-7*) Moody.

Lutzer, Erwin W. How You Can Be Sure You Will Spend Eternity with God. LC 96-207824. pap. 8.99 (*0-8024-2719-7*, 177) Moody.

***Lutzer, Erwin W.** Issues of Eternity, 3, 1. 225p. 1999. boxed set 29.97 (*0-8024-9081-6*) Moody.

Lutzer, Erwin W. Living with Your Passions. 156p. 1983. 9.99 (*0-88207-294-3*, 6-2294, Victor Bks) Chariot Victor.

— Measuring Morality: A Comparison of Ethical Systems. LC 89-29503. Orig. Title: The Necessity of Ethical Absolutes. 120p. (C). 1989. reprint ed. pap. 8.99 (*0-945241-04-6*) Probe Bks.

— The Necessity of Ethical Absolutes (CFUC) 112p. (Orig.). 1981. pap. 7.95 (*0-310-35791-8*, 12659P) Zondervan.

— One Minute after You Die: A Preview of Your Final Destination. LC 97-147274. 144p. 1997. pap. 8.99 (*0-8024-6322-3*, 237); pap. 11.99 (*0-8024-6323-1*, 238) Moody.

— Pastor to Pastor: Trackling the Problems of Ministry. expanded rev. ed. LC 97-41096. 128p. 1997. pap. 8.99 (*0-8254-3164-6*) Kregel.

— The Serpent of Paradise: The Incredible Story of How Satan's Rebellion Serves God's Purposes. LC 97-147275. pap. 10.99 (*0-8024-2720-0*, 283) Moody.

***Lutzer, Erwin W.** Seven Miracles That Should Convince You. 1999. 16.99 (*0-8024-7741-0*) Moody.

Lutzer, Erwin W. Seven Miracles That Should Convince You: The Claims of Christ & Today's Culture. 1999. 19.99 (*0-8024-7846-8*) Moody.

— Seven Reasons Why I Believe the Bible Is God's Word. 200p. 1998. 19.95 (*0-8024-8442-5*); pap. 5.99 (*0-8024-8443-3*) Moody.

***Lutzer, Erwin W.** Seven Reasons Why You Can Trust the Bible. 1998. 19.99 (*0-8024-8444-1*) Moody.

— Ten Lies about God: And How You May Already Be Decieved. 2000. 19.99 (*0-8499-1627-5*) Word Pub.

— Tu Eterno Galardon. (SPA.). 128p. 1999. pap. 5.99 (*0-8254-1409-1*, Edit Portavoz) Kregel.

— Tu Primer Minuto Despues de Morir. (SPA.). 112p. 1999. pap. 5.99 (*0-8254-1425-3*, Edit Portavoz) Kregel.

Lutzer, Erwin W. Twelve Myths Americans Believe. (Orig.). 1993. pap. 10.99 (*0-8024-9017-4*) Moody.

— Why the Cross Can Do What Politics Can't: When They See You, Do They See Jesus? LC 98-41131. 184p. 1999. pap. 9.99 (*1-56507-998-1*) Harvest Hse.

— Your Eternal Reward: Triumph & Tears at the Judgment Seat of Christ. (Orig.). 1998. pap. 8.99 (*0-8024-4192-0*); mass mkt. 5.99 (*0-8024-4193-9*); mass mkt. 11.99 (*0-8024-4194-7*) Moody.

Lutzer, Erwin W., jt. auth. see Van Stone, Doris.

Lutzin, Sidney G., ed. Managing Municipal Leisure Services. LC 80-17378. (Municipal Management Ser.). 271p. 1980. pap. text 21.00 (*0-87326-023-6*) Intl City-Cnty Mgt.

Lutzker, Arnold P. Copyrights & Trademarks for Media Professionals. LC 96-52114. (Broadcasting & Cable Ser.). 208p. 1997. pap. 24.95 (*0-240-80276-4*, Focal) Buttrwrth-Heinemann.

Lutzker, John R., ed. Handbook of Child Abuse Research & Treatment. LC 97-39967. (Issues in Clinical Child Psychology Ser.). 612p. (C). 1997. 95.00 (*0-306-45659-1*, Plenum Trade) Perseus Pubng.

Lutzker, John R. & Campbell, Randy. Ecobehavioral Family Interventions in Development Disabilities. LC 94-3954. 126p. 1994. 20.75 (*0-534-24396-7*) Brooks-Cole.

Lutzker, Marilyn. Criminal Justice Research in Libraries: Strategies & Resources. LC 85-17765. (Illus.). 183p. 1986. lib. bdg. 55.00 (*0-313-24490-1*, LCJ/, Greenwood Pr) Greenwood.

— Multiculturalism in the College Curriculum: A Handbook of Strategies & Resources for Faculty. LC 94-37880. (Greenwood Educators' Reference Collection). 160p. 1995. lib. bdg. 55.00 (*0-313-28918-2*, Greenwood Pr) Greenwood.

— Research Projects for College Students: What to Write Across the Curriculum. LC 87-37549. 152p. 1988. lib. bdg. 47.95 (*0-313-25149-5*, LRW/, Greenwood Pr) Greenwood.

Lutzow, Franz. Lectures on the Historians of Bohemia. LC 72-173174. 128p. 1972. reprint ed. 18.95 (*0-405-08756-X*, Pub. by Blom Pubns) Ayer.

— The Life & Times of Master John Hus. LC 77-84728. (Illus.). reprint ed. 57.50 (*0-404-16128-6*) AMS Pr.

Lutzvick, Margaret S. Going to Palmyra; Sherman Deeds. (Illus.). xxviii, 335p. 1996. mass mkt. 39.95 (*0-9655764-0-X*) M S Lutzvick.

Luu, Le. A Time Far Past. Hai, Ngo V. et al, eds. Chung, Nguyen B. et al, trs. from VIE. LC 96-47787.Tr. of Thoi Xa Vang. 296p. 1997. 24.95 (*1-55849-085-X*) U of Mass Pr.

Luukkanen, Eino. Fighter over Finland: The Memoirs of a Fighter Pilot. Gilbert, James B. & Green, William, eds. Salo, Mauno A., tr. LC 79-7282. (Flight: Its First Seventy-Five Years Ser.). (Illus.). 1980. reprint ed. lib. bdg. 30.95 (*0-405-12191-1*) Ayer.

Luurila, Olavi J. Sauna & the Heart: Arrhythmias & Other Cardiovascular Responses During Finnish Sauna & Exercise Testing in Healthy Men & Post-Myocardial Infarction Patients. 60p. 1980. pap. 12.50 (*951-99256-6-X*) Sauna Soc.

***Luus, Rein.** Iterative Dynamic Programming. LC 99-58886. 324p. 2000. 89.95 (*1-58488-148-8*, Chap & Hall CRC) CRC Pr.

Luv, Bud E. You Oughta Be Me: How to be a Lounge Singer & Live Like One. (Illus.). 256p. (Orig.). 1993. pap. 10.95 (*0-312-09947-9*) St Martin.

Luvaas, Jay. The Military Legacy of the Civil War: The European Inheritance. LC 88-27800. (Modern War Studies). (Illus.). xxx, 258p. 1988. pap. 14.95 (*0-7006-0379-4*) U Pr of KS.

— U. S. Army War College Guide to the Battles of Chancellorsville & Fredericksburg. (U. S. Army War College Guides to Civil War Battles Ser.). 364p. 1996. pap. text 14.95 (*0-7006-0785-4*) U Pr of KS.

Luvaas, Jay, ed. Dear Miss Em: General Eichelberger's War in the Pacific, 1942-1945, 2. LC 71-176429. (Contributions in Military History Ser.: No. 2). 322p. 1972. 59.95 (*0-8371-6278-5*, LDM/, Greenwood Pr) Greenwood.

Luvaas, Jay, ed. from ENG. Frederick the Great on the Art of War. LC 98-16791. 416p. 1998. reprint ed. pap. 16.95 (*0-306-80861-7*) Da Capo.

— Frederick the Great on the Art of War. 400p. 1999. reprint ed. mass mkt. 16.95 (*0-306-80908-7*, Pub. by Da Capo) HarpC.

— Napoleon on the Art of War. LC 99-13248. 208p. 1999. 25.00 (*0-684-85185-7*) S&S Trade.

Luvaas, Jay, et al, eds. The U. S. Army War College Guide to the Battle of Shiloh. LC 96-24199. (U. S. Army War College Guides to Civil War Battles). (Illus.). 253p. 1996. pap. 12.95 (*0-7006-0783-8*) U Pr of KS.

— The U. S. Army War College Guide to the Battle of Shiloh. LC 96-24199. (Illus.). 232p. 1996. 29.95 (*0-7006-0782-X*) U Pr of KS.

Luvaas, Jay & Cullen, Joseph. Appomattox Court House. LC 80-607775. (Official National Park Handbook Ser.: No. 109). 1980. pap. 8.00 (*0-912627-06-9*) Natl Park Serv.

Luvaas, Jay & Nelson, Harold W. The U. S. Army War College Guide to the Battle of Gettysburg. (Illus.). 240p. 1994. pap. 12.95 (*0-7006-0686-6*) U Pr of KS.

Luvaas, Jay & Nelson, Harold W., eds. Guide to the Battle of Antietam. LC 96-15563. (Illus.). 336p. 1996. pap. 14.95 (*0-7006-0784-6*) U Pr of KS.

Luvaas, Jay, ed. see Henderson, G. F.

Luvaas, Jay, ed. see Henderson, George F.

Luvasik, Stephen. Review & Analysis of the Report of the President's Commission on Critical Infrastructure. 34p. 1998. pap. 5.00 (*0-935371-49-4*) CFISAC.

Luvera, Paul N., Jr. Attorney's Guidebook of Trial Forms & Techniques for Successful Handling of Personal Injury Cases. 1979. 89.50 (*0-13-050294-4*) Exec Reports.

Luvera, Paul N. How to Prepare & Try a Plaintiff's Soft Tissue Neck Injury Case: A Practice Primer for Preparing & Trying a Plaintiff's "Whiplash" Case. (Illus.). xii, 346p. write for info. (*0-318-57762-3*) P N Luvera.

Luvera, Paul N., jt. auth. see Trine, William A.

Luvmour, Josette & Luvmour, Sambhava. Natural Learning Rhythms: Discovering How & When Your Child Learns. 320p. 1997. pap. 16.95 (*0-89087-840-4*) Celestial Arts.

— Tiger by the Tail: Essays on the Inherent Spirituality of Natural Learning Rhythms. 176p. 1998. pap. 14.95 (*0-9667584-0-4*) EnCompass Pr.

Luvmour, Josette, jt. auth. see Luvmour, Sambhava.

Luvmour, Sambhava & Luvmour, Josette. Everyone Wins! Cooperative Games & Activities. 128p. pap. 8.95 (*0-86571-190-9*) New Soc Pubs.

Luvmour, Sambhava, jt. auth. see Luvmour, Josette.

Luvoncn, David J. Japan : A Documentary History: The Late Tokugawa Period to the Present, Vol. II. LC 96-24433. (Illus.). 410p. (C). (gr. 13). 1996. pap. text 24.95 (*0-7656-0036-6*, East Gate Bk) M E Sharpe.

Lux, David S. Patronage & Royal Science in 17th-Century France: The Academie de Physique in Caen. LC 89-1002. 256p. 1989. 37.50 (*0-8014-2334-1*) Cornell U Pr.

Lux, Harm. Francesca Woodman: Photography. (Illus.). 1994. pap. 25.00 (*1-881616-13-4*) Dist Art Pubs.

Lux, Ivan & Koblinger, Laszlo. Monte Carlo Particle Transport Methods: Neutron & Photon Calculations. 448p. 1991. lib. bdg. 119.95 (*0-8493-6074-9*, QC793) CRC Pr.

Lux, J. Richard & Pieters, Richard S. Basic Exercises in Algebra & Trigonometry. 1979. 8.48 (*0-8013-0068-1*); pap. text 8.22 (*0-88334-122-0*, 76096) Longman.

Lux, Jonathan, ed. Classification Societies. 132p. 1993. 110.00 (*1-85044-491-9*) LLP.

Lux, Jonathan, jt. auth. see Fisher, Christopher.

Lux, K., jt. auth. see Hiss, G.

Lux, Kenneth, jt. auth. see Lutz, Mark.

***Lux, Lawrance George.** Aggravated Assault. LC 99-64385. 252p. 1999. 25.00 (*0-7388-0444-4*); pap. 18.00 (*0-7388-0445-2*) Xlibris Corp.

— Plans for the Future: A Study on Future Trends. LC 99-91913. 187p. 2000. 25.00 (*0-7388-1294-3*); pap. 18.00 (*0-7388-1295-1*) Xlibris Corp.

— Prognosis 2000: Evaluation of Current Trends. LC 99-91198. 1999. 25.00 (*0-7388-0660-9*); pap. 18.00 (*0-7388-0661-7*) Xlibris Corp.

Lux, Scott. Natural Pain Relief: Techniques for Miraculous Healing. ix, 112p. 1997. pap. 10.95 (*0-9609324-1-0*) Wisdom of Pain.

Lux, Thomas. The Blind Swimmer: Selected Early Poems 1970-1975. 64p. (Orig.). 1996. pap. 10.00 (*0-938566-73-3*) Adastra Pr.

— The Drowned River. 68p. (C). 1993. reprint ed. pap. 8.00 (*0-938566-60-1*) Adastra Pr.

— The Drowned River: New Poems. 80p. 1990. pap. 8.95 (*0-685-29459-5*) HM.

— Half Promised Land. LC 94-70469. (Classic Contemporaries Ser.). 100p. 1994. reprint ed. pap. 12.95 (*0-88748-205-8*) Carnegie-Mellon.

— Massachusetts: Ten Poems. 15p. (C). 1981. pap. 5.00 (*0-913219-32-0*) Pym-Rand Pr.

— Massachusetts: Ten Poems. deluxe ed. 15p. (C). 1981. 10.00 (*0-913219-33-9*) Pym-Rand Pr.

— New & Selected Poems, 1975-1995. 192p. 1999. pap. 14.00 (*0-395-92488-X*) HM.

— New & Selected Poems of Lux. LC 97-430. 160p. 1997. 23.00 (*0-395-85832-1*) HM.

— Split Horizon. LC 93-46333. 96p. 1995. pap. 9.95 (*0-395-70097-3*) HM.

— Sunday. LC 88-63541. (Classic Contemporaries Ser.). 1989. pap. 12.95 (*0-88748-089-6*) Carnegie-Mellon.

***Lux, Thomas, ed.** Ploughshares Winter, 1998-99: Poems & Stories Edited by Thomas Lux. 243p. 1998. pap. 9.95 (*0-933277-24-5*) Ploughshares.

***Lux Verbi Staff.** Joy at The Workplace. 1999. 4.95 (*0-86997-774-1*) Lux Verbi.

— Joy for A Friend. 1999. 4.95 (*0-86997-773-3*) Lux Verbi.

Lux, William. An Engineer in the Courtroom. 364p. 1995. 49.00 (*1-56091-672-9*, R-155) Soc Auto Engineers.

Luxan, Diego P. De, see De Luxan, Diego P.

***Luxbacher, Joe.** Becoming Fit: How to Trim Down. (Illus.). 160p. 2000. pap. 16.95 (*1-57167-457-8*) Coaches Choice.

Luxbacher, Joe. Fun Games for Soccer Training. LC 86-27198. (Illus.). 144p. 1987. reprint ed. pap. 44.70 (*0-608-04288-9*, 206506700012) Bks Demand.

Luxbacher, Joseph A. Soccer: Steps to Success. 2nd ed. LC 95-44483. (Steps to Success Activity Ser.). (Illus.). 168p. (Orig.). 1996. pap. 15.95 (*0-87322-763-8*, PLUX0763) Human Kinetics.

***Luxbacher, Joseph A.** Soccer: Winning Techniques. (Illus.). 162p. 1998. pap. 16.95 (*0-945483-77-5*) E Bowers Pub.

Luxbacher, Joseph A. Soccer Practice Games. 2nd ed. LC 94-12525. 160p. 1994. pap. 14.95 (*0-87322-554-6*, PLUX0554) Human Kinetics.

***Luxbacher, Joseph A., ed.** Attacking Soccer. LC 99-28703. (Illus.). 208p. 1999. pap. 16.95 (*0-7360-0123-9*, PLUX0123) Human Kinetics.

Luxbacher, Joseph A. & Klein, Gene. The Soccer Goalkeeper. 2nd ed. LC 93-6290. 176p. 1993. pap. 15.95 (*0-87322-397-7*, PLUX0397) Human Kinetics.

Luxemborg, Rosa. Reform Or Revolution. LC 73-79783. 79p. 1970. reprint ed. pap. 10.95 (*0-87348-303-0*) Pathfinder NY.

Luxemburg, Rosa. Comrade & Lover: Rosa Luxemburg's Letters to Leo Jogiches. Ettinger, Elzbieta, ed. 242p. 1979. 22.50 (*0-262-05021-8*) MIT Pr.

— Letters to Karl & Luise Kautsky, 1896-1918. 1974. 250.00 (*0-87968-190-X*) Gordon Pr.

— The National Question: Selected Writings by Rosa Luxemburg. Davis, Horace B., ed. LC 74-2148. 318p. 1976. reprint ed. pap. 98.60 (*0-7837-3913-3*, 204376100010) Bks Demand.

— Reform or Revolution. 1973. 250.00 (*0-87968-069-5*) Gordon Pr.

— Reform or Revolution. Integer, tr. LC 73-79783. 79p. 1970. reprint ed. lib. bdg. 30.00 (*0-87348-302-2*) Pathfinder NY.

— Rosa Luxemburg Speaks. Waters, Mary-Alice, ed. LC 90-70745. 473p. 1970. reprint ed. pap. 26.95 (*0-87348-146-1*) Pathfinder NY.

— The Russian Revolution, & Leninism or Marxism? 120p. 1961. pap. text 14.95 (*0-472-06057-0*, 06057, Ann Arbor Bks) U of Mich Pr.

— The Russian Revolution, & Leninism or Marxism?, AA 57. LC 80-24374. (Ann Arbor Paperbacks for the Study of Communism & Marxism). 109p. 1981. reprint ed. lib. bdg. 38.50 (*0-313-22429-3*, LURR, Greenwood Pr) Greenwood.

— Theory & Practice. Wolff, David, tr. from GER. (Illus.). 67p. (Orig.). 1980. pap. 2.00 (*0-914441-22-1*) News & Letters.

Luxemburg, Rosa & Bukharin, Nikolai I. The Accumulation of Capital: An Anti-Critique Imperialism & the Accumulation of Capital. Wichmann, Rudolf, tr. LC 72-81768. 299p. reprint ed. pap. 92.70 (*0-8357-6001-4*, 203433900089) Bks Demand.

Luxemburg, Rut Blees. London - A Modern Project. (Illus.). 64p. 1997. pap. 19.95 (*1-901033-50-3*, Pub. by Black Dog Pubg) RAM Publications.

Luxemburg, W. A., jt. ed. see Huijsmans, C. B.

Luxenberg, Larry. Walking the Appalachian Trail. (Illus.). 256p. 1994. pap. 16.95 (*0-8117-3095-6*) Stackpole.

***Luxenberg, Susan Diamond.** Fearless Remodeling! A Planning Guide for the Homeowner. LC 99-95451. (Illus.). 232p. 2000. pap. 24.95 (*0-9673383-0-1*, Pub. by HomeSmart Cons) IPG Chicago.

Luxenburg, Joan. Probation Casework: The Convergence of Theory with Practice. (Illus.). 174p. (Orig.). (C). 1983. pap. text 21.00 (*0-8191-3271-3*) U Pr of Amer.

Luxenburg, Norman, ed. & frwd. see Skrjabina, Elena.

Luxenburg, Norman, tr. see Skriabina, Elena.

Luxenburg, Norman, tr. see Skrjabina, Elena.

Luxenburg, Norman, tr. & intro. see Skrjabina, Elena.

Luxford, Lucy A., ed. see Phillips, R. C.

Luxford, Michael. Children with Special Needs. (Rudolf Steiner's Ideas in Practice Ser.). (Illus.). 128p. (Orig.). 1994. pap. 9.95 (*0-88010-381-7*) Anthroposophic.

Luxiang, Wang, jt. auth. see Xiaokang, Su.

Luxleacher, Jim. Conditioning for Soccer. LC 97-30050. (Illus.). 160p. (Orig.). 1997. pap. 12.95 (*1-57028-146-7*, 81467H, Mstrs Pr) NTC Contemp Pub Co.

Luxmoore, Charles F. English Saltglazed Earthenware. (Illus.). 99.95 (*0-685-53309-3*) Ars Ceramica.

Luxmoore, Jonathan. The Helsinki Agreement: Dialogue or Delusion? (C). 1990. 35.00 (*0-907967-76-0*, Pub. by Inst Euro Def & Strat) St Mut.

— Vatican & the Red Flag. LC 99-197761. 1999. 39.95 (*0-225-66772-X*, Pub. by G Chapman) Bks Intl VA.

***Luxmoore, Jonathan.** Vatican & the Red Flag: The Struggle for the Soul of Eastern Europe. (Illus.). 368p. 2000. pap. 27.95 (*0-225-66883-1*) G Chapman.

***Luxmoore, Nick.** Listening to Young People in School, Youth Work & Counselling. LC 00-41265. (Illus.). 2000. pap. write for info. (*1-85302-909-2*, Pub. by Jessica Kingsley) Taylor & Francis.

Luxmoore, R. A., ed. A Directory of Crocodilian Farming Operation. 2nd ed. 352p. 1992. 40.00 (*2-8317-0078-7*, Pub. by IUCN) Island Pr.

Luxmoore, R. J., jt. ed. see Zelazny, Lucian W.

Luxner, Karla. Maternal - Infant Nursing Care Plans. unabridged ed. (Nursing Care Plans Ser.). 309p. 1999. pap. 39.95 (*1-56930-099-2*) Skidmore Roth Pub.

Luxon, James T. & Parker, David E. Industrial Lasers & Their Applications, No. 209. (Illus.). 248p. (C). 1985. text 66.00 (*0-13-461369-4*) P-H.

Luxon, Linda M., jt. ed. see Davies, Rosalyn A.

Luxon, S. G., jt. auth. see Collings, A. J.

Luxon, Thomas H. Literal Figures: Puritan Allegory & the Reformation Crisis in Representation. LC 94-30412. 262p. 1995. 28.00 (*0-226-49785-2*) U Ch Pr.

Luxrado, Herve. French Revolution. (Illus.). (J). write for info. (*0-237-60269-5*) EVN1 UK.

Luxton, Donald, jt. auth. see D'Acres, Lilia.

Luxton, Meg. More Than a Labour of Love: Three Generations of Women's Work in the Home. 260p. pap. 14.95 (*0-88961-062-2*, Pub. by Womens Pr) LPC InBook.

Luxton, Peter & Wilkie, Margaret. Commercial Leases. 380p. 1998. 152.00 (*1-85811-165-X*, Pub. by CLT Prof) Gaunt.

— Commercial Property, 1993-94. (Legal Practice Course Guides Ser.). 225p. 1994. pap. 34.00 (*1-85431-351-7*, Pub. by Blackstone Pr) Gaunt.

Luxton, Peter, et al. Equity & Trusts: Blackstone's Law Questions & Answers. 2nd ed. 226p. 1996. pap. 22.00 (*1-85431-495-5*, Pub. by Blackstone Pr) Gaunt.

***Luxton, R.** Clinical Biochemistry. LC 99-30077. 264p. 1999. pap. text 36.00 (*0-7506-2878-2*) Buttrwrth-Heinemann.

Luxton, Richard N., tr. from MYN. The Book of Chumayel: The Counsel Book of the Yucatec Maya, 1539-1638. 335p. 1996. pap. 38.80 (*0-89412-244-4*) Aegean Park Pr.

Luy, J. F. & Russer, P. Silicon-Based Millimeter-Wave Devices: Series in Electronics & Photonics. LC 94-12946. 1994. 75.95 (*0-387-58047-6*) Spr-Verlag.

Luyben, Michael L. & Luyben, William L. Essentials of Process Control. LC 96-8642. 1997. write for info. (*0-07-039173-4*) McGraw.

Luyben, Michael L., jt. auth. see Luyben, William L.

Luyben, William L. Process Modeling, Simulation & Control. 2nd ed. (Chemical Engineering Ser.). 725p. (C). 1989. 98.13 (*0-07-039159-9*) McGraw.

Luyben, William L. & Luyben, Michael L. Essentials of Process Control. LC 96-8642. (Illus.). 624p. (C). 1996. 86.88 (*0-07-039172-6*) McGraw.

Luyben, William L., et al. Plantwide Process Control. LC 98-16167. 395p. 1998. 79.95 (*0-07-006779-1*) McGraw.

Luyben, William L., jt. auth. see Luyben, Michael L.

Luyendijk-Elshout, A. M. The Four Seasons of Human. (History of Science Ser.). (Illus.). 100p. 1999. 110.00 (*90-5235-136-8*, Pub. by Erasmus Pub) Balogh.

Luyken, Jan. Vonken der Liefde Jesu. (GER.). xvi, 232p. 1982. reprint ed. write for info. (*3-487-06955-5*) G Olms Pubs.

Luykx, Aurolyn. The Citizen Factory: Schooling & Cultural Production in Bolivia. LC 98-13843. (SUNY Series, Power, Social Identity, & Education). 370p. (C). 1998. pap. text 24.95 (*0-7914-4038-9*) State U NY Pr.

— The Citizen Factory: Schooling & Cultural Production in Bolivia. LC 98-13843. (SUNY Series, Power, Social Identity, & Education). 370p. (C). 1999. text 74.50 (*0-7914-4037-0*) State U NY Pr.

Luykx, Felix F., ed. see Frissel, M. J.

Luyten, Mark, et al. Mark Luyten: On a Balcony: A Novel. LC 96-52684. (Illus.). 112p. (Orig.). 1997. pap. 16.95 (*0-935640-54-1*) Walker Art Ctr.

Luyten, Meredith. Prayerwheels. Kaplan, Peter, ed. LC 76-14544. 1976. 3.00 (*0-915176-14-9*) Pourboire.

Luyters, Mary. Years of Awakening. 1991. pap. 9.95 (*0-380-00734-7*, Avon Bks) Morrow Avon.

Luythen, S. J., ed. see International Astronomical Union Staff.

Luz, Antonio De La, see De La Luz, Antonio.

Luz, George A., jt. ed. see De Pauw, John W.

***Luz, Ulrich.** Matthew 8-20: Hermeneia. 2000. 62.00 (*0-8006-6034-X*, Fortress Pr) Augsburg Fortress.

Luz, Ulrich. Matthew One - Seven: A Continental Commentary. Linss, Wilhelm C., tr. from GER. LC 92-23792. 416p. 1992. text 49.50 (*0-8006-9600-X*, 1-9600, Fortress Pr) Augsburg Fortress.

— The Theology of the Gospel of Matthew. Robinson, J. Bradford, tr. (New Testament Theology Ser.). 180p. (C). 1995. text 54.95 (*0-521-43433-5*) Cambridge U Pr.

— The Theology of the Gospel of Matthew. Robinson, J. Bradford, tr. (New Testament Theology Ser.). 180p. (C). 1995. pap. text 16.95 (*0-521-43576-5*) Cambridge U Pr.

Luz Villanueva, Alma. Weeping Woman: La Llorona & Other Stories. LC 93-29735. 168p. 1994. 15.00 (*0-927534-38-X*) Biling Rev-Pr.

Luza, Radomir, Jr. Airports & Railroads: A Collection of Vigrettes & Essays. LC 98-104169. (Illus.). 62p. 1997. pap. 5.00 (*0-9643783-5-3*) R Luza.

***Luza, Radomir, Jr.** A Prayer for Monica: A Little Ditty for a Child of the City, 1999. (Illus.). 13p. 1999. pap. 5.00 (*0-9643783-6-1*) R Luza.

Luza, Radomir v., Jr. Broken Headlights: Selected Poems 1995-1996. LC 98-104161. vi, 36p. (Orig.). 1997. pap. 5.00 (*0-9643783-4-5*) R Luza.

Luza, Radomir V., Jr. The Harahan Journal: Selected Poems 1986-91. 50p. 1991. pap. 10.00 (*0-9643783-0-2*) R Luza.

— Porch Light Blues: Selected Poems, 1993-1994. LC 98-104090. 80p. 1995. pap. 12.95 (*0-9643783-3-7*) R Luza.

Luza, Radomir V. The Resistance in Austria, 1938-1945. LC 83-6714. 383p. reprint ed. pap. 118.80 (*0-7837-2936-7*, 205751800006) Bks Demand.

Luza, Radomir V., Jr. This 'n That: Handwriting from a Wounded Heart 1991-1993. 66p. 1993. pap. 6.00 (*0-9643783-1-0*) R Luza.

Luzadder, Patrick K., jt. auth. see Marsh, Valerie.

Luzadder, Warren J. & Duff, Jon M. The Fundamentals of Engineering Drawing: With an Introduction to Interactive Computer Graphics for Design & Production. 11th ed. 692p. 1992. 91.00 (*0-13-335050-9*) P-H.

— Introduction to Engineering Drawing: The Foundations of Engineering Design & Computer Aided Drafting. 2nd ed. 323p. 1992. pap. text 64.00 (*0-13-480849-5*, Pub. by P-H) S&S Trade.

Luzader, Susan, jt. auth. see Prust, Randall.

Luzatto, Moshe C. Derech HaShem: The Way of G-D. Kaplan, Aryeh, tr. from HEB. LC 96-30224. 1978. pap. 19.95 (*0-87306-344-9*) Feldheim.

— Derech HaShem: The Way of God. Kaplan, Aryeh, tr. from HEB. LC 96-30224. (Torah Classics Library). 1978. 23.95 (*0-87306-769-X*) Feldheim.

Luzbetak, Louis J. The Church & Cultures: New Perspectives in Missiological Anthropology. rev. ed. LC 89-2880. (American Society of Missiology Ser.). 384p. 1989. pap. 30.00 (*0-88344-625-1*) Orbis Bks.

Luzeng, Song, tr. see Mao, Li, ed.

Luzhkov, Y. M. Moscow Does Not Believe in Tears: Reflections of Moscow's Mayor. Esterman, Gary, ed. Davidov, M., tr. from RUS.Tr. of Nash dom- Moskva. (RUS., Illus.). 7300p. 1996. 20.00 (*0-9653464-0-4*) J M Martin.

Luzi, Anthony. Timeslipping. LC 98-91757. (Illus.). 120p. 1998. pap. write for info. (*1-57502-911-1*, PO2515) Morris Pubng.

Luzi, Anthony & Luzi, Antoinette D. Auntie Ann's Ancient & Contemporary Recipes Vol. 1: Cakes & Cookies. LC 97-39013. 72p. 1998. pap. 14.95 (*1-889059-11-0*, XaNova) Regent Pr.

Luzi, Antoinette D., jt. auth. see Luzi, Anthony.

Luzi, Marina. The Story of Baby Jesus. Daughters of St. Paul Staff, tr. from ITA. LC 95-115626. (Illus.). 61p. (J). (ps). 1995. 12.95 (*0-8198-6972-4*) Pauline Bks.

Luzi, Mario. After Many Years. (C). 1990. 26.00 (*0-948268-77-8*, Pub. by Dedalus); pap. 25.00 (*0-948268-76-X*, Pub. by Dedalus)

— For the Baptism of Our Fragments, Vol. 1. (Essential Poets Ser.: No. 46). 190p. 1993. pap. 12.00 (*0-920717-55-1*) Guernica Editions.

— In the Dark Body of Metamorphosis & Other Poems. Salomon, I. L., tr. from ITA. 110p. 1975. 6.95 (*0-393-04391-6*); pap. 2.50 (*0-393-04403-3*) Norton.

— Phrases & Passages of a Salutary Song. Bonaffini, Luigi, tr. 150p. 1999. pap. write for info. (*1-77051-077-X*) Guerilla Poetics.

— Phrases & Passages of a Salutary Song. Bonaffini, Luigi, tr. from ITA. LC 98-74234. (Essential Poets Ser.: No. 84). 150p. 1999. pap. 15.00 (*1-55071-077-X*) Guernica Editions.

Luzier, J. Michael, jt. auth. see Brandes, Donald H., Jr.

Luzikov, Valentin N. Mitochondrial Biogenesis & Breakdown. Galkin, Alexander V., tr. from RUS. LC 84-12157. 378p. 1985. 95.00 (*0-306-10979-4*, Kluwer Plenum) Kluwer Academic.

— Mitochondrial Biogenesis & Breakdown. Roodyn, Donald B., ed. Galkin, Alexander V., tr. LC 84-12157. (Illus.). 378p. 1985. reprint ed. pap. 117.20 (*0-608-05420-8*, 206588900006) Bks Demand.

Luzio, Aldo Di, see Auer, Peter & Di Luzio, Aldo, eds.

Luzio, Eduardo. The Microcomputer Industry in Brazil: The Case of a Protected High Technology Industry. LC 94-36640. 192p. 1996. 62.95 (*0-275-94923-0*, Praeger Pubs) Greenwood.

Luzio, J. P. & Thompson, R. J. Macromolecular Aspects of Medical Biochemistry. (Illus.). 278p. (C). 1990. text 85.00 (*0-521-26083-3*); pap. text 30.95 (*0-521-27828-7*) Cambridge U Pr.

Luzio, N. R. Di, see International Symposium on Atherosclerosis Staff.

Luzmeier, Tom & Taylor, Jesse. Making Your Living from the Stockmarket: A How-To Book for the Novice Investor. LC 93-74997. 184p. (Orig.). pap. 24.95 (*0-9639975-0-5*) Blue Walrus.

Luzor, ed. Myanmar Newspaper Reader. LC 96-86039. 328p. 1997. 54.00 (*1-881265-48-X*) Dunwoody Pr.

Luzot, Muriel, tr. see Hindman, Sandra.

Luzot, Muriel, tr. see Hindman, Sandra & Rowe, Nina A.

Luzsa, G. X-Ray Anatomy of the Vascular System. 388p. (C). 1975. 75.00 (*963-05-0060-4*, Pub. by Akade Kiado) St Mut.

Luzuriaga, Carlos & Zuvekas, Clarence, Jr. Income Distribution & Poverty in Rural Ecuador: 1950-1979, A Survey of the Literature. LC 83-5174. 243p. (C). 1983. 19.00 (*0-87918-054-4*) ASU Lat Am St.

Luzuriaga, Gerardo & Reeve, Richard, eds. Los Clasicos del Teatro Hispanoamerican, I (The Classics of Latin American Theater, I) (SPA.). 543p. 1975. pap. 17.99 (*968-16-4006-3*, Pub. by Fondo) Continental Bk.

— Los Clasicos del Teatro Hispanoamericano, II (The Classics of Latin American Theater, II) (SPA.). 562p. 1975. pap. 17.99 (*968-16-4486-7*, Pub. by Fondo) Continental Bk.

Luzz. Making Career Decisions That Count: A Practical Guide. 148p. (C). 1996. pap. text 26.60 (*0-13-777731-0*) P-H.

Luzzaro, Susan. Complicity: Poems. 32p. (Orig.). 1996. pap. 7.00 (*0-932264-17-4*) Trask Hse Bks.

— Flesh Envelope. 1997. pap. text 8.95 (*0-931122-88-0*) West End.

Luzzati, Daniel, et al, eds. Le Dialogique: Colloque International sur les Formes Philosophiques, Linguistiques, Litteraires, et Cognitives du Dialogue Universite du Maine, 15-16 Septembre, 1994. (Sciences pour la Communication Ser.: Vol. 51). (FRE.). 410p. 1997. 51.95 (*3-906759-11-3*, Pub. by P Lang) P Lang Pubng.

Luzzato. The Path of the Just-Mesilath Yesharim. 1982. pap. 15.95 (*0-87306-115-2*) Feldheim.

Luzzato, Moshe Chaim. The Path of the Just-Mesilath Yesharim. Silverstein, Shraga, tr. 1990. 8.95 (*0-87306-239-6*) Feldheim.

Luzzatti, M. Nautics an English Reader. 275p. 1976. pap. text 49.95 (*0-8288-5744-X*, M9295) Fr & Eur.

Luzzatto & La Penna, eds. Babrii. (GRE.). 1986. 75.00 (*3-322-00339-6*, T1112, Pub. by B G Teubner) U of Mich Pr.

Luzzatto, Moshe C. Daat Tevnoth: The Knowing Heart. Silverstein, Shraga, tr. from HEB. (Torah Classics Library). 357p. 1982. 18.95 (*0-87306-194-2*) Feldheim.

— The Path of the Upright: Mesillat Yesharim. Kaplan, Mordecai Menaheim, tr. LC 94-40542. 504p. 1995. 30.00 (*1-56821-427-8*) Aronson.

— Ways of Reason: Guide to Talmudic Reasoning & Logic. 1992. 24.95 (*0-87306-495-X*) Feldheim.

Luzzatto, Moshe Chaim. The Book of Logic. Sackton, David & Tcholkowsky, Chaim, trs. (ENG & HEB.). 264p. 1995. 24.95 (*0-87306-707-X*) Feldheim.

— Serving Our Creator. Kaplan, Aryeh, tr. 9.95 (*1-58330-124-0*) Feldheim.

Luzzi, D. E., et al, eds. Beam-Solid Interactions for Materials Synthesis & Characterization, Vol. 354. (MRS Symposium Proceedings Ser.). 746p. 1995. 85.00 (*1-55899-255-3*) Materials Res.

***Luzzo, Darrell A.** Career Counseling of College Students: An Empirical Guide to Strategies That Work. LC 00-44751. 2000. boxed set. write for info. (*1-55798-708-4*) Am Psychol.

LVA Basic Reading Task Force Staff. Basic Reading Tutor Training Workshop. Lawson, V. K., ed. 1981. student ed. 550.00 incl. audio, sl. (*0-930713-42-7*); 2.75 (*0-318-41707-3*) Lit Vol Am.

***Lvfgren, Orvar.** On Holiday: A History of Vacationing. LC 99-31304. 347p. 1999. 29.95 (*0-520-21767-5*, Pub. by U CA Pr) Cal Prin Full Svc.

LVIS, Cookbook Committee Staff. The East Hampton LVIS Centennial Cookbook: Celebrating the 100th Anniversary of the Ladies' Village Improvement Society of East Hampton, Long Island. LC 94-76712. 304p. 1994. 10.00 (*0-9641759-0-8*) Ladies Village.

L'vov-Anokhin, B. Galina Ulanova. (RUS.). 350p. 1984. 42.00 (*0-7855-0921-6*) St Mut.

Lvov, Arkady A., ed. see Vysotskii, Vladimir.

Lvov, Dmitri K., jt. auth. see Zhdanov, V. M.

Lvov, Dmitri K., ed. see Balandin, I. G., et al.

Lvov, Dmitri K., ed. see Frolov, A. V., et al.

Lvov, Dmitri K., jt. ed. see Mahy, Brian W.

Lvov, N., jt. auth. see Davats, V.

L'Vov, V. S. & Fuchssteiner, B., eds. Wave Turbulence under Parametric Excitation. LC 94-25113. (Nonlinear Dynamics Ser.). 352p. 1994. 108.95 (*0-387-51991-2*) Spr-Verlag.

***Lvov, Yurij & Mhohwald, H.** Protein Architecture. LC 99-38871. 394p. 1999. 175.00 (*0-8247-8236-4*) Dekker.

Lvov, Yurij, jt. auth. see Eaton, Joseph W.

L'Vovich, M. I. World Water Resources & Their Future. LC 79-67029. (Illus.). 416p. 1979. 34.00 (*0-87590-224-3*) Am Geophysical.

Lvovich, Natasha. The Multilingual Self: An Inquiry into Language Learning. LC 97-6164. 1997. pap. 16.50 (*0-8058-2320-4*) L Erlbaum Assocs.

Lwanga, Stephen K. & Lemeshow, S. Sample Size Determination in Health Studies: A Practical Manual. (ENG, FRE & SPA.). viii, 80p. 1991. pap. text 16.00 (*92-4-154405-8*, 1150336) World Health.

Lwanga, Stephen K. & Tye, Cho-Yook, eds. Teaching Health Statistics: Twenty Lesson & Seminar Outlines. (ARA, FRE & SPA.). 230p. 1986. pap. text 39.00 (*92-4-156090-8*, 1150261) World Health.

***Lwin, Claudia S.** The Food of Burma: Authentic Recipes from the Land of the Golden Pagoda. (Food of the World Series). (Illus.). 144p. 1999. pap. 16.95 (*962-593-411-1*) Periplus.

***Lwin, Claudia Saw.** The Food of Burma: Authentic Recipes from the Land of the Golden Pagoda. (Illus.). 120p. 1999. 18.95 (*962-593-812-5*, Pub. by Periplus) Tuttle Pubng.

— Food of Burma: Authentic Recipes from the Land of the Golden Pagodas. (World Foods sER.). (Illus.). 144p. 2000. 18.95 (*962-593-600-9*) Periplus.

Lwin, Claudia Saw, jt. auth. see Periplus Editions Staff.

Ly, Filip De, see De Ly, Filip.

Ly, Judith, jt. auth. see Lewins, Frank.

Ly Kim Tran, jt. auth. see Song Nhi.

Ly Kim Tran, ed. see Thanh-Thanh (Nhuan Le X), et al.

Ly, Tran D. American Clocks Vol. 1: A Guide to Identification & Prices. (Illus.). 320p. 1989. pap. 49.50 (*0-930163-39-7*) Arlington Bk.

— American Clocks Vol. 1: Price Guide Up-Date, 2000. 16p. 1995. pap. 10.00 (*0-930163-52-4*) Arlington Bk.

— American Clocks Vol. 2: With a Special Section on Self-Winding Clocks. (Illus.). 336p. 1991. pap. 49.50 (*0-930163-44-3*) Arlington Bk.

— American Clocks Vol. 2: 1996 Price Guide Up-Date. 12p. 1996. pap. 5.00 (*0-930163-54-0*) US Bks.

— French Clocks & Bronzes: Price Guide Up-Date, 1995. 12p. 1995. pap. 5.00 (*0-9647406-3-X*) US Bks.

— Gustav Becker Clocks: A Guide to Identification & Prices. (Illus.). 248p. 1997. 35.00 (*0-9647406-5-6*); pap. 29.50 (*0-9647406-6-4*) US Bks.

— Longcase Clocks & Standing Regulators Pt. 1: Machine Made Clocks. (Illus.). 1994. 69.50 (*0-930163-60-5*) Arlington Bk.

— Seth Thomas Clock & Movements: 1996 Revised & Price Up-Date. 2nd enl. ed. (Illus.). 496p. (C). 1996. reprint ed. 49.50 (*0-9647406-0-5*) US Bks.

— Seth Thomas Clock & Movements: 1996 Revised & Price Up-Date. 2nd enl. rev. ed. (Illus.). 496p. (C). 1996. pap. 39.50 (*0-9647406-1-3*) US Bks.

— Seth Thomas Clocks & Movements: Price Guide Up-Date, 1995. 12p. 1995. pap. 5.00 (*0-9647406-2-1*) US Bks.

— Ulysse Nardin Chronometers, Pocket Watches & Wrist Watches with 1988 Price Guide. (Illus.). 20p. 1988. pap. 4.95 (*0-930163-66-4*) Arlington Bk.

— Waterbury Clocks: Price Guide Up-Date, 1996. (Illus.). 12p. 1996. pap. 5.00 (*0-930163-69-9*) Arlington Bk.

— Welch Clocks. (Illus.). 304p. 1992. pap. 32.95 (*0-685-60154-4*) Arlington Bk.

— Welch Clocks: Price Guide Up-Date, 1992. 8p. 1992. pap. 5.00 (*0-930163-64-8*) Arlington Bk.

Ly, Tran D., tr. Calendar Clocks. (Illus.). 360p. 1993. 49.50 (*0-930163-43-5*) Arlington Bk.

Ly, Xeng, tr. see Leyman, Jean.

Lyakhovich, L. S. Thermochemical Treatment of Metals & Alloys. 1986. 36.00 (*81-205-0049-0*, Pub. by Oxford IBH) S Asia.

Lyal, Richard, jt. auth. see Farmer, Paul.

Lyall. Space Law. 79.95 (*1-85521-104-1*) Ashgate Pub Co.

Lyall, ed. Diwans of Abid Ibn Al-Abras of Asad & Amir Ibn At-Tufail of Amir Ibn Sa Sa Ah. (Gibb Memorial Ser.: Vol. 21). 1980. 38.50 (*0-906094-13-5*, Pub. by Aris & Phillips) David Brown.

Lyall, A. C. Whakatohea of Opotiki. LC 97-200099. 220p. 1997. write for info. (*0-7900-0570-0*) Reed Pubng.

Lyall, Alan. The First Descent of the Matterhorn: A Bibliographical Guide to the 1865 Accident & Its Aftermath. 1998. 135.00 (*0-8464-4805-X*) Beekman Pubs.

Lyall, Alfred. Tennyson. LC 76-53034. (Studies in Tennyson: No. 27). 1977. lib. bdg. 75.00 (*0-8383-2164-X*) M S G Haskell Hse.

Lyall, Alfred C. History of India from the Close of the Seventeenth Century to the Present Time. LC 72-14391. (History of India Ser.: No. 8). reprint ed. 110.00 (*0-404-09008-7*) AMS Pr.

— The Rise & Expansion of the British Dominion in India. 5th ed. (Illus.). reprint ed. text 28.50 (*0-685-13409-1*) Coronet Bks.

— Studies in Literature & History. LC 68-29227. (Essay Index Reprint Ser.). 1977. reprint ed. 23.95 (*0-8369-0637-3*) Ayer.

— Warren Hastings. LC 73-140364. (Select Bibliographies Reprint Ser.). 1977. reprint ed. 20.95 (*0-8369-5607-9*) Ayer.

Lyall, Beth, jt. ed. see Funk, Kenneth.

Lyall, Bob. The Tokens, Checks, Metallic Tickets, Passes, & Tallies of the British Caribbean & Bermuda. Schenkman, David E., ed. (Illus.). 210p. 1989. text 35.00 (*0-918492-08-4*) TAMS.

Lyall, David. Counselling in the Pastoral & Spiritual Context. LC 94-26387. (Counselling in Context Ser.). 176p. 1994. pap. 29.95 (*0-335-19162-2*) OpUniv Pr.

Lyall, Ernie. Arctic Man. 239p. 1979. mass mkt. 6.95 (*0-88780-106-4*, Pub. by Formac Publ Co) Formac Dist Ltd.

Lyall, Fiona & El Haj, A. J., eds. Biomechanics & Cells. LC 93-42046. (Society for Experimental Biology Seminar Ser.: No. 54). (Illus.). 287p. (C). 1994. text 90.00 (*0-521-45454-9*) Cambridge U Pr.

Lyall, Francis. A Death in Time. large type ed. (Lythway Ser.). 267p. 1991. 24.95 (*0-7451-1307-9*, G K Hall Lrg Type) Mac Lib Ref.

— The I Am Sayings of Jesus. 10.99 (*0-614-11568-X*, Pub. by Christian Focus) Spring Arbor Dist.

— The I Am Sayings of Jesus. unabridged ed. 176p. 1996. 150.99 (*1-85792-185-2*, Pub. by Christian Focus) Spring Arbor Dist.

— Law & Space Telecommunications. 1989. text 129.95 (*1-85521-039-8*, Pub. by Dartmth Pub) Ashgate Pub Co.

— Of Presbyters & Kings: Church & State in the Law of Scotland. 220p. 1980. 27.00 (*0-08-025715-1*, Pergamon Pr) Elsevier.

— Slaves, Citizens, Sons: Legal Metaphors in the Epistles. 320p. 1984. pap. 14.95 (*0-310-45191-4*, 12452P) Zondervan.

***Lyall, G.** All Honourable Men. (J). 1998. mass mkt. 13.95 (*0-340-70855-7*, Pub. by Hodder & Stought Ltd) Trafalgar.

Lyall, Gavin. The Crocus List. large type ed. 512p. 1986. 11.50 (*0-7089-8327-8*, Charnwood) Ulverscroft.

— Judas Country. large type ed. 1977. 27.99 (*0-7089-0069-0*) Ulverscroft.

— Uncle Target. large type ed. 487p. 1989. 27.99 (*0-7089-1945-6*) Ulverscroft.

— Venus with Pistol. large type ed. 1975. 27.99 (*0-85456-370-9*) Ulverscroft.

Lyall, John & Anisfeld, Michael H. Audit by Mail: Time & Cost-Effective GMP Audit Tools. 143p. 1995. ring bd. 247.00 (*0-935184-66-X*) Interpharm.

Lyall, Katharine C., jt. auth. see Rossi, Peter H.

***Lyall, Leslie.** Three of China's Mighty Men: Leaders of the Chinese Church under Persecution. 2000. pap. 7.99 (*1-85792-493-2*) Christian Focus.

Lyall, Leslie T. God Reigns in China. 1985. pap. 6.95 (*0-340-36199-9*) OMF Bks.

Lyall, Leslie T., ed. The Phoenix Rises: The Phenomenal Growth of Eight Chinese Churches. 145p. (Orig.). 1992. pap. 5.95 (*981-3009-04-7*) OMF Bks.

Lyall, R. Coun in Pastoral Con. LC 94-26387. (Counselling in Context Ser.). 1994. write for info. (*0-335-19163-0*) OpUniv Pr.

Lyall, R. J. Ane Resonyng of Ane Scottis & Inglis Merchand Betuix Rowand & Lionis: William Lamb (c. 1494 - c. 1550) Ane Resonyng. 250p. 1985. pap. text 18.50 (*0-08-028485-X*, Pergamon Pr) Elsevier.

Lyall, Robert. Travels in Russia, the Krimea, the Caucasus & Georgia. LC 74-115560. (Russia Observed Ser., No. 1). 1970. reprint ed. 52.95 (*0-405-03046-0*) Ayer.

Lyall, Roderick J. Ane Resonyng of Ane Scottis & Inglis Merchand Betuix Rowand & Lionis: William Lamb (c. 1494 - c. 1550) Ane Resonyng. 250p. 1985. text 35.00 (*0-08-030386-2*, Pergamon Pr) Elsevier.

Lyall, Sutherland. Designing the New Landscape. LC 97-61180. (Illus.). 240p. 1998. pap. 29.95 (*0-500-28033-9*, Pub. by Thames Hudson) Norton.

— Imagination Headquarters: London 1990 Herron Associates. (Architecture in Detail Ser.). (Illus.). 60p. (C). 1993. pap. 29.95 (*0-7148-2764-9*, Pub. by Phaidon Press) Phaidon Pr.

— The Lady & the Unicorn. (Temporis Ser.). (Illus.). 220p. 2000. 55.00 (*1-85995-519-3*) Parkstone Pr.

— Waters of Life: Impressions of Water in Russian Painting. (Temporis Ser.). 200p. 1999. 55.00 (*1-85995-567-3*) Parkstone Pr.

Lyall, Victoria & Schweke, William. Using Alliance-Based Development Strategies for Economic Empowerment. 81p. 1996. pap. 15.00 (*1-883187-11-7*) Corp Ent Dev.

Lyan, David, jt. auth. see Harris, Patricia.

Lyapunov, A. M. The General Problem of the Stability of Motion. Fuller, A. T., ed. & tr. by. (Control Theory & Applications Ser.). 280p. 1992. 65.00 (*0-7484-0062-1*, Pub. by Tay Francis Ltd) Taylor & Francis.

Lyas, Colin. Aesthetics. (Fundamentals of Philosophy Ser.). (Illus.). 256p. 1993. pap. 19.95 (*0-7735-1647-6*, Pub. by McG-Queens Univ Pr) CUP Services.

— Aesthetics. (Fundamentals of Philosophy Ser.). (Illus.). 256p. 1997. 60.00 (*0-7735-1646-8*, Pub. by McG-Queens Univ Pr) CUP Services.

***Lyas, Colin.** Peter Winch. (Philosophy Now Ser.). 2000. 57.50 (*1-902683-01-3*); pap. text 19.95 (*1-902683-02-1*) Acumen Pub.

Lyas, Colin, tr. see Croce, Benedetto.

Lyatsky, Henry V. Continental-Crust Structures on the Continental Margin of Western North America. LC 96-2184. (Lecture Notes in Earth Sciences Ser.: Vol. 62). (Illus.). 352p. 1996. pap. 117.00 (*3-540-60842-7*) Spr-Verlag.

***Lyatsky, Henry V. & Lyatsky, Vadim B.** The Cordilleran Miogeosyncline in North America: Geologic Evolution & Tectonic Nature. LC 99-34037. (Lecture Notes in Earth Sciences Ser.: Vol. 86). (Illus.). xx, 384p. 1999. pap. 120.00 (*3-540-66197-2*) Spr-Verlag.

Lyatsky, Vadim B., jt. auth. see Lyatsky, Henry V.

Lyback-Dahl, Susui M. Klara's Beautiful Isle of Love. (Illus.). 81p. (Orig.). (J). 1996. pap. write for info. (*1-57579-027-0*) Pine Hill Pr.

Lyback, Johanna R. Indian Legends. (Long Ago Ser.). (Illus.). 279p. (J). (gr. 3 up). 1994. reprint ed. pap. 7.95 (*1-877976-15-6*, 406-0012) Tipi Pr.

This collection of stories represents the origin, myths & legends of American Indians from over 15 major tribes, & 48 states of the U.S.A. These timeless tales tell of the Native American's sacred beliefs passed down from generation to generation. "The American Indian was a natural storyteller. Seeing, as he did, an omen in every shifting shade of the clouds, a sign in the changing leaf, a token of beauty or ugliness in different places in the wildwood, he knew no rock nor river, lake nor mountain, valley nor hillside that did not speak of some attraction, some vision of race, some deed of valor, incident of love or remembrance of wrong. These memories lived in stories that were told & retold to each succeeding generation, from time immemorial." - Johanna R. M. Lyback. INDIAN LEGENDS was originally published in 1925 by Lyons & Carnahan & reprinted by Tipi Press of St. Joseph's Indian School in its original form in hopes of keeping wonderful myths & legends of the American Indian alive for generations to come. The 279-page book features over 100 illustrations. Available from Tipi Press, St. Joseph's Indian School, Chamberlain, SD 57326; 605-734-3300; FAX: 605-734-3480. *Publisher Paid Annotation.*

Lyback, Phyllis. Fifty Thousand Holes. (Illus.). 112p. 1996. pap. write for info. (*1-57579-036-X*) Pine Hill Pr.

Lybar & Fry. Cowboys: Thematic Unit. 80p. (Orig.). (J). (gr. 3-5). 1996. pap., wbk. ed. 9.95 (*1-55734-593-7*) Tchr Create Mat.

Lybarger, Donald F. Dowler: Story of the Dowler-Hartshorne Fisher-Lybarger Families. 63p. 1997. reprint ed. pap. 13.50 (*0-8328-8350-6*); reprint ed. lib. bdg. 23.50 (*0-8328-8349-2*) Higginson Bk Co.

Lybarger, Jeffrey A., et al, eds. Priority Health Conditions: An Integrated Strategy to Evaluate the Relationship Between Illness & Exposure to Hazardous Substances. 214p. (Orig.). (C). 1994. pap. text 50.00 (*0-7881-0530-2*) DIANE Pub.

Lybbert, Blair. Transforming Learning with Block Scheduling: A Guide for Principals. LC 98-9075. (Illus.). 164p. 1998. 45.95 (*0-8039-6657-1*); pap. 19.95 (*0-8039-6658-X*) Corwin Pr.

Lybeck, Johan, jt. auth. see Engstrom, Peter.

Lybeck, Kevin L., et al. The Law of Payment Bonds. LC 97-47681. 1998. 99.95 (*1-57073-532-8*) Amer Bar Assn.

Lyberg, Lars & Biemer, Paul. Survey Measurement & Process Quality. LC 96-44720. 808p. 1997. 109.95 (*0-471-16559-X*) Wiley.

Lyberg, M. D., ed. Source Book for Energy Auditors, 2 vols., Set. 694p. (Orig.). 1987. pap. 170.00 (*91-540-4763-3*) Coronet Bks.

Lybrand & IFR Publishing Copper Staff. 855 Coopers & Lybrand Set. 1994. per. 200.00 (*1-55738-855-5*, Irwn Prfssnl) McGraw-Hill Prof.

Lybrand, jt. auth. see Coopers.

Lybrand, Carole. Cultivating Your Christian Life. 128p. (Orig.). 1994. pap. 6.95 (*0-89114-209-6*) Baptist Pub Hse.

Lybrand, Fred, Jr. Heavenly Citizenship. 140p. (Orig.). 1993. pap. 9.99 (*1-56043-785-5*, Treasure Hse) Destiny Image.

Lybrand, Fred R., Jr. The Absolute Quickest Way to Help Your Child Change. Ross, Todd, ed. 200p. (Orig.). 1996. pap. text 15.00 (*0-9652497-0-0*) Kauffman Burgess.

Lybrand, William A., et al. A Study on Evaluation of Driver Education. LC 75-121262. 225p. 1968. 19.00 (*0-403-04515-0*) Scholarly.

Lybrand, William A., jt. ed. see Lipkin, Mack, Jr.

Lybyer, Albert H. The Government of the Ottoman Empire in the Time of Suleiman the Magnificent. LC 75-41305. reprint ed. 39.50 (*0-404-14681-3*) AMS Pr.

Lybyer, J. M. David Copperfield Notes. (Cliffs Notes Ser.). 80p. 1959. pap. 4.95 (*0-8220-0364-3*, Cliff) IDG Bks.

— Lord Jim Notes. (Cliffs Notes Ser.). 80p. 1962. pap. 4.95 (*0-8220-0762-2*, Cliff) IDG Bks.

— Poe's Short Stories: Notes. (Cliffs Notes Ser.). 72p. (Orig.). (C). 1981. pap. text 4.95 (*0-8220-1046-1*, Cliff) IDG Bks.

— The Red Badge of Courage Notes. (Cliffs Notes Ser.). 88p. 1964. pap. 4.95 (*0-8220-1120-4*, Cliff) IDG Bks.

— Uncle Tom's Cabin Notes. (Cliffs Notes Ser.). 72p. 1984. pap. text 4.95 (*0-8220-1313-4*, Cliff) IDG Bks.

Lycan, William, ed. Mind & Cognition: An Anthology. 2nd ed. LC 98-35450. (Blackwell Philosophy Anthologies Ser.). 630p. 1999. 64.95 (*0-631-21204-3*); pap. 34.95 (*0-631-20545-4*) Blackwell Pubs.

Lycan, William G. Consciousness. (Illus.). 181p. 1995. pap. text 16.00 (*0-262-62096-0*, Bradford Bks) MIT Pr.

— Consciousness & Experience. 231p. 1996. 35.00 (*0-262-12197-2*, Bradford Bks) MIT Pr.

— Logical Form in Natural Language. 360p. 1984. 39.50 (*0-262-12108-5*, Bradford Bks) MIT Pr.

— Logical Form in Natural Language. 360p. 1986. pap. text 12.50 (*0-262-62053-7*, Bradford Bks) MIT Pr.

L

An Asterisk (*) at the beginning of an entry indicates that the title is appearing for the first time.

— Mind & Cognition. 340p. 1990. pap. text 34.95 (*0-631-16763-3*) Blackwell Pubs.

— Modality & Meaning. (Studies in Linguistics & Philosophy). 334p. (C). 1994. lib. bdg. 117.50 (*0-7923-3006-4*, Pub. by Kluwer Academic) Kluwer Academic.

— Modality & Meaning. (Studies in Linguistics & Philosophy). 334p. (C). 1995. pap. text 64.00 (*0-7923-3007-2*, Pub. by Kluwer Academic) Kluwer Academic.

***Lycan, William G.** Philosophy of Language: Contemporary Introduction. LC 99-29547. (Contemporary Introductions to Philosophy Ser.). 224p. (C). 1999. text 65.00 (*0-415-17115-6*) Routledge.

— Philosophy of Language: Contemporary Introduction. LC 99-29547. (Contemporary Introductions to Philosophy Ser.). 224p. 2000. pap. 19.99 (*0-415-17116-4*) Routledge.

Lycan, William G., jt. auth. see Boer, Steven E.

Lycan, William G., jt. auth. see Pospesel, Howard.

***Lycett, Andrew.** Ian Fleming: The Man Behind James Bond. (Illus.). 486p. 1999. reprint ed. text 25.00 (*0-7881-6656-5*) DIANE Pub.

Lycett, G. W., jt. ed. see Ginerson, D.

Lycett, Simon. Candle Creations. LC 98-23211. (Illus.). 112p. 1999. pap. 19.95 (*0-8092-2782-7*, 278270, Contemporary Bks) NTC Contemp Pub Co.

***Lycett, Simon.** Decorating with Herbs: Beautiful & Fragrant Projects for Your Home. LC 98-45013. 1999. 24.95 (*0-7621-0126-1*, Pub. by RD Assn) Penguin Putnam.

— Flowers with a Flourish: Floral Designs for Every Season. LC 98-51605. (Illus.). 192p. 1999. 22.95 (*1-57145-641-4*, Laurel Glen Pub) Advantage Pubs.

Lycett, Simon. Served with a Flourish: Novel Ways to Present Food for Every Occasion. LC 99-40453. (Illus.). 176p. 1999. 22.95 (*1-57145-646-5*, Laurel Glen Pub) Advantage Pubs.

Lychack, William. England. LC 95-10109. (Games People Play Ser.). (Illus.). 64p. (J). (gr. 4-6). 1995. lib. bdg. 23.50 (*0-516-04436-2*) Childrens.

— Russia. LC 96-31126. (Games People Play Ser.). 64p. (J). (gr. 4-6). 1996. lib. bdg. 23.50 (*0-516-04441-9*) Childrens.

Lychagin, V. V., ed. The Interplay Between Differential Geometry & Differential Equations. LC 91-640741. (American Mathematical Society Translations Ser.: Series 2, Vol. 167). 294p. 1995. 98.00 (*0-8218-0428-6*, TRANS2/167C) Am Math.

Lychak, M., jt. auth. see Kuntzevich, V. M.

Lyche, T., jt. ed. see Goldman, R. N.

Lycholat, Tony. The Complete Book of Stretching. (Illus.). 96p. 1995. pap. 17.95 (*1-85223-917-4*, Pub. by Crolwood) Trafalgar.

Lyck, L. & Boyko, V. I., eds. Management, Technology, & Human Resources Policy in the Artic (the North) (NATO ASI Ser.: Vol. 4). 1996. text 276.00 (*0-7923-4023-X*) Kluwer Academic.

Lycke, Ruth E. Y2K Why Me? Everything You Need to Ask Yourself to Prepare for January 1, 2000. (Illus.). 96p. 1999. pap. 9.95 (*1-928858-01-5*) Edgemont Inc.

Lyco Press Development Team Staff. Internet Games Directory. 1996. pap. text 29.99 incl. cd-rom (*1-56276-463-2*, Ziff-Davis Pr) Que.

Lycophron. Alexandra. 427p. 1973. reprint ed. write for info. (*3-487-04686-5*) G Olms Pubs.

— Alexandra, Vol. I. Scheer, Eduard, ed. xxxii, 148p. 1958. write for info. (*3-296-14501-X*) G Olms Pubs.

— Alexandra, Vol. II. Scheer, Eduard, ed. lxiv, 398p. 1958. write for info. (*3-296-14502-8*) G Olms Pubs.

— The Alexandra of Lycophron. Connor, W. R., ed. LC 78-18587. (Greek Texts & Commentaries Ser.). (ENG & GRE., Illus.). 1979. reprint ed. lib. bdg. 21.95 (*0-405-11429-X*) Ayer.

Lycos Development Group Staff. Most Popular Web Sites. 2nd ed. 1997. 39.99 (*0-7897-1246-6*) Macmillan.

Lycos, Kimon. Plato on Justice & Power: Reading Book I of Plato's Republic. LC 86-19166. (SUNY Series in Philosophy). 201p. (C). 1987. text 21.50 (*0-88706-415-9*) State U NY Pr.

Lycos Press Development Staff. Business Resources Web Directory. (Lycos Insites Ser.). 1997. pap. text 39.99 incl. cd-rom (*1-56276-466-7*, Lycos Pr) Que.

— Internet International Directory, 1997. 1996. pap. text 39.99 incl. cd-rom (*0-7897-1054-4*, Ziff-Davis Pr) Que.

Lycos Press Staff. Most Popular Web Sites: The Best of the Net from A2Z. 1272p. 1996. 49.99 (*0-7897-0792-6*) Que.

— Most Popular Web Sites: The/Best of the Net from A to Z. 2nd ed. LC 97-69185. 1128p. 1997. 39.99 (*0-7897-1348-9*) Que.

Lyczkowski, Robert W., ed. see American Society of Mechanical Engineers Staff.

Lyda, Hap C. History of Biblical Judaism: An Introductory Study of the Bible. 3rd ed. LC 93-39503. 1994. pap. 19.95 (*0-9630629-2-1*) Twenty Fst Century.

Lydall. Critique of Orthodox Economics: An Alternative Model. LC 97-38377. 208p. 1998. text 69.95 (*0-312-21143-0*) St Martin.

Lydall, Harold F. Trade & Employment: A Study of the Effects of Trade Expansion on Employment in Developing & Developed Countries (WEP Study) x, 140p. 1975. 24.75 (*92-2-101240-9*); pap. 15.75 (*92-2-101239-5*) Intl Labour Office.

— Yugoslav Socialism: Theory & Practice. (Illus.). 302p. 1987. pap. text 22.00 (*0-19-828583-3*) OUP.

Lydamore, Margaret, tr. see Hamman, Adalbert.

Lyday, Bruce W. How to Pass Your Police Oral Interview. (Orig.). 1997. pap. 11.95 (*0-9657506-0-4*) W Coast Police.

Lyday, Cookie. Country Ribbon Crafts: Delightful Projects Using Easy Techniques. LC 94-35542. (Illus.). 144p. 1995. 27.95 (*0-8069-0990-0*, Chapelle) Sterling.

— Country Ribbon Crafts: Delightful Projects Using Easy Techniques. (Illus.). 144p. 1996. pap. 14.95 (*0-8069-0991-9*) Sterling.

Lyday, Leon F., jt. auth. see Dauster, F.

Lyday, Richard W., jt. auth. see Wheeler, Donald J.

Lyddon, Eileen. Door Through Darkness: John of the Cross & Mysticism in Everyday Life. 176p. (Orig.). 1995. pap. 9.95 (*1-56548-037-6*) New City.

Lyddon, Jan W., jt. auth. see Layzell, Daniel T.

***Lydecker, Beatrice.** Seasons: My Journey Through the Three Dimensions of Natural Healing. McNeil, Beth, ed. (Illus.). 272p. 1999. pap. 16.95 (*0-9622094-9-X*, Living Free Pubns) B Lydecker.

— Stories the Animals Tell Me. 2nd ed. 158p. 1979. reprint ed. pap. 8.95 (*0-9622094-0-6*) B Lydecker.

Lydecker, Beatrice C. Stories Animals Tell Me: 17 Stories of Animals Ben Lydecker Talked to Who Have Related Their Life Story As They "See It" (Illus.). 160p. 1988. reprint ed. 8.95 (*0-06-250550-5*) B Lydecker.

— What the Animals Tell Me: A Noted Expert Tells You How to Understand What Your Pet Wants You to Know . . . Psychological Handbook for Pets & How to Tell They Have a Psychological Problem & What to Do about It. LC 76-9997. 160p. 1989. reprint ed. pap. 7.95 (*0-06-091557-9*, PL 1557) B Lydecker.

Lydecker, Toni. Serves One: Super Meals for Solo Cooks. LC 98-65710. 192p. 1998. pap. text 14.95 (*1-891105-01-9*) Lake Isle Pr.

Lydeen, Lottie F. Human Concepts of Self in Life, Love & Work: Index of New Information with Authors, Subjects & Bibliography. 180p. 1993. 47.50 (*1-55914-790-3*); pap. 44.50 (*1-55914-791-1*) ABBE Pubs Assn.

— Incest - Acts, Myths & Facts: Index of Modern Authors & Subjects with Guide for Rapid Research. LC 90-56269. 200p. 1991. 47.50 (*1-55914-312-6*); pap. 44.50 (*1-55914-313-4*) ABBE Pubs Assn.

— Psychology of Attachment & Bonding: Index of Modern Information. LC 88-47600. 150p. 1988. 47.50 (*0-88164-790-X*); pap. 44.50 (*0-88164-791-8*) ABBE Pubs Assn.

— Sexology Encyclopedia Vol. 9: Incest: Index & Reference Books of New Information. Bartone, John C., ed. (Illus.). 163p. 1996. pap. 39.95 (*0-7883-0867-X*) ABBE Pubs Assn.

— Sexology Encyclopedia Vol. 9: Incest: Index & Reference Books of New Information, 25 vols., Set. Bartone, John C., ed. (Illus.). 163p. 1996. 49.95 (*0-7883-0866-1*) ABBE Pubs Assn.

— Sexual Abuse of Children: Index of Modern Information. LC 89-47967. 150p. 1990. 47.50 (*1-55914-038-0*); pap. 44.50 (*1-55914-039-9*) ABBE Pubs Assn.

Lydekker, Richard. The Great & Small Game of India, Burma & Tibet. LC 98-902763. xviii, 416 p. 1996. write for info. (*81-206-1162-4*) Asian Educ Servs.

Lydekker, Richard & Dollman, J. G. Game Animals of Indian Sub-Continents. 412p. 1985. pap. 175.00 (*0-7855-0362-5*, Pub. by Intl Bks & Periodicals) St Mut.

Lydekker, Richard, jt. auth. see Flower, William H.

Lyden, Fremont J. & Legters, Lyman H., eds. Native Americans & Public Policy. (Orig.). 1988. pap. 15.00 (*0-944285-02-3*) Pol Studies.

Lyden, Fremont J. & Miller, Ernest G. Public Budgeting: Program Planning & Implementation. 4th ed. (Illus.). 384p. (C). 1982. pap. text 16.95 (*0-13-737403-8*) P-H.

Lyden, Fremont J., et al. Training of Good Physicians: Critical Factors in Career Choices. LC 68-21977. (Commonwealth Fund Publications). (Illus.). 262p. 1968. 36.50 (*0-674-90285-8*) HUP.

Lyden, Fremont J., jt. ed. see Legters, Lyman H.

Lyden, Jacki. Daughter of the Queen of Sheba: A Memoir. LC 97-19952. 288p. 1997. 24.00 (*0-395-76531-5*) HM.

— Daughter of the Queen of Sheba: A Memoir. 257p. 1998. pap. 12.95 (*0-14-027684-X*) Viking Penguin.

Lyden, John, ed. Enduring Issues in Religion. (Enduring Issues Ser.). 312p. (C). 1995. pap. text 17.45 (*1-56510-259-2*, 2592); lib. bdg. 27.45 (*1-56510-260-6*, 2606) Greenhaven.

Lyden, John P., jt. auth. see Arnold, William D.

***Lyden, Patrick, ed.** Thrombolytic Therapy for Stroke. 400p. 2000. 125.00 (*0-89603-746-0*) Humana.

***Lyden, Rob.** Distance Running. (Illus.). 320p. 2000. pap. 19.95 (*1-57167-449-7*) Coaches Choice.

Lydenberg, Harry M. & Archer, John. The Care & Repair of Books. 4th rev. ed. LC 60-11980. 128p. reprint ed. pap. 39.70 (*0-608-11159-7*, 201367900087) Bks Demand.

Lydenberg, Robin. Word Cultures: Radical Theory & Practice in William S. Burroughs' Fiction. LC 86-30719. 224p. 1987. text 24.95 (*0-252-01413-8*) U of Ill Pr.

Lydenberg, Robin, jt. ed. see Skerl, Jennie.

Lyders, Josette A. Journal & Newsletter Editing. (Illus.). xv, 209p. 1993. lib. bdg. 35.00 (*0-87287-917-8*) Libs Unl.

Lyders, Richard, jt. auth. see Fingerman, Joel.

Lydersen, Aksel. Mass Transfer in Engineering Practice. LC 82-7086. (Illus.). 335p. 1983. reprint ed. pap. 103.90 (*0-608-05288-4*, 206582600001) Bks Demand.

Lydersen, Bjorn K., ed. Large Scale Cell Culture Technology. 252p. 1993. 110.00 (*0-471-03732-X*) Wiley.

Lydersen, S., et al, eds. Safety & Reliability: Proceedings of the ESREL '98 Conference, Trondheim, Norway, 16-19 June 1998, 2 vols. (Illus.). 1474p. (C). 1998. text 146.00 (*90-5410-966-1*, Pub. by A A Balkema) Ashgate Pub Co.

Lyderson, Bjorn K., ed. see Nelson, Kim L.

Lydgate, Barry, et al. French in Action, Study Guide: A Beginning Course in Language & Culture. 1987. 12.00 (*0-300-03939-5*) Yale U Pr.

Lydgate, J., tr. see De Deguileville, Guillaume.

Lydgate, John. Assembly of Gods, or, the Accord of Reason & Sensuality in the Fear of Death. LC 77-136399. (University of Chicago Studies in English: No. 1). 1970. reprint ed. 37.50 (*0-404-50261-X*) AMS Pr.

— Here Endeth the Book of the Lyf of Our Lady. LC 73-38207. (English Experience Ser.: No. 473). 192p. 1972. reprint ed. 75.00 (*90-221-0473-7*) Walter J Johnson.

— Lydgate's Fall of Princes Pt. 4: Bibliographical Introduction, Notes, & Glossary. Bergen, Henry, ed. LC 23-17910. (Carnegie Institution of Washington Publication Ser.: Vol. 262). 538p. reprint ed. pap. 166.80 (*0-608-06206-5*, 206644300004) Bks Demand.

— Lydgate's Minor Poems: The Two Nightingale Poems. Glauning, Otto, ed. (EETS, ES Ser.: No. 80). 1969. reprint ed. 36.00 (*0-527-00282-8*) Periodicals Srv.

— Lydgate's Reson & Sensuallyte: Studies & Notes, Vol. II. Sieper, Ernst, ed. (ES 89 Ser.). 1967. reprint ed. 9.95 (*0-19-722534-9*) OUP.

— Lydgate's Siege of Thebes, Pt. 2. Erdmann, Axel, ed. (EETS, ES Ser.: No. 125). 1969. reprint ed. 40.00 (*0-527-00311-5*) Periodicals Srv.

— Lydgate's Temple of Glass. Schick, J., ed. (EETS, ES Ser.: No. 60). 1969. reprint ed. 54.00 (*0-527-00263-1*) Periodicals Srv.

— Lydgate's Troy Book, Pt. 1. Bergen, Henry, ed. (EETS, ES Ser.: Nos. 97, 103, 106, 126). 1969. reprint ed. 90.00 (*0-527-00298-4*) Periodicals Srv.

— Lydgate's Troy Book, Pt. 4. Bergen, Henry, ed. (EETS, ES Ser.: Nos. 97, 103, 106, 126). 1969. reprint ed. 70.00 (*0-527-00300-X*) Periodicals Srv.

— Lydgate's Troy Book, Pts. 2-3. Bergen, Henry, ed. (EETS, ES Ser.: Nos. 97, 103, 106, 126). 1969. reprint ed. 65.00 (*0-527-00299-2*) Periodicals Srv.

— The Minor Poems of John Lydgate. (BCL1-PR English Literature Ser.). 1992. reprint ed. lib. bdg. write for info. (*0-7812-7185-1*) Rprt Serv.

— The Minor Poems of John Lydgate, Pt. I. MacCracken, J. N., ed. (EETS, OS Ser.: Nos. 107 & 192). 1974. reprint ed. 40.00 (*0-527-00308-5*) Periodicals Srv.

— The Minor Poems of John Lydgate, Pt. II. MacCracken, J. N., ed. (EETS, OS Ser.: Nos. 107 & 192). 1974. reprint ed. 30.00 (*0-527-00193-7*) Periodicals Srv.

Lydgate, John & Edwards, Robert R. Troy Book: Selections. LC 97-47781. (Middle English Texts Ser.). (ENM.). 430p. 1998. pap. 20.00 (*1-879288-99-0*) Medieval Inst.

Lydgate, Tony. The Art of Making Elegant Jewelry Boxes: Design & Techniques. LC 96-11988. (Illus.). 144p. 1996. pap. 19.95 (*0-8069-4287-8*, Chapelle) Sterling.

— The Art of Making Elegant Wood Boxes: Award Winning Designs. LC 92-38556. (Illus.). 144p. 1993. pap. 17.95 (*0-8069-8838-X*) Sterling.

— The Art of Making Fine Wood Jewelry. LC 97-51566. (Illus.). 144p. 1998. pap. 19.95 (*0-8069-0361-9*) Sterling.

— The Art of Making Small Wood Boxes: Award-Winning Designs. LC 97-15268. (Illus.). 144p. 1997. 19.95 (*0-8069-9576-9*) Sterling.

— Award-Winning Wood Boxes: Design & Techniques. LC 94-48062. (Illus.). 144p. 1995. 17.95 (*0-8069-8841-X*, Chapelle) Sterling.

Lydgate, Tony & Leong, Po Shun. Art Boxes. LC 97-35569. (Illus.). 128p. 1998. pap. 19.95 (*0-8069-9967-5*) Sterling.

***Lydiard, Arthur.** Distance Training for Masters, 1. 2000. pap. text 17.95 (*1-84126-018-5*) Meyer & Meyer.

— Distance Training for Young Athletes. 1998. pap. text 17.95 (*3-89124-533-5*) Meyer & Meyer.

Lydiard, Arthur. Running the Lydiard War. 1978. 12.95 (*0-02-499720-X*, Macmillan Coll) P-H.

Lydiard, Arthur. Running to the Top. 1997. pap. text 17.95 (*3-89124-440-1*) Meyer & Meyer.

— Running with Lydiard. 2000. pap. 17.95 (*1-84126-026-6*) Meyer & Meyer.

Lydiard, Arthur & Gilmour, Garth. Running the Lydiard Way. LC 78-360. (Illus.). 241p. 1978. 12.95 (*0-89037-096-6*) Anderson World.

Lydiard, Teri. The British Columbia Bicycling Guide. (Illus.). 76p. (Orig.). 1984. pap. 9.95 (*0-9691693-0-2*) Gordon Soules Bk.

Lydiate, Liz, ed. Professional Practice in Design Consultancy: A Design Business Association Guide. (Illus.). 208p. (C). 1992. pap. 46.95 (*0-85072-304-3*, Pub. by Design Council Bks) Ashgate Pub Co.

***Lydiatt, William & Johnson, Perry.** Cancers of the Head & Neck: A Guide to Diagnosis & Treatment. (Illus.). 152p. 2000. pap. 14.95 (*1-886039-48-8*, Pub. by Addicus Bks) LPC Group.

— Cancers of the Mouth & Throat: A Patient's Guide to Treatment. 160p. 2000. pap. 14.95 (*1-886039-44-5*, Pub. by Addicus Bks) LPC Group.

Lydic, Ralph, ed. Molecular Regulation of Arousal States. LC 97-21353. (Cellular & Molecular Neuropharmacology Ser.). 256p. 1997. per. 94.95 (*0-8493-3361-X*) CRC Pr.

Lydic, Ralph & Baghdoyan, Helen A. Handbook of Behavioral State Control Molecular & Physiological Mechanisms. LC 98-34858. 688p. 1998. 89.95 (*0-8493-3151-X*, 3151) CRC Pr.

Lydic, Ralph & Biebuyck, Julian F., eds. Clinical Physiology of Sleep. (Clinical Physiology Series - An American Physiological Society Book). (Illus.). 254p. 1988. text 49.00 (*0-19-520780-7*) OUP.

***Lydick, Kelly.** We Once Were. unabridged ed. 29p. 1999. pap. 5.00 (*0-9676887-0-1*) Pure Carbon Pubg.

Lydolph, Paul E. Geography of the U. S. S. R. Includes Supplement Updated to July, 1995. 5th ed. LC 89-63699. (Illus.). 500p. (C). 1990. text 37.50 (*0-9624933-0-9*) Misty Val Pub.

— Weather & Climate. LC 84-18080. (Illus.). 232p. (C). 1985. 47.50 (*0-86598-120-5*, R3924) Rowman.

Lydon, Betsy. The Shoppers' Guide to Better Food Choices: By Betsy Lydon & Mothers & Others for a Livable Planet. Pennybacker, Mindy, ed. (Illus.). x, 100p. (Orig.). 1996. pap. 15.00 (*0-9653607-0-9*, 8883264636) Mothers & Others.

Lydon, James, ed. Law & Disorder in Medieval Ireland: Essays Celebrating the Parliament of 1297. 160p. 1997. boxed set 45.00 (*1-85182-257-7*, Pub. by Four Cts Pr) Intl Spec Bk.

Lydon, James F. The Making of Ireland: A History. LC 98-13707. 432p. 1998. pap. 22.99 (*0-415-01348-8*) Routledge.

— The Making of Ireland: A History. LC 98-13707. 432p. (C). 1998. 75.00 (*0-415-01347-X*) Routledge.

Lydon, John. Rotten: No Irish, No Blacks, No Dogs. 332p. 1995. pap. 14.00 (*0-312-11883-X*) St Martin.

Lydon, Kelly K. The M-Boats of World War I. (Illus.). xii, 124p. 1998. pap. 20.00 (*0-9663091-0-3*) New Eng Seafarer.

Lydon, Mary. Skirting the Issue: Essays in Literary Theory. LC 94-27062. 1995. 48.00 (*0-299-14460-7*); pap. 24.95 (*0-299-14464-X*) U of Wis Pr.

***Lydon, Michael.** Ray Charles: Man & Music. (Illus.). 448p. 2000. pap. 14.95 (*1-57322-780-3*, Riverhd Trade) Berkley Pub.

Lydon, Michael. Ray Charles: Man & Music. LC 98-29602. (Illus.). 448p. 1999. 27.95 (*1-57322-132-5*, Riverhead Books) Putnam Pub Group.

— Rock Folk. 1990. pap. 9.95 (*0-8065-1206-7*, Citadel Pr) Carol Pub Group.

— Writing & Life. LC 95-13843. 110p. 1995. pap. 9.95 (*0-87451-730-3*) U Pr of New Eng.

Lydon, Michael & Mandel, Ellen. Boogie Lightning: How Music Became Electric. (Illus.). 1980. pap. 6.95 (*0-306-80123-X*) Da Capo.

Lydon, Peggy, jt. auth. see Kovac, Lesle.

Lydon, Peter, jt. ed. see Rogers, Peter.

Lydon, Sandy. Chinese Gold: The Chinese in the Monterey Bay Region. LC 84-72699. (Illus.). 550p. (C). 1985. pap. text 24.95 (*0-932319-01-7*) Capitola Bk.

— The Japanese in the Monterey Bay Region: A Brief History. (Illus.). 150p. 1997. pap. 19.95 (*0-932319-05-X*) Capitola Bk.

Lydon, Susan G. The Knitting Sutra. LC 96-34368. 2000. pap. 9.00 (*0-06-251203-X*) Harper SF.

— The Knitting Sutra: Craft as a Spiritual Practice. LC 96-34368. (Illus.). 176p. 1997. 19.00 (*0-06-251202-1*, Pub. by Harper SF) HarpC.

Lydon, William T. & McGraw, M. Loretta. Concept Development for Visually Handicapped Children: A Resource Guide for Teachers & Other Professionals Working in Educational Settings. rev. ed. 80p. 1973. pap. 16.95 (*0-89128-018-9*) Am Foun Blind.

Lydtin, H. & Trenkwalder, P. Calcium Antagonists. (Illus.). 272p. 1989. 86.95 (*0-387-51372-8*, 3257) Spr-Verlag.

Lydtin, Hans, ed. see International Conference on Chemical Vapor Deposit.

***Lydyard, Peter M., et al.** Instant Notes in Immunology. LC 99-58028. (Instant Notes Ser.). (Illus.). 250p. 2000. pap. text 24.95 (*0-387-91586-9*) Spr-Verlag.

— Pathology Integrated: An A-Z of Disease & Its Pathologenesis. (An Arnold Publication). 2000. pap. text 32.50 (*0-340-74063-9*, Pub. by E A) OUP.

***Lye, Keith.** Atlas in the Round: Our Planet as You've Never Seen Before. 32p. (J). (gr. 4-6). 1999. 15.95 (*0-7624-0657-7*) Running Pr.

Lye, Keith. Coasts. Furstinger, Nancy, ed. (Our World Ser.). (Illus.). 48p. (J). (gr. 5-8). 1989. lib. bdg. 12.95 (*0-382-09790-4*) Silver Burdett Pr.

— Cold Climates. LC 96-32759. (The World's Climate Ser.). 48p. (J). 1997. lib. bdg. 24.26 (*0-8172-4825-0*) Raintree Steck-V.

— The Complete Atlas of the World. LC 94-19316. (Illus.). 160p. (J). (gr. 5-12). 1994. lib. bdg. 37.11 (*0-8114-5804-0*) Raintree Steck-V.

— Deserts. (Our World Ser.). (Illus.). 48p. (J). (gr. 5-8). 1987. lib. bdg. 12.95 (*0-382-09501-4*) Silver Burdett Pr.

— Dry Climates. LC 96-31161. (World's Climate Ser.). 48p. (J). 1997. 24.26 (*0-8172-4828-5*) Raintree Steck-V.

— The Earth. (Young Readers' Nature Library). (Illus.). 64p. (J). (gr. 4-6). 1991. lib. bdg. 21.90 (*1-56294-025-2*) Millbrook Pr.

— Earthquakes. 32p. (J). (gr. 1-4). 1996. pap. text 4.95 (*0-8114-9657-0*) Raintree Steck-V.

— Equatorial Climates. LC 96-32758. (World's Climate Ser.). 48p. (J). 1997. lib. bdg. 24.26 (*0-8172-4826-9*) Raintree Steck-V.

— Mountains. (What about Ser.). 32p. (J). (gr. 1-4). 1996. pap. text 4.95 (*0-8114-9659-7*) Raintree Steck-V.

— Mountains. (Our World Ser.). (Illus.). 48p. (J). (gr. 5-8). 1987. lib. bdg. 12.95 (*0-382-09498-0*) Silver Burdett Pr.

***Lye, Keith.** The New Children's Illustrated Atlas of the World. LC 99-75105. (Illus.). 56p. (J). (gr. 4-7). 2000. 9.98 (*0-7624-0643-7*, Courage) Running Pr.

Lye, Keith. The Portable World Factbook. 352p. (Orig.). 1996. pap. 12.00 (*0-380-78570-6*, Avon Bks); pap. 14.00 (*0-380-73051-0*, Avon Bks) Morrow Avon.

— Rocks & Minerals. 32p. (J). (gr. 1-4). 1994. pap. 4.95 (*0-8114-6441-5*) Raintree Steck-V.

— Rocks, Minerals & Fossils. (Our World Ser.). (Illus.). 48p. (J). (gr. 5-8). 1991. lib. bdg. 12.95 (*0-382-24226-2*) Silver Burdett Pr.

— Spain. (Getting to Know Ser.). (Illus.). 48p. (J). (gr. 4-7). 1994. 9.95 (*0-8442-7627-8*, 76278, Natl Textbk Co) NTC Contemp Pub Co.

— Temperate Climates. LC 96-31162. (The World's Climate Ser.). 48p. (J). 1997. lib. bdg. 24.26 (*0-8172-4827-7*) Raintree Steck-V.

An Asterisk (*) at the beginning of an entry indicates that the title is appearing for the first time.

— Volcanoes. 32p. (J). (gr. 1-4). 1996. pap. 4.95 (*0-8114-9665-1*) Raintree Steck-V.

— The World Today. (World of Science Ser.). (Illus.). 64p. (YA). 1985. 15.95 (*0-8160-1072-2*) Facts on File.

Lye, Keith, jt. auth. see Dempsey, Michael W.

Lye, Keith, jt. auth. see Mason, Antony.

Lye, Keith, jt. auth. see Passport Books Editors.

Lyell, Andrew, ed. Memoirs of an Air Observation Post Officer. 162p. (C). 1990. pap. 36.00 (*0-948251-06-9*, Pub. by Picton) St Mut.

***Lyell, Anne M. & Worcester Historical Museum Staff.** Wish You Were Here: Worcester Postcards, CA. 1905-1920 LC 98-61630. 95 Pp. 1998. write for info. (*1-884292-01-1*) Worcester Hist.

Lyell, Anne M., ed. see Lyell, Nan.

Lyell, Charles. Geological Evidence of the Antiquity of Man. 4th ed. LC 72-1728. (Illus.). reprint ed. 72.50 (*0-404-08138-X*) AMS Pr.

— Life, Letters & Journals, 2 vols., Set. Lyell, Katharine M., ed. LC 72-1728. (Darwin Ser.). (Illus.). 488p. (C). 1983. reprint ed. 115.00 (*0-404-08156-8*) AMS Pr.

— Principles of Geology. Secord, James A., ed. & intro. by. LC 98-165644. xlvii, 472p. 1998. pap. 15.95 (*0-14-043528-X*) Viking Penguin.

— Principles of Geology, 4 vols. 11th unabridged ed. (Classic Reprint Ser.). (Illus.). 1323p. 1997. reprint ed. 120.00 (*0-936128-60-7*) De Young Pr.

— Principles of Geology, 3 vols., Set. (Illus.). 1970. reprint ed. text 100.00 (*3-7682-0685-8*) Lubrecht & Cramer.

— Principles of Geology, Vol. 1. LC 90-11008. (Illus.). 586p. 1990. pap. text 22.00 (*0-226-49794-1*) U Ch Pr.

— Principles of Geology, Vol. 1. LC 90-11008. (Illus.). 576p. 1995. lib. bdg. 48.00 (*0-226-49793-3*) U Ch Pr.

— Principles of Geology, Vol. 3. LC 90-11008. (Illus.). 620p. 1991. pap. text 21.00 (*0-226-49799-2*) U Ch Pr.

— Principles of Geology, Vol. 3. LC 90-11008. (Illus.). 620p. 1991. lib. bdg. 46.00 (*0-226-49798-4*) U Ch Pr.

— Principles of Geology, Vol. 2: An Inquiry How Far the Former Changes of the Earth's Surface Are Referable to Causes Now in Operation, Vol. 2. (Illus.). 352p. 1991. lib. bdg. 42.00 (*0-226-49796-8*) U Ch Pr.

— Principles of Geology, Vol. 2: An Inquiry How Far the Former Changes of the Earth's Surface Are Referable to Causes Now in Operation, Vol. 2. (Illus.). 352p. 1991. pap. text 19.50 (*0-226-49797-6*) U Ch Pr.

— A Second Visit to North America, 2 vols., Set. 1955. 79.00 (*0-403-00357-1*) Scholarly.

— A Second Visit to North America, 2 vols., Set. (BCL1 - U. S. History Ser.). 1991. reprint ed. lib. bdg. 150.00 (*0-7812-6012-4*) Rprt Serv.

— Sir Charles Lyell's Scientific Journals on the Species Question. Wilson, Leonard G., ed. LC 77-99848. (Yale Studies in the History of Science & Medicine: No. 5). (Illus.). 636p. reprint ed. pap. 197.20 (*0-8357-8322-7*, 203392200087) Bks Demand.

— Travels in North America, the Years, 1841-2: Geological Observations on the United States, Canada & Nova Scotia, 2 vols. Albritton, Claude C., Jr., ed. LC 77-6525. (History of Geology Ser.). (Illus.). 1978. reprint ed. lib. bdg. 44.95 (*0-405-10447-2*) Ayer.

Lyell, Don, et al. Financial Institutions & Markets. 269p. 1997. pap. 39.00 (*0-455-21450-6*, Pub. by LawBk Co) Gaunt.

Lyell, Katharine M., ed. see Lyell, Charles.

Lyell, Nan. Nonquitt, a Summer Album, 1872-1985. Lyell, Anne M., ed. LC 87-71240. (Illus.). 288p. 1987. 35.00 (*0-9618732-0-5*) Barekneed Pubs.

Lyell, William A., tr. see Lao, She.

Lyell, William A., tr. see Lu Hsun, pseud.

Lyell, William A., tr. see Zhang Henshui.

Lyell, William J., Jr., compiled by. A Lu Hsun Reader. 1976. 14.95 (*0-88710-046-5*) Yale Far Eastern Pubns.

Lyer, V. R. Krishna, see Krishna Lyer, V. R.

Lyerly, Betty C. The Best of Mayberry: The Best of the Best, Home Economists Tested Recipes. LC 94-12045. (Illus.). 288p. 1996. 18.99 (*0-9650515-0-1*, Pub. by B C Lyerly) D Gibson.

***Lyerly, Cynthia L.** Methodism & the Southern Mind, 1770-1810. (Religion in America Ser.). 264p. 1998. text 45.00 (*0-19-511429-9*) OUP.

Lyerly, H. Kim, jt. auth. see Sabiston, David C.

Lyerly, H. Kim, jt. ed. see Sabiston, David C., Jr.

Lyerly, Kim, jt. auth. see Clavien, Pierre-Alain.

Lyeskov, Nicolai. The Enchanted Wanderer. Paschkoff, A. G., tr. 251p. 1985. reprint ed. pap. 14.95 (*0-948166-04-5*, Pub. by Soho Bk Co) Dufour.

Lyfareff, Robert, ed. see Kasturi, Rajeev & Nagpal, Arvind.

Lyford, Carrie A. Iroquois: Their Arts & Crafts. (Illus.). 100p. 1989. pap. 9.95 (*0-88839-135-8*) Hancock House.

— Iroquois Crafts. (Illus.). 100p. 1982. reprint ed. pap. 5.95 (*0-936984-02-3*) Schneider Pubs.

— Ojibwa Crafts. (Illus.). 216p. 1982. reprint ed. pap. 8.95 (*0-936984-01-5*) Schneider Pubs.

— Quill & Beadwork of the Western Sioux. (Illus.). 116p. 1979. reprint ed. pap. 9.95 (*0-933472-00-5*) Johnson Bks.

— Quill & Beadwork of the Western Sioux. LC 99-32836. (Illus.). 116p. 1984. reprint ed. pap. 9.95 (*0-936984-08-2*) Schneider Pubs.

Lyford, William. The Instructed Christian. 345p. 1999. reprint ed. 27.95 (*1-57358-092-9*) Soli Deo Gloria.

Lyftogt, Kenneth L. From Blue Mills to Columbia: Cedar Falls & the Civil War. LC 93-24495. (Illus.). 200p. 1993. 32.95 (*0-8138-1399-9*) Iowa St U Pr.

Lygeros, jt. auth. see Godbole, Narhar.

Lygidakis, N. J., et al, eds. Pitfalls & Complications in the Diagnosis & Management of Hepatobiliary & Pancreatic Diseases. LC 93-11759. 1993. 259.00 (*0-86577-487-0*) Thieme Med Pubs.

Lygidakis, N. J. & Tytgat, Guido N., eds. Hepatobiliary & Pancreatic Malignancies. (Illus.). 472p. 1989. text 175.00 (*0-86577-327-0*) Thieme Med Pubs.

Lygon, Myriam, jt. auth. see Miles, Andrew.

Lygre, David G. General, Organic & Biologic Chemistry. (Chemistry Ser.). 1995. mass mkt., student ed. 20.75 (*0-534-24254-5*) Brooks-Cole.

— General, Organic & Biological Chemistry. LC 94-8083. 670p. 1994. mass mkt. 99.95 (*0-534-24252-9*) Brooks-Cole.

— General, Organic & Biological Chemistry. 1994. mass mkt., teacher ed. write for info. (*0-534-24255-3*) Brooks-Cole.

— Organic & Biochemistry. (Chemistry Ser.). 1995. pap., lab manual ed. 28.95 (*0-534-34253-1*) Brooks-Cole.

Lyina, T. Masterworks of Russian Painting from Soviet Museums. (Illus.). 295p. (C). 1989. text 350.00 (*0-569-09218-3*, Pub. by Collets) St Mut.

Lyiubarskii, Yu, tr. see Feldman, G. M.

***Lyke, Edward.** Zoology-1301 Lab Manual. 1999. pap. text 16.08 (*1-56870-360-0*) RonJon Pub.

Lyke, Evelyn M. Assessing for Nursing Diagnoses: A Human Needs Approach. (Illus.). 222p. 1992. pap. text 21.00 (*0-397-54819-2*) Lppncott W & W.

***Lyke, Howie L.** It Automation: The Quest for "Lights Out" (Harris Kern's Enterprise Computing Institute Ser.). 190p. 1999. 39.99 (*0-13-013786-3*) P-H.

Lyke, James. Ensemble Music for Group Piano, 1. 1976. spiral bd. 12.40 (*0-87563-120-7*) Stipes.

— Ensemble Music for Group Piano, 2. 1976. spiral bd. 14.80 (*0-87563-128-2*) Stipes.

— Keyboard Musicianship Bk. 1: Group Piano for Adults. 7th ed. 1998. spiral bd. 34.80 (*0-87563-787-6*) Stipes.

Lyke, James & Kocour, Mike. Irving Berlin Melodies for Student & Teacher: The Bass Clef Book. 23p. (C). 1992. pap. text 4.00 (*0-87563-398-6*) Stipes.

— Irving Berlin Melodies for Student & Teacher: The Treble Clef Book. 23p. (C). 1992. pap. text 4.00 (*0-87563-399-4*) Stipes.

Lyke, James, et al. Creative Piano Teaching. 3rd ed. 1996. pap. 27.80 (*0-87563-640-3*) Stipes.

— Keyboard Fundamentals. 274p. 1996. spiral bd. 26.80 (*0-87563-639-X*) Stipes.

— Keyboard Musicianship: Group Piano for Adults, Bk. 2. 6th ed. 1994. spiral bd. 28.80 (*0-87563-504-0*) Stipes.

***Lyke, James, et al.** Keyboard Musicianship Bk. 2: Piano for Adults. 7th ed. 380p. (C). 1999. spiral bd. 38.80 (*0-87563-877-5*) Stipes.

Lyke, James P. What We Have Seen & Heard: A Pastoral Letter on Evangelization from the Black Bishops of the United States. 40p. (Orig.). 1984. pap. text 1.95 (*0-86716-040-3*) St Anthony Mess Pr.

Lyke, Larry L. King David with the Wise Woman of Tekoa: The Resonance of Tradition in Parabolic Narrative. LC 98-102963. (Journal for the Study of the Old Testament Supplement Ser.: Vol. 255). 211 p. 1997. 60.00 (*1-85075-826-3*, Pub. by Sheffield Acad) CUP Services.

Lyke, William L., ed. see National Symposium on the Future Availability of G.

Lykes, Aimee, tr. see Zong-Pu, Feng.

Lykes, Brinton M., jt. ed. see Stewart, Abigail J.

Lykes, Dorothy R. Cobalt Blue. (Illus.). 64p. 1995. 20.00 (*0-933313-24-1*); pap. 12.95 (*0-933313-25-X*) SUN Gemini Pr.

— Cobalt Blue. deluxe limited ed. (Illus.). 64p. 1995. 30.00 (*0-933313-23-3*) SUN Gemini Pr.

Lykes, M. Brinton, et al, eds. Myths about the Powerless. LC 95-47188. 336p. (C). 1996. pap. 22.95 (*1-56639-422-8*); lib. bdg. 69.95 (*1-56639-421-X*) Temple U Pr.

Lykiard, Alexis. Catkin. 60p. 1985. 21.00 (*0-947612-08-4*, Pub. by Rivelin Grapheme Pr) St Mut.

Lykiard, Alexis. Selected Poems, 1956-96. 80p. pap. write for info. (*3-7052-0960-4*, Pub. by Poetry Salzburg) Intl Spec Bk.

Lykiard, Alexis, tr. see Apollinaire, Guillaume.

Lykiard, Alexis, tr. see Aragon, Louis.

Lykiard, Alexis, tr. see De Lautreamont, Comte.

Lykiard, Alexis, tr. see Jarry, Alfred.

Lykins, Benjamin W., Jr., et al. Point-of-Use - Point-of-Entry. 368p. 1991. lib. bdg. 89.95 (*0-87371-354-0*, L354) Lewis Pubs.

Lykins, Benjamin W., Jr., jt. auth. see Clark, Robert M.

***Lykins, Elizabeth.** Respirando Bien: Su Guia Para Vivir con Asma & Alergias. (SPA., Illus.). 118p. 1999. pap. 18.95 (*0-9701963-1-8*) B L Enter.

***Lykins, Elizabeth M.** Asthma Treatment Guide: Step-by-Step Instructions on Asthma Management. Baptiste, Gurline J., ed. (Illus.). 51p. 1999. pap. 11.95 (*0-9701963-2-6*) B L Enter.

— Breathing Easy: Your Guide to Living with Asthma & Allergies. Baptiste, Gurline J., ed. (Illus.). 117p. 1999. pap. 18.95 (*0-9701963-0-X*) B L Enter.

— Tratando El Asma: El Manejo de Asma Paso a Paso. (SPA., Illus.). 59p. 1999. pap. 11.95 (*0-9701963-3-4*) B L Enter.

Lykins, Jenny. Distant Dreams. 1998. mass mkt. 5.99 (*0-515-12368-4*, Jove) Berkley Pub.

— Echoes of Tomorrow. 352p. 1997. mass mkt. 5.99 (*0-515-12079-0*, Jove) Berkley Pub.

— Lost Yesterday. (Time Passages Ser.). 352p. 1997. mass mkt. 5.99 (*0-515-12013-8*, Jove) Berkley Pub.

— River of Dreams. 1999. mass mkt. 5.99 (*0-515-12607-1*, Jove) Berkley Pub.

— Waiting for Yesterday. 336p. 1997. mass mkt. 5.99 (*0-515-12129-0*, Jove) Berkley Pub.

Lykke, Anne M. The Vegetation of Delta du Saloum National Park, Senegal. LC 95-216870. (AAU Reports: No. 33). (Illus.). 90p. (C). 1994. pap. 12.95 (*87-87600-42-0*, Pub. by Aarhus Univ Pr) David Brown.

Lykke, Anne M., et al, eds. Sustainable Development in the Sahel: Proceedings of the 4th Sahel Workshop, January 6 - 8, 1992. (AAU Reports: No. 29). 132p. (C). 1992. pap. text 12.95 (*0-614-12694-0*, Pub. by Aarhus Univ Pr) David Brown.

Lykke, Erik, ed. Achieving Environmental Goals: The Concept & Practice of Environmental Performance Review. 274p. 1992. 72.95 (*1-85293-263-5*, TD153) CRC Pr.

— Achieving Environmental Goals: The Concept & Practice of Environmental Performance Review. LC 92-24768. 224p. 1994. 145.00 (*0-471-94709-1*) Wiley.

Lykke, Nina, jt. auth. see Bryld, Mette.

Lykken, David T. The Antisocial Personalities. 272p. 1995. text 49.95 (*0-8058-1941-X*); pap. text 24.50 (*0-8058-1974-6*) L Erlbaum Assocs.

***Lykken, David T.** Happiness. 288p. 2000. pap. 13.95 (*0-312-26333-3*) St Martin.

Lykken, David T. A Tremor in the Blood: Uses & Abuses of the Lie Detector. 2nd ed. LC 98-9702. (Illus.). 326p. (C). 1998. 27.50 (*0-306-45782-2*, Plenum Trade) Perseus Pubng.

Lyklema. Fundamentals of Interface & Colloid Science. 1997. write for info. (*0-12-460527-3*) Acad Pr.

***Lyklema, Hans.** Fundamentals of Interface & Colloid Science: Interface Tension, Vol. 3. 750p. 2000. 135.00 (*0-12-460523-0*) Acad Pr.

Lyklema, J. Fundamentals of Interface & Colloid Science. (Illus.). 744p. 1991. text 123.00 (*0-12-460525-7*) Acad Pr.

Lyklema, J., ed. Fundamentals of Interface & Colloid Science Vol. II: Solid-State Interfaces, Vol. 2. (Illus.). 768p. 1995. text 105.00 (*0-12-460524-9*) Acad Pr.

Lykos, Peter, ed. Computer Modeling of Matter. LC 78-25828. (ACS Symposium Ser.: No. 86). 1978. 32.95 (*0-8412-0463-2*) Am Chemical.

— Computer Modeling of Matter. LC 78-25828. (ACS Symposium Ser.: Vol. 86). 282p. 1978. reprint ed. pap. 87.50 (*0-608-03098-6*, 206355100007) Bks Demand.

Lykos, Peter & Shavitt, Isaiah, eds. Supercomputers in Chemistry. LC 81-17630. (ACS Symposium Ser.: No. 173). 1981. 38.95 (*0-8412-0666-X*) Am Chemical.

— Supercomputers in Chemistry. LC 81-17630. (ACS Symposium Ser.: No. 173). (Illus.). 288p. 1981. reprint ed. pap. 89.30 (*0-608-03239-5*, 206375800007) Bks Demand.

Lyle, jt. auth. see Aspland.

Lyle, jt. auth. see Carlson.

Lyle, Alexandra. Keepsakes. 1991. mass mkt. 4.95 (*1-55817-539-3*, Pinncle Kensgtn) Kensgtn Pub Corp.

Lyle, Anna C. Poetic Justice: A Memoir of My Father Roy Campbell. 156p. 1986. 100.00 (*0-930126-17-3*) Typographeum.

Lyle, David. The Book of Masonry Stoves: Rediscovering an Old Way of Warming. LC 83-3897. (Illus.). 192p. 1996. pap. 24.95 (*0-931790-57-3*) Brick Hse Pub.

— The Book of Masonry Stoves: Rediscovering an Old Way of Warming. LC 97-35544. 1997. pap. 24.95 (*1-890132-09-8*) Chelsea Green Pub.

Lyle, Denis. The Good, the Bad & the Lukewarm. 1999. pap. text 9.99 (*1-84030-014-0*) Ambassador Prodns Ltd.

***Lyle, Dennis.** Countdown to Apocalypse. 1999. pap. 9.99 (*1-84030-064-7*) Ambassador Prodns Ltd.

Lyle, Dorothy S. & Brinkley, Jeanne. Contemporary Clothing. 1983. text 47.44 (*0-02-663140-7*) Glencoe.

Lyle, E. B., jt. auth. see Shaw, P. Shuldham.

Lyle, E. S., Jr. Surface Mine Reclamation Manual. 299p. 1986. 66.50 (*0-444-01014-9*) P-H.

Lyle, Elizabeth. Cassy. large type ed. 512p. 1982. 11.50 (*0-7089-0862-4*) Ulverscroft.

Lyle, Emily. Archaic Cosmos. 1991. 19.95 (*0-7486-6047-X*, Pub. by Polygon) Subterrancan Co.

Lyle, Emily B., ed. Scottish Ballads. (Classics Ser.). 224p. 1994. pap. 13.95 (*0-86241-477-6*, Pub. by Canongate Books) Interlink Pub.

Lyle, Emily B., jt. ed. see Shuldham-Shaw, Patrick.

Lyle, Fred F. Stress-Corrosion Cracking Susceptibility of Weldments in Duplex Stainless Steels. LC 89-50344. (MTI Publication Ser.: No. 33). (Illus.). 86p. reprint ed. pap. 30.00 (*0-608-06691-5*, 206688800009) Bks Demand.

***Lyle, Garry.** England: Major World Nations. LC 99-19240. (Major World Nations Ser.). (Illus.). 144p. 1999. 19.95 (*0-7910-5383-0*) Chelsea Hse.

Lyle, Garry. Greece: Major World Nations. LC 99-19154. (Illus.). 144p. 1999. 19.95 (*0-7910-5385-7*) Chelsea Hse.

— Hong Kong: Major World nations. LC 98-15073. (Major World Nations Ser.). (Illus.). 144p. (YA). (gr. 5 up). 1999. lib. bdg. 19.95 (*0-7910-4990-6*) Chelsea Hse.

— Indonesia: Major World Nations. LC 98-15072. (Major World Nations Ser.). (Illus.). 144p. (YA). (gr. 5 up). 1999. lib. bdg. 19.95 (*0-7910-4987-6*) Chelsea Hse.

— Peru: Major World Nations. LC 98-6401. (Major World Nations Ser.). (Illus.). 144p. (YA). (gr. 5 up). 1999. lib. bdg. 19.95 (*0-7910-4971-X*) Chelsea Hse.

— Turkey: Major World Nations. LC 99-11867. (Major World Nations Ser.). (Illus.). 144p. 1999. 19.95 (*0-7910-5401-2*) Chelsea Hse.

Lyle, Gary. Iran: Major World Nations. LC 97-23832. (Major World Nations Ser.). (Illus.). 144p. (YA). (gr. 5 up). 1999. lib. bdg. 19.95 (*0-7910-4740-7*) Chelsea Hse.

Lyle, Jack & McLeod, Douglas B. Communication, Media & Change. LC 92-19127. xix, 264p. (C). 1993. pap. text 34.95 (*0-87484-935-7*, 935) Mayfield Pub.

Lyle, James R. & Torras, Hoyt W. The Managed Care Handbook: How to Prepare Your Medical Practice for the Managed Care Revolution. 2nd ed. Swanson, Kathryn & Lynch, Maureen, eds. LC 96-21217. 428p. (Orig.). 1996. pap. 49.95 (*1-57066-055-7*, ME074) Practice Mgmt Info.

— 1996 Physicians Fee & Coding Guide. 1996. pap. 109.95 (*1-879249-14-6*) HlthCare Consult.

— Part B Billing Guide. 1995. pap. 99.00 (*1-879249-16-2*) HlthCare Consult.

— Physicians Guide to Managed Care. 2nd ed. 1995. pap. 49.95 (*1-879249-17-0*) HlthCare Consult.

Lyle, James R., jt. auth. see Torras, Hoyt W.

Lyle, Jane. The Fortune Teller's Deck. 160p. 1996. text 22.95 (*0-312-13668-4*) St Martin.

— The Lover's Tarot: For Affairs of the Heart. (Illus.). 144p. 1992. text 28.95 (*0-312-08258-4*) St Martin.

— The Renaissance Tarot: Legends of the Past Now Reveal the Future. (Illus.). 192p. 1998. pap. 25.00 (*0-684-85490-2*) S&S Trade.

Lyle, Jean K., ed. see Donn, Elizabeth R.

Lyle, Jim. SBus: TELOS: The Electronic Library of Science. LC 92-18701. (Illus.). ix, 351p. 1992. 59.95 (*0-387-97862-3*) Spr-Verlag.

***Lyle, Jim.** Things Seen in the Desert. LC 00-41062. (Illus.). 2000. write for info. (*1-887400-29-X*) Earthen Vessel Prodns.

Lyle, John, jt. auth. see Cross, Neville R.

Lyle, John T. Design for Human Ecosystems: Landscape, Land Use & Natural Resources. LC 99-10752. 288p. (C). 1999. pap. 30.00 (*1-55963-720-X*) Island Pr.

— Regenerative Design for Sustainable Development. LC 93-21637. 352p. 1996. pap. 44.95 (*0-471-17843-8*) Wiley.

Lyle, Katie L. The Foraging Gourmet. LC 97-19. (Illus.). 192p. (Orig.). 1997. pap. 16.95 (*1-55821-529-8*) Lyons Pr.

— Scalded to Death by the Steam: Authentic Stories of Railroad Disasters & the Ballads That Were Written about Them. LC 88-830. (Illus.). 224p. 1988. pap. text 12.95 (*0-945575-01-7*) Algonquin Bks.

— When the Fighting Is All Over: The Memoir of a Marine Corps General's Daughter. LC 97-71939. 320p. 1997. 21.95 (*1-56352-426-0*) Longstreet.

— The Wild Berry Book: Romance. Recipes & Remedies. LC 93-48078. (Camp & Cottage Ser.). (Illus.). 144p. 1994. pap. 14.95 (*1-55971-221-X*, NorthWord Pr) Creat Pub Intl.

Lyle, Katie L., ed. see Letcher, John S.

Lyle, Katie Letcher. The Man Who Wanted Seven Wives: The Greenbrier Ghost & the Famous Murder Mystery of 1897. 2nd ed. LC 99-61240. (Illus.). 227p. 1999. 22.95 (*1-891852-04-3*) Quarrier Pr.

***Lyle, Katie Letcher.** The Man Who Wanted Seven Wives: The Greenbrier Ghost & the Famous Murder Mystery of 1897. 2nd rev. ed. LC 99-61240. (Illus.). 170p. 1999. pap. 12.95 (*1-891852-05-1*) Quarrier Pr.

Lyle, Kenneth R., Jr. Ethical Admonition in the Epistle of Jude. (Studies in Biblical Literature: Vol. 4). XVII, 152p. (C). 1998. text 40.95 (*0-8204-3838-3*) P Lang Pubng.

Lyle, Linda & Doty, Howard. Legal Transcription. 1994. text 150.00 incl. audio (*1-56118-673-2*) Paradigm MN.

— Legal Transcription. 500p. 1994. pap. text 25.95 (*1-56118-671-6*) Paradigm MN.

— Legal Transcription. 200p. 1995. teacher ed. 8.00 (*1-56118-672-4*) Paradigm MN.

Lyle, Linda R. & Doty, Howard G. Legal Transcription: Instructor's guide with forms disk, 3.5 IBM. 69.00 (*1-56118-847-6*) EMC-Paradigm.

Lyle, M. C. Nourse: James Nourse & His Descendants. (Illus.). 167p. 1991. reprint ed. pap. 22.50 (*0-8328-1823-2*); reprint ed. lib. bdg. 32.50 (*0-8328-1822-4*) Higginson Bk Co.

Lyle, Molly. The LD Teacher's IEP Companion: Goals, Strategies & Activities for LD Students. LC 99-162563. 169 p. 1998. spiral bd. 37.95 (*0-7606-0168-2*) LinguiSystems.

***Lyle, Oscar K.** Lyle Family, the Ancestry & Posterity of Matthew, John, Daniel & Samual Lyle, Pioneer Settlers in Virginia. 361p. 2000. reprint ed. pap. 38.50 (*0-8063-4986-7*, Pub. by Clearfield Co) ACCESS Pubs Network.

Lyle, P. K. How to Buy or Lease a Car Without Getting Ripped Off. LC 98-49364. (Illus.). 224p. 1999. pap. 10.95 (*1-58062-129-5*) Adams Media.

Lyle, Rob. Mistral. 1953. 49.50 (*0-686-50050-4*) Elliots Bks.

Lyle, Royster, Jr., jt. auth. see Crawford, Barbara.

Lyle, S., tr. see Royer, D. & Dieulesaint, E.

Lyle, Stephen, tr. see Prantzos, Nikos.

Lyle, Tony, jt. auth. see Sargent, Michael.

Lyle, Watson. Camille Saint-Saens: His Life & Art. 210p. 1990. reprint ed. lib. bdg. 69.00 (*0-7812-9083-X*) Rprt Serv.

— Rachmaninoff. LC 74-24140. 1976. reprint ed. 42.50 (*0-404-13003-8*) AMS Pr.

Lyles, Anne, jt. auth. see Wilton, Andrew.

Lyles, Annie & Hamlyn, Robin. British Watercolours from the Oppe Collection. (Illus.). 240p. 1997. pap. 60.00 (*1-85437-240-8*, Pub. by Tate Gallery) U of Wash Pr.

***Lyles, Dick.** Winning Ways: Four Secrets for Getting Great Results by Working Well with People. LC 99-58057. 96p. 2000. 19.95 (*0-399-14606-7*) Putnam Pub Group.

Lyles, Glynn P. Earth-Ladyman: A Book of Faction. 132p. (Orig.). 1995. pap. 9.95 (*0-944851-07-X*) Earth Star.

Lyles, Jean. Ducks & Geese. 48p. 1987. pap. text 6.50 (*1-56770-172-8*) S Scheewe Pubns.

***Lyles, Kevin.** Vietnam: U. S. Uniforms in Color Photographs. (Europa Militaria Ser.: Vol. 3). (Illus.). 96p. 2000. pap. 22.95 (*1-86126-305-8*, 130138AE, Pub. by Crowood) Motorbooks Intl.

Lyles, Kevin. Vietnam: U. S. Uniforms in Colour Photographs. (Europa Militaria Ser.: Vol. 3). (Illus.). 96p. 1992. pap. 19.95 (*1-872004-52-0*, Pub. by Windrow & Green) Motorbooks Intl.

Lyles, Kevin L. The Gatekeepers: Federal District Courts in the Political Process. LC 97-25900. 328p. 1997. 65.00 (*0-275-96082-X*, Praeger Pubs) Greenwood.

Lyles, Lois, jt. auth. see McClean, Vernon.

Lyles, Milton. Cruelest Lie. LC 96-43954. 1998. pap. 14.95 (*1-887492-01-1*) Hi I Que Pub.

Lyles, Peggy. Red Leaves in the Air. 20p. 1979. pap. 2.00 (*0-913719-37-4*, High Coo Pr) Brooks Books.

Lyles, Richard I. & Joiner, Carl. Supervision in the Health Care Organizations. LC 85-17799. 245p. 1989. text 33.50 (*0-8273-4294-2*) Delmar.

Lyles, Sharon. Law Enforcement & Criminal Justice Associations & Research Centers. 62p. 1996. pap. 5.00 (*0-16-060857-0*) USGPO.

Lyles, Sharon, et al. Directory of Law Enforcement & Criminal Justice Associations & Research Centers. 57p. 1997. reprint ed. pap. text 20.00 (*0-7881-4730-7*) DIANE Pub.

Lyles, William H. Putting Dell on the Map: A History of the Dell Paperbacks, 5. LC 83-1641. (Contributions to the Study of Popular Culture Ser.: No. 5). 178p. 1983. 49.95 (*0-313-23667-4*, LPD/, Greenwood Pr) Greenwood.

Lyles, William H., compiled by. Dell Paperbacks, Nineteen Forty-Two to Mid-Nineteen Sixty-Two: A Catalog-Index. LC 82-25505. (Illus.). 471p. 1983. lib. bdg. 75.00 (*0-313-23668-2*, LYE/, Greenwood Pr) Greenwood.

Lyly, John. Complete Works of John Lyly, 3 vols., Set. (BCL1-PR English Literature Ser.). 1992. reprint ed. lib. bdg. 225.00 (*0-7812-7212-2*) Rprt Serv.

— Endymion. Bevington, David M., ed. (Illus.). 224p. 1997. pap. 19.95 (*0-7190-3091-9*) St Martin.

— Euphues: The Anatomy of Wit: Euphues & His England. (BCL1-PR English Literature Ser.). 473p. 1992. reprint ed. lib. bdg. 99.00 (*0-7812-7213-0*) Rprt Serv.

— Euphues, the Anatomy of Wit. Arber, Edward, ed. 205p. 1960. reprint ed. pap. 25.00 (*0-87556-213-2*) Saifer.

— Gallathea & Midas. Lancashire, Anne B., ed. LC 69-11445. (Regents Renaissance Drama Ser.). 206p. reprint ed. pap. 63.90 (*0-7837-6465-0*, 204646900001) Bks Demand.

— Gallathea, 1592. Scragg, Leah, ed. & intro. by. LC 99-191755. (Malone Society Reprints Ser.: No. 161). 70p. 1999. text 39.95 (*0-19-729037-X*) OUP.

***Lyly, John, et al.** Galatea & Midas. LC 99-54909. 2000. write for info. (*0-7190-3095-1*, Pub. by Manchester Univ Pr) St Martin.

Lyman. The Police: An Introduction. LC 98-20842. 502p. 1998. 73.00 (*0-13-260365-9*) P-H.

***Lyman & Potter.** Organized Crime. 2nd ed. LC 99-13095. (Illus.). 536p. 1999. 71.00 (*0-13-010020-X*) P-H.

Lyman, et al. Clinical, Instruction & Supervision for Accountability. 2nd ed. 176p. 1987. per. 31.95 (*0-8403-4418-X*) Kendall-Hunt.

Lyman Allyn Art Museum Staff, jt. auth. see Cuming, Beatrice.

Lyman, Amy R. Personnel Decisions in the Family Farm Business. 64p. 1993. 6.00 (*1-879906-13-9*, 3357) ANR Pubns CA.

Lyman, C. E., et al. Scanning Electron Microscopy, X-Ray Microanalysis & Analytical Electron Microscopy. (Illus.). 420p. (C). 1990. spiral bd., wbk. ed., lab manual ed. 39.50 (*0-306-43591-8*, Kluwer Plenum) Kluwer Academic.

Lyman, Caron A., jt. auth. see Sugar, Alan M.

Lyman, Charles P. & Lynch, David W. The Massachusetts Society for Promoting Agriculture, 1942-1992. (Illus.). 128p. 1992. 20.00 (*0-938864-16-5*) Ipswich Pr.

Lyman, Chester S. Around the Horn to the Sandwich Islands & California 1845-1850. (American Biography Ser.). 328p. 1991. reprint ed. lib. bdg. 79.00 (*0-7812-8255-1*) Rprt Serv.

— Around the Horn to the Sandwich Islands & California 1845-50. Teggart, Frederick J., ed. LC 70-152992. (Select Bibliographies Reprint Ser.). 1977. reprint ed. 25.95 (*0-8369-5744-X*) Ayer.

Lyman, Clara, jt. ed. see Core, Lucy.

Lyman, Darius, Jr. Leaven for Doughfaces: Parables Touching Slavery. LC 78-146266. (Black Heritage Library Collection). 1977. 28.95 (*0-8369-8741-1*) Ayer.

Lyman, Darryl. Civil War Quotations. 208p. 1995. pap. 11.95 (*0-938289-45-4*, 289454) Combined Pub.

— Civil War Wordbook: Including Sayings, Phrases, & Expletives. 240p. 1993. pap. 11.95 (*0-938289-25-X*, 28925X) Combined Pub.

— The Dictionary of Animal Words & Phrases. enl. rev. ed. LC 94-10106. Orig. Title: The Animal Things We Say. 1994. 19.95 (*0-8246-0378-8*) Jonathan David.

— Great African-American Women. LC 98-51973. 1999. 29.95 (*0-8246-0412-1*) Jonathan David.

***Lyman, Darryl.** Great African-American Women. (Illus.). 352p. 2000. 14.99 (*0-517-16216-4*) Random Hse Value.

Lyman, Darryl. Great Jewish Families. LC 97-18940. 1997. 24.95 (*0-8246-0400-8*) Jonathan David.

— Great Jews in Music. 500p. 1986. 29.95 (*0-8246-0315-X*) Jonathan David.

***Lyman, Darryl.** Great Jews in the Performing Arts. LC 99-28219. 1999. 29.95 (*0-8246-0419-9*) Jonathan David.

Lyman, Darryl. Great Jews on Stage & Screen. 288p. 1987. 24.95 (*0-8246-0328-1*) Jonathan David.

— Holocaust Rescuers: Ten Stories of Courage. LC 98-21584. (Collective Biographies Ser.). 128 p. (YA). (gr. 6 up). 1999. lib. bdg. 20.95 (*0-7660-1114-3*) Enslow Pubs.

— Jewish Heroes & Heroines: Their Unique Achievements. LC 96-728. (Illus.). 1996. 24.95 (*0-8246-0388-5*) Jonathan David.

Lyman, David. The Ernst Haas Memorial Collection. Gallant, Aprile, ed. (Illus.). 48p. 1998. pap. 10.00 (*0-916857-15-8*) Port Mus Art.

Lyman, Dean B. Last Lutanist & Other Poems. LC 73-144722. (Yale Series of Younger Poets: No. 15). reprint ed. 18.00 (*0-404-53815-0*) AMS Pr.

***Lyman, Dianna L. J.** Spoken Heart: Poems Thru the Spirit. LC 99-73023. 60p. 1999. pap. 9.95 (*1-890622-83-4*) Leathers Pub.

Lyman, E. R., ed. see Wong, Theodore R.

Lyman, Edward L. Political Deliverance: The Mormon Quest for Utah Statehood. LC 85-1204. (Illus.). 352p. 1986. text 22.95 (*0-252-01239-9*) U of Ill Pr.

— San Bernardino: The Rise & Fall of a California Community. LC 95-9698. (Illus.). 484p. 1996. 24.95 (*1-56085-067-1*) Signature Bks.

***Lyman, Edward Leo.** Victor Valley: An Illustrated History. LC 00-103660. (Illus.). 200p. (C). 2000. 39.95 (*1-886483-47-7*) Heritge Media.

Lyman, Francesca. Inside the Dzanga Sangha Rain Forest: Exploring the Heart of Central Africa. LC 97-51335. 128p. (J). (gr. 3-7). 1999. pap. 12.95 (*0-7611-0870-X*) Workman Pub.

Lyman, George D. Ralston's Ring: California Plunders the Comstock Lode. 1992. reprint ed. lib. bdg. 75.00 (*0-7812-5062-5*) Rprt Serv.

Lyman, Henry. Bluefishing. (Illus.). 160p. (Orig.). 1997. reprint ed. 16.95 (*0-941130-57-6*); reprint ed. pap. 12.95 (*0-941130-58-4*) Lyons Pr.

Lyman, Henry, ed. After Frost: An Anthology of Poetry from New England. LC 96-20905. 256p. 1996. pap. 16.95 (*1-55849-041-8*) U of Mass Pr.

Lyman, Henry & Woolner, Frank. Bottom Fishing. (Illus.). 128p. 1988. pap. 10.95 (*0-941130-63-0*) Lyons Pr.

Lyman, Henry, jt. auth. see Woolner, Frank.

Lyman, Howard. Mad Cowboy. LC 97-51961. 224p. 1998. 22.50 (*0-684-84516-4*) S&S Trade.

Lyman, Howard B. Test Scores & What They Mean. 4th ed. (Illus.). 204p. (C). 1986. pap. text 20.50 (*0-13-903832-9*) P-H.

— Test Scores & What They Mean. 6th ed. LC 97-30509. 190p. (C). 1997. pap. text 35.00 (*0-205-17539-2*) Allyn.

Lyman, Irene P. Dark Isle of Love. large type ed. (Linford Romance Library). 320p. 1986. pap. 16.99 (*0-7089-6233-5*, Linford) Ulverscroft.

Lyman, J. Rebecca. Christology & Cosmology: Models of Divine Activity in Origen, Eusebius, & Athanasius. LC 92-32481. (Oxford Theological Monographs). (C). 1993. 42.00 (*0-19-826745-2*, Clarendon Pr) OUP.

***Lyman, Jon & Hull, Cheryl, eds.** Alaska Sport Fishing Guide. rev. ed. (Illus.). 110p. 2000. pap. text 25.00 (*0-7881-8602-7*) DIANE Pub.

Lyman, K. Basic Nursing Education Programmes: A Guide to Their Planning. (Public Health Papers: No. 7). 81p. 1961. 3.00 (*92-4-130007-8*) World Health.

Lyman, Karen A. Day in, Day Out with Alzheimer's: Stress in Caregiving Relationships. LC 93-9157. (Health, Society, & Policy Ser.). 256p. 1993. 69.95 (*1-56639-097-4*); pap. 22.95 (*1-56639-098-2*) Temple U Pr.

Lyman, Kennie, ed. see Bigon, Maria, et al.

Lyman, Kennie, ed. see Cippriani, Curzio & Borelli, Alessando.

Lyman, Lawrence & Foyle, Harvey C. Cooperative Grouping for Interactive Learning: Students, Teachers, & Administrators. 96p. 1990. pap. 11.95 (*0-8106-1842-7*) NEA.

Lyman, Lawrence, et al. Cooperative Learning in the Elementary Classroom. LC 93-4125. (Developments in Classroom Instruction Ser.). 160p. 1993. pap. 14.95 (*0-8106-3042-7*, NEA Prof Lib) NEA.

***Lyman, Linda L.** How Do They Know You Care? The Principal's Challenge. LC 99-58623. 192p. 2000. write for info. (*0-8077-3930-8*); pap. 21.95 (*0-8077-3929-4*) Tchrs Coll.

Lyman, M. Practical Aspects of Drug Enforcement: Procedures & Administration. (Practical Aspects of Criminal & Forensic Investigations Ser.). iix, 450p. 1989. 49.50 (*0-444-01455-1*) CRC Pr.

Lyman, Mary E. Death & the Christian Answer. LC 60-9784. (C). 1960. pap. 4.00 (*0-87574-107-X*) Pendle Hill.

Lyman-Mersereau, Marion, jt. auth. see Heidel, John.

Lyman-Mersereau, Marion, jt. auth. see Janke, Jennifer E.

Lyman, Michael D. Criminal Investigation: The Art & the Science. 2nd ed. LC 98-20841. 580p. 1998. 72.00 (*0-13-080980-2*) P-H.

— Narcotics & Crime Control. (Illus.). 206p. 1987. 45.95 (*0-398-05347-2*); pap. 29.95 (*0-398-06252-8*) C C Thomas.

— Practical Drug Enforcement: Procedures & Administration. LC 93-19071. 416p. 1992. boxed set 83.95 (*0-8493-9514-3*, HV8079) CRC Pr.

Lyman, Michael D. & Potter, Gary W. Drugs in Society: Causes, Concepts & Control. 3rd ed. LC 98-19028. 512p. 1998. pap. 40.95 (*0-87084-522-5*) Anderson Pub Co.

Lyman, Nanci A. Paul Bunyan. LC 79-66320. (Illus.). 48p. (J). (gr. 3-6). 1980. pap. 3.95 (*0-89375-309-2*); lib. bdg. 15.85 (*0-89375-310-6*) Troll Communs.

— Pecos Bill. LC 79-66319. (Illus.). 48p. (J). (gr. 3-6). 1980. pap. 3.95 (*0-89375-307-6*) Troll Communs.

Lyman, Patricia. Beads & Cabochons: How to Create Fashion Earrings & Jewelry. Knight, Denise, ed. LC 90-86227. (Illus.). 92p. (Orig.). 1992. pap. 10.95 (*0-943604-32-X*, BOO/23) Eagles View.

Lyman, Paul D. National Directory for the Service of Civil Process. 587p. (Orig.). 1990. pap. 49.95 (*1-878337-24-6*) Knowles Pub Inc.

Lyman, Payson W. History of Easthampton, Its Settlement & Growth: With a Genealogical Record of Its Original Families. vi, 209p. 1985. reprint ed. 20.00 (*0-917890-58-2*) Heritage Bk.

Lyman, Phineas, jt. auth. see Loudon, Archibald.

Lyman, Princeton N., jt. auth. see Cole, David C.

Lyman, R. D. & Hembree-Kigin, T. L. Mental Health Interventions with Preschool Children. (Issues in Clinical Child Psychology Ser.: 1). (Illus.). 312p. (C). 1994. 47.50 (*0-306-44860-2*, Plenum Trade) Perseus Pubng.

Lyman, R. D., et al. Residential & Inpatient Treatment of Children & Adolescents. (Illus.). 390p. (C). 1989. text 75.00 (*0-306-43161-0*, Kluwer Plenum) Kluwer Academic.

Lyman, R. L., et al. Americanist Culture History: Fundamentals of Time, Space, & Form. LC 97-22167. (Illus.). 508p. (C). 1997. 102.00 (*0-306-45539-0*, Plenum Trade) Perseus Pubng.

Lyman, R. L., et al. The Rise & Fall of Culture History. LC 97-14507. (Illus.). 286p. (C). 1997. 53.00 (*0-306-45537-4*, Kluwer Plenum) Kluwer Academic.

Lyman, R. L., et al. The Rise & Fall of Culture History. LC 97-14507. (Illus.). 286p. (C). 1997. pap. 29.00 (*0-306-45538-2*, Plenum Trade) Perseus Pubng.

Lyman, R. Lee. Prehistory of the Oregon Coast: The Effects of Excavation Strategies & Assemblage Size on Archaeological Inquiry. (Illus.). 391p. (C). 1991. text 74.95 (*0-12-460415-3*) Acad Pr.

— Vertebrate Taphonomy. LC 93-28675. (Manuals in Archaeology Ser.). (Illus.). 550p. (C). 1994. pap. text 39.95 (*0-521-45840-4*) Cambridge U Pr.

— White Goats, White Lies: The Abuse of Science in Olympic National Park. LC 97-46727. 1998. 29.95 (*0-87480-555-4*) U of Utah Pr.

Lyman, R. Lee, et al, eds. Americanist Culture History: Fundamentals of Time, Space & Form. LC 97-22167. (Illus.). 508p. (C). 1997. pap. 54.00 (*0-306-45540-4*, Kluwer Plenum) Kluwer Academic.

Lyman, R. Lee, jt. auth. see O'Brien, Michael J.

Lyman, Ralph. Binding & Finishing: An Introduction. 2nd rev. ed. (Illus.). 250p. (C). 1998. text 75.00 (*0-88362-224-6*, 15422) GATFPress.

Lyman, Ralph, jt. auth. see Kotok, Alan.

Lyman, Rebecca. Early Christian Traditions. LC 99-22972. (New Church's Teaching Ser.: Vol. 6). 180p. 1999. pap. 11.95 (*1-56101-161-4*) Cowley Pubns.

Lyman, Richard. In the Silence of Scorpions. 32p. 1971. write for info. (*0-318-64120-8*) Poets Pr.

Lyman, Robert D. & Campbell, Nancy R. Treating Children & Adolescents in Residential & Inpatient Settings. LC 96-10054. (Developmental Clinical Psychology & Psychiatry Ser.: Vol. 36). 160p. 1996. 30.00 (*0-8039-7046-3*) Sage.

— Treatment of Children & Adolescents in Residential & Inpatient Settings, No. 36. LC 96-10054. (Developmental Clinical Psychology & Psychiatry Ser.: Vol. 36). 160p. 1996. pap. 12.99 (*0-8039-7047-1*) Sage.

Lyman, Samuel & Marshall, Atwood. Bastogne: The Story of the First Eight Days. LC 79-18262. 1981. reprint ed. 23.95 (*0-89201-060-6*) Zenger Pub.

Lyman, Stanford M. Civilization: Contents, Discontents, Malcontents & Other Essays in Social Theory. LC 89-20221. 352p. 1990. text 38.00 (*1-55728-136-X*) U of Ark Pr.

— Color, Culture, Civilization: Race & Minority Issues in American Society. 408p. (C). 1995. pap. text 19.95 (*0-252-06475-5*) U of Ill Pr.

Lyman, Stanford M. Militarism, Imperialism, & Racial Accommodation: An Analysis & Interpretation of the Early Writings of Robert E. Park. 360p. 1992. text 38.00 (*1-55728-219-6*) U of Ark Pr.

Lyman, Stanford M. NATO & Germany: A Study in the Sociology of Supranational Relations. LC 95-12243. Vol. 4. (Illus.). 384p. 1995. text 40.00 (*1-55728-389-3*) U of Ark Pr.

— Postmodernism & a Sociology of the Absurd: And Other Essays on the "Nouvelle Vague" in American Social Science. LC 96-50984. (Studies in American Sociology). 1997. 34.00 (*1-55728-453-9*) U of Ark Pr.

— The Seven Deadly Sins: Society & Evil. rev. ed. LC 88-82176. 368p. 1989. pap. text 24.95 (*0-930390-81-4*) Gen Hall.

— The Seven Deadly Sins: Society & Evil. 2nd rev. ed. LC 88-82176. 368p. 1989. text 39.95 (*0-930390-82-2*) Gen Hall.

Lyman, Stanford M., et al, eds. Social Movements: Critiques, Concepts, Case Studies. (Main Trends of the Modern World Ser.). 340p. (C). 1994. text 50.00 (*0-8147-5085-0*); pap. text 18.50 (*0-8147-5086-9*) NYU Pr.

Lyman, Stanford M. & Scott, Marvin B. A Sociology of the Absurd. 2nd ed. LC 89-80378. 256p. 1989. text 36.95 (*0-930390-86-5*); pap. text 22.95 (*0-930390-85-7*) Gen Hall.

Lyman, Stanley D. Wounded Knee, 1973: A Personal Account. O'Neil, Floyd A. et al, eds. LC 90-12653. (Illus.). xxxx, 196p. 1991. text 40.00 (*0-8032-2889-9*) U of Nebr Pr.

— Wounded Knee, 1973: A Personal Account. O'Neil, Floyd A. et al, eds. LC 90-12653. (Illus.). xxxx, 196p. 1993. pap. 16.00 (*0-8032-7933-7*, Bison Books) U of Nebr Pr.

Lyman, Stephen, photos by. Into the Wilderness: An Artist's Journey. LC 95-9421. (Illus.). 180p. 1995. 40.00 (*1-885183-31-3*) Artisan.

Lyman, Taylor, ed. see American Society for Metals Staff.

Lyman, Theodore. Meade's Headquarters, 1863 to 1865: Letters of Colonel Theodore Lyman from the Wilderness to Appomattox. Agassiz, George R., ed. LC 71-137381. (Select Bibliographies Reprint Ser.). 1977. reprint ed. 32.95 (*0-8369-5582-X*) Ayer.

— Meade's Headquarters, 1863-1865: Letters of Colonel Theodore Lyman from the Wilderness to Appomattox. (American Biography Ser.). 371p. 1991. reprint ed. lib. bdg. 79.00 (*0-7812-8256-X*) Rprt Serv.

Lyman, Theodore R., jt. auth. see Gardiner, John A.

Lyman, Thomas A. Dictionary of Mong Njua: A Miao (Meo) Language of Southeast Asia. LC 72-94484. (Janua Linguarum, Ser. Practica: No. 123). (MON., Illus.). 403p. (Orig.). 1974. pap. text 115.40 (*90-279-2696-4*) Mouton.

Lyman, Thomas W. & Smartt, Daniel. French Romanesque Sculpture: An Annotated Bibliography. 464p. 1987. 60.00 (*0-8161-8330-9*, Hall Reference) Macmillan.

Lyman, W. D. Lyman's History of Old Walla Walla County: Embracing Walla Walla, Columbia, Garfield & Asotin Counties, 2 vols. (Illus.). 1577p. 1997. reprint ed. lib. bdg. 144.50 (*0-8328-6938-4*) Higginson Bk Co.

Lyman, Warren J. Mobility & Degradation of Organic Contaminants in Subsurface Environments. 416p. 1992. boxed set 104.95 (*0-87371-800-3*) Lewis Pubs.

Lyman, Warren J., et al. Cleanup of Petroleum Contaminated Soils at Underground Storage Tanks. 216p. 1990. 48.00 (*0-8155-1258-9*) Noyes.

Lyman, Warren J., et al. Handbook of Chemical Property Estimation Methods: Environmental Behavior of Organic Compounds. 960p. 1990. reprint ed. text 105.00 (*0-8412-1761-0*, Pub. by Am Chemical) OUP.

Lymbery, A. J., jt. ed. see Thompson, R. C.

Lymbery, Sylvia. Colloquial Italian: Complete Language Course. (Illus.). 336p. 1996. pap. 14.99 (*0-415-12086-1*); pap. 27.99 incl. audio (*0-415-12088-8*) Routledge.

***Lymbery, Sylvia.** Teach Yourself Italian Extra! (Teach Yourself Ser.). 256p. 2000. pap. 10.95 (*0-8442-2672-6*, Teach Yrslf) NTC Contemp Pub Co.

Lympany, Moura & Strickland, Margot. Moura Lympany: Her Autobiography. (Illus.). 186p. 1991. 40.00 (*0-7206-0824-4*, Pub. by P Owen Ltd) Dufour.

Lyn, Charisse Van Der, see Van Der Lyn, Charisse.

Lyn, Craig. The Macintosh 3D Handbook. Orig. Title: Macintosh 3D. (Illus.). 450p. 1997. pap. 39.95 (*1-886801-63-0*) Thomson Learn.

Lyn, Craig & Long, Ben. The Macintosh 3D Handbook. 3rd ed. Orig. Title: Macintosh 3D. (Illus.). 530p. 1999. pap. 49.95 (*1-886801-83-5*) Chrles River Media.

Lyn, Judy. The Sun Always Rises. 77p. 1990. pap. 9.95 (*0-9638550-0-X*) Judy Lyn.

***Lyn You, E. R.** FAQs - Frequently Asked Questions. 1000p. 1999. 39.95 (*0-9666737-1-9*) Amer Readers Pubg.

Lyna, Bill & Carter, Detra. North Carolina Retirement & Relocation Guide. large type ed. (Retirement & Relocation Guides Ser.). (Illus.). 350p. (Orig.). Date not set. pap. 24.95 (*1-56559-112-7*) HGI-Over Fifty.

Lynam, Joss. Best Irish Walks. 210p. (Orig.). 1995. pap. text 12.95 (*0-8442-9713-5*, Passprt Bks) NTC Contemp Pub Co.

Lynam, Joss, ed. Best Irish Walks. 2nd ed. LC 97-195681. (Illus.). 208p. (Orig.). 1997. pap. 12.95 (*0-8442-9707-0*, 97070, Natl Textbk Co) NTC Contemp Pub Co.

Lynam, Marshall L. Stories I Never Told the Speaker: The Chaotic Adventures of a Capitol Hill Aide. LC 97-61458. (Illus.). 267p. 1998. 25.00 (*0-9637629-7-4*) Three Forks.

Lynam, P. J., jt. auth. see McConnell, Sarah.

Lynam, Shevawn. Humanity Dick Martin: "King of Connemara," Seventeen Fifty-Four to Eighteen Thirty-Four. (Illus.). 300p. 1989. reprint ed. pap. 13.95 (*0-946640-36-X*, Pub. by Lilliput Pr) Irish Bks Media.

***Lynar, A.** Lost to the World. 1998. pap. text 35.00 (*1-84018-066-8*, Pub. by Mainstream Pubng) Trafalgar.

Lynas, Helen, ed. Out of the Mouths of Babes: The Unforgettable Things Children Say. (Illus.). 112p. 1998. pap. 15.95 (*0-233-99101-8*, Pub. by Andre Deutsch) Trafalgar.

Lynas, Steve, ed. The Complete Book of Gold. (Illus.). 1999. 45.00 (*0-233-99090-9*) Trafalgar.

Lynas, Wendy. Communication Options in the Education of Deaf Children. LC 95-108460. 126p. (Orig.). (C). 1994. pap. text 34.95 (*1-56593-373-7*, 0750) Singular Publishing.

Lynaugh, Joan E. American Nursing: From Hospitals to Health Systems. LC 96-45993. 100p. 1997. pap. 28.95 (*1-57718-046-1*) Blackwell Pubs.

— The Community Hospitals of Kansas City, Missouri, 1870-1915. (Medical Care in the United States Ser.). 200p. 1989. text 15.00 (*0-8240-8337-7*) Garland.

Lynaugh, Joan E., ed. Nursing History Review: Official Journal of the American Association for the History of Nursing, Vol. 2. (Illus.). 208p. 1993. pap. text 35.00 (*0-8122-1451-X*) U of Pa Pr.

— Nursing History Review: Official Journal of the American Association for the History of Nursing, Vol. 3. (Illus.). 312p. 1994. pap. text 35.00 (*0-8122-1452-8*) U of Pa Pr.

— Nursing History Review: Official Journal of the American Association for the History of Nursing, Vol. 4. (Illus.). 224p. 1995. pap. text 36.00 (*0-8122-1453-6*) U of Pa Pr.

— Nursing History Review: Official Journal of the American Association for the History of Nursing, Vol. 5. (Illus.). 256p. 1996. pap. text 36.00 (*0-8122-1454-4*) U of Pa Pr.

Lynaugh, Joan E., jt. auth. see Fairman, Julie.

Lynberg, Michael. Pocketful of Wisdom. 160p. 1996. pap. 6.95 (*0-312-14392-3*) St Martin.

Lynberg, Michael, compiled by. Winning! Great Coaches & Athletes Share Their Secrets of Success. LC 92-40069. 160p. 1993. pap. 6.99 (*0-385-47017-7*) Doubleday.

***Lynch.** HIV/AIDS at Year 2000: A Sourcebook for Social Workers. LC 98-47766. 268p. (C). 1999. pap. 29.00 (*0-205-29006-X*, Longwood Div) Allyn.

Lynch. International Trade Documents/Regulations. (GB - Basic Business Ser.). 1996. pap. 60.95 (*0-8273-6832-1*) S-W Pub.

— Math Matters. (MA - Academic Math Ser.: Bk. 2). 1994. text, teacher ed. 72.95 (*0-538-63730-7*) S-W Pub.

— Math Matters. (MA - Academic Math Ser.: Bk. 2). (SPA.). 1996. mass mkt., suppl. ed. 12.95 (*0-538-65888-6*) S-W Pub.

— Math Matters, Bk. 2. (MA - Academic Math Ser.). (C). 1997. reprint ed. 38.95 (*0-538-68109-8*) S-W Pub.
— Math Matters: An Integrated Approach. (MA - Academic Math Ser.: Bk. 1). 1992. mass mkt. 12.95 (*0-538-61101-4*) S-W Pub.
— Math Matters: An Integrated Approach. (MA - Academic Math Ser.: Bk. 2). 1993. pap., wbk. ed. 12.95 (*0-538-61113-8*) S-W Pub.
— Math Matters: An Integrated Approach. (MA - Academic Math Ser.: Bk. 1). 1993. 221.95 (*0-538-61107-3*) S-W Pub.
— Math Matters: An Integrated Approach. (MA - Academic Math Ser.: Bk. 3). 1995. pap. 52.95 (*0-538-61124-3*) S-W Pub.
— Math Matters: Integral Approach, Copyright Update. (MA - Academic Math Ser.: Bk. 2). 1997. text 52.95 (*0-538-63952-0*) S-W Pub.
— Math Matters Bk. 1: Assessment Options. 1994. text 53.95 (*0-538-63729-3*) S-W Pub.
— Math Matters Bk. 1: Copyright Update. (Academic Math Ser.). 1995. text 59.95 (*0-538-63953-9*) S-W Pub.
— Negotiation Made Simple. 208p. Date not set. pap. text 19.95 (*0-7506-3473-1*) Buttrwrth-Heinemann.
— Organization Theory & Management. (Public Administration & Public Policy Ser.: Vol. 20). (Illus.). 280p. 1983. text 75.00 (*0-8247-7021-8*) Dekker.
Lynch. Scotland. pap. 19.95 (*0-7126-9893-0*, Pub. by Random) Trafalgar.
Lynch. Voices in Democracy: Telecourse Studyguide. (C). 1998. pap. text, student ed. 21.00 (*0-15-507923-9*, Pub. by Harcourt Coll Pubs) Harcourt.
— Your Key to Success. 168p. 1998. pap. text 12.00 (*0-536-01376-4*) Pearson Custom.
Lynch & Olmstead. Math Matters: Tests, 1. (Academic Math Ser.). 1992. 2.50 (*0-538-61102-2*) S-W Pub.
Lynch & Pickett. General & Oral Pathology for the Dental Hygienist. (Illus.). 500p. 1991. 35.00 (*0-8016-3101-7*) Mosby Inc.
Lynch & Warfel, eds. Enjoy. (Illus.). 304p. 1981. spiral bd. 10.00 (*0-9607538-0-X*) Womens Com Buffalo.
***Lynch, et al.** Liaison Psychiatry & Teamwork. 256p. 2000. pap. text 40.00 (*0-7506-4298-X*) Buttrwrth-Heinemann.
Lynch, jt. auth. see Fucile.
Lynch, jt. auth. see Olmstead.
Lynch, Robert G. & Economic Policy Institute Staff. Do State & Local Tax Incentives Work? LC 96-84244. 34 p. 1996. write for info. (*0-944826-66-0*) Economic Policy Inst.
Lynch, Aaron. Thought Contagion: How Belief Spreads Through Society. 256p. 1996. 24.00 (*0-465-08466-4*, Pub. by Basic) HarpC.
— Thought Contagion: When Ideas Act Like Viruses. 208p. 2000. pap. 14.00 (*0-465-08467-2*, Pub. by Basic) HarpC.
Lynch, Acklyn. Nightmare Overhanging Darkly: Essays on Black Culture & Resistance. rev. ed. 276p. 1993. reprint ed. pap. 14.95 (*0-88378-142-5*) Third World.
Lynch, Alfred F., jt. auth. see Newman, Pamela.
Lynch, Allen. Guide to Museums & Art Galleries of Nova Scotia. LC 99-169341. (Illus.). 112p. 1999. pap. text 10.95 (*1-55109-250-6*) Nimbus Publ.
Lynch, Allen C. Does Russia Have a Democratic Future? Hoepli-Phalon, Nancy, ed. LC 97-60997. (Headline Ser.: No. 313). (Illus.). 72p. 1997. pap. 5.95 (*0-87124-177-3*) Foreign Policy.
— The Soviet Breakup & U. S. Foreign Policy. Hoepli, Nancy L., ed. LC 92-71574. (Headline Ser.: No. 297). (Illus.). 72p. (Orig.). 1992. pap. 5.95 (*0-87124-146-3*) Foreign Policy.
— The Soviet Study of International Relations. (Soviet & East European Studies). 256p. (C). 1989. pap. text 19.95 (*0-521-36763-8*) Cambridge U Pr.
Lynch, Allen C. & Thompson, Kenneth W., eds. Soviet & Post-Soviet Russia in a World of Change. LC 93-35876. (Miller Center Series on a World in Change. Vol. 5). 238p. (Orig.). 1994. pap. text 23.50 (*0-8191-8706-2*, Pub. by White Miller Center); lib. bdg. 52.00 (*0-8191-8705-4*, Pub. by White Miller Center) U Pr of Amer.
Lynch, Allen C., jt. auth. see Lukic, Reneo.
Lynch, Amanda K. Sane Living. 52p. (Orig.). 1997. pap. 6.95 (*1-891210-88-2*, SL03) Bartlett Pub.
Lynch, Amy. Nashville. LC 90-41611. (Downtown America Ser.). (Illus.). 60p. (J). (gr. 3 up). 1991. lib. bdg. 13.95 (*0-87518-453-7*) Silver Burdett Pr.
— Nashville: Downtown America. (Illus.). 64p. (J). (gr. 4-7). 1996. pap. text 7.95 (*0-382-24792-2*) Silver Burdett Pr.
Lynch, Andrew. Malory's Book of Arms: The Narrative of Combat in Le Morte D'Arthur. LC 96-47724. (Arthurian Studies: Vol. 39). 192p. 1997. 60.00 (*0-85991-511-5*) Boydell & Brewer.
Lynch, Andrew & Maddern, Philippa, eds. Venus & Mars: Engendering Love & War in Medieval & Early Modern Europe. LC 96-138983. 216p. (C). 1995. pap. 24.95 (*1-875560-45-9*, Pub. by Univ of West Aust Pr) Intl Spec Bk.
Lynch, Anne & Discoveries Library Staff. Great Buildings. LC 95-32821. (Illus.). 64p. (J). (gr. 4-7). 1996. 16.00 (*0-8094-9371-3*) Time-Life.
Lynch, Anne B. Two Years in Russia - A Joint Venture in a Soviet Village, 1925-1927. rev. ed. LC 97-69240. (Illus.). 288p. 1999. pap. 18.95 (*1-57197-082-7*) Pentland Pr.
Lynch, Annette. Dress, Gender & Cultural Change: Asian-American & African-American Rites of Passage. (Dress, Body, Culture Ser.). (Illus.). 192p. 1999. pap. 19.50 (*1-85973-979-2*, Pub. by Berg Pubs) NYU Pr.
***Lynch, Annette.** Dress, Gender & Cultural Change: Asian-American & African-American Rites of Passage. (Dress, Body, Culture Ser.). (Illus.). 192p. 1999. 55.00 (*1-85973-974-1*, Pub. by Berg Pubs) NYU Pr.
— Redesigning School Health Services. LC 82-12178. (Illus.). 351p. 1983. 45.95 (*0-89885-102-5*, Kluwer Acad Hman Sci) Kluwer Academic.
Lynch, Anthony. Resident Evil No. 2: Prima's Official Strategy Guide. LC 98-67883. (Prima Games Ser.). 96p. 1998. per. 12.99 (*0-7615-1919-X*) Prima Pub.
— Toh Shin Den Fighters Companion. 1995. pap. text 9.99 (*1-56686-341-4*) Brady Pub.
— Totally Unauthorized Sega Games Guide II. (Illus.). 176p. (Orig.). 1995. pap. 9.99 (*1-56686-342-2*) Brady Pub.
Lynch, Anthony, jt. ed. see Millett, Benignus.
Lynch, Arthur J. George Rainsford Fairbanks: A Man of Many Facets. LC 98-91054. (Illus.). xxii, 192p. 1999. pap. 14.95 (*0-9669699-0-1*) Shambles.
***Lynch, Audry.** Steinbeck Remembered. LC 99-50842. (Illus.). 144p. 2000. pap. 12.95 (*1-56474-326-8*) Fithian Pr.
Lynch, Audry. With Steinbeck in the Sea of Cortez: A Memoir of the Steinbeck - Ricketts Expedition. (Illus.). 96p. (Orig.). 1991. pap. 7.95 (*0-944627-56-0*) Sand River Pr.
Lynch, Barbara S., ed. see Institute of Medicine Staff.
Lynch, Barry. The BBC Diet: The Easiest, Healthiest Diet Ever. 178p. 1992. pap. 4.95 (*0-563-20689-6*, Pub. by BBC) Parkwest Pubns.
Lynch, Barry. Complete BBC Diet. 1994. pap. 11.95 (*0-14-023722-4*, Pub. by Pnguin Bks Ltd) Trafalgar.
Lynch, Barry, ed. Ada: Experiences & Prospects: Proceedings of the Ada-Europe International Conference, Dublin, 1990. (Ada Companion Ser.). (Illus.). 374p. (C). 1990. text 89.95 (*0-521-39522-4*) Cambridge U Pr.
Lynch, Betsy, jt. auth. see Bennett, Dwight.
Lynch, Betty. Artist en Route. Deats, Suzanne, ed. LC 97-72397. (Illus.). 128p. 1998. 40.00 (*0-9673062-0-5*, Pub. by Lynch Pr) Herveys Bklink.
Lynch, Betty. Artist en Route. limited ed. Deats, Suzanne, ed. LC 99-72397. (Illus.). 124p. 1997. 250.00 (*0-9673062-1-3*, Pub. by Lynch Pr) Herveys Bklink.
Lynch, Beverly P., ed. Academic Library in Transition: Planning for the 1990s. 400p. (Orig.). (C). 1989. pap. text 49.95 (*1-55570-043-8*) Neal-Schuman.
— Information Technology & the Remaking of the University Library. LC 85-644752. (New Directions for Higher Education Ser.: No. HE 90). 112p. 1995. pap. 22.00 (*0-7879-9918-0*) Jossey-Bass.
— Management Strategies for Libraries: A Basic Reader. LC 85-5668. 682p. 1985. pap. text 55.00 (*0-918212-86-3*) Neal-Schuman.
***Lynch, Bohun.** Menace from the Moon. 1999. reprint ed. 28.00 (*1-55246-218-8*) Battered Silicon.
Lynch, Brian. Easter Snow: An Island off Ireland. 150p. 1993. pap. 19.95 (*3-89429-265-2*, Pub. by Poolbeg Pr) Dufour.
— Voices from the Nettle-Way. 60p. 1990. pap. 10.95 (*1-85186-055-X*) Dufour.
Lynch, Brian, ed. Tony O'Malley. (Illus.). 324p. 1996. 86.95 (*1-85928-235-0*, Pub. by Scolar Pr) Ashgate Pub Co.
— Tony O'Malley. limited ed. (Illus.). 324p. 1996. 800.00 (*1-85928-328-4*, Pub. by Scolar Pr) Ashgate Pub Co.
Lynch, Brian K. Language Program Evaluation: Theory & Practice. (Cambridge Applied Linguistics Ser.). (Illus.). 208p. (C). 1995. text 54.95 (*0-521-48191-0*); pap. text 20.95 (*0-521-48438-3*) Cambridge U Pr.
Lynch-Brown, Carol. Essentials of Children's Literature. 1999. pap. 36.50 (*0-205-30288-2*) Allyn.
Lynch-Brown, Carol, ed. International Children's Literature: A Special Issue of the Journal of Early Child Development & Care. 80p. 1989. pap. text 128.00 (*0-677-25910-7*) Gordon & Breach.
***Lynch-Brown, Carol & Tomlinson, Carl M.** Essentials of Children's Literature. 3rd ed. LC 98-7939. 379p. 1998. pap. text 36.00 (*0-205-28136-2*) Allyn.
Lynch-Brown, Carol, jt. auth. see Tomlinson, Carl M.
Lynch, Carl, III, ed. Clinical Cardiac Electrophysiology: Perioperative Considerations. LC 94-2130. (Society of Cardiovascular Anesthesiologists Monograph Ser.). (Illus.). 372p. 1994. reprint ed. pap. 115.40 (*0-608-05772-X*, 205973700007) Bks Demand.
Lynch, Carmen, jt. auth. see Blinder, Martin.
Lynch, Cecelia. Beyond Appeasement: Interpreting Interwar Peace Movements in World Politics. 240p. 1998. 32.50 (*0-8014-3548-X*) Cornell U Pr.
***Lynch, Cecelia & Loriaux, Michael, eds.** Law & Moral Action in World Politics. LC 99-42360. 272p. 1999. pap. 19.95 (*0-8166-3171-9*, Pub. by U of Minn Pr); lib. bdg. 49.95 (*0-8166-3170-0*, Pub. by U of Minn Pr) Chicago Distribution Ctr.
Lynch, Charles A. I Should Forgive But... LC 98-23652. 1998. pap. text 12.99 (*0-8499-4001-X*) Word Pub.
Lynch, Charles T., ed. Handbook of Materials Science. Incl. Vol. I. General Properties. 760p. 1974. lib. bdg. 159.00 (*0-87819-231-X*, TA403); Vol. II. Metals, Composites & Refractory Materials. 448p. 1975. lib. bdg. 139.00 (*0-87819-232-8*); Vol. III. Nonmetallic Materials & Applications. 642p. 1975. lib. bdg. 139.00 (*0-87819-233-6*, TA403); write for info. (*0-318-51462-1*) CRC Pr.
— Practical Handbook of Materials Science. 648p. 1989. boxed set 110.00 (*0-8493-3702-X*, TA403) CRC Pr.
Lynch, Chris. Babes in the Woods, 2. (He-Man Women Haters Club Ser.). 1997. 9.60 (*0-606-11445-9*, Pub. by Turtleback) Demco.
Lynch, Chris. Blood Relations. LC 94-18728. (Blue-Eyed Son Ser.: No. 2). (Illus.). 224p. (YA). (gr. 8 up). 1996. pap. 4.50 (*0-06-447122-5*, HarpTrophy) HarpC Child Bks.
— Blood Relations. LC 94-18728. (Blue-Eyed Son Ser.: No. 2). (Illus.). 224p. (YA). (gr. 12 up). 1996. lib. bdg. 13.89 (*0-06-025399-1*, HarpTrophy) HarpC Child Bks.
— Blood Relations. LC 94-18728. 1996. 9.60 (*0-606-09090-8*, Pub. by Turtleback) Demco.
— Chiller. 218p. 1995. pap. 8.95 (*1-85371-512-3*, Pub. by Poolbeg Pr) Dufour.
— Dog Eat Dog. LC 95-34691. (Blue-Eyed Son Ser.: Vol. 3). 144p. (YA). (gr. 7 up). 1996. pap. 4.50 (*0-06-447123-3*, HarpTrophy) HarpC Child Bks.
— Dog Eat Dog. (Blue-Eyed Son Ser.). 1996. 9.60 (*0-606-09091-6*, Pub. by Turtleback) Demco.
— Extreme Elvin. LC 98-28820. 240p. (gr. 7-12). 1999. 15.95 (*0-06-028040-9*) HarpC Child Bks.
— Extreme Elvin. LC 98-28820. 240p. (gr. 7-12). 1999. lib. bdg. 15.89 (*0-06-028210-X*) HarpC Child Bks.
— Extreme Elvin. LC 98-28820. 240p. (YA). (gr. 12 up). 2000. mass mkt. 4.95 (*0-06-447142-X*, HarpTrophy) HarpC Child Bks.
Lynch, Chris. Freewill. 192p. mass mkt. 4.95 (*0-06-447202-7*) HarpC.
— Freewill. (J). 2001. write for info. (*0-06-028176-6*); lib. bdg. write for info. (*0-06-028177-4*) HarpC Child Bks.
— Gold Dust. 192p. (gr. 4 up). mass mkt. 4.95 (*0-06-447201-9*) HarpC.
— Gold Dust. 208p. (J). (gr. 5 up). 2000. 15.95 (*0-06-028174-X*); lib. bdg. 15.89 (*0-06-028175-8*) HarpC Child Bks.
— Gypsy Davey. LC 94-2674. (Illus.). 192p. (J). 1998. pap. 11.00 (*0-06-440730-6*) HarpC.
Lynch, Chris. Gypsy Davey. LC 94-2674. 160p. (YA). (gr. 7 up). 1994. 14.00 (*0-06-023586-1*) HarpC Child Bks.
— Iceman. LC 93-7776. 160p. (YA). (gr. 7 up). 1994. 15.00 (*0-06-023340-0*) HarpC Child Bks.
— Iceman. LC 93-7776. (Trophy Bk.). 192p. (J). (gr. 12 up). 1995. pap. 4.95 (*0-06-447114-4*, HarpTrophy) HarpC Child Bks.
— Iceman. (J). 1995. 10.05 (*0-606-08461-4*, Pub. by Turtleback) Demco.
Lynch, Chris. Johnny Chesthair, 1. (He-Man Women Haters Club Ser.). 1997. 9.60 (*0-606-11444-0*, Pub. by Turtleback) Demco.
— Ladies' Choice, 4. (He-Man Women Haters Club Ser.). 1997. 9.60 (*0-606-11447-5*, Pub. by Turtleback) Demco.
Lynch, Chris. Mick. LC 94-18725. (Trophy Bk.: Bk. 1). 160p. (YA). (gr. 7 up). 1996. pap. 4.50 (*0-06-447121-7*, HarpTrophy) HarpC Child Bks.
— Mick. LC 94-18725. 1996. 9.60 (*0-606-09089-4*, Pub. by Turtleback) Demco.
— Political Timber. LC 96-5750. 176p. (J). (gr. 7 up). 1996. lib. bdg. 14.89 (*0-06-027361-5*) HarpC Child Bks.
— Political Timber. LC 96-5750. (Illus.). 176p. (YA). (gr. 7 up). 1996. 14.95 (*0-06-027360-7*) HarpC Child Bks.
— Political Timber. 1997. 10.05 (*0-606-11758-X*, Pub. by Turtleback) Demco.
— Political Timber. LC 96-5750. (Trophy Bk.). 176p. (YA). (gr. 7 up). 1997. reprint ed. pap. 4.95 (*0-06-447141-1*, HarpTrophy) HarpC Child Bks.
Lynch, Chris. Scratch & the Sniffs, 3. (He-Man Women Haters Club Ser.). 1997. 9.60 (*0-606-11446-7*, Pub. by Turtleback) Demco.
Lynch, Chris. Shadow Boxer. LC 92-47490. 224p. (J). (gr. 5 up). 1993. lib. bdg. 14.89 (*0-06-023028-2*) HarpC Child Bks.
— Shadow Boxer. LC 92-47490. (Trophy Bk.). 224p. (YA). (gr. 5 up). 1995. pap. 4.95 (*0-06-447112-8*, HarpTrophy) HarpC Child Bks.
— Shadow Boxer. (YA). (gr. 9-12). 1996. 18.50 (*0-8446-6886-9*) Peter Smith.
— Shadow Boxer. 1995. 10.05 (*0-606-08147-X*) Turtleback.
— Slot Machine. LC 94-48235. 256p. (YA). (gr. 7 up). 1995. lib. bdg. 14.89 (*0-06-023585-3*) HarpC Child Bks.
— Slot Machine. LC 94-48235. (Trophy Bk.). (Illus.). 256p. (YA). (gr. 4-7). 1996. pap. 4.95 (*0-06-447140-3*, HarpTrophy) HarpC Child Bks.
Lynch, Chris. Slot Machine. (J). 1996. 10.05 (*0-606-09867-4*, Pub. by Turtleback) Demco.
Lynch, Chris. Whitechurch. LC 98-54799. 256p. (J). (gr. 12 up). 1999. 14.95 (*0-06-028330-0*) HarpC Child Bks.
***Lynch, Chris.** Whitechurch. LC 98-54799. 256p. (YA). (gr. 12 up). 1999. lib. bdg. 14.89 (*0-06-028331-9*) HarpC Child Bks.
— Whitechurch. LC 98-54799. (Illus.). 256p. (YA). (gr. 7 up). 2000. pap. 7.95 (*0-06-447143-8*, HarpTrophy) HarpC Child Bks.
Lynch, Chris. Wolf Gang. LC 97-41954. (He-Man Women Haters Club Ser.). 128p. (YA). (gr. 3-7). 1998. pap. 4.50 (*0-06-440659-8*) HarpC Child Bks.
— Wolf Gang, 5. (He-Man Women Haters Club Ser.). (J). 1998. 9.70 (*0-606-12964-2*, Pub. by Turtleback) Demco.
Lynch, Christopher. Selling Catholicism: Bishop Sheen & the Power of Television. LC 98-17426. (Illus.). 216p. 1998. 24.95 (*0-8131-2067-5*) U Pr of Ky.
Lynch, Chuck. You Can Work It Out, Vol. 1. LC 99-37225. 1999. pap. 12.99 (*0-8499-3773-6*) Word Pub.
Lynch, Clare A. White Chocolate. 1999. write for info. (*0-345-42572-3*) Ballantine Pub Grp.
Lynch, Claudia. "I Do" Veils - So Can You! A Step-by-Step Guide to Making Bridal Headpieces, Hats, & Veils with Professional Results. (Illus.). 120p. (Orig.). 1996. pap. 19.95 (*0-9650813-6-2*) Harpagon.
***Lynch, Connie.** Don't Lose Your Mind: Four Components of Superior Mental Fitness. (Illus.). 51p. 2000. spiral bd. 10.00 (*1-885587-70-8*) Bridge Lrn Systs.
***Lynch, Constance A.** It takes a Kitongoji. 61p. 1999. pap. 8.95 (*0-9621659-1-3*) CAL Pubs.
Lynch, Constance A. Reflections: Poems by Constance Anderson Lynch. (Illus.). 40p. 1988. pap. text 7.95 (*0-9621659-0-5*) CAL Pubs.
Lynch, Cyprian J., ed. A Poor Man's Legacy: An Anthology of Franciscan Poverty. (Franciscan Pathway Ser.). 759p. 1988. pap. 45.00 (*1-57659-069-0*) Franciscan Inst.
Lynch, D. Bad Fortune. 1989. pap. 4.50 (*1-55817-182-7*) Kensgtn Pub Corp.
Lynch, D., et al. Powder Metallurgy: A New Process for Manufacturing Gears. (Technical Papers: Vol. P249.02). (Illus.). 17p. 1951. pap. text 30.00 (*1-55589-346-5*) AGMA.
Lynch, D. O., ed. Studies of Law in Social Change & Development: Legal Roles in Columbia, No. 4. 1981. 14.00 (*91-7106-180-0*); pap. 7.00 (*91-7106-177-0*) Intl Ctr Law.
Lynch, Daniel. Native & Naturalized Woody Plants of Austin & the Hill Country. Mosely, Jane, ed. LC 80-53737. (Illus.). 180p. (Orig.). 1981. pap. 7.95 (*0-938472-00-3*) St Edwards Univ.
Lynch, Daniel C. After the Propaganda State: Media, Politics & "Thought Work" in Reformed China. LC 99-11807. 327p. 1999. 45.00 (*0-8047-3461-5*) Stanford U Pr.
— Ventry. 1990. 16.95 (*1-55972-049-2*, Birch Ln Pr) Carol Pub Group.
Lynch, Daniel C. & Lundquist, Leslie. Digital Money: The New Era of Internet Commerce. 304p. 1995. pap. 24.95 (*0-471-14178-X*) Wiley.
Lynch, Daniel C. & Rose, Marshall T. Internet System Handbook. (Illus.). 832p. (C). 1992. 67.95 (*0-201-56741-5*) Addison-Wesley.
Lynch, Daniel R. & Davies, Alan M., eds. Quantitative Skill Assessment for Coastal Ocean Models. LC 95-9943. (Coastal & Estuarine Studies: Vol. 49). 510p. 1995. 70.00 (*0-87590-261-8*) Am Geophysical.
Lynch, David. Yeats: The Poetics of the Self. LC 78-13242. 1992. lib. bdg. 19.50 (*0-226-49816-6*) U Ch Pr.
— Yeats: The Poetics of the Self. LC 78-13242. 256p. 1993. pap. text 7.50 (*0-226-49812-3*) U Ch Pr.
Lynch, David & Gifford, Barry. Lost Highway. LC 97-161340. (Illus.). 128p. (Orig.). 1997. pap. 13.95 (*0-571-19150-9*) Faber & Faber.
***Lynch, David A. & Newell, John D.** Imaging of Diffuse Lung Disease. 288p. 1999. boxed set 92.95 incl. cd-rom (*1-55009-092-5*) DEKR.
Lynch, David W. & Olson, Clifford G. Photoemission Studies of High-Temperature Superconductors. LC 98-7169. (Cambridge Studies in Low Temperature Physics: No. 5). (Illus.). 450p. (C). 1998. 110.00 (*0-521-55189-7*) Cambridge U Pr.
Lynch, David W., jt. auth. see Lyman, Charles P.
Lynch, Declan. Ireland on Three Million Pounds a Day. 200p. 1995. pap. 11.95 (*1-874597-29-4*, Pub. by New Island Books) Irish Bks Media.
Lynch, Deidre. The Economy of Character: Novels, Market Culture & the Business of Inner Meaning. LC 97-40313. 320p. 1998. pap. text 18.00 (*0-226-49820-4*); lib. bdg. 45.00 (*0-226-49819-0*) U Ch Pr.
***Lynch, Deidre.** Janeites: Austen's Disciples & Devotees. LC 00-21205. (Illus.). 248p. 2000. 55.00 (*0-691-05005-8*, Pub. by Princeton U Pr) Cal Prin Full Svc.
— Janeites: Austen's Disciples & Devotees. LC 00-21205. (Illus.). 248p. 2000. pap. 17.95 (*0-691-05006-6*) Princeton U Pr.
Lynch, Deidre & Warner, William B., eds. Cultural Institutions of the Novel. LC 96-19761. 472p. 1996. text 59.95 (*0-8223-1854-7*); pap. text 21.95 (*0-8223-1843-1*) Duke.
Lynch, Denis P., jt. auth. see Eisen, Drore.
Lynch, Denis T. Boss Tweed: Story of a Grim Generation. LC 73-19157. (Politics & People Ser.). (Illus.). 448p. 1974. reprint ed. 34.95 (*0-405-05879-9*) Ayer.
— Boss Tweed: The Story of a Grim Generation. (BCL1 - United States Local History Ser.). 433p. 1991. reprint ed. lib. bdg. 99.00 (*0-7812-6277-1*) Rprt Serv.
Lynch, Don, text. Titanic: An Illustrated History. (Illus.). (J). 1997. 39.45 (*0-7868-6401-X*, Pub. by Hyperion) Time Warner.
Lynch, Don & Thompson, David. Battle Born Nevada: People History Stories. 2nd rev. ed. Bean, James H., ed. LC 93-79470. (Illus.). 356p. (YA). (gr. 7-8). 1998. text 27.09 (*0-913205-20-6*) Grace Dangberg.
Lynch, Don, ed. see Hittman, Michael.
Lynch, Don, ed. see Sanger, David.
Lynch, Don, ed. see Sodaro, Craig & Adams, Randy L.
Lynch, Donald. Titanic: An Illustrated History. (Illus.). 224p. (J). 1995. pap. 29.45 (*0-7868-8147-X*, Pub. by Hyperion) Time Warner.
Lynch, Dov & Royal Institute of International Affairs. Russian Peacekeeping Stragegies in the CIS: The Cases of Moldova, Georgia & Tajikistan. LC 99-14621. 2000. text 65.00 (*0-312-22422-2*) St Martin.
Lynch, Dov, jt. auth. see Kalyuzhnova, Yelena.
Lynch, Dudley. Your Dolphin High-Performance Business Brain - An Operator's Manual: 21st Century Thinking Skills for Ambitious People under Challenge or under Fire. (Illus.). 260p. 1993. pap. 25.00 (*0-945822-04-9*) Brain Technologies.
Lynch, Dudley & Kordis, Paul L. DolphinThink: The Workbook: Mastering the Skills You Need to Get Tough, Get Free, Get Focused & Get Going As a New Kind of Winner. (Illus.). 122p. (Orig.). 1989. pap. 24.95 (*0-945822-02-2*) Brain Technologies.
Lynch, E. K. The Scapular of Carmel. 2nd rev. ed. 45p. 1996. 1.00 (*0-911988-11-4*, 42972) AMI Pr.
Lynch, Edith M. Decades: Lifestyle Changes in Career Expectations. LC 80-65703. 154p. reprint ed. pap. 47.80 (*0-608-12860-0*, 202357900033) Bks Demand.
Lynch, Edmund C., jt. ed. see Lynch, Peggy Z.
Lynch, Edward A. Latin America's Christian Democratic Parties: A Political Economy. LC 92-23069. 224p. 1992. 57.95 (*0-275-94464-6*, C4464, Praeger Pubs) Greenwood.
— Religion & Politics in Latin America: Liberation Theology & Christian Democracy. LC 90-48694. 216p. 1991. 55.00 (*0-275-93774-7*, C3774, Praeger Pubs) Greenwood.

L

Lynch, Eleanor W. & Hanson, Marci J. Developing Cross-Cultural Competence: A Guide for Working with Children. 2nd ed. LC 97-41733. 1998. 39.95 (*1-55766-331-9*) P H Brookes.

Lynch, Eleanor W., jt. auth. see Hanson, Marci J.

Lynch, Elizabeth. Dear Deceiver. 272p. (Orig.). 1995. mass mkt. 3.99 (*0-380-78046-1*, Avon Bks) Morrow Avon.

Lynch, Elizabeth C. Lynch Record, Containing Biographical Sketches of Men of the Name Lynch, 16th-20th Century, Together with Information Regarding the Origin of the Name. 154p. 1993. reprint ed. pap. 25.00 (*0-8328-3150-6*); reprint ed. lib. bdg. 35.00 (*0-8328-3149-2*) Higginson Bk Co.

Lynch, Eugene F., et al. California Negotiation & Settlement Handbook. 1991. ring bd. write for info. (*0-327-00064-3*) LEXIS Pub.

Lynch, F. D. Clozentropy: A Technique for Studying Audience Response to Films. LC 77-22911. (Illus.). 1978. lib. bdg. 11.95 (*0-405-10754-4*) Ayer.

Lynch, Frances. A Guide to Ancient & Historic Wales: Gwynedd. LC 96-143547. (Guide to Ancient & Historic Wales Ser.). (Illus.). x, 220p. 1995. pap. 24.00 (*0-11-701574-1*, Pub. by Statnry Office) Balogh.

Lynch, Frances. Megalithic Tombs & Long Barrows in Britain. (Illus.). 64p. pap. 10.50 (*0-7478-0341-2*, Pub. by Shire Pubns) Parkwest Pubns.

Lynch, Frances M. France & the International Economy: From Vichy to the Treaty of Rome. LC 96-17106. (Explorations in Economic History Ser.). 248p. (C). 1997. 80.00 (*0-415-14219-9*) Routledge.

Lynch, Francis. Draw the Line: A Sexual Harassment-Free Workplace. Doyle, Kathleen, ed. (Successful Business Library). (Illus.). 172p. (Orig.). 1995. pap. 17.95 (*1-55571-370-X*, Oasis Pr) PSI Resch.

Lynch, Francis T. The Book of Yields: Food Facts for Accurate Recipe Costing. 4th ed. 72p. 1998. reprint ed. pap. 89.00 (*1-892735-02-4*, CDP18) Chef Desk.

— ChefDesk Management Guides for Foodservice. 110p. 1997. pap. 39.00 (*1-892735-00-8*, CDMG1) Chef Desk.

— Garnishing. LC 87-8714. 143p. 1987. pap. 16.95 (*0-89586-476-2*, HP Books) Berkley Pub.

***Lynch, Frank.** Oracle: DBA. (Oracle Manuals Ser.). 180p. 1999. 150.00 (*1-930245-09-2*) Pinnacle Soft Solut.

Lynch-Fraser, Diane. Life's Little Miseries: Helping Your Child with the Disasters of Everyday Life. LC 92-12816. 246p. 1992. 20.95 (*0-02-919323-0*) Jossey-Bass.

Lynch, Fred D., ed. see Lady J.

Lynch, Frederick R. Diversity Industry. LC 96-43919. 432p. 1997. 27.00 (*0-684-82283-0*) Free Pr.

***Lynch, Frederick R.** The Diversity Machine: The Drive to Change the "White Male Workplace" 430p. 2000. pap. 24.95 (*0-7658-0731-9*) Transaction Pubs.

Lynch, Frederick R. Invisible Victims: White Males & the Crisis of Affirmative Action. LC 91-15288. (Illus.). 256p. 1991. pap. 18.95 (*0-275-94102-7*, B4102, Praeger Pubs) Greenwood.

— Invisible Victims: White Males & the Crisis of Affirmative Action, 80. LC 89-1899. (Contributions in Sociology Ser.: No. 80). 253p. 1989. 62.95 (*0-313-26496-1*, LYN, Greenwood Pr) Greenwood.

Lynch, Gary. Synapses, Circuits, & the Beginnings of Memory. (Cognitive Neuroscience Ser.). (Illus.). 136p. (C). 1986. 25.00 (*0-262-12114-X*, Bradford Bks) MIT Pr.

Lynch, Gary, et al. Brain & Memory: Modulation & Mediation of Neuroplasticity. (Illus.). 368p. 1995. text 85.00 (*0-19-508294-X*) OUP.

***Lynch, Gary G., et al.** Corporate Governance Institute: Blueprint for Good Governance in the 1990s. LC 98-166405. (Corporate Law & Practice Course Handbook Ser.). 872 p. 1998. write for info. (*0-87224-455-5*) PLI.

Lynch, George. Desktop Publishing Word for Windows. 1993. pap. 12.00 (*1-56243-112-9*, T18) DDC Pub.

— OS/2 2.1: IBM PC Quick Reference Guide. 1993. pap. 12.00 (*1-56243-119-6*, Y-18) DDC Pub.

— OS/2 2 Quick Reference Guide. 1993. pap. 12.00 (*1-56243-091-2*, OS-17) DDC Pub.

— QR/Word for Windows for Dummies. (Illus.). 175p. 1993. spiral bd. 8.95 (*1-56884-029-2*) IDG Bks.

— Quick Reference Guide for OS-2 Version 2.1 Warp. 1995. pap. 12.00 (*1-56243-273-7*, Y-19) DDC Pub.

Lynch, George & Lynch, Helen. Clarisworks 5.0 Step by Step: Macintosh Version. LC 97-48863. (Illus.). 156p. 1998. spiral bd. 26.60 (*1-57426-079-0*) Computer Lit Pr.

— Microsoft Works Step-by-Step: Macintosh Version 4.0. LC 94-46423. (Illus.). 34p. 1995. pap., teacher ed. 21.25 (*0-941681-81-5*); spiral bd. 26.60 (*0-941681-80-7*) Computer Lit Pr.

Lynch, George & Lynch, Helen. Microsoft Works Step-by-Step: Windows 95 Version 4.0/4.5. LC 96-38139. (Illus.). 124p. 1996. spiral bd. 26.60 (*1-57426-004-9*) Computer Lit Pr.

Lynch, George C. Canaries. (Colorguide Ser.). 1982. pap. 6.95 (*0-940842-10-6*) South Group.

Lynch, Gerald. Roughnecks, Drillers, & Tool Pushers: Thirty-three Years in the Oil Fields. (Personal Narratives of the West Ser.). (Illus.). 278p. 1987. 24.95 (*0-292-71553-6*) U of Tex Pr.

— Roughnecks, Drillers, & Tool Pushers: Thirty-Three Years in the Oil Fields. LC 87-13857. (Personal Narratives of the West Ser.). (Illus.). 278p. 1991. reprint ed. pap. 12.95 (*0-292-77052-9*) U of Tex Pr.

— Stephen Leacock: Humour & Humanity. 216p. (C). 1988. text 60.00 (*0-7735-0652-7*, Pub. by McG-Queens Univ Pr) CUP Services.

Lynch, Gerald J., jt. auth. see Barron, John.

Lynch, Gerald J., jt. auth. see Barron, John M.

***Lynch, Gerald W.** Human Dignity & the Police: Ehtics & Integrity in Police Work. LC 99-20328. 184p. 1999. pap. 29.95 (*0-398-06967-0*); text 41.95 (*0-398-06958-1*) C C Thomas.

Lynch, Gerard. Gauged Brickwork: A Technical Handbook. 150p. 1990. text 69.95 (*0-566-09057-0*, Pub. by Gower) Ashgate Pub Co.

Lynch, Gloria E., ed. see Thibodaux Service League Members Staff.

***Lynch, Gordon.** Clinical Counselling in Pastoral Settings. LC 99-18232. (Clinical Counselling in Context Ser.). 1999. pap. write for info. (*0-415-19676-0*) Routledge.

***Lynch, Gordon, ed.** Clinical Counselling in Pastoral Settings. LC 99-18232. (Clinical Counselling in Context Ser.). 160p. (C). 1999. text. write for info. (*0-415-19675-2*) Routledge.

Lynch, Grayston L. Decision for Disaster: Betrayal at the Bay of Pigs. LC 98-5234. (Association of the U. S. Army Book Ser.). (Illus.). 208p. 1998. 24.95 (*1-57488-148-5*) Brasseys.

***Lynch, Grayston L.** Decision for Disaster: Betrayal at the Bay of Pigs. 2000. pap. 15.95 (*1-57488-237-6*) Brasseys.

Lynch, H. Math Matters. 1993. teacher ed. 350.00 (*0-538-61941-4*) Sth-Wstrn College.

Lynch, H. Toledo: The Story of an Old Spanish Capital. (Mediaeval Towns Ser.: Vol. 5). 1974. reprint ed. pap. 35.00 (*0-8115-0847-1*) Periodicals Srv.

Lynch, H. F. Armenia: Travels & Studies, 2 vols., Set. 1990. reprint ed. 75.00 (*0-86685-461-4*) Intl Bk Ctr.

Lynch, H. T., ed. see Kullander, S.

Lynch, Hannah. George Meredith. LC 73-128572. (Studies in George Meredith: No. 21). 1972. reprint ed. lib. bdg. 75.00 (*0-8383-0906-2*) M S G Haskell Hse.

Lynch, Harry, ed. Catching the Crow: A Collection of Winning Entries from 1982 WV Writers Awards Competition. 160p. 1983. pap. 5.95 (*0-941092-39-9*) Mtn St Pr.

Lynch, Helen, jt. auth. see Lynch, George.

Lynch, Henry T., ed. Cancer Genetics in Women, Vol. I. 184p. 1987. 107.00 (*0-8493-5183-9*, CRC Reprint) Franklin.

— Cancer Genetics in Women, Vol. II. 192p. 1987. 113.00 (*0-8493-5184-7*, CRC Reprint) Franklin.

— Hereditary Malignant Melanoma. 128p. 1991. 223.00 (*0-8493-6051-X*, RC280, CRC Reprint) Franklin.

Lynch, Henry T. & Takeshi Hirayama, eds. Genetic Epidemiology of Cancer. 336p. 1989. lib. bdg. 249.00 (*0-8493-6756-5*, RC268) CRC Pr.

Lynch, Henry T. & Tautu, P., eds. Recent Progress in the Genetic Epidemiology of Cancer. (Illus.). 160p. 1991. 79.95 (*0-387-53022-3*) Spr-Verlag.

Lynch, Ida Phillips, jt. auth. see Fields, Margaret.

***Lynch, Jack.** A Bibliography of Johnsonian Studies, 1986-1998. LC 99-55818. (Studies in the Eighteenth Century). 1999. write for info. (*0-404-63533-4*) AMS Press.

***Lynch, Jacqueline.** Sketching the Soul. 75p. 2000. pap. 5.60 (*0-87129-965-8*, SE5) Dramatic Pub.

Lynch, James. Corporate Compassion: Succeeding with Care. LC 98-185447. (Illus.). 160p. 1998. 80.00 (*0-304-70044-4*) Continuum.

***Lynch, James.** Cry Unheard: New Insights into the Medical Consequences of Loneliness. 333p. 2000. 26.95 (*1-890862-11-8*) Bancroft MD.

Lynch, James. Multicultural Education: A Global Approach. 220p. 1989. 29.95 (*1-85000-557-5*, Falmer Pr) Taylor & Francis.

— Multicultural Education: Principles & Practice. (Education Bks.). 256p. (C). 1986. text 37.50 (*0-7102-0411-6*, Routledge Thoemms); pap. text 19.95 (*0-7102-0768-9*, Routledge Thoemms) Routledge.

— Provision for Children with Special Educational Needs in the Asia Region. LC 94-34138. (Technical Papers: No. 261). 116p. 1995. pap. 22.00 (*0-8213-3036-5*, 13036) World Bank.

Lynch, James, ed. Education & Development: A Human Rights Analysis. LC 97-169438. (International Debates Ser.). 160p. 1997. text 85.00 (*0-304-33497-9*) Continuum.

Lynch, James, et al, eds. Concepts, Approaches & Assumptions. LC 97-169438. (International Debates Ser.). 440p. 1997. text 130.00 (*0-304-32889-8*) Continuum.

— Cultural Diversity & the Schools, 4 vols., Set. 1992. 385.00 (*0-7507-0149-8*, Falmer Pr) Taylor & Francis.

— Education for Cultural Diversity: Convergence & Divergence. (Cultural Diversity & the Schools Ser.: Vol. 1). 500p. 1992. 110.00 (*1-85000-989-9*, Falmer Pr) Taylor & Francis.

— Equity & Excellence in Education for Development. LC 97-169450. (International Debates Ser.). 352p. 1997. text 130.00 (*0-304-32896-0*) Continuum.

— Human Rights, Education, & Global Responsibilities. (Cultural Diversity & the Schools Ser.: Vol. 4). 400p. 1992. 110.00 (*1-85000-995-3*, Falmer Pr) Taylor & Francis.

— Innovations in Delivering Primary Education Vol. 3: Tradition & Innovations in Delivering Primary Education. (International Debates Ser.). 352p. 1997. text 130.00 (*0-304-32888-X*) Continuum.

— Non-Formal Educational Strategies Vol. 4: Tradition & Innovation: Non-Formal & Non-Governmental Approaches. (International Debates Ser.). 352p. 1996. text 130.00 (*0-304-32894-4*) Continuum.

— Prejudice, Polemic or Progress? (Cultural Diversity & the Schools Ser.: Vol. 2). 500p. 1992. 110.00 (*1-85000-991-0*, Falmer Pr) Taylor & Francis.

Lynch, James A. & Tasch, Edward B. Food Production & Public Policy in Developing Countries: Case Studies. LC 83-2155. 360p. 1983. 69.50 (*0-275-91038-5*, C1038, Praeger Pubs) Greenwood.

Lynch, James B., Jr. The Custis Chronicles: The Virginia Generations. LC 92-62069. (Illus.). 304p. 1997. 34.50 (*0-89725-221-7*, 1598) Picton Pr.

— The Custis Chronicles: The Years of Migration. LC 92-62069. (Illus.). 288p. 1993. 32.50 (*0-929539-70-2*, 1170) Picton Pr.

Lynch, James C. The Barkeeper Pocket Peeker. 16p. 1998. ring bd. 9.99 (*0-9670452-0-7*) N American.

Lynch, James D. Kemper County Vindicated, & a Peep at Radical Rule in Mississippi. LC 70-91663. 416p. 1970. reprint ed. lib. bdg. 38.50 (*0-8371-2069-1*, LYK&) Greenwood.

Lynch, James F., ed. see NSF Science & Technology Center in Discrete Mathem & DIMACS Staff.

Lynch, James J. Banking & Finance: Managing the Moral Dimension. 272p. 1994. 89.95 (*1-85573-176-2*, Pub. by Woodhead Pubng) Am Educ Systs.

— Corporate Compassion: Succeeding with Care. LC 98-185447. 244p. 1998. 29.95 (*0-304-70045-2*, Pub. by Cassell) LPC InBook.

— Henry Fielding & the Heliodoran Novel: Romance, Epic & Fielding's New Province of Writing. LC 85-27402. 128p. 1986. 28.50 (*0-8386-3268-8*) Fairleigh Dickinson.

— Psychology of Relationship Banking: Profiting in the Psyche. 240p. 1996. 135.00 (*1-85573-244-0*, Pub. by Woodhead Pubng) Am Educ Systs.

— Sustaining Quality Advantages in Financial Services. (C). 1994. 125.00 (*0-7478-1828-2*, Pub. by S Thornes Pubs) Trans-Atl Phila.

Lynch, James J., jt. auth. see Evans, Bertrand.

Lynch, James M. & Wiseman, Alan, eds. Environmental Biomonitoring: The Biotechnology Ecotoxicology Interface. LC 97-14837. (Biotechnology Research Ser.: No. 7). (Illus.). 320p. (C). 1998. text 95.00 (*0-521-62141-0*) Cambridge U Pr.

Lynch, James M., jt. ed. see Hokkanen, Heikki M.

Lynch, James R. Checkmate. Choppin, Hazel & Frost, Anne, eds. (Illus.). 150p. 1995. pap. text 5.95 (*0-318-68542-6*) Frost Pub.

— Jimmy Boy. Choppin, Hazel, ed. (Illus.). 229p. 1991. 19.95 (*0-9614624-7-7*) Frost Pub.

Lynch, Jeffrey. Computerized Fuel Injection - Engine Control: GM. 352p. 1991. pap. 13.50 (*0-8273-4526-7*); mass mkt. 35.00 (*0-8273-4525-9*) Delmar.

Lynch, Jeremiah, jt. auth. see Lipton, Sydney.

***Lynch, Jerry.** Creative Coaching. (Illus.). 232p. 2001. pap. write for info. (*0-7360-3327-0*) Human Kinetics.

***Lynch, Jerry & Huang, Chungliang Al.** Working Out, Working Within: The Tao of Inner Fitness Through Sports & Exercise. 263p. 2000. reprint ed. text 24.00 (*0-7881-9205-1*) DIANE Pub.

Lynch, Jerry & Scott, Warren. Running Within. LC 99-11547. (Illus.). 216p. 1999. pap. 15.95 (*0-88011-832-6*, PLYN0832) Human Kinetics.

Lynch, Jerry, et al. Working Out, Working Within: The Tao of Inner Fitness Through Sports & Exercise. LC 97-36671. 288p. 1999. reprint ed. pap. 13.95 (*0-87477-968-5*, Tarcher Putnam) Putnam Pub Group.

Lynch, Jerry, jt. auth. see Huang, Al Chung-liang.

Lynch, Jerry, jt. auth. see Huang, Chungliang A.

Lynch, Jerry, jt. auth. see Huang, Chungliang Al.

Lynch, Joanna R. & Gillespie, Greg. Process & Practice of Radio Programming. LC 98-4847. 336p. (C). 1998. pap. 39.00 (*0-7618-1045-5*) U Pr of Amer.

Lynch, John. Caudillos in Spanish America, 1800-1850. (Illus.). 486p. 1992. text 85.00 (*0-19-821135-X*) OUP.

Lynch, John. For King & Parliament: Bristol & the English Civil War. 1999. 45.95 (*0-7509-2021-1*) Bks Intl VA.

— Hispanic World in Crisis & Change: 1598-1700. 1994. pap. 29.95 (*0-631-19397-9*) Blackwell Pubs.

— Massacre in the Pampas, 1872: Britain & Argentina in the Age of Migration. LC 97-35259. (Illus.). xiii, 256p. 1998. 28.95 (*0-8061-3018-0*) U of Okla Pr.

— Max Beerbohm in Perspective. LC 73-21682. (English Biography Ser.: No. 31). 1974. lib. bdg. 75.00 (*0-8383-1788-X*) M S G Haskell Hse.

— Pacific Languages: An Introduction. LC 97-24552. xix, 359p. 1998. pap. text 35.00 (*0-8248-1898-9*) UH Pr.

— Spain 1516-1598: From Nation State to World Empire. 1994. pap. 33.95 (*0-631-19398-7*) Blackwell Pubs.

Lynch, John. The Spanish-American Revolutions 1808-1826. 2nd ed. (C). 1986. pap. text 17.50 (*0-393-95537-0*) Norton.

Lynch, John. Spanish Colonial Administration, 1782-1810: The Intendant System in the Viceroyalty of the Rio De la Plata, 5. LC 69-13979. 335p. 1969. reprint ed. lib. bdg. 69.50 (*0-8371-0546-3*, LYSC, Greenwood Pr) Greenwood.

— Troubled Journey: Sermons for Pentecost, Middle Third - Gospel. LC 94-999. 1994. pap. 8.50 (*0-7880-0015-2*) CSS OH.

Lynch, John, ed. Latin American Revolutions, 1808-1826: Old & New World Origins. LC 94-16521. 424p. 1994. 27.95 (*0-8061-2661-2*) U of Okla Pr.

— Latin American Revolutions, 1808-1826: Old & New World Origins. LC 94-16521. 1996. pap. 16.95 (*0-8061-2663-9*) U of Okla Pr.

— Plant Closures & Community Recovery. 208p. (Orig.). 1990. pap. 39.50 (*0-317-04839-2*) Natl Coun Econ Dev.

Lynch, John & Kilmartin, Christopher T. The Pain Behind the Mask: Overcoming Masculine Depression. LC 98-45944. (Illus.). 226p. 1999. pap. 19.95 (*0-7890-0558-1*); lib. bdg. 39.95 (*0-7890-0557-3*) Haworth Pr.

Lynch, John, et al. Outcome Measures for Health Education & Other Health Care Interventions. 168p. (C). 1996. 38.00 (*0-7619-0066-7*); pap. 16.95 (*0-7619-0067-5*) Sage.

Lynch, John, jt. ed. see Aulich, James.

Lynch, John, jt. ed. see Corfman, Kim.

Lynch, John A., Jr. & Bourne, Richard W. Modern Maryland Civil Procedure. 1,166p. 1993. 95.00 (*1-55834-077-7*, 64520-10, MICHIE) LEXIS Pub.

— Modern Maryland Civil Procedure: 1998 Cumulative Supplement. 225p. 1998. write for info. (*0-327-00239-5*, 64521-14) LEXIS Pub.

— Modern Maryland Civil Procedure, 1999 Cumulative Supplement. 250p. 1999. write for info. (*0-327-01495-4*, 6452115) LEXIS Pub.

Lynch, John D. Leptodactylid Frogs of the Genus Eleutherodactylus from the Andes of Southern Ecuador. (Miscellaneous Publications: No. 66). 62p. 1979. pap. 3.25 (*0-686-80375-2*) U KS Nat Hist Mus.

— Leptodactylid Frogs of the Genus Eleutherodactylus in the Andes of Northern Ecuador & Adjacent Colombia. (Miscellaneous Publications: No. 72). 46p. 1981. 2.75 (*0-317-04880-5*) U KS Nat Hist Mus.

— New Species of Frogs (Leptodactylidae Eleutherodactylus) from the Pacific Versant of Ecuador. (Occasional Papers: No. 55). 33p. 1976. pap. 1.00 (*0-686-80372-8*) U KS Nat Hist Mus.

— A Re-Assessment of the Telmatobiine Leptodactylid Frogs of Patagonia. (Occasional Papers: No. 72). 57p. 1978. pap. 1.00 (*0-686-80373-6*) U KS Nat Hist Mus.

— A Review of the Andean Leptodactylid Frog Genus Phrynopus. (Occasional Papers: No. 35). 51p. 1975. pap. 1.00 (*0-686-80370-1*) U KS Nat Hist Mus.

— A Review of the Broad-Headed Eleutherodactyline Frogs of South America (Leptodactylidae) (Occasional Papers: No. 38). 46p. 1975. pap. 1.00 (*0-686-80371-X*) U KS Nat Hist Mus.

Lynch, John D. & Duellman, William E. The Eleutherodactylus of the Amazonian Slopes of the Ecuadorian Andes: (Anura: Lepodactylidae) (Miscellaneous Publications: No. 69). 86p. 1980. 4.75 (*0-317-04879-1*) U KS Nat Hist Mus.

— A Review of the Centrolenid Frogs of Ecuador, with Descriptions of New Species. (Occasional Papers: No. 16). (Illus.). 66p. 1973. 1.00 (*0-317-04877-5*) U KS Nat Hist Mus.

Lynch, John D. & Duellman, William Edward. Frogs of the Genus Eleutherodactylus (Leptodactylidae) in Western Ecuador: Systematics, Ecology, & Biogeography. LC 97-191501. (Illus.). 1997. write for info. (*0-89338-054-7*) U KS Nat Hist Mus.

Lynch, John E. The Theory of Knowledge of Vital du Four. (Philosophy Ser.). 215p. 1972. pap. 17.00 (*1-57659-103-4*) Franciscan Inst.

Lynch, John F., jt. auth. see Bellomo, Charles.

Lynch, John G. Prophets' Bread. 1989. pap. 7.25 (*1-55673-131-0*, 9856) CSS OH.

Lynch, John I. Therapeutic Madness. LC 97-91126. 214p. 1998. pap. 12.95 (*0-9660249-0-7*, 1-888-626-6575) Verlager Bks.

Lynch, John J., jt. auth. see Joseph, Lou.

Lynch, John M. Real Estate Tax Abatement Practice & Procedure. LC 92-81121. 162p. 1992. pap. text 45.00 (*0-944490-45-X*) Mass CLE.

Lynch, John R. Facts of Reconstruction. LC 68-29009. (American Negro: His History & Literature, Ser. 1). 1969. reprint ed. 30.95 (*0-405-01828-2*) Ayer.

— Reminiscences of an Active Life: The Autobiography of John Roy Lynch. Franklin, John H., ed. LC 70-110669. (Negro American Biographies & Autobiographies Ser.). 1970. lib. bdg. 30.00 (*0-226-49818-2*) U Ch Pr.

Lynch, John W. A Woman Wrapped in Silence. 288p. 1976. pap. 12.95 (*0-8091-1905-6*) Paulist Pr.

Lynch, John W., tr. see Laurentin, Rene.

Lynch, Joseph. Pockets. large type ed. (Illus.). (J). pap. 16.98 (*0-932970-83-4*) Prinit Pr.

Lynch, Joseph H. Christianizing Kinship: Ritual Sponsorship in Anglo-Saxon England. LC 98-3806. 376p. 1998. 49.95 (*0-8014-3527-7*) Cornell U Pr.

— Godparents & Kinship in Early Medieval Europe. LC 85-43297. 393p. reprint ed. pap. 121.90 (*0-608-06319-3*, 206668100008) Bks Demand.

— The Medieval Church: A Brief History. LC 91-45261. 385p. (C). 1995. pap. 50.00 (*0-582-49467-2*, 79361) Longman.

— Medieval Church Hist. (C). 1992. text 66.50 (*0-582-49466-4*) Addison-Wesley.

Lynch, Joseph M. Negotiating the Constitution: The Earliest Debates over Original Intent. LC 98-43447. 1999. 42.50 (*0-8014-3558-7*) Cornell U Pr.

Lynch, Joseph P., III, jt. auth. see Kahn, M. Gabriel.

Lynch, Judith, jt. auth. see Bell, Mary T.

Lynch, Judy. Easy Lessons for Teaching Word Families: Hands-On Lessons That Build Phonemic Awareness, Phonics. (Illus.). 128p. 1998. pap. text 14.95 (*0-590-68570-8*) Scholastic Inc.

Lynch, K., jt. auth. see Willigan, Dennis J.

Lynch, K. A., ed. see Jaworski, Ron, et al.

Lynch, Kate, jt. auth. see Healey, Michael.

Lynch, Katherine A. Family, Class & Ideology: In Early Industrial France: Social Policy & the Working-Class Family, 1825-1848. LC 88-40198. 352p. (C). 1988. text 39.50 (*0-299-11790-1*) U of Wis Pr.

Lynch, Kathleen. Athabascan Prehistory. (Illus.). 29p. (J). 1995. pap. 6.95 (*1-878051-40-7*) Circumpolar Pr.

Lynch, Kathleen. Early Times. (Early Alaskan People Ser.: Vol. 2). (Illus.). 34p. (Orig.). 1981. reprint ed. pap. 6.95 (*1-878051-37-7*, CP077) Circumpolar Pr.

— Eskimo Prehistory. (Early Alaskan People Ser.: Vol. 3). (Illus.). 41p. (Orig.). 1981. reprint ed. pap. 6.95 (*1-878051-38-5*, CP078) Circumpolar Pr.

— The Hidden Curriculum: Reproduction in Education, A Reappraisal. 240p. 1989. pap. 34.95 (*1-85000-574-5*, Falmer Pr) Taylor & Francis.

— Making Snowshoes. (Alaska Ser.: Vol. 9). 46p. (Orig.). 1974. pap. 4.95 (*1-878051-06-7*, CP053) Circumpolar Pr.

An Asterisk (*) at the beginning of an entry indicates that the title is appearing for the first time.

— Northern Eskimo Stories. (Illus.). 30p. (Orig.). 1974. reprint ed. pap. 7.95 (*1-878051-30-X*, CP058) Circumpolar Pr.

— Southeastern Prehistory. (Early Alaskan Peoples Ser.: Vol. 4). (Illus.). 34p. (Orig.). 1982. reprint ed. pap. 6.95 (*1-878051-31-8*, CP073) Circumpolar Pr.

— Southeastern Stories. (Illus.). 26p. (Orig.). 1978. reprint ed. pap. 7.95 (*0-614-16022-7*, CP062) Circumpolar Pr.

— Stories of Aleutians & Kodiak. (Illus.). (Orig.). 1978. reprint ed. pap. 7.95 (*1-878051-33-4*, CP063) Circumpolar Pr.

Lynch, Kathleen, ed. & illus. see Lastufka, Francine.

Lynch, Kathleen K., jt. ed. see Goldberg, Steven S.

Lynch, Kathleen M. Jacob Tonson, Kit-Cat Publisher. LC 77-111046. 256p. reprint ed. pap. 79.40 (*0-608-11122-8*, 202221800025) Bks Demand.

— Roger Boyle, First Earl of Orrery. LC 65-17348. 328p. reprint ed. pap. 101.70 (*0-608-14395-2*, 202178000023) Bks Demand.

— The Social Mode of Restoration Comedy. LC 65-23483. 1926. pap. 21.00 (*0-8196-0164-0*) Biblo.

— The Social Mode of Restoration Comedy. (BCL1-PR English Literature Ser.). 242p. 1992. reprint ed. lib. bdg. 79.00 (*0-7812-7109-6*) Rprt Serv.

Lynch, Kathleen M., ed. see Congreve, William.

Lynch, Kathryn L. The High Medieval Dream Vision: Poetry, Philosophy, & Literary Form. LC 87-18042. 280p. 1988. 39.50 (*0-8047-1275-1*) Stanford U Pr.

Lynch, Kathy. Aleut Basket Weaving. (Alaska Ser.: Vol. 1). (Illus.). 25p. (Orig.). 1974. reprint ed. pap. 4.95 (*1-878051-24-5*, CP037) Circumpolar Pr.

— Aleut Prehistory. (Early Alaskan Peoples Ser.: Vol. 1). (Illus.). 25p. (Orig.). 1982. pap. 6.95 (*1-878051-35-0*, CP071) Circumpolar Pr.

— Building a Log Cabin. (Alaska Ser.: Vol. 5). (Illus.). 43p. (Orig.). 1976. reprint ed. pap. 5.95 (*1-878051-21-0*, CP038) Circumpolar Pr.

— How to Build Fishwheels. (Alaska Ser.: Vol. 6). 45p. (Orig.). 1979. reprint ed. pap. 4.95 (*1-878051-19-9*, CP056) Circumpolar Pr.

***Lynch, Ken.** Biblical Music in a Contemporary World. 194p. 1999. pap. 8.95 (*0-7392-0394-0*, PO3619) Morris Pubng.

Lynch, Ken. Soul Stirring Sermons: Evangelistic Voices from the Past & Present. 295p. (Orig.). 1996. pap. 12.00 (*1-57502-221-4*, PO875) Morris Pubng.

Lynch, Kermit. Adventures on the Wine Route: A Wine Buyer's Tour of France. (Illus.). 274p. 1990. pap. 14.00 (*0-374-52266-9*) FS&G.

Lynch, Kerry. Butterworths Investigations Service. 1996. ring bd. write for info. (*0-406-99839-6*, BISASET, MICHIE) LEXIS Pub.

Lynch, Kevin. City Sense & City Design: Writings & Projects of Kevin Lynch. Banerjee, Tridib & Southworth, Michael, eds. (Illus.). 872p. 1995. pap. text 37.00 (*0-262-62095-2*) MIT Pr.

— Good City Form. 528p. 1984. reprint ed. pap. text 26.00 (*0-262-62046-4*) MIT Pr.

— Image of the City. (Illus.). 1960. pap. text 12.50 (*0-262-62001-4*, 11) MIT Pr.

— What Time Is This Place? LC 72-7059. 288p. 1976. pap. text 18.95 (*0-262-62032-4*) MIT Pr.

Lynch, Kevin & Hack, Gary. Site Planning. 3rd ed. (Illus.). 450p. (C). 1984. 60.00 (*0-262-12106-9*) MIT Pr.

Lynch, Kevin R. Identification & Expression of G-Protein Coupled Receptors. LC 97-18388. (Receptor Biochemistry & Methodology Ser.). 222p. 1998. 149.95 (*0-471-18310-5*, Wiley-Liss) Wiley.

***Lynch, Kevin R.** Identification & Expression of G-Protein Coupled Receptors. LC 97-18388. (Receptor Biochemistry & Methodology Ser.). 222p. 1999. pap. 75.00 (*0-471-19493-X*, Wiley-Liss) Wiley.

Lynch, Kilian F. The Sacrament of Confirmation in the Early-Middle Scholastic Period. (Theology Ser.). 1xxv, 256p. 1957. pap. 17.00 (*1-57659-025-9*) Franciscan Inst.

Lynch, Killian F., ed. John de la Rochelle, Eleven Marian Sermons. xxiv, 103p. 1961. pap. 7.00 (*1-57659-054-2*) Franciscan Inst.

Lynch, L. R. Educational Approaches to High Level Wellness: An Annotated Bibliography. 1982. pap. 3.95 (*0-685-06384-4*) R Bernard.

Lynch, L. Riddick. The Complete Guide to Selected Health & Health-Related Careers. Chatman, Urella et al, eds. (Illus.). (Orig.). 1980. pap. 10.45 (*0-685-04204-9*) R Bernard.

Lynch, L. Riddick, ed. Cross-Cultural Approach to Health Behavior. LC 73-84199. 364p. 1975. 38.50 (*0-8386-7439-9*); pap. 17.95 (*0-8386-1377-2*) Fairleigh Dickinson.

Lynch, Larry. Set Dances of Ireland: Tradition & Evolution. (Illus.). 316p. (Orig.). 1991. reprint ed. 35.00 (*0-9623366-0-2*) Seadna Bks.

Lynch, Lawrence L. Dangerous Ground: The Rival Detectives. LC 75-32764. (Literature of Mystery & Detection Ser.). (Illus.). 1976. reprint ed. 39.95 (*0-405-07885-4*) Ayer.

Lynch, Lawrence W. Eighteenth Century French Novelists & the Novel. 3rd ed. LC 79-88359. 190p. 1979. 17.95 (*0-917786-16-5*) Summa Pubns.

Lynch, Lee. Cactus Love. LC 94-15979. 224p. 1994. pap. 9.95 (*1-56280-071-X*) Naiad Pr.

— Home in Your Hands. 240p. 1986. pap. 7.95 (*0-930044-80-0*) Naiad Pr.

— Rafferty Street. LC 98-6890. 192p. 1998. pap. 10.95 (*0-934678-93-6*) New Victoria Pubs.

— That Old Studebaker. 272p. (Orig.). 1991. pap. 9.95 (*0-941483-82-7*) Naiad Pr.

Lynch, Lee & Woods, Akia, eds. Off the Rag: Lesbians Writing on Menopause. LC 96-19898. 250p. 1996. pap. 12.95 (*0-934678-77-4*) New Victoria Pubs.

Lynch, Liam. The Pale Moon of Morning. LC 95-231231. 218p. 1998. pap. 11.95 (*0-86327-310-6*, Pub. by Wolfhound Press) Irish Amer Bk.

— Shell, Sea Shell. 176p. 1997. pap. 10.95 (*0-86327-030-1*, Pub. by Wolfhound Press) Irish Amer Bk.

— Tenebrae. 160p. 1997. pap. 10.95 (*0-86327-036-0*, Pub. by Wolfhound Press) Irish Amer Bk.

Lynch, Lisa M. The Impact of Private-Sector Training on Race & Gender Wage Differentials & the Career Patterns of Young Workers. (Illus.). 65p. (C). 1998. reprint ed. pap. text 20.00 (*0-7881-3912-6*) DIANE Pub.

Lynch, Lisa M., ed. Training & the Private Sector: International Comparisons. LC 93-46425. (National Bureau of Economic Research Comparative Labor Markets Ser.). 336p. (C). 1994. 47.00 (*0-226-49810-7*) U Ch Pr.

Lynch, Lonnie T. Master the Art of Carving Melon Centerpieces: Carving Watermelons. Barry, Bob, ed. (Mastering the Art of Ser.). (Illus.). 112p. (C). 1992. reprint ed. pap. 9.95 (*0-9629277-0-8*) L Lynch.

— Mastering the Art of Carving Melon Centerpieces. large type ed. Barry, Bob, ed. (Carving Melons Ser.: Vol. 2). (Illus.). 112p. 1997. pap. 9.95 (*0-9629277-1-6*) L Lynch.

— Mastering the Art of Cooking Florida Seafood. (Illus.). 160p. (Orig.). 1996. pap. 9.95 (*0-9629277-2-4*) L Lynch.

— Mastering the Art of Florida Seafood. LC 99-26592. (Illus.). 200p. 1999. pap. 12.95 (*1-56164-176-6*) Pineapple Pr.

***Lynch, Lydia.** Paradoxia: A Predator's Diary. 1999. pap. text 13.95 (*1-84068-008-3*) Creation Books.

Lynch, Lydia. Paradoxia: A Predator's Story. 160p. 1997. 16.95 (*1-871592-49-6*) Creation Books.

Lynch, M. & Roberts, J. C. The Consequences of Child Abuse. 1982. text 99.00 (*0-12-460570-2*) Acad Pr.

Lynch, M. Elizabeth, jt. auth. see Webb-Vignery, June.

Lynch, M. Kelly, ed. see O'Neill, Joseph.

Lynch, M. Nadine. Business Plus Strategy Equals Success: Business Plannign Made Easier. LC 94-96613. (Illus.). 203p. (Orig.). pap. 19.95 (*0-9645674-0-7*) MNL Pub.

Lynch, Malcolm A., ed. Burket's Oral Medicine. 8th ed. (Illus.). 875p. 1983. text 55.00 (*0-397-52106-5*, 65-07131, Lippncott) Lppncott W & W.

Lynch, Malcolm A., et al, eds. Burket's Oral Medicine. 9th ed. (Illus.). 816p. 1994. text 84.00 (*0-397-51242-2*) Lppncott W & W.

Lynch, Marc. State Interests & Public Spheres: The International Politics of Jordan's Identity. LC 99-12186. 368p. 1999. pap. 18.50 (*0-231-11323-4*) Col U Pr.

***Lynch, Marc, ed.** State Interests & Public Spheres: The International Politics of Jordan's Identity. LC 99-12186. 368p. 1999. 50.00 (*0-231-11322-6*) Col U Pr.

Lynch, Marcella O. Cooking by the Book. (Illus.). 312p. 1993. 19.95 (*0-9639118-0-5*) Marcella Lynch.

Lynch, Margaret. Health Insurance Terminology: A Glossary of Health Insurance Terms. 112p. 1992. pap. text 10.00 (*1-879143-13-5*) Health Ins Assn Am.

Lynch, Margaret, jt. auth. see Lewis, Peter.

Lynch, Marietta & Perry, Patricia. No More Monkeys: A Photographic Version of the Children's Finger Game. (Orig.). (J). (ps-3). pap. 2.95 (*0-9610962-0-9*) M Lynch.

Lynch, Marina A. & O'Mara, Shane M., eds. Neuroscience Labfax. LC 96-47962. (Labfax Ser.). (Illus.). 288p. 1997. text 59.95 (*0-12-460490-0*) Morgan Kaufmann.

Lynch, Martha. Reminiscences of Adams, Jay & Randolph Cos., Ind., 1896. 363p. 1979. 19.00 (*0-686-27819-4*) Bookmark.

Lynch, Mary Ann, jt. auth. see Christena, Karol.

Lynch, Mary G., ed. College Admissions Index of Majors & Sports: 1996-1997 Edition. 600p. 1996. pap. 30.00 (*1-878172-63-8*, Wintergreen-Orchard) Riverside Pub Co.

Lynch, Mary G. & Beattie, Don, eds. Technical, Trade & Business School Data Handbook, 1994-96: National Edition. 4 vols. 5th ed. 2950p. (Orig.). 1994. pap. 150.00 (*1-878172-28-X*, Wintergreen-Orchard) Riverside Pub Co.

Lynch, Mary J. Non-Tax Sources of Revenue for Public Libraries. 1988. 6.00 (*0-8389-7253-5*) ALA.

Lynch, Mary J., ed. Academic Libraries: Research Perspectives. LC 90-32120. (ACRL Publications in Librarianship: No. 47). 279p. reprint ed. pap. 86.50 (*0-7837-5906-1*, 204570400007) Bks Demand.

Lynch, Mary J. & Eckard, Helen M., eds. Library Data Collection Handbook. LC 82-147483. 236p. reprint ed. pap. 73.20 (*0-608-12586-5*, 202394800034) Bks Demand.

Lynch, Mary J., et al. ALA Survey of Librarian Salaries, 1991. LC Z 0682.3.L92. 63p. reprint ed. pap. 30.00 (*0-7837-5913-4*, 204571200007) Bks Demand.

Lynch, Mary J., jt. auth. see Drake, Sandra L.

***Lynch, Mary Jo.** ALA Survey of Librarian Salaries 1998. 55p. 1999. pap. 55.00 (*0-8389-7992-0*) ALA.

Lynch, Mary L. On Your Own: Professional Growth Through Independent Nursing Practice. LC 81-19702. 250p. 1983. 33.75 (*0-8185-0507-9*) Jones & Bartlett.

***Lynch, Maureen, et al, eds.** Health & Medicine on the Internet, 2000: Annual Guide to the World Wide Web for Consumers. 2nd rev. ed. (Illus.). 950p. 1999. pap. 19.95 (*1-885987-18-8*, ME093, Health Info Pr) Practice Mgmt Info.

Lynch, Maureen & Swanson, Kathryn, eds. Health Insurance Carrier Directory, 1999: Time Saver. 425p. 1998. ring bd. 59.95 (*1-57066-128-6*, 9942) Practice Mgmt Info.

Lynch, Maureen, ed. see Boyle, Anthony.

Lynch, Maureen, ed. see Knaus, Denise L.

Lynch, Maureen, ed. see Lyle, James R. & Torras, Hoyt W.

Lynch, Maureen, ed. see Nily, Gisela, et al.

Lynch, Maureen, jt. ed. see Swanson, Kathryn M.

Lynch, Maureen, jt. ed. see Swanson, Kathryn.

***Lynch, Mervin D. & Harris, Carole Ruth.** Fostering Creativity in Children, K-8: Theory & Practice. LC 99-52536. 288p. 2000. pap. text. write for info. (*0-205-30600-4*) Allyn.

Lynch, Michael. Art & Artifact in Laboratory Science: A Study of Shop Work & Shop Talk in a Laboratory. (Studies in Ethnomethodology). (Illus.). 180p. 1985. 45.00 (*0-7100-9753-0*, Routledge Thoemms) Routledge.

— Computer Numerical Control Accessory Devices. LC 93-8902. 262p. 1994. 53.00 (*0-07-039226-9*) McGraw.

— Computer Numerical Controls for Machining. 422p. 1992. 60.00 (*0-07-039223-4*) McGraw.

— Edinburgh & the Reformation. (Modern Revivals in History Ser.). 432p. 1993. 72.95 (*0-7512-0203-7*, Pub. by Gregg Revivals) Ashgate Pub Co.

— Scientific Practice & Ordinary Action: Ethnomethodology & Social Studies of Science. (Illus.). 355p. (C). 1994. text 59.95 (*0-521-43152-2*) Cambridge U Pr.

— Scientific Practice & Ordinary Action: Ethnomethodology & Social Studies of Science. (Illus.). 355p. 1997. pap. text 21.95 (*0-521-59742-0*) Cambridge U Pr.

— These Waves of Dying Friends. Kenny, Maurice & Gosciak, J. G., eds. (Illus.). 80p. (Orig.). 1988. pap. 5.00 (*0-936556-19-6*) Contact Two.

Lynch, Michael & Edgar, William. American Sports Car Racing in the 1950'S. Parravano, John, ed. LC 98-24688. (Illus.). 172p. 1998. 39.95 (*0-7603-0367-3*) MBI Pubg.

Lynch, Michael & Walsh, Bruce. Genetics & Analysis of Quantitative Traits. LC 97-17666. (Illus.). 980p. (C). 1997. text 72.95 (*0-87893-481-2*) Sinauer Assocs.

Lynch, Michael & Woolgar, Steve, eds. Representation in Scientific Practice. 376p. 1990. pap. text 22.00 (*0-262-62076-6*) MIT Pr.

Lynch, Michael, et al. The Spectacle of History: Speech, Text, & Memory at the Iran-Contra Hearings. LC 95-35529. (Post-Contemporary Interventions Ser.). 352p. 1996. text 49.95 (*0-8223-1729-X*); pap. text 18.95 (*0-8223-1738-9*) Duke.

***Lynch, Michael C.** Doing Well by Doing Good? Oil Industry Responses to Kyoto. 18p. 1999. pap. 10.00 (*0-918714-57-5*) Intl Res Ctr Energy.

Lynch, Michael C. Facing the Elephant: Oil Market Evolution & Future Oil Crises. (Illus.). 24p. 1998. pap. 10.00 (*0-918714-55-9*) Intl Res Ctr Energy.

Lynch, Michael F. Creative Revolt: A Study of Wright, Ellison, & Dostoevsky. (American University Studies: American Literature: Ser. XXIV, Vol. 12). 202p. (C). 1990. text 42.95 (*0-8204-1018-7*) P Lang Pubng.

***Lynch, Michael J.** Three Wishes. LC 99-91863. 2000. 25.00 (*0-7388-1318-4*); pap. 18.00 (*0-7388-1319-2*) Xlibris Corp.

Lynch, Michael J., ed. Radical Criminology. LC 96-19705. (International Library of Criminology, Criminal Justice & Penology). 544p. 1997. text 179.95 (*1-85521-858-5*, Pub. by Dartmth Pub) Ashgate Pub Co.

Lynch, Michael J. & Groves, W. Byron. A Primer in Radical Criminology: Special Edge Supplementary Texts. 2nd rev. ed. LC 89-24402. 150p. 1989. pap. text 19.90 (*0-911577-15-7*, Criminal Justice) Willow Tree NY.

Lynch, Michael J. & Patterson, E. Britt, eds. Race & Criminal Justice. LC 91-20028. (C). 1991. pap. text 25.50 (*0-911577-20-3*, Criminal Justice) Willow Tree NY.

***Lynch, Michael J., et al.** The New Primer in Radical Criminology: Critical Perspectives on Crime, Power & Identity. 3rd rev. ed. LC HV6018.L95 1989. 154p. 2000. pap. text 19.90 (*1-881798-21-6*, Pub. by Willow Tree NY) Lib Res.

Lynch, Michael P. Truth in Context: An Essay on Pluralism & Objectivity. LC 98-18000. (Illus.). 192p. 1998. 30.00 (*0-262-12212-X*, Bradford Bks) MIT Pr.

Lynch, Michel A. Microprogrammed State Machine Design. 512p. 1993. boxed set 89.95 (*0-8493-4464-6*, QA76) CRC Pr.

Lynch, Mike. Advanced CNC Techniques. (Illus.). 305p. 1992. pap. text. write for info. (*1-930861-10-9*) C N C Con.

— Machining Center Programming & Operation Answers. (Illus.). 90p. 1998. pap. text. write for info. (*1-930861-02-8*, CC-MCPO-A) C N C Con.

— Machining Center Programming & Operation Manual. (Illus.). 205p. 1998. pap. text. write for info. (*1-930861-00-1*, CC-MCPO-M) C N C Con.

— Machining Center Programming & Operation Workbook. rev. ed. (Illus.). 90p. 1998. pap. text. write for info. (*1-930861-01-X*, CC-MCPO-W) C N C Con.

Lynch, Mike. Managing Computer Numerical Control Operations: How to Get the Most Out of Your CNC Machine Tools. LC 95-70370. 372p. 1995. 83.00 (*0-87263-466-3*) SME.

Lynch, Mike. Parametric Programming for CNC Machining & Turning Centers Answers. 67p. 1996. pap. text. write for info. (*1-930861-09-5*) C N C Con.

— Parametric Programming for CNC Machining & Turning Centers Manual. (Illus.). 233p. 1996. pap. text. write for info. (*1-930861-07-9*) C N C Con.

— Parametric Programming for CNC Machining & Turning Centers Workbook. (Illus.). 68p. 1996. pap. text. write for info. (*1-930861-08-7*) C N C Con.

Lynch, Mike. Parametric Programming for Computer Numerical Control Machine Tools & Touch Probes: CNC's Best-Kept Secret. LC 96-70115. (Illus.). 433p. 1996. 83.00 (*0-87263-481-7*, 2544) SME.

Lynch, Mike. Probe Programming for CNC Machining & Turning Centers. (Illus.). 211p. 1995. pap. text. write for info. (*1-930861-11-7*) C N C Con.

— Programming & Operating CNC Routers. (Illus.). 224p. 1999. pap. text. write for info. (*1-930861-12-5*) C N C Con.

— Setup & Cycle Time Reduction for CNC. (Illus.). 175p. 1996. pap. text. write for info. (*1-930861-06-0*) C N C Con.

— Turning Center Programming & Operation Answers. 2nd rev. ed. (Illus.). 104p. 1998. pap. text. write for info. (*1-930861-05-2*) C N C Con.

— Turning Center Programming & Operation Manual. 2nd ed. (Illus.). 342p. 1998. pap. text. write for info. (*1-930861-03-6*, CC-TCPO-M) C N C Con.

— Turning center Programming & Operation Workbook. 2nd rev. ed. (Illus.). 104p. 1998. pap. text, wbk. ed. write for info. (*1-930861-04-4*, CC-TCPO-W) C N C Con.

***Lynch, N. Timothy & Krogh, B., eds.** Hybrid Systems: Computation & Control: Proceedings of the Third International Workshop, HSCC 2000, Pittsburgh, PA, March 23-25, 2000. (Lecture Notes in Computer Science Ser.: Vol. 1790). xii, 465p. 2000. pap. 73.00 (*3-540-67259-1*) Spr-Verlag.

Lynch, N. Timothy & Vasudevan, Sridhar V., eds. Persistent Pain: Psychosocial Assessment & Intervention. (Current Management of Pain Ser.). (C). 1988. text 140.50 (*0-89838-363-3*) Kluwer Academic.

Lynch, Nancy A. Distributed Algorithms. LC 97-41375. 872p. 1996. text 79.95 (*1-55860-348-4*) Morgan Kaufmann.

Lynch, Nancy A., et al. Atomic Transactions. LC 93-32236. 476p. (C). 1993. text 59.95 (*1-55860-104-X*) Morgan Kaufmann.

Lynch, Nick. The Arties Draw. (Illus.). 32p. (J). (gr. 1-6). 1998. pap. 8.95 (*0-233-99133-6*, Pub. by Andre Deutsch) Trafalgar.

— The Arties Paint. (Illus.). 32p. (J). (gr. 1-6). 1998. pap. 8.95 (*0-233-99132-8*) Trafalgar.

***Lynch, Olmstead.** Enrichment & Chapter Investigation Masters. 2nd ed. 2000. pap. 14.95 (*0-538-69350-9*); pap. 14.95 (*0-538-69447-5*); pap. 14.95 (*0-538-69470-X*) Thomson Learn.

— Enrichment & Chapter Investigation Masters, Math Matters, Vol. 3. 2nd ed. 2000. pap. 14.95 Thomson Learn.

— Math Matters. 1997. pap. 43.75 (*0-538-68107-1*) Sth-Wstrn College.

— Math Matters. 3rd ed. 1994. pap. text 9.75 (*0-538-61126-X*) Sth-Wstrn College.

Lynch, Olmstead. Math Matters, Bk. 1. 2nd ed. (Academic Math Ser.). 2000. mass mkt. 43.95 (*0-538-68659-6*) S-W Pub.

— Math Matters, Bk. 2. 2nd ed. (Academic Math Ser.). 2000. mass mkt. 43.95 (*0-538-68661-8*) S-W Pub.

— Math Matters, Bk. 3. 2nd ed. (Academic Math Ser.). 2000. mass mkt. 43.95 (*0-538-68663-4*) S-W Pub.

***Lynch, Olmstead.** Reteaching Masters, Math Matters, Vol. 3. 2nd ed. 2000. pap. 14.95 (*0-538-69471-8*) S-W Pub.

— Technology Activity Masters, Math Matters. 2nd ed. 2000. pap. 14.95 (*0-538-69472-6*) S-W Pub.

Lynch, Otto E. Finding Gold in the Desert: The Art of Dry Washing. Fessler, Diane M., ed. (Illus.). 32p. 1994. pap. 4.95 (*0-935810-53-6*) R H Pub.

Lynch, Owen J. & Talbot, Kirk. Balancing Acts: Community-Based Forest Management & National Law in Asia & the Pacific. 200p. 1995. pap. 20.00 (*1-56973-033-4*) World Resources Inst.

Lynch, Owen M., ed. Divine Passions: The Social Construction of Emotion in India. 340p. 1990. 50.00 (*0-520-06647-2*, Pub. by U CA Pr) Cal Prin Full Svc.

Lynch, P. J. The Candlewick Book of Fairy Tales. LC 92-54961. 96p. (J). (ps up). 1993. 16.95 (*1-56402-260-9*) Candlewick Pr.

Lynch, P. W., jt. auth. see Foale, M. A.

Lynch, Pat, ed. Compendium of State Laws on Insurance Topics. 277p. (C). 1997. ring bd. 175.00 (*0-89382-444-5*, CSL-ZM) Nat Assn Insurance.

Lynch, Patricia. Back of Beyond. 180p. (J). (gr. 4 up). 1993. pap. 9.95 (*1-85371-206-X*, Pub. by Poolbeg Pr) Dufour.

— Brogeen & the Green Shoes. 208p. 1993. pap. 8.95 (*1-85371-051-2*, Pub. by Poolbeg Pr) Dufour.

— Brogeen & the Princess of Sheen. 155p. (J). (gr. 1 up). 1986. pap. 11.95 (*0-85105-905-8*, Pub. by Smyth) Dufour.

— Brogeen Follows the Magic Flute. 191p. (J). (ps-8). 1993. pap. 7.95 (*1-85371-022-9*, Pub. by Poolbeg Pr) Dufour.

— Sally from Cork. 230p. 1990. pap. 8.95 (*1-85371-070-9*, Pub. by Poolbeg Pr) Dufour.

— The Turf-cutter's Donkey. 224p. 1984. 22.00 (*0-85105-900-7*, Pub. by Smyth) Dufour.

— Turf Cutter's Donkey. 243p. (J). (ps-8). 1988. pap. 7.95 (*1-85371-016-4*, Pub. by Poolbeg Pr) Dufour.

— The Turf-Cutter's Donkey. 242p. (YA). (gr. 5 up). pap. 8.95 (*1-85371-808-4*, Pub. by Poolbeg Pr) Dufour.

Lynch, Patricia, et al. Fiddler's Quest. 309p. (J). (gr. 3-9). 1994. reprint ed. pap. 9.95 (*1-85371-333-3*, Pub. by Poolbeg Pr) Dufour.

Lynch, Patricia L. Communication Skill Book: Practice to Theory. 224p. 1995. per. 39.20 (*0-7872-0336-X*) Kendall-Hunt.

Lynch, Patrick. Carriers. 1996. mass mkt. 6.99 (*0-425-15488-2*) Berkley Pub.

***Lynch, Patrick.** Figure of Eight. LC 99-36121. 320p. 2000. 24.95 (*0-525-94510-5*, Dutt) Dutton Plume.

Lynch, Patrick. Omega. 1998. mass mkt. 6.99 (*0-451-19323-7*, Sig) NAL.

***Lynch, Patrick.** The Policy. 1999. reprint ed. mass mkt. 6.99 (*0-451-19326-1*, Sig) NAL.

Lynch, Patrick, tr. see Ott, Ludwig.

Lynch, Patrick J. & Horton, Sarah. Web Style Guide: Basic Design Principles for Creating Web Sites. LC 98-45282. 176p. 1999. 35.00 (*0-300-07674-6*) Yale U Pr.

— Web Style Guide: Basic Design Principles for Creating Web Sites. LC 98-45282. (Illus.). 164p. 1999. pap. text 14.95 (*0-300-07675-4*) Yale U Pr.

L

Lynch, Patrick J. & Simon, Phillip I. The Official Internet World Manual of Web Style. 200p. 1995. 19.99 (*1-57207-016-1*) Mecklermedia.

Lynch, Patrick J., jt. auth. see Jaffe, C. Carl.

Lynch, Patrick J., jt. auth. see Proctor, Noble S.

Lynch, Patti. Gourmet Inspirations: The Art of Healthy Cooking. (Illus.). 170p. 1993. pap. 12.95 (*0-9620469-1-4*) Sweet Inspirations.

— Kids' Stuffin's: Good & Healthy Snacks for Kids to Make & Eat. (Illus.). (J). 1995. pap. 12.95 (*0-9620469-2-2*) Sweet Inspirations.

— Sweet Inspirations: A Sugar Free Dessert Cookbook. 4th ed. (Illus.). 150p. 1992. reprint ed. pap. 12.95 (*0-9620469-0-6*) Sweet Inspirations.

Lynch, Peggy Z. Lean Forward, Catch the Echo. 32p. 1998. pap. 5.00 (*1-878149-43-1*) Counterpoint Pub.

Lynch, Peggy Z. & Lynch, Edmund C., eds. The Many-Eyed Landscapes. (Illus.). 88p. 1991. lib. bdg. 10.95 (*1-878149-05-9*) Counterpoint Pub.

Lynch, Penelope. Financial Modelling for Project Finance: Self-Study Workbook. 1997. 295.00 (*1-85564-544-0*, Pub. by Euromoney) Am Educ Systs.

Lynch, Peter. Learn to Earn: A Beginner's Guide to the Basics of Investing & Business. LC 96-44480. 272p. 1997. 21.95 (*0-471-18003-3*) Wiley.

Lynch, Peter & Rothchild, John. Beating the Street: The Best-Selling Author of One Up on Wall Street Shows You How to Pick Winning Stocks & Mutual Funds. 320p. 1993. 23.00 (*0-671-75915-9*) S&S Trade.

— Beating the Street: The Best-Selling Author of (One up on Wall Street) Shows You How to Pick Winning Stocks & Mutual Funds. rev. ed. (Illus.). 336p. 1994. per. 14.00 (*0-671-89163-4*) S&S Trade Pap.

— Learn to Earn: An Introduction to the Basics of Investing & Business. (Illus.). 272p. 1996. per. 13.00 (*0-684-81163-4*) S&S Trade Pap.

— One up on Wall Street: How to Use What You Already Know to Make Money in the Market. 304p. 2000. pap. 14.00 (*0-7432-0040-3*, Fireside) S&S Trade Pap.

Lynch, Peter & Rothchild, John. One up on Wall Street: How to Use What You Already Know to Make Money in the Market. 320p. 1990. pap. 13.95 (*0-14-012792-5*, Penguin Bks) Viking Penguin.

Lynch, Peter E. Silvio: Congressman for Everyone, a Biography of Silvio Conti. LC 96-44316. (Illus.). 192p. 1997. 24.95 (*0-86534-256-3*) Sunstone Pr.

Lynch, Peter J. Dermatology. 3rd ed. LC 92-48556. (House Officer Ser.). (Illus.). 448p. 1994. 21.95 (*0-683-05252-7*) Lppncott W & W.

— Genital Dermatology. LC 94-19068. 292p. 1994. text 163.00 (*0-443-08885-3*) Church.

Lynch, Peter J., jt. auth. see Dahl, Mark V.

Lynch, Peter J., jt. ed. see Sams, W. Mitchell.

Lynch, Peter S. Minority Nationalism & European Integration. LC 97-140251. 228p. 75.00 (*0-7083-1377-9*, Pub. by Univ Wales Pr) Paul & Co Pubs.

Lynch, Peter S., jt. auth. see Boyle, Raymond.

***Lynch, Philip.** The Politics of Nationhood: Sovereignty, Britishness, & Conservative Politics. LC 98-28308. 33p. 1999. text 65.00 (*0-312-21835-4*) St Martin.

Lynch, Philip F. Downhole Operations. LC 81-4254. (Primer in Drilling & Production Equipment Ser.: No. 3). (Illus.). 128p. (Orig.). 1981. reprint ed. pap. 39.70 (*0-7837-8147-4*, 204795500008) Bks Demand.

— Rig Equipment. fac. ed. LC 80-24533. (His a Primer in Drilling & Production Equipment: No. 2). (Illus.). 142p. pap. 44.10 (*0-7837-7426-5*, 204722100006) Bks Demand.

Lynch, Phillip, ed. Lesbian & Gay Wedding Album: A Documentary Planner for Lesbian & Gay Couples. LC 96-40112. (Illus.). 1998. 23.00 (*0-934172-23-4*) WIM Pubns.

— Lesbian & Gay Wedding Album: An All-in-One Photo Documentary Planner. LC 96-40112. (Illus.). 1998. 45.00 (*0-934172-24-2*) WIM Pubns.

Lynch, Priscilla. Using Big Books & Predictable Books.Tr. of Comment Utiliser les Grands Livres et la Litterature Enfantine. (FRE.). pap. 7.99 (*0-590-71984-X*) Scholastic Inc.

Lynch, Priscilla & Laraja, Taryn. Stories of the States Activity Book. (Illus.). 72p. (gr. 4-7). 1995. pap. 8.95 (*1-881889-83-1*) Silver Moon.

Lynch, R. G., ed. FC Receptors Symposium: Journal: Immunologic Research, Vol. 11, Nos. 3-4, 1992. (Illus.). iv, 144p. 1992. pap. 35.00 (*3-8055-5695-0*) S Karger.

Lynch, R. L. & Plessman, C. K. Financial Services. 2nd ed. 1989. pap. write for info. (*0-07-039204-8*) McGraw.

— Financial Services. 2nd ed. 1990. 12.84 (*0-07-039205-6*) McGraw.

Lynch, Ransom V. & Ostberg, Donald R. Calculus: A First Course. LC 82-23300. 704p. (C). 1983. reprint ed. text 53.50 (*0-89874-597-7*) Krieger.

Lynch, Ransom V., et al. Calculus, with Computer Applications. LC 72-86514. 975p. reprint ed. pap. 200.00 (*0-8357-7972-6*, 205597900042) Bks Demand.

Lynch, Richard. Adobe Photoshop 5 How-To. LC 98-85293. 704p. 1998. pap. 39.99 (*1-57169-156-1*) Sams.

— Corporate Strategy. 848p. 1997. pap. 59.50 (*0-273-60753-7*, Pub. by Pitman Pub) Trans-Atl Phila.

— Getting Out of Your Own Way. Abbott, Helen, ed. 112p. (Orig.). 1989. pap. 8.00 (*0-933445-02-4*) Abbott Pr WA.

Lynch, Richard. Health & Spiritual Healing. 140p. 1992. pap. 12.00 (*0-89540-146-0*, SB-146) Sun Pub.

— How to Use Adobe Photoshop 5.5. 256p. 1999. pap. 24.99 (*0-672-31719-2*) Sams.

Lynch, Richard. Precision Management: How to Build & Manage the Winning Organization. 2nd ed. 230p. (Orig.). 1988. reprint ed. pap. 10.00 (*0-933445-00-8*) Abbott Pr WA.

— Private Investigator's Guide for the Investigation & Location of Missing & Abducted Children. (Private Investigation Ser.). (Illus.). 90p. (C). 1996. pap. text 35.00 (*0-918487-88-9*) Thomas Investigative.

***Lynch, Richard.** Special Edition Using Adobe Photoshop X. (Special Edition Using... Que Ser.). 2000. pap. 39.99 (*0-7897-2425-1*) Que.

Lynch, Richard, jt. ed. see Leibovitz, Maury.

Lynch, Richard, ed. see Mason, Ralph, et al.

Lynch, Richard C. Broadway, Movie, TV & Studio Cast Musicals on Record: A Discography of Recordings, 1985-1995, 68. LC 96-24975. (Discographies Ser.: No. 68). 272p. 1996. lib. bdg. 67.95 (*0-313-29855-6*) Greenwood.

Lynch, Richard C., compiled by. Broadway on Record: A Directory of New York Cast Recordings of Musical Shows, 1931-1986, 28. LC 87-11822. (Discographies Ser.: No. 28). 312p. 1987. lib. bdg. 45.00 (*0-313-25523-7*, LBR/, Greenwood Pr) Greenwood.

— Movie Musicals on Record: A Directory of Recordings of Motion Picture Musicals, 1927-1987, 32. LC 89-2137. (Discographies Ser.: No. 32). 455p. 1989. lib. bdg. 59.95 (*0-313-26540-2*, LMV/, Greenwood Pr) Greenwood.

Lynch, Richard C., ed. TV & Studio Cast Musicals on Record: A Discography of Television Musicals & Studio Recordings of Stage & Film Musicals, 38. LC 90-40205. (Discographies Ser.: No. 38). 344p. 1990. lib. bdg. 65.00 (*0-313-27324-3*, LTV, Greenwood Pr) Greenwood.

Lynch, Richard L. Marketing Education: A Future Perspective. 86p. 1983. 8.75 (*0-318-22150-0*, SN37) Ctr Educ Trng Employ.

Lynch, Richard L. & Cross, Kelvin F. Measure Up! Yardsticks for Continuous Improvement. 2nd ed. LC 95-1580. 1995. pap. 30.95 (*1-55786-718-6*) Blackwell Pubs.

Lynch, Richard L. & Lunch, Richard L., eds. Food Marketing. (Career Competencies in Marketing Ser.). (Illus.). 1979. text 12.04 (*0-07-051483-6*) McGraw.

Lynch, Richard L., jt. auth. see Crawford, Lucy.

Lynch, Richard L., ed. see Mathisen, Marilyn.

Lynch, Richard L., ed. see Smith, William O.

Lynch, Richard L., ed. see Vorndran, Barbara S. & Litchfield, Carolyn.

Lynch, Richard L., ed. see Wray, Ralph.

Lynch, Rick. 180 Seconds at Willow Park. 1998. 21.95 (*0-7871-1601-7*, NewStar Pr) NewStar Media.

Lynch, Rick, jt. auth. see McCurley, Steve.

Lynch, Rick, jt. auth. see Vineyard, Sue.

***Lynch, Rita Frost.** A Glimpse of News Past: The Courier, Murfreesboro, Tennessee, 1830-1832. LC 99-66569. (Tennessee Heritage Library Bicentennial Collection). (Illus.). 160p. 1999. 22.95 (*1-57736-162-8*, Hillsboro Pr) Providence Hse.

Lynch, Robert E., jt. auth. see Birkhoff, Garrett D.

Lynch, Robert F., jt. auth. see Werner, Thomas J.

Lynch, Robert M. The Sonoma Valley Story: Pages Through the Ages. LC 97-91567. (Illus.). xviii, 312p. 1997. 29.95 (*0-9653857-0-1*) Sonoma Index-Tribune.

Lynch, Robert N., jt. ed. see Poggie, John J., Jr.

Lynch, Robert P. Business Alliances Guide: The Hidden Competitive Weapon. LC 92-15341. 352p. 1993. 42.95 (*0-471-57030-3*) Wiley.

— The Practical Guide to Joint Ventures & Corporate Alliances: How to Form How to Organize How to Operate. LC 89-8893. 416p. 1989. 158.95 (*0-471-62456-X*) Wiley.

Lynch, Rodney. Altar Work 101. 2000. pap. 6.99 (*1-57794-015-6*) Dake Pub.

Lynch, Ronald C. The Police Manager. 3rd ed. 352p. (C). 1986. 61.88 (*0-07-554818-6*) McGraw.

Lynch, Ronald G. The Police Manager. 5th rev. ed. LC 98-24145. 273p. (C). 1998. pap. 33.95 (*0-87084-710-4*) Anderson Pub Co.

Lynch, S., jt. auth. see Brown, Ray.

***LYNCH, SAM.** Small Hotels of Sydney. (Illus.). 152p. 1999. pap. 14.95 (*1-86315-109-5*) Little Hills.

Lynch, Samuel E., et al, eds. Tissue Engineering: Dental Applications & Future Directions. LC 98-35196. (Illus.). 297p. 1999. text 98.00 (*0-86715-346-6*) Quint Pub Co.

Lynch, Sarah, ed. Designing Green Support Programs. (Policy Studies Program Report: No. 4). (Illus.). 119p. 1994. pap. 10.00 (*1-893182-04-5*) H A Wallace Inst.

Lynch, Sarah & Smith, Katherine R. Lean, Mean & Green... Designing Farm Support Programs in a New Era. (Policy Study Program Report: No. 3). (Illus.). 27p. 1994. pap. 7.50 (*1-893182-09-6*) H A Wallace Inst.

Lynch, Sarah, jt. auth. see CFNPP Staff.

***Lynch, Sharon J.** Equity & Science Education Reform. LC 99-38080. 266p. 1999. write for info. (*0-8058-3248-3*) L Erlbaum Assocs.

— Equity & Science Education Reform. LC 99-38080. 266p. 2000. pap. write for info. (*0-8058-3249-1*) L Erlbaum Assocs.

Lynch, Sherry, ed. The Librarian's Guide to Partnerships. LC 99-14137. (Handbook Ser.). (Illus.). 99p. 1999. pap. 19.00 (*1-57950-002-1*, 95681) Highsmith Pr.

Lynch, Stacy & Smith, Michael P., eds. The Newsroom Brain: A Working Guide to Journalism Decisions. 62p. 1998. pap. 35.00 (*0-9656018-2-X*) NMC.

Lynch, Stacy C. Classical Music for Beginners. (Illus.). 176p. 1994. pap. 9.95 (*0-86316-162-6*) Writers & Readers.

***Lynch, Stephen J.** Dynamical Systems with Applications Using Maple. (Illus.). 2000. 54.50 (*0-8176-4150-5*) Birkhauser.

Lynch, Stephen J. Shakespearean Intertextuality: Studies in Selected Sources & Plays, 86. LC 98-22910. (Contributions in Drama & Theatre Studies: Vol. 86). 136p. 1998. 49.95 (*0-313-30726-1*, Greenwood Pr) Greenwood.

Lynch, Steve. Arrogance & Accords: The Inside Story of the Honda Scandal. LC 97-91854. (Illus.). 326p. 1997. 24.00 (*0-9657766-1-1*, 003) Pecos Press.

Lynch, Sylvia D. Harvey Logan in Knoxville. LC 98-44384. 1998. 25.95 (*1-57208-001-9*) Creative Texas.

Lynch, Ted, ed. see International SAMPE Technical Conference Staff.

Lynch, Ted, ed. see International SAMPE Technical Conference Staff, et al.

***Lynch, Thomas.** Bodies in Motion & at Rest: On Metaphor & Mortality. LC 00-21355. 192p. 2000. 23.95 (*0-393-04927-2*) Norton.

Lynch, Thomas. Still Life in Milford: Poems. LC 98-5934. 96p. 1998. 21.00 (*0-393-04659-1*) Norton.

— Still Life in Milford: Poems. 144p. 1999. pap. 11.00 (*0-393-31973-3*, Norton Paperbks) Norton.

— The Undertaking: Life Studies from the Dismal Trade. LC 96-40900. (Illus.). 160p. 1997. 23.00 (*0-393-04112-3*) Norton.

— The Undertaking: Life Studies from the Dismal Trade. annuals 224p. 1998. pap. 12.95 (*0-14-027623-8*) Viking Penguin.

Lynch, Thomas, ed. High Speed Rail in the U. S. Super Trains for the Millennium. (Illus.). 142p. 1998. text 45.00 (*90-5699-605-3*); pap. text 24.00 (*90-5699-606-1*) Gordon & Breach.

Lynch, Thomas D. Federal Budget & Financial Management Reform. LC 90-20711. 232p. 1991. 57.95 (*0-89930-538-5*, LFF/, Quorum Bks) Greenwood.

— Public Budgeting in America. 4th ed. LC 94-519. 400p. 1994. 56.00 (*0-13-735846-6*) P-H.

Lynch, Thomas D. & Dicker, Todd J., eds. Handbook of Organization Theory & Management: The Philosophical Approach. LC 97-45543. (Public Administration & Public Policy Ser.). (Illus.). 504p. 1997. text 195.00 (*0-8247-0113-5*) Dekker.

Lynch, Thomas D. & Martin, Lawrence L., eds. Handbook of Comparative Public Budgeting & Financial Management. LC 92-36823. (Public Administration & Public Policy Ser.: Vol. 50). (Illus.). 328p. 1992. text 175.00 (*0-8247-8773-0*) Dekker.

Lynch, Thomas J., jt. auth. see Bowman, Fred Q.

Lynch, Tim, ed. see Morin, William J.

***Lynch, Timothy, ed.** After Prohibition: An Adult Approach to Drug Policies in the 21st Century. 2000. pap. 9.95 (*1-882577-94-9*) Cato Inst.

–After Prohibition: An Adult Approach to Drug Policies in the 21st Century. 150p. 2000. 18.95 (*1-882577-93-0*) Cato Pub.

More than 10 years ago, federal officials boldly claimed that they would create a drug-free America by 1995. To reach that objective, Congress spent billions of dollars to disrupt the drug trade. Despite thousands of arrests & seizures, America is not drug-free. Illegal drugs are as readily available today as ever before. Drug prohibition has created more problems than it has solved. The drug war has shattered our cities, corrupted law enforcement & distorted our foreign policy. Yet drug prohibition is still seen as a viable strategy by most police officers, prosecutors & political leaders. Paradoxically alternative drug policies--such as legalization--fall outside the parameter of serious debate in our nation's capital. Still, the politics of drug policy are shifting. Rejecting the never ending call to escalate the drug war, voters in several states have approved referendum that would legalize marijuana for medicinal purposes. And two state governors have confounded the political pundits by openly expressing skepticism about drug wars. To illuminate this ongoing debate, the distinguished contributors to this volume examine the harmful consequences of drug prohibition & assess alternative policies. *Publisher Paid Annotation.*

***Lynch, Tom.** Fables of Aesop. LC 00-8088. (Illus.). 32p. (J). (ps up). 2000. 15.99 (*0-670-88948-2*, Viking Child) Peng Put Young Read.

— Tom Lynch's Watercolor Secrets. King, Jennifer & Dodd, Terri, eds. (Illus.). 128p. 2000. 27.95 (*1-929834-01-2*) Intl Artist Pubg.

Lynch, Tom, jt. auth. see Bowman, Fred Q.

Lynch, Tom, jt. ed. see Willis, John.

Lynch, Tony. Communication in the Language Classroom: Input, Interaction & Negotiation. (Illus.). 190p. 1996. pap. text 15.95 (*0-19-433522-4*) OUP.

Lynch, Tony, jt. auth. see Anderson, Anne.

Lynch, Tony, jt. auth. see Wells, David.

Lynch, U. S., jt. auth. see Stover, Catherine.

Lynch, V. E. Trails to Successful Trapping. 170p. 1935. pap. 4.00 (*0-936622-23-7*) A R Harding Pub.

Lynch, Vincent. American Jukebox: The Classic Years. (Illus.). 120p. (Orig.). 1990. 29.95 (*0-87701-722-0*); pap. 16.95 (*0-87701-678-X*) Chronicle Bks.

Lynch, Vincent J., et al, eds. The Changing Face of Aids: Implications for Social Work Practice. LC 92-42902. 288p. 1995. pap. 20.95 (*0-86569-260-2*, Auburn Hse) Greenwood.

— The Expanding Face of AIDS: Implications for Social Work Practice. LC 92-42902. 288p. 1993. 55.00 (*0-86569-205-X*, T205, Auburn Hse) Greenwood.

Lynch, Vincent J. & Wilson, Paul A., eds. Caring for the HIV/AIDS Caregiver. LC 96-15503. 176p. 1996. 57.95 (*0-86569-239-4*, Auburn Hse) Greenwood.

Lynch, Vivian Valvano. Portraits of Artists. LC 99-19545. 296p. 1999. 52.00 (*1-57309-364-5*) Intl Scholars.

Lynch, Wayne. A Is for Arctic: Natural Wonders of a Polar World. (Illus.). 144p. 1996. pap. 24.95 (*1-55209-048-5*) Firefly Bks Ltd.

— A Is for Arctic: Natural Wonders of a Polar World. (Illus.). 143p. 1999. reprint ed. pap. text 25.00 (*0-7881-6416-3*) DIANE Pub.

— Arctic Alphabet: Exploring the North from A to Z. LC 99-930385. (Illus.). 32p. (YA). (gr. 4-6). 1999. pap. 6.95 (*1-55209-334-4*) Firefly Bks Ltd.

— Arctic Alphabet: Exploring the North from A to Z. LC 99-930382. (Illus.). 32p. (YA). (gr. 4 up). 1999. lib. bdg. 19.95 (*1-55209-336-0*) Firefly Bks Ltd.

— Bears: Monarchs of the Northern Wilderness. LC 93-666. (Illus.). 256p. 1993. 40.00 (*0-89886-372-4*) Mountaineers.

— Bears, Bears, Bears. (Illus.). 64p. (YA). (gr. 5 up). 1995. pap. 9.95 (*1-895565-69-3*); lib. bdg. 19.95 (*1-895565-72-3*) Firefly Bks Ltd.

— Mountain Bears. 1999. pap. text 14.95 (*1-894004-28-0*) Fifth Hse Publ.

— Penguins! (Illus.). 64p. (YA). (gr. 4 up). 1999. pap. 9.95 (*1-55209-424-3*); lib. bdg. 19.95 (*1-55209-421-9*) Firefly Bks Ltd.

— Penguins of the World. (Illus.). 144p. (J). 1997. 35.00 (*1-55209-180-5*) Firefly Bks Ltd.

***Lynch, Wayne.** Whose Baby Is This? 32p. 2000. pap. 6.95 (*1-55285-064-1*) Carlton Bks Ltd.

Lynch, Wayne. Whose Feet Are These? (Illus.). 32p. pap. write for info. (*1-55110-860-7*) Whitecap Bks.

***Lynch, Wayne.** Whose House Is This? (Illus.). 32p. (J). (ps-2). 1999. pap. 6.95 (*1-55110-861-5*) Whitecap Bks.

— Wild Birds Across the Prairies. 1999. pap. text 24.95 (*1-894004-21-3*) Fifth Hse Publ.

Lynch, Wayne, jt. auth. see Lang, Aubrey.

***Lynch, Wendy.** Bach. LC 99-37330. (Lives & Times Ser.). 2000. lib. bdg. write for info. (*1-57572-214-3*) Heinemann Lib.

— Beethoven. LC 99-37329. (Lives & Times Ser.). 2000. lib. bdg. write for info. (*1-57572-215-1*) Heinemann Lib.

— Dr. Seuss. LC 99-44283. (Lives & Times Ser.). (Illus.). (J). 2000. write for info. (*1-57572-216-X*) Heinemann Lib.

— Mozart. LC 99-37280. (Lives & Times Ser.). 2000. lib. bdg. write for info. (*1-57572-219-4*) Heinemann Lib.

— Prokofiev. LC 99-37331. (Lives & Times Ser.). 2000. lib. bdg. write for info. (*1-57572-220-8*) Heinemann Lib.

Lynch, Wendy. Walt Disney. LC 97-51775. (Lives & Times Ser.). (J). 1998. 12.95 (*1-57572-671-8*) Heinemann Lib.

Lynch, William. Parksville. 120p. 1994. pap. text 10.95 (*0-88982-132-1*, Pub. by Oolichan Bks) Genl Dist Srvs.

Lynch, William, jt. ed. see Kearsley, Greg P.

Lynch, William F. Approach to the Metaphysics of Plato Through the Parmenides. LC 59-7530. 255p. 1968. reprint ed. lib. bdg. 59.50 (*0-8371-4833-2*, LYMP, Greenwood Pr) Greenwood.

— Images of Hope: Imagination as Healer of the Hopeless. LC 73-20418. (C). 1987. reprint ed. pap. text 15.00 (*0-268-00537-0*) U of Notre Dame Pr.

— Narrative of the United States' Expedition to the River Jordan & the Dead Sea. Davis, Moshe, ed. LC 77-70719. (America & the Holy Land Ser.). (Illus.). 1977. reprint ed. lib. bdg. 50.95 (*0-405-10264-X*) Ayer.

Lynch, Yvonne G. . . . Wait for the Wave. LC 97-90707. 1998. 17.95 (*0-533-12464-6*) Vantage.

Lynchard, Danny. Sure to Endure. 43p. 1983. pap. 1.95 (*0-88144-043-4*) Christian Pub.

Lynchburg College Faculty Staff. Lynchburg College Symposium Readings Vol. I: Tyranny & Freedom. LC 93-26942. 408p. (Orig.). 1993. pap. 24.95 (*0-8191-9284-8*); lib. bdg. 45.00 (*0-8191-9323-2*) U Pr of Amer.

— War & Peace: Toynbee, Hawtrey, Wright. 366p. (Orig.). (C). 1993. pap. text 24.95 (*0-8191-9285-6*) U Pr of Amer.

— War & Peace: Toynbee, Hawtrey, Wright. (Lynchburg College Symposium Readings Ser.: Vol. II). 366p. (Orig.). (C). 1993. lib. bdg. 45.00 (*0-8191-9324-0*) U Pr of Amer.

Lynchburg College Faculty Staff, ed. The Nature of Man: Series One, Volume I, Series 1, Vol. I. LC 82-45158. (Classical Selections on Great Issues, Symposium Readings Ser.). 480p. (Orig.). (C). 1982. pap. text 16.50 (*0-8191-2463-X*) U Pr of Amer.

***Lyncheski, Stephanie.** Huron River Hunting & Fishing Club Celebrates Seventy-Five Years. Myers, Karen, ed. 88p. 2000. 30.00 (*0-929690-50-8*) Herit Pubs AZ.

Lynd, Alice & Lynd, Staughton. Liberation Theology for Quakers. 1996. pap. 4.00 (*0-87574-326-9*) Pendle Hill.

Lynd, Alice & Lynd, Staughton, eds. Rank & File: Personal Histories by Working-Class Organizers. 320p. (YA). (gr. 9-12). 1988. reprint ed. pap. 12.00 (*0-85345-752-2*, Pub. by Monthly Rev) NYU Pr.

Lynd, Alice, jt. auth. see Lynd, Staughton.

Lynd, Alice, jt. ed. see Lynd, Staughton.

Lynd, Deborah. Lotus Notes & Domino 5 Development Unleashed. (Unleashed Ser.). 1400p. 1999. pap. 49.99 (*0-672-31414-2*) Sams.

Lynd, Helen M. England in the Eighteen-Eighties: Toward a Social Basis for Freedom. 518p. 1984. 49.95 (*0-88738-004-2*) Transaction Pubs.

Lynd, Helen M., jt. auth. see Lynd, Robert S.

Lynd, Louise. Creative Fund Raising. LC 87-60658. 94p. 1987. pap. 9.95 (*0-9618773-0-8*) PC Ltd.

Lynd, Robert. Art of Letters. LC 71-152191. (Essay Index Reprint Ser.). 1977. reprint ed. 19.95 (*0-8369-2239-5*) Ayer.

An Asterisk (*) at the beginning of an entry indicates that the title is appearing for the first time.

— Blue Lion, & Other Essays. LC 68-55848. (Essay Index Reprint Ser.). 1977. 19.95 (*0-8369-0638-1*) Ayer.

— Books & Authors. LC 73-90659. (Essay Index Reprint Ser.). 1977. 19.95 (*0-8369-1209-8*) Ayer.

— Books & Writers. LC 71-105028. (Essay Index Reprint Ser.). 1977. 29.95 (*0-8369-1525-9*) Ayer.

— Dr. Johnson & Company. LC 73-21749. (English Biography Ser.: No. 31). 1974. lib. bdg. 75.00 (*0-8383-1836-3*) M S G Haskell Hse.

— Galway of the Races. 1996. 19.95 (*0-946640-48-3*, Pub. by Lilliput Pr) Irish Bks Media.

— Money-Box. LC 70-84321. (Essay Index Reprint Ser.). 1977. 18.95 (*0-8369-1091-5*) Ayer.

— Old & New Masters. LC 79-111845. (Essay Index Reprint Ser.). 1977. 20.95 (*0-8369-1616-6*) Ayer.

— Passion of Labour. LC 73-76909. (Essay Index Reprint Ser.). 1977. 19.95 (*0-8369-0025-1*) Ayer.

— Peal of Bells. LC 78-90660. (Essay Index Reprint Ser.). 1977. 20.95 (*0-8369-1226-8*) Ayer.

— Peal of Bells. LC 75-131772. 1971. reprint ed. 16.00 (*0-403-00659-7*) Scholarly.

Lynd, Robert S. Knowledge for What? The Place of Social Science in American Culture. LC 86-7795. 287p. 1986. reprint ed. pap. 89.00 (*0-608-02320-5*, 206296100004) Bks Demand.

— Solomon in All His Glory. LC 72-86769. (Essay Index Reprint Ser.). 1977. 21.95 (*0-8369-1420-1*) Ayer.

Lynd, Robert S. & Lynd, Helen M. Middletown. 562p. (C). 1959. pap. 15.00 (*0-15-659550-8*, Harvest Bks) Harcourt.

Lynd, Staughter. Solidarity Unionism. 64p. (Orig.). 1992. pap. 9.00 (*0-88286-208-1*) C H Kerr.

Lynd, Staughton. Class Conflict, Slavery & the United States Constitution: Ten Essays. LC 80-18219. 288p. 1980. reprint ed. lib. bdg. 59.50 (*0-313-22672-5*, LYCC, Greenwood Pr) Greenwood.

— Fight Against Shutdowns: Youngstown's Fight Against Steelmill Closings. LC 82-60169. 256p. (Orig.). 1982. pap. 10.95 (*0-917300-14-9*) Singlejack Bks.

— The Fight Against Shutdowns: Youngstown's Steel Mill Closings. 244p. 1992. reprint ed. pap. 10.00 (*0-88286-217-0*) C H Kerr.

— Labor Law for the Rank & Filer. 64p. 1994. pap. 10.00 (*0-88286-222-7*) C H Kerr.

— Labor Law for the Rank & Filer. rev. ed. LC 77-95429. 1982. pap. 2.95 (*0-917300-04-1*) Singlejack Bks.

— Living Inside Our Hope: A Steadfast Radical's Thoughts on Rebuilding the Movement. LC 96-39270. (ILR Press Book). (Illus.). 1996. text 39.95 (*0-8014-3363-0*); pap. text 15.95 (*0-8014-8402-2*) Cornell U Pr.

— Living Inside Our Hope: A Steadfast Radical's Thoughts on Rebuilding the Movement. 1997. 37.50 (*0-614-27584-9*); pap. 14.95 (*0-614-27583-0*) Cornell U Pr.

Lynd, Staughton, ed. We Are All Leaders: The Alternative Unionism of the Early 1930s. 1995. write for info. (*0-614-96404-0*) U of Ill Pr.

— "We Are All Leaders" The Alternative Unionism of the Early 1930s. (Working Class in American History Ser.). 336p. 1996. text 44.95 (*0-252-02243-2*) U of Ill Pr.

— "We Are All Leaders" The Alternative Unionism of the Early 1930s. (Working Class in American History Ser.). 336p. 1996. pap. text 19.95 (*0-252-06547-6*) U of Ill Pr.

***Lynd, Staughton & Lynd, Alice.** The New Rank & File. LC 00-9146. 2000. pap. write for info. (*0-8014-8676-9*) Cornell U Pr.

***Lynd, Staughton & Lynd, Alice, eds.** The New Rank & File. 2000. pap. 15.95 (*0-8014-3806-3*, ILR Press) Cornell U Pr.

Lynd, Staughton & Lynd, Alice, eds. Nonviolence in America: A Documentary History. rev. ed. LC 94-41973. 576p. reprint ed. pap. 178.60 (*0-608-20192-8*, 207145100012) Bks Demand.

— Nonviolence in America: A Documentary History. rev. ed. LC 94-41973. 600p. 1995. 45.00 (*1-57075-013-0*); pap. 25.00 (*1-57075-010-6*) Orbis Bks.

Lynd, Staughton, et al. Homeland: Oral Histories of Palestine & Palestinians. LC 93-8075. 288p. 1994. 35.00 (*1-56656-133-7*, Olive Branch Pr); pap. 14.95 (*1-56656-132-9*, Olive Branch Pr) Interlink Pub.

Lynd, Staughton, jt. auth. see Lynd, Alice.

Lynd, Staughton, jt. ed. see Lynd, Alice.

Lynd, Sylvia. Mulberry Bush. LC 78-142886. (Short Story Index Reprint Ser.). 1977. 19.95 (*0-8369-3751-1*) Ayer.

Lyndaker Lindsey, Susan, et al. The Okapi: Mysterious Animal of Cong-Zaire. LC 98-28740. 140p. 1999. pap. 17.95 (*0-292-74707-1*) U of Tex Pr.

Lyndall, Terri M. Law Office Management. (Paralegal Ser.). 1992. pap., teacher ed. 9.00 (*0-8273-4866-5*) Delmar.

Lyndall, Terri M., jt. auth. see Lynton, Jonathan S.

Lynde, Bill. From a Journalist's Notebook: Unforgettable Characters I Have Known. LC 98-71010. 208p. 1998. pap. 12.95 (*1-58151-004-7*) BookPartners.

Lynde, Denyse, ed. see Pickard, Liz, et al.

Lynde Dix, Dorothea, jt. auth. see Lightner, David L.

Lynde, Eleanor. Daylight in the Canyon: The Memoirs of Eleanor Lynde. 2nd ed. (Illus.). 231p. reprint ed. pap. text. write for info. (*0-9639967-0-3*) Daylght MT.

Lynde, Francis. Cripple Creek, Nineteen Hundred. Jones, William R., ed. (Illus.). 20p. 1976. reprint ed. pap. 2.00 (*0-89646-001-0*) Vistabooks.

— The Grafters. LC 68-20017. (Americans in Fiction Ser.). 408p. reprint ed. pap. text 7.95 (*0-89197-774-0*); reprint ed. lib. bdg. 30.50 (*0-8398-1177-2*) Irvington.

***Lynde-Recchia, Molly.** Prose, Verse & Truth-Telling in the Thirteenth Century: An Essay on Form & Function in Selected Texts, Accompanied by an Edition of the Prose Thebes as Found in the Histoire Ancienne Jusqu'a Cesar. LC 99-75745. (Edward C. Armstrong Monographs on Medieval Literature: Vol. 10). 206p. 2000. pap. 34.50 (*0-917058-92-5*) French Forum.

Lynde, Rob, jt. auth. see Curtin, Dave.

Lynde, Stan. The Bodacious Kid. Prezeau, Jael, ed. LC 95-68395. (Illus.). 256p. 1996. 24.95 (*1-886370-10-9*, BK71) Cttnwd Pub.

— Careless Creek. unabridged ed. Prezeau, Jael, ed. (Illus.). 296p. 1998. pap. 16.95 (*1-886370-12-5*) Cttnwd Pub.

— Grass Roots: The Complete Cartoon Series. 2nd rev. ed. LC 91-77329. (Illus.). 152p. 1993. pap. 13.00 (*0-9626999-4-2*, BK51) Cttnwd Pub.

***Lynde, Stan.** Grass Roots, 1998-1999. LC 99-94843. (Illus.). 128p. 1999. pap. 15.95 (*1-886370-15-X*, Pub. by Cttnwd Pub) Mountain Pr.

Lynde, Stan. Latigo, 1979-1980, Bk. 1. LC 91-77330. (Illus.). 88p. (Orig.). 1991. pap. 9.95 (*0-9626999-3-4*, BK20) Cttnwd Pub.

— Latigo, 1980-1981, Bk. 2. LC 91-77330. (Illus.). 72p. (Orig.). 1992. pap. 9.95 (*0-9626999-7-7*, BK21) Cttnwd Pub.

— Latigo, 1981-1983, Bk. 3. LC 94-72092. (Illus.). 168p. (Orig.). 1994. pap. 18.95 (*0-9626999-9-3*, BK22) Cttnwd Pub.

— A Month of Sundays: The Best of Rick O'Shay & Hipshot. 2nd ed. LC 92-72285. (Illus.). 64p. (Orig.). 1993. reprint ed. pap. 15.00 (*0-9626999-8-5*, BK60) Cttnwd Pub.

— New Adventures of Rick O'Shay & Hipshot Bks. 1 & 2: Price of Fame, 2 vols., Set. 64p. 1992. pap. text 10.00 (*1-886370-13-3*) Cttnwd Pub.

— Pardners, Bks. 1 & 2. LC 90-84936. (Illus.). 88p. (J). (gr. 3 up). 1991. pap. 14.95 (*1-886370-14-1*) Cttnwd Pub.

— Rick O'Shay: The Dailies, 1961-1962, No. 2. LC 95-68475. 160p. 1995. pap. text 20.00 (*1-886370-01-X*, BK62) Cttnwd Pub.

— Rick O'Shay, Hipshot & Me: A Memoir. 2nd ed. Gold, Mike, ed. LC 90-82941. (Illus.). 264p. (J). 1990. reprint ed. pap. 18.95 (*0-9626999-0-X*, BK02) Cttnwd Pub.

— Rick O'Shay, the Dailies, 1958. (Illus.). 88p. (Orig.). 1997. reprint ed. pap. 14.95 (*1-886370-09-5*, BK-70) Cttnwd Pub.

— Rick O'Shay, the Dailies, 1963-1964. (Illus.). 176p. 1996. reprint ed. pap. 18.95 (*1-886370-02-8*, BK-63) Cttnwd Pub.

Lynden-Bell, D., ed. Cosmical Magnetism: Proceedings of the NATO Advanced Research Workshop, Cambridge, England, July 5-9, 1993. LC 94-668. (NATO Advanced Study Institutes Series C, Mathematical & Physical Sciences: Vol. 422). 228p. (C). 1994. text 136.00 (*0-7923-2730-6*) Kluwer Academic.

Lynden-Bell, D. & Gilmore, Gerry, eds. Baryonic Dark Matter. (C). 1990. text 155.00 (*0-7923-0699-6*) Kluwer Academic.

Lynden, Frederick C. & Chapman, E. A., eds. Advances in Librarianship, Vol. 22. (Illus.). 189p. (C). 1998. text 89.95 (*0-12-024622-8*) Acad Pr.

***Lynden, Frederick C. & Chapman, Elizabeth, eds.** Advances in Librarianship Vol. 23. 385p. 1999. 99.95 (*0-12-024623-6*) Acad Pr.

Lynden, Frederick C., jt. ed. see Chapman, Elizabeth A.

***Lyndon B. Johnson School of Public Affairs. Policy Research Project on Colonia Housing and Infrastructure.** Colonia Housing & Infrastructure. LC 97-74582. (Illus.). 1998. write for info. (*0-89940-737-4*) LBJ Sch Pub Aff.

Lyndon Baines Johnson Library. Lyndon B. Johnson National Security Files: National Security Files, November 1963-june 1965. LC 89-955812. (The Presidential Documents Ser.). 17 p. 1985. write for info. (*0-89093-461-4*) U Pubns Amer.

— The Lyndon B. Johnson National Security Files, 1963-1969: Project Coordinator, Robert E. Lester. LC 98-159189. (National Security Files Ser.). 18 p. 1996. write for info. (*1-55655-643-8*) U Pubns Amer.

Lyndon Baines Johnson Library Staff, jt. auth. see Johnson, Lyndon B.

Lyndon, Donlyn & Moore, Charles W. Chambers for a Memory Palace. (Illus.). 338p. 1996. reprint ed. pap. text 19.00 (*0-262-62105-3*) MIT Pr.

Lyndon, R. F. The Shoot Apical Meristem: Its Growth & Development. LC 98-10719. (Developmental & Cell Biology Ser.: No. 34). (Illus.). 288p. (C). 1998. 90.00 (*0-521-40457-6*) Cambridge U Pr.

Lyndon, Robert. Plant Development: The Cellular Basis. (Topics in Plant Physiology Ser.: No. 3). (Illus.). 220p. (C). 1990. text 75.00 (*0-04-581032-X*) Routledge.

— Plant Development: The Cellular Basis. (Topics in Plant Physiology Ser.: No. 3). (Illus.). 220p. (C). 1990. pap. 49.95 (*0-04-581033-8*) Thomson Learn.

Lyndon, Sonja & Paskin, Sylvia, eds. The Slow Mirror & Other Stories: New Fiction by Jewish Writers. LC 97-176056. 240p. (Orig.). 1997. pap. 15.00 (*0-907123-81-3*, Pub. by Five Leaves) AK Pr Dist.

Lynds, Beverly T., ed. Dark Nebulae, Globules, & Protostars. LC 73-152040. 160p. reprint ed. pap. 49.60 (*0-608-15937-9*, 203098100073) Bks Demand.

Lynds, Dennis. Talking to the World: And Other Stories. LC 94-26635. 176p. (Orig.). 1995. 18.95 (*1-880284-10-3*) J Daniel.

— Why Girls Ride Sidesaddle. LC 79-50801. (Illus.). 115p. 1980. pap. 15.00 (*0-913204-13-7*) December Pr.

Lynds, Gayle. Masquerade. 464p. 1997. mass mkt. 6.99 (*0-425-16019-X*) Berkley Pub.

***Lynds, Gayle.** Mesmerized. 2000. write for info. (*0-671-02407-8*) PB.

Lynds, Gayle. Mosaic. 1999. per. 6.99 (*0-671-02406-X*) PB.

— Mosaic. 480p. 1998. 24.00 (*0-671-02405-1*) S&S Trade.

Lynds, Gayle, jt. auth. see Ludlum, Robert.

Lynds, Joe, jt. auth. see Debetta, Peter.

Lynds, Sheila, ed. see Hanson, A. E.

Lyne, Alice. A, My Name Is... LC 96-29262. (Illus.). 32p. (J). (ps-2). 1997. 14.95 (*1-879085-40-2*, Whispering Coyote) Charlesbridge Pub.

— A, My Name Is Alex... LC 96-29262. (Illus.). 32p. (J). (ps-2). 1997. pap. 5.95 (*1-879085-41-0*, Whispering Coyote) Charlesbridge Pub.

Lyne, Andrew G. & Graham-Smith, Francis. Pulsar Astronomy. 2nd rev. ed. LC 97-16354. (Cambridge Astrophysics Ser.: No. 31). (Illus.). 276p. (C). 1998. text 80.00 (*0-521-59413-8*) Cambridge U Pr.

Lyne, G. M. Personae Comicae. (C). 1982. pap. text 39.00 (*0-900269-11-1*, Pub. by Old Vicarage) St Mut.

— Personae Comicae. 48p. 1992. reprint ed. 6.00 (*0-86516-031-7*) Bolchazy-Carducci.

***Lyne, Jack.** Schoolhouse Dreams Deferred: Decay, Hope, & Desegregation in a Core-City School System. LC 98-68411. ix, 321p. 1999. pap. 18.00 (*0-87367-738-2*) Phi Delta Kappa.

Lyne, Lawrence S., ed. A Cross Section of Educational Research: Journal Articles for Discussion & Evaluation. LC 99-229045. (Illus.). 192p. (C). 1999. pap. text 23.95 (*1-884585-16-7*) Pyrczak Pub.

Lyne, Patricia M., et al. Collins & Lyne's Microbiological Methods. 7th ed. LC 94-21648. (Illus.). 480p. 1995. pap. text 73.00 (*0-7506-0653-3*) Buttrwrth-Heinemann.

Lyne, R. N. Zanzibar in Contemporary Times. 384p. 1987. 270.00 (*1-85077-173-1*, Pub. by Darf Pubs Ltd) St Mut.

Lyne, R. O. Further Voices in Virgil's Aeneid. 262p. 1992. pap. text 29.95 (*0-19-814092-4*) OUP.

Lyne, R. O. Horace: Public Poet & Private Self. LC 94-43759. 1995. 32.50 (*0-300-06322-9*) Yale U Pr.

Lyne, R. O. Words & the Poet: Characteristic Techniques of Style in Vergil's Aeneid. 224p. 1990. text 60.00 (*0-19-814896-8*) OUP.

— Words & the Poet: Characteristic Techniques of Style in Vergil's Aeneid. 224p. 1998. reprint ed. pap. text 25.00 (*0-19-815261-2*) OUP.

Lyne, R. O., ed. see Catullus, Gaius Valerius.

Lyne, Sandford, ed. Ten-Second Rainshowers: Poems by Young People. LC 95-1071. (Illus.). 124p. (J). (gr. 3 up). 1996. per. 16.00 (*0-689-80113-0*) S&S Bks Yung.

Lyne, Sandy. The Lion & the Boy. (Illus.). 48p. (J). (gr. 4-7). 1988. 12.95 (*0-933905-04-1*); pap. 9.95 (*0-933905-15-7*) Claycomb Pr.

Lyne, William R. The Tanoan-Egyptian Djed Festival Stone: Thothmes III's Expedition to America, c. 1475 B.C. (Illus.). 112p. (YA). 1999. pap. 10.00 (*0-9637467-3-1*) Creatopia Prods.

— Voyage to Quiburio Vol. 1: Dawn at Galistea. (Illus.). 264p. (Orig.). (YA). 1998. pap. 18.00 (*0-9637467-4-X*) Creatopia Prods.

Lyne, Wm. R. Free Energy Surprise. (Illus.). 20p. 1998. pap. 10.00 (*0-9637467-5-8*) Creatopia Prods.

Lyneham, Paul, jt. ed. see Olle, Annette.

Lyneis, M. M., et al. Journal of California & Great Basin Anthropology, No. 10:2. (Malki Museum, Journal of California & Great Basin Anthropology Ser.). (Illus.). 142p. 1988. pap. text 15.63 (*1-55567-840-8*) Coyote Press.

Lyneis, Margaret M. The Main Ridge Community at Lost City: Virgin Anasazi Architecture, Ceramics, & Burials. LC 92-53608. (Anthropological Papers: No. 117). (Illus.). 120p. 1992. pap. 25.00 (*0-87480-411-6*) U of Utah Pr.

Lyneis, Margaret M., et al. Impacts: Damage to Cultural Resources in the California Desert. (Illus.). 180p. (C). 1980. reprint ed. pap. text 19.38 (*1-55567-403-8*) Coyote Press.

Lynes, John. Cycling in Ontario. Ulysses Travel Guide Staff, ed. (Illus.). 320p. 1999. 16.95 (*2-89464-191-5*) Ulysses Travel.

***Lynes, John.** Ontario's Bike Paths & Railtrails. 2000. pap. 14.95 (*2-89464-263-6*, Pub. by Ulysses Travel) Globe Pequot.

Lynes, Barbara B. O'Keefe, Stieglitz & the Critics, 1916 to 1929. LC 90-48860. (Illus.). 392p. 1998. pap. 17.95 (*0-226-49824-7*) U Ch Pr.

Lynes, Carlos, Jr., ed. see Camus, Albert.

Lynes, Carlos, Jr., ed. see Proust, Marcel.

Lynes, John W. Themes in the Current Reformation in Religious Thinking: The Covenantal Friendship of God. LC 97-2069. (Studies in Religion & Society: Vol. 36). 220p. 1997. text 89.95 (*0-7734-8674-7*) E Mellen.

Lynes, Robert. Teaching English in Eastern & Central Europe: Finding Work, Teaching & Living in Europe. LC 95-68431. (Illus.). 304p. 1995. pap. 14.95 (*0-8442-0876-0*, 08760, Passprt Bks) NTC Contemp Pub Co.

Lynes, Russell. The Art Makers: An Informal History of Painting, Sculpture, & Architecture in 19th Century America. (Illus.). 526p. 1982. reprint ed. pap. 10.95 (*0-486-24239-0*) Dover.

— The Tastemakers. LC 82-25116. (Illus.). 362p. (C). 1983. reprint ed. lib. bdg. 67.50 (*0-313-23843-X*, LYTA, Greenwood Pr) Greenwood.

Lyness, James. Multiple Choice Questions in Preparation for the AP Computer Science ("A" & "AB") Examination. 2nd ed. 69p. 1989. student ed. 15.95 (*1-878621-18-1*) D & S Mktg Syst.

Lyness, Jeffrey M. Psychiatric Pearls. LC 96-29495. (Illus.). 328p. 1997. pap. 21.95 (*0-8036-0280-4*) Davis Co.

Lyness, Stephanie, tr. see Maniere, Jacques.

Lyng. Career Mathematics. 1988. text, student ed. 52.04 (*0-395-48342-5*) HM.

— Career Mathematics. (C). 1988. pap., teacher ed. 45.08 (*0-395-48343-3*) HM.

Lyng, Merwin J. Dancing Curves: A Dynamic Demonstration of Geometric Principles. LC 78-2781. (Illus.). 16p. 1978. pap. 8.95 (*0-87353-124-8*) NCTM.

Lyng, Stephen. Holistic Health & Biomedical Medicine: A Countersystem Analysis. LC 89-11531. (SUNY Series in the Political Economy of Health Care). 268p. (C). 1990. text 64.50 (*0-7914-0255-X*); pap. text 21.95 (*0-7914-0256-8*) State U NY Pr.

Lyngaae-Jorgensen, J., jt. ed. see Sondergaard, K.

Lyngdoh, Mary P. The Festival in the History & Culture of the Khasi. 1991. text 30.00 (*0-7069-5615-X*, Pub. by Vikas) S Asia.

***Lynge, Dana & Weiss, Barry.** 20 Common Procedures in Primary Care. (Illus.). 512p. 2000. Price not set. (*0-07-136002-6*) McGraw.

Lynge, Johannes. Rules, Language Games & the Autonomy of Understanding. 208p. 1997. pap. 26.00 (*82-00-12680-3*) Scandnvan Univ Pr.

Lyngheim, Linda. California Gold Rush Projects & Activities. (California Junior Heritage Ser.). (Illus.). 56p. (J). (gr. 3-12). 1998. pap. 9.95 (*0-915369-07-9*) Langtry Pubns.

— California Mission Projects & Activities. LC 93-79027. (California Junior Heritage Ser.). (Illus.). 54p. (Orig.). (J). (gr. 3-6). 1993. pap. 9.95 (*0-915369-05-2*) Langtry Pubns.

— Gold Rush Adventure. rev. ed. LC 87-82679. (California Junior Heritage Ser.). (Illus.). 96p. (J). (gr. 3-6). 1997. 13.95 (*0-915369-03-6*); pap. 10.95 (*0-915369-02-8*) Langtry Pubns.

— The Indians & the California Missions. rev. ed. LC 84-80543. (California Junior Heritage Ser.). (Illus.). 160p. (J). (gr. 4-6). 1990. 14.95 (*0-915369-04-4*); pap. 10.95 (*0-915369-00-1*) Langtry Pubns.

Lyngheim, Linda, et al. Father Junipero Serra, the Traveling Missionary. LC 85-82131. (Illus.). 64p. (J). (gr. 3-5). 1986. 13.95 (*0-915369-01-X*) Langtry Pubns.

Lyngheim, Lynda, jt. auth. see Scagnetti, Jack.

Lyngso. Danish Insurance Law. 1992. pap. text 70.50 (*90-6544-657-5*) Kluwer Academic.

Lyngstad, Alexandra & Lyngstad, Sverre. Ivan Goncharov. 184p. 1971. 49.50 (*0-685-63210-5*) Elliots Bks.

Lyngstad, Alexandra H. Dostoevskij & Schiller. 1975. pap. text 32.35 (*3-10-800094-2*) Mouton.

Lyngstad, Sverre. Jonas Lie. LC 76-50007. (Twayne's World Authors Ser.). 223p. (C). 1977. lib. bdg. 17.95 (*0-8057-6274-4*) Irvington.

— Sigurd Hoel's Fiction: Cultural Criticism & Tragic Vision, 6. LC 83-26470. (Contributions to the Study of World Literature Ser.: No. 6). 198p. 1984. 49.95 (*0-313-24343-3*, LSH/, Greenwood Pr) Greenwood.

Lyngstad, Sverre, et al, eds. Norway. (Review of National Literatures Ser.: Vol. 12). 240p. 1983. pap. 6.95 (*0-918680-17-4*) Griffon House.

Lyngstad, Sverre, jt. auth. see Hamsun, Knut.

Lyngstad, Sverre, jt. auth. see Lyngstad, Alexandra.

Lyngstad, Sverre, ed. & tr. see Hamsun, Knut.

Lyngstad, Sverre, tr. see Askildsen, Kjell.

Lyngstad, Sverre, tr. see Garborg, Arne.

Lyngstad, Sverre, tr. see Haff, Bergljot.

Lyngstad, Sverre, tr. see Hamsun, Knut.

Lyngstad, Sverre, tr. see Hoel, Sigurd.

Lyngstad, Sverre, tr. & afterword by see Faldbakken, Knut.

Lynip, Ryllis G., jt. auth. see Garrick, David.

Lynk, Miles V. The Black Troopers. LC 70-153875. reprint ed. 29.50 (*0-404-00196-3*) AMS Pr.

Lynk, William M. Dinner Theatre: A Survey & Directory. LC 92-36607. 160p. 1993. lib. bdg. 59.95 (*0-313-28442-3*, LDE, Greenwood Pr) Greenwood.

Lynlee, J. L. All That Glitters. rev. ed. LC 86-61197. (Illus.). 128p. 1996. pap. 16.95 (*0-88740-969-5*) Schiffer.

***Lynn.** Battle. 2000. pap. 18.00 (*0-8133-3372-5*, Pub. by Westview) HarpC.

Lynn. Introduction to Environmental Biology. 2nd ed. 46p. (C). 1997. student ed., spiral bd. 16.00 (*0-7872-4301-9*) Kendall-Hunt.

— Introductory Musicianship. 5th ed. LC 96-77246. (C). 1996. pap. text 63.50 (*0-15-501612-1*) Harcourt.

Lynn, ed. Introduction to Literature. (C). 1998. pap. text, teacher ed. write for info. (*0-321-40037-2*) Addson-Wesley Educ.

Lynn, jt. auth. see Darling.

Lynn, Adele B. In Search of Honor: Lessons from Workers on How to Build Trust & Spark Inspiration. LC 98-71506. (Illus.). 200p. 1998. 22.95 (*0-9664084-4-6*) BajonHse Pub.

Lynn, Amy. Bits of Heaven: Life's Lessons & God's Miracles. 184p. 1999. pap. 10.95 (*1-58169-029-0*, Evergrn Pr AL) Genesis Comm Inc.

— Hidden Castle: A Message of Hope & Recovery. 144p. 1998. pap. 7.95 (*0-9637311-9-X*) Genesis Comm Inc.

— Seeds of the Heart: A Daily Guide to Hope & Recovery. 288p. 1998. pap. 12.95 (*0-9637311-4-9*) Genesis Comm Inc.

***Lynn, Amy.** When the Petal Falls: A Woman's Guide to Hope & Healing. 160p. 2000. pap. 9.95 (*1-58169-051-7*, Evergrn Pr AL) Genesis Comm Inc.

***Lynn, Andrea.** Shadow Lovers. 256p. 2000. 25.00 (*0-8133-3394-6*, Pub. by Westview) HarpC.

Lynn, Andrew J. Small Business Tax Guide: Guide to Small Business Tax. (Illus.). (Orig.). 1992. pap. 24.95 (*1-877983-04-7*) Data-Lynn Bk.

— Starting a Small Business Handbook: How to Start & Operate Your Own Small Business. 2nd rev. ed. (Illus.). 190p. (Orig.). 1992. pap. 24.95 (*1-877983-05-5*) Data-Lynn Bk.

Lynn, Ann. Beautiful Dreamer. (Historical Ser.). 1994. per. 3.99 (*0-373-28834-4*, 1-28834-9) Harlequin Bks.

Lynn-Ann, ed. see Valenti, Vince & Jaeger, Jag.

Lynn, Arthur D., Jr., ed. The Property Tax & Its Administration. LC 69-16110. 260p. 1969. reprint ed. pap. 80.60 (*0-608-01925-9*, 206258000003) Bks Demand.

— Property Taxation, Land Use & Public Policy: Proceedings of a Symposium Sponsored by the Committee on Taxation, Resources & Economic Development (TRED) at the University of Wisconsin-Madison, 1973. LC 75-12210. (Publications

L

of the Committee on Taxation, Resources & Economic Development: Vol. 8). 267p. 1976. reprint ed. pap. 82.80 (0-608-01960-7, 20626150003) Bks Demand.

Lynn, B. W. & Verzegnassi, C., eds. Tests of Electroweak Theories, Polarized Processes & Other Phenomena: Proceedings of the 2nd ICTP Conference on Tests of Electroweak Physics, Trieste, Italy, June 1985. 476p. 1987. pap. 51.00 (9971-5-0305-0); text 124.00 (9971-5-0300-X) World Scientific Pub.

Lynn, B. W. & Wheater, J. F., eds. Radiative Corrections in SU (2) L X U (1) Proceedings of the Workshop on Radiative Corrections in SU (2) O X U (1), Miramore, Trieste, Italy, June 6-8. 340p. 1984. 55.00 (9971-966-26-3); pap. 33.00 (9971-966-28-X) World Scientific Pub.

Lynn, Bari. Eclectic Living: Ideas for Creating Your Own Unique Home Style. LC 98-17610. (Illus.). 192p. 1998. 26.00 (0-06-019117-1) HarpC.

— Weekends with Bari Lynn. Date not set. 27.50 (0-06-019118-X) HarpC.

Lynn-Barnes, Diana. Celebrity Parenting: Famous Parents Share Personal Stories. 240p. (Orig.). 1992. pap. 12.95 (0-9633286-3-8) F Charles Pubns.

Lynn, Barry, et al. Your Right to Religious Liberty: A Basic Guide to Religious Rights. LC 94-13635. (ACLU Handbook Ser.). 128p. (C). 1995. pap. 9.95 (0-8093-1967-5) S Ill U Pr.

Lynn, Barry W. Polluting the Censorship Debate: A Summary & Critique of the Final Report of the Attorney General's Commission on Pornography. 188p. 1986. 5.00 (0-86566-040-9) ACLU DC.

Lynn, Brendan. Holding the Ground: The Nationalist Party in Northern Ireland. LC 97-7846. 288p. 1997. text 72.95 (1-85521-980-8, Pub. by Ashgate Pub) Ashgate Pub Co.

Lynn, Cari, jt. auth. see Gugliemo, Anthony.

Lynn, Caroline. Kentucky Wildlife Viewing Guide. LC 94-38073. (Falcon Guides Ser.). (Illus.). 80p. (Orig.). 1994. pap. 8.95 (1-56044-304-9) Falcon Pub Inc.

Lynn, Catherine. Wallpaper in America: From the Seventeenth Century to World War I. (Illus.). 1980. 45.00 (0-393-01448-7) Norton.

— The White Dress. Johnson, Marilyn, ed. (Illus.). (Orig.). 1996. pap. 15.00 (0-943795-30-3) Chiron Rev.

Lynn, Cathy, ed. Expressions. 32p. (Orig.). 1984. pap. write for info. (0-318-57742-9) Myriad.

Lynn Chao, Yenshew, intro. Card Catalog of the Rubel Asiatic Research Collection: Harvard University Fine Arts Library, 7 Vols. 3680p. 1989. lib. bdg. 1720.00 (0-86291-852-9) U Pubns Amer.

***Lynn, Claudia.** All about Life: To My Children. 2000. pap. 15.95 (0-9674225-0-7) Bequest Bks.

Lynn, Cynthia. No More Hotels in Paris: How to Find Alternative Accommodations. LC 98-65293. 140p. 1999. per. 14.95 (1-879899-08-6) Newjoy Pr.

— No More Hotels in Rome Vol. 2: How to Find Alternative Accommodations. 210p. 2000. pap. 14.95 (1-879899-22-1) Newjoy Pr.

Lynn, D. M. & Sulmeyer, Irving. Collier Handbook for Trustees & Debtors in Possession. text 110.00 (0-8205-4169-9) Bender.

Lynn, David. Fortune Telling. LC 97-777971. (Short Fiction Ser.). 221p. 1998. pap. 15.95 (0-88748-283-X) Carnegie-Mellon.

— High School Talk Sheets: 50 Creative Discussions for High School Youth Groups. 112p. 1987. pap. 12.99 (0-310-20931-5, 13262P) Zondervan.

— Junior High Talksheets. 112p. 1988. pap. 12.99 (0-310-20941-2, 13263P) Zondervan.

— More High School Talksheets: Fifty All-New Creative Discussions for High School Youth Groups. 112p. (YA). 1992. pap. 12.99 (0-310-57491-9) Zondervan.

— More Junior High Talksheets: Fifty All-New Creative Discussions for Junior High Youth Groups. 112p. (YA). 1992. pap. 12.99 (0-310-57481-1) Zondervan.

— Twisters: Questions You Never Thought to Ask. 176p. 1990. pap. 8.99 (0-310-52262-5) Zondervan.

Lynn, David. Zingers: Twenty-Five Real-Life Character Builders. 64p. 1990. mass mkt. 9.99 (0-310-52511-X) Zondervan.

Lynn, David & Lynn, Kathy. Great Games for Kids. 128p. 1990. pap. 10.99 (0-310-52541-1) Zondervan.

— More Great Fundraising Ideas for Youth Ministry: Over 150 More Easy-to-Use Money-Makers That Really Work. LC 95-41234. 144p. 1996. pap. 12.99 (0-310-20780-0) Zondervan.

Lynn, David & Lynn, Kathy, eds. Great Fundraising Ideas for Youth Groups. 208p. 1993. pap. 12.99 (0-310-67171-X) Zondervan.

Lynn, David & Yaconelli, Mike. Grow for It! Journal Through the Scriptures: Your Personal Spiritual Growth Diary Through 52 Important Bible Passages. 128p. 1994. pap. 9.99 (0-310-49031-6) Zondervan.

Lynn, David H. The Kenyon Review. 231p. (Orig.). 1999. pap. 8.00 (1-883840-00-7) Kenyon Review.

Lynn, Donald, jt. auth. see Menhart, John.

Lynn, Duke, jt. auth. see Lichtman, Kevin.

Lynn, Dyanna. Wildheart's Wishupons: Believe in Your Magic. LC 97-51444. (Illus.). 48p. (J). (gr. k-7). 1998. 17.95 (0-9658863-0-1) Tail Feather Bks.

Lynn-Dyson, Karen, jt. ed. see Ellwood, David.

Lynn, Elizabeth A. The Chronicles of Tornor: The Complete Trilogy. 560p. 1998. pap. 16.00 (0-441-00559-4) Ace Bks.

***Lynn, Elizabeth A.** The Dancers of Arun. (Chronicles of Tornor Ser.: Bk. 2). 2000. reprint ed. pap. 13.00 (0-441-00687-6) Ace Bks.

Lynn, Elizabeth A. Dragon's Winter. LC 97-21543. 352p. 1998. pap. 21.95 (0-441-00502-0) Ace Bks.

— Dragon's Winter, 1 vol. 352p. 1999. reprint ed. mass mkt. 6.50 (0-441-00611-6) Ace Bks.

***Lynn, Elizabeth A.** The Northern Girl. (Chronicles of Tornor Ser.: Vol. 3). 470p. 2000. pap. 14.00 (0-441-00727-9) Berkley Pub.

Lynn, Elizabeth A. Watchtower. (Chronicles of Tornor Ser.: Bk. 1). 1999. reprint ed. pap. 12.00 (0-441-00647-7) ACE.

Lynn, Gary S. Breaking Through Bureaucracy: How Corporate Entrepreneurs Create, Protect & Commercialize. 1993. per. 21.95 (1-55738-521-1, Irwn Prfssnl) McGraw-Hill Prof.

— From Concept to Market. LC 88-27851. 256p. 1989. pap. 27.95 (0-471-50125-5) Wiley.

Lynn, George T. Survival Strategies for Parenting Your ADD Child: Dealing with Obsessions, Compulsions, Depression, Explosive Behavior & Rage. (Illus.). 290p. (Orig.). 1996. pap. 12.95 (1-887424-19-9) Underwood Bks.

Lynn, Greg. Animate Form. LC 97-10076. (Illus.). 128p. 1998. 40.00 incl. cd-rom (1-56898-083-3) Princeton Arch.

Lynn, Heloise B., jt. auth. see McBeth, Colin.

Lynn Historical Society Staff. Lynn: Postcards. LC 98-87445. (Postcard History Ser.). (Illus.). 128p. 1998. pap. 16.99 (0-7524-1278-7) Arcadia Publng.

— Records of Ye Towne Meetings of Lynn, 7 vols. 1971. pap. 30.00 (1-882162-10-2) Lynn Hist Soc.

— Records of Ye Towne Meetings of Lynn, 1717-1730, Pt. 3. 97p. 1960. pap. 5.00 (1-882162-05-6) Lynn Hist Soc.

— Records of Ye Towne Meetings of Lynn, 1730-1742, Pt. 4. 94p. 1964. pap. 5.00 (1-882162-06-4) Lynn Hist Soc.

— Records of Ye Towne Meetings of Lynn, 1742-1759, Pt. 5. 98p. 1966. pap. 5.00 (1-882162-07-2) Lynn Hist Soc.

— Records of Ye Towne Meetings of Lynn, 1759-1771, Pt. 6. 98p. 1970. pap. 5.00 (1-882162-08-0) Lynn Hist Soc.

— Records of Ye Towne Meetings of Lynn, 1771-1783, Pt. 7. 100p. 1971. pap. 5.00 (1-882162-09-9) Lynn Hist Soc.

— Records of Ye Towne Meetings of Lynn, 1701-1717, Vol. 2. 107p. 1956. pap. 5.00 (1-882162-04-8) Lynn Hist Soc.

— Records of Ye Towne Meetings of Lynn, 1691-1701, Pt. I. 83p. 1949. pap. 5.00 (1-882162-03-X) Lynn Hist Soc.

Lynn, Holly. Disease: The Cause & Cure. 32p. pap. 3.00 (0-942494-67-9) Coleman Pub.

— Happiness in Five Easy Steps. 19p. pap. 3.00 (0-942494-34-2) Coleman Pub.

Lynn, Hugh. Head over Heels. 1993. 24.95 (0-7022-2418-9, Pub. by Univ Queensland Pr) Intl Spec Bk.

Lynn, I. H. & Crippen, T. F. Rock Type Classification for the NZ Land Resource Inventory. 1991. 30.00 (0-477-02624-9, Pub. by Manaaki Whenua) Balogh.

***Lynn, Irene.** Duty Nurse. large type ed. 320p. 1999. pap. 20.99 (1-85389-955-0, Dales) Ulverscroft.

Lynn, Irene & Wills, Loan L. School Lessons, Work Lessons: Recruiting & Sustaining Employer Involvement in School-to-Work Programs. 100p. 1994. 12.00 (0-937846-48-1) Inst Educ Lead.

Lynn, J. W., et al, eds. High-Temperature Superconductivity. (Graduate Texts in Contemporary Physics Ser.). xv, 403p. 1990. 69.96 (0-387-96770-2) Spr-Verlag.

Lynn, J. W., jt. auth. see Sen Gupta, D. P.

Lynn, Jack. The Hallelujah Flight: The Compelling Story of an Epic Journey. 237p. 1998. text 20.00 (0-7881-5280-7) DIANE Pub.

Lynn, Jack M. Bio-Finishing: The Manual. (Illus.). 205p. (C). 1987. pap. 75.00 (0-9618586-0-5) Five Star Assocs.

Lynn, James, ed. see Von La Roche, Sophie.

Lynn, James, tr. see Schlaffer, Heinz.

Lynn, Jennifer, ed. see Sky, Steve.

Lynn, Jermyn C. Political Parties in China. LC 75-42523. (Studies in Chinese Government & Law). 255p. 1975. reprint ed. lib. bdg. 62.50 (0-313-26961-0, U6961, Greenwood Pr) Greenwood.

Lynn, Joanna & Harrold, Joan. Handbook for Mortals: Guidance for People Facing Serious Illness. LC 98-33691. (Illus.). 256p. 1999. 25.00 (0-19-511662-3) OUP.

Lynn, Joanne. A Good Dying: Shaping Health Care for the Last Months of Life. Harrold, Joan K., ed. LC 98-10051. 188p. 1998. 49.95 (0-7890-0399-6) Haworth Pr.

Lynn, Joanne, ed. By No Extraordinary Means: The Choice to Forgo Life-Sustaining Food & Water. LC 85-45781. (Medical Ethics Ser.). 323p. 1989. pap. 6.75 (0-253-20517-4, MB-517) Ind U Pr.

Lynn, Joanne & Schuster, Janice Lynch, eds. Improving Care for the End of Life: A Sourcebook for Health Care Managers & Clinicians. LC 99-45308. (Illus.). 464p. 2000. 39.95 (0-19-511661-5) OUP.

Lynn, Joanne, jt. ed. see Harrold, Joan K.

Lynn, Jodie. DR. (Doing-Reruns) Mommy: A New Millennium Mom. (Illus.). 200p. 2001. pap. 12.95 (0-9659125-5-8) Martin-Ola.

— Mommy - CEO (Constantly Evaluating Others) 5 Golden Rules. unabridged ed. (Illus.). v, 120p. (Orig.). 1997. pap. 10.95 (0-9659125-3-1) Martin-Ola.

Lynn, John. 800 Paces to Hell: The Story of Andersonville. LC 97-40676. (Illus.). 540p. 1998. 35.00 (1-887901-19-1) Sergeant Kirk.

Lynn, John & Bloom, Stephen. Surgical Endocrinology. (Illus.). 592p. 1993. 265.00 (0-7506-1390-4) Buttrwrth-Heinemann.

Lynn, John A. The Bayonets of the Republic: Motivation & Tactics in the Army of Revolutionary France, 1791-94. (History & Warfare Ser.). 368p. (C). 1996. pap. text 32.00 (0-8133-2945-0, Pub. by Westview) HarpC.

— Giant of the Grand Siecle: The French Army, 1610-1715. 671p. (C). 1997. text 64.95 (0-521-57273-8) Cambridge U Pr.

***Lynn, John A.** The Wars of Louis the XIV, 1667-1714. LC 98-52972. 421p. (C). 1999. pap. 34.60 (0-582-05629-2) Addison-Wesley.

— The Wars of Louis XIV, 1667-1714. (C). 1999. text 75.95 (0-582-05628-4) Addison-Wesley.

Lynn, John A., ed. Feeding Mars: Logistics in Western Warfare from the Middle Ages to the Present. 344p. (C). 1994. pap. 30.00 (0-8133-1865-3, Pub. by Westview) HarpC.

— Tools of War: Instruments, Ideas, & Institutions of Warfare, 1445-1871. fac. ed. LC 89-4887. 276p. 1990. reprint ed. pap. 85.60 (0-7837-8077-X, 204783000008) Bks Demand.

***Lynn, John Worth.** Confederate Commando & Fleet Surgeon: Doctor Burr Conrad. (Illus.). 240p. 2000. 29.95 (1-57249-220-1, Burd St Pr) White Mane Pub.

Lynn-Jones, Sean M., ed. The Cold War & After: Prospects for Peace. 2nd expanded ed. LC 93-77977. (Illus.). 400p. 1993. pap. text 21.50 (0-262-62088-X) MIT Pr.

Lynn-Jones, Sean M., et al, eds. Nuclear Diplomacy & Crisis Management: An International Security Reader. 364p. 1990. 36.00 (0-262-12152-2); pap. text 18.00 (0-262-62078-2) MIT Pr.

— Soviet Military Policy: An International Security Reader. 350p. (Orig.). 1989. pap. text 14.95 (0-262-62066-9) MIT Pr.

Lynn-Jones, Sean M. & Miller, Steven E., eds. America's Strategy in a Changing World. (International Security Reader Ser.). (Illus.). 410p. 1992. pap. text 21.00 (0-262-62085-5) MIT Pr.

— Global Dangers: Changing Dimensions of International Security. LC 94-24037. (International Security Readers Ser.). 1995. pap. text 21.50 (0-262-62097-9) MIT Pr.

Lynn-Jones, Sean M., jt. auth. see Layne, Christopher.

Lynn, Judith. Feminist Sex Slave. (Orig.). 1994. pap. 20.00 (0-9645883-9-0) Estrum Pr.

Lynn, Kathy, jt. auth. see Lynn, David.

Lynn, Kathy, jt. ed. see Lynn, David.

Lynn, Kenneth S. The Air-Line to Seattle: Studies in Literary & Historical Writing about America. LC 83-13459. 240p. 1983. lib. bdg. 17.50 (0-226-49832-8) U Ch Pr.

— The Air-Line to Seattle: Studies in Literary & Historical Writing about America. LC 83-13459. 238p. 1984. pap. text 11.00 (0-226-49833-6) U Ch Pr.

— Charlie Chaplin & His Times. LC 96-30978. 1997. 34.50 (0-684-80851-X) S&S Trade.

— A Divided People, 30. LC 76-25779. (Contributions in American Studies: No. 30). 113p. 1977. 42.95 (0-8371-9271-4, LYD/, Greenwood Pr) Greenwood.

— Hemingway. (Illus.). 712p. 1995. pap. 19.95 (0-674-38732-5, LYNHEX) HUP.

— Mark Twain & Southwestern Humor. LC 70-176135. (Illus.). 300p. 1972. reprint ed. lib. bdg. 59.75 (0-8371-6270-X, LMTPB, Greenwood Pr) Greenwood.

— William Dean Howells: An American Life. LC 71-142091. 372p. 1971. write for info. (0-15-142177-3, NIPI Bks) Natl Intermedia.

Lynn, Kenneth S., ed. Houghton Books in Literature. Incl. Designs for Reading: Level I., 4 bks. pap. 6.76 Short Stories., 001 pap. 21.20 (0-395-02780-2); write for info. (0-318-53415-0) HM.

Lynn, Kristie. Early American Cookbook. (Orig.). 1983. mass mkt. 6.95 (0-89709-047-0) Liberty Pub.

Lynn, Kristie & Pelton, Robert W. Early American Cookbook. LC 83-81148. (Illus.). 176p. (Orig.). 1983. pap. 8.95 (0-89709-199-X) Liberty Pub.

Lynn, Laurel. Chasing Rainbows: A Search for Family Ties. 16072p. (Orig.). 1992. pap. 9.95 (0-934896-19-4) Adopt Aware Pr.

Lynn, Laurence E., Jr. Public Management As Art, Science, & Profession. LC 95-41793. (Illus.). 208p. (C). 1996. pap. text 22.95 (1-56643-034-8, Chatham House Pub) Seven Bridges.

***Lynn, Laurence E., Jr.** Teaching & Learning with Cases: A Guidebook. LC 98-25376. 192p. (C). 1998. pap. text 22.95 (1-56643-066-6, Chatham House Pub) Seven Bridges.

Lynn, Laurence E., Jr & McGeary, Michael G., eds. Inner-City Poverty in the United States. LC 90-45776. 288p. 1990. reprint ed. pap. 89.30 (0-608-02445-7, 206308800004) Bks Demand.

Lynn, Laurence E., Jr., ed. see Heinrich, Carolyn J.

Lynn, Lawrence. How to Invest Today: A Beginner's Guide to the World of Investments. LC 95-10838. 1995. 23.00 (0-8050-3733-0) H Holt & Co.

— How to Invest Today: A Beginner's Guide to the World of Investments. 288p. 1996. pap. 15.95 (0-8050-5025-6) H Holt & Co.

***Lynn, Lawrence.** Public Management: As Art, Science & Profession. 2nd ed. 2001. pap. text 27.95 (1-889119-45-8, Chatham House Pub) Seven Bridges.

Lynn, Lawrence, ed. Taking Charge of Your Financial Future. LC 97-51634. 464p. 1998. pap. 19.95 (0-8092-2908-0, 290800, Contemporary Bks) NTC Contemp Pub Co.

Lynn, Leonard H. & McKeown, Timothy J. Organizing Business: Trade Associations in America & Japan. LC 87-17468. (AEI Studies: No. 459). 214p. (Orig.). (C). 1988. lib. bdg. 21.75 (0-8447-3629-5) U Pr of Amer.

***Lynn, Les.** Environmental Biology & Ecology Laboratory Manual. 3rd ed. 184p. (C). 1999. spiral bd. 41.95 (0-7872-6145-9, 41614502) Kendall-Hunt.

— Study Guide for Introduction to Enviromental Biology. 3rd ed. 48p. (C). spiral bd. write for info. (0-7872-6749-X) Kendall-Hunt.

Lynn, Les M. Environmental Biology. 168p. (C). 1995. pap. text, ring bd. 34.95 (0-7872-0974-0) Kendall-Hunt.

Lynn, Leslie, et al. A Regency Christmas. (Orig.). 1994. mass mkt. 3.99 (0-449-22267-5, Crest) Fawcett.

Lynn, Less. Intro to Environmental Biology. 52p. (C). 1995. student ed., spiral bd. 11.95 (0-7872-1072-2) Kendall-Hunt.

Lynn, Loretta. Selected from Coal Miner's Daughter. abr. ed. Literacy Volunteers of New York City Staff & Vecsey, George, eds. (Writers' Voices Ser.). 64p. (Orig.). 1990. pap. text 3.95 (0-929631-11-0, Signal Hill) New Readers.

Lynn, Loretta & Vecsey, George. Coal Miner's Daughter. Orig. Title: Loretta Lynn: Coal Miner's Daughter. (Illus.). 236p. 1996. reprint ed. pap. 13.95 (0-306-80680-0) Da Capo.

Lynn, M. Stuart. Hawaii International Conference on Systems Sciences, (HICSS-29) Vol. 5: Digital Documents. LC 10-603425. 200p. 1996. pap. 50.00 (0-8186-7426-1, PRO7426) IEEE Comp Soc.

— Preservation & Access Technology: A Structured Glossary of Technical Terms. 68p. 1990. pap. 5.00 (1-887334-03-3) Coun Lib & Info.

Lynn, Mac. Churches of Christ in the United States, 1994. 750p. 1994. pap. 14.95 (1-885836-00-7) Morrison & Phillips.

Lynn, Madeleine, ed. Yangtze River: The Wildest, Wickedest River on Earth. (Illus.). 294p. 1997. pap. 32.00 (0-19-586920-6) OUP.

Lynn, Marjorie Heaton. Dear Family. rev. ed. LC 98-66448. (Illus.). 491p. 1998. 29.95 (1-878044-59-1) Mayhaven Pub.

Lynn, Martin. Commerce & Economic Change in West Africa: The Palm Oil Trade in the Nineteenth Century. LC 97-7352. (African Studies Ser.: Vol. 93). 288p. (C). 1998. text 64.95 (0-521-59074-4) Cambridge U Pr.

Lynn, Mary. Every Page Perfect: A Full-Size Writer's Manual for Manuscript Format & Submission Protocol. rev. ed. LC 97-138805. (Illus.). 185p. 1997. pap. 14.95 (0-9637498-2-X) Toad Hall PA.

Lynn, Mary, ed. see Red, James.

Lynn, Mary C., ed. An Eyewitness Account of the American Revolution & New England Life: The Journal of J. F. Wasmus, German Company Surgeon, 1776-1783, 106. Doblin, Helga, tr. LC 90-3631. (Contributions in Military Studies Ser.: No. 106). 344p. 1990. 65.00 (0-313-27355-3, WEH/, Greenwood Pr) Greenwood.

— The Specht Journal: A Military Journal of the Burgoyne Campaign, 158. Doblin, Helga et al, trs. LC 94-23828. (Contributions in Military Studies Ser.: Vol. 158). 224p. 1995. 59.95 (0-313-29446-1, Greenwood Pr) Greenwood.

Lynn, Mary C., jt. tr. see Doblin, Helga.

Lynn, Matthew. Birds of Prey: Boeing vs. Airbus: A Battle for the Skies. LC 96-47592. 244p. 1997. 24.95 (1-56858-086-X) FWEW.

— Birds of Prey: Boeing vs. Airbus: A Battle for the Skies. 2nd rev. ed. LC 96-47592. 256p. 1998. reprint ed. pap. 14.95 (1-56858-107-6) FWEW.

Lynn, Monty L. & Moberg, David O., eds. Research in the Social Scientific Study of Religion, Vol. 1. 260p. 1989. 73.25 (0-89232-882-7) Jai Pr.

— Research in the Social Scientific Study of Religion, Vol. 2. 247p. 1990. 73.25 (0-89232-933-5) Jai Pr.

— Research in the Social Scientific Study of Religion, Vol. 3. 279p. 1991. 73.25 (1-55938-276-7) Jai Pr.

— Research in the Social Scientific Study of Religion, Vol. 4. 305p. 1992. 73.25 (1-55938-359-3) Jai Pr.

— Research in the Social Scientific Study of Religion, Vol. 5. 258p. 1993. 73.25 (1-55938-301-1) Jai Pr.

— Research in the Social Scientific Study of Religion, Vol. 6. 256p. 1994. 73.25 (1-55938-762-9) Jai Pr.

— Research in the Social Scientific Study of Religion, Vol. 7. 277p. 1996. 73.25 (1-55938-893-5) Jai Pr.

Lynn, N. M., jt. auth. see Gates, P. J.

Lynn, Naomi B., ed. United Nations Decade for Women World Conference. LC 84-4559. (Women & Politics Ser.: Vol. 4, No. 1). 93p. 1984. text 32.95 (0-86656-150-1) Haworth Pr.

— Women, Politics & the Constitution. LC 90-37948. (Women & Politics Ser.: Vol. 10, No. 2). 161p. 1990. text 4.95 (1-56024-029-6) Haworth Pr.

— Women, Politics & the Constitution. LC 90-37948. (Women & Politics Ser.: Vol. 10, No. 2). 161p. 1994. pap. text 22.95 (0-918393-75-2, Harrington Park) Haworth Pr.

Lynn, Naomi B. & McClure, Arthur F. The Fulbright Premise: Senator J. William Fulbright's Views on Presidential Power. LC 72-14248. 224p. 1973. 20.00 (0-8387-1358-0) Bucknell U Pr.

Lynn, Patricia, tr. see Kraay, Robert & Kiefer, Jan, eds.

Lynn, Paul A. Electronic Signals & Systems. 347p. (C). 1987. pap. 32.50 (0-333-39164-0); text 50.00 (0-333-39163-2) Scholium Intl.

— An Introduction to the Analysis & Processing of Signals. 3rd ed. 263p. (C). 1989. 49.95 (0-89116-981-4) Hemisp Pub.

— Radar Systems. (Illus.). 144p. 1987. text 17.98 (0-442-23684-0) Chapman & Hall.

***Lynn, Paul A. & Fuerst, Wolfgang.** Introductory Digital Signal Processing with Computer Applications. 2nd ed. LC 97-22235. 494p. 1998. pap. 59.95 (0-471-97631-8) Wiley.

Lynn, Peny, ed. see Lewis, Victoria.

Lynn, Raina. L' Amour A Reapprendre. (Amours d'Aujourd'Hui Ser.). 1999. mass mkt. 4.99 (0-373-38326-6, 1-38326-4) Harlequin Bks.

***Lynn, Raina.** Haunting Hope. 1999. mass mkt. 5.99 (0-515-12655-1) Berkley Pub.

Lynn, Raina. A Marriage to Fight For. 1997. per. 3.99 (0-373-07804-8, 1-07804-7) Silhouette.

— Partners in Parenthood. (Intimate Moments Ser.). 1998. per. 4.25 (0-373-07869-2, 1-07869-0) Silhouette.

Lynn, Richard. Dysgenics: Genetic Deterioration in Modern Populations. LC 96-2802. (Human Evolution, Behavior & Intelligence Ser.). 256p. 1996. 65.00 (0-275-94917-6, Praeger Pubs) Greenwood.

Lynn, Richard, et al. A Shortcut Through Adventureland Vol. 2: Infocom. write for info. (*0-318-58218-X*) P-H.

Lynn, Richard J., tr. The Classic of Changes: A New Translation of the I Ching As Interpreted by Wang Bi. LC 93-43999. (Translations from the Asian Classics Ser.). 688p. (C). 1994. 23.50 (*0-231-08294-0*) Col U Pr.

Lynn, Richardson R. Apellate Litigation. 2nd ed. 418p. 1993. pap. 54.95 (*1-880921-00-6*) Austin & Winfield.

— Appellate Litigation. 2nd ed. 418p. 1993. 74.95 (*1-880921-02-2*) Austin & Winfield.

Lynn, Richardson R., jt. auth. see Cody, W. J.

Lynn, Robert, jt. auth. see Sindel, Stan.

Lynn, Robert B. & Koch, Klaus-Peter. Valentin Haussmann (1565 70-Ca. 1614) A Thematic-Documentary Catalogue of His Works. LC 96-39598. (Thematic Catalogues Ser.). (GER.). 1997. 62.00 (*0-945193-91-2*) Pendragon NY.

Lynn, Robert E., ed. Chicorel Abstracts to Reading & Learning Disabilities. 1983rd ed. (Chicorel Index Ser.: Vol. 19). 325p. 1984. text 125.00 (*0-934598-85-1*) Am Lib Pub Co.

— Chicorel Abstracts to Reading & Learning Disabilities, 1981. (Chicorel Index Ser.: Vol. 19). 490p. 1983. 125.00 (*0-934598-83-5*) Am Lib Pub Co.

— Chicorel Abstracts to Reading & Learning Disabilities, 1982. (Chicorel Index Ser.: Vol. 19). 424p. 1984. 125.00 (*0-934598-84-3*) Am Lib Pub Co.

Lynn, Robert H. All the Kings Men Notes. (Cliffs Notes Ser.). 80p. 1964. pap. 4.95 (*0-8220-0146-2*, Cliff) IDG Bks.

Lynn, Robert J. Introduction to Estate Planning in a Nutshell. 4th ed. (Nutshell Ser.). 352p. (C). 1992. pap. 21.00 (*0-314-00809-8*) West Pub.

Lynn, Robert W. Understanding Religious Giving Styles. 1998. pap. 12.25 (*1-56699-204-4*, AL201) Alban Inst.

Lynn, Ruth. Ester: The Story of a Small Ghost. Wagner, R. M., ed. LC 81-69693. (Illus.). 28p. (J). (gr. 5 up). 1981. 12.95 (*0-941674-00-2*) Woodcock Pr.

Lynn, Ruth N., ed. Fantasy Literature for Children & Young Adults: An Annotated Bibliography. 4th rev. ed. LC 94-42529. 770p. 1995. 55.00 (*0-8352-3456-8*) Bowker.

Lynn, Sandra. I Must Hold These Strangers. Oliphant, David, ed. (Illus.). 1980. pap. 5.00 (*0-933384-04-1*) Prickly Pear.

— Where Rainbows Wait for Rain: The Big Bend Country. LC 89-39975. (Illus.). 90p. 1989. 22.00 (*0-940352-06-0*) Mesa Hse.

— Windows on the Past: Historic Lodgings of New Mexico. LC 98-48956. (Illus.). xiv, 209p. 1999. 24.95 (*0-8263-2000-7*) U of NM Pr.

Lynn, Sara. Big Book of Cool Crafts: Working with Paper, Paint, & Models. LC 99-18097. (Illus.). 76p. (J). (gr. k-3). 1999. pap. text 5.95 (*1-57505-409-4*, Carolrhoda) Lerner Pub.

— Clothes. (Aladdin Board Bks.). (Illus.). 14p. (J). (ps). 1986. pap. 2.95 (*0-689-71095-X*) Aladdin.

Lynn, Sara. Jungle Friends. LC QL112.L95 1996. (Illus.). (J). bds. write for info. (*0-7636-0042-3*) Candlewick Press.

— Rain & Shine. rev. ed. (Play & Discover Ser.). (Illus.). (J). 2000. 9.95 (*1-58728-042-6*); pap. 4.95 (*1-58728-046-9*) Two Can Pub.

Lynn, Sara & James, Diane. Play with Paint. (Play with Crafts Ser.). (Illus.). 24p. (J). (ps-2). 1992. lib. bdg. 19.95 (*0-87614-755-4*, Carolrhoda) Lerner Pub.

— Play with Paper. (J). (ps-2). 1992. lib. bdg. 19.95 (*0-87614-754-6*, Carolrhoda) Lerner Pub.

Lynn, Sarah, jt. auth. see English, Laura M.

Lynn, Sheri & Washington, J. W., Jr. What Married Men Say & Why Women Stupidly Fall. (Illus.). 85p. 1998. write for info. (*1-892652-01-3*) Poorboy FiveJay.

Lynn-Sherow, Bonnie. Mechanization, Land Use, & Ownership: Oklahoma in the Early Twentieth Century. (LTC Paper Ser.: Vol. 155). (Illus.). iii, 16p. (C). 1996. pap. 4.00 (*0-934519-73-0*, LTC155) U of Wis Land.

Lynn, Sheryl. The Bodyguard: Elk River, Colorado. (Intrigue Ser.: No. 514). 1999. per. 3.99 (*0-373-22514-8*, 1-22514-3) Harlequin Bks.

Lynn, Stacey, ed. see Davis, Carolyn O.

Lynn, Stephan G. & Weintraub, Pamela. Medical Emergency! The St. Luke's-Roosevelt Hospital Center Book of Emergency Medicine. 1996. pap. 19.95 (*0-614-97846-7*, Wm Morrow) Morrow Avon.

***Lynn, Stephen G. & Weintraub, Pamela.** Medical Emergency! The St. Luke's-Roosevelt Hospital Center Book of Emergency Medicine. (Illus.). 385p. 1999. pap. text 20.00 (*0-7881-6067-2*) DIANE Pub.

Lynn, Steven. A Short Guide to Writing. LC 96-30523. 176p. 1996. pap. text 25.00 (*0-205-18934-2*) Allyn.

Lynn, Steven. Texts & Contexts. 2nd ed. 272p. (C). 1999. pap. text 31.60 (*0-321-06724-X*) Addison-Wesley.

Lynn, Steven J. Samuel Johnson after Deconstruction: Rhetoric & "The Rambler" LC 91-4951. 208p. (C). 1992. 26.95 (*0-8093-1770-2*) S Ill U Pr.

Lynn, Steven J., et al, eds. Casebook of Clinical Hypnosis. LC 96-11150. 429p. 1996. 49.95 (*1-55798-365-8*) Am Psychol.

Lynn, Steven J. & McConkey, Kevin M., eds. Truth in Memory. LC 98-6870. 508p. 1998. 52.00 (*1-57230-345-X*) Guilford Pubns.

Lynn, Steven J. & Rhue, Judith W., eds. Theories of Hypnosis: Current Models & Perspectives. LC 91-28531. (Clinical & Experimental Hypnosis Ser.). 626p. 1991. lib. bdg. 68.00 (*0-89862-343-X*) Guilford Pubns.

Lynn, Steven Jay & Rhue, Judith W., eds. Dissociation: Clinical & Theoretical Perspectives. LC 94-12041. 477p. 1994. lib. bdg. 55.00 (*0-89862-186-0*) Guilford Pubns.

Lynn, Susan. Progressive Women in Conservative Times: Racial Justice, Peace, & Feminism, 1945-1960s. LC 92-7978. 220p. (C). 1993. text 40.00 (*0-8135-1867-9*); pap. text 17.00 (*0-8135-1868-7*) Rutgers U Pr.

Lynn, Teri. Journey to the Cross: A Lenten Devotional. LC 98-14680. (Illus.). 112p. 1998. pap. 12.95 (*1-880090-71-6*) Galde Pr.

Lynn, Terri. Uncommon Stock. (Superromance Ser.). 1993. per. 3.39 (*0-373-70534-4*, 1-70534-2) Harlequin Bks.

— Valentine's Summer. (Superromance Ser.). 1993. per. 3.50 (*0-373-70555-7*, 1-70555-7) Harlequin Bks.

Lynn, Theodore S. & Bloomfield, Micah. Real Estate Investment Trust. 1088p. 145.00 (*0-7913-1932-6*) Warren Gorham & Lamont.

Lynn, Thomas H. The Hidden Dangers in Tap Water & the Best Solutions. LC 96-94029. 1996. pap. 13.95 (*1-885676-09-3*) Meltdown Intl.

Lynn, Tish, ed. see Weihs, Karen M.

Lynn, Vera, et al. Unsung Heroines: The Women Who Won the War. large type ed. 222p. 1993. 22.95 (*1-85089-596-1*, Pub. by ISIS Lrg Prnt) Transaction Pubs.

***Lynn, Walter W.** Havens for Travelers. (Illus.). xvi, 240p. 1999. pap. 14.50 (*0-9674746-0-4*) Agape.

Lynn, William S., ed. Inflammatory Cells & Lung Disease. 120p. 1983. 74.00 (*0-8493-5792-6*, RC771, CRC Reprint) Franklin.

Lynn, William S., jt. auth. see Wong, Paul K.

Lynn, William S., jt. ed. see Wong, Paul K.

Lynne, Alma. Alma Lynne's Country Needlecrafts: From Cross-Stitch to Bunnies to Easy Christmas Quilts, over 50 Projects to Warm Hearts & Homes. 1997. pap. 16.95 (*0-87596-959-3*) Rodale Pr Inc.

— Alma Lynne's Cross-Stitch for Special Occasions. LC 93-84607. 144p. 1993. 24.99 (*0-8487-1121-1*) Oxmoor Hse.

Lynne, Erica. Angora: A Handbook for Spinners. LC 92-367. (Illus.). 120p. (Orig.). 1992. pap. 14.95 (*0-934026-75-0*) Interweave.

***Lynne, Gloria & Chilton, Karen.** I Wish You Love. LC 99-55103. 240p. 2000. 24.95 (*0-312-87031-0*, Pub. by Forge NYC) St Martin.

— I Wish You Love. 2001. pap. write for info. (*0-312-87029-9*) St Martin.

Lynne, Heather. Golden Girl. large type ed. (Linford Romance Library). 1993. pap. 14.95 (*0-685-67906-3*, Linford) Ulverscroft.

Lynne, James B. Rogue Diamond. large type ed. 534p. 1982. 11.50 (*0-7089-8044-9*) Ulverscroft.

Lynne, Janice. Courtney's Alaska Cruise. (Courtney Travel Adventure Ser.: Bk. 2). (Illus.). 32p. (J). 1996. pap. 6.95 (*0-9649522-1-1*) Destiny Pub FL.

— Courtney's First Cruise. (Courtney Travel Adventure Ser.). 32p. (J). (ps-3). 1996. pap. write for info. (*0-9649522-0-3*) Destiny Pub FL.

Lynne, Mary. Galaxy of Scents: The Ancient Art of Perfune Making. 291p. 1994. reprint ed. pap. 29.95 (*1-56459-458-0*) Kessinger Pub.

Lynne, Rita, jt. auth. see Prato, Peter J.

Lynne, Sandi. 1999 Wall Street in Advance: A Full Year's Schedule of Market Moving Events for Strategic Investors. (Illus.). 32p. 1998. mass mkt. 21.95 (*0-9664730-0-0*) S Lynne.

Lynne, Terry, jt. auth. see Graham.

Lynne, Victoria. With This Kiss. 384p. 1999. mass mkt. 5.99 (*0-440-22334-2*) Dell.

***Lynnford, Janet.** Bride of Hearts. (Lords of Desire Ser.). 2000. mass mkt. 3.99 (*0-451-40831-4*) Signet.

Lynnford, Janet. Firebrand Bride. 320p. 1999. mass mkt. 5.99 (*0-451-40830-6*, Topaz) NAL.

Lynnlee, J. L. All That Glitters. 3rd rev. ed. (Illus.). 128p. 1999. pap. 16.95 (*0-7643-0850-5*) Schiffer.

— Purrrfection: The Cat. LC 90-61743. (Illus.). 96p. (Orig.). 1990. pap. 16.95 (*0-88740-269-0*) Schiffer.

Lynns, Richard. Classic of Changes I Ching. 1996. 49.95 incl. cd-rom (*0-231-10806-0*) Col U Pr.

Lynnworth, Lawrence C. Ultrasonic Measurements for Process Control: Theory, Techniques, Applications. 694p. 1989. text 154.00 (*0-12-460585-0*) Acad Pr.

***Lynons.** Adjunct Professor Guide: Surviving & Thriving in the College Classroom. LC 98-29466. 202p. 1998. pap. text 29.95 (*0-205-28774-3*) P-H.

Lynott, Bob. The Weather Tomorrow: Why Can't They Get It Right? LC 86-83330. 190p. (Orig.). 1987. pap. 15.00 (*0-9618077-0-9*) Gadfly Pr.

Lynott, Philip. Philip Lynott: Songs for While I'm Away. (Illus.). 96p. 1996. pap. 17.99 (*1-886894-82-5*, MBS Paperbk) Mus Bk Servs.

Lynott, Robert E. How Weather Works, & Why. LC 93-81357. (Illus.). 144p. (C). 1994. pap. text 40.00 (*0-9618077-1-7*) Gadfly Pr.

Lynott, William J. Power Letters for Service Executives. 109p. 1994. pap. 19.95 (*1-930797-30-3*) Appliance Univ.

Lynskey, Edward C. The Tree Surgeon's Gift. 1990. 22.50 (*0-916379-75-2*) Scripta.

Lynton, Ernest, jt. ed. see Driscoll, Amy.

Lynton, Ernest A. Making the Case for Professional Service. 120p. 1995. pap. 12.00 (*1-56377-033-4*, FR9501) Am Assn Higher Ed.

— Missing Connection Between Business & Universities. (ACE-Oryx Series on Higher Education). (Illus.). 192p. 1984. 27.95 (*0-02-919280-3*) Free Pr.

Lynton, Jonathan, et al. Law Office Management for Paralegals. 1992. pap. 37.95 (*0-8273-4865-7*) Delmar.

Lynton, Jonathan S. Ballentine's Legal Dictionary & Thesaurus. LC 94-33514. 768p. (C). 1994. mass mkt. 48.95 (*0-8273-6526-8*) Delmar.

— Ballentine's Thesaurus for Legal Research & Writing. LC 93-13825. (Paralegal Ser.). 401p. (C). 1993. mass mkt. 28.95 (*0-8273-6208-0*) Delmar.

— Law Office Management. 2nd ed. (C). 1996. text 39.95 (*0-8273-7975-7*) Delmar.

Lynton, Jonathan S. & Lyndall, Terri M. Legal Ethics & Professional Responsibility. LC 92-36136. (Illus.). 392p. (C). 1993. pap. 30.25 (*0-8273-5504-1*) Delmar.

— Legal Ethics & Professional Responsibility: Instructor's Guide. 34p. 1993. 12.50 (*0-8273-5506-8*) Delmar.

Lynton, Jonathan S., et al. Law Office Management. 2nd rev. ed. (Paralegal Ser.). 496p. (C). 1996. mass mkt. 65.95 (*0-8273-7139-X*) Delmar.

Lynton, Linda. The Sari: Styles, Patterns, History, Techniques. 1995. 58.00 (*0-500-01672-0*) Thames Hudson.

Lynton, Lyndall & Masinter Staff. Law Office Management - IML. 2nd ed. (Paralegal Ser.). 48p. 1996. teacher ed. 17.95 (*0-8273-7140-3*) Delmar.

Lynton, Mark. Accidental Journey: A Cambridge Internee's Memoir of World War II. 352p. 1995. 23.95 (*0-87951-577-5*, Pub. by Overlook Pr) Penguin Putnam.

— Accidental Journey: A Cambridge Internee's Memoir of World War II. 352p. 1998. pap. 13.95 (*0-87951-848-0*, Pub. by Overlook Pr) Penguin Putnam.

Lynton, Norbert. Ben Nicholson. (Illus.). 472p. (C). 1993. reprint ed. text 125.00 (*0-7148-2813-0*, Pub. by Phaidon Press) Phaidon Pr.

— Ben Nicholson. 2nd ed. (Colour Library). (Illus.). 240p. 1998. pap. 34.95 (*0-7148-3750-4*, Pub. by Phaidon Press) Phaidon Pr.

— Henry Moore: The Human Dimension. (Illus.). 160p. 1991. pap. 35.00 (*0-906909-04-X*, Pub. by Lund Humphries) Antique Collect.

— The Story of Modern Art. 2nd ed. (Illus.). 400p. 1997. pap. 19.95 (*0-7148-2422-4*, Pub. by Phaidon Press) Phaidon Pr.

— Victor Pasmore: Paintings & Graphics, 1980-92. (Illus.). 156p. (C). 1992. 95.00 (*0-85331-606-6*, Pub. by Lund Humphries) Antique Collect.

Lynton, Norbert, jt. auth. see Langmuir, Erika.

Lynton, Rolf P. Social Science in Actual Practice: Themes on My Blue Guitar. LC 97-30581. 1997. write for info. (*0-7619-9207-3*); pap. write for info. (*0-7619-9208-1*) Sage.

Lynton, Rolf P. & Pareek, Udai. Training for Development. 2nd fac. ed. LC 89-7989. (Kumarian Press Library of Management for Development). (Illus.). 364p. 1990. pap. 112.90 (*0-7837-7584-9*, 204733700007) Bks Demand.

Lynton, Rolf P. & Pareek, Udai, eds. Facilitating Development: Readings for Trainers, Consultants & Policy-Makers. LC 92-17104. 1992. 38.50 (*0-8039-9417-6*) Sage.

***Lynton, Rolf P. & Pareek, Udai Narain.** Training for Organizational Transformation. 3rd ed. LC 00-24861. 2000. write for info. (*0-7619-9428-9*) Sage.

Lynwander, P. Gear Tooth Scoring Design Considerations. (Technical Papers: Vol. P219.10). (Illus.). 29p. 1981. pap. text 30.00 (*1-55589-255-8*) AGMA.

Lynwander, Peter. Gear Drive Systems: Design & Application. (Mechanical Engineering Ser.: Vol. 20). (Illus.). 432p. 1983. text 135.00 (*0-8247-1896-8*) Dekker.

Lynx, David & Martin, Alvin. Setting the Stage & the House That Jack Built. LC 92-70719. (Illus.). 16p. (Orig.). (C). 1992. pap. 5.95 (*1-880269-08-2*) D H Sheehan.

Lynx, David, jt. ed. see Munns, J. Frank.

Lynx, David, ed. see Schuyler, Steven.

Lynx, David, ed. see Siebol, Michael.

Lyon. Earth Science. 1976. teacher ed. 28.75 (*0-697-05059-9*, WCB McGr Hill) McGrw-H Hghr Educ.

— Sixty Minute Tax Planner 2000. (60 Minute Ser.). 320p. 1999. pap. text 15.00 (*0-7352-0106-4*) PH Pr.

Lyon & Rao. Java Digital Signal Processing. 1997. 44.95 (*0-8055-1568-2*, M&T Bks) IDG Bks.

Lyon, jt. auth. see Curtay.

Lyon, ed. see De Molina, Tirso.

Lyon, A. B., et al. Lyon Memorial: Massachusetts Families, Including Descendants of the Immigrant William Lyon of Roxbury, Peter & George of Dorchester, with an Introduction Treating the English Ancestry of the American Families. (Illus.). 491p. 1989. reprint ed. pap. 73.50 (*0-8328-0796-6*); reprint ed. lib. bdg. 81.50 (*0-8328-0795-8*) Higginson Bk Co.

***Lyon, Aaron.** Dock Designs. (Residential Ser.). (Illus.). 100p. 2000. 44.50 (*0-9702939-0-9*) Shore Prod.

Lyon, Adrian, jt. auth. see Lyon, C. M.

***Lyon, Al.** Welcome to My World. LC 99-65308. 64p. 2000. pap. 9.95 (*1-56315-256-8*, Pub. by SterlingHse) Natl Bk Netwk.

Lyon, Albert. No More Tomorrow. 232p. mass mkt. 4.99 (*1-55197-158-5*) Picasso Publ.

Lyon, Amy. In a Vermont Kitchen: Foods, Fresh from Farms, Forests & Orchards. LC 99-35935. 1999. 23.95 (*1-55788-316-5*, HP Books) Berkley Pub.

Lyon, Andrew B. Cracking the Code: Making Sense of the Corporate Alternative Minimum Tax. LC 97-4641. 168p. 1997. 38.95 (*0-8157-5324-1*); pap. 16.95 (*0-8157-5323-3*) Brookings.

Lyon, Arabella. Intentions: Negotiated, Contested, & Ignored. LC 97-49173. (Literature & Philosophy Ser.). 215p. 1998. 45.00 (*0-271-01797-X*); pap. 17.95 (*0-271-01798-8*) Pa St U Pr.

Lyon, Bill, jt. auth. see Zordich, Cynthia.

Lyon, Bob, ed. see Hale, C. Clark.

Lyon, Brenda G., jt. ed. see Civille, Gail V.

Lyon, Bryce, ed. The High Middle Ages 1,000-1300. LC 64-21207. (Orig.). 1964. pap. 17.95 (*0-02-919480-6*) Free Pr.

Lyon, Bryce, tr. see Ganshof, Francois L.

Lyon, Bryce D. Medieval Finance: A Comparison of Financial Institutions in Northwestern Europe. LC 67-19657. 100p. reprint ed. 31.00 (*0-608-16575-1*, 202751600055) Bks Demand.

Lyon, Brynolf & Smith, Archie, Jr., eds. Tending the Flock: Congregations & Family Ministry. LC 98-7434. 240p. 1998. pap. text 18.00 (*0-664-25627-9*) Westminster John Knox.

Lyon, Buck. The Crow Horse. large type ed. (Linford Western Library). 320p. 1993. pap. 16.99 (*0-7089-7361-2*) Ulverscroft.

Lyon, C. A., et al. Summary of Low-Speed Airfoil Data, No. 2. (Illus.). 274p. (Orig.). 1996. pap. 25.00 (*0-9646747-2-6*) Soartech.

Lyon, C. M. & De Cruz, Stephen. Lyon & de Cruz: Parents, Children & the Law. 400p. 1994. pap. 36.00 (*0-406-50800-3*, MICHIE) LEXIS Pub.

Lyon, C. M. & Lyon, Adrian. Butterworths Family Law Handbook. 1130p. 1991. pap. 50.00 (*0-406-60980-2*, U.K., MICHIE) LEXIS Pub.

Lyon, Carol B. Darling, I'm Still Alive & Recovering from Love. 38p. (Orig.). 1993. pap. 3.95 (*1-879559-07-2*) Galaxy OH.

Lyon, Charleen C. The Tale of Halley's Comet: An Educational Coloring Book. (Illus.). 32p. (Orig.). (J). (gr. 3-6). 1985. pap. 2.95 (*0-9614973-0-0*) Niota Pr.

Lyon, Charles, et al. Jaws Maui. Cannon, Peter W., ed. (Illus.). 227p. 1998. 39.95 (*0-9658986-0-1*) Jaws Maui.

Lyon, Charles, jt. auth. see Lyon, Leslie Connell.

Lyon, Christina M., jt. auth. see Freeman, Michael D.

Lyon, Christopher. International Dictionary of Films & Filmmakers, 5 vols. Incl. Vol. I. Films. 650p. 1984. 60.00 (*0-912289-04-X*); Vol. II. Directors-Filmakers. 650p. 1986. 115.00 (*0-912289-05-8*); Vol. III. Actors & Actresses. 650p. 1986. 115.00 (*0-912289-08-2*); 250.00 (*0-685-06728-9*) St James Pr.

Lyon, Christopher A., et al. Summary of Low-Speed Airfoil Data, No. 3. (Illus.). 440p. 1997. pap. 35.00 (*0-9646747-3-4*) Soartech.

Lyon, Christy, jt. auth. see Pavlicin, Karen.

Lyon, Clyde. Early Part of This Century in What Is Now the Land Between the Lakes: Or, 1913 to 1929 in What Is Now the Land Between the Lakes. 228p. 1994. pap. 9.95 (*0-9640691-0-5*) Country Life.

Lyon, D. G. Beginner's Assyrian. 185p. 1998. reprint ed. pap. 11.95 (*0-7818-0677-1*) Hippocrene Bks.

Lyon, D. J., jt. ed. see Green, M. B.

Lyon, D. W., jt. auth. see Steinberg, J. B.

***Lyon, Dan D.** Gourmet Cannabis Cookery: The High Art of Marijuana Cuisine. (Illus.). 96p. 1999. pap. text 10.00 (*1-55950-192-8*, 85299) Loompanics.

Lyon, Danny. The Bikeriders. 2nd ed. (Illus.). 104p. 1998. reprint ed. 50.00 (*0-944092-46-2*) Twin Palms Pub.

— I Like to Eat Right on the Dirt: A Child's Journey Back in Space & Time. Wolff, Daniel, ed. LC 89-91769. (Illus.). 56p. (Orig.). 1989. spiral bd. 35.00 (*0-9620992-2-8*) Bleak Beauty.

— Knave of Hearts. (Illus.). 156p. 1999. 60.00 (*0-944092-63-2*) Twin Palms Pub.

— Knave of Hearts. limited ed. (Illus.). 156p. 1999. 250.00 (*0-944092-64-0*) Twin Palms Pub.

— Memories of the Southern Civil Rights Movement. LC 92-5961. (Lyndhurst Series on the South. Published for the Duke University Center for Documentary Studies). (Illus.). vii, 185p. (C). 1992. pap. 27.50 (*0-8078-4386-5*) U of NC Pr.

— Merci Gonaives: A Photgrapher's Account of Haiti & the February Revolution. (Illus.). 64p. 1994. pap. 19.95 (*1-881616-28-2*) Dist Art Pubs.

— Merci Gonaives: A Photographer's Account of Haiti & the February Revolution. LC 87-73298. (Illus.). 64p. (Orig.). (C). 1988. pap. 20.00 (*0-9620992-0-1*) Bleak Beauty.

Lyon, David. The Biggest Truck. LC 87-22640. (Illus.). 32p. (J). (ps-3). 1988. lib. bdg. 13.88 (*0-688-05514-1*) Lothrop.

— The Electronic Eye: The Rise of Surveillance Society. LC 93-35598. (C). 1994. pap. 18.95 (*0-8166-2515-8*) U of Minn Pr.

— The First Destroyers: The Turtleback Torpedo Boat Destroyers of the 1890s. (Chatham Shipshape Ser.). (Illus.). 128p. 1997. 55.00 (*1-55750-271-4*) Naval Inst Pr.

***Lyon, David.** Guidelines for Sensory Analysis. 2nd ed. LC 99-27341. 192p. 1999. 65.00 (*0-8342-1642-6*) Aspen Pub.

Lyon, David. The Information Society: Issues & Illusions. (Illus.). 200p. 1988. pap. text 22.95 (*0-7456-0369-6*) Blackwell Pubs.

***Lyon, David.** Jesus in Disneyland: Religion in Postmodern Times. 224p. 2000. text 59.95 (*0-7456-1488-4*, Pub. by Polity Pr); pap. text 24.95 (*0-7456-1489-2*, Pub. by Polity Pr) Blackwell Pubs.

Lyon, David. Living Stones: St. James Church, Kingston, 1845-1995: From Stuartville to Queen's Campus. (Illus.). 196p. 1995. pap. 19.95 (*1-55082-160-1*, Pub. by Quarry Pr) LPC InBook.

— Nelson Against Napoleon: From the Nile to Copenhagen, 1798-1801. LC 97-68138. (Chatham Pictorial Histories Ser.). (Illus.). 192p. 1997. 49.95 (*1-55750-642-6*) Naval Inst Pr.

— Postmodernity. Parkin, Frank, ed. (Concepts in the Social Sciences Ser.). 112p. 1994. 9.00 (*0-335-19149-5*); pap. 2.00 (*0-335-19148-7*) OpUniv Pr.

— Postmodernity. LC 94-14630. (Concepts in Social Thought Ser.). 112p. 1994. text 39.95 (*0-8166-2612-X*) U of Minn Pr.

— Postmodernity. 2nd ed. 1999. pap. text 18.95 (*0-335-20144-X*) OpUniv Pr.

***Lyon, David.** Postmodernity. 2nd ed. 1999. pap. text 14.95 (*0-8166-3227-8*) U of Minn Pr.

Lyon, David. Postmodernity 2nd ed. 1999. 69.95 (*0-335-20145-8*) OpUniv Pr.

— The Runaway Duck. LC 84-5677. (Illus.). 32p. (J). (ps up). 1987. reprint ed. mass mkt. 4.95 (*0-688-07334-4*, Wm Morrow) Morrow Avon.

L

An Asterisk (*) at the beginning of an entry indicates that the title is appearing for the first time.

L

— Sea Battles in Close-Up: The Age of Nelson. LC 96-67493. (Illus.). 224p. 1996. 29.95 (*1-55750-746-5*) Naval Inst Pr.

— The Silicon Society. LC 86-194046. (London Lectures in Contemporary Christianity: 1979). 127p. (Orig.). reprint ed. pap. 39.40 (*0-608-18115-3*, 203274000081) Bks Demand.

— The Sound of Horns. LC 82-24968. 63p. 1984. pap. 4.95 (*0-934332-38-X*) LEpervier Pr.

Lyon, David & Zureik, Elia T., eds. Computers, Surveillance, & Privacy. LC 95-38820. 1996. pap. 19.95 (*0-8166-2653-7*); text 49.95 (*0-8166-2652-9*) U of Minn Pr.

***Lyon, David, et al.** Boston. LC 00-34629. (Travel Guides Ser.). (Illus.). 2001. write for info. (*0-7894-6645-7*) DK Pub Inc.

Lyon, David, jt. auth. see Harris, Pat.

Lyon, David, jt. auth. see Harris, Patricia.

Lyon, David D. Practical CM. unabridged ed. (Illus.). 301p. 1996. spiral bd. 45.00 (*0-9661248-7-1*) Raven Publ.

***Lyon, David D.** Practical CM: Best Configuration Management Practices for the 21st Century. 208p. 2000. 59.95 (*0-7506-4724-8*) Buttrwrth-Heinemann.

Lyon, David D. Practical CM: Best Configuration Management Practices for the 21st Century. 2nd rev. ed. (Illus.). 210p. 1999. spiral bd. 55.00 (*0-9661248-4-7*) Raven Publ.

***Lyon, David D.** Practical Project: Guidelines for Project Engineers. 2nd rev. ed. (Illus.). 210p. 1999. spiral bd. 55.00 (*0-9661248-5-5*) Raven Publ.

Lyon, David D. Practical Project: Guidelines for Project Engineers & Program Management Personnel. (Illus.). 210p. 1999. spiral bd. 55.00 (*0-9661248-1-2*) Raven Publ.

***Lyon, Doris.** My Personal Prayer Journal. 162p. 1999. pap. 9.99 (*1-57921-173-9*, Pub. by WinePress Pub) BookWorld.

Lyon, Dorothy M. The Wheel of Life. 1989. 75.00 (*0-7223-2167-8*, Pub. by A H S Ltd) St Mut.

Lyon, E. Stina, jt. ed. see Morris, Lydia.

Lyon, E. Wilson, ed. see Barbe-Marboi, Francois.

Lyon, Edward A. 60-Minute Tax Planner. LC 98-30377. (Illus.). 268p. (C). 1998. 34.95 (*0-13-095293-1*) P-H.

— 60-Minute Tax Planner: Fast & Easy Plans to Save on Taxes & Add Cash to Your Next Paycheck. LC 98-30377. (Illus.). 320p. 1998. pap. text 15.00 (*0-7352-0045-9*) PH Pr.

Lyon, Edward E., et al. Earth Science. 6th ed. 240p. (C). 1993. text, teacher ed. write for info. (*0-697-05474-8*, WCB McGr Hill) McGrw-H Hghr Educ.

Lyon, Edwin A. A New Deal for Southeastern Archaeology. LC 95-11101. (SPA., Illus.). 304p. (Orig.). (C). 1996. pap. text 29.95 (*0-8173-0791-5*) U of Ala Pr.

***Lyon, Eileen Groth.** Politicians in the Pulpit: Christian Radicalism in Britain from the Fall of the Bastille to the Disintegration of Chartism. 310p. 1999. 78.95 (*0-7546-0029-7*, Pub. by Ashgate Pub) Ashgate Pub Co.

***Lyon, Elizabeth.** Nonfiction Book Proposal Anybody Can Write: A Contract & Advance Before You Write Your Book. 2nd ed. 2000. pap. 18.95 (*0-936085-45-2*) Blue Heron OR.

Lyon, Elizabeth. The Sell-Your-Novel Tool Kit: Everything You Need to Know About Queries, Synopses, Marketing & Breaking In. 352p. (Orig.). 1997. pap. 17.95 (*0-936085-40-1*) Blue Heron OR.

Lyon, Elizabeth C. Nonfiction Book Proposals Anybody Can Write: How to Get a Contract & Advance Before You Write Your Book. LC 96-167212. 240p. (Orig.). (C). 1995. pap. 17.95 (*0-936085-31-2*) Blue Heron OR.

Lyon, Eugene. The Enterprise of Florida: Pedro Menendez de Aviles & the Spanish Conquest of 1565-1568. LC 76-29612. (Illus.). 253p. 1976. pap. 24.95 (*0-8130-0777-1*) U Press Fla.

— Search for the Atocha: Concluding the Seventeen Year Search for the Atocha. (Illus.). 1995. pap. 16.95 (*0-912451-20-3*) Florida Classics.

Lyon, Eugene, ed. Pedro Menendez de Aviles. LC 94-10710. (Spanish Borderlands Sourcebooks Ser.: Vol. 24). (Illus.). 640p. 1995. text 25.00 (*0-8240-2099-5*) Garland.

Lyon, F. H., tr. see Schnitzler, Arthur.

Lyon, Francis D. Twists of Fate. 256p. (Orig.). 1993. pap. 14.95 (*1-879260-10-7*) Evanston Pub.

Lyon, G., ed. Vallejo: El Tragaluz. (Bristol Spanish Texts Ser.). (SPA.). 1995. pap. 18.95 (*1-85399-412-X*, Pub. by Brist Class Pr) Focus Pub-R Pullins.

— Virus Infection & the Developing Nervous System. (C). 1988. text 132.50 (*0-7462-0053-6*) Kluwer Academic.

Lyon, G. F. A Narrative of Travels in Northern Africa in the Years, 1816-1820. 400p. 1990. 135.00 (*1-85077-032-8*, Pub. by Darf Pubs Ltd) St Mut.

Lyon, G. Reid, et al, eds. Developmental Neuroimaging: Mapping the Development of Brain & Behavior. (Illus.). 312p. 1996. text 139.95 (*0-12-686070-X*) Acad Pr.

Lyon, G. Reid & Krasnegor, Norman A. Attention, Memory, & Executive Function. LC 95-2540. 432p. 1995. boxed set 45.00 (*1-55766-198-7*) P H Brookes.

Lyon, G. Reid & Rumsey, Judith M., eds. Neuroimaging: A Window to the Neurological Foundations of Learning & Behavior in Children. 288p. (Orig.). 1996. pap. text 49.95 (*1-55766-256-8*, 2568) P H Brookes.

***Lyon, George.** One Lucky Girl. LC 98-41149. (Illus.). 32p. (J). (gr. k-3). 2000. 15.95 (*0-7894-2613-7*, D K Ink) DK Pub Inc.

Lyon, George E. A B Cedar. LC 88-22797. (Illus.). 32p. (J). (ps-1). 1996. pap. 6.95 (*0-531-07080-8*) Orchard Bks Watts.

— Ada's Pal. LC 95-53732. (Illus.). 32p. (J). (ps-1). 1996. 14.95 (*0-531-09528-2*); lib. bdg. 15.99 (*0-531-08878-2*) Orchard Bks Watts.

— Catalpa: Poems by George Ella Lyon. 63p. (Orig.). 1993. pap. 9.95 (*0-9636545-2-7*) Wind Pubns.

— Cecil's Story. LC 90-7775. (Illus.). 32p. (J). (gr. k-2). 1991. 15.95 (*0-531-05912-X*) Orchard Bks Watts.

— Cecil's Story. LC 90-7775. (Illus.). 32p. (J). (gr. k-2). 1995. pap. text 5.95 (*0-531-07063-8*) Orchard Bks Watts.

— Choices. LC 89-38082. (New Books for New Readers). 64p. 1989. pap. 5.95 (*0-8131-0900-0*) U Pr of Ky.

— Come a Tide. LC 89-35650. (Illus.). 32p. (J). (ps-3). 1990. lib. bdg. 16.99 (*0-531-08454-X*) Orchard Bks Watts.

— Come a Tide. LC 89-35650. (Illus.). 32p. (J). (ps-2). 1993. pap. 6.95 (*0-531-07036-0*) Orchard Bks Watts.

— Come a Tide. 1993. 12.15 (*0-606-05212-7*, Pub. by Turtleback) Demco.

— Counting on the Woods. LC 97-34117. (Illus.). 32p. (J). (ps-3). 1998. 15.95 (*0-7894-2480-0*) DK Pub Inc.

— A Day at Damp Camp. LC 95-20848. (Illus.). 24p. (J). (ps-3). 1996. 15.95 (*0-531-09504-5*) Orchard Bks Watts.

— Dreamplace. LC 92-25102. (Illus.). 32p. (J). (ps-2). 1993. 15.95 (*0-531-05466-7*) Orchard Bks Watts.

— Dreamplace. LC 92-25102. (Illus.). 32p. (J). (ps-2). 1998. pap. 6.95 (*0-531-07101-4*) Orchard Bks Watts.

Lyon, George-E. Father Time & the Day Boxes. LC 93-25201. (Illus.). 32p. (J). (gr. k-3). 1994. reprint ed. pap. 4.95 (*0-689-71792-X*) Aladdin.

Lyon, George E. Five Live Bongos. (Illus.). 40p. (J). (ps-3). 1994. 15.95 (*0-590-46654-2*, Scholastic Hardcover) Scholastic Inc.

— Here & Then. LC 94-6921. 128p. (J). (gr. 5-7). 1994. 15.95 (*0-531-06866-8*) Orchard Bks Watts.

— Mama Is a Miner. LC 93-49398. (Illus.). 32p. (J). (gr. k-3). 1994. 15.95 (*0-531-06853-6*); lib. bdg. 16.99 (*0-531-08703-4*) Orchard Bks Watts.

— The Outside Inn. LC 90-14285. (Illus.). 32p. (J). (ps-1). 1997. pap. 6.95 (*0-531-07086-7*) Orchard Bks Watts.

— A Regular Rolling Noah. LC 90-39984. (Illus.). 32p. (J). (gr. k-3). 1991. reprint ed. mass mkt. 4.95 (*0-689-71449-1*) Aladdin.

— The Stranger I Left Behind. LC 96-31631. (J). 1997. pap. 3.95 (*0-8167-4026-7*) Troll Communs.

— Together. LC 89-2892. (Illus.). 32p. (J). (ps-1). 1989. 15.95 (*0-531-05831-X*) Orchard Bks Watts.

— Together. LC 89-2892. (Illus.). 32p. (J). (ps-3). 1993. pap. 5.95 (*0-531-07047-6*) Orchard Bks Watts.

— Who Came down That Road? LC 91-20742. (Illus.). 32p. (J). (ps-2). 1996. pap. 5.95 (*0-531-07073-5*) Orchard Bks Watts.

— With a Hammer for My Heart. LC 97-36074. 224p. 1997. 21.95 (*0-7894-2460-6*) DK Pub Inc.

***Lyon, George E.** With a Hammer for My Heart. 224p. 1999. reprint ed. pap. 12.00 (*0-380-73217-3*, Avon Bks) Morrow Avon.

Lyon, George E. A Wordful Child. LC 96-866. (Meet the Author Ser.). (Illus.). 32p. (J). (gr. 2-5). 1996. 14.95 (*1-57274-016-7*, 715) R Owen Pubs.

Lyon, George E. & Soentpiet, Chris K. A Sign. LC 97-26878. 32p. (J). (gr. k-4). 1998. 15.95 (*0-531-30073-0*) Orchard Bks Watts.

— A Sign. LC 97-26878. (Illus.). 32p. (J). (gr. k-4). 1998. lib. bdg. 16.99 (*0-531-33073-7*) Orchard Bks Watts.

Lyon, George Ella. A B Cedar, an Alphabet of Trees. LC 88-22797. 1996. 12.15 (*0-606-10732-0*, Pub. by Turtleback) Demco.

— Book. LC 98-19835. (Illus.). 32p. (J). (ps-2). 1999. 16.95 (*0-7894-2560-2*, D K Ink) DK Pub Inc.

***Lyon, George Ella.** Borrowed Children. LC 99-32579. 176p. (J). (gr. 4-8). 1999. pap. 9.95 (*0-8131-0972-8*) U Pr of Ky.

Lyon, George Ella. Cecil's Story. 1995. 11.15 (*0-606-08712-5*, Pub. by Turtleback) Demco.

***Lyon, George Ella.** Counting on the Woods. LC 97-34117. (Illus.). 32p. (J). (ps-2). 2000. pap. text 5.95 (*0-7894-2662-5*, D K Ink) DK Pub Inc.

Lyon, George Ella. Dreamplace. (J). 1998. 12.15 (*0-606-13348-8*, Pub. by Turtleback) Demco.

— Here & Then. 1997. pap. 3.95 (*0-8167-4207-3*) Troll Communs.

— A Traveling Cat. LC 98-13796. (Illus.). 32p. (J). (ps-2). 1998. 15.95 (*0-531-30102-8*); lib. bdg. 16.99 (*0-531-33102-4*) Orchard Bks Watts.

— Who Came Down That Road? LC 91-20742. 1996. 11.15 (*0-606-10065-2*, Pub. by Turtleback) Demco.

Lyon, Gilles, et al. Neurology of Hereditary Metabolic Diseases of Children. 2nd ed. LC 95-23487. (Illus.). 512p. 1996. text 79.00 (*0-07-000389-0*) McGraw-Hill HPD.

Lyon, H., ed. Theory & Strategy in Histochemistry: A Guide to the Selection & Understanding of Techniques. (Illus.). xviii, 591p. 1991. 107.00 (*0-387-19311-1*) Spr-Verlag.

Lyon, H. Curtis & Juern, John. Pressed down but Not Forgotten: Depression. LC 93-84289. 112p. 1993. 11.99 (*0-8100-0490-9*, 15N2001) Northwest Pub.

Lyon, Harris M. Graphics. LC 72-4458. (Short Story Index Reprint Ser.). 1977. reprint ed. 23.95 (*0-8369-4182-9*) Ayer.

Lyon, Hastings & Block, Herman. Edward Coke, Oracle of the Law. LC 92-773. (Illus.). xii, 385p. 1992. reprint ed. lib. bdg. 47.50 (*0-8377-2413-9*, Rothman) W S Hein.

***Lyon, Henry C.** "Desolating the Fair Country" The Civil War Diary & Letters of Lt. Henry C. Lyon, 34th New York. Radigan, Emily N., ed. LC 99-16707. (Illus.). 221p. 1999. lib. bdg. 27.50 (*0-7864-0690-9*) McFarland & Co.

Lyon, Howard H., et al. Plant-Parasitic Nematodes: A Pictorial Key to Genera. 5th ed. (Comstock Bk.). (Illus.). 288p. 1996. text 49.95 (*0-8014-3116-6*) Cornell U Pr.

Lyon, Howard H., jt. auth. see Johnson, Warren T.

Lyon, Ida. Wonders of Life (1910) 236p. 1998. reprint ed. pap. 18.95 (*0-7661-0548-2*) Kessinger Pub.

Lyon, Isaac. Recollections of an Old Cartman: Old New York Street Life. (Illus.). 114p. 1983. reprint ed. 17.50 (*0-9608788-4-X*) NY Bound.

***Lyon, J. G.** Wetland Landscape Characterization: Techniques & Applications for GIS, Mapping, Remote Sensing & Image Analysis. LC 00-9454. 2000. write for info. (*1-57504-121-9*, Ann Arbor Press) Sleepng Bear.

Lyon, J. Noel & Atkey, Ronald G., eds. Canadian Constitutional Law in a Modern Perspective. LC 78-18165. 1403p. reprint ed. pap. 200.00 (*0-8357-7993-9*, 201427600089) Bks Demand.

Lyon, Jack, ed. see Harrison, Conrad B.

Lyon, Jack M. Best-Loved Poems of the LDS People. LC 96-32020. vii, 373p. 1996. 21.95 (*1-57345-212-2*) Deseret Bk.

***Lyon, Jack M.** Inspirational Classics for Latter-Day Saints. LC 00-27981. 2000. write for info. (*1-57345-778-7*) Deseret Bk.

Lyon, Jack M. Poems That Lift the Soul: A Treasury of Faith & Inspiration. LC 97-43382. 1998. pap. 19.95 (*1-57345-364-1*, Shadow Mount) Deseret Bk.

Lyon, Jack M., et al. Best-Loved Stories of the LDS People. LC 97-24195. xv, 472p. 1997. 23.95 (*1-57345-266-1*) Deseret Bk.

***Lyon, James.** Lonely Planet Maldives. 4th ed. (Travel Guides Ser.). (Illus.). 208p. 2000. pap. 15.95 (*0-86442-700-X*) Lonely Planet.

Lyon, James. Urania: A Choice Collection of Psalm-Tunes, Anthems & Hymns. LC 69-11667. (Music Reprint Ser.). 198p. 1974. reprint ed. lib. bdg. 37.50 (*0-306-71198-2*) Da Capo.

Lyon, James, et al. Lonely Planet Maldives. 3rd ed. (Illus.). 160p. 1997. pap. 14.95 (*0-86442-497-3*) Lonely Planet.

***Lyon, James, et al.** Lonely Planet South America on a Shoestring. 7th ed. (Illus.). 1176p. 2000. pap. 29.95 (*0-86442-656-9*) Lonely Planet.

Lyon, James, et al. Lonely Planet U. S. A. (Illus.). 1200p. 1999. pap. 24.95 (*0-86442-513-9*) Lonely Planet.

— South America. 7th ed. (Illus.). 1176p. 1997. pap. 29.95 (*0-86442-401-9*) Lonely Planet.

Lyon, James B., contrib. by. Report & Proceedings of the Senate Appointed to Investigate the Police Department of the City of New York, 5 vols. 1997. reprint ed. 595.00 (*1-57588-278-7*, 310930) W S Hein.

Lyon, James K. Bertolt Brecht & Rudyard Kipling: A Marxist's Imperialist. LC 73-94231. (Studies in General & Comparative Literature: No. 3). 138p. 1975. pap. text 58.50 (*90-279-3411-8*) Mouton.

— Bertolt Brecht in America. LC 80-7543. (Illus.). 438p. (Orig.). reprint ed. pap. 135.80 (*0-608-06360-6*, 206672100008) Bks Demand.

Lyon, James K. & Breuer, Hans-Peter, eds. Brecht Unbound. LC 95-1992. 1995. write for info. (*0-87413-537-0*) U Delaware Pr.

Lyon, James K. & Inglis, Craig M., eds. Benn Gottfried: Konkordanz Zur Lyrik Gottfried Benns. (Alpha-Omega, Reihe D Ser.). 524p. 1971. write for info. (*3-487-04037-9*) G Olms Pubs.

Lyon, Janet. Manifestoes & the Trouble with the Modern. LC 98-36507. 1999. write for info. (*0-8014-3635-4*); pap. write for info. (*0-8014-8591-6*) Cornell U Pr.

Lyon, Jean. Becoming Bilingual: Language Acquisition in a Bilingual Community. LC 96-15893. (Bilingual Education & Bilingualism Ser.: Vol. 11). 271p. 1996. 99.00 (*1-85359-318-4*, Pub. by Multilingual Matters); pap. 34.95 (*1-85359-317-6*, Pub. by Multilingual Matters) Taylor & Francis.

Lyon, Jeff. Altered Fates: Gene Therapy & the Retooling of Human Life. 636p. 1996. pap. 15.95 (*0-393-31528-2*) Norton.

Lyon, Jeff & Gorner, Peter. Altered Fates: The Genetic Re-Engineering of Human Life. 800p. 1995. 27.50 (*0-393-03596-4*) Norton.

Lyon-Jenness, Cheryl, compiled by. From the Homestead Kitchen. (Illus.). 233p. 1982. pap. 25.00 (*0-939294-12-5*, TX-715-F7) Beech Leaf.

Lyon, John. Teares for the Death of Alexander, Earle of Dunfermeling, Lord Chancellar of Scotland. LC 79-172760. (Bannatyne Club, Edinburgh. Publications: No. 4). reprint ed. 29.50 (*0-404-52704-3*) AMS Pr.

— The Theatre of Valle-Inclan. LC 83-7368. (Cambridge Iberian & Latin American Studies). 241p. reprint ed. pap. 68.70 (*0-608-15263-3*, 2029222) Bks Demand.

Lyon, John & Sloan, Philip. From Natural History to the History of Nature: Readings from Buffon & His Critics. LC 81-1320. 432p. 1981. text 31.00 (*0-268-00955-4*) U of Notre Dame Pr.

Lyon, John, ed. see Valle-Inclan, Ramon Del.

Lyon, John, ed. & intro. see Conrad, Joseph.

Lyon, John, ed. & intro. see James, Henry.

Lyon, John, tr. see Duhem, Pierre.

Lyon, John F. & Lee, Siu-Lam. Laboratory Manual for Life Science I. 100p. (C). 1996. spiral bd. 20.95 (*0-7872-2325-5*) Kendall-Hunt.

Lyon, John G. & McCarthy, Jack, eds. Wetland & Environmental Applications of GIS. LC 95-10772. (Mapping Sciences Ser.). 400p. 1995. lib. bdg. 85.00 (*0-87371-897-6*, L897) Lewis Pubs.

Lyon, John Grimson. Practical Handbook for Wetland Identification & Delineation. (Mapping Sciences Ser.). 176p. 1993. boxed set 85.00 (*0-87371-590-X*, L590) Lewis Pubs.

Lyon, John H. Study of the New Metamorphosis. LC 20-3786. reprint ed. 27.50 (*0-404-04087-X*) AMS Pr.

Lyon, Jon G. Coping with Aphasia. LC 97-29700. (Coping with Aging Ser.). (Illus.). 422p. (Orig.). 1997. pap. 49.95 (*1-879105-75-6*, 0338) Thomson Learn.

Lyon, Jonathan, jt. auth. see Horwich, Robert H.

Lyon, Kathryn. Witch Hunt: A True Story of Social Hysteria & Abused Justice. LC 97-94318. 512p. 1998. mass mkt. 5.99 (*0-380-79066-1*, Avon Bks) Morrow Avon.

Lyon, Kathryn, et al. Post-Soviet Eurasia: Anthropological Perspectives on a World in Transition. (Michigan Discussions in Anthropology Ser.). (Illus.). vi, 102p. (Orig.). (C). 1996. pap. 17.00 (*1-889480-00-2*) U MI Dept Anthropol.

Lyon, Kenneth S., jt. auth. see Sedjo, Roger A.

Lyon, Kevin. Psalm-Prayers for Every Mood. 176p. (Orig.). 1996. pap. 10.95 (*1-85607-164-2*, Pub. by Columba Press) Whitecap Bks.

***Lyon, Larry.** The Community in Urban Society. 320p. (C). 1999. pap. 17.95 (*1-57766-071-4*) Waveland Pr.

Lyon, Larry B., Jr. Before the Morning Calm: A Novel of Korea. (Illus.). 140p. 1997. pap. 4.95 (*0-9656601-0-9*) L B Lyon.

***Lyon, Leslie Connell & Lyon, Charles.** Surf Clowns. LC 99-67773. (Illus.). 176p. (gr. 3-10). 2000. pap. 29.95 (*0-9675214-4-0*) Bad Cat Bks.

Lyon, Leverett S. Hand-to-Mouth Buying: A Study in the Organization, Planning & Stabilization of Trade. LC 75-39259. (Getting & Spending: The Consumer's Dilemma Ser.). (Illus.). 1976. reprint ed. 41.95 (*0-405-08032-8*) Ayer.

— Salesman in Marketing Strategy. Assael, Henry, ed. LC 78-240. (Century of Marketing Ser.). 1979. reprint ed. lib. bdg. 36.95 (*0-405-11183-5*) Ayer.

Lyon, Leverett S., et al. Government & Economic Life: Development & Current Issues of American Public Policy, 2 vols., 79 and 83. LC 78-16476. (Institute of Economics of Brookings Institution Publication: No. 79). 1978. reprint ed. lib. bdg. 95.00 (*0-313-20601-5*, LYGE) Greenwood.

— Government & Economic Life: Development & Current Issues of American Public Policy, 2 vols., Vol. 1. LC 78-16476. (Institute of Economics of Brookings Institution Publication: No. 79). 1978. reprint ed. lib. bdg. 55.00 (*0-313-20600-7*, LYGE1) Greenwood.

— Government & Economic Life: Development & Current Issues of American Public Policy, 2 vols., Vol. 2. LC 78-16476. (Institute of Economics of Brookings Institution Publication: No. 79). 1978. reprint ed. lib. bdg. 55.00 (*0-313-20599-X*, LYGE2) Greenwood.

— The National Recovery Administration. LC 71-171386. (FDR & the Era of the New Deal Ser.). 1972. reprint ed. lib. bdg. 95.00 (*0-306-70385-8*) Da Capo.

Lyon, Lockwood. Migrating to DB2. 254p. 1993. 52.00 (*0-471-58180-1*) Wiley.

***Lyon, Lynn Boyer.** The Unforgiving Minute: The Triumphant Life of Rory David Boyer. (Illus.). 1999. pap. write for info. (*0-9663764-3-9*) Reivers Pr.

Lyon, Mack. Paul's Sermon on Mars' Hill. 110p. 1997. pap. 6.99 (*0-89225-466-1*, G54661) Gospel Advocate.

Lyon, Marcus W., Jr. Mammals of Indiana. LC 73-17829. (Natural Sciences in America Ser.). (Illus.). 388p. 1974. reprint ed. 33.95 (*0-405-05747-4*) Ayer.

Lyon, Margaret & Reynolds, Flora E. The Flying Cloud & Her First Passengers. (Illus.). 168p. 1998. reprint ed. pap. 25.00 (*0-9648938-2-7*) Mills Coll Ctr Bk.

Lyon, Margaret, ed. see Fayrfax, Robert.

Lyon, Mary. The Frazzled Working Woman's Practical Guide to Motherhood. LC 97-68723. (Illus.). 208p. 1997. pap. 14.95 (*0-914984-75-6*) Starburst.

Lyon, Mary, tr. see Ganshof, Francois L.

Lyon, Mary F., et al, eds. Genetic Variants & Strains of the Laboratory Mouse, 2 vols. 3rd ed. (Illus.). 1996. text 295.00 (*0-19-854869-9*) OUP.

Lyon, Matthew, jt. auth. see Hafner, Katie.

Lyon, Melvin E. Symbol & Idea in Henry Adams. LC 67-20597. 338p. reprint ed. pap. 104.80 (*0-7837-6019-1*, 204583100008) Bks Demand.

Lyon, Nancy. The Mystery of Stonehenge. (Great Unsolved Mysteries Ser.). 1997. pap. 4.95 (*0-8114-6862-3*) Raintree Steck-V.

Lyon, Pamela. We Are Staying: The Alyawarre Struggle for Land at Lake Nash. 240p. (C). 1990. 60.00 (*0-7316-7458-8*, Pub. by Pascoe Pub) St Mut.

Lyon, Pamela, ed. French Short Stories. 286p. 1966. pap. 12.95 (*0-14-002385-2*, Penguin Bks) Viking Penguin.

Lyon, Patricia J. Native South Americans: Ethnology of the Least Known Continent. (Illus.). 433p. (C). 1985. reprint ed. pap. text 19.95 (*0-88133-133-3*) Waveland Pr.

Lyon, Patricia J., tr. see Bonavia, Duccio.

Lyon, Peter, ed. Britain & Canada. (Studies in Commonwealth Politics & History: No. 4). 191p. 1976. 35.00 (*0-7146-3052-7*, Pub. by F Cass Pubs) Intl Spec Bk.

Lyon, Philip A., ed. Desorption Mass Spectrometry: Are SIMS & FAB the Same? LC 85-20151. (ACS Symposium Ser.: Vol. 291). 256p. 1985. reprint ed. pap. 79.40 (*0-608-03919-5*, 206436600009) Bks Demand.

Lyon, Reid, ed. Frames of Reference for the Assessment of Learning Disabilities: New Views on Measurement Issues. 672p. 1994. pap. 55.00 (*1-55766-138-3*) P H Brookes.

***Lyon, Richard H.** Designing for Product Sound Quality. LC 00-37689. (Mechanical Engineering Ser.). (Illus.). 2000. pap. write for info. (*0-8247-0400-2*) Dekker.

Lyon, Richards. Vine & Wine '95. (Yearly Datebook Journals Ser.). 162p. (Orig.). (C). 1994. pap. text 14.95 (*0-9616004-6-2*) Stonecrest Pr.

Lyon, Richards. Vine to Wine. LC 85-62333. (Illus.). 120p. 1985. pap. 9.95 (*0-9616004-0-3*) Stonecrest Pr.

— Vine to Wine, Vol. 1. 2nd rev. ed. (Vine to Wine Ser.). (Illus.). 128p. 1999. 14.95 (*0-9616004-8-9*, Pub. by Stonecrest Pr) Wine Appreciation.

Lyon, Richards & Ruyet, Jake. 100 Napa County Roadside Wildflowers, Vol. 1. unabridged ed. LC 96-92461. 1996. pap., per. 14.95 (*0-9616004-7-0*) Stonecrest Pr.

Lyon, Rick. Bell Eight. LC 94-70457. (New Poets of America Ser.). 70p. 1994. pap. 12.50 (*1-880238-09-8*) BOA Edns.

An Asterisk (*) at the beginning of an entry indicates that the title is appearing for the first time.

L

*Lyon, Robert. Water Marked: Stories of a Naked Fly Fisherman. 200p. 1998. pap. 16.95 (1-888345-14-4) Paper Jam.
Lyon, Rod, ed. Everyday Cornish. (C). 1989. pap. 45.00 (0-907566-82-0, Pub. by Dyllansow Truran) St Mut.
Lyon, Rod & Pengilly, John. Notes on Spoken Cornish. (C). 1989. 30.00 (1-85022-034-4, Pub. by Dyllansow Truran) St Mut.
Lyon, Ron & Paschall, Jenny. Beyond Belief!! Bizarre Facts & Incredible Stories from All over the World. (Illus.). 96p. 1997. reprint ed. pap. text 10.00 (0-7881-5089-8) DIANE Pub.
Lyon, Ron, jt. auth. see Paschall, Jenny.
Lyon, Roy B. Bosquejos Utiles para Laicos: Useful Outlines for Laymen. (SPA., Illus.). 96p. 1971. reprint ed. pap. 6.50 (0-311-42401-5) Casa Bautista.
Lyon, Sandra, ed. see Hale, C. Clark.
Lyon, Steve, jt. auth. see Wilson, F. Paul.
Lyon, Suzanne. Bandit Invincible: Butch Cassidy. LC 99-41704. 1999. 19.95 (0-7862-1843-6) Mac Lib Ref.
Lyon, T. Edgar. John Lyon: The Life of a Pioneer Poet. (Specialized Monographs: Vol. 6). 1989. 14.95 (0-88494-708-4) Bookcraft Inc.
Lyon, Talia. Girls on the Run. (Scarlet Ser.). (Orig.). 1997. mass mkt. 3.99 (1-85487-976-6, Pub. by Scarlet Bks) London Brdge.
Lyon, Tammie. Little Red Hen. LC 97-221420. (Illus.). 1997. write for info. (0-7853-2297-3) Pubns Intl Ltd.
Lyon, Tammie. Miriam & the Baby Moses. LC 99-203960. 12p. (J). (ps). 1999. bds. 3.99 (0-310-97577-8) Zondervan.
Lyon, Thomas & Williams, Terry T., eds. Great & Peculiar Beauty: A Utah Reader. LC 95-13281. (Illus.). 1024p. 1995. 35.00 (0-87905-691-6) Gibbs Smith Pub.
Lyon, Thomas E., Jr. Juan Godoy. LC 73-161825. (Twayne's World Authors Ser.). 161p. (C). 1972. lib. bdg. 17.95 (0-8290-1732-1) Irvington.
Lyon, Thomas J. John Muir. LC 72-619587. (Western Writers Ser.: No. 3). (Illus.). 48p. (Orig.). (C). 1972. pap. 4.95 (0-88430-002-1) Boise St U W Writ Ser.
Lyon, Thomas J., ed. The Literary West: An Anthology of Western American Literature. LC 98-10579. (Illus.). 464p. 1999. 35.00 (0-19-512460-X); pap. 18.95 (0-19-512461-8) OUP.
Lyon, Thomas J., et al, eds. Updating the Literary West: Western Literature Association. LC 97-9120. 1032p. 1997. 79.50 (0-87565-175-5) Tex Christian.
Lyon, Thomas J., et al. Places, Shadows, Dancing People. LC 71-632230. (Utah State University, Monograph Ser.: Vol. 17, No. 1). 70p. reprint ed. pap. 30.00 (0-8357-6264-5, 203460700090) Bks Demand.
Lyon, Thomas J., ed. see Bass, Rick, et al.
Lyon, Thomas J., ed. see Waters, Frank.
Lyon, Todd. Chic Simple: Paint. 1994. 12.50 (0-679-43217-5) Knopf.
— Chic Simple Desk. 104p. 1994. 12.50 (0-679-43220-5) Knopf.
— Hugs & Kisses. LC 97-32509. (Tiny Folio Ser.). (Illus.). 288p. 1998. 11.95 (0-7892-0427-4) Abbeville Pr.
— The New Year's Eve Compendium: Toasts, Tips, Trivia & Tidbits for Bringing in the New Year. 1998. pap. write for info. (0-609-80341-7) C Potter.
— The New Year's Eve Compendium: Toasts, Tips, Trivia & Tidbits for Bringing in the New Year. LC 98-16943. (Illus.). 112p. 1998. 12.00 (0-609-60374-4) C Potter.
Lyon, Todd, ed. The Family of Women: Voices Across the Generations. LC 98-31560. (Illus.). 144p. 1999. 24.95 (0-7892-0338-3) Abbeville Pr.
Lyon, Todd, jt. auth. see George, Judy.
Lyon, Tolbert J. Lyon Hunts & Humor: True Life Hunting & Adventure Stories. LC 90-37549. 1990. pap. 12.95 (0-86534-148-6) Sunstone Pr.
Lyon, Wanda S. & Sutton, Cynthia E. Osteoporosis: How to Make Your Bones Last a Lifetime. 240p. 1993. pap. 10.99 (1-56943-005-5) NTC Contemp Pub Co.
Lyon, Wanda S., jt. auth. see Sutton, Cynthia E.
Lyon, Wendy. A Mother's Dilemma. 123p. 1993. 8.95 (1-878526-44-8) Pineapple MI.
Lyon, Wendy & Clark, Sheree. Creative Direct Mail Design: The Guide & Showcase. (Illus.). 160p. 1995. 29.99 (1-56496-143-5) Rockport Pubs.
Lyon, William F., jt. auth. see Davidson, Ralph H.
Lyon, William F., jt. auth. see Sherman, M. L.
Lyon, William H. Those Old Yellow Dog Days: Frontier Journalism in Arizona, 1859-1912. LC 93-49523. (Illus.). 272p. 1994. 29.95 (0-910037-32-9) AZ Hist Soc.
Lyon, William H., ed. Journalism in the West. (Illus.). 108p. 1980. pap. text 15.00 (0-89745-008-6) Sunflower U Pr.
Lyon, William S. Encyclopedia of Native American Healing. 360p. 1996. lib. bdg. 70.00 (0-87436-852-9) ABC-CLIO.
— Encyclopedia of Native American Healing. (Illus.). 416p. 1998. pap. 15.95 (0-393-31735-8) Norton.
— Encyclopedia of Native American Shamanism: Sacred Ceremonies of North America. LC 98-34582. 512p. 1998. lib. bdg. 65.00 (0-87436-933-9, FN-1719) ABC-CLIO.
Lyonga, Lynne N., ed. see Ngeyi, Stanley-Pierre.
Lyongrun, Arnold. Masterpieces of Art Nouveau Stained Glass Design. (Illus.). 32p. 1989. pap. 7.95 (0-486-25953-6) Dover.
*Lyonharte, Richard L. Anna's Story: New, Effective Treatments for Rheumatoid Arthritis. 153p. 1999. pap. 15.95 (0-7414-0204-1) Buy Books.
Lyonnet, P. Maintenance Planning: Methods & Mathematics. (Illus.). 224p. (C). (gr. 13). 1991. text 48.96 (0-412-37680-6, Chap & Hall NY) Chapman & Hall.
Lyonnet, Stanislas & Sabarin, Leopold. Sin, Redemption & Sacrifice: A Biblical & Patristic Study. (Analecta Biblica Ser.: Vol. 48). 1971. pap. 27.00 (88-7653-048-7, Pub. by Biblical Inst Pr) Loyola Pr.
Lyons. America Government Chapter. Date not set. suppl. ed. write for info. (0-314-06465-6) West Pub.
— American Government Overview. Date not set. write for info. (0-314-06721-3) West Pub.
— American Government Survey. 1995. wbk. ed. 9.50 (0-314-06131-2) West Pub.
— Castles Burning. 1981. pap. 2.50 (0-671-41864-5) PB.
Lyons. Emotion. 248p. 1993. 61.95 (0-7512-0132-4) Ashgate Pub Co.
Lyons. GED Math Book. (YA - Adult Education Ser.). 1995. pap. 10.95 (0-538-71103-5) S-W Pub.
— Letters from Slave Girl. (J). 1998. pap. 3.95 (0-87628-518-3) Ctr Appl Res.
*Lyons, ed. Graphic Communication Dictionary. LC 99-34860. (Against the Clock Ser.). 328p. 1999. pap. 26.00 (0-13-012226-2) P-H.
Lyons, ed. A Transect Through the New England Appalachians. (IGC Field Trip Guidebooks Ser.). 72p. 1989. 21.00 (0-87590-607-9, T162) Am Geophysical.
Lyons & Scheb. American Government: Politics & Political Culture. (Political Science Ser.). 1995. mass mkt., student ed. 17.75 (0-314-05251-8) West Pub.
— Study Politics. (Political Science Ser.). 1995. 12.00 (0-314-06040-5) Wadsworth Pub.
Lyons, jt. auth. see Nicoles.
Lyons, jt. auth. see Richardson.
Lyons, Douglas A. Image Processing in Java. LC 99-10044. 574p. 1999. pap. text 49.99 (0-13-974577-7) P-H.
Lyons, A. B., jt. ed. see Miller, R. B.
Lyons, Alana. Now It's Your Turn: How Women Can Transform Their Lives & Save the Planet. LC 98-26346. 1998. pap. 13.95 (0-9663694-0-8) Jaguar Bks Inc.
Lyons, Albert C. Abergavenny Nine Hundred: A Pictorial Celebration. (C). 1989. 70.00 (1-870402-55-3, Pub. by D Brown & Sons Ltd) St Mut.
Lyons, Albert M. Fifty-Fifty: A Blend of Old & New. LC 73-178445. (Short Story Index Reprint Ser.). 1977. reprint ed. 23.95 (0-8369-4046-6) Ayer.
Lyons, Albert S. & Petrucelli, R. Joseph. Medicine: An Illustrated History. (Illus.). 1978. text 42.95 (0-8109-1054-3) Abrams.
Lyons, Allan S. Enhanced Convertibles: Uncommon Profits with Low Risk. (C). 1995. text 29.95 (0-13-320615-7) P-H.
— Winning in the Options Market: A Streetwise Trader Shows You How to Outsmart the Pros. LC 94-172543. 250p. 1994. text 42.50 (1-55738-431-2, Irwn Prfssnl) McGraw-Hill Prof.
Lyons, Anna. The Bunny Meets Ann Peacock. (Illus.). 16p. (J). (gr. k-3). 1998. pap. 6.00 (0-8059-4362-5) Dorrance.
Lyons, Anne. Values for Your Son, Your Daughter, & Yourself. 52p. 1993. pap. 12.95 (0-9638076-0-9) Fulton Freeman Pubs.
Lyons, Anne K. Anthony Trollope: An Annotated Bibliography of Periodical Works by & about Him in the United States & Great Britain to 1900. 175p. 1985. 25.00 (0-913283-04-5) Penkevill.
Lyons, Art & Seraydarian, Patricia E. Paradigm Reference Manual. 372p. (C). 1993. pap. text 16.95 (1-56118-370-9) Paradigm MN.
— Paradigm Reference Manual. 372p. (C). 1994. pap. text, teacher ed. 8.00 (1-56118-371-7) Paradigm MN.
Lyons, Art, et al. Paradigm Reference Manual: Workbook. 256p. (C). 1994. student ed. 10.00 (1-56118-372-5) Paradigm MN.
Lyons, Art, jt. auth. see McLean, Gary.
*Lyons, Arthur. Death on the Cheap: The Lost B Movies of Film Noir. (Illus.). 2000. pap. 17.50 (0-306-80996-6, Pub. by Da Capo) HarpC.
Lyons, Arthur. Fast Fade: A Jacob Asch Mystery. 224p. 1987. 15.45 (0-89296-216-X, Pub. by Mysterious Pr) Little.
— Other People's Money. 1989. 17.45 (0-89296-218-6, Pub. by Mysterious Pr) Little.
Lyons, Arthur, jt. auth. see Gray, Dudley.
Lyons, Barbara, jt. ed. see Rowland, Diane.
Lyons, Barbara Ann, jt. auth. see Muma, Richard D.
Lyons, Beth. African American: Harriet Tubman. (Graphic Learning Multicultural Literature Program Ser.). (ENG & SPA., Illus.). (J). (gr. k-5). 1994. teacher ed. 45.00 (0-87746-401-4) Graphic Learning.
— Asian American: Minoru Yasui. (Graphic Learning Multicultural Literature Program Ser.). (ENG & SPA., Illus.). (J). (gr. k-5). 1994. teacher ed. 45.00 (0-87746-416-2) Graphic Learning.
— Federal Control of Business: Antitrust Laws. rev. ed. LC 72-84857. (Antitrust Ser.). 1972. 135.00 (0-685-59804-7) West Group.
— Me & My World: Teachers Manual. (Graphic Learning Integrated Social Studies Ser.). 200p. 1997. teacher ed. 125.00 (0-87746-364-6) Graphic Learning.
Lyons, Beth, retold by. African American: The Name of the Tree. (Graphic Learning Multicultural Literature Program Ser.). (ENG & SPA., Illus.). (J). (gr. k-5). 1994. teacher ed. 45.00 (0-87746-410-3) Graphic Learning.
— Native American: When Coyote Stole Fire. (Graphic Learning Multicultural Literature Program Ser.). (ENG & SPA., Illus.). (J). (gr. k-5). 1994. teacher ed. 45.00 (0-87746-440-5) Graphic Learning.
Lyons, Beverly P. Sociocultural Differences Between America-Born & West Indian-Born Elderly Blacks: A Comparative Study of Health & Social Service Use. Bruchey, Stuart, ed. LC 97-22284. (Garland Studies on the Elderly in America). 135p. 1997. text 43.00 (0-8153-3042-1) Garland.
Lyons, Blythe & Janes, Missy. Choosing the Right School for Your Child: A Guide to Selected Elementary Schools in the Washington Area. 344p. (Orig.). 1990. pap. 14.95 (0-8191-7682-6) Madison Bks UPA.
Lyons, Bonnie & Oliver, Bill. Passion & Craft: Conversations with Notable Writers. LC 97-33749. 232p. 1998. 19.95 (0-252-06687-1); text 39.95 (0-252-02387-0) U of Ill Pr.
Lyons, Bonnie G., jt. auth. see Stuth, Jerry W.
*Lyons, Brian. Canadian Macroeconomics: Problems & Policies. 6th ed. 400p. 2000. pap. 59.93 (0-13-086377-7) P-H.
— Canadian Microeconomics: Problems & Policies. 6th ed. 384p. 2000. pap. 59.93 (0-13-086378-5) P-H.
Lyons, Bridget G., ed. Chimes at Midnight. (Films in Print Ser.). (Illus.). 225p. (C). 1988. text 40.00 (0-8135-1338-3) Rutgers U Pr.
— Reading in an Age of Theory. LC 96-45633. 256p. (C). 1997. text 45.00 (0-8135-2430-X) Rutgers U Pr.
Lyons, Brooke, et al. Scoliosis: Ascending the Curve. LC 99-28380. 256p. 1999. 24.95 (0-87131-883-0) M Evans.
Lyons, C. P. Trees & Shrubs Of Washington. (Illus.). 160p. 1999. pap. 12.95 (1-55105-094-3) Lone Pine.
— Trees, Shrubs & Flowers to Know in British Columbia & Washington. rev. ed. (Illus.). 376p. 1995. pap. 15.95 (1-55105-044-7) Lone Pine.
*Lyons, C. P. Wildflowers of Washington. 2000. pap. 15.95 (1-55105-207-5) Lone Pine.
Lyons, Carol, et al. Partners in Learning: Teachers & Children in Reading Recovery. (Language & Literacy Ser.). 256p. (C). 1993. text 38.00 (0-8077-3298-2); pap. text 19.95 (0-8077-3297-4) Tchrs Coll.
Lyons, Carol, ed. see Roberts, John.
*Lyons, Carol A. & Pinnell, Gay Su. Learning How to Make a Difference: A Practical Guide for the Professional Development of Literacy Teachers. 2001. pap. text. write for info. (0-325-00282-7) Heinemann.
Lyons, Cat. Death in the Wind. LC 96-96998. 192p. 1996. 18.95 (0-8034-9184-0, Avalon Bks) Bouregy.
— Murder for Reasons Unknown. LC 96-95287. 192p. 1997. 18.95 (0-8034-9193-X, Avalon Bks) Bouregy.
*Lyons, Cat. Murder in Palm Beach. LC 00-190021. 192p. 2000. 18.95 (0-8034-9418-1, Avalon Bks) Bouregy.
Lyons, Cathie. Journey Toward Wholeness. 1987. pap. 4.95 (0-377-00171-6) Friendship Pr.
Lyons, Champ, Jr. Alabama Practice Series, 2 vols. 2nd ed. 1250p. 1986. 120.00 (0-317-52097-0) West Pub.
*Lyons, Channy. Verda & Me: My Grandmother Takes Me with Her to Draw in the Garden... (Illus.). 50p. 2000. pap. 8.00 (0-9625879-1-5) Wilde Pr.
Lyons, Charles. The New Censors: Movies & the Culture Wars. LC 96-36587. (Culture & the Moving Image Ser.). 248p. (C). 1997. 69.95 (1-56639-511-9) Temple U Pr.
— The New Censors: Movies & the Culture Wars. LC 96-36587. (Culture & the Moving Image Ser.). 248p. (C). 1997. pap. text 17.95 (1-56639-512-7) Temple U Pr.
Lyons, Charles, ed. see Robinson, Marcus S.
Lyons, Charles H., et al. Education for What? British Policy Versus Local Initiative. (Foreign & Comparative Studies Program, Eastern Africa Ser.: No. 13). 100p. 1973. pap. 3.00 (0-915984-10-5) Syracuse U Foreign Comp.
Lyons, Charles R. Critical Essays on Henrik Ibsen. (Critical Essays on World Literature Ser.). 264p. 1987. 48.00 (0-8161-8835-1, G K Hall & Co) Mac Lib Ref.
— Hedda Gabler: Gender, Role & the World. Lecker, Robert, ed. (Twayne's Masterworks Ser.). 168p. 1990. 23.95 (0-8057-9417-4, MWS 62) Macmillan.
— Samuel Beckett. King, Bruce & King, Adele, eds. (Modern Dramatists Ser.). 209p. 1990. pap. 13.95 (0-333-29466-1) St Martin.
— Shakespeare & the Ambiguity of Love's Triumph. (Studies in English Literature: No. 68). 213p. 1971. text 64.65 (90-279-1751-5) Mouton.
Lyons, Charlotte. Mary Engelbreit's Christmas Companion: The Mary Engelbreit Look & How to Get It. (Illus.). 136p. 1995. 24.95 (0-8362-4627-6) Andrews & McMeel.
— Mary Engelbreit's Home Companion: The Mary Engelbreit Look & How to Get It. (Illus.). 128p. 1994. 24.95 (0-8362-4621-7) Andrews & McMeel.
*Lyons, Charlotte. Mothers & Daughters at Home: 35 Projects to Make Together. LC 99-54522. (Illus.). 160p. 2000. 24.00 (0-684-86273-5) Simon & Schuster.
— The New Ebony Cookbook. LC 99-49232. (Illus.). 120p. 1999. 19.95 (0-87485-090-8) Johnson Chicago.
Lyons, Charlotte, ed. Practical Grammar. 1980. 4.95 (1-55708-325-8, MCR459) McDonald Pub Co.
Lyons, Charlotte, jt. auth. see Engelbreit, Mary.
Lyons, Chess & Merilees, William J. Trees, Shrubs & Flowers to Know in Washington & British Columbia, Vol. 1. rev. ed. (Illus.). 376p. (Orig.). 1995. pap. 15.95 (1-55105-062-5, 1-55105) Lone Pine.
Lyons, Christine, jt. auth. see Schaefer, Dan.
Lyons, Christine, jt. auth. see Schaefer, Daniel.
Lyons, Christopher. Definiteness. (Textbooks in Linguistics Ser.). (Illus.). 320p. (C). 1998. 74.95 (0-521-36282-2); pap. 27.95 (0-521-36835-9) Cambridge U Pr.
Lyons, Claire L. The Archaic Cemeteries. LC 96-7100. (Morgantina Studies: No. 5). 378p. 1996. text 90.00 (0-691-04016-8, Pub. by Princeton U Pr) Cal Prin Full Svc.
Lyons, Claire L., et al. Irresistible Decay: Ruins Reclaimed. Roth, Michael S., ed. LC 97-14118. (Bibliographies & Dossiers Ser.). 124p. 1997. pap. 19.95 (0-89236-468-8, Pub. by J P Getty Trust) OUP.
Lyons, Claire L., jt. ed. see Kolowski-Ostrow, Ann O.
Lyons, Dan. Cars of 1957 - Lyons. LC 98-169949. 144 p. 1997. write for info. (0-7853-2450-X) Pubns Intl Ltd.
*Lyons, Dan. Democracy, Rights & Freedoms: What Are They? What Good Are They? (Studies in Theoretical & Applied Ethics: Vol. 3). 200p. (C). 2000. 47.95 (0-8204-4513-4) P Lang Pubng.
Lyons, Dan. Sixties American Cars. LC 97-43431. (Illus.). 96p. 1998. pap. 13.95 (0-7603-0327-4) MBI Pubg.
Lyons, Dan, jt. auth. see Olsen, Byron D.
Lyons, Dana. Cows with Guns. LC 98-167586. 64p. 1998. pap. 14.95 (0-670-87890-1) Viking Penguin.
Lyons, Daniel. Dog Days. 304p. 1999. pap. 12.95 (0-452-28096-6, Plume) Dutton Plume.
— Dog Days. LC 98-10949. 224p. (YA). 1998. 23.00 (0-684-84000-6) S&S Trade.
— The Last Good Man. LC 93-3464. 176p. (C). 1993. 22.95 (0-87023-865-5) U of Mass Pr.
— The Last Good Man. LC 93-3464. (Associated Writing Programs Award for Short Fiction Ser.). 176p. 1995. pap. 15.95 (0-87023-978-3) U of Mass Pr.
Lyons, Daniel, tr. see Bosco, John.
Lyons, David. English Lakes. (Land of the Poets Ser.). (Illus.). 64p. 1996. 9.99 (1-57215-143-9, JG1142) World Pubns.
— Ethics & the Rule of Law. LC 83-7687. 240p. 1984. pap. text 20.95 (0-521-27712-4) Cambridge U Pr.
— In the Interest of the Governed: A Study in Bentham's Philosophy of Utility & Law. 2nd rev. ed. 176p. 1991. text 49.95 (0-19-823964-5) OUP.
— Ireland: Land of the Poets. (Land of the Poets Ser.). (Illus.). 64p. 1996. 9.99 (1-57215-142-0, JG1141) World Pubns.
— Land of the Poets Ireland. (Illus.). 64p. 1998. 7.98 (1-85648-324-X, Thunder Bay) Advantage Pubs.
— Land of the Poets Lake District. (Land of the Poets Ser.). (Illus.). 64p. 1998. 7.98 (1-85648-325-8, Thunder Bay) Advantage Pubs.
— Land of the Poets Scotland. (Illus.). 64p. 1998. 7.98 (1-85648-323-1, Thunder Bay) Advantage Pubs.
— Moral Aspects of Legal Theory: Essays on Law, Justice, & Political Responsibility. LC 92-28985. 233p. (C). 1993. text 64.95 (0-521-43244-8) Cambridge U Pr.
— Rights, Welfare & Mill's Moral Theory. 208p. 1994. pap. text 19.95 (0-19-508218-4) OUP.
— Scotland. (Land of the Poets Ser.). (Illus.). 64p. 1996. 9.99 (1-57215-141-2, JG1140) World Pubns.
Lyons, David, ed. Mill's Utilitarianism: Critical Essays. LC 97-29038. (Critical Essays on the Classics Ser.). 244p. 1998. 36.00 (0-8476-8783-X); pap. 15.95 (0-8476-8784-8) Rowman.
Lyons, David, ed. see Bailey, D'Army.
Lyons, Deborah. Edward Hopper: A Journal of His Work. LC 95-308. (Illus.). 128p. 1997. 25.00 (0-393-31330-1) Norton.
— Gender & Immortality: Heroines in Ancient Greek Myth & Cult. LC 96-19562. 296p. 1997. text 39.50 (0-691-01100-1, Pub. by Princeton U Pr) Cal Prin Full Svc.
Lyons, Deborah, et al, eds. Addison Gallery of American Art: 65 Years. LC 95-83554. (Illus.). 512p. 1996. 75.00 (1-879886-40-5, 620172); pap. 60.00 (1-879886-42-1, 620173) Addison Gallery.
Lyons, Deborah & Weinberg, Adam D. Edward Hopper & the American Imagination. (Illus.). 272p. 1997. pap. 25.00 (0-393-31329-8) Norton.
Lyons, Dianne J. Planning Your Career in Alternative Medicine: A Guide to Degree & Certificate Programs in Alternative Health Care. LC 98-108399. 444p. 1997. pap. 19.95 (0-89529-802-3, Avery) Penguin Putnam.
Lyons, Douglas B., jt. auth. see Lyons, Jeffrey.
Lyons, Edward, ed. see Jurado, Eunice S.
Lyons, Edward T. The Walk. (Orig.). 1997. pap. write for info. (1-57553-484-3) Watermrk Pr.
Lyons, Elizabeth & Peters, Heather. Buddhism: History & Diversity of a Great Tradition. (Illus.). 64p. 1985. pap. 9.95 (0-934718-76-8) U Museum Pubns.
Lyons, Elizabeth G., jt. auth. see Lyons, Richard A.
Lyons, Emily B. How to Use Your Power of Visualization. (Lyons Visualization Ser.). (Illus.). 145p. (Orig.). 1980. pap. 10.00 (0-9604374-0-1) Lyons Visual.
Lyons, Enda. Jesus: Self-Portrait by God. LC 95-12265. 208p. (Orig.). 1995. pap. 9.95 (0-8091-3583-3) Paulist Pr.
Lyons, Eric R. Black Art of Windows Game Programming: Developing High-Speed Games with Win C. (Illus.). 650p. 1995. pap. 34.95 (1-878739-95-6) Sams.
Lyons, Ernest. Last Cracker Barrel. LC 75-7562. (Florida Classics Ser.). 201p. (Orig.). 1976. pap. 6.95 (0-912451-02-5) Florida Classics.
— My Florida. LC 69-14559. (Florida Classics Ser.). (Illus.). 136p. 1977. reprint ed. pap. 9.95 (0-912451-01-7) Florida Classics.
Lyons, Eugene. Assignment in Utopia. 290p. (C). 1990. pap. 29.95 (0-88738-856-6) Transaction Pubs.
— Assignment in Utopia. LC 76-110271. 658p. 1971. reprint ed. lib. bdg. 85.00 (0-8371-4497-3, LYAU, Greenwood Pr) Greenwood.
Lyons, Eugene, ed. Six Soviet Plays. LC 68-8937. 468p. 1968. reprint ed. lib. bdg. 75.00 (0-8371-0154-9, LYSP, Greenwood Pr) Greenwood.
Lyons, Evanthia, jt. auth. see Breakwell, Glynis M.
Lyons, Evanthia, jt. ed. see Breakwell, Glynis M.
Lyons, F. S. L. John Dillon: A Biography. LC 73-354502. xi, 516 p. 1968. write for info. (0-7100-2887-3) Routledge.
Lyons, Francis S. John Dillon: A Biography. LC 68-8594. 544p. reprint ed. pap. 168.70 (0-608-30166-3, 202011200016) Bks Demand.
Lyons, G. & Russell, I. F., eds. Clinical Problems in Obstetric Anaesthesia. (Illus.). 352p. 1997. text 60.00 (0-412-71600-3, Pub. by E A) OUP.
Lyons, Gail G., ed. Como Superar a la Competencia en el Negocio Inmobiliario.Tr. of Real Estate Sales Handbook. (SPA.). 208p. 1996. pap. 19.95 (0-7931-2151-5, 1913-4401) Dearborn.
— The Real Estate Sales Handbook. 10th ed. 273p. 1994. pap. 21.95 (0-7931-0947-7, 1913-2310) Dearborn.
Lyons, Gail G. & Harlan, Donald L. Buyer Agency: Your Competitive Edge in Real Estate. 3rd ed. LC 97-10586. 216p. 1997. pap. 24.95 (0-7931-2674-6, 1978-0303, Real Estate Ed) Dearborn.

An Asterisk (*) at the beginning of an entry indicates that the title is appearing for the first time.

Lyons, Gail G., et al. The Future of Real Estate: Profiting from the Revolution. 202p. 1996. pap. 21.95 (*0-7931-1584-1*, 1907-1701, Real Estate Ed) Dearborn.

*__Lyons, Gary.__ Desert Gardens. 176p. 2000. text 50.00 (*0-8478-2187-0*) Rizzoli Intl.

Lyons, Gene. Fools for Scandal: How the Media Invented Whitewater. 240p. 1996. pap. text 9.95 (*1-879957-52-3*, Franklin Sq Pr) Harpers Mag Found.

— The Higher Illiteracy: Essays on Bureaucracy, Propaganda, & Self-Delusion. LC 87-34013. 278p. (Orig.). 1988. pap. 18.00 (*1-55728-004-5*) U of Ark Pr.

Lyons, Gene & Harpers Magazine Staff. Fools for Scandal: How the Media Invented Whitewater. Rosenbush, Ellen, ed. 240p. 1996. pap. 9.95 (*0-614-15844-3*, Franklin Sq Pr) Harpers Mag Found.

Lyons, Gene, jt. auth. see Conason, Joe.

Lyons, Gene M. Putting ACUNS Together. LC 99-219053. (ACUNS Reports & Papers). 56p. 1999. pap. text 5.00 (*1-880660-18-0*) Acad Coun UN Syst.

— The Uneasy Partnership: Social Science & the Federal Government in the Twentieth Century. LC 72-93761. 394p. 1969. 39.95 (*0-87154-561-6*) Russell Sage.

Lyons, Gene M. & Lambert, Richard D. Social Science & the Federal Government. LC 76-148005. (Annals of the American Academy of Political & Social Science Ser.: No. 394). 1971. 28.00 (*0-87761-137-8*); pap. 18.00 (*0-87761-136-X*) Am Acad Pol Soc Sci.

Lyons, Gene M. & Masland, John W. Education & Military Leadership: A Study of the R. O. T. C. LC 75-18401. (Illus.). 283p. 1975. reprint ed. lib. bdg. 65.00 (*0-8371-8335-9*, LYED, Greenwood Pr) Greenwood.

Lyons, Gene M. & Mastanduno, Michael, eds. Beyond Westphalia? State Sovereignty & International Invention. LC 94-32440. 360p. 1995. text 48.50 (*0-8018-4953-5*) Johns Hopkins.

Lyons, Genevieve. Alice's Awakening. 224p. 26.00 (*0-7278-5506-9*) Severn Hse.

— Alice's Awakening. large type ed. LC 00-39522. 2000. write for info. (*0-7838-9109-1*, G K Hall & Co) Mac Lib Ref.

Lyons, Genevieve. Daniella's Decision. 224p. 1999. 25.00 (*0-7278-2267-5*, Pub. by Severn Hse) Chivers N Amer.

— Daniella's Decision. large type ed. LC 99-22229. 1999. 19.95 (*0-7838-8661-6*, G K Hall Lrg Type) Mac Lib Ref.

— Lucy Leighton's Journey. large type ed. LC 96-53886. 258p. 1997. lib. bdg. 21.95 (*0-7838-8075-8*, G K Hall Lrg Type) Mac Lib Ref.

— The Other Cheek. large type ed. LC 98-41738. 411p. 1998. pap. write for info. (*0-7540-2163-7*, G K Hall Lrg Type) Mac Lib Ref.

— The Other Cheek. large type ed. LC 98-41738. 1998. 25.95 (*0-7838-0389-3*, G K Hall Lrg Type) Mac Lib Ref.

— The Palucci Vendetta. large type ed. 625p. 1993. 27.99 (*0-7505-0510-9*, Pub. by Mgna Lrg Print) Ulverscroft.

— Perdita's Passion. large type ed. LC 98-5510. (Romance Ser.). 224 p. 1998. write for info. (*0-7540-3275-2*) Chivers N Amer.

— Perdita's Passion. large type ed. LC 98-5510. 265p. 1998. 18.95 (*0-7838-8459-1*, G K Hall Lrg Type) Mac Lib Ref.

— Poppy Penhaligon's Progress. 288p. 1996. 22.00 (*0-7278-4894-1*) Severn Hse.

Lyons, Geoffrey, jt. auth. see Jirasinghe, Dilum.

Lyons, George. Holiness in Everyday Life. 48p. 1992. pap. 5.99 (*0-8341-1432-1*) Beacon Hill.

— More Holiness in Everyday Life. LC 97-3826. 120p. (Orig.). 1997. pap. 8.99 (*0-8341-1661-8*) Beacon Hill.

Lyons, Graham, ed. The Russian Version of the Second World War: The History of the War As Taught to Soviet Schoolchildren. Vanston, Marjorie, tr. from RUS. LC 82-24236. (Illus.). 168p. reprint ed. pap. 52.10 (*0-7837-1572-2*, 204186400024) Bks Demand.

Lyons, Graham, et al. Is the End Nigh? Internationalism, Global Chaos & the Destruction of the Earth. 283p. 1995. 82.95 (*1-85972-218-0*, Pub. by Avebry) Ashgate Pub Co.

Lyons, Graham, jt. auth. see Smith, Joseph W.

Lyons Graphic Design Staff, ed. see Perry, Katy.

Lyons Graphic Designs Staff, ed. see Perry, Kate.

Lyons, H. P. Praying Our Prayers. 72p. 1976. 4.95 (*0-8199-0598-4*, Frncscn Herld) Franciscan Pr.

Lyons, Harold, jt. auth. see Bolch, Ben W.

Lyons, Harriet, ed. see Roth, Joan.

Lyons, Henry G. Royal Society, 1660-1940: A History of Its Administration under Its Charters. LC 69-10124. (Illus.). 354p. 1968. reprint ed. lib. bdg. 35.00 (*0-8371-0155-7*, LYRS, Greenwood Pr) Greenwood.

Lyons, Irish J., jt. auth. see McMichael, Joe.

Lyons, Ivan, jt. auth. see Lyons, Nan.

Lyons, J. B. Oliver St. John Gogarty. (Irish Writers Ser.). 89p. 1976. 8.50 (*0-8387-1359-9*); pap. 1.95 (*0-8387-1397-1*) Bucknell U Pr.

— Surgeon Major Parke's African Journey, 1887-1889. LC 94-158925. 282p. 1994. 39.95 (*1-874675-20-1*) Dufour.

— What Did I Die Of? The Deaths of Parnell, Wilde, Synge & Other Literary Pathologies. (Illus.). 234p. 1999. reprint ed. pap. text 15.00 (*0-7881-6126-1*) DIANE Pub.

Lyons, James. Legends of Cork. 144p. 1992. pap. 8.95 (*0-947962-29-8*) Dufour.

Lyons, James, jt. auth. see Howard, John T., Jr.

Lyons, James E., ed. Winning Strategies & Techniques for Civil Litigators. 339p. 1992. 105.00 (*0-685-69515-8*, H3-3004) PLI.

Lyons, James R., ed. The Intellectual Legacy of Paul Tillich. LC 68-63714. (Slaughter Foundation Lectures: 1966). 119p. reprint ed. pap. 36.90 (*0-608-16490-9*, 202763600055) Bks Demand.

*__Lyons, Jeffrey.__ Out of Left Field 2. 2000. pap. write for info. (*0-8129-3315-X*, Times Bks) Crown Pub Group.

Lyons, Jeffrey & Lyons, Douglas B. Out of Left Field: Over 1,134 Newly Discovered Amazing Baseball Records. 1998. pap. 12.00 (*0-8129-2993-4*) Random.

Lyons, Jim. How to Find Buried Treasure. rev. ed. (Illus.). 42p. 1986. reprint ed. pap. 7.95 (*0-9616231-0-1*) Jim Lyons.

Lyons, Joan. My Mother's Book. (Illus.). 48p. (Orig.). 1993. pap. 10.00 (*0-89822-104-8*) Visual Studies.

— Twenty-Five Years Ago. (Illus.). 24p. 1998. pap. 10.00 (*0-89822-075-0*) Visual Studies.

Lyons, Joan, intro. Artists' Books: A Critical Anthology & Sourcebook. 3rd ed. LC 85-3180. (Research, Fine Arts Ser.). (Illus.). 274p. (C). 1993. reprint ed. pap. text 19.95 (*0-89822-041-6*, N74333A75) Visual Studies.

Lyons, Jodi & Stevenson, Lanelle. P. O. P. S. Principles of Pop Singing. 320p. 1990. spiral bd. 32.00 incl. audio (*0-02-871971-9*, Schirmer Books) Mac Lib Ref.

*__Lyons, John.__ Communicating with Cues Pt. I: The Rider's Guide to Training & Problem Solving. Gallatin, Maureen, ed. (John Lyons' The Making of a Perfect Horse Ser.: Vol. I). (Illus.). 208p. 1998. 26.95 (*1-879620-55-3*) Belvoir Pubns.

— Communicating with Cues Pt. II: The Rider's Guide to Training & Problem Solving. Gallatin, Maureen, ed. (John Lyons' The Making of a Perfect Horse Ser.: Vol. II). 208p. 1999. 26.95 (*1-879620-56-1*) Belvoir Pubns.

— Communicating with Cues Pt. III: The Rider's Guide to Training & Problem Solving. Gallatin, Maureen, ed. (John Lyons' The Making of a Perfect Horse Ser.: Vol. IV). (Illus.). viii, 208p. 1999. 26.95 (*1-879620-58-8*) Belvoir Pubns.

Lyons, John. Introduction to Theoretical Linguistics. (Illus.). 520p. (Orig.). (C). 1968. pap. text 37.95 (*0-521-09510-7*) Cambridge U Pr.

— Language & Linguistics. LC 80-42002. (Illus.). 366p. (C). 1981. pap. text 21.95 (*0-521-29775-3*) Cambridge U Pr.

— Linguistic Semantics: An Introduction. 394p. (C). 1996. pap. text 20.95 (*0-521-43877-2*) Cambridge U Pr.

— Lyons on Horses. 240p. 1991. 29.95 (*0-385-41398-X*) Doubleday.

*__Lyons, John.__ Perfect Horsekeeping: Expert Advice on Tack & Barn. Gallatin, Maureen, ed. (John Lyons Perfect Horse Library Ser.). (Illus.). viii, 200p. 1999. 26.95 (*1-879620-62-6*) Belvoir Pubns.

— Perfectly Practical Advice on Horsemanship. Gallatin, Maureen, ed. (John Lyons' The Making of a Perfect Horse Ser.: Vol. VI). (Illus.). viii, 200p. 1999. 26.95 (*1-879620-60-X*) Belvoir Pubns.

— Private Lessons: John Lyons Answers Your Questions about Care & Training. Gallatin, Maureen, ed. (John Lyons Perfect Horse Library Ser.). (Illus.). viii, 200p. 2000. 26.95 (*1-879620-63-4*) Belvoir Pubns.

— Raising & Feeding the Perfect Horse. Gallatin, Maureen, ed. (John Lyons' The Making of a Perfect Horse Ser.: Vol. V). (Illus.). viii, 200p. 1999. 26.95 (*1-879620-59-6*) Belvoir Pubns.

Lyons, John. Semantics One. LC 76-40838. (Illus.). 384p. 1977. pap. text 31.95 (*0-521-29165-8*) Cambridge U Pr.

— Semantics Two. LC 76-40838. (Illus.). 460p. 1977. pap. text 31.95 (*0-521-29186-0*) Cambridge U Pr.

*__Lyons, John.__ Veterinary Care for the Perfect Horse. Gallatin, Maureen, ed. (John Lyons' The Making of a Perfect Horse Ser.: Vol. III). (Illus.). viii, 200p. 1999. 26.95 (*1-879620-57-X*) Belvoir Pubns.

Lyons, John, ed. see De Lafayette, Madame.

Lyons, John, tr. see Cardenal, Ernesto.

Lyons, John D. Kingdom of Disorder: Theory of Tragedy in Classical France. LC 98-55267. (Studies in Romance Literatures). 1999. 38.95 (*1-55753-160-9*) Purdue U Pr.

— The Listening Voice: An Essay on the Rhetoric of Saint-Amant. LC 82-82429. (French Forum Monographs: No. 40). 138p. (Orig.). 1982. pap. 10.95 (*0-917058-39-9*) French Forum.

— The Tragedy of Origins: Pierre Corneille & Historical Perspective. LC 95-33608. 1996. 37.50 (*0-8047-2616-7*) Stanford U Pr.

Lyons, John D. & McKinley, Mary B., eds. Critical Tales: New Studies of the Heptameron & Early Modern Culture. LC 93-26575. 296p. (C). 1994. text 38.95 (*0-8122-3206-2*) U of Pa Pr.

Lyons, John D. & Nichols, Stephen G., Jr., eds. Mimesis, from Mirror to Method, Augustine to Descartes. LC 82-40340. 287p. 1982. reprint ed. pap. 89.00 (*0-608-02322-1*, 206296300004) Bks Demand.

Lyons, John D. & Vickers, Nancy J., eds. The Dialectic of Discovery: Essays on the Teaching & Interpretation of Literature Presented to Lawrence E. Harvey. LC 83-81598. (French Forum Monographs: No. 50). 192p. (Orig.). 1984. pap. 17.95 (*0-917058-50-X*) French Forum.

Lyons, John F. The Life & Times of Louis-Amadeus Rappe, First Bishop of Cleveland. (Illus.). 300p. 1997. 29.95 (*0-9656426-0-7*) Bishop Pr OH.

Lyons, John S., et al. The Measurement & Management of Clinical Outcomes in Mental Health. LC 96-42269. 304p. 1997. 75.00 (*0-471-15429-6*) Wiley.

Lyons, John S., jt. ed. see Hultmand, Cheryl I.

Lyons, Johnny. Joking Off. LC 99-165083. 128p. 1998. pap. 4.99 (*0-8217-5907-8*, Zebra Kensgtn) Kensgtn Pub Corp.

*__Lyons, Johnny.__ Joking off Again. (Zebra Bks.). 128p. 1999. mass mkt. 4.99 (*0-8217-6408-X*, Zebra Kensgtn) Kensgtn Pub Corp.

Lyons, Johnny. Joking Off II. 128p. 1998. mass mkt. 4.99 (*0-8217-6002-5*, Zebra Kensgtn) Kensgtn Pub Corp.

— More Joking Off. 128p. 1999. mass mkt. 4.99 (*0-8217-6117-X*) Kensgtn Pub Corp.

— Still Joking Off. 128p. 1999. mass mkt. 4.99 (*0-8217-6223-0*, Knsington) Kensgtn Pub Corp.

Lyons, Joseph. Ecology of the Body: Styles of Behavior in Human Life. LC 87-9080. 339p. (C). 1987. text 49.95 (*0-8223-0710-3*) Duke.

Lyons, Joy M. Mammoth Cave: The Story Behind the Scenery. LC 91-60037. (Illus.). 48p. (Orig.). 1991. 7.95 (*0-88714-050-5*) KC Pubns.

Lyons, Joyce V. & Huddart, Jenny A. Integrating Reproductive Health into NGO Programs Vol. 1: Family Planning. 2nd ed. (Illus.). 160p. 1997. pap. write for info. (*0-9664963-0-2*) Initiatives Inc.

— Integrating Reproductive Health into NGO Programs Vol. 1: Family Planning Trainer's Guide. 120p. 1998. pap. write for info. (*0-9664963-2-9*) Initiatives Inc.

— Integrer la Sante Reproductive aux Programmes des ONG Vol. 1: Planification Familiale. 2nd ed. (FRE.). 146p. 1998. pap. write for info. (*0-9664963-1-0*) Initiatives Inc.

*__Lyons, Joyce V., et al.__ Integrating Reproductive Health into NGO Programs: PIR - The Performance Improvement Review Package: A Quality Assurance Tool for Community Based Programs. 2nd ed. 171p. 2000. pap. write for info. (*0-9664963-4-5*) Initiatives Inc.

*__Lyons, Judith.__ Awakened by His Kiss. Vol. 1296. 251p. 2000. mass mkt. 4.25 (*0-373-24296-4*, 1-24296-5) Silhouette.

*__Lyons, Julie, ed.__ The Heritage of Dallas County, Alabama. (Heritage of Alabama Ser.: Vol. 24). 320p. 2001. 50.00 (*1-891647-46-6*) Herit Pub Consult.

Lyons, Karen. International Social Work: Themes & Perspectives. LC 98-35470. 12p. (C). 1999. text 59.95 (*1-85742-389-5*, Pub. by Arena) Ashgate Pub Co.

*__Lyons, Karen.__ Social Work in Higher Education: Demise or Development? (Center for Evaluative & Development Research Ser.). 278p. 1999. text 69.95 (*0-7546-1007-1*, Pub. by Ashgate Pub) Ashgate Pub Co.

Lyons, Kathleen & Cooney-Lazaneo, Mary B. Plants of the Coast Redwood Region. (Illus.). (Orig.). (C). 1988. pap. text 15.00 (*0-9626961-0-2*) Looking Pr.

Lyons, Keith, ed. N Scale Product Guide. 1997. per. 24.95 (*0-945434-26-X*) Hundman Pub.

Lyons, Kenneth P. Cardiovascular Nuclear Medicine. (Illus.). 334p. (C). 1992. pap. text 120.00 (*0-8385-1052-3*, A1052-8, Apple Lange Med) McGraw.

*__Lyons, Kevin J.__ Buying for the Future: Contract Management & the Environmental Challenge. LC 99-37471. 240p. 2000. 75.00 (*0-7453-1346-9*, Pub. by Pluto GBR); pap. 24.95 (*0-7453-1341-8*, Pub. by Pluto GBR) Stylus Pub VA.

Lyons, Kevin J., jt. auth. see Gitlin, Laura N.

Lyons, Kim. In Padua. 32p. 1991. pap. 4.00 (*0-685-56987-X*) St Lazaire.

*__Lyons, Kimberly.__ Abracadabra. 104p. 2000. pap. 12.00 (*1-887123-31-8*, Pub. by Granary Bks) SPD-Small Pr Dist.

Lyons, Kimberly. Mettle. (Illus.). 45p. 1997. 200.00 (*1-887123-10-5*) Granary Bks.

Lyons, Kimberly C. Promises. 203p. 1998. pap. 10.00 (*0-9666027-0-6*) Lyons Den MI.

Lyons, Laura. Lyons' Guide to the Career Jungle: Workplace Ethics. LC 89-91730. 85p. 1989. pap. text 12.95 (*0-9623216-0-5*, Pub. by Odenwald Pr) Career Dynamics Inter.

Lyons, Laurence, jt. auth. see Birchall, David.

Lyons, Lawrence, jt. auth. see Gutmann, Felix.

Lyons, Lawrence W. Dan Quayle Meets the Last Judgement: Why It Happened. LC 90-85362. 238p. (Orig.). 1992. pap. 11.88 (*0-942121-33-3*) Grammar Pub.

— The Language Crystal: The Complete Solution to Civilization's Oldest Puzzle. LC 87-80516. (Illus.). 510p. (Orig.). 1988. pap. 14.76 (*0-942121-18-X*) Grammar Pub.

Lyons, Len. The Commodore 64 Connection. 256p. 1985. pap. write for info. (*0-201-17631-9*) Addison-Wesley.

Lyons, Leonard S. The Great Jazz Pianists. (Quality Paperbacks Ser.). (Illus.). 320p. 1989. reprint ed. pap. 13.95 (*0-306-80343-7*) Da Capo.

Lyons, Letitia M. Francis Norbet Blanchet & the Founding of the Oregon Missions (1838-1848) LC 73-3585. (Catholic University of America. Studies in Romance Languages & Literatures: No. 31). reprint ed. 41.00 (*0-404-57781-4*) AMS Pr.

Lyons, Linda B. A Handbook to the Pension Building: Home of the National Building Museum. 2nd ed. LC 93-27937. 1993. pap. write for info. (*0-9619752-2-9*) Natl Bldg Mus.

*__Lyons, Lisa.__ Departures: 11 Artists at the Getty. LC 99-57616. 56p. 2000. pap. 24.95 (*0-89236-582-X*) J P Getty Trust.

Lyons, Lisa, ed. see Arlen, Alice.

Lyons, Lisa, ed. see Perry, Katy.

Lyons, Lona, ed. see Treadgold, Richard.

Lyons, Lorenzo. Makua Laiana: Story of Lorenzo Lyons. (American Autobiography Ser.). 278p. 1995. reprint ed. lib. bdg. 79.00 (*0-7812-8583-6*) Rprt Serv.

Lyons, Louis. All You Wanted to Know about Mathematics but Were Afraid to Ask, 2 vols. (C). 1999. pap. 44.95 (*0-521-62763-X*) Cambridge U Pr.

— All You Wanted to Know about Mathematics but Were Afraid to Ask Vol. 1: Mathematics Applied to Science. (Illus.). 343p. (C). 1995. text 69.95 (*0-521-43465-3*); pap. text 27.95 (*0-521-43600-1*) Cambridge U Pr.

— All You Wanted to Know about Mathematics but Were Afraid to Ask Vol. 2: Mathematics for Science Students. (Illus.). 398p. (C). 1998. text 69.95 (*0-521-43466-1*); pap. text 27.95 (*0-521-43601-X*) Cambridge U Pr.

— A Practical Guide to Data Analysis for Physical Science Students. (Illus.). 107p. (C). 1991. text 49.95 (*0-521-41415-6*); pap. text 16.95 (*0-521-42463-1*) Cambridge U Pr.

Lyons, M. C. The Arabian Epic: Heroic & Oral Storytelling. (University of Cambridge Oriental Publications: No. 52). 350p. (C). 1995. text 200.00 (*0-521-48354-9*) Cambridge U Pr.

— The Arabian Epic Vol. 1: Heroic & Oral Storytelling: Introduction. (University of Cambridge Oriental Publications: 49). 198p. (C). 1995. text 54.95 (*0-521-47428-0*) Cambridge U Pr.

— The Arabian Epic Vol. 2: Heroic & Oral Storytelling: Analysis. (University of Cambridge Oriental Publications: No. 49). 500p. (C). 1995. text 85.00 (*0-521-47449-3*) Cambridge U Pr.

— The Arabian Epic Vol. 3: Heroic & Oral Storytelling: Texts. (University of Cambridge Oriental Publications: No. 49). 671p. (C). 1995. text 100.00 (*0-521-47450-7*) Cambridge U Pr.

*__Lyons, M. C.__ Identification & Identity in Classical Arabic Poetry. (Literary Studies: Vol. 2). 384p. (C). 1999. 90.00 (*0-906094-38-0*, Pub. by Gibb Memorial Trust) David Brown.

Lyons, M. E. Electroactive Polymer Electrochemistry Pt. 1: Fundamentals. (Illus.). 504p. (C). 1995. text 125.00 (*0-306-44792-4*, Kluwer Plenum) Kluwer Academic.

— Electroactive Polymer Electrochemistry Pt. 2: Methods & Applications. (Illus.). 328p. (C). 1996. text 102.00 (*0-306-45158-1*, Kluwer Plenum) Kluwer Academic.

Lyons, M. T. & Johnson, A. Preparing the Winning Bid. 352p. 1992. 60.00 (*0-85314-377-3*, Pub. by Tolley Pubng) St Mut.

Lyons, Malcolm C. & Jackson, D. E. Saladin: The Politics of the Holy War. 466p. 1997. pap. 13.95 (*0-521-58562-7*) Cambridge U Pr.

Lyons, Marjorie A., jt. ed. see VandeCreek, Larry.

*__Lyons, Mark.__ Defining the Nonprofit Sector: Australia. (Working Papers of the Johns Hopkins Comparative Nonprofit Sector Project: Vol. 30). (Illus.). 20p. 1998. pap. text 6.00 (*1-886333-35-1*) JH Univ Inst Pol Studies.

Lyons, Mark. The Good Parishioner. 73p. 1983. pap. 1.95 (*0-8199-0830-4*, Frncscn Herld) Franciscan Pr.

Lyons, Mark J. Background for Belief. 74p. (Orig.). 1990. pap. 1.95 (*0-8199-0957-2*, Frncscn Herld) Franciscan Pr.

*__Lyons, Marlena & Psaris, Jett.__ Undefended Love. (Illus.). 176p. 2000. pap. 13.95 (*1-57224-208-6*, Pub. by New Harbinger) Publishers Group.

Lyons, Mary. Baby Included! (The Big Event!) (Presents Ser.: No. 1997). 1998. per. 3.75 (*0-373-11997-6*, 1-11997-3) Harlequin Bks.

— Cara de Angel: Husband Not Included! (Bianca Ser.: Vol. 122).Tr. of Looks Like an Angel. 1998. per. 3.50 (*0-373-33472-9*, 1-33472-1) Harlequin Bks.

— Empezo con un Beso. (Bianca Ser.). 1996. per. 3.50 (*0-373-33372-2*, 1-33372-3) Harlequin Bks.

*__Lyons, Mary.__ En el Dia de los Enamorados. (Bianca Ser.: Bk. 205).Tr. of In St. Valentine's Day. (SPA.). 155p. 2000. per. 3.50 (*0-373-33555-5*, 1-33555-3) Harlequin Bks.

Lyons, Mary. Fiancailles pour la Saint-Valentin. (Azur Ser.: No. 747). (FRE.). 1999. mass mkt. 3.50 (*0-373-34747-2*, 1-34747-5) Harlequin Bks.

— Husband Not Included! 1997. per. 3.50 (*0-373-11904-6*, 1-11904-9) Harlequin Bks.

— It Started with a Kiss. LC 96-675. 186p. 1996. per. 3.50 (*0-373-11801-5*, 1-11801-7) Harlequin Bks.

*__Lyons, Mary.__ The Italian Seduction. Vol. 212. (Harlequin Presents Ser.). 2000. mass mkt. 3.99 (*0-373-12120-2*, 1121201) Harlequin Bks.

Lyons, Mary. Keeping Secrets. (J). 1995. 15.95 (*0-8050-3065-4*) H Holt & Co.

*__Lyons, Mary.__ Loca Pasion. (Bianca Ser.: No. 181).Tr. of Crazy Passion. (SPA.). 1999. per. 3.50 (*0-373-33531-8*, 1-33531-4) Harlequin Bks.

Lyons, Mary. Love Is the Key. (Presents Ser.). 1994. per. 2.99 (*0-373-11633-0*, 1-11633-4) Harlequin Bks.

*__Lyons, Mary.__ Maine's Achieving Women: Conversations with Entrepreneurs. (Illus.). 176p. 2000. pap. 11.95 (*0-9678276-0-4*) Lilac River.

Lyons, Mary. Memoirs of Mrs. Leeson, Madam, 1727-1797. LC 95-235679. 280p. 1995. pap. 19.95 (*1-874675-52-X*, Pub. by Lilliput Pr) Irish Bks Media.

— Mr. Loverman. 1997. per. 3.50 (*0-373-11868-6*, 1-11868-6) Harlequin Bks.

— Mr. Loverman. large type ed. (Mills & Boon Large Print Ser.). 288p. 1997. 23.99 (*0-263-14852-1*) Ulverscroft.

— No Surrender. large type ed. 215p. 1992. 11.50 (*0-7505-0313-0*, Pub. by Mgna Lrg Print) Ulverscroft.

*__Lyons, Mary.__ Novio de Alta Sociedad. Vol. 209.Tr. of High Society Groom. (SPA.). 2000. per. 3.50 (*0-373-33559-8*, 1-33559-5) Harlequin Bks.

Lyons, Mary. The Playboy's Baby: Expecting! (Presents Ser.: No. 2028). 1999. per. 3.75 (*0-373-12028-1*, 1-12028-6) Harlequin Bks.

— The Poison Place. (J). 1997. 16.00 (*0-614-29300-6*) Atheneum Yung Read.

*__Lyons, Mary.__ Reform of the Playboy. large type ed. 288p. 2000. 25.99 (*0-263-16311-3*, Pub. by Mills & Boon) Ulverscroft.

— Reform of the Playboy: (Notting Hill Grooms) (Presents Ser.: No. 2083). 2000. per. 3.99 (*0-373-12083-4*, 1-12083-1, Harlequin) Harlequin Bks.

Lyons, Mary. Silver Lady. 1993. per. 2.99 (*0-373-11610-1*, 1-11610-2) Harlequin Bks.

*__Lyons, Mary.__ The Society Groom. (Presents Ser.: No. 2066). 1999. per. 3.75 (*0-373-12066-4*, 1-12066-6) Harlequin Bks.

Lyons, Mary. The Valentine Affair! (Presents Ser.: No. 1940). 1998. per. 3.75 (*0-373-11940-2*, 1-11940-3) Harlequin Bks.

— The Yuletide Bride. LC 96-302. 188p. 1995. per. 3.25 (*0-373-11781-7*, 1-11781-1) Harlequin Bks.

An Asterisk (*) at the beginning of an entry indicates that the title is appearing for the first time.

Lyons, Mary A. Gearboid Bog, Ninth Earl of Kildare. LC 99-158465. (Historical Association of Ireland / Life & Times Ser.). vi, 77 p. 1998. write for info. (*0-85221-135-X*) Dundalgon Pr.

***Lyons, Mary Ann.** Church & Society in County Kildare, 1480-1547. (Maynooth History Studies Ser.). 208p. 1999. 55.00 (*1-85182-459-6*, Pub. by Four Cts Pr) Intl Spec Bk.

Lyons, Mary D. Poetry in the Latin Class. 9p. 1991. spiral bd. 1.60 (*0-939507-15-3*, B16) Amer Classical.

Lyons, Mary E. Catching the Fire: Philip Simmons, Blacksmith. LC 96-38643. (Illus.). 48p. (J). 1997. 16.00 (*0-395-72033-8*) HM.

— Letters from a Slave Girl: The Story of Harriet Jacobs. (J). (gr. 7). 1996. mass mkt. 3.95 (*0-689-80015-0*) Aladdin.

— Letters from a Slave Girl: The Story of Harriet Jacobs. LC 91-45778. (Illus.). 176p. (YA). (gr. 7 up). 1992. 16.00 (*0-684-19446-5*) Scribner.

— Letters from a Slave Girl: The Story of Harriet Jacobs. LC 91-45778. 1996. 9.05 (*0-606-09551-9*, Pub. by Turtleback) Demco.

— Master of Mahogany: The Story of Tom Day, Free Black Cabinetmaker. LC 93-37900. (Illus.). 48p. (J). (gr. 3-6). 1994. mass mkt. 15.95 (*0-684-19675-1*, Scribners Ref) Mac Lib Ref.

— Painting Dreams: Minnie Evans, Visionary Artist. LC 95-3994. (Illus.). 48p. (J). (gr. 3-7). 1995. 14.95 (*0-395-72032-X*) HM.

— The Poison Palace. LC 96-53678. (Illus.). 160p. (J). (gr. 7 up). 1997. 16.00 (*0-689-81146-2*) S&S Childrens.

— The Poison Place. LC 96-53678. 160p. (J). (gr. 5 up). 1999. per. 4.50 (*0-689-82678-8*, 076714004993) Aladdin.

— Raw Head, Bloody Bones: African-American Tales of the Supernatural. LC 91-10690. (Illus.). 96p. (J). 1995. pap. 3.95 (*0-689-80306-0*) Aladdin.

— Raw Head, Bloody Bones: African-American Tales of the Supernatural. (J). 1995. 9.30 (*0-606-08057-0*) Turtleback.

— Sorrow's Kitchen: The Life & Folklore of Zora Neale Hurston. LC 92-30600. (Great Achievers Ser.). (Illus.). 160p. (YA). (gr. 7 up). 1993. mass mkt. 7.99 (*0-02-044445-1*) Macmillan.

— Sorrow's Kitchen: The Life & Folklore of Zora Neale Hurston. LC 90-8058. (Illus.). 144p. (YA). (gr. 7 up). 1990. 15.00 (*0-684-19198-9*) Scribner.

— Sorrow's Kitchen: The Life & Folklore of Zora Neale Hurston. (Great Achievers Ser.). (J). 1993. 12.05 (*0-606-05615-7*, Pub. by Turtleback) Demco.

— Starting Home: The Story of Horace Pippin, Painter. LC 92-26990. (African-American Artists & Artisans Ser.). (Illus.). 48p. (J). (gr. 3-6). 1993. 15.95 (*0-684-19534-8*) Scribner.

— Stitching Stars: The Story Quilts of Harriet Powers. (J). 1998. pap. 6.99 (*0-87628-344-X*) Ctr Appl Res.

— Stitching Stars: The Story Quilts of Harriet Powers. LC 92-38561. (Illus.). 42p. (YA). 1993. mass mkt. 6.99 (*0-689-81707-X*) S&S Childrens.

— Stitching Stars: The Story Quilts of Harriet Powers. LC 92-38561. (African-American Artists & Artisans Ser.). (Illus.). 48p. (J). (gr. 3-6). 1993. 17.00 (*0-684-19576-3*) Scribner.

Lyons, Mary E. Stitching Stars: The Story Quilts of Harriet Powers. 1997. 12.19 (*0-606-13041-1*, Pub. by Turtleback) Demco.

Lyons, Mary E., selected by. Raw Head, Bloody Bones: African-American Tales of the Supernatural. LC 91-10690. (Illus.). 112p. (YA). (gr. 5 up). 1991. 15.00 (*0-684-19333-7*) Scribner.

***Lyons, Mary E. & Branch, Muriel M.** Ellen Bee: A Scrapbook Of The Civil War. LC 99-42050. (J). (gr. 4-6). 2000. 17.00 (*0-689-82379-7*) Atheneum Yung Read.

Lyons, Mary E., jt. auth. see Hunter, Clementine.

Lyons, Maryinez. A Colonial Disease: A Social History of Sleeping Sickness in Northern Zaire, 1900-1940. (History of Medicine Ser.). (Illus.). 351p. (C). 1992. text 85.00 (*0-521-40350-2*) Cambridge U Pr.

— Histories of Sexually Transmitted Diseases & HIV/AIDS in Sub-Saharan Africa, 44. Setel, Philip & Lewis, Milton, eds. LC 98-38207. (Contributions in Medical Studies: Vol. 44). 280p. 1999. 75.00 (*0-313-29715-0*, Greenwood Pr) Greenwood.

Lyons, Matthew N. Rose Kohn Goldsen Papers: A Descriptive Guide. (Illus.). 32p. 1992. pap. text. write for info. (*0-935995-02-1*) Cornell Manu.

Lyons, Matthew N., et al. Eyes Right! Challenging the Right Wing Backlash. Berlet, Chip, ed. 400p. (Orig.). (C). 1995. 40.00 (*0-89608-524-4*) South End Pr.

Lyons, Matthew N., jt. auth. see Berlet, Chip.

Lyons, Melvin K. The Care & Feeding of Dirt Archaeologists: A Manual of Sanitation, Hygiene, & Medicine for Archaeological Field Expeditions in the Near East. x, 76p. 1978. pap. text 5.95 (*0-317-04130-4*) Am Sch Orient Res.

Lyons, Michael C., jt. auth. see Alexander, James A.

Lyons, Michael J. World War I: A Short History. 2nd ed. LC 99-23061. 354p. 1999. pap. text 34.00 (*0-13-020551-6*) P-H.

— World War II: A Short History. 3rd ed. LC 97-52325. 367p. (C). 1998. pap. text 34.00 (*0-13-095477-2*) P-H.

Lyons, Morgan, et al. Key Organizational Issues in Intergenerational Mentoring. 71p. 1993. 10.00 (*0-86510-067-5*) Natl Inst Work.

***Lyons, Nan.** ACCESSWalks London: Jones,&Simon, Set. 1999. audio 18.00 (*0-694-52141-8*) HarperAudio.

— ACCESSWalks NEW YORK CITY: Post,&Steve, Set. 1999. audio 18.00 (*0-694-52120-5*) HarperAudio.

— ACCESSWalks PARIS: LeClere,&Jean, Set. 1999. audio 18.00 (*0-694-52140-X*) HarperAudio.

Lyons, Nan. Fielding's New York Agenda. 1996. pap. text 16.95 (*1-56952-124-7*) Fielding Wrldwide.

— Fielding's Sydney Agenda. Knoles, Kathy, ed. (Illus.). 256p. 1997. pap. 16.95 (*1-56952-123-9*) Fielding Wrldwide.

— Gluttony: More Is More. (Sin Series). (Illus.). 128p. 1999. 24.95 (*0-9669573-0-X*) Red Rock.

Lyons, Nan & Lyons, Ivan. Imperial Taste. (Illus.). 184p. 1991. 27.95 (*4-7700-1513-5*) Kodansha.

— Someone Is Killing the Great Chefs of Europe. LC 75-45140. 240p. 1990. 19.95 (*0-15-183760-0*) Harcourt.

Lyons, Nathan. Notations in Passing. 121p. 1974. 23.95 (*0-262-12067-4*); pap. text 12.50 (*0-262-62028-6*) MIT Pr.

***Lyons, Nathan.** Riding First Class on the Titanic: Photographs by Nathan Lyons. LC 99-48724. (Illus.). 248p. 1999. pap. 20.00 (*0-262-62135-5*) MIT Pr.

— Riding 1st Class on the Titanic: Photographs by Nathan Lyons. (Illus.). 2000. pap. 20.00 (*0-262-18135-5*) MIT Pr.

Lyons, Nathan. Verbal Landscape - Dinosaur Sat Down. LC 98-101587. (Illus.). 30p. 1987. pap. 10.00 (*0-939784-16-5*) CEPA Gall.

Lyons, Nathan, ed. see Denison, Herbert.

Lyons, Nathan, ed. see Story, Alfred T.

Lyons, Nene W. The Healing Touch. 80p. (C). 1988. pap. 35.00 (*0-7212-0743-X*, Pub. by Regency Pr GBR) St Mut.

Lyons, Nick. Confessions of a Fly Fishing Addict. LC 98-45974. (Illus.). 240p. 1999. pap. 12.00 (*0-87113-745-3*, Atlntc Mnthly) Grove-Atltic.

— A Flyfisher's World. (Illus.). 304p. 1998. pap. 12.00 (*0-87113-713-5*, Atlntc Mnthly) Grove-Atltic.

— A Flyfisher's World: Further Reflections of a Fly-Fishing Addict. LC 95-39206. (Illus.). 304p. 1996. 23.00 (*0-87113-628-7*, Atlntc Mnthly) Grove-Atltic.

***Lyons, Nick.** Full Creel. (Illus.). 464p. 2000. 25.00 (*0-87113-813-1*, Atlntc Mnthly) Grove-Atltic.

Lyons, Nick. My Secret Fishing Line. LC 99-13921. (Illus.). 208p. 1999. 23.00 (*0-87113-750-X*, Atlntc Mnthly) Grove-Atltic.

— The Seasonable Angler: Journeys Through a Fisherman's Year. LC 98-45975. (Illus.). 192p. 1999. pap. 12.00 (*0-87113-744-5*, Atlntc Mnthly) Grove-Atltic.

— Spring Creek. (Illus.). 169p. 2000. pap. 125.00 (*1-56416-182-X*); lthr. 350.00 (*1-56416-181-1*) Derrydale Pr.

Lyons, Nick. Spring Creek. LC 92-13026. (Illus.). 176p. 1995. pap. 11.00 (*0-87113-612-0*, Atlntc Mnthly) Grove-Atltic.

Lyons, Nick, ed. In Praise of Wild Trout. LC 97-32694. 112p. 1998. 20.00 (*1-55821-671-5*) Lyons Pr.

— In Praise of Wild Trout. deluxe ed. 112p. 1998. lthr. 750.00 (*1-55821-676-6*) Lyons Pr.

— The Quotable Fisherman. LC 98-3424. (Illus.). 176p. 1998. 20.00 (*1-55821-717-7*) Lyons Pr.

Lyons, Nick, ed. & intro. see Hemingway, Ernest.

Lyons, Nona. With Portfolio in Hand: Validating the New Teacher Professionalism. LC 97-49365. 288p. 1998. 54.00 (*0-8077-3717-8*); pap. 24.95 (*0-8077-3716-X*) Tchrs Coll.

Lyons, Oren, et al. Exiled in the Land of the Free: Democracy, Indian Nations & the U. S. Constitution. LC 91-72479. 428p. (C). 1992. 24.95 (*0-940666-15-4*) Clear Light.

— Exiled in the Land of the Free: Democracy, Indian Nations & the U.S. Constitution. LC 91-72479. (Illus.). 428p. (C). 1997. pap. 14.95 (*0-940666-50-2*) Clear Light.

Lyons, P., et al. Involving Parents: A Handbook for Participation in Schools. 248p. 1984. pap. 12.95 (*0-931114-19-5*, F1008) High-Scope.

Lyons, Paddy, ed. Lord Rochester. (Everyman's Poetry Ser.). 116p. 1997. pap. 1.95 (*0-460-87819-0*, Everyman's Classic Lib) Tuttle Pubng.

Lyons, Paddy, ed. The Complete Poems & Plays of John Wilmot, Second Earl of Rochester. 288p. 1993. 8.95 (*0-460-87223-0*, Everyman's Classic Lib) Tuttle Pubng.

Lyons, Paddy & Morgan, Fideles, eds. Female Playwrights of the Restoration: Five Comedies. 365p. (Orig.). 1994. 9.95 (*0-460-87427-6*, Everyman's Classic Lib) Tuttle Pubng.

Lyons, Paddy, ed. see Shelley, Mary Wollstonecraft.

Lyons, Patrick J. Applying Expert System Technology to Business. 269p. (C). 1994. pap. 37.95 (*0-534-20538-0*); pap. 39.95 (*0-534-20541-0*) Course Tech.

Lyons, Paul. Class of '66: Living in Suburban Middle America. LC 93-50899. 272p. (C). 1994. text 69.95 (*1-56639-213-6*); pap. text 22.95 (*1-56639-214-4*) Temple U Pr.

— New Left, New Right, & the Legacy of the Sixties. LC 96-13397. 256p. (C). 1996. pap. 22.95 (*1-56639-478-3*) Temple U Pr.

— New Left, New Right, & the Legacy of the Sixties. LC 96-13397. 256p. (C). 1996. 69.95 (*1-56639-477-5*) Temple U Pr.

— Thirty-Five Lesson Formats: A Sourcebook of Instructional Alternatives. LC 91-45289. 160p. (Orig.). 1992. pap. 24.95 (*0-87778-244-X*) Educ Tech Pubns.

Lyons, Paul, ed. The Quotable Gambler. LC 99-48169. 1999. 20.00 (*1-55821-949-8*) Lyons Pr.

Lyons, Paul C., et al, eds. Historical Perspective of Early Twentieth Century Carboniferous Paleobotany in North America: In Memory of William Culp Darrah. LC 95-15891. (Memoir Ser.: No. 185). (Illus.). 1995. 105.00 (*0-8137-1185-1*) Geol Soc.

Lyons, Paul C. & Brownlow, Arthur H., eds. Studies in New England Geology: A Memoir in Honor of C. Wroe Wolfe. LC 75-30494. (Geological Society of America, Memoir Ser.: No. 146). (Illus.). 410p. reprint ed. pap. 127.10 (*0-8357-3149-9*, 203941200012) Bks Demand.

Lyons, Paul C. & Rice, Charles L., eds. Paleoenvironmental & Tectonic Controls in Coal-Forming Basins of the United States. LC 86-25716. (Geological Society of America Ser.: Vol. 210). (Illus.). 213p. 1986. reprint ed. pap. 66.10 (*0-608-07737-2*, 206782500010) Bks Demand.

Lyons, Paul J. Managing Contributed Funds & Assets: The Tax-Exempt Financial Planning Manual. LC 85-24991. 350p. 1985. 135.00 (*0-914756-27-3*, 600009) Taft Group.

Lyons, Pauline D., jt. auth. see Marzano, Kathryn M.

Lyons, Pete. Can-Am History. (Illus.). 268p. 1995. 39.95 (*0-7603-0017-8*) MBI Pubg.

— Can-Am Photohistory. LC 99-49088. (Illus.). 192p. 1999. 34.95 (*0-7603-0806-3*, 129238AP, Pub. by MBI Pubg) Motorbooks Intl.

Lyons, Pete, jt. auth. see Consumer Guide Editors.

Lyons, Phyllis I. The Saga of Dazai Osamu: A Critical Study with Translations. LC 83-42542. (Illus.). 432p. 1985. 49.50 (*0-8047-1197-6*) Stanford U Pr.

Lyons, Ponsonby, jt. ed. see Hart, William.

***Lyons Press Staff.** American Boy's Book of Sports & Games: A Practical Guide to Indoor & Outdoor Amusements. 2000. pap. 16.95 (*1-58574-115-9*) Lyons Pr.

— Century of Seafaring: A Maritime History of the Twentieth Century. 2000. 24.95 (*1-55821-990-0*) Lyons Pr.

Lyons, Renee F., et al. Relationships, Chronic Illness, & Disability. (Series on Close Relationships: Vol. 11). 176p. 1995. 42.00 (*0-8039-4703-8*) Sage.

Lyons, Rex & Lyons, Rose. Holly Hill Inn Cookbook. (Illus.). 248p. 1989. pap. 11.95 (*0-9621134-0-9*) Cider Pr KY.

Lyons, Richard. Captives. 92p. 1997. pap. text 7.50 (*1-881604-29-2*) Scopcraeft.

***Lyons, Richard.** Divisible by One. LC 99-54425. 195p. 2001. 24.00 (*0-9657639-9-4*) Van Neste.

Lyons, Richard. The Edge of Things. LC 97-51819. 231 p. 1999. 24.00 (*0-9657639-2-7*) Van Neste.

— Enough to Be a Woman. LC 95-128016. 68p. 1994. 7.50 (*1-881604-01-2*) Scopcraeft.

— Fable from a North Window. 160p. 1995. 8.00 (*1-881604-18-7*) Scopcraeft.

— Hours of the Cardinal. LC 99-50777. (James Dickey Contemporary Poetry Ser.). 2000. pap. 15.95 (*1-57003-320-X*); pap. 9.95 (*1-57003-321-8*) U of SC Pr.

— My World at War. 158p. 1998. pap. text 7.50 (*1-881604-33-0*) Scopcraeft.

— Paintings in Taxicabs: Characteristics of Certain Art Consumers. LC 64-64377. 160p. 1965. pap. 3.00 (*0-911042-09-1*) NDSU Inst Reg.

— Scanning the Land: Poems in North Dakota. LC 80-149876. (Illus.). 157p. 1980. 11.75 (*0-911042-23-7*) NDSU Inst Reg.

— These Modern Nights: Poems. LC 87-26355. 80p. (Orig.). 1988. pap. 12.95 (*0-8262-0672-7*) U of Mo Pr.

— A Wilderness of Faith & Love. LC 87-73429. (Contemporary Fiction Ser.). 130p. (Orig.). 1988. pap. 7.95 (*0-935306-42-0*) Barnwood Pr.

Lyons, Richard, et al. Schooling to Working: Exploring the Connections. LC 90-40764. (American University Studies: Vol. 30). 207p. (C). 1991. text 34.95 (*0-8204-1344-5*) P Lang Pubng.

Lyons, Richard, jt. auth. see Gorenstein, Daniel.

Lyons, Richard, ed. see Chambers, George.

Lyons, Richard A. Making Miniature Furniture. LC 99-48937. 128p. 1999. pap. text 7.95 (*0-486-40719-5*) Dover.

***Lyons, Richard A.** Restoring Antique Furniture: A Complete Guide. 2000. pap. text 8.95 (*0-486-40954-6*) Dover.

Lyons, Richard A. & Lyons, Elizabeth G. Making Miniature Furniture. 240p. 1988. pap. 14.95 (*0-13-547258-X*) P-H.

Lyons, Richard G. Understanding Digital Signal Processing. 544p. 1996. 61.95 (*0-201-63467-8*) Addison-Wesley.

Lyons, Richard G., et al, eds. Struggles over the Purposes of Schooling in a Democratic State: Selected Readings in the History of Amereican Education. 292p. 1998. 52.00 (*0-7618-1174-5*); pap. 32.50 (*0-7618-1175-3*) U Pr of Amer.

Lyons, Richard M. Camp Baseball. 95p. (Orig.). 1993. pap. 10.00 (*0-9638099-0-3*) SPSHR.

***Lyons, Robert.** A CPA's Guide to Getting Started with Not-for-Profit Organization Tax Issues. 252p. 2000. pap. 45.00 (*0-87051-297-8*, 091003) Am Inst CPA.

— A CPA's Guide to Tackling Tough Tax Issues for Not-for-Profit Organizations. 252p. 2000. pap. 45.00 (*0-87051-298-6*, 091002) Am Inst CPA.

Lyons, Robert. In the Reeds. 52p. 1998. pap. 11.00 (*0-944920-28-4*) Bellowing Ark Pr.

Lyons, Robert, ed. Autobiography: A Reader for Writers. 2nd ed. 398p. (C). 1984. pap. text 25.95 (*0-19-503401-5*) OUP.

Lyons, Robert E. The Conquest of Mexico by Hernan Cortez, 1518-1521: Selected Translations & a Portfolio of Etchings. (Illus.). 16p. (Orig.). 1987. 785.00 (*0-943435-00-5*) Cartographer Ink.

Lyons, Robert J. Michelangelo Antonioni's Neo-Realism: A World View. LC 75-21433. (Dissertations on Film Ser.). 1976. lib. bdg. 19.95 (*0-405-07618-5*) Ayer.

***Lyons, Robin.** Introduction to Physical Geography: Lab Manual & Workbook. 280p. (C). 2000. ring bd. 19.95 (*0-7872-7112-8*) Kendall-Hunt.

Lyons, Roderick. How Progression Is Recorded. (Orig.). 1991. pap. text 10.50 (*0-913412-55-4*) Brandon Hse.

Lyons, Rose, jt. auth. see Lyons, Rex.

Lyons, Ruth, jt. ed. see Gold, Charlotte.

Lyons-Scott, Laurice. God, the Ultimate Euphoric Experience. Jenkins, Patricia & Graphicana Design Staff, eds. (Illus.). 376p. 1998. 49.98 (*0-9662660-0-5*) L Lyons.

***Lyons, Shawn.** A Walk-About Guide to Alaska Vol. 2: A First Person Hiking Guide. LC 99-62672. (Illus.). 438p. 1999. pap. 16.95 (*1-888125-47-0*) Publ Consult.

Lyons, Sherrie L. Thomas Henry Huxley: The Evolution of a Scientist. LC 99-39254. 339p. 1999. 54.95 (*1-57392-706-6*) Prometheus Bks.

Lyons, Stanely & Beigel, Renate. Carpet & Floorcoverings for Your Home. 1995. 8.95 (*1-899163-09-3*) Cimino Pub Grp.

Lyons, Stanley L. Lighting for Industry & Security: A Handbook for Providers & Users of Lighting. LC 92-10329. (Illus.). 320p. 1993. 160.00 (*0-7506-1084-0*) Buttrwrth-Heinemann.

Lyons, Stephen D., jt. auth. see Christopherson, Richard I.

Lyons, Stephen J. Landscape of the Heart: Writings on Daughters & Journeys. LC 95-26672. 144p. (C). 1996. pap. 12.95 (*0-87422-133-1*) Wash St U Pr.

***Lyons, Steve.** The Final Sanction. (Doctor Who Ser.). 288p. 2000. mass mkt. 6.95 (*0-563-55584-X*, Pub. by BBC Bks) Genl Dist Srvs.

Lyons, Steve. Kiling Ground. (Dr. Who New Adventures Ser.). 280p. 1996. mass mkt. 5.95 (*0-426-20474-3*, Pub. by Virgin Bks) London Brdge.

— Murder Game. (Doctor Who Ser.). 1998. pap. 5.95 (*0-563-40565-1*) BBC.

— Salvation. 1999. mass mkt. 5.95 (*0-563-55566-1*) BBC Worldwide.

***Lyons, Steve.** Space Age. (Doctor Who Ser.). (Illus.). 288p. (J). 2000. mass mkt. 6.95 (*0-563-53800-7*) BBC Worldwide.

Lyons, Steve. Steve Lyons: Psychoanalysis. LC 95-69132. (Illus.). 224p. 1995. 19.95 (*1-57167-013-0*) Sports Pub.

— Witch Hunters. (Doctor Who Ser.). 1998. pap. 5.95 (*0-563-40579-1*) BBC.

Lyons, Steve & Howarth, Chris. The Completely Useless Star Trek Encyclopedia. (Virgin Ser.). (Orig.). 1997. mass mkt. 5.95 (*0-7535-0198-8*, Pub. by Virgin Bks) London Brdge.

Lyons, Steve, jt. auth. see Howarth, Chris.

***Lyons, Sue.** Sixteen Weeks until Death. LC 99-93888. 2000. pap. 13.95 (*0-533-13182-0*) Vantage.

Lyons, T. J. & Scott, W. D. Principles of Air Pollution Meteorology. 1990. 49.95 (*0-8493-7106-6*, QC) CRC Pr.

Lyons, T. P. Personnel Function in a Changing Environment. (Times Management Library). 1971. pap. 22.95 (*0-8464-0710-8*) Beekman Pubs.

Lyons, T. P., et al, eds. The Alcohol Textbook. 332p. 1997. 120.00 (*1-897676-55-7*, Pub. by Univ Nottingham) St Mut.

***Lyons, T. P. & Cole, D. J. A., eds.** Concepts in Pig Science: The 1st Annual Turtle Lake Pig Science Conference. 177p. 1999. text 105.00 (*1-897676-27-1*, Pub. by Nottingham Univ Pr) St Mut.

Lyons, T. P. & Jacques, K. A., eds. Biotechnology in the Feed Industry: Proceedings of Alltech's Eleventh Annual Symposium. 496p. 1995. 150.00 (*1-897676-56-5*, Pub. by Univ Nottingham) St Mut.

— Biotechnology in the Feed Industry: Proceedings of Alltech's Tenth Annual Symposium. 344p. 1994. 150.00 (*1-897676-51-4*, Pub. by Univ Nottingham) St Mut.

— Biotechnology in the Feed Industry: Proceedings of Alltech's Thirteenth Annual Symposium. 440p. 1997. 165.00 (*1-897676-64-6*, Pub. by Univ Nottingham) St Mut.

— Biotechnology in the Feed Industry: Proceedings of Alltech's Twelfth Annual Symposium. 350p. 1996. 150.00 (*1-897676-59-X*, Pub. by Univ Nottingham) St Mut.

Lyons, Teresa S., jt. auth. see Jordan, K. Forbis.

Lyons, Terrence. Somalia: State Collapse, Multilateral Intervention, & Strategies for Political Reconstruction. LC 95-70292. 99p. 1995. pap. 11.95 (*0-8157-5351-9*) Brookings.

— Voting for Peace. LC 99-40205. (Studies in Foreign Policy). vii, 104 p. 1998. pap. 14.95 (*0-8157-5353-5*) Brookings.

Lyons, Terrence, jt. ed. see Deng, Francis M.

Lyons, Thomas P. The Economic Geography of Fujian: A Sourcebook, Vol. I. (Cornell East Asia Ser.: No. 82). (Illus.). 234p. 1995. ring bd. 42.50 (*1-885445-82-2*, 82) Cornell East Asia Pgm.

— The Economic Geography of Fujian Vol. 2: A Sourcebook. (Cornell East Asia Ser.: Vol. 89). (Illus.). 216p. (C). 1997. ring bd. 42.50 (*1-885445-89-X*, CEAS 89) Cornell East Asia Pgm.

— Poverty & Growth in a South China County: Anxi, Fujian, 1949-1992. (Cornell East Asia Ser.: No. 72). (Illus.). 174p. 1994. pap. 11.90 (*0-939657-72-4*, 72); lib. bdg. 18.70 (*0-939657-81-3*, 72) Cornell East Asia Pgm.

Lyons, Thomas P., jt. ed. see Nee, Victor G.

Lyons, Thomas S. & Hamlin, Roger E. Creating an Economic Development Action Plan: A Guide for Development Professionals. LC 90-38845. 224p. 1990. 57.95 (*0-275-93648-1*, C3648, Praeger Pubs) Greenwood.

Lyons, Thomas S., jt. auth. see Hamlin, Roger E.

Lyons, Thomas T., ed. The President: Preacher, Teacher, Salesman-Selected Presidential Speeches, 1933-1983. LC 84-51315. (Illus.). 206p. (Orig.). (C). 1985. pap. text 11.95 (*0-9608014-4-8*) World Eagle.

Lyons, Tim. Astrology Beyond Ego. LC 86-40123. 204p. 1986. pap. 6.95 (*0-8356-0612-0*, Quest) Theos Pub Hse.

Lyons, Timothy J. The Silent Partner: The History of the American Film Manufacturing Company 1910-1921. Vol. 7. LC 73-21590. 266p. 1974. 18.95 (*0-405-04872-6*) Ayer.

L

L

Lyons, Timothy J., ed. Ida Survival Guide & Membership Directory: The Millennial Edition, 1999-2000. (Illus.). 384p. 1999. pap. 50.00 (*0-9660269-6-9*) Intl Docum Assoc.
— The IDA Survival Guide & Membership Directory, 1997-98. 368p. 1997. 49.95 (*0-9660269-0-X*) Intl Docum Assoc.
Lyons, Tom W. The Pelican & After: A Novel about Emotional Disturbance. LC 83-3283. 268p. 1983. 22.00 (*0-9609506-0-5*) Prescott Durrell & Co.
Lyons, Tony, jt. auth. see Crawford, Tad.
Lyons, V. & Ziegler, C. Business Desktop Publishing Applications: Job-Based Tasks. 200p. (C). 1994. pap. text 16.95 incl. 3.5 hd (*1-56118-400-4*) Paradigm MN.
Lyons, Victoria & Ziegler, C. Business Desktop Publishing Applications: Job-Based Tasks. 200p. (C). 1994. pap. text 16.95 incl. disk (*1-56118-398-9*) Paradigm MN.
— Business Desktop Publishing Applications: Job-Based Tasks. 200p. (C). 1994. teacher ed. 8.00 (*1-56118-399-7*) Paradigm MN.
Lyons, Vonnie. Keikilani, the Kona Nightingale. (Illus.). 32p. (J). (ps-6). 1994. lib. bdg. 8.95 (*0-9643512-0-X*) Mouse Pubng.
Lyons, W., ed. Standard Handbook of Petroleum & Natural Gas Engineering, Vol. 2. 6th ed. 1088p. 1996. 220.00 (*0-88415-643-5*, 5643) Gulf Pub.
Lyons, W. B., et al, eds. Ecosystems Processes in Antarctic Ice-Free Landscapes: Proceedings of an International Workshop, Christchurch, 1-4 July 1996. (Illus.). 294p. (C). 1997. text 104.00 (*90-5410-925-4*, Pub. by A A Balkema) Ashgate Pub Co.
Lyons, W. E., et al. The Politics of Dissatisfaction: Citizens, Services & Urban Institutions. LC 91-35287. (Bureaucracies, Public Administration & Public Policy Ser.). 248p. (C). (gr. 13). 1992. text 74.95 (*0-87332-898-1*) M E Sharpe.
— The Politics of Dissatisfaction: Citizens, Services & Urban Institutions. LC 91-35287. (Bureaucracies, Public Administration & Public Policy Ser.). 248p. (C). (gr. 13). 1993. pap. text 35.95 (*1-56324-378-4*) M E Sharpe.
Lyons, Walter A. Handy Weather Answer Book. (Illus.). 398p. 1996. 16.95 (*0-7876-1034-8*) Visible Ink Pr.
Lyons, Wendy, jt. auth. see Clark, Sheree.
Lyons, William. Approaches to Intentionality. 274p. 1995. text 49.95 (*0-19-823526-7*) OUP.
— Approaches to Intentionality. 274p. 1998. reprint ed. pap. text 19.95 (*0-19-875222-9*) OUP.
— The Disappearance of Introspection. 224p. 1986. 25.00 (*0-262-12115-8*, Bradford Bks) MIT Pr.
— The Disappearance of Introspection. 211p. 1988. pap. 12.50 (*0-262-62062-6*, Bradford Bks) MIT Pr.
Lyons, William, ed. Modern Philosophy of Mind. 336p. (Orig.). 1995. pap. 8.50 (*0-460-87558-2*, Everyman's Classic Lib) Tuttle Pubng.
Lyons, William, et al. American Government: Politics & Political Culture. LC 94-38187. 648p. (C). 1995. 78.95 (*0-314-04558-9*) West Pub.
Lyons, William, jt. auth. see Hopkins, Anne H.
Lyons, William, ed. see Elder, Crawford.
***Lyons, William C.** Air & Gas Drilling Manual. (Professional Engineering Ser.). (Illus.). 640p. 2000. 99.95 (*0-07-039312-5*) McGraw-Hill Prof.
Lyons, William C., ed. Standard Handbook of Petroleum & Natural Gas Engineering, Vol. 1. 6th ed. LC 96-13965. 1440p. 1996. 275.00 (*0-88415-642-7*, 5642) Gulf Pub.
Lyons, William E. The Politics of City-County Merger: The Lexington-Fayette County Experience. LC 77-73706. 192p. 1977. reprint ed. pap. 59.60 (*0-608-02125-3*, 206277400004) Bks Demand.
Lyons, William H, jt. auth. see Duncan, Richard F.
Lyons, William T. The Politics of Community Policing: Rearranging the Power to Punish. LC 98-40135. (Law, Meaning & Violence Ser.). 256p. 1999. text 39.50 (*0-472-10953-7*, 10953) U of Mich Pr.
Lyotard, Jean F. The Postmodern Explained. Pefanis, Julian & Thomas, Morgan, eds. Barry, Don et al, trs. from FRE. LC 92-10408.Tr. of Le/Postmoderne Explique Aux Enfants. 104p. (C). 1992. pap. 12.95 (*0-8166-2211-6*) U of Minn Pr.
— Postmodern Fables. Van Den Abbeele, Georges, tr. from ENG. LC 97-25953. 1997. 24.95 (*0-8166-2554-9*) U of Minn Pr.
***Lyotard, Jean F., et al.** Toward the Postmodern. LC 98-49225. 256p. 1998. 24.95 (*1-57392-585-3*, Humanity Bks) Prometheus Bks.
***Lyotard, Jean-Francois.** The Confession of Augustine. LC 00-22883. (Meridian Ser.). 2000. pap. write for info. (*0-8047-3793-2*) Stanford U Pr.
Lyotard, Jean-Francois. The Differend: Phrases in Dispute. Van Den Abbeele, Georges, tr. from FRE. LC 88-4780. (Theory & History of Literature Ser.: Vol. 46). 224p. (Orig.). 1989. pap. 16.95 (*0-8166-1611-6*) U of Minn Pr.
— Heidegger & "the Jews" Michel, Andreas & Roberts, Mark S., trs. 144p. (C). 1990. pap. 14.95 (*0-8166-1857-7*) U of Minn Pr.
— The Inhuman: Reflections on Time. Bennington, Geoffrey & Bowlby, Rachel, trs. from FRE. LC 91-66838. 224p. (C). 1992. 39.50 (*0-8047-2006-1*); pap. 13.95 (*0-8047-2008-8*) Stanford U Pr.
— Lesson on Analytic Sublime. LC 96-37014. (Deridian Ser.). 1997. pap. 24.95 (*0-8047-2763-5*) Stanford U Pr.
— Lessons on the Analytic of the Sublime. LC 93-10683. 208p. (C). 1993. 39.50 (*0-8047-2241-2*); pap. 14.95 (*0-8047-2242-0*) Stanford U Pr.
— The Libidinal Economy. Grant, Iain H., tr. LC 91-32761. (Theories of Contemporary Culture Ser.). 320p. 1993. text 51.95 (*0-253-33614-7*); pap. text 22.95 (*0-253-20728-2*, MB-728) Ind U Pr.
— Phenomenology. Beakley, Brian, tr. from FRE. LC 90-19828. (SUNY Series in Contemporary Continental Philosophy). 153p. (C). 1991. pap. text 19.95 (*0-7914-0806-X*) State U NY Pr.
— Phenomenology. Beakley, Brian, tr. from FRE. LC 90-19828. (SUNY Series in Contemporary Continental Philosophy). 153p. (C). 1991. text 59.50 (*0-7914-0805-1*) State U NY Pr.
— Political Writings. Readings, Bill & Geiman, Kevin P., trs. 380p. (C). 1993. pap. 19.95 (*0-8166-2045-8*) U of Minn Pr.
— Political Writings. Readings, Bill & Geiman, Kevin P., trs. 380p. (C). 1993. text 49.95 (*0-8166-2043-1*) U of Minn Pr.
— The Post-Modern Condition: A Report on Knowledge. Bennington, Geoff & Massumi, Brian, trs. from FRE. LC 83-14717. (Theory & History of Literature Ser.: Vol. 10). 131p. (C). 1984. pap. 12.95 (*0-8166-1173-4*) U of Minn Pr.
— Postmodern Fables. 1999. pap. 16.95 (*0-8166-2555-7*) U of Minn Pr.
— Signed, Malraux. Harvey, Robert, tr. from FRE. LC 98-53762. 346p. 1999. 29.95 (*0-8166-3106-9*) U of Minn Pr.
— Toward the Postmodern. Harvey, Robert & Roberts, Mark S., eds. LC 92-719. (Philosophy & Literary Theory Ser.). 280p. (C). 1995. pap. 17.50 (*0-391-03890-7*) Humanities.
Lyotard, Jean-Francois & Gruber, Eberhard. The Hyphen: Between Judaism & Christianity. Brault, Pascale-Anne & Naas, Michael, trs. from FRE. (Philosophy & Literary Theory Ser.). 120p. 1998. 39.95 (*0-391-04051-0*) Humanities.
***Lyotard, Jean-Francois & Gruber, Eberhard.** The Hyphen: Between Judaism & Christianity. LC 97-27122. (Philosophy & Literature Theory Ser.). 120p. 1998. 39.95 (*1-57392-635-3*, Humanity Bks) Prometheus Bks.
***Lyotard, Jean Francois & Monory, Jacques.** Assassination of Experience. (Illus.). 238p. 1998. pap. 29.95 (*1-901033-06-6*, Pub. by Black Dog Pubg) RAM Publications.
Lyotard, Jean-Francois & Thebaud, Jean-Loup. Just Gaming. Massumi, Brian, tr. LC 85-1109. (Theory & History of Literature Ser.: Vol. 20). vi, 129p. 1985. pap. 12.95 (*0-8166-1277-3*) U of Minn Pr.
Lyotard, Jean-Francois & Van Den Abbeele, George. Driftworks. LC 88-193957. 128p. Date not set. 7.00 (*0-936756-04-7*) Autonomedia.
Lyovin, Anatole V. An Introduction to the Languages of the World. (Illus.). 512p. 1997. pap. text 35.00 (*0-19-508116-1*) OUP.
Lyovina, Valentina V., tr. see Kavelin, Archimandrite L.
Lyovina, Valentina V., tr. see St. Theophan the Recluse.
***Lypen, John.** Motor Air Bag Manual. (Illus.). 1999. 76.00 (*1-58251-020-2*) Motor Info Sys.
Lypny, Gregory J., jt. auth. see Burger, Albert E.
Lypyns'kyi, Viacheslav. Ukraina Na Perelomi, 1657-1659: Zamitky do Istorii Ukrains'koho Derzhavnoho Budivnyctva v XVII-im Stolittiu. (Viacheslav Lypyns'kyi, Tvory Ser.: Vol. 3). 400p. 1992. text 39.95 (*0-9631165-0-9*) WKL East Europ.
Lyr, Guyette. La Fuite end Douce. (FRE.). 1979. pap. 10.95 (*0-7859-4121-5*) Fr & Eur.
— L' Herbe des Fous. (FRE.). 1982. pap. 10.95 (*0-7859-4170-3*) Fr & Eur.
Lyr, Horst. Modern Selective Fungicides: Properties, Applications, Mechanisms of Action. 2nd rev. ed. (Illus.). 600p. 1995. 108.00 (*3-334-60455-1*) Balogh.
***Lyr, Horst, et al, eds.** Modern Fungicides & Antifungal Compounds II. (Illus.). 520p. 1999. 153.00 (*1-898298-60-2*, Pub. by Intercept UK) Spr-Verlag.
***Lyra, Carmen.** The Subversive Voice of Carmen Lyra: Selected Works. Horan, Elizabeth Rosa, ed. & tr. by. LC 99-87011. (Illus.). 144p. 2000. 49.95 (*0-8130-1767-X*) U Press Fla.
Lyra, F., tr. see Dzielska, Maria.
Lyra, Maria & Valsiner, Jane. Advances in Child Development Within Culturally Structures Environments Vol. 4: Construction of Psychological Processes in Interpersonal Communication. LC 97-20464. (Child Development Within Culturally Structured Environments Ser.: Vol. 4). 1998. 73.25 (*1-56750-296-2*) Ablx Pub.
Lyra, Maria C. & Valsiner, Jaan. Construction of Psychological Processes in Interpersonal Communication. LC 97-20464. (Child Development Within Culturally Structured Environments Ser.). 1997. pap. 39.50 (*1-56750-415-9*) Ablx Pub.
Lyrand, L., jt. auth. see Coopers, C.
Lyren, Delon, jt. auth. see Hickman, Jane W.
Lyric Publishing Staff. Treasure of Skeleton Reef. (Wishbone Mysteries Ser.). 144p. (J). 1998. pap. 1.99 (*1-57064-481-0*) Lyrick Pub.
Lyric Staff. Release. Ingram, Keisha A. & Horne, Barbara E., eds. LC 99-60309. 100p. 1999. pap. 12.50 (*1-893608-02-6*) Sincerity Pubg.
***Lyrick Publishing Staff.** Adventures of Wishbone. (Illus.). (J). 1999. mass mkt. 11.97 (*1-57064-755-0*, Big1 Red Chair) Lyrick Pub.
— Barney Christmas Plush Clip Strips. (Barney Ser.). (J). (ps-k). 2000. 71.40 (*1-57064-775-5*) Lyrick Pub.
— Barney Halloween Plush Clip Strips. (Illus.). 2000. 71.40 (*1-58668-010-2*) Lyrick Pub.
Lyrick Publishing Staff. Barney's Count to 10. (Barney Ser.). (Illus.). 24p. (J). (ps-3). 1999. pap. 6.95 incl. audio (*1-57064-623-6*, Barney Publ) Lyrick Pub.
— Case Of The Disappearing Dinosaurs, 10. 1999. pap. text 1.99 (*1-57064-763-1*) Lyrick Pub.
— Case Of The Unsolved Case, 13. 1999. pap. text 1.99 (*1-57064-760-7*) Lyrick Pub.
— Dave & the Giant Pickle. (Veggietales Ser.). (Illus.). 30p. (ps-3). 1999. pap. 6.95 (*1-57064-626-0*) Lyrick Pub.
— Disoriented Express, Vol. 14. 1999. pap. text 1.99 (*1-57064-764-X*) Lyrick Pub.
***Lyrick Publishing Staff.** Dog Days of the West. (Super Adventures of Wishbone Ser.). 2000. pap. text 1.99 (*1-57064-966-9*) Lyrick Pub.
Lyrick Publishing Staff. Forgotten Horses, Vol. 12. 1999. pap. text 1.99 (*1-57064-761-5*) Lyrick Pub.
***Lyrick Publishing Staff.** Ghost of Camp Ka Nowata, Vol. 2. (Wishbone Super Mysteries Ser.). (Illus.). 2000. pap. text 1.99 (*1-57064-970-7*) Lyrick Pub.
Lyrick Publishing Staff. Haunted Clubhouse. (Wishbone Mysteries Ser.). 144p. (J). 1998. pap. 1.99 (*1-57064-482-9*) Lyrick Pub.
***Lyrick Publishing Staff.** Haunting of Hathaway House, Vol.3. (Wishbone Super Mysteries Ser.). (Illus.). 2000. pap. text 1.99 (*1-57064-971-5*) Lyrick Pub.
— Larry Boy & the Fib from Outer Space. (Veggietales Ser.). (Illus.). 30p. (ps-3). 1999. pap. 6.95 (*1-57064-625-2*) Lyrick Pub.
— Let's Have Fun with Barney. (J). (ps-3). 2000. pap. text 9.99 (*1-57064-953-7*) Lyrick Pub.
Lyrick Publishing Staff. Lights! Camera! Action Dog!, Vol. 11. Vol. 11. (gr. 4-7). 1999. pap. text 1.99 (*1-57064-762-3*) Lyrick Pub.
— The Maltese Dog. (Wishbone Mysteries Ser.). 144p. (J). 1998. pap. 1.99 (*1-57064-486-1*) Lyrick Pub.
— The Riddle of the Wayward Books. (Wishbone Mysteries Ser.). 144p. (J). 1998. pap. 1.99 (*1-57064-483-7*) Lyrick Pub.
— Stage Invader, Vol. 15. 1999. pap. 1.99 (*1-57064-765-8*) Lyrick Pub.
***Lyrick Publishing Staff.** Story of Flibbe-O-Loo. (Veggietales Ser.). (Illus.). (ps-3). 1999. pap. 6.95 (*1-57064-627-9*) Lyrick Pub.
— Tails of Terror, Vol. 4. (Super Adventures of Wishbone Ser.: Vol. 4). (Illus.). (gr. 4-7). 2000. pap. text 1.99 (*1-57064-969-3*) Lyrick Pub.
Lyrick Publishing Staff. Tale of the Missing Mascot. LC 97-74835. (Wishbone Mysteries Ser.: Vol. 4). 144p. (J). (gr. 4-7). 1998. pap. 1.99 (*1-57064-484-5*) Lyrick Pub.
***Lyrick Publishing Staff.** Unleashed in Space, Vol. 3. (Super Adventures of Wishbone Ser.). (Illus.). 2000. pap. text 1.99 (*1-57064-968-5*) Lyrick Pub.
— The Wishbone Mysteries. (Illus.). (J). 1999. mass mkt. 11.97 (*1-57064-756-9*, Big1 Red Chair) Lyrick Pub.
Lyrick Publishing Staff, ed. Barney's I Love You. LC 99-66251. (Barney Ser.). (Illus.). 10p. (J). (ps-k). 2000. 6.95 (*1-57064-707-0*, Barney Publ) Lyrick Pub.
***Lyrick Publishing Staff, ed.** Barney's Puppet Show. (Barney Ser.). (Illus.). (J). (ps-3). 2000. pap. 9.99 (*1-57064-952-9*) Lyrick Pub.
— Huckleberry Dog. (The Adventures of Wishbone Ser.). (Illus.). 144p. (J). (gr. 3-6). 2000. pap. 3.99 (*1-57064-389-X*) Lyrick Pub.
***Lyrick Publishing Staff & Halfmann, Janet.** Barney's Run, Jump, Skip & Sing! (Barney Ser.). (Illus.). 84p. (J). (ps-k). 2000. pap. 1.99 (*1-57064-729-1*, 97980) Lyrick Pub.
***Lyrick Studios Staff.** Barney's Favorite Christmas Stories. LC 00-100421. (Illus.). 104p. (J). (ps-k). 2000. 6.95 (*1-57064-988-X*) Lyrick Pub.
— Barney's Favorite Halloween Stories. LC 00-100420. (Illus.). 48p. (J). (ps-k). 2000. 4.95 (*1-57064-987-1*, Barney Publ) Lyrick Pub.
Lyrick Studios Staff. Barney's Great Adventure: A Super-Dee-Duper Color & Activity Book. (Barney Ser.). 112p. (J). (ps-k). 1998. pap. text 3.25 (*1-57064-314-8*) Lyrick Pub.
— Barney's Great Adventure: The Chase Is On! LC 97-75559. (Barney Ser.). 24p. (J). (ps-k). 1998. pap. text 3.25 (*1-57064-247-8*) Lyrick Pub.
— Barney's Great Adventure Activity Pad. (Barney Ser.). (J). (ps-k). 1998. pap. text 1.95 (*1-57064-333-4*) Lyrick Pub.
— Barney's Great Adventure Singalong. (Barney Ser.). (J). (ps-3). 1998. pap. 7.95 incl. audio (*1-57132-313-9*, 9445) Lyrick Studios.
— Barney's Great Adventure Sticker Book. (Barney Ser.). (J). (ps-k). 1997. pap. text 1.95 (*1-57064-316-4*) Lyrick Pub.
— Fun on the Farm: A Super-Dee-Duper Color & Activity Book. 112p. (J). 1998. pap. text 3.25 (*1-57064-315-6*) Lyrick Pub.
***Lyrick Studios Staff.** Legend of Sleepy Hollow, Vol. 2. (Super Adventures of Wishbone Ser.). (Illus.). (J). 2000. pap. text 1.99 (*1-57064-967-7*) Lyrick Pub.
Lyrick Studios Staff. Storytime Three: Three Billy Goats Gruff. (Barney Ser.). (Illus.). (J). 1998. pap. text 7.95 incl. audio (*1-57132-150-0*, 9570) Lyrick Studios.
Lyricks Studios Staff. Fun with Friends: A Dino-Mite Color & Activity Book. 80p. (J). 1998. pap. text 1.95 (*1-57064-313-X*) Lyrick Pub.
— Parade & Carnival Fun: A Dino-Mite Color & Activity Book. 80p. (J). 1998. pap. text 1.95 (*1-57064-312-1*) Lyrick Pub.
Lys, Thomas, ed. see Brunner, Karl.
Lysaght. Revenge Is a Dish Best Eaten Cold. 1999. write for info. (*0-671-52026-1*) S&S Trade.
Lysaght, Alan, jt. auth. see Pritchard, David.
Lysaght, Brian. Dealing. 1999. text 13.95 (*0-312-18534-0*) St Martin.
— Eye of the Beholder. 1997. per. 5.99 (*0-671-00115-9*) PB.
Lysaght, M. J., et al, eds. Disputed Issues in Renal Failure Therapy. (Contributions to Nephrology Ser.: Vol. 44). (Illus.). xii, 294p. 1985. 29.75 (*3-8055-3938-X*) S Karger.
Lysaght, M. J., jt. ed. see Gurland, H. J.
Lysaght, Patricia. The Banshee: The Irish Death Messenger. (Illus.). 352p. 1997. pap. 16.95 (*1-57098-138-8*) Roberts Rinehart.
— A Pocket History of the Banshee. 144p. 1997. pap. 7.95 (*0-86278-501-4*, Pub. by OBrien Pr) Irish Amer Bk.
Lysaght, Patrick, ed. see International Workshop on Field Programmable Logic & Applications Staff.
Lysaght, Sean. The Clare Island Survey. 46p. 1991. pap. 12.95 (*1-85235-077-6*) Dufour.
— Noah's Irish Art. (C). 1990. 30.00 (*0-948268-63-8*, Pub. by Dedalus); pap. 15.00 (*0-948268-62-X*, Pub. by Dedalus) St Mut.
— Robert Lloyd Praeger: And the Culture of Science in Ireland, 1865-1953. 256p. 1999. boxed set 45.00 (*1-85182-422-7*) Intl Spec Bk.
— Scarecrow. LC 98-181420. 64p. 1998. 24.95 (*1-85235-217-5*, Pub. by Gallery Pr); pap. 14.95 (*1-85235-216-7*) Gallery Pr.
Lysaght, Sidney R. Reading of Life. LC 70-142659. (Essay Index Reprint Ser.). 1977. 20.95 (*0-8369-2060-0*) Ayer.
Lysak, Robert L., ed. Auroral Plasma Dynamics. LC 93-43462. (Geophysical Monograph Ser.: No. 80). 1993. 57.00 (*0-87590-039-9*) Am Geophysical.
Lysakowski, Rich & Gregg, Charles E., eds. Computerized Chemical Data Standards: Databases, Data Interchange, & Information Systems, STP 1214. LC 94-31856. (Special Technical Publication Ser.: Vol. 1214). (Illus.). 175p. 1994. text 53.00 (*0-8031-1876-7*, STP1214) ASTM.
Lysanov, Y. P., jt. auth. see Brekhovskikh, L. M.
Lysaught, Jerome P. Action in Affirmation: Towards an Unambiguous Profession of Nursing. (Illus.). 224p. 1981. text 27.95 (*0-07-039271-4*) McGraw.
Lyse, Simon, tr. see Zvyagin, Boris B.
Lysek, G., jt. auth. see Jennings, D. H.
Lysek, G., jt. auth. see Kloidt, Martina.
Lysen, Lucinda K., ed. Quick Reference to Clinical Dietetics. LC 96-50455. 292p. 1997. pap. 34.00 (*0-8342-0629-3*) Aspen Pub.
Lysengen, Janet D. & Rathke, Ann M., eds. The Centennial Anthology of North Dakota History: Journal of the Northern Plains. (Illus.). xv, 526p. 1996. pap. 24.95 (*1-891419-03-X*) State Hist ND.
Lysenko, V. On the Way to Knowledge: Man, the Earth, Outer Space, Acceleration. 266p. (C). 1988. 40.00 (*0-7855-4996-X*, Pub. by Collets) St Mut.
Lyshak-Stelzer, Francie. The Secret: Art & Healing from Sexual Abuse. LC 99-20781. (Illus.). 48p. 1999. pap. write for info. (*1-884444-56-3*, WPO74) Safer Soc.
Lysheha, Oleh. The Selected Poems of Oleh Lysheha. Brasfield, James, tr. (Research Institute Monograph Ser.). (ENG & UKR., Illus.). 160p. 2000. pap. text 12.95 (*0-916458-90-3*, Pub. by Harvard Ukrainian) HUP.
***Lyshevski, Sergey E.** Electromechanical Systems, Electric Machines & Applied Mechatronics. LC 99-15197. (Electric Power Engineering Ser). 800p. 1999. boxed set 89.95 (*0-8493-2275-8*) CRC Pr.
Lysiak, Lynne D., jt. ed. see Baker, Barry B.
Lysias. Ausgewahlt Reden, 2 vols. in 1. viii, 310p. 1963. write for info. (*3-296-14510-9*) G Olms Pubs.
— Lysia Epitaphios, Pts. I & II. Connor, W. R., ed. LC 78-18608. (Greek Texts & Commentaries Ser.). 1979. reprint ed. lib. bdg. 21.95 (*0-405-11448-6*) Ayer.
***Lysias.** Lysias. LC 99-6344. 462p. 2000. 24.95 (*0-292-78166-0*); 55.00 (*0-292-78165-2*) U of Tex Pr.
Lysias. Orationes. Hude, Karl, ed. (Oxford Classical Texts Ser.). (GRE.). 290p. 1979. reprint ed. text 29.95 (*0-19-814538-1*) OUP.
— Orations. (Loeb Classical Library: No. 244). 734p. 1930. 19.95 (*0-674-99269-5*) HUP.
— Selected Speeches. Carey, Christopher, ed. (Cambridge Greek & Latin Classics Ser.). 256p. (C). 1990. text 65.00 (*0-521-26435-9*); pap. text 22.95 (*0-521-26988-1*) Cambridge U Pr.
Lysik, David, ed. The Liturgy Documents, Vol. 2. 395p. 1999. pap. 15.00 (*1-56854-245-3*, LDOCZ) Liturgy Tr Pubns.
Lysik, David A., ed. Lectionary for Masses with Children: Sundays, Year A. American Bible Society Staff, tr. (Illus.). 1995. 35.00 (*0-929650-71-9*, LEC/CA); pap. text 10.00 (*1-56854-000-0*, CLA/SE) Liturgy Tr Pubns.
— The Many Presences of Christ. LC 99-25798. 214p. 1999. pap. 16.00 (*1-56854-313-1*) Liturgy Tr Pubns.
Lyskawa, jt. auth. see Barron.
Lyskawa, Chet, jt. auth. see Barron, Ann.
Lyskawa, Chet, jt. auth. see Barron, Mary Kemper.
Lysko, J. M., tr. see Arhangel'skii, A. V., ed.
Lysman, Frederick D. Being Public. 4th ed. 30p. pap. text 15.00 (*0-936093-37-4*) Packard Pr Fin.
Lysne, D. K., jt. ed. see Broch, E.
Lysne, Robin H. Sacred Living: A Daily Guide. rev. ed. LC 97-15645. 250p. 1997. 14.95 (*1-57324-099-0*) Conari Press.
Lysne, Robin Heernes. Living a Sacred Life: 365 Meditations & Celebrations. 240p. 1999. pap. 13.95 (*1-57324-185-7*) Conari Press.
Lyson, Thomas A. Two Sides of the Sunbelt: The Growing Divergence Between the Rural & Urban South. LC 88-31928. 163p. 1989. 52.95 (*0-275-93201-X*, C3201, Praeger Pubs) Greenwood.
Lyson, Thomas A. & Falk, William W., eds. Forgotten Places: Uneven Development in Rural America. LC 92-43847. (Rural America Ser.). 298p. 1993. 35.00 (*0-7006-0592-4*); pap. 15.95 (*0-7006-0593-2*) U Pr of KS.
Lyson, Thomas A., jt. ed. see Falk, William W.
Lyson, Thomas A., jt. ed. see Olson, Richard.
Lysons, C. K. Purchasing Handbook. 211p. (C). 1989. 130.00 (*0-7855-5757-1*, Pub. by Inst Pur & Supply) St Mut.
Lysons, Kenneth. Earning Money in Retirement. (C). 1991. 50.00 (*0-86242-103-9*, Pub. by Age Concern Eng) St Mut.
— Earning More in Retirement. large type ed. 21.95 (*1-85695-070-0*, Pub. by ISIS Lrg Prnt) Transaction Pubs.

An Asterisk (*) at the beginning of an entry indicates that the title is appearing for the first time.

— Learning Difficulties & Business Administration. (Special Needs & Business Administration Ser.). 76p. 1993. pap. 27.50 (*1-85302-198-9*) Taylor & Francis.
— Purchasing. 4th ed. 320p. 2000. pap. 39.50 (*0-273-63422-4*) F T P H.
— Understanding Hearing Loss. rev. ed. 150p. 1995. pap. 18.95 (*1-85302-214-4*, Pub. by Jessica Kingsley) Taylor & Francis.
***Lysons, Patrick L.** The Elohoic Verses "Mythos of Elohim" Bk. 1: Variations on a Dream. LC 99-91589. 1999. 25.00 (*0-7388-0914-4*); pap. 18.00 (*0-7388-0915-2*) Xlibris Corp.
Lyssiotis, Peter. Three Cheers for Civilization. 96p. (C). 1990. 120.00 (*0-7855-6623-6*, Pub. by Pascoe Pub) St Mut.
Lyssiotis, Peter, jt. auth. see Couani, Anna.
Lystad, Mary. At Home in America: As Seen Through Its Books for Children. LC 81-21272. (Illus.). 154p. 1984. 18.95 (*0-87073-378-8*); pap. 13.25 (*0-87073-379-6*) Schenkman Bks Inc.
Lystad, Mary, ed. Mental Health Response to Mass Emergencies: Theory & Practice. LC 88-5025. (Psychosocial Stress Ser.: No. 12). 454p. 1988. text 56.95 (*0-87630-514-1*) Brunner-Mazel.
Lystad, Mary H. From Dr. Mather to Dr. Seuss: 200 Years of American Books for Children. LC 79-16949. 276p. 1980. reprint ed. pap. 85.60 (*0-608-05347-3*, 206505200012) Bks Demand.
Lyster, Jim, ed. see Peterson, Eugene.
Lyster, Martin. The Strange Adventures of the Dangerous Sports Club. LC 99-189169. 176p. 1998. pap. 16.95 (*1-899344-28-4*, Pub. by Do-Not Press) Dufour.
Lyster, Mimi E. Child Custody: Building Agreements That Work. 2nd ed. Leonard, Robin, ed. LC 96-8279. (Illus.). 208p. 1996. pap. 24.95 (*0-87337-345-6*) Nolo com.
— Child Custody: Building Parenting Agreements That Work 3rd ed. LC 99-13950. 1999. 29.95 (*0-87337-521-1*) Nolo com.
Lyster, Simon. International Wildlife Law. 493p. (C). 1985. 46.00 (*0-906496-46-2*, Pub. by Grotius Pubns Ltd); pap. 23.00 (*0-906496-22-5*, Pub. by Grotius Pubns Ltd) St Mut.
Lystra, Helen P., ed. Kitchen Sampler, a Heritage Cookbook. (Illus.). 192p. (Orig.). 1982. pap. 6.95 (*0-9608642-0-2*) UMCD.
Lystra, Karen. Searching the Heart: Women, Men, & Romantic Love in Nineteenth-Century America. 352p. 1992. pap. text 19.95 (*0-19-507476-9*) OUP.
***Lysymy, Paul.** Ground Zero. LC 99-65325. 192224p. 2000. pap. 11.95 (*1-56315-261-4*, Pub. by SterlingHse) Natl Bk Netwk.
Lytch, William E. The Cradle of Texas Presbyterianism: Memorial Presbyterian Church, San Augustine, Texas. (Illus.). 224p. 1993. 19.95 (*1-881576-19-1*) Providence Hse.
Lyte, Charles. The Royal Gardens in Windsor Great Park. LC 97-223868. (Illus.). 50.00 (*0-85628-261-8*, Pub. by Aidan Ellis Pub) Antique Collect.
Lytel, Allan H. & Buckmaster, Lawrence W. ABC's of Computer Programming. 2nd ed. LC 73-75079. 112p. 1973. write for info. (*0-672-20841-5*) Sams.
Lytel, Robert B. & Botterbusch, Karl F. Physical Demands Job Analysis: A New Approach. (Illus.). 166p. (Orig.). 1981. pap. write for info. (*0-916671-34-8*) TRR.
Lyth, David H., jt. auth. see Liddle, Andrew R.
Lyth, Peter, ed. Air Transport. (Studies in Transport History). 180p. 1996. 61.95 (*1-85928-309-8*, Pub. by Scolar Pr) Ashgate Pub Co.
Lyth, Peter, tr. see Schmidt, Elfriede.
Lyth, Peter J. Inflation & the Merchant Economy: The Hamburg Mittelstand, 1914-1924. LC 89-18118. 212p. 1990. 19.95 (*0-85496-592-0*) Berg Pubs.
Lythe, S. G. The Economy of Scotland in Its European Setting, 1550-1625. LC 75-31475. 277p. 1977. reprint ed. lib. bdg. 38.50 (*0-8371-8333-5*, LYES, Greenwood Pr) Greenwood.
Lythgoe, Dennis L. Let'em Holler: A Political Biography of J. Bracken Lee. LC 82-60039. (Illus.). xii, 343p. 1982. 17.50 (*0-913738-33-6*) Utah St Hist Soc.
Lythgoe, Gillian, jt. auth. see Lythgoe, John N.
Lythgoe, J. N. The Ecology & Vision. (Illus.). 256p. 1980. text 65.00 (*0-19-854529-0*) OUP.
Lythgoe, John N. & Lythgoe, Gillian. Fishes of the Sea: The North Atlantic & Mediterranean. (Illus.). 256p. 1991. 42.00 (*0-262-12162-X*) MIT Pr.
Lytinen, Kalle & Tahvananinen, Veli-Pekka, eds. Next Generation CASE Tools. LC 91-59042. (Studies in Computer & Communications Systems: Vol. 3). 240p. (gr. 12). 1992. pap. 70.00 (*90-5199-076-6*, Pub. by IOS Pr) IOS Press.
Lytle. General Zoology. 13th ed. 400p. 1999. spiral bd., lab manual ed. 50.00 (*0-07-012220-2*) McGraw.
— Uncivil War. 2001. 35.00 (*0-07-039278-1*) McGraw.
Lytle, Andrew. At the Moon's Inn. (Library of Alabama Classics). 416p. (Orig.). 1990. pap. 15.95 (*0-8173-0511-4*) U of Ala Pr.
— Kristin: A Reading by Andrew Lytle. LC 92-7255. 112p. 1992. text 19.95 (*0-8262-0847-9*) U of Mo Pr.
— The Long Night. LC 88-12101. (Library of Alabama Classics). 336p. 1988. reprint ed. pap. 14.95 (*0-8173-0415-0*) U of Ala Pr.
— Southerners & Europeans: Essays in a Time of Disorder. LC 87-24169. (Library of Southern Civilization). xix, 308p. 1988. text 42.50 (*0-8071-1420-0*) La State U Pr.
— Velvet Horn. 370p. 1987. pap. 10.95 (*0-918769-03-5*) Univ South Pr.
Lytle, Andrew N. Bedford Forrest & His Critter Company. 402p. 1984. reprint ed. 120.00 (*0-918450-16-0*) C Elder.
— Bedford Forrest & His Critter Company. LC 91-67518. (Southern Classics Ser.). 431p. 1992. reprint ed. pap. 15.95 (*1-879941-09-0*) J S Sanders.
— Stories: Alchemy & Others. 192p. 1984. pap. 9.95 (*0-918769-00-0*) Univ South Pr.
— A Wake for the Living. LC 92-89829. (Southern Classics Ser.). 308p. 1992. reprint ed. pap. 13.95 (*1-879941-10-4*) J S Sanders.
Lytle, Andrews. Reflections of a Ghost. deluxe limited ed. 35.00 (*0-686-78139-2*) New London Pr.
Lytle, Arthur. Beating Tantra at Its Own Game: Spiritual Sexuality. LC 89-81551. 200p. (Orig.). 1990. pap. 12.95 (*0-941404-89-7*) New Falcon Pubns.
Lytle, Arthur C. So You Want to Be a Channel! 2nd ed. LC 87-83572. 256p. (Orig.). 1988. pap. 12.95 (*1-56184-106-4*) New Falcon Pubns.
— A Spiritual Psychology for the Aquarian Age. LC 91-68304. 256p. (Orig.). 1992. pap. 12.95 (*1-56184-052-1*) New Falcon Pubns.
***Lytle, Casey.** Alien in the Mirror: Homeworld: Book One. 218p. (YA). (gr. 5-8). 2000. mass mkt. 5.99 (*0-9678933-0-5*) Mcnarn Grp.
Lytle, Charles F., jt. auth. see Wodsedalek, J. E.
***Lytle, Chris.** The Accidental Salesperson: How to Take Control of Your Sales Career & Earn the Respect & Income You Deserve. LC 00-38092. 192p. 2000. pap. 17.95 (*0-8144-7083-1*) AMACOM.
Lytle, Clifford M. The Warren Court & Its Critics. LC 66-28788. 149p. reprint ed. pap. 46.20 (*0-608-13462-7*, 202275600029) Bks Demand.
Lytle, Clifford M., jt. auth. see Deloria, Vine, Jr.
Lytle, Clyde F. Leaves of Gold: An Inspirational Classic. 198p. 1983. 16.99 (*0-915720-74-4*) Brownlow Pub Co.
Lytle, Clyde F., ed. Leaves of Gold: An Inspirational Classic. deluxe ed. 198p. 1983. 19.99 (*0-915720-84-1*) Brownlow Pub Co.
Lytle, Douglas. Pink Tanks & Velvet Hangovers: An American in Prague. LC 94-41644. (Illus.). 250p. (Orig.). (C). 1995. pap. 16.95 (*1-883319-24-2*) Frog Ltd CA.
Lytle, Eldon G. A Grammar of Subordinate Structures in English. (Janua Linguarum, Series Practica: No. 175). 1974. pap. text 42.35 (*90-279-2630-1*) Mouton.
Lytle, Elizabeth S. Careers in Plumbing, Heating, & Cooling. LC 94-13577. (Careers Ser.). (Illus.). (YA). (gr. 7-12). 1995. lib. bdg. 16.95 (*0-8239-2052-6*) Rosen Group.
— Exploring Careers As an Electrician. rev. ed. LC 93-12776. (YA). (gr. 7-12). 1996. 16.95 (*0-8239-2143-3*) Rosen Group.
Lytle, Guy F., ed. Reform & Authority in the Medieval & Reformation Church. LC 79-17380. 351p. reprint ed. pap. 108.90 (*0-608-17238-3*, 202949600061) Bks Demand.
Lytle, Guy F. & Orgel, Stephen, eds. Patronage in the Renaissance. LC 81-47143. (Folger Institute Essays Ser.). (Illus.). 405p. reprint ed. pap. 125.60 (*0-8357-4199-0*, 203697700006) Bks Demand.
Lytle, Horace. Point! A Book about Bird Dogs. 2nd ed. (Fifty Greatest Bks.). (Illus.). 200p. 1992. reprint ed. 50.00 (*1-56416-036-X*) Derrydale Pr.
***Lytle, J. Horace.** Point! (Illus.). 208p. 2000. 24.95 (*1-58667-031-X*, Pub. by Derrydale Pr) Natl Bk Netwk.
Lytle, Jesse H., tr. see Stavans, Ilan.
Lytle, John F. What Do Your Customers Really Want? Here's a Simple, Sure-Fire Way to Find Out. 250p. 1992. text 24.95 (*1-55738-456-8*, 456, Irwn Prfssnl) McGraw-Hill Prof.
— What Do Your Customers Really Want? Here's a Sure-Fire Way to Find Out. 240p. 1994. per. 19.95 (*1-55738-829-6*, Irwn Prfssnl) McGraw-Hill Prof.
Lytle, Joyce, ed. see Anderson, Alex.
Lytle, Joyce, ed. see Barickman, Amy.
Lytle, Joyce, ed. see James, Michael.
Lytle, Joyce, ed. see Lose, Patrick.
Lytle, Joyce, ed. see Phalen, Diane.
Lytle, Joyce, ed. see Sienkiewicz, Elly.
Lytle, Joyce, ed. see Wells, Joan & Wells, Valori.
Lytle, Joyce, ed. see Wells, Valori & Wells, Jean.
Lytle, Joyce, ed. see Wolfrom, Joen.
Lytle, Joyce, ed. see Young, Blanche & Stone, Dalene Y.
Lytle, Joyce E., ed. see Anderson, Alex.
Lytle, Joyce E., ed. see Collins, Sally.
Lytle, Joyce E., ed. see Porcella, Yvonne.
Lytle, Joyce E., ed. see Sienkiewicz, Elly.
Lytle, Joyce E., ed. see Speckmann, Doreen.
Lytle, Joyce E., ed. see Wolfrom, Joen.
Lytle, Mark H. The Origins of the Iranian-American Alliance, 1941-1953. 254p. 1987. 49.50 (*0-8419-1060-X*) Holmes & Meier.
Lytle, Mark H., jt. auth. see Davidson, James W.
Lytle, Milton S. History of Huntingdon County, Pennsylvania: From the Earliest Times to the Centennial Anniversary of American Independence. (Illus.). 361p. 1992. reprint ed. lib. bdg. 39.50 (*0-8328-1416-4*) Higginson Bk Co.
***Lytle, Patricia M., ed.** 101 Essays from Across America: The Happy Marriage Book. (Illus.). 134p. 2000. pap. 19.95 (*0-9679830-0-2*) Lytle Research.
Lytle, Robert A. Mackinac Passage: A Summer Adventure. (Illus.). 184p. 1995. pap. 11.95 (*1-882376-11-0*) Thunder Bay Pr.
— Mackinac Passage: The Boathouse Mystery. (Illus.). 172p. (J). (gr. 3-10). 1996. pap. 11.95 (*1-882376-29-3*) Thunder Bay Pr.
— Mackinac Passage: The General's Treasure. (Illus.). 172p. (YA). (gr. 9-12). 1997. pap. 12.95 (*1-882376-45-5*) Thunder Bay Pr.
— Med Chek. LC 92-63337. 140p. 1993. pap. 12.95 (*1-882792-01-7*) Proctor Pubns.
***Lytle, Robert A.** Three Rivers Crossing. 180p. (J). (gr. 4-8). 2000. 15.95 (*0-938682-55-5*) River Rd Pubns.
Lytle, Robert J. Live Free, Don't Become a Corporate Mule. (Illus.). 200p. (Orig.). 1990. pap. text 15.95 (*0-9626082-0-3*) Tana Starr Pub.
***Lytle, Shawn P.** Lost Souls: A Bizarre Voyage into the Lives of the Desolate That Run Wild in Search of Deliverance. 112p. 1999. pap. 18.00 (*0-9668764-1-5*) One Way Out.
***Lytle, Shawn P.** Twisted Dreams: How Far Would You Go To Reach Your Dreams?, 1. LC 98-94234. 53p. 1999. pap. 10.00 (*0-9668764-0-7*) One Way Out.
Lytle, Stephen, tr. see Gonzalez-Rubio, Javier.
Lytle, Susan L. & Wolfe, Marcie. Adult Literacy Education: Program Evaluation & Learner Assessment. 1989. 8.75 (*0-317-03008-6*, IN338) Ctr Educ Trng Employ.
Lytle, Susan L., jt. ed. see Cochran-Smith, Marilyn.
Lytle, Tom, et al. 101 Ways to Be Family Friendly. 112p. (Orig.). 1996. pap. 7.99 (*0-8341-1659-6*) Beacon Hill.
Lytle, William S., et al. A Summary of Oil & Gas Developments in Pennsylvania, 1955-1959. (Mineral Resource Reports: No. 45). (Illus.). 133p. 1984. reprint ed. pap. 15.40 (*0-8182-0036-7*) Commonweal PA.
Lytle, William S., jt. auth. see Wagner, Walter R.
***Lyttelton, Humphrey.** Best of Jazz. 424p. 1999. pap. 15.95 (*1-86105-187-5*) Robson.
Lyttle. Mental Disorders. 2nd ed. 1994. pap. text 55.00 (*0-7020-1416-8*) Harcourt.
Lyttle, Bradford. The Chicago Anti-Vietnam War Movement. (Illus.). 173p. (Orig.). 1988. pap. text 4.95 (*0-9620611-0-7*) Midwest Pacifist Ctr.
— You Come with Naked Hands: The Story of the San Francisco to Moscow March for Peace. LC 66-1279. (Illus.). 289p. 1966. 25.00 (*0-934676-08-9*) Greenlf Bks.
Lyttle, C. R., jt. ed. see Strauss, Jerome F., III.
Lyttle, Gerlind, tr. see Fritsch, Gustav.
Lyttle, Jeff. Gorillas in Our Midst: The Story of the Columbus Zoo Gorillas. LC 97-26066. 199p. 1997. 24.95 (*0-8142-0766-9*) Ohio St U Pr.
Lyttle, Richard B. Mark Twain: The Man & His Adventures. LC 93-11247. (Illus.). 192p. (YA). (gr. 5 up). 1994. write for info. (*0-689-31712-3*) Atheneum Yung Read.
Lyttle, Thomas, compiled by. Psychedelics. LC 93-19655. 272p. 1993. pap. 14.95 (*0-9623032-2-4*) Barricade Bks.
Lyttle, William H. For Honor, Glory, & Union: The Mexican & Civil War Letters of Brig. Gen. William Haines Lytle. Carter, Ruth C., ed. LC 98-37536. (Illus.). 264p. 1999. 27.50 (*0-8131-2108-6*) U Pr of Ky.
***Lyttleton, Chris.** Endangered Relations: Negotiating Sex & AIDS in Thailand. 260p. 2000. text 42.00 (*90-5702-421-7*, Harwood Acad Pubs) Gordon & Breach.
Lyttleton, David, jt. auth. see McDonald, Ian.
Lyttleton, Raymond A. The Earth & Its Mountains. LC 82-13701. (Illus.). 232p. reprint ed. pap. 72.00 (*0-8357-3079-4*, 203933600012) Bks Demand.
Lytton, ed. see Royal Society of Literature, United Kingdom Staff.
Lytton, Constance. Prisons & Prisoners. 1989. 10.95 (*0-86068-682-5*) Random.
Lytton, H., jt. auth. see Grusec, J. E.
Lytton, Henry. The Secrets of a Savoyard. LC 80-17086. (Music Reprint Ser.). 1980. reprint ed. 29.50 (*0-306-76048-7*) Da Capo.
Lytton, Robert L., et al. Development & Validation of Performance Prediction Models & Specifications for Asphalt Binders & Paving Mixes. 500p. (Orig.). (C). 1993. pap. text 20.00 (*0-309-05617-9*, SHRP-A-357) SHRP.
Lytton, Rosina B. A Blighted Life: A True Story, 1880 Edition. 18th ed. Roberts, Marie M., ed. & intro. by. LC 94-222404. (Subversive Women Ser.). 124p. 1996. reprint ed. pap. 19.95 (*1-85506-248-8*) Bks Intl VA.
— Shells from the Sands of Time: 1876 Edition. Roberts, Marie M., ed. & intro. by. (Her Write His Name Ser.). 272p. 1996. reprint ed. pap. 29.95 (*1-85506-386-7*) Bks Intl VA.
Lyu, Michael R. The Handbook on Software Reliability. 875p. 1996. 72.50 (*0-614-25306-3*, RS30) Inst Electrical.
— McGraw-Hill Software Reliability Engineering Handbook. 850p. 1996. 79.99 (*0-07-039400-8*) McGraw.
Lyubarev, A. E., jt. ed. see Kurganov, Boris I.
Lyubarskii, Yu I., tr. see Govorov, N. V.
***Lyubashenko, Volodymyr V.** Squared HOPF Algebras LC 99-39861. (Memoirs Ser.). 1999. write for info. (*0-8218-1361-7*) Am Math.
Lyubich, Y. I. Functional Analysis One: Linear Functional Analysis. Nikol'skij, N. K. & Gamkrelidze, R. V., eds. Tweddle, I., tr. from RUS. (Encyclopedia of Mathematical Sciences Ser.: Vol. 19). xi, 278p. 1992. 118.95 (*0-387-50584-9*) Spr-Verlag.
— Introduction to the Theory of Banach Representations of Groups. (Operator Theory Ser.: No. 30). 232p. 1988. 146.50 (*0-8176-2207-1*) Birkhauser.
— Mathematical Structures in Population Genetics. Akin, E. & Levin, S. A., eds. (Biomathematics Ser.: Vol. 22). (Illus.). x, 373p. 1992. 149.95 (*0-387-53337-0*) Spr-Verlag.
Lyubich, Y. I., jt. auth. see Belitskii, G. R.
Lyubimov, D. V., et al. Universal Scenarios of Transitions to Chaos Via Homoclinic Bifurations, Vol. 8. (SSR: SEC Mathematical Physics Review Ser.: Vol. 8, Pt. 4). ii, 78p. 1989. pap. text 85.00 (*3-7186-4867-9*) Gordon & Breach.
Lyubomirskaya, Nataliya V., ed. see Arkhipova, Irina R.
Lyubutin, I. S., jt. auth. see Kagan, Yu M.
Lyubutin, I. S., jt. ed. see Kagan, Yu M.
Lyuksyutov, Igor, et al. Two-Dimensional Crystals. (Illus.). 423p. 1992. text 123.00 (*0-12-460590-7*) Acad Pr.
Lyusternik, L. & Chervonenkis, O. Handbook for Computing Elementary Functions. LC 64-22370. (International Series of Monographs on Pure & Applied Mathematics: Vol. 76). 1965. 117.00 (*0-08-010844-X*, Pub. by Pergamon Repr) Franklin.
Lyusternik, L. & Collins, P. Shortest Paths Variational Problems: Survey of Recent East European Mathematical Literature. LC 64-14145. (Popular Lectures in Mathematics: Vol. 13). 1964. 49.00 (*0-08-010647-1*, Pub. by Pergamon Repr) Franklin.
Lyusternik, L. & Yanpol'skii, A. Mathematical Analysis: Functions Limits Series Continued Fractions. LC 63-19330. (International Series of Monographs on Pure & Applied Mathematics: Vol. 69). 1965. 185.00 (*0-08-010133-X*, Pub. by Pergamon Repr) Franklin.
Lyutovich, Klara, jt. ed. see Kasper, Erich.
Lyuu, Yuh-Dauh. Information Dispersal & Parallel Computation. (International Series on Parallel Computation: No. 3). 197p. (C). 1993. text 44.95 (*0-521-43226-X*) Cambridge U Pr.
Lyver, Des. Basics of Video Lighting. 2nd ed. LC 99-14609. (Illus.). 144p. 1999. pap. 19.95 (*0-240-51559-5*, Focal) Buttrwrth-Heinemann.
— The Basics of Video Production. 2nd ed. LC 99-29843. 144p. 1999. pap. 19.95 (*0-240-51560-9*, Focal) Buttrwrth-Heinemann.
— Basics of Video Sound. (Illus.). 128p. 1995. pap. text 19.95 (*0-240-51410-6*, Focal) Buttrwrth-Heinemann.
— Basics of Video Sound. 2nd ed. LC 99-30576. 144p. 1999. pap. 19.95 (*0-240-51561-7*, Focal) Buttrwrth-Heinemann.
Lyver, Des & Swainson, Graham. Basics of Video Lighting. (Illus.). 128p. 1995. pap. 19.95 (*0-240-51414-9*, Focal) Buttrwrth-Heinemann.
Lyver, Margaret. Amelia Everything Will Be Alright: A Woman of Steel - A Heart of Gold - A Soul Made of Platinum. LC 98-91234. 230p. 1998. pap. 17.50 (*1-57502-964-2*, PO2643) Morris Pubng.
Lyytinen, Heikki, ed. Comorbidity & Developmental Neurocognitive Disorders. 104p. 1995. pap. 20.00 (*0-8058-9941-3*) L Erlbaum Assocs.
— Psychological Correlates of Infant Cognition: A Special Issue of "Developmental Neuropsychology" 1997. pap. 100.00 (*0-8058-9871-9*) L Erlbaum Assocs.
Lyzlova, Sussana N. & Stefanv. Phosphagen Kinases. 240p. 1990. lib. bdg. 190.00 (*0-8493-6467-1*, QP606) CRC Pr.
L[0081]ders, Hans. The Supplementary Sensorimotor Area, No. 70. 544p. 1995. text, suppl. ed. 131.00 (*0-7817-0268-2*) Lppncott W & W.

M

M. Cartoons by M. (Illus.). 64p. 1992. pap. 12.00 (*0-9635101-0-X*) A V A Pr.
— The International Directory of Names Men Call Their... (Illus.). 80p. (Orig.). 1989. pap. 5.95 (*0-9621447-3-8*) Little Sam.
— Lord God of Truth Within. 1976. reprint ed. 18.00 (*0-911662-56-1*) Yoga.
M. Abdul Hamid Siddiqi, tr. see Sunnah.
M., Catherine. A Message from the Future. iv, 187p. 1997. pap. 14.99 (*0-9660558-0-2*) Theuism.
M. D. Anderson Cancer Center Department of Surgica & Feig, Barry W. The M. D. Anderson Surgical Oncology Handbook. 2nd ed. LC 98-37038. 448p. 1998. pap. text 42.95 (*0-7817-1581-4*) Lppncott W & W.
M. E. R. Mary Jones & Her Bible. (Victorian Children's Classics Ser.). 96p. 1985. pap. 5.99 (*1-85030-012-7*) Bridge-Logos.
M., Eduardo Zepeda, jt. ed. see Clement, Norris C.
M. Evans & Company Staff. The Any Diet Diary: Count Your Way to Success. 192p. 1998. pap. 7.95 (*0-87131-865-2*) M Evans.
M Friedman Pub Grp Inc Staff. Assorted Notes/Gestures. 1998. pap. text 12.50 (*1-56799-841-0*) M Friedman Pub Grp Inc.
M. Garvelmann, Donald, ed. see Herz, Henri.
***M., Joe.** Boozing & Losing... And Drugging, Too. LC 99-93817. 2000. 12.95 (*0-533-13153-7*) Vantage.
M. K. Graphic & Design Editorial Dept. Staff, ed. see Donaldson, Peter.
M. K. Graphics Staff & Kozak, Donald P. A Guide to Computer Music: Electronic Music Resource. 2nd ed. (Illus.). 100p. 1991. pap. 19.95 (*0-9621514-1-6*) Sound Mgmt Prodns.
***M. K. Publishing Group Staff.** New York at Night. 2nd ed. (Illus.). 2000. pap. 11.95 (*0-9666057-2-1*) Nightlife Inc.
M. L. French & Son Inc. Staff. Uniforms, Accessories & Equipment for U. S. Army Officers & Enlisted Men. (World War II Monograph Ser.: Vol. 33). (Illus.). 22p. 1998. 14.95 (*1-57638-122-6*, M33); pap. 4.95 (*1-57638-121-8*, M33) Merriam Pr.
M, Mary. How to Have a No-Hands Orgasm: Having Orgasms Through Intercourse. 133p. (Orig.). 1986. pap. 8.95 (*0-9618974-0-6*) Books NY.
M. McHenry, Deni, ed. see Marquardt-Cherry, Janet.
M, Mike, jt. auth. see K, Dave.
M., Sara & Johnson Institute (Minneapolis, Minn.) Staff. Trapped by Love: When Your Partner Has a Drinking Problem. LC 97-7459. (Illus.). 31p. 1997. pap. 2.95 (*1-56246-141-9*, 3216, HazeldenJohnson Inst) Hazelden.
***M. Sara Rosenthal.** Thyroid Sourcebook for Women. LC 99-39865. 336p. 1999. pap. 17.95 (*0-7373-0264-X*, 0264XW) NTC Contemp Pub Co.

An Asterisk (*) at the beginning of an entry indicates that the title is appearing for the first time.

M., Stanley. The Glumlot Letters: A Devil's Discourse on Sobriety, Recovery & the Twelve Steps of A. A. LC 97-92399. 192p. 1997. pap. 12.00 (*0-9659672-3-9*) CAPIZON Pub.

M. T. A Sponsorship Guide for All Twelve-Step Programs. LC 97-47262. 224p. 1998. pap. 12.95 (*0-312-18182-5*) St Martin.

M. T. Vasudevan Nair, et al. The Demon Seed & Other Writings. LC 98-908651. xiv, 470 p. 1998. 22.00 (*0-14-027659-9*) Viking Penguin.

M. Tayyib Bakhsh Budayuni, tr. see Allama Shibli Numani.

M-USA Business Systems, Inc. Staff. Understanding Computer Accounting. (VideoNotes Ser.). (Illus.). (Orig.). 1988. pap. text 24.95 incl. VHS (*0-929978-02-1*, T03) M-USA Busn Systs.

— Understanding Computer Project Management. (VideoNotes Ser.). (Illus.). (Orig.). 1988. pap. text 24.95 incl. VHS (*0-929978-04-8*, T04) M-USA Busn Systs.

— Understanding Lotus 1-2-3. (VideoNotes Ser.). (Illus.). (Orig.). 1988. pap. text 24.95 incl. VHS (*0-929978-01-3*, T02) M-USA Busn Systs.

M-USA Business Systems, Inc. Staff, ed. Understanding MS-DOS. (VideoNotes Ser.). (Illus.). (Orig.). 1988. pap. 24.95 incl. VHS (*0-929978-00-5*, T01) M-USA Busn Systs.

M-USA Video Staff. Lotus 1-2-3 Version 2.3. (LogicNotes Ser.). 1991. 24.95 (*0-929978-57-9*) M-USA Busn Systs.

— MS-DOS 5.0. (LogicNotes Ser.). 1991. 24.95 (*0-929978-60-9*) M-USA Busn Systs.

— 1-2-3 for Kids, Set. (LogicNotes Ser.). (Illus.). (Orig.). 1990. pap. text 24.95 (*0-929978-53-6*) M-USA Busn Systs.

— Using IBM Displaywrite 5. (LogicNotes Ser.). (Illus.). (Orig.). 1991. pap. text 24.95 (*0-929978-32-3*) M-USA Busn Systs.

— Using Microsoft's Word for DOS 5.0. (LogicNotes Ser.). (Illus.). (Orig.). 1991. pap. text 24.95 (*0-929978-63-3*) M-USA Busn Systs.

— WordPerfect for Windows. (LogicNotes Ser.). 1991. 24.95 (*0-929978-52-8*) M-USA Busn Systs.

Ma & Rittner, C. Modern Organic Elemental Analysis. (Illus.). 512p. 1979. text 225.00 (*0-8247-6786-1*) Dekker.

Ma, Anand N. & Sambuddha, D. From Death to Deathlessness: Answers to the Seekers of the Path. LC 97-216036. (Talks in America Ser.). 520p. 1990. 24.95 (*3-89338-074-4*, Pub. by Rebel Hse) Oshos.

Ma Baolin, jt. auth. see Mao, Cindy.

Ma, Benjamin. Nuclear Reactor Materials & Applications. 592p. (gr. 13). 1982. text 84.95 (*0-442-22559-8*) Chapman & Hall.

Ma Chengyuan. Ancient Chinese Bronzes. Hsio-Yen Shih, ed. (Illus.). 224p. 1986. 85.00 (*0-19-583795-9*) OUP.

Ma, Christina, jt. auth. see Weinofen, Donnah.

Ma, D. C., ed. Sloshing, Fluid-Structure Interaction & Structural Response due to Shock & Impact Loads 1994: Proceedings of the Pressure Vessels & Piping Conference, Minneapolis, MN, 1994. LC 94-71745. (PVP Ser.: Vol. 272). 233p. 1994. pap. 60.00 (*0-7918-1195-6*) ASME.

Ma, D. C., et al, eds. Fluid Sloshing & Fluid-Structure Interaction - 1995. (Proceedings of the 1995 ASME/JSME Pressure Vessels & Piping Conference Ser.: PVP-Vol. 314). 180p. 1995. 80.00 (*0-7918-1345-2*, H00977) ASME.

— Seismic Engineering, 1995. LC 88-71134. (Proceedings of the 1995 ASME/JSME Pressure Vessels & Piping Conference Ser.: PVP-Vol. 312). 472p. 1995. 140.00 (*0-7918-1343-6*, H00975) ASME.

Ma, D. C., jt. ed. see Au-Yang, M. K.

Ma Deva Sarito, ed. see Osho.

Ma Dexian, jt. ed. see Hong, Wang.

Ma Dhyan Sagar, ed. see Osho.

Ma, Dong M., jt. auth. see Liveson, Jay A.

Ma, E., et al, eds. Chemistry & Physics of Nanostructures & Related Non-Equilibrium Materials. LC 96-79955. (Illus.). 414p. 1997. 90.00 (*0-87339-353-8*, 3538) Minerals Metals.

— Phase Transformations & Systems Driven Far from Equilibrium Vol. 481: Materials Research Society Symposium Proceedings. LC 98-19423. 686p. 1998. text 80.00 (*1-55899-386-X*) Materials Res.

***Ma, Eric K.** Culture, Politics, & Television in Hong Kong. LC 99-210149. (Culture & Communication in Asia Ser.). 242p. 1999. 0.00 (*0-415-17998-X*) Routledge.

Ma, Grace Xueqin & Henderson, George. Rethinking Ethnicity & Health Care: A Sociocultural Perspective. LC 99-25016. 346p. 1999. 46.95 (*0-398-06957-3*) C C Thomas.

Ma, Grace Xuequin. The Culture of Health: Asian Communities in the United States. LC 99-19224. 184p. 1999. 55.00 (*0-89789-625-4*, Bergin & Garvey) Greenwood.

***Ma, Grace Xuequin & Henderson, George.** Rethinking Ethnicity & Health Care: A Sociocultural Perspective. LC 99-25016. (Illus.). 346p. 1999. text 62.95 (*0-398-06956-5*) C C Thomas.

Ma, Ho-t'ien. Chinese Agent in Mongolia. De Francis, John, tr. LC 49-11857. 231p. reprint ed. pap. 71.70 (*0-608-18534-5*, 200391300037) Bks Demand.

***Ma, J. & Yong, J.** Forward-Backward Stochastic Differential Equations & Their Applications. Dold, A. et al, eds. LC 99-23640. (Lecture Notes in Mathematics Ser.: Vol. 1702). x, 270p. 1999. pap. 49.00 (*3-540-65960-9*) Spr-Verlag.

Ma, J. Meimei, jt. auth. see Calvert, William S.

Ma Jaya Sati Bhagavati. Bones & Ash. (Illus.). 147p. 1995. 21.95 (*0-9640469-2-X*); pap. 12.95 (*0-9640469-3-8*) Jaya Commns.

— Hidden under the Breast of the Mother. 64p. pap. 6.95 (*0-9640469-1-1*) Jaya Commns.

— The River. (Illus.). 85p. 15.95 (*0-9640469-0-3*) Jaya Commns.

Ma, Jing-heng. At Middle Age: A Learning Guide for Students of Advanced Chinese. 2nd ed. 262p. (C). 1991. pap. text 25.00 (*0-89264-103-7*) Ctr Chinese Studies.

Ma, Jing-heng. A Great Wall: A Learning Guide. 2nd ed. 320p. 1993. pap. text 25.00 (*0-89264-112-6*) Ctr Chinese Studies.

Ma, Jing-heng. Strange Friends: A Learning Guide for Students of Intermediate Chinese. 2nd ed. 224p. (C). 1991. pap. text 25.00 (*0-89264-102-9*) Ctr Chinese Studies.

— The True Story of Ah Q: A Learning Guide. 230p. 1992. pap. text 25.00 (*0-89264-105-3*) Ctr Chinese Studies.

***Ma, John.** Antiochus III & the Cities of Western Asia Minor. LC 99-23236. (Illus.). 450p. 2000. text 98.00 (*0-19-815219-1*) OUP.

***Ma, Julie C.** When the Spirit Meets the Spirits: Pentecostal Ministry among the Kankana-ey Tribe in the Phillipines. 2000. 45.95 (*3-631-34858-4*) P Lang Pubng.

— When the Spirit Meets the Spirits: Pentecostal Ministry among the Kankana-ey Tribe in the Phillipines. (Studies in the Intercultural History of Christianity: Vol. 118). 273p. 2000. pap. 45.95 (*0-8204-4332-8*) P Lang Pubng.

***Ma, Jun.** The Chinese Economy in the 1990s. LC 99-23358. (Studies on the Chinese Economy). 197p. 1999. text 69.95 (*0-312-22556-3*) St Martin.

Ma, Jun. Intergovernmental Relations & Economic Management in China. (Studies on the Chinese Economy). 192p. 1997. text 69.95 (*0-312-16111-5*) St Martin.

Ma, Karen. The Modern Madame Butterfly: Fantasy & Reality in Japanese Cross-Cultural Relationships. LC 95-60955. 286p. 1996. pap. 12.95 (*0-8048-2041-4*) Tuttle Pubng.

— The Modern Madame Butterfly: Fantasy & Reality in Japanese Cross-Cultural Relationships. 296p. 1999. reprint ed. pap. text 14.00 (*0-7881-6263-2*) DIANE Pub.

Ma, Kee M. Chinese American Food Practices, Customs, & Holidays. (Ethnic & Regional Food Practices Ser.). 36p. 1990. ring bd. 10.00 (*0-88091-077-1*, 0868) Am Dietetic Assn.

Ma, L. Eve. Revolutionaries, Monarchists, & Chinatowns: Chinese Politics in the Americas & the 1911 Revolution. LC 89-28021. (Illus.). 240p. 1990. reprint ed. pap. 68.40 (*0-608-04392-3*, 2065173) Bks Demand.

Ma, L. Eve Armentrout, ed. Farms, Firms & Runways: Perspectives on U. S. Military Bases in the Western Pacific. 200p. (Orig.). 1999. pap. 19.95 (*1-879176-34-3*) Imprint Pubns.

A timely collection of essays, with a balance of viewpoints, by well-informed sources who have been intimately connected with the issue of U.S. military bases in the Western Pacific. The volume examines the origins of these bases & presents diverse perspectives on whether they should be maintained at their current & recent levels. Separate sections focus on the cases of Okinawa, the Philippines, & Guam, which include contributions from experts native to the regions. They also assess the impact of base-closing, inquire into legal issues associated with the treaties that have enabled the United States to maintain the bases, & shed light on the political implications of the kinds of treaties which have supported U.S. military installations in many parts of the world. Paper, ISBN 1-879176-34-3, $19.95, 200+ pp., index, September 1998. Order from Imprint Publications, 230 East Ohio St., Chicago, IL 60611. 312-337-9268, FAX: 312-337-9622, e-mail: imppub@aol.com, add $5 for single copy shipping, credit cards accepted. www.imprint-chicago.com

Publisher Paid Annotation.

***Ma, Li, et al.** Engineering Properties of Foods & Other Biological Materials: A Laboratory Manual. LC 98-93807. (Illus.). 198p. 1998. pap., lab manual ed. 34.50 (*1-892769-00-X*, M1498) Am Soc Ag Eng.

Ma, Liping. Knowing & Teaching Elementary Mathematics: Teachers' Understanding of Fundamental Mathematics in China & the United States. LC 99-17342. (Studies in Mathematical Thinking & Learning). 192p. 1999. 45.00 (*0-8058-2908-3*); pap. 19.95 (*0-8058-2909-1*) L Erlbaum Assocs.

Ma, Liwang, jt. ed. see Selim, H. Magdi.

Ma, M. T. Theory & Application of Antenna Arrays. LC 73-15615. 429p. pap. 133.00 (*0-608-18554-X*, 202249100027) Bks Demand.

Ma Mpolo, Jean M. & Nwachuku, Daisy, eds. Pastoral Care & Counselling in Africa Today. (African Pastoral Studies: Vol. 1). (Illus.). 194p. 1991. pap. 36.80 (*3-631-44131-2*) P Lang Pubng.

Ma Prem Lisa, ed. see Osho.

Ma Prem Mangla, ed. see Osho.

Ma Prem Taranga, ed. see Osho.

Ma, Qingsheng. Life in Beijing: Easy Chinese Readings in 500 Characters. Zhu, Jian, ed. Luethi, Molly, tr. from CHI. LC 97-74382. (CHI., Illus.). 262p. (C). 1997. pap. 14.95 (*1-891107-02-X*) BIGI Intl.

Ma Renu, ed. see Baba Hari Dass.

Ma Rhea, Zane, jt. auth. see Teasdale, G. R.

Ma Rialp, Rosa, jt. auth. see Suris Jorda, Jordi.

Ma, S. Marshall, ed. Effects of Deterioration on Safety & Reliability of Structures. (Sessions Proceedings Ser.). 49p. 1986. 3.00 (*0-87262-519-2*) Am Soc Civil Eng.

Ma, Shang-Keng. Modern Theory of Critical Phenomena. LC 76-8386. (Frontiers in Physics Ser.: Vol. 46). (Illus.). (C). 1976. pap. 55.00 (*0-8053-6671-7*) Addison-Wesley.

***Ma, Shang-Keng.** Modern Theory of Critical Phenomena. 582p. 2000. pap. text 39.00 (*0-7382-0301-7*) Perseus Pubng.

Ma, Shang-Keng. Statistical Mechanics. 576p. 1985. text 38.00 (*9971-966-06-9*); pap. text 53.00 (*9971-966-07-7*) World Scientific Pub.

***Ma, Sheng-Mei.** The Deathly Embrace: Orientalism & Asian American Identity. LC 00-8866. 2000. pap. write for info. (*0-8166-3711-3*) U of Minn Pr.

Ma, Sheng-Mei. Immigrant Subjectivities in Asian American & Asian Diaspora Literatures. LC 97-30819. 224p. (C). 1998. text 59.50 (*0-7914-3829-5*); pap. text 19.95 (*0-7914-3830-9*) State U NY Pr.

Ma Shivam Suvarna, ed. see Osho.

Ma Shivan Suvarna, ed. see Osho.

MA Soc. of the Mayflower Desc. Staff. The Mayflower Descendant, Vol. 17, 1915. (Illus.). 315p. 1996. 27.00 (*0-7884-0377-X*, MD17) Heritage Bk.

— The Mayflower Descendant, Vol. 18, 1916. (Illus.). x, 295p. 1996. 27.00 (*0-7884-0378-8*, MD18) Heritage Bk.

MA Society of Mayflower Descendants Staff. The Mayflower Descendant, Vol. 26, 1924. (Illus.). viii, 224p. 1996. reprint ed. 27.00 (*0-7884-0524-1*, MD26) Heritage Bk.

— The Mayflower Descendant, 1913, Vol. 15. 301p. 1995. reprint ed. 25.00 (*0-7884-0334-6*, MD15) Heritage Bk.

— The Mayflower Descendant, 1914, Vol. 16. 300p. 1995. reprint ed. 25.00 (*0-7884-0335-4*, MD16) Heritage Bk.

Ma, Stephen K. Administrative Reform in Post-Mao China: Efficiency or Ethics? LC 95-39301. 228p. 1996. lib. bdg. 34.00 (*0-7618-0499-4*) U Pr of Amer.

Ma, T. P. & Dressendorfer, Paul V. Radiation Effects in MOS Devices & Circuits. LC 88-29180. 608p. 1989. 198.50 (*0-471-84893-X*) Wiley.

Ma, Tom. Chinese Fables & Wisdom. LC 97-29987. 128p. 1997. pap. 10.00 (*1-56980-123-1*) Barricade Bks.

— Chinese Fables & Wisdom: Insights for Better Living. 126p. 1996. pap. 16.95 (*0-89876-211-1*) Gardner Pr.

— Chinese Ghost Stories. LC 99-32289. 2000. pap. 12.00 (*1-56980-142-8*) Barricade Bks.

Ma, Tsoy-Wo. Classical Analysis on Normed Spaces. LC 94-44467. 376p. 1995. text 74.00 (*981-02-2137-1*) World Scientific Pub.

Ma, Tsu-Sheng. Quantitative Analysis of Organic Mixtures: General Principles, Pt. 1. LC 78-23202. 384p. reprint ed. pap. 119.10 (*0-608-10031-5*, 205560100029) Bks Demand.

Ma, Wei-Yi. A Bibliography of Chinese-Language Materials on the People's Communes. LC 82-14617. (Michigan Monographs in Chinese Studies: No. 44). xxviii, 301p. (C). 1982. pap. text 25.00 (*0-89264-044-8*) Ctr Chinese Studies.

Ma, Weihua, ed. see Gong, James L.

Ma, Weihua, ed. see Wenbing, Fam.

Ma, Wen-Hwan. American Policy Toward China. LC 73-111743. (American Imperialism: Viewpoints of United States Foreign Policy, 1898-1941 Ser.). 1977. reprint ed. 25.95 (*0-405-02037-6*) Ayer.

Ma Wong, Angi. Night of the Red Moon. LC 94-68680. (Illus.). 96p. (J). (gr. 4 up). 1994. text 16.00 (*0-9635906-1-8*) Pacific Herit.

Ma, Wonsuk. Until the Spirit Comes: The Spirit of God in the Book of Isaiah. LC 99-207552. (JSOTS Ser.: Vol. 271). 247p. 1999. 70.00 (*1-85075-981-2*, Pub. by Sheffield Acad) CUP Services.

Ma, Wonsuk & Menzies, Robert P., eds. Pentecostalism in Context: Essays in Honor of William W. Menzies. (JPTS Ser.: Vol. 11). 373p. 1997. pap. 21.95 (*1-85075-803-4*, Pub. by Sheffield Acad) CUP Services.

Ma, X. & Bai, J., eds. Precambrian Crustal Evolution of China. LC 98-4244. (Illus.). 336p. 1998. 159.00 (*3-540-61710-8*) Spr-Verlag.

Ma, X. W. Introduction to Theoretical Computer Science. 120p. (C). 1990. text 36.00 (*981-02-0193-1*) World Scientific Pub.

***Ma, Xiaoying & Ortolano, Leonard.** Environmental Regulation in China: Institutions, Enforcement & Compliance. LC 99-86906. 272p. 2000. text 67.00 (*0-8476-9398-8*) Rowman.

— Environmental Regulation in China: Institutions, Enforcement & Compliance. LC 99-86906. 272p. 2000. pap. 24.95 (*0-8476-9399-6*) Rowman.

Ma, Y. W. & Lau, Joseph S., eds. Traditional Chinese Stories: Themes & Variations. LC 86-71550. (C & T Asian Literature Ser.). 619p. (C). 1991. reprint ed. pap. text 22.95 (*0-88727-071-9*) Cheng & Tsui.

Ma Yin-Ch'u. Finances of the City of New York. LC 68-56669. (Columbia University, Studies in the Social Sciences: No. 149). reprint ed. 29.50 (*0-404-51149-X*) AMS Pr.

Ma Yoga Sudha, jt. auth. see Osho.

Ma, Yu, jt. auth. see Greene, Felix.

Ma, Z., et al. Earthquake Prediction. (Illus.). 344p. 1990. 76.95 (*0-387-50271-8*) Spr-Verlag.

Ma, Z. M., et al, eds. Dirichlet Forms & Stochastic Processes: Proceedings of the International Conference, Beijing, China, October 25-31, 1993. xii, 444p. (C). 1995. lib. bdg. 152.95 (*3-11-014284-8*) De Gruyter.

Ma, Z. Q. Yang-Baxter Equation & Quantum Enveloping Algebras. 328p. 1993. text 86.00 (*981-02-1383-2*) World Scientific Pub.

Ma, Zhi-Ming, jt. auth. see Rockner, Michael.

Ma Zhong Lin, et al. Readings from Chinese Writers, 1949-1986, Vol. 1. 342p. 1991. 14.95 (*0-8351-1916-5*) China Bks.

— Readings from Chinese Writers, 1919-1949, Vol. 1. 333p. 1990. 14.95 (*0-8351-1927-0*) China Bks.

— Readings from Chinese Writers, 1949-1986, Vol. 2. 690p. 1991. 14.95 (*0-8351-1948-3*) China Bks.

— Readings from Chinese Writers, 1919-1949, Vol. 2. 360p. 1991. 14.95 (*0-8351-1928-9*) China Bks.

— Readings from Chinese Writers, up to 1919, Vol. 1. 417p. 1982. 17.95 (*0-8351-1942-4*) China Bks.

— Readings from Chinese Writers, up to 1919, Vol. 2. 449p. 1982. 17.95 (*0-8351-2660-9*) China Bks.

Maab, Ingrid. Regression und Individuation: Alfred Doblins Naturphilosophie und Spate Romane vor dem Hintergrund Einer Affinitat zu Freuds Metapsychologie. (Hamburger Beitrage zur Germanistik Ser.: Bd. 24). (GER.). 208p. 1997. 42.95 (*3-631-30876-0*) P Lang Pubng.

***Maack, Annelore.** Protected by the Enemy. LC 00-102828. 2000. 19.95 (*1-880710-51-X*) Monterey Pacific.

— Protected by the Enemy. 225p. 2000. 19.95 (*1-885003-51-X*, Pub. by R D Reed Pubs) Midpt Trade.

Maack, Mary N. & Passet, Joanne. Aspirations & Mentoring in an Academic Environment: Women Faculty in Library & Information Science, 75. LC 93-16200. (Contributions in Librarianship & Information Science Ser.: No. 75). 232p. 1994. 59.95 (*0-313-27836-9*, MRL, Greenwood Pr) Greenwood.

Maag, John. Parenting Without Punishment: Making Problem Behavior Work for You. LC 95-47277. 260p. (Orig.). 1996. pap. 17.95 (*0-914783-78-5*) Charles.

Maag, John W. Behavior Management: From Theoretical Implications to Practical Applications. LC 98-46619. (Illus.). 640p. (Orig.). 1999. pap. text 49.95 (*0-7693-0001-4*, 1980) Thomson Learn.

— Questions & Answers about Childhood Depression & Its Treatment. 224p. 2000. pap. text 18.95 (*0-914783-88-2*) Charles.

— Teaching Children & Youth Self-Control: Applications of Perceptual Control Therapy. 48p. 1997. pap. text 11.40 (*0-86586-310-5*) Coun Exc Child.

Maag, Karin. Seminary or University? The Genevan Academy & Reformed Higher Education, 1560-1620. LC 95-24368. (St. Andrews Studies in Reformation History). 224p. 1996. 86.95 (*1-85928-166-4*, Pub. by Scolar Pr) Ashgate Pub Co.

***Maag, Karin, ed.** Melanchthon in Europe: His Work & Influence Beyond Wittenberg. LC 99-31488. (Texts & Studies in Reformation & Post-Reformation Thought). 192p. (YA). 1999. pap. 17.99 (*0-8010-2223-1*) Baker Bks.

Maag, Karin, ed. The Reformation in Eastern & Central Europe. LC 96-41760. (St. Andrews Studies in Reformation History). (Illus.). 256p. 1997. text 83.95 (*1-85928-358-6*, Pub. by Scolar Pr) Ashgate Pub Co.

Maag, Karin, jt. ed. see Gilmont, Jean-Francois.

Maag, Marilyn J. The Simple Will in Ohio. 2nd ed. (Ohio Practice Manual Ser.). 131p. 1997. pap. 38.00 (*0-87084-547-0*) Anderson Pub Co.

Maag, Marilyn J., et al. Anderson's Ohio Probate Practice & Procedure. LC 99-13902. 1999. write for info. (*0-87084-387-7*) Anderson Pub Co.

Maaga, Mary M. Hearing the Voices of Jonestown. LC 97-45194. (Religion & Politics Ser.). 200p. 1998. 29.95 (*0-8156-0515-3*) Syracuse U Pr.

Maahs, Iris, ed. see Moore, Mary E.

Maahs, Kenneth H. Of Angels, Beasts, & Plagues: The Message of Revelation for a New Millennium. LC 98-32059. 1999. pap. 16.00 (*0-8170-1299-0*) Judson.

Maaler, Josua. Die Teutsch Spraach. (GER.). xvi, 1072p. 1971. reprint ed. write for info. (*0-318-70473-0*) G Olms Pubs.

Maaloe, S. Principles of Igneous Petrology. (Illus.). 415p. 1985. 167.95 (*0-387-13520-0*) Spr-Verlag.

Maalouf, Amin. Crusades Through Arab Eyes. 1989. pap. 16.00 (*0-8052-0898-4*) Schocken.

— The First Century after Beatrice. Blair, Dorothy S., tr. from FRE. LC 95-21365. 192p. 1995. 18.50 (*0-8076-1373-8*) Braziller.

— The Gardens of Light. Blair, Dorothy S., tr. LC 98-23334. (Emerging Voices Ser.). 256p. 1999. 25.00 (*1-56656-247-3*, Interlink Bks) Interlink Pub.

— The Gardens of Light. Blair, Dorothy, tr. (Emerging Voices Ser.). 256p. 1999. pap. 15.00 (*1-56656-248-1*, Interlink Bks) Interlink Pub.

— Leo Africanus. 360p. 1992. reprint ed. pap. 15.95 (*1-56131-022-0*, Pub. by I R Dee) Natl Bk Netwk.

— Ports of Call. Manguel, Alberto, tr. from FRE. LC 99-490291. 224p. 1999. 24.00 (*1-86046-446-7*, Pub. by Harvill Press) FS&G.

— Samarkand. Harris, Russell, tr. from FRE. LC 95-42496. (Emerging Voices Ser.). 320p. 1996. 35.00 (*1-56656-200-7*) Interlink Pub.

— Samarkand. 2nd ed. Harris, Russell, tr. from FRE. LC 95-42496. (Emerging Voices Ser.). 320p. 1999. pap. 14.95 (*1-56656-293-7*) Interlink Pub.

Maalouf, Jean. Bold Prayers from the Heart. (Illus.). 96p. (Orig.). 1995. pap. 9.95 (*1-55612-850-9*) Sheed & Ward WI.

— Bold Prayers from the Heart. (Illus.). 96p. (Orig.). 1995. pap. 9.95 (*1-55612-773-1*) Sheed & Ward WI.

***Maalouf, Jean.** The Divine Milien: A Spiritual Clinic for Today & Tomorrow. (Teilhard Studies Ser.: Vol. 38). 1999. 3.50 (*0-89012-081-1*) Am Teilhard.

— I Can Tell God Anything: Living Prayer. LC 99-55493. 160p. 2000. pap. 14.95 (*1-58051-071-X*) Sheed & Ward WI.

Maalouf, Jean. Jesus Laughed & Other Reflections on Being Human. 160p. (Orig.). 1996. pap. 14.95 (*1-55612-911-4*, LL1911) Sheed & Ward WI.

***Maalouf, Jean.** Praying with Mother Teresa. LC 99-50865. (Companions for the Journey Ser.). (Illus.). 136p. (C). 2000. pap. 8.95 (*0-88489-640-4*) St Marys.

An Asterisk (*) at the beginning of an entry indicates that the title is appearing for the first time.

Maamiry, Al. Economics in Islam. (C). 1987. 17.50 (*0-8364-2135-3*, Pub. by Lancer India) S Asia.

***Maan, Ajit K.** Internarrative Identity. LC 99-16281. 136p. 1999. 35.00 (*0-7618-1455-8*) U Pr of Amer.

Maan, Bashir. The New Scots. 200p. (C). 1996. pap. 30.00 (*0-85976-357-9*, Pub. by J Donald) St Mut.

Maan, H. S. Scientific Reviews on Arid Zone Research, 5 vols., 4. (C). 1991. 350.00 (*0-7855-6760-7*, Pub. by Scientific Pubs) St Mut.

— Scientific Reviews on Arid Zone Research, 5 vols., Set, Vols. 1-6. (C). 1991. write for info. (*81-85046-06-9*, Pub. by Scientific Pubs) St Mut.

— Scientific Reviews on Arid Zone Research, 5 vols., Vols. 1-3 & 5-6. (C). 1991. 250.00 (*0-7855-7071-3*, Pub. by Scientific Pubs) St Mut.

***Maan, Tony & Rembrandt Harmenszoon van Rijn Staff.** Rembrandt's Jesus: Meditations on the Life of Christ. LC 99-40242. 140p. 1999. 24.95 (*1-56212-402-1*, 160415) CRC Pubns.

Maanen, G. E. Van, see Van Maanen, G. E., ed.

Maanen, M. A. van, compiled by. Catalogue of Books Printed Before the Seventeenth Century Now in the Library of the Royal Netherlands Academy of Arts & Sciences. xii, 156p. 1979. pap. text 28.25 (*0-7204-8496-0*) Elsevier.

Ma'ani, Baharieh R. Asiyih Khanum: The Most Exalted Leaf. (Illus.). 88p. 1993. 12.25 (*0-85398-353-4*) G Ronald Pub.

Maani, Sholeh A. & Victoria University of Wellington. Institute of Policy Studies. Investing in Minds: The Economics of Higher Education in New Zealand. LC 98-151748. (Illus.). 1997. write for info. (*0-908935-11-0*) Vict U Well IPS.

Maanum, Armand & Montgomery, Herb. The Complete Book of Swedish Massage. 96p. (Orig.). 1985. 12.95 (*0-86683-864-3*) Harper SF.

***Maaps, Carl.** The Shadow Horse. (Illus.). 80p. (J). 1999. pap. 6.95 (*0-89992-146-9*) Coun India Ed.

Maar, Harko G. De, see De Maar, Harko G.

Maar, Paul. Home Sweet Home. (Illus.). 32p. (J). (ps-1). 1995. pap. 5.95 (*1-55037-382-X*, Pub. by Annick); lib. bdg. 15.95 (*1-55037-383-8*, Pub. by Annick) Firefly Bks Ltd.

Maaranen, S., jt. auth. see Garrity, P. J.

Maarbjerg, John P. Scandinavia in the European World-Economy, ca. 1570-1625: Some Local Evidence of Economic Integration. (American University Studies, Series IX: Vol. 169). (Illus.). XIV, 300p. (C). 1995. text 49.95 (*0-8204-2532-X*) P Lang Pubng.

Maarel, E. Van Der, see Van Der Maarel, E.

Maarouf, Osama. Electronic Devices. 4th ed. 1995. pap. text, student ed. 25.80 (*0-13-398454-0*) P-H.

Maarse, F. J. The Study of Handwriting Movement: Peripheral Models & Signal Processing Techniques. 160p. 1987. pap. 26.75 (*90-265-0812-3*) Swets.

Maarse, F. J., et al, eds. Computers in Psychology: Applications, Methods & Instrumentation. (Computers in Psychology Ser.: Vol. 5). 286p. 1994. 65.00 (*90-265-1415-8*) Swets.

— Computers in Psychology: Tools for Experimental & Applied Psychology. LC 92-49200. 246p. 1992. 52.00 (*90-265-1268-6*) Swets.

Maarse, F. J., et al. Computers in Psychology: Methods, Instrumentation, & Psychodiagnostics. 220p. 1988. 31.50 (*90-265-0896-4*) Swets.

Maarse, H. & Belz, R. Isolation, Separation & Identification of Volatile Compounds in Aroma Research. 1982. text 184.00 (*90-277-1432-0*) Kluwer Academic.

Maarse, H. & Van der Heij, D. G., eds. Trends in Flavour Research: Proceedings of the 7th Weurman Flavour Research Symposium, Noordwijkerhout, The Netherlands, 15-18 June, 1993. LC 93-50139. (Developments in Food Science Ser.: No. 35). 528p. 1994. 204.50 (*0-444-81587-2*) Elsevier.

Maarse, Henk, ed. Volatile Compounds in Foods & Beverages. (Food Science & Technology Ser.: Vol. 44). (Illus.). 784p. 1991. text 245.00 (*0-8247-8390-5*) Dekker.

Maarsen, Jacqueline Van, see Van Maarsen, Jacqueline.

Maarseveen, Henc Van, see Holterman, Thom, ed.

Maarseveen, Henc Van, see Holterman, Thom & Van Maarseveen, Henc, eds.

Maarsingh, B. Numbers: A Practical Commentary. LC 86-29263. (Text & Interpretation Ser.). 128p. reprint ed. pap. 39.70 (*0-7837-3189-2*, 204279300006) Bks Demand.

Maarten van Bemmelen, Peter. Issues in Biblical Inspiration: Sanday & Warfield. (Andrews University Seminary Doctoral Dissertation Ser.: Vol. 13). 430p. (Orig.). 1988. pap. 19.99 (*0-943872-49-9*) Andrews Univ Pr.

Maas. Atlas on Facial Plastic Surgery. 1998. pap. text 190.00 (*0-8385-0286-5*, Medical Exam) Appleton & Lange.

— Psychology 101. 368p. 1998. pap. text 29.75 (*0-536-01389-6*) Pearson Custom.

***Maas, ed.** Psychology 101. 346p. 1999. pap. text 30.00 (*0-536-02647-5*) P-H.

Maas, Curt, jt. photos by see Bristol, Larsh K.

Maas, David E. The Return of the Massachusetts Loyalists. (Outstanding Studies in Early American History). 596p. 1989. reprint ed. 35.00 (*0-8240-6189-6*) Garland.

Maas, David F. The Images of Order. (American University Studies: Language: Ser. XIV, Vol. 15). XIV, 262p. (C). 1988. text 37.50 (*0-8204-0680-5*) P Lang Pubng.

Maas, David R. North American Game Animals. LC 95-18908. (Hunting & Fishing Library). (Illus.). 128p. 1995. 19.95 (*0-86573-048-2*) Creat Pub Intl.

Maas, Dieter. Naehrstoffstress, Stoerung und Konkurrenz in Ihrer Wirkung Auf Ausgewaehlte Arten der Kopfbinsenriede. (Dissertationes Botanicae Ser.: Band 254). (Illus.). x, 186p. 1995. pap. 48.00 (*3-443-64166-0*, Pub. by Gebruder Borntraeger) Balogh.

Maas, Elaine H. The Jews of Houston: An Ethnographic Study. LC 89-45444. (Immigrant Communities & Ethnic Minorities in the U. S. & Canada Ser.: No. 66). 1989. 52.50 (*0-404-19476-1*) AMS Pr.

Maas, Elton R. Twentieth Century in Prophecy. LC 98-90802. 1999. 18.95 (*0-533-12922-2*) Vantage.

Maas, Erich, ed. see Palermo, Blinky.

Maas, Ernst. Philologische Untersuchungen Heft 3: De Biographis Graecis Quaestiones Selectae. 169p. write for info. (*0-318-70817-5*) G Olms Pubs.

Maas, Ernst, ed. Commentariorum in Aratum Reliquiae. lxxi, 750p. 1958. write for info. incl. 3.5 hd (*3-296-11900-0*) G Olms Pubs.

Maas Geesteranus, R. A. Die Terrestrischen Stachelpilze Europas. (Verhandelingen der Koninklijke Nederlandse Akademie van Wetenschappen, Afd. Natuurkunde Ser.: No. 65).Tr. of Terrestrial Hydnums of Europe. (GER.). 128p. 1975. pap. text 41.50 (*0-7204-8286-0*) Elsevier.

— Hydnaceous Fungi of the Eastern Old World. (Verhandelingen der Koninklijke Nederlandse Akademie van Wetenschappen, Afd. Natuurkunde Ser.: No. 60(3)). 176p. pap. 37.50 (*0-7204-8222-4*) Elsevier.

Maas, Georgia S., ed. see Baay, Dirk.

Maas, Gideon, jt. auth. see Fox, William.

Maas, Henry. Letters of A. E. Housman. 1979. 25.00 (*0-8464-0090-1*) Beekman Pubs.

Maas, Henry, et al, eds. Letters of Aubrey Beardsley. LC 68-11571. (Illus.). 472p. 1975. 65.00 (*0-8386-6884-4*) Fairleigh Dickinson.

Maas, Henry, ed. see Dowson, Ernest.

Maas, Henry, tr. see Goldmann, Lucien.

Maas, Henry S. & Kuypers, Joseph A. From Thirty to Seventy. LC 74-6742. (Jossey-Bass Behavioral Science Ser.). 256p. reprint ed. pap. 79.40 (*0-7837-0182-9*, 204047800017) Bks Demand.

Maas, Jacob Van Lutsenburg, see Karmokolias, Yannis & Van Lutsenburg Maas, Jacob.

Maas, James B. Power Sleep. abr. ed. 1998. 14.00 incl. audio (*0-375-40201-2*) Random.

— Power Sleep: The Revolutionary Program That Prepares Your Mind for Peak Performance. LC 98-34045. 304p. 1999. pap. 13.00 (*0-06-097760-4*) HarpC.

Maas, James B. & Kleiber, Douglas A. Directory of Teaching Innovations in Psychology. LC BF0077.M25. 610p. reprint ed. pap. 189.10 (*0-7837-0485-2*, 204080900018) Bks Demand.

Maas, James W. Industrial Electronics. LC 94-34333. 962p. 1995. text 78.75 (*0-02-373023-4*) Macmillan.

Maas, James W., jt. ed. see Davis, John M.

Maas, Jane. Better Brochures, Catalogs & Mailing Pieces. (Illus.). 128p. 1984. pap. 8.95 (*0-312-07731-9*) St Martin.

Maas, Jane, jt. auth. see Roman, Kenneth.

Maas, Jeremy. Victorian Fairy Painting. LC 98-119100. (Illus.). 160p. 1997. 40.00 (*1-85894-043-5*, Pub. by Merrell Holberton) U of Wash Pr.

Maas, Jeremy, et al. Victorian Fairy Painting. LC 98-119100. (Illus.). 1997. write for info. (*0-900946-58-X*) Royal Academy of Arts.

Maas, Jim. DC - AC Fundamentals. 383p. 1992. student ed. 15.95 (*1-881483-03-7*) HyperGraphics.

Maas, John L., ed. Compendium of Strawberry Diseases. 2nd ed. (Illus.). 128p. 1998. pap. 42.00 (*0-89054-194-9*) Am Phytopathol Soc.

Maas, Jonathon. Airport Humor. 120p. 1992. pap. 6.95 (*0-9632230-0-3*) Travelers Pub.

***Maas, Kathleen, et al, eds.** Teaching for Justice: Concepts & Models for Service-Learning in Peace Studies. (Service-Learning in the Disciplines Ser.: Vol. 11). 200p. 2000. pap. 28.50 (*1-56377-015-6*) Am Assn Higher Ed.

Maas, Martha & Snyder, Jane M. Stringed Instruments of Ancient Greece. LC 87-2103. 288p. (C). 1989. 50.00 (*0-300-03686-8*) Yale U Pr.

Maas, Meridean. Health Care Rationing: Dilemma & Paradox. Kelly, Kathleen, ed. Vol. 6. 1994. write for info. (*0-318-72368-9*) Mosby Inc.

Maas, Meridean & Kelly, Kathleen. Health Care Work Redesign. (Series on Nursing Administration: 7). 256p. 1995. text 39.95 (*0-8039-7164-8*) Sage.

Maas, Meridean, et al. Nursing Diagnosis & Interventions for the Elderly. McCormick, Mark, ed. 736p. (C). 1991. pap. text 45.25 (*0-201-12679-6*) Addison-Wesley.

Maas, Meridean, jt. ed. see Johnson, Marion.

***Maas, Michael.** Readings in Late Antiquity: Sourcebook. LC 99-21404. 512p. 1999. pap. 32.99 (*0-415-15988-1*) Routledge.

***Maas, Michael, ed.** Readings in Late Antiquity: A Sourcebook. LC 99-21404. 448p. (C). 2000. text 99.99 (*0-415-15987-3*) Routledge.

***Maas, P. J. M. & Westra, L. Y., eds.** Familias de Plantas Neotropicales. (SPA., Illus.). 315p. 1998. text 25.00 (*3-904144-08-1*, Pub. by Gantner) Lubrecht & Cramer.

Maas, P. J. Van der, see Van der Maas, P. J.

Maas, Paul J. Flora of Ecuador No. 222: Zingiberaceae. (Opera Botanica Series B). 49p. 1976. pap. 15.00 (*91-546-0214-9*, Pub. by Coun Nordic Pubs) Balogh.

Maas, Paul J. & Westra, Lubbert Y. Neotropical Plant Families: A Concise Guide to Families of Vascular Plants in the Neotropics. (Illus.). viii, 289p. 1992. pap. 34.00 (*3-87429-342-4*, 049967, Pub. by Koeltz Sci Bks) Lubrecht & Cramer.

Maas, Paul J., et al. Flora of Ecuador Nos. 223 & 224: Cannaceae, Maranthaceae. (Opera Botanica Series B). 191p. 1988. pap. 70.00 (*87-88702-28-6*, Pub. by Coun Nordic Pubs) Balogh.

— Saprophytes Pro Parte. (Flora Neotropica Monographs: No. 40-42). (Illus.). 1986. pap. 49.50 (*0-89327-271-X*) NY Botanical.

Maas, Paul J., jt. auth. see Maas-van de Kamer, H.

Maas, Peter. China White. 320p. 1995. mass mkt. 5.99 (*0-7860-0204-2*, Pinncle Kensgtn) Kensgtn Pub Corp.

— China White. large type ed. LC 95-5406. (Large Print Bks.). 1995. pap. 22.95 (*1-56895-096-9*) Wheeler Pub.

Maas, Peter. Flood. 15.00 (*0-06-093280-5*) HarpC.

— In a Child's Name. abr. ed. (Illus.). 1990. 15.95 incl. audio (*0-671-72627-7*) S&S Audio.

Maas, Peter. In a Child's Name. Rubenstein, Julie, ed. 352p. 1991. reprint ed. mass mkt. 5.99 (*0-671-74619-7*) PB.

— Serpico. 416p. 1997. mass mkt. 6.99 (*0-06-101214-9*, Harp PBks) HarpC.

***Maas, Peter.** The Terrible Hours. 320p. 2000. mass mkt. 6.99 (*0-06-101459-1*, Torch) HarpC.

Maas, Peter. The Terrible Hours: The Man Behind the Greatest Submarine Rescue in History. LC 99-27195. 272p. 1999. 25.00 (*0-06-019480-4*) HarpC.

— The Terrible Hours: The Man Behind the Greatest Submarine Rescue in History. 272p. 2001. pap. 13.00 (*0-06-093277-5*) HarpC.

***Maas, Peter.** The Terrible Hours: The Man Behind the Greatest Submarine Rescue in History. large type ed. LC 99-58957. (Americana Series). 2000. 30.95 (*0-7862-2427-4*) Thorndike Pr.

— The Terrible Hours: The Man Behind the Greatest Submarine Rescue in History. large type ed. LC 99-58957. 2001. pap. 28.95 (*0-7862-2428-2*) Thorndike Pr.

— Underboss: Bosco,&Philip. abr. ed. 1997. audio. write for info. (*0-694-51870-0*, Pub. by HarperAudio) Lndmrk Audiobks.

Maas, Peter. Underboss: Sammy the Bull Gravano's Story of Life in the Mafia. 512p. 1997. mass mkt. 6.99 (*0-06-109664-4*) HarpC.

— Underboss: Sammy the Bull Gravano's Story of Life in the Mafia. LC 97-157286. (Illus.). 336p. 1999. pap. 13.00 (*0-06-093096-9*) HarpC.

Maas, Peter, ed. The Natural Health Guide to Headache Relief. LC 97-144755. 304p. 1997. per. 14.00 (*0-671-51899-2*, PB Trade Paper) PB.

Maas, Robert W. Tolley's Anti-Avoidance Provisions. 632p. 1992. 150.00 (*0-85459-519-8*, Pub. by Tolley Pubng) St Mut.

— Tolley's Property Taxes, 1993-1994. 460p. 1993. 80.00 (*0-85459-788-3*, Pub. by Tolley Pubng) St Mut.

— Tolley's Property Taxes, 1995-1996. 450p. 1995. 195.00 (*1-86012-036-9*, Pub. by Tolley Pubng) St Mut.

— Tolley's Taxation of Employments. 352p. 1991. 120.00 (*0-85459-578-3*, Pub. by Tolley Pubng) St Mut.

— Tolley's Taxation of Employments. 420p. 1995. 195.00 (*1-86012-044-X*, Pub. by Tolley Pubng) St Mut.

— Tolley's Taxation of Employments. 3rd ed. 352p. (C). 1994. 120.00 (*0-85459-904-5*, Pub. by Tolley Pubng) St Mut.

Maas, Robin. Living Hope: Baptism & the Cost of Christian Witness. LC 97-69412. 96p. 1999. pap. 15.95 (*0-88177-238-0*, DR238) Discipleship Res.

Maas, Robin, jt. auth. see O'Donnell, Gabriel.

Maas, Stephen A. C NL: Linear & Nonlinear Microwave Circuit Analysis & Optimization Software & Users Manual. (Microwave Library). 100p. 1990. 550.00 incl. disk (*0-89006-428-8*) Artech Hse.

— Microwave Mixers. 2nd ed. (Microwave Library). 375p. 1992. text 93.00 (*0-89006-605-1*) Artech Hse.

— Nonlinear Microwave Circuits. LC 96-9355. 504p. 1996. 69.95 (*0-7803-3403-5*) IEEE Standards.

— The RF & Microwave Cookbook. LC 98-28219. 267p. 1998. 75.00 (*0-89006-973-5*) Artech Hse.

Maas, Terry. Bluewater Hunting & Freediving. 2nd rev. ed. LC 98-70237. (Illus.). 220p. 1998. reprint ed. 39.85 (*0-9644966-3-1*) BlueWtr Freedivers.

Maas, Terry & Sipperly, David. Freedive. LC 97-78090. (Illus.). 1998. 39.85 (*0-9644966-1-5*) BlueWtr Freedivers.

Maas, Utz & Van Reijen, Willem, eds. Geteilte Sprache: Festschrift fur Rainer Marten. (GER.). vi, 349p. 1988. 69.00 (*90-6032-314-9*, Pub. by B R Gruner) Humanities.

Maas-van de Kamer, H. & Maas, Paul J. Phanerogams: Burmanniaceae. Goerts-van-Rijn, A. R. A., ed. (Flora of the Guianas Ser.: Series A, Fascicle 6). (Illus.). 45p. 1989. pap. 35.00 (*3-87429-290-8*, 036458, Pub. by Koeltz Sci Bks) Lubrecht & Cramer.

— Phanerogams: Truridacea. Goerts-van-Rijn, A. R. A., ed. (Flora of the Guianas Ser.: Series A, Fascicle 5, No. 174). (Illus.). 18p. 1989. pap. 30.00 (*3-87429-289-4*, 036456, Pub. by Koeltz Sci Bks) Lubrecht & Cramer.

Maas, Virginia. Niddy Noddy the Noodlemaker. (Color-A-Story Ser.). (Illus.). 12p. (J). (ps-2). 1981. pap. 2.75 (*0-933992-15-7*) Coffee Break.

***Maas, Werner.** Gene Action: A Historical Account. (Illus.). 176p. 2000. 31.95 (*0-19-514131-8*) OUP.

Maas, Willard, jt. ed. see Van Ghent, Dorothy B.

***Maas, Winy.** Costa Iberica: Datascape. (SPA.). 2000. pap. 34.95 (*84-95273-19-5*) Actar.

Maasbach, M. J. & Wilding, L. P. Spatial Variabilities of Soils & Landforms. (SSSA Special Publications: No. 28). 270p. 1991. 30.00 (*0-89118-798-7*) Soil Sci Soc Am.

Maasen, Sabine. Biology As Society, Society As Biology: Metaphors. Mendelsohn, Everett I. et al, eds. LC 94-36251. (Sociology of the Sciences (Yearbook) Ser.). 364p. (C). 1995. lib. bdg. 176.50 (*0-7923-3174-5*, Pub. by Kluwer Academic) Kluwer Academic.

***Maasen, Sabine & Weingart, Peter.** Metaphors & the Dynamics of Knowledge. 256p. 2000. 90.00 (*0-415-20802-5*) Routledge.

Maasik. Signs of Life: Critical Thinking. 2nd ed. 1997. pap. text 35.55 (*0-312-18512-X*) St Martin.

Maasik, Sonia. California: Critical Thinking & Reading. 2000. pap. text 36.45 (*0-312-13735-4*) St Martin.

— California Dreams & Realities. LC 98-87535. 1999. pap. text 33.95 (*0-312-19419-6*) St Martin.

— Signs of Life. 2nd ed. 1996. pap. text 27.00 (*0-312-16718-0*) St Martin.

— Signs of Life. 2nd ed. 1997. pap. text 2.40 (*0-312-14913-1*); pap. text 5.00 (*0-312-14915-8*) St Martin.

— Signs of Life in U. S. A. 2nd ed. LC 96-86776. 795p. 1997. pap. text 35.95 (*0-312-13631-5*) St Martin.

— Signs of Life with Rules. 3rd ed. 1996. pap. text 30.15 (*0-312-14959-X*) St Martin.

Maasik, Sonia & Solomon, Jack, eds. Signs of Life in the U.S.A. Readings on Popular Culture for Writers. 3rd ed. 1999. pap. text 35.95 (*0-312-19582-6*) St Martin.

Maaskant-Kleibrink, Marianne. Settlement Excavations at Borgo le Ferriere (Satricum), Vol. 1. (Illus.). viii, 356p. (C). 1987. 93.00 (*90-6980-013-6*, Pub. by Egbert Forsten) Hod1der & Stoughton.

— Settlement Excavations at Borgo le Ferriere (Satricum) Vol. 2: The Campaigns 1983, 1985, 1987. (Illus.). 384p. 1993. 130.00 (*90-6980-048-9*, Pub. by Egbert Forsten) Hod1der & Stoughton.

Maaskant-Kleibrink, Marianne, ed. Papers on Mediterranean Archaeology. (Caelcvlvs: Images of Ancient Latin Culture Ser.: Vol. I). 172p. 1993. pap. 40.00 (*0-685-68014-2*, Pub. by Egbert Forsten) Hod1der & Stoughton.

M

Maass, Arthur. Muddy Waters: The Army Engineers & the Nation's Rivers. LC 73-20238. (FDR & the Era of the New Deal Ser.). 306p. 1974. reprint ed. lib. bdg. 39.50 (*0-306-70607-5*) Da Capo.

Maass, Arthur & Anderson, Raymond L. And the Desert Shall Rejoice: Conflict, Growth, & Justice in Arid Environments. LC 85-24157. 456p. (C). 1986. reprint ed. lib. bdg. 38.50 (*0-89874-908-5*) Krieger.

— And the Desert Shall Rejoice Part 2: A Simulation of Irrigation Systems. LC 86-20027. 56p. 1987. reprint ed. pap. 10.50 (*0-89874-978-6*) Krieger.

Maass, Bruno. The Organization of the German Air Force High Command & Higher Echelon Headquarters within the German Air Force. (USAF Historical Studies: No. 190). 247p. 1955. reprint ed. pap. text 38.95 (*0-89126-151-6*) MA-AH Pub.

Maass, David & Hill, Gene. A Gallery of Waterfowl & Upland Birds. LC 78-61769. (Illus.). 1978. text 44.95 (*0-8227-8019-4*) Petersen Pub.

Maass, Donald. The Career Novelist: A Literary Agent Offers Strategies for Succes. LC 96-17148. 245p. 1996. pap. 15.95 (*0-435-08693-6*) Heinemann.

Maass, Eliezer. Stand Firm: A Survival Guide for the New Jewish Believer. rev. ed. Anderson, Fran, ed. 202p. 1995. reprint ed. pap. 8.00 (*1-878678-02-7*) A M F Intl.

Maass, Ernst, ed. see Aratus.

Maass Hill, Peggy, jt. auth. see Miller, Saul.

***Maass, John.** The Victorian Home in America. (Illus.). 2000. pap. 14.95 (*0-486-41252-0*) Dover.

Maass, Martin, ed. see Groner, Erich.

Maass, Michael. Die Geometrischen Dreifuesse. (Olympische Forschungen Ser.: Bd. X). (C). 1978. 153.85 (*3-11-006703-X*) De Gruyter.

Maass, Peter. Love Thy Neighbor: A Story of War. LC 95-39250. 305p. 1996. 25.00 (*0-679-44433-5*) Knopf.

— Love Thy Neighbor: A Story of War. LC 95-39250. 305p. 1997. pap. 13.00 (*0-679-76389-9*) Vin Bks.

Maass, Richard A., et al. Supplier Certification: A Continuous Improvement Strategy. (Supplier Quality Ser.). 141p. (Orig.). 1990. pap. 27.00 (*0-87389-083-3*, H0592) ASQ Qual Pr.

Maass, Robert. Fire Fighters. (Illus.). 32p. (J). (gr. k-3). 1992. pap. 4.99 (*0-590-41460-7*) Scholastic Inc.

— Fire Fighters. 1989. 10.19 (*0-606-01835-2*, Pub. by Turtleback) Demco.

***Maass, Robert.** Garbage. LC 99-32144. (Illus.). 32p. (gr. k-3). 1999. 15.95 (*0-8050-5951-2*) H Holt & Co.

Maass, Robert. Garden. LC 97-23425. (Illus.). 32p. (J). (gr. 2-4). 1998. 15.95 (*0-8050-5477-4*) H Holt & Co.

— Tugboats. LC 96-17884. (J). 1995. 15.95 (*0-8050-3116-2*) H Holt & Co.

— U. N. Ambassador: A Behind-the-Scenes Look at Madeleine Albright's World. (Illus.). 48p. (J). (gr. 3-7). 1995. 16.95 (*0-8027-8355-4*); lib. bdg. 17.85 (*0-8027-8356-2*) Walker & Co.

— When Autumn Comes. LC 90-32069. (Illus.). 32p. (J). (ps-3). 1995. pap. 5.95 (*0-8050-2349-6*, Owlet BYR) H Holt & Co.

— When Autumn Comes. (J). 1992. 11.15 (*0-606-02980-X*, Pub. by Turtleback) Demco.

— When Spring Comes. LC 93-29816. 89p. (J). 1995. 14.95 (*0-8050-2085-3*, Bks Young Read) H Holt & Co.

— When Spring Comes. (Illus.). 32p. (J). (gr. k-3). 1995. pap. 5.95 (*0-8050-4705-0*, Owlet BYR) H Holt & Co.

— When Spring Comes. 1996. 11.15 (*0-606-10969-2*, Pub. by Turtleback) Demco.

— When Summer Comes. (Illus.). 32p. (J). (gr. k-3). 1995. pap. 5.95 (*0-8050-4706-9*, Owlet BYR) H Holt & Co.

— When Summer Comes. LC 92-26955. (Illus.). 32p. (J). (gr. 1-3). 1995. 14.95 (*0-8050-2087-X*, Bks Young Read) H Holt & Co.

— When Summer Comes. 1996. 11.15 (*0-606-10970-6*, Pub. by Turtleback) Demco.

— When Winter Comes. LC 93-7146. (Illus.). 32p. (J). (gr. 1-3). 1995. 14.95 (*0-8050-2086-1*, Bks Young Read) H Holt & Co.

— When Winter Comes. LC 93-7146. (Illus.). 32p. (J). (ps-3). 1996. pap. 5.95 (*0-8050-4926-6*, B Martin BYR) H Holt & Co.

— When Winter Comes. 1996. 11.15 (*0-606-10971-4*, Pub. by Turtleback) Demco.

Maass, Vera S., jt. auth. see Neely, Margery A.

An Asterisk (*) at the beginning of an entry indicates that the title is appearing for the first time.

Maass, Wolfgang & Bishop, Christopher M., eds. Pulsed Neural Networks. LC 98-38511. (Illus.). 400p. 1999. 45.00 (*0-262-13350-4*, Bradford Bks) MIT Pr.

Maassen, Bernhard & Whaite, Robin, eds. In Vitro Diagnostic Medical Devices: Law & Practice in Five EU Member States. LC 94-3568. 140p. (C). 1994. text 119.00 (*0-7923-2996-1*) Kluwer Academic.

Maassen, Irmgard, jt. auth. see St. Clair, William.

Maassen, P., jt. ed. see Huisman, J.

Maassen, Pierce. Heavenly Comfort. 1959. pap. 0.70 (*0-686-23473-1*) Rose Pub MI.

— Motherhood. 1959. pap. 0.70 (*0-686-23476-6*) Rose Pub MI.

Maassen, Ruth. Picking Raspberries. (Chapbook Ser.: No. 4). 40p. (Orig.). 1997. pap. 8.95 (*0-9649463-3-5*) Folly Cove.

Maassen van den Brink, Henriette. Female Labor Supply: Child Care & Marital Conflict. 225p. (Orig.). 1994. pap. 34.50 (*90-5356-072-6*, Pub. by Amsterdam U Pr) U of Mich Pr.

Maaster, Roger D. & Schubertt, Glendon A., eds. Primate Politics. LC 90-9611. 224p. (C). 1991. 42.00 (*0-8093-1611-0*) S Ill U Pr.

Maatman, Russell. The Bible, Natural Science, & Evolution. (Orig.). 1980. pap. 4.95 (*0-932914-03-9*) Dordt Coll Pr.

— The Impact of Evolutionary Theory: A Christian View. 318p. (Orig.). 1993. pap. 12.95 (*0-932914-28-4*) Dordt Coll Pr.

— The Unity in Creation. 143p. (Orig.). 1978. pap. 4.95 (*0-932914-00-4*) Dordt Coll Pr.

Maatz, R., et al. Intramedullary Nailing & Other Intermedullary Osteosyntheses. 230p. 1986. text 145.00 (*0-7216-1279-2*, W B Saunders Co) Harcrt Hlth Sci Grp.

Maaz, W., ed. see Onnerfors, Alf.

Maaz, Wolfgang. Lateinische Epigrammatik im Hohen Mittelalter. (Spolia Berolinensia Ser.: Bd. 2). (GER.). viii, 306p. 1992. write for info. (*3-615-00075-7*) G Olms Pubs.

Maaz, Wolfgang, jt. auth. see Wagner, Fritz.

Maaz, Wolfgang, ed. see Schroder, Werner.

***Mabana, Kahiudi Claver.** L'Univers Mythique de Tchicaya U Tam'si a Travers Son Oeuvre en Prose. (Publications Universitaires Europeennes: Vol. 237). xii, 400p. 1998. 52.95 (*3-906760-76-6*, Pub. by P Lang) P Lang Pubng.

Mabandla, Oyama, jt. auth. see Ellis, Stephen.

***Mabanglo, Elynia S.** Invitation of the Imperialist: Poems. 228p. 1998. pap. text 20.00 (*971-542-201-2*) UH Pr.

Mabank Sesquicentennial Committee. History of Mabank Texas. (Illus.). 445p. 1987. 55.00 (*0-88107-080-7*) Curtis Media.

Mabbe, James, tr. see Aleman, Mateo.

Mabbe, James, tr. see Rojas, Fernando De.

Mabberley, D. J. Jupiter Botanicus: Robert Brown of the British Museum. (Illus.). 500p. 1985. lib. bdg. 120.00 (*3-7682-1408-7*) Lubrecht & Cramer.

— The Plant-Book: A Portable Dictionary of the Vascular Plants. 2nd ed. LC 96-30091. 874p. (C). 1997. text 52.95 (*0-521-41421-0*) Cambridge U Pr.

— Tropical Rain Forest Ecology. 2nd ed. (Tertiary Level Biology Ser.). 200p. 1991. 87.50 (*0-412-02881-6*, A6375); mass mkt. 34.95 (*0-412-02891-3*, A6379) Chapman & Hall.

***Mabberley, David.** Arthur Harry Church: The Anatomy of Flowers. (Illus.). 128p. 2000. 45.00 (*1-85894-116-4*, Pub. by Merrell Holberton) Rizzoli Intl.

— Ferdinand Bauer. 45.00 (*1-85894-087-7*, Pub. by Merrell Holberton) U of Wash Pr.

Mabberley, David & White, James J. Paradisus: Hawaiian Plant Watercolors by Geraldine King Tam. LC 98-75731. (Illus.). 152p. 1999. 49.95 (*0-937426-42-3*) Honolu Arts.

Mabberley, David, jt. auth. see Lack, H. W.

Mabberley, Julie. Activity Based Costing in Financial Institutions: How to Develop Your Products More Cost Effectively. 2nd ed. 1998. 59.95 (*0-273-63753-3*, Finc Times) F T P-H.

— Managing the Future in Financial Institutions: Meeting the Challenge with Better Information. (Illus.). 336p. 1996. 50.00 (*0-273-61975-6*) F T P-H.

— The Price Waterhouse Guide to Activity-Based Costing for Financial Institutions. 240p. 1996. 75.00 (*0-7863-0143-0*, Irwn McGrw-H) McGrw-H Hghr Educ.

Mabbett, Andy. Pink Floyd. (Complete Guides to the Music Of...Ser.). (Illus.). 150p. (Orig.). 1995. pap. 8.95 (*0-7119-4301-X*, OP 47735, Pub. by Omnibus Press) Omnibus NY.

Mabbett, Andy, jt. auth. see Miles.

Mabbett, D., jt. auth. see Bolderson, H.

Mabbett, Deborah. Trade, Employment, & Welfare: A Comparative Study of Trade & Labour Market Policies in Sweden & New Zealand, 1880-1980. (Illus.). 248p. 1995. text 52.00 (*0-19-828379-2*) OUP.

Mabbett, Ian & Chandler, David. The Khmers. (PeopleTalk Ser.). (Illus.). 288p. 1995. 60.95 (*0-631-17582-2*) Blackwell Pubs.

— The Khmers. Bellwood, Peter & Glover, Ian, eds. (The Peoples of South East Asia & the Pacific Ser.). (Illus.). 276p. 1996. pap. 28.95 (*0-631-20298-6*) Blackwell Pubs.

Mabbitt, J. H. The Health Services of Glamorgan. 232p. (C). 1989. 39.00 (*0-9500789-5-6*, Pub. by D Brown & Sons Ltd) St Mut.

Mabble, Scott, ed. Abstract 95/96. (Illus.). (C). 1996. text 19.95 (*1-883584-07-8*) CUGSA.

Mabbott, Maureen C. Mabbott As Poe Scholar: The Early Years. Kadis, Averil J., ed. (Orig.). 1980. pap. 2.95 (*0-910556-14-8*) Enoch Pratt.

Mabbott, Thomas O., ed. see Poe, Edgar Allan.

Mabbott, Thomas Ollive, ed. see Poe, Edgar Allan.

Mabbs, F. E. & Collison, D. Electron Paramagnetic Resonance of d Transition Metal Compounds. LC 92-36527. (Studies in Inorganic Chemistry: Vol. 16). 1326p. 1992. 731.50 (*0-444-89852-2*) Elsevier.

Mabbutt. Desert Landforms. (Australian National University Press Ser.). 1996. text. write for info. (*0-08-032875-X*, Pergamon Pr); pap. text. write for info. (*0-08-032929-2*, Pergamon Pr) Elsevier.

Mabbutt, Anita, jt. auth. see Mabbutt, Bill.

Mabbutt, Bill & Mabbutt, Anita. North American Wild Game Cookbook. (Illus.). 212p. (Orig.). 1992. reprint ed. pap. 12.95 (*0-9634334-0-7*); reprint ed. spiral bd. 12.95 (*0-9634334-1-5*) B & A Mabbutt.

Mabe, Joni. Everything Elvis. LC 96-24702. (Illus.). 144p. 1996. 29.95 (*1-56025-107-7*, Thunders Mouth) Avalon NY.

— Everything Elvis. (Illus.). 144p. 1998. pap. text 19.95 (*1-56025-178-6*, Thunders Mouth) Avalon NY.

— Everything Elvis. (Illus.). 135p. 1998. text 30.00 (*0-7881-5636-5*) DIANE Pub.

— Joni Mabe's Museum Book. 1988. pap. 25.00 (*0-932526-18-7*) Nexus Pr.

Mabe, Mitzi. A Community of Writers. 1998. text 23.28 (*1-56870-306-6*) RonJon Pub.

***Mabee, Carleton.** The American Leonardo: A Life of Samuel F. Morse. rev. ed. LC 00-29056. (Illus.). 500p. 2000. pap. 25.00 (*1-930098-08-1*) Purple Mnt Pr.

Mabee, Carleton. Black Education in New York State: From Colonial to Modern Times. LC 79-21262. (New York State Study Ser.). (Illus.). 356p. 1979. reprint ed. pap. 110.40 (*0-608-06945-0*, 206715300009) Bks Demand.

— Listen to the Whistle: An Anecdotal History of the Wallkill Valley Railroad in Orange & Ulster Counties, New York. Jacobs, John K., ed. LC 95-42950. (Illus.). 168p. 1995. lib. bdg. 29.00 (*0-935796-69-X*) Purple Mnt Pr.

Mabee, Carleton & Newhouse, Susan M. Sojourner Truth: Slave, Prophet, Legend. LC 93-9370. (Illus.). 320p. (C). 1993. text 45.00 (*0-8147-5484-8*) NYU Pr.

— Sojourner Truth: Slave, Prophet, Legend. LC 93-9370. (Illus.). 320p. (C). 1995. pap. text 17.50 (*0-8147-5525-9*) NYU Pr.

Mabee, Carleton H. A Guide to Croquet Court Planning, Building & Maintenance. Senghas, Richard, ed. (Illus.). 120p. (Orig.). 1991. pap. 45.00 (*0-9630074-0-8*) Bass Cove.

Mabee, Charles. Reading Sacred Texts Through American Eyes: Biblical Interpretation As Cultural Critique. LC 91-14356. (Studies in American Biblical Hermeneutics). 128p. (C). 1991. 24.95 (*0-86554-385-2*, H313); pap. text 16.95 (*0-86554-403-4*, MUP/P095) Mercer Univ Pr.

— Reimagining America: A Theological Critique of the American Mythos & Biblical Hermeneutics. LC 84-27335. xvi, 156p. 1985. 15.95 (*0-86554-148-5*, MUP/H139) Mercer Univ Pr.

Mabee, Charles, ed. see Mercer, Calvin R.

***Mabee, Kerri.** If Spiders Were Purple & Sparkly. Wise, Noreen, ed. (Book-a-Day Collection). (Illus.). 32p. (YA). 2000. pap. 5.95 (*1-58584-401-2*) Huckleberry CT.

— The Lemon Dilemna. Wise, Noreen, ed. (Book-a-Day Collection). 32p. (YA). (ps up). 2000. pap. 5.95 (*1-58584-430-6*) Huckleberry CT.

***Mabee, Stephanie.** Internet Fundamentals: Module 1. Dietz, Kevin C., ed. (Illus.). 187p. (C). 1999. pap. write for info. (*0-7423-0294-6*) ComputerPREP.

Maben, Laura. Homework for Thinkers: A Year's Worth of Creative Assignments to Stimulate Critical Thinking. Britt, Leslie, ed. & intro. by. (Illus.). 64p. (Orig.). (J). (gr. 3-6). 1995. pap. text 7.95 (*0-86530-300-2*, 1P300-2) Incentive Pubns.

Maben, Manly. Vanport, Oregon. (Illus.). (C). 1987. pap. 15.95 (*0-87595-118-X*) Oregon Hist.

Maber, Richard G. The Poetry of Pierre Le Moyne (1602-1671) 311p. 1982. pap. 45.00 (*3-261-04945-6*) P Lang Pubng.

Maberry, Grace. It Came to Pass. LC 97-75412. (Illus.). 64p. 1997. pap. 10.95 (*1-57736-071-0*) Providence Hse.

Mabert. Production Operation Management. 1997. write for info. (*0-02-373032-3*) P-H.

— Production Operation Management CTB IBM. 1997. write for info. (*0-02-373035-8*) P-H.

— Production Operation Management TB. 1997. write for info. (*0-02-373034-X*) P-H.

Mabert, Vincent A. & Jacobs, F. Robert, eds. Integrated Production Systems: Design, Planning, Control, & Scheduling. 4th ed. 277p. 1991. pap. text 39.95 (*0-89806-119-9*, MOTVTG) Eng Mgmt Pr.

Mabery-Foster, Lucy. Women & the Church. LC 99-24524. 1999. 24.99 (*0-8499-1360-8*); 19.97 (*0-8499-1594-5*) Word Pub.

Mabery, Ken, compiled by. Natural History of El Malpais National Monument. (Bulletin Ser.: No. 156). (Illus.). 186p. 1997. pap. 24.95 (*1-883905-01-X*) NM Bureau Mines.

Mabery, Marilyne V. El Malpais National Monument. Priehs, T. J. & Houk, Rose, eds. LC 90-60723. (Illus.). 16p. (Orig.). 1990. pap. 3.95 (*0-911408-89-4*) SW Pks Mnmts.

— Right after Sundown: Teaching Stories of the Navajo. 1991. pap. 14.95 (*0-912586-69-9*) Dine College Pr.

Mabey, Bill, jt. auth. see Bain, Neville.

Mabey, Chris, jt. auth. see Thomson, Rosemary.

Mabey, Christopher. Graduates into Industry. 1986. text 63.95 (*0-566-00886-6*, Pub. by Avebry) Ashgate Pub Co.

Mabey, Christopher & Iles, Paul. Managing Learning. (Bus Press-New). 320p. 1994. pap. 20.99 (*1-86152-198-7*) Thomson Learn.

Mabey, Christopher & Iles, Paul, eds. Managing Learning. LC 94-17871. 208p. (C). 1994. mass mkt. 31.95 (*0-415-11984-7*, C0461) Routledge.

— Managing Learning. LC 94-17871. 320p. (C). (gr. 13). 1994. mass mkt. 77.95 (*0-415-11983-9*, C0111) Routledge.

Mabey, Christopher, et al. Human Resource Management: A Strategic Introduction. 2nd rev. ed. LC 98-36600. 512p. 1998. 79.95 (*0-631-21145-4*) Blackwell Pubs.

— Human Resource Management: A Strategic Introduction. 2nd rev. ed. LC 98-36600. 512p. (C). 1998. pap. 49.95 (*0-631-20823-2*) Blackwell Pubs.

— Strategic Human Resource Management: A Reader. LC 98-61093. viii, 334p. 1998. 27.95 (*0-7619-6033-3*) Sage.

Mabey, David. Good Cider. (Illus.). 144p. text 19.95 (*0-905483-34-0*, Pub. by Whittet Bks) Diamond Farm Bk.

Mabey, David & Collison, David. The Perfect Pickle Book. 3rd rev. ed. 1995. pap. 9.95 (*0-563-37068-8*, BBC-Parkwest) Parkwest Pubns.

Mabey, Don R. & Budding, Karin E. High-Temperature Geothermal Resources of Utah. (Bulletin of the Utah Geological Survey Ser.: No. 123). (Illus.). 64p. (Orig.). 1987. pap. 7.00 (*1-55791-090-1*, B-123) Utah Geological Survey.

Mabey, Jay, ed. Repeater Directory, 1997-1998. 1997. pap. 8.00 (*0-87259-617-6*) Am Radio.

Mabey, Judith & Sorensen, Bernice. Counselling for Young People. LC 94-41293. 160p. 1995. pap. 26.95 (*0-335-19298-X*) OpUniv Pr.

Mabey, Juliet. God's Big Book of Virtues: A Treasury of Wisdom for Living a Good Life. (Illus.). 160p. 1999. text 11.95 (*1-85168-171-X*, Pub. by Onewrld Pubns) Penguin Putnam.

— God's Big Instruction Book: Timeless Wisdom on How to Follow the Spiritual Path. rev. ed. (Illus.). 160p. 1999. text 11.95 (*1-85168-170-1*, Pub. by Onewrld Pubns) Penguin Putnam.

***Mabey, Juliet.** Rumi: Spiritual Treasury. 2000. 14.95 (*1-85168-215-5*, Pub. by Onewrld Pubns) Penguin Putnam.

Mabey, Juliet. Words to Comfort, Words to Heal: Poems & Meditations for Those Who Grieve. 128p. 1998. 10.95 (*1-85168-154-X*, Pub. by Element MA) Penguin Putnam.

Mabey, Juliet, compiled by. God's Big Handbook for the Soul: An Owner's Manual. (Illus.). 160p. 2000. 11.95 (*1-85168-187-6*, Pub. by Onewrld Pubns) Element MA.

— The Oneworld Book of Prayer: A Treasury of Prayers from Around the World. 160p. 1999. text 12.95 (*1-85168-203-1*, Pub. by Element MA) Penguin Putnam.

Mabey, Martha. Artists Die Best in Black. (Wallace Mysteries Ser.). 204p. 1996. 22.95 (*0-9638639-4-0*) Nimrod Hse.

Mabey, Nick. Argument in the Greenhouse: The International Economics of Controlling Global Warming. LC 96-8982. (Global Environmental Change Ser.). (Illus.). 464p. (C). 1997. 85.00 (*0-415-14908-8*); pap. 27.99 (*0-415-14909-6*) Routledge.

***Mabey, Richard.** Book of Spring Flowers. 1998. pap. 17.95 (*1-85619-728-X*, Pub. by Sinclair-Stevenson) Trafalgar.

— Book of Wild Herbs. 1998. pap. 17.95 (*1-85619-723-9*, Pub. by Sinclair-Stevenson) Trafalgar.

Mabey, Richard. Collins Food for Free. (Illus.). 240p. 1989. 19.95 (*0-00-219865-7*, Pub. by HarpC) Trafalgar.

***Mabey, Richard.** Flora Britannica. 1998. pap. 29.95 (*0-7011-6731-9*, Pub. by Random) Trafalgar.

Mabey, Richard. Flora Britannica: The Definitive New Guide to Britain's Wild Flowers, Plants & Trees. (Illus.). 480p. 1998. 55.00 (*1-85619-377-2*) Phoenix Hse.

— Home Country. large type ed. 250p. 1992. 22.95 (*1-85089-580-5*, Pub. by ISIS Lrg Prnt) Transaction Pubs.

— A Nature Journal. (Illus.). 152p. 1992. 24.95 (*0-7011-3507-7*, Pub. by Chatto & Windus) Trafalgar.

— The New Age Herbalist. 1988. per. 21.00 (*0-684-81577-X*) S&S Trade.

Mabey, Richard. The Oxford Book of Nature Writing. 272p. 1995. pap. 15.00 (*0-19-282519-4*) OUP.

Mabey, Richard. The Yorkshire Dales. (Illus.). 96p. 1997. 29.95 (*1-900455-09-9*, Pub. by Colin Baxter Ltd) Voyageur Pr.

Mabey, Richard, ed. Class, a Symposium. (Great Society Ser.). 1967. 10.00 (*0-218-51456-5*) Dufour.

— The Oxford Book of Nature Writing. 272p. 1995. 30.00 (*0-19-214172-4*) OUP.

Mabey, Richard, ed. see White, Gilbert.

Mabie, Caroline W. Behold I Show You a Mystery. LC 80-82229. 150p. (Orig.). 1980. pap. 4.95 (*0-9601416-5-0*) J C Print.

Mabie, Caroline W., ed. see Wilson, J. Eugene.

Mabie, Grace. A Picture Book of Animal Opposites. LC 91-33596. (Picture Book of...Ser.). (Illus.). 24p. (J). (gr. 1-4). 1992. pap. 2.95 (*0-8167-2439-3*); text 14.50 (*0-8167-2438-5*) Troll Communs.

— A Picture Book of Baby Animals. LC 92-26264. (Picture Book of...Ser.). (Illus.). 24p. (J). (gr. 1-4). 1992. lib. bdg. 14.50 (*0-8167-2468-7*) Troll Communs.

— A Picture Book of Baby Animals. LC 92-26264. (Picture Book of...Ser.). (Illus.). 24p. (J). (gr. 1-4). 1997. pap. 2.95 (*0-8167-2469-5*) Troll Communs.

— A Picture Book of Night-Time Animals. LC 91-33597. (Picture Book of...Ser.). (Illus.). 24p. (J). (gr. 1-4). 1992. lib. bdg. 14.50 (*0-8167-2432-6*) Troll Communs.

— A Picture Book of Night-Time Animals. LC 91-33597. (Picture Book of...Ser.). (Illus.). 24p. (J). (gr. 1-4). 1997. pap. 2.95 (*0-8167-2433-4*) Troll Communs.

— A Picture Book of Water Birds. LC 91-34129. (Picture Book of...Ser.). (Illus.). 24p. (J). (gr. 1-4). 1992. lib. bdg. 14.50 (*0-8167-2436-9*) Troll Communs.

Mabie, Grace, ed. see Baum, L. Frank.

Mabie, Grace, ed. & adapted by see Baum, L. Frank.

Mabie, H. W. In the Forest of Arden. 34p. 1989. pap. 6.95 (*0-912132-22-1*) Dominion Pr.

Mabie, Hamilton H. & Reinholtz, Charles F. Mechanisms & Dynamics of Machinery. 4th ed. LC 86-11115. 656p. 1987. text 106.95 (*0-471-80237-9*) Wiley.

Mabie, Hamilton W. American Ideals, Character & Life. LC 74-157965. (Essay Index Reprint Ser.). 1977. reprint ed. 23.95 (*0-8369-2240-9*) Ayer.

— Backgrounds of Literature. LC 72-111846. (Essay Index Reprint Ser.). 1977. 31.95 (*0-8369-1617-4*) Ayer.

— Essays in Lent. LC 69-18931. (Essay Index Reprint Ser.). 1977. 15.95 (*0-8369-0046-4*) Ayer.

— Essays in Literary Interpretation. LC 72-293. (Essay Index Reprint Ser.). 1977. reprint ed. 20.95 (*0-8369-2802-4*) Ayer.

— Fruits of the Spirit. LC 67-22103. (Essay Index Reprint Ser.). 1977. 20.95 (*0-8369-0639-X*) Ayer.

— Myths Every Child Should Know. 1990. pap. 20.00 (*0-8195-1235-4*) Biblo.

— The Writers of Knickerbocker, New York. 121p. 1993. reprint ed. lib. bdg. 69.00 (*0-7812-5278-4*) Rprt Serv.

Mabie, Hamilton W., compiled by. Book of Old English Ballads. LC 79-121929. (Granger Index Reprint Ser.). 1977. 19.95 (*0-8369-6170-6*) Ayer.

— Book of Old English Love Songs. LC 73-121930. (Granger Index Reprint Ser.). 1977. 19.95 (*0-8369-6171-4*) Ayer.

Mabie, Hamilton W., ed. Norse Stories. (Illus.). Date not set. 14.95 (*0-7818-0770-0*) Hippocrene Bks.

Mabie, Margot C. Bioethics & the New Medical Technology. LC 92-22642. 160p. (YA). (gr. 7 up). 1993. 15.00 (*0-689-31637-2*) Atheneum Yung Read.

Mabileau, Albert, et al, eds. Local Politics & Participation in France & Britain. (Illus.). 284p. (C). 1990. text 69.95 (*0-521-34576-6*) Cambridge U Pr.

***Mabille, Gerard.** Views of the Gardens at Marly: Louis XIV: Royal Gardener. (Illus.). 248p. 1998. 95.00 (*2-909838-28-5*, Pub. by A Gourcuff) Antique Collect.

Mabille, Pierre. The Mirror of the Marvelous: The Classic Surrealist Work on Myth. Gladding, Jody, tr. from FRE. LC 98-14998. (Illus.). 256p. 1998. 25.00 (*0-89281-650-3*, Inner Trad) Inner Tradit.

Mabin, Alan, ed. Organisation & Economic Change. 220p. (Orig.). 1989. pap. text 17.95 (*0-86975-382-7*, Pub. by Ravan Pr) Ohio U Pr.

Mabin, Geraldine. Cookie Magic. (Illus.). 32p. (J). (gr. k-3). 1994. pap. write for info. (*0-614-17734-0*) Stoddart Publ.

Mabin, Geraldine & Seligman, Lynn. Cookie Magic. unabridged ed. (Illus.). 32p. (J). (ps-2). 1996. pap. 4.95 (*0-19-540994-9*) STDK.

***Mabin, Victoria J. & Balderstone, Steven J.** The World of the Theory of Constraints: A Review of He International Literature. LC 99-42146. 223p. 1999. 39.95 (*1-57444-276-7*) St Lucie Pr.

Mablekos, Carole M. Presentations That Work, Vol. 1. (Engineers Guide to Business Ser.). (Illus.). 1991. 19.95 (*0-7803-0305-9*, EG101) Inst Electrical.

Mablekos, Carole M., ed. Technical Writing & Communication. 174p. 1988. 510.00 incl. audio (*0-8412-1484-0*, A3); teacher ed. 39.00 (*0-8412-1501-4*) Am Chemical.

Mably, Gabriel B. De, see De Mably, Gabriel B.

Mabogunje, Akin L. The Development Process: A Spatial Perspective. LC 80-19939. 357p. 1980. 39.95 (*0-8419-0659-9*) Holmes & Meier.

— Perspective on Urban Land & Urban Management Policies in Sub-Saharan Africa. LC 92-43900. (Technical Papers: No. 196). 65p. 1993. pap. 22.00 (*0-8213-2355-5*, 12355) World Bank.

— The State of the Earth: Contemporary Geographic Perspectives. LC 96-36188. (Contemporary Social Sciences Ser.). 1997. 78.95 (*0-631-20243-9*); pap. 34.95 (*0-631-20244-7*) Blackwell Pubs.

— Urbanization in Nigeria. LC 76-80853. 353p. 1969. 44.50 (*0-8419-0002-7*, Africana); pap. 12.00 (*0-8419-0097-3*, Africana) Holmes & Meier.

***Mabokela, Reitumetse Obakeng & King, Kimberly Lenease, eds.** Apartheid No More: Case Studies of Southern African Universities in the Process of Transformation. 2001. write for info. (*0-89789-713-7*) Greenwood.

Mabon, Bonnie J., ed. see Mabon, Lon T. & Lively, Scott.

Mabon, E., tr. see Godwin, Francis.

Mabon, George, compiled by. Caring in Homes Initiative: A Policies & Foundation Training. (C). 1991. 55.00 (*0-7855-0083-9*, Pub. by Natl Inst Soc Work) St Mut.

— Caring in Homes Initiative: An Induction Programme. (C). 1991. 50.00 (*0-7855-0082-0*, Pub. by Natl Inst Soc Work) St Mut.

Mabon, Lon T. & Lively, Scott. God Is Politically Involved: A Scriptural Foundation Revealing God's Sovereign Will Requiring Public & Social Activism from His People. Mabon, Bonnie J., ed. 203p. 1998. pap. 12.00 (*0-9647609-4-0*) Fndrs Pubng.

Mabourguet, Patrice. Larousse Dictionnaire General. (FRE.). 1690p. 1993. 69.95 (*0-7859-7124-6*, 203320300X) Fr & Eur.

Mabrey, Robert. Engineering Graphics. (Illus.). 1997. teacher ed. write for info. (*0-8053-6483-8*) Benjamin-Cummings.

— Engineering Graphics Toolkit. 300p. (C). 1997. pap. text 40.00 (*0-8053-6482-X*) Addison-Wesley.

Mabro, Judy. Veiled Half Truths. rev. ed. 288p. 1996. pap. 24.50 (*1-86064-027-3*) St Martin.

Mabro, Judy, jt. ed. see El-Solh, Camillia F.

Mabro, Robert, ed. An International Perspective: Proceedings of the Oxford Energy Seminar 1982-1985. (Institute for Energy Studies). (Illus.). 170p. (C). 1986. text 38.00 (*0-19-730002-2*) OUP.

— OPEC & the World Oil Market: The Genesis of the 1986 Price Crisis. (Institute for Energy Studies). (Illus.). 282p. 1987. text 55.00 (*0-19-730003-0*) OUP.

***Mabro, Robert & Wybrew-Bond, Ian, eds.** Gas to Europe: The Strategies of Four Major Suppliers. (Illus.). 288p. 1999. text 65.00 (0-19-730022-7) OUP.

Mabrouk, Layla, tr. Soul's Journey after Death. 40p. 1996. pap. 3.95 (0-614-21347-9, 1407) Kazi Pubns.

Mabrouk, Patricia A. Analytical Chemistry No. 1: Problem Solver. (C). 1993. student ed. 30.12 (1-56870-089-X) RonJon Pub.

— Analytical Chemistry Lab Manual. (C). 1993. student ed. 20.65 (1-56870-088-1) RonJon Pub.

Mabrouk, Suzanne T. The Organic Chemistry Survival Manual. LC 94-47102. 115p. (C). 1996. pap. text 17.96 (0-395-83869-X) HM.

Mabry. Economics, 2 vols. (C). 1994. pap., teacher ed. 6.76 (0-395-66998-7) HM.

— Economics, 2 vols. 2nd ed. LC 93-78685. (C). 1993. text 57.96 (0-395-66996-0) HM.

— Economics, 2 vols. 2nd ed. (C). 1994. pap. text, student ed. 19.96 (0-395-66997-9) HM.

Mabry, Bevars D. The Development of Labor Institutions in Thailand. LC 79-113663. (Cornell University, Southeast Asia Program, Data Paper Ser.: No. 112). 164p. reprint ed. pap. 50.90 (0-8357-6090-1, 203459500090) Bks Demand.

Mabry, Celia H., ed. Philosophies of Reference Service. LC 97-36870. 246p. 1997. 49.95 (0-7890-0371-6) Haworth Pr.

Mabry, Donald J. The Mexican University & the State: Student Conflicts, 1910-1971. LC 81-48377. 344p. 1982. 28.95 (0-89096-128-X) Tex A&M Univ Pr.

Mabry, Donald J., ed. The Latin American Narcotics Trade & U. S. National Security, 240. LC 89-12030. (Contributions in Political Science Ser.: No. 240). 216p. 1989. 59.95 (0-313-26786-3, MLJ/, Greenwood Pr) Greenwood.

Mabry, E. Scott. Promises Made, Promises Kept: The Source of Staying Power in Marriage. 208p. (Orig.). 1996. pap. 12.95 (1-883893-50-X) WinePress Pub.

— Triangle Power: A Source of Staying Power in Marriage. LC 94-65479. 210p. (Orig.). 1994. pap. 11.95 (0-9639732-0-7) St Croix Pubns.

Mabry, Eddie. Balthasar Hubmaier's Doctrine of the Church. 236p. 1994. lib. bdg. 39.50 (0-8191-9472-7) U Pr of Amer.

— Balthasar Hubmaier's Understanding of Faith. LC 98-34815. 200p. 1998. 37.00 (0-7618-1220-2) U Pr of Amer.

Mabry, Hunter P., jt. auth. see Oommen, T. K.

Mabry, J. God As Nature Sees God: A Christian Reading of the Tao Te Ching. 1994. pap. 14.95 (1-85230-594-0, Pub. by Element MA) Penguin Putnam.

Mabry, John. Little Book of the Tao Te Ching. (Illus.). 48p. 1995. pap. 5.95 (1-85230-707-2, Pub. by Element MA) Penguin Putnam.

Mabry, Jonathan B., ed. Archaeological Investigations at Early Village Sites in the Middle Santa Cruz Valley Vol. I: Analyses & Synthesis, 2 vols. (Anthropological Papers: No. 19). (Illus.). 700p. 1996. pap. 49.95 (1-886398-27-5) Desert Archaeol.

— Archaeological Investigations at Early Village Sites in the Middle Santa Cruz Valley Vol. II: Analyses & Synthesis, 2 vols. (Anthropological Papers: No. 19). (Illus.). 500p. 1996. pap. 49.95 (1-886398-28-3) Desert Archaeol.

— Canals & Communities: Small-Scale Irrigation Systems. LC 96-9958. (Arizona Studies in Human Ecology). 300p. 1996. 47.50 (0-8165-1592-1) U of Ariz Pr.

Mabry, Jonathan B., et al. Archaeological Investigations at Early Village Sites in the Middle Santa Cruz Valley: Site & Feature Descriptions, 2 vols. (Anthropological Papers: No. 18). (Illus.). 600p. 1995. pap. 39.95 (1-886398-26-7) Desert Archaeol.

— Tucson at the Turn of the Century: The Archaeology of a City Block. (Illus.). 198p. (Orig.). 1994. pap. 15.00 (1-886398 11 3) Desert Archaeol.

Mabry, Linda. Portfolios Plus: A Critical Guide to Alternative Assessment. LC 99-6169. (1-Off Ser.). (Illus.). 136p. 1999. 61.95 (0-8039-6610-5); pap. 27.95 (0-8039-6611-3) Corwin Pr.

Mabry, Linda & Stake, Robert E., eds. Evaluation in the Post-Modern Dilemma. (Advances in Program Evaluation Ser.: Vol. 3). 216p. 1997. 78.50 (1-55938-770-X) Jai Pr.

Mabry, Marcus. White Bucks & Black-Eyed Peas: Coming of Age Black in White America. 303p. 1998. text 23.00 (0-7881-5879-1) DIANE Pub.

Mabry, Richard L. Skin Endpoint Titration. 2nd ed. LC 93-50108. (AAOA Monographs). (Illus.). 104p. 1994. text 23.00 (0-86577-525-7) Thieme Med Pubs.

Mabry, Richard L., jt. auth. see King, Hueston C.

Mabry, Steve, jt. auth. see McNabb, Bill.

Mabry, Tom J. & Wagenitz, G. W. Research Advances in the Compositae. (Plant Systematics & Evolution Ser.: Suppl. 4). (Illus.). 120p. 1990. 111.95 (0-387-82174-0) Spr-Verlag.

Mabry, Tom J., jt. ed. see Behnke, H. D.

Mabry, William A. Negro in North Carolina Politics since Reconstruction. LC 75-110130. (Duke University. Trinity College Historical Society. Historical Papers: No. 23). reprint ed. 30.00 (0-404-51773-0) AMS Pr.

Mabry, William E. The Wildness of Worship. 1994. pap. 4.95 (1-55673-826-9, 7997) CSS OH.

Mabuchi, K., ed. International Symposium on Advanced Techniques & Clinical Applications in Biomedical Thermology. 324p. 1995. pap. text 61.00 (3-7186-5628-0, Harwood Acad Pubs) Gordon & Breach.

Mabuchi, T., et al. Geometry & Analysis on Complex Manifolds: Festschrift for S. Kobayashi's 60th Birthday. 260p. 1994. text 74.00 (981-02-2067-7) World Scientific Pub.

Mabuchi, Toshiki & Mukai, Shigeru, eds. Einstein Metrics & Yang-Mills Connections. LC 93-18074. (Lecture Notes in Pure & Applied Mathematics Ser.: Vol. 145). (Illus.). 240p. 1993. pap. text 135.00 (0-8247-9069-3) Dekker.

Mabunda, L. Mpho. Contemporary Black Biography. (Contemporary Black Biography Ser.: Vol. 11). 275p. 1996. text 60.00 (0-8103-9319-0) Gale.

— Contemporary Black Biography, Vol. 9. (Contemporary Black Biography Ser.). 275p. 1995. text 60.00 (0-8103-5740-2) Gale.

— Contemporary Black Biography, Vol. 10. 275p. 1995. text 60.00 (0-8103-9318-2) Gale.

Mabunda, L. Mpho, ed. African-American Almanac. 7th ed. 1450p. 1996. 165.00 (0-8103-7867-1) Gale.

Maby. Electronic Circuits. (C). 2000. text. write for info. (0-471-12470-2) Wiley.

Mac. Desert Storm. 1994. 21.79 (1-57251-006-4) Little.

Mac Adam, Alfred, tr. see Fuentes, Carlos.

Mac Adam, Alfred, tr. see Machado de Assis, Joaquim Maria.

Mac Adam, Alfred, tr. see Vargas Llosa, Mario.

Mac an Ghaill, Mairtin. The Making of Men: Masculinities, Sexualities & Schooling. LC 93-37338. 1994. pap. 32.95 (0-335-15781-5) OpUniv Pr.

Mac An Ghaill, Mairtin. Understanding Masculinities: Social Relations & Cultural Arenas. 224p. 1996. pap. 29.95 (0-335-19460-5) OpUniv Pr.

Mac Aonghusa, Proinsas, ed. What Connolly Said. 94p. (Orig.). 1995. pap. 9.95 (1-874597-11-1, Pub. by New Island Books) Irish Bks Media.

Mac Arthur, John. La Gloria Del Cielo. 160p. 1997. pap. 6.99 (0-8254-1452-0) Kregel.

Mac Arthur, Margaret & Sharrow, Gregory. The Vermont Heritage Songbook. 108p. 1994. 9.95 (0-916718-13-1) VT Folklife Ctr.

Mac Austin, Hilary, jt. ed. see Thompson, Kathleen.

Mac Cammon, Art. Web Bound. 2nd ed. 180p. 1996. pap. 14.95 (0-9650520-0-1) Web Bound Inc.

— Web Bound 2000: The Essential Web Resource. (WebBound Ser.). 536p. 1999. pap. 19.95 (0-9650520-1-X) Web Bound Inc.

***Mac Chombaich De Colquhoun, Patrick.** A Summary of the Roman Civil Law: Illustrated by Commentaries on & Parallels from the Mosaic, Canon, Mohammedan, English & Foreign Law, 4 vols. 2182p. 2000. reprint ed. 495.00 (1-56169-598-X) Gaunt.

Mac Chombaich De Colquhoun, Patrick. Summary of the Roman Civil Law: Illustrated Commentaries on & Parallels from the Mosaic, Canon, Mohammedan, English, & Foreign Law, 4 vols., Set. (Illus.). 1988. reprint ed. 195.00 (0-8377-2036-2, Rothman) W S Hein.

Mac Conghail, Muiris. The Blaskets: People & Literature. rev. ed. (Illus.). 176p. 1995. pap. 16.95 (1-57098-033-0) Roberts Rinehart.

Mac Connell, Robert, jt. auth. see Naroola, Gurmeet.

Mac Cormack, Karen. Marine Snow. LC 96-118782. 64p. 1995. pap. 12.00 (1-55022-258-9, Pub. by ECW) Genl Dist Srvs.

— Quirks & Quillets. (Illus.). 56p. (Orig.). 1990. pap. 8.00 (0-925904-04-X) Chax Pr.

— The Tongue Moves Talk. LC 97-278. 1997. pap. write for info. (0-925904-12-0) Chax Pr.

Mac Cragh, Esteban. Nuevo Diccionario Ingles-Espanol y Espanol-Ingles: New Spanish-English & English-Spanish Dictionary. 5th ed. 1990. 29.95 (0-7859-5037-0) Fr & Eur.

Mac Curtain, Margaret & O'Corrain, Donncha, eds. Women in Irish Society: The Historical Dimension, 11. LC 79-964. (Contributions in Women's Studies: No. 11). 125p. 1979. 38.50 (0-313-21254-6, MWI/, Greenwood Pr) Greenwood.

***Mac Donald, Heather.** The Burden of Bad Ideas: How Modern Intellectuals Misshape Our Society. 256p. 2000. 26.00 (1-56663-337-0, Pub. by I R Dee) Natl Bk Netwk.

Mac Donald, Hugh, tr. see Debussy, Claude.

Mac Dougall, David S., ed. European Community Energy Law: Selected Topics. (International Energy & Resources Law & Policy Ser.). 304p. (C). 1994. lib. bdg. 131.50 (1-85333-962-8, Pub. by Graham & Trotman) Kluwer Academic.

Mac Eoin, Gearailt, tr. see O'Conaire, Padraic.

Mac, Freddy, pseud. How to Buy Gold & Silver for Half Price. (Illus.). 80p. (Orig.). 1984. pap. 20.00 (0-9614202-0-0) Golden Aloha.

Mac Gillivray, H. T., ed. Digitised Optical Sky Surveys: Proceedings of the Conference on Digitised Optical Sky Surveys, Held in Edinburgh, Scotland, June 18-21, 1991. (Astrophysics & Space Science Library). 544p. (C). 1992. text 236.00 (0-7923-1642-8) Kluwer Academic.

Mac Gregor, Felipe E., ed. Coca & Cocaine: An Andean Perspective, 37. LC 92-12282. (Contributions in Criminology & Penology Ser.: No. 37). 168p. 1993. 55.00 (0-313-28530-6, ACN/, Greenwood Pr) Greenwood.

Mac Harg, Marcia L., ed. International Survey of Investment Adviser Regulation. 368p. 1994. lib. bdg. 145.50 (1-85966-078-9, Pub. by Graham & Trotman) Kluwer Academic.

Mac Kay, James A. Enciclopedia Mundial del Sello 1945-1975. (SPA.). 112p. 1976. 87.50 (0-8288-5670-2, S50553) Fr & Eur.

Mac Knight, Lynne. Celebration of Motherhood: With Love & Laughter. LC 98-83106. 365p. 1999. 25.00 (0-7388-0339-1); pap. 15.00 (0-7388-0340-5) Xlibris Corp.

Mac Lane, Jude. Heart Messages: From Archangel Michael & Jude Mac Lane. 75p. (Orig.). (C). 1989. pap. 8.00 (0-9622052-0-6) Turtle Prints.

Mac Lane, S. & Moerdijk, Izak. Sheaves in Geometry & Logic: A First Introduction to Topos Theory. (Universitext Ser.). (Illus.). 616p. 1994. 60.95 (0-387-97710-4) Spr-Verlag.

Mac Lane, Saunders. Homology. LC 94-47666. 422p. 1995. 35.00 (3-540-58662-8) Spr-Verlag.

Mac Lane, Saunders & Birkhoff, Garrett D. Algebra. 3rd ed. xv, 630p. (C). 1987. text 32.50 (0-8284-0330-9) Chelsea Pub.

Mac Lane, Saunders, jt. auth. see Birkhoff, Garrett D.

***Mac Laughlin, Jim.** Reimagining the Nation State: The Contested Terrains of Nation-Building. LC 00-9418. 2000. write for info. (0-7453-1369-8, Pub. by Pluto GBR) Stylus Pub VA.

Mac Laverty, Bernard. Walking the Dog. 200p. 1996. pap. 11.00 (0-393-31453-7, Norton Paperbks) Norton.

Mac Lean, Norman, tr. see Pischinger, Alfred.

Mac Liammoir, Micheal & Boland, Eavan. W. B. Yeats. LC 85-51360. (Literary Lives Ser.). (Illus.). 144p. 1998. reprint ed. pap. 12.95 (0-500-26022-2, Pub. by Thames Hudson) Norton.

Mac Low, Jackson. Forty-Two Merzgedichte in Memoriam Kurt Schwitters: February, 1987 - September, 1989. LC 94-2575. 1994. 14.95 (0-88268-145-1) Station Hill Pr.

— From Pearl Harbor Day to FDR's Birthday. LC 82-61709. (Sun & Moon Classics Ser.: Vol. 126). 72p. 1982. pap. 10.95 (0-940650-19-3) Sun & Moon CA.

— Pieces O' Six. (Sun & Moon Classics Ser.: No. 17). 188p. 1989. pap. 11.95 (1-55713-060-4) Sun & Moon CA.

***Mac Low, Jackson.** 20 Forties. 49p. 2000. pap. 14.95 (84-87467-35-0, Pub. by Zasterle Pr) SPD-Small Pr Dist.

Mac Mathuna, Seamus & Corrain, Aibhe O. Collins Gem Irish Dictionary. (Collins Gem Ser.). 640p. 1995. pap. 6.95 (0-00-470753-2, Perennial) HarperTrade.

Mac Orlan, Pierre. Le Chant de l'Equippage. (FRE.). 1979. pap. 10.95 (0-7859-4112-6) Fr & Eur.

— Chronique des Jours Desesperes Suivi de les Voisins. (FRE.). 148p. 1985. pap. 10.95 (0-7859-4236-X, 2070376915) Fr & Eur.

— Sous la Lumiere Froide. (FRE.). 224p. 1979. pap. 10.95 (0-7859-4124-X, 2070371530) Fr & Eur.

Mac Poilin, Aodan. Irish Is Fun! (IRI.). 1987. reprint ed. pap. 6.95 (0-86243-143-3) Intl Spec Bk.

Mac Poilin, Aodan, ed. see Fiacc, Padraic.

***Mac Productions Staff.** Golfing in Oregon. 10th ed. (Illus.). 2000. pap. text 10.95 (1-878591-53-3) Mac Prodns.

— Golfing in Washington. 15th ed. 2000. pap. text 11.95 (1-878591-52-5) Mac Prodns.

***Mac Productions Staff, ed.** Golfing in Arizona. (Illus.). 2000. pap. 11.95 (1-878591-54-1) Mac Prodns.

— Golfing in Hawaii. (Illus.). 2000. pap. 11.95 (1-878591-55-X) Mac Prodns.

Mac Uistin, Liam. Post-Mortem. (Irish Play Ser.). 1977. pap. 2.50 (0-912262-43-5) Proscenium.

***Mac Uistn, Liam.** Exploring Newgrange. LC 99-492095. (Illus.). 112p. (J). 2000. 14.95 (0-86278-600-2, Pub. by OBrien Pr) IPG Chicago.

Mac, Viccie, jt. auth. see Collura, Mario A.

Macadam. Blue Guide Tuscany. 3rd ed. (Illus.). 448p. 1999. pap. 24.95 (0-393-31949-0) Norton.

— Sicily. 5th ed. (Blue Guide Ser.). (Illus.). 384p. 1999. pap. 22.95 (0-393-31935-0) Norton.

MacAdam, A., tr. see Arenas, Reinaldo.

MacAdam, Alfred, tr. see Fuentes, Carlos.

MacAdam, Alfred, tr. see Pessoa, Fernando.

MacAdam, Alfred, tr. see Vargas Llosa, Mario.

MacAdam, Alfred, tr. & intro. see Cortazar, Julio.

MacAdam, Alfred J. Modern Latin American Narratives: The Dreams of Reason. LC 76-8098. 1993. lib. bdg. 15.00 (0-226-49993-6) U Ch Pr.

— Textual Confrontations: Comparative Readings in Latin American Literature. LC 86-24913. 288p. 1987. 23.95 (0-226-49990-1) U Ch Pr.

MacAdam, Alfred J., tr. see Fuentes, Carlos.

MaCadam, Alta. Blue Guide Northern Italy. 10th ed. 576p. 1997. pap. 25.95 (0-393-31745-5) Norton.

Macadam, Alta. Blue Guide Rome. 6th ed. (Illus.). 448p. 1998. pap. 21.95 (0-393-31804-4) Norton.

— Blue Guide Venice. 6th ed. (Illus.). 224p. 1998. pap. 21.95 (0-393-31805-2) Norton.

***MacAdam, Alta.** Florence. 7th ed. (Blue Guide Ser.). (Illus.). 300p. 1998. pap. 21.95 (0-393-31871-0, Norton Paperbks) Norton.

***Macadam, Alta.** Umbria. 3rd ed. (Blue Guide Ser.). (Illus.). 288p. 2000. pap. 20.95 (0-393-32016-2) Norton.

MacAdam, Barbara J. Clark G.Voorhees 1871-1933. (Illus.). 32p. (Orig.). 1981. pap. 8.00 (1-880897-13-X) Lyme Hist.

— Looking for America: Prints of Rural Life from the 1930s & 1940s. LC 94-45118. (Illus.). 1994. 3.00 (0-944722-18-0) Hood Mus Art.

MacAdam, Barbara J., et al. Winter's Promise: Willard Metcalf in Cornish, New Hampshire, 1909-1920. LC 98-41971. 1998. pap. 25.00 (0-944722-22-9) Hood Mus Art.

MacAdam, D. L., ed. see Reimer, L.

MacAdam, David L. Color Measurement. 2nd rev. ed. (Optical Sciences Ser.: Vol. 27). (Illus.). 256p. 1985. 84.95 (0-387-15573-2) Spr-Verlag.

MacAdam, David L., ed. Selected Papers on Colorimetry-Fundamentals. LC 93-10037. (Milestone Ser.: Vol. MS 77). 1993. pap. 45.00 (0-8194-1295-3) SPIE.

— Selected Papers on Colorimetry-Fundamentals. LC 93-10037. (Milestone Ser.: Vol. MS 77/HC). 1993. 55.00 (0-8194-1296-1) SPIE.

MacAdam, David L., ed. see Cotter, David, et al.

MacAdam, Don & Reynolds, Gail. Hockey Fitness: Year-Round Conditioning on & off the Ice. LC 88-681. (Illus.). 152p. (Orig.). 1988. pap. 14.95 (0-88011-314-6, PMAC0314) Human Kinetics.

Macadam, Heather D., jt. auth. see Gelissen, Rena K.

MacAdam, Henry I. West Windor Then & Now: Commemorating the Bicentennial of West Windsor Township (1797-1997) Currie, Ruth H., tr. LC 98-164933. (Illus.). vi, 116p. 1997. pap. 26.95 (0-9662560-0-X, Book #1) Princeton Corridor.

Macadam, John. South West Coast Path: Padstow to Falmouth. (National Trail Guides Ser.). (Illus.). 168p. 1995. pap. 19.95 (1-85410-098-X, Pub. by Aurum Pr) London Brdge.

***MacAdam, Kimberly.** Michigan Law & Practice Encyclopedia Vol. 3: 1999 Replacement. 2nd ed. 500p. 1999. write for info. (0-327-01770-8, 6383311) LEXIS Pub.

— Michigan Law & Practice Encyclopedia Vol. 4: 1999 Replacement. 2nd ed. 500p. 1999. write for info. (0-327-01771-6, 6383511) LEXIS Pub.

***MacAdam, Kimberly, ed.** Michigan Law & Practice Encyclopedia: Interim Index. 2nd ed. 150p. 1999. pap. write for info. (0-327-04986-3, 6387010) LEXIS Pub.

— Michigan Law & Practice Encyclopedia Vol. 8: 1999 Replacement. 2nd ed. 500p. 1999. write for info. (0-327-04966-9, 6384111) LEXIS Pub.

MacAdam, Robert K., jt. auth. see McIlvaine, Charles.

MacAdams, Lewis, Jr. The Poetry Room. LC 73-123978. 65p. 1970. 12.50 (0-89366-104-X) Ultramarine Pub.

MacAdams, Phoebe. Ordinary Snake Dance. 62p. 1994. pap. 10.00 (0-9649240-3-X) Cahuenga Pr.

— Sunday. 100p. (Orig.). 1983. pap. 6.00 (0-939180-20-0) Tombouctou.

MacAdams, William & Nelson, Paul. 701 Toughest Movie Trivia Questions of All Time. LC 95-19763. 224p. 1995. pap. 9.95 (0-8065-1700-X, Citadel Pr) Carol Pub Group.

Macafee, Caroline. Glasgow. (Varieties of English Around the World (VEAW) Text Ser.: No. 3). v, 167p. (Orig.). 1983. 38.00 (90-272-4711-0) J Benjamins Pubng Co.

— The Nuttis Schell: Essays on the Scots Language Presented to a J Aitken. 240p. 1987. text 39.00 (0-08-034530-1, Pergamon Pr) Elsevier.

MacAfee, Helen, ed. see Yale Review Staff.

***Macafee, R. D.** History of Monroe Township & Borough P.A. (By Clement F. Heverly) Genealogical Index & Abstract. 69p. 1999. reprint ed. pap. 14.00 (0-8328-9842-2) Higginson Bk Co.

Macagba. Medical Motifs. 1998. pap. 1.00 (0-486-28256-2) Dover.

Macagba, Jonathan. Go Figure, Vol. 1. LC 94-70879. 120p. (Orig.). 1994. 14.95 (0-88108-140-X) Art Dir.

— Go Figure, Vol. 2. LC 94-73085. 120p. (Orig.). 1994. 14.95 (0-88108-123-X) Art Dir.

MacAgy, Jermayne & Sourian, Etienne. Out of This World: An Exhibition of Fantastic Landscapes from the Renaissance to the Present: March 20-April 30, 1964, Fine Arts Gallery, University of St. Thomas. (Illus.). 1964. pap. 5.00 (0-914412-23-X, Inst Arts Catalogues) Menil Found.

Macaire, D. & Nicolas, G. Wirtschaftsdeutsch fuer Anfaenger: Lehr- und Arbeitsbuch. (GER.). 225p. (C). 1995. pap. text 27.00 (3-12-675128-8, Pub. by Klett Edition); audio 40.50 (3-12-675130-X, Pub. by Klett Edition) Intl Bk Import.

Macaire, Von D. & Hosch, W. Bilder in der Landeskunde. (Fernstudieneinheit Ser.: No. 11). (GER.). 192p. 1997. pap. 11.25 (3-468-49660-5) Langenscheidt.

Macaj, Peter. 1999 Import Performance Directory, Vol. 1. 250p. 1999. pap. 9.95 (0-9668418-0-8) A Marketing.

Macalady, Donald L., ed. Perspectives in Environmental Chemistry. LC 97-4123. (Topics in Environmental Chemistry Ser.). (Illus.). 528p. 1997. text 68.00 (0-19-510208-8); pap. text 47.95 (0-19-510209-6) OUP.

MacAlan, Peter. Fireball. large type ed. (Magna Adventure Suspense Ser.). 403p. 1992. 27.99 (0-7505-0286-X) Ulverscroft.

MacAlister, Robert A. Ancient Ireland: A Study in the Lessons of Archeology & History. LC 72-83747. (Illus.). 1978. reprint ed. 26.95 (0-405-08757-8, Pub. by Blom Pubns) Ayer.

— The Archaeology of Ireland. rev. ed. LC 70-172160. (Illus.). 1972. reprint ed. 36.95 (0-405-08758-6, Pub. by Blom Pubns) Ayer.

Macalister, Robert A. A Century of Excavation in Palestine. Davis, Moshe, ed. LC 77-70720. (America & the Holy Land Ser.). (Illus.). 1977. reprint ed. lib. bdg. 35.95 (0-405-10265-8) Ayer.

— Corpus Inscriptionum Insularum Celticarum Vol. I: The Ogham Inscriptions of Ireland & Britain. 2nd ed. 544p. 1996. reprint ed. boxed set 75.00 (1-85182-242-9, Pub. by Four Cts Pr) Intl Spec Bk.

MacAlister, Robert A. Ireland in Pre-Celtic Times. LC 68-56469. (Illus.). 1972. reprint ed. 34.95 (0-405-08759-4, Pub. by Blom Pubns) Ayer.

Macalister, Robert A. The Philistines: Their History & Civilization. (British Academy, London, Schweich Lectures on Biblical Archaeology Series, 1930). 1974. reprint ed. pap. 25.00 (0-8115-1253-3) Periodicals Srv.

MacAlister, Robert A. The Secret Languages of Ireland. LC 78-72637. (Celtic Language & Literature). reprint ed. 29.50 (0-404-17566-X) AMS Pr.

Macalister, Robert A., tr. from IRI. Life of St. Finan. 1987. reprint ed. pap. 1.95 (0-89979-035-6) British Am Bks.

Macalister-Smith, Peter. International Humanitarian Assistance: Disaster Relief Action in International Law & Organization. 1985. lib. bdg. 113.50 (90-247-2993-9) Kluwer Academic.

Macalister, Suzanne. Dreams & Suicides. 248p. (C). 1996. 80.00 (0-415-07005-8) Routledge.

M

Macallair-Schiraldi. Pak: Reforming Juvenile Justice: Reasons & Strategies. 314p. (C). 1997. pap. text 63.95 (0-7872-4550-X, 41455001) Kendall-Hunt.

Macallan. Shorts: The Macallan. 192p. 1998. pap. 12.95 (0-7486-6245-6, Pub. by Polygon) Subterranean Co.

MacAllan, Andrew. Diamond Hard. 672p. 1992. pap. 11.95 (0-7472-3513-9, Pub. by Headline Bk Pub) Trafalgar.

— Speculator. 608p. 1994. pap. 13.95 (0-7472-4181-3, Pub. by Headline Bk Pub) Trafalgar.

MacAllister, Carol L. Windows to My Soul: Reflections of an "Inner" Traveler. (Illus.). 100p. (Orig.). 1990. pap. 6.95 (0-9624856-0-8) Handsome Bks.

MacAllister, Dawson & Kimmel, Tim. Student Relationships, Vol. 3. (J). (gr. 5-12). 1981. pap., teacher ed. 6.95 (0-923417-19-2) Shepherd Minst.

MacAllister, Heather. Un Amour Capricieux. (Horizon Ser.). 1999. mass mkt. 3.50 (0-373-39515-9, 1-39515-1) Harlequin Bks.

— A Bachelor & the Babies: Bachelor Territory. (Romance Ser.: Vol. 3513). 1998. per. 3.50 (0-373-03513-6, 1-03513-8) Harlequin Bks.

— The Bachelor & the Babies: Bachelor Territory. large type ed. (Larger Print Ser.: Vol. 359). 1998. per. 3.50 (0-373-15759-2, 1-15759-3) Harlequin Bks.

Macallister, Heather. Bedded Bliss. (Promo Ser.). 1999. per. 4.50 (0-373-21984-9, 1-21984-9) Harlequin Bks.

MacAllister, Heather. Bedded Bliss (The Wrong Bed) (Temptation Ser.). 1996. per. 3.50 (0-373-25683-3, 1-25683-3) Harlequin Bks.

— The Boss & the Plain Jayne Bride. (Romance Ser.: No. 3555). 1999. per. 3.50 (0-373-03555-1, 1-03555-9, Harlequin) Harlequin Bks.

— The Boss & the Plain Jayne Bride. large type ed. (Larger Print Ser.: No. 401). 1999. per. 3.50 (0-373-15801-7, 1-15801-3, Harlequin) Harlequin Bks.

— Bride Overboard. (Temptation Ser.: No. 637). 1997. per. 3.50 (0-373-25737-6, 1-25737-7) Harlequin Bks.

***Macallister, Heather.** Un Celibataire pour Cadeau. (Rouge Passion Ser.: No. 540). (FRE.). 2000. mass mkt. 3.99 (0-373-37540-9, 1-37540-1, Harlequin French) Harlequin Bks.

MacAllister, Heather. Christmas Male. 1996. per. 3.50 (0-373-25716-3, 1-25716-1) Harlequin Bks.

— Un Fiance pour la Saint-Valentin. (Rouge Passion Ser.: No. 499). (FRE.). 1999. mass mkt. 3.50 (0-373-37499-2, 1-37499-0) Harlequin Bks.

***MacAllister, Heather.** The Good, the Bad & the Cuddly: Bachelors & Babies. (Harlequin Temptation Ser.). 1999. mass mkt. 3.75 (0-373-25857-7, Harlequin) Harlequin Bks.

MacAllister, Heather. Hand-Picked Husband: Texas Grooms Wanted! 1998. per. 3.50 (0-373-03535-7, 1-03535-1, Mira Bks) Harlequin Bks.

Macallister, Heather. Hand-Picked Husband: Texas Grooms Wanted! large type ed. Vol. 429. 253p. 1999. per. 3.50 (0-373-15829-7, 1-15829-4, Mira Bks) Harlequin Bks.

MacAllister, Heather. Hand-Picked Husband: Texas Grooms Wanted!, No. 381. large type ed. (Larger Print Ser.). 1999. mass mkt. 3.50 (0-373-15781-9, 1-15781-7) Harlequin Bks.

— Indomptable Sirene. (Rouge Passion Ser.: Bk. 491). 1999. mass mkt. 3.50 (0-373-37491-7, 1-37491-7) Harlequin Bks.

Macallister, Heather. Long Southern Nights. 1997. per. 3.50 (0-373-25756-2, 1-25756-7) Harlequin Bks.

MacAllister, Heather. Manhunting in Memphis. (Temptation Ser.: No. 669). 1998. per. 3.75 (0-373-25769-4, 1-25769-0) Harlequin Bks.

Macallister, Heather. Mr. December: (Mail Order Men) (Temptation Ser.: No. 711). 1998. per. 3.75 (0-373-25811-9, 1-25811-0) Harlequin Bks.

***MacAllister, Heather.** Moonlighting: Sweet Talkin' Guys. (Temptation Ser.: Bk. 785). 2000. per. 3.99 (0-373-25885-2, 1-25885-4) Harlequin Bks.

MacAllister, Heather. Papa a l'Essai. (Horizon Ser.: Vol. 501). (FRE.). 1999. mass mkt. 3.50 (0-373-39501-9, 1-39501-1) Harlequin Bks.

***MacAllister, Heather.** The Paternity Plan: Project: Pregnancy. (Romance Ser.: Bk. 3625). 2000. mass mkt. 3.50 (0-373-03625-6, 1-03625-4) Harlequin Bks.

MacAllister, Heather. The Rancher & the Rich Girl. (Heart of the West Ser.: Bk. 7). 1999. per. 4.50 (0-373-82591-9, 1-82591-8) Harlequin Bks.

MacAllister, Heather, et al. Temptation Blaze. (Promo Ser.). 1998. per. 5.99 (0-373-83369-5, 1-83369-8) Harlequin Bks.

Macallister, Heather, jt. auth. see Early, Margot.

MacAloon, John J. Brides of Victory: Nationalism & Gender in Olympic Ritual. 122p. 49.50 (0-85496-718-4) Berg Pubs.

— This Great Symbol: Pierre de Coubertin & the Origins of the Modern Olympic Games. LC 80-21898. (Illus.). xiv, 360p. (C). 1995. pap. text 12.00 (0-226-50001-2) U Ch Pr.

— This Great Symbol: Pierre de Coubertin & the Origins of the Modern Olympic Games. LC 80-21898. (Illus.). 381p. reprint ed. pap. 118.20 (0-608-09468-4, 205462800005) Bks Demand.

— This Great Symbol: Pierre De Courbertin & the Origins of the Modern Olympic Games. LC 80-21898. (C). 1992. lib. bdg. 28.00 (0-226-50000-4) U Ch Pr.

MacAloon, John J., ed. General Education in the Social Sciences: Centennial Reflections on the College of the University of Chicago. LC 91-42118. (Centennial Publication Ser.). 304p. 1992. pap. text 15.00 (0-226-50003-9) U Ch Pr.

— General Education in the Social Sciences: Centennial Reflections on the College of the University of Chicago. LC 91-42118. (Centennial Publication Ser.). 304p. 1992. lib. bdg. 48.50 (0-226-50002-0) U Ch Pr.

MacAlpin, Miles. Book of the Living: A Handbook of Self-Directed Consciousness. 1989. pap. 7.00 (0-913004-65-0) Point Loma Pub.

Macalpine. Inside Kidvid. 1999. pap. write for info. (0-670-84690-2) Viking Penguin.

Macalpine, Ida, jt. auth. see Hunter, Richard.

Macaluso, Christelle. God Knows Best about Joy: Biblical Reflections to Lift up the Heart. LC 98-96129. xi, 170p. 1998. pap. 9.95 (0-9663462-0-3) Fun Nun.

Macaluso, Donald G. The Financial Advantage of Multinational Firm During Tight Credit Periods in Host Countries. Bruchey, Stuart, ed. LC 80-582. (Multinational Corporations Ser.). 1981. lib. bdg. 19.95 (0-405-13374-X) Ayer.

Macaluso, Gregory J. Morris, Orange & King William Artillery. (Virginia Regimental Histories Ser.). (Illus.). 122p. 1991. 19.95 (1-56190-011-7) H E Howard.

***Macaluso, Mary C.** One-Liners from God: Biblical Affirmations to Lift up the Heart. LC 99-90612. xi, 170p. 1999. pap. 9.95 (0-9663462-1-1) Fun Nun.

Macaluso, Nora, ed. see Pendlum, David W.

Macaluso, Pamela. Christmas Wedding. 1995. per. 3.25 (0-373-05970-1, 1-05970-8) Silhouette.

— The Cowboy Who Came in from the Cold. 1998. per. 3.75 (0-373-76152-X, 1-76152-7) Silhouette.

— Dream Wedding: (Just Married) (Desire Ser.). 1995. per. 3.25 (0-373-05928-0, 1-05928-6) Silhouette.

— Hometown Wedding. (Desire Ser.). 1994. per. 2.99 (0-373-05897-7, 1-05897-3) Silhouette.

***Macaluso, Pamela.** Intima Atraccion: The Cowboy Who Came in from the Cold. (Deseo Ser.: No. 149).Tr. of Close Attraction. (SPA.). 1999. per. 3.50 (0-373-35279-4, 1-35279-8) Harlequin Bks.

Macaluso, Pamela. The Loneliest Cowboy. 1997. per. 3.50 (0-373-76048-5, 1-76048-7) Silhouette.

— Noviazgo Fingido (False Engagement), No. 136. (Harlequin Deseo Ser.). (SPA.). 1998. mass mkt. 3.50 (0-373-35266-2, 1-35266-5) Harlequin Bks.

— Solo un Hombre - Just a Man. (SPA.). 1997. per. 3.50 (0-373-35195-X, 1-35195-6) Harlequin Bks.

Macalypse The Younger. Principia Discordia: or How I Found Goddess & What I Did to Her When I Found Her. 1976. lib. bdg. 250.00 (0-685-75085-X) Revisionist Pr.

***Macan, Darko.** Vader's Quest. (Star Wars Ser.). (Illus.). (J). 2000. pap. 11.95 (1-56971-415-0) Dark Horse Comics.

Macan, Edward L. Rocking the Classics: English Progressive Rock & the Counterculture. (Illus.). 320p. 1997. pap. 17.95 (0-19-509888-9); text 49.95 (0-19-509887-0) OUP.

Macan, T. T. A Key to the Adults of the British Trichoptera. 1973. 35.00 (0-900386-19-3) St Mut.

— A Key to the British Fresh - And Brackish-Water Gastropods. 4th ed. 1977. 30.00 (0-900386-30-4) St Mut.

— A Key to the Nymphs of British Ephemeroptera. 3rd ed. 1979. 50.00 (0-900386-35-5) St Mut.

— A Revised Key to the British Water Bugs (Hempitera-Heteroptera) 2nd ed. 1976. 45.00 (0-900386-07-X) St Mut.

Macan, T. T., ed. Symposium: Factors That Regulate the Sizes of Natural Populations in Fresh Water. (International Association of Theoretical & Applied Limnology, Communications Ser.: No. 13). (Illus.). 211p. (Orig.). 1965. pap. 31.00 (3-510-52013-0, Pub. by E Schweizerbartsche) Balogh.

Macan, Thomas T. Freshwater Ecology. 2nd ed. LC 75-300630. (Longman Text Ser.). (Illus.). 351p. reprint ed. pap. 108.90 (0-8357-6121-5, 203450700090) Bks Demand.

MacAndrew, A. R., tr. see Babel, Isaac.

MacAndrew, Andrew R. Diary of a Madman & Other Stories. 1961. mass mkt. 5.95 (0-451-52403-9, CE1824, Sig Classics) NAL.

MacAndrew, Andrew R., tr. see Dostoyevsky, Fyodor.

MacAndrew, Elizabeth. The Gothic Tradition in Fiction. LC 79-9447. 303p. reprint ed. pap. 86.40 (0-685-20374-3, 2029829) Bks Demand.

MacAndrew, Jane, et al. Strange Worlds, Fantastic Places. LC 97-38045. (The Earth, Its Wonders, Its Secrets Ser.). 160p. 1997. write for info. (0-7621-0071-0) RD Assn.

MacAndrew, Marie-Christine, ed. see Zaleski, Eugene.

MacAndrew, Ronald, ed. see Patterson, William R.

MacAndrews, Colin. Land Policy in Modern Indonesia: A Study of Land Issues in the New Order Period. LC 86-5144. (Lincoln Institute of Land Policy Bk.). (Illus.). 127p. reprint ed. pap. 39.40 (0-7837-5764-6, 204542700006) Bks Demand.

***MacAnghaill, Mairtin.** Contemporary Racisms & Ethnicities: Social & Cultural Transformations. LC 98-49830. (Sociology & Social Change Ser.). 1999. pap. 26.95 (0-335-19672-1) OpUniv Pr.

MacAninch, Jack W., jt. auth. see Tanagho, Emil A.

Macann, Christopher E. Four Phenomenological Philosophers: Hesserl, Heidegger, Sartre, Merleau-Ponty. LC 93-16569. 240p. (C). 1993. pap. 20.99 (0-415-07354-5) Routledge.

— Presence & Coincidence: The Transformation of Transcendental into Ontological Phenomenology. 152p. (C). 1991. lib. bdg. 102.00 (0-7923-0923-5, Pub. by Kluwer Academic) Kluwer Academic.

Macann, Christopher E., ed. Martin Heidegger: Critical Assessments, 4 vols., Set. LC 91-46751. (Illus.). 1472p. (C). (gr. 13). 1992. text, boxed set 655.00 (0-415-04982-2, A7593) Routledge.

Macann, Christopher E., ed. see Heidegger, Martin.

Macansantos, Francis C. The Words & Other Poems. LC 97-947031. (Philippine Writers Ser.). 168 p. 1997. write for info. (971-542-156-3) U of Philippines Pr.

MacAoidh, Aonghus. Manuscript of Dove, Vol. 1. 186p. 1992. pap. 34.00 (0-685-62622-9) A MacRaonuill.

— Manuscript of Dove, Vol. 2. 200p. 1992. pap. 36.00 (0-685-62623-7) A MacRaonuill.

— Manuscript of Dove, Vol. 3. 162p. 1992. pap. 30.00 (0-685-66249-7) A MacRaonuill.

MacAoidh, Caoimhin. Between the Jigs & the Reels: The Donegal Fiddle Tradition. LC 94-229031. (Illus.). 320p. 1994. pap. 21.95 (1-873437-08-0, Pub. by Drumlin Pubns Ltd) Irish Bks Media.

MacAonghas, Pol. An Guth Aoibhneach. (C). 1993. pap. 36.00 (0-85411-054-2, Pub. by Saltire Soc) St Mut.

***MacAonghuis, Iain & O'Maolalaigh, Roibeard.** Hugo Scottish Gaelic in Three Months: Simplified Language Course. LC 98-48004. (Hugo Ser.). (GAE & ENG.). 1999. 24.95 incl. audio (0-7894-4439-9) DK Pub Inc.

MacAormick, Neil, jt. ed. see Amselek, Paul.

Macapagal, Lawrence. The Last Laugh. 324p. (Orig.). 1996. mass mkt. 5.99 (0-9655332-0-4) Bravo Pr CA.

Macar, Francoise, et al, eds. Time, Action & Cognition Towards Bridging the Gap: Proceedings of the NATO Advanced Research Workshop, Held in St. Malo, France, 22-25 October, 1991. LC 92-10966. (NATO Advanced Study Institutes Series D, Behavioural & Social Sciences: No. 66). 432p. (C). 1992. lib. bdg. 218.00 (0-7923-1783-1, Pub. by Kluwer Academic) Kluwer Academic.

Macaraeg, Doug. Nibbles: Schoolbound. (Illus.). 22p. (J). (gr. k-3). 1997. pap. 6.95 (0-9666833-0-7) Coconut Works.

Macaranas, Natividad. Bravely They Fought. 344p. 1997. pap. 12.95 (1-57087-323-2) Prof Pr NC.

Macaraya, Batua A., jt. auth. see McKaughan, Howard P.

Macardle, Donald W., jt. auth. see Schindler, Anton F.

MacArdle, Donald W., tr. see Beethoven, Ludwig van.

Macardle, Dorothy. The Unforeseen. reprint ed. lib. bdg. 23.95 (0-89190-113-2, Rivercity Pr) Amereon Ltd.

— The Uninvited. adapted ed. 1979. pap. 5.25 (0-8222-1196-3) Dramatists Play.

— The Uninvited. 342p. 1976. reprint ed. lib. bdg. 25.95 (0-89244-068-6, Queens House) Amereon Ltd.

Macardle, Melanie T. Biotechnology: Index of Modern Information. LC 88-47996. 150p. 1990. 47.50 (1-55914-230-8); pap. 44.50 (1-55914-231-6) ABBE Pubs Assn.

Macaree, David. Daniel Defoe: His Political Writings & Literary Devices. LC 90-25038. (Studies in British Literature: Vol. 14). 164p. 1991. lib. bdg. 79.95 (0-88946-590-8) E Mellen.

Macaree, David, jt. auth. see MacAree, Mary.

MacAree, Mary & Macaree, David. 103 Hikes in Southwestern British Columbia. 4th ed. 224p. 1994. pap. 14.95 (0-89886-395-3) Mountaineers.

***Macari, Anne Marie.** Ivory Cradle. 96p. 2000. pap. 14.00 (0-9663395-5-X) Amer Poet.

— Ivory Cradle. 96p. 2000. 23.00 (0-9663395-4-1, Pub. by Amer Poet); pap. 14.00 (0-9663395-6-8, Pub. by Amer Poet) Copper Canyon.

Macari, Emir J., et al, eds. Geo-Environmental Issues Facing the Americas: Proceedings of a Workshop. LC 95-34324. 205p. 1995. 28.00 (0-7844-0098-9) Am Soc Civil Eng.

Macari, Emir J. & Saunders, F. Michael, eds. Environmental Quality, Innovative Technologies, & Sustainable Economic Development: A NAFTA Perspective. LC 97-157. 168p. 1997. 20.00 (0-7844-0224-8) Am Soc Civil Eng.

Macari, Mario, jt. auth. see Tally, Taz.

***Macario, Carla, et al.** Export Growth in Latin America: Policies & Performance. LC 00-28260. 200p. 2000. lib. bdg. 49.95 (1-55587-759-1) L Rienner.

Macario, Raymond C. Cellular Radio. 2nd rev. ed. (Telecommunications Ser.). (Illus.). 276p. 1997. 50.00 (0-07-044433-1) McGraw.

Macario, Raymond C., ed. Modern Personal Radio Systems. LC 96-140440. (I. E. E. Telecommunications Ser.: No. 33). (Illus.). 336p. 1995. boxed set 92.00 (0-85296-861-2) INSPEC Inc.

Macario, Raymond C., jt. ed. see Balston, D. M.

Macarius. Fifty Spiritual Homilies. 1974. reprint ed. 12.50 (0-89981-035-7) Eastern Orthodox.

Macarius, Staretz, jt. auth. see Marcarius Starets of Optina.

Macaro, E. A. Radio France. 1985. pap. text 9.63 (0-582-35400-5, 72218); audio 16.96 (0-582-37684-X, 72581) Longman.

Macaro, Ernesto. Target Language, Collaborative Learning & Autonomy. LC 96-33004. (Modern Languages in Practice Ser.). 220p. 1997. 85.00 (1-85359-369-9, Pub. by Multilingual Matters); pap. 29.95 (1-85359-368-0, Pub. by Multilingual Matters) Taylor & Francis.

Macarov, David. Certain Change: Social Work Practice in the Future. LC 90-27568. 185p. 1991. pap. 21.95 (0-87101-191-3) Natl Assn Soc Wkrs.

— Incentives to Work. LC 71-110629. (Jossey-Bass Behavioral Science Ser.). 270p. reprint ed. 83.70 (0-8357-9326-5, 201382900087) Bks Demand.

— The Structure of Social Welfare. 344p. 1995. text 52.00 (0-8039-4939-1); pap. text 25.50 (0-8039-4940-5) Sage.

MacArov, David, jt. auth. see Dixon, John.

Macarow, Leo. New Math - Or New Myth? LC 81-90343. 70p. 1981. pap. text 4.95 (0-9606994-1-4) Greenview Pubns.

Macarro, Luis N., jt. ed. see Lopez, Antonio C.

MacArtain, Aonghus. Manuscript by Aonghus MacArtain. 105p. 1992. pap. 19.00 (0-685-67869-5) A MacRaonuill.

Macarther Study Staff. MacArthur Study Bible, 1. 1998. 49.99 (0-8499-5421-5) Word Pub.

Macarthue, John F. Glory of Heaven. 1997. pap. 9.99 (1-85792-299-9, Pub. by Christian Focus) Spring Arbor Dist.

MacArthur, A. Anton Rubinstein. 1971. 35.00 (0-87968-650-2) Gordon Pr.

MacArthur, Antonia. His Majesty's Bark Endeavour. LC 97-166099. (Illus.). 86p. 1998. pap. 14.95 (0-207-19180-8) HarpC.

MacArthur, Barbara. Canten Navidad. (ENG & SPA., Illus.). 15p. (Orig.). (J). (ps-12). 1993. pap. 12.95 incl. audio (1-881120-09-0) Frog Pr WI.

— Chantez Noel. (ENG & FRE., Illus.). 14p. (J). (ps-12). 1993. pap. 12.95 incl. audio (1-881120-10-4) Frog Pr WI.

— Sing, Dance, Laugh & Eat Cheeseburgers. (Illus.). 35p. (Orig.). (J). (ps-12). 1992. pap. 17.95 incl. audio (1-881120-06-6) Frog Pr WI.

— Sing, Dance, Laugh & Eat Quiche. rev. ed. (FRE., Illus.). 35p. (J). (ps-12). 1990. reprint ed. pap. 15.88 incl. audio (1-881120-00-7) Frog Pr WI.

— Sing, Dance, Laugh & Eat Quiche 3. (ENG & FRE., Illus.). 35p. (Orig.). (J). (ps-12). 1992. pap. 15.88 incl. audio (1-881120-07-4) Frog Pr WI.

— Sing, Dance, Laugh & Eat Quiche 2. (ENG & FRE., Illus.). 35p. (Orig.). (J). (ps-12). 1989. pap. text 15.88 incl. audio (1-881120-01-5) Frog Pr WI.

— Sing, Dance, Laugh & Eat Tacos. (ENG & SPA., Illus.). 35p. (Orig.). (J). (ps-12). 1990. pap. text 15.88 incl. audio (1-881120-04-X) Frog Pr WI.

— Sing, Dance, Laugh & Eat Tacos 3. (ENG & SPA., Illus.). 35p. (J). (ps-12). 1993. pap. 15.88 incl. audio (1-881120-13-9) Frog Pr WI.

— Sing, Dance, Laugh & Eat Tacos 2. (ENG & SPA., Illus.). 36p. (Orig.). (J). (ps-12). 1991. pap. text 15.88 incl. audio (1-881120-05-8) Frog Pr WI.

— Sing, Dance, Laugh & Learn German. (ENG & GER., Illus.). 18p. (Orig.). (J). (ps-12). 1993. pap. 12.95 incl. audio (1-881120-11-2) Frog Pr WI.

— Sing, Dance, Laugh & Learn Spanish. (ENG & SPA., Illus.). 18p. (Orig.). (J). (ps-12). 1993. pap. 12.95 incl. audio (1-881120-08-2) Frog Pr WI.

— Singen Weihnachten. (ENG & GER., Illus.). 14p. (Orig.). (J). (ps-12). 1993. pap. 12.95 incl. audio (1-881120-12-0) Frog Pr WI.

MacArthur, Blair. The Love Formula: A Unique Way to Evaluate Your Love Partner. 2nd ed. 287p. 1990. 15.95 (0-944052-00-2) Cayman Isle Ent.

MacArthur, Brian. Historical Speeches. 1997. pap. 13.95 (0-14-017619-5) Viking Penguin.

***MacArthur, Brian.** Penguin Book of Twentieth Century Speeches. 525p. 2000. pap. 15.95 (0-14-028500-8) Viking Penguin.

MacArthur, Brian. Requiem: Diana, Princess of Wales, 1961-1997, Memories & Tributes. LC 97-77561. 1997. 22.95 (1-55970-442-X, Pub. by Arcade Pub Inc) Time Warner.

MacArthur, Brian, ed. The Penguin Book of 20th-Century Speeches. 512p. (C). 1994. pap. 15.95 (0-14-023234-6) Viking Penguin.

— Requiem: Diana, Princess of Wales, 1961-1997: Memories & Tributes. 224p. 1998. pap. 13.45 (1-55970-456-X, Pub. by Arcade Pub Inc) Time Warner.

MacArthur, Catherine. The Flight of the Dove. large type ed. 341p. 1982. 27.99 (0-7089-0791-1) Ulverscroft.

— George's Women. large type ed. 283p. 1980. 27.99 (0-7089-0451-3) Ulverscroft.

— It Was the Lark. large type ed. 1979. 27.99 (0-7089-0370-3) Ulverscroft.

MacArthur, D. A., jt. ed. see Ho, K. C.

MacArthur, David. Tasting It. (Illus.). 104p. (Orig.). 1984. pap. 9.95 (0-9612674-0-2) Wine Country.

MacArthur, E. Mairi. Columba's Island: Iona from Past to Present. (Illus.). 220p. 1996. pap. 23.00 (0-7486-0737-4, Pub. by Edinburgh U Pr) Col U Pr.

— Iona Island Guide. (Scotland's Island Guides Ser.). (Illus.). 128p. 1997. 19.95 (1-900455-11-0, Pub. by Colin Baxter Ltd) Voyageur Pr.

MacArthur, Elizabeth, tr. see Serres, Michael.

MacArthur, Elizabeth J. Extravagant Narratives: Closure & Dynamics in the Epistolary Form. 299p. 1990. text 45.00 (0-691-06793-7, Pub. by Princeton U Pr) Cal Prin Full Svc.

MacArthur, Erika. Precious Little One, 1. 1998. 20.00 (1-58134-001-X) Crossway Bks.

MacArthur, John. Alone with God. 192p. 1995. pap. 9.99 (1-56476-488-5, 6-3488, Victor Bks) Chariot Victor.

MacArthur, John, Jr. Anxiety Attacked. LC 93-3721. (MacArthur Study Ser.). (Illus.). 192p. (Orig.). 1993. pap. 9.99 (1-56476-128-2, 6-3128, Victor Bks) Chariot Victor.

MacArthur, John. The Body Dynamic: How in the World Is the Church to Work? LC 96-228000. 192p. 1996. pap. 9.99 (1-56476-586-5, Victor Bks) Chariot Victor.

— The Charismatics: A Doctrinal Perspective LC 78-5297. 224 p. 1978. write for info. (0-310-28490-2) Zondervan.

— Different by Design. LC 94-22011. 192p. (Orig.). 1994. pap. 9.99 (1-56476-247-5, 6-3247, Victor Bks) Chariot Victor.

***MacArthur, John.** Ephesians. (MacArthur Bible Study Guides Ser.). 2000. pap. 7.99 (0-8499-5541-6) Word Pub.

MacArthur, John. First Love. LC 94-41137. (MacArthur Study Ser.). 208p. (Orig.). 1995. pap. 9.99 (1-56476-334-X, Victor Bks) Chariot Victor.

***MacArthur, John.** 1 Samuel. (MacArthur Bible Study Guides Ser.). 2000. pap. 7.99 (0-8499-5538-6) Word Pub.

Macarthur, John, Jr. Found God's Will. 64p. 1977. pap. 3.50 (0-88207-503-9, 6-2503, Victor Bks) Chariot Victor.

MacArthur, John. Found: God's Will: Find the Direction & Purpose God Wants for Your Life. LC 98-164392. 1998. pap. text 3.99 (1-56476-740-X, Victor Bks) Chariot Victor.

— The Freedom & Power of Forgiveness. LC 98-11274. 256p. 1998. 19.99 (0-89107-979-3) Crossway Bks.

An Asterisk (*) at the beginning of an entry indicates that the title is appearing for the first time.

MacArthur, John, Jr. God: Coming to Face with His Majesty. (MacArthur Study Ser.). 192p. (Orig.). 1993. pap. 9.99 (*1-56476-071-5*, 6-3071, Victor Bks) Chariot Victor.

— God's High Calling for Women. (John MacArthur Bible Study Ser.). pap. 6.99 (*0-8024-5308-2*, 155) Moody.

***MacArthur, John.** Gospel According to the Apostles: The Role of Works in the Life of Faith. 2000. pap. 12.99 (*0-8499-4212-8*) Word Pub.

MacArthur, John. How to Get the Most From God's Word. LC 97-27916. 1997. 10.99 (*0-8499-4093-1*) Word Pub.

MacArthur, John, Jr. How to Meet the Enemy. (MacArthur Study Ser.). 216p. (Orig.). 1992. pap. 9.99 (*1-56476-016-2*, 6-3016, Victor Bks) Chariot Victor.

— How to Study the Bible. (John MacArthur Bible Study Ser.). pap. 6.99 (*0-8024-5105-5*, 174) Moody.

MacArthur, John. How to Study the Bible. 1997. pap. 15.99 (*0-8499-1529-5*) Word Pub.

***MacArthur, John.** I Believe in Jesus: Leading Your Child to Christ. LC 99-462432. (Illus.). (J). 1999. write for info. (*0-8499-7541-7*) Tommy Nelson.

MacArthur, John. I Believe in Jesus: Leading Your Child to Christ. LC 99-23599. (Illus.). 32p. (J). 1999. 12.99 (*0-8499-7511-5*) Tommy Nelson.

MacArthur, John, Jr. James. LC 99-173615. (MacArthur New Testament Commentary Ser.). 1998. 21.99 (*0-8024-0900-8*) Moody.

MacArthur, John. MacArthur Study Bible. 1998. 69.99 (*0-8499-1562-7*) Word Pub.

***MacArthur, John.** MacArthur Topical Bible. 1632p. 1999. 34.99 (*0-8499-1572-4*) Word Pub.

— Mark. (MacArthur Bible Study Guides Ser.). 2000. pap. 7.99 (*0-8499-5539-4*) Word Pub.

MacArthur, John, Jr. The Master's Plan for the Church. pap. 12.99 (*0-8024-7841-7*, 213) Moody.

— Matthew 8-15. 1986. 23.99 (*0-88469-172-1*) BMH Bks.

***MacArthur, John.** Murder of Jesus, 1. 320p. 2000. 19.99 (*0-8499-1554-6*) J Countryman.

— The Murder of Jesus: A Study of How Jesus Died. LC 00-20515. 2000. write for info. (*0-8499-6303-6*) Word Pub.

— Murder of Jesus: EZ Lesson Plan. (Illus.). 2000. 39.99 (*0-8499-8796-2*) Word Pub.

— Murder of Jesus: Student's Guide. (Illus.). (J). 2000. pap. 7.99 (*0-8499-8797-0*) Word Pub.

MacArthur, John. Our Sufficiency in Christ. LC 98-20910. 1998. 12.99 (*1-58134-013-3*) Crossway Bks.

MacArthur, John, Jr. Philippians. 2000. 12.99 (*0-8024-5262-0*) Moody.

MacArthur, John. The Power of Suffering: LGI. (MacArthur Study Ser.: No. 7). 192p. 1995. pap. 9.99 (*1-56476-429-X*, 6-3429, Victor Bks) Chariot Victor.

MacArthur, John, Jr. Rediscovering Pastoral Ministry. LC 95-6452. (MacArthur Resource Library). 400p. 1995. 24.99 (*0-8499-1092-7*) Word Pub.

— Revelations 1-11. (MacArthur New Testament Commentary Ser.). 344p. 1999. 21.99 (*0-8024-0773-0*) Moody.

***MacArthur, John.** Revelation 12-22. 2000. 23.99 (*0-8024-0774-9*) Moody.

— Romans. (MacArthur Bible Study Guides Ser.). 2000. pap. 7.99 (*0-8499-5540-8*) Word Pub.

MacArthur, John, Jr. Romans 9-16. (MacArthur New Testament Commentaries Ser.). 23.99 (*0-8024-0768-4*, 507) Moody.

— Saved Without a Doubt. (MacArthur Study Ser.). 192p. (Orig.). 1992. pap. 9.99 (*1-56476-017-0*, 6-3017, Victor Bks) Chariot Victor.

MacArthur, John. Silent Shepherd. LC 96-18173. 168p. 1996. 9.99 (*1-56476-579-2*, 6-3579) Chariot Victor.

— Spiritual Warfare: Fighting to Win. 75p. 1989. pap. 3.95 (*0-318-42572-6*) Grace You.

— Successful Christian Parenting, Vol. 1. (Successful Christian Parents Ser.). 300p. 1999. pap. 12.99 (*0-8499-3775-2*) Word Pubng.

— Successful Christian Parenting: Raising Your Child with Care, Compassion, & Common Sense. LC 98-50176. 240p. 1999. 19.99 (*0-8499-1082-X*) Word Pub.

MacArthur, John, Jr. The Ultimate Priority. pap. 10.99 (*0-8024-0186-4*, 307) Moody.

MacArthur, John. The Vanishing Conscience. 1995. pap. 10.99 (*0-8499-3678-0*) Word Pub.

***MacArthur, John.** What the Bible Says about Parenting, 1. 180p. 2000. pap. text 14.99 (*0-8499-4202-0*); pap. text 10.99 (*0-8499-4203-9*); pap. text 99.99 (*0-8499-8806-3*) J Countryman.

— Whose Money Is It Anyway? A Biblical Guide to Using God's Wealth. LC 00-26813. 224p. 2000. pap. write for info. (*0-8499-5554-8*) Word Pub.

MacArthur, John, ed. MacArthur Study Bible. 1998. 89.99 (*0-8499-1563-5*); 69.99 (*0-8499-5422-3*); lthr. 129.99 (*0-8499-5423-1*) Word Pub.

MacArthur, John, Jr. & MacArthur, John F. Charismatic Chaos. 1992. 14.99 incl. audio (*0-310-57578-8*) Zondervan.

MacArthur, John, et al. Onward Christian Soldiers: Protestants Affirm the Church. 309p. 1999. pap. 16.95 (*1-57358-102-X*) Soli Deo Gloria.

MacArthur, John D. & Weiss, John. Agriculture, Projects & Development: Papers in Honour of David Edwards. 400p. 1994. 82.95 (*1-85628-647-9*, Pub. by Avebry) Ashgate Pub Co.

***MacArthur, John F.** Acts. (MacArthur Bible Study Guides Ser.: Vol. 7). 128p. 2000. pap. 7.99 (*0-8499-5544-0*) Word Pub.

MacArthur, John F., Jr. Ashamed of the Gospel: When the Church Becomes Like the World. LC 93-23849. 1993. 17.99 (*0-89107-729-4*) Crossway Bks.

MacArthur, John F. Ashamed of the Gospel: When the Church Becomes Like the World. 254p. 1999. reprint ed. pap. 12.99 (*1-58134-077-X*) Crossway Bks.

— Los Carismaticos: Una Perspectiva Doctrinal.Tr. of Charismatic Chaos. (SPA.). 1994. 15.50 (*0-311-09069-9*) Casa Bautista.

Macarthur, John F. Charismatic Chaos: Signs & Wonders; Speaking in Tongues; Health, Wealth & Prosperity. 432p. 1993. mass mkt. 5.99 (*0-310-57572-9*) Zondervan.

MacArthur, John F. The Charismatics. 1980. pap. 9.99 (*0-310-28491-0*, 12645P) Zondervan.

Macarthur, John F. Christmas Celebrations. 1993. 4.99 (*0-310-96264-1*) Zondervan.

— Colossians-Philemon. 1992. 19.99 (*0-88469-236-1*) BMH Bks.

MacArthur, John F., Jr. Cuidado con los Falaces!Tr. of Beware the Pretenders. (SPA.). 96p. 1992. pap. 3.99 (*0-8254-1453-9*, Edit Portavoz) Kregel.

***MacArthur, John F.** Daniel. (MacArthur Bible Study Guides Ser.: Vol. 5). 128p. 2000. pap. 7.99 (*0-8499-5542-4*) Word Pub.

MacArthur, John F., Jr. Drawing Near: Daily Readings for a Deeper Faith. LC 93-5469. 384p. 1993. 17.99 (*0-89107-758-8*) Crossway Bks.

— Ephesians. 1986. 23.99 (*0-88469-171-3*) BMH Bks.

— El Evangelio Segun Jesucristo. DeBustamante, Rafael C., tr. from ENG.Tr. of Gospel According to Jesus. (SPA.). 256p. (Orig.). 1991. pap. 8.99 (*0-311-09138-5*) Casa Bautista.

***MacArthur, John F.** A Faith to Grow on. 192p. (J). (gr. k up). 2000. 14.99 (*0-8499-7512-3*) Tommy Nelson.

— 1 & 2 Peter. (MacArthur Bible Study Guides Ser.: Vol. 8). 128p. 2000. pap. 7.99 (*0-8499-5545-9*) Word Pub.

Macarthur, John F. First Corinthians. 1984. 23.99 (*0-88469-161-6*) BMH Bks.

***MacArthur, John F.** Galatians. (MacArthur Bible Study Guides Ser.: Vol. 10). 128p. 2000. pap. 7.99 (*0-8499-5547-5*) Word Pub.

Macarthur, John F. Glory of Heaven: The Truth about Heaven, Angels & Eternal Life. 1998. pap. 12.99 (*1-58134-034-6*) Crossway Bks.

— God with Us. 144p. 1989. 12.99 (*0-310-28690-5*) Zondervan.

MacArthur, John F., Jr. Gospel According to Jesus. 1989. pap. 12.99 (*0-310-28651-4*) Zondervan.

MacArthur, John F. The Gospel According to Jesus: Salvation Without Obedience? 272p. 1988. 14.95 (*0-310-28650-6*, 12646) Zondervan.

MacArthur, John F., Jr. The Gospel According to Jesus: What Does Jesus Mean When He Says "Follow Me" exp. rev. ed. 304p. 1994. 14.99 (*0-310-39491-0*) Zondervan.

— Hebrews. 1983. 21.99 (*0-88469-155-1*) BMH Bks.

MacArthur, John F. In the Footsteps of Faith: Lessons From the Lives of Great Men & Women of the Bible. LC 98-34849. 192p. 1998. pap. text 10.99 (*1-58134-019-2*) Crossway Bks.

***MacArthur, John F.** John. (MacArthur Bible Study Guides Ser.: Vol. 6). 128p. 2000. pap. 7.99 (*0-8499-5543-2*) Word Pub.

***MacArthur, John F., Jr.** La Libertad y el Poder del Perdon. (SPA.). 256p. 1999. pap. 9.99 (*0-8254-1469-5*, Edit Portavoz) Kregel.

MacArthur, John F., Jr. Matthew One-Seven. 1985. 23.99 (*0-88469-168-3*) BMH Bks.

MacArthur, John F. Nothing but the Truth: Defending the Gospel in a Disturbing Age. LC 99-37022. 192p. 1999. pap. 10.99 (*1-58134-090-7*) Crossway Bks.

MacArthur, John F., Jr. Una Nueva Mirada a la Consejeria Biblica.Tr. of Introduction to Biblical Counselling. (SPA.). 384p. 1996. 13.99 (*0-89922-572-1*, C008-5721) Caribe Betania.

MacArthur, John F. The Pillars of Christian Character: The Basic Essentials of a Living Faith. LC 98-16146. 192p. 1998. pap. 10.99 (*0-89107-950-5*) Crossway Bks.

***MacArthur, John F., Jr.** El Poder de la Integridad. (SPA.). 192p. 1999. pap. 8.99 (*0-8254-1468-7*, Edit Portavoz) Kregel.

MacArthur, John F. The Power of Integrity: Building a Life Without Compromise. LC 97-7861. 192p. 1997. pap. 10.99 (*0-89107-942-4*) Crossway Bks.

MacArthur, John F., Jr. Reckless Faith: When the Church Loses It's Will to Discern. LC 94-39874. 256p. 1994. 17.99 (*0-89107-793-6*) Crossway Bks.

MacArthur, John F. El Redescubrimiento de la Predicacion Expositiva.Tr. of Rediscovering Expository Preaching. (ENG & SPA.). 400p. 1995. pap. text 18.99 (*0-89922-528-4*) Caribe Betania.

***MacArthur, John F.** Ruth & Esther. (MacArthur Bible Study Guides Ser.: Vol. 9). 128p. 2000. pap. 7.99 (*0-8499-5546-7*) Word Pub.

MacArthur, John F. The Second Coming: Signs of Christ's Return & the End of the Age. LC 99-30666. 239p. 1999. 19.99 (*1-58134-121-0*) Crossway Bks.

MacArthur, John F., Jr. Strength for Today: Daily Readings for a Deeper Faith. LC 97-29635. 1997. 19.99 (*0-89107-969-6*) Crossway Bks.

***MacArthur, John F.** Why Government Can't Save You: An Alternative to Political Activism. 200p. 2000. pap. 12.99 (*0-8499-5555-6*) Word Pub.

MacArthur, John F., Jr., ed. The MacArthur Study Bible. (Illus.). 2200p. 1997. bond lthr. 59.99 (*0-8499-1223-7*) Word Pub.

MacArthur, John F., jt. auth. see MacArthur, John, Jr.

MacArthur, John F., Jr., jt. auth. see Master's Seminary Faculty Staff.

MacArthur, John J., Jr. Acts 1-12. (MacArthur New Testament Commentaries Ser.). 21.99 (*0-8024-0759-5*, 504) Moody.

— Acts 13-28. LC 97-157582. (MacArthur New Testament Commentaries Ser.). 23.99 (*0-8024-0760-9*, 505) Moody.

MacArthur, John J., Jr. Colossians & Philemon. (MacArthur New Testament Commentaries Ser.). 19.99 (*0-8024-0761-7*, 511) Moody.

— Ephesians. (MacArthur New Testament Commentaries Ser.). 23.99 (*0-8024-2358-2*, 510) Moody.

— First Corinthians. (MacArthur New Testament Commentaries Ser.). 23.99 (*0-8024-0754-4*, 508) Moody.

— First Timothy. LC 96-202657. (MacArthur New Testament Commentaries Ser.). 21.99 (*0-8024-0756-0*, 512) Moody.

— Galatians. (MacArthur New Testament Commentaries Ser.). 19.99 (*0-8024-0762-5*, 509) Moody.

— Hebrews. (MacArthur New Testament Commentaries Ser.). 23.99 (*0-8024-0753-6*, 515) Moody.

— MacArthur New Testament Commentary Series, 9 bks., Set. 174.91 (*0-8024-7587-6*) Moody.

— Matthew 8-15. (MacArthur New Testament Commentaries Ser.). 23.99 (*0-8024-0763-3*, 501) Moody.

— Matthew 1-7. (MacArthur New Testament Commentaries Ser.). 23.99 (*0-8024-0755-2*, 500) Moody.

— Matthew 16-23. (MacArthur New Testament Commentaries Ser.). 23.99 (*0-8024-0764-1*, 502) Moody.

— Matthew 24-28. (MacArthur New Testament Commentary Ser.). 1989. 21.99 (*0-8024-0765-X*) Moody.

— Romans 1-8. (MacArthur New Testament Commentaries Ser.). 23.99 (*0-8024-0767-6*, 506) Moody.

— Second Timothy. LC 95-219887. (MacArthur New Testament Commentaries Ser.). 19.99 (*0-8024-0757-9*, 513) Moody.

— Titus. LC 96-200716. (MacArthur New Testament Commentaries Ser.). 19.99 (*0-8024-0758-7*, 514) Moody.

MacArthur, John Jr. The Gospel According to Jesus: What Does Jesus Mean When He Says "Follow Me" 1994. 14.99 incl. audio (*0-310-39498-8*) Zondervan.

MacArthur, John R. Second Front: Censorship & Propaganda in the Gulf War. 224p. 1992. 20.00 (*0-8090-8517-8*) Hill & Wang.

— Second Front: Censorship & Propaganda in the Gulf War. LC 93-19604. 1993. reprint ed. 15.95 (*0-520-08398-9*, Pub. by U CA Pr) Cal Prin Full Svc.

***MacArthur, John R.** The Selling of "Free Trade" NAFTA, Washington & the Subversion of American Democracy. LC 99-55541. 368p. 2000. text 25.00 (*0-8090-8531-3*) Hill & Wang.

MacArthur, John R., ed. The MacArthur Study Bible. (Illus.). 1997. cd-rom 39.99 (*0-8499-5335-9*) Word Pub.

MacArthur, Jr., John. The Only Way to Happiness. LC 98-209031. (Foundations of the Faith: The Beatitudes Ser.). 1998. pap. 8.99 (*0-8024-3054-6*) Moody.

***MacArthur, Loren.** Audubon Guide to National Wildlife Refuges: California & Hi. (Illus.). 240p. 2000. pap. 19.95 (*0-312-20689-5*) St Martin.

***MacArthur, Loren & Miller, Debbie S.** The Audubon Guide to the National Wildlife Refuge: Pacific Northwest & Alaska. (Illus.). 272p. 2000. pap. 19.95 (*0-312-25372-9*) St Martin.

MacArthur, Mairi. Iona. 1991. text 35.00 (*0-7486-0214-3*, Pub. by Edinburgh U Pr) Col U Pr.

MacArthur, Margaret, ed. see Veira, Stanford M.

MacArthur, Mary, jt. ed. see Clark, LaVerne H.

MacArthur, Nancy. Adventure of the Big Snow. (J). (gr. 2-4). 1998. pap. text 3.50 (*0-590-37209-2*) Scholastic Inc.

***MacArthur, Nancy.** Adventure of the Big Snow. (J). 1998. 8.70 (*0-606-12868-9*, Pub. by Turtleback) Demco.

MacArthur, Robert C. Room at the Mark: A History of the Development of Yachts, Yacht Clubs, Yacht Racing & the Racing Rules. (Illus.). 340p. 1990. 40.00 (*0-915953-03-X*) Yacht Owners.

MacArthur, Roger H. & Wilson, Edward O. Theory of Island Biogeography. (Monographs in Population Biology: Vol. 1). (Illus.). 218p. 1967. pap. text 24.95 (*0-691-08050-X*, Pub. by Princeton U Pr) Cal Prin Full Svc.

MacArthur Study Group Staff. MacArthur Study Bible, 1. 1997. 39.97 (*0-8499-1635-6*) Word Pub.

MacArthur, William J., Jr. Knoxville, Crossroads of the New South. LC 82-71491. (Illus.). 192p. 1982. 11.00 (*0-941199-06-1*) ETHS.

Macartney, C. A. Studies on Early Hungarian & Pontic History. Peter, Laszlo, ed. LC 97-45791. (Variorum Collected Studies: Vol. 588). 656p. 1998. text 128.95 (*0-86078-644-7*, Pub. by Ashgate Pub) Ashgate Pub Co.

Macartney, Carlile A. The Magyars in the Ninth Century. LC 31-19298. 253p. reprint ed. pap. 72.20 (*0-608-12055-3*, 2024496) Bks Demand.

— The Medieval Hungarian Historians: A Critical & Analytical Guide. LC 53-7690. 206p. reprint ed. pap. 58.80 (*0-608-30151-5*, 2050792) Bks Demand.

Macartney, Clarence E. Chariots of Fire. 160p. 1994. pap. 10.99 (*0-8254-3274-X*) Kregel.

— The Faith Once Delivered. 160p. 1995. pap. 10.99 (*0-8254-3281-2*) Kregel.

— Grant & His Generals. LC 75-142660. (Essay Index Reprint Ser.). 1977. 23.95 (*0-8369-2171-2*) Ayer.

— Great Characters of the Bible. 112p. 1996. pap. 9.99 (*0-8254-3282-0*) Kregel.

— Great Interviews of Jesus. LC 95-32063. 144p. 1996. pap. 9.99 (*0-8254-3283-9*) Kregel.

— Great Nights of the Bible. LC 96-28984. 144p. 1997. pap. 9.99 (*0-8254-3287-1*) Kregel.

— Great Women of the Bible. LC 91-21648. 160p. 1992. pap. 10.99 (*0-8254-3268-5*) Kregel.

— The Greatest Men of the Bible. LC 96-31496. 144p. 1997. pap. 9.99 (*0-8254-3286-3*) Kregel.

— The Greatest Questions of the Bible & of Life. LC 93-36683. 152p. 1995. pap. 10.99 (*0-8254-3273-1*) Kregel.

— The Greatest Texts of the Bible. LC 92-16136. 160p. 1992. reprint ed. pap. 10.99 (*0-8254-3266-9*) Kregel.

— The Greatest Words of the Bible & in Human Speech. LC 93-36682. 144p. 1995. pap. 9.99 (*0-8254-3271-5*) Kregel.

— The Lamb of God: Sermons by Clarence Macartney. Bodey, Richard A., ed. LC 94-23031. 144p. 1994. pap. 9.99 (*0-8254-2151-9*) Kregel.

— Lincoln & His Generals. LC 70-124241. (Select Bibliographies Reprint Ser.). (Illus.). 1977. reprint ed. 18.95 (*0-8369-5429-7*) Ayer.

— The Parables of the Old Testament. 160p. 1995. pap. 10.99 (*0-8254-3278-2*) Kregel.

— Parallel Lives of the Old & New Testaments. LC 95-8799. 128p. 1995. pap. 9.99 (*0-8254-3280-4*) Kregel.

— Paul the Man: His Life & His Ministry. LC 92-16135. 176p. 1992. reprint ed. pap. 10.99 (*0-8254-3269-3*) Kregel.

— The Prayers of the Old Testament. LC 95-8722. 120p. 1995. pap. 9.99 (*0-8254-3279-0*) Kregel.

— Six Kings of the American Pulpit. LC 75-152192. (Essay Index Reprint Ser.). 1977. reprint ed. 18.95 (*0-8369-2323-5*) Ayer.

— Strange Texts but Grand Truths. 144p. 1994. pap. 9.99 (*0-8254-3272-3*) Kregel.

— The Trials of Great Bible Characters. 144p. 1996. pap. 9.99 (*0-8254-3285-5*) Kregel.

— Twelve Great Questions about Christ. LC 92-23990. 152p. 1993. pap. 10.99 (*0-8254-3267-7*) Kregel.

— The Wisest Fool: Sermons on Bible Characters. 160p. 1996. pap. 10.99 (*0-8254-3284-7*) Kregel.

Macartney, Clarence E., ed. Men Who Missed It. LC 76-128274. (Essay Index Reprint Ser.). 1977. 18.95 (*0-8369-1835-5*) Ayer.

Macartney, Elke S. Be YourSelf Boldly: Honoring the Free Spirit Within. rev. ed. LC 95-62029. 96p. (Orig.). 1995. pap. 9.95 (*0-9649454-0-1*) Voyage Pubng.

Macartney, F. J., ed. Congenital Heart Disease. (Current Status of Clinical Cardiology Ser.). 1985. text 155.50 (*0-85200-719-1*) Kluwer Academic.

***MacArtney, Hilary.** Scotland. (Collins Pocket Reference Ser.). (Illus.). 256p. 1999. pap. 13.00 (*0-00-472210-8*, Pub. by HarpC) Trafalgar.

Macartney, Mike, jt. auth. see Taylor, James.

Macartney, W. J. Self-Determination in the Commonwealth. 128p. 1988. pap. text 25.90 (*0-08-034525-5*, Pergamon Pr) Elsevier.

Macarulla, D. Diccionario Lexicon Ingles-Espanol, Espanol-Ingles. (ENG & SPA.). 384p. 1974. pap. 13.95 (*0-8288-5996-5*, S31391) Fr & Eur.

Macary, Leonce, jt. auth. see Crispin, M. Jackson.

MacAskill, jt. auth. see Williams.

Macaskill, C. Against the Odds: Adopting Mentally Handicapped Children. (C). 1989. 60.00 (*0-903534-58-4*, Pub. by Brit Ag for Adopt & Fost) St Mut.

MacAtasney, Gerard. The Famine in Lurgan/Portadown: This Dreadful Visitation. LC 97-184532. (Illus.). 126p. (Orig.). 1997. pap. 13.95 (*1-900960-02-8*, Pub. by Beyond the Pale) Irish Bks Media.

MacAtasney, Gerard, jt. auth. see Kinealy, Christine.

MaCaughrean, Geraldine & Kemp, Moira. Grandma Chickenlegs. LC 99-19161. (Picture Bks). 32p. (J). (gr. k-3). 1999. lib. bdg. 15.95 (*1-57505-415-9*, Carolrhoda) Lerner Pub.

Macaulay. Being Human. 1997. pap. 9.99 (*1-900507-07-2*, Pub. by Enitha Pr) Dufour.

Macaulay, Alistair. Margot Fonteyn. (Illus.). 128p. 1998. pap. 9.95 (*0-7509-1579-X*, Pub. by Sutton Pub Ltd) Intl Pubs Mktg.

Macaulay, Ambrose. William Crolly, Archbishop of Armagh, 1835-1849. 496p. 1994. 35.00 (*1-85182-147-3*, Pub. by Four Cts Pr) Intl Spec Bk.

Macaulay, Catharine. On Burke's Reflections on the French Revolution, 1790. LC 96-34848. (Revolution & Romanticism Ser.). 1997. 55.00 (*1-85477-204-X*) Continuum.

MaCaulay, Cathlin, jt. auth. see Cree, Viviene F.

MacAulay, Craig. Dix Hommes et une Echelle - Ten Men on a Ladder. (Picture Bks.). (FRE., Illus.). 32p. (J). (ps-3). 1996. pap. 5.95 (*1-55037-342-0*, Pub. by Les Editions) Firefly Bks Ltd.

Macaulay, Craig. Ten Men on a Ladder. (Illus.). 32p. (J). (ps). 1993. text 14.95 (*1-55037-341-2*, Pub. by Annick) Firefly Bks Ltd.

— Ten Men on a Ladder. (Illus.). 32p. (J). (ps up). 1996. pap. 4.95 (*1-55037-340-4*, Pub. by Annick) Firefly Bks Ltd.

Macaulay, David. Baaa, 001. LC 85-2316. (Illus.). 64p. (J). (gr. 6 up). 1985. 13.95 (*0-395-38948-8*) HM.

— Baaa, 001. LC 85-2316. (Illus.). 64p. (J). (ps up). 1985. pap. 5.95 (*0-395-39588-7*) HM.

— Black & White. (Illus.). 32p. (J). 1990. 17.00 (*0-395-52151-3*) HM.

***Macaulay, David.** Building Big. (Illus.). 192p. 2000. 30.00 (*0-395-96331-1*) HM.

— Building the Book Cathedral. LC 99-17975. 112p. 1999. 29.95 (*0-395-92147-3*) HM.

Macaulay, David. Castle, 001. LC 77-7159. (Illus.). 80p. (J). (gr. 1 up). 1977. 18.00 (*0-395-25784-0*) HM.

— Castle, 001. LC 77-7159. (Illus.). 80p. (J). (gr. 1 up). 1982. pap. 8.95 (*0-395-32920-5*) HM.

— Castle. 1977. 13.15 (*0-606-02292-9*, Pub. by Turtleback) Demco.

Cathedral, 001. (Illus.). 80p. (J). (gr. k up). 1981. pap. 8.95 (*0-395-31668-5*) HM.

— Cathedral: The Story of Its Construction, 001. LC 73-6634. (Illus.). 80p. (J). (gr. 1-5). 1973. 18.00 (*0-395-17513-5*) HM.

— Cathedral: The Story of Its Construction. 1973. 13.15 (*0-606-00413-0*, Pub. by Turtleback) Demco.

— City: A Story of Roman Planning & Construction, 001. (Illus.). 112p. (YA). (gr. 6 up). 1974. 18.00 (*0-395-19492-X*) HM.

— City: A Story of Roman Planning & Construction, 001. (Illus.). 112p. (YA). (gr. 2 up). 1983. pap. 7.95 (*0-395-34922-2*) HM.

An Asterisk (*) at the beginning of an entry indicates that the title is appearing for the first time.

— City: A Story of Roman Planning & Construction. 1974. 13.05 (*0-606-00581-1*, Pub. by Turtleback) Demco.
— Great Moments in Architecture, 001. (Illus.). 128p. 1978. 22.95 (*0-395-25500-7*); pap. 13.95 (*0-395-26711-0*) HM.
— Mill, 001. (Illus.). 128p. (J). (gr. 6 up). 1983. 18.00 (*0-395-34830-7*) HM.
— Mill. 128p. (J). (ps up). 1989. pap. 8.95 (*0-395-52019-3*, Sandpiper) HM.
— The Motel of the Mysteries, 001. 96p. 1979. pap. 13.00 (*0-395-28425-2*) HM.
— The New Way Things Work. LC 98-14224. (Illus.). 400p. 1998. 35.00 (*0-395-93847-3*) HM.
— Pyramid, 001. (Illus.). 80p. (J). (gr. 7 up). 1975. 18.00 (*0-395-21407-6*) HM.
— Pyramid. 1975. 13.15 (*0-606-00557-9*, Pub. by Turtleback) Demco.
— Pyramid PA, 001. (Illus.). 80p. (J). (gr. 5 up). 1982. pap. 8.95 (*0-395-32121-2*) HM.
— Rome Antics. LC 97-20941. (Illus.). 80p. (J). 1997. 18.00 (*0-395-82279-3*) HM.
— Ship. 96p. (J). (gr. 4-7). 1993. 19.95 (*0-395-52439-3*) HM.
— Ship. (Illus.). 96p. (YA). (gr. 5 up). 1995. pap. 8.95 (*0-395-74518-7*, Sandpiper) HM.
— Ship. (J). 1993. 14.30 (*0-606-08159-3*) Turtleback.
— Shortcut. LC 95-2542. (Illus.). 64p. (J). 1995. 15.95 (*0-395-52436-9*) HM.

M

***Macaulay, David.** Shortcut. LC 95-2542. (Illus.). 64p. (J). (ps-3). 1999. pap. 7.95 (*0-618-00607-9*, W Lorraine) HM.
Macaulay, David. Unbuilding, 001. (Illus.). 80p. (J). (gr. 3 up). 1980. 18.00 (*0-395-29457-6*) HM.
— Unbuilding. 80p. (J). (gr. k-3). 1987. pap. 8.95 (*0-395-45425-5*) HM.
— Unbuilding. LC 80-15491. (Sandpipers Ser.). (Illus.). 128p. (J). (gr. 5 up). 1987. pap. 6.95 (*0-395-45360-7*) HM.
— Underground, 001. (Illus.). 112p. (J). (gr. 1 up). 1976. 18.00 (*0-395-24739-X*) HM.
— Underground, 001. (Illus.). 112p. (J). (gr. 1 up). 1983. pap. 9.95 (*0-395-34065-9*) HM.
— The Way Things Work, 2 vols. (YA). 1996. 39.95 incl. cd-rom (*0-7894-1599-2*) DK Pub Inc.
— The Way Things Work. (Illus.). 400p. (J). (ps up). 1988. 29.95 (*0-395-42857-2*) HM.
Macaulay, David. Way Things Work 2.0. 1997. 29.00 (*0-7894-1253-5*) DK Pub Inc.
Macaulay, David. Why the Chicken Crossed the Road. (Illus.). 32p. (J). (gr. 4-6). 1987. 16.00 (*0-395-44241-9*, Clarion Bks) HM.
— Why the Chicken Crossed the Road. 32p. (J). 1991. pap. 6.95 (*0-395-58411-6*) HM.
MacAulay, Donald, ed. The Celtic Languages. (Language Surveys Ser.). (Illus.). 484p. (C). 1993. text 105.00 (*0-521-23127-2*) Cambridge U Pr.
— Modern Scottish Gaelic Poems: A Bilingual Anthology. 224p. 1995. pap. 12.95 (*0-86241-494-6*, Pub. by Canongate Books) Interlink Pub.
MacAulay, Donald, et al, eds. Modern Scottish Gaelic Poems-Nua-Bhardach Ghaidhlig. LC 76-21270. 220p. 1977. 16.00 (*0-8112-0631-9*, Pub. by New Directions) Norton.
Macaulay, E. J. The Soul of Cambria. rev. ed. LC 88-71795. (Illus.). 128p. 1989. reprint ed. pap. 7.00 (*0-934666-28-8*) Artisan Pubs.
Macaulay, F. S. The Algebraic Theory of Modular Systems. (Mathematical Library). 144p. (C). 1994. pap. text 22.95 (*0-521-45562-6*) Cambridge U Pr.
Macaulay, Frederick R. The Smoothing of Time Series. (General Ser.: No. 19). 172p. 1931. reprint ed. 44.80 (*0-87014-018-3*) Natl Bur Econ Res.
— Some Theoretical Problems Suggested by the Movements of Interest Rates, Bond Yields & Stock Prices in the United States Since 1856. Bruchey, Stuart, ed. LC 80-1161. (Rise of Commercial Banking Ser.). (Illus.). 1981. reprint ed. lib. bdg. 33.95 (*0-405-13668-4*) Ayer.
— Some Theoretical Problems Suggested by the Movements of Interest Rates, Bond Yields & Stock Prices in the United States since 1856. (General Ser.: No. 33). 625p. 1938. reprint ed. 160.00 (*0-87014-032-9*) Natl Bur Econ Res.
Macaulay, G. C., ed. see Gower, John.
Macaulay, H. M., jt. auth. see Llewelyn-Davies, R.
Macaulay, James. Glasgow School of Art, Glasgow 1897-1909: Charles Mackintosh. (Architecture in Detail Ser.). 1993. pap. 29.95 (*0-7148-2778-9*, Pub. by Phaidon Press) Phaidon Pr.
— Hill House: Helensburgh 1903 Charles Rennie MacKintosh. LC 95-148651. (Architecture in Detail Ser.). (Illus.). 60p. (C). 1994. pap. 29.95 (*0-7148-2780-0*, Pub. by Phaidon Press) Phaidon Pr.
MacAulay, John. Birlinn: Longships of the Hebrides. (Illus.). 128p. 1997. pap. 15.95 (*1-874267-30-8*, Pub. by White Horse Pr) Paul & Co Pubs.
***MacAulay, John M.** Seal-Folk & Ocean Paddlers: Sliochd Nan Ron. 128p. 1999. pap. 14.95 (*1-874267-39-1*, Pub. by White Horse Pr) Paul & Co Pubs.
Macaulay, Kenneth. Colony of Sierra Leone Vindicated from the Misrepresentations of Mr. MacQueen of Glasgow. 127p. 1968. reprint ed. 45.00 (*0-7146-1831-4*, Pub. by F Cass Pubs) Intl Spec Bk.
Macaulay, Linda. Requirements Engineering. LC 95-51545. (Applied Computing Ser.). 216p. 1996. pap. 34.95 (*3-540-76006-7*) Spr-Verlag.
Macaulay, Linda, jt. ed. see Sutcliffe, Alistair G.
Macaulay, Lord. The Lays of Ancient Rome. LC 97-43667. (Gateway Ser.). 190p. 1997. pap. 12.95 (*0-89526-403-X*, Gateway Editions) Regnery Pub.
Macaulay, Monica. A Grammar of Chalcatongo Mixtec. (Publications in Linguistics: Vol. 127). (Illus.). 300p. (C). 1996. pap. 30.00 (*0-520-09807-2*, Pub. by U CA Pr) Cal Prin Full Svc.
Macaulay, Neill. Dom Pedro: The Struggle for Liberty in Brazil & Portugal, 1798-1834. LC 86-16711. xiv, 362p. 1986. text 49.95 (*0-8223-0681-6*) Duke.
— A Rebel in Cuba: An American's Memoir. 199p. 1991. pap. 11.95 (*1-879915-01-4*) Affil Writers America.
— A Rebel in Cuba: An American's Memoir. 2nd annot. ed. LC 72-101072. (Illus.). 212p. 1999. reprint ed. pap. 17.95 (*0-9653864-2-2*) Wacahoota Pr.
— The Sandino Affair. LC 85-20430. (Illus.). 320p. 1985. reprint ed. pap. text 19.95 (*0-8223-0696-4*) Duke.
— The Sandino Affair. 2nd ed. (Illus.). 320p. 1998. reprint ed. pap. 19.95 (*0-9653864-4-9*) Wacahoota Pr.
MacAulay, Neill, jt. auth. see Bushnell, David.
Macaulay, Ranald & Barrs, Jerram. Being Human: The Nature of Spiritual Experience. 216p. 1998. reprint ed. pap. 15.99 (*0-8308-1502-3*, 1502) InterVarsity.
Macaulay, Richard, jt. auth. see Wald, Jerry.
Macaulay, Ronald K. The Social Art: Language & Its Uses. (Illus.). 256p. 1996. pap. 16.95 (*0-19-510657-1*) OUP.
Macaulay, Ronald K., jt. ed. see Brenneis, Donald.
Macaulay, Ronald K. S. Standards & Variation in Urban Speech: Some Examples from Lowland Scots. LC 97-23074. (Varieties of English Around the World General Ser.: No. 20). x, 201p. 1997. lib. bdg. 64.00 (*1-55619-717-9*) J Benjamins Pubng Co.
Macaulay, Rose. Life among the English. (Writers' Britain Ser.). (Illus.). 96p. 1997. 11.95 (*1-85375-231-2*) Prion.
— Milton. LC 74-7050. (Studies in Milton: No. 22). 1974. lib. bdg. 75.00 (*0-8383-1911-4*) M S G Haskell Hse.
— Orphan Island. 1971. reprint ed. 39.00 (*0-403-01081-0*) Scholarly.
— Personal Pleasures. LC 79-152193. (Essay Index Reprint Ser.). 1977. 23.95 (*0-8369-2195-X*) Ayer.
— The Shadow Flies. LC 70-145153. (Literature Ser.). 484p. 1972. reprint ed. 59.00 (*0-403-01082-9*) Scholarly.
— Some Religious Elements in English Literature. LC 72-158506. 160p. 1972. reprint ed. 13.00 (*0-403-01305-4*) Scholarly.
MacAulay, Rose. Some Religious Elements in English Literature. (BCL1-PR English Literature Ser.). 160p. 1992. reprint ed. lib. bdg. 69.00 (*0-7812-7027-8*) Rprt Serv.
Macaulay, Rose. The Towers of Trebizond. 288p. 1995. pap. 12.95 (*0-7867-0266-4*) Carroll & Graf.
Macaulay, Ruth Marris & Chaney, John. Warren. LC 97-158188. (Images of America Ser.). 1997. pap. 16.99 (*0-7524-0447-4*) Arcadia Publng.
Macaulay, Stewart. Law & the Balance of Power: The Automobile Manufacturers & Their Dealers. LC 66-26503. 224p. 1966. 29.95 (*0-87154-574-8*) Russell Sage.
Macaulay, Stewart, et al. Contracts: Law in Action. abr. ed. 1995. 56.00 (*1-55834-225-7*, 12469-10, MICHIE) LEXIS Pub.
— Law & Society: Readings on the Social Study of Law. 700p. (C). 1995. pap. text 41.75 (*0-393-96713-1*) Norton.
Macaulay, Susan Shaefer. For the Children's Sake: Foundations of Education for Home & School. LC 83-72043. 192p. 1984. pap. 12.99 (*0-89107-290-X*) Crossway Bks.
— For the Family's Sake: The Value of the Home in Everyone's Life. LC 99-33107. 224p. 1999. pap. 12.99 (*1-58134-111-3*) Crossway Bks.
***MacAulay, Suzanne Pollock.** Stitching Rites: Colcha Embroidery along the Northern Rio Grande. LC 00-8200. (Illus.). 220p. 2000. 35.00 (*0-8165-2029-1*) U of Ariz Pr.
Macaulay, Teresa. Non-Violent Stories & Poems for Children. LC 96-67651. (Illus.). 128p. (Orig.). (J). (ps-3). 1996. 16.95 (*1-56167-244-0*) Noble Hse MD.
Macaulay, Thomas Babington. Essay on Frederic the Great. LC 73-137257. reprint ed. 24.50 (*0-404-04100-0*) AMS Pr.
— The History of England. Roper, Hugh T., ed. & abr. by. (English Library). 576p. 1979. pap. 14.95 (*0-14-043133-0*, Penguin Classics) Viking Penguin.
— History of England from the Accession of James Second, 6 vols. Firth, C. H., ed. LC 14-14308. reprint ed. 425.00 (*0-404-04110-8*) AMS Pr.
— Milton. (BCL1-PR English Literature Ser.). 155p. 1992. reprint ed. lib. bdg. 69.00 (*0-7812-7386-2*) Rprt Serv.
— Napoleon & the Restoration of the Bourbons: The Complete Portion of Macaulay's Projected History of France from the Restoration of the Bourbons to the Accession of Louis Phillipe. LC 77-7107. 117p. 1977. text 44.00 (*0-231-04376-7*) Col U Pr.
— Speeches by Lord Macaulay, with His Minute on Indian Education. Young, G. M., ed. LC 76-29441. 1935. 55.00 (*0-404-15348-8*) AMS Pr.
— The Works of Lord Macaulay Complete: The Albany Edition, 12 vols., Set. LC 76-42708. reprint ed. 900.00 (*0-404-59480-8*) AMS Pr.
Macaulay, Vincent A., jt. ed. see Buck, Brian.
Macauley, David. Minding Nature: The Philosophers of Ecology. LC 95-39862. (Democracy & Ecology Ser.). 355p. 1996. pap. text 18.95 (*1-57230-059-0*, 0059); lib. bdg. 43.95 (*1-57230-058-2*, 0058) Guilford Pubns.
MacAuley, Domhnall. A Guide to Cycling Injuries: Prevention & Treatment. LC 95-76303. (Illus.). 128p. (Orig.). 1996. pap. 5.98 (*0-933201-73-7*) MBI Pubg.
— Sports Medicine: Practical Guidelines for General Practice. 288p. 2000. pap. text 37.50 (*0-7506-3730-7*) Buttrwrth-Heinemann.
***MacAuley, Domhnall, ed.** Benefits & Hazards of Exercise. (Illus.). 383p. 1999. pap. text 62.95 (*0-7279-1412-X*) BMJ Pub.
***Macauley, Dunstan L. D.** Baa Salaka: Sacrificial Lamb. LC 99-91771. 2000. 25.00 (*0-7388-1254-4*); pap. 18.00 (*0-7388-1255-2*) Xlibris Corp.
Macauley, Dylan, jt. auth. see Garvey, Hugh.
Macauley, Ed, jt. auth. see Friedl, Francis.
Macauley, Heather. Children of Light. 238p. (Orig.). 1995. pap. 12.95 (*0-9648093-3-8*) HOME Pubng.
— The Lovers. 96p. (Orig.). (C). 1996. pap. 9.95 (*0-9648093-7-0*) HOME Pubng.
***Macauley, Irene.** Best Practices in Customer Care for Financial Services. 50p. 1999. spiral bd. 77.00 (*0-89258-362-2*, D087) Assn Inform & Image Mgmt.
Macauley, Melissa A. Social Power & Legal Culture: Litigation Masters in Late Imperial China. LC 98-23869. (Law, Society, & Culture in China Ser.). 456p. 1999. 55.00 (*0-8047-3135-7*) Stanford U Pr.
Macauley, Molly K., et al. Using Economic Incentives to Regulate Toxic Substances. 143p. 1992. lib. bdg. 24.95 (*0-915707-65-9*) Resources Future.
Macauley, Robie & Lanning, George. Technique in Fiction. 288p. 1990. pap. 10.95 (*0-312-05168-9*) St Martin.
Macauliff, Dan, ed. Effective Technical Communications. 2nd ed. (C). 1989. pap. text 19.40 (*0-536-57614-9*) Pearson Custom.
MacAuliffe, Max A. The Sikh Religion, 6 vols. in 3. 1963. text 125.00 (*0-685-13749-X*) Coronet Bks.
— The Sikh Religion: Its Gurus Sacred Writings & Authors, 3 vols., Set. 1990. reprint ed. 68.00 (*81-85395-94-2*, Pub. by Low Price) S Asia.
Macauliffe, Max A. The Sikhs: Their Religion, Gurus, Sacred Writings & Authors, 6 vols., Set. (C). 1988. 500.00 (*0-7855-0054-5*, Pub. by Print Hse) St Mut.
MacAuslan, Janna & Aspen, Kristan, compiled by. Guitar Music by Women Composers: An Annotated Catalog, 61. LC 97-10404. (Music Reference Collection: Vol. 61). 224p. 1997. lib. bdg. 72.95 (*0-313-29385-6*, Greenwood Pr) Greenwood.
MacAvlay, Lex. Battle Bismarck Sea. 1992. mass mkt. write for info. (*0-312-92750-9*) Tor Bks.
***MaCavoy, Jim.** Aretha Franklin. (Black Americans of Achievement Ser.). 2000. 19.95 (*0-7910-5808-5*) Chelsea Hse.
— Aretha Franklin. (Black Americans of Achievement Ser.). (Illus.). 2000. pap. 9.95 (*0-7910-5809-3*) Chelsea Hse.
MacAvoy, Paul W. Energy Policy: An Economic Analysis. (Illus.). (C). 1983. pap. text 7.75 (*0-393-95321-1*) Norton.
— The Failure of Antitrust & Regulation to Establish Competition in Long-Distance Telephone Services. LC 96-21011. 1996. 50.00 (*0-262-13332-6*) MIT Pr.
— Industry Regulation & the Performance of the American Economy. (C). 1992. pap. text 12.50 (*0-393-96186-9*) Norton.
— Price Formation in Natural Gas Fields, No. 14--14. LC 76-43984. (Yale Studies in Economics: No. 14). (Illus.). 281p. 1977. reprint ed. lib. bdg. 49.50 (*0-8371-8981-0*, MAPF, Greenwood Pr) Greenwood.
MacAvoy, Paul W. Regulated Industries & the Economy. LC 79-15457. 160p. (C). 1979. pap. text 7.75 (*0-393-95094-8*) Norton.
— Sixty Years of Natural Gas Regulation & Deregulation. LC 00-40837. 2001. write for info. (*0-300-08381-5*) Yale U Pr.
Macavoy, Paul W., ed. Deregulation & Privatization in the U. S. A. 120p. 1996. pap. 16.00 (*0-7486-0738-2*, Pub. by Edinburgh U Pr) Col U Pr.
MacAvoy, Paul W., jt. auth. see Carron, Andrew S.
MacAvoy, R. A. King of the Dead Bk. II: Lens of the World Trilogy. 288p. 1992. mass mkt. 4.50 (*0-380-71017-X*, Avon Bks) Morrow Avon.
— Lens of the World. 288p. 1991. reprint ed. mass mkt. 4.99 (*0-380-71016-1*, Avon Bks) Morrow Avon.
— Lens of the World Bk. 3: The Belly of the Wolf. 224p. 1995. mass mkt. 4.99 (*0-380-71018-8*, Avon Bks) Morrow Avon.
MacBain, A. Etymological Dictionary of the Gaelic Language. 1991. lib. bdg. 45.00 (*0-8288-3342-7*, M12095) Fr & Eur.
MacBain, Alexander. Etymological Dictionary of Scottish-Gaelic. 2nd ed. 412p. 1998. reprint ed. pap. 14.95 (*0-7818-0632-1*) Hippocrene Bks.
MacBain, Alexander, ed. see Cameron, Alexander.
MacBain, Alexander, ed. see MacKenzie, Alexander.
MacBain, William. De Sainte Katerine: An Anonymous Picard Version of the Life of St. Catherine of Alexandria. 232p. (C). 1987. text 47.50 (*0-8026-0010-7*) Univ Pub Assocs.
***MacBay, Shannon & Rhys-Gruffydd, Karol.** Albion - There & Back. (Follow the Legend Ser.: Vol. 1). (Illus.). 200p. 2000. pap. 24.95 (*0-9700439-1-0*) ADRI Pub.
MacBean, Alasdair I. Export Instabilty & Economic Development. LC 67-1818. (Center for International Affairs Ser.). (Illus.). 367p. 1966. 40.50 (*0-674-28600-6*) HUP.
***MacBean, Alasdair I., ed.** Trade & Transition: Trade Promotion in Transitional Economies. LC 99-38240. (Illus.). 208p. 2000. 49.50 (*0-7146-5034-X*, Pub. by F Cass Pubs); pap. 24.50 (*0-7146-8088-5*, Pub. by F Cass Pubs) Intl Spec Bk.
MacBean, Alasdair I. & Nguyen, D. T. Commodity Policies: Problems & Prospects. 464p. 1987. lib. bdg. 95.00 (*0-7099-1708-2*, Pub. by C Helm) Routldge.
MacBean, Alasdair I. & Snowden, N. International Institutions in Trade & Finance. (Studies in Economics: No. 18). (Illus.). 272p. (C). 1981. pap. text 18.95 (*0-04-382033-6*) Routledge.
MacBean, E. Craig, jt. auth. see Simmons, Henry C.
Macbean, James R. Film & Revolution. LC 75-1936. 347p. reprint ed. pap. 107.60 (*0-608-13200-4*, 205604500044) Bks Demand.
Macbeath, Alexander. Experiments in Living: A Study of the Nature & Foundation of Ethics or Morals in the Light of Recent Work in Social Anthropology. LC 77-27180. (Gifford Lectures: 1948-49). reprint ed. 34.50 (*0-404-60503-6*) AMS Pr.
MacBeath, John. Personal & Social Education. 90p. 1989. pap. 26.00 (*0-7073-0531-4*, Pub. by Mercat Pr Bks) St Mut.
MacBeath, John E. Schools Speak for Themselves, Again. LC 98-31538. 1999. 20.99 (*0-415-20580-8*) Routledge.
***MacBeath, John E. C.** Self-Evaluation in European Schools: A Story of Change. LC 00-31138. 2000. write for info. (*0-415-23014-4*) Routledge.
MacBeath, Murray. The Philosophy of Time. Le Poidevin, Robin, ed. LC 92-26125. (Readings in Philosophy Ser.). (Illus.). 236p. 1993. pap. text 19.95 (*0-19-823999-8*) OUP.
Macbeth, ed. Foundations of Multicomponent VSP Processing. Date not set. text. write for info. (*0-08-042439-2*, Pergamon Pr) Elsevier.
MacBeth, A. School Boards: From Purpose to Practice. 160p. 1989. pap. 26.00 (*0-7073-0598-5*, Pub. by Mercat Pr Bks) St Mut.
MacBeth, A. & Ramsey, S. Emergency Reporting Requirements for Environmental Spills & Releases. 1989. ring bd. 150.00 (*0-13-834698-4*) P-H.
MacBeth, Alastair, et al, eds. Collaborate or Compete? Educational Partnership in a Market Economy. 208p. 1995. 85.00 (*0-7507-0383-0*, Falmer Pr); pap. 34.95 (*0-7507-0384-9*, Falmer Pr) Taylor & Francis.
Macbeth, Angus, et al. Reporting Requirements for Environmental Releases, 2 vols. 1264p. 1992. ring bd. 185.00 (*0-13-010083-8*) Aspen Law.
MacBeth, D. K. Advanced Manufacturing Strategy & Management. 180p. 1989. 94.95 (*0-387-51113-X*) Spr-Verlag.
MacBeth, D. K. & Southern, G., eds. Operations Management in Advanced Manufacture & Services. 300p. 1989. 118.95 (*0-387-51009-5*) Spr-Verlag.
Macbeth, Fergus R. Lung Cancer: A Practical Guide to Management. 148p. 1996. pap. text 15.00 (*3-7186-5860-7*, Harwood Acad Pubs) Gordon & Breach.
Macbeth, Fergus R., et al. Lung Cancer: A Practical Guide to Management. 148p. 1996. text 39.00 (*3-7186-5859-3*, Harwood Acad Pubs) Gordon & Breach.
Macbeth, Fiona & Fine, Nic. Playing with Fire: Creative Conflict Resolution for Young Adults. (Illus.). 192p. 1995. pap. 19.95 (*0-86571-306-5*) New Soc Pubs.
MacBeth, George. Poetry, 1900-1975. 1980. pap. text. write for info. (*0-582-35149-9*, Pub. by Addison-Wesley) Longman.
MacBeth, George & Booth, Martin, eds. The Book of Cats. (Illus.). 360p. 1992. reprint ed. pap. 19.95 (*1-85224-163-2*, Pub. by Bloodaxe Bks) Dufour.
Macbeth, Helen, ed. Health Outcomes: Biological, Social & Economic Perspectives. (Biosocial Society Ser.: No. 8). (Illus.). 176p. 1996. text 98.50 (*0-19-854879-6*) OUP.
MacBeth, Helen M. Food Preference & Taste: Continuity & Change. LC 97-28668. (Anthropology of Food & Nutrition Ser.). 224p. 1997. 49.00 (*1-57181-958-4*) Berghahn Bks.
Macbeth, Helen M. Food Preference & Taste: Continuity & Change. LC 97-28668. (The Anthropology of Food & Nutrition Ser.). 1997. pap. 19.50 (*1-57181-970-3*) Berghahn Bks.
***Macbeth, Hillard.** Investment Traps & How to Avoid Them: A Canadian Guide to Savvy Investing. 240p. 1999. pap. 21.95 (*0-13-022258-5*) P-H.
MacBeth, James L. Jesus Healer (1919) 130p. 1998. reprint ed. pap. 14.95 (*0-7661-0586-5*) Kessinger Pub.
Macbeth, Jessica. Sun over Mountain: A Course in Creative Imagination. 3rd ed. (Illus.). 288p. 1991. pap. write for info. (*0-946551-67-7*) ACCESS Pubs Network.
Macbeth, Jessica, jt. auth. see Froud, Brian.
Macbeth, Norman. Darwin Retried: An Appeal to Reason. LC 73-160418. 184p. 1979. reprint ed. pap. 14.95 (*0-87645-105-9*, Gambit) Harvard Common Pr.
— Darwinism: A Time for Funerals. (Broadside Editions Ser.). 32p. (C). 1985. reprint ed. pap. 4.95 (*0-9609850-8-5*) Rob Briggs.
Macbeth, Norman, tr. see Steiner, Rudolf.
MacBeth, Tannis M., ed. Tuning in to Young Viewers: Social Science Perspectives on Television. LC 95-50231. 296p. (C). 1996. 48.00 (*0-8039-5825-0*); pap. 22.95 (*0-8039-5826-9*) Sage.
MacBrayne, jt. auth. see Picton Publishing Staff.
MacBrayne, Edna. Alida: An Erotic Novel. LC 81-80486. 180p. (Orig.). 1981. pap. 9.00 (*0-939500-00-0*) Parkhurst.
MacBrayne, Lewis & Ramsey, James P. One More Chance: An Experiment with Human Salvage. LC 73-156023. reprint ed. 47.50 (*0-404-09124-5*) AMS Pr.
Macbride, A. S. Speculative Masonry Its Mission, Its Evolution & Its Landmarks. 254p. 1986. reprint ed. pap. text 7.50 (*0-88053-040-5*, M-89) Macoy Pub.
MacBride, Andrew & Susser, Joshua. Byte Guide to OpenDoc. (Byte Ser.). 416p. 1996. pap. text 29.95 (*0-07-882118-5*) McGraw.
MacBride, Dexter, ed. Opportunities in Appraising-Valuation Sciences. (Illus.). 149p. 1993. pap. 10.95 (*0-8442-6660-4*, VGM Career) NTC Contemp Pub Co.
— Opportunities in Appraising-Valuation Sciences. (Illus.). 149p. 1995. 13.95 (*0-8442-6659-0*, VGM Career) NTC Contemp Pub Co.
MacBride, J. D. Handbook of Practical Shipbuilding. 1973. lib. bdg. 75.00 (*0-8490-1932-X*) Gordon Pr.
Macbride, James F. Flora of Peru. LC 36-10426. (Field Museum of Natural History, Publication 680, Anthropological Ser.: Vol. 13, Pt. 3A, No. 1). 290p. 1951. reprint ed. pap. 89.90 (*0-608-03770-2*, 206459300009) Bks Demand.
— Flora of Peru Pt. 3, No. 2. LC 36-10426. (Field Museum of Natural History Botanical Ser.: Vol. 13). (Illus.). 271p. 1949. reprint ed. pap. 84.10 (*0-608-02728-6*, 206339300003) Bks Demand.

An Asterisk (*) at the beginning of an entry indicates that the title is appearing for the first time.

MacBride, Maud G. The Autobiography of Maud Gonne: A Servant of the Queen. rev. ed. Jeffares, A. Norman & White, Anna M., eds. LC 94-39713. 396p. 1995. pap. 18.00 (0-226-30252-0); lib. bdg. 32.00 (0-226-30251-2) U Ch Pr.

MacBride, Robert. Timesharing: What's in It for You. LC 76-10858. 26p. reprint ed. pap. 30.00 (0-608-30421-2, 200461700045) Bks Demand.

MacBride, Roger L. Bachelor Girl. LC 99-10604. (Little House). (Illus.). 256p. (J). (gr. 3-7). 1999. 15.95 (0-06-027755-6); pap. 4.95 (0-06-440691-1); lib. bdg. 15.89 (0-06-028434-X) HarpC Child Bks.

— In the Land of the Big Red Apple. LC 94-33646. (Little House). (Illus.). 352p. (J). (gr. 3-7). 1995. 15.95 (0-06-024963-3) HarpC.

— In the Land of the Big Red Apple. (Little House). (Illus.). 352p. (J). (gr. 3-6). 1995. lib. bdg. 15.89 (0-06-024964-1) HarpC Child Bks.

— In the Land of the Big Red Apple. LC 94-33646. (Little House). (Illus.). 352p. (J). (gr. 4-7). 1995. pap. 4.95 (0-06-440574-5, HarpTrophy) HarpC Child Bks.

— Little Farm in the Ozarks. (Little House). (Illus.). 256p. (J). (gr. 3-6). 1994. 15.95 (0-06-024245-0) HarpC Child Bks.

— Little Farm in the Ozarks. LC 93-23688. (Little House). (Illus.). 304p. (J). (gr. 4-7). 1994. pap. 4.95 (0-06-440510-9, HarpTrophy) HarpC Child Bks.

— Little House on Rocky Ridge. LC 92-39132. (Little House). (Illus.). 368p. (J). (gr. 3-7). 1993. pap. 4.95 (0-06-440478-1, HarpTrophy) HarpC Child Bks.

— Little House on Rocky Ridge. (Little House). (Illus.). (J). (gr. 3-6). 1993. 10.05 (0-606-05432-4, Pub. by Turtleback) Demco.

— Little House on Rocky Ridge. 305th ed. LC 92-39132. (Little House). (Illus.). 368p. (J). (gr. 4-7). 1993. 16.95 (0-06-020842-2) HarpC Child Bks.

— Little Town in the Ozarks. (Little House). (Illus.). 352p. (J). (gr. 3-6). 1996. 15.95 (0-06-024977-3) HarpC Child Bks.

— Little Town in the Ozarks. LC 95-47590. (Little House). (Illus.). 352p. (J). (gr. 4-7). 1996. pap. 4.95 (0-06-440580-X, HarpTrophy); lib. bdg. 15.89 (0-06-024970-6) HarpC Child Bks.

— Missouri Bound. LC PZ7.M12255Mi 1999. (Little House Chapter Bks.: No. 1). (Illus.). 80p. (J). (gr. k-2). 1999. lib. bdg. 14.89 (0-06-027953-2) HarpC.

— Missouri Bound. LC PZ7.M12255Mi 1999. (Little House Chapter Bks.: No. 1). (Illus.). 80p. (J). (gr. k-2). 1999. mass mkt. 4.25 (0-06-442087-6) HarpC Child Bks.

Macbride, Roger L. A New Dawn for America: The Libertarian Challenge. LC 76-174402. 111p. 1976. 5.95 (0-916054-03-9) Jameson Bks.

MacBride, Roger L. New Dawn on Rocky Ridge. LC PZ7.M12255Nj 1997. (Little House). (Illus.). 384p. (J). (gr. 3-6). 1997. 15.95 (0-06-024971-4) HarpC.

— New Dawn on Rocky Ridge. LC 97-4990. (Little House). (Illus.). 384p. (J). (gr. 3-7). 1997. pap. 4.95 (0-06-440581-8, HarpTrophy) HarpC Child Bks.

— On the Banks of the Bayou. LC 98-5573. (Little House: Vol. 1). (Illus.). 240p. (J). (gr. 3-7). 1998. pap. 4.95 (0-06-440582-6) HarpC.

— On the Banks of the Bayou. LC 98-5573. (Little House: Vol. 1). (Illus.). 240p. (J). (gr. 3-7). 1998. 15.95 (0-06-024973-0) HarpC Child Bks.

— On the Other Side of the Hill. LC 95-14263. (Little House). (Illus.). 352p. (J). (gr. 4-7). 1995. pap. 4.95 (0-06-440575-3, HarpTrophy) HarpC Child Bks.

***MacBride, Roger L.** Rose at Rocky Ridge. (Little House Chapter Bks.: No. 2). (Illus.). 80p. (J). (gr. k-2). 2000. pap. 4.25 (0-06-442093-0) HarpC Child Bks.

— Rose at Rocky Ridge. LC 99-31386. (Little House Chapter Bks.: No. 2). (Illus.). 80p. (J). (gr. 2-5). 2000. lib. bdg. 14.89 (0-06-028156-1) HarpC Child Bks.

MacBride, Roger L., ed. see Wilder, Laura Ingalls.

***Macbride, Roger Lea.** The Adventures of Rose & Swiney. LC 99-87633. (Little House Chapter Bks.: No. 4). (Illus.). 80p. (J). (gr. k-2). 2000. mass mkt. 4.25 (0-06-442108-2, HarpTrophy) HarpC Child Bks.

— The Adventures of Rose & Swiney: Adapted from The Rose Years. LC 99-87633. (Little House Chapter Bks.: No. 4). (Illus.). 80p. (J). (gr. k-2). 2000. lib. bdg. 14.89 (0-06-028553-2) HarpC Child Bks.

— Bachelor Girl. (Little House Ser.). (Illus.). (J). 1999. 10.30 (0-606-18676-X) Turtleback.

— Brookfield Days. (Little House Ser.). (Illus.). (J). 1999. 9.70 (0-606-18680-8) Turtleback.

— Frontier Family. (Little House Ser.). (Illus.). (J). 1999. 9.70 (0-606-18681-6) Turtleback.

Macbride, Roger Lea. In the Land of the Big Red Apple. (Little House). (Illus.). (J). (gr. 3-6). 1995. 10.05 (0-606-07702-2, Pub. by Turtleback) Demco.

— The Little Farm in the Ozarks. (Little House). (Illus.). (J). (gr. 3-6). 1994. 10.05 (0-606-06537-7, Pub. by Turtleback) Demco.

***Macbride, Roger Lea.** Little House Chapter Book, No. 32. 2002. lib. bdg. write for info. (0-06-029178-8) HarpC Child Bks.

— Little House Chapter Book, No. 32. (J). 2002. pap. write for info. (0-06-442142-2, HarpTrophy) HarpC Child Bks.

— Missouri School Days. (J). 2001. pap. write for info. (0-06-442110-4, HarpTrophy); lib. bdg. write for info. (0-06-028555-9) HarpC Child Bks.

— New Dawn on Rocky Ridge. (Little House). (Illus.). (J). (gr. 3-6). 1997. 10.05 (0-606-11678-8, Pub. by Turtleback) Demco.

Macbride, Roger Lea. On the Other Side of the Hill. LC 95-14263. (Little House). (Illus.). 356p. (J). (gr. 4-7). 1995. 15.95 (0-06-024967-6) HarpC Child Bks.

— On the Other Side of the Hill. (Little House). (Illus.). (J). (gr. 3-6). 1995. 10.05 (0-606-08450-9, Pub. by Turtleback) Demco.

***Macbride, Roger Lea.** Rose & Alva. LC PZ7.M478275Ro 2000. (Little House Chapter Bks.: No. 3). (Illus.). 80p. (J). (gr. k-2). 2000. pap. 4.25 (0-06-442095-7, HarpTrophy) HarpC Child Bks.

***Macbride, Roger Lea & Ettlinger, Doris.** Rose & Alva. LC PZ7.M478275RO. (Little House Chapter Bks.: No. 3). 80p. (J). (gr. k-2). 2000. lib. bdg. 14.89 (0-06-028158-8) HarpC Child Bks.

MacBridge, P. K. Programming in Visual BASIC. 208p. 1994. pap. 59.95 (1-85805-092-8, Pub. by DP Publns) St Mut.

MacBroom, James G. The River Book: The Nature & Management of Streams in Glaciated Terranes, Vol. XXVIII. LC 98-29653. (DEP Bulletin Ser.: No. 28). (Illus.). 241p. 1998. 39.95 (0-942085-06-X) CT Dep Environ.

M.A.C.C. Team Staff. Bilingual Rite of Baptism. (SPA.). 47p. 1991. write for info. (0-614-04879-6) Mex Am Cult.

— Cantos Para Pedir Posadas y Otras Canciones de Navidad. (SPA.). 24p. 1982. write for info. (0-614-04893-1) Mex Am Cult.

— Celebremos la Cuaresma y la Pascua. (SPA., Illus.). 8p. 1980. write for info. (0-614-04887-7) Mex Am Cult.

— Celebremos la Cuaresma y la Semana Santa. (SPA.). 82p. 1982. write for info. (0-614-04895-8) Mex Am Cult.

— Expresiones de Fe de los Hispanos en el Sur Oeste. (SPA.). 68p. 1994. write for info. (0-614-04885-0) Mex Am Cult.

— Faith Expressions of Hispanics in the Southwest. 64p. 1977. write for info. (0-614-04884-2) Mex Am Cult.

— The Family Novena of Guadalupe. (SPA.). 50p. write for info. (0-614-04898-2) Mex Am Cult.

— Fronteras. 469p. 1983. write for info. (0-614-04897-4) Mex Am Cult.

— Guia Practica para Ayudar a Sacerdotes a Celebrar la Misa en Espanol. (SPA.). 16p. write for info. incl. audio (0-614-04882-6) Mex Am Cult.

— La Historia de la Virgen de Guadalupe. (SPA.). 11p. 1980. write for info. (0-614-04889-3) Mex Am Cult.

— The Image of Our Lady of Guadalupe. (Illus.). 4p. 1977. write for info. (0-614-04894-X) Mex Am Cult.

— M. A. C. C. en Fiesta. (SPA.). 96p. 1982. write for info. (0-614-04891-5) Mex Am Cult.

— Manual para Comunidades Eclesiales de Base. (SPA.). 36p. 1991. write for info. (0-614-04890-7) Mex Am Cult.

— Matrimony in Christ, the New Rite. (SPA.). 20p. 1970. write for info. (0-614-04880-X) Mex Am Cult.

— Ojo de Dios. 6p. write for info. (0-614-04896-6) Mex Am Cult.

— Oraciones del Corazon (Prayers of the Heart) (SPA.). 34p. 1992. write for info. (0-614-04892-3) Mex Am Cult.

— Pastoral Care of the Sick. (SPA.). 205p. 1986. write for info. (0-614-04883-4) Mex Am Cult.

MACC Team Staff. Que Es Ser Catolico?Tr. of About Being Catholic. (SPA., Illus.). 36p. 1976. write for info. (0-614-04901-6) Mex Am Cult.

M.A.C.C. Team Staff. R. I. C. A. Rito Para Iniciar los Cristianos Adultos. (SPA., Illus.). 68p. 1989. write for info. (0-614-04886-9) Mex Am Cult.

— Religious Celebration of the Quinceanera. (SPA.). 50p. 1980. write for info. (0-614-04881-8) Mex Am Cult.

— The Story of Our Lady of Guadalupe. 11p. 1978. write for info. (0-614-04888-5) Mex Am Cult.

Maccabe, Arthur B. Computer Systems: Architecture, Organization, Programming. LC 92-27699. 792p. (C). 1993. text 69.75 (0-256-11456-0, Irwn McGrw-H) McGrw-H Hghr Educ.

***MacCabe, Colin.** The Eisenstein Reader. Taylor, Richard, ed. LC 99-215415. 160p. 1998. pap. 22.50 (0-85170-676-2) Ind U Pr.

MacCabe, Colin. The Eloquence of the Vulgar: Language, Cinema & the Politics of Culture. LC 99-229766. 160p. 1998. 60.00 (0-85170-677-0) Ind U Pr.

— Eloquence of the Vulgar: Language, Cinema & the Politics of Culture. LC 99-229766. 1998. pap. text 22.50 (0-85170-678-9) British Film Inst.

— Performance. LC 98-215547. (Film Classics Ser.). 1998. pap. 10.95 (0-85170-670-3) Ind U Pr.

MacCabe, Colin, ed. The Talking Cure: Essays in Psychoanalysis & Language. LC 79-28551. 243p. 1986. pap. 12.95 (0-312-78475-9) St Martin.

MacCabe, Colin, et al, eds. Who Is Andy Warhol? (Illus.). 224p. 1998. 59.95 (0-85170-588-X, Pub. by British Film Inst); pap. 22.50 (0-85170-589-8, Pub. by British Film Inst) Ind U Pr.

MacCabe, Colin, jt. auth. see Julien, Isaac.

MacCabe, S. L., ed. Seismic Engineering, 1994: Proceedings of the Pressure Vessels & Piping Conference. LC 88-71134. (PVP Ser.: Vol. 275-1,275-2). 382p. 1994. pap. 115.00 (0-7918-1198-0) ASME.

***Maccabee, Bruce S.** The U. F. O.-F. B. I. Connection: The Secret History of the Government's Conspiracy. LC 00-28277. (Illus.). 336p. 2000. pap. 14.95 (1-56718-493-6) Llewellyn Pubns.

Maccabee, Jordan B. God's Last Message. 200p. mass mkt. 4.99 (1-55197-871-7) Picasso Publ.

Maccabee, Paul. John Dillinger Slept Here: A Crooks' Tour of Crime & Corruption in St. Paul, 1920-1936. LC 95-5236. xx, 362p. 1995. pap. 24.95 (0-87351-316-9) Minn Hist.

— John Dillinger Slept Here: A Crooks' Tour of Crime & Corruption in St. Paul, 1920-1936. LC 95-5236. (Illus.). xx, 362p. 1995. 45.00 (0-87351-315-0) Minn Hist.

***Maccaferri, Elena.** A Bench on Which to Rest: The Diary of an Emigrant. Phillips, Maria C., tr. from ITA. LC 99-32971.Tr. of Diario Di Una Emigrante. 128p. 1999. 15.00 (1-928746-02-0) Herodias.

MacCaffrey, Isabel G. Paradise Lost As Myth. LC 59-9282. 239p. reprint ed. pap. 74.10 (0-7837-4169-3, 205901800012) Bks Demand.

— Spenser's Allegory: The Anatomy of Imagination. LC 75-30197. 457p. reprint ed. pap. 141.70 (0-8357-3548-6, 203429600089) Bks Demand.

MacCaffrey, Isabel G., ed. see Milton, John.

MacCaffrey, James. History of the Catholic Church: From the Renaissance to the French Revolution, Vol. I. LC 75-130558. 419p. reprint ed. lib. bdg. 28.50 (0-8290-0463-7) Irvington.

— History of the Catholic Church: From the Renaissance to the French Revolution, Vol. II. LC 75-130558. 470p. reprint ed. lib. bdg. 25.50 (0-8290-0464-5) Irvington.

— History of the Catholic Church from the Renassaince to the French Revolution, 2 vols, 1. LC 75-130558. (Select Bibliographies Reprint Ser.). 1977. reprint ed. 29.95 (0-8369-9984-3) Ayer.

— History of the Catholic Church from the Renassaince to the French Revolution, 2 vols, Set. LC 75-130558. (Select Bibliographies Reprint Ser.). 1977. reprint ed. 58.95 (0-8369-5551-5) Ayer.

— History of the Catholic Church from the Renassaince to the French Revolution, 2 vols, Vol. 2. LC 75-130558. (Select Bibliographies Reprint Ser.). 1977. reprint ed. 29.95 (0-8369-9985-1) Ayer.

MacCaffrey, Wallace. Elizabeth I. 496p. 1995. pap. text 19.95 (0-340-61455-2, B4719, Pub. by E A) OUP.

MacCaffrey, Wallace T. Elizabeth I & Religion. LC 93-3568. (Illus.). 512p. 1993. 35.00 (0-340-56167-X, B2317, Pub. by E A) Routldge.

— Elizabeth I & Religion. LC 93-3568. (Illus.). 512p. (C). (gr. 13). 1993. pap. 11.99 (0-415-07352-9, B2460, Pub. by E A) Routldge.

— Exeter, Fifteen Forty to Sixteen Forty: The Growth of an English County Town. 2nd ed. (Historical Monographs: No. 35). (Illus.). 328p. 1975. 37.95 (0-674-27501-2) HUP.

— Queen Elizabeth & the Making of Policy, 1572-1588. LC 80-8564. 540p. reprint ed. pap. 167.40 (0-608-06420-3, 206663300008) Bks Demand.

— Shaping of the Elizabethan Regime. LC 68-27409. 517p. reprint ed. 160.30 (0-8357-9513-6, 201463600093) Bks Demand.

— The Shaping of the Elizabethan Regime: Elizabethan Politics, 1558-1572. LC 68-27409. (Princeton Paperbacks Ser.). 519p. reprint ed. pap. 160.90 (0-608-07366-0, 206759400009) Bks Demand.

MacCaffrey, Wallace T., ed. see Camden, William.

Maccall, A. Dynamic Geog Fish. 200p. 1990. pap. 15.00 (0-295-96912-1) U of Wash Pr.

MacCall, Alec D. Dynamic Geography of Marine Fish Populations. 200p. 1990. text 25.00 (0-295-96911-3) U of Wash Pr.

Maccall, William. Foreign Biographies, 2 vols, Set. LC 72-5617. (Essay Index Reprint Ser.). 1977. reprint ed. 39.95 (0-8369-2999-3) Ayer.

MacCalla, Amanda. Fitful Tracings: Stories. 148p. (Orig.). 1996. pap. 12.00 (0-945131-03-8) Terrace Pr.

Maccalla, G., jt. ed. see Cercone, N. J.

MacCallum, Anne C. Pumpkin, Pumpkin! Lore, History, Outlandish Facts & Good Eating. LC 84-81831. (Illus.). 200p. (Orig.). 1986. pap. 8.95 (0-9600300-9-3) Heather Foun.

MacCallum, Gerald C., Jr. Legislative Intent & Other Essays on Politics, Law, & Morality. Singer, Marcus G. & Martin, Rex, eds. LC 93-841. 288p. (C). 1993. text 45.00 (0-299-13860-7) U of Wis Pr.

MacCallum, Hugh. Milton & the Sons of God: The Divine Image in Milton's Epic Poetry. 335p. 1986. text 40.00 (0-8020-5679-2) U of Toronto Pr.

MacCallum, Hugh, ed. see Woodhouse, Arthur S.

MacCallum, Iain. UCSD Pascal for the IBM PC. write for info. (0-318-59632-6) S&S Trade.

MacCallum, Malcolm A. & Wright, Francis J. Algebraic Computing with REDUCE. 320p. 1992. 65.00 (0-19-853444-2); pap. 32.00 (0-19-853443-4) OUP.

MacCallum, Malcolm A., et al. Algebraic Computing in General Relativity: Lecture Notes from the First Brazilian School on Computer Algebra, Vol. 2. Rebouças, Marcelo J., ed. (Illus.). 400p. 1995. text 65.00 (0-19-853646-1) OUP.

Maccallum, Mungo W. Tennyson's Idylls of the King & Arthurian Story from the Sixteenth Century. LC 73-154159. (Select Bibliographies Reprint Ser.). 1977. reprint ed. 26.95 (0-8369-5775-X) Ayer.

MacCallum, Neil R. A World of Folk Tales from Multi-Cultural Scotland. 80p. 1990. pap. 21.00 (1-898218-70-6) St Mut.

MacCallum, Reid. Imitation & Design: And Other Essays. Blissett, William, ed. LC 54-7922. 227p. reprint ed. pap. 70.40 (0-608-11250-X, 201608700004) Bks Demand.

MacCallum, Spencer H. Art of Community. LC 78-112866. 118p. 1970. 10.00 (0-9600300-4-3) Heather Foun.

MacCallum, Spencer H., ed. see Riegel, E. C.

MacCallum-Whitcomb, Susan, jt. auth. see Tharp, Julie.

MacCallum-Whitcomb, Susan, jt. ed. see Tharp, Julie.

MacCallum, William G. William Stewart Halsted, Surgeon. LC 30-31890. 263p. reprint ed. pap. 81.60 (0-608-13405-8, 205574400034) Bks Demand.

Maccalous, Sarah & Phillips, Althea. Directory of Transportation Data Sources (1996) 708p. (C). 1998. pap. text 60.00 (0-7881-7509-2) DIANE Pub.

Maccalous, Sarah, jt. ed. see Bradley, Kathleen.

MacCambridge, Michael. The Franchise: A History of Sports Illustrated Magazine. 448p. (J). 1998. pap. 14.45 (0-7868-8357-X, Pub. by Hyperion) Time Warner.

MacCameron, Robert. Bananas, Labor, & Politics in Honduras: 1954-1963. LC 82-24946. (Foreign & Comparative Studies Program, Latin American Ser.: No. 5). (Illus.). (Orig.). (C). 1983. pap. text 14.00 (0-915984-96-2) Syracuse U Foreign Comp.

MacCann, Donnarae. White Supremacy in Children's Literature: Characterizations of African Americans, 1830-1900. Zipes, Jack D., ed. LC 97-37620. (Children's Literature & Culture Ser.: Vol. 4). 312p. 1997. text 80.00 (0-8153-2056-6, SS1043) Garland.

MacCann, Donnarae & Woodard, Gloria, eds. The Black American in Books for Children: Readings in Racism. 2nd ed. LC 85-10893. (Illus.). 310p. 1985. 31.00 (0-8108-1826-4) Scarecrow.

— Cultural Conformity in Books for Children: Further Readings in Racism. LC 77-22174. 215p. 1977. 26.50 (0-8108-1064-6) Scarecrow.

MacCann, Donnarae, jt. auth. see Maddy, Yulisa A.

MacCann, Lyndon. Casebook on Company Law. 1991. pap. 68.00 (1-85475-023-2, UK, MICHIE) LEXIS Pub.

— Companies Acts, 1963-1990. LC 96-231716. 1993. pap. text 120.00 (1-85475-148-4, IE, MICHIE) LEXIS Pub.

— Company Secretarial Manual. 1994. pap. text 99.00 (0-85475-238-2, IE, MICHIE) LEXIS Pub.

MacCann, Richard D. Films of the 1920s. LC 96-43027. (American Movies: The First Thirty Years Ser.: Vol. 5). (Illus.). 144p. 1996. 32.50 (0-8108-3255-0); pap. 23.50 (0-8108-3256-9) Scarecrow.

— The First Film Makers. (American Movies: The First Thirty Years Ser.). (Illus.). 335p. 1989. 36.00 (0-8108-2229-6); pap. 25.00 (0-8108-2230-X) Scarecrow.

— The First Tycoons. LC 86-22064. (Illus.). 269p. 1987. 29.50 (0-8108-1949-X); pap. 22.50 (0-8108-1950-3) Scarecrow.

— Hollywood in Transition. LC 77-5314. 208p. 1977. reprint ed. lib. bdg. 59.50 (0-8371-9616-7, MAHT, Greenwood Pr) Greenwood.

— A New Vice Presidency for a New Century. LC 91-76548. (Illus.). vi, 90p. (Orig.). 1991. pap. write for info. (0-934570-01-9) Image & Idea.

— The Silent Comedians. LC 93-11399. (American Movies: The First Thirty Years Ser.). (Illus.). 257p. 1993. 35.00 (0-8108-2725-5); pap. 22.50 (0-8108-2730-1) Scarecrow.

— The Silent Screen. LC 97-26270. (American Movies Ser.). 1997. 44.50 (0-8108-3368-9) Scarecrow.

— The Silent Screen. LC 97-26270. (American Movies Ser.). 1997. pap. 22.50 (0-8108-3392-1) Scarecrow.

— The Stars Appear. LC 91-42748. (American Movies: The First Thirty Years Ser.: No. 3). (Illus.). 339p. 1992. 45.00 (0-8108-2527-9); pap. 25.00 (0-8108-2528-7) Scarecrow.

— To Save Us from Ourselves: The Vision of a Future President. 226p. (Orig.). 1994. pap. 19.95 (0-934570-02-7) Image & Idea.

MacCann, William. Two Thousand Miles' Ride Through the Argentine Provinces, 2 vols. LC 70-128433. reprint ed. 97.00 (0-404-04102-7) AMS Pr.

MacCannell, Dean. Empty Meeting Grounds: The Tourist Papers. LC 91-32508. 240p. (C). 1992. pap. 24.99 (0-415-05693-4, A6836) Routledge.

— The Tourist: A New Theory of the Leisure Class. LC 98-38832. 245p. 1999. pap. 12.95 (0-520-21892-2, Pub. by U CA Pr) Cal Prin Full Svc.

MacCannell, Dean. The Tourist: A New Theory of the Leisure Class LC 75-7770. vi, 214 p. 1976. 8.95 (0-8052-3595-7) Schocken.

MacCannell, Dean & MacCannell, Juliet F. The Time of the Sign: A Semiotic Interpretation of Modern Culture. LC 81-47960. (Advances in Semiotics Ser.). 224p. reprint ed. pap. 69.50 (0-608-18257-5, 205670900081) Bks Demand.

MacCannell, Juliet F. Figuring Lacan. Criticism & the Cultural Unconscious. LC 86-11217. (Critics of the Twentieth Century Ser.). 204p. reprint ed. pap. 63.30 (0-7837-6884-2, 204671400003) Bks Demand.

— The Hysteric's Guide to the Future Female Subject. LC 99-17021. 288p. 1999. pap. 18.95 (0-8166-3296-0, Pub. by U of Minn Pr) Chicago Distribution Ctr.

— The Hysteric's Guide to the Future Female Subject. LC 99-17021. 288p. 1999. lib. bdg. 47.95 (0-8166-3295-2, Pub. by U of Minn Pr) Chicago Distribution Ctr.

— The Other Perspective in Gender & Culture: Rewriting Woman & the Symbolic. 1990. text 46.00 (0-231-07256-2) Col U Pr.

MacCannell, Juliet F. & Zakarin, Laura, eds. Thinking Bodies. LC 93-34805. (Irvine Studies in the Humanities). 288p. 1994. 39.50 (0-8047-2306-0); pap. 15.95 (0-8047-2304-4) Stanford U Pr.

MacCannell, Juliet F., jt. auth. see MacCannell, Dean.

MacCannell, Juliet F., tr. see Cixous, Helene.

MacCannell, Linda, photos by. Riders of the West: Portraits from Indian Rodeo. LC 98-55931. (Illus.). 120p. 1999. pap. 24.95 (0-295-97786-8) U of Wash Pr.

***Maccaro, Janet C.** 90 Day Immune System Makeover. 2000. pap. 12.99 (0-88419-692-5) Creation House.

Maccaro, Karen, jt. auth. see Edmunds, John C.

MacCaroll, Amber. Kaleidoscope of Day Dreams: A Spiritual Journey Through the Tarot. LC 98-75048. 218p. 1998. pap. 16.95 (0-9667767-9-8) JJay Pubg.

Maccarone, Grace. Cars! Cars! Cars! LC 94-18389. (Story Corner Ser.). (Illus.). 24p. (J). 1995. 6.95 (0-590-47572-X) Scholastic Inc.

***Maccarone, Grace.** A Child Was Born: A First Nativity Book. (Illus.). 32p. (J). (ps-1). 2000. 10.95 (0-439-18296-4) Scholastic Inc.

Maccarone, Grace. The Class Trip. LC 99-10687. (Hello Reader Ser.: Level 1). (Illus.). 32p. (J). (ps-3). 1999. pap. 3.99 (0-439-06755-3, Pub. by Scholastic Inc) Penguin Putnam.

M

***Maccarone, Grace.** Class Trip. (Hello, Reader! Ser.). (Illus.). (J). 1999. 9.44 (*0-606-18533-X*) Turtleback.

Maccarone, Grace. The Classroom Pet. LC 95-13151. (Hello Reader! Ser.: Bk. 3). (Illus.). 32p. (J). (ps-3). 1995. pap. 2.95 (*0-590-26264-5*, Cartwheel) Scholastic Inc.

— Classroom Pet. (Hello, Reader! Ser.). 1995. 8.70 (*0-606-09279-X*, Pub. by Turtleback) Demco.

— First Grade Friends: Recess Mess. LC 95-36016. (Hello Reader! Ser.: Level 1). (Illus.). (J). (ps-1). 1996. 3.50 (*0-614-08619-1*) Scholastic Inc.

— The Gym Day Winner. LC 95-10285. (Hello Reader! Ser.: Bk. 2). (Illus.). 32p. (J). (ps-1). 1996. pap. 3.99 (*0-590-26263-7*, Cartwheel) Scholastic Inc.

— Gym Day Winner. (Hello, Reader! Ser.). 1996. 9.19 (*0-606-09280-3*, Pub. by Turtleback) Demco.

— The Haunting of Grade Three. 96p. (Orig.). (J). (gr. 4-7). 1987. pap. 2.99 (*0-590-43868-9*) Scholastic Inc.

Maccarone, Grace. Haunting of Grade Three. (Lucky Star Ser.). (J). 1987. 7.85 (*0-606-03589-3*, Pub. by Turtleback) Demco.

Maccarone, Grace. I Have a Cold. LC 98-20284. (Hello Reader! Ser.: Level 1). (Illus.). 32p. (J). (ps-3). 1999. mass mkt. 3.50 (*0-590-39638-2*, Pub. by Scholastic Inc) Penguin Putnam.

***Maccarone, Grace.** I Shop with My Daddy. (Hello, Reader! Ser.). (J). 1998. 8.70 (*0-606-13510-3*, Pub. by Turtleback) Demco.

MacCarone, Grace. I Shop with My Daddy, Level 1. LC 97-14308. (Hello Reader! Ser.). (Illus.). (J). 1998. 3.50 (*0-590-50196-8*) Scholastic Inc.

Maccarone, Grace. Itchy, Itchy Chicken Pox. (Hello, Reader! Ser.). (J). 1992. 8.70 (*0-606-01857-3*, Pub. by Turtleback) Demco.

— Itchy, Itchy Chickenpox. LC 91-16695. (Illus.). 32p. (J). (ps-3). 1992. pap. 3.50 (*0-590-44948-6*) Scholastic Inc.

Maccarone, Grace. Looking At Space: First-Grade Friends. LC 95-36016. (Hello Reader! Ser.). (Illus.). 32p. (J). (ps-3). 1996. pap. 3.50 (*0-590-73878-X*, Cartwheel) Scholastic Inc.

Maccarone, Grace. The Lunch Box Surprise. LC 95-10284. (Hello Reader! Ser.: Bk. 1). (Illus.). 32p. (J). (ps-3). 1995. pap. 2.95 (*0-590-26267-X*, Cartwheel) Scholastic Inc.

Maccarone, Grace. The Lunch Box Surprise. (First-Grade Friends Ser.). (J). 1995. 8.70 (*0-606-07517-8*, Pub. by Turtleback) Demco.

Maccarone, Grace. Monster Math. LC 95-12133. (Hello Math Reader Level 1 Ser.). (Illus.). 32p. (J). (ps-3). 1995. pap. 3.50 (*0-590-22712-2*, Cartwheel) Scholastic Inc.

— Monster Math. (J). 1995. 8.70 (*0-606-07882-7*, Pub. by Turtleback) Demco.

***Maccarone, Grace.** Monster Math Picnic. 1998. 8.70 (*0-606-13617-7*, Pub. by Turtleback) Demco.

— Monster Math School Time. (Hello Math Reader Ser.). (J). 1997. 8.70 (*0-606-11634-6*, Pub. by Turtleback) Demco.

***MacCarone, Grace.** Monster Money. (Hello Math Reader Ser.). (J). (ps-1). 1998. 8.70 (*0-606-13618-5*, Pub. by Turtleback) Demco.

Maccarone, Grace. My Tooth Is about to Fall Out. LC 94-9772. (Hello Reader! Ser.).Tr. of Ma Dent Va Tomber. (Illus.). 32p. (J). (ps-1). 1995. 3.50 (*0-590-48376-5*, Cartwheel) Scholastic Inc.

Maccarone, Grace. My Tooth Is about to Fall Out.Tr. of Ma Dent Va Tomber. (J). 1995. 8.70 (*0-606-07912-2*, Pub. by Turtleback) Demco.

Maccarone, Grace. Oink! Moo! How Do You Do? LC 93-45962. (Illus.). 24p. (J). 1994. 6.95 (*0-590-48161-4*) Scholastic Inc.

— Oink! Moo! How Do You Do? (Illus.). 24p. (J). (ps). 1994. 6.95 (*0-590-20655-9*) Scholastic Inc.

— Our Solar System. LC 95-36015. (Hello Reader! Ser.: Level 1). (Illus.). (J). 1997. pap. 3.50 (*0-590-73879-8*) Scholastic Inc.

MacCarone, Grace. Un Partido de Futbol. (Mariposa Ser.). (SPA., Illus.). 32p. (J). (ps-1). 1998. pap. text 3.50 (*0-590-27499-6*, Cartwheel) Scholastic Inc.

— Un Partido de Futbol. (Mariposa Scholastica en Espanol Ser.). (J). 1998. 8.70 (*0-606-13882-X*, Pub. by Turtleback) Demco.

Maccarone, Grace. Pica, Pica Varicela: Itchy, Itchy Chicken Pox. (Hola Lector! Ser.).Tr. of Itchy, Itchy Chicken Pox. 1996. 8.70 (*0-606-08844-X*, Pub. by Turtleback) Demco.

— Pica, Pica Varicela (Itchy, Itchy Chicken Pox) Noda, Yolanda, tr. LC 97-102383.Tr. of Itchy, Itchy Chicken Pox. (SPA., Illus.). 30p. (J). (ps-3). 1996. mass mkt. 3.50 (*0-590-69817-6*) Scholastic Inc.

— Pizza Party. LC 93-19732. (Hello Reader! Ser.). (Illus.). 32p. (J). (ps-4). 1994. pap. 3.50 (*0-590-47563-0*, Cartwheel) Scholastic Inc.

Maccarone, Grace. Pizza Party! LC 93-19732. (Hello, Reader! Ser.). 1994. 8.70 (*0-606-06672-1*, Pub. by Turtleback) Demco.

— Recess Mess. (Hello, Reader! Ser.). 1996. 8.70 (*0-606-09281-1*, Pub. by Turtleback) Demco.

Maccarone, Grace. Return of the Third-Grade Ghosthunters. 64p. (J). (gr. 2-5). 1989. pap. 2.99 (*0-590-41944-7*). Scholastic Inc.

Maccarone, Grace. Sharing Time Troubles. (First-Grade Friends Ser.). (J). 1997. 8.70 (*0-606-11331-2*, Pub. by Turtleback) Demco.

Maccarone, Grace. Silly Story of Goldie Locks & the Three Squares. (Hello Math Reader Ser.). 1996. 8.70 (*0-606-09856-9*, Pub. by Turtleback) Demco.

— The Silly Story of Goldilocks & the Three Squares. LC 95-13226. (Hello Math Reader Ser.: Level 2). (Illus.). 32-40p. (J). (gr. k-2). 1996. pap. 3.50 (*0-590-54344-X*, Cartwheel) Scholastic Inc.

Maccarone, Grace. Soccer Game! (Hello, Reader! Ser.). (YA). 1994. 8.70 (*0-606-06748-5*, Pub. by Turtleback) Demco.

MacCarone, Grace. Soccer Game! LC 93-43742. (Illus.). 32p. (J). (ps-3). 1994. 2.95 (*0-590-48369-2*) Scholastic Inc.

Maccarone, Grace. The Sword in the Stone. LC 91-39947. (Hello Reader! Ser.). (Illus.). 32p. (J). (ps-3). 1992. pap. 3.50 (*0-590-45527-3*, 043, Cartwheel) Scholastic Inc.

— The Sword in the Stone. (Hello, Reader! Ser.). (J). 1992. 8.70 (*0-606-01957-X*, Pub. by Turtleback) Demco.

***Maccarone, Grace.** What is That? Said the Cat. (J). 1998. 8.95 (*0-606-13900-1*) Turtleback.

Maccarone, Grace. "What Is That?" Said the Cat, Level 1. LC 94-39100. (Hello Reader! Ser.). (Illus.). (J). 1995. 3.50 (*0-590-25945-8*, Cartwheel) Scholastic Inc.

MacCarone, Grace & Burns, Marilyn. Four Pigs, One Wolf & Seven Magic Shapes. LC 97-5040. (Hello Math Reader Ser.). (Illus.). (J). (gr. 3). 1997. write for info. (*0-590-30857-2*) Scholastic Inc.

— Monster Math School Time. LC 97-5035. (Hello Math Reader Ser.). (Illus.). 32p. (J). (ps-1). 1997. 3.50 (*0-590-30859-9*) Scholastic Inc.

***Maccarone, Grace & Burns, Marilyn.** Monster Money. LC 97-43658. (Hello Reader! Math Ser.: Level 1). (Illus.). 32p. (J). (ps-3). 1998. pap. 3.50 (*0-590-12007-7*) Scholastic Inc.

***Maccarone, Grace & Courtney, Richard.** Dinosaurs. LC 00-25984. (Hello Reader! Ser.). (Illus.). (J). 2001. pap. write for info. (*0-439-20060-1*) Scholastic Inc.

***Maccarone, Grace & Johnson, Meredith.** Mr. Rover Takes Over. LC 99-462281. (Hello Reader! Ser.). (Illus.). (J). 2000. pap. write for info. (*0-439-20057-1*) Scholastic Inc.

***Maccarone, Grace & Lewin, Betsy.** First Grade Friends: Softball Practice. LC 00-25455. (Hello Reader! Ser.). (Illus.). (J). 2000. write for info. (*0-439-20139-X*) Scholastic Inc.

***Maccarone, Grace & Williams, Sam.** A Child Was Born: A Christmas Story. LC 99-88022. (J). 2000. write for info. (*0-439-14087-0*) Scholastic Inc.

MacCarone, Grace, et al. Monster Math Picnic. LC 97-12854. (Hello Math Reader Ser.). (Illus.). (J). (ps-4). 1998. 3.50 (*0-590-37127-4*) Scholastic Inc.

Maccarone, Grace, jt. auth. see Chardiet, Bernice.

Maccarone, Sal. How to Make $40,000 a Year with Your Woodworking. LC 98-26021. (Illus.). 128p. 1998. pap. 19.99 (*1-55870-480-9*, Popular Woodwkng Bks) F & W Pubns Inc.

— Tune up Your Tools. (Illus.). 144p. (Orig.). 1996. pap. 22.99 (*1-55870-409-4*, Betrwy Bks) F & W Pubns Inc.

Maccarone, Sandra F., jt. illus. see White, Kathleen.

MacCarron, Donald. Step Together! The Story of Ireland's Emergency Army As Told by Its Veterans. LC 99-176034. (Illus.). 192p. 1999. text 29.95 (*0-7165-2619-0*, Pub. by Irish Acad Pr) Intl Spec Bk.

***Maccarrone, Betsy.** First-Grade Friends: The Class Trip. (Hello, Reader! Ser.). (Illus.). (J). 1999. 9.44 (*0-606-18543-7*) Turtleback.

MacCarter, Jane S. New Mexico Wildlife Viewing Guide. LC 93-42965. (Watchable Wildlife Ser.). (Illus.). 96p. 1994. pap. 8.95 (*1-56044-213-1*) Falcon Pub Inc.

***MacCarter, Jane S.** New Mexico Wildlife Viewing Guide. 2nd ed. LC 99-89042. (Illus.). 2000. 9.95 (*1-56044-991-8*) Falcon Pub Inc.

MacCarthy, Alan W., Jr. How to Save Big Bucks on Your Pet's Veterinary Bills. 128p. 1992. pap. 14.95 (*1-882822-00-5*) First-Care.

MacCarthy, B., tr. see Oengus the Culdee.

MacCarthy, Bartholomew, ed. The Codex Palatino-Vaticanus. LC 78-72679. (Royal Irish Academy. Todd Lecture Ser.: Vol. 3). reprint ed. 35.00 (*0-404-60563-X*) AMS Pr.

MacCarthy, Catherine P. The Blue Globe: Poems. LC 98-145427. 96p. 1998. pap. 14.95 (*0-85640-619-8*, Pub. by Blackstaff Pr) Dufour.

MacCarthy, Desmond. Court Theatre, 1904-1907: A Commentary & Criticism. Weintraub, Stanley, ed. LC 66-27969. (Books of the Theatre: No. 6). 182p. 1966. 19.95 (*0-87024-068-4*) U of Miami Pr.

Maccarthy, Desmond. Criticism. LC 78-97710. (Essay Index Reprint Ser.). 1977. 23.95 (*0-8369-1360-4*) Ayer.

MacCarthy, Desmond. Experience. LC 68-54357. (Essay Index Reprint Ser.). 1977. 21.95 (*0-8369-0640-3*) Ayer.

— Portraits. LC 72-5613. (Essay Index Reprint Ser.). 1977. reprint ed. 21.95 (*0-8369-7299-6*) Ayer.

MacCarthy, Fiona. Stanley Spencer: English Visions. LC 97-61407. (Illus.). 192p. 1997. 45.00 (*0-300-07337-2*) Yale U Pr.

MacCarthy, Mary. The Crafter's Pattern Sourcebook: 1,000 Classic Motifs for Every Craft from Around the World & Though the Ages. (Illus.). 1999. 27.50 (*1-57076-141-8*) Trafalgar.

— Decorative Stencils for Your Home. (Illus.). 128p. 1996. 27.99 (*0-89134-767-4*, North Lght Bks) F & W Pubns Inc.

— Handicaps: Six Studies. LC 67-26756. (Essay Index Reprint Ser.). 1977. 18.95 (*0-8369-0642-X*) Ayer.

MacCarthy, Mike, jt. auth. see Meek, Doris.

MacCarthy, Mor & Count of Clandemond. An Irish Miscellany: Essays Heraldic, Historical & Genealogical. (Illus.). 350p. 1998. lib. bdg. 40.00 (*0-9654220-3-8*) Gryfons Pubs & Dist.

MacCarthy, P., ed. Humic Substances in Soil & Crop Sciences: Selected Readings. 304p. 1990. 30.00 (*0-89118-104-0*) Soil Sci Soc Am.

MacCarthy, Patricia, jt. auth. see Mahy, Margaret.

MacCarthy, Patrick & Suffet, Irwin H., eds. Aquatic Humic Substances: Influence on Fate & Treatment of Pollutants. LC 88-38029. (Advances in Chemistry Ser.: Vol. 219). 896p. 1989. reprint ed. pap. 200.00 (*0-608-03896-2*, 206434300008) Bks Demand.

— Aquatic Humic Substances: Influence on Fate & Treatment of Pollution. LC 88-38029. (Advances in Chemistry Ser.: No. 219). (Illus.). 898p. 1989. text 109.95 (*0-8412-1428-X*, Pub. by Am Chemical) OUP.

MacCarthy, R. B. The Trinity College Estates, 1800-1923: Corporate Management in an Age of Reform. LC 92-233413. ix, 27p. 1992. write for info. (*0-85221-118-X*) Dundalgon Pr.

MacCarthy, Robert. Ancient & Modern: A Short History of the Church of Ireland. 64p. 1995. pap. 5.95 (*1-85182-205-4*, Pub. by Four Cts Pr) Intl Spec Bk.

MacCartney, Clarence E., ed. Great Sermons of the World. LC 97-23007. 416p. 1997. reprint ed. 19.95 (*1-56563-302-4*) Hendrickson MA.

MacCartney, Mike. BMW '02 Restoration Guide. (Illus.). 224p. 1998. pap. 29.95 (*1-85520-451-7*, Pub. by Brooklands Bks) Motorbooks Intl.

MacCary, W. Thomas. Childlike Achilles: Ontogeny & Phylogeny in the Iliad. LC 82-4458. (Illus.). 294p. reprint ed. pap. 91.20 (*0-7837-0422-4*, 204074500018) Bks Demand.

— Friends & Lovers: The Phenomenology of Desire in Shakespearean Comedy. LC 84-17605. 276p. reprint ed. pap. 85.60 (*0-8357-3443-9*, 203970000013) Bks Demand.

— Hamlet: A Guide to the Play. LC 97-38987. (Greenwood Guides to Shakespeare Ser.). 168p. 1998. lib. bdg. 55.00 (*0-313-30082-8*, Greenwood Pr) Greenwood.

MacCashill, Libby & Novak, David. Ladies on the Field: Two Civil War Nurses from Maine on the Battlefields of Virginia. (Illus.). 100p. 1996. pap. 10.00 (*0-9651858-1-8*) Signal Tree.

MacCaskey, Michael. Gardening for Dummies. National Gardening Association Editors, ed. LC SB453.M238 1999. (For Dummies Ser.). (Illus.). 432p. 1999. pap. 16.99 (*0-7645-5130-2*) IDG Bks.

— Gardening for Dummies, Mini Edition. 1999. 4.95 (*0-7624-0634-8*) Running Pr.

MacCaskey, Michael, jt. auth. see Haas, Cathy.

MacCaskill, Bridget. The Blood Is Wild. pap. 19.95 (*0-224-03697-1*, Pub. by Jonathan Cape) Trafalgar.

— The Blood Is Wild. (Illus.). 176p. 1996. 35.00 (*0-224-03698-X*, Pub. by Jonathan Cape) Trafalgar.

— The Blood Is Wild. (Illus.). 160p. 1997. pap. 19.95 (*0-244-03697-7*, Pub. by Jonathan Cape) Trafalgar.

***MacCaskill, Don.** Listen to the Trees. 2000. pap. 19.95 (*0-946487-65-0*) Luath Pr Ltd.

Maccaulay, Teresa. Reach for the Stars & Read. (Illus.). (J). (gr. 1-6). 1999. pap. 14.95 (*1-56167-482-6*) Am Literary Pr.

***MacCauley, Clay.** Seminole Indians of Florida. (Southeastern Classics in Archaeology, Anthropology & History). (Illus.). 96p. 2000. pap. 29.95 (*0-8130-1792-0*) U Press Fla.

MacCauley, Nancy L. Diana: A Modern Metaphysical Fairy Tale. Teasdale, Carrie, ed. LC 85-73902. 320p. (Orig.). 1986. pap. 9.95 (*0-251-93702-X*) Another Way.

MacCharles, D. C. Trade among Multinationals: Intra-Industry Trade & National Competitiveness. 224p. 1987. lib. bdg. 65.00 (*0-7099-4618-X*, Pub. by C Helm) Routldge.

Maccherone, Christina. The Greatest Roanoke Region: Your Open Door. (Illus.). 190p. 1997. 34.95 (*1-890291-06-4*) Platinum Pubng.

Macchi, jt. auth. see Frenzel.

***Macchi, Jean-Daniel.** Israel et Ses Tribus Selon Genese 49. (Orbis Biblicus et Orientalis Ser.: No. 171). xiv, 380p. 1999. text 69.00 (*3-7278-1259-1*, Pub. by Ed Univ Fri) Eisenbrauns.

Macchi, John W. & Kane, Art. Choosing the Right Cruise for You: The Bon Voyage Guide. LC 94-29665. (Illus.). 112p. 1994. pap. 9.95 (*0-942963-52-0*) Distinctive Pub.

Macchi, Odile. Adaptive Processing: The Least Mean Squares Approach with Applications in Transmission. 476p. 1995. 270.00 (*0-471-93403-8*) Wiley.

Macchi, V. Italian-English - English-Italian Dictionary (Sansoni) 3rd ed. (ENG & ITA.). 2277p. 1991. 110.00 (*88-383-1437-3*, Pub. by Sansoni) IBD Ltd.

Macchi, Vladimiro. Collins-Sansoni Italian Dictionary. 3rd ed. (ENG & ITA.). 2277p. 1988. 50.00 (*0-7859-7399-0*, 0060178035) Fr & Eur.

— Harrap's Standard Italian Dictionary, Vol. 4: English-Italian M-Z. 1991. pap. 59.95 (*0-13-382573-6*) P-H.

— Italian-German Dictionary: Woerterbuch Italienisch-Deutsch. 5th ed. (GER & ITA.). 600p. 1986. 17.95 (*0-8288-0374-9*, F42340) Fr & Eur.

— Langenscheidt Large German-Italian Dictionary: Langenscheidt Grosswoerterbuch Deutsch-Italienisch. 2nd ed. (GER & ITA.). 938p. 1984. 135.00 (*0-8288-0373-0*, F41300) Fr & Eur.

— Sansoni Woerterbuch der Italienischen und Deutschen Sprache. 2nd ed. (GER & ITA.). 3178p. 1989. 795.00 (*0-7859-8578-6*, 8838314535) Fr & Eur.

— Woerterbuch Italienisch-Deutsch, Deutsch-Italienisch. (GER & ITA.). 1114p. 1989. 29.95 (*0-7859-8442-9*, 3572037522) Fr & Eur.

Macchi, Vladimiro, ed. see Sansoni.

Macchia, Stephen A., et al. Becoming a Healthy Church: 10 Characteristics to Pursue in the Process. LC 98-33826. 240p. (gr. 13). 1999. 16.99 (*0-8010-1177-9*) Baker Bks.

Macchiavelli, A., et al, eds. Nuclear Physics: Proceedings of the Ninth Workshop, Buenos Aire, Argentina June 23-July 4, 1986. 608p. 1987. text 138.00 (*9971-5-0204-6*) World Scientific Pub.

Macchiavelli, M. Decoupage: Ideas & Projects to Decorate Your Home. (Illus.). 160p. 1996. pap. 19.95 (*0-7063-7462-2*, Pub. by WrLock) Sterling.

***Macchiavelli, Mariarita.** Quick & Easy Mosaics: Innovative Projects & Techniques. (Illus.). 160p. 1999. pap. 14.95 (*0-8069-4475-7*) Sterling.

Macchiavelli, Niccolo. The Arte of Warre, (Certain Waies of the Orderyng of Souldiours) Whitehorne, P., tr. LC 79-26097. (English Experience Ser.: No. 135). 1969. reprint ed. 65.00 (*90-221-0135-5*) Walter J Johnson.

***Macchiavello, C., et al, eds.** Quantum Computation & Quantum Information Theory. 450p. 1999. 84.00 (*981-02-4117-8*) World Scientific Pub.

Macchio, Ralph. Independence Day. (Illus.). 96p. 1996. pap. text 6.95 (*0-7851-0226-4*) Marvel Entrprs.

— X-Men Adventures, Vol. 2. LC 95-119843. (Illus.). 96p. 1994. pap. 4.95 (*0-7851-0028-8*) Marvel Entrprs.

Macchio, William J., ed. Hurricane Andrew: Path of Destruction. 100p. (Orig.). pap. 11.95 (*1-882526-00-7*) BD Pub.

Macci, Joy E. Serendipity of Success: Treasure Hunt Unlocking the Keys to Your Personal Success System. LC 98-87972. (Illus.). 160p. 1998. pap. 14.98 (*0-9667337-0-3*) JOS Unlmtd Pubns.

MacCiarnain, Seamus, ed. see National Graves Association of Ireland Staff.

Maccini, Robert G. Her Testimony Is True: Women As Witnesses According to John. (JSNT Supplement Ser.: No. 125). 278p. 1996. 80.00 (*1-85075-588-4*, Pub. by Sheffield Acad) CUP Services.

Macciocchi, Maria A. Daily Life in Revolutionary China. LC 72-81757. 512p. 1973. pap. 10.00 (*0-85345-282-2*, Pub. by Monthly Rev) NYU Pr.

Maccioli, Gerald A., ed. Theory & Practice of Intra-Aortic Balloon Pump Therapy. LC 96-14625. 206p. 1996. 39.95 (*0-683-05302-7*) Lppncott W & W.

Macciomei, Nancy R. & Ruben, Douglas H. Behavioral Management in the Public Schools: An Urban Approach. LC 99-21600. 176p. 1999. 55.00 (*0-275-96327-6*, C6327, Praeger Pubs) Greenwood.

Macciomei, Nancy R., jt. ed. see Douglas, Ruben H.

***Maccioni, Alvaro.** Mama Toscana: The Authentic Tuscan Cookbook. (Illus.). 224p. 2000. 45.00 (*1-86205-174-7*, Pub. by Pavilion Bks Ltd) Trafalgar.

MacClancy, Jeremy. Consuming Culture. 256p. 1995. 23.00 (*0-8050-2578-2*) H Holt & Co.

— Consuming Culture: Why You Eat What You Eat. 1995. pap. 13.95 (*0-8050-3587-7*) H Holt & Co.

***MacClancy, Jeremy.** Consuming Culture: Why You Eat What You Eat. (Illus.). 246p. 1999. reprint ed. text 23.00 (*0-7881-6240-3*) DIANE Pub.

— The Decline of Carlism. (Basque Ser.). 384p. 2000. 49.95 (*0-87417-344-2*) U of Nev Pr.

MacClancy, Jeremy, ed. Contesting Art. LC 98-120911. 1997. 55.00 (*1-85973-134-1*, Pub. by Berg Pubs); pap. 19.50 (*1-85973-139-2*, Pub. by Berg Pubs) NYU Pr.

MacClancy, Jeremy, et al, eds. Sport, Identity & Ethnicity. (Ethnic Identity Ser.). (Illus.). 203p. 1996. 55.00 (*1-85973-140-6*, Pub. by Berg Pubs); pap. 19.50 (*1-85973-145-7*, Pub. by Berg Pubs) NYU Pr.

MacClancy, Jeremy & McDonaugh, Chris, eds. Popularizing Anthropology. 272p. (C). 1996. 85.00 (*0-415-13612-1*); pap. 25.99 (*0-415-13613-X*) Routledge.

MacClancy, Jeremy, jt. auth. see Pocock, David F.

MacCleery, Douglas W. American Forests: A History of Resiliency & Recovery. (Illus.). 58p. (YA). (gr. 12 up). 1994. pap. text 40.00 (*0-7881-0858-1*) DIANE Pub.

— American Forests: A History of Resiliency & Recovery. 2nd rev. ed. LC 92-29771. (Issues Ser.). (Illus.). vi, 58p. (C). 1996. pap. 6.95 (*0-89030-048-8*) Forest Hist Soc.

MacClennan, Carole. Learning by Doing: Eighty Activities to Enrich Religion Classes for Young Children. LC 93-60026. (Illus.). 136p. (Orig.). 1993. pap. 14.95 (*0-89622-562-3*) Twenty-Third.

MacClintock, Carol, ed. Readings in the History of Music in Performance. LC 78-8511. (Illus.). 448p. 1994. pap. 18.95 (*0-253-20285-X*); text 35.00 (*0-253-14495-7*) Ind U Pr.

MacClintock, Lucy, ed. see Klein, David.

MacCluer, Barbara I., jt. auth. see Cowen, Carl C., Jr.

MacCluer, C. R. Boundary Value Problems & Orthogonal Expansions: Physical Problems from a Sobolev Viewpoint. LC 94-20004. 368p. 1994. 79.95 (*0-7803-1071-3*, PC04226) Inst Electrical.

— Mathematical Modeling for Industry, Science & Government. LC 99-27073. 308p. 1999. 76.00 (*0-13-949199-6*) P-H.

***MacClure, Terrence.** Golf Ching. 2001. 6.99 (*0-517-16267-9*) Crown Pub Group.

Maccluskie, Ingersoll. Counseling in Community Agencies. (Counseling Ser.). 2000. pap. text 40.50 (*0-534-35605-2*) Brooks-Cole.

Maccluskie, Tom. Ships: From the Harland & Wolfe Archives. 1998. 15.99 (*0-7858-0949-X*) Bk Sales Inc.

Maccoby, Annie & Church, Jeff. Alien Equation. 47p. 1986. reprint ed. pap. 3.50 (*0-87129-024-3*, A45) Dramatic Pub.

MacCoby, Eleanor E. The Two Sexes: Growing up Apart, Coming Together. LC 97-30594. (Family & Public Policy Ser.). 384p. 1999. text 39.95 (*0-674-91481-3*) Belknap Pr.

Maccoby, Eleanor E. Two Sexes: Growing up, Apart, Coming Together. (Family & Public Policy Ser.). 384p. 1999. pap. text 19.95 (*0-674-91482-1*) HUP.

Maccoby, Eleanor E. & Jacklin, Carol N. The Psychology of Sex Differences, 2 vols., Vol. I. LC 73-94488. xv, 634p. 1974. pap. 17.95 (*0-8047-0974-2*) Stanford U Pr.

— The Psychology of Sex Differences, 2 vols., Vol. II. LC 73-94488. xv, 634p. 1974. pap. 11.95 (*0-8047-0975-0*) Stanford U Pr.

An Asterisk (*) at the beginning of an entry indicates that the title is appearing for the first time.

Maccoby, Eleanor E. & Mnookin, Robert H. Dividing the Child: Social & Legal Dilemmas of Custody. (Illus.). 416p. 1992. 52.00 (*0-674-21294-0*) HUP.
— Dividing the Child: Social & Legal Dilemmas of Custody. (Illus.). 384p. 1994. pap. text 22.50 (*0-674-21295-9*, MACDIX) HUP.
Maccoby, Hyam. Ritual & Morality: The Ritual Purity Systems & Its Place in Judaism. LC 98-35975. 265p. (C). 1999. text 54.95 (*0-521-49540-7*) Cambridge U Pr.
Maccoby, Hyam Z. Judas Iscariot & the Myth of Jewish Evil. 280p. 1992. 27.95 (*0-02-919555-1*) Free Pr.
— Revolution in Judaea: Jesus & the Jewish Resistance. LC 80-16752. 256p. 1980. 9.95 (*0-8008-6784-X*) Taplinger.
Maccoby, Hyam Z., ed. Judaism on Trial: Jewish-Christian Disputations in the Middle Ages. 246p. 1993. reprint ed. pap. 19.95 (*1-874774-16-1*, Pub. by Littman Lib) Intl Spec Bk.
Maccoby, Michael. Why Work? Motivating the New Workforce. 2nd ed. 155p. 1995. pap. 24.95 (*0-917917-05-7*) Miles River.
Maccoby, Michael, ed. Sweden at the Edge: Lessons for American & Swedish Managers. LC 90-44875. (Innovations in Organizations Ser.). 260p. (C). 1991. text 35.00 (*0-8122-8153-5*) U of Pa Pr.
Maccoby, Michael, jt. ed. see Cortina, Maruicio.
MacCoby, Simon, ed. The English Radical Tradition, 1763-1914. LC 78-681. 236p. 1978. reprint ed. lib. bdg. 65.00 (*0-313-20284-2*, MAER, Greenwood Pr) Greenwood.
MacColl, E. Kimbark & Stein, Harry H. Merchants, Money & Power: The Portland Establishment, 1843-1913. Brunsman, Philippa, ed. LC 88-24653. (Illus.). 550p. 1988. 29.95 (*0-9603408-3-1*); pap. 19.95 (*0-9603408-4-X*) Georgian Pr.
MacColl, Ewan. Folk Songs & Ballads of Scotland. (Illus.). 96p. 1965. pap. 11.95 (*0-8256-0057-X*, OK61341, Oak) Music Sales.
MacColl, Ewan & Seeger, Peggy, eds. Travellers' Songs from England & Scotland. LC 76-2854. 399p. 1977. reprint ed. pap. 123.70 (*0-608-01433-8*, 206219500002) Bks Demand.
***MacColl, Gail.** The Book of Card Games for Little Kids. (Illus.). 112p. 2000. pap. 12.95 (*0-7611-0708-8*) Workman Pub.
MacColl, Gail S. The Book of Cards for Kids. LC 91-50962. (Illus.). 128p. (J). (ps-4). 1992. 12.95 (*1-56305-240-7*, 3240) Workman Pub.
MacColl, Gail S. & Wallace, Carol M. To Marry an English Lord: or How Anglomania Really Got Started. LC 85-40529. (Illus.). 416p. 1986. pap. 14.95 (*0-89480-939-3*, 939) Workman Pub.
MacColl, Gail S., et al. Hispanics' Schooling: Risk Factors for Dropping Out & Barriers to Resuming Education. (Illus.). 40p. (C). 1999. reprint ed. pap. text 15.00 (*0-7881-7567-X*) DIANE Pub.
MacColl, L. A., ed. see Applied Mathematics Symposium Staff.
Maccoll, R. & Guard-Friar, D. Phycobiliproteins. LC 85-32567. 224p. 1986. 132.00 (*0-8493-5525-7*, CRC Reprint) Franklin.
MacColla, Charles J. Breach of Promise: Its Historical & Social Considerations, to Which Are Added a Few Pages on the Law of Breach of Promise & a Glance at Many Amusing Cases since the Reign of Queen Elizabeth. xi, 93p. 1993. reprint ed. 30.00 (*0-8377-2445-7*, Rothman) W S Hein.
MacColla, Fionn. And the Cock Crew. 192p. 1995. pap. 11.95 (*0-86241-536-5*, Pub. by Canongate Books) Interlink Pub.
MacCollum, David V. Construction Safety Planning. 304p. 1995. text 60.95 (*0-442-01940-8*, VNR) Wiley.
MacCollum, David V. Construction Safety Planning. (Industrial Health & Safety Ser.). 285p. 1995. 80.00 (*0-471-28669-9*, VNR) Wiley.
MacCollum, David V. Crane Hazards & Their Prevention. LC 93-39816. (Illus.). 172p. (Orig.). 1993. pap. 34.95 (*0-939874-95-4*, 4348) ASSE.
***MacComb, Debra Ann.** Tales of Liberation, Strategies of Containment: Divorce & the Representation of Womanhood in American Fiction, 1880-1920. LC 00-26133. (Studies in American Popular History & Culture). 2000. write for info. (*0-8153-3804-X*) Garland.
MacCombie, Turi. Create Your Own Rain Forest Sticker Picture. (Illus.). (J). 1995. pap. 3.50 (*0-486-28407-7*) Dover.
MacCombie, Turi. Ready-to-Use Whimsical Illustrations of Animals. (Clip Art Ser.). (Illus.). 64p. 1990. pap. 5.95 (*0-486-26268-5*) Dover.
Maccombie, Turi. Realistic Dinosaurs Stickers. (Illus.). (J). (gr. k-3). 1994. pap. 1.00 (*0-486-28066-7*) Dover.
MacCombie, Turi. My First Book of Animals from A to Z: More Than 150 Animals Every Child Should Know. LC 92-19284. (Cartwheel Learning Bookshelf Ser.). 64p. (J). (ps-2). 1994. 13.95 (*0-590-46305-5*, Cartwheel) Scholastic Inc.
MacCombie, Turi, jt. auth. see Black, Sonia W.
MacConaill, M. A., jt. auth. see Basmajian, John V.
MacConaill, P. A., et al, eds. Mechatronics & Robotics. (Advances in Design & Manufacturing Ser.: No. 1). 346p. 1991. 90.00 (*90-5199-057-X*, Pub. by IOS Pr) IOS Press.
Macconaill, P. A., jt. ed. see Rathmill, K.
Maccone, Claudio. Telecommunications, KLT & Relativity. Blade, Richard A., ed. (Textbooks in Science & Mathematics Ser.). (Illus.). x, 238p. (Orig.). (C). 1994. pap. 35.00 (*1-880930-04-8*) IPI Pr.
MacConnell. Florida Motor Vehicle Liability Law 98-4, 4 vols. 350p. 1998. write for info. (*0-327-00816-4*, 8071721) LEXIS Pub.
— Florida Motor Vehicle Liability Law 99-1, 4 vols. 422p. 1999. ring bd. 48.00 (*0-327-01168-8*, 8071722) LEXIS Pub.
***MacConnell.** Florida Motor Vehicle Liability Law 99-3. 200p. 1999. ring bd. write for info. (*0-327-01706-6*, 8071724) LEXIS Pub.
— Florida Motor Vehicle Liability Law 99-2, 4 vols., Set. 268p. 1999. ring bd. write for info. (*0-327-01530-6*, 8071723) LEXIS Pub.
— Florida Traffic & DUI Practice Manual 99-3, 3 vols., Set. 240p. 1999. ring bd. write for info. (*0-327-01652-3*, 8081224) LEXIS Pub.
MacConnell. Florida Traffic & DUI Practice Manual 99-1, Issue 99-1. 474p. 1999. ring bd., suppl. ed. write for info. (*0-327-01066-5*, 8081222) LEXIS Pub.
— Florida Traffic & DUI Practice Manual 99-2, 3 vols. 262p. 1999. ring bd. write for info. (*0-327-01351-6*, 8081223) LEXIS Pub.
MacConnell, James D. Dr. Mac, Planner for Schools: Memoirs of My First 80 Years. (Illus.). vi, 194p. 1988. 17.95 (*0-929558-00-6*) Johnson-Dole.
MacConnell, Marcia. Florida Motor Vehicle Liability Law Service, 1981. 1994. ring bd., suppl. ed. 45.00 (*0-685-14238-8*, MICHIE) LEXIS Pub.
— Florida Motor Vehicle Liability Law Service, 1981, 4 vols., Set. 310p. 1997. ring bd. 280.00 (*0-409-26142-4*, 80710-10, MICHIE) LEXIS Pub.
— Florida Negligence Law Manual. 1987. ring bd., suppl. ed. 45.00 (*0-685-14241-8*, MICHIE) LEXIS Pub.
— Florida Negligence Law Manual, 2 vols., Set. 900p. 1995. ring bd. 160.00 (*0-409-26454-7*, 80723-10, MICHIE) LEXIS Pub.
— Florida Traffic & DUI Practice. 1994. suppl. ed. 47.00 (*0-318-59843-4*, MICHIE) LEXIS Pub.
— Florida Traffic & DUI Practice, 3 vols., Set. 1000p. 1995. spiral bd. 270.00 (*0-409-26131-9*, 80805-10, MICHIE) LEXIS Pub.
Maccord, Howard A., Sr. The Archeological Society of Virginia, a Forty-Year History, No. 21. 66p. 1990. pap. 13.50 (*1-884626-07-6*) Archeolog Soc.
MacCord, Howard A., Sr. Falls Zone Archaeology in Virginia, No. M1. 142p. 1985. pap. 15.00 (*1-884626-21-1*) Archeolog Soc.
— The Lewis Creek Mound Culture in Virginia, No. M3. 92p. 1986. pap. 17.00 (*1-884626-20-3*) Archeolog Soc.
— Prehistory of the Gathright Dam Area, Virginia, No. M2. 75p. 1975. pap. 15.00 (*1-884626-19-X*) Archeolog Soc.
Maccord, Howard A., Sr. & Buchanan, William T., Jr. The Crab Orchard Site: Tazewell County, Virginia, No. 8. 156p. 1980. pap. 9.00 (*1-884626-02-5*) Archeolog Soc.
MacCorkle, Douglas B. God's Special Secret: The Case Paul Argues in the Epistle to the Ephesians. (Illus.). 300p. (Orig.). 1994. pap. text 14.95 (*0-9639865-0-3*) D B MacCorkle.
MacCorkle, Lyn. Cubans in the United States: A Bibliography for Research in the Social & Behavioral Science, 1. LC 84-6675. (Bibliographies & Indexes in Sociology Ser.: No. 1). 227p. 1984. lib. bdg. 59.95 (*0-313-24509-6*, MKC/, Greenwood Pr) Greenwood.
MacCorkle, Stuart A. American Policy of Recognition Toward Mexico. LC 72-131774. 1971. reprint ed. 9.00 (*0-403-00661-9*) Scholarly.
— American Policy of Recognition Towards Mexico. LC 70-155620. reprint ed. 27.50 (*0-404-04108-6*) AMS Pr.
MacCormac, Earl & Stamenov, Maxim I., eds. Fractals of Brain, Fractals of Mind: In Search of a Symmetry Bond. LC 96-17605. (Advances in Consciousness Research Ser.: Vol. 7). x, 359p. 1996. pap. 34.95 (*1-55619-187-1*) J Benjamins Pubng Co.
MacCormac, Earl R. A Cognitive Theory of Metaphor. 264p. 1989. reprint ed. pap. text 16.00 (*0-262-63124-5*, Bradford Bks) MIT Pr.
— Metaphor & Myth in Science & Religion. LC 75-23941. 187p. reprint ed. pap. 58.00 (*0-608-15267-6*, 205220700060) Bks Demand.
MacCormac, John P. This Time for Keeps. LC 72-4584. (Essay Index Reprint Ser.). 1977. reprint ed. 20.95 (*0-8369-2962-4*) Ayer.
MacCormack, Bill, ed. see Trollope, Anthony.
MacCormack, Carol & Strathern, Marilyn, eds. Nature, Culture & Gender. (Illus.). 235p. 1980. pap. text 22.95 (*0-521-28001-X*) Cambridge U Pr.
MacCormack, Carol P., ed. Ethnography of Fertility & Birth. 2nd rev. ed. (Illus.). 283p. (C). 1994. pap. text 13.95 (*0-88133-817-6*) Waveland Pr.
MacCormack, Ellen, jt. auth. see Janda, Louis.
MacCormack, Geoffrey. The Spirit of Traditional Chinese Law. LC 94-39610. (Spirit of the Laws Ser.). 1995. 45.00 (*0-8203-1722-5*) U of Ga Pr.
— Traditional Chinese Penal Law. 1991. text 76.50 (*0-7486-0211-9*, Pub. by Edinburgh U Pr) Col U Pr.
MacCormack, Harry. Call of the Mountains. LC 99-14760. 72p. 1999. pap. 14.95 (*0-7734-3097-0*) E Mellen.
MacCormack, John R. Revolutionary Politics in the Long Parliament. LC 72-93952. 352p. 1973. 32.00 (*0-674-76775-6*) HUP.
MacCormack, Karen & Halsey, Alan. Fit to Print. 62p. 1998. pap. 16.95 (*1-55245-032-5*) Coach Hse Bks.
MacCormack, Sabine. Religion in the Andes: Vision & Imagination in Early Colonial Peru. (Illus.). 531p. 1991. text 69.50 (*0-691-09468-3*, Pub. by Princeton U Pr); pap. text 22.95 (*0-691-02106-6*, Pub. by Princeton U Pr) Cal Prin Full Svc.
— The Shadows of Poetry: Vergil in the Mind of Augustine. LC 97-45014. (Transformation of the Classical Heritage Ser.). 273p. 1998. 40.00 (*0-520-21187-1*, Pub. by U CA Pr) Cal Prin Full Svc.
MacCormick. Shark Attacks, Vol. 1. 1998. 5.99 (*0-312-96618-0*, Pub. by Tor Bks) St Martin.
MacCormick, Alec. Papier Mache Style: 100 Step-by-Step Designs for Bowls, Jewelry, Toys, Vases, Mirrors & Other Creations. (Illus.). 128p. 1995. pap. 15.95 (*0-8019-8755-5*) Krause Pubns.
MacCormick, Austin H. The Education of Adult Prisoners. LC 73-38668. (Foundations of Criminal Justice Ser.). reprint ed. 64.50 (*0-404-09178-4*) AMS Pr.
MacCormick, D. Neil. Enlightenment, Rights & Revolutions: Essays in Philosophy of Law & Social Philosophy. 396p. 1989. pap. text 60.00 (*0-08-037734-3*, Pub. by Aberdeen U Pr) Macmillan.
— H. L. A. Hart. Twining, William, ed. LC 81-50790. (Jurists: Profiles in Legal Theory Ser.). 192p. 1981. 32.50 (*0-8047-1107-0*) Stanford U Pr.
— Legal Reasoning & Legal Theory. (Clarendon Law Ser.). 322p. 1994. pap. text 32.00 (*0-19-876384-0*) OUP.
— Legal Right & Social Democracy: Essays in Legal & Political Philosophy. 1984. pap. 18.95 (*0-19-825502-0*) OUP.
MacCormick, D. Neil & Birks, Peter B. H., eds. The Legal Mind: Essays for Tony Honore. 336p. 1986. text 79.00 (*0-19-876196-1*) OUP.
MacCormick, D. Neil & Summers, Robert S. Interpreting Statutes: A Comparative Study. (Applied Legal Philosophy Ser.). 567p. 1991. text 131.95 (*1-85521-183-1*, Pub. by Dartmth Pub) Ashgate Pub Co.
MacCormick, D. Neil & Summers, Robert S., eds. Interpreting Precedents: A Comparative Study. LC 96-39520. (Applied Legal Philosophy Ser.). 608p. 1997. text 109.95 (*1-85521-686-8*, Pub. by Dartmth Pub) Ashgate Pub Co.
MacCormick, D. Neil & Weinberger, Ota. An Institutional Theory of Law. 240p. 1986. text 129.50 (*90-277-2079-7*, D Reidel) Kluwer Academic.
MacCormick, D. Neil, jt. ed. see Aarnio, Aulis.
MacCormick, D. Neil, ed. see Wroblewski, Jerzy.
MacCormick, Neil. Constructing Legal Systems: European Union in Legal Theory. LC 97-37681. 140p. 1997. lib. bdg. 80.00 (*0-7923-4731-5*) Kluwer Academic.
MacCormick, Neil & Atria, Fernando. Interpretation of Law. 185.95 (*0-7546-2021-2*) Ashgate Pub Co.
MacCornack, Katharine G. Mental Representation Theory in Old French Allegory from the Twelfth & Thirteenth Centuries. LC 96-17599. (Studies in French Literature: Vol. 26). 184p. 1996. text 79.95 (*0-7734-8815-4*) E Mellen.
MacCorquodale, Patricia, jt. auth. see DeLamater, John.
MacCorquondale, Patricia L. Engineers & Economic Conversion: From the Military to the Marketplace. LC 92-40393. (Illus.). 273p. 1993. 44.95 (*0-387-94005-7*) Spr-Verlag.
MacCoskey, Michael & National Gardening Association Editors. Gardening for Dummies. (Illus.). 384p. 1996. pap. 16.99 (*1-56884-644-4*) IDG Bks.
MacCoull, Leslie S. Coptic Perspective on Late Antiquity. LC 92-41249. (Collected Studies: Vol. CS398). 256p. 1993. 101.95 (*0-86078-364-2*, Pub. by Variorum) Ashgate Pub Co.
— Discorus of Aphrodito: His Works & His World. (Transformation of the Classical Heritage Ser.: Vol. XVI). 225p. 1988. 42.50 (*0-520-06226-4*, Pub. by U CA Pr) Cal Prin Full Svc.
MacCrach, E. Spanish-English - English-Spanish. 5th ed. 758p. 1990. 22.00 (*84-261-0079-1*) IBD Ltd.
MacCracken, C. U. S.-U. S. S. R. Report on Climate & Climate Change. 288p. 1990. boxed set 82.00 (*0-87371-440-7*, L440) Lewis Pubs.
MacCracken, H. N., ed. John Lydgate: The Minor Poems, Vol. I. (ES 107 Ser.). 1963. reprint ed. 30.00 (*0-19-722563-2*, Pub. by EETS) Boydell & Brewer.
Maccracken, H. N., ed. Lydgate's Minor Poems Pt. 1: Religious Poems. (EETS, ES Ser.: Vol. 107). 1969. reprint ed. 30.00 (*0-8115-3409-X*) Periodicals Srv.
— Lydgate's Minor Poems Pt. 2: Secular Poems. (EETS, OS Ser.: Vol. 192). 1969. reprint ed. 30.00 (*0-8115-3380-8*) Periodicals Srv.
MacCracken, J. N., ed. see Lydgate, John.
MacCracken, Joan. The Sun, the Rain & the Insulin: Growing up with Diabetes. Hoel, Donna & Hoel, Greg, eds. LC 96-90047. (Illus.). 250p. (Orig.). 1996. pap. 12.95 (*0-9646018-5-0*) Tiffin Pr ME.
MacCracken, John H. College & Commonwealth, & Other Educational Papers & Addresses. LC 67-26757. (Essay Index Reprint Ser.). 1977. 21.95 (*0-8369-0644-6*) Ayer.
MacCracken, Linda. Market-Driven Strategy: An Executive Guide to Health Care's Integrated Environment. LC 97-28826. 210p. 1997. 55.00 (*1-55648-211-6*) AHPI.
MacCracken, Thomas G., ed. A Directory of Historical-Instrument Makers in North America. 2nd rev. ed. (Early Music America Information Resource Ser.). 36p. 1995. pap. 15.00 (*1-878206-09-5*) Early Music.
— Early-Music Degree Programs in North America. (Early Music America Information Resource Ser.). 10p. (Orig.). 1992. pap. 5.00 (*1-878206-05-2*) Early Music.
MacCracken, Thomas G., ed. see Baratz, Lewis R.
MacCracken, Thomas G., ed. see Chancey, Tina & Neely, Patricia A.
MacCracken, Thomas G., ed. see Houle, George, et al.
***MacCrae, Melissa.** It Takes a Woman: Women Shaping Public Policy. 104p. 1999. pap. 12.00 (*0-9659377-1-2*) Goddess ME.
MacCrae, Melissa & Bradford, Maureen, eds. No Place for Little Boys: Civil War Letters of a Union Soldier. LC 97-94233. (Illus.). v, 119p. 1997. pap. 14.95 (*0-9659377-0-4*) Goddess ME.
MacCready, Jean & Quade, Vicki. Two under the Covers. (Illus.). (Orig.). 1981. pap. 2.95 (*0-9602604-1-2*) V Quade.
MacCreagh, Gordon. White Waters & Black. LC 85-8745. (Illus.). xxxii, 336p. 1992. pap. 11.95 (*0-226-50016-0*) U Ch Pr.
MacCregor, Geddes, ed. Immortality & Human Destiny: A Variety of Views. LC 85-12436. 235p. 1986. pap. 12.95 (*0-913757-61-6*) Paragon Hse.
Maccubbin, Robert P., ed. 'Tis Nature's Fault: Unauthorized Sexuality During the Enlightenment. 272p. 1988. pap. text 20.95 (*0-521-34768-8*) Cambridge U Pr.
Maccubbin, Robert P. & Hamilton-Phillips, Martha, eds. The Age of William Third & Mary the Second: Power, Politics, & Patronage, 1688-1702. (Illus.). (Orig.). 1988. pap. 26.95 (*0-317-93141-5*) Col Wm & Mary Eng Dept.
Maccubbin, Robert P., jt. ed. see Hamilton-Phillips, Martha.
MacCubbin, Tom. The Edible Landscape. rev. ed. O'Meara, Lynn & Mott, Margaret, eds. LC 98-9368. (Illus.). 320p. 1998. pap. 19.95 (*1-883114-08-X*); lib. bdg. 26.95 (*1-883114-09-8*) Waterview Pr.
— Florida Home Grown. rev. ed. LC 97-375. (Illus.). 144p. 1997. pap. 11.95 (*1-883114-06-3*); lib. bdg. 18.95 (*1-883114-07-1*) Waterview Pr.
***MacCubbin, Tom.** Month-by-Month Gardening in Florida. LC 99-51669. 1999. 19.95 (*1-888608-24-2*) Cool Springs Pr.
— My Florida Garden: A Gardener's Journal. (Illus.). 2000. spiral bd. 19.95 (*1-930604-03-3*) Cool Springs Pr.
MacCubbin, Tom, jt. auth. see Tasker, Georgia.
MacCuish & Flyn. Crofting Law. 186p. text 116.00 (*0-406-17912-3*, UK, MICHIE) LEXIS Pub.
MacCuish, D. Luther & His Katie. Date not set. pap. 4.99 (*0-906731-34-8*, Pub. by Christian Focus) Spring Arbor Dist.
MacCuish, Dolina. Augustine, a Mother's Son: The Influence of Augustine's Mother on His Ministry. 1999. pap. text 7.99 (*1-85792-437-1*) Christian Focus.
MacCuish, Marianne R. Into Another Country: Poetry. LC 90-33838. 64p. (Orig.). 1990. pap. 7.50 (*0-931832-59-4*) Fithian Pr.
MacCulloch, Diarmaid. Groundwork of Christian History. 1987. pap. text 20.00 (*0-7162-0434-7*) Epworth Pr.
— The Later Reformation in England, 1547-1603. 2nd ed. LC 00-42056. (British History in Perspective Ser.). (Illus.). 2000. pap. write for info. (*0-312-23737-5*) St Martin.
MacCulloch, Diarmaid. Suffolk & the Tudors: Politics & Religion in an English County 1500-1600. (Illus.). 360p. 1987. text 79.00 (*0-19-822914-3*) OUP.
— Thomas Cranmer: A Life. LC 95-49593. (Illus.). 704p. (C). 1996. 42.00 (*0-300-06688-0*) Yale U Pr.
***MacCulloch, Diarmaid.** Thomas Cranmer: A Life. LC 95-49593. (Illus.). 704p. 1998. pap. 18.00 (*0-300-07448-4*) Yale U Pr.
MacCulloch, Diarmaid, ed. The Reign of Henry VIII: Politics, Policy, & Piety. LC 95-19514. (Problems in Focus Ser.). 256p. 1995. pap. 21.95 (*0-312-12900-9*); text 55.00 (*0-312-12892-4*) St Martin.
MacCulloch, Diarmaid, jt. auth. see Fletcher, Anthony.
MacCulloch, Jennifer. Creatures of Culture: The Animal Protection & Preservation Movements in Sydney, 1880-1930. 256p. 1996. pap. 39.95 (*0-522-84687-4*, Pub. by Melbourne Univ Pr) Paul & Co Pubs.
MacCulloch, John A. Celtic & Scandinavian Religions. Date not set. pap. text 14.95 (*0-89733-434-5*) Academy Chi Pubs.
— The Celtic & Scandinavian Religions. LC 72-11739. 180p. 1973. reprint ed. lib. bdg. 38.50 (*0-8371-6705-1*, MCSR, Greenwood Pr) Greenwood.
— Celtic Mythology. 1996. pap. text 16.95 (*0-89733-433-7*) Academy Chi Pubs.
— Celtic Mythology & Slavic Mythology. LC 63-19088. (Mythology of All Races Ser.: Vol. 3). (Illus.). 477p. reprint ed. 40.00 (*0-8154-0142-6*) Cooper Sq.
— Medieval Faith & Fable. 1977. 17.95 (*0-8369-7118-3*, 7952) Ayer.
— The Religion of the Ancient Celts. 400p. 1998. pap. 19.95 (*0-09-471330-8*, Pub. by Constable & Co) Trafalgar.
Macculluch, John A. The Harrowing of Hell: A Comparative Study of an Early Christian Doctrine. LC 79-8113. 1983. reprint ed. 42.50 (*0-404-18426-X*) AMS Pr.
MacCumaill, Finn. Fianaigecht. LC 78-72614. (Royal Irish Academy. Todd Lecture Ser.: Vol. 16). reprint ed. 27.50 (*0-404-60576-1*) AMS Pr.
MacCumber, Mathew. Management of Ocular Traumas & Other Emergencies. 4th ed. LC 97-26482. 380p. 1997. pap. text 57.95 (*0-397-51496-4*) Lppncott W & W.
MacCunn, John. Six Radical Thinkers: Bentham, J.S. Mill, Codden, Carlyle, Massine, T.H. Green. Mayer, J. P., ed. LC 78-67370. (European Political Thought Ser.). 1979. reprint ed. lib. bdg. 21.95 (*0-405-11720-5*) Ayer.
MacCurdy, Doug & Tully, Shawn. Sports Illustrated Tennis: Strokes for Success. LC 93-28170. (Illus.). 1993. pap. 12.95 (*1-56800-006-5*, Pub. by Sports Illus Bks) Natl Bk Netwk.
MacCurdy, George G. A Study of Chiriquian Antiquities. (Connecticut Academy of Arts & Sciences Ser., Trans.: Vol. 3). 1911. pap. 300.00 (*0-685-22870-3*) Elliots Bks.
MacCurdy, George G., ed. Early Man. LC 77-86770. (Essay Index Reprint Ser.). 1977. 30.95 (*0-8369-1184-9*) Ayer.
MacCurdy, Rahno M., et al. Selling the Gold Vol. III: History of Sunkist & Pure Gold. Barker, Richard H., ed. (Citrus Roots... Our Legacy Ser.: Vol. I). (Illus.). 76p. 1999. pap. 15.00 (*0-9669508-1-X*) Upland Public.
MacCurdy, Raymond R. Francisco de Rojas Zorrilla. LC 68-9514. (Twayne's World Authors Ser.). 1968. lib. bdg. 20.95 (*0-8057-2770-1*) Irvington.
MacCurdy, Raymond R., ed. Spanish Drama of the Golden Age. (SPA.). 1985. reprint ed. 49.50 (*0-89197-985-9*); reprint ed. pap. text 24.95 (*0-89197-986-7*) Irvington.
MacCurdy, Tim. Caesar of Santa Fe: A Novel from History. LC 89-85379. 240p. (Orig.). 1993. pap. 11.95 (*0-938513-07-9*) Amador Pubs.
MacCurely, Marian M., jt. ed. see Anderson, Charles M.
MacCurtain, Margaret & O'Dowd, Mary, eds. Women in Early Modern Ireland, 1500-1800. 1991. text 68.00 (*0-7486-0223-2*, Pub. by Edinburgh U Pr) Col U Pr.

M

— Women in Early Modern Ireland, 1500-1800. (Illus.). 240p. 1992. pap. 34.00 (*0-7486-0241-0*, Pub. by Edinburgh U Pr) Col U Pr.

MacCuspie, P. Ann. Promoting Acceptance of Children with Disabilities: From Tolerance to Inclusion. 235p. 1996. pap. 27.95 (*0-9680388-0-8*) Am Foun Blind.

Macdaid, Gerald P., et al. Atlas of Type Tables. LC 86-32635. 595p. 1986. 50.00 (*0-935652-13-2*) Ctr Applications Psych.

MacDairmid, Hugh. The Raucle Tongue. LC 97-172673. 580p. 1998. 65.00 (*1-85754-271-1*, Pub. by Carcanet Pr) Paul & Co Pubs.

— The Raucle Tongue III. 400p. 1998. 65.00 (*1-85754-378-5*, Pub. by Carcanet Pr) Paul & Co Pubs.

MacDaniels, Carol, jt. auth. see Cox, Gerry R.

MacDaniels, L. H. Study of the Fe'i Banana & Its Distribution with Reference to Polynesian Migrations. (BMB Ser.: No. 190). 1947. 25.00 (*0-527-02298-5*) Periodicals Srv.

MacDari, Conor. The Bible: An Irish Book. 84p. 1996. spiral bd. 15.50 (*0-7873-0576-6*) Hlth Research.

— The Bible: An Irish Book of Pre-Roman Spiritual Culture. 102p. 1996. spiral bd. 15.50 (*0-7873-0577-4*) Hlth Research.

— Irish Wisdom Preserved in Bible & Pyramids. 235p. 1993. reprint ed. spiral bd. 16.50 (*0-7873-0575-8*) Hlth Research.

— Irish Wisdom Preserved in Bible & Pyramids (1923) 240p. 1996. reprint ed. pap. 15.95 (*1-56459-754-7*) Kessinger Pub.

MacDermid, Shelley, jt. auth. see DeHaan, Laura.

MacDermot, Brian. The Irish Catholic Petition of 1805: The Diary of Denys Scully. 230p. (C). 1993. 29.95 (*0-7165-2497-X*, Pub. by Irish Acad Pr) Intl Spec Bk.

MacDermot, Brian, ed. The Catholic Question in Ireland & England, 1798-1822: The Papers of Denys Scully. 776p. 1988. 39.50 (*0-7165-2423-6*, Pub. by Irish Acad Pr) Intl Spec Bk.

***MacDermot, Molly.** Britney Spears: The Unofficial Book. (Illus.). 64p. 1999. pap. 12.95 (*0-8230-7864-7*, Billboard Bks) Watsn-Guptill.

— Christina Aguilera: The Unofficial Book. (Illus.). (YA). 2000. pap. 12.95 (*0-8230-8308-X*, Billboard Bks) Watsn-Guptill.

— Mandy Moore: The Unofficial Book. (Illus.). (J). 2000. pap. 12.95 (*0-8230-8374-8*, Billboard Bks) Watsn-Guptill.

MacDermot, Niall & Fahlander, Inger. Report of Mission to Uruguay in April-May, 1974. LC KZ0166.. 10p. reprint ed. pap. 30.00 (*0-608-14354-5*, 205190800013) Bks Demand.

MacDermot, Violet. The Cult of the Seer in the Ancient Middle East: A Contribution to Current Research on Hallucinations Drawn from Coptic & Other Texts. LC 79-152047. 841p. reprint ed. pap. 200.00 (*0-7837-4674-1*, 204442000003) Bks Demand.

MacDermott, Barbara & Deglin, Judith H. Understanding Basic Pharmacology: Practical Approaches for Effective Application. 546p. (C). 1994. pap. text 29.95 (*0-8036-5714-5*) Davis Co.

MacDermott, Charles P. & Shenoy, Aroon V. Selecting Thermoplastics in Engineering. 2nd ed. LC 97-4020. (Plastics Engineering Ser.: Vol. 42). (Illus.). 328p. 1997. text 135.00 (*0-8247-9845-7*) Dekker.

MacDermott, Eithne. Clann Na Poblachta. 240p. 2000. 60.00 (*1-85918-186-4*, Pub. by Cork Univ); pap. 22.50 (*1-85918-187-2*, Pub. by Cork Univ) Stylus Pub VA.

MacDermott, Mercia. Bulgarian Folk Customs. LC 98-199769. 264p. 1997. write for info. (*1-85302-485-6*, Pub. by Jessica Kingsley); pap. write for info. (*1-85302-486-4*, Pub. by Jessica Kingsley) Taylor & Francis.

MacDermott, Richard. Inflammatory Bowel Disease. (Illus.). 658p. (C). 1992. pap. text 110.00 (*0-8385-4069-4*, A4069-9, Appleton Lange Med) McGraw.

MacDevitt, Margaret L., jt. auth. see Brault, Margaret A.

MacDhomhnuill, Domhnull. Manuscript by Domhnull MacDhomhnuill. 282p. 1992. pap. 51.00 (*0-685-67870-9*) A MacRaonuill.

MacDiarmid, Alan G. The Bond to Halogens & Halogenoids, Pt. 1. LC QD0165.M33. (Organometallic Compounds of the Group IV Elements Ser.: Vol. 2). (Illus.). 392p. reprint ed. pap. 121.60 (*0-8357-7338-8*, 205506800001) Bks Demand.

MacDiarmid, Alan G., ed. Organometallic Compounds of the Group Four Elements, Vol. 1 Part 2: The Bond to Carbon. LC 68-11573. 275p. 1968. reprint ed. pap. 85.30 (*0-608-08448-4*, 202783100054) Bks Demand.

— Organometallic Compounds of the Group Four Elements, Vol. 2, Pt. 2: The Bond of Halogens & Halogenoids. LC 68-11573. 248p. 1972. reprint ed. pap. 76.90 (*0-608-08449-2*, 202707600054) Bks Demand.

— Organometallic Compounds of the Group Four Elements Vol. 1, Pt. 1: The Bond to Carbon. LC 68-11573. (Illus.). 619p. reprint ed. pap. 191.90 (*0-608-18013-0*, 202900200001) Bks Demand.

***MacDiarmid, Hugh.** Annals of the Five Senses. 304p. 2000. 55.00 (*1-85754-272-X*, Pub. by Carcanet Pr) Paul & Co Pubs.

MacDiarmid, Hugh. Lucky Poet: A Self-Study in Literature & Political Ideas: Being the Autobiography of Hugh MacDiarmid (Christopher Murray Grieve) LC 73-152431. xxiv, 43p. 1972. write for info. (*0-224-00715-7*) Jonathan Cape.

— Selected Poems. Riach, Alan & Grieve, Michael, eds. LC 93-5312. 320p. 1993. 23.95 (*0-8112-1248-3*, Pub. by New Directions) Norton.

MacDiarmid, Hugh, ed. The Golden Treasury of Scottish Poetry. 448p. 1995. 19.95 (*0-86241-446-6*, Pub. by Canongate Books) Interlink Pub.

MacDiarmid, Hugh, jt. auth. see Chiari, Joseph.

MacDiarmid, Jim. Akerta. Manutoli, Sophie, tr.Tr. of Sun. (ESK., Illus.). 16p. (J). (gr. k-3). 1998. pap. text 6.00 (*1-58084-047-7*) Lower Kuskokwim.

— Neqem Ayuqucia Nallunritellruan-qaa... Nega! large type ed. Collidge, Joseph, tr.Tr. of Meet... a Fish!. (ESK., Illus.). 20p. (J). (gr. 3-5). 1999. pap. text 7.00 (*1-58084-176-7*) Lower Kuskokwim.

Macdicken, Kenneth G. & Vergara, Napoleon T., eds. Agroforestry: Classification & Management. 400p. 1990. 175.00 (*0-471-83781-4*) Wiley.

MacDicken, Kenneth G., jt. ed. see Taylor, David Conrad.

MacDonagh, Donagh. Warning to Conquerors. LC 68-26023. 69p. 1968. 15.95 (*0-8023-1167-9*) Dufour.

MacDonagh, Oliver. Irish Culture & Nationalism. (Australian National University Press Ser.). 1996. text. write for info. (*0-08-032874-1*, Pergamon Pr) Elsevier.

— Jane Austen: Real & Imagined Worlds. 240p. (C). 1993. reprint ed. pap. 15.00 (*0-300-05449-1*) Yale U Pr.

— A Pattern of Government Growth, 1800-1860. (Modern Revivals in History Ser.). 368p. 1993. 69.95 (*0-7512-0165-0*, Pub. by Gregg Revivals) Ashgate Pub Co.

MacDonagh, Oliver, jt. auth. see Dennison, S. R.

MacDonagh, Sandra. Victorian Patchwork Patterns: Instructions & Full-Size Templates for 12 Quilts. (Illus.). 64p. (Orig.). 1988. pap. 5.95 (*0-486-25543-3*) Dover.

MacDonagh, Thomas. Literature in Ireland: Studies Irish & Anglo-Irish. 209p. 1996. pap. 15.95 (*0-946327-16-5*, Pub. by Relay Pubns) Irish Bks Media.

— The Poetical Works of Thomas MacDonagh. LC 75-28822. reprint ed. 24.00 (*0-404-13814-4*) AMS Pr.

MacDonagh, Tom. My Green Age. 148p. 1986. pap. 8.95 (*0-905169-76-X*, Pub. by Poolbeg Pr) Dufour.

MacDonald. Agricultural Technology in Developing Countries. 1976. 59.95 (*90-237-6259-2*) Ashgate Pub Co.

— Beastly Boys & Ghastly Girls. 48p. (J). (gr. 2-5). 1998. lib. bdg. 14.89 (*0-06-024953-6*) HarpC Child Bks.

MacDonald. Contact Lens Design & Fitting. (Home Care Aide Ser.). 1995. pap. 29.95 (*0-8273-6376-1*) Delmar.

— Contemporary Moral Issues in a Diverse Society. 2nd ed. (Philosophy Ser.). 1919. pap. 33.75 (*0-534-53604-2*) Wadsworth Pub.

MacDonald. Effective Interventions for Child Abuse & Neglect. text. write for info. (*0-471-49146-2*); pap. text. write for info. (*0-471-49147-0*) Wiley.

MacDonald. International Business. (ITBP Acquisitions Ser.). 2000. pap. 24.99 (*1-86152-452-8*) Thomson Learn.

— Introductory Philosophy for a Diverse World. 1919. pap. 3800.00 (*0-534-56709-6*) Thomson Learn.

Macdonald. Islands of the Pacific Rim & Their People. (And Its People Ser.). 48p. (J). (gr. 5-6). 1994. lib. bdg. 24.26 (*0-8172-4670-3*) Raintree Steck-V.

***MacDonald.** Lunches. (J). 2000. 29.95 (*0-385-40765-3*, Pub. by Transworld Publishers Ltd) Trafalgar.

MacDonald. Macroeconomics & Business: An Interactive Approach. (ITBP Acquisitions Ser.). 400p. 1999. pap. 22.99 (*1-86152-450-1*) Thomson Learn.

***MacDonald.** Managing Police Operations: Nypd Crime Control Model Compstat. 2000. pap. 32.00 (*0-534-53991-2*) Thomson Learn.

MacDonald. The Marketing Plan. 96p. 1987. pap. text 34.95 (*0-7506-0678-9*) Buttrwrth-Heinemann.

***MacDonald.** MCSD Visual Basic 6.0 Desktop Exam Cram. (Programming Ser.). (C). 1999. pap. 15.60 (*0-619-01607-8*) Course Tech.

MacDonald. On a Far Wild Shore. mass mkt. write for info. (*0-312-90295-6*) Tor Bks.

— The Princess & the Goblin. LC 99-21546. (Illus.). 192p. (J). 1999. pap. text 2.50 (*0-486-40787-X*) Dover.

— Reciprocity among Private Multiemployer Pension Plans. (C). 1975. 12.95 (*0-256-01736-0*, Irwn McGrw-H) McGrw-H Hghr Educ.

***Macdonald.** Riding to Music. 2000. 10.95 (*0-85131-567-4*, Pub. by J A Allen) Trafalgar.

MacDonald. Russia & U. S. S. R., 1905-1964. 1994. pap. text. write for info. (*0-582-22672-4*, Pub. by Addison-Wesley) Longman.

— The Son of the Day & the Daughter of the Night. (J). 1998. pap. 7.95 (*0-671-75230-8*) S&S Bks Yung.

***MacDonald.** Speaking to Miranda. LC 91-47901. (Keypoint Book Ser.). 192p. (YA). (gr. 7 up). 1999. pap. 3.95 (*0-06-447088-1*) HarpC Child Bks.

MacDonald. The Squeaky Door. 32p. (J). (ps-1). Date not set. pap. 4.95 (*0-06-443566-0*) HarpC Child Bks.

— Squeaky Door. 32p. (J). (ps-1). Date not set. 12.95 (*0-06-028373-4*); lib. bdg. 12.89 (*0-06-028374-2*) HarpC Child Bks.

— Vancouver: A Visual History. (Illus.). 96p. 1992. text 42.00 (*0-88922-311-4*) Genl Dist Srvs.

— Western Motifs. 1998. pap. 1.00 (*0-486-28257-0*) Dover.

— The Wind & the Moon. (J). 2002. text 15.95 (*0-8050-4127-3*) St Martin.

MacDonald, ed. The Allyn & Bacon Sourcebook for College Writing Teachers. 2nd ed. 433p. 1999. pap. text 37.00 (*0-205-31603-4*) Allyn.

***MacDonald, ed.** The Radio Broadcaster's Big Book: Control Room, Public File Workbooks. rev. ed. (Broadcaster's Big Bks.). (Illus.). 200p. 1999. 249.00 (*0-938023-19-5*) Wind River Inst Pr.

MacDonald & Rogers. Key Account Management. LC 98-197726. 224p. 2000. text 49.95 (*0-7506-3278-X*) Buttrwrth-Heinemann.

MacDonald, jt. auth. see Bohm.

MacDonald, jt. auth. see Bohm, Ralph C.

MacDonald, jt. auth. see Bohn.

MacDonald, jt. auth. see Fravel.

MacDonald, jt. auth. see Kessler.

MacDonald, jt. auth. see May.

MacDonald, jt. auth. see Salomone.

MacDonald, Janet. Living & Working in London. rev. ed. 256p. 1999. pap. 21.95 (*1-901130-11-8*, Pub. by Survival Books) Seven Hills Bk.

MacDonald, Janet, jt. auth. see Hampshire, David.

MacDonald, A. Creation in Crisis? Date not set. pap. 5.99 (*1-871676-86-X*, Pub. by Christian Focus) Spring Arbor Dist.

Macdonald, A. Love Minus Zero. 8.50 (*0-906731-92-5*, Pub. by Christian Focus) Spring Arbor Dist.

MacDonald, A. A., et al, eds. The Broken Body: Passion & Devotion in Late-Medieval Culture. (Mediaevalia Groningana Ser.: Vol. XXI). 239p. 1998. pap. text 58.00 (*90-6980-111-6*, Pub. by Egbert Forsten) Hod1der & Stoughton.

— The Renaissance in Scotland: Studies in Literature, Religion, History & Culture Offered to John Durkan. LC 94-26032. (Studies in Intellectual History: 54). 1994. 113.00 (*90-04-10097-0*) Brill Academic Pubs.

MacDonald, A. A., jt. ed. see Drijvers, J. W.

MacDonald, A. A., jt. ed. see Houwen, L. A.

MacDonald, A. D. Mabou Pioneers: A Genealogical, 2 vols., Vol. 1. 880p. text 29.95 (*0-88780-005-X*, Pub. by Formac Publ Co) Formac Dist Ltd.

MacDonald, A. F. Federal Aid: A Study of the American Subsidy System. (American Federalism-the Urban Dimension Ser.). (Illus.). 1978. reprint ed. lib. bdg. 29.95 (*0-405-10494-4*) Ayer.

MacDonald, A. G. Effects of High Pressure on Biological Systems. (Advances in Comparative & Environmental Physiology Ser.: Vol. 17). (Illus.). 260p. 1993. 227.95 (*0-387-54845-9*) Spr-Verlag.

MacDonald, A. H., ed. Quantum Hall Effect. (C). 1990. pap. text 96.00 (*0-7923-0538-8*); lib. bdg. 163.00 (*0-7923-0537-X*) Kluwer Academic.

MacDonald, A. R. Prison Secrets: Things Seen, Suffered, & Recorded During Seven Years in Ludlow Street Jail. LC 70-90185. (Mass Violence in America Ser.). 1977. reprint ed. 17.95 (*0-405-01327-2*) Ayer.

***Macdonald, A. S.** Marine Corps Gallantry: Or Psychosis Sgt. Macdonald. 244p. 2000. per. 15.00 (*0-9676941-0-8*) ASM Pubng.

MacDonald, A. W. Mandala & Landscape. (Illus.). xiv, 460p. (C). 1997. 99.00 (*81-246-0060-0*, Pub. by D K Printwrld) Nataraj Bks.

MacDonald, Agnes, jt. auth. see MacDonald, Kenneth B.

MacDonald, Aileen A. The Figure of Merlin in Thirteenth Century French Romance. (Studies in Medieval Literature: Vol. 3). 260p. 1990. lib. bdg. 89.95 (*0-88946-317-4*) E Mellen.

***MacDonald, Alan.** Al Capone & His Gang. (Illus.). 192p. (gr. 4-7). 2000. pap. text 4.50 (*0-439-21124-7*) Scholastic Inc.

— Beware of the Bears. (Illus.). 32p. (J). (ps-2). 1999. pap. 5.95 (*1-58431-008-1*, Pub. by Little Tiger) Futech Educ Prods.

MacDonald, Alan. Essential Christmas Book: Family Crafts & Activities to Get to the Heart of Christmas. 1997. pap. text 10.00 (*0-687-06299-3*) Abingdon.

***MacDonald, Alan.** Henry the VIII & His Chopping Block. (Illus.). 192p. (gr. 4-7). 2000. pap. text 4.50 (*0-439-21125-5*) Scholastic Inc.

MacDonald, Alan. The Jacobean Kirk, 1567-1625: Sovereignty, Polity & Liturgy. LC 98-19314. (St. Andrews Studies in Reformation History). (Illus.). 217p. 1998. text 83.95 (*1-85928-373-X*, BX9071.M24, Pub. by Scolar Pr) Ashgate Pub Co.

— King Next Door. LC 98-216946. 1998. pap. text 5.99 (*0-7459-3897-3*) Lion USA.

***MacDonald, Alan.** The Not-So-Wise Man: A Christmas Story. LC 99-31745. (Illus.). 32p. (J). (ps-4). 1999. 15.00 (*0-8028-5196-7*, Eerdmans Bks) Eerdmans.

— The Pig in a Wig. LC 98-51318. (Illus.). 32p. (J). (ps-1). 1999. 15.95 (*1-56145-197-5*) Peachtree Pubs.

Macdonald, Alan. Whispering in God's Ear: Inspirational Poetry for Children. (J). 1998. 7.99 (*0-88486-217-8*) Arrowood Pr.

MacDonald, Alan & Stickley, Janet. The Essential Christmas Book. 100.00 (*0-687-09540-9*) Abingdon.

MacDonald, Alan & Williamson, Gwyneth. Beware of the Bears! LC 97-33222. (Illus.). 32p. (J). (ps-2). 1998. 14.95 (*1-888444-28-2*, 21026) Little Tiger.

MacDonald, Alasdair A., jt. ed. see Aertsen, Henk.

MacDonald, Alex. Alex in Wonderland. 210p. 1993. pap. 11.95 (*0-921586-28-0*, Pub. by New Star Bks) Genl Dist Srvs.

Macdonald, Alexander, ed. Letters to the Argyll Family from Elizabeth Queen of England, Mary Queen of Scots, & Others. LC 77-12765. (Maitland Club, Glasgow. Publications: No. 50). reprint ed. 37.50 (*0-404-53031-1*) AMS Pr.

— Papers Relative to the Royal Guard of Scottish Archers in France. LC 79-175588. (Maitland Club, Glasgow. Publications: No. 36). reprint ed. 27.50 (*0-404-53007-9*) AMS Pr.

— Reports on the State of Certain Parishes in Scotland. LC 79-175588. (Maitland Club, Glasgow. Publications: No. 34). reprint ed. 32.50 (*0-404-53003-6*) AMS Pr.

MacDonald, Alexander, ed. see Blackwood, Adam.

Macdonald, Alexander, ed. see James First King of England.

Macdonald, Alexander, ed. see Maitland Club Staff.

MacDonald, Alexander, ed. see Miles, Dorothy.

MacDonald, Alexander W. Essays on the Enthnology of Nepal & South Asia. 1984. 75.00 (*0-7855-0224-6*, Pub. by Ratna Pustak Bhandar) St Mut.

— Essays on the Enthnology of Nepal & South Asia, Vol. 2. 1987. 75.00 (*0-7855-0225-4*, Pub. by Ratna Pustak Bhandar) St Mut.

— Essays on the Ethnology of Nepal & South Asia. 1984. 85.00 (*0-7855-0311-0*, Pub. by Ratna Pustak Bhandar) St Mut.

MacDonald, Alexander W., ed. Essays on the Ethnology of Nepal & South Asia, Vol. I. 318p. (C). 1984. 125.00 (*0-89771-119-X*, Pub. by Ratna Pustak Bhandar) St Mut.

— Essays on the Ethnology of Nepal & South Asia, Vol. II. 147p. (C). 1987. 200.00 (*0-89771-120-3*, Pub. by Ratna Pustak Bhandar) St Mut.

Macdonald, Alexandra, ed. see Jackson, Mildred & Teague, Terri.

MacDonald, Alister G. Physiological Aspects of Deep Sea Biology. LC 73-90652. (Physiological Society Monographs: No. 31). 464p. reprint ed. pap. 132.30 (*0-608-15748-1*, 2031685) Bks Demand.

MacDonald, Allan. Allan MacDonald's Old Time Fiddle Tunes. Weber, Beth, ed. 22p. 1998. pap. 9.95 (*0-9659942-3-6*, Erda Music) Erda Pub.

MacDonald, Allan J. Berengar & the Reform of the Sacramental System. 444p. 1977. reprint ed. lib. bdg. 30.00 (*0-915172-25-9*) Richwood Pub.

— Hildebrand: A Life of Gregory the Seventh. (Great Medieval Churchmen Ser.). 254p. 1977. reprint ed. lib. bdg. 17.50 (*0-915172-26-7*) Richwood Pub.

— Lanfranc, a Study of His Life, Work & Writing. LC 80-2223. reprint ed. 37.50 (*0-404-18768-4*) AMS Pr.

MacDonald, Amy. Cousin Ruth's Tooth. LC 94-26426. (Illus.). 32p. (J). (gr. k-3). 1996. 16.00 (*0-395-71253-X*) HM.

— Let's Go. LC 92-46095. (Let's Explore Board Bks.). (Illus.). 12p. (J). (ps up). 1994. bds. 5.95 (*1-56402-202-1*) Candlewick Pr.

— Let's Play. LC 91-71838. (Let's Explore Board Bks.). (Illus.). 12p. (J). (ps). 1992. bds. 5.95 (*1-56402-023-1*) Candlewick Pr.

— Let's Try. LC 91-71839. (Let's Explore Board Bks.). (Illus.). 12p. (J). (ps). 1992. bds. 5.95 (*1-56402-022-3*) Candlewick Pr.

— Little Beaver & the Echo. (CHI & ENG., Illus.). 32p. (J). (ps-2). 1997. write for info. (*1-85430-507-7*, Pub. by MAGI1 UK); write for info. (*1-85430-509-3*, Pub. by MAGI1 UK); write for info. (*1-85430-511-5*, Pub. by MAGI1 UK) Midpt Trade.

— Little Beaver & the Echo. (Illus.). 32p. (J). (ps-3). 1990. 15.95 (*0-399-22203-0*, G P Putnam) Peng Put Young Read.

— Little Beaver & the Echo. (Illus.). 32p. (J). (ps-3). 1998. pap. 6.99 (*0-698-11628-3*, PapStar) Peng Put Young Read.

***MacDonald, Amy.** No More Nice. LC 96-7661. (Illus.). 144p. (gr. 3-7). 1998. mass mkt. 3.99 (*0-380-73055-3*, Avon Bks) Morrow Avon.

MacDonald, Amy. No More Nice. LC 96-7661. (Illus.). 128p. (J). (gr. 3-7). 1996. 14.95 (*0-531-09542-8*); lib. bdg. 15.99 (*0-531-08892-8*) Orchard Bks Watts.

— Rachel Fister's Blister. (Illus.). 32p. (J). (ps-3). 1990. 15.00 (*0-395-52152-1*) HM.

— Rachel Fister's Blister. (Illus.). 32p. (J). (gr. k-3). 1993. pap. 5.95 (*0-395-65744-X*) HM.

— Rachel Fister's Blister. (Carry-Along Book & Cassette Favorites Ser.). (Illus.). 32p. (J). (ps-3). 1996. pap. 9.95 incl. audio (*0-395-77978-2*, 491162) HM.

— Rachel Fister's Blister. (J). 1990. 11.15 (*0-606-05560-6*, Pub. by Turtleback) Demco.

— The Spider Who Created the World. LC 95-23181. (Illus.). 32p. (J). (ps-3). 1996. 15.95 (*0-531-09505-3*); lib. bdg. 16.99 (*0-531-08855-3*) Orchard Bks Watts.

MacDonald, Amy, et al. The Presumpscot River Watch Guide to the Presumpscot River: Its History, Ecology, & Recreational Uses. 80p. (Orig.). 1994. pap. 9.99 (*0-9639872-0-8*) Presumpscot River.

***MacDonald, Andrew.** Building a Geodatabase: ArcInfo 8. 336p. 2000. pap. 29.95 (*1-879102-72-2*, Pub. by ESR Inst) IPG Chicago.

Macdonald, Andrew. The Turner Diaries: A Novel. LC 80-82692. 224p. 1996. reprint ed. pap. 12.00 (*1-56980-086-3*) Barricade Bks.

MacDonald, Andrew & MacDonald, Gina. Mastering Writing Essentials. (Illus.). 464p. (C). 1996. pap. text 32.80 (*0-205-15010-1*) P-H.

Macdonald, Andrew & Pierce, William L. Hunter. 2nd ed. LC 89-69872. 259p. 1998. pap. 12.95 (*0-937944-09-2*) Natl Vanguard.

— The Turner Diaries. 2nd ed. LC 80-82692. 216p. (Orig.). 1999. pap. write for info. (*0-937944-12-2*) Natl Vanguard.

***Macdonald, Andrew, et al.** Shape-Shifting: Images of Native Americans in Popular Fiction, 71. LC 00-21048. (Contributions to the Study of Popular Culture: Vol. 71). 400p. 2000. 69.00 (*0-313-30842-X*, GM0842, Greenwood Pr) Greenwood.

MacDonald, Andrew S. Nowhere to Go but Down? 232p. 1989. text 44.95 (*0-04-445408-2*) Routledge.

MacDonald, Andy. Don't Slip on the Soap: More Crazy Capers from the Best-Selling Author of Bread & Molasses. 177p. 1997. pap. 8.00 (*0-7737-1021-3*) Genl Dist Srvs.

***MacDonald, Angus.** The Highlands & Islands of Scotland. (Illus.). 160p. 2000. pap. 16.95 (*0-7538-0544-8*) Phoenix Hse.

MacDonald, Angus & MacDonald, Patricia. Granite & Green: Above North-East Scotland. (Illus.). 168p. 1993. 34.95 (*1-85158-465-X*, Pub. by Mainstream Pubng) Trafalgar.

Macdonald, Angus & Macdonald, Patricia. The Highlands & Islands of Scotland. (Illus.). 160p. 1996. pap. 17.95 (*0-297-83213-1*, Pub. by Weidenfeld & Nicolson) Trafalgar.

MacDonald, Angus A. The Spirit of Service: Recollections of a Pioneer. Macdonald, Eleanor J., ed. (Illus.). 131p. (Orig.). 1988. 20.00 (*0-9637172-0-0*) E J Macdonald.

MacDonald, Angus J. Structure & Architecture. LC 94-1101. (Illus.). 144p. 1994. pap. text 39.95 (*0-7506-1798-5*) Buttrwrth-Heinemann.

An Asterisk (*) at the beginning of an entry indicates that the title is appearing for the first time.

***MacDonald, Angus J.** Structure & Architecture. 2nd ed. (Illus.). 160p. 2001. pap. 37.95 (*0-7506-4793-0*, Architectural Pr) Buttrwrth-Heinemann.

MacDonald, Angus W. Building Your Own Earth-Tempered Home: A Construction Manual. (Illus.). 96p. (Orig.). 1984. pap. 11.95 (*0-938432-19-2*) Mother Earth.

MacDonald, Ann-Marie. Fall on Your Knees: A Novel. LC 96-34186. 512p. 1998. per. 13.00 (*0-684-83868-0*) Scribner.

— Goodnight Desdemona, Good Morning Juliet. LC 98-8447. 112p. 1998. pap. 13.00 (*0-8021-3577-3*, Grove) Grove-Atltic.

— Goodnight Desdemona, Good Morning Juliet. LC 96-931991. 96p. 1997. pap. text 11.95 (*0-88754-513-0*) Theatre Comm.

MacDonald, Anna, ed. Buon Appetito! Regional Italian Recipes - Ricette Regionali Italiane. LC 96-198142. (ITA., Illus.). 1995. spiral bd. 49.95 (*0-7305-8919-6*) Intl Spec Bk.

MacDonald, Anne, jt. auth. see Whitehead, Hector F.

MacDonald, Anne L. Nanny-Mac's Cat. (Illus.). 24p. (J). (ps-3). 1996. pap. 5.95 (*0-921556-54-3*, Pub. by Gynergy-Ragweed) U of Toronto Pr.

MacDonald, Arley R. Managers View Information. LC 82-19570. (Illus.). 96p. reprint ed. pap. 30.00 (*0-7837-6302-6*, 204601700010) Bks Demand.

MacDonald, Arline. Complete Book of Vitamins & Minerals. LC 98-208800. (Consumer Information Ser.). 384p. 1997. write for info. (*0-7853-2575-1*) Pubns Intl Ltd.

MacDonald, Arthur. Criminology. LC 75-156960. reprint ed. 57.50 (*0-404-09123-7*) AMS Pr.

MacDonald, Austin F. Government of the Argentine Republic. LC 71-180411. reprint ed. 47.50 (*0-404-56136-5*) AMS Pr.

Macdonald, Barbara & Rich, Cynthia. Look Me in the Eye: Old Women, Aging, & Ageism. 2nd ed. LC 91-36595. 192p. (Orig.). 1991. pap. 8.95 (*0-933216-87-4*) Spinsters Ink.

MacDonald, Barbara J., jt. ed. see Lawson, V. K.

MacDonald, Barrie. Broadcasting in the United Kingdom: A Guide to Information Sources. 2nd ed. 304p. 1993. text 100.00 (*0-7201-2086-1*) Continuum.

MacDonald, Barrie I. & Petheram, Michel. Keyguide to Information Sources in Media Ethics. LC 97-40767. 352p. 1998. 140.00 (*0-7201-2128-0*, Pub. by Mansell Pub) Cassell.

MacDonald-Bayne, Murdo. Beyond the Himalayas. 1973. 250.00 (*0-87968-063-6*) Gordon Pr.

***MacDonald-Bayne, Murdo.** Divine Healing of Mind & Body. 2000. pap. 17.95 (*0-85207-332-1*) C W Daniel.

***MacDonald, Bernadette & Amatt, John, eds.** Voices from the Summit. 2000. 30.00 (*0-7922-7958-1*) Natl Geog.

MacDonald, Betty. The Egg & I. 23.95 (*0-89190-959-1*) Amereon Ltd.

— The Egg & I. 103p. 1958. pap. 5.50 (*0-87129-642-X*, E14) Dramatic Pub.

— The Egg & I. LC 45-336. 1963. 14.95 (*0-397-00279-3*, Lippncott) Lppncott W & W.

— The Egg & I. LC 87-45068. 288p. 1987. reprint ed. pap. 13.00 (*0-06-091428-9*, PL/1428, Perennial) HarperTrade.

— Nancy & Plum. 1993. reprint ed. lib. bdg. 31.95 (*1-56849-017-8*) Buccaneer Bks.

— Nancy & Plum. (Illus.). 190p. (YA). (gr. 5 up). 1997. reprint ed. pap. 9.95 (*0-944309-00-3*) J Keil Enterp.

— Onions in the Stew. Dalzell, William, ed. 1984. pap. 5.50 (*0-87129-383-8*, O16) Dramatic Pub.

***MacDonald, Betty.** The Plague & I. large type ed. LC 00-39600. 314p. 2000. 23.95 (*0-7838-9106-7*, G K Hall & Co) Mac Lib Ref.

— The Plague & I. (Common Reader Edition Ser.). 2000. reprint ed. pap. 15.95 (*1-888173-29-7*, Pub. by Akadine Pr) Trafalgar.

MacDonald, Betty B. Hello, Mrs. Piggle-Wiggle. LC 57-5613. (Illus.). (J). (gr. k-3). 1957. 15.95 (*0-397-31715-8*) HarpC Child Bks.

— Hello, Mrs. Piggle-Wiggle. LC 57-5613. (Trophy Bk.). (Illus.). 128p. (J). (gr. 1-5). 1985. pap. 4.95 (*0-06-440149-9*, HarpTrophy) HarpC Child Bks.

— Mrs. Piggle-Wiggle. (J). 1957. 10.05 (*0-606-00728-8*, Pub. by Turtleback) Demco.

— Mrs. Piggle-Wiggle. rev. ed. LC 47-1876. (Illus.). (J). (gr. k-3). 1957. 15.95 (*0-397-31712-3*) HarpC Child Bks.

— Mrs. Piggle-Wiggle. rev. ed. LC 47-1876. (Trophy Bk.). (Illus.). 128p. (J). (gr. 1-5). 1985. pap. 4.95 (*0-06-440148-0*, HarpTrophy) HarpC Child Bks.

— Mrs. Piggle-Wiggle's Farm. (Illus.). (J). (gr. 2-6). 14.95 (*0-397-30273-8*, 592801) HarpC Child Bks.

— Mrs. Piggle-Wiggle's Farm. LC 54-7299. (Illus.). 132p. (J). (gr. k-3). 1954. 15.95 (*0-397-31713-1*) HarpC Child Bks.

— Mrs. Piggle-Wiggle's Farm. LC 54-7299. (Trophy Bk.). (Illus.). 128p. (J). (gr. 1-5). 1985. pap. 4.95 (*0-06-440150-2*, HarpTrophy) HarpC Child Bks.

— Mrs. Piggle-Wiggle's Farm. (J). 1985. 10.05 (*0-606-00729-6*, Pub. by Turtleback) Demco.

— Mrs. Piggle-Wiggle's Magic. 136p. (J). 1976. 17.95 (*0-8488-1087-2*) Amereon Ltd.

— Mrs. Piggle-Wiggle's Magic. LC 49-11124. (Illus.). 144p. (J). (gr. k-3). 1957. 15.95 (*0-397-31714-X*) HarpC Child Bks.

— Mrs. Piggle-Wiggle's Magic. LC 49-11124. (Trophy Bk.). (Illus.). 144p. (J). (gr. 1-5). 1985. pap. 4.95 (*0-06-440151-0*, HarpTrophy) HarpC Child Bks.

— Mrs. Piggle-Wiggle's Magic. (J). 1957. 10.05 (*0-606-00731-8*, Pub. by Turtleback) Demco.

— The Won't-Pick-up-Toys Cure. LC 96-43610. (Mrs. Piggle-Wiggle Adventure Ser.). (Illus.). (J). 1998. lib. bdg. write for info. (*0-06-027629-0*) HarpC Child Bks.

— The Won't-Take-a-Bath-Cure. LC 96-43425. (Mrs. Piggle-Wiggle Adventure Ser.). (Illus.). 40p. (J). (ps-2). 1998. lib. bdg. 14.89 (*0-06-027631-2*) HarpC Child Bks.

MacDonald, Betty B., ed. Mrs. Piggle-Wiggle's Bad Table-Manners Cure. LC 97-18055. (Mrs. Piggle-Wiggle Adventure Ser.). (Illus.). (J). 2000. 12.95 (*0-06-027632-0*) HarpC.

Macdonald, Betty Bard. Hello, Mrs. Piggle-Wiggle. (J). 1985. 10.05 (*0-606-07636-0*, Pub. by Turtleback) Demco.

***Macdonald, Betty Bard.** Onions in the Stew. LC 00-31965. (Illus.). 2000. write for info. (*0-7838-9107-5*, G K Hall & Co) Mac Lib Ref.

***MacDonald, Betty C.** Mrs. Piggle-Wiggle's Bad Table-Manners Cure. LC 97-18055. (Mrs. Piggle-Wiggle Adventure Ser.). (Illus.). (J). 2000. lib. bdg. 12.89 (*0-06-027633-9*) HarpC.

MacDonald, Beverly. The Madigal. LC 97-221126. 410 p. 1995. write for info. (*0-330-35644-5*) Pan.

MacDonald, Bob & Grace, Eric. Wonderstruck I. (Illus.). 96p. 1991. pap. 10.95 (*0-7737-5477-6*) Genl Dist Srvs.

— Wonderstruck II. (Illus.). 96p. 1991. pap. 10.95 (*0-7737-5478-4*) Genl Dist Srvs.

MacDonald, Bonney. Henry James's "Italian Hours" Revelatory & Resistant Impression. Litz, A. Walton, ed. LC 89-20128. (Studies in Modern Literature: No. 106). 145p. reprint ed. pap. 45.00 (*0-8357-2025-X*, 207073300004) Bks Demand.

MacDonald, Bradley J. William Morris & the Aesthetic Constitution of Politics. LC 99-11558. 208p. 1999. 45.00 (*0-7391-0055-6*) Lxngtn Bks.

MacDonald, Bradley J., ed. see MacDonald, James B.

MacDonald, Brian W. Tribal Rugs: Treasures of the Black Tent. (Illus.). 180p. 1997. 69.50 (*1-85149-268-2*) Antique Collect.

MacDonald, Brooks & Griffin, Martha. Lobster Tales: Recipes & Recitations Featuring the Maine Attraction. (Orig.). 1995. pap. 14.95 (*0-9649367-0-4*) Lobster Tales.

MacDonald, Brooks, jt. auth. see Griffin, Martha.

Macdonald, Bruce. Practical Woody Plant Propagation for Nursery Growers, Vol. I. (Illus.). 660p. 1987. 69.95 (*0-88192-062-2*) Timber.

MacDonald, Bruce A., ed. see Metallurgical Society of AIME Staff.

MacDonald, Bruce K., ed. see Meyerowitz, Joel.

MacDonald, Bruno, ed. Pink Floyd Through the Eyes of . . . The Band, Its Fans, Friends & Foes. LC 97-5216. (Illus.). 400p. 1997. reprint ed. pap. 14.95 (*0-306-80780-7*) Da Capo.

***MacDonald, Bryden.** Divinity Bash - Nine Lives. large type ed. 128p. 1999. pap. 11.95 (*0-88922-408-0*, Pub. by Talonbks) Genl Dist Srvs.

MacDonald, Bryden. The Weekend Healer. LC 96-106341. 128p. 1996. pap. 11.95 (*0-88922-360-2*) Genl Dist Srvs.

— Whale Riding Weather. LC 94-241874. 128p. 1995. pap. 11.95 (*0-88922-353-X*, Pub. by Talonbks) Genl Dist Srvs.

***MacDonald, Burton.** East of the Jordan: Territories & Sites of the Hebrew Scriptures. (ASOR Bks.: Vol. 5). (Illus.). 304p. 2000. pap. write for info. (*0-89757-031-6*) Am Sch Orient Res.

***MacDonald, Burton & Younker, Randall W.** Ancient Ammon. LC 99-24375. (Studies in the History & Culture of the Ancient Near East.). 30p. 1999. 97.50 (*90-04-10762-2*) Brill Academic Pubs.

MacDonald, Byron J. Calligraphy: The Art of Lettering with the Broad Pen. pap. 5.95 (*0-8008-1182-8*) Taplinger.

MacDonald, C., ed. Cicero: De Imperio. (Bristol Latin Texts Ser.). (LAT.). 1991. pap. 18.95 (*0-86292-182-1*, Pub. by Brist Class Pr) Focus Pub-R Pullins.

— Cicero: Pro Murena. (Bristol Latin Texts Ser.). (LAT.). 220p. 1982. reprint ed. 20.95 (*0-86292-010-8*, Pub. by Brist Class Pr) Focus Pub-R Pullins.

MacDonald, Callum. The Killing of Reinhard Heydrich: The SS "Butcher of Prague" LC 98-7844. Orig. Title: The Killing of SS Obergruppenfuhrer Reinhard Heydrich. (Illus.). 239p. 1998. reprint ed. pap. 14.95 (*0-306-80860-9*) Da Capo.

MacDonald, Callum A. Korea: The War Before Vietnam. LC 86-22943. 320p. 1987. 32.95 (*0-02-919621-3*) Free Pr.

Macdonald, Cameron. Could It Be Stress? Reflections on Psychosomatic Illness. 192p. (C). 1992. pap. write for info. (*1-874640-10-6*, Pub. by Argyll Pubng) St Mut.

Macdonald, Cameron & Sirianni, Carmen, eds. Working in the Service Society. LC 96-23091. (Labor & Social Change Ser.). 362p. (C). 1996. pap. 24.95 (*1-56639-480-5*) Temple U Pr.

Macdonald, Carol. Using the Target Language. 1994. pap. 24.00 (*1-85234-507-1*, Pub. by S Thornes Pubs) Trans-Atl Phila.

MacDonald, Caroline. Hostilities. (J). 1997. mass mkt. 3.99 (*0-590-46064-1*) Scholastic Inc.

MacDonald, Caroline. Hostilities. LC 93-19019. 1991. 9.09 (*0-606-11480-7*, Pub. by Turtleback) Demco.

MacDonald, Caroline. Hostilities: Nine Bizarre Stories. LC 93-19019. 144p. (YA). (gr. 7-9). 1994. 13.95 (*0-590-46063-3*) Scholastic Inc.

— Speaking to Miranda. LC 91-47901. (Willa Perlman Bks.). 256p. (YA). (gr. 7 up). 1992. 14.00 (*0-06-021102-4*); lib. bdg. 13.89 (*0-06-021103-2*) HarpC Child Bks.

MacDonald, Carolyn A. Advanced Concepts for Geriatric Nursing Assistants. LC 94-61648. (Illus.). 224p. 1994. pap. 28.95 (*0-910251-71-1*, ACG73) Venture Pub PA.

MacDonald, Catherine. Reaching the Summit. LC 09-889656. 200p. 2000. pap. 14.95 (*0-88739-227-X*) Creat Arts Bk.

MacDonald, Cathryn. Danger: Divorce in Progress: One Woman's Story. 225p. 1998. pap. 12.95 (*0-9661563-0-7*) Ocean Tree Pubns.

MacDonald, Catriona. Unionist Scotland, 1800-1997. LC 98-200768. 152p. 1998. pap. 45.00 (*0-85976-471-0*, Pub. by J Donald) St Mut.

MacDonald, Charles. Scotland's Gift - Golf. rev. ed. (Classics of Golf Ser.). (Illus.). 340p. 1988. 28.00 (*0-940889-07-2*) Classics Golf.

MacDonald, Charles & Pierce, Richard. The Productive Supervisor: A Program of Practical Managerial Skills. Incl. Career Counseling Skills. 1985. lab manual ed. 5.00 (*0-914234-36-6*); Career Counseling Skills. 1985. (*0-87425-006-4*); Coaching Skills. 1985. lab manual ed. 5.00 (*0-914234-34-X*); Coaching Skills. 1985. (*0-87425-004-8*); Controlling Skills. 1985. lab manual ed. 5.00 (*0-87425-001-3*); Delegating Skills. 1985. (*0-914234-93-5*); Delegating Skills. 1985. (*0-87425-013-7*); Feedback Skills. 1985. lab manual ed. 5.00 (*0-87425-003-X*); Group Communication Skills. 1985. (*0-914234-39-0*); Group Communication Skills. 1985. (*0-87425-009-9*); Managing by Standards Skills. 1985. (*0-914234-96-X*); Managing by Standards Skills. 1985. (*0-87425-016-1*); Motivative Skills. 1985. lab manual ed. 5.00 (*0-914234-37-4*); Motivative Skills. 1985. (*0-87425-007-2*); Performance Appraisal Skills. 1985. lab manual ed. 5.00 (*0-914234-35-8*); Performance Appraisal Skills. 1985. (*0-87425-005-6*); Person-to-Person Communication Skills. 1985. (*0-914234-38-2*); Person-to-Person Communication Skills. 1985. (*0-87425-008-0*); Planning Skills. 1985. lab manual ed. 5.00 (*0-914234-30-7*); Planning Skills. 1985. (*0-87425-000-5*); Priority Setting Skills. 1985. (*0-914234-92-7*); Priority Setting Skills. 1985. (*0-87425-012-9*); Problem-Solving Skills. 1985. lab manual ed. 5.00 (*0-914234-32-3*); Problem-Solving Skills. 1985. (*0-87425-002-1*); Public Relations Skills. 1985. (*0-914234-60-9*); Public Relations Skills. 1985. (*0-87425-011-0*); Self-Development Skills. 1985. (*0-914234-95-1*); Self-Development Skills. 1985. (*0-87425-015-3*); Time Management Skills. 1985. (*0-914234-94-3*); Time Management Skills. 1985. (*0-87425-014-5*); Written Communication Skills. 1985. (*0-87425-010-2*); 1985. write for info. (*0-318-59244-4*) HRD Press.

Macdonald, Charles & Pierce, Richard. The Productive Supervisor: A Program of Practical Managerial Skills. 1985. pap. 85.00 (*0-685-73696-2*) HRD Press.

MacDonald, Charles & Watt, John. Moidart among the Clanranalds. LC 97-130697. (Illus.). 270p. pap. 19.95 (*1-874744-65-3*, Pub. by Birlinn Ltd) Dufour.

MacDonald, Charles B. Company Commander: The Classic Infantry Memoir of World War II. 320p. 24.95 (*0-8488-2570-5*) Amereon Ltd.

— Company Commander: The Classic Infantry Memoir of World War II. LC 99-32573. 288p. 1999. reprint ed. pap. 16.95 (*1-58080-038-6*) Burford Bks.

— The Mighty Endeavor: The American War in Europe. (Illus.). 621p. 1992. reprint ed. pap. 16.95 (*0-306-80486-7*) Da Capo.

— A Time for Trumpets: The Untold Story of the Battle of the Bulge. (Illus.). 720p. 1997. reprint ed. pap. 17.00 (*0-688-15157-4*, Quil) HarperTrade.

MacDonald, Charles B. United States Army in World War 2, European Theater of Operations, the Last Offensive. 552p. 1994. pap. 42.00 (*0-16-061316-7*) USGPO.

— United States Army in World War 2, Three Battles, Arnaville, Altuzzo & Schmidt. 443p. 1993. per. 29.00 (*0-16-061308-6*) USGPO.

MacDonald, Charles G. Iran, Saudi Arabia, & the Law of the Sea: Political Interaction & Legal Development in the Persian Gulf, 48. LC 79-6186. (Contributions in Political Science Ser.: No. 48). 226p. 1980. 59.95 (*0-313-20768-2*, MLS/) Greenwood.

MacDonald, Charles R. Twenty-Four Ways to Greater Business Productivity: Master Checklists for Marketing, Advertising, Sales, Distribution & Customer Service. LC 81-7096. 446p. 1981. text 49.50 (*0-87624-203-4*, Inst Busn Plan) P-H.

Macdonald, Charlotte, jt. ed. see Porter, Frances.

Macdonald, Chris & Nichol, John. Modern America. (Key History for GCSE Ser.). (Illus.). 96p. 1996. pap. 19.95 (*0-7487-2597-0*, Pub. by S Thornes Pubs) Trans-Atl Phila.

Macdonald, Christine. Lewis the Story of an Island. (C). 1992. text 45.00 (*0-86152-804-2*, Pub. by Acair Ltd) St Mut.

MacDonald, Claire. Quick & Easy Desserts & Puddings. (Illus.). 130p. (Orig.). 1994. pap. 9.95 (*0-563-36443-2*, BBC-Parkwest) Parkwest Pubns.

MacDonald, Claire. Suppers LC 99-164375. 256p. 1996. write for info. (*0-552-14209-3*, Pub. by Corgi Bks Ltd) Doubleday.

MacDonald, Claire, jt. auth. see Gough, Richard.

MacDonald, Claire, jt. ed. see Gough, Richard.

MacDonald-Clark, Margaret & Munn, Pamela. Education in Scotland: Policy & Practice from Pre-School to Secondary. LC 97-14247. 208p. (C). 1997. 60.00 (*0-415-15835-4*); pap. write for info. (*0-415-15836-2*) Routledge.

MacDonald, Colin. Down to Earth: Life in the Highlands & Islands of Scotland. (Aberdeen University Press Bks.). (Illus.). 352p. 1991. pap. 17.90 (*0-08-041224-6*, Pub. by Aberdeen U Pr) Macmillan.

— Highland Life & Lore. LC 98-187790. 320p. 1996. pap. 44.00 (*1-873644-72-8*, Pub. by Mercat Pr Bks) St Mut.

Macdonald, Copthorne. Toward Wisdom: Finding Our Way to Inner Peace, Love, & Happiness. 208p. (Orig.). 1996. pap. 11.95 (*1-57174-044-9*) Hampton Roads Pub Co.

Macdonald, Cynthia. I Can't Remember: Poems. 96p. 1999. pap. 14.00 (*0-679-76608-1*) Knopf.

— Living Wills: New & Selected Poems. LC 90-52737. 160p. 1992. pap. 12.00 (*0-679-74278-6*) Knopf.

MacDonald, Cynthia. Mind-Body Identity Theories. 256p. 1989. 45.00 (*0-415-03347-0*, A3659) Routledge.

MacDonald, Cynthia & Laurence, Stephen. Contemporary Readings in the Foundations of Metaphysics. 416p. 1998. 29.95 (*0-631-20172-6*) Blackwell Pubs.

MacDonald, Cynthia & Laurence, Stephen, eds. Contemporary Readings in the Foundations of Metaphysics. LC 97-47397. 416p. 1998. 64.95 (*0-631-20171-8*) Blackwell Pubs.

MacDonald, Cynthia & MacDonald, Graham. Philosophy of Psychology: Debates on Psychological Explanation. 401p. 1995. pap. 31.95 (*0-631-18542-9*) Blackwell Pubs.

Macdonald, Cynthia & Macdonald, Graham, eds. Connectionism: Debates on Psychological Exploration. (Illus.). (C). 1995. pap. 31.95 (*0-631-19745-1*) Blackwell Pubs.

Macdonald, D. Sedimentation, Tectonics & Eustasy. 1991. pap. 125.00 (*0-632-03017-8*) Blackwell Sci.

Macdonald, D. & Barrett, P. Collins Field Guide: Mammals of Britain & Europe. (Illus.). 312p. 1995. 35.95 (*0-00-219779-0*, Pub. by HarpC) Trafalgar.

MacDonald, D. A., jt. ed. see Bruford, A. J.

MacDonald, D. B. The Development of Muslim Theology, Jurisprudence & Constitution Theory. 400p. 1985. 280.00 (*1-85077-066-2*, Pub. by Darf Pubs Ltd) St Mut.

— The Religious Attitude & Life in Islam. 336p. 1985. 265.00 (*1-85077-050-6*, Pub. by Darf Pubs Ltd) St Mut.

MacDonald, D. J. Chi Mi. 1998. pap. 19.95 (*1-874744-85-8*, Pub. by Birlinn Ltd) Dufour.

Macdonald, D. L. Poor Polidor: A Critical Biography of the Author of the Vampyre. 400p. 1991. text 60.00 (*0-8020-2774-1*) U of Toronto Pr.

Macdonald, D. L., ed. see Polidori, John W.

MacDonald, D. L., ed. see Shelley, Mary Wollstonecraft.

***MacDonald, D. R.** Cape Breton Road. LC 00-29555. 288p. 2001. 23.00 (*0-15-100523-0*) Harcourt.

MacDonald, D. R. Eyestone. LC 87-83285. 1988. 15.95 (*0-916366-48-0*, Pub. by Pushcart Pr) Norton.

Macdonald, D. Ross. Mercantile Law of Scotland. 1995. pap. text. write for info. (*0-406-10585-5*, UK, MICHIE) LEXIS Pub.

MacDonald, Dan, jt. auth. see Smith, Kelvin.

MacDonald, Daniel & Smith, Kelvin. Chess for Kids. (YA). (gr. 4-7). Date not set. boxed set 14.95 (*1-55850-792-2*) Adams Media.

***Macdonald, David.** Foxes. LC 99-89098. (WorldLife Library). (Illus.). 72p. 2000. pap. 16.95 (*0-89658-467-4*) Voyageur Pr.

MacDonald, David. Twenty Years in Tibet. (C). 1991. reprint ed. 36.00 (*81-85326-50-9*, Pub. by Vintage) S Asia.

***MacDonald, David S.** Brookman Stamp Price Guide 2001. (Brookman Stamp Price Guide Ser.). (Illus.). 350p. 2000. pap. 22.95 (*0-936937-50-5*) Brookman Stamp.

MacDonald, David S. Brookman 1996: Price Guide for United States Stamps & Postal Collectibles. 1995. pap. 14.95 (*0-936937-39-4*) Brookman Stamp.

— 1995 Brookman: Price Guide for United States Stamps & Postal Collectibles. 1995. pap. text 14.95 (*0-936937-38-6*) Brookman Stamp.

— Traveler Stamp Album. (Illus.). 272p. 1986. pap. 18.95 (*0-937458-42-2*) Harris & Co.

MacDonald, David S., ed. Canada Stamp Album. (Illus.). 416p. 1984. pap. 42.95 (*0-937458-08-2*) Harris & Co.

— U. S. Plate Blocks, Vol. A. (Illus.). 480p. 1983. pap. text 37.95 (*0-937458-18-X*) Harris & Co.

— U. S. Plate Blocks, Vol. B. (Illus.). 416p. 1984. reprint ed. pap. text 37.95 (*0-937458-19-8*) Harris & Co.

MacDonald, David W. Rabies & Wildlife: A Biologist's Perspective. (Illus.). 1980. write for info. (*0-318-54886-0*) OUP.

MacDonald, David W., ed. The Encyclopedia of Mammals. (Illus.). 960p. 1984. 80.00 (*0-87196-871-1*) Facts on File.

Macdonald, David W., et al, eds. Chemical Signals in Vertebrates. (Illus.). 688p. 1991. 110.00 (*0-19-857731-1*) OUP.

MacDonald, David W., jt. ed. see Brown, Richard E.

***MacDonald, Davis S.** Brookman Stamp Price Guide 2001. (Illus.). 2000. pap. 17.95 (*0-936937-49-1*) Brookman Stamp.

***MacDonald, Davis S., ed.** 2000 Brookman Stamp Price Guide. (Illus.). 300p. 1999. pap. 16.95 (*0-936937-46-7*) Brookman Stamp.

***MacDonald, Dennis Ronald.** The Homeric Epics & the Gospel of Mark. LC 99-46344. 272p. 2000. 30.00 (*0-300-08012-3*) Yale U Pr.

MacDonald, Diane B., jt. auth. see Ramaglia, Judith A.

MacDonald, Diane L. Transgressive Corporeality: The Body, Poststructuralism & the Theological Imagination. LC 94-24727. 170p. (C). 1995. text 57.50 (*0-7914-2487-1*); pap. text 18.95 (*0-7914-2488-X*) State U NY Pr.

Macdonald, Digby D., ed. Transient Techniques in Electrochemistry. LC 77-24603. 330p. 1977. 75.00 (*0-306-31010-4*, Plenum Trade) Perseus Pubng.

MacDonald, Donald. Ancient Martial Music of Caledonia. MacRaonuill, Alasdair, ed. & intro. by. 132p. 1995. pap. 24.00 (*0-614-24065-4*) A MacRaonuill.

— Christian Experience. 160p. 1988. 17.99 (*0-85151-527-4*) Banner of Truth.

— Democratic Architecture: Practical Solutions to Today's Housing Crisis. LC 96-39042. (Illus.). 176p. 1996. pap. text 35.00 (*0-8230-1343-X*) Watsn-Guptill.

— The Diaries of Donald MacDonald. LC 72-77060. 233p. 1973. reprint ed. lib. bdg. 35.00 (*0-678-00914-7*) Kelley.

Macdonald, Donald F. Fasti Ecclesiae Vol. X: Scoticanae. 530p. (C). 1989. 150.00 (*0-7855-6822-0*, Pub. by St Andrew) St Mut.

— Fasti Ecclesiae Scoticanae. 530p. (C). 1988. text 125.00 (*0-7152-0495-5*) St Mut.

— Scotland's Shifting Population, 1770-1850. LC 78-15153. (Illus.). vii, 172p. 1978. reprint ed. lib. bdg. 35.00 (*0-87991-860-8*) Porcupine Pr.

M

Macdonald, Donald S. The Koreans: Contemporary Politics & Society. 3rd ed. Clark, Donald N., ed. & rev. by. (C). 1996. pap. 30.00 (*0-8133-2888-8*, Pub. by Westview) HarpC.

***MacDonald, Dora M.** This Is Duluth. LC 98-94255. (Historic Preservation Ser.). iii, 281p. 1999. write for info. (*1-889924-03-2*) Paradigm Pr WI.

Macdonald, Dorothy, compiled by. Cumulative Index to American Book Collector. 7.50 (*0-89679-008-8*) Moretus Pr.

***MacDonald, Dorothy M.** Brittany: Ideal Companion at Home & Afield. 224p. 1999. text 27.95 (*1-58245-000-5*) Howell Bks.

MacDonald, Dougald, ed. The Best of Rock & Ice: An Anthology. LC 99-6455. 1999. pap. 17.95 (*0-89886-665-0*) Mountaineers.

Macdonald, Dougald, jt. auth. see Soles, Clyde.

MacDonald, Douglas. Spirals. (Offset Offshoot Ser.: No.4). 34p. 1979. pap. 10.00 (*0-317-06440-1*) Ommation Pr.

Macdonald, Douglas J. Adventures in Chaos: American Intervention for Reform in the Third World. 376p. 1992. 51.95 (*0-674-00577-5*) HUP.

MacDonald, Douglas M., jt. auth. see Edwards, James C.

MacDonald, Duncan & Sagendorph, Robb. Old-Time New England Cookbook. LC 92-47279. Orig. Title: Rain, Hail, & Baked Beans: A New England Seasonal Cookbook. (Illus.). 224p. 1993. reprint ed. pap. 6.95 (*0-486-27630-9*) Dover.

Macdonald, Duncan B. Aspects of Islam. LC 77-179530. (Select Bibliographies Reprint Ser.). 1980. reprint ed. 28.95 (*0-8369-6659-7*) Ayer.

— The Religious Attitude & Life in Islam. LC 70-121277. reprint ed. 32.50 (*0-404-04125-6*) AMS Pr.

MacDonald, Dwight. The Root Is Man. 187p. Date not set. 7.00 (*1-57027-017-1*) Autonomedia.

Macdonald, Dwight & Sutton, Francis X. The Ford Foundation: The Men & the Millions. 212p. (Orig.). 1988. pap. 29.95 (*0-88738-748-9*) Transaction Pubs.

MacDonald, Dwight, ed. see Herzen, Aleksandr.

MacDonald, Dwight, tr. see Camus, Albert.

MacDonald, Edgar E. & Inge, Tonette B. Ellen Glasgow: A Reference Guide. (Reference Guides to Literature Ser.). 328p. 1986. 55.00 (*0-8161-8218-3*, Hall Reference) Macmillan.

MacDonald, Edgar E., ed. see Lazarus, Rachel M.

MacDonald, Edward E. An Atoll Called Tarawa. rev. ed. 1999. mass mkt. 12.99 (*1-891371-00-2*) Angel Ministries.

MacDonald, Edward E. Forever Yours. unabridged ed. 1997. mass mkt. 6.95 (*1-891371-02-9*) Angel Ministries.

— It's Christmas Time Again. unabridged ed. 1997. mass mkt. 6.95 (*1-891371-05-3*) Angel Ministries.

— Other Times Fading Faces. unabridged ed. 1996. mass mkt. 9.95 (*1-891371-01-0*) Angel Ministries.

— Reflections. unabridged ed. (Illus.). 1995. mass mkt. 12.95 (*1-891371-04-5*) Angel Ministries.

— A Time. unabridged ed. 1993. mass mkt. 6.95 (*1-891371-03-7*) Angel Ministries.

— You Out There. unabridged ed. (Illus.). 1997. mass mkt. 12.95 (*1-891371-06-1*) Angel Ministries.

Macdonald, Eleanor J., ed. see MacDonald, Angus A.

MacDonald, Eleanor K. A Window into History: Family Memory in Children's Literature. LC 95-40621. 248p. 1995. pap. 27.50 (*0-89774-879-4*) Oryx Pr.

Macdonald, Elisabeth. Bring down the Sun. 352p. (Orig.). 1996. mass mkt. 5.50 (*0-380-77960-9*, Avon Bks) Morrow Avon.

MacDonald, Elisabeth. Voices on the Wind. 352p. (Orig.). 1994. mass mkt. 4.99 (*0-380-77376-7*, Avon Bks) Morrow Avon.

***MacDonald, Elizabeth.** Dilly-Dally & the Nine Secrets. LC 99-32212. (Illus.). 32p. (J). 2000. 15.99 (*0-525-46006-3*, Dutton Child) Peng Put Young Read.

Macdonald, Elizabeth. John's Picture. (J). 1999. pap. 3.95 (*0-14-054344-9*) NAL.

MacDonald, Elizabeth. The Wolf Is Coming! LC 97-26758. (Illus.). (J). 1998. 15.99 (*0-525-45952-9*, Dutton Child) Peng Put Young Read.

Macdonald, Elizabeth & Rowland, Diane. Information Technology Law: Text, Cases & Materials. LC 97-218108. xxvi, 405p. 1997. pap. 54.00 (*1-85941-225-4*, Pub. by Cavendish Pubng) Gaunt.

MacDonald, Elizabeth, jt. auth. see Koffman, Laurence.

Macdonald, Elspeth T. & Macdonald, J. B. Drug Treatment in the Elderly. LC 82-1913. (Wiley Series on Disease Management in the Elderly: No. 1). 259p. reprint ed. pap. 80.30 (*0-8357-8623-4*, 203504600091) Bks Demand.

MacDonald, F. & Ford, C. H. Oncogenes & Tumor Suppressor Genes. (Medical Perspectives Ser.). 112p. (Orig.). 1991. pap. 46.50 (*1-872748-55-4*, Pub. by Bios Sci) Coronet Bks.

MacDonald, Finlay J. & Ford, C. Molecular Biology of Cancer. (Medical Perspectives Ser.). (Illus.). 160p. (Orig.). 1996. pap. text 39.95 (*1-85996-225-4*, Pub. by Bios Sci) Bks Intl VA.

MacDonald, Finlay J., jt. ed. see Buckingham, John B.

***MacDonald, Fiona.** Abraham Lincoln. (World in the Time of... Ser.). (Illus.). (J). 2000. 17.95 (*0-7910-6028-4*) Chelsea Hse.

— Albert Einstein: Genius Beyond the Theory of Relativity. (Giants of Science Ser.). 64p. (gr. 4-7). 2000. 19.95 (*1-56711-330-3*) Blackbirch.

— Alexander the Great. (World in the Time of... Ser.). (Illus.). (J). 2000. 17.95 (*0-7910-6029-2*) Chelsea Hse.

MacDonald, Fiona. Ancient African Town. LC 98-6722. (Metropolis Ser.). (Illus.). 45p. (J). (gr. 4-7). 1998. 24.00 (*0-531-14480-1*) Watts.

— An Ancient African Town. (Metropolis Ser.). (Illus.). 48p. (J). (gr. 3-7). 1999. pap. text 8.95 (*0-531-15360-6*) Watts.

— The Ancient Aztecs Treasure Chest: Secrets of a Lost Civilization to Unlock & Discover. LC 95-70146. (Treasure Chest Ser.). (Illus.). 32p. (J). 1996. 19.95 (*1-56138-619-7*) Running Pr.

***MacDonald, Fiona.** Castles. LC 00-35903. (Topic Bks.). (Illus.). (J). 2001. write for info. (*0-531-14551-4*) Watts.

MacDonald, Fiona. Celtic World. Anness Publishing Staff, ed. (Step into Ser.). (Illus.). 64p. (J). 1999. 12.95 (*0-7548-0215-9*, Lorenz Bks) Anness Pub.

***MacDonald, Fiona.** Charlemagne. (World in the Time of... Ser.). (Illus.). (J). 2000. 17.95 (*0-7910-6030-6*) Chelsea Hse.

MacDonald, Fiona. Child's Eye View of History. LC 97-10507. 64p. (J). (gr. 5 up). 1998. per. 16.95 (*0-689-81378-3*) S&S Childrens.

— Cities: Citizens & Civilizations. (Timelines Ser.). (Illus.). 48p. (J). (gr. 5-8). 1992. 24.00 (*0-531-14408-9*) Watts.

— Cities: Citizens & Civilizations. (Timelines Ser.). (Illus.). 48p. (J). (gr. 5-8). 1996. reprint ed. pap. 7.95 (*0-531-15287-1*) Watts.

— Crime & Punishment: Law & Order. LC 95-1038. (Timelines Ser.). (Illus.). 48p. (J). (gr. 5-8). 1995. pap. 7.95 (*0-531-15280-4*) Watts.

***MacDonald, Fiona.** Einstein. (World in the Time of... Ser.). (Illus.). (J). 2000. 17.95 (*0-7910-6031-4*) Chelsea Hse.

MacDonald, Fiona. Explorers: Expeditions & Pioneers. LC 94-14040. (Timelines Ser.). (Illus.). 48p. (J). (gr. 5-8). 1994. lib. bdg. 24.00 (*0-531-14332-5*) Watts.

— Exploring the World. LC 96-1925. (Voyages of Discovery Ser.). (Illus.). 48p. (YA). (gr. 4 up). 1996. 18.95 (*0-87226-487-4*, P Bedrick Books) NTC Contemp Pub Co.

— First Facts about the American Frontier. LC 96-12297. (First Facts Ser.). (Illus.). 32p. (YA). (gr. 5-9). 1996. 14.95 (*0-87226-498-X*, 6498XB, P Bedrick Books) NTC Contemp Pub Co.

— First Facts about the Ancient Greeks. LC 97-7209. (First Facts Ser.). (Illus.). 32p. (J). (gr. 5-9). 1997. 14.95 (*0-87226-532-3*, 65323B, P Bedrick Books) NTC Contemp Pub Co.

— First Facts about the Ancient Romans. (First Facts Ser.). (Illus.). 32p. (YA). (gr. 4 up). 1996. 14.95 (*0-87226-496-3*, 64963B, P Bedrick Books) NTC Contemp Pub Co.

— First Facts about the Middle Ages. LC 97-7208. (First Facts Ser.). (Illus.). 32p. (YA). (gr. 4 up). 1997. 14.95 (*0-87226-533-1*, 65331B, P Bedrick Books) NTC Contemp Pub Co.

— Houses: Habitats & Home Life. (Timelines Ser.). (Illus.). 48p. (J). (gr. 5-8). 1994. lib. bdg. 24.00 (*0-531-14333-3*) Watts.

— How Would You Survive As an Ancient Greek? LC 95-3177. (How Would You Survive? Ser.). (Illus.). 48p. (J). (gr. 5-8). 1995. lib. bdg. 24.00 (*0-531-14342-2*) Watts.

— How Would You Survive As an Ancient Greek? LC 95-3177. (How Would You Survive? Ser.). (Illus.). 48p. (J). (gr. 5-8). 1996. pap. 7.95 (*0-531-15307-X*) Watts.

— How Would You Survive as an Aztec? LC 94-28068. (How Would You Survive? Ser.). (Illus.). 48p. (J). (gr. 5-8). lib. bdg. 24.00 (*0-531-14348-1*) Watts.

— How Would You Survive As an Aztec? (How Would You Survive? Ser.). 32p. (J). (gr. 5-8). 1997. pap. 7.95 (*0-531-15304-5*) Watts.

— How Would You Survive in the Middle Ages? LC 95-3176. (How Would You Survive? Ser.). (Illus.). 48p. (J). (gr. 5-8). 1995. lib. bdg. 24.00 (*0-531-14343-0*) Watts.

— How Would You Survive in the Middle Ages? (How Would You Survive? Ser.). 32p. (J). 1997. pap. 7.95 (*0-531-15306-1*) Watts.

— I Wonder Why Greeks Built Temples & Other Questions about Ancient Greece. LC 96-34095. (I Wonder Why Ser.). (Illus.). 32p. (J). (gr. k-3). 1997. 11.95 (*0-7534-5056-9*) LKC.

— I Wonder Why Romans Wore Togas & Other Questions about Ancient Rome. LC 96-34547. (I Wonder Why Ser.). (Illus.). 32p. (J). (gr. k-3). 1997. 11.95 (*0-7534-5057-7*, Kingfisher) LKC.

— Inca Town. (Metropolis Ser.). (Illus.). 48p. (J). (gr. 3-7). 1999. pap. text 8.95 (*0-531-15361-4*) Watts.

— Island Voices. 176p. 1995. pap. 13.95 (*0-86241-469-5*, Pub. by Canongate Books) Interlink Pub.

— Kings & Queens: Rulers & Despots. (Timelines Ser.). (Illus.). 48p. (J). (gr. 5-8). 1995. lib. bdg. 22.00 (*0-531-14369-4*) Watts.

***MacDonald, Fiona.** Leonardo Da Vinci. (World in the Time of... Ser.). (Illus.). (J). 2000. 17.95 (*0-7910-6032-2*) Chelsea Hse.

MacDonald, Fiona. Magellan: A Voyage around the World. (Expedition Ser.). (Illus.). 32p. (J). (gr. 2-9). 1998. pap. 7.95 (*0-531-15341-X*) Watts.

***MacDonald, Fiona.** Marco Polo. (World in the Time of... Ser.). (Illus.). (J). 2000. 17.95 (*0-7910-6033-0*) Chelsea Hse.

— Marie Antoinette. (World in the Time of... Ser.). (Illus.). (J). 2000. 17.95 (*0-7910-6034-9*) Chelsea Hse.

MacDonald, Fiona. A Medieval Castle. (Inside Story Ser.). (Illus.). 48p. (YA). (gr. 5 up). 1990. lib. bdg. 18.95 (*0-87226-340-1*, 63401B, P Bedrick Books) NTC Contemp Pub Co.

— A Medieval Cathedral. LC 91-16415. (Inside Story Ser.). (Illus.). 48p. (YA). (gr. 4-7). 1994. 18.95 (*0-87226-350-9*, 63509B, P Bedrick Books) NTC Contemp Pub Co.

— The Middle Ages. (Illustrated History of the World Ser.). (Illus.). 80p. (J). (gr. 4-9). 1993. 19.95 (*0-8160-2788-9*) Facts on File.

— Plains Indians. (Insights Ser.). (Illus.). 60p. (J). (gr. 4 up). 1993. 15.95 (*0-8120-6376-7*) Barron.

***MacDonald, Fiona.** Rain Forest. (Topic Bks.). (Illus.). (J). 2000. pap. 6.95 (*0-531-15425-4*) Watts.

MacDonald, Fiona. The Roman Colosseum. LC 96-15138. (Inside Story Ser.). (Illus.). 48p. (YA). (gr. 5 up). 1996. lib. bdg. 18.95 (*0-87226-275-8*, 62758B, P Bedrick Books) NTC Contemp Pub Co.

— A Roman Fort. LC 93-16397. (Inside Story Ser.). (Illus.). 48p. (YA). (gr. 4-7). 1993. 18.95 (*0-87226-370-3*, 63703B, P Bedrick Books) NTC Contemp Pub Co.

— A Roman Fort. LC 93-16397. (Inside Story Ser.). (Illus.). 48p. (YA). (gr. 5 up). 1993. 9.95 (*0-87226-259-6*, P Bedrick Books) NTC Contemp Pub Co.

— A Sixteenth Century Mosque. LC 94-20008. (Inside Story Ser.). (Illus.). 48p. (YA). (gr. 4-7). 1994. 18.95 (*0-87226-310-X*, 6310XB, P Bedrick Books) NTC Contemp Pub Co.

— 16th Century Mosque. 58p. (J). 1996. pap. 14.95 (*0-614-20979-X*, 1648) Kazi Pubns.

— So You Want to Be a Roman Soldier. LC 98-27984. (So You Want to Be... Ser.). (Illus.). 32p. (J). (gr. 4-6). 1999. lib. bdg. 18.90 (*0-7613-1421-0*, Copper Beech Bks) Millbrook Pr.

***MacDonald, Fiona.** Space. LC 99-46361. (Topic Bks.). 2000. 22.50 (*0-531-14542-5*) Watts.

— Space. (Topic Bks.). (Illus.). (J). 2000. pap. 6.95 (*0-531-15426-2*) Watts.

MacDonald, Fiona. Step Into Ancient Japan. 1999. 12.95 (*1-85967-917-X*, Lorenz Bks) Anness Pub.

— The Traveler's Guide to Ancient Greece. LC 98-7363. (J). 1998. write for info. (*0-590-11762-9*); pap. write for info. (*0-590-11920-6*) Scholastic Inc.

***MacDonald, Fiona.** Tutankhamen. (World in the Time of... Ser.). (Illus.). (J). 2000. 17.95 (*0-7910-6035-7*) Chelsea Hse.

MacDonald, Fiona. Vikings. (Insights Ser.). (Illus.). 60p. (J). (gr. 4 up). 1993. 15.95 (*0-8120-6375-9*) Barron.

— Vikings Treasure Chest. (Treasure Chest Ser.). (Illus.). 32p. (J). (gr. 3-8). 1997. 19.95 (*0-7624-0147-8*) Running Pr.

***MacDonald, Fiona.** Water. LC 99-43053. (Topic Bks.). 1999. 22.50 (*0-531-14543-3*) Watts.

— Water. (Topic Bks.). (Illus.). (J). 2000. pap. 6.95 (*0-531-15427-0*) Watts.

— Weather. LC 99-45291. (Topic Bks.). 2000. 22.50 (*0-531-14544-1*) Watts.

— Weather. (Topic Bks.). (Illus.). (YA). 2000. pap. 6.95 (*0-531-15428-9*) Watts.

MacDonald, Fiona. Women in Ancient Egypt. LC 99-11857. (Other Half of History Ser.). 48p. (J). (gr. 4-7). 1999. 17.95 (*0-87226-567-6*, 65676B, P Bedrick Books) NTC Contemp Pub Co.

— Women in Ancient Greece. LC 99-21091. (Other Half of History Ser.). 48p. (J). (gr. 4-7). 1999. lib. bdg. 17.95 (*0-87226-568-4*, 65684B, P Bedrick Books) NTC Contemp Pub Co.

***MacDonald, Fiona.** Women in Ancient Rome. (Other Half of History Ser.). (Illus.). 48p. (J). (gr. 3-7). 2000. 17.95 (*0-87226-570-6*, 65706B, P Bedrick Books) NTC Contemp Pub Co.

— Women in Medieval Times. (Other Half of History Ser.). 48p. (J). 2000. 17.95 (*0-87226-569-2*, 65692B, P Bedrick Books) NTC Contemp Pub Co.

MacDonald, Fiona. Women in 19th Century America. LC 98-42644. (Other Half of History Ser.). (Illus.). 48 p. (J). (gr. 3-7). 1999. 17.95 (*0-87226-566-8*, 65668B, P Bedrick Books) NTC Contemp Pub Co.

— Women in 19th-Century Europe. LC 98-42170. (Other Half of History Ser.). 48p. (J). (gr. 4-8). 1999. lib. bdg. 17.95 (*0-87226-565-X*, 6565XB, P Bedrick Books) NTC Contemp Pub Co.

***MacDonald, Fiona.** Women in Peace & War, 1900-1945. (Other Half of History Ser.). (YA). 2000. 17.95 (*0-87226-666-4*, P Bedrick Books) NTC Contemp Pub Co.

MacDonald, Fiona. The World in the Time of Abraham Lincoln. LC 96-53372. (World in the Time of Ser.). (J). 1997. pap. write for info. (*0-382-39744-4*, Dillon Silver Burdett); lib. bdg. 19.95 (*0-382-39745-2*) Silver Burdett Pr.

— The World in the Time of Albert Einstein. LC 97-44780. (J). 1998. pap. 9.95 (*0-382-39738-X*, Dillon Silver Burdett) Silver Burdett Pr.

— The World in the Time of Albert Einstein: 1879-1955. LC 97-44780. 48p. (YA). (gr. 6-12). 1998. lib. bdg. 9.95 (*0-382-39739-8*, Dillon Silver Burdett) Silver Burdett Pr.

— The World in the Time of Alexander the Great. LC 96-53371. (World in the Time of Ser.). (J). 1997. pap. write for info. (*0-382-39742-8*, Dillon Silver Burdett); lib. bdg. 19.95 (*0-382-39743-6*, Dillon Silver Burdett) Silver Burdett Pr.

— The World in the Time of Charlemagne. LC 97-39931. (World in the Time of Ser.). 1998. pap. write for info. (*0-382-39736-3*) Silver Burdett Pr.

— The World in the Time of Charlemagne: AD 700-900. LC 97-39931. (The World in the Time of Ser.). 48p. (YA). (gr. 6-12). 1998. 9.95 (*0-382-39737-1*) Silver Burdett Pr.

— The World in the Time of Leonardo da Vinci. LC 97-20216. (World in the Time of Ser.). 1998. pap. write for info. (*0-382-39740-1*, Dillon Silver Burdett); lib. bdg. 19.95 (*0-382-39741-X*, Dillon Silver Burdett) Silver Burdett Pr.

— The World in the Time of Marco Polo. (World in the Time of Ser.). (Illus.). 48p. (J). (gr. 4-8). 1997. pap. 9.95 (*0-382-39748-7*, Dillon Silver Burdett); lib. bdg. 16.95 (*0-382-39749-5*, Dillon Silver Burdett) Silver Burdett Pr.

— The World in the Time of Marie Antoinette. LC 97-22085. (World in the Time of Ser.). 1998. pap. write for info. (*0-382-39734-7*, Dillon Silver Burdett); lib. bdg. 19.95 (*0-382-39735-5*, Dillon Silver Burdett) Silver Burdett Pr.

— The World in the Time of Tutankhamun. (World in the Time of Ser.). (Illus.). 48p. (J). (gr. 4-8). 1997. pap. 9.95 (*0-382-39746-0*, Dillon Silver Burdett); lib. bdg. 16.95 (*0-382-39747-9*, Dillon Silver Burdett) Silver Burdett Pr.

— The World of Islam up to 1500s. 64p. 1996. pap. 12.95 (*0-614-21045-3*, 1335) Kazi Pubns.

MacDonald, Fiona & Bergin, Mark. A Greek Temple. LC 92-10712. (Inside Story Ser.). (Illus.). 48p. (YA). (gr. 5 up). 1992. 18.95 (*0-87226-361-4*, 63614B, P Bedrick Books) NTC Contemp Pub Co.

— Marco Polo: A Journey Through China. (Expedition Ser.). (Illus.). 32p. (J). (gr. 2-9). 1998. pap. 7.95 (*0-531-15340-1*) Watts.

MacDonald, Fiona & Roberts, Alison. The Stone Age News. LC 97-41255. (Illus.). 32p. (J). (gr. 4-9). 1998. 16.99 (*0-7636-0451-8*) Candlewick Pr.

MacDonald, Fiona & Salariya, David. Inca Town. LC 98-18516. (Metropolis Ser.). (Illus.). 45p. (J). (gr. 4-7). 1998. 24.00 (*0-531-14481-X*) Watts.

— Marco Polo: A Journey Through China. LC 97-7533. (Expedition Ser.). (Illus.). 32p. (J). (gr. 5 up). 1998. 21.00 (*0-531-14453-4*) Watts.

***MacDonald, Fiona, et al.** Rain Forest. LC 99-45292. 2000. 22.50 (*0-531-14541-7*) Watts.

MacDonald, Fiona, et al. A Samurai Castle. LC 95-2181. (Inside Story Ser.). (Illus.). 48p. (YA). (gr. 4-7). 1995. lib. bdg. 18.95 (*0-87226-381-9*, 63819B, P Bedrick Books) NTC Contemp Pub Co.

Macdonald, Frederick. Bishop Stirling of the Falklands. 1976. lib. bdg. 59.95 (*0-8490-1509-X*) Gordon Pr.

Macdonald, G. The Little Island. (Illus.). 48p. (J). 1993. pap. 5.99 (*0-440-40830-X*) Dell.

MacDonald, G. Silver Coinage of Crete. (Illus.). 1974. pap. 9.00 (*0-932106-30-7*) S J Durst.

Macdonald, G. The Silver Coinage of Crete: A Metrological Note. (Illus.). 29p. 1974. pap. 5.00 (*0-916710-13-0*) Obol Intl.

***MacDonald, G., et al.** Discovering Character in God. 320p. 1999. pap. 12.99 (*0-7642-2181-7*) Bethany Hse.

MacDonald, G. J. & Sertorio, L. Global Climate & Ecosystem Change. LC 90-47793. (NATO ASI Series B, Physics: Vol. 240). (Illus.). 262p. (C). 1991. 89.50 (*0-306-43715-5*, Plenum Trade) Perseus Pubng.

***MacDonald, Gail.** High Call, High Privilege. 240p. 2000. pap. 10.95 (*1-56563-557-4*) Hendrickson MA.

MacDonald, Gail. High Call, High Privilege: A Pastor's Wife Speaks to Every Woman in a Place of Responsibility. rev. ed. LC 98-24345. 226p. 1998. 16.95 (*1-56563-367-9*) Hendrickson MA.

***MacDonald, Gail.** In His Everlasting Arms: Learning to Trust God in All Circumstances. 194p. 2000. pap. 10.99 (*1-56955-188-X*) Servant.

MacDonald, Gail, jt. auth. see MacDonald, Gordon.

MacDonald, Gayle. Medicine Hands: Massage Therapy for People with Cancer. (Illus.). 192p. 1999. pap. 23.95 (*1-899171-77-0*) Words Distrib.

MacDonald, Gaynor, jt. ed. see Maher, John C.

MacDonald, George. Adela Cathcart. (George MacDonald Original Works Ser.: Series IV). 462p. 1994. reprint ed. 22.00 (*1-881084-23-X*) Johannesen.

— Alec Forbes & His Friend Annie. Phillips, Michael R., ed. (George MacDonald Classics for Young Readers Ser.). 256p. (J). (gr. 2-7). 1990. text 10.99 (*1-55661-140-4*) Bethany Hse.

— Alec Forbes of Howglen. LC 87-82627. (Sunrise Centenary Editions Ser.: Vol. 1). 489p. 1988. 27.50 (*0-940652-50-1*) Sunrise Bks.

— Alec Forbes of Howglen. (George MacDonald Original Works Ser.: Series V). 440p. 1995. reprint ed. 22.00 (*1-881084-33-7*) Johannesen.

— Annals of a Quiet Neighbourhood. deluxe ed. 1992. 37.50 (*0-940652-60-9*) Sunrise Bks.

— Annals of a Quiet Neighbourhood. (George MacDonald Original Works Ser.: Series V). 600p. 1995. reprint ed. 24.00 (*1-881084-29-9*) Johannesen.

— At the Back of the North Wind. (Victorian Children's Classics Ser.). 370p. (YA). 1989. pap. 6.99 (*0-88270-556-3*) Bridge-Logos.

— At the Back of the North Wind. LC 88-63292. (Books of Wonder). (Illus.). 252p. (YA). (gr. 4-7). 1989. 22.00 (*0-688-07808-7*, Wm Morrow) Morrow Avon.

— At the Back of the North Wind. (J). 1992. pap. 2.95 (*0-8167-2877-1*) Troll Communs.

— At the Back of the North Wind. large type ed. 437p. 1997. reprint ed. lib. bdg. 24.00 (*0-939495-21-X*) North Bks.

— At the Back of the North Wind. 1995. reprint ed. lib. bdg. 29.95 (*1-56849-660-5*) Buccaneer Bks.

— At the Back of the North Wind. 280p. 1998. reprint ed. lib. bdg. 24.00 (*1-58287-015-2*) North Bks.

— At the Back of the North Wind: With Colour Plates. (George MacDonald Original Works Ser.: Series II). (Illus.). 378p. (YA). 1998. reprint ed. 26.00 (*1-881084-07-8*) Johannesen.

— At the Back of the Northwind. 1998. mass mkt. 3.99 (*0-8125-6712-9*, Pub. by Tor Bks) St Martin.

— The Baronet's Song. abr. rev. ed. Phillips, Michael, ed. LC 83-6417. 28p. 1983. pap. 7.99 (*0-87123-291-X*) Bethany Hse.

— Belgium. (Illustrated Travel Guides from Thomas Cook Ser.). (Illus.). 192p. 1994. pap. 12.95 (*0-8442-9059-9*, Passprt Bks) NTC Contemp Pub Co.

— Belgium. 3rd ed. (Passport's Illustrated Travel Guides from Thomas Cook Ser.). (Illus.). 192p. 1999. pap. 14.95 (*0-658-00032-2*, 000322, Passprt Bks) NTC Contemp Pub Co.

— Castle Warlock. LC 94-65868. (Centenary Ser.: No. 14). 731p. 1998. 45.00 (*0-940652-63-3*) Sunrise Bks.

— Castle Warlock. (George MacDonald Original Works Ser.: Series I). 379p. 1998. reprint ed. 22.00 (*1-881084-03-5*) Johannesen.

An Asterisk (*) at the beginning of an entry indicates that the title is appearing for the first time.

— The Christmas Stories of George MacDonald. LC 81-68187. (J). (gr. 3-7). 1981. 12.99 (*0-89191-491-9*, 54916, Chariot Bks) Chariot Victor.

***MacDonald, George.** The Complete Fairy Tales. Knoepflmacher, U. C., ed. & intro. by. LC 98-55673. (Penguin Classics Ser.). 352p. 1999. pap. 13.95 (*0-14-043737-1*) Viking Penguin.

MacDonald, George. A Daughter's Devotion. rev. ed. Phillips, Michael, ed. LC 88-19256. (George MacDonald Classics for Young Readers Ser.). 32p. 1988. pap. 8.99 (*0-87123-906-X*) Bethany Hse.

— David Elginbrod. (George MacDonald Original Works Ser.: Series VI). 459p. 1995. reprint ed. 22.00 (*1-881084-40-X*) Johannesen.

— David Elginbrod. LC 88-61686. (Centenary Ser.: Vol. 2). 470p. 1999. reprint ed. 27.50 (*0-940652-51-X*) Sunrise Bks.

— Diary of an Old Soul: Reflections for Each Day of the Year. LC 94-21982. 128p. 1994. pap. 10.99 (*0-8066-2734-4*, 9-2734, Augsburg) Augsburg Fortress.

— The Disciple & Other Poems. deluxe ed. 1989. 27.50 (*0-940652-87-0*) Sunrise Bks.

— Dish of Orts. (George MacDonald Original Works Ser.: Series VII). 322p. 1996. reprint ed. 22.00 (*1-881084-45-0*) Johannesen.

— Donal Grant. 1990. 47.50 (*0-940652-56-0*) Sunrise Bks.

— Donal Grant. (George MacDonald Original Works Ser.: Series I). 397p. 1998. reprint ed. 22.00 (*1-881084-02-7*) Johannesen.

— The Elect Lady. 1989. 26.50 (*0-940652-79-X*) Sunrise Bks.

— The Elect Lady (a duplex) (Series II). 373p. 1992. reprint ed. 20.00 (*1-881084-61-2*) Johannesen.

— England's Antiphon. (George MacDonald Original Works Ser.: Series VII). 332p. 1996. reprint ed. 22.00 (*1-881084-46-9*) Johannesen.

— The Evolution of Coinage. viii, 148p. 1980. 20.00 (*0-916710-73-4*) Obol Intl.

— Far above Rubies (a duplex) (Series VII). 450p. 1996. reprint ed. 24.00 (*1-881084-60-4*) Johannesen.

— Flight of the Shadow. (George MacDonald Original Works Ser.: Series IV). 337p. 1994. reprint ed. 20.00 (*1-881084-26-4*) Johannesen.

***MacDonald, George.** Frommer's Belgium, Holland & Luxembourg. 6th ed. (Frommer's Belgium, Holland & Luxembourg Ser.). 514p. 1999. pap. 17.95 (*0-02-862601-X*, Pub. by Macmillan) S&S Trade.

MacDonald, George. The Gentlewoman's Choice. 2nd ed. Phillips, Mike, ed. LC 87-6556. 224p. 1987. pap. 7.99 (*0-87123-941-8*) Bethany Hse.

— George MacDonald: An Anthology. Lewis, C. S., ed. LC 96-18404. 192p. 1996. per. 9.00 (*0-684-82375-6*) S&S Trade Pap.

— George MacDonald: Selections from His Greatest Works. 2nd ed. Neuhouser, David L., ed. 185p. 1997. reprint ed. pap. 6.00 (*1-881084-58-2*) Johannesen.

Macdonald, George. George MacDonald: The Parish Papers: Edited for Today's Readers. Hamilton, Dan, ed. LC 96-43541. 500p. 1997. write for info. (*1-56476-618-7*, Victor Bks) Chariot Victor.

MacDonald, George. George MacDonald Complete Original Unedited 48 Works: With Colour Plates & Black & White Illustrations, 44 vols., Set. (Illus.). 1997. 908.00 (*1-881084-55-8*) Johannesen.

— George MacDonald in the Pulpit: Compilation of Spoken Sermons from 1871-1901. 376p. 1999. 26.00 (*1-881084-57-4*) Johannesen.

— George MacDonald Original Works: Series VI: Hope of the Gospel/Miracles of Our Lord (a duplex), Mary Marston, David Elginbrod, Robert Falconer, Tragedie of Hamlet, 5 vols., Set. 1995. reprint ed. 102.00 (*1-881084-41-8*) Johannesen.

— George MacDonald Original Works: Series VII: Heather & Snow - Far Above Rubies (a duplex), Weighed & Wanting, Salted with Fire, A Dish of Orts, England's Antiphon, 5 vols., Set. 1996. 104.00 (*1-881084-47-7*) Johannesen.

— George MacDonald Original Works: Series VIII: Unspoken Sermons (Series 1, 2, 3), Wilfrid Cumbermede, Thomas Wingfold, St. George & St. Michael, Poetical Works Vol. I, Poetical Works Vol. II, 6 vols., Set. 1997. reprint ed. 128.00 (*1-881084-54-X*) Johannesen.

— George MacDonald Original Works Series I: What's Mine's Mine, Sir Gibbie, Donal Grant, Castle Warlock, A Rough Shaking, There & Back, 6 vols., Set. (Illus.). 1992. reprint ed. 120.00 (*1-881084-06-X*) Johannesen.

— George MacDonald Original Works Series II: At the Back of the North Wind, Paul Faber, Vicar's Daughter, Guild Court, Home Again/Elect Lady (a duplex), 5 vols., Set. (Illus.). 1992. reprint ed. 100.00 (*1-881084-12-4*) Johannesen.

— George MacDonald Original Works Series III: Black & White Illustrated: The Light Princess & Other Fairy Tales, The Wise Woman/Gutta Percha Willie (a duplex), 2 vols., Series III. (Illus.). 354p. (YA). (gr. 5 up). 1993. reprint ed. 40.00 (*1-881084-21-3*) Johannesen.

— George MacDonald Original Works Series III: Colour Plates: Ranald Bannerman's Boyhood, Princess & the Goblin, Princess & Curdie, At the Back of North Wind, 4 vols., Set. (Illus.). (YA). (gr. 5 up). 1998. reprint ed. 96.00 (*1-881084-20-5*) Johannesen.

— George MacDonald Original Works Series III: Ranald Bannerman's Boyhood, Princess & the Goblin, Princess & Curdie, The Light Princess & Other Fairy Tales, The Wise Woman/Gutta Percha Willie (a duplex), 5 vols., Set. (Illus.). (YA). (gr. 5 up). 1993. reprint ed. 112.00 (*1-881084-18-3*) Johannesen.

— George MacDonald Original Works Series IV: Phantastes, Lilith, Adela Cathcart, Portent & Other Stories, Stephen Archer & Other Tales, Flight of the Shadow, 6 vols., Set. (Illus.). 1994. reprint ed. 118.00 (*1-881084-28-0*) Johannesen.

— George MacDonald Original Works Series V: Annals of a Quiet Neighbourhood, Seaboard Parish, Malcolm, Marquis of Lossie, Alec Forbes, Rampolli, 6 bks., Set. 1995. reprint ed. 124.00 (*1-881084-35-3*) Johannesen.

— The Gifts of the Child Christ. 2nd ed. Sadler, Glenn E., ed. (Illus.). 584p. 1996. pap. 20.00 (*0-8028-4165-1*) Eerdmans.

— The Gifts of the Child Christ: Fairytales & Stories for the Childlike. LC 75-302609. (J). 1973. write for info. (*0-264-66049-8*) A R Mowbray.

— Gold Coast, Past & Present: A Short Description of the Country & Its People. LC 70-94483. (Illus.). 352p. 1969. reprint ed. lib. bdg. 35.00 (*0-8371-2370-4*, MGC&) Greenwood.

— The Golden Key. (Illus.). 1993. 19.50 (*0-8446-6661-0*) Peter Smith.

— The Golden Key. 2nd ed. LC 67-6087. (Illus.). 96p. (J). (gr. 1 up). 1984. pap. 5.95 (*0-374-42590-6*) FS&G.

— The Golden Key. 2nd ed. LC 67-6087. (Illus.). 96p. (J). (ps-3). 1984. 15.00 (*0-374-32706-8*) FS&G.

— Guild Court, a London Story. (George MacDonald Original Works Ser.: Series II). 382p. 1999. reprint ed. 22.00 (*1-881084-10-8*) Johannesen.

— Gutta Percha Willie (a duplex) (Illus.). 384p. 1998. reprint ed. 22.00 (*1-881084-62-0*) Johannesen.

— The Heart of George MacDonald: A One-Volume Collection of His Most Important Fiction, Essays, Sermons, Drama, Poetry, & Letters. Hein, Rolland, ed. (Wheaton Literary Ser.). 448p. 1994. 24.99 (*0-87788-371-8*, H Shaw Pubs) Waterbrook Pr.

— Heather & Snow. Hamilton, Dan, ed. 288p. 1987. pap. 5.95 (*0-89693-760-7*, Victor Bks) Chariot Victor.

— Heather & Snow. (George MacDonald Original Works Ser.: Series VII). 450p. reprint ed. 24.00 (*1-881084-42-6*) Johannesen.

— A Hidden Life & Other Poems. 1989. 27.50 (*0-940652-86-2*) Sunrise Bks.

— Home Again. Hamilton, Dan, ed. 192p. 1988. pap. text 5.95 (*0-89693-464-0*, Victor Bks) Chariot Victor.

— Home Again. (George MacDonald Original Works Ser.: Series II). 373p. reprint ed. 20.00 (*1-881084-11-6*) Johannesen.

— The Hope of the Gospel. 1989. 24.50 (*0-940652-84-6*) Sunrise Bks.

— Hope of the Gospel. (George MacDonald Original Works Ser.: Series VI). 440p. reprint ed. 24.00 (*1-881084-36-1*) Johannesen.

— Life Essential: The Hope of the Gospel. 2nd ed. Hein, Rolland, ed. LC 74-16732. (Wheaton Literary Ser.). 104p. 1978. pap. 6.99 (*0-87788-499-4*, H Shaw Pubs) Waterbrook Pr.

— The Light Princess. LC 86-33636. (Illus.). 44p. (J). (ps up). 1988. 13.95 (*0-15-245300-8*, Harcourt Child Bks) Harcourt.

MacDonald, George. The Light Princess. 110p. (J). (gr. 4-5). pap. 5.95 (*0-8072-1396-9*) Listening Lib.

MacDonald, George. The Light Princess. rev. ed. LC 69-14981. (Illus.). 120p. (J). (gr. 4-7). 1969. 15.00 (*0-374-34455-8*) FS&G.

— The Light Princess. rev. ed. LC 69-14981. (Illus.). 120p. (J). (gr. 4-7). 1984. pap. 5.95 (*0-374-44458-7*) FS&G.

— The Light Princess & Other Fairy Tales. (George MacDonald Original Works Ser.: Series III). (Illus.). 305p. (YA). (gr. 5 up). 1997. reprint ed. 22.00 (*1-881084-16-7*) Johannesen.

— The Light Princess & Other Fantasy Stories. Sadler, George G., ed. 176p. 1980. pap. 7.00 (*0-8028-1861-7*) Eerdmans.

— Lilith. 1981. pap. 8.00 (*0-8028-6061-3*) Eerdmans.

— Lilith A & Lilith, 1896: A Duplex. (George MacDonald Original Works Ser.: Series IV). 388p. 1998. reprint ed. 24.00 (*1-881084-27-2*) Johannesen.

— Lilith Variorum, 2 vols., Set. Hein, Rolland, ed. 800p. 1996. 48.00 (*1-881084-56-6*) Johannesen.

***MacDonald, George.** The Lost Princess. Sadler, Glenn Edward, ed. (Illus.). 134p. (J). 1999. reprint ed. text 25.00 (*0-7881-6847-9*) DIANE Pub.

MacDonald, George. The Maiden's Bequest. Phillips, Michael, ed. LC 85-4024. 288p. (Orig.). 1985. pap. 8.99 (*0-87123-823-3*) Bethany Hse.

— The Maiden's Bequest; The Minister's Restoration; The Laird's Inheitance. Phillips, Michael, ed. (George MacDonald Collection). 672p. 1998. text 12.99 (*0-7642-2148-5*) Bethany Hse.

— Malcolm. deluxe ed. 1988. 27.50 (*0-940652-53-6*) Sunrise Bks.

— Malcolm. (George MacDonald Original Works Ser.: Series V). 450p. 1995. reprint ed. 22.00 (*1-881084-31-0*) Johannesen.

— The Marquis of Lossie. 1994. 27.50 (*0-940652-54-4*) Sunrise Bks.

— The Marquis of Lossie. (George MacDonald Original Works Ser.: Series V). 390p. 1995. reprint ed. 22.00 (*1-881084-32-9*) Johannesen.

— Mary Marston. (George MacDonald Original Works Ser.: Series VI). 355p. 1995. reprint ed. 22.00 (*1-881084-37-X*) Johannesen.

— Miracles of Our Lord (a duplex) 440p. 1995. reprint ed. 24.00 (*1-881084-59-0*) Johannesen.

— The Musician's Quest. Phillips, Michael, ed. LC 84-18508. Orig. Title: Robert Falconer. 272p. 1984. reprint ed. pap. 8.99 (*0-87123-444-0*) Bethany Hse.

— Paul Faber, Surgeon. (George MacDonald Original Works Ser.: Series II). 396p. 1998. reprint ed. 22.00 (*1-881084-08-6*) Johannesen.

— Phantastes. 1981. pap. 8.00 (*0-8028-6060-5*) Eerdmans.

— Phantastes. (George MacDonald Original Works Ser.: Series IV). (Illus.). 324p. 1998. reprint ed. 22.00 (*1-881084-22-1*) Johannesen.

— The Poetical Works of George MacDonald, Vol. I. (George MacDonald Original Works Ser.: Series VIII). 448p. 1997. reprint ed. 22.00 (*1-881084-50-7*) Johannesen.

— The Poetical Works of George MacDonald, Vol. II. (George MacDonald Original Works Ser.: Series VIII). 424p. 1997. reprint ed. 22.00 (*1-881084-51-5*) Johannesen.

— The Portent & Other Stories. (George MacDonald Original Works Ser.: Series IV). 340p. 1999. reprint ed. 22.00 (*1-881084-24-8*) Johannesen.

— The Princess & Curdie. (Illus.). (YA). (gr. 5 up). 1996. pap. 4.99 (*0-14-036762-4*, Viking) Viking Penguin.

— Princess & Curdie. (J). 1997. pap. 1.95 (*0-8167-0473-2*) Troll Communs.

— The Princess & Curdie. large type ed. 274p. 1997. reprint ed. lib. bdg. 22.00 (*0-939495-22-8*) North Bks.

— The Princess & Curdie. 306p. (J). 1989. reprint ed. lib. bdg. 26.95 (*0-89966-591-8*) Buccaneer Bks.

— The Princess & Curdie. 177p. 1998. reprint ed. lib. bdg. 22.00 (*1-58287-059-4*) North Bks.

— The Princess & Curdie: With Colour Plates. (George MacDonald Original Works Ser.: Series III). (Illus.). 320p. (YA). (gr. 5 up). 1997. reprint ed. 26.00 (*1-881084-15-9*) Johannesen.

— Princess & Goblin. (Illus.). (YA). (gr. 5 up). 1997. pap. 3.99 (*0-14-036746-2*, Viking) Viking Penguin.

— Princess & the Goblin. (Airmont Classics Ser.). (J). (gr. 3 up). 1967. mass mkt. 1.50 (*0-8049-0156-2*, CL-156) Airmont.

— Princess & the Goblin. (J). 1997. pap. 2.95 (*0-8167-0472-4*) Troll Communs.

— Princess & the Goblin. (Puffin Classics). 1997. 9.09 (*0-606-12489-6*, Pub. by Turtleback) Demco.

— The Princess & the Goblin. 160p. (J). 1998. 24.95 (*1-85149-701-3*) Antique Collect.

— The Princess & the Goblin. LC 93-11264. (Everyman's Library of Children's Classics). (J). (gr. 2 up). 1993. 12.95 (*0-679-42810-0*) Everymns Lib.

— The Princess & the Goblin. LC 86-2532. (Books of Wonder). (Illus.). 208p. (J). (ps up). 1986. 22.95 (*0-688-06604-6*, Wm Morrow) Morrow Avon.

— The Princess & the Goblin. large type ed. 260p. 1998. lib. bdg. 22.00 (*0-939495-24-4*) North Bks.

— The Princess & the Goblin. (J). 1989. reprint ed. lib. bdg. 26.95 (*0-89966-598-5*) Buccaneer Bks.

— The Princess & the Goblin. 154p. 1998. reprint ed. lib. bdg. 22.00 (*1-58287-060-8*) North Bks.

— The Princess & the Goblin: With Colour Plates. (George MacDonald Original Works Ser.: Series III). (Illus.). 308p. (YA). (gr. 5 up). 1997. reprint ed. 26.00 (*1-881084-14-0*) Johannesen.

— Rampolli. (George MacDonald Original Works Ser.: Series V). 330p. 1995. reprint ed. 22.00 (*1-881084-34-5*) Johannesen.

— Ranald Bannerman's Boyhood: With Colour Plates. (George MacDonald Original Works Ser.: Series III). (Illus.). 335p. (YA). (gr. 5 up). 1999. reprint ed. 26.00 (*1-881084-13-2*) Johannesen.

— Robert Falconer. 1990. 33.50 (*0-940652-52-8*) Sunrise Bks.

— Robert Falconer. (George MacDonald Original Works Ser.: Series VI). 417p. 1995. reprint ed. 22.00 (*1-881084-39-6*) Johannesen.

— A Rough Shaking. (George MacDonald Original Works Ser.: Series I). (Illus.). 384p. 1999. reprint ed. 22.00 (*1-881084-04-3*) Johannesen.

— St. George & St. Michael. (George MacDonald Original Works Ser.: Series VIII). 432p. 1997. reprint ed. 22.00 (*1-881084-49-3*) Johannesen.

— Salted with Fire. deluxe ed. 1989. 26.50 (*0-940652-98-6*) Sunrise Bks.

— Salted with Fire. (George MacDonald Original Works Ser.: Series VII). 325p. 1996. reprint ed. 22.00 (*1-881084-44-2*) Johannesen.

— The Seaboard Parish. (George MacDonald Original Works Ser.: Series V). 650p. 1995. reprint ed. 24.00 (*1-881084-30-2*) Johannesen.

— Sir Gibbie. 1989. 27.50 (*0-940652-55-2*) Sunrise Bks.

— Sir Gibbie. (George MacDonald Original Works Ser.: Series I). 450p. 1996. reprint ed. 22.00 (*1-881084-01-9*) Johannesen.

— Stephen Archer & Other Tales. (George MacDonald Original Works Ser.: Series IV). 354p. 1994. reprint ed. 20.00 (*1-881084-25-6*) Johannesen.

— The Story of Little Christmas. abr. ed. (Illus.). 32p. (J). (gr. 2-6). 1995. 14.99 (*0-7814-0233-6*, Chariot Bks) Chariot Victor.

— There & Back. (George MacDonald Original Works Ser.: Series I). 392p. 1999. reprint ed. 22.00 (*1-881084-05-1*) Johannesen.

— Thomas Wingfold, Curate. 1989. 29.50 (*0-940652-57-9*) Sunrise Bks.

— Thomas Wingfold, Curate. (George MacDonald Original Works Ser.: Series VIII). 518p. 1997. reprint ed. 24.00 (*1-881084-53-1*) Johannesen.

— A Time to Harvest. Phillips, Michael, ed. (George MacDonald Classic Devotionals Ser.: Bk. 2). 128p. (Orig.). 1991. pap. 6.99 (*1-55661-207-9*) Bethany Hse.

— The Tragedie of Hamlet. (George MacDonald Original Works Ser.: Series VI). 1995. reprint ed. 22.00 (*1-881084-38-8*) Johannesen.

— Unspoken Sermons, Series I, II & III. (George MacDonald Original Works Ser.: Series VIII). 619p. 1999. reprint ed. 26.00 (*1-881084-48-5*) Johannesen.

— Unspoken Sermons, Vol. 1. 1989. 24.50 (*0-940652-80-3*) Sunrise Bks.

— Unspoken Sermons, Vol. 2. 1989. 24.50 (*0-940652-81-1*) Sunrise Bks.

— Unspoken Sermons, Vol. 3. 1996. 24.50 (*0-940652-82-X*) Sunrise Bks.

— Unspoken Sermons (Series Three) The Sermons of George MacDonald. 250p. (C). 1987. reprint ed. pap. 14.95 (*0-944724-06-X*) J J Flynn.

— Unspoken Sermons (Series Two) The Sermons of George MacDonald. 250p. (C). 1987. reprint ed. pap. 14.95 (*0-944724-05-1*) J J Flynn.

— The Vicar's Daughter. (George MacDonald Original Works Ser.: Series II). 389p. 1998. reprint ed. 22.00 (*1-881084-09-4*) Johannesen.

— Wee Sir Gibbie of the Highlands. Phillips, Michael R., ed. (George MacDonald Classics for Young Readers Ser.). 24p. (J). (gr. 2-7). 1990. text 10.99 (*1-55661-139-0*) Bethany Hse.

— Weighed & Wanting. (George MacDonald Original Works Ser.: Series VII). 625p. 1996. reprint ed. 24.00 (*1-881084-43-4*) Johannesen.

— What's Mine's Mine. 1994. 33.50 (*0-940652-64-1*) Sunrise Bks.

— What's Mine's Mine. (George MacDonald Original Works Ser.: Series I). 387p. 1995. reprint ed. 22.00 (*1-881084-00-0*) Johannesen.

— Wilfrid Cumbermede. (George MacDonald Original Works Ser.: Series VIII). 540p. 1997. reprint ed. 24.00 (*1-881084-52-3*) Johannesen.

— Wisdom to Live By. 218p. 1996. 19.95 (*0-940652-39-0*) Sunrise Bks.

— The Wise Woman. (George MacDonald Original Works Ser.: Series III). 384p. 1998. reprint ed. 22.00 (*1-881084-17-5*) Johannesen.

— Wise Woman & Other Fantasy Stories. Sadler, Glenn G., ed. 176p. 1980. pap. 7.00 (*0-8028-1860-9*) Eerdmans.

***MacDonald, George & Phillips, M. J.** Knowing the Heart of God. 368p. 1999. pap. 12.99 (*0-7642-2312-7*) Bethany Hse.

MacDonald, George & Phillips, Michael. The Baron's Apprenticeship. LC 86-11734. 272p. 1986. pap. 8.99 (*0-87123-655-9*) Bethany Hse.

MacDonald, George & Phillips, Michael R. The Poet's Homecoming. 192p. 1990. pap. 7.99 (*1-55661-135-8*) Bethany Hse.

MacDonald, George, et al. Champions: The Super Hero Role Playing Game. rev. ed. (Illus.). 352p. (C). 1989. 32.00 (*1-55806-043-X*, 400) Hero Games.

— The Gold Key & the Green Life: Some Fantasies & Celtic Tales LC 87-208337. 222 p. 1986. write for info. (*0-09-467110-9*) Constable & Co.

Macdonald, George A. How Successful Lawyers Were Educated: Addressed to Students, to Those Who Expect to Become Students & to Their Parents & Teachers. 168p. 1985. reprint ed. 37.50 (*0-8377-0853-2*, Rothman) W S Hein.

Macdonald, George E. England's Antiphon. 1977. 18.95 (*0-8369-7227-9*, 8026) Ayer.

— Fifty Years of Freethought, Being the Story of the Truth Seeker with the Natural History of Its Third Editor, 2 vols. LC 76-161334. (Atheist Viewpoint Ser.). (Illus.). 1224p. 1972. reprint ed. 80.95 (*0-405-03793-7*) Ayer.

— Stephen Archer & Other Tales. LC 79-152946. (Short Story Index Reprint Ser.). 1977. reprint ed. 23.95 (*0-8369-3805-4*) Ayer.

— Thumbscrew & Rack. rev. ed. (Illus.). 26p. 1991. reprint ed. 6.00 (*0-910309-68-X*, 5232) Am Atheist.

MacDonald, George F. Chiefs of the Sea & Sky: Haida Heritage Sites of the Queen Charlotte Islands. (Illus.). 96p. 1989. pap. 19.95 (*0-7748-0331-2*) U of Wash Pr.

***MacDonald, George F.** Haida Art. (Illus.). 256p. 2000. pap. 50.00 (*1-55054-743-7*, Pub. by DGL) Orca Bk Pubs.

MacDonald, George F. Haida Art. LC 96-7727. (Illus.). 256p. 1996. 60.00 (*0-295-97561-X*) U of Wash Pr.

— Haida Monumental Art: Villages of the Queen Charlotte Islands. LC 94 3977. (Illus.). 228p. 1994. pap. 45.00 (*0-295-97362-5*) U of Wash Pr.

— Kitwanga Fort Report. (Mercury Ser.: Directorate No. 4). (Illus.). 132p. 1988. pap. 12.95 (*0-660-10777-5*, Pub. by CN Mus Civilization) U of Wash Pr.

— Ninstints: Haida World Heritage Site. (Illus.). 64p. 1986. pap. 15.95 (*0-7748-0163-8*) U of Wash Pr.

MacDonald, George F. & Alsford, Stephen. A Museum for the Global Village. (Illus.). 244p. 1989. pap. 19.95 (*0-660-10787-2*, Pub. by CN Mus Civilization) U of Wash Pr.

MacDonald, George F. & Cove, John J., eds. Tsimshian Narratives No. 2: Trade & Warfare. LC 87-99106. (Mercury Ser.: Directorate No. 3, Pt. 2). (Illus.). 244p. 1993. pap. 17.95 (*0-660-10770-8*, Pub. by CN Mus Civilization) U of Wash Pr.

MacDonald, George F. & Inglis, Richard I. The Dig: An Archaeological Reconstruction of a West Coast Village. (Canadian Prehistory Ser.). (Illus.). 100p. 1976. pap. 12.95 (*0-660-00007-5*, Pub. by CN Mus Civilization) U of Wash Pr.

Macdonald, Geraldine M., jt. auth. see Hudson, Barbara L.

MacDonald, GHeorge. Haida Art. 1997. text 60.00 (*90-5703-261-9*, Pub. by Craftsman House) Gordon & Breach.

Macdonald, Gina. James Clavell: A Critical Companion. LC 95-43265. (Critical Companions to Popular Contemporary Writers Ser.). 240p. 1996. 29.95 (*0-313-29494-1*, Greenwood Pr) Greenwood.

— Robert Ludlum. LC 96-50289. (Critical Companions to Popular Contemporary Writers Ser.). 248p. 1997. 29.95 (*0-313-29971-4*, Greenwood Pr) Greenwood.

MacDonald, Gina, jt. auth. see MacDonald, Andrew.

MacDonald, Ginger, jt. auth. see Brammer, Lawrence W.

MacDonald, Glenn M., jt. auth. see Davies, James B.

MacDonald, Glynn. The Complete Illustrated Guide to Alexander Technique. (Illus.). 224p. 1998. pap. 24.95 (*1-86204-226-8*, Pub. by Element MA) Penguin Putnam.

M

MacDonald, Gordon. Christ Followers in the Real World: Developing a Faith That Works in the 90's. 240p. 1991. pap. 10.99 (*0-8407-9119-4*) Nelson.
— The Effective Father. 256p. 1983. mass mkt. 5.99 (*0-8423-0669-2*) Tyndale Hse.
— Good-Bye, Grant Street. 300p. (Orig.). 1999. pap. text 5.99 (*0-8423-3288-X*) Tyndale Hse.
Macdonald, Gordon. The Life God Blesses. LC 94-28151. 1994. 18.99 (*0-8407-9155-0*, Oliver-Nelson) Nelson.
MacDonald, Gordon. The Life God Blesses: Weathering the Storms of Life That Threaten the Soul. LC 97-6538. 276p. 1997. pap. 12.99 (*0-7852-7160-0*) Nelson.
***MacDonald, Gordon.** Mid-Course Correction: Re-Ordering Your Private World for the Next Part of Your Journey. LC 99-88448. 224p. 2000. 16.99 (*0-7852-7841-9*) Nelson.
MacDonald, Gordon. Ordering Your Private World. LC 97-6545. 228p. 1997. pap. 12.99 (*0-7852-7161-9*) Nelson.
— Ordering Your Private World. 1995. pap. 12.95 (*1-880828-94-4*) Touch Pubns.
MacDonald, Gordon. Plan de Accion para Ser un Mejor Papa. (Serie Guia de Bolsillo - Pocket Guides Ser.).Tr. of Action Plan for Great Dads. (SPA.). 2.79 (*0-7899-0010-6*, 498076) Editorial Unilit.
MacDonald, Gordon. Plan de Accion para Ser un Mejor Papa - Action Plan for Great Dads. (SPA.). 1990. write for info. (*1-56063-033-7*) Editorial Unilit.
— Ponga Orden en Su Mundo Interior. Araujo, Juan S., tr. from ENG.Tr. of Ordering Your Private World. (SPA.). 176p. (C). 1989. pap. 7.99 (*0-88113-246-2*) Caribe Betania.
— Rebuilding Your Broken World. enl. ed. 1988. pap. 12.99 (*0-8407-9576-9*) Nelson.
— Renewing Your Spiritual Passion. LC 97-6544. 240p. 1997. pap. 12.99 (*0-7852-7162-7*) Nelson.
— Restoring Joy, 3 vols. in 1. 608p. 1996. pap. 14.99 (*0-88486-137-6*) Arrowood Pr.
— Restoring Joy to Your Inner World. (Guidelines for Living Ser.). 1992. 10.98 (*0-88486-059-0*) Arrowood Pr.
— When Men Think Private Thoughts. 272p. 1996. 19.99 (*0-7852-7839-7*) Nelson.
— When Men Think Private Thoughts. LC 97-6543. 288p. 1997. pap. 12.99 (*0-7852-7163-5*) Nelson.
Macdonald, Gordon & Hubbard, Douglass. Volcanoes of the National Parks in Hawaii. rev. ed. (Illus.). 64p. (C). 1989. pap. text 6.95 (*0-940295-01-6*) HI Natural Hist.
***MacDonald, Gordon & MacDonald, Gail.** Quiet Moments with Gordon & Gail MacDonald. 2001. 14.99 (*1-56955-189-8*) Servant.
MacDonald, Gordon, jt. auth. see Davies, John K.
Macdonald, Gordon A., et al. Volcanoes in the Sea: The Geology of Hawaii. 2nd ed. LC 82-23685. (Illus.). 528p. 1983. 34.95 (*0-8248-0832-0*) UH Pr.
MacDonald, Gordon J. Climate Change: A Challenge to the Means of Technology Transfer. (IGCC Policy Papers: No. 2). 51p. (Orig.). 1992. pap. 3.50 (*0-934637-17-2*) U of CA Inst Global.
MacDonald, Grace E., compiled by. Check-List of Legislative Journals of States of the United States of America. LC 79-92126. (Legal Bibliographic & Research Reprint Ser.: Vol. 3). 274p. 1980. reprint ed. lib. bdg. 42.00 (*0-89941-034-0*, 300900) W S Hein.
MacDonald, Graham & Pettit, Philip. Semantics & the Social Sciences. 224p. (C). 1981. pap. 13.95 (*0-7100-0784-1*, Routledge Thoemms) Routledge.
MacDonald, Graham, jt. auth. see MacDonald, Cynthia.
MacDonald, Graham, jt. ed. see Macdonald, Cynthia.
MacDonald, Greville. George MacDonald & His Wife. 583p. 1998. reprint ed. 26.00 (*1-881084-63-9*) Johannesen.
— Sanity of William Blake. (Studies in Blake: No. 3). 1970. reprint ed. pap. 24.95 (*0-8383-0097-9*) M S G Haskell Hse.
Macdonald, H. Malcolm, ed. The Intellectual in Politics. LC 66-29160. (Quarterly Ser.). 1966. 15.00 (*0-87959-074-2*) U of Tex H Ransom Ctr.
MacDonald-Haig, Caroline, jt. auth. see Kennett, Frances.
Macdonald, Hamish. Mussolini & Italian Fascism. (Pathfinder History Ser.). (Illus.). 64p. (YA). (gr. 11 up). 1999. pap. 15.95 (*0-7487-3386-8*, Pub. by S Thornes Pubs) Trans-Atl Phila.
MacDonald, High. Chung Lee Loves Lobsters. (Illus.). 24p. (J). (gr. k-3). 1992. pap. 4.95 (*1-55037-214-9*, Pub. by Annick); lib. bdg. 14.95 (*1-55037-217-3*, Pub. by Annick) Firefly Bks Ltd.
MacDonald, Hope. Discovering How to Pray. 160p. 1976. pap. 3.95 (*0-310-28512-7*, 10050P) Zondervan.
— Discovering How to Pray: Revised with Study Guide. 144p. 1990. pap. 10.99 (*0-310-28361-2*) Zondervan.
— The Flip Side of Liberation: A Call to Traditional Values. 176p. 1990. pap. 8.95 (*0-310-28351-5*) Zondervan.
— Letters from Heaven. LC 98-22233. 1998. 13.00 (*1-57683-098-5*) NavPress.
— Traditional Values for Today's Woman. Orig. Title: Flip Side of Liberation. 160p. 1992. reprint ed. pap. 9.99 (*0-310-54831-4*) Zondervan.
— When Angels Appear. (Orig.). 1996. pap. 5.99 (*0-310-21508-0*) Zondervan.
Macdonald, Hugh. Portraits in Prose. LC 71-101830. (Biography Index Reprint Ser.). 1977. 30.95 (*0-8369-8004-2*) Ayer.
MacDonald, Hugh, ed. Selected Letters of Berlioz. Nichols, Roger, tr. LC 96-47015. 496p. (C). 1997. 35.00 (*0-393-04062-3*) Norton.
MacDonald, Hugh, ed. see Gasgoinge, George & Etchells, Frederick.
MacDonald, I., ed. Effect of Carbohydrates on Lipid Metabolism. (Progress in Biochemical Pharmacology Ser.: Vol. 8). (Illus.). 1973. 125.25 (*3-8055-1600-2*) S Karger.
Macdonald, I, ed. Metabolic Effects of Dietary Carbohydrates. (Progress in Biochemical Pharmacology Ser.: Vol. 21). (Illus.). x, 274p. 1986. 186.25 (*3-8055-4229-1*) S Karger.
Macdonald, I & Davitt, M., compiled by. Modern Gaelic Poetry from Scotland & Ireland. 256p. 1995. 29.95 (*0-86241-356-7*, Pub. by Canongate Books) Interlink Pub.
***MacDonald, I. G.** Symmetric Functions & Hall Polynomials. 2nd ed. 486p. 1999. pap. text 65.00 (*0-19-850450-0*) OUP.
Macdonald, I. G. Symmetric Functions & Hall Polynomials. 2nd ed. (Mathematical Monographs). 488p. 1995. 95.00 (*0-19-853489-2*) OUP.
MacDonald, I. G. Symmetric Functions & Orthogonal Polynomials. LC 97-26100. (University Lectures). 53p. 1997. pap. 19.00 (*0-8218-0770-6*) Am Math.
Macdonald, I. G., jt. ed. see Pietrzik, K.
MacDonald, Iain, ed. Saint Brendan. (Celtic Studies Ser.). 62p. 1992. pap. 6.95 (*0-86315-141-8*) Dufour.
— Saint Bride. (Celtic Studies Ser.). 62p. 1992. pap. 6.95 (*0-86315-142-6*) Dufour.
— Saint Columba. (Celtic Studies Ser.). 62p. 1992. pap. 6.95 (*0-86315-143-4*) Dufour.
— Saint Patrick. (Celtic Studies Ser.). 62p. 1992. pap. 6.95 (*0-86315-144-2*) Dufour.
— Saints of Northumbria: Cuthbert, Aidan, Oswald, Hilda. 144p. 1997. pap. 10.95 (*0-86315-252-X*, 2052, Pub. by Floris Bks) Anthroposophic.
MacDonald, Iain, ed. see Aelred of Rievaulx.
MacDonald, Iain, ed. see Jocelinus of Furness.
MacDonald, Iain, ed. see Robert of Orkney.
MacDonald, Iain, ed. see Turgot.
Macdonald, Iain A. Representing the Debtor in a Chapter 7 Business Bankruptcy Pts. 1 & 2: Summer 1992 Action Guide. Hagelstein, Marie & Johnson, Elizabeth M., eds. 213p. 1992. pap. 52.00 (*0-88124-529-1*, BU-11311) Cont Ed Bar-CA.
Macdonald, Ian. Birds, Beasts & Fishes. 1995. 30.00 (*0-8050-3623-7*) H Holt & Co.
— Key Words German. 1989. pap. text 9.48 (*0-582-20349-X*, 70715) Longman.
— Revolution in the Head: The Beatles' Records & the Sixties. 373p. 1995. 25.00 (*0-8050-2780-7*); pap. 14.95 (*0-8050-4245-8*) H Holt & Co.
MacDonald, Ian & Low, John. Fruit & Vegetables. (Illus.). 137p. 1991. pap. write for info. (*0-237-50790-0*) EVN1 UK.
Macdonald, Ian & O'Keefe, Betty. The Mulligan Affair: Top Cop on the Take. LC 98-174195. 160p. 1997. pap. 16.95 (*1-895811-45-7*) Heritage Hse.
Macdonald, Ian, jt. auth. see O'Keefe, Betty.
Macdonald, Ian, ed. see European Nutritionists Staff.
MacDonald, Ian A. & Blake, Nicholas J. MacDonald's Immigration Law & Practice. 1996. suppl. ed. write for info. (*0-406-99903-1*, MBIL4S, MICHIE) LEXIS Pub.
Macdonald, Ian D. Alex. LC 85-2418. 32p. 1985. pap. 3.95 (*0-936428-10-4*) Polygonal Pub.
Macdonald, Ian R. Gabriel Miro: His Private Library & His Literary Blackground. (Monografias A Ser.: Vol. XLI). 250p. (Orig.). (C). 1975. pap. 51.00 (*0-900411-91-0*, Pub. by Tamesis Bks Ltd) Boydell & Brewer.
MacDonald, Ingrid. Catherine, Catherine: Lesbian Short Stories. 144p. reprint ed. pap. 9.95 (*0-88961-164-5*, Pub. by Womens Pr) LPC InBook.
***Macdonald, Irene M.** Littleriver's Yesteryears, 1853-1965. Escola, Emery, tr. LC 99-95194. (Illus.). 220p. 1999. pap. 20.00 (*0-9672398-3-4*) Mendocino Graph.
Macdonald, Isobel. A Family in Skye. 1985. 35.00 (*0-86152-055-6*, Pub. by Acair Ltd) St Mut.
MacDonald, J. The Compleat Theory of Scots Higland Bagpipe: Manuscript of J. MacDonald. MacRaonuill, Alasdair, ed. (Illus.). 177p. 1992. pap. 32.00 (*0-685-59540-4*) A MacRaonuill.
MacDonald, J. & Renton, R. Abair: Pocket Gaelic-English-Gaelic Dictionary. (AKK, ENG & GAE.). 1990. pap. 19.95 (*0-8288-3376-1*, F132981) Fr & Eur.
Macdonald, J. A., ed. The Time Projection Chamber: AIP Conference Proceedings, TRIUMF, Vancover, 1983, No. 108. LC 83-83445. 264p. 1984. lib. bdg. 39.00 (*0-88318-307-2*) Am Inst Physics.
MacDonald, J. A., jt. auth. see Renton, R. W.
Macdonald, J. B., jt. auth. see Macdonald, Elspeth T.
***Macdonald, J. D.** Peter Crossman 1. 2001. text 23.95 (*0-312-86988-6*) St Martin.
MacDonald, J. E. The Barbados Journal, 1932. (Illus.). 144p. 1989. 15.95 (*0-921254-03-2*, Pub. by Penumbra Pr) U of Toronto Pr.
— Sketchbook, 1915-1922. Bishop, Hunter, ed. 134p. 1979. pap. 9.95 (*0-920806-07-4*, Pub. by Penumbra Pr) U of Toronto Pr.
MacDonald, J. Fred. Television & the Red Menace: The Video Road to Vietnam. LC 84-18302. 217p. 1985. 55.00 (*0-275-90141-6*, C0141, Praeger Pubs); pap. 19.95 (*0-275-91807-6*, B1807, Praeger Pubs) Greenwood.
— Who Shot the Sheriff? The Rise & Fall of the Television Western. LC 86-18230. 172p. 1986. 49.95 (*0-275-92326-6*, C2326, Praeger Pubs) Greenwood.
MacDonald, J. Fred, ed. Richard Durham's Destination Freedom: Scripts from Radio's Black Legacy, 1948-50. LC 88-35686. 280p. 1989. 65.00 (*0-275-93138-2*, C3138, Praeger Pubs) Greenwood.
Macdonald, J. Ross. Annotated Topical Guide to U. S. Income Tax Treaties: A Service, 6 vols. 6618p. 1988. ring bd. 790.00 (*0-13-103037-X*) Aspen Law.
— Impedance Spectroscopy Emphasizing Solid Materials & Systems. LC 86-32582. 368p. 1987. 120.00 (*0-471-83122-0*) Wiley.
MacDonald, Jack. Handbook of Radio Publicity & Promotion. LC 73-114020. 1970. 34.95 (*0-8306-0213-5*, 213AH) McGraw-Hill Prof.
MacDonald, Jack, jt. auth. see Clifford, Angela.
MacDonald, Jake. Lakes, Lures & Lodges: An Angler's Guide to Western Canada. 1993. per. 14.95 (*0-88801-176-8*) LPC InBook.
— Raised by the River. 275p. 1997. pap. 12.95 (*0-88801-166-0*, Pub. by Turnstone Pr) Genl Dist Srvs.
MacDonald, James. Food from the Far West: American Agriculture. 1980. lib. bdg. 69.95 (*0-8490-3187-7*) Gordon Pr.
— Food from the Far West: American Agriculture with Special Reference to Beef Production & Importation of Dead Meat from America to Great Britain. LC 72-89059. (Rural America Ser.). 1973. reprint ed. 31.00 (*0-8420-1490-X*) Scholarly Res Inc.
— I Want to Change... So Help Me God. LC 99-58539. 2000. pap. 12.99 (*0-8024-3423-1*) Moody.
— Religion & Myth. LC 74-82059. 240p. 1969. reprint ed. lib. bdg. 35.00 (*0-8371-1550-7*, MAR&) Greenwood.
MacDonald, James, et al. Programming with Comal 1: Lab Pack 1. Schroeder, Bonnie, ed. (Illus.). teacher ed. 19.95 (*1-56177-131-7*, TE403-1); student ed. 9.95 (*1-56177-125-2*, 403-1); teacher ed., student ed. 159.95 incl. disk (*1-56177-129-5*, L403-1); disk 6.95 (*0-685-45809-1*, D403-1) CES Compu-Tech.
— Programming with Comal 1: Lab Pack 2. Schroeder, Bonnie, ed. (Illus.). teacher ed. 19.95 (*0-685-45810-5*, T403-2); student ed. 9.95 (*1-56177-126-0*, 403-2); teacher ed., student ed. 159.95 incl. disk (*1-56177-130-9*, L403-2); disk 6.95 (*1-56177-128-7*, D403-2) CES Compu-Tech.
MacDonald, James, jt. auth. see Kennedy, Sandra.
MacDonald, James B. Theory As a Prayerful Act: The Collected Essays of James B. Macdonald, Vol. 22. MacDonald, Bradley J., ed. (Counterpoints Studies & Concepts in the Postmodern Theory of Education). XII, 202p. (C). 1995. 29.95 (*0-8204-2792-6*) P Lang Pubng.
MacDonald, James D., jt. auth. see Doyle, Debra.
MacDonald, Janet. The Complete Handbook of Gardening Tips. 1997. pap. 12.95 (*1-887053-10-7*) United Res CA.
— Riding to Music. 95p. 1990. pap. 24.00 (*0-85131-433-3*, Pub. by J A Allen) St Mut.
— Teaching Side-Saddle. 100p. (C). 1990. pap. 24.00 (*0-85131-556-9*, Pub. by J A Allen) Trafalgar.
— Writing Non-Fiction & Getting Published. (Teach Yourself Ser.). 192p. 1998. pap. 12.95 (*0-8442-0180-4*, 01804, Teach Yrslf) NTC Contemp Pub Co.
MacDonald, Janet W. Riding Side-Saddle. 96p. 1995. 45.00 (*0-85131-621-2*, Pub. by J A Allen) Trafalgar.
— Running a Stable As a Business. 112p. 1984. pap. 20.00 (*0-87556-544-1*) Saifer.
Macdonald, Janet W. Running a Tack Shop As a Business. 112p. (C). 1990. pap. 30.00 (*0-85131-425-2*, Pub. by J A Allen) Trafalgar.
MacDonald, Jeffery L. Transnational Aspects of Iu-Mien Refugee Identity. LC 97-38689. (Asian Americans Ser.). (Illus.). 348p. 1997. text 83.00 (*0-8153-2994-6*) Garland.
MacDonald, Jeffery L., jt. ed. see Krulfeld, Ruth M.
MacDonald, Jeffrey A. & Bingham, Anne. Pension Handbook for Union Negotiators. LC 85-29959. 203p. 1986. reprint ed. pap. 63.00 (*0-608-04275-7*, 206502700012) Bks Demand.
MacDonald, Jennifer, jt. auth. see Waldrop, Rosmarie.
MacDonald, Joan B. The Holiness of Everyday Life. LC 95-19817. 146p. 1995. 14.95 (*0-87579-938-8*) Deseret Bk.
***MacDonald, Joan V.** Tobacco & Nicotine Drug Dangers. LC 99-36405. (Drug Dangers Ser.). (Illus.). 64p. (gr. 4-10). 2000. lib. bdg. 19.95 (*0-7660-1317-0*) Enslow Pubs.
***MacDonald, John.** The Arctic Sky: Inuit Star Lore, Legend & Astronomy. (Illus.). 272p. 1998. pap. 29.95 (*0-88854-427-8*) Royal Ontario.
MacDonald, John. The Beach Girls. 1999. lib. bdg. 19.95 (*1-56723-166-7*) Yestermorrow.
— Calling a Halt to Mindless Change: A Plea for Commonsense Management. LC 97-48808. 256p. 1998. 24.95 (*0-8144-0349-2*) AMACOM.
— The Coming of War in the Pacific. 1996. 25.00 (*0-02-919626-4*) Free Pr.
— The Coming of War in the Pacific. 1997. 25.00 (*0-684-82799-9*) Free Pr.
— Czar Ferdinand & His People. LC 74-135815. (Eastern Europe Collection). 1971. reprint ed. 26.95 (*0-405-02757-5*) Ayer.
— Great Battlefields of the World. LC 85-332. 200p. 1988. pap. 25.95 (*0-02-044464-8*) Macmillan.
— Great Battles of the Civil War. (Illus.). 336p. 1992. pap. 24.95 (*0-02-034554-2*) Macmillan.
***MacDonald, John.** Great Battles of the Civil War. (Illus.). 200p. 2000. reprint ed. pap. 32.00 (*0-7881-9220-5*) DIANE Pub.
MacDonald, John. Memar Marqah: The Teaching of Marqah, 2 vols., Set. (C). 1963. 89.25 (*3-11-005567-8*) De Gruyter.
— On the Run. 1999. lib. bdg. 19.95 (*1-56723-165-9*) Yestermorrow.
— Samaritan Chronicle: or Sepher Ha-Yamim No. 2: From Joshua to Nebuchadnezzar. (Beiheft zur Zeitschrift fuer die Alttestamentliche Wissenschaft Ser.: No. 107). (C). 1969. 92.35 (*3-11-002582-5*) De Gruyter.
Macdonald, John, tr. from FRE. Instructions for the Conduct of Infantry on Actual Service. 785p. 1997. reprint ed. pap. 35.00 (*1-58545-028-6*) Nafziger Collection.
MacDonald, John & Livesay, Anthony. Great Battles of World War I. (Great Battles of the World Wars Ser.). (Illus.). 192p. 1997. 24.98 (*0-7651-9337-X*) Smithmark.
— The Great Battles of World War II. (Great Battles of the World Wars Ser.). (Illus.). 192p. 1997. 24.98 (*0-7651-9336-1*) Smithmark.
MacDonald, John, jt. auth. see Mouroulis, Pantazis.
MacDonald, John, jt. ed. see Ahlgren, James.
MacDonald, John A. Due South: The Official Compendium. (Illus.). 128p. 1998. pap. 12.95 (*1-55013-966-5*) Firefly Bks Ltd.
— Troublous Times in Canada: A History of the Fenian Raids of 1866 & 1870. 255p. (C). 1987. 91.00 (*0-7855-2217-4*, Pub. by Picton) St Mut.
MacDonald, John D. Bright Orange for the Shroud. (Travis McGee Mystery Ser.). 1996. reprint ed. mass mkt. 5.99 (*0-449-22444-9*, Crest) Fawcett.
— Bright Orange for the Shroud. (Travis McGee Mystery Ser.). 1996. reprint ed. mass mkt. 5.99 (*0-449-45615-3*, Crest) Fawcett.
— Cape Fear. 1987. mass mkt. 5.99 (*0-449-13190-4*, GM) Fawcett.
— Cinnamon Skin: A Travis McGee Novel. 1996. mass mkt. 5.99 (*0-449-22484-8*) Fawcett.
— Condominium. 1985. mass mkt. 5.99 (*0-449-20737-4*, Crest) Fawcett.
***MacDonald, John D.** The Damned. 1999. lib. bdg. 20.95 (*1-56723-167-5*) Yestermorrow.
MacDonald, John D. Darker Than Amber. 1996. mass mkt. 5.99 (*0-449-22446-5*) Fawcett.
— Darker Than Amber. 1997. mass mkt. 5.99 (*0-449-45637-4*) Fawcett.
— A Deadly Shade of Gold. 1996. mass mkt. 5.99 (*0-449-22442-2*) Fawcett.
— Death Trap. 254p. Date not set. 22.95 (*0-8488-2358-3*) Amereon Ltd.
— The Deep Blue Goodbye. 320p. 1995. mass mkt. 6.99 (*0-449-22383-3*) Fawcett.
— The Dreadful Lemon Sky. 1996. mass mkt. 5.99 (*0-449-22479-1*) Fawcett.
— Dress Her in Indigo. (Travis McGee Mystery Ser.). 1996. mass mkt. 5.99 (*0-449-22462-7*) Fawcett.
— Dress Her in Indigo. 1997. pap. text 5.99 (*0-449-45716-8*) Fawcett.
— The Empty Copper Sea. 21.95 (*0-89190-778-5*) Amereon Ltd.
— The Empty Copper Sea. 1996. mass mkt. 5.99 (*0-449-22480-5*) Fawcett.
***MacDonald, John D.** End of the Tiger. 1999. lib. bdg. 21.95 (*1-56723-168-3*) Yestermorrow.
MacDonald, John D. A Flash of Green. (Travis McGee Mystery Ser.). 1984. mass mkt. 5.99 (*0-449-12692-7*, GM) Fawcett.
— Free Fall in Crimson. 1996. mass mkt. 5.99 (*0-449-22482-1*) Fawcett.
— The Girl in the Plain Brown Wrapper. 1996. mass mkt. 5.99 (*0-449-22461-9*) Fawcett.
— The Girl in the Plain Brown Wrapper. 1997. mass mkt. 5.99 (*0-449-45715-X*) Fawcett.
— The Green Ripper. 21.95 (*0-89190-779-3*) Amereon Ltd.
— The Green Ripper. 1996. mass mkt. 5.99 (*0-449-22481-3*) Fawcett.
— Judge Me Not. 20.95 (*0-89190-776-9*) Amereon Ltd.
— A Key to the Suite. 1989. 17.95 (*0-89296-393-X*) Mysterious Pr.
— The Lonely Silver Rain. LC 96-96201. 1996. mass mkt. 5.99 (*0-449-22485-6*) Fawcett.
— The Long Lavender Look. 1996. mass mkt. 5.99 (*0-449-22474-0*) Fawcett.
— The Long Lavender Look. (Travis McGee Mystery Ser.). 1998. mass mkt. 5.99 (*0-449-45717-6*) Fawcett.
— Nightmare in Pink. 1996. mass mkt. 5.99 (*0-449-22414-7*) Fawcett.
— One Fearful Yellow Eye. 1996. mass mkt. 5.99 (*0-449-22458-9*) Fawcett.
— One Fearful Yellow Eye. 1997. mass mkt. 5.99 (*0-449-45639-0*) Fawcett.
— Pale Gray for Guilt. 1996. mass mkt. 5.99 (*0-449-22460-0*) Fawcett.
— Pale Gray for Guilt. 1997. mass mkt. 5.99 (*0-449-45721-4*) Fawcett.
— The Price of Murder. 1976. 19.95 (*0-8488-0569-0*) Amereon Ltd.
— A Purple Place for Dying. 1995. mass mkt. 5.99 (*0-449-22438-4*) Fawcett.
— The Quick Red Fox. 1995. mass mkt. 5.99 (*0-449-22440-6*) Fawcett.
— The Quick Red Fox. 1996. mass mkt. 5.99 (*0-449-45613-7*, Crest) Fawcett.
— The Scarlet Ruse. 1996. mass mkt. 5.99 (*0-449-22477-5*) Fawcett.
— Seven. 20.95 (*0-89190-775-0*) Amereon Ltd.
— A Tan & Sandy Silence. 1996. mass mkt. 5.99 (*0-449-22476-7*, Crest) Fawcett.
— The Turquoise Lament. 1996. mass mkt. 5.99 (*0-449-22478-3*, Crest) Fawcett.
— The Turquoise Lament. LC 73-14806. 1973. 15.00 (*0-397-00987-9*, Lippncott) Lppncott W & W.
— Wine of the Dreamers. 20.95 (*0-89190-777-7*) Amereon Ltd.
MacDonald, John D., ed. Dictionary of Organometallic Compounds, 5 vols., Set. 2nd ed. (Illus.). 6192p. (C). (gr. 13). 1994. ring bd. 1575.95 (*0-412-43060-6*, Chap & Hall CRC) CRC Pr.
MacDonald, John D., et al. Manual of Oncologic Therapeutics. 3rd ed. 576p. 1995. spiral bd. 49.00 (*0-397-51394-1*) Lppncott W & W.
MacDonald, John D., jt. auth. see Moore, Lewis D.
Macdonald, John M. The Murderer & His Victim. 2nd ed. 342p. 1986. pap. 42.95 (*0-398-06254-4*) C C Thomas.
— The Murderer & His Victim. 2nd ed. 342p. (C). 1986. text 57.95 (*0-398-05205-0*) C C Thomas.

An Asterisk (*) at the beginning of an entry indicates that the title is appearing for the first time.

— Rape: Controversial Issues: Criminal Profiles, Date Rape, False Reports & False Memories. 218p. (C). 1995. pap. text 41.95 (*0-398-06546-2*) C C Thomas.
— Rape Controversial Issues: Criminal Profiles, Date Rape, False Reports & False Memories. 218p. (C). 1995. text 59.95 (*0-398-06545-4*) C C Thomas.
Macdonald, John M. & Haney, Thomas P. Criminal Investigation. LC 90-82052. 320p. (Orig.). (C). 1990. pap. text 12.00 (*0-9618230-1-1*) Apache Pr.
Macdonald, John M. & Kennedy, Jerry. Criminal Investigation of Drug Offenses: The Narcs' Manual. 422p. (C). 1983. 71.95 (*0-398-04915-7*) C C Thomas.
— Criminal Investigation of Drug Offenses: The Narcs' Manual. 422p. 1987. pap. 50.95 (*0-398-06253-6*) C C Thomas.
Macdonald, John M. & Michaud, David L. Criminal Interrogation. enl. rev. ed. LC 92-70604. Orig. Title: The Confession: Interrogation & Criminal Profiles for Police Officers. 232p. (C). 1992. pap. text 12.00 (*0-9618230-2-X*) Apache Pr.
Macdonald, John S., ed. Gastrointestinal Oncology. (Cancer Treatment & Research Ser.). 1987. text 241.50 (*0-89838-829-5*) Kluwer Academic.
MacDonald, John Stuart. Plan Implementation. (Progress in Planning Ser.). 1979. pap. 35.00 (*0-08-024307-X*, Pergamon Pr) Elsevier.
MacDonald, Jon. Great Battles of the Civil War. (Illus.). 1988. 19.95 (*0-02-577300-3*) Macmillan.
MacDonald, Joseph P. Redesigning School: Lessons for the 21st Century. LC 96-25339. (Education Ser.). 320p. 1996. 30.95 (*0-7879-0321-3*) Jossey-Bass.
MacDonald, Joyce G. Race, Ethnicity, & Power in the Renaissance. 1996. write for info. (*0-318-61237-2*) Fairleigh Dickinson.
MacDonald, Joyce G., ed. Race, Ethnicity, & Power in the Renaissance. LC 96-14655. (Illus.). 192p. 1997. 34.50 (*0-8386-3656-X*) Fairleigh Dickinson.
MacDonald, Julie, jt. ed. see Burns, Yvonne R.
MacDonald, June F., ed. NABC Report 5, Agricultural Biotechnology: A Public Conversation about Risk. 135p. 1993. pap. 5.00 (*0-9630907-3-9*) Natl Agri Biotech.
— NABC Report 4, Animal Biotechnology: Opportunities & Challenges. 181p. 1992. pap. 5.00 (*0-9630907-2-0*) Natl Agri Biotech.
— NABC Report 6, Agricultural Biotechnology & the Public Good. 213p. 1994. pap. 5.00 (*0-9630907-5-5*) Natl Agri Biotech.
— NABC Report 3, Agricultural Biotechnology at the Crossroads: Biological, Social & Institutional Concerns. 307p. 1991. pap. 7.00 (*0-9630907-4-7*) Natl Agri Biotech.
— NABC Report 3, Agricultural Biotechnology at the Crossroads: Biological, Social & Institutional Concerns. 307p. 1992. pap. text 5.00 (*0-685-60015-7*) Natl Agri Biotech.
Macdonald, K. Sociobiological Perspectives on Human Development. (Illus.). 450p. 1987. 94.95 (*0-387-96581-5*) Spr-Verlag.
MacDonald, K. B. Social & Personality Development: An Evolutionary Synthesis. (Perspectives in Developmental Psychology Ser.). (Illus.). 340p. (C). 1988. 70.00 (*0-306-42891-1*, Plenum Trade) Perseus Pubng.
MacDonald, K. L. Small Gasoline Engines Student's Workbook. 2nd ed. 1973. pap. write for info. (*0-672-97632-3*) Macmillan.
Macdonald, K. R. The Palace of Time: The Proof of God & Immortality. (Illus.). 106p. 1999. pap. 15.00 (*0-9670022-0-6*) Rain Bks.
Macdonald, Kate. Anne of Green Gables Cookbook. 48p. (YA). 1988. pap. 5.95 (*0-7704-2258-6*) Bantam.
— Anne of Green Gables Cookbook. (Illus.). 48p. (J). 1987. 14.95 (*0-19-540496-3*) OUP.
Macdonald, Kate, ed. see Buchan, John.
MacDonald, Katherine, jt. auth. see Weingarten, Jan.
MacDonald, Kathleen. When Writers Write. 2nd ed. (Illus.). 320p. (C). 1987. pap. text 32.20 (*0-13-956509-4*) P-H.
MacDonald, Kathryn, photos by. Living in America by James Snydal. (Illus.). 36p. 1997. pap. 4.95 (*0-9648133-7-8*) New Thght Jour Pr.
MacDonald, Kathryn & Morgan, Mar Lou. The Farm & City Cookbook. (Illus.). 296p. 1995. pap. 14.95 (*0-929005-67-8*) LPC InBook.
MacDonald, Kathy, et al. Counselling for Sexual Abuse: A Therapist's Guide to Working with Adults, Children & Families. 336p. 1995. pap. text 49.95 (*0-19-558315-9*) OUP.
Macdonald, Keith M. The Sociology of the Professions. 224p. 1995. 69.95 (*0-8039-8633-5*); pap. 26.95 (*0-8039-8634-3*) Sage.
MacDonald, Keith N. The Practice of Medicine among the Burmese. LC 77-87505. reprint ed. 42.50 (*0-404-16837-X*) AMS Pr.
MacDonald, Kenneth B. & MacDonald, Agnes. The Second Coming: Tough Questions Answered. 300p. (Orig.). (YA). 1991. pap. 9.95 (*0-9626490-0-7*) Revivals & Missions.
MacDonald, Kenneth D. On Fire with Selling: A Rich Analysis of Sales Experiences Mixed with Amazing Real-Life Stories. LC 94-30534. (Illus.). 80p. 1995. pap. 9.95 (*0-942963-54-7*) Distinctive Pub.
MacDonald, Kevin. The Culture of Critique: An Evolutionary Analysis of Jewish Involvement in Twentieth-Century Intellectual & LC 98-14905. (Human Evolution, Behavior & Intelligence Ser.). 392p. 1998. 65.00 (*0-275-96113-3*, Praeger Pubs) Greenwood.
***MacDonald, Kevin.** Imagining Reality: The Faber Book of Documentary. 400p. 1998. pap. 16.95 (*0-571-19202-5*) Faber & Faber.
MacDonald, Kevin. Parent-Child Play: Descriptions & Implications. LC 92-20562. (SUNY Series, Children's Play in Society). 389p. (C). 1993. pap. text 21.95 (*0-7914-1464-7*) State U NY Pr.
Macdonald, Kevin. A People That Shall Dwell Alone: Judaism as an Evolutionary Group Strategy. LC 94-16446. (Human Evolution, Behavior & Intelligence Ser.). 320p. 1994. 65.00 (*0-275-94869-2*, Praeger Pubs) Greenwood.
MacDonald, Kevin. Separation & Its Discontents: Toward an Evolutionary Theory of Anti-Semitism. LC 97-26901. (Human Evolution, Behavior & Intelligence Ser.). 336p. 1998. 65.00 (*0-275-94870-6*, Praeger Pubs) Greenwood.
MacDonald, Kevin, ed. Parent-Child Play: Descriptions & Implications. LC 92-20562. (SUNY Series, Children's Play in Society). 389p. (C). 1993. text 64.50 (*0-7914-1463-9*) State U NY Pr.
MacDonald, L. Ian. From Bourassa to Bourassa: A Pivotal Decade in Canadian History. LC 85-103559. (Illus.). 328p. reprint ed. pap. 101.70 (*0-8357-6438-9*, 203580900097) Bks Demand.
Macdonald, L. O. A Unique & Glorious Mission: Women & Presbyterianism in Scotland, 1830-1930. 300p. 1998. pap. 60.00 (*0-85976-478-8*, Pub. by J Donald) St Mut.
***MacDonald, L. W. & Luo, Ronnier.** Colour Imaging: Vision & Technology. LC 98-53330. 440p. 1999. 115.00 (*0-471-98531-7*) Wiley.
MacDonald, L. W., jt. auth. see Heaton, Nigel.
MacDonald, Lachlan, jt. ed. see Gilmore, Elaine.
MacDonald, Lachlan P. The Guide to Whale Watching: The Grey Whale. (Illus.). 96p. (Orig.). 1990. pap. 4.95 (*0-936940-06-9*) Helm Pub.
— The Hunter & Other Stories. 1989. write for info. (*0-318-65384-2*) Pr MacDonald & Reinecke.
— Uncommon Guide to Carmel, Monterey & Big Sur. (Illus.). 1990. pap. 8.95 (*0-939919-03-6*) Bear Flag Bks.
— An Uncommon Guide to San Luis Obispo County California. 2nd rev. ed. LC 75-2794. (Illus.). 1990. pap. 8.95 (*0-939919-00-1*) Bear Flag Bks.
MacDonald, Lachlan P., ed. Channel X Short-Short Stories, Vol. 1, No. 1. (Illus.). 64p. 1990. pap. 6.95 (*1-877947-06-7*) Pr MacDonald & Reinecke.
MacDonald, Lachlan P., ed. see Angel, Myron F.
MacDonald, Lady C. Lady MacDonald's Scotland: The Best of Scottish Food & Drink. (Illus.). 160p. 1996. pap. 16.95 (*0-8212-2309-7*, Pub. by Bulfinch Pr) Little.
***Macdonald, Larry.** Nortel Networks: How Innovation & Vision Created a Network Giant. 2000. 27.95 (*0-471-64542-7*) Wiley.
MacDonald, Laura. Drastic Measures. large type ed. (Mills & Boon Large Print Ser.). 288p. 1997. 23.99 (*0-263-15083-6*, Pub. by Mills & Boon) Ulverscroft.
— False Pretences. large type ed. (Mills & Boon Large Print Ser.). 288p. 1997. 23.99 (*0-263-14834-3*) Ulverscroft.
***MacDonald, Laura.** Holding the Baby. 288p. 2000. 26.99 (*0-263-16322-9*, Pub. by Mills & Boon) Ulverscroft.
MacDonald, Laura. In at the Deep End. large type ed. 288p. 1995. 23.99 (*0-263-14623-5*, Pub. by Mills & Boon) Ulverscroft.
***MacDonald, Laura.** To Love & to Cherish. large type ed. 1999. 25.99 (*0-263-15945-0*, Pub. by Mills & Boon) Ulverscroft.
— Village Partners. large type ed. 288p. 1999. 25.99 (*0-263-16145-5*, Pub. by Mills & Boon) Ulverscroft.
Macdonald, Laura A. Island Partner. large type ed. 246p. 1993. 27.99 (*0-7505-0574-5*) Ulverscroft.
MacDonald, Laurence E. The Invisible Art of Film Music: A Comprehensive History. (Illus.). 431p. 1998. pap. text 31.95 (*1-880157-56-X*) Ardsley.
Macdonald, Lawrence W. The Collected Works of Lawrence W. Macdonald, Vol. 1. Shapiro, Abraham, ed. (Illus.). 299p. (C). 1992. lib. bdg. 18.00 (*0-943599-56-3*) OEPF.
— The Collected Works of Lawrence W. Macdonald, Vol. 2. Schwartz, Ira & Shapiro, Abraham, eds. (Illus.). 350p. (C). 1992. lib. bdg. 18.00 (*0-943599-58-X*) OEPF.
MacDonald, Linda D., et al. Teaching Technologies in Libraries. (Professional Librarian Ser.). 198p. (C). 1990. 40.00 (*0-8161-1906-6*, Hall Reference); 30.00 (*0-8161-1907-4*, Hall Reference) Macmillan.
MacDonald, Lindsay, jt. ed. see Brown, Sarah.
MacDonald, Lindsay W. Getting the Best from State-of-the-Art Display Systems. LC 97-173741. 446p. 1997. 120.00 (*0-471-95870-0*) Wiley.
MacDonald, Lindsay W. & Vince, John, eds. Interacting with Virtual Environments. LC 93-33676. 314p. 1994. 100.00 (*0-471-93941-2*) Wiley.
MacDonald, Lisa, ed. Jazz: The National Gallery Pocket Address Book. (Illus.). 144p. 1985. 7.95 (*0-939456-12-5*) Galison.
— Winterthur's Twelve Months of Flowers. (Illus.). 32p. 1985. 12.95 (*0-939456-11-7*) Galison.
MacDonald, Lorna. A Grammar of Tauya. (Mouton Grammar Library: No. 6). (Illus.). xiii, 385p. (C). 1990. lib. bdg. 152.35 (*3-11-012673-7*) Mouton.
MacDonald, Lorne. Basic Circuit Analysis for Electronics Through Experimentation. 3rd ed. 360p. 1998. pap. text 20.00 (*0-911908-25-0*) Tech Ed Pr.
— Basic Circuit Analysis for Electronics Using Electronics Workbench. (Illus.). 160p. 1998. pap. text 12.50 (*0-911908-26-9*) Tech Ed Pr.
***MacDonald, Lorne.** Basic Solid State Electronic Circuit Analysis. 4th rev. ed. 480p. 2000. pap. text 25.00 (*0-911908-28-5*, 911908-28-5) Tech Ed Pr.
MacDonald, Lorne. Practical Analysis of Advanced Electronic Circuits Through Experimentation. 2nd ed. 384p. 1984. pap. text 20.00 (*0-911908-18-8*) Tech Ed Pr.
— Practical Circuit Analysis of Amplifiers. 544p. 1994. pap. text 25.00 (*0-911908-22-6*) Tech Ed Pr.
MacDonald, Lucille. Two Lives. LC 95-62162. (Illus.). 272p. 1996. pap. 16.95 (*0-936029-43-9*) Western Bk Journ.
MacDonald, Lyn. The First Year of Fighting. 1988. 24.95 (*0-318-37460-9*) Atheneum Yung Read.
***MacDonald, Lyn.** 1914-1918: Voices & Images of the Great War. (Illus.). 346p. 2000. pap. 27.50 (*0-14-014674-1*, Pub. by Pnguin Bks Ltd) Trafalgar.
MacDonald, Lyn. 1915: The Death of Innocence. LC 94-25654. 1995. write for info. (*0-8050-3499-4*) H Holt & Co.
***MacDonald, Lyn.** To the Last Man: Spring 1918. (Illus.). 416p. 2001. reprint ed. pap. 15.95 (*0-7867-0797-6*, Pub. by Carroll & Graf) Publishers Group.
Macdonald, Lyn. To the Last Man: Spring 1918. 416p. 1999. 27.95 (*0-7867-0663-5*) Carroll & Graf.
***Macdonald, Madeline.** The Last Year of the Gang: A Diary from a Girl's School. (Illus.). 234p. 2000. 30.00 (*1-85776-437-4*, Pub. by Book Guild Ltd) Trans-Atl Phila.
MacDonald, Malcolm. Brahms. LC 90-8545. 490p. 1993. per. 25.00 (*0-02-872851-3*) Music Sales.
MacDonald, Malcolm. Dancing on Snowflakes. large type ed. 1995. 27.99 (*0-7089-3316-5*) Ulverscroft.
— John Foulds & His Music: An Introduction. (Illus.). 162p. (Orig.). 1989. pap. 21.95 (*0-912483-02-4*) Pro-Am Music.
— Like a Diamond. 2nd ed. 384p. 1999. text 23.95 (*0-312-20557-0*) St Martin.
— Ronald Stevenson: A Musical Biography. 1990. 21.95 (*0-912483-62-8*) Pro-Am Music.
***MacDonald, Malcolm.** Tamsin Harte. LC 99-88104. 384p. 2000. text 24.95 (*0-312-20628-3*) St Martin.
MacDonald, Malcom. Tomorrows Tide. LC 97-8189. 1997. text 23.95 (*0-312-15676-6*) St Martin.
MacDonald, Mandy. The Andes: A Quest for Justice. 128p. (C). 1993. pap. 9.95 (*0-85598-200-4*, Pub. by Oxfam Pub) Stylus Pub VA.
MacDonald, Mandy, ed. Gender Planning in Development Agencies. (Gender & Development Ser.). (Illus.). 232p. (C). 1994. pap. 15.95 (*0-85598-263-2*, Pub. by Oxfam Pub) Stylus Pub VA.
MacDonald, Mandy & Gatehouse, Mike. In the Mountains of Morazan: Portrait of a Returned Refugee Community in El Salvador. (Illus.). 220p. 1994. pap. 19.00 (*0-85345-957-6*, PB9576, Pub. by Monthly Rev) NYU Pr.
— In the Mountains of Morazban: Portrait of a Returned Refugee Community in El Salvador LC 95-232576. iii, 216p. 1995. write for info. (*0-906156-94-7*) Lat Am Bur.
MacDonald, Mandy, jt. auth. see MacDonald, Neil.
MacDonald, Mandy, jt. ed. see Marsden, Hilary.
***MacDonald, Margaret.** The Old Woman & Her Pig. (J). (ps-1). 2001. lib. bdg. 15.89 (*0-06-028090-5*) HarpC Child Bks.
— The Old Woman & Her Pig. 32p. (J). (ps-1). 2001. 15.95 (*0-06-028089-1*) HarpC Child Bks.
MacDonald, Margaret F. James McNeill Whistler: Watercolors, Pastels, & Drawings: A Catalogue Raisonne. LC 94-10253. (Illus.). 688p. 1995. 160.00 (*0-300-05987-6*) Yale U Pr.
MacDonald, Margaret F., jt. auth. see Dorment, Richard.
MacDonald, Margaret R. Bookplay: One Hundred-One Creative Themes to Share with Young Children. LC 94-25146. (Illus.). xx, 225p. (C). 1995. lib. bdg. 35.00 (*0-208-02280-5*, Lib Prof Pubns) Shoe String.
— Booksharing: One Hundred One Programs to Use with Preschoolers. LC 87-35777. (Illus.). x, 236p. (C). 1988. lib. bdg. 35.00 (*0-208-02159-0*, Lib Prof Pubns) Shoe String.
— Booksharing: One Hundred One Programs to Use with Preschoolers. LC 87-35777. (Illus.). x, 236p. (C). 1991. pap. text 27.50 (*0-208-02314-3*, Lib Prof Pubns) Shoe String.
— Celebrate the World: Twenty Tellable Folktales for Multicultural Festivals. LC 94-6682. (Illus.). 225p. 1994. 40.00 (*0-8242-0862-5*) Wilson.
— Earth Care: World Folktales to Talk About. LC 99-29785. (Illus.). 128p. (YA). 1999. 26.50 (*0-208-02416-6*, Linnet Bks) Shoe String.
— Earth Care: World Folktales to Talk About. LC 99-29785. (Illus.). 128p. (YA). (ps up). 1999. pap. 17.50 (*0-208-02426-3*, Linnet Bks) Shoe String.
— Ghost Stories of the Pacific Northwest. (American Storytelling Ser.). 256p. (YA). 1995. 24.95 (*0-87483-436-8*) August Hse.
— The Girl Who Wore Too Much: A Folktale from Thailand. LC 97-38807. (THA & ENG., Illus.). 32p. (J). (ps-4). 1998. 15.95 (*0-87483-503-8*) August Hse.
— Look Back & See: Twenty Lively Tales for Gentle Tellers. (Illus.). 178p. (Orig.). 1991. 35.00 (*0-8242-0810-2*) Wilson.
— The Old Woman Who Lived in a Vinegar Bottle. LC 94-46967. (Illus.). (J). (ps-3). 1995. 15.95 (*0-87483-415-5*) August Hse.
— Peace Tales: World Folktales to Talk About. LC 92-8994. 128p. (J). (gr. 1-6). 1992. pap. text 17.50 (*0-208-02329-1*, Linnet Bks); lib. bdg. 25.00 (*0-208-02328-3*, Linnet Bks) Shoe String.
— Pickin' Peas. LC 95-26133. (Illus.). 32p. (J). (ps-3). 1998. lib. bdg. 15.89 (*0-06-027970-2*) HarpC.
— Scipio Storytelling: Talk in a Southern Indiana Community. LC 96-15649. 248p. 1996. pap. text 34.00 (*0-7618-0350-5*); lib. bdg. 54.00 (*0-7618-0349-1*) U Pr of Amer.
— The Skit Book: One Hundred & One Skits from Kids. LC 89-29654. (Illus.). 152p. (J). (gr. 1-9). 1990. pap. 18.00 (*0-208-02283-X*, Linnet Bks); lib. bdg. 25.00 (*0-208-02258-9*, Linnet Bks) Shoe String.
— Slop! A Welsh Folktale. LC 96-53359. (Illus.). 24p. (J). (gr. k-6). 1997. 15.95 (*1-55591-352-0*) Fulcrum Pub.
— Storyteller's Start-up Book: Finding, Learning, Performing, & Using Folktales. 215p. 1993. 26.95 (*0-87483-304-3*); pap. 14.95 (*0-87483-305-1*) August Hse.
— Tuck-Me-In Tales: Bedtime Stories from Around the World. (Illus.). 64p. (J). 1996. 19.95 (*0-87483-461-9*, Aug Hse LittleFolk) August Hse.
— When the Lights Go Out: Twenty Scary Tales to Tell. (Illus.). 176p. 1988. 35.00 (*0-8242-0770-X*); pap. 20.00 (*0-8242-0823-4*) Wilson.
MacDonald, Margaret R., ed. Storyteller's Sourcebook. (Neal Schuman Bk.). 818p. 1995. 99.00 (*0-8103-0471-6*) Gale.
— Tom Thumb. LC 93-21. (Multicultural Folktale Ser.). 184p. 1993. pap. 29.50 (*0-89774-728-3*) Oryx Pr.
— Traditional Storytelling Today: An International Sourcebook. 627p. 1999. lib. bdg. 95.00 (*1-57958-011-4*) Fitzroy Dearborn.
— Twenty Tellable Tales: Audience Participation Folktales for the Beginning Storyteller. LC 85-26565. (Illus.). 220p. 1986. 35.00 (*0-8242-0719-X*) Wilson.
MacDonald, Margaret R. & Jaeger, Winifred. The Round Book: Rounds Kids Love to Sing. LC 99-214628. (Illus.). 128p. (J). (gr. 1-4). 1999. pap. 16.50 (*0-208-02472-7*, Linnet Bks); lib. bdg. 22.50 (*0-208-02441-7*, Linnet Bks) Shoe String.
MacDonald, Margaret R., ed. see Vathanaprida, Supaporn.
***MacDonald, Margaret Read.** Mabela the Clever. LC 00-8307. (Illus.). (J). 2000. write for info. (*0-8075-4902-9*) A Whitman.
— Shake-It-Up Tales! Stories to Sing, Dance, Drum & Act Out. 192p. 2000. 24.95 (*0-87483-590-9*); pap. 14.95 (*0-87483-570-4*) August Hse.
MacDonald, Margaret Y. Early Christian Women & Pagan Opinion: The Power of Hysterical Woman. LC 96-36627. 290p. (C). 1996. text 64.95 (*0-521-56174-4*); pap. text 22.95 (*0-521-56728-9*) Cambridge U Pr.
MacDonald, Marguerite D., jt. ed. see Hammond, Robert M.
MacDonald, Marian L., jt. auth. see Anastas, Jean W.
MacDonald, Marianne. Death's Autograph: A Mystery. 352p. 1999. mass mkt. 5.99 (*0-06-109742-X*) HarpC.
— Death's Autograph: A Mystery. LC 97-19587. 224p. 1997. 22.95 (*0-312-16815-2*, Thomas Dunne) St Martin.
Macdonald, Marianne. Dragon for Sale. (Planet Reader First Chapter Bks.). (Illus.). 64p. (J). (gr. 2-5). 1998. pap. 2.95 (*0-8167-4340-1*) Troll Communs.
MacDonald, Marianne. Ghost Walk. LC 98-31260. 256p. 1998. text 21.95 (*0-312-19417-X*) St Martin.
***MacDonald, Marianne.** Ghost Walk: An Antiquarian Book Mystery. 304p. 2000. mass mkt. 5.99 (*0-06-101426-5*) HarpC.
— Road Kill. 2000. 22.95 (*0-312-24234-4*) St Martin.
MacDonald, Marianne. Smoke Screen. LC 99-47894. 288p. 1999. text 23.95 (*0-312-24243-3*) St Martin.
Macdonald, Marion E. The Significance of Various Kinds of Preparation for the City-Elementary School Principalship in Pennsylvania with Implications for a Program for Preparing for the Elementary-School Principalship in. LC 77-177020. (Columbia University. Teachers College. Contributions to Education Ser.: No. 416). reprint ed. 37.50 (*0-404-55416-4*) AMS Pr.
MacDonald, Mark. Pokemon Trainers Survival Guide. 1999. pap. 11.95 (*1-884364-33-0*) Sandwich Islands.
— True North Canadian Essays for Composition. (C). 1999. pap. text. write for info. (*0-201-61373-5*) Addison-Wesley.
MacDonald, Mark, et al. Pokemon Trainer's Survival Guide. rev. ed. 144p. 1999. pap. 12.95 (*1-884364-25-X*) Sandwich Islands.
MacDonald, Mark, jt. auth. see Arnold, J. Douglas.
MacDonald, Mark R., jt. auth. see Doern, Bruce G.
MacDonald, Mark R., jt. auth. see Doern, G. Bruce.
MacDonald, Mary. Shared Hope: Environment & Development Agendas for the 21st Century. LC 97-35355. 208p. (C). 1998. 65.00 (*0-415-15491-X*) Routledge.
Macdonald, Mary A. Hedgehog Bakes a Cake - Bank Street. 32p. (J). (ps-3). 1990. pap. 4.50 (*0-553-34890-6*) Bantam.
Macdonald, Mary E. Federal Grants for Vocational Rehabilitation. Phillips, William R. & Rosenberg, Janet, eds. LC 79-6914. (Physically Handicapped in Society Ser.). 1980. reprint ed. lib. bdg. 44.95 (*0-405-13123-2*) Ayer.
MacDonald, Mary L. Literature & Society in the Canadas, 1817-1850. LC 92-11215. 368p. 1992. lib. bdg. 99.95 (*0-7734-9524-X*) E Mellen.
MacDonald, Mary N. Mararoko: A Study in Melanesian Religion. LC 90-35291. (American University Studies: Anthropology & Science: Ser. XI, Vol. 45). (Illus.). XVII, 592p. (C). 1991. text 85.95 (*0-8204-1194-9*) P Lang Pubng.
MacDonald, Maryann. No Room for Francie. LC 94-8596. (Lots of O'Leary's Ser.). (J). 1995. 9.15 (*0-606-09693-0*, Pub. by Turtleback) Demco.
— No Room for Francie, No. 2. LC 94-8596. (Lots of O'Learys Ser.). (Illus.). 64p. (J). (gr. 2-4). 1995. 13.95 (*0-7868-0032-1*, Pub. by Hyprn Child) Little.
— The Pink Party. LC 93-20989. (Illus.). 40p. (J). (gr. k-3). 1994. lib. bdg. 10.89 (*1-56282-621-2*, Pub. by Hyprn Child) Little.
— Princess Josie's Pets. LC 96-27186. (Hyperion Chapters Ser.). (Illus.). 64p. (J). (gr. 1-3). 1997. lib. bdg. 14.49 (*0-7868-2263-5*, Pub. by Hyprn Ppbks) Little.
— Princess Josie's Pets. LC 96-27186. (Hyperion Chapters Ser.). (Illus.). 64p. (J). (gr. 1-3). 1998. pap. 3.95 (*0-7868-1134-X*, Pub. by Hyprn Ppbks) Little.
— Princess Josie's Pets. (Hyperion Chapters Ser.). 1998. 9.05 (*0-606-13724-6*, Pub. by Turtleback) Demco.
— Rosie & the Poor Rabbits. LC 92-42766. (Illus.). 32p. (J). (ps-2). 1994. 13.95 (*0-689-31832-4*) Atheneum Yung Read.

M

— Rosie's Baby Tooth. LC 90-35923. (Illus.). 32p. (J). (ps-2). 1991. lib. bdg. 12.95 (*0-689-31626-7*) Atheneum Yung Read.
Macdonald, Maryann. Sam's Worries. 1994. 10.15 (*0-606-06711-6*, Pub. by Turtleback) Demco.
— Second Hand Star. LC 93-31812. (Hyperion Chapters Ser.). (Illus.). 64p. (J). (gr. 2-4). 1997. pap. 3.99 (*0-7868-1168-4*, Pub. by Hyprn Ppbks) Little.
MacDonald, Maryann. Secondhand Star. LC 93-31812. (Lots of O'Leary's Ser.). (J). 1997. 19.50 (*0-7868-2316-X*) Hyperion.
— Secondhand Star. LC 93-31812. (Lots of O'Learys Ser.). (Illus.). 64p. (J). (gr. 2-5). 1994. 11.95 (*1-56282-616-6*, Pub. by Hyprn Child) Little.
— Secondhand Star. (Lots of O'Leary's Ser.). 1998. 9.15 (*0-606-13769-6*, Pub. by Turtleback) Demco.
MacDonald, Maryellen C., ed. Lexical Representations & Sentence Processing. LC 97-202451. (Illus.). 403p. 1997. write for info. (*0-86377-962-X*, Pub. by Psychol Pr) Taylor & Francis.
MacDonald, Marylee. Repairing Historic Flat Plaster: Walls & Ceilings. 14p. 1990. pap. 1.00 (*0-16-003573-2*) USGPO.
MacDonald, Marylee, jt. auth. see Konzo, Seichi.
MacDonald, Melody. Caught in the Act: The Feldberg Investigation. 1994. pap. 9.95 (*1-897766-05-X*, Pub. by Jon Carpenter) Paul & Co Pubs.
MacDonald, Mhairi G. Emergency Transport of the Perinatal Patient. 1989. 55.00 (*0-316-54198-2*, Little Brwn Med Div) Lppncott W & W.
MacDonald, Mhairi G., jt. ed. see Fletcher, Mary Ann.
MacDonald, Mia. Reinventing Systems: Collaborations to Support Families. Harvard Family Research Project Staff, ed. LC 94-167390. 92p. 1994. pap. text 7.50 (*0-9630627-3-5*) Harvard Fam.
MacDonald, Michael & Benfield, Steve, eds. Power Builder 4.0: Secrets of the Power Builder Masters: Creating Mission Critical Applications in Power Builder 4. 0. (Power Engineering Ser.). (Illus.). 600p. 1995. pap. 49.95 (*1-886141-00-2*) SYS-Con Pubns.
MacDonald, Michael & Griffith, Michael. PowerBuilder 5.0: Secrets of the PowerBuilder Masters: PowerBuilder Developer's Journal. 2nd rev. ed. (PowerBuilder Training Ser.). (Illus.). 1104p. 1996. pap. 59.95 incl. cd-rom (*1-886141-01-0*) SYS-Con Pubns.
MacDonald, Michael & Murphy, Terence R. Sleepless Souls: Suicide in Early Modern England. (Oxford Studies in Social History). (Illus.). 400p. 1991. text 95.00 (*0-19-822919-4*) OUP.
MacDonald, Michael, et al. Home of the Brave. (Cyberpunk Ser.). (Illus.). 144p. (Orig.). 1993. pap. 14.00 (*0-937279-36-6*, CP3221) Talsorian.
— Operation: Rimfire. (Mekton Ser.). (Illus.). 104p. (Orig.). 1993. pap. 14.00 (*0-937279-37-4*, MK1501) Talsorian.
MacDonald, Michael, jt. auth. see Celko, Joe.
MacDonald, Michael, jt. auth. see Garbus, Jeff.
MacDonald, Michael, ed. see Ackerman, David, et al.
MacDonald, Michael D. High Performance Client/Server with Visual Basic 6. LC 98-34264. (High Performance Ser.). 699p. 1998. pap. 49.99 (*1-57610-282-3*) Coriolis Grp.
— MCSD Visual Basic 6 Desktop Exam Cram. LC 98-33444. (Exam Cram Ser.). 1999. pap. 29.99 (*1-57610-376-5*) Coriolis Grp.
Macdonald, Michael H. Europe, a Tantalizing Romance: Past & Present Europe for Students & the Serious Traveler. 2nd ed. LC 96-20526. 400p. 1996. pap. text 37.50 (*0-7618-0411-0*); lib. bdg. 64.50 (*0-7618-0410-2*) U Pr of Amer.
***MacDonald, Michael Patrick.** All Souls. 2000. pap. 14.00 (*0-345-44177-X*) Ballantine Pub Grp.
MacDonald, Michael Patrick. All Souls: A Family Story from Southie. LC 99-30692. (Illus.). 224p. 1999. 24.00 (*0-8070-7212-5*) Beacon Pr.
MacDonald, Michele. Alexander Technique. (Illus.). 64p. 1999. 9.95 (*1-85967-896-3*) Anness Pub.
MacDonald, Mike, et al. Mekton Z. (Mekton Ser.). (Illus.). 160p. (Orig.). 1995. pap. 20.00 (*0-937279-54-4*, MK1003) Talsorian.
MacDonald, Murdo. Nothing Is Altogether Trivial: An Anthology of Writing from the Edinburgh Review. (Illus.). 240p. 1996. pap. 22.00 (*0-7486-0698-X*, Pub. by Edinburgh U Pr) Col U Pr.
***MacDonald, Murdo.** Scottish Art. LC 99-65174. (World of Art Ser.). (Illus.). 224p. 2000. pap. 14.95 (*0-500-20333-4*, Pub. by Thames Hudson) Norton.
MacDonald, Myra. Representing Women: Myths of Feminity in the Popular Media. LC 95-17544. 1995. text. write for info. (*0-340-63221-6*, Pub. by E A); pap. text 18.95 (*0-340-58016-X*, Pub. by E A) OUP.
MacDonald, N. REDUCE for Physicists. (Illus.). 167p. 1994. 57.00 (*0-7503-0277-1*) IOP Pub.
— Time Lags in Biological Models. (Lecture Notes in Biomathematics Ser.: Vol. 27). (Illus.). 1978. pap. 23.00 (*0-387-09092-4*) Spr-Verlag.
MacDonald, N. P. The Making of Brazil: Portuguese Roots, 1500-1822. LC 97-121666. (Illus.). 520p. 1996. 62.50 (*1-85776-068-9*, Pub. by Book Guild Ltd) Trans-Atl Phila.
MacDonald, Nancy. Homage to the Spanish Exiles: Voices from the Spanish Civil War. LC 86-10541. 358p. 1987. 28.95 (*0-89885-325-7*, Kluwer Acad Hman Sci) Kluwer Academic.
MacDonald, Nancy, tr. see Paz, Abel.
MacDonald, Neil. The Caribbean: Making Our Own Choices. (Illus.). 64p. (C). 1990. pap. 7.95 (*0-85598-086-9*, Pub. by Oxfam Pub) Stylus Pub VA.
MacDonald, Neil, et al, eds. Palliative Medicine: A Case-Based Manual. (Illus.). 330p. 1998. pap. text 29.95 (*0-19-262657-4*) OUP.
MacDonald, Neil & MacDonald, Mandy. Brazil: A Mask Called Progress. (Illus.). 128p. (C). 1991. pap. 9.95 (*0-85598-091-5*, Pub. by Oxfam Pub) Stylus Pub VA.
MacDonald, Norbert. Distant Neighbors: A Comparative History of Seattle & Vancouver. LC 86-30892. 291p. 1987. reprint ed. pap. 90.30 (*0-608-01840-6*, 206249000003) Bks Demand.
MacDonald, Oliver, ed. Polish August: Documents from the Beginnings of the Polish Workers' Rebellion. (Illus.). 177p. 1982. pap. 2.00 (*0-939306-02-6*) Left Bank.
MacDonald, Pat, ed. see Beach, Lynn.
MacDonald, Pat, ed. see Bennett, Cherie.
MacDonald, Pat, ed. see Carris, Joan D.
MacDonald, Pat, ed. see Clayton, Ed.
MacDonald, Pat, ed. see Cohen, Daniel.
MacDonald, Pat, ed. see Coville, Bruce.
MacDonald, Pat, ed. see Gilson, Jamie.
MacDonald, Pat, ed. see Gorman, S. S.
MacDonald, Pat, ed. see Hermes, Patricia.
MacDonald, Pat, ed. see Hiser, Constance.
MacDonald, Pat, ed. see Kehret, Peg.
MacDonald, Pat, ed. see Lewis, Linda.
MacDonald, Pat, ed. see Miller, Judi.
MacDonald, Pat, ed. see Murrow, Liza K.
MacDonald, Pat, ed. see Pike, Christopher, pseud.
MacDonald, Pat, ed. see Posner, Richard.
MacDonald, Pat, ed. see Ragz, M. M.
MacDonald, Pat, ed. see Siegal, Barbara & Seigel, Scott.
MacDonald, Pat, ed. see Siegal, Barbara & Siegel, Scott.
MacDonald, Pat, ed. see Smith, L. J.
MacDonald, Pat, ed. see Stine, R. L., pseud.
MacDonald, Pat, ed. see Wallace, Bill.
MacDonald, Patricia. Lost Innocents. 368p. 1999. mass mkt. 7.50 (*0-446-60759-2*, Pub. by Warner Bks) Little.
***MacDonald, Patricia.** Pablo Picasso: Genius! The Artist & the Process. (Illus.). 128p. (YA). (gr. 7-9). 1999. text 20.00 (*0-7881-6842-8*) DIANE Pub.
MacDonald, Patricia. Secret Admirer. 384p. 1997. mass mkt. 6.50 (*0-446-60368-6*, Pub. by Warner Bks) Little.
— Secret Admirer. large type ed. (Large Print Ser.). 456p. 1996. lib. bdg. 23.95 (*1-57490-039-0*, Beeler LP Bks) T T Beeler.
Macdonald, Patricia, jt. auth. see Macdonald, Angus.
MacDonald, Patricia, jt. auth. see MacDonald, Angus.
MacDonald, Patricia, ed. see Auch, Mary J.
MacDonald, Patricia, ed. see Baker, Barbara.
MacDonald, Patricia, ed. see Beach, Lynn.
MacDonald, Patricia, ed. see Bennett, Cherie.
MacDonald, Patricia, ed. see Bennett, Cherrie.
MacDonald, Patricia, ed. see Cohen, Daniel.
MacDonald, Patricia, ed. see Coville, Bruce.
MacDonald, Patricia, ed. see Cusick, Richie T.
MacDonald, Patricia, ed. see Garden, Nancy.
MacDonald, Patricia, ed. see Gorman, S. S.
MacDonald, Patricia, ed. see Haas, Dorothy.
MacDonald, Patricia, ed. see Helldorfer, M. C.
MacDonald, Patricia, ed. see Hiser, Constance.
MacDonald, Patricia, ed. see Hodgman, Ann.
MacDonald, Patricia, ed. see Hollands, Judith.
MacDonald, Patricia, ed. see Kehret, Peg.
MacDonald, Patricia, ed. see Lawlor, Laurie.
MacDonald, Patricia, ed. see Leroe, Ellen.
MacDonald, Patricia, ed. see Monsell, Mary E.
MacDonald, Patricia, ed. see Murrow, Liza K.
MacDonald, Patricia, ed. see Nash, Bruce & Zullo, Allan.
MacDonald, Patricia, ed. see Pike, Christopher, pseud.
MacDonald, Patricia, ed. see Poploff, Michelle.
MacDonald, Patricia, ed. see Posner, Richard.
MacDonald, Patricia, ed. see Ragz, M. M.
MacDonald, Patricia, ed. see Ransom, Candice F.
MacDonald, Patricia, ed. see Rubinstein, Gillian.
MacDonald, Patricia, ed. see Shirts, Morris A.
MacDonald, Patricia, ed. see Siegal, Barbara & Siegal, Scott.
MacDonald, Patricia, ed. see Siegal, Barbara & Siegel, Scott.
MacDonald, Patricia, ed. see Smith, L. J.
MacDonald, Patricia, ed. see Smith, L. T.
MacDonald, Patricia, ed. see Smith, Lisa.
MacDonald, Patricia, ed. see Stine, R. L., pseud.
MacDonald, Patricia, ed. see Thompson, Joan.
MacDonald, Patricia, ed. see Wallace, Bill.
***MacDonald, Patricia J.** Lost Innocents. LC 99-43651. 1999. 26.95 (*1-57490-216-4*) T T Beeler.
MacDonald, Patricia J. Lost Innocents. LC 97-23306. 304p. 1998. 24.00 (*0-446-51687-2*, Pub. by Warner Bks) Little.
— No Way Home. large type ed. 1991. 27.99 (*0-7089-2484-0*) Ulverscroft.
MacDonald, Patty V. Long Lost Recipes: Of Aunt Susan. (Illus.). 198p. 1989. 15.95 (*0-9624490-0-8*) P V MacDonald.
MacDonald, Patty V., ed. Spiced with Wit: Will Rogers' Tomfoolery More Aunt Susan Recipes. (Illus.). 220p. 1992. 15.95 (*0-9624490-1-6*) P V MacDonald.
MacDonald, Patty Vineyard, ed. see Corbitt, Helen.
***MacDonald, Paul S.** Descartes & Husserl: The Philosophical Project of Radical Beginnings. LC 99-15027. (SUNY Series in Philosophy). 320p. (C). 1999. text 65.50 (*0-7914-4369-8*); pap. text 21.95 (*0-7914-4370-1*) State U NY Pr.
MacDonald, Pauline, jt. auth. see Brown, Doris V.
***MacDonald, Paxson C. & Conte, Cynthia M.** A Taste of the 18th Century. LC 99-74156. 160p. 1999. spiral bd. 12.95 (*0-9672351-0-3*) Michie Tavern.
MacDonald, Peter. Court Jesters Cartoons. LC 99-192510. 1991. pap. 7.95 (*0-7736-7320-2*) Genl Dist Srvs.
— From the Cop Shop. 224p. 1997. pap. 13.95 (*0-7737-5918-2*) Stoddart Publ.
— Giap: The Victor in Vietnam. 352p. 1993. 25.00 (*0-393-03401-1*) Norton.
— Special Forces: A History of the World's Elite Fighting Units. 1988. 12.98 (*1-55521-112-7*) Bk Sales Inc.
MacDonald, Peter V. From the Cop Shop: Hilarious Tales from Our Men & Women of the Badge. LC 97-138576. (Illus.). 224p. 1996. 19.95 (*0-7737-2912-7*) Stoddart Publ.
MacDonald, Philip. The List of Adrian Messenger. 1976. 20.95 (*0-8488-0570-4*) Amereon Ltd.
— The List of Adrian Messenger. 1993. reprint ed. lib. bdg. 16.95 (*1-56849-210-3*) Buccaneer Bks.
— The Rasp. 23.95 (*0-89190-094-2*) Amereon Ltd.
— The Rasp. 288p. 1979. reprint ed. pap. 5.95 (*0-486-23864-4*) Dover.
MacDonald, Philip E., jt. ed. see Shah, Vikram N.
MacDonald, R. The International Law & Policy of Human Welfare. 708p. 1978. lib. bdg. 200.00 (*90-286-0808-7*) Kluwer Academic.
MacDonald, R. & McGill, D. Drafting. (Butterworths Skills Ser.). 260p. 1996. pap. write for info. (*0-409-30827-7*, MICHIE) LEXIS Pub.
MacDonald, R. & Travis, C. Libraries & Special Collections on Latin America & the Caribbean: A Directory of European Resources. 2nd ed. LC 87-24114. (Institute of Latin American Studies Monographs). 256p. (C). 1988. text 75.00 (*0-485-17714-5*, Pub. by Athlone Pr) Humanities.
MacDonald, R. H. A Broadcast News Manual of Style. 202p. (C). 1989. pap. text 27.33 (*0-582-99865-4*, 75290) Longman.
MacDonald, R. J., et al. Surface Science: Principles & Current Applications. LC 96-31370. 374p. 1996. 109.50 (*3-540-61405-2*) Spr-Verlag.
Macdonald, R. S., jt. ed. see Djwa, Sandra.
MacDonald, Ranald. Ranald MacDonald: The Narrative of His Life, 1824-1894. 2nd ed. Lewis, William S. & Murakami, Naojiro, eds. (North Pacific Studies: No. 16). Orig. Title: Ranald MacDonald 1824-1894. (Illus.). 384p. 1990. reprint ed. 30.00 (*0-87595-229-1*) Oregon Hist.
MacDonald, Randall M. The Internet & the School Library Media Specialist: Transforming Traditional Services. LC 96-37045. (Greenwood Professional Guides in School Librarianship). 224p. 1997. 39.95 (*0-313-30028-3*, Greenwood Pr) Greenwood.
***MacDonald, Randall M. & MacDonald, Susan Priest.** Successful Keyword Searching: Initiating Research on Popular Topics using Electronic Databases. LC 00-35323. 2000. write for info. (*0-313-30676-1*) Greenwood.
Macdonald, Rob & Wilent, Steve. RDO & ODBC: Client Server Database Programming with Visual BASIC. LC 96-32364. (Special Reports). 1996. pap. write for info. (*1-880935-50-3*) Pinnacle WA.
MacDonald, Robbyn. Victorian Embroidery. (Illus.). 128p. 1994. 24.95 (*1-86351-110-5*, Pub. by Sally Milner) Sterling.
MacDonald, Robert. Creating Writers. 2nd ed. LC 96-12958. 352p. (C). 1996. pap. text 36.56 (*0-8013-1578-6*) Addison-Wesley.
— Handbook of Basic Skills & Strategies for Beginner Teachers Facing the Challenge. 2nd ed. LC 98-2663. 288p. (C). 1998. pap. 52.00 (*0-8013-1574-3*) Addison-Wesley.
Macdonald, Robert. Islands of the Pacific Rim & Their People. LC 94-7541. (People & Places Ser.). 48p. (J). (gr. 5-8). 1994. lib. bdg. 24.26 (*1-56847-167-X*) Raintree Steck-V.
— Maori. LC 93-35530. (Threatened Cultures Ser.). (Illus.). 48p. (J). (gr. 4-6). 1994. lib. bdg. 24.26 (*1-56847-151-3*) Raintree Steck-V.
— Transitions: Military Pathways to Civilian Careers. Rosen, Roger, ed. (Military Opportunities Ser.). (YA). (gr. 7-12). 1988. lib. bdg. 15.95 (*0-8239-0777-5*) Rosen Group.
MacDonald, Robert, ed. The Lay of the Land: The Golf Writings of Pat Ward-Thomas. (Illus.). 253p. 1990. 28.00 (*0-940889-28-5*) Classics Golf.
— Youth, the Underclass & Social Exclusion. LC 97-1608. (Illus.). 240p. (C). 1997. 80.00 (*0-415-15829-X*); pap. 24.99 (*0-415-15830-3*) Routledge.
MacDonald, Robert & Coffield, Frank. Risky Business? Youth, Enterprise & Policy for the 1990s. 224p. 1991. pap. 34.95 (*1-85000-898-1*, Falmer Pr) Taylor & Francis.
MacDonald, Robert, jt. auth. see Boske, Leigh.
Macdonald, Robert, jt. ed. see Wind, Herbert W.
MacDonald, Robert A., ed. Libro de las Tahuererias. (Spanish Legal Texts Ser.). xii, 485p. 1995. 50.00 (*1-56954-027-6*) Hispanic Seminary.
— Text & Concordance of Especulo, Alfonso el Sabio, MS10.123: Biblioteca Nacional de Madrid. (Spanish Legal Texts Ser.: No. 4). (SPA.). 12p. 1989. 10.00 incl. fiche (*0-940639-37-8*) Hispanic Seminary.
MacDonald, Robert D. Chinchilla. (Phoenix Theatre Ser.). 1982. pap. 2.95 (*0-912262-73-7*) Proscenium.
***MacDonald, Robert D.** Great Speeches from European Drama. (Oberon Bks.). 2000. pap. 14.95 (*1-84002-002-4*) Theatre Comm.
MacDonald, Robert D. Ice House. 80p. 1998. pap. 10.95 (*1-84002-030-X*, Pub. by Oberon Bks Ltd) Theatre Comm.
— In Quest of Conscience. (Oberon Bks.). 70p. 1997. pap. 12.95 (*1-870259-55-6*) Theatre Comm.
MacDonald, Robert D., tr. see Durrenmatt, Friedrich.
MacDonald, Robert D., tr. see Goethe, Johann Wolfgang Von.
MacDonald, Robert D., tr. see Goldoni, Carlo.
MacDonald, Robert D., tr. see Ibsen, Henrik.
MacDonald, Robert D., tr. see Racine, Jean.
MacDonald, Robert H. The Library of Drummond of Hawthornden. LC 68-22845. xii, 245p. 1971. write for info. (*0-85224-019-8*) Edinburgh U Pr.
— Sons of the Empire: The Frontier & the Boy Scout Movement 1890-1918. LC 93-93285. 258p. 1993. text 35.00 (*0-8020-2843-8*) U of Toronto Pr.
Macdonald, Robert M. Collective Bargaining in the Automobile Industry: A Study of Wage Structure & Competitive Relations. LC 63-13967. (Yale Studies in Economics: No. 17). 424p. reprint ed. pap. 131.50 (*0-608-14020-1*, 202201700024) Bks Demand.
Macdonald, Robert S. The Catherine. 356p. 1982. 12.95 (*0-89433-181-7*) Petrocelli.
Macdonald, Robert S., ed. The Darwin Sketchbook: Portraits of Golf's Greatest Players & Other Selections from Bernard Darwin's Writings, 1910-55. 2nd ed. (Illus.). 410p. 1992. lib. bdg. 28.00 (*0-940889-39-0*) Classics Golf.
MacDonald, Rod. Dive Scapa Flow. rev. ed. (Illus.). 160p. 1998. 29.95 (*1-85158-983-X*, Pub. by Mainstream Pubng) Trafalgar.
Macdonald, Roderick & Thomas, Huw, eds. Nationality & Planning in Scotland & Wales. LC 97-187097. 312p. 1997. 65.00 (*0-7083-1398-1*, Pub. by Univ Wales Pr) Paul & Co Pubs.
MacDonald, Roger. Provence & the Cote D'Azur. 1995. pap. 16.95 (*0-8442-9938-3*, Passprt Bks) NTC Contemp Pub Co.
Macdonald, Roger. Provence & the Cote D'Azur. (Regional Guides of France Ser.). (Illus.). 192p. 1994. pap. 16.95 (*0-8442-9087-4*, 90874, Passprt Bks) NTC Contemp Pub Co.
MacDonald, Ronald. Floating Exchange Rates: Theories & Evidence. (Illus.). 260p. (C). 1988. text 49.95 (*0-04-338134-0*); pap. text 25.00 (*0-04-338135-9*) Routledge.
— From a Northern Window: A Personal Remembrance of George MacDonald. 1989. 11.95 (*0-940652-33-1*) Sunrise Bks.
— From a Northern Window: A Personal Remembrance of George MacDonald. 1989. 7.95 (*0-940652-30-7*) Sunrise Bks.
***MacDonald, Ronald & Marsh, Ian.** Exchange Rate Modelling. LC 99-50109. (Advanced Studies in Theoretical & Applied Econometrics). 1999. write for info. (*0-7923-8668-X*) Kluwer Academic.
MacDonald, Ronald & Taylor, Mark P., eds. Exchange Rate Economics, 2 vols. (International Library of Critical Writings in Economics: Vol. 16). 1184p. 1991. text 465.00 (*1-85278-409-1*) E Elgar.
MacDonald, Ronald, jt. auth. see Hallwood, C. Paul.
Macdonald, Ronald R. The Burial-Places of Memory: Epic Underworlds in Vergil, Dante, & Milton. LC 86-19216. 240p. 1987. 30.00 (*0-87023-558-3*) U of Mass Pr.
— William Shakespeare: The Comedies. (Twayne's English Authors Ser.: No. 489). 200p. (C). 1992. 32.00 (*0-8057-7010-0*) Macmillan.
MacDonald, Ronald S., ed. Essays in Honour of Wang Tieya. 960p. (C). 1994. lib. bdg. 238.00 (*0-7923-2469-2*) Kluwer Academic.
MacDonald, Ronald S., et al, eds. Canadian Perspectives on International Law & Organization. LC 72-98024. 992p. reprint ed. pap. 200.00 (*0-608-12880-5*, 202364700033) Bks Demand.
— The European System for the Protection of Human Rights. LC 93-26605. (International Studies on Human Rights). 968p. (C). 1993. lib. bdg. 208.00 (*0-7923-2431-5*) Kluwer Academic.
MacDonald, Ronald S. & Johnston, Douglas M., eds. The Structure & Process of International Law. 1986. lib. bdg. 147.50 (*90-247-3273-5*) Kluwer Academic.
***MacDonald, Rose.** Taping Techniques: Principles & Practice. 2nd ed. (Illus.). 224p. 2000. pap. 47.50 (*0-7506-4150-9*) Buttrwrth-Heinemann.
MacDonald, Rose, ed. Taping Techniques: Principles & Practice. (Illus.). 263p. 1994. pap. text 48.50 (*0-7506-0577-4*) Buttrwrth-Heinemann.
MacDonald, Rosemary. Arabic Cookery. 192p. 1996. pap. text 22.50 (*0-572-02145-3*, Pub. by W Foulsham) Trans-Atl Phila.
MacDonald, Ross, jt. auth. see Molyneux, Bill.
MacDonald, Ross B. The Master Tutor: A Guidebook for More Effective Tutoring. (Illus.). 64p. (Orig.). (C). 1994. teacher ed. 64.95 (*0-935637-20-6*); student ed. 19.95 (*0-935637-19-2*); trans. 85.00 (*0-935637-21-4*) Cambridge Strat.
MacDonald, Ross, pseud. Archer in Jeopardy, 3 bks., Set. Incl. Zebra-Striped Hearse. LC 79-63807. 1979. LC 79-63807. 1979. 24.95 (*0-394-50804-1*) Knopf.
— Black Money. (Lew Archer Mystery Ser.). 1996. pap. 11.00 (*0-679-76810-6*) Random.
— The Blue Hammer. 23.95 (*0-89190-095-0*); pap. 16.95 (*0-8488-1722-2*) Amereon Ltd.
MacDonald, Ross, pseud. The Chill. 1983. mass mkt. 2.75 (*0-553-24282-2*) Bantam.
Macdonald, Ross, pseud. The Chill. (Lew Archer Mystery Ser.). 1996. pap. 11.00 (*0-679-76807-6*) Random.
— The Chill: A Lew Archer Novel. large type ed. LC 95-7490. 436p. 1995. 21.95 (*0-7862-0461-3*) Thorndike Pr.
— The Doomsters. LC 79-63807. 1979. write for info. (*0-318-54004-5*) Knopf.
— The Drowning Pool. (Lew Archer Mystery Ser.). 1996. pap. 12.00 (*0-679-76806-8*) Random.
— The Galton Case. LC 97-118474. 1996. pap. 11.00 (*0-679-76864-5*) McKay.
— The Instant Enemy. LC 79-63807. 1979. write for info. (*0-318-54005-3*) Knopf.
***MacDonald, Ross, pseud.** The Ivory Grin. 192p. 1998. 19.50 (*0-7540-8519-8*, Black Dagger) Chivers N Amer.

An Asterisk (*) at the beginning of an entry indicates that the title is appearing for the first time.

MacDonald, Ross, pseud. Meet Me at the Morgue. 1984. mass mkt. 2.95 (*0-553-24033-1*) Bantam.

— The Moving Target. LC 97-47422. 245p. 1998. pap. 11.00 (*0-375-70146-X*) Vin Bks.

— Self-Portrait: Ceaselessly into the Past. Sipper, Ralph B., ed. LC 95-1610. (Brownstone Mystery Guides Ser.: Vol. 13). iv, 131p. 1995. pap. 19.00 (*0-941028-26-7*) Millefleurs.

— Sleeping Beauty. 23.95 (*0-89190-096-9*) Amereon Ltd.

— The Underground Man. 1984. mass mkt. 3.95 (*0-553-27183-0*) Bantam.

— The Underground Man. LC 97-120675. (SPA.). 1996. pap. 11.00 (*0-679-76808-4*) Vin Bks.

— The Wycherly Woman. 1984. mass mkt. 2.95 (*0-553-23855-8*) Bantam.

— The Wycherly Woman. LC 97-50178. 278p. 1998. pap. 11.00 (*0-375-70144-3*) Vin Bks.

— The Zebra-Striped Hearse. LC 97-47424. 278p. 1998. pap. 11.00 (*0-375-70145-1*) Vin Bks.

MacDonald, Ross, pseud, et al. Inward Journey. Sipper, Ralph B., ed. 176p. 1987. reprint ed. 8.95 (*0-89296-902-4*) Mysterious Pr.

MacDonald, Ruth K. Beatrix Potter. (English Authors Ser.: No. 422). 168p. 1986. 28.95 (*0-8057-6917-X*, Twyne) Mac Lib Ref.

— Christian's Children: The Influence of John Bunyan's The Pilgrim's Progress on American Children's Literature. (American University Studies: American Literature: Ser. XXIV, Vol. 10). XV, 208p. (C). 1989. text 35.10 (*0-8204-1003-9*) P Lang Pubng.

MacDonald, Ruth K. Literature for Children in England & America from 1646-1774. LC 81-52810. viii, 204p. 1982. 35.00 (*0-87875-227-7*) Whitston Pub.

MacDonald, Ruth K. Louisa May Alcott, No. 457. (United States Authors Ser.). 128p. 1983. 21.95 (*0-8057-7397-5*, Twayne) Mac Lib Ref.

— Shel Silverstein. LC 97-15204. (Twayne's United States Authors Ser.). 1997. 28.95 (*0-8057-1606-8*) Irvington.

Macdonald, S. & Roman, P. Research Advances in Alcohol & Drug Problems Vol. 11: Drug Testing in the Workplace. (Research Advances in Alcohol & Drug Problems: Vol. 11). (Illus.). 356p. (C). 1994. 100.00 (*0-306-44557-3*, Plenum Trade) Perseus Pubng.

MacDonald, S. C. Understanding Your Bible: An Introduction to Dispensationalism. (Illus.). 177p. (Orig.). 1995. pap. 10.95 (*0-912340-05-3*) Grace Bible Coll.

MacDonald, S. O., jt. auth. see Myhrman, Matts.

MacDonald, Sandra. Ben of Colonial Newport. (Geronimo Pack Ser.). 8p. (J). (gr. k-2). 1993. pap. write for info. (*1-882563-08-5*) Lamont Bks.

— Birds at the Sanctuary. (Birds Pack Ser.). 8p. (J). (gr. k-2). 1993. pap. write for info. (*1-882563-03-4*) Lamont Bks.

***Macdonald, Sandy.** Quick Escapes - Boston: 25 Weekend Getaways from the Hub. (Quick Escapes Ser.). (Illus.). 320p. 2000. pap. 15.95 (*0-7627-0708-9*) Globe Pequot.

Macdonald, Sandy. Toys R Us Toy Guide. LC 96-232651. 1996. mass mkt. 6.99 (*0-671-52598-0*) PB.

MacDonald, Scott. Avant-Garde Film: Motion Studies. LC 92-17446. (Cambridge Film Classics Ser.). (Illus.). 209p. (C). 1993. text 54.95 (*0-521-38129-0*); pap. text 15.95 (*0-521-38821-X*) Cambridge U Pr.

— A Critical Cinema 3: Interviews with Independent Filmmakers. (Illus.). 456p. 1998. pap. text 19.95 (*0-520-20943-5*, Pub. by U CA Pr) Cal Prin Full Svc.

— Critical Cinema Two: Interviews with Independent Filmmakers. 1992. pap. 19.95 (*0-520-07918-3*, Pub. by U CA Pr) Cal Prin Full Svc.

— A Critical Cinema 3: Interviews with Independent Filmmakers. (Illus.). 456p. 1998. 55.00 (*0-520-08705-4*, Pub. by U CA Pr) Cal Prin Full Svc.

Macdonald, Scott. Frames of Mind. (Illus.). 24p. 1986. pap. 1.00 (*0-915895-04-8*) Munson Williams.

MacDonald, Scott. The Global Debt Crisis: Forecasting the Future from Regional Perspectives. 256p. 1990. text 49.00 (*0-86187-742-X*) St Martin.

***Macdonald, Scott.** Rolling the Iron Dice: Historical Analogies & Decisions to Use Military Force in Regional Contingencies, 199. (Contributions in Military Studies Ser.: Vol. 199). 264p. 2000. 69.50 (*0-313-31421-7*, GM1421, Greenwood Pr) Greenwood.

MacDonald, Scott, ed. Being & Goodness: The Concept of Good in Metaphysics & Philosophical Theology. LC 90-55197. 336p. 1991. 49.95 (*0-8014-2312-0*); pap. text 17.95 (*0-8014-9779-5*) Cornell U Pr.

— Screen Writings: Scripts & Texts from Independent Filmmakers. LC 92-30429. 1994. 55.00 (*0-520-08024-6*, Pub. by U CA Pr); pap. 24.95 (*0-520-08025-4*, Pub. by U CA Pr) Cal Prin Full Svc.

MacDonald, Scott & Oden, Chester W., Jr. Moose: The Story of a Very Special Person. 2nd ed. 200p. (Orig.). (YA). (gr. 8 up). 1978. pap. 10.95 (*0-03-043936-1*) Brookline Bks.

MacDonald, Scott & Stump, Eleonore, eds. Aquinas's Moral Theory: Essays in Honor of Norman Kretzmann. LC 98-38623. (Illus.). 296p. 1998. 49.95 (*0-8014-3436-X*) Cornell U Pr.

MacDonald, Scott, jt. auth. see Coxeter, Harold.

MacDonald, Scott, jt. auth. see Fauriol, Georges A.

MacDonald, Scott A. Complete Job Finder's Guide for the 90's: Marketing Yourself in the New Job Market. 224p. 1993. pap. 13.95 (*0-942710-84-3*) Impact VA.

MacDonald, Scott B. Dancing on a Volcano: The Latin American Drug Trade. LC 88-9950. 177p. 1988. 42.95 (*0-275-92752-0*, C2752, Praeger Pubs); pap. 19.95 (*0-275-93105-6*, B3105, Praeger Pubs) Greenwood.

— European Destiny, Atlantic Transformations: Portuguese Foreign Policy under the Second Republic, 1974-1992. LC 92-20671. 192p. (C). 1992. 44.95 (*1-56000-078-3*) Transaction Pubs.

— Mountain High, White Avalanche: Cocaine & Power in the Andean States & Panama, 137. LC 88-39214. (Washington Papers: No. 137). (Illus.). 166p. 1989. 49.95 (*0-275-93234-6*, C3234, Praeger Pubs); pap. 13.95 (*0-275-93235-4*, B3235, Praeger Pubs) Greenwood.

— Trinidad & Tobago: Democracy & Development in the Caribbean. LC 86-639. 240p. 1986. 59.95 (*0-275-92004-6*, C2004, Praeger Pubs) Greenwood.

MacDonald, Scott B., et al, eds. The Caribbean after Grenada: Revolution, Conflict, & Democracy. LC 88-11986. 304p. 1988. 69.50 (*0-275-92722-9*, C2722, Praeger Pubs) Greenwood.

MacDonald, Scott B., et al, eds. Latin American Debt in the 1990s: Lessons from the Past & Forecasts for the Future. LC 91-2244. 168p. 1991. 52.95 (*0-275-93903-0*, C3903, Praeger Pubs) Greenwood.

MacDonald, Scott B. & Fauriol, Georges A. Fast Forward: Latin America on the Edge of the Twenty-First Century. LC 98-38648. 428p. 1999. pap. 29.95 (*0-7658-0495-6*) Transaction Pubs.

MacDonald, Scott B. & Fauriol, Georges A., eds. The Politics of the Caribbean Basin Sugar Trade. LC 90-20868. 176p. 1991. 52.95 (*0-275-93052-1*, C3052, Praeger Pubs) Greenwood.

MacDonald, Scott B. & Hughes, Jane E. New Tigers & Old Elephants: The Development Game in the 1990s & Beyond. LC 99-53931. 364p. 1999. pap. 29.95 (*0-7658-0633-9*) Transaction Pubs.

MacDonald, Scott B. & Zagaris, Bruce, eds. International Handbook on Drug Control. LC 91-35118. 463p. 1992. lib. bdg. 99.50 (*0-313-27375-8*, MHB/, Greenwood Pr) Greenwood.

MacDonald, Scott B., et al. New Tigers & Old Elephants: The Development Game in the 1990s & Beyond. LC 95-18142. 1995. 44.95 (*1-56000-204-2*) Transaction Pubs.

MacDonald, Sebastian, jt. ed. see Stuhlmueller, Carroll.

MacDonald, Sebastian K. Moral Theology & Suffering. LC 93-41341. (AUS VII: Vol. 171). XIV, 185p. (C). 1995. text 39.95 (*0-8204-2371-8*) P Lang Pubng.

MacDonald, Shane. Diary of a Broken Heart. LC 96-37677. 1996. pap. text 2.25 (*0-921411-51-0*) Genl Dist Srvs.

MacDonald, Shari. Diamonds. LC 96-47444. 235p. 1996. pap. 9.99 (*0-88070-982-0*, Palisades OR) Multnomah Pubs.

***MacDonald, Shari.** Love on the Run. LC 00-34720. 2000. write for info. (*0-7862-2708-7*) Five Star.

— Love on the Run. LC 98-231258. (Salinger Sisters Romantic Comedy Ser.: Bk. 1). 256p. 1998. pap. 6.95 (*1-57856-084-5*) Waterbrook Pr.

MacDonald, Shari. A Match Made in Heaven. (Salinger Sisters Romantic Comedy Ser.: Bk. 2). 256p. 1999. pap. 6.95 (*1-57856-137-X*) Waterbrook Pr.

— The Perfect Wife. LC 99-14976. (Salinger Sisters Romantic Comedy Ser.: Vol. 3). 256p. 1999. pap. 6.95 (*1-57856-138-8*) Waterbrook Pr.

— Sierra. 264p. 1995. pap. 9.99 (*0-88070-726-7*, Palisades OR) Multnomah Pubs.

— Stardust. LC 97-6687. 286p. 1997. pap. 9.99 (*1-57673-109-X*, Palisades OR) Multnomah Pubs.

— Stardust. large type ed. LC 98-54662. 1999. 23.95 (*0-7862-1806-1*) Thorndike Pr.

***Macdonald, Sharman.** After Juliet. (Connections Ser.). (Illus.). 112p. (YA). 2000. pap. 17.95 (*0-7487-4288-3*, Pub. by S Thornes Pubs) Trans-Atl Phila.

Macdonald, Sharman. Shades. 96p. (Orig.). 1993. pap. 8.95 (*0-571-16884-1*) Faber & Faber.

— Sharman Macdonald Plays, No. 1. 384p. (Orig.). 1995. pap. 14.95 (*0-571-17621-6*) Faber & Faber.

Macdonald, Sharman, jt. auth. see Rickman, Alan.

MacDonald, Sharon. Everyday Discoveries: Amazingly Easy Science & Math Using Stuff You Already Have. LC 98-17151. 246p. 1998. pap. 19.95 (*0-87659-196-9*) Gryphon Hse.

— The Politics of Display: Museums, Science & Culture. LC 97-3319. (Illus.). 264p. (C). 1998. 85.00 (*0-415-15325-5*); pap. 29.99 (*0-415-15326-3*) Routledge.

— Reimagining Culture. LC 98-115323. 297p. 1997. 55.00 (*1-85973-980-6*, Pub. by Berg Pubs); pap. 19.50 (*1-85973-985-7*, Pub. by Berg Pubs) NYU Pr.

— Squish, Sort, Paint, & Build: Over 200 Learning Center Activities. LC 96-9099. (Illus.). 127p. (Orig.). 1996. pap., teacher ed. 19.95 (*0-87659-180-2*) Gryphon Hse.

— We Learn All about Community Helpers. (J). (ps-1). 1988. pap. 7.99 (*0-8224-4599-9*) Fearon Teacher Aids.

— We Learn All about Dinosaurs. (J). (ps-1). 1988. pap. 7.99 (*0-8224-4595-6*) Fearon Teacher Aids.

— We Learn All about Endangered Species. 1992. pap. 9.99 (*0-86653-944-1*) Fearon Teacher Aids.

— We Learn All about Fall. (J). (ps-1). 1988. pap. 7.95 (*0-8224-4596-4*) Fearon Teacher Aids.

— We Learn All about Farms. (J). (ps-1). 1988. pap. 7.99 (*0-8224-4594-8*) Fearon Teacher Aids.

Macdonald, Sharon. We Learn All about Machines. 1991. 7.99 (*0-8224-4590-5*) Fearon Teacher Aids.

MacDonald, Sharon. We Learn All about Protecting Our Environment. 1992. pap. 9.99 (*0-86653-942-5*) Fearon Teacher Aids.

— We Learn All about Series, 9 bks., Set. (J). (ps-1). 55.99 (*1-56417-740-8*, FE0020) Fearon Teacher Aids.

Macdonald, Sharon. We Learn All about Spring. 1991. 7.99 (*0-8224-4591-3*) Fearon Teacher Aids.

MacDonald, Sharon. We Learn All about the Circus. (J). (ps-1). 1988. pap. 7.99 (*0-8224-4598-0*) Fearon Teacher Aids.

— We Learn All about the Earth's Habitats. 1992. pap. 9.99 (*0-86653-943-3*) Fearon Teacher Aids.

— We Learn All about the Environment Series, 3 bks., Set. (J). (ps-1). 25.99 (*1-56417-756-4*, FE7564) Fearon Teacher Aids.

Macdonald, Sharon. We Learn All about Transportation. 1991. 7.99 (*0-8224-4592-1*) Fearon Teacher Aids.

MacDonald, Sharon. We Learn All about Winter. (J). (ps-1). 1988. pap. 7.99 (*0-8224-4597-2*) Fearon Teacher Aids.

Macdonald, Sharon, et al, eds. Images of Women in Peace & War: Cross-Cultural & Historical Perspectives. LC 87-40518. 256p. (C). 1988. pap. text 14.95 (*0-299-11764-2*) U of Wis Pr.

— Inside European Identities: Ethnography in Western Europe. LC 92-14740. (Ethnicity & Identity Ser.). 224p. 1993. 49.50 (*0-85496-723-0*, Pub. by Berg Pubs); pap. 19.50 (*0-85496-888-1*, Pub. by Berg Pubs) NYU Pr.

MacDonald, Sharon & Fyfe, Gordon, eds. Theorizing Museums: Representing Identity & Diversity in a Changing World. LC 96-6174. (Sociological Review Monograph: No. 43). 1996. pap. 24.95 (*0-631-20151-3*) Blackwell Pubs.

MacDonald, Sheila & Mason, Chris. Otters: An Action Plan for Their Conservation. Foster-Turley, Pat et al, eds. (Illus.). 130p. (Orig.). 1991. pap. 20.00 (*2-8317-0013-2*, Pub. by IUCN) Island Pr.

MacDonald, Simon, ed. see Buckmaster, Charles.

Macdonald-Smith, Ian, photos by. Bermuda: Gardens & Houses. LC 95-48923. (Illus.). 204p. 1996. 50.00 (*0-8478-1930-2*, Pub. by Rizzoli Intl) St Martin.

Macdonald, Stephen C. A German Revolution: Local Change & Continuity in Prussia, 1918-1920. LC 91-12411. (Modern European History Outstanding Studies & Dissertations). 376p. 1991. text 20.00 (*0-8240-2544-X*) Garland.

MacDonald, Steve. Historic Warplanes. 1995. 6.98 (*0-7858-0337-8*) Bk Sales Inc.

***MacDonald, Steven.** Just Clowning Around: Two Stories. (Green Light Readers Ser.). (Illus.). 20p. (J). 2000. 10.95 (*0-15-202512-X*) Harcourt.

— Just Clowning Around: Two Stories. (Illus.). (J). 2000. 9.40 (*0-606-18180-6*) Turtleback.

***MacDonald, Steven & McPhail, David M.** Just Clowning Around. LC 99-6798. (Green Light Readers Ser.). (Illus.). 20p. (J). (gr. k-2). 2000. pap. 3.95 (*0-15-202518-9*, Harcourt Child Bks) Harcourt.

MacDonald, Steven A. Landlord-Tenant Solutions in California. 196p. 1999. 24.95 (*0-9654726-6-3*) Investment Pub.

MacDonald, Stuart. Information for Innovation: Managing Change from an Information Perspective. LC 97-18064. (Illus.). 306p. 1998. text 75.00 (*0-19-828825-5*) OUP.

***Macdonald, Stuart.** Information for Innovation: Managing Change from an Information Perspective. (Illus.). 312p. 2000. pap. 24.95 (*0-19-924147-3*) OUP.

MacDonald, Stuart & Madden, gary. Telecommunications & Socio-Economic Development. LC 98-18016. 1998. write for info. (*0-444-82648-3*) Elsevier.

Macdonald, Stuart & Nightingale, John. Information & Organization: A Tribute to the Work of Don Lamberton. LC 99-17587. 536p. 1999. 127.00 (*0-444-82886-9*, North Holland) Elsevier.

MacDonald, Sue, jt. auth. see Rossiter, Richard H.

MacDonald, Susan. Nanta's Lion: A Search-&-Find Adventure. LC 94-16634. (Illus.). 24p. (J). (ps up). 1995. 15.00 (*0-688-13125-5*, Wm Morrow) Morrow Avon.

MacDonald, Susan P. Anthony Trollope. (Twayne's English Authors Ser.: No. 441). 167p. 1987. 32.00 (*0-8057-6945-5*, TEAS 441, Twyne) Mac Lib Ref.

— Professional Academic Writing in the Humanities & Social Sciences. LC 93-11093. 256p. (C). 1994. 31.95 (*0-8093-1930-6*) S Ill U Pr.

MacDonald, Susan Priest, jt. auth. see MacDonald, Randall M.

MacDonald, Suse. Alphabatics. (J). 1998. pap. 6.95 (*0-87628-366-0*) Ctr Appl Res.

— Alphabatics. LC 85-31429. (Illus.). 64p. (J). (ps up). 1986. text, lib. bdg. 16.95 (*0-02-761520-0*, Bradbury S&S) S&S Childrens.

— Alphabatics. (J). 1992. 12.15 (*0-606-01991-X*, Pub. by Turtleback) Demco.

— Alphabatics. LC 91-38497. (Illus.). 56p. (J). (ps-1). 1992. reprint ed. mass mkt. 6.95 (*0-689-71625-7*) Aladdin.

— Award Puzzles: The Caldecott Collection - Alphabatics. (Illus.). 1992. 6.95 (*0-938971-71-9*) JTG Nashville.

— Elephants on Board. LC 98-13397. (Illus.). 32p. (J). 1999. 14.00 (*0-15-200951-5*) Harcourt.

***MacDonald, Suse.** Look Whooo's Counting. LC 99-87552. (Illus.). (J). (ps-1). 2000. 14.95 (*0-590-68320-9*) Scholastic Inc.

MacDonald, Suse. Peck, Slither & Slide. LC 96-18439. (Illus.). 48p. (ps-1). 1997. 15.00 (*0-15-200079-8*) Harcourt.

— Sea Shapes. LC 93-27957. (Illus.). 32p. (J). 1998. pap. 6.00 (*0-15-201700-3*, Harcourt Child Bks) Harcourt.

— Sea Shapes. 1998. 11.10 (*0-606-13765-3*, Pub. by Turtleback) Demco.

— Sea Shapes. abr. ed. LC 93-27957. (Illus.). 32p. (J). (ps-2). 1997. 13.95 (*0-15-200027-5*, Gulliver Bks) Harcourt.

MacDonald, T. C., ed. Immunology of Gastrointestinal Diseases. (Immunology & Medicine Ser.). (C). 1992. text 223.00 (*0-7923-8961-1*) Kluwer Academic.

MacDonald, T. C., et al, eds. Advances in Mucosal Immunology. (C). 1990. text 418.00 (*0-7462-0115-5*) Kluwer Academic.

Macdonald, Theodore. Ethnicity & Culture Amidst New "Neighbors" The Runa of Ecuador's Amazon Region. LC 99-230085. 176p. 1998. pap. 20.00 (*0-205-19821-X*) P-H.

MacDonald, Theodore. Rethinking Health Promotion: Global Approach. LC 97-41764. (Illus.). 248p. (C). 1998. 85.00 (*0-415-16474-5*) Routledge.

MacDonald, Theodore H., ed. A Developmental Analysis of Cuba's Health Care System since 1959. LC 99-22943. (Studies in Health & Human Services: Vol. 32). 13p. 1999. 99.95 (*0-7734-8049-8*) E Mellen.

MacDonald, Thomas T. Ontogeny of the Immune System of the Gut. 128p. 1990. lib. bdg. 142.00 (*0-8493-6084-6*, QR185) CRC Pr.

MacDonald, Thomas T., ed. Mucosal T Cells. (Chemical Immunology Ser.: Vol. 71 (1998)). (Illus.). xii, 242p. 1998. 208.75 (*3-8055-6722-7*) S Karger.

MacDonald, Thoreau. Thoreau MacDonald's Notebooks. Flood, John, ed. 224p. 1980. 14.95 (*0-920806-05-8*, Pub. by Penumbra Pr) U of Toronto Pr.

MacDonald, W. A. Trout Tales & Salmon Stories. 240p. 1993. per. 14.95 (*0-88982-121-6*, Pub. by Oolichan Bks) Genl Dist Srvs.

MacDonald, W. A., jt. auth. see Cameron, C.

Macdonald, W. C. Elder-Character & Duties. 1993. pap. 30.00 (*0-7152-0658-3*) St Mut.

MacDonald, W. D. Fraud on the Widow's Share. (Michigan Legal Publications). xviii, 477p. 1971. 47.50 (*1-57588-292-2*, 300910) W S Hein.

MacDonald, W. S., ed. Roll of Graduates of the University of Aberdeen, 1956-1970: With Supplement, 1860-1955. 1982. 70.00 (*0-08-028469-8*, Pergamon Pr) Elsevier.

Macdonald, Webster. Memoirs of a Maverick Lawyer. (Illus.). 237p. (Orig.). 1993. pap. 19.95 (*1-55059-068-5*) Temeron Bks.

MacDonald, Wilbert L. Pope & His Critics. LC 74-30369. (English Literature Ser.: No. 33). 1974. lib. bdg. 75.00 (*0-8383-1990-4*) M S G Haskell Hse.

MacDonald, William. The Architecture of the Roman Empire: An Urban Appraisal, Vol. 2. rev. ed. LC 81-16513. Vol. 2. 320p. (C). 1988. reprint ed. pap. 25.00 (*0-300-03470-9*) Yale U Pr.

— Be Holy: The Forgotten Command. 1996. pap. 10.99 (*0-946351-37-6*, Pub. by John Ritchie) Loizeaux.

— Believer's Bible Commentary: Old & New Testaments, 2 vols. Farstad, Arthur L., ed. & intro. by. LC 94-24086. 2464p. 1995. 39.99 (*0-8407-1972-8*) Nelson.

— Las Buenas Nuevas. Orig. Title: Good News. (SPA.). 96p. 1972. pap. 3.99 (*0-8254-1451-2*, Edit Portavoz) Kregel.

— Christ Loved the Church. 1956. pap. 6.50 (*0-937396-09-5*) Walterick Pubs.

— Cual Es la Diferencia? Orig. Title: What Is the Difference?. (SPA.). 112p. 1981. mass mkt. 3.99 (*0-8254-1450-4*, Edit Portavoz) Kregel.

— Enjoying Ecclesiastes. 1988. pap. 6.00 (*0-937396-07-9*) Walterick Pubs.

— Enjoying the Proverbs. 1982. pap. 6.00 (*0-937396-23-0*) Walterick Pubs.

— Ephesians. 1988. pap. 6.00 (*0-937396-74-5*) Walterick Pubs.

— First Peter. 1988. pap. 6.00 (*0-937396-75-3*) Walterick Pubs.

— First Steps to Discovering God. (Christian Life Application Ser.). 1995. pap. 7.99 (*1-56570-054-6*) Meridian MI.

MacDonald, William. George Washington: A Brief Biography. 2nd ed. LC 87-34823. (Illus.). 40p. 1987. pap. 2.00 (*0-931917-14-X*) Mt Vernon Ladies.

MacDonald, William. God's Answers to Man's Questions. 1958. pap. 3.00 (*0-937396-16-8*) Walterick Pubs.

— Grace of God. 1960. pap. 3.00 (*0-937396-18-4*) Walterick Pubs.

— Grasping for Shadows. 1972. pap. 3.00 (*0-937396-19-2*) Walterick Pubs.

— Here's the Difference. 1975. pap. 6.00 (*0-937396-55-9*) Walterick Pubs.

— Here's the Difference: A Study of Important Biblical Distinctives. Orig. Title: What's the Difference. 1998. pap. 11.99 (*1-882701-45-3*) Uplook Min.

— Jacksonian Democracy, 1829-37. LC 74-169921. reprint ed. 42.50 (*0-404-04126-4*) AMS Pr.

— Let Me Introduce You to the Bible. 1980. pap. 4.00 (*0-937396-22-2*) Walterick Pubs.

— Lord, Break Me. 1972. pap. 3.00 (*0-937396-24-9*) Walterick Pubs.

Macdonald, William. Mandamiento Olvidado: Sed Santos. 176p. 1997. pap. 8.99 (*0-8254-1460-1*) Kregel.

MacDonald, William. Matthew: Behold Your King. 1988. pap. 9.00 (*0-937396-26-5*) Walterick Pubs.

— My Heart, My Life, My All: Love's Response: A Living Sacrifice. 1997. pap. 8.95 (*1-882701-44-5*) Uplook Min.

— Now That Is Amazing Grace. 96p. (Orig.). 1995. pap. 3.95 (*1-882701-21-6*) Uplook Min.

— Old Testament Digest Vol. 3: Job-Malachi. 1981. pap. 7.95 (*0-937396-29-X*) Walterick Pubs.

— Once in Christ in Christ Forever: More Than 100 Biblical Reasons Why a True Believer Cannot Be Lost. 1997. pap. 10.95 (*1-882701-43-7*) Uplook Min.

— One Day at a Time. 2nd ed. 1998. reprint ed. 24.99 (*1-882701-48-8*) Uplook Min.

***MacDonald, William.** Our God Is Wonderful. 154p. 1999. pap. 7.99 (*1-882701-60-7*, Gospel Folio Pr) Uplook Min.

— Ranger Man. 1999. 19.00 (*0-7540-8080-3*) Chivers N Amer.

MacDonald, William. Second Peter & Jude. 1988. pap. 6.00 (*0-937396-77-X*) Walterick Pubs.

— Seek Ye First. 1972. pap. 3.00 (*0-937396-38-9*) Walterick Pubs.

— That's a Good Question. 30p. (Orig.). 1995. pap. 1.50 (*1-884838-02-2*) Walterick Pubs.

— There's a Way Back to God. 1986. reprint ed. pap. 3.00 (*0-937396-42-7*) Walterick Pubs.

— Think of Your Future. 1956. pap. 3.00 (*0-937396-44-3*) Walterick Pubs.

— To What Should We Be Loyal. 1981. pap. 3.00 (*0-937396-47-8*) Walterick Pubs.

— True Discipleship. 1975. pap. 6.50 (*0-937396-50-8*) Walterick Pubs.

— Winning Souls the Bible Way. 1988. pap. 6.00 (*0-937396-56-7*) Walterick Pubs.

M

An Asterisk (*) at the beginning of an entry indicates that the title is appearing for the first time.

— The Wonders of God. 122p. (Orig.). 1996. pap. 7.95 (*1-882701-25-9*) Uplook Min.

— Worlds Apart. 76p. (Orig.). 1993. pap. 4.95 (*1-882701-05-4*) Uplook Min.

MacDonald, William, ed. Select Charters & Other Documents: Illustrative of American History, 1606-1775. (Illus.). ix, 401p. 1993. reprint ed. 52.00 (*0-8377-2443-0*, Rothman) W S Hein.

***MacDonald, William & Farstad, Arthur L.** Enjoy Your Bible: Practical Pointers to Make Your Bible Study a Pleasure. 124p. 1999. pap. 6.99 (*1-882701-58-5*, Gospel Folio Pr) Uplook Min.

MacDonald, William & Farstad, Arthur L., eds. Believer's Bible Commentary New Testament. 1205p. 1989. 24.95 (*0-945681-00-3*) A&O Pr.

MacDonald, William & Hamel, Mike. Old Testament Digest: Gen-Deut., Vol. 1. 1981. pap. 7.95 (*0-937396-59-1*) Walterick Pubs.

— Old Testament Digest Vol. 2: Joshua-Esther. 1982. pap. 7.95 (*0-937396-61-3*) Walterick Pubs.

MacDonald, William B. Sketch of Coptic Grammar: Adapted for Self-Tuition. 1987. reprint ed. pap. 12.95 (*0-89979-047-X*) British Am Bks.

***MacDonald, William C.** Alias Dix Ryder. large type ed. LC 99-41714. (Thorndike Western Ser.). 1999. 20.95 (*0-7862-2193-3*) Thorndike Pr.

MacDonald, William C. The Comanche Scalp: A Gregory Quist Story. large type ed. LC 97-47175. 1998. 18.95 (*0-7862-1351-5*) Thorndike Pr.

— Powdersmoke Range. large type ed. LC 96-48190. (Nightingale Ser.). 283p. 1997. lib. bdg. 17.95 (*0-7838-2048-8*, G K Hall Lrg Type) Mac Lib Ref.

— Restless Guns. large type ed. LC 94-35253. 300p. 1995. pap. 16.95 (*0-7838-1148-9*, G K Hall Lrg Type) Mac Lib Ref.

— The Shadow Rider. 1996. 17.50 (*0-7451-4697-X*, Gunsmoke) Chivers N Amer.

— Sunrise Guns. large type ed. LC 94-33672. (Nightingale Ser.). 264p. 1995. pap. 16.95 (*0-7838-1151-9*, G K Hall Lrg Type) Mac Lib Ref.

***MacDonald, William Colt.** Blind Cartridges. large type ed. LC 99-58226. (Paperback Ser.). 2000. pap. 23.95 (*0-7838-8937-2*, G K Hall Lrg Type) Mac Lib Ref.

MacDonald, William Colt. Ridin' Through. large type ed. LC 98-33774. 228p. 1999. write for info. (*0-7540-3538-7*) Chivers N Amer.

— Ridin' Through. large type ed. LC 98-33774. 1999. 30.00 (*0-7838-0357-5*, G K Hall Lrg Type) Mac Lib Ref.

MacDonald, William G. Greek Enchiridion: A Concise Handbook of Grammar for Translation & Exegesis. 218p. 1986. spiral bd. 14.95 (*0-913573-18-3*) Hendrickson MA.

Macdonald, William K. Digging for Gold: Papers on Archaeology for Profit. (Technical Reports Ser.: No. 5). 1976. pap. 2.00 (*0-932206-14-X*) U Mich Mus Anthro.

MacDonald, William L. The Architecture of the Roman Empire: An Introductory Study. rev. ed. LC 81-16513. (Publications in the History of Art: No. 17). (Illus.). 372p. 1982. pap. 25.00 (*0-300-02819-9*, Y-429) Yale U Pr.

— Early Christian & Byzantine Architecture. LC 62-7531. (Great Ages of World Architecture Ser.). 128p. 1965. pap. 10.95 (*0-8076-0338-4*) Braziller.

— The Pantheon: Design, Meaning & Progeny. (Harvard Paperbacks Ser.). (Illus.). 160p. (C). 1976. pap. text 15.95 (*0-674-65346-7*) HUP.

— Piranesi's Carceri: Sources of Invention. (Illus.). 18p. (Orig.). (C). 1979. pap. 5.00 (*1-880269-01-5*) D H Sheehan.

MacDonald, William L. & Pinto, John A. Hadrian's Villa & Its Legacy. LC 94-28183. 1995. 60.00 (*0-300-05381-9*) Yale U Pr.

Macdonald, William W. The Making of an English Revolutionary: The Early Parliamentary Career of John Pym. LC 80-65867. 208p. 1982. 32.50 (*0-8386-3018-9*) Fairleigh Dickinson.

***MacDonald, Ziggy & Pyle, David J.** Illicit Activity: The Economics of Crime, Drugs & Tax Fraud. LC 00-44165. 2000. write for info. (*0-7546-2047-6*, Pub. by Ashgate Pub) Ashgate Pub Co.

Macdonell, A., jt. auth. see Martin, W.

Macdonell, A. A. India's Past: A Survey of Her Literature, Religions, Languages & Antiquities. (C). 1995. reprint ed. 28.00 (*81-206-0570-5*, Pub. by Asian Educ Servs) S Asia.

***Macdonell, A. A.** Vedic Grammar. 2nd ed. (Illus.). 2000. reprint ed. 44.50 (*81-215-0946-7*, Pub. by M Manoharial) S Asia.

Macdonell, A. A. Vedic Mythology. (C). 1995. reprint ed. 19.50 (*81-208-1113-5*, Pub. by Motilal Bnarsidass) S Asia.

***Macdonell, A. A.** Vedic Mythology. 2nd ed. 2000. reprint ed. 24.00 (*81-215-0949-1*, Pub. by M Manoharial) S Asia.

Macdonell, A. G. Napoleon & His Marshals: Prion Lost Treasures. 325p. 1997. pap. 16.95 (*1-85375-222-3*) Prion.

Macdonell, Annie. Thomas Hardy. LC 77-148276. reprint ed. 36.00 (*0-404-08885-6*) AMS Pr.

Macdonell, Arthur A. Brhad Devata, 2 pts. (C). 1994. text 44.00 (*81-208-1141-0*, Pub. by Motilal Bnarsidass) S Asia.

MacDonell, Arthur A. History of Sanskrit Literature. 472p. reprint ed. text 34.00 (*0-685-13411-3*) Coronet Bks.

— History of Sanskrit Literature. LC 68-24966. (Studies in Comparative Literature: No. 35). 1969. reprint ed. lib. bdg. 75.00 (*0-8383-0211-4*) M S G Haskell Hse.

— Practical Sanskrit Dictionary. (C). 1996. 46.00 (*81-215-0715-4*, Pub. by M Manoharial) Coronet Bks.

Macdonell, Arthur A. A Sanskrit Grammar for Students. (SAN.). (C). 1997. 13.00 (*81-246-0094-5*, Pub. by DK Pubs Ind); pap. 9.00 (*81-246-0095-3*, Pub. by DK Pubs Ind) S Asia.

— Sanskrit Grammar for Students. (C). 12.50 (*81-208-0504-6*, Pub. by Motilal Bnarsidass); pap. 8.50 (*81-208-0505-4*, Pub. by Motilal Bnarsidass) S Asia.

— A Sanskrit Grammar for Students. 3rd ed. 284p. 1986. pap. text 35.00 (*0-19-815466-6*) OUP.

MacDonell, Arthur A. Vedic Mythology. 1973. 300.00 (*0-87968-153-5*) Gordon Pr.

Macdonell, Arthur A. A Vedic Reader for Students. 296p. 1992. pap. 14.95 (*0-19-560038-X*) OUP.

— Vedic Reader for Students: Containing Thirty Hymns of the Rigveda in the Original Samhita & Pada Texts, with Transliteration, Translation, Explanatory Notes, Introduction, Vocabulary. (C). 1992. reprint ed. text 18.00 (*81-208-1017-1*, Pub. by Motilal Bnarsidass); reprint ed. pap. text 12.00 (*81-208-1018-X*, Pub. by Motilal Bnarsidass) S Asia.

MacDonell, John & Manson, Edward, eds. Great Jurists of the World, 1914. LC 97-8298. (Illus.). xxxii, 607p. 1997. reprint ed. 95.00 (*1-886363-28-5*) Lawbk Exchange.

***Macdonell, John, et al.** Early Fur Trade on the Northern Plains: Canadian Traders among the Mandan & Hidatsa Indians, 1738-1818; The Narratives of John Macdonell, David Thompson, Francois-Antoine Larocque & Charles McKenzie. Wood, W. Raymond & Thiessen, Thomas D., eds. (The American Exploration & Travel Ser.: Vol. 68). (Illus.). 376p. 1999. pap. 26.95 (*0-8061-3198-5*) U of Okla Pr.

Macdonell, Richard, jt. auth. see Georgiades, Nick.

MacDonnel, Anna. Margery Nahl: California Impressionist. (Illus.). 140p. 1994. 37.50 (*0-9640481-0-8*) M W Morse.

Macdonnell, Anna M. Ting Shao Kuang. (Illus.). 192p. 1989. text 100.00 (*0-685-27816-6*) Segal Fine Art.

Macdonnell, Arthur A. The Brhad-Devata, Attributed to Saunaka: A Summary of the Deities & Myths of the RgVeda, Vols. 5-6. (Harvard Oriental Ser.). (C). 1965. 27.50 (*0-8364-2357-7*, Pub. by Motilal Bnarsidass) S Asia.

— A History of Sanskrit Literature. vi, 406p. 1990. reprint ed. 16.00 (*81-208-0035-4*, Pub. by Motilal Bnarsidass) S Asia.

MacDonnell, Arthur A. Practical Sanskrit Dictionary: With Transliteration Accentuation & Etymological Analysis Throughout. (SAN.). 396p. 1984. reprint ed. text 95.00 (*0-19-864303-9*) OUP.

MacDonnell, Francis. Insidious Foes: The Axis Fifth Column & the American Home Front. (Illus.). 264p. 1995. 49.95 (*0-19-509268-6*) OUP.

MacDonnell, Hector. The Wild Geese of the Antrim MacDonnells. 176p. 1999. text 37.50 (*0-7165-2609-3*, Pub. by Irish Acad Pr) Intl Spec Bk.

Macdonnell, John. Historical Trials. Lee, R. W., ed. xvi, 234p. 1983. reprint ed. 37.50 (*0-8377-0848-6*, Rothman) W S Hein.

***Macdonnell, John.** Law of Master & Servant, 1 vol. xxxiv, 717p. 2000. reprint ed. 188.00 (*1-56169-628-5*) Gaunt.

MacDonnell, John D. King Leopold Second: His Rule in Belgium & the Congo. (Illus.). 1970. reprint ed. 17.50 (*0-87266-041-9*) Argosy.

MacDonnell, Joseph. Gospel Illustrations: A Reproduction of the 153 Images Taken from Jerome Nadal's 1595 Book, Adnotationes et Meditationes in Evangelia. (Illus.). 171p. 1998. pap. 20.00 (*0-9657731-2-4*) Clavius Grp.

— Jesuit Geometers: A Study of Fifty-Six Prominent Jesuit Geometers During the First Two Centuries of Jesuit History. LC 89-80568. (Studies on Jesuit Topics IV: No. 11). (Illus.). iv, 106p. 1989. pap. 8.00 (*0-912422-94-7*) Inst Jesuit.

MacDonnell, Joseph F. Galerie Illustree Revisited: Alfred Hamy's 405 Jesuit Portraits. LC 97-77118. (FRE., Illus.). 130p. 1998. pap. 35.00 (*0-9657731-1-6*) Clavius Grp.

— Jesuit Family Album: Sketches of Chivalry from the Early Society. Ryan, Joseph, ed. LC 97-66543. (Illus.). xiv, 222p. (Orig.). 1997. pap. 10.00 (*0-9657731-0-8*) Clavius Grp.

Macdonnell, Justin. Fifty Years in the Bush: A History of the Arts Council of NSW. (Illus.). 1997. pap. 29.95 (*0-86819-521-9*, Pub. by Currency Pr) Accents Pubns.

MacDonnell, Kenneth F. & Segal, Maurice S. Current Respiratory Care. 489p. 1977. pap. text 15.95 (*0-316-54191-5*, Little Brwn Med Div) Lppncott W & W.

MacDonnell, Kenneth F., et al. Respiratory Intensive Care. 478p. 1987. 100.00 (*0-316-54193-1*, Little Brwn Med Div) Lppncott W & W.

***MacDonnell, Lawrence J.** From Reclamation to Sustainability: Water, Agriculture, & the Environment in the American West. LC 99-41006. (Illus.). 344p. 1999. 34.95 (*0-87081-533-4*) Univ Pr Colo.

MacDonnell, Lawrence J. & Bates, Sarah F., eds. Natural Resources Policy & Law: Trends & Directions. LC 93-8388. 280p. 1993. text 45.00 (*1-55963-245-3*); pap. text 25.00 (*1-55963-246-1*) Island Pr.

MacDonnell, Margaret & Shaw, John, eds. Luirgean Eachainn Nill: Folktales from Cape Breton. 1985. 35.00 (*0-86152-086-6*, Pub. by Acair Ltd); pap. 25.00 (*0-7855-1321-3*, Pub. by Acair Ltd) St Mut.

***MacDonnell, Michele.** Health & Well-being. 64p. 2000. pap. 6.95 (*1-84215-123-1*) Anness Pub.

MacDonnell, Ray, jt. auth. see MacNamee, Brian.

MacDonogh. Berlin. 544p. 1999. pap. 18.95 (*0-312-24437-1*) St Martin.

MacDonogh, Giles. Brillat-Savarin: The Judge & His Stomach. LC 93-13879. 256p. 1993. text 27.50 (*1-56663-028-2*) I R Dee.

***MacDonogh, Giles.** Frederick the Great: A Life in Deed & Letters. (Illus.). 464p. 2000. text 27.95 (*0-312-25318-4*) St Martin.

Macdonogh, Giles. A Good German: Adam von Trott zu Solz. (Illus.). 358p. 1992. 25.00 (*0-87951-449-3*, Pub. by Overlook Pr) Penguin Putnam.

MacDonogh, Giles. A Good German: Adam von Trott Zu Solz. 368p. 1993. pap. 13.95 (*0-87951-496-5*, Pub. by Overlook Pr) Penguin Putnam.

— Prussia. Date not set. pap. 12.99 (*0-7493-2435-X*) Heinemann.

***MacDonogh, Katharine.** Reigning Cats & Dogs: A History of Pets at Court Since the Renaissance. LC 99-37440. (Illus.). 288p. 1999. text 26.95 (*0-312-22837-6*) St Martin.

***MacDonogh, Steve.** Open Book: One Publisher's War. (Illus.). 288p. 1999. pap. 18.95 (*0-86322-263-3*, Pub. by Brandon Bk Pubs) Irish Bks Media.

— The Story of Irish Dance. (Illus.). 256p. 1999. pap. 31.95 (*0-86322-244-7*, Pub. by Brandon Bk Pubs) Irish Bks Media.

MacDonogh, Steve, ed. The Rushdie Letters: Freedom to Speak, Freedom to Write. LC 92-46585. (Stages Ser.). 190p. (C). 1993. pap. text 9.95 (*0-8032-8198-6*, Bison Books) U of Nebr Pr.

MacDonough, Glen, jt. auth. see Herbert, Victor.

MacDonough, R. MacDonough-Hackstaff Ancestry. (Illus.). 526p. 1989. reprint ed. pap. 79.00 (*0-8328-0847-4*); reprint ed. lib. bdg. 87.00 (*0-8328-0846-6*) Higginson Bk Co.

MacDorman, John, jt. auth. see Leary, Brian.

MacDorman, Marian F., jt. auth. see Pastore, Lisa M.

MacDougal, Bonnie. Angle of Impact. LC 97-18183. 355p. 1998. 24.00 (*0-345-41445-4*) Ballantine Pub Grp.

Macdougal, Bonnie. Angle of Impact. 1999. mass mkt. 6.99 (*0-345-41446-2*) Ballantine Pub Grp.

MacDougal, Bonnie. Breach of Trust. 384p. 1996. 23.00 (*0-671-53720-2*, PB Hardcover) PB.

Macdougal, Bonnie. Breach of Trust. 1998. per. 6.99 (*0-671-53719-9*) PB.

— Out of Order. LC 99-13477. 1999. 24.50 (*0-345-43444-7*) Ballantine Pub Grp.

***MacDougal, Bonnie.** Out of Order. 2000. mass mkt. 6.99 (*0-345-43445-5*) Ballantine Pub Grp.

MacDougal, Dennis. In the Best of Families: The Anatomy of a True Tragedy. 360p. 1996. mass mkt. 7.50 (*0-446-60235-3*, Pub. by Warner Bks) Little.

***MacDougal, Gary.** Make a Difference: How One Man Helped to Solve America's Poverty Problem. LC 99-55710. 368p. 2000. text 29.95 (*0-312-25223-4*, Thomas Dunne) St Martin.

MacDougal, John M. Revision of Passiflora Subgenus Decaloba Section Pseudodysosmia (Passifloraceae) Anderson, Christiane, ed. (Systematic Botany Monographs: Vol. 41). (Illus.). 146p. 1994. pap. 19.00 (*0-912861-41-X*) Am Soc Plant.

MacDougal, P. Paullette. Two Husbands in Heaven. 76p. 1998. pap. 5.60 (*0-87129-825-2*, TA7) Dramatic Pub.

***MacDougall, Alan.** Inland Sailing. rev. ed. (Illus.). 96p. 2000. reprint ed. per. 12.95 (*1-884898-19-X*) Eden Pubng OR.

— Jokers Wild: The Las Vegas Scene. (Illus.). 64p. 2000. per. 10.95 (*1-884898-15-7*) Eden Pubng OR.

MacDougall, Alan F. & Chaney, Michael. Security & Crime Prevention in Libraries. 250p. 1992. 86.95 (*1-85742-014-4*, Pub. by Gower) Ashgate Pub Co.

MacDougall, Alan F. & Prytherch, Raymond John. Cooperative Training in Libraries. (Illus.). 289p. 1990. text 74.95 (*0-566-05709-3*, Pub. by Gower) Ashgate Pub Co.

— Handbook of Library Co-Operation. 300p. 1991. text 78.95 (*0-566-03627-4*, Pub. by Gower) Ashgate Pub Co.

***Macdougall, Alan Scott.** Poetry Grand Slam Finale. Dan, Barbara G., ed. LC 99-97407. (Illus.). 164p. 2000. pap. 19.95 (*1-884898-09-2*) Eden Pubng OR.

MacDougall, Alice F. The Autobiography of a Business Woman. Baxter, Annette K., ed. LC 79-8800. (Signal Lives Ser.). (Illus.). 1980. reprint ed. lib. bdg. 26.95 (*0-405-12847-9*) Ayer.

MacDougall, Arthur R. If It Returns with Scars: Dud Dean Stories. LC 81-9293. 1981. reprint ed. 5.95 (*0-89621-065-0*) Thorndike Pr.

MacDougall, B. R., et al, eds. Proceedings of the Symposium on Oxide Films on Metals & Alloys. LC 92-74173. (Proceedings Ser.: Vol. 92-22). 624p. 1992. 55.00 (*1-56677-023-8*) Electrochem Soc.

MacDougall, Carl. The Devil & the Giro: Two Centuries of Scottish Stories. LC 90-103334. 568 p. 1989. write for info. (*0-86241-207-2*) Canongate Books.

MacDougall, Carl, ed. The Devil & the Giro: The Scottish Short Story. 732p. 1996. pap. 14.95 (*0-86241-359-1*, Pub. by Canongate Books) Interlink Pub.

MacDougall, Curtis D. Reporters Report Reporters. LC 68-15283. (Illus.). 193p. reprint ed. pap. 59.90 (*0-608-18767-4*, 202978100065) Bks Demand.

— Superstition & the Press. LC 83-61115. (Science & the Paranormal Ser.). 628p. 1983. 41.95 (*0-87975-211-4*); pap. 26.95 (*0-87975-212-2*) Prometheus Bks.

MacDougall, David & Taylor, Lucien. Transcultural Cinema. LC 98-21197. 528p. 1998. text 59.50 (*0-691-01235-0*, Pub. by Princeton U Pr); pap. text 18.95 (*0-691-01234-2*, Pub. by Princeton U Pr) Cal Prin Full Svc.

MacDougall, Edward B. Computer Programming for Spatial Problems. LC 77-368680. vii, 160p. 1976. write for info. (*0-7131-5865-4*) Arnld Pub.

— Computer Programming for Spatial Problems. LC 76-46976. vii, 158p. 1976. write for info. (*0-470-99011-2*) Halsted Pr.

MacDougall, Elisabeth B. Fountains, Statues & Flowers: Studies in Italian Gardens of the Sixteenth & Seventeenth Centuries. LC 93-9546. (Illus.). 356p. 1994. 50.00 (*0-88402-216-1*) Dumbarton Oaks.

MacDougall, Elisabeth B., ed. Medieval Gardens. LC 85-29343. (Colloquium on the History of Landscape Architecture Ser.: No. 9). (Illus.). 352p. 1986. 35.00 (*0-88402-146-7*) Dumbarton Oaks.

MacDougall, Elisabeth B. & Jashemski, Wilhelmina F., eds. Ancient Roman Gardens. LC 81-4510. (Colloquium on the History of Landscape Architecture Ser.: No. 7). (Illus.). 212p. 1981. 22.00 (*0-88402-100-9*) Dumbarton Oaks.

— Ancient Roman Villa Gardens. LC 86-24255. (Dumbarton Oaks Colloquium on the History of Landscape Architecture Ser.: No. 10). (Illus.). 268p. 1987. 36.00 (*0-88402-162-9*, MAVG) Dumbarton Oaks.

MacDougall, Elisabeth B., jt. ed. see Tatum, George B.

MacDougall, Hamilton C. Early New England Psalmody: An Historical Appreciation, 1620-1820. LC 79-87398. (Music Reprint Ser.). 1969. reprint ed. lib. bdg. 29.50 (*0-306-71542-2*) Da Capo.

MacDougall, Hugh A. Racial Myth in English History: Trogans, Teutons, & Anglo-Saxons. LC 81-69941. 156p. Date not set. reprint ed. pap. 48.40 (*0-608-20684-9*, 207179100002) Bks Demand.

MacDougall, Ian. Voices from the Hunger Marches, Vol. II. 11.99 (*0-7486-6101-8*, Pub. by Polygon) Subterranean Co.

— Voices from War. 416p. 1997. pap. 65.00 (*1-873644-45-0*, Pub. by Mercat Pr Bks) St Mut.

MacDougall, J. A. & Koerner, Robert M., eds. Elements of Briquetting & Agglomeration No. II. 171p. 40.00 (*0-318-17372-7*) Inst Briquetting.

MacDougall, J. D. A Short History of Planet Earth: Mountains, Mammals, Fire, & Ice. LC 95-46399. (Illus.). 272p. 1996. 24.95 (*0-471-14805-9*) Wiley.

— A Short History of Planet Earth: Mountains, Mammals, Fire & Ice. 266p. 1998. pap. 15.99 (*0-471-19703-3*) Wiley.

MacDougall, J. Duncan, et al, eds. Physiological Testing of the High-Performance Athlete. 2nd ed. LC 90-35488. 448p. (C). 1990. text 46.00 (*0-87322-300-4*, BMAC0300) Human Kinetics.

MacDougall, James. Folk Tales & Fairy Lore in Gaelic & English: Collected from Oral Tradition. Dorsen, Richard M., ed. LC 77-70587. (International Folklore Ser.). 1977. reprint ed. lib. bdg. 28.95 (*0-405-10106-6*) Ayer.

MacDougall, James, ed. Folk & Hero Tales. LC 75-144456. (Waifs & Strays of Celtic Tradition: Argyllshire Ser.: No. 3). (Illus.). reprint ed. 41.50 (*0-404-53533-X*) AMS Pr.

***MacDougall, Jane & Jennings, Madeleine, eds.** Pregnancy Week-by-Week: Everything You Need to Know about Yourself & Your Developing Baby. (Illus.). 96p. 2000. reprint ed. pap. 17.00 (*0-7881-9247-7*) DIANE Pub.

MacDougall, Jean. Highland Postbag: Correspondence of Four MacDougal Chiefs 1715-1865. (Illus.). 304p. 1985. 22.50 (*0-85683-071-2*, Pub. by Shepheard-Walwyn Pubs) Paul & Co Pubs.

MacDougall, Jennifer, jt. auth. see Kinnell-Evans, Margaret.

MacDougall, Jill & Yoder, P. Stanley, eds. Contaminating Theatre: Intersections of Theatre, Therapy, & Public Health. LC 98-7121. (Psychosocial Issues Ser.). (Illus.). 256p. 1998. pap. text 19.95 (*0-8101-1535-2*) Northwestern U Pr.

MacDougall, Jill, tr. see Bonal, Denise, et al.

MacDougall, Jill, tr. see Farhoud, Abla, et al.

MacDougall, Jill, tr. see Micone, Marco.

MacDougall, Jill R. Performing Identities on the States of Quebec. LC 95-22893. (Francophone Cultures & Literatures Ser.: Vol. 15). (Illus.). X, 231p. (C). 1998. text 47.95 (*0-8204-3004-8*) P Lang Pubng.

MacDougall, Jill R. & Yoder, P. Stanley, eds. Contaminating Theatre: Intersections of Theatre, Therapy, & Public Health. LC 98-7121. (Psychosocial Issues Ser.). (Illus.). 256p. 1998. 89.95 (*0-8101-1534-4*) Northwestern U Pr.

MacDougall, John. Land or Religion? The Sardar & Kherwar Movements in Bihar, 1858-1895. 1986. 27.00 (*0-8364-1591-4*, Pub. by Manohar) S Asia.

MacDougall, Margaret O. The Clan MacKay. (Johnston & Bacon Clan Histories Ser.). (Illus.). 32p. 1993. reprint ed. pap. 8.95 (*0-8063-5014-8*, 9614) Clearfield Co.

MacDougall, Mary K. Se Sano Ahora! rev. ed. LC 93-61519. (SPA.). 292p. 1994. 12.95 (*0-87159-195-2*) Unity Bks.

MacDougall, Mary Katheine. Dear Me, I Love You. 176p. (Orig.). 1986. pap. 9.95 (*0-940175-00-2*) Now Comns.

MacDougall, Mary-Katherine. Black Jupiter. Gruver, Kate E., ed. (Illus.). 181p. (YA). (gr. 5 up). 1983. 8.95 (*0-940175-01-0*) Now Comns.

MacDougall, Mary Katherine. Dear Friend, I Love You. 176p. (Orig.). 1986. pap. 9.95 (*0-87707-226-4*) Now Comns.

MacDougall, Mary-Katherine. Making Love Happen. Liepa, Alex, ed. 236p. 1980. 8.95 (*0-940175-02-9*) Now Comns.

MacDougall, Norman. Scotland & War. 232p. 1991. text 66.00 (*0-685-58963-3*) B&N Imports.

— Scotland & War, AD 79-1918. 200p. (C). 1997. text 50.00 (*0-85976-248-3*, Pub. by J Donald) St Mut.

MacDougall, Pauleena M., ed. see Chaney, Michael.

MacDougall, Pauleena M., ed. see McKenna, Joseph.

MacDougall, Phillip. Royal Dockyards. (Album Ser.: No. 231). (Illus.). 32p. 1989. pap. 6.25 (*0-7478-0033-2*, Pub. by Shire Pubns) Parkwest Pubns.

MacDougall, Ranald & Cain, James M. Mildred Pierce. LaValley, Albert J., ed. LC 80-5107. (Warner Bros. Screenplay Ser.). (Illus.). 264p. 1980. 14.95 (*0-299-08370-5*) U of Wis Pr.

An Asterisk (*) at the beginning of an entry indicates that the title is appearing for the first time.

MacDougall, Ruth D. The Cheerleader. LC 98-92550. 288p. 1998. reprint ed. pap. 12.95 (*0-9663352-0-1*) Frigate Bks.

***Macdougall, Ruth D.** The Cost of Living. 2000. per. 95.76 (*0-671-78359-9*, Pocket Books) PB.

MacDougall, Ruth D., jt. auth. see Doan, Daniel.

MacDougall, Ruth D., ed. see Doan, Daniel.

***MacDougall, Stewart.** Find Your Swing: Stewart MacDougall's Golf Book. 2nd rev. ed. (Illus.). 96p. 1999. 19.00 (*0-9669811-1-1*) MacDougall & Co Inc.

— Stewart MacDougall's Complete Instruction Book "No-Swing Golf Swing" Golf: Autumn. (Illus.). 144p. 1999. 19.00 (*0-9669811-0-3*) MacDougall & Co Inc.

MacDougall, Terry E., ed. Political Leadership in Contemporary Japan. LC 82-9634. (Michigan Papers in Japanese Studies: No. 1). xiv, 146p. 1982. pap. 7.00 (*0-939512-06-8*) U MI Japan.

***Macdougall, Walter M.** The Old Somerset Railroad: A Lifeline for Northern Maine 1874-1929. LC 99-87562. 176p. 2000. 24.95 (*0-89272-492-7*) Down East.

MacDougall, William L. American Revolutionary: A Biography of General Alexander McDougall, 57. LC 76-15324. (Contributions in American History Ser.: No. 57). (Illus.). 186p. 1977. 45.00 (*0-8371-9035-5*, MAR/, Greenwood Pr) Greenwood.

— The Search for Virginia Dare. (Illus.). 40p. (C). 1995. text 19.50 (*0-930329-95-3*) Kabel Pubs.

MacDowall, David W. Indian Numismatics, History, Art & Culture: Essays in Honour of Dr. Parmeshwari Lal Gupta, 2 vols., Set. (Agam Indological Ser.: No. 14). (C). 1992. 200.00 (*0-8364-2833-1*, Pub. by Agam Kala Prakashan) S Asia.

— The Western Coinages of Nero. LC 74-82869. (Numismatic Notes & Monographs: No. 161). (Illus.). 281p. (Orig.). 1979. pap. 40.00 (*0-89722-176-1*) Am Numismatic.

Macdowall, M. W., tr. see Franzos, Karl E.

MacDowall, Simon. Germanic Warrior: 236-568 AD. (Warrior Ser.: No. 17). (Illus.). 64p. 1996. pap. 12.95 (*1-85532-586-1*, Pub. by Ospry) Stackpole.

— Late Roman Cavalryman, 236-565 AD. (Warrior Ser.). (Illus.). 64p. 1995. pap. 12.95 (*1-85532-567-5*, Pub. by Ospry) Stackpole.

— Late Roman Infantry, 236-565 A.D. (Warrior Ser.). (Illus.). 64p. 1994. pap. 12.95 (*1-85532-419-9*, 9608, Pub. by Ospry) Stackpole.

MacDowell, Betty, jt. auth. see Harley, Rachel B.

MacDowell, D. M. Gorgias: Encomium of Helen. (GRE.). 48p. 1982. 14.95 (*0-86292-053-1*, Pub. by Brist Class Pr) Focus Pub-R Pullins.

MacDowell, D. M., ed. see Harrison, A. R.

MacDowell, Douglas M. Aristophanes & Athens: An Introduction to the Plays. 376p. 1995. pap. text 19.95 (*0-19-872159-5*) OUP.

— The Law in Classical Athens. LC 78-54141. (Aspects of Greek & Roman Life Ser.). 280p. 1978. pap. text 16.95 (*0-8014-9365-X*) Cornell U Pr.

MacDowell, Douglas M., ed. see Demosthenes.

MacDowell, Douglas M., tr. see Antiphon & Andocides.

MacDowell, Edward. Critical & Historical Essays. 2nd ed. LC 69-11289. 1969. reprint ed. lib. bdg. 37.50 (*0-306-71098-6*) Da Capo.

— Etudes & Technical Exercises for Piano. (Earlier American Music Ser.: No. 29). 140p. 1987. reprint ed. 27.50 (*0-306-77325-2*) Da Capo.

— Piano Pieces, Opus 51, 55, 61, 62. LC 70-170391. (Earlier American Music Ser.: No. 8). 144p. 1972. reprint ed. lib. bdg. 32.50 (*0-306-77308-2*) Da Capo.

— Piano Works: Woodland Sketches, Complete Sonatas & Other Pieces. 224p. 1990. pap. 12.95 (*0-486-26293-6*) Dover.

— Songs (Opus 40, 47, 56, 58, 60) LC 73-170392. (Earlier American Music Ser.). 1972. 23.50 (*0-685-45908-X*) Da Capo.

MacDowell, Edward & Thalberg, Sigismond. The Nineteenth Century Piano Ballade: An Anthology. Parakilas, James, ed. (Recent Researches in Music of the 19th & Early 20th Centuries Ser.: No. RRN9). (Illus.). 92, xxiip. 1990. pap. 40.00 (*0-89579-249-4*) A-R Eds.

MacDowell, Edward A. Critical & Historical Essays: Lectures Delivered at Columbia University. 293p. 1990. reprint ed. lib. bdg. 69.00 (*0-7812-9014-7*) Rprt Serv.

MacDowell, Edwin C. Size Inheritance in Rabbits. LC 14-9001. (Carnegie Institution of Washington Publication Ser.: Vol. 196). (Illus.). 55p. reprint ed. pap. 30.00 (*0-608-06218-9*, 206654700008) Bks Demand.

MacDowell, John F., jt. ed. see Boyd, David C.

MacDowell, Laurel S. Remember Kirkland Lake: The Gold-Miners' Strike of 1941-42. (State & Economic Life Ser.). 308p. 1983. pap. 14.95 (*0-8020-6457-4*); text 35.00 (*0-8020-5585-0*) U of Toronto Pr.

— Remember Kirkland Lake: The History & Effects of the Kirkland Lake Gold Miners' Strike, 1941-42. LC 83-132702. (State & Economic Life Ser.: No. 5). (Illus.). 308p. reprint ed. pap. 95.50 (*0-8357-6386-2*, 203574100096) Bks Demand.

MacDowell, Lloyd W. Alaska Glaciers & Ice Fields. fac. ed. (Shorey Historical Ser.). (Illus.). 16p. 1906. reprint ed. pap. 10.00 (*0-8466-0064-1*, S-64) Shoreys Bkstore.

MacDowell, Mark. Comparative Study of Don Juan & Madhyamaka Buddhism. 116p. 1986. 10.95 (*0-317-60565-8*, Pub. by Motilal Bnarsidass) S Asia.

— A Comparative Study of Teachings of Don Juan & Madhyamaka Buddhism. xv, 116p. (C). 1991. reprint ed. 11.00 (*81-208-0162-8*, Pub. by Motilal Bnarsidass) S Asia.

MacDowell, Marsha. Stories in Thread. Fitzgerald, Ruth D. & Caltrider, Sue, eds. (Illus.). (Orig.). 1989. spiral bd. 20.00 (*0-944311-02-4*) MSU Museum.

MacDowell, Marsha, ed. African American Quiltmaking in Michigan. LC 97-17124. (Illus.). 375p. 1998. 45.00 (*0-87013-410-8*) Mich St U Pr.

***MacDowell, Marsha & Benz, Charmaine M., eds.** E'aawiyaang (Who We Are) (Illus.). 64p. 1999. pap. write for info. (*0-9672331-0-0*) Saginaw Chippewa.

MacDowell, Marsha & Fitzgerald, Ruth D. Michigan Quilts: One Hundred & Fifty Years of a Textile Tradition. LC 87-62538. (Illus.). 175p. (Orig.). (C). 1987. 34.95 (*0-944311-00-8*); pap. 24.95 (*0-944311-01-6*) MSU Museum.

MacDowell, Marsha & Reed, Janice. Sisters of the Great Lakes: Art of American Indian Women. (Illus.). 68p. (Orig.). 1996. pap. 24.95 (*0-944311-08-3*) MSU Museum.

MacDowell, Marsha, et al. Anishnaabek: Artists of Little Traverse Bay. (Illus.). 88p. (Orig.). 1997. pap. 14.95 (*0-944311-09-1*) MSU Museum.

— Contemporary Great Lakes Pow Wow Regalia: Nda Maamawigaami (Together We Dance) (Illus.). 80p. (Orig.). 1997. pap. 24.95 (*0-944311-10-5*) MSU Museum.

MacDowell, Michael A. Public Understanding of Economic Policies: The Tax Cuts of 1962 & 1964. LC 77-14765. (Dissertations in American Economic History Ser.). 1978. 33.95 (*0-405-11048-0*) Ayer.

***Macdowell, Ruth B.** Pieced Flowers. Kuhn, Barb & MacFarland, Sara, eds. (Illus.). 112p. 2000. pap. 24.95 (*1-57120-091-6*, 10208, Pub. by C & T Pub) Watsn-Guptill.

***MacDowell, Wayne G.** Not Just Another Love Story. LC 99-62148. 370p. 1999. pap. 19.95 (*1-889131-42-3*) CasAnanda.

Macduff, Nancy. Building Effective Volunteer Committees. 2nd ed. Millgard, Janie, ed. (Illus.). 82p. (C). 1986. pap. 20.70 (*0-945795-01-7*) MBA Pub.

— Episodic Volunteering: Building the Short-Term Volunteer Program. Millgard, Janie & Ricketts, Jennifer, eds. 24p. 1991. pap. 9.25 (*0-945795-09-2*) MBA Pub.

— Slide Shows on a Shoe String. Millgard, Janie, ed. (Illus.). 54p. (C). 1986. pap. 12.00 (*0-945795-02-5*) MBA Pub.

— Volunteer Recruiting & Retention: A Marketing Approach. 2nd rev. ed. Millgard, Janie, ed. (Illus.). 196p. (C). 1996. pap. 37.00 (*0-945795-08-4*) MBA Pub.

— Volunteer Screening: An Audio Workbook. 24p. 1996. pap., wbk. ed. 20.00 incl. audio (*0-945795-12-2*) MBA Pub.

Macduff, Nancy, ed. see Henson, Sarah & Larson, Bruce.

MacDugall, Elizabeth B., jt. ed. see Tatum, George B.

Mace, Alice E. Ortho's Guide to the Birds Around Us. Sherman, Suzanne, ed. LC 95-68607. (Illus.). 352p. 1996. 29.95 (*0-89721-290-8*, Ortho Bks) Meredith Bks.

Mace, Angela. Architecture in Manuscript, 1601-1996. LC 97-6588. (Illus.). 704p. 1998. 175.00 (*0-7201-2195-7*) Continuum.

Mace, Ann. Los Edificios de Nueva York. Romo, Alberto, tr. (Books for Young Learners).Tr. of New York City Buildings. (SPA., Illus.). 12p. (J). (gr. k-2). 1997. pap. text 5.00 (*1-57274-182-1*, A2855) R Owen Pubs.

***Mace, Ann.** Looking for Bears. (Books for Young Learners). (Illus.). 12p. (J). (gr. k-2). 1999. pap. text 5.00 (*1-57274-268-2*, A2468) R Owen Pubs.

Mace, Ann. New York City Buildings. (Books for Young Learners). (Illus.). 12p. (J). (gr. k-2). 1997. pap. text 5.00 (*1-57274-077-9*, A2475) R Owen Pubs.

Mace, Arthur C. & Winlock, Herbert E. The Tomb of Senebtisi at Lisht: Metropolitan Museum of Art Egyptian Expedition Publications, Vol. 1. LC 73-168408. (Metropolitan Museum of Art Publications in Reprint). (Illus.). 228p. 1973. reprint ed. 35.95 (*0-405-02241-7*) Ayer.

Mace, Arthur C., jt. auth. see Carter, Howard.

Mace, Aurelia G. The Aletheia. 2nd ed. (Illus.). 146p. 1992. reprint ed. 14.95 (*0-915836-23-8*) United Soc Shakers.

— The Aletheia: Spirit of Truth. 2nd ed. LC 72-2989. reprint ed. 34.50 (*0-404-10751-6*) AMS Pr.

Mace, Carroll E. Two Spanish-Quiche Dance Dramas of Rabinal, Vol. 3. 221p. 1970. pap. 7.00 (*0-912788-02-X*) Tulane Romance Lang.

Mace, Chris. Heart & Soul: The Therapeutic Face of Philosophy. LC 98-34501. 1999. 85.00 (*0-415-17000-1*); pap. 27.99 (*0-415-17001-X*) Routledge.

Mace, Chris J., ed. The Art & Science of Assessment in Psychotherapy. LC 94-46785. 208p. (C). 1995. pap. 27.99 (*0-415-10539-0*, C0465) Routledge.

— The Art & Science of Assessment in Psychotherapy. LC 94-46785. 208p. (C). (gr. 13). 1995. 80.00 (*0-415-10538-2*, C0459) Routledge.

Mace, David R. Getting Ready for Marriage. LC 84-28320. 128p. 1985. reprint ed. pap. 6.95 (*0-687-14136-2*) Abingdon.

— Sexual Difficulties in Marriage. LC 72-75652. (Pocket Counsel Bks.). 64p. (Orig.). reprint ed. pap. 30.00 (*0-608-16309-0*, 202717800054) Bks Demand.

Mace, David R., ed. Modern Marriage & the Clergy. LC 74-19593. (Special Issue of Pastoral Psychology Ser.). 84p. 1978. 16.95 (*0-87705-368-5*, Kluwer Acad Hman Sci) Kluwer Academic.

Mace, David R. & Mace, Vera. How to Have a Happy Marriage. 1987. reprint ed. pap. 8.95 (*0-687-17832-0*) Abingdon.

Mace, Emden C. The Lord of Glory. 1986. pap. 5.99 (*0-88019-182-1*) Schmul Pub Co.

Mace, George, jt. auth. see Melone, Albert P.

Mace, Georgina M., et al, eds. Conservation in a Changing World. LC 98-24393. (Conservation Biology Ser.: No. 1). (Illus.). 308p. (C). 1999. pap. 34.95 (*0-521-63445-8*) Cambridge U Pr.

— Conservation in a Changing World. LC 98-24393. (Conservation Biology Ser.: No. 1). (Illus.). 320p. (C). 1999. 80.00 (*0-521-63270-6*) Cambridge U Pr.

Mace, Gerard. Wood Asleep. 1997. pap. 19.95 (*1-85224-432-1*, Pub. by Bloodaxe Bks) Dufour.

Mace, Gillian S., et al. The Bereaved Child: Analysis, Education, & Treatment - An Abstracted Bibliography. LC 81-8637. 292p. 1981. 95.00 (*0-306-65197-1*, Kluwer Plenum) Kluwer Academic.

Mace, Gordon & Belanger, Louis. The Americas in Transition: The Contours of Regionalism LC 99-10363. 1999. 55.00 (*1-55587-717-6*) L Rienner.

Mace, Gordon & Therien, Jean-Philippe, eds. Foreign Policy & Regionalism in the Americas. 264p. 1996. pap. 19.95 (*1-55587-637-4*); lib. bdg. 49.95 (*1-55587-513-0*) L Rienner.

Mace, Harvey F. The Highs & Lows of Flying. Frisque, Tom, ed. (Illus.). 149p. 1994. pap. 19.95 (*0-9623080-5-6*) Aviation Usk.

Mace, James D. Radographic Pathology for Technologists. 3rd ed. LC 97-23176. (Illus.). 352p. (C). (gr. 13). 1997. pap. text 39.00 (*0-8151-4568-3*, 30347) Mosby Inc.

Mace, James E. Communism & the Dilemmas of National Liberation: National Communism in Soviet Ukraine, 1918-1933. LC 83-4361. (Harvard Ukrainian Research Institute Monograph). 334p. 1990. text 27.00 (*0-916458-09-1*) Harvard Ukrainian.

Mace, Jane. Playing with Time: Mothers & the Meaning of Literacy. LC 99-159373. 1998. 85.00 (*1-85728-890-4*) Taylor & Francis.

— Playing with Time: Mothers & the Meaning of Literacy. LC 99-159373. 185p. 1998. 24.95 (*1-85728-891-2*) UCL Pr Ltd.

— Talking about Literacy: Principles & Practices of Adult Literacy Education. 192p. (C). 1992. pap. 22.99 (*0-415-06655-7*, A9638) Routledge.

— Working with Words: Literacy Beyond School. (Chameleon Education Ser.). 144p. 1981. pap. 4.95 (*0-906495-15-6*) Writers & Readers.

Mace, Jane, ed. Literacy, Language & Community Publishing: Essays in Adult Education. LC 94-47982. 1995. 84.95 (*1-85359-280-3*, Pub. by Multilingual Matters); pap. 34.95 (*1-85359-279-X*, Pub. by Multilingual Matters) Taylor & Francis.

Mace, Jean. Home Fairy Tales. Booth, Mary L., tr. from FRE. LC 78-74517. (Children's Literature Reprint Ser.). (Illus.). (J). (gr. 4-5). 1979. reprint ed. 30.00 (*0-8486-0220-X*) Roth Pub Inc.

Mace, John. Arabic Grammar: A Reference Guide. 192p. 1999. pap. text 23.00 (*0-7486-1079-0*, Pub. by Edinburgh U Pr) Col U Pr.

***Mace, John.** Arabic Grammar: A Reference Guide. 192p. 1999. 72.00 (*0-7486-1078-2*, Pub. by Edinburgh U Pr) Col U Pr.

Mace, John. Arabic Today: A Student, Business & Professional Course. LC 97-113000. 288p. 1996. pap. 35.00 (*0-7486-0616-5*, Pub. by Edinburgh U Pr) Col U Pr.

— Teach Yourself Arabic Verbs & Essential Grammar. (Teach Yourself Ser.). 256p. 1999. pap. 14.95 (*0-8442-2685-8*) NTC Contemp Pub Co.

***Mace, John.** Teach Yourself Beginners Arabic Script. (Teach Yourself Beginner's...Ser.). 176p. 2000. pap. 10.95 (*0-658-00077-2*, 000772) NTC Contemp Pub Co.

Mace, John. Teach Yourself Modern Persian: A Complete Course for Beginners. (PER., Illus.). 272p. 1995. pap. 15.95 (*0-8442-3815-5*, Teach Yrslf) NTC Contemp Pub Co.

— Teach Yourself Persian, Modern. (Teach Yourself Ser.). 1992. 14.95 (*0-685-63252-0*) Fr & Eur.

***Mace, K. C.** The Walnut Man. 160p. 2000. pap. 14.95 (*1-893162-16-8*) Erica Hse.

Mace, Mary E. Memory Storage Patterns in Parallel Processing. (C). 1987. text 78.00 (*0-89838-239-4*) Kluwer Academic.

Mace-Matluck, Betty J., et al. Through the Golden Door: Educational Approaches for Immigrant Adolescents with Limited Schooling. LC 98-17091. (Language in Education Ser.). 1998. pap. 20.95 (*1-887744-07-X*) Delta Systems.

Mace, Myles L. Directors: Myth & Reality. 224p. 1986. pap. 11.96 (*0-07-103253-3*) McGraw.

Mace, Nancy A. Henry Fielding's Novels & the Classical Tradition. LC 95-42482. 200p. 1996. 34.50 (*0-87413-585-0*) U Delaware Pr.

***Mace, Nancy L.** The 36-Hour Day: A Family Guide to Caring for Persons with Alzheimer Disease, Related Dementing Illnesses & Memory Loss in Later Life. 3rd large type ed. (Health Book Ser.). (Illus.). 496p. 2000. pap. 19.95 (*0-8018-6521-2*) Johns Hopkins.

Mace, Nancy L., ed. Dementia Care: Patient, Family, & Community. LC 89-8106. 416p. 1991. reprint ed. pap. text 19.95 (*0-8018-4314-6*) Johns Hopkins.

Mace, Nancy L. & Rabins, Peter V. The Thirty-Six Hour Day. (C). 1989. 45.00 (*0-340-37012-2*, Pub. by Age Concern Eng) St Mut.

— The 36-Hour Day. large type ed. 1995. 29.50 (*0-7089-5801-X*) Ulverscroft.

***Mace, Nancy L. & Rabins, Peter V.** The 36-Hour Day: A Family Guide to Caring for Persons with Alzheimer Disease. 3rd ed. LC 98-43608. 352p. 1999. 39.95 (*0-8018-6148-9*) Johns Hopkins.

Mace, Nancy L. & Rabins, Peter V. The 36-Hour Day: A Family Guide to Caring for Persons with Alzheimer Disease, Related Dementing Illnesses & Memory Loss in Later Life. 3rd ed. LC 98-43608. (Press Health Book Ser.). xx, 339 p. 1999. 13.95 (*0-8018-6149-7*) Johns Hopkins.

— The Thirty-Six Hour Day: A Family Guide to Caring for Persons with Alzheimer's Disease, Related Dementing Illnesses & Memory Loss in Later Life. rev. ed. 448p. 1992. mass mkt. 7.50 (*0-446-36104-6*, Pub. by Warner Bks) Little.

— The Thirty-Six Hour Day: A Family Guide to Caring for Persons with Alzheimer's Disease, Related Dementing Illnesses & Memory Loss in Later Life. 2nd rev. ed. LC 90-49523. 352p. 1991. text 38.95 (*0-8018-4033-3*) Johns Hopkins.

Mace, Nigel, ed. see Lindsay, David.

Mace, O. Henry. Collector's Guide to Early Photographs. 2nd ed. LC 89-51557. (Illus.). 224p. 1999. per. 19.95 (*0-87341-720-8*) Krause Pubns.

— Collector's Guide to Victoriana. LC 90-50637. (Illus.). 240p. 1991. pap. 18.95 (*0-87069-576-2*, Wllce-Homestd) Krause Pubns.

Mace, Patrick B. The Silver Whistle. (J). (gr. k up). 1986. pap. 6.00 (*0-87602-250-6*) Anchorage.

Mace, Paul. The Paul Mace Guide to Data Recovery. 2nd ed. 1991. pap. 24.95 (*0-13-654500-9*) P-H.

Mace, Rodney. British Trade Union Posters: An Illustrated History. 1999. 44.95 (*0-7509-2158-7*) Sutton Pub Ltd.

***Mace, Rodney.** F. M. Alexander - The Coming Man: An Intellectual Biography of the Originator of "The Alexander Technique" 250p. 1999. 60.00 (*1-85343-409-4*, Pub. by Free Assoc Bks); pap. 24.50 (*1-85343-410-8*, Pub. by Free Assoc Bks) NYU Pr.

Mace, Rodney. Trafalgar Square: Emblem of Empire. (C). 1976. pap. 22.50 (*0-85315-367-1*, Pub. by Lawrence & Wishart) NYU Pr.

Mace, Ruth, jt. auth. see Milner-Gulland, E. J.

Mace, Shirley. 1996-97 Price Guide for Encyclopedia of Silhouette Collectibles on Glass. Ekvall, Angela, ed. 12p. 1996. 5.00 (*0-9633674-0-4*) Shadow Enter.

— Silhouette Collectibles: On Glass. (Illus.). 160p. 1992. 24.95 (*0-9633674-5-5*) Shadow Enter.

***Mace, Shirley.** Vintage Silhouettes on Glass & Reverse Paintings. Jeppson, Deborah & Waddington, Bernice, eds. (Illus.). 176p. 2000. 40.00 (*0-9633674-6-3*) Shadow Enter.

Mace, Suzanne, jt. auth. see Mace, Tony.

Mace, Thomas. Musick's Monument. fac. ed. (Monuments of Music & Music Literature in Facsimile, II Ser.: Vol. 17). (Illus.). 1966. lib. bdg. 75.00 (*0-8450-2217-2*) Broude.

Mace, Tony & Mace, Suzanne. Cactus & Succulents. LC 98-18395. (Care Manual Ser.). (Illus.). 128p. 1998. 19.95 (*1-57145-619-8*, Laurel Glen Pub) Advantage Pubs.

Mace, Vera, jt. auth. see Mace, David R.

***Mace, William, ed.** How are Affordances Related to Events? An Exchange of Views, A Special Issue of Ecological Psychology. 103p. 2000. pap. write for info. (*0-8058-9766-6*) L Erlbaum Assocs.

Mace, William J. The Weekend Golfer. LC 96-69829. 86p. (Orig.). 1997. pap. 11.95 (*1-57197-038-X*) Pentland Pr.

MacEachen, Dougald B. Keats & Shelley Notes. (Cliffs Notes Ser.). 80p. (Orig.). 1971. pap. 4.50 (*0-8220-0702-9*, Cliff) IDG Bks.

MacEacher, Dougald B. Don Juan Notes. (Cliffs Notes Ser.). 96p. 1970. pap. 4.50 (*0-8220-0411-9*, Cliff) IDG Bks.

MacEachern, Diane. Enough Is Enough: The Hell-Raiser's Guide to Community Activism. 176p. (Orig.). 1994. pap. 10.00 (*0-380-77335-X*, Avon Bks) Morrow Avon.

MacEachern, Doug, jt. auth. see Stein, Lincoln.

MacEachern, Kim, jt. auth. see Walker, Judy.

MacEachern, Kim, jt. auth. see Walker, Judy Hille.

***MacEachim, Douglas J.** The Final Months of the War with Japan: Signals Intelligence, U. S. Invasion Planning & the A-Bomb Decision. (Illus.). 250p. (C). 1999. pap. text 50.00 (*0-7881-8325-7*) DIANE Pub.

***MacEachin, Douglas J.** CIA Assessments of the Soviet Union: The Record Versus the Charges, An Intelligence Monograph. 47p. 1999. pap. 4.25 (*0-16-058831-6*) USGPO.

— Final Months of the War with Japan: Signals Intelligence, United States Invasion Planning & the A-bomb Decision. 300p. 1999. per. 25.00 (*0-16-058822-7*) USGPO.

MacEachren, Alan M. How Maps Work: Representation, Visualization & Design. LC 94-31138. 513p. 1995. lib. bdg. 47.95 (*0-89862-589-0*, 2589) Guilford Pubns.

— How to Tell Some Truth with Maps: A Primer on Symbolization & Design. Cromley, Robert & Cromley, Ellen, eds. (Resource Publications in Geography). (Illus.). 136p. (C). 1994. pap. 15.00 (*0-89291-214-6*) Assn Am Geographers.

— Visualization in Modern Cartography. LC 94-19075. (Modern Cartography Ser.: No. 2). 368p. 1994. pap. text. write for info. (*0-08-042415-5*, Pergamon Pr) Elsevier.

MacEachren, Alan M. & Taylor, Fraser, eds. Visualization in Modern Cartography. LC 94-19075. (Modern Cell Biology Ser.: No. 2). 368p. 1994. text. write for info. (*0-08-042416-3*, Pergamon Pr) Elsevier.

MacEachren, Alan M., jt. ed. see Monmonier, Mark.

***MacEarlean, Neasa.** Get More from Work & More Fun. 224p. 2000. pap. 29.95 (*0-8464-5064-X*) Beekman Pubs.

Macebuh, Stanley. James Baldwin: A Critical Study. LC 72-93679. 194p. 1973. 24.95 (*0-89388-064-7*) Okpaku Communications.

***Maceda, Jose.** Gongs & Bamboo: A Panorama of Philippine Music Instruments. LC 98-947898. (Illus.). 342p. 1999. pap. text 90.00 (*971-542-124-5*, Pub. by U of Philippines Pr) UH Pr.

Macedo. Dancing with Bigotry. LC 99-27682. 2000. text 35.00 (*0-312-21608-4*) St Martin.

Macedo, Donaldo, tr. see Freire, Paulo.

Macedo, Donaldo P. Literacies of Power: What Americans Are Not Allowed to Know. LC 94-3375. (Edge Ser.). (C). 1994. pap. 24.00 (*0-8133-2253-7*, Pub. by Westview) HarpC.

Macedo, Donaldo P. & Koike, Dale A. Romance Linguistics: The Portuguese Context. LC 92-19868. 216p. 1992. 49.95 (*0-89789-297-6*, H297, Bergin & Garvey) Greenwood.

Macedo, Donaldo P., jt. auth. see Freire, Paulo.

M

An Asterisk (*) at the beginning of an entry indicates that the title is appearing for the first time.

Macedo, Donaldo P., ed. & intro. see Chomsky, Noam.

Macedo, Donaldo P., tr. see Freire, Paulo.

Macedo, E. A. & Rasmussen, P. Liquid-Liquid Equilibrium Data Collection Suppl. 1: Tables, Diagrams & Model Parameters for Binary, Ternary & Quaternary Systems. (Dechema Chemistry Data Ser.: Vol. V, Pt. 4). (Illus.). 340p. 1987. text 260.00 (*3-921567-73-4*, Pub. by Dechema) Scholium Intl.

Macedo, Helder, ed. Studies in Portuguese Literature & History in Honour of Luis de Sousa Rebelo. (Monografias A Ser.: No. 147). (POR., Illus.). 208p. (C). 1993. 75.00 (*1-85566-012-1*) Boydell & Brewer.

Macedo, Helder, jt. ed. see Lisboa, Eugenio.

Macedo, Jorge. The Theoretical Basis of the Living System. LC 75-17399. (Illus.). 84p. 1979. 10.50 (*0-87527-158-8*) Green.

Macedo, Jorge B. De, see Bliss, Christopher & De Macedo, Jorge B., eds.

Macedo, Sergio. Lakota: An Illustrated History. 56p. 1996. pap. 12.95 (*1-887896-02-3*) Treas Chest Bks.

***Macedo, Stephen.** Diversity & Distrust. LC 99-41461. 384p. 1999. 45.00 (*0-674-21311-4*) HUP.

Macedo, Stephen. Liberal Virtues: Citizenship, Virtue, & Community in Liberal Constitutionalism. 320p. 1991. reprint ed. pap. 19.95 (*0-19-827872-1*) OUP.

Macedo, Stephen. Reassessing the Sixties. Date not set. pap. write for info. (*0-393-31700-5*) Norton.

Macedo, Stephen. Reassessing the Sixties. (C). 1997. pap. text 14.50 (*0-393-97142-2*) Norton.

Macedo, Stephen, ed. Democratic Disagreement: Essays on Deliberative Democracy. LC 98-50040. (Practical & Professional Ethics Ser.). 304p. 1999. pap. 19.95 (*0-19-513199-1*); text 49.95 (*0-19-513191-6*) OUP.

Macedonius Consul. The Epigrams. Madden, John A., ed. LC 96-178668. (Spudasmata Ser.: Bd. 60). xviii, 321p. 1995. write for info. (*3-487-10059-2*) G Olms Pubs.

Macek, Carl. Heavy Metal: The Movie. 2nd rev. ed. (Illus.). 144p. 1996. pap. 24.95 (*0-87816-524-X*) Kitchen Sink.

Macek, Ellen A. The Loyal Opposition: Tudor Traditionalist Polemics, 1535-1558. (Studies in Church History: Vol. 7). XV, 299p. (C). 1996. text 53.95 (*0-8204-3059-5*) P Lang Pubng.

***Macek, Ivana.** War Within: Everyday Life in Sarajevo under Seige. (Studies in Cultural Anthropology Twenty-Eight). 313p. 2000. pap. 32.50 (*91-554-4695-7*, Pub. by Uppsala Universitet) Coronet Bks.

Macek, Josef. The Hussite Movement in Bohemia. Fried, Vilem & Milner, Ian, trs. LC 78-63207. (Heresies of the Early Christian & Medieval Era Ser.: Second Ser.). reprint ed. 54.00 (*0-404-16237-1*) AMS Pr.

Macek, Vladko. In the Struggle for Freedom. LC 68-8182. (Illus.). 1968. 30.00 (*0-271-00069-4*) Pa St U Pr.

Macel, Otakar, jt. auth. see Van Bergeijk, Herman.

Macel, Otokar, jt. auth. see Van Bergeijk, Herman.

MacEllven, Douglass T. Legal Research Handbook. 440p. 1993. pap. text, student ed. 35.00 (*0-409-91116-X*, MICHIE) LEXIS Pub.

MacElrevey, Daniel H. Shiphandling for the Mariner. 3rd ed. LC 95-5938. (Illus.). 344p. 1995. text 35.00 (*0-87033-464-6*) Cornell Maritime.

Macelroy, R. D. Life Science & Space Research XXV: Natural & Artificial Ecosystems. (Advances in Space Research Ser.). 466p. 1994. pap. 165.00 (*0-08-042488-0*, Pergamon Pr) Elsevier.

MacElroy, R. D., et al, eds. Life Sciences & Space Research XXIV (4) Natural & Artificial Ecosystems: Proceedings of the Topical Meeting of the COSPAR Interdiscplinary Scientific Commission F (Meetings F10, F11, F1 & F12) of the COSPAR 28th Plenary Meeting Held in The Hague, The Netherlands, 25 June-6 July, 1990. (Advances in Space Research Ser.: Vol. 12). 280p. 1992. pap. 165.00 (*0-08-041849-X*, Pergamon Pr) Elsevier.

— Life Sciences & Space Research XXIII (3) Natural & Artificial Ecosystems: Proceedings of the Topical Meetings of COSPAR Interdisciplinary Scientific Commission F (Meetings F9, F10, F11 & F12) of the COSPAR 27th Plenary Meeting Held in Espoo, Finland, 18-29 July, 1988, No. XXIII. (Advances in Space Research Ser.: Vol. 9). (Illus.). 196p. 1989. pap. 92.75 (*0-08-040150-3*, Pergamon Pr) Elsevier.

MacElroy, R. D., et al. Natural & Artificial Ecosystems. (Advances in Space Research (RJ) Ser.: Vol. 18). 288p. 1995. 194.50 (*0-08-042668-9*, Pergamon Pr) Elsevier.

Macelwane, James B. When the Earth Quakes. LC 76-29402. reprint ed. 32.50 (*0-404-15340-2*) AMS Pr.

Macentee, Michael I. The Complete Denture: A Clinical Pathway. LC 98-27920. 126p. 1999. 48.00 (*0-86715-350-4*) Quint Pub Co.

MacEoin, Beth. Homeopathy for Menopause. LC 97-6962. 256p. 1997. pap. 14.95 (*0-89281-648-1*) Inner Tradit.

***MacEoin, Beth.** Natural Medicine: A Practical Guide to Family Health. 512p. 2000. 35.00 (*0-7475-3023-8*, Pub. by Blmsbury Pub) Trafalgar.

MacEoin, Denis. Rituals in Babism & Baha'ism. (Pembroke Persian Papers). 192p. 1995. text 65.00 (*1-85043-654-1*, Pub. by I B T) St Martin.

— The Sources for Early Babi Doctrine & History: A Survey. LC 91-43294. ix, 274p. 1992. 94.50 (*90-04-09462-8*) Brill Academic Pubs.

MacEoin, G., et al, eds. Third International Conference on Minority Languages, Galway 1986: General Papers. 240p. 1987. 59.00 (*0-905028-78-3*, MM31, Pub. by Multilingual Matters) Taylor & Francis.

MacEoin, Gary, ed. The Papacy & the People of God. LC 97-39381. 176p. (Orig.). 1998. pap. 15.00 (*1-57075-178-1*) Orbis Bks.

Macer, Daryl, ed. The Human Genome Project, Vol. 1. Date not set. 128.50 (*0-7623-0398-0*) Jai Pr.

Macer-Story, Eugenia. Angels of Time. 88p. 1984. 30.00 (*0-7212-0697-2*, Pub. by Regency Pr GBR) St Mut.

— Awakening to the Light: After the Longest Night. 55p. 1995. pap. 13.00 (*1-879980-07-X*) Magick Mirror.

— Battles with Dragons: Certain Tales of Political Yoga. 180p. (Orig.). 1994. pap. 25.00 (*1-879980-03-7*) Magick Mirror.

— Crossing Jungle River. 72p. 1998. pap. 15.00 (*1-879980-11-8*) Magick Mirror.

— The Dark Frontier. LC 98-126670. (Illus.). 250p. (Orig.). 1997. pap. 20.00 (*1-879980-08-8*) Magick Mirror.

— Dr. Fu Man Chu Meets the Lonesome Cowboy: Sorcery & the UFO Experience. 300p. 1991. 35.00 (*1-879980-02-9*) Magick Mirror.

— Gypsy Fair. 49p. 1990. 12.95 (*1-879980-00-2*) Magick Mirror.

— Legacy of Daedalus. 94p. 1995. pap. 6.00 (*1-879980-05-3*) Magick Mirror.

— Sea Condor - Dusty Sun. 62p. 1994. pap. 12.95 (*1-879980-06-1*) Magick Mirror.

— The Strawberry Man & 27 Love Poems. 1992. 12.95 (*1-879980-01-0*) Magick Mirror.

***Macer-Story, Eugenia.** Troll & Other Interdimensional Invasions. 79p. 1999. pap. 6.00 (*1-879980-13-4*) Magick Mirror.

— Vanishing Questions. 40p. 2000. pap. 6.00 (*1-879980-14-2*, Yanker) Magick Mirror.

***Macer-Story, Eugenia, ed.** Yankee Oracle Gazette. (Quarterly Journal Ser.). 90p. 2000. pap. 55.00 (*1-879980-12-6*) Magick Mirror.

Maceri, Domenico. Dalla Novellas Alla Commedia Pirandelliana. LC 90-26478. (American University Studies: Romance Languages & Literature: Ser. II, Vol. 165). XII, 179p. (C). 1991. text 34.95 (*0-8204-1483-2*) P Lang Pubng.

Maceri, Eileen, ed. see Andrade, Gene.

Maceri, Franco, jt. ed. see Del Piero, G.

Macesich, George. Commercial Banking & Regional Development in the United States, 1950-1960. LC 65-64030. (Florida State University Studies: No. 45). 178p. reprint ed. pap. 55.20 (*0-7837-4932-5*, 204459800004) Bks Demand.

— Integration & Stabilization: A Monetary View. LC 95-30654. 152p. 1996. 52.95 (*0-275-95242-8*, Praeger Pubs) Greenwood.

— The International Monetary Economy & the Third World. LC 81-7298. 296p. 1981. 75.00 (*0-275-90674-4*, C0674, Praeger Pubs) Greenwood.

***Macesich, George.** Issues in Money & Banking. LC 99-55877. 160p. 2000. 49.95 (*0-275-96777-8*, Praeger Pubs) Greenwood.

Macesich, George. Monetarism: Theory & Policy. Zecher, J. Richard & Wilford, D. Sykes, eds. LC 82-19040. (Praeger Studies in International Monetary Economics & Finance). 269p. 1983. 55.00 (*0-275-91039-3*, C1039, Praeger Pubs) Greenwood.

— Monetary Policy & Politics: Rules vs. Discretion. LC 92-3379. 176p. 1992. 52.95 (*0-275-94335-6*, Praeger Pubs) Greenwood.

— Monetary Policy & Rational Expectations. LC 86-20538. 164p. 1987. 52.95 (*0-275-92327-4*, C2327, Praeger Pubs) Greenwood.

— Monetary Reform & Cooperation Theory. LC 88-25883. 142p. 1989. 57.95 (*0-275-93109-9*, C3109, Praeger Pubs) Greenwood.

— Money & Democracy. LC 89-26540. 184p. 1990. 52.95 (*0-275-93480-2*, C3480, Greenwood Pr) Greenwood.

— Money, Systems & Growth: A New Economic Order? LC 98-23554. 128p. 1999. 49.95 (*0-275-96171-0*, Praeger Pubs) Greenwood.

— Political Economy of Money: Emerging Fiat Monetary Regime. LC 99-17922. 152p. 1999. 49.95 (*0-275-96572-4*) Greenwood.

— The Politics of Monetarism: Its Historical & Institutional Development. (Illus.). 170p. 1984. 50.00 (*0-8476-7344-8*) Rowman.

— Reform & Market Democracy. LC 91-10179. 160p. 1991. 47.95 (*0-275-93989-8*, C3989, Praeger Pubs) Greenwood.

— Successor States & Cooperation Theory. LC 94-6377. 192p. 1994. 59.95 (*0-275-94936-2*, Praeger Pubs) Greenwood.

— Transformation & Emerging Markets. LC 96-16273. 144p. 1996. 52.95 (*0-275-95518-4*, Praeger Pubs) Greenwood.

— The United States in the Changing Global Economy: Policy Implications & Issues. LC 96-44686. 136p. 1997. 49.95 (*0-275-95705-5*, Praeger Pubs) Greenwood.

— World Banking & Finance: Cooperation Versus Conflict. LC 84-17908. 177p. 1984. 42.95 (*0-275-91220-5*, C1220, Praeger Pubs) Greenwood.

— World Debt & Stability. LC 90-37787. 128p. 1991. 52.95 (*0-275-93669-4*, C3669, Praeger Pubs) Greenwood.

— World Economy at the Crossroads. LC 97-19210. 152p. 1997. 52.95 (*0-275-95902-3*) Greenwood.

Macesich, George, ed. Yugoslavia in the Age of Democracy: Essays on Economic & Political Reform. LC 91-34495. 250p. 1992. 55.00 (*0-275-94175-2*, C4175, Praeger Pubs) Greenwood.

Macesich, George, et al, eds. Essays on the Yugoslav Economic Model. LC 87-38474. 261p. 1989. 65.00 (*0-275-92670-2*, C2670, Praeger Pubs) Greenwood.

Macesich, George & Dimitrejevic, Dimitrije. Monetary Reform in Former Socialist Economies. LC 94-25042. 160p. 1994. 55.00 (*0-275-95008-5*, Praeger Pubs) Greenwood.

Macesich, George & Tsai, Hui-Liang. Money in Economic Systems. Zecher, J. Richard & Wilford, D. Sykes, eds. LC 81-20977. (Studies in International Monetary Economics & Finances). 236p. 1982. 49.95 (*0-275-90852-6*, C0852, Praeger Pubs) Greenwood.

Macesich, George, jt. auth. see Dimitrijevic, Dimitrije.

MacEwan, Arthur. Debt & Disorder: International Economic Instability & U. S. Imperial Decline. 144p. (C). 1989. 26.00 (*0-85345-795-6*, Pub. by Monthly Rev); pap. 12.00 (*0-85345-796-4*, Pub. by Monthly Rev) NYU Pr.

***MacEwan, Arthur.** Neo-Liberalism or Democracy. LC 99-51918. 1999. text 69.50 (*1-85649-724-0*) Zed Books.

— Neo-Liberalism or Democracy? Economic Strategy Markets & Alter. LC 99-51918. 288p. 1999. pap. 25.00 (*1-85649-725-9*) Zed Books.

MacEwan, Arthur & Tabb, William K., eds. Instability & Change in the World Economy. 377p. (C). 1989. 36.00 (*0-85345-782-4*, Pub. by Monthly Rev); pap. 22.00 (*0-85345-783-2*, Pub. by Monthly Rev) NYU Pr.

MacEwan, Bonnie, jt. ed. see Johnson, Peggy.

***MacEwan, Dave.** The Spark of Life Trilogy. LC 99-69508. 176p. 2000. pap. 15.95 (*0-9677236-0-4*) Offbay Pubng.

MacEwan, Elias J., tr. see Freytag, Gustav.

MacEwan, Gwendolyn. Mermaids & Ikons: A Greek Summer. 112p. (Orig.). 1978. pap. 6.95 (*0-88784-062-0*, Pub. by Hse of Anansi Pr) Genl Dist Srvs.

MacEwan, Malcolm, jt. auth. see MacEwen, Ann.

MacEwen, Ann & MacEwan, Malcolm. National Parks: Conservation or Cosmetics. (Resource Management Ser.). 1982. pap. text 24.95 (*0-04-719004-3*) Routledge.

MacEwen, Ann & MacEwen, Malcolm. Greenprints for the Countryside: The Story of Britain's National Parks. 304p. 1987. text 65.00 (*0-04-719013-2*) Routledge.

MacEwen, Caroline J., jt. ed. see Loran, Donald F.

MacEwen, E. Gregory, jt. auth. see Withrow, Stephen J.

Macewen, Florence L. Natick: A Town with Character. Coverly, Carol J., ed. & compiled by by. LC 97-164679. (Illus.). xvi, 193p. (Orig.). 1997. pap. 24.00 (*0-9653848-0-2*) Morse Inst Lib.

MacEwen, G. Dean, et al, eds. Pediatric Fractures: A Practical Approach to Assessment & Treatment. LC 92-48218. (Illus.). 464p. 1993. 120.00 (*0-683-05310-8*) Lppncott W & W.

MacEwen, Gwendolyn. The Honeydrum: Seven Tales from Arab Lands. 77p. (J). 1983. reprint ed. 9.95 (*0-88962-228-0*) Mosaic.

— The Honeydrum: Seven Tales from Arab Lands. 77p. (J). 1995. reprint ed. pap. 7.95 (*0-88962-227-2*) Mosaic.

— Noman. 120p. 1985. pap. 4.95 (*0-7736-7086-6*) Genl Dist Srvs.

***MacEwen, Gwendolyn.** Poetry of Gwendolyn MacEwen Vol. 1: The Early Years, 2nd ed. (Picas Ser.: No. 18). 176p. 1999. reprint ed. pap. 7.00 (*1-55096-543-3*, Pub. by Exile Edns) Paul & Co Pubs.

— Poetry of Gwendolyn Macewen Vol. 2: The Later Years, 2nd ed. (Picas Ser.: No. 19). 148p. 1999. reprint ed. pap. 7.00 (*1-55096-547-6*, Pub. by Exile Edns) Paul & Co Pubs.

MacEwen, Gwendolyn. The T. E. Lawrence Poems. 80p. 1994. reprint ed. pap. 9.95 (*0-88962-172-1*) Mosaic.

MacEwen, Malcolm. Greening of a Red. 306p. (C). 54.95 (*0-7453-0440-0*, Pub. by Pluto GBR); pap. 19.95 (*0-7453-0441-9*, Pub. by Pluto GBR) Stylus Pub VA.

MacEwen, Malcolm, jt. auth. see MacEwen, Ann.

MacEwen, Martin. Housing, Race & Law. 512p. (C). 1990. 120.00 (*0-415-00063-7*, A4887) Routledge.

— Tackling Racism in Europe: An Examination of Anti-Discrimination Law in Practice. 224p. 1995. 49.50 (*0-85496-857-1*); pap. 16.50 (*1-85973-047-7*) Berg Pubs.

MacEwen, Martin, ed. Anti-Discrimination Law Enforcement: A Comparative Perspective. (Research in Ethnic Relations Ser.). 250p. 1997. 78.95 (*1-85972-404-3*, Pub. by Avebry) Ashgate Pub Co.

MacEwen, Philip, ed. Ethics, Metaphysics & Religion in the Thought of F. H. Bradley. LC 96-44917. (Studies in the History of Philosophy: Vol. 42). 256p. 1997. text 89.95 (*0-7734-8767-0*) E Mellen.

MacEwen, Sally, ed. Views of Clytemnestra, Ancient & Modern. LC 89-28420. (Studies in Comparative Literature: Vol. 9). (Illus.). 154p. 1990. lib. bdg. 69.95 (*0-88946-627-0*) E Mellen.

MacEwen, Sally & Tarkow, Theodore A. Euripides: Iphigenia at Aulis. (Greek Commentaries Ser.). 120p. (Orig.). (C). 1989. pap. text 7.00 (*0-929524-55-1*) Bryn Mawr Commentaries.

MacEwen, William A. & Lewis, A. H. Encyclopedia of Nautical Knowledge. LC 53-9685. 626p. 1953. 38.50 (*0-87033-010-1*) Cornell Maritime.

MacEwen, William A., jt. auth. see Turpin, Edward A.

Macey & Miller. Costly Policies: State Regulation & Antitrust Exemption in Insurance Markets. 100p. 1993. pap. 9.75 (*0-8447-3830-1*) Am Enterprise.

Macey, David, tr. see Lemaire, Anika.

Macey, David, tr. see Maffesoli, Michel.

Macey, David, tr. see Touraine, Alain.

Macey, David, tr. see Whitford, Margaret, ed.

Macey, David A. Government & Peasant in Russia, 1861-1906: The Prehistory of the Stolypin Reforms. 1987. text 38.00 (*0-87580-122-6*) N Ill U Pr.

Macey, J. Bank Law Regulations. 1992. 53.00 (*0-316-54208-3*, Aspen Law & Bus) Aspen Pub.

Macey, Jonathan R. Insider Trading: Economics, Politics & Policy. 150p. (C). 1991. pap. 9.75 (*0-8447-7010-8*, AEI Pr) Am Enterprise.

— Model Business Corporation Act. 530p. 1991. ring bd. 95.00 (*0-13-596628-0*) Aspen Law.

— Third Party Legal Opinions: Evaluation & Analysis. 332p. 1992. ring bd. 95.00 (*0-13-110470-5*) Aspen Law.

— Wealth Creation As a "Sin" (Independent Policy Reports). 37p. 1996. pap. 5.95 (*0-945999-44-5*) Independent Inst.

Macey, Jonathan R. & Miller, Geoffrey P. Banking Law & Regulation. 2nd ed. 800p. 1997. boxed set 60.00 (*1-56706-518-X*, 6518X) Panel Pubs.

Macey, Jonathan R. & Miller, Geoffrey P. Banking Law & Regulation: Statutory Supplement with Recent Cases & Developments: 1997 Edition. 280p. 1997. pap. text, suppl. ed. 21.95 (*1-56706-572-4*, 65724) Panel Pubs.

***Macey, Jonathan R. & Miller, Geoffrey P.** Banking Law & Regulation: Statutory Supplement with Recent Cases & Developments, 2000 Edition. 280p. 2000. pap., suppl. ed. write for info. (*0-7355-1321-X*, 1321X) Panel Pubs.

Macey, Jonathan R., jt. auth. see Butler, Henry N.

Macey, Neil, jt. auth. see Williams, Kathi.

Macey, Patrick. Savonarolan Music in Early Modern Europe: Savonarola's Musical Legacy. LC 97-50600. (Oxford Monographs on Music). (Illus.). 380p. 1999. text 60.00 (*0-19-816669-9*) OUP.

Macey, Samuel L. Time: A Bibliographic Guide. LC 91-25934. (Reference Books on Sociology & Science Ser.). 448p. 1991. text 20.00 (*0-8153-0646-6*, H1506) Garland.

Macey, Samuel L., ed. Encyclopedia of Time. LC 93-43355. (Illus.). 724p. 1994. text 100.00 (*0-8153-0615-6*, SS810) Garland.

Macey, Samuel L., intro. A Learned Dissertation on Dumpling: With a Word upon Pudding: And Pudding & Dumpling Burnt to Pot: or a Compleat Way to the Dissertation on Dumpling. LC 92-22731. (Augustan Reprints Ser.: No. 140). 1970. reprint ed. 14.50 (*0-404-70140-X*, PR3291) AMS Pr.

Macfadden, Barnarr. Natural Cure for Rupture. 125p. 1996. reprint ed. spiral bd. 11.50 (*0-7873-0578-2*) Hlth Research.

***Macfadden, Bernar.** Hair Culture: Rational Methods for Growing the Hair & for Developing Its Strength & Beauty. (Illus.). 212p. 2000. pap. 12.95 (*1-55709-502-7*) Applewood.

Macfadden, Bernar. The Walking Cure. (Illus.). 179p. 1984. reprint ed. pap. text 15.00 (*0-87556-391-0*) Saifer.

MacFadden, Bruce J. Fossil Horses: Systematics, Paleobiology & Evolution of the Family Equidae. (Illus.). 383p. (C). 1992. text 80.00 (*0-521-34041-1*) Cambridge U Pr.

— Fossil Horses: Systematics, Paleobiology & Evolution of the Family Equidae. (Illus.). 383p. (C). 1994. pap. text 33.95 (*0-521-47708-5*) Cambridge U Pr.

MacFadden, Bruce J., jt. ed. see Damuth, John D.

Macfadden, Clifford H. A Bibliography of Pacific Area Maps. LC 75-30119. (International Research Series of the Institute of Pacific Relations). 1976. reprint ed. 37.50 (*0-404-59542-1*) AMS Pr.

MacFaddin, Jean F. Biochemical Tests for Identification of Medical Bacteria. 3rd ed. 800p. spiral bd. 56.00 (*0-683-05318-3*) Lppncott W & W.

MacFadyen, A. & Ford, E. David, eds. Advances in Ecological Research, Vol. 13. (Serial Publication Ser.). 1983. text 104.00 (*0-12-013913-8*) Acad Pr.

MacFadyen, A. J. & MacFadyen, H. W., eds. Economic Psychology: Intersections in Theory & Application. 698p. 1986. 242.75 (*0-444-70072-2*, North Holland) Elsevier.

MacFadyen, Bruce V., Jr. & Ponsky, Jeffrey L., eds. Operative Laparoscopy & Thoracoscopy. LC 95-20399. (Illus.). 768p. 1996. text 235.00 (*0-7817-0279-8*) Lppncott W & W.

MacFadyen, David. Joseph Brodsky & the Baroque. 320p. 1999. 65.00 (*0-7735-1779-0*) McG-Queens Univ Pr.

MacFadyen, H. W., jt. ed. see MacFadyen, A. J.

MacFadyen, John A. & Hurst, Barbara. Rhode Island Criminal Procedure, 1988-1991. 530p. 1993. ring bd. 125.00 (*0-88063-075-2*, MICHIE); suppl. ed. 55.00 (*0-250-40700-0*, MICHIE) LEXIS Pub.

MacFall, Haldane. Aubrey Beardsley, the Man & His Work. (Illus.). 109p. 1977. 21.95 (*0-8369-9918-5*) Ayer.

***MacFalls, Sean.** Between the Leaves: There Are Little Stars. 2nd rev. ed. LC 99-91046. (Illus.). v, 40p. 1998. pap. 8.00 (*1-929812-02-7*) Peregrine Pr Wa.

— Gentle House Poems. LC 99-91047. v, 40p. (C). 1999. pap. 8.00 (*1-929812-03-5*) Peregrine Pr Wa.

— Under Blue Mountain. deluxe ed. LC 99-91048. v, 60p. 2000. 12.00 (*1-929812-04-3*) Peregrine Pr Wa.

— What Her Name Was: Requiem for a Dream. 30p. 1996. pap. 8.00 (*1-929812-01-9*) Peregrine Pr Wa.

Macfarlan, Allan & Macfarlan, Paulette. Handbook of American Indian Games. (American Indians Ser.). 288p. 1985. reprint ed. pap. 8.95 (*0-486-24837-2*) Dover.

MacFarlan, Allan & MacFarlan, Paulette. Knotcraft: The Practical & Entertaining Art of Tying Knots. (Crafts Ser.). (Illus.). 192p. (YA). (gr. 6 up). 1983. reprint ed. pap. 5.95 (*0-486-24515-2*) Dover.

Macfarlan, Allan A. Exploring the Outdoors with Indian Secrets. LC 82-5466. (Illus.). 224p. 1982. pap. 12.95 (*0-8117-2183-3*) Stackpole.

— Living Like Indians: A Treasury of North American Indian Crafts, Games & Activities. unabridged ed. LC 99-25168. (Illus.). 320p. 1999. pap. text 7.95 (*0-486-40671-7*) Dover.

Macfarlan, Duncan. The Revivals of the Eighteenth Century, Particularly at Cambuslang: With Three Sermons by the Rev. George Whitefield. (Revival Library). (Illus.). 312p. (C). 1980. reprint ed. lib. bdg. 16.00 (*0-940033-14-3*) R O Roberts.

Macfarlan, Paulette, jt. auth. see Macfarlan, Allan.

MacFarlan, Paulette, jt. auth. see MacFarlan, Allan.

Macfarlan, Susan T. Menopause: The Age of Choice. 110p. (Orig.). 1997. mass mkt. 4.00 (*0-9628604-0-9*) Sumac Pub.

MacFarland. Future Radio Programming Strategies: Cultivating Listenership in the Digital Age. 2nd ed. 1997. pap. 45.00 incl. audio (*0-8058-2987-3*) L Erlbaum Assocs.

MacFarland, Beverly, et al, eds. A Line of Cutting Women. LC 98-42510. 256p. (C). 1998. pap. 16.95 (*0-934971-62-5*) Calyx Bks.

***MacFarland, Beverly, et al, eds.** A Line of Cutting Women. LC 98-42510. 256p. (C). 1998. 32.00 (*0-934971-63-3*) Calyx Bks.

MacFarland, Charles S. The New Church & the New Germany: A Study of Church & State. LC 78-63691. (Studies in Fascism: Ideology & Practice). 224p. reprint ed. 39.50 (*0-404-16953-8*) AMS Pr.

An Asterisk (*) at the beginning of an entry indicates that the title is appearing for the first time.

MacFarland, David T. Contemporary Radio Programming Strategies. (CTS Broadcasting Ser.). 224p. 1990. pap. text 24.95 (*0-8058-0665-2*) L Erlbaum Assocs.

— Development of the Top Forty Radio Format. Sterling, Christopher H., ed. LC 78-21726. (Dissertations in Broadcasting Ser.). (Illus.). 1980. lib. bdg. 48.95 (*0-405-11765-5*) Ayer.

Macfarland, David T. Future Radio Programming Strategies. 2nd ed. LC 97-7737. (LEA's Communication Ser.). 264p. 1997. write for info. (*0-8058-2105-8*); pap. write for info. (*0-8058-2106-6*) L Erlbaum Assocs.

MacFarland, David T., ed. Contemporary Radio Programming Strategies. 224p. (C). 1990. text 49.95 (*0-8058-0664-4*) L Erlbaum Assocs.

MacFarland, Diane, ed. see Holbrook, Sally.

MacFarland, Elaine. Protestants First: Orangeism in Nineteenth-Century Scotland. (Illus.). 224p. 1991. 55.00 (*0-7486-0202-X*, Pub. by Edinburgh U Pr) Col U Pr.

MacFarland, Frank. Studies of Opisthobranchiate Mollusks of the Pacific Coast of North America. Kessell, Howard L., ed. (Memoirs of the California Academy of Sciences Ser.: No. 6). (Illus.). 546p. 1966. 25.00 (*0-940228-10-6*) Calif Acad Sci.

MacFarland, Gerald D. Malpractice in Health Occupations: Index of New Information. 150p. 1994. 47.50 (*0-7883-0050-4*); pap. 44.50 (*0-7883-0051-2*) ABBE Pubs Assn.

MacFarland, Julie, ed. see Noone, Michael.

MacFarland, Paul. How to Build Frameshop Worktables, Fixtures & Jigs. (Illus.). 64p. 1991. 19.00 (*0-938655-36-1*) Columba Pub.

MacFarland, Sam, ed. see Gilbert, Jennifer.

MacFarland, Sara, ed. see Armstrong, Carol.

MacFarland, Sara, ed. see Baker, Cozy.

MacFarland, Sara, ed. see Brackman, Barbara Ann.

MacFarland, Sara, ed. see Macdowell, Ruth B.

MacFarland, Sara, ed. see Oroyan, Susanna.

MacFarland, Sara, ed. see Walner, Hari.

MacFarlane. Diets to Help Arthritis. 1995. mass mkt. 3.99 (*0-7225-2871-X*) Thorsons PA.

MacFarlane, jt. auth. see Jeffcoat, William.

Macfarlane, A. & Gurung, Ganesh M. Gurungs of Nepal: A Guide to the Gurungs. 1992. 20.00 (*0-7855-0227-0*, Pub. by Ratna Pustak Bhandar) St Mut.

MacFarlane, A. G., jt. auth. see De Silva, C. W.

MacFarlane, A. G., jt. auth. see Hung, Y. S.

MacFarlane, Aidan. The Psychology of Childbirth. (Developing Child Ser.). (Illus.). 160p. 1977. pap. text 8.95 (*0-674-72106-3*) HUP.

— User: The Truth about Drugs, What They Do, How They Feel, & Why People Take Them. 174p. 1996. pap. 10.20 (*0-19-286179-4*, M2807) OUP.

Macfarlane, Aidan, et al. Child Health: The Screening Tests. (Practical Guides for General Practice Ser.: No. 11). (Illus.). 64p. 1989. pap. 12.95 (*0-19-261768-0*) OUP.

MacFarlane, Aidan, jt. auth. see Sefi, Sue.

Macfarlane, Alan. A Guide to English Historical Records. LC 82-25102. 144p. reprint ed. pap. 41.10 (*0-608-16853-X*, 2027238) Bks Demand.

***Macfarlane, Alan.** The Riddle of the Modern World: Liberty Wealth & Equality. LC 00-35260. 272p. 2000. text 65.00 (*0-312-23204-7*) St Martin.

Macfarlane, Alan. The Savage Wars of Peace: England, Japan & the Malthusian Trap. LC 96-28823. 1997. 66.95 (*0-631-18117-2*) Blackwell Pubs.

Macfarlane, Alan, ed. see Josselin, Ralph.

***Macfarlane, Alison & Mugford, Miranda.** Birth Counts Vol. 1: Statistics of Pregnancy & Childbirth. 2nd ed. 2000. 59.00 (*0-11-621049-4*, Pub. by Statnry Office) Balogh.

***Macfarlane, Alison, et al.** Birth Counts Vol. 2: Statistics of Pregnancy & Childbirth. 2nd ed. (Illus.). 2000. 59.00 (*0-11-620917-8*, Pub. by Statnry Office) Balogh.

— Birth Counts Vols. 1 & 2: Statistics of Pregnancy & Childbirth. 2 vols., Set. 2nd ed. 2000. 90.00 (*0-11-621050-8*, Pub. by Statnry Office) Balogh.

MacFarlane, Allison, et al. Himalaya & Tibet: Mountain Roots To Mountain Tops. LC 98-43984. (Special Paper Ser.). 330p. 1999. write for info. (*0-8137-2328-0*) Geol Soc.

MacFarlane, Bert, jt. auth. see Myles, Elizabeth.

MacFarlane, Bob. Advancing with Autocad R14 for Windows 95 & Windows Nt. 256p. 1999. pap. 39.95 (*0-470-35238-8*) Halsted Pr.

MacFarlane, Brian. Australian Cinema. (Illus.). 304p. 1988. text 46.00 (*0-231-06728-3*) Col U Pr.

Macfarlane, Brian A. MVS Capacity Planning for a Balanced System. LC 94-21735. (IBM Ser.). 1994. write for info. (*0-07-709053-5*) McGraw.

MacFarlane, Bud, Jr. Conceived Without Sin. 608p. 1997. pap. text 3.99 (*0-9646316-1-X*) St Jude Media.

***Macfarlane, Bud, Jr.** House of Gold. 501p. 1999. pap. write for info. (*0-9646316-3-6*) St Jude Media.

Macfarlane, Bud, Jr. Pierced by a Sword: A Chronicle of the Coming Tribulations. 592p. (Orig.). 1995. mass mkt. 3.99 (*0-9646316-0-1*) St Jude Media.

MacFarlane, Craig, et al. Inner Vision: The Story of the World's Greatest Blind Athlete. LC 97-52666. 220p. 1997. 22.95 (*1-886110-30-1*, Pub. by Addax Pubng) Midpt Trade.

MacFarlane, D. & Shelton, M. Pastures in Vanuatu. (C). 1986. text 50.00 (*0-949511-15-3*, Pub. by ACIAR) St Mut.

MacFarlane, David. Summer Gone: A Novel. LC 99-47955. 288p. 2000. 23.00 (*0-517-70262-2*, FIC019000, Crown) Crown Pub Group.

Macfarlane, David, jt. auth. see Cohon, George.

MacFarlane, David, jt. auth. see Goodwin, Gabrielle.

Macfarlane, Deborah, jt. auth. see White, Merran.

MacFarlane, Doug, jt. auth. see Harding, Vicki.

Macfarlane, Eleanor C. Boost Family Involvement: How to Make Your Program Succeed under the New Title I Guidelines. 80p. (Orig.). 1995. pap. 18.00 (*1-883790-15-8*, 100-1273, EDINFO Pr) Grayson Bernard Pubs.

Macfarlane, Eleanor C., jt. auth. see Simic, Marjorie R.

MacFarlane, Ellen B. & Burstein, Patricia. Legwork: An Inspiring Journey Through a Chronic Illness. LC 94-11726. 1994. write for info. (*0-02-578001-8*) Macmillan.

Macfarlane, Eric. Education 16-19: In Transition. LC 92-24739. (Educational Management Ser.). 160p. 1992. pap. write for info. (*0-415-08086-X*) Routledge.

Macfarlane, G. Layman's Dictionary of Law. 256p. 1984. pap. 10.00 (*0-08-039157-5*, Pergamon Pr) Elsevier.

Macfarlane, George T., jt. ed. see Gibson, Glenn R.

Macfarlane, Gwyn. Alexander Fleming: The Man & the Myth. LC 83-18358. (Illus.). 352p. 1984. 32.00 (*0-674-01490-1*) HUP.

MacFarlane, Gwyn. Howard Florey: The Making of a Great Scientist. (Illus.). 1979. 39.95 (*0-19-858161-0*) OUP.

MacFarlane, I. A., jt. auth. see Eyes, B.

MacFarlane, I. G. Complete Electrocardiology, 3 vols. 1988. 395.00 (*0-08-035567-6*, Pergamon Pr) Elsevier.

MacFarlane, I. G., jt. auth. see Johnson.

MacFarlane, Ivan C., ed. see National Research Council of Canada, Associate Com.

Macfarlane, Jean W. Studies in Child Guidance. (SRCD M Ser.: Vol. 3, No. 6). 1938. 25.00 (*0-527-01506-7*) Periodicals Srv.

***MacFarlane, John.** Ernest Lapointe & Quebec's Influence on Canada's Foreign Policy. 288p. 1999. text 50.00 (*0-8020-4487-5*) U of Toronto Pr.

MacFarlane, Julie, ed. Rethinking Disuptes: The Mediation Alternative. LC 97-102644. (Lecture Notes...Ser.). 400p. 1996. write for info. (*1-85941-151-7*, Pub. by Cavendish Pubng) Gaunt.

Macfarlane, Julie, ed. see Boon, Andy.

Macfarlane, Julie, ed. see Chapman, Jenny.

Macfarlane, Julie, ed. see Costanzo, Margot.

Macfarlane, Julie, ed. see Doonan, Elmer.

Macfarlane, Julie, ed. see Stott, David.

Macfarlane, Julie, ed. see Tribe, Diana.

MacFarlane, Kee & Cunningham, Carolyn. Steps to Healthy Touching. (Illus.). 144p. (Orig.). (J). (gr. k-7). 1988. student ed. 19.95 (*0-685-20041-8*, 1400) Kidsrights.

MacFarlane, Kee, jt. auth. see Cunningham, Carolyn.

MacFarlane, L. J. Socialism, Social Ownership, & Social Justice. LC 98-19809. 344p. 1998. text 69.95 (*0-312-21622-X*) St Martin.

MacFarlane, L. W. Dr. Mac: The Man, His Land & His People. LC 85-79991. (Illus.). 466p. 1985. 29.95 (*0-935615-00-8*) S Utah U Pr.

MacFarlane, Leslie J. ISS BRIT POLS SINCE 1945. 3rd ed. (Political Realities Ser.). 160p. (C). 1986. pap. text 18.95 (*0-582-35560-5*, 72241) Longman.

— William Elphinstone & the Kingdom of Scotland, 1431-1514: The Struggle for Order. (Illus.). 540p. 1985. text 60.00 (*0-08-030408-7*, Pub. by Aberdeen U Pr) Macmillan.

MacFarlane, Linda, jt. auth. see Macfarlane, Stuart.

MacFarlane, Lisa, ed. This World Is Not Conclusion: Faith in Nineteenth-Century New England Fiction. LC 98-9308. (Hardscrabble Bks.). 301p. 1998. pap. 19.95 (*0-87451-862-8*) U Pr of New Eng.

MacFarlane, Lisa, ed. see Juster, Susan.

MacFarlane, Lisa, ed. & intro. see Adams, Henry (Brooks).

MacFarlane, M. H., jt. ed. see Hwang, W-Y. P.

Macfarlane, Michael. Urology. 2nd ed. (House Officer Ser.). (Illus.). 336p. 1994. 21.95 (*0-683-05325-6*) Lppncott W & W.

— Urology for the House Officer. (House Officer Ser.). (Illus.). 300p. (Orig.). (C). 1988. pap. 20.00 (*0-683-05324-8*) Lppncott W & W.

***MacFarlane, Muriel.** Heal Your Aura Finding True Love by Generating A Positive Personal Energy Field. LC 99-40383. 1999. pap. text 12.95 (*0-8065-2132-5*) Carol Pub Group.

MacFarlane, Muriel. Your Psychic Self. LC 99-181983. 288p. 1998. pap. 13.00 (*1-57566-328-7*, Knsington) Kensgtn Pub Corp.

Macfarlane, Muriel K. The Panic Attack, Anxiety & Phobia Solutions Handbook. LC 95-60774. 336p. (Orig.). 1996. pap. 12.95 (*1-887053-00-X*) United Res CA.

MacFarlane, Muriel K. The Psoriasis Handbook: A Self-Help Guide. LC 95-61640. (Illus.). 224p. (Orig.). 1995. pap. 12.95 (*1-887053-01-8*) United Res CA.

— The Sinus Handbook: A Self-Help Guide. LC 96-61828. (Illus.). 312p. 1997. pap. 12.95 (*1-887053-08-5*) United Res CA.

MacFarlane, Nigel. A Paper Journey: Travels among the Village Papermakers of India & Nepal. limited ed. (Illus.). 90p. 1993. 240.00 (*0-938768-45-X*) Oak Knoll.

MacFarlane, P. W. & De Padva, F. Electrocardiology 92. 400p. 1993. text 121.00 (*981-02-1387-5*) World Scientific Pub.

MacFarlane, P. W. & Rautarharju, P. Electrocardiology 1993. LC 95-108388. 364p. 1994. text 86.00 (*981-02-1793-5*) World Scientific Pub.

MacFarlane, Peter. Health Law: Commentary & Materials. 240p. 1993. pap. 39.00 (*1-86287-098-5*, Pub. by Federation Pr) Gaunt.

— Health Law: Commentary & Materials. 2nd ed. 250p. 1995. pap. 39.00 (*1-86287-162-0*, Pub. by Federation Pr) Gaunt.

***MacFarlane, Peter.** Health Law: Commentary & Materials. 3rd ed. 318p. 2000. pap. 39.95 (*1-86287-357-7*, Pub. by Federation Pr) Gaunt.

MacFarlane, Peter & Fisher, Simon. Churches, Clergy & the Law. 292p. 1996. pap. 29.00 (*1-86287-210-4*, Pub. by Federation Pr) Gaunt.

***Macfarlane, Peter S., et al.** Pathology Illustrated. 5th ed. LC 99-28979. 2000. write for info. (*0-443-05957-8*) Church.

Macfarlane, Peter W. & Lawrie, T. D., eds. Comprehensive Electrocardiology: Theory & Practice in Health & Disease, 3 vols., Set. LC 88-17891. (Illus.). 1900p. 1988. 715.00 (*0-08-035568-4*, Pergamon Pr) Elsevier.

Macfarlane, Peter W., jt. ed. see Bacharova, Ljuba.

Macfarlane, Quentin. Alison: A Father's Search for His Missing Daughter. 2nd ed. (Illus.). 192p. 1994. pap. 17.95 (*1-85158-624-5*, Pub. by Mainstream Pubng) Trafalgar.

***MacFarlane, Richard.** Canada's Newspaper Legend: The Biography of J. Douglas MacFarlane. (Illus.). 2000. pap. 17.95 (*1-55022-413-1*, Pub. by ECW) LPC InBook.

Macfarlane, Robert & Hardy, David, eds. Outcome after Head, Neck, & Spinal Trauma: A Medico-Legal Guide. 456p. 1997. text 135.00 (*0-7506-2178-8*) Buttrwrth-Heinemann.

MacFarlane, Ruth B. Collecting & Preserving Plants. unabridged ed. LC 94-11884. (Illus.). 192p. 1994. pap. text 5.95 (*0-486-28281-3*) Dover.

MacFarlane, S. Neil. Superpower Rivalry & Third World Radicalism: The Idea of National Liberation. LC 84-43081. 248p. reprint ed. pap. 76.90 (*0-608-06698-2*, 206689500009) Bks Demand.

MacFarlane, S. Neil, jt. ed. see Cambell, Kurt M.

***Macfarlane, Stuart & MacFarlane, Linda.** Old Wrecks' Jokes. Exley, Helen, ed. (Joke Bks.). (Illus.). 64p. 1999. 8.50 (*1-86187-124-4*) Exley Giftbooks.

— Over 30s' Jokes. Exley, Helen, ed. (Joke Bks.). (Illus.). 64p. 1999. 8.50 (*1-86187-123-6*) Exley Giftbooks.

MacFarquhar, Roderick. The Origins of the Cultural Revolution Vol. 1: Contradictions Among the People, 1956-1957. LC 73-15793. (Studies of the East Asian Institute). (Illus.). 470p. 1987. pap. text 25.50 (*0-231-08385-8*, King's Crown Paperbacks) Col U Pr.

— The Origins of the Cultural Revolution Vol. 2: The Great Leap Forward, 1958-1960. (Studies of the East Asian Institute). (Illus.). 439p. 1987. pap. text 29.00 (*0-231-05717-2*) Col U Pr.

— The Origins of the Cultural Revolution Vol. III: The Coming of the Cataclysm, Vol. 3. 480p. 1997. 50.00 (*0-231-11082-0*) Col U Pr.

— The Origins of the Cultural Revolution Vol. III: The Coming of the Cataclysm, 1961-1966. 1999. pap. 18.50 (*0-231-11083-9*) Col U Pr.

MacFarquhar, Roderick, ed. The Politics of China: The Eras of Mao & Deng. 2nd ed. 608p. 1997. text 69.95 (*0-521-58141-9*); pap. text 25.95 (*0-521-58863-4*) Cambridge U Pr.

MacFarquhar, Roderick, et al, eds. The Secret Speeches of Chairman Mao: From the Hundred Flowers to the Great Leap Forward. (Contemporary China Ser.: No. 6). 400p. 1989. pap. 18.00 (*0-674-79673-X*) HUP.

MacFarquhar, Roderick & Fairbank, John K., eds. The Cambridge History of China Vol. 14: The People's Republic of China, Pt. 1: The Emergence of Revolutionary China, 1949-1965. LC 76-29852. (Illus.). 748p. 1987. text 145.00 (*0-521-24336-X*) Cambridge U Pr.

— The Cambridge History of China Vol. 15: The People's Republic, Pt. 2: Revolutions Within the Chinese Revolution, 1966-1982. (Illus.). 1134p. (C). 1991. text 149.95 (*0-521-24337-8*) Cambridge U Pr.

MacFarquhar, Roderick, jt. auth. see Goldman, Merle.

MacFate, Robert P., jt. auth. see Levinson, Samuel A.

Macfayden, A. & Ford, E. D., eds. Advances in Ecological Research, Vol. 15. (Serial Publication Ser.). 448p. 1986. text 104.00 (*0-12-013915-4*) Acad Pr.

— Advances in Ecological Research, Vol. 16. (Serial Publication Ser.). 300p. 1987. text 104.00 (*0-12-013916-2*) Acad Pr.

Macfie, A. L. Atat Urk. LC 93-33763. (Profiles in Power Ser.). (C). 1995. pap. text 27.19 (*0-582-07863-6*) Longman.

— Ataturk. LC 93-33763. (Profiles in Power Ser.). (C). 1994. text 50.95 (*0-582-07862-8*) Longman.

— The Eastern Question, 1774-1923. 2nd rev. ed. LC 96-33924. (Seminar Studies in History). 152p. (C). 1996. pap. text 14.06 (*0-582-29195-X*, Pub. by Addison-Wesley) Longman.

MacFie, A. L. End Ottoman Empire. LC 97-50575. 272p. (C). 1998. 75.00 (*0-582-28762-6*) Longman.

Macfie, Alec L. Theories of the Trade Cycle. LC 78-119544. (Reprints of Economic Classics Ser.). ix, 198p. 1971. reprint ed. lib. bdg. 35.00 (*0-678-00699-7*) Kelley.

Macfie, H. J. H., jt. auth. see Thomson, D. M. H.

Macfie, J. M. Myths & Legends of India: An Introduction to the Study of Hinduism. (C). 1994. pap. 9.50 (*81-7167-131-4*, Pub. by Rupa) S Asia.

Macfie, Matthew. Vancouver Island & British Columbia: Their History, Resources & Prospects. LC 72-9458. (Far Western Frontier Ser.). (Illus.). 600p. 1973. reprint ed. 41.95 (*0-405-04986-2*) Ayer.

MacFloner, Niles. Life's Hidden Meaning. (Illus.). 763p. 1999. pap. 39.95 (*0-9648483-0-9*) Ageless Wisdom.

***MacGaffey, Janet, et al.** Congo-Paris: Transnational Traders on the Margins of the Law. LC 00-27282. 2000. pap. write for info. (*0-253-21402-5*) Ind U Pr.

MacGaffey, Janet, et al. The Real Economy of Zaire: The Contribution of Smuggling & Other Unofficial Activities to National Wealth. LC 91-3844. 192p. (Orig.). (C). 1991. text 31.95 (*0-8122-3140-6*); pap. text 20.95 (*0-8122-1365-3*) U of Pa Pr.

***MacGaffey, Wyatt.** Kongo Political Culture: The Conceptual Challenge of the Particular. LC 99-43432. (Illus.). 272p. 2000. 39.95 (*0-253-33698-8*) Ind U Pr.

MacGaffey, Wyatt. Modern Kongo Prophets: Religion in a Plural Society. LC 82-48554. (African Systems of Thought Ser.). (Illus.). 301p. reprint ed. pap. 93.40 (*0-608-18264-8*, 205672900081) Bks Demand.

— Religion & Society in Central Africa: The BaKongo of Lower Zaire. LC 85-31805. (Illus.). xii, 296p. 1986. pap. text 16.95 (*0-226-50030-6*) U Ch Pr.

— Religion & Society in Central Africa: The BaKongo of Lower Zaire. LC 85-31805. (Illus.). xii, 296p. 1995. lib. bdg. 54.00 (*0-226-50029-2*) U Ch Pr.

MacGaffey, Wyatt & Barnett, Clifford R. Cuba: Its People, Its Society, Its Culture. 10--10. LC 73-19296. (Survey of World Cultures Ser.: No. 10). (Illus.). 392p. 1974. reprint ed. lib. bdg. 35.00 (*0-8371-7319-1*, MCUB, Greenwood Pr) Greenwood.

MacGaffey, Wyatt & Harris, Michael D. Astonishment & Power: Kongo Minkisi/The Art of Renee Stout. (Illus.). 224p. (Orig.). 1993. pap. 34.95 (*1-56098-274-8*) Smithsonian.

MacGahan, J. A. Campaigning on the Oxus & the Fall of Khiva. LC 78-115561. (Russia Observed Ser.). 1970. reprint ed. 28.95 (*0-405-03047-9*) Ayer.

MacGarrigle, George L. Aleutian Islands: The United States Army Campaigns of World War 2. 26p. 1992. pap. 1.25 (*0-16-035882-5*) USGPO.

— Central Burma: The United States Army Campaigns of World War 2. 22p. 1996. pap. 2.00 (*0-16-048137-6*) USGPO.

— Combat Operations: Taking the Offensive, October 1966 to October 1967. (CMH Publication Ser.: Vol. 91-4). (Illus.). 507p. 1998. boxed set 44.00 (*0-16-049540-7*) USGPO.

Macgee, Thomas D. Gallery of Irish Writers: The Irish Writers of the Seventeenth Century. LC 75-28823. reprint ed. 39.50 (*0-404-13815-2*) AMS Pr.

MacGibbon, David & Ross, Thomas, eds. Castellated & Domestic Architecture of Scotland, 5 vols. (C). 1996. 500.00 (*0-901824-18-6*, Pub. by Mercat Pr Bks) St Mut.

MacGibbon, Duncan A. The Canadian Grain Trade. LC 32-18135. 237p. reprint ed. pap. 73.50 (*0-8357-7996-3*, 201430700089) Bks Demand.

MacGibbon, James, ed. see Smith, Stevie.

MacGibbon, Jean. I Meant to Marry Him. large type ed. 368p. 1986. 27.99 (*0-7089-1473-X*) Ulverscroft.

Macgibbon, Lian & Ross, Fitzroy, eds. Ecclesiastical Architecture of Scotland, 3 vols. 1996. 400.00 (*1-873644-00-0*, Pub. by Mercat Pr Bks) St Mut.

MacGilchrist, Barbara. Managing Access & Entitlement in Primary Education. 32p. 1992. pap. 6.00 (*0-948080-76-0*, Trentham Bks) Stylus Pub VA.

MacGilchrist, Barbara, et al. The Intelligent School. LC 97-223063. (One-Off Ser.). (Illus.). 144p. 1997. pap. 25.95 (*1-85396-342-9*) Corwin Pr.

MacGill-Callahan, Sheila. And Still the Turtle Watched. (Illus.). 32p. (J). (gr. k). 1996. pap. 6.99 (*0-14-055836-5*, PuffinBks) Peng Put Young Read.

— And Still the Turtle Watched. LC 90-37377. 1996. 11.19 (*0-606-10123-3*, Pub. by Turtleback) Demco.

***MacGill-Callahan, Sheila.** Last Snake in Ireland. (Illus.). (J). 2000. pap. 6.95 (*0-8234-1555-4*) Holiday.

Macgill-Callahan, Sheila. The Last Snake in Ireland: A Story about St. Patrick. LC 98-33504. (Illus.). (YA). (gr. k-6). 1999. 16.95 (*0-8234-1425-6*) Holiday.

***MacGill, Patrick.** Children of the Dead End. 323p. 1999. pap. 15.95 (*1-84158-000-7*, Pub. by Birlinn Ltd) Dufour.

— The Rat-Pit. 319p. 1999. pap. 15.95 (*1-84158-004-X*, Pub. by Birlinn Ltd) Dufour.

***MacGill, Peter.** Irving Pen. (Illus.). 64p. 1999. pap. write for info. (*1-878283-87-1*) PaceWildenstein.

MacGillavry, et al. International Tables for X-Ray Crystallography. (Mathematical Tables Ser.: Vol. I). 1983. lib. bdg. 85.00 (*90-277-1532-7*) Kluwer Academic.

MacGillivray, Alex, jt. ed. see Jackson, Tim.

MacGillivray, Catherine A., tr. see Cixous, Helene.

MacGillivray, Catherine A., tr. & intro. see Cixous, Helene.

MacGillivray, Evan James & Leigh-Jones, Nicholas. Macgillivray on Insurance Law: Relating to All Risks Other Than Marine. 9th ed. LC 98-198138. (Insurance Practitioners Library). 1024 p. 1997. write for info. (*0-421-50480-3*) Sweet & Maxwell.

MacGillivray, H. T., ed. Astronomy from Wide-Field Imaging: Proceedings of the 161st Symposium of the International Astronomical Union, Held in Potsdam, Germany, August 23-27, 1993. LC 94-12286. (International Astronomical Union Symposia Ser.). 792p. (C). 1994. pap. text 127.00 (*0-7923-2879-5*); lib. bdg. 257.00 (*0-7923-2878-7*) Kluwer Academic.

MacGillivray, Ian, ed. Twinning & Twins. fac. ed. LC 88-14385. (Wiley Medical Publications). 331p. 1988. reprint ed. pap. 102.70 (*0-7837-8268-3*, 204904900009) Bks Demand.

MacGillivray, J. A. Knossos: Pottery Groups of the Old Palace Period. (BSA Studies: Vol. 5). (Illus.). 195p. 1999. lib. bdg. 79.50 (*0-904887-32-4*, Pub. by Brit Sch Athens) David Brown.

MacGillivray, James R. Keats: A Bibliography & Reference Guide. LC Z 8461.M3. (Toronto University Dept. of English, Studies & Texts: No. 3). 292p. reprint ed. pap. 90.60 (*0-608-11454-5*, 201430800089) Bks Demand.

***MacGillivray, Joseph Alexander.** Minotaur: Sir Arthur Evans & the Archaeology of the Minoan Myth. (Illus.). 352p. 2000. text 26.00 (*0-8090-3035-7*) FS&G.

MacGillivray, Lois. Decision-Related Research on the Organization of Service Delivery Systems in Metropolitan Areas: Fire Protection. LC 79-83819. 1979. write for info. (*0-89138-985-7*) ICPSR.

***MacGillivray, Roxane.** Florida Student Supplement for Litigation. LC 99-44778. 1999. pap. text 21.95 (*0-7355-1181-0*) Panel Pubs.

An Asterisk (*) at the beginning of an entry indicates that the title is appearing for the first time.

MacGillivray, Scott. Laurel & Hardy: From the Forties Forward. LC 98-16059. (Illus.). 216p. 1998. 40.00 (*1-879511-35-5*, Vestal Pr); pap. 19.95 (*1-879511-41-X*, Vestal Pr) Madison Bks UPA.

MacGillivray, W. R., et al, eds. Physics of Electronic & Atomic Collisions: Proceedings of ICPEAC XVII Brisbane, 10-16 July 1991. (Illus.). 720p. 1992. 326.00 (*0-7503-0167-8*) IOP Pub.

***MacGillivray, William & Ralph, Robert.** A Hebridean Naturalist's Journal, 1817-1818. LC 98-188999. 252p. 1999. 66.00 (*0-86152-122-6*) Acair Ltd.

MacGinitie, Harry D. The Eocene Green River Flora of Northwestern Colorado & Northeastern Utah. LC 73-626230. (University of California Publications in Social Welfare: Vol. 83). (Illus.). 210p. reprint ed. pap. 65.10 (*0-608-17935-3*, 201500300093) Bks Demand.

MacGinitie, Walter H., ed. Assessment Problems in Reading. LC 73-84793. 107p. reprint ed. pap. 33.20 (*0-8357-5809-5*, 202681400052) Bks Demand.

Macginley, T. J. Steel Structures: Practical Design Studies. 2nd ed. LC 98-171439. (Illus.). 352p. (Orig.). 1997. mass mkt. 39.95 (*0-419-17930-5*, E & FN Spon) Routledge.

MacGinley, T. J., jt. auth. see Choo, B. S.

MacGinty, Roger, jt. auth. see Darby, John.

MacGiorman, Jack W. Romanos: El Evangelio para Todo Hombre, Vol. 6. (Estudios Biblicos Basicos Ser.).Tr. of Romans: Every Man's Gospel. (SPA.). 152p. 1973. pap. 7.99 (*0-311-04343-7*) Casa Bautista.

***MacGivney, Joseph.** Place Names of the County of Longford. 224p. 2000. cd-rom 19.95 (*1-58211-235-5*) Quintin Pub RI.

MacGlashan, M. E. Iran-U. S. Claims Tribunal Reports, Vols. 8-22. (C). 1992. text 400.00 (*0-7855-0125-8*, Pub. by Grotius Pubns Ltd) St Mut.

MacGlashing, John W. Batmen: Night Air Group 90 in World War II. Lambert, John W., ed. LC 96-144529. (Gold Wings Ser.: Vol. 1). (Illus.). 48p. (Orig.). 1995. pap. 12.95 (*1-883809-08-8*, 4023) Specialty Pr.

MacGorman, Donald R. & Rust, W. David. The Electrical Nature of Storms. (Illus.). 432p. 1998. text 85.00 (*0-19-507337-1*) OUP.

MacGorman, J. W. The Layman's Bible Commentary: Romans, I Corinthians, Vol. 20. LC 79-51501. 154p. 1980. 11.99 (*0-8054-1190-9*) Broadman.

MacGougan, Denny & Reynolds, J. B. Tacoma: Tomorrow's City - Today. LC 96-4821. (Urban Tapestry Ser.). (Illus.). 192p. 1996. 39.50 (*1-881096-28-9*) Towery Pub.

MacGowan, Christopher. William Carlos William's Early Poetry: The Visual Arts Background. 160p. 1984. pap. 49.95 (*0-7734-1986-1*) E Mellen.

MacGowan, Christopher, ed. see Levertov, Denise & Williams, William Carlos.

MacGowan, Christopher J., ed. see Williams, William Carlos.

***MacGowan, Craig.** Mac's Field Guide to Denali National Park. 2000. per. 4.95 (*0-89886-745-2*) Mountaineers.

— Mac's Field Guide to Midwest Garden Bugs. 2000. per. 4.95 (*0-89886-746-0*) Mountaineers.

MacGowan, Craig. Mac's Field Guide to Mount Rainier National Park: Flowers & Trees. (Mac's Field Guide Ser.). (Illus.). 1998. pap. 4.95 (*0-89886-596-4*) Mountaineers.

— Mac's Field Guide to Mount Rainier National Park: Mammals & Birds. (Mac's Field Guide Ser.). (Illus.). 1998. pap. 4.95 (*0-89886-595-6*) Mountaineers.

***MacGowan, Craig.** Mac's Field Guide to Southeast Garden Bugs. 2000. per. 4.95 (*0-89886-747-9*) Mountaineers.

— Mac's Field Guide to Yellowstone & Grand Teton National Parks: Trees & Wildflowers. 2nd ed. LC 99-6541. (Field Guide Ser.). (Illus.). 1999. pap. 4.95 (*0-89886-673-1*) Mountaineers.

MacGowan, Craig. Mac's Field Guide to Yosemite National Park: Birds & Mammals. (Mac's Field Guide Ser.). 1999. 4.95 (*0-89886-674-X*) Mountaineers.

— Mac's Field Guide to Yosemite National Park: Trees & Wildflowers. (Orig.). 1999. pap. 4.95 (*0-89886-675-8*) Mountaineers.

— MAC's Field Guides: Alaskan Wildlife. (Illus.). 1997. pap. 4.95 (*0-89886-393-7*) Mountaineers.

— MAC's Field Guides: California Coastal Birds. (Illus.). 1990. pap. 4.95 (*0-89886-261-2*) Mountaineers.

— Mac's Field Guides: California Coastal Fish. (Illus.). 1997. pap. 4.95 (*0-89886-570-0*) Mountaineers.

— MAC's Field Guides: California Coastal Invertebrates. (Illus.). 1997. pap. 4.95 (*0-89886-532-8*) Mountaineers.

— MAC's Field Guides: North America/Birds of Prey. (Illus.). 1990. pap. 4.95 (*0-89886-260-4*) Mountaineers.

— MAC's Field Guides: North America/Dinosaurs. (Illus.). 1997. pap. 4.95 (*0-89886-530-1*) Mountaineers.

— MAC's Field Guides: North America/Freshwater Fish. (Illus.). 1998. pap. 4.95 (*0-89886-217-5*) Mountaineers.

— MAC's Field Guides: North America/Land Mammals. (Illus.). 1990. pap. 4.95 (*0-89886-243-4*) Mountaineers.

— MAC's Field Guides: North America/Marine Mammals. (Illus.). 1988. pap. 4.95 (*0-89886-218-3*) Mountaineers.

— MAC's Field Guides: North America/Reptiles. (Illus.). 1992. pap. 4.95 (*0-89886-339-2*) Mountaineers.

— MAC's Field Guides: North America/Salmon & Trout. (Illus.). 1994. pap. 4.95 (*0-89886-392-9*) Mountaineers.

— MAC's Field Guides: Northeast Coast Water Birds. (Illus.). 1988. pap. 4.95 (*0-89886-214-0*) Mountaineers.

— MAC's Field Guides: Northeast Coastal Fish. (Illus.). 1990. pap. 4.95 (*0-89886-244-2*) Mountaineers.

— MAC's Field Guides: Northeast Coastal Invertebrates. (Illus.). 1988. pap. 4.95 (*0-89886-215-9*) Mountaineers.

— MAC's Field Guides: Northeast Park/Backyard Birds. (Illus.). 1990. pap. 4.95 (*0-89886-245-0*) Mountaineers.

— MAC's Field Guides: Northeast Wildflowers. (Illus.). 1992. pap. 4.95 (*0-89886-337-6*) Mountaineers.

— MAC's Field Guides: Northern California Park/Garden Birds. (Illus.). 1991. pap. 4.95 (*0-89886-314-7*) Mountaineers.

— MAC's Field Guides: Northern California Wildflowers. (Illus.). 1991. pap. 4.95 (*0-89886-288-4*) Mountaineers.

— MAC's Field Guides: Northwest Coast Water Birds. (Illus.). 1988. pap. 4.95 (*0-89886-213-2*) Mountaineers.

— MAC's Field Guides: Northwest Coastal Fish. (Illus.). 1988. pap. 4.95 (*0-89886-211-6*) Mountaineers.

— MAC's Field Guides: Northwest Coastal Invertebrates. (Illus.). 1997. pap. 4.95 (*0-89886-212-4*) Mountaineers.

— MAC's Field Guides: Northwest Garden Bugs. (Illus.). 1997. pap. 4.95 (*0-89886-531-X*) Mountaineers.

— MAC's Field Guides: Northwest Park/Backyard Birds. (Illus.). 1990. pap. 4.95 (*0-89886-246-9*) Mountaineers.

— MAC's Field Guides: Northwest Trees. (Illus.). 1994. pap. 4.95 (*0-89886-391-0*) Mountaineers.

— MAC's Field Guides: Pacific Northwest Wildflowers. (Illus.). 1991. pap. 4.95 (*0-89886-287-6*) Mountaineers.

— MAC's Field Guides: San Juan Islands. (Illus.). 1992. pap. 4.95 (*0-89886-338-4*) Mountaineers.

— MAC's Field Guides: Southern California - Wildflowers. (Illus.). 1991. pap. 4.95 (*0-89886-289-2*) Mountaineers.

— MAC's Field Guides: Southern California Park/Garden Birds. (Illus.). 1991. pap. 4.95 (*0-89886-315-5*) Mountaineers.

— MAC's Field Guides: Southwest Cacti, Shrubs, Trees. (Illus.). 1991. pap. 4.95 (*0-89886-295-7*) Mountaineers.

— MAC's Field Guides: Southwest Park/Garden Birds. (Illus.). 1991. pap. 4.95 (*0-89886-294-9*) Mountaineers.

MacGowan, Craig & Sauskojus. MAC's Field Guides: Rocky Mountain Wildflowers. (Illus.). 1992. pap. 4.95 (*0-89886-336-8*) Mountaineers.

MacGowan, Douglas. Murder in Victorian Scotland: The Trial of Madeleine Smith. LC 99-13792. 192p. 1999. 35.00 (*0-275-96431-0*, C6431, Praeger Pubs) Greenwood.

MacGowan-Gilhooly, Adele. Achieving Clarity in English: A Whole-Language Book. 156p. (C). 1996. pap. text, per. 13.95 (*0-7872-2096-5*) Kendall-Hunt.

MacGowan-Gilhooly, Adele M. Achieving Fluency in English: A Whole-Language Book. 116p. (C). 1996. pap. 13.95 (*0-7872-2039-6*) Kendall-Hunt.

MacGowan, Kenneth & Hester, Joseph. Early Man in the New World. 1990. 16.50 (*0-8446-2501-9*) Peter Smith.

MacGowan, Kenneth & Jones, Robert E. Continental Stagecraft. LC 64-14711. (Illus.). 249p. 1972. 20.95 (*0-405-08765-9*, Pub. by Blom Pubns) Ayer.

MacGowan, S. Douglas. The Real World of Engineering: Case History, No. 44. 3.50 (*0-614-05212-2*, CHN04305913.5M) ASFE.

MacGowan, Sandra, ed. see Faiola, Theodora & Pullen, J. A.

Macgowen, Kenneth. A Primer of Playwriting. 2nd ed. LC 80-39768. 199p. 1981. reprint ed. lib. bdg. 67.50 (*0-313-22896-5*, MACP, Greenwood Pr) Greenwood.

***Macgoye, Marjorie.** Coming to Birth. 2000. 30.00 (*1-55861-253-X*); pap. 11.95 (*1-55861-249-1*) Feminist Pr.

— The Present Moment. 2000. 30.00 (*1-55861-254-8*); pap. 11.95 (*1-55861-248-3*) Feminist Pr.

MacGrath, Harold. The Man on the Box. LC 70-124776. reprint ed. 29.50 (*0-404-04130-2*) AMS Pr.

— The Man on the Box. LC 78-145155. 361p. 1972. reprint ed. 16.00 (*0-403-01083-7*) Scholarly.

MacGrath, Michelle. Art of Teaching Peacefully: Improving Behavior & Reducing Conflict in the Classroom, 1. LC 98-215122. 1998. pap. text 24.95 (*1-85346-560-7*) Taylor & Francis.

MacGreevy, Thomas. Collected Poems of Thomas MacGreevy. Schreibman, Susan, ed. 180p. 1992. text 24.95 (*0-8132-0756-8*) Cath U Pr.

***MacGregor.** Florida Commercial Landlord Tenant Law 99-2. 116p. 1999. ring bd. write for info. (*0-327-01473-3*, 8053319) LEXIS Pub.

MacGregor. Florida Commercial Landlord Tenant Law 99-1. 146p. 1999. lib. bdg. write for info. (*0-327-00962-4*, 8053318) LEXIS Pub.

— Florida Condominium Law, Issue 99-1. 178p. 1999. ring bd., suppl. ed. write for info. (*0-327-01063-0*, 8054122) LEXIS Pub.

— Florida Condominium Law 98-4, 3 vols. 322p. 1998. write for info. (*0-327-00817-2*, 8054121) LEXIS Pub.

***MacGregor.** Florida Condominium Law 99-2. 190p. 1999. ring bd. write for info. (*0-327-01474-1*, 8054123) LEXIS Pub.

— Florida Condominium Law 99-3. 138p. 1999. ring bd. write for info. (*0-327-01704-X*, 8054124) LEXIS Pub.

MacGregor. Florida Rules of Court Service, Issue 99-1. 324p. 1999. ring bd. write for info. (*0-327-01049-5*, 8078625) LEXIS Pub.

— Florida Rules of Court Service 98-5, 4 vols. 168p. 1998. write for info. (*0-327-00815-6*, 8078624) LEXIS Pub.

— Florida Rules of Court Service 99-2, 4 vols. 170p. 1999. ring bd. 48.00 (*0-327-01170-X*, 8078626) LEXIS Pub.

***MacGregor.** Florida Rules of Court Service 99-3, 4 vols., Set. 190p. 1999. ring bd. write for info. (*0-327-01649-3*, 8078627) LEXIS Pub.

MacGregor. Florida Workers' Compensation Manual 99-1, 2 vols. 450p. 1999. ring bd. write for info. (*0-327-01352-4*, 8081917) LEXIS Pub.

***MacGregor.** Florida Workers' Compensation Manual 99-2. 250p. 1999. ring bd. write for info. (*0-327-01709-0*, 8081918) LEXIS Pub.

MaCgregor. Higher Chemistry. 1993. pap. text. write for info. (*0-05-005080-X*) Addison-Wesley.

Macgregor. Wilder's Wilderness. 1994. per. 2.99 (*0-373-17172-2*) Harlequin Bks.

MacGregor, Douglas A. & Center for Strategic & International Studies Staff. Breaking the Phalanx: A New Design for Landpower in the 21st Century. LC 96-34012. 304p. 1997. 65.00 (*0-275-95793-4*, Praeger Pubs) Greenwood.

MacGregor, A. J. Graphics Simplified: How to Plan & Prepare Effective Charts, Graphs, Illustrations, & Other Visual Aids. LC 79-10358. 1979. pap. 9.95 (*0-8020-6363-2*) U of Toronto Pr.

MacGregor, Alexander P., Jr. Ten Years of Classicists: Dissertations & Statistics, 1986-1996. LC 97-45995. vii, 105p. 1997. pap. 20.00 (*0-86516-405-3*) Bolchazy-Carducci.

***MacGregor, Anne.** Is HRT Right for You? LC 99-234027. 160p. 1998. pap. 9.95 (*0-85969-803-3*, Pub. by Sheldon Pr) Intl Pubs Mktg.

MacGregor, Anne. Managing Migraine in Primary Care. LC 98-46293. (Illus.). 239p. 1998. pap. 39.95 (*0-632-05083-7*) Blackwell Sci.

***MacGregor, Anne.** Migraine in Women. 90p. 1999. 39.95 (*1-85317-744-X*, Pub. by Martin Dunitz) Blackwell Sci.

MacGregor, Anne, jt. auth. see Wilkinson, Marcia.

MacGregor, Arthur, ed. Antiquities from Europe & the Near East - Collection of the Lord McAlpine. (Illus.). 142p. 1995. pap. 29.95 (*0-907849-70-9*, 709, Pub. by Ashmolean Mus) A Schwartz & Co.

MacGregor, Arthur, ed. Tradescant's Rarities: Essays on the Foundation of the Ashmolean Museum, 1683, with a Catalogue of the Surviving Early Collections. (Illus.). 1983. 150.00 (*0-19-813405-3*) OUP.

MacGregor, Arthur, jt. auth. see Hook, Moira.

Macgregor, Brent. Live, Direct & Biased? Making Television News in the Satellite Age. LC 96-37949. 1997. text 60.00 (*0-340-66224-7*, Pub. by E A) St Martin.

MacGregor, Brent. Live, Direct & Biased? Making Television News in the Satellite Age. LC 96-37949. 248p. 1997. text 19.95 (*0-340-66225-5*, Pub. by E A) OUP.

MacGregor, C. The Equine Foot. (Illus.). 510p. 2000. text. write for info. (*0-7020-1766-3*, Pub. by W B Saunders) Saunders.

Macgregor, Carol L. The Journals of Patrick Gass: Member of the Lewis & Clark Expedition. LC 97-15350. 460p. 1997. 36.00 (*0-87842-350-8*); pap. 20.00 (*0-87842-351-6*) Mountain Pr.

MacGregor, Chip & MacGregor, Patti. Family Times: Gazillions of Great Ideas for Growing Together in Fun & Faith. LC 98-43194. 250p. 1999. pap. 9.99 (*0-7369-0028-4*) Harvest Hse.

MacGregor, Covey. Bethump'd with Words: Book Edition. LC 98-92125. x, 270p. 1998. pap. 15.00 (*0-9667604-0-9*, MLR-005) MLR Bks.

MacGregor, Cynthia. Creative Family Projects: Exciting & Practical Activities You Can Do Together. 240p. 1995. pap. 9.95 (*0-8065-1636-4*, Citadel Pr) Carol Pub Group.

— Everybody Wins! 150 Non-Competitive Games for Kids. LC 98-8592. 224p. 1998. pap. text 10.95 (*1-58062-063-9*) Adams Media.

— Family Customs & Traditions. 224p. 1995. 21.95 (*0-925190-49-7*) Fairview Press.

Macgregor, Cynthia. Family Customs & Traditions. 224p. 1996. pap. 12.95 (*1-57749-004-5*) Fairview Press.

***MacGregor, Cynthia.** Fun Family Traditions: 100 Fun Activities to Keep Your Family Close. 200p. 2000. per. 9.00 (*0-671-31816-0*) S&S Trade.

MacGregor, Cynthia. Kids During the Age of Exploration. LC 98-2612. (Kids Throughout History Ser.). 24p. (J). (gr. k-4). 1999. 15.93 (*0-8239-5257-6*, PowerKids) Rosen Group.

***MacGregor, Cynthia.** Listen to Your Instincts. LC 97-49227. (Abduction Prevention Library). (J). 1998. 15.93 (*0-8239-5249-5*, PowerKids) Rosen Group.

MacGregor, Cynthia. Mommy I'm Bored: One Hundred & Twenty Six Fun Filled & Educational Games Your Child Can...Play Alone. 160p. 1995. pap. 8.95 (*0-8065-1662-3*, Citadel Pr) Carol Pub Group.

***MacGregor, Cynthia.** Mommy's Little Helper Christmas Crafts. (Illus.). (J). 1999. 8.00 (*0-689-83071-8*, Meadowbrook Pr) S&S Childrens.

MacGregor, Cynthia. Raising a Creative Child: Challenging Activities & Games for Young Minds. 142p. 1999. reprint ed. 26.95 (*0-7351-0099-3*) Replica Bks.

— Raising a Creative Child: Challenging Activities for Growing Young Minds. 160p. 1995. pap. 9.95 (*0-8065-1741-7*, Citadel Pr) Carol Pub Group.

— Staying Safe at Home & On-Line. LC 97-47364. (Abduction Prevention Library). 24p. (J). 1999. 17.26 (*0-8239-5251-7*, PowerKids) Rosen Group.

***MacGregor, Cynthia.** Staying Safe by Saying No. LC 97-53216. (Abduction Prevention Library). 24p. (J). 1999. 17.26 (*0-8239-5252-5*, PowerKids) Rosen Group.

MacGregor, Cynthia. Stranger Danger. LC 97-32957. (Abduction Prevention Library). 24p. (J). 1999. 17.26 (*0-8239-5247-9*, PowerKids) Rosen Group.

***MacGregor, Cynthia.** Ten Steps to Staying Safe. LC 97-53215. (Abduction Prevention Library). 24p. (J). 1999. 17.26 (*0-8239-5248-7*, PowerKids) Rosen Group.

MacGregor, Cynthia. 365 After-School Activities You Can Do with Your Child. LC 99-27507. 416p. 1999. pap. 10.95 (*1-58062-212-7*) Adams Media.

— What Do You Know about Manners. (Illus.). 200p. (J). (gr. 1-7). 2000. pap. 6.99 (*0-689-83292-3*) S&S Childrens.

***MacGregor, Cynthia.** What Do You Know about Manners? A Funny Quiz for Kids. LC 99-89731. 2000. write for info. (*0-88166-354-9*) Meadowbrook.

— What to Do If You Get Lost. LC 97-49268. (Abduction Prevention Library). 24p. (J). 1999. 17.26 (*0-8239-5250-9*, PowerKids) Rosen Group.

MacGregor, Cynthia. Why Do People Die? Helping Your Child Understand with Love & Illustrations. LC 98-47097. (Illus.). (J). 1999. 14.95 (*0-8184-0598-8*, L Stuart) Carol Pub Group.

— Why Do We Have to Move? Helping Your Child Adjust-with Love & Illustrations. LC 96-26092. (Illus.). 1996. 14.95 (*0-8184-0583-X*, L Stuart) Carol Pub Group.

— Why Do We Need Another Baby? Helping Your Child Welcome a New Arrival. (Illus.). 1996. pap. 13.95 (*0-8065-1757-3*, Citadel Pr) Carol Pub Group.

— Why Do We Need Another Baby? Helping Your Child Welcome a New Arrival - with Love & Illustrations. (Illus.). 1996. 13.95 (*0-8184-0578-3*, L Stuart) Carol Pub Group.

MacGregor, Cynthia, jt. auth. see O's, Mr.

MacGregor, D. H. Industrial Combination: London School of Economics. (LSE Scarce Tracts in Economics Ser.). 246p. (C). 1997. 90.00 (*0-415-14390-X*) Routledge.

Macgregor, D. S., et al, eds. Petroleum Geology of North Africa. (Geological Society Special Publication Ser.: No. 132). 448p. 1998. 142.00 (*1-86239-004-5*, Pub. by Geol Soc Pub Hse) AAPG.

MacGregor, David. The Communist Ideal in Hegel & Marx. 320p. 1984. text 40.00 (*0-8020-5616-4*); pap. text 19.95 (*0-8020-6816-2*) U of Toronto Pr.

— Hegel & Marx: After the Fall of Communism. LC 98-211648. (Political Philosophy Now Ser.). 192p. 1998. 55.00 (*0-7083-1429-5*, Pub. by Univ Wales Pr); pap. 25.00 (*0-7083-1430-9*, Pub. by Univ Wales Pr) Paul & Co Pubs.

— Hegel, Marx & the English State. 360p. 1996. reprint ed. pap. text 19.95 (*0-8020-7842-7*) U of Toronto Pr.

MacGregor, David R. British & American Clippers: A Comparison of Their Design, Construction & Performance. LC 93-86142. (Illus.). 192p. 1993. 47.50 (*1-55750-084-3*) Naval Inst Pr.

— The Schooner: Its Design & Development from 1600 to the Present. (Illus.). 192p. 1997. 42.95 (*1-55750-847-X*) Naval Inst Pr.

— The Tea Clippers: Their History & Development, 1833-1875. LC 82-61670. (Illus.). 255p. 1982. 36.95 (*0-87021-884-0*) Naval Inst Pr.

MacGregor, Doug. Florida Rules of Court Service, 98-4. 650p. 1998. ring bd. write for info. (*0-327-00608-0*, 8078623) LEXIS Pub.

— The Refrigerator Door Gallery: Cartoons from the News-Press. (Illus.). 192p. (Orig.). 1996. pap. 12.95 (*0-9654843-0-0*) D MacGregor.

MacGregor, Douglas. A Collection of MacGregor Editorial Cartoons from the Norwich Bulletin. LC 88-92529. (Illus.). 196p. (Orig.). (J). (gr. 6-8). 1988. pap. text 10.00 (*0-9621270-0-0*) Norwich Bulletin.

MacGregor, Douglas, jt. auth. see Glover, Nicholas C.

Macgregor, Douglas A. The Soviet-East German Military Alliance. (Illus.). 192p. (C). 1989. text 54.95 (*0-521-36562-7*) Cambridge U Pr.

MacGregor, Douglas A. & Center for Strategic & International Studies Staff. Breaking the Phalanx: A New Design for Landpower in the 21st Century. LC 96-34012. 304p. 1997. pap. 24.95 (*0-275-95794-2*, Praeger Pubs) Greenwood.

MacGregor, Douglas S. Florida Condominium Law Manual, 1987-1991, 3 vols., Set. 1200p. 1995. spiral bd. 270.00 (*0-409-26137-8*, MICHIE) LEXIS Pub.

— Virginia Condominium Law, 1990-1991. 250p. 1991. ring bd. 50.00 (*0-409-26579-9*, MICHIE) LEXIS Pub.

MacGregor, Douglas S. & Glover, Nicholas C. Florida Commercial Landlord-Tenant Law, 1985-1994, Set. 440p. 1997. ring bd. 90.00 (*0-409-26326-5*, 80530-10, MICHIE) LEXIS Pub.

MacGregor, Douglas S., jt. auth. see Brown, Barry.

MacGregor, Douglas S., jt. auth. see Glover, Nicholas C.

MacGregor, Edward. Shadow War. (Vampire Ser.). (Illus.). 104p. 1999. pap. 15.95 (*1-56504-227-1*, 2903) White Wolf.

MacGregor, Elizabeth A. & Greenwood, C. T. Polymers in Nature. LC 79-41787. (Illus.). 399p. reprint ed. pap. 123.70 (*0-8357-3737-3*, 203646300003) Bks Demand.

MacGregor, Forbes. MacGregor's Mixture. 144p. (C). 1989. 35.00 (*0-903065-15-0*, Pub. by G Wright Pub) St Mut.

Macgregor, Forbes. More MacGregor's Mixture. 144p. (C). 1989. 40.00 (*0-903065-42-8*, Pub. by G Wright Pub) St Mut.

— Scots Proverbs & Rhymes. 80p. (C). 1989. 30.00 (*0-903065-39-8*, Pub. by G Wright Pub) St Mut.

Macgregor, Forbes, ed. Famous Scots. 344p. (C). 1989. 65.00 (*0-903065-47-9*, Pub. by G Wright Pub) St Mut.

Macgregor, Frances C. After Plastic Surgery: Adaptation & Adjustment. LC 79-11808. (Praeger Special Studies). 136p. 1979. 47.95 (*0-275-90383-4*, C0383, Praeger Pubs) Greenwood.

MacGregor, Francis C. After Plastic Surgery: Adaptation & Adjustment. 160p. (C). 1979. 45.00 (*0-03-052131-9*) Phoenix Soc.

MacGregor, G. Ethnology of Tokelau Islands. (BMB Ser.: No. 146). 1972. reprint ed. 30.00 (*0-527-02254-3*) Periodicals Srv.

MacGregor, G. A. & De Wardener, H. E. Salt, Diet & Health. (Illus.). 248p. (C). 1998. pap. 24.95 (*0-521-63545-4*); text 64.95 (*0-521-58352-7*) Cambridge U Pr.

MacGregor, G. A., jt. auth. see Beevers, D. G.

MacGregor, Geddes. Angels: Ministers of Grace. LC 87-11243. (Illus.). 230p. 1987. pap. 12.95 (*1-55778-001-3*) Paragon Hse.

— Apostles Extraordinary: A Celebration of Saints & Sinners. LC 85-22118. (Illus.). 168p. (Orig.). 1986. pap. 8.95 (*0-89407-065-7*) Strawberry Hill.

— Dictionary of Religion & Philosophy. LC 89-3404. 624p. 1995. 22.95 (*1-55778-019-6*) Paragon Hse.

An Asterisk (*) at the beginning of an entry indicates that the title is appearing for the first time.

— Dictionary of Religion & Philosophy. 624p. (C). 1991. reprint ed. pap. 19.95 (*1-55778-441-8*) Paragon Hse.
— He Who Lets Us Be: A New Theology of Love. LC 86-30335. 194p. 1987. pap. 8.95 (*0-913729-61-2*) Paragon Hse.
— Images of Afterlife: Beliefs from Antiquity to Modern Times. (Illus.). 256p. 1992. 21.95 (*1-55778-396-9*) Paragon Hse.
— The Nicene Creed, Illumined by Modern Thought. LC 80-19348. 163p. reprint ed. pap. 50.60 (*0-608-11916-4*, 202322000032) Bks Demand.
— Reincarnation in Christianity: A New Vision of the Role of Rebirth in Christian Thought. 1989. pap. 9.95 (*0-8356-0501-9*, Quest) Theos Pub Hse.
— Scotland: An Intimate Portrait. 288p. 1990. pap. 15.00 (*0-395-56236-8*) HM.
MacGregor, Geddes, ed. Immortality & Human Destiny: A Variety of Views. 256p. 1986. pap. 12.95 (*0-913757-46-2*) Paragon Hse.
MacGregor, Graham A. Current Advances in Ace Inhibition. 3rd ed. 1993. text 105.00 (*4-89370-071-5*) Church.
— Diagnostic Picture Tests in Hypertension. 1996. 14.95 (*0-7234-2477-2*, Pub. by Martin Dunitz) Mosby Inc.
MacGregor, Graham A. & Sever, Peter S., eds. Current Advances in Ace Inhibition 2. 2nd ed. (Illus.). 320p. 1991. text 144.00 (*0-443-04600-X*) Church.
MacGregor, Greg. Overland: The California Emigrant Trail of 1841-1870. LC 95-32470. (Illus.). 168p. (C). 1996. 75.00 (*0-8263-1703-0*); pap. 24.95 (*0-8263-1704-9*) U of NM Pr.
MacGregor, Gregory M. Deadspin. 544p. 1998. reprint ed. mass mkt. 5.99 (*0-553-57811-1*) Bantam.
MacGregor-Hastie, Roy, ed. Anthology of Contemporary Romanian Poetry. 166p. 1969. 30.00 (*0-7206-0280-7*, Pub. by P Owen Ltd) Dufour.
Macgregor, Helen. Tom Thumb's Musical Mathematics. (Illus.). 64p. (J). (gr. 1-2). 1998. spiral bd. 13.95 (*0-7136-4971-2*, Pub. by A & C Blk) Midpt Trade.
MacGregor, Herbert C. Working with Animal Chromosomes. 2nd ed. LC 88-14397. 306p. 1988. 250.00 (*0-471-92028-2*) Wiley.
MacGregor, I. J. & Doyle, A. T., eds. Nuclear & Particle Physics, 1993: Proceedings of the Conference Held in Glasgow, U. K., 30 March-1 April 1993. (Institute of Physics Conference Ser.: No. 133). (Illus.). 288p. 1993. 200.00 (*0-7503-0289-5*) IOP Pub.
MacGregor, J. G. Peter Fidler: Canada's Forgotten Explorer, 1769-1822. 1999. pap. 9.95 (*1-894004-19-1*) Fifth Hse Publ.
MacGregor, J. J. Forest Economic Research at Oxford: 1945-1974. 1974. 32.00 (*0-7855-7179-5*) St Mut.
MacGregor, James G. Reinforced Concrete: Mechanics & Design. 3rd ed. LC 96-14925. 939p. (C). 1996. 105.00 (*0-13-233974-9*) P-H.
***MacGregor, Janet.** Introduction to Anatomy & Physiology of Children. LC 99-34182. 192p. (C). 2000. text. write for info. (*0-415-21508-0*) Routledge.
— Introduction to the Anatomy & Physiology of Children. LC 99-34182. 192p. 2000. pap. 25.99 (*0-415-21509-9*) Routledge.
MacGregor, Jean, ed. Student Self-Evaluation: Fostering Reflective Learning. LC 85-644763. (New Directions for Teaching & Learning Ser.: No. TL 56). 123p. (Orig.). 1994. pap. 22.00 (*1-55542-683-2*) Jossey-Bass.
MacGregor, Jerry, jt. auth. see Waltke, Bruce.
MacGregor, Jimmie. Jimmie MacGregor's Scotland. (Illus.). 192p. 1994. 27.95 (*0-563-36316-9*, BBC-Parkwest) Parkwest Pubns.
— MacGregor Across Scotland: A Long-Distance Walk from Montrose to Ardnamurchan. LC 92-80836. (Illus.). 96p. (Orig.). 1992. pap. 7.95 (*0-563-36187-5*, BBC-Parkwest) Parkwest Pubns.
Macgregor, Jimmie. The Moray Coast Speyside & the Cairngorms. (Illus.). 88p. 1991. pap. 7.95 (*0-563-20560-1*, Pub. by BBC) Parkwest Pubns.
***MacGregor, John.** A Thousand Miles in the Rob Roy Canoe. LC 99-86904. (Illus.). 2000. 16.99 (*1-929516-06-1*) Dixon-Price.
MacGregor, John C. A Portfolio of Rose Hips. (Illus.). 20p. 1981. 35.00 (*0-936736-01-1*); pap. 25.00 (*0-936736-02-X*) Sweetbrier.
MacGregor, John M. The Discovery of the Art of the Insane. (Illus.). 512p. (C). 1989. pap. text 39.50 (*0-691-00036-0*, Pub. by Princeton U Pr) Cal Prin Full Svc.
***MacGregor, John M.** Metamorphosis - The Fiber Art of Judith Scott: The Outsider Artist & the Experience of Down's Syndrome. unabridged ed. (Illus.). 208p. 1999. 45.00 (*0-9673160-0-6*) Creative Growth Art Ctr.
***MacGregor, Kenley.** Master of Seduction. 352p. 2000. mass mkt. 5.99 (*0-06-108712-2*) HarpC.
MacGregor, Kinley. A Pirate of Her Own. 320p. 1999. mass mkt. 5.99 (*0-06-108711-4*) HarpC.
MacGregor, Lona, jt. auth. see Orwell, George.
MacGregor, Lorri. What You Need to Know about Jehovah's Witnesses. rev. ed. (Conversations with the Cults Ser.). 160p. 1992. pap. 6.99 (*0-89081-944-0*) Harvest Hse.
MacGregor, Malcolm & Baldwin, Stanley C. Your Money Matters. LC 76-56123. 176p. 1977. pap. 7.99 (*0-87123-662-1*) Bethany Hse.
MacGregor, Malcolm B. The Sources & Literature of Scottish Church History. LC 76-1125. 260p. 1977. reprint ed. lib. bdg. 20.00 (*0-915172-10-0*) Richwood Pub.
MacGregor, Malcolm H. The Enigmatic Electron. LC 92-31829. (Fundamental Theories of Physics Ser.: Vol. 49). 1992. text 138.00 (*0-7923-1982-6*) Kluwer Academic.
Macgregor, Margaret E., jt. ed. see Chase, Mary E.
***MacGregor, Mariam G.** Designing Student Leadership Programs: Transforming the Leadership Potential of Youth. 153p. 1999. pap. 25.00 (*0-9677981-2-4*) Youthleadership.
— Leadership 101: Developing Leadership Skills for Resilient Youth, Facilitator's Guide) 135p. 1997. pap., teacher ed. 30.00 (*0-9677981-0-8*) Youthleadership.
— Leadership 101: Developing Your Leadership Skills, Student Workbook. 80p. 1997. pap., wbk. ed. 14.00 (*0-9677981-1-6*) Youthleadership.
MacGregor-Mendoza, Patricia. Spanish & Academic Achievement among Midwest Mexican Youth: The Myth of the Barrier. rev. ed. LC 99-18527. (Latino Communities Ser.). 200p. 1999. 51.00 (*0-8153-3345-5*) Garland.
MacGregor, Miles. The Sunflower. Thatch, Nancy R., ed. (Books for Students by Students). (Illus.). 29p. (J). (gr. 3-6). 1994. lib. bdg. 15.95 (*0-933849-52-4*) Landmark Edns.
MacGregor, Miriam. Boss of Brightland. large type ed. 304p. 1993. 27.99 (*0-7505-0554-0*, Pub. by Mgna Lrg Print) Ulverscroft.
— The Glowing Dark. large type ed. 336p. 1987. 27.99 (*0-7089-1613-9*) Ulverscroft.
— The House At Lake Taupo. large type ed. 304p. 1987. 27.99 (*0-7089-1730-5*) Ulverscroft.
— Lord of the Lodge. large type ed. 285p. 1992. 11.50 (*0-7505-0315-7*) Ulverscroft.
Macgregor, Miriam. Master of Marshlands. large type ed. 288p. 1991. reprint ed. lib. bdg. 18.95 (*0-263-12718-4*) Mac Lib Ref.
MacGregor, Miriam. The Orchard King. 1993. per. 2.89 (*0-373-03255-2*, 1-03255-6) Harlequin Bks.
Macgregor, Miriam. The Orchard King. large type ed. 1993. reprint ed. lib. bdg. 18.95 (*0-263-13182-3*) Mac Lib Ref.
— Riddell of Rivermoon. large type ed. 1990. lib. bdg. 18.95 (*0-263-12348-0*) Mac Lib Ref.
MacGregor, Miriam. A Sigh on the Breeze. large type ed. 336p. 1986. 27.99 (*0-7089-1423-3*) Ulverscroft.
Macgregor, Miriam. The Stairway to Destiny. large type ed. 303p. 1994. 27.99 (*0-7505-0661-X*) Ulverscroft.
MacGregor, Miriam. Winter at Whitecliffs. large type ed. (Magna Romance Ser.). 301p. 1992. 27.99 (*0-7505-0411-0*) Ulverscroft.
Macgregor, Miriam, ed. Cat Cuts: A Collection of Engravers' Cats. 64p. 1992. 12.95 (*1-55109-007-4*) Nimbus Publ.
MacGregor, Molly. Magnificent Trickster: The Story of Milarepa. LC 88-92347. 1992. pap. 9.99 (*0-929929-01-2*) MM Pr.
— Mississippi Headwaters Guide Book: A Guide to the Natural, Cultural, Scenic, Scientific & Recreational Values of the Mississippi River's First 400 Miles. LC 96-127602. (Illus.). 88p. (Orig.). 1995. pap. 15.00 (*0-9645849-1-3*) MS Headwaters.
— Sky Goes on Forever. 165p. 1988. pap. 5.95 (*0-929929-00-4*) MM Pr.
MacGregor, Morna. Early Celtic Art in North Britain: A Study of the Decorative Metalwork from the Third Century BC to the Third Century AD, 2 vols. Incl. Vol. 1. (Illus.). 240p. 1975. Vol. 2. (Illus.). 322p. 1975. 1975. Set text 57.50 (*0-7185-1135-2*) St Martin.
***MacGregor, Morris J.** The Emergence of a Black Catholic Community: St. Augustine's in Washington. LC 98-46476. (Illus.). 543p. 1999. pap. 24.95 (*0-8132-0943-9*); text 39.95 (*0-8132-0942-0*) Cath U Pr.
MacGregor, Morris J. A Parish for the Federal City: St. Patrick's in Washington, 1794-1994. LC 93-49694. (Illus.). 475p. (C). 1994. 29.95 (*0-8132-0801-7*); pap. 19.95 (*0-8132-0802-5*) Cath U Pr.
MacGregor, Morris J., jt. ed. see Nalty, Bernard C.
MacGregor-Morris, Pamela. The History of the H. I. S. Eighteen Eighty-Five to Nineteen Eighty-Five: 100 Years of the Hunters' Improvement & National Light Horse Breeding Society. 277p. (C). 1988. 100.00 (*0-9509663-1-2*) St Mut.
MacGregor, Neil. A Victim of Anonymity. LC 93-60981. (Walter Neurath Memorial Lectures). (Illus.). 48p. 1994. 14.95 (*0-500-55026-3*, Pub. by Thames Hudson) Norton.
MacGregor, Neil, frwd. Treasures of the National Gallery, London. (SPA., Illus.). 288p. 1996. 11.95 (*0-7892-0482-7*) Abbeville Pr.
***MacGregor, Neil & Langmuir, Erika.** Seeing Salvation: Images of Christ in Art. (Illus.). 240p. 2000. 35.00 (*0-300-08478-1*) Yale U Pr.
MacGregor, Patti, jt. auth. see MacGregor, Chip.
MacGregor, Rob. The Genesis Deluge. 320p. 1992. mass mkt. 5.50 (*0-553-29502-0*) Bantam.
— Hawk Moon. 192p. (J). (gr. 7 up). 1996. per. 16.00 (*0-689-80171-8*) S&S Bks Yung.
— Hawk Moon. (J). 1998. 9.60 (*0-606-13469-7*, Pub. by Turtleback) Demco.
— Hawk Moon. 192p. (YA). (gr. 7 up). 1998. reprint ed. mass mkt. 4.50 (*0-440-22741-0*, LLL BDD) BDD Bks Young Read.
— Indiana Jones & the Dance of the Giants. 256p. 1991. mass mkt. 4.99 (*0-553-29035-5*) Bantam.
— Indiana Jones & the Interior World. 272p. 1992. mass mkt. 4.99 (*0 553 29966 2*) Bantam.
— Indiana Jones & the Seven Veils. 304p. 1991. mass mkt. 5.50 (*0-553-29334-6*) Bantam.
— Indiana Jones & the Unicorn's Legacy. 304p. 1992. mass mkt. 4.99 (*0-553-29666-3*) Bantam.
— The Peril at Delphi. (Indiana Jones Ser.: No. 1). 272p. 1991. mass mkt. 4.99 (*0-553-28931-4*) Bantam.
***MacGregor, Rob.** Peter Benchley's Amazon: The Ghost Tribe, No. 1. 384p. 2000. mass mkt. 6.99 (*0-380-81403-X*, Torch) HarpC.
MacGregor, Rob. Phantom. 1996. mass mkt. 5.99 (*0-380-78887-X*, Avon Bks) Morrow Avon.
— Prophecy Rock. LC 94-33163. 208p. (YA). (gr. 7 up). 1995. mass mkt. 16.00 (*0-689-80056-8*) S&S Bks Yung.
— Prophecy Rock. (J). 1998. 9.60 (*0-606-13725-4*, Pub. by Turtleback) Demco.
— Prophecy Rock. 208p. (YA). (gr. 7 up). 1998. reprint ed. mass mkt. 4.50 (*0-440-22738-0*, LLL BDD) BDD Bks Young Read.
— Spawn: Born in Darkness, Sworn to Justice. 1997. mass mkt. 5.99 (*0-380-79441-1*, Avon Bks) Morrow Avon.
— Spawn: Born in Darkness, Sworn to Justice. (J). (gr. 3-7). 1997. pap. 4.99 (*0-380-79443-8*, Avon Bks) Morrow Avon.
***MacGregor, Rob.** The Unofficial Star Wars Episode One: The Phantom Menace Internet Guide. 50p. 1999. pap. 10.00 (*1-883573-20-3*, Lightning Rod) Pride & Imprints.
MacGregor, Rob, jt. auth. see MacGregor, Trish.
MacGregor, Rob, jt. auth. see Williams, Billy Dee.
MacGregor, Rob R., jt. ed. see Rossman, Milton D.
Macgregor, Robert S. World Wide Web Security: How to Build a Secure World Wide Web Connection. LC 97-118461. 224p. 1996. pap. 29.80 (*0-13-612409-7*) P-H.
MacGregor, Roger, tr. see Phleps, Herman.
MacGregor, Ronald J. Theoretical Mechanics of Biological Neural Networks. (Neural Networks: Foundations to Applications Ser.). (Illus.). 377p. 1993. text 59.00 (*0-12-464255-1*) Acad Pr.
Macgregor, Roy. Danger in Dinosaur Valley, Vol. 10. (Screech Owls Ser.: No. 10). 120p. (YA). (gr. 5-8). 1998. mass mkt. 5.99 (*0-7710-5620-6*) McCland & Stewart.
***MacGregor, Roy.** The Ghost of the Stanley Cup. (Screech Owls Ser.: No. 11). 112p. (YA). (gr. 5-8). 2000. mass mkt. 3.95 (*0-7710-5622-2*) McCland & Stewart.
— Road Games: A Year in the Life of the NHL. (Illus.). 336p. 1994. 24.95 (*0-921912-58-7*) MW&R.
MacGregor, Roy. The Screech Owls Series Boxed Set: Murder at Hockey Camp; Kidnapped in Sweden; Terror in Florida. Incl. Kidnapped in Sweden. 120p. (YA). (gr. 5-8). 1997. mass mkt. 3.95 (*0-7710-5615-X*); Murder at Hockey Camp. 120p. (YA). (gr. 6-9). 1996. mass mkt. 3.95 (*0-7710-5629-X*); Terror in Florida. 120p. (YA). (gr. 4-7). 1997. mass mkt. 3.95 (*0-7710-5616-8*); (Screech Owls Ser.: Nos. 4-6). (YA). (gr. 5-8). 1998. pap., boxed set. write for info. (*0-7710-5621-4*) McCland & Stewart.
— The Screech Owls Series Boxed Set: Mystery at Lake Placid; The Night They Stole the Stanley Cup; The Screech Owls' Northern Adventure. Incl. Mystery at Lake Placid. (Illus.). 208p. (YA). (gr. 5-8). Date not set. pap. 3.95 (*0-7710-5625-7*); Night They Stole the Stanley Cup. 120p. (YA). (gr. 6-9). 1996. mass mkt. 3.95 (*0-7710-5626-5*); Screech Owls' Northern Adventure. (Illus.). 112p. (YA). (gr. 6-9). Date not set. pap. 3.95 (*0-7710-5628-1*); (Screech Owls Ser.: Nos. 1-3). (YA). (gr. 5-8). 1996. pap., boxed set. write for info. (*0-7710-5636-2*) McCland & Stewart.
***MacGregor, Roy.** The Screech Owls Series Boxed Set: The Quebec City Crisis; The Screech Owls' Home Loss; Nightmare in Nagano. Incl. Nightmare in Nagano. 120p. (YA). (gr. 4-7). 1999. pap. 5.99 (*0-7710-5619-2*); Quebec City Crisis. 120p. (YA). (gr. 5-8). 1998. pap. 5.99 (*0-7710-5617-6*); Screech Owls' Home Loss. 120p. (YA). (gr. 8-12). 1998. pap. 4.99 (*0-7710-5618-4*); (Screech Owls Ser.: Nos. 7-9). (YA). (gr. 5-8). 1998. Set pap., boxed set 11.85 (*0-7710-5639-7*) McCland & Stewart.
— The Seven A. M. Practice: Stories of Family Life. 160p. 1997. 19.99 (*0-7710-5600-1*) McCland & Stewart.
***Macgregor, Roy.** The West Coast Murders, Vol. 12. (Screech Owls Ser.: Vol. 12). 112p. (gr. 4-7). 2000. mass mkt. 3.95 (*0-7710-5623-0*) McCland & Stewart.
MacGregor, Sandy, jt. auth. see Abraham, Marilyn.
MacGregor, Stewart. The Sinner. LC 72-95425. 256p. 1973. 7.95 (*0-87955-903-9*) O'Hara.
MacGregor, Susanne & Lipow, Arthur, eds. The Other City: People & Politics in New York & London. LC 94-24212. 256p. (C). 1995. pap. 18.50 (*0-391-03885-0*) Humanities.
— The Other City: People & Politics in New York & London. LC 94-24212. 256p. (C). 1995. text 49.95 (*0-391-03852-4*) Humanities.
MacGregor, Susanne & Pimlott, Ben, eds. Tackling the Inner Cities: The Nineteen Eighties Reviewed, Prospects for the 1990s. (Illus.). 304p. 1990. text 79.00 (*0-19-827737-7*) OUP.
Macgregor, Susanne, jt. auth. see Jewson, Nick.
MacGregor, Susanne, jt. auth. see Jones, Helen.
MacGregor, Suzanne. Drugs & British Society: Responses to a Social Problem in the 1980s. 208p. 1989. 52.50 (*0-415-03064-1*) Routledge.
MacGregor, T. J. Blue Pearl. LC 93-49700. 384p. 1994. 21.45 (*0-7868-6061-8*, Pub. by Hyperion) Time Warner.
— Dark Fields. 1987. mass mkt. 5.99 (*0-345-33756-5*) Ballantine Pub Grp.
— Death Flats. (Florida Mysteries Ser.). (Orig.). 1991. mass mkt. 4.99 (*0-345-35768-X*) Ballantine Pub Grp.
— Hanged Man. 352p. 1999. mass mkt. 5.99 (*0-7860-0646-3*) Pinnacle Books.
— Kill Flash. 1987. mass mkt. 4.99 (*0-345-33754-9*) Ballantine Pub Grp.
— Kin Dread. 320p. (Orig.). 1990. mass mkt. 4.95 (*0-345-35766-3*) Ballantine Pub Grp.
— Mistress of the Bones. LC 95-10123. 352p. 1995. 21.45 (*0-7868-6106-1*, Pub. by Hyperion) Time Warner.
— The Seventh Sense. 272p. 1999. text 23.00 (*1-57566-411-9*) Kensgtn Pub Corp.
***MacGregor, T. J.** Seventh Sense. 2000. mass mkt. 6.99 (*0-7860-1083-5*, Pinncle Kensgtn) Kensgtn Pub Corp.
MacGregor, T. J. Storm Surge. LC 92-42516. 336p. (YA). 1993. 19.45 (*1-56282-789-8*, Pub. by Hyperion) Time Warner.
MacGregor, Trish. The Hanged Man. 320p. 1998. text 23.00 (*1-57566-266-3*, Knsington) Kensgtn Pub Corp.
— Your Cosmic Kids: Using Astrology to Understand Your Children. LC 98-73903. (Illus.). 328p. 1999. pap. 13.95 (*1-57174-127-5*) Hampton Roads Pub Co.
MacGregor, Trish & MacGregor, Rob. Everything Dreams Book. LC 97-24590. (Illus.). 304p. 1997. pap. 12.95 (*1-55850-806-6*) Adams Media.
MacGregor-Villarreal, Mary. Brazilian Folk Narrative Scholarship: A Critical Survey & Selective Annotated Bibliography. LC 94-20707. (Folklore Library: Vol. 8). 264p. 1994. reprint ed. text. write for info. (*0-8153-1243-1*, H1683) Garland.
MacGregor, William B., tr. see Rouquette, Max.
MacGregory, Alastair R. & Lechner, Sybille K. Removable Partial Prosthodontics. LC 93-2006. (Case Oriented Manual of Treatment). 160p. (gr. 13). 1994. 51.95 (*0-7234-1960-4*) Mosby Inc.
MacGreil, Michael. Prejudice & Tolerance in Ireland. LC 79-49275. 600p. 1980. 75.00 (*0-275-90515-2*, C0515, Praeger Pubs) Greenwood.
MacGrogan, Robert, et al. Prep Pak for FLMI 361. Stone, Gene, ed. (FLMI Insurance Education Program Ser.). 281p. spiral bd., wbk. ed. 24.00 (*0-939921-88-X*, Pub. by Life Office) PBD Inc.
MacGrory, Yvonne. The Ghost of Susannah Parry. 126p. (J). 1996. pap. 8.95 (*0-947962-90-5*) Dufour.
***MacGrory, Yvonne.** Quest of the Ruby Ring. 144p. 2000. pap. 8.95 (*1-901737-15-2*, Pub. by Anvil Books Ltd) Dufour.
MacGrory, Yvonne. The Secret of the Ruby Ring. LC 93-35950. (Illus.). 192p. (Orig.). (J). (gr. 4-7). 1994. reprint ed. pap. 6.95 (*0-915943-92-1*) Milkweed Ed.
MacGruer, Malcolm S. Horse-Horse Tiger-Tiger. LC 94-77797. 352p. 1994. 22.00 (*0-9642624-0-1*) Mereside Hse.
MacGuigan, Mark R. Cases & Materials on Creditors' Rights. 2nd ed. LC 67-108724. (Illus.). 724p. reprint ed. pap. 200.00 (*0-8357-8058-9*, 203406400088) Bks Demand.
MacGuire, Anne. Manual of Patient Care Standards. ring bd. 249.00 (*0-87189-765-2*, S15) Aspen Pub.
Macguire, G. Q. & Noz, Marilyn E. Radiation Protection - In the Health Sciences. 300p. 1995. text 66.00 (*981-02-2406-0*) World Scientific Pub.
Macguire, Gregory. Missing Sisters. LC 97-24112. 164p. (J). 1998. pap. 4.95 (*0-7868-1273-7*, Pub. by Hyperion) Time Warner.
***Macguire, Gregory.** Missing Sisters. 1998. 10.05 (*0-606-13612-6*, Pub. by Turtleback) Demco.
MacGuire, Jack. Hopscotch, Hangman, Hot-Potato, & HA, HA, HA. (Illus.). 320p. 1990. pap. 15.00 (*0-671-76332-6*, Fireside) S&S Trade Pap.
MacGuire, James, jt. auth. see Buckley, Christopher.
MacGuire, John W., jt. auth. see Parker, Harry.
MacGuire, M., jt. auth. see Fliegel, S. W.
Macguire, Meade. Does God Care? LC 97-60845. 96p. 1997. reprint ed. per. 7.95 (*1-57258-087-9*) Teach Servs.
***MacGunnigle, Bruce C.** Rhode Island Freemen, 1747-1755: A Census of Registered Voters. 49p. 1999. 9.00 (*0-8063-0754-4*, Pub. by Clearfield Co) ACCESS Pubs Network.
Macgyver, Wilson. Kickass Windows NT 4 Programming. 1997. pap. text 49.99 incl. cd-rom (*1-57610-116-9*) Coriolis Grp.
Mach. Contemporary Class Piano. 5th ed. (C). 1996. pap. text 63.50 (*0-15-501738-1*) Harcourt.
Mach, Bogdan W. & Weslowski, Wlodzimierz. Social Mobility & Social Structure. 180p. 1987. text 47.50 (*0-7100-9982-7*, Routledge Thoemms) Routledge.
Mach, Elyse. Great Contemporary Pianists Speak for Themselves. (Illus.). 480p. 1991. pap. 12.95 (*0-486-26695-8*) Dover.
Mach, Ernst. Contributions to the Analysis of the Sensations. 220p. 90.00 (*1-85506-675-0*) Thoemmes Pr.
Mach, Ernst. Principles of the Theory of Heat. 1986. lib. bdg. 294.00 (*90-277-2206-4*) Kluwer Academic.
Mach III Plus Staff. Airliners in Colour. (C). 1993. pap. 70.00 (*0-9515462-4-4*, Pub. by Mach III Plus) St Mut.
— European Air Arms, 1993. (C). 1993. pap. 35.00 (*0-9515462-8-7*, Pub. by Mach III Plus) St Mut.
— European Military Aircraft Directory, 1993. (C). 1993. pap. 30.00 (*0-9515462-6-0*, Pub. by Mach III Plus) St Mut.
— United Kingdom Air Arms, 1993. (C). 1993. 35.00 (*0-9515462-7-9*, Pub. by Mach III Plus) St Mut.
— United States Military Aircraft Directory, 1993. (C). 1993. pap. 55.00 (*0-9515462-5-2*, Pub. by Mach III Plus) St Mut.
Mach III Plus Staff, ed. United States Air Force, 1993. (C). 1993. pap. 40.00 (*0-9515462-9-5*, Pub. by Mach III Plus) St Mut.
Mach, J. L., et al. Paradigm Skillbuilding: Keyboarding with Speed & Control. LC 97-52310. 1998. text 24.95 incl. cd-rom (*0-7638-0027-9*) Paradigm MN.
Mach, J. L., et al. Paradigm Skillbuilding: Keyboarding with Speed & Control, Instructor's guide. 8.00 (*0-7638-0029-5*) EMC-Paradigm.
Mach, Jean-Pierre, ed. From Basic Cancer Research to Clinical Application: International Society for Oncodevelopmental Biology & Medicine, 25th Anniversary Meeting, Montreux, September 1997: Abstracts. (Tumor Biology Ser.: Vol. 18, Suppl. 2, 1997). 138p. 1997. pap. 41.75 (*3-8055-6596-8*) S Karger.
Mach, K. A. & Mitchell, William. Paradigm Keyboarding & Applications: A Mastery Approach for Microcomputers & Typewriters: Text with Student Disks, 3.5. 3rd ed. text 29.95 incl. 3.5 hd (*1-56118-157-9*) EMC-Paradigm.
Mach, Kaye, et al. Advanced. teacher ed. write for info. SRA.

An Asterisk (*) at the beginning of an entry indicates that the title is appearing for the first time.

— College Typewriting: A Mastery Approach. Incl. Advanced. text 15.95 (*0-574-20655-8*, 13-3655); Beginning. pap. text 13.95 (*0-574-20695-7*, 13-3695); Beginning. 4.95 (*0-574-20541-1*, 13-3541); Intermediate. pap. text 14.95 (*0-574-20700-7*, 13-3592); Intermediate. 6.95 (*0-574-20543-8*, 13-3543); Set. Intermediate., 45 vols. 27.50 (*0-574-20548-9*, 13-3548); teacher ed. 3.95 (*0-574-20658-2*, 13-3658); 150.00 (*0-686-66313-6*) SRA.

Mach, Pavel, jt. auth. see Harman, George G.

Mach, R., jt. ed. see Truhlik, E.

Mach, Zdzislaw. Symbols, Conflict, & Identity: Essays in Political Anthropology. LC 92-22553. (SUNY Series in Anthropological Studies of Contemporary Issues). 297p. (C). 1993. pap. text 21.95 (*0-7914-1466-3*) State U NY Pr.

Macha, Gary P. Aircraft Wrecks in the Mountains & Deserts of California, 1909-1996. LC 96-79070. (Illus.). 232p. (Orig.). 1997. pap. 19.95 (*0-924272-08-2*) Info Net Pub.

Machac, Kathy, jt. auth. see McWaid, Helen.

Machacek, David W., jt. auth. see Hammond, Phillip E.

Machado. IML to Accompany Early Childhood Experiences in Language Arts. 6th ed. 112p. 1998. text, teacher ed. 10.00 (*0-8273-8362-2*) Delmar.

Machado, jt. auth. see Domino.

Machado, jt. auth. see Ibarra.

Machado, Adam. Key to the Highway: A Collection of American Songs Linking Present Culture to the Past Transcribed for Classroom Singing with History, Biography, & Education Notes. (Illus.). 90p. 1998. pap. 17.95 (*0-935432-13-2*) Kodaly Ctr Am.

Machado, Ana M. Explorations into Latin America. LC 94-28624. (Exploration Into Ser.). (Illus.). 48p. (J). (gr. 4 up). 1995. lib. bdg. 15.95 (*0-02-718084-0*, Dillon Silver Burdett); pap. 7.95 (*0-382-24971-2*) Silver Burdett Pr.

— Explorations into Latin America. LC 93-28624. (Exploration Into Ser.). 48p. (J). (gr. 1-8). 1995. pap. 7.95 (*0-382-24970-4*) Silver Burdett Pr.

— Historia Medio Al Reves (Half-Tale Told Backwards) Mansour, Monica, tr. (SPA., Illus.). 54p. (J). (gr. 3-4). 1992. pap. 5.99 (*968-16-4545-6*, Pub. by Fondo) Continental Bk.

— Nina Bonita. (SPA., Illus.). 24p. (J). (ps-3). pap. 6.95 (*980-257-165-2*, Pub. by Ediciones Ekare) Kane-Miller Bk.

— Nina Bonita. Iribarren, Elena, tr. from POR. LC 95-81577. (Illus.). 24p. (J). (ps-3). 1996. 9.95 (*0-916291-63-4*) Kane-Miller Bk.

— Un Parajito Me Conto (A Little Bird Told Me) (SPA.). 44p. (J). (gr. 3-4). 1992. pap. 5.99 (*968-16-3769-0*, Pub. by Fondo) Continental Bk.

***Machado, Ana Maria.** Latin America. (Exploration Into... Ser.). (Illus.). (J). 2000. 17.95 (*0-7910-6024-1*) Chelsea Hse.

Machado, Ana Maria. El Perro del Cerro y la Rana de la Sabana.Tr. of Hound from the Mound & the Frog from the Bog. (SPA.). (J). 1998. pap. 6.95 (*980-257-021-4*, Pub. by Ediciones Ekare) Kane-Miller Bk.

Machado, Antonio. Antonio Machado: Selected Poems. Trueblood, Alan S., ed. & tr. by. from SPA. LC 81-13481. 332p. 1988. reprint ed. pap. 18.50 (*0-674-04066-X*) HUP.

— Canciones. Bly, Robert, tr. from SPA. LC 80-27641. 15p. 1980. pap. 4.00 (*0-915124-46-7*) Toothpaste.

— Del Camino. Smith, Michael, tr. 30p. 1974. pap. 6.95 (*0-902996-12-6*) Dufour.

— I Never Wanted Fame. Bly, Robert, tr. from SPA. 1979. pap. 4.00 (*0-915408-19-8*) Ally Pr.

— The Landscape of Soria. Maloney, Dennis, tr. from SPA. 24p. 1985. pap. 4.00 (*0-934834-57-1*) White Pine.

— Poesia. (SPA.). pap. 10.95 (*84-206-1602-8*, Pub. by Alianza Editorial) Continental Bk.

— Poesias Completas. Alvar, Manuel, ed. (Nueva Austral Ser.: Vol. 33). (SPA.). 1991. pap. text 29.95 (*84-239-1833-5*) Elliots Bks.

— Times Alone: Selected Poems of Antonio Machado. Bly, Robert, tr. LC 83-6955. (Wesleyan Poetry in Translation Ser.). (ENG & SPA.). 187p. 1983. pap. 15.95 (*0-8195-6081-2*, Wesleyan Univ Pr) U Pr of New Eng.

Machado, Antonio A., jt. ed. see Solimeo, Gustavo.

Machado, Antonio C., et al. Our Lady at Fatima: Prophecies of Tragedy or Hope for America & the World? LC 85-70673. (Illus.). 128p. (Orig.). (J). (gr. 8). 1986. pap. 7.95 (*1-877905-10-0*) Am Soc Defense TFP.

Machado, Calixto, ed. see International Symposium on Brain Death Staff.

***Machado de Assis, Joaquim Maria.** The Alienist. limited ed. Mac Adam, Alfred, tr. from POR. Orig. Title: O Alienista. (Illus.). 58p. 1998. 450.00 (*0-910457-38-7*) Arion Pr.

Machado de Assis, Joaquim Maria. Counselor Ayres' Memorial. Caldwell, Helen, tr. from POR. LC 72-187876. 1973. pap. 13.95 (*0-520-04775-3*, Pub. by U CA Pr) Cal Prin Full Svc.

— Dom Casmurro. Caldwell, Helen, tr. 269p. 1991. pap. 12.00 (*0-374-52303-7*) FS&G.

— Dom Casmurro. Gledson, John A., tr. LC 96-44126. (Library of Latin America). 288p. 1997. 25.00 (*0-19-510308-4*) OUP.

— Dom Casmurro. Scott-Buccleuch, Robert L., tr. from POR. 160p. 1992. 30.00 (*0-7206-0845-7*, Pub. by P Owen Ltd) Dufour.

— Don Casmurro. Gledson, John A., tr. (Library of Latin America). 288p. 1998. reprint ed. pap. 10.95 (*0-19-510309-2*) OUP.

— Epitaph of a Small Winner. 224p. 1990. pap. 12.00 (*0-374-52192-1*) FS&G.

***Machado de Assis, Joaquim Maria.** Esau & Jacob. Moises, Carlos Felipe & Borges, Dain, eds. Lowe, Elizabeth, tr. (Library of Latin America). 368p. 2000. 30.00 (*0-19-510810-8*); pap. 16.95 (*0-19-510811-6*) OUP.

Machado de Assis, Joaquim Maria. Helena. Caldwell, Helen, tr. from POR. LC 83-17966. 197p. (C). 1984. 45.00 (*0-520-04812-1*, Pub. by U CA Pr); pap. 14.95 (*0-520-06025-3*, Pub. by U CA Pr) Cal Prin Full Svc.

— Iaia Garcia. Bagby, Albert I., Jr., tr. LC 76-24338. (Studies in Romance Languages: No. 17). 188p. reprint ed. pap. 58.30 (*0-8357-4291-1*, 203709000007) Bks Demand.

— Philosopher or Dog? Wilson, Clotilde, tr. 288p. 1992. pap. 12.00 (*0-374-52328-2*) FS&G.

— Philosopher or Dog? 288p. 1982. pap. 3.95 (*0-380-58982-6*, 58982-6, Avon Bks) Morrow Avon.

— The Posthumous Memoirs of Bras Cubas. Rabassa, Gregory, tr. LC 96-44125. (Library of Latin America). 240p. 1997. 25.00 (*0-19-510169-3*) OUP.

— The Posthumous Memoirs of Bras Cubas. Rabassa, Gregory, tr. (Library of Latin America). 240p. 1998. reprint ed. pap. 12.95 (*0-19-510170-7*) OUP.

— Quincas Borba. Favaretto, Celso & Haberly, David T., eds. Rabassa, Gregory, tr. (Library of Latin America). 320p. 1998. 25.00 (*0-19-510681-4*) OUP.

— Quincas Borba. 320p. 1999. pap. 13.95 (*0-19-510682-2*) OUP.

— The Wager: Aires' Journal. Scott-Buccleuch, Robert L., tr. from POR. LC 90-80799. 160p. 1990. 30.00 (*0-7206-0772-8*) Dufour.

Machado de Assis, Joaquim Maria, see Machado de Assis, Joaquim Maria.

Machado, Diamantino P. The Structure of Portuguese Society: The Failure of Fascism. LC 91-9646. 240p. 1991. 62.95 (*0-275-93784-4*, C3784, Praeger Pubs) Greenwood.

Machado, Donna P. Skills for Success: Working & Studying in English: Teacher's Edition. 286p. (C). 1998. pap. text, teacher ed. 18.95 (*0-521-65714-8*) Cambridge U Pr.

Machado, Ed. One Tree Island. LC 94-67585. 264p. (J). (gr. 5-10). 1994. pap. 5.99 (*0-9642652-0-6*) Reef Pubng.

Machado, Eduardo. The Floating Island Plays. LC 91-25117. 232p. 1991. 24.95 (*1-55936-035-6*); pap. 13.95 (*1-55936-034-8*) Theatre Comm.

Machado, Felix. Jnaneshvari: Path to Liberation. LC 98-915267. xxxviii, 156p. 1998. write for info. (*81-7039-233-0*) Somaiya Publns.

Machado, Francisco. Mirror of the New Christians. Talmage, F. & Vieira, M., eds. 344p. pap. text 45.14 (*0-88844-036-7*) Brill Academic Pubs.

Machado, George, photos by. 4 Men by George Machado. (Illus.). 200p. 1997. 50.00 (*0-9652009-3-0*) Alluvial Ent.

Machado, Gerson A., ed. Low-Power HF Microelectronics: A Unified Approach. (IEE Circuits & Systems Ser.: No. 8). 960p. 1996. boxed set 99.00 (*0-85296-874-4*) INSPEC Inc.

Machado, Jeanne M. Early Childhood Experience in Language Arts. 5th ed. (Early Childhood Education Ser.). 100p. 1995. text, teacher ed. 14.00 (*0-8273-5881-4*) Delmar.

— Early Childhood Experiences in Language Arts. 4th ed. 416p. 1990. pap., teacher ed. 10.00 (*0-8273-3505-9*) Delmar.

— Early Childhood Experiences in Language Arts. 4th ed. 416p. 1990. pap. 28.50 (*0-8273-3504-0*) Delmar.

— Early Childhood Experiences in Language Arts: Emerging Literacy. 5th ed. LC 94-25760. (Illus.). 496p. (C). 1994. mass mkt. 40.50 (*0-8273-5880-6*) Delmar.

— Early Childhood Experiences in Language Arts: Emerging Literacy. 6th abr. rev. ed. LC 98-11429. 576p. (C). 1998. pap. 58.95 (*0-8273-8361-4*) Delmar.

— Student Teaching: Early Childhood Practicum Guide. 3rd ed. (Early Childhood Education Ser.). (C). 1996. teacher ed. 10.50 (*0-8273-7620-0*) Delmar.

Machado, Jeanne M. & Botnarescue, Helen M. Student Teaching: Early Childhood Practicum Guide. 2nd ed. LC 92-10647. 456p. 1993. pap. 27.95 (*0-8273-5242-5*) Delmar.

Machado, Jeanne M. & Meyer-Botnaerescue, Helen. Student Teaching: Early Childhood Practicum Guide. 3rd ed. LC 96-13121. (Early Childhood Education Ser.). 464p. (C). 1996. text 50.95 (*0-8273-7619-7*) Delmar.

Machado, Jeanne M. & Meyer-Botnarescue, Helen. Instructor's Guide for Student Teaching: Early Childhood Practicum Guide. 2nd ed. 70p. 1993. 12.95 (*0-8273-5243-3*) Delmar.

***Machado, Jeanne M. & Meyer-Botnarescue, Helen.** Student Teaching: Early Childhood Practicum Guide. 4th ed. LC 00-30684. 2000. pap. write for info. (*0-7668-1056-9*) Delmar.

Machado, Jeanne M. & Meyer, Helen C. Early Childhood Practicum Guide. LC 83-71047. (Illus.). 400p. 1984. pap. 27.75 (*0-8273-2080-9*) Delmar.

— Early Childhood Practicum Guide. LC 83-71047. (Illus.). 400p. 1984. teacher ed. 10.50 (*0-8273-2081-7*) Delmar.

Machado, Luis A. The Right to Be Intelligent. 85p. 1980. text 40.00 (*0-08-025781-X*, CRC Reprint) Franklin.

Machado, M. A. & Narducci, L. M., eds. Optics in Four Dimensions, 1980: ICO Ensenada. LC 80-70771. (AIP Conference Proceedings Ser.: No. 65). 745p. 1981. lib. bdg. 40.75 (*0-88318-164-9*) Am Inst Physics.

Machado, M. E., jt. ed. see Pick, M.

Machado, Manuel. Antologia. 11th ed. 152p. 1979. pap. 8.95 (*0-7859-5189-X*) Fr & Eur.

— Diccionario Tecnico de la Construccion, Edificacion y Obras Publicas Frances-Espanol y Espanol-Frances. (SPA.). 576p. 1969. 59.95 (*0-8288-6577-9*, S-50242) Fr & Eur.

Machado, Manuel A. Barbarians of the North: Modern Chihuahua & the Mexican Political System. (Illus.). 224p. 1993. 19.95 (*0-89015-839-8*) Sunbelt Media.

— An Industry in Crisis: Mexican-United States Cooperation in the Control of Foot & Mouth Disease. LC 68-64741. (University of California Publications in Social Welfare: Vol. 80). 110p. reprint ed. pap. 34.10 (*0-608-13932-7*, 202143900021) Bks Demand.

Machado, Manuel A., Jr. The North Mexican Cattle Industry, 1910-1975: Ideology, Conflict & Change. LC 80-5515. (Illus.). 168p. 1981. 24.95 (*0-89096-104-2*) Tex A&M Univ Pr.

Machado, Manuel Y. Las Adelfas. La Lola Se Va a los Puertos. Chicharro Chamorro, Damaso, ed. (Nueva Austral Ser.: Vol. 271). (SPA.). 1993. pap. text 34.95 (*84-239-7271-2*) Elliots Bks.

— Desdichas de la Fortuna O Julianillo Valcarcel. Juan de Manara. Chicharro Chamorro, Damaso, ed. (Nueva Austral Ser.: Vol. 236). (SPA.). 1991. pap. text 24.95 (*84-239-7236-4*) Elliots Bks.

***Machado, Michael J. & Costa, Jim, eds.** Summary of the Joint Information Hearing on El Nino: California Legislature. (Illus.). 101p. (C). 2000. reprint ed. pap. text 20.00 (*0-7881-8657-4*) DIANE Pub.

***Machado, Nora.** Using the Bodies of the Dead: Legal, Ethical & Organisational Dimensions of Organ Transplantation. LC 98-19209. 264p. 1998. 74.95 (*1-85521-973-5*) Ashgate Pub Co.

Machado, Roberto. Cuba, 1930-1958: Pearl of the Antilles. 1996. 45.00 (*0-9638703-1-9*) Shade Tree Pr.

— Cuba, 1930-1958: The Pearl of the Antilles. (Illus.). 96p. 1996. 45.00 (*0-614-18267-0*) Shade Tree Pr.

— Pearl of the Antilles. 1996. 45.00 (*0-9638703-9-4*) Shade Tree Pr.

Machado, Rod. Rod Machado's Instrument Pilot's Survival Manual. rev. ed. 232p. (C). 1992. reprint ed. pap. text 29.95 (*0-9631229-0-8*) Av Speak Bur.

— Rod Machado's Private Pilot Handbook: The Ultimate Private Pilot Book. Titterington, Diane & Weiss, Brian, eds. (Illus.). 572p. (C). 1996. pap. text 34.95 (*0-9631229-9-1*) Av Speak Bur.

Machado, Rodolfo & El-Khoury, Rodolphe. Monolithic Architecture. (Illus.). 173p. 1995. 60.00 (*3-7913-1609-5*, Pub. by Prestel) te Neues.

Machado, William C. Uniforms & Equipment of the Last Campaign, 1916: The Pursuit of Pancho Villa. (Illus.). 112p. (Orig.). (C). 1993. pap. 20.00 (*0-9636005-0-8*) W C Machado.

Machado y Ruiz, Antonio. Antologia de la Novela Realista. (Clasicos Esenciales Ser.). (SPA.). (C). 1998. pap. 9.95 (*84-294-4562-5*) Santillana.

— Solitudes, Galleries, & Other Poems. Predmore, Richard L., tr. from SPA. LC 86-32758. ix, 237p. 1987. text 39.95 (*0-8223-0713-8*) Duke.

MacHaffie, Barbara J. Her Story: Women in Christian Tradition. LC 85-45494. 192p. 1986. pap. 16.00 (*0-8006-1893-9*, 1-1893, Fortress Pr) Augsburg Fortress.

MacHaffie, Barbara J., ed. Readings in Her Story: Women in Christian Tradition. LC 92-3693. 256p. (Orig.). 1992. pap. 20.00 (*0-8006-2575-7*, 1-2575, Fortress Pr) Augsburg Fortress.

Machairas, Leontios. Recital Concerning the Sweet Land of Cyprus, 2 vols., Set. Dawkins, R. M., ed. LC 78-63351. (Crusades & Military Orders Ser.: Second Series). reprint ed. 92.50 (*0-404-17030-7*) AMS Pr.

***Machale.** Wit - Humorous Quotations from Woody Allen to Oscar Wilde. 320p. 1999. 7.98 (*1-56731-356-6*, MJF Bks) Fine Comms.

Machale, Carlos F. Vox New College Spanish-English Dictionary. (SPA., Illus.). 1536p. 21.95 (*0-8442-7999-4*, 79994, Natl Textbk Co) NTC Contemp Pub Co.

MacHale, D. J. East of the Sun West of the Moon. LC 91-15220. (Illus.). 36p. (J). (ps-3). 1995. pap. 10.95 incl. audio (*0-689-80361-3*, Rabbit Ears) Little Simon.

Machale, D. J. & Derby, Kathleen. The Tale of the Nightly Neighbors. (Are You Afraid of the Dark? Ser.: No. 4). (YA). (gr. 4-7). 1995. pap. 3.99 (*0-671-53445-9*, PB Trade Paper) PB.

MacHale, Des. Best Irish Humorous Quotations. 88p. 1997. pap. 9.95 (*1-85635-138-6*, Pub. by Mercier Pr) Irish Amer Bk.

— Irish Love & Marriage Jokes. 1991. pap. 4.95 (*0-85342-500-0*) Dufour.

Machale, Des. Mind-Bending Lateral Thinking Puzzles by Des Machale, No. 1. (Mind-Bending Puzzle Bks.). (Illus.). 96p. 1998. 6.95 (*1-899712-23-2*, Pub. by Lagoon Bks) Midpt Trade.

MacHale, Des. Spiritual & Thought Provoking Quotations. 160p. 1997. pap. 12.95 (*1-85635-169-6*, Pub. by Mercier Pr) Irish Amer Bk.

— Wit: Humorous Quotations. LC 97-42465. 320p. 1998. 14.95 (*1-57098-213-9*) Roberts Rinehart.

— The World's Best Scottish Jokes. 96p. 1998. pap. 6.95 (*0-00-638264-9*, Pub. by HarpC) Trafalgar.

— Yet More Wit LC 98-215645. x, 310p. 1998. write for info. (*1-85635-239-0*) Mercier Pr.

MacHale, Des, jt. auth. see Sloane, Paul.

***Machalek, Jan.** Eva's Summer Vacation: A Story of the Czech Republic. LC 99-19243. (Illus.). 32p. (J). (gr. k-3). 1999. pap. 5.95 (*1-56899-803-1*) Soundprints.

— Eva's Summer Vacation: A Story of the Czech Republic. LC 99-19243. (Illus.). 32p. (J). (ps-3). 1999. 15.95 (*1-56899-802-3*) Soundprints.

Machalek, Jan. Eva's Summer Vacation: A Story of the Czech Republic - Includes Doll. (Illus.). 32p. (J). (gr. k-3). 1999. pap. 16.95 (*1-56899-806-6*) Soundprints.

Machalow, Robert. Using Lotus 1-2-3 for Windows: A How-to-Do-It Manual for Librarians. LC 94-25790. 268p. 1994. pap. 38.50 (*1-55570-187-6*) Neal-Schuman.

— Using Microsoft Excel: A How-to-Do-It Manual for Librarians. LC 90-21524. 175p. 1991. 38.50 (*1-55570-075-6*) Neal-Schuman.

— Using Microsoft Works: A How-to-Do-It Manual for Librarians. 276p. 1992. 38.50 (*1-55570-110-8*) Neal-Schuman.

Machamer, Gene. Final Farewells. (Illus.). 160p. 1998. pap. 9.95 (*0-9627369-5-3*) Carlisle Pr.

***Machamer, Gene.** The Lost Avenger. LC 99-74432. (Illus.). 176p. 1999. pap. 9.00 (*0-9627369-6-1*) Carlisle Pr.

Machamer, Gene. Native American Profiles. LC 95-95329. (Illus.). 170p. (Orig.). 1996. pap. 10.00 (*0-9627369-3-7*) Carlisle Pr.

— One Hundred One Uses for a Crooked Politician. LC 92-90220. (Illus.). 104p. (Orig.). 1992. pap. 6.95 (*0-9627369-1-0*) Carlisle Pr.

Machamer, Peter, ed. The Cambridge Companion to Galileo. LC 98-13357. (Cambridge Companions to Philosophy Ser.). (Illus.). 496p. (C). 1998. text 59.95 (*0-521-58178-8*); pap. text 19.95 (*0-521-58841-3*) Cambridge U Pr.

Machamer, Peter, et al, eds. Scientific Controversies: Philosophical & Historical Perspectives. LC 98-38234. (Illus.). 288p. 2000. text 45.00 (*0-19-511987-8*) OUP.

***Machamer, Peter, et al, eds.** Theory & Method in the Neurosciences. (The Pittsburgh-Konstanz Series in the Philosophy & History of Science). 400p. 2000. 65.00 (*0-8229-4140-6*) U of Pittsburgh Pr.

Machamer, Peter, jt. ed. see Carrier, Martin.

Machamer, Peter K., jt. ed. see Fine, Arthur.

***Machan, Tibor R.** Ayn Rand. LC 99-28015. (Masterworks in the Western Tradition Ser.). 176p. 1999. pap. text 24.95 (*0-8204-4144-9*) P Lang Pubng.

Machan, Tibor R. Classical Individualism: The Supreme Importance of Each Human Being. LC 98-9404. (Routledge Studies in Social & Political Thought). 272p. (C). 1998. 85.00 (*0-415-16572-5*) Routledge.

MaChan, Tibor R. Generosity: Virtue in the Civil Society. LC 97-51252. 116p. 16.95 (*1-882577-53-1*) Cato Inst.

— Generosity: Virtue in the Civil Society. LC 97-51252. 1998. 8.95 (*1-882577-54-X*) Cato Inst.

Machan, Tibor R. Liberty & Culture: Essays on the Idea of a Free Society. LC 88-32183. 288p. 1989. 27.95 (*0-87975-524-5*) Prometheus Bks.

— The Moral Case for the Free Market Economy: A Philosophical Argument. LC 88-37917. (Problems in Contemporary Philosophy Ser.: Vol. 15). 140p. 1989. lib. bdg. 69.95 (*0-88946-343-3*) E Mellen.

***Machan, Tibor R.** Morality & Work. LC 00-21785. 2000. write for info. (*0-8179-9852-7*) Hoover Inst Pr.

Machan, Tibor R. A Primer on Ethics. LC 96-6502. 1997. 19.95 (*0-8061-2946-8*) U of Okla Pr.

— Private Rights & Public Illusions. LC 93-45616. 379p. (C). 1994. 34.95 (*1-56000-176-3*); pap. 19.95 (*1-56000-749-4*) Transaction Pubs.

— Why Freedom Must Be First. LC 97-31176. (Hoover Essays Ser.: No. 20). 1997. pap. 5.00 (*0-8179-3832-X*) Hoover Inst Pr.

Machan, Tibor R., ed. Business Ethics in the Global Market. LC 99-25882. (Publication Ser.: Vol. 455). 141p. 1999. pap. 17.95 (*0-8179-9632-X*) Hoover Inst Pr.

— Commerce & Morality: Alternative Essays in Business Ethics. 264p. 1988. 59.00 (*0-8476-7586-6*); pap. 25.00 (*0-8476-7587-4*) Rowman.

***Machan, Tibor R., ed.** The Commons--It's Tragedies & Othe Follies. (Philosophic Reflections on a Free Society Ser.). 2000. 17.95 (*0-8179-9922-1*) Hoover Inst Pr.

MaChan, Tibor R., ed. Education in a Free Society. LC 99-55365. (Publication Ser.: No. 475). Date not set. 16.95 (*0-8179-9832-2*) Hoover Inst Pr.

***Machan, Tibor R., ed.** Individual Rights Reconsidered: Lasting Truths of the U. S. Declaration of Independence. (Philosophic Reflections on a Free Society Ser.). 2000. 17.95 (*0-8179-9932-9*) Hoover Inst Pr.

Machan, Tibor R. & Johnson, M. Bruce, eds. Rights & Regulation: Ethical, Political, & Economic Issues. LC 83-11309. (Illus.). 309p. (C). 1983. pap. 14.95 (*0-936488-61-1*) PRIPP.

Machan, Tibor R. & Nelson, John O. A Dialogue Partly on Political Liberty. 82p. (Orig.). (C). 1989. pap. text 13.50 (*0-8191-7736-9*) U Pr of Amer.

Machan, Tibor R. & Rasmussen, Douglas B., eds. Liberty for the 21st Century: Contemporary Libertarian Thought. LC 95-19310. (Studies in Social, Political, & Legal Philosophy). 416p. (C). 1995. pap. text 26.95 (*0-8476-8058-4*); lib. bdg. 67.50 (*0-8476-8057-6*) Rowman.

Machan, Tibor R., jt. auth. see Chesher, James E.

Machan, Tibor R., jt. auth. see Skoble, Aeon J.

Machan, Tim W. Techniques of Translation: Chaucer's Boece. LC 85-524. 163p. (C). 1985. 29.95 (*0-937664-68-5*) Pilgrim Bks OK.

— Textual Criticism & Middle English Texts. LC 94-5441. 1994. text 40.00 (*0-8139-1508-2*) U Pr of Va.

Machan, Tim W., ed. Medieval Literature: Texts & Interpretation. (Medieval & Renaissance Texts & Studies: Vol. 79). 208p. 1991. 24.00 (*0-86698-090-3*, MR79) MRTS.

Machan, Tim W. & Scott, Charles T., eds. English in Its Social Contexts: Essays in Historical Sociolinguistics. (Oxford Studies in Sociolinguistics). (Illus.). 288p. (C). 1992. pap. text 23.95 (*0-19-506500-X*) OUP.

Machan, Wayne & Bruggen, Bill. The Corvair, 1960-1969. LC 89-63378. (Authenticity Ser.). (Illus.). 128p. (Orig.). (YA). 1991. pap. 19.95 (*0-929758-07-2*) Beeman Jorgensen.

Machann, Clinton. Czech-Americans in Transition. LC 99-10925. 136p. 1999. 18.95 (*1-57168-298-8*, Eakin Pr) Sunbelt Media.

— The Essential Matthew Arnold: An Annotated Bibliography of Major Modern Studies. LC 92-36565. (Reference Ser.). 177p. 1993. 55.00 (*0-8161-9087-9*, G K Hall & Co) Mac Lib Ref.

MacHann, Clinton. Matthew Arnold: A Literary Life. LC 97-18187. 1998. text 35.00 (*0-312-21031-0*) St Martin.

An Asterisk (*) at the beginning of an entry indicates that the title is appearing for the first time.

Machann, Clinton. Victorian Autobiography The Genre of Autobiography in Victorian Literature. 128p. (C). 1995. text 42.50 (0-472-10565-5, 10565) U of Mich Pr.

Machann, Clinton & Burt, Forrest D., eds. Matthew Arnold in His Time & Ours: Centenary Essays. LC 87-25271. 220p. 1988. text 35.00 (0-8139-1173-7) U Pr of Va.

Machann, Clinton & Clark, William B., eds. Katherine Anne Porter & Texas: An Uneasy Relationship. LC 89-20667. (Illus.). 216p. 1990. 31.50 (0-89096-441-6) Tex A&M Univ Pr.

Machann, Clinton & Mendl, James W. Krasna Amerika: A Study of Texas Czechs, 1851-1939. (Illus.). 288p. 1983. 16.95 (0-89015-391-4) Sunbelt Media.

Machann, Clinton & Mendl, James W., Jr., eds. Czech Voices: Stories from Texas in the "Amerikan Narodni Kalendar" LC 90-43294. (Centennial Series of the Association of Former Students: No. 39). (Illus.). 184p. 1998. pap. 16.95 (0-89096-846-2) Tex A&M Univ Pr.

Machann, Clinton, jt. ed. see Burt, Forrest D.

MacHardy, William E. Apple Scab: Biology, Epidemiology, & Management. LC 95-80654. (Illus.). 545p. 1995. 95.00 (0-89054-206-6) Am Phytopathol Soc.

MacHarg, Marcia L. & Clark, Barton B. International Survey of Investment Adviser Regulation. 2nd ed. LC 98-51087. 1999. 150.00 (90-411-9688-9) Kluwer Law Intl.

Macharg, Kenneth D. Don't Rush the Lord! A Pilgrimage to God's Purpose. LC 97-9430. 102p. 1997. pap. 8.95 (0-87808-254-9, WCL254-9) William Carey Lib.

Macharia, Kinuthia. Social & Political Dynamics of the Informal Economy in African Cities: Nairobi & Harare. LC 97-13284. 238p. (C). 1997. 57.00 (0-7618-0840-X); pap. 34.50 (0-7618-0841-8) U Pr of Amer.

Macharia, Laila N. Models of Election Commissions in Africa: December, 1995. ii, 34p. 1996. pap. text 5.00 (1-879720-05-1) Intl Fndt Elect.

Macharzina, Klaus & Staehle, Wolfgang H., eds. European Approaches to International Management. xiv, 386p. 1986. 82.95 (3-11-009827-X) De Gruyter.

MacHaster, Eve B. God Comforts His People, Vol. 11. LC 95-835. (Story Bible Ser.: Vol. 7). (Illus.). 176p. (Orig.). (J). (gr. 3 up). 1985. pap. 6.99 (0-8361-3393-5) Herald Pr.

Machat, Jeffery, et al. The Art of Lasik. 2nd ed. LC 98-28025. (Illus.). 544p. 1998. text 215.00 (1-55642-386-1, 63861) SLACK Inc.

Machat, Jeffery J. Excimer Laser Refractive Surgery: Practice & Principles. (Illus.). 480p. 1996. 195.00 (1-55642-274-1, 62741) SLACK Inc.

***Machat, Jeffery J., et al.** The Art of Lasik. 2nd ed. (SPA., Illus.). 544p. 1999. 215.00 (1-55642-421-3) SLACK Inc.

Machatschke, Roland. Islam. Bowden, John, tr. from GER. LC 96-12387. (Basics Ser.: Vol. 2). 96p. (Orig.). 1996. pap. 10.00 (1-56338-162-1) TPI PA.

Machaut, Guillaume De, see Guillaume de Machaut.

MacHay, John. Knuckleheads in the News. LC 96-96851. 1996. pap. 8.95 (0-345-40988-4) Ballantine Pub Grp.

Mache, Francois-Bernard. Music, Myth, & Nature, or, the Dolphins of Arion. rev. ed. Delaney, Susan, tr. from FRE. LC 92-39112. (Contemporary Music Studies: Vol. 6). 200p. 1993. text 46.00 (3-7186-5321-4); pap. text 20.00 (3-7186-5322-2) Gordon & Breach.

— Music, Society & Imagination in Contemporary France. (Contemporary Music Review Ser.). 212p. 1994. pap. text 25.00 (3-7186-5421-0, Harwood Acad Pubs) Gordon & Breach.

Mache, R., et al, eds. The Translational Apparatus of Photosynthetic Organelles. (NATO ASI Series H: Cell Biology: Vol. 55). (Illus.). 241p. 1991. 119.95 (0-387-51779-0) Spr-Verlag.

Mache, Ulrich, et al, eds. Saemtliche Werke: Ausgaben Deutscher Literatur des 15 bis 18 Jahrhunderts. Incl. Vol. 6. Afrikanische Sofonisbe. Meid, Volker, ed. 1972. 500.00 (3-11-003918-4), Vol. 8. Simson. 1970. 444.00 (3-11-006364-6); Vol. 9. Deutscher Helicon. Meid, Volker, ed. 1971. 393.00 (3-11-003598-7); Vol. 11. Sprach-Vebung, Rosen-Mand, Helikonische Hechell, Sendeschreiben a Den Kreutztragenden. Meid, Volker, ed. 1973. 304.00 (3-11-004525-7); (C). write for info. (0-318-51645-4) De Gruyter.

Mache, Wolfgang W. Lexikon der Textkommunikation und Datenkommunikation: Lexicon of Text & Data Communication. 3rd ed. (GER.). 580p. 1993. 195.00 (0-8288-1358-2, M15282) Fr & Eur.

Machedlover, Helene, jt. auth. see Connor, Billie M.

Machedon, Luminita & Scoffham, Ernie. Romanian Modernism: The Architecture of Bucharest, 1920-1940. LC 98-37573. (Illus.). 352p. 1999. 50.00 (0-262-13348-2) MIT Pr.

Machefert-Tassin, Yves & Semmens, Peter W. Channel Tunnel Trains: Channel Tunnel Rolling Stock & the Euro Tunnel System. LC 97-152478. (Illus.). 160p. 40.00 (1-872009-33-6, Pub. by Boston Mills) Genl Dist Srvs.

MacHeix, Jeans-Jacques, ed. Fruit Phenolics. 392p. 1990. lib. bdg. 269.00 (0-8493-4968-0, SB357) CRC Pr.

Machek, Josef, et al, eds. Prague Studies in Mathematical Linguistics, Vol. 7. (Linguistic & Literary Studies in Eastern Europe: No. 9). 255p. 1981. 65.00 (90-272-1511-1) J Benjamins Pubng Co.

Machel, Kelly. Month of Meals: One Day to a Freezerful of Entrees. Engstrom, Judith A. & Engstrom, Ron, eds. LC 97-92239. 140p. 1997. ring bd. 21.95 (0-9659528-0-0) KRM.

Machell, Carolyn, jt. auth. see Fielder, Ron.

Machell, Keith, jt. auth. see Potts, Kathryn H.

Machelon, Jean-Pierre, jt. auth. see De Lolme, J. L.

Machem, J. Gresham. The New Testament: An Introduction to Its History & Literature. 1976. pap. 15.99 (0-85151-449-9) Banner of Truth.

Machemehi, Jerry L., jt. ed. see Bennett, F. Lawrence.

Machemer, Corona, ed. see Lane, Harlan, et al.

Machen, Arthur. The Angels of Mon: The Bowmen & Other Legends of the War. 77p. 1977. 15.95 (0-8369-4183-7) Ayer.

— The Children of the Pool & Other Stories. Reginald, R. & Menville, Douglas A., eds. LC 76-1366. (Supernatural & Occult Fiction Ser.). 1976. reprint ed. lib. bdg. 24.95 (0-405-08424-2) Ayer.

— Dreads & Drolls. LC 67-28757. (Essay Index Reprint Ser.). 1977. 28.95 (0-8369-0648-9) Ayer.

— The Great God Pan. LC 79-128737. (Short Story Index Reprint Ser.). 1977. 24.95 (0-8369-3628-0) Ayer.

— The Great God Pan. unabridged ed. (Creation Classics Ser.). (Illus.). 128p. 1996. reprint ed. pap. 12.95 (1-871592-11-9) Creation Books.

— Guinevere & Lancelot & Others. Brooks, Cuyler W., Jr. & Shoemaker, Michael, eds. (Illus.). 50p. 1987. pap. 10.00 (0-9603300-2-X) Purple Mouth.

— The Hill of Dreams. (Illus.). 196p. 1998. reprint ed. 49.95 (1-872621-31-7, Pub. by Tartarus Pr) Firebird Dist.

— House of Souls. LC 72-152947. (Short Story Index Reprint Ser.). 1977. reprint ed. 27.95 (0-8369-3806-2) Ayer.

— Ornaments in Jade. 54p. 1997. 29.95 (1-872621-24-4, Pub. by Tartarus Pr) Firebird Dist.

— The Secret Glory. 253p. 1999. 49.95 (1-872621-36-8, Pub. by Tartarus Pr) Firebird Dist.

— Tales of Horror & the Supernatural. 2nd ed. 391p. 1998. 49.95 (1-872621-25-2, Pub. by Tartarus Pr) Firebird Dist.

— Three Imposters & Other Stories. 320p. 1998. pap. text 12.95 (1-56882-132-8) Chaosium.

Machen, Arthur & Buck, Mitchell S. On Paganism/ Afterglow. 58p. 1998. reprint ed. 25.95 (1-872621-30-9, Pub. by Tartarus Pr) Firebird Dist.

Machen, Arthur, et al. Blood & Roses: The Vampire in 19th Century Literature. unabridged ed. Gladwell, Adele O. & Havoc, James, eds. (Creation Classics Ser.). (Illus.). 268p. 1996. reprint ed. pap. 15.95 (1-871592-14-3) Creation Books.

Machen, Arthur W., Jr. A Venerable Assembly: The History of Venable, Baetjer & Howard. 240p. 1991. write for info. (0-9631294-0-6) V B & H.

Machen, Christopher, jt. see Hill, Kyl.

Machen, Christopher, jt. auth. see Kingsmore, Richard.

Machen, Eli, jt. auth. see Lasser, Mark R.

Machen, J. Gresham. The Christian View of Man. 254p. 1995. reprint ed. pap. 10.99 (0-85151-112-0) Banner of Truth.

— Christianity & Liberalism. 1946. pap. 11.00 (0-8028-1121-3) Eerdmans.

— Education, Christianity & the State. 2nd rev. ed. Robbins, John W., ed. & intro. by. 165p. 1994. pap. 9.95 (0-940931-89-3) Trinity Found.

— God Transcendent. 208p. 1982. pap. 9.99 (0-85151-355-7) Banner of Truth.

— Griego del Nuevo Testamento. (SPA.). 10.99 (0-8297-1682-3) Vida Pubs.

***Machen, J. Gresham.** The New Testament Greek for Beginners. 300p. 1998. pap. 25.00 (1-57910-180-1) Wipf & Stock.

— New Testament Greek for Beginners. rev. ed. Robbins, John W., ed. 287p. (C). 2000. 16.95 (0-940931-77-X); pap. 10.95 (0-940931-55-9) Trinity Found.

— New Testament Greek for Beginners. 2nd abr. ed. LC 99-21889. 416p. 2000. 19.99 (0-8010-2211-8) Baker Bks.

Machen, J. Gresham. Vision Cristiana del Hombre. (SPA.). 257p. 1996. reprint ed. pap. 6.25 (0-85151-709-9) Banner of Truth.

— What Is Faith? 264p. 1991. pap. text 9.99 (0-85151-594-0) Banner of Truth.

***Machen, M. Marge, ed.** Academic Research & Development Expenditures: Fiscal Year 1997. 210p. (C). 1999. pap. text 35.00 (0-7881-8227-7) DIANE Pub.

Machenaud, Dennis. Golf: How to Play Each Shot by the Professionals. 168p. 1995. 17.98 (0-7858-0214-2) Bk Sales Inc.

Machenzie, J. Lachlan & Todd, Richard, eds. In Other Words: Festschrift H. H. Meier. (Illus.). 346p. (C). 1989. pap. 76.95 (90-6765-413-2) Mouton.

Macher, Alan, jt. auth. see Murphy, Stephanie.

Macher, E., jt. ed. see Klippel, K. F.

Macher, Janet, ed. Bio Aerosols: Assessment & Control. 526p. 1998. text 89.00 (1-882417-29-1, 3180) Am Conf Govt Indus Hygienist.

Macher, Ron. Making Your Small Farm Profitable: 20 Guiding Principles, New Crops & New Markets, Maximize Net Profits Per Acre. LC 99-16219. (Illus.). 288p. 1999. pap. 19.95 (1-58017-161-3) Storey Bks.

Macherey, Pierre. In a Materialist Way: Selected Essays. LC 98-30211. 1998. 45.00 (1-85984-949-0, Pub. by Verso) Norton.

— The Object of Literature. (Literature, Culture, Theory Ser.: No. 14). 254p. (C). 1995. text 64.95 (0-521-41955-7); pap. text 19.95 (0-521-47678-X) Cambridge U Pr.

— A Theory of Literary Production. Wall, Geoffrey, tr. from FRE. 1978. pap. 15.95 (0-7100-0087-1) Routledge.

— A Theory of Literary Production LC 78-40559. 326 p. 1978. write for info. (0-7100-8978-3, Routledge Thoemms) Routledge.

Maches, Richard. Travel, Entertainment & Gifts. 4th rev. ed. LC 98-212415. 178p. 1997. pap. 69.95 (1-57801-015-2) Western Schls.

***Maches, Richard.** Travel, Entertainment & Gifts 99. 5th ed. (Illus.). 178p. 1999. pap. write for info. (1-57801-040-3) Western Schls.

Macheski, Cecilia. Quilt Stories. LC 93-33292. 304p. 1994. 29.95 (0-8131-1849-2) U Pr of Ky.

Macheski, Cecilia, jt. ed. see Schofield, Mary A.

***Machette, Alan.** CCTV for Security Professionals. (Illus.). 2000. pap. text 64.95 (0-7506-7303-6) Buttrwrth-Heinemann.

Machette, Michael N., ed. In the Footsteps of G. K. Gilbert - Lake Bonneville & Neotectonics of the Eastern Basin & Range Province: Guidebook for GSA Annual Meeting. (Miscellaneous Publication Ser.: Vol. 88-1). (Illus.). 120p. 1988. pap. 8.50 (1-55791-298-X, MP-88-1) Utah Geological Survey.

Machi, Antonio, tr. see De Finetti, Bruno.

Machi, Junji & Sigel, Bernard, eds. Ultrasound for Surgeons. LC 96-9300. (Illus.). 384p. 1997. 98.50 (0-89640-321-1) Igaku-Shoin.

Machi, Mario. Under the Rising Sun: Memories of a Japanese Prisoner of War. (Illus.). 176p. (Orig.). 1995. pap. 12.95 (0-9642521-0-4) Wolfenden.

Machi, S., ed. Radiation Processing for Environmental Conservation. 202p. 1985. pap. 30.00 (0-08-031435-X, Pergamon Pr) Elsevier.

Machia, Jim. The Road to Retirement. 73p. 1998. pap. 7.95 (0-9637794-4-3) Machia.

Machiavelli, Mariarita. Quick & Easy Mosaics: Innovative Project & Techniques. LC 98-3571. (Illus.). 160p. 1998. 27.95 (0-8069-3895-1) Sterling.

***Machiavelli, Niccolo.** Art of War. 1998. lib. bdg. 20.00 (0-226-50040-3) U Ch Pr.

Machiavelli, Niccolo. The Art of War. Whitehorne, Peter, tr. LC 73-172705. (Tudor Translations, First Ser.: No. 39). (Orig.). reprint ed. 115.00 (0-404-51951-2) AMS Pr.

— The Art of War. rev. ed. Farneworth, Ellis, tr. LC 64-66078. (Orig.). (C). 1965. pap. write for info. (0-672-60434-5, LLA196, Bobbs) Macmillan.

— The Art of War: A Revised Edition Ellis Farneworth Translation. Farneworth, Ellis, tr. (Quality Paperbacks Ser.). 336p. 1990. reprint ed. pap. 13.95 (0-306-80412-3) Da Capo.

— Clizia. Gallagher, Daniel T., tr. & notes by. 90p. (C). 1996. pap. text 6.50 (0-88133-902-4) Waveland Pr.

— The Discourses. Crick, Bernard, ed. Walker, Leslie J., tr. (Classics Ser.). 544p. 1984. pap. 10.95 (0-14-044428-9, Penguin Classics) Viking Penguin.

— Discourses on Livy. Bondanella, Julia Conway & Bondanella, Peter, trs. (Oxford World's Classics Ser.). 448p. 2000. pap. 10.95 (0-19-283950-0) OUP.

— Discourses on Livy. Mansfield, Harvey C. & Tarcov, Nathan, trs. LC 95-50910. 400p. 1996. 34.95 (0-226-50035-7) U Ch Pr.

— Discourses on Livy. 368p. 1998. pap. text 14.00 (0-226-50036-5) U Ch Pr.

— First Decennale. LC 77-91630. 33p. reprint ed. pap. 30.00 (0-7837-2293-1, 205738100004) Bks Demand.

— Florentine Histories. Banfield, Laura, tr. from ITA. 412p. (C). 1988. pap. text 19.95 (0-691-00863-9, Pub. by Princeton U Pr) Cal Prin Full Svc.

— Florentine Histories. Banfield, Laura F. & Mansfield, Harvey C., Jr., trs. LC 87-38503. 410p. 1988. reprint ed. pap. 127.10 (0-608-07801-8, 205986800010) Bks Demand.

— Florentine History. Bedingfeld, T., tr. LC 73-172705. (Tudor Translations, First Ser.: No. 40). reprint ed. 57.50 (0-404-51952-0) AMS Pr.

— The History, Political & Diplomatic Writings of Niccolo Machiavelli, 4 vols. 1981. 1200.00 (0-87968-405-4) Gordon Pr.

— The Letters of Machiavelli: A Selection. Gilbert, Allan H., ed. & tr. by. 252p. 1988. pap. text 13.50 (0-226-50041-1) U Ch Pr.

— The Literary Works of Machiavelli: With Selections from the Private Correspondence. Hale, John Rigby, ed. LC 79-4216. 202p. 1979. reprint ed. lib. bdg. 35.00 (0-313-21248-1, MALW) Greenwood.

— The Living Thoughts of Machiavelli. Sforza, Carlo, ed. LC 74-28758. (Illus.). 161p. 1975. reprint ed. lib. bdg. 35.00 (0-8371-7923-8, MALIT, Greenwood Pr) Greenwood.

— Machiavelli: The History of Florence & Other Selections. Gilmore, Myron P., ed. Rawson, Judith A., tr. 1970. 32.50 (0-671-48364-1) Irvington.

— Mandragola. Paolucci, Henry & Paolucci, Anne A., trs. LC 57-14629. 64p. 1957. pap. 10.00 (0-672-60231-8, LLA58, Bobbs) Macmillan.

— Mandragola. Flaumenhaft, Mera J., tr. from ITA. LC 80-54106. 64p. (C). 1981. pap. text 5.25 (0-917974-57-3) Waveland Pr.

— La Mandragola. Luciani, Vincent, ed. (ITA & ENG.). (C). 1997. pap. 10.95 (0-913298-19-0) S F Vanni.

— The Mandrake. Shawn, Wallace, tr. 1978. pap. 5.25 (0-8222-0728-1) Dramatists Play.

— Oeuvres Completes. (FRE.). 1978. lib. bdg. 105.00 (0-8288-3524-1, F30070) Fr & Eur.

— Oeuvres Completes: La Mandragore, le Prince, Etc. 1664p. 42.95 (0-686-56535-5) Fr & Eur.

— The Other Machiavelli: Republican Writings by the Author of "The Prince" Taylor, Quentin P., ed. LC 97-43868. 136p. (C). 1998. text 46.00 (0-7618-1014-5); pap. text 24.50 (0-7618-1015-3) U Pr of Amer.

— The Portable Machiavelli. Bondanella, Peter E. & Musa, Mark, trs. from ITA. (Portable Library: No. 92). 576p. (Orig.). 1979. pap. 15.95 (0-14-015092-7, Penguin Bks) Viking Penguin.

— The Prince. (C). 1997. pap. text 10.00 (0-321-02595-4) Addson-Wesley Educ.

— The Prince. 1998. pap. text 2.00 (0-451-62755-5) Addson-Wesley Educ.

— The Prince. (Airmont Classics Ser.). (YA). (gr. 11 up). 1965. mass mkt. 2.95 (0-8049-0056-6, CL-56) Airmont.

— The Prince. 17.95 (0-89190-547-2) Amereon Ltd.

Machiavelli, Niccolo. The Prince. 1994. lib. bdg. 18.95 (1-56849-500-5) Buccaneer Bks.

Machiavelli, Niccolo. The Prince. Price, Russell & Skinner, Quentin, eds. (Cambridge Texts in the History of Political Thought Ser.). 192p. 1988. pap. text 8.95 (0-521-34993-1) Cambridge U Pr.

— The Prince. Price, Russell & Skinner, Quentin, eds. (Cambridge Texts in the History of Political Thought Ser.). 192p. 1989. text 29.95 (0-521-34240-6) Cambridge U Pr.

— The Prince. Wootton, David, tr. from ITA. LC 94-44698. (HPC Classics Ser.). 128p. (C). 1995. pap. text 3.95 (0-87220-316-6); lib. bdg. 24.95 (0-87220-317-4) Hackett Pub.

— The Prince. Bergin, Thomas G., ed. & tr. by. (Crofts Classics). 96p. 1947. pap. text 4.95 (0-88295-053-3) Harlan Davidson.

— The Prince. Sonnino, Paul, tr. & intro. by. LC 95-17621. 144p. (C). 1995. pap. 9.95 (0-391-03940-7) Humanities.

— The Prince. Atkinson, James, ed. LC 75-15946. (Library of Liberal Arts: Vol. 172). 448p. 1976. pap. write for info. (0-672-61244-5) Macmillan.

— The Prince. 1992. 16.00 (0-679-41044-9) McKay.

— The Prince. LC 99-21656. 1999. mass mkt. 3.95 (0-451-52746-1, Sig Classics) NAL.

— The Prince. 1999. audio. write for info. (0-14-086109-2) NAL.

— The Prince. Bondanella, Peter, ed. & tr. by. Musa, Mark, tr. (Oxford World's Classics Ser.). 126p. 1998. pap. 4.95 (0-19-283397-9) OUP.

— The Prince. Thompson, H. H., tr. LC 86-70377. (Great Books in Philosophy). 92p. 1986. pap. 4.95 (0-87975-344-7) Prometheus Bks.

Machiavelli, Niccolo. The Prince. 1995. pap. 11.95 (1-57392-423-7) Prometheus Bks.

Machiavelli, Niccolo. The Prince. (Bantam Classics Ser.). 1985. 9.05 (0-606-02466-2, Pub. by Turtleback) Demco.

— The Prince. Bull, George, tr. & intro. by. (Penguin Classics Ser.). 96p. (YA). (gr. 9 up). 1961. pap. 5.95 (0-14-044107-7) Viking Penguin.

— The Prince. Bull, George, tr. LC 99-228739. (Penguin Classics Ser.). 107p. 1999. pap. 5.95 (0-14-044752-0) Viking Penguin.

— The Prince. (Classics of World Literature Ser.). 1998. pap. 5.95 (1-85326-775-9, 7759WW, Pub. by Wrdsworth Edits) NTC Contemp Pub Co.

— Le Prince. (FRE.). 192p. 1986. pap. 10.95 (0-7859-4477-X, 204016653X) Fr & Eur.

— The Prince. Dacres, Edward, tr. LC 73-172705. (Tudor Translations, First Ser.). reprint ed. write for info. (0-318-50527-4) AMS Pr.

— The Prince. Thompson, Hill, tr. from ITA. 186p. 1988. reprint ed. 19.95 (0-88280-115-5); reprint ed. pap. 15.95 (0-88280-116-3) ETC Pubns.

— The Prince. De Alvarez, Leo P., tr. from ITA. (Illus.). 168p. (C). 1989. reprint ed. pap. text 7.95 (0-88133-444-8) Waveland Pr.

— The Prince. unabridged ed. 80p. 1992. reprint ed. pap. text 1.00 (0-486-27274-5) Dover.

— The Prince. unabridged ed. Bull, George, tr. (Classics on Cassette Ser.). 1994. 24.00 incl. audio (0-453-00893-3, Pub. by Penguin-HghBrdg) Penguin Putnam.

— The Prince. 2nd ed. Adams, Robert M., ed. & tr. by. LC 91-32538. (Critical Editions Ser.). 288p. (C). 1992. pap. text 9.25 (0-393-96220-2) Norton.

— The Prince. 2nd ed. Mansfield, Harvey C., tr. LC 98-5772. 152p. 1998. 24.00 (0-226-50043-8); pap. text 8.00 (0-226-50044-6) U Ch Pr.

— The Prince: A New Translation. Mansfield, Harvey C., Jr., tr. from ITA. LC 85-2536. xxviii, 144p. 1999. pap. text 8.00 (0-226-50038-1) U Ch Pr.

— The Prince: And Selected Discourses. Donno, Daniel, ed. 160p. (YA). (gr. 9-12). 1984. mass mkt. 3.95 (0-553-21278-8, Bantam Classics) Bantam.

***Machiavelli, Niccolo.** The Prince: Wordsworth Classics of World Literature. Detmold, C. E., tr. 143p. 2000. reprint ed. pap. text 15.00 (0-7881-9159-4) DIANE Pub.

Machiavelli, Niccolo. The Prince & Other Political Writings. Milner, Stephen, ed. 288p. 1995. 5.50 (0-460-87629-5, Everyman's Classic Lib) Tuttle Pubng.

— The Prince & Other Works. Gilbert, Alan H., ed. & tr. by. (University Classics Ser.). 332p. 1964. pap. 12.95 (0-87532-101-1) Hendricks House.

— Le Prince, Suivi de l'Antiprince. (FRE.). 1996. pap. 7.95 (2-87714-327-9, Pub. by Bookking Intl) Distribks Inc.

— Il Principe. 1999. 14.95 (88-17-12037-5) CE27.

***Machiavelli, Niccolo.** Il Principe by Nicole Machiavelli, Vol. 4. Falyhera, Maurizio & Giocometti, Cristina, eds. (ITA.). 1999. 19.95 incl. audio (1-58214-106-1) Mltilingl Bks.

— Il Principle by Nicole Machiavelli, Vol. 4. Falyhera, Maurizio & Giocometti, Cristina, eds. (ITA.). 1999. 29.95 incl. audio compact disk (1-58214-107-X) Mltilingl Bks.

Machiavelli, Niccolo. Selected Political Writings. Wootton, David et al, eds. LC 94-21202. (Hackett Classics Ser.). 272p. (Orig.). (C). 1994. lib. bdg. 34.95 (0-87220-248-8) Hackett Pub.

— Selected Political Writings. Wootton, David, tr. from ITA. LC 94-21202. (Hackett Classics Ser.). 272p. (Orig.). (C). 1994. pap. 8.95 (0-87220-247-X) Hackett Pub.

Machiavelli, Niccolo, et al. Ariosto's The Supposes, Machiavelli's The Mandrake, Intronati's The Deceived: Three Italian Renaissance Comedies. Cairns, Christopher & Accademia Senese Degli Intronati Staff, eds. Lorch, Jennifer, tr. from ITA. & intro. by. LC 96-19456. 452p. 1996. text 109.95 (0-7734-8821-9) E Mellen.

— The Prince. Codevilla, Angelo, tr. LC 96-50047. (Rethinking the Western Tradition Ser.). 192p. 1997. 25.00 (0-300-06402-0); pap. 11.00 (0-300-06403-9) Yale U Pr.

M

— The Prince & Other Discourses. Ricci, Luigi, tr. (Modern Library College Editions). 540p. (C). 1950. pap. 6.25 (*0-07-553577-7*, T25) McGraw.

Machiavelli, Niccolo, jt. auth. see Hale, John Rigby.

Machiavelli, Niccolo, jt. auth. see Jisten, Remon L.

Machida, Curtis A., ed. Adrenergic Receptor Protocols. LC 99-34211. (Methods in Molecular Biology Ser.: Vol. 136). 592p. 1999. 125.00 (*0-89603-602-2*) Humana.

***MacHida, Katsunosuke.** The Principles of Molecular Mechanics. 328p. 1999. 149.95 (*0-471-35727-8*) Wiley.

Machida, Margo, et al. Asia - America: Identities in Contemporary Asian American Art. LC 93-83676. 128p. 1994. pap. 22.00 (*1-56584-090-9*, Pub. by New Press NY) Norton.

Machida, Robert. Eritrea: The Struggle for Independence. (Current Issues Ser.: No. 2). 100p. 1987. pap. 5.95 (*0-932415-24-5*) Red Sea Pr.

Machida, Soho & Mentzas, Ioannis. Renegade Monk: Honen & Japanese Pure Land Buddhism. LC 98-22139. 214p. 1999. 40.00 (*0-520-21179-0*, Pub. by U CA Pr) Cal Prin Full Svc.

Machiels, L. & Monkewitz, P. A. Advances in Turbulence Vol. VI: Proceedings of the Sixth European Turbulence Conference Held in Lausanne, Switzerland, 2-5 July 1996. Gavrilakis, S., ed. LC 96-27922. (Fluid Mechanics & Its Applications Ser.). 652p. (C). 1996. text 291.00 (*0-7923-4132-5*) Kluwer Academic.

M

Machievelli, Lorenzo Niccio. History of Florence & of the Affairs of Italy: From the Earliest Times to the Death of Lorenzo. 1999. pap. text 16.95 (*1-56886-073-0*, Pub. by Marsilio Pubs) Consort Bk Sales.

Machin, D., et al. Sample Size Tables for Clinical Studies. 2nd ed. (Illus.). 1997. 99.95 (*0-86542-870-0*) Blackwell Sci.

Machin, David, jt. auth. see Parmar, Mahesh K.

Machin, David, jt. auth. see Tunstall, Jeremy.

***Machin, Doris.** Excelente Es Tu Nombre. 2000. audio 6.99 (*0-8297-2503-2*) Vida Pubs.

Machin, E., ed. National Communism in Western Europe: A Third Way for Socialism? LC 82-24945. 1983. pap. 13.95 (*0-416-73440-5*, NO. 3854) Routledge.

Machin, E. Anthony, jt. auth. see Fife, Ian.

Machin, G. I. Churches & Social Issues in Twentieth-Century Britain. 282p. 1998. text 65.00 (*0-19-821780-3*) OUP.

— Politics & the Churches in Great Britain, 1869-1921. LC 87-1620. 386p. 1987. text 72.00 (*0-19-820106-0*) OUP.

***Machin, G. I. T.** The Rise of Democracy In Britain, 1830-1918. LC 00-40448. 2000. write for info. (*0-312-23544-5*) St Martin.

Machin, Geoffrey A. & Keith, Louis G. An Atlas of Multiple Pregnancy: Biology & Pathology. LC 97-20395. (Encyclopedia of Visual Medicine Ser.). (Illus.). 216p. 1999. 139.95 (*1-85070-918-1*) Prthnon Pub.

Machin, Henry. Diary of Henry Machyn. Nichols, John G., ed. (Camden Society, London. Publications, First Ser.: No. 42). reprint ed. 105.00 (*0-404-50142-7*) AMS Pr.

Machin, Ian. Disraeli. LC 94-11277. (Profiles in Power Ser.). 208p. (C). 1995. text 45.75 (*0-582-09806-8*, 76875, Pub. by Addison-Wesley); pap. text 22.50 (*0-582-09805-X*, 76874, Pub. by Addison-Wesley) Longman.

Machin, S. J., jt. auth. see Pittilo, R. M.

***Machina.** Foundations Book, 1999-2000. 196p. 1999. pap. text 15.00 (*0-536-02829-X*) Pearson Custom.

Machina, Mark, jt. ed. see Gollier, Christian.

Machinability Data Center Technical Staff, ed. Machining Data Handbook, 2 vols., Set. 3rd ed. LC 80-81480. (Illus.). 1980. 150.00 (*0-936974-00-1*) Inst Adv Manuf.

***Machine Tools Limited Hidustan Press.** Mechatronics & Machine Tools. LC 98-51794. 1998. 69.95 (*0-07-134634-1*) McGraw.

Machinist, Peter, ed. see Baltzer, Klaus.

Machinist, Peter, jt. ed. see Cole, Steven W.

Machle, Edward J. Nature & Heaven in the Xunzi: A Study of the Tian Lun. LC 92-31573. (SUNY Series in Chinese Philosophy & Culture). 224p. (C). 1993. text 64.50 (*0-7914-1553-8*); pap. text 21.95 (*0-7914-1554-6*) State U NY Pr.

***Machle, Rick.** Ester's Easter Tale: How the Easter Bunny Came to Be. LC 99-90104. (Illus.). 36p. (J). 1999. pap. 7.99 (*0-9670375-0-6*) Growing Ideas.

Machleder, Herbert I., ed. Vascular Disorders of the Upper Extremity. 3rd ed. LC 98-21934. (Illus.). 515p. 1998. 98.00 (*0-87993-409-3*, Futura Media) Futura Pub.

***Machlin, Dan.** This Side Facing You. 35p. 2000. 5.00 (*0-9675754-0-0*) Heart Hammer.

Machlin, E. S. An Introduction to Aspects of Thermodynamics & Kinetics Relevant to Materials Science. (Illus.). 352p. (C). 1991. text 65.00 (*1-878857-02-9*) Giro Pr.

— Materials Science in Microelectronics Vol. I: The Relationships Between Thin Film Processing & Structure. (Materials Science Ser.). (Illus.). 240p. (C). 1995. text 65.00 (*1-878857-07-X*) Giro Pr.

Machlin, E. S., ed. see Metallurgical Society of AIME Staff.

Machlin, Edda S. Child of the Ghetto: Coming of Age in Fascist Italy: A Memoir, 1926-1946. LC 95-20714. (Illus.). 320p. 1995. 27.50 (*1-878857-08-8*) Giro Pr.

— The Classic Cuisine of the Italian Jews, No. I. rev. ed. (Illus.). 254p. 1993. 35.00 (*1-878857-05-3*) Giro Pr.

— The Classic Cuisine of the Italian Jews, No. II. (Illus.). 272p. 1992. 35.00 (*1-878857-03-7*) Giro Pr.

— Classic Dolci of the Italian Jews: A World of Jewish Desserts. (Illus.). 256p. 1999. 35.00 (*1-878857-12-6*) Giro Pr.

Machlin, Eugene S. Materials Science in Microelectronics Vol. II: Effects of Structure on Properties in Thin Films. (Illus.). 240p. (C). 1998. 75.00 (*1-878857-10-X*) Giro Pr.

Machlin, Evangeline. Dialects for the Stage, Set. LC 75-7880. 182p. 1987. spiral bd. 54.99 (*0-87830-040-6*, Thtre Arts Bks) Routledge.

— Speech for the Stage. LC 80-51639. 1980. 17.95 (*0-87830-120-8*, Thtre Arts Bks) Routledge.

— Speech for the Stage. 2nd ed. (Illus.). 248p. (C). (gr. 13). 1992. pap. 19.99 (*0-87830-015-5*, Thtre Arts Bks) Routledge.

— Teaching Speech for the Stage: A Manual for Classroom Instruction. 1980. pap. 4.95 (*0-87830-573-4*, Thtre Arts Bks) Routledge.

Machlin, I., ed. see Symposium on Metallurgy & Technology of Refractory.

Machlin, Jennifer L. & Young, Tomme R. Managing Environmental Risk: Real Estate & Business Transactions. LC 88-17497. (Environmental Law Ser.). 1988. ring bd. 145.00 (*0-87632-603-3*) West Group.

Machlin, Jerome S. Tournament Bridge: An Uncensored Memoir. LC 84-223705. 121p. 1980. pap. 5.95 (*0-939460-06-8*) Devyn Pr.

***Machlin, Mikki.** My Name Is Not Gussie. LC 99-19160. (Illus.). 32p. (J). (gr. k-3). 1999. 16.00 (*0-395-95646-3*) HM.

***Machlin, Steven R.** Design, Methods & Field Results of the 1996 Medical Expenditure Panel Survey Medical Provider Component. 12p. 2000. pap. write for info. (*1-58763-002-8*) Agency Healthcare.

***Machlis.** Enjoyment of Music Shorter Version with Norton Recordings on 4 Cds. 8th ed. 1999. pap. text. write for info. (*0-393-99045-1*) Norton.

Machlis, Gary E., ed. Interpretive Views: Opinions on Evaluating Interpretation. LC 86-61991. (Illus.). (Orig.). 1986. pap. 9.95 (*0-940091-15-1*) Natl Parks & Cons.

Machlis, Gary E. & Field, Donald R., eds. On Interpretation: Sociology for Interpreters of Natural & Cultural History. rev. ed. LC 92-3386. (Illus.). 320p. (C). 1992. pap. text 21.95 (*0-87071-365-5*) Oreg St U Pr.

Machlis, Joseph. Allegro: A Novel. LC 96-53542. 224p. 1997. 23.00 (*0-393-04075-5*) Norton.

— American Composers of Our Time. LC 88-31968. 237p. 1990. reprint ed. lib. bdg. 65.00 (*0-313-22141-3*, MACT, Greenwood Pr) Greenwood.

— Introduction to Contemporary Music. 2nd ed. (Illus.). 694p. (C). 1979. text 41.00 (*0-393-09026-4*) Norton.

— Lisa's Boy: A Novel. 416p. 1982. 13.95 (*0-393-01606-4*) Norton.

— Stefan in Love: A Novel. 240p. 1991. 19.95 (*0-393-03005-9*) Norton.

Machlis, Joseph & Forney, Kristine. The Enjoyment of Music: An Introduction to Perceptive Listening. 8th ed. LC 98-34249. 650p. 1998. 62.50 (*0-393-97299-2*); pap. 48.75 (*0-393-97301-8*) Norton.

— The Enjoyment of Music: An Introduction to Perceptive Listening. 8th ed. LC 98-34248. 650p. 1999. 62.50 (*0-393-97290-9*) Norton.

Machlis, Leonard, ed. Annual Review of Plant Physiology, Vol. 17. LC 51-1660. 1966. text 40.00 (*0-8243-0617-1*) Annual Reviews.

— Annual Review of Plant Physiology, Vol. 18. LC 51-1660. 1967. text 40.00 (*0-8243-0618-X*) Annual Reviews.

— Annual Review of Plant Physiology, Vol. 19. LC 51-1660. 1968. text 40.00 (*0-8243-0619-8*) Annual Reviews.

— Annual Review of Plant Physiology, Vol. 20. LC 51-1660. 1969. text 40.00 (*0-8243-0620-1*) Annual Reviews.

— Annual Review of Plant Physiology, Vol. 22. LC 51-1660. 1971. text 40.00 (*0-8243-0622-8*) Annual Reviews.

— Annual Review of Plant Physiology & Plant Molecular Biology, Vol. 21. LC 51-1660. 1970. 44.00 (*0-8243-0621-X*) Annual Reviews.

— Annual Review of Plant Physiology & Plant Molecular Biology, Vol. 23. LC 51-1660. 1972. 44.00 (*0-8243-0623-6*) Annual Reviews.

Machlis, Paul. Union Catalog of Letters to Clemens. LC 92-1225. (UC Publications in Catalogs & Bibliographies: Vol. 8). 407p. 1992. 65.00 (*0-520-09743-2*, Pub. by U CA Pr) Cal Prin Full Svc.

Machlis, Sally, jt. auth. see Field, Nancy.

Machlowitz, Marilyn. Advanced Career Strategies: Corporate Smarts for Women on the Way Up. 220p. 1984. 15.95 (*0-943066-04-2*) CareerTrack Pubns.

Machlup, Fritz. The Alignment of Foreign Exchange Rates. LC 72-169260. (Special Studies in International Economics & Development). 1972. 22.50 (*0-8290-0384-3*); pap. text 9.95 (*0-89197-655-8*) Irvington.

— The Book Value of Monetary Gold. LC 72-38795. (Essays in International Finance Ser.: Vol. 91). 24p. reprint ed. pap. 30.00 (*0-8357-7344-2*, 203231500079) Bks Demand.

— The Branches of Learning. LC 82-3695. (Knowledge, Its Creation, Distribution, & Economic Significance Ser.: Vol. 2). 219p. 1982. reprint ed. pap. 67.90 (*0-608-04583-7*, 206535300003) Bks Demand.

— Economic Semantics. 2nd ed. 368p. (C). 1990. pap. 24.95 (*0-88738-836-1*) Transaction Pubs.

— The Economics of Information & Human Capital. LC 83-42588. (Knowledge, Its Creation, Distribution, & Economic Significance Ser.: No. 3). (Illus.). 665p. 1984. reprint ed. pap. 200.00 (*0-608-02550-X*, 206319400004) Bks Demand.

— The Economics of Sellers' Competition: Model Analysis of Sellers' Conduct. LC 53-6339. (Illus.). 602p. reprint ed. pap. 186.70 (*0-608-06167-0*, 206650000008) Bks Demand.

— International Trade & the National Income Multiplier. LC 65-18335. (Reprints of Economic Classics Ser.). xvi, 237p. 1965. reprint ed. 35.00 (*0-678-00083-2*) Kelley.

— The Political Economy of Monopoly: Business, Labor, & Government Policies. LC 53-6338. 560p. reprint ed. pap. 173.60 (*0-8357-8274-3*, 203412100088) Bks Demand.

— Remaking the Internaitonal Monetary System: The Rio Agreement & Beyond. LC 68-31419. 176p. 1968. pap. 3.00 (*0-87186-224-7*) Comm Econ Dev.

— Remaking the International Monetary System: The Rio Agreement & Beyond. LC 68-31419. (Committee For Economic Development, CED Supplementary Papers: No. 24). 171p. reprint ed. pap. 53.10 (*0-608-11902-4*, 202312500032) Bks Demand.

Machlup, Fritz, et al, eds. International Mobility & Movement of Capital. (Universities-National Bureau Conference Ser.: No. 24). 719p. 1972. text 160.00 (*0-87014-249-6*) Natl Bur Econ Res.

— International Mobility & Movement of Capital: A Conference of the Universities - National Bureau Committee for Economic Research. LC 76-188342. (Universities-National Burear Conference Ser.: No. 24). 719p. reprint ed. pap. 200.00 (*0-8357-3242-8*, 205713600011) Bks Demand.

Machlup, Fritz & Leeson, Kenneth W. Information Through the Printed Word The Dissemination of Scholarly, Scientific, & Intellectual Knowledge. Incl. Vol. 1. Book Publishing. LC 78-19460. 320p. 1978. 69.50 (*0-275-90301-X*, C03011, Praeger Pubs); Vol. 2. Journals. LC 78-19460. 1978. 62.95 (*0-275-90302-8*, C03022, Praeger Pubs); Vol. 3. Libraries. LC 78-19460. 219p. 1978. 55.00 (*0-275-90303-6*, C03033, Praeger Pubs); Vol. 4. Book, Journals, & Bibliographic Services. LC 78-19460. 342p. 1980. 69.50 (*0-275-90516-0*, C05164, Praeger Pubs); LC 78-19460. 363p. 1978. write for info. (*0-318-55346-5*, Praeger Pubs) Greenwood.

Machmer, Richard S. & Machmer, Rosemarie B. Just for Nice: Carving & Whittling Magic of Southeastern PA. (Illus.). 87p. 1991. text 11.98 (*1-887762-02-7*) His Soc Brks Cnty.

— Just for Nice: Carving & Whittling Magic of Southeastern Pennsylvania. (Illus.). 88p. (C). 1992. text 35.00 (*0-8122-3209-7*) U of Pa Pr.

Machmer, Richard S. & Machmer, Rosemarie B., contrib. by. Berks County Tall-Case Clocks: 1750-1850. (Illus.). 104p. 1995. spiral bd. 25.00 (*1-887762-01-9*) His Soc Brks Cnty.

Machmer, Rosemarie B., jt. auth. see Machmer, Richard S.

Machmer, Rosemarie B., jt. contrib. by see Machmer, Richard S.

Machner, Hartmut & Jahn, J., eds. Coincident Particle Emission from Continuum States in Nuclei (COPECOS) Proceedings of the Workshop on Coincident Particle Emission from Continuum States in Nucle (COPECOS), F R, Germany, June 1984. 642p. 1984. 121.00 (*9971-966-98-0*) World Scientific Pub.

Machner, Hartmut & Sistemich, Knornel. Physics with GeV-Particle Beams: Proceedings of the International Conference. 550p. 1995. text 128.00 (*981-02-2279-3*) World Scientific Pub.

Machnik, Joe & Harris, Paul. So You Want to Be a Goalkeeper: The No. 1 Handbook for Soccer Coaches & Players. (Illus.). 62p. 1980. pap. 7.95 (*0-916802-18-3*) Soccer for Am.

Macho, James & Cable, Greg. Everyone's Guide to Outpatient Surgery. (Illus.). 192p. pap. 19.95 (*1-895897-41-6*) Somerville Hse.

Macho, Linda. Crocheting Ruffled Doilies. (Knitting, Crocheting, Tatting Ser.). (Illus.). 48p. (Orig.). 1983. pap. 3.95 (*0-486-24400-8*) Dover.

— Patterns for Quilting. 80p. 1984. pap. 6.95 (*0-486-24632-9*) Dover.

Macho, Linda, jt. auth. see Weiss, Rita.

Macho-Stadler, Ines & Perez-Castrillo, J. David. An Introduction to the Economics of Information: Incentives & Contracts. (Illus.). 292p. 1997. text 75.00 (*0-19-877467-2*) OUP.

— An Introduction to the Economics of Information: Incentives & Contracts. Watt, Richard, tr. (Illus.). 292p. 1997. pap. text 28.00 (*0-19-877466-4*) OUP.

Machoian, Jeannette. A Teaching Guide to "Roll of Thunder, Hear My Cry" (Discovering Literature Ser.). (Illus.). 61p. (YA). (gr. 5 up). 1999. pap., teacher ed. 6.95 (*0-931993-94-6*, GP-094) Garlic Pr OR.

— A Teaching Guide to "The Outsiders" (Discovering Literature Ser.). (Illus.). 54p. 1998. pap. text, teacher ed. 6.95 (*0-931993-93-8*, GP-093) Garlic Pr OR.

Machon, Kirsty. Immortality. LC 96-229686. 1997. pap. text 10.95 (*1-875243-22-4*, Pub. by Blackwattle) LPC InBook.

Machonis, Peter A. Histoire de la Langue: Du Latin a L'Ancien Francais. 290p. (Orig.). (C). 1990. pap. text 25.00 (*0-8191-7874-8*); lib. bdg. 46.50 (*0-8191-7873-X*) U Pr of Amer.

Machor, James L. Pastoral Cities: Urban Ideals & the Symbolic Landscape of America. LC 87-2171. (History of American Thought & Culture Ser.). 288p. (C). 1987. pap. text 14.95 (*0-299-11284-5*) U of Wis Pr.

Machor, James L., ed. Readers in History: Nineteenth-Century American Literature & the Contexts of Response. LC 92-14471. 304p. 1993. pap. text 16.95 (*0-8018-4437-1*) Johns Hopkins.

***Machor, James L. & Goldstein, Philip.** Reception Study: From Literary Theory to Cultural Studies. LC 00-36593. 2000. write for info. (*0-415-92650-5*) Routledge.

Machoski, Brenda, ed. see Martin, Charles L. & Hackett, Donald.

Machosky, Brenda, ed. see Burke, Mary A. & Liljenstolpe, Carl.

Machosky, Brenda, ed. see Dickson, Mary.

Machosky, Brenda, ed. see Fritz, Roger.

Machosky, Brenda, ed. see Gerson, Richard F.

Machosky, Brenda, ed. see Tompkins, Neville C.

Machotka, Pavel. Cezanne: Landscape into Art. LC 96-62232. (Illus.). 156p. 1996. 50.00 (*0-300-06701-1*) Yale U Pr.

— Cezanne: Motif into Form. (Illus.). (C). 1996. 45.00 (*0-614-95687-0*) Yale U Pr.

— The Nude: Perception & Personality. (Illus.). 352p. (C). 1979. text 39.50 (*0-8290-0868-3*) Irvington.

— Style & Psyche: The Art of Lundy Siegriest & Terry St. John. LC 99-10559. (Perspectives on Creativity Ser.). (Illus.). 1999. pap. 21.95 (*1-57273-148-6*) Hampton Pr NJ.

Machotka, Pavel & Spiegel, John P. Articulate Body. (Illus.). 250p. 1982. 32.50 (*0-8290-0229-4*) Irvington.

— The Articulate Body. (Illus.). 250p. (C). 1985. reprint ed. pap. text 12.95 (*0-8290-1662-7*) Irvington.

Machova, Lenka, ed. see Swedenborg, Emanuel.

MacHovec, et al. The Aware Bears, Set. Downey, John & Cohen, Lois, eds. (Children's Personal Safety Ser.). (Illus.). (Orig.). (J). (gr. k-2). 1991. pap. 39.50 (*0-89976-236-0*) Oceana Educ Comm.

MacHovec, Frank. Becoming Street Smart: How to Protect Yourself & Your Love Ones from Being Crime Victims. 1993. pap. 13.95 (*0-88282-081-8*) New Horizon NJ.

MacHovec, Frank J. Cults & Personality. 210p. 1989. pap. 35.95 (*0-398-06255-2*) C C Thomas.

— Cults & Personality. 210p. (C). 1989. text 47.95 (*0-398-05607-2*) C C Thomas.

— The Expert Witness Survival Manual. 186p. 1987. 45.95 (*0-398-05374-X*); pap. 31.95 (*0-398-06256-0*) C C Thomas.

***MacHovec, Frank J.** Four Pillars Of Leadership-Management: A Leadership Skills Training Manual. LC 00-191056. 122p. 2000. pap. 18.00 (*0-7388-2052-0*) Xlibris Corp.

MacHovec, Frank J. Hypnosis Complications: Prevention & Risk Management. 172p. 1986. pap. 23.95 (*0-398-06257-9*) C C Thomas.

— Hypnosis Complications: Prevention & Risk Management. 172p. (C). 1986. text 37.95 (*0-398-05271-9*) C C Thomas.

— Interview & Interrogation: A Scientific Approach. 176p. (C). 1989. text 35.95 (*0-398-05578-5*) C C Thomas.

— Private Investigation: Methods & Materials. 134p. 1991. pap. 23.95 (*0-398-06258-7*) C C Thomas.

— Private Investigation: Methods & Materials. 134p. (C). 1991. text 34.95 (*0-398-05749-4*) C C Thomas.

— Security Services, Security Science. 154p. 1992. pap. 23.95 (*0-398-06259-5*) C C Thomas.

— Security Services, Security Science. 154p. (C). 1992. text 37.95 (*0-398-05811-3*) C C Thomas.

Machovec, Frank M. Perfect Competition & the Transformation of Economics. LC 94-32765. (Foundations of the Market Economy Ser.). 360p. (C). (gr. 13). 1995. 90.00 (*0-415-11580-9*, C0028) Routledge.

Machovec, George S. Telecommunications & Networking Glossary. (LITA Guides Ser.: No. 3). 68p. 1990. pap. 6.00 (*0-8389-7476-7*) ALA.

— Telecommunications, Networking, & Internet Glossary. LC 94-30839. (LITA Monographs: No. 4). 124p. 1993. pap. 18.00 (*0-8389-7697-2*) Lib Info Tech.

***Machover, Alexandra.** The Little Brave Son. (J). (gr. 1-3). 2000. 10.95 (*0-533-13474-9*) Vantage.

Machover, Carl. The C Handbook: CAD, CAM, CAE, CIM. (Computer Graphics Technology & Management Ser.). (Illus.). 400p. 1989. 44.50 (*0-8306-9398-X*, 3098) McGraw-Hill Prof.

— CAD - CAM Handbook. 3rd ed. 1995. 69.50 (*0-07-039375-3*) McGraw.

— The Economics of PC Graphics & Peripherals: An Audiocassette Briefing. 42.95 (*0-317-65608-2*) TBC Inc.

Machover, Carl & Sherr, Sol. Computer Graphics Displays: Technology & Applications. (Series on Information Display: Vol. 4). 400p. 1998. 78.00 (*981-02-3314-0*) World Scientific Pub.

Machover, Jacobo. El Heraldo de Malas Noticias: Guillermo Cabrera Infante: Ensayo a dos Voces. LC 96-83779. (SPA.). 151p. (Orig.). 1996. pap. 16.00 (*0-89729-802-0*) Ediciones.

Machover, Karen. Personality Projection in the Drawing of the Human Figure: A Method of Personality Investigation. (Illus.). 192p. 1980. 37.95 (*0-398-01184-2*); pap. 24.95 (*0-398-06260-9*) C C Thomas.

Machover, Moshe. Set Theory, Logic & Their Limitations. 297p. (C). 1996. pap. text 26.95 (*0-521-47998-3*) Cambridge U Pr.

— Set Theory, Logic & Their Limitations. 295p. (C). 1996. text 69.95 (*0-521-47493-0*) Cambridge U Pr.

Machover, Moshe, jt. auth. see Bell, . L.

Machover, Reinisch J., jt. ed. see Bancroft, John.

Machover, Tod. Musical Thought at Ircam, Vol. 1, No. 1. (Contemporary Music Review Ser.). ii, 230p. 1984. pap. text 48.00 (*3-7186-0272-5*) Gordon & Breach.

Machover, Wilma & Uszler, Marienne. Sound Choices: Guiding Your Child's Musical Experiences. (Illus.). 400p. 1996. pap. 19.95 (*0-19-509208-2*); text 35.00 (*0-19-509207-4*) OUP.

Machovich, R. & Owen, W. G., eds. Enzymology of Plasminogen Activation. (Journal: Enzymology: Vol. 40, No. 2-3, 1988). (Illus.). 116p. 1988. pap. 75.00 (*3-8055-4854-0*) S Karger.

Machovich, Raymond. Blood Vessel Wall & Thrombosis: Thrombotic Processes in Atherogenesis, 2 vols., Vol. 2. LC 87-24298. 280p. 1988. 112.00 (*0-8493-5627-X*, RC694, CRC Reprint) Franklin.

Machovich, Raymond, ed. Blood Vessel Wall & Thrombosis: Hemostasis, 2 vols., Vol. 1. LC 87-24298. 320p. 1988. 145.00 (*0-8493-5626-1*, RC694, CRC Reprint) Franklin.

Machovich, Raymond, ed. see Salunkhe, D. K., et al.

Machovich, Raymund, ed. The Thrombin, 2 vols., Vol. I. 176p. 1984. 104.00 (*0-8493-6186-9*, QP93, CRC Reprint) Franklin.

An Asterisk (*) at the beginning of an entry indicates that the title is appearing for the first time.

— The Thrombin, 2 vols., Vol. II. 128p. 1984. 76.00 (*0-8493-6187-7*, QP93, CRC Reprint) Franklin.

*__Machowicz, Richard J.__ Unleashing the Warrior Within: Using 7 Principles of Combat to Achieve Your Goals. LC 99-27699. 272p. 2000. text 21.95 (*0-7868-6569-5*, Pub. by Hyperion) Time Warner.

Machowski, Jan & Bialek, Janusz. Power System Dynamics & Stability. LC 96-39033. 484p. 1997. pap. 79.95 (*0-471-95643-0*) Wiley.

Machray, Alex, jt. auth. see Thorne, Kaye.

Macht, J. Poor Eaters: Helping Children Who Refuse to Eat. LC 89-26514. (Illus.). 328p. (C). 1990. 19.95 (*0-306-43451-2*, Plenum Trade) Perseus Pubng.

Macht, Joel. Special Education's Failed System: A Question of Eligibility. LC 98-9535. 224p. 1998. 57.95 (*0-89789-589-4*, Bergin & Garvey) Greenwood.

Macht, Norman. Roberto Alomar. LC 98-48048. (Latinos in Baseball Ser.). (Illus.). 64p. (YA). (gr. 5 up). 1999. lib. bdg. 18.95 (*1-883845-84-X*) M Lane Pubs.

Macht, Norman & Chelsea House Publishing Staff. Greg Maddux. LC 97-5109. (Baseball Legends Ser.). (Illus.). 64p. (J). (gr. 3 up). 1997. 15.95 (*0-7910-4378-9*) Chelsea Hse.

Macht, Norman, jt. auth. see Bartell, Dick.

Macht, Norman, jt. auth. see Kavanagh, Jack.

Macht, Norman L. Babe Ruth. (Baseball Legends Ser.). (Illus.). 64p. (J). (gr. 3 up). 1991. lib. bdg. 15.95 (*0-7910-1189-5*) Chelsea Hse.

— Baseball. LC 97-30934. (Composite Guide Ser.). (Illus.). 64p. (YA). (gr. 3 up). 1999. lib. bdg. 7.95 (*0-7910-4723-7*) Chelsea Hse.

*__Macht, Norman L.__ Baseball. (Composite Guide Ser.). (Illus.). 1999. pap. 7.95 (*0-7910-5751-8*) Chelsea Hse.

Macht, Norman L. Christy Mathewson. (Baseball Legends Ser.). (Illus.). 64p. (J). (gr. 3 up). 1991. lib. bdg. 15.95 (*0-7910-1182-8*) Chelsea Hse.

— Clarence Thomas: Supreme Court Justice. Huggins, Nathan I., ed. LC 94-44353. (Black Americans of Achievement Ser.). (Illus.). 124p. (YA). (gr. 5 up). 1995. lib. bdg. 19.95 (*0-7910-1883-0*) Chelsea Hse.

— Clarence Thomas: Supreme Court Justice. Huggins, Nathan I., ed. LC 94-44353. (Black Americans of Achievement Ser.). 124p. (YA). (gr. 5 up). 1995. pap. 8.95 (*0-7910-1912-8*) Chelsea Hse.

— Cy Young. (Baseball Legends Ser.). (Illus.). 64p. (J). (gr. 3 up). 1992. lib. bdg. 15.95 (*0-7910-1196-8*) Chelsea Hse.

— Frank Robinson. (Baseball Legends Ser.). (Illus.). 64p. (J). (gr. 3 up). 1991. lib. bdg. 15.95 (*0-7910-1187-9*) Chelsea Hse.

— The History of Slavery. LC 96-45640. (World History Ser.). (Illus.). (J). (gr. 4-12). 1997. lib. bdg. 22.45 (*1-56006-302-5*) Lucent Bks.

— Jim Abbott: The Major Leaguer Who Was Born Without a Right Hand. LC 93-31838. (Great Achievers Ser.). (Illus.). 120p. (YA). (gr. 5 up). 1994. lib. bdg. 19.95 (*0-7910-2079-7*) Chelsea Hse.

— Lou Gehrig. (Baseball Legends Ser.). (Illus.). 64p. (J). (gr. 3 up). 1992. lib. bdg. 15.95 (*0-7910-1176-3*) Chelsea Hse.

— Roberto Clemente: Baseball Great. LC 93-26178. (Junior Hispanics of Achievement Ser.). (Illus.). 76p. (J). (gr. 4-7). 1993. pap. 4.95 (*0-7910-2541-1*); lib. bdg. 15.95 (*0-7910-1764-8*) Chelsea Hse.

*__Macht, Norman L.__ Roger Clemens. (Baseball Legends Ser.). 64p. (gr. 4-7). 1999. pap. text 9.95 (*0-7910-5455-1*) Chelsea Hse.

Macht, Norman L. Sojourner Truth: Crusader for Civil Rights. LC 91-37268. (Junior Black Americans of Achievement Ser.). (Illus.). 76p. (J). (gr. 4-7). 1993. lib. bdg. 15.95 (*0-7910-1754-0*) Chelsea Hse.

— Tom Seaver. (Baseball Legends Ser.). (Illus.). 64p. (J). (gr. 3 up). 1994. lib. bdg. 15.95 (*0-7910-1951-9*) Chelsea Hse.

— Track & Field. LC 97-47684. (Composite Guide Ser.). (Illus.). 64p. (YA). (gr. 3 up). 1999. lib. bdg. 15.95 (*0-7910-4720-2*) Chelsea Hse.

— Ty Cobb. (Baseball Legends Ser.). (Illus.). 64p. (J). (gr. 3 up). 1992. lib. bdg. 15.95 (*0-7910-1172-0*) Chelsea Hse.

Macht, Norman L., jt. auth. see Bagli, Vince.

Macht, Norman L., jt. auth. see Barney, Rex.

Macht, Philip. Circles in the Sand. LC 84-90597. (Illus.). 64p. (YA). (gr. 7 up). 1985. 12.95 (*0-930339-00-2*) Maxrom Pr.

— Great Mountain. (Illus.). 30p. (Orig.). (J). 1991. pap. 15.00 (*0-930339-01-0*) Maxrom Pr.

— Pumpkin Art. (Illus.). 48p. (Orig.). 1991. pap. 20.00 (*0-930339-02-9*) Maxrom Pr.

— Wonderpup. (Illus.). 40p. (J). (gr. 4-6). 1992. 15.00 (*0-930339-03-7*) Maxrom Pr.

Machtig, Brett. Wealth in a Decade: Brett Machtig's Proven System for Creating Wealth, Living Off Your Investments & Attaining a Financially Secure Life. LC 96-9322. 256p. 1996. text 24.95 (*0-7863-1072-3*, Irwn Prfssnl) McGraw-Hill Prof.

Machtinger, Edward, jt. auth. see American Academy of Pediatrics Staff.

Machtley, Ronald K., et al. Telecommunications Act Handbook: A Complete Reference for Business. Knauer, Leon, ed. LC 96-24661. 620p. 1996. text 89.00 (*0-86587-545-6*) Gov Insts.

MacHuisdean, W. Hamish. The Great La Vol. 1: First Two Visits. 53p. 1993. reprint ed. spiral bd. 9.00 (*0-7873-0579-0*) Hlth Research.

Machulla, Hans-Jhurgen. Imaging of Hyposia: Tracer Developments. LC 98-49717. (Developments in Nuclear Medicine Ser.). 17p. 1999. write for info. (*0-7923-5529-6*) Kluwer Academic.

Machulsky, E., jt. auth. see Topornin, B.

Machura, Stefan, jt. ed. see Rohl, Klaus F.

*__Machus, Gary E. & Field, Donald R., eds.__ National Parks & Rural Development: Practice & Policy in the United States. (Illus.). 296p. 2000. 55.00 (*1-55963-814-1*, Shearwater Bks); pap. 27.50 (*1-55963-815-X*, Shearwater Bks) Island Pr.

Machutta, Stephen T., Sr. Acne? Try Nature's Remedy. LC 88-92625. 90p. (Orig.). (J). (gr. 3-11). 1991. pap. 9.95 (*0-9621489-0-3*) New Begin Life.

Machy, Patrick & Leserman, Lee. Liposomes in Cell Biology & Pharmacology. (Research in Ser.). 192p. 1987. 51.00 (*2-85598-327-4*) S M P F Inc.

MacIan, Janice Lynn, jt. auth. see Long, Donna Reseigh.

MacIan, Paula S. It Was the Year of the Scalping: Poems about Emotional Incest, Sexually Motivated Abuse, Mother-Daughter Incest, Father-Daughter Incest. LC 91-65735. (Illus.). 56p. (Orig.). 1991. 14.95 (*0-9629497-6-0*); pap. 6.95 (*0-9629497-4-4*) Still Wtrs Pr.

Maciariello, Joseph A. Lasting Value: Lessons from a Century of Agility at Lincoln Electric. 240p. 1999. 39.95 (*0-471-33025-6*) Wiley.

— Management Control Systems. (Illus.). 720p. (C). 1984. text. write for info. (*0-318-57575-2*) P-H.

Maciariello, Joseph A. & Kirby, Calvin J. Management Control Systems: Using Adaptive Systems to Attain Control. 2nd ed. LC 93-29228. 560p. 1994. pap. text 98.00 (*0-13-098146-X*) P-H.

Macias, Anna. Against All Odds: The Feminist Movement in Mexico to 1940, 30. LC 81-6201. (Contributions in Women's Studies: No. 30). 195p. 1982. 49.95 (*0-313-23028-5*, MAO/, Greenwood Pr) Greenwood.

Macias, Benjamin. One Hundred One Bible Riddles for All Ages. (Illus.). 112p. (Orig.). (J). (gr. 1 up). 1993. pap. 7.95 (*0-9638277-1-5*) Fam of God.

Macias, Cheryl. Citizen's Guide to Food Recovery. 66p. 1997. pap. text 20.00 (*0-7881-4561-4*) DIANE Pub.

Macias, Edward S. & Hopke, Philip K., eds. Atmospheric Aerosol: Source/Air Quality Relationships. LC 81-10960. (Illus.). 368p. 1981. reprint ed. pap. 114.10 (*0-608-03247-6*, 206376600007) Bks Demand.

Macias, Edward S. & Hopke, Phillip K., eds. Atmospheric Aerosol: Source-Air Quality Relationships. LC 81-10960. (ACS Symposium Ser.: No. 167). 359p. 1981. 43.95 (*0-8412-0646-5*) Am Chemical.

Macias Goytia, Angelina, ed. La Arqueologia en los Anales del Museo Michoacano: Epocas I & II. (SPA.). 600p. 1993. pap. 17.00 (*968-29-4506-2*, IN070) UPLAAP.

Macias-Lopez, Antonio. An Assessment of Agricultural Education in Mexico, Central America, & the Caribbean. (Studies in Technology & Social Change: No. 18). (Illus.). 133p. (Orig.). (C). 1990. pap. 12.00 (*0-945271-26-3*) ISU-CIKARD.

Macias, Nelinda Galvan. Leyendas Mexicanas. 1996. pap. text 6.98 (*968-403-911-5*) Selector.

Macias, Regina, ed. see Burrill, Richard L.

Macias, Ricky. Porcelain Draped Dolls. (Illus.). 40p. (Orig.). 1996. pap. text 4.95 (*0-916809-90-0*) Scott Pubns MI.

Macias, Shirley, tr. see Mahmud-i-Zarqani.

Macias, Susan. First Mate. large type ed. (Black Satin Romance Ser.). 290p. 1997. 27.99 (*1-86110-034-5*) Ulverscroft.

— Honeysuckle DeVine. 384p. 1996. mass mkt. 4.99 (*0-06-108406-9*) HarpC.

— Master of the Chase. large type ed. (Black Satin Romance Ser.). 287p. 1997. 27.99 (*1-86110-025-6*) Ulverscroft.

*__Macias, Trinidad Red.__ Always Faithful: Philosophic Realism.Tr. of Semper Fidelis. 2000. 7.95 (*0-533-13333-5*) Vantage.

Maciaszek. Database Design & Implementation. (C). 1990. pap. 41.00 (*0-13-203233-3*, Macmillan Coll) P-H.

*__Maciaszek, Joseph.__ The Life & Times of Byron O'Tool. LC 99 93749. 2000. 13.95 (*0 533 13132 4*) Vantage.

Macidull, John. Alien Legacy. 216p. 1999. 16.00 (*0-8059-4589-X*) Dorrance.

Macie, Michelle, ed. see Damp, Dennis V.

Macie, Michelle, ed. see Wood, Patricia B.

Macieira-Coelho, A. The Biology of Normal Proliferating Cells in Vitro Relevance for in Vivo Aging. (Interdisciplinary Topics in Gerontology Ser.: Vol. 23). (Illus.). vi, 218p. 1987. 148.00 (*3-8055-4660-2*) S Karger.

*__Macieira-Coelho, Alvaro.__ Signaling Through the Cell Matrix. LC 00-35750. (Progress in Molecular & Subcellular Biology Ser.). 2000. write for info. (*3-540-67220-6*) Spr-Verlag.

Macieira-Coelho, Alvaro, ed. Cell Immortalization. LC 99-15705. (Progress in Molecular & Subcellular Biology Ser.: Vol. 24). (Illus.). viii, 190p. 1999. 125.00 (*3-540-65618-9*) Spr-Verlag.

Macieira-Coelho, Alvaro, et al, eds. Inhibitors of Cell Growth. LC 98-11893. (Progress in Molecular & Subcellular Biology Ser.: Vol. 20). (Illus.). 275p. 1998. 129.00 (*3-540-64092-4*) Spr-Verlag.

Maciejonski, Jan. Predictive Control with Constraints. 256p. (C). 2000. 84.95 (*0-201-39823-0*) Addison-Wesley.

Maciejowski, J. M. The Modelling of Systems with Small Observation Sets. (Lecture Notes in Control & Information Sciences: Vol. 10). (Illus.). 1978. 24.95 (*0-387-09004-5*) Spr-Verlag.

*__Maciejowski, Jan.__ Multivariable Feedback Design. 2nd ed. (C). 2000. text. write for info. (*0-201-40364-1*) Addison-Wesley.

Maciejunes, Nannette V. & Fleischman, Lawrence A. Thirty-Eight Rare Drawings: By Charles Burchfield. (Illus.). 32p. 1992. pap. 15.00 (*0-87920-017-0*) Kennedy Gall.

Maciejunes, Nannette V. & Fleischman, Martha. Charles Burchfield Watercolors, 1915-1920. (Illus.). 48p. 1990. pap. 15.00 (*0-87920-016-2*) Kennedy Gall.

Maciejunes, Nannette V., et al. The American Collections, Columbus Museum of Art. Roberts, Norma J., ed. LC 88-23774. (Illus.). 288p. (Orig.). 1988. 35.00 (*0-8109-1811-0*) Columbus Mus Art.

— The Paintings of Charles Burchfield North by Midwest. Murphy, Diana, ed. LC 96-33433. (Illus.). 278p. 1997. 60.00 (*0-8109-3148-6*, Pub. by Abrams) Time Warner.

Maciel & Sob. Culture Across Borders: Mexican Immigration & Popular Culture. LC 97-33899. (Illus.). 312p. 1998. 40.00 (*0-8165-1832-7*); pap. 16.95 (*0-8165-1833-5*) U of Ariz Pr.

Maciel, Agnaldo S., et al. Another Venice: Ciao, Anarchici - Images from an International Rendez-Vous. (Illus.). 111p. 1986. 48.99 (*0-920057-73-X*, Pub. by Black Rose); pap. 19.99 (*0-920057-71-3*, Pub. by Black Rose) Consort Bk Sales.

Maciel, David & Ortiz, Isidro D., eds. Chicanas - Chicanos at the Crossroads: Social, Economic, & Political Change. LC 95-41767. 258p. 1996. 42.00 (*0-8165-1343-0*); pap. 17.95 (*0-8165-1634-0*) U of Ariz Pr.

*__Maciel, David R., et al, eds.__ The Chicano Renaissance: Contemporary Cultural Trends. LC 00-8073. (Illus.). 370p. 2000. 45.00 (*0-8165-2020-8*); pap. 19.95 (*0-8165-2021-6*) U of Ariz Pr.

Maciel, David R., ed. see Hershfield, Joanne.

Maciel, Gary E., ed. Nuclear Magnetic Resonance in Modern Technology: Proceedings of the NATO Advanced Study Institute, Sarigerme Park (Dalaman), Turkey, August 16-September 4, 1992. (NATO ASI, Series C, Mathematical & Physical Sciences: Vol. 447). 620p. (C). 1995. text 374.00 (*0-7923-3167-2*) Kluwer Academic.

Maciel, Jairo. A Traveller's Road. Sacchette, Reinaldo, ed. & tr. by. from POR. Borges, Renato, ed. Kowarick, Margaret P., tr. from POR. 135p. (Orig.). 1994. pap. write for info. (*0-9642230-0-7*) J Maciel.

*__Maciel, Olivia.__ Luna de Cal.Tr. of Limestone Moon. (SPA & ENG.). 2000. pap. 16.00 (*0-9678808-0-7*, El Cisne) Black Swan Pr IL.

Maciel, Olivia, ed. Shards of Light (Astillas de Luz) 120p. 1998. pap. 12.95 (*1-882688-18-X*) Tia Chucha Pr.

Macierira-Coelho, Alvaro, ed. Molecular Basis of Aging. LC 95-15170. 576p. 1995. boxed set 199.95 (*0-8493-4786-6*, 4786) CRC Pr.

Macierowski, Edward, tr. see Apollonius.

Macierowski, Edward M., tr. & contrib. by see Aquinas, Thomas, Saint.

Maciha, John. The Apartment Manager's Desk Reference. (Illus.). 550p. 1995. student ed. 89.00 (*1-883422-34-5*) Adams-Blake.

— Code 911: Emergency Procedures for Apartment Communities: A Guideline for Disaster Management. LC 94-74383. (Illus.). 240p. (Orig.). 1995. pap. 49.00 (*1-883422-33-7*) Adams-Blake.

Macillwain, Charles H., ed. see Wraxall, Peter.

Macilwaine, P. S., jt. auth. see Plumpton, C. A.

Macin, Enrique. Adan Se Despide. Dos Pasos, ed. (Palabra Nueva Ser.). (SPA.). (Orig.). 1988. pap. 12.00 (*0-9615403-3-8*) Dos Pasos Ed.

MacInaugh, Edmond A. Disguise Techniques: Fool All of the People Some of the Time. (Illus.). 88p. 1984. pap. 18.00 (*0-87364-307-0*) Paladin Pr.

MacInaugh, Edmund A. Disguise Techniques. (Illus.). 88p. 1988. reprint ed. pap. 5.95 (*0-8065-1098-6*, Citadel Pr) Carol Pub Group.

Macinko, George, jt. ed. see Platt, Rutherford H.

MacInnes. Interior Structures: Museums. text. write for info. (*0-471-48958-1*) Wiley.

— Office Builders. text. write for info. (*0-471-49148-9*) Wiley.

MacInnes, Colin. Les Blanc-Becs. (FRE.). 1985. pap. 13.95 (*0-7859-4218-1*) Fr & Eur.

— Mr. Love & Justice. 128p. 1995. pap. write for info. (*0-7490-0186-0*) Allison & Busby.

Macinnes, D., ed. Folk & Hero Tales. (Folk-Lore Society, London Monographs: Vol. 25). (ENG & GAE.). 1972. reprint ed. pap. 45.00 (*0-8115-0511-1*) Periodicals Srv.

MacInnes, Duncan. Folk & Hero Tales. Nutt, Alfred T., ed. LC 71-144455. (Waifs & Strays of Celtic Tradition: Argyllshire Ser.: No. 2). (Illus.). reprint ed. 52.50 (*0-404-53532-1*) AMS Pr.

MacInnes, Fiona. To Step among Wrack. (C). 1986. 40.00 (*0-907618-17-0*, Pub. by Orkney Pr) St Mut.

Macinnes, Gordon. Wrong for All the Right Reasons: How White Liberals Have Been Undone by Race. 320p. (C). 1996. text 27.50 (*0-8147-5543-7*) NYU Pr.

MacInnes, Hamish. International Mountain Rescue Handbook. (Illus.). 1999. 35.00 (*0-09-475360-1*, Pub. by Constable & Co) Trafalgar.

— The Price of Adventure: Mountain Rescue Stories from Four Continents. (Illus.). 200p. 1988. 15.95 (*0-89886-174-8*) Mountaineers.

MacInnes, Helen. Above Suspicion. LC 54-928. 1954. 24.95 (*0-15-102707-2*) Harcourt.

— Agent in Place. 25.95 (*0-89190-106-X*) Amereon Ltd.

— Assignment in Brittany. LC 42-17993. 1971. 24.95 (*0-15-109620-1*) Harcourt.

— Decision at Delphi. 442p. 28.95 (*0-8488-2683-3*) Amereon Ltd.

— Decision at Delphi. LC 60-15705. 1960. 24.95 (*0-15-124221-6*) Harcourt.

— The Double Image. 24.95 (*0-89190-105-1*) Amereon Ltd.

Macinnes, Helen. Helen Macinnes: Three Bestselling Novels of Terror & Suspense. 1993. 11.98 (*0-88365-814-3*) Galahad Bks.

MacInnes, Helen. Home Is the Hunter. 20.95 (*0-89190-102-7*) Amereon Ltd.

— Horizon. LC 46-3853. 1971. 24.95 (*0-15-142171-4*) Harcourt.

— Horizon. large type ed. LC 93-17775. 275p. 1993. lib. bdg. 20.95 (*1-56054-454-6*) Thorndike Pr.

— I & My True Love. LC 52-13765. 1953. 24.95 (*0-15-143403-4*) Harcourt.

— I & My True Love. large type ed. LC 92-41149. 524p. 1993. reprint ed. lib. bdg. 21.95 (*1-56054-453-8*) Thorndike Pr.

— Neither 5 nor 3. LC 51-1551. 1951. 24.95 (*0-15-165069-1*) Harcourt.

— North from Rome. LC 58-5922. 1958. 24.95 (*0-15-167001-3*) Harcourt.

— Pray for a Brave Heart. LC 55-5241. 1955. 24.95 (*0-15-173901-3*) Harcourt.

— Rest & Be Thankful. 320p. Date not set. 24.95 (*0-8488-2359-1*) Amereon Ltd.

— Ride a Pale Horse. LC 84-9037. 352p. 1984. 15.95 (*0-15-177268-1*) Harcourt.

— The Salzburg Connection. large type ed. LC 92-23906. (All-Time Favorites Ser.). 698p. 1993. reprint ed. lib. bdg. 20.95 (*1-56054-455-4*) Thorndike Pr.

— The Snare of the Hunter. 24.95 (*0-89190-103-5*) Amereon Ltd.

— Triple Threat. 27.95 (*0-89190-104-3*) Amereon Ltd.

— While Still We Live. LC 44-2182. 1971. 24.95 (*0-15-196090-9*) Harcourt.

— While Still We Live. large type ed. LC 92-27926. 830p. 1992. reprint ed. lib. bdg. 20.95 (*1-56054-456-2*) Thorndike Pr.

MacInnes, Hugh. Turbochargers. pap. write for info. (*0-912656-49-2*) Berkley Pub.

Macinnes, J. The End of Masculinity: The Confusion of Sexual Genesis & Sexual Difference in Modern Society. LC 97-20463. 192p. 1998. 79.95 (*0-335-19659-4*) OpUniv Pr.

MacInnes, John. The End of Masculinity: The Confusion of Sexual Genesis & Sexual Difference in Modern Society. LC 97-20463. 192p. 1998. pap. 25.95 (*0-335-19658-6*) OpUniv Pr.

MacInnes, John W. The Comical As Textual Practice in Les Fleurs du Mal. LC 87-14269. 165p. 1988. 49.95 (*0-8130-0866-2*) U Press Fla.

MacInnes, Kenneth, tr. see Kruglov, Vladimir & Lenyashin, Vladimir.

MacInnes, M. J. Nature to Advantage Dress'd. spiral bd. 3.75 (*0-87018-043-6*) Ross.

MacInnes, Mairi. Elsewhere & Back: New & Selected Poems. 80p. 1993. pap. 13.95 (*1-85224-199-3*, Pub. by Bloodaxe Bks) Dufour.

*__MacInnes, Mairi.__ Ghostwriter. 78p. 2000. pap. 15.95 (*1-85224-474-7*, Pub. by Bloodaxe Bks) Dufour.

MacInnes, Mairi. Herring, Oatmeal, Milk & Salt. (QRL Poetry Bks.: Vol. XXII). 1981. 20.00 (*0-614-06386-8*) Quarterly Rev.

*__MacInnes, Mairi.__ The Pebble: Old & New Poems. 2000. pap. 19.95 (*0-252-06794-0*) U of Ill Pr.

— Pebble: Old & New Poems. 2000. 40.00 (*0-252-02571-7*) U of Ill Pr.

MacInnes, Ranald. Building a Nation. 1999. 30.00 (*0-86241-830-5*) Interlink Pub.

MacInnes, Sheldon. Journey in Celtic Music: Cape Breton Style. LC 98-114774. (Illus.). 170p. 1997. pap. 17.95 (*0-920336-55-8*, Pub. by U Coll Cape Breton) Genl Dist Srvs.

MacInnis, Craig. Remembering the Rocket: A Celebration. (Peter Goddard Bks.). 1998. 19.95 (*0-7737-3128-8*) Genl Dist Srvs.

*__MacInnis, Craig, ed.__ Remembering Bobby Orr: A Celebration. large type ed. (Original Six Ser.). (Illus.). 128p. 1999. text 19.95 (*0-7737-3196-2*, Pub. by Stoddart Publ) Genl Dist Srvs.

MacInnis, Debbie, jt. ed. see Brucks, Merrie.

MacInnis, Donald E. Religion in China Today: Policy & Practice. LC 89-38900. 450p. 1989. pap. 21.00 (*0-88344-645-6*) Orbis Bks.

MacInnis, Donald E., jt. ed. see Kaiyuan, Zhang.

MacInnis, Donald E., tr. see Zhufeng, Luo, ed.

MacInnis, Jamie. Practicing. 88p. (Orig.). 1980. pap. 5.00 (*0-939180-13-8*) Tombouctou.

MacInnis, Jeff & Rowland, Wade. Polar Passage. 224p. 1990. mass mkt. 4.95 (*0-8041-0650-9*) Ivy Books.

MacInnis, Joseph. Fitzgerald's Storm: The Wreck of the Edmund Fitzgerald. 1997. pap. text 13.95 (*1-882376-53-6*) Thunder Bay Pr.

MacInnis, Joseph, ed. Saving the Oceans. 1992. 50.00 (*1-55013-416-7*) U of Toronto Pr.

MacInta, Tim, jt. auth. see Sonnenreich, Wes.

MacIntire, Douglas. Veterinary Emergency & Critical Care. 560p. 1999. pap. text 45.95 (*0-397-58463-6*) Lppncott W & W.

Macintire, Elizabeth J., tr. see Gad, Carl.

Macintosh, A. A. A Critical & Exegetical Commentary on Hosea. Emerton, J. A., ed. (International Critical Commentary Ser.). 704p. 1997. 69.95 (*0-567-08545-7*, Pub. by T & T Clark) Bks Intl VA.

Macintosh, Brownie. New England Artists & Writers: In Their Own Words. (New England Gift Bks.: Vol. 5). (Illus.). 64p. 2000. 4.95 (*1-58066-017-7*, Covered Brdge Pr) Douglas Charles Ltd.

— The Streamlined Double Decker Bus. (Illus.). 16p. (Orig.). (J). (gr. 2-5). 1995. pap. 9.95 (*0-924771-57-7*, Covered Brdge Pr) Douglas Charles Ltd.

Macintosh, Brownie, jt. auth. see Thompson, Julie.

MacIntosh, Craig, jt. auth. see Howard, Greg.

*__Macintosh, Donald.__ Travels in Galloway: Memoirs from Southwest Scotland. 2000. 15.00 (*1-897784-92-9*, Pub. by N Wilson Pubng) Interlink Pub.

Macintosh, Donald & Hawes, Michael. Sport & Canadian Diplomacy. 248p. 1994. 55.00 (*0-7735-1161-X*, Pub. by McG-Queens Univ Pr) CUP Services.

Macintosh, Donald & Whitson, David. The Game Planners: Transforming Canada's Sport System. 176p. (C). 1990. 65.00 (*0-7735-0758-2*, Pub. by McG-Queens Univ Pr) CUP Services.
— The Game Planners: Transforming Canada's Sport System. 180p. (C). 1994. pap. text 24.95 (*0-7735-1211-X*, Pub. by McG-Queens Univ Pr) CUP Services.
Macintosh, Donald, et al. Sport & Politics in Canada: Federal Government Involvement since 1961. 224p. (C). 1987. text 55.00 (*0-7735-0609-8*, Pub. by McG-Queens Univ Pr) CUP Services.
— Sport & Politics in Canada: Federal Government Involvement since 1961. 224p. (C). 1988. pap. text 27.95 (*0-7735-0665-9*, Pub. by McG-Queens Univ Pr) CUP Services.
MacIntosh, Doug. God up Close: How to Meditate on His Word. LC 99-182088. 176p. 1998. pap. 11.99 (*0-8024-7079-3*) Moody.
Macintosh, Douglas C. Theology As an Empirical Science. Gaustad, Edwin S., ed. LC 79-52601. (Baptist Tradition Ser.). 1980. reprint ed. lib. bdg. 25.95 (*0-405-12466-X*) Ayer.
Macintosh, Duncan. Chinese Blue & White Porcelain. LC 95-140600. (Illus.). 238p. 1994. 59.50 (*1-85149-210-0*) Antique Collect.
Macintosh, Fiona. Dying Acts: Death in Ancient Greek & Modern Irish Tragic Drama. LC 95-128053. 212p. 1995. text 65.00 (*0-312-12555-0*) St Martin.
Macintosh, Jeffrey G., jt. auth. see Briaudo, Richard J.
Macintosh, John. Life of Robert Burns. LC 78-144517. (Illus.). reprint ed. 37.50 (*0-404-08519-9*) AMS Pr.
Macintosh, Norman B. Management Accounting & Control Systems: Organisational & Behavioural Approach. LC 94-31614. 281p. 1995. 115.00 (*0-471-94409-2*) Wiley.
— Management Accounting & Control Systems: Organisational & Behavioural Approach. LC 94-31614. 294p. 1995. pap. 79.00 (*0-471-94411-4*) Wiley.
Macintosh, Sara. Marijuana: Health Effects. rev. ed. 2000. pap. 0.50 (*0-89230-161-9*) Do It Now.
— Marijuana: Personality & Behavior. rev. ed. 2000. pap. 0.50 (*0-89230-160-0*) Do It Now.
Macintosh-Smith, Tim. Yemen: Travels in Dictionary Land. (Illus.). 280p. 1998. 35.00 (*0-7195-5622-8*, Pub. by John Murray) Trafalgar.
***MacIntrye, Ewan.** Blackstone's LLB Cases & Materials: Consumer Law. 375p. 1999. pap. 38.00 (*1-85431-989-2*, Pub. by Blackstone Pr) Gaunt.
— Blackstone's LLB Learning Texts: Consumer Law. 332p. 1999. pap. 38.00 (*1-85431-988-4*, Pub. by Blackstone Pr) Gaunt.
MacIntyre. A Corner of a Foreign Field. text (*0-374-12985-1*) FS&G.
MacIntyre, ed. Dictionary of Inorganic Compounds, Vol. 6. (Illus.). 476p. (C). (gr. 13). 1993. ring bd., suppl. ed. 624.95 (*0-412-49090-0*, Chap & Hall CRC) CRC Pr.
— Dictionary of Inorganic Compounds, Vol. 8. (Illus.). 650p. (C). (gr. 13). 1995. ring bd., suppl. ed. 624.95 (*0-412-49110-9*, Chap & Hall CRC) CRC Pr.
MacIntyre, Alasdair C. After Virtue: A Study in Moral Theory. 2nd ed. LC 83-40601. 320p. 1984. pap. text 15.00 (*0-268-00611-3*) U of Notre Dame Pr.
— Against the Self-Images of the Age: Essays on Ideology & Philosophy. LC 78-1571. 1978. reprint ed. pap. text 15.00 (*0-268-00587-7*) U of Notre Dame Pr.
***MacIntyre, Alasdair C.** Dependent Rational Animals: Why Human Beings Need the Virtues. LC 99-11357. (Paul Carus Lectures: Vol. 20). 184p. 1999. 26.95 (*0-8126-9397-3*) Open Court.
MacIntyre, Alasdair C. First Principles, Final Ends & Contemporary Philosophical Issues. LC 89-64321. (Aquinas Lectures). 1990. 15.00 (*0-87462-157-7*) Marquette.
— Hume's Ethical Writings: Selections from David Hume. LC 79-1346. 1979. reprint ed. pap. text 15.00 (*0-268-01073-0*) U of Notre Dame Pr.
— Marxism & Christianity. LC 83-40600. 143p. 1984. reprint ed. pap. text 9.50 (*0-268-01358-6*) U of Notre Dame Pr.
— A Short History of Ethics. 280p. 1966. pap. 11.00 (*0-02-087260-7*) Macmillan.
— A Short History of Ethics. LC 97-22280. (C). 1997. reprint ed. pap. 18.00 (*0-268-01759-X*) U of Notre Dame Pr.
— A Short History of Ethics: A History of Moral Philosophy from the Homeric Age to the Twentieth Century. 1995. per. 13.00 (*0-684-82677-1*, Scribners Ref) Mac Lib Ref.
— Three Rival Versions of Moral Enquiry: Encyclopaedia, Genealogy, & Tradition. LC 89-29275. 256p. (C). 1990. text 29.00 (*0-268-01871-5*) U of Notre Dame Pr.
— Three Rival Versions of Moral Enquiry: Encyclopaedia, Genealogy, & Tradition. LC 89-29275. (C). 1991. pap. text 15.00 (*0-268-01877-4*) U of Notre Dame Pr.
— The Unconscious: A Conceptual Analysis. (Key Texts Ser.). 109p. 1997. reprint ed. pap. 15.00 (*1-85506-520-7*) Thoemmes Pr.
— Whose Justice? Which Rationality? LC 87-40354. 432p. (C). 1989. text 17.50 (*0-268-01942-8*); pap. text 17.50 (*0-268-01944-4*) U of Notre Dame Pr.
MacIntyre, Alasdair C. & Ricoeur, Paul. The Religious Significance of Atheism. LC 68-28398. (Bampton Lectures in America: No. 18). 106p. reprint ed. pap. 32.90 (*0-8357-4569-4*, 203747900008) Bks Demand.
MacIntyre, Alasdair C., jt. ed. see Hauerwas, Stanley.
MacIntyre, Alex, jt. auth. see Scott, Doug.
MacIntyre, Andrew, ed. Business & Government in Industrializing Asia. LC 94-1663. 1994. text 42.50 (*0-8014-3062-3*); pap. text 17.95 (*0-8014-8227-5*) Cornell U Pr.
MacIntyre, Andrew J. Business & Politics in Indonesia. 176p. pap. 24.95 (*0-04-442330-6*, Pub. by Allen & Unwin Pty) Paul & Co Pubs.
MacIntyre, Angus, jt. auth. see Picton Publishing Staff.
Macintyre, Ben. The Napoleon of Crime: The Life & Times of Adam Worth, Master Thief. 368p. 1998. pap. 12.95 (*0-385-31993-2*) Doubleday.
— The Napoleon of Crime: The Life & Times of Adam Worth, Master Thief. LC 97-520. 304p. 1997. 24.00 (*0-374-21899-4*) FS&G.
MacIntyre, Bruce C. The Viennese Concerted Mass of the Early Classic Period. LC 85-20872. (Studies in Musicology: No. 89). (Illus.). 788p. reprint ed. pap. 200.00 (*0-8357-1673-2*, 207060900005) Bks Demand.
MacIntyre, C. E., tr. from FRE. Poems of Tristan Corbiere. (Illus.). 105p. 1989. 185.00 (*0-933861-03-6*) H Berliner.
MacIntyre, C. F., tr. French Symbolist Poetry. (C). 1958. pap. 14.95 (*0-520-00784-0*, Pub. by U CA Pr) Cal Prin Full Svc.
MacIntyre, C. F., tr. see Goethe, Johann Wolfgang Von.
MacIntyre, C. F., tr. see Mallarme, Stephane.
MacIntyre, C. F., tr. see Rilke, Rainer Maria.
MacIntyre, C. F., tr. see Verlaine, Paul.
***MacIntyre, David, et al.** College 101: More Than 300 Tips We Wish Someone Would Have Told Us Before Starting College. large type ed. (Illus.). 160p. 1999. pap. 12.00 (*0-9674004-0-6*) Eductional Endeav.
***MacIntyre, Deirdre & Carr, Alan.** Prevention of Child Sexual Abuse in Ireland: The Development & Evaluation of the Stay Safe Programme. LC 00-34864. (Studies in Health & Human Services). 2000. write for info. (*0-7734-7715-2*) E Mellen.
Macintyre, Deluca D., ed. Essays on Creativity & Science. (Illus.). 308p. (Orig.). 1986. pap. 5.00 (*0-9616581-0-X*) Hawaii CTE.
MacIntyre, Donald G. Fighting Ships & Seamen. LC 78-2703. (Illus.). 192p. 1978. lib. bdg. 49.75 (*0-313-20357-1*, MFSS, Greenwood Pr) Greenwood.
***MacIntyre, Donald G.** U-Boat Killer: Fighting the U-Boats in the Battle of the Atlantic. (Military Classics). (Illus.). 2000. pap. 9.95 (*0-304-35235-7*) Continuum.
MacIntyre, Gertrude A. Active Partners: Education & Local Development. x, 197p. 1996. pap. 18.95 (*0-920336-68-X*, Pub. by U Coll Cape Breton) Genl Dist Srvs.
MacIntyre, Gertrude A., ed. Perspectives on Communities: A Community Economic Development Roundtable. 160p. 1997. pap. 19.95 (*0-920336-57-4*, Pub. by U Coll Cape Breton) Genl Dist Srvs.
MacIntyre, Gordon. Accreditation of Teacher Education: The Story of CATE 1984-1989. 224p. 1991. pap. 34.95 (*1-85000-981-3*, Falmer Pr) Taylor & Francis.
MacIntyre, Iain. Vancouver Canucks. LC 93-48447. (NHL Today Ser.). (Illus.). 32p. (YA). (gr. 3 up). 1996. lib. bdg. 21.30 (*0-88682-745-0*, Creat Educ) Creative Co.
Macintyre, Ian G., jt. auth. see James, Noel P.
Macintyre, Ian G., jt. auth. see Miller, James A.
MacIntyre, Ian G., jt. ed. see Ruetzler, Klaus.
MacIntyre, James. Three Men on an Island. LC 97-115993. 150p. 1997. 39.95 (*0-85640-582-5*, Pub. by Blackstaff Pr) Dufour.
MacIntyre, Jane E., ed. Dictionary of Organometallic Compounds: Fifth Supplement, 2 vols. 1125p. (gr. 13). 1989. ring bd. write for info. (*0-412-28180-5*, A3821, Chap & Hall CRC) CRC Pr.
— Dictionary of Organometallic Compounds: Fourth Supplement. (Illus.). 600p. (gr. 13). 1988. ring bd. write for info. (*0-412-28170-8*, A1997, Chap & Hall CRC) CRC Pr.
— Dictionary of Organometallic Compounds: Third Supplement. 600p. 1987. ring bd. write for info. (*0-412-26340-8*, Chap & Hall CRC) CRC Pr.
Macintyre, Lorn. Cruel in the Shadow. large type ed. 576p. 1982. 27.99 (*0-7089-0867-5*) Ulverscroft.
MacIntyre, Lynn. Easy Guide to Sewing Pants. LC 97-32736. (Sewing Companion Library). (Illus.). 144p. (Orig.). 1998. pap. 19.95 (*1-56158-233-6*, 070361) Taunton.
***MacIntyre, Marion E.** Pennsylvania Criminal Lawsource: The Collected Pennsylvania Statutes & Rules. LC 99-72786. 856p. 1999. pap. 64.50 (*1-887024-78-6*) Bisel Co.
MacIntyre, Neil R. & Branson, Richard D. Mechanical Ventilation. LC 99-25457. (Illus.). 700p. 2000. text. write for info. (*0-7216-7361-9*, W B Saunders Co) Harcrt Hlth Sci Grp.
Macintyre, Pamela, jt. auth. see Lees, Stella.
Macintyre, Pamela E. Acute Pain Management. (C). 1995. pap. text 34.00 (*0-7020-1990-9*) Harcourt.
MacIntyre, R. J. Molecular Evolutionary Genetics. LC 85-19312. (Monographs in Evolutionary Biology). (Illus.). 632p. (C). 1985. text 135.00 (*0-306-42042-2*, Kluwer Plenum) Kluwer Academic.
MacIntyre, Richard. Mortal Men: Living with Asymptomatic HIV. LC 98-8501. 256p. (C). 1999. 26.00 (*0-8135-2596-9*) Rutgers U Pr.
***Macintyre, Stuart.** A Concise History of Australia. LC 99-45570. (Cambridge Concise Histories Ser.). (Illus.). 272p. 2000. 54.95 (*0-521-62359-6*); pap. 17.95 (*0-521-62577-7*) Cambridge U Pr.
Macintyre, Stuart. The Oxford History of Australia, 1901-1942 Vol. 4: The Succeeding Age. (Illus.). 420p. 1993. reprint ed. pap. text 21.00 (*0-19-553518-9*) OUP.
MacIntyre, Stuart. A Proletarian Science: Marxism in Britain, 1917-1933. (C). 1986. pap. 22.50 (*0-85315-667-0*, Pub. by Lawrence & Wishart) NYU Pr.
Macintyre, Stuart. The Reds: The Communist Party of Australia from Origins to Illegality. (Illus.). 520p. 1998. 49.95 (*1-86448-580-9*, Pub. by Allen & Unwin Pty) Paul & Co Pubs.
***Macintyre, Stuart.** The Reds: The Communist Party of Australia from Origins to Illegality. (Illus.). 496p. 2000. 29.95 (*1-86508-180-9*, Pub. by Allen & Unwin Pty) Paul & Co Pubs.
Macintyre, Stuart & Thomas, Julian, eds. The Discovery of Australian History 1890-1939: 1890-1939. 256p. 1995. pap. 24.95 (*0-522-84699-8*, Pub. by Melbourne Univ Pr) Paul & Co Pubs.
Macintyre, Stuart, ed. & intro. see Deakin, Alfred.
MacIntyre, Stuart F., ed. The Oxford History of Australia: 1901 - 1942, the Succeeding Age, 5 vols., Vol. 4. LC 87-107443. (Illus.). 420p. 1987. text 45.00 (*0-19-554612-1*) OUP.
Macintyre, Stuart F. & Mitchell, Richard P., eds. Foundations of Arbitration: The Origins & Effects of State Compulsory Arbitration, 1890-1914. (Australian Studies on Labour Relations). 396p. 1990. pap. text 26.00 (*0-19-554996-1*) OUP.
MacIntyre, Tom. Fleurs-du Lit. (C). 1990. 25.00 (*0-948268-84-0*, Pub. by Dedalus) St Mut.
— Fleurs-du-Lit. 54p. 1990. pap. 30.00 (*0-948268-83-2*, Pub. by Dedalus) St Mut.
— A Glance Will Tell You & a Dream Confirm. 48p. 1994. pap. 11.95 (*1-873790-58-9*) Dufour.
— The Harper's Turn. 66p. 1982. 21.00 (*0-904011-29-1*) Dufour.
— I Bailed Out at Ardee. (C). 1987. pap. 30.00 (*0-948268-28-X*, Pub. by Dedalus) St Mut.
— The Word for Yes: New & Selected Stories. 126p. 1991. pap. 14.95 (*1-85235-069-5*) Dufour.
MacIntyre, Tom, tr. see Rose, Catherine & Rose, Neil.
MacIntyre, Wendy. Mairi. 236p. 1992. pap. text 12.95 (*0-88982-122-4*, Pub. by Oolichan Bks) Genl Dist Srvs.
Macioce, Frank M., et al. Conducting Due Diligence 1995. LC 95-212425. (Corporate Law & Practice Course Handbook Ser.). 872p. 1994. 129.00 (*0-87224-178-5*) PLI.
Maciocha, Teresa, ed. see Wilson, Edwin H.
Macioci, Nikolas. Why Dance? 72p. 1996. pap. 8.50 (*1-880286-22-X*) Singular Speech Pr.
Macioci, R. Nikolas. Cafes of Childhood. 52p. (Orig.). 1992. pap. 6.95 (*0-9627501-9-0*) Event Horizon.
— Cafes of Childhood. 44p. (Orig.). 1991. pap. 7.00 (*0-9628094-2-X*) Pearl Edit.
Maciocia, Giovanni. Chinese Medicine. (C). 1996. pap. 225.00 incl. cd-rom (*0-443-07821-1*) Harcourt.
— The Foundations of Chinese Medicine: A Comprehensive Text for Acupuncturists & Herbalists. (Illus.). 528p. 1989. write for info. (*0-443-03980-1*) Church.
— Tongue Diagnosis in Chinese Medicine. 2nd rev. ed. LC 94-61961. (Illus.). 210p. (C). 1995. text 45.00 (*0-939616-19-X*) Eastland.
Maciolek, Cindi R. The Basics of Buying Art. 150p. (Orig.). 1995. pap. 15.00 (*0-9647911-0-2*) Grand Arbor Pr.
MacIonis. Film Video Guide Society. 3rd ed. 1996. text. write for info. (*0-13-437831-8*) Allyn.
Macionis. Sociology. 6th ed. 1996. pap. text, student ed. 20.80 (*0-13-465303-3*) P-H.
— Sociology. 6th ed. 1999. 59.00 (*0-13-020664-4*) P-H.
MacIonis. Sociology. 6th ed. 1997. pap. text, suppl. ed. write for info. (*0-13-463754-2*) P-H.
Macionis. Sociology. 7th ed. 288p. 1998. pap., student ed. 21.00 (*0-13-095766-6*) P-H.
MacIonis. Sociology & Time Dollar Concepts. 6th ed. 1997. text 87.00 (*0-13-673724-2*) P-H.
Macionis, John J. Society: The Basics. 3rd ed. LC 95-2839. 512p. (C). 1995. pap. text 39.40 (*0-13-435819-8*) P-H.
— Society Study Guide. 5th ed. LC 99-20609. (Illus.). 499p. 1999. pap. text 46.67 incl. audio compact disk (*0-13-020748-9*) P-H.
MacIonis, John J. Sociology. 5th ed. LC 94-13021. 708p. 1994. text 72.00 (*0-13-101155-3*) P-H.
Macionis, John J. Sociology. 6th ed. LC 96-22938. 708p. (C). 1996. 66.00 (*0-13-237264-9*) P-H.
***MacIonis, John J.** Sociology. 6th ed. (Prentice Hall College Titles Ser.). 1999. 30.40 (*0-13-465668-7*) P-H.
***Macionis, John J.** Sociology. 8th ed. 736p. 2000. 69.33 (*0-13-018495-0*) P-H.
Macionis, John J. Sociology: Student Media Version. 7th ed. LC 97-43779. 700p. (C). 1998. pap. text 70.00 (*0-13-095391-1*) P-H.
Macionis, John J. & Benokraitis, Nijole V. Seeing Ourselves: Classic, Contemporary, & Cross-Cultural Readings in Sociology. 4th ed. LC 97-14965. 500p. 1997. pap. text 33.00 (*0-13-610684-6*) P-H.
***Macionis, John J. & Benokraitis, Nijole V.** Seeing Ourselves: Classic, Contemporary & Cross-Cultural Readings in Sociology. 5th ed. LC 00-38561. 2000. write for info. (*0-13-081358-3*) Aspen Law.
Macionis, John J. & Parrillo, Vincent J. Cities & Urban Life. LC 97-37717. 432p. (C). 1998. 63.00 (*0-13-736323-0*) P-H.
***Macionis, John J. & Parrillo, Vincent N.** Cities & Urban Life. 2nd ed. LC 00-22778. 504p. 2000. 58.67 (*0-13-088416-2*) P-H.
Maciora, Joseph G. The Maciora & Mik Families Genealogy: Historia Rodzin Mikow i Maciorow. LC 83-62000. (Illus.). 30p. (Orig.). 1983. pap. 7.00 (*0-9613407-0-3*) J G V Maciora.
MacIsaac, David, ed. The Defeat of the German Air Force: United States Strategic Bombing Survey, 10 vols. Incl. Vol. 1. LC 75-26396. 1976. (*0-8240-2026-X*); Vol. 2. LC 75-26396. 1976. (*0-8240-2027-8*); Vol. 3. LC 75-26396. 1976. (*0-8240-2028-6*); Vol. 4. LC 75-26396. 1976. (*0-8240-2029-4*); Vol. 5. LC 75-26396. 1976. (*0-8240-2030-8*); Vol. 6. LC 75-26396. 1976. (*0-8240-2031-6*); Vol. 7. LC 75-26396. 1976. (*0-8240-2032-4*); Vol. 8. LC 75-26396. 1976. (*0-8240-2033-2*); Vol. 9. LC 75-26396. 1976. (*0-8240-2034-0*); Vol. 10. LC 75-26396. 1976. (*0-8240-2035-9*); LC 75-26396. 1976. Set lib. bdg. 53.00 (*0-685-01848-2*) Garland.
MacIsaac, David S., jt. auth. see Rowe, Crayton E.
MacIsaac, Duncan, ed. see Campbell, John G.
MacIsaac, Maryellen. Handbook of IS Management. rev. ed. 1992. suppl. ed. 54.95 (*0-7913-0648-8*) Warren Gorham & Lamont.
— Handbook of IS Management. 3rd rev. ed. 1991. per. 150.00 (*0-87769-285-8*) Warren Gorham & Lamont.
MacIsaac, Maryellen, jt. ed. see Gilhooley, Ian A.
MacIsaac, Robert, ed. see Traubel, Horace.
MacIsaac, Ron & Champagne, Anne, eds. Clayoquot Mass Trials: Defending the Rainforest. LC 95-177403. (Illus.). 192p. 1995. pap. 17.95 (*0-86571-321-9*) New Soc Pubs.
MacIsaac, Sharon. Freud & Original Sin. LC 73-92232. 176p. reprint ed. pap. 54.60 (*0-608-11158-9*, 200904200072) Bks Demand.
Macisco, John J., Jr., jt. auth. see Powers, Mary G.
Macisco, John J., Jr., jt. ed. see Powers, Mary G.
Maciuika, John V., jt. auth. see Wayne, Kathryn M.
Maciunas, Robert J., ed. Advanced Techniques in Central Nervous System Metastases. 323p. 1998. 95.00 (*1-879284-47-2*) Am Assn Neuro.
Maciunas, Robert J., jt. auth. see Alexander, Eben.
Maciuszko, Jerzy J. The Polish Short Story in English: A Guide & Critical Bibliography. LC 68-12253. 474p. reprint ed. pap. 147.00 (*0-7837-3617-7*, 204348300009) Bks Demand.
MacIver, D. Chinese-English Dictionary: Hakka-Dialect. (CHI & ENG.). 1982. reprint ed. 55.00 (*0-89986-344-2*) Oriental Bk Store.
Maciver, D. Chinese-English Dictionary, Hakka-Dialect. 1982. 53.25 (*957-638-077-4*, Pub. by SMC Pub) Antique Collect.
MacIver, Dan & McCarroll, Les. Initiatives, Games, Activities. 134p. 1999. spiral bd. 35.95 (*0-7872-5747-8*, 41574701) Kendall-Hunt.
MacIver, Douglas J., jt. auth. see Epstein, Joyce L.
MacIver, Ian. Urban Water Supply Alternatives: Perception & Choice in the Grand Basin, Ontario. LC 70-115926. (University of Chicago, Department of Geography, Research Paper Ser.: No. 126). (Illus.). 193p. reprint ed. pap. 59.90 (*0-7837-0402-X*, 204072300018) Bks Demand.
MacIver, Joyce. The Glimpse. LC 82-90994. 160p. 1983. 12.95 (*0-87212-174-7*) Libra.
MacIver, Mary. Pilgrim Souls. 1990. text 28.00 (*0-08-037978-8*, Pergamon Pr) Elsevier.
MacIver, Mathew E. & Schreiber, Jan, eds. Planning with the Small Computer: An Applications Reader. LC 86-8462. (Lincoln Institute of Land Policy Bk.). 182p. reprint ed. pap. 56.50 (*0-7837-3270-8*, 204328900007) Bks Demand.
MacIver, R. M. Community: A Sociological Study. LC 70-172924. 452p. 1972. reprint ed. 24.95 (*0-405-08766-7*, Pub. by Blom Pubns) Ayer.
MacIver, R. M., ed. see Institute for Religious & Social Studies Staff.
MacIver, Robert. Robert M. MacIver on Community, Society & Power. Bramson, Leon, ed. LC 70-123374. (Heritage of Sociology Ser.). (C). 1993. pap. text 3.45 (*0-226-50048-9*, P375) U Ch Pr.
— Robert M. MacIver on Community, Society & Power. Bramson, Leon, ed. LC 70-123374. (Heritage of Sociology Ser.). (C). 1995. lib. bdg. 24.00 (*0-226-50047-0*) U Ch Pr.
MacIver, Robert M. Academic Freedom in Our Time. LC 67-18441. 329p. 1967. reprint ed. 75.00 (*0-87752-065-8*) Gordian.
— Community: A Sociological Study Being an Attempt to Set Out the Fundamental Laws of Social Life. 446p. 1970. reprint ed. 30.00 (*0-7146-1581-1*, BHA-01581, Pub. by F Cass Pubs) Intl Spec Bk.
— Group Relations & Group Antagonisms. 1990. 16.50 (*0-8446-1294-4*) Peter Smith.
— The Nations & the United Nations. LC 74-7382. (National Studies on International Organization-Carnegie Endowment for International Peace). (Illus.). 186p. 1974. reprint ed. lib. bdg. 55.00 (*0-8371-7535-6*, MANU) Greenwood.
— Social Causation. 1990. 16.50 (*0-8446-2504-3*) Peter Smith.
MacIvor, Daniel. House Humans. LC 96-931998. (Orig.). 1997. pap. 11.95 (*0-88754-521-1*) Theatre Comm.
— Marion Bridge. 128p. 1999. pap. 11.95 (*0-88922-407-2*) Talonbks.
— Never Swim Alone & This Is a Play: 2 Plays by Daniel Macivor, 2 bks. in 1. LC 94-173034. 1997. pap. 10.95 (*0-88754-524-6*) Theatre Comm.
— See Bob Run, 2 bks. in 1. LC 90-175665. 64p. (Orig.). 1997. pap. 10.95 (*0-88754-486-X*) Theatre Comm.
MacIvor, Daniel & Brooks, Daniel. Here Lies Henry. LC 97-169909. (Orig.). 1997. pap. 12.95 (*0-88754-519-X*) Theatre Comm.
MacIvor, Heather. Women in Politics in Canada: An Introductory Text. 360p. (C). 1996. pap. text 19.95 (*1-55111-036-9*) Broadview Pr.
Mack. California Estate Administration. (Paralegal Ser.). 1997. teacher ed. 9.95 (*0-8273-7306-6*) Delmar.
— European Witch Craze. 2000. pap. text. write for info. (*0-312-17100-5*) St Martin.
— Lineman's & Cableman's Field Manual. LC 99-87049. 300p. 2000. pap. 49.95 (*0-07-135470-0*) McGraw-Hill Prof.
Mack, ed. Aggression & Its Alternatives in the Conduct of International Relations. (Psychoanalytic Inquiry Ser.: Vol. 6, No. 2). 1995. 20.00 (*0-88163-970-2*) Analytic Pr.
Mack, Adrienne. A+ Parents: Help Your Child Learn & Succeed in School. LC 97-3145. (Illus.). 144p. (Orig.). 1997. pap. 12.95 (*0-935526-36-6*) McBooks Pr.

An Asterisk (*) at the beginning of an entry indicates that the title is appearing for the first time.

Mack, Al. Calligraphy & Lettering, No. 2. (How to Draw & Paint Ser.). (Illus.). 32p. (Orig.). 1989. pap. 6.95 (*1-56010-024-9*, HT211) W Foster Pub.

Mack, Alison. Dry All Night: The Picture Book Technique That Stops Bedwetting. (Illus.). 175p. 1990. pap. 16.95 (*0-316-54225-3*, Pub. by Little) Time Warner.

***Mack, Alison.** Marijuana as Medicine: The Science Beyond the Controversy. 240p. 1999. pap. 16.95 (*0-309-06531-3*, Joseph Henry Pr) Natl Acad Pr.

Mack, Alison. Toilet Learning: The Picture Book Technique for Children & Parents. 109p. 1983. pap. 13.00 (*0-316-54237-7*, Little Brwn Med Div) Lppncott W & W.

Mack, Andrew, ed. Asian Flashpoint: Security & the Korean Peninsula. 175p. 1994. pap. 24.95 (*1-86373-401-3*, Pub. by Allen & Unwin Pty) Paul & Co Pubs.

— A Peaceful Ocean? Maritime Security in the Pacific in the Post-Cold War Era. 200p. 1994. pap. 24.95 (*1-86373-593-3*, Pub. by Allen & Unwin Pty) Paul & Co Pubs.

Mack, Andrew, et al. Beyond the Cold War in the Pacific. Kahler, Miles, ed. (IGCC Studies in Global Conflict & Cooperation: No. 2). 155p. (Orig.). 1991. pap. 5.00 (*0-934637-14-8*) U of CA Inst Global.

— The Northeast Asian Cooperation Dialogue No. II: Confidence-Building & Crisis Prevention. (IGCC Policy Papers: No. 9). 88p. (Orig.). 1994. pap. 3.50 (*0-934637-24-5*) U of CA Inst Global.

Mack, Andrew, jt. ed. see Harris, Stuart.

Mack, Andrew L., et al. A Biological Assessment of the Lakekamu Basin, Papua, New Guinea. (RAP Working Papers: No. 9). 150p. (C). 1999. pap. write for info. (*1-881173-20-8*, Pub. by Conser Intl) U Ch Pr.

***Mack, Angela & Robinson, Brenda.** For That Special Day: A Guidebook for Planning Your Wedding. (Illus.). 44p. 1999. pap. 7.95 (*0-9675616-1-2*, ANDOKI Pubns) Angela Mack.

— For That Special Day: A Guidebook to Planning Your Wedding. 40p. 1999. pap. 8.50 (*0-7392-0471-8*, P03795) Morris Pubng.

Mack, Anna E. For His Sake. LC 74-86800. (Granger Index Reprint Ser.). 1977. 15.95 (*0-8369-6083-1*) Ayer.

Mack, Anna E., compiled by. Because I Love You. LC 77-121931. (Granger Index Reprint Ser.). 1977. 19.95 (*0-8369-6172-2*) Ayer.

Mack, Arien, ed. Home: A Place in the World. LC 92-44279. (Illus.). 281p. (C). 1993. text 47.50 (*0-8147-5483-X*) NYU Pr.

— Home: A Place in the World. (Illus.). 281p. (C). 1995. pap. text 19.50 (*0-8147-5526-7*) NYU Pr.

— Humans & Other Animals. LC 98-37449. (Illus.). 450p. 1999. text 50.00 (*0-8142-0817-7*); pap. text 21.95 (*0-8142-5017-3*) Ohio St U Pr.

— In Time of Plague: The History & Social Consequences of Lethal Epidemic Disease. 272p. (C). 1991. text 45.00 (*0-8147-5467-8*) NYU Pr.

— In Time of Plague: The History & Social Consequences of Lethal Epidemic Disease. 272p. (C). 1992. pap. text 18.50 (*0-8147-5485-6*) NYU Pr.

Mack, Arien & Rock, Irvin. Inattentional Blindness. LC 97-28254. (Cognitive Psychology Ser.). (Illus.). 296p. 1998. 40.50 (*0-262-13339-3*) MIT Pr.

***Mack, Arien & Rock, Irvin.** Inattentional Blindness. (Illus.). 288p. (C). 2000. pap. 27.00 (*0-262-63203-9*) MIT Pr.

Mack, Arthur C. Enjoying the Catskills. 1972. pap. 4.95 (*0-939166-01-1*) Outdoor Pubns.

— The Palisades of the Hudson. (Illus.). 64p. 1982. reprint ed. pap. 6.95 (*0-915850-05-2*) Walking News Inc.

***Mack, Benjamin.** Fire Eating: A Manual of Instruction. rev. ed. LC 00-31455. 2000. write for info. (*0-917643-12-7*) B Dube.

***Mack, Beverly B. & Boyd, Jean.** One Woman's Jihad: Nana Asma'u, Scholar & Scribe. LC 99-53817. (Illus.). 192p. 2000. pap. 13.95 (*0-253-21398-3*); lib. bdg. 35.00 (*0-253-33707-0*) Ind U Pr.

Mack, Burton L. The Lost Gospel: The Book of Q & Christian Origins. LC 92-53921. 288p. 1994. reprint ed. pap. 15.00 (*0-06-065375-2*, Pub. by Harper SF) HarpC.

— A Myth of Innocence: Mark & Christian Origins. LC 86-45906. (Foundations & Facets Ser.). 448p. 1991. pap. 25.00 (*0-8006-2549-8*, 1-2549) Augsburg Fortress.

— Who Wrote the New Testament: The Making of the Christian Myth. LC 95-8937. 336p. 1996. pap. 16.00 (*0-06-065518-6*, Pub. by Harper SF) HarpC.

— Wisdom & the Hebrew Epic: Ben Sira's Hymn in Praise of the Fathers. LC 85-8564. (Chicago Studies in the History of Judaism). xiv, 264p. 1994. lib. bdg. 27.50 (*0-226-50049-7*) U Ch Pr.

Mack, C. J., jt. auth. see Enoeda, K.

Mack, Carol K. & Mack, Dinah. A Field Guide to Demons, Fairies, Fallen Angels & Other Subversive Spirits. LC 98-34584. (Illus.). 336p. 1998. 26.95 (*1-55970-447-0*, Pub. by Arcade Pub Inc) Time Warner.

— A Field Guide to Demons, Fairies, Fallen Angels & Other Subversive Spirits. LC 99-20481. 336p. 1999. 15.00 (*0-8050-6270-X*) H Holt & Co.

Mack, Charles. Encyclopedia of Matchbox Toys. LC 97-22931. 240p. 1997. pap. 29.95 (*0-7643-0325-2*) Schiffer.

Mack, Charles, jt. auth. see Enoeda, Keinosuke.

Mack, Charles R. Paper Pleasures: Five Centuries of Drawings & Watercolors. 168p. (C). 1995. pap. 19.95 (*1-57003-065-0*) U of SC Pr.

— Pienza: The Creation of a Renaissance City. LC 86-24269. (Illus.). 256p. 1987. text 52.50 (*0-8014-1699-X*) Cornell U Pr.

Mack, Charles R. & Robertson, Lynn, eds. The Roman Remains: John Izard Middleton's Visual Souvenirs of 1820-1823, with Addition Views in Italy, France, & Switzerland. LC 97-4726. (Illus.). 175p. 1997. 24.95 (*1-57003-169-X*) U of SC Pr.

Mack, Charles S. Business, Politics & the Practice of Government Relations. LC 97-19230. 288p. 1997. 69.50 (*1-56720-057-5*, Quorum Bks) Greenwood.

— The Executive Handbook of Trade & Business Associations: How They Work & How To Make Them Work Effectively for You. LC 90-8957. 272p. 1990. 65.00 (*0-89930-531-8*, MEJ/, Quorum Bks) Greenwood.

— Lobbying & Government Relations: A Guide for Executives. LC 88-35730. 244p. 1989. 65.00 (*0-89930-390-0*, MGV/, Quorum Bks) Greenwood.

Mack, Charlie. Encyclopedia of Matchbox Toys, 1947-1996. 2nd rev. ed. (Illus.). 352p. 1999. pap. 29.95 (*0-7643-0866-1*) Schiffer.

— Lesney's Matchbox Toys: Regular Wheel Years, 1947-1969. LC 92-60637. (Illus.). 144p. 1992. pap. 16.95 (*0-88740-434-0*) Schiffer.

— Lesney's Matchbox Toys: The Superfast Years, 1969-1982. LC 92-63103. (Illus.). 128p. (Orig.). 1993. pap. 19.95 (*0-88740-463-4*) Schiffer.

— Lesney's Matchbox Toys: The Superfast Years, 1969-1982. 2nd rev. ed. (Illus.). 128p. (Orig.). 1999. pap. 19.95 (*0-7643-0772-X*) Schiffer.

— Matchbox Toys: The Universal Years, 1982-1992. (Illus.). 256p. 1993. pap. 19.95 (*0-88740-550-9*) Schiffer.

— Matchbox Toys: The Universal Years, 1982-1992. 2nd rev. ed. (Illus.). 256p. 1999. pap. 19.95 (*0-7643-0771-1*) Schiffer.

— Matchbox Toys, the Tyco Years, 1993-1994. LC 95-19425. (Illus.). 144p. (Orig.). 1995. pap. 19.95 (*0-88740-865-6*) Schiffer.

Mack, Charlotte W. & Feldt, Constance C. Spatial Reasoning with Soma Cube Activities. 79p. (J). (gr. 5-8). 1993. pap. 19.95 (*0-939765-61-6*, G157) Janson Pubns.

Mack, Chester. Punchdrunk Man Reader. LC 87-51416. (Illus.). 140p. 1988. 14.95 (*0-9605630-1-6*) Thistlerose.

Mack, Chris A. Inside Prolith: A Comprehensive Guide to Optical Lithography Simulation. 2nd ed. (Illus.). 175p. (Orig.). 1997. reprint ed. pap. 95.00 (*0-9650922-0-8*) Finle Technol.

***Mack, Chris A. & Stevenson, Tom, eds.** Lithography for Semiconductor Manufacturing. (Europto Ser.: Vol. 3741). 270p. 1999. pap. text 72.00 (*0-8194-3221-0*) SPIE.

Mack, Connie. Connie Mack's Baseball Book. 1976. 23.95 (*0-8488-1591-2*) Amereon Ltd.

— My 66 Years in the Big Leagues. Date not set. lib. bdg. 21.95 (*0-8488-1587-4*) Amereon Ltd.

***Mack, Connie, ed.** The Multifamily Assisted Housing Reform & Affordability Act of 1997 - S.513: Congressional Hearing. (Illus.). 155p. (C). 2000. reprint ed. pap. text 30.00 (*0-7881-8691-4*) DIANE Pub.

Mack, Connie, jt. ed. see Faircloth, Lauch.

Mack, D., jt. auth. see Lackes, R.

Mack, Dan. Log Cabin Living: Simply Log. LC 99-30624. (Illus.). 160p. 1999. 39.95 (*0-87905-920-6*) Gibbs Smith Pub.

Mack, Dana. The Assault on Parenthood: How Our Culture Undermines the Family. LC 97-3903. 256p. 1997. 24.50 (*0-684-80774-2*) Simon & Schuster.

— The Assault on Parenthood: How Our Culture Undermines the Family. LC 97-3903. 368p. 2000. reprint ed. pap. 15.95 (*1-893554-11-2*) Encounter Bks.

Mack, Daniel. The Jems EMT-B Certification Preparation & Review. 2nd ed. LC 95-23166. (Illus.). 200p. (C). (gr. 13). 1995. pap. text 21.95 (*0-8151-6204-9*, 25664) Mosby Inc.

— Making Rustic Furniture: The Tradition, Spirit & Technique with Dozens of Project Ideas. LC 90-4517. (Illus.). 160p. 1992. pap. 19.95 (*1-887374-12-4*, Pub. by Lark Books) Sterling.

— The Rustic Furniture Companion: Traditions, Techniques & Inspirations. Morgenthal, Deborah, ed. LC 95-40314. (Illus.). 144p. 1996. 26.95 (*0-937274-97-6*) Lark Books.

— The Rustic Furniture Companion: Traditions, Techniques & Inspirations. Morgenthal, Deborah, ed. LC 95-40314. (Illus.). 144p. 1999. pap. 19.95 (*1-887374-65-5*) Lark Books.

— Simple Rustic Furniture: A Weekend Workshop with Dan Mack. Morgenthal, Deborah, ed. LC 98-34719. (Illus.). 112p. 1999. 19.95 (*1-57990-086-0*, Pub. by Lark Books) Random.

Mack, David. Kabuki: Circle of Blood. (Illus.). 272p. (Orig.). 1998. pap. 29.95 (*1-58240-048-2*) Image Comics.

— Kabuki: Circle of Blood. limited ed. (Illus.). 272p. (Orig.). 1998. pap. 49.95 (*1-58240-049-0*) Image Comics.

— Kabuki: Masks of the Noh. (Illus.). 128p. 1998. pap. 10.95 (*1-887279-99-7*) Image Comics.

— Kabuki: Masks of the Noh. (Illus.). 128p. 1998. 19.95 (*1-58240-068-7*) Image Comics.

— Kabuki: Masks of the Noh. limited ed. (Illus.). 128p. 1998. 39.95 (*1-58240-069-5*) Image Comics.

— Kabuki: Skin Deep. (Illus.). 112p. 1998. 23.95 (*1-58240-073-3*); pap. 9.95 (*1-58240-000-8*) Image Comics.

— Kabuki: Skin Deep. limited ed. (Illus.). 112p. 1998. 39.95 (*1-58240-074-1*) Image Comics.

— Kabuki Vol. I: Circle of Blood. (Illus.). 272p. 1997. pap. 17.95 (*1-887279-80-6*) Image Comics.

Mack, David, jt. auth. see Francis, Gary.

Mack, Deni, jt. ed. see Karaban, Roslyn A.

Mack, Dinah, jt. auth. see Mack, Carol K.

Mack, Donald, ed. see Cole, George W.

Mack, Donald, ed. see Dunnigan, William.

Mack, Donald, ed. see Schabacker, Richard.

Mack, Donald, ed. see Wetsel Market Bureau Staff.

Mack, Donald R. The Unofficial IEEE Brainbuster Gamebook: Mental Workouts for the Technically Inclined. LC 92-4724. (Illus.). 144p. 1992. pap. 12.95 (*0-7803-0423-3*, PP03186) Inst Electrical.

Mack, Donald W. Lenin & the Russian Revolution. Reeves, Marjorie, ed. (Then & There Ser.). (Illus.). 104p. (Orig.). (gr. 7-12). 1970. pap. text 8.76 (*0-582-20457-7*, 70766) Longman.

Mack, Dorothy. Gamester's Daughter. 224p. 1998. mass mkt. 4.99 (*0-451-19529-9*, Sig) NAL.

***Mack, Dorothy.** The Gold Scent Bottle. 215p. 2000. mass mkt. 4.99 (*0-451-20003-9*, Sig) NAL.

Mack, Douglas S., ed. see Hogg, James.

Mack, Douglas S., ed. see Scott, Sir Walter.

Mack, Edward C. Public Schools & British Opinion since 1860: The Relationship Between Contemporary Ideas & the Evolution of an English Institution. LC 75-109777. 511p. 1971. reprint ed. lib. bdg. 75.00 (*0-8371-4267-9*, MAPS, Greenwood Pr) Greenwood.

Mack, Eric, jt. auth. see Spencer, Herbert.

***Mack, Ernest W.** Keep the Faith: The Biography of a Nevada Brain Surgeon & Avid Fisherman. Starmer, Heather, ed. 229p. 1998. 25.00 (*0-9649759-6-3*) Greasewood.

Mack, F. M. & Zettersten, A., eds. The English Text of the Ancrene Riwle, BM MS Cotton Titus Dxviii. (EETS Original Ser.: Vol. 252). 1963. 30.00 (*0-19-722252-8*, Pub. by EETS) Boydell & Brewer.

Mack, Faite. Assessment Resources for Teachers of Young Children. (Illus.). 343p. (Orig.). (C). 1996. pap. text 34.80 (*0-87563-663-2*) Stipes.

— Resources for Educational Testing & Measurement. 352p. (Orig.). (C). 1994. pap. text 19.80 (*0-87563-489-3*) Stipes.

Mack, Frances, ed. Seinte Marherete. (EETS, OS Ser.: Vol. 193). 1974. reprint ed. 40.00 (*0-8115-3381-6*) Periodicals Srv.

Mack, G. H., et al, eds. Cretaceous & Laramide Tectonic Evolution of Southwestern New Mexico. (Guidebook Ser.: No. 39). (Illus.). 216p. 1988. 40.00 (*1-58546-074-5*) NMex Geol Soc.

— Las Cruces County, Vol. II. (Guidebook Ser.: No. 49). (Illus.). 325p. 1998. pap. 45.00 (*1-58546-084-2*) NMex Geol Soc.

***Mack, Gerhard.** Art Museums: Into the 21st Century. (Illus.). 112p. 1999. pap. 29.95 (*3-7643-5963-3*, Pub. by Birkhauser) Princeton Arch.

Mack, Gerhard. Herzog & de Meuron Vol. 2: The Complete Works, 1989-1991. (Illus.). 208p. 1996. 85.00 (*3-7643-5187-X*, Pub. by Birkhauser) Princeton Arch.

— Herzog & De Meuron 1978-1988 Vol. 1: The Complete Works, Vol. 1. (Illus.). 240p. 1997. 85.00 (*3-7643-5616-2*, Pub. by Birkhauser) Princeton Arch.

***Mack, Gerhard, ed.** Herzog & de Meuron 1992-1996: The Complete Works, Vol. 3. (GER & ENG., Illus.). 272p. 2000. 98.00 (*3-7643-6264-2*, Pub. by Birkhauser) Princeton Arch.

Mack, Gerstle. Gustave Courbet: A Biography. (Quality Paperbacks Ser.). (Illus.). 494p. 1989. pap. 14.95 (*0-306-80375-5*) Da Capo.

— Paul Cezanne: A Biography. (Illus.). 462p. 1994. pap. 14.95 (*1-56924-904-0*) Marlowe & Co.

***Mack, Gerstle & Gibson, Thomas.** Architectural Details of Northern & Central Spain: One Hundred & Four Measured Drawings, Fifty-Five Photographs. deluxe fac. ed. (Illus.). 151p. 2000. reprint ed. 55.00 (*0-7404-0024-X*) Higginson Bk Co.

Mack, Glenn. Adventures in Improvisation at the Keyboard. 64p. 1970. pap. text 9.95 (*0-87487-076-3*) Summy-Birchard.

— Adventures in Modes & Keys. 32p. 1991. pap. text 5.95 (*0-87487-625-7*) Summy-Birchard.

Mack, Grace C. My Special Book of Jewish Celebrations. (Illus.). 36p. (Orig.). (J). (ps-2). 1984. pap. 8.95 (*0-9602338-4-9*) Rockdale Ridge.

Mack, Greg H. Geology of Southern New Mexico: A Beginner's Guide, Including El Paso. LC 96-35688. (Illus.). 176p. 1997. pap. 19.95 (*0-8263-1794-4*) U of NM Pr.

Mack, Hananel. The Aggadic Midrash Literature. 144p. 1989. pap. 12.00 (*965-05-0486-9*, Pub. by Israel Ministry Def) Gefen Bks.

Mack, Harold C., ed. see Symposium on the Physiology & Pathology of Human R.

Mack, Heinz, jt. auth. see Piene, Otto.

Mack, James A. In Pictures Rocky Mountain: The Continuing Story. LC 95-75098. (Illus.). 48p. 1995. pap. 7.95 (*0-88714-085-8*) KC Pubns.

— In Pictures Rocky Mountain: The Continuing Story. Morales, Brigitte, tr. (GER., Illus.). 48p. 1995. pap. 8.95 (*0-88714-800-X*) KC Pubns.

— In Pictures Rocky Mountain: The Continuing Story. Le Bras, Yvon, tr. (FRE., Illus.). 48p. 1995. pap. 8.95 (*0-88714-801-8*) KC Pubns.

— In Pictures Rocky Mountain: The Continuing Story. Petzinger, Saori, tr. (JPN., Illus.). 48p. 1995. pap. 8.95 (*0-88714-802-6*) KC Pubns.

Mack, James A., jt. auth. see Liggett, Diane T.

Mack, Jane. Excel for Windows 95 Essentials, IM. 1996. text, teacher ed. 49.99 (*1-57576-268-4*) Que Educ & Trng.

— Excel for Windows 95 Essentials: Level II. LC 95-72187. 164p. 1996. pap. text 22.99 (*1-57576-269-2*) Que Educ & Trng.

Mack, Jane. Excel for Windows 95 Essential, IM, Level 2. 1996. text, teacher ed. 49.99 (*1-57576-270-6*) Que Educ & Trng.

Mack, Janis. All Day Singin' & Dinner on the Ground: "A Southern Tradition" (Illus.). 150p. (Orig.). 1997. pap. 12.95 (*0-9656762-1-8*) Mack Enterprises.

— All Day Singin' & Dinner on the Ground: A Southern Tradition. (Illus.). 150p. 1997. 14.95 (*0-9656762-3-4*) Mack Enterprises.

— Arkansas Recipes, Legends, & Such from Pickles Gap, Skunk Hollow, & Toad Suck. 2nd ed. (Illus.). 140p. 1996. reprint ed. pap. 9.95 (*0-9656762-0-X*) Mack Enterprises.

Mack, Jefferson. Running a Ring of Spies: Spycraft & Black Operations in the Real World of Espionage. 216p. 1996. pap. 20.00 (*0-87364-902-8*) Paladin Pr.

— The Safe House: Setting up & Running Your Own Sanctuary. LC 99-189161. 96p. 1998. pap. 12.00 (*0-87364-989-3*) Paladin Pr.

Mack, Jim. Haleakala: The Story Behind the Scenery. rev. ed. LC 92-70431. (Illus.). 48p. (Orig.). 1992. pap. 7.95 (*0-88714-052-1*) KC Pubns.

***Mack, John.** Ascending the Heights: A Layman's Guide to the Ladder of Divine Ascent. 176p. 2000. pap. 14.95 (*1-888212-17-9*) Conciliar Pr.

Mack, John. Celtic Portraits. unabridged ed. Howard, Greg, ed. 35p. 1998. write for info. (*0-9663601-0-9*) Green Hill Prodns.

— Malagasy Textiles. (Ethnography Ser.: No. 14). (Illus.). 60p. 1989. pap. 10.50 (*0-7478-0015-4*, Pub. by Shire Pubns) Parkwest Pubns.

— Nightmares & Human Conflict. 288p. 1989. text 64.50 (*0-231-07102-7*); pap. text 22.50 (*0-231-07103-5*) Col U Pr.

— Preserve Them, O Lord: A Guide for Couples Preparing for Marriage in the Orthodox Church. (Illus.). 1996. wbk. ed. 11.95 (*1-888212-01-2*) Conciliar Pr.

Mack, John, ed. Ethnic Jewelry. (Illus.). 208p. 1988. 49.50 (*0-8109-0891-3*) Abrams.

— Masks & the Art of Expression. LC 93-48524. (Illus.). 224p. 1994. 49.50 (*0-8109-3641-0*, Pub. by Abrams) Time Warner.

Mack, John & Robertshaw, P., eds. Culture History in the Southern Sudan: Archaeology, Linguistics, Ethnohistory. 1982. pap. 27.00 (*1-872566-04-9*, Pub. by Brit Inst Estrn Africa) David Brown.

Mack, John, jt. auth. see Hine, Robert V.

Mack, John, jt. auth. see McLeod, Malcolm.

Mack, John E. Abduction: Human Encounters with Aliens. 1995. mass mkt. 6.99 (*0-345-39300-7*) Ballantine Pub Grp.

— Abduction: Human Encounters with Aliens. large type ed. LC 94-32723. 1994. pap. 21.95 (*1-56895-082-9*) Wheeler Pub.

— Passport to the Cosmos: Human Transformation & Alien Encounters. LC 99-35412. 320p. 1999. 24.00 (*0-517-70568-0*, Crown) Crown Pub Group.

***Mack, John E.** Passport to the Cosmos: Human Transformation & Alien Encounters. 224p. 2000. pap. 14.00 (*0-609-80557-6*, Three Riv Pr) Crown Pub Group.

Mack, John E. Prince of Our Disorder: The Life of T. E. Lawrence. LC 98-141432. 609p. 1999. pap. text 19.50 (*0-674-70494-0*) HUP.

Mack, John E. & Ablon, Steven L., eds. The Development & Sustaining of Self-Esteem in Childhood. LC 83-22726. xiv, 304p. 1984. 47.50 (*0-8236-1255-4*) Intl Univs Pr.

Mack, John E. & Rogers, Rita S. The Alchemy of Survival: One Woman's Journey. (Radcliffe Biography Ser.). (Illus.). 1988. 17.26 (*0-201-12682-6*) Addison-Wesley.

— The Alchemy of Survival: One Woman's Journey. (Radcliffe Biography Ser.). (Illus.). 1989. pap. 13.41 (*0-201-51800-7*) Addison-Wesley.

Mack, Judy B. My Daddy & Me. (Illus.). 40p. (Orig.). (J). (gr. k-4). 2000. pap. write for info. (*0-9637795-7-5*) MinervaPress.

Mack, Karen. The Magical Adventures of Sun Beams. (Illus.). 32p. (J). (ps-4). 1992. pap. 5.95 (*0-9631644-0-6*) Shooting Star.

Mack, Karin & Skjei, Eric. Overcoming Writing Blocks. 1980. 10.00 (*0-685-02301-X*); pap. 6.95 (*0-685-02302-8*) HM.

Mack, Kibibi C. Parlor Ladies & Ebony Drudges: African American Women, Class, & Woek in a South Carolina Community. LC 98-25345. (Illus.). 264p. 1999. text 34.00 (*1-57233-030-9*) U of Tenn Pr.

Mack, Kibibi V., ed. The African American Encyclopedia: Supplement, 2 vols. 558p. 1997. pap. text 214.21 (*0-7614-0563-1*, E185) Marshall Cavendish.

Mack, Leo. Handicap a Winner at the Hounds: Quinelas Trifectas Daily Doubles. 99p. 1991. pap. text 15.95 (*0-9630208-1-1*) Macks Bks.

— Handicap a Winning Bet at the Greyhounds. abr. ed. 103p. 1991. pap. text 16.95 (*0-9630208-2-X*) Macks Bks.

— How to Win at the Greyhounds. 145p. 1990. pap. text 20.00 (*0-9630208-0-3*) Macks Bks.

Mack, Loffie. Making the Most of Work Spaces. LC 95-67264. (Illus.). 80p. 1995. 19.95 (*0-8478-1897-7*, Pub. by Rizzoli Intl) St Martin.

Mack, Lois. Rules for Medical Terminology. 2nd ed. 256p. (C). 1996. spiral bd. 40.95 (*0-7872-2844-3*, 41284401) Kendall-Hunt.

***Mack, Lorrie.** Art of Home Conversion: Transforming Uncommon Properties into Stylish Homes. (Illus.). 2000. pap. 21.95 (*1 84188 023-X*) Seven Dials.

— Calm Working Spaces. (Illus.). 176p. 2000. 35.00 (*0-688-17462-0*, HarpRes) HarpInfo.

Mack, Lorrie. Conran's Living in Small Spaces. 1988. 29.95 (*0-316-54383-7*) Little.

***Mack, Lorrie.** Living in Small Spaces. 1999. pap. 14.95 (*1-85029-800-9*) Conran Octopus.

— Setting Up Home: The Essential Guide to Creating a Home from Scratch. (Illus.). 224p. 2000. 29.95 (*1-84222-059-4*) Carlton Bks Ltd.

Mack, Lorrie, et al. Laura Ashley Guide to Country Decorating. 208p. (YA). 1993. 34.00 (*1-56282-745-6*, Pub. by Hyperion) Time Warner.

M

An Asterisk (*) at the beginning of an entry indicates that the title is appearing for the first time.

— Laura Ashley Guide to Country Decorating. (Illus.). 208p. (J). 1994. pap. 17.45 (0-7868-8086-4, Pub. by Hyperion) Time Warner.

Mack, Mark. Stremmel House. LC 97-39001. (One House Ser.). (Illus.). 64p. 1997. pap. 19.95 (1-885254-49-0, Pub. by Monacelli Pr) Penguin Putnam.

Mack, Maureen. To Die While Living: My Journey. 424p. pap. write for info. (965-222-960-1, Pub. by Maureen Mack) BookMasters.

Mack, Maynard. Alexander Pope: A Life. LC 85-2941. (Illus.). 1986. 25.95 (0-393-02208-0) Norton.

— Alexander Pope: A Life. LC 85-2941. (Illus.). 1988. pap. 14.95 (0-393-30529-5) Norton.

— Alexander Pope: A Life. LC 85-40466. (Illus.). 976p. 1988. pap. 25.00 (0-300-04303-1) Yale U Pr.

— Collected in Himself: Essays, Critical, Biographical & Bibliographical on Pope & Some of His Contemporaries. LC 79-57524. 576p. 1982. 70.00 (0-87413-182-0) U Delaware Pr.

— Everybody's Shakespeare: Reflections Chiefly on Tragedies. LC 92-25122. xii, 279p. 1993. reprint ed. pap. 14.00 (0-8032-8214-1, Bison Books) U of Nebr Pr.

— Killing the King: Three Studies in Shakespeare's Tragic Structure. LC 72-91301. (Yale Studies in English: No. 180). 220p. reprint ed. pap. 68.20 (0-8357-8197-6, 203380900087) Bks Demand.

*__Mack, Maynard.__ N. A. Wild Exlporation (C). 1999. pap. text. write for info. (0-393-98038-3) Norton.

Mack, Maynard. The Norton Anthology of World Masterpieces. LC 96-39009. 3052p. (C). 1997. pap. text 53.50 (0-393-97143-0) Norton.

— The World of Alexander Pope. (Illus.). 70p. (Orig.). 1988. pap. 5.00 (0-685-59700-8) Yale Ctr Brit Art.

Mack, Maynard, ed. The Last & Greatest Art: Some Unpublished Poetical Manuscripts of Alexander Pope. LC 81-50304. 448p. 1984. 85.00 (0-87413-183-9) U Delaware Pr.

Mack, Maynard, et al, eds. Norton Anthology of World Masterpieces. 5th ed. (C). 1987. pap. write for info. (0-393-95486-2) Norton.

— Norton Anthology of World Masterpieces: Instructor's Guide. (C). 1987. pap., teacher ed. 10.50 (0-393-95489-7) Norton.

Mack, Maynard & Lord, George D., eds. Poetic Traditions of the English Renaissance. LC 82-1941. 336p. 1982. 40.00 (0-300-02785-0) Yale U Pr.

Mack, Maynard & Winn, James A., eds. Pope: Recent Essays by Several Hands. LC 79-26345. (Essential Articles Ser.). iv, 768p. (C). 1979. lib. bdg. 57.50 (0-208-01769-0, Archon Bks) Shoe String.

Mack, Maynard, jt. auth. see Boynton, Robert W.

Mack, Maynard, ed. see Homer.

Mack, Maynard, ed. see Shakespeare, William.

Mack, Michael. Free Indeed: Lessons from Jesus' Miracles. Eichenberger, Jim, ed. (Solid Foundation Bible Studies). 64p. 1999. 9.99 (0-7847-0902-5, 41102) Standard Pub.

Mack, Michael J., jt. auth. see Krasna, Mark J.

*__Mack, Michele.__ The Ten Commitments of Love: A Journal for Life on Planet Earth. LC 98-93707. 176p. 1999. pap. 12.95 (0-9667747-0-1, TCOL1) Coven Light.

Mack, Nancy, ed. Words from the Heart. LC 93-85719. 52p. 1993. pap. 4.95 (0-89821-113-1, 12314) Reiman Pubns.

Mack, Pamela E. From Engineering Science to Big Science: The NACA & NASA Collier Trophy Research Project Winners. (NASA History Ser.). (Illus.). 451p. 1998. boxed set 35.00 (0-16-049640-3) USGPO.

— Viewing the Earth: The Social Construction of the Landsat Satellite System. Bijker, Wiebe E. et al, eds. (Inside Technology Ser.). 280p. 1990. 32.50 (0-262-13259-1) MIT Pr.

*__Mack, Patricia.__ Corn. (Produce Cookbook Ser.). (Illus.). 144p. 1999. 16.75 (0-9654733-8-4, Pub. by Record Bks) Brodart.

Mack, Patricia. The 15 Minute Chef. LC 98-46903. 304p. (Orig.). 1999. pap. 15.95 (1-55788-300-9, HP Books) Berkley Pub.

— Tomatoes. (Produce Cookbook Ser.: Vol. 1). (Illus.). 144p. 1999. 16.75 (0-9654733-7-6, Pub. by Record Bks) Brodart.

Mack, Pauline B. & Urbach, C. Study of Institutional Children with Particular Reference to the Caloric Value As Well As Other Factors of the Dietary. (SRCD M Ser.: Vol. 13, No. 1). 1948. pap. 25.00 (0-527-01543-1) Periodicals Srv.

Mack, Pauline B., et al. Study of Two Levels of Bread Enrichment in Children's Diets. (SRCD M Ser.: Vol. 18, No. 2). 1953. pap. 25.00 (0-527-01558-X) Periodicals Srv.

Mack, Peter. Renaissance Argument: Valla & Agricola in the Traditions of Rhetoric & Dialectic. LC 93-26623. (Brill's Studies in Intellectual History: Vol. 43). xi, 395p. 1993. 134.50 (90-04-09879-8) Brill Academic Pubs.

Mack, Peter & Magwood, Chris. Straw Bale Building: How to Plan, Design & Build with Straw. (Illus.). 256p. 2000. pap. 24.95 (0-86571-403-7) New Soc Pubs.

Mack, Phyllis. Visionary Women: Ecstatic Prophecy in Seventeenth-Century England. 1992. pap. 17.95 (0-520-08937-5, Pub. by U CA Pr) Cal Prin Full Svc.

Mack, Phyllis, jt. ed. see Bartov, Omer.

Mack, R. Dictionary of Veterinary Medicine German-English - English-German. 2nd ed. (ENG & GER.). 823p. 1997. 146.00 (3-8263-3055-2, Pub. by Blckwell Wissenschafts) IBD Ltd.

— Russian-English Veterinary Dictionary. 104p. (Orig.). (C). 1972. 50.00 (0-89771-927-1, Pub. by Collets) St Mut.

— Russian-English Veterinary Dictionary. 104p. (Orig.). 1972. pap. text 35.00 (0-85198-255-7) OUP.

Mack, Raneta Lawson. A Layperson's Guide to Criminal Law. LC 98-53382. 216p. 1999. lib. bdg. 65.00 (0-313-30556-0) Greenwood.

Mack, Raymond W., ed. Changing South. LC 72-91467. 115p. 1970. 34.95 (0-87855-060-7); pap. 19.95 (0-87855-557-9) Transaction Pubs.

Mack, Richard, Jr. Bittersweet: Poems. LC 94-6754. 64p. 1996. 10.95 (0-944957-45-5) Rivercross Pub.

*__Mack, Richard E.__ Memoir of a Cold War Soldier. LC 00-36878. 2001. write for info. (0-87338-675-2) Kent St U Pr.

Mack, Richard I., jt. auth. see Walters, Timothy R.

Mack, Robert, ed. Thomas Gray. (Everyman's Poetry Ser.). 116p. 1997. pap. 1.95 (0-460-87805-0, Everyman's Classic Lib) Tuttle Pubng.

*__Mack, Robert C.__ Repointing Mortar Joints in Historic Masonry Buildings. 16p. 1998. pap. 2.00 (0-16-061691-3) USGPO.

Mack, Robert D. Appeal to Immediate Experience. LC 68-58803. (Essay Index Reprint Ser.). 1977. 17.95 (0-8369-0085-5) Ayer.

*__Mack, Robert L.__ Thomas Gray. (Illus.). 578p. 2000. 39.95 (0-300-08499-4) Yale U Pr.

Mack, Robert L., ed. Arabian Night's Entertainments. (World's Classics Ser.). 976p. 1995. pap. 15.95 (0-19-282832-0) OUP.

Mack, Robert L., ed. Arabian Night's Entertainments. (Oxford World's Classics Ser.). 974p. 2000. pap. 15.95 (0-19-283479-7) OUP.

Mack, Robert L., jt. auth. see Nielsen, Jakob.

Mack, Roy. Dictionary for Veterinary Science & Biosciences. (ENG & GER.). 324p. 1987. pap. 85.00 (0-8288-2385-5, M4375) Fr & Eur.

— Dictionary of Veterinary Medicine & Biosciences, German-English, English-German, 4 Language Index. 2nd ed. (ENG, FRE, GER & LAT.). 824p. 1996. 195.00 (0-7859-9807-1) Fr & Eur.

— Dictionnaire des Termes Veterinaires et Animlaiers: French-English, English-French. (ENG & FRE.). 576p. 1991. 195.00 (0-7859-8134-9, 2863260863) Fr & Eur.

— Veterinary Dictionary: Russian-English. (ENG & RUS.). 104p. 1972. pap. 35.00 (0-8288-6425-X, M-9710) Fr & Eur.

Mack, Roy, ed. Dictionary of Animal Health Terminology. LC 92-9212. (ENG, FRE, GER, LAT & SPA.). 434p. 1992. 178.50 (0-444-88085-2) Elsevier.

Mack, Roy, ed. see Office International des Epizooties Staff.

Mack, Ruth P. Consumption & Business Fluctuations: A Case Study of the Shoe, Leather, Hide Sequence. (Studies in Business Cycles; No. 7). 318p. 1956. reprint ed. 82.70 (0-87014-090-6) Natl Bur Econ Res.

— Controlling Retailers. LC 77-76646. (Columbia University. Studies in the Social Sciences: No. 423). reprint ed. 34.00 (0-404-51423-5) AMS Pr.

— Factors Influencing Consumption: An Experimental Analysis of Shoe Buying. (Technical Papers: No. 10). 132p. 1954. reprint ed. 34.40 (0-87014-416-2) Natl Bur Econ Res.

— Information, Expectations, & Inventory Fluctuation: A Study of Materials Stock on Hand & on Order. (Studies in Business Cycles: No. 16). 320p. 1967. reprint ed. 83.20 (0-87014-478-2) Natl Bur Econ Res.

Mack, Sara. Ovid. LC 87-37157. 180p. (C). 1988. pap. 15.00 (0-300-04295-7) Yale U Pr.

Mack, Scarlett. Good-Bye Diet Demon: You Can Become Sophisticated at Permanent Weight Control! LC 88-50008. 176p. 1989. pap. 14.95 (0-945654-00-6) Aroc Pub.

Mack Smith, Denis. Italy: A Modern History. enl. rev. ed. LC 69-15851. (History of the Modern World Ser.). (Illus.). 584p. 1957. text 29.95 (0-472-07051-7, 07051) U of Mich Pr.

— Mazzini. LC 93-38313. (Illus.). 352p. 1994. 37.50 (0-300-05884-5) Yale U Pr.

Mack-Smith, Denis M. Garibaldi: A Great Life in Brief. LC 82-6271. (Great Lives In Brief Ser.). 214p. 1982. reprint ed. lib. bdg. 55.00 (0-313-23618-6, MSGA, Greenwood Pr) Greenwood.

— Italy & Its Monarchy. (Illus.). 413p. (C). 1992. reprint ed. pap. 22.00 (0-300-05132-8) Yale U Pr.

Mack, Stan, jt. auth. see Bode, Janet.

Mack, Stanely, jt. illus. see Bode, Janet.

Mack, Stanley. Stan Mack's Out-Takes. LC 84-42756. (Illus.). 128p. 1985. pap. 7.95 (0-87951-997-5, Pub. by Overlook Pr) Penguin Putnam.

— Stan Mack's Real Life American Revolution. LC 94-17808. (Illus.). 144p. (Orig.). 1994. pap. 10.00 (0-380-77223-X, Avon Bks) Morrow Avon.

— The Story of the Jews: A 4,000 Year Adventure. (Illus.). 288p. 1999. pap. 14.95 (0-375-75336-2) Villard Books.

Mack, Stanley L. Cartwright: Edward Cartwright of Nantucket, Massachusetts, Some of His Descendants & Their Allied Families. (Illus.). 38p. 1997. reprint ed. pap. 8.00 (0-8328-7876-6); reprint ed. lib. bdg. 18.00 (0-8328-7875-8) Higginson Bk Co.

Mack, Stephen & Platt, Janan. HTML 4.0 - No Experience Required. LC 97-69202. 704p. 1997. pap. text 29.99 (0-7821-2143-8) Sybex.

Mack, Stevie. Gente del Sol. (J). (gr. 3-8). 1991. 129.00 incl. VHS (0-945666-16-0) Crizmac.

Mack, Stevie & Phillips, Lori. Island Worlds: Art & Culture in the Pacific. (J). (gr. 4-12). 1998. 92.95 incl. VHS (0-945666-62-4) Crizmac.

Mack, Stevie, et al. The Days of the Dead: A Curriculum Resource. (J). (gr. 4-12). 1998. ring bd. 42.95 (0-945666-63-2) Crizmac.

Mack, Stevie, jt. auth. see Christine, Deborah.

Mack, Stevie, jt. auth. see Fiore, Jennifer.

Mack, Stevie, ed. see Albany Institute of History & Art Staff.

Mack, Stevie, ed. see Kordich, Diane D.

Mack, Sue. Fertility Counselling. 1996. pap. text 28.00 (0-7020-1977-1, W B Saunders Co) Harcrt Hlth Sci Grp.

Mack, Sue, jt. auth. see Tiran, Denise.

Mack, Sue, jt. ed. see Tiran, Denise.

Mack, Timothy C., jt. ed. see Hunter, Kenneth W.

*__Mack, Tracy.__ Drawing Lessons. LC 99-27254. (Illus.). 176p. (YA). (gr. 7-12). 2000. 15.95 (0-439-11202-8, Scholastic Ref) Scholastic Inc.

*__Mack, Vicki.__ Capture the Moment: Picture Perfect Tips Every Bride Should Know. (Illus.). 132p. 2000. pap. 12.95 (0-9645392-6-8, Pub. by Pinale Pr) Partners Pubs Grp.

Mack, Vicki. The Groom's Guide: Almost Everything a Man Needs to Know. 2nd rev. ed. (Illus.). 118p. 1998. per. 11.95 (0-9645392-2-5) Pinale Pr.

Mack, W., ed. Worldwide Guide to Equivalent Nonferrous Metals & Alloys. 3rd rev. ed. 500p. 1995. 198.00 (0-87170-540-0, 6331) ASM.

Mack, Wayne A. Fortaleciendo el Matrimonio. Orig. Title: Strengthening Your Marriage. (SPA.). 176p. 1992. pap. 7.99 (0-8254-1454-7, Edit Portavoz) Kregel.

— Homework Manual for Biblical Living: Family & Marital Problems, Vol. 2. 1980. pap. 5.99 (0-87552-357-9) P & R Pubng.

— Homework Manual for Biblical Living: Personal & Interpersonal Problems, Vol. 1. 1979. pap. 6.99 (0-87552-356-0) P & R Pubng.

*__Mack, Wayne A.__ Preparando el Matrimonio en el Camino de Dios (Preparing for Marriage God's Way) 163p. 1999. pap. 14.99 (1-56322-066-0) Hensley Pub.

Mack, Wayne A. Preparing for Marriage God's Way. 153p. pap. 12.99 (1-56322-019-9) Hensley Pub.

— The Saga of the Saints: An Illustrated History of the First 25 Seasons. LC 92-13809. 1992. 29.95 (0-930892-18-6) A Hardy & Assocs.

*__Mack, Wayne A.__ Strengthening Your Marriage. 2nd ed. LC 99-13189. 1999. pap. 8.99 (0-87552-385-4) P & R Pubng.

Mack, Wayne A. Your Family, God's Way: Developing & Sustaining Relationships in the Home. 239p. 1991. pap. 8.99 (0-87552-358-7) P & R Pubng.

Mack, Wayne A. & Swavely, David. Life in the Father's House: A Member's Guide to the Local Church. LC 96-20257. 224p. (Orig.). 1996. pap. 9.99 (0-87552-355-2) P & R Pubng.

Mack, William P. Captain Kilburnie: A Novel. LC 99-27386. 1999. 25.95 (1-55750-586-1) Naval Inst Pr.

— Checkfire! LC 92-50363. (Destroyer Ser.). 1992. 22.95 (1-877853-17-8) Nautical & Aviation.

— Lieutenant Christopher. LC 97-43810. 1998. 24.95 (1-877853-53-4) Nautical & Aviation.

*__Mack, William P.__ Lieutenant Christopher: A Novel of the Sea. 316p. 1999. reprint ed. pap. 19.95 (1-877853-57-7) Nautical & Aviation.

Mack, William P. New Guinea. (Destroyer Ser.). 320p. 1993. 22.95 (1-877853-32-1) Nautical & Aviation.

— Normandy. (Destroyer Ser.: Bk. 6). 250p. 1995. 22.95 (1-877853-38-0) Nautical & Aviation.

— Pursuit of the Seawolf. LC 91-22050. (Destroyer Ser.). 419p. 1991. 22.95 (1-877853-12-7) Nautical & Aviation.

— Straits of Messina. LC 94-22931. (Destroyer Ser.). 1994. 22.95 (1-877853-34-8) Nautical & Aviation.

Mack, William P. & Connell, Royal W. Naval Ceremonies, Customs, & Traditions. 5th ed. LC 79-92236. (Illus.). 386p. 1980. 28.95 (0-87021-412-8) Naval Inst Pr.

Mack, William P. & Mack, William P., Jr. South to Java. LC 87-24768. (Destroyer Ser.). 460p. 1987. 22.95 (0-933852-70-3) Nautical & Aviation.

Mack, William P. & Paulsen, Thomas D. The Naval Officer's Guide. 10th ed. LC 90-22820. (Illus.). 528p. 1991. 25.95 (0-87021-296-6) Naval Inst Pr.

Mack, William P., et al. The Naval Officer's Guide. 11th ed. LC 98-29988. (Illus.). 512p. 1998. 27.95 (1-55750-645-0) Naval Inst Pr.

Mack, William P., Jr., jt. auth. see Mack, William P.

Mack, William P., jt. auth. see Stavridis, James.

Mack-Williams, Kibibi. Food & Our History. (African American Life Ser.). 48p. (J). (gr. 4-8). Date not set. lib. bdg. 17.95 (0-86625-033-6) Rourke Pubns.

Mack-Williams, Kibibi V. Food & Our History. LC 95-6590. (African American Life Ser.). 48p. (J). (gr. 4-6). 1995. lib. bdg. 23.93 (1-57103-033-6) Rourke Pr.

— Malcolm X. LC 92-46767. (Pioneers Ser.). 112p. (J). 1993. lib. bdg. 25.27 (0-86625-493-5) Rourke Pubns.

— Mossi. LC 95-20839. (Heritage Library of African Peoples: Set 2). (Illus.). 64p. (YA). (gr. 7-12). 1996. lib. bdg. 16.95 (0-8239-1984-6) Rosen Group.

— People of Faith. LC 95-11444. (African American Life Ser.). (J). (gr. 2-6). 1995. lib. bdg. 23.93 (1-57103-031-X) Rourke Pr.

Mack, Zelb. California Paralegal's Guide, 2 vols. 5th rev. ed. LC 98-67073. 1401p. 1998. ring bd. 145.00 (0-327-00122-4, 80249-11) LEXIS Pub.

Mack, Zella. California Paralegal's Guide, Issue 1. 250p. 1999. ring bd. write for info. (0-327-01355-9, 8025321) LEXIS Pub.

Mack, Zella E. California Estate Administration. LC 95-49736. (Paralegal Ser.). 384p. (C). 1996. mass mkt. 62.95 (0-8273-7305-8) Delmar.

Mack, Zella E. California Paralegal's Guide, 2 vols., 1. 4th ed. 300p. 1993. 35.00 (0-250-47215-5, MICHIE) LEXIS Pub.

— California Paralegal's Guide, 2 vols., 2. 4th ed. 1993. write for info. (0-250-47216-3, MICHIE) LEXIS Pub.

— California Paralegal's Guide, 2 vols., No. 1. 4th ed. 1994. suppl. ed. 41.00 (0-685-66642-5, MICHIE) LEXIS Pub.

Mackaay, Ejan, ed. see Basque, Guy.

Mackaay, Ejan, jt. tr. see Haanappel, Peter P.

Mackail, Denis G. Barrie: The Story of J. M. B. LC 73-37896. (Select Bibliographies Reprint Ser.). 1977. reprint ed. 37.95 (0-8369-6734-8) Ayer.

— How Amusing: And a Lot of Other Fables. LC 76-144160. (Short Story Index Reprint Ser.). 1977. reprint ed. 30.95 (0-8369-3775-9) Ayer.

— Tales from Greenery Street. LC 75-140335. (Short Story Index Reprint Ser.). 1977. 23.95 (0-8369-3727-9) Ayer.

Mackail, J. W. Lectures on Greek Poetry. LC 66-23520. 1910. 28.00 (0-8196-0180-2) Biblo.

MacKail, J. W. The Life of William Morris. 1996. 26.75 (0-8446-6878-8) Peter Smith.

Mackail, J. W. The Life of William Morris. unabridged ed. LC 95-17066. (Illus.). 800p. 1995. reprint ed. pap. text 18.95 (0-486-28793-9) Dover.

MacKail, John W. Approach to Shakespeare. LC 75-109655. (Select Bibliographies Reprint Ser.). 1977. 20.95 (0-8369-5264-2) Ayer.

Mackail, John W. Classical Studies. LC 68-16950. (Essay Index Reprint Ser.). 1977. 19.95 (0-8369-0649-7) Ayer.

— Lectures on Poetry. LC 67-23242. (Essay Index Reprint Ser.). 1977. 22.95 (0-8369-0650-0) Ayer.

— The Life of William Morris, 2 vols., Set. LC 79-118180. (English Biography Ser.: No. 31). 1970. reprint ed. lib. bdg. 150.00 (0-8383-1070-2) M S G Haskell Hse.

— Studies in Humanism. LC 73-84322. (Essay Index Reprint Ser.). 1977. 20.95 (0-8369-1092-3) Ayer.

— Studies of English Poets. LC 68-25604. (Essay Index Reprint Ser.). 1977. reprint ed. 20.95 (0-8369-0651-9) Ayer.

— William Morris & His Circle. LC 79-117585. (English Literature Ser.: No. 33). 1970. reprint ed. lib. bdg. 75.00 (0-8383-1018-4) M S G Haskell Hse.

Mackal, Roy P. A Living Dinosaur? In Search of Mokele-mbembe. unabridged ed. (Illus.). 340p. (YA). (gr. 5 up). 1987. 29.95 (90-04-08543-2) Brill Academic Pubs.

Mackall, Dandi Daley. The Case of the Disappearing Dirt. LC 96-14003. (Cinnamon Lake Mysteries Ser.). (Illus.). 80p. (J). (gr. 1-4). 1996. pap. 4.99 (0-570-04793-5, 56-1813) Concordia.

*__Mackall, Dandi Daley.__ Case of the Missing Memory, Vol. 8. 80p. (J). (gr. 1-5). 1999. pap. text 5.00 (0-570-05558-X) Concordia.

Mackall, Dandi Daley. The Cinnamon Lake-Ness Monster. LC 97-44230. (Cinnamon Lake Mysteries Ser.). 80p. (J). (ps-2). 1998. 4.99 (0-570-05336-6, 12-3384) Concordia.

*__Mackall, Dandi Daley.__ Easter Adventure. (Puzzle Club Mysteries Ser.). (Illus.). 32p. (J). (ps-2). 1998. 7.00 (0-570-05474-5, 56-1937GJ) Concordia.

— Easter Adventure. (Puzzle Club Mysteries Ser.). (Illus.). 80p. (J). (ps-5). 1998. pap. 4.99 (0-570-05479-6, 56-1942GJ) Concordia.

Mackall, Dandi Daley. God Made Me. LC 92-72745. 32p. (J). 1992. pap. 5.99 (0-8066-2633-X, 9-2633) Augsburg Fortress.

*__Mackall, Dandi Daley.__ Horse Cents, 1, 2. (Horsefeathers Ser.: Vol. 2). 191p. (J). (gr. 7-11). 2000. pap. text 5.99 (0-570-07007-4) Concordia.

— Horse of a Different Color. LC 99-50885. (Horsefeathers Ser.: Vol. 4). 192p. (J). (gr. 7-11). 2000. pap. text 5.99 (0-570-07009-0) Concordia.

— Horse Whispers in the Air. LC 99-50884. (Horsefeathers Ser.: Vol. 3). 191p. (J). (gr. 7-11). 2000. pap. text 5.99 (0-570-07008-2) Concordia.

— Horsefeathers, 1. Vol. 1. (Illus.). 189p. (J). (gr. 7-11). 2000. pap. text 5.99 (0-570-07006-6) Concordia.

Mackall, Dandi Daley. Jesus Loves Me. LC 94-71206. (Illus.). 32p. (J). (ps-3). 1994. pap. 5.99 (0-8066-2695-X, 9-2695, Augsburg) Augsburg Fortress.

— Kidnap Kid Mystery. LC 98-147738. (Puzzle Club Mystery Ser.). (gr. 1-5). 1998. pap. text 4.99 (0-570-05051-0, 56-1875) Concordia.

— Kids Are Still Saying the Darndest Things. 224p. 1994. pap. 7.95 (1-55958-575-7) Prima Pub.

— Kids Say the Cutest Things about Love. LC 98-170157. (Kids Say the Cutest Things about . . . Ser.). 1998. 8.99 (1-57757-034-0) Honor Bks OK.

— Kids Say the Greatest Things about God: A Kid's-Eye View of Life's Biggest Subject. 150p. 1995. pap. 6.99 (0-8423-2009-1) Tyndale Hse.

— Kindred Sisters: New Testament Women Speak to Us Today. 160p. 1996. pap. 12.99 (0-8066-2828-6, 9-2828, Augsburg) Augsburg Fortress.

— Meets the Jigsaw Kids, 1, 7. Vol. 7. 80p. (J). (gr. 1-5). 1999. pap. text 4.99 (0-570-05475-3) Concordia.

— Musical Mystery. LC 98-169815. (Puzzle Club Mystery Ser.). 80p. (J). (ps-3). 1998. pap. 4.99 (0-570-05059-6) Concordia.

— Mystery of Great Price. (Puzzle Club Mystery Ser.). 1997. pap. text 4.99 (0-570-05027-8, 56-1851) Concordia.

— Of Spies & Spider Webs. (Cinnamon Lake Mysteries Ser.). (gr. 1-4). 1997. pap. text 4.99 (0-570-04984-9, 12-3334) Concordia.

*__Mackall, Dandi Daley.__ Off to Bethlehem! 24p. (ps-k). 1999. pap. 8.95 (0-694-01505-9) HarpC.

Mackall, Dandi Daley. Poison Pen Mystery. LC 98-147736. (Puzzle Club Mystery Ser.). (gr. 1-5). 1998. pap. text 4.99 (0-570-05052-9, 56-1876) Concordia.

— The Presidential Mystery. LC 98-30769. (Cinnamon Lake Mysteries Ser.). 80p. (J). (gr. 1-4). 1999. pap. 4.99 (0-570-05354-4, 12-3405GJ) Concordia.

— Puzzle Club Activity Book. (Puzzle Club Mystery Ser.). 1997. pap. text 0.99 (0-570-05025-1, 56-1849) Concordia.

— Puzzle Club Picture Book. LC 97-215582. 1997. pap. text 6.99 (0-570-05024-3, 56-1848) Concordia.

— The Secret Society of the Left Hand. LC 96-14503. (Cinnamon Lake Mysteries Ser.: Vol. 1). (Illus.). 80p. (J). (gr. 1-4). 1996. pap. 4.99 (0-570-04792-7, 56-1812) Concordia.

— Soup Kitchen Suspicion. LC 97-30163. (Cinnamon Lake Mysteries Ser.). (Illus.). (J). (gr. 1-4). 1998. 4.99 (0-570-05312-9, 12-3362) Concordia.

An Asterisk (*) at the beginning of an entry indicates that the title is appearing for the first time.

***Mackall, Dandi Daley.** Why I Believe in God: And Other Reflections by Children. LC 99-37229. 1999. 9.95 (*0-7615-1649-2*) Prima Pub.

MacKall, John W. The Life of William Morris, 2 vols., 1 bk. LC 68-57988. 1972. reprint ed. 36.95 (*0-405-08767-5*, Pub. by Blom Pubns) Ayer.

Mackall, Phyllis, ed. see Barkey, Tom.

Mackall, Phyllis, ed. see Crist, Terry M., Jr.

MacKall, Phyllis, ed. see Dalessandro, Gloria.

Mackall, Phyllis, ed. see Gomez, Derrick P.

Mackall, Phyllis, ed. see McCallum, Brian K.

Mackall, Phyllis, ed. see Piper, Mel L.

MacKall, Phyllis, ed. see Renner, Rick.

Mackaman, Douglas P. Leisure Settings: Bourgeois Culture, Medicine & the Spa in Modern France. LC 98-15570. 256p. 1998. pap. text 18.00 (*0-226-50075-6*) U Ch Pr.

***Mackaman, Douglas P.** Leisure Settings: Bourgeois Culture, Medicine & the Spa in Modern France. LC 98-15570. 256p. 1998. lib. bdg. 46.00 (*0-226-50074-8*) U Ch Pr.

***Mackaman, Douglas P. & Mays, Michael, eds.** World War I & the Cultures of Modernity. LC 99-57734. (Illus.). 240p. 2000. text 35.00 (*1-57806-243-8*) U Pr of Miss.

Mackaman, Julie. Filmmaker's Resource: The Watson-Guptill Guide to Workshops, Conferences, Artists' Colonies & Academic Programs. LC 97-14384. (Getting Your Act Together Ser.). (Illus.). 224p. 1997. 19.95 (*0-8230-7653-9*) Watsn-Guptill.

Mackan, Donald, tr. see Sehlin, Gunhild.

Mackavey, Maria G. & Levin, Richard J. Shared Purpose: Working Together to Build Strong Families & Higher Performance Companies. LC 97-33530. 244p. 1997. 24.95 (*0-8144-0388-3*) AMACOM.

Mackay. Computer Exercises: Mac & Microsoft Works. 1992. pap. text. write for info. (*0-582-87647-8*, Pub. by Addison-Wesley) Longman.

MacKay, jt. auth. see Puddey.

Mackay, A. & Texter, John. Electrochemistry in Colloids & Dispersions. 546p. 1992. 175.00 (*0-471-18840-9*) Wiley.

MacKay, A. L. A Dictionary of Scientific Quotations. (Illus.). 312p. 1991. pap. 34.00 (*0-7503-0106-6*) IOP Pub.

Mackay, A. L., jt. auth. see Barrett, A. N.

Mackay, Adrian, jt. auth. see Wilmshurst, John.

Mackay, Agnes E. An Anatomy of Solitude: Towards a New Interpretation of the Sources of Creative Inspiration. 235p. 1982. 35.00 (*0-85335-229-1*, Pub. by Stuart Titles Ltd) St Mut.

— The Universal Self: A Study of Paul Valery. 263p. 1982. 45.00 (*0-85335-235-6*, Pub. by Stuart Titles Ltd) St Mut.

Mackay, Alexander. Western World: Or, Travels in the United States in 1846-47, Vol. 1. LC 68-55900. 1970. reprint ed. lib. bdg. 45.00 (*0-8371-0549-8*, MAWF, Greenwood Pr) Greenwood.

— Western World: Or, Travels in the United States in 1846-47, Vol. 2. LC 68-55900. 1970. reprint ed. lib. bdg. 45.00 (*0-8371-0823-3*, MAWG, Greenwood Pr) Greenwood.

— Western World: Or, Travels in the United States in 1846-47, Vol. 3. LC 68-55900. 1970. reprint ed. lib. bdg. 45.00 (*0-8371-0824-1*, MAWH, Greenwood Pr) Greenwood.

— The Western World: or Travels in the United States in 1846-47, 3 vols. 2nd ed. LC 68-55900. (Illus.). 1970. reprint ed. lib. bdg. 95.00 (*0-8371-2586-3*, MAWE, Greenwood Pr) Greenwood.

MacKay, Alfred F. Arrow's Theorem, the Paradox of Social Choice: A Case Study in the Philosophy of Economics. LC 79-26445. 152p. reprint ed. pap. 47.20 (*0-8357-5754-4*, 205664400078) Bks Demand.

MacKay, Alfred F., ed. see Oberlin Colloquium in Philosophy Staff.

Mackay, Allen. Team up for Excellence. (Illus.). 216p. 1993. pap. text 29.95 (*0-19-558268-3*) OUP.

MacKay, Angus. Brontes: Fact & Fiction. LC 70-148277. reprint ed. 21.50 (*0-404-08886-4*) AMS Pr.

— Society, Economy & Religion in Late Medieval Castile. (Collected Studies: No. CS261). (ENG & SPA., Illus.). 334p. (C). 1987. reprint ed. lib. bdg. 117.95 (*0-86078-209-3*, Pub. by Variorum) Ashgate Pub Co.

Mackay, Angus & Ditchburn, David, eds. Atlas of Medieval Europe. LC 96-257. (Illus.). 240p. (C). 1996. 85.00 (*0-415-01923-0*) Routledge.

— Atlas of Medieval Europe. (Illus.). 288p. (C). 1997. pap. 27.99 (*0-415-12231-7*) Routledge.

MacKay, Angus & MacPherson, Ian R. Love, Religion, & Politics in Fifteenth Century Spain. LC 98-36907. (Medieval Iberian Peninsula Ser.). 1998. 97.25 (*90-04-10810-6*) Brill Academic Pubs.

MacKay, Angus, jt. ed. see Bartlett, Robert.

Mackay, Angus, jt. ed. see Goodman, Anthony.

MacKay, Anne, ed. Wolf Girls at Vassar: Lesbian & Gay Experiences, 1930-1990. 128p. 1992. pap. 10.95 (*0-9631911-0-1*) Ten Percent.

Mackay, B. Pet Owner's Guide to the Yorkshire Terrier. (Pet Owner's Guide Ser.). (Illus.). 80p. 1997. 8.00 (*0-948955-39-2*, Pub. by Ringpr Bks) Seven Hills Bk.

***Mackay, Barry Kent.** Bird Sounds. 2001. pap. 19.95 (*0-8117-2787-4*) Stackpole.

***Mackay, Belinda.** China's Dancer: Cameos of Life in China. 301p. 1999. reprint ed. mass mkt. 9.99 (*1-898938-76-8*, Pub. by Alpha GBR) OM Literature.

Mackay, Brent. The King of Bean. 44p. 1981. pap. 5.50 (*0-919626-16-5*, Pub. by Brick Bks) Genl Dist Srvs.

MacKay, Brian. Hiking, Cycling, & Canoeing in Maryland: A Family Guide. LC 94-36543. (Illus.). 544p. 1995. pap. 18.95 (*0-8018-5035-5*); text 40.00 (*0-8018-5033-9*) Johns Hopkins.

MacKay, Bruce, et al. Tumors of the Lung, Vol. 24. (Illus.). 432p. 1990. text 92.00 (*0-7216-5807-5*, W B Saunders Co) Harcrt Hlth Sci Grp.

MacKay, Carol H. Soliloquy in 19th-Century Fiction. 208p. 1987. 48.00 (*0-389-20710-1*, N8268) B&N Imports.

***MacKay, Carolyn.** A Grammar of Misantla Totonac. LC 99-33235. (Illus.). 459p. 1999. 55.00 (*0-87480-455-8*) U of Utah Pr.

Mackay, Charles. Extraordinary Pop Delusions. 1995. pap. 14.00 (*0-517-88433-X*) Random.

MacKay, Charles. Extraordinary Popular Delusions. 1976. 37.95 (*0-8488-1421-5*) Amereon Ltd.

Mackay, Charles. Extraordinary Popular Delusions & the Madness of Crowds. 1991. lib. bdg. 300.00 (*0-8490-4713-7*) Gordon Pr.

***Mackay, Charles.** Extraordinary Popular Delusions & the Madness of Crowds. 1998. 27.95 (*0-934405-00-X*) Templeton Fnd.

— Extraordinary Popular Delusions & the Madness of Crowds. 750p. 2000. pap. 19.95 (*1-890151-40-8*) Templeton Fnd.

MacKay, Charles. Extraordinary Popular Delusions & the Madness of Crowds. 774p. 1986. reprint ed. lib. bdg. 36.95 (*0-89966-516-0*) Buccaneer Bks.

Mackay, Charles. Poetical Works of Charles Mackay. LC 70-144452. reprint ed. 37.50 (*0-404-08564-4*) AMS Pr.

Mackay, Charles, ed. Medora Leigh: A History & an Autobiography. LC 78-37700. reprint ed. 39.50 (*0-404-56759-2*) AMS Pr.

Mackay, Charles & LeBon, Gustav. Extraordinary Popular Delusions & the Madness of Crowds & The Crowd, A Study of the Popular Mind: Twin Classics of Crowd Psychology, 2 bks. abr. ed. 324p. (Orig.). 1993. reprint ed. pap. 19.95 (*0-934380-23-6*, 551) Traders Pr.

Mackay, Charles W., jt. ed. see Hall, Burton.

MacKay, Claire. The Toronto Story. (Illus.). 112p. (Orig.). (J). (gr. 5 up). 1991. 34.95 (*1-55037-137-1*, Pub. by Annick); pap. 24.95 (*1-55037-135-5*, Pub. by Annick) Firefly Bks Ltd.

Mackay, Claire, ed. Laughs: Funny Stories Selected by Claire Mackay. LC 96-61148. 208p. (J). (gr. 5-9). 1997. pap. 6.95 (*0-88776-393-6*) Tundra Bks.

MacKay, Claire, jt. auth. see Hewitt, Marsha.

Mackay, Constance D. Plays of the Pioneers: A Book of Historical Pageant Plays. LC 76-40389. (One-Act Plays in Reprint Ser.). 1976. reprint ed. 20.00 (*0-8486-2005-4*) Roth Pub Inc.

MacKay, D. B. Seed Technology in Tropics. 1997. pap. 90.00 (*81-7233-162-2*, Pub. by Scientific Pubs) St Mut.

Mackay, D. G. The Organization of Perception & Action. (Cognitive Science Ser.). (Illus.). xxii, 233p. 1987. 60.95 (*0-387-96509-2*) Spr-Verlag.

Mackay, David. The Modern House: Designed by the World's Leading Architects. (Illus.). 160p. 1991. 29.95 (*0-8038-9276-4*) Archit CT.

— A Place of Exile: The European Settlement of New South Wales. 184p. 1986. 29.95 (*0-19-554632-6*) OUP.

Mackay, David N., ed. Trial of James Stewart: The Appin Murder, No. 1. 2nd rev. ed. (Notable British Trials Ser.). xxiv, 390p. 1995. reprint ed. 124.00 (*1-56169-122-4*, 15165) Gaunt.

— Trial of Simon, Lord Lovat of the '45. (Notable British Trials Ser.). lv, 314p. 1995. reprint ed. 112.00 (*1-56169-120-8*) Gaunt.

MacKay, Don. The Handbook of Property Conservation. 300p. 1999. lib. bdg. 69.95 (*0-8493-4108-6*) CRC Pr.

***MacKay, Don.** Handbook of Property Estimation Methods for Chemicals: Enviornmental & Health Sciences. LC 99-58377. 504p. 2000. boxed set 69.95 (*1-56670-456-1*) Lewis Pubs.

— Messerschmitt Bf110. (Illus.). 192p. 2000. 44.95 (*1-86126-313-9*, 130057AE, Pub. by Cro1wood) Motorbooks Intl.

Mackay, Donald. The Asian Dream: Canada's National Railway & the Pacific Trade. (Illus.). 224p. 1986. 25.00 (*0-88894-501-9*, Pub. by DGL) Sterling.

Mackay, Donald. Environmental Fate & Degradation, CRCnetBASE, 1999 1998. 424.95 (*0-8493-9757-X*) CRC Pr.

— Flight from Famine: The Coming of the Irish to Canada. 368p. 1996. pap. text 16.95 (*0-7710-5445-9*) McCland & Stewart.

Mackay, Donald. Illustrated Handbook of Environmental Fate for Organic Chemicals, Vol. 3. 928p. 1993. lib. bdg. 120.00 (*0-87371-973-5*) Lewis Pubs.

— The Malayan Emegency: The Domino That Stood Still. LC 97-25794. (Illus.). 174p. 1997. 29.95 (*1-85753-118-3*, Pub. by Brasseys) Brasseys.

— Multimedia Environmental Models: The Fugacity Approach. 272p. 1991. boxed set 85.00 (*0-87371-242-0*, L242) Lewis Pubs.

Mackay, Donald & Perry, Lorne. Train Country. (Illus.). 192p. 1995. pap. 24.95 (*0-911581-37-5*) Heimburger Hse Pub.

MacKay, Donald, et al. Illustrated Handbook of Environmental Fate for Organic Chemicals, Vol. II. 608p. 1992. lib. bdg. 110.00 (*0-87371-583-7*, L583) Lewis Pubs.

Mackay, Donald, et al. Illustrated Handbook of Physical-Chemical Properties & Environmental Fate for Organic Chemicals Vol. 4: Oxygen, Nitrogen, & Sulfur-Containing Compounds. (Illus.). 976p. 1995. lib. bdg. 110.00 (*1-56670-035-3*, L1035) Lewis Pubs.

— Illustrated Handbook of Physical-Chemical Properties of Environmental Fate for Organic Chemicals: Pesticides, Vol. V. 800p. 1997. lib. bdg. 99.95 (*1-56670-255-0*) CRC Pr.

Mackay, Donald G. Scotland's Rural Land Use Agencies: The History & Effectiveness in Scotland of the Forestry Commission Nature Conservancy Council & Countryside Commission. 240p. 1990. pap. 45.00 (*1-898218-31-5*) St Mut.

MacKay, Donald M. Science & the Quest for Meaning. LC 81-17504. 87p. reprint ed. pap. 30.00 (*0-608-14502-5*, 202533300043) Bks Demand.

MacKay, Douglas. Honourable Company. LC 73-124242. (Select Bibliographies Reprint Ser.). 1977. 25.95 (*0-8369-5430-0*) Ayer.

Mackay, Duncan. Linford Christie. (Illus.). 96p. 1996. 24.95 (*0-297-83530-0*, Pub. by Weidenfeld & Nicolson) Trafalgar.

Mackay, Duncan, jt. auth. see Downes, Steven.

MacKay, E. Anne. Signs of Orality: The Oral Tradition & Its Influence in the Greek & Roman World. LC 98-41718. (Mnemosyne, Bibliotheca Classica Batava Ser.). 1998. 85.50 (*90-04-11273-1*) Brill Academic Pubs.

Mackay, E. J. Chanhu-Daro Excavations, 1935-1936. (American Folklore Society Memoirs Ser.: Vol. 20). 1972. reprint ed. 70.00 (*0-527-02694-8*) Periodicals Srv.

Mackay, Eric V., et al. Illustrated Textbook of Gynaecology. 2nd ed. (Illus.). 605p. 1992. pap. text 69.00 (*0-7295-1211-8*) Bailliere Tindall.

MacKay, Ernest J. The Indus Civilization. LC 77-86434. (Illus.). 240p. 1983. reprint ed. 42.50 (*0-404-16673-3*) AMS Pr.

MacKay, Ernest J., et al. Further Excavations at Mohenjo-Daro: Being an Official Account of Archaeological Excavations at Mohenjo-Daro Carried out by the Government of India Between 1927 & 1931, 2 vols., Set. LC 77-87006. reprint ed. 127.00 (*0-404-16670-9*) AMS Pr.

Mackay, Fergus. International Law. 320p. 1997. 29.99 (*90-6224-969-8*, Pub. by Uitgeverij Arkel) LPC InBook.

***Mackay, Francis.** Asiago: Italy. 2000. pap. 16.95 (*0-85052-759-7*, Pub. by Pen & Sword) Combined Pub.

Mackay, G. A., jt. auth. see Lind, T.

Mackay, G. R., jt. ed. see Bradshaw, J. E.

Mackay, Gilbert F. & Dunn, William R. Early Communicative Skills. 224p. 1989. pap. 16.95 (*0-415-03205-9*) Routledge.

MacKay, Graham, jt. ed. see Sargent, Mike.

Mackay, Harold G. Christian Woman in God's Church & Family. 1988. pap. 4.00 (*0-937396-70-2*) Walterick Pubs.

— Coming of Christ. 1989. 4.00 (*0-937396-79-6*) Walterick Pubs.

MacKay, Harold G. Morning in My Heart. (Illus.). 120p. (Orig.). 1993. pap. 5.95 (*1-882701-04-6*) Uplook Min.

Mackay, Harold G. Story of Your Bible. 1985. pap. 4.00 (*0-937396-65-6*) Walterick Pubs.

— The Study of Your Bible. 1988. pap. 4.00 (*0-937396-68-0*) Walterick Pubs.

Mackay, Harvey. Beware the Naked Man Who. LC 89-28354. 324p. 1990. 19.95 (*0-688-09229-2*, Wm Morrow) Morrow Avon.

— Beware the Naked Man Who Offers You His Shirt: Do What You Love, Love What You Do, & Deliver More Than You Promise. LC HF5381.M197. 1996. pap. 12.95 (*0-449-91184-5*) Fawcett.

— Beware the Naked Man Who Offers You His Shirt: Do What You Love, Love What You Do, & Deliver More Than You Promise. LC HF5381.M197. 416p. 1991. mass mkt. 5.95 (*0-8041-0583-9*) Ivy Books.

— Dig Your Well Before You're Thirsty: The Only Networking Book You'll Ever Need. LC HD69.S8M25. 336p. 1999. pap. 14.95 (*0-385-48546-8*) Doubleday.

— The Harvey Mackay Rolodex Network Builder. 62p. 1993. pap. 8.95 (*0-9637967-0-4*) MacKay Envelope.

— Pushing the Envelope: All the Way to the Top. LC 98-45526. 418p. 1999. 24.95 (*0-345-43295-9*) Ballantine Pub Grp.

***Mackay, Harvey.** Pushing the Envelope: All the Way to the Top. 368p. 2000. pap. 16.00 (*0-449-00669-7*, Ballantine) Ballantine Pub Grp.

Mackay, Harvey. Pushing the Envelope: What I've Learned in 40 Years of Business. 1999. 24.95 (*0-449-00445-7*) Fawcett.

— Sharkproof: Get the Job You Want, Keep the Job You Love...in Today's Frenzied Job Market. LC 92-53494. 288p. 1993. 22.00 (*0-88730-619-5*, HarpBusn) HarpInfo.

— Swim W Sharks Without. LC 87-24757. 224p. 1988. 20.00 (*0-688-07473-1*, Wm Morrow) Morrow Avon.

— Swim with the Sharks. 1996. pap. 12.95 (*0-449-91148-9*) Fawcett.

— Swim with the Sharks Without Being Eaten Alive: Outsell, Outmanage, Outmotivate, & Outnegotiate Your Competition. 352p. 1989. mass mkt. 6.99 (*0-8041-0426-3*) Ivy Books.

Mackay, Harvey, jt. auth. see Hartman, John W.

Mackay, Helen G. Chill Hours. LC 77-178446. (Short Story Index Reprint Ser.). 1977. reprint ed. 19.95 (*0-8369-4047-4*) Ayer.

Mackay, Henry F. Followers in the Way. LC 71-93359. (Essay Index Reprint Ser.). 1977. 19.95 (*0-8369-1304-3*) Ayer.

MacKay, Hugh. Memoirs of the War Carried on in Scotland & Ireland. LC 70-172707. (Maitland Club, Glasgow. Publications: No. 22). reprint ed. 37.50 (*0-404-52755-8*) AMS Pr.

Mackay, Hugh, ed. Consumption & Everyday Life. LC 97-65515. (Culture, Media & Identities Ser.). 368p. 1997. 75.00 (*0-7619-5437-6*); pap. 23.95 (*0-7619-5438-4*) Sage.

Mackay, Hughie & Beynon, John, eds. Understanding Technology in Education. 272p. 1991. 75.00 (*1-85000-887-6*, Falmer Pr); pap. 29.95 (*1-85000-888-4*, Falmer Pr) Taylor & Francis.

Mackay, Hughie, jt. auth. see Beynon, John.

Mackay, I. R., ed. Multidisciplinary Gerontology: A Structure for Research in Gerontology in a Developed Country. (Interdisciplinary Topics in Gerontology Ser.: Vol. 11). (Illus.). 1977. 53.25 (*3-8055-2679-2*) S Karger.

Mackay, Ian. Appraisal Discussion. (C). 1992. pap. 18.00 (*0-85171-099-9*, Pub. by IPM Hse) St Mut.

***MacKay, Ian.** Asking Questions. 96p. 2000. pap. 17.95 (*0-8464-5003-8*) Beekman Pubs.

Mackay, Ian. Choosing Staff: A Guide to Better Selection Interviewing. 72p. (C). 1991. pap. 21.00 (*0-85171-092-1*, Pub. by IPM Hse) St Mut.

— Expecting Answers? An Introduction to the Skills of Questioning & Listening. (C). 1989. pap. 30.00 (*0-7855-2656-0*, Pub. by IPM Hse) St Mut.

MacKay, Ian. 40 Checklists for Managers & Team Leaders. 221p. 1997. pap. 34.95 (*0-566-07984-4*, Pub. by Gower) Ashgate Pub Co.

Mackay, Ian. A Guide to Asking Questions. (C). 1980. pap. 18.00 (*0-85171-075-1*, Pub. by IPM Hse) St Mut.

— A Guide to Listening. (C). 1984. pap. 40.00 (*0-85171-080-8*, Pub. by IPM Hse) St Mut.

— A Guide to Managing Time. (C). 1990. pap. 60.00 (*0-85171-090-5*, Pub. by IPM Hse) St Mut.

— Handbook of Training Activities Interpersonal Skills. 253p. (C). 1992. ring bd. 300.00 (*0-85171-100-6*, Pub. by IPM Hse) St Mut.

***MacKay, Ian.** Listening Skills. 80p. 2000. pap. 17.95 (*0-8464-5105-0*) Beekman Pubs.

MacKay, Ian. Thirty-Five Checklists for Human Resource Development. (Illus.). 179p. 1989. text 86.95 (*0-566-02823-9*, Pub. by Gower) Ashgate Pub Co.

MacKay, Ian R., jt. ed. see Rose, Noel R.

Mackay, J. Collecting Local History. Date not set. pap. text. write for info. (*0-582-40613-7*, Pub. by Addison-Wesley) Longman.

MacKay, J. G. Sgeulachd a Choire. Date not set. 21.95 (*0-9516022-8-4*, Pub. by Maclean Pr) Dufour.

Mackay, J. L. Haggai, Zechariah & Malachi. (Focus on the Bible Commentary Ser.). 13.50 (*1-85792-067-8*, Pub. by Christian Focus) Spring Arbor Dist.

— Jonah, Micah & Nahum. (Focus on the Bible Commentary Ser.). 11.99 (*1-85792-030-9*, Pub. by Christian Focus) Spring Arbor Dist.

Mackay, James. Allan Pinkerton: The First Private Eye. LC 97-21271. (Illus.). 256p. 1997. 27.95 (*0-471-19415-8*) Wiley.

MacKay, James. Beginner's Guide to Coin Collecting. 96p. 9.99 (*1-57215-247-8*, JG2478) World Pubns.

***Mackay, James.** Clans & Tartans of Scotland. (Illus.). 128p. 2000. 12.99 (*0-517-16240-7*) Random Hse Value.

Mackay, James. The Dictionary of Sculptors in Bronze. LC 96-175047. 414p. 1992. reprint ed. 69.50 (*1-85149-110-4*) Antique Collect.

— The Guinness Book of Stamps: Facts & Feats. 224p. 1992. 19.95 (*1-55859-432-9*) Abbeville Pr.

— I Have Not Yet Begun to Fight: A Life of John Paul Jones. LC 99-25542. 320p. 1999. 30.00 (*0-87113-756-9*, Atlntc Mnthly) Grove-Atltic.

— Michael Collins: A Life. (Illus.). 320p. 1997. pap. 19.95 (*1-85158-949-X*, Pub. by Mainstream Pubng) Trafalgar.

— Vagabond of Verse: A Biography of Robert Service. (Illus.). 432p. 1996. pap. 22.95 (*1-85158-849-3*, Pub. by Mainstream Pubng) Trafalgar.

MacKay, James. William Wallace: Brave Heart. LC 96-139812. 288p. 1996. pap. 16.95 (*1-85158-823-X*, Pub. by Mainstream Pubng) Trafalgar.

MacKay, James & Godwin, James Gowing. Betrayal in High Places. LC 97-151069. xii, 271 p. 1996. write for info. (*1-897666-41-1*) Lane Pubs.

Mackay, James & HMSO Staff. The Land O'Burns: A Guide to the Burns Country. (Illus.). 52p. 1996. pap. text 18.00 (*0-11-495766-5*, Pub. by Statnry Office) Balogh.

Mackay, James A. British Stamps. 1985. pap. text. write for info. (*0-582-40620-X*, Pub. by Addison-Wesley) Longman.

— Burnsiana. (C). 1988. 150.00 (*0-907526-35-7*, Pub. by Alloway Pub) St Mut.

***MacKay, James A.** In My End Is My Beginning: A Life of Mary Queen of Scots. 2000. text 25.95 (*0-312-25249-8*) St Martin.

MacKay, James A. Kilmarnock. 204p. (C). 1989. text 75.00 (*0-907526-52-7*, Pub. by Alloway Pub) St Mut.

Mackay, James A., ed. The Complete Poetical Works of Robert Burns. 640p. 1993. 45.00 (*0-907526-64-0*, Pub. by Alloway Pub) St Mut.

— The Complete Poetical Works of Robert Burns. deluxe ed. 640p. 1993. boxed set 75.00 (*0-907526-62-4*, Pub. by Alloway Pub) St Mut.

Mackay, James A., jt. auth. see Kytle, Calvin.

Mackay, John. Hibernian: The Complete Story. 250p. (C). 1989. text 30.00 (*0-85976-321-8*, Pub. by J Donald) St Mut.

— Hibernian: The Easter Road Story. 230p. 1996. pap. 26.00 (*0-85976-426-5*, Pub. by J Donald) St Mut.

— Life of Lieutenant-General Hugh Mackay. LC 74-172708. (Bannatyne Club, Edinburgh. Publications: No. 53). reprint ed. 27.50 (*0-404-52763-9*) AMS Pr.

— New Jersey Business Corporations, 1996, 2 vols. 2nd ed. LC 96-79308. 1996. text 160.00 (*1-55834-435-7*, 83000-11, MICHIE) LEXIS Pub.

Mackay, John, jt. auth. see Erickson, Robert.

MacKay, John H. The Anarchists. LC 77-185840. 1972. reprint ed. lib. bdg. 300.00 (*0-87700-059-X*) Revisionist Pr.

***Mackay, John Henry.** The Anarchists. 201p. 1999. pap. 12.00 (*1-57027-066-X*, Pub. by Autonomedia) SPD-Small Pr Dist.

***Mackay, John L.** Jonah, Micah, Nahum, Habakkuk & Zephaniah. (Focus on the Bible Commentary Ser.). 1999. pap. 14.99 (*1-85792-392-8*) Christian Focus.

MacKay, John R., II. New Jersey Business Corporations, 1998 Cumulative Supplement, 2 vols. 2nd ed. Incl. Vol. 1. New Jersey Business Corporations: 1998 Cumulative Supplement. 2nd ed. 50p. 1998. 160.00 (*0-327-00620-X*, 8299611); Vol. 2. New Jersey Business Corporations: 1998 Cumulative Supplement. 2nd ed. 50p. 1998. (*0-327-00621-8*, 8299711); 50p. 1998. 45.00 (*0-327-00576-9*, 8299511) LEXIS Pub.

M

Mackay, Joy. Raindrops Keep Falling on My Tent. 20p. 1981. pap. 4.95 (*0-87603-060-6*) Am Camping.

***MacKay, Judith.** Penguin Atlas of Human Sexual Behavior. 2000. pap. 18.95 (*0-14-051479-1*) Viking Penguin.

MacKay, Judith, et al. The State of Health Atlas. LC 92-27298. 128p. 1993. pap. 16.00 (*0-671-79375-6*, Touchstone) S&S Trade Pap.

MacKay, Judy F. Tales of a Nuf in the Land of Doon. (Illus.). 84p. (Orig.). (J). (gr. 4-7). 1992. per. 9.95 (*1-882748-00-X*) MacKay-Langley.

MacKay, June, tr. see Jackins, Harvey.

MacKay, Karen. Dear Sisters: Break Free from Domestic Violence. (Illus.). 160p. 1997. pap. 14.95 (*0-9654553-1-9*) Hilton Pub.

Mackay, Kris. The Ultimate Love. 1994. 10.95 (*0-88494-926-5*) Bookcraft Inc.

Mackay, Kris, jt. auth. see Jones, Barbara B.

Mackay, Lesley. Conflicts in Care: Medicine & Nursing. LC 92-49096. 1993. 44.75 (*1-56593-120-3*, 0423) Singular Publishing.

MacKay, Lesley. Nursing a Problem. 1989. 110.00 (*0-335-09902-5*); pap. 32.95 (*0-335-09901-7*) OpUniv Pr.

Mackay, Lesley & Torrington, Derek. The Changing Nature of Personnel Management. 160p. (C). 1986. 120.00 (*0-85292-377-5*) St Mut.

M

Mackay, Lesley, et al. Classic Texts: Health, the Professionals & the NHS. LC 98-15950. 352p. 1998. pap. text 35.00 (*0-7506-2738-7*) Buttrwrth-Heinemann.

MacKay, Linda G., jt. auth. see Fisher, Elizabeth.

Mackay, Louis, tr. see Brantenberg, Gerd.

MacKay, Louise L. & Ralston, Elizabeth W. Creating Better Schools: What Authentic Principals Do. LC 98-19762. (Principals Taking Action (PTA) Ser.). (Illus.). 144p. 1998. pap. 21.95 (*0-8039-6602-4*, 81270) Corwin Pr.

Mackay, Louise Layne & Ralston, Elizabeth Welch. Creating Better Schools: What Authentic Principals Do. LC 98-19762. (Principals Taking Action (PTA) Ser.). (Illus.). 144p. 1998. 49.95 (*0-8039-6601-6*, 81269) Corwin Pr.

***MacKay-Lyons, Brian.** Brian MacKay-Lyons: Selected Projects 1986-1997. (Illus.). 120p. 1998. pap. 24.50 (*0-929112-39-3*) Baker & Taylor.

Mackay, M. Burns Lore of Dumfries & Galloway. (C). 1988. 75.00 (*0-907526-36-5*, Pub. by Alloway Pub) St Mut.

— The Complete Letters of Robert Burns: Souvenir Edition. (C). 1988. 160.00 (*0-907526-32-2*, Pub. by Alloway Pub) St Mut.

— Complete Works & Letters of Burns, 2 vols., Set. (C). 1988. 290.00 (*0-907526-33-0*, Pub. by Alloway Pub) St Mut.

— The Complete Works of Robert Burns: Presentation Edition. (C). 1988. 350.00 (*0-907526-29-2*, Pub. by Alloway Pub) St Mut.

— The Complete Works of Robert Burns: Souvenir Edition. (C). 1988. 110.00 (*0-907526-23-3*, Pub. by Alloway Pub) St Mut.

Mackay, Mac, jt. auth. see Corsan, John.

Mackay, Marguerite, ed. see Benjamin, Linda W.

Mackay, Marguerite, ed. see Hill, Roger.

MacKay, Marguerite, ed. see Sage, Jewel R.

MacKay, Mary. The Strange Visitation of Josiah McNason: A Christmas Ghost Story. Reginald, R. & Menville, Douglas A., eds. LC 75-46262. 1976. reprint ed. lib. bdg. 17.95 (*0-405-08120-0*) Ayer.

Mackay, Mary Alice, ed. see Groft, Tammis Kane, et al.

Mackay, Nancy & Pisano, Vivian M. Swim Bay Area: A Guide to Swimming Pools in the San Francisco Bay Area. (Illus.). 192p. (Orig.). 1988. pap. 8.95 (*0-943937-00-0*) Swimming Across West.

Mackay, Niall. By Steam Boat & Steam Train. (Illus.). 80p. 1994. pap. 14.95 (*0-919822-73-8*, Pub. by Boston Mills) Genl Dist Srvs.

MacKay, Niall. Over the Hills to Georgian Bay: The Ottawa, Arnprior & Parry Sound Railway. LC 97-154681. (Illus.). 136p. 1995. pap. text 15.95 (*0-919783-06-6*, Pub. by Boston Mills) Genl Dist Srvs.

Mackay, Nicci. Spoken in Whispers: The Autobiography of a Horse Whisperer. LC 98-27673. 327 p. 1999. write for info. (*0-7540-3484-4*) Chivers N Amer.

— Spoken in Whispers: The Autobiography of a Horse Whisperer. LC 98-15037. 192p. 1998. pap. 11.00 (*0-684-85298-5*, Fireside) S&S Trade Pap.

— Spoken in Whispers: The Autobiography of a Horse Whisperer. large type ed. LC 98-27673. 370p. 1999. 30.00 (*0-7862-1601-8*) Thorndike Pr.

Mackay, Nigel. Motivation & Explanation: An Essay on Freud's Philosophy of Science. (Psychological Issues Monographs: No. 56). 260p. 1989. 37.50 (*0-8236-3474-4*) Intl Univs Pr.

Mackay, Noel. Go For the Gold in Real Estate Sales & Exchanges: A Mental & Physical Approach to Excellence in Real Estate Performance. 100p. (Orig.). 1986. pap. 13.95 (*0-9616070-0-9*) Mountain Pr CA.

MacKay, P. Computers Arabic Language. 1990. 160.00 (*0-89116-563-0*) Hemisp Pub.

Mackay, Pierre A., jt. auth. see Angiolello, Giovan M.

Mackay, R. D. Mental Condition Defences in the Criminal Law. (Oxford Monographs on Criminal Law & Justice). (Illus.). 280p. 1996. text 62.00 (*0-19-825995-6*) OUP.

MacKay, R. S. Renormalization in Area-Preserving Maps. (Advanced Series in Nonlinear Dynamics). 324p. 1993. text 61.00 (*981-02-1371-9*) World Scientific Pub.

Mackay, R. S. & Meiss, J. D. Hamiltonian Dynamical Systems: A Reprint Selection. (Illus.). 800p. 1987. 229.00 (*0-85274-205-3*); pap. 82.00 (*0-85274-216-9*) IOP Pub.

Mackay, R. W. Federal Europe: Being the Case for European Federation Together with a Draft Constitution of a United States of Europe. 323p. 1995. reprint ed. 96.00 (*1-56169-462-2*) Gaunt.

Mackay, Raymond A. & Texter, John, eds. Electrochemistry in Colloids & Dispersions. LC 92-11403. 546p. 1992. 115.00 (*1-56081-573-6*, Wiley-VCH) Wiley.

Mackay, Robert. Letters of Robert MacKay to His Wife. (American Autobiography Ser.). 325p. 1995. reprint ed. lib. bdg. 89.00 (*0-7812-8584-4*) Rprt Serv.

— Test of War: Inside Britain from 1939-1945. 1998. pap. 24.95 (*1-85728-635-9*) UCL Pr Ltd.

Mackay, Robert, jt. auth. see Thompson, Moira.

Mackay, Robert A., ed. Newfoundland: Economic, Diplomatic & Strategic Studies. LC 76-46180. reprint ed. 49.50 (*0-404-15366-6*) AMS Pr.

MacKay-Robinson, Christina. Edd the Astronaut. (Illus.). 32p. (J). (gr. k-3). 1992. pap. 3.95 (*0-563-36062-3*, BBC-Parkwest) Parkwest Pubns.

— Edd's Ghost Story. (Illus.). 32p. (J). (gr. k-3). 1992. pap. 3.95 (*0-563-36063-1*, BBC-Parkwest) Parkwest Pubns.

MacKay-Robinson, Christina & Faulkner, Keith. Edd the Duck in Storyland. (Illus.). 32p. (J). (gr. k-3). 1992. 12.95 (*0-563-36046-1*, BBC-Parkwest) Parkwest Pubns.

Mackay, Roderick & Reynolds, William. Algonquin. (Illus.). 119p. 32.00 (*1-55046-088-9*, Pub. by Boston Mills) Genl Dist Srvs.

MacKay, Roderick & Reynolds, William. Algonquin. 2nd ed. 119p. 1995. 40.00 (*1-55046-143-5*) Boston Mills.

***MacKay, Ron.** BF110G Walk Around. (Walk Around Ser.: VOl. 24). (Illus.). 80p. 2000. pap. 14.95 (*0-89747-420-1*, 5524) Squad Sig Pubns.

MacKay, Ron. Hurricane Walk Around. (Walk Around Ser.: Vol. 14). (Illus.). 80p. 1998. pap. 14.95 (*0-89747-388-4*, 5514) Squad Sig Pubns.

Mackay, Ron. Mosquito Walk Around. LC 99-189609. (Walk Around Ser.: Vol. 15). (Illus.). 80p. 1998. pap. 14.95 (*0-89747-396-5*, 5515) Squad Sig Pubns.

***MacKay, Ron.** Ridgewell's Flying Fortresses, 381st Bombardment Group (h) in WWII. (Illus.). 256p. 2000. 59.95 (*0-7643-1063-1*) Schiffer.

MacKay, Ron. 381st Bomb Group. LC 94-168212. (Fighter Groups - Squadrons Ser.). (Illus.). 64p. 1994. pap. 10.95 (*0-89747-314-0*) Squad Sig Pubns.

— 20th Fighter Group. (Illus.). 80p. (Orig.). 1996. pap. 12.95 (*0-89747-368-X*, 6176) Squad Sig Pubns.

Mackay, Ronald & Mountford, A. J., eds. English for Specific Purposes: A Case Study Approach. LC 78-319777. (Applied Linguistics & Language Studies). 239p. reprint ed. pap. 74.10 (*0-608-30141-8*, 202098800020) Bks Demand.

Mackay, Ronald W. Towards a United States of Europe. LC 75-31435. 160p. 1976. reprint ed. lib. bdg. 65.00 (*0-8371-8509-2*, MATU, Greenwood Pr) Greenwood.

MacKay, Ruth. The Limits of Royal Authority: Resistance & Obedience in Seventeenth-Century Castile. LC 98-38428. (Cambridge Studies in Early Modern History). (Illus.). 200p. (C). 1999. text 59.95 (*0-521-64343-0*) Cambridge U Pr.

MacKay, Ruth, et al, eds. Empathy in the Helping Relationship. LC 89-11408. 208p. 1989. 29.95 (*0-8261-6140-5*) Springer Pub.

Mackay, S. E., jt. auth. see Trzeciak, John.

Mackay, Scott. Night City Stories. (Cyberpunk Ser.). 144p. 1992. pap. 15.00 (*1-887801-34-0*, Atlas Games) Trident MN.

— Outpost. LC 97-36367. 352p. 1998. text 24.95 (*0-312-86467-1*) St Martin.

***Mackay, Scott.** Outpost. 352p. 1999. pap. 14.95 (*0-312-86842-1*, Pub. by Tor Bks) St Martin.

Mackay, Sheila. Bridge Across the Century. (C). 1989. 45.00 (*0-948473-00-2*) St Mut.

— Faces of Leith. (Illus.). (C). 1989. 30.00 (*0-948473-01-0*) St Mut.

— The Forth Bridge: A Picture History. (Illus.). 112p. (C). 1989. 140.00 (*0-948473-13-4*) St Mut.

Mackay, Shena. An Advent Calendar. LC 97-10023. 160p. 1997. 19.95 (*1-55921-211-X*) Moyer Bell.

— The Artist's Widow. LC 98-41720. 176p. 1999. 21.95 (*1-55921-229-2*) Moyer Bell.

***Mackay, Shena.** The Artist's Widow. large type unabridged ed. 2000. 25.95 (*0-7531-6025-0*, 160250, Pub. by ISIS Lrg Prnt) ISIS Pub.

Mackay, Shena. Dreams of Dead Women's Handbags: Collected Stories. LC 97-18477. 1997. 14.00 (*0-15-600533-6*, Harvest Bks) Harcourt.

— Dreams of Dead Women's Handbags: Collected Stories. LC 94-15578. 480p. 1994. 24.95 (*1-55921-121-0*) Moyer Bell.

— The Orchard Fire. LC 97-18478. 1997. pap. 12.00 (*0-15-600532-8*, Harvest Bks) Harcourt.

— The Orchard on Fire. LC 96-8420. 215p. 1996. 19.95 (*1-55921-175-X*) Moyer Bell.

***Mackay, Shena.** The World's Smallest Unicorn. LC 99-87267. 223p. 2000. 22.95 (*1-55921-247-0*) Moyer Bell.

Mackay-Smith, Alexander. American Foxhunting Stories. Fine, Norman M., ed. 257p. 1996. 75.00 (*0-9645282-1-5*) Millwood Hse.

***Mackay-Smith, Alexander.** Speed & the Thoroughbred: How the Racehorse Got Its Speed. (Illus.). 221p. 2000. 50.00 (*1-58667-040-9*, Pub. by Derrydale Pr) Natl Bk Netwk.

***Mackay, Stephen.** The Fairies' Ring: A Book of Fairy Stories & Poems. LC 99-32230. 96p. 1999. 24.99 (*0-525-46045-4*, Dutton Child) Peng Put Young Read.

MacKay, Susan, et al. Burning Wood & Coal. LC 85-25966. (Illus.). 90p. 1985. pap. text 5.00 (*0-935817-00-X*, 23) NRAES.

MacKay, Susan E. Field Glossary of Agricultural Terms in French & English. Drenkhahn, Betty Jo, ed. LC 84-82622. (International Programs in Agriculture Ser.). 197p. (Orig.). 1985. pap. text 4.00 (*0-9614109-0-6*) Intl Prog Agricult.

Mackay, T. F., jt. ed. see Hill, W. G.

Mackay, Thomas, ed. A Plea for Liberty. LC 81-80950. 565p. 1982. reprint ed. 20.00 (*0-913966-95-9*); reprint ed. pap. 7.00 (*0-913966-96-7*) Liberty Fund.

MacKay, Virginia. Northern Delights. (Illus.). 108p. 1994. pap. text 8.00 (*1-885781-00-8*) Soapstone Pr.

Mackay, Virginia. Rainy Days Are for Pulling Weeds. (Illus.). 176p. 1996. pap. 10.00 (*1-885781-01-6*) Soapstone Pr.

Mackay, W. P. Grace & Truth: Under Twelve Different Aspects. Austin, Bobby W., ed. 288p. 1995. pap. write for info. (*0-9639640-4-6*) Grace Vision.

— La Gracia y la Verdad. Austin, Bobby W., ed. Arancibia, Rene, tr. from ENG. 288p. 1995. pap. write for info. (*0-9639640-5-4*) Grace Vision.

MacKay, William M. & Conte, Mario. An Introduction to the Physics of Particle Accelerators. 250p. (C). 1994. text 74.00 (*981-02-0812-X*) World Scientific Pub.

MacKay, William M. & Conte, Mario. An Introduction to the Physics of Particle Accelerators. 250p. (C). 1994. pap. text 36.00 (*981-02-0813-8*) World Scientific Pub.

MacKaye, Arvia. The Battle for the Sunlight. 2nd ed. 62p. 1983. reprint ed. pap. 6.50 (*0-932776-07-8*) Adonis Pr.

MacKaye, Arvia, tr. see Steffen, Albert.

MacKaye, Benton. The New Exploration: A Philosophy of Regional Planning. 3rd ed. 284p. 1991. reprint ed. pap. 8.95 (*0-917953-43-6*) Appalachian Trail.

MacKaye Ege, Arvia. A Biography of Percy & Marion MacKaye. (Illus.). 730p. 1991. write for info. (*0-318-66785-1*) Kennebec River.

MacKaye, Maria E. The Abbess of Port Royal, & Other French Studies. 1977. 12.95 (*0-8369-7228-7*, 8027) Ayer.

MacKaye, Percy. Epoch: The Life of Steele MacKaye Genius of the Theatre, in Relation to His Time & Contemporaries, a Memoir, 2 vols., Set. LC 27-25140. reprint ed. 69.00 (*0-403-00077-7*) Scholarly.

— Epoch: The Life of Steele MacKaye, Genius of the Theatre, in Relation to His Times & Contemporaries, a Memoir, 2 vols., Set. (BCL1-PS American Literature Ser.). 1992. reprint ed. lib. bdg. 150.00 (*0-7812-6790-0*) Rprt Serv.

MacKaye, Percy & Torrence, Ridgely. Miami Poets: Percy MacKaye & Ridgely Torrence. Pratt, William, ed. (Keepsakes Ser.). (Illus.). 74p. (Orig.). 1988. pap. text. write for info. (*0-918761-02-6*) Miami U Pubns.

MacKaye, Percy, tr. see Steffen, Albert.

Mackaye, W., jt. auth. see Lutwiniak, W.

Mackaye, William R. Washington Post: Crossword, Vol. 7. 1996. pap. 9.00 (*0-8129-3024-X*, Times Bks) Crown Pub Group.

— The Washington Post Sunday Crossword Puzzles, Vol. 4. 64p. 1994. pap. 9.00 (*0-8129-2396-0*, Times Bks) Crown Pub Group.

MacKaye, William R. Washington Post Sunday Crossword Puzzles, Vol. 8. 1999. pap. 9.50 (*0-8129-3039-8*, Times Bks) Crown Pub Group.

MacKaye, William R., ed. The Washington Post Sunday Crossword Puzzles, Vol. 5. Vol. 5. 64p. 1996. pap. 9.00 (*0-8129-2648-X*, Times Bks) Crown Pub Group.

Mackaye, William R., jt. ed. see Lutwiniak, William.

MacKeand, J. Crawford. Sparks & Flames: Ignition in Engines: An Historical Approach. LC 97-90492. (Illus.). viii, 168p. 1997. pap. 14.95 (*0-9659066-4-7*, T 003) Tyndar Pr.

Mackechnie, John, compiled by. Catalogue of Gaelic Manuscripts in Selected Libraries in Great Britain & Ireland, 2 vols, Set. 1973. 265.00 (*0-8161-0832-3*, G K Hall & Co) Mac Lib Ref.

Mackee, Barbara G. 72 Crafty Scrollsaw Patterns. LC 99-62072. (Illus.). 128p. 1999. pap. 14.95 (*0-7643-0840-8*) Schiffer.

MacKeen, Leslie A. Who Can Fix It? Thatch, Nancy R., ed. LC 89-31819. (Books for Students by Students). (Illus.). 26p. (J). (gr. 4-7). 1989. lib. bdg. 15.95 (*0-933849-19-2*) Landmark Edns.

MacKeever, Frank C. Native & Naturalized Plants of Nantucket. Ahles, Harry E., ed. LC 68-19673. 160p. 1968. 22.50 (*0-87023-037-9*) U of Mass Pr.

Mackeever, Samuel A., ed. see Sutton, Charles.

MacKeigan, John M. & Cataldo, Peter A., eds. Intestinal Stomas: Principles, Techniques, & Management. LC 93-7281. (Illus.). 484p. 1993. 85.00 (*0-942219-40-6*) Quality Med Pub.

MacKeigan, John M. & Hillary, Kathleen M. Colon & Rectal Cancer. Grin, Oliver D. & Bouwman, Dorothy L., eds. (Patient Education Ser.). (Illus.). 30p. 1990. pap. text 4.00 (*0-929689-44-5*) Ludann Co.

— Rectal Bleeding & Colon Polyps. Grin, Oliver D. & Bouwman, Dorothy L., eds. (Patient Education Ser.). (Illus.). 26p. 1990. pap. text 4.00 (*0-929689-43-7*) Ludann Co.

Mackel, Kathy. Alien in a Bottle. 160p. 14.89 (*0-06-029282-2*) HarpC.

Mackel, Kathy. Can of Worms. LC 98-53346. 160p. (J). (gr. 3-7). 1999. 15.00 (*0-380-97681-1*, Wm Morrow) Morrow Avon.

***Mackel, Kathy.** Can of Worms. (Illus.). 160p. (J). (gr. 3-7). 2000. mass mkt. 3.99 (*0-380-80050-0*, Avon Bks) Morrow Avon.

— Can of Worms. (Illus.). (J). 2000. 9.34 (*0-606-17962-3*) Turtleback.

— Eggs in One Basket. 144p. (J). 2000. 14.95 (*0-380-97847-4*) Morrow Avon.

— Eggs in one Basket. 144p. (J). 2000. 14.89 (*0-06-029213-X*) Morrow Avon.

Mackel, Kathy. A Season of Comebacks. LC 96-6882. 112p. (J). (gr. 3-7). 1997. 15.95 (*0-399-23026-2*, G P Putnam) Peng Put Young Read.

— A Season of Comebacks. 126p. (J). (gr. 4-6). 1998. pap. 4.99 (*0-698-11637-2*, PapStar) Peng Put Young Read.

— A Season of Comebacks. (J). 1998. 10.09 (*0-606-13767-X*, Pub. by Turtleback) Demco.

Mackell, Phyllis, ed. see Penn-Brown, Adelle.

Mackellar, Colin. Racing Hondas. (Illus.). 200p. 1998. 34.95 (*1-86126-073-3*, Pub. by Crolwood) Motorbooks Intl.

— Yamaha Racing Motorcycle: Factory & Production Road Racing Two-Strokes 1955-93. (Illus.). 192p. 1995. 34.95 (*1-85223-920-4*, Pub. by Crolwood) Motorbooks Intl.

MacKellar, Robin. The Challenge of Parenthood. LC 97-73700. (Orig.). 1997. pap. 8.99 (*0-88270-726-4*) Bridge-Logos.

Mackellar, Thompson, ed. see Martin, Joyce L.

Mackelprang. Human Services & Persons with Disability. LC 98-22619. (Social Work Ser.). 1998. pap. 32.95 (*0-534-34494-1*) Brooks-Cole.

Mackelprang, Romel W., ed. see Valentine, Deborah.

MacKelvie, Charles F. & Handler, Marcia S. The Trustee's Guide to Board Duties, Responsibilities & Liabilities. LC 92-48301. 92p. 1993. per. 24.95 (*1-882198-15-8*) Hlthcare Fin Mgmt.

MacKelvie, Jock. Yanqui Guajiro. LC 97-91638. 504p. 1997. 27.00 (*0-9656624-1-1*) Condor Pub.

Macken, C. A. & Perelson, Alan S. Branching Processes Applied to Cell Surface Aggregation Phenomena. (Lecture Notes in Biomathematics Ser.: Vol. 58). vii, 122p. 1985. 31.95 (*0-387-15656-9*) Spr-Verlag.

Macken, C. A., et al. Stem Cell Proliferation & Differentiation. (Lecture Notes in Biomathematics Ser.: Vol. 76). viii, 113p. 1988. 31.95 (*0-387-50183-5*) Spr-Verlag.

Macken, Cara A., jt. auth. see Larsen, Earnie.

Macken, J. J. The Employment Revolution. iv, 138p. 1992. pap. 33.00 (*1-86287-099-3*, Pub. by Federation Pr) Gaunt.

Macken, James, et al. Macken, McCarry & Sappideen: The Law of Employment. 4th ed. 650p. 1997. pap. 80.00 (*0-455-21454-9*, 14604, Pub. by LawBk Co) Gaunt.

Macken, Jim. Australia's Unions: A Death or a Difficult Birth? 225p. 1997. pap. 29.00 (*1-86287-260-0*, Pub. by Federation Pr) Gaunt.

Macken, JoAnn Easly. Cats on Judy. LC 96-44939. (Illus.). 32p. (J). (ps-2). 1997. 15.95 (*1-879085-73-9*, Whispering Coyote) Charlesbridge Pub.

Macken, John S. The Autonomy Theme in the Church Dogmatics: Karl Barth & His Critics. 242p. (C). 1990. text 80.00 (*0-521-34626-6*) Cambridge U Pr.

***Macken, Lynda Lee.** Adirondack Ghosts. (Illus.). 80p. 2000. pap. 7.95 (*0-9700718-1-7*) Black Cat Pr NJ.

— Haunted History of Staten Island. (Illus.). 80p. 2000. pap. 7.95 (*0-9700718-0-9*) Black Cat Pr NJ.

Macken, Walter. The Bogman. LC 95-123579. 288p. 1998. reprint ed. pap. 13.95 (*0-86322-184-X*, Pub. by Brandon Bk Pubs) Irish Bks Media.

— Brown Lord of the Mountain. 284p. 1995. reprint ed. pap. 11.95 (*0-86322-201-3*, Pub. by Brandon Bk Pubs) Irish Bks Media.

— God Made Sunday & Other Stories. 222p. 1996. reprint ed. pap. 11.95 (*0-86322-217-X*, Pub. by Brandon Bk Pubs) Irish Bks Media.

— The Grass of the People. LC 98-235750. 248 p. 1998. write for info. (*0-86322-248-X*) Brandon Bk Pubs.

— The Green Hills & Other Stories. 220p. 1996. reprint ed. pap. 11.95 (*0-86322-216-1*, Pub. by Brandon Bk Pubs) Irish Bks Media.

***Macken, Walter.** I Am Alone. 272p. 2000. 23.95 (*0-86322-266-8*, Pub. by Brandon Bk Pubs) Irish Bks Media.

Macken, Walter. The Island of the Great Yellow Ox. LC 90-22515. 192p. (J). (gr. 5-9). 1991. pap. 14.00 (*0-671-73800-3*) S&S Bks Yung.

— Quench the Moon. LC 95-219585. 412p. 1995. pap. 11.95 (*0-86322-202-1*, Pub. by Brandon Bk Pubs) Irish Bks Media.

— Rain on the Wind. 288p. 1994. reprint ed. pap. 11.95 (*0-86322-185-8*, Pub. by Brandon Bk Pubs) Irish Bks Media.

Mackendrick, John, tr. see Buchner, Georg.

MacKendrick, Karmen. Counterpleasures. LC 98-26067. (SUNY Series in Postmodern Culture). 224p. (C). 1999. text 59.50 (*0-7914-4147-4*); pap. text 19.95 (*0-7914-4148-2*) State U NY Pr.

***MacKendrick, Karmen.** Immemorial Silence. LC 00-36568. (C). 2001. pap. text 16.95 (*0-7914-4878-9*) State U NY Pr.

— Immemorial Silence. LC 00-36568. (C). 2001. text 49.50 (*0-7914-4877-0*) State U NY Pr.

MacKendrick, Louis K. Al Purdy & His Works. 56p. (C). 1990. pap. 9.95 (*1-55022-058-6*, Pub. by ECW) Genl Dist Srvs.

— Robert Harlow & His Works. (Canadian Author Studies). 57p. (C). 1989. pap. text 9.95 (*0-920763-90-1*, Pub. by ECW) Genl Dist Srvs.

— Some Other Reality: Alice Munro's Something I've Been Meaning to Tell You. (Canadian Fiction Studies: No. 25). 120p. (C). 1993. pap. text 14.95 (*1-55022-129-9*, Pub. by ECW) Genl Dist Srvs.

MacKendrick, Mary, ed. see Martin, Charles V.

MacKendrick, Paul. The Greek Stones Speak: The Story of Archaeology in Greek Lands. 2nd ed. (Illus.). 576p. 1983. pap. 15.95 (*0-393-30111-7*) Norton.

— The Mute Stones Speak: The Story of Archaeology in Italy. 2nd ed. (Illus.). 1983. pap. 14.95 (*0-393-30119-2*) Norton.

An Asterisk (*) at the beginning of an entry indicates that the title is appearing for the first time.

MacKendrick, Paul L. The Athenian Aristocracy, 399 to 31 B. C. LC 69-12728. (Martin Classical Lectures: No. 23). 125p. 1969. reprint ed. pap. 38.80 (*0-7837-2294-X*, 205738200004) Bks Demand.

— The Dacian Stones Speak. LC 73-16210. (Illus.). 270p. reprint ed. pap. 83.70 (*0-7837-3753-X*, 204357000010) Bks Demand.

— The North African Stones Speak. LC 79-18534. (Illus.). 456p. reprint ed. pap. 141.40 (*0-7837-6860-5*, 204668900003) Bks Demand.

Mackendrick, Paul L. Qui Miscuit Utile Dulci: Fetschrift Essays for Paul Lachlan MacKendrick. Schmeling, Gareth L. & Mikalson, Jon D., eds. LC 97-32620. xvi, 400p. 1997. pap. 50.00 (*0-86516-406-1*) Bolchazy-Carducci.

MacKendrick, Paul L. The Roman Mind at Work. LC 80-13022. (Anvil Ser.). 192p. 1980. reprint ed. pap. text 10.50 (*0-89874-200-5*) Krieger.

Mackenfuss, Pam, jt. auth. see Abbott, Fran W.

Mackenna, B. R. & Callander, Robin. Illustrated Physiology. 6th ed. LC 96-27920. (Illus.). (C). 1996. pap. text 38.95 (*0-443-05060-0*) Church.

MacKenna, David W. Field Training for Medium & Small City Police Departments: A Program Planning Manual. 118p. (Orig.). 1985. pap. text 10.00 (*0-936440-69-4*) U TX SUPA.

***MacKenna, Dolores.** William Trevor: The Writer & His Work. LC 99-196856. 250p. 1999. pap. 18.95 (*1-874597-74-X*, Pub. by New Island Books) Dufour.

MacKenna, John. The Fallen & Other Stories. 169p. 1993. pap. 15.95 (*0-85640-495-0*, Pub. by Blackstaff Pr) Dufour.

MacKenna, John, et al. Clare: A Novel. 181p. 1994. pap. 13.95 (*0-85640-467-5*, Pub. by Blackstaff Pr) Dufour.

Mackenna, Robert W. As Shadows Lengthen: Later Essays. LC 67-26759. (Essay Index Reprint Ser.). 1977. 18.95 (*0-8369-0653-5*) Ayer.

MacKenna, Stephen. The Enneads. 768p. 1992. reprint ed. 65.00 (*0-943914-55-8*) Larson Pubns.

— Plotinus on the Beautiful (1908) 50p. 1998. reprint ed. pap. 9.95 (*0-7661-0345-5*) Kessinger Pub.

MacKenna, Stephen, tr. see Dillon, John, ed.

Mackenna, Stephen, tr. see Turnbull, Grace R., ed.

***MacKenna, Wolf.** Dust Riders. 2000. mass mkt. 5.99 (*0-425-17698-3*) Berkley Pub.

***MacKenney, Linda.** The Activities of Popular Dramatists & Drama Groups in Scotland, 1900-1952. LC 99-48819. (Studies in Theatre Arts: Vol. 9). 320p. 2000. text 99.95 (*0-7734-7905-8*) E Mellen.

MacKenney, Richard. City-State, 1500-1700. 1996. text 11.95 (*0-333-38702-3*, Pub. by Macmillan) St Martin.

Mackenney, Richard. Sixteenth Century Europe: Expansion & Conflict. 1993. pap. 18.95 (*0-312-06739-9*) St Martin.

MacKenney, Richard. Tradesmen & Traders: The World of the Guilds in Venice & Europe, c. 1250-c. 1650. LC 89-10963. 1990. write for info. (*0-415-02656-3*) Routledge.

— Tradesmen & Traders: The World of the Guilds in Venice & Europe, C. 1250-C. 1650. LC 87-672566. xv, 289 p. 1987. write for info. (*0-7099-1763-5*) C Helm.

Mackenroth, Donald R. HP 48SX Programming Examples. (Illus.). 224p. 1991. pap. text 26.95 (*0-685-49803-4*) Addison-Wesley.

— Practical Examples for HP48 Calculator. 1992. pap. text 24.95 (*0-201-56325-8*) Addison-Wesley.

Mackenroth, Donald R. & Sands, Leo G. Illustrated Encyclopedia of Solid State Circuits & Applications. LC 84-23077. (Illus.). 353p. 1984. text 32.95 (*0-13-450537-9*, Busn) P-H.

Mackensen, G., ed. see Ophthalmic Microsurgery Study Group Staff.

Mackensen, Lutz. Deutsches Woerterbuch. (GER.). 1263p. 1986. 69.93 (*0-8288-1978-5*, M7339) Fr & Eur.

— Ursprung der Woerter: Etymologisches Woerterbuch der Deutschen Sprache. (GER.). 446p. 1985. 49.95 (*0-7859-8406-2*, 3517008583) Fr & Eur.

Mackensie, Iain M. The Anachronism of Time: A Theological Study into the Nature of Time. 191p. 1995. pap. 29.95 (*1-85311-089-2*, 6302, Pub. by Canterbury Press Norwich) Morehouse Pub.

MacKenthun, Carole & Dwyer, Paulinus. Peace. (Fruit of the Spirit Ser.). (Illus.). 48p. (J). (gr. 2-7). 1986. student ed. 7.95 (*0-86653-365-6*, SS 877, Shining Star Pubns) Good Apple.

MacKenthun, Carole & Thoresen, Kathy. 100 Best Ideas for Primary Language Arts. (One Hundred Best Ideas Ser.). (Illus.). 112p. (J). (gr. k-3). 1994. pap., teacher ed. 9.95 (*1-57310-001-3*) Teachng & Lrning Co.

Mackenthun, Gesa. Metaphors of Dispossession: American Beginnings & the Translation of Empire, 1492-1637. LC 96-52787. 370p. 1997. 32.95 (*0-8061-2953-0*) U of Okla Pr.

***MacKenthun, Kenneth Marsh.** Basic Concepts in Environmental Management. LC 98-37469. 176p. 1999. 69.95 (*1-56670-380-8*) Lewis Pubs.

MacKenthun, Kenneth Marsh & Bregman, Jacob I. Environmental Regulations Handbook. 320p. 1991. boxed set 95.00 (*0-87371-494-6*, L494) Lewis Pubs.

MacKenty, John E. Apportionment of Death Taxes. 1988. write for info. (*0-318-61708-0*) Am Coll Trust & Est.

MacKenzie. Bessie Head. LC 98-55671. 12p. 1999. 28.95 (*0-8057-1629-7*, Twyne) Mac Lib Ref.

Mackenzie. Boy Who Listened: Samuel. 1996. pap. 2.99 (*1-85792-199-2*, Pub. by Christian Focus) Spring Arbor Dist.

MacKenzie. Dancing Murder. 1992. pap. text. write for info. (*0-17-556003-X*) Addison-Wesley.

Mackenzie. The Empire of Nature: Hunting, Conservation & British Imperialism. 320p. 1997. pap. 29.95 (*0-7190-5227-0*) St Martin.

Mackenzie. Essentials of the American Presidency. 200p. Date not set. 55.00 (*0-8133-3065-3*) Westview.

MacKenzie. Essentials of the American Presidency. 200p. Date not set. pap. 18.95 (*0-8133-3066-1*) Westview.

Mackenzie. Fearless Fighter: David. 1996. pap. 2.99 (*1-85792-198-4*, Pub. by Christian Focus) Spring Arbor Dist.

***MacKenzie.** Non Western Art. 2nd ed. LC 99-86441. (Illus.). 256p. 2000. pap. 26.67 (*0-13-900036-4*) P-H.

Mackenzie. Nuestro Bebe: Regalo.Tr. of Our Baby Book: Gift. (SPA.). write for info. (*0-614-27087-1*) Editorial Unilit.

MacKenzie. Reconstructing Social Criticis. LC 98-34977. 1999. text 65.00 (*0-312-21742-0*) St Martin.

— Russia & the U. S. in the Twentieth Century. 4th ed. (History Ser.). 2000. 41.25 (*0-534-57195-6*) Wadsworth Pub.

Mackenzie. Science & Technical Writers Reference, Vol. 1. 1997. pap. text 40.50 (*0-312-18966-4*) St Martin.

— Science & Technology Today. 1994. pap. text, teacher ed. 5.00 (*0-312-09690-9*) St Martin.

***MacKenzie.** Second World War. LC 98-39608. 160p. (C). 1999. pap. 14.20 (*0-582-32692-3*) Addison-Wesley.

Mackenzie. A Theory of Group Structures, 2 vols., Vol. 2. 550p. 1976. text 198.00 (*0-677-05330-4*) Gordon & Breach.

— Voice in the Dark. 1997. pap. 5.99 (*1-85792-298-0*, Pub. by Christian Focus) Spring Arbor Dist.

MacKenzie & Guilford. Atlas of Rock-Forming Minerals in Thin Sections. 1980. pap. text. write for info. (*0-582-45591-X*, Pub. by Addison-Wesley) Longman.

MacKenzie, jt. auth. see Hart.

MacKenzie, A. History of the Frasers of Lovat with Genealogy of the Principal Families of the Name: To Which Is Added Those of Dunballock & Phopacy. (Illus.). 761p. 1990. reprint ed. pap. 105.00 (*0-8328-1465-2*); reprint ed. lib. bdg. 113.00 (*0-8328-1464-4*) Higginson Bk Co.

— Munroe: History of the Munros of Fowlis, with Genealogies of the Principal Families of the Names, to Which Are Added Those of Lexington & New England. 632p. 1992. reprint ed. pap. 95.00 (*0-8328-2695-2*); reprint ed. lib. bdg. 105.00 (*0-8328-2694-4*) Higginson Bk Co.

MacKenzie, A., et al. Instant Notes in Ecology. (Instant Notes Ser.). 352p. 1998. pap. 24.95 (*0-387-91561-3*) Spr-Verlag.

MacKenzie, A. D. Gazzam-DeBleen. History of the Gazzam Family, Together with a Biographical Sketch of the American Branch of the Family of DeBleen. (Illus.). 72p. 1997. reprint ed. pap. 15.00 (*0-8328-8715-3*); reprint ed. lib. bdg. 25.00 (*0-8328-8714-5*) Higginson Bk Co.

Mackenzie, A. Fiona D. Land, Ecology & Resistance in Kenya, 1880-1952. LC 98-135453. (Social History of Africa Ser.). 286p. 1998. pap. 26.00 (*0-325-00024-7*) Heinemann.

MacKenzie, A. R., jt. auth. see Colbeck, I.

Mackenzie, Agnes M. David One: On the Declaration of Arbroath. 26p. 1985. 22.00 (*0-7855-0773-6*, Pub. by Saltire Soc) St Mut.

— The Foundations of Scotland: From the Earliest Times to 1286. LC 75-41505. 316p. 1979. reprint ed. lib. bdg. 59.75 (*0-8371-8703-6*, MAFN, Greenwood Pr) Greenwood.

— Robert Bruce, King of Scots. LC 78-128880. (Select Bibliographies Reprint Ser.). 1977. reprint ed. 24.95 (*0-8369-5500-5*) Ayer.

— The Scotland of Queen Mary & the Religious Wars, 1513-1638. LC 75-41506. (Illus.). 404p. 1976. reprint ed. lib. bdg. 75.00 (*0-8371-8704-4*, MASQ, Greenwood Pr) Greenwood.

Mackenzie, Alec. Managing Your Goals. 1993. 16.00 incl. audio (*0-671-87995-6*) S&S Trade.

— Time for Success: A Goal-Getter's Strategy. 192p. 1991. pap. 9.95 (*0-07-044656-3*) McGraw.

Mackenzie, Alec, jt. auth. see Engstrom, Ted W.

Mackenzie, Alec, jt. auth. see Mackenzie, Melody.

Mackenzie, Alec R. The Time Trap: The Classic Book on Time Management. 3rd ed. LC 97-20780. 240p. 1997. pap. 17.95 (*0-8144-7926-X*) AMACOM.

— The Time Trap: The New Version of the Classic Book on Time Management. LC 89-46217. 176p. 1991. pap. 14.95 (*0-8144-7760-7*) AMACOM.

Mackenzie, Alec R., jt. auth. see Engstrom, Ted W.

Mackenzie, Alexander. The History of the Highland Clearances. LC 98-188449. 560p. 1996. pap. 44.00 (*0-901824-96-8*, Pub. by Mercat Pr Bks) St Mut.

— History of the Highland Clearances. 532p. (C). 1883. pap. 45.00 (*0-9505884-7-4*, Pub. by Mercat Pr Bks) St Mut.

— Journal of the Voyage to the Pacific. unabridged ed. Sheppe, Walter, ed. (Illus.). 384p. 1996. reprint ed. pap. text 10.95 (*0-486-28894-3*) Dover.

— Mackenzie's Rock. (Shorey Historical Ser.). 39p. reprint ed. pap. 10.00 (*0-8466-0048-X*, S48) Shoreys Bkstore.

MacKenzie, Alexander. Matheson. History of the Mathesons, with Genealogies of the Various Familes (with 1998 Index by Marlene Sue Van Horne) enl. ed. MacBain, Alexander, ed. (Illus.). 201p. 1998. reprint ed. pap. 32.00 (*0-8328-9681-0*); reprint ed. lib. bdg. 42.00 (*0-8328-9680-2*) Higginson Bk Co.

Mackenzie, Alexander. Voyages from Montreal Through the Continent of North America to the Frozen & Pacific Oceans in 1789 & 1793, with an Account of the Rise & State of the Fur Trade, 2 vols. LC 72-2721. (American Explorers Ser.). reprint ed. 115.00 (*0-404-54912-8*) AMS Pr.

Mackenzie, Alexander S. First Man West. Sheppe, Walter, ed. LC 76-3568. (Illus.). 366p. 1976. reprint ed. lib. bdg. 65.00 (*0-8371-8789-3*, SHFM, Greenwood Pr) Greenwood.

— The Life of Paul Jones. LC 70-160981. (Select Bibliographies Reprint Ser.). 1977. reprint ed. 23.95 (*0-8369-5849-7*) Ayer.

Mackenzie, Alison M. Adult Age Differences in Memory. (C). 1991. 35.00 (*1-85041-037-2*, Pub. by Univ Nottingham) St Mut.

Mackenzie, Alistair. Golf Architecture. rev. ed. 1997. 24.95 (*0-940889-16-1*) Classics Golf.

Mackenzie, Alister. The Spirit of St. Andrews. (Illus.). 270p. 1995. 24.95 (*1-886947-00-7*) Sleepng Bear.

MacKenzie, Alister. The Spirit of St. Andrews. LC 97-37063. (Illus.). 288p. 1998. pap. 15.00 (*0-7679-0169-X*) Broadway BDD.

MacKenzie, Andrew. Adventures in Time: Encounters with the Past. LC 97-460. (Studies in Psychic Research Ser.). (Illus.). 180p. 1997. 36.50 (*0-485-82001-3*, Pub. by Athlone Pr) Humanities.

***Mackenzie, Andrew P.** Superconductors: The Metallic State of the Cuprates & Other Oxide Metals. (Frontiers in Physics Ser.). 2000. pap. 65.00 (*0-7382-0177-4*) Perseus Pubng.

Mackenzie, Angus. Secrets: The CIA's War at Home. LC 96-22685. (Illus.). 241p. 1997. 27.50 (*0-520-20020-9*, Pub. by U CA Pr) Cal Prin Full Svc.

***Mackenzie, Angus.** Secrets: The CIA's War at Home. 254p. 1999. pap. 17.95 (*0-520-21955-4*, Pub. by U CA Pr) Cal Prin Full Svc.

MacKenzie, Ann L., tr. see Calderon de la Barca, Pedro.

Mackenzie, Anne, ed. see Nelson, Mary C.

Mackenzie, Barbara A. Shakespeare's Sonnets: Their Relation to His Life. LC 78-6965. reprint ed. 21.50 (*0-404-04135-3*) AMS Pr.

Mackenzie, Bridget. Piping Traditions of the North of Scotland. 360p. 1998. pap. 30.00 (*0-85976-476-1*, Pub. by J Donald) St Mut.

Mackenzie, C. Big Sister's Secret-Miriam. (Biblewise Ser.). (J). 1995. 2.99 (*1-85792-098-8*, Pub. by Christian Focus) Spring Arbor Dist.

MacKenzie, C. Caring Creator. (J). 1995. 12.99 (*0-906731-05-4*, Pub. by Christian Focus) Spring Arbor Dist.

Mackenzie, C. Children of the Bible. (J). 101. 12.99 (*1-85792-032-5*, Pub. by Christian Focus) Spring Arbor Dist.

— Children of the Bible. 1995. pap. 6.99 (*0-906731-13-5*, Pub. by Christian Focus) Spring Arbor Dist.

— El Elias Siervo de Dios/Hacia Milagros.Tr. of God's Miracle Man. (SPA.). (J). 1.99 (*1-56063-699-8*, 497730) Editorial Unilit.

— Esther - the Brave Queen. (BibleTime Bks.). (J). 1995. 2.99 (*0-906731-64-X*, Pub. by Christian Focus) Spring Arbor Dist.

— Flying Away. 1995. 4.99 (*1-871676-93-2*, Pub. by Christian Focus) Spring Arbor Dist.

— Followers of Jesus. (Jesus Ser.). 1995. 12.99 (*1-871676-89-4*, Pub. by Christian Focus) Spring Arbor Dist.

— Gideon - Soldier of God. (BibleTime Bks.). (J). 1995. 2.99 (*0-906731-02-X*, Pub. by Christian Focus) Spring Arbor Dist.

— God's Miracle Man-Elijah. (Biblewise Ser.). (J). 1995. 2.99 (*1-85792-097-X*, Pub. by Christian Focus) Spring Arbor Dist.

— Hannah: The Mother Who Prayed. (BibleTime Bks.). (J). 1995. 2.99 (*0-906731-10-0*, Pub. by Christian Focus) Spring Arbor Dist.

— In the Lord's Army. Date not set. 2.50 (*1-871676-65-7*, Pub. by Christian Focus) Spring Arbor Dist.

— Jesus & His Kingdom. (Jesus Ser.). 1995. 12.99 (*1-871676-62-2*, Pub. by Christian Focus) Spring Arbor Dist.

— Jethro & Co. Date not set. pap. 4.99 (*1-85792-057-0*, Pub. by Christian Focus) Spring Arbor Dist.

— John - the Baptist. (BibleTime Bks.). (J). 1995. 2.99 (*0-906731-44-5*, Pub. by Christian Focus) Spring Arbor Dist.

— Jonah - The Runaway Preacher. (BibleTime Bks.). (J). 1995. 2.99 (*0-906731-66-6*, Pub. by Christian Focus) Spring Arbor Dist.

— Joseph's Great Adventure: Sticker Book. (Jesus Ser.). (J). 1995. 12.99 (*1-85792-118-6*, Pub. by Christian Focus) Spring Arbor Dist.

— Joshua - The Brave Leader. (BibleTime Bks.). (J). 1995. 2.99 (*0-906731-12-7*, Pub. by Christian Focus) Spring Arbor Dist.

— Life of Jesus. (Jesus Ser.). 1995. 12.99 (*0-906731-89-5*, Pub. by Christian Focus); pap. 6.99 (*1-85792-061-9*, Pub. by Christian Focus) Spring Arbor Dist.

MacKenzie, C. Martha & Mary: Friends of Jesus. (BibleTime Bks.). (J). 1995. 2.99 (*0-906731-67-4*, Pub. by Christian Focus) Spring Arbor Dist.

— Mary: Mother of Jesus. (BibleTime Bks.). (J). 1995. 2.99 (*0-906731-06-2*, Pub. by Christian Focus) Spring Arbor Dist.

Mackenzie, C. Names of Jesus. Date not set. pap. 1.75 (*0-906731-61-5*, Pub. by Christian Focus) Spring Arbor Dist.

— Nuestro Bebe (Our Baby Book) (SPA.). 10.99 (*1-56063-613-0*, 494014) Editorial Unilit.

— Our Baby Book. 9.99 (*1-85792-026-0*, Pub. by Christian Focus) Spring Arbor Dist.

— People Jesus Met. Date not set. pap. 1.75 (*0-906731-84-4*, Pub. by Christian Focus) Spring Arbor Dist.

— Peter - The Apostle. (BibleTime Bks.). (J). 1995. 2.99 (*0-906731-65-8*, Pub. by Christian Focus) Spring Arbor Dist.

— Peter - The Fisherman. (BibleTime Bks.). (J). 1995. 2.99 (*0-906731-08-9*, Pub. by Christian Focus) Spring Arbor Dist.

— The Praying Prince. (Biblewise Ser.). (J). 1995. 2.99 (*1-85792-155-0*, Pub. by Christian Focus) Spring Arbor Dist.

— Puzzling Through Mark. Date not set. pap. 4.99 (*1-85792-056-2*, Pub. by Christian Focus) Spring Arbor Dist.

— Rebekah: The Mother of Twins. (BibleTime Bks.). (J). 1995. 2.99 (*0-906731-45-3*, Pub. by Christian Focus) Spring Arbor Dist.

— Ruth: The Harvest Girl. (BibleTime Bks.). (J). 1995. 2.99 (*0-906731-07-0*, Pub. by Christian Focus) Spring Arbor Dist.

— El Secreto de la Hermana Mayor, el Maria.Tr. of Big Sister's Secret. (SPA.). (J). 1.99 (*1-56063-700-5*, 497731) Editorial Unilit.

MacKenzie, C. Seek & Find. 2.99 (*0-906731-78-X*, Pub. by Christian Focus) Spring Arbor Dist.

Mackenzie, C. Simon Peter - The Disciple. (BibleTime Bks.). (J). 1995. 2.99 (*0-906731-09-7*, Pub. by Christian Focus) Spring Arbor Dist.

MacKenzie, C. Talking to You. 3.99 (*1-871676-45-2*, Pub. by Christian Focus) Spring Arbor Dist.

— Two Margarets. 5.99 (*0-906731-43-7*, Pub. by Christian Focus) Spring Arbor Dist.

Mackenzie, C. We Are Loved. (J). 1995. 2.99 (*1-871676-53-3*, Pub. by Christian Focus) Spring Arbor Dist.

— The Wonderful Promise. (Biblewise Ser.). (J). 1995. 2.99 (*1-85792-156-9*, Pub. by Christian Focus) Spring Arbor Dist.

Mackenzie, Calvin G. The Irony of Reform: Roots of American Political Disenchantment. (Transforming American Politics Ser.). 240p. (C). 1996. pap. text 25.00 (*0-8133-2839-X*, Pub. by Westview) HarpC.

Mackenzie, Campbell, tr. see Bonnechose, Emile de.

MacKenzie, Carine. El Amoroso Creador.Tr. of Caring Creator. (SPA.). 40p. (J). 1992. pap. 5.99 (*1-56063-305-0*, 490445) Editorial Unilit.

***MacKenzie, Carine.** Bible Stories for Bedtime. (Illus.). (J). 2000. 12.99 (*1-85792-467-3*) Christian Focus.

MacKenzie, Carine. God Has Power. 1999. 3.99 (*1-85792-477-0*) Christian Focus.

— God Is Everywhere. 1999. 3.99 (*1-85792-480-0*) Christian Focus.

— God Is Faithful. 1999. 3.99 (*1-85792-481-9*) Christian Focus.

— God Is Kind. 1999. 3.99 (*1-85792-476-2*) Christian Focus.

— God Knows Everything. 1999. 3.99 (*1-85792-479-7*) Christian Focus.

— God Never Changes. 1999. 3.99 (*1-85792-478-9*) Christian Focus.

***MacKenzie, Carine.** Journeys of Adventure - Paul. 1999. pap. 2.99 (*1-85792-465-7*) Christian Focus.

— Little Hands Story Bible. (Illus.). (J). 1999. 9.99 (*1-85792-342-1*) Christian Focus.

— Long, Long Ago, in Bethlehem the Birth of Jesus. 1999. 12.99 (*1-85792-386-3*) Christian Focus.

Mackenzie, Carine. Ninos de la Biblia.Tr. of Children of the Bible. (SPA.). 48p. (J). 1993. 9.99 (*1-56063-546-0*, 498748) Editorial Unilit.

— Women of the Bible: The Stories of Rebekah, Hannah & Esther. (Illus.). 96p. 1998. 7.99 (*0-88486-203-8*, Inspirational Pr) Arrowood Pr.

MacKenzie, Catherine. Alexander Graham Bell: The Man Who Contracted Space. LC 77-150193. (Select Bibliographies Reprint Ser.). 1977. reprint ed. 33.95 (*0-8369-5706-7*) Ayer.

— Hudson Taylor: An Adventure Begins. 1999. pap. text 5.99 (*1-85792-423-1*) Christian Focus.

***MacKenzie, Catriona & Stoljar, Natalie, eds.** Relational Autonomy: Feminist Essays on Autonomy, Agency & the Social Self. LC 99-12792. 328p. 2000. 49.95 (*0-19-512333-6*) OUP.

***MacKenzie, Catriona & Stoljar, Natalie, eds.** Relational Autonomy: Feminist Essays on Autonomy, Agency & the Social Self. LC 99-12792. 328p. 2000. pap. 19.95 (*0-19-512334-4*) OUP.

Mackenzie, Chalmers J. The Mackenzie-McNaughton Wartime Letters. Thistle, Mel, ed. LC 72-185741. 192p. reprint ed. pap. 59.60 (*0-608-30165-5*, 201443300094) Bks Demand.

Mackenzie, Charles E. Coded-Character Sets: History & Development. LC 77-90165. (IBM Systems Programming Ser.). 1980. text. write for info. (*0-201-14460-3*) Addison-Wesley.

MacKenzie, Charlotte. Psychiatry for the Rich: A History of Ticehurst Private Asylum, 1792-1917. LC 92-49160. (Wellcome Institute Series in the History of Medicine). (Illus.). 224p. (C). 1993. 85.00 (*0-415-08891-7*, A9941) Routledge.

MacKenzie, Christine L. & Iberall, Thea. The Grasping Hand. LC 93-47171. 500p. 1994. 162.50 (*0-444-81746-8*, North Holland) Elsevier.

***MacKenzie, Clayton G.** Emblems of Mortality: Econographic Experiments in Shakespeare's Theatre. 212p. 2000. 42.50 (*0-7618-1660-7*) U Pr of Amer.

Mackenzie, Clyde L., Jr. Fisheries of Raritan Bay. LC 91-43031. (Illus.). 304p. (C). 1992. text 45.00 (*0-8135-1839-3*); pap. text 16.95 (*0-8135-1840-7*) Rutgers U Pr.

— History, Present Condition & Future of the Molluscan Fisheries of North & Central America & Europe. 244p. 1997. per. 21.00 (*0-16-054582-X*) USGPO.

MacKenzie, Clyde L. History, Present Condition & Future of the Molluscan Fisheries of North & Central America & Europe: Atlantic & Gulf Coasts, Vol. 1. 240p. 1997. per. 22.00 (*0-16-060914-3*) USGPO.

— History, Present Condition & Future of the Molluscan Fisheries of North & Central America & Europe: Pacific Coast & Supplemental Topics, Vol.2. 221p. 1998. per. 18.00 (*0-16-060917-8*) USGPO.

M

MacKenzie, Clyde L., Jr., et al, eds. The History, Present Condition, & Future of the Molluscan Fisheries of North & Central America & Europe Vol. 3: Europe. (Illus.). 248p. 1997. reprint ed. 31.00 (*0-89904-698-3*, Seascape Res Alliance); reprint ed. pap. 25.40 (*0-89904-699-1*, Seascape Res Alliance) Crumb Elbow Pub.

MacKenzie, Clyde L., Jr., et al. History, Present Condition, & Future of the Molluscan Fisheries of North & Central America & Europe Vol. 2: Pacific Coast & Supplement Topics. (Illus.). 230p. 1997. 29.00 (*0-89904-875-7*, Seascape Res Alliance); spiral bd. 24.00 (*0-89904-876-5*, Seascape Res Alliance) Crumb Elbow Pub.

Mackenzie, Compton. Greek Memories. LC 86-13217. (Foreign Intelligence Book Ser.). 587p. 1987. lib. bdg. 49.95 (*0-313-27006-6*, U7006, Greenwood Pr) Greenwood.

MacKenzie, Compton. Guy & Pauline. 1988. reprint ed. lib. bdg. 69.00 (*0-7812-0377-5*) Rprt Serv.

Mackenzie, Compton. Guy & Pauline. LC 71-145156. (Literature Ser.). 396p. 1972. reprint ed. 69.00 (*0-403-01084-5*) Scholarly.

— Literature in My Time. LC 67-28758. (Essay Index Reprint Ser.). 1977. 18.95 (*0-8369-0654-3*) Ayer.

— Realms of Silver. Wilkins, Mira, ed. LC 78-3934. (International Finance Ser.). (Illus.). 1979. reprint ed. lib. bdg. 35.95 (*0-405-11236-X*) Ayer.

MacKenzie, Craig, ed. see Head, Bessie.

***MacKenzie, Cynthia, ed.** A Concordance to the Letters of Emily Dickinson. 850p. 2000. 225.00 (*0-87081-568-7*, Pub. by Univ Pr Colo) U of Okla Pr.

Mackenzie, D. Califate of the West. 368p. 1987. 290.00 (*1-85077-163-4*, Pub. by Darf Pubs Ltd) St Mut.

— Myths of Pre-Columbian America. 1972. 75.00 (*0-8490-0701-1*) Gordon Pr.

MacKenzie, D. N., jt. auth. see Blumhardt, J. F.

MacKenzie, D. Scott, jt. ed. see Bains, Trilochan.

Mackenzie, Dave. Bird Boxes & Feeders for the Garden. LC 98-140552. (Illus.). 176p. 1998. 17.95 (*1-86108-065-4*, Pub. by Guild Master) Sterling.

— Pine Furniture Projects for the Home. LC 97-198854. (Illus.). 128p. 1997. pap. text 14.95 (*1-86108-035-2*, Pub. by Guild Master) Sterling.

— Space-Saving Furniture Projects for the Home. LC 99-199265. 176p. 1999. pap. 17.95 (*1-86108-099-9*, Pub. by Guild Master) Sterling.

Mackenzie, David. Apis: The Congenial Conspirator. (East European Monographs: No. 265). 401p. 1989. text 72.00 (*0-88033-162-3*, Pub. by East Eur Monographs) Col U Pr.

MacKenzie, David. Arthur Irwin: A Biography. LC 93-93699. 323p. 1993. text 45.00 (*0-8020-2632-X*) U of Toronto Pr.

Mackenzie, David. The "Black Hand" on Trial: Salonika, 1917. LC 95-60872. 447p. 1995. 59.00 (*0-88033-320-0*, 423, Pub. by East Eur Monographs) Col U Pr.

MacKenzie, David. Canada & International Civil Aviation, 1932-1948. 228p. 1989. text 40.00 (*0-8020-5828-0*) U of Toronto Pr.

— From Messianism to Collapse. LC 93-80890. (C). 1994. pap. text 44.50 (*0-15-501303-3*, Pub. by Harcourt Coll Pubs) Harcourt.

— Goat Husbandry. 5th ed. Goodwin, Ruth, ed. (Illus.). 384p. 1993. pap. 16.95 (*0-571-16595-8*) Faber & Faber.

— Ilija Garasnin. 1985. text 79.50 (*0-88033-073-2*, 181, Pub. by East Eur Monographs) Col U Pr.

— Imperial Dreams, Harsh Realities: Tsarist Russian Foreign Policy, 1815-1917. LC 93-77106. 196p. (C). 1994. pap. text 49.00 (*0-15-500934-6*) Harcourt.

— Inside the Atlantic Triangle: Canada & the Entrance of Newfoundland into Confederation 1939-1949. 304p. 1986. text 35.00 (*0-8020-2587-0*) U of Toronto Pr.

— Serbs & Russians. 435p. 1997. 56.00 (*0-88033-356-1*, 459, Pub. by East Eur Monographs) Col U Pr.

MacKenzie, David & Curran, Michael W. A History of Russia & the Soviet Union. 3rd ed. 924p. (C). 1990. pap. write for info. (*0-534-10687-0*) Wadsworth Pub.

Mackenzie, David & Curran, Michael W. A History of Russia, the Soviet Union, & Beyond. 4th ed. 912p. (C). 1992. pap. 46.75 (*0-534-17970-3*) Wadsworth Pub.

***Mackenzie, David & Curran, Michael W.** A History of Russia, the Soviet Union, & Beyond. 5th ed. LC 98-6694. 1998. pap. 73.95 (*0-534-54891-1*) Wadsworth Pub.

MacKenzie, David & Curran, Michael W. History of the Soviet Union. 458p. (C). 1989. pap. write for info. (*0-534-10691-9*) Wadsworth Pub.

— A History of the Soviet Union. 2nd ed. 550p. (C). 1990. mass mkt. 37.25 (*0-534-14910-3*) Wadsworth Pub.

— Russia & the U. S. S. R. in the 20th Century. 3rd ed. LC 96-44924. (C). 1996. 67.95 (*0-534-51688-2*) Wadsworth Pub.

MacKenzie, David, ed. see Denny, Steven.

MacKenzie, David R. Principles of Agricultural Research Management. LC 95-45495. 342p. (C). 1995. pap. text 42.00 (*0-7618-0198-7*); lib. bdg. 59.00 (*0-7618-0197-9*) U Pr of Amer.

— Violent Solutions: Revolutions, Nationalism, & Secret Societies in Europe to 1918. LC 96-2999. (Illus.). 332p. 1996. pap. text 34.50 (*0-7618-0400-5*); lib. bdg. 62.50 (*0-7618-0399-8*) U Pr of Amer.

MacKenzie, David S. Perennial Ground Covers. LC 96-23737. (Illus.). 452p. 1997. 49.95 (*0-88192-368-0*) Timber.

MacKenzie, Dolly. Bargain Hunting in New Jersey: A Guide. (Illus.). 184p. (Orig.). 1988. pap. 7.95 (*0-929211-00-6*) Directories NJ.

MacKenzie, Donald. By Any Illegal Means. large type ed. 296p. 1992. 14.95 (*0-7451-1360-5*, G K Hall Lrg Type) Mac Lib Ref.

Mackenzie, Donald. Deep, Dark & Dead. large type ed. (Linford Mystery Library). 304p. 1997. pap. 16.99 (*0-7089-5111-2*, Linford) Ulverscroft.

MacKenzie, Donald. Folk Tales from Russia. LC 98-27813. (Library of Folklore). (Illus.). 192p. (J). (gr. 3-4). 1999. 12.50 (*0-7818-0696-8*) Hippocrene Bks.

— Inventing Accuracy: A Historical Sociology of Nuclear Missile Guidance. (Illus.). 480p. 1993. pap. text 23.00 (*0-262-63147-4*) MIT Pr.

— Knowing Machines: Essays on Technical Change. (Inside Technology Ser.). (Illus.). 360p. (C). 1996. 37.50 (*0-262-13315-6*) MIT Pr.

— Knowing Machines: Essays on Technical Change. (Inside Technology Ser.). (Illus.). 352p. 1998. pap. text 17.50 (*0-262-63188-1*) MIT Pr.

— Loose Cannon. large type ed. LC 93-28769. 269p. 1994. lib. bdg. 16.95 (*0-8161-5859-2*, G K Hall Lrg Type) Mac Lib Ref.

Mackenzie, Donald. Raven Feathers His Nest. large type ed. 317p. 1982. 27.99 (*0-7089-0787-3*) Ulverscroft.

— Raven's Longest Night. large type ed. 336p. 1985. 27.99 (*0-7089-1381-4*) Ulverscroft.

MacKenzie, Donald. Salute from a Dead Man. large type ed. (Linford Mystery Library). 416p. 1997. pap. 16.99 (*0-7089-5165-1*) Ulverscroft.

— A Savage State of Grace. large type ed. 272p. 1991. 19.95 (*0-7451-0932-2*, G K Hall Lrg Type) Mac Lib Ref.

— Spreewald Collection. LC 75-327749. 189p. 1975. write for info. (*0-333-17933-1*) Macmillan.

Mackenzie, Donald. Statistics in Britain, 1865-1930: The Social Construction of Scientific Knowledge. 306p. 1981. 26.50 (*0-85224-369-3*, Pub. by Edinburgh U Pr) Col U Pr.

MacKenzie, Donald, ed. see Kipling, Rudyard.

MacKenzie, Donald A. India: Myths & Legends. (Illus.). 463p. (Orig.). 1997. reprint ed. pap. text 20.00 (*0-7881-5044-8*) DIANE Pub.

MacKenzie, Donald A. Migration of Symbols & Their Relations to Beliefs & Customs. LC 73-121283. reprint ed. 28.00 (*0-404-04136-1*) AMS Pr.

Mackenzie, Donald A. Myths of Pre-Columbian America. (LC History-America-E). 351p. 1999. reprint ed. lib. bdg. 99.00 (*0-7812-4299-1*) Rprt Serv.

— Myths of Pre-Columbian America. unabridged ed. LC 96-32395. (Illus.). 416p. 1996. reprint ed. pap. text 9.95 (*0-486-29379-3*) Dover.

— Otfrid Von Weissenburg: Narrator or Commentator. (Stanford University. Stanford Studies in Language & Literature: Vol. 6, Pt. 3). reprint ed. 27.50 (*0-404-51812-5*) AMS Pr.

MacKenzie, Donald A. Scottish Fairy Tales. LC 97-19553. (Children's Thrift Classics Ser.). (Illus.). (J). (gr. 5). 1997. pap. 1.00 (*0-486-29900-7*) Dover.

Mackenzie, Donald A. Scottish Wonder Tales from Myth & Legend. LC 96-42204. (Illus.). 40p. 1997. reprint ed. pap. text 6.95 (*0-486-29677-6*) Dover.

MacKenzie, Donald A. & Wajcman, Judy. The Social Shaping of Technology. 2nd ed. LC 98-41239. 1999. 85.00 (*0-335-19914-3*); pap. 27.95 (*0-335-19913-5*) OpUniv Pr.

Mackenzie, Donald G. Planning Educational Facilities. LC 89-14610. 102p. (Orig.). (C). 1989. pap. text 20.00 (*0-8191-7480-7*) U Pr of Amer.

MacKenzie, Donald M. Fish. LC 98-55446. 1999. pap. 5.00 (*0-88734-789-4*) Players Pr.

Mackenzie, Donald R. & Kerst, Erna W. A Bibliographic Overview of Housing in Developing Countries: Annotated, Nos. 1225-1227. 1977. 12.50 (*0-686-19686-4*, Sage Prdcls Pr) Sage.

MacKenzie, Doris L. & Hebert, Eugene E., eds. Correctional Boot Camps: A Tough Intermediate Sanction. (Illus.). 307p. (Orig.). (C). 1996. pap. text 40.00 (*0-7881-3511-2*) DIANE Pub.

MacKenzie, Doris L. & Uchida, Craig, eds. Drugs & Crime: Evaluating Public Policy Initiatives. LC 93-36738. 316p. (C). 1994. text 42.00 (*0-8039-4456-X*); pap. text 19.95 (*0-8039-4457-8*) Sage.

MacKenzie, Dorothy. Green Design: Design for the Environment. 2nd ed. (Illus.). 176p. 1997. 35.00 (*1-85669-096-2*, Pub. by L King Pubng) Bks Nippan.

MacKenzie, Dorothy, jt. ed. see Silverman, Phyllis R.

Mackenzie, Drew. Sunday Bloody Sunday. 1996. mass mkt. 4.99 (*1-85782-018-5*, Pub. by Blake Publng) Seven Hills Bk.

MacKenzie, Duncan. MCSD Fast Track: Solution Architectures. (Fast Tracks Ser.). 400p. 1999. pap. text 44.95 (*0-7357-0029-X*) New Riders Pub.

Mackenzie, Duncan & Martins, Felipe. Word 2000 VBA Programmer's Reference. 650p. 1999. pap. 24.99 (*1-86100-255-6*) Wrox Pr Inc.

MacKenzie, E. T. Neurotransmitters & the Cerebral Circulation. LC 84-15098. (L. E. R. S. Monograph Ser.: Vol. 2). (Illus.). 270p. 1984. reprint ed. pap. 83.70 (*0-608-00679-3*, 206126600009) Bks Demand.

Mackenzie, Elizabeth R. Healing the Social Body: A Holistic Approach to Public Health Policy. LC 97-11610. (Health Care Policy in the United States Ser.). 256p. 1998. text 67.00 (*0-8153-2909-1*) Garland.

***Mackenzie, F. A., ed.** The Trial of Harry Thaw. (Famous Trials Ser.). 300p. 2000. 75.00 (*1-56169-618-8*) Gaunt.

MacKenzie, Fred T. Our Changing Planet. 2nd ed. LC 97-31347. 486p. 1997. pap. text 46.00 (*0-13-271321-7*) P-H.

MacKenzie, Fred T., jt. auth. see Woodwell, George M.

Mackenzie, Fred T., jt. ed. see Morse, J. W.

MacKenzie, Frederick. British Fusilier in Revolutionary Boston. French, Allen, ed. LC 79-102237. (Select Bibliographies Reprint Ser.). 1977. 21.95 (*0-8369-5122-0*) Ayer.

— Diary of Frederick MacKenzie. 2 vols., Set. LC 67-29038. (Eyewitness Accounts of the American Revolution Ser.). 1968. reprint ed. 36.95 (*0-405-01132-6*) Ayer.

— Diary of Frederick MacKenzie, 2 vols., Vol. 1. LC 67-29038. (Eyewitness Accounts of the American Revolution Ser.). 1968. reprint ed. 19.95 (*0-405-01130-X*) Ayer.

— Diary of Frederick MacKenzie, 2 vols., Vol. 2. LC 67-29038. (Eyewitness Accounts of the American Revolution Ser.). 1968. reprint ed. 19.95 (*0-405-01131-8*) Ayer.

MacKenzie, G. & Line, Maurice B., eds. Librarianship & Information Work Worldwide, 1998. 1997. pap. 95.00 (*1-85739-169-1*) Bowker-Saur.

Mackenzie, G. A., et al. The Composition of Fiscal Adjustment & Growth: Lessons from Fiscal Reforms in Eight Economies, Vol. 149. LC 96-30022. (Occassional Papers). 1997. write for info. (*1-55775-629-5*) Intl Monetary.

— Pension Regimes & Saving, Vol. 153. LC 97-33432. (Occasional Papers). 1997. write for info. (*1-55775-640-6*) Intl Monetary.

Mackenzie, G. Calvin. Government & Public Policy in America. 352p. 1986. 8.25 (*0-685-10335-8*) McGraw.

Mackenzie, G. Calvin, ed. The In-&-Outers: Presidential Appointees & Transient Government in Washington. LC 86-46281. (Illus.). 262p. reprint ed. pap. 81.30 (*0-608-06168-9*, 206650100008) Bks Demand.

Mackenzie, G. Calvin & Thornton, Saranna. Bucking the Deficit: Economic Policymaking in America. (Dilemmas in American Politics Ser.). 208p. (C). 1996. pap. 20.00 (*0-8133-2061-5*, Pub. by Westview) HarpC.

Mackenzie, G. Calvin, et al. Under the Microscope: The Report of the Twentieth Century Fund Task Force on Presidential Appointments; with Background Papers. LC 96-27236. 1996. write for info. (*0-87078-401-3*) Century Foundation.

MacKenzie, G. Calvin, jt. ed. see Cooper, Joseph.

MacKenzie, Gareth. Theseus & the Minotaur. LC 97-167303. (Illus.). 24p. (YA). (gr. 7 up). 1997. 17.95 (*0-7887-1153-9*) Recorded Bks.

Mackenzie, Gavin. The Aristocracy of Labor: The Position of Skilled Craftsmen in the American Class Structure. LC 73-80484. (Cambridge Studies in Sociology: Vol. 7). 218p. reprint ed. pap. 62.20 (*0-8357-5732-3*, 2027244) Bks Demand.

Mackenzie, George A., ed. see Muir, Alexander.

Mackenzie, George H., et al. Beam Instrumentation Workshop: Proceedings: Beam Instrumentation Workshop (1994: Vancouver, B. C., Canada) LC 95-79635. (AIP Conference Proceedings Ser.: No. 333). 592p. 1995. 140.00 (*1-56396-352-3*) Am Inst Physics.

Mackenzie, George N. Colonial Families of the United States of America Vol. I: Main Families. (Illus.). 730p. 1995. reprint ed. 45.00 (*0-8063-0223-2*) Genealog Pub.

— Colonial Families of the United States of America Vol. II: Main Families. (Illus.). 941p. 1995. reprint ed. 50.00 (*0-8063-0224-0*) Genealog Pub.

— Colonial Families of the United States of America Vol. III: Main Families. (Illus.). 740p. 1995. reprint ed. 45.00 (*0-8063-0225-9*) Genealog Pub.

— Colonial Families of the United States of America Vol. V: Main Families. (Illus.). 719p. 1995. reprint ed. 40.00 (*0-8063-0227-5*) Genealog Pub.

— Colonial Families of the United States of America Vol. VI: Main Families. (Illus.). 600p. 1995. reprint ed. 40.00 (*0-8063-0228-3*) Genealog Pub.

— Colonial Families of the United States of America Vol. VII: Main Families. (Illus.). 605p. 1995. reprint ed. 40.00 (*0-8063-0229-1*) Genealog Pub.

Mackenzie, George Norbury. Colonial Families of the United States of America, 7 vols., Set. (Illus.). 6119p. 1995. reprint ed. 225.00 (*0-8063-1453-2*, 3590) Genealog Pub.

Mackenzie, Georgena M. & Irby, A. P. Travels in the Slavonic Provinces of Turkey-in-Europe. LC 78-135816. (Eastern Europe Collection). 1971. reprint ed. 44.95 (*0-405-02758-3*) Ayer.

MacKenzie, Gordene O. Transgender Nation. LC 94-71363. (Illus.). 182p. (C). 1994. 41.95 (*0-87972-596-6*); pap. 14.95 (*0-87972-597-4*) Bowling Green Univ Popular Press.

MacKenzie, Gordon. Orbiting the Giant Hairball: A Corporate Fool's Guide to Surviving with Grace. LC 96-92018. (Illus.). 224p. 1996. 44.40 (*0-9650249-0-3*) OpusPocus.

— Orbiting the Giant Hairball: A Corporate Fool's Guide to Surviving with Grace. LC 97-52991. (Illus.). 224p. 1998. 22.00 (*0-670-87983-5*) Viking Penguin.

***MacKenzie, Gordon.** The Watercolorist's Essential Notebook. (Illus.). 144p. 2000. 24.99 (*0-89134-946-4*, North Lght Bks) F & W Pubns Inc.

Mackenzie-Grieve, Averil. Clara Novello, Eighteen Eighteen to Nineteen Eight. LC 79-24421. (Music Reprint Ser.). 1980. reprint ed. lib. bdg. 39.50 (*0-306-76009-6*) Da Capo.

— Last Years of the English Slave Trade, Liverpool, 1705-1807. 331p. 1968. reprint ed. 35.00 (*0-7146-1895-0*, Pub. by F Cass Pubs) Intl Spec Bk.

***MacKenzie, H. F.** Contemporary Canadian Marketing Cases. 304p. 1999. pap. 66.60 (*0-13-084091-2*) P-H.

***Mackenzie, Harry.** The Directory of AFRS Series, 82. LC 99-36378. (Discographies Ser.). 280p. 1999. lib. bdg. 79.50 (*0-313-30812-8*) Greenwood.

Mackenzie, Harry, compiled by. Command Performance, U. S. A.! A Discography, 64. LC 95-43112. (Discographies Ser.: No. 64). 280p. 1996. lib. bdg. 79.50 (*0-313-29828-9*, Greenwood Pr) Greenwood.

Mackenzie, Harry & Polomski, Lothar, compiled by. One Night Stand Series, 1-1001, Vol. 44. LC 91-7317. (Discographies Ser.: No. 44). 448p. 1991. lib. bdg. 75.00 (*0-313-27729-X*, MKZ, Greenwood Pr) Greenwood.

Mackenzie, Harry, jt. auth. see Kiner, Larry F.

MacKenzie, Hector, ed. see International Trade Staff.

Mackenzie, Henry. The Man of Feeling. (C). 1958. pap. 12.50 (*0-393-00214-4*) Norton.

MacKenzie, Henry. The Novels of Henry Mackenzie, 4 vols. Incl. 2. Man of the World. 1976. reprint ed. 30.00 (*0-404-04092-6*); 3. Man of the World. 1976. reprint ed. 30.00 (*0-404-04093-4*); Vol. 1. Man of Feeling. 1976. 30.00 (*0-404-04091-8*); Vol. 4. Julia de Roubigne. 1976. reprint ed. 30.00 (*0-404-04094-2*); 1976. write for info. (*0-318-50676-9*) AMS Pr.

— The Novels of Henry Mackenzie, 4 vols., Set. Incl. 2. Man of the World. 1976. reprint ed. 30.00 (*0-404-04092-6*); 3. Man of the World. 1976. reprint ed. 30.00 (*0-404-04093-4*); Vol. 1. Man of Feeling. 1976. 30.00 (*0-404-04091-8*); Vol. 4. Julia de Roubigne. 1976. reprint ed. 30.00 (*0-404-04094-2*); 1976. 120.00 (*0-404-04090-X*) AMS Pr.

Mackenzie, Henry, ed. The Mirror & the Lounger. LC 78-67534. (Scottish Enlightenment Ser.). Orig. Title: The Mirrors, Nos. 1-110, the Lounger, Nos. 1-101. reprint ed. 32.50 (*0-404-17675-5*) AMS Pr.

Mackenzie, Hettie M. Hegel's Educational Theory & Practice. LC 79-122985. (Studies in Philosophy: No. 40). 1971. reprint ed. lib. bdg. 75.00 (*0-8383-1118-0*) M S G Haskell Hse.

MacKenzie-Hook, Derek. Ireland for Kids: The All-Year Guide. (Illus.). 288p. 1997. 17.95 (*1-85158-920-1*, Pub. by Mainstream Pubng) Trafalgar.

Mackenzie, I. E. Introduction to Linguistic Philosophy. LC 97-4608. 256p. 1997. text 47.95 (*0-7619-0174-4*); pap. text 22.95 (*0-7619-0175-2*) Sage.

MacKenzie, I. Scott. The 8051 Microcontroller. 3rd ed. LC 98-19475. 366p. 1998. 91.00 (*0-13-780008-8*) P-H.

— The 8051 Microprocessor. 2nd ed. (Illus.). 384p. 1994. write for info. (*0-614-32036-4*, Merrill Pub Co) Macmillan.

— The Eighty Fifty-One Microprocessor. 2nd ed. (Illus.). 384p. 1994. write for info. (*0-614-32069-0*, Merrill Pub Co) Macmillan.

MacKenzie, I. Scott. Microprocessor 68000. 1995. 74.25 (*0-13-018266-4*) P-H.

MacKenzie, I. Scott. The 6800 Microprocessor. LC 94-32687. 608p. 1995. pap. text 99.00 (*0-02-373654-2*, Macmillan Coll) P-H.

Mackenzie, Iain M. The Dynamism of Space: A Theological Study into the Nature of Space. 212p. (Orig.). 1996. pap. 28.95 (*1-85311-117-1*, 6332, Pub. by Canterbury Press Norwich) Morehouse Pub.

MacKenzie, Iain M., ed. Archaeological Theory: Progress or Posture? (Worldwide Archaeology Ser.). 192p. 1994. 61.95 (*1-85628-710-6*, Pub. by Avebry) Ashgate Pub Co.

Mackenzie, Iain M., ed. Cathedrals Now: Their Use & Place in Society. 104p. 1997. pap. 19.95 (*1-85311-143-0*, 6313, Pub. by Canterbury Press Norwich) Morehouse Pub.

Mackenzie, Ian. Ancient Landscapes: A Photographic Journey Through the Remaining Wilderness of British Columbia. (Illus.). 128p. 1995. pap. 19.95 (*1-55105-043-9*) Lone Pine.

MacKenzie, Ian. British Prints. (Illus.). 376p. 1998. 79.50 (*1-85149-235-6*) Antique Collect.

Mackenzie, Ian. British Prints: Dictionary & Price Guide. (Illus.). 360p. 1988. 89.50 (*0-902028-96-0*) Antique Collect.

MacKenzie, Ian, ed. see Radha, Sivananda.

***Mackenzie, Ian E.** Semantics of Spanish Verbal Categories. LC 99-31520. 202p. (C). 1999. pap. text 37.95 (*0-8204-4243-7*) P Lang Pubng.

MacKenzie, J. One Day We Met the Lions. 1995. 2.99 (*1-871676-79-7*, Pub. by Christian Focus) Spring Arbor Dist.

***Mackenzie, J. S., ed.** Hantaviruses: Emerging Viral Diseases. (Illus.). 67p. 1999. pap. text 20.00 (*0-7881-8078-9*) DIANE Pub.

Mackenzie, J. S. & Van Halm, J. Innovation in the Information Chain: The Effects of Technological Development on the Provision of Scientific & Technical Information. 224p. 1989. 35.00 (*0-415-03871-5*, A3645) Routledge.

MacKenzie, James. The History of Health, & the Art of Preserving It. Kastenbaum, Robert J., ed. LC 78-22208. (Aging & Old Age Ser.). 1979. reprint ed. lib. bdg. 37.95 (*0-405-11822-8*) Ayer.

MacKenzie, James J. Breathing Easier: Taking Action on Climate Change, Air Pollution & Energy Insecurity. 24p. 1988. pap. text 10.00 (*0-915825-35-X*) World Resources Inst.

MacKenzie, James J. Climate Protection & the National Interest. LC 97-80336. 56p. 1997. pap. 20.00 (*1-56973-228-0*) World Resources Inst.

MacKenzie, James J. Keys to the Car: Electric & Hydrogen Vehicles for the 21st Century. large type ed. 128p. 1994. pap. 20.00 (*0-915825-93-7*) World Resources Inst.

MacKenzie, James J. & El-Ashry, Mohamed T. Air Pollution's Toll on Forests & Crops. 384p. (C). 1992. reprint ed. pap. 25.00 (*0-300-05232-4*) Yale U Pr.

— Ill Winds: Airborne Pollution's Toll on Trees & Crops. LC 88-51128. 84p. 1988. pap. text 15.00 (*0-915825-29-5*) World Resources Inst.

MacKenzie, James J., et al. The Going Rate: What It Really Costs to Drive. 32p. 1992. pap. 20.00 (*0-915825-77-5*, MACTP) World Resources Inst.

Mackenzie, Jean G. A Lexicon of the Fourteenth-Century Aragonese Manuscripts of Juan Fernandez de Heredia. (Dialect Ser.: No. 8). xlii, 234p. 1984. 35.00 (*0-942260-48-1*) Hispanic Seminary.

MacKenzie, Jeanne, ed. see Webb, Beatrice Potter.

MacKenzie, Jeff L. Financial Engineering with Basic Trading: Customizing Yield-Enhancement. rev. ed. 350p. 1994. 55.00 (*1-55738-802-4*, Irwn Prfssnl) McGraw-Hill Prof.

An Asterisk (*) at the beginning of an entry indicates that the title is appearing for the first time.

MacKenzie, Jennie. Sunset Creative Fun Crafts for Kids. (Arts-Crafts-Cooking-Drawing Books for Children Ser.). (Illus.). 80p. (J). (ps-3). 1995. lib. bdg. 17.95 (*1-56674-085-1*) Forest Hse.

MacKenzie, Jennifer. Ward Management in Practice. LC 97-51523. (C). 1998. pap. text 35.00 (*0-443-05702-8*) Church.

MacKenzie, John. Be Good to Yourself. (Illus.). 150p. 1981. 12.95 (*0-89496-027-X*) Ross Bks.

MacKenzie, John. Be Good to Yourself. (Illus.). 150p. 1981. pap. 9.95 (*0-89496-026-1*) Ross Bks.

Mackenzie, John M. Diary, 1851. (C). 1992. text 75.00 (*0-86152-872-7*, Pub. by Acair Ltd) St Mut.

MacKenzie, John M. Propaganda & Empire: The Manipulation of British Public Opinion, 1880-1960. LC 83-25325. (Illus.). 320p. (C). 1988. text 32.00 (*0-7190-1869-2*, Pub. by Manchester Univ Pr) St Martin.

MacKenzie, John M., ed. Imperialism & Popular Culture. LC 85-13657. (Studies in Imperialism). (Illus.). 256p. 1989. reprint ed. pap. 32.00 (*0-7190-1868-4*, Pub. by Manchester Univ Pr) St Martin.

***Mackenzie, John M. & Chamberlain of the Lews Staff.** Diary, 1851. 168p. 1999. 52.00 (*0-86152-908-1*, Pub. by Acair Ltd) St Mut.

Mackenzie, John M. & Chamberlain of the Lews Staff. Diary, 1851. LC 98-188837. 168p. 1999. pap. 32.00 (*0-86152-923-5*) Acair Ltd.

Mackenzie, John M. & Hiery, Herman, eds. European Impact & Pacific Influence: British & German Policy in the Pacific Islands & the Indigenous Response. LC 96-60435. (Tauris Academic Studies). (Illus.). 256p. 1997. text 59.50 (*1-86064-059-1*, Pub. by I B T) St Martin.

Mackenzie, John M., et al. David Livingstone & the Victorian Encounter with Africa. LC 96-189083. (Illus.). 239p. 1996. 69.50 (*1-85514-177-9*, Pub. by Natl Port Gall) Antique Collect.

MacKenzie, John M., jt. auth. see Richards, Jeffrey.

Mackenzie, John P. Seabirds. (Birds of the World Ser.). (Illus.). 144p. 1997. 19.95 (*1-55013-787-5*, Pub. by Key Porter) Firefly Bks Ltd.

— Wading Birds. (Birds of the World Ser.). 1993. 24.95 (*1-55013-279-2*) U of Toronto Pr.

***MacKenzie, John P. S.** Seabirds: Birds of the World. (Illus.). 142p. 2000. reprint ed. pap. text 20.00 (*0-7881-6914-9*) DIANE Pub.

MacKenzie, John R. Organized Labor Education & Training Programs. 45p. 1984. 5.50 (*0-318-22163-2*, IN286) Ctr Educ Trng Employ.

Mackenzie, John W. Chronicle of the Kings of Scotland. LC 72-1037. (Maitland Club, Glasgow. Publications: No. 8). reprint ed. 40.00 (*0-404-52935-6*) AMS Pr.

MacKenzie, Joy. The Big Book of Bible Crafts & Projects. (Illus.). 224p. (Orig.). (J). (ps-4). 1981. pap. 19.99 (*0-310-70151-1*, 14019P) Zondervan.

— Solving Bible Mysteries: 101 Games, Puzzles, Projects, Crafts, Experiments & More. 112p. (J). 1994. 10.99 (*0-310-59761-7*) Zondervan.

MacKenzie, Joy & Bledsoe, Shirley. The Bible Book of Lists. 128p. (YA). (gr. 7-9). 1984. pap. 6.95 (*0-310-70321-2*, 14035P) Zondervan.

Mackenzie, Joy, et al. A Big Book of Bible Games & Puzzles. 192p. (J). (gr. 1-6). 1982. reprint ed. pap. 19.99 (*0-310-70271-2*, 14029P) Zondervan.

MacKenzie, Joy, jt. auth. see Forle, Imogene.

MacKenzie, Joy, jt. auth. see Forte, Imogene.

MacKenzie, Judith-Anne & Phillips, Mary. A Practical Approach to Land Law. 332p. (C). 1989. 160.00 (*1-85431-046-1*, Pub. by Blackstone Pr) St Mut.

— A Practical Approach to Land Law. 5th ed. 374p. 1994. text 36.00 (*1-85431-354-1*, Pub. by Blackstone Pr) Gaunt.

— A Practical Approach to Land Law. 6th ed. 380p. 1996. pap. 38.00 (*1-85431-550-1*, Pub. by Blackstone Pr) Gaunt.

— A Practical Approach to Land Law. 7th rev. ed. LC 99-160193. 399p. 1997. pap. 38.00 (*1-85431-683-4*, Pub. by Blackstone Pr) Gaunt.

***MacKenzie, Judith-Anne & Phillips, Mary.** Textbook on Land Law. 8th ed. 546p. 1999. pap. 36.00 (*1-85431-875-6*, Pub. by Blackstone Pr) Gaunt.

MacKenzie, Julia, jt. auth. see Corey, D. Steven.

Mackenzie, Julie. Horse Law. 1988. pap. 100.00 (*0-7219-1130-7*, Pub. by Scientific) St Mut.

MacKenzie, K. Roy. Classics in Group Psychotherapy. LC 91-35412. 356p. 1992. lib. bdg. 55.00 (*0-89862-799-0*) Guilford Pubns.

— Introduction to Time-Limited Group Psychotherapy. 317p. 1990. text 44.00 (*0-88048-168-4*, 8168) Am Psychiatric.

— Time-Managed Group Psychotherapy: Effective Clinical Applications. 466p. 1997. text 69.50 (*0-88048-863-8*, 8863) Am Psychiatric.

MacKenzie, K. Roy, ed. Effective Use of Group Therapy in Managed Care. (Clinical Practice: No. 29). 1994. 31.00 (*0-88048-492-6*, 8492) Am Psychiatric.

MacKenzie, K. Roy, jt. ed. see Bernard, Harold S.

MacKenzie, K. Roy, jt. ed. see Dies, Robert R.

MacKenzie, K. Roy, jt. ed. see Harper-Giuffre, Heather.

MacKenzie, Kathleen. Advertising ... It's a Gamble! How to Roll the Odds in Favor of Your Small Business. (Illus.). vi, 90p. 1997. spiral bd. 24.95 (*0-9661342-0-6*) Wiz Words.

Mackenzie-Kennedy, C. The Atlantic Blue Riband. 1999. pap. 26.00 (*1-85072-133-5*, Pub. by W Sessions) St Mut.

Mackenzie, Kenneth. Turkey in Transition: The West's Neglected Ally. (C). 1984. 35.00 (*0-907967-20-5*, Pub. by Inst Euro Def & Strat) St Mut.

Mackenzie, Kenneth D. Organizational Design: The Organizational Audit & Analysis Technology. Voigt, Melvin J., ed. LC 85-13454. (Communication & Information Science Ser.). 304p. 1986. text 73.25 (*0-89391-348-0*) Ablx Pub.

— Organizational Design: The Organizational Audit & Analysis Technology. 304p. 1993. pap. 39.50 (*1-56750-072-2*) Ablx Pub.

Mackenzie, Kenneth D. The Organizational Hologram: The Effective Management of Organizational Change. 528p. 1990. lib. bdg. 186.00 (*0-7923-9082-2*) Kluwer Academic.

Mackenzie, Kenneth D. Practitioner's Guide for Improving an Organization. LC 95-94247. 159p. (Orig.). 1995. pap. text 39.95 (*0-9646185-0-8*) Mackenzie & Co.

Mackenzie, Kenneth D., ed. see Jabes, Jak.

Mackenzie, Kenneth D., ed. see Kiesler, Sara B.

Mackenzie, Kenneth D., ed. see Pfeffer, Jeffrey.

Mackenzie, Kenneth D., ed. see Simmons, Richard E.

Mackenzie, Kenneth D., ed. see Tuggle, Francis D.

Mackenzie, Kenneth R. The Royal Masonic Cyclopaedia. 790p. 1994. reprint ed. pap. 49.95 (*1-56459-420-3*) Kessinger Pub.

Mackenzie, Kenneth R., jt. auth. see Fell, Bryan H.

Mackenzie, Kennety R., tr. see Mickiewicz, Adam.

Mackenzie, Kirill. The General Theory of Lie Groupoids & Lie Algebroids. (London Mathematical Society Lecture Note Ser.: No. 213). 300p. (C). 1999. pap. text 37.95 (*0-521-49928-3*) Cambridge U Pr.

MacKenzie, Kyle. Making It Happen: A Non-Technical Guide To Project Management. 256p. 1998. pap. 29.95 (*0-471-64234-7*) Wiley.

MacKenzie, L. H. Squeaky Toys: Possibly the First Toy to Grab Your Attention. 128p. 1998. pap. 24.95 (*0-7643-0622-7*) Schiffer.

***Mackenzie, Leeann.** Garden Decoration from Junk: Transform Household Junk into Fabulous Garden Features. (Illus.). 2000. 24.95 (*1-85585-761-8*) Collins & Br.

MacKenzie, Leslie, ed. The Complete Directory for People with Chronic Illness, 1998. 3rd rev. ed. 1009p. 1998. 190.00 (*1-891482-04-1*); pap. 165.00 (*0-939300-93-1*) Grey Hse Pub.

Mackenzie, Leslie, et al, eds. The National Housing Directory for People with Disabilities. 1429p. (Orig.). 1993. pap. 150.00 (*0-939300-13-3*) Grey Hse Pub.

Mackenzie, Leslie & Lignor, Amy, eds. The Directory of Overseas Catalogs, 1997. (Illus.). 522p. 1997. pap. 165.00 (*0-939300-75-3*) Grey Hse Pub.

— The Directory of Overseas Catalogs, 1997. 2nd ed. (Illus.). 522p. 1997. 190.00 (*0-939300-36-2*) Grey Hse Pub.

Mackenzie, Lewis. Autumn Wind Haiku: Selected Poems by Kobayashi Issa. 146p. 1999. pap. 10.00 (*4-7700-2473-8*, Pub. by Kodansha Intl) Kodansha.

***Mackenzie, Linda.** Help Yourself Heal with Self-Hypnosis. LC 99-87964. 192p. 2000. pap. 14.95 (*0-8069-4969-4*) Sterling.

Mackenzie, Linda. How to Self-Publish & Market Your Personal Growth Book. LC 98-55164. 1999. pap. 12.95 (*0-89594-981-4*) Crossing Pr.

— Inner Insights - The Book of Charts: Alternative Medicine & Awareness Quick Reference Charts. (Illus.). 112p. (Orig.). 1999. pap. 18.95 (*0-9656432-1-2*, Pub. by Creat Hlth & Spirit) ACCESS Pubs Network.

Mackenzie, Lord. Studies in Roman Law with Comparative View of the Laws of France, England & Scotland. 7th ed. Kirkpatrick, John, ed. LC 90-56337. 524p. 1991. reprint ed. 130.00 (*0-912004-88-6*) Gaunt.

Mackenzie, Lorrie, jt. auth. see Farrell, Ted.

MacKenzie, Louis A., Jr. Pascal's Lettres Provinciales: The Motif & Practice of Fragmentation. LC 88-61122. (ENG & FRE.). 146p. 1988. lib. bdg. 24.95 (*0-917786-63-7*) Summa Pubns.

Mackenzie, Lynn. Non-Western Art: A Brief Guide. LC 94-44273. 176p. (C). 1995. pap. text 17.33 (*0-13-104894-5*) P-H.

Mackenzie, M. W., ed. Advances in Applied Fourier Transform Infrared Spectroscopy. LC 88-14404. (Illus.). 362p. 1988. reprint ed. pap. 112.30 (*0-608-06835-7*, 206703200009) Bks Demand.

MacKenzie, Malcolm S. Selected Poems, 1981-1984. 103p. 1984. 4.95 (*0-89697-180-5*) Intl Univ Pr.

MacKenzie, Malcolm S., jt. auth. see Williams, Kim-Eric.

MacKenzie, Manfred. Communities of Honor & Love in Henry James. 247p. 1975. 31.00 (*0-674-15160-7*) HUP.

MacKenzie, Margaret & MacKenzie, Roderick. The Ultimate Guide to Toronto. (Illus.). 240p. 1992. pap. 11.95 (*0-8118-0151-9*) Chronicle Bks.

MacKenzie, Marlin M. & Denlinger, Ken. Golf: The Mind Game. 224p. 1990. pap. 12.95 (*0-440-50209-8*, Dell Trade Pbks) Dell.

MacKenzie, Maureen A. Androgynous Objects: String Bags & Gender in Central New Guinea. (Studies in Anthropology & History). 272p. 1991. text 87.00 (*3-7186-5155-6*, Harwood Acad Pubs) Gordon & Breach.

— Androgynous Objects: String Bags & Gender in Central New Guinea. (Studies in Anthropology & History). 272p. 1998. pap. text 14.00 (*90-5702-270-2*, Harwood Acad Pubs) Gordon & Breach.

MacKenzie, Maxwell. The Beatles: Every Little Thing. LC 98-28641. 224p. 1998. pap. 10.00 (*0-380-79698-8*, Avon Bks) Morrow Avon.

Mackenzie, Melody & Mackenzie, Alec. Investing Time for Maximum Return. Spectrum Communications Staff, ed. LC 94-73037. (AMI How-to Ser.). 93p. 1995. pap. 12.95 (*1-884926-28-2*, TRAP) Amer Media.

Mackenzie, Michael. Lower Denture Problems? The Worlds Only Self-Help Book on Dentures. LC 98-74385. (Illus.). 136p. 1999. 19.95 (*0-9668234-9-4*) First Bite Pubg.

***MacKenzie, Myrna.** At the Billionaire's Bidding: The Wedding Auction. 2000. per. 3.50 (*0-373-19442-0*) Silhouette.

MacKenzie, Myrna. Babies & a Blue-Eyed Man. (Romance Ser.). 1996. per. 3.25 (*0-373-19182-0*, 1-19182-4) Silhouette.

***MacKenzie, Myrna.** Contractually His: Wedding Auction. (Romance Ser.: Bk. 1454). 2000. per. 3.50 (*0-373-19454-4*, 1-19454-7) Silhouette.

Mackenzie, Myrna. The Daddy List. (Romance Ser.). 1995. per. 2.99 (*0-373-19090-5*, 1-19090-9) Silhouette.

MacKenzie, Myrna. Prince Charming's Return: Fabulous Fathers. 1999. per. 3.50 (*0-373-19361-0*, 1-19361-4) Silhouette.

— The Scandalous Return of Jake Walker. 1997. per. 3.25 (*0-373-19256-8*, 1-19256-6) Silhouette.

Mackenzie, Myrna. The Secret Groom. (Surprise Brides Ser.). 1997. per. 3.25 (*0-373-19225-8*, 1-19225-1) Silhouette.

***MacKenzie, Myrna.** Simon Says... Marry Me! (Romance Ser.: Vol. 143). 2000. mass mkt. 3.50 (*0-373-19429-3*) Silhouette.

MacKenzie, Nancy. Science & Technology Today. 553p. 1994. pap. text 38.95 (*0-312-09692-5*) St Martin.

Mackenzie, Neil D. Ayyubid Cairo: A Topographical Study. (Illus.). 208p. 1992. text 35.00 (*977-424-275-0*, Pub. by Am Univ Cairo Pr) Col U Pr.

MacKenzie, Norman, ed. see Wells, H. G.

MacKenzie, Norman H., ed. see Hopkins, Gerard Manley.

MacKenzie, Norman H., ed. see Webb, Beatrice Potter.

MacKenzie, Osgood H. & Sawyer, M. T. A Hundred Years in the Highlands. (Illus.). 222p. pap. 11.95 (*1-874744-29-7*, Pub. by Birlinn Ltd) Dufour.

MacKenzie, Patricia & Gillen, William. New York Chocolate Lover's Guide: The Best Candy, Cakes, & Chocolate Treats in Town. LC 97-152384. 144p. 1996. 16.00 (*1-885492-36-7*) City & Co.

Mackenzie, Patricia L. Stained Glass Patterns. (Illus.). 95p. 1997. pap. 18.95 (*0-9657552-8-2*) P L Mackenzie.

Mackenzie, Patricia L., ed. Organic Living Designs. (Illus.). Date not set. pap. write for info. (*0-9657552-9-0*) P L Mackenzie.

MacKenzie, Patrick. Lawful Occasions. 1992. pap. 14.95 (*1-85635-024-X*) Dufour.

Mackenzie, Patrick T. The Problems of Philosophers: An Introduction. LC 88-17724. 316p. (C). 1989. pap. text 24.95 (*0-87975-486-9*) Prometheus Bks.

***Mackenzie, R., et al, eds.** Solitons: Properties, Dynamics, Interactions, Applications. LC 99-16040. (CRM Series in Mathematical Physics). (Illus.). 400p. 1999. 49.95 (*0-387-98895-5*) Spr-Verlag.

Mackenzie, R. Alec. New Time Management Methods for You & Your Staff. 2nd ed. 250p. 1990. ring bd. 91.50 (*0-85013-168-5*) Dartnell Corp.

— Teamwork Through Time Management: New Time Management Methods for Everyone in Your Organization. 257p. 1991. pap. 23.95 (*0-85013-182-0*) Dartnell Corp.

MacKenzie, R. Sheldon. The Isolated Jesus: Seven Messages for Good Friday or Lent. LC 93-39814. 68p. 1993. pap. 7.95 (*1-55673-703-3*) CSS OH.

Mackenzie, Rachel. The Wine of Astonishment. LC 96-83495. 176p. (Orig.). 1997. pap. 13.95 (*1-885983-17-4*) Turtle Point Pr.

MacKenzie, Ralph E., jt. auth. see Finch, Robert.

MacKenzie, Ralph E., jt. auth. see Geisler, Norman L.

Mackenzie, Richard. The Caddie Master. (Illus.). 136p. 1998. 18.95 (*1-886947-56-2*) Sleepng Bear.

— A Wee Nip at the 19th Hole: A History of the St. Andrews Caddie. (Illus.). 144p. 1998. 18.95 (*0-553-10824-7*) Bantam.

— A Wee Nip at the 19th Hole: A History of the St. Andrews Caddie. LC 97-43960. (Illus.). 150p. 1997. 18.95 (*1-886947-38-4*) Sleepng Bear.

Mackenzie, Robert E., jt. auth. see Auslander, Louis.

Mackenzie, Robert H. The Trafalgar Roll. 354p. 1989. 27.95 (*0-87021-990-1*) Naval Inst Pr.

Mackenzie, Robert J. Setting Limits: How to Raise Responsible, Independent Children by Providing Clear Boundaries. 2nd expanded rev. ed. LC 97-48667. 368p. 1998. per. 15.00 (*0-7615-1212-8*) Prima Pub.

Mackenzie, Robert J. Setting Limits in the Classroom: How to Move Beyond Classroom Dance. 304p. 1996. pap., per. 15.00 (*0-7615-0033-2*) Prima Pub.

MacKenzie, Robert K. The Author of the Apocalypse: A Review of the Prevailing Hypothesis of Jewish-Christian Authorship. LC 96-52268. (Biblical Press Ser.: Vol. 51). 208p. 1997. text 89.95 (*0-7734-2423-7*, Mellen Biblical Pr) E Mellen.

MacKenzie, Roderick, jt. auth. see MacKenzie, Margaret.

MacKenzie, Roderick A. Faith & History in the Old Testament. LC 63-10585. 127p. 1963. reprint ed. pap. 39.40 (*0-7837-4524-9*, 205751900006) Bks Demand.

Mackenzie, Ross. Brief Points: An Almanac for Parents & Friends of U. S. Naval Academy Midshipmen, Updated. rev. ed. LC 96-11801. (Illus.). 232p. 1996. 21.95 (*1-55750-584-5*) Naval Inst Pr.

MacKenzie, Ross & Culbertson, Todd, eds. Eyewitness: Writings from the Ordeal of Communism. 492p. (C). 1992. lib. bdg. 27.95 (*0-932088-77-5*) Freedom Hse.

— Eyewitness: Writings from the Ordeal of Communism. LC 92-30861. (Focus on Issues Ser.: No. 15). 1992. pap. write for info. (*0-932088-76-7*) Freedom Hse.

Mackenzie, Ross, jt. ed. see Borg, Marcus J.

MacKenzie, S. P. The Home Guard: A Military & Political History. (Illus.). 276p. 1995. text 32.00 (*0-19-820577-5*) OUP.

— The Home Guard: A Military & Political History. LC 96-19278. (Illus.). 276p. 1997. pap. 15.95 (*0-19-285331-7*) OUP.

— Politics & Military Morale: Current Affairs & Citizenship Education in the British Army 1914-1950. (Oxford Historical Monographs). (Illus.). 258p. 1992. text 65.00 (*0-19-820244-X*) OUP.

MacKenzie, Samuel L. & Taylor, David C., eds. Seed Oils for the Future. LC 93-7118. 190p. 1993. 60.00 (*0-935315-46-2*) Am Oil Chemists.

***MacKenzie, Scott & Stewart, Jimmy, eds.** Graphics Interface Proceedings, 1988-99. 1999. pap. 50.00 (*1-55860-632-7*) Morgan Kaufmann.

MacKenzie, Scott, jt. auth. see Hjort, Mette.

MacKenzie, Scott B., jt. ed. see Goodstein, Ronald C.

Mackenzie, Scotty & Goode, Ruth. My Love Affair with the State of Maine. 2nd ed. LC 97-929. (Illus.). 328p. 1997. reprint ed. pap. 14.95 (*0-89272-407-2*) Down East.

MacKenzie, Shea. The Bread Machine Gourmet: Simple Recipes for Extraordinary Breads. LC 93-977. (Illus.). 324p. Date not set. pap. 14.95 (*0-89529-697-7*, Avery) Penguin Putnam.

— The Garden of Earthly Delights Cookbook: Gourmet Vegetarian Cooking. LC 93-8339. (Illus.). 480p. pap. 14.95 (*0-89529-530-X*, Avery) Penguin Putnam.

— Garden of Earthly Delights Cookbook: Gourmet Vegetarian Cooking. 468p. 1995. pap. 14.95 (*0-89529-673-X*, Avery) Penguin Putnam.

— The Pizza Gourmet: Simple Recipes for Spectacular Pizzas. LC 95-4860. (Illus.). 232p. pap. 14.95 (*0-89529-656-X*, Avery) Penguin Putnam.

MacKenzie, Stephen. Decoys & Aggression: A Police K9 Training Manual. (Illus.). 96p. 1996. write for info. (*1-55059-132-0*) Detselig Ents.

Mackenzie, Stephen A. Equine Safety. LC 97-7257. (Agriculture Ser.). 160p. 1997. mass mkt. 35.95 (*0-8273-7231-0*) Delmar.

— Equine Safety. (Agriculture Ser.). 1998. teacher ed. 10.00 (*0-8273-7232-9*) Delmar.

MacKenzie, Steve. Fundamentals of Free Lungeing: An Introduction to Tackless Training. (Illus.). 98p. 1994. 20.95 (*0-939481-35-9*) Half Halt Pr.

— SEALs No. 1: Ambush. 192p. 1987. pap. 2.50 (*0-380-75189-5*, Avon Bks) Morrow Avon.

— SEALs No. 4: Target. 192p. 1987. pap. 2.95 (*0-380-75193-3*, Avon Bks) Morrow Avon.

— SEALs No. 7: Recon. 160p. 1988. pap. 2.95 (*0-380-75529-7*, Avon Bks) Morrow Avon.

— SEALs No. 8: Infiltrate. 160p. (Orig.). 1988. pap. 2.95 (*0-380-75530-0*, Avon Bks) Morrow Avon.

— SEALs No. 9: Assault! 160p. 1988. pap. 2.95 (*0-380-75532-7*, Avon Bks) Morrow Avon.

— SEALs No. 10: Sniper. 1988. pap. 2.95 (*0-380-75533-5*, Avon Bks) Morrow Avon.

— SEALs No. 11: Attack. 160p. 1989. pap. 2.95 (*0-380-75582-3*, Avon Bks) Morrow Avon.

— SEALs No. 12: Stronghold. 160p. (Orig.). 1989. pap. 2.95 (*0-380-75583-1*, Avon Bks) Morrow Avon.

— SEALs No. 13: Crisis! 160p. (Orig.). 1989. pap. 2.95 (*0-380-75771-0*, Avon Bks) Morrow Avon.

— SEALs No. 14: Treasure. 176p. 1989. pap. 2.95 (*0-380-75772-9*, Avon Bks) Morrow Avon.

Mackenzie, Susan, jt. ed. see Gold, Charlotte.

MacKenzie, Susan H. Integrated Resource Planning & Management: The Ecosystem Approach in the Great Lakes Basin. 240p. (Orig.). (C). 1996. text 50.00 (*1-55963-423-5*); pap. text 27.00 (*1-55963-424-3*) Island Pr.

Mackenzie, Suzanne. Visible Histories: Women & Environments in a Post-War British City. 240p. (C). 1989. text 65.00 (*0-7735-0712-4*, Pub. by McG-Queens Univ Pr) CUP Services.

Mackenzie, Talitha & Kopka, Matthew, prods. Ba Ba Ba Mo Leanabh: Hush, Hush, Little Baby. (Illus.). 32p. (J). 1996. 23.95 incl. cd-rom (*1-55961-391-2*, Ellipsis Kids) Relaxtn Co.

Mackenzie, Vance. Hodder Goes Home. large type ed. (Linford Western Large Print Ser.). 208p. 1997. pap. 16.99 (*0-7089-5091-4*, Linford) Ulverscroft.

Mackenzie, Vicki. Cave in the Snow: Tenzin Palmo's Quest for Enlightenment. (Illus.). 210p. 1998. 24.95 (*1-58234-004-8*) Bloomsbury Pubg.

— Cave in the Snow: Tenzin Palmo's Quest for Enlightenment. 224p. 1999. pap. 14.95 (*1-58234-045-5*) Bloomsbury Pubg.

— Reborn in the West: The Reincarnation Masters. (Illus.). 215p. 1996. pap. 13.95 (*1-56924-804-4*) Marlowe & Co.

***Mackenzie, Vicki.** Reborn in the West: The Reincarnation Masters. (Illus.). 214p. 1999. reprint ed. text 28.00 (*0-7881-6253-5*) DIANE Pub.

Mackenzie, Vicki. Reincarnation: The Boy Lama. 2nd rev. ed. LC 95-51032. (Illus.). 192p. 1996. pap. 16.95 (*0-86171-108-4*) Wisdom MA.

MacKenzie, W., et al. Canadiens, Canadians & Quebecoi's. 1974. pap. text 7.40 (*0-13-112888-4*) P-H.

MacKenzie, W. J. Power, Violence, Decision LC 76-361447. (Peregrine Bks.). 272 p. 1975. write for info. (*0-14-055098-4*) Penguin Putnam.

MacKenzie, W. Mackay. The Medieval Castle in Scotland. LC 75-174843. (Illus.). 260p. 1972. reprint ed. 24.95 (*0-405-08769-1*, Pub. by Blom Pubns) Ayer.

MacKenzie, W. Mackay. Poems of William Dunbar. 272p. 1989. pap. 21.00 (*0-901824-94-1*, Pub. by Mercat Pr Bks) St Mut.

MacKenzie, W. Roy. Quest of the Ballad. LC 68-815. (Studies in Poetry: No. 38). 1969. reprint ed. lib. bdg. 75.00 (*0-8383-0591-1*) M S G Haskell Hse.

MacKenzie, W. S. & Adams, A. E. A Color Atlas of Rocks & Minerals in Thin Section. LC 93-6167. 192p. 1996. text 49.50 (*0-470-23628-0*) Halsted Pr.

— A Color Atlas of Rocks & Minerals in Thin Section. LC 93-6167. (Illus.). 192p. 1994. pap. 49.95 (*0-470-23338-9*) Wiley.

M

Mackenzie, W. S. & Guilford, C. Atlas of Rock-Forming Minerals in Thin Sections. LC 79-27822. 98p. 1980. pap. text 64.95 (0-470-26921-9) Halsted Pr.

MacKenzie, W. S., et al. Atlas of Igneous Rock & Their Textures. 148p. 1982. pap. text 59.95 (0-470-27339-9) Halsted Pr.

Mackenzie, W. S., jt. auth. see Adams, A. E.

MacKenzie, Warren. For Women Only: A Woman's Guide to Financial Security. rev. ed. LC 86-70681. (Financial & Business Services Ser.). 196p. 1987. pap. text 5.50 (0-938125-04-4); 5.25 (0-938125-05-2) Crystal Rainbow.

Mackenzie, William. Practical Treatise on the Diseases of the Eye. deluxe ed. LC 78-31614. 732p. 1979. reprint ed. 49.50 (0-88275-947-7) Krieger.

— Practical Treatise on the Diseases of the Eye. LC 78-31614. 732p. 1979. reprint ed. 44.50 (0-88275-841-1) Krieger.

Mackenzie, William & MacLean, Alasdair. Old Skye Tales: Traditions, Reflections & Memories. (Illus.). 94p. pap. 19.95 (1-899272-01-1, Pub. by Maclean Pr) Dufour.

Mackenzie, William C. The Highlands & Isles of Scotland: A Historical Survey. LC 75-41183. reprint ed. 37.50 (0-404-14682-1) AMS Pr.

***Mackenzie, William C. & ASM International Staff.** Worldwide Guide to Equivalent Irons & Steels. 4th ed. LC 99-47360. 1999. write for info. (0-87170-635-0) ASM.

Mackenzie, William L. Eighteen Thirty-Seven: Revolution in the Canadas. 240p. 1974. 8.95 (0-919600-22-0, Pub. by NC Ltd) U of Toronto Pr.

MacKenzie, William R. English Moralities from the Point of View of Allegory. LC 66-29466. 278p. 1966. reprint ed. 75.00 (0-87752-066-6) Gordian.

MacKenzie, William R. English Moralities from the Point of View of Allegory. LC 68-54172. (Studies in Drama: No. 39). 1969. reprint ed. lib. bdg. 75.00 (0-8383-0592-X) M S G Haskell Hse.

— English Moralities from the Point of View of Allegory. (BCL1-PR English Literature Ser.). 278p. 1992. reprint ed. lib. bdg. 79.00 (0-7812-7099-5) Rprt Serv.

Mackenzie-Wintle, Hector. Renault. (Illus.). 160p. 1999. pap. 21.95 (0-7509-1924-8, Pub. by Sutton Pub Ltd) Intl Pubs Mktg.

MacKeown, P. K. Stochastic Simulation in Physics. LC 97-10647. 440p. (C). 1997. pap. 59.00 (981-3083-26-3, Pub. by Spr-Verlag) Spr-Verlag.

MacKeown, P. K. & Newman, D. J. Computational Techniques in Physics. (Illus.). 240p. 1987. disk 59.00 (0-85274-429-3) IOP Pub.

— Computational Techniques in Physics. LC 87-21116. (Illus.). 240p. 1987. pap. 41.00 (0-85274-548-6) IOP Pub.

Macker, John. Burroughs at Santo Domingo. 27p. 1998. pap. 8.00 (0-9623013-3-7) Long Road Pr.

— The First Gangster. (Illus.). 28p. 1994. pap. 6.00 (0-9623013-2-9) Long Road Pr.

Mackereth, F. J. Ion-Exchange Procedures for the Estimation of (I) Total Ionic Concentration, (II) Chlorides & (III) Sulphates in Natural Waters. (International Association of Theoretical & Applied Limnology, Communications Ser.: No. 4). (Illus.). 16p. 1955. pap. 15.00 (3-510-52004-1, Pub. by E Schweizerbartsche) Balogh.

Mackereth, F. J., et al. Water Analysis: Some Revised Methods for Limnologists. 1978. 39.00 (0-900386-31-2) St Mut.

Mackereth, F. J., jt. auth. see Heron, J.

Mackerian, Gail. Dissolved Oxygen in the Chesapeake Bay: Processes & Effects. 1987. 6.95 (0-943676-26-6) MD Sea Grant Col.

Mackerle, M. The Boundary Element Reference Book. LC 87-72284. 350p. 1987. 77.00 (0-931215-67-6) Computational Mech MA.

Mackerness, Eric D. A Social History of English Music. LC 75-40994. (Illus.). 307p. 1976. reprint ed. lib. bdg. 38.50 (0-8371-8705-2, MAHEM, Greenwood Pr) Greenwood.

MacKerras. Asia Since 1945: History Through Documents. 1992. pap. text. write for info. (0-582-87137-9, Pub. by Addison-Wesley) Longman.

— China in Revolution. 1993. pap. text. write for info. (0-582-91060-9, Pub. by Addison-Wesley) Longman.

— China since 1978. 2nd ed. 287p. (C). 1998. pap. 25.66 (0-582-81026-4) Longman.

— China Since 1978. 1994. pap. text. write for info. (0-582-80183-4, Pub. by Addison-Wesley) Longman.

— Eastern Asia an Introduction to History. 1995. pap. text. write for info. (0-582-80660-7, Pub. by Addison-Wesley) Longman.

Mackerras, Colin. China in Transformation 1900-1949. LC 97-50298. (Seminar Studies in History). 144p. (C). 1998. pap. 16.80 (0-582-31209-4) Longman.

— China's Minorities: Integration & Modernization in the Twentieth Century. LC 93-43882. (Illus.). 364p. (C). 1994. text 85.00 (0-19-585988-X) OUP.

MacKerras, Colin. China's Minority Culture. 1995. text. write for info. (0-582-80671-2, Pub. by Addison-Wesley) Longman.

***MacKerras, Colin.** Eastern Asia: An Introductory History. 3rd ed. (Illus.). 704p. 2000. pap. text 29.00 (0-7339-0192-1) Addison-Wesley.

Mackerras, Colin. Peking Opera. LC 97-6887. (Images of Asia Ser.). (Illus.). 80p. 1997. text 18.95 (0-19-587729-2) OUP.

***Mackerras, Colin.** Western Images of China. 2nd ed. LC 99-34631. 220p. 2000. text 29.95 (0-19-590738-8) OUP.

Mackerras, Colin, ed. Chinese Theater: From Its Origins to the Present Day. LC 83-6687. (Illus.). 228p. (C). 1983. reprint ed. pap. text 16.00 (0-8248-1220-4) UH Pr.

— East & Southeast Asia: A Multidisciplinary Survey. LC 95-8986. 640p. 1995. 29.95 (1-55587-612-9) L Rienner.

MacKerras, Colin & McMillen, Donald H., eds. Dictionary of the Politics of the People's Republic of China. (Routledge in Asia Ser.). 288p. (C). 1998. 100.00 (0-415-15450-2) Routledge.

Mackerras, Colin & Yorke, Amanda. The Cambridge Handbook of Contemporary China. (Illus.). 276p. (C). 1992. pap. text 24.95 (0-521-38755-8) Cambridge U Pr.

Mackerras, Colin, et al. China since 1978: Reform, Modernisation & Socialism with Chinese Characteristics. LC 93-24509. 1994. pap. 20.95 (0-312-10306-9); text 55.00 (0-312-10252-6) St Martin.

Mackerras, Colin, jt. ed. see Maidment, Richard.

Mackerras, Colin, jt. ed. see Tung, Constantine.

Mackerras, Patrick. Medicine: A Guide for Prospective Students. 137p. 1996. 17.95 (0-644-36056-9, Pub. by Aust Gov Pub) Accents Pubns.

MacKerron, Conrad B. Business in the Rain Forests: Corporations, Deforestation & Sustainability. Cogan, Douglas G., ed. (Illus.). 256p. 1993. pap. 20.00 (1-879775-08-5) IRRC Inc DC.

MacKerron, D. K., jt. ed. see Haverkort, A. J.

MacKerron, G. & Pearson, P., eds. The U. K. Energy Experience: A Model or a Warning? Proceedings of the British Institute of Energy Economics. LC 96-218393. 524p. 1996. lib. bdg. 86.00 (1-86094-022-6) World Scientific Pub.

Mackersey, Ian. Tom Rolt & the Cressy Years. 106p. (C). 1989. 45.00 (0-947712-01-1, Pub. by S A Baldwin) St Mut.

Mackervoy, Susan, et al, trs. Knopf Guide to the Louvre. LC 95-18403. (Guides Ser.). 392p. (YA). 1995. pap. 25.00 (0-679-76452-6) Knopf.

Mackesy, Piers. Could the British Have Won the War of Independence? Billias, George A., ed. LC 76-41409. (Bland-Lee Lectures in History Ser.). 1976. pap. 1.00 (0-914206-08-7) Clark U Pr.

— The Coward of Minden: The Affair of Lord George Sackville. LC 78-26204. (Illus.). 279p. 1979. text 25.00 (0-312-17060-2) St Martin.

— The War for America, 1775-1783. LC 92-37789. (Illus.). xxx, 569p. (C). 1993. pap. 24.00 (0-8032-8192-7, Bison Books) U of Nebr Pr.

— The War in the Mediterranean, 1803 to 1810. LC 81-6457. (Illus.). 430p. 1981. reprint ed. lib. bdg. 75.00 (0-313-22913-9, MAWM, Greenwood Pr) Greenwood.

MacKethan, Lucinda H. Daughters of Time: Creating Woman's Voice in Southern Story. LC 89-4824. (Brown Thrasher Bks.). 144p. 1992. pap. 14.00 (0-8203-1444-7) U of Ga Pr.

MacKethan, Lucinda H., jt. auth. see Bacon, Eugenia J.

MacKethan, Lucinda H., ed. see Pond, Cornelia J.

Mackett, M. & Williamson, J. Human Vaccines & Vaccination. (Medical Perspectives Ser.). 160p. (Orig.). 1994. pap. 52.50 (1-872748-77-5, Pub. by Bios Sci) Coronet Bks.

Mackewn, Jennifer. Developing Gestalt Counselling. LC 97-66577. (Developing Counselling Ser.). 128p. 1996. 59.95 (0-8039-7860-X); pap. 16.95 (0-8039-7861-8) Sage.

Mackey. Copper 1991, 4 vols., Set. (Proceedings of the Metallurgical Society of Canada Ser.). 1992. 963.00 (0-08-041432-X, Pergamon Pr); 595.00 (0-08-041434-6, Pergamon Pr) Elsevier.

— Year the Horses Came. LC 92-56119. pap. 10.00 (0-06-250736-2, Perennial) HarperTrade.

Mackey, A. G. Jurisprudence of Freemasonry. 21.95 (0-685-22001-X) Wehman.

Mackey, Agnes E. The Universal Self: A Study of Paul Valery. LC 61-65142. 279p. reprint ed. pap. 86.50 (0-608-16296-5, 202653000050) Bks Demand.

Mackey, Aidan, ed. Collected Works of G. K. Chesterton: Collected Poetry, Vol. X, Pt. 1. LC 85-81511. Vol. 1. 565p. 1994. 39.95 (0-89870-390-5) Ignatius Pr.

Mackey, Albert G. The Book of the Chapter on Monitorial Instructions in the Degrees of Mark, Past & Most Excellent Master of the Royal Arch. 262p. 1997. reprint ed. pap. 24.95 (0-7661-0034-0) Kessinger Pub.

— Encyclopedia of Free Masonry. 1046p. 1991. reprint ed. pap. 75.00 (1-56459-099-2) Kessinger Pub.

— The History of Freemasonry. 576p. 1996. 19.99 (0-517-14982-6) Random Hse Value.

— Jurisprudence of Freemasonry. 1994. pap. 17.00 (0-911164-14-6) Powner.

— A Lexicon of Freemasonry. 527p. 1994. reprint ed. pap. 39.95 (1-56459-463-7) Kessinger Pub.

— Mackey's Jurisprudence of Freemasonry. 406p. 1994. reprint ed. 16.50 (0-88053-026-X, M 073) Macoy Pub.

— A Manual of the Lodge (1898): or Monitorial Instructions in the Degrees of Entered Apprentice, Fellow Craft, & Master Mason Arranged in Accordance with the American System of Lectures: To Which Are Added the Ceremonies of the Order Past Master, Relating to Installations, Dedications, Consecrations, Laying of Corner-Stones, Etc. 275p. 1995. reprint ed. pap. 24.95 (1-56459-518-8) Kessinger Pub.

— Symbolism of Freemasonry. 17.00 (0-911164-32-4) Powner.

— Symbolism of Freemasonry: Its Science, Philosophy, Legends, Myths & Symbols. 375p. 1994. reprint ed. pap. 24.95 (1-56459-469-6) Kessinger Pub.

***Mackey, Albert G. & Morris, Rob.** Lights & Shadows of the Mystic Tie (1889) 634p. 1999. reprint ed. pap. 45.00 (0-7661-0770-1) Kessinger Pub.

Mackey, Alison, jt. auth. see Gass, Susan M.

Mackey, Allison, jt. auth. see Westheimer, Patricia.

Mackey, Arthur. Biblical Principles of Success. 1995. pap. 9.99 (1-56229-454-7) Pneuma Life Pub.

Mackey, Arthur L. Biblical Principles of Success: A Practical Guide for Living. 1993. pap. 8.00 (0-927936-47-X) Vincom Pubng Co.

Mackey, Arthur L., Jr. Walking Through the Doorways of Destiny: A Motivational Guide for Living. LC 97-214432. 158p. 1996. pap. 9.99 (1-56229-455-5) Pneuma Life Pub.

Mackey, B., et al. Culture Change along the Eastern Sierra Nevada/Cascade Front Vol. VIII: Jackrabbit Tamale: Recipe for Historic Era Homesteading. fac. ed. (Far Western Anthropological Research Group, Inc. Ser.). (Illus.). 605p. (C). 1997. reprint ed. pap. text 61.88 (1-55567-718-5) Coyote Press.

Mackey, Bertha. A Saloon Keeper's Daughter Saved. 15p. 1982. pap. 0.50 (0-686-36264-0); pap. 0.25 (0-686-37285-9) Faith Pub Hse.

Mackey, Betty. The Herb Collector's Notebook. (Illus.). 1998. pap. 9.50 (0-9616338-8-3) B B Mackey Bks.

Mackey, Betty B. Garden Notes Through the Years: Four-Year Comparative Garden Diary. rev. ed. (Illus.). 118p. 1995. pap. 10.95 (0-9616338-4-0) B B Mackey Bks.

— The Plant Collector's Notebook. rev. ed. 150p. 1996. pap. 7.95 (0-9616338-5-9) B B Mackey Bks.

Mackey, Betty B., et al. The Gardener's Home Companion. 608p. 1991. 34.95 (0-02-578035-2) Macmillan.

Mackey, Betty B., jt. auth. see Halpin, Anne M.

Mackey, Betty B., ed. & illus. see Brandies, Monica M.

Mackey, Cleo. The Cowboy & Rodeo Evolution. (Illus.). 120p. 1980. reprint ed. 7.95 (0-9608176-0-3); reprint ed. pap. 5.95 (0-9608176-1-1) C Mackey.

Mackey, Daphne. More Grammar Plus. 224p. 1996. pap. text, student ed. 13.23 (0-201-89884-5) Addison-Wesley.

— More Grammar Plus. 224p. 1996. pap. text, wbk. ed. 15.44 (0-201-87677-9) Addison-Wesley.

— More Grammar Plus, Bk. A. 1996. pap. text, student ed. 13.23 (0-201-89883-7) Addison-Wesley.

— More Grammar Plus, Bk. A. 112p. 1996. pap. text, wbk. ed. 8.13 (0-201-89885-3) Addison-Wesley.

— More Grammar Plus, Bk. B. 112p. 1996. pap. text, wbk. ed. 8.13 (0-201-89886-1) Addison-Wesley.

Mackey, Daphne & DeFillippo, J. Grammar Plus. 2nd ed. (C). 1994. pap. text, teacher ed. 12.51 (0-201-53496-7) Addison-Wesley.

— Grammar Plus: A Basic Skills Course. 2nd ed. 176p. (C). 1994. student ed., ring bd., wbk. ed. 15.44 (0-201-53497-5) Addison-Wesley.

— Grammar Plus: A Basic Skills Course. 2nd ed. 320p. (C). 1994. pap. text, student ed. 26.46 (0-201-53495-9) Addison-Wesley.

Mackey, Daphne & Sokmen, Anita J. More Grammar Plus. Hilles, Sharon, ed. LC 95-24396. 1996. pap. text, student ed. 26.46 (0-201-87675-2) Addison-Wesley.

Mackey, Daphne, jt. auth. see Abraham, Paul.

Mackey, Daphne, jt. auth. see Abraham, Paul F.

Mackey, Daphne, jt. auth. see DeFillippo, J.

Mackey, Daphne, jt. auth. see Sokmen, Anita.

Mackey, David. Multiple Family Housing. (Illus.). 1977. 32.50 (0-8038-0164-5) Archit CT.

***Mackey, David.** The New Architecture of Learning: Strategies & Solutions in Training & Development. 240p. 2000. pap. 29.95 (0-7494-3120-2, Pub. by Kogan Page Ltd) Stylus Pub VA.

Mackey, David, jt. auth. see Taylor, Bryan.

MacKey, David, jt. auth. see Thorne, Kaye.

Mackey, Donald R., jt. auth. see Jensen, Rue.

Mackey, Douglas A. D. H. Lawrence: The Poet Who Was Not Wrong. LC 84-291. (Milford Series: Popular Writers of Today: Vol. 42). 149p. 1986. pap. 19.00 (0-89370-271-4) Millefleurs.

— The Dance of Consciousness: Enlightenment in Modern Literature. LC 94-27641. (I. O. Evans Studies in the Philosophy & Criticism of Literature: No. 16). 157p. 1994. pap. 19.00 (0-89370-405-9) Millefleurs.

— Philip K. Dick. (United States Authors Ser.). 168p. 1988. 22.95 (0-8057-7515-3, Twyne) Mac Lib Ref.

— The Work of Ian Watson: An Annotated Bibliography & Guide. Clarke, Boden, ed. LC 88-36646. (Bibliographies of Modern Authors Ser.: No. 18). 148p. (C). 1989. pap. 19.00 (0-8095-1512-1) Millefleurs.

Mackey, Douglas A., jt. auth. see Spayde, Sydney H.

Mackey, Douglas A., ed. see Early, Lewis & Mantle, Mickey.

***Mackey, Eva.** The House of Difference: Cultural Politics & National Identity in Canada. LC 98-33939. 4p. 1999. write for info. (0-415-18166-6) Routledge.

***Mackey, Frank.** Steamboat Connections: Montreal to Upper Canada, 1816-1843. (Illus.). 440p. 2000. 44.95 (0-7735-2055-4, Pub. by McG-Queens Univ Pr) CUP Services.

Mackey, G. W. Theory of Unitary Group Representation. Kaplansky, Irving, ed. LC 76-17697. (Chicago Lectures in Mathematics). 382p. 1999. pap. text 12.00 (0-226-50052-7) U Ch Pr.

Mackey, G. W., ed. The Scope & History of Commutative & Noncommutative Harmonic Analysis. LC 92-12857. (History of Mathematics Ser.: Vol. 5). 370p. 1992. text 52.00 (0-8218-9903-1, HMATH/5C) Am Math.

Mackey, G. W., jt. auth. see Segal, I. E.

Mackey, Gale. Mirame, Puedo Cantar Mas! Look, I Can Sing More!, Vol. 5. (Look, I Can Talk! Ser.: Vol. 5). (SPA.). xx, 59p. (gr. 4-12). 1997. pap. 12.95 incl. audio Command Performance.

Mackey, Gale & Seely, Contee. Mirame, Puedo Cantar Mas! Look, I Can Sing More!, Vol. 5. (Look, I Can Talk! Ser.: Vol. 5). (SPA.). xx, 59p. (gr. 4-12). 1997. pap. 19.95 incl. audio (0-929724-31-3, 31-3) Command Performance.

Mackey, Henry B., tr. see De Sales, Francis.

Mackey, Henry B., tr. see St. Francis de Sales.

Mackey, Howard & Perry, Candy M., eds. Vestry Book of Hungar's Parish: Northampton County, Virginia, 1757-1875. LC 97-80359. 160p. 1997. 28.50 (0-89725-331-0, 1837) Picton Pr.

Mackey, James P. Power & Christian Ethics. (New Studies in Christian Ethics: No. 3). 251p. (C). 1994. text 69.95 (0-521-41595-0) Cambridge U Pr.

— The Religious Imagination. 256p. 1986. 50.00 (0-85224-512-2, Pub. by Edinburgh U Pr) Col U Pr.

Mackey, James P., ed. An Introduction to Celtic Christianity. 432p. 1993. pap. text 34.95 (0-567-29507-9, Pub. by T & T Clark) Bks Intl VA.

***Mackey, James Patrick.** The Critique of Theological Reason. LC 99-57403. 388p. (C). 2000. write for info. (0-521-77293-1) Cambridge U Pr.

***Mackey, James T. & Thomas, Michael F.** Management Accounting: A Road of Discovery. LC 99-24166. (SWC-Accounting Ser.). 561p. 1999. pap. 67.95 (0-538-87189-X) S-W Pub.

Mackey, Kitty. How to Make Perfect Dollhouse Figures. LC 98-157274. (Illus.). 48p. 1998. pap. 11.95 (0-89024-341-7, 12203, Kalmbach Books) Kalmbach.

Mackey, Laura. Math in the Garden. (Math Is Everywhere Ser.). (Illus.). 48p. (J). (gr. k-1). 1994. pap. text, teacher ed. 6.45 (1-55799-320-3, EMC 092) Evan-Moor Edu Pubs.

— Math in the Kitchen. (Math Is Everywhere Ser.). (Illus.). 48p. (J). (gr. 2-3). 1994. pap. text, teacher ed. 6.45 (1-55799-327-0, EMC 099) Evan-Moor Edu Pubs.

Mackey, Lloyd. Like Father, Like Son. LC 97-168937. (Illus.). 200p. 1997. pap. 16.95 (1-55022-299-6, Pub. by ECW) Genl Dist Srvs.

Mackey, Louis. Fact, Fiction & Representation: Four Novels by Gilbert Sorrentino. (ENG Ser.). xii, 98p. 1997. 45.00 (1-57113-100-0) Camden Hse.

— Peregrinations of the Word: Essays in Medieval Philosophy. LC 96-45815. 248p. (C). 1997. text 44.50 (0-472-10736-4, 10736) U of Mich Pr.

Mackey, Louis H. Points of View: Readings of Kierkegaard. LC 85-22713. (Kierkegaard & Postmodernism Ser.). 240p. (Orig.). 1986. pap. 24.95 (0-8130-0824-7) U Press Fla.

MacKey, M., jt. auth. see Kotsonis, Frank N.

Mackey, M. A., jt. auth. see Kotsonis, Frank N.

Mackey, M. C. Time's Arrow: Origins of Thermodynamic Behavior. (Illus.). 150p. 1991. 49.00 (0-387-97702-3) Spr-Verlag.

— Time's Arrow: Origins of Thermodynamic Behavior. (Illus.). 192p. 1994. reprint ed. 39.95 (0-387-94093-6) Spr-Verlag.

— Time's Arrow: Origins of Thermodynamic Behavior. 2nd ed. (Illus.). 190p. 1993. write for info. (3-540-94093-6) Spr-Verlag.

Mackey, M. C., jt. ed. see Rensing, L.

Mackey, Margaret. The Case of Peter Rabbit: Changing Conditions of Literature for Children. LC 98-6480. (Children's Literature & Culture Ser.: Vol. 7). (Illus.). 240p. 1998. 49.00 (0-8153-3094-4) Garland.

— The Case of Peter Rabbit: Changing Conditions of Literature for Children. LC 98-6480. (Children's Literature & Culture Ser.: No. 7). (Illus.). 240p. 1999. pap. 19.95 (0-8153-3264-5, H2115) Garland.

Mackey, Mary. The Dear Dance of Eros. LC 86-76612. (International Poetry Ser.: No. 2). 150p. (Orig.). 1987. pap. 7.95 (0-940242-17-6) Fjord Pr.

— The Fires of Spring. 1998. mass mkt. 5.99 (0-451-19589-2, Sig) NAL.

— Horses at the Gate. 416p. 1996. mass mkt. 5.99 (0-451-40723-7, Onyx) NAL.

Mackey, Mary. The Year the Horses Came. 400p. 1995. mass mkt. 5.99 (0-451-18298-7, Onyx) NAL.

Mackey, Mary S. & Mackey, Maryette G. The Pronunciation of Ten Thousand Proper Names: Giving Geographical & Biographical Names, Names of Books, Works of Art, Characters in Fiction, Foreign Titles, Etc. LC 89-71138. xiii, 329p. 1993. reprint ed. lib. bdg. 48.00 (1-55888-918-3) Omnigraphics Inc.

Mackey, Maryette G., jt. auth. see Mackey, Mary S.

Mackey, Mik, ed. Remembering Heart Mountain: Essays on Japanese American Internment in Wyoming. LC 98-207964. (Illus.). 241p. 1998. pap. 15.95 (0-9661556-1-0) Western Hist.

Mackey, Mike. Black Gold: Patterns in the Development of Wyoming's Oil Industry. (Illus.). 160p. 1997. pap. 9.95 (0-9661556-0-2) Western Hist.

***Mackey, Mike.** Heart Mountain: Life in Wyoming's Concentration Camp. (Illus.). 182p. (C). 2000. pap. 15.95 (0-9661556-3-7) Western Hist.

***Mackey, Mike, ed.** The Equality State: Essays on Intolerance & Inequality in Wyoming. 122p. 1999. pap. 10.95 (0-9661556-2-9) Western Hist.

Mackey, Nathaniel. Bedouin Hornbook. (Classics Ser.: No. 113). 216p. 1997. pap. 12.95 (1-55713-246-1) Sun & Moon CA.

— Bedouin Hornbook. LC 86-1471. (From a Broken Bottle Traces of Perfume Still Emanate Ser.: No. 1). 216p. reprint ed. pap. 67.00 (0-7837-6485-5, 204651200001) Bks Demand.

— Discrepant Engagement: Dissonance, Cross-Culturality, & Experimental Writing. LC 93-626. (Cambridge Studies in American Literature & Culture: No. 71). 325p. (C). 1993. text 69.95 (0-521-44453-5) Cambridge U Pr.

***Mackey, Nathaniel.** Discrepant Engagement: Dissonance, Cross-Culturality & Experimental Writing. LC 99-45460. (Modern & Contemporary Poetics Ser.). 2000. pap. 24.95 (0-8173-1032-0) U of Ala Pr.

Mackey, Nathaniel. Djbot Baghostus's Run. (New American Fiction Ser.: No. 29). 208p. (Orig.). 1993. pap. 12.95 (1-55713-055-8) Sun & Moon CA.

— School of UDHRA. LC 93-21774. 144p. (Orig.). 1993. pap. 9.95 (0-87286-278-X) City Lights.

— Song of the Andoumboulou: 18-20. LC 94-199892. (Illus.). 24p. (Orig.). 1994. pap. 66.00 (0-939952-16-5) Moving Parts.

An Asterisk (*) at the beginning of an entry indicates that the title is appearing for the first time.

— Whatsaid Serif. LC 98-11042. 114p. 1998. pap. 12.95 (*0-87286-341-7*) City Lights.

Mackey, Nathaniel, jt. ed. see Lange, Art.

Mackey, P. J., jt. ed. see Lehner, T.

Mackey, Peter Francis. Chaos Theory & James Joyce's Everyman. LC 99-31507. 232p. 1999. 49.95 (*0-8130-1708-4*) U Press Fla.

Mackey, Philip E., jt. auth. see Hansen, Barbara J.

Mackey, R. Scott. Barbary Baseball: The Pacific Coast League of the 1920s. LC 94-44985. (Illus.). 237p. 1995. pap. 28.50 (*0-7864-0055-2*) McFarland & Co.

Mackey, Richard A. & O'Brien, Bernard A. Lasting Marriages: Men & Women Growing Together. LC 95-3336. 208p. 1995. 59.95 (*0-275-95075-1*, Praeger Pubs); pap. 19.95 (*0-275-95076-X*, Praeger Pubs) Greenwood.

Mackey, Richard A., et al. Gay & Lesbian Couples: Voices from Lasting Relationships. LC 97-11079. 224p. 1997. 57.95 (*0-275-95846-9*, Praeger Pubs); pap. 20.95 (*0-275-95847-7*, Praeger Pubs) Greenwood.

Mackey, Richard T. Bowling. 5th rev. ed. LC 92-12893. 97p. (C). 1993. pap. text 13.95 (*1-55934-161-0*, 1161) Mayfield Pub.

Mackey, Richard W. The Zabern Affair, 1913-1914. 268p. (C). 1991. lib. bdg. 44.50 (*0-8191-8408-X*) U Pr of Amer.

Mackey, Robert, jt. auth. see Mitcham, Carl.

Mackey, Robert, jt. ed. see Mitcham, Carl.

Mackey, Rochelle, ed. see Wood, MacDonald.

Mackey, Rosella, ed. see Daniel, Patricia A.

Mackey, Rosella, ed. see Daniels, Patricia A.

***Mackey, Sally & Cooper, Simon.** Theatre Studies. rev. exp. ed. (Illus.). 384p. (YA). 2000. pap. 49.50 (*0-7487-5168-8*, Pub. by S Thornes Pubs) Trans-Atl Phila.

Mackey, Sally, et al. Diet & Exercise for Elevated Risk Reduction. Breitrose, Prue, ed. 68p. 1997. ring bd. 54.95 (*1-879552-21-3*) SCRDP.

Mackey, Sally, jt. auth. see Cooper, Simon.

Mackey, Samatha. Today's a Good Day. (Illus.). 16p. (J). (gr. k-3). 1997. pap. 7.00 (*0-8059-4125-8*) Dorrance.

Mackey, Samson A. Mythological Astronomy of the Ancients Demonstrated, Pt. 1. LC 73-84043. (Secret Doctrine Reference Ser.). 380p. 1973. reprint ed. 17.00 (*0-913510-06-8*) Wizards.

Mackey, Sandra. Better Than Gold & Silver. 1975. pap. 6.95 (*0-89137-407-8*) Quality Pubns.

— The Iranians. LC 98-167695. 448p. 1998. pap. 15.95 (*0-452-27563-6*, Plume) Dutton Plume.

— The Iranians: Portrait of a Nation in Chaos. 1996. 24.95 (*0-614-95750-8*, Dutt) Dutton Plume.

Mackey, Scott R. Constitutional Amendment to Require a Balanced Federal Budget. (State Legislative Reports: Vol. 17, No. 11). 8p. 1992. pap. text 15.00 (*1-55516-283-5*, 7302-1711) Natl Conf State Legis.

— State & Local Tax Levels: Fiscal Year, 1991. (Legislative Finance Papers: No. 80). 24p. 1992. pap. text 25.00 (*1-55516-080-8*, 5101-80) Natl Conf State Legis.

— State-Local Tax Levels: Fiscal Year, 1992. (Legislative Finance Papers: No. 92). 7p. 1994. 10.00 (*1-55516-552-4*, 5105-92) Natl Conf State Legis.

— State Programs to Assist Distressed Local Governments. (Legislative Finance Papers: No. 86). 37p. 1993. 15.00 (*1-55516-083-2*, 5101-86) Natl Conf State Legis.

— State Property Tax Relief Programs for Homeowners & Renters. (Legislative Finance Papers: No. 81). 21p. 1992. pap. text 15.00 (*1-55516-081-6*, 5101-81) Natl Conf State Legis.

— State Tax Actions, 1995. 55p. Date not set. 35.00 (*1-55516-014-X*, 5101-00ZZ) Natl Conf State Legis.

— State Tax Actions, 1994. (Legislative Finance Papers: No. ZZ). 56p. 1994. 35.00 (*1-55516-001-8*, 5101-94) Natl Conf State Legis.

— State Tax Actions, 1996. 56p. 1996. 35.00 (*1-55516-555-9*, 5101-0102) Natl Conf State Legis.

Mackey, Scott R. & Carter, Karen. State Tax Policies & Senior Citizens. 2nd ed. LC 95-620886. 78p. 1994. 25.00 (*1-55516-523-0*, 5323) Natl Conf State Legis.

Mackey, Scott R. & National Conference of State Legislatures Staff. Tax Policy Handbook for State Legislators. LC 98-175034. 54 p. 1996. write for info. (*1-55516-563-X*) Natl Conf State Legis.

Mackey, Scott R. & Snell, Ronald K. Amending the Federal Constitution to Require a Balance Budget. (Legislative Finance Papers: No. 96). 17p. 1994. 15.00 (*1-55516-008-5*, 5101-96) Natl Conf State Legis.

Mackey, Sharon, ed. see Patterson, Robert.

Mackey, Sylvia E. Echoes from the Prairie. (Illus.). 260p. (Orig.). 1992. pap. 14.95 (*0-9632931-0-9*) Kiitos Pub.

Mackey, Thomas. Accounting: A Road of Discovery. (SWC-Accounting Ser.). 2001. pap. 60.00 (*0-324-02808-3*) Thomson Learn.

— Financial Accounting, Vol. 1. (Swc-Accounting Ser.). 2001. pap., student ed. 15.00 (*0-324-02806-7*) Sth-Wstrn College.

— Financial Accounting, Vol. II. (SWC-Accounting). 2001. pap. 15.00 (*0-324-02807-5*) Thomson Learn.

— Financial Accounting: A Road of Discovery. (SWC-Accounting Ser.). 2001. pap. 50.00 (*0-324-02805-9*) Thomson Learn.

Mackey, Thomas S., ed. see Minerals, Metals & Materials Society Staff.

Mackey, Tomas, tr. see Streett, R. Alan.

Mackey, Wade C. The American Father: Biocultural & Developmental Aspects. (Plenum Series in Adult Development & Aging: Adult Development & Aging Ser.). (Illus.). 278p. (C). 1996. 51.00 (*0-306-45337-1*, Plenum Trade) Perseus Pubng.

— Fathering Behaviors: The Dynamics of the Man-Child Bond. LC 85-6599. (Perspectives in Developmental Psychology Ser.). (Illus.). 220p. (C). 1985. 59.00 (*0-306-41868-1*, Plenum Trade) Perseus Pubng.

***Mackey, Wade C. & Coney, Nancy S.** Gender Roles, Traditions & Generations to Come: The Collision of Competing Interests & the Feminist Paradox. LC 00-40106. 2000. write for info. (*1-56072-825-6*) Nova Sci Pubs.

Mackey, William F. & Ornstein, Jacob, eds. Sociolinguistic Studies in Language Contact. (Trends in Linguistics, Studies & Monographs: No. 6). 1979. text 65.40 (*90-279-7866-2*) Mouton.

Mackey, William F., jt. auth. see Beebe, Von N.

Mackey, William J., et al. Urbanism as Delinquency: Compromising the Agenda for Social Change. 184p. (C). 1993. lib. bdg. 49.50 (*0-8191-9102-7*) U Pr of Amer.

Macki, J. & Strauss, A. Introduction to Optimal Control Theory, Vol. XIII. Ewing, J. H. et al, eds. LC 95-22684. (Undergraduate Texts in Mathematics Ser.). (Illus.). 165p. (C). 1995. reprint ed. 49.95 (*0-387-90624-X*) Spr-Verlag.

MacKichan, Margaret A. & Ross, Bob. In the Kingdom of Grass. LC 91-34853. (Great Plains Photography Ser.). 143p. 1992. reprint ed. pap. 44.40 (*0-608-01410-9*, 206217300002) Bks Demand.

Mackichan, N. D. The GP & the Primary Health Care Team. (Illus.). 1976. pap. 29.00 (*0-8464-0453-2*) Beekman Pubs.

MacKie. Europe Votes, Vol.2. 1985. 77.95 (*0-900178-24-8*) Ashgate Pub Co.

MacKie. Florida Contract Law. 1991. pap. 15.00 (*0-409-27212-4*, MICHIE) LEXIS Pub.

— Florida Evidence Rules & Cases. 1991. pap. 15.00 (*0-409-27337-6*, MICHIE) LEXIS Pub.

— Florida Real Property Manual. 1991. pap. 15.00 (*1-56257-861-8*, MICHIE) LEXIS Pub.

Mackie. Greater Heights. 160p. 2000. 14.95 (*0-88962-603-0*, 863154, Sundial NY) Mosaic.

***Mackie.** Guidebook to Organic Synthesis. 408p. (Orig.). 2000. pap. 32.98 (*0-582-29093-7*, Prentice Hall) P-H.

Mackie. Melanoma, Vol. 51. 1996. text 99.00 (*0-443-05335-9*, W B Saunders Co) Harcrt Hlth Sci Grp.

— Nana's Garden. large type ed. (Illus.). 72p. (Orig.). 1997. pap. 18.95 (*0-922705-92-5*) Quilt Day.

MacKie, et al. For Henry Kucera Studies in Slavic Philology & Computational Linguistics. (Papers in Slavic Philology: Vol. 6). 1992. 29.50 (*0-930042-72-7*) Mich Slavic Pubns.

Mackie, Alastair. Ingaidherins: Selected Poems. 100p. 1987. pap. text 13.75 (*0-08-035071-2*, Pub. by Aberdeen U Pr) Macmillan.

Mackie, Alwynne. Art-Talk: Theory & Practice in Abstract Expressionism. (Illus.). 288p. 1989. text 41.50 (*0-231-06648-1*) Col U Pr.

Mackie, B. Allan. Building with Logs. rev. ed. (Illus.). 128p. 1997. pap. 24.95 (*1-55209-102-3*) Firefly Bks Ltd.

— Log House Plans. rev. ed. (Illus.). 200p. 1997. pap. 24.95 (*1-55209-103-1*) Firefly Bks Ltd.

Mackie, B. Allan, et al. Log Span Tables: For Floor Joists, Beams & Roof Supports. 3rd rev. ed. (Illus.). 117p. (C). 1993. pap. 15.00 (*0-9636902-0-5*) CN Log Builders.

Mackie, Benita & Rompf, Shirley J. Building Sentences. 3rd ed. LC 94-16909. 384p. 1994. pap. text 42.00 (*0-13-150138-0*) P-H.

Mackie, Beverly J. Afrocentric Shopping Guide: Where to Find African-American Products in Houston & Surrounding Areas. 44p. (Orig.). 1994. pap. 6.95 (*1-884509-05-3*) Creat Info.

***Mackie, Carole & Brattle, Sue.** Me & My Shadow: Living with Multiple Sclerosis. 224p. 1999. 24.95 (*1-85410-627-9*, Pub. by Aurum Press Ltd) London Brdge.

Mackie, Christine. Life & Food in the Caribbean. 188p. 1995. pap. 11.95 (*1-56131-064-6*, NAB) I R Dee.

Mackie, Christopher D. Canonizing Economic Theory: How Theories & Ideas Are Selected in Economics. LC 98-9241. 216p. (C). (gr. 13). 1998. text 62.95 (*0-7656-0284-9*) M E Sharpe.

***Mackie, Christopher D.** Canonizing Economic Theory: How Theories & Ideas Are Selected in Economics. LC 98-9241. 216p. (C). (gr. 13). 1998. pap. text 28.95 (*0-7656-0285-7*) M E Sharpe.

Mackie, Clare. The Cat Notebook: Being an Illustrated Book with Quotes. rev. ed. 96p. 1995. pap. 5.95 (*1-56138-635-9*) Running Pr.

Mackie, Cristine. Life & Food in the Caribbean. 188p. 1996. pap. 15.95 (*976-8100-49-4*, Pub. by Ian Randle) Paul & Co Pubs.

Mackie, Diane & Hamilton, David, eds. Affect, Cognition, & Stereotyping: Interactive Processes in Group Perception. (Illus.). 389p. 1993. text 69.95 (*0-12-464410-4*) Acad Pr.

Mackie, Diane, jt. auth. see Smith, Elliott.

Mackie, Diane M., jt. auth. see Smith, Eliot R.

Mackie, Dianne. Affirmations for Adult Children. 1991. 6.95 (*0-9622150-0-7*) Aurora VA.

Mackie, Erin S. Market a la Mode: Fashion, Commodity, & Gender in the Tatler & the Spectator. LC 97-4442. 328p. 1997. text 39.95 (*0-8018-5588-8*) Johns Hopkins.

Mackie, Fiona. The Status of Everyday Life: A Sociological Excavation of the Prevailing Framework of Perception. (International Library of Sociology Ser.). 288p. 1985. 49.95 (*0-7102-0154-0*, Routledge Thoemms) Routledge.

Mackie, Gerald L., jt. auth. see Claudi, Renata.

Mackie, Hilary. Talking Trojan: Speech & Community in the Iliad. 208p. 1996. pap. text 23.95 (*0-8476-8255-2*); lib. bdg. 55.50 (*0-8476-8254-4*) Rowman.

Mackie, Howard. Gambit. (Illus.). 96p. 1995. pap. 12.95 (*0-7851-0109-8*) Marvel Entrprs.

— Rogue. (Illus.). 96p. 1995. pap. 12.95 (*0-7851-0140-3*) Marvel Entrprs.

MacKie, Howard, et al. Ghost Rider: Resurrected. (Illus.). 192p. 1991. pap. 12.95 (*0-87135-803-4*) Marvel Entrprs.

Mackie, J. A., ed. Australia in the New World Order: Foreign Policy in the 1970s. LC 76-378596. 164p. reprint ed. pap. 50.90 (*0-7837-1455-6*, 205243100022) Bks Demand.

— The Chinese in Indonesia: Five Essays. LC 76-139. 295p. reprint ed. pap. 91.50 (*0-608-12566-0*, 202397100035) Bks Demand.

Mackie, J. D. History of Scotland. 1984. pap. 14.95 (*0-14-013649-5*) Viking Penguin.

Mackie, J. L. Ethics. 1990. pap. 13.95 (*0-14-013558-8*, Viking) Viking Penguin.

— Hume's Moral Theory. (International Library of Philosophy). 176p. (C). 1980. pap. 25.99 (*0-415-10436-X*) Routledge.

***Mackie, Joan.** Classic Chic: Timeless Decorating That's Always in Style. (Chatelaine Home Decor Ser.). (Illus.). 128p. 1999. pap. 19.95 (*0-7710-2009-0*) McCland & Stewart.

Mackie, Joan. Garden Rooms: Nature-Inspired Decorating Indoors & Out. (Chatelaine Home Focus Ser.). (Illus.). 128p. 1998. pap. 19.95 (*0-7710-2008-2*) McCland & Stewart.

— The New Modern: Anything Goes in Today's Decorating. (Illus.). 128p. 1998. pap. 19.95 (*0-7710-2013-9*) McCland & Stewart.

Mackie, Joan, jt. auth. see Crowley, Marilyn Bentz.

Mackie, John D. Earlier Tudors, 1485-1558. (Oxford History of England Ser.). (Illus.). 722p. 1952. text 65.00 (*0-19-821706-4*) OUP.

Mackie, John L. The Cement of the Universe: A Study of Causation. (Clarendon Library of Logic & Philosophy). (Illus.). 340p. 1980. pap. text 32.00 (*0-19-824642-0*) OUP.

Mackie, John L. The Miracle of Theism. 276p. 1983. pap. text 24.95 (*0-19-824682-X*) OUP.

Mackie, John L. Problems from Locke. (Illus.). 248p. (C). 1976. pap. text 24.00 (*0-19-875036-6*) OUP.

Mackie, Joyce. Basic Ballet. 127p. 1980. pap. 8.95 (*0-14-046445-X*) Viking Penguin.

Mackie, K. The Application of Learning Theory to Adult Teaching. (C). 1988. text 40.00 (*0-7855-3182-3*, Pub. by Univ Nottingham) St Mut.

Mackie, K. & Burton, M. Outline of Succession. LC 95-135572. 300p. 1994. pap. write for info. (*0-409-30491-3*, MICHIE) LEXIS Pub.

Mackie, Karl. The Application of Learning Theory to Adult Teaching. (C). 1981. 35.00 (*0-902031-88-0*, Pub. by Univ Nottingham) St Mut.

Mackie, Karl & Miles, David. Commercial Dispute Resolution: An ADR Practice Guide. 224p. 1994. boxed set 121.00 (*0-406-02011-6*, UK, MICHIE) LEXIS Pub.

Mackie, Karl, jt. auth. see Carroll, Eileen.

Mackie, Keith. Golf at St. Andrews. (Illus.). 192p. 1995. 45.00 (*1-56554-129-4*) Pelican.

— Open Championship Golf Courses of Britain. (Illus.). 192p. 1997. pap. 49.95 (*1-56554-296-7*) Pelican.

Mackie, Keith, jt. auth. see Smith, Peter.

Mackie, Louise W. The Splendor of Turkish Weaving: An Exhibition of Silks & Carpets of the 13th-18th Centuries. (Illus.). 86p. 1973. 8.00 (*0-87405-002-2*) Textile Mus.

Mackie, Louise W. & Thompson, Jon, eds. Turkmen: Tribal Carpets & Traditions. LC 80-53159. (Illus.). 240p. 1980. 75.00 (*0-87405-014-6*) Textile Mus.

Mackie, Louise W., jt. auth. see Straka, Jerome A.

MacKie, Marie D., tr. see Prunieres, Henry.

Mackie, Mary. Castle Kintyle. large type ed. LC 94-3349. 263p. 1994. lib. bdg. 16.95 (*0-8161-7452-0*, G K Hall Lrg Type) Mac Lib Ref.

— The Clouded Land. 608p. 1995. mass mkt. 11.95 (*0-7472-4684-X*, Pub. by Headline Bk Pub) Trafalgar.

— Cobwebs & Cream Teas. (Illus.). 176p. 1995. pap. 13.95 (*0-575-05980-X*, Pub. by V Gollancz) Trafalgar.

— Counterfeit Love. large type ed. (Linford Romance Library). 272p. 1992. pap. 16.99 (*0-7089-7205-5*) Ulverscroft.

— The Dark Days of Spring. large type ed. (Dales Large Print Ser.). 240p. 1996. pap. 18.99 (*1-85389-608-X*, Dales) Ulverscroft.

— Dark Ruby. large type ed. (Dales Large Print Ser.). 258p. 1996. pap. 18.99 (*1-85389-652-7*, Dales) Ulverscroft.

— Dry Rot & Daffodils. (Illus.). 192p. 1995. pap. 13.95 (*0-575-05934-6*, Pub. by V Gollancz) Trafalgar.

— Dry Rot & Daffodils. large type ed. 368p. 1995. 27.99 (*0-7089-3394-7*) Ulverscroft.

***Mackie, Mary.** Elusive Victory. large type ed. LC 00-28682. 2000. write for info. (*0-7862-2566-1*) Thorndike Pr.

MacKie, Mary. Enigma for a Nurse. large type ed. (Linford Romance Library). 336p. 1994. pap. 16.99 (*0-7089-7514-3*, Linford) Ulverscroft.

Mackie, Mary. Falconer's Wood. large type ed. 304p. 1994. 27.99 (*0-7089-3079-4*) Ulverscroft.

— Flame in the Forest. large type ed. (Linford Romance Library). 320p. 1995. pap. 16.99 (*0-7089-7681-6*, Linford) Ulverscroft.

— The Flower & the Storm. large type ed. (Linford Romance Library). 1991. pap. 16.99 (*0-7089-7045-1*) Ulverscroft.

— Give Me No Rubies. large type ed. (Linford Romance Large Print Ser.). 224p. 1995. pap. 16.99 (*0-7089-7726-X*, Linford) Ulverscroft.

— Into the Twilight. large type ed. (Linford Romance Library). 336p. 1994. pap. 16.99 (*0-7089-7527-5*, Linford) Ulverscroft.

— A Light in the Valley. large type ed. 1991. 27.99 (*0-7089-2464-6*) Ulverscroft.

— A Man Like Matthew. large type ed. (Linford Romance Library). 1991. pap. 16.99 (*0-7089-7118-0*) Ulverscroft.

— Mist Around the Moon. large type ed. (Dales Large Print Ser.). 1996. pap. 18.99 (*1-85389-609-8*, Dales) Ulverscroft.

— Nicola's Winter. large type ed. (Linford Romance Library). 336p. 1996. pap. 16.99 (*0-7089-7967-X*, Linford) Ulverscroft.

— Nightflower. large type ed. 1990. pap. 16.99 (*0-7089-6883-X*, Linford) Ulverscroft.

***Mackie, Mary.** Pamela. large type ed. LC 99-49387. (General Ser.). 2000. pap. 22.95 (*0-7862-2308-1*) Thorndike Pr.

Mackie, Mary. A Return to Love. large type ed. (Linford Romance Library). 208p. 1997. pap. 16.99 (*0-7089-5116-3*, Linford) Ulverscroft.

— Robin's Song. large type ed. (Linford Romance Library). 304p. 1996. pap. 16.99 (*0-7089-7898-3*, Linford) Ulverscroft.

— Season of Mists. large type ed. (Linford Romance Large Print Ser.). 256p. 1998. pap. 17.99 (*0-7089-5245-3*, Linford) Ulverscroft.

— Shadow on the Lake. large type ed. LC 98-31300. 1999. 30.00 (*0-7862-1669-7*) Thorndike Pr.

— Shadows of Yesterday. large type ed. 224p. 1996. pap. 17.95 (*0-7838-1627-8*, G K Hall Lrg Type) Mac Lib Ref.

— Spring Fever. 192p. 1996. 22.00 (*0-7278-5156-X*) Severn Hse.

— Spring Fever. large type ed. (Ulverscroft Large Print Ser.). 288p. 1997. 27.99 (*0-7089-3778-0*) Ulverscroft.

— Still Weeps the Willow. large type ed. (Linford Romance Library). 336p. 1992. pap. 16.99 (*0-7089-7242-X*) Ulverscroft.

— Straw in the Wind. large type ed. LC 94-33451. (Nightingale Ser.). 216p. 1995. pap. 16.95 (*0-8161-7453-9*, G K Hall Lrg Type) Mac Lib Ref.

— Sweeter Than Wine. 192p. 1997. 24.00 (*0-7278-5231-0*) Severn Hse.

— A Voice in the Fog. large type ed. (Romance Ser.). 288p. 1992. 27.99 (*0-7089-2695-9*) Ulverscroft.

— The Waiting Web. large type ed. (Linford Romance Library). 272p. 1992. pap. 16.99 (*0-7089-7287-X*) Ulverscroft.

— The Whispering Well. large type ed. (Nightingale Ser.). 1996. pap. 17.95 (*0-7838-1622-7*, G K Hall Lrg Type) Mac Lib Ref.

***Mackie, Mary.** The Wolf of Weirdmoor. large type ed. LC 99-14892. 197p. 1999. 21.95 (*0-7862-1980-7*) Mac Lib Ref.

MacKie, Mary-Frances L. Avon Connecticut: An Historical Story. LC 88-5999. (Illus.). 336p. 1988. 22.50 (*0-914659-33-2*) Phoenix Pub.

Mackie-Mason, Jeffrey K. & Lee, Christopher. Telecommunications Guide to the Internet. 241p. 1998. pap. text 59.00 (*0-86587-601-0*, 601) Gov Insts.

MacKie-Mason, Jeffrey K., jt. ed. see Waterman, David.

Mackie, Peter & Preston, John. The Local Bus Market: A Case Study of Regulatory Change. LC 96-83233. 248p. 1996. 72.95 (*1-85628-267-8*, Pub. by Avebry) Ashgate Pub Co.

Mackie, Peter J. Peter J. Mackie, jt. auth. see Gwilliam, K. M.

Mackie, R. M., ed. Primary & Secondary Prevention of Malignant Melanoma. (Pigment Cell Ser.: Vol. 11, 1996). (Illus.). viii, 130p. 1996. 158.25 (*3-8055-6273-X*) S Karger.

Mackie, R. M., jt. auth. see Grob, J. J.

Mackie, Richard. Operation New Life: The Untold Story. (Illus.). 86p. (Orig.). 1997. pap. 14.95 (*1-885372-09-4*) Solution CA.

— Publishing on the Internet. 96p. (Orig.). 1997. pap. 9.85 (*1-885372-03-1*) Solution CA.

— Take This Job & Sell It! The Recruiter's Handbook. LC 93-33890. (Illus.). 176p. (Orig.). 1994. pap. 24.95 (*0-936609-30-3*) QED Ft Bragg.

Mackie, Richard A. Beat the Devil: How to Get Government Regulators Off Your Back - Permanently! 288p. 1994. pap. 19.95 (*1-885372-01-9*) Solution CA.

Mackie, Richard A., ed. The Journals of John Davidson Mackie. (Illus.). 298p. (Orig.). 1996. lib. bdg. write for info. (*1-885372-04-3*) Solution CA.

Mackie, Richard S. Trading Beyond the Mountains: The British Fur Trade on the Pacific, 1793-1843. LC 97-144799. 440p. 1997. 75.00 (*0-7748-0559-5*) U of Wash Pr.

— Trading Beyond the Mountains: The British Fur Trade on the Pacific, 1793-1843. (Illus.). 368p. 1997. pap. 29.95 (*0-7748-0613-3*) U of Wash Pr.

Mackie, Robert. In Love & in Laugh. LC 96-144470. 1996. pap. text 17.90 (*0-7152-0716-4*) St Mut.

Mackie, Roderick, et al. Gastrointestinal Microbiology, Vol. 1. LC 96-30506. 672p. 1997. write for info. (*0-412-98361-3*) Kluwer Academic.

— Gastrointestinal Microbiology: Gastrointestinal Microbes & Host Interactions, Vol. 2. LC 96-30506. 1997. write for info. (*0-412-98371-0*) Kluwer Academic.

Mackie, Ron. A Wild Garden: The Monterey Peninsula. (Illus.). 1985. pap. 7.95 (*0-910286-99-X*) Boxwood.

MacKie, Rona M. Clinical Dermatology. 4th ed. (Illus.). 334p. 1996. pap. text 39.95 (*0-19-262761-9*) OUP.

Mackie, Rona M. Healthy Skin: The Facts: Good Skin Care Throughout Life. (Facts Ser.). (Illus.). 160p. 1992. text 21.95 (*0-19-262246-3*) OUP.

Mackie, Rona M., ed. Malignant Melanoma. (Pigment Cell Ser.: Vol. 6). (Illus.). viii, 204p. 1983. 121.00 (*3-8055-3690-9*) S Karger.

Mackie, Sam A. Florida Civil Procedure Guide. Stephens, Mark, ed. 606p. write for info. (*1-878337-46-7*) Knowles Pub Inc.

M

Mackie, Thomas. Europe Votes Three. 2nd ed. (Parliamentary Research Services Ser.). 442p. 1990. text 82.95 (0-900178-35-3, Pub. by Dartmth Pub) Ashgate Pub Co.

Mackie, Thomas T. & Rohds, Richard. The International Almanac of Electoral History. 3rd ed. 511p. 1991. 105.00 (0-87187-575-6) Congr Quarterly.

Mackie, Vera. Creating Socialist Women in Japan: Gender, Labour & Activism, 1900-1937. (Illus.). 262p. (C). 1997. text 54.95 (0-521-55137-4) Cambridge U Pr.

Mackie, Vera. Fighting Women: A History of Feminism in Japan. 224p. 1997. 93.50 (0-7103-0594-X, Pub. by Kegan Paul Intl) Col U Pr.

Mackie, William. The Diary of a Canny Man 1818-1828: Adam Mackie, Farmer, Merchant & Innkeeper in Fyvie. (Aberdeen University Press Bks.). (Illus.). 96p. 1991. pap. 13.90 (0-08-041213-0, Pub. by Aberdeen U Pr) Macmillan.

MacKiernan, Elizabeth. Ancestors Maybe: Anovel. (Burning Deck Fiction Ser.). 160p. 1993. pap. 8.00 (0-930901-81-9) Burning Deck.

— Ancestors Maybe: Anovel. limited ed. (Burning Deck Fiction Ser.). 160p. 1993. pap. 15.00 (0-930901-82-7) Burning Deck.

Mackiewicz, A., jt. auth. see Breborowicz, J.

Mackiewicz, Andrea. The Economist Intelligence Unit Guide to Building a Global Image. (Illus.). 184p. (C). 1998. text 40.00 (0-7881-5710-8) DIANE Pub.

Mackiewicz, Andrzej, et al, eds. Acute Phase Proteins: Molecular Biology, Biochemistry, & Clinical Applications. 704p. 1993. lib. bdg. 269.00 (0-8493-6913-4, RB131) CRC Pr.

— Interleukin-6-Type Cytokines. LC 95-30188. (Annals of the New York Academy of Sciences Ser.: Vol. 762). 1995. write for info. (0-89766-931-2) NY Acad Sci.

— Interleukin-6-Type Cytokines. LC 95-30188. (Annals of the New York Academy of Sciences Ser.: Vol. 762). 522p. 1995. pap. 150.00 (0-89766-932-0) NY Acad Sci.

Mackiewicz, Andrzej & Sehgal, Pravinkumar B. Molecular Aspects of Cancer & Its Therapy. LC 97-32691. (Molecular & Cell Biology Updates Ser.). 1998. write for info. (0-8176-5724-X) Birkhauser.

Mackiewicz, Andrzej & Sehgal, Pravinkumar B., eds. Molecular Aspects of Cancer & Its Therapy. LC 97-32691. (Molecular & Cell Biology Updates Ser.). (Illus.). 300p. 1997. text 118.00 (3-7643-5724-X) Birkhauser.

Mackiewicz, Edward R., jt. auth. see Veal, Edward T.

Mackiewicz, S. Dostoievski. LC 73-21635. (Studies in Dostoyevsky: No. 86). 1974. lib. bdg. 75.00 (0-8383-1818-5) M S G Haskell Hse.

Mackillop, Ian. F. R. Leavis: A Life in Criticism. LC 96-45528. (Illus.). 493p. 1997. text 35.00 (0-312-16357-6) St Martin.

Mackillop, Ian & Storer, Richard, eds. F R Leavis: Essays & Documents. (Sheffield Academic Press Ser.). 300p. 1995. 39.50 (1-85075-564-7, Pub. by Sheffield Acad) CUP Services.

MacKillop, James. Dictionary of Celtic Mythology. LC 97-19398. 432p. 1998. 49.95 (0-19-869157-2) OUP.

***MacKillop, James.** Dictionary of Celtic Mythology. 432p. 2000. pap. 15.95 (0-19-280120-1) OUP.

MacKillop, James. Fionn MacCumhaill: Celtic Myth in English Literature. LC 85-22116. (Irish Studies). 256p. (Orig.). 1986. pap. text 44.95 (0-8156-2344-5) Syracuse U Pr.

***MacKillop, James, ed.** Contemporary Irish Cinema. LC 98-52456. 256p. 1999. 49.95 (0-8156-2798-X) Syracuse U Pr.

MacKillop, James & Woolfolk, Donna. Speaking of Words: A Language Reader. 3rd ed. LC 81-6734. 324p. (C). 1986. pap. text 32.50 (0-03-003953-3, Pub. by Harcourt Coll Pubs) Harcourt.

MacKillop, James, jt. ed. see Murphy, Maureen O.

***MacKillop, Linda, ed.** Making the Connection: A Personal Guide to Help You Through the Detours of Life. 1999. 19.95 (0-9675839-0-X); pap. 14.95 (0-9675839-1-8) Creative Pr Pubng.

MacKillop, Mary & Press, Margaret M. Julian Tension Woods, A Life. LC 98-110000. xii, 228p. 1997. write for info. (1-86371-696-3) Clns Dove.

***MacKillop, Rob.** Scottish Traditional Music for Guitar. 68p. 2000. pap. 15.95 (0-946868-23-9, 99357, Pub. by Hardie Pr) Mel Bay.

— Scottish Traditional Music for Guitar. 64p. 2000. pap. 15.95 (0-7866-5791-X, 99357) Mel Bay.

Mackin. Hunter's Rehabillitation Handbook. 45th ed. 2001. pap. 225.00 (0-323-01094-6) Mosby Inc.

— Rehabilitation of Arthritic Hand & Wrist. 2000. write for info. (0-443-08997-3) Church.

***Mackin, Bob.** Record-Breaking Baseball Trivia. (Illus.). 128p. 2000. pap. 6.95 (1-55054-757-7) DGL.

Mackin, David, ed. see Boe, Susan.

Mackin, Edward. The Nominative Case. 192p. 1991. 18.95 (0-8027-5780-4) Walker & Co.

Mackin, James A., Jr. Community over Chaos: An Ecological Perspective on Communication Ethics. LC 96-34776. (Studies in Rhetoric & Communication). 288p. 1997. text 34.95 (0-8173-0860-1) U of Ala Pr.

Mackin, Jeanne. Cornell Book of Herbs & Edible Flowers. Calvert, Trudie, ed. (Illus.). 110p. 1993. pap. 15.75 (1-57753-015-2, 132HB) Corn Coop Ext.

— The Cornell Book of Herbs & Edible Flowers. (Illus.). 104p. (C). 1999. reprint ed. pap. text 30.00 (0-7881-8092-4) DIANE Pub.

Mackin, Jeanne. Dreams of Empire. 256p. 1996. 21.00 (1-57566-020-2) Kensgtn Pub Corp.

— Dreams of Empire. 256p. 1997. mass mkt. 4.99 (1-57566-133-0, Knsington) Kensgtn Pub Corp.

Mackin, Jeanne, jt. ed. see Ackerman, Diane.

Mackin, Karey, ed. see Brown, Milli.

***Mackin, Robert E.** Property & Casualty Insurance: State Legislation. 220p. 1999. pap. 75.00 (0-8080-0323-2) CCH INC.

— State Insurance Legislation: 1999 Yearbook. 400p. 2000. pap. 99.00 (0-8080-0476-X) CCH INC.

Mackin, Ronald. A Short Course in Spoken English. 1975. pap. 5.95 (0-87789-137-0); audio 55.00 (0-87789-140-0) ELS Educ Servs.

Mackin, Ronald, jt. auth. see Eastwood, John.

Mackinder, Halford John. Britain & the British Seas. LC 69-13982. 377p. 1970. reprint ed. lib. bdg. 65.00 (0-8371-2754-8, MABR, Greenwood Pr) Greenwood.

— Britain & the British Seas. LC 68-25248. (British History Ser.: No. 30). 1969. reprint ed. lib. bdg. 75.00 (0-8383-0212-2) M S G Haskell Hse.

Mackinder, Halford John. Democratic Ideals & Reality: Politics of Reconstruction by the Right Honourable Sir Halford J. Mackinder. 239p. 1996. per. 13.00 (0-16-061145-8) USGPO.

Mackinder, Halford John. Democratic Ideals & Reality. LC 81-12797. 278p. 1981. reprint ed. lib. bdg. 69.50 (0-313-23150-8, MADM, Greenwood Pr) Greenwood.

Mackinder, Jack. Celtic Design & Ornament for Calligraphers. LC 98-61185. (Illus.). 96p. 1999. pap. 15.95 (0-500-28094-0, Pub. by Thames Hudson) Norton.

***MacKiney, Millie.** African American Excellence. 78p. 1999. 7.95 (1-56245-391-2) Great Quotations.

— African American Wisdom. 1999. pap. 5.95 (1-56245-380-7) Great Quotations.

MacKiney, Millie. African-American Wisdom: Seeing Strength in Our Heritage. Caton, Patrick, ed. LC 97-71652. 168p. 1997. pap. 5.95 (1-56245-310-6) Great Quotations.

***MacKiney, Millie.** Memories for My Grandchild. 2000. 19.99 (1-56245-419-6) Great Quotations.

Mackiney, Millie. Only a Sister: Could Be Such a Good Friend. Caton, Patrick, ed. LC 97-77654. (Illus.). 168p. 1998. pap. 5.95 (1-56245-338-6) Great Quotations.

MacKiney, Millie. Servant's Heart. 1999. pap. text 5.95 (1-56245-352-1) Great Quotations.

Mackinlay, John. Peacekeepers: An Assessment of Peacekeeping Operations at the Arab-Israel Interface. 208p. 1989. 29.95 (0-685-29202-9) Routledge.

Mackinlay, Leila. Broken Armour. large type ed. 346p. 1989. 27.99 (0-7089-1961-8) Ulverscroft.

— Farewell to Sadness. large type ed. (Romance Ser.). 304p. 1992. 27.99 (0-7089-2729-7) Ulverscroft.

— Guilt's Pavilions. large type ed. (Romance Suspense Ser.). 416p. 1992. 27.99 (0-7089-2664-9) Ulverscroft.

— Midnight Is Mine. large type ed. 1991. 27.99 (0-7089-2540-5) Ulverscroft.

— Pilot's Point. large type ed. 464p. 1987. 27.99 (0-7089-1601-5) Ulverscroft.

— Restless Dream. large type ed. 1988. 15.95 (0-7089-1746-1) Ulverscroft.

— Spring Rainbow. large type ed. 384p. 1987. 27.99 (0-7089-1702-X) Ulverscroft.

— The Third Boat. large type ed. 1989. 27.99 (0-7089-2106-X) Ulverscroft.

— Uneasy Conquest. large type ed. 368p. 1987. 27.99 (0-7089-1643-0) Ulverscroft.

— Unwise Wanderer. large type ed. 432p. 1986. 27.99 (0-7089-1492-6) Ulverscroft.

— Vain Delights. large type ed. 400p. 1988. 27.99 (0-7089-1902-2) Ulverscroft.

Mackinlay, Sterling. Origin & Development of Light Opera. 1972. 59.95 (0-8490-0772-0) Gordon Pr.

Mackinley, Malcolm S. Garcia the Centenarian & His Times. LC 75-40206. (Music Reprint Ser.). 1975. reprint ed. lib. bdg. 42.50 (0-306-70671-7) Da Capo.

MacKinney, Archie A., Jr., ed. Pathophysiology of Blood. LC 83-26040. (Wiley Pathophysiology Ser.). (Illus.). 462p. (Orig.). reprint ed. pap. 143.30 (0-8357-4660-7, 203759000008) Bks Demand.

MacKinney, Loren C. Early Medieval Medicine: With Special Reference to France & Charters. 1979. 25.95 (0-405-10613-0) Ayer.

MacKinney, Loren C., ed. see University of North Carolina, Division of the Huma.

MacKinnon. Ethics: Theory & Contemporary Issues. (Philosophy Ser.). 1994. pap., teacher ed. 24.50 (0-534-20311-6) Wadsworth Pub.

— Ethics: Theory & Contemporary Issues. 3rd ed. (Philosophy Ser.). 2000. pap. text 39.25 (0-534-54632-3) Thomson Learn.

MacKinnon, ed. Oil in the California Monterey Formation. (IGC Field Trip Guidebooks Ser.). 64p. 1989. 21.00 (0-87590-600-1, T311) Am Geophysical.

***MacKinnon, Alison.** Education into the 21st Century: Dangerous Terrain for Women. LC 98-203730. 208p. 1998. pap. text 26.95 (0-7507-0657-0) Taylor & Francis.

MacKinnon, Alison. Love & Freedom: Professional Women & the Reshaping of Personal Life. LC 96-28526. (Illus.). 314p. 1997. text 59.95 (0-521-49736-1); pap. text 22.95 (0-521-49761-2) Cambridge U Pr.

MacKinnon, Alison, jt. ed. see Gatens, Moira.

MacKinnon, Andy, et al. Plants of Northern British Columbia Revised. 2nd rev. ed. 1999. pap. 19.95 (1-55105-108-7) Lone Pine.

MacKinnon, Andy, jt. auth. see Pojar, Jim.

MacKinnon, Barbara. American Philosophy: A Historical Anthology. LC 84-2458. (SUNY Series in Philosophy). 688p. (C). 1985. pap. text 24.95 (0-87395-923-X) State U NY Pr.

— Ethics: Theory & Contemporary Issues. LC 94-12192. 473p. 1994. mass mkt. 41.95 (0-534-20310-8) Wadsworth Pub.

— Ethics: Theory & Contemporary Issues. 2nd ed. LC 97-12685. (Philosophy Ser.). (C). 1997. 56.95 (0-534-52504-0) Wadsworth Pub.

***MacKinnon, Barbara, ed.** Human Cloning: Science, Ethics, & Public Policy. LC 99-50519. 184p. 2000. 29.95 (0-252-02491-5) U of Ill Pr.

MacKinnon, Bernard. Seven Mourners: Depression & the Needs of Human Nature. LC 98-48629. 2000. 18.95 (1-56072-633-4) Nova Sci Pubs.

Mackinnon, Bernie. Song for a Shadow. LC 90-39647. 320p. (YA). (gr. 7 up). 1991. 18.00 (0-395-55419-5) HM.

***Mackinnon, Billy.** Hideous Kinky. 1999. pap. text 12.95 (1-901680-25-8) Screen Communs.

MacKinnon, Catharine A. Feminism Unmodified: Discourses on Life & Law. LC 86-25694. 328p. 1988. pap. text 16.50 (0-674-29874-8) HUP.

— Feminism Unmodified: Discourses on Life & Law. LC 86-25694. 352p. 1987. reprint ed. 37.95 (0-674-29873-X) HUP.

— Only Words. LC 93-13600. 112p. 1993. text 14.95 (0-674-63933-2) HUP.

— Only Words. 160p. 1996. pap. 10.00 (0-674-63934-0) HUP.

— Sexual Harassment of Working Women: A Case of Sex Discrimination. LC 78-9645. (Fastback Ser.: No. 19). 312p. 1979. pap. 18.00 (0-300-02299-9) Yale U Pr.

— Toward a Feminist Theory of the State. 352p. (C). 1991. pap. text 14.95 (0-674-89646-7) HUP.

— Toward a Feminist Theory of the State. LC 89-7540. 352p. 1991. text 27.50 (0-674-89645-9) HUP.

MacKinnon, Catharine A. & Dworkin, Andrea, eds. In Harm's Way: The Pornography Civil Rights Hearings. LC 97-30374. (Illus.). 512p. 1998. 45.00 (0-674-44578-3); pap. 24.95 (0-674-44579-1) HUP.

***Mackinnon, Christopher.** Mountain Biking in New Jersey: 37 Off-Road Rides in the Garden State. (Illus.). 2000. pap. 13.95 (0-9652733-5-0) Freewheeling.

MacKinnon, Christy. Silent Observer. (Awareness & Caring Ser.). (Illus.). 48p. (J). (gr. k-6). 1997. lib. bdg. 17.95 (1-56674-075-4) Forest Hse.

— Silent Observer. LC 93-4510. (Illus.). 48p. (J). 1993. 15.95 (1-56368-022-X, Pub. by K Green Pubns) Gallaudet Univ Pr.

MacKinnon, D. I., et al, eds. Brachiopods Through Time: Proceedings of the Second International Brachiopods Congress, University of Otago, Dunedin, New Zealand, 5-9 February 1990. 580p. (C). 1990. text 136.00 (90-6191-160-5, Pub. by A A Balkema) Ashgate Pub Co.

MacKinnon, Debbie. Daniel's Duck. (Illus.). (J). (ps-k). 1997. bds. 4.99 (0-614-28685-9, Dial Yng Read) Peng Put Young Read.

Mackinnon, Debbie. Eye Spy Colors. LC 97-43260. (Illus.). 24p. (YA). (ps-k). 1998. 8.95 (0-88106-334-7) Charlesbridge Pub.

***MacKinnon, Debbie.** Eye Spy Shapes. LC 99-51654. (Illus.). 24p. (YA). (ps up). 2000. 8.95 (0-88106-135-2) Charlesbridge Pub.

— Find Kitty! 10p. (J). 1999. write for info. (0-7112-0921-9, Pub. by F Lincoln) Antique Collect.

— Find My Boots! 10p. (J). 1999. write for info. (0-7112-0922-7, Pub. by F Lincoln) Antique Collect.

— Find My Cake! 10p. (J). 1999. write for info. (0-7112-0920-0, Pub. by F Lincoln) Antique Collect.

***Mackinnon, Debbie.** Let's Play: I Can Do It. (Illus.). 8p. (J). (ps-3). 1999. 7.95 (0-316-64897-3) Little.

— My Day. (Illus.). 8p. (J). (ps-3). 1999. 7.95 (0-316-64898-1) Little.

MacKinnon, Debbie. My World of Spanish Words. LC 94-42967.Tr. of Mi Mundo de Palabras. (Illus.). 128p. (J). 1995. 8.95 (0-8120-6505-0) Barron.

— My World of Words. LC 94-42966.Tr. of Mon Monde de Mots. (ENG & FRE., Illus.). 128p. (J). 1995. 8.95 (0-8120-6506-9) Barron.

— My World of Words. LC 94-43792.Tr. of Mon Monde de Mots. (Illus.). 128p. (J). (ps). 1995. 7.95 (0-8120-6507-7) Barron.

— Pippa's Puppy. (Illus.). (J). (ps-k). 1997. bds. 4.99 (0-614-28686-7, Dial Yng Read) Peng Put Young Read.

— Sarah's Shovel. (Illus.). (J). (ps-k). 1997. bds. 4.99 (0-614-28687-5, Dial Yng Read) Peng Put Young Read.

— Tom's Train. (Illus.). (J). (ps-k). 1997. bds. 4.99 (0-614-28688-3, Dial Yng Read) Peng Put Young Read.

***MacKinnon, Debbie.** What Am I? (Right Start Ser.). 24p. (J). 1999. 7.99 (0-7112-1276-7) F Lincoln.

MacKinnon, Debbie. What Shape? 1999. pap. 4.99 (0-14-055744-X) NAL.

MacKinnon, Debbie & Sieveking, Anthea. All about Me. LC 93-23143. (Illus.). 32p. (J). (ps). 1994. 11.95 (0-8120-6348-1) Barron.

MacKinnon, Donald D. Fingon, Memoirs of Clan Fingon, with Family Tree. 246p. 1993. reprint ed. pap. 39.00 (0-8328-3591-9); reprint ed. lib. bdg. 49.00 (0-8328-3590-0) Higginson Bk Co.

MacKinnon, Donald M. Themes in Theology: The Three-Fold Chord. 256p. 1996. 47.95 (0-567-09446-4) Bks Intl VA.

MacKinnon, Donald W. In Search of Human Effectiveness: Identifying & Developing Creativity. LC 78-62345. 1978. pap. 14.95 (0-930222-03-2) Creat Educ Found.

MacKinnon, Douglas. First Victim. LC 96-53350. 320p. 1997. 19.95 (0-87131-824-5) M Evans.

MacKinnon, Edward M. Scientific Explanation & Atomic Physics. LC 82-2702. 460p. reprint ed. pap. 142.60 (0-608-09475-7, 205427500005) Bks Demand.

MacKinnon, Flora I., ed. see More, Henry.

MacKinnon, Frank. Church Politics & Education in Canada: The P. E. I. Experience. 144p. (Orig.). 1995. pap. text. write for info. (1-55059-104-5) Detselig Ents.

MacKinnon, Frank D. On Circuit, 1924-1937. 313p. 1997. reprint ed. 80.00 (1-56169-342-1) Gaunt.

MacKinnon, Herbert C., jt. ed. see Rechcigl, Jack E.

Mackinnon, I. D. & Mumpton, Frederick A., eds. Electron - Optical Methods in Clay Science, No. 2. (CMS Workshop Lectures). (Illus.). 159p. (Orig.). (C). 1990. pap. text 18.00 (1-881208-02-8) Clay Minerals.

Mackinnon, J. P. & Shadbolt, S. H. The South African Campaign, 1879. (Illus.). 384p. 1995. 50.00 (1-85367-203-3, Pub. by Greenhill Bks) Stackpole.

Mackinnon, James. Calvin & the Reformation. LC 83-45648. reprint ed. 37.50 (0-404-19841-4) AMS Pr.

— Luther & the Reformation, 4 vols., Set. LC 83-45648. reprint ed. 157.50 (0-404-19857-0) AMS Pr.

MacKinnon, James G., jt. auth. see Davidson, Russell.

MacKinnon, Jamie. Great Lakes Beer Guide: An Affectionate, Opinionated Guide to the Beers of Michigan, New York, Ontario. LC 98-222094. 1997. pap. text 14.50 (1-55046-209-1, Pub. by Boston Mills) Genl Dist Srvs.

MacKinnon, Jan, ed. see Smedley, Agnes.

MacKinnon, Janice R. & MacKinnon, Stephen R. Agnes Smedley: The Life & Times of an American Radical. 460p. (C). 1988. 45.00 (0-520-05966-2, Pub. by U CA Pr); pap. 15.95 (0-520-06614-6, Pub. by U CA Pr) Cal Prin Full Svc.

MacKinnon, John. NHL Hockey: An Official Fan's Guide. 128p. 1998. 23.95 (1-892049-04-X) Triumph Bks.

— NHL Hockey: The Official Fans' Guide: The NHL's Complete Authorized Guide. 2nd rev. ed. LC 98-1528. (Illus.). 128p. 1997. 19.95 (1-57243-215-2) Triumph Bks.

***MacKinnon, John.** NHL Hockey: An Offical Fans' Guide: The NHL's Complete Authorized Guide. 4th ed. 1999. pap. 23.95 (1-57243-338-8) Triumph Bks.

MacKinnon, John. Wild China. LC 96-16953. (Illus.). 208p. (C). 1996. 45.00 (0-262-13329-6) MIT Pr.

MacKinnon, John & Hicks, Nigel. Birds of China Including Hong Kong. (Photographic Wildlife Pocket Guides Ser.). (Illus.). 144p. 1996. pap. 15.95 (1-85368-764-2, RCB-764P, Pub. by New5 Holland) Chelsea Green Pub.

***MacKinnon, John & McDermott, John.** NHL Hockey: An Official Fans' Guide. (Illus.). 128p. 2000. 19.95 (1-84222-101-9) Carlton Bks Ltd.

MacKinnon, John, et al. A Field Guide to the Birds of Borneo, Sumatra, Java, & Bali, the Greater Sunda Islands. LC 92-30340. (Illus.). 507p. 1993. pap. 55.00 (0-19-854034-5); text 95.00 (0-19-854035-3) OUP.

MacKinnon, John R. & Stuart, Simon N., eds. The Kouprey: An Action Plan for Its Conservation. (Illus.). 20p. (Orig.). 1988. pap. 7.00 (2-88032-972-8, Pub. by IUCN) Island Pr.

***MacKinnon, John Ramsay, et al.** A Field Guide to the Birds of China. LC 99-50044. 848p. 2000. 100.00 (0-19-854941-5) OUP.

Mackinnon, K. Love Breaks Through. 6.99 (1-85792-027-9, Pub. by Christian Focus) Spring Arbor Dist.

MacKinnon, K., jt. auth. see Neilands, L.

MacKinnon, Kathy, et al, eds. Managing Protected Areas in the Tropics. (International Union for the Conservation of Nature & Natural Resources: A Belhaven Press Book Ser.). (Illus.). 320p. 1986. pap. 51.00 (2-88032-808-X, Pub. by IUCN) Island Pr.

MacKinnon, Kathy, et al. The Ecology of Kalimantan (Indonesian Borneo), Vol. III. (Ecology of Indonesia Ser.). (Illus.). 826p. 1997. text 49.95 (0-945971-73-7) Periplus.

MacKinnon, Kenneth. Gaelic: A Past & Future Prospect. (C). 1993. pap. 32.00 (0-85411-047-X, Pub. by Saltire Soc) St Mut.

— Greek Tragedy into Film. LC 86-13420. 256p. 1987. 36.50 (0-8386-3301-3) Fairleigh Dickinson.

— Hollywood's Small Towns: An Introduction to the American Small-Town Movie. LC 83-27113. 218p. 1984. 23.50 (0-8108-1678-4) Scarecrow.

— Misogyny in the Movies: The De Palma Question. LC 88-40607. (Illus.). 224p. 1990. 38.50 (0-87413-376-9) U Delaware Pr.

— The Politics of Popular Representation: Reagan, Thatcher, AIDS, & the Movies. LC 91-58581. 256p. 1992. 38.50 (0-8386-3474-5) Fairleigh Dickinson.

— Uneasy Pleasures: The Male As Erotic Object. LC 97-46621. (Illus.). 264p. 1998. 39.50 (0-8386-3797-3) Fairleigh Dickinson.

MacKinnon, L. Mechanics & Motion. (Oxford Physics Ser.). (Illus.). 1978. 23.50 (0-19-851825-0); pap. 10.95 (0-19-851843-9) OUP.

Mackinnon, Lachlan. Experimental Physics at Low Temperatures: An Introductory Survey. LC 65-14928. (Illus.). 282p. reprint ed. pap. 87.50 (0-7837-3606-1, 204347100009) Bks Demand.

MacKinnon, Laurel T. Advances in Exercise Immunology. LC 98-38767. (Illus.). 376p. 1999. 49.00 (0-88011-562-9) Human Kinetics.

MacKinnon, Laurie K. Trust & Betrayal in the Treatment of Child Abuse. LC 97-43972. 260p. 1998. lib. bdg. 30.00 (1-57230-298-4) Guilford Pubns.

***MacKinnon, Laurie K.** Trust & Betrayal in the Treatment of Child Abuse. 260p. 1999. pap. text 21.00 (1-57230-523-1) Guilford Pubns.

MacKinnon, Lilias. Music by Heart. (Music Book Index Ser.). 141p. 1992. reprint ed. lib. bdg. 69.00 (0-7812-9459-2) Rprt Serv.

Mackinnon, Lillias. Music by Heart. LC 80-26551. 141p. 1981. reprint ed. lib. bdg. 49.50 (0-313-22810-8, MAMB, Greenwood Pr) Greenwood.

MacKinnon, Mary H. & McIntyre, Moni. Readings in Ecology & Feminist Theology. 360p. (Orig.). 1995. pap. 19.95 (1-55612-762-6) Sheed & Ward WI.

***MacKinnon, Michael.** The Evolution of U. S. Peacekeeping Policy under Clinton. LC 99-17425. (Series on Peacekeeping: No. 6). 203p. 1999. 49.50 (0-7146-4937-6, Pub. by F Cass Pubs); pap. 22.50 (0-7146-4497-8, Pub. by F Cass Pubs) Intl Spec Bk.

An Asterisk (*) at the beginning of an entry indicates that the title is appearing for the first time.

MacKinnon, Neil. This Unfriendly Soil: The Loyalist Experience in Nova Scotia, 1783-1791. 244p. (C). 1989. pap. text 19.95 (0-7735-0719-1, Pub. by McG-Queens Univ Pr) CUP Services.

MacKinnon, Neil, et al. Economics: A Guide for the Financial Markets. 350p. 1992. 75.00 (1-873446-06-3, Pub. by IFR Pub) Am Educ Systs.

MacKinnon, Neil J. Symbolic Interactionism As Affect Control. LC 93-38563. (SUNY Series in the Sociology of Emotions). 245p. (C). 1994. pap. text 21.95 (0-7914-2042-6) State U NY Pr.

— Symbolic Interactionism As Affect Control. LC 93-38563. (SUNY Series in the Sociology of Emotions). 245p. (C). 1994. text 64.50 (0-7914-2041-8) State U NY Pr.

Mackinnon, Niall. The British Folk Scene: Musical Performance & Social Identity. LC 93-4036. (Popular Music in Britain Ser.). 224p. 1994. 122.00 (0-335-09774-X); pap. 31.95 (0-335-09773-1) OpUniv Pr.

MacKinnon, Pamela C. & Morris, John B. Oxford Textbook of Functional Anatomy, Vol. 1. 2nd rev. ed. LC 92-48317. (Oxford Medical Publications). (Illus.). 174p. (C). 1994. pap. text 24.95 (0-19-262195-5) OUP.

— Oxford Textbook of Functional Anatomy Vol. 2: Thorax & Abdomen. (Illus.). 150p. 1988. pap. text 27.95 (0-19-261518-1) OUP.

Mackinnon, Pamela C. & Morris, John F. Oxford Textbook of Functional Anatomy Vol. 3: Head & Neck, Vol. 2. rev. ed. (Illus.). 162p. 1991. pap. text 35.00 (0-19-261519-X) OUP.

MacKinnon, R. J. BLT-EC (Breach, Leach & Transport-equilibrium Chemistry) Data Input Guide: Computer Model for Simulating Release & Coupled Geochemical Transport of Contaminants. 368p. 1997. per. 33.00 (0-16-062846-6) USGPO.

MacKinnon, Richard M. World Place Location Learning System. 8th rev. ed. 104p. (C). 1996. pap. 14.00 (1-57182-410-3) Hayden-McNeil.

Mackinnon, Roderick. Teach Yourself Gaelic. (Teach Yourself Ser.). 1992. 15.95 (0-8288-8333-5) Fr & Eur.

MacKinnon, Roger A. & Michels, Robert. Psychiatric Interview in Clinical Practice. LC 70-151680. 1971. text 52.00 (0-7216-5973-X, W B Saunders Co) Harcrt Hlth Sci Grp.

MacKinnon, Roger A. & Yudofsky, Stuart C. Principles of the Psychiatric Evaluation. (Illus.). 325p. 1991. pap. text 39.95 (0-397-51064-0) Lppncott W & W.

Mackinnon, S. E. Surgery of the Peripheral Nerve. (Illus.). 662p. 1988. 189.00 (0-86577-283-5) Thieme Med Pubs.

MacKinnon, Stephen R. & Friesen, Oris. China Reporting: An Oral History of American Journalism in the 1930's & 1940's. 200p. (C). 1987. pap. 15.95 (0-520-06967-6, Pub. by U CA Pr) Cal Prin Full Svc.

MacKinnon, Stephen R., jt. auth. see MacKinnon, Janice R.

MacKinnon, Steve, ed. see Smedley, Agnes.

Mackinson, Larry & Goldstein, Joshua F. Open Secrets: The Encyclopedia of Congressional Money & Politics. 4th ed. 1348p. 1996. text 120.00 (1-56802-229-8) Congr Quarterly.

Mackintosh. Damascus & Its People: Sketches of Modern Life in Syria. LC 77-87617. reprint ed. 39.50 (0-404-16444-7) AMS Pr.

Mackintosh & Nolan. Cardiac Emergencies. 208p. 1998. pap. text 30.00 (0-7506-3833-8) Buttrwrth-Heinemann.

Mackintosh, A. Symbolism & Art Nouveau. LC 77-76764. (Modern Movements in Art Ser.). 1978. reprint ed. pap. 3.50 (0-8120-0882-0) Barron.

Mackintosh, Allan, ed. Advanced Telescope Making Techniques, Vol. 1: Optics. LC 86-18935. (Illus.). 320p. 1993. 24.95 (0-943396-11-5) Willmann-Bell.

— Advanced Telescope Making Techniques, Vol. 2: Mechanical. LC 86-18935. (Illus.). 320p. 1993. 24.95 (0-943396-12-3) Willmann-Bell.

Mackintosh, C. H. Short Papers. 477p. 1995. 14.95 (0-88172-205-7) Believers Bkshelf.

Mackintosh, Carlos H. La Oracion y los Cultos de Oracion. 2nd ed. Daniel, Roger P., ed. Bautista, Sara, tr. from ENG. (Serie Diamante).Tr. of Prayer & the Prayer Meeting. (SPA., Illus.). 40p. 1982. pap. 0.85 (0-942504-08-9) Overcomer Pr.

— El Perdon de los Pecados. 2nd ed. Bennett, Gordon H., ed. Bautista, Sara, tr. from ENG. (Serie Diamante).Tr. of Forgiveness of Sins. (SPA.). 36p. 1982. pap. 0.85 (0-942504-02-X) Overcomer Pr.

Mackintosh, Charles Rennie. Nikolaus Pevsner. 1998. pap. text 7.99 (88-86502-89-3, Pub. by Canal & Stamperia) Antique Collect.

Mackintosh, David, jt. auth. see Gray, Nigel.

Mackintosh, Douglas R. The Economics of Airborne Emissions. LC 72-89646. (Special Studies in U. S. Economic, Social & Political Issues). 1973. 42.50 (0-275-28668-1) Irvington.

Mackintosh, Duncan R. A Further Collection of Chinese Lyrics & Other Poems: Rendered into Verse by Alan Ayling from the Translations of the Chinese by Duncan Mackintosh in Collaboration with Ch'eng Hsi & T'ung Ping-cheng. LC 73-112602. (Illus.). 293p. reprint ed. pap. 90.90 (0-7837-6195-3, 204591700009) Bks Demand.

Mackintosh, Graham. Into a Desert Place: A 3000 Mile Walk Around the Coast of Baja California. (Illus.). 336p. 1995. pap. 15.95 (0-393-31289-5, Norton Paperbks) Norton.

MacKintosh, Graham. Into a Desert Place: A 3000 Mile Walk Around the Coast of Baja California. 2nd rev. ed. LC 90-91690. (Illus.). 312p. 1990. reprint ed. 24.95 (0-9626109-0-9) Graham Macintosh.

*__Mackintosh, Graham.__ Journey with a Baja Burro. Lindsay, Lowell, ed. (Cultural Heritage Bks.). (Illus.). 336p. 2000. pap. 17.95 (0-932653-41-3) Sunbelt Pubns.

Mackintosh, H. R., ed. see Schleiermacher, Friedrich Daniel Ernst.

Mackintosh, Ian. Architecture, Actor & Audience. LC 92-18625. (Illus.). 176p. (C). 1993. pap. 27.99 (0-415-03183-4, A7960) Routledge.

Mackintosh, J. J. Birds of Darjeling & India. 226p. 1986. pap. 150.00 (81-7089-147-7, Pub. by Intl Bk Distr) St Mut.

Mackintosh, J. W. The Hunts & the Hunted. 237p. (C). 1989. text 50.00 (1-872795-67-6, Pub. by Pentland Pr) St Mut.

Mackintosh, James. Memoirs of the Life of the Right Honorable Sir James Mackintosh, 2 vols. LC 76-172711. reprint ed. 40.00 (0-404-07433-2) AMS Pr.

— Roman Law in Modern Practice. xii, 202p. 1995. reprint ed. 35.00 (0-8377-2477-5, Rothman) W S Hein.

— The Roman Law of Sale: With Modern Illustrations Digest XVII.1 & XIX.1 Translated with Notes & References to Cases & the Sale of Goods Act. 2nd enl. ed. LC 93-79722. (Illus.). 318p. 1994. reprint ed. 80.00 (1-56169-080-5) Gaunt.

— The Roman Law of Sale: With Notes & References to Cases & the Sale of Goods Bill. LC 93-79721. (Illus.). 292p. 1994. reprint ed. 75.00 (1-56169-079-1) Gaunt.

Mackintosh, John J. Scotland: From the Earliest Times to the Present Century. LC 75-39198. (Select Bibliographies Reprint Ser.). 1977. reprint ed. 29.95 (0-8369-6800-X) Ayer.

Mackintosh, John P. & Fawley Foundation Staff. Britain's Malaise, Political or Economic? LC 78-319427. (Fawley Foundation Lecture Ser.). 26p. 1977. write for info. (0-85432-182-9) Univ of Southampton.

Mackintosh, L. J. Birds of Darjeeling & India. 226p. 1986. reprint ed. 175.00 (81-7089-047-0, Pub. by Intl Bk Distr) St Mut.

Mackintosh, M., et al. Economics & Changing Economies. 1152p. 1996. mass mkt. 24.95 (0-412-62840-6) Chapman & Hall.

Mackintosh, Maureen. Gender, Class & Rural Transition: Agribusiness & the Food Crisis in Senegal. LC 89-5836. 192p. (C). 1989. pap. 17.50 (0-86232-841-1, Pub. by Zed Books); text 55.00 (0-86232-840-3, Pub. by Zed Books) St Martin.

Mackintosh, Maureen & Roy, Rathin, eds. Economic Decentralization & Public Management Reform. LC 99-21718. (New Horizons in Public Policy Ser.). 304p. 1999. 95.00 (1-85898-995-7) E Elgar.

Mackintosh, N. J. IQ & Human Intelligence. (Illus.). 430p. 1998. text 98.00 (0-19-852368-8); pap. text 35.00 (0-19-852367-X) OUP.

— Psychology of Animal Learning. 1974. text 125.00 (0-12-464650-6) Acad Pr.

Mackintosh, N. J., ed. Cyril Burt: Fraud or Framed? (Illus.). 168p. 1995. text 30.00 (0-19-852336-X) OUP.

Mackintosh, Paul S., tr. see Oe, Kenzaburo.

Mackintosh, Prudence. Just As We Were: A Narrow Slice of Texas Womanhood. (Southwestern Writers Collection). 184p. 1996. 19.95 (0-292-75200-8) U of Tex Pr.

Mackintosh, Robert. Hegel & Hegelianism: 1903 Edition. 314p. 1996. reprint ed. 48.00 (1-85506-060-4) Bks Intl VA.

— Heritage of Lies. 1995. mass mkt. 4.99 (0-8217-5100-X, Zebra Kensgtn) Kensgtn Pub Corp.

— Silk. 1992. pap. 4.99 (0-685-53101-5) Pinnacle MO.

Mackintosh, Robert, jt. auth. see Short, Bobby.

Mackintosh, Robert H., Jr. Selected Bibliography of County, City & Town History & Related Published Records in the South Carolina Archives Reference Library. 43p. 1994. pap. text 2.00 (1-880067-27-7) SC Dept of Arch & Hist.

Mackintosh, Sherwin, jt. ed. see Fawcett, Geoff.

*__Mackintosh-Smith, Tim.__ Yemen: The Unknown Arabia. LC 99-59752. 280p. 2000. 35.00 (1-58567-001-4, Pub. by Overlook Pr) Penguin Putnam.

Mackintosh-Smith, Tim, tr. see Al-Hibshi, Abdullah M., ed.

Mackintosh Staff. Mackintosh Postcard Book. 1996. pap. 5.99 (3-8228-8630-0) Taschen Amer.

Mackintosh, William H. & Goliwas, Ruth M. The Stained Glass Coloring Book. (Illus.). 48p. (J). (ps-2). 1990. pap. 2.95 (0-671-69477-4) Litle Simon.

Mackinzie, Carine. Our Loving God. 1997. 12.99 (1-85792-294-8) Christian Focus.

Macklean, G. Helen of the Glen. (Flamingo Ser.). Date not set. 3.99 (0-906731-80-1, Pub. by Christian Focus) Spring Arbor Dist.

Macklem, Peter T. & Permutt, S., eds. The Lung in Transition Between Health & Disease. (Lung Biology in Health & Disease Ser.: Vol. 12). (Illus.). 464p. 1979. text 190.00 (0-8247-7750-6) Dekker.

Macklem, Peter T., ed. see Mead, Jere.

Macklem, Peter T., jt. ed. see Roussos, Charis.

Macklen, E. D. Thermistors. 226p. 1980. 150.00 (0-901150-07-X) St Mut.

*__Mackler, Carolyn.__ Love & Other Four-Letter Words. 2000. 14.95 (0-385-32743-9) Delacorte.

Mackler, Tasha. Murder . . . by Category: A Subject Guide to Mystery Fiction. LC 91-37638. 484p. 1991. 55.50 (0-8108-2463-9) Scarecrow.

Mackley, George. Confessions of a Woodpecker. deluxe ed. 1981. 250.00 (0-905418-92-1, Pub. by Gresham Bks) St Mut.

— George Mackley: Wood Engraver. 136p. 1984. 110.00 (0-905418-90-5, Pub. by Gresham Bks) St Mut.

Mackley, George E. Wood Engraving. 128p. 1984. 90.00 (0-905418-84-0, Pub. by Gresham Bks) St Mut.

— Wood Engraving. 144p. 1985. 45.00 (0-946095-18-3, Pub. by Gresham Bks) St Mut.

Mackley, Jim, III. Flue Covers - Collector's Value Guide. LC 98-114028. (Illus.). 160p. 1997. pap. 12.95 (1-57432-017-3, 4944) Collector Bks.

Mackley, Lesley. Book of Afternoon Tea. (Illus.). 120p. 1992. pap. 12.00 (1-55788-046-8, HP Books) Berkley Pub.

*__Mackley, Lesley.__ Book of Caribbean Cooking. (Illus.). 120p. 2000. pap. 12.00 (1-55788-328-9, HP Books) Berkley Pub.

Mackley, Lesley. Book of Greek Cooking. (Illus.). 120p. (Orig.). 1993. pap. 12.00 (1-55788-062-X, HP Books) Berkley Pub.

— The Book of North African Cooking. LC 99-180926. 120p. 1998. pap. 12.00 (1-55788-295-9, HP Books) Berkley Pub.

Mackley, Lesley, jt. auth. see Morris, Sallie.

Mackley-Smith, Gary B., jt. auth. see Noakes, Patrick.

*__Mackley, Tim A.__ Uncommon Sense: Core Knowledge in the Classroom. LC 99-6820. 66p. 1999. pap. 11.95 (0-87120-361-8) ASCD.

Macklin, ed. see De Cervantes Saavedra, Miguel.

Macklin, Alys E., ed. Twenty-Nine Tales from the French. Herrick, Robert, tr. & intro. by. LC 72-157785. (Short Story Index Reprint Ser.). 1977. reprint ed. 21.95 (0-8369-3897-6) Ayer.

Macklin, Barbara J. Structural Stability & Culture Change in a Mexican-American Community. Cortes, Carlos E., ed. LC 76-1249. (Chicano Heritage Ser.). 1977. 25.95 (0-405-09513-9) Ayer.

Macklin, Carole, ed. Proceedings of the Conference of the American Academy of Advertising, 1997. 1997. pap. 25.00 (0-931030-20-X) Am Acad Advert.

Macklin, Charles. The Covent Garden Theatre. LC 93-20862. (Augustan Reprints Ser.: No. 116). 1993. reprint ed. 14.50 (0-404-70116-7) AMS Pr.

— A Will & No Will: or A Bone for the Lawyers: And the New Play Criticized: or the Plague of Envy. LC 92-23648. (Augustan Reprints Ser.: Nos. 127-128). 1967. reprint ed. 21.50 (0-404-70127-2, PR3543) AMS Pr.

Macklin, Eleanor. AIDS & Families. LC 89-32929. 1994. pap. 19.95 (0-918393-60-4, Harrington Park) Haworth Pr.

Macklin, Eleanor, ed. AIDS & Families. 284p. 1989. 49.95 (0-86656-879-4) Haworth Pr.

Macklin, Eleanor D. & Rubin, Roger H., eds. Contemporary Families & Alternative Lifestyles: Handbook on Research & Theory. LC 82-10717. (Illus.). 416p. 1983. reprint ed. pap. 129.00 (0-608-01118-5, 205942200001) Bks Demand.

Macklin, Elizabeth. A Woman Kneeling in the Big City. 96p. 1994. pap. 8.95 (0-393-31105-8) Norton.

*__Macklin, Elizabeth.__ You've Just Been Told. LC 99-59714. 112p. 2000. 22.00 (0-393-04867-5) Norton.

*__Macklin, F. Anthony & Pici, Nick.__ Voices from the Set: The Film Heritage Interviews. LC 00-35784. (Filmmakers Ser.). (Illus.). 2000. write for info. (0-8108-3795-1) Scarecrow.

Macklin, Gerald. A Study of Theatrical Vision in Arthur Rimbaud's Illuminations. LC 93-32574. (Studies in French Literature: Vol. 16). 290p. 1993. 89.95 (0-7734-9349-2) E Mellen.

Macklin, Jenenne R. Faith the Size of a Mustard Seed: A Companion for Daily Living. LC 98-93824. 198p. 1999. pap. 12.95 (0-9667001-3-9) InnerWisdom Pubg.

Macklin, John. The World's Strangest "True" Ghost Stories. LC 89-26125. (Illus.). 96p. (J). (gr. 4 up). 1991. pap. 4.95 (0-8069-5785-9) Sterling.

Macklin, John J. The Window & the Garden: The Modernist Fictions of Ramon Perez de Ayala. LC 87-62378. 206p. 1988. pap. 30.00 (0-89295-053-6) Society Sp & Sp-Am.

Macklin, M. Carolin & Carlson, Les. Advertising to Children: Concepts & Controversies. LC 99-6231. 1999. 29.95 (0-7619-1285-1) Sage.

Macklin, Mark G., jt. ed. see Needham, Stuart.

Macklin, Michael. Agricultural Extension in India. LC 92-38463. (Technical Papers: No. 190). 43p. 1993. pap. 22.00 (0-8213-2291-5, 12291) World Bank.

Macklin, R., jt. auth. see Gaylin, W.

Macklin, Ronald R. The Logging Business Management Handbook. LC 82-83344. (Forest Industries Book). (Illus.). 176p. 1983. pap. 42.00 (0-87930-146-5) Miller Freeman.

Macklin, Ruth. Against Relativism: Cultural Diversity & the Search for Ethical Universals in Medicine. LC 98-44063. 304p. 1999. text 32.95 (0-19-511632-1) OUP.

— Surrogates & Other Mothers: The Debates over Assisted Reproduction. LC 93-5988. 240p. 1994. pap. 22.95 (1-56639-180-6) Temple U Pr.

Macklin, Ruth & Gaylin, Willard, eds. Mental Retardation & Sterilization: A Problem of Competency & Paternalism. LC 81-7393. (Hastings Center Series in Ethics). 274p. 1981. 39.50 (0-306-40689-6, Plenum Trade) Perseus Pubng.

Macklis, Roger M. Introduction to Medicine ISE, No. 2. 1988. 15.95 (0-316-54249-0, Little Brwn Med Div) Lppncott W & W.

— Macklis-Wash Package. 1984. 26.90 (0-316-54248-2) Little.

Macklis, Roger M., et al. Introduction to Clinical Medicine: A Student-to-Student Manual. 3rd ed. LC 94-14222. 320p. 1994. spiral bd. 29.95 (0-316-54243-1, Little Brwn Med Div) Lppncott W & W.

Mackmin, David. The Valuation & Sale of Residential Property. 2nd ed. 272p. (C). 1994. pap. 31.95 (0-415-09329-5, B3723) Thomson Learn.

Mackmin, David, jt. auth. see Baum, Andrew.

Mackness, M.I. & Clerc, M., eds. Esterases, Lipases & Phospholipases: From Structure to Clinical Significance, Vol. 266. (NATO ASI Ser.: 266). (Illus.). 290p. (C). 1994. text 115.00 (0-306-44802-5, Kluwer Plenum) Kluwer Academic.

Mackness, Robin. Oradour: Massacre & Aftermath. large type ed. (Illus.). 1991. 11.50 (0-7089-2503-0) Ulverscroft.

*__Mackniak, Michael.__ Milton Moose Finds a Home. large type ed. (Illus.). 36p. (J). (gr. 1-4). 2000. 18.95 (1-57532-221-8) Press-Tige Pub.

Macknight, Anthony D. & Leader, John P., eds. Epithelial Ion & Water Transport. fac. ed. LC 80-5542. (Illus.). 392p. pap. 121.60 (0-7837-7209-2, 204709000005) Bks Demand.

Macknight, James, ed. see Drummond, John.

*__MacKnight, Lynne.__ Celebration of Motherhood: With Love & Laughter. 220p. 2000. pap. 12.95 (0-9675757-9-6) PebbleCreek.

Macknight, Nancy, ed. see Sackville-West, Vita.

Macknight, Nigel. Modern Formula One Race Car: From Concept to Competition, Design & Development of the Lola BMS-Ferrari Grand Prix Car. (Illus.). 192p. 1993. 39.95 (0-87938-823-4) MBI Pubg.

MacKnight, Nigel. Showroom Stock Race Car Preparation. (Illus.). 160p. 1992. pap. 6.98 (0-87938-652-5) MBI Pubg.

MacKnight, Scott D., jt. auth. see Mudroch, Alena.

MacKnight, Scott D., jt. ed. see Mudroch, Alena.

MacKnight, William J., jt. auth. see Aklonis, John J.

Macko, John L., jt. auth. see Chidester, Jane E.

Macko, S., jt. auth. see Engel, M.

Mackoff, Barbara. Growing a Girl: Seven Strategies for Raising a Strong, Spirited Daughter. LC 96-21993. 320p. 1996. pap. 12.95 (0-440-50661-1, Dell Trade Pbks) Dell.

*__Mackoff, Barbara & Wenet, Gary Alan.__ The Inner Work of Leaders: Leadership as a Habit of Mind. LC 00-38048. 2000. 24.95 (0-8144-0590-8) AMACOM.

*__MacKonochie, Alison.__ Baby's 1st Year: Practical Handbook. 1999. pap. 8.95 (0-7548-0014-8, Lorenz Bks) Anness Pub.

— Caring for New Baby. (Practical Handbook Ser.). 1999. pap. 8.95 (0-7548-0016-4, Lorenz Bks) Anness Pub.

MacKonochie, Alison. Complete Book of Pregnancy & Babycare. 1998. pap. text 27.50 (1-85967-665-0, Lorenz Bks) Anness Pub.

*__MacKonochie, Alison.__ Complete Book on Pregnancy & Babycare. 256p. 2000. pap. 19.95 (1-84215-077-4) Anness Pub.

MacKonochie, Alison. Perfect Pregnancy Week by Week: Practical Handbook. 1999. pap. 8.95 (0-7548-0011-3, Lorenz Bks) Anness Pub.

Mackowiak, Katja. Angstlichkeit, Selbstregulation und Problemlosen Im Vorschulalter. (Psychologie Ser.: Bd. 609). (Illus.). 313p. 1998. 51.95 (3-631-32802-8) P Lang Pubng.

Mackowiak, Paula. Relief of Pain from Headaches & TMJ. LC 89-927914. (Illus.). 200p. (Orig.). 1989. pap. 11.95 (0-9625508-2-5) Solomon Bks.

Mackowiak, Philip A. Fever: Basic Mechanisms & Management. 2nd ed. LC 96-9374. 480p. 1996. text 104.00 (0-397-51715-7) Lppncott W & W.

Mackowski, Richard M. Jerusalem: City of Jesus: An Exploration of the Traditions, Writings, & Remains of the Holy City from the Time of Christ. LC 79-28093. 231p. reprint ed. pap. 71.70 (0-608-14503-3, 202533400043) Bks Demand.

Mackrell, Alice. An Illustrated History of Fashion: 500 Years of Fashion Illustration. LC 97-19634. (Illus.). 225p. 1997. 45.00 (0-89676-216-5, Costume & Fashion Pr) QSMG Ltd.

— Paul Poiret. LC 90-4086. (Illus.). 100p. (Orig.). (C). 1990. 39.95 (0-8419-1279-3); pap. 25.95 (0-8419-1280-7) Holmes & Meier.

Mackrell, Alice, jt. auth. see Ewing, Elizabeth.

Mackrell, Brian. Hariru Vikitoria! An Illustrated History of the Maori Tour of England, 1863. (Illus.). 1985. pap. 27.00 (0-19-558072-9) OUP.

Mackrell, Gerald. Thoughts for Religious. (C). 1988. 39.00 (0-85439-234-3, Pub. by St Paul Pubns) St Mut.

MacKrell, John & Albert, David. MCAD Buyer's Guide: Solids-Based Systems for Mechanical CAD/CAM. 3rd rev. ed. (Illus.). 600p. 1999. ring bd. 795.00 (1-889760-06-4) CIMdata Inc.

MacKrell, John, jt. auth. see Al-Timimi, Kais.

MacKrell, John, jt. auth. see Port, Stanley.

Mackrell, Judith. Out of Line: The Story of British New Dance. (Illus.). 160p. (Orig.). 1992. pap. 17.95 (1-85273-038-2, Pub. by Dance Bks) Princeton Bk Co.

Mackrell, Judith, jt. auth. see Craine, Debra.

*__MacKrell, Thomas.__ Words Are Friends. 1999. pap. write for info. (1-58235-330-1) Watermrk Pr.

Mackreth, Donald. Peterborough: History & Guide. (History & Guide Ser.). (Illus.). 128p. 1994. pap. 13.95 (0-7509-0235-3, Pub. by Sutton Pub Ltd) Intl Pubs Mktg.

Mackridge, Peter. A Descriptive Analysis of Standard Modern Greek. (Illus.). 412p. 1987. pap. text 35.00 (0-19-815854-8) OUP.

— Dionysios Solomos. (Studies in Modern Greek). 114p. (Orig.). (C). 1989. pap. text 16.00 (0-89241-488-X); lib. bdg. 25.00 (0-89241-487-1) Caratzas.

Mackridge, Peter, ed. Ancient Greek Myth in Modern Greek Poetry: Essays in Memory of C. A. Trypanis. LC 96-218410. 220p. (C). 1996. text 35.00 (0-7146-4751-9, Pub. by F Cass Pubs) Intl Spec Bk.

Mackridge, Peter & Holton, David. Greek: Comprehensive Grammar of the Modern Language. LC 97-224324. (GRE & ENG., Illus.). 544p. (C). 1997. 85.00 (0-415-10001-1); pap. 32.99 (0-415-10002-X) Routledge.

Mackridge, Peter, tr. see Prevelakis, Pandelis.

Mackridge, Peter A. & Yannakakis, Eleni, eds. Ourselves & Others: The Development of a Greek Macedonian Cultural Identity since 1912. LC 96-35258. 224p. 1997. 49.50 (1-85973-133-3, Pub. by Berg Pubs); pap. 19.50 (1-85973-138-4, Pub. by Berg Pubs) NYU Pr.

M

***Mackrill, Sue.** Triumphant Faith. LC 99-61366. 208p. 2000. pap. 12.95 (*1-57921-153-4*, Pub. by WinePress Pub) BookWorld.

Mackrodt, jt. ed. see Catlow, C. R.

***Macks.** Altos. 2001. write for info. (*0-7432-0471-9*) S&S Trade.

Macks. From Soup to Nuts. LC 99-42446. 144p. 1999. 12.00 (*0-684-86984-5*) S&S Trade.

Macks, Jon. Heaven Talks Back: An Uncommon Conversation. LC 98-37843. 144p. 1998. 12.95 (*0-684-85272-1*) Simon & Schuster.

Macksey, Catherine C., tr. see Descombes, Vincent.

Macksey, Kenneth. For Want of a Nail: The Impact on War of Logistics & Communications. (Illus.). 203p. 1990. 42.00 (*0-08-036268-0*, Pub. by Brasseys) Brasseys.

— From Triumph to Disaster: The Fatal Flaws of German Generalship from Moltke to Guderian. LC 96-32215. 240p. 1996. 34.95 (*1-85367-244-0*) Stackpole.

— Guderian: Panzer General. 254p. 1992. 35.00 (*1-85367-059-6*, 5517) Stackpole.

— Guderian, Panzer General. LC 97-15562. (Illus.). 240p. 1997. pap. 19.95 (*1-85367-286-6*) Greenhill Bks.

— Invasion: The Alternate History of the German Invasion of England, July 1940. LC 98-49190. 1999. pap. 19.95 (*1-85367-361-7*) Stackpole.

— Invasion: The German Invasion of England, July 1940. 256p. 1990. 35.00 (*1-85367-065-0*, 5535) Stackpole.

— Kesselring: German Master Strategist of the Second World War. LC 96-32214. 264p. 1996. 34.95 (*1-85367-256-4*) Stackpole.

M

***Macksey, Kenneth.** Kesselring: German Master Strategist of the Second World War. LC 00-38078. (Greenhill Military Ser.). 2000. pap. write for info. (*1-85367-422-2*) Stackpole.

Macksey, Kenneth. Military Errors of World War II. (Illus.). 256p. 1993. pap. 16.95 (*1-85409-199-9*) Sterling.

— Military Errors of World War Two. (Illus.). 262p. 1998. pap. 9.95 (*0-304-35083-4*) Sterling.

— Rommel: Battles & Campaigns. LC 97-10973. (Illus.). 226p. 1997. pap. 15.95 (*0-306-80786-6*) Da Capo.

— Tank Versus Tank: The Illustrated Story of Armoured Battlefield Conflict in the Twentieth Centry. (Illus.). 196p. 1999. pap. 26.95 (*1-902304-30-6*, Pub. by Grub St) Seven Hills Bk.

— Why the Germans Lose at War: The Myth of German Military Superiority. LC 99-16559. (Illus.). 240p. 1999. pap. text 18.95 (*1-85367-383-8*, Pub. by Greenhill Bks) Stackpole.

Macksey, Kenneth, ed. The Hitler Options: Alternate Decisions of World War II. LC 94-40997. (Illus.). 240p. 1995. 29.95 (*1-85367-192-4*, Pub. by Greenhill Bks) Stackpole.

— The Hitler Options: Alternate Decisions of World War II. LC 99-162040. (Illus.). 208p. 1998. pap. 18.95 (*1-85367-312-9*, Pub. by Greenhill Bks) Stackpole.

Macksey, Richard & Donato, Eugenio, eds. The Language of Criticism & the Sciences of Man: The Structuralist Controversy. LC 78-95789. 367p. reprint ed. pap. 113.80 (*0-608-10122-2*, 200419700041) Bks Demand.

— The Structuralist Controversy: The Languages of Criticism & the Sciences of Man. LC 78-95789. 365p. reprint ed. pap. 113.20 (*0-7837-3390-9*, 204334800008) Bks Demand.

Macksey, Richard A., ed. Velocities of Change: Critical Essays from MLN. LC 72-12343. 397p. 1974. pap. 17.95 (*0-8018-1495-2*) Johns Hopkins.

Mackson, Racheal. Catholic Homeschool Treasury. 1999. pap. text 14.95 (*0-89870-725-0*) Ignatius Pr.

Mackta, Jayne S., jt. auth. see Weiss, Joan O.

MacKuen, Michael B. & Coombs, Steven L. More Than News: Media Power in Public Affairs. LC 81-183. (People & Communication Ser.: No. 12). (Illus.). 231p. reprint ed. pap. 71.70 (*0-8357-4767-0*, 203770400009) Bks Demand.

Mackway-Jones, Kevin, ed. Emergency Triage - Manchester Triage Group. 156p. 1996. pap. text 22.00 (*0-7279-1126-0*, 340300460, Pub. by BMJ Pub) Login Brothers Bk Co.

Mackway-Jones, Kevin & Walker, Mike, eds. Pocket Guide to Teaching for Medical Instructors. 91p. 1998. pap. text 18.95 (*0-7279-1380-8*) Login Brothers Bk Co.

Mackworth, Alan K., jt. ed. see Freuder, Eugene C.

Mackworth, Cecily, ed. Mirror for French Poetry, 1840 to 1940. LC 71-76946. (Granger Index Reprint Ser.). 1977. 19.95 (*0-8369-6027-0*) Ayer.

Mackworth-Praed, Humphrey. Conservation Pieces. 220p. (C). 1991. pap. text 120.00 (*1-85341-046-2*, Pub. by Surrey Beatty & Sons) St Mut.

Macky, Peter W. The Centrality of Metaphors to Biblical Thought: A Method for Interpreting the Bible. LC 89-49023. (Studies in the Bible & Early Christianity: Vol. 19). 312p. 1990. lib. bdg. 99.95 (*0-88946-619-X*) E Mellen.

— St. Paul's Cosmic War Myth: A Military Version of the Gospel. LC 97-13443. (Westminster College Library of Biblical Symbolism). XIV, 309p. 1998. 53.95 (*0-8204-3829-4*) P Lang Pubng.

***Maclachlan.** Iceberg. 32p. 1999. 14.95 (*0-06-025454-8*) HarpC Child Bks.

MacLachlan. Iceberg. 32p. lib. bdg. 14.89 (*0-06-025458-0*) HarpC Child Bks.

MacLachlan, Alastair. The Rise & Fall of Revolutionary England: An Essay on the Fabrication of Seventeenth-Century History. LC 95-31667. (British History in Perspective Ser.). 352p. 1996. text 49.95 (*0-312-12841-X*) St Martin.

Maclachlan, Anne & Ferguson, Lindy. Robert Takes Over: An Interactive Intermediate Reading & Grammar Text. (Illus.). 128p. 1998. pap. text 18.95 (*1-879440-26-1*) Optima CA.

MacLachlan, Bonnie. The Age of Grace: Charis in Early Greek Poetry. LC 92-37031. (Illus.). 192p. (C). 1993. text 37.50 (*0-691-06974-3*, Pub. by Princeton U Pr) Cal Prin Full Svc.

MacLachlan, Cheryl. Bringing France Home. 1995. 40.00 (*0-517-59806-X*); pap. 25.00 (*0-517-88165-9*) Crown Pub Group.

— Bringing it Home, England: The Ultimate Guide to Creating the Feeling of England in Your Home. LC 97-35941. (Illus.). 192p. 1998. 40.00 (*0-517-70782-9*) C Potter.

MacLachlan, Cheryl & Niles, Bo. Bringing Sweden Home: The Ultimate Guide to Creating the Feeling of Sweden in Your Home. LC 96-26002. 1997. 40.00 (*0-517-70783-7*) C Potter.

Maclachlan, Cheryl, jt. ed. see Harvey, W. J.

MacLachlan, Christopher, ed. Scotlands Issue 2: Gender & Identity. 120p. 1996. pap. 22.50 (*0-7486-0702-1*, Pub. by Edinburgh U Pr) Col U Pr.

— Scotlands Issue One: Canons. 120p. 1996. pap. 22.50 (*0-7486-0486-3*, Pub. by Edinburgh U Pr) Col U Pr.

MacLachlan, Colin M. & Beezley, William H. El Gran Pueblo: A History of Greater Mexico. 2nd ed. LC 97-44273. 536p. (C). 1998. pap. text 44.00 (*0-13-778374-4*) P-H.

MacLachlan, Colin M. & Rodriguez, Jaime E. The Forging of the Cosmic Race: A Reinterpretation of Colonial Mexico. LC 78-68836. (Illus.). 408p. 1980. pap. 17.95 (*0-520-04280-8*, Pub. by U CA Pr) Cal Prin Full Svc.

MacLachlan, Colin M., jt. auth. see Beezley, William H.

Maclachlan, D. F., ed. see Sopcak, James E.

***MacLachlan, Hugh.** Great Melnikov. 2000. pap. 14.95 (*0-946487-42-1*) Luath Pr Ltd.

***MacLachlan, Ian.** Roger Laporte: The Orphic Text. (Legenda Ser.). 200p. (C). 2000. pap. 49.50 (*1-900755-38-6*, Pub. by E H R C) David Brown.

MacLachlan, James. Galileo Galilei: First Physicist. (Oxford Portraits in Science Ser.). (Illus.). 128p. (J). 1997. 22.00 (*0-19-509342-9*) OUP.

— Galileo Galilei: First Physicist. (Oxford Portraits in Science Ser.). (Illus.). 128p. 1999. pap. 11.95 (*0-19-513170-3*) OUP.

MacLachlan, James, jt. auth. see Collier, Bruce.

Maclachlan, John M. & Floyd, Joe S., Jr. This Changing South. LC 56-12858. 166p. reprint ed. pap. 51.50 (*0-8357-6720-5*, 203535500095) Bks Demand.

Maclachlan, John M., ed. see Southern Conference on Gerontology Staff.

MacLachlan, Malcolm. Culture & Health: Psychological Perspectives on Problems & Practice. LC 97-8648. (Wiley Series in Culture & Professional Practice). 332p. 1997. pap. 52.95 (*0-471-96626-6*) Wiley.

Maclachlan, Malcolm. An Introduction to Marine Drilling. (Illus.). 354p. 1992. pap. 125.00 (*1-870945-44-1*) Oilfield Publns.

Maclachlan, Morag. Fort Langley Journals, 1827-30: Journals. LC 98-211625. 1999. pap. text 17.95 (*0-7748-0665-6*) U BC Pr.

MacLachlan, Patricia. All the Places to Love. LC 92-794. (Charlotte Zolotow Bk.). (Illus.). 32p. (J). (gr. 1 up). 1994. 16.95 (*0-06-021098-2*) HarpC Child Bks.

— All the Places to Love. LC 92-794. (Charlotte Zolotow Bk.). (Illus.). 32p. (J). (ps-3). 1994. lib. bdg. 16.89 (*0-06-021099-0*) HarpC Child Bks.

— Arthur, for the Very First Time. LC 79-2007. (Illus.). 128p. (J). (gr. 4-7). 1980. lib. bdg. 15.89 (*0-06-024047-4*) HarpC Child Bks.

— Arthur, for the Very First Time. LC 79-2007. (Trophy Bk.). (Illus.). 128p. (J). (gr. 3-6). 1989. pap. 4.95 (*0-06-440288-6*, HarpTrophy) HarpC Child Bks.

MacLachlan, Patricia. Arthur, for the Very First Time. (J). 1980. 9.60 (*0-606-04038-2*, Pub. by Turtleback) Demco.

MacLachlan, Patricia. Baby. 132p. (J). (gr. 4-7). 1995. pap. 4.99 (*0-440-41145-9*, Yearling) BDD Bks Young Read.

— Baby. LC 93-22117. 144p. (J). (gr. 4-7). 1993. 15.95 (*0-385-31133-8*) Delacorte.

MacLachlan, Patricia. Baby. 1995. 9.60 (*0-606-07220-9*, Pub. by Turtleback) Demco.

MacLachlan, Patricia. Cassie Binegar. LC 81-48641. (Charlotte Zolotow Bk.). 128p. (J). (gr. 3-7). 1982. lib. bdg. 14.89 (*0-06-024034-2*) HarpC Child Bks.

— Cassie Binegar. LC 81-48641. (Trophy Bk.). 128p. (J). (gr. 4-7). 1987. pap. 4.95 (*0-06-440195-2*, HarpTrophy) HarpC Child Bks.

— Cassie Binegar. (J). 1987. 10.05 (*0-606-01155-2*, Pub. by Turtleback) Demco.

— The Facts & Fictions of Minna Pratt. LC 85-45388. (Charlotte Zolotow Bk.). 144p. (J). (gr. 4-7). 1988. lib. bdg. 14.89 (*0-06-024117-9*) HarpC Child Bks.

— The Facts & Fictions of Minna Pratt. LC 85-45338. (Trophy Bk.). 144p. (J). (gr. 3-7). 1990. pap. 4.95 (*0-06-440265-7*, HarpTrophy) HarpC Child Bks.

— The Facts & Fictions of Minna Pratt. 1988. 9.60 (*0-606-00994-9*, Pub. by Turtleback) Demco.

— The Facts & Fictions of Minna Pratt. large type ed. 1995. 37.50 (*0-614-09578-6*, L-34832-00) Am Printing Hse.

— Five Writers. (J). 1998. write for info. (*0-385-32136-8*) BDD Bks Young Read.

— Journey. (Illus.). 96p. (J). (gr. 4-7). 1993. pap. 4.50 (*0-440-40809-1*) Dell.

— Journey. 96p. (J). (gr. 4-6). 1991. 14.95 (*0-385-30427-7*) Doubleday.

MacLachlan, Patricia. Journey. (J). 1991. 9.19 (*0-606-05387-5*, Pub. by Turtleback) Demco.

MacLachlan, Patricia. Mama One, Mama Two. LC 81-47795. (Charlotte Zolotow Bk.). (Illus.). 32p. (J). (ps-3). 1982. lib. bdg. 15.89 (*0-06-024082-2*) HarpC Child Bks.

MacLachlan, Patricia. MAMA 1 MAMA 2. LC 81-47795. (Charlotte Zolotow Bk.). (Illus.). 32p. (J). (gr. 1-3). 1982. 13.00 (*0-06-024081-4*) HarpC Child Bks.

MacLachlan, Patricia. Sarah, Plain & Tall. LC 83-49481. (Charlotte Zolotow Bk.). 64p. (J). (gr. 3-5). 1985. 14.95 (*0-06-024101-2*) HarpC Child Bks.

— Sarah, Plain & Tall. LC 83-49481. (Charlotte Zolotow Bk.). 64p. (J). (gr. 4-7). 1985. lib. bdg. 14.89 (*0-06-024102-0*) HarpC Child Bks.

— Sarah, Plain & Tall. LC 83-49481. (Trophy Bk.). 64p. (J). (gr. 4-7). 1987. pap. 4.95 (*0-06-440205-3*, HarpTrophy) HarpC Child Bks.

— Sarah, Plain & Tall. LC 83-49481. (J). 1987. 10.15 (*0-606-03453-6*, Pub. by Turtleback) Demco.

— Sarah, Plain & Tall. large type ed. (LRS Large Print Cornerstone Ser.). 72p. (J). (gr. 3-8). 1999. lib. bdg. 19.95 (*1-58118-049-7*, 22773) LRS.

MacLachlan, Patricia. Sarah, Plain & Tall. 5th ed. 86p. (J). (gr. 3-6). 14.95 (*0-06-027560-X*) HarpC Child Bks.

MacLachlan, Patricia. Sarah, Sencilla y Alta (Sarah, Plain & Tall) (J). (gr. 5). 1996. pap. text 7.50 (*84-279-3421-1*) Lectorum Pubns.

— Sarah, Sencilla y Alta (Sarah, Plain & Tall) 1988. 13.15 (*0-606-10504-2*, Pub. by Turtleback) Demco.

— Seven Kisses in a Row. LC 82-47718. (Charlotte Zolotow Bk.). (Illus.). 64p. (J). (ps-3). 1983. lib. bdg. 14.89 (*0-06-024084-9*) HarpC Child Bks.

— Seven Kisses in a Row. LC 82-47718. (Charlotte Zolotow Bk.). (Illus.). 64p. (J). (gr. 2-5). 1988. pap. 4.95 (*0-06-440231-2*, HarpTrophy) HarpC Child Bks.

— Seven Kisses in a Row. 1983. 9.70 (*0-606-03912-0*, Pub. by Turtleback) Demco.

***MacLachlan, Patricia.** The Sick Day. (J). 2001. mass mkt. (*0-385-90007-4*) BDD Bks Young Read.

— The Sick Day. (J). 2001. mass mkt. 12.95 (*0-385-32150-3*, Pub. by Random Bks Yng Read) Random.

MacLachlan, Patricia. Skylark. (J). (gr. 5). 1995. 9.32 (*0-395-73258-1*) HM.

— Skylark. LC 93-33211. 96p. (J). (gr. 3-5). 1994. 12.95 (*0-06-023328-1*); lib. bdg. 12.89 (*0-06-023333-8*) HarpC Child Bks.

— Skylark. LC 93-33211. 112p. (J). (gr. 3-5). 1997. pap. 4.95 (*0-06-440622-9*, HarpTrophy) HarpC Child Bks.

— Skylark. 1997. 10.15 (*0-606-10930-7*, Pub. by Turtleback) Demco.

— Skylark. large type ed. 118p. (J). (gr. 5). 29.50 (*0-614-20620-0*, L-38193-00 APHB) Am Printing Hse.

— Three Names. LC 90-4444. (Charlotte Zolotow Bk.). (Illus.). 32p. (J). (gr. k-4). 1991. lib. bdg. 16.89 (*0-06-024036-9*) HarpC Child Bks.

— Three Names. LC 90-4444. (Illus.). 32p. (J). (gr. k-4). 1994. pap. 5.95 (*0-06-443360-9*, HarpTrophy) HarpC Child Bks.

MacLachlan, Patricia. Three Names. 1991. 11.15 (*0-606-06810-4*, Pub. by Turtleback) Demco.

MacLachlan, Patricia. Through Grandpa's Eyes. (Illus.). (J). (gr. 2-5). 1983. 13.89 (*0-06-024044-X*, 595015) HarpC Child Bks.

— Through Grandpa's Eyes. (Reading Rainbow Bks.). (J). 1983. 10.15 (*0-606-01956-1*, Pub. by Turtleback) Demco.

— Thru Grandpa's Eyes. LC 79-2019. (Illus.). 40p. (J). (gr. 2-4). 1980. lib. bdg. 15.89 (*0-06-024043-1*) HarpC.

— Thru Grandpa's Eyes. LC 79-2019. (Trophy Picture Bk.). (Illus.). 40p. (J). (gr. 1-4). 1983. pap. 5.95 (*0-06-443041-3*, HarpTrophy) HarpC Child Bks.

— Tomorrow's Wizard. LC 95-33453. 80p. (J). (gr. 3 up). 1996. pap. 6.00 (*0-15-201276-1*) Harcourt.

— Tomorrow's Wizard. LC 81-47733. (Charlotte Zolotow Bk.). (Illus.). 96p. (J). (gr. 3-6). 1982. 12.95 (*0-06-024073-3*); lib. bdg. 13.89 (*0-06-024074-1*) HarpC Child Bks.

— Unclaimed Treasures. LC 83-47714. (Trophy Bk.). 128p. (J). (gr. 5-7). 1987. pap. 4.95 (*0-06-440189-8*, HarpTrophy) HarpC Child Bks.

— Viaje (Journey) (SPA.). (YA). 1996. pap. 6.99 (*968-16-4722-X*, Pub. by Fondo) Continental Bk.

— What You Know First. LC 94-38341. (Joanna Cotler Bks.). (Illus.). 32p. (J). (gr. 2 up). 1995. 14.95 (*0-06-024413-5*); lib. bdg. 14.89 (*0-06-024414-3*, J Cotler) HarpC Child Bks.

— What You Know First. LC 94-38341. (Trophy Picture Bk.). (Illus.). 32p. (J). (ps-3). 1998. pap. 5.95 (*0-06-443492-3*) HarpC Child Bks.

— What You Know First. (Trophy Picture Bks.). (J). 1998. 11.15 (*0-606-13905-2*, Pub. by Turtleback) Demco.

Maclachlan, Simon, ed. Life after Big Bang. (C). 1988. lib. bdg. 68.50 (*0-86010-982-8*, Pub. by Graham & Trotman) Kluwer Academic.

Maclachlin, Cheryl. Bringing Italy Home. 1995. 40.00 (*0-517-59807-8*) Crown Pub Group.

MacLafferty, Robert L., et al. Social Security Disability: Alternatives Would Boost Cost-Effectiveness of Continuing Disability Reviews. (Illus.). 112p. (Orig.). (C). 1997. pap. text 30.00 (*0-7881-4053-1*) DIANE Pub.

— Social Security Disability: Improvements Needed to Continuing Disability Review Process. (Illus.). 112p. (Orig.). (C). 1997. pap. text 30.00 (*0-7881-4050-7*) DIANE Pub.

Maclagan, David. Creation Myths: Man's Introduction to the World. (Art & Imagination Ser.). (Illus.). 1977. pap. 15.95 (*0-500-81010-9*, Pub. by Thames Hudson) Norton.

Maclagan, Patrick. Management & Morality: A Developmental Perspective. LC 97-62444. vi, 212p. 1998. pap. write for info. (*0-8039-7680-1*) Sage.

MacLagan, Robert C., compiled by. The Games & Diversions of Argyleshire. (Folk-Lore Society, London Monographs: Vol. 47). 1969. reprint ed. pap. 30.00 (*0-8115-0521-9*) Periodicals Srv.

Maclagen, Robert C., compiled by. Games & Diversions of Argyleshire. LC 75-34848. (Studies in Play & Games). (Illus.). 1976. reprint ed. 25.95 (*0-405-07927-3*) Ayer.

MacLain, M., ed. see Reider, Barbara E.

MacLaine, Allan, intro. The Beginnings to Fifteen Fifty-Eight. (Great Writers Library). 86p. pap. 6.00 (*0-312-34700-6*) Academy Chi Pubs.

MacLaine, Allan H. Robert Fergusson. LC 65-18225. (Twayne's English Authors Ser.). 178p. (C). 1965. lib. bdg. 20.95 (*0-8057-1192-9*) Irvington.

***MacLaine, Shirley.** The Camino: A Journey of the Spirit. LC 00-28347. 320p. 2000. 24.95 (*0-7434-0072-0*, PB Hardcover); per. 24.95 (*0-7434-0921-3*) PB.

MacLaine, Shirley. Don't Fall off the Mountain. 304p. 1985. mass mkt. 6.99 (*0-553-27438-4*) Bantam.

— Going Within. 1989. 18.95 (*0-685-24546-2*) S&S Trade.

— It's All in the Playing. 352p. 1988. mass mkt. 6.99 (*0-553-27299-3*) Bantam.

— My Lucky Stars: A Hollywood Memoir. 400p. 1996. mass mkt. 6.99 (*0-553-57233-4*) Bantam.

— My Lucky Stars: A Hollywood Memoir. large type ed. LC 95-24495. 552p. 1995. 24.95 (*0-7838-1476-3*, G K Hall Lrg Type) Mac Lib Ref.

— You Can Get There from Here. 224p. 1976. mass mkt. 6.99 (*0-553-26173-8*) Bantam.

— You Can Get There from Here. 249p. 1975. 17.95 (*0-393-07489-7*) Norton.

MacLam, Helen, ed. Choice Reviews in Women's Studies, 1990-96. LC 96-52113. 454p. 1997. pap. 45.50 (*0-8389-7881-9*) Assn Coll & Res Libs.

Macland, Susan, jt. auth. see Ireland, Liz.

MacLane, Mary. I, Mary MacLane: A Diary of Human Days. (American Biography Ser.). 317p. 1991. reprint ed. lib. bdg. 79.00 (*0-7812-8257-8*) Rprt Serv.

Maclane, Mary. The Story of Mary Maclane & Other Writings. Rosemont, Penelope, ed. (Illus.). 192p. 1998. pap. 15.00 (*0-88286-233-2*) C H Kerr.

MacLane, Mary. The Story of Mary MacLane by Herself. (American Biography Ser.). 322p. 1991. reprint ed. lib. bdg. 79.00 (*0-7812-8258-6*) Rprt Serv.

— Tender Darkness: A Mary MacLane Anthology. Pruitt, Elisabeth A., ed. (Illus.). 208p. 1993. reprint ed. pap. 14.95 (*1-883304-01-6*) Abernathy & Brown.

MacLane, S. Categories for the Working Mathematician. LC 78-166080. (Graduate Texts in Mathematics Ser.: Vol. 5). 272p. 1994. 48.95 (*0-387-90035-7*) Spr-Verlag.

— Homology. (Grundlehren der Mathematischen Wissenschaften Ser.: Vol. 114). (Illus.). x, 422p. 1994. 89.95 (*0-387-03823-X*) Spr-Verlag.

MacLane, S. & Siefkes, D. J., eds. The Collected Works of J. Richard Buchi. (Illus.). 705p. 1989. 102.95 (*0-387-97064-9*, 3061) Spr-Verlag.

MacLane, Saunders. Categories for the Working Mathematician. 2nd ed. Axler, S. et al, eds. LC 97-45229. (Graduate Texts in Mathematics Ser.: Vol. 5). (Illus.). 352p. 1998. 49.95 (*0-387-98403-8*) Spr-Verlag.

— Selected Papers: Saunders MacLane. Kaplansky, Irving, ed. LC 79-10105. 1979. 107.95 (*0-387-90394-1*) Spr-Verlag.

Maclaran, Andrew. Dublin: The Shaping of a Capital. LC 92-43255. (World Cities Ser.). 224p. 1993. 105.00 (*0-471-94711-3*) Wiley.

MacLaren, et al. Maternal, Neonatal & Women's Health Nursing Student's Activity Book. 304p. 1991. pap., student ed. 17.95 (*0-87434-360-7*) Springhouse Corp.

MacLaren, Aileen. Maternal & Neonatal Nursing. LC 93-37753. (Concepts & Activities Ser.). (Illus.). 448p. 1993. pap. 23.95 (*0-87434-576-6*) Springhouse Corp.

MacLaren, Aileen & Kenner, Carole A. Essentials of Maternal & Neonatal Nursing. 208p. 1992. pap., teacher ed. write for info. (*0-87434-472-7*) Springhouse Corp.

Maclaren, Alexander. After the Resurrection. LC 91-21642. 160p. 1992. pap. 10.99 (*0-8254-3199-9*) Kregel.

— Best of Alexander Maclaren. Atkins, Gaius G., ed. LC 74-179733. (Biography Index Reprint Ser.). 1977. reprint ed. 17.95 (*0-8369-8101-4*) Ayer.

MacLaren, Alexander. Expositions of Holy Scripture, 17. 13128p. (gr. 11). 1977. reprint ed. 495.00 (*0-8010-5967-4*) Baker Bks.

Maclaren, Alexander. Music for the Soul. LC 96-79878. (Walk in the Word Ser). 400p. 1996. 24.99 (*0-89957-218-9*) AMG Pubs.

— Sermons for All Seasons. 550p. 1995. reprint ed. 19.99 (*0-529-10481-4*, SFS) World Publng.

MacLaren, Alexander. Sermons for All Seasons: A Year's Ministry. (Bible Sermon Ser.: Pulpit Legends Collection). 497p. 1995. 19.99 (*0-89957-207-3*) AMG Pubs.

MacLaren, Angus, jt. auth. see Hammer, David L.

MacLaren, Catharine, jt. auth. see Ellis, Albert.

MacLaren, Dorothy H. Esopus Hodie, Aesop Today, Vol. 1. (ENG & LAT.). 64p. (YA). (gr. 9-12). 9.75 (*0-939507-06-4*, B20) Amer Classical.

— Esopus Hodie, Aesop Today, Vol. II. (LAT.). 68p. 1991. pap. text 9.75 (*0-939507-25-0*, B21) Amer Classical.

MacLaren, Ian. Beside the Bonnie Brier Bush. 1976. 23.95 (*0-8488-0290-X*) Amereon Ltd.

— Days of Auld Lang Syne. 1976. 23.95 (*0-8488-0291-8*) Amereon Ltd.

— Kate Carnegie. 1976. 23.95 (*0-8488-0292-6*) Amereon Ltd.

Maclaren, J. M. Surface Crystallography. 1987. lib. bdg. 152.00 (*90-277-2503-9*) Kluwer Academic.

MacLaren, J. M., et al. Surface Crystallographic Information Service: A Handbook of Surface Structures. (C). 1987. pap. text 122.00 (*90-277-2554-3*) Kluwer Academic.

MacLaren, James. Beginner's Gaelic. (Hippocrene Beginner's Language Ser.). (ENG & GAE.). 20p. 1999. pap. 14.95 (*0-7818-0726-3*) Hippocrene Bks.

An Asterisk (*) at the beginning of an entry indicates that the title is appearing for the first time.

— Gaelic Self-Taught. 1991. pap. 19.95 (*0-8288-3344-3*, M4217) Fr & Eur.

— Gaelic Self-Taught. (C). 1989. pap. 30.00 (*0-901771-20-1*, Pub. by Gairm Pubns) St Mut.

Maclaren, James. Gaelic Self Taught. 4th ed. 1992. pap. 24.50 (*0-901771-84-8*) Colton Bk.

MacLaren, James. Learn to Surf. LC 97-1394. (Illus.). 144p. (Orig.). 1997. pap. 12.95 (*1-55821-568-9*) Lyons Pr.

MacLaren, Margaret. The MacLarens: A History of Clan Labhran. 153p. (C). 1989. text 60.00 (*0-946270-10-4*, Pub. by Pentland Pr) St Mut.

MacLaren, Margaret, jt. auth. see Hills, P. J.

MacLaren, Neil. Dutch School, 2 vol. exp. rev. ed. (National Gallery Publications). (Illus.). 1990. pap. 190.00 (*0-300-06137-4*) Yale U Pr.

— The Spanish School. rev. ed. (National Gallery Publications). (Illus.). 1989. pap. 25.00 (*0-300-06143-9*) Yale U Pr.

MacLaren-Ross, J. Doomsday Book. 1961. 11.95 (*0-8392-1027-2*) Astor-Honor.

Maclaren-Ross, J., tr. see Simenon, Georges.

MacLaren, Roy, ed. African Exploits: The Diaries of William Stairs, 1887-1892. (Illus.). 520p. 1998. 49.95 (*0-7735-1640-9*, Pub. by McG-Queens Univ Pr) CUP Services.

MacLaren, Terrence F. Eckstrom's Licensing in Foreign & Domestic Operations: Joint Ventures, 3 vols., Set. LC 85-10934. (IP Ser.). 1985. ring bd. 425.00 (*0-87632-466-9*) West Group.

MacLaren, Terrence F., ed. Worldwide Trade Secrets Law. LC 93-27434. (IP Ser.). 1993. ring bd. 425.00 (*0-87632-921-0*) West Group.

Maclaren, W. A. Rubber, Tea & Cacao with Special Sections on Coffee, Spices & Tobacco. 1980. lib. bdg. 75.00 (*0-8490-3110-9*) Gordon Pr.

***MacLarnon, Ann & Ross, Caroline, eds.** Evolution of Non-Maternal Care in Primates. (Folia Primatologica Ser.: Vol. 71, Nos. 1-2). 114p. 2000. pap. 34.00 (*3-8055-6968-8*) S Karger.

MacLauchlan, Andrew. Classic Desserts. 256p. 1994. 54.95 (*0-471-28605-2*, VNR) Wiley.

MacLauchlan, Andrew. The Making of a Pastry Chef: Recipes & Inspirations from America's Best Pastry Chefs. LC 99-13033. 352p. 1999. pap. 29.95 (*0-471-29320-2*) Wiley.

— New Classic Deserts. (Illus.). 288p. 1994. text 52.95 (*0-442-01735-9*, VNR) Wiley.

MacLauchlan, Andrew, jt. auth. see Miller, Mark.

MacLaughlin, David. Structural Steel Design/Fabric Drawing. LC 97-10389. (Construction & Building Trades Ser.). 352p. (C). 1997. mass mkt. 56.95 (*0-8273-7313-9*) Delmar.

MacLaughlin, Dawn & McEwen, Susan, eds. Proceedings of the 19th Annual Boston University Conference on Language Development, 2 vols. (BUCLD Proceedings Ser.: Vol. 19). (Illus.). 688p. (C). 1995. pap. 42.00 (*1-57473-002-9*); lib. bdg. 92.00 (*1-57473-102-5*) Cascadilla Pr.

MacLaughlin, Jim. Ireland. 96p. 1994. pap. 7.50 (*1-85918-028-0*, Pub. by Cork Univ) Stylus Pub VA.

MacLaughlin, Jim. Location & Dislocation in Contemporary Irish Society: Perspectives on Irish Emigration & Irish Identities in a Global Context. LC 97-27245. 1997. pap. 24.00 (*0-268-01317-9*) U of Notre Dame Pr.

Maclaughlin, Jim. Travellers & Ireland: Whose Country, Whose History? LC 96-111665. (Undercurrents Ser.). 90p. 1995. pap. text 7.50 (*1-85918-094-9*, Pub. by Cork Univ) Intl Spec Bk.

MacLaughlin, Jim, ed. Location & Dislocation in Contemporary Irish Society: Perspectives on Irish Emmigration & Irish Identities in a Global Context. 256p. 1997. 69.95 (*1-85918-054-X*, Pub. by Cork Univ); pap. 27.95 (*1-85918-055-8*, Pub. by Cork Univ) Intl Spec Bk.

MacLaughlin, Margaret L. Math for Business Applications. 2nd ed. 400p. (Orig.). 2000. pap. 59.95 (*0-201-61446-4*) Addison-Wesley.

MacLaughlin, Margaret L., jt. ed. see Cody, Michael J.

MacLaughlin, Robert, et al. Cthulhu Live. (Illus.). (Orig.). 1997. pap. 16.95 (*1-56882-041-0*, 6502) Chaosium.

Maclauries. A Narrative or Journal of Voyages & Travels Through the Northwest Continent in the Years 1789 & 1793. 93p. 1980. 16.95 (*0-87770-231-4*) Ye Galleon.

Maclaurin, Colin, ed. An Account of Sir Isaac Newton's Philosophical Discoveries. (Anglistica & Americana Ser.: No. 87). (Illus.). 440p. 1971. reprint ed. 83.20 (*3-487-04002-6*) G Olms Pubs.

MacLaurin, Diane. The Magic Horn. Karcher, Pamela, ed. (Illus.). 75p. (Orig.). (YA). (gr. 6 up). 1993. pap. write for info. (*0-934549-01-X*) Laurin Hse.

Maclaurin, W. Rupert. Invention & Innovation in the Radio Industry. LC 74-161146. (History of Broadcasting: Radio to Television Ser.). 1976. reprint ed. 25.95 (*0-405-03567-5*) Ayer.

MacLaury, Jean. Selected Federal & State Publications of Interest to Planning Librarians, No. 4. 1976. 5.50 (*0-686-20413-1*, Sage Prdcls Pr) Sage.

— Selected Federal & State Publications of Interest to Planning Librarians, No. 8. 1977. 2.50 (*0-686-19123-4*, 1246, Sage Prdcls Pr) Sage.

— Selected Federal & State Publications of Interest to Planning Librarians, No. 9. 1977. 2.50 (*0-686-19104-8*, 1268, Sage Prdcls Pr) Sage.

— Selected Federal & State Publications of Interest to Planning Librarians, No. 1, No. 1092. 1976. 7.00 (*0-686-20404-2*, Sage Prdcls Pr) Sage.

— Selected Federal & State Publications of Interest to Planning Librarians, No. 2, No. 1115. 1976. 5.00 (*0-686-20405-0*, Sage Prdcls Pr) Sage.

— Selected Federal & State Publications of Interest to Planning Librarians, No. 5, No. 1174. 1976. 6.00 (*0-686-20417-4*, Sage Prdcls Pr) Sage.

MacLaury, Robert E. Color & Cognition in Mesoamerica: Constructing Categories As Vantages. LC 96-10072. 1997. 85.00 (*0-292-75193-1*) U of Tex Pr.

MacLaury, Robert E., jt. ed. see Taylor, John R.

MacLaverty, Bernard. Cal: A Novel. 160p. 1995. pap. 13.00 (*0-393-31332-8*, Norton Paperbks) Norton.

— Columba. 1994. pap. 21.00 (*1-899827-46-3*) St Mut.

— Grace Notes: A Novel. LC 97-22090. 224p. 1997. 23.00 (*0-393-04542-0*) Norton.

— Grace Notes: A Novel. 288p. 1998. pap. 13.00 (*0-393-31841-9*, Norton Paperbks) Norton.

— Lamb. LC 98-35738. 200p. 1999. pap. write for info. (*0-7540-3476-3*) Chivers N Amer.

— Lamb. 160p. 1997. pap. 11.00 (*0-393-31701-3*) Norton.

— Lamb. large type ed. LC 98-35738. 214p. 1999. 30.00 (*0-7862-1609-3*, G K Hall Lrg Type) Mac Lib Ref.

MaClay, Charlotte. Accidental Roommates, Vol. 29. (Love & Laughter Ser.). 1997. per. 3.50 (*0-373-44029-4*) Harlequin Bks.

Maclay, Charlotte. The Bewitching Bachelor. (American Romance Ser.). 1996. per. 3.75 (*0-373-16620-6*, 1-16620-6) Harlequin Bks.

— Courting Cupid. 1999. per. 3.50 (*0-373-44061-8*, Harlequin) Harlequin Bks.

— The Cowboy & the Belly Dancer. LC 95-13560. (American Romance Ser.). 251p. 1995. per. 3.50 (*0-373-16585-4*, 1-16585-1) Harlequin Bks.

— Daddy & the Mermaid: Once upon a Kiss. (American Romance Ser.: No. 709). 1998. per. 3.75 (*0-373-16709-1*, 1-16709-7) Harlequin Bks.

— A Daddy for Becky. (American Romance Ser.: Bk. 806). 2000. per. 3.99 (*0-373-16806-3*, 1-16806-1) Harlequin Bks.

— Daddy's Little Cowgirl (Sexy Single Dads) (American Romance Ser.: No. 766). 1999. per. 3.99 (*0-373-16766-0*, 1-16766-7) Harlequin Bks.

MaClay, Charlotte. Deputy Daddy. 1999. per. 3.99 (*0-373-16788-1*, 1-16788-1) Harlequin Bks.

Maclay, Charlotte. Elusive Treasure. (American Romance Ser.). 1993. per. 3.50 (*0-373-16503-X*, 1-16503-4) Harlequin Bks.

***Maclay, Charlotte.** Expecting at Christmas, No. 140. (Romance Ser.). 1999. per. 3.50 (*0-373-19409-9*) Silhouette.

Maclay, Charlotte. A Ghostly Affair. (American Romance Ser.). 1993. mass mkt. 3.39 (*0-373-16488-2*, 1-16488-8) Harlequin Bks.

— The Hog-Tied Groom: The Brides of Grazer's Corners. (American Romance Ser.: Vol. 743). 1998. per. 3.99 (*0-373-16743-1*, 1-16743-6) Harlequin Bks.

— How to Marry a Millionaire. (American Romance Ser.). 1995. per. 3.50 (*0-373-16566-8*, 1-16566-1) Harlequin Bks.

***Maclay, Charlotte.** In a Cowboy's Embrace, (American Romance Ser.: Vol. 825). 2000. mass mkt. 4.25 (*0-373-16825-X*) Harlequin Bks.

Maclay, Charlotte. The Kidnapped Bride. 1994. per. 3.50 (*0-373-16537-4*, 1-16537-2) Harlequin Bks.

— A Little Bit Pregnant. (American Romance Ser.). 1998. per. 3.99 (*0-373-16728-8*, 1-16728-7) Harlequin Bks.

— The Littlest Angel. 1996. per. 3.75 (*0-373-16657-5*, 1-16657-8) Harlequin Bks.

— Michael's Magic. (American Romance Ser.). 1994. per. 3.50 (*0-373-16532-3*, 1-16532-3) Harlequin Bks.

— Only Bachelors Need Apply. 1997. per. 3.25 (*0-373-19249-5*, 1-19249-1) Silhouette.

***Maclay, Charlotte.** The Right Cowboy's Bed: Caught with a Cowboy. 2000. per. 4.25 (*0-373-16821-7*) Harlequin Bks.

Maclay, Charlotte. Stealing Samantha. (American Romance Ser.: No. 684). 1997. per. 3.75 (*0-373-16684-2*, 1-16684-2) Harlequin Bks.

— The Villain's Lady. (American Romance Ser.). 1993. per. 3.39 (*0-373-16474-2*, 1-16474-8) Harlequin Bks.

— Wanted: A Dad to Brag About. (American Romance Ser.). 1996. per. 3.75 (*0-373-16643-5*, 1-16643-8) Harlequin Bks.

***Maclay, Charlotte & Jarrett, Liz.** Duets 2-in-1: Not Exactly Pregnant; Darn Near Perfect. (Duets Ser.: No. 20). 2000. mass mkt. 5.99 (*0-373-44086-3*, 1-44086-6, Harlequin) Harlequin Bks.

Maclay, Charlotte, jt. auth. see Diamond, Jacqueline.

Maclay, Edgar S. A History of American Privateers. LC 74-119937. (Select Bibliographies Reprint Ser.). 1977. reprint ed. 36.95 (*0-8369-5380-0*) Ayer.

Maclay, Elise. The Forest Has Eyes. LC 98-7800. (Illus.). 32p. (J). (ps-2). 1999. 16.95 (*0-86713-055-5*, 85132) Greenwich Wrkshop.

— Green Winter: Celebrations of Later Life. 88p. 1995. pap. 8.95 (*0-8050-3805-1*, Owl) H Holt & Co.

Maclay, Elise, jt. auth. see Doolittle, Bev.

Maclay, Elise, ed. see Blish, Carolyn.

Maclay, John, intro. Voices from the Night. deluxe limited ed. LC 93-80782. 320p. 1994. 60.00 (*0-940776-29-4*) Maclay Assoc.

Maclay, John, ed. & intro. see Castle, Mort, et al.

Maclay, Michael. The European Union. Briggs, Asa, ed. LC 99-163553. (Pocket Histories Ser.). 128p. 1998. pap. 9.95 (*0-7509-1952-3*, Pub. by Sutton Pub Ltd) Intl Pubs Mktg.

Maclay, Phyllis. Whose Birthday Is It Anyway? A Children's Christmas Program. 12p. (Orig.). 1997. pap. 4.75 (*0-7880-1055-7*) CSS OH.

Maclay, Timothy D. & Allahdadi, Firooz A., eds. Characteristics & Consequences of Orbital Debris & Natural Space Impactors, Vol. 2813. 266p. 1996. 66.00 (*0-8194-2201-0*) SPIE.

Maclay, William. The Journal of William Maclay: United States Senator from Pennsylvania, 1789-1791. (American Biography Ser.). 429p. 1991. reprint ed. lib. bdg. 89.00 (*0-7812-8259-4*) Rprt Serv.

MacLead, Norman. The Gold Thread. unabridged ed. Clarkson, Clay, ed. (Illus.). 120p. (J). (gr. 3-8). 1999. reprint ed. 13.95 (*1-888692-06-5*) Whole Heart.

Maclean. Compendium of Kaffir Laws & Customs. (Illus.). 171p. 1968. reprint ed. 39.50 (*0-7146-1907-8*, Pub. by F Cass Pubs) Intl Spec Bk.

— Desert Leader: Moses. 1997. pap. 2.99 (*1-85792-304-9*, Pub. by Christian Focus) Spring Arbor Dist.

— Happy Harvest. 1996. mass mkt. 2.99 (*1-85792-246-8*, Pub. by Christian Focus) Spring Arbor Dist.

— Joseph's Journal. 1997. pap. 4.99 (*1-85792-293-X*, Pub. by Christian Focus) Spring Arbor Dist.

— Man Who Ran: Jonah. 1996. mass mkt. 2.99 (*1-85792-228-X*, Pub. by Christian Focus) Spring Arbor Dist.

— Shepherd King. 1997. pap. 2.99 (*1-85792-303-0*, Pub. by Christian Focus) Spring Arbor Dist.

MacLean. Solomon. large type ed. (Illus.). 75p. (J). 1996. spiral bd. 10.00 (*0-940178-47-8*) Sitare.

MacLean, ed. see Sitare Ltd. Staff.

MacLean, Alair, jt. auth. see Rennie, Caroline.

Maclean, Alan. No, I Tell a Lie, It Was the Tuesday . . . A Trudge Through His Life & Times. (Illus.). 182p. 1998. 35.00 (*1-85626-248-0*, Pub. by Cathie Kyle) Trafalgar.

MacLean, Alasdair. A MacDonald for the Prince. 104p. 1999. pap. 26.00 (*0-86152-002-5*, Pub. by Acair Ltd) St Mut.

MacLean, Alasdair, jt. auth. see Buchanan, John L.

MacLean, Alasdair, jt. auth. see Mackenzie, William.

MacLean, Alasdair, jt. auth. see Nicolson, Alexander.

MacLean, Alasdair R., jt. ed. see Brown, S. Moira.

***MacLean, Alex S., photos by.** Taking Measures Across the American Landscape. (Illus.). 208p. 2000. pap. 35.00 (*0-300-08696-2*) Yale U Pr.

MacLean, Alex S., jt. auth. see Sexton, Richard.

MacLean, Alistair. Caravan to Vaccares. large type ed. 1972. 27.99 (*0-85456-099-8*) Ulverscroft.

***MacLean, Alistair.** Caravan to Vaccares. large type unabridged ed. 1999. 25.95 (*0-7531-5977-5*, 159775, Pub. by ISIS Lrg Prnt) ISIS Pub.

MacLean, Alistair. Circus. 24.95 (*0-89190-672-X*) Amereon Ltd.

— Fear Is the Key. 1976. 22.95 (*0-89190-171-X*) Amereon Ltd.

— Force Ten from Navarone. LC 68-18084. 1968. 4.95 (*0-385-02759-1*) Doubleday.

— Force Ten from Navarone. large type ed. 1975. 12.00 (*0-85456-345-8*) Ulverscroft.

— The Golden Gate. 1976. 21.95 (*0-8488-0571-2*) Amereon Ltd.

— Goodbye California. 24.95 (*0-89190-671-1*) Amereon Ltd.

MacLean, Alistair. The Guns of Navarone. 1984. 11.09 (*0-606-00780-6*, Pub. by Turtleback) Demco.

MacLean, Alistair. The Guns of Navarone. 1994. reprint ed. lib. bdg. 27.95 (*1-56849-306-1*) Buccaneer Bks.

***MacLean, Alistair.** Guns of Navarone; Force 10 from Navarone. 320p. 2000. 8.99 (*0-517-20640-4*) Random Hse Value.

MacLean, Alistair. Hollywood. large type ed. (Yesterday & Tomorrow Fantasy Cartoon Ser.). (FRE., Illus.). 75p. (YA). 1999. 10.00 (*0-940178-89-3*) Sitare.

***MacLean, Alistair.** Ice Station Zebra. large type unabridged ed. 352p. 1999. 26.95 (*0-7531-5978-3*, 159783, Pub. by ISIS Lrg Prnt) ISIS Pub.

MacLean, Alistair. Instant Comedy: The Toughest Nut in Show Business, Cracks. large type ed. (Opening the Million Dollar Doors of Show Business Ser.). (Illus.). 75p. (YA). 1997. spiral bd. 10.00 (*0-940178-21-4*) Sitare.

— Night Without End. LC 60-6893. (J). 1960. 6.95 (*0-385-00546-6*) Doubleday.

— Night Without End. reprint ed. lib. bdg. 21.95 (*0-89190-174-4*, Rivercity Pr) Amereon Ltd.

— Puppet on a Chain. reprint ed. lib. bdg. 21.95 (*0-89190-175-2*, Rivercity Pr) Amereon Ltd.

***MacLean, Alistair.** River of Death. large type unabridged ed. 2000. 25.95 (*0-7531-5979-1*, 159791, Pub. by ISIS Lrg Prnt) ISIS Pub.

MacLean, Alistair. Samson. large type ed. (Yesterday & Tomorrow Bible Cartoon Ser.: Vol. 1, Bk. III). (Illus.). 75p. (YA). 1996. spiral bd. 10.00 (*0-940178-04-4*) Sitare.

***MacLean, Alistair.** The Satan Bug. 2000. 21.95 (*0-7540-8571-6*, Black Dagger) Chivers N Amer.

MacLean, Alistair. The Satan Bug. 1994. reprint ed. lib. bdg. 27.95 (*1-56849-305-3*) Buccaneer Bks.

— Seawitch. 21.95 (*0-89190-673-8*) Amereon Ltd.

— Secret Ways. 1976. 22.95 (*0-89190-172-8*) Amereon Ltd.

— South by Java Head. 1976. 23.95 (*0-89190-173-6*) Amereon Ltd.

— The Unexpected Show Business: Unexpected Surprises You Can Avoid. large type ed. (Opening the Million Dollar Doors of Show Business Ser.). (Illus.). 75p. 1997. spiral bd. 10.00 (*0-940178-22-2*) Sitare.

— What the Hell...? large type ed. Sitare Ltd. Staff, ed. (Illus.). 369p. 1998. lib. bdg. 20.00 (*0-940178-18-4*) Sitare.

MacLean, Alistair, ed. A to Z Tap: The Alphabet of Tap Dancing. large type ed. (Opening the Million Dollar Doors of Show Business Ser.). (Illus.). 100p. 1997. spiral bd. 10.00 (*0-940178-98-2*) Sitare.

— Animals of the Bible. large type ed. (Yesterday & Tomorrow Bible Cartoon Ser.). (Illus.). 75p. (YA). 1996. spiral bd. 10.00 (*0-940178-75-3*) Sitare.

— Job: The Good Servant. large type ed. (Yesterday & Tomorrow Bible Cartoon Ser.). (Illus.). 75p. (YA). 1996. spiral bd. 10.00 (*0-940178-79-6*) Sitare.

— My Back is Normal: Back Problems. large type ed. (Illus.). 100p. 1999. spiral bd. 10.00 (*0-940178-01-X*) Sitare.

MacLean, Alistair, jt. auth. see Bowser, M.

MacLean, Alistair, jt. auth. see Maclean-Bowser.

MacLean, Alistair, ed. see Sitare Ltd. Staff.

Maclean, Amanda. Everlasting. 320p. 1996. pap. 9.99 (*0-88070-929-4*, Palisades OR) Multnomah Pubs.

MacLean, Amanda. Kingdom Come. LC 97-479. 286p. 1997. pap. 9.99 (*1-57673-120-0*, Palisades OR) Multnomah Pubs.

— Stonehaven. 303p. 1995. pap. 9.99 (*0-88070-757-7*, Multnomah Bks) Multnomah Pubs.

MacLean, Ana, jt. ed. see Weller, Marc.

MacLean, Angus. The Beginning of Time & Other Stories. (Illus.). 233p. (Orig.). 1984. 14.95 (*0-914598-67-8*); pap. 8.95 (*0-914598-68-6*) Bear Flag Bks.

— The Ghosts of Frank & Jesse James & Other Stories. (Illus.). 124p. (Orig.). 1987. 10.95 (*0-914598-72-4*); pap. 7.95 (*0-914598-73-2*) Bear Flag Bks.

— Legends of the California Bandidos. (Illus.). 256p. 1989. reprint ed. 12.50 (*0-939919-21-4*); reprint ed. pap. 8.95 (*0-939919-20-6*) Bear Flag Bks.

Maclean, Anne. The Elimination of Morality: Reflections on Utilitarianism & Bioethics. LC 93-20281. 256p. (C). 1993. pap. 24.99 (*0-415-09538-7*, B2372) Routledge.

MacLean, Annie M. Wage-Earning Women. LC 74-3962. (Women in America Ser.). (Illus.). 218p. 1974. reprint ed. 24.95 (*0-405-06111-0*) Ayer.

MacLean, Barbara H. I Can't Do What? Profiles of Pathfinding Women. Wheeler, Eugene D., ed. LC 96-28005. (Illus.). 240p. (Orig.). 1996. pap. 14.95 (*0-934793-62-X*) Pathfinder CA.

Maclean-Bowser. Show Business, Business: Basics for Keeping Your Sanity in the Maze of Big Deals. large type ed. (Opening the Million Dollar Doors of Show Business Ser.). (Illus.). 75p. (YA). 1996. spiral bd. 10.00 (*0-940178-20-6*) Sitare.

Maclean-Bowser & MacLean, Alistair. Rules of the Road: Travel with Caution by Being Prepared. (Opening the Million Dollar Doors of Show Business Ser.). (Illus.). 100p. 1998. 5.00 (*0-940178-23-0*) Sitare.

Maclean, Brenda. A Pioneering Plantsman: A. K. Bulley & the Great Plant Hunters. (Illus.). 200p. 1997. pap. 58.00 (*0-11-250018-8*, Pub. by Statnry Office) Balogh.

MacLean, Brian D., jt. ed. see Lowman, John.

MacLean, Brian K. & Osberg, Lars, eds. The Unemployment Crisis. LC 97-187309. (Critical Perspectives on Public Affairs Ser.). 280p. 1996. 65.00 (*0-7735-1417-1*, Pub. by McG-Queens Univ Pr); pap. 24.95 (*0-7735-1418-X*, HD5707, Pub. by McG-Queens Univ Pr) CUP Services.

MacLean, C., jt. auth. see Hilbers, C. W.

Maclean, C. D. Manual of the Administration of the Madras Presidency, 3 vols., Set, Vols. I-III. (C). 1987. reprint ed. 168.50 (*0-8364-2415-8*, Pub. by Asian Educ Servs) S Asia.

Maclean, Cailean. Skyescape. (Traditional Scotland Ser.). (Illus.). 36p. pap. 13.95 (*0-9516022-9-2*, Pub. by Maclean Pr) Dufour.

Maclean, Caleb. Sammy Sosa: Cubs Clubber. LC 99-23005. (Sports Stars Ser.). 48p. (J). (gr. 3-4). 1999. 19.00 (*0-516-21662-7*) Childrens.

***Maclean, Caleb.** Sammy Sosa: Cubs Clubber. (Sports Stars Ser.). (J). 2000. pap. text 5.95 (*0-516-27005-2*) Childrens.

— Terrell Davis: Bronco Buster. LC 99-23009. (Sports Stars Ser.). 48p. (J). (gr. 3-4). 1999. 19.00 (*0-516-21663-5*) Childrens.

***Maclean, Caleb.** Terrell Davis: Bronco Buster. (Sports Stars Ser.). (J). 2000. pap. text 5.95 (*0-516-27006-0*) Childrens.

MacLean, Carter D. Interpreting Anaphors in Natural Language Texts. LC 87-26250. (Artificial Intelligence Ser.). 290p. 1987. text 78.95 (*0-470-21009-5*) P-H.

Maclean, Catherine H. Dorothy & William Wordsworth. LC 71-39678. (English Biography Ser.: No. 31). 1972. reprint ed. lib. bdg. 75.00 (*0-8383-1403-1*) M S G Haskell Hse.

Maclean, Catherine M. Dorothy Wordsworth: The Early Years. LC 77-124243. (Select Bibliographies Reprint Ser.). 1977. reprint ed. 25.95 (*0-8369-5431-9*) Ayer.

Maclean, Charles. A Little Book of Scottish Castles. Maclean, Sheila, ed. (Little Irish Bookshelf Ser.). (Illus.). 60p. 1995. 9.95 (*0-86281-546-0*, Pub. by Appletree Pr) Irish Bks Media.

— Malt Whisky. (Illus.). 176p. 1997. 40.00 (*1-85732-683-0*, Pub. by Millers Pubns) Antique Collect.

MacLean, Charles. Pocket Guide to Scotch Whisky. 224p. 1998. pap. 14.95 (*1-84000-022-8*, Pub. by Mitchell Beazley) Antique Collect.

— Pocket Whiskey Book: A Guide to Malt, Grain, Liquor & Leading Blended Whiskies. LC 96-139074. 192p. 1993. 12.95 (*1-85732-171-5*, Pub. by Reed Illust Books) Antique Collect.

***MacLean, Charles.** Romantic Scotland. (Illus.). 2000. pap. 16.95 (*0-7538-0509-X*) Phoenix Hse.

MacLean, Charles. Romantic Scotland, No. 32. (Country Ser.). (Illus.). 160p. 1995. pap. 17.95 (*0-297-83396-0*, Pub. by Orion Pubng Grp) Trafalgar.

Maclean, Charles. St. Kilda: Island on the Edge of the World. (Classics Ser.). (Illus.). 196p. 1996. pap. 12.95 (*0-86241-388-5*, Pub. by Canongate Books) Interlink Pub.

Maclean, Charles R. The Natal Papers of 'John Ross' Gray, Stephen, ed. & intro. by. (Killie Campbell Africana Library Publication: No. 7). 228p. 1992. pap. 35.00 (*0-86980-851-6*, Pub. by Univ Natal Pr) Intl Spec Bk.

Maclean, Christina. Whispers of Love. 82p. 1997. pap. 7.99 (*1-84030-002-7*) Emerald House Group Inc.

M

Maclean, Colin & Maclean, Moira. Baby's First Bible. LC 95-81113. (First Bible Collection Ser.). 20p. (J). (ps-3). 1996. bds. 10.99 (*1-57584-033-2*, Pub. by Rdrs Digest) Random.

Maclean, Colin, jt. illus. see Maclean, Moira.

MacLean Craig, Jane, jt. auth. see Feder, Lewis M.

MacLean Craig, Jane, jt. auth. see Warren, Kaile R.

MacLean, D. J. Optical Line Systems: Transmission Aspects. LC 95-4908. 642p. 1996. 210.00 (*0-471-95083-1*) Wiley.

Maclean, D. M. Trusts & Powers. xx, 139p. 1989. 43.00 (*0-455-20910-3*, Pub. by LawBk Co) Gaunt.

Maclean, Derryl N. Religion & Society in Arab Sind. LC 88-24064. (Monographs & Theoretical Studies in Sociology & Anthropology in Honour of Nels Anderson: Vol. 25). x, 191p. (Orig.). 1989. pap. text 56.50 (*90-04-08551-3*) Brill Academic Pubs.

Maclean, Donald, tr. see Goethe, Johann Wolfgang Von.

Maclean, Donald, tr. see Reinckens, Sunnhild.

MacLean, Dorothy. Choices of Love. LC 98-5096. 224p. 1998. pap. 16.95 (*0-940262-90-8*, 2073, Lindisfarne) Anthroposophic.

Maclean, Dorothy. To Hear the Angels Sing: An Odyssey of Co-creation with the Devic Kingdom. 230p. 1990. reprint ed. pap. 10.95 (*0-940262-37-1*, Lindisfarne) Anthroposophic.

M

Maclean, Doug & Gould, Sue. The Helping Process: An Introduction. 224p. 1988. lib. bdg. 52.50 (*0-7099-4682-1*, Pub. by C Helm) Routldge.

MacLean, Douglas, ed. The Security Gamble: Deterrence Dilemmas in the Nuclear Age. 1984. pap. 22.75 (*0-317-05231-4*) IPPP.

— The Security Gamble: Deterrence Dilemmas in the Nuclear Age. LC 84-15080. (Maryland Studies in Public Philosophy). 190p. (C). 1984. 29.95 (*0-8476-7329-4*) IPPP.

— Values at Risk. 1986. 49.00 (*0-317-05233-0*) IPPP.

— Values at Risk. (Maryland Studies in Public Philosophy). 192p. (C). 1986. 49.00 (*0-8476-7414-2*) IPPP.

— Values at Risk. (Maryland Studies in Public Philosophy). 192p. (C). 1986. pap. 25.00 (*0-8476-7415-0*) Rowman.

MacLean, Douglas & Brown, Peter G., eds. Energy & the Future. 1983. 59.50 (*0-317-05527-5*); pap. 27.25 (*0-317-05223-3*) IPPP.

— Energy & the Future. LC 82-18609. (Illus.). 218p. (C). 1983. pap. text 27.25 (*0-8476-7225-5*, R7225) IPPP.

— Energy & the Future. LC 82-18609. (Illus.). 218p. (C). 1983. text 65.00 (*0-8476-7149-6*, R7149) Rowman.

MacLean, Douglas & Mills, Claudia, eds. Liberalism Reconsidered. 1983. 55.75 (*0-317-05227-6*); pap. 24.00 (*0-317-05228-4*) IPPP.

— Liberalism Reconsidered. LC 83-8623. (Maryland Studies in Public Philosophy). 160p. (C). 1983. 55.75 (*0-8476-7279-4*) IPPP.

— Liberalism Reconsidered. LC 83-8623. (Maryland Studies in Public Philosophy). 160p. (C). 1983. pap. 26.50 (*0-8476-7280-8*) Rowman.

MacLean, E. Avilaitqatigiik (The Two Friends) (ESK.). 50p. (J). 1974. pap. 4.00 (*0-933769-41-5*) Alaska Native.

— Savaaksrat I (Workbook I) (ESK.). 30p. (J). 1974. pap., wbk. ed. 2.00 (*0-933769-43-1*) Alaska Native.

— Suva Una? (What Is It Doing?) rev. ed. (ESK.). 31p. 1976. pap. 2.50 (*0-933769-44-X*) Alaska Native.

MacLean, Edna, ed. Ataatalugiik. (ESK.). 99p. 1975. pap. 4.00 (*0-933769-39-3*) Alaska Native.

— Avaqqanam Quliaqtuaqtanik. (ESK.). 19p. 1975. pap. 2.00 (*0-933769-40-7*) Alaska Native.

MacLean, Edna A. Inupiallu Tannillu Uqalunisa Ilanich: Abridged Inupiaq & English Dictionary. (ESK., Illus.). xx, 168p. (C). 1981. pap. 16.00 (*0-933769-19-9*) Alaska Native.

— North Slope Inupiaq Dialogues. 13p. (C). 1985. pap. 3.00 (*1-55500-014-2*) Alaska Native.

— North Slope Inupiaq Grammar: First Year. 3rd rev. ed. (Illus.). xii, 279p. 1986. pap. text 18.00 (*1-55500-026-6*) Alaska Native.

— Quliaqtuat Mumiaksrat: Ilisaqtuanun Savaaksriat. (ESK., Illus.). 35p. (Orig.). (C). 1986. pap. 4.50 (*1-55500-027-4*) Alaska Native.

MacLean, Eleanor. Between the Lines: How to Detect Bias & Propaganda in the News & Everyday Life. 296p. 1981. 48.99 (*0-919619-14-2*, M23, Pub. by Black Rose); pap. 19.99 (*0-919619-12-6*, Pub. by Black Rose) Consort Bk Sales.

MacLean, Elizabeth K. Joseph E. Davies: Envoy to the Soviets. LC 91-44445. 264p. 1992. 59.95 (*0-275-93580-9*, C3580, Praeger Pubs) Greenwood.

Maclean, Fitzroy. Eastern Approaches. (Illus.). 543p. 2000. pap. 19.95 (*0-14-013271-6*, Pub. by Pnguin Bks Ltd) Trafalgar.

— Highlanders: A History of the Scottish Clans. (Illus.). 256p. 1995. 40.00 (*0-670-86644-X*, Viking Studio) Studio Bks.

MacLean, Fitzroy. Josip Broz Tito, a Pictorial Biography. LC 80-18683. (Illus.). 127p. 1980. write for info. (*0-07-044660-1*) McGraw.

Maclean, Fitzroy. Scotland: A Concise History. 2nd rev. ed. LC 92-62136. (Illus.). 240p. 1993. pap. 16.95 (*0-500-27706-0*, Pub. by Thames Hudson) Norton.

***Maclean, Fitzroy.** Scotland: A Concise History. 3rd ed. LC 00-101118. (Illus.). 256p. 2001. reprint ed. 16.95 (*0-500-28233-1*, Pub. by Thames Hudson) Norton.

MacLean, Fitzroy. West Highland Tales. (Illus.). 194p. 1996. pap. 19.50 (*0-86241-278-1*, Pub. by Canongate Books) Interlink Pub.

MacLean, French L. The Camp Men: The SS Officers Who Ran the Nazi Concentration Camp System. LC 98-85646. (Illus.). 384p. 1999. 59.95 (*0-7643-0636-7*) Schiffer.

Maclean, French L. The Cruel Hunters, SS-Sonderkommando Dirlewanger: Hilter's Most Notorious Anti-Partisan Unit. LC 97-80402. (Illus.). 256p. 1998. 29.95 (*0-7643-0483-6*) Schiffer.

MacLean, French L. The Field Men: The SS Officers who Led the Einsatzkommandos/the Nazi Mobile Killing Units. LC 99-60334. (Illus.). 232p. 1999. 59.95 (*0-7643-0754-1*) Schiffer.

— Quiet Flows the Rhine: German General Officer Casualties in World War II. 1996. 29.00 (*0-921991-32-0*) J J Fedorowicz.

Maclean, Gary E. Documenting Quality for ISO 9000 & Other Industry Standards. LC 93-27743. 231p. 1993. text 30.00 (*0-87389-212-7*, H0761) ASQ Qual Pr.

Maclean, Gerald, ed. Culture & Society in the Stuart Restoration: Literature, Drama, History. (Illus.). 308p. (C). 1995. pap. text 21.95 (*0-521-47566-X*) Cambridge U Pr.

MacLean, Gerald, et al, eds. The Country & the City Revisited: England & the Politics of Culture, 1550-1850. LC 98-36169. (Illus.). 272p. (C). 1999. text 59.95 (*0-521-59201-1*) Cambridge U Pr.

MacLean, Gerald, ed. see Spivak, Gayatri Chakravorty.

MacLean, Gerald M. Time's Witness: Historical Representation in English Poetry. LC 89-40532. (Illus.). 374p. reprint ed. pap. 116.00 (*0-608-20450-1*, 207170300002) Bks Demand.

— Time's Witness: Historical Representation in English Poetry, 1603- 1660. LC 89-40532. (Illus.). 336p. (C). 1990. pap. text 17.50 (*0-299-12394-4*) U of Wis Pr.

Maclean, Gordon L. Aids to Bird Identification in Southern Africa. 2nd enl. rev. ed. (Illus.). 72p. 1988. pap. 9.95 (*0-86980-586-X*, Pub. by Univ Natal Pr) Intl Spec Bk.

— The Ecophysiology of Desert Birds. LC 95-34589. (Adaptation of Desert Organisms Ser.). 192p. 1995. 141.95 (*3-540-59269-5*) Spr-Verlag.

— Ornithology for Africa. 310p. 1991. 45.00 (*0-86980-737-4*, Pub. by Univ Natal Pr); pap. 35.00 (*0-86980-771-4*, Pub. by Univ Natal Pr) Intl Spec Bk.

— Roberts Birds of Southern Africa. 600p. (C). 1988. 275.00 (*1-85368-037-0*, Pub. by New5 Holland) St Mut.

MacLean, Grant. Walk Historic Halifax: Walking Guide to an Historic Capital. (Illus.). 128p. 1996. pap. 12.95 (*1-55109-135-6*) Nimbus Publ.

Maclean, Heather. Women's Experience of Breastfeeding. 208p. 1990. pap. 13.95 (*0-8020-6756-5*) U of Toronto Pr.

Maclean, Heather & Oram, Barbara. Living with Diabetes. xii, 154p. 1988. pap. 11.95 (*0-8020-6693-3*) U of Toronto Pr.

Maclean, Hector. Photography for Artists. LC 72-9218. (Literature of Photography Ser.). 1979. reprint ed. 15.95 (*0-405-04925-0*) Ayer.

MacLean, Helene. Pediatric Nutrition in Clinical Practice. (Illus.). 300p. 1984. write for info. (*0-318-58157-4*) Addison-Wesley.

Maclean, Hugh & Smythe, Emma. Yukon Lady: A Tale of Loyalty & Courage. (Illus.). 180p. 1985. pap. text 11.95 (*0-88839-186-2*) Hancock House.

Maclean, Hugh, ed. see Jonson, Ben, et al.

Maclean, Ian. Interpretation & Meaning in the Renaissance: The Case of Law. (Ideas in Context Ser.: No. 21). (Illus.). 253p. (C). 1992. text 59.95 (*0-521-41546-2*) Cambridge U Pr.

Maclean, Ian, jt. auth. see McFarlane, I. D.

Maclean, Ian, ed. & tr. see Moliere.

MacLean, J. H. Elsevier's Dictionary of Building Construction: English - French. (ENG & FRE.). 390p. 1989. 225.00 (*0-8288-9283-0*) Fr & Eur.

Maclean, J. H. Elsevier's Dictionary of Building Construction: English-French. 400p. 1989. 182.25 (*0-444-42966-2*) Elsevier.

MacLean, J. H. Elsevier's Dictionary of Building Construction: French - English. (ENG & FRE.). 346p. 1988. 225.00 (*0-8288-9282-2*, M801) Fr & Eur.

— Elsevier's Dictionary of Building Construction: French-English. 356p. 1988. 182.25 (*0-444-42931-X*) Elsevier.

Maclean, J. L. & Temprosa, R. M. Bibliography on Indo-Pacific Red Tides. 1990. pap. text 5.00 (*971-10-2259-1*, Pub. by ICLARM) Intl Spec Bk.

Maclean, J. L., et al. The Bibliographic Impact of ICLARM. (ICLARM Technical Reports: No. 26). 19p. 1990. write for info. (*971-10-2280-X*, Pub. by ICLARM) Intl Spec Bk.

MacLean, J. L., jt. ed. see Hallegraeff, Gustaff M.

***MacLean, J. P.** A History of the Clan MacLean: From Its First Settlement at Duard Castle, in the Isle of Mull, to the Present Period, Including a Genealogical Account of Some of the Principle Families Together with Their Heraldry, Legends, Superstitions, Etc. 498p. 1999. reprint ed. pap. 35.50 (*0-7884-1316-3*, M020) Heritage Bk.

MaClean, James H. & Scott, John S. Penguin Dictionary of Building. (Illus.). pap. 17.95 (*0-14-051239-X*, Pub. by Pnguin Bks Ltd) Trafalgar.

MacLean, Jan. An Island Loving. large type ed. (Linford Romance Library). 416p. 1985. pap. 16.99 (*0-7089-6099-5*) Ulverscroft.

Maclean, Jan. White Fire. large type ed. (Linford Romance Library). 368p. 1985. pap. 16.99 (*0-7089-6051-0*) Ulverscroft.

MacLean, Jim, jt. auth. see Daniels, Steve.

Maclean, Joan. English in Basic Medical Science. (English in Focus Ser.). (Illus.). 124p. 1975. pap. text 12.95 (*0-19-437515-3*); pap. text, teacher ed. 14.95 (*0-19-437503-X*) OUP.

MacLean, Joan, tr. see Benitez, Fernando.

MacLean, John. Historical & Traditional Sketches of Highland Families & of the Highlands. 250p. 1998. reprint ed. pap. 19.00 (*0-7884-0809-7*, M014) Heritage Bk.

— History of the College of New Jersey from Its Origin in 1746 to the Commencement of 1854, 2 vols., Set. LC 74-89198. (American Education: Its Men, Institutions, & Ideas. Series 1). 1970. reprint ed. 38.95 (*0-405-01435-X*) Ayer.

Maclean, John. Idea of Immortality As Known to the Jews, Greeks, St. Paul, Modern Times (1907) 50p. 1998. reprint ed. pap. 7.95 (*0-7661-0675-6*) Kessinger Pub.

MacLean, John. Mac. 192p. 1989. reprint ed. pap. 2.95 (*0-380-70700-4*, Avon Bks) Morrow Avon.

MacLean, John, ed. see Salisbury, Robert C.

Maclean, John, ed. see Totnes, George C.

MacLean, John C. A Rich Harvest: The History, Buildings & People of Lincoln, Massachusetts. (Illus.). 680p. 1987. 30.00 (*0-944856-01-2*) Lincoln Hist Soc.

MacLean, John C. & Faran, Palmer. Voices of the Battle Road: A Performance, Student Activity & Resource Kit for Teachers. 42p. (J). (gr. 2-12). 1996. ring bd. 29.95 (*1-882063-40-6*) Cottage Pr MA.

MacLean, John C. & Martin, Margaret M. Lincoln Libraries, 1798-1984. (Illus.). 112p. (Orig.). 1984. pap. 15.00 (*0-944856-06-3*) Lincoln Hist Soc.

***Maclean, John N.** Fire on the Mountain: The True Story of the South Canyon Fire. (Illus.). 288p. 2000. 13.95 (*0-7434-1038-6*, WSP) PB.

***Maclean, John N., ed.** Fire on the Mountain: The True Story of the Sourth Canyon Fire. LC 99-20188. (Illus.). 288p. 1999. 24.00 (*0-688-14477-2*, Wm Morrow) Morrow Avon.

MacLean, John P. An Historical Account of the Settlements of Scotch Highlanders in America Prior to the Peace of 1783. (Illus.). 455p. 1997. reprint ed. pap. 36.50 (*0-8063-0230-5*, 3610) Clearfield Co.

***MacLean, Julianne.** Prairie Bride. (Historical Ser.). 2000. mass mkt. 4.99 (*0-373-29126-4*, 1-29126-9) Harlequin Bks.

***MacLean, Kath.** For a Cappuccino on Bloor. (New Muse Award Ser.). 80p. 1998. pap. 10.25 (*0-921411-74-X*) Genl Dist Srvs.

MacLean, Katy, jt. auth. see Leigh, Margaret.

MacLean, Kenneth. Blue Heron's Sky. 80p. 1991. pap. 10.00 (*0-941179-28-1*) Latitudes Pr.

Maclean, Kerry L. Pigs over Boulder. (Illus.). 32p. (Orig.). (J). (ps-k). 1996. pap. 12.95 (*0-9652998-0-5*) On the Spot.

MacLean, Kerry L. Pigs over Colorado. 1997. pap. text 14.95 (*0-9652998-1-3*) On the Spot.

Maclean, Kerry L. Sophie's Not Afraid! A Bubble-Bug Book. LC 98-91443. (Illus.). 32p. (J). (gr. k-4). 1999. 16.95 (*0-9652998-2-1*) On the Spot.

MacLean, Loraine. Old Inverness in Pictures. 1978. 24.95 (*0-8464-0682-9*) Beekman Pubs.

Maclean, Magnus. The Literature of the Highlands. LC 70-144492. reprint ed. 32.50 (*0-404-08595-4*) AMS Pr.

Maclean, Mairi, jt. auth. see Trouille, Jean-Marc.

MacLean, Margaret, ed. Cultural Heritage in Asia & the Pacific: Conservation & Policy. LC 93-25491. 131p. 1993. pap. 35.00 (*0-89236-248-0*, Pub. by J P Getty Trust) OUP.

***MacLean, Margaret, et al.** Time & Bits: Managing Digital Continuity. LC 99-46692. (Illus.). 84p. 2000. pap. 9.95 (*0-89236-583-8*) J P Getty Trust.

Maclean, Marie & MacLean, Marie. Narrative As Performance: The Baudelairean Experiment. 220p. 1988. pap. 14.95 (*0-415-00664-3*); text 49.95 (*0-415-00663-5*) Routledge.

MacLean, Marie, jt. auth. see Maclean, Marie.

MacLean, Marion S., jt. auth. see Mohr, Marian M.

MacLean, Mavis & Kurczewski, Jacek, eds. Families, Politics, & the Law: Perspectives for East & West Europe. (Oxford Socio-Legal Studies). 336p. 1994. text 59.00 (*0-19-825810-0*) OUP.

Maclean, Mavis, jt. ed. see Eekelaar, John M.

MacLean, Mavis, jt. ed. see Weitzman, Lenore J.

***MacLean, Moira.** Baby's First Bible Songs. (Illus.). 20p. (J). (ps-k). 2000. bds. 10.99 (*0-7847-0966-1*, 03540) Standard Pub.

***Maclean, Moira.** Baby's First Bible Songs & Cassette. (J). 2000. 10.99 (*1-57584-702-7*, Pub. by Rdrs Digest) S&S Trade.

— In My Garden. (Magic Lanterns Ser.). (J). 7.98 (*1-57717-115-2*) Todtri Prods.

— In the Woods. (Magic Lanterns Ser.). (J). 7.98 (*1-57717-116-0*) Todtri Prods.

— On the Farm. (Magic Lanterns Ser.). (J). 7.98 (*1-57717-114-4*) Todtri Prods.

— Under the Sea. (Magic Lanterns Ser.). (J). 7.98 (*1-57717-117-9*) Todtri Prods.

Maclean, Moira & Maclean, Colin. The Nursery Treasury: A Collection of Rhymes, Poems, Lullabies & Games. 128p. (J). 1988. 24.95 (*0-385-24650-1*) Doubleday.

Maclean, Moira, jt. illus. see Maclean, Colin.

MacLean, Mrs. Alistair, pseud. Action Acting: Releasing the Inner Power to Convince Your Audience. large type ed. (Opening the Million Dollar Doors of Show Business Ser.). (Illus.). 75p. 1997. spiral bd. 10.00 (*0-940178-32-X*) Sitare.

— Boondini. large type ed. (Illus.). 75p. (J). 1998. spiral bd. 10.00 (*0-940178-60-5*) Sitare.

— Brotherly Love: The Story of Joseph. large type ed. (Follow Me to Yesterday Bible Cartoon Ser.). (CHI, ENG, FRE, GER & JPN., Illus.). 100p. (J). 1996. spiral bd. 10.00 (*0-940178-80-X*) Sitare.

— David & Bathsheba (Bible) large type ed. (Yesterday & Tomorrow Bible Cartoon Ser.). (Illus.). 75p. (YA). 1998. spiral bd. 10.00 (*0-940178-77-X*) Sitare.

— Elijah. large type ed. (Yesterday & Tomorrow Bible Cartoon Ser.). (Illus.). 75p. (YA). 1996. spiral bd. 10.00 (*0-940178-78-8*) Sitare.

— The Five Dollar Memory Course. large type ed. (Opening the Million Dollar Doors of Show Business Ser.). (Illus.). 75p. 1997. spiral bd. 10.00 (*0-940178-58-3*) Sitare.

— Getting Ready for 70 (And 80) Making It Through Those Difficult Senior Years. large type ed. (Self Help Ser.). (Illus.). 100p. 1996. spiral bd. 10.00 (*0-940178-69-9*) Sitare.

— The Good Servant: The Story of Job. large type ed. (Yesterday & Tomorrow Bible Cartoon Ser.: Vol. 1, Bk. IV). (Illus.). 75p. (J). 1996. spiral bd. 10.00 (*0-940178-51-6*) Sitare.

— Joshua. large type ed. (Follow Me to Yesterday Bible Cartoon Ser.). (Illus.). 100p. (YA). 1996. spiral bd. 10.00 (*0-940178-81-8*) Sitare.

— Noah & the Rainbow. large type ed. (Yesterday & Tomorrow Bible Cartoon Ser.). (Illus.). 75p. (YA). 1996. spiral bd. 10.00 (*0-940178-82-6*) Sitare.

— Relaxed Singing: Overcoming Basic Obstacles for Smoother Singing, 12 vols. large type rev. ed. (Opening the Million Dollar Doors of Show Business Ser.: Vol. 6). (Illus.). 75p. 1999. 10.00 (*0-940178-33-8*) Sitare.

— St. Fife (Calypso Cartoon) large type ed. (Yesterday & Tomorrow Fantasy Cartoon Ser.). (Illus.). 75p. (YA). 1996. spiral bd. 10.00 (*0-940178-92-3*) Sitare.

— Saul. large type ed. (Yesterday & Tomorrow Bible Cartoon Ser.). (Illus.). 75p. (YA). 1996. spiral bd. 10.00 (*0-940178-84-2*) Sitare.

— The Soul of All Mankind: A Wealthy Man Refuses to Die! large type ed. (Yesterday & Tomorrow Fantasy Cartoon Ser.). (Illus.). 75p. (YA). 1996. spiral bd. 10.00 (*0-940178-90-7*) Sitare.

— Target Family: A Circus Family Tames the West. large type ed. (Illus.). 75p. (J). 1996. spiral bd. 10.00 (*0-940178-53-2*) Sitare.

— The Ten Plagues (Bible) large type ed. (Yesterday & Tomorrow Bible Cartoon Ser.). (Illus.). 75p. (J). 1998. spiral bd. 5.00 (*0-940178-86-9*) Sitare.

— Tobias (Bible) Translations: Chinese, French, German, Japanese, Korean, Spanish. 2nd large type ed. Linz, Wes, ed. (Follow Me to Yesterday Bible Cartoon Ser.). (GER, KOR & SPA., Illus.). 75p. (YA). 1998. spiral bd. 10.00 (*0-940178-85-0*) Sitare.

— Wilhe the Spaceman: A Space Traveler Strikes Out on Earth. large type ed. (Yesterday & Tomorrow Fantasy Cartoon Ser.). (Illus.). 75p. (YA). 1996. spiral bd. 10.00 (*0-940178-93-1*) Sitare.

MacLean, Mrs. Alistair, pseud, ed. Writing for Show Business. large type ed. (Opening the Million Dollar Doors of Show Business Ser.). (Illus.). 75p. 1997. spiral bd. 10.00 (*0-940178-52-4*) Sitare.

MacLean, Mrs. Alistair, pseud & Sitare Ltd. Staff. Opening the Million Dollar Doors of Show Business. large type ed. (Illus.). 100p. 1999. 10.00 (*0-940178-64-8*) Sitare.

MacLean, Murray. New Hedges for the Countryside. (Illus.). 288p. 1992. text 34.95 (*0-85236-242-0*, Pub. by Farming Pr) Diamond Farm Bk.

Maclean, N. Discovering Inverness-Shire. (Discovering Ser.). 1996. pap. 22.50 (*0-85976-228-9*, Pub. by J Donald) St Mut.

MacLean, Nadine. It's a Whale of a Tale. 152p. 2000. pap. 13.00 (*0-8059-4467-2*) Dorrance.

MacLean, Nancy F., jt. auth. see Ahern, Lawrence R.

MacLean, Nancy K. Behind the Mask of Chivalry: The Making of the Second Ku Klux Klan. (Illus.). 336p. 1995. pap. 15.95 (*0-19-509836-6*) OUP.

MacLean, Neil, intro. Food for All Seasons: The New Scottish Cooking. 130p. (C). 1989. 110.00 (*0-948473-10-X*) St Mut.

Maclean, Norman, ed. Animals with Novel Genes. LC 94-11728. (Illus.). 282p. (C). 1995. text 59.95 (*0-521-43256-1*) Cambridge U Pr.

— Oxford Surveys on Eukaryotic Genes, Vol. 7. (Illus.). 184p. 1991. 75.00 (*0-19-854256-9*) OUP.

— Oxford Surveys on Eukaryotic Genes, 1987, Vol. 4. (Illus.). 216p. 1988. 49.95 (*0-19-854231-3*) OUP.

Maclean, Norman, tr. see Lungwitz, Hans.

Maclean, Norman F. Norman Maclean. McFarland, Ron & Nichols, Hugh, eds. LC 87-72517. (American Authors Ser.). 200p. 1988. pap. 15.00 (*0-917652-71-1*) Confluence Pr.

— A River Runs Through It. (Illus.). vi, 168p. 1989. 27.50 (*0-226-50060-8*) U Ch Pr.

Maclean, Norman F. A River Runs Through It & Other Stories. LC 76-20484. xviii, 422 p. 1976. write for info. (*0-8161-6398-7*) Mac Lib Ref.

Maclean, Norman F. A River Runs Through It & Other Stories. LC 75-20895. 232p. 1976. 20.00 (*0-226-50055-1*) U Ch Pr.

— A River Runs Through It & Other Stories. LC 75-20895. 232p. 1979. pap. 11.00 (*0-226-50057-8*, P821) U Ch Pr.

— A River Runs Through It & Other Stories. Peters, Sally, ed. 237p. 1992. reprint ed. mass mkt. 6.99 (*0-671-77697-5*) PB.

— Young Men & Fire. LC 92-11890. (Illus.). 310p. 1992. 19.95 (*0-226-50061-6*) U Ch Pr.

— Young Men & Fire. LC 92-11890. (Illus.). 316p. 1993. pap. 12.00 (*0-226-50062-4*) U Ch Pr.

— Young Men & Fire. large type ed. LC 92-45046. (General Ser.). 417p. 1993. lib. bdg. 21.95 (*0-8161-5734-0*, G K Hall Lrg Type) Mac Lib Ref.

MacLean, P. D. The Triune Brain in Evolution: Role in Paleocerebral Functions. LC 89-22899. (Illus.). 696p. (C). 1990. text 115.00 (*0-306-43168-8*, Kluwer Plenum) Kluwer Academic.

An Asterisk (*) at the beginning of an entry indicates that the title is appearing for the first time.

MacLean, Philip S. Explorations in Technical Math: Using the TI-85 Graphing Calculator. (Illus.). 201p. (C). 1997. pap. text, wbk. ed. 10.31 (*1-889766-08-9*) Columbus State Bks.
MacLean, R., jt. auth. see Matthews, P.
MacLean, Rebecca, ed. The Foundation Grants Index, 1998. 26th ed. 2130p. 1997. 165.00 (*0-87954-724-3*, GI26) Foundation Ctr.
MacLean, Rebecca, ed. see Foundation Center Staff.
MaClean, Richard, jt. auth. see Penner, Peter.
MacLean, Rick. Terror: Murder & Panic in New Brunswick. 1990. mass mkt. 5.95 (*0-7710-5592-7*) McCland & Stewart.
Maclean, Robert, ed. Teachers' Career & Promotional Patterns: A Sociological Analysis. 284p. 1992. 95.00 (*0-7507-0000-9*, Falmer Pr) Taylor & Francis.
***MacLean, Robert & Volpi, Bettina.** EU Trade Barrier Regulation: Pursuing & Defending Investigations. 152p. 2000. pap. 92.00 (*1-902558-36-7*, Pub. by Palladian Law) Gaunt.
MacLean, Robert M. European Community Law. 250p. (C). 1991. pap. 70.00 (*1-85352-787-4*, Pub. by HLT Pubns) St Mut.
— Narcissus & the Voyeur: Three Books & Two Films. (Approaches to Semiotics Ser.: No. 48). 1979. text 60.00 (*90-279-7838-7*) Mouton.
— Public International Law Cases. 276p. 1996. pap. 110.00 (*0-7510-0665-3*, Pub. by HLT Pubns) St Mut.
MacLean, Robert M., ed. European Union Law. 298p. 1996. pap. 95.00 (*0-7510-0695-5*, Pub. by HLT Pubns) St Mut.
— European Union Law Cases. 248p. 1996. pap. 95.00 (*0-7510-0661-0*, Pub. by HLT Pubns) St Mut.
— Public International Law. 316p. (C). 1990. pap. 40.00 (*1-85352-752-1*, Pub. by HLT Pubns) St Mut.
— Public International Law. 325p. (C). 1991. 90.00 (*1-85352-398-4*, Pub. by HLT Pubns) St Mut.
— Public International Law. 430p. 1996. pap. 110.00 (*0-7510-0699-8*, Pub. by HLT Pubns) St Mut.
MacLean, Robert M. & Rossiter, Sean. Flying Cold: The Adventures of Russel Merrill, Pioneer Alaskan Aviator. LC 94-27416. (Illus.). 192p. 1994. 34.95 (*0-945397-32-1*); pap. 24.95 (*0-945397-33-X*) Epicenter Pr.
MacLean, Roy. Stalin's Nose. large type ed. 1993. 39.95 (*0-7066-1002-4*, Pub. by Remploy Pr) St Mut.
Maclean, Rupert, ed. Teacher's Career & Promotional Patterns: A Sociological Analysis. 284p. 1991. 55.00 (*0-685-50669-X*, Falmer Pr); pap. 25.00 (*0-685-50670-3*, Falmer Pr) Taylor & Francis.
Maclean, Rupert & McKenzie, Phillip. Australian Teachers Careers. (C). 1990. 80.00 (*0-86431-077-3*, Pub. by Aust Council Educ Res) St Mut.
Maclean, Ruth. Snapshots N.t. 1999. pap. text 5.99 (*1-85792-347-2*) Christian Focus.
MacLean, Ruth E., jt. ed. see Cohen, M. Michael.
MacLean, Sally-Beth. Chester Art: A Subject List of Extant & Lost Art Including Items Relevant to Early Drama. (Early Drama, Art & Music Monograph: No. 3). 1982. pap. 7.95 (*0-918720-21-4*); boxed set 14.95 (*0-918720-20-6*) Medieval Inst.
MacLean, Sally-Beth, jt. auth. see McMillin, Scott.
MacLean, Sally-Beth, jt. ed. see Carpenter, Jennifer.
Maclean, Sheila, ed. see Maclean, Charles.
***MacLean, Sorley.** From Wood to Ridge: Collected Poems in Gaelic & English. 320p. 2000. pap. 19.95 (*1-903101-00-X*, Pub. by Carcanet Pr) Paul & Co Pubs.
MacLean, Sorley, et al. Sorley Maclean Poems 1932-82. Gillis, Daniel, ed. & intro. by. Smith, Iain C. et al, intros. LC 87-2755. (Columban Celtic Ser.: Vol. 2). 180p. (Orig.). 1986. 12.95 (*0-941638-01-4*); pap. 8.95 (*0-941638-02-2*) Iona Phila.
***MacLean Staff.** Oraciones Para los Pequenitos with Other. (SPA.). (J). (ps-k). 2000. 10.99 (*0-7899-0744-5*) Spanish Hse Distributors.
MacLean, Susan, ed. see Jagin, Mary, et al.
MacLean, Susan L. 1998 Annual Survey Report. 1999. 500.00 (*0-935890-33-5*) Emerg Nurses IL.
— 1998 Ed Database Summary. 1999. 30.00 (*0-935890-32-7*) Emerg Nurses IL.
— 1997 Annual Survey Report. (Illus.). 1999. 500.00 (*0-935890-31-9*) Emerg Nurses IL.
— 1997 Ed Database Summary. (Illus.). 1999. 30.00 (*0-935890-30-0*) Emerg Nurses IL.
MacLean, Susan L., et al, contrib. by. 1996 National Emergency Department Annual Survey Report Summary. unabridged ed. 78p. 1997. pap. 30.00 (*0-935890-16-5*) Emerg Nurses IL.
— 1996 National Emergency Department Database Survey. unabridged ed. 311p. 1997. pap. 500.00 (*0-935890-17-3*) Emerg Nurses IL.
MacLean, William E., Jr., ed. Handbook of Mental Deficiency, Psychological Theory & Research. 688p. 1996. text 75.00 (*0-8058-1407-8*) L Erlbaum Assocs.
Maclean, Williams. Computing in School. 200p. (C). 1987. 50.00 (*81-85017-35-2*, Pub. by Interprint) St Mut.
Maclear, jt. auth. see Srivastava, Vinita.
Maclear, Anne B. Early New England Towns. LC 08-18393. (Columbia University. Studies in the Social Sciences: No. 78). reprint ed. 34.50 (*0-404-51078-7*) AMS Pr.
Maclear, George F. Apostles of Mediaeval Europe. LC 72-624. (Essay Index Reprint Ser.). 1977. reprint ed. 23.95 (*0-8369-2803-2*) Ayer.
Maclear, J. F. Church & State in the Modern Age: A Documentary History. 528p. 1995. text 75.00 (*0-19-508681-3*) OUP.
Maclear, Kyo. Beclouded Visions: Hiroshima-Nagasaki & the Art of Witness. LC 98-3383. (SUNY Series, Interruptions). (Illus.). 224p. (C). 1998. text 59.50 (*0-7914-4005-2*); pap. text 19.95 (*0-7914-4006-0*) State U NY Pr.
MacLear, Michael. The Ten Thousand Day War: Vietnam, 1945-1975. 384p. 1982. pap. 10.95 (*0-380-60970-3*, Avon Bks) Morrow Avon.
MacLeary, A. National Taxation for Property Management & Valuation. 240p. 1990. pap. write for info. (*0-419-15320-9*, E & FN Spon) Routledge.
MacLehose, Alexander, tr. see Vercors.
Maclehose, Christopher. Leopard IV: Bearing Witness. 352p. 1999. pap. text 15.00 (*1-86046-067-4*) Harvill Press.
Maclehose, Louisa S., tr. see Vasari, Giorgio.
Macleira, A., ed. Cancer & Aging. 304p. 1990. lib. bdg. 149.00 (*0-8493-6878-2*, RC262) CRC Pr.
Macleish, A., ed. see Frankfurter, Felix.
MacLeish, A. Bruce, ed. & intro. see Guldbeck, Per E.
MacLeish, Andrew. Middle English Subject-Verb Cluster: A Quantitative Synchronic Description. LC 68-23809. (Janua Linguarum, Ser. Practica: No. 26). (Orig.). (C). 1969. pap. text 73.10 (*90-279-0689-0*) Mouton.
Macleish, Archibald. Champion of a Cause: Essays & Addresses on Librarianship. LC 70-150577. 262p. reprint ed. pap. 81.30 (*0-608-12609-8*, 202419100035) Bks Demand.
— Collected Poems: 1917-1984. 544p. 1985. pap. 18.00 (*0-395-39569-0*) HM.
— Freedom Is the Right to Choose. LC 72-142662. (Essay Index Reprint Ser.). 1977. 19.95 (*0-8369-2172-0*) Ayer.
— The Great American Fourth of July Parade. LC 74-24682. (Poetry Ser.). 51p. 1976. pap. 12.95 (*0-8229-5272-6*) U of Pittsburgh Pr.
— J. B. The Pulitzer Prize Winning Play in Verse. 160p. 2000. pap. 12.95 (*0-395-08353-2*, 4, SenEd) HM.
— Land of the Free. LC 77-9353. (Photography Ser.). (Illus.). 1977. reprint ed. pap. 7.95 (*0-306-80080-2*) Da Capo.
— Nobodaddy. LC 74-1356. (Studies in Poetry: No. 38). 1974. lib. bdg. 75.00 (*0-8383-2034-1*) M S G Haskell Hse.
— Poetry & Opinion. LC 74-2189. (Studies in Poetry: No. 38). (C). 1974. lib. bdg. 75.00 (*0-8383-2043-0*) M S G Haskell Hse.
— Three Short Plays: Manuscript Edition. 1961. pap. 13.00 (*0-8222-0600-5*) Dramatists Play.
— Time to Act. LC 71-117820. (Essay Index Reprint Ser.). 1977. 20.95 (*0-8369-1713-8*) Ayer.
Macleish, Archibald, jt. auth. see Friend, William L.
MacLeish, Joyce, et al. Video English Course Junior: Call Workbook 3. (EFL Non-Sequential Ser.). (Illus.). 144p. (J). (gr. 4-6). 1996. pap., wbk. ed. 21.17 (*1-928882-25-0*) CCLS Pubg Hse.
— Video English Course Junior: Call Workbook 4. (EFL Non-Sequential Ser.). (Illus.). 168p. (J). (gr. 4-6). 1996. pap., wbk. ed. 22.37 (*1-928882-28-5*) CCLS Pubg Hse.
MacLeish, Kenneth, tr. see Aristotle.
MacLeish, Rod. Crossing at Ivalo. 320p. 1992. reprint ed. mass mkt. 4.99 (*0-8217-3961-1*, Zebra Kensgtn) Kensgtn Pub Corp.
MacLeish, Roderick. Prince Ombra. 320p. 1994. pap. 12.95 (*0-312-89024-9*) Orb NYC.
MacLeish, Sumner. Seven Words for Wind: Essays & Field Notes from Alaska's Pribilof Islands. Griffith, Valerie, ed. LC 97-75309. (Illus.). 160p. 1997. 16.95 (*0-945397-35-6*, 749721) Epicenter Pr.
***MacLellan, Alec.** The Hollow Earth Enigma. (Illus.). 240p. 1999. pap. 12.95 (*0-285-63498-4*, Pub. by Souvenir Pr Ltd) IPG Chicago.
MacLellan, Alec. The Lost World of Agharti: The Mystery of Vril Power. (Illus.). 236p. 1997. pap. 12.95 (*0-285-63314-7*, Pub. by Souvenir Pr Ltd) IPG Chicago.
MacLellan, Angus. The Furrow Behind Me: The Autobiography of a Hebridean Crofter. Campbell, John L., tr. from GAE. LC 98-214513. 222p. 1998. pap. 13.95 (*1-874744-27-0*, Pub. by Birlinn Ltd) Dufour.
— Stories from South Uist. Campbell, John L., tr. from GAE. LC 98 131209. 284p. 1998. pap. 13.95 (*1-874744-26-2*, Pub. by Birlinn Ltd) Dufour.
MacLellan, D. G. & Ermini, M., eds. Asian Pacific Congress on Antisepsis: Proceedings, 3rd Congress, Sydney, January 1997. (Dermatology Ser.: Vol. 195, Suppl. 2, 1997). (Illus.). iv, 160p. 1997. pap. 69.75 (*3-8055-6627-1*) S Karger.
MacLellan, Gordon. Sacred Animals. (Illus.). (Orig.). 1997. pap. 22.95 (*1-898307-69-5*, Pub. by Capall Bann Pubng) Holmes Pub.
***MacLellan, Gordon.** Shamanism. (Guides Ser.). 144p. 2000. pap. 6.95 (*0-7499-2023-8*, Pub. by Piatkus Bks) London Brdge.
MacLellan, Gordon. Talking to the Earth. (Illus.). (Orig.). 1995. pap. 19.95 (*1-898307-43-1*) Holmes Pub.
MacLellan, Nic. After Moruroa. 1998. pap. text 18.95 (*1-876175-05-2*) Ocean Pr NJ.
MacLellan, Scott N. Amanda's Gift: One Family's Journey Through the Maze of Serious Childhood Illness. (Illus.). 151p. 1999. pap. 12.95 (*0-9665271-6-X*) Hlth Aware Comm.
MacLelland, Bruce. Prosperity Through Thought Force. 158p. 1997. pap. 12.00 (*0-89540-276-9*, SB-276) Sun Pub.
MacLelland, Jackie. High Heels. Tilton, Marquetta H., ed. (Illus.). 34p. (Orig.). 1992. pap. 6.50 (*0-942186-04-4*) Paperbacks Plus.
MacLenan, Bruce J. Principles of Programming Languages: Design, Evaluation & Implementation. 3rd ed. LC 98-27755. (Illus.). 528p. 1999. text 77.95 (*0-19-511306-3*) OUP.
***MacLennan.** Counselling for Managers. 296p. 1998. pap. 39.95 (*0-566-08092-3*) Ashgate Pub Co.
MacLennan, Alastair H., et al, eds. Progress in Relaxin Research: Proceedings of the 2nd International Congress on the Hormone Relaxin. LC 94-31284. 696p. 1995. text 106.00 (*981-3049-02-2*) World Scientific Pub.
MacLennan, Andres, ed. see Barston, R. P.
MacLennan, Beryce W. & Dies, Kathryn R. Group Counseling & Psychotherapy with Adolescents. 2nd ed. LC 92-13564. 224p. 1992. text 40.50 (*0-231-07834-X*) Col U Pr.
MacLennan, Beryce W. & Felsenfeld, Naomi. Group Counseling & Psychotherapy with Adolescents. LC 68-18998. 208p. reprint ed. pap. 64.50 (*0-8357-8669-2*, 205682500091) Bks Demand.
MacLennan, Bruce J. Functional Programming: Practice & Theory. (Illus.). 608p. (C). 1990. 45.95 (*0-201-13744-5*) Addison-Wesley.
MacLennan, Bruce J. Principles of Programming Languages: Design, Evaluation & Implementation. 2nd ed. (Illus.). 592p. 1995. reprint ed. text 76.00 (*0-19-510583-4*) OUP.
***MacLennan, C.** Hothead. 1998. mass mkt. 6.95 (*0-7472-5954-2*, Pub. by Headline Bk Pub) Trafalgar.
Maclennan, David, ed. A Pocket Book of Healing. (C). 1990. pap. 35.00 (*0-85305-220-4*, Pub. by Arthur James) St Mut.
MacLennan, David N. & Simmonds, E. John. Fisheries Acoustics. 344p. 1992. 79.95 (*0-442-31472-8*) Chapman & Hall.
Maclennan, Don. Solstice. LC 98-109018. 1994. pap. 21.00 (*1-874923-40-X*) St Mut.
MacLennan, Donald. Gaidhlig Blasad (A Taste of Gaelic) unabridged ed. 22p. pap. 21.95 incl. audio (*0-88432-615-2*, AFSG10) Audio-Forum.
Maclennan, Duncan. Housing Economics: An Applied Approach. LC 80-42053. (Illus.). 304p. reprint ed. pap. 94.30 (*0-7837-1588-9*, 204188000024) Bks Demand.
Maclennan, Duncan & Gibb, Kenneth, eds. Housing Finance & Subsidies in Britain. LC 93-21587. 230p. 1993. 67.95 (*1-85628-423-9*, Pub. by Avebry) Ashgate Pub Co.
Maclennan, Elizabeth. The Moon Belongs to Everyone: Making Theatre with 7:84. 214p. (Orig.). (C). 1990. pap. write for info. (*0-413-64150-3*, A0478, Methuen Drama) Methn.
MacLennan, George. Achanult. 352p. (C). 1995. pap. write for info. (*1-874640-20-3*, Pub. by Argyll Pubng) St Mut.
— Lucid Interval: Subjective Writing & Madness in History. 232p. 1992. 38.50 (*0-8386-3505-9*) Fairleigh Dickinson.
MacLennan, Gill. Quick & Easy Calorie Counting: With Easy-to-Use Charts Plus 150 Low-Calorie Recipes. LC 95-83718. (Illus.). 272p. 1996. pap. 7.99 (*0-563-37031-9*, BBC-Parkwest) Parkwest Pubns.
Maclennan, Gordon W. Seanchas Annie Bhan: The Lore of Annie Bhan. (IRI & ENG.). 270p. 1998. 23.95 (*1-898473-84-6*, Pub. by Town Hse) Roberts Rinehart.
MacLennan, Hugh. Barometer Rising. 240p. 1996. pap. text 6.95 (*0-7710-9991-6*) McCland & Stewart.
MacLennan, J. M., tr. see Sukachev, V. & Dylis, N.
MacLennan, Janice, jt. auth. see Lidstone, John.
***MacLennan, Julio Crespo.** Spain & the Process of European Integration, 1957-85. LC 00-33355. 2000. write for info. (*0-312-23576-3*) St Martin.
MacLennan, Malcolm. Gaelic Dictionary: Gaelic-English English-Gaelic. (ENG & GAE.). 632p. 1980. 38.00 (*0-08-025713-5*, Pergamon Pr); pap. 22.00 (*0-685-04003-8*, Pergamon Pr) Elsevier.
***MacLennan, Malcolm.** Gaelic Dictionary: Gaelic-English English Gaelic. 616p. 1999. pap. 50.00 (*0-86152-171-4*, Pub. by Acair Ltd) St Mut.
MacLennan, Malcolm. Gaelic-English - English-Gaelic Dictionary: A Pronouncing & Etymological Dictionary of Scots Gaelic. 632p. 1991. pap. 25.00 (*0-08-025712-7*, Pub. by Aberdeen U Pr) Macmillan.
Maclennan, Malcolm. Gaelic-English, English-Gaelic Dictionary. (ENG & GAE.). 613p. 1991. reprint ed. 39.95 (*0-8288-7881-1*, F45412) Fr & Eur.
— Maclennan's Gaelic-English - English-Gaelic Dictionary. 1985. 125.00 (*0-317-54667-8*, Pub. by Acair Ltd); pap. 80.00 (*0-7855-2996-9*, Pub. by Acair Ltd) St Mut.
MacLennan, Malcolm, ed. see Wilson, Thomas W.
***MacLennan, Michael L.** Beat the Sunset. 96p. 1998. pap. 13.95 (*0-88754-549-1*) Theatre Comm.
MacLennan, Nigel. Awesome Purpose. LC 98-19795. 175p. 1998. 67.95 (*0-566-08040-0*, Pub. by Gower) Ashgate Pub Co.
— Counselling for Managers. LC 95-49159. (Illus.). 294p. 1996. 61.95 (*0-566-07661-6*, Pub. by Gower) Ashgate Pub Co.
***MacLennan, Nigel.** Opportunity Spotting. LC 97-32767. 160p. 1998. 29.95 (*0-566-08004-4*, Pub. by Gower) Ashgate Pub Co.
MacLennan, Nigel. Opportunity Spotting: Creativity for Corporate Growth. (Illus.). 160p. 1994. 83.95 (*0-566-07497-4*, Pub. by Gower) Ashgate Pub Co.
MacLennan, Robert, et al. Cancer Registration & Its Techniques. Davis, W., ed. LC 80-471857. (IARC Scientific Publications: No. 21). 248p. reprint ed. pap. 76.90 (*0-7837-3999-0*, 204383000011) Bks Demand.
MacLennan, Toby. One Walked Out of Two & Forgot It. LC 75-189887. 1972. 15.00 (*0-87110-083-5*) Ultramarine Pub.
MacLennan, W. J. Old Age: A Guide for Professional & Lay Careers. 141p. (C). 1989. pap. 40.00 (*0-7855-6815-8*, Pub. by St Andrew) St Mut.
— Old Age: A Guide for Professional & Lay Careers. 141p. 1993. pap. 24.00 (*0-7152-0640-0*) St Mut.
MacLennan, W. J., tr. Old Age: A Guide for Professional & Lay Careers. 141p. (C). 1991. pap. text 50.00 (*86-15-30640-0*, Pub. by St Andrew) St Mut.
MacLennan, W. J. & Peden, N. R. Metabolic & Endocrine Problems in the Elderly. (Illus.). 210p. 1989. 80.95 (*0-387-19541-6*) Spr-Verlag.
MacLennan, W. J., et al. Infections in Elderly Patients. 176p. 1994. text 56.00 (*0-340-55933-0*, Pub. by E A) OUP.
MacLennan, W. J., jt. auth. see Paterson, Colin R.
MacLeod. Age of the Child: Children in America, 1890-1920. LC 97-49321. 1998. 33.00 (*0-8057-4105-4*, Hall Reference) Macmillan.
— Analytical Modelling Structural Systems. 1990. pap. write for info. (*0-318-68283-4*) P-H.
Macleod. Behold Your God. 1991. 19.99 (*1-871676-09-6*, Pub. by Christian Focus) Spring Arbor Dist.
MacLeod. Corpse Oozak's. 1992. 3.95 (*0-446-77517-7*) Warner Bks.
— Practicing Nursing. 1996. text 29.95 (*0-443-05279-4*, W B Saunders Co) Harcrt Hlth Sci Grp.
Macleod. Technology & the Human Prospect. (C). 1992. text 59.00 (*0-86187-530-3*) St Martin.
— The Treatment of Cattle by Homeopathy. 129p. 1981. pap. 17.95 (*0-85207-247-3*, Pub. by C W Daniel) Natl Bk Netwk.
MacLeod. The Treatment of Cattle by Homeopathy. 1997. pap. 26.95 (*0-8464-1210-1*) Beekman Pubs.
Macleod, jt. auth. see Peters.
MacLeod, A. J., jt. ed. see Morton, I. D.
MacLeod, Alan. Senlac. 243p. 1997. pap. write for info. (*1-86106-497-7*, Pub. by Minerva Pr) Unity Dist.
MacLeod, Alison. Changeling. LC 96-25854. 336p. 1996. 23.95 (*0-312-14564-0*) St Martin.
***MacLeod, Alistair.** Island: The Complete Stories. 320p. 2000. 25.95 (*0-393-05035-1*) Norton.
— No Great Mischief. LC 00-21801. (Illus.). 288p. 2000. 23.95 (*0-393-04970-1*) Norton.
MacLeod, Anne. Just the Caravaggio. 1999. 12.95 (*3-901993-00-2*, Pub. by Poetry Salzburg) Intl Spec Bk.
MacLeod, Anne S. American Childhood: Essays on Children's Literature of the Nineteenth & Twentieth Centuries. LC 92-38269. (C). 1995. pap. text 20.00 (*0-8203-1803-5*) U of Ga Pr.
— A Moral Tale: Children's Fiction & American Culture, 1820-1860. LC 75-12533. 196p. (Orig.). (C). 1975. lib. bdg. 30.00 (*0-208-01552-3*, Archon Bks) Shoe String.
— A Moral Tale: Children's Fiction & American Culture, 1820-1860. LC 75-12533. 196p. (Orig.). (C). 1990. reprint ed. pap. text 21.50 (*0-208-02292-9*, Archon Bks) Shoe String.
MacLeod, Anne S. & Kidd, Jerry S., eds. Children's Literature: Selected Essays & Bibliographies. LC 77-620023. (Student Contribution Ser.: No. 9). 1977. pap. 9.75 (*0-911808-13-2*) U of Md Lib Serv.
MacLeod, Arlene. Accommodating Protest: Working Women, the New Veiling, & Change in Cairo. 240p. (C). 1990. text 40.50 (*0-231-07280-5*) Col U Pr.
— Accommodating Protest: Working Women, the New Veiling, & Change in Cairo. 240p. (C). 1993. pap. 18.00 (*0-231-07281-3*) Col U Pr.
MacLeod, B. An Epigrapher's Annotated Index to Cholan & Yucatecan Verb Morphology. xi, 107p. 1987. 10.00 (*0-913134-28-7*) Mus Anthro MO.
MacLeod, Bruce A. Club Date Musicians: Playing the New York Party Circuit. LC 92-10010. (Illus.). 232p. (C). 1993. text 29.95 (*0-252-01954-7*) U of Ill Pr.
Macleod-Brudenell, Iain, jt. auth. see Deshpande, Chris.
Macleod, C. W., ed. see Homer.
MacLeod, Calbraith. Practical Reformation: A Realistic Approach to the Reformation of the Self. 1999. pap. 10.95 (*1-879418-68-1*, Pub. by Audenreed Pr) Baker & Taylor.
MacLeod, Calum. Uzbekistan. LC 98-51858. 1999. pap. 19.95 (*962-217-582-1*) Norton.
MacLeod, Calum & Mayhew, Bradley. Uzbekistan. (Illus.). 328p. 1997. pap. 19.95 (*0-8442-4852-5*, 48525, Natl Textbk Co) NTC Contemp Pub Co.
MacLeod, Calum, jt. auth. see Creighton, Helen.
MacLeod, Calum, jt. auth. see Zhang, Lijia.
MacLeod, Catriona. Embodying Ambiguity: Androgyny & Aesthetics from Wincklemann to Keller. LC 97-47168. (Kritik Ser.). (Illus.). 304p. 1998. 39.95 (*0-8143-2539-4*) Wayne St U Pr.
MacLeod, Celeste L. Horatio Alger, Farewell: The End of the American Dream. LC 80-5201. 310p. 1980. 6.95 (*0-87223-611-0*) Temescal Bks.
MacLeod, Charlotte. The Balloon Man. LC 98-6199. 240p. 1998. 23.00 (*0-89296-657-2*, Pub. by Mysterious Pr) Little.
— The Balloon Man. LC 98-56115. 1999. 27.95 (*0-7862-1835-5*) Thorndike Pr.
— The Balloon Man. 288p. 2000. mass mkt. 6.50 (*0-446-60835-1*, Pub. by Warner Bks) Little.
— The Bilbao Looking Glass. 208p. 1984. pap. 3.50 (*0-380-67454-8*, Avon Bks) Morrow Avon.
— The Convivial Codfish. 224p. 1985. pap. 3.50 (*0-380-69865-X*, Avon Bks) Morrow Avon.
— Curse of the Giant Hogweed. (Peter Shandy Ser.). 176p. 1986. pap. 3.50 (*0-380-70051-4*, Avon Bks) Morrow Avon.
— Exit the Milkman. Vol. 10. 256p. 1997. mass mkt. 5.99 (*0-446-40398-9*, Pub. by Mysterious Pr) Little.
— Exit the Milkman. large type ed. LC 96-44393. 1996. 22.95 (*1-56895-388-7*) Wheeler Pub.
— The Family Vault. 240p. 1980. mass mkt. 4.50 (*0-380-49080-3*, Avon Bks) Morrow Avon.
— Grab Bag. 224p. 1986. pap. 3.50 (*0-380 75099 6*, Avon Bks) Morrow Avon.
— The Luck Runs Out. 192p. 1981. pap. 3.50 (*0-380-54171-8*, Avon Bks) Morrow Avon.
— The Odd Job. 272p. 1996. mass mkt. 5.99 (*0-446-40397-0*, Pub. by Warner Bks) Little.
— An Owl Too Many. large type ed. (General Ser.). 355p. 1991. lib. bdg. 20.95 (*0-8161-5235-7*, G K Hall Lrg Type) Mac Lib Ref.
— The Palace Guard. 176p. 1982. mass mkt. 3.99 (*0-380-59857-4*, Avon Bks) Morrow Avon.
— The Plain Old Man. 224p. 1986. mass mkt. 3.99 (*0-380-70148-0*, Avon Bks) Morrow Avon.

M

— The Recycled Citizen. 1992. 4.50 (*0-446-77518-5*) Warner Bks.

— The Resurrection Man: A Sarah Kelling & Max Bittersohn Mystery. large type ed. LC 92-16313. 386p. 1992. reprint ed. lib. bdg. 18.95 (*1-56054-457-0*) Thorndike Pr.

— The Silver Ghost: A Sarah Kelling Mystery. LC 87-40383. (Sarah Kelling Mystery Ser.). 224p. 1988. 15.45 (*0-89296-189-9*, Pub. by Mysterious Pr) Little.

— Something the Cat Dragged In. 208p. 1984. mass mkt. 3.99 (*0-380-69096-9*, Avon Bks) Morrow Avon.

— The Withdrawing Room. 192p. 1982. mass mkt. 3.99 (*0-380-56473-4*, Avon Bks) Morrow Avon.

— Wrack & Rune. 208p. 1983. mass mkt. 3.99 (*0-380-61911-3*, Avon Bks) Morrow Avon.

MacLeod, Charlotte, compiled by. Christmas Stalkings. 272p. 1992. mass mkt. 5.50 (*0-446-40303-2*, Pub. by Warner Bks) Little.

— Christmas Stalkings: Tales of Yuletide Murder. large type ed. LC 93-16770. 339p. 1993. lib. bdg. 22.95 (*0-8161-5576-3*, G K Hall Lrg Type) Mac Lib Ref.

— Mistletoe Mysteries. 256p. 1989. 16.45 (*0-89296-400-6*) Mysterious Pr.

— Mistletoe Mysteries. 256p. 1990. mass mkt. 5.50 (*0-445-40920-7*, Pub. by Warner Bks) Little.

MacLeod, Charlotte, see Craig, Alisa, pseud.

Macleod, Colin. Collected Essays. Taplin, Oliver, ed. 1984. 65.00 (*0-19-814025-8*) OUP.

— Collected Essays. (Illus.). 370p. 1997. pap. text 38.00 (*0-19-815084-9*) OUP.

M

MacLeod, Colin, et al. Cognitive Psychology & Emotional Disorders. 2nd ed. LC 96-32464. (Clinical Psychology Ser.). 416p. 1997. pap. 69.95 (*0-471-94430-0*) Wiley.

MacLeod, Colin M. Liberalism, Justice, & Markets: A Critique of Liberal Equality. 248p. 1998. text 55.00 (*0-19-829397-6*) OUP.

MacLeod, Colin M., jt. auth. see Golding, Jonathan M.

Macleod, D. Behold Your God. 13.50 (*1-871676-50-9*, Pub. by Christian Focus) Spring Arbor Dist.

MacLeod, D. Rome & Canterbury. 5.99 (*0-906731-88-7*, Pub. by Christian Focus) Spring Arbor Dist.

Macleod, D. Shared Life. 5.99 (*1-85792-128-3*, Pub. by Christian Focus) Spring Arbor Dist.

— Spirit of Promise. 1995. 6.99 (*0-906731-48-8*, Pub. by Christian Focus) Spring Arbor Dist.

Macleod, D., et al, eds. Exercise: Benefits, Limits & Adaptations. 416p. 1987. pap. text 27.50 (*0-419-14140-5*, E & FN Spon) Routledge.

Macleod, D. A., jt. auth. see Hendries, W. F.

MacLeod, Dan. The Ergonomics Edge: Improving Safety, Quality, & Productivity. (Industrial Health & Safety Ser.). 278p. 1994. 80.00 (*0-471-28511-0*, VNR) Wiley.

MacLeod, Dan. The Ergonomics Edge: Improving Safety, Quality, & Productivity. (Illus.). 278p. 1995. pap. 55.95 (*0-442-01259-4*, VNR) Wiley.

— The Industrial Ergonomics Tool Kit with Training Disc. LC 98-30908. 1998. 79.95 (*1-56670-332-8*) Lewis Pubs.

— The Office Ergonomics Tool Kit with Training Disk. LC 98-28650. 272p. 1999. lib. bdg. 79.95 (*1-56670-318-2*) Lewis Pubs.

MacLeod, Dan & Saunders, H. Duane. Cumulative Trauma: Reducing the Risk. Pollock, Richard A., ed. (Illus.). (Orig.). 1990. pap. text 2.75 (*0-9616461-7-9*) Saunders Grp.

Macleod, Dan, et al. The Ergonomics Manual. Pollock, Richard A., ed. (Illus.). (Orig.). 1990. pap. text 5.00 (*0-9616461-9-5*) Saunders Grp.

MacLeod, David, jt. auth. see McKay, Sharon.

MacLeod, David, jt. auth. see McKay, Sharon E.

MacLeod, David I. Age of the Child: Children in America, 1890-1920. LC 97-49321. 219p. 1998. 29.95 (*0-8057-4106-2*, Twyne) Mac Lib Ref.

Macleod, David I. Building Character in the American Boy: The Boy Scouts, YMCA & Their Forerunners, 1870-1920. LC 83-47763. 424p. reprint ed. pap. 131.50 (*0-608-20451-X*, 207170400002) Bks Demand.

MacLeod, Dawn. Oasis of the North. 276p. (C). 1985. pap. 39.00 (*0-906664-02-0*, Pub. by Mercat Pr Bks) St Mut.

Macleod, Dianne S. Art & the Victorian Middle Class: Money & the Making of Cultural Identity. (Illus.). 550p. (C). 1996. text 99.95 (*0-521-55090-4*) Cambridge U Pr.

Macleod, Dianne Sachko, see Codell, Julie F. & Sachko Macleod, Dianne, eds.

MacLeod, Don. The Internet Guide for the Legal Researcher: The Complete Guide to Finding & Retrieving Legal Information on the Internet. 2nd ed. LC 97-209581. 400p. (Orig.). 1997. 55.00 (*0-939486-46-6*) Infosources.

***MacLeod, Donald.** Faith to Live By: Christian Teaching That Makes a Difference. 2000. pap. text 22.99 (*1-85792-428-2*) Christian Focus.

Macleod, Donald. The Humiliated & Exalted Lord: A Study of Philippians 2 & Christology. Duncan, J. Ligon, III, ed. 80p. (C). 1993. pap. text 6.95 (*1-884416-03-9*) A Press.

MacLeod, Donald. The Person of Christ. LC 98-40356. (Contours of Christian Theology Ser.). 288p. 1998. pap. 16.99 (*0-8308-1537-6*, 1537) InterVarsity.

MacLeod, Donald, jt. auth. see Martin, Martin.

Macleod, Donald A., jt. auth. see Hendrie, William F.

MacLeod, Douglas, jt. ed. see Moser, Mary A.

MacLeod, Elizabeth. Alexander Graham Bell: An Inventive Life. unabridged ed. (Illus.). 32p. (J). (gr. 2-6). 1999. 16.95 (*1-55074-456-9*, Pub. by Kids Can Pr); pap. 6.95 (*1-55074-458-5*, Pub. by Kids Can Pr) Genl Dist Srvs.

— Bake It & Build It. (Kids Can Do It Ser.). (Illus.). 40p. (J). (gr. 4-6). 1998. pap. 5.95 (*1-55074-427-5*, Pub. by Kids Can Pr) Genl Dist Srvs.

Macleod, Elizabeth. Dinosaurs. LC 97-4937. (Illus.). 32p. (J). 1997. pap. 5.99 (*0-14-056162-5*) Viking Penguin.

MacLeod, Elizabeth. Dinosaurs: The Fastest, the Fiercest, the Most Amazing. (Illus.). 32p. (J). 1994. 12.95 (*1-55074-145-4*) Kids Can Pr.

MacLeod, Elizabeth. Dinosaurs: The Fastest, the Fiercest, the Most Amazing. (Illus.). 32p. (J). (gr. 1-4). 1995. 11.99 (*0-670-86026-3*, Viking Child) Peng Put Young Read.

— Dinosaurs: The Fastest, the Fiercest, the Most Amazing. 1997. 11.19 (*0-606-11260-X*, Pub. by Turtleback) Demco.

— Grow It Again. unabridged ed. LC 98-93222. (Kids Can Do It Ser.). (Illus.). 40p. (J). (gr. 3-6). 1999. 5.95 (*1-55074-558-1*, Pub. by Kids Can Pr) Genl Dist Srvs.

— I Heard a Little Baa. (Illus.). 24p. (J). (ps-1). 1998. 10.95 (*1-55074-496-8*, Pub. by Kids Can Pr) Genl Dist Srvs.

— The Phone Book: Instant Communication from Smoke Signals to Satellites & Beyond... unabridged ed. (Illus.). 64p. (J). (gr. 3-7). 1997. pap. 12.95 (*1-55074-220-5*, Pub. by Kids Can Pr) Genl Dist Srvs.

MacLeod, Elizabeth. Stamp Collecting: For Canadian Kids. (Illus.). 40p. (J). 1996. pap. 6.95 (*1-55074-313-9*) Kids Can Pr.

Macleod, Emma V. A War of Ideas: British Attitudes to the Wars Against Revolutionary France, 1792-1802. LC 98-19310. 240p. 1999. text 78.95 (*1-84014-614-1*, DC158.8.M215, Pub. by Ashgate Pub) Ashgate Pub Co.

MacLeod, Evelyn J., ed. One Woman's Charlottetown: Diaries of Margaret Gray Lord, 1863, 1876, 1890. (Mercury Ser.: History No. 42). (Illus.). 212p. 1988. pap. 19.95 (*0-660-10780-5*, Pub. by CN Mus Civilization) U of Wash Pr.

Macleod, Finlay, ed. Togail Tir Marking Time: The Map for the Western Isles. 160p. (C). 1999. pap. 32.00 (*0-86152-842-5*, Pub. by Acair Ltd) St Mut.

MacLeod, Flora. Motivating & Managing Today's Volunteers: How to Build & Lead a Terrific Team. (Reference Ser.). 192p. 1993. pap. 11.95 (*0-88908-275-8*) Self-Counsel Pr.

Macleod, Flora, ed. Parents & Schools: The Contemporary Challenge. 200p. 1989. 75.00 (*1-85000-498-6*, Falmer Pr); pap. 37.95 (*1-85000-499-4*, Falmer Pr) Taylor & Francis.

***MacLeod, Flora & Hogarth, Sarah.** Leading Today's Volunteers: Motivate & Manage Your Team. 1999. pap. 13.95 (*1-55180-247-3*) Self-Counsel Pr.

MacLeod, G. The Treatment of Horses by Homeopathy. rev. ed. 182p. 1993. pap. 26.95 (*0-8464-1284-5*) Beekman Pubs.

Macleod, G. A Veterinary Materia Medica & Clinical Repertory. 165p. 1983. pap. 17.95 (*0-85207-257-0*) C W Daniel.

Macleod, Gael S., jt. auth. see Macleod, William M.

MacLeod, Gail. Choice Neighborhoods - Your Relocation Guide: San Diego's Best Communities. rev. ed. (Illus.). 64p. 1999. pap. 4.95 (*0-9657990-1-8*) MacLeod Consult.

— Choice Neighborhoods - Your Relocation Guide: San Diego's Fairway Living. (Illus.). 64p. 1997. mass mkt. 5.95 (*0-9657990-0-X*, Choice Neigh) MacLeod Consult.

Macleod, George. Cats: Homoeopathic Remedies. 156p. (Orig.). 1990. pap. 19.95 (*0-8464-1335-3*) Beekman Pubs.

— Cats: Homoeopathic Remedies. 128p. (Orig.). 1990. pap. 11.95 (*0-85207-190-6*, Pub. by C W Daniel) Natl Bk Netwk.

— Dogs: Homoeopathic Remedies. 156p. (Orig.). 1990. pap. 20.95 (*0-8464-1334-5*) Beekman Pubs.

— Dogs: Homoeopathic Remedies. 128p. (Orig.). 1990. pap. 13.95 (*0-85207-218-X*, Pub. by C W Daniel) Natl Bk Netwk.

MacLeod, George. Goats: Homoeopathic Remedies. 192p. (Orig.). pap. 29.95 (*0-8464-4178-0*); pap. 29.95 (*0-8464-4217-5*) Beekman Pubs.

— Goats: Homoeopathic Remedies. 128p. (Orig.). 1992. pap. 19.95 (*0-85207-244-9*, Pub. by C W Daniel) Natl Bk Netwk.

— Pigs. 129p. 1994. pap. 19.95 (*0-85207-278-3*, Pub. by C W Daniel) Natl Bk Netwk.

— Pigs: Homoeopathic Approach to the Treatment & Prevention. 1994. pap. 29.95 (*0-8464-4336-8*) Beekman Pubs.

— The Treatment of Cattle by Homeopathy. 160p. (Orig.). pap. 26.95 (*0-8464-4303-1*) Beekman Pubs.

Macleod, George. The Treatment of Horses by Homeopathy. 130p. 1979. pap. 17.95 (*0-85207-249-X*, Pub. by C W Daniel) Natl Bk Netwk.

MacLeod, George. A Veterinary Material Medical & Clincial Repertory. 208p. (Orig.). pap. 26.95 (*0-8464-4309-0*) Beekman Pubs.

Macleod, George, jt. auth. see Hawkins, M. Raymonde.

MacLeod, George F. The Whole Earth Shall Cry Glory. 1987. 35.00 (*0-947988-04-1*, Pub. by Wild Goose Pubns); pap. 30.00 (*0-947988-01-7*, Pub. by Wild Goose Pubns) St Mut.

MacLeod, Glen G. Wallace Stevens & Company: The Harmonium Years, 1913-1923. LC 83-3624. (Studies in Modern Literature: No. 3). 133p. reprint ed. pap. 41.30 (*0-8357-1405-5*, 207050400097) Bks Demand.

— Wallace Stevens & Modern Art: From the Armory Show to Abstract Expressionism. LC 92-25358. 253p. (C). 1993. 40.00 (*0-300-05360-6*) Yale U Pr.

MacLeod, Gregory. From Mondragon to America: Experiments in Community Economic Development. (Illus.). 250p. 1998. 19.95 (*0-920336-53-1*, Pub. by Goose Ln Edits) Genl Dist Srvs.

MacLeod, Gregory. New Age Business: Community Corporations that Work. 82p. 1986. pap. 9.95 (*0-88810-354-9*, Pub. by J Lorimer) Formac Dist Ltd.

MacLeod, Heather. City Birds. LC 95-12940. (Rookie Readers Ser.). (Illus.). 32p. (J). (ps-2). 1995. lib. bdg. 17.00 (*0-516-02028-5*) Childrens.

— My Flesh the Sound of Rain. LC 99-487822. 96p. 1999. pap. 7.95 (*1-55050-141-0*) Genl Dist Srvs.

MacLeod, I., et al. The External Relations of the European Communities: A Manual of Law & Practice. LC 95-42356. (Oxford European Community Law Library Ser.). 514p. 1996. pap. text 38.00 (*0-19-825930-1*, Clarendon Pr) OUP.

Macleod, I., jt. auth. see Brander, M.

Macleod, I. M. & Heher, A. D., eds. Software for Computer Control (SOCOCO 1988) Selected Papers from the Fifth IFAC-IFIP Symposium, Johannesburg, South Africa, 26-28 April, 1988. (IFAC Proceedings Ser.). (Illus.). 164p. 1989. 94.00 (*0-08-035724-5*) Elsevier.

MacLeod, I. M., et al. Distributed Computer Control Systems, 1997 (DCCS '97) A Proceedings Volume from the 14th IFAC Workshop, Seoul, Korea, 28-30 July, 1997. LC 97-51595. 1997. 67.00 (*0-08-042933-5*) Elsevier.

Macleod, I. M., jt. auth. see De Paoli, F.

MacLeod, Ian. Talks for Children. 108p. (C). 1992. pap. 39.00 (*0-7855-6835-2*, Pub. by St Andrew) St Mut.

MacLeod, Ian, compiled by. More Talks for Children. 128p. (C). 1992. pap. 39.00 (*0-7855-6836-0*, Pub. by St Andrew) St Mut.

— More Talks for Children. 128p. 1993. pap. 24.00 (*0-7152-0657-5*, Pub. by St Andrew) St Mut.

MacLeod, Ian, jt. auth. see Surtees, Beatrice.

MacLeod, Ian, jt. ed. see Surtees, Beatrice.

MacLeod, Ian R. The Great Wheel: A Novel. LC 96-53365. 352p. 1997. 24.00 (*0-15-100293-2*) Harcourt.

— Voyages by Starlight. LC 96-24237. 288p. 1997. 22.95 (*0-87054-171-4*, Arkham Hse) Arkham.

Macleod, Innes & Gilroy, Margaret. Discovering the River Clyde. (Discovering Ser.). 180p. (C). 1996. pap. 26.85 (*0-85976-333-1*, Pub. by J Donald) St Mut.

***MacLeod, Isabail, et al, eds.** A Compact Dictionary. (J). (gr. 4-8). 1999. pap. 45.00 (*0-7217-0653-3*, Pub. by Schofield) St Mut.

— A Compact Dictionary: Exercises. (J). (gr. 4-8). 1999. pap. 45.00 (*0-7217-0654-1*, Pub. by Schofield) St Mut.

— A Concise Junior Dictionary. (J). (gr. 2-4). 1999. pap. 35.00 (*0-7217-0646-0*, Pub. by Schofield) St Mut.

— A Concise Junior Dictionary: Exercises. (J). (gr. 2-4). 1999. pap. 35.00 (*0-7217-0647-9*, Pub. by Schofield) St Mut.

MacLeod, Isabail, jt. auth. see McLaughlin, Patrick.

MacLeod, Isabail, jt. ed. see Anderson, Alasdair.

MacLeod, Iseabail. Edinburgh Pocket Guide. (Illus.). 80p. (Orig.). 1996. pap. 9.95 (*1-900455-01-3*, Pub. by Colin Baxter Ltd) Voyageur Pr.

Macleod, Iseabail, et al, eds. The Scots Thesaurus. (Illus.). 556p. 1991. 37.00 (*0-08-036582-5*, Pub. by Aberdeen U Pr); pap. 19.90 (*0-08-036583-3*, Pub. by Aberdeen U Pr) Macmillan.

— The Scots Thesaurus. deluxe ed. (Illus.). 556p. 1991. lib. bdg. 76.50 (*0-08-040926-1*, Pub. by Aberdeen U Pr) Macmillan.

MacLeod, Iseabail, intro. Mrs. McLintock's Recipes for Cookery & Pastry-Work. 96p. 1986. pap. 3.90 (*0-08-034519-0*, Pub. by Aberdeen U Pr) Macmillan.

Macleod, Iseabail, et al. The Pocket Scots Dictionary. 320p. 1988. pap. 9.95 (*0-08-036581-7*, Pub. by Aberdeen U Pr) Macmillan.

MacLeod, Iseaball, jt. auth. see McLaughlin, Patrick.

Macleod, J. K. Consumer Sales Law. 911p. 1989. pap. 72.00 (*0-406-50388-5*, UK, MICHIE) LEXIS Pub.

MacLeod, J. S. MacLeod & Levitt: Taxation of Insurance Business. 4th ed. 1997. write for info. (*0-406-04606-9*, MLTI4, MICHIE) LEXIS Pub.

MacLeod, J. S. & Levitt, A. R. Taxation of Insurance Business. 3rd ed. 356p. 1992. boxed set 175.00 (*0-406-50882-8*, U.K., MICHIE) LEXIS Pub.

MacLeod, Jalerie, ed. Search INFORM. 4th ed. 1990. 65.00 (*0-914604-00-7*) UMI Louisville.

MacLeod, James. The Great Doctor Waddel: A Study of Moses Waddel, 1770-1840, As Teacher & Puritan. 194p. 1985. pap. 12.50 (*0-89308-546-4*) Southern Hist Pr.

MacLeod, Jay. Ain't No Makin' It: Aspirations & Attainment in a Low-Income Neighborhood. 2nd expanded rev. ed. 336p. (C). 1995. pap. 25.00 (*0-8133-1515-8*, Pub. by Westview) HarpC.

MacLeod, Jean B. If I'd Only Listened to Mom. 3rd ed. LC 97-7595. 1997. pap. 14.95 (*0-312-15589-1*) St Martin.

MacLeod, Jean S. Lovesome Hill. 224p. 1996. 22.00 (*0-7278-4981-6*) Severn Hse.

MacLeod, Joan. Amigo's Blue Guitar. 3rd ed. 80p. 1997. pap. 10.95 (*0-88922-371-8*, Pub. by Talonbks) Genl Dist Srvs.

***MacLeod, Joan.** The Hope Slide/Little Sister. 2nd rev. ed. LC 95-106986. 128p. (J). 1999. pap. 11.95 (*0-88922-411-0*, Pub. by Talonbks) Genl Dist Srvs.

MacLeod, Joan. Toronto, Mississippi & Jewel, 2 bks. in 1 LC 90-175678. 144p. (Orig.). 1989. pap. 12.95 (*0-88754-474-6*) Theatre Comm.

— 2000. LC 98-120130. 128p. 1997. pap. 11.95 (*0-88922-373-4*, Pub. by Talonbks) Genl Dist Srvs.

Macleod, John. Highlanders: A History of the Gaels. (Illus.). 324p. 1998. mass mkt. 15.95 (*0-340-63991-1*, Pub. by Hodder & Stought Ltd) Trafalgar.

— No Great Mischief If You Fall: The Highland Experience. (Illus.). 240p. 1994. 34.95 (*1-85158-540-0*, Pub. by Mainstream Pubng) Trafalgar.

— Scottish Theology: In Relation to Church History since the Reformation. 350p. (C). 1995. reprint ed. pap. text 10.95 (*1-884416-14-4*, Reformed Acad Pr) A Press.

— Some Favourite Books. 128p. 1989. pap. 4.50 (*0-85151-538-X*) Banner of Truth.

MacLeod, Joseph. Beauty & the Beast. LC 74-30346. (Studies in Comparative Literature: No. 35). 1974. lib. bdg. 75.00 (*0-8383-1884-3*) M S G Haskell Hse.

MacLeod, Kathryn. Mouthpiece. 104p. 1996. pap. 8.95 (*0-921331-23-1*, Pub. by Tsunami Edits) Barnholden.

MacLeod, Ken. The Cassini Division. LC 99-26544. 1999. 22.95 (*0-312-87044-2*, Pub. by Tor Bks) St Martin.

***MacLeod, Ken.** The Cassini Division. 2000. mass mkt. 6.99 (*0-8125-6858-3*) Tor Bks.

— The Sky Road. 304p. 2000. 24.95 (*0-312-87335-2*, Pub. by Tor Bks) St Martin.

— Stone Canal. 2000. mass mkt. write for info. (*0-8125-6864-8*) Tor Bks.

— The Stone Canal. 320p. 2000. 24.95 (*0-312-87053-1*, Pub. by Tor Bks) St Martin.

Macleod, M. Discovering Galloway. (Discovering Ser.). 288p. (C). 1996. pap. 26.85 (*0-85976-114-2*, Pub. by J Donald) St Mut.

MacLeod, M. God Hears Me. (J). 1995. 2.99 (*1-871676-61-4*, Pub. by Christian Focus) Spring Arbor Dist.

MacLeod, M. D., ed. Opera: Tomus One, Libelli 1-25. (Oxford Classical Texts Ser.). 358p. (C). 1972. text 39.95 (*0-19-814656-6*) OUP.

— Opera: Tomus Two, Libelli 26-43. (Oxford Classical Texts Ser.). 384p. (C). 1975. text 49.95 (*0-19-814580-2*) OUP.

Macleod, M. D., ed. see Lucian.

MacLeod, Malcolm. A Bridge Built Halfway: A History of Memorial University College, 1925-1950. 400p. (C). 1990. text 60.00 (*0-7735-0761-2*, Pub. by McG-Queens Univ Pr) CUP Services.

Macleod, Malcolm L. Concordance to the Poems of Robert Herrick. LC 76-92974. (Studies in Poetry: No. 38). 1970. reprint ed. lib. bdg. 75.00 (*0-8383-0991-7*) M S G Haskell Hse.

Macleod, Margaret A., ed. see Hargrave, Letitia M.

MacLeod, Marian B. Dancing Through Pentecost: Dance Language for Worship from Pentecost to Thanksgiving. Adams, Doug, ed. (Orig.). 1981. pap. 3.00 (*0-941500-23-3*) Sharing Co.

MacLeod, Morna. Wish in the Bottle. 136p. (J). (gr. 2-6). 1997. mass mkt. 3.99 (*0-590-62970-0*) Scholastic Inc.

— Wish in the Bottle. 1997. 9.09 (*0-606-12103-X*, Pub. by Turtleback) Demco.

***MacLeod, Murdo J. & Rawski, Evelyn S., eds.** European Intruders & Changes in Behaviour & Customs in Africa, America & Asia Before 1800. LC 98-23610. (Expanding World Ser.: No. 30). 464p. 1998. text 135.95 (*0-86078-522-X*) Ashgate Pub Co.

MacLeod, Murdo J. & Wasserstrom, Robert, eds. Spaniards & Indians in Southeastern Mesoamerica: Essays on the History of Ethnic Relations. LC 82-23725. (Latin American Studies). (Illus.). xviii, 291p. 1983. text 40.00 (*0-8032-3082-6*) U of Nebr Pr.

MacLeod, Murdo J., et al. Indian-Religious Relations in Colonial Spanish America. Ramirez, Susan E. et al, eds. LC 88-39611. (Foreign & Comparative Studies Program, Latin American Ser.: No. 9). (Illus.). (Orig.). (C). 1989. pap. text 13.00 (*0-915984-32-6*) Syracuse U Foreign Comp.

MacLeod, Murdo J., jt. ed. see Adams, Richard E. W.

MacLeod, Murdo J., jt. ed. see Adams, Richard E.

MacLeod, Neil. The Real Paradise: Flora & Fauna of the Gold Coast & Hinterland. 112p. (C). 1990. 60.00 (*0-86439-049-1*, Pub. by Boolarong Pubns) St Mut.

Macleod, Norman. German Lyric Poetry. LC 74-164696. reprint ed. 31.50 (*0-404-04138-8*) AMS Pr.

— Selected Poems of Norman Macleod. 3rd ed. Trusky, Tom, ed. LC 75-21690. (Ahsahta Press Modern & Contemporary Poets of the West Ser.). 60p. 1975. pap. 6.95 (*0-916272-00-1*) Ahsahta Pr.

MacLeod, Norman, jt. auth. see Keller, Gerta.

Macleod, Norman, jt. auth. see Scott, Ron.

MacLeod, Olive. Chiefs & Cities of Central Africa: Across Lake Chad by Way of British, French, & German Territories. LC 78-161269. (Illus.). 408p. 1977. reprint ed. 36.95 (*0-8369-8828-0*) Ayer.

MacLeod, Paul K., jt. auth. see Field, Ben T.

Macleod, Pegi N. Daffodils in Winter. Murray, Joan, ed. 346p. 1984. 27.50 (*0-920806-48-1*, Pub. by Penumbra Pr) U of Toronto Pr.

MacLeod, R. & Friday, J. Archives of British Men of Science. 1972. 500.00 incl. fiche (*0-7201-0281-2*) Continuum.

MacLeod, R., jt. auth. see Brook, W.

MacLeod, R. C. MacLeod: A Short Sketch of Their Clan, History, Folk-Lore, Tales & Biographical Notices of Some Eminent Clansmen. 118p. 1992. reprint ed. pap. 19.00 (*0-8328-2681-2*); reprint ed. lib. bdg. 29.00 (*0-8328-2680-4*) Higginson Bk Co.

Macleod, R. C. The NWMP & Law Enforcement, Eighteen Seventy-Three to Nineteen Hundred Five. LC 76-3709. 230p. reprint ed. pap. 71.30 (*0-8357-8254-9*, 203401100088) Bks Demand.

MacLeod, R. C. & Schneiderman, David, eds. Police Powers in Canada: The Evolution & Practice of Authority. 370p. 1994. text 50.00 (*0-8020-2863-2*); pap. text 24.95 (*0-8020-7362-X*) U of Toronto Pr.

MacLeod, R. M., jt. ed. see Muller, E. E.

***MacLeod-Ralls, Karen.** Quest for the Celtic Key. 256p. 2000. pap. 18.95 (*0-946487-73-1*) Luath Pr Ltd.

MacLeod, Robert. All Other Perils. large type ed. 1978. 27.99 (*0-7089-0138-7*) Ulverscroft.

— Ambush at Junction Rock. 1979. mass mkt. 1.75 (*0-449-14303-1*, GM) Fawcett.

Macleod, Robert. Ambush at Junction Rock. large type ed. 1982. 15.95 (*0-7089-0855-1*) Ulverscroft.

— The Californio. large type ed. 1980. 12.00 (*0-7089-0588-9*) Ulverscroft.

MacLeod, Robert. Dragonship. large type ed. 1978. 27.99 (*0-7089-0182-4*) Ulverscroft.

— A Killing in Malta. large type ed. 1979. 27.99 (*0-7089-0320-7*) Ulverscroft.

— A Legacy from Tenerife. large type ed. 1985. 27.99 (*0-7089-1351-2*) Ulverscroft.

An Asterisk (*) at the beginning of an entry indicates that the title is appearing for the first time.

— The Money Mountain. large type ed. 400p. 1988. 11.50 (0-7089-1838-7) Ulverscroft.

— Path of Ghosts. large type ed. 248p. 1980. 27.99 (0-7089-0458-0) Ulverscroft.

— A Property in Cyprus. large type ed. 1978. 27.99 (0-7089-0092-5) Ulverscroft.

Macleod, Robert. The Running Gun. 1980. mass mkt. 1.75 (0-449-14302-3, GM) Fawcett.

MacLeod, Robert. A Witchdance in Bavaria. large type ed. 1977. 27.99 (0-7089-0010-0) Ulverscroft.

MacLeod, Robert B. The Persistent Problems of Psychology. LC 75-15636. 207p. 1975. pap. text 19.50 (0-8207-0254-4) Duquesne.

MacLeod, Robert B., jt. frwd. see Ketchum, John D.

Macleod, Rod, jt. auth. see Beal, Bob.

Macleod, Roderick, ed. see Ironside, Edmund.

MacLeod, Roy, ed. The Commonwealth of Science: ANZAAS & the Scientific Enterprise in Australasia 1888-1988. (Illus.). 432p. 1988. text 49.95 (0-19-554683-0) OUP.

Macleod, Roy, ed. The Commonwealth of Science: ANZAAS & the Scientific Enterprise in Australia, 1888-1988. (Illus.). 417p. 1999. reprint ed. text 25.00 (0-7881-6273-X) DIANE Pub.

MacLeod, Roy, ed. Library of Alexandria. 196p. 1999. text 55.00 (1-86064-428-7) St Martin.

MacLeod, Roy & Kumar, Deepak, eds. Technology & the Raj: Western Technology & Technical Transfers to India, 1700-1947. LC 95-17152. 348p. (C). 1995. 45.00 (0-8039-9237-8) Sage.

Macleod, Roy & Lewis, Milton, eds. Disease, Medicine & Empire. 302p. (C). 1989. lib. bdg. 79.95 (0-415-00685-6) Routledge.

MacLeod, Roy M. The Creed of Science in Victorian England. (Variorum Collected Studies Ser.: Vol. 598). 300p. 1998. text 89.95 (0-86078-669-2, Pub. by Ashgate Pub) Ashgate Pub Co.

— Public Science & Public Policy in Victorian England. (Collected Studies: Vol. CS509). 352p. 1996. 106.95 (0-86078-535-1, Pub. by Variorum) Ashgate Pub Co.

***MacLeod, Roy M.** Science & the Pacific War: Science & Survival in the Pacific, 1939-1945 LC 99-16758. 1999. write for info. (0-7923-5851-1) Kluwer Academic.

MacLeod, Roy M. & Rehbock, Philip F., eds. Darwin's Laboratory: Evolutionary Theory & Natural History in the Pacific. LC 94-20341. (Illus.). x, 540p. 1995. text 32.00 (0-8248-1613-7) UH Pr.

MacLeod, Ruairidth H. Flora MacDonald: The Jacobite Heroine in Scotland & North America. (Illus.). 256p. pap. 18.95 (0-85683-147-6, Pub. by Shepheard-Walwyn Pubs) Paul & Co Pubs.

Macleod, S. & Giltinan, D. Child Care Law: A Summary of the Law in Scotland. (C). 1989. 50.00 (0-903534-70-3, Pub. by Brit Ag for Adopt & Fost) St Mut.

MacLeod, Scott. Snakes in the Lobby. 105p. 1997. pap. 1997.00 (1-878327-76-3, SM2-001) Morning NC.

MacLeod, Scott, jt. auth. see Sancton, Thomas.

MacLeod, V. & Thornberry, S., eds. Business Dateline Controlled Vocabulary. 1990. 25.00 (0-914604-41-4) UMI Louisville.

MacLeod, Virge. Lovelife: Entries. 3rd rev. ed. 435p. 1996. pap. write for info. (0-9610402-1-1) Solus Impress.

MacLeod, Wendell, et al. Bethune the Montreal Years: An Informal Portrait. 167p. 1978. pap. 4.99 (0-88862-213-9, Pub. by J Lorimer) Formac Dist Ltd.

MacLeod, Wendy. Apocalyptic Butterflies. 1990. pap. 5.25 (0-8222-0060-0) Dramatists Play.

— The House of Yes. 1996. pap. 5.25 (0-8222-1516-0) Dramatists Play.

Macleod, Wendy. The Shallow End & the Lost Colony. 1992. pap. 5.25 (0-8222-1346-X) Dramatists Play.

MacLeod, Wendy. Sin. LC 98-222979. 1997. pap. 5.25 (0-8222-1561-6) Dramatists Play.

— The Water Children. LC 99-222947. 1998. pap. 5.25 (0-8222-1662-0) Dramatists Play.

Macleod, William. Harper's New York & Erie Railroad Guide. (Illus.). 180p. 10.95 (0-941567-47-8) J C & A L Fawcett.

***Macleod, William C.** The American Indian Frontier. (LC History-America-E). 598p. 1999. reprint ed. lib. bdg. 129.00 (0-7812-4262-2) Rprt Serv.

Macleod, William M. & Macleod, Gael S. M. I. N. D. over Weight: How to Stay Slim the Rest of Your Life. 126p. (Orig.). 1985. reprint ed. 19.95 incl. audio (0-934439-05-2); reprint ed. pap. 9.95 (0-934439-03-6); reprint ed. 9.95 (0-934439-04-4) W G M Pub.

MacLeoid, Tormod, et al. Invention of the Cremona Hoax/Canntaireachd - Articulate Music/Piobaireachd As Verbally Taught, 3 vols. in 1. MacRaonuill, Alasdair, tr. from GAE. & intro. by. 96p. 1992. pap. 18.00 (0-685-66248-9) A MacRaonuill.

Maclera. Dr. Luke's Casebook. 1996. pap. 4.99 (1-85792-192-5, Pub. by Christian Focus) Spring Arbor Dist.

MacLiam, Thomas, ed. Lazy Way to Irish. (IRI., Illus.). 1994. pap. 9.95 (0-86243-287-1) Intl Spec Bk.

MacLiammoir, Michael. All for Hecuba. (Illus.). 25.95 (0-8283-1137-4) Branden Bks.

MacLiammoir, Michael & Barrett, John. Selected Plays of Michael MacLiammoir. LC 96-37909. (Irish Drama Selections Ser.). 319p. 1998. pap. 16.95 (0-8132-0889-0); text 39.95 (0-8132-0888-2) Cath U Pr.

MacLiammoir, Micheal. The Importance of Being Oscar: An Entertainment on the Life & Works of Oscar Wilde. 72p. 1996. pap. 11.95 (0-85105-510-9, Pub. by Smyth) Dufour.

MacLimore, Guy. Mekton Empire. Quintanar, Derek, ed. (Mekton Ser.). (Illus.). 120p. (C). 1990. pap. 14.00 (0-937279-15-3, MK1301) Talsorian.

Maclin, A. P., et al, eds. Magnetic Phenomena. (Lecture Notes in Physics Ser.: Vol. 337). vi, 142p. 1989. 41.00 (0-387-51428-7) Spr-Verlag.

Maclin-Bynum, Valerie J. G. I. F. T. S. - God Inspires Faith Through Salvation. 1997. pap. write for info. (1-57553-509-2) Watermrk Pr.

Maclin, H. T. The Faith That Compels Us. 128p. 1997. pap. 9.95 (1-885224-13-3) Bristol Hse.

Maclin, Victoria M., jt. auth. see Bieber, Eric J.

Macliver, C. & Thom, M. Family Talk: Picture Sheets for Children Whose Family Is Adopting or Fostering. 1990. 50.00 (0-903534-89-4, Pub. by Brit Ag for Adopt & Fost) St Mut.

MacLochlainn, Alf. The Corpus in the Library: Stories & Novellas. LC 94-8746. (Illus.). 151p. (Orig.). 1996. pap. 11.95 (1-56478-068-6) Dalkey Arch.

— Out of Focus. LC 85-72481. 64p. 1985. 20.00 (0-916583-12-0); pap. 7.95 (0-916583-13-9) Dalkey Arch.

MacLoughlin, Shaun. Writing for Radio: How to Create Successful Radio Plays, Features & Short Stories. 144p. 1998. pap. 19.95 (1-85703-284-5, Pub. by How To Bks) Trans-Atl Phila.

MacLow, Jackson. Barnesbook: Four Poems Derived from Sentences by Djuna Barnes, Vol. 127. LC 96-35905. (Sun & Moon Classics Ser.: No. 127). 56p. 1996. pap. 9.95 (1-55713-235-6) Sun & Moon CA.

Maclow, Jackson. Bloomsday. (Illus.). 112p. 1984. pap. 9.95 (0-88268-008-0) Station Hill Pr.

***MacLow, Jackson.** 42 Merzgedichte: In Memoriam of Kurt Schwitters. (Orig.). 1998. pap. 14.95 (1-886449-70-8, P9708, Pub. by Barrytown Ltd) Consort Bk Sales.

MacLow, Jackson. French Sonnets. (Illus.). 62p. 1989. pap. 8.00 (0-87924-064-4) Membrane Pr.

— The Pronouns: A Collection of Forty Dances for the Dancers-February 3rd to March 22nd 1964. LC 79-64919. 88p. 1979. pap. 15.00 (0-930794-06-0) Station Hill Pr.

— The Pronouns: A Collection of Forty Dances for the Dancers-February 3rd to March 22nd 1964. deluxe limited ed. LC 79-64919. 88p. 1979. boxed set 50.00 (0-930794-74-5) Station Hill Pr.

— Representative Works, 1938-1985. LC 85-61392. (Roof Bks.). 350p. (Orig.). 1985. 18.95 (0-937804-19-3); pap. 12.95 (0-937804-18-5) Segue NYC.

— Twenties. (Roof Bks.). 112p. 1991. pap. text 8.95 (0-937804-42-8) Segue NYC.

— The Virginia Woolf Poems. 44p. 1985. pap. 5.00 (0-930901-28-2) Burning Deck.

— Words & Ends from E-Z. LC 89-80484. (Illus.). 96p. (Orig.). 1989. pap. 7.50 (0-939691-03-5) Avenue B.

Maclulich, T. D. Between Europe & America: The Canadian Tradition in Fiction. 266p. (C). 1988. text 25.00 (0-920763-96-0, Pub. by ECW); pap. text 15.00 (0-920763-95-2, Pub. by ECW) Genl Dist Srvs.

MacLulich, T. D. Hugh MacLennan. (World Authors Ser.: No. 708). 166p. 1983. 28.95 (0-8057-6555-7) Macmillan.

MacLure, Margaret, et al. Oracy Matters. 224p. 1988. pap. 34.95 (0-335-15855-2) OpUniv Pr.

MacLure, Millar, ed. Marlowe: The Critical Heritage, Fifteen Eighty-Eight to Eighteen Ninety-Six. 1979. 69.50 (0-7100-0245-9, Routledge Thoemms) Routledge.

MacLure, Millar & Watt, F. W., eds. Essays in English Literature from The Renaissance to the Victorian Age: Presented to A. S. P. Woodhouse, 1964. LC 64-55295. 352p. reprint ed. pap. 109.20 (0-608-16306-6, 202653200050) Bks Demand.

Maclure, Stuart & Davies, Peter, eds. Learning to Think, Thinking to Learn: Proceedings of the 1989 OECD Conference Organized by the Centre for Educational Research & Innovation. (Illus.). 266p. 1991. 87.75 (0-08-040646-7, Pergamon Pr); pap. 38.50 (0-08-040657-2, Pergamon Pr) Elsevier.

Maclure, W. Observations on the Geology of the United States of America. 1966. reprint ed. text 44.00 (0-934454-67-1) Lubrecht & Cramer.

Maclure, William. Opinions on Various Subjects: Dedicated to the Industrious Producers, 3 vols. LC 68-18220. 1971. reprint ed. 150.00 (0-678-00712-8) Kelley.

Maclure, William & Fretageot, Marie D. Partnership for Posterity: The Correspondence of William Maclure & Marie Duclos Fretageot, 1820-1833. Elliott, Josephine M., ed. LC 94-15045. (Illus.). xxx, 1151p. 1994. 95.00 (0-87195-104-5) Ind Hist Soc.

MacIver, D. N., ed. The Liberal Democrats. LC 96-1620. 256p. (C). 1996. pap. text 32.00 (0-13-227802-2) P-H.

MacLysaght, Edward. Irish Families: Their Names, Arms & Origins. 4th ed. (Illus.). 248p. 1991. reprint ed. 39.50 (0-7165-2364-7, Pub. by Irish Acad Pr) Intl Spec Bk.

— More Irish Families. LC 96-216061. (Illus.). 254p. 1996. pap. 19.95 (0-7165-2604-2, Pub. by Irish Acad Pr) Intl Spec Bk.

— The Surnames of Ireland. 314p. 1991. reprint ed. pap. 9.50 (0-7165-2366-3, Pub. by Irish Acad Pr) Intl Spec Bk.

MacMahon. The Imagination of Jean Genet. 18.50 (0-685-34133-X) Fr & Eur.

MacMahon, A. W., et al. The Administration of Federal Work Relief. LC 73-167845. (FDR & the Era of the New Deal Ser.). 408p. 1971. reprint ed. lib. bdg. 49.50 (0-306-70326-2) Da Capo.

MacMahon, Alice T. All about Childbirth: A Manual for Prepared Childbirth. 4th ed. LC 94-27717. (Illus.). 208p. 1994. pap. 6.95 (0-931128-04-8) Family Pubns.

— Women & Hormones: An Essential Guide to Being Female. MacMahon, James R., ed. LC 90-81214. (Illus.). 208p. (Orig.). 1990. pap. 9.95 (0-931128-03-X) Family Pubns.

Macmahon, Arthur W. Memorandum on the Postwar International Information Program of the United States. LC 72-4673. (International Propaganda & Communications Ser.). 135p. 1972. reprint ed. 18.95 (0-405-04757-6) Ayer.

Macmahon, Arthur W. & Millett, John D. Federal Administrators: A Biographical Approach to the Problems of Departmental Administration. LC 70-181953. reprint ed. 31.00 (0-404-04139-6) AMS Pr.

***MacMahon, Bill, ed.** The Architecture of East Australia. (Illus.). 270p. 2001. 42.00 (3-930698-90-0) Edition A Menges.

MacMahon, Brian & Sugimura, Takashi, eds. Coffee & Health. LC 84-14199. (Banbury Reports: Vol.17). 259p. 1984. 47.50 (0-87969-217-0) Cold Spring Harbor.

MacMahon, Brian & Trichopoulos, Dimitrios. Epidemiology: Principles & Practice. 2nd ed. LC 96-5095. 288p. 1996. text 42.50 (0-316-54222-9, Little Brwn Med Div) Lppncott W & W.

Macmahon, Brian, jt. ed. see Clark, Duncan W.

MacMahon, Bryan. The Honey Spike. 247p. 1993. reprint ed. pap. 14.95 (1-85371-310-4, Pub. by Poolbeg Pr) Dufour.

— The Master. (Illus.). 187p. 1994. 30.00 (1-85371-222-1, Pub. by Poolbeg Pr); pap. 14.95 (1-85371-254-X, Pub. by Poolbeg Pr) Dufour.

— Patsy-O. LC 89-51016. 128p. (Orig.). (J). (gr. 4-7). 1989. pap. 6.95 (1-85371-036-9, Pub. by Poolbeg Pr) Dufour.

— The Tallystick: And Other Stories. LC 94-165342. 256p. 1995. 29.00 (1-85371-338-4, Pub. by Poolbeg Pr) Dufour.

— The Tallystick & Other Stories. 248p. 1997. pap. 14.95 (1-85371-447-X, Pub. by Poolbeg Pr) Dufour.

MacMahon, Bryan, tr. see Sayers, Peig.

MacMahon, Candace W. Elizabeth Bishop: A Bibliography, 1927-1979. LC 79-13063. 247p. reprint ed. pap. 76.60 (0-7837-2150-1, 204243600004) Bks Demand.

MacMahon, Darcie A., jt. auth. see Deagan, Kathleen A.

MacMahon, Desmond. Brass, Wood-Wind & Strings: The Instruments of the Orchestra: Music Book Index. 101p. 1993. reprint ed. lib. bdg. 69.00 (0-7812-9705-2) Rprt Serv.

MacMahon, Heber, et al. Chest Disease (Fifth Series) Test & Syllabus, Vol. 40. Choplin, Robert H., ed. (Professional Self-Evaluation Ser.). (Illus.). 660p. 1996. 220.00 (1-55903-040-2) Am Coll Radiology.

MacMahon, Horace. Stereo Book of Contours. LC 74-188860. 32p. (J). (gr. 1 up). 1972. spiral bd. 7.75 (0-8331-1705-X, 456) Hubbard Sci.

MacMahon, James R., ed. see MacMahon, Alice T.

MacMahon, Percy A. Combinatory Analysis, 2 Vols. in 1. LC 59-10267. 49.50 (0-8284-1137-9) Chelsea Pub.

— Percy Alexander McMahon - Collected Papers: Combinatorics, Vol. 1. Andrews, George E., ed. LC 77-28962. (Mathematicians of Our Time Ser.). 1978. 125.00 (0-262-13121-8) MIT Pr.

— Percy Alexander McMahon - Collected Papers Vol. II: Number Theory, Invariants & Applications. Andrews, George E., ed. (Mathematicians of Our Time Ser.: No. 24). (Illus.). 904p. 1986. 105.00 (0-262-13214-1) MIT Pr.

MacMahon, Robert A., ed. An Aid to Pediatric Surgery. 2nd ed. (Illus.). 272p. (Orig.). 1991. pap. text 36.95 (0-443-04185-7) Church.

Macmanamon, Francis P. Cultural Resource Management in Contemporary Society: Perspectives on Managing & Presenting the Past. LC 98-49060. 1999. write for info. (0-415-11785-2) Routledge.

MacManiman, Gen. Dry It-You'll Like It, Vol. 1. 3rd ed. (Illus.). 80p. 1997. reprint ed. pap. 6.95 (0-9611998-0-6) MacManiman.

MacManus, Dermot. Middle Kingdom. The Faerie World of Ireland. (Illus.). 191p. 1973. 6.95 (0-317-65888-3, Pub. by Smyth) Dufour.

— The Middle Kingdom: The Faerie World of Ireland. (Illus.). 191p. 1979. pap. 12.95 (0-900675-82-9, Pub. by Smyth) Dufour.

MacManus, Diarmuid. Irish Earth Folk. (Illus.). 1959. 10.95 (0-8159-5814-5) Devin.

Macmanus, Elizabeth R. & Macmanus, Susan A. Sawmills, Citrus, Critters & Crackers: Life in Early Lutz & Central Pasco County. LC 98-25437. 1998. write for info. (1-879852-58-6) Univ Tampa.

MacManus, Francis. Men Withering. 1988. pap. 7.95 (0-85342-115-3) Dufour.

MacManus, Jeffrey. Database Access with Visual Basic 5.X. LC 98-84227. 736p. 1998. 39.99 (1-56276-567-1) Que.

MacManus, Judith. How to Write & Deliver an Effective Speech. LC 97-80139. (Illus.). 116p. 1997. pap. 9.95 (0-02-862191-3, Arc) IDG Bks.

Macmanus, Mariquita. Rules for Living. (New Poets Ser.). 40p. 1998. mass mkt. 8.00 (0-932616-62-3) Brick Hse Bks.

Macmanus, Seumas. Dark Patrick. LC 70-178447. (Short Story Index Reprint Ser.). 1977. reprint ed. 15.95 (0-8369-4048-2) Ayer.

***MacManus, Seumas.** Favorite Irish Folk Tales. LC 98-43821. 192p. 1999. pap. text 5.95 (0-486-40549-4) Dover.

MacManus, Seumas. The Rocky Road to Dublin. 9.95 (0-8159-6712-8) Devin.

Macmanus, Seumas. The Story of the Irish Race. 768p. 1990. 14.99 (0-517-06408-1) Random Hse Value.

MacManus, Seumas. The Story of the Irish Race: A Popular History of Ireland. 41st rev. ed. 740p. 1990. 24.95 (0-8159-6827-2) Devin.

Macmanus, Seumas. Through the Turf Smoke. LC 72-81273. (Short Story Index Reprint Ser.). 1977. 20.95 (0-8369-3025-8) Ayer.

MacManus, Seumas, ed. Donegal Fairy Stories. (Illus.). 256p. (J). (gr. 4-6). 1968. pap. 6.95 (0-486-21971-2) Dover.

MacManus, Susan A. Federal Aid to Houston. LC 82-74101. 59p. 1983. pap. 8.95 (0-8157-5425-6) Brookings.

— Revenue Patterns in U. S. Cities & Suburbs: A Comparative Analysis. LC 77-27499. (Praeger Special Studies). 265p. 1978. 59.95 (0-275-90304-4, C0304, Praeger Pubs) Greenwood.

***MacManus, Susan A.** Targeting Senior Voters: Campaign Outreach to Elders & Others with Special Needs. 256p. 2000. 59.00 (0-7425-0111-6); pap. 19.95 (0-7425-0112-4) Rowman.

Macmanus, Susan A., jt. auth. see Macmanus, Elizabeth R.

MacManus, Theodore. Advertising: Sword Arm of Business. 9.50 (0-8159-6832-9) Devin.

MacManus, Yvonne. Deadly Legacy. large type ed. LC 99-11202. 1999. pap. 20.95 (0-7862-1873-8) Mac Lib Ref.

— With Fate Conspire. large type ed. LC 98-5563. (Candlelights Ser.). 1998. 19.95 (0-7862-1430-9) Thorndike Pr.

— You Can Write a Romance & Get It Published. 2nd rev. ed. 240p. (Orig.). 1997. pap. 14.95 (0-9637498-1-1) Toad Hall PA.

Macmartin, D. F. Thirty Years in Hell: or The Confessions of a Drug Fiend. Grob, Gerald N., ed. LC 80-1256. (Addiction in America Ser.). 1981. reprint ed. lib. bdg. 27.95 (0-405-13606-4) Ayer.

MacMaster, Eve B. God Builds His Church. LC 87-2875. (Story Bible Ser.: Vol. 10). (Illus.). 184p. (Orig.). (J). (gr. 3 up). 1987. pap. 6.99 (0-8361-3446-X) Herald Pr.

— God Gives the Land: Stories of God & His People: Joshua. LC 83-182. (Story Bible Ser.: Vol. 3). (Illus.). 168p. (Orig.). (J). (ps-1). 1983. pap. 6.99 (0-8361-3332-3) Herald Pr.

— God Rescues His People: Stories of God & His People: Exodus, Leviticus, Numbers & Deuteronomy. LC 82-2849. (Story Bible Ser.: Vol. 2). (Illus.). 176p. (J). (ps-1). 1982. pap. 6.99 (0-8361-1994-0) Herald Pr.

— God Sends His Son. LC 86-18342. (Story Bible Activity Ser.: Vol. 8). (Illus.). 160p. (Orig.). (J). (gr. 3-9). 1986. pap. 6.99 (0-8361-3420-6) Herald Pr.

— God's Chosen King: Stories of God & His People: I Samuel. LC 83-12736. (Story Bible Ser.: Vol. 4). (Illus.). 190p. (Orig.). (J). (gr. 5-6). 1983. pap. 6.99 (0-8361-3344-7) Herald Pr.

— God's Family. LC 81-6551. (Story Bible Ser.: Vol. 1). (Illus.). 168p. (J). (gr. 3 up). 1981. pap. 6.99 (0-8361-1964-9) Herald Pr.

— God's Justice. LC 84-20514. (Story Bible Ser.: Vol. 6). (Illus.). 168p. (Orig.). (J). (ps-1). 1984. pap. 6.99 (0-8361-3381-1) Herald Pr.

— God's Suffering Servant. LC 86-19526. (Story Bible Activity Ser.: Vol. 9). (Illus.). 120p. (Orig.). (J). (gr. 3-9). 1987. pap. 6.99 (0-8361-3422-2) Herald Pr.

— God's Wisdom & Power. LC 84-8974. (Story Bible Ser.: Vol. 5). (Illus.). 168p. (Orig.). (J). (gr. 3-8). 1984. pap. 6.99 (0-8361-3362-5) Herald Pr.

MacMaster, Richard K. History of Hardy County, WV, Seventeen Eighty-Six to Nineteen Eighty-Six. 338p. 1986. 35.00 (0-317-54414-4) Hardy Cnty Lib.

— Land, Piety & Peoplehood. LC 84-15790. (Mennonite Experience in America Ser.: Vol. 1). 344p. (Orig.). 1985. pap. 19.99 (0-8361-1261-X) Herald Pr.

MacMaster, Richard K. & Hiebert, Ray E. A Grateful Remembrance: The Story of Montgomery County, Maryland. (Illus.). 440p. 1996. reprint ed. pap. 16.95 (0-9643819-8-2) Innovat Game.

MacMaster, Richard K., et al. Conscience in Crisis. LC 78-27530. (Studies in Anabaptist & Mennonite History: Vol. 20). 528p. 1979. 19.99 (0-8361-1213-X) Herald Pr.

MacMaster, Richard K., jt. auth. see Copeland, Pamela C.

MacMasters, Eve B. Story Bible Series Set, 10 bks. 1987. pap. text 69.90 (0-8361-1009-9) Herald Pr.

***MacMath, Fiona.** Saints' Names for Your Baby. LC 99-16137. 136p. 2000. pap. 5.95 (0-8146-2703-X) Liturgical Pr.

MacMathuna, Sean. Atheist: And Other Stories. 172p. 1993. pap. 11.95 (0-86327-103-0, Pub. by Wolfhound Press) Irish Amer Bk.

MacMichael, D. B., jt. auth. see Reay, David A.

Macmichael, H. A. History of the Arabs in Sudan, 2 vols., Set. 1967. reprint ed. 145.00 (0-7146-1041-0, Pub. by F Cass Pubs) Intl Spec Bk.

— Tribes of Northern & Central Kordofan. 260p. 1967. reprint ed. 57.50 (0-7146-1113-1, Pub. by F Cass Pubs) Intl Spec Bk.

MacMichael, William. Journal from Moscow to Constantinople in the Years 1817 & 1818. LC 71-135817. (Eastern Europe Collection). 1971. reprint ed. 21.95 (0-405-02759-1) Ayer.

Macmill. Preacher & Teacher. 1997. 24.99 (1-85792-240-9, Pub. by Christian Focus) Spring Arbor Dist.

MacMillan. American Heart Association 92-94. 1997. 150.00 (0-8385-0195-8) Appleton & Lange.

— Appleton & Lange Guide for Authors. (C). 1980. write for info. (0-8385-0196-6) Appleton & Lange.

***MacMillan.** College Blue Book, 27. 1999. 347.25 (0-02-865300-9) Holiday.

— College Blue Book, 27. 1999. 625.00 (0-02-865307-6) Holiday.

— Dermatology Primary Care, Vol. 1. 1999. 185.00 (0-8385-1570-3) Appleton & Lange.

— Dermatology Primary Care, Vol. 2. 1997. 185.00 (0-8385-1571-1) Appleton & Lange.

— Elizabeth Blackadder. (Illus.). 128p. 1999. student ed. 54.95 (0-7546-0063-7) Ashgate Pub Co.

— Elizabeth Blackadder. limited ed. 393.95 (1-84014-669-9) Ashgate Pub Co.

Macmillan. Encyclopedia of Philosophy, 4, 1. 1973. 120.00 (*0-02-894960-9*) Macmillan.
— Encyclopedia of Philosophy, 4 vols., Vol. 3. 1973. 120.00 (*0-02-894980-3*) Mac Lib Ref.
MacMillan. Encyclopedia of Philosophy, Vol. 4. 1973. 120.00 (*0-02-894990-0*) Macmillan.
— Golfing in Idaho & Montana. 1998. 10.95 (*1-878591-24-X*) Mac Prodns.
— Golfing in Oregon. 1998. 9.95 (*1-878591-23-1*) Mac Prodns.
Macmillan. Golfing in Washington. 1998. 11.95 (*1-878591-22-3*) Mac Prodns.
— Law & Other Things. vii, 284p. 1997. reprint ed. 87.50 (*1-56169-299-9*) Gaunt.
***MacMillan.** Macintosh. 216p. 1998. pap. text 33.33 incl. cd-rom (*0-13-013161-X*) P-H.
MacMillan. Travel & Leisure. 1997. pap. text 334.80 (*0-02-862094-1*) Macmillan.
***Macmillan.** World Meetings: Social & Behavioral Science Human Service Management. 2nd ed. 1998. per. 45.00 (*0-02-864999-0*) Macmillan.
Macmillan. World Meetings: Social & Behavioral Science Human Service Management. 3rd ed. 1998. per. 45.00 (*0-02-865000-X*) Macmillan.
MacMillan. World Meetings: United States & Canada , Vol. 1, Vol. 35. 1997. per. 48.75 (*0-02-864793-9*) Mac Lib Ref.
— World Meetings: United States & Canada, Vol. 2, Vol. 35. 1997. per. 48.75 (*0-02-864794-7*) Mac Lib Ref.
Macmillan. World Meetings: United States & Canada 1998. 36th ed. 1997. per. 195.00 (*0-02-864987-7*) Macmillan.
Macmillan & Gilleasbuig. On Reflection: A Workable Relief. 90p. 1993. pap. 21.00 (*0-7152-0683-4*, Pub. by St Andrew) St Mut.
Macmillan, jt. auth. see Twist.
MacMillan, Angus. The International Aluminum Trade. (International Trade Ser.). (Illus.). 192p. Date not set. 225.00 (*1-85573-151-7*, Pub. by Woodhead Pubng) Am Educ Systs.
— Steel Alloying Metals & Their Markets. 200p. Date not set. write for info. (*1-85573-374-9*, Pub. by Woodhead Pubng) Am Educ Systs.
MacMillan, Angus, ed. The Base Metals Handbook: The Definitive Reference Source to the Major Base Metals. (Illus.). 406p. 1998. 890.00 (*1-85573-047-2*, Pub. by Woodhead Pubng) Am Educ Systs.
MacMillan, Arnold J., et al. The Clan MacMillan - History, Vol. I. Burtt, M. Edward, ed. (Illus.). vi, 357p. (Orig.). 1994. pap. write for info. (*1-888913-10-X*) M E Burtt.
Macmillan, B. H. Checklist of the Mosses of Banks Peninsula, New Zealand. (Landcare Research Science Ser.: No. 17). (Illus.). 80p. 1996. pap. 25.00 (*0-478-09302-0*, Pub. by Manaaki Whenua) Balogh.
Macmillan, Bonnie. Why Schoolchildren Can't Read. (IEA Studies in Education: No. 2). 211p. 1997. pap. 34.50 (*0-255-36403-2*, Pub. by Inst Economic Affairs) Coronet Bks.
Macmillan Books Staff. The Baseball Encyclopedia: The Complete & Definitive Record of Major... 10th ed. 1996. 99.95 incl. cd-rom (*0-02-861435-6*) Macmillan.
— Baseball Encyclopedia Update: Complete Career Records for All Players Who Played In The 1997 Sea. 224p. 1998. pap. text 14.95 (*0-02-862148-4*) Macmillan.
— The Macmillan World Atlas. 1996. 75.00 incl. cd-rom (*0-02-861445-3*) Macmillan.
— The Way Nature Works. (Illus.). 360p. 1998. pap. text 24.95 (*0-02-862281-2*, Pub. by Macmillan) S&S Trade.
MacMillan, C. J. & Garrison, James W. A Logical Theory of Teaching: Erotetics & Intentionality. (Philosophy & Education Ser.: No. 1). 254p. (C). 1988. text 137.50 (*90-277-2813-5*) Kluwer Academic.
MacMillan, C. Michael. The Practice of Language Rights in Canada. LC 99-179457. (Illus.). 272p. 1998. text 50.00 (*0-8020-4279-1*); pap. text 19.95 (*0-8020-8115-0*) U of Toronto Pr.
MacMillan, Carrie, et al. Silenced Sextet: Six Nineteenth-Century Canadian Women Novelists. (Illus.). 240p. 1993. 60.00 (*0-7735-0945-3*, Pub. by McG-Queens Univ Pr) CUP Services.
Macmillan Children's Book Staff. Children. LC 97-210025. (Illus.). 12p. (J). (ps-3). 1997. 12.00 (*0-679-88422-X*, Pub. by Knopf Bks Yng Read) Random.
— Food. LC 97-210026. (Illus.). 12p. (J). (ps-3). 1997. 12.00 (*0-679-88424-6*, Pub. by Knopf Bks Yng Read) Random.
***Macmillan Children's Book Staff.** Little Guide to Babies. (Illus.). (J). 2000. 3.99 (*0-333-73422-X*) Mcm Child Bks.
— Little Guide to Dads. (Illus.). (J). 2000. 3.99 (*0-333-73420-3*) Mcm Child Bks.
— Little Guide to Mums. (Illus.). (J). 2000. 3.99 (*0-333-73419-X*) Mcm Child Bks.
— Little Guide to Pets. (Illus.). (J). 2000. 3.99 (*0-333-73421-1*) Mcm Child Bks.
Macmillan Children's Book Staff. Pets. (Illus.). 12p. (J). (ps-3). 1997. 12.00 (*0-679-88421-1*, Pub. by Knopf Bks Yng Read) Random.
MacMillan Computer Publishing Staff. Teach Yourself Windows 95 in 24 Hours. 2nd ed. 1997. pap. 29.98 (*0-672-31270-0*) Sams.
MacMillan, Daniel. Golfing in Oregon. 7th ed. 1997. pap. text 9.95 (*1-878591-21-5*) Mac Prodns.
— Golfing in Oregon. 9th ed. 1999. pap. text 10.95 (*1-878591-51-7*) Mac Prodns.
— Golfing in Washington. 12th ed. 1997. pap. text 10.95 (*1-878591-20-7*) Mac Prodns.
— Golfing in Washington. 14th ed. 1999. pap. text 11.95 (*1-878591-50-9*) Mac Prodns.
MacMillan, David, ed. Casting Couch Confessions: Erotic Tales Anthology. 192p. 1999. pap. 14.95 (*1-889138-17-7*) Companion Press.
***MacMillan, David, ed.** The Freshman Club: Gay Virgin Tales Anthology. 192p. 2000. pap. 14.95 (*1-889138-27-4*, Pub. by Companion Press) SCB Distributors.
— Rent Boys: Hustlers & Escorts - Gay Erotic Tales. 192p. 2000. pap. 14.95 (*1-889138-25-8*, Pub. by Companion Press) SCB Distributors.
— Skin Flicks Vol. 2: Naked Auditions & Other Gay Erotic Tales. 192p. 2000. pap. 14.95 (*1-889138-26-6*, Pub. by Companion Press) SCB Distributors.
Macmillan Development Team. New Riders' Official Internet & World Wide Web Yellow Pages. 7th ed. 1998. pap. text 29.99 (*1-56205-874-6*) New Riders Pub.
MacMillan, Dianne. Destination Los Angeles. LC 96-37407. (Port Cities of North America Ser.). (J). 1997. lib. bdg. 22.60 (*0-8225-2786-3*) Lerner Pub.
— Missions of Los Angeles. (J). (gr. 4-7). 1999. pap. 5.95 (*0-8225-9834-5*) Lerner Pub.
— Missions of the Los Angeles Area. LC 95-16717. (California Missions Ser.). 80p. (J). (gr. 4-7). 1996. lib. bdg. 23.93 (*0-8225-1927-5*, Lerner Publctns) Lerner Pub.
Macmillan, Dianne M. Cheetahs. LC 96-28554. (J). (gr. 2-5). 1997. 19.93 (*1-57505-044-7*, Carolrhoda) Lerner Pub.
MacMillan, Dianne M. Cheetahs. LC 96-28554. (Illus.). 48p. (gr. 2-5). 1997. pap. 19.93 (*1-57505-225-3*, Carolrhoda) Lerner Pub.
— Chinese New Year. LC 93-46183. (Best Holiday Bks.). (Illus.). 48p. (J). (gr. 1-4). 1994. lib. bdg. 18.95 (*0-89490-500-7*) Enslow Pubs.
— Diwali: Hindu Festival of Lights. LC 96-32344. (Best Holiday Bks.). 48p. (J). (gr. 1-4). 1997. lib. bdg. 18.95 (*0-89490-817-0*) Enslow Pubs.
— Elephants: Our Last Land Giants. LC 92-35268. (Nature Watch Ser.). (J). (gr. 2-5). 1993. lib. bdg. 19.93 (*0-87614-770-8*, Carolrhoda) Lerner Pub.
— Japanese Children's Day & the Obon Festival. LC 96-39170. (Best Holiday Bks.). (Illus.). 48p. (J). (gr. 1-4). 1997. lib. bdg. 18.95 (*0-89490-818-9*) Enslow Pubs.
— Mardi Gras. LC 96-43563. (Best Holiday Bks.). (Illus.). 48p. (J). (gr. 1-4). 1997. lib. bdg. 18.95 (*0-89490-819-7*) Enslow Pubs.
— Martin Luther King, Jr. Day. LC 91-43097. (Best Holiday Bks.). (Illus.). 48p. (J). (gr. 1-4). 1992. lib. bdg. 18.95 (*0-89490-382-9*) Enslow Pubs.
— Mexican Independence Day & Cinco de Mayo. LC 96-47244. (Best Holiday Bks.). (Illus.). 48p. (J). (gr. 1-4). 1997. lib. bdg. 18.95 (*0-89490-816-2*) Enslow Pubs.
— Presidents Day. LC 96-27290. (Best Holiday Bks.). (Illus.). 48p. (J). (gr. 1-4). 1997. lib. bdg. 18.95 (*0-89490-820-0*) Enslow Pubs.
— Ramadan & Id Al-Fitr. LC 93-46185. (Best Holiday Bks.). (Illus.). 48p. (J). (gr. 1-4). 1994. lib. bdg. 18.95 (*0-89490-502-3*) Enslow Pubs.
— Tet: Vietnamese New Year. LC 93-46184. (Best Holiday Bks.). (Illus.). 48p. (J). (gr. 1-4). 1994. lib. bdg. 18.95 (*0-89490-501-5*) Enslow Pubs.
— Thanksgiving Day. LC 96-31395. (Best Holiday Bks.). 48p. (J). (gr. 1-4). 1997. lib. bdg. 18.95 (*0-89490-822-7*) Enslow Pubs.
MacMillan, Dianne M., jt. auth. see Freeman, Dorothy R.
***Macmillan, Don.** The Big Book of John Deere Tractors: The Complete Model-by-Model Encyclopedia, Plus Classic Toys, Brochures, & Collectibles. LC 99-22716. (Town Square Bks.). (Illus.). 256p. 1999. 39.95 (*0-89658-378-3*) Voyageur Pr.
Macmillan, Don. John Deere Tractors Worldwide: A Century of Progress, 1893-1993. LC 94-78879. (Illus.). 248p. 1994. 34.95 (*0-929355-55-5*) Am Soc Ag Eng.
Macmillan, Don & Harrington, Roy. John Deere Tractors & Equipment, 1960-1990, Vol. 2. LC 88-71413. (Illus.). 392p. 1991. 39.95 (*0-929355-19-9*, H0190) Am Soc Ag Eng.
Macmillan, Don & Jones, Russell. John Deere Tractors & Equipment, 1837-1959, Vol. 1. LC 88-71413. (Illus.). 370p. 1996. 39.95 (*0-916150-95-X*, H0388) Am Soc Ag Eng.
MacMillan, Donald. Smoke Wars: Anaconda Copper, Montana Air Pollution, & the Courts, 1890. LC 99-24153. (Illus.). 304p. 2000. 40.00 (*0-917298-62-4*) MT Hist Soc.
— Smoke Wars: Anaconda Copper, Montana Air Pollution & the Courts, 1890. (Illus.). 304p. 2000. pap. 18.95 (*0-917298-65-9*) MT Hist Soc.
Macmillan, Duncan. The Paintings of Steven Campbell: The Story So Far. (Illus.). 120p. 1994. 35.00 (*1-85158-546-X*, Pub. by Mainstream Pubng) Trafalgar.
***Macmillan, Duncan.** Scottish Art, 1460-2000. (Illus.). 2000. 90.00 (*1-84018-255-5*, Pub. by Mainstream Pubng) Trafalgar.
Macmillan, Duncan. Scottish Art in the 20th Century. (Illus.). 192p. 1996. 40.00 (*1-85158-630-X*, Pub. by Mainstream Pubng) Trafalgar.
— Scottish Art 1460-1990. (Illus.). 432p. 1992. 95.00 (*1-85158-251-7*, Pub. by Mainstream Pubng) Trafalgar.
— Scottish Art 1460-1990. (Illus.). 432p. 1996. pap. 40.00 (*1-85158-862-0*, Pub. by Mainstream Pubng) Trafalgar.
MacMillan, Duncan. Symbols of Survival: The Art of Will MacLean. (Illus.). 120p. 1993. 34.95 (*1-85158-419-6*, Pub. by Mainstream Pubng) Trafalgar.
Macmillan Educational Company Staff. Collier's Encyclopedia, 1991, 24 vols., Set. 1991. 499.00 (*0-02-942517-4*) Free Pr.
Macmillan Educational Company Staff, ed. Merit Students Encyclopedia, 1991, 20 vols., Set. 1991. text 579.00 (*0-02-943752-0*) Free Pr.
Macmillan, Ernest. Music in Canada. 1988. reprint ed. lib. bdg. 49.00 (*0-7812-0198-5*) Rprt Serv.
Macmillan, Ernest, ed. Music in Canada. LC 77-18206. 232p. 1955. reprint ed. 49.00 (*0-403-01616-9*) Scholarly.
***Macmillan, Fiona, ed.** International Corporate Law, Vol. 1. 256p. 1999. 74.95 (*1-84113-037-0*, Pub. by Hart Pub) Intl Spec Bk.
MacMillan, Floyd B. The Clan MacMillan - History, Vol. II. Burtt, M. Edward, ed. v, 324p. (Orig.). 1994. pap. write for info. (*1-888913-14-2*) M E Burtt.
Macmillan, Gail. Breed Apart: Novia Scotia's Duck Tolling Retriever. LC 99-160803. (Illus.). 112p. 1998. 24.95 (*1-55109-231-X*) Nimbus Publ.
MacMillan, Gail. Held Accountable. LC 99-90147. 192p. 1997. lib. bdg. 18.95 (*0-8034-9357-6*, Avalon Bks) Bouregy.
***MacMillan, Gail.** The Hermit of Hart's Hollow. LC 99-91310. 192p. 2000. 18.95 (*0-8034-9397-5*, Avalon Bks) Bouregy.
MacMillan, Gail. Promise Pending. LC 98-96066. 192p. 1998. 18.95 (*0-8034-9292-8*) Bouregy.
— Someone Special. LC 98-96333. 192p. 1998. lib. bdg. 18.95 (*0-8034-9313-4*, Avalon Bks) Bouregy.
MacMillan, Gail & Strang, Alison. The Nova Scotia Duck Tolling Retriever. LC 95-8602. (Illus.). 288p. 1996. 49.95 (*0-931866-73-1*) Alpine Pubns.
Macmillan General Reference Staff. Complete Computer: Library Reference Set. 1998. 832.71 (*0-02-865082-4*) Macmillan.
— Complete Idiot'a Guide to Healthy Stretching. 1998. 18.95 (*0-02-865113-8*, Pub. by Macmillan) S&S Trade.
— Complete Idiot'a Guide to Yoga. 1998. 17.95 (*0-02-865112-X*, Pub. by Macmillan) S&S Trade.
— The Complete Idiot's Guide Almanac of Business Letters Memos. 1998. 16.95 (*0-02-865093-X*, Pub. by Macmillan) S&S Trade.
— The Complete Idiot's Guide to a Perfect Wedding. 1998. 17.95 (*0-02-865126-X*, Pub. by Macmillan) S&S Trade.
— The Complete Idiot's Guide to Adoption. 1998. 18.95 (*0-02-865127-8*, Pub. by Macmillan) S&S Trade.
— The Complete Idiot's Guide to Antiques & Collectibles. 1998. 16.95 (*0-02-865154-5*, Pub. by Macmillan) S&S Trade.
— The Complete Idiot's Guide to Assertiveness. 1998. 16.95 (*0-02-865146-4*, Pub. by Macmillan) S&S Trade.
— Complete Idiot's Guide to Breaking Bad Habits. 1998. 16.95 (*0-02-865148-0*, Pub. by Macmillan) S&S Trade.
— Complete Idiot's Guide to Bridge. 1998. 16.95 (*0-02-865156-1*, Pub. by Macmillan) S&S Trade.
— Complete Idiot's Guide to Bringing up Baby. 1998. 16.95 (*0-02-865125-1*, Pub. by Macmillan) S&S Trade.
— Complete Idiot's Guide to Business Management. 1998. 16.95 (*0-02-865099-9*, Pub. by Macmillan) S&S Trade.
— Complete Idiot's Guide to Buying & Leasing a Car. 1998. 14.95 (*0-02-865104-9*, Pub. by Macmillan) S&S Trade.
— Complete Idiot's Guide to Buying Insurance Annuities. 1998. 16.95 (*0-02-865103-0*, Pub. by Macmillan) S&S Trade.
— Complete Idiot's Guide to Buying Selling a Home. 1998. 17.95 (*0-02-865117-0*, Pub. by Macmillan) S&S Trade.
— Complete Idiot's Guide to Changing Careers. 1998. 17.95 (*0-02-865137-5*, Pub. by Macmillan) S&S Trade.
— Complete Idiot's Guide to Chess. 1998. 16.95 (*0-02-865155-3*, Pub. by Macmillan) S&S Trade.
— Complete Idiot's Guide to Choosing Training a Dog. 1998. 16.95 (*0-02-865150-2*, Pub. by Macmillan) S&S Trade.
— Complete Idiot's Guide to College Planning. 1998. 14.95 (*0-02-865123-5*, Pub. by Macmillan) S&S Trade.
— Complete Idiot's Guide to Cooking Basics. 1998. 18.95 (*0-02-865121-9*, Pub. by Macmillan) S&S Trade.
— Complete Idiot's Guide to Creating New Products. 1998. 16.95 (*0-02-865090-5*, Pub. by Macmillan) S&S Trade.
— Complete Idiot's Guide to Dating. 1998. 16.95 (*0-02-865129-4*) Macmillan.
— Complete Idiot's Guide to Dealing with Your Inlaws. 1998. 16.95 (*0-02-865136-7*) Macmillan.
— Complete Idiot's Guide to Decorating Your Home. 1998. 16.95 (*0-02-865120-0*, Pub. by Macmillan) S&S Trade.
— Complete Idiot's Guide to Doing Income Taxes 98. 1998. 12.95 (*0-02-865107-3*, Pub. by Macmillan) S&S Trade.
— Complete Idiot's Guide to Dynamic Selling. 1998. 16.95 (*0-02-865097-2*, Pub. by Macmillan) S&S Trade.
— Complete Idiot's Guide to Eating Smart. 1998. 16.95 (*0-02-865111-1*, Pub. by Macmillan) S&S Trade.
— Complete Idiot's Guide to Entertaining. 1998. 16.95 (*0-02-865119-7*, Pub. by Macmillan) S&S Trade.
— Complete Idiot's Guide to Etiquette. 1998. 16.95 (*0-02-865142-1*, Pub. by Macmillan) S&S Trade.
— Complete Idiot's Guide to Finance Accounting. 1998. 16.95 (*0-02-865106-5*, Pub. by Macmillan) S&S Trade.
— Complete Idiot's Guide to Fun Tricks with Your Dog. 1998. 14.95 (*0-02-865151-0*, Pub. by Macmillan) S&S Trade.
— Complete Idiot's Guide to Gardening. 1998. 16.95 (*0-02-865153-7*, Pub. by Macmillan) S&S Trade.
— Complete Idiot's Guide to Genealogy. 1998. 17.95 (*0-02-865159-6*, Pub. by Macmillan) S&S Trade.
— Complete Idiot's Guide to Getting along with Difficult People. 1998. 16.95 (*0-02-865131-6*) Macmillan.
— Complete Idiot's Guide to Getting the Job You Want. 1998. 24.95 (*0-02-865138-3*, Pub. by Macmillan) S&S Trade.
— Complete Idiot's Guide to Golf. 1998. 18.95 (*0-02-865157-X*, Pub. by Macmillan) S&S Trade.
— Complete Idiot's Guide to Grandparenting. 1998. write for info. (*0-02-865134-0*) Macmillan.
— Complete Idiot's Guide to Great Customer Service. 1998. 16.95 (*0-02-865096-4*, Pub. by Macmillan) S&S Trade.
— Complete Idiot's Guide to Home Repair. 1998. 16.95 (*0-02-865118-9*, Pub. by Macmillan) S&S Trade.
MacMillan General Reference Staff. Complete Idiot's Guide to Leadership. 1998. 16.95 (*0-02-865147-2*, Pub. by Macmillan) S&S Trade.
Macmillan General Reference Staff. The Complete Idiot's Guide to Life Science. 352p. 2000. pap. 16.95 (*0-02-863199-4*) Macmillan.
— Complete Idiot's Guide to Making Money on Wall Street. 1998. 18.95 (*0-02-865100-6*, Pub. by Macmillan) S&S Trade.
— Complete Idiot's Guide to Making Money with Mutual Funds. 1998. 16.95 (*0-02-865102-2*, Pub. by Macmillan) S&S Trade.
— Complete Idiot's Guide to Managed Health Care. 1998. 17.95 (*0-02-865115-4*, Pub. by Macmillan) S&S Trade.
— Complete Idiot's Guide to Managing People. 1998. 18.95 (*0-02-865087-5*, Pub. by Macmillan) S&S Trade.
— Complete Idiot's Guide to Managing Your Money. 1998. 16.99 (*0-02-865101-4*, Pub. by Macmillan) S&S Trade.
— Complete Idiot's Guide to Managing Your Time. 1998. 14.95 (*0-02-865139-1*, Pub. by Macmillan) S&S Trade.
— Complete Idiot's Guide to Marketing Basics. 1998. 18.95 (*0-02-865091-3*, Pub. by Macmillan) S&S Trade.
— The Complete Idiot's Guide to Near Death Experience. 400p. 2000. pap. text 16.95 (*0-02-863234-6*) Macmillan.
— Complete Idiot's Guide to Organizing Your Life. 1998. 16.95 (*0-02-865143-X*, Pub. by Macmillan) S&S Trade.
— Complete Idiot's Guide to Parenting a Preschooler. 1998. 16.95 (*0-02-865132-4*) Macmillan.
— Complete Idiot's Guide to PCs. 6th ed. 1998. 19.99 (*0-02-865241-X*, Pub. by Macmillan) S&S Trade.
— Complete Idiot's Guide to Photography. 1998. 16.95 (*0-02-865152-9*, Pub. by Macmillan) S&S Trade.
— Complete Idiot's Guide to Project Management. 1998. 16.95 (*0-02-865098-0*, Pub. by Macmillan) S&S Trade.
— Complete Idiot's Guide to Protecting Yourself from Legal Hassles. 1998. 16.99 (*0-02-865094-8*, Pub. by Macmillan) S&S Trade.
— The Complete Idiot's Guide to Raising a Smart Kid. 352p. 1999. pap. text 16.95 (*0-02-863230-3*) Macmillan.
— Complete Idiot's Guide to Raising a Teenager. 1998. 16.95 (*0-02-865130-8*) Macmillan.
— Complete Idiot's Guide to Reaching Your Goals. 1998. 16.95 (*0-02-865149-9*, Pub. by Macmillan) S&S Trade.
— Complete Idiot's Guide to Smart Moving. 1998. 16.95 (*0-02-865122-7*, Pub. by Macmillan) S&S Trade.
— Complete Idiot's Guide to Speaking in Public with Confidence. 1998. 16.95 (*0-02-865140-5*, Pub. by Macmillan) S&S Trade.
— Complete Idiot's Guide to Starting a Home Based Business. 1998. 16.95 (*0-02-865092-1*, Pub. by Macmillan) S&S Trade.
— Complete Idiot's Guide to Starting Your Own Business. 1998. 18.95 (*0-02-865086-7*, Pub. by Macmillan) S&S Trade.
— Complete Idiot's Guide to Stress. 1998. 16.95 (*0-02-865110-3*, Pub. by Macmillan) S&S Trade.
— Complete Idiot's Guide to Successful Business Presentations. 1998. 16.95 (*0-02-865095-6*, Pub. by Macmillan) S&S Trade.
— Complete Idiot's Guide to Surviving Divorce. 1998. 16.95 (*0-02-865124-3*, Pub. by Macmillan) S&S Trade.
— Complete Idiot's Guide to Terrific Business Writing. 1998. 16.95 (*0-02-865089-1*, Pub. by Macmillan) S&S Trade.
— Complete Idiot's Guide to the Perfect Cover Letter. 1998. 14.95 (*0-02-865144-8*, Pub. by Macmillan) S&S Trade.
— Complete Idiot's Guide to the Perfect Interview. 1998. 14.95 (*0-02-865145-6*, Pub. by Macmillan) S&S Trade.
— Complete Idiot's Guide to the Perfect Marriage. 1998. 16.95 (*0-02-865133-2*) Macmillan.
— Complete Idiot's Guide to the Perfect Resume. 1998. 16.95 (*0-02-865141-3*, Pub. by Macmillan) S&S Trade.
— Complete Idiot's Guide to The World's Religions. 1998. 16.95 (*0-02-865128-6*, Pub. by Macmillan) S&S Trade.
— Complete Idiot's Guide to Trouble Free Car Repair. 1998. 16.95 (*0-02-865105-7*, Pub. by Macmillan) S&S Trade.
— Complete Idiot's Guide to Understanding Football Like a Pro. 1998. 16.95 (*0-02-865158-8*, Pub. by Macmillan) S&S Trade.
— Complete Idiot's Guide to Vitamins. 1998. 16.95 (*0-02-865116-2*, Pub. by Macmillan) S&S Trade.
— Complete Idiot's Guide to Windows 95. 2nd ed. 1998. 19.99 (*0-02-865235-5*, Pub. by Macmillan) S&S Trade.
— Complete Idiot's Guide to Wine. 1998. 16.95 (*0-02-865160-X*, Pub. by Macmillan) S&S Trade.
— Complete Idiot's Guide to Winning Through Negotiation. 1998. 16.95 (*0-02-865088-3*, Pub. by Macmillan) S&S Trade.
— The Complete Idiot's Guide to 401 (k) Plans. 1998. 17.95 (*0-02-865108-1*, Pub. by Macmillan) S&S Trade.
— Complete Idiot's Guides for Business: Library Reference Set. 1998. 241.30 (*0-02-865070-0*, Pub. by Macmillan) S&S Trade.
— Complete Idiot's Guides to Careers: Library Reference Set. 1998. 223.35 (*0-02-865076-X*, Pub. by Macmillan) S&S Trade.
— Complete Idiot's Guides to Health & Fitness: Library Reference Set, 7 vols., Set. 1998. 123.65 (*0-02-865072-7*, Pub. by Macmillan) S&S Trade.
— Complete Idiot's Guides to Hobbies Library Reference, 11 vols., Set. 1998. 180.45 (*0-02-865077-8*, Pub. by Macmillan) S&S Trade.
— Complete Idiot's Guides to Home & Family: Library Reference Set, 12 vols., Set. 1998. 207.40 (*0-02-865073-5*, Pub. by Macmillan) S&S Trade.
— Complete Idiot's Guides to Relationships Library Reference, 8 vols., Set. 1998. 136.60 (*0-02-865075-1*, Pub. by Macmillan) S&S Trade.
— Complete Idiot's to Wills & Estates. 1998. 16.95 (*0-02-865109-X*, Pub. by Macmillan) S&S Trade.

An Asterisk (*) at the beginning of an entry indicates that the title is appearing for the first time.

— Compleys Idiot's Guide to Losing Weight. 1998. 17.95 (*0-02-865114-6*, Pub. by Macmillan) S&S Trade.

— Computers Today & Tomorrow. 1998. 29.99 (*0-02-865251-7*, Pub. by Macmillan) S&S Trade.

— Designing Campus Networks. 1998. 55.00 (*0-02-865283-5*, Pub. by Macmillan) S&S Trade.

— DSL Specialization Techniques Standards. 1998. 54.99 (*0-02-865284-3*, Pub. by Macmillan) S&S Trade.

— Easy Windows 95. 2nd ed. 1998. 19.99 (*0-02-865239-8*, Pub. by Macmillan) S&S Trade.

— Economics of Electronic Commerce. 1998. 49.99 (*0-02-865285-1*, Pub. by Macmillan) S&S Trade.

— Essential Computer: Library Reference Set. 1998. 580.78 (*0-02-865083-2*, Pub. by Macmillan) S&S Trade.

— Frommer's Arizona 98. 1998. 16.95 (*0-02-865161-8*, Pub. by Macmillan) S&S Trade.

— Frommer's Australia. 4th ed. 1998. 18.95 (*0-02-865215-0*, Pub. by Macmillan) S&S Trade.

— Frommer's Bahamas 98. 1998. 16.95 (*0-02-865216-9*, Pub. by Macmillan) S&S Trade.

— Frommers Basic: Library Reference Set, 50, Set. 1998. 883.50 (*0-02-865080-8*, Pub. by Macmillan) S&S Trade.

— Frommer's Bermuda 99. 1998. 15.95 (*0-02-865217-7*, Pub. by Macmillan) S&S Trade.

— Frommer's California 98. 1998. 18.95 (*0-02-865162-6*, Pub. by Macmillan) S&S Trade.

— Frommer's Canada. 10th ed. 1998. 19.95 (*0-02-865171-5*, Pub. by Macmillan) S&S Trade.

— Frommer's Cancun Cozumel the Yucatan 99. 1998. 14.95 (*0-02-865192-8*, Pub. by Macmillan) S&S Trade.

— Frommer's Caribbean Cruises Ports of Call 98. 1998. 19.95 (*0-02-865173-1*, Pub. by Macmillan) S&S Trade.

— Frommer's Caribbean 99. 1998. 19.95 (*0-02-865172-3*, Pub. by Macmillan) S&S Trade.

— Frommer's Chicago 98. 1998. 14.95 (*0-02-865186-3*, Pub. by Macmillan) S&S Trade.

— Frommer's China. 1998. 21.95 (*0-02-865193-6*, Pub. by Macmillan) S&S Trade.

— Frommer's Colorado. 4th ed. 1998. 15.95 (*0-02-865211-8*, Pub. by Macmillan) S&S Trade.

— Frommer's Costa Rica 98. 1998. 15.95 (*0-02-865194-4*, Pub. by Macmillan) S&S Trade.

— Frommer's England 98. 1998. 19.95 (*0-02-865174-X*, Pub. by Macmillan) S&S Trade.

— Frommer's Europe. 1998. 21.95 (*0-02-865175-8*, Pub. by Macmillan) S&S Trade.

— Frommer's Florida 98. 1998. 18.95 (*0-02-865163-4*, Pub. by Macmillan) S&S Trade.

— Frommer's France 98. 1998. 19.95 (*0-02-865176-6*, Pub. by Macmillan) S&S Trade.

— Frommer's Germany 98. 1998. 19.95 (*0-02-865195-2*, Pub. by Macmillan) S&S Trade.

— Frommer's Greece. 1998. 19.95 (*0-02-865218-5*, Pub. by Macmillan) S&S Trade.

— Frommer's Hawaii. 1998. 18.95 (*0-02-865164-2*, Pub. by Macmillan) S&S Trade.

— Frommer's Hong Kong. 4th ed. 1998. 14.95 (*0-02-865219-3*, Pub. by Macmillan) S&S Trade.

— Frommer's Honolulu Waikiki Oahu. 5th ed. 1998. 14.95 (*0-02-865212-6*, Pub. by Macmillan) S&S Trade.

— Frommer's Ireland. 2nd ed. 1998. 18.95 (*0-02-865196-0*, Pub. by Macmillan) S&S Trade.

— Frommer's Israel. 2nd ed. 1998. 18.95 (*0-02-865220-7*, Pub. by Macmillan) S&S Trade.

— Frommer's Italy 99. 1998. 19.95 (*0-02-865177-4*, Pub. by Macmillan) S&S Trade.

— Frommer's Jamaica Barbados. 3rd ed. 1998. 14.95 (*0-02-865221-5*, Pub. by Macmillan) S&S Trade.

— Frommer's Japan. 4th ed. 1998. 21.95 (*0-02-865222-3*, Pub. by Macmillan) S&S Trade.

— Frommer's Las Vegas 98. 1998. 14.95 (*0-02-865165-0*, Pub. by Macmillan) S&S Trade.

— Frommer's London 98. 1998. 14.95 (*0-02-865178-2*, Pub. by Macmillan) S&S Trade.

— Frommer's Los Angeles 98. 11th ed. 1998. 14.95 (*0-02-865187-1*, Pub. by Macmillan) S&S Trade.

— Frommer's Maui 99. 2nd ed. 1998. 14.95 (*0-02-865166-9*, Pub. by Macmillan) S&S Trade.

— Frommer's Mexico 98. 1998. 19.95 (*0-02-865179-0*, Pub. by Macmillan) S&S Trade.

— Frommer's Miami, the Keys. 4th ed. 1998. 13.95 (*0-02-865213-4*, Pub. by Macmillan) S&S Trade.

— Frommer's Mini Travel Guides: Library Reference Set, 25, Set. 1998. 451.75 (*0-02-865078-6*, Pub. by Macmillan) S&S Trade.

— Frommer's Montreal Quebec. 9th ed. 1998. 14.95 (*0-02-865223-1*, Pub. by Macmillan) S&S Trade.

— Frommer's National Parks of the American West. 1998. 21.95 (*0-02-865167-7*, Pub. by Macmillan) S&S Trade.

— Frommer's New England 98. 1998. 18.95 (*0-02-865214-2*, Pub. by Macmillan) S&S Trade.

— Frommer's New Orleans 98. 1998. 14.95 (*0-02-865168-5*, Pub. by Macmillan) S&S Trade.

— Frommer's New York City with Kids. 5th ed. 1998. 15.95 (*0-02-865209-6*, Pub. by Macmillan) S&S Trade.

— Frommer's New York City 99. 1998. 14.95 (*0-02-865169-3*, Pub. by Macmillan) S&S Trade.

— Frommer's Nova Scotia, New Brunswick. 2nd ed. 1998. 14.95 (*0-02-865224-X*, Pub. by Macmillan) S&S Trade.

— Frommer's Paris 98. 1998. 14.95 (*0-02-865180-4*, Pub. by Macmillan) S&S Trade.

— Frommer's Portugal. 15th ed. 1998. 18.95 (*0-02-865225-8*, Pub. by Macmillan) S&S Trade.

— Frommer's Prague the Best of the Czech Republic. 2nd ed. 1998. 14.95 (*0-02-865226-6*, Pub. by Macmillan) S&S Trade.

— Frommer's Puerto Rico. 3rd ed. 1998. 14.95 (*0-02-865197-9*, Pub. by Macmillan) S&S Trade.

— Frommer's San Diego 98. 1998. 14.95 (*0-02-865170-7*, Pub. by Macmillan) S&S Trade.

— Frommer's San Francisco 98. 1998. 14.95 (*0-02-865188-X*, Pub. by Macmillan) S&S Trade.

MacMillan General Reference Staff. Frommer's Scandinavia. 17th ed. 1998. 19.95 (*0-02-865227-4*, Pub. by Macmillan) S&S Trade.

Macmillan General Reference Staff. Frommer's Scotland. 4th ed. 1998. 18.95 (*0-02-865198-7*, Pub. by Macmillan) S&S Trade.

— Frommer's Singapore, Malaysia. 1998. 16.95 (*0-02-865228-2*, Pub. by Macmillan) S&S Trade.

— Frommer's South Pacific. 5th ed. 1998. 19.95 (*0-02-865229-0*, Pub. by Macmillan) S&S Trade.

— Frommer's Spain. 17th ed. 1998. 19.95 (*0-02-865199-5*, Pub. by Macmillan) S&S Trade.

— Frommer's Switzerland. 8th ed. 1998. 19.95 (*0-02-865200-2*, Pub. by Macmillan) S&S Trade.

— Frommer's Toronto. 5th ed. 1998. 14.95 (*0-02-865230-4*, Pub. by Macmillan) S&S Trade.

— Frommer's U. S. A. 5th ed. 1998. 21.95 (*0-02-865189-8*, Pub. by Macmillan) S&S Trade.

— Frommer's Unofficial Guide to Disneyland 99. 1998. 13.95 (*0-02-865208-8*, Pub. by Macmillan) S&S Trade.

— Frommer's Unofficial Guide to Las Vegas 98. 1998. 16.95 (*0-02-865236-3*, Pub. by Macmillan) S&S Trade.

— Frommer's Unofficial Guide to Walt Disney World 98. 1998. 15.95 (*0-02-865185-5*, Pub. by Macmillan) S&S Trade.

— Frommer's Vancouver Victoria. 4th ed. 1998. 14.95 (*0-02-865201-0*, Pub. by Macmillan) S&S Trade.

— Frommer's Walt Disney World Orlando 98. 1998. 14.95 (*0-02-865190-1*, Pub. by Macmillan) S&S Trade.

— Frommer's Washington D. C. with Kids. 4th ed. 1998. 15.95 (*0-02-865210-X*, Pub. by Macmillan) S&S Trade.

— Frommer's Washington, D. C. 98. 1998. 14.95 (*0-02-865191-X*, Pub. by Macmillan) S&S Trade.

— Handbook of Programming Languages, Vol. 1. 1998. 49.99 (*0-02-865288-6*, Pub. by Macmillan) S&S Trade.

— Handbook of Programming Languages, Vol. 2. 1998. 49.99 (*0-02-865289-4*, Pub. by Macmillan) S&S Trade.

— Handbook of Programming Languages, Vol. 3. 1998. 49.99 (*0-02-865290-8*, Pub. by Macmillan) S&S Trade.

— Handbook of Programming Languages, Vol. 4. 1998. 49.99 (*0-02-865291-6*, Pub. by Macmillan) S&S Trade.

— How Computers Work. deluxe ed. 1998. 29.99 (*0-02-865240-1*, Pub. by Macmillan) S&S Trade.

— How to Use the Internet. 4th ed. 1998. 24.99 (*0-02-865244-4*, Pub. by Macmillan) S&S Trade.

— Internet Routing Architectures. 1998. 55.00 (*0-02-865282-7*, Pub. by Macmillan) S&S Trade.

— Interworking Technologies Handbook. 1998. 50.00 (*0-02-865287-8*, Pub. by Macmillan) S&S Trade.

— MCSE Training Guide: Exchange Server 5.0. 1998. 49.99 (*0-02-865274-6*, Pub. by Macmillan) S&S Trade.

— MCSE Training Guide: Internet Explorer 4. 1998. 49.99 (*0-02-865277-0*, Pub. by Macmillan) S&S Trade.

— MCSE Training Guide: Internet Information Sever 4. 1998. 49.99 (*0-02-865271-1*, Pub. by Macmillan) S&S Trade.

— MCSE Training Guide: Microsoft Exchange Server 5.5. 1998. 49.99 (*0-02-865278-9*, Pub. by Macmillan) S&S Trade.

— MCSE Training Guide: Networking Essentials. 1998. 49.99 (*0-02-865266-5*, Pub. by Macmillan) S&S Trade.

— MCSE Training Guide: SQL Server 6.5 Administration. 1998. 49.99 (*0-02-865275-4*, Pub. by Macmillan) S&S Trade.

— MCSE Training Guide: SQL Server 6.5 Design & Implementation. 1998. 49.99 (*0-02-865276-2*, Pub. by Macmillan) S&S Trade.

— MCSE Training Guide: Systems Management Server 1. 2. 1998. 49.99 (*0-02-865272-X*, Pub. by Macmillan) S&S Trade.

— MCSE Training Guide: Windows NT Server 4. 1998. 49.99 (*0-02-865267-3*, Pub. by Macmillan) S&S Trade.

— MCSE Training Guide: Windows NT Workstation 4. 1998. 49.99 (*0-02-865269-X*, Pub. by Macmillan) S&S Trade.

— MCSE Training Guide: Windows 95. 2nd ed. 1998. 49.99 (*0-02-865273-8*, Pub. by Macmillan) S&S Trade.

— Peter Nortons Inside the PC. 1998. 29.99 (*0-02-865317-3*, Pub. by Macmillan) S&S Trade.

— Residential Broadband. 1998. 55.00 (*0-02-865293-2*, Pub. by Macmillan) S&S Trade.

— Sam's Teach Yourself C in 21 Days. 2nd ed. 1998. 29.99 (*0-02-865262-2*, Pub. by Macmillan) S&S Trade.

— Sam's Teach Yourself C in 24 Hours. 1998. 24.99 (*0-02-865261-4*, Pub. by Macmillan) S&S Trade.

— Sam's Teach Yourself Excel 97 in 24 Hours. 1998. 19.99 (*0-02-865257-6*, Pub. by Macmillan) S&S Trade.

— Sam's Teach Yourself Networking in 24 Hours. 1998. 19.99 (*0-02-865263-0*, Pub. by Macmillan) S&S Trade.

— Sam's Teach Yourself Office 97 in 24 Hours. 2nd ed. 1998. 19.99 (*0-02-865255-X*, Pub. by Macmillan) S&S Trade.

— Sam's Teach Yourself PCs in 10 Minutes. 1998. 12.99 (*0-02-865258-4*, Pub. by Macmillan) S&S Trade.

— Sam's Teach Yourself PCs in 24 Hours. 1998. 19.99 (*0-02-865253-3*, Pub. by Macmillan) S&S Trade.

— Sam's Teach Yourself the Internet in 24 Hours. 2nd ed. 1998. 19.99 (*0-02-865254-1*, Pub. by Macmillan) S&S Trade.

— Sam's Teach Yourself Visual Basics in 21 Days. 4th ed. 1998. 29.99 (*0-02-865260-6*, Pub. by Macmillan) S&S Trade.

— Sam's Teach Yourself Visual Basics in 24 Hours. 1998. 19.99 (*0-02-865259-2*, Pub. by Macmillan) S&S Trade.

— Sam's Teach Yourself Windows 95 in 24 Hours. 2nd ed. 1998. 19.99 (*0-02-865252-5*, Pub. by Macmillan) S&S Trade.

— Sam's Teach Yourself Windows 98 in 24 Hours. 1998. 19.99 (*0-02-865264-9*, Pub. by Macmillan) S&S Trade.

— Sam's Teach Yourself Word 97 in 10 Minutes. 1998. 12.99 (*0-02-865299-1*, Pub. by Macmillan) S&S Trade.

— Sam's Teach Yourself Word 97 in 24 Hours. 1998. 19.99 (*0-02-865256-8*, Pub. by Macmillan) S&S Trade.

— Solaris Advanced Systems Administrators Guide. 2nd ed. 1998. 39.99 (*0-02-865294-0*, Pub. by Macmillan) S&S Trade.

— Solaris System Administrators Guide. 2nd ed. 1998. 34.99 (*0-02-865295-9*, Pub. by Macmillan) S&S Trade.

— Technical Publishing: Library Reference Set. 1998. 835.92 (*0-02-865084-0*) Macmillan.

— Upgrading & Repairing PCs. 10th ed. 1998. 49.99 (*0-02-865250-9*, Pub. by Macmillan) S&S Trade.

— Using HTML 4. 4th ed. 1998. 29.99 (*0-02-865245-2*, Pub. by Macmillan) S&S Trade.

— Using Office 97. 3rd ed. 1998. 29.99 (*0-02-865246-0*, Pub. by Macmillan) S&S Trade.

— Using Office 97 Professional: Special Edition. 1998. 39.99 (*0-02-865247-9*, Pub. by Macmillan) S&S Trade.

— Using the Internet. 1998. 29.99 (*0-02-865242-8*, Pub. by Macmillan) S&S Trade.

— Using the Internet with Windows 95: Special Edition. 1998. 49.99 (*0-02-865243-6*, Pub. by Macmillan) S&S Trade.

— Using Windows 95. 1998. 29.99 (*0-02-865237-1*, Pub. by Macmillan) S&S Trade.

— Using Windows 98. 1998. 29.99 (*0-02-865249-5*, Pub. by Macmillan) S&S Trade.

— Using Word 97: Special Edition. 1998. 34.99 (*0-02-865248-7*, Pub. by Macmillan) S&S Trade.

— Windows NT Automated Deployment Customization. 1998. 32.00 (*0-02-865297-5*, Pub. by Macmillan) S&S Trade.

— Windows NT Server 4 Enterprise. 1998. 49.99 (*0-02-865268-1*, Pub. by Macmillan) S&S Trade.

— Windows NT Shell Scripting. 1998. 32.00 (*0-02-865298-3*, Pub. by Macmillan) S&S Trade.

— Windows NT Unix Integration. 1998. 32.00 (*0-02-865296-7*, Pub. by Macmillan) S&S Trade.

MacMillan, Gordon. At the End of the Rainbow? Gold, Land, & People in the Brazilian Amazon. LC 95-139. (Methods & Cases in Conservation Science Ser.). 1995. 50.00 (*0-231-10354-9*); pap. 25.00 (*0-231-10355-7*) Col U Pr.

MacMillan, Greg. PC Lab:exper/basic Cir. (Primarily Tech Material). 316p. 1992. pap. text 34.95 incl. disk (*0-8273-4821-5*) Delmar.

Macmillan, Harold. War Diaries: Politics & War in the Mediterranean, January 1943 - May 1945. (Illus.). 804p. 1984. 67.50 (*0-333-37198-4*, Pub. by Macmillan) Trans-Atl Phila.

MacMillan, Harriet L., jt. auth. see Dawson, David L.

MacMillan, Hugh. Africa & Empire: W. H. MacMillan, Historian & Social Critic. Marks, Shula, ed. (Commonwealth Papers: No. 25). 351p. 1989. 79.95 (*0-566-05494-9*, Pub. by Dartmth Pub) Ashgate Pub Co.

***MacMillan, Hugh.** Zion in Africa: The Jews of Zambia. LC 99-229267. 1999. 59.50 (*1-86064-405-8*, Pub. by I B T) St Martin.

Macmillan, Hugh & Christophers, Mike. Strategic Issues in the Life Assurance Industry. LC 98-136170. 256p. 1997. pap. text 89.95 (*0-7506-3280-1*) Buttrwrth-Heinemann.

Macmillan, Hugh P. Law & Other Things. LC 76-152195. (Essay Index Reprint Ser.). 1977. 18.95 (*0-8369-2196-8*) Ayer.

— Roman Mossaics: or Studies in Rome & Its Neighbourhood. 1977. 18.95 (*0-8369-7322-4*, 8115) Ayer.

MacMillan, I. C., jt. auth. see Birley, Susan.

MacMillan, Ian. Exiles from Time - Stories of Hawaii. 150p. 1998. pap. 12.95 (*0-9653971-6-5*) Anoai Pr.

— The Red Wind: Makani'Ula. 464p. 1998. 22.95 (*1-56647-205-9*); pap. 14.95 (*1-56647-203-2*) Mutual Pub HI.

***MacMillan, Ian.** Village of a Million Spirits: A Novel of the Treblinka Uprising. LC 99-18847. 272p. 2000. pap. 12.95 (*0-14-029033-8*) Penguin Putnam.

MacMillan, Ian. Village of a Million Spirits: A Novel of the Treblinka Uprising. LC 99-18847. 257p. 1999. 24.00 (*1-883642-84-1*) Steerforth Pr.

MacMillan, Ian C., jt. auth. see Birley, Susan.

MacMillan, Ian C., jt. auth. see Block, Zenas.

MacMillan, Ian C., jt. auth. see McGrath, Rita Gunther.

MacMillan, Ian C., jt. ed. see Birley, Susan.

Macmillan, J., ed. Hormonal Regulation of Development I: Molcular Aspects of Plant Hormones. (Encyclopedia of Plant Physiology Ser.: Vol. 9). (Illus.). 681p. 1980. 256.95 (*0-387-10161-6*) Spr-Verlag.

MacMillan, J. A. The Authority of the Believer: A Classic Which Includes Encounter with Darkness. LC 80-68065. 181p. 1997. pap. 9.99 (*0-87509-636-0*) Chr Pubns.

Macmillan, J. D., jt. auth. see Campbell, M.

MacMillan, John. The Authority of the Believer. rev. ed. 1998. pap. 5.99 (*0-87509-811-8*) Chr Pubns.

— On Liberal Peace: Democracy, War, & the International Order. 256p. 1998. text 59.50 (*1-86064-010-9*, Pub. by I B T) St Martin.

— On Liberal Peace: Democracy, War & the International Order LC 95-61532. (Library of International Relations). 306p. 1998. write for info. (*1-86064-080-X*) I B T.

MacMillan, John & Linklater, Andrew, eds. Boundaries in Question: New Directions in International Relations. LC 95-3441. 288p. 1995. 79.50 (*1-85567-265-0*); pap. 24.95 (*1-85567-266-9*) Bks Intl VA.

MacMillan, Judith. This Gift. 34p. 1998. pap. 8.95 (*0-533-12458-1*) Vantage.

***MacMillan, Judith.** Wright, Austin - A Celebration. (Illus.). 1999. pap. 21.00 (*1-85072-160-2*, Pub. by W Sessions) St Mut.

Macmillan, Kathleen, tr. see Prezzolini, Giuseppe.

Macmillan, Katie, jt. ed. see Allen, Kristen.

MacMillan, Laurie. Santa Barbara - Secrets & Side Trips. 2nd rev. ed. (Illus.). 139p. 1997. pap. 8.95 (*1-885375-03-4*, Shore Line Pr) Pacific Books.

— Santa Barbara Secrets & Sidetrips. (Illus.). 128p. (Orig.). 1991. pap. 8.95 (*0-945092-17-2*) EZ Nature.

Macmillan Library Reference Staff. The Constitution & Its Amendments, 4 vol., set. LC 98-8570. 1998. 225.00 (*0-02-864858-7*) Macmillan Gen Ref.

— Encyclopedia on the American Presidency, 2 vols. unabridged ed. 1998. 250.00 (*0-02-865052-2*) Macmillan Info.

— Macmillan Compendium: African-American History. LC 98-36730. 1153p. 1998. per. 115.00 (*0-02-864979-6*) Macmillan Gen Ref.

— Macmillan Compendium: American History. LC 98-36732. 1198p. 1998. per. 115.00 (*0-02-864978-8*) Macmillan Gen Ref.

— Macmillan Compendium: Everyday Life: A Social History. LC 98-35920. 1078p. 1998. 115.00 (*0-02-864976-1*) Macmillan Gen Ref.

Macmillan Library Reference Staff, ed. Biographical Dictionary of Mathematicians, Vol. 2, Vol. 2. 1991. 70.00 (*0-684-19289-6*) Mac Lib Ref.

Macmillan Library Reference Staff, ed. see Cook, Will.

***MacMillan Lifestyle Group Staff.** Learn to Quilt the Lazy Way. (Lazy Way Ser.). 304p. 1999. pap. 12.95 (*0-02-863174-9*) Free Pr.

MacMillan Lifestyles Group Staff. Plant a Garden the Lazy Way. (Lazy Way Ser.). (Illus.). 304p. 1999. pap. 12.95 (*0-02-863161-7*) Glencoe.

Macmillan, M. Freud Evaluated: The Completed Arc. (Advances in Psychology Ser.: No. 75). 688p. 1991. 189.50 (*0-444-88717-2*, North Holland) Elsevier.

Macmillan, M. A., tr. see Von Bredow, Ilse.

Macmillan, Malcolm. Freud Evaluated: The Completed Arc. (Illus.). 786p. (C). 1996. pap. text 39.50 (*0-262-63171-7*) MIT Pr.

***Macmillan, Malcolm.** An Odd Kind of Fame: Stories of Phineas Gage. LC 99-56640. (Illus.). 526p. 2000. 37.50 (*0-262-13363-6*) MIT Pr.

MacMillan, Margaret. Women of the Raj. LC 87-50183. (Illus.). 256p. 1996. pap. 18.95 (*0-500-27898-9*, Pub. by Thames Hudson) Norton.

MacMillan, Maya K. Curried Favors: Family Recipes from South India. LC 96-15281. (Illus.). 160p. 1996. 35.00 (*0-7892-0055-4*) Abbeville Pr.

***Macmillan, Maya Kaimal.** Curried Favors: Family Recipes from South India. 160p. 2000. pap. text 24.95 (*0-7892-0628-5*) Abbeville Pr.

Macmillan, Michael E., ed. Hawaiian Journal of History, Vol. 26. pap. 12.00 (*0-681-26847-6*) Booklines Hawaii.

— Hawaiian Journal of History, Vol. 28. pap. 12.00 (*0-681-30642-4*) Booklines Hawaii.

MacMillan, Michael E., ed. see Castle, Alfred L.

MacMillan, N. H., jt. auth. see Kelly, A.

MacMillan, Norma. In a Shaker Kitchen: One Hundred of the Best Shaker Recipes. LC 94-41491. 1995. 25.00 (*0-684-80110-8*) S&S Trade.

— A Little New Orleans Cookbook. (Illus.). 60p. 1995. 7.95 (*0-8118-0906-4*) Chronicle Bks.

Macmillan, Norman. Into the Blue. LC 79-169430. (Literature & History of Aviation Ser.). 1972. reprint ed. 25.95 (*0-405-03773-2*) Ayer.

Macmillan Publishing Company Staff. African American History. LC 98-43733. (Macmillan Information Now Encyclopedias Ser.). 700p. 1998. per. 39.95 (*0-02-865017-4*) Macmillan.

— Baedeker Barcelona. 1997. 16.95 (*0-02-861910-2*) Macmillan.

— Baedeker Berlin. 4th ed. 304p. 1998. pap. text 17.95 (*0-02-861905-6*, Pub. by Macmillan) S&S Trade.

— Baedeker New Zealand. 400p. 1998. pap. text 24.95 (*0-02-861911-0*, Pub. by Macmillan) S&S Trade.

— College Blue Book, 5 vols. 26th ed. 1997. 550.00 (*0-02-864760-2*) Macmillan.

— College Blue Book, 1-3. 25th ed. 1995. 150.00 (*0-02-895144-1*) Macmillan.

— College Blue Book, 1-4. 25th ed. 1995. 200.00 (*0-02-895145-X*) Macmillan.

— College Blue Book, Vol. 1-3 & 5. 25th ed. 1995. 200.00 (*0-02-895146-8*) Macmillan.

— Consumer's Guide Assortment. 1998. 334.80 (*0-02-862733-4*) Macmillan.

— Information Now Encyclopedia of the American West. 700p. 1999. 39.95 (*0-02-865332-7*) Macmillan.

— Israel: Yesterday & Today: A Photographic Survey of the Building of a Nation. LC 98-5343. 256p. 1998. 39.95 (*0-02-862585-4*) Macmillan.

— The Macmillan Atlas of War & Peace: Bosnia Herzegovina. 48p. 1996. 12.95 (*0-02-861265-5*) Macmillan.

— Macmillan Baseball Encyclopedia Update, 1997, Update 1. 208p. 1997. pap. text 14.95 (*0-02-861512-3*) Macmillan.

— Macmillan Dictionary. 1973. write for info. (*0-02-195340-6*) Macmillan.

— Macmillan Dictionary for Students. LC 84-3880. (Illus.). 1216p. (YA). (gr. 6-12). 1984. lib. bdg. 19.95 (*0-02-761560-X*, Mac Bks Young Read) S&S Childrens.

— MacMillan Health Encyclopedia, 9 Vols. LC 99-23432. 1999. write for info. (*0-02-865036-0*) Macmillan.

***Macmillan Publishing Company Staff.** Macmillan Quick Reference Encyclopedia: Alcohol. 1998. 24.95 (*0-02-864959-1*) Macmillan.

— Macmillan Quick Reference Encyclopedia: Drugs. 1998. 24.95 (*0-02-864958-3*) Macmillan.

Macmillan Publishing Company Staff. Macmillan School Dictionary. 1974. 21.04 (*0-02-195310-4*) Macmillan.

M

— MacMillan Transportation Encyclopedia, 6 Vols. LC 99-33371. 649p. 1999. write for info. (*0-02-865361-0*) Macmillan.

— The Macmillan Visual Dictionary, Multilingual Edition: English, French, Spanish, German. (Illus.). 928p. 1994. 65.00 (*0-02-578115-4*) Macmillan.

— The New York Public Library American History Desk Reference. Faux, Marian, ed. LC 96-16054. (Illus.). 640p. 1997. 39.95 (*0-02-861322-8*) Macmillan.

— The Tea Companion. LC 97-5770. (Illus.). 192p. 1997. 22.00 (*0-02-861727-4*) Macmillan.

— Twayne's English Authors. 1996. 1243.75 (*0-7838-1716-9*) Macmillan USA.

— The Unofficial Guide to Alternative Medicine. 400p. 1998. pap. 22.95 (*0-02-862526-9*) Macmillan.

— The Unofficial Guide to Buying a Car. 400p. 1998. pap. text 22.95 (*0-02-862524-2*) Macmillan.

— The Unofficial Guide to Cosmetic Surgery. LC 99-232066. 400p. 1998. pap. text 22.95 (*0-02-862522-6*, Pub. by Macmillan) S&S Trade.

— The Unofficial Guide to Dieting Safely. LC 99-230985. 400p. 1998. pap. text 22.95 (*0-02-862521-8*, Pub. by Macmillan) S&S Trade.

— The Unofficial Guide to Firing & Hiring People. 400p. 1998. pap. text 22.95 (*0-02-862523-4*, Pub. by Macmillan) S&S Trade.

— The Unofficial Guide to Starting a Business. 400p. 1998. pap. 16.00 (*0-02-862525-0*, Pub. by Macmillan) S&S Trade.

— Visual Dictionary, Four Languages. 928p. 1993. 60.00 (*0-685-70478-5*) Macmillan.

— World Meetings: Medicine, Vol. 21. 1998. pap. 43.75 (*0-02-865003-4*) Macmillan.

— World Meetings: Medicine, Vol. 21. 2nd ed. 1998. per. 43.75 (*0-02-865004-2*) Macmillan.

— World Meetings: Medicine, Vol. 21. 3rd ed. 1998. per. 43.75 (*0-02-865005-0*) Macmillan.

— World Meetings: Medicine, Vol. 21. 4th ed. 1998. per. 43.75 (*0-02-865006-9*) Macmillan.

— World Meetings: Medicine 1998, Vol. 21. 1997. per. 175.00 (*0-02-865002-6*) Macmillan.

— World Meetings: Outside United States & Canada, Vol. 31. 1998. per. 48.75 (*0-02-864993-1*) Macmillan.

— World Meetings: Outside United States & Canada, Vol. 31. 2nd ed. 1998. per. 48.75 (*0-02-864994-X*) Macmillan.

— World Meetings: Outside United States & Canada, Vol. 31. 3rd ed. 1998. per. 48.75 (*0-02-864995-8*) Macmillan.

— World Meetings: Outside United States & Canada, Vol. 31. 4th ed. 1998. per. 48.75 (*0-02-864996-6*) Macmillan.

— World Meetings: Outside United States & Canada 1998, Vol. 31. 1997. per. 195.00 (*0-02-864992-3*) Macmillan.

— World Meetings: Social & Behavioral Sciences Human Resources & Management 1998, Vol. 28. 1997. per. 180.00 (*0-02-864997-4*) Macmillan.

— World Meetings: Social & Behavioral Sciences Human Services Management, Vol. 28. 1998. per. 45.00 (*0-02-864998-2*) Macmillan.

— World Meetings: United States & Canada, Vol. 36. 1998. per. 48.75 (*0-02-864988-5*) Macmillan.

— World Meetings: United States & Canada, Vol. 36. 2nd ed. 1998. per. 48.75 (*0-02-864989-3*) Macmillan.

— World Meetings: United States & Canada, Vol. 36. 3rd ed. 1998. per. 48.75 (*0-02-864990-7*) Macmillan.

— World Meetings: United States & Canada, Vol. 36. 4th ed. 1998. per. 48.75 (*0-02-864991-5*) Macmillan.

— World Meetings Vol. 19: Medicine, 1996, 4 vols. 1995. per. 175.00 (*0-02-864646-0*) Macmillan.

— World Meetings Vol. 19 No. 1: Medicine. 1996. per. 43.75 (*0-02-864647-9*) Macmillan.

— World Meetings Vol. 19 No. 2: Medicine. 1996. per. 43.75 (*0-02-864648-7*) Macmillan.

— World Meetings Vol. 19 No. 3: Medicine. 1996. per. 43.75 (*0-02-864649-5*) Macmillan.

— World Meetings Vol. 19 No. 4: Medicine. 1996. per. 43.75 (*0-02-864650-9*) Macmillan.

— World Meetings Vol. 26: Social & Behavorial Sciences Human Service & Management 1996, 4 vols. 1995. per. 180.00 (*0-02-864641-X*) Macmillan.

— World Meetings Vol. 26 No. 1: Social & Behavioral Sciences Human Services & Management. 1996. per. 45.00 (*0-02-864642-8*) Macmillan.

— World Meetings Vol. 26, No. 2: Social & Behavioral Sciences, Human Services & Management. 1996. per. 45.00 (*0-02-864643-6*) Macmillan.

— World Meetings Vol. 26 No. 4: Social & Behavorial Sciences, Human Service & Mgmt. 1996. per. 45.00 (*0-02-864645-2*) Macmillan.

— World Meetings Vol. 26 No.3: Social & Behavorial Sciences, Human Services & Management. 1996. per. 45.00 (*0-02-864644-4*) Macmillan.

— World Meetings Vol. 29: Outside United States & Canada 1996, 4 vols. 1995. per. 195.00 (*0-02-864636-3*) Macmillan.

— World Meetings Vol. 29 No. 1: Outside United States & Canada. 1996. per. 48.75 (*0-02-864637-1*) Macmillan.

— World Meetings Vol. 29 No. 2: Outside United States & Canada. 1996. per. 48.75 (*0-02-864638-X*) Macmillan.

— World Meetings Vol. 29 No. 3: Outside United States & Canada. 1996. pap. 48.75 (*0-02-864639-8*) Macmillan.

— World Meetings Vol. 29 No. 3: Outside United States & Canada. 1996. per. 48.75 (*0-02-864640-1*) Macmillan.

— World Meetings Vol. 34: United States & Canada, 1996, 4 vols. 1995. per. 195.00 (*0-02-864631-2*) Macmillan.

— World Meetings Vol. 34 No. 1: United States & Canada. 1996. per. 48.75 (*0-02-864632-0*) Macmillan.

— World Meetings Vol. 34 No. 2: United States & Canada. 1996. per. 48.75 (*0-02-864633-9*) Macmillan.

— World Meetings Vol. 34 No. 3: United States & Canada. 1996. per. 48.75 (*0-02-864634-7*) Macmillan.

— World Meetings Vol. 34 No. 4: United States & Canada. 1996. per. 48.75 (*0-02-864635-5*) Macmillan.

Macmillan Publishing Company Staff, ed. Atlas Package, 4 bks., Set. large type ed. (Illus.). 1991. 385.00 (*0-02-897301-1*) Macmillan.

— The Book of the World: With Digital Atlas Cdrom. (Illus.). 608p. 1995. 450.00 (*0-02-860811-9*) Macmillan.

— Cowboy Almanac. 1997. 12.95 (*0-02-860408-3*) Macmillan.

— Explore BBQ Cooking. 1985. 9.32 (*0-02-663710-3*) Macmillan.

— Forensic Handbook. 1995. 25.00 (*0-02-860409-1*) Macmillan.

— International Encyclopedia of Social Sciences, Vols. 16 & 17. 1996. 60.00 (*0-02-864733-5*) Mac Lib Ref.

— Seventeen Teen Body Book. (YA). Date not set. 14.95 (*0-02-043975-X*) Macmillan.

***Macmillan Publishing Company Staff & Koch, Ed T.** Investing Like a Pro. (Complete Idiot's Guides (Lifestyle) Ser.). (Illus.). 330p. 1999. 16.95 (*0-02-862044-5*) Macmillan Gen Ref.

Macmillan Publishing Company Staff, et al. Macmillan Field Guides: Rocks & Minerals. (Illus.). 192p. 1985. pap. 12.95 (*0-02-079640-4*) Macmillan.

***Macmillan, R. & Lisansky, S. G., eds.** Global Cosmetic Regulatory Harmonization: An Impetus to the Development of Export Markets: Proceedings of an International Cosmetic Industry Congress, Florence, 1998. (Illus.). 120p. 1998. 90.00 (*1-872691-81-1*, CPL Pr) CPL Sci Pub.

Macmillan Reference Library. Macmillan Profiles: Heroes of the Holocaust. LC 98-56458. (Profiles Ser.). 1999. 75.00 (*0-02-865362-9*) Macmillan.

***Macmillan Reference Library.** Understanding the Holocaust: A Student's Guide. (Illus.). (YA). 2000. 325.00 (*0-02-865536-2*, Macmillan Ref) Mac Lib Ref.

Macmillan Staff. A to Z Guide to Alcohol. 1998. per. 75.00 (*0-02-864967-2*) Macmillan.

— A to Z Guide to Drugs. 1998. per. 75.00 (*0-02-864968-0*) Macmillan.

— A to Z Guide Tobacco Caffeine. 1998. per. 75.00 (*0-02-864969-9*) S&S Trade.

— Artists & Musicians. (Macmillan Profiles Ser.). 1998. per. 75.00 (*0-02-864980-X*) Macmillan.

— Career Information Center, 13 vols. 7th ed. LC 95-4929. 2080p. 1999. 275.00 (*0-02-864915-X*) Macmillan.

— College Blue Book. 26th ed. (College Blue Book (5 Vol.)). 1997. 245.00 (*0-02-864758-0*) Macmillan.

— Compendium of World Religions: Mac Comp World Relig. LC 97-25525. 1200p. 1997. 125.00 (*0-02-864918-4*) Mac Lib Ref.

— Macmillan Compendium: Sex, Genetics & Human Reproduction. LC 97-25526. 1152p. 1997. 125.00 (*0-02-864919-2*) Mac Lib Ref.

— Macmillan Compendium: The Confederacy. LC 97-23462. 1200p. 1997. 125.00 (*0-02-864920-6*) Mac Lib Ref.

— Macmillan Compendium America at War: Selected Biographies from the Three-Volume Encyclopedia of the American Military. LC 98-41961. 846p. 1998. 115.00 (*0-02-865061-1*) Mac Lib Ref.

***Macmillan Staff.** Macmillan Compendium of How Government Works. LC 98-49352. 1200p. 1998. per. 125.00 (*0-02-864975-3*) Macmillan Gen Ref.

Macmillan Staff. Macmillan Quick Reference Encyclopedia: Tobacco & Caffeine. 1998. 24.95 (*0-02-864957-5*) Macmillan.

— The Macmillan World Atlas. LC 95-34908. (Illus.). 440p. 1996. 59.95 (*0-02-860812-7*) Macmillan.

— Military Leaders. (Macmillan Profiles Ser.). 1998. per. 75.00 (*0-02-864981-8*) Macmillan.

— Pique, Vol. 2. 1992. pap. 10.00 (*0-688-11974-3*, Wm Morrow) Morrow Avon.

Macmillan Staff, ed. School Dictionary, 2 vols., No. 1. (J). (gr. 3-5). 1989. pap. 25.00 (*0-02-195003-2*) Macmillan.

— School Dictionary, 2 vols., No. 2. (YA). (gr. 6-8). 1989. pap. 23.93 (*0-02-195004-0*) Macmillan.

MacMillan, Stuart B. The Creeping Crud. LC 90-232129. 33p. 1990. write for info. (*0-573-69211-4*) S French Trade.

***Macmillan Technical Publishing Staff.** Cisco IOS. (CCIE Professional Development Ser.). 2000. pap. 55.00 (*1-57870-181-3*) Cisco Press.

Macmillan Technical Publishing Staff. MBONE: Interactive Multimedia on the Internet. 2nd ed. 350p. 44.99 (*1-57870-019-1*) Macmillan Tech.

Macmillan Travel Staff. The Complete Idiot's Guide to Mexico's Resorts. LC 97-1156. (Complete Idiot's Travel Guide Ser.). (Illus.). 464p. 1998. pap. 18.95 (*0-02-862579-X*) Macmillan Gen Ref.

Macmillan Travel Staff, ed. Barcelona, Madrid & Seville. 2nd ed. (Frommer's Barcelona, Madrid & Seville Ser.). 1999. pap. 14.95 (*0-02-862368-1*, Frommer) Macmillan Gen Ref.

— Ireland. 1999th ed. (Frommer's Travel Guides Ser.). 560p. 1999. pap. write for info. (*0-02-862326-6*, Frommer) Macmillan Gen Ref.

— Los Angeles. 1999th ed. (Frommer's Travel Guides Ser.). 320p. 1999. pap. 14.95 (*0-02-862358-4*, Frommer) Macmillan Gen Ref.

— Munich & the Bavarian Alps. 2nd ed. (Frommer's Travel Guides Ser.). 1999. pap. 14.95 (*0-02-862369-X*, Frommer) Macmillan Gen Ref.

— New Mexico. 5th ed. (Frommer's New Mexico Ser.). 1999. pap. 15.95 (*0-02-862371-1*, Frommer) Macmillan Gen Ref.

— Rome. 1999th ed. (Frommer's Travel Guides Ser.). 272p. 1999. pap. write for info. (*0-02-862365-7*, Frommer) Macmillan Gen Ref.

Macmillan Travel Staff & Graham, Rick. The Complete Idiot's Travel Guide to Las Vegas. (Complete Idiot's Travel Guide Ser.). 256p. 1998. pap. 15.95 (*0-02-862299-5*) Macmillan Gen Ref.

Macmillan Travel Staff & Tevis, Paula. The Complete Idiot's Travel Guide to San Francisco & the Wine Country. (Complete Idiot's Travel Guide Ser.). 253p. 1998. pap. 15.95 (*0-02-862304-5*) Macmillan Gen Ref.

Macmillan Travel Staff & Wohlforth, Charles P. Family Vacations in the National Parks. (Frommer's National Park Guides Ser.). (Illus.). 528p. 1999. pap. 18.95 (*0-02-861845-9*, Frommer) Macmillan Gen Ref.

Macmillan Travel Staff, et al. The Complete Idiot's Travel Guide to New Orleans. (Complete Idiot's Guide Ser.). (Illus.). 286p. 1998. pap. text 15.95 (*0-02-862303-7*) Macmillan Gen Ref.

— The Complete Idiot's Travel Guide to New York City. (Complete Idiot's Travel Guide Ser.). 284p. 1998. pap. 15.95 (*0-02-862297-9*) Macmillan Gen Ref.

— The Complete Idiot's Travel Guide to Walt Disney World. (Complete Idiot's Travel Guide Ser.). 288p. 1998. pap. 15.95 (*0-02-862298-7*) Macmillan Gen Ref.

Macmillan United Kingdom Staff & The Daily Telegraph Staff, eds. Diana Remembered 1961-1997. (Illus.). 120p. 1997. 19.95 (*0-333-73474-2*, Pub. by Macmillan) Trans-Atl Phila.

MacMillan, W. Duncan, et al. MacMillan: The American Grain Family. LC 98-10694. xi, 336 p. 1998. 30.00 (*1-890434-04-3*) Afton Hist Soc.

Macmillan, William M. Bantu, Boer, & Briton: The Making of the South African Native Problem. LC 78-27446. (Illus.). 382p. 1979. reprint ed. lib. bdg. 35.00 (*0-313-20906-5*, MABB, Greenwood Pr) Greenwood.

— The Road to Self-Rule: A Study in Colonial Evolution. LC 77-140365. (Select Bibliographies Reprint Ser.). 1977. reprint ed. 21.95 (*0-8369-5608-7*) Ayer.

— Warning from the West Indies. LC 73-160982. (Select Bibliographies Reprint Ser.). 1977. reprint ed. 25.95 (*0-8369-5850-0*) Ayer.

Macmillian & Library Reference Staff. Macmillian Profiles: African American Women. LC 98-56447. (Profiles Ser.). 1999. 75.00 (*0-02-865363-7*, Macmillan Coll) P-H.

Macmillian & Library Reference Staff. World Meetings no. 2: Medicine, vol. 20. 1997. per. 43.75 (*0-02-864809-9*) Macmillan.

— World Meetings no. 3: Outside United States & Canada , vol. 30. 1997. per. 48.75 (*0-02-864800-5*) Macmillan.

— World Meetings no. 30: Medicine , vol. 20. 1997. per. 43.75 (*0-02-864810-2*) CDG Bks.

— World Meetings no.1-4: United States & Canada,1997, vol.35. 1996. per. 195.00 (*0-02-864797-1*) S&S Trade.

— World Meetings no.3: United States & Canada , vol.35. 1997. per. 48.75 (*0-02-864795-5*) S&S Trade.

— World Meetings No.4, Vol.20. 1997. per. 43.75 (*0-02-864811-0*) Macmillan.

— World Meetings no.4: Medicine , 1997, vol.20. 1996. per. 175.00 (*0-02-864812-9*) S&S Trade.

MacMillian, Daniel. Golfing in Idaho & Montana. 1996. pap. text 10.95 (*1-878591-17-7*) Mac Prodns.

Macmillian, H. F. A Handbook for Tropical Planting & Gardening. 560p. 1984. 400.00 (*81-85046-12-3*, Pub. by Scientific) St Mut.

MacMillian, Margaret & Kislenko, Arne. The Uneasy Century: International Relations, 1900-1990. 244p. (C). 1996. pap. text, per. 40.95 (*0-7872-2217-8*, 41221701) Kendall-Hunt.

Macmillian Publishing Company, Inc. Staff. American Life. LC 98-49351. (Macmillan Information Now Encyclopedias Ser.). 700p. 1998. per. 39.95 (*0-02-865015-8*) Macmillan.

— United States History. (Macmillan Information Now Encyclopedias Ser.). 700p. 1998. 39.95 (*0-02-865016-6*) Macmillan.

MacMillian Publishing Company Staff. Maximum Windows 2000 Security. 1000p. 1999. 39.99 (*0-672-31581-5*) Macmillan.

MacMillian Publishing Company Staff, ed. Stranger. 1969. 3.95 (*0-671-00757-2*, Arco) Macmillan Gen Ref.

MacMinn, Ney, et al. Bibliography of the Published Writings of John Stuart Mill: Edited from His Manuscript with Corrections & Note (1945 Edition) 120p. 1996. reprint ed. 36.00 (*1-85506-046-9*) Bks Intl VA.

MacMirr, Richard, ed. see Koertge, Ron & Rocamona, Mary.

MacMitchell, Melanie. Sacred Footsteps: A Traveler's Guide to Spiritual Places of Italy & France. (Illus.). 164p. (Orig.). 1991. pap. 9.95 (*0-9629727-0-3*) Opal Star Pr.

***MacMorran, Kenneth M.** Handbook for Churchwardens & Parochial Church Councilors. (Illus.). 2000. pap. 16.95 (*0-264-67486-3*) A R Mowbray.

MacMullan, Jackie, jt. auth. see Bird, Larry.

MacMullen, Grace R. Pain: The Gift Nobody Wants. (Joyful Living Ser.). 1986. pap. 2.50 (*0-912623-00-4*) Joyful Woman.

MacMullen, Jerry, jt. auth. see McNairn, Jack.

MacMullen, Ramsay. Christianity & Paganism in the Fourth to Eighth Centuries. LC 97-7786. 272p. 1997. 40.00 (*0-300-07148-5*) Yale U Pr.

***MacMullen, Ramsay.** Christianity & Paganism in the Fourth to Eighth Centuries. (Illus.). 288p. 1999. 16.00 (*0-300-08077-8*) Yale U Pr.

MacMullen, Ramsay. Christianizing the Roman Empire: A.D. 100-400. LC 84-3694. 200p. 1986. pap. 16.00 (*0-300-03642-6*, Y-571) Yale U Pr.

— Constantine. (Classical Lives Ser.). 272p. 1987. pap. 14.95 (*0-7099-4685-6*, Pub. by C Helm) Routldge.

— Corruption & the Decline of Rome. 331p. (C). 1990. reprint ed. pap. 18.00 (*0-300-04799-1*) Yale U Pr.

— Enemies of the Roman Order. LC 92-18399. 384p. (C). 1993. pap. 27.99 (*0-415-08621-3*, A9752) Routledge.

— Enemies of the Roman Order: Treason, Unrest, & Alienation in the Empire. LC 66-18250. (Illus.). 386p. reprint ed. pap. 119.70 (*0-7837-1717-2*, 205724600024) Bks Demand.

— Paganism in the Roman Empire. LC 80-54222. 384p. 1983. pap. 16.00 (*0-300-02984-5*) Yale U Pr.

— Roman Government's Response to Crisis, A.D. 235-337. LC 75-43324. 320p. reprint ed. pap. 99.20 (*0-8357-8311-1*, 203381000087) Bks Demand.

— Roman Social Relations, 50 B. C to A. D. 284. LC 73-86909. 317p. 1981. pap. 16.00 (*0-300-02702-8*, Y-392) Yale U Pr.

***MacMullen, Ramsay.** Romanization in the Time of Augustus. LC 00-28108. (Illus.). 240p. 2000. 25.00 (*0-300-08254-1*) Yale U Pr.

MacMullen, Ramsay. Sisters of the Brush: Their Family, Art, Life & Letters 1797-1833. LC 97-92193. (Illus.). 550p. 1997. 29.00 (*0-9658780-0-7*) PastTimes Pr.

— Soldier & Civilian in the Later Roman Empire. LC 63-7591. (Historical Monographs: No. 52). (Illus.). 224p. 1963. 15.00 (*0-674-81690-0*) HUP.

MacMullen, Ramsay & Lane, Eugene N., eds. Paganism & Christianity, 100-425 C.E. A Sourcebook. LC 92-3069. 224p. (Orig.). 1992. pap. 20.00 (*0-8006-2647-8*, 1-2647, Fortress Pr) Augsburg Fortress.

MacMunn, George & Falls, Cyril. Military Operations, Egypt & Palestine, Vol. I. (Great War Ser.: Vol. 46). (Illus.). 469p. 1996. reprint ed. 49.95 (*0-89839-241-1*) Battery Pr.

MacMunn, George F. Leadership Through the Ages. LC 68-16951. (Essay Index Reprint Ser.). 1977. 19.95 (*0-8369-0657-8*) Ayer.

MacMurray, J. W., ed. see Pearson, Jonathan, et al.

MacMurray, Jessica M., ed. 101 Opera Librettos: Complete Texts with English Translations of the World's Best Loved Operas. 1482p. 1996. 29.98 (*1-884822-79-7*) Blck Dog & Leventhal.

MacMurray, John. By Chance? Landscapes from the Canvas of the Creator. LC 97-42935. (Landscapes from the Canvas of the Creator Ser.). (Illus.). 80p. 1998. 21.99 (*1-57673-297-5*, Multnomah Gift Bks) Multnomah Pubs.

***MacMurray, John.** By Chance Calendar. 1998. pap. 11.99 (*1-57673-461-7*) Multables.

Macmurray, John. Conditions of Freedom. LC 93-9222. 108p. (C). 1993. reprint ed. pap. 15.00 (*0-391-03714-5*) Humanities.

MacMurray, John. The Form of the Personal, 2 vols., Set. LC 77-27175. (Gifford Lectures: 1953-54). reprint ed. 37.50 (*0-404-60550-8*) AMS Pr.

Macmurray, John. Freedom in the Modern World. LC 91-32303. 200p. (C). 1992. pap. 15.00 (*0-391-03728-5*) Humanities.

— Interpreting the Universe. LC 93-20101. 112p. (C). 1996. reprint ed. pap. 15.00 (*0-391-03818-4*) Humanities.

— Persons in Relation. LC 91-21420. 256p. (C). 1991. pap. 17.50 (*0-391-03716-1*) Humanities.

— Persons in Relation. LC 98-54284. 1998. write for info. (*1-57392-625-6*, Humanity Bks) Prometheus Bks.

— Reason & Emotion. LC 91-32302. 232p. (C). 1992. pap. 17.50 (*0-391-03729-3*) Humanities.

— Self As Agent. LC 91-21419. 232p. (C). 1991. pap. 17.50 (*0-391-03715-3*) Humanities.

MacMurray, John. Self as Agent. 1991. pap. 23.00 (*1-57392-337-0*) Prometheus Bks.

Macmurray, John, ed. Some Makers of the Modern Spirit: A Symposium. LC 68-22926. (Essay Index Reprint Ser.). 1977. reprint ed. 18.95 (*0-8369-0658-6*) Ayer.

MacMurray, Robert R. Technological Change in the American Cotton Spinning Industry, 1790-1836. Bruchey, Stuart, ed. LC 76-39835. (Nineteen Seventy-Seven Dissertations Ser.). (Illus.). 1977. lib. bdg. 62.95 (*0-405-09915-0*) Ayer.

***MacMurrough, Sorcha.** Call Home the Heart. 244p. 2000. 18.95 (*1-58345-072-6*) Domhan Bks.

— The Sea of Love. 148p. 2000. 15.95 (*1-58345-032-7*); pap. 10.00 (*1-58345-033-5*) Domhan Bks.

MacMurrough, Sorcha. The Sea of Love: An Historical Romance. LC 98-66689. 325p. 1998. 25.00 (*0-7388-0069-4*); pap. 15.00 (*0-7388-0070-8*) Xlibris Corp.

MacNab. Care of the Critically Ill Child. 1999. text 79.00 (*0-443-05394-4*, W B Saunders Co) Harcrt Hlth Sci Grp.

MacNab, Alan A., jt. auth. see Sherf, Arden F.

***Macnab, Angus.** Spain under the Crescent Moon. 1999. pap. 35.00 (*1-887752-21-8*) Fons Vitae.

Macnab, Angus, tr. see Guenon, Rene.

MacNab, F. A Ride in Morocco. 400p. 1985. 220.00 (*1-85077-071-9*, Pub. by Darf Pubs Ltd) St Mut.

Macnab, Francis. Brief Psychotherapy: CMT. 342p. 1993. pap. 89.95 (*0-471-94078-X*) Wiley.

Macnab, Geoffrey. J. Arthur Rank & the British Film Industry. (Cinema & Society Ser.). (Illus.). 320p. (C). 1994. pap. 22.99 (*0-415-11711-9*, B4597) Routledge.

***Macnab, Geoffrey.** Searching for Stars: Stardom & Screen Acting in British Cinema LC 99-27248. (Rethinking British Cinema Ser.). 2000. 24.95 (*0-304-33352-2*) Continuum.

Macnab, Ian. Neck Ache & Shoulder Pain. (Illus.). 528p. 1994. 69.00 (*0-683-05354-X*) Lppncott W & W.

Macnab, Ian & McCulloch, John A. Backache. 2nd ed. (Illus.). 448p. 1989. 62.00 (*0-683-05352-3*) Lppncott W & W.

Macnab, Peter. Highways & Byways in Mull & Iona. LC 99-185028. (C). 1989. pap. 9.95 (*0-946487-16-2*) Luath Pr Ltd.

An Asterisk (*) at the beginning of an entry indicates that the title is appearing for the first time.

***Macnab, Peter.** Mull & Iona: Highways & Byways, the Fairest of the Inner Hebridean Isles & Scotland's Great Centre of "Celtic Christianity" (Guides to Scotland Ser.). (Illus.). 128p. 1999. pap. 9.95 (0-946487-58-8, Pub. by Luath Pr Ltd) Midpt Trade.

Macnab, Peter. Tall Tales from an Island. (Illus.). 192p. 1999. pap. 14.95 (0-946487-07-3, Pub. by Luath Pr Ltd) Midpt Trade.

MacNabb, Elizabeth L. The Fractured Family: The Second Sex & Its (Dis) Connected Daughters. LC 92-34830. (Writing about Women Ser.: Vol. 5). XII, 210p. (C). 1993. text 46.95 (0-8204-1881-1) P Lang Pubng.

***MacNabb, Elizabeth L.** Transforming the Disciplines: A Women's Studies Primer. LC 00-40739. 2000. pap. write for info. (1-56023-960-3) Haworth Pr.

Macnaghten, Angus. Haunted Berkshire. 96p. 1987. pap. 30.00 (0-905392-58-2) St Mut.

MacNaghten, Hugh. Emile Coue: The Man & His Work. 52p. 1993. pap. 5.00 (0-89540-230-0, SB-230) Sun Pub.

Macnaghten, Phil & Urry, John. Contested Natures. LC 97-62443. (Theory, Culture & Society Ser.). viii, 307p. 1998. pap. write for info. (0-7619-5313-2) Sage.

MacNair, Donald J. The Challenge of the Eldership: A Handbook for the Elders of the Church. (Orig.). 1984. pap. 1.95 (0-934688-12-5) Great Comm Pubns.

— The Living Church: A Guide for Revitalization. (Illus.). 167p. (Orig.). 1980. pap. 5.95 (0-934688-00-1) Great Comm Pubns.

MacNair, Donald J. & Meek, Esther L. The Practices of a Healthy Church: Biblical Strategies for Vibrant Church Life & Ministry. LC 99-26138. 256p. 1999. pap. 11.99 (0-87552-390-0) P & R Pubng.

MacNair, Edward A., et al, eds. Winter Simulation Conference Proceedings: Washington, DC, 1989. 1140p. 1989. 130.00 (0-911801-58-8, WSC-89) Soc Computer Sim.

MacNair, Harley F. The Real Conflict Between China & Japan: An Analysis of Opposing Ideologies. LC DS0721.M3. (Double-Page Reprint Ser.). 116p. reprint ed. pap. 36.00 (0-608-14351-0, 202011400016) Bks Demand.

MacNair, Harley F., ed. China. LC 71-134111. (Essay Index Reprint Ser.). 1977. 39.95 (0-8369-1987-4) Ayer.

Macnair, Ian. Teach Yourself New Testament Greek. LC 94-45016. 512p. 1995. pap., student ed. 16.99 (0-8407-1151-4) Nelson.

MacNair, Mary W. American Doctoral Dissertations. 1973. 250.00 (0-87968-598-0) Gordon Pr.

Macnair, Peter L., et al. The Legacy. (Illus.). 194p. 1984. reprint ed. pap. 29.95 (0-295-96166-X) U of Wash Pr.

MacNair, Rachel, et al. Prolife Feminism: Yesterday & Today. 380p. (Orig.). 1995. pap. 14.99 (0-945819-62-5) Sulzburger & Graham Pub.

MacNair, Ray & McKinney, Elizabeth. Assessment of Child & Adolescent Functioning: A Practitioner's Instrument for Assessing Clients. LC 83-26602. 75p. 1983. pap. 4.50 (0-911847-02-2) U GA Inst Community.

MacNair, Ray H., ed. Research Strategies in Community Practice. LC 98-27529. 123p. 1998. 29.95 (0-7890-0529-8) Haworth Pr.

MacNair, William. Computer Fact Book, 3 vols., Set. Incl. Vol. I. 39p. lib. bdg. 39.95 (0-941303-31-4); Vol. I. 39p. pap. 12.50 (0-941303-01-2); Vol. II. 40p. lib. bdg. 39.95 (0-941303-32-2); Vol. II. 40p. pap. text 12.50 (0-941303-02-0); Vol. III. 41p. lib. bdg. 39.95 (0-941303-33-0); Vol. III. 41p. pap. 12.50 (0-941303-03-9); (Illus.). (Orig.). Set pap. 37.50 (0-941303-21-7); Set lib. bdg. 99.95 (0-941303-22-5) Comput & Arts Pubns.

— Dictionary of Computer & Video Terms. (Illus.). 87p. (Orig.). 1987. pap. 14.50 (0-941303-05-5); lib. bdg. 49.95 (0-941303-35-7) Comput & Arts Pubns.

MacNair, Wilmer. Basic Thinking: On Beginning at the Beginning in Thinking about Social & Economic Problems. LC 94-44029. 360p. (C). 1995. pap. text 32.50 (0-8191-9841-2); lib. bdg. 59.00 (0-8191-9840-4) U Pr of Amer.

MacNally, Lea. The Highland Year. LC 98-218269. 144p. 1998. pap. 19.95 (1-874744-77-7, Pub. by Birlinn Ltd) Dufour.

MacNally, Ralph C. Ecological Versatility & Community Ecology. (Studies in Ecology). (Illus.). 453p. (C). 1995. text 85.00 (0-521-40553-X) Cambridge U Pr.

Macnamara, Angela. Ready Steady Grow! 1989. pap. 22.00 (0-86217-166-0, Pub. by Veritas Pubns) St Mut.

MacNamara, Brinsley. The Clanking of Chains. Date not set. pap. 8.95 (0-900068-48-5) Dufour.

— The Clanking of Chains. 174p. 1965. 14.95 (0-900068-91-4) Dufour.

— The Valley of the Squinting Windows. 1996. pap. 14.95 (0-900068-83-3) Dufour.

— The Valley of the Squinting Windows. 2nd ed. 224p. 1996. reprint ed. pap. 13.95 (0-947962-01-8, Pub. by Anvil Books Ltd) Irish Bks Media.

— The Various Lives of Marcus Igoe. LC 96-772. 237p. 1996. pap. 13.95 (0-8023-1303-3) Dufour.

MacNamara, Desmond. The Book of Intrusions. LC 93-36126. 214p. 1994. 19.95 (1-56478-041-4) Dalkey Arch.

MacNamara, Donal E. & Karmen, Andrew, eds. Deviants: Victims or Victimizers? LC 83-17825. (Sage Annual Reviews of Studies in Deviance: No. 7). (Illus.). 256p. reprint ed. pap. 79.40 (0-8357-4768-9, 203770500009) Bks Demand.

MacNamara, Donal E. & McCorkle, Llyod. Crime, Criminals & Corrections. LC 81-84361. 304p. 1982. pap. text 15.00 (0-89444-033-0); lib. bdg. 17.00 (0-89444-032-2) John Jay Pr.

MacNamara, Donal E. & Stead, Philip J. New Dimensions in Transnational Crime. 154p. 1982. lib. bdg. 10.00 (0-89444-035-7) John Jay Pr.

Macnamara, Ellen. The Etruscans. (British Museum Ser.). (Illus.). 72p. 1991. pap. 14.00 (0-674-26907-1, MACETX) HUP.

MacNamara, H. Practical Treatise on Nullities & Irregularities in Law: Their Character, Distinctions, & Consequences. xx, 231p. 1996. reprint ed. 37.50 (0-8377-2481-3, Rothman) W S Hein.

Macnamara, Jim. The Modern Presenters Handbook. 144p. (C). 1996. pap. text 14.95 (0-13-842154-4) P-H.

MacNamara, John. A Border Dispute: The Place of Logic in Psychology. (Learning, Development & Conceptual Change Ser.). 230p. 1986. 27.50 (0-262-13216-8, Bradford Bks) MIT Pr.

Macnamara, John. Through the Rearview Mirror: Historical Reflections on Psychology. LC 98-50264. (Illus.). 361p. 1999. 37.50 (0-262-13352-0) MIT Pr.

Macnamara, N. C. The Story of an Irish Sept: The Origin & History of the MacNamaras. LC 99-221959. 1999. reprint ed. 45.00 (0-9519551-1-X) M Breen.

Macnamara, Paul. Those Were the Days, My Friend: My Life in Hollywood with David O. Selznick & Others. LC 93-32129. (Filmmakers Ser.: No. 35). (Illus.). 207p. 1993. 32.00 (0-8108-2694-1) Scarecrow.

MacNamara, Rejda. Personal Financial Planning. 6th ed. LC 97-21669. 648p. (C). 1997. 92.00 (0-321-00927-4) Addson-Wesley Educ.

MacNamara, Roger D. Creating Abuse-Free Caregiving Environments for Children, the Disabled, & the Elderly: Preparing, Supervising, & Managing Caregivers for the Emotional Impact of Their Responsibilities. 270p. 1992. pap. 35.95 (0-398-06261-7) C C Thomas.

— Creating Abuse-Free Caregiving Environments for Children, the Disabled, & the Elderly: Preparing, Supervising, & Managing Caregivers for the Emotional Impact of Their Responsibilities. 270p. (C). 1992. text 49.95 (0-398-05761-3) C C Thomas.

— Freedom from Abuse in Organized Care Settings for the Elderly & Handicapped: Lessons from Human Service Administration. 104p. 1988. pap. 23.95 (0-398-06262-5) C C Thomas.

— Freedom from Abuse in Organized Care Settings for the Elderly & Handicapped: Lessons from Human Service Administration. 104p. (C). 1988. text 35.95 (0-398-05493-2) C C Thomas.

MacNamara, Thomas J., jt. auth. see Plant, Jeremy F.

MacNamara, Vincent. Faith & Ethics: Recent Roman Catholicism. LC 85-5539. 261p. reprint ed. pap. 81.00 (0-7837-6701-3, 204633300011) Bks Demand.

MacNamee, Brian & MacDonnell, Ray. The Marketing Casebase: Short Examples of Marketing Practice. LC 94-31229. 240p. (C). 1995. pap. 14.99 (0-415-10321-5, C0029) Thomson Learn.

MacNamee, Verda. Verda: An Artist Sketches Europe, 1951. LC 90-70192. 100p. (Orig.). 1990. pap. 14.95 (0-9625879-0-7) Wilde Pr.

MacNaughto, Mary Davis, et al. Revolution in Clay: The Marer Collection of Contemporary Ceramics. (Ruth Chandler Williamson Gallery Ser.). (Illus.). 181p. 1994. pap. 29.95 (0-295-97405-2) Williamson Gallery.

MacNaughton, Edgar. Elementary Steam Power Engineering. LC 48-7834. 654p. reprint ed. pap. 200.00 (0-608-30505-7, 205526300011) Bks Demand.

MacNaughton, Jane, jt. auth. see Downie, Robin.

MacNaughton, Mary. Larger Than Life: Robert Rahway Zakanitch's Big Bungalow Suite. LC 98-119042. (Illus.). 46p. 1998. pap. 14.95 (0-295-97672-1) U of Wash Pr.

MacNaughton, Mary D. Art at Scripps: The Early Years. (Illus.). 48p. 1987. 6.00 (0-915478-56-0) Williamson Gallery.

— Crossing the Line: Word & Image in Art, 1960-1990. (Illus.). 14p. 1990. 3.00 (0-685-51609-1) Montgomery Gallery.

— New California Printmaking: Selections from Northern & Southern California. (Illus.). 20p. 1987. 3.00 (0-915478-55-2) Williamson Gallery.

MacNaughton, Mary D., jt. auth. see Alloway, Lawrence.

MacNaughton, Robert D. Seventh Goswami: Biography of Bhaktivinode Thakur. (Lives of Vaisnava Acaryas Ser.: Vol. 2). (Illus.). 300p. (C). 1989. pap. 12.95 (0-923519-02-5) New Jaipur.

MacNaughton, Robert D., see Rupa Vitasa Dasa, pseud.

MacNaughton, Robert L. Yankee Team. 76p. 1996. reprint ed. pap. 12.00 (0-923135-31-6) Dalley Bk Service.

MacNaughton, Robin. Goddess Power: A Woman's Sun Sign Guide to Help Rediscover Feminine Strengths. 1996. mass mkt. 5.99 (0-671-88181-7) PB.

— How to Seduce Any Man in the Zodiac. Todd, Rebecca, ed. 128p. 1995. mass mkt. 5.99 (0-671-86803-9) PB.

— Power Astrology: Make the Most of Your Sun Sign. 287p. 1990. mass mkt. 6.99 (0-671-67181-2) PB.

— Robin MacNaughton's Sun Sign Personality Guide. 512p. 1997. mass mkt. 7.99 (0-553-27380-9) Bantam.

Macnaughton, Robin. Why Does He Say One Thing & Do Another? LC 97-114959. 1997. per. 5.99 (0-671-00207-4) PB.

MacNaughton, William R. Mark Twain's Last Years As a Writer. LC 78-19846. 264p. reprint ed. pap. 81.90 (0-7837-3201-5, AU0042900007) Bks Demand.

MacNaughtton, Don. They Stood in the Door. 413p. 1985. 35.00 (0-7223-1752-2, Pub. by A H S Ltd) St Mut.

MacNeacail, Aonghas. A Proper Schooling: And Other Poems. 88p. 1996. pap. 13.95 (0-7486-6218-9, Pub. by Polygon) Subterranean Co.

— Rock & Water. 1990. 12.95 (0-7486-6065-8, Pub. by Polygon) Subterranean Co.

Macneacail, Aonghas. An Seachnadh: The Avoiding & Other Poems. (C). 1989. 39.00 (0-86334-058-X, Pub. by Saltire Soc) St Mut.

MacNeal, Donald L. The Flora of the Upper Cretaceous Woodbine Sand in Denton County, Texas. (Monograph: No. 10). (Illus.). 152p. (Orig.). 1958. pap. 6.00 (0-910006-17-2) Acad Nat Sci Phila.

MacNeal, Edward. MacNeal's Master Atlas of Decision Making: A New Kind of Guide to the Maps People Use in Making up Their Minds. Joyner, Russell, ed. & comment by. LC 97-2441. (Illus.). 144p. (Orig.). 1997. pap. 19.95 (0-918970-44-X) Intl Gen Semantics.

— The Semantics of Air Passenger Transportation. LC 80-85432. (Illus.). 132p. 1981. 19.95 (0-9605682-0-4) Norfolk Port.

MacNeal, Kenneth. Truth in Accounting. LC 74-75709. 1970. reprint ed. text 30.00 (0-914348-04-3) Scholars Bk.

Macneal, Patricia M., et al, eds. Headwaters & Hardwoods. LC 96-70566. (Illus.). 208p. (Orig.). 1997. pap. 14.50 (0-9654340-0-1) Nrthrn Tier Cultural.

MacNeal, Richard H. Electric Circuit Analogies for Elastic Structures. LC 62-17465. (Airplane, Missile & Spacecraft Structures Ser.: Vol. 2). 278p. reprint ed. pap. 86.20 (0-608-30693-2, 200740100062) Bks Demand.

— Finite Elements: Their Design & Performance. (Illus.). 552p. 1993. text 155.00 (0-8247-9162-2) Dekker.

Macneal, W. Douglas, ed. Centre County Heritage 1976-1985. (Illus.). 424p. 1996. 15.00 (1-887315-09-8) Centre Cty Hist Soc.

MacNealy, Mary S. Strategies for Empirical Research in Writing. LC 98-4890. 260p. (C). 1998. pap. text 38.00 (0-205-27253-3) Allyn.

MacNealy, Mary S. & Kreuz, Roger J., eds. Empirical Approaches to Literature & Aesthetics. (Advances in Discourse Processes Ser.: Vol. 52). (Illus.). 729p. 1996. pap. 42.50 (1-56750-124-9) Ablx Pub.

MacNealy, Mary S., jt. ed. see Kreuz, Roger J.

MacNee, Marie J. Science Fiction, Fantasy, & Horror Writers, 2 vols. LC 94-32459. 480p. (J). 1994. text 55.00 (0-8103-9865-6, UXL) Gale.

Macnee, Marie J. & Hoehner, Jane. Outlaws, Mobsters & Crooks: From the Old West to the Internet. LC 98-14861. (J). 1998. 84.00 (0-7876-2806-9, UXL) Gale.

MacNee, Marie J. & Hoehner, Janes. Outlaws, Mobsters & Crooks: From the Old West to the Internet. LC 98-14861. (J). 1998. 84.00 (0-7876-2804-2, UXL); pap. 84.00 (0-7876-2805-0, UXL) Gale.

MacNee, Marie J., jt. auth. see Stein, Gordon.

Macnee, Patrick. The Avengers: Dead Duck. 160p. 1998. reprint ed. pap. 9.99 (1-57500-071-7, Pub. by TV Bks) HarpC.

MacNee, Patrick. Avengers: Deadline. LC 99-201998. (Illus.). 192p. 1998. pap. 9.99 (1-57500-072-5, Pub. by TV Bks) HarpC.

Macnee, Patrick. The Avengers & Me. (Illus.). 144p. 1998. pap. 22.00 (1-57500-059-8, Pub. by TV Bks) HarpC.

— Blind in One Ear: The Avenger Returns. LC 89-32147. 304p. 1992. pap. 9.95 (0-916515-85-0) Mercury Hse Inc.

Macneely, Jeff. Golf Tips: How to Succeed in Golf Without Really Trying. 1999. pap. text 9.95 (1-57243-327-2) Triumph Bks.

MacNeice, Corinna, jt. auth. see Dolphin, Johnny.

MacNeice, Louis. Modern Poetry: A Personal Essay. LC 77-95439. (Studies in Poetry: No. 38). (C). 1969. reprint ed. lib. bdg. 75.00 (0-8383-0992-5) M S G Haskell Hse.

— Selected Plays of Louis MacNeice. Heuser, Alan & McDonald, Peter, eds. 420p. 1994. text 58.00 (0-19-811245-9) OUP.

— Selected Prose of Louis MacNeice. Heuser, Alan, ed. 328p. 1990. text 55.00 (0-19-818525-1) OUP.

— Varieties of Parable. LC 66-10036. (Clark Lectures, 1963). 165p. reprint ed. pap. 47.10 (0-608-12053-7, 2024498) Bks Demand.

MacNeil. Burden of Desire. 576p. 1993. mass mkt. 7.99 (0-440-28000-1) Dell.

— Federal Arbitration Act. LC 93-77669. 1994. 150.00 (0-316-54291-1, Aspen Law & Bus) Aspen Pub.

— Federal Arbitration Act, Chapter 44. 1995. 70.00 (0-316-54334-9, Aspen Law & Bus) Aspen Pub.

— Federal Arbitration Act, Vol. 2. 1994. 150.00 (0-316-54293-8, Aspen Law & Bus) Aspen Pub.

— Federal Arbitration Act, Vol. 5. 1994. 150.00 (0-316-54307-1, Aspen Law & Bus) Aspen Pub.

MacNeil, Brian, tr. see Rise, Svein.

MacNeil, Duncan. By Command of the Viceroy. large type ed. 1979. 27.99 (0-7089-0341-X) Ulverscroft.

MacNeil, Greg. 200 Funniest Sports. 224p. 1995. mass mkt. 6.99 (0-7704-2720-0) Bantam.

MacNeil, Heather. Without Consent: The Ethics of Disclosing Personal Information in Public Archives. LC 92-16754. (Society of American Archivists Ser.). 230p. 1992. 31.50 (0-8108-2581-3) Scarecrow.

MacNeil Hesmer, Elizabeth, ed. see Cohen, Bruce P., et al.

MacNeil, Ian, jt. auth. see Sport Medicine Council of British Columbia Staff.

MacNeil, Ian B. & Umphrey, Gary J., eds. Advances in the Statistical Sciences, Vol. I: Applied Probability, Stochastic Processes & Sampling Theory. (C). 1986. lib. bdg. 139.00 (90-277-2393-1) Kluwer Academic.

— Advances in the Statistical Sciences, Vol. II: Foundations of Statistical Inference, Vol. II. 308p. (C). 1986. lib. bdg. 124.50 (90-277-2394-X, D Reidel) Kluwer Academic.

— Advances in the Statistical Sciences, Vol. IV: Stochastic Hydrology. (C). 1986. lib. bdg. 106.00 (90-277-2396-6) Kluwer Academic.

— Advances in the Statistical Sciences, Vol. V: Biostatistics. (C). 1986. lib. bdg. 124.50 (90-277-2397-4) Kluwer Academic.

— Advances in the Statistical Sciences, Vol. VI: Actuarial Science. (C). 1986. lib. bdg. 115.50 (90-277-2398-2) Kluwer Academic.

Macneil, Ian R. American Arbitration Law: Reformation - Nationalization - Internationalization. 288p. 1992. text 65.00 (0-19-507062-3) OUP.

MacNeil, Ian R. Contracts: Exchange Transactions & Relations, Cases & Materials. 2nd ed. (University Casebook Ser.). 1320p. 1989. reprint ed. text 42.00 (0-88277-432-8) Foundation Pr.

Macneil, Ian R. The New Social Contract: An Inquiry into Modern Contractual Relations. LC 80-5395. 180p. reprint ed. pap. 55.80 (0-7837-6218-6, 208022000004) Bks Demand.

MacNeil, James L. A Study of Gaudium et Spes 19-22, the Second Vatican Council Response to Contemporary Atheism. LC 97-42273. 396p. 1997. 99.95 (0-7734-8431-0) E Mellen.

***MacNeil, Joan & MacNeil, Robin.** Twin Babies, Twin Babies. (Illus.). 16p. (J). 2000. pap. 5.95 (1-891846-17-5) Busn Word.

MacNeil, Joe N. Tales until Dawn: The World of a Cape Breton Gaelic Story-Teller. Shaw, John W., ed. (ENG & GAE.). 528p. 1987. 75.00 (0-7735-0559-8, Pub. by McG-Queens Univ Pr); pap. 24.95 (0-7735-0560-1, Pub. by McG-Queens Univ Pr) CUP Services.

***MacNeil, Karen.** The Wine Bible. 676p. 2001. pap. 17.95 (1-56305-434-5) Workman Pub.

MacNeil, Kevin. Love & Zen in the Outer Hebrides. 1998. pap. 12.95 (0-86241-812-7, Pub. by Canongate Books) Interlink Pub.

***MacNeil, Madeline.** Shall We Gather/Hymns Arranged for Hammered Dulcimer. 56p. 1999. pap. 12.95 (0-7866-3844-3, 97204) Mel Bay.

MacNeil, Madeline. You Can Teach Yourself Dulcimer. 1989. audio 9.98 (0-87166-322-8, 94304C) Mel Bay.

— You Can Teach Yourself Dulcimer. 100p. 1989. pap. 9.95 (0-87166-266-3, 94304) Mel Bay.

— You Can Teach Yourself Dulcimer. 1993. pap. 18.95 incl. audio (0-87166-309-0, 94304P) Mel Bay.

— You Can Teach Yourself Dulcimer. 1995. VHS 29.95 (0-7866-0617-7, 94304VX) Mel Bay.

— You Can Teach Yourself Dulcimer. 100p. 1996. 24.95 incl. audio compact disk (0-7866-0987-7, 94304CDP); audio compact disk 15.98 (0-7866-0376-3, 94304CD) Mel Bay.

MacNeil, Madeline. You Can Teach Yourself Hammered Dulcimer. 88p. 1995. pap. 18.95 incl. audio (0-7866-0878-1, 95440P) Mel Bay.

— You Can Teach Yourself Hammered Dulcimer. 88p. 1999. pap. 17.95 incl. audio compact disk (0-7866-4850-3, 95440BCD) Mel Bay.

MacNeil, Maeline. You Can Teach Yourself Hammered Dulcimer. 88p. 1995. pap. 9.95 (0-7866-0456-5, 95440) Mel Bay.

MacNeil, N. The President's Medals. LC 76-49563. (Illus.). 1977. lib. bdg. 15.00 (0-517-52918-1) S J Durst.

MacNeil, Neil. Levon West. (Illus.). 16p. (Orig.). (C). 1968. pap. 6.00 (0-943526-33-7) Parrish Art.

MacNeil of Barra. MacNeil: The Clan MacNeil (Clann Niall) of Scotland. (Illus.). 227p. 1993. reprint ed. pap. 34.00 (0-8328-3370-3); reprint ed. lib. bdg. 44.00 (0-8328-3369-X) Higginson Bk Co.

MacNeil, Robert. Breaking News. LC 99-29222. 1999. pap. 13.00 (0-15-600763-0) Harcourt.

— Breaking News: A Novel. LC 98-19562. 384p. 1998. 24.95 (0-385-42020-X) Doubleday.

Macneil, Robert. Burden of Desire. LC 98-20927. (C). 1998. pap. 14.00 (0-15-600609-X, Harvest Bks) Harcourt.

MacNeil, Robert. Burden of Desire. large type ed. 1996. pap. 23.95 (1-56895-303-8) Wheeler Pub.

— The Canadian Feeling. 1999. pap. write for info. (0-14-013082-9); pap. write for info. (0-670-83179-4) Viking Penguin.

— Eudora Welty: Seeing Black & White. LC 90-12640. 1990. pap. 9.95 (0-87805-471-5) U Pr of Miss.

— The Voyage. 1997. mass mkt. 8.99 (0-7704-2736-7) Bantam.

— The Voyage. 1995. 23.95 (0-614-15473-1, N A Talese) Doubleday.

— The Voyage. large type ed. LC 96-28001. (Harvest Bks.). 304p. 1996. pap. 12.00 (0-15-600463-1) Harcourt.

— Wordstruck. 256p. 1990. pap. 12.95 (0-14-010401-1, Penguin Bks) Viking Penguin.

MacNeil, Robin, jt. auth. see MacNeil, Joan.

MacNeil, Sylvia. The Paris Collection: French Doll Fashions & Accessories. LC 92-203522. (Illus.). 192p. 1992. 29.95 (0-87588-372-9) Hobby Hse.

MacNeilage, P. F., ed. The Production of Speech. (Illus.). 302p. 1983. 107.00 (0-387-90735-1) Spr-Verlag.

***Macneill, Alastair.** The Devil's Door. large type ed. 512p. 2000. write for info. (0-7505-1525-2, Pub. by Mgna Lrg Print) Ulverscroft.

MacNeill, Alyson. Twenty-Three Wood Engravings. 1993. boxed set 80.00 (0-907664-16-4, Pub. by Old Stiles) St Mut.

— Twenty Three Wood Engravings from the Song of the Forest by Colin Mackay. 1993. 180.00 (0-907664-15-6, Pub. by Old Stiles) St Mut.

MacNeill, Alyson, contrib. by. Benedicite Omnia Opera. 64p. 1993. 190.00 (0-907664-11-3, Pub. by Old Stiles) St Mut.

MacNeill, Arthur, et al, eds. The Neuropsychology Handbook: Treatment Issues & Special Populations, Vol. 2. 2nd ed. (Illus.). 408p. 1997. 52.95 (0-8261-9731-0) Springer Pub.

MacNeill, Brian, tr. see Nordstokke, Kjell.

MacNeill, Debra J. Customer Service Excellence. LC 93-6. 112p. 1993. pap. 10.95 (1-55623-969-6, Irwn Prfssnl) McGraw-Hill Prof.

MacNeill, Debra J., jt. auth. see Schwartz, Roberta.

MacNeill, Dorothy. 22 Ready-to-Use Programs for Women's Groups. 136p. 1996. pap. 9.95 (0-687-05089-8) Abingdon.

M

M

Macneill, Hector. Poetical Works of Hector Macneill, 2 vols. LC 74-144453. reprint ed. 13.50 (*0-404-08565-2*) AMS Pr.

MacNeill, James H., jt. auth. see Roy, Robert H.

MacNeill, Jim, et al. Beyond Interdependence: The Meshing of the World's Economy & the Earth's Ecology. (Illus.). 192p. 1991. pap. text 8.95 (*0-19-507126-3*) OUP.

— CIDA & Sustainable Development: How Canada's Aid Policies Can Support Sustainable Development in the Third World More Effectively. 110p. 1990. 17.95 (*0-88645-097-7*, Pub. by Inst Res Pub) Ashgate Pub Co.

MacNeill, M. Everyday Gaelic. 1991. pap. 19.95 (*0-8288-3346-X*, F132984) Fr & Eur.

***MacNeill, Mary.** The Widow down by the Brook. large type unabridged ed. 300p. 1999. 25.95 (*0-7531-5717-9*, 157179, Pub. by ISIS Lrg Prnt) ISIS Pub.

MacNeill, Mary I. The Widow down by the Brook: A Memoir from a Time Gone By. LC 98-54771. 208p. 1999. 21.50 (*0-684-85969-6*) S&S Trade.

Macneill, Seumas, jt. auth. see Richardson, F.

MacNeish, Jerry. The Definitive, Nineteen Sixty-Seven to Nineteen Sixty-Eight Camaro Z-28 Book. (Illus.). 148p. 1990. pap. 21.95 (*0-9626399-0-7*) J MacNeish.

— The Definitive 1969 Camaro Z-28/SS396 Fact Book. (Illus.). 235p. (Orig.). 1993. pap. text 25.95 (*0-9626399-1-5*) J MacNeish.

MacNeish, R. First Annual Report of the Ayacucho Project. (Reports of the Ayacucho Archaeological-Botanical Project Ser.). 1969. pap. text 10.00 (*0-939312-15-8*) Peabody Found.

Macneish, R., et al. The Central Peruvian Prehistoric Interaction Sphere, Vol. 7. 1975. pap. 15.00 (*0-939312-08-5*) Peabody Found.

MacNeish, R., et al. First Annual Report of the Belize Archaic Archaeological Reconnaissance. 1980. pap. 10.00 (*0-939312-17-4*) Peabody Found.

MacNeish, Richard S. The Origins of Agriculture & Settled Life. LC 91-50304. (Illus.). 448p. 1992. text 75.00 (*0-8061-2364-8*) U of Okla Pr.

MacNeish, Richard S., et al. The Prehistory of the Ayacucho Basin, Peru: Nonceramic Artifacts, Vol. III. (Illus.). 360p. 1980. text 57.50 (*0-472-02707-7*, 02707) U of Mich Pr.

— Prehistory of the Ayacucho Basin, Peru Vol. II: Excavations & Chronology. LC 80-13960. (Illus.). 296p. (C). 1981. text 57.50 (*0-472-04907-0*, 04907) U of Mich Pr.

MacNeish, Richard S., jt. auth. see Wray, Donald E.

***MacNelly, Jeff.** From Coach Potato to Mouse Potato. (Illus.). 128p. 2000. pap. 9.95 (*1-57243-384-1*) Triumph Bks.

MacNelly, Jeff. A Golf Handbook: All I Ever Learned I Forgot by the Third Fairway. (Illus.). 128p. 1997. pap. 9.95 (*1-57243-189-X*) Triumph Bks.

— A Golf Handbook: Everything I Ever Learned I Forgot by the Third Fairway. (Illus.). 144p. 1996. 9.95 (*1-57243-115-6*) Triumph Bks.

— Shoe Goes to Wrigley Field: How Many Next Years Do You Get in Baseball? (Illus.). 59p. (Orig.). 1988. pap. 5.95 (*0-933893-51-5*) Bonus Books.

MacNevin. Building Rainbow Bridge: Educational Diversity in America. 382p. 1998. pap. text 46.00 (*0-536-01871-5*) Pearson Custom.

Macnew, T. Ultra Fine Pitch Gears. (Technical Papers: Vol. P379.01). (Illus.). 4p. (Orig.). 1956. pap. text 30.00 incl. audio compact disk (*1-55589-394-5*) AGMA.

MacNicholas, John. James Joyce's Exiles: A Textual Companion. LC 78-67061. (Reference Library Ser.). 1979. text 20.00 (*0-8240-9781-5*) Garland.

MacNicholas, John, ed. Twentieth-Century American Dramatists, 2 vols., Set. (Dictionary of Literary Biography Ser.: Vol. 7). (Illus.). 848p. 1996. text 296.00 (*0-8103-0928-9*) Gale.

MacNicol, Eona K. Lamp in the Night Wind: St. Columba Story. 256p. (C). 1988. 50.00 (*0-85335-006-X*, Pub. by Stuart Titles Ltd) St Mut.

MacNicol, Fred. Hungarian Cookery LC 78-326347. xxix, 257 p. 1978. 4.95 (*0-7139-1102-6*, A Lane) Viking Penguin.

Macnicol, Fred, tr. see Karpati, Janos.

Macnicol, John. The Politics of Retirement in Britain, 1878-1948. LC 97-41842. 416p. (C). 1998. text 74.95 (*0-521-62273-5*) Cambridge U Pr.

Macnicol, Malcolm F. The Problem Knee. 2nd ed. LC 94-45158. (Illus.). 224p. 1995. 100.00 (*0-7506-0487-5*) Buttrwrth-Heinemann.

MacNicoll, Murray G., ed. & tr. see Azevedo, Aluisio.

MacNiece, Louis, tr. see Goethe, Johann Wolfgang Von.

***MacNiocaill, C. & Ryan, P., eds.** Continental Tectonics. (Geological Society Special Publications: No. 164). 300p. 1999. 125.00 (*1-86239-051-7*, Pub. by Geol Soc Pub Hse) AAPG.

MacNiven Cameron, Sheila. The Best from New Mexico Kitchens. 1994. spiral bd. 9.95 (*0-937206-35-0*) New Mexico Mag.

MacNiven, Don. Bradley's Moral Psychology. LC 87-1731. (Studies in the History of Philosophy: Vol. 3). 288p. 1987. lib. bdg. 89.95 (*0-88946-306-9*) E Mellen.

— Creative Morality: An Introduction to Theoretical & Practical Ethics. LC 92-30808. 256p. (C). 1993. pap. 25.99 (*0-415-00030-0*, B0418) Routledge.

MacNiven, Ian S. Lawrence Durrell: A Biography. (Illus.). 768p. 1998. 36.95 (*0-571-17248-2*) Faber & Faber.

MacNiven, Ian S., ed. see Durrell, Lawrence & Miller, Henry.

Macnow, Glen. David Robinson: Star Center. LC 94-15647. (Sports Reports Ser.). (Illus.). 104p. (J). (gr. 4-10). 1994. lib. bdg. 20.95 (*0-89490-483-3*) Enslow Pubs.

***MacNow, Glen.** The Denver Broncos Football Team. LC 00-9112. (Great Sports Teams Ser.). (Illus.). 2000. pap. write for info. (*0-7660-1489-4*) Enslow Pubs.

MacNow, Glen. Ken Griffey, Jr. Star Outfielder. LC 96-52742. (Sports Reports Ser.). 104p. (J). (gr. 4-10). 1997. lib. bdg. 20.95 (*0-89490-802-2*) Enslow Pubs.

***Macnow, Glen.** The Philadelphia Flyers Hockey Team. LC 99-12581. (Great Sports Teams Ser.). (Illus.). 48p. (gr. 4-10). 2000. lib. bdg. 18.95 (*0-7660-1279-4*) Enslow Pubs.

Macnow, Glen. The Philadelphia 76ers Basketball Team. LC 97-20378. (Great Sports Teams Ser.). (Illus.). 48p. (YA). (gr. 4-10). 1998. lib. bdg. 18.95 (*0-7660-1063-5*) Enslow Pubs.

***Macnow, Glen.** The Philadelphia 76ers Basketball Team. LC 97-20378. (Great Sports Teams Ser.). (Illus.). 48p. (YA). (gr. 4-10). 1998. pap. 9.95 (*0-7660-1751-6*) Enslow Pubs.

Macnow, Glen. Shaquille O'Neal: Star Center. LC 96-3425. (Sports Reports Ser.). (Illus.). 104p. (J). (gr. 4-10). 1996. lib. bdg. 20.95 (*0-89490-656-9*) Enslow Pubs.

— Sports Great Cal Ripken, Jr. LC 92-24158. (Sports Great Bks.). (Illus.). 64p. (J). (gr. 4-10). 1993. lib. bdg. 17.95 (*0-89490-387-X*) Enslow Pubs.

— Sports Great Charles Barkley. LC 91-45827. (Sports Great Bks.). (Illus.). 64p. (J). (gr. 4-10). 1992. lib. bdg. 17.95 (*0-89490-386-1*) Enslow Pubs.

— Sports Great Charles Barkley. rev. ed. LC 97-22844. (Sports Great Bks.). (Illus.). 64p. (J). (gr. 4-10). 1998. lib. bdg. 17.95 (*0-7660-1004-X*) Enslow Pubs.

— Sports Great Chris Webber. LC 98-35039. (Sports Great Bks.). 64p. (J). (gr. 4-10). 1999. lib. bdg. 17.95 (*0-7660-1069-4*) Enslow Pubs.

— Sports Great Deion Sanders. LC 98-14942. (Sports Great Bks.). 64p. (J). (gr. 4-10). 1999. lib. bdg. 17.95 (*0-7660-1068-6*) Enslow Pubs.

***Macnow, Glen.** Sports Great Kevin Garnett. LC 99-40390. (Sports Great Bks.). (Illus.). 64p. (gr. 4-10). 2000. lib. bdg. 17.95 (*0-7660-1263-8*) Enslow Pubs.

— Sports Great Kobe Bryant. LC 99-15908. (Sports Great Bks.). (Illus.). 64p. (gr. 4-10). 2000. lib. bdg. 17.95 (*0-7660-1264-6*) Enslow Pubs.

Macnow, Glen. Sports Great Troy Aikman. LC 94-30537. (Sports Great Bks.). (Illus.). 64p. (J). (gr. 4-10). 1995. lib. bdg. 17.95 (*0-89490-593-7*) Enslow Pubs.

***Macnulty, Shirley.** Knitting for Fun & Profit. LC 99-39230. (Illus.). 292p. 1999. pap. 16.99 (*0-7615-2108-9*) Prima Pub.

MacNulty, W. Kirk. Freemasonry: A Journey Through Ritual & Symbol. LC 91-65320. (Art & Imagination Ser.). (Illus.). 96p. (Orig.). 1991. pap. 15.95 (*0-500-81037-0*, Pub. by Thames Hudson) Norton.

MacNutt, Francis. Deliverance from Evil Spirits: A Practical Manual. LC 95-5150. 288p. (Orig.). (gr. 10). 1995. pap. 14.99 (*0-8007-9232-7*) Chosen Bks.

— Healing: 25th Anniversary Edition. 25th anniversary rev. expanded ed. LC 99-11944. 268p. 1999. pap. 12.95 (*0-87793-676-5*) Ave Maria.

— Overcome by the Spirit. LC 90-44727. 192p. (gr. 10). 1990. pap. 11.99 (*0-8007-9170-3*) Chosen Bks.

MacNutt, Francis A. Bartholome de las Casas: His Life, His Apostolate, & His Writings. LC 70-172712. reprint ed. 55.00 (*0-404-07146-5*) AMS Pr.

— Bartolome de las Casas. 1972. 59.95 (*0-87968-708-8*) Gordon Pr.

MacNutt, Francis A. & Greenway, John, intros. Fernando Cortes: His Five Letters of Relation to the Emperor Charles V of Spain, 2 vols. LC 77-1155. (Beautiful Rio Grande Classics Ser.). 895p. 1977. reprint ed. lib. bdg. 50.00 (*0-87380-125-3*) Popular E Commerce.

MacNutt, Francis S. Healing. rev. ed. LC 88-71068. 1988. pap. 9.99 (*0-88419-217-2*) Creation House.

— The Power to Heal. LC 77-77845. 256p. 1977. pap. 9.95 (*0-87793-133-X*) Ave Maria.

— Prayer That Heals: Praying for Healing in the Family. LC 80-69770. 120p. (Orig.). 1981. pap. 6.95 (*0-87793-219-0*) Ave Maria.

— Praying for Your Unborn Child. 176p. 1989. pap. 10.00 (*0-385-23282-9*) Doubleday.

MacNutt, J. Scott. A Manual for Health Officers. Rosenkrantz, Barbara G., ed. LC 76-40634. (Public Health in America Ser.). (Illus.). 1977. reprint ed. lib. bdg. 54.95 (*0-405-09825-1*) Ayer.

MacNutt, Karen L. Ladies Legal Companion. (Illus.). 87p. (Orig.). 1993. pap. 8.95 (*0-9622534-1-3*) MacNutt Art Trust.

— A Sketch of Glenn G. MacNutt. (Illus.). 24p. 1989. 9.52 (*0-9622534-0-5*) MacNutt Art Trust.

MacNutt, William S. Days of Lorne: Impressions of a Governor-General. LC 77-16170. (Illus.). 272p. 1978. reprint ed. lib. bdg. 65.00 (*0-313-20021-1*, MADL, Greenwood Pr) Greenwood.

Macoboy, Stirling. The Illustrated Encyclopedia of Camellias. LC 97-39345. (Illus.). 304p. 1998. 39.95 (*0-88192-421-0*) Timber.

— The Ultimate Rose Book: One Thousand Five Hundred Roses--Antique, Modern (Including Miniature), & Wild--All Shown in Color & Selected for Their Beauty, Fragrance, & Enduring Popularity. LC 93-10419. (Illus.). 472p. 1993. 49.50 (*0-8109-3920-7*, Pub. by Abrams) Time Warner.

Macoff & Associates Staff, ed. see Nance, Kimi.

Macom, D. C. First Lady Last Lady. 269p. 1999. pap. 15.95 (*0-7414-0053-7*) Buy Books.

Macomber, Debbie. All Things Considered. (Western Lovers Ser.). 1996. per. 3.99 (*0-373-88535-0*, 1-88535-9) Harlequin Bks.

— The Apartment. (To Mother with Love Ser.). 1993. pap. 4.99 (*0-685-61545-6*) Silhouette.

— Baby Blessed. 1994. per. 3.50 (*0-373-09895-2*, 1-09895-3) Harlequin Bks.

— The Bachelor Prince. (Silhouette Romance Ser.). 1994. per. 2.75 (*0-373-19012-3*, 5-19012-9) Harlequin Bks.

— The Bachelor Prince. 1997. per. 168.00 (*0-373-91012-6*, 5-91012-0) Harlequin Bks.

— Because of the Baby. LC 95-22610. (Romance Ser.). 185p. 1996. per. 3.25 (*0-373-03395-8*, 1-03395-0) Harlequin Bks.

— Because of the Baby. large type ed. (Harlequin Romance Ser.). 1997. 20.95 (*0-263-15007-0*) Mac Lib Ref.

— Borrowed Dreams. (Men Made in America Ser.). 1993. per. 3.59 (*0-373-45152-0*, 1-45152-5) Harlequin Bks.

— Bride on the Loose. (Special Ser.: No. 756). 1992. per. 3.39 (*0-373-09756-5*) Silhouette.

— Bride on the Loose. large type ed. (Silhouette Romance Ser.). 1995. lib. bdg. 18.95 (*0-373-59421-6*) Thorndike Pr.

— Bride Wanted from This Day Forward. 1993. per. 3.50 (*0-373-09836-7*, 5-09836-3) Silhouette.

— Brides for Brothers. LC 96-452. 187p. 1995. per. 2.99 (*0-373-03379-6*, 1-03379-4) Harlequin Bks.

— Can This Be Christmas? 1998. 12.95 (*1-55166-455-0*, 1-66455-6, Mira Bks) Harlequin Bks.

— Caroline's Child. (Promo Ser.). 1998. per. 4.50 (*0-373-83344-X*, 1-83344-1) Harlequin Bks.

***Macomber, Debbie.** Caroline's Child. large type ed. 288p. 1999. 25.99 (*0-263-16104-8*, Pub. by Mills & Boon) Ulverscroft.

— Country Brides. 2000. pap. 9.99 (*1-55166-626-X*, 1-66626-2, Mira Bks) Harlequin Bks.

Macomber, Debbie. Country Brides: A Little Bit Country; Country Bride. 1998. mass mkt. 5.99 (*1-55166-475-5*, 1-66475-4, Mira Bks) Harlequin Bks.

— Daddy's Little Helper. LC 96-297. 185p. 1995. per. 2.99 (*0-373-03387-7*, 1-03387-7) Harlequin Bks.

— Daddy's Little Helper. large type ed. (Harlequin Romance Ser.). 1997. 20.95 (*0-263-14974-9*) Thorndike Pr.

— Dakota Born. 2000. mass mkt. 6.99 (*1-55166-576-X*, Mira Bks) Harlequin Bks.

— Dakota Born. 2000. 21.95 (*1-55166-560-3*, 1-66560-3, Mira Bks) Harlequin Bks.

***Macomber, Debbie.** Dakota Home. 2000. mass mkt. 6.99 (*1-55166-602-2*, 1-66602-3, Mira Bks) Harlequin Bks.

Macomber, Debbie. Denim & Diamonds. 1997. per. 5.50 (*1-55166-284-1*) Harlequin Bks.

— Dr. Texas. (Heart of Texas Mini Ser.). 216p. 1998. per. 4.50 (*0-373-83345-8*, 1-83345-8) Harlequin Bks.

***Macomber, Debbie.** Dr. Texas. large type ed. 1998. 6.25 (*0-263-16130-7*) Mills & Boon.

— Dr. Texas. large type ed. 288p. 1999. 25.99 (*0-263-16141-2*, Pub. by Mills & Boon) Ulverscroft.

Macomber, Debbie. Ending in Marriage. LC 96-2371. (Romance Ser.). 186p. 1996. per. 3.25 (*0-373-03403-2*, 1-03403-2) Harlequin Bks.

— Fallen Angel. 256p. 1996. per. 5.50 (*1-55166-180-2*, 1-66180-0, Mira Bks) Harlequin Bks.

***Macomber, Debbie.** Fallen Angel. LC 00-37744. 2000. write for info. (*0-7862-2601-3*) Thorndike Pr.

Macomber, Debbie. Falling for Him (Midnight Sons) LC 96-720. (Romance Ser.). 184p. 1996. per. 3.25 (*0-373-03399-0*, 1-03399-2) Harlequin Bks.

***Macomber, Debbie.** Family Men: Daddy's Little Helper & Because of the Baby, 2 bks. in 1. Vol. 2. 2000. mass mkt. 5.99 (*0-373-83435-7*, 1-83435-7) Harlequin Bks.

Macomber, Debbie. Father's Day. (Romance Ser.: No. 3130). 1991. per. 2.75 (*0-373-03130-0*) Harlequin Bks.

— First Comes Marriage. (Romance Ser.: No. 3113). 1991. per. 2.75 (*0-373-03113-0*) Harlequin Bks.

— For All My Tomorrows. 256p. 1996. per. 5.50 (*1-55166-156-X*, 1-66156-0, Mira Bks) Harlequin Bks.

***Macomber, Debbie.** For All My Tomorrows. LC 00-39681. 2000. pap. write for info. (*0-7838-9048-6*, G K Hall & Co) Mac Lib Ref.

Macomber, Debbie. The Forgetful Bride. (Romance Ser.: No. 166). 1991. per. 2.79 (*0-373-03166-1*) Harlequin Bks.

— Groom Wanted: From This Day Forward. (Special Edition Ser.). 1993. mass mkt. 3.50 (*0-373-09831-6*, 5-09831-4) Silhouette.

— Hasty Wedding. 1993. per. 3.39 (*0-373-09798-0*, 5-09798-5) Silhouette.

— Here Comes Trouble. (Romance Ser.: No. 3148). 1991. per. 2.79 (*0-373-03148-3*) Harlequin Bks.

— Just Married. 1995. per. 3.75 (*0-373-24003-1*, 1-24003-5) Silhouette.

— Just Married. large type ed. (Large Print Ser.). 384p. 1997. 20.95 (*0-373-59851-3*) Harlequin Bks.

— Legendary Lovers. 1995. per. 5.50 (*0-373-20114-1*) Harlequin Bks.

— Lone Star Baby. (Harlequin Ser.). 1998. per. 4.50 (*0-373-83347-4*) Harlequin Bks.

***Macomber, Debbie.** Lone Star Baby. large type ed. 288p. 1999. 25.99 (*0-263-16208-7*, Pub. by Mills & Boon) Ulverscroft.

Macomber, Debbie. Lone Star Lovin' (Romance Ser.). 1993. mass mkt. 2.99 (*0-373-03271-4*, 1-03271-3) Harlequin Bks.

— Lonesome Cowboy. (Promo Ser.). 1998. per. 4.50 (*0-373-83342-3*, 1-83342-5) Harlequin Bks.

***Macomber, Debbie.** Lonesome Cowboy. large type ed. 1999. 25.99 (*0-263-16058-0*, Pub. by Mills & Boon) Ulverscroft.

Macomber, Debbie. Mail-Order Marriages. Vol. 1. 384p. 2000. per. 5.99 (*0-373-83434-9*) Harlequin Bks.

— The Man You'll Marry. (Romance Ser.: No. 196). 1992. per. 2.89 (*0-373-03196-3*, 1-03196-2) Harlequin Bks.

— The Marriage Risk. LC 96-455. 189p. 1995. per. 2.99 (*0-373-03383-4*) Harlequin Bks.

— Marriage Wanted: From This Day Forward. (Special Edition Ser.). 1993. per. 3.50 (*0-373-09842-1*, 5-09842-1) Silhouette.

— Montana. LC 97-17245. 299p. 1997. pap. 21.95 (*1-55166-316-3*, 1-66316-0, Mira Bks) Harlequin Bks.

— Montana. (Mira Bks.). 1998. per. 6.99 (*1-55166-434-8*, 1-66434-1, Mira Bks) Harlequin Bks.

— Moon over Water. (Mira Bks.). 1998. 21.95 (*1-55166-319-8*, 1-66319-4, Mira Bks) Harlequin Bks.

***Macomber, Debbie.** Moon over Water. 378p. 1999. mass mkt. 6.99 (*1-55166-533-6*, 1-66533-0, Mira Bks) Harlequin Bks.

Macomber, Debbie. Mrs. Miracle. large type ed. LC 98-26228. (G. K. Hall Romance (Large Print) Ser.). 1998. 26.95 (*0-7838-0318-4*, G K Hall Lrg Type) Mac Lib Ref.

— My Hero. (Romance Ser.: No. 180). 1992. per. 2.79 (*0-373-03180-7*, 1-03180-6) Harlequin Bks.

— Nell's Cowboy. (Promo Ser.: No. 5). 1998. per. 4.50 (*0-373-83346-6*, 1-83346-6) Harlequin Bks.

***Macomber, Debbie.** Nell's Cowboy. large type ed. 288p. 1999. 25.99 (*0-263-16173-0*, Pub. by Mills & Boon) Ulverscroft.

Macomber, Debbie. One Night. 336p. 1994. mass mkt. 6.50 (*0-06-108185-X*) HarpC.

***Macomber, Debbie.** One Night. large type ed. (G. K. Hall Romance Ser.). 2000. 28.95 (*0-7838-8972-0*, G K Hall Lrg Type) Mac Lib Ref.

— Orchard Valley. 1999. per. 5.99 (*1-55166-308-2*, 1-66308-7, Mira Bks) Harlequin Bks.

Macomber, Debbie. Orchard Valley Trilogy: Nora; Stephanie; Valerie, 3 bks. 1997. mass mkt. write for info. (*0-373-15269-8*, 1-15269-3) Harlequin Bks.

— Orchard Valley Weddings. (By Request Ser.). 1997. mass mkt. 5.99 (*2-273-20156-7*, 1-20156-5) Harlequin Bks.

— The Playboy & the Widow. (Mira Bks.). 256p. 1996. per. 5.50 (*1-55166-080-6*, 1-66080-2, Mira Bks) Harlequin Bks.

***Macomber, Debbie.** The Playboy & the Widow. LC 00-37799. 2000. pap. write for info. (*0-7862-2607-2*) Thorndike Pr.

Macomber, Debbie. Promise Me Forever. 256p. 1999. mass mkt. write for info. (*1-55166-052-0*, 0-66052-2, Mira Bks) Harlequin Bks.

— Promise,Texas. 384p. 1999. per. 6.99 (*1-55166-502-6*, Mira Bks) Harlequin Bks.

— Rainy Day Kisses. (Romance Ser.: No. 3076). 1990. pap. 2.50 (*0-373-03076-2*) Harlequin Bks.

***Macomber, Debbie.** Ready for Love. 2001. pap. 9.99 (*1-55166-792-4*, Mira Bks) Harlequin Bks.

Macomber, Debbie. Ready for Marriage. (Romance Ser.). 1994. per. 2.99 (*0-373-03307-9*, 1-03307-5); per. 2.99 (*0-373-15553-0*) Harlequin Bks.

— Ready for Marriage. (Promo Ser.). 1999. per. 4.50 (*0-373-21957-1*, 1-21957-5) Harlequin Bks.

— Ready for Marriage. large type ed. 206p. 1995. pap. 19.95 (*0-7838-1176-4*, G K Hall Lrg Type) Mac Lib Ref.

— Ready for Romance. (Romance Ser.). 1993. mass mkt. 2.99 (*0-373-03288-9*, 1-03288-7); per. 2.99 (*0-373-15534-4*) Harlequin Bks.

— Reflections of Yesterday. (Mira Bks.). 256p. 1995. per. 4.99 (*1-55166-070-9*, 1-66070-3, Mira Bks) Harlequin Bks.

***Macomber, Debbie.** Return to Promise. 2000. 12.95 (*1-55166-613-8*, 1-66613-0, Mira Bks) Harlequin Bks.

Macomber, Debbie. Same Time, Next Year. (Special Edition Ser.). 1995. per. 3.75 (*0-373-09937-1*, 1-09937-3) Silhouette.

— Same Time, Next Year. large type ed. (Silhouette Ser.). 1996. 19.95 (*0-373-59754-1*) Thorndike Pr.

— A Season of Angels: Season of Angels, A. 336p. 1999. mass mkt. 5.99 (*0-06-108184-1*, Harp PBks) HarpC.

— Shadow Chasing. (Mira Bks.). 256p. 1997. per. 5.50 (*1-55166-263-9*, 1-66263-4, Mira Bks) Harlequin Bks.

***Macomber, Debbie.** Shadow Chasing. LC 00-39642. 2001. pap. write for info. (*0-7838-9053-2*, G K Hall & Co) Mac Lib Ref.

Macomber, Debbie. Shirley, Goodness & Mercy. 1999. mass mkt. 6.99 (*1-55166-562-X*, 1-66562-9, Mira Bks) Harlequin Bks.

***Macomber, Debbie.** Shirley, Goodness & Mercy. 136p. 1999. 12.95 (*1-55166-529-8*, 1-66529-8, Mira Bks) Harlequin Bks.

Macomber, Debbie. Someday Soon. 352p. 1995. mass mkt. 6.50 (*0-06-108309-7*, Harp PBks) HarpC.

— Sooner or Later. 368p. 1996. mass mkt. 6.50 (*0-06-108345-3*, Harp PBks) HarpC.

— Starlight. 256p. 1995. per. 4.99 (*1-55166-021-0*, Mira Bks) Harlequin Bks.

— Stephanie. 1992. per. 2.89 (*0-373-03239-0*, 1-03239-0) Harlequin Bks.

— Texas Two-Step. (Heart of Texas Mini Ser.). 219p. 1998. per. 4.50 (*0-373-83343-1*, 1-83343-3) Harlequin Bks.

***Macomber, Debbie.** Texas Two-Step. large type ed. 288p. 1999. 25.99 (*0-263-16081-5*, Pub. by Mills & Boon) Ulverscroft.

Macomber, Debbie. This Matter of Marriage. 1999. mass mkt. write for info. (*1-55166-260-4*, 0-66260-1, Mira Bks) Harlequin Bks.

— Three Brides, No Groom. 1997. per. 6.99 (*0-373-48352-X*) Harlequin Bks.

— Touched by Angels. 320p. 1999. mass mkt. 5.99 (*0-06-108344-5*, Harp PBks) HarpC.

— The Trouble with Angels. 352p. 1999. mass mkt. 5.99 (*0-06-108308-9*, Harp PBks) HarpC.

— Wanted: Perfect Partner. (Yours Truly Ser.). 1995. per. 3.50 (*0-373-52001-8*, 1-52001-4) Silhouette.

— Yours & Mine. (Harlequin Promotion Ser.). 1997. per. 3.99 (*0-373-83355-5*, 1-83355-7) Harlequin Bks.

Macomber, Debbie & Jackson, Lisa. 'Tis the Season: Christmas Masquerade; Snowbound. (By Request Ser.). 1999. per. 4.99 (*0-373-48395-3*, 1-48395-7, Harlequin) Harlequin Bks.

***Macomber, Debbie & Quinn, Tara Taylor.** The First Man You Meet, Jacob's Girls, 2 bks. 2000. mass mkt. 4.99 (*0-373-83454-3*, 1834548) Harlequin Bks.

An Asterisk (*) at the beginning of an entry indicates that the title is appearing for the first time.

Macomber, Debbie & Roszel, Renee. Love by Degree & The Boardroom Bridegroom, 2 bks. in 1, Bk. 1. 50th anniversary ed. (Harlequin 50th Anniversary Collection Ser.). 377p. 1999. mass mkt. 6.99 (*0-373-83409-8*, 1-83409-2, Harlequin) Harlequin Bks.

***Macomber, Debbie, et al.** Born in a Small Town: Midnight Sons & Daughters; The Glory Girl; Promise Me Picket Fences, 3 bks. in 1. (Superromance Ser.: Vol. 936). 304p. 2000. mass mkt. 4.50 (*0-373-70936-6*, 1-70936-9) Harlequin Bks.

Macomber, Debbie, et al. By Request: Men in Uniform. 1994. per. 5.50 (*0-373-20100-1*) Silhouette.

— Home for Christmas. 1996. per. 5.99 (*0-373-20130-3*, 1-20130-0) Harlequin Bks.

— Runaway Brides. 1996. per. 5.99 (*0-373-20124-9*, 1-20124-3) Harlequin Bks.

— Three Mothers & a Cradle: Rock-a-Bye Baby; Cradle Song; Beginnings. (Silhouette Promo Ser.). 1995. per. 4.99 (*0-373-48335-X*, 1-48335-3) Harlequin Bks.

Macomber, Debbie, jt. auth. see Wisdom, Linda Randall.

Macomber, Frank, jt. auth. see Fleming, William.

Macomber, J. D., jt. ed. see Lippert, E.

Macomber, James D. The Dynamics of Spectroscopic Transitions: Illustrated by Magnetic Resonance & Laser Effects. LC 75-25852. (Wiley-Interscience Monographs in Chemical Physics). (Illus.). 358p. reprint ed. pap. 111.00 (*0-608-18544-2*, 201307800084) Bks Demand.

Macomber, Roger. Organic Chemistry, Vol. I. LC 96-60221. (Illus.). 319p. (C). 1996. pap. text 36.50 (*0-935702-90-3*) Univ Sci Bks.

— Organic Chemistry, Vol. 2. (Illus.). 410p. (C). 1996. pap. text 38.50 (*0-935702-93-8*) Univ Sci Bks.

Macomber, Roger S. College Outline: Organic Chemistry. (C). 1995. pap. text 13.50 (*0-15-600044-X*) Harcourt Coll Pubs.

— A Complete Introduction to Modern NMR Spectroscopy. LC 97-17106. 400p. 1997. pap. 59.95 (*0-471-15736-8*) Wiley.

Macomber, William F. A Catalogue of Ethiopian Manuscripts Microfilmed for the Ethiopian Manuscript Microfilm Library, Addis Ababa, & the Hill Monastic Manuscript Library, Collegeville: Project Numbers 1-300, Vol. 1. (Illus.). ix, 355p. (Orig.). 1975. pap. 15.00 (*0-940250-51-9*) Hill Monastic.

— A Catalogue of Ethiopian Manuscripts Microfilmed for the Ethiopian Manuscript Microfilm Library, Addis Ababa, & the Hill Monastic Manuscript Library, Collegeville: Project Numbers 301-700, Vol. 2. v, 524p. (Orig.). 1976. pap. 25.00 (*0-940250-52-7*) Hill Monastic.

Macomber, William F., jt. auth. see Haile, Getatchew.

Macon, James H. Little House on the Prairie: A Study Guide. (Novel-Ties Ser.). (J). (gr. 3-5). 1989. pap. text, teacher ed., student ed. 15.95 (*0-88122-051-5*) Lrn Links.

— Responses to Literature, Grades K-8. 32p. 1990. pap. 5.95 (*0-87207-747-0*) Intl Reading.

— Treasure Island: A Study Guide. (Novel-Ties Ser.). (J). (gr. 6-8). 1989. pap. text, teacher ed., student ed. 15.95 (*0-88122-060-4*) Lrn Links.

Macon, Larry. The United Pastors Mission: Messages for Modern Times. LC 98-66441. 96p. 1998. per. 14.95 (*0-7872-2410-3*) Kendall-Hunt.

Macon, Larry L. The Religious Ethics of Martin Luther King, Jr. & Malcolm X. (Illus.). 180p. 2001. pap. 22.00 (*1-893435-09-1*) Lakeshore Comm.

Macon, Myra, ed. School Library Media Services to the Handicapped. LC 81-4262. (Illus.). 208p. 1982. 49.95 (*0-313-22684-9*, MAL/, Greenwood Pr) Greenwood.

Macon, Perry, jt. auth. see Hagedorn, John M.

***Macon, Steven C.** What Color Is Your Wallpaper? (Illus.). 24p. 1999. 3.25 (*1-57688-013-3*, 80133) Branch & Vine.

Maconie, Robin. The Concept of Music. (Illus.). 198p. 1993. reprint ed. pap. text 22.00 (*0-19-816388-6*) OUP.

— The Science of Music. LC 96-43398. (Illus.). 232p. (C). 1997. text 29.95 (*0-19-816648-6*) OUP.

— Stockhausen. LC 79-56837. (Illus.). 352p. 1981. pap. 20.00 (*0-7145-2706-8*) M Boyars Pubs.

— The Works of Karlheinz Stockhausen. 2nd ed. (Illus.). 332p. 1990. text 90.00 (*0-19-315477-3*) OUP.

***Maconie, Stuart.** 3862 Days: The Official History of Blur. 1999. pap. 17.95 (*0-7535-0287-9*, Pub. by Virgin Bks) London Brdge.

Maconochie. MRCP Pediactrics. (C). 1998. pap. text 39.00 (*0-7020-2381-7*) Harcourt.

Macor, Alida. And Sew On... rev. ed. LC 82-91121. (Illus.). 96p. 1995. pap. 7.50 (*0-9610632-0-3*) Alida Macor.

Macorini, Edgardo, ed. The History of Science & Technology: A Narrative Chronology, 2 vols., Set. 960p. 1988. 160.00 (*0-87196-477-5*) Facts on File.

MacOrlan, Pierre. Le Bandera. (FRE.). 1972. pap. 8.95 (*0-7859-3994-6*) Fr & Eur.

— Le Quai des Brumes. (FRE.). 1972. pap. 8.95 (*0-7859-3985-7*) Fr & Eur.

Macosko, Christopher W. Rheology: Principles, Measurements & Applications. LC 93-31652. (Advances in Interfacial Engineering Ser.). 1994. 95.00 (*1-56081-579-5*, Wiley-VCH) Wiley.

Macosko, Christopher W. Rheology: Principles, Measurements & Applications. 568p. 1994. 115.00 (*0-471-18575-2*) Wiley.

Macosko, Christopher W. Rim: Fundamentals of Reaction Injection Molding. 246p. 1989. 59.95 (*1-56990-055-8*) Hanser-Gardner.

Macoun, Michael J. Wrong Place, Right Time. LC 96-60444. (Illus.). 224p. 1996. text 39.50 (*1-86064-019-2*) St Martin.

Macoupon County Homemakers Extension Association S. The Homemaker's Sampler. 350p. 1980. pap. 6.50 (*0-918544-45-9*) MCH.

Macourek, Chris. Heart to Heart: Low-Fat Cooking Made Easy. (Illus.). 200p. 1992. 11.95 (*0-9635418-0-3*) Chris Kitchen.

Macourek, Milos. Max & Sally & the Phenomenal Phone. Herrmann, Dagmar, tr. from CZE. LC 88-33871. (Illus.). 82p. (J). (gr. 2-4). 1989. 16.95 (*0-922984-00-X*) Wellington IL.

Macovei, Catalina. Grigorescu. (Great Painters Ser.). (Illus.). 176p. 1999. 40.00 (*1-85995-537-1*) Parkstone Pr.

Macovski, Albert. Medical Imaging Systems. (Illus.). 256p. (C). 1983. text 65.20 (*0-13-572685-9*) P-H.

Macovski, Michael. Dialogue & Critical Discourse: Language, Culture, Critical Theory. LC 92-28231. (Illus.). 256p. 1997. pap. text 21.00 (*0-19-508124-2*) OUP.

— Dialogue & Critical Discourse: Language, Culture, Critical Theory. LC 92-28231. (Illus.). 288p. 1997. text 55.00 (*0-19-507063-1*) OUP.

Macovski, Michael S. Dialogue & Literature: Apostrophe, Auditors & the Collapse of Romantic Discourse. 256p. 1994. text 49.95 (*0-19-506965-X*) OUP.

Macoy, jt. auth. see Simons.

Macoy Publishing & Masonic Supply Co. Staff. Book of the Scarlet Line: Heroines of Jericho Ritual & Ceremonies. 152p. 1994. reprint ed. text 8.75 (*0-88053-304-8*, S 077) Macoy Pub.

Macoy Publishing Staff. Book of the Scarlet Line Heroines of Jericho (1948) 150p. 1999. reprint ed. pap. 17.95 (*0-7661-0827-9*) Kessinger Pub.

Macoy, Robert. The Adoptive Rite. 8.50 (*0-911164-01-4*) Powner.

— The Adoptive Rite. rev. ed. LC 98-219086. 303p. 1998. reprint ed. text 10.00 (*0-88053-300-5*, S 073) Macoy Pub.

— Amaranth Ritual. 169p. 1994. reprint ed. text 7.50 (*0-88053-301-3*, S 074) Macoy Pub.

— Christmas, Easter, Ascension & Burial Services for Knights Templar. rev. ed. 111p. 1978. pap. 4.60 (*0-88053-011-1*, M 036) Macoy Pub.

— Dictionary of Freemasonry. 704p. 1989. 9.99 (*0-517-69213-9*) Random Hse Value.

— General History, Cyclopedia & Dictionary of Freemasonry: Containing an Elaborate Account of the Rise & Progress of Freemasonry, & Its Kindred Associations, Ancient & Modern. Also, Definitions of the Technical Terms Used by the Fraternity. (Illus.). 710p. 1994. reprint ed. pap. 49.95 (*1-56459-428-9*) Kessinger Pub.

— The Masonic Manual: A Pocket Companion for the Initiated Containing the Rituals of Freemasonry. 322p. 1997. reprint ed. pap. 24.95 (*0-7661-0067-7*) Kessinger Pub.

***Macoy, Robert.** Obituary Rites of Freemasonry. 106p. 1999. reprint ed. pap. 14.95 (*0-7661-0742-6*) Kessinger Pub.

Macoy, Robert. Worshipful Master's Assistant. rev. ed. xiv, 253p. 1997. reprint ed. 17.95 (*0-88053-008-1*, M-026) Macoy Pub.

— Worshipful Master's Assistant: The Encyclopedia of Useful Knowledge. 304p. 1998. reprint ed. pap. 16.50 (*0-7661-0214-9*) Kessinger Pub.

Macoy, Robert, jt. auth. see Addison, C. G.

MacPhail, Anna. The Well-Dressed Child. LC 99-17204. (Illus.). 160p. 1999. 39.95 (*0-7643-0858-0*) Schiffer.

MacPhail, Catherine. Fighting Back. (Illus.). 128p. (J). pap. 7.95 (*0-14-038270-4*, Pub. by Pnguin Bks Ltd) Trafalgar.

MacPhail, Elizabeth C. The Story of New San Diego & of Its Founder Alonzo E. Horton. 2nd rev. ed. LC 79-63134. (Illus.). 63p. 1979. pap. 8.95 (*0-918740-01-0*) San Diego Hist.

MacPhail, Elizabeth R. The Infuence of German Immigrants on the Growth of San Diego. (Illus.). 104p. 1986. 14.95 (*0-918740-05-3*) San Diego Hist.

MacPhail, Eric. Voyage to Rome in French Renaissance Literature. (Stanford French & Italian Studies: Vol. 68). 224p. 1991. pap. 56.50 (*0-915838-84-2*) Anma Libri.

MacPhail, Euan. The Evolution of Consciousness. (Illus.). 272p. 1998. text 75.00 (*0-19-850325-3*); pap. text 29.95 (*0-19-850324-5*) OUP.

MacPhail, Euan M. Brain & Intelligence in Vertebrates. (Illus.). 423p. 1982. pap. text 24.95 (*0-19-854551-7*) OUP.

Macphail, Euan M. The Neuroscience of Animal Intelligence: From the Seahare to the Seahorse. Terrace, Herbert S., ed. LC 92-31167. (Animal Intelligence Ser.). (Illus.). 506p. (C). 1993. text 75.50 (*0-231-06144-7*) Col U Pr.

Macphail, I. M. The Crofters War. 252p. (C). 1999. 66.00 (*0-86152-860-3*, Pub. by Acair Ltd) St Mut.

MacPhail, I. M. A Short History of Dumbartonshire. 136p. (C). 1986. 45.00 (*0-907590-01-2*) St Mut.

MacPhail, J. R. Highland Papers, Vol. IV. 290p. 1994. reprint ed. pap. text 25.00 (*0-7884-0220-X*) Heritage Bk.

MacPhail, J. R., ed. Highland Papers, Vol. 2. (Illus.). 375p. 1994. pap. text 25.00 (*0-7884-0043-6*) Heritage Bk.

— Highland Papers, Vol. III. 338p. 1995. pap. text 25.00 (*0-7884-0186-6*) Heritage Bk.

MacPhail, Jannetta, jt. auth. see Kerr, Janet R.

Macphail, Jannetta, jt. auth. see Kerr, Janet Ross.

MacPhail, Jessica. Yesterday's Papers: The Rolling Stones in Print, 1963-1984. (Rock & Roll Reference Ser.: No. 19). (Illus.). 236p. 1986. 39.50 (*0-87650-209-5*) Popular Culture.

MacPhail, Lee. My Nine Innings: An Autobiography of 50 Years in Baseball. 1989. 21.95 (*0-88736-387-3*) Mecklermedia.

MacPhail, Mary. Pet Owner's Guide to the Rottweiler. (Pet Owner's Guide Ser.). (Illus.). 80p. 1997. 8.00 (*0-948955-38-4*, Pub. by Ringpr Bks) Seven Hills Bk.

MacPhail, R. M., ed. Campbell's English-Santali Dictionary. 1984. 40.00 (*0-8364-1137-4*, Pub. by Mukhopadhyaya) S Asia.

MacPhedran, Gabrielle & Hopkins, Adam. Essential Berlin. (Essential Travel Guides Ser.). (Illus.). 128p. (Orig.). 1996. pap. 8.95 (*0-8442-8897-7*, 88977, Passprt Bks) NTC Contemp Pub Co.

Macphedran, Gabrielle, jt. auth. see Hopkins, Adam.

MacPhee, John S. Fundamentals of Lithographic Printing: Mechanics of Printing. LC 97-78414. (Illus.). 378p. (C). 1998. text 75.00 (*0-88362-214-9*, 1440) GATFPress.

MacPhee, R. D. Auditory Regions of Primates & Eutherian Insectivores. (Contributions to Primatology Ser.: Vol. 18). (Illus.). xvi, 288p. 1981. pap. 57.50 (*3-8055-1963-X*) S Karger.

— Primates & Their Relatives in Phylogenetic Perspective. (Advances in Primatology Ser.). (Illus.). 398p. (C). 1993. text 95.00 (*0-306-44422-4*, Kluwer Plenum) Kluwer Academic.

MacPhee, R. D., ed. Extinctions in Near Time: Causes, Contexts & Consequences. LC 99-30048. (Advances in Vertebrate Paleobiology Ser.). (Illus.). 380p. (C). 1999. text. write for info. (*0-306-46092-0*, Kluwer Plenum) Kluwer Academic.

MacPhee, Roberta, jt. auth. see Sawyer, Joan.

MacPhee, Rosalind. Picasso's Woman: A Breast Cancer Story. Baker, Deborah, ed. LC 95-42781. 288p. 1996. 20.00 (*1-56836-138-6*) Kodansha.

MacPhee, Ross. Endangered! Exploring a World at Risk. Boggs, Jessie, ed. (Illus.). 64p. (Orig.). 1997. pap. 2.95 (*0-913424-20-X*) Am Mus Natl Hist.

— Endangered! Exploring a World at Risk. Boggs, Jessie, ed. Chiappe, Luis, tr. (SPA., Illus.). 64p. (Orig.). 1997. pap. 2.95 (*0-913424-21-8*) Am Mus Natl Hist.

MacPhee, Tracey H. & DeBruyn, Robert L. School Promotion, Publicity & Public Relations...Nothing but Benefits. LC 87-60751. 320p. 1997. text 29.95 (*0-914607-25-1*) Master Tchr.

MacPherson. Map Reading for the Caribbean. Date not set. pap. text. write for info. (*0-582-76609-5*, Pub. by Addison-Wesley) Longman.

— A Model-Perinatal Autopsy Protocol. (Illus.). 60p. 1995. pap. text 10.00 (*1-881041-16-6*) Am Registry Path.

Macpherson, ed. see Garcia Lorca, Federico.

MacPherson, Andrew. International Telecommunication Standards Organizations. (Artech House Telecom Management Library). 240p. 1990. text 36.00 (*0-89006-365-6*) Artech Hse.

Macpherson, Angus. Landscapes Angus Macpherson. 1993. pap. write for info. (*0-9637700-0-4*) AM DSG Pr.

MacPherson, Anne, jt. auth. see Schendel, Shirley.

MacPherson, Bryan. An International Criminal Court: Applying World Law to Individuals. (U. N. Reform Series Monograph: No. 10). 70p. 1992. pap. 5.00 (*1-881520-00-5*) Ctr U N Reform Educ.

MacPherson, Bryan F. World Court Enhancements to Advance the Rule of Law. (CURE Monographs: No. 13). 78p. (Orig.). 1994. pap. text 5.00 (*1-881520-03-X*) Ctr U N Reform Educ.

Macpherson, C. Sugar Gliders. LC 97-14543. (Complete Pet Owner's Manual Ser.). (Illus.). 120p. 1997. pap. 6.95 (*0-7641-0172-2*) Barron.

MacPherson, C. & MacPherson, L. Samoan Medical Belief & Practice. 280p. 1990. 32.95 (*1-86940-045-3*, Pub. by Auckland Univ) Paul & Co Pubs.

Macpherson, C. B. Democracy in Alberta: Social Credit & the Party System. LC 54-4046. (Social Credit in Alberta Ser.). 1953. pap. text 13.95 (*0-8020-6009-9*) U of Toronto Pr.

— Real World of Democracy. 78p. 1972. pap. text 9.95 (*0-19-501534-7*) OUP.

Macpherson, C. B., ed. Property: Mainstream & Critical Positions. LC 78-2311. (Controversy Ser.). 216p. 1978. pap. text 15.95 (*0-8020-6336-5*) U of Toronto Pr.

Macpherson, C. B., jt. ed. see Crepeau, P. A.

Macpherson, C. B., ed. see Hobbes, Thomas.

Macpherson, C. B., ed. see Locke, John.

***MacPherson, C. N. L., et al, eds.** Dogs, Zoonoses & Public Health. (CABI Publishing Ser.). (Illus.). 350p. 2000. text. write for info. (*0-85199-436-9*) OUP.

MacPherson, C. N. L., jt. ed. see Craig, P.

MacPherson, Camilia G. A Critical Reading of the Development of Raimon Panikkar's Thought on the Trinity. LC 95-43443. 174p. 1996. pap. text 34.00 (*0-7618-0184-7*); lib. bdg. 54.00 (*0-7618-0183-9*) U Pr of Amer.

Macpherson, Charles. Memoirs of the Life & Travels of the Late Charles Macpherson, Esq. in Asia, Africa & America. 1977. 19.95 (*0-8369-9229-6*, 9083) Ayer.

Macpherson, Colin, jt. auth. see Pierce, Steven R.

Macpherson, Crawford B., ed. Property, Mainstream & Critical Positions. LC 78-2311. 217p. reprint ed. pap. 67.30 (*0-8357-8290-5*, 203406200088) Bks Demand.

MacPherson, Dave. The Incredible Cover-Up. 171p. (C). 1980. pap. text 6.99 (*0-931608-06-6*) Omega Pubns OR.

Macpherson, David. The Rapture Plot. 290p. (Orig.). 1995. pap. 14.95 (*0-9625220-2-3*) Millennium Three Pubs.

Macpherson, David & Bay, Tom. CYA-Change Your Attitude: Creating Success One Thought at a Time. Date not set. pap. 14.95 (*0-9659497-0-2*) MacBay Prsntations.

Macpherson, David, jt. auth. see Bay, Tom.

MacPherson, David A., jt. auth. see Hirsch, Barry T.

MacPherson, Don. Leading Ladies. LC 86-13833. (Illus.). 1986. 25.00 (*0-312-47649-3*) St Martin.

MacPherson, Duncan. Bullet Penetration: Modeling the Dynamics & the Incapacitation Resulting from Wound Trauma. LC 94-79577. (Illus.). 303p. 1994. 39.95 (*0-9643577-0-4*) Ballistic Pubns.

***Macpherson, Edie, ed.** Bridges To The Heart (1999 Youth Devotional) A Collection Of 28 Devotionals For Teens. 32p. 1998. 3.99 (*0-8341-1761-4*) Beacon Hill.

Macpherson, G., ed. Our NHS: Celebration of 50 Years. (Illus.). 227p. 1998. text 36.00 (*0-7279-1279-8*, Pub. by BMJ Pub) Login Brothers Bk Co.

MacPherson, George. Home-Grown Energy from Short-Rotation Coppice. (Illus.). 250p. (C). 1995. 32.95 (*0-85236-289-7*, Pub. by Farming Pr) Diamond Farm Bk.

MacPherson, Glenn J., jt. ed. see Marvin, Ursula B.

MacPherson, Gordon. Black's Medical Dictionary. 39th ed. 1999. 39.95 (*1-56833-129-0*) Madison Bks UPA.

Macpherson, Gordon, ed. Black's Medical Dictionary. 656p. (C). 1992. text 95.00 (*0-389-20989-9*) B&N Imports.

Macpherson, H. D., jt. auth. see Kaye, R. W.

Macpherson, Hugh & Kaptchuk, Ted J. Acupuncture in Practice: Case Histories from the West. LC 96-26153. 1996. text 55.00 (*0-443-05049-X*) Church.

Macpherson, Ian. Wild Harbour. (Classics Ser.). (Illus.). 208p. 1996. pap. 9.95 (*0-86241-234-X*, Pub. by Canongate Books) Interlink Pub.

Macpherson, Ian, ed. Juan Manuel Studies. (Monografias A Ser.: Vol. LX). (SPA.). 199p. (C). 1977. 51.00 (*0-7293-0024-2*, Pub. by Tamesis Bks Ltd) Boydell & Brewer.

MacPherson, Ian, ed. Western Canada. (Illus.). 80p. 1985. pap. text 15.00 (*0-89745-064-7*) Sunflower U Pr.

Macpherson, Ian, tr. see Garcia Lorca, Federico.

MacPherson, Ian R., jt. auth. see MacKay, Angus.

Macpherson, James. Fragments of Ancient Poetry, Collected in the Highlands of Scotland, & Translated from the Galic or Erse Language. LC 92-1719. (Augustan Reprints Ser.: No. 122). 1966. reprint ed. 14.50 (*0-404-70122-1*, PR3544) AMS Pr.

M

MacPherson, James. The Highlander: An Heroic Poem in Six Cantos. LC 78-67535. reprint ed. 37.50 (*0-404-17198-2*) AMS Pr.

Macpherson, James. Poems of Ossian, 2 vols. LC 76-144459. reprint ed. 195.00 (*0-404-08697-7*) AMS Pr.

MacPherson, James. Poems of Ossian. (BCL1-PR English Literature Ser.). 298p. 1992. reprint ed. lib. bdg. 79.00 (*0-7812-7370-6*) Rprt Serv.

Macpherson, James. The Poems of Ossian & Related Works. Gaskill, Howard et al, eds. 480p. 1996. pap. 28.00 (*0-7486-0707-2*, Pub. by Edinburgh U Pr) Col U Pr.

— Poems of Ossian in the Original Gaelic, 3 vols. M'Arthur, John, ed. LC 70-144460. reprint ed. 185.00 (*0-404-08730-2*) AMS Pr.

Macpherson, James & Ossian. Ossian's Fingal, 1792. LC 96-2989. (Revolution & Romanticism, 1789-1834 Ser.). 224p. 1996. 75.00 (*1-85477-208-2*) Continuum.

Macpherson, James, ed. see Ossian.

MacPherson, James L. & Kasprisin, Duke O. Therapeutic Hemapheresis, 2 vols., Vol. 1. LC 84-17637. 224p. 1985. 132.00 (*0-8493-6148-6*, RB173) Franklin.

MacPherson, James L., jt. ed. see Kasprisin, Duke O.

Macpherson, Jay. The Spirit of Solitude: Conventions & Continuities in Late Romance. LC 81-11462. (Illus.). 364p. 1982. 50.00 (*0-300-02632-3*) Yale U Pr.

Macpherson, Jay, tr. see Marmeladov, Yuri.

MacPherson, Jena. Travel Smart: Pacific Northwest. 2nd rev. ed. (Travel Smart Ser.). (Illus.). 272p. 1999. pap. 16.95 (*1-56261-455-X*) Avalon Travel.

MacPherson, Jennifer B. As They Burn the Theater Down. LC 98-75648. 96p. 1998. pap. 10.00 (*0-9643477-6-8*) Hale Mary Pr.

— Cute & Perky, Slim & Sexy: A Poet's Guide to Personal Ads. LC 96-27264. 68p. 1996. pap. 14.95 (*0-7734-2669-8*, Mellen Poetry Pr) E Mellen.

MacPherson, John. Tales from Barra Told by The Coddy. 160p. pap. 11.95 (*1-874744-03-3*, Pub. by Birlinn Ltd) Dufour.

Macpherson, Kay. When in Doubt, Do Both: The Times of My Life. (Illus.). 298p. 1994. pap. 18.95 (*0-8020-7473-1*); text 50.00 (*0-8020-0454-7*) U of Toronto Pr.

Macpherson, Ken. Frigates of the Royal Canadian Navy, 1943-1974. (Illus.). 112p. 1993. 24.95 (*0-920277-22-5*, Vanwell Pub) Howell Pr VA.

— Minesweepers of the Royal Canadian Navy, 1938-1945. (Illus.). 110p. 1993. 24.95 (*0-920277-55-1*, Pub. by Vanwell Publ) Howell Pr VA.

Macpherson, Ken, jt. auth. see Barrie, Ron.

Macpherson, Ken, jt. auth. see Milner, Marc.

MacPherson, Kenneth & Bryher, Winifred, eds. Close-up: A Magazine Devoted to the Art of Films, Set, Vols 1[00ad]10. LC 70-88572. (Contemporary Art Ser.). reprint ed. 330.00 (*0-405-00732-9*) Ayer.

MacPherson, Kerrie. Asian Department Stores. LC 97-38823. (ConsumAsiaN Ser.). (Illus.). 288p. 1998. text 45.00 (*0-8248-1987-X*) UH Pr.

Macpherson, Kerrie L. A Wilderness of Marshes: The Origins of Public Health in Shanghai, 1843-1893. (East Asian Historical Monographs). (Illus.). 356p. 1987. text 39.95 (*0-19-584019-4*) OUP.

Macpherson, Kevin D. Fill Your Oil Paintings with Light & Color. LC 96-25743. (Illus.). 144p. 1997. 28.99 (*0-89134-687-2*, North Lght Bks) F & W Pubns Inc.

***Macpherson, Kevin D.** Fill Your Oil Paintings with Light & Color. (Illus.). 144p. 2000. pap. 19.99 (*1-58180-053-3*, North Lght Bks) F & W Pubns Inc.

MacPherson, L., jt. auth. see MacPherson, C.

MacPherson, Lillian, jt. auth. see DeCoste, F. C.

***Macpherson, M. A.** Outlaws & Lawmen of the American West. 232p. 2000. pap. 10.95 (*1-55105-164-8*) Lone Pine.

— Outlaws of the Canadian West. 232p. 1999. pap. 11.95 (*1-55105-166-4*) Lone Pine.

***MacPherson, Malcolm.** Cowboy & the Elephant. 2000. text. write for info. (*0-312-25209-9*) St Martin.

— Deadlock. 180p. 1998. 16.95 incl. audio (*1-56431-230-5*) Sunset Prod.

MacPherson, Malcolm, ed. The Black Box: All-New Cockpit Voice Recorder Accounts of In-Flight Accidents. rev. ed. LC 98-9888. 224p. 1998. pap. 15.00 (0-688-15892-7, Wm Morrow) Morrow Avon.

MacPherson, Malcolm C. Deadlock. LC 97-39747. 1998. 22.50 (0-684-83157-0) S&S Trade.

MacPherson, Mary. Best of Ontario. (Illus.). 240p. 1994. pap. 19.95 (1-55111-052-0) Broadview Pr.

Macpherson, Michael C. Family Years: A Guide to Positive Parenting. 146p. (Orig.). 1983. 5.95 (0-86683-772-8) Harper SF.

MacPherson, Michael C. Homecoming. LC 96-75496. 256p. (Orig.). 1996. pap. 13.00 (0-9642136-1-3) Green Duck Pr.

Macpherson, Michael C. Remembering. LC 94-96488. 224p. (Orig.). 1995. pap. 12.00 (0-9642136-0-5) Green Duck Pr.

MacPherson, Myra. She Came to Live Out Loud: An Inspiring Family Journey Through Illness, Loss & Grief. LC 98-28125. (Illus.). 384p. 1999. 24.50 (0-684-82264-4) Scribner.

Macpherson, Neill. Business Guide to Myanmar. 200p. 1997. pap. 17.95 (981-00-6795-X, Pub. by Select Bks) Weatherhill.

Macpherson, R., jt. auth. see Goresky, M.

MacPherson, R. D. Raoul Bott Vol. 2: Collected Papers: Differential Operators (the 1960s) (Contemporary Mathematicians Ser.). (Illus.). xxxiii, 802p. 1996. 104.50 (0-8176-3646-3) Birkhauser.

MacPherson, R. D., ed. The Collected Works of Raoul Bott: Topology of Lie Groups - the 1950s, Vol. 1. (Contemporary Mathematicians Ser.). (Illus.). 450p. 1995. 104.50 (0-8176-3613-7) Birkhauser.

— Raoul Bott: Collected Papers. 485p. 1994. 104.50 (0-8176-3647-1) Birkhauser.

— Raoul Bott: Collected Papers. (Contemporary Mathematicians Ser.: Vol. 4). 484p. 1994. 104.50 (0-8176-3648-X) Birkhauser.

MacPherson, R. D., jt. auth. see Brylinski, Jean-Luc.

MacPherson, R. J. Educative Accountability: Theory, Practice, Policy & Research in Educational Administration. LC 96-41875. ix, 388p. 1996. 78.00 (0-08-042768-5, Pergamon Pr) Elsevier.

Macpherson, R. J., jt. ed. see Duignan, P. A.

Macpherson, R. J., jt. ed. see Martin, Yvonne M.

MacPherson, Rett. A Comedy of Heirs. 2nd ed. LC 99-22065. 214p. 1999. text 21.95 (0-312-20513-9) St Martin.

— Family Skeletons, Vol. 1. 1998. 5.99 (0-312-96602-4, Pub. by Tor Bks) St Martin.

***MacPherson, Rett.** Misty Mourning. 2000. 22.95 (0-312-26619-7) St Martin.

MacPherson, Rett. Veiled Antiquity. LC 98-6929. 224p. 1998. text 20.95 (0-312-18677-0) St Martin.

— Veiled Antiquity, Vol. 1. Vol. 1. 240p. 1999. 5.99 (0-312-96701-2, Pub. by Tor Bks) St Martin.

Macpherson, Reynold J. The Politics of Accountability: Educative & International Perspectives. LC 98-154496. (Yearbook of the Politics of Education Association Ser.). 240p. 1998. pap. 24.95 (0-8039-6687-3) Corwin Pr.

MacPherson, Robert, jt. auth. see Fulton, William.

MacPherson, Robert D., ed. Collected Works of Raoul Bott, Set. LC 93-36938. (Contemporary Mathematicians Ser.). 1993. write for info. (3-7643-3701-X) Birkhauser.

— Collected Works of Raoul Bott, Set. LC 93-36938. (Contemporary Mathematicians Ser.). 1995. 324.50 (0-8176-3701-X) Birkhauser.

MacPherson, Rod. Guide to Caribbean Reef Fish. 2p. 1995. 4.75 (0-939560-10-0) Natural World.

— Guide to Hawaiian Flowers. 2p. 1995. 4.75 (0-939560-17-8) Natural World.

— Guide to Hawaiian Reef Fish. 2p. 1994. 4.75 (0-939560-04-6) Natural World.

— Guide to Pacific Coast Inshore Fish. 2p. 1996. 4.75 (0-939560-18-6) Natural World.

— Guide to Reef Fish of Florida. 2p. 1995. 4.75 (0-939560-05-4) Natural World.

— Guide to Reef Fish of Micronesia. 2p. 1995. 4.75 (0-939560-15-1) Natural World.

— Guide to Reef Fish of the Bahamas. 2p. 1995. 4.75 (0-939560-06-2) Natural World.

— Guide to Reef Fish of the Cayman Islands. 2p. 1995. 4.75 (0-939560-08-9) Natural World.

— Guide to Reef Fish of the Indian Ocean. 2p. 1995. 4.75 (0-939560-12-7) Natural World.

— Guide to Reef Fish of the Red Sea. 2p. 1995. 4.75 (0-939560-11-9) Natural World.

— Guide to Reef Fish of the West Central Pacific. 2p. 1995. 4.75 (0-939560-13-5) Natural World.

— Guide to Reef Fish of the Western Pacific. 2p. 1995. 4.75 (0-939560-14-3) Natural World.

— Guide to the Birds of Hawaii. 2p. 1995. 4.75 (0-939560-16-X) Natural World.

— Guide to the Birds of Hawaii Volcanoes National Park. 2p. 1996. 4.75 (0-939560-20-8) Natural World.

— Guide to the Fish of the Sea of Cortez. 2p. 1996. 4.75 (0-939560-19-4) Natural World.

— Guide to the Reef Fish of the Coastal Caribbean. 2p. 1995. 4.75 (0-939560-09-7) Natural World.

MacPherson, Selina. Conquer the Night. 384p. (Orig.). 1995. mass mkt. 4.99 (0-380-77252-3, Avon Bks) Morrow Avon.

— Embrace the Wild Dawn. 368p. (Orig.). 1994. mass mkt. 4.50 (0-380-77251-5, Avon Bks) Morrow Avon.

— Forbidden Flame. 400p. (Orig.). 1993. mass mkt. 4.50 (0-380-77250-7, Avon Bks) Morrow Avon.

— Rough & Tender. 384p. 1991. pap. 3.95 (0-380-76322-2, Avon Bks) Morrow Avon.

***MacPherson, Selina.** Scandalous Bride. 2000. mass mkt. 5.99 (0-8217-6861-1, Zebra Kensgtn) Kensgtn Pub Corp.

MacPherson, Stewart. Social Policy in the Third World: The Social Dilemmas of Underdevelopment. LC 82-6837. 220p. (C). 1983. pap. text 20.00 (0-86598-090-X, R3890) Rowman.

MacPherson, Stewart & Cheng, Joseph Y., eds. Economic & Social Development in South China. LC 96-4212. (Illus.). 344p. 1996. 95.00 (1-85898-301-0) E Elgar.

MacPherson, Stewart & Wong, Hoi K., eds. Social Development & Societies in Transition. LC 97-77893. (Illus.). 302p. 1998. text 67.95 (1-84014-136-0, Pub. by Ashgate Pub) Ashgate Pub Co.

MacPherson, Stewart, jt. auth. see Bandyopadhyay, Mridula.

MacPherson, Stewart, jt. ed. see Wong, Linda.

Macpherson, W. J. The Economic Development of Japan, 1868-1941. (New Studies in Economic & Social History: Vol. 2). 106p. (C). 1995. text 34.95 (0-521-55261-3); pap. text 10.95 (0-521-55792-5) Cambridge U Pr.

Macpherson, W. J., ed. The Industrialization of Japan. LC 93-43724. (Industrial Revolutions Ser.: No. 7). 1994. 124.95 (0-631-18074-5) Blackwell Pubs.

Macpherson, William. The Stephen Lawrence Inquiry. (Command Papers (All) Ser.: No. 4262-I). xii, 342p. 1999. pap. 55.00 (0-10-142622-4, HM26224, Pub. by Statnry Office) Balogh.

MacPherson, Winnie. Cheetahs for Kids. LC 98-15942. (Wildlife for Kids Ser.). (Illus.). 48p. (J). (gr. 3-7). 1998. pap. 6.95 (1-55971-665-7, NorthWord Pr) Creat Pub Intl.

***MacPherson, Winnie.** Cheetahs for Kids. (Wildlife for Kids Ser.). (Illus.). (J). 1998. 12.40 (0-606-18076-1) Turtleback.

MacPhie, Les, jt. auth. see Harris, Graham.

***MacPhillamy, Daizui.** Roar of the Tigress: The Oral Teachings of Rev. Master Jiyu-Kennet: Western Woman & Zen Master. 2001. pap. 17.00 (0-930066-21-9) Shasta Abbey.

MacPhillamy, Daizui, ed. see Great Master Dogen.

MacPhillamy, Daizui, jt. ed. see Jiyu-Kennett, P. T.

MacPike, Loralee, ed. There's Something I've Been Meaning to Tell You: An Anthology about Lesbians & Gay Men Coming Out to Their Children. 288p. 1989. 16.95 (0-941483-54-1); pap. 9.95 (0-941483-44-4) Naiad Pr.

***Macquarie Corporate Finance Ltd. Staff.** Guide to Financing Transport Projects. 120p. 2000. pap. text 225.00 (1-85564-752-4, Pub. by Euromoney) Am Educ Systs.

Macquarrie, A. The Saints of Scotland: Essays in Scottish Church History, AD 450-1093. LC 97-146852. 200p. 1996. pap. 75.00 (0-85976-446-X, Pub. by J Donald) St Mut.

— Scotland & the Crusades, 1095-1560. 168p. 1996. pap. 75.00 (0-85976-445-1, Pub. by J Donald) St Mut.

MacQuarrie, Gordon. Flyfishing with MacQuarrie: Sixteen Classic Tales. (Illus.). 254p. 1995. 19.50 (1-57223-025-8, 0258) Willow Creek Pr.

— The Gordon MacQuarrie Trilogy, 3 vols. Taylor, Zack, ed. (Illus.). 572p. 1985. boxed set 49.00 (1-57223-006-1, 1507) Willow Creek Pr.

MacQuarrie, Gordon. Gordon MacQuarrie Trilogy. abr. ed. 1994. 45.00 incl. audio (1-57223-017-7, 0177) Willow Creek Pr.

MacQuarrie, Gordon. The Last Stories of the Old Duck Hunters, Vol. 3. (Illus.). 151p. 1994. 19.50 (1-57223-005-3, 1510) Willow Creek Pr.

MacQuarrie, Gordon. Last Stories of the Old Duck Hunters Audio, Vol. 3. abr. ed. (Gordon MacQuarrie Trilogy Ser.). 1994. 16.95 incl. audio (1-57223-016-9, 0169) Willow Creek Pr.

— More Stories of the Old Duck Hunters Audio, Vol. 2. abr. ed. (Gordon MacQuarrie Trilogy Ser.). 1994. 16.95 incl. audio (1-57223-015-0, 0150) Willow Creek Pr.

MacQuarrie, Gordon. Stories of the Old Duck Hunters & Other Drivel, Vol. 1. Taylor, Zack, ed. (Illus.). 223p. 1994. 19.50 (1-57223-003-7, 1508) Willow Creek Pr.

MacQuarrie, Gordon. Stories of the Old Duck Hunters Audio, Vol. 1. abr. ed. (Gordon MacQuarrie Trilogy Ser.). 1994. 16.95 incl. audio (1-57223-014-2, 0142) Willow Creek Pr.

MacQuarrie, Heath. Red Tory Blues: A Political Memoir. 320p. 1992. text 35.00 (0-8020-5958-9) U of Toronto Pr.

Macquarrie, John. Christology Revisited. LC 98-39835. 128p. 1998. pap. 13.00 (1-56338-252-0) TPI PA.

— The Concept of Peace. LC 90-34038. 96p. (Orig.). (C). 1990. pap. text 8.00 (0-334-02449-8) TPI PA.

— An Existentialist Theology: A Comparison of Heidegger & Bultmann. LC 79-4604. 252p. 1979. reprint ed. lib. bdg. 35.00 (0-313-20795-X, MAAE, Greenwood Pr) Greenwood.

— God-Talk: An Examination of the Language & Logic of Theology. 1982. 9.95 (0-8164-2205-2) Harper SF.

— A Guide to the Sacraments. 256p. 1998. pap. 16.95 (0-8264-1100-2) Continuum.

— Heidegger & Christianity: The Hensley Henon Lectures, 1993-94. 144p. (C). 1999. pap. 15.95 (0-8264-1171-1) Continuum.

— Jesus Christ in Modern Thought. LC 90-31831. 464p. (C). 1991. pap. 24.00 (0-334-02446-3) TPI PA.

— Mary for All Christians. 160p. 1992. reprint ed. 21.95 (0-00-599219-2, Pub. by T & T Clark) Bks Intl VA.

— Mediators Between Human & Divine: From Moses to Muhammad. LC 79-5052. 180p. 1999. pap. 15.95 (0-8264-1170-3) Continuum.

***MacQuarrie, John.** Mediators Between Human & Divine: From Moses to Muhammad. 171p. 2000. reprint ed. 20.00 (0-7881-9343-0) DIANE Pub.

— On Being a Theologian. 1998. pap. 23.00 (0-334-02771-3) TPI PA.

Macquarrie, John. Paths in Spirituality. 2nd ed. LC 93-8172. 176p. 1993. pap. 12.95 (0-8192-1602-X) Morehouse Pub.

MacQuarrie, John. Principles of Christian Theology. 1985. 24.00 (0-684-14777-7) S&S Trade.

Macquarrie, John. Principles of Christian Theology. 2nd ed. LC 76-23182. 544p. (C). 1977. pap. text 36.00 (0-02-374510-X, Macmillan Coll) P-H.

MacQuarrie, John & Macquarrie, John. Mystery & Truth. (Pere Marquette Lectures). 1970. 15.00 (0-87462-518-1) Marquette.

Macquarrie, John, jt. auth. see MacQuarrie, John.

Macquarrie, John, jt. ed. see Childress, James F.

MacQuarrie, Kate, jt. auth. see McAskill, J. Dan.

MacQueen, Bruce D. Myth, Rhetoric, & Fiction: A Reading of Longus's Daphnis & Chloe. LC 90-12054. 297p. 1990. reprint ed. pap. 92.10 (0-608-01856-2, 206250600003) Bks Demand.

Macqueen, Chris. Getting Ahead in Tertiary Studies: A Practical Guide for Business, Social Science & Arts Students. LC 98-170580. 160p. 1998. pap. 14.95 (0-86840-592-2, Pub. by New South Wales Univ Pr) Intl Spec Bk.

MacQueen, Hector L. Copyright, Competition & Industrial Design. (David Hume Papers: No. 14). 117p. 1990. pap. text 14.00 (0-08-037965-6, Pub. by Aberdeen U Pr) Macmillan.

— Copyright, Competition & Industrial Design. 128p. 1996. pap. 16.00 (0-7486-0733-1, Pub. by Edinburgh U Pr) Col U Pr.

— MacQueen: Studying Scots Law. 170p. 1993. pap. 20.00 (0-406-00013-1, U.K., MICHIE) LEXIS Pub.

MacQueen, Hector L. & Thomson, J. M. MacQueen & Thomson: Contract Law in Scotland. 1997. write for info. (0-406-05397-9, MSLC, MICHIE) LEXIS Pub.

MacQueen, Hector L., et al. The Reform of Civil Justice. LC 98-128930. (Hume Papers on Public Policy Ser.). x, 115 p. 1997. write for info. (0-7486-1123-1) Edinburgh U Pr.

MacQueen, Hector L., jt. ed. see Kiralfy, Albert.

Macqueen, J. G. The Hittites: And Their Contemporaries in Asia Minor. 4th rev. ed. LC 85-51750. (Ancient Peoples & Places Ser.). (Illus.). 180p. 1996. pap. 15.95 (0-500-27887-3, Pub. by Thames Hudson) Norton.

MacQueen, Jack. Numerology: Theory & Outline of a Literary Mode. 163p. 1985. 25.00 (0-85224-492-4, Pub. by Edinburgh U Pr) Col U Pr.

MacQueen, John. Humanism in Renaissance Scotland. 224p. 1990. 68.00 (0-7486-0111-2, Pub. by Edinburgh U Pr) Col U Pr.

MacQueen, Megan, ed. see Mills, Kenneth G.

MacQueen, Neal, jt. auth. see Armstrong-Hansche, Melissa.

MacQueen, Neil. Computers, Kids & Christian Education. LC 98-135619. 1998. pap. text 14.99 (0-8066-3638-6, 15-8665, Augsburg) Augsburg Fortress.

MacQueen, Norrie. The Decolonization of Portuguese Africa: Metropolitan Revolution & the Dissolution of Empire. LC 96-34685. 288p. (C). 1997. 63.00 (0-582-25994-0) Longman.

Macqueen, Norrie. The United Nations since 1945. LC 98-39611. (Seminar Studies in History). 149p. 1999. pap. text 13.00 (0-582-35673-3) Longman.

MacQueen, Peter. In Wildest Africa. 1909. 29.00 (0-403-00353-9) Scholarly.

MacQueen, Roger W. & Leckie, Dale A., eds. Foreland Basins & Fold Belts. (AAPG Memoir Ser.: No. 55). (Illus.). x, 460p. 1992. 89.00 (0-89181-334-9, 578) AAPG.

Macqueen, Roger W., jt. ed. see Hutchinson, R. W.

***Macquet, Dominique.** Dominique's Fresh Flavors: Contemporary French Cuisine in New Orleans. (Illus.). 208p. 2000. 24.95 (1-58008-153-3) Ten Speed Pr.

MacQuitty, Jane. Jane MacQuitty's Guide to Champagne & Sparkling Wines. 318p. 1993. pap. 14.95 (1-85732-948-1, Pub. by Reed Illust Books) Antique Collect.

MacQuitty, Mirand A. Ocean. LC 97-18889. (Inside Guides Ser.). (J). 1997. write for info. (0-7894-2035-X) DK Pub Inc.

***MacQuitty, Miranda.** Desert. (Eyewitness Books). (Illus.). (J). (gr. 4-7). 2000. 19.99 (0-7894-6600-7) DK Pub Inc.

— Desert. (Eyewitness Books). (J). (gr. 4-7). 2000. 15.95 (0-7894-5862-4) DK Pub Inc.

— Ocean. (Eyewitness Books). (Illus.). (J). (gr. 4-7). 2000. 19.99 (0-7894-6611-2) DK Pub Inc.

— Ocean. (Eyewitness Books). (J). (gr. 4-7). 2000. 15.95 (0-7894-6034-3) DK Pub Inc.

— Ocean. (Illus.). 64p. (J). (gr. 5). 1995. 19.00 (0-679-87331-7); lib. bdg. 20.99 (0-679-97331-1) Random.

— Shark. (Eyewitness Books). (Illus.). (J). (gr. 4-7). 2000. 19.99 (0-7894-6589-2) DK Pub Inc.

— Shark. (Eyewitness Books). (J). (gr. 4-7). 2000. 15.95 (0-7894-5778-4) DK Pub Inc.

***Macrae.** Presenting Young Adult Fantasy. LC 98-12896. 464p. 1998. 26.95 (0-8057-8220-6, Twyne) Mac Lib Ref.

Macrae, Alasdair D. W. B. Yeats: A Literary Life. LC 94-20524. (Literary Lives Ser.). 1994. text 45.00 (0-312-12310-8) St Martin.

Macrae, Alexander. Macrae: History of the Clan Macrae, with Genealogies. (Illus.). xxii, 442p. 1992. reprint ed. pap. 71.00 (0-8328-2683-9); reprint ed. lib. bdg. 81.00 (0-8328-2682-0) Higginson Bk Co.

MacRae, Allan A. The Gospel of Isaiah. LC 92-71421. 192p. 1992. pap. 9.95 (0-944788-94-7) IBRI.

— JEDP: Lectures on the Higher Criticism of the Pentateuch. LC 89-81338. 294p. 1994. pap. 12.95 (0-944788-89-0) IBRI.

— Studies in Isaiah. LC 95-80673. vi, 358p. (Orig.). 1995. pap. 13.95 (0-944788-88-2) IBRI.

MacRae, C. Neil, et al, eds. Stereotypes & Stereotyping. LC 95-37283. 462p. 1996. lib. bdg. 58.00 (1-57230-053-1) Guilford Pubns.

MacRae-Campbell, Linda & McKisson, Micki. Endangered Species: Their Struggle to Survive. (Our Only Earth Ser.). 104p. (J). (gr. 4-12). 1990. 25.00 (0-913705-54-3) Zephyr Pr AZ.

Macrae-Campbell, Linda & McKisson, Micki. The Future of Our Tropical Rainforests. (Our Only Earth Ser.). 104p. (J). (gr. 4-12). 1990. pap. text 25.00 (0-913705-49-7) Zephyr Pr AZ.

MacRae-Campbell, Linda, et al. The Ocean Crisis. (Our Only Earth Ser.). 104p. (J). (gr. 4-12). 1990. pap. 25.00 (0-913705-53-5) Zephyr Pr AZ.

MacRae-Campbell, Linda, jt. auth. see McKisson, Micki.

MacRae, Cara. Psychosocial Occupational Therapy: A Clinical Practice. LC 97-46388. (Teaching Methods Ser.). 704p. (C). 1997. pap. 37.95 (0-8273-6283-8) Delmar.

Macrae, Chris. Brand Chartering Handbook: How Brand Organizations Learn Living Scripts. 1996. 30.00 (0-201-87743-0) Addison-Wesley.

MacRae, Diann. Birder's Guide to Washington. LC 95-1573. (Illus.). 336p. 1995. pap. 17.95 (0-88415-126-3, 5126) Gulf Pub.

MacRae, Donald L. Television Production: An Introduction. 2nd ed. (Illus.). 1982. pap. 17.95 (0-458-93930-7, 6508) Routledge.

MacRae, Donald L. & Hartleib, Carl J. Relating Styles Participant Kit. 1981. pap. text 65.00 (0-07-092327-2) McGraw.

MacRae, Duncan, Jr. Policy Indicators: Links Between Social Science & Public Debate. LC 84-17294. (Urban & Regional Policy & Development Studies). xvi, 414p. 1985. 59.95 (0-8078-1628-0) U of NC Pr.

MacRae, Duncan, Jr. & Whittington, Dale. Expert Advice for Policy Choice: Analysis & Discourse. Rabe, Barry & Tierney, John, eds. LC 96-46602. (American Governance & Public Policy Ser.). 432p. 1997. 65.00 (0-87840-640-9); pap. 25.00 (0-87840-641-7) Georgetown U Pr.

MaCrae, Duncan, Jr. & Wilde, James A. Policy Analysis for Public Decisions. 344p. 1985. reprint ed. pap. text 25.50 (0-8191-4835-0) U Pr of Amer.

MacRae, George W. The Epistle to the Hebrews. Karris, Robert J., ed. (Collegeville Bible Commentary - New Testament Ser.: No. 10). 64p. (C). 1983. pap. 4.95 (0-8146-1310-1) Liturgical Pr.

MacRae, George W., ed. see Conzelmann, Hans.

Macrae-Gibson, Gavin. The Secret Life of Buildings: An American Mythology for Modern Architecture. (Graham Foundation Architecture Ser.). 223p. 1985. 35.00 (0-262-13203-6) MIT Pr.

Macrae-Gibson, O. D., ed. Of Arthour & of Merlin Vol. I: Text, Vol. I, Text. (OS 268 Ser.: No. 26). 1973. 29.95 (0-19-722270-6) OUP.

— Of Arthour & of Merlin Vol. II: Introduction, Notes & Glossary, Vol. II, Intro., Notes & Glossary. (OS 279 Ser.: No. 279). 1979. 29.95 (0-19-722281-1) OUP.

Macrae, Janet. Therapeutic Touch: A Practical Guide. LC 87-45444. (Illus.). 112p. 1988. pap. 10.00 (0-394-75588-X) Knopf.

Macrae, Janet A., jt. ed. see Calabria, Michael D.

Macrae, John, ed. see Abbey, Edward.

MacRae, Joyce. Showcase of Interior Design: Pacific Edition 2. LC 95-44671. 235p. 1996. 39.00 (1-883065-08-9) Rockport Vitae Pub.

MacRae, Julia. Window. 1992. write for info. (1-85681-010-0, Pub. by Julia MacRae) Random House.

Macrae, Mason. The Distant Hills. large type ed. (Linford Western Library). 352p. 1985. pap. 16.99 (0-7089-6188-6) Ulverscroft.

Macrae, Neil, jt. auth. see Ellis, Hadyn D.

MacRae, Norma M. Canning & Preserving Without Sugar. 4th rev. ed. LC 96-41194. (Illus.). 240p. (Orig.). 1996. pap. 15.95 (1-56440-992-9) Globe Pequot.

Macrae, Robert. HPLC in Food Analysis. 2nd ed. 502p. 1988. text 121.00 (0-12-464781-2) Acad Pr.

Macrae, Robert, et al, eds. Encyclopedia of Food Science, Food Technology & Nutrition, 8 vols. LC 92-15557. (Illus.). 5500p. 1993. text 2414.00 (0-12-226850-4) Acad Pr.

— Encyclopedia of Food Science, Food Technology, & Nutrition, 8 vols., 1. LC 92-15557. (Illus.). 1993. text 314.00 (0-12-226851-2) Acad Pr.

— Encyclopedia of Food Science, Food Technology, & Nutrition, 8 vols., 2. LC 92-15557. (Illus.). 1993. text 314.00 (0-12-226852-0) Acad Pr.

— Encyclopedia of Food Science, Food Technology, & Nutrition, 8 vols., 3. LC 92-15557. (Illus.). 1993. text 314.00 (0-12-226853-9) Acad Pr.

— Encyclopedia of Food Science, Food Technology, & Nutrition, 8 vols., 4. LC 92-15557. (Illus.). 1993. text 314.00 (0-12-226854-7) Acad Pr.

— Encyclopedia of Food Science, Food Technology, & Nutrition, 8 vols., 5. LC 92-15557. (Illus.). 1993. text 314.00 (0-12-226855-5) Acad Pr.

— Encyclopedia of Food Science, Food Technology, & Nutrition, 8 vols., 6. LC 92-15557. (Illus.). 1993. text 314.00 (0-12-226856-3) Acad Pr.

— Encyclopedia of Food Science, Food Technology, & Nutrition, 8 vols., 7. LC 92-15557. (Illus.). 1993. text 314.00 (0-12-226857-1) Acad Pr.

— Encyclopedia of Food Science, Food Technology, & Nutrition, 8 vols., 8. LC 92-15557. (Illus.). 1993. text 314.00 (0-12-226858-X) Acad Pr.

***Macrae, Scott, et al.** Customized Corneal Ablation. 400p. (C). 2000. text 180.00 (1-55642-488-4) SLACK Inc.

MacRae, Sheila & Jeffers, H. Paul. Hollywood Mother of the Year: Sheila MacRae's Own Story. (Illus.). 256p. 1992. 18.95 (1-55972-112-X, Birch Ln Pr) Carol Pub Group.

MacRae, Thomas H., et al, eds. Biochemistry & Cell Biology of Artemia. 272p. 1988. 156.00 (0-8493-4897-8, QL444, CRC Reprint) Franklin.

***MacRaild, Donald M.** The Great Famine & Beyond: Irish Migrants in Britain in the Nineteenth & Twentieth Centuries. LC 99-47584. 208p. 2000. pap. 24.50 (0-7165-2720-0, Pub. by Irish Acad Pr) Intl Spec Bk.

MacRaild, Donald M. Irish Migrants in Modern Britain, 1750-1922. LC 98-42418. (Social History in Perspective Ser.). 240p. 1999. text 59.95 (0-312-22032-4) St Martin.

***MacRaild, Donald M.** Labour in British Society 1830. LC 99-45253. 2000. text 65.00 (0-312-23313-2) St Martin.

***MacRaild, Donald M., ed.** The Great Famine & Beyond: Irish Migrants in Britain in the Nineteenth & Twentieth Centuries. 208p. 2000. 49.50 (0-7146-5009-9, Pub. by F Cass Pubs); pap. 24.50 (0-7146-8065-6, Pub. by F Cass Pubs) Intl Spec Bk.

***MacRaild, Donald M. & Hepburn, A. C., eds.** The Great Famine & Beyond: Irish Immigrants in Britain in the Nineteenth & Twentieth Centuries. LC 99-47584. 208p. 2000. 52.50 (0-7165-2706-5, Pub. by Irish Acad Pr) Intl Spec Bk.

Macrakis, Kristie. Surviving the Swastika: Scientific Research in Nazi Germany. LC 93-19919. (Illus.). 320p. 1993. text 49.95 (0-19-507010-0) OUP.

Macrakis, Kristie & Hoffman, Dieter. Science under Socialism: East Germany in Comparative Perspective. LC 98-41275. xiv, 380p. 1999. 55.00 (0-674-79477-X) HUP.

Macrakis, Michael S. Scarcity's Ways: The Origins of Capital: A Critical Essay on THermodynamics, Statistical Mechanics & Economics. LC 97-35847. (Boston Studies in the Philosophy of Science: No. 176). 240p. 1997. 107.00 (0-7923-4760-9) Kluwer Academic.

Macrakis, Michael S., ed. Greek Letters: From Tablets to Pixels. LC 96-36875. 300p. 1996. 49.95 (1-884718-27-2, 45576) Oak Knoll.

Macran, Henry S., ed. Harmonika Stoicheia - The Harmonics of Aristoxenus. 303p. 1990. reprint ed. 70.00 (3-487-05254-7) G Olms Pubs.

Macrander, Albert T., et al, eds. Crystal & Multilayer Optics, Vol. 3448. LC 99-200343. 1998. 80.00 (0-8194-2903-1) SPIE.

Macrander, Albert T. & Khounsary, Ali M., eds. High Heat Flux & Synchrotron Radiation Beamlines, Vol. 3151. LC 98-143982. 352p. 1997. 80.00 (0-8194-2573-7) SPIE.

MacRaois, Cormac. Battle below Giltspur. (Illus.). 1989. pap. 8.95 (0-86327-198-7, Pub. by Wolfhound Press) Irish Amer Bk.

— Dance of the Midnight Fire. 1990. pap. 8.95 (0-86327-262-2) Dufour.

MacRaonuill, Alasdair. Eachdraidh a' Chiuil Mhoir - History of the Music Great. 380p. 1988. 69.00 (0-9621754-0-4); pap. 69.00 (0-9621754-1-2) A MacRaonuill.

MacRaonuill, Alasdair, ed. see MacDonald, J.

MacRaonuill, Alasdair, ed. & intro. see Glen, David.

MacRaonuill, Alasdair, ed. & intro. see MacDonald, Donald.

MacRaonuill, Alasdair, ed. & intro. see Ross, William.

MacRaonuill, Alasdair, ed. & intro. see Thomason, Charles S.

MacRaonuill, Alasdair, tr. & intro. see MacLeoid, Tormod, et al.

MacRauch, Earl. Buckaroo Banzai. 1984. pap. 4.95 (0-671-50574-2) S&S Trade.

Macray, W. Dunn, ed. see Hyde, Edward.

Macray, William D., ed. Charters & Documents Illustrating the History of the Cathedral: City & Diocese of Salisbury in the 12th & 13th Centuries. (Rolls Ser.: No. 97). 1972. reprint ed. 70.00 (0-8115-1176-6) Periodicals Srv.

— Chronicon Abbatiae de Evesham Ad Annum, 1418. (Rolls Ser.: No. 29). 1972. reprint ed. 70.00 (0-8115-1057-3) Periodicals Srv.

— Chronicon Abbatiae Rameseinesis. (Rolls Ser.: No. 83). 1972. reprint ed. 70.00 (0-8115-1156-1) Periodicals Srv.

***Macre, Norman.** John Von Neumann. LC 99-37303. 1999. write for info. (0-8218-2064-8) Am Math.

Macrea, Joanna & Zwi, Anthony, eds. War & Hunger: Rethinking International Responses to Complex Emergencies. LC 94-41463. 256p. (C). 1994. text 54.00 (1-85649-291-5, Pub. by Zed Books) St Martin.

Macready, Norra, ed. Protease Inhibitors: Therapeutic Application & Development. (Biomedical Library). 1997. pap. 795.00 (1-57936-022-X) IBC USA.

Macready, Sarah & Thompson, F. H. Archaeological Field Survey in Britain & Abroad. (Illus.). 250p. 1985. pap. 15.98 (0-85431-247-1, Pub. by Soc Antiquaries) David Brown.

Macready, Sarah, jt. ed. see Thompson, F. H.

MacReady, William C. The Diaries of William Charles MacReady, 2 vols., 1. Toynbee, William C., ed. LC 78-84519. 1972. 24.95 (0-405-08773-X, Pub. by Blom Pubns) Ayer.

— The Diaries of William Charles MacReady, 2 vols., 2. Toynbee, William C., ed. LC 78-84519. 1972. 24.95 (0-405-08774-8, Pub. by Blom Pubns) Ayer.

— The Diaries of William Charles MacReady, 2 vols., Set. Toynbee, William C., ed. LC 78-84519. 1026p. 1972. 48.95 (0-405-08772-1, Pub. by Blom Pubns) Ayer.

MacReamoinn, Sean, ed. Authority in the Church. LC 96-102161. 96p. (Orig.). 1996. pap. 9.95 (1-85607-154-5, Pub. by Columba Press) Whitecap Bks.

Macredie, R., et al, eds. Modelling for Added Value. LC 98-3911. (Illus.). 260p. 1998. pap. 89.95 (3-540-76108-X) Spr-Verlag.

MacReynolds, George, compiled by. Place Names in Bucks County, Pennsylvania, Alphabetically Arranged in an Historical Narrative. 474p. 1996. reprint ed. lib. bdg. 49.00 (0-8328-5218-X) Higginson Bk Co.

***Macri, Anthony.** A Medical Malpractice Case. LC 99-91027. 1999. 25.00 (0-7388-0596-3); pap. 18.00 (0-7388-0597-1) Xlibris Corp.

***Macricol.** Problem Knee. 224p. 1998. pap. text 60.00 (0-7506-4044-8) Buttrwrth-Heinemann.

***Macrides, Ruth.** Kinship & Justice in Byzantium, 11th-15th Centuries. LC 99-67231. (Variorum Collected Studies: Vol. 642). 320p. 2000. text 105.95 (0-86078-799-0, Pub. by Ashgate Pub) Ashgate Pub Co.

Macridis, Roy C. Contemporary Political Ideologies. 5th ed. (C). 1991. text 36.50 (0-673-52165-6) Addson-Wesley Educ.

— Foreign Policy in World Politics. 8th ed. 432p. (C). 1991. pap. text 43.60 (0-13-335084-3) P-H.

— Greek Politics at a Crossroads: What Kind of Socialism? (Publication Ser.: No. 299). 72p. (Orig.). (C). 1984. pap. text 3.98 (0-8179-7992-1) Hoover Inst Pr.

— Modern Political Systems: Europe. 7th ed. 528p. (C). 1990. text 48.00 (0-13-595356-1) P-H.

Macridis, Roy C. & Burg, Steven L. Introduction to Comparative Politics: Regimes & Change. 2nd ed. 224p. (C). 1997. pap. text 50.00 (0-673-52035-8) Addson-Wesley Educ.

Macridis, Roy C. & Hulliung, Mark. Contemporary Political Ideologies: Movements & Regimes. 6th ed. 320p. (C). 1997. pap. text 55.00 (0-673-52458-2) Addson-Wesley Educ.

Macrina, Francis L. Scientific Integrity: An Introductory Text with Cases. 2nd ed. LC 99-54234. (Illus.). 350p. (C). 2000. pap. text 39.95 (1-55581-152-3) ASM Pr.

Macris & Woodard. ERISA & Benefits Law Journal, Vol. 5, No. 3. 1998. pap. text 125.00 (0-327-00146-1, 80426-20) LEXIS Pub.

Macris, C. J., ed. see NATO Advanced Study Institute Staff.

Macris, George P. The Orthodox Church & the Ecumenical Movement During the Period 1920-1969. (Illus.). 196p. (Orig.). 1986. pap. 12.50 (0-913026-74-3) St Nectarios.

Macris, Georgia, ed. A Greek Feast: A Book of Greek Recipes. LC 93-72818. (Illus.). 254p. (Orig.). 1993. pap. 12.00 (0-9638023-0-5) Daugh of Penelope.

Macris, Michael, ed. ERISA & Benefits Law Journal. 1992. pap. 125.00 (1-56257-322-5, 80425-10, MICHIE) LEXIS Pub.

Macris, Ursula. Otto Furth, das Dramatische Werk der Wiener Jahre und Prosa im Exil, Vol. 10. (Austrian Culture Ser.). (GER.). VIII, 182p. (C). 1995. 45.95 (0-8204-2230-4) P Lang Pubng.

Macriss, R. A., et al. Physical & Thermodynamic Properties of Ammonia-Water Mixtures. (Research Bulletin Ser.: No. 34). iv, 42p. 1964. pap. 25.00 (1-58222-033-6) Inst Gas Tech.

MacRitchie, David. Accounts of the Gypsies of India. LC 97-179582. 254 p. 1997. write for info. (0-9656299-9-6) Glennfrey Pub.

— Scottish Gypsies under the Stewarts. LC 75-3463. reprint ed. 27.50 (0-404-16892-2) AMS Pr.

MacRitchie, David, ed. Accounts of the Gypsies of India. LC 75-3461. (Illus.). reprint ed. 34.50 (0-404-16893-0) AMS Pr.

MacRitchie, Finlay. Chemistry at Interfaces. 283p. 1990. text 81.00 (0-12-464785-5) Acad Pr.

MacRitchie, Finlay, jt. auth. see Bekes, Ferenc.

MacRitchie, James. HE Chi-Kung: Cultivating Personal Energy. (Health Essentials Ser.). 128p. 1997. pap. 9.95 (1-86204-064-8, Pub. by Element MA) Penguin Putnam.

Macro Systems, Inc. Staff. Social Skills on the Job Computer Software Manual. (Social Skills on the Job Ser.). 1989. pap. text 8.95 (0-88671-347-1, 4704) Am Guidance.

MacRobbie, Bill. All Aboard, Set Sail, Let's Go. (Illus.). 216p. 1994. pap. 14.95 (0-931541-39-5) Mancorp Pub.

MacRobert, Alan M. Star-Hopping for Backyard Astronomers. LC 93-25106. (Illus.). 160p. 1993. pap. 21.95 (0-933346-68-9) Sky Pub.

***MacRobert, C. M., et al, eds.** Oxford Slavonic Papers. (Illus.). 161p. 1999. text 65.00 (0-19-815966-8) OUP.

MacRobert, C. M., et al, eds. Oxford Slavonic Papers, Vol. 28. 28th ed. LC Vol. 28. (New Ser.). (Illus.). 143p. (C). 1996. text 65.00 (0-19-815916-1) OUP.

— Oxford Slavonic Papers, Vol. 29. (New Ser.). (Illus.). 136p. 1997. text 65.00 (0-19-815673-1) OUP.

— Oxford Slavonic Papers, New Series, Vol. XXV. (New Ser.). (Illus.). 176p. 1993. text 75.00 (0-19-815670-7) OUP.

— Oxford Slavonic Papers, New Series, Vol. XXVI (1993) (New Ser.). (Illus.). 108p. 1994. text 65.00 (0-19-815671-5) OUP.

***MacRobert, C. M. & Smith, G. S., eds.** Oxford Slavonic Papers, New Series. 136p. 2000. text 60.00 (0-19-815990-0) OUP.

Macrobert, T. M., ed. see Bromwich, T. J.

MacRoberts, Barbara R., jt. auth. see MacRoberts, Michael H.

MacRoberts, Michael H. & MacRoberts, Barbara R. Social Organization & Behavior of the Acorn Woodpecker in Central Coastal California. 115p. 1976. 10.00 (0-943610-21-4) Am Ornithologists.

Macromedia, Inc. Staff. Director Multimedia Studio Authorized. LC 97-175311. 264p. 1997. pap. 39.95 incl. cd-rom (0-201-68829-8, T1228) Peachpit Pr.

***Macromedia, Inc. Staff.** FreeHand 8 Authorized. 432p. 1998. pap. 39.95 incl. cd-rom (0-201-69691-6) Peachpit Pr.

Macromedia, Inc. Staff. FreeHand Graphics Studio & Interactive, Macromedia, Inc. 208p. 1997. pap. 49.95 incl. cd-rom (0-201-68837-9) Peachpit Pr.

— Lingo for Director 5 Authorized. LC 97-164748. 288p. 1997. pap. 39.95 incl. cd-rom (0-201-68830-1) Peachpit Pr.

Macromedia Press Staff. Authorware 4 Authorized. LC 99-190544. ix, 445p. 1997. write for info. incl. cd-rom (0-201-69634-7) Macromedia CA.

***MacRone, Michael.** Animalogies: A Fine Kettle of Fish & 150 Other Animal Expressions. (Illus.). 150p. 2000. 15.00 (0-7881-9346-5) DIANE Pub.

Macrone, Michael. Brush Up on Your Mythology. LC 98-8608. 1999. 6.99 (0-517-20287-5) Random Hse Value.

— Brush up Your Bible. LC 98-12328. 384p. 1998. 7.99 (0-517-20189-5) Random Hse Value.

— Brush Up Your Bible! (Illus.). 384p. 1995. pap. 11.00 (0-06-272020-1, Perennial) HarperTrade.

— Brush up Your Poetry. LC 96-43989. 256p. 1996. 18.95 (0-8362-2145-1, Cader Bks) Andrews & McMeel.

— Brush up Your Shakespeare. LC 97-43651. 256p. 1998. 6.99 (0-517-18935-6) Random Hse Value.

— Brush Up Your Shakespeare! LC 89-46105. (Illus.). 256p. 1994. pap. 13.00 (0-06-272018-X, Harper Ref) HarpC.

***Macrone, Michael.** Brush Up Your Shakespeare! An Infectious Tour Through the Most Famous & Quotable Words & Phrases from the Bard. rev. ed. LC 99-58223. 272p. 2000. pap. 14.00 (0-06-273732-5) HarpC.

Macrone, Michael. By Jove. LC 92-52541. (Illus.). 256p. 1994. reprint ed. pap. 13.00 (0-06-272019-8, Harper Ref) HarpC.

— It's Greek to Me. LC 98-30350. 256p. 1999. 6.99 (0-517-20284-0) Random Hse Value.

— It's Greek to Me. LC 91-55004. (Illus.). 256p. 1994. reprint ed. pap. 13.00 (0-06-272044-9, Harper Ref) HarpC.

Macrone, Michael. Naughty Shakespeare. LC 97-2728. (Illus.). 192p. 1997. 16.95 (0-8362-2757-3, Cader Bks) Andrews & McMeel.

***Macrone, Michael.** Naughty Shakespeare. 2000. 7.99 (0-517-20960-8) Random Hse Value.

MacRorie, K. T. Hoosier Hauntings. (Illus.). 158p. 1997. pap. 12.95 (1-882376-37-4) Thunder Bay Pr.

Macrorie, Ken. The I-Search Paper: Revised Edition of Searching Writing. rev. ed. LC 88-10329. 376p. (C). 1988. pap. text 25.00 (0-86709-223-8, 0223, Pub. by Boynton Cook Pubs) Heinemann.

— Telling Writing. 4th ed. LC 84-29296. 300p. (YA). (gr. 10). 1985. pap. text 21.50 (0-86709-153-3, 0153, Pub. by Boynton Cook Pubs) Heinemann.

— Twenty Teachers. (Illus.). 272p. 1987. pap. 10.95 (0-19-504982-9) OUP.

— Uptaught. LC 97-100486. (Innovators in Education Ser.). 188p. 1996. pap. 14.95 (0-86709-396-X, 0396, Pub. by Boynton Cook Pubs) Heinemann.

— Writing to Be Read. 3rd rev. ed. LC 84-14922. 287p. (YA). (gr. 9-12). 1986. pap. text 21.50 (0-86709-133-9, 0133, Pub. by Boynton Cook Pubs) Heinemann.

Macrory, Richard & Hollins, Steve. A Source Book of European Community Environmental Law. 226p. 1995. text 45.00 (0-19-825937-9) OUP.

MacRostie, Don, jt. auth. see Erlewine, Dan.

***Macsai, Gwen.** Lipshtick: Life as a Girl. LC 99-24462. 288p. 2000. 23.00 (0-06-019101-5) HarpC.

Macsai, Gwen. Lipstick. Date not set. pap. 13.00 (0-06-093061-6) HarpC.

Macsai, John, et al. Housing. 2nd ed. (Illus.). 590p. 1982. 125.00 (0-471-08126-4) Wiley.

MacShane, Denis. International Labour & the Origins of the Cold War. 334p. 1992. text 75.00 (0-19-827366-5) OUP.

— Solidarity. LC 81-16515. 1982. 40.00 (0-85124-319-3) Dufour.

— Solidarity: Poland's Independent Trade Union. LC 81-16515. 1982. 37.50 (0-685-38820-4, Pub. by Spkesman) Dufour.

— Solidarity: Poland's Independent Trade Union. 172p. 1987. 75.00 (0-7855-2942-X); pap. 20.00 (0-7855-2943-8) St Mut.

MacShane, Denis, et al. Power! Black Workers, Their Unions & the Struggle for Freedom in South Africa. 195p. 1984. 30.00 (0-89608-245-8) South End Pr.

— Power! Black Workers, Their Unions, & the Struggle for Freedom in South Africa. 195p. (Orig.). 1984. pap. 8.00 (0-89608-244-X) South End Pr.

MacShane, Frank. Noblesse Oblige. 1999. text 19.95 (0-670-81527-6) Viking Penguin.

MacShane, Frank, ed. Ford Madox Ford: The Critical Heritage. (Critical Heritage Ser.). 1972. 69.50 (0-7100-6957-X, Routledge Thoemms) Routledge.

— Selected Letters of Raymond Chandler. LC 81-4852. 616p. 1981. text 57.50 (0-231-05080-1) Col U Pr.

MacShane, Frank & Carlson, Lori, eds. Return Trip Tango & Other Stories from Abroad. (Columbia Collection). 320p. (C). 1992. pap. 19.00 (0-231-07993-1); text 44.00 (0-231-07992-3) Col U Pr.

MacShane, Frank, ed. see Ford, Ford Madox.

MacSiccar, I. John F. Kennedy. (Illus.). 64p. 1995. 9.98 (1-57215-029-7) World Pubns.

Macsich, George. Economic Nationalism & Stability. LC 85-12342. 176p. 1985. 45.00 (0-275-90215-3, C0215, Praeger Pubs) Greenwood.

MacSkimming, Roy. Gordie: A Hockey Legend. (Illus.). 240p. 1995. pap. 9.95 (1-55054-455-1) Sterling.

— Hockey War: The Great Canada-Soviet Hockey Series of 1972. (Illus.). 240p. 1996. 22.95 (1-55054-473-X, Pub. by Greystone Bks) Sterling.

Macsolis. Baile de Luna: Dance Moon. (SPA., Illus.). 25p. (J). (ps-2). 1991. 12.95 (84-261-2583-2) Donars.

MacSporran, Jane, jt. auth. see Cuccione, Michael.

***MacStravic, R. Scott.** Creating Consumer Loyalty in Healthcare. LC 99-26390. (Ache Management Ser.). 203p. 1999. pap. 40.00 (1-56793-108-1) Health Admin Pr.

MacStravic, Robin E., et al. Managing Health Care Demand. LC 97-47204. 576p. 1998. 65.00 (0-8342-0927-6, 09276) Aspen Pub.

MacStravic, Sue, ed. see Ryder, Tracie R.

***MacSwan, Jeff.** A Minimalist Approach to Intrasentential Code Switching. rev. ed. LC 98-51959. (Outstanding Dissertations in Linguistics Ser.). 329p. 1999. 71.00 (0-8153-3274-2) Garland.

Macsween. Muir's Path. 13th ed. 1994. 150.00 (0-340-55145-3, Pub. by E A) Routldge.

MacSween, Ann, jt. ed. see Cooke, Anthony.

MacSween, Morag. Anorexic Bodies: A Feminist & Sociological Perspective on Anorexia. LC 95-9185. 280p. (C). 1995. pap. 27.99 (0-415-02847-7) Routledge.

MacSween, Robert, et al, eds. Pathology of the Liver. 2nd ed. (Illus.). 717p. 1987. 230.00 (0-443-03049-9) Church.

MacSween, Roderick N., et al, eds. Pathology of the Liver. 3rd ed. LC 94-33377. 1994. text 270.00 (0-443-04454-6) Church.

MacSween, Roderick N., jt. ed. see Anthony, Peter P.

MacSweeney, Barry. The Book of Demons. 110p. 1998. pap. 17.95 (1-85224-414-3, Pub. by Bloodaxe Bks) Dufour.

MacSweeney, David. The Crazy Ape: Sanity, Madness, Your Brain & You. 244p. 1982. 27.00 (0-7206-0565-2, Pub. by P Owen Ltd) Dufour.

Macsyma, Inc. Staff. PDEase2D Lite. 40p. 1999. pap. 97.00 incl. cd-rom (3-540-14768-3) Spr-Verlag.

***Mactaggart, Ross.** Golden Century: Classic Motor Yachts, 1830-1930. (Illus.). 2000. 45.00 (0-393-04949-3) Norton.

Mactaggart, Terrence J. Seeking Excellence Through Independence: Liberating Colleges & Universities from State Regulations. LC 97-48664. 212p. 1998. 29.95 (0-7879-0922-X) Jossey-Bass.

MacTaggart, Terrence J., ed. Restructuring Higher Education: What Works & What Doesn't in Reorganizing Governing Systems. LC 95-40654. (Higher & Adult Education Ser.). 286p. 1996. 36.95 (0-7879-0193-8) Jossey-Bass.

MacTague, Bendan, jt. auth. see Majors, Ken.

Mactas, David J. Alcohol, Tobacco & Other Drug Abuse: Challenges & Responses for Faith Leaders. 102p. (C). 1997. reprint ed. pap. text 40.00 (0-7881-3760-3) DIANE Pub.

— Checklist for Monitoring Alcohol & Other Drug Confidentiality Compliance. 52p. (C). 1998. pap. text 20.00 (0-7881-4779-X) DIANE Pub.

MacTavish, David, jt. auth. see Heron, Michal.

Mactavish, Sandy. For Struggling Golfers Only: A Simplified Swing Which Will Have You Scoring in the 80's. (Illus.). 64p. (Orig.). 1994. pap. 12.85 (0-9641095-0-6) Supreme Pubng.

MacThomais, R. Gaelic Learner's Handbook. 1991. pap. 10.95 (0-8288-3347-8, F132987) Fr & Eur.

Mactier, R. A. & Nolph, K. D., eds. Current Concepts of CAPD Vol. 7, No. 2-3: Journal: Blood Purification, 1989. (Illus.). 120p. 1989. pap. 74.00 (3-8055-5009-X) S Karger.

Mactire, Sean P. Malicious Intent: A Writer's Guide to How Murderers, Robbers, Rapists & Other Criminals Think. (Howdunit Ser.). 240p. 1995. pap. 16.99 (0-89879-648-2, Wrtrs Digest Bks) F & W Pubns Inc.

MacTurk, Robert H. & Morgan, George A. Mastery Motivation Vol. 12: Origins, Conceptualizations & Applications. Gallaudet University Press Staff & Colorado State University Staff, eds. LC 96-136371. (Advances in Applied Developmental Psychology Ser.: Vol. 12). (Illus.). 336p. 1995. text 73.25 (1-56750-146-X) Ablx Pub.

MacTurk, Robert H. & Morgan, George A., eds. Mastery Motivation Vol. 12: Origins, Conceptualizations & Applications. LC 96-136371. (Advances in Applied Developmental Psychology: Vol. 12). (Illus.). 336p. 1995. pap. 39.50 (1-56750-203-2) Ablx Pub.

Macuch, Rudolf. Geschichte der Neusyrischen Literatur. (C). 1976. 292.30 (3-11-005959-2) De Gruyter.

— Grammatik des Samaritanischen Hebraeisch. (Studia Samaritana: Band 1). (C). 1969. 280.75 (3-11-000133-0) De Gruyter.

— Handbook of Classical & Modern Mandaic. (C). 1965. 246.15 (3-11-000261-2) De Gruyter.

— Zur Sprache und Literatur der Mandaer: Mit Beitraegen von Kurt Rudolph & Eric Segelberg. (C). 1976. 192.30 (3-11-004838-8) De Gruyter.

Macuga, Linda. Harvest of Hope. 414p. 1999. pap. 15.95 (1-891929-29-1) Four Seasons.

— "No!" Is an Option: A Second Story in Recovery. 363p. 1999. pap. 12.95 (1-891929-11-9) Four Seasons.

— Promises in a New Life: Available to All Who Walk a Twelve Step Path. 346p. 1998. pap. 12.95 (1-891929-03-8) Four Seasons.

— United We Stand: One Story in Recovery. 448p. 1998. pap. 12.95 (0-9656811-5-7) Four Seasons.

***MacUistin, Liam.** Celtic Magic Tales. (Illus.). 96p. (J). (gr. 3-7). 2000. pap. 0.95 (0-86278-341-0, Pub. by OBrien Pr) IPG Chicago.

MacUistin, Liam. The Tain: The Great Celtic Epic. (Illus.). 96p. (YA). (gr. 3 up). 1997. pap. 6.95 (0-86278-238-4, Pub. by OBrien Pr) Irish Amer Bk.

MacUistin, Liam & Cronin, Laura. The Hunt for Diarmaid & Grainne. (Illus.). 80p. 1997. pap. 6.95 (0-86278-480-8) Irish Amer Bk.

Maculaitis, Jean D. Maculaitis Assessment Batteries. 1982. 19.10 (0-88084-079-X); 21.85 (0-88084-088-9); 33.70 (0-88084-089-7); 26.00 (0-88084-094-3); 26.00 (0-88084-099-4); 43.90 (0-88084-104-4); 34.50 (0-88084-109-5); 19.75 (0-88084-108-7) Alemany Pr.

M

Maculiffe, Max A. Sikh Religion, 6 vols., Set. 1270p. 1986. 400.00 (*0-7855-1203-9*) St Mut.

Macunovich, Janet. Caring for Perennials: What to Do & When to Do It. LC 96-27505. (Illus.). 200p. (Orig.). 1997. pap. 17.95 (*0-88266-957-5*, 9575) Storey Bks.

— Easy Garden Design: Twelve Simple Steps to Creating Successful Gardens & Landscapes. Art, Pam, ed. LC 91-58926. (Illus.). 176p. 1992. pap. 16.95 (*0-88266-791-2*, Garden Way Pub) Storey Bks.

***Macunovich, Janet.** Easy Landscape Design: 12 Simple Steps for Planning Successful Gardens & Landscapes. rev. ed. 176p. 2001. 18.95 (*1-58017-315-2*) Storey Bks.

Macur, Juliet, jt. auth. see Martin, Mark.

Macur, Mary. Curious What You Might Find When You Go Out to Look for Elephants. LC 48-29. pap. 5.00 (*0-686-28865-3*) First Amend.

Macura, Miroslav & Coleman, David, eds. International Migration: Regional Processes & Responses. (ECE Economic Studies: No. 7). 200p. 27.00 (*92-1-100688-0*) UN.

Macura, Paul. Dictionary of Botany Vol. 2: General Terms. (ENG, FRE, GER & RUS.). 750p. 1982. 247.75 (*0-444-41977-2*) Elsevier.

— Elsevier's Dictionary of Botany Vol. 1: Plant Names. LC 79-15558. 588p. 1984. 247.75 (*0-444-41787-7*) Elsevier.

— Elsevier's Dictionary of Botany Vol. 1: Plant Names. 580p. 1979. 295.00 (*0-8288-9210-5*, M8804) Fr & Eur.

— Elsevier's Dictionary of Botany Vol. 2: General Terms. 744p. 1982. 295.00 (*0-8288-9211-3*, M14277) Fr & Eur.

— Elsevier's Dictionary of Chemistry. 932p. 1993. 227.25 (*0-444-89628-7*) Elsevier.

— Elsevier's Dictionary of Chemistry: Russian - English. (ENG & RUS.). 1000p. 1993. write for info. (*0-8288-9225-3*) Fr & Eur.

— Elsevier's Russian - English Dictionary. (ENG & RUS.). 3264p. 1990. 495.00 (*0-8288-9306-3*, F30420) Fr & Eur.

— Elsevier's Russian-English Dictionary. 3264p. 1990. 389.00 (*0-444-88467-X*) Elsevier.

— Russian-English Dictionary of Electrotechnology & Applied Sciences. LC 85-8653. 958p. 1986. reprint ed. lib. bdg. 99.50 (*0-89874-869-0*) Krieger.

***Macura, Paul & Elsevier Science Publishers Staff.** Russian-English Dictionary. 2nd rev. ed. LC 99-31050. (ENG & RUS.). 3630p. 2000. 431.50 (*0-444-82483-9*) Elsevier.

Macurda, D. B., jt. auth. see Breimar, A.

Macurdy, Grace H. Chronology of the Extant Plays of Euripides. LC 68-936. (Studies in Drama: No. 39). 1969. reprint ed. lib. bdg. 75.00 (*0-8383-0590-3*) M S G Haskell Hse.

— Hellenistic Queens. (Illus.). xv, 250p. 1985. reprint ed. pap. 20.00 (*0-89005-542-4*) Ares.

— Hellenistic Queens, No. 14--14. LC 75-16848. (Johns Hopkins University Studies in Archaeology: No. 14). (Illus.). 250p. 1975. reprint ed. lib. bdg. 35.00 (*0-8371-8271-9*, MAHQ, Greenwood Pr) Greenwood.

— Hellenistic Queens: A Study of Woman-Power in Macedonia, Seleucid Syria, & Ptolemaic Egypt. LC 75-41184. reprint ed. 37.50 (*0-404-14683-X*) AMS Pr.

— Troy & Paeonia: With Glimpses of Ancient Balkan History & Religion. xi, 259p. 1989. reprint ed. text 50.00 (*0-89241-439-1*) Caratzas.

Macurdy, Grace H., jt. auth. see Forrer, L.

MaCurdy, Thomas E. & O'Brien-Strain, Margaret. Reform Reversed? The Restoration of Welfare Benefits to Immigrants in California. LC 98-39690. (Illus.). 75p. 1998. pap. 10.00 (*1-58213-002-7*) Pub Policy Inst.

MaCurdy, Thomas E. & O'Brien'Strain, Margaret. Who Will Be Affected by Welfare Reform in California? LC 97-29762. (Illus.). xxi, 185p. 1997. pap. 15.00 (*0-9653184-3-5*) Pub Policy Inst.

***Macurdy, Thomas E., et al.** The Rise & Fall of California's Welfare Caseload: Types & Regions, 1980-1999. LC 00-40313. 2000. write for info. (*1-58213-053-1*) Pub Policy Inst.

Macurdy, Thomas E., et al. Who Benefits & Who Pays for Minimum Wage Increases in California? A Perspective on Proposition 210. LC 97-18745. (Essays in Public Policy Ser.: No. 78). 51p. (C). 2000. pap. 5.00 (*0-8179-5832-0*) Hoover Inst Pr.

Macurdy, Thomas E., jt. auth. see O'Brien-Strain, Margaret.

Macvannel, John A. The Educational Theories of Herbart & Froebel. LC 72-177043. (Columbia University. Teachers College. Contributions to Education Ser.: No. 4). reprint ed. 37.50 (*0-404-55004-5*) AMS Pr.

— Hegel's Doctrine of the Will. LC 03-12358. reprint ed. 27.50 (*0-404-04146-9*) AMS Pr.

Macve, Richard. A Conceptual Framework for Financial Accounting & Reporting: Vision, Tool, or Threat? LC 97-35910. (New Works in Accounting History Ser.). (Illus.). 280p. 1997. text 72.00 (*0-8153-3035-9*) Garland.

MacVeagh, Lincoln. Ambassador MacVeagh Reports: Greece, 1933-1947. Iatrides, John O., ed. LC 79-19079. 784p. 1980. reprint ed. pap. 200.00 (*0-7837-9352-9*, 206009400004) Bks Demand.

Macveagh, Rogers. The Transportation Act, 1920. Bruchey, Stuart, ed. LC 80-1330. (Railroads Ser.). 1981. reprint ed. lib. bdg. 93.95 (*0-405-13804-0*) Ayer.

MacVean, Jean, ed. see Blackburn, Thomas.

MacVicar, Angus. The Singing Spider. (Black Dagger Crime Ser.). 192p. 1997. 19.50 (*0-7451-8941-5*, Black Dagger) Chivers N Amer.

— Stranger at Xmas. LC 98-54739. 1999. pap. 5.00 (*0-88734-825-4*) Players Pr.

MacVicar, Thaddeus. Franciscan Spirituals & the Capuchin Reform. (History Ser.). 173p. 1987. pap. 9.00 (*1-57659-086-0*) Franciscan Inst.

MacVicar, W. M. A Short History of Annapolis Royal: The Port Royal of the French, from Its Settlement in 1604 to the Withdrawal of the British Troops in 1854. (Illus.). 133p. 1998. reprint ed. pap. 14.95 (*1-58211-061-1*, 097642) Quintin Pub RI.

Macviocia, Giovanni. Chinese Medicine: The Treatment of Disease with Acupuncture & Chinese Herbs. LC 93-10311. 1994. text 121.00 (*0-443-04305-1*) Church.

MacVittie. Vascular Surgery. (Perioperative Nursing Ser.). (Illus.). 272p. (C). (gr. 13). 1997. text 54.95 (*0-8151-7031-9*, 27475) Mosby Inc.

MacVittie, T. J., jt. ed. see Broerse, J. J.

MacWalter. ICH in Clinical Medicine. (Illus.). 128p. (C). (gr. 13). 1994. pap. text 29.00 (*0-8151-5805-X*, 22958) Mosby Inc.

MacWeeney, Alen, ed. Book of Days Nineteen Ninety. (Illus.). 120p. 1989. 9.95 (*0-945618-03-4*) Dorsoduro Pr.

MacWethy, Lou D. The Book of Names: Especially Relating to the Early Palatines & the First Settlers in the Mohawk Valley. (Illus.). 209p. 1999. pap. 22.50 (*0-8063-0231-3*, 3620) Clearfield Co.

MacWhinney, Brian. The Childes Project: Tools for Analyzing Talk. 2nd ed. 472p. 1995. text 35.00 (*0-8058-2027-2*) L Erlbaum Assocs.

***MacWhinney, Brian.** The Childes Project: Tools for Analyzing Talk. 3rd ed. LC 00-24971. 2000. write for info. (*0-8058-3572-5*) L Erlbaum Assocs.

MacWhinney, Brian. The Emergence of Language. LC 98-47001. (Carnegie Mellon Symposia on Cognition Ser.). 520p. 1998. 99.95 (*0-8058-3010-3*); pap. 45.00 (*0-8058-3011-1*) L Erlbaum Assocs.

— Mechanisms of Language Acquisition. (Carnegie-Mellon Symposium Ser.). 480p. (C). 1987. pap. 55.00 (*0-89859-973-3*) L Erlbaum Assocs.

MacWhinney, Brian, ed. Hungarian Language Acquisition As an Exemplification of a General Model of Grammatical Development: The Crosslinguistic Study of Language, Vol. 2. (Crosslinguistic Study of Language Acquisition Ser.). 80p. 1986. pap. 14.95 (*0-89859-850-8*) L Erlbaum Assocs.

MacWhinney, Brian, jt. auth. see Higginson, Roy.

MacWhinney, Brian, jt. ed. see Fletcher, Paul.

Macwhinnie, Ian. The Radiant Kingdom: An Allegorical Study of Meditation. LC 95-47990. 96p. 1996. pap. 8.95 (*0-89087-789-0*) Celestial Arts.

MacWilliams, Ed J. The Apostates: A Biblical Study for Local Churches. 1995. ring bd. 12.95 (*1-878897-03-9*) Blueprint Pubns.

— Ghana Diary: The Revival Begins. 1995. pap. 12.95 (*1-878897-04-7*) Blueprint Pubns.

— The Last Days of God's Church: Is True Christianity Being Forgotten? 1995. pap. 12.95 (*0-926557-09-2*) Blueprint Pubns.

— The New Rapture Scenario: It's Not Like Your Daddy Pictured It. 1995. pap. 7.95 (*1-878897-01-2*) Blueprint Pubns.

— Without Natural Affection: Is Criminal Hardness Replacing Natural Feelings? 1995. pap. 7.95 (*1-878897-02-0*) Blueprint Pubns.

MacWilliams, F. J. & Sloane, N. J. The Theory of Error Correcting Codes, 2 pts. in 1 vol. (Mathematical Library: Vol. 16). 782p. 1983. 130.00 (*0-444-85193-3*, North Holland) Elsevier.

Macy. A Whole New Ball Game. (J). 1995. 14.95 (*0-8050-2741-6*) H Holt & Co.

***Macy, David.** I Believe in Angels. 30p. 1999. pap. 3.95 (*0-9668443-4-3*, 5706) Macy Intl.

Macy, David. I Believe in the Power. 209p. 1999. 19.95 (*0-9668443-2-7*) Macy Intl.

— Love Will Find a Way: Poems for Soul Seekers. 40p. 1999. pap. 3.95 (*0-9668443-3-5*) Macy Intl.

***Macy, David.** Poems from the Heart. 36p. 1999. pap. 3.95 (*0-9668443-5-1*) Macy Intl.

— Soft Gentle Rain. 40p. 1999. pap. 3.95 (*0-9668443-6-X*) Macy Intl.

***Macy, Caitlin.** The Fundamentals of Play. LC 99-86625. 320p. 2000. 24.95 (*0-375-50413-3*) Random.

Macy, David. America Wake Up. 2nd ed. 41p. 1998. reprint ed. pap. 3.95 (*0-9668443-1-9*) Macy Intl.

Macy, Deborah K. Gyp! LC 96-90508. 1997. pap. 12.95 (*0-533-12083-7*) Vantage.

Macy, Eliot E. Captain's Daughters of Martha's Vineyard. LC 78-62650. (How We Lived Ser.: No. 1). 1979. 12.95 (*0-85699-141-4*); pap. 7.95 (*0-85699-142-2*) Chatham Pr.

Macy, Gary. Treasures from the Storeroom: Medieval Religion & the Eucharist. LC 98-32330. 1999. 24.95 (*0-8146-6053-3*) Liturgical Pr.

Macy, Gary, ed. Theology & the New Histories Vol. 44: The Annual Publication of the College Theology Society. LC 99-214231. 292p. 1999. pap. 18.00 (*1-57075-239-7*) Orbis Bks.

Macy, Harry, Jr. & Mocete, Melissa, eds. Index to Baptismal Surnames: In the Reformed Churches of Claverack, Cortlandt, Fishkill, Gallatin, Gravesend, Hillsdale, Kaatsbaan, Kinderhook, Linlithgo, Phillipsburgh, Poughkeepsie, Red Hook - Old, Red Hook - Upper, Reyn Beeck, Rhinebeck Flatts & Rochester. 228p. 1991. 35.00 (*0-9628194-0-9*) Holland Soc NY.

Macy, Howard R. Rhythms of the Inner Life: Yearning for Closeness with God. LC 99-17424. 187p. 1999. pap. text 10.99 (*1-56476-777-9*, Victor Bks) Chariot Victor.

Macy, Howard R., jt. ed. see Anderson, Paul N.

Macy, Jesse. Anti-Slavery Crusade: A Chronicle of the Gathering Storm. (History - United States Ser.). 245p. 1992. reprint ed. lib. bdg. 79.00 (*0-7812-6154-6*) Rprt Serv.

— Civil Government in Iowa. (Notable American Authors Ser.). 1999. reprint ed. lib. bdg. 125.00 (*0-7812-3907-9*) Rprt Serv.

— Comparative Free Government. (Notable American Authors Ser.). 1999. reprint ed. lib. bdg. 125.00 (*0-7812-3913-3*) Rprt Serv.

— The English Consitution. (Notable American Authors Ser.). 1999. reprint ed. lib. bdg. 125.00 (*0-7812-3910-9*) Rprt Serv.

— English Constitution: A Commentary on Its Nature & Growth. xxiii, 534p. 1988. reprint ed. 52.50 (*0-8377-2438-4*, Rothman) W S Hein.

— Institutional Beginnings in a Western State. (Notable American Authors Ser.). 1999. reprint ed. lib. bdg. 125.00 (*0-7812-3908-7*) Rprt Serv.

— Our Government: What It Does & How It Does It. (Notable American Authors Ser.). 1999. reprint ed. lib. bdg. 125.00 (*0-7812-3909-5*) Rprt Serv.

— Party Organization & Machinery. LC 73-19159. (Politics & People Ser.). 336p. 1974. reprint ed. 25.95 (*0-405-05881-0*) Ayer.

— Party Organization & Machinery. (Notable American Authors Ser.). 1999. reprint ed. lib. bdg. 125.00 (*0-7812-3912-5*) Rprt Serv.

— Political Parties in the United States. (Notable American Authors Ser.). 1999. reprint ed. lib. bdg. 125.00 (*0-7812-3911-7*) Rprt Serv.

— Political Parties in the United States, 1846-1861. LC 73-19160. (Politics & People Ser.). 344p. 1974. reprint ed. 26.95 (*0-405-05882-9*) Ayer.

Macy, Joanna. Dharma & Development: Religion As Resource in the Sarvodaya Self-Help Movement. fac. rev. ed. LC 85-236. (Illus.). 119p. 1985. pap. 36.90 (*0-7837-7573-3*, 204732600007) Bks Demand.

— Mutual Causality in Buddhism & General Systems Theory: The Dharma of Natural Systems. LC 90-39937. (SUNY Series in Buddhist Studies). 254p. (C). 1991. pap. text 21.95 (*0-7914-0637-7*) State U NY Pr.

***Macy, Joanna.** Widening Circles: A Memoir. (Illus.). 240p. 2000. pap. 16.95 (*0-86571-420-7*, Pub. by New Soc Pubs) Consort Bk Sales.

Macy, Joanna. World As Lover, World As Self. LC 91-681. 280p. (Orig.). 1991. pap. 15.00 (*0-938077-27-9*) Parallax Pr.

Macy, Joanna, tr. see Rilke, Rainer Maria.

Macy, Joanna R. & Brown, Molly Y. Coming Back to Life: Practices to Reconnect Our Lives, Our World. 240p. 1998. pap. 16.95 (*0-86571-391-X*) New Soc Pubs.

Macy, John. Edgar Allan Poe. LC 75-3089. (Studies in Poe: No. 23). 1975. lib. bdg. 75.00 (*0-8383-2090-2*) M S G Haskell Hse.

Macy, John A. The Spirit of American Literature. (BCL1-PS American Literature Ser.). 347p. 1992. reprint ed. lib. bdg. 89.00 (*0-7812-6604-1*) Rprt Serv.

Macy, Jon. Tropo, Vol. I. (Illus.). 132p. (Orig.). 1994. pap. 5.95 (*1-883611-04-0*) Blckbird Comics.

Macy, Jonathan R., jt. ed. see Brown, J. Robert, Jr.

Macy, Mark, ed. Solutions for a Troubled World. LC 87-8859. (Peace Ser.: Vol. I). (Illus.). 314p. (Orig.). 1987. pap. 8.95 (*0-930705-03-3*) M H Macy & Co.

Macy, Mark, ed. see Harsch-Fischbach, Maggy & Locher, Theo.

Macy, Melinda, jt. auth. see Macy, Robert.

Macy, Obed & Macy, William F. History of Nantucket, Being a Compendious Acct. of the First Settlement of the Island by the English, Together with the Rise & Progress of the Whale Fishery, & Other Historical Facts. 2nd ed. 313p. 1995. reprint ed. lib. bdg. 39.50 (*0-8328-4466-7*) Higginson Bk Co.

Macy, Ralph. The Interim Pastor. pap. 7.25 (*1-56699-000-9*) Alban Inst.

Macy, Randy D., ed. Macy Family Cookbook. 2nd large type ed. (Illus.). 100p. 1996. pap. 19.95 (*0-9674622-0-7*) Macy Family.

Macy, Robert & Macy, Melinda. Destination Baghdad. 100p. 1991. pap. 10.00 (*0-9649096-1-8*) M M Graphics.

— Las Vegas: A New Dimension . . . a New Destiny. 3rd ed. 78p. 1996. pap. 10.00 (*0-9649096-2-6*) M M Graphics.

Macy, Robert B., jt. auth. see Pandya, Abhijit S.

Macy, Silvanus J. Genealogy of the Macy Family, 1635-1868. (Illus.). 457p. 1989. reprint ed. pap. 68.50 (*0-8328-0849-0*); reprint ed. lib. bdg. 76.50 (*0-8328-0848-2*) Higginson Bk Co.

***Macy, Sue.** Shooting Hoops. (Barbie Amazing Athlete Look-Look Bks.). (Illus.). 24p. (J). 1999. pap. 3.29 (*0-307-13256-0*, Goldn Books) Gldn Bks Pub Co.

Macy, Sue. A Whole New Ball: The Story of the All-American Girls Professional Baseball League. large type ed. 1995. 42.50 (*0-614-09616-2*, L-81917-00) Am Printing Hse.

— A Whole New Ball Game: The Story of the All-American Girls Professional Baseball League. LC 92-31813. (Illus.). 160p. (YA). (gr. 5 up). 1995. 14.95 (*0-8050-1942-1*, Bks Young Read) H Holt & Co.

— A Whole New Ball Game: The Story of the All-American Girls Professional Baseball League. LC 94-46789. (J). 1995. pap. 4.99 (*0-14-037423-X*, PuffinBks) Peng Put Young Read.

Macy, Sue. Whole New Ball Game: The Story of the All-American Girls Professional Baseball League. 1995. 10.09 (*0-606-08381-2*, Pub. by Turtleback) Demco.

Macy, Sue. Winning Ways. (J). 1998. pap. 5.99 (*0-590-76336-9*) Scholastic Inc.

— Winning Ways: A Photohistory of American Women in Sports. LC 95-44969. (Illus.). 160p. (J). (gr. 7-12). 1995. 15.95 (*0-8050-4147-8*) H Holt & Co.

— Winning Ways: A Photohistory of American Women in Sports. 1998. 11.09 (*0-606-13922-2*, Pub. by Turtleback) Demco.

Macy, Sue & Gottesman, Jane. Play Like a Girl: A Celebration of Women in Sports. LC 98-47754. 32p. (J). (gr. 4). 1999. 15.95 (*0-8050-6071-5*) H Holt & Co.

Macy, William F., jt. auth. see Macy, Obed.

MacYoung, Marc A. Cheap Shots, Ambushes, & Other Lessons: A Down & Dirty Book on Streetfighting & Survival. (Illus.). 264p. 1988. pap. 25.00 (*0-87364-496-4*) Paladin Pr.

— Fists, Wits, & a Wicked Right: Surviving on the Wild Side of the Street. (Illus.). 152p. 1991. pap. 14.00 (*0-87364-611-8*) Paladin Pr.

— Floor Fighting: Stompings, Maimings, & Other Things to Avoid When a Fight Goes to the Floor. (Illus.). 200p. 1993. pap. 19.00 (*0-87364-716-5*) Paladin Pr.

— Knives, Knife Fighting, & Related Hassles: How to Survive a Real Knife Fight. (Illus.). 128p. 1990. pap. 12.00 (*0-87364-544-8*) Paladin Pr.

— Pool Cues, Beer Bottles & Baseball Bats: Animal's Guide to Improvised Weapons for Self-Defense & Survival. (Illus.). 152p. 1990. pap. 20.00 (*0-87364-545-6*) Paladin Pr.

— A Professional's Guide to Ending Violence Quickly: How Bouncers, Bodyguards, & Other Security Professionals Handle Ugly Situations. LC 96-216344. (Illus.). 256p. 1996. pap. 21.00 (*0-87364-899-4*) Paladin Pr.

— Street E&E: Evading, Escaping, & Other Ways to Save Your Ass When Things Get Ugly. (Illus.). 192p. 1993. pap. 16.00 (*0-87364-743-2*) Paladin Pr.

— Violence, Blunders, & Fractured Jaws: Advanced Awareness Techniques & Street Etiquette. 344p. 1992. pap. 22.95 (*0-87364-671-1*) Paladin Pr.

MacYoung, Marc A. & Pfouts, Chris. Safe in the City: A Streetwise Guide to Avoid Being Robbed, Raped, Ripped off, or Run Over. 312p. 1994. pap. 22.95 (*0-87364-775-0*) Paladin Pr.

Maczak, Antoni. Money, Prices & Power in Poland 16th-17th Centuries: A Comparative Approach. LC 94-43313. (Collected Studies: No. CS487). 312p. 1995. 109.95 (*0-86078-478-9*, Pub. by Variorum) Ashgate Pub Co.

— Travel in Early Modern Europe. Phillips, Ursula, tr. from POL. 368p. 1995. 74.95 (*0-7456-0840-X*) Blackwell Pubs.

Maczak, Antoni & Parker, William N., eds. Natural Resources in European History: A Conference Report. LC 78-24688. (RFF Research Paper Ser.: No. R-13). 238p. pap. 73.80 (*0-8357-4683-6*, 203763000008) Bks Demand.

Maczek, Andrew. Statistical Thermodynamics. (Oxford Chemistry Primers Ser.: No. 58). (Illus.). 96p. (C). 1998. pap. text 12.95 (*0-19-855911-9*) OUP.

Maczka, Kathleen. Assessing Physically Disabled People at Home. Campling, Jo, ed. (Therapy in Practice Ser.: No. 12). 128p. 1990. pap. 28.95 (*0-412-32480-6*, A4417) Chapman & Hall.

MacZura, Jason, jt. auth. see Scott, David.

***Maczynski, Andrew R. & Talar, Maciej P.** Three Centuries with Mary Immaculate as Patroness. 2000. pap. write for info. (*0-944203-30-2*) Marian Pr.

Mad, Aztec. Baseball Sabermetric 1991. 1991. pap. 15.95 (*0-9625846-4-9*) Mad Aztec Pr.

***Mad Dog, pseud.** Skywriting at Night. 304p. 2000. pap. 16.00 (*0-7388-2115-2*) Xlibris Corp.

***Mad German.** Politically Incorrect Poetry. (Illus.). 48p. 1999. pap. 13.00 (*1-883821-15-0*) Mother Bird.

Mad Magazine Editors. Mad about the Buoy. Feldstein, Albert B., ed. (Mad Ser.: No. 53). 1986. mass mkt. 3.95 (*0-446-30506-5*) Warner Bks.

— Mad about the Sixties: The Best of the Decade, Vol. 1. LC 95-22337. (Illus.). 240p. 1995. pap. 20.00 (*0-316-33418-9*) Little.

— Mad in Orbit. (Mad Ser.). (Illus.). 192p. 1981. mass mkt. 1.75 (*0-446-94591-9*, Pub. by Warner Bks) Little.

— A Mad Look at the Sixties. Meglin, Nick, ed. (Illus.). 192p. (Orig.). 1989. mass mkt. 3.95 (*0-446-35499-6*, Pub. by Warner Bks) Little.

— Mad Overboard. (Mad Ser.: No. 47). (Illus.). 192p. (Orig.). 1983. mass mkt. 1.95 (*0-446-30407-7*, Pub. by Warner Bks) Little.

— Mad Spy vs. Spy: The Updated Files. 192p. (Orig.). 1989. mass mkt. 3.95 (*0-446-35400-7*, Pub. by Warner Bks) Little.

— The Medicine Mad. (Mad Ser.: No. 44). (Illus.). (Orig.). 1987. mass mkt. 3.99 (*0-446-34853-8*, Pub. by Warner Bks) Little.

— Polyunsaturated MAD. 192p. 1976. mass mkt. 3.50 (*0-446-86179-0*, Pub. by Warner Bks) Little.

— Sing along with Mad. 192p. 1989. mass mkt. 3.50 (*0-446-35995-5*, Pub. by Warner Bks) Little.

— Soaring MAD. 192p. (Orig.). 1989. mass mkt. 3.50 (*0-446-35498-8*, Pub. by Warner Bks) Little.

— The Spring Training MAD. 192p. 1993. mass mkt. 3.99 (*0-446-36452-5*, Pub. by Warner Bks) Little.

— Til MAD Do Us Part. 1987. mass mkt. 3.99 (*0-446-34369-2*, Pub. by Warner Bks) Little.

— The Wet & Wisdom of Mad. 192p. (Orig.). 1987. mass mkt. 3.99 (*0-446-34366-8*, Pub. by Warner Bks) Little.

Mad Magazine Editors, ed. Stamp Out Mad. (Mad Ser.: No. 66). 1990. mass mkt. 3.50 (*0-446-35415-5*, Pub. by Warner Bks) Little.

***Mad Science Staff.** Go Mad. 2000. 10.95 (*0-07-135248-1*) McGraw.

***Madach, Imre.** The Tragedy of Man. 272p. 1999. pap. 22.00 (*963-13-4533-5*, Pub. by Corvina Bks) St Mut.

Madach, Imre. The Tragedy of Man. 148p. 1989. text 31.00 (*0-88033-169-0*, Pub. by East Eur Monographs) Col U Pr.

— The Tragedy of Man. 1973. 300.00 (*0-8490-1225-2*) Gordon Pr.

— The Tragedy of Man. (Illus.). 272p. 1989. reprint ed. pap. 54.00 (*963-13-3994-7*, Pub. by Corvina Bks) St Mut.

Madachy, Joseph S. Madachy's Mathematical Recreations. LC 78-74116. (Illus.). 1979. pap. 4.95 (*0-486-23762-1*) Dover.

An Asterisk (*) at the beginning of an entry indicates that the title is appearing for the first time.

Madahil, Antonio Gomes da Rocha, tr. see Schaub-Koch, Emile.

Madaj, E. J., Jr., jt. auth. see Truce, W. E.

Madala, Hema R. Inductive Learning Algorithms for Complex Systems Modeling. 384p. 1993. boxed set 99.95 (*0-8493-4438-7*) CRC Pr.

Madaliyar, C. Rasanayagam. Ancient Jaffna. (Illus.). 478p. 1986. reprint ed. 22.00 (*0-8364-1744-5*, Pub. by Manohar) S Asia.

Madama. Pulmonary Function Testing & Cardiopulmonary Stress Testing - IML. 2nd ed. 76p. 1997. teacher ed. 14.95 (*0-8273-8411-4*) Delmar.

Madama, John. Desktop Publishing: The Art of Communication. (Media Workshop Ser.). (Illus.). 80p. (YA). (gr. 5 up). 1993. lib. bdg. 21.27 (*0-8225-2303-5*, Lerner Publctns) Lerner Pub.

— Desktop Publishing: The Art of Communication. (Media Workshop Ser.). (Illus.). 80p. (YA). (gr. 5 up). 1995. pap. 8.95 (*0-8225-9626-1*, First Ave Edns) Lerner Pub.

Madama, Vince. Pulmonary Function Testing & Cardiopulmonary Stress Testing. 2nd ed. LC 97-37682. 528p. (C). 1997. mass mkt. 45.95 (*0-8273-8410-6*) Delmar.

Madama, Vincent C. Principles of Arterial Blood Gases. (Respiratory Care Ser.). 1994. teacher ed. 12.00 (*0-8273-5560-2*) Delmar.

— Principles of Arterial Blood Gases. (Respiratory Care Ser.). 1997. pap. 46.95 (*0-8273-5559-9*) Delmar.

— Pulmonary Function Testing & Cardiopulmonary Stress Testing Transparency Masters. 126p. 1990. pap. 26.25 (*0-8273-3864-3*) Delmar.

— Pulmonary Function Testing & Cardiovascular Stress Testing. LC 92-18604. 590p. (C). 1993. mass mkt. 33.00 (*0-8273-3863-5*) Delmar.

Madamba, Anna B. Underemployment among Asians in the United States: Asian Indian, Filipino & Vietnamese Workers. rev. ed. LC 98-15137. (Studies in the History of American Labor). 250p. 1998. 50.00 (*0-8153-3006-5*) Garland.

***Madame d'Aulnoy's Collection Staff.** Beauty & the Beast. LC 99-29992. (Illus.). 48p. (YA). (gr. 5-12). 2000. 17.95 (*1-56846-129-1*, Creative Eds) Creative Co.

Madame de Stael. Corinne: Or Italy. Isbell, John, ed. Raphael, Sylvia, tr. LC 98-10540. (Oxford World's Classics Ser.). 450p. 1999. pap. 14.95 (*0-19-282505-4*) OUP.

Madan, A., et al, eds. Amorphous Silicon Semiconductors: Pure & Hydrogenated. (MRS Symposium Proceedings Ser.: Vol. 95). 1987. text 17.50 (*0-931837-62-6*) Materials Res.

Madan, A., et al, eds. Amorphous Silicon Technology. (Symposium Proceedings Ser.: Vol. 118). 1988. text 17.50 (*0-931837-88-X*) Materials Res.

Madan, A., et al, eds. Amorphous Silicon Technology - 1991 Vol. 219: Materials Research Society Symposium Proceedings. 885p. 1991. text 17.50 (*1-55899-113-1*) Materials Res.

Madan, Arun & Shaw, Melvin P. The Physics & Applications of Amorphous Semiconductors. 545p. 1988. text 123.00 (*0-12-464960-2*) Acad Pr.

Madan, Brij M. Engine Electrical Equipment - U. S. Markets & Opportunities: 1991-1996 Analysis. (Illus.). 220p. 1992. pap. text 1900.00 (*1-878218-27-1*) World Info Tech.

Madan, Falconer. Books in Manuscript. LC 68-25315. (Reference Ser.: No. 44). (Illus.). (C). 1972. reprint ed. lib. bdg. 75.00 (*0-8383-0213-0*) M S G Haskell Hse.

Madan, G. Swahili English Dictionary. (ENG & SWA.). 442p. 1992. 59.95 (*0-8288-8458-7*) Fr & Eur.

Madan, G., jt. auth. see Steere.

Madan, G. R. Indian Social Problems, 2 vols., Set. 505p. 1981. 24.95 (*0-318-36851-X*) Asia Bk Corp.

— India's Social Transformation: Problems of Welfare & Planning, Vol. II. 2nd enl. rev. ed. 324p. reprint ed. 15.95 (*0-317-39863-6*, Pub. by Allied Pubs) Asia Bk Corp.

Madan, Geoffrey. Geoffrey Madan's Notebooks. Gere, J. A. & Sparrow, John, eds. 1981. 29.95 (*0-19-215870-8*) OUP.

Madan, K. D. Life & Travels of Vasco Da Gama. LC 98-909888. xxix, 140p. 1998. write for info. (*81-206-1360-0*) Asian Educ Servs.

Madan, N. L. Indian Political System. 1989. 38.50 (*81-202-0246-5*, Pub. by Ajanta) S Asia.

Madan, P. L. Indian Cartography: Historical Perspective. LC 97-904245. (Illus.). (C). 1997. 38.00 (*81-7304-177-6*, Pub. by Manohar) S Asia.

Madan, R. Chua's Circuit: A Paradigm for Chaos. 1088p. 1993. text 213.00 (*981-02-1366-2*) World Scientific Pub.

Madan, Rabinder N., jt. ed. see Indo-U. S. Workshop on Parallel & Distributed Sign.

Madan, Raj, compiled by. Colored Minorities in Great Britain: A Comprehensive Bibliography, 1970-1977. LC 78-74656. 199p. 1979. lib. bdg. 49.95 (*0-313-20705-4*, MCM/, Greenwood Pr) Greenwood.

Madan, S. N. Dictionary of Anthropology. 328p. 1989. 80.00 (*81-7041-163-7*, Pub. by Scientific Pubs) St Mut.

***Madan, Sada Nand.** Srimad Bhagavata & Medieval Hindi Poets. LC 99-940248. 1998. 42.50 (*81-7646-024-9*, Pub. by BR Pub) S Asia.

Madan, T. N. Modern Myths, Locked Minds: Secularism & Fundamentalism in India. (Oxford India Paperbacks Ser.). 340p. 1998. reprint ed. pap. text 13.95 (*0-19-564707-6*) OUP.

Madan, Triloki N. Family & Kinship: A Study of the Pandits of Rural Kashmir. 2nd ed. (Illus.). 352p. 1990. text 28.00 (*0-19-562138-7*) OUP.

— Non-Renunciation: Themes & Interpretations of Hindu Culture. 196p. 1988. text 22.50 (*0-19-562040-2*) OUP.

— Non-Renunciation: Themes & Interpretations of Hindu Culture. 198p. 1996. pap. text 10.95 (*0-19-563809-3*) OUP.

— Pathways: Approaches to the Study of Society in India. (Illus.). 304p. 1996. pap. text 12.95 (*0-19-563650-3*) OUP.

Madan, Triloki N., ed. Muslim Communities of South Asia: Culture, Society, & Power. LC 95-906177. (C). 1995. reprint ed. 28.50 (*81-7304-090-7*, Pub. by Manohar) S Asia.

— Religion in India. (Oxford in India Readings in Sociology & Social & Cultural Anthropology Ser.). (Illus.). 478p. 1993. reprint ed. pap. text 16.95 (*0-19-563092-0*) OUP.

— Way of Life: King, Householder, Renouncer: Essays in Honour of Louis Dumont. (C). 1988. reprint ed. 31.00 (*81-208-0527-5*, Pub. by Motilal Bnarsidass) S Asia.

Madancy, Joyce A., jt. auth. see Lampton, David M.

Madanes, Cloe. Secret Meaning of Money: How to Prevent Financial Affairs from Destroying Our Most Intimate Relationships. 1998. pap. text 17.95 (*0-7879-4116-6*) Jossey-Bass.

Madanes, Cloe. Sex. Love, & Violence: Strategies for Transformation. (C). 1990. 25.95 (*0-393-70096-8*) Norton.

Madanes, Cloe. Strategic Family Therapy. LC 80-26286. (Social & Behavioral Science Ser.). 272p. 1991. pap. 22.95 (*1-55542-363-9*) Jossey-Bass.

Madanes, Cloe, et al. The Violence of Men: New Techniques for Working with Abusive Families: A Therapy of Social Action. LC 95-12239. (Psychology Ser.). 233p. 1995. 29.95 (*0-7879-0117-2*) Jossey-Bass.

Madani, Ali. Design of Urban Space: An Inquiry into a Socio-Spatial Process. LC 96-21431. 1996. text 110.00 (*0-471-96672-X*) Wiley.

— Design of Urban Space: An Inquiry into a Socio-Spatial Process. LC 96-21431. 254p. 1996. pap. 49.95 (*0-471-96673-8*) Wiley.

Madani, Mohammed I. Hijab. 2nd ed. Sadiq, Mohammed, tr. LC 96-41574. 128p. 1996. pap. text 5.00 (*1-881963-50-0*) Al-Saadawi Pubns.

Madani, Mohsan Saeidi, see Saeidi Madani, Mohsan.

Madanipour, Ali. Social Exclusion in European Cities. LC 98-186340. 301p. 1998. pap. 32.95 (*1-85302-609-3*, Pub. by Jessica Kingsley) Taylor & Francis.

— Tehran: The Making of a Metropolis. LC 98-15968. (World Cities Ser.). 302p. 1998. 95.00 (*0-471-95779-8*) Wiley.

Madansky, A. Prescriptions for Working Statisticians. (Texts in Statistics Ser.). (Illus.). 350p. 1988. 53.95 (*0-387-96627-7*) Spr-Verlag.

Madansky, Albert, ed. see Antelman, Gordon.

Madany, B. M. The Bible & Islam. 1989. 5.25 (*0-685-74119-2*) Chr Lit.

***Madar, Daniel R.** Heavy Traffic: Deregulation, Trade & Transformation in North American Trucking. LC 00-36776. 2000. write for info. (*0-87013-556-2*) Mich St U Pr.

— Heavy Traffic: Deregulation, Trade & Transformation in North American Trucking. 240p. 2000. 75.00 (*0-7748-0769-5*) UBC Pr.

Madar, Wendy, jt. auth. see Wilson, Charis.

Madar, Z. & Odes, S. H. Dietary Fiber Research. (Progress in Biochemical Pharmacology Ser.: Vol. 24). (Illus.). viii, 148p. 1990. 116.75 (*3-8055-5043-X*) S Karger.

Madara, Edward J., ed. see American Self-Help Clearinghouse Staff.

***Madara, John S.** Nine Keys to Happiness: Collected Speeches & Writings of Dr. John S. Madara, M. D. LC 99-91727. 2000. 25.00 (*0-7388-1202-1*); pap. 18.00 (*0-7388-1203-X*) Xlibris Corp.

Madaraka, Jelani M. African Origins of Law & Justice: The Concept of Maat in Ancient Egypt. 45p. 1994. pap. write for info. (*1-884897-00-2*) Zamani Pr.

Madaras. Taking Sides: American History, Vol. 1. 8th ed. 408p. 1999. pap. 18.44 (*0-07-303188-7*) McGraw.

Madaras, Area & Madaras, Lynda. My Body, My Self for Girls: The "What's Happening to My Body?" Workbook for Girls. LC 93-19189. (Illus.). 128p. (YA). (gr. 6-12). 1993. pap., wbk. ed. 11.95 (*1-55704-150-4*, Pub. by Newmarket) Norton.

Madaras, Area, jt. auth. see Madaras, Lynda.

Madaras, Larry & SoRelle, James M. Clashing Views on Controversial Issues in American History, Vol. I. 7th ed. (Taking Sides Ser.). (Illus.). 416p. 1997. pap. text 13.00 (*0-697-37529-3*, Dshkn McG-Hill) McGrw-H Hghr Educ.

— Clashing Views on Controversial Issues in American History, Vol. II. 7th ed. (Taking Sides Ser.). (Illus.). 432p. 1997. pap. text 13.00 (*0-697-37533-1*, Dshkn McG-Hill) McGrw-H Hghr Educ.

Madaras, Larry & SoRelle, James M., eds. The Colonial Period to Reconstruction, Vol. 1. 6th ed. LC 94-48862. (C). 1995. text 13.95 (*1-56134-326-9*, Dshkn McG-Hill) McGrw-H Hghr Educ.

— Reconstruction to the Present, Vol. 2. 6th ed. LC 94-48862. (C). 1995. text 13.95 (*1-56134-327-7*, Dshkn McG-Hill) McGrw-H Hghr Educ.

— Taking Sides Vol. I: Clashing Views on Controversial Issues in American History: The Colonial Period to Reconstruction. 5th ed. LC 92-74291. (Illus.). 396p. (C). 1993. text 12.95 (*1-56134-121-5*, Dshkn McG-Hill) McGrw-H Hghr Educ.

***Madaras, Lynda & Madaras, Area.** My Body, My Self for Boys: A "What's Happening to My Body?" Quizbook. (Illus.). 2000. reprint ed. pap. 12.95 (*1-55704-440-6*) Newmarket.

Madaras, Lynda & Madaras, Area. My Body, My Self for Boys: The "What's Happening to My Body?" Workbook for Boys. LC 95-40401. (Illus.). 112p. (YA). (gr. 6-12). 1995. pap., wbk. ed. 11.95 (*1-55704-230-6*, Pub. by Newmarket) Norton.

***Madaras, Lynda & Madaras, Area.** My Body, My Self for Girls: A "What's Happening to My Body?" Quizbook. (Illus.). 2000. reprint ed. pap. 12.95 (*1-55704-441-4*) Newmarket.

Madaras, Lynda & Madaras, Area. My Feelings, My Self: A Growing-Up Guide for Girls. rev. ed. LC 93-9877. Orig. Title: Lynda Madaras' Growing-Up Guide for Girls. (Illus.). 160p. (J). (gr. 3-10). 1993. pap. 11.95 (*1-55704-157-1*, Pub. by Newmarket) Norton.

***Madaras, Lynda & Madaras, Area.** The "What's Happening to My Body?" Book for Boys: A Growing-Up Guide for Parents & Sons. 3rd ed. (Illus.). 2000. 22.95 (*1-55704-447-3*) Newmarket.

— The "What's Happening to My Body?" Book for Boys: A Growing-Up Guide for Parents & Sons. 3rd ed. (Illus.). 2000. reprint ed. pap. 12.95 (*1-55704-443-0*) Newmarket.

— The "What's Happening to My Body?" Book for Girls: A Growing-Up Guide for Parents & Daughters. 3rd ed. (Illus.). 2000. reprint ed. 22.95 (*1-55704-448-1*); reprint ed. pap. 12.95 (*1-55704-444-9*) Newmarket.

Madaras, Lynda & Madaras, Area. What's Happening to My Body? Book for Girls: A Growing Up Guide for Parents & Daughters. rev. ed. LC 87-28117. (Illus.). 304p. 1988. 18.95 (*1-55704-001-X*, Pub. by Newmarket); pap. 11.95 (*0-937858-98-6*) Newmarket.

Madaras, Lynda & Patterson, Jane. Womancare: A Gynecological Guide to Your Body. 960p. 1983. pap. 15.00 (*0-380-87643-4*, Avon Bks) Morrow Avon.

Madaras, Lynda & Saavedra, Dane. What's Happening to My Body? Book for Boys: A Growing Up Guide for Parents & Sons. rev. ed. LC 87-28116. (Illus.). 288p. 1988. pap. 11.95 (*0-937858-99-4*) Newmarket.

— What's Happening to My Body? Book for Boys: A Growing Up Guide for Parents & Sons. 2nd rev. ed. LC 87-28116. (Illus.). 288p. 1988. 18.95 (*1-55704-002-8*, Pub. by Newmarket) Norton.

Madaras, Lynda, jt. auth. see Madaras, Area.

Madarasz, Norman, ed. & intro. see Badiou, Alian.

Madarasz, Norman, tr. see Badiou, Alian.

Madaraza, Brent. 1998 Supercross: Collectors Edition, 1. 136 p. 1998. 19.95 (*0-9683708-0-2*) Aspire Ent.

***Madariaga.** Politics & Culture in 18th Century Russia. LC 98-18989. 312p. (C). 1998. pap. 29.06 (*0-582-32255-3*) Longman.

Madariaga. Politics & Culture 18TH Century Russia. LC 98-53064. (C). 1998. text 68.44 (*0-582-32256-1*) Longman.

Madariaga, Juan, jt. ed. see Dionigi, R.

Madariaga, L. Thematic Dictionary of Literary Terms: Diccionario Tematico des Terminos Literarios. (SPA.). 572p. 1980. 29.95 (*0-8288-1578-X*, S39853) Fr & Eur.

Madariaga, Salvador de. Christopher Columbus: Being the Life of the Very Magnificent Lord Don Cristobal Colon. LC 79-16973. (Illus.). 534p. 1979. reprint ed. lib. bdg. 95.00 (*0-313-22031-X*, MACB, Greenwood Pr) Greenwood.

— El Corazon de Piedra Verde, I. (Nueva Austral Ser.: Vol. 55). (SPA.). 1991. pap. text 34.95 (*84-239-1855-6*) Elliots Bks.

— El Corazon de Piedra Verde, II. (Nueva Austral Ser.: Vol. 56). (SPA.). 1991. pap. text 29.95 (*84-239-1864-5*) Elliots Bks.

— Don Quixote: An Introductory Essay in Psychology. LC 79-16911. 159p. 1980. reprint ed. lib. bdg. 35.00 (*0-313-22011-5*, MADQ, Greenwood Pr) Greenwood.

— Hernan Cortes: Conqueror of Mexico. LC 79-2570. (Illus.). 554p. 1979. reprint ed. lib. bdg. 41.50 (*0-313-22030-1*, MACM, Greenwood Pr) Greenwood.

Madariaga, Salvador De, see De Madariaga, Salvador.

Madaris, Don. Scrap-Paper Miracle. Butler, Cathy, ed. 85p. 1993. reprint ed. pap. text 6.95 (*1-56309-022-8*, N934111, New Hope) Womans Mission Union.

Madaris, Don L. Little Donald Lee, Miss Etta G, & the Two Room Schoolhouse. (Illus.). 112p. (Orig.). 1991. pap. 7.95 (*0-943487-34-X*) Sevgo Pr.

Madaris, Don L., jt. auth. see Miller, Sarah W.

Madas, A. World Consumption of Wood, Trends & Prognoses. 130p. (C). 1974. 30.00 (*963-05-0183-X*, Pub. by Akade Kiado) St Mut.

Madathanus, Hinricus. Parabola, a Rosicrucian Tale. 50p. 1992. reprint ed. pap. 7.00 (*1-56459-035-6*) Kessinger Pub.

Madaule, ed. see Claudel, Paul.

Madaule, Jacques. The Albigensian Crusade: An Historical Essay. Wall, Barbara, tr. LC 66-23621. 191p. reprint ed. pap. 59.30 (*0-7837-0455-0*, 204077800018) Bks Demand.

Madaule, Paul. When Listening Comes Alive: A Guide to Effective Learning & Communication. (Illus.). 224p. 1996. pap. write for info. (*0-9697079-0-8*) Moulin Publ.

— When Listening Comes Alive: A Guide to Effective Learning & Communication. 2nd ed. 204p. 1997. pap. text 14.95 (*0-9697079-1-6*) Moulin Publ.

Madaus, George F., ed. Evaluation Models: Viewpoints on Educational & Human Services Evaluation (Text Edition) (C). 1983. lib. bdg. 90.00 (*0-89838-123-1*) Kluwer Academic.

Madaus, George F. & Scriven, Michael S., eds. Evaluation Models: Viewpoints on Educational & Human Services Evaluation (Text Edition) 440p. (C). 1983. lib. bdg. 58.50 (*0-89838-132-0*) Kluwer Academic.

Madaus, George F. & Stufflebeam, Daniel L., eds. Educational Evaluation: Classic Works of Ralph W. Tyler. (C). 1988. lib. bdg. 91.50 (*0-89838-273-4*) Kluwer Academic.

Madaus, Gerhard. Lehrbuch der Biologischen Heilmittel. (GER.). 1997. reprint ed. 498.00 (*3-487-05889-8*) G Olms Pubs.

Madaus, Howard. The Guns of Remington: Historic Firearms Spanning Two Centuries. Tafoya, Renee, ed. LC 97-73476. (Illus.). 352p. 1997. 99.95 (*0-9659503-0-1*) Biplane Prodns.

Madaus, Howard M., jt. auth. see Murphy, John M.

Madaus, Howard M., jt. auth. see Zeitlin, Richard H.

Madauss, M. Martyria. Turning Defeat into Victory. 124p. 1995. pap. 3.25 (*1-897647-09-3*) Evang Sisterhood Mary.

Madauss, Martyria. Jesus: A Portrait of Love. 1983. 6.50 (*3-87209-603-6*) Evang Sisterhood Mary.

— The Shield of Faith. deluxe ed. 1974. 0.95 (*3-87209-659-1*) Evang Sisterhood Mary.

Madavan, Vijay. Cooking the Indian Way. (Easy Menu Ethnic Cookbooks Ser.). (Illus.). 52p. (J). (gr. 5 up). 1985. lib. bdg. 19.93 (*0-8225-0911-3*, Lerner Publctns) Lerner Pub.

Maday, Bela C., jt. auth. see Hollos, Marida.

Maday, Michael, ed. see Cady, H. Emilie.

Maday, Michael, ed. see Fillmore, Charles.

Maday, Michael, ed. see Gatlin, Dana.

Maday, Michael, ed. see Jafolla, Mary-Alice & Jafolla, Richard.

Maday, Michael, ed. see Shanklin, Imelda O.

Maday, Michael, ed. see Turner, Elizabeth S.

Maday, Michael, ed. see Unity School of Christianity Staff.

Maday, Michael, ed. see West, Georgiana T.

Maday, Michael A., ed. New Thought for a New Millennium: Twelve Powers for the 21st Century. LC 97-26296. 235p. 1998. 19.95 (*0-87159-205-3*, 001) Unity Bks.

Maday, Stefan Von, see Von Maday, Stefan.

Maday, Tom & Landers, Sam. Great Chicago Stories. LC 94-60776. (Illus.). 232p. 1996. reprint ed. 40.00 (*0-9641703-0-2*) TwoPress Pubng.

— Great Chicago Stories. 2nd ed. (Illus.). 232p. 1996. pap. 30.00 (*0-9641703-1-0*) TwoPress Pubng.

Maday, Yvon, jt. ed. see Bernardi, Christine.

Maddala, G. S. Econometric Methods & Applications, 2 vols. (Economists of the Twentieth Century Ser.). 1168p. 1994. text 240.00 (*1-85278-804-6*) E Elgar.

— Introduction to Econometrics. (Illus.). 656p. (C). 1992. teacher ed. write for info. (*0-318-69329-1*) Macmillan.

— Limited-Dependent & Qualitative Variables in Economometrics. LC 82-9554. (Econometric Society Monographs: No. 3). 401p. 1986. pap. text 29.95 (*0-521-33825-5*) Cambridge U Pr.

Maddala, G. S., ed. The Econometrics of Panel Data, 2 vols., Set. (International Library of Critical Writings in Economics: Vol. 1). 1000p. 1993. 415.00 (*1-85278-585-3*) E Elgar.

Maddala, G. S., et al, eds. Econometrics. LC 93-12857. (Handbook of Statistics Ser.: Vol. 11). 804p. 1993. 190.00 (*0-444-89577-9*, North Holland) Elsevier.

Maddala, G. S. & Kim, In-Moo. Unit Roots, Cointegration & Structural Change. LC 98-17325. (Themes in Modern Econometrics Ser.: No. 4). (Illus.). 505p. (C). 1998. pap. 24.95 (*0-521-58782-4*); text 69.95 (*0-521-58257-1*) Cambridge U Pr.

Maddala, G. S. & Rao, C. R., eds. Handbook of Statistics Vol. 14: Statistical Methods in Finance. LC 97-165202. 750p. 1996. 175.00 (*0-444-81964-9*) Elsevier.

— Robust Inference, Vol. 15. (Handbook of Statistics Ser.). 716p. 1997. 148.75 (*0-444-82172-4*, North Holland) Elsevier.

Maddams, W. F., jt. auth. see Bower, D. I.

Maddaus, William O. Water Conservation. 100p. 1987. pap. 36.00 (*0-89867-387-9*, 20238) Am Water Wks Assn.

Madden. Abdominal Wall Hernias. 368p. 1989. text 145.00 (*0-7216-1288-1*, W B Saunders Co) Harcrt Hlth Sci Grp.

— Fiction Tutor Nineteen Ninety-One. 200p. (C). 1991. pap. text. write for info. (*0-318-69146-9*) Harcourt Coll Pubs.

— Introduction to Sectional Anatomy. (Radiographic Technology Ser.). 1997. wbk. ed. 17.95 (*0-8273-6999-9*) Delmar.

— Introduction to Sectional Anatomy. (Radiographic Technology Ser.). 1998. teacher ed. 16.00 (*0-8273-7000-8*); text 45.95 (*0-8273-6998-0*) Delmar.

— Lecture Notes. 108p. (C). 1998. pap. text 10.75 (*0-536-01485-X*) Pearson Custom.

— Pocketful of Prose Poems & Plays. (C). 1995. 34.00 (*0-15-503786-2*) Harcourt.

— Spelling. 1983. pap., wbk. ed. 12.25 (*0-15-328550-8*) Harcourt Schl Pubs.

— Spelling: Grade 3. 1983. 26.00 (*0-15-328558-3*) Harcourt Schl Pubs.

— Spelling 85. (Illus.). 1983. 26.75 (*0-15-328561-3*) Harcourt Schl Pubs.

— Spelling 83. 1983. 28.25 (*0-15-328564-8*) Harcourt Schl Pubs.

— Spelling 83. 1983. 67.25 (*0-15-328567-2*); 67.25 (*0-15-328568-0*); 67.25 (*0-15-328569-9*) Harcourt Schl Pubs.

— Spelling 83. (Illus.). 1983. 56.25 (*0-15-328565-6*) Harcourt Schl Pubs.

— Spelling 1987. 1983. 26.00 (*0-15-328559-1*) Harcourt Schl Pubs.

— Spelling 83: Grade 6. 1983. 26.75 (*0-15-328562-1*) Harcourt Schl Pubs.

— Spelling 83: Grade 6. 1989. 67.25 (*0-15-328570-2*) Harcourt Schl Pubs.

— Spelling 83: Grade 7. 1983. 73.00 (*0-15-328571-0*) Harcourt Schl Pubs.

— Spelling 83: Grade 7. 1983. 28.00 (*0-15-328563-X*) Harcourt Schl Pubs.

Madden, ed. A Bridge to Literature. (C). 1998. text. write for info. (*0-321-01183-X*) Addson-Wesley Educ.

Madden & Wydeven, Joseph F. Wright Morris Revisited. LC 98-10001. 212p. 1998. 28.95 (*0-8057-4531-9*, Twyne) Mac Lib Ref.

Madden, et al. Women in Evangelization: Memories of the Past, Visions of the Future. 158p. (C). 1992. pap. text 9.95 (*0-9629051-1-9*) Barry Univ.

Madden, A. F. & Morris-Jones, W. H., eds. Australia & Britain: Studies in a Changing Relationship. (Studies in Commonwealth Politics & History: No. 8). (Illus.). 214p. 1983. 32.50 (*0-7146-3149-3*, Pub. by F Cass Pubs) Intl Spec Bk.

Madden, Ann. The Yahweh Encounters: Bible Astronauts, Ark Radiations & Temple Electronics. Jones, Joanye P., ed. (Illus.). 373p. (Orig.). 1995. pap. 13.95 (*0-9615111-2-5*) Sandbird Pub.

***Madden, Annette.** In Her Footsteps: 101 Remarkable Black Women from the Queen of Sheba to Queen Latifa. 2001. pap. 15.95 (*1-57324-553-4*) Conari Press.

Madden, B., jt. ed. see Jeffrey, D. W.

Madden, Bartley J. CFROI Cash Flow Return on Investment Valuation: A Total System Approach to Valuing the Firm. LC 99-219974. 352p. 1998. 64.95 (*0-7506-3865-6*) Buttrwrth-Heinemann.

Madden, Bill. Damned Yankees: A No-Holds-Barred Account of Life with Boss Steinbrenner. 1991. mass mkt. 5.95 (*0-446-36089-9*, Pub. by Warner Bks) Little.

— Gering High Athletics: A Sportswriter's View. 100p. 1994. write for info. (*0-9644166-0-3*) Sports Amer.

Madden, Bob. Nuclear Missiles & a Justification for a Crazy Life. 170p. (Orig.). 1982. pap. 2.50 (*0-9608256-0-6*) R Madden.

— Pray for All the Children of the Universe & Death Ends Desire. 126p. (Orig.). 1995. pap. 6.99 (*0-9608256-1-4*) R Madden.

Madden, Carl H. Clash of Culture: Management & the Age of Changing Values. LC 72-88236. 132p. 1976. 5.00 (*0-685-03540-9*) Natl Planning.

Madden, Carl H., ed. The Case for the Multinational Corporation. LC 76-12863. (Special Studies). 234p. 1976. 45.00 (*0-275-90248-X*, C0248, Praeger Pubs) Greenwood.

Madden, Carolyn G. & Myers, Cynthia L., eds. Discourse & Performance of International Teaching Assistants. 252p. 1994. pap. 25.95 (*0-939791-52-8*) Tchrs Eng Spkrs.

Madden, Carolyn G. & Reinhart, Susan M. Pyramids: Structurally Based Tasks for E. S. L. Learners. (English As a Second Language Ser.). (Illus.). 120p. (C). 1987. pap. text 12.95 (*0-472-08073-3*, 08073); pap. text, teacher ed. 12.95 (*0-472-08072-5*, 08072) U of Mich Pr.

Madden, Carolyn G. & Rohlck, Theresa N. Discussion & Interaction in the Academic Community. (Michigan Series in English for Academic & Professional Purposes). 152p. (Orig.). 1997. pap., teacher ed. 10.95 (*0-472-08455-0*, 08455); pap. text 16.95 (*0-472-08290-6*, 08290) U of Mich Pr.

Madden, Charles. Fractals in Music: Introductory Mathematics for Musical Analysis. LC 99-90421. (In Music Ser.: No. 1). (Illus.). 224p. 1999. text 39.95 (*0-9671727-5-6*, 1001) High Art Pr.

— Freemasonry - Mankind's Hidden Enemy: With Current Official Catholic Statements. 66p. 1995. pap. 5.00 (*0-89555-534-4*) TAN Bks Pubs.

Madden, Charles S., ed. Proceedings of the Conference of the American Academy of Advertising, 1995. 1995. pap. text, per. 25.00 (*0-931030-18-8*) Am Acad Advert.

Madden, Chris C. Baby Hints Handbook. (Illus.). 144p. (Orig.). 1982. pap. 3.95 (*0-941298-05-1*) M E Pinkham.

— Baby's First Helping. (Family Bk. Ser.). (Illus.). 159p. pap. 5.95 (*0-318-19492-9*) M E Pinkham.

— Bathrooms. LC 95-12991. 1996. 32.50 (*0-517-59938-4*) C Potter.

— Chris Madden's Guide to Personalizing Your Home: Simple, Beautiful Ideas for Every Room. LC 97-7679. 1997. 20.00 (*0-609-60083-4*) C Potter.

— Kitchens. LC 92-16444. (Illus.). 288p. 1993. 45.00 (*0-517-58160-4*) C Potter.

— Rooms with a View: Two Decades of Outstanding American Interior Design from the Kips Bay. (Illus.). 192p. 1995. pap. 39.95 (*0-86636-289-4*) PBC Intl Inc.

Madden, Chris C. & Showhouse, Kips B. Rooms with a View: Two Decades of Outstanding American Interior Design. LC 92-35193. 1993. 45.00 (*0-86636-190-1*) PBC Intl Inc.

Madden, Chris Carson. Getaways. LC 99-24606. (Illus.). 224p. 2000. 35.00 (*0-609-60320-5*) C Potter.

Madden, Chris Casson. Room of Her Own: Women's Personal Spaces. LC 97-22643. (Illus.). 224p. 1997. 30.00 (*0-517-59939-2*) C Potter.

Madden, Christine W., ed. see Madden, Yvonne M.

Madden, Cindy, jt. auth. see Lockwood, Lisa.

***Madden, Dano.** Drop. LC 99-200358. 45p. 1998. write for info. (*0-573-62256-6*) French.

Madden, David. Cain's Craft. LC 84-20215. 176p. 1985. 21.00 (*0-8108-1750-0*) Scarecrow.

— Cassandra Singing. LC 99-10582. 288p. 1999. pap. 18.95 (*1-57233-035-X*) U of Tenn Pr.

— Fiction Tutor-Custom Pupil. (C). 1996. pap. 22.00 (*0-15-504422-2*, Pub. by Harcourt Coll Pubs) Harcourt.

— James M. Cain. LC 86-72297. 200p. (C). 1987. pap. 9.95 (*0-88748-045-4*) Carnegie-Mellon.

— James M. Cain. (Twayne's United States Authors Ser.). 1974. lib. bdg. 20.95 (*0-8057-0128-1*) Irvington.

— A Pocketful of Plays: Sample Edition. (C). 1995. pap. text 8.00 (*0-15-503630-0*) Harcourt Coll Pubs.

— A Pocketful of Plays: Vintage. (C). 1995. pap. text 12.00 (*0-15-502543-0*, Pub. by Harcourt Coll Pubs) Harcourt.

— A Pocketful of Poems: Sample Edition. (C). 1995. pap. text 8.00 (*0-15-503628-9*) Harcourt Coll Pubs.

— A Pocketful of Poetry: Vintage. LC 95-79366. (C). 1995. pap. text 12.00 (*0-15-502544-9*, Pub. by Harcourt Coll Pubs) Harcourt.

— A Pocketful of Prose: Contemporary Short Fiction. 236p. (C). 1991. pap. text. write for info. (*0-318-69117-5*) Harcourt Coll Pubs.

— A Pocketful of Prose: Contemporary Short Fiction. 230p. (C). 1992. pap. text 12.00 (*0-03-054934-5*, Pub. by Harcourt Coll Pubs); 13.50 (*0-03-014289-X*) Harcourt Coll Pubs.

— A Pocketful of Prose: Vintage. (C). 1995. pap. text 12.00 (*0-15-502545-7*, Pub. by Harcourt Coll Pubs) Harcourt.

— A Pocketful of Prose: Vintage Short Fiction. 288p. (C). 1992. pap. text 11.50 (*0-03-054937-X*, Pub. by Harcourt Coll Pubs); disk. write for info. (*0-318-69139-6*) Harcourt Coll Pubs.

— A Primer of the Novel: For Readers & Writers. LC 79-21881. 466p. 1980. lib. bdg. 29.00 (*0-8108-1265-7*) Scarecrow.

— Revising Nonfiction. 1999. pap. 11.95 (*0-452-27456-7*, Plume) Dutton Plume.

— Sharpshooter: A Novel of the Civil War. LC 96-9994. (Illus.). 176p. 1996. 19.95 (*0-87049-948-3*) U of Tenn Pr.

***Madden, David, ed.** Beyond the Battlefield: The Ordinary Lives & Extraordinary Times of the Civil War Soldiers. LC 99-89055. 304p. 2000. per. 16.00 (*0-684-85633-6*) S&S Trade.

— The Legacy of Robert Penn Warren. LC 00-28726. (Southern Literary Studies). 200p. 2000. 34.95 (*0-8071-2592-X*) La State U Pr.

Madden, David, ed. The World of Fiction. LC 89-11088. 1200p. (C). 1989. pap. text 46.00 (*0-03-014292-X*, Pub. by Harcourt Coll Pubs) Harcourt.

Madden, David & Folks, Jeffrey J., eds. Remembering James Agee. 2nd ed. LC 97-8507. 1997. 29.95 (*0-8203-1913-9*) U of Ga Pr.

Madden, David & Scott, Virgil, eds. Studies in the Short Story. 6th ed. LC 83-8590. 540p. (C). 1984. pap. text 36.50 (*0-03-063644-2*, Pub. by Harcourt Coll Pubs) Harcourt.

Madden, David W. Critical Essays on Thomas Berger. (Critical Essays on American Literature Ser.). 1995. 49.00 (*0-7838-0029-0*, Twyne) Mac Lib Ref.

— Understanding Paul West. LC 93-12537. (Understanding Contemporary British Literature Ser.). 183p. (C). 1993. text 29.95 (*0-87249-886-7*) U of SC Pr.

Madden, Deborah, jt. ed. see Bartnett, Joy.

Madden, Denise, jt. auth. see Eckstein, Warren.

Madden, Dodgson H. Diary of Master William Silence. (BCL1-PR English Literature Ser.). 386p. 1992. reprint ed. lib. bdg. 89.00 (*0-7812-7309-9*) Rprt Serv.

— Diary of Master William Silence: A Study of Shakespeare & Elizabethan Sport. LC 78-89018. 386p. 1970. reprint ed. lib. bdg. 69.50 (*0-8371-2322-4*, MAMS, Greenwood Pr) Greenwood.

— Diary of Master William Silence: A Study of Shakespeare & Elizabethan Sport. LC 71-95440. (Studies in Shakespeare: No. 24). 1970. reprint ed. lib. bdg. 75.00 (*0-8383-0993-3*) M S G Haskell Hse.

Madden, Don. Wartville Wizard. (J). 1993. 11.19 (*0-606-02970-2*, Pub. by Turtleback) Demco.

— The Wartville Wizard. LC 92-22246. (Illus.). 32p. (J). (gr. k-3). 1993. reprint ed. mass mkt. 5.99 (*0-689-71667-2*) Aladdin.

Madden, Donald L. & Holmes, James R. Management Accountants: Responding to Change. Barth, Claire, ed. 63p. (Orig.). 1990. pap. 20.00 (*0-86641-185-2*, 90246) Inst Mgmt Account.

Madden, Dorothy. You Call Me Louis, Not Mr. Horst. (Choreography & Dance Studies). 192p. 1997. text 89.00 (*3-7186-5877-1*, Harwood Acad Pubs); pap. text 28.00 (*3-7186-5887-9*, Harwood Acad Pubs) Gordon & Breach.

Madden, Edward F. Carpe Diem. 128p. 1993. pap. text 12.50 (*0-86720-782-5*) Jones & Bartlett.

Madden, Edward H. Philosophical Problems of Psychology. LC 72-11481. 149p. 1973. reprint ed. lib. bdg. 38.50 (*0-8371-6668-3*, MAPH, Greenwood Pr) Greenwood.

Madden, Edward H. & Hamilton, James E. Freedom & Grace: The Life of Asa Mahan. LC 82-5724. (Studies in Evangelicalism: No. 3). 287p. 1982. 26.50 (*0-8108-1555-9*) Scarecrow.

Madden, Edward H., jt. auth. see Hare, Peter H.

Madden, Edward H., jt. ed. see Ryan, Frank X.

Madden, Etta M. Bodies of Life: Shaker Literature & Literacies, 52. LC 97-30110. (Contributions to the Study of Religion: Vol. 52). 208p. 1998. 55.00 (*0-313-30303-7*, Greenwood Pr) Greenwood.

Madden, F. W. History of Jewish Coinage. (Illus.). 1967. lib. bdg. 25.00 (*0-932106-32-3*) S J Durst.

Madden, F. W., jt. auth. see Herman, H. A.

Madden, Frederic. Syr Gawayne. 1972. 59.95 (*0-8490-1171-X*) Gordon Pr.

Madden, Frederic, ed. Matthaei Parisiensis, Monachi Sancti Albani, Historia Anglorum Sive, ut Vulgo Dicitur, Historia Minor, 3 vols. (Rolls Ser.: No. 44). 1969. reprint ed. 210.00 (*0-8115-1103-0*) Periodicals Srv.

— Syr Gawayne: A Collection of Ancient Romance Poems by Scottish & English Authors. LC 71-144420. (Bannatyne Club. Edinburgh. Publications: No. 61). reprint ed. 49.50 (*0-404-52772-8*) AMS Pr.

Madden, Frederic, tr. see Layamon.

Madden, Frederic W. Coins of the Jews. (International Numismata Orientalia Ser.: Vol. II). (Illus.). viii, 1703p. 1976. reprint ed. write for info. incl. 3.5 hd (*3-487-06006-X*) G Olms Pubs.

***Madden, Frederick, ed.** The End of Empire: Dependencies Since 1948 Part 1: The West Indies, British Honduras, Hong Kong, Fiji, Cyprus, Gibraltar & the Falklands Select Documents on the Constitutional History of the British Empire & Commonwealth, Vol. 8. 2000. lib. bdg. write for info. (*0-313-29072-5*, Quorum Bks) Greenwood.

Madden, Frederick & Darwin, John. The Dependent Empire: Colonies, Protectorates & Mandates Select Documents, 7. LC 84-21213. (Documents in Imperial History Ser.: Vol. 7). 912p. 1994. lib. bdg. 145.00 (*0-313-27318-9*, Greenwood Pr) Greenwood.

Madden, Frederick & Darwin, John, eds. The Dominions & India since 1900: Select Documents on the Constitutional History of the British Empire & Commonwealth, 6. LC 84-21213. 906p. 1993. lib. bdg. 145.00 (*0-313-27317-0*, Greenwood Pr) Greenwood.

Madden, Frederick & Fieldhouse, David, eds. Advance & Retreat in Representative Self-Government, 1840-1900: Select Documents on the Constitutional History of the British Empire & Commonwealth, 5. LC 84-21213. (Documents in Imperial History Ser.: Vol. 5, No. 5). 848p. 1991. lib. bdg. 145.00 (*0-313-27757-5*, MNT/, Greenwood Pr) Greenwood.

— The Classical Period of the First British Empire, 1689-1783: The Foundations of a Colonial System of Government: Select Documents on the Constitutional History of the British Empire with Commonwealth, 2. LC 84-21213. (Documents of Imperial History Ser.: No. 2). 628p. 1985. lib. bdg. 115.00 (*0-313-25176-2*, MDL/) Greenwood.

— The Dependent Empire & Ireland, 1840-1900: Advance & Retreat in Representative Self-Government - Select Documents on the Constitutional History of the British Empire & Commonwealth, Vol. V. (Documents in Imperial History Ser.: No. 5). 864p. 1991. 95.00 (*0-685-54256-4*, MNT/, Greenwood Pr) Greenwood.

— The Empire of the Bretaignes, Eleven Seventy-Five to Sixteen Eighty-Eight: Foundations of a Colonial System of Government; Select Documents on the Constitutional History of the British Empire & Commonwealth, 1. LC 84-21213. (Documents in Imperial History Ser.: No. 1). (Illus.). 669p. 1985. lib. bdg. 115.00 (*0-313-23897-9*, MFI/) Greenwood.

Madden, Frederick & Fieldhouse, David, eds. Imperial Reconstruction, 1763-1840: The Evolution of Alternative Systems of Colonial Government: Select Documents on the Constitutional History of the British Empire & Commonwealth, 3. LC 84-21213. (Documents in Imperial History Ser.: No. 3). 933p. 1987. lib. bdg. 145.00 (*0-313-25916-X*, MRN/) Greenwood.

Madden, Frederick & Fieldhouse, David, eds. Settler Self-Government, 1840-1900: Select Documents on the Constitutional History of the British Empire & Commonwealth, 4. LC 84-21213. (Documents in Imperial History Ser.: No. 4). 864p. 1990. lib. bdg. 125.00 (*0-313-27326-X*, MGO/) Greenwood.

Madden, Frederick, jt. ed. see Robinson, Kenneth.

Madden, Gail. High Key Portraiture of Children, Seniors & Families. 2nd ed. (Illus.). 83p. 1995. pap. 29.50 (*0-934420-20-3*) Studio Pr NE.

Madden, gary, jt. auth. see MacDonald, Stuart.

Madden, Henry. Strasburg Tapes. write for info. (*0-318-62725-6*) Daedalus Act.

Madden, Isabel B., jt. auth. see Bozzi, Aldo.

Madden, J. Patrick, et al. Beyond Pesticides: Biological Approaches to Pest Management in California. LC 92-61146. (Illus.). 220p. 1992. pap. 14.00 (*1-879906-10-4*, 3354) ANR Pubns CA.

— For All Generations: Making World Agriculture More Sustainable. LC 96-71652. (Illus.). 642p. 1997. pap. 30.00 (*0-9655767-0-1*) OM Pub Cnslts.

Madden, James J., jt. auth. see Schwartz, Niels.

Madden, James J., jt. ed. see Delzell, Charles N.

Madden, James W. The Art of Throwing Weapons. LC 91-60071. (Illus.). 104p. (Orig.). 1991. pap. 8.95 (*0-9628825-3-4*) Paladin Pr.

Madden, Janet. Emerging Voices. 3rd ed. (C). 1996. pap. text. write for info. (*0-15-502922-3*); pap. text, teacher ed. 26.75 (*0-15-502923-1*) Harcourt Coll Pubs.

Madden, Janet & Blake, Sara M. Crosscurrents: Themes for Developing Writers. 400p. (C). 1992. teacher ed. write for info. (*0-03-055853-0*); pap. text 36.00 (*0-03-055852-2*, Pub. by Harcourt Coll Pubs) Harcourt.

Madden, Janet & Blake, Sara M. Emerging Voices. 2nd ed. 512p. (C). 1993. pap. text 37.00 (*0-15-500303-8*, Pub. by Harcourt Coll Pubs) Harcourt.

Madden, Janet & Blake, Sara M. Emerging Voices: Reading in the American Experience. 2nd ed. 512p. (C). 1993. pap. text 5.50 (*0-15-500729-7*) Harcourt Coll Pubs.

Madden, Janet, jt. auth. see Blake, Sara M.

Madden, Janet, jt. auth. see Eula, Michael J.

***Madden, Janice F.** Changes in Income Inequality Within U. S. Metropolitan Areas. LC 00-23017. 186p. 2000. 34.00 (*0-88099-204-2*); pap. 15.00 (*0-88099-203-4*) W E Upjohn.

Madden, Janice F. & Stull, William J. Work, Wages, & Poverty: Income Distribution in Post-Industrial Philadelphia. LC 91-22426. 240p. (Orig.). (C). 1991. pap. text 22.95 (*0-8122-1348-3*) U of Pa Pr.

Madden, Janice F., jt. auth. see Stull, William J.

Madden, John, IV. Neurobiology of Learning, Emotion, & Affect. LC 91-18296. (Illus.). 368p. 1991. reprint ed. pap. 114.10 (*0-608-07190-0*, 206741500009) Bks Demand.

Madden, John & Anderson, Dave. All Madden: Hey, I'm Talking Pro Football! 22.00 (*0-614-23033-0*) HarpC.

— One Knee Equals Two Feet (And Everything Else You Need to Know about Football) 1987. mass mkt. 5.99 (*0-515-09193-6*, Jove) Berkley Pub.

— One Size Doesn't Fit All. 256p. 1989. pap. 5.50 (*0-515-10146-X*, Jove) Berkley Pub.

Madden, John A., ed. see Macedonius Consul.

Madden, John L. Federal & State Lands in Louisiana. 1972. 35.00 (*0-87511-078-9*) Claitors.

Madden, John T. & Nadler, Marcus. International Money Markets. LC 68-23311. 548p. 1969. reprint ed. lib. bdg. 45.50 (*0-8371-0552-8*, MAIM, Greenwood Pr) Greenwood.

Madden, Joseph P. A Documentary History of Yonkers, New York Vol. 2, Pt. 1: The Unsettled Years, 1853-1860. LC 92-167800. 342p. 1994. pap. text 30.50 (*1-55613-930-6*) Heritage Bk.

— A Documentary History of Yonkers, New York Vol. 2, Pt. 2: The Dutch, the English & an Incorporated American Village, 1609-1860. LC 92-167800. 286p. (Orig.). 1994. pap. text 27.50 (*1-55613-946-2*) Heritage Bk.

***Madden, Kristin.** Pagan Parenting: Spiritual, Magical & Emotional Development of the Child. 2000. pap. 14.95 (*1-56718-492-8*) Llewellyn Pubns.

— Shamanic Guide to Death & Dying. LC 99-47186. 288p. 1999. pap. 16.95 (*1-56718-494-4*) Llewellyn Pubns.

Madden, Laurence V., jt. auth. see Campbell, C. Lee.

Madden, Lawrence J., ed. The Joseph Campbell Phenomenon: Implications for the Contemporary Church. 168p. 1992. pap. 12.95 (*0-912405-89-9*, Pastoral Press) OR Catholic.

Madden, Lionel, ed. Robert Southey: The Critical Heritage. 1972. 69.50 (*0-7100-7375-5*, Routledge Thoemms) Routledge.

Madden, Lionel & Storey, Richard. Primary Sources for Victorian Studies. (C). 1977. 30.00 (*0-85033-252-4*) St Mut.

Madden-Lunsford, Kerry. Offsides: A Novel. LC 96-17164. 288p. 1996. 22.00 (*0-688-14935-9*, Wm Morrow) Morrow Avon.

Madden, Lynne R., jt. auth. see Forster, Jas. H.

Madden, M. Stuart. Toxic Torts Deskbook. 240p. 1992. boxed set 99.95 (*0-87371-508-X*, L508) Lewis Pubs.

Madden, M. Stuart, jt. auth. see Boston, Gerald W.

Madden, M. Stuart, ed. see Boston, Gerald W.

Madden, Mary. The Pagan Divinities & Their Worship As Depicted in the Work of St. Augustine. 1972. 59.95 (*0-8490-0796-8*) Gordon Pr.

Madden, Mary J. Thinward Bound: Medical Management & Weight Loss. Hoel, Donna, ed. LC 82-17679. (Illus.). 112p. 1982. pap. text 11.50 (*0-89303-228-X*) P-H.

***Madden, Matt.** Odds Off. 2000. pap. 9.95 (*0-9665363-9-8*) Highwater Bks.

Madden, Maxine A. & Spencer, Harry O. Sounds on Strings: Getting to Know Your Cello. (Illus.). 32p. (J). (gr. k-6). 1998. pap. text 4.95 (*1-893178-02-1*) AMSER.

— Sounds on Strings: Getting to Know Your String Bass. (Illus.). 32p. (J). (gr. k-6). 1998. pap. text 4.95 (*1-893178-03-X*) AMSER.

— Sounds on Strings: Getting to Know Your Viola. (Illus.). 32p. (J). (gr. k-6). 1998. pap. text 4.95 (*1-893178-01-3*) AMSER.

— Sounds on Strings: Getting to Know Your Violin. (Illus.). 32p. (J). (gr. k-6). 1998. pap. text 4.95 (*1-893178-00-5*) AMSER.

— Sounds on Strings: Piano - Teachers Manual. (Illus.). 32p. (J). (gr. k-6). 1998. pap. text, teacher ed. 3.00 (*1-893178-04-8*) AMSER.

Madden, Mickee. Dusk Before Dawn. 352p. 1996. pap. 5.99 (*0-7860-0240-9*, Pinncle Kensgtn) Kensgtn Pub Corp.

— Everlastin' 1994. mass mkt. 5.99 (*0-7860-0003-1*, Pinncle Kensgtn) Kensgtn Pub Corp.

— Everlastin' 384p. 1995. mass mkt. 5.99 (*0-8217-0003-0*, Zebra Kensgtn) Kensgtn Pub Corp.

— Love Everlastin' 352p. 1998. pap. 5.99 (*0-7860-0527-0*, Pinncle Kensgtn) Kensgtn Pub Corp.

— One Bright Star. 352p. 1997. mass mkt. 5.99 (*0-7860-0273-5*, Pinncle Kensgtn) Kensgtn Pub Corp.

Madden, Mickie. Hope Everlastin' 1999. 5.99 (*0-7860-0653-6*) Kensgtn Pub Corp.

Madden, Moss, jt. ed. see Hewings, Geoffrey J.

***Madden, Myron C.** The Power to Bless. rev. ed. LC 99-33213. 130p. 1999. reprint ed. pap. 15.00 (*0-914520-39-3*) Insight Pr.

Madden, Onyx. The Mysterious Chronicles of Oz: or Tip & the Sawhorse of Oz. LC 83-73621. (Illus.). 240p. 1985. 14.95 (*0-930422-34-1*) Dennis-Landman.

Madden, P. J. Wigglesworth Standard. 240p. 1993. mass mkt. 5.99 (*0-88368-261-3*) Whitaker Hse.

Madden, Patrick J. Jesus' Walking on the Sea: An Investigation of the Origin of the Narrative Account. LC 96-6543. (Beiheft zur Zeitschrift fuer die Neuetestamentliche Wissenschaft Ser.: Vol. 81). i, 156p. (C). 1997. lib. bdg. 80.00 (*3-11-015247-9*) De Gruyter.

Madden, Paul. Adolf Hitler & the Nazi Epoch: An Annotated Bibliography of English-Language Works on the Origins, Nature, & Structure of the Nazi State. LC 98-41703. (Magill Bibliographies Ser.). 768p. 1998. 75.00 (*0-8108-3558-4*) Scarecrow.

— Fidel Castro. LC 92-46482. (World Leaders Ser.). 112p. (YA). 1993. lib. bdg. 25.27 (*0-86625-479-X*) Rourke Pubns.

***Madden, Peter J.** The Secret of Wigglesworth's Power. LC 00-39245. 164p. 2000. pap. 10.99 (*0-88368-586-8*) Whitaker Hse.

— The Wigglesworth Standard. LC 00-36653. 2000. pap. write for info. (*0-88368-612-0*) Whitaker Hse.

Madden, Richard. HBJ Spelling Signature Edition Gold Level 8. 88th ed. (J). 1988. text 30.00 (*0-15-327084-5*) Harcourt.

— Spelling. 1983. 26.00 (*0-15-328560-5*) Harcourt Schl Pubs.

Madden, Richard & Australian Bureau of Statistics Staff. National Aboriginal & Torres Strait Islander Survey, 1994: Detailed Findings. LC 98-180477. vi, 103 p. 1995. write for info. (*0-642-20735-6*) Aust Inst Criminology.

Madden, Richard C. Catholics in South Carolina: A Record. 428p. (Orig.). 1985. pap. text 29.00 (*0-8191-4458-4*); lib. bdg. 54.00 (*0-8191-4457-6*) U Pr of Amer.

An Asterisk (*) at the beginning of an entry indicates that the title is appearing for the first time.

Madden, Richard R. Literary Life & Correspondence of the Countess of Blessington. 3 vols. reprint ed. 210.00 (*0-404-07720-X*) AMS Pr.

Madden, Robert E. Tax Planning for Highly Compensated Individuals. 2nd ed. 816p. 1989. suppl. ed. 160.00 (*0-7913-0210-5*); suppl. ed. 45.75 (*0-7913-0902-9*) Warren Gorham & Lamont.

— Tax Planning for Highly Compensated Individuals. 3rd ed. LC 96-61694. 1120p. 1997. suppl. ed. 185.00 (*0-7913-3014-1*, TPH) Warren Gorham & Lamont.

Madden, Robert G. Legal Issues in Social Work, Counseling, & Mental Health. LC 97-45285. (Sourcebooks for the Human Services). 1998. write for info. (*0-7619-1232-0*); pap. write for info. (*0-7619-1233-9*) Sage.

***Madden, Sonya.** These Strange Lives of Poetic Madness. 40p. 1999. pap. 5.00 (*1-889289-39-6*) Ye Olde Font Shoppe.

***Madden, Steven J.** Service Learning Across the Curriculum: Case Applications in Higher Education. 176p. 2000. 47.00 (*0-7618-1583-X*); pap. 27.50 (*0-7618-1584-8*) U Pr of Amer.

Madden, Stuart M. Products Liability: 1985 Pocket Part. 130p. 1985. pap. text. write for info. (*0-318-59390-4*) West Pub.

Madden, Susan. Nobody Overeats. LC 97-61705. 176p. 1997. pap. 12.95 (*1-890394-10-6*, Sage Creek) Rhodes & Easton.

Madden, Susan L. The Preemie Parents' Companion: The Essential Guide to Caring for Your Premature Baby in the Hospital, at Home & Through the First Years. LC 99-25790. (Illus.). 336p. 2000. pap. 14.95 (*1-55832-135-7*) Harvard Common Pr.

— The Preemie Parents' Companion: The Essential Guide to Caring for Your Premature Baby in the Hospital, at Home & Through the First Years. LC 99-25790. (Illus.). 336p. 2000. 27.95 (*1-55832-134-9*) Harvard Common Pr.

Madden, Tara R. Romance on the Run: Five Minutes of Quality Sex for Busy Couples. 96p. 1995. pap. 10.00 (*0-8217-4885-8*, Zebra Kensgtn) Kensgtn Pub Corp.

Madden, Thomas. Graves in Wheat. (Ice River Regional Writers Ser.: Vol. 2). 60p. 1998. pap. 7.95 (*1-877655-22-8*) Wordcraft Oregon.

Madden, Thomas E., jt. auth. see Giorgianni, Edward J.

***Madden, Thomas F.** Concise History of the Crusades. LC 99-27012. 192p. 1999. 50.00 (*0-8476-9429-1*); pap. 12.95 (*0-8476-9430-5*) Rowman.

Madden, Thomas F., jt. auth. see Queller, Donald E.

Madden, Thomas J. King of the Condo: A Hilarious Whodunit with an Oceanview. (Illus.). 160p. 1998. pap. 9.95 (*1-890819-05-0*) TransMedia FL.

— Spin Man: The Topsy-Turvy World of Public Relations . . . a Tell-All Tale. (Illus.). 208p. 1997. 21.95 (*1-890819-00-X*) TransMedia FL.

Madden, W. C. The AAGPBL Record Book: Comprehensive Hitting, Fielding & Pitching Statistics for the All-American Girls Professional. LC 99-37844. (Illus.). 302p. 2000. boxed set 35.00 (*0-7864-0597-X*) McFarland & Co.

— The Dutiful Dozen. 74p. (Orig.). (C). 1997. pap. 9.95 (*0-9645819-1-4*) Madden Pub.

— The Women of the All-American Girls Professional Baseball League: A Biographical Dictionary. LC 97-9158. (Illus.). 295p. 1997. boxed set 35.00 (*0-7864-0304-7*) McFarland & Co.

Madden, Wayne & Woodbury, Carol. Implementing AS/400 Security. 3rd rev. ed. LC 98-8864. 400p. 1998. pap. 69.00 (*1-882419-78-2*) News Four-Hund.

Madden, Wayne, jt. auth. see Yergin, Jonathan.

Madden, William. Hoosiers of Summer. LC 94-75209. 200p. 24.95 (*1-878208-44-6*) Guild Pr IN.

Madden, Yvonne M. Black Magic & Stolen Timber. Madden, Christine W., ed. audio, digital audio 50.00 (*0-9619080-2-5*) Vonnie Pub.

Madden, Yvonne M. Black Magic & Stolen Timber. Madden, Christine W., ed. 296p. 1993. text 25.00 (*0-9619080-0-9*); pap. text 20.00 (*0-9619080-1-7*) Vonnie Pub.

Madderlake, et al. Flowers Rediscovered. rev. ed. LC 94-20401. (Illus.). 232p. 1994. pap. 24.95 (*1-885183-03-8*) Artisan.

Maddern, Guy J., et al. Hernia Repair: Open vs. Laparoscopic Approaches. LC 97-133. 1997. text 80.00 (*0-443-05523-8*) Church.

Maddern, Philippa, jt. ed. see Lynch, Andrew.

Maddern, Philippa C. Violence & Social Order: East Anglia, 1422-1442. (Oxford Historical Monographs). (Illus.). 280p. 1992. text 69.00 (*0-19-820235-0*) OUP.

***Madderom, Chuck.** Los Angeles City Fire Apparatus: Photo Archive. LC 99-76048. (Illus.). 128p. 2000. pap. 29.95 (*1-58388-012-7*, 129956AE, Pub. by Iconografix) Motorbooks Intl.

Madders, Kevin. A New Force at a New Frontier: Europe's Development in the Space Field in the Light of Its Main Actors, Policies, Law & Activities from Its Beginnings up to the Present. LC 96-15202. (Illus.). 628p. (C). 1997. text 155.00 (*0-521-57096-4*) Cambridge U Pr.

Maddex, Diane. Architects Make Zigzags: Looking at Architecture from A to Z. LC 84-9679. (Illus.). 64p. (Orig.). (YA). (gr. 3 up). 1995. pap. 11.95 (*0-471-14357-X*) Wiley.

***Maddex, Diane.** Fifty Favorite Furnishings: By Frank Lloyd Wright. LC 99-29716. (Illus.). 128p. 1999. 17.98 (*0-7651-1670-7*) Smithmark.

— Fifty Favorite Rooms: By Frank Lloyd Wright. LC 98-7285. (Illus.). 128p. 1998. 17.98 (*0-7651-0839-9*) Smithmark.

— Fifty Great American Rooms. (Illus.). 128p. 2001. 17.98 (*0-7651-1669-3*) Smithmark.

Maddex, Diane. Frank Lloyd Wright's House Beautiful. Beautiful House Editors, ed. LC 99-36733. (Illus.). 176p. 2000. 40.00 (*0-688-16736-5*, Hearst) Hearst Commns.

***Maddex, Diane & Wright, Frank Lloyd.** Fifty Favorite Houses by Frank Lloyd Wright. LC 99-47522. (Illus.). 128p. 2000. 17.98 (*0-7651-1763-0*) Smithmark.

Maddex, Diane, ed. see National Trust for Historic Preservation Staff.

Maddex, Robert L., Jr. Constitutions of the World. LC 95-11374. 338p. (C). 1995. text 95.00 (*0-87187-992-1*) Congr Quarterly.

***Maddex, Robert L.** The Encyclopedia of Human Rights & Remedies. 400p. 2000. 120.00 (*1-56802-490-8*) CQ Pr.

Maddex, Robert L., Jr. Illustrated Dictionary of Constitutional Concepts. LC 96-32484. (Illus.). 335p. (C). (gr. 11). 1996. text 95.00 (*1-56802-170-4*) Congr Quarterly.

***Maddex, Robert L.** State Constitutions of the United States. LC 98-36835. 500p. (C). 1998. text 115.00 (*1-56802-373-1*) Congr Quarterly.

Maddi. Personality Theories. 6th ed. 1996. teacher ed. write for info. (*0-534-34078-4*) Thomson Learn.

Maddi, Salvatore R. Personality Theories: A Comparative Analysis. 5th ed. 749p. (C). 1989. text 45.00 (*0-534-10696-X*) Brooks-Cole.

Maddicott, J. R. Simon de Montfort. (Illus.). 430p. 1996. pap. text 24.95 (*0-521-37636-X*) Cambridge U Pr.

***Maddicott, John Robert, et al.** The Medieval State: Essays Presented to James Campbell. LC 99-43948. 2001. write for info. (*1-85285-195-3*) Hambledon Press.

Maddieson, Ian & Hinnebusch, Thomas J. Language History & Linguistic Description in Africa. (Trends in African Linguistics Ser.). 316p. 1997. write for info. (*0-86543-631-2*) Africa World.

Maddieson, Ian & Hinnenbusch, Thomas J. Language History & Linguistic Description in Africa. (Trends in African Linguistics Ser.). 316p. 1997. pap. 29.95 (*0-86543-632-0*) Africa World.

Maddieson, Ian, jt. auth. see Ladefoged, Peter.

Maddigan, Judi. Soft Toys for Babies. Fanning, Robbie, ed. (Stitch & Enrich Ser.). (Illus.). 200p. (Orig.). 1991. pap. 17.95 (*0-932086-29-2*) Open Chain Pub.

Maddin, Stuart. Current Dermatologic Therapy. 2nd ed. 1991. text 72.00 (*0-7216-1053-6*, W B Saunders Co) Harcrt Hlth Sci Grp.

Maddison, Angus. Dynamic Forces in Capitalist Development. (Illus.). 350p. 1991. pap. text 28.00 (*0-19-828398-9*) OUP.

— Explaining the Economic Performance of Nations: Essays in Time & Space. (Economists of the Twentieth Century Ser.). 496p. 1995. 110.00 (*1-85278-600-0*) E Elgar.

— Monitoring the World Economy, 1820-1992. 255p. 1995. pap. 30.00 (*92-64-14549-4*, 41-95-09-1, Pub. by Org for Econ) OECD.

Maddison, Angus & Organisation for Economic Co-operation & Development Staff. Chinese Economic Performance in the Long Run. LC 98-203988. (Development Centre Studies). 194p. 1998. write for info. (*92-64-16180-5*) Org for Econ.

Maddison, Dorothy, jt. auth. see Sullivan, Gail.

Maddison, John. Education in the Microelectronics Era. LC 99-943832. 208p. 1983. pap. 25.00 (*0-335-10182-8*) OpUniv Pr.

— Information Technology & Education. 320p. 1982. 99.00 (*0-335-10183-6*) OpUniv Pr.

Maddison, Lauren. Deceptions: A Connor Hawthorne Mystery. LC 98-49284. 352p. 1999. pap. 12.95 (*1-55583-490-6*, Pub. by Alyson Pubns) Consort Bk Sales.

Maddison, Lowinger, jt. auth. see Holst, Imogen.

Maddison, P. J., et al, eds. Oxford Textbook of Rheumatology, 1. LC 92-48994. (Illus.). 240p. 1996. text (*0-19 262432 6*) OUP.

— Oxford Textbook of Rheumatology, 2. LC 92-48994. 1993. write for info. (*0-19-262343-5*) OUP.

Maddison, Peter J., et al, eds. Oxford Textbook of Rheumatology, 2 vols. 2nd ed. LC 98-149774. (Illus.). 1998. text 375.00 (*0-19-262697-3*) OUP.

Maddison, R. & Darnton, G. Information Systems in Organizations: Improving Business Processes. (Illus.). 464p. 1995. mass mkt. 25.99 (*0-412-62530-X*) Chapman & Hall.

Maddison, R. N., jt. auth. see Bhabuta, Love.

Maddison, Ralph. Englands Looking In & Out: Presented to the High Court of Parliament Now Assembled. LC 76-57397. (English Experience Ser.: No. 813). 1977. reprint ed. lib. bdg. 15.00 (*90-221-0813-9*) Walter J Johnson.

***Maddison, Stephen.** Fags, Hags & Queer Sisters: Gender Dissent & Heterosocial Bonds in Gay Culture. LC 00-33306. 2000. pap. write for info. (*0-312-23637-9*) St Martin.

Maddix, Frank & Morgan, Gareth. Systems Software: An Introduction to Language Processors & Operating Systems. 1989. text 49.95 (*0-470-21422-8*) P-H.

Maddock, Alfred G. Mossbauer Spectroscopy: Principles & Applications of the Techniques. 250p. 1998. 89.00 (*1-898563-16-0*, Pub. by Horwood Pub) Paul & Co Pubs.

Maddock, James W., ed. Sexuality Education in Postsecondary & Professional Training Settings. LC 97-14977. 193p. 1997. 39.95 (*0-7890-0027-X*) Haworth Pr.

Maddock, James W., et al, eds. Families Before & after Perestroika: Russian & U. S. Perspectives. LC 93-23409. (Perspectives on Marriage & the Family Ser.). 240p. 1993. lib. bdg. 35.00 (*0-89862-085-6*) Guilford Pubns.

— Human Sexuality & the Family. LC 83-13013. (Marriage & Family Review Ser.: Vol. 6, Nos. 3-4). 159p. 1984. text 49.95 (*0-86656-159-5*) Haworth Pr.

Maddock, James W. & Larson, Noel R. Child Sexual Abuse: An Ecological Approach to Treating Victims & Perpetrators. 400p. 1996. 40.00 (*0-393-70211-1*) Norton.

— Incestuous Families: An Ecological Approach to Understanding & Treatment. 380p. (C). 1995. 40.00 (*0-393-70193-X*) Norton.

Maddock, Jerome T., jt. ed. see Drancsak, Marina.

Maddock, John. History of Road Trains in the Northern Territory. (Illus.). 176p. 1993. reprint ed. pap. 21.95 (*0-86417-187-0*, Pub. by Kangaroo Pr) Seven Hills Bk.

— People Movers: A History of the Private Bus Companies. (Illus.). 214p. (Orig.). 1994. 39.95 (*0-86417-412-8*, Pub. by Kangaroo Pr) Seven Hills Bk.

Maddock, Kenneth, jt. ed. see Buchler, Ira R.

Maddock, Linda, et al, eds. Mechanics & Physiology of Animal Swimming. (Illus.). 260p. (C). 1995. text 59.95 (*0-521-46078-6*) Cambridge U Pr.

Maddock, Nicholas & Wilson, Frank. Project Design for Agricultural Development. 236p. 1994. 72.95 (*1-85628-413-1*, Pub. by Avebry) Ashgate Pub Co.

Maddock, R. J. & Calcutt, D. M. Electronics Engineers. 2nd ed. (Illus.). 720p. (C). 1994. pap. 69.95 (*0-582-21583-8*, Pub. by Addison-Wesley) Trans-Atl Phila.

Maddock, R. T., jt. auth. see Phillips, G. A.

Maddock, Richard C. Motigraphics: Measuring Human Motivation. LC 99-27546. 320p. 2000. 69.50 (*1-56720-284-5*, Quorum Bks) Greenwood.

Maddock, Richard C. & Fulton, Richard L. Marketing to the Mind: Right Brain Strategies for Advertising & Marketing. LC 95-50743. 304p. 1996. 59.95 (*1-56720-031-1*, Quorum Bks) Greenwood.

— Motivation, Emotions & Leadership: The Silent Side of Management. LC 98-6021. 224p. 1998. 59.95 (*1-56720-151-2*, Quorum Bks) Greenwood.

Maddock, Rodney & King, Stephen. Unlocking the Infrastructure: The Reform of Public Utilities in Australia. 200p. 1997. pap. 29.95 (*1-86448-114-5*, Pub. by Allen & Unwin Pty) Paul & Co Pubs.

***Maddock, Su.** Challenging Women: Gender, Culture & Organization. 224p. 1999. 82.00 (*0-7619-5150-4*); pap. 26.50 (*0-7619-5151-2*) Sage.

***Maddocks, Graham.** Montauban: Somme. (Battleground Europe Ser.). 1998. pap. text 16.95 (*0-85052-579-9*, Pub. by Leo Cooper) Trans-Atl Phila.

Maddocks, Graham, jt. auth. see Davies, Frank.

Maddocks, Hugh C. Deep-Sky Name Index 2000.0. LC 90-84968. 125p. (Orig.). 1991. pap. 16.95 (*0-9628305-0-X*) Foxon-Maddocks.

— Generic Markup of Electronic Index Manuscripts. LC 88-10896. 1988. pap. text 15.00 (*0-936547-04-9*) Am Soc Index.

***Maddocks, Ian, et al.** Primary Care of Landmine Injuries in Africa. (Illus.). 72p. 2000. pap. 10.00 (*1-893368-03-3*) Intl Phys PONW.

Maddocks, Margaret. Fair Shines the Day. large type ed. (Ulverscroft). 464p. 1994. 27.99 (*0-7089-3026-3*) Ulverscroft.

— The Frozen Fountain. large type ed. 352p. 1994. 27.99 (*0-7089-3080-8*) Ulverscroft.

— November Tree. large type ed. 1989. 27.99 (*0-7089-2058-6*) Ulverscroft.

— Piper's Tune. large type ed. 384p. 1994. 27.99 (*0-7089-3097-2*) Ulverscroft.

— Remembered Spring. large type ed. (Ulverscroft). 400p. 1994. 27.99 (*0-7089-3062-X*) Ulverscroft.

— The Silver Answer. large type ed. 1990. 27.99 (*0-7089-2126-4*) Ulverscroft.

Maddocks, Morris. The Christian Healing Ministry. 432p. 1995. pap. 21.95 (*0-687-06627-1*) Abingdon.

***Maddocks, Peg.** Cambridge Girl. 338p. 1999. pap. 14.95 (*0-9674339-0-8*) Trefoil Bks.

Maddocks, Peter. Cartooning for Beginners. 1994. 8.98 (*0-7858-0090-5*) Bk Sales Inc.

Maddoux, Marlin. Seal of Gaia. LC 98-36612. 476 p. 1998. pap. 13.99 (*0-8499-3715-9*) Word Pub.

Maddow, Ben. Edward Weston: His Life. rev. ed. (Illus.). 288p. 1989. reprint ed. pap. 25.95 (*0-89381-369-9*) Aperture.

— A False Autobiography: Poems, 1940-1990. 88p. 1991. 15.00 (*0-9629909-0-6*); pap. 9.00 (*0-9629909-1-4*) Other Shores Pr.

Maddox. American History. 13th ed. 1995. 12.74 (*1-56134-344-7*) McGraw.

— American History, 2. 13th ed. 1995. 12.74 (*1-56134-345-5*) McGraw.

— Annual Editions: American History, Vol. I. 14th ed. 256p. (C). 1996. text. write for info. (*0-697-36303-1*) Brown & Benchmark.

— Australian Democracy. 2nd ed. 1991. pap. text. write for info. (*0-582-87024-0*, Pub. by Addison-Wesley) Longman.

Maddox. Master Classes 6. 176p. 1997. 20.00 (*0-465-04517-0*, Pub. by Basic) HarpC.

Maddox, A. J. The Work of a Magistrate. (C). 1980. pap. 70.00 (*0-7219-0561-7*, Pub. by Scientific) St Mut.

Maddox, Brenda. D. H. Lawrence: The Married Man. LC 94-28960. (Illus.). 621p. 1994. 30.00 (*0-671-68712-3*) S&S Trade.

— D. H. Lawrence: The Story of a Marriage. (Illus.). 656p. 1996. pap. 17.00 (*0-393-31454-5*, Norton Paperbks) Norton.

***Maddox, Brenda.** Nora: The Real Life of Molly Bloom. 512p. 2000. pap. 14.00 (*0-618-05700-5*) HM.

— Yeats's Ghosts: The Secret Life of W. B. Yeats. LC 99-12858. (Illus.). 474p. 1999. 32.00 (*0-06-017494-3*, G Carr Bks) HarpC.

***Maddox, Brenda.** Yeats's Ghosts: The Secret Life of W. B. Yeats. 496p. 2000. pap. 16.00 (*0-06-098504-6*, Perennial) HarperTrade.

Maddox, Bryan. The Cache la Poudre River User's Guide. 2nd rev. ed. Titterington, Scott, ed. (Illus.). 80p. 1997. pap. 12.95 (*1-881663-07-8*) Poudre Canyon Pr.

Maddox, Connie, jt. auth. see Maddox, Ed.

Maddox, David. Budgeting for Not-for-Profit Organizations. LC 99-12223. (Nonprofit Law, Finance, & Management Ser.). 269p. 1999. 85.00 (*0-471-25397-9*) Wiley.

Maddox, Don. The Official ISRA Baseball Handbook: How to Beg, Borrow & Steal Your Way to a Pennant. (International Sports Replay Association Handbooks Ser.). (Illus.). 243p. (Orig.). 1994. pap. 16.95 (*1-883358-18-3*) R&D Pub NJ.

Maddox, Don, jt. auth. see Bisguier, Arthur.

Maddox, Don, jt. auth. see Henley, Ron.

Maddox, Don, ed. see Henley, Ron & Hodges, Paul H.

Maddox, Don, ed. see Wolff, Patrick.

***Maddox, Donald.** Fictions of Identity in Medieval France. 260p. (C). 2000. text Price not set. (*0-521-78105-1*) Cambridge U Pr.

Maddox, Donald. Semiotics of Deceit: Language, Drama, & Culture in Maistre Pierre Pathelin. LC 82-74491. (Illus.). 232p. 1984. 35.00 (*0-8387-5040-0*) Bucknell U Pr.

— Structure & Sacring: The Systematic Kingdom in Chretien's Erec et Enide. LC 77-93405. (French Forum Monographs: No. 8). 221p. (Orig.). 1978. pap. 10.95 (*0-917058-07-0*) French Forum.

Maddox, Donald & Sturm-Maddox, Sara. Jean D'Arras: Roman de Melusine. Wilhelm, James J., ed. (Garland Library of Medieval Literature). 350p. Date not set. text 52.50 (*0-8153-1180-X*) Garland.

Maddox, Donald & Sturm-Maddox, Sara, eds. Froissart Across the Genres. LC 98-30124. 224p. 1998. 55.00 (*0-8130-1619-3*) U Press Fla.

— Melusine of Lusignan: Founding Fiction in Late Medieval France. LC 95-52471. (C). 1996. 50.00 (*0-8203-1823-X*) U of Ga Pr.

Maddox, Donald, jt. ed. see Sturm-Maddox, Sara.

Maddox, Ed & Maddox, Connie. Pike County, Kentucky: A Pictorial History. LC 98-2624. 1998. write for info. (*1-57864-026-1*) Donning Co.

Maddox, Everette. American Waste. 92p. 1993. 10.00 (*0-614-05039-1*) Portals Pr.

— Bar Scotch. LC 87-63109. 57p. (Orig.). 1988. pap. 7.00 (*0-944100-01-5*) Pirogue Pub.

— The Everette Maddox Songbook. Cassin, Maxine, ed. (Journal Press Bks.: Louisiana Legacy). (Illus.). 80p. 1982. pap. 25.00 (*0-938498-02-9*) New Orleans Poetry.

Maddox, Everette, ed. see Maxine, Cassin.

Maddox, George L., ed. The Domesticated Drug. 1970. 29.95 (*0-8084-0108-4*); pap. 24.95 (*0-8084-0109-2*) NCUP.

— The Encyclopedia of Aging. 2nd ed. (Illus.). 1256p. 1995. 159.00 (*0-8261-4841-7*) Springer Pub.

Maddox, George L., et al, eds. Normal Aging 3: Reports from the Duke Longitudinal Studies, 1975-84. LC 85-1598. (Illus.). xx, 468p. (C). 1985. text 49.95 (*0-8223-0624-7*) Duke.

Maddox, George L., frwd. Social Patterns in Normal Aging: Findings from the Duke Longitudinal Studies. LC 81-9800. xii, 135p. 1981. text 32.95 (*0-8223-0458-9*) Duke.

Maddox, George L. & Lawton, M. Powell, eds. The Annual Review of Gerontology & Geriatrics: Kinship, Aging, & Social Change. (Annual Review of Gerontology Ser.: Vol. 13). 280p. 1993. text 46.00 (*0-8261-6495-1*) Springer Pub.

— Annual Review of Gerontology & Geriatrics: Varieties of Aging, Vol. 8. 320p. 1988. 56.00 (*0-8261-6490-0*) Springer Pub.

Maddox, George L. & McCall, Bevode C. Drinking among Teen-Agers. 1964. pap. 15.95 (*0-8084-0413-X*) NCUP.

— Drinking Among Teen-Agers. LC 64-63392. (Monographs: No. 4). 1964. 14.95 (*0-911290-31-1*) Rutgers Ctr Alcohol.

Maddox, George L., jt. auth. see Busse, Ewald W.

Maddox, George L., jt. auth. see Lawton, M. Powell.

Maddox, George T. & Norton, Richard L. Hard Trials & Tribulations of an Old Confederate Soldier. Massey, J. Troy, ed. (Illus.). 82p. 1997. reprint ed. pap. 8.95 (*1-891959-02-6*) Oak Hills Pubg.

Maddox, Graham. Religion & the Rise of Democracy. LC 95-19599. 304p. (C). 1996. 90.00 (*0-415-02603-2*) Routledge.

Maddox, Gregory, ed. African Nationalism & Revolution. LC 93-11080. (Articles on Colonialism & Nationalism in Africa Ser.: Vol. 4). (Illus.). 400p. 1993. text 79.00 (*0-8153-1391-8*) Garland.

— The Colonial Epoch in Africa. LC 93-17822. (Articles on Colonialism & Nationalism in Africa Ser.: Vol. 2). 408p. 1993. text 83.00 (*0-8153-1389-6*) Garland.

— Conquest & Resistance to Colonialism in Africa. LC 93-19790. (Articles on Colonialism & Nationalism in Africa Ser.: Vol. 1). 384p. 1993. text 77.00 (*0-8153-1388-8*) Garland.

Maddox, Gregory, et al, eds. Custodians of the Land: Environment & Hunger in Tanzanian History. LC 95-22932. (Eastern African Studies). 285p. (C). 1995. text 44.95 (*0-8214-1133-0*); pap. text 19.95 (*0-8214-1134-9*) Ohio U Pr.

Maddox, Gregory H., ed. & tr. see Mnyampala, Mathias E.

Maddox, Hugh. Alabama Rules of Criminal Procedure, 2 vols. 2nd ed. LC 94-79597. 1994. text 130.00 (*1-55834-199-4*, 64564-11, MICHIE) LEXIS Pub.

— Alabama Rules of Criminal Procedure. 2nd ed. 1995. suppl. ed. 40.00 (*0-614-25251-2*, 64561-11, MICHIE) LEXIS Pub.

M

*__Maddox, Hugh.__ Alabama Rules of Criminal Procedure, 2 vols. 3rd ed. Incl. Vol. 1. Alabama Rules of Criminal Procedure. 3rd ed. 1999. (0-327-04915-4); Vol. 2. Alabama Rules of Criminal Procedure. 3rd ed. 1999. (0-327-04916-2); 900p. 1999. 180.00 (0-327-04914-6) LEXIS Pub.

Maddox, Hugh. Alabama Rules of Criminal Procedure, 2 vols., Set. 2nd ed. 1994. suppl. ed. 130.00 (0-87473-636-6, MICHIE) LEXIS Pub.

— Alabama Rules of Criminal Procedure: 1992 Supplement. 296p. 1992. write for info. (0-87473-971-3, 64565-10, MICHIE) LEXIS Pub.

— Alabama Rules of Criminal Procedure, 1998 Cumulative Supplement. 2nd ed. 400p. 1998. write for info. (0-327-00400-2, 6456114) LEXIS Pub.

Maddox, I. J. Infinite Matrices of Operators. (Lecture Notes in Mathematics Ser.: Vol. 786). 122p. 1980. 29.95 (0-387-09764-3) Spr-Verlag.

Maddox, Ian S. Practical Sanitation in the Food Industry. xii, 182p. 1994. text 73.00 (2-88449-005-1); pap. text 29.00 (2-88124-992-2) Gordon & Breach.

Maddox, Irene & Cobb, Rosalyn, eds. Campfire Songs. 3rd ed. (Illus.). 1998. pap. 10.95 (0-7627-0318-0) Globe Pequot.

Maddox, J., jt. auth. see Capers, Roberta M.

Maddox, John. What Remains to Be Discovered? Mapping the Secrets of the Universe, the Origins of Life & the Future of the Human Race. LC 98-29137. 448p. 1998. 25.50 (0-684-82292-X) Free Pr.

— What Remains to Be Discovered ? Mapping the Secrets of the Universe, the Origins of Life & the Future of the Human Race. 448p. 1999. per. 15.00 (0-684-86300-6) S&S Trade Pap.

Maddox, John, jt. auth. see Beaton, Leonard.

Maddox, John L. The Medicine Man: A Sociological Study of the Character & Evolution of Shamanism. LC 75-23737. reprint ed. 45.00 (0-404-13294-4) AMS Pr.

Maddox, Karen. From Beneath the Surface. LC 90-82946. (Illus.). 74p. (Orig.). 1994. reprint ed. 10.00 (0-9620375-6-7) Faith Unlimited.

*__Maddox, Karl.__ SB: 1 or God. LC 99-93933. 2000. pap. 12.95 (0-533-13193-6) Vantage.

*__Maddox, Kate.__ Web Commerce: Building a Digital Business. LC 98-13347. (Upside Bks.). 288p. 1998. 29.95 (0-471-29282-6, VNR) Wiley.

Maddox, Kathleen B. Collected Poems & One Essay. Orth, Jane, ed. (Illus.). 97p. 1995. pap. 6.00 (1-885761-01-5) Turner Geriatric.

Maddox, Kenneth W. An Unprejudiced Eye: The Drawings of Jasper F. Cropsey. LC 79-90970. (Illus.). 72p. (Orig.). 1979. pap. 5.00 (0-943651-07-7) Hudson Riv.

Maddox, Lucy. Locating American Studies: The Evolution of a Discipline. LC 98-18959. (Illus.). 456p. 1998. 19.95 (0-8018-6056-3) Johns Hopkins.

— Removals: Nineteenth-Century American Literature & the Politics of Indian Affairs. 216p. 1991. text 60.00 (0-19-506931-5) OUP.

Maddox, Margaret, jt. auth. see Gottschalk, Louis.

Maddox, Maris, ed. see Maddox, Suzan.

*__Maddox, Mary, et al, eds.__ El Lenguaje es la Clave: El Hablar y los Libros & El Hablar y el Jugar, Vol. II. (SPA.). 92p. 1999. student ed. 95.00 (1-930690-01-0) Wash Resrch Instit.

*__Maddox, Mary, et al.__ Language is the Key: Talking & Books & Talking & Play, Vol. I. (Illus.). 92p. 1998. student ed. 95.00 (1-930690-00-2) Wash Resrch Instit.

Maddox, Michael. Human Factors Guide for Aviation Maintenance. 576p. 1995. ring bd. 45.00 (0-16-042643-X) USGPO.

— Supplement to Human Factors Guide for Aviation Maintenance. 190p. 1997. ring bd. 20.00 (0-16-062399-5) USGPO.

Maddox, Mike, jt. auth. see Anderson, Jeff.

Maddox, Mike, ed. see Anderson, Jeff.

Maddox, Muriel. Captain from Corfu: A Novel. LC 98-52306. 256p. 1999. 22.95 (0-86534-287-3) Sunstone Pr.

— Llantarnam: A Novel. Smith, James C., Jr., ed. LC 91-38366. 416p. (Orig.). 1992. pap. 16.95 (0-86534-173-7) Sunstone Pr.

— Love & Betrayal: A Novel. LC 96-16304. 288p. 1997. 22.95 (0-86534-249-0) Sunstone Pr.

*__Maddox, Muriel.__ Noela: Two Novellas. 288p. 2000. 22.95 (0-86534-309-8) Sunstone Pr.

*__Maddox, Randall A.__ Distributed Application Programming in C++ 400p. 2000. pap. 49.99 incl. cd-rom (0-13-087133-8, Prentice Hall) P-H.

Maddox, Randy L. Aldersgate Reconsidered. 1990. pap. 14.95 (0-687-00984-7) Abingdon.

— Responsible Grace: John Wesley's Practical Theology. (Kingswood Ser.). 400p. (Orig.). 1994. pap. 19.95 (0-687-00334-2) Abingdon.

— Rethinking Wesley's Theology for Contemporary Methodism. Matthews, Rex, ed. LC 98-6005. 256p. 1998. pap. 21.95 (0-687-06045-1) Abingdon.

Maddox, Richard. El Castillo: The Politics of Tradition in an Andalusian Town. 368p. 1993. pap. text 17.95 (0-252-06339-2) U of Ill Pr.

— El Castillo: The Politics of Tradition in an Andalusian Town. (Illus.). 368p. (C). 1993. text 49.95 (0-252-01946-6) U of Ill Pr.

— DAT Technical Service Handbook. (Illus.). 256p. 1994. text 52.95 (0-442-01423-6, VNR) Wiley.

Maddox, Robert. Annual Editions: American History, Vol. II. 14th ed. 256p. (C). 1996. text. write for info. (0-697-36308-2) Brown & Benchmark.

— The Purposes of Luke-Acts. 228p. pap. text 27.95 (0-567-29270-3, Pub. by T & T Clark) Bks Intl VA.

Maddox, Robert B. & Conrad, Pamela J. Guide to Affirmative Action: A Primer for Supervisors & Managers. 2nd rev. ed. LC 96-85071. (Fifty-Minute Ser.). (Illus.). 79p. 1996. pap. 10.95 (1-56052-382-4) Crisp Pubns.

Maddox, Robert C. Cross-Cultural Problems in International Business: The Role of the Cultural Integration Function. LC 92-43086. 160p. 1993. 49.95 (0-89930-581-4, MOK, Quorum Bks) Greenwood.

Maddox, Robert F. The Senatorial Career of Harley Martin Kilgore. rev. ed. LC 96-207268. (Illus.). 351p. (C). 1996. reprint ed. pap. text 16.95 (0-943025-81-8) Cummngs & Hath.

Maddox, Robert J. American History: Fifteenth Edition, Vol. 1. 15th ed. (Annual Ser.). (Illus.). 240p. 1998. pap. text 12.25 (0-697-39380-1, Dshkn McG-Hill) McGrw-H Hghr Educ.

— Weapons for Victory: The Hiroshima Decision Fifty Years Later. 200p. (C). 1995. 19.95 (0-8262-1037-6) U of Mo Pr.

Maddox, Robert J., ed. American History: Fifteenth Edition, Vol. 2. 15th ed. (Annual Ser.). (Illus.). 240p. 1998. pap. text 12.25 (0-697-39379-8, Dshkn McG-Hill) McGrw-H Hghr Educ.

Maddox, Robert L. Prostate Cancer: What I Found Out & What You Should Know. LC 97-20186. 160p. 1997. pap. text 11.99 (0-87788-566-4, H Shaw Pubs) Waterbrook Pr.

Maddox, Robert N. Process Engineer's Absorption Pocket Handbook. LC 85-852. 96p. 1985. reprint ed. pap. 30.00 (0-608-01336-6, 206208000001) Bks Demand.

Maddox, Robert N., jt. auth. see Hines, Anthony L.

Maddox, Robert P. The Black Hills of Deadwood. (Illus.). 125p. 1998. pap. 10.00 (0-9668394-0-4, 100001) Rogue River.

Maddox, Ruth P. Building SMU: 1915-1957. 1995. pap. 27.00 (1-884363-07-5) Odenwald Pr.

Maddox, S. & Aragon-Salamanca, A. Wide Field Spectroscopy & the Distant Universe: Proceedings of the 35th Herstmonceux Conference. 400p. 1995. text 99.00 (981-02-2031-6) World Scientific Pub.

Maddox, S. J. Fatigue Strength of Welded Structures. 2nd ed. (Illus.). 208p. 1991. 153.00 (1-85573-013-8, Pub. by Woodhead Pubng) Am Educ Systs.

Maddox, S. J., ed. see Welding Institute Staff.

Maddox, Sam. The Quest for Cure: Restoring Function after Spinal Cord Injury. LC 92-50575. (Illus.). 200p. (Orig.). 1993. pap. 22.45 (0-929819-03-9) Paralyzed Vets.

*__Maddox, Sarah O. & Webb, Patricia F.__ A Mother's Garden of Prayer: Cultivating a Lifestyle of Praying for Your Children. LC 98-31067. 128p. 1999. pap. 13.99 (0-8054-1768-0) Broadman.

Maddox, Suzan. The Complete Family Health & Medical Record Book. Maddox, Maris, ed. 52p. pap. text 7.95 (0-9660678-5-1, 007) TEK Pubns.

Maddox, Sylvia, jt. auth. see Earle, Mary C.

Maddox, Tom. Halo. 224p. 1992. mass mkt. 3.99 (0-8125-1096-8) Tor Bks.

Maddox, Tony. Fergus the Farmyard Dog. (Illus.). 28p. (J). 1993. pap. 4.95 (0-8120-1763-3) Barron.

— Fergus's Big Splash. LC 96-7357. (Illus.). 32p. (J). (ps-3). 1996. pap. 4.95 (0-8120-9786-5) Barron.

— Fergus's Big Splash. 1996. 10.15 (0-606-11323-1, Pub. by Turtleback) Demco.

— Fergus's Upside-Down Day. LC 94-16656. (Illus.). 32p. (J). 1994. pap. 4.95 (0-8120-9074-8) Barron.

— Fergus's Upside-Down Day. LC 94-16656. (Illus.). 32p. (J). 1995. 12.95 (0-8120-6471-2) Barron.

— Spike's Best Nest. LC 97-40812. (Illus.). 32p. (J). 1998. pap. 5.95 (0-7641-0548-5) Barron.

— Spike's Best Nest. 1998. 11.15 (0-606-13795-5, Pub. by Turtleback) Demco.

Maddox, William. Profits in Building Spec Homes. (Illus.). 232p. (Orig.). 1994. pap. 27.25 (0-934041-93-8) Craftsman.

— Scacciato. 128p. (Orig.). 1996. pap. 10.00 (0-916620-97-2) Portals Pr.

Maddox, William A. The Free School Idea in Virginia Before the Civil War: A Phase of Political & Social Evolution. LC 70-177045. (Columbia University. Teachers College. Contributions to Education Ser.: No. 93). reprint ed. 37.50 (0-404-55093-2) AMS Pr.

— Free School Idea in Virginia Before the Civil War: A Phase of Poltiical & Social Evolution. LC 75-89202. (American Education, It's Men, Institutions, & Ideas. Series 1). 1978. reprint ed. 18.95 (0-405-01436-8) Ayer.

Maddoxs, Anson. Freak Legion: A Players Guide to Fomori. (Warewolf Ser.). 1995. pap., per. 12.00 (1-56504-350-2, 3066) White Wolf.

*__Maddrey, Willis C.__ Conquering Hepatitis. 100p. 2000. pap. 9.95 (1-896998-06-2, Empowering Pr) Decker.

— Transplantation of the Liver. 3rd ed. 700p. text 139.00 (0-7817-2039-7) Lppncott W & W.

*__Maddrey, Willis C., ed.__ Atlas of the Liver. 2nd ed. LC 99-34180. (Gastroenterology & Hepatology Ser.: Vol. 1). 320p. 2000. text 124.95 (1-57340-134-X) Current Med.

Maddrey, Willis C. & Sorrell, Michael F. Transplantation of the Liver. 2nd ed. LC 94-25108. (Illus.). 640p. (C). 1996. pap. text 175.00 (0-8385-8990-1, A8990-2, Apple Lange Med) McGraw.

Maddrey, Willis C., ed. see Feldman, Mark.

Madduc, jt. auth. see Johnson.

Maddux, Carolyn. Remembering Water. 89p. (Orig.). 1996. pap. 10.00 (0-944920-22-5) Bellowing Ark Pr.

Maddux, Cleborne, jt. auth. see LaMont Johnson, D.

Maddux, Cleborne D. Distance Education: A Selected Bibliography. Milheim, William D., ed. LC 92-24055. (Educational Technology Selected Bibliography Ser.: Vol. 7). 71p. (Orig.). 1992. pap. 24.95 (0-87778-249-0) Educ Tech Pubns.

Maddux, Cleborne D., ed. LOGO in the Schools. LC 85-8411. (Computers in the Schools Ser.: Vol. 2. Nos. 2-3). 305p. 1985. text 9.95 (0-86656-424-1); pap. text 24.95 (0-86656-425-X) Haworth Pr.

*__Maddux, Cleborne D. & Johnson, D. L.__ Educational Computing: Learning with Tomorrow's Technologies. 3rd ed. 351p. 2001. pap. 56.00 (0-205-31842-8) Allyn.

Maddux, Cleborne D. & Johnson, D. LaMont, eds. Logo: A Retrospective. LC 97-32264. 212p. 1997. 49.95 (0-7890-0374-0) Haworth Pr.

Maddux, Cleborne D., jt. auth. see Kass, Corrine E.

Maddux, Dorothy, jt. auth. see Maddux, Robert B.

Maddux, Earle H., ed. A Manual for Priests. 301p. 1996. reprint ed. 29.95 (1-886412-19-7) Preserv Press.

Maddux, J. E., et al, eds. Social Processes in Clinical & Counseling Psychology. (Illus.). 392p. 1987. 52.00 (0-387-96533-5) Spr-Verlag.

Maddux, James E., ed. Self-Efficacy, Adaptation, & Adjustment: Theory, Research, & Application. LC 95-3668. (Plenum Series in Social-Clinical Psychology). (Illus.). 414p. (C). 1995. 57.50 (0-306-44875-0, Plenum Trade) Perseus Pubng.

Maddux, Mike. MASM: Tips & Techniques for Unisys 1100-2200 Systems. Drolet, Michele, ed. 260p. 1990. student ed. 45.00 (0-9627241-0-6) PCI TX.

Maddux, Rachel. Communication: The Autobiography of Rachel Maddux, & Her Novella, Turnips Blood. Walker, Nancy A., ed. LC 91-7248. (Rachel Maddux Ser.). (Illus.). 240p. (C). 1991. 28.95 (0-87049-699-9) U of Tenn Pr.

— Green Kingdom. LC 92-26664. (Rachel Maddux Ser.: Vol. 4). 576p. (C). 1993. 37.95 (0-87049-780-4) U of Tenn Pr.

— A Walk in the Spring Rain & the Orchard Children. LC 92-4980. 344p. 1992. 31.95 (0-87049-757-X) U of Tenn Pr.

— The Way Things Are: The Stories of Rachel Maddux. LC 91-40099. 296p. 1992. 28.95 (0-87049-751-0) U of Tenn Pr.

Maddux, Robert. Delegating for Results. 2nd rev. ed. LC 97-66609. (Fifty Minute Ser.). (Illus.). 120p. 1997. pap. 10.95 (1-56052-455-3) Crisp Pubns.

— Team Building: An Exercise in Leadership. 70p. (Orig.). 1988. 7.95 (0-318-33263-9, 116) Am Bartenders.

Maddux, Robert, jt. auth. see Chapman, Elwood.

Maddux, Robert B. Building Teams for Your Small Business. Paris, Janis, ed. LC 95-74820. (Small Business & Entrepreneurship Ser.). 100p. (Orig.). 1996. pap. 15.95 (1-56052-365-4) Crisp Pubns.

*__Maddux, Robert B.__ Effective Performance Appraisals. 4th ed. Godding, Carol, ed. LC 99-75961. (Fifty-Minute Ser.). (Illus.). 80p. 2000. pap. 12.95 (1-56052-504-5) Crisp Pubns.

Maddux, Robert B. Effective Performance Appraisals: A Practice Guide for More Productive & Positive Performance Appraisals. 3rd rev. ed. Crisp, Michael, ed. LC 92-73962. (Fifty-Minute Ser.). 79p. (Orig.). 1993. reprint ed. pap. 10.95 (1-56052-196-1) Crisp Pubns.

— Quality Interviewing: A Step-by-Step Action Plan for Success. 3rd rev. ed. Crisp, Michael, ed. LC 93-7049. (Fifty-Minute Ser.). (Illus.). 72p. 1994. pap. 10.95 (1-56052-262-3) Crisp Pubns.

— Successful Negotiation: Effective "Win-Win" Strategies & Tactics. 3rd rev. ed. LC 94-74330. (Fifty-Minute Ser.). (Illus.). 74p. (Orig.). 1995. pap. 10.95 (1-56052-348-4) Crisp Pubns.

— Team Building. 2nd ed. (Better Management Skills Ser.). 1994. pap. 12.95 (0-7494-1411-1) Kogan Page Ltd.

— Team Building: An Exercise in Leadership. rev. ed. Crisp, Michael G., ed. LC 91-77080. (Fifty-Minute Ser.). (Illus.). 77p. (Orig.). 1992. pap. 10.95 (1-56052-118-X) Crisp Pubns.

— Tworzenie Zespolu: Rozwijanie Umiejetnosci Zarzadzania. Grycz, Czeslaw J., ed. Salski, Andrzej, ed. & tr. by. from ENG. (POL., Illus.). iv, 74p. (Orig.). (C). 1991. pap. 7.95 (1-56513-002-2) W Poniecki Charit.

Maddux, Robert B. & Maddux, Dorothy. Ethics in Business: A Guide for Managers. Sanders, Marian, ed. LC 88-63799. (Fifty-Minute Ser.). (Illus.). 70p. (Orig.). 1989. pap. 10.95 (0-931961-69-6) Crisp Pubns.

Maddux, Robert B. & Voorhees, Lynda. Job Performance & Chemical Dependency: A Guide for Supervisors & Managers. Crisp, Michael G., ed. LC 86-73172. (Fifty-Minute Ser.). (Illus.). 79p. (Orig.). 1987. pap. 10.95 (0-931961-27-0) Crisp Pubns.

Maddux, Thomas R. Years of Estrangement: American Relations with the Soviet Union. LC 79-26489. 248p. 1980. reprint ed. pap. 76.90 (0-608-04458-X, 206520200001) Bks Demand.

Maddy, Agnes. Puzzles, the Bible Has the Answers. (Illus.). 48p. (Orig.). 1993. pap. 3.25 (0-915374-75-7, 75-7) Rapids Christian.

Maddy, Olive. Maddy - Us Maddys: An Account of the Family in England & the Descendants of William Maddy of Fairfax of Fairfax County, Virginia, & James Maddy of Fairfax & Orange County. (Illus.). 280p. 1994. reprint ed. pap. 44.00 (0-8328-4036-X); reprint ed. lib. bdg. 54.00 (0-8328-4035-1) Higginson Bk Co.

Maddy, Penelope. Naturalism in Mathematics. LC 97-12665. 264p. (C). 1998. text 35.00 (0-19-823573-9) OUP.

*__Maddy, Penelope.__ Naturalism in Mathematics. 264p. 2000. pap. 19.95 (0-19-825075-4) OUP.

Maddy, Penelope. Realism in Mathematics. (Illus.). 216p. 1992. pap. text 24.00 (0-19-824035-X) OUP.

Maddy-Weitzman, Bruce. The Crystalization of the Arab State System: Inter-Arab Politics, 1945-1954. (Contemporary Issues in the Middle East Ser.). 400p. 1992. pap. text 18.95 (0-8156-2580-4) Syracuse U Pr.

*__Maddy-Weitzman, Bruce.__ Middle East Contemporary Survey Vol. XX: 1996. 800p. 1998. text 135.00 (0-8133-3582-5, Pub. by Westview) HarpC.

*__Maddy-Weitzman, Bruce, ed.__ Middle East Contemporary Survey, Vol. 21. LC 78-648245. 840p. 2000. 99.00 (0-8133-3762-3) Westview.

Maddy-Weitzman, Bruce & Inbar, Efraim, eds. Religious Radicalism in the Greater Middle East. LC 96-42105. (Besa Study in Mideast Securitye). 272p. (C). 1997. text 49.50 (0-7146-4769-1, Pub. by F Cass Pubs); pap. text 24.50 (0-7146-4326-2, Pub. by F Cass Pubs) Intl Spec Bk.

Maddy, Y. No Past, No Present, No Future. 1997. pap. 13.95 (0-435-90522-8) Heinemann.

Maddy, Yulisa A. & MacCann, Donnarae. African Images in Juvenile Literature: Commentaries on Neocolonialist Fiction. LC 96-38596. 160p. 1996. lib. bdg. 37.50 (0-7864-0241-5) McFarland & Co.

*__Made E-Z Staff.__ Business Plans Made E-Z. (Made E-Z Ser.). 2000. pap. text 17.95 (1-56382-461-2) E-Z Legal.

Made E-Z Staff. Buying/Selling a Business Made Easy. 224p. 2000. pap. 17.95 (1-56382-440-X) E-Z Legal.

*__Made E-Z Staff.__ Profitable Mail Order Made E-Z. 316p. 2000. pap. 17.95 (1-56382-442-6) E-Z Legal.

Made E-Z Staff. Raising Venture Capital Made E-Z. 220p. 2000. pap. 17.95 (1-56382-441-8) E-Z Legal.

*__Made E-Z Staff.__ Your Profitable Small Business Made E-Z. (Made E-Z Ser.). 2000. pap. 17.95 (1-56382-460-4) E-Z Legal.

Madean, Charles, et al. Clans & Tartans. LC 97-712. 60p. 1997. 8.95 (1-56554-291-6) Pelican.

Madeira, Louis C., compiled by. Annals of Music in Philadelphia & History of the Musical Fund Society. LC 78-169650. (Music Reprint Ser.). (Illus.). 234p. 1973. reprint ed. lib. bdg. 29.50 (0-306-70260-6) Da Capo.

Madej, Bruce. Michigan: Champions of the West. 274p. 1997. 39.95 (1-57167-115-3) Sports Pub.

Madeja, Stanley S., ed. Gifted & Talented in Art Education. (Illus.). 128p. (Orig.). (C). 1983. pap. text 16.00 (0-937652-00-8, 231) Natl Art Ed.

Madeja, W. Victor. Hitler's Elite Guards, The Waffen SS & Parachutists: Between Fascism & Genocide. LC 84-80623. (Illus.). 211p. 1992. pap. 16.00 (0-941052-55-9) Valor Pub.

— Italian Army Handbook, 1940-1944. LC 84-8059. (Illus.). 176p. (Orig.). 1984. 16.00 (0-941052-60-5) Valor Pub.

— U. S. Army Order of Battle: Pacific Divisions. 1984. 14.00 (0-941052-72-9) Valor Pub.

Madeja, W. Victor, ed. Dictionary of German Military Terms, Abbreviations & Map Symbols. (ENG & GER.). 146p. 1992. 18.00 (0-941052-75-3) Valor Pub.

— German Field Army & Officer Corps. 4th ed. LC 84-80623. (Illus.). 200p. 1998. 16.00 (0-941052-53-2) Valor Pub.

— German Replacement Army. LC 84-80673. (Illus.). 184p. (Orig.). 1998. 16.00 (0-941052-54-0, 54) Valor Pub.

— The German War Machine: German Weapons & Manpower. LC 84-80626. (Illus.). 180p. 1984. pap. 14.00 (0-941052-21-4) Valor Pub.

— The German War Machine: German Weapons & Manpower. LC 84-80626. (Illus.). 180p. 1985. 14.00 (0-941052-58-3) Valor Pub.

— Hitler's Dying Ground: Disintegration of the German Armed Forces in WW2. 4th ed. LC 84-80623. (Illus.). 212p. 1992. pap. 16.00 (0-941052-52-4) Valor Pub.

— Italian Army Order of Battle, 1940-1944: Between Monarchy & Fascism. 3rd ed. (Europe's Axis Powers Ser.). (Illus.). 202p. 1991. 14.00 (0-941052-59-1) Valor Pub.

— Japanese Armed Forces Order of Battle, 1937-1945: Divisions. (Illus.). 1993. pap. 14.00 (0-941052-67-2) Valor Pub.

— Japanese Mobilization & Pacific Campaign. LC 84-80624. (Illus.). 200p. 1985. 16.00 (0-941052-69-9); pap. 16.00 (0-941052-27-3) Valor Pub.

— The Motorization Myth. LC 84-8625. (Illus.). 176p. 1984. 14.00 (0-941052-57-5); pap. 14.00 (0-941052-20-6) Valor Pub.

— The Polish 2nd Corps & the Italian Campaign. LC 84-81892. (Illus.). 186p. 1984. 14.00 (0-941052-51-6) Valor Pub.

— The Polish 2nd Corps & the Italian Campaign. LC 84-81892. (Illus.). 186p. 1985. pap. 14.00 (0-941052-34-6) Valor Pub.

— Russo-German War: Small Unit Actions. 194p. 1986. 14.00 (0-941052-74-5) Valor Pub.

— Russo-German War: Small Unit Actions. (East Front Handbooks Ser.). (Illus.). 192p. 1997. pap. 14.00 (0-941052-36-2) Valor Pub.

— Russo-German War - Balkans, November 1940-November, 1944. (Battle Situation - East Front Ser.). (Illus.). 128p. 1989. pap. 18.00 (0-941052-91-5) Valor Pub.

— The Russo-German War, Autumn 1941. (Battle Situation - East Front Ser.). (GER., Illus.). 80p. 1988. pap. 18.00 (0-941052-82-6) Valor Pub.

— The Russo-German War, Summer-Autumn, 1942. (Ost-Lage Ser.: No. 29). 80p. 2001. pap. 18.00 (0-941052-79-6) Valor Pub.

— The Russo-German War, Summer-Fall, 1943. (Battle Situation - East Front Ser.). (Illus.). 100p. 2000. pap. text 18.00 (0-941052-86-9, 31) Valor Pub.

— The Russo-German War, Summer, 1941. (Battle Situation - East Front Ser.). (GER., Illus.). 138p. 2000. pap. text 18.00 (0-941052-76-1) Valor Pub.

— The Russo-German War, Summer, 1944. (Battle Situation - East Front Ser.). (GER., Illus.). 80p. 2000. reprint ed. pap. text 18.00 (0-941052-88-5) Valor Pub.

— The Russo-German War, Winter-Spring, 1944. (Battle Situation - East Front Ser.). (GER., Illus.). 92p. (Orig.). 1988. pap. text 18.00 (0-941052-87-7) Valor Pub.

— The Russo-German War, Winter-Spring, 1942. (Battle Situation - East Front Ser.). (GER., Illus.). 80p. 2001. pap. text 18.00 (0-941052-78-8) Valor Pub.

— The Russo-German War, Winter-Spring, 1943. (Battle Situation - East Front Ser.). (Illus.). 80p. 2001. pap. text 18.00 (*0-941052-85-0*) Valor Pub.
— U. S. Army Order of Battle: Mediterranean & Europe 1942-1945. 190p. 1984. 14.00 (*0-941052-70-2*); pap. 14.00 (*0-941052-26-5*) Valor Pub.
— U. S. Army Order of Battle: Pacific Divisions. (U. S. Army Units Ser.). 1984. pap. 14.00 (*0-941052-19-2*) Valor Pub.

Madelaine, Richard, ed. see Shakespeare, William.

Madeleine, Fredric. The Drug Controversy & the Rise of Antichrist. 2nd ed. 43p. (C). 1994. pap. 7.00 (*0-9627423-3-3*) Candlestick.

Madeleva, M. Grace. Chaucer's Nuns & Other Essays. reprint ed. 39.00 (*0-403-04008-6*) Somerset Pub.

Madeley. Religion & Politics. 127.95 (*1-85521-906-9*) Ashgate Pub Co.

Madeley, C. Guide to the Collection & Transport of Virological Specimens, Including Chlamydial & Rickettsial Specimens. (Nonserial Publication). 40p. 1977. pap. text 10.00 (*92-4-154055-9*, 1150061) World Health.

Madeley, John. American Iridescent Stretch Glass: Identification & Value Guide. 1998. pap. text 19.95 (*1-57432-032-7*) Collector Bks.
— Big Business, Poor Peoples: The Impact of Transnational Corporations in the World's Poor LC 99-17549. 1999. pap. 19.95 (*1-85649-672-4*) St Martin.
— Big Business, Poor Peoples: The Impact of Transnational Corporations in the World's Poor LC 99-17549. 1999. 55.00 (*1-85649-671-6*) Zed Books.
— Trade & the Poor: The Impact of International Trade on Developing Countries. LC 92-39846. 224p. 1993. text 39.95 (*0-312-09236-9*) St Martin.

Madelin, Louis. Consulate & Empire, 2 vols. LC 34-10700. (National History of France Ser.: No. 7). reprint ed. 90.00 (*0-404-50810-3*) AMS Pr.
— Figures of the Revolution. Curtis, R., tr. LC 68-22221. (Essay Index Reprint Ser.). 1977. 21.95 (*0-8369-0663-2*) Ayer.
— French Revolution. LC 73-181954. (National History of France Ser.: No. 6). reprint ed. 45.00 (*0-404-50796-4*) AMS Pr.

Madeline. The Life Story of a Manic Depressive. 32p. 1998. pap. 7.00 (*0-8059-4271-8*) Dorrance.

***Madeline, Laurence.** Musee d'Orsay: 100 Impressionist Masterpieces. (Illus.). 144p. 2000. pap. 19.95 (*2-86656-209-7*, Pub. by Scala Edit) Antique Collect.

Madeline, X. How to Become a Vampire in Six Easy Lessons. 1986. pap. 3.99 (*0-9611944-3-X*) Dracula Pr.

Madeling, O., ed. Semiconductors: Group IV-Elements & III-V-Compounds. (Data in Science & Technology Ser.). 200p. 1991. pap. 49.50 (*0-387-53150-5*) Spr-Verlag.

Madell, Geoffrey. Mind & Materialism. 176p. 1988. 45.00 (*0-85224-575-0*, Pub. by Edinburgh U Pr) Col U Pr.
— Mind & Materialism. 160p. 1991. pap. text 22.00 (*0-85224-602-1*, Pub. by Edinburgh U Pr) Col U Pr.

Madell, Jane R. Behavioral Audiologic Evaluation of Infants & Young Children. pap. 59.00 incl. vdisk (*0-86577-804-3*) Thieme Med Pubs.
— Behavioral Audiologic Evaluation of Infants & Young Children. LC 98-4647. (Illus.). 300p. 1998. pap. 35.00 (*0-86577-692-X*) Thieme Med Pubs.
— Behavioral Evaluation of Hearing in Infants & Young Children. LC 98-4647. 1998. 35.00 (*3-13-107981-9*) Thieme Med Pubs.

Madell, Thomas. Disk & File Management Tasks on HP-UX. LC 96-30626. 208p. (C). 1996. pap. 29.40 (*0-13-518861-X*) P-H.

***Madelung, O., et al, eds.** Non-Tetrahedrally Bonded Binary Compounds II: Supplement to Vol. III/17g (Print Version) Revised & Updated Edition of Vol. III/17g (CD-ROM) (Numerical Data & Functional Relationships in Science & Technology - New Ser.: Pt. D). 2000. 3883.00 incl. cd-rom (*3-540-64966-2*) Spr-Verlag.
— Non-Tetrahedrally Bonded Elements & Binary Compounds I. 470p. 1999. 2943.00 (*3-540-64583-7*) Spr-Verlag.

Madelung, O., ed. see Predel, B.

Madelung, Otfried. Introduction to Solid-State Theory. LC 77-26263. (Solid-State Sciences Ser.: Vol. 2). (Illus.). 1988. 54.50 (*0-387-08516-5*) Spr-Verlag.
— Introduction to Solid-State Theory. Taylor, B. C., tr. (Series in Solid-State Sciences: Vol. 2). 501p. 1995. 44.50 (*3-540-60443-X*) Spr-Verlag.

Madelung, Otfried, ed. Basic Data of Semiconductors. 2nd rev. ed. LC 96-17680. 328p. 1996. 69.00 (*3-540-60883-4*) Spr-Verlag.
— Phase Equilibria, Crystallographic Data & Values of Thermodynamic Properties of Binary Alloys. (Numerical Data & Functional Relationships in Science & Technology Ser.: Vol. 5). 385p. 1994. 1540.95 (*0-387-56073-4*) Spr-Verlag.

Madelung, Otfried & Martienssen, W. Theoretical Structures of Molecules. (Atomic & Molecular Physics Ser.: Vol. 22). 160p. 1994. 610.95 (*0-387-56332-6*) Spr-Verlag.

Madelung, Otfried & Martienssen, W., eds. Landolt-Bornstein: Comprehensive Index 1996. (Numerical Data & Functional Relationships in Science & Technology Ser.). 352p. 1996. 1562.00 incl. cd-rom (*3-540-60804-4*) Spr-Verlag.

Madelung, Otfried & Poerschke, R., eds. Semiconductors: Others Than Group IV Elements & III-V Compounds. LC 92-8630. (Data in Science & Technology Ser.). vii, 153p. 1992. write for info. (*3-540-55373-8*); 64.95 (*0-387-55373-8*) Spr-Verlag.

Madelung, Otfried & Voigt, H. H., eds. Lanolt-Boernstein Numerical Data & Functional Relationships in Science & Technology: Astronomy, Astrophysics & Space Research; Astronomy & Astrophysics; Methods, Constants, the Solar System, Group VI; Vol. 3; Subvol. A. 240p. 1993. 720.95 (*3-540-56079-3*) Spr-Verlag.

Madelung, Otfried, ed. see Predel, B.

Madelung, Wilferd. Advent of the Fatimids: A Contemporary Shi'i Witness. text 45.00 (*1-86064-551-8*, Pub. by I B T) St Martin.

Madelung, Wilferd. Religious Schools & Sects in Medieval Islam. (Collected Studies: No. CS213). 352p. (C). 1985. reprint ed. lib. bdg. 124.95 (*0-86078-161-5*, Pub. by Variorum) Ashgate Pub Co.
— The Succession to Muhammad: A History of Early Islam. LC 95-26105. 464p. (C). 1996. text 69.95 (*0-521-56181-7*) Cambridge U Pr.
— The Succession to Muhammad: A Study of the Early Caliphate. (Illus.). 429p. (C). 1998. pap. text 24.95 (*0-521-64696-0*) Cambridge U Pr.

Madelung, Wilferd & Walker, Paul E. An Ismaili Heresiography: The "B Ab Al-Shay T An" From Ab U Tamm Am's Kit Ab Al-Shajara. LC 98-4196. (Islamic History & Civilization Studies & Texts). xii, 286p. 1998. 85.50 (*90-04-11072-0*) Brill Academic Pubs.

Madelung, Wilfred. Religious & Ethnic Movements in Medieval Islam. (Collected Studies: Vol. CS364). 352p. 1992. 117.95 (*0-86078-310-3*, Pub. by Variorum) Ashgate Pub Co.

Madely, John. Trade & the Poor: The Impact of International Trade on Developing Countries. 2nd ed. 230p. (Orig.). 1996. pap. 23.95 (*1-85339-324-X*, Pub. by Intermed Tech) Stylus Pub VA.

Mademoiselles Noires, Inc., Staff. The Black Gourmet Cookbook. (Illus.). 80p. (Orig.). 1987. spiral bd. 19.95 (*0-9643335-0-3*) Mmlle Noires.

Maden, Anthony. Women, Prisons, & Psychiatry: Mental Disorder Behind Bars. LC 95-39178. 224p. 1995. pap. text 45.00 (*0-7506-2003-X*) Buttrwrth-Heinemann.

Maden, Chris, jt. auth. see Ray, Eric.

Maden, Mary. A Dolphin Adventure: Touched by a Dolphin. (Earth/Ocean Adventures Ser.: Vol. 3). (Illus.). (J). (gr. 1-7). 1999. pap. 5.95 (*1-890479-59-4*) Dog & Pony Pub.
— Flying High with the Wright Brothers: The Story of Their First Flight - a Dog's Tale. LC 95-92331. (Illus.). 20p. (J). (gr. 1-4). 1995. pap. 5.95 (*0-9646970-0-9*) Dog & Pony Pub.
— The Great Manatee Rescue. Schroeder, Eric, ed. (Earth/Ocean Adventures Ser.: Vol. 2). (Illus.). (J). (gr. 1-7). 1999. pap. 5.95 (*1-890479-58-6*) Dog & Pony Pub.
— The Great Pirate Adventure. Schroeder, Eric, ed. (Outer Banks Animals Adventure Ser.: Vol. 7). (Illus.). 24p. (J). (gr. k-6). 1999. pap. 5.95 (*1-890479-56-X*) Dog & Pony Pub.
— The Great Shark Adventure. (Earth/Ocean Adventures Ser.: Vol. 1). (Illus.). (J). (gr. 1-7). 1999. pap. 5.95 (*1-890479-60-8*) Dog & Pony Pub.
— Hurricane! Schroeder, Eric, ed. (Illus.). 20p. (Orig.). (J). (gr. 1-6). 1997. pap. 5.95 (*1-890479-51-9*) Dog & Pony Pub.
— In Search of the Lost Colony. LC 95-71831. (Outer Banks Animals Adventure Ser.: No. 3). (Illus.). 20p. (Orig.). (J). (gr. 2-5). 1996. pap. 5.95 (*0-9646970-2-5*) Dog & Pony Pub.
— A Lighthouse Adventure, No. 4. Schroeder, Eric, ed. LC 95-83720. (Outer Banks Animals Adventure Ser.). (Illus.). 20p. (Orig.). (J). (gr. 1-4). 1996. pap. 5.95 (*0-9646970-3-3*) Dog & Pony Pub.
— My Outer Banks Coloring Book. (Illus.). 24p. (Orig.). (J). (gr. k-5). 1996. pap. 2.95 (*0-9646970-4-1*) Dog & Pony Pub.
— My Pirate Coloring Book. Schroeder, Eric, ed. (Illus.). (J). (ps-6). 1999. pap. 3.95 (*1-890479-57-8*) Dog & Pony Pub.
— My Smoky Mountain Coloring Book. (Illus.). 16p. (Orig.). (J). (gr. k-5). 1997. pap. 2.95 (*1-890479-54-3*) Dog & Pony Pub.
— The Secret of Blackbeard's Treasure: A Pony's Tale. LC 95-92332. (Outer Banks Animal Ser.). (Illus.). 20p. (Orig.). (J). (gr. 1-4). 1995. pap. 5.95 (*0-9646970-1-7*) Dog & Pony Pub.
— Shipwreck! Stories of the Graveyard of the Atlantic. Schroeder, Eric, ed. LC 97-65801. (Illus.). 20p. (Orig.). (J). (gr. 1-6). 1997. pap. 5.95 (*1-890479-50-0*) Dog & Pony Pub.

Maden, Sue. Greetings from Jamestown, Rhode Island: Picture Post Card Views, 1900-1950. (Illus.). 152p. (Orig.). 1988. pap. 16.00 (*0-9620875-0-5*) West Ferry Pr.

Maden, Tony, et al. The Treatment & Security Needs of Special Hospital Patients. 150p. 1995. pap. text 150.00 (*1-56593-501-2*, 1160) Singular Publishing.

Madenwald, Abbie M. Arctic Schoolteacher: Kulukak, Alaska, 1931-1933. LC 92-54129. (Western Frontier Library: Vol. 59). (Illus.). 224p. 1992. 24.95 (*0-8061-2469-5*) U of Okla Pr.
— Arctic Schoolteacher: Kulukak, Alaska, 1931-1933. LC 92-54129. (Western Frontier Library: Vol. 59). (Illus.). 224p. 1994. pap. 13.95 (*0-8061-2611-6*) U of Okla Pr.

Madeo, Silvia A., et al. Sommerfeld's Concepts of Taxation, 1995 Edition. 95th ed. 272p. (C). 1994. pap. text, student ed. 33.75 (*0-03-006834-7*) Dryden Pr.

Mader. Biology. 4th ed. 1994. 16.50 (*0-697-25484-4*, WCB McGr Hill) McGrw-H Hghr Educ.
— Biology. 5th ed. 1995. teacher ed. 29.37 (*0-697-21820-1*, WCB McGr Hill); pap. text 353.43 (*0-697-21837-6*, WCB McGr Hill) McGrw-H Hghr Educ.
— Biology. 5th ed. 1996. lab manual ed. 13.75 (*0-697-21829-5*, WCB McGr Hill) McGrw-H Hghr Educ.
— Biology. 6th ed. 1997. pap. 39.74 (*0-697-34083-X*) McGraw.
— Biology. 6th ed. 1997. write for info. (*0-697-34086-4*, WCB McGr Hill) McGrw-H Hghr Educ.

***Mader.** Biology 7th ed. 2000. 65.00 (*0-07-013657-2*) McGraw.

Mader. Biology: Ex-7. 4th ed. 1993. lab manual ed. 11.25 (*0-697-22689-1*, WCB McGr Hill) McGrw-H Hghr Educ.
— Biology: 10 Exercises. 4th ed. 1993. lab manual ed. 20.00 (*0-697-22679-4*) McGraw.
— Biology: 15 Exercises. 4th ed. 1993. lab manual ed. 18.50 (*0-697-22796-0*) McGraw.
— Biology Custom Lab: Custom Lab 8. 3rd ed. 1991. 20.00 (*0-697-14769-X*) McGraw.
— Cpsh Cps(cin St C) Clr Bio Lm. 6th ed. 1999. pap. text 17.50 (*0-07-236015-1*) McGraw.

***Mader.** Crichton College Biology. 6th ed. 1999. 44.00 (*0-07-236920-5*) McGraw.

Mader. Custom Biology Lab. 3rd ed. 1991. 12.25 (*0-697-15139-5*, WCB McGr Hill) McGrw-H Hghr Educ.
— Electronic Text to Accompany Introduction to Biology. (C). 1995. pap. write for info. (*0-697-24726-0*, WCB McGr Hill) McGrw-H Hghr Educ.
— Human Biology. 4th ed. 1994. teacher ed. 25.62 (*0-697-15972-8*) McGraw.
— Human Biology. 7th ed. 2001. 44.74 (*0-07-232481-3*); student ed. 16.50 (*0-07-232482-1*) McGraw.
— Human Biology: Lab Resource Guide. 4th ed. 1994. 14.68 (*0-697-15960-4*) McGraw.
— Human Biology: Student Study Guide. 1997. student ed. 15.50 (*0-697-27824-7*) McGraw.
— Inquiry into Life. 7th ed. 1993. wbk. ed. 4.74 (*0-697-13700-7*) McGraw.
— Inquiry into Life. 7th ed. 1994. lab manual ed. 12.00 (*0-697-13687-6*) McGraw.
— Inquiry into Life. 7th ed. 1994. pap. text, teacher ed. 21.87 (*0-697-13684-1*) McGraw.
— Inquiry into Life. 7th ed. 1993. text, student ed. 53.25 (*0-697-24828-3*, WCB McGr Hill) McGrw-H Hghr Educ.
— Inquiry into Life. 7th ed. 1994. 277.50 (*0-697-13701-5*, WCB McGr Hill) McGrw-H Hghr Educ.
— Inquiry into Life. 7th ed. 1994. student ed. 66.50 (*0-697-25678-2*, WCB McGr Hill) McGrw-H Hghr Educ.
— Inquiry into Life. 7th ed. 1996. 254.50 (*0-697-26502-1*, WCB McGr Hill) McGrw-H Hghr Educ.
— Inquiry into Life. 8th ed. 1996. 14.06 (*0-697-25192-6*, WCB McGr Hill); text 58.25 incl. audio (*0-697-39369-0*, WCB McGr Hill) McGrw-H Hghr Educ.
— Inquiry into Life: Answer Study Questions. 7th ed. 1994. 8.74 (*0-697-20531-2*, WCB McGr Hill) McGrw-H Hghr Educ.
— Inquiry into Life: Laboratory Research Guide. 8th ed. 1996. 11.25 (*0-697-25184-5*, WCB McGr Hill) McGrw-H Hghr Educ.
— Inquiry into Life Lecture Enrichment Kit. 7th ed. 1994. 14.68 (*0-697-13685-X*) McGraw.
— Inquiry into Life Visual Testbank. 7th ed. 1994. 12.74 (*0-697-13688-4*) McGraw.
— Inquiry Labman. 6th ed. 1991. 22.00 (*0-697-15024-0*) McGraw.
— Inquiry Labman. 6th ed. 1991. 15.25 (*0-697-16030-0*) McGraw.
— Introduction to Biology. 1993. teacher ed. 11.25 (*0-697-16876-X*, WCB McGr Hill) McGrw-H Hghr Educ.
— Introduction to Biology: Art Masters. 1994. 45.94 (*0-697-16877-8*) McGraw.
— Masters of Biology. 5th ed. 1995. 43.00 (*0-697-21831-7*, WCB McGr Hill) McGrw-H Hghr Educ.
— Understanding Human Anatomy. 3rd ed. 1996. 306.25 (*0-697-25174-8*, WCB McGr Hill) McGrw-H Hghr Educ.
— Understanding One Another. 2nd ed. 1996. 37.74 (*0-07-039443-1*) McGraw.

***Mader, A.** Almost Completely Decomposable Groups. (Algebra, Logic & Applications Ser.: Vol. 13). 368p. 1999. text 90.00 (*90-5699-225-2*) Gordon & Breach.

Mader, A., tr. see Booss, B. & Bleecker, D. D.

Mader, Carol. Blends, Digraphs, & More No. 2295: Phonics Without Worksheets. Hults, Alaska B., ed. (Phonics Without Worksheets Ser.). (Illus.). 80p. 1999. pap. text 9.98 (*1-57471-536-4*) Creat Teach Pr.
— Consonants No. 2293: Phonics Without Worksheets. Hults, Alaska B., ed. (Phonics Without Worksheets Ser.). (Illus.). 80p. 1999. pap. text 9.98 (*1-57471-534-8*) Creat Teach Pr.

***Mader, Carol.** Crazy Clothesline Characters: Plus 39 More Creative Ways to Ten Bible Stories. LC 99-17016. (Illus.). (J). 2000. 16.99 (*0-7644-2140-9*) Group Pub.
— Emotion Explosion! 40 Devotions for Preteen Ministry. (Illus.). (J). 2000. pap. 14.99 (*0-7644-2221-9*) Group Pub.

Mader, Carol. Vowels No. 2294: Phonics Without Worksheets. Hults, Alaska B., ed. (Phonics Without Worksheets Ser.). 80p. 1999. pap. text 9.98 (*1-57471-535-6*) Creat Teach Pr.

Mader, Charles L. Numerical Modeling of Explosives & Propellants. 2nd ed. LC 97-21340. 464p. 1997. boxed set 119.95 (*0-8493-3149-8*) CRC Pr.

Mader, Detlef. Aeolian & Adhesion Morphodynamics & Phytoecology in Recent Coastal & Inland Sand & Snow Flats & Dunes from Mainly North Sea & Baltic Sea to Mars & Venus, 2 vols. LC 94-41210. (Illus.). LIV, 2348p. 1995. 225.95 (*0-8204-2814-0*) P Lang Pubng.
— Taphonomy, Sedimentology, & Genesis of Plant Fossil Deposit Types in Lettenkohle (Lower Keuper) & Schilfsandstein (Middle Keuper) in Lower Franconia (Germany) (Illus.). XVI, 164p. 1995. 23.95 (*0-8204-2813-2*) P Lang Pubng.

Mader, Diane C., jt. auth. see Mader, Thomas F.

Mader, Douglas P., et al. Ssri Process Ctrl Method. LC 92-41667. (Six Sigma Research Institute Ser.). 1993. pap. 25.95 (*0-201-63410-4*) Addison-Wesley.

Mader, Douglas R. Reptile Medicine & Surgery. LC 95-9672. (Illus.). 624p. 1995. text 98.00 (*0-7216-5208-5*, W B Saunders Co) Harcrt Hlth Sci Grp.

Mader, George G., jt. auth. see Lagorio, Henry J.

Mader, Gerald L., ed. Permanent Satellite Tracking Networks for Geodesy & Geodynamics. (International Association of Geodesy Symposia Ser.: Vol. 109). (Illus.). 210p. 1993. pap. write for info. (*3-540-55827-6*) Spr-Verlag.
— Permanent Satellite Tracking Networks for Geodesy & Geodynamics: Symposium No. 109, Vienna, Austria, August 11-24, 1991. LC 93-2186. (International Association of Geodesy Symposia Ser.: No. 109). 1993. 86.95 (*0-387-55827-6*) Spr-Verlag.

***Mader, Gottfried.** Flavius Josephus & the Politics of Historiography: Apologetic & Impression Management in the Bellum Judaicum. (Mnemosyne, Supplements Ser.). 216p. 2000. 65.00 (*90-04-11446-7*) Brill Academic Pubs.

Mader, Gunter & Neubert-Mader, Laila. The English Formal Garden: Five Centuries of Design. Taylor, Ingrid, tr. (Illus.). 232p. 1997. 65.00 (*0-8478-2025-4*, Pub. by Rizzoli Intl) St Martin.

Mader, Jan. My Brother Wants to Be Like Me. large type ed. (Illus.). 16p. (J). (gr. k-2). 1998. text 4.95 (*1-879835-27-4*, Kaeden) Kaeden Corp.

Mader, Katherine, jt. auth. see Wolf, Marvin J.

Mader, Robert D., jt. auth. see Adams, James R.

Mader, Ron & Gollin, James. Adventures in Nature: Honduras. LC 97-29401. (Adventures in Nature Ser.). (Illus.). 272p. 1998. pap. 17.95 (*1-56261-341-3*) Avalon Travel.

Mader, Sylvia. Biology. 3rd ed. 880p. (C). 1990. student ed. write for info. (*0-697-11247-0*, WCB McGr Hill) McGrw-H Hghr Educ.
— Biology. 3rd ed. 880p. (C). 1990. text. write for info. (*0-697-05638-4*, WCB McGr Hill) McGrw-H Hghr Educ.
— Biology. 3rd ed. 880p. (C). 1990. text, student ed. 28.12 (*0-697-05640-6*, WCB McGr Hill) McGrw-H Hghr Educ.
— Biology, 6 pts. 4th ed. 896p. (C). 1992. text. write for info. (*0-697-15096-8*, WCB McGr Hill); text, student ed. write for info. (*0-697-12383-9*, WCB McGr Hill) McGrw-H Hghr Educ.
— Biology, 6 pts. 4th ed. 896p. (C). 1992. text, student ed. 25.00 (*0-697-12384-7*, WCB McGr Hill); text, student ed. write for info. (*0-697-12386-3*, WCB McGr Hill) McGrw-H Hghr Educ.
— Biology. 4th ed. (C). 1993. text. write for info. (*0-697-17063-2*, WCB McGr Hill) McGrw-H Hghr Educ.
— Biology. 5th ed. (C). 1995. text, student ed. write for info. (*0-697-28182-5*, WCB McGr Hill); text, student ed. write for info. (*0-697-29002-6*, WCB McGr Hill); per. write for info. (*0-697-21819-8*, WCB McGr Hill) McGrw-H Hghr Educ.
— Biology. 5th ed. (C). 1995. text, student ed. write for info. (*0-697-29001-8*, WCB McGr Hill) McGrw-H Hghr Educ.
— Biology. 5th ed. 320p. (C). 1995. text, student ed. 25.00 (*0-697-21832-5*, WCB McGr Hill); text, lab manual ed. write for info. (*0-697-21828-7*, WCB McGr Hill) McGrw-H Hghr Educ.

***Mader, Sylvia.** Biology. 7th ed. (Illus.). (C). 2000. pap., student ed. 28.13 (*0-07-013659-9*); spiral bd., lab manual ed. 42.81 (*0-07-013658-0*) McGrw-H Hghr Educ.

Mader, Sylvia. Biology, 6 pts., Pt. I: The Cell. 4th ed. 896p. (C). 1992. text. write for info. (*0-697-15098-4*, WCB McGr Hill) McGrw-H Hghr Educ.
— Biology, 6 pts., Pt. II: Genetic Basics of Life. 4th ed. 896p. (C). 1992. text. write for info. (*0-697-15099-2*, WCB McGr Hill) McGrw-H Hghr Educ.
— Biology, 6 pts., Pt. III: Evolution & Diversity. 4th ed. 896p. (C). 1992. text. write for info. (*0-697-15100-X*, WCB McGr Hill) McGrw-H Hghr Educ.
— Biology, 6 pts., Pt. IV: Plant Structure & Function. 4th ed. 896p. (C). 1992. text. write for info. (*0-697-15101-8*, WCB McGr Hill) McGrw-H Hghr Educ.
— Biology, 6 pts., Pt. V: Biology of Animal Structure & Function. 4th ed. 896p. (C). 1992. text. write for info. (*0-697-15102-6*, WCB McGr Hill) McGrw-H Hghr Educ.
— Biology, 6 pts., Pt. VI: Biology of Behavior & Ecology. 4th ed. 896p. (C). 1992. text. write for info. (*0-697-15103-4*, WCB McGr Hill) McGrw-H Hghr Educ.
— Human Biology. 544p. (C). 1988. student ed. write for info. (*0-697-05341-5*, WCB McGr Hill) McGrw-H Hghr Educ.
— Human Biology. 2nd ed. 576p. (C). 1989. text, student ed. write for info. (*0-697-10194-0*, WCB McGr Hill) McGrw-H Hghr Educ.
— Human Biology. 4th ed. 528p. (C). 1994. text, student ed. 18.75 (*0-697-16236-2*, WCB McGr Hill); text, student ed. write for info. (*0-697-24182-3*, WCB McGr Hill); text, student ed. write for info. (*0-697-26485-8*, WCB McGr Hill); student ed., spiral bd. write for info. (*0-697-15961-2*, WCB McGr Hill) McGrw-H Hghr Educ.
— Human Biology. 5th ed. LC 97-13872. 576p. (C). 1997. text 49.50 (*0-697-27821-2*, WCB McGr Hill) McGrw-H Hghr Educ.
— Human Biology. 5th ed. 288p. (C). 1997. text, lab manual ed. write for info. (*0-697-27825-5*, WCB McGr Hill) McGrw-H Hghr Educ.

M

— Human Reproductive Biology. 2nd ed. 224p. (C). 1991. text. write for info. (0-697-11805-3, WCB McGr Hill) McGrw-H Hghr Educ.
— Inquiry into Life. 6th ed. 848p. (C). 1990. text. write for info. (0-697-13280-3, WCB McGr Hill) McGrw-H Hghr Educ.
— Inquiry into Life. 6th ed. 848p. (C). 1991. text. write for info. (0-697-13747-3, WCB McGr Hill) McGrw-H Hghr Educ.
— Inquiry into Life, 2 vols. 6th ed. 864p. (C). 1991. text, student ed. write for info. (0-697-13752-X, WCB McGr Hill) McGrw-H Hghr Educ.
— Inquiry into Life. 8th ed. 304p. (C). 1997. text, student ed. 23.12 (0-697-25190-X, WCB McGr Hill) McGrw-H Hghr Educ.
— Inquiry into Life, Vol. II. 6th ed. 288p. (C). 1991. write for info. (0-697-13750-3, WCB McGr Hill) McGrw-H Hghr Educ.
— Inquiry into Life with Student Study Art Notebook. 7th ed. (Illus.). 784p. (C). 1993. text, student ed. write for info. (0-697-23117-8, WCB McGr Hill) McGrw-H Hghr Educ.
— Inquiry into Life with Student Study Art Notebook. 7th ed. (Illus.). 784p. (C). 1993. text. write for info. (0-697-13680-9, WCB McGr Hill) McGrw-H Hghr Educ.
— Inquiry into Life with Student Study Art Notebook. 7th ed. (Illus.). 784p. (C). 1993. text. write for info. (0-697-13679-5, WCB McGr Hill) McGrw-H Hghr Educ.
— Inquiry into Life with Student Study Art Notebook. 7th ed. (Illus.). 784p. (C). 1993. text, student ed. 23.12 (0-697-13702-3, WCB McGr Hill) McGrw-H Hghr Educ.
— Introduction to Biology & Student Study Art Notebook. 416p. (C). 1993. text, student ed. write for info. (0-697-23170-4, WCB McGr Hill) McGrw-H Hghr Educ.
— Introduction to Biology & Student Study Art Notebook. 416p. (C). 1993. text. write for info. (0-697-16626-0, WCB McGr Hill) McGrw-H Hghr Educ.
— Introduction to Biology & Student Study Art Notebook. 416p. (C). 1993. text. write for info. (0-697-21002-2, WCB McGr Hill) McGrw-H Hghr Educ.
— Introduction to Biology & Student Study Art Notebook. 416p. (C). 1994. text, student ed. 19.37 (0-697-16879-4, WCB McGr Hill) McGrw-H Hghr Educ.
— Introduction to Biology & Student Study Art Notebook. 416p. 1994. write for info. (0-697-27031-9, WCB McGr Hill) McGrw-H Hghr Educ.
— Understanding Human Anatomy & Physiology. 2nd ed. 464p. (C). 1994. text, student ed. 24.37 (0-697-13673-6, WCB McGr Hill) McGrw-H Hghr Educ.

Mader, Sylvia & Templin, Jay M. Understanding Human Anatomy & Physiology. 3rd ed. 160p. (C). 1996. text, student ed. 20.62 (0-697-25173-X, WCB McGr Hill) McGrw-H Hghr Educ.

Mader, Sylvia, et al. Exercises for Human Biology. 4th ed. 132p. (C). 1995. student ed., spiral bd. write for info. (0-697-32668-3, WCB McGr Hill) McGrw-H Hghr Educ.

Mader, Sylvia S. Biology. 6th ed. LC 97-29147. 1997. write for info. (0-697-34079-1, WCB McGr Hill); pap. write for info. (0-697-34080-5, WCB McGr Hill) McGrw-H Hghr Educ.
— Human Biology. 3rd ed. 528p. (C). 1991. text. write for info. (0-697-12333-2, WCB McGr Hill) McGrw-H Hghr Educ.
— Human Biology. 3rd ed. 528p. (C). 1991. text. write for info. (0-697-13837-2, WCB McGr Hill); text, student ed. 25.62 (0-697-12335-9, WCB McGr Hill) McGrw-H Hghr Educ.
— Human Biology. 3rd ed. 528p. (C). 1991. text, student ed. write for info. (0-697-12336-7, WCB McGr Hill) McGrw-H Hghr Educ.
— Human Biology. 6th ed. 224p. 1999. pap., student ed. 21.25 (0-07-290586-7) McGraw.
— Human Biology. 6th ed. 288p. 1999. spiral bd., lab manual ed. 42.81 (0-07-290585-9) McGraw.

***Mader, Sylvia S.** Human Biology. 6th ed. 576p. 1999. 79.55 incl. cd-rom (0-07-233823-7, McGrw-H College) McGrw-H Hghr Educ.
— Human Biology 6th ed. LC 99-14988. 2000. write for info. (0-07-290584-0) McGrw-H Hghr Educ.

Mader, Sylvia S. Human Reproductive Biology. 3rd ed. 2000. 37.00 (0-697-15948-5) McGraw.
— Inquiry into Life. 8th ed. 816p. (C). 1996. text. write for info. (0-697-34329-4, WCB McGr Hill) McGrw-H Hghr Educ.
— Inquiry into Life. 8th ed. 816p. (C). 1996. text. write for info. (0-697-34330-8, WCB McGr Hill); text, lab manual ed. write for info. (0-697-25183-7, WCB McGr Hill) McGrw-H Hghr Educ.
— Inquiry into Life 9th ed. LC 99-14024. 1999. write for info. (0-07-36070-9) McGraw.
— Martha's Vineyard Nature Guide. (Illus.). 96p. (Orig.). 1985. pap. 7.99 (0-317-40346-X) Mader Enter.
— Understanding Human Anatomy & Physiology. 3rd ed. LC 95-83238. 480p. (C). 1996. text. write for info. (0-697-25170-5, WCB McGr Hill) McGrw-H Hghr Educ.

Mader, Sylvia S., ed. Understanding Human Anatomy & Physiology. 4th ed. LC 99-86647. 2000. 38.25 (0-07-290756-8) McGraw.

Mader, T. R. The Wolf: Myth, Legend & Misconception. rev. ed. (Illus.). 32p. (C). 1997. pap. 5.00 (0-944402-06-2) Cmmn Man Inst.

Mader, Thomas F. & Mader, Diane C. Understanding One Another: Communicating Interpersonally. 416p. (C). 1989. text. write for info. (0-697-06779-3) Brown & Benchmark.

Mader, Troy R. The Death Sentence of AIDS: A Comprehensive Source Book of Quotes by the World's Leading Physicians, Scientists & Researchers. LC 87-72211. (Orig.). 1987. pap. 9.94 (0-944402-00-3) Cmmn Man Inst.
— Unnatural Wolf Transplant in Yellowstone National Park. (C). 1990. pap. text 3.50 (0-944402-04-6) Cmmn Man Inst.
— Wolves & Humans in Conflict: A Pictorial History of Wolves in North America. (Illus.). (C). text 24.95 (0-944402-05-4) Cmmn Man Inst.

Mader, Ueli. Gewaltfreie Revolution in Entwicklungslandern. 1984. 20.95 (3-906764-18-4, Pub. by P Lang) P Lang Pubng.

Madera, Joseph A., jt. auth. see Baker, Jeanne C.

Madere, Henry. The Mailman Would Not Kill. 226p. (Orig.). 1997. pap. 11.95 (0-9656529-0-4) Madere Ent.

Madero, Francisco I. The Presidential Succession of 1910. Davis, Thomas, tr. from SPA. (American University Studies: Ser. IX, Vol. 89). XXII, 307p. (C). 1990. text 51.50 (0-8204-1250-3) P Lang Pubng.

***Madero, Pino.** My Book of Psalms. Wickenhiser, Mary David, tr. (Illus.). 56p. (J). (gr. 2-5). 2000. pap. 3.95 (0-8198-4807-7) Pauline Bks.
— Prayers from My Heart. Wickenhiser, Mary David, tr. (Illus.). 32p. (J). (gr. 2-5). 2000. pap. 3.95 (0-8198-5916-8) Pauline Bks.

Madero, Ramon A. Tu Nueva Vida. (Serie Realidades - Realities Ser.).Tr. of Your New Life. (SPA.). 36p. 1989. pap. 1.79 (1-56063-005-1, 498109) Editorial Unilit.

Madeson, J. J., jt. auth. see Moser, Charles.

Madewell, Bruce R., jt. ed. see Theilen, Gordon H.

Madewell, Terry. Glory Holes: An Expert's Guide to Tennessee's Best Fishing. Reeser, Jacki, ed. (Illus.). 120p. (Orig.). 1985. pap. 9.95 (0-9615455-1-8) J T Pub Co.
— Terry Madewell's Catfishing from A to Z: A Manual of Modern Catfishing Techniques. Reeser, Jacki, ed. 52p. 1993. 8.00 (0-9615455-4-2) J T Pub Co.

Madey, Doren L., jt. auth. see Hill, Paul T.

Madey, R., jt. auth. see Jaroniec, M.

***Madey, Scott, ed.** The Social Psychology of Aging: A special Issue of Basic & Applied Social Psychology. 128p. 2000. pap. write for info. (0-8058-9749-6) L Erlbaum Assocs.

Madey, T. E., jt. auth. see Yates, J. T., Jr.

***Madfes, Tania J. & Muench, Ann.** Learning from Assessment - Tools for Examining Assessment Through Standards: A Middle School Mathematics Professional Development Resource. viii, 99p. 1999. 25.00 (0-914409-11-5) WestEd.

***Madfes, Tania J. & Shulman, Judith H., eds.** Dilemmas in Professional Development: A Case-Based Approach to Improving Practice. 78p. 1999. pap. 24.00 (0-914409-00-X) WestEd.

Madgalena, Flo A. I Remember Union: The Story of Mary Magdalena. 2nd rev. ed. Zopf, Jayn A., ed. (Illus.). 496p. 1996. pap. 19.95 (1-880914-07-7) All Worlds Pub.

Madge, Charles. Of Love, Time & Places: Selected Poems. 216p. 1994. 39.95 (0-85646-231-4, Pub. by Anvil Press) Dufour.

Madge, Charles, ed. see Jennings, Humphrey.

Madge, Nicola, et al. The National Childhood Encephalopathy Study: A 10-Year Follow-Up. (Illus.). 121p. (C). 1993. pap. text 19.95 (0-521-45883-8) Cambridge U Pr.

Madge, Peter. Civil Engineering Insurance & Bonding. (C). 1987. 185.00 (0-7855-4257-4, Pub. by Witherby & Co) St Mut.
— Concise Guide to the JCT Insurance Clauses, 1986. (C). 1987. 110.00 (0-7855-4247-7, Pub. by Witherby & Co) St Mut.
— Guide to the Indemnity & Insurance Aspects of Building Contracts. (C). 1989. 150.00 (0-7855-4159-4, Pub. by Witherby & Co) St Mut.
— Liability Policy Wording & Cover. 150p. 1973. 75.00 (0-948691-04-2, Pub. by Witherby & Co) St Mut.
— Liability Policy Wording & Cover. 2nd ed. (C). 1973. 85.00 (0-7855-4100-4, Pub. by Witherby & Co) St Mut.

Madge, Peter, jt. auth. see Eaglestone, Frank N.

Madge, Sara, jt. auth. see Singh, Surinder.

Madge, Sidney J. Domesday of Crown Lands. (Illus.). 499p. 1968. 39.50 (0-7146-1341-X, Pub. by F Cass Pubs) Intl Spec Bk.

Madge, Sidney J., ed. Abstracts of Inquisitiones Post Mortem for Gloucestershire Returned into the Court of Chancery During the Plantagenet Period, Pt. IV: 20 Henry III to 29 Edward I, 1236-1300. (British Record Society Index Library: Vol. 30). 1972. reprint ed. pap. 25.00 (0-8115-1475-7) Periodicals Srv.
— Abstracts of Inquisitiones Post Mortem for the City of London Returned into the Court of Chancery During the Tudor Period, Pt. II: 4-9, Elizabeth, 1561-1577. (British Record Society Index Library: Vol. 26). 1972. reprint ed. pap. 25.00 (0-8115-1471-4) Periodicals Srv.

Madge, Steve, jt. auth. see Kightley, Chris.

Madge, Steven. Waterfowl: An Identification Guide to the Ducks, Geese & Swans of the World. (Illus.). 298p. 1992. pap. 29.95 (0-395-46726-8) HM.

Madge, Steven & Beaman, Mark. An Identification Guide to the Birds of Europe & the Western Palearctic. LC 96-13626. 784p. 1998. 99.50 (0-691-02726-9, Pub. by Princeton U Pr) Cal Prin Full Svc.

Madge, Tim. Last Hero - Bill Tilman: A Biography of the Explorer. (Illus.). 288p. 1995. 24.95 (0-89886-452-6) Mountaineers.

Madges, William. God & the World: Christian Texts in Perspective. LC 98-42940. 300p. 1998. pap. 25.00 (1-57075-212-5) Orbis Bks.

Madges, William, jt. auth. see Hill, Brennan R.

Madgett, Mary Ann. Poetic Feelings. LC 95-94235. (Illus.). 60p. (Orig.). 1995. pap. 7.95 (0-9645227-9-9) Madgett Pub.

Madgett, Naomi L. Exits & Entrances. LC 77-91712. (Illus.). 69p. (YA). (gr. 9-12). 1978. per. 5.00 (0-916418-13-8) Lotus.
— Pink Ladies in the Afternoon. 2nd ed. LC 90-60605. 75p. (YA). (gr. 7-10). 1990. pap. 7.00 (0-916418-78-2) Lotus.
— Remembrances of Spring: Collected Early Poems. LC 93-34603. (Lotus Poetry Ser.: Vol. 1). 170p. 1993. 24.95 (0-87013-345-4) Mich St U Pr.
— Star by Star. 2nd ed. LC 77-143900. 61p. (YA). (gr. 7-12). 1970. reprint ed. per. 5.00 (0-916418-00-6) Lotus.
— A Student's Guide to Creative Writing. LC 79-93055. 134p. (C). 1980. pap. 11.00 (0-916418-24-3, Penway Bks) Lotus.

Madgett, Naomi L., ed. A Milestone Sampler: 15th Anniversary Anthology. (Illus.). 130p. (Orig.). (YA). (gr. 9-12). 1988. pap., per. 9.00 (0-916418-74-X) Lotus.

Madgett, Naomi L., intro. Adam of Ife: Black Women in Praise of Black Men. LC 91-61410. (Illus.). 235p. (Orig.). 1992. pap. 15.00 (0-916418-80-4) Lotus.

Madgic, Bob. A Guide to California's Freshwater Fishes. LC 98-32180. (Illus.). 1999. pap. 19.95 (0-87961-254-1) Naturegraph.
— Pursuing Wild Trout: A Journey in Wilderness Values. unabridged ed. LC 97-92758. (Illus.). 192p. 1998. pap. 14.95 (0-9660743-1-9) River Bend Bks.

Madgwick, H. I., jt. auth. see Sattoo, T.

Madgwick, Peter J. Introduction to British Politics. 3rd ed. LC 84-4481. 456p. 1991. pap. 35.00 (0-7487-0335-7) Dufour.
— A New Introduction to British Politics. 550p. 1994. pap. 37.50 (0-7487-1592-4, Pub. by S Thornes Pubs) Trans-Atl Phila.

Madgwick, Peter J., jt. auth. see Woodhouse.

Madgwick, Wendy. Light & Dark. 1999. pap. text 5.95 (0-8172-5882-5) Raintree Steck-V.
— Light & Dark. LC 98-7002. (Science Starters Ser.). (J). 1999. 22.83 (0-8172-5556-7) Raintree Steck-V.
— Living Things. LC 98-30065. (Science Starters Ser.). 1999. 5.95 (0-8172-5883-3) Raintree Steck-V.

***Madgwick, Wendy.** Living Things. (J). 1999. 22.83 (0-8172-5332-7) Raintree Steck-V.

Madgwick, Wendy. Magnets & Sparks. LC 98-14618. (Science Starters Ser.). (J). 1999. 22.83 (0-8172-5328-9) Raintree Steck-V.
— Museum Maze. 48p. (J). (gr. 4-6). 1999. write for info. (0-7613-0961-6, Copper Beech Bks); pap. write for info. (0-7613-0385-5, Copper Beech Bks) Millbrook Pr.

***Madgwick, Wendy.** On the Move. LC 98-30064. (Science Starters Ser.). 32 p. 1999. 5.95 (0-8172-5884-1) Raintree Steck-V.

Madgwick, Wendy. On the Move. 1999. 22.83 (0-8172-5333-5) Raintree Steck-V.
— Super Materials. 1999. pap. text 5.95 (0-8172-5881-7) Raintree Steck-V.
— Super Materials. LC 98-7005. (Science Starters Ser.). (J). 1999. 22.83 (0-8172-5555-9) Raintree Steck-V.
— Super Sound. LC 98-14444. (Science Starters Ser.). (J). 1999. 22.83 (0-8172-5327-0) Raintree Steck-V.

Madgwick, Wendy & Courtney, Don. Citymaze! A Collection of Amazing City Mazes. (Illus.). 40p. (J). (gr. 3 up). 1995. pap. 7.95 (1-56294-846-6) Millbrook Pr.
— Citymaze! A Collection of Amazing City Mazes. LC 94-26291. (Illus.). 40p. (YA). (gr. 3 up). 1995. lib. bdg. 17.90 (1-56294-561-0) Millbrook Pr.

Madgwick, Wendy, jt. auth. see Huddleston, Ruth.

Madhava, K. G. History of the Freedom Movement in India (1857-1947) (C). 1995. 28.00 (81-7013-138-3, Pub. by Navarang) S Asia.
— Western Karnataka: Its Agrarian Relations A.D. 1500-1800. (C). 1991. 29.50 (81-7013-073-5, Pub. by Navarang) S Asia.

Madhava Rao, A. G., jt. ed. see Dover, W. D.

Madhava-Vidyaranya. Sankara Digvijaya: The Traditional Life of Sri Sankaracharya. Tapasyananda, tr. xxxvi, 195p. 1979. pap. 8.95 (81-7120-434-1, Pub. by Ramakrishna Math) Vedanta Pr.

Madhavan, C. E., jt. ed. see Nori, K. V.

Madhavan, Shobhana, jt. auth. see Barrass, Robert.

Madhavananda, Swami, tr. Minor Upanishads. 1970. pap. 2.00 (81-7505-104-3, Pub. by Advaita Ashrama) Vedanta Pr.
— Uddhava Gita: The Last Message of Sri Krishna. 425p. pap. 6.95 (81-7505-115-9, Pub. by Advaita Ashrama) Vedanta Pr.

Madhavananda, Swami & Majumdar, Ramesh, eds. Great Women of India. 553p. 1987. 15.00 (81-85301-30-1, Pub. by Advaita Ashrama) Vedanta Pr.

Madhavananda, Swami, tr. see Adhvarindra, Dharmaraja.

Madhavananda, Swami, tr. see Shankara.

Madhaven, C. E., ed. Foundations of Software Technology & Theoretical Computer Science. (Lecture Notes in Computer Science Ser.: Vol. 405). xiii, 339p. 1989. 40.00 (0-387-52048-1) Spr-Verlag.

Madhavi, D. L., et al. Food Antioxidants, No. 71. (Food Science & Technology Ser.: Vol. 71). (Illus.). 512p. 1995. text 185.00 (0-8247-9351-X) Dekker.

Madhere, Serge. Piti Piti Plen Kay. 90p. 1987. pap. text. write for info. (1-881686-00-0) Madhere.
— Silo Sajes: Prensip Filozofi Lavi. 103p. 1992. pap. text. write for info. (1-881686-02-7) Madhere.
— Tezen. 72p. 1989. pap. text. write for info. (1-881686-01-9) Madhere.

Madhihassan, S. Indian Alchemy or Rasayana. (C). 1991. 12.50 (81-208-0788-X, Pub. by Motilal Bnarsidass) S Asia.

Madhok, Bal R. Kashmir: The Storm Center of the World. 280p. 1992. 10.00 (0-9611614-8-5); pap. 17.95 (0-9611614-9-3) A Ghosh.

Madhok, R., et al, eds. Blood, Blood Products, & AIDS. LC 87-21530. (Johns Hopkins Series in Contemporary Medicine & Public Health). (Illus.). 244p. reprint ed. pap. 75.70 (0-608-06169-7, 206650200008) Bks Demand.

Madhu Bazaz Wangu. Hinduism. (World Religions Ser.). (Illus.). 128p. (J). (gr. 4-9). 1991. 19.95 (0-8160-2447-2) Facts on File.

Madhu, Swaminathan. Linear Circuits Analysis. (Illus.). 850p. 1988. text. write for info. (0-318-62359-5) P-H.

Madhubuti, Haki R. Black Men, Obsolete, Single, Dangerous? Essays in Discovery, Solution & Hope. LC 89-51325. 1990. 29.95 (0-88378-134-4) Third World.
— Black Men, Obsolete, Single, Dangerous? Essays in Discovery, Solution & Hope. LC 89-51325. 300p. 1990. pap. 14.95 (0-88378-135-2) Third World.
— Claiming Earth: Race, Rage, Rape, Redemption: Blacks Seeking a Culture of Enlightened Empowerment. 175p. 1994. 22.00 (0-88378-095-X) Third World.
— Developmental Manual for Young Black Males. 1996. pap. 9.95 (0-88378-170-0) Third World.
— Don't Cry, Scream. 1992. pap. 8.00 (0-88378-016-X) Third World.
— Enemies: The Clash of Races. LC 77-12275. (Orig.). 1978. pap. 12.95 (0-88378-073-9) Third World.
— From Plan to Planet: Life Studies: The Need for Afrikan Minds & Institutions. LC 72-94350. (Orig.). 1992. pap. 7.95 (0-88378-066-6) Third World.
— Groundwork: Selected Poems of Haki R. Madhubuti Don L. Lee (1966-1996) LC 96-30118. 1996. write for info. (0-88378-173-5); pap. 14.95 (0-88378-172-7) Third World.
— Heart Love: Wedding & Love Poems. LC 98-15418. 80p. 1998. 16.95 (0-88378-202-2); pap. 8.95 (0-88378-201-4) Third World.
— Killing Memory, Seeking Ancestors. (Orig.). 1992. pap. 8.00 (0-88378-093-3) Third World.
— Kwanzaa: A Progressive & Uplifting African-American Holiday. 4th ed. (Orig.). 1987. reprint ed. pap. 2.50 (0-88378-012-7) Third World.

Madhubuti, Haki R., ed. Black Books Bulletin - Words Work: Black Intellectual Mercenaries. 80p. 1993. pap. 4.95 (0-685-69762-2) Third World.
— Confusion by Any Other Name: Essays Exploring the Negative Impact of the Blackman's Guide to Understanding the Blackwoman. 26p. 1992. 3.95 (0-88378-148-4) Third World.
— Say That the River Turns: The Impact of Gwendolyn Brooks. (Orig.). 1987. pap. 8.95 (0-88378-118-2) Third World.

Madhubuti, Haki R., intro. Why L. A. Happened: Implications of the '92 Los Angeles Rebellion. LC 92-63015. 287p. (Orig.). 1993. pap. 14.95 (0-88378-094-1) Third World.

Madhubuti, Haki R. & Karenga, Maulana, eds. Million Man March - Day of Absence: A Commemorative Anthology Speeches, Commentary, Photography. 172p. 1996. pap. text 19.95 (0-88378-188-3) Third World.

Madhubuti, Haki R. & Madhubuti, Safisha. African-Centered Education: Its Value, Importance, & Necessity in the Development of Black Children. 32p. pap. 5.00 (0-88378-151-4) Third World.

Madhubuti, Safisha. The Story of Kwanzaa. (J). (gr. 1). 1989. reprint ed. pap. 5.95 (0-88378-001-1) Third World.

Madhubuti, Safisha, jt. auth. see Madhubuti, Haki R.

Madhukar, B. B. & Srivastava, S. N. Mica & Mica Industry. LC 99-227034. (Illus.). 212p. (C). 1995. text 104.00 (90-5410-209-8, TN953, Pub. by A A Balkema) Ashgate Pub Co.

Madhuri, Desai, ed. see Gordon, Douglas H.

Madhurima. Violence Against Women: Dynamics of Conjugal Relations. LC 96-904828. (Illus.). 264p. (C). 1996. 32.00 (81-212-0527-1, Pub. by Gyan Publishing Hse) Nataraj Bks.

Madhurima, jt. auth. see Mahajan, Amarjit.

Madhusudana, C. V. Thermal Contact Conductance. Ling, F. F., ed. LC 95-19291. (Mechanical Engineering Ser.). (Illus.). 176p. 1995. 69.95 (0-387-94534-2) Spr-Verlag.

Madhusudana, C. V., jt. auth. see Leonardi, E.

Madi, Linda. The Scotsman's Lady. 352p. 1998. pap. 4.99 (0-8217-5989-2) Kensgtn Pub Corp.

Madi, Phinda M. Affirmative Action in Corporate South Africa: Surviving in the Jungle. 134p. 1993. pap. 23.00 (0-7021-3040-0, Pub. by Juta & Co) Intl Spec Bk.

Madiebo, Alexander. Memoirs of a Biafran General. LC 75-18600. 350p. 1976. 20.00 (0-89388-206-2) Okpaku Communications.

Madigan. Brock Biology Micro Organ. 500p. 1998. pap. text 59.00 (0-536-01531-7) Pearson Custom.
— Dorothy Canfield Fisher. 1996. 24.95 (0-8057-7645-1, Twyne) Mac Lib Ref.
— Instructional Resource Manual for Radiograhic Anatomy & Positioning. 576p. (C). 1997. pap., teacher ed. 25.00 (0-8385-8245-1, A-8245-1, Apple Lange Med) McGraw.

Madigan. Pocket Manual for Radiographic Anatomy & Positioning. 320p. (C). 1997. pap. 23.95 (0-8385-8237-0, A-8237-8, Apple Lange Med) McGraw.

Madigan, Arthur, tr. see Alexander of Aphrodisias.

Madigan, Arthur, tr. & comment see Aristotle.

Madigan, Brian C. The Temple of Apollo Bassitas Vol. 2: The Sculpture. LC 92-23979. (Illus.). 144p. 1992. 50.00 (0-87661-947-2) Am Sch Athens.

Madigan, C. O. & Elmwood, A. When They Were Kids: Over 400 Sketches of Famous Childhoods. LC 98-17690. 352p. 1998. pap. 14.95 (0-375-70389-6) Random Ref & Info.

An Asterisk (*) at the beginning of an entry indicates that the title is appearing for the first time.

Madigan, Carol O. & Elmwood, Ann. Life's Big Instruction Book: The Almanac of Indispensable Information. 1995. pap. write for info. (*0-446-67157-6*) Warner Bks.

Madigan, Carol O. & Elwood, Ann. Test Your 1980s Literacy. 288p. 1990. pap. 8.95 (*0-685-32623-3*) P-H.

Madigan, Charles & Martinez, Arthur C. The Hard Road to the Softer Side: Lessons from the Transformation of Sears. LC 98-24237. 1999. 25.00 (*0-8129-2960-8*, Times Bks) Crown Pub Group.

Madigan, Charles, jt. auth. see Greenwald, Gerald.

Madigan, Charles, jt. auth. see O'Shea, James.

Madigan, Dan & Bancroft, Ann. Many Hands, Many Miracles. LC 97-1801. 1997. pap. 16.00 (*0-268-01426-4*) U of Notre Dame Pr.

Madigan, Dan & Koivu-Rybicki, Victoria T. The Writing Lives of Children. LC 96-51055. (Illus.). 128p. (Orig.). (C). 1997. pap. text 16.00 (*1-57110-011-3*) Stenhse Pubs.

***Madigan, Gerry.** The Five Plateaus of Progress: Practical Lessons in Self-Development, Personal Leadership & Positive Living. 180p. 2000. pap. 16.95 (*1-86076-145-3*, Pub. by Oak Tr) Midpt Trade.

Madigan, John E. Manual of Equine Neonatal Medicine. 2nd rev. ed. (Illus.). 363p. 1994. pap. text 29.95 (*0-9629517-0-6*) Live Oak CA.

— Manual of Equine Neonatal Medicine. 3rd ed. (Illus.). 415p. 1997. pap. 42.00 (*0-9629517-1-4*) Live Oak CA.

Madigan, Julian. The Agony of Ecstasy. LC 96-151146. 282p. 1996. pap. 12.95 (*1-85371-682-0*, Pub. by Poolbeg Pr) Dufour.

Madigan, Leo. The Catholic Quiz Book. 140p. 1996. pap. 9.95 (*0-85244-264-5*, 921, Pub. by Gra1cewing) Morehouse Pub.

Madigan, Mark J., ed. Keeping Fires Night & Day: Selected Letters of Dorothy Canfield Fisher. (Illus.). 384p. (C). 1993. 34.95 (*0-8262-0884-3*) U of Mo Pr.

Madigan, Mark J., ed. see Fisher, Dorothy Canfield.

Madigan, Mark J., ed. & afterword by see Fisher, Dorothy Canfield.

Madigan, Mary G. & Nilcae, Grace S., eds. Concert Artists Guild 1998 Guide to Competitions. 135p. 1997. pap. 17.95 (*0-9629075-8-8*) Concert Artists.

Madigan, Michael T., et al. Brock's Biology of Microorganism. 9th ed. LC 99-30064. 1046p. (C). 1999. 101.33 (*0-13-081922-0*) P-H.

***Madigan, Mike.** The Twisted Badge: An Inside Look at Politics in Law Enforcement. 3rd ed. LC 99-91142. 168p. 1999. pap. 11.95 (*0-924309-01-6*) Integrity Pubns.

Madigan, Mike, jt. auth. see Wright, George.

Madigan, Patrick. Christian Revelation & the Completion of the Aristotelian Revolution. 136p. (Orig.). (C). 1988. pap. text 19.50 (*0-8191-7091-7*); lib. bdg. 34.00 (*0-8191-7090-9*) U Pr of Amer.

— The Modern Project to Rigor: Descartes to Nietzsche. LC 85-22564. (Illus.). 224p. (Orig.). (C). 1986. lib. bdg. 49.50 (*0-8191-5080-0*) U Pr of Amer.

— Penance, Contemplation, & Service: Pivotal Experiences of Christian Spirituality. 232p. (Orig.). 1994. pap. text 14.95 (*0-8146-5911-X*, M Glazier) Liturgical Pr.

Madigan, Patrick, jt. auth. see Baumert, Norbert.

Madigan, Patrick, tr. see Adam, Adolf.

Madigan, Patrick, tr. see Larere, Philippe.

Madigan, Shawn. Liturgical Spirituality & the Rite of Christian Initiation of Adults. LC 97-22387. (Forum Essays Ser.: No. 5). 120p. 1997. pap. 6.00 (*0-929650-80-8*, LITSPI) Liturgy Tr Pubns.

***Madigan, Shawn.** Spirituality Rooted in Liturgy. 2nd rev. ed. LC 99-26635. 248p. (C). 1999. pap. 15.95 (*1-56929-029-6*, Pastoral Press) OR Catholic.

Madigan, Shawn, ed. Mystics, Visionaries & Prophets: A Historical Anthology of Women's Spiritual Writings. LC 98-36261. 512p. 1998. 39.00 (*0-8006-3145-5*, 9-3145) Augsburg Fortress.

Madigan, Timothy J., ed. see Kurtz, Paul.

Madill. Applied Mechanics Level 3. 1985. pap. text. write for info. (*0-582-41292-7*, Pub. by Addison-Wesley) Longman.

Madin, Douglas L., ed. The Psychology of Learning & Motivation, Vol. 30. (Illus.). 328p. 1993. text 99.95 (*0-12-543330-1*) Acad Pr.

***Madin, Kate.** Down to a Sunless Sea: The Strange World of Hydrothermal Vents. 64p. (J). 1999. pap. 8.95 (*0-7398-1239-4*) Raintree Steck-V.

— Down to a Sunless Sea: The Strange World of Hydrothermal Vents. LC 99-26962. (Turnstone Ocean Explorers Ser.). 64p. (YA). (gr. 6-8). 1999. 27.11 (*0-7398-1238-6*) Raintree Steck-V.

Madin, Kate, jt. auth. see Kovacs, Deborah.

Madina, Alex & Berry, Mary. Tales from Times Past: Sinister Stories of the 19th Century. (Cambridge School Anthologies Ser.). 128p. (C). 1998. pap. 9.95 (*0-521-58566-X*) Cambridge U Pr.

Madina, Marta, tr. see Sadasivam, Bharati, ed.

Madinaveitia, Catherine. J. D. Salinger's The Catcher in the Rye. rev. ed. (Brodie's Notes Ser.). 91p. 1992. pap. 5.95 (*0-333-58167-9*, Pub. by Macmillan) Trans-Atl Phila.

Madinaveitia, Horacio. La Gran Aventura de Don Roberto. (SPA., Illus.). 32p. (J). (gr. k-4). 1992. lib. bdg. 13.95 (*1-879567-02-4*, Valeria Bks) Wonder Well.

— Sir Robert's Little Outing. (Illus.). 32p. (J). (gr. k-4). 1991. pap. text 7.95 (*1-879567-00-8*, Valeria Bks); lib. bdg. 13.95 (*1-879567-01-6*, Valeria Bks) Wonder Well.

Madine, Margaret W. Fondue Cooking. LC 77-95289. 1970. 5.95 (*0-88351-010-3*) Test Recipe.

***Madinger, John.** Confidential Informant: Law Enforcement's Most Valuable Tool. LC 99-39503. 352p. 1999. boxed set 69.95 (*0-8493-0709-0*) CRC Pr.

— Money Laundering: A Guide to Criminal Investigations. LC 98-45932. 445p. 1999. boxed set 69.95 (*0-8493-0710-4*) CRC Pr.

Madino, Og. The Spellbinder's Gift. 1996. pap. 10.00 (*0-449-91224-8*) Fawcett.

Madis, George. The Winchester Book. 3rd ed. LC 79-8991. (Illus.). 1985. 49.50 (*0-910156-03-4*) Art & Ref.

— Winchester Dates of Manufacture. 1984. 6.00 (*0-910156-05-0*) Art & Ref.

— The Winchester Era. (Illus.). 1985. 19.95 (*0-910156-08-5*) Art & Ref.

— The Winchester Handbook. (Illus.). 320p. (YA). 1981. 24.95 (*0-910156-04-2*) Art & Ref.

— The Winchester Model 12. (Illus.). 1982. 24.95 (*0-910156-06-9*) Art & Ref.

Madisetti, Avanindra. Digital Subscriber Loop DSL Technologies. (DSP & Communications Technology Ser.). 1999. 99.95 (*0-8493-3731-3*) CRC Pr.

Madisetti, Vijay. Digital Signal Processing Handbook. LC 97-21848. 1776p. 1997. boxed set 139.95 (*0-8493-8572-5*) CRC Pr.

— Digital Signal Processing Handbook. 1999. cd-rom 129.00 (*0-8493-2135-2*) CRC Pr.

Madisetti, Vijay, ed. Modeling & Simulation on Microcomputers, 1990. 138p. 1990. pap. 40.00 (*0-911801-64-2*, MSM90) Soc Computer Sim.

Madisetti, Vijay, et al, eds. Fifth Workshop on Parallel & Distributed Simulation (PADS '91) (Simulation Ser.: Vol. 23, No. 1). 250p. 1991. 60.00 (*0-911801-78-2*, SS-23-1) Soc Computer Sim.

Madisetti, Vijay, et al. Quick-Turnaround ASIC Design in VHDL: Core-Based Behavioral Synthesis, Vol. 367. LC 96-1910. (Kluwer International Series in Engineering & Computer Science). 216p. (C). 1996. text 115.00 (*0-7923-9744-4*) Kluwer Academic.

Madisetti, Vijay K., ed. see Williams, Ed D.

Madison. Born on the Edge. Date not set. write for info. (*0-395-29109-7*) Ticknor & Fields.

— Just Enough Fortran 90. (C). 1998. text. write for info. (*0-673-99396-5*) Addison-Wesley.

— Just Enough Fortran 90: Solutions Manual. (C). 1998. pap. text, teacher ed. write for info. (*0-673-55822-3*) Addison-Wesley.

— Real Estate Finance. 1312p. 1991. 57.00 (*0-316-54363-2*, Aspen Law & Bus) Aspen Pub.

Madison, Arnold, jt. auth. see Wyndham, Lee.

***Madison, Bob.** American Horror Writers. LC 99-41494. (Collective Biographies Ser.). 2000. lib. bdg. write for info. (*0-7660-1379-0*) Enslow Pubs.

Madison, Bob, ed. Dracula: The First Hundred Years. LC 97-73132. (Illus.). 324p. (Orig.). 1997. pap. 20.00 (*1-887664-14-9*) Midnght Marquee Pr.

Madison, Brian. Alleged Imagery Errors. (C). 1992. pap. text 10.95 (*0-913412-56-2*) Brandon Hse.

— Rectification of Memory-Errors. (C). 1991. pap. text 9.99 (*0-913412-57-0*) Brandon Hse.

***Madison, Carolyn.** Scotsman & the Spinster. (Regency Romance Ser.). 2000. mass mkt. 4.99 (*0-8217-6654-6*, Zebra Kensgtn) Kensgtn Pub Corp.

Madison, Charles L., jt. auth. see Gauthier, Sharon V.

Madison, Cheri C. Nevada's Red Rock Canyon: The Story Behind the Scenery. LC 88-81169. (Illus.). 48p. (Orig.). 1988. pap. 7.95 (*0-88714-025-4*) KC Pubns.

Madison County Farm Bureau Women's Committee. Cookbook 25 Years: Women of the Farm Bureau. 473p. 1981. pap. 16.95 (*0-9644914-0-0*) Madison Cty Farm Bur.

— Cookbook 25 Years: Women of the Farm Bureau. 490p. 1995. text 18.95 (*0-9644914-1-9*) Madison Cty Farm Bur.

Madison, Curt, jt. ed. see Yarber, Yvonne.

Madison, D. Soyini. The Woman That I Am. 720p. 1997. pap. 19.95 (*0-312-15296-5*) St Martin.

Madison, Deborah. Deborah Madison's Essential Vegetable Cookbook. 1996. 39.95 (*0-614-19355-9*) Bantam.

— Savory Way. 464p. 1990. 27.50 (*0-553-05780-4*) Bantam.

— The Savory Way. LC 97-45596. (Illus.). 464p. 1998. pap. 20.00 (*0-7679-0166-5*) Broadway BDD.

***Madison, Deborah.** This Can't Be Tofu! 75 Innovative Recipes. LC 99-40281. (Illus.). 144p. 2000. pap. 15.00 (*0-7679-0419-2*) Broadway BDD.

Madison, Deborah. Vegetarian Cooking for Everyone. LC 97-11138. (Illus.). 752p. 1997. 40.00 (*0-7679-0014-6*) Broadway BDD.

— The Vegetarian Table: America. LC 95-50303. (Illus.). 144p. 1996. 22.95 (*0-8118-0888-2*) Chronicle Bks.

Madison, Deborah, jt. auth. see Brown, Edward E.

***Madison, Deborah L.** A Slimy Frog Who Went to School. (J). (gr. k-3). 1999. pap. 5.95 (*0-533-13013-1*) Vantage.

Madison, Elaine. How to Use America Online. 3rd ed. LC 98-159626. 240p. 1996. 24.99 (*1-56276-432-2*, Ziff-Davis Pr) Que.

— How to Use America Online. 4th ed. LC 97-80915. 240p. 1999. 24.99 (*1-56276-543-4*, Ziff-Davis Pr) Que.

Madison, G. B. The Logic of Liberty, 30. LC 85-27278. (Contributions in Philosophy Ser.: No. 30). 307p. 1986. 55.00 (*0-313-25018-9*, MLG/, Greenwood Pr) Greenwood.

— The Phenomenology of Merleau-Ponty: A Search for the Limits of Consciousness. LC 84-5080. (Series in Continental Thought : Vol. 3). 377p. 1981. pap. text 17.95 (*0-8214-0644-2*) Ohio U Pr.

Madison, Gary B. The Political Economy of Civil Society & Human Rights. LC 97-8645. 320p. (C). 1998. 85.00 (*0-415-16677-2*) Routledge.

Madison, Gary B., intro. Working Through Derrida. (Studies in Phenomenology & Existential Philosophy). 294p. (Orig.). 1993. 69.95 (*0-8101-1054-7*); pap. 22.50 (*0-8101-1079-2*) Northwestern U Pr.

Madison, Gary B. & Fairbairn, Marty, eds. The Ethics of Postmodernity: Current Trends in Continental Thought. LC 99-21665. (Studies in Phenomenology & Existential Philosophy). 216p. 1998. 69.95 (*0-8101-1375-9*) Northwestern U Pr.

— The Ethics of Postmodernity: Current Trends in Continental Thought. LC 99-21665. (Studies in Phenomenology & Existential Philosophy). 216p. 1999. pap. 22.50 (*0-8101-1376-7*) Northwestern U Pr.

Madison, Guy M. The Res, 3 vols. Mary, Floreda, ed. (Illus.). 372p. 1998. per. 12.95 (*0-9657032-9-0*) G M Madison.

— Ward 7. Mary, Floreda, ed. 108p. 1997. pap. 5.95 (*0-9657032-0-7*) G M Madison.

Madison Historical Comm. Staff, ed. Madison County History, Vol. 2. (Illus.). 280p. 1997. 79.50 (*0-9660880-5-0*) Madison Cty Hist.

Madison Historical Society Staff. Madison in the Twentieth Century. LC 98-86604. (Images of America Ser.). (Illus.). 128p. 1998. pap. 16.99 (*0-7524-0940-9*) Arcadia Publng.

Madison, James. CNC Machining Handbook. (Illus.). 396p. (C). 1996. text 41.95 (*0-8311-3064-4*) Indus Pr.

***Madison, James.** CNC Program Design. 1999. 39.95 (*0-8311-3117-9*) Indus Pr.

Madison, James. The Debates in the Federal Convention of 1787, 2 vols., Set. LC 86-63352. 677p. 1987. 81.95 (*0-87975-388-9*) Prometheus Bks.

— Federalist, No. 10. (Reprint Series in Social Sciences). (C). 1993. reprint ed. pap. text 5.00 (*0-8290-3200-2*, PS-397) Irvington.

— Federalist, No. 51. (Reprint Series in Social Sciences). (C). 1993. reprint ed. pap. text 1.00 (*0-8290-3708-X*, PS-396) Irvington.

***Madison, James.** Internet/PC User's Workout Handbook. 127p. 2000. pap. 17.95 (*1-56072-487-0*, Nova Kroshka Bks) Nova Sci Pubs.

Madison, James. James Madison: A Biography in His Own Words. Peterson, Merrill D., ed. (Founding Fathers Ser.). 1974. 15.00 (*0-06-013332-5*) HarpC.

— James Madison: Writings. Rakove, Jack N., ed. LC 98-50372. 928p. 1999. 40.00 (*1-883011-66-3*, Pub. by Library of America) Penguin Putnam.

— James Madison's "Advice to My Country" Mattern, David B., ed. LC 96-28149. 144p. 1997. 17.95 (*0-8139-1717-4*) U Pr of Va.

— Journal of the Federal Convention. Scott, E. H., ed. LC 78-119938. (Select Bibliographies Reprint Ser.). 1977. reprint ed. 36.95 (*0-8369-5381-9*) Ayer.

— The Mind of the Founder: Sources of the Political Thought of James Madison. rev. ed. Meyers, Marvin, ed. LC 80-54466. 516p. 1981. pap. 23.00 (*0-87451-201-8*) U Pr of New Eng.

— Notes of Debates in the Federal Convention of 1787. 720p. 1987. reprint ed. pap. 19.95 (*0-393-30405-1*) Norton.

— Notes of Debates in the Federal Convention of 1787. rev. ed. LC 84-5080. 718p. 1985. text 50.00 (*0-8214-0777-5*) Ohio U Pr.

— The Papers of James Madison, 10 vols. Hutchinson, William T. et al, eds. Incl. March-December, 1781. Rachal, William H., ed. LC 62-9114. 381p. 1993. lib. bdg. 25.00 (*0-226-36295-7*); May 3, 1783-February 20, 1784. Rachal, William M., ed. LC 62-9114. 1971. lib. bdg. 35.00 (*0-226-36300-7*); May 27, 1787-March 3, 1788. Rachal, William H., ed. LC 62-9114. 1993. lib. bdg. 35.00 (*0-226-50107-8*); Vol. 8. March 10, 1784 - March 28, 1786. Rachal, William M., ed. LC 62-9114. 1992. lib. bdg. 30.00 (*0-226-50104-3*); Vol. 4. 1 January-31 July, 1782. Rachal, William M., ed. LC 62-9114. 486p. 1992. lib. bdg. 25.00 (*0-226-36296-5*); Vol. 5. 1 August-31 December 1782. Rachal, William M., ed. LC 62-9114. 1967. lib. bdg. 35.00 (*0-226-36297-3*); 1 January 1783-30 April, 1783. Rachal, William M., ed. LC 62-9114. 548p. 1969. lib. bdg. 35.00 (*0-226-36298-1*); LC 62-9114. (Illus.). write for info. (*0-318-56067-4*) U Ch Pr.

— The Papers of James Madison: August 1, 1801-February 28, 1802. Cross, Jeanne K. et al, eds. (Secretary of State Ser.: Vol. 2). 576p. (C). 1993. text 60.00 (*0-8139-1403-5*) U Pr of Va.

— The Papers of James Madison: March 1789 to January 1790. with a supplement 24 October 1775-24 January 1789. Rutland, Robert A. & Hobson, Charles F., eds. LC 62-9114. (Vol. 12). 498p. 1979. text 42.50 (*0-8139-0803-5*) U Pr of Va.

— The Papers of James Madison: 1 March-30 September 1809. Rutland, Robert A. & Mason, Thomas A., eds. LC 83-6953. (Presidential Ser.: Vol. 1). 414p. 1984. text 42.50 (*0-8139-0991-0*) U Pr of Va.

— The Papers of James Madison: 1 October 1809 - 2 November 1810. Cross, Jeanne K. et al, eds. (Presidential Ser.: Vol. 2). 681p. (C). 1992. text 55.00 (*0-8139-1345-4*) U Pr of Va.

— The Papers of James Madison: 8 October 1802 - 15 May 1803. Hackett, Mary A. et al, eds. (Secretary of State Ser.: Vol. 4). Date not set. 65.00 (*0-8139-1747-6*) U Pr of Va.

— The Papers of James Madison Vol. 3: 1 March 1802-6 October 1802: Secretary of State Series. Mattern, David B. et al, eds. 608p. (C). 1995. text 50.00 (*0-8139-1541-4*) U Pr of Va.

— The Papers of James Madison Vol. 11: 7 March 1788 to 1 March 1789. Rutland, Robert A. & Hobson, Charles F., eds. LC 62-9114. 471p. 1977. text 42.50 (*0-8139-0739-X*) U Pr of Va.

— The Papers of James Madison Vol. 16: 27 April 1795-27 March 1797. Stagg, John C. et al, eds. LC 62-9114. (Papers of James Madison). 576p. 1989. text 47.50 (*0-8139-1212-1*) U Pr of Va.

— The Papers of James Madison Vol. 17: 31 March 1797-3 March 1801, with a Supplement. Stagg, J. C. et al, eds. (Papers of James Madison). 656p. 1991. text 49.50 (*0-8139-1288-1*) U Pr of Va.

— The Virginia Report of 1799-1800, Touching the Alien & Sedition Laws. LC 75-107626. (Civil Liberties in American History Ser.). 1970. reprint ed. lib. bdg. 35.00 (*0-306-71860-X*) Da Capo.

— A Vocabulary of New Jersey Delaware. LC 99-19305. (American Language Reprints Ser.: Vol. 10). 51p. 1998. 16.00 (*1-889758-03-5*) Evol Pubng & Manuf.

Madison, James, et al. The Federalist Papers. 1961. 24.75 (*0-8446-6842-7*) Peter Smith.

— The Papers of James Madison. Brugger, Robert J. et al, eds. LC 85-29516. (Secretary of State Series, 4 March-31 July 1801: Vol. 1). xxx, 526p. 1987. text 42.50 (*0-8139-1093-5*) U Pr of Va.

Madison, James H. Eli Lilly: A Life, 1885-1977. (Illus.). xiii, 342p. 1989. 24.95 (*0-87195-047-2*) Ind Hist Soc.

— Indiana Through Tradition & Change: A History of the Hoosier State & Its People, 1920-1945. (History of Indiana Ser.: Vol. 5). (Illus.). xx, 453p. 1982. 27.50 (*0-87195-043-X*); pap. 9.95 (*0-87195-042-1*) Ind Hist Soc.

— The Indiana Way: A State History. LC 85-45071. (Illus.). xviii, 364p. 1986. pap. 14.95 (*0-253-20609-X*) Ind U Pr.

Madison, James H., ed. Heartland: Comparative Histories of the Midwestern States. LC 87-45835. (Midwestern History & Culture Ser.). 318p. 1988. 14.95 (*0-253-31423-2*) Ind U Pr.

Madison, James H., ed. Wendell Willkie: Hoosier Internationalist. LC 91-12758. (Illus.). 214p. 1992. text 8.95 (*0-253-33619-8*) Ind U Pr.

***Madison, James Neal.** Scottish Clans Notecards with Envelope & Other. 1999. pap. 7.95 (*1-56554-633-4*) Pelican.

Madison, James T., ed. see Venkstern, Tat'kilana.

Madison, Joseph E. Black Man's Hell. (Illus.). 304p. 1997. 22.95 (*1-56924-712-9*) Marlowe & Co.

Madison, Kathy. Fun Guide to Anchorage. Lauzen, Elizabeth, ed. (Illus.). 32p. (Orig.). (J). (gr. 1-6). 1987. pap., wbk. ed. 3.50 (*0-942553-00-4*) Madison Aves.

Madison, Lloyd. Boomer Sawbones. large type ed. (Linford Western Library). 304p. 1986. pap. 16.99 (*0-7089-6279-3*, Linford) Ulverscroft.

— The Rainmaker of Deadman. large type ed. (Linford Western Library). 304p. 1987. pap. 16.99 (*0-7089-6353-6*, Linford) Ulverscroft.

Madison, Louis E. San Francisco on a Shoestring. 10th rev. ed. 224p. 1997. pap. 8.95 (*0-912125-08-X*) L E Madison.

Madison, Lynda. Keep Talking: A Mother-Daughter Guide to the Pre-Teen Years. LC 96-52078. 208p. (YA). 1997. 19.95 (*0-8362-2752-2*) Andrews & McMeel.

— Keep Talking: A Mother-Daughter Guide to the Pre-Teen Years. (YA). 1999. pap. text 12.95 (*0-8362-8736-3*) Andrews & McMeel.

— Parenting with Purpose: Progressive Discipline in the Toddler Years. LC 98-19803. xiii, 235 p. 1998. pap. 12.95 (*0-8362-6768-0*) Andrews & McMeel.

Madison, Malcolm. Numerology. 23p. 1985. reprint ed. spiral bd. 8.00 (*0-7873-1243-6*) Hlth Research.

Madison, Maria. The Reckoning. 1993. mass mkt. 5.95 (*1-56201-042-5*) Blue Moon Bks.

***Madison, Michael, et al.** Modern Real Estate Finance & Land Transfer: A Transactional Approach. 2nd ed. LC 99-37775. 1999. boxed set 64.00 (*0-7355-0327-3*) Panel Pubs.

Madison, Michael, jt. ed. see Chapman, Michael W.

Madison, Michael T. & Dwyer, Jeffrey R. Law of Real Estate Financing. LC 80-53430. 916p. 1981. suppl. ed. 160.00 (*0-88262-516-0*) Warren Gorham & Lamont.

Madison, Michael T. & Zinman, Robert M. Modern Real Estate Financing: A Transactional Approach. 1312p. 1991. teacher ed. write for info. (*0-316-54364-0*, 43640) Aspen Law.

Madison, Mike. Growing Flowers for Market: A Practical Manual for Small-Scale Field Production & Marketing of Fresh Flowers. (Illus.). 270p. 1998. pap. 19.95 (*0-9662908-0-1*) Yolo Pr.

Madison, Olivia M., et al, eds. Bibliographic Control of Conference Proceedings, Papers & Conference Materials. LC 96-30103. (ALCTS Papers on Library Technical Services & Collections: Vol. 7). 130p. (C). 1996. pap. 21.00 (*0-8389-7860-6*) Assn Coll & Res Libs.

Madison, Olivia M., jt. ed. see Byram, John D., Jr.

Madison Public Library Staff & Causley, Monroe. Arthur Rushmore & the Golden Hind Press: Catalog of the Exhibition October 1-October 31, 1994. (Illus.). ix, 31p. (Orig.). 1994. pap. 10.00 (*0-9646103-0-2*) Madison Libr.

Madison, Richard. Rivers of Living Water. 64p. 1997. pap. 6.99 (*1-885857-21-7*) Four Wnds Pubng.

— Signs of Jesus' Return. Eldredge, A., ed. 70p. (Orig.). 1994. pap. 6.99 (*1-885857-00-4*) Four Wnds Pubng.

Madison, Richard L. Healing from God. LC 98-10161. (Illus.). 142p. 1998. pap. 6.99 (*0-88368-485-3*) Whitaker Hse.

Madison, Roger A., et al. Federal Support for Training Foreign Language & Area Specialists: The Education & Careers of FLAS Fellowship Recipients. LC 83-17761. 1983. pap. 15.00 (*0-8330-0524-3*, R-3070-ED) Rand Corp.

Madison, Ron. Have You Ever Heard a Young Child Rhyme? That Child Will Read in Half the Time. (Poetry - A Friend in the Classroom Ser.). (Illus.). 60p. (J). (ps-4). 1998. teacher ed., spiral bd. 14.00 (*1-887206-19-1*) Neds Head Prodns.

— Ned & Crow: A Lesson in Diversity. LC 96-171529. (Ned & Friends Ser.). (Illus.). 12p. (J). (ps-2). 1996. pap. 2.95 (*1-887206-11-6*) Neds Head Prodns.

— Ned & Crow Set: Packaged with 8" Doll. (Ned & Friends Ser.). (Illus.). 12p. (J). (ps-2). 1997. pap. 19.95 incl. audio (*1-887206-13-2*) Neds Head Prodns.

— Ned & Fred: A Lesson in Loyalty. (Ned & Friends Ser.). (Illus.). 12p. (J). (ps-2). 1995. pap. 2.95 (*1-887206-02-7*) Neds Head Prodns.

— Ned & Fred Set: Packaged with 8" Doll. (Illus.). 12p. (J). (ps-2). 1996. pap. 19.95 incl. audio (*1-887206-09-4*) Neds Head Prodns.

— Ned & Friends Reading & Rhyming Supplement: Books, Dolls & Cassettes for the Classroom. (Ned & Friends Ser.). (Illus.). 492p. 1998. pap., spiral bd. 158.00 (*1-887206-14-0*) Neds Head Prodns.

— Ned, Fred & Friend: A Lesson in Compassion. LC 95-237932. (Ned & Friends Ser.). (Illus.). 12p. (J). (ps-2). 1995. pap. 2.95 (*1-887206-03-5*) Neds Head Prodns.

— Ned's Folks: A Lesson in Love. (Ned & Friends Ser.). (Illus.). 12p. (J). (ps-4). 1996. pap. 2.95 (*1-887206-12-4*) Neds Head Prodns.

— Ned's Friend: A Lesson in Friendship. (Ned & Friends Ser.). (Illus.). 12p. (J). (ps-2). 1995. pap. 2.95 (*1-887206-01-9*) Neds Head Prodns.

— Ned's Friend Set: Packaged with 8" Doll. (Ned & Friends Ser.). (Illus.). 12p. (J). (ps-2). 1996. pap. 19.95 incl. audio (*1-887206-10-8*) Neds Head Prodns.

— Ned's Head: A Lesson in Self-Esteem. (Ned & Friends Ser.). (Illus.). 12p. (J). (ps-2). 1993. pap. 2.95 (*1-887206-00-0*) Neds Head Prodns.

— Ned's Head Set: Packaged with 14" Pillow-Doll. (Ned & Friends Ser.). (Illus.). 24p. (J). (ps-2). 1995. pap. 19.95 incl. audio (*1-887206-04-3*) Neds Head Prodns.

— Teaching Safety Can Be Fun: Let Ned Show You How It's Done. (Poetry - A Friend in the Classroom Ser.). (Illus.). 24p. (J). (ps-2). 1999. teacher ed., spiral bd. 14.00 (*1-887206-20-5*) Neds Head Prodns.

***Madison, Ronald & Schmidt, Corey.** Talking Pictures: A Parent's Guide to Using Movies to Discuss Ethics, Values & Everyday Problems. (Illus.). 2001. pap. text 12.95 (*0-7624-0803-0*) Running Pr.

Madison-Shaw, Tamara. Sistuh's Sermon on the Mount: The Blood Still Boils. LC XLittlebook. 42p. (Orig.). 1993. 6.00 (*0-940880-43-1*) Open Hand.

Madison Square Press. Festival Graphics. 1924. 45.00 (*0-688-16048-4*, Wm Morrow) Morrow Avon.

— International Logos & Trademarks, No. 4. (Illus.). 196p. 1999. 37.50 (*0-942604-62-8*) Madison Square.

Madison Square Press Staff. Atlanta Graphic Design. 240p. 1998. 39.95 (*0-942604-61-X*) Madison Square.

***Madison Square Press Staff.** Extreme Fonts. 1999. 35.00 (*0-688-16934-1*, Wm Morrow) Morrow Avon.

— Hot California Graphics. (Illus.). 256p. 2000. 39.95 (*0-942604-76-8*, Pub. by Madison Square) BHB Intl.

Madison Square Press Staff. International Logos. 4th ed. 1998. 37.50 (*0-688-16624-5*, Wm Morrow) Morrow Avon.

— International Logos & Trademarks. 1997. 34.95 (*0-688-14257-5*, Wm Morrow) Morrow Avon.

— Labels of Distiction. 1999. pap. 19.95 (*0-688-16225-8*, Wm Morrow) Morrow Avon.

Madison Square Press Staff. Model Making. 1924. 35.00 (*0-688-16924-4*, Wm Morrow) Morrow Avon.

— Times Square. 1999. 40.00 (*0-688-17261-X*, Wm Morrow) Morrow Avon.

— Typefaces. 1996. 32.50 (*0-688-14532-9*, Wm Morrow) Morrow Avon.

Madison Square Press Staff. Web Art. (Illus.). 1999. pap. 39.95 (*0-688-16491-9*, Wm Morrow) Morrow Avon.

Madison, Susan. The Color of Hope. mass mkt. write for info. (*0-312-97545-7*) St Martin.

— The Color of Hope. LC 00-25361. 384p. 2000. text 24.95 (*0-312-25186-6*) St Martin.

Madison, Virginia & Stillwell, Hallie. How Come It's Called That? Place Names in the Big Bend Country. 3rd ed. (Illus.). 164p. 1997. reprint ed. pap. 12.95 (*0-9657985-0-X*) Iron Mountain.

Madix, Robert J., ed. Surface Reactions. LC 93-49867. (Surface Sciences Ser.: Vol. 34). 1994. 75.95 (*0-387-57605-3*) Spr-Verlag.

Madjar, H., et al, eds. Breast Ultrasound Update. (Illus.). x, 376p. 1995. 100.00 (*3-8055-5860-0*) S Karger.

***Madjar, H. & Jellins, Jack.** The Practice of Breast Ultrasound: Techniques, Findings, Differential Diagnosis. LC 99-52543. (Illus.). 2000. 99.00 (*0-86577-898-1*) Thieme Med Pubs.

***Madjar, Irena.** Nursing & the Experience of Illness: Phenomenology in Practice. LC 98-33321. 1999. 85.00 (*0-415-20782-7*); pap. 25.99 (*0-415-20783-5*) Routledge.

Madjenovic, Paul J., ed. How to Achieve Credit Card Merchant Status. 64p. 1996. pap. 35.00 (*0-915344-50-5*) Todd Pubns.

Madjiji, Azita, tr. see Aiach, Gilbert.

Madkins, Jerry. The Challenge of Modern Management. (C). 1994. pap. text 31.72 (*1-56870-119-5*) RonJon Pub.

— Corporate Social Responsibility. 106p. (C). 1994. 34.97 (*1-56870-140-3*) RonJon Pub.

Madl, Ferenc. The Law of the European Economic Community: Enterprises, Economic Competition & the Economic Function of the State in the Process of Economic Integration. 329p. (C). 1978. 60.00 (*963-05-1330-7*, Pub. by Akade Kiado) St Mut.

Madl, Ferenc & Vekas, L. The Law of Conflicts & Foreign Trade. 379p. (C). 1987. 114.00 (*963-05-4274-9*, Pub. by Akade Kiado) St Mut.

***Madl, Ferenc & Vekas, Lajos.** The Law of Conflicts & of International Economic Relations. 565p. 1998. 110.00 (*963-05-7525-6*, Pub. by Akade Kiado) Intl Spec Bk.

Madl, Linda. Bayou Rose. 384p. 1996. mass mkt. 4.99 (*0-8217-5268-5*, Zebra Kensgtn) Kensgtn Pub Corp.

***Madl, Linda.** Brighter Than Gold. 368p. 2000. mass mkt. 5.99 (*0-8217-6755-0*, Zebra Kensgtn) Kensgtn Pub Corp.

Madl, Linda. Scotsman's Bride. 352p. 1999. mass mkt. 4.99 (*0-8217-6151-X*) Kensgtn Pub Corp.

— A Whisper of Violets. 384p. 1997. mass mkt. 4.99 (*0-8217-5633-8*, Zebra Kensgtn) Kensgtn Pub Corp.

Madlala, Nozizwe, jt. auth. see Lund, Francie.

Madland, Helga S. Marianne Ehrmann: Reason & Emotion in Her Life & Works. (Women in German Literature Ser.: Vol. 1). X, 340p. (C). 1998. text 57.95 (*0-8204-3929-0*) P Lang Pubng.

— Non-Aristotelian Drama in Eighteenth Century Germany & its Modernity: J. M. R. Lenz. (European University Studies: German Language & Literature: Ser. 1, Vol. 621). 308p. 1982. pap. 53.00 (*3-261-05079-9*) P Lang Pubng.

Madland, Helga S., jt. ed. see Leidner, Alan C.

Madlem. Power Investing with Sector Funds. 368p. 1998. boxed set 39.95 (*0-910944-09-1*) St Lucie Pr.

Madlem, Melody, et al. Managing Stress: A Mindset for Health. LC 96-8732. 1996. write for info. (*1-56796-151-7*) WRS Group.

***Madlem, Peter V. & Sykes, Thomas K.** International Dictionary of Mutual Funds, Closed-End Funds & REITs. 412p. 2000. 55.00 (*1-888998-87-3*, 98-87-3) Glenlake Pub.

Madlem, Peter W. Power Investing with Sector Funds: Mutual Fund Timing & Allocation Strategies. LC 97-39485. 1997. write for info. (*0-910944-05-9*) St Lucie Pr.

Madnick, Stuart E., ed. The Strategic Use of Information Technology. (Executive Bookshelf-Sloan Management Review Ser.). (Illus.). 220p. 1987. text 35.00 (*0-19-505048-7*) OUP.

Mado, Michio. The Animals: Selected Poems. LC 92-10356. (ENG & JPN., Illus.). 48p. (J). (ps up). 1992. text, lib. bdg. 16.95 (*0-689-50574-4*) McElderry Bks.

— The Magic Pocket. Michiko, U., tr. LC 97-75774. (Illus.). 32p. (J). (ps-3). 1998. per. 16.00 (*0-689-82137-9*) S&S Childrens.

Madoc-Jones, Beryl. An Introduction to Women's Studies. Coates, Jennifer, ed. & intro. by. (Illus.). 288p. (C). 1996. pap. 30.95 (*0-631-19255-7*) Blackwell Pubs.

— An Introduction to Women's Studies. Coates, Jennifer, ed. & intro. by. (Illus.). 288p. (C). 1996. 58.95 (*0-631-19254-9*) Blackwell Pubs.

Madocks, Susan, tr. see Pedrocco, Filippo.

Madoff, Pamela, jt. auth. see Lai, David C.

Madoff, Steven H. Michael Gitlin: Sculptures Drawings, 1982-1985. (Illus.). 23p. (Orig.). 1985. pap. 10.00 (*0-913263-11-7*) Exit Art.

Madoff, Steven H., ed. Pop Art: A Critical History. LC 97-2587. (Documents of Twentieth Century Art Ser.). (Illus.). 413p. 1997. 55.00 (*0-520-21018-2*, Pub. by U CA Pr); pap. 24.95 (*0-520-21243-6*, Pub. by U CA Pr) Cal Prin Full Svc.

***Madoff, Steven H. & Mamet, David.** Donald Sultan: In the Still Life Tradition. (Illus.). 80p. 2000. 25.00 (*0-915525-06-2*) Memphis Brooks Museum.

***Madoff, Steven Henry.** While We're Here. 70p. 1999. pap. 12.95 (*1-889097-37-3*, Pub. by Hard Pr MA) SPD-Small Pr Dist.

Madoff, Steven Henry. Works & Days. 72p. 1999. 15.95 (*1-889097-28-4*, Pub. by Hard Pr MA) Consort Bk Sales.

Madole, Juanita M. & American Bar Association, Tort & Insurance Practic. The Government Contractor Defense: A Fair Defense or the Contractor's Shield? LC 86-71631. 80p. 1986. 29.95 (*0-89707-252-9*, 519-0055) Amer Bar Assn.

***Madon, Suzanne.** French Villages. (Illus.). 136p. 2000. 29.95 (*2-907670-30-1*, Pub. by La Maison) IPG Chicago.

***Madonick, Michael D.** Waking the Deaf Dog. LC 99-39891. 78p. 2000. pap. 12.95 (*0-9661072-8-4*) Avocet Pr.

Madonna, John M., jt. auth. see Ciottone, Robert A.

Madonna, Margo, jt. auth. see Madonna, Salvino.

Madonna, Richard G. Orbital Mechanics. LC 88-29051. (Foundation Ser.). 126p. (C). 1997. 52.50 (*0-89464-010-0*) Krieger.

***Madonna, Salvino & Madonna, Margo.** A Pinch of This & a Pinch of That: The Cooking Treasures of Our Fairytale Italian Restaurant, Mama Lena's Italian Kitchen. (Illus.). 280p. 1999. pap. 29.95 (*0-7392-0457-2*, PO3762) Morris Pubng.

Madore, Barry F. & Tully, Brent R., eds. Galaxy Distances & Deviations from Universal Expansion. 1986. text 169.50 (*90-277-2277-3*) Kluwer Academic.

Madore, Barry F, jt. auth. see Arp, Halton C.

***Madore, Georges.** The Rosary: Contemplating the Mystery. 112p. 2000. pap. 4.95 (*0-8198-6471-4*) Pauline Bks.

Madore, J. An Introduction to Noncommutative Differential Geometry & Its Physical Applications. LC 99-11964. (London Mathematical Society Lecture Note Ser.: No. 257). 330p. (C). 1999. pap. text 35.95 (*0-521-65991-4*) Cambridge U Pr.

Madore, Michael, ed. see Acker, Kathy, et al.

***Madott, Darlene.** Mazilli's Shoes. (Drama Ser.: Vol. 17). (ENG & ITA.). 128p. 1999. pap. 13.00 (*1-55071-097-4*, Pub. by Guernica Editions) Paul & Co Pubs.

Madou, Marc. Fundamentals of Microfabrication. LC 96-43344. 608p. (C). 1997. boxed set 99.95 (*0-8493-9451-1*, 9451) CRC Pr.

Madou, Marc J. & Morrison, S. Roy. Chemical Sensing with Solid State Devices. 556p. 1989. text 166.00 (*0-12-464965-3*) Acad Pr.

Madous, H. Michael & Newman, Eric P. The First Official U. S. Coins: The Flag Connection. 3rd ed. Alberts, Robert C. et al, eds. (Flag Plaza Standard Ser.: Third Special Edition). 6p. 1989. reprint ed. pap. 1.50 (*0-934021-33-3*) Natl Flag Foun.

Madow, Glenn. MCSE Exam Notes: Networking Essentials. LC 98-85670. (Illus.). 368p. 1998. pap. 19.99 (*0-7821-2291-4*) Sybex.

Madow, Leo. Anger. LC 75-162773. 132p. 1974. pap. 6.95 (*0-684-13688-0*, Scribners Ref) Mac Lib Ref.

Madox, Ford B. The Diary of Madox Brown. Surtees, Virginia, ed. LC 81-51344. (Paul Mellon Centre for Studies in British Art). (Illus.). 320p. (C). 1981. 47.50 (*0-300-02743-5*) Yale U Pr.

Madox, Thomas. Baronia Anglica. LC 79-8369. reprint ed. 78.50 (*0-404-18358-1*) AMS Pr.

— History & Antiquities of the Exchequer, 2 Vols, Set. 2nd ed. 1969. reprint ed. 60.00 (*0-8377-2426-0*, Rothman) W S Hein.

***Madra, Amandeeps.** Warrior Saints: Three Centuries of the Sikh Military Tradition. 182p. 1999. 49.50 (*1-86064-490-2*, Pub. by I B T) St Martin.

Madras, Neal & Slade, G. The Self-Avoiding Walk. (Illus.). 448p. 1996. pap. 36.50 (*0-8176-3891-1*) Birkhauser.

Madras, Neal & Slade, Gordon. The Self-Avoiding Walk. LC 92-28276. (Probability & Its Applications Ser.). xiv, 425p. 1992. 68.00 (*0-8176-3589-0*) Birkhauser.

***Madras, Neal Noah.** Monte Carlo Methods. LC 00-39810. (Fields Institute Communications Ser.: Vol. 26). 228p. 2000. 69.00 (*0-8218-1992-5*) Am Math.

Madras, Ronald. The Catholic Church & Antisemitism: Poland, 1933-1939. LC 94-4488. (Studies in Antisemitism: Vol. 1). 429p. 1994. text 59.00 (*3-7186-5568-3*) Gordon & Breach.

Madray, George. The End. LC 97-60595. 208p. 1997. pap. 9.95 (*1-883893-91-7*) WinePress Pub.

Madrazo, Beatrice, jt. auth. see Shirkhoda, Ali.

Madrazo, Gerry M., Jr., ed. Sourcebook for Science Supervisors. 4th ed. 134p. 1993. pap. text 17.95 (*0-87355-114-1*) Natl Sci Tchrs.

Madrelle, Alexandre. Strength Calculations for Oil Country Tubular Goods. 1956. pap. 60.00 (*2-7108-0003-9*, Pub. by Edits Technip) Enfield Pubs NH.

Madreperla, Steven A. & McCuen, Brooks. Macular Hole: Pathogenesis, Diagnosis, & Treatment. LC 98-20598. (Illus.). 192p. 1998. pap. text 59.95 (*0-7506-9960-4*) Buttrwrth-Heinemann.

Madrick, Jeffrey. The End of Affluence: The Causes & Consequences of America's Economic Dilemma. LC 97-14372. 240p. 1997. pap. 12.00 (*0-375-75033-9*) Random.

***Madrick, Jeffrey.** Perspectives on Economics. 2000. pap. 12.95 (*0-87078-444-7*) Century Foundation.

Madrid Conference on Optimun Currency Areas Staff. The Economics of Common Currencies: Proceedings. Johnson, Harry G. & Swoboda, Alexander K., eds. LC 73-76382. (Illus.). 302p. reprint ed. pap. 93.70 (*0-8357-8109-7*, 203393500087) Bks Demand.

Madrid, Luis, ed. see Lenin, Vladimir Il'ich.

Madrid, Luis, ed. see Marx, Karl & Engels, Friedrich.

Madrid, Luis, ed. & intro. see Mandela, Nelson.

Madrid, Mary. Patterns of Rogerian Knowing. LC 96-29676. 1996. 25.95 (*0-88737-688-6*) Natl League Nurse.

Madrid, Mary & Manhart Barrett, Elizabeth A., eds. Rogers' Scientific Art of Nursing Practice. LC 94-202074. 451p. 1994. 33.95 (*0-88737-608-8*, 15-2610, NLN Pr) Natl League Nurse.

Madrid, Patrick. Any Friend of God's Is a Friend of Mine. 134p. 1996. pap. 9.99 (*0-9642610-9-X*) Basilica Pr.

— Pope Fiction: Answers to 30 Myths & Misconceptions about the Papacy. 345p. 1999. pap. 14.99 (*0-9642610-0-6*) Basilica Pr.

Madrid, Patrick, ed. Surprised by Truth: 11 Converts Give the Biblical & Historical Reasons for Becoming Catholic. 280p. (Orig.). 1994. pap. 13.99 (*0-9642610-8-1*) Basilica Pr.

Madrid, Philip E. & Sun, Shih W. Ssri Dev Desgn Procs Win. LC 92-23863. (Six Sigma Research Institute Ser.). 1992. pap. text 16.95 (*0-201-63424-4*) Addison-Wesley.

Madrid, Raul M. Overexposed: U. S. Banks Confront the Third World Debt Crisis. 260p. 1990. pap. 35.00 (*0-931035-50-3*) IRRC Inc DC.

Madrid, Renato E. DevilWings. LC 96-946567. 270p. 1997. pap. text 19.00 (*971-550-228-8*, Pub. by Ateneo de Manila Univ Pr) UH Pr.

— Southern Harvest: A Collection of Stories. viii, 187p. (Orig.). 1987. pap. 15.00 (*971-10-0297-3*, Pub. by New Day Pub) Cellar.

Madrigal. Immunogenetics: Advances & Education the First Congress of the Slovak Foundation, No. 35. LC 97-17214. 292p. 1997. text 174.00 (*0-7923-4613-0*) Kluwer Academic.

Madrigal, Antonio, tr. see Krudwig, Vickie L.

Madrigal, Antonio, tr. see Krudwig, Vickie L. & Brown, Craig McFarland.

Madrigal, Antonio H. Eagle & the Rainbow: Timeless Tales from Mexico. LC 96-46159. (Fulcrum Kids Ser.). (Illus.). 1997. 15.95 (*1-55591-317-2*) Fulcrum Pub.

— Erandi's Braids. LC 97-49631. (Illus.). 32p. (J). (ps-3). 1999. 15.99 (*0-399-23212-5*) Putnam Pub Group.

***Madrigal, Antonio Hernandez.** Blanca's Feather. (Illus.). 32p. (J). (gr. k-3). 2000. 15.95 (*0-87358-743-X*, Rising Moon Bks) Northland AZ.

Madrigal, Johnny, jt. ed. see Schifter, Jacobo.

Madrigal, Jose A., ed. New Historicism & the Comedia: Poetics, Politics & Praxis. LC 97-66177. (ENG & SPA.). 236p. 1997. pap. 30.00 (*0-89295-087-0*) Society Sp & Sp-Am.

Madrigal, Jose A., jt. auth. see McCrary, William C.

Madrigal, Jose A., ed. see Muzaurrieta, Jose M.

Madrigal, Jose A., ed. see Valerio, Juan F.

Madrigal, Lorena. Statistics for Anthropology. (Illus.). 252p. (C). 1998. text 64.95 (*0-521-57116-2*); pap. text 24.95 (*0-521-57786-1*) Cambridge U Pr.

Madrigal, M. & Ramondino, Salvatore. See It & Say It in Itallian. 1961. mass mkt. 6.99 (*0-451-16821-6*) NAL.

Madrigal, Margarita. First Steps in Spanish. 1987. pap. text 16.20 (*0-13-319153-2*) P-H.

— Madrigal's Magic Key to Spanish. (Illus.). 512p. 1989. pap. 11.95 (*0-385-41095-6*) Doubleday.

— Open Door to Spanish, Bk. 1. (Illus.). 223p. (C). (gr. 7-12). 1980. audio 45.00 (*0-686-77563-5*, 58471) Prentice ESL.

— Open Door to Spanish, Bk. 1. (Illus.). 223p. (YA). (gr. 7-12). 1980. pap. text 5.25 (*0-88345-420-3*, 18469) Prentice ESL.

— Open Door to Spanish, Bk. 2. (Open Door to Spanish Ser.). 222p. (J). (gr. 7-12). 1981. teacher ed. 1.50 (*0-88345-487-4*, 18474); pap. text 5.25 (*0-88345-427-0*, 18470); audio 45.00 (*0-686-77684-4*, 58472) Prentice ESL.

— Open Door to Spanish: A Conversation Course for Beginners, Level 1, Bk. 1. 2nd ed. LC 94-22581. 256p. 1994. pap. 37.60 (*0-13-181520-2*) P-H.

— Open Door to Spanish: A Conversation Course for Beginners, Level 2, Vol. 2. 2nd ed. (Illus.). 272p. (C). 1994. pap. text 39.60 (*0-13-181538-5*) P-H.

— See It & Say It in Spanish. (Orig.). 1961. mass mkt. 6.99 (*0-451-16837-2*, Sig) NAL.

Madrigal, Margarita & Dulac. Open the Door to French. (C). 1987. pap. text 19.20 (*0-13-637232-5*) P-H.

Madrigal, Margarita & Dulac, Colette. First Steps in French. (Illus.). (gr. 4-7). 1964. pap. text 3.25 (*0-88345-176-X*, 17473) Prentice ESL.

— See It & Say It in French. 1963. mass mkt. 6.99 (*0-451-16347-8*) NAL.

Madrigal, Margarita & Halpert, Inge. See It & Say It in German. (Orig.). 1962. mass mkt. 6.99 (*0-451-16678-7*) NAL.

Madrigal Pana, Johnny, jt. auth. see Schifter, Jacobo.

Madrigal, Sylvia. Farms: Big Book. (Wonders! Ser.). (Illus.). 24p. (Orig.). (J). (gr. 1-3). 1992. pap. text 29.95 (*1-56334-063-1*) Hampton-Brown.

— Farms: Small Book. (Wonders! Ser.). (Illus.). 24p. (Orig.). (J). (gr. 1-3). 1992. pap. text 6.00 (*1-56334-069-0*) Hampton-Brown.

— Granjas: Big Book. (Que Maravilla! Ser.). (SPA., Illus.). 24p. (Orig.). (J). (gr. 1-3). 1992. pap. 29.95 (*1-56334-024-0*) Hampton-Brown.

— Granjas: Small Book. (Que Maravilla! Ser.). (SPA., Illus.). 24p. (Orig.). (J). (gr. 1-3). 1992. pap. 6.00 (*1-56334-038-0*) Hampton-Brown.

Madrigana, Rosa M. Whiplash Injuries: Medical Subject Analysis & Research Guide with Bibliography. LC 83-45539. 140p. 1985. 47.50 (*0-88164-094-8*); pap. 44.50 (*0-88164-095-6*) ABBE Pubs Assn.

Madriz, Esther. Nothing Bad Happens to Good Girls: Fear of Crime in Women's Lives. LC 96-37659. 192p. 1997. 40.00 (*0-520-20291-0*, Pub. by U CA Pr); pap. 15.95 (*0-520-20855-2*, Pub. by U CA Pr) Cal Prin Full Svc.

Madron, Frantisek, jt. auth. see Veverka, Vladimir.

Madron, Thomas W. Local Area Networks: New Technologies, Emerging Standards. 3rd ed. 400p. 1994. pap. 29.95 (*0-471-00959-8*) Wiley.

Madron, Thomas W. Network Security in the 90's: Issues & Solutions for Managers. LC 92-7427. 304p. 1992. pap. 32.95 (*0-471-54777-8*) Wiley.

Madron, Thomas W., et al. Using Microcomputers in Research. (Quantitative Applications in the Social Sciences Ser.: Vol. 52). 1985. 10.95 (*0-8039-2457-7*) Sage.

***Madrona, Enrique.** Global Distributed Applications with Windows DNA. LC 99-89512. (Computing Library). 352p. 2000. 69.00 (*1-58053-086-9*) Artech Hse.

***Madrone, Hawk.** Weeding at Dawn: A Lesbian Country Life. LC 00-33142. 2000. pap. write for info. (*1-56023-207-2*, Alice St Edns) Harrington Pk.

Madry, Bobbi R. Job Seekers Guide. 1988. student ed. 10.95 (*0-87350-901-3*); pap. 19.95 (*0-87350-900-5*) Thomson Learn.

— Job Seekers Guide Curriculum. (Career Education Ser.). 1989. write for info. (*0-87350-369-4*) Milady Pub.

— Lesson Plans for Professional Estheticians. 1982. student ed. 17.95 (*0-87350-357-0*) Milady Pub.

— Milady Illustrated Cosmetology Dictionary. (Illus.). 1985. 27.95 (*0-87350-412-7*) Milady Pub.

Madry, Bobbi R., jt. auth. see Vega, Jo-Ann.

Madry, Bobbi R., ed. see Martel, Gloria.

Madsen. Engineering Drawing & Design. 976p. 1997. pap. text 19.95 (*0-8273-8155-7*) Delmar.

— Engineering Drawing & Design. 2nd ed. 976p. 1996. text 69.95 (*0-8273-8156-5*) Delmar.

***Madsen.** Engineering Drawing & Design. 3rd ed. (Drafting Ser.). 2001. 66.75 (*0-7668-1634-6*); 18.50 (*0-7668-1636-2*) Delmar.

Madsen. Secrets Cat Language Premium. 1998. pap. text 4.95 (*0-13-020720-9*) P-H.

Madsen, jt. auth. see Jefferis.

Madsen, tr. see Jackins, Harvey & Meyer.

Madsen, Albert A., jt. auth. see Curtis, Edward L.

Madsen, Axel. Chanel: A Woman of Her Own. (Illus.). 400p. 1995. pap. 15.95 (*0-8050-1639-2*, Owl) H Holt & Co.

— The Deal Maker: How William C. Durant Made General Motors. LC 99-11639. 310p. 1999. 30.00 (*0-471-28327-4*) Wiley.

— Forbidden Lovers: Hollywood's Greatest Secret--Female Stars Who Loved Other Women. (Illus.). 368p. 1995. 19.95 (*1-55972-275-4*, Birch Ln Pr) Carol Pub Group.

— Forbidden Lovers: Hollywood's Greatest Secret--Female Stars Who Loved Other Women. (Illus.). 240p. 1996. mass mkt. 5.99 (*0-8065-8005-4*, Citadel Stars) Carol Pub Group.

***Madsen, Axel.** John Jacob Astor: America's First Multimillionaire. 336p. 2001. 30.00 (*0-471-38503-4*) Wiley.

An Asterisk (*) at the beginning of an entry indicates that the title is appearing for the first time.

Madsen, Benedicte & Willert, Soren. Survival in the Organization: Gunnar Hjelholt Looks Back at the Concentration Camp from an Organizational Perspective. Matteson, Edith, tr. (Illus.). 96p. (C). 1996. pap. 9.95 (*87-7288-539-4*, Pub. by Aarhus Univ Pr) David Brown.

Madsen, Betty M. & Madsen, Brigham D. North to Montana! Jehus, Bullwackers, & Mule Skinners on the Montana Trail. LC 78-60240. (University of Utah Publications in the American West: No. 13). (Illus.). 318p. reprint ed. pap. 98.60 (*0-8357-4376-4*, 203720700007) Bks Demand.

— North to Montana! Jehus, Bullwhackers & Mule Skinners on the Montana Trail. 320p. 1998. pap. 21.95 (*0-87421-259-6*) Utah St U Pr.

Madsen, Bjarne, et al, eds. Modelling the Economy & the Environment. LC 96-13010. (Illus.). 352p. 1996. text 127.00 (*3-540-60780-3*) Spr-Verlag.

Madsen, Borg. Structural Behaviour of Timber. 456p. 1992. 72.00 (*0-614-16836-8*, TEL01-1) Am Soc Civil Eng.

Madsen, Brigham D. Against the Grain: Memoirs of a Western Historian. LC 98-17518. (Illus.). 400p. 1998. 31.95 (*1-56085-113-9*) Signature Bks.

— Bannock of Idaho. LC 96-214885. (Idaho Yesterdays Ser.). 1996. reprint ed. pap. 15.95 (*0-89301-189-4*) U of Idaho Pr.

***Madsen, Brigham D.** Chief Pocatello: The White Plume. LC 99-45149. (Idaho Yesterdays Ser.). 150p. 1999. pap. 14.95 (*0-89301-222-X*) U of Idaho Pr.

Madsen, Brigham D. Chief Pocatello: The "White Plume" LC 86-6719. (Bonneville Bks.). 154p. reprint ed. pap. 47.80 (*0-7837-3963-X*, 204379200011) Bks Demand.

— Corinne, the Gentile Capital of Utah. LC 80-50202. (Illus.). xii, 331p. 1980. 17.50 (*0-913738-30-1*) Utah St Hist Soc.

— The Lemhi: Sacajawea's People. LC 78-53137. (Illus.). (Orig.). 1980. pap. 7.95 (*0-87004-267-X*) Caxton.

— The Lemhi: Sacajawea's People. LC 78-53137. (Illus.). 214p. (Orig.). reprint ed. pap. 66.40 (*0-8357-4120-6*, 203695100005) Bks Demand.

— The Northern Shoshoni. LC 78-53138. (Illus.). 262p. 2000. pap. 18.95 (*0-87004-266-1*) Caxton.

Madsen, Brigham D., ed. The Shoshoni Frontier & the Bear River Massacre. (Illus.). 304p. 1995. reprint ed. pap. 17.95 (*0-87480-494-9*) U of Utah Pr.

Madsen, Brigham D., jt. auth. see Madsen, Betty M.

Madsen, Brigham D., ed. see Hudson, John.

Madsen, Brigham D., ed. see Roberts, B. H.

Madsen, Brigham D., ed. & intro. see Roberts, B. H.

Madsen, C. K. & Zhao, J.H. Optical Filter Design & Analysis: A Signal Processing Approach. LC 98-34993. (Wiley Series in Microwave & Optical Engineering). 432p. 1999. 84.95 (*0-471-18373-3*) Wiley.

Madsen, Carol C. In Their Own Words: The Women & the Story of Nauvoo. LC 93-41762. 250p. 1994. 14.95 (*0-87579-770-9*) Deseret Bk.

— Journey to Zion: Voices from the Mormon Trail. LC 97-2043. xvii, 750p. 1997. 25.95 (*1-57345-244-0*) Deseret Bk.

Madsen, Carol C., ed. Battle for the Ballot: Essays on Woman Suffrage in Utah, 1870-1896. LC 96-51229. 336p. 1997. 39.95 (*0-87421-222-7*); pap. 19.95 (*0-87421-223-5*) Utah St U Pr.

Madsen, Charles H., Jr. & Madsen, Clifford K. Teaching Discipline: A Positive Approach for Educational Development. 4th ed. LC 99-230186. 350p. (C). 1981. pap. text 29.95 (*0-89892-178-3*) Contemp Pub Co of Raleigh.

Madsen, Charles H., Jr., jt. auth. see Madsen, Clifford K.

Madsen, Chris. Natural Cats. LC 96-30487. 128p. 1997. 14.95 (*0-87605-679-6*) Howell Bks.

— Natural Dogs. LC 97-31267. 128p. 1998. 17.95 (*0 87605 585 4*) Howell Bks.

— The Royal Navy & German Naval Disarmament, 1942-47. LC 97-30156. (Naval Policy & History Ser.: Vol. 4). 304p. (C). 1998. text 59.50 (*0-7146-4823-X*, Pub. by F Cass Pubs); pap. text 26.50 (*0-7146-4373-4*, Pub. by F Cass Pubs) Intl Spec Bk.

Madsen, Christine. Drinking & Driving. LC 89-31584. (Understanding Drugs Ser.). (Illus.). 32p. (J). (gr. 5-7). 1989. lib. bdg. 20.80 (*0-531-10799-X*) Watts.

***Madsen, Clifford K.** Vision 2020: The Housewright Symposium on the Future of Music Education. 240p. (Orig.). 2000. pap. 26.00 (*1-56545-128-7*, 1660) MENC.

Madsen, Clifford K. & Kuhn, Terry L. Contemporary Music Education. 2nd rev. ed. LC 77-90672. 186p. (C). 1994. pap. text 17.95 (*0-89892-119-8*) Contemp Pub Co of Raleigh.

Madsen, Clifford K. & Madsen, Charles H., Jr. Experimental Research in Music. 3rd ed. (Illus.). 1996. reprint ed. pap. text 27.95 (*0-89892-152-X*) Contemp Pub Co of Raleigh.

Madsen, Clifford K. & Moore, Randall S. Experimental Research in Music - Workbook in Design & Statistical Tests. rev. ed. 1978. 34.95 (*0-89892-017-5*) Contemp Pub Co of Raleigh.

Madsen, Clifford K. & Prickett, Carol A., eds. Applications of Research in Music Behavior. LC 85-24690. (Illus.). 384p. 1991. pap. text 24.95 (*0-8173-0542-4*) U of Ala Pr.

Madsen, Clifford K. & Yarbrough, Cornelia. Competency-Based Music Education. 185p. (C). 1985. reprint ed. pap. text 27.95 (*0-89892-061-2*) Contemp Pub Co of Raleigh.

Madsen, Clifford K., et al. Research in Music Behavior: Modifying Music Behavior in the Classroom. LC 74-16362. (Illus.). 285p. reprint ed. pap. 88.40 (*0-608-10898-7*, 202032500017) Bks Demand.

Madsen, Clifford K., jt. auth. see Madsen, Charles H., Jr.

Madsen, Clifford K., jt. auth. see Yarbrough, Cornelia.

Madsen, Daniel. Forgotten Fleet: The Mothball Navy. LC 99-30936. 1999. 36.95 (*1-55750-543-8*) Naval Inst Pr.

Madsen, David. Confessions of a Flesh-Eater. (Dedalus Original Fiction in Paperback Ser.). 224p. (Orig.). 1998. pap. 12.99 (*1-873982-47-X*, Pub. by Dedalus) Subterranean Co.

— The National University: Enduring Dream of the U. S. A. LC 66-22036. 179p. reprint ed. pap. 55.50 (*0-608-16645-6*, 202768300055) Bks Demand.

— Successful Dissertations & Theses: A Guide to Graduate Student Research from Proposal to Completion. LC 82-49039. (Joint Publication in the Jossey-Bass Higher Education Series & the Jossey-Bass Social & Behavioral Science Ser.). 192p. reprint ed. pap. 59.60 (*0-7837-2550-7*, 204270900006) Bks Demand.

— Successful Dissertations & Theses: A Guide to Graduate Student Research from Proposal to Completion. 2nd ed. LC 91-21687. (Higher & Adult Education - Social & Behavioral Science Ser.). 238p. 1991. reprint ed. text 25.00 (*1-55542-389-2*) Jossey-Bass.

Madsen, David & Jefferis, Alan. Print Reading for Architecture & Construction Technology. 415p. 1994. mass mkt. 31.75 (*0-8273-5429-0*) Delmar.

***Madsen, David & Rawls.** AutoCAD LT 2000: Basics Through Advanced. 800p. 2000. pap. 54.00 (*0-13-018174-9*) P-H.

Madsen, David & Rhode, David, eds. Across the West: Human Population Movement & the Expansion of the Numa. 256p. (C). 1994. text 50.00 (*0-87480-465-5*) U of Utah Pr.

Madsen, David A. AutoCAD LT for Windows 95: Basics Through Advanced. LC 97-9271. 740p. 1997. pap. 66.00 (*0-13-596644-2*) P-H.

— AutoCAD LT 98: Basics Through Advanced. LC 99-31018. (Illus.). 800p. 1999. pap. 60.00 (*0-13-085100-0*) P-H.

— Drafting: Syllabus. 1974. pap. text 10.95 (*0-89420-070-4*, 107015); audio 104.35 (*0-89420-140-9*, 107000) Natl Book.

— Engineering Drawing & Design. 2nd ed. (Drafting (w-o Blueprint Rdg.) Ser.). 976p. (C). 1995. mass mkt. 104.95 (*0-8273-6720-1*) Delmar.

— Engineering Drawing & Design. 2nd ed. (IU-Mechanical Technology Ser.). 976p. 1996. teacher ed. 10.00 (*0-8273-7429-1*) Delmar.

— Fundamentals of Engineering Drawing I. (Drafting Ser.). 1993. 25.00 (*0-8273-5239-5*) Delmar.

— Geometric Dimensioning & Tolerancing: Basic Fundamentals. rev. ed. LC 98-46353. (Illus.). 351p. 1999. pap. text, teacher ed. 34.64 (*1-56637-537-1*) Goodheart.

— Print Reading for Engineering & Manufacturing Technology. 96p. 1994. pap. text, teacher ed. 15.50 (*0-8273-5236-0*) Delmar.

— Print Reading for Engineering & Manufacturing Technology. 407p. 1994. pap. 32.75 (*0-8273-5235-2*) Delmar.

— Problems Workbook, Engineering Drawing & Design. 2nd ed. (Mechanical Technology Ser.). 976p. (C). 1996. text, student ed. 19.95 (*0-8273-7525-5*) Delmar.

Madsen, David A. & Jefferis, Alan. Architectural Drafting & Design. 3rd ed. (Drafting Ser.). 800p. (C). 1995. mass mkt. 86.95 (*0-8273-6749-X*) Delmar.

— Print Reading for Architecture & Construction Technology. 72p. (C). 1994. text, teacher ed. 16.50 (*0-8273-5430-4*) Delmar.

***Madsen, David A. & Palma, Ronald M.** Architectural Autocad / LC 00-42944. 2000. write for info. (*1-56637-748-X*) Goodheart.

Madsen, David A. & Rawls, Rod R. AutoCAD LT 97: Basics Through Advanced. 2nd ed. LC 98-11897. 758p. (C). 1998. pap. 63.00 (*0-13-080896-2*) P-H.

Madsen, David A. & Shumaker, Terence M. AutoCAD & Its Applications: Advanced, Release 13 for Windows. LC 96-23891. (Illus.). 560p. (Orig.). (C). 1996. pap. text 32.80 (*1-56637-183-X*) Goodheart.

Madsen, David A. & Shumaker, Terence M. AutoCAD & Its Applications: Basics, Release 13 for Windows. LC 95-9502. (Illus.). 1119p. (Orig.). (C). 1995. pap. text 39.96 (*1-56637-182-1*) Goodheart.

Madsen, David A. & Shumaker, Terence M. Civil Drafting Technolgy. 3rd ed. LC 97-9270. 295p. 1997. pap. text 52.00 (*0-13-751181-7*, Pub. by P-H) S&S Trade.

***Madsen, David A. & Shumaker, Terence M.** Civil Drafting Technology. 4th ed. 350p. 2000. pap. text 53.33 (*0-13-087155-9*) P-H.

Madsen, David A., et al. Engineering Drawing & Design. 1024p. 13.95 (*0-685-56321-9*) Delmar.

— Engineering Drawing & Design. 1024p. 1991. pap. 20.50 (*0-8273-4747-2*); trans. 107.13 (*0-8273-4749-9*) Delmar.

— Engineering Drawing & Design. 1024p. 1992. disk 53.60 (*0-8273-4748-0*) Delmar.

— Engineering Drawing & Design, Vol. 1. 1024p. 1991. pap., teacher ed. 27.00 (*0-8273-2603-3*) Delmar.

— Engineering Drawing & Design, Vol. II. 1024p. teacher ed. write for info. (*0-8273-4765-0*) Delmar.

— Fundamentals of Drafting Technology. rev. ed. LC 93-10536. Orig. Title: Engineering Drawing & Design. 604p. (C). 1993. pap. text 67.95 (*0-8273-5238-7*) Delmar.

Madsen, David A., jt. auth. see Jefferis, Alan.

Madsen, David A., jt. auth. see Shumaker, Terence M.

Madsen, David B. Exploring the Fremont. pap. 15.00 (*0-940378-35-3*) Utah Mus Natural Hist.

— A Preliminary Assessment of Archeological Resources Within the Grand Staircase-Escalante National Monument, Utah. LC 97-150128. (Circular of the Utah Geological Survey Ser.: Vol. 95). (Illus.). 23p. 1997. pap. 3.00 (*1-55791-605-5*, C-95) Utah Geological Survey.

***Madsen, David B. & Metcalf, Michael D.** Intermountain Archaeology. LC 99-46478. (Anthropological Papers). 219p. 2000. pap. 45.00 (*0-87480-611-9*) U of Utah Pr.

Madsen, David B. & O'Connell, James F., eds. Man & Environment in the Great Basin. (SAA Papers: No. 2). 248p. 1982. pap. 25.00 (*0-932839-02-9*) Soc Am Arch.

Madsen, David B., jt. auth. see Hawkins, Bruce R.

Madsen, David B., jt. auth. see Janetski, Joel.

Madsen, Deborah L. American Exceptionalism. LC 98-22620. 186p. 1998. pap. text 18.00 (*1-57806-108-3*) U Pr of Miss.

***Madsen, Deborah L.** Feminist Theory & Literary Practice. LC 00-9133. 2000. pap. write for info. (*0-7453-1601-8*, Pub. by Pluto GBR) Stylus Pub VA.

Madsen, Deborah L. Post-Colonial Literatures: Expanding the Canon LC 99-21628. 1999. write for info. (*0-7453-1515-1*) Pluto GBR.

***Madsen, Deborah L.** Post-Colonial Literatures: Expanding the Canon. LC 99-21628. 1999. pap. 22.50 (*0-7453-1510-0*) Pluto GBR.

Madsen, Deborah L. Rereading Allegory: A Narrative Approach to Genre. LC 94-25350. 1994. text 45.00 (*0-312-12298-5*) St Martin.

Madsen, Deborah L., ed. Visions of America since 1492. LC 94-12856. 1994. text 45.00 (*0-312-12281-0*) St Martin.

Madsen, Donna L. & Nelson, Lynda B. Micro-Typewriter: Tutorial Guide. 56p. 1986. pap. text 5.95 (*1-57094-041-X*) S E Warner Sftware.

— Micro-Typewriter: Tutorial Guide. 2nd ed. 58p. 1987. pap. text 5.95 (*1-57094-042-8*) S E Warner Sftware.

— Micro-Typewriter: Tutorial Guide. 3rd ed. 60p. 1988. pap. text 5.95 (*1-57094-043-6*) S E Warner Sftware.

— Micro-Typewriter: Tutorial Guide. 4th ed. 62p. 1989. pap. text 5.95 (*1-57094-044-4*) S E Warner Sftware.

— Micro-Typewriter: Tutorial Guide. 5th ed. 64p. 1992. pap. text 5.95 (*1-57094-045-2*) S E Warner Sftware.

Madsen, Douglas & Snow, Peter G. The Charismatic Bond: Political Behavior in Time of Crisis. (Illus.). 200p. 1996. pap. 18.50 (*0-674-10988-0*) HUP.

Madsen, Douglas, jt. auth. see Snow, Peter G.

Madsen, George F. Marshall's Iowa Title Opinions & Standards Annotated. 2nd ed. 65.00 (*0-327-12319-2*) LEXIS Pub.

Madsen, Harold S. Techniques in Testing. (Techniques in Teaching English As a Second Language Ser.). (Illus.). 224p. (C). 1983. pap. text 13.50 (*0-19-434132-1*) OUP.

Madsen, Henrick O., jt. auth. see Ditlevsen, Ove.

Madsen, Henrik, jt. auth. see Heclo, Hugh.

Madsen, Ib & Tornehave, Jergen. From Calculus to Cohomology: De Rham Cohomology & Characteristic Classes. 293p. (C). 1997. text 69.95 (*0-521-58059-5*); pap. text 27.95 (*0-521-58956-8*) Cambridge U Pr.

Madsen, Ib H. & Milgram, R. James. The Classifying Spaces for Surgery & Cobordism of Manifolds. LC 78-70311. (Annals of Mathematics Studies: No. 92). 292p. 1979. reprint ed. pap. 90.60 (*0-608-06634-6*, 206683100009) Bks Demand.

Madsen, J. B. & Cold, G. E. The Effects of Anaesthetics upon Cerebral Circulation & Metabolism. (Illus.). 150p. 1991. 71.95 (*0-387-82198-8*) Spr-Verlag.

Madsen, J. E. Flora of Ecuador No. 45: Cactaceae. (Opera Botanica Series B). 78p. 1989. pap. 40.00 (*87-88702-37-5*, Pub. by Coun Nordic Pubs) Balogh.

Madsen, James A., jt. illus. see Robinson, Timothy M.

Madsen, James H., Jr. Allosaurus Fragilis: A Revised Osteology. LC QE169.A3. (Bulletin Ser.: Vol. 109). (Illus.). 163p. 1976. pap. 9.00 (*1-55791-076-6*, B-109) Utah Geological Survey.

Madsen, Jane M., jt. auth. see Chunko, Shelby E.

Madsen, Jean. Educational Reform at the State Level: The Politics & Problems of Implementation. LC 93-9072. 1993. write for info. (*0-7507-0280-X*, Falmer Pr) Taylor & Francis.

— Educational Reform at the State Level: The Politics & Problems of Implementation. (Education Policy Perspectives Ser.). 192p. 1994. 75.00 (*0-7507-0206-0*, Falmer Pr) Taylor & Francis.

— Private & Public School Partnerships: Sharing Lessons about Decentralization. LC 96-12658. 240p. 1996. 79.95 (*0-7507-0536-1*, Falmer Pr); pap. 27.95 (*0-7507-0537-X*, Falmer Pr) Taylor & Francis.

Madsen, John. Geol 107: General Geology Course Notebook. 80p. (C). 1997. spiral bd. 18.95 (*0-7872-4407-4*, 41440701) Kendall-Hunt.

Madsen, Jon. The New Testament: A Rendering. pap. 29.50 (*0-86315-184-1*, 1869, Pub. by Floris Bks) Anthroposophic.

Madsen, Joyce & Madsen, Larry. Babe the Gallant Pig: A Study Guide. Friedland, J. & Kessler, R., eds. (Novel-Ties Ser.). (J). (gr. 4-5). 1996. pap. text 15.95 (*1-56982-634-X*) Lrn Links.

***Madsen, Julie.** Inner Views: Stories on the Strength of America. LC 99-37779. (Illus.). 352p. 1999. pap. 14.95 (*0-9633083-9-4*) Quixote Pubns.

Madsen, K. B. Theories of Motivation: A Comparative Study of Modern Theories of Motivation. 4th ed. LC 68-22338. 366p. reprint ed. pap. 113.50 (*0 608-11170-8*, 205086100062) Bks Demand.

Madsen, K. B. & Mos, Leendert P., eds. Annals of Theoretical Psychology, Vol. 3. LC 84-644088. 368p. 1985. 85.00 (*0-306-41972-6*, Plenum Trade) Perseus Pubng.

Madsen, Kate. Dog Days: A Scrapbook for My Best Friend. (Illus.). 80p. 1999. 12.95 (*0-87905-895-1*) Gibbs Smith Pub.

Madsen, Ken. Wild Rivers, Wild Lands. LC 97-153013. (Illus.). 120p. 1996. pap. text 24.95 (*1-896758-01-0*, Pub. by Lost Moose) Genl Dist Srvs.

Madsen, Larry, jt. auth. see Madsen, Joyce.

Madsen, Louise. Christian Community: An Introduction. pap. 3.95 (*0-86315-220-1*, 1913, Pub. by Floris Bks) Anthroposophic.

Madsen, Lynn. Rebounding from Childbirth: Toward Emotional Recovery. LC 93-40162. 192p. 1994. pap. 14.95 (*0-89789-348-4*, Bergin & Garvey) Greenwood.

Madsen, Mark S. The Dynamic Cosmos: Exploring the Physical Evolution of the Universe. LC 95-70841. (Illus.). 144p. (gr. 13). 1995. lib. bdg. 39.95 (*0-412-62300-5*) Chapman & Hall.

Madsen, Mark T. Medical Physics Handbook of Nuclear Medicine. (Illus.). 114p. (Orig.). (C). 1992. pap. text 16.95 (*0-944838-14-6*) Med Physics Pub.

Madsen, Michael. Burning in Paradise. 156p. 1998. pap. text 14.00 (*1-888277-06-8*) Incommcdo San Diego.

Madsen, Norman P. Basic Bible Commentary Vol. 20: John. Deming, Lynne M., ed. LC 94-10965. 160p. (Orig.). 1994. pap. 5.95 (*0-687-02639-3*) Abingdon.

— Basic Bible Commentary Vol. 23: First & Second Corinthians. Deming, Lynne M., ed. LC 94-10965. 160p. (Orig.). 1994. pap. 5.95 (*0-687-02643-1*) Abingdon.

Madsen, O. Lehrmann, et al, eds. Proceedings: ECOOP 'Ninety-Two, European Conference on Object-Oriented Programming, Utrecht, The Netherlands, June 29-July 3, 1992. LC 92-19991. (Lecture Notes in Computer Science Ser.: Vol. 615). x, 426p. 1992. 63.95 (*0-387-55668-0*) Spr-Verlag.

Madsen, R. Scott. The Bomber Mountain Crash: A Wyoming Mystery. rev. ed. LC 90-62431. (Illus.). 104p. 1990. 16.95 (*0-9624665-1-4*); pap. text 7.95 (*0-9624665-0-6*) Mtn Man Pub.

Madsen, Richard. China & the American Dream: A Moral Inquiry. LC 93-45003. (C). 1995. 35.00 (*0-520-08613-9*, Pub. by U CA Pr) Cal Prin Full Svc.

— China's Catholics: Tragedy & Hope in an Emerging Civil Society. LC 97-50613. (Illus.). 204p. 1998. 27.50 (*0-520-21326-2*, Pub. by U CA Pr) Cal Prin Full Svc.

Madsen, Richard E. The Sealed Book: An Interpretation of the Book of Revelation. 83p. 1998. pap. 14.95 (*1-890622-35-4*) Leathers Pub.

Madsen, Richard W. & Moeschberger, Melvin L. Statistical Concepts with Applications to Business & Economics. 2nd ed. (Illus.). 672p. (C). 1986. text 33.95 (*0-317-38353-1*) P-H.

Madsen, Richard W., jt. auth. see Isaacson, Dean L.

Madsen, Rick, ed. see Lisech, Howard & Lisech, Bonnie.

Madsen, Rick, ed. see Lisech, Howard, et al.

Madsen, Ross Martin. Perrywinkle's Magic Match. LC 95-45185. (Illus.). 40p. (J). (gr. 1-4). 1997. 13.99 (*0-8037-1108-5*, Dial Yng Read) Peng Put Young Read.

***Madsen, Ross Martin.** Perrywinkle's Magic Match, Vol. 1. (Easy-to-Read Ser.). 1999. pap. 3.99 (*0-14-038215-1*, PuffinBks) Peng Put Young Read.

Madsen, Roy P. Animated Film: Concepts, Methods, Uses. 1976. 26.95 (*0-8488-0830-4*) Amereon Ltd.

Madsen, Sharon, jt. ed. see McCulloch, Myrna T.

Madsen, Sheila & Gould, Bette. The Teacher's Book of Lists. 2nd ed. (Illus.). 336p. (J). (gr. k-6). 1994. pap. 19.95 (*0-673-36074-1*, GoodYrBooks) Addson-Wesley Educ.

Madsen, Stephan T. Sources of Art Nouveau. LC 75-26819. (Quality Paperbacks Ser.). (Illus.). 1976. pap. 10.95 (*0-306-80024-1*) Da Capo.

— Sources of Art Noveau. Christopherson, Ragnar, tr. LC 74-34464. (Architecture & Decorative Art Ser.). (Illus.). 488p. 1975. reprint ed. lib. bdg. 59.50 (*0-306-70733-0*) Da Capo.

Madsen, Steven K., jt. auth. see Crampton, C. Gregory.

Madsen, Stig T. State, Society, & Human Rights in South Asia. LC 96-900157. (C). 1996. 38.00 (*81-7304-138-5*, Pub. by Manohar) S Asia.

Madsen, Stig T., ed. State, Society & the Environment in South Asia. LC 98-128434. (Man & Nature Ser.: Vol. 3). 337p. 1999. text 55.00 (*0-7007-0614-3*, Pub. by Curzon Pr Ltd) UH Pr.

Madsen, Susan A. Growing up in Zion: True Stories of Young Pioneers Building the Kingdom. LC 96-22032. 1996. 14.95 (*1-57345-189-4*) Deseret Bk.

— I Walked to Zion: True Stories of Young Pioneers on the Mormon Trail. LC 94-404. ix, 182p. (YA). (gr. 6-12). 1994. 12.95 (*0-87579-848-9*) Deseret Bk.

— The Lord Needed a Prophet. 2nd ed. LC 96-31. (Illus.). 250p. (J). (gr. 3-6). 1996. 14.95 (*1-57345-088-X*) Deseret Bk.

— Second Rescue. LC 97-49662. xii, 148 p. 1998. write for info. (*1-57345-362-5*) Deseret Bk.

***Madsen, Susan Arrington & Woods, Fred E.** I Sailed to Zion: True Stories of Young Pioneers Who Crossed the Ocean. LC 00-23599. 2000. write for info. (*1-57345-651-9*) Deseret Bk.

Madsen, Svend A. Days with Diam. Jones, Glyn W., tr. 246p. 1995. pap. 24.00 (*1-870041-26-7*) Dufour.

— Virtue & Vice in the Middle Time. Ogier, James M., tr. LC 92-10596. (Library of World Literature in Translation: Vol. 29). (DAN & ENG.). 584p. 1992. text 20.00 (*0-8153-0606-7*) Garland.

Madsen, Tage K., ed. Advances in International Marketing: I, Vol. 8. 1996. 78.50 (*0-7623-0164-3*) Jai Pr.

Madsen, Torsten, ed. Multivariate Archaeology: Numerical Approaches in Scandinavian Archaeology. (Jutland Archaeological Society Publications: No. 21). (Illus.). 150p. (C). 1988. pap. 16.95 (*87-7288-047-3*, Pub. by Aarhus Univ Pr) David Brown.

Madsen, Truman G. Defender of the Faith: The B. H. Roberts Story. deluxe ed. 1994. 11.95 (*0-88494-950-8*) Bookcraft Inc.

— Four Essays on Love. 1995. pap. 4.95 (*1-57008-179-4*) Bookcraft Inc.

— Joseph Smith the Prophet. 1989. 16.95 (*0-88494-704-1*) Bookcraft Inc.

M

— The Radiant Life. 1994. 10.95 (*0-88494-938-9*) Bookcraft Inc.

Madsen, Wayne, ed. Genocide & Covert Operations in Africa, 1993-1999. LC 99-26128. (African Studies: Vol. 50). 568p. 1999. text 119.95 (*0-7734-8002-1*) E Mellen.

Madsen, Willard J. Conversational Sign Language II: An Intermediate-Advanced Manual of American Sign Language. 236p. 1972. pap. text 13.95 (*0-913580-00-7*, Clerc Bks) Gallaudet Univ Pr.

— Intermediate Conversational Sign Language. LC 82-81440. (Illus.). 400p. 1982. pap. text 21.95 (*0-913580-79-1*) Gallaudet Univ Pr.

Madsen, William. Virgin's Children: Life in an Aztec Village Today. LC 74-88900. 248p. 1970. reprint ed. lib. bdg. 69.50 (*0-8371-2098-5*, MAVC, Greenwood Pr) Greenwood.

***Madsen, William C.** Collaborative Therapy with Multi-Stressed Families: From Old Problems to New Futures. LC 99-39708. (Family Therapy Ser.). 350p. 1999. lib. bdg. 36.00 (*1-57230-490-1*) Guilford Pubns.

Madsen, William G., ed. see Milton, John.

Madson, Arthur. Blue-Eyed Boy. Spelius, Carol, ed. 59p. (Orig.). pap. 7.95 (*0-941363-13-9*) Lake Shore Pub.

— Coming up Sequined. 46p. (Orig.). 1991. pap. 7.50 (*1-878660-11-X*) Fireweed WI.

Madson, J. Outdoor Life Deer Hunter's Encyclopedia. 1985. 49.95 (*0-943822-53-X*) Times Mir Mag Bk Div.

Madson, John. Stories from under the Sky. LC 87-34486. (Iowa Heritage Collection). (Illus.). 206p. 1988. reprint ed. pap. 12.95 (*0-8138-0077-3*) Iowa St U Pr.

***Madson, John.** Up on the River: With the People & Wildlife of the Upper Mississippi. 2000. pap. 16.95 (*1-58574-188-4*) Lyons Pr.

Madson, John. Where the Sky Began: Land of the Tallgrass Prairie. rev. ed. LC 95-38585. (Illus.). 340p. 1995. pap. 24.95 (*0-8138-2515-6*) Iowa St U Pr.

Madtes, Richard E. The Ithaca Chapter of Joyce's Ulysses. LC 83-9248. (Studies in Modern Literature: No. 27). 172p. reprint ed. pap. 53.40 (*0-8357-1460-8*, 207050500097) Bks Demand.

Madu, Christian N. Managing Green Technologies for Global Competitiveness. LC 95-19468. 280p. 1996. 67.95 (*0-89930-827-9*, Quorum Bks) Greenwood.

— Strategic Planning in Technology Transfer to Less Developed Countries. LC 91-22020. 224p. 1992. 57.95 (*0-89930-629-2*, MTY, Quorum Bks) Greenwood.

Madu, Christian N., ed. Management of New Technologies for Global Competitiveness. LC 92-31712. 400p. 1993. 65.00 (*0-89930-713-2*, MNH, Quorum Bks) Greenwood.

Madu, Christian N. & Kuei, Chu-Hua. Experimental Statistical Designs & Analysis in Simulation Modeling. LC 92-37467. 224p. 1993. 69.50 (*0-89930-695-0*, MXS/, Quorum Bks) Greenwood.

— Strategic Total Quality Mangement: Corporate Performance & Product Quality. LC 94-32082. 224p. 1995. 55.00 (*0-89930-817-1*, Quorum Bks) Greenwood.

Madu, Raphael O. African Symbols, Proverbs & Myths: The Hermeneutics of Destiny. LC 91-42866. (Studies in African & African-American Culture: Vol. 3). 327p. (C). 1992. text 59.80 (*0-8204-1863-3*) P Lang Pubng.

***Maduakor, Casmir.** Towards a Peaceful Resolution of Conflicts in Nigeria: With Particular Reference to Some Aspects of Martin Luther King, Jr.'s & Catholic Social Teachings on Nonviolence. (European University Studies: Vol. 679). 218p. 1999. pap. 35.95 (*3-631-35585-8*) P Lang Pubng.

Maduell, Charles R., Jr. The Census Tables for the French Colony at Louisiana from 1699 through 1732. LC 76-183748. (Illus.). 181p. 2000. reprint ed. pap. 21.00 (*0-8063-0490-1*, Pub. by Clearfield Co) ACCESS Pubs Network.

Madugula, I. S. The Acarya: Sankara of Kaladi, a Story. 143p. (C). 1991. reprint ed. text 16.00 (*81-208-0009-5*, Pub. by Motilal Bnarsidass) S Asia.

Madugula, Marty K. & Kennedy, J. B. Single & Compound Angle Members: Structural Analysis & Design. (Illus.). 372p. 1986. mass mkt. 141.50 (*0-85334-364-0*) Elsevier.

Maduno, Chukwudi O. Nnamdi Azikiwe: The Vision of the New Africa. (Ekumeku Universal Foundation Ser.). 72p. (Orig.). 1996. pap. text 10.00 (*0-9644596-4-7*) Ekumeku Commun.

— Ohacracy: The Undercurrent of Africa-Centered Nationalism. (Illus.). 118p. (Orig.). 1995. pap. text 11.99 (*0-9644596-2-0*) Ekumeku Commun.

— White Magic: The Origins & Ideas of Black Mental & Cultural Colonialism. LC 95-201562. 279p. (Orig.). 1994. pap. 12.00 (*1-56411-085-0*) Untd Bros & Sis.

Madupu, Gangadhur, jt. auth. see Hanrahan, Edward J.

Madura. Financial Markets & Institutions. 5th ed. (SWC-Economics Ser.). 2000. pap., student ed. 18.00 (*0-324-02745-1*) Sth-Wstrn College.

— Intermediate Accounting 1/e. (SWC-Accounting). (C). 1995. pap. 17.95 (*0-314-05878-8*) S-W Pub.

— International Financial Management. 5th ed. LC 97-21527. (FN - Financial Mangement Ser.). 1997. pap. 68.95 (*0-538-87787-1*) S-W Pub.

***Madura.** International Financial Management. 6th ed. LC 99-26766. 660p. 1999. pap. 95.95 (*0-324-00955-0*) Sth-Wstrn College.

— International Financial Management. 6th ed. (SWC-Finance Ser.). 1999. pap., student ed. 19.75 (*0-324-01556-9*) Thomson Learn.

— International Financial Management. 7th ed. 2001. pap. 51.00 (*0-324-07174-4*) Sth-Wstrn College.

Madura. Introduction to Business. LC 96-26938. (GB - Business Basics Ser.). (C). 1997. text 78.95 (*0-538-87883-5*) S-W Pub.

***Madura.** Introduction To Business. 2000. 28.00 (*0-324-06474-8*) Sth-Wstrn College.

— Introduction to Business. 2nd ed. 2000. pap. 46.75 (*0-324-00675-6*) Thomson Learn.

— Web Tutor on Webct to Accompany Introduction to Business. 2000. pap. 19.00 (*0-324-06485-3*) Sth-Wstrn College.

Madura, Henryk, jt. ed. see Jankiewicz, Zdzislaw.

Madura, Jeff. Financial Markets & Institns 3. 3rd ed. LC 94-17238. (SWC-Finance). 786p. (C). 1995. mass mkt. 58.25 (*0-314-04160-5*) West Pub.

— Financial Markets & Institutions. 2nd ed. Fenton & Craig, eds. 717p. (C). 1992. text 61.00 (*0-314-87735-5*) West Pub.

— Financial Markets & Institutions. 4th ed. LC 97-23570. (FI - Financial Institutions Ser.). 1997. mass mkt. 119.25 (*0-538-87756-1*) S-W Pub.

— Financial Markets & Institutions. 5th ed. LC 99-52078. (SWC-Economics Ser.). 698p. 2000. pap. 91.95 (*0-324-02744-3*) Sth-Wstrn College.

— Global Portfolio Management for Institutional Investors. LC 95-44349. 192p. 1996. 57.95 (*1-56720-032-X*, Quorum Bks) Greenwood.

— International Financial Management, 3d. 3rd ed. Fenton & Craig, eds. LC 85-29501. (SWC-Finance). 728p. (C). 1991. mass mkt. 60.50 (*0-314-86272-2*) West Pub.

— International Financial Mgmt 4. 4th ed. LC 94-17237. (SWC-Finance). 784p. (C). 1994. mass mkt. 62.25 (*0-314-04161-3*) West Pub.

— Introduction to Business. LC 96-26938. 1997. mass mkt. 32.50 (*0-538-87884-3*) S-W Pub.

— Introduction to Business. LC 96-26938. 650p. 1997. write for info. (*0-314-09978-6*) West Pub.

— Introduction to Finite Management. Date not set. pap. text, student ed. 20.50 (*0-314-65704-5*); pap. text, student ed. write for info. (*0-314-65724-X*) West Pub.

Madura, Jeffrey M. Basic Accounting. (Illus.). 200p. (C). 1981. pap. text 14.95 (*0-916780-16-3*) CES Assocs.

— Interpreting Financial Reports for Decision Making. (Illus.). 170p. 1984. 37.95 (*0-916780-22-8*) CES Assocs.

***Madureira, Joe.** Battle Chasers: A Gathering of Heroes. 160p. 1999. pap. text 14.95 (*1-56389-538-2*, Pub. by DC Comics) Time Warner.

***Madureira, Joe & Sharrieff, Munier.** Battle Chasers: A Gathering of Heroes. (Illus.). 160p. 1999. 24.95 (*1-56389-597-8*, Pub. by DC Comics) Time Warner.

Madureira, Joe & Sharrieff, Munier. Battle Chasers No. 1: Collected Edition. (Illus.). 56p. 1998. pap. 5.95 (*1-58240-039-3*) Image Comics.

Madurga, G. & Lozano, M. Heavy-Ion Collision, La Rabida, Spain, 1982: Proceedings. (Lecture Notes in Physics Ser.: Vol. 168). 429p. 1982. 42.95 (*0-387-11945-0*) Spr-Verlag.

Madurga, G., jt. auth. see Garcia-Leon, M.

Madurga, G., jt. ed. see Garcia-Leon, M.

Madurga, G., jt. ed. see Lozano, M.

Maduro, Miguel P. We the Court: The European Court of Justice & the European Economic Constitution. LC 98-196487. 256p. 1997. pap. 45.00 (*1-901362-25-6*, Pub. by Hart Pub) Northwestern U Pr.

***Maduro, Otto.** Mapas para la Fiesta. (SPA.). 214p. 1999. pap. 14.95 (*0-9657839-6-0*) AETH Bks.

Maduro, Otto. Religion & Social Conflicts. Barr, Robert R., tr. from SPA. LC 82-3439. Orig. Title: Religion y Lucha de Clase. 189p. (Orig.). reprint ed. pap. 58.60 (*0-7837-5512-0*, 204528200005) Bks Demand.

Maduro, Otto, ed. Judaism, Christianity, & Liberation: An Agenda for Dialogue. LC 90-22940. 160p. 1991. reprint ed. pap. 49.60 (*0-7837-9850-4*, 206057900005) Bks Demand.

Maduro, Otto, jt. ed. see Ellis, Marc H.

Maduro, Roger & Schauerhammer, Ralf. The Holes in the Ozone Scare: The Scientific Evidence That the Sky Isn't Falling. (Illus.). 357p. (Orig.). 1992. pap. 15.00 (*0-9628134-0-0*) Twenty Fst Sci.

Madvig, Donald, tr. see Schweizer, Eduard.

Madvig, Johan N. Adversaria Critica Ad Scriptores Graecos et Latinos, 3 vols., Set. viii, 1703p. 1967. reprint ed. write for info. (*0-318-70779-9*) G Olms Pubs.

— Kleine Philologische Schriften. vii, 560p. 1966. reprint ed. write for info. (*0-318-70780-2*) G Olms Pubs.

— Opuscula Academica. xi, 779p. 1977. reprint ed. write for info. (*3-487-06456-1*) G Olms Pubs.

Madwed, Sidney. How to Use Poetry to Get Better Results in Your Life. 117p. 1991. pap. 11.95 (*0-9629490-0-0*) S Madwed.

Madyan, Abu. The Way of Abu Madyan. Cornell, Vincent, ed. & tr. by. (Golden Palm Ser.). (ARA.). (C). 1995. 39.95 (*0-946621-34-9*, Pub. by Islamic Texts) Intl Spec Bk.

— The Way of Abu Madyan. Cornell, Vincent J., ed. & tr. by. (Golden Palm Ser.). (ARA.). (C). 1996. pap. text 35.00 (*0-946621-35-7*, Pub. by Islamic Texts) Intl Spec Bk.

Mae, Linda. One Too Many Candles of Repentance: Poetry & Prose by Linda Mae. (Illus.). 48p. (Orig.). 1994. pap. 4.95 (*0-9642130-0-1*) Fountain Pen.

Mae-Wan Ho. The Rainbow & the Worm: The Physics of Organisms. 220p. 1993. text 40.00 (*981-02-1486-3*) World Scientific Pub.

Maebius, Nancy K. & Linton, Adrianne D. Examaster for Linton, Matteson, & Maebius: Introductory Nursing Care of Adults. (Illus.). 100p. Date not set. write for info. (*0-7216-8075-5*, W B Saunders Co) Harcrt Hlth Sci Grp.

— Test Manual for Introductory Nursing Care of Adults. 155p. Date not set. write for info. (*0-7216-8073-9*, W B Saunders Co) Harcrt Hlth Sci Grp.

Maebius, Nancy K., jt. auth. see Herlihy, Barbara.

Maecha, Alberto, ed. see Bourgeois, Jean-Francois.

Maeck, Klaus. Hor Mit Schmerzen (Listen with Pain) 136p. pap. 25.00 (*3-931126-09-9*, Pub. by Die Gestalten) Consort Bk Sales.

Maeda, Anthony C. Angels of Twilight: Selected Poems & Songs by Tony Maeda. 20p. (Orig.). 1992. pap. 5.00 (*0-9633301-0-1*) Mustang Pr.

Maeda, Daisaku. Honorable Elders Revisited. LC 85-16138. (Illus.). xix, 136p. 1985. text 39.95 (*0-8223-0261-6*); pap. text 18.95 (*0-8223-0263-2*) Duke.

Maeda, F. Y. Dirichlet Integrals on Harmonic Spaces. (Lecture Notes in Mathematics Ser.: Vol. 803). 180p. 1980. 33.95 (*0-387-09995-6*) Spr-Verlag.

Maeda, H., et al. Neocarzinostatin: The Past, Present, & Future of an Anticancer Drug. LC 96-47101. 1997. 197.00 (*4-431-70187-7*) Spr-Verlag.

Maeda, H., jt. ed. see Koprowski, Hilary.

Maeda, Hiroshi & Tagano, Kazumasa. Bismuth-Based High-Temperature Superconductors. LC 96-18858. (Applied Physics Ser.: Vol. 6). (Illus.). 656p. 1996. text 250.00 (*0-8247-9690-X*) Dekker.

Maeda, Ivy, et al. Kids' Trips in Tokyo: City Walks & Family Outings. 1998. pap. 19.00 (*4-7700-2040-6*, Pub. by Kodansha Intl) Kodansha.

Maeda, John. Design by Numbers. LC 98-37583. (Illus.). 250p. 1999. 45.00 (*0-262-13354-7*) MIT Pr.

***Maeda, John.** Maeda @ Media. (Illus.). 480p. 2000. 75.00 (*0-8478-2295-8*) Rizzoli Intl.

Maeda, Jun. Fluid Power: Proceedings of the Second JHPS International Symposiumon Fluid Power. (Illus.). 800p. (C). 1994. 350.00 (*0-419-19100-3*, E & FN Spon) Routledge.

— Let's Study Japanese. LC 64-24949. (JPN., Illus.). 130p. (YA). (gr. 9 up). 1965. pap. 6.95 (*0-8048-0362-5*) Tuttle Pubng.

Maeda, Jun, ed. see NHK Overseas Broadcasting Department Staff & Mizutani, Nobuko.

Maeda, K., et al, eds. Recent Advances in Renal Research: Contributions from Japan. (Contributions to Nephrology Ser.: Vol. 9). (Illus.). 127p. 1978. 29.75 (*3-8055-2826-4*) S Karger.

— Vitamin D & Calcium Metabolism in the Renal Diseases. (Contributions to Nephrology Ser.: Vol. 22). (Illus.). vi, 122p. 1980. 29.75 (*3-8055-0389-X*) S Karger.

Maeda, K. & Shinzato, T., eds. Dialysis-Related Amyloidosis. (Contributions to Nephrology Ser.: Vol. 112). (Illus.). viii, 176p. 1995. 172.25 (*3-8055-6046-X*) S Karger.

— Effective Hemodiafiltration: New Methods. (Contributions to Nephrology Ser.: Vol. 108). (Illus.). viii, 136p. 1994. 49.75 (*3-8055-5886-4*) S Karger.

Maeda, Kei-ichiro, et al, eds. Neural Control of Reproduction: Physiology & Behavior. LC 97-183208. (Illus.). xii, 254p. 1997. 235.00 (*3-8055-6513-5*) S Karger.

Maeda, Misayo G. & Craft, Lucille. Japanese Secrets of Beautiful Skin. LC 89-50660. (Illus.). 204p. 1989. pap. 15.95 (*0-8048-1543-7*) Tuttle Pubng.

Maeda, Mizuo, jt. ed. see Bartsch, Richard A.

Maeda, Shintaro. Thomas Raccoon's Fantastic Airshow. Thatch, Nancy R., ed. (Books for Students by Students). (Illus.). 29p. (J). (gr. k-3). 1994. lib. bdg. 15.95 (*0-933849-51-6*) Landmark Edns.

Maeda, Shinzo, photos by. A Tree, a Blade of Grass, Okumikawa, the Nippon Alps: Photographs by Shinzo Maeda. (Illus.). 287p. 1998. text 40.00 (*0-7881-5751-5*) DIANE Pub.

Maeda, Tetsuo. The Hidden Army: The Untold Story of Japan's Military Forces. Kenney, David J., ed. Karpa, Steven, tr. LC 94-40937. (Illus.). 344p. 1995. 24.95 (*1-883695-01-5*) Edition Q.

***Maeda, Toshio.** Urotsukidoji: Legend of the Overfiend. Newman, Dan, tr. from JPN. (Illus.). i, 189p. 1999. pap. 16.95 (*1-56219-917-X*, CMX 06111) Central Pk Media.

Maeda, Yoshiaki, et al, eds. Symplectic Geometry & Quantization: A Symposium on Symplectic Geometry & Quantization Problems, July 1993, Japan. LC 94-25115. (Contemporary Mathematics Ser.: Vol. 179). 285p. 1994. pap. 51.00 (*0-8218-0302-6*, CONM/179) Am Math.

Maedel, Lynn & Sommer, Sandra. Blood Cell Morphology. 1993. sl. write for info. (*0-89189-329-6*) Am Soc Clinical.

— Blood Cell Morphology, 6 vols., Set. 1993. 540.00 incl. sl. (*0-685-74782-4*) Am Soc Clinical.

Maeder, Andre & Renzini, Alvio, eds. Observational Tests of the Stellar Evolution Theory. 1984. pap. text 84.50 (*90-277-1775-3*); lib. bdg. 186.00 (*90-277-1774-5*) Kluwer Academic.

Maeder, Andre, jt. ed. see De Jong, T.

***Maeder, Beverly.** Wallace Stevens' Experimental Language: The Lion in the Lute. LC 99-12847. 1999. text 45.00 (*0-312-21334-4*) St Martin.

Maeder, Clara F. Autobiography of Clara Fisher Maeder. (American Biography Ser.). 138p. 1991. reprint ed. lib. bdg. 69.00 (*0-7812-8260-8*) Rprt Serv.

Maeder, Jay, jt. ed. see New York Daily News Staff.

Maeder, Robert. The Cross & Crown: Thoughts for Lent, Christ's Sufferings, Christ the King. Kunze, Eileen, tr. from GER. LC 98-61890. 160p. 1999. pap. 9.95 (*0-9639032-2-5*) Sarto Hse.

Maeder, Roman. Computer Science with Mathematica. LC 99-38932. 400p. (C). 2000. 69.95 (*0-521-63172-6*) Cambridge U Pr.

***Maeder, Roman.** Computer Science with Mathematica. LC 99-38932. 400p. (C). 2000. pap. 24.95 (*0-521-66395-4*) Cambridge U Pr.

Maeder, Roman. The Mathematica Programmer - Mathematica Programmer II. 1997. pap. text 59.95 incl. cd-rom, disk (*0-12-799060-7*) Acad Pr.

Maeder, Roman E. Computer Science with Mathematica: Theory & Practice for Science, Mathematics & Engineering. (Illus.). 384p. (C). 1997. text. write for info. (*0-201-56940-X*) Addison-Wesley.

— The Mathematica Programmer II. (Illus.). 296p. 1996. pap. text 44.95 (*0-12-464992-0*) Acad Pr.

— Programming in Mathematica. 1989. 35.50 (*0-685-31411-1*) Addison-Wesley.

— Programming in Mathematica. 2nd ed. (Advanced Book Program Ser.). (Illus.). 304p. (C). 1991. 46.95 (*0-201-54877-1*) Addison-Wesley.

— Programming in Mathematica. 2nd ed. 1995. 31.25 (*0-201-54578-0*) Addison-Wesley.

— Programming in Mathematica. 3rd ed. LC 96-5714. 384p. (C). 1996. pap. text 34.95 (*0-201-85449-X*) Addison-Wesley.

— Programming in Mathematics. 1989. text 35.50 (*0-201-51002-2*) Addison-Wesley.

— Programming in Mathematics. 2nd ed. 304p. (C). 1991. pap. text 36.95 (*0-201-54878-X*) Addison-Wesley.

Maeder, Susan. White Song: Poems. LC 98-66173. 110 p. 1998. 0.00 (*0-9650522-1-4*) Paper Tribe.

— White Song: Poems. LC 98-66173. 110p. 1998. pap. 12.95 (*0-9656052-2-1*) Pot Shard.

Maeder, Tom, jt. auth. see Crimmins, Cathy.

Maedke, Wilmer O., et al. Consumer Education. LC 77-73301. 528p. (gr. 11-12). 1984. teacher ed. 10.67 (*0-02-475740-3*, Macmillan Coll); text 27.96 (*0-02-475720-9*, Macmillan Coll); student ed. 7.72 (*0-02-475730-6*, Macmillan Coll) P-H.

Maehder, Jurgen, ed. see Langer, Arne.

Maehl, William H. August Bebel: Shadow Emperor of the German Workers. LC 79-51544. (Memoirs of the American Philosophical Society Ser.: Vol. 138). 576p. reprint ed. pap. 178.60 (*0-7837-0542-5*, 204087000019) Bks Demand.

— The German Socialist Party: Champion of the First Republic, 1918-1933. LC 84-5903. (Memoirs Ser.: Vol. 169). 400p. 1986. 40.00 (*0-87169-169-8*, M169-MAW) Am Philos.

***Maehl, William H.** Lifelong Learning at Its Best: Innovative Practices in Adult Credit Programs. LC 99-6469. (Higher & Adult Education Ser.). 384p. 1999. 34.95 (*0-7879-4603-6*) Jossey-Bass.

Maehler, ed. Pindari Pt. II: Fragmenta, Indices. (GRE.). 1989. 44.50 (*3-322-00673-5*, T1586, Pub. by B G Teubner) U of Mich Pr.

Maehler & Snell, eds. Pindari Pt. I: Epinicia. (GRE.). 1997. 29.95 (*3-8154-1585-3*, T1585, Pub. by B G Teubner) U of Mich Pr.

Maehler, ed. see Snell.

Maehler, jt. ed. see Snell.

Maehler, H. Die Lieder des Bakchylides. 440p. 1997. pap. 156.50 (*90-04-10761-4*) Brill Academic Pubs.

Maehler, Herwig. Die Lieder des Bakchylides: Zweiter Teil. Die Dithyramben Und Fragmente. Text, Bersetzung Und Kommentar. Vol. 167. (GER., Illus.). Xxvi, 382p. 1997. text 182.50 (*90-04-10671-5*) Brill Academic Pubs.

Maehler, Margaret, tr. from FRE. Alexandria Rediscovered. LC 98-73413. (Illus.). 256p. 1998. 60.00 (*0-8076-1442-4*) Braziller.

Maehling, Rita F., jt. auth. see Hale, Roger L.

Maehlis, Sally, jt. auth. see Field, Nancy.

Maehly, A. & Williams, R. L., eds. Forensic Science Progress, Vol. 3. (Illus.). 140p. 1988. 119.95 (*0-387-18447-3*) Spr-Verlag.

Maehly, A., ed. see Seller, K.

Maehr, David S. The Florida Panther: Life & Death of a Vanishing Carnivore. LC 97-14844. 320p. 1997. text. write for info. (*1-55963-506-1*); pap. text. write for info. (*1-55963-507-X*) Island Pr.

Maehr, David S., jt. auth. see Kale, Herbert W., II.

Maehr, J. M. K-3 Language & Literacy. LC 90-22885. (K-Three Curriculum Ser.). 256p. 1991. pap. 22.95 (*0-929816-23-4*, E3001) High-Scope.

Maehr, Martin L., et al, eds. Advances in Motivation & Achievement: Motivation & Adolescent Development, Vol. 8. 304p. 1994. 78.50 (*1-55938-436-0*) Jai Pr.

— Advances in Motivation & Achievement: Motivation & Adulthood, Vol. 4. 408p. 1985. 78.50 (*0-89232-544-5*) Jai Pr.

— Advances in Motivation & Achievement: Motivation Enhancing Environments, Vol. 6. 312p. 1989. 78.50 (*0-89232-889-4*) Jai Pr.

— Advances in Motivation & Achievement: Motivation Enhancing Environments, Vol. 7. 432p. 1991. 78.50 (*1-55938-122-1*) Jai Pr.

— Advances in Motivation & Achievement: Motivation Enhancing Environments, Vol. 9. 328p. 1995. 78.50 (*1-55938-769-6*) Jai Pr.

— Advances in Motivation & Achievement: The Development of Achievement Motivation. (Advances in Motivation & Achievement Ser.: Vol. 3). 368p. 1984. 78.50 (*0-89232-289-6*) Jai Pr.

— Advances in Motivation & Achievement: The Effects of School Desegregation on Motivation & Achievement, Vol. 1. 344p. 1984. 78.50 (*0-89232-290-X*) Jai Pr.

— Advances in Motivation & Achievement: Women in Science, Vol. 2. 400p. 1984. 78.50 (*0-89232-288-8*) Jai Pr.

— Enhancing Motivation. (Advances in Motivation & Achievement Ser.: Vol. 5). 352p. 1987. 78.50 (*0-89232-621-2*) Jai Pr.

Maehr, Martin L. & Pintrich, Paul R., eds. Advances in Motivation & Achievement, Vol. 10. 496p. 1997. 78.50 (*0-7623-0103-1*) Jai Pr.

— Advances in Motivation & Achievement, Vol. 11. Date not set. 78.50 (*0-7623-0430-8*) Jai Pr.

Maeijer, J. M. & Geens, Koen, eds. Defensive Measures Against Hostile Takeovers in the Common Market. 232p. 1991. lib. bdg. 107.00 (*0-7923-0834-4*) Kluwer Academic.

Maeir, Clifford L. The Role of Spectroscopy in the Acceptance of the Internally Structured Atom. Cohen, I. Bernard, ed. LC 80-2093. (Development of Science Ser.). (Illus.). 1981. lib. bdg. 55.95 (*0-405-13858-X*) Ayer.

Maekawa. Ironfist Chimini: Kung Fu Boy. (Ironfist Chimini Ser.: Vol. 1). Date not set. 4.99 (*0-385-32507-X*) Delacorte.

Maekawa, Koichi, et al. Modelling of Concrete Performance: Hydration, Microstructure Formation, & Mass Transport. LC 98-31036. 1999. 110.00 (*0-419-24200-7*, E & FN Spon) Routledge.

***Maekawa, Kumiko.** Narrative & Experience: Innovations in Thirteenth-Century Picture Books. 349p. 2000. text 52.95 (*0-8204-4365-4*) P Lang Pubng.

Maekawa, M. & Belady, L. A., eds. Operating Systems Engineering, Amagi, Japan 1980: Proceedings. (Lecture Notes in Computer Science Ser.: Vol. 143). 465p. 1982. 40.00 (*0-387-11604-4*) Spr-Verlag.

Maekawa, S., ed. Physics of Magnetic Materials: Proceedings of the International Symposium on Physics of Magnetic Materials. 620p. (C). 1987. text 153.00 (*9971-5-0358-1*) World Scientific Pub.

Maekawa, Shin, ed. Oxygen-Free Museum Cases. LC 98-15964. (Research in Conservation Ser.). (Illus.). 100p. 1998. pap. 30.00 (*0-89236-529-3*, Pub. by J P Getty Trust) OUP.

Maekawa, Shin, jt. auth. see Selwitz, Charles.

Maekawa, Zenichiro, ed. Environmental & Architectural Acoustics. 400p. (C). (gr. 13). 1994. 160.00 (*0-419-15980-0*) Chapman & Bkman.

Maelicke, A., ed. Molecular Biology of Neuroreceptors & Ion Channels. (NATO ASI Series H: Vol. 32). (Illus.). 670p. 1989. 251.95 (*0-387-50380-3*) Spr-Verlag.

— Nicotinic Acetylcholine Receptor. (NATO ASI Series H: Vol. 3). xvi, 489p. 1986. 165.95 (*0-387-17168-1*) Spr-Verlag.

Maelzer, G., ed. Bibliographie zur Geschichte des Pietismus, Vol. 1, Die Werke der Wuerttembergischen Pietisten. 415p. (C). 1972. 104.60 (*3-11-002219-2*) De Gruyter.

Maempa, John T. Combating the Darkness. (Spiritual Discovery Ser.). 124p. 1996. pap., teacher ed. 9.95 (*0-88243-214-1*, 02-0214); pap., student ed. 4.95 (*0-88243-114-5*, 02-0114) Gospel Pub.

Maenchen-Helfen, Otto J. The World of the Huns: Studies in Their History & Culture. Knight, Max, ed. LC 79-94985. (Illus.). 634p. reprint ed. pap. 196.60 (*0-7837-4764-0*, 204451100003) Bks Demand.

Maendel, Rachel. Rachel, a Hutterite Girl. LC 99-29922. 48p. (J). (ps-4). 1999. pap. 12.99 (*0-8361-9119-6*) Herald Pr.

Maennchen, Julis & Waschke, Ernst-Joachim, eds. Altes Testament - Literatursammlung und Heilige Schrift: Gesammelte Aufsaetze zur Entstehung, Geschichte und Auslegung des Alten Testaments. (Beiheft zur Zeitschrift fuer die Alttestamentliche Wissenschaft Ser.: Bd. 212). (GER.). viii, 306p. (C). 1993. lib. bdg. 106.15 (*3-11-013982-0*) De Gruyter.

Maeno, Itoko, jt. auth. see Talley, Carol.

Maenpaa, Pasi, jt. auth. see Falk, Pasi.

***Maenza, David J.** Chicago U. S. A. A Quality Pictorial of Yesterday, Today & Tomorrow. (Illus.). 1999. 19.95 (*0-929520-24-6*) D J Maenza Assocs.

Maenza, David J. Chicago Usa: Yesterday Today & Tomorrow. (Illus.). 1999. write for info. (*0-929520-22-X*) D J Maenza Assocs.

Maercken Zu Geerath, Ernst F. Von, see Von Maercken Zu Geerath, Ernst F.

***Maercker, A.** Posttraumatische Belastungsstorungen: Stand und Perspektiven des Wissens uber Effektive Therapien. (Verhaltenstherapie Ser.). 60p. 1999. 35.00 (*3-8055-7028-7*) S Karger.

Maercker, A., et al. Post-Traumatic Stress Disorder: A Lifespan Developmental Perspective. LC 98-36649. viii, 264p. 1998. 39.00 (*0-88937-187-3*) Hogrefe & Huber Pubs.

Maerd, Dorvshka. Sipapu Odyssey. 2nd ed. (Illus.). 128p. 1995. reprint ed. pap. 6.00 (*1-56935-045-0*) Phoenix Source.

Maerk, T. D. & Dunn, G. H., eds. Electron Impact Ionization. (Illus.). 400p. 1985. 140.95 (*0-387-81778-6*) Spr-Verlag.

Maeroff. Altered Destinies: Making Life Better For Schoolchildren in Need. 228p. 1999. pap. 15.95 (*0-312-22080-4*) St Martin.

Maeroff, Gene I. Altered Destinies: Making Life Better for Schoolchildren in Need. LC 97-38747. 352p. 1998. text 26.95 (*0-312-17543-4*) St Martin.

— The Empowerment of Teachers: Overcoming the Crisis of Confidence. 152p. (Orig.). (C). 1988. pap. text 16.95 (*0-8077-2908-6*) Tchrs Coll.

— Team Building for School Change: Equipping Teachers for New Roles. LC 93-19983. (Series on School Reform). 192p. (C). 1993. text 36.00 (*0-8077-3268-0*); pap. text 17.95 (*0-8077-3267-2*) Tchrs Coll.

Maeroff, Gene I., ed. Sources of Inspiration: Fifteen Modern Religious Leaders. LC 92-27494. 308p. (Orig.). 1992. 29.95 (*1-55612-602-6*); pap. 19.95 (*1-55612-556-9*, LL1556) Sheed & Ward WI.

Maeroff, Gene I. & Hechinger Institute on Education & the Media Staff. Imaging Education: The Media & Schools in America. LC 97-51286. 1998. 50.00 (*0-8077-3735-6*); pap. 23.95 (*0-8077-3734-8*) Tchrs Coll.

Maerowitz, Marlene A., jt. auth. see Mauet, Thomas A.

Maertz, Gregory, ed. Cultural Interactions in the Romantic Age: Critical Essays in Comparative Literature. LC 97-7314. (SUNY Series, The Margins of Literature). 258p. (C). 1998. text 59.50 (*0-7914-3559-8*); pap. text 19.95 (*0-7914-3560-1*) State U NY Pr.

Maerz, George C., jt. ed. see Harlow, Giles D.

Maes, A. A., jt. ed. see Van Rossum, J. H.

Maes, Alex. Regional Myocardial Blood Flow & Metabolism in Chronic & Acute Heart Disease: A Study with Positron Emission Tomography. (Acta Biomedica Loveniensia Ser.: No. 131). (Illus.). 129p. (Orig.). 1996. pap. 39.50 (*90-6186-747-9*, Pub. by Leuven Univ) Coronet Bks.

***Maes, Francis, ed.** The Empire Resounds: Music in the Days of Charles V. (Illus.). 176p. 1999. pap. 37.50 (*90-6186-981-1*, Pub. by Leuven Univ) Coronet Bks.

Maes, Fred. The Frustrated Cartoonist's Handbook. (Illus.). 95p. (Orig.). 1997. pap. 12.95 (*1-890462-00-4*) J Francisco.

— Nobody Can Kick You Unless You Bend Over: A Book about People, Problems, & Personal Pride. (Illus.). (Orig.). 1997. pap. write for info. (*1-890462-01-2*) J Francisco.

— Profound Thoughts from the World's Deepest Thinkers. (Illus.). (Orig.). 1997. pap. write for info. (*1-890462-03-9*) J Francisco.

— Taking the Guilt & Fear Out of Faith. (Illus.). (Orig.). 1997. pap. write for info. (*1-890462-02-0*) J Francisco.

Maes, Greg, ed. see Hurrey, Clair, et al.

Maes, John L. Suffering: A Care Giver's Guide. LC 89-27485. 224p. 1990. pap. 12.95 (*0-687-40570-X*) Abingdon.

***Maes, M., et al.** European Society for Paediatric Endocrinology (ESPE) 39th Annual Meeting, Brussels, September 2000: Abstracts. (Hormone Research Ser.: 53). (Illus.). 188p. 2000. pap. 45.25 (*3-8055-7121-6*) S Karger.

Maes, Michael & Coccaro, Emil F. Neurobiology of Aggression & Impulsivity. LC 98-19062. (Series on Clinical & Neurobiological Advances in Psychiatry). 228p. 1998. 137.95 (*0-471-98101-X*) Wiley.

Maes, Pattie, ed. Designing Autonomous Agents: Theory & Practice from Biology to Engineering & Back. (Illus.). 200p. 1991. pap. text 26.50 (*0-262-63135-0*) MIT Pr.

Maes, Pattie, et al, eds. From Animals to Animates 4: Proceedings of the Fourth International Conference on Simulation of Adaptive Behavior. LC 96-213435. (Illus.). 600p. 1996. pap. text 68.00 (*0-262-63178-4*, Bradford Bks) MIT Pr.

Maes, Pattie, jt. ed. see Brooks, Rodney A.

Maes, Reuben O. About the Underlying Scheme of Things. 1997. pap. 11.95 (*1-878406-10-8*, Paintbrsh) Parker Dstb.

Maes, Robert A., jt. ed. see Brandenberger, Hans.

Maes, Stan, et al, eds. International Review of Health Psychology, Vol. 1. 240p. 1992. 445.00 (*0-471-92754-6*) Wiley.

— International Review of Health Psychology, 3 vols., Vol. 3. 280p. 1994. 445.00 (*0-471-94456-4*) Wiley.

— International Review of Health Psychology, Vol. 2, Vol. 2. 246p. 1993. 445.00 (*0-471-93826-2*) Wiley.

— Topics in Health Psychology. LC 88-5646. (Illus.). 330p. 1988. reprint ed. pap. 102.30 (*0-608-05264-7*, 206580200001) Bks Demand.

***Maes, Yvonne.** The Cannibal's Wife: A Memoir. LC 99-32952. 256p. 1999. 25.00 (*1-928746-03-9*) Herodias.

Maesaka, Cheryl. Networks That Work: A Guide to Dental Networking. 100p. 1999. pap. 15.95 (*0-88100-105-8*) Natl Writ Pr.

Maese, Lorraine. How to Get Your Kids in Show Biz: A Guide Book. (Illus.). 68p. (Orig.). 1997. pap. 10.95 (*0-9657789-0-8*) Talent Bks.

Maesen, L. J. Van Der, see Hanum, I. Faridah, ed.

Maeshino, Hiroshi, tr. see Cassidy, T. K.

Maest, Ann S., jt. ed. see Kharaka, Yousif K.

Maestas, Bobby. Kawai K-One Sound Making Book. Alexander, Peter L., ed. (Kawai K-One Support Ser.). (Illus.). 138p. (C). 1988. pap. text 19.95 (*0-939067-08-0*) Alexander Pub.

— Korg M-1 Sound Making Book, Level 1. Alexander, Peter L., ed. (Korg M-One Support Ser.). (Illus.). 167p. (C). 1989. pap. 21.95 (*0-939067-39-0*) Alexander Pub.

Maestas, Bobby & Goldfield, Paul. Sampling Basics. Alexander, Peter L., ed. 125p. (C). 1989. pap. text 14.95 (*0-939067-82-X*) Alexander Pub.

Maestas, Lily & Snyder, Lorelei. Unlimited Options: Career Strategies to Last a Lifetime. 256p. (Orig.). 1996. pap., per. 14.97 (*0-9651077-5-2*) Prsprity Pr.

***Maestas, Lily, et al.** Get Clear on Your Career: Meeting the School-To-Career Needs for Today's Workforce. 100p. 2000. pap. 19.95 (*0-9651077-6-0*) Prsprity Pr.

Maestas, Roberto, jt. ed. see Johansen, Bruce.

Maestas, Ronald W., jt. auth. see Ross, Steven C.

Maestri, George. Digital Character Animation. LC 96-47533. 400p. 1996. pap. 55.00 (*1-56205-559-3*) New Riders Pub.

***Maestri, George.** Digital Character Animation 2: Essential Techniques, Vol. 1. (Digital Character Animation Ser.). (Illus.). 280p. 1999. pap. 50.00 incl. cd-rom (*1-56205-930-0*) New Riders Pub.

Maestri, William F. Choose Life & Not Death: A Primer on Abortion, Euthanasia, & Suicide. LC 85-28687. 1986. pap. 9.95 (*0-8189-0490-9*) Alba.

***Maestri, William F.** Do Not Lose Hope: Healing the Wounded Heart of Women Who Have Had an Abortion. LC 99-37223. xii, 82p. 2000. pap. 5.95 (*0-8189-0830-0*) Alba.

Maestri, William F. A Guide for the Study of Familiaris Consortio. 104p. 1995. pap. 1.75 (*0-8198-3074-7*) Pauline Bks.

— My Advent Journal. 110p. 1990. pap. 5.95 (*0-8189-0599-9*) Alba.

— My Lenten Journal. 132p. 1990. pap. 6.95 (*0-8189-0576-X*) Alba.

— My Rosary Journal: The Great Mysteries. (Illus.). 112p. (Orig.). 1993. pap. 7.95 (*0-8189-0673-1*) Alba.

— My Way of the Cross Journal: A Lenten Journey with Jesus. 98p. (Orig.). 1993. pap. 5.95 (*0-8189-0663-4*) Alba.

— Paul's Pastoral Vision: Pastoral Letters for a Pastoral Church Today. LC 89-203. 240p. (Orig.). 1989. pap. 12.95 (*0-8189-0556-5*) Alba.

— Portraits of Extraordinary Women. LC 96-53060. (Illus.). 120p. 1997. 19.95 (*1-56554-242-8*) Pelican.

— A Priest to Turn To: Biblical & Pastoral Reflections on the Priesthood. LC 88-31418. 256p. (Orig.). 1989. pap. 12.95 (*0-8189-0546-8*) Alba.

— What the Church Teaches: A Guide for the Study of Veritatis Splendor. 87p. 1994. pap. 1.50 (*0-8198-3072-0*) Pauline Bks.

— A Word in Season. LC 84-11026. 153p. (Orig.). 1983. pap. 6.95 (*0-8189-0459-3*) Alba.

Maestri, William F., ed. Mary: Model of Justice. LC 86-22304. 92p. (Orig.). 1987. pap. 4.95 (*0-8189-0511-5*) Alba.

Maestrini, Nicholas. Forever Love: God's Plan for Happiness. LC 97-91612. 298p. 1997. pap. 11.95 (*0-9642010-3-8*) Pime Wrld Pr.

— Forever Love: God's Plan for Happiness. rev. ed. LC 97-68069. 298p. 1997. pap. 11.95 (*0-9642010-5-4*) Pime Wrld Pr.

Maestrini, Nicholas, tr. see Vismara, Clement.

Maestro, Betsy. Big City Port. (Reading Rainbow Bks.). (J). 1983. 10.15 (*0-606-01784-4*, Pub. by Turtleback) Demco.

— Bike Trip. LC 90-35935. (Illus.). 32p. (J). (gr. k-4). 1992. 16.00 (*0-06-022731-1*); lib. bdg. 15.89 (*0-06-022732-X*) HarpC Child Bks.

— Ferryboat. LC 85-47887. (Illus.). 32p. (J). (ps-3). 1986. lib. bdg. 15.89 (*0-690-04520-4*) HarpC Child Bks.

— How Do Apples Grow? (Let's-Read-And-Find-Out Book Ser.). (J). 1993. 10.15 (*0-606-05357-3*, Pub. by Turtleback) Demco.

— How Do Apples Grow. LC 91-9468. (Let's-Read-&-Find-Out Science Bks.). (Illus.). 32p. (J). (gr. k-4). 1992. lib. bdg. 15.89 (*0-06-020056-1*) HarpC Child Bks.

— How Do Apples Grow. LC 91-9468. (Trophy Let's Read-&-Find-Out Science Bk.: Stage 2). (Illus.). 32p. (J). (gr. k-4). 1993. pap. 4.95 (*0-06-445117-8*, HarpTrophy) HarpC Child Bks.

— A More Perfect Union: The Story of Our Constitution. (J). 1987. 13.15 (*0-606-04750-6*, Pub. by Turtleback) Demco.

— Sea Full of Sharks. (Illus.). 32p. (gr. k-3). 1997. pap. 4.99 (*0-590-43101-3*) Scholastic Inc.

— The Story of Money. (J). 1995. 12.15 (*0-606-08208-5*, Pub. by Turtleback) Demco.

— Story of the Statue of Liberty. 1989. 11.15 (*0-606-09905-0*, Pub. by Turtleback) Demco.

— Taxi: A Book of City Words. LC 88-22867. (Illus.). 32p. (J). (ps-3). 1990. reprint ed. pap. 6.95 (*0-395-54811-X*, Clarion Bks) HM.

— Traffic: A Book of Opposites. 1999. 6.99 (*0-517-80071-3*) Crown Pub Group.

Maestro, Betsy. What Is a Skeleton. 40p. (ps-1). 15.95 (*0-06-029006-4*); pap. 4.95 (*0-06-445215-8*); lib. bdg. 15.89 (*0-06-029007-2*) HarpC.

— Why Do Leaves Change Color? (Let's Read-&-Find-Out Science Ser.). (J). 1994. 10.15 (*0-606-06879-1*, Pub. by Turtleback) Demco.

Maestro, Betsy. Why Do Leaves Change Color. LC 93-9611. (Illus.). 32p. (J). (ps-3). 1996. pap. 7.95 incl. audio (*0-694-70080-0*) HarpC.

Maestro, Betsy. Why Do Leaves Change Color. LC 93-9611. (Let's-Read-&-Find-Out Science Bks.). (Illus.). 32p. (J). (gr. k-4). 1994. pap. 4.95 (*0-06-445126-7*, HarpTrophy) HarpC Child Bks.

— Why Do Leaves Change Color. LC 93-9611. (Let's-Read-&-Find-Out Science Bks.). (Illus.). 32p. (J). (ps-3). 1994. lib. bdg. 15.89 (*0-06-022874-1*) HarpC Child Bks.

Maestro, Betsy & Maestro, Giulio. Exploration & Conquest. LC 93-48618. (Illus.). 48p. (J). (gr. 4-7). 1997. mass mkt. 5.95 (*0-688-15474-3*, Wm Morrow) Morrow Avon.

— A Sea Full of Sharks.Tr. of Mer Pleine de Requins. (FRE., Illus.). (J). pap. 7.99 (*0-590-74409-7*) Scholastic Inc.

***Maestro, Betsy & Maestro, Giulio.** The Story of Religion. (Illus.). 48p. (J). (gr. k-4). 1999. pap. 5.95 (*0-688-17146-X*, Wm Morrow) Morrow Avon.

Maestro, Betsy & Maestro, Giulio. Una Union Mas Perfecta: La Historia de Nuestra Constitucion (A More Perfect Union) Marcuse, Aida E., tr. (Illus.). 48p. (J). (gr. 5). 1993. 13.95 (*0-9625162-8-7*) Lectorum Pubns.

— Una Union Mas Perfecta (A More Perfect Union) La Historia de Nuestra Constitucion. Marcuse, Aida E., tr. (Illus.). 48p. (J). (gr. 5). 1993. pap. 6.95 (*1-880507-29-3*) Lectorum Pubns.

Maestro, Betsy C. Bats. LC 93-26153. (Illus.). 32p. (J). (gr. 3 up). 1994. 15.95 (*0-590-46150-8*) Scholastic Inc.

— Coming to America: The Story of Immigration. LC 94-31110. (Illus.). 40p. (J). (gr. k-4). 1996. 15.95 (*0-590-44151-5*) Scholastic Inc.

— The Discovery of the Americas. LC 89-32375. (Illus.). (J). (gr. 4-7). 1991. 16.00 (*0-688-06837-5*) Lothrop.

— The Discovery of the Americas. 1992. 11.15 (*0-606-12257-5*, Pub. by Turtleback) Demco.

— A More Perfect Union: The Story of Our Constitution. LC 87-4083. (Illus.). 48p. (J). (gr. 1-5). 1987. lib. bdg. 15.93 (*0-688-06840-5*) Lothrop.

— The New Americans: Colonial Times, 1620-1689. LC 95-19636. (Illus.). 48p. (J). (gr. k up). 1998. 16.00 (*0-688-13448-3*); lib. bdg. 15.93 (*0-688-13449-1*) Lothrop.

— The New Nation. 1924. lib. bdg. write for info. (*0-688-16016-6*) Lothrop.

— A Sea Full of Sharks. 1997. 10.19 (*0-606-11820-9*, Pub. by Turtleback) Demco.

***Maestro, Betsy C.** The Story of Clocks & Calendars: Marking a Millennium. LC 98-21305. 48p. (J). 1999. lib. bdg. 15.89 (*0-688-14549-3*) Morrow Avon.

Maestro, Betsy C. The Story of Money. (Illus.). 48p. (J). (gr. 1 up). 1993. 17.00 (*0-395-56242-2*, Clarion Bks) HM.

— The Story of Money. LC 94-26607. (Illus.). 48p. (J). (ps-3). 1995. reprint ed. pap. 6.95 (*0-688-13304-5*, Wm Morrow) Morrow Avon.

— The Story of the Statue of Liberty. LC 85-11324. (Illus.). 40p. (J). (ps-3). 1986. lib. bdg. 16.93 (*0-688-05774-8*) Lothrop.

— The Story of the Statue of Liberty. LC 85-11324. (Illus.). 48p. (J). (ps-3). 1989. pap. 5.95 (*0-688-08746-9*, Wm Morrow) Morrow Avon.

— Struggle for a Continent: The French & Indian Wars 1689-1763. LC 99-11500. (Illus.). 48p. (J). (gr. 1-7). 2000. 15.95 (*0-688-13450-5*); 15.89 (*0-688-13451-3*) Morrow Avon.

— The Voice of the People. (J). (gr. 1 up). 1998. mass mkt. 5.95 (*0-688-16157-X*, Wm Morrow) Morrow Avon.

— The Voice of the People: American Democracy in Action. LC 95-12672. (Illus.). 48p. (J). (ps-3). 1996. 16.00 (*0-688-10678-1*); lib. bdg. 15.93 (*0-688-10679-X*) Lothrop.

Maestro, Betsy C. & DelVecchio, Ellen. Big City Port. LC 85-4339. (Illus.). 32p. (J). (gr. k-3). 1984. lib. bdg. 14.95 (*0-02-762110-3*, Four Winds Pr) S&S Childrens.

Maestro, Betsy C. & Maestro, Giulio. The Discovery of the Americas. LC 89-32375. (Illus.). 48p. (J). (gr. k up). 1992. mass mkt. 6.95 (*0-688-11512-8*, Wm Morrow) Morrow Avon.

— Exploration & Conquest: The Americas After Columbus, 1500-1620. LC 93-48618. (J). 1994. 16.00 (*0-688-09267-5*) Lothrop.

— A More Perfect Union: The Story of Our Constitution. LC 87-4083. (Illus.). 48p. (J). (ps-3). 1990. mass mkt. 7.95 (*0-688-10192-5*, Wm Morrow) Morrow Avon.

— The Story of Religion. LC 92-38980. (Illus.). 48p. (J). (gr. 2-4). 1993. 15.95 (*0-395-62364-2*, Clarion Bks) HM.

Maestro, Betsy C., jt. auth. see Maestro, Giulio.

Maestro, Betty. Take a Look at Snakes. (J). 1997. pap. text 5.99 (*0-590-44936-2*) Scholastic Inc.

Maestro, Giulio. Geese Find the Missing Piece: School Time Riddle Rhymes. LC 98-41513. (I Can Read Bks.). (Illus.). 48p. (J). (ps-3). 1999. lib. bdg. 14.89 (*0-06-026221-4*) HarpC Child Bks.

***Maestro, Giulio.** Geese Find the Missing Piece: School Time Riddle Rhymes. LC 98-41513. (I Can Read Bks.). (Illus.). 48p. (J). (ps-3). 1999. 14.95 (*0-06-026220-6*) HarpC Child Bks.

— Geese Find the Missing Piece: School Time Riddle Rhymes. LC 98-41513. (I Can Read Bks.). (Illus.). 48p. (J). (ps-3). 2000. pap. 3.95 (*0-06-443707-8*, HarpTrophy) HarpC Child Bks.

Maestro, Giulio. Halloween Howls: Riddles That Are a Scream. (Picture Puffin Ser.). (Illus.). (J). 1992. 10.19 (*0-606-01701-1*, Pub. by Turtleback) Demco.

— Riddle Roundup: A Wild Bunch to Beef up Your Word Power. LC 86-33404. (Illus.). 64p. (J). (gr. 2-5). 1989. pap. 6.95 (*0-89919-537-7*, Clarion Bks) HM.

***Maestro, Giulio & Maestro, Betsy C.** The Story of Clocks & Calendars: Marking a Millennium. LC 98-21305. 48p. (J). 1999. 15.95 (*0-688-14548-5*) Morrow Avon.

Maestro, Giulio, jt. auth. see Maestro, Betsy.

Maestro, Giulio, jt. auth. see Maestro, Betsy C.

Maestro, Giulio, jt. auth. see Maestro, Marco.

Maestro, Marco. What Do You Hear When Cows Sing? And Other Silly Riddles. (I Can Read Bks.). (J). (ps-1). 1997. 8.95 (*0-606-10966-8*, Pub. by Turtleback) Demco.

Maestro, Marco & Maestro, Giulio. What Do You Hear When Cows Sing? And Other Silly Riddles. (I Can Read Bks.). (Illus.). 48p. (J). (ps-1). 1996. 14.95 (*0-06-024948-X*) HarpC Child Bks.

— What Do You Hear When Cows Sing: And Other Silly Riddles. (I Can Read Bks.). (Illus.). 48p. (J). (ps-1). 1996. lib. bdg. 14.89 (*0-06-024949-8*) HarpC Child Bks.

Maestro, Marco, et al. What Do You Hear When Cows Sing: And Other Silly Riddles. LC 94-18686. (I Can Read Bks.). (Illus.). 48p. (J). (ps-1). 1997. pap. 3.95 (*0-06-444227-6*, HarpTrophy) HarpC Child Bks.

Maestro, Vittorio, ed. see Dingus, Lowell, et al.

Maestro, Vittorio, ed. see Maisey, John, et al.

***Maestroni, G. J. M. & Conti, A., eds.** International Society of Neuroimmunomodulation: 4th International Congress, Lugano, September 1999: Abstracts. (Neuroimmunomodulation Ser.: Vol. 6, No. 6). iv, 114p. 1999. pap. 34.00 (*3-8055-6972-6*) S Karger.

***Maeterlinck, M.** Maeterlinck: Pelleas et Melisande: With Les Aveugles, l'Intruse & Interieur. Hodson, Leighton, ed. (FRE.). 140p. (C). 1999. pap. text 18.95 (*1-85399-551-7*, Pub. by Brist Class Pr) Focus Pub-R Pullins.

Maeterlinck, Maurice. Before the Great Silence. Kastenbaum, Robert J., ed. LC 76-19580. (Death & Dying Ser.). 1977. reprint ed. lib. bdg. 21.95 (*0-405-09593-7*) Ayer.

— The Blue Bird. (Illus.). 271p. (YA). (gr. 1 up). 1984. 16.95 (*0-932785-02-6*); pap. 10.95 (*0-932785-01-8*) Philos Pub.

— Le Bourgmestre de Stilmonde. (FRE.). 216p. 1967. reprint ed. pap. 11.95 (*0-7859-0931-1*) Fr & Eur.

— Bulles Bleues. (FRE.). 236p. 1948. 14.95 (*0-7859-0014-4*, F66680) Fr & Eur.

— Death. Kastenbaum, Robert J., ed. LC 76-19581. (Death & Dying Ser.). 1977. reprint ed. lib. bdg. 19.95 (*0-405-09577-5*) Ayer.

— Devant Dieu. (FRE.). 224p. 1967. reprint ed. pap. 11.95 (*0-7859-4684-5*) Fr & Eur.

M

An Asterisk (*) at the beginning of an entry indicates that the title is appearing for the first time.

— Five Modern Plays. Incl. Intruder. Set pap. 5.95 (*0-8283-1435-7*) Branden Bks.

— The Great Secret. (Citadel Library of the Mystic Arts). 1989. pap. 7.95 (*0-8065-1155-9*, Citadel Pr) Carol Pub Group.

— L' Hote Inconnu. (FRE.). 196p. 1967. reprint ed. pap. 11.95 (*0-7859-4685-3*) Fr & Eur.

— L' Intelligence des Fleurs. (FRE.). 316p. 1951. 9.95 (*0-7859-0025-X*, F67720) Fr & Eur.

— Light Beyond. De Mattos, Alexander T., tr. LC 70-37844. (Essay Index Reprint Ser.). 1977. reprint ed. 20.95 (*0-8369-2607-2*) Ayer.

— Monna Vanna. (FRE.). 186p. 1967. reprint ed. pap. write for info. (*0-7859-4686-1*) Fr & Eur.

— Monna Vanna: A Play in Three Acts. Coleman, Alexis I., tr. from FRE. LC 93-10174. 102p. 1993. reprint ed. pap. 11.95 (*1-56114-166-6*) Second Renaissance.

— L' Oiseau Bleu: Feerie en Cinq Actes et Douze Tableaux. (FRE.). 186p. 1976. 34.95 (*0-8288-9898-7*, F118590) Fr & Eur.

— On Emerson & Other Essays. Moses, Montrose J., tr. from FRE. LC 78-58262. (Essay Index in Reprint Ser.). 1978. reprint ed. 25.00 (*0-8486-3024-6*) Roth Pub Inc.

— Pelleas et Melisande. (FRE.). 70p. 1968. 14.95 (*0-7859-0018-7*, F66750) Fr & Eur.

— La Princesse Isabelle. (FRE.). 196p. 1967. reprint ed. pap. 11.95 (*0-7859-4687-X*) Fr & Eur.

— Le Sablier. (FRE.). 224p. 1967. reprint ed. pap. 11.95 (*0-7859-4633-0*) Fr & Eur.

— Serres Chaudes, Quinze Chansond: La Princesse Maleine. (FRE.). 320p. 1983. pap. 16.95 (*0-7859-4688-8*) Fr & Eur.

— Serres Chaudes, Quinze Chansond: La Princesse Maleine. (Poesie Ser.). (FRE.). 320p. 1983. pap. 13.95 (*2-07-032245-9*) Schoenhof.

— Theatre Inedit. (FRE.). 1967. reprint ed. pap. 11.95 (*0-7859-4703-5*) Fr & Eur.

— The Treasure of the Humble. Sutro, Alfred, tr. LC 77-10276. reprint ed. 27.50 (*0-404-16328-9*) AMS Pr.

— Le Tresor des Humbles. (FRE.). 180p. 1986. pap. 13.95 (*0-7859-4662-4*) Fr & Eur.

— La Vie des Abeilles. 9.95 (*0-686-56293-3*) Fr & Eur.

— La Vie des Fourmis. (FRE.). 260p. 1969. 39.95 (*0-7859-0021-7*, F66832) Fr & Eur.

— La Vie des Termites. (FRE.). 210p. 1969. 39.95 (*0-8288-9743-3*, 2246009294) Fr & Eur.

— Women, & Four Other Essays. 1991. lib. bdg. 75.00 (*0-8490-4190-2*) Gordon Pr.

Maeterlinck, Maurice, et al. Three Pre-Surrealist Plays. Slater, Maya, tr. & intro. by. LC 96-52367. (The World's Classics Ser.). (Illus.). 272p. 1997. pap. 11.95 (*0-19-283217-4*) OUP.

— What Is Civilization? LC 68-57342. (Essay Index Reprint Ser.). 1977. 19.95 (*0-8369-0986-0*) Ayer.

Maeusbacher, R., jt. ed. see Barsch, D.

Maeusbacher, Roland & Schulte, Achim, eds. High Mountain Geomorphology: Dedicated to D. Barsch on the Occasion of His 60th Anniversary. (Zeitschrift fuer Geomorphologie - Annals of Geomorphology Ser.: Supplementband 104). (Illus.). vi, 202p. 1996. pap. 70.00 (*3-443-21104-6*, Pub. by Gebruder Borntraeger) Balogh.

Maevis, Alfred c. Unknown in the Underground. 5.00 (*0-614-05243-2*, UNK10791M) ASFE.

***Maex, K., et al, eds.** Materials, Technology & Reliability for Advanced Interconnects & Low-k Dielectrics: Materials Research Society Symposium Proceedings, Vol. 612. 2000. text 82.00 (*1-55899-520-X*) Materials Res.

Maex, Karen, et al, eds. Materials Synthesis & Processing Using Ion Beams Vol. 316: Materials Research Society Symposium Proceedings. LC 94-3152. 1077p. 1994. text 80.00 (*1-55899-215-4*) Materials Res.

Maex, Karen & Van Rossum, Marc, eds. Properties of Metal Silicides. (EMIS Datareviews Ser.: No. 14). 380p. 1995. boxed set 195.00 (*0-85296-859-0*) INSPEC Inc.

Maex, R. Direction-Selective Simplee Cells in Cat Striate Cortex. No. 100. 142p. (Orig.). 1994. pap. 33.50 (*90-6186-649-9*, Pub. by Leuven Univ) Coronet Bks.

Maeyama, Y., ed. see Hartner, Willy.

Maezumi, Hakuyu T. & Glassman, Bernard T. The Hazy Moon of Enlightenment: On Zen Practice III. LC 77-81974. (Zen Writings Ser.: Vol. 4). (Illus.). 1978. pap. 8.95 (*0-916820-05-X*) Center Pubns.

Maezumi, Hakuyu T. & Glassman, Bernard T., eds. On Zen Practice: Foundations of Practice. LC 76-9463. (Zen Writings Ser.: Vol. 1). (Illus.). 1976. pap. 5.00 (*0-916820-02-5*) Center Pubns.

Maezumi, Hakuyu T. & Loori, John D. The Way of Everyday Life. LC 78-8309. (Illus.). 1978. pap. 9.95 (*0-916820-06-8*) Center Pubns.

Maezumi, Hakuyu T., jt. auth. see Merzel, Dennis G.

MaFarlane, Gavin. ABC of VAT: And Customs & Excise Terms. 250p. (C). 1991. 34.00 (*1-85431-163-8*, Pub. by Blackstone Pr) Gaunt.

Mafeje, Archie. Science, Ideology & Development: Three Essays on Development Theory. 86p. 1978. write for info. (*91-7106-134-7*, Pub. by Nordic Africa) Transaction Pubs.

Mafeje, Archie & Radwan, Samir, eds. Economic & Demographic Change in Africa. (International Studies in Demography). (Illus.). 184p. 1995. text 45.00 (*0-19-828892-1*) OUP.

Mafera, G., jt. auth. see Anderson, K.

Maffei, Anthony C. Classroom Computers: A Practical Guide for Effective Teaching. (Illus.). 266p. 1986. 38.95 (*0-89885-251-X*, Kluwer Acad Hman Sci); pap. 20.95 (*0-89885-255-2*, Kluwer Acad Hman Sci) Kluwer Academic.

Maffei, Anthony C. & Buckley, Patricia. Teaching Preschool Math: Foundations & Activities. LC 79-27448. 176p. 1980. 26.95 (*0-87705-492-4*, Kluwer Acad Hman Sci) Kluwer Academic.

Maffei, Anthony C., jt. auth. see Hauck, Theresa M.

Maffei, L., ed. Pathophysiology of the Visual System. (Documenta Ophthalmologica Proceedings Ser.: No. 30). 304p. 1981. text 171.00 (*90-6193-726-4*) Kluwer Academic.

Maffei, Maria C., et al, eds. Participation in World Treaties on the Protection of the Environment: A Collection of Data. LC 97-113541. (International Environmental Law & Policy Ser.). 290p. 1997. text 114.00 (*90-411-0879-3*, K3583) Kluwer Law Intl.

Maffei, Nick. Money Management Worksheets - IBM. 1991. 24.95 (*0-8306-6621-4*) McGraw-Hill Prof.

— Money Management Worksheets - IBM PC. 1991. 24.95 (*0-8306-6622-2*) McGraw-Hill Prof.

Maffei, Paolo. Monsters in the Sky. (Illus.). 1980. 35.00 (*0-262-13153-6*) MIT Pr.

Maffei, Xavier. English - Konkani Dictionary. 566p. 1990. 49.95 (*0-8288-8459-5*) Fr & Eur.

— Konkani English Dictionary. 160p. 1990. 29.95 (*0-8288-8460-9*) Fr & Eur.

— Konkani Grammar. 456p. 1986. 39.95 (*0-8288-8461-7*) Fr & Eur.

***Maffeo, Steven E.** Most Secret & Confidential: Intelligence in the Age of Nelson. LC 99-48837. (Illus.). 368p. 2000. 32.95 (*1-55750-545-4*) Naval Inst Pr.

Maffesoli, Michel. The Contemplation of the World: Figures of Community Style. Emanuel, Susan, tr. 1996. pap. 19.95 (*0-8166-2689-8*); text 49.95 (*0-8166-2688-X*) U of Minn Pr.

— Ordinary Knowledge: An Introduction to Interpretative Sociology. Macey, David, tr. 192p. 1996. 76.95 (*0-7456-1118-4*) Blackwell Pubs.

— The Shadow of Dionysus: A Contribution to the Sociology of the Orgy. Linse, C. & Palmquist, M. K., trs. LC 91-41828. 167p. (C). 1992. pap. text 21.95 (*0-7914-1240-7*) State U NY Pr.

— The Shadow of Dionysus: A Contribution to the Sociology of the Orgy. Linse, C. & Palmquist, M. K., trs. LC 91-41828. 167p. (C). 1993. text 64.50 (*0-7914-1239-3*) State U NY Pr.

— The Time of the Tribes: The Decline of Individualism in Mass Societies. (Theory, Culture & Society Ser.). 224p. 1996. 69.95 (*0-8039-8473-1*); pap. 26.95 (*0-8039-8474-X*) Sage.

Maffesoli, Michel, jt. auth. see Nancy, Jean L.

Maffetone, Phillip. Complementary Sports Medicine. LC 98-52399. (Illus.). 440p. 1999. text 55.00 (*0-88011-869-5*) Human Kinetics.

Maffetone, Andrea, ed. see Schaufele, Nancy L. & Kennedy, Donna B.

Maffetone, Philip. In Fitness & in Health. 3rd rev. ed. 296p. Date not set. pap. text 16.95 (*0-9642062-2-6*) D Barmore Prods.

***Maffetone, Philip.** The Maffetone Method: The Holistic, Low-Stress, No-Pain Way to Exceptional Fitness. LC 99-22495. 208p. 1999. pap. 14.95 (*0-07-134331-8*) McGraw.

Maffetone, Philip & Mantell, Matthew E. High Performance Heart: Effective Training with the HRM for Health, Fitness & Competition. 2nd rev. ed. (Illus.). 160p. 1996. pap. 12.95 (*0-933201-64-8*) MBI Pubg.

Maffetone, Philip B. Training for Endurance. Fitzgerald, Matthew, ed. LC 96-83504. 160p. (Orig.). 1996. pap. 12.95 (*0-9642062-1-8*) D Barmore Prods.

Maffett, Andrew L. Topics for a Statistical Description of Radar Cross Section. LC 88-20698. (Remote Sensing & Image Processing Ser.). 373p. 1989. 170.00 (*0-471-61357-6*) Wiley.

Maffett, Michael. Neptune's Account. 348p. 1995. 23.95 (*0-9644618-0-3*) Woodvale Pr.

Maffezzoni, C., ed. Modeling & Control of Electric Power Plants: Proceedings of the IFAC Workshop, Como, Italy, 22-23 September 1983. (IFAC Publication). 176p. 1984. 78.00 (*0-08-031163-6*, Pub. by Pergamon Repr) Franklin.

Maffi, Luisa, jt. ed. see Hardin, C. L.

Maffi, Mario. Gateways to the Promised Land: Ethnicity & Culture in New York's Lower East Side. (Illus.). 350p. (C). 1995. text 47.50 (*0-8147-5509-7*); pap. text 19.00 (*0-8147-5508-9*) NYU Pr.

Maffin, June. Disturbed by God: A Journey of Spiritual Discovery. 128p. 1996. 9.95 (*1-55126-153-7*) Forward Movement.

Maffini, Mary Jane. Speak Ill of the Dead: A Camilla MacPhee Mystery. (Rendezvous Crime Ser.). 304p. 1999. pap. 9.95 (*0-929141-65-2*, Rendezvous) Napoleon Publ.

Maffioli, C. S. Out of Galileo No. 49: The Science of Waters 1628-1718. xx, 509p. 1994. 63.00 (*90-5235-071-X*, Pub. by Erasmus Pub) Balogh.

Maffioli, Len, jt. auth. see Norton, Bruce H.

Maffioli, Leonard J., jt. auth. see Norton, Bruce H.

Maffit, Rocky. Rhythm & Beauty: The Art of Percussion. (Illus.). 136p. 1999. text 35.00 (*0-8230-8406-X*) Watsn-Guptill.

Maffly-Kipp, Laurie R. Religion & Society in Frontier California. LC 93-24808. (Yale Historical Publications). 256p. 1994. 32.50 (*0-300-05377-0*) Yale U Pr.

***Mafi, Maryam & Kolin, Azima Melita.** Rumi: Whispers of the Beloved. 2000. pap. 9.95 (*0-7225-3981-9*, Pub. by Thorsons PA) HarpC.

Mafi, Maryam, tr. & afterword by see Danishvar, Simin.

Mafi, Perry. The Now That Never Was. 119p. (Orig.). 1992. pap. text 7.95 (*0-9631372-1-2*) P Mafi Writs.

— Wake up from Your Dream. 83p. 1990. pap. text 7.95 (*0-9631372-0-4*) P Mafi Writs.

Mafico, Christopher J. Urban Low Income Housing in Zambabwe. 176p. 1991. 82.95 (*1-85628-226-0*, Pub. by Avebry) Ashgate Pub Co.

Mafinezam, Alidad, tr. see Khatami, Mohammad.

Maflin, Andrea. Decorative Paper: Projects, Techniques, Pull-Out Designs. (Illus.). 108p. 1995. pap. 22.95 (*1-57076-027-6*, Trafalgar Sq Pub) Trafalgar.

— Easy & Elegant Home Decorating: 25 Stylish Projects for Your Home. LC 98-9360. (Easy & Elegant Ser.). (Illus.). 128p. 1998. 24.95 (*0-8160-3829-5*) Facts on File.

Maflower Culinary Editors. Picnics & Barbecues. LC 98-134052. (The Everyday Chef Ser.). 64p. 1997. pap. text 5.99 (*1-58029-012-4*, Everywhere) Hambleton-Hill.

Mafor, Andrew. Return to Empire: Punjab under the Sikhs & British in the Mid-19th Century. 1996. write for info. (*81-207-1806-2*) Sterling Pubs.

Mafrou, Edisyon, ed. see Large, Josaphat.

Maga, Joseph A. Smoke in Food Processing. LC 87-24231. 176p. 1988. 101.00 (*0-8493-5155-3*, TP371, CRC Reprint) Franklin.

Maga, Joseph A. & Tu, Anthony T., eds. Food Additive Toxicology. (Illus.). 552p. 1994. text 199.00 (*0-8247-9245-9*) Dekker.

***Maga, Tim.** Judgment at Tokyo: The Japanese War Crimes Trials. (Illus.). 240p. 2001. 25.00 (*0-8131-2177-9*) U Pr of Ky.

Maga, Timothy P. Defending Paradise: The United States & Guam, 1898-1950. 1988. 15.00 (*0-8240-4336-7*) Garland.

— Hands Across the Sea? U. S. - Japan Relations, 1961-1981. LC 97-25016. 194p. 1997. text 29.95 (*0-8214-1210-8*) Ohio U Pr.

— John F. Kennedy & New Frontier Diplomacy, 1961-1963. LC 92-43248. 170p. (C). 1993. lib. bdg. 19.50 (*0-89464-829-2*) Krieger.

— The Perils of Power: Crises in American Foreign Relations since World War II. 189p. (Orig.). 1995. pap. 10.99 (*0-936285-25-7*) U New Haven Pr.

— The World of Jimmy Carter: U. S. Foreign Policy, 1977-1981. Katsaros, Thomas, ed. 200p. (Orig.). 1994. pap. text 10.99 (*0-936285-23-0*) U New Haven Pr.

Magad, Eugene L. & Amos, John M. Total Materials Management: Achieving Maximum Profits Through Materials-Logistics Operations. LC 94-47941. (Materials Management-Logistics Ser.). 1995. write for info. (*0-614-32192-1*, Chap & Hall NY) Chapman & Hall.

Magadini, P. Learn to Play the Drum Set, Bk. 1. 48p. 1980. pap. 5.95 (*0-7935-1199-2*, 06620000) H Leonard.

Magadini, P. Learn to Play the Drum Set, Bk. 1. 48p. 1984. pap. 12.95 (*0-7935-1749-4*, 06620002) H Leonard.

Magadini, P. Learn to Play the Drum Set, Bk. 2. 48p. 1981. pap. 5.95 (*0-7935-1200-X*, 06620001) H Leonard.

Magadini, P. Learn to Play the Drum Set, Bk. 2. 48p. 1988. pap. 12.95 (*0-7935-1750-8*, 06620005) H Leonard.

— Polyrhythms. rev. ed. 68p. 1988. pap. 19.95 (*0-7935-2124-6*, 06620611) H Leonard.

Magadini, P. Polyrhythms, Bk. 1. rev. ed. 68p. 1988. pap. 14.95 (*0-7935-2123-8*, 06620612) H Leonard.

***Magadini, Peter.** Learn to Play the Drumset BK.1: A Professional's Unique Approach to Playing the Drumset. 48p. 1999. pap. 14.95 incl. audio compact disk (*0-634-00524-3*) H Leonard.

— Learn to Play the Drumset BK.2: A Professional's Unique Approach to Playing the Drumset. 48p. 1999. pap. 14.95 incl. audio compact disk (*0-634-00525-1*) H Leonard.

Magadini, Peter. Poly Rhythms for the Drum Set. 60p. (Orig.). 1995. pap. text 21.95 (*0-89724-821-X*, EL9591CD) Wrner Bros.

***Magagna, Anna M.** Best-Loved Bible Verses for Children. (Timothy R. Botts Collection). (Illus.). 12p. 1999. ring bd. 19.99 (*0-8423-3522-6*) Tyndale Hse.

Magagna, Jeanne, ed. see Rey, Henri.

Magagna, Victor V. Communities of Grain: Rural Rebellion in Comparative Perspective. LC 90-55720. (Wilder House Series in Politics, History, & Culture). 312p. 1991. text 47.50 (*0-8014-2361-9*) Cornell U Pr.

Magahem, Jimmy. Smart Drugs: Food for Thought. rev. ed. 1999. pap. 0.50 (*0-89230-246-1*) Do It Now.

Magai, Carol & McFadden, Susan H. The Role of Emotions in Social & Personality Development: History, Theory & Research. (Emotions, Personality, & Psychotherapy Ser.: Vol. 1). (Illus.). 380p. (C). 1995. 49.50 (*0-306-44866-1*, Plenum Trade) Perseus Pubng.

Magai, Carol & McFadden, Susan H., eds. Handbook of Emotion, Adult Development, & Aging. LC 96-22522. (Illus.). 470p. 1996. text 75.00 (*0-12-464995-5*) Acad Pr.

Magaia, Lina. Dumba Nengue: Run for Your Life: Peasant Tales of Tragedy in Mozambique. Wolfers, Michael, tr. from POR. LC 87-72780. (Illus.). 115p. (C). 1988. 14.95 (*0-86543-073-X*); pap. 6.95 (*0-86543-074-8*) Africa World.

Magal Institute Staff, tr. see Porter, Jack N., ed.

Magal, Lily, pseud & Arbel, Rachel. In the Land of the Golden Fleece: The Jews of Georgia-History & Culture. (Illus.). 1993. 38.00 (*965-05-0650-0*, Pub. by Israel Ministry Def) Gefen Bks.

Magalaner, Marvin. Time of Apprenticeship: The Fiction of Young James Joyce. LC 70-140366. (Select Bibliographies Reprint Ser.). 1977. reprint ed. 18.95 (*0-8369-5609-5*) Ayer.

Magalas. Mechanical Spectroscopy of Materials. 1000p. 1997. text. write for info. (*0-412-58450-6*, Chap & Hall NY) Chapman & Hall.

Magalas, L. B. & Gorczyca, S., eds. Internal Friction & Ultrasonic in Solids, Including High-Temperature Superconductors. 876p. (C). 1993. text 283.00 (*0-87849-623-8*, Pub. by Trans T Pub) Enfield Pubs NH.

Magalashivili, Lily, see Magal, Lily, pseud.

Magalhaes, Antonio R. & McKaughan, Sean. Sustainable Development: Implications for World Peace. LC 96-80015. (Tom Slick World Peace Ser.). 248p. 1997. pap. 17.50 (*0-89940-007-8*) LBJ Sch Pub Aff.

Magalhaes, Antonio R. & Schmandt, Jurgen. The Road to Sustainable Development: A Guide for Non-Governmental Organizations. LC 97-70395. (Policy Research Project Reports). 246 p. 1998. pap. 18.00 (*0-89940-730-7*) LBJ Sch Pub Aff.

Magalhaes, Hulda, ed. see American Association of Laboratory Animal Science.

Magalhaes, Jose Calvet De, see Calvet De Magalhaes, Jose.

Magalhaes, Luis, et al, eds. Equadiff, '95: Proceedings of the International Conference on Differential Equations Lisboa, Portugal 24 - 29 July 1995. LC 98-215312. 550p. 1998. 98.00 (*981-02-3421-X*) World Scientific Pub.

Magalini, Sabina I. & Magalini, Sergio C. Dictionary of Medical Syndromes. 4th ed. LC 96-41119. 976p. 1996. text 99.00 (*0-397-58418-0*) Lppncott W & W.

Magalini, Sergio C., jt. auth. see Magalini, Sabina I.

Magalit, Isabelo F. Can a Christian Be a Nationalist? 35p. (Orig.). 1993. pap. 5.00 (*971-10-0517-4*, Pub. by New Day Pub) Cellar.

Magallanes, Eduardo. Querido Alberto: Biografia Autorizado de Juan Gabriel. (SPA., Illus.). 208p. 1995. per. 12.00 (*0-684-81548-6*) S&S Trade Pap.

Magallon, Ana & Betran, J. Antonio, eds. Isidorus Hispaliensis: Concordantia in Isidori Hispaliensis Etymolog, 2 vols. 1200p. write for info. (*0-318-71154-0*) G Olms Pubs.

Magallon, Ana, ed. see Hispaliensis, Isidorus.

Magallon, Linda L. Mutual Dreaming. LC 97-3114. 384p. 1997. per. 12.00 (*0-671-52684-7*) PB.

Magalnick, B. English Reader. 1979. pap. text 6.84 (*0-07-039470-9*) McGraw.

Magaloni, Diana I. Metodologia para el Analisis de la Tecnica Pictorica Mural Prehispanica: El Templo Rojo de Cacaxtla. 88p. 1994. pap. 11.00 (*968-29-5129-1*, IN053) UPLAAP.

Magan, Geralyn G., ed. Aging, Race & Culture: Issues in Long Term Care. LC 82-72776. 77p. 1982. 6.50 (*0-685-06337-2*) Am Assn Homes.

Magan, Margaret A. Brain-Compatible Science. LC 98-60466. (Illus.). 256p. 1998. pap. 36.95 (*1-57517-081-7*, 1594) SkyLght.

Magan, William. The Story of Ireland: A History of an Ancient Irish Family & Their Country from 1690-1914. (Illus.). 428p. 2000. pap. 19.95 (*1-86204-729-4*, Pub. by Element MA) Penguin Putnam.

Magana. Guia Rapida Impresoras Laser.Tr. of Spanish Guide to Laser Printers. (SPA.). 1990. 12.95 (*0-7859-3700-5*, 8428317801) Fr & Eur.

Magana, Lisa, ed. Mexican Americans: Are They an Ambivalent Minority? LC 95-117322. 138p. (YA). (gr. 12 up). 1994. pap. text 15.00 (*1-57240-000-5*) T Rivera Ctr.

Magana, Raoul D., jt. auth. see Gelfand, Leo.

Magana Solis, Luis F. Los Superconductores. (Ciencia para Todos Ser.). (SPA.). pap. 6.99 (*968-16-2920-5*, Pub. by Fondo) Continental Bk.

Magann, Julia H. Municipal Financial Disclosure: An Empirical Investigation. Farmer, Richard N., ed. LC 83-1106. (Research for Business Decisions Ser.: No. 58). 110p. reprint ed. 34.10 (*0-8357-1394-6*, 207040200088) Bks Demand.

Maganza, Dennis M., ed. see Fielding, Henry.

Maganzini, Christy. Almanac of Dungeons, Prisons & Jails. LC 97-18653. (KidBacks Ser.). (J). 1998. pap. 5.99 (*0-679-88353-3*, Pub. by Random Bks Yng Read) Random.

— Cool Math: Math Tricks, Awesome Activities, Amazing Factoids & More. LC 96-40484. (Illus.). 96p. (J). (gr. 4 up). 1997. pap. 6.99 (*0-8431-7857-4*, Price Stern) Peng Put Young Read.

Magarello, Anthony. Good Reading-Good Writing, A. (Effective Language Arts Program Ser.). (Illus.). 59p. 1981. 4.75 (*0-9602800-7-3*) Comp Pr.

— Good Reading-Good Writing, C. (Effective Language Arts Program Ser.). 61p. 1983. 4.75 (*0-9602800-8-1*) Comp Pr.

Magaret, Pat M. & Slusser, Donna I. Watercolor Impressions. 1995. pap. 26.95 (*1-56477-116-4*, B233) Martingale & Co.

— Watercolor Quilts. Weiland, Barbara, ed. LC 93-8551. (Illus.). 118p. (Orig.). 1993. pap. 24.95 (*1-56477-031-1*, B161) Martingale & Co.

Magaret, Patricia Maixner, jt. auth. see Slusser, Donna Ingram.

Magarey, D. R. Buying & Selling Businesses & Companies. 2nd ed. 316p. 1989. 69.00 (*0-409-49535-2*, Austral, MICHIE) LEXIS Pub.

Magarey, Susan, et al, eds. Debutante Nation: Feminism Rewrites History of the 1890's. 224p. 1993. pap. 19.95 (*1-86373-296-9*, Pub. by Allen & Unwin Pty) Paul & Co Pubs.

Magarey, Susan, jt. ed. see Edwards, Anne.

Magargal, Bill, jt. auth. see Spodek, Marie S.

Magarian-Gold, Judi, jt. auth. see Mogensen, Sandra.

Magarian-Gold, Judy, jt. auth. see Mogensen, Sandra.

Magarick, Pat. Casualty Insurance Claims: Coverage-Investigation-Law, 2 vols. 3rd ed. LC 87-16624. 1988. ring bd. 215.00 (*0-87632-559-2*) West Group.

— Casualty Investigation Checklists. 3rd ed. LC 84-23135. 1985. spiral bd. 62.50 (*0-87632-457-X*) West Group.

— Excess Liability: The Law of Extracontractual Liability of Insurers. 3rd ed. LC 88-17495. 1989. ring bd. 135.00 (*0-87632-604-1*) West Group.

An Asterisk (*) at the beginning of an entry indicates that the title is appearing for the first time.

— Insurance Law Review. 1990. 125.00 (*0-87632-847-8*) West Group.

Magarick, Pat & Brownlee, Ken. Casualty Investigation Checklists. 4th ed. LC 94-17154. 1994. spiral bd. 80.00 (*0-87632-073-6*) West Group.

Magaro, Peter A. Cognition in Schizophrenia & Paranoia: The Integration of Cognitive Processes. LC 80-13870. 351p. 1980. text 69.95 (*0-89859-028-0*) L Erlbaum Assocs.

Magaro, Peter A., ed. Cognitive Bases of Mental Disorders. (Annual Review of Psychopathology Ser.: Vol. 1). 352p. (C). 1990. text 56.00 (*0-8039-4009-2*); pap. text 26.00 (*0-8039-4010-6*) Sage.

Magaro, Peter A., et al. The Mental Health Industry: A Cultural Phenomenon. LC 77-14434. (Wiley Series on Personality Processes). 288p. reprint ed. pap. 89.30 (*0-608-13282-9*, 205576100037) Bks Demand.

Magarrell, Elaine. Blameless Lives. LC 91-66080. 84p. (Orig.). 1991. pap. 10.00 (*0-915380-28-5*) Word Works.

— On Hogback Mountain. LC 84-52606. (Series Nine). 54p. 1985. pap. 7.00 (*0-931846-27-7*) Wash Writers Pub.

Magarshack, David, ed. Chekhov: Uncle Vanya (Dyadya Vanya) (Bristol Russian Texts Ser.). (RUS.). 110p. (C). 1992. reprint ed. pap. 18.95 (*1-85399-259-3*, Pub. by Brist Class Pr) Focus Pub-R Pullins.

Magarshack, David, tr. see Chekhov, Anton.

Magarshack, David, tr. see Dostoyevsky, Fyodor.

Magarshack, David, tr. see Gogol, Nikolai Vasilevich.

Magarshack, David, tr. see Goncharov, Ivan A.

Magarshack, David, tr. see Ostrovskii, Aleksandr N.

Magarshack, David, tr. see Ostrovsky, Alexander.

Magarshack, David, tr. see Pasternak, Boris.

Magarshack, David, tr. see Tolstoy, Leo.

Magarshack, David, tr. & intro. see Gogol, Nikolai Vasilevich.

Magarshack, David, tr. & intro. see Saltykov-Shchedrin, Mikhail Evgrafovich.

Magarshack, David, tr. & selected by see Dostoyevsky, Fyodor.

Magas, Branca. The Destruction of Yugoslavia: Tracing the Breakup 1980-1992. LC 92-30825. 384p. (gr. 13). 1993. pap. 23.00 (*0-86091-593-X*, A3754, Pub. by Verso) Norton.

— The Widening Gyre: Class & Nation in Yugoslavia. 256p. 1990. 50.00 (*0-86091-262-0*, A3750); pap. 17.95 (*0-86091-975-7*, A3754) Routledge.

Magasi, P. Surgery of the Neurogenic Bladder. 148p. (C). 1982. 75.00 (*963-05-2892-4*, Pub. by Akade Kiado) St Mut.

Magat, Richard. Unlikely Partners: Philanthropic Foundations & the Labor Movement. LC 98-28132. (Illus.). 272p. 1999. 39.95 (*0-8014-3552-8*, ILR Press) Cornell U Pr.

Magat, Richard, ed. An Agile Servant: Community Leadership by Community Foundations. LC 89-38377. 1989. 24.95 (*0-87954-330-2*); pap. 15.95 (*0-87954-332-9*) Foundation Ctr.

Magat, Wesley A. & Viscusi, W. Kip. Informational Approaches to Regulation. (REA Ser.). (Illus.). 294p. 1992. 37.50 (*0-262-13277-X*) MIT Pr.

Magat, Wesley A., et al. Rules in the Making: A Statistical Analysis of Regulatory Agency Behavior. LC 85-43555. 182p. 1986. text 22.50 (*0-915707-24-1*) Resources Future.

Magat, Wesley A., jt. auth. see Viscusi, W. Kip.

Magaw, John W., ed. Federal Firearms Regulations Reference Guide. 114p. (Orig.). 1996. pap. text 30.00 (*0-7881-2821-3*) DIANE Pub.

Magay, M. I. Hungarian-English & English-Hungarian Dictionary for Tourists. 8th ed. (ENG & HUN.). 629p. 1986. 14.95 (*0-8288-1655-7*, M10680) Fr & Eur.

Magay, T., et al. Hungarian-English & English Hungarian Dictionary for Tourists. 630p. (C). 1991. pap. 21.00 (*963-05-5984-6*, Pub. by Akade Kiado) St Mut.

Magay, T., jt. auth. see Orszagh, L.

Magay, T., ed. see Futasz, D. & Kovecses, Z.

Magay, Tamas. English-Hungarian Concise Dictionary. 17th ed. (HUN.). 703p. 1991. 30.50 (*0-7859-8935-8*, 3426266253) Fr & Eur.

— Hungarian-English Concise Dictionary. 3rd ed. (ENG & HUN.). 1991. 30.50 (*0-7859-8942-0*) Fr & Eur.

Magay, Tamas, et al, eds. English-Hungarian Dictionary of Science & Technology. 1995. 995.00 incl. cd-rom (*963-05-6962-0*, Pub. by Akade Kiado) St Mut.

Magay, Tamas & Kiss, L. English-Hungarian Dictionary of Technology & Science. 1670p. 1993. 180.00 (*963-05-6480-7*, Pub. by Akade Kiado) St Mut.

Magay, Tamas & Kiss, L., eds. Hungarian-English & English Hungarian Paperback Dictionary, 2 vols. 1186p. (C). 1991. pap. 60.00 (*963-05-6056-9*, Pub. by Akade Kiado) St Mut.

Magay, Tamas & Kiss, Laszlo. English-Hungarian Standard Dictionary. 541p. 1995. pap. 40.00 (*0-7818-0391-8*) Hippocrene Bks.

— NTC's Hungarian & English Dictionary. LC 96-12536.Tr. of Angol-Magyar Kisszotar. (ENG & HUN., Illus.). 840p. 1996. 29.95 (*0-8442-4968-8*, 49688, Natl Textbk Co) NTC Contemp Pub Co.

— NTC's Hungarian & English Dictionary. LC 96-12536.Tr. of Angol-Magyar Kisszotar. (HUN & ENG.). 848p. 1998. pap. 23.95 (*0-8442-4969-6*, 49696, Natl Textbk Co) NTC Contemp Pub Co.

Magay, Tamas & Lang, I. L. Anglicisms, Americanisms. 320p. (C). 1993. 24.00 (*963-05-6043-7*, Pub. by Akade Kiado) St Mut.

— Anglicisms, Americanisms. (ENG & HUN.). 320p. 1991. 14.95 (*0-8288-7190-6*, F88860) Fr & Eur.

Magay, Tamas & Orszagh, Laszlo. A Concise English-Hungarian Dictionary. 1052p. (C). 1992. 100.00 (*963-05-6338-X*, Pub. by Akade Kiado) St Mut.

— A Concise Hungarian-English Dictionary. 3rd rev. ed. 1152p. (C). 1993. 65.00 (*963-05-6547-1*, Pub. by Akade Kiado) St Mut.

— English-Hungarian Concise Dictionary. 17th ed. 1045p. 1991. 38.00 (*963-05-6669-9*) IBD Ltd.

— Hungarian-English Concise Dictionary. rev. ed. 1152p. 1996. 52.00 (*963-05-6907-8*) IBD Ltd.

Magay, Tamas & Orszagh, Laszlo, eds. A Concise Hungarian-English Dictionary. rev. ed. (HUN & ENG.). 1152p. 1990. 55.00 (*0-19-864169-9*) OUP.

Magay, Tamas & Zigany, J., eds. Budalex 88 Proceedings. 580p. (C). 1990. pap. 180.00 (*963-05-5863-7*, Pub. by Akade Kiado) St Mut.

Magazine, Alan H. Environmental Management in Local Government: A Study of Local Response to Federal Mandate. LC 77-12818. (Special Studies). 148p. 1977. 45.00 (*0-275-90269-2*, C0269, Praeger Pubs) Greenwood.

Magazine Marketing Service Staff. M. M. S. County Buying Power Index. LC 75-22826. (America in Two Centuries Ser.). 1976. reprint ed. 20.95 (*0-405-07698-3*) Ayer.

Magazine of Wall Street Staff. Fourteen Methods of Operating in the Stock Market. LC 68-29698. 1968. reprint ed. 13.00 (*0-87034-027-1*) Fraser Pub Co.

Magaziner, Allan. Complete Idiot's Guide to Living Longer & Healthier. LC 98-89624. (Illus.). 400p. 1998. 16.95 (*0-02-862934-5*) Macmillan Gen Ref.

***Magaziner, Allan.** Total Health Handbook. (Illus.). 2000. pap. 17.00 (*1-57566-483-6*) Kensgtn Pub Corp.

Magaziner, Ira C. & Hout, Thomas M. Japanese Industrial Policy. LC 81-80791. (Policy Papers in International Affairs: No. 15). (Illus.). 120p. 1981. pap. text 9.50 (*0-87725-515-6*) U of Cal IAS.

Magda, Kovacs. Microelectronics Dictionary in Three Languages. 1990. pap. 28.50 (*0-7859-8964-1*) Fr & Eur.

Magda, Matthew S., ed. Monessen: Industrial Boomtown & Steel Community, 1898-1980. (American Places Ser.). (Illus.). 152p. 1985. pap. text 6.95 (*0-89271-029-2*) Pa Hist & Mus.

Magdalany, Philip. Criss-Crossing & Watercolor: Manuscript Edition. 1970. pap. 13.00 (*0-8222-0251-4*) Dramatists Play.

Magdalen. Children in the Church Today: An Orthodox Perspective. (Illus.). 104p. (Orig.). 1990. pap. 8.95 (*0-88141-104-3*) St Vladimirs.

Magdalena. The Real Preacher. 1986. 30.00 (*0-946270-23-6*, Pub. by Pentland Pr) St Mut.

Magdalena, Flo A. Sunlight on Water: A Manual for Soul-Full Living. Zopf, Jayn A. & McInnis, Noel, eds. (Illus.). 434p. (Orig.). 1996. pap. 19.95 (*1-880914-12-3*) All Worlds Pub.

Magdaleno, Mauricio. El Ardiente Verano. (SPA.). pap. 7.99 (*968-16-0260-9*, Pub. by Fondo) Continental Bk.

— Jose Marti. 1976. lib. bdg. 250.00 (*0-8490-2108-1*) Gordon Pr.

— Sunburst. Brenner, Anita, tr. from SPA. LC 74-25390. reprint ed. 34.50 (*0-404-58449-7*) AMS Pr.

Magdalino, Paul. The Empire of Manuel I Komnenos, 1142-1180. LC 92-13501. (Illus.). 583p. (C). 1993. text 95.00 (*0-521-30571-3*) Cambridge U Pr.

— Tradition & Transformation in Medieval Byzantium. (Collected Studies: No. CS 343). 350p. 1991. text 117.95 (*0-86078-295-6*, Pub. by Variorum) Ashgate Pub Co.

Magdalino, Paul, ed. New Constantines: The Rhythm of Imperial Renewal in Byzantium, 4th-13th Centuries. LC 94-5125. (Publications - Society for the Promotion of Byzantine Studies: Vol. 2). 324p. 1994. text 77.95 (*0-86078-409-6*, Pub. by Variorum) Ashgate Pub Co.

— The Perception of the Past in Twelfth-Century Europe. 256p. 1992. 55.00 (*1-85285-066-3*) Hambledon Press.

Magdalino, Paul, jt. ed. see Ricks, David.

Magdanz, James. Go Home, River. LC 96-5769. (Illus.). 32p. (J). (ps up). 1996. 15.95 (*0-88240-476-8*, Alaska NW Bks) Gr Arts Ctr Pub.

Magdanz, Lee. Color the Inside of Your Brain. (Illus.). 22p. 1989. pap. 9.95 (*0-9613949-2-7*) R S Pr.

Magdaong-Manginsay, Edna G., jt. auth. see Alonto, Zafrullah M.

Magdassi, Shlomo. Surface Activities of Proteins: Chemical & Physical Modifications. LC 96-25981. (Illus.). 336p. 1996. text 150.00 (*0-8247-9532-6*) Dekker.

Magdassi, Shlomo & Touitou, Elka, eds. Novel Cosmetic Delivery Systems. LC 98-31683. (Cosmetic Science & Technology Ser.: Vol. 19). (Illus.). 376p. 1998. text 165.00 (*0-8247-1703-1*) Dekker.

Magdelen, Margaret. Transformed by Love: The Way of Mary Magdalen. LC 90-61562. 96p. (Orig.). 1990. pap. 5.95 (*0-9623410-5-3*, Resurrection Pr) Catholic Bk Pub.

Magden, Ronald. Fursato. (Illus.). 248 p. 1998. 49.95 (*0-9629616-4-7*) Magden Assocs.

Magden, Ronald E. A History of Seattle Waterfront Workers 1884-1934. (Illus.). 280p. (Orig.). 1991. pap. 10.00 (*0-9629578-0-1*) Magden Assocs.

— The Working Longshoreman. (Illus.). 208p. (Orig.). 1991. 10.00 (*0-9629616-1-2*) Magden Assocs.

Magden, Ronald E. & Martinson, A. D. The Working Waterfront: The Story of Tacoma's Ships & Men. (Illus.). 181p. (Orig.). 1982. pap. 10.00 (*0-9629578-2-8*) Intl Long WA.

Magder, Ted. Canada's Hollywood: The Canadian State & Feature Films. (State & Economic Life Ser.). 368p. 1993. text 50.00 (*0-8020-2970-1*); pap. text 22.95 (*0-8020-7433-2*) U of Toronto Pr.

Magdi Wahba. English-Arabic Dictionary: Al-Mukhtar. 1989. 39.95 (*0-86685-535-1*) Intl Bk Ctr.

Magdich, L. N. & Molchanov, V. Y. Acousto-optical Devices & Their Applications. viii, 160p. 1989. text 218.00 (*2-88124-677-X*) Gordon & Breach.

Magdics, Klara. Studies in the Acoustic Characteristics of Hungarian Speech Sounds. LC 68-65314. (Uralic & Altaic Ser.: Vol. 97). (Illus.). 141p. 1969. pap. text 12.00 (*0-87750-041-X*) Res Inst Inner Asian Studies.

Magdoff, F. R., et al. Soil Organic Matter: Analysis & Interpretation. (SSSA Special Publications: No. 46). 67p. 1996. 24.00 (*0-89118-822-3*) Soil Sci Soc Am.

Magdoff, Fred. Hungry for Profit: The Agribusiness Threat to Farmers, Food & the Environment. 1999. pap. 19.00 (*1-58367-016-5*, Pub. by Monthly Rev) NYU Pr.

***Magdoff, Fred, et al, eds.** Hungry for Profit: The Agribusiness Threat to Farmers, Food & the Environment. 220p. 1999. 45.00 (*1-58367-015-7*, Pub. by Monthly Rev) NYU Pr.

***Magdoff, Fred & Vanes, Harold.** Building Soils for Better Crops. 2nd ed. (Illus.). 240p. 2000. pap. 19.95 (*1-888626-05-4*) Sustnble Agri.

Magdoff, Harry. Imperialism: From the Colonial Age to the Present. LC 77-76167. 279p. 1979. pap. 12.00 (*0-85345-498-1*, Pub. by Monthly Rev) NYU Pr.

Magdoff, Harry & Sweezy, Paul M. The End of Prosperity: The American Economy in the 1970's. LC 77-76168. 136p. 1977. 25.00 (*0-85345-422-1*, Pub. by Monthly Rev) NYU Pr.

— The Irreversible Crisis. 96p. (Orig.). (C). 1989. pap. 10.00 (*0-85345-776-X*, Pub. by Monthly Rev) NYU Pr.

— Stagnation & the Financial Explosion. 224p. 1987. 24.00 (*0-85345-716-6*); pap. 10.00 (*0-85345-715-8*, Pub. by Monthly Rev) NYU Pr.

Magdoff, Harry, jt. auth. see Sweezy, Paul M.

Magdoff, Harry, jt. ed. see Sweezy, Paul M.

Magdol, Edward. The Antislavery Rank & File: A Social Profile of the Abolitionists' Constituency, 117. LC 85-30191. (Contributions in American History Ser.: No. 117). 188p. 1986. 52.95 (*0-313-24723-4*, MRK/, Greenwood Pr) Greenwood.

— A Right to the Land: Essays on the Freedmen's Community, 61. LC 76-39707. (Contributions in American History Ser.: No. 61). (Illus.). 290p. 1977. 59.95 (*0-8371-9409-1*, MFC/, Greenwood Pr) Greenwood.

Magdol, Edward & Wakelyn, Jon L. The Southern Common People: Studies in Nineteenth-Century Social History, 86. LC 79-7724. (Contributions in American History Ser.: No. 86). (Illus.). 386p. (C). 1980. 69.50 (*0-313-21403-4*, MLL/, Greenwood Pr) Greenwood.

Magee. Grammar Workbook Mosaics. 1997. pap. text 6.67 (*0-13-918509-7*) P-H.

— Mosaics: Focusing on Sentences in Context. (C). 1997. wbk. ed. 6.67 (*0-13-919481-9*, Macmillan Coll) P-H.

Magee, jt. auth. see Weiss.

Magee, Anthony I., ed. Protein Targeting: A Practical Approach. (Practical Approach Ser.). (Illus.). 288p. 1992. pap. text 49.95 (*0-19-963210-3*) OUP.

Magee, Bernard. Quiz & Puzzle Book. 1998. pap. 9.95 (*0-572-02392-8*, Pub. by W Foulsham) Trans-Atl Phila.

Magee, Brian. In the Light of Christ: The Old Testament Readings at the Easter Vigil. 1994. pap. 21.00 (*1-85390-296-9*, Pub. by Veritas Pubns) St Mut.

— Reading for the Funeral Mass. 72p. 1989. pap. 22.00 (*0-86217-222-5*, Pub. by Veritas Pubns) St Mut.

— Readings for Your Wedding. 88p. 1989. pap. 22.00 (*0-86217-211-X*, Pub. by Veritas Pubns) St Mut.

— The Story of Philosophy. LC 98-3780. 240p. (YA). (gr. 6 up). 1998. 29.95 (*0-7894-3511-X*) DK Pub Inc.

Magee, Brian, intro. Psalm Prayers for Morning & Evening. 65p. (Orig.). 1991. pap. 5.95 (*1-85390-121-0*, Pub. by Veritas Pubns) St Mut.

Magee, Bryan. Aspects of Wagner. 2nd ed. 112p. 1988. pap. 12.95 (*0-19-284012-6*) OUP.

— Confessions of a Philosopher: A Personal Journey Through Western Philosophy from Plato to Popper. LC 98-32048. 1999. pap. 13.95 (*0-375-75036-3*) Modern Library Prakashan.

— Democratic Revolution. LC 64-25509. 1964. 18.95 (*0-8023-1075-3*) Dufour.

— The Great Philosophers. (Illus.). 352p. 1988. pap. text 13.95 (*0-19-282201-2*) OUP.

***Magee, Bryan.** The Great Philosophers: An Introduction to Western Philosophy. (Illus.). 352p. 2000. pap. 15.95 (*0-19-289322-X*) OUP.

Magee, Bryan. The Philosophy of Schopenhauer. 2nd enl. rev. ed. LC 97-220691. 476p. 1997. pap. text 18.95 (*0-19-823722-7*) OUP.

Magee, Bryan & Milligan, Martin. On Blindness: Letters Between Bryan Magee & Martin Milligan. 200p. (C). 1996. 22.00 (*0-19-823543-7*) OUP.

Magee, Christopher S., jt. auth. see Baldwin, Robert E.

Magee, D. F. & Dalley, A. F. Digestion & the Structure & Function of the Gut. (Continuing Education Ser.: Vol. 8). (Illus.). viii, 360p. 1986. 128.75 (*3-8055-4204-6*) S Karger.

Magee, David. The Grabhorn Press, Nineteen Fifteen to Nineteen Fifty-Six: A Bibliography. LC 75-14603. 1975. 150.00 (*0-915346-04-4*) A Wofsy Fine Arts.

— The Lifeforce Maximizer. LC 86 81432. (Illus.). 164p. (Orig.). 1986. pap. 39.50 (*0-938811-00-2*) Life Survival Digest.

Magee, David J. Orthopedic Physical Assessment. 3rd ed. LC 96-41121. (Illus.). 815p. 1997. text 51.95 (*0-7216-6290-0*, W B Saunders Co) Harcrt Hlth Sci Grp.

— Physiological Basis Musculoskeletal Therapy. 1997. text. write for info. (*0-7216-5982-9*, W B Saunders Co) Harcrt Hlth Sci Grp.

Magee, David J., et al. Athletic Injuries & Rehabilitation. Biblis, Margaret, ed. LC 95-23428. (Illus.). 992p. 1996. text 99.00 (*0-7216-4946-7*, W B Saunders Co) Harcrt Hlth Sci Grp.

Magee, David S. Everything Your Heirs Need to Know: Organizing Your Assets, Family History & Final Wishes. 3rd ed. LC 98-228209. 1998. pap. 19.95 (*0-7931-2987-7*) Dearborn.

Magee, Dennis W. Freshwater Wetlands: A Guide to Common Indicator Plants of the Northeast. LC 80-26876. (Illus.). 240p. 1981. pap. text 18.95 (*0-87023-317-3*) U of Mass Pr.

Magee, Dennis W. & Ahles, Harry E. Flora of the Northeast: A Manual of the Vascular Flora of New England & Adjacent New York. LC 98-49300. (Illus.). 1248p. 1999. 69.95 (*1-55849-189-9*) U of Mass Pr.

Magee, Doug & Newman, Robert. All Aboard ABC. (Illus.). 48p. (J). (ps-3). 1994. pap. 6.99 (*0-14-055351-7*, PuffinBks) Peng Put Young Read.

Magee, Elaine. Alphabet Cooking. LC 97-26731. 144p. 1998. pap. 14.95 (*0-8092-2970-6*, 297060, Contemporary Bks) NTC Contemp Pub Co.

***Magee, Elaine.** Around the World in 80 Recipes: A Children's Tour of Cultures & Cuisines. (Illus.). 224p. (J). 2000. pap. 16.95 (*1-58182-049-6*, Cumberland Hearthside) Cumberland Hse.

Magee, Elaine. Bible Lessons in the Kitchen: Activities for Children Ages 5+ LC 98-230255. 112p. (Orig.). 1997. pap. 11.95 (*1-56561-124-1*) Wiley.

***Magee, Elaine.** Chez Moi: Lightening up Recipes from Famous Restaurants. LC 99-50113. (Illus.). 288p. 1999. pap. 16.95 (*1-58182-041-0*, Cumberland Hearthside) Cumberland Hse.

Magee, Elaine. Eat Well for a Healthy Menopause: The Low-Fat, High-Nutrition Guide. 288p. 1997. pap. 5.99 (*0-471-19360-7*) Wiley.

— The Good News Eating Plan for Type II Diabetes. LC 97-38639. (Illus.). 240p. 1997. pap. 15.95 (*0-471-17624-9*) Wiley.

***Magee, Elaine.** Recipe Doctor. LC 99-56128. 356p. 2000. pap. 12.95 (*1-58062-342-5*) Adams Media.

Magee, Elaine. Someone's in the Kitchen with Mommy. LC 96-29326. 160p. 1997. bds. 15.95 (*0-8092-3142-5*, 314250, Contemporary Bks) NTC Contemp Pub Co.

Magee, Elaine. Taste Vs. Fat: How to Save Money, Time, & Your Taste Buds by Knowing Which Brand-name Products Rate the Highest on Taste & Nutrition. 208p. 1997. pap. 12.95 (*0-471-34708-6*) Wiley.

Magee, Elaine. Tell Me What to Eat If I Have Diabetes: Nutrition You Can Live With. LC 99-38601. 160p. 1999. pap. 10.99 (*1-56414-426-7*) Career Pr Inc.

***Magee, Elaine.** Tell Me What to Eat If I Have Irritable Bowel Syndrome: Nutrition You Can Live With. (Tell Me What to Eat Ser.). 160p. 2000. pap. 10.99 (*1-56414-444-5*) Career Pr Inc.

— Tell Me What to Eat to Help Prevent Breast Cancer: Nutrition You Can Live With. LC 00-20749. 160p. 2000. pap. 10.99 (*1-56414-447-X*) Career Pr Inc.

— Tell Me What to Eat to Help Prevent Colon Cancer: Nutrition You Can Live With. 160p. 2001. pap. 10.99 (*1-56414-514-X*, New Page Bks) Career Pr Inc.

— Tell Me What to Eat When I Approach Menopause: Nutrition You Can Live With. LC 99-16766. 160p. 1999. pap. text 10.99 (*1-56414-425-9*) Career Pr Inc.

Magee, Elanie. Bible Lessons in the Kitchen: Activities for Children Ages 5 & Up. 112p. 1997. pap. 11.95 (*0-471-34662-4*) Wiley.

Magee, Elizabeth. Richard Wagner & the Nibelungs. 242p. 1991. text 65.00 (*0-19-816190-5*) OUP.

Magee, Frances T., jt. auth. see Magee, Stephen P.

Magee, Gary B. Productivity & Performance in the Paper Industry: Labour, Capital & Technology in Britain & America, 1860-1914. LC 96-26082. (Cambridge Studies in Modern Economic History: No. 4). 309p. 1997. text 59.95 (*0-521-58197-4*) Cambridge U Pr.

Magee, Gordon. Is Jesus in the Godhead or Is the Godhead in Jesus? 48p. 1998. pap. 3.99 (*0-932581-32-3*) Word Aflame.

Magee, Gregory H. Facilities Maintenance Management. (Illus.). 280p. (C). 1988. 86.95 (*0-87629-100-0*, 67249) R S Means.

Magee, Heno. Hatchet. 76p. 1988. pap. 12.95 (*0-902996-67-3*) Dufour.

— Hatchet. 1978. pap. 2.95 (*0-912262-48-6*) Proscenium.

— Hatchet. deluxe ed. 1978. 7.50 (*0-912262-47-8*) Proscenium.

MaGee, Herman J. Unit Costs of Salaries in Teachers College & Normal Schools. LC 73-177046. (Columbia University. Teachers College. Contributions to Education Ser.: No. 489). reprint ed. 37.50 (*0-404-55489-X*) AMS Pr.

Magee, J. H. Night of Affliction & Morning of Recovery. LC 77-89397. (Black Heritage Library Collection). 1977. 15.95 (*0-8369-8622-9*) Ayer.

Magee, J. O. Company Accounts. 445p. (C). 1982. 85.00 (*0-7855-5664-8*, Pub. by Inst Pur & Supply) St Mut.

Magee, J. Robert. Japan Cheap & Easy: A Practical Guide to Daily Life in Japan. 168p. (Orig.). 1993. pap. 11.95 (*4-89684-231-6*, Pub. by Yohan Pubns) Weatherhill.

Magee, J. Robert, adapted by. Japanese Fairy Tales: Warashibe Chaja, a Fortune from Straw & Other Stories. (Illus.). 154p. (J). 1996. pap. 11.95 (*4-89684-247-2*, Pub. by Yohan Pubns) Weatherhill.

Magee, J. Robert, tr. from JPN. Japanese Fairy Tales I. 161p. 1995. pap. text 11.95 (*4-89684-245-6*, Pub. by Yohan Pubns) Weatherhill.

Magee, J. S. & Dolbear, Geoffrey E. Petroleum Catalysis in Nontechnical Language. LC 98-12063. 1998. 64.95 (*0-87814-661-X*) PennWell Bks.

Magee, J. S. & Mitchell, M. M., Jr., eds. Fluid Catalytic Cracking: Science & Technology. LC 93-20742. (Studies in Surface Science & Catalysis: Vol. 76). 624p. 1993. 302.00 (*0-444-89037-8*) Elsevier.

M

An Asterisk (*) at the beginning of an entry indicates that the title is appearing for the first time.

M

Magee, James E. Your Place in the Cosmos Vol. I: A Layman's Book of Astronomy & the Mythology of the Eighty-Eight Celestial Constellations & Registry. (Illus.). 530p. (YA). 1985. text 34.45 (*0-9614354-0-2*) Mosele & Assocs.
— Your Place in the Cosmos Vol. II: A Layman's Book of Astronomy & the Mythology of the Eighty-Eight Celestial Constellations & Registry. (Illus.). 508p. (YA). 1988. text 34.45 (*0-9614354-1-0*) Mosele & Assocs.
— Your Place in the Cosmos Vol. III: A Layman's Book of Astronomy & the Mythology of the Eighty-Eight Celestial Constellations & Registry. (Illus.). 388p. (YA). 1992. text 49.45 (*0-9614354-2-9*) Mosele & Assocs.
Magee, James J. Mr. Justice Black, Absolutist on the Court. LC 79-11555. (Virginia Legal Studies). 232p. reprint ed. pap. 72.00 (*0-608-18803-4*, 203018800067) Bks Demand.
Magee, Jarlon. Sanctuary of Illusion. LC 91-60468. 1991. pap. 12.95 (*0-87212-248-4*) Libra.
Magee, Jeff. Bounceback. 1992. pap. 12.95 (*0-932845-50-9*) Lowell Pr.
***Magee, Jeff & Kramer, Jeff.** Concurrency: State Models & Java Programs. LC 98-51717. (Worldwide Series in Computer Science). (Illus.). 374p. 1999. 64.99 incl. cd-rom (*0-471-98710-7*) Wiley.
Magee, Jeffrey, jt. auth. see Crawford, Richard.
Magee, Jeffrey L. Enough Already! The 50 Fastest Ways to Deal with, Manage & Eliminate Negativity at Work & Home. (Illus.). 162p. (C). 1998. pap. 12.95 (*0-9641240-9-2*) J Magee Intl.
— The Leadership Alternative: The Ultimate Management Handbook 9-Steps to High Impact Leadership. 1996. pap. text 19.95 (*0-9641240-2-5*) J Magee Intl.
— The P Factor: The Personality Jumpstart Advantage. Spaith, Nancey, ed. 250p. 1993. pap. 19.95 (*0-9641240-0-9*) J Magee Intl.
— Power Charged for Life! Designing a Championship Attitude. Drissel, Nancy, ed. 80p. (Orig.). (C). 1994. pap. 12.95 (*0-9641240-1-7*) J Magee Intl.
— Yield Management: The Leadership Alternative for Performance & Net Profit Improvement. LC 97-45717. (Illus.). 327p. 1998. 29.95 (*1-57444-206-6*) St Lucie Pr.
***Magee, Jeffrey L. & Kent-Fessaro, Jay.** Coaching for Impact: Leadership & the Art of Coaching, the New Rules of Engagement & How They Impact the Generational Segmentations at Work! 254p. 2000. 19.95 (*0-9641240-3-3*) J Magee Intl.
Magee, John. Analyzing Bar Charts for Profits. McDermott, Richard J., ed. & illus. by. LC 99-25084. 248p. 1997. per. 29.95 (*0-910944-03-2*) St Lucie Pr.
— Boethius on Signification & Mind. LC 89-37962. (Philosophia Antiqua Ser.: Vol. LII). xiv, 165p. (Orig.). 1989. pap. 71.00 (*90-04-09096-7*) Brill Academic Pubs.
— Microbe Base - Apple. 1986. text 1049.00 incl. disk (*0-12-465014-7*) Acad Pr.
***Magee, John.** Winning the Mental Game on Wall Street: The Psychology & Philosophy of Successful Investing. (John Magee Investment Ser.). 464p. 2000. boxed set 44.95 (*0-910944-17-2*) St Lucie Pr.
Magee, John, ed. Anicii Manlii Severini Boethii de Divisione Liber: Critical Edition, Translation, Prolegomena, & Commentary. LC 97-50500. (Philosophia Antiqua Ser.: No. 77). (Illus.). 344p. 1998. 117.50 (*90-04-10873-4*) Brill Academic Pubs.
Magee, John, jt. auth. see Edwards, Robert D.
Magee, Joseph H., jt. auth. see Horwitz, Orville.
Magee, Kathleen, jt. auth. see Brewer, John D.
Magee, Kenneth R. & Saper, Joel R. Clinical & Basic Neurology for Health Professionals. LC 80-27146. 311p. reprint ed. pap. 96.50 (*0-608-15894-1*, 203079200074) Bks Demand.
Magee, Kenneth R., jt. auth. see Simpson, John F.
Magee, Kevin. Recent Events. 1995. pap. 10.00 (*0-9649595-0-X*) Hypobololemaioi.
Magee, Linda. 201 Group Games. (Game & Party Bks.). 72p. (gr. 10). 1984. pap. 5.99 (*0-8010-6154-7*) Baker Bks.
Magee, Maggie & Miller, Diana C. Lesbian Lives: Psychoanalytic Narratives Old & New. LC 97-35034. 448p. 1997. 55.00 (*0-88163-269-4*) Analytic Pr.
Magee, Mary L., jt. auth. see Magee, Tom.
Magee, Matthew. Dublin on a Shoestring: The Insider's Guide. (Illus.). 256p. 1998. pap. 9.95 (*1-899047-30-1*, Pub. by A A Farmar) Irish Bks Media.
Magee, Mike. The Principles of Positive Leadership: Lessons for Positive Living. 116p. 1995. 14.95 (*1-889793-01-9*) Spencer Bks.
Magee, Mike, ed. The 50 Most Positive Doctors in America. (Illus.). 152p. 1996. 49.95 (*1-889793-00-0*) Spencer Bks.
Magee, Patricia. Raising a Happy, Confident & Successful Child: 52 Principles to Help Parents Grow. 120p. (Orig.). 1996. pap. 9.95 (*1-889793-02-7*) Spencer Bks.
Magee, Patricia, et al. Building Blocks: Year One. (Illus.). 93p. (Orig.). 1996. pap. 9.95 (*1-889793-03-5*) Spencer Bks.
— Building Blocks: Year Three. (Illus.). 93p. (Orig.). 1997. pap. 9.95 (*1-889793-05-1*) Spencer Bks.
— Building Blocks: Year Two. (Illus.). 93p. (Orig.). 1997. pap. 9.95 (*1-889793-04-3*) Spencer Bks.
MaGee, Patrick. Brain Dancing: Work Smarter, Learn Faster & Manage Information More Effectively. rev. ed. Walsh, Caitilin, ed. LC 96-94115. (Illus.). 300p. 1998. pap. 19.95 (*0-9646260-2-0*) BrainDance.
Magee, Paul. Focus on Society. 2nd ed. 164p. (C). 1987. pap. text 8.95 (*0-87901-375-3*) Worth.
***Magee, Paul.** From Here to Tierra Del Fuego. LC 99-6942. (Transnational Cultural Studies). 200p. 2000. text 29.95 (*0-252-02555-5*) U of Ill Pr.
Magee, Peter N., ed. Nitrosamines & Human Cancer. LC 82-12952. (Banbury Reports: Vol. 12). 599p. 1982. 67.00 (*0-87969-211-1*) Cold Spring Harbor.
Magee, Philip S., et al, eds. Pesticide Synthesis Through Rational Approaches: Based on a Symposium Sponsored by the Division of Pesticide Chemistry at the 186th Meeting of the American Chemical Society, Washington, DC, August 28-September 2, 1983. LC 84-11062. (ACS Symposium Ser.: No. 255). (Illus.). 368p. reprint ed. pap. 114.10 (*0-7837-1965-5*, 205244300001) Bks Demand.
Magee, R. Dale, ed. see Boucher, David.
Magee, Richard D., jt. ed. see Marsh, Diane T.
Magee, Richard S., et al. Innovative Site Remediation Technology Vol. 7: Thermal Destruction. Anderson, William C., ed. LC 93-20786. 128p. 1994. 79.95 (*1-883767-07-5*) Am Acad Environ.
Magee, Robert J. Japan Cheap & Easy: A Practical Guide to Daily Life in Japan. LC 97-51892. 1998. 9.95 (*0-8348-0422-0*) Weatherhill.
Magee, Robert P. Reading Japanese Around You. (JPN.). 160p. (Orig.). 1994. pap. 11.95 (*4-89684-240-5*, Pub. by Yohan Pubns) Weatherhill.
Magee, Rosemary M., ed. Conversations with Flannery O'Connor. LC 86-22381. (Literary Conversations Ser.). 146p. 1987. pap. 17.00 (*0-87805-265-8*); text 39.50 (*0-87805-264-X*) U Pr of Miss.
— Friendship & Sympathy: Communities of Southern Women Writers. LC 91-25615. 1992. pap. text 16.95 (*0-87805-545-2*) U Pr of Miss.
Magee, Sean. That's Racing. O'Sullevan, Peter, ed. (Illus.). 208p. 1996. pap. 22.95 (*1-85158-828-0*, Pub. by Mainstream Pubng) Trafalgar.
Magee, Sean, compiled by. The Race of My Life. (Illus.). 168p. 1997. 40.00 (*0-7472-1259-7*, Pub. by Headline Bk Pub) Trafalgar.
— The Race of My Life. (Illus.). 176p. 1998. pap. 29.95 (*0-7472-7778-8*, Pub. by Headline Bk Pub) Trafalgar.
***Magee, Sean, ed.** Coming to the Last: A Tribute to Peter O'Sullevan. 2000. 22.95 (*1-85225-263-4*, Pub. by Transworld Publishers Ltd) Trafalgar.
Magee, Stephen P. International Trade & Distortions in Factor Markets. LC 75-25163. (Business Economics & Finance Ser.: No. 6). 158p. reprint ed. pap. 49.00 (*0-7837-0701-0*, 204103300019) Bks Demand.
Magee, Stephen P., et al, eds. Black Hole Tariffs & Endogenous Policy Theory: Political Economy in General Equilibrium. (Illus.). 464p. (C). 1989. text 89.95 (*0-521-36247-4*); pap. text 27.95 (*0-521-37700-5*) Cambridge U Pr.
Magee, Stephen P. & Magee, Frances T. A Plague of Lawyers: Greed & the American Legal System. 1994. write for info. (*0-446-51811-5*) Warner Bks.
Magee, Susan F., jt. auth. see Pachter, Barbara.
Magee, Tim, et al. A Solar Greenhouse Guide for the Pacific Northwest. 2nd ed. Stewart, Annie & Sassaman, Richard, eds. (Illus.). 91p. 1979. pap. 6.00 (*0-934478-26-0*) Ecotope.
Magee, Tom & Hoy, Ray. Opportunities Do Not Knock. large type ed. (Illus.). 300p. Date not set. pap. 24.95 (*1-56559-902-0*) HGI-Over Fifty.
Magee, Tom & Magee, Mary L. Baja California Business & Retirement Guide. large type rev. ed. (Retirement & Relocation Guide Ser.). (Illus.). 350p. (Orig.). 1999. pap. 24.95 (*1-56559-903-9*) HGI-Over Fifty.
— RV'ing for Fun & Profit. large type ed. LC 96-75992. (For Fun & Profit Ser.). (Illus.). 300p. (Orig.). 1996. pap. 24.95 (*1-56559-901-2*) HGI-Over Fifty.
Magee, Trish. Raising a Happy Confident Successful Child: 52 Lessons to Help Parents Grow. LC 97-39261. 144p. 1998. 7.95 (*1-55850-836-8*) Adams Media.
Magee, Veda. To Emma. LC 95-60146. 250p. 1995. text. write for info. (*1-882194-14-4*) TN Valley Pub.
Magee, Veda H. Tass. LC 96-61333. 226p. 1996. 21.00 (*1-882194-28-4*) TN Valley Pub.
***Magee, Vishu.** Archetype Design: House As a Vehicle for Spirit. LC 99-90459. (Illus.). 224p. 1999. pap. 19.95 (*0-9672163-0-3*) Archetype Design.
Magee, Wes. Dark Age. 56p. 1982. pap. 11.95 (*0-85640-256-7*, Pub. by Blackstaff Pr) Dufour.
— Legend of the Ragged Boy. (Illus.). 32p. (J). (ps-3). 1993. 14.45 (*1-55970-228-1*, Pub. by Arcade Pub Inc) Time Warner.
Magee, Wes. Madtail Miniwhale & Other Shape Poems. (Illus.). 1991. pap. 9.95 (*0-14-034031-9*, Pub. by Pnguin Bks Ltd) Trafalgar.
***Magee, William.** The Nature of Things: Emptiness & Essence in the Geluk World. LC 00-22590. 244p. 2000. pap. 19.95 (*1-55939-145-6*) Snow Lion Pubns.
Magee, William A. & Napper, Elizabeth S. Fluent Tibetan: A Proficiency Oriented Learning System, Novice & Intermediate Levels, 18 tapes, Set of 3. Hopkins, Jeffrey, ed. LC 93-4076. 1025p. 1993. pap. 250.00 incl. audio (*1-55939-021-2*) Snow Lion Pubns.
Magee, William H. Convention & the Art of Jane Austen's Heroines. 199p. (Orig.). 1995. text 69.95 (*1-883255-85-6*); pap. text 49.95 (*1-883255-84-8*) Intl Scholars.
Magee, William K. Anglo-Irish Essays. LC 67-26738. (Essay Index Reprint Ser.). 1977. reprint ed. 17.95 (*0-8369-0664-0*) Ayer.
— Irish Literary Portraits. LC 67-23243. (Essay Index Reprint Ser.). 1977. 17.95 (*0-8369-0665-9*) Ayer.
Magee, William N., ed. see Poplin, Robert L. & Ritchie, Thomas E.
Magel, Charles, ed. see Gompertz, Lewis.
Magel, Charles R. A Bibliography on Animal Rights & Related Matters. LC 80-5636. 622p. (C). 1981. lib. bdg. 75.00 (*0-8191-1488-X*) U Pr of Amer.
Magel, Emil. Folktales from the Gambia: Wolof Fictional Narratives. LC 81-51649. 208p. 1984. 14.95 (*0-89410-220-6*, Three Contnts); pap. 8.00 (*0-89410-221-4*, Three Contnts) L Rienner.
***Magel, John.** The Wordlanders: The World's Greatest Reading Challenge. (Illus.). 144p. 1999. pap. 9.95 (*0-9675247-0-9*, Pub. by J Magel) BkMstrs TX.
Mageli, Eldrid. Organising Women's Protest: A Study of Political Styles in Two South Indian Activist Groups. LC 96-229335. (NIAS Monographs in Asian Studies: No. 72). 288p. (C). 1996. text 48.00 (*0-7007-0431-0*, Pub. by Curzon Pr Ltd); pap. text 24.95 (*0-7007-0440-X*, Pub. by Curzon Pr Ltd) UH Pr.
Mageli, Paul D. The Immigrant Experience. (Magill Bibliographies Ser.). 183p. 1991. 42.00 (*0-8108-2793-X*) Scarecrow.
Magellan, Mauro. Home at Last. LC 89-19994. (Illus.). 32p. (J). (ps-3). 1990. 10.95 (*0-89334-119-3*) Humanics Ltd.
— Max, the Apartment Cat. LC 88-32067. (Illus.). 32p. (J). 1989. 10.95 (*0-89334-117-7*) Humanics Ltd.
***Magellan Press.** World History Atlas. (History Ser.). 1999. 11.00 (*0-534-56866-1*) Wadsworth Pub.
Magellan, Romayne. Pocket Prophecy. (Illus.). 64p. 1997. 7.95 (*1-86204-131-8*, Pub. by Element MA) Penguin Putnam.
Magellanic Clouds Symposium Staff. The Magellanic Clouds: Proceedings of the Symposium, Santiago De Chile, March 1969. Muller, A. B., ed. LC 73-154743. (Astrophysics & Space Science Library: No.23). 189p. 1971. text 94.00 (*90-277-0205-5*) Kluwer Academic.
Magen, Ursula & Rashad, Mahmoud, eds. Vom Halys Zum Euphrat. 311p. 1996. text 92.00 (*3-927120-41-3*, Pub. by Ugarit-Verlag) Eisenbrauns.
Magen, Ursula, jt. auth. see Mauer, Gerlinde.
Magen, Zipora. Exploring Adolescent Happiness: Commitment, Purpose, & Fulfillment. LC 98-8973. 248p. 1998. 28.00 (*0-7619-0730-0*); pap. 12.99 (*0-7619-0731-9*) Sage.
Magenau, John M., III, jt. auth. see Hunt, Raymond G.
Magenda, Burhan. East Kalimantan No. 70: The Decline of a Commercial Aristocracy. (Modern Indonesia Project Ser.). 120p. 1991. pap. 11.00 (*0-87763-036-4*) Cornell Mod Indo.
Magendans, J. F. Elongation & Contraction of the Plant Axis & Development of Spongy Tissues in the Radish Tuber: (Raphanus Sativus L. cv. Saxa Nova) (Wageningen Agricultural University Papers: No. 91-1). 64p. 1991. pap. 17.00 (*90-6754-184-2*, Pub. by Backhuys Pubs) Balogh.
Magendans, J. F. C. & Van Veenendaal, W. L. H. Morphology of Pits in Hardwood Fibres: (1) Nomenclature of Axial Xylary Elements: A Morphological & Physiological Approach, (2) Bordered Pits & Funnel Pits: Further Evidence of Convergent Evolution. (Wageningen Agricultural University Papers). (Illus.). 100p. 1999. pap. 39.00 (*90-5782-036-6*, Pub. by Backhuys Pubs) Balogh.
Magendanz, Thomas & Popescu-Zeletin, Radu. Intelligent Networks: Basic Technology, Standards & Evolution. 172p. 1996. mass mkt. 31.95 (*1-85032-293-7*) ITCP.
Magendie, Francois. Elementary Treatise on Human Physiology, 4. Revere, John, tr. from FRE. LC 77-72191. (Contributions to the History of Psychology Ser.: Vol. IV, Pt. E, Physiological Psychology). 280p. 1978. reprint ed. lib. bdg. 75.00 (*0-313-26952-1*, U6952, Greenwood Pr) Greenwood.
Magenes, E., jt. auth. see Lions, J. L.
***Magenheimer, Heinz.** Hitler's War: Germany's Key Strategic Decisions, 1940-1945, Could Germany Have Won World War Two? 2000. pap. 19.95 (*0-304-35339-6*) Continuum.
Magenheimer, Kay. First Light to Dawn: A Collection of Poems in Three Parts. LC 92-85139. (Illus.). 496p. 1992. 29.95 (*0-9634972-0-0*) Runnymede Pr.
Magenheiner, Heinz. Hitler's War: Germany's Key Strategic Decisions, 1940-1945. (Illus.). 352p. 1999. 29.95 (*1-85409-472-6*, Pub. by Arms & Armour) Sterling.
***Magennis, Eoin.** The Irish Political System, 1740-1765: The Golden Age Of The Undertakers? 192p. 1999. 55.00 (*1-85182-484-7*, Pub. by Four Cts Pr) Intl Spec Bk.
Magennis, Eoin, jt. auth. see Jupp, Peter.
Magennis, Hugh. Anglo-Saxon Appetites: Food & Drink & Their Consumption in Old English & Related Literature. LC 99-198486. 260p. 1998. boxed set 65.00 (*1-85182-382-4*, Pub. by Four Cts Pr) Intl Spec Bk.
— Images of Community in Old English Poetry. LC 95-26344. (Studies in Anglo-Saxon England: No. 18). 221p. (C). 1996. text 64.95 (*0-521-49566-0*) Cambridge U Pr.
Mageo, Jeannette M. Theorizing Self in Samoa: Emotions, Genders, & Sexualities. LC 98-9016. (Illus.). 312p. (C). 1998. pap. text 22.95 (*0-472-08518-2*, 08518) U of Mich Pr.
— Theorizing Self in Samoa: Emotions, Genders, & Sexualities. LC 98-9016. (Illus.). 312p. (C). 1998. text 59.50 (*0-472-10920-0*, 10920) U of Mich Pr.
Mageo, Jeannette M. & Howard, Alan, eds. Spirits in Culture, History & Mind. LC 95-23713. 282p. (C). 1996. pap. 20.99 (*0-415-91368-3*) Routledge.
— Spirits in Culture, History & Mind. LC 95-23713. 282p. (C). (gr. 13). 1996. 75.00 (*0-415-91367-5*) Routledge.
Mager. The Complete Letter Writer. 320p. 1999. write for info. (*0-671-00430-1*) S&S Trade.
Mager, Alison, ed. Children of the Past in Photographic Portraits: An Album with 165 Prints. (Illus.). 89p. 1978. pap. 8.95 (*0-486-23697-8*) Dover.
Mager, Anne Kelk. Gender & the Making of a South African Bantustan: A Social History of the Ciskei, 1945-1959. LC 98-43081. (Social History of Africa Ser.). 272p. 1999. 59.95 (*0-325-00111-1*, Bergin & Garvey); pap. 24.95 (*0-325-00110-3*) Greenwood.
Mager, Don. Borderings. 24p. 1998. pap. 6.00 (*1-890644-38-2*) Union Cnty.
— Glosses. Date not set. pap. 7.95 (*1-879934-38-8*) St Andrews NC.
— That Which Is Owed to Death. (Illus.). 56p. 1998. pap. 6.95 (*0-9663293-0-9*) Main St Rag.
Mager, Gerald M. & Myers, Betty. Developing a Career in the Academy. (SPE Monographs). 1983. 10.00 (*0-933669-22-4*) Soc Profs Ed.
Mager, Hugo. Elizabeth, Grand Duchess of Russia. (Illus.). 400p. 1998. 27.50 (*0-7867-0509-4*) Carroll & Graf.
— Elizabeth, Grand Duchess of Russia. 432p. 1999. pap. text 14.95 (*0-7867-0678-3*) Carroll & Graf.
***Mager, Marcia Zina.** Believing in Faeries. (Illus.). 2000. pap. 25.95 (*0-85207-331-3*) C W Daniel.
Mager, Mike. The Medical School Manual: A Practical Guide to Admission to American Medical Schools. 100p. (Orig.). (C). 1996. pap. 9.95 (*1-889793-06-X*) Spencer Bks.
Mager, Nathan H. The Kondratieff Waves. LC 86-9319. 256p. 1986. 67.95 (*0-275-92149-2*, C2149, Praeger Pubs) Greenwood.
Mager, Nathan H. & Mager, Sylvia K. Complete Letter Writer. 1991. mass mkt. 5.99 (*0-671-74419-4*) PB.
Mager, Robert F. Developing Attitude Toward Learning: Or Smats 'n' Smuts. 2nd ed. (Illus.). 116p. 1996. reprint ed. pap. text 17.95 (*1-879618-05-2*) Ctr Effect Perf.
— Goal Analysis 2nd ed. LC 83-60501. (Mager Library). viii, 139p. 1984. write for info. (*0-8224-4339-2*) Globe Fearon.
— Mager Six-Pack, 6 vols. Incl. Analyzing Performance Problems: Or You Really Oughta Wanna. 3rd rev. ed. Pipe, Peter. LC 96-72446. (Illus.). 187p. 1997. pap. 19.95 (*1-879618-17-6*, 404); Goal Analysis: How to Clarify Your Goals So You Can Actually Achieve Them. 3rd rev. ed. LC 96-72445. (Illus.). 170p. 1997. pap. 19.95 (*1-879618-04-4*, 405); How to Turn Learners on... Without Turning Them Off: Ways to Ignite Interest in Learning. 3rd rev. ed. LC 96-72444. (Illus.). 161p. 1997. pap. 19.95 (*1-879618-18-4*, 406); Making Instruction Work: A Step-by-Step Guide to Designing & Developing Instruction That Works. 2nd rev. ed. LC 96-72447. (Illus.). 288p. 1997. pap. 19.95 (*1-879618-02-8*, 407); Measuring Instructional Results: How to Find Out If Your Instructional Objectives Have Been Achieved. 3rd rev. ed. LC 96-72448. (Illus.). 192p. 1997. pap. 19.95 (*1-879618-16-8*, 403); Preparing Instructional Objectives: A Critical Tool in the Development of Effective Instruction. 3rd rev. ed. LC 96-72449. (Illus.). 202p. 1997. pap. 19.95 (*1-879618-03-6*, 402); 95.00 (*1-879618-15-X*) Ctr Effect Perf.
— Making Instruction Work. 1988. pap. 17.95 (*1-56103-467-3*) Ctr Effect Perf.
— Measuring Instructional Results. 2nd ed. LC 83-60502. 1984. pap. 18.95 (*1-56103-340-5*) Ctr Effect Perf.
— Preparing Instructional Objectives. 2nd rev. ed. LC 83-60503. 1984. pap. 17.95 (*1-56103-341-3*) Ctr Effect Perf.
— Troubleshooting the Troubleshooting Course: Debug d'Bugs. LC 82-81980. 1983. pap. 18.95 (*1-56103-370-7*) Ctr Effect Perf.
— What Every Manager Should Know about Training: An Insider's Guide to Getting Your Money's Worth. 2nd rev. ed. 139p. 1999. pap. 19.95 (*1-879618-19-2*, 412-8192, Pub. by Ctr Effect Perf) IPG Chicago.
— What Every Manager Should Know about Training: Or I've Got a Training Problem & Other Odd Ideas. LC 91-78265. 160p. 1996. reprint ed. pap. 17.95 (*1-879618-08-7*) Ctr Effect Perf.
Mager, Robert F. & Beach, Kenneth, Jr. Developing Vocational Instruction. 1986. pap. 17.95 (*1-56103-060-0*) Ctr Effect Perf.
Mager, Robert F. & Pipe, Peter. The How to Write a Book Book. (Illus.). 137p. (C). 1991. reprint ed. pap. text 17.95 (*1-879618-00-1*) Ctr Effect Perf.
— A Quick Reference Checklist: For Use in Analyzing Performance Problems, pkg. of 25. 4p. 1996. reprint ed. 16.95 (*1-879618-12-5*) Ctr Effect Perf.
Mager Stellman, Jeanne. Encyclopaedia of Occupational Health & Safety, 4 vols. 4th ed. 4000p. 1998. 990.00 (*92-2-110403-6*) Intl Labour Office.
Mager Stellman, Jeanne, ed. Encyclopaedia of Occupational Health & Safety, 4 vols. in 1. 4th ed. 4000p. 1998. 491.00 (*92-2-109203-8*, Pub. by Statnry Office) Balogh.
Mager, Sylvia K., jt. auth. see Mager, Nathan H.
Magere, Philippe. Dictionnaire de l'Allemand dD'Aujourd'hui: German-French, French-German. (FRE & GER.). 743p. 1987. pap. 19.95 (*0-7859-8009-1*, 2737002699) Fr & Eur.
Magerovskii, Lev. Bibliografiia Gazetnykh Sobranii Russkogo Istoricheskogo Arkhiva za Gody 1917-1921. LC 91-67666. (RUS.). vi, 136p. 1995. reprint ed. lib. bdg. 60.00 (*0-88354-352-4*) N Ross.
***Magers, Boyd & Fitzgerald, Michael G.** Western Women: Interviews with 50 Leading Ladies of Movie & Television Westerns from the 1930s to the 1960s. LC 99-25467. (Illus.). 288p. 1999. boxed set 36.50 (*0-7864-0672-0*) McFarland & Co.
Magers, Bernard. Seventy-Five Years of Western Electric Tube Manufacturing: A Log Book History of over 750 W.E. Tubes Including Dates of Manufacture. 148p. 1992. pap. 16.95 (*0-9632440-1-9*) Antique Elect.
Magers-Rankin, Deborah. California Liability Insurance Practice: Claims & Litigation, 2 vols. LC 90-84639. 285p. 1996. ring bd. 80.00 (*0-7626-0028-4*, CP-39265) Cont Ed Bar-CA.
— California Liability Insurance Practice: Claims & Litigation - 8/97 Update, 2 vols. LC 90-84639. 520p. 1997. ring bd. 82.00 (*0-7626-0137-X*, CP-39266) Cont Ed Bar-CA.
Magers-Rankin, Deborah. California Liability Insurance Practice: Claims & Litigation: August 1994 Update, Set, Vols. 1 & 2. LC 90-84639. 474p. 1994. 64.00 (*0-88124-790-1*, CP-39263) Cont Ed Bar-CA.
Magers-Rankin, Deborah, ed. see Grover, Margaret J. & Carson, Joseph J.

An Asterisk (*) at the beginning of an entry indicates that the title is appearing for the first time.

Magers-Rankin, Deborah, ed. see Huchting, Stephen H.

Magers-Rankin, Deborah, ed. see Slocumb, William H., et al.

Magers-Rankin, Deborah, ed. see Tidus, Jeffrey A.

Magerstadt, Michael. Antibody Conjugates & Malignant Disease. (Illus.). 248p. 1991. lib. bdg. 190.00 (*0-8493-6089-7*, RC270) CRC Pr.

Mages, Michael J. The Dark Stain: The Role of Innate Depravity in American Literature, 1620-1940. 363p. (C). 1996. text 64.95 (*1-57292-027-0*); pap. text 44.95 (*1-57292-026-2*) Austin & Winfield.

— Magnalia Christi Americana: America's Literary Old Testament. LC 98-48854. (Illus.). 415p. 1999. 89.95 (*1-57309-358-0*) Intl Scholars.

Magesa, Laurenti. African Religion: The Moral Traditions of Abundant Life. LC 97-19051. 200p. (Orig.). 1997. pap. 20.00 (*1-57075-105-6*) Orbis Bks.

Maget, E., jt. auth. see Le Lionnais, Francois.

Maget, M. Le Pain Anniversaire a Villard d'Arene en Oisans. 237p. 1989. pap. text 51.00 (*2-88124-263-4*) Gordon & Breach.

Magezis, Joy. Teach Yourself Women's Studies. (Illus.). 192p. 1996. pap., student ed. 12.95 (*0-8442-3113-4*, Teach Yrslf) NTC Contemp Pub Co.

Maggard, Bill N. TPM That Works: The Theory & Design of Total Productive Maintenance. LC 92-41792. (Illus.). 202p. (C). 1992. text 44.95 (*1-882258-01-0*, TPMTW) TPM Pr.

***Maggard, John & LaFever, Greg.** Name That Train. 10p. (J). (ps-3). 1998. 7.95 (*1-929174-07-1*) Oshkosh BGosh.

Maggard, Margaret, ed. Guide to Private Fortunes, 1993. 93rd ed. 727p. 1992. 255.00 (*1-879784-29-7*, 600356) Taft Group.

Maggard, Michael J., jt. auth. see Harris, Roy D.

Maggard, Shawna. Outskirts of Bethlehem: A Collection of Selected Poetry. 110p. 1997. pap. write for info. (*1-57502-558-2*, PO1616) Morris Pubng.

Maggart, Rita J. In the Growing Places. LC 96-69159. (Illus.). 96p. (Orig.). 1996. 18.95 (*1-881576-96-5*) Providence Hse.

Maggart, Zelda R. & Zintz, Miles V. The Reading Process: The Teacher & the Learner. 6th ed. 720p. (C). 1992. text. write for info. (*0-697-12581-5*) Brown & Benchmark.

Maggart-Zintz. Reading Process. 6th ed. 1992. 23.12 (*0-697-12582-3*, WCB McGr Hill) McGrw-H Hghr Educ.

Maggay, Melba P., ed. Communicating Cross-Culturally: Towards a New Context for Missions in the Philippines. 61p. (Orig.). (C). 1989. pap. 7.50 (*971-10-0350-3*, Pub. by New Day Pub) Cellar.

Maggenti, A. R. General Nematology. (Microbiology Ser.). (Illus.). 372p. 1981. 76.00 (*0-387-90588-X*) Spr-Verlag.

***Maggi, Annette & Boucher, Jackie.** What You Can Do to Prevent Diabetes: Simple Changes to Improve Your Life. LC 99-52765. 160p. 2000. pap. 12.95 (*0-471-34796-5*) Wiley.

Maggi, Annette, jt. auth. see Labat, Jackie.

Maggi, Armando. Uttering the Word: The Mystical Performances of Maria Maddalena de' Pazzi, a Renaissance Visionary. LC 97-38498. 224p. (C). 1998. text 59.50 (*0-7914-3901-1*); pap. text 19.95 (*0-7914-3902-X*) State U NY Pr.

***Maggi, Armando, tr.** Maria Maddalena de' Pazzi: Selected Revelations. LC 99-88285. (CWS Ser.: Vol. 98). 365p. 2000. pap. 39.95 (*0-8091-0509-8*); pap. 29.95 (*0-8091-3923-5*) Paulist Pr.

Maggi, C. A., ed. Nervous Control of the Urogenital System. Vol. 3. 1992. write for info. (*0-318-69520-0*) Gordon & Breach.

Maggi, Maria T. The Rings Around Saturn. 66p. 1996. pap. 12.00 (*1-891033-05-0*, Rainshadow Editns) Black Rock Pr.

***Maggiano, David.** CGI Programming with TCL. LC 99-54109. (Illus.). 352p. 1999. pap. text 44.95 (*0-201-60629-1*) Addison-Wesley.

Maggied, Hal S. Transportation for the Poor: Research in Rural Mobility. (Studies in Applied Regional Science). 1982. lib. bdg. 73.50 (*0-89838-081-2*) Kluwer Academic.

Maggin, Donald L. Bio of Dizzy Gillespie. 1924. write for info. (*0-688-17088-9*, Wm Morrow) Morrow Avon.

Maggin, Donald L. Stan Getz: A Life in Jazz. 1996. 25.00 (*0-614-95806-7*, Wm Morrow) Morrow Avon.

— Stan Getz: A Life in Jazz. (Illus.). 432p. 1997. reprint ed. pap. 15.00 (*0-688-15555-3*, Quil) HarperTrade.

Maggin, Elliot S. Kingdom Come. LC 97-32286. (Illus.). 256p. 1998. 20.00 (*0-446-52234-1*, Pub. by Warner Bks) Little.

— Kingdom Come. 416p. 1999. mass mkt. 6.50 (*0-446-60669-3*, Pub. by Warner Bks) Little.

— Superman: Last Son of Krypton. 22.95 (*0-8488-0118-0*) Amereon Ltd.

Maggin, Elliot S., jt. auth. see Lobdell, Scott.

Magginetti, Robert T., et al. Early Permian Fusulinids from the Owens Valley Group, East-Central California. LC 87-30901. (Geological Society of America Ser.: Vol. 217). (Illus.). 68p. 1988. reprint ed. pap. 30.00 (*0-608-07743-7*, 206783100010) Bks Demand.

Maggini, George B., ed. The Greater Cincinnati Relocation Guide. (Illus.). 152p. 1998. pap. 9.00 (*0-9666092-0-4*) Morada Pubg.

***Maggio.** Consumer Letter Book. LC 99-10586. 1999. text 34.95 (*0-13-082782-7*) P-H.

— Quotations on Education. 1998. text 13.95 (*0-13-973355-8*) P-H.

— Quotations on Love. 1998. 13.95 (*0-13-973363-9*) P-H.

Maggio. Right Books Are Fun Say It. 448p. 1999. pap. text 7.98 (*0-13-021483-3*) P-H.

***Maggio.** Sicily Nana Never Saw. 2000. pap. 22.00 (*0-7382-0342-4*, Pub. by Perseus Pubng) HarpC.

Maggio, C. A. & Scriabine, A., eds. Alpha-Glucosidease Inhibition: Potential Use in Diabetes: Proceedings of the First Preclinical Workshop on Acarbose. (Drugs in Development Ser.). (Illus.). 285p. (Orig.). 1994. pap. text 75.00 (*0-9637603-0-0*) Neva Pr.

Maggio, Carole & Roderick, Kyle. Facercise: The Dynamic Muscle-Toning Program for Renewed Vitality & a More Youthful Appearance. (Illus.). 85p. (Orig.). 1995. pap. 12.00 (*0-399-51960-2*, Perigee Bks) Berkley Pub.

Maggio, Chris, ed. The Pet Ferret Owners' Manual. (Illus.). 72p. (Orig.). 1995. pap. write for info. (*0-9646477-2-9*); lib. bdg. write for info. (*0-9646477-1-0*) C Maggio.

Maggio, Edward T. Enzyme-Immunoassay. 304p. 1980. 173.00 (*0-8493-5617-2*, QP519, CRC Reprint) Franklin.

Maggio, Joseph A., jt. auth. see Dahlgren, Emily.

Maggio, Margk & Maze, T. H., eds. Transportation Policy. (Orig.). 1993. pap. 15.00 (*0-944285-33-3*) Pol Studies.

Maggio, Michael. Quotations for a Man's Soul. LC 98-25270. 208p. 1998. text 14.95 (*0-7352-0054-8*) PH Pr.

— Sex, Money & Sports: Quotations on the Only Things Men Talk About. LC 98-26087. 208p. 1998. 14.95 (*0-7352-0053-X*) PH Pr.

Maggio, Rosalie. The Best Letters for All Occasions. LC 99-10586. 480p. 1999. pap. 16.00 (*0-7352-0081-5*) PH Pr.

— How They Said It: Wise & Witty Letters from the Famous & Infamous. LC 99-42540. 256p. 1999. text 16.00 (*0-7352-0132-3*) PH Pr.

— How to Say It: Choice Words, Phrases, Sentences & Paragraphs for Every Situation. LC 90-38681. 448p. (C). 1990. pap. 15.95 (*0-13-424375-7*); text 29.95 (*0-13-424367-6*) P-H.

— A Journal with Quotations for the Soul. 160p. (C). 1997. text 8.95 (*0-13-776212-7*) P-H.

— A Journal with Quotations from Women on Life. 160p. (C). 1997. text 8.95 (*0-13-673997-0*) P-H.

— A Journal with Quotations on Education. 160p. (C). 1997. text 8.95 (*0-13-776220-8*) P-H.

— A Journal with Quotations on Love. 160p. (C). 1997. text 8.95 (*0-13-776238-0*) P-H.

— The New Beacon Book of Quotations by Women. 864p. 1996. 35.00 (*0-8070-6782-2*) Beacon Pr.

— Quotations for the Soul. LC 97-35714. 192p. (C). 1997. text 13.95 (*0-13-769159-9*) P-H.

— Quotations from Women about Life. LC 97-35713. 192p. (C). 1997. text 13.95 (*0-13-671489-7*) P-H.

— Quotations on Education. 192p. (C). 1997. text 13.95 (*0-13-769134-3*) P-H.

— Quotations on Education. 192p. (C). 1999. pap. text 7.95 (*0-13-025780-X*) S&S Trade.

— Quotations on Love. LC 97-35711. 192p. (C). 1997. 13.95 (*0-13-769142-4*) P-H.

— Talking about People: A Guide to Fair & Accurate Language. 3rd ed. LC 97-30047. Orig. Title: Dictionary of Bias-Free Usage. 440p. 1997. pap. 27.50 (*1-57356-069-3*) Oryx Pr.

***Maggio, Rosalie, ed.** Quotations on Love. 180p. 1999. pap. text 14.00 (*0-7881-6397-3*) DIANE Pub.

Maggio, Rosalie & Hooks, Tisha, eds. The New Beacon Book of Quotations by Women. 864p. 1998. pap. 20.00 (*0-8070-6783-0*) Beacon Pr,

***Maggio, Theresa.** Mattanza: Love & Death in the Sea of Sicily. (Illus.). 288p. 2000. text 25.00 (*0-7382-0269-X*) Perseus Pubng.

Maggio, Viqui. Absolutely Angels: Poems for Children & Other Believers. LC 97-77906. 32p. (J). (gr. k-3). 1998. 14.95 (*1-56397-708-7*) Boyds Mills Pr.

Maggiolini, M., et al. Endocrine Disorders in Thalassemia: Physiological Therapeutic Aspects. LC 94-23058. 1994. 86.00 (*0 387 58390 4*) Spr-Verlag.

— Endocrine Disorders in Thalassemia: Physiological Therapeutic Aspects. LC 94-23058. 1996. 99.00 (*3-540-58390-4*) Spr-Verlag.

***Maggiolo, Paulette B.** The Guilty Teacher. Cottrell, Elizabeth H., ed. LC 99-61783. 272p. 1999. pap. 15.00 (*0-9665319-2-2*) Grnlf Ent.

Maggioni, M. Julie. Pensees of Pascal: A Study in Baroque Style. LC 79-94181. (Catholic University of America. Studies in Romance Languages & Literatures: No. 39). reprint ed. 37.50 (*0-404-50339-X*) AMS Pr.

Maggiora, Carl J. & Nastasi, Michael A. High Energy & Heavy Ion Beams in Materials Analysis. (MRS Conference Proceedings Ser.: Vol. HIB). 1990. text 17.50 (*1-55899-091-7*) Materials Res.

Maggiora, Gerald M., jt. ed. see Johnson, Mark A.

***Maggiore, Christine.** What If Everything You Thought You Knew about AIDS Was Wrong? The Book That Will Change Your View of HIV & AIDS... And possibly Change Your Life. 4th rev. ed. (Illus.). 126p. (C). 2000. pap. 12.95 (*0-9674153-0-6*, Pub. by Alive & Well Altern) IPG Chicago.

Maggiore, Dolores J. Lesbianism: An Annotated Bibliography & Guide to the Literature, 1976-1986. 2nd ed. LC 92-34699. 271p. 1992. 34.50 (*0-8108-2617-8*) Scarecrow.

Maggiore, Dolores J., ed. Lesbians & Child Custody: A Casebook, Vol. 8. LC 92-5398. (Gay & Lesbian Studies). 280p. 1992. text 15.00 (*0-8153-0229-0*) Garland.

Maggiore, MaryAnn. Salt: A Book of Poems by MaryAnn Maggiore. (Orig.). 1989. pap. 6.95 (*0-9623396-0-1*) Express PA.

Maggiore, Quirino & Pizzarelli, Francesco, eds. International Society of Blood Purification: 15th Annual Meeting, Florence, September 1997: Abstracts. (Blood Purification Ser.: Vol. 15, Suppl. 2, 1997). (Illus.). xiv, 52p. 1997. pap. 39.25 (*3-8055-6592-5*) S Karger.

Maggiori, Herman J. How to Make the World Your Market: The International Sales & Marketing Handbook. LC 91-73712. (Illus.). 480p. (Orig.). 1992. pap. 24.95 (*1-878179-06-3*) ALLSTORY.

Maggiotto. Politics in the American Democracy. (C). 1999. pap. text 37.50 (*0-15-502199-0*, Pub. by Harcourt Coll Pubs) Harcourt.

***Maggiotto, Michael A. & Wekkin, Gary D.** Partisan Linkages in Southern Politics: Elites, Voters & Identifiers. LC 00-8218. 208p. 2000. 38.00 (*1-57233-088-0*) U of Tenn Pr.

Maggipinto, Donata. Halloween Treats: Recipes & Crafts for the Whole Family. LC 98-4547. (Holiday Celebrations Book Ser.). (Illus.). 96p. 1998. pap. 14.95 (*0-8118-2197-8*) Chronicle Bks.

Maggipinto, Donna. Real-Life Entertaining. LC 97-46875. (Illus.). 1998. 30.00 (*0-609-60111-3*) C Potter.

Maggitti, Phil. Bulldogs. LC 97-20248. (Barron's Complete Pet Owner's Manuals). (Illus.). 120p. 1997. pap. text 6.95 (*0-8120-9309-7*) Barron.

Maggitti, Phil. Before You Buy That Kitten. 1995. pap. 8.95 (*0-8120-1336-0*) Barron.

— Birman Cats: Everything about Acquisition, Care, Nutrition, Behavior, Health Care, & Breeding. LC 96-3265. (Illus.). 112p. 1996. pap. 6.95 (*0-8120-9584-7*) Barron.

— Guide to a Well-Behaved Cat. LC 93-8751. 138p. 1993. pap. 10.95 (*0-8120-1476-6*) Barron.

— Owning the Right Cat. 1993. 29.95 (*1-56465-111-8*, 16003) Tetra Pr.

— Owning the Right Dog. 1993. 29.95 (*1-56465-110-X*, 16001) Tetra Pr.

***Maggitti, Phil.** Pugs: Everything about Purchase, Care, Nutrition, Breeding, Behavior & Training. 2nd ed. LC 99-40285. (Complete Pet Owner's Manual Ser.). (Illus.). 64-104p. 2000. 6.95 (*0-7641-1045-4*) Barron.

Maggitti, Phil. Scottish Fold Cats: Everything about Acquisition, Care, Nutrition, Behavior, Health Care, & Breeding. LC 92-36729. (Complete Pet Owner's Manual Ser.). 88p. 1993. pap. 6.95 (*0-8120-4999-3*) Barron.

Maggitti, Phil & Helgren, J. Anne. It's Showtime! LC 98-20370. (Illus.). 96p. 1998. pap. 8.95 (*0-7641-0253-2*, 835900Q) Barron.

Maggitti, Phil, jt. auth. see Benson, Gary J.

Magglund, Clarence E., et al. Real Estate Agent & Appraiser Liability: In Plain Language. 261p. 1993. 49.50 (*0-9631290-1-5*) Common Law.

Maggs, Bruce, jt. auth. see Leighton, Thomson F.

Maggs, Christine A. & Hommersand, Max H. Rhodophyta Pt. 3a: Ceramiales. (Seaweeds of the British Isles Ser.: Vol. 1). (Illus.). 464p. 1993. pap. 69.95 (*0-11-310045-0*, HM00450, Pub. by Statnry Office) Balogh.

Maggs, Christopher J., ed. Nursing History: The State of the Art. LC 86-32802. 208p. pap. 25.00 (*0-7099-4637-6*, Pub. by C Helm) Routldge.

Maggs, Colin G. Bath to Weymouth Line. 74p. (C). 1985. 45.00 (*0-85361-289-7*) St Mut.

— Branch Lines of Dorset. (Illus.). 160p. 1996. 30.95 (*0-7509-1147-6*, Pub. by Sutton Pub Ltd) Intl Pubs Mktg.

— Branch Lines of Hampshire. (Branch Lines Ser.). (Illus.). 160p. 1997. pap. 30.95 (*0-7509-1297-9*, Pub. by Sutton Pub Ltd) Intl Pubs Mktg.

— Colin Magg's West of England. LC 99-182488. (Illus.). 184p. 1998. 49.95 (*0-7509-1618-4*, Pub. by Sutton Pub Ltd) Intl Pubs Mktg.

***Maggs, Colin G.** Steam Tales from the Footplate. 1999. 36.00 (*0-7509-1769-5*) Bks Intl VA.

Maggs, Colin G. Taunton to Barnstaple Line: Devon & Somerset Railway. 60p. (C). 1985. 39.00 (*0-85361-266-8*) St Mut.

Maggs, Colin G., ed. Highbridge in Its Heyday: Home of the Somerset & Dorset Railway. 88p. (C). 1985. 50.00 (*0-85361-324-9*, Pub. by Oakwood) St Mut.

Maggs, John, jt. auth. see Thyer, Dennis.

Maggs, Margaret M. English Across the Curriculum: Content-Area Vocabulary & Skills. 2nd ed. 1993. pap., teacher ed. 9.82 (*0-8442-0292-4*) NTC Contemp Pub Co.

— English Across the Curriculum: Content-Area Vocabulary & Skills, Bk. 1. 2nd ed. 64p. 1993. pap. 9.82 (*0-8442-0289-4*) NTC Contemp Pub Co.

— English Across the Curriculum: Content-Area Vocabulary & Skills, Bk. 2. 2nd ed. 64p. 1993. pap. 9.82 (*0-8442-0290-8*) NTC Contemp Pub Co.

— English Across the Curriculum: Content-Area Vocabulary & Skills, Bk. 3. 2nd ed. 64p. 1993. pap. 9.82 (*0-8442-0291-6*) NTC Contemp Pub Co.

Maggs, Peter B. The Mandelstam & 'Der Nister' Files: An Introduction to Stalin-Era Prison & Labor Camp Records. LC 95-41480. (Illus.). 184p. (C). (gr. 13). 1995. text 69.95 (*1-56324-175-7*) M E Sharpe.

Maggs, Peter B., ed. from RUS. The Civil Code of the Russian Federation. LC 97-16587. 536p. (C). (gr. 13). 1997. text 225.00 (*0-7656-0175-3*) M E Sharpe.

Maggs, Peter B., et al. Computer Law - Cases, Comments, & Questions, Teacher's Manual to Accompany. (American Casebook Ser.). 106p. (C). 1992. pap. text. write for info. (*0-314-01065-3*) West Pub.

— Computer Law, Cases - Comments - Questions, 1996 Supplement To. (American Casebook Ser.). 230p. (C). 1996. pap. 16.50 (*0-314-20241-2*) West Pub.

— Computer Law, Cases - Comments, & Questions. (American Casebook Ser.). 731p. (C). 1991. 57.50 (*0-314-92197-4*) West Pub.

Maggs, R. J., jt. ed. see Knapman, C. E.

***Maggs, Sue.** Chicken. 96p. 2000. 12.95 (*1-84215-056-1*) Anness Pub.

— Healthy Life - Low Fat Pasta. 96p. 2000. 12.95 (*1-84215-081-2*) Anness Pub.

Maghan, Jess, jt. ed. see Kelly, Robert J.

Maghimbi, S., jt. auth. see Forster, P. G.

Maghimbi, Sam, jt. ed. see Forster, Peter G.

Maghroori, Ray, jt. auth. see Gurtov, Melvin.

Maghsoud, Moulana S. A Meditation: Payam-e-del. Angha, Nahid, tr. from PER. (Illus.). 65p. (Orig.). 1994. pap. 10.00 (*0-918437-05-9*) Intl Sufism.

— Psalms of Gods: Avaz-e-Khodayan. Angha, Nahid, tr. from PER. (Illus.). 32p. (Orig.). 1991. pap. 8.00 (*0-918437-09-1*) Intl Sufism.

Maghsoud, Shah & Angha, Sadegh. Al-Salat: The Reality of Prayer in Islam. LC 97-69664. 100p. 1998. pap. 9.95 (*0-910735-73-5*) MTO Printing & Pubn Ctr.

— Manifestations of Thought. LC 97-69690. 87p. (Orig.). 1997. pap. 9.95 (*0-910735-70-0*) MTO Printing & Pubn Ctr.

Magi, Aldo P. & Walser, Richard, eds. Thomas Wolfe Interviewed, 1929-1938. LC 84-25083. (Southern Literary Studies). (Illus.). viii, 135p. 1985. text 25.00 (*0-8071-1229-1*) La State U Pr.

Magi, Giovanna. Masterpieces of Louvre. Hollingworth, Michael, tr. 64p. pap. text 9.95 (*88-7009-151-1*, Pub. by Bonechi) Eiron.

Magi Society Staff. Astrology Really Works! Kramer, Jill, ed. LC 95-7644. (Illus.). 336p. (Orig.). 1995. pap. 12.95 (*1-56170-134-3*, 170) Hay House.

— MAGI Astrology: The Key to Success in Love & Money. LC 98-46503. (Illus.). 448p. (Orig.). 1999. pap. 14.95 (*1-56170-128-9*, 168) Hay House.

— Magi Society Ephemeris. LC 96-19651. 752p. 1996. 30.00 (*1-56170-331-1*, 150) Hay House.

MagicWeb Staff, tr. see Rau, Robert.

Magid. Critical Thinking. (C). 2000. pap. text 29.50 (*0-03-022237-0*) Harcourt Coll Pubs.

Magid, Alvin. Private Lives - Public Surfaces: Grassroots Perspectives & the Legitimacy Question in Yugoslav Socialism. 500p. 1992. text 66.50 (*0-88033-211-5*, Pub. by East Eur Monographs) Col U Pr.

— Urban Nationalism: A Study of Political Development in Trinidad. LC 86-33978. 314p. 1988. 49.95 (*0-8130-0853-0*) U Press Fla.

Magid, Alvin, jt. ed. see Schoolman, Morton.

Magid, Andy R. Lectures on Differential Galois Theory. LC 94-10431. (University Lectures: Vol. 7). 105p. 1994. pap. 19.00 (*0-8218-7004-1*, ULECT/7) Am Math.

— The Separable Galois Theory of Commutative Rings. LC 74-80286. (Pure & Applied Mathematics Ser.: No. 27). 156p. reprint ed. pap. 48.40 (*0-7837-0872-6*, 204118000019) Bks Demand.

Magid, Andy R., jt. auth. see Goldman, W.

Magid, Andy R., jt. auth. see Lubotsky, Alexander.

Magid, Barry. Freud's Case Studies: Self-Psychological Perspectives. 216p. 1993. text 39.95 (*0-88163-132-9*) Analytic Pr.

Magid, Barry, ed. see Williams, William Carlos & Tomlinson, Charles.

Magid, Dubner. Alle Mesholim Fun, 2 vols., Set. 25.00 (*0-88482-720-8*) Hebrew Pub.

Magid, Henry M. English Political Pluralism: The Problem of Freedom & Organization. LC 41-15264. reprint ed. 20.00 (*0-404-04149-3*) AMS Pr.

Magid, Isam Mohamed Abdel, see Rowe, Donald R. & Mohamed Abdel Magid, Isam.

Magid, Ken. The Advice Book: A Question-Answer Book for Those Who Love. 247p. (Orig.). 1993. pap. 19.95 (*1-883590-50-7*) K M Prods.

Magid, Ken & McKelvey, Carole A. High Risk: Children Without a Conscience. 384p. (Orig.). 1989. pap. 14.95 (*0-553-34667-9*) Bantam.

Magid, Larry. The Economic Importance of Transportation Infrastructure Investment. 16p. 1997. pap. 15.00 (*1-55877-280-4*) Natl Governor.

***Magid, Lawrence J.** The Little PC Book. 3rd ed. LC 99-204285. 380p. (C). 1998. pap. text 19.99 (*0-201-35366-0*, Pub. by Peachpit Pr) Addison-Wesley.

Magid, Lynn H. Guide to Dallas Private Schools. Watson, Cristine L., ed. 466p. (Orig.). 1990. pap. 19.95 (*0-9627445-0-6*) Private-in-Print.

— Guide to Dallas Private Schools. 2nd ed. 550p. (Orig.). 1993. reprint ed. pap. text 24.95 (*0-9627445-2-2*) Private-in-Print.

— Guide to Dallas Private Schools. 3rd ed. LC 97-150017. 729p. (Orig.). 1996. reprint ed. pap. text 24.95 (*0-9627445-1-4*) Private-in-Print.

Magid, Lynn H. & Kahn, Beth F. A Guide to Dallas Learning Specialists. Lively, Ken, ed. LC 95-113565. 250p. (Orig.). 1993. pap. text 5.95 (*0-9627445-3-0*) Private-in-Print.

Magid, Peter G. OS/2 Warp Uncensored. 848p. 1995. pap. 39.99 (*1-56884-474-3*) IDG Bks.

Magid, Renee Y. & Codkind, Melissa. Work & Personal Life: Managing the Issues. Reider, Andrea, ed. LC 94-68577. (Fifty-Minute Ser.). (Illus.). 74p. (Orig.). 1995. pap. 10.95 (*1-56052-269-0*) Crisp Pubns.

Magid, Renee Y. & Fleming, Nancy E. When Mothers & Fathers Work: Creative Strategies for Balancing Career & Family. LC 86-47817. 208p. reprint ed. pap. 64.50 (*0-7837-4240-1*, 204392900012) Bks Demand.

— When Mothers & Fathers Work: Creative Ways to Succeed with Both Family & Career. 224p. 1989. reprint ed. pap. 3.95 (*0-380-70753-5*, Avon Bks) Morrow Avon.

Magid, Shaul, jt. auth. see Cohen, Aryeh.

Magida, Arthur. The Land of the Poison Wind. 2000. 25.00 (*0-465-01419-4*) HarpC.

Magida, Arthur J. Prophet of Rage: A Life of Louis Farrakhan & His Nation. 1997. pap. 13.00 (*0-465-06437-X*, Pub. by Basic) HarpC.

Magida, Arthur J., ed. How to Be a Perfect Stranger Vol. 1: A Guide to Etiquette in Other People's Religious Ceremonies. LC 95-37474. 432p. 1995. 24.95 (*1-879045-39-7*) Jewish Lights.

M

Magida, Arthur J. & Matlins, Stuart M., eds. How to Be a Perfect Stranger Vol. 1: A Guide to Etiquette in Other People's Religious Ceremonies. 432p. 1999. pap. 19.95 (*1-893361-01-2*) SkyLight Paths.
— How to Be a Perfect Stranger Vol. 2: A Guide to Etiquette in Other People's Religious Ceremonies. 416p. 1999. pap. 19.95 (*1-893361-02-0*) SkyLight Paths.
Magida, Arthur J., jt. ed. see Matlins, Stuart M.
Magida, Daniel L. The Rules of Seduction. 432p. 1994. pap. 10.00 (*0-449-90852-6*, Columbine) Fawcett.
Magida, Phyllis & Grunes, Barbara. Gourmet Fish on the Grill. 192p. (Orig.). 1989. pap. 12.95 (*0-8092-4596-5*, 459650, Contemporary Bks) NTC Contemp Pub Co.
Magida, Phyllis & Spitler, Sue. Skinny Vegetarian Entrees: Over 100 Delicious, Low-Fat, Quick & Easy Meatless Main Dishes from Soups, Stews, Casseroles & Ethnic Specialties to Bean, Grain & Dairy Delights. 2nd ed. LC 96-24481. (Skinny Cookbook Ser.). 205p. 1996. pap. 12.95 (*1-57284-007-2*) Surrey Bks.
Magida, Phyllis, jt. auth. see Grunes, Barbara.
Magidoff, Robert, jt. auth. see Pinza, Ezio.
Magidson, Jane & Harney, Susan. Shopwalks Paris: Shopping Maps & Guide. (Illus.). 1994. pap. 5.95 (*0-9638326-0-3*) Shopwalks.
Magidson, Mark. Baraka: A Visual Journal. 120p. 2000. 50.00 (*0-9671744-0-6*, Pub. by St Anns Pr) Dist Art Pubs.
Magie, David. Roman Rule in Asia Minor to the End of the Third Century After Christ, 2 vols. LC 75-7328. (Roman History Ser.). 1975. reprint ed. 121.95 (*0-405-07098-5*) Ayer.
— Roman Rule in Asia Minor to the End of the Third Century After Christ, 2 vols., Vol. 1. LC 75-7328. (Roman History Ser.). 1975. reprint ed. 60.95 (*0-405-07099-3*) Ayer.
— Roman Rule in Asia Minor to the End of the Third Century After Christ, 2 vols., Vol. 2. LC 75-7328. (Roman History Ser.). 1975. reprint ed. 60.95 (*0-405-07100-0*) Ayer.
Magie, David, tr. see Warmington, E. H., ed.
Magie, Dian, jt. auth. see Korza, Pam.
Magie, William F. A Source Book in Physics. LC 63-21307. (Source Books in the History of the Sciences). (Illus.). 634p. reprint ed. pap. 196.60 (*0-7837-4118-9*, 205794100011) Bks Demand.
***Magiera, Janet M.** Enriched in Everything: Biblical Lessons on Giving. (Searchlight Ser.: Vol. I). 2000. 12.00 (*0-9679613-0-0*) Lite of the Word.
Magill. Freedom & Experience. LC 96-30255. 256p. 1997. text 55.00 (*0-312-16474-2*) St Martin.
— Motor Learning. 5th ed. 1997. lab manual ed. write for info. (*0-697-38953-7*) McGrw-H Hghr Educ.
— Motor Learning Concepts & Appl. 4th ed. 1992. 63.75 (*0-697-12645-5*) McGraw.
Magill, Anne. Designing & Gardening with the Plant Materials & Conditions of North Central Florida (New USDA Zone 9) A Companion Volume to Landscape Design & Gardening Procedures for the Not So Rich. 118p. (Orig.). 1990. pap. 10.95 (*0-9627632-1-7*) Melrose Garden Pr.
— Landscape Design & Gardening Procedures for the Not So Rich. (Illus.). 104p. (Orig.). 1989. pap. 8.95 (*0-9627632-0-9*) Melrose Garden Pr.
Magill, Arthur W. Assessing Public Concern for Landscape Quality: A Potential Model to Identify Visual Thresholds. (Illus.). 48p. (Orig.). (C). 1993. pap. text 30.00 (*0-7881-0017-3*) DIANE Pub.
***Magill, Barbara, et al, eds.** Accessible Computer Technology: Meeting the Needs of People with Disabilities. 40p. 1999. 29.00 (*0-9670470-3-X*) Thompson Pub Grp.
***Magill, Barbara Gamble.** Workplace Accommodations under the ADA. Smith, Allen & Woodworth, Anne H., eds. 1999. pap. 79.00 (*0-9670470-7-2*) Thompson Pub Grp.
Magill, C. W., jt. auth. see McNiel, N. A.
Magill, Dan. Dan Magill's Bull-Doggerel: Fifty Years of Anecdotes from the Greatest Bulldog Ever. LC 93-79659. (Illus.). 192p. 1993. 16.95 (*1-56352-089-3*) Longstreet.
— Match Pointers: Courtside with the Winningest Coach in Tennis History. 192p. 1995. 19.95 (*1-56352-194-6*) Longstreet.
Magill, E., jt. ed. see Calder, M.
Magill, Frank, ed. Chronology of 20th-Century History: Arts & Culture, 2 vols. 1998. lib. bdg. 275.00 (*1-884964-66-4*) Fitzroy Dearborn.
— International Encyclopedia of Propaganda. (Illus.). 1998. lib. bdg. 175.00 (*1-57958-023-8*) Fitzroy Dearborn.
Magill, Frank N. Great Events from History II, 5 vols., Set. LC 93-28381. (Arts & Culture Series). 2878p. 1993. lib. bdg. 375.00 (*0-89356-807-4*) Salem Pr.
— Great Women Writers. 1995. write for info. (*0-8050-2932-X*) H Holt & Co.
— Magill's Literary Annual, 1984: Books of 1983, 2 vols. LC 77-99209. 996p. 1984. lib. bdg. 55.00 (*0-89356-284-X*) Salem Pr.
— Masterplots II: British & Commonwealth Fiction, 4 vols., Set. LC 87-4639. 2024p. 1987. lib. bdg. 365.00 (*0-89356-468-0*) Salem Pr.
— Masterplots II: Short Story, 6 vols., Set. LC 86-22025. 2856p. 1986. lib. bdg. 425.00 (*0-89356-461-3*) Salem Pr.
— The Nobel Prize Winners: Literature, 3 vols., Set. (Literature Ser.). (Illus.). 1090p. 1988. lib. bdg. 210.00 (*0-89356-541-5*) Salem Pr.
— Survey of Social Science: Government & Politics, 5 vols., Set. LC 95-30408. 2371p. (YA). (gr. 9-12). 1995. lib. bdg. 375.00 (*0-89356-745-0*) Salem Pr.
Magill, Frank N., ed. Chronology of 20th-Century History: Business & Commerce, 2 vols., Set. 1996. lib. bdg. 275.00 (*1-884964-42-7*) Fitzroy Dearborn.
— Chronology of 20th-Century History: Ecology & the Environment, 2 vols. 1997. lib. bdg. 275.00 (*1-884964-57-5*) Fitzroy Dearborn.
— Critical Survey of Drama, 7 vols., Set. rev. ed. 3212p. (J). (gr. 9-12). 1994. lib. bdg. 425.00 (*0-89356-851-1*) Salem Pr.
— Critical Survey of Drama: Foreign Language Series, 6 vols., Set. LC 86-11884. (Foreign Language Series, Written in English). 2628p. (YA). (gr. 9-12). 1986. lib. bdg. 350.00 (*0-89356-382-X*) Salem Pr.
— Critical Survey of Literary Theory, 4 vols., Set. 1900p. 1988. lib. bdg. 300.00 (*0-317-67452-8*) Pan-Am Publishing Co.
— Critical Survey of Poetry, 5 vols., Set. LC 84-5365. (Foreign Language Ser.). 2383p. 1984. lib. bdg. 275.00 (*0-89356-350-1*) Salem Pr.
— Critical Survey of Poetry, 8 vols., Set. rev. ed. LC 92-3727. (Critical Survey of Poetry). 4254p. 1992. lib. bdg. 475.00 (*0-89356-834-1*) Salem Pr.
— Critical Survey of Short Fiction, 7 vols., Set. rev. ed. LC 92-41950. 2948p. 1993. lib. bdg. 425.00 (*0-89356-843-0*) Salem Pr.
— Great Events from History II: Ecology & the Environment, 5 vols., Set. LC 95-5035. 2296p. (YA). (gr. 9 up). 1995. lib. bdg. 375.00 (*0-89356-751-5*) Salem Pr.
— Great Events from History II: Human Rights, 5 vols., Set. LC 92-12896. 2880p. 1992. lib. bdg. 375.00 (*0-89356-643-8*) Salem Pr.
— Great Events from History II: Science & Technology, 5 vols., Set. LC 91-23313. 2610p. 1991. lib. bdg. 375.00 (*0-89356-637-3*) Salem Pr.
— Great Lives from History: American, 5 vols., Set. LC 86-31561. (American Ser.). 2670p. 1987. lib. bdg. 365.00 (*0-89356-529-6*) Salem Pr.
— Great Lives from History: Ancient & Medieval, 5 vols., Set. LC 88-18514. (Ancient & Medieval Ser.). 2502p. (J). 1988. lib. bdg. 365.00 (*0-89356-545-8*) Salem Pr.
— Great Lives from History: British & Commonwealth, 5 vols., Set. LC 87-26511. (British & Commonwealth Ser.). 2760p. 1987. lib. bdg. 365.00 (*0-89356-535-0*) Salem Pr.
— Great Lives from History: Renaissance to 1900, 5 vols., Set. LC 89-24039. (Renaissance to 1900 Ser.). 2632p. (J). 1989. lib. bdg. 365.00 (*0-89356-551-2*) Salem Pr.
— Great Lives from History: Twentieth Century, 5 vols., Set. (Twentieth Century Ser.). 2604p. 1990. lib. bdg. 365.00 (*0-89356-565-2*) Salem Pr.
Magill, Frank N., ed. Great Lives from History Index. rev. ed. 266p. 1995. pap. 12.95 (*0-89356-891-0*) Salem Pr.
Magill, Frank N., ed. International Encyclopedia of Economics, 2 vols. 1997. 275.00 (*1-884964-83-4*) Fitzroy Dearborn.
— International Encyclopedia of Government & Politics, 2 vols. 1996. 275.00 (*1-884964-63-X*) Fitzroy Dearborn.
— International Encyclopedia of Psychology, 2 vols., Set. 1996. lib. bdg. 275.00 (*1-884964-60-5*) Fitzroy Dearborn.
— International Encyclopedia of Sociology, 2 vols., Set. 1996. lib. bdg. 275.00 (*1-884964-54-0*) Fitzroy Dearborn.
— Magill's Literary Annual, 1981: Books of 1980, 2 vols., Set. LC 77-99209. 950p. 1981. lib. bdg. 55.00 (*0-89356-281-5*) Salem Pr.
— Magill's Literary Annual, 1982: Books of 1981, 2 vols., Set. LC 77-99209. 1007p. 1982. lib. bdg. 55.00 (*0-89356-282-3*) Salem Pr.
— Magill's Literary Annual, 1983: Books of 1982, 2 vols., Set. LC 77-99209. 938p. 1983. lib. bdg. 55.00 (*0-89356-283-1*) Salem Pr.
— Magill's Literary Annual, 1985: Books of 1984, 2 vols., Set. LC 77-99209. 1067p. 1985. lib. bdg. 60.00 (*0-89356-285-8*) Salem Pr.
— Magill's Literary Annual, 1986: Books of 1985, 2 vols., Set. LC 77-99209. 988p. 1986. lib. bdg. 60.00 (*0-89356-286-6*) Salem Pr.
— Magill's Literary Annual, 1987: Books of 1986, 2 vols., Set. LC 77-99209. 1026p. 1987. lib. bdg. 65.00 (*0-89356-287-4*) Salem Pr.
— Magill's Literary Annual, 1988: Books of 1987, 2 vols., Set. LC 77-99209. 1013p. 1988. lib. bdg. 65.00 (*0-89356-288-2*) Salem Pr.
— Magill's Literary Annual, 1989: Books of 1988, 2 vols., Set. LC 79-99209. 938p. 1989. lib. bdg. 65.00 (*0-89356-289-0*) Salem Pr.
— Magill's Literary Annual, 1978, 2 vols., Set. LC 77-99209. 946p. 1978. lib. bdg. 55.00 (*0-89356-278-5*) Salem Pr.
— Magill's Literary Annual, 1990: Books of 1989, 2 vols., Set. LC 77-99209. 933p. 1990. lib. bdg. 70.00 (*0-89356-290-4*) Salem Pr.
— Magill's Literary Annual, 1991: Books of 1990, 2 vols., Set. LC 77-99209. 924p. 1991. lib. bdg. 70.00 (*0-89356-291-2*) Salem Pr.
— Magill's Literary Annual, 1992: Books of 1991, 2 vols., Set. LC 77-99209. 937p. 1992. lib. bdg. 70.00 (*0-89356-292-0*) Salem Pr.
— Magill's Literary Annual, 1993: Books of 1992, 2 vols., Set. LC 77-99209. 899p. 1993. lib. bdg. 70.00 (*0-89356-293-9*) Salem Pr.
— Magill's Literary Annual, 1994: Books of 1993, 2 vols., Set. LC 77-99209. 876p. 1994. lib. bdg. 70.00 (*0-89356-294-7*) Salem Pr.
— Magill's Literary Annual, 1995: Books of 1994, 2 vols., Set. LC 77-99209. 1067p. 1995. lib. bdg. 75.00 (*0-89356-295-5*) Salem Pr.
— Magill's Literary Annual, 1979: Books of 1978, 2 vols., Set. LC 77-99209. 926p. 1979. lib. bdg. 55.00 (*0-89356-279-3*) Salem Pr.
— Magill's Survey of American Literature, 6 vols., Set. LC 91-28113. (Illus.). 2160p. 1991. lib. bdg. 542.79 (*1-85435-437-X*) Marshall Cavendish.
— Magill's Survey of Science: Applied Science, 6 vols., Set. LC 92-35688. 3107p. 1991. lib. bdg. 475.00 (*0-89356-705-1*) Salem Pr.
— Magill's Survey of Science: Life Science, 6 vols., Set. 2964p. 1991. lib. bdg. 475.00 (*0-89356-612-8*) Salem Pr.
— Magill's Survey of Science: Physical Science, 6 vols., Set. LC 91-32962. 2981p. 1992. lib. bdg. 475.00 (*0-89356-618-7*) Salem Pr.
— Magill's Survey of World Literature, 6 vols. LC 92-11198. 1992. 389.95 (*1-85435-482-5*) Marshall Cavendish.
— Masterpieces of American Literature. LC 93-15940. 640p. 1993. 47.50 (*0-06-270072-3*, Harper Ref) HarpC.
— Masterpieces of Women's Literature. LC 95-26601. (Masterpieces of...Ser.). 608p. 1996. 50.00 (*0-06-270138-X*, Harper Ref) HarpC.
— Masterpieces of World Literature. LC 89-45052. 992p. 1991. 55.00 (*0-06-270050-2*) HarperTrade.
— Masterplots: Revised Category Edition, 3 vols. rev. ed. (British Fiction Ser.). 1832p. 1985. lib. bdg. 120.00 (*0-89356-504-0*) Salem Pr.
— Masterplots Revised Category Edition: American Fiction, 3 vols., Set. rev. ed. LC 85-1936. 1532p. 1985. lib. bdg. 120.00 (*0-89356-500-8*) Salem Pr.
— Masterplots Revised Category Edition: European Fiction, 3 vols., Set. rev. ed. LC 85-18297. 1482p. 1986. lib. bdg. 120.00 (*0-89356-508-3*) Salem Pr.
— Masterplots II: African American Literature, 3 vols., Set. LC 93-33876. 1568p. (YA). (gr. 9-12). 1994. lib. bdg. 275.00 (*0-89356-594-6*) Salem Pr.
— Masterplots II: Drama, 4 vols., Set. LC 89-10989. 1864p. 1990. lib. bdg. 365.00 (*0-89356-491-5*) Salem Pr.
— Masterplots II: Juvenile & Young Adult Fiction, 4 vols., Set. LC 91-4509. 1792p. (YA). (gr. 6 up). 1991. lib. bdg. 365.00 (*0-89356-579-2*) Salem Pr.
— Masterplots II: Nonfiction, 4 vols., Set. LC 89-5877. 1810p. 1989. lib. bdg. 365.00 (*0-89356-478-8*) Salem Pr.
— Masterplots II: Poetry, 6 vols., Set. LC 91-44341. 2630p. 1992. lib. bdg. 425.00 (*0-89356-584-9*) Salem Pr.
— Masterplots II: Short Story Series Supplement, 4 vols., Set. LC 88-6469. 1746p. (YA). (gr. 9-12). 1996. lib. bdg. 325.00 (*0-89356-769-8*) Salem Pr.
— Masterplots II: Women's Literature, 6 vols. LC 94-25180. 2698p. 1995. lib. bdg. 500.00 (*0-89356-898-8*) Salem Pr.
— The Nobel Prize Winners: Chemistry, 3 vols., Set. LC 90-8092. (Chemistry Ser.). (Illus.). 1306p. 1990. lib. bdg. 210.00 (*0-89356-561-X*) Salem Pr.
— The Nobel Prize Winners: Physics, 3 vols., Set. LC 89-6409. (Illus.). 1427p. 1989. lib. bdg. 210.00 (*0-89356-557-1*) Salem Pr.
— The Nobel Prize Winners: Physiology or Medicine, 3 vols., Set. LC 91-12143. (Physiology or Medicine Ser.). (Illus.). 1659p. 1991. lib. bdg. 210.00 (*0-89356-571-7*) Salem Pr.
***Magill, Frank N., ed.** The 17th & 18th Centuries. LC 97-51154. (Dictionary of World Biography Ser.: Vol. 4). (Illus.). 1515p. 1999. lib. bdg. 125.00 (*0-89356-316-1*) Salem Pr.
Magill, Frank N., ed. Survey of Social Science: Economics, 5 vols., Set. LC 91-29798. (Economics Ser.). 2656p. (YA). (gr. 9-12). 1991. lib. bdg. 375.00 (*0-89356-725-6*) Salem Pr.
Magill, Frank N., ed. Survey of Social Science: Psychology, 6 vols., Set. LC 93-34708. 2923p. 1993. lib. bdg. 425.00 (*0-89356-732-9*) Salem Pr.
Magill, Frank N., et al, eds. Magill's Literary Annual, 1977, 2 vols., Set. LC 77-99209. 960p. 1977. lib. bdg. 55.00 (*0-89356-077-4*) Salem Pr.
***Magill, Frank N., et al, eds.** Magill's Survey of Science, Applied Science Supplement (1998) Applied Science Supplement. (Applied Science Series, Supplement). 448p. (YA). (gr. 9 up). 1998. lib. bdg., suppl. ed. 90.00 (*0-89356-934-8*) Salem Pr.
— Magill's Survey of Science, Earth Science Supplement (1998) Earth Science Supplement. (Earth Science Series, Supplement). 448p. (YA). (gr. 9 up). 1998. lib. bdg., suppl. ed. 90.00 (*0-89356-933-X*) Salem Pr.
— Magill's Survey of Science, Life Science Supplement (1998) Life Science Supplement. (Life Science Series, Supplement). 448p. (gr. 9 up). 1998. lib. bdg., suppl. ed. 90.00 (*0-89356-936-4*) Salem Pr.
— Magill's Survey of Science, Physical Science Supplement (1998) Physical Science Supplement. (Physical Science Series, Supplement). 448p. (YA). (gr. 9 up). 1998. lib. bdg., suppl. ed. 90.00 (*0-89356-935-6*) Salem Pr.
Magill, Frank N. & Mazzeno, Laurence W., eds. Masterplots, 12 vols. 2nd rev. ed. 7680p. 1996. lib. bdg. 600.00 (*0-89356-084-7*) Salem Pr.
Magill, Frank N. & Roth, John, eds. Masterpieces of World Philosophy: More Than 100 Classics of the World's Greatest Philosophers Analyzed & Explained. LC 15-8176. 704p. 1991. 47.00 (*0-06-270051-0*, Harper Ref) HarpC.
Magill, Frank N. & Salem Press Editors. Masterplots II: Juvenile & Young Adult Literature, Supplement, 1997, 3 vols. LC 96-39759. 1536p. (YA). (gr. 6-12). 1997. lib. bdg. 275.00 (*0-89356-916-X*) Salem Pr.
***Magill, Frank N., et al.** The American Presidents. rev. ed. LC 99-38924. (Illus.). 852p. (YA). (gr. 6 up). 1999. lib. bdg. 135.00 (*0-89356-224-6*) Salem Pr.
Magill, Frank N., ed. see Salem Press Editors.
Magill, Gerard, ed. Discourse & Context: An Interdisciplinary Study of John Henry Newman. LC 92-17309. 232p. (C). 1993. 36.95 (*0-8093-1836-9*) S Ill U Pr.
— Personality & Belief: Interdisciplinary Essays on John Henry Newman. 228p. (C). 1994. lib. bdg. 44.00 (*0-8191-9757-2*) U Pr of Amer.
Magill, Gerard & Hoff, Marie D., eds. Values & Public Life: An Interdisciplinary Study. LC 95-17930. 328p. (C). 1995. 49.50 (*0-8191-9974-5*) U Pr of Amer.
Magill, Gerard, jt. ed. see Rainey, R. Randall.
Magill, Harry B. Biography of Francis Schlatter, the Healer. 198p. 1996. reprint ed. spiral bd. 15.00 (*0-7873-0580-4*) Hlth Research.
— The Biography of Francis Schlatter, the Healer: Life, Works & Wanderings - 5000 Healings a Day. 1991. lib. bdg. 75.95 (*0-8490-4130-9*) Gordon Pr.
Magill, Harry T., et al. The CPA Profession: Opportunities, Responsibilities & Services. LC 97-40486. 252p. 1997. pap. text 39.80 (*0-13-737792-4*) P-H.
Magill, Jane M. & Moore, John B., Jr. Experiments in Biochemistry. (Illus.). 100p. 1978. spiral bd. 10.95 (*0-89641-007-2*) American Pr.
— Experiments in Metabolism. (Illus.). 100p. 1979. spiral bd. 10.95 (*0-89641-013-7*) American Pr.
Magill, Jerry. I Hate Selling. LC 95-94820. 80p. (Orig.). 1995. pap. 8.95 (*0-9648142-0-X*) J Magill.
Magill, John, jt. text see Adams, Lynn.
Magill, Kathleen. Kate. LC 99-13504. (Five Star Original Romance Ser.). 1999. 24.95 (*0-7862-1885-1*, Five Star MI) Mac Lib Ref.
— Megan. LC 99-24656. 1999. 26.95 (*0-7838-8629-2*) Mac Lib Ref.
Magill, Michael & Quinzii, Martine. Theory of Incomplete Markets, Vol. 1. (Illus.). 504p. (C). 1996. 62.50 (*0-262-13324-5*) MIT Pr.
Magill, Michael A., jt. auth. see Neathery, Raymond F.
Magill, Michele M. Repertoire des References aux Arts et a la Litterature dans "A la Recherche du Temps Perdu" de Marcel Proust. LC 91-65734. (Marcel Proust Studies: Vol. 2). (FRE.). 272p. 1991. lib. bdg. 38.95 (*0-917786-85-8*) Summa Pubns.
Magill, Mike. Transline. 2000. 34.99 (*0-310-22803-4*) HarpC.
Magill, R. E. Bryophyta Pt. 1: Mosses. Fascicle 1. (Flora of Southern Africa Ser.). (Illus.). 291p. 1981. 38.00 (*0-621-06951-5*, Pub. by Natl Botanical Inst) Balogh.
— Bryophyta Pt. 1: Mosses. Fascicle 2. (Flora of Southern Africa Ser.). (Illus.). 152p. 1987. 17.00 (*0-621-10325-X*, Pub. by Natl Botanical Inst) Balogh.
Magill, R. E. & Schelpe, E. A. The Bryophytes of Southern Africa. An Annotated Checklist. (Memoirs of the Botanical Survey of South Africa Ser.: No. 43). (Illus.). 39p. 1979. 15.00 (*0-621-04718-X*, Pub. by Natl Botanical Inst) Balogh.
Magill, Richard A. Motor Learning: Concepts & Application. 4th ed. 480p. (C). 1996. text. write for info. (*0-697-38984-7*, WCB McGr Hill) McGrw-H Hghr Educ.
— Motor Learning: Concepts & Application. 5th ed. LC 97-16623. 352p. (C). 1997. text. write for info. (*0-697-24652-3*, WCB McGr Hill) McGrw-H Hghr Educ.
***Magill, Richard A.** Motor Learning: Concepts & Application. 6th ed. (Illus.). 384p. 2001. Price not set. (*0-07-232936-X*) McGraw.
Magill, Richard A. Motor Learning: Concepts & Applications. 4th ed. 480p. (C). 1992. text. write for info. (*0-697-12643-9*) Brown & Benchmark.
Magill, Richard A., et al, eds. Children in Sport. LC 82-82668. 327p. reprint ed. pap. 101.40 (*0-608-15855-0*, 203147000074) Bks Demand.
Magill, Robert E., jt. auth. see Crosby, Marshall R.
Magill, Robert E., jt. ed. see Coosey, Marshall R.
Maginel, Robert, jt. auth. see Rose, Frank.
Magini, Mauro, ed. X-Ray Diffraction of Ions in Aqueous Solutions: Hydration & Complex Formation. 288p. 1988. 158.00 (*0-8493-6945-2*, QD561, CRC Reprint) Franklin.
Magini, Mauro, jt. ed. see Fiorani, Dino.
Maginn, John L. & Tuttle, Donald L., eds. Managing Investment Portfolios: A Dynamic Process. 2nd ed. LC 89-50465. 775p. (C). 1991. text 165.00 (*0-7913-0322-5*) Warren Gorham & Lamont.
Maginn, Michael D. Effective Teamwork: A Practical Guide to Team Membership. LC 93-5. 112p. 1993. pap. 10.95 (*1-55623-880-0*, Irwn Prfssnl) McGraw-Hill Prof.
***Maginnes, Al.** The Light in Our Houses. 72p. 2000. pap. 12.00 (*0-8071-2622-5*) La State U Pr.
Maginnis, Hayden B. Painting in the Age of Giotto: A Historical Reevaluation. LC 96-11306. 1997. 55.00 (*0-271-01599-3*) Pa St U Pr.
***Maginnis, Hayden B. J., et al.** The Early Painters of Siena LC 99-35892. 2000. write for info. (*0-271-02004-0*) Pa St U Pr.
Maginnis, John. Cross to Bear: Louisiana Politics 1991 from David Duke to Edwin Edwards. (Illus.). 320p. 1992. 19.95 (*0-9614138-2-4*) Darkhorse Pr.
— The Last Hayride. Phillips, Barbara, ed. LC 84-80875. (Illus.). 354p. (C). 1994. pap. 9.95 (*0-9614138-1-6*) Darkhorse Pr.
Maginnis, John H., Jr., ed. see Button, Chris.
Maginnis, Matthew, jt. auth. see Carpenter, Allan.
***Maginnis, Tobin.** Level I Networking: Sair Linux & GNU Certification. 304p. 2000. pap. text 34.99 (*0-471-36977-2*) Wiley.
— Sair Linux & GNU Certification. 304p. 2000. pap. text 34.99 (*0-471-36975-6*) Wiley.
— Sair Linux & GNU Certification Level I: System Administration. 448p. 2000. pap. text 39.99 (*0-471-36976-4*) Wiley.
— SAIR Linux & GNU Certification Level I: Installation & Configuration. LC 99-49095. 304p. 1999. pap. 34.99 (*0-471-36978-0*) Wiley.
Magisa, Lenore, ed. see Beil, Drake.
Magison, Ernest C. Electrical Instruments in Hazardous Locations. 4th ed. LC 98-12645. xiv, 583 p. 1998. 57.00 (*1-55617-638-4*) ISA.
— Intrinsic Safety. LC 84-10852. (Independent Learning Module from the Instrument Society of America Ser.). (Illus.). 191p. 1984. reprint ed. pap. 59.30 (*0-7837-9045-7*, 204979600003) Bks Demand.

An Asterisk (*) at the beginning of an entry indicates that the title is appearing for the first time.

Magison, Ernest C., jt. auth. see Calder, William.

Magisos, Joel H., et al. Excellence in Vocational Education: Four Levels, Four Perspectives. 39p. 1984. 4.75 (*0-318-22101-2*, IN287) Ctr Educ Trng Employ.

Magister, Thomas. Ecloga Vocum Atticarum. cxlvi, 504p. 1970. reprint ed. write for info. (*0-318-71053-6*) G Olms Pubs.

Magistrale, Anthony S. Landscape of Fear: Stephen King's American Gothic. LC 87-72642. 139p. (C). 1988. 26.95 (*0-87972-404-8*) Bowling Green Univ Popular Press.

— The Moral Voyages of Stephen King. LC 88-1076. (Starmont Studies in Literary Criticism: No. 25). iv, vi, 157p. 1989. pap. 21.00 (*1-55742-070-X*) Millefleurs.

— Obsessions. (Illus.). 40p. 1989. pap. 3.95 (*0-910619-05-0*) Niekas Pubns.

— Stephen King - The Second Decade: Danse Macabre to the Dark Half. (United States Authors Ser.). 208p. 1992. 32.00 (*0-8057-3957-2*, 599) Macmillan.

Magistrale, Anthony S., ed. Casebook on "The Stand" LC 93-214779. (Starmont Studies in Literary Criticism: No. 38). xii, 210p. 1992. pap. 23.00 (*1-55742-250-8*) Millefleurs.

— The Dark Descent: Essays Defining Stephen King's Horrorscape, 48. LC 91-36705. (Contributions to the Study of Science Fiction & Fantasy Ser.: No. 48). 248p. 1992. 47.95 (*0-313-27297-2*, MDU/, Greenwood Pr) Greenwood.

Magistrale, Anthony S. & Warner, Kenneth. Writing Across Culture: An Introduction to Study Abroad & the Writing Process. 176p. (C). 1995. pap. text 19.95 (*0-8204-1923-0*) P Lang Pubng.

Magistrale, Anthony S., jt. auth. see Frank, Frederick S.

Magistrale, Tony. Discovering Stephen King's the Shining: Essays on the Bestselling Novel by America's Premier Horror Writer. 2nd ed. LC 98-38108. (I. O. Evans Studies in the Philosophy & Criticism of Literature). 1998. pap. write for info. (*1-55742-133-1*) Millefleurs.

***Magistrale, Tony & Poger, Sidney.** Poe's Children: Connections Between Tales of Terror & Detection. LC 98-53779. 148p. (C). 1999. pap. text 25.95 (*0-8204-4070-1*) P Lang Pubng.

Magistro, Cynthia, jt. auth. see Spurlock, John.

Magitskii, Efim. Galereiia Vymysla - Stikhi. LC 87-82249. (RUS.). 112p. 1987. 10.00 (*0-911971-27-0*) Effect Pub.

Maglacas, A. Mangay & Simons, J., eds. The Potential of the Traditional Birth Attendant. (WHO Offset Publications: No. 95). 105p. 1986. pap. text 16.00 (*92-4-170095-5*, 1120095) World Health.

Maglalang, Demetrio M. Agricultural Approach to Family Planning. 159p. 1976. pap. text 3.00 (*0-942717-01-5*) Intl Inst Rural.

Magleby, David B. Direct Legislation: Voting on Ballot Propositions in the United States. LC 83-22265. 284p. reprint ed. pap. 88.10 (*0-7837-4275-4*, 204396700012) Bks Demand.

***Magleby, David B., ed.** Outside Money: Soft Money & Issue Advocacy in the 1998 Congressional Elections. LC 99-49349. 192p. 2000. 55.00 (*0-7425-0042-X*); pap. 19.95 (*0-7425-0043-8*) Rowman.

Magleby, David B. & Nelson, Candice J. The Money Chase: Congressional Campaign Finance Reform. 250p. 1990. 34.95 (*0-8157-5434-5*); pap. 14.95 (*0-8157-5433-7*) Brookings.

Magleby, Richard, jt. ed. see Anderson, Margot.

Magley, Beverley. Scenic Byways: East & South. rev. ed. LC 99-17803. (Illus.). 216p. 1999. pap. 14.95 (*1-56044-734-6*) Falcon Pub Inc.

***Magley, Beverley.** Scenic Byways: Rocky Mountains. rev. ed. (Illus.). 272p. 1999. pap. 16.95 (*1-56044-735-4*) Falcon Pub Inc.

Magley, Beverly. Arizona Wildflowers. LC 91-58054. (Interpreting the Great Outdoors Ser.). (Illus.). 32p. 1991. pap. 5.95 (*1-56044-096-1*) Falcon Pub Inc.

— California Wildflowers. 2nd ed. LC 88-83883. (Illus.). 32p. 1996. pap. 6.95 (*1-56044-385-5*) Falcon Pub Inc.

— Montana Wildflowers. LC 91-58876. (Interpreting the Great Outdoors Ser.). (Illus.). 32p. 1992. pap. 6.95 (*1-56044-118-6*) Falcon Pub Inc.

— Oregon Wildflowers: Beginner's Field Guide. LC 91-77419. (Interpreting the Great Outdoors Ser.). (Illus.). 32p. 1992. pap. 6.95 (*1-56044-035-X*) Falcon Pub Inc.

— Scenic Byways Far West. LC 99-29290. 272p. 1998. pap. 14.95 (*1-56044-653-6*) Falcon Pub Inc.

— Scenic Byways I. LC 90-80040. (Falcon Guide Ser.). (Illus.). 240p. (Orig.). 1990. pap. 14.95 (*0-937959-94-4*) Falcon Pub Inc.

— Texas Wildflowers. LC 92-55083. (Illus.). 32p. 1993. pap. text 6.95 (*1-56044-386-3*) Falcon Pub Inc.

Magliano, James, jt. auth. see McLoughlin.

Magliaro, Susan G., jt. auth. see Shambaugh, R. Neal.

Maglic, K. D., et al. Compendium of Thermophysical Property Measurement Methods Vol. 2: Recommended Measurement Techniques & Practices. (Illus.). 661p. (C). 1991. text 159.50 (*0-306-43854-2*, Kluwer Plenum) Kluwer Academic.

Maglic, Kosta D., ed. Compendium of Thermophysical Property Measurement Methods, Vol. 1: Survey of Measurement Techniques. (Illus.). 806p. (C). 1984. text 210.00 (*0-306-41424-4*, Kluwer Plenum) Kluwer Academic.

Maglin, Nan B. & Schniedewind, Nancy, eds. Women & Stepfamilies. (Women in the Political Economy Ser.). (Illus.). 448p. 1990. pap. 22.95 (*0-87722-782-9*) Temple U Pr.

— Women & Stepfamilies: Voices of Anger & Love. LC 88-11719. (Women in the Political Economy Ser.). 448p. (C). 1988. 49.95 (*0-87722-586-9*) Temple U Pr.

Maglin, Nan B., jt. ed. see Perry, Donna.

Maglinte, jt. auth. see Herlinger.

Maglio, Vincent J. & Cooke, H. B., eds. Evolution of African Mammals. LC 77-19318. (Illus.). 656p. 1979. 98.95 (*0-674-27075-4*) HUP.

Magliocchetti, Bruno & Verna, Anthony, eds. The Motif of the Journey in Nineteenth-Century Italian Literature. LC 94-8388. 210p. 1994. 49.95 (*0-8130-1291-0*) U Press Fla.

Magliocco, Maurine, jt. ed. see Hargrove, Anne C.

Magliola, Robert R. On Deconstructing Life-Worlds: Buddhism, Christianity, Culture. LC 96-27889. (American Academy of Religion Cultural Criticism Ser.). 202p. 1997. 29.95 (*0-7885-0295-6*, 010703) OUP.

Maglione, Connie A. & Fiore, Carmen A. Voices of the Daughters. LC 89-5031. (Illus.). 335p. 1989. 18.95 (*0-939219-05-0*) Townhouse Pub.

Maglione, Harry, jt. ed. see Emmens, Carol A.

Maglione, Robin S. Alyndoria: Tales of Inner Magic. (Illus.). 71p. (Orig.). (J). (gr. k-12). 1986. pap. 12.00 (*0-910609-11-X*) Gifted Educ Pr.

Magliozzi, Ray, jt. auth. see Magliozzi, Tom.

Magliozzi, Ronald S. Treasures from the Film Archives: A Catalog of Short Silent Fiction Films Held by FIAF Archives. LC 88-13500. 856p. 1988. 66.00 (*0-8108-2180-X*) Scarecrow.

Magliozzi, Tom & Magliozzi, Ray. Car Talk. 224p. 1991. pap. 13.95 (*0-440-50364-7*) Dell.

— A Haircut in Horse Town: And Other Great Car Talk Puzzlers. LC 99-21131. 1999. pap. text 15.95 (*0-399-52561-0*) Berkley Pub.

***Magliozzi, Tom & Magliozzi, Ray.** In Our Humble Opinion: Car Talk's Click & Clack Rant & Rave. 224p. 2000. 19.95 (*0-399-52600-5*, Perigee Bks) Berkley Pub.

Maglischo, Cheryl W. Biomechanics Workbook to Accompnay Software. 137p. (C). 1991. text. write for info. (*0-697-14842-4*) Brown & Benchmark.

Maglischo, Ernest W. Swimming Even Faster: A Comprehensive Guide to the Science of Swimming. 2nd ed. LC 92-41324. 755p. (C). 1993. text 48.95 (*1-55934-036-3*, 1036) Mayfield Pub.

Maglischo, Ernest W. & Ferguson Brennan, Cathy. Swim for the Health of It. LC 84-60886. 144p. (Orig.). (C). 1985. pap. text 17.95 (*0-87484-588-2*, 588) Mayfield Pub.

***Magliveras, Konstantinos D.** Exclusion from Participation in International Organizations: The Law & Practice Behind Member States' Expulsion & Suspension of Membership. LC 99-31738. (Studies & Materials on the Settlement of International Disputes: Vol. 5). 336p. 1999. 135.00 (*90-411-1239-1*) Kluwer Law Intl.

Magliveras, S. & Kramer, Edna E. Finite Geometries & Combinatorial Designs: (Special Session) LC 90-45302. (Contemporary Mathematics Ser.: Vol. 111). 312p. 1990. pap. 55.00 (*0-8218-5118-7*, CONM/111) Am Math.

***Magloire, Kim.** Cracking the Regents Biography 2000. 3rd ed. 552p. 2000. pap. 6.95 (*0-375-75553-5*) Random.

Maglott, D. R. & Nierman, W. C., eds. American Type Culture Collection Catalogue of Recombinant DNA Materials. 3rd ed. 150p. 1993. pap. text. write for info. (*0-930009-51-7*) ATCC.

Maglott, D. R., jt. ed. see Nierman, W. C.

Magnabosco, Jennifer L., jt. ed. see Mullen, Edward J.

Magnaghi, Russell M. Herbert E. Bolton & the Historiography of the Americas, 5. LC 97-38566. (Studies in Historiography: Vol. 5). 240p. 1998. 59.95 (*0-313-29895-5*, Greenwood Pr) Greenwood.

— Indian Slavery, Labor, Evangelization, & Captivity in the Americas: An Annotated Bibliography. LC 97-25956. (Native American Bibliography Ser.: No. 22). 768p. 1998. 110.00 (*0-8108-3355-7*) Scarecrow.

— Miners, Merchants & Midwives: Michigan's Upper Peninsula Italians. LC 87-70604. 113p. (Orig.). 1987. pap. 7.95 (*0-942879-00-7*) Belle Fontaine Pr.

Magnaghi, Russell M., compiled by. A Sense of Time: The Encyclopedia of Northern Michigan University. 450p. 1999. write for info. (*0-918616-25-5*) Northern Mich.

Magnaghi, Russell M. & Marsden, Michael T., eds. A Sense of Place: Michigan's Upper Peninsula: Essays in Honor of William & Margery Vandament. LC 97-197532. (Illus.). 270p. 1997. 21.25 (*0-918616-20-4*); pap. 11.75 (*0-918616-21-2*) Northern Mich.

Magnago-Lampugnani, Vittorio, et al, eds. Dam: Architectural Annual 1995. (ENG & GER., Illus.). 200p. 1995. pap. 45.00 (*3-7913-1498-X*, Pub. by Prestel) te Neues.

Magnaint-Lopez, Bernard, jt. auth. see Pelletier, Sophie.

Magnan. Endoscopy in Neuro-Otology. LC 98-32395. (Illus.). 119p. 1999. 129.00 (*0-86577-828-0*) Thieme Med Pubs.

— Paroles. (C). 1999. pap. text, wbk. ed., lab manual ed. 41.50 (*0-03-020797-5*) Harcourt.

— Planning for Proficiency. (Teaching Methods Ser.). (J). 1990. mass mkt. 27.95 (*0-8384-2924-6*) Heinle & Heinle.

***Magnan, Jacques.** Endoscopy in Neuro-Otology. LC 98-32395. 1999. write for info. (*3-13-113061-X*, Pub. by G Thieme) Thieme Med Pubs.

Magnan, Marcella C., jt. auth. see Magnan, William B.

Magnan, Pierre. L' Amant du Poivre d'Ane. (FRE.). 416p. 1991. pap. 13.95 (*0-7859-4379-X*, 2070384292) Fr & Eur.

— La Maison Assassinee. (FRE.). 1985. pap. 13.95 (*0-7859-4224-6*) Fr & Eur.

***Magnan, Pierre.** Murdered House. 2000. 26.00 (*1-86046-649-4*) Harvill Press.

Magnan, Richard A. Software User Interface Compatibility after Lotus Development Corporation vs Paperback Software International. (Illus.). 49p. (Orig.). 1993. pap. text. write for info. (*1-879716-04-6*, P-93-4) Ctr Info Policy.

Magnan, Robert, ed. 147 Practical Tips for Teaching Professors. 63p. 1990. reprint ed. pap. text 12.50 (*1-891859-01-3*) Atwood Pub LLC.

— One Hundred Forty-Seven Practical Tips for Teaching Professors. LC 92-9593. 45p. 1990. pap. 12.50 (*0-912150-09-2*) Atwood Pub LLC.

Magnan, Robert & Santovec, Mary Lou. 1001 Commonly Misspelled Words: What Your Spell Checker Won't Tell You. 272p. 2000. pap. 12.95 (*0-07-135736-X*) McGraw.

Magnan, Robert, jt. auth. see Schoenfeld, A. Clay.

Magnan, Rudy A., ed. Reinventing American Education. (Orig.). pap. write for info. (*0-943025-47-8*) Cummngs & Hath.

***Magnan, Sally S.** Paroles. 1998. 82.00 (*0-03-021243-X*) H Holt & Co.

Magnan, Sally S., ed. Shifting the Instructional Focus to the Learner. LC 55-34379. (Reports of the Northeast Conference on the Teaching of Foreign Languages). 177p. 1990. pap. 10.95 (*0-915432-90-0*) NE Conf Teach Foreign.

Magnan, Sally S., et al. Paroles. (C). 1998. text 44.50 (*0-03-022782-8*) Harcourt Coll Pubs.

Magnan, William B. & Magnan, Marcella C. The Streets of St. Louis: A History of St. Louis Street Names. LC 96-160203. 232p. 1996. pap. 16.95 (*0-9631448-6-3*) VA Pub Corp.

Magnani, David & McMurtry, Newell. Breaking the Boardom: An Annotated Bibliography on Boards & Councils. (Illus.). (Orig.). 1983. pap. 10.00 (*0-934210-08-X*) Devlp Commy.

Magnani, Denise. Discover the Winterthur Garden. (Discover Winterthur Ser.). (Illus.). 48p. 1998. pap. 7.95 (*0-912724-45-5*) Winterthur.

— The Winterthur Garden: Henry Francis du Pont's Romance with the Land. LC 94-14976. (Illus.). 192p. 1995. 39.95 (*0-8109-3779-4*, Pub. by Abrams) Time Warner.

Magnani, Duane. Another Jesus, 2 vols., I. 1990. pap. 12.95 (*1-883858-01-1*) Witness CA.

— Another Jesus, 2 vols., II. 1990. pap. 12.95 (*1-883858-02-X*) Witness CA.

— Another Jesus, 2 vols., Set. 1990. pap. 19.95 (*1-883858-00-3*) Witness CA.

— Bible Students? 1983. pap. 12.95 (*1-883858-03-8*) Witness CA.

— Charles Taze Russell - Child Molester. 1986. pap. 4.95 (*1-883858-04-6*) Witness CA.

— Cruel & Unusual Punishment. 1986. pap. 13.95 (*1-883858-05-4*) Witness CA.

— Danger at Your Door. 1987. pap. 13.95 (*1-883858-06-2*, 687) Witness CA.

— Dialogue with Jehovah's Witnesses, 2 vols., I. 1983. pap. 13.95 (*1-883858-08-9*) Witness CA.

— Dialogue with Jehovah's Witnesses, 2 vols., II. 1983. pap. 13.95 (*1-883858-09-7*) Witness CA.

— Dialogue with Jehovah's Witnesses, 2 vols., Set. 1983. pap. 22.95 (*1-883858-07-0*) Witness CA.

— Divine Minds. 178p. 1990. pap. 5.95 (*1-883858-63-1*) Witness CA.

— The Heavenly Weatherman. 1987. pap. 12.95 (*1-883858-12-7*) Witness CA.

— The Moneymakers. 1986. pap. 8.95 (*1-883858-14-3*) Witness CA.

— Point-Counterpoint Vol. 1: False Prophets. 1986. pap. 8.95 (*1-883858-16-X*) Witness CA.

— A Problem of Communication. 1989. pap. 7.95 (*1-883858-17-8*) Witness CA.

— Refutation of Preparing for Child Custody Cases. 1988. pap. 12.95 (*1-883858-18-6*) Witness CA.

— Resurrection of the Gods. 79p. 1990. pap. 2.95 (*1-883858-64-X*) Witness CA.

— Saleskids. 1986. pap. 14.95 (*1-883858-19-4*) Witness CA.

— The Secret Doctrine of Jehovah's Witnesses. 1983. pap. 4.95 (*1-883858-20-8*) Witness CA.

— Super Index. 1993. pap. 9.95 (*1-883858-21-6*) Witness CA.

— What Makes a Minister? 1986. pap. 4.95 (*1-883858-23-2*) Witness CA.

— Where Are the 144,000? (Illus.). 25p. 1990. pap. 4.95 (*1-883858-67-4*) Witness CA.

— Where Is Michael? 1984. pap. 7.95 (*1-883858-24-0*) Witness CA.

— Who Is the Faithful & Wise Servant? rev. ed. 1992. pap. 12.95 (*1-883858-25-9*) Witness CA.

Magnani, Duane & Barrett, Arthur. Eyes of Understanding. 1977. pap. 7.95 (*1-883858-10-0*) Witness CA.

— From Kingdom Hall to Kingdom Come. rev. ed. 1987. pap. 12.95 (*1-883858-11-9*) Witness CA.

Magnani, Gregorio, jt. ed. see Buchholz, Daniel.

Magnani, Joseph L. & Peters, Vincent F. How to Conduct Doctor Dinner Meetings. 60p. (Orig.). 1998. pap. 24.95 (*0-9656231-1-4*) Black Dog Pub.

***Magnani, Lorenzo, et al.** Model-Based Reasoning in Scientific Discovery. LC 99-44860. 354p. 1999. write for info. (*0-306-46292-3*) Kluwer Academic.

***Magnani, Loris & LaRosa, Theodore.** Physics of the Solar System: A Companion to Introductory Astronomy Textbooks. (Physics of the Solar System). 210p. (C). 1998. per. 28.95 (*0-7872-4890-8*, 41489001) Kendall-Hunt.

Magnani, M. & De Flora, A., eds. Red Blood Cell Aging. (Advances in Experimental Medicine & Biology Ser.). (Illus.). 400p. (C). 1991. text 156.00 (*0-306-44021-0*, Kluwer Plenum) Kluwer Academic.

Magnani, M. & DeLoach, J. R. The Use of Resealed Erthrocytes As Carriers & Bioreactors. (Advances in Experimental Medicine & Biology Ser.: Vol. 326). (Illus.). 357p. (C). 1993. text 110.00 (*0-306-44345-7*, Kluwer Plenum) Kluwer Academic.

Magnani, Nanette, jt. auth. see Kabbucho, Kamau.

Magnanti. Applied Mathematical Programming. 2nd ed. (C). 1996. text. write for info. (*0-201-60971-1*) Addison-Wesley.

Magnarella. Justice in Africa. 61.95 (*0-7546-1073-X*) Ashgate Pub Co.

Magnarella, Paul, ed. Middle East & North Africa: Governance, Democratization, Human Rights. (Contemporary Perspectives on Developing Societies Ser.). 240p. 1999. text 65.95 (*1-84014-913-2*, Pub. by Ashgate Pub) Ashgate Pub Co.

Magnarella, Paul J. Human Materialism: A Model of Sociocultural Systems & a Strategy for Analysis. LC 93-11146. (Illus.). 192p. 1993. 49.95 (*0-8130-1233-3*); pap. 19.95 (*0-8130-1245-7*) U Press Fla.

— The Peasant Venture: Tradition, Migration & Change among Georgian Peasants in Turkey. (Illus.). 175p. 1979. pap. 13.95 (*0-87073-821-6*) Schenkman Bks Inc.

— Tradition & Change in a Turkish Town. 2nd ed. (Illus.). 210p. 1982. 19.95 (*0-87073-153-X*); pap. 15.95 (*0-87073-152-1*) Schenkman Bks Inc.

Magnarelli, Sharon. The Lost Rib. LC 83-46157. 232p. 1985. 38.50 (*0-8387-5074-5*) Bucknell U Pr.

— Understanding Jose Donoso. LC 92-19103. (Understanding Modern European & Latin American Literature Ser.). (Illus.). 204p. 1992. text 29.95 (*0-87249-844-1*) U of SC Pr.

Magnasco. From College to Career. 1997. pap. 32.81 (*0-07-032953-2*) McGraw.

Magnavita, Jeffrey J. Relational Therapy for Personality Disorders. LC 99-11517. (Series in Couples & Family Dynamics & Treatment). 291p. 1999. 45.00 (*0-471-29566-3*) Wiley.

— Restructuring Personality Disorders: A Short-Term Dynamic Approach. LC 96-44159. (Assessment of Personality & Psychopathology Ser.). 349p. 1997. lib. bdg. 40.00 (*1-57230-185-6*, 0185) Guilford Pubns.

Magne, Emile, ed. see De La Fayette, Marie-Madeleine.

Magne, Lawrence. RDI Evaluates the Sony ICF-2010 Receiver. (Radio Database International White Paper). (Illus.). 22p. (Orig.). 1988. pap. 6.95 (*0-914941-06-2*) IBS PA.

Magne, Lawrence, et al, eds. Passport to World Band Radio: 2000 Edition. (Illus.). 560p. 1999. pap. 19.95 (*0-914941-49-6*, PAW00P, Pub. by IBS PA) Natl Bk Netwk.

Magne, Lawrence, et al. Passport Evaluation of the ICOM IC-R9000 Receiver. (Radio Database International White Paper). (Illus.). 28p. (Orig.). 1990. pap. 6.95 (*0-914941-21-6*, WP14) IBS PA.

***Magnenat-Thalmann, N., et al, eds.** Computer Animation & Simulation '99: Proceedings of the Eurographics Workshop in Milano, Italy, September 7-8, 1999. (Eurographics Ser.). (Illus.). x, 230p. 1999. pap. 54.95 (*3-211-83392-7*) Spr-Verlag.

Magnenat-Thalmann, N. & Thalmann, Daniel. Image Synthesis Theory & Practice. (Computer Science Workbench Ser.). (Illus.). 400p. 1987. 59.00 (*0-387-70023-4*) Spr-Verlag.

— Synthetic Actors in Computer-Generated 3D Films. Kunii, Toshiyasu L., ed. (Computer Science Workbench Ser.). (Illus.). 144p. 1990. 82.74 (*0-387-52214-X*) Spr-Verlag.

Magnenat-Thalmann, N. & Thalmann, Daniel, eds. Computer Animation '90. (Illus.). viii, 242p. 1990. 107.95 (*0-387-70061-7*) Spr-Verlag.

— Computer Animation '91. (Illus.). viii, 256p. 1991. 139.95 (*0-387-70077-3*) Spr-Verlag.

— Computer-Generated Images. (Illus.). x, 497p. 1986. 79.00 (*0-387-70010-2*) Spr-Verlag.

— State-of-the-Art in Computer Animation. (Illus.). viii, 227p. 1989. 109.00 (*0-387-70046-3*) Spr-Verlag.

***Magnenat-Thalmann, Nadia & Volino, Pascal.** Dressing Virtual Humans. Barsky, Brian A., ed. (Computer Graphics & Geometric Modeling Ser.). 400p. 1999. text 59.95 incl. cd-rom (*1-55860-590-8*, Pub. by Morgan Kaufmann) Harcourt.

Magnenat-Thalmann, Nadia, et al. 1998 Multimedia Modeling: Mmm '98 : October 12-15, 1998, Lausanne, Switzerland : Proceedings. LC 98-86890. x, 231 p. 1998. write for info. (*0-8186-8911-0*) IEEE Comp Soc.

Magner, Blake A. Start Exploring the Civil War. (Start Exploring Ser.). (Illus.). 128p. (J). (gr. 4-7). 1997. 8.95 (*0-7624-0163-X*) Running Pr.

Magner, Carolyn. Life Moses: My Bible Sticker Storybook. 24p. (J). (ps-3). 1994. pap. 2.99 (*0-7814-0141-0*) Chariot Victor.

***Magner, E. C. & Magner, Rose M.** Bittersweet. 188p. (C). 1999. pap. 10.95 (*1-929416-10-5*) Magner Pubg.

— The Headstone. 221p. (C). 1999. pap. 10.95 (*1-929416-15-6*) Magner Pubg.

— I'll Never Say Goodbye. 160p. 1999. pap. 10.95 (*1-929416-06-7*) Magner Pubg.

— A Time for Tears. 190p. 1999. pap. 10.95 (*1-929416-14-8*) Magner Pubg.

— Whispers from the River. 166p. (C). 1999. pap. 10.95 (*1-929416-07-5*) Magner Pubg.

Magner, Eilis. Joske's Law & Procedure at Meetings in Australia. 8th ed. 220p. 1994. 60.00 (*0-455-21276-7*, Pub. by LawBk Co); pap. 36.00 (*0-455-21277-5*, Pub. by LawBk Co) Gaunt.

Magner, George. Chiropractic: The Victim's Perspective. Barrett, Stephen, ed. LC 95-21978. (Illus.). 252p. 1995. 25.95 (*1-57392-041-X*) Prometheus Bks.

Magner, James, Jr. The Temple of the Bell of Silence. 176p. (Orig.). 1992. pap. 5.00 (*0-937393-12-6*) Fred Pr.

Magner, James A. Men of Mexico. LC 68-55849. (Essay Index Reprint Ser.). 1977. 44.95 (*0-8369-0666-7*) Ayer.

Magner, L. N. History of Medicine in the Americas. Date not set. write for info. (*0-8247-9905-4*) Dekker.

Magner, Lee. Banished. (Intimate Moments Ser.). 1994. per. 3.50 (*0-373-07556-1*, 5-07556-9) Silhouette.

M

— Dangerous. LC 96-7303. (Intimate Moments Ser.). 251p. 1996. per. 3.99 (*0-373-07699-1*, 1-07699-1) Silhouette.

— Owen's Touch: Try to Remember. 1998. per. 4.25 (*0-373-07891-9*, 1-07891-4) Silhouette.

— Song of the Mourning Dove. (Intimate Moments Ser.: No. 420). 1992. per. 3.29 (*0-373-07420-4*, 5-07420-8) Harlequin Bks.

— Standoff. (Intimate Moments Ser.). 1993. per. 3.50 (*0-373-07507-3*, 5-07507-2) Silhouette.

Magner, Lois N. A History of the Life Sciences. 2nd ed. LC 93-34946. (Illus.). 512p. 1993. text 45.00 (*0-8247-8942-3*) Dekker.

Magner, Lois N., ed. Doctors, Nurses & Medical Practitioners: A Bio-Bibliographical Sourcebook. LC 97-2232. 384p. 1997. lib. bdg. 85.00 (*0-313-29452-6*, Greenwood Pr) Greenwood.

— A History of Medicine. (Illus.). 400p. 1992. text 59.75 (*0-8247-8673-4*) Dekker.

*__Magner Publishing Staff.__ Color the Hummingbirds. (Illus.). 20p. (J). (ps-7). 1999. pap. 4.95 (*1-929416-05-9*) Magner Pubg.

— Color the Owl Family. (Illus.). 20p. (J). (ps-7). 1999. pap. 4.95 (*1-929416-02-4*) Magner Pubg.

— Meet Your Backyard Friends. (Illus.). 16p. (J). (ps-7). 1999. pap. 4.95 (*1-929416-04-0*) Magner Pubg.

Magner Publishing Staff, ed. see Johnston, Nick.

Magner Publishing Staff, ed. see Kellum, Rose.

Magner Publishing Staff, ed. see Taylor, Ron.

Magner Publishing Staff, ed. see Wright, Herbert.

Magner, Rose M., jt. auth. see Magner, E. C.

Magner, Thomas F. Introduction to Croatian & Serbian Languages. 1995. pap. text 25.00 (*0-271-01536-5*) Pa St U Pr.

Magner, Thomas F. Introduction to the Croatian & Serbian Language. rev. ed. LC 89-37132. 448p. 1990. lib. bdg. 49.50 (*0-271-00685-4*) Pa St U Pr.

— Introduction to the Croatian & Serbian Language. rev. ed. LC 89-37132. 400p. 1995. pap. 25.00 (*0-271-01467-9*) Pa St U Pr.

Magnes, Beatrice. Episodes: A Memoir. 124p. 1977. 10.00 (*0-943376-07-6*) Magnes Mus.

Magnes, Martin. Weltmonographie der Triblidiaceae. (Bibliotheca Mycologica Ser.: Vol. 165). (SPA., Illus.). ii, 178p. 1997. 56.00 (*3-443-59067-5*, DM 95, Pub. by Gebruder Borntraeger) Balogh.

Magnes, Martin & Hafellner, Josef. Ascomyceten Auf Gefuesspflanzen an Ufern Von Gebirgsseen in Den Ostalpen. (Bibliotheca Mycologica: Vol. 139). (GER., Illus.). 186p. 1991. 48.00 (*3-443-59040-3*, Pub. by Gebruder Borntraeger) Balogh.

Magness, J. Lee. At the Foot of the Cross: Meditations on the Meal of Remembrance. LC 96-7301. 112p. 1996. 6.99 (*0-7847-0463-5*, 23023) Standard Pub.

Magness, Jodi. Jerusalem Ceramic Chronology. (Journal for the Study of the Old Testament Supplement Monographs Ser.: Vol. 9). 277p. 1993. 80.00 (*1-85075-413-6*, Pub. by Sheffield Acad) CUP Services.

Magness, John M. Pilot Vision: And Other Pilot Secrets to Succeed in the Business World. LC 98-27851. 128p. 1998. 17.95 (*0-944708-50-1*) Adams Hall.

Magness, Perre M. Past Times: Stories of Early Memphis. (Illus.). 288p. 1994. 25.00 (*0-9642929-0-4*) Parkway Press.

*__Magnet, Myron.__ The Dream & the Nightmare: The Sixties' Legacy to the Underclass. LC 92-23260. 256p. 2000. reprint ed. pap. 15.95 (*1-893554-02-3*) Encounter Bks.

*__Magnet, Myron, ed.__ The Millennial City: A New Urban Paradigm for 21st Century America. LC 99-88326. 448p. 2000. text 27.50 (*1-56663-285-4*, Pub. by I R Dee) Natl Bk Netwk.

— What Makes Charity Work? A Century of Public & Private Philanthropy. 256p. 2000. 24.95 (*1-56663-334-6*, Pub. by I R Dee) Natl Bk Netwk.

Magnetic Resonance Annual Staff. Magnetic Resonance Annual, 1988. fac. ed. Kressel, Herbert Y., ed. LC 85-646023. (Illus.). 357p. pap. 110.70 (*0-7837-7223-8*, 204707500005) Bks Demand.

— Magnetic Resonance Annual, 1985. LC 85-646023. 334p. 1985. reprint ed. pap. 103.60 (*0-608-00365-4*, 206108200007) Bks Demand.

Magni, Jean-Fran C., et al. Robust Flight Control, Vol. 224. LC 97-1194. (Lecture Notes in Control & Information Sciences). 1997. pap. 88.00 (*3-540-76151-9*) Spr-Verlag.

Magni, Laura. Two Little Monkeys. LC 92-70226. (Illus.). 18p. (J). (ps-k). 1992. bds. 3.95 (*1-56397-154-2*) Boyds Mills Pr.

Magnien, E., ed. Biomolecular Engineering in the European Community. 1986. text 445.50 (*90-247-3400-2*) Kluwer Academic.

Magnien, E. & De Nettancourt, D., eds. Genetic Engineering of Plants & Micro-Organisms Important for Agriculture. (Advances in Agricultural Biotechnology Ser.). 1985. text 145.50 (*90-247-3131-3*) Kluwer Academic.

Magnien, Robert. State of the Chesapeake Bay, 1995. 47p. 1995. pap. 3.75 (*0-16-042627-8*) USGPO.

Magnien, Victor & Lacroix, M. Dictionnaire Grec-Francais.Tr. of Greek-French Dictionary. (FRE & GRE.). 2168p. 1969. 79.95 (*0-8288-6592-2*, M-6382) Fr & Eur.

*__Magnier, Thierry & Hallensleben, Georg.__ Isabelle & the Angel. LC 99-18344. (J). 2000. 15.95 (*0-8118-2526-4*) Chronicle Bks.

Magnin, Andre, ed. Malick Sidibe. (Illus.). 256p. 1998. 49.95 (*3-931141-93-4*, Pub. by Scalo Pubs) Dist Art Pubs.

Magnin, Andre, pref. Seydou Keita: African Photographer. (Illus.). 288p. 1997. 49.95 (*3-931141-46-2*, Pub. by Scalo Pubs) Dist Art Pubs.

Magnin, Andre & Soulillou, Jacques, eds. Contemporary Art of Africa. LC 94-42674. (Illus.). 192p. 1996. 60.00 (*0-8109-4032-9*, Pub. by Abrams) Time Warner.

Magnin, John D. San Diego County Practical Guide to Divorce. 237p. (Orig.). 1994. 34.95 (*1-885558-00-7*) CA Pract Law.

— San Diego County Practical Guide to Divorce. Rose, Donna L., ed. 237p. (Orig.). 1994. pap. text 29.95 (*1-885558-14-7*) CA Pract Law.

Magnin, Thierry. Advances in Corrosion-Deformation Interactions. (Materials Science Forum Ser.: Vol. 202). (Illus.). 188p. 1996. text 88.00 (*0-87849-707-2*, Pub. by Trans T Pub) Enfield Pubs NH.

Magnin, Thierry, ed. Corrosion-Deformation Interactions CDI '96: 2nd International Conference on Corrosion-Deformation Interactions in Conjunction with EUROCORR '96. (European Federation of Corrosion Publications Ser.: Vol. 21). (Illus.). 560p. 1998. 170.00 (*1-86125-048-7*, Pub. by Inst Materials) Ashgate Pub Co.

Magnini, Michael, ed. North of Infinity: Futurity Visions. LC 99-460571. 216p. 1997. pap. 12.95 (*0-88962-634-0*, 734083Q) Mosaic.

Magno, Cettina T. & Erdman, David V., eds. The Four Zoas by William Blake: A Photographic Facsimile of the Manuscript. LC 84-45891. (Illus.). 1987. 85.00 (*0-8387-5083-4*) Bucknell U Pr.

*__Magno, Joseph A.__ Self-Love: The Heart of Healing. 224p. 1999. pap. 29.50 (*0-7618-1574-0*) U Pr of Amer.

— Self-Love: The Heart of Healing. 224p. 2000. 52.00 (*0-7618-1573-2*) U Pr of Amer.

Magno, Rosa M. Always There's a Thud: Poems. 115p. (Orig.). 1987. pap. 10.00 (*971-10-0328-7*, Pub. by New Day Pub) Cellar.

Magnon, Leonor V. De, see De Magnon, Leonor V.

Magnor, Mary, et al, texts. Jesus Teaches Us. 141p. pap. 6.50 (*0-8198-3924-8*) Pauline Bks.

Magnor, Mary & Magnor, Thomas. Jesus Teaches Us. 244p. teacher ed., spiral bd. 16.95 (*0-8198-3926-4*) Pauline Bks.

Magnor, Thomas, jt. auth. see Magnor, Mary.

Magnotta, George, jt. auth. see Price, Robert S.

Magnotti, Shirley. Library Science Research, 1974-1979. viii, 179p. 1983. 45.00 (*0-87875-235-8*) Whitston Pub.

— Master's Theses in Library Science, 1970-1974. LC 75-8232. iii, 198p. 1976. 35.00 (*0-87875-100-9*) Whitston Pub.

Magnou, Jacqueline. Robert Musil: De "Torless" a "Noces" ou le Vertige du Moi. (Contacts Ser.: Series III, Vol. 31). (FRE.). xiii, 586p. 1995. 62.95 (*3-906754-08-1*, Pub. by P Lang) P Lang Pubng.

*__Magnum.__ GMT 2000: A Portrait of Britain in a Week. 2000. pap. 14.95 (*0-00-220172-0*, Pub. by HarpC) Trafalgar.

Magnum, A. Fletcher, ed. Conference on Assessing the Effects of Legislation on the Workload of the Courts: Papers & Proceedings. (Illus.). 173p. (C). 1998. pap. text 35.00 (*0-7881-4991-1*) DIANE Pub.

Magnum, Abbas. Allah O Akbar: A Journey Through Militant Islam. LC 95-163312. (Illus.). 320p. (C). 1994. text 69.95 (*0-7148-3162-X*, Pub. by Phaidon Press) Phaidon Pr.

Magnum Photo Agency Staff. Israel: 50 Years. (Illus.). 256p. 1998. 91.00 (*0-89381-774-0*) Aperture.

*__Magnum Photographers Staff.__ Magnum Degrees. (Illus.). 535p. 2000. 69.95 (*0-7148-3821-7*) Phaidon Pr.

Magnum Photographers Staff, photos by. In Our Time: The Last Five Decades as Seen by the Photographers of Magnum. (Illus.). 1989. 85.00 (*0-393-02767-8*) Norton.

Magnum Photos Agency Staff, ed. Birth. (Terrail Photo Ser.). (Illus.). 64p. 1998. pap. text 11.95 (*2-87939-167-9*, Pub. by Pierre Terrail) Rizzoli Intl.

— Desert. (Terrail Photo Ser.). (Illus.). 64p. 1998. pap. text 11.95 (*2-87939-158-X*, Pub. by Pierre Terrail) Rizzoli Intl.

— Night. (Terrail Photo Ser.). (Illus.). 64p. 1998. pap. text 11.95 (*2-87939-155-5*, Pub. by Pierre Terrail) Rizzoli Intl.

— Struggle. (Terrail Photo Ser.). (Illus.). 64p. 1998. pap. text 11.95 (*2-87939-164-4*, Pub. by Pierre Terrail) Rizzoli Intl.

— Walls. (Terrail Photo Ser.). (Illus.). 64p. 1998. pap. text 11.95 (*2-87939-170-9*, Pub. by Pierre Terrail) Rizzoli Intl.

— Writers. (Terrail Photo Ser.). (Illus.). 64p. 1998. pap. text 11.95 (*2-87939-161-X*, Pub. by Pierre Terrail) Rizzoli Intl.

Magnum Photos Staff, jt. photos by see Economopoulos, Nikos.

Magnum School, Inc. Staff. Curso Completo de Tiro de Defensa. (SPA., Illus.). 1987. student ed. 24.95 (*0-945406-01-0*) Magnum Schl.

Magnum School Inc. Staff. Firearms: A Complete Guide for Their Proper Use & Care. 2nd ed. (Illus.). 103p. (YA). 1994. student ed. 24.95 (*0-945406-02-9*) Magnum Schl.

Magnum School, Inc. Staff & Zylberglait, Tobias, eds. Manual Didactico para Investigadores de Delitos Financieros. (SPA.). 134p. (Orig.). 1995. lab manual ed. 29.95 (*0-945406-03-7*) Magnum Schl.

Magnus, Alfred. Non-Spherical Principal Series Representations of a Semisimple Lie Group. LC 79-10157. (Memoirs Ser.: No. 19/216). 52p. 1979. pap. 17.00 (*0-8218-2216-0*, MEMO/19/216) Am Math.

— Non-Spherical Principal Series Representations of a Semisimple Lie Group. LC 79-10157. (American Mathematical Society Ser.: No. 216). 58p. reprint ed. pap. 30.00 (*0-608-09215-0*, 205271900005) Bks Demand.

Magnus, B. Heidegger's Metahistory of Philosophy: Amor Fati, Being & Truth. 159p. 1970. pap. text 50.50 (*90-247-5052-0*, Pub. by M Nijhoff) Kluwer Academic.

Magnus, Bernd. Nietzsche's Existential Imperative. LC 77-9864. (Studies in Phenomenology & Existential Philosophy). 254p. reprint ed. pap. 78.80 (*0-8357-6686-1*, 205686500094) Bks Demand.

— Postmodern Turn. (C). (gr. 13). 1999. 55.00 (*0-415-90726-8*) Routledge.

Magnus, Bernd & Cullenberg, Stephen, eds. Whither Marxism? Global Crises in International Perspective. 288p. (C). (gr. 13). 1994. pap. 23.99 (*0-415-91043-9*, B4463) Routledge.

Magnus, Bernd & Higgins, Kathleen, eds. The Cambridge Companion to Nietzsche. (Companions to Philosophy Ser.). 415p. (C). 1996. text 59.95 (*0-521-36586-4*); pap. text 20.95 (*0-521-36767-0*) Cambridge U Pr.

Magnus, Bernd, et al. Nietzsche's Case: Philosophy As - And Literature. 350p. (C). 1992. pap. 23.99 (*0-415-90095-6*, A2728) Routledge.

Magnus, George A., jt. auth. see Kettell, Brian.

Magnus, Hugo, jt. ed. see Connor, W. R.

Magnus, I. B. & Kjellstorn, B. Musical Motifs in Swedish Church Art: The Pictorial Representations of Music & Music-Making in Sweden's Medieval Churches up to 1630. Stevens, Michael, tr. from SWE. (ENG & SWE., Illus.). 408p. 1993. 82.50 (*91-972117-0-2*) Coronet Bks.

*__Magnus, J. R. & Neudecker, H.__ Matrix Differential Calculus with Applications in Statistics & Econometrics. 2nd ed. LC QA188.M345 1999. 422p. 1999. pap. 64.95 (*0-471-98633-X*) Wiley.

Magnus, Jan R. Linear Structures. (Charles Griffin Book). 218p. 1988. text 60.00 (*0-19-520655-X*) OUP.

Magnus, Joann & Bogot, Howard I. An Artist You Don't Have to Be! A Jewish Arts & Crafts Book. (Illus.). 1990. pap. 10.95 (*0-8074-0422-5*, 168504) UAHC.

Magnus, Katie. Jewish Portraits. LC 72-3396. (Essay Index Reprint Ser.). 1977. reprint ed. 20.95 (*0-8369-2912-8*) Ayer.

Magnus, Laurie. English Literature in Its Foreign Relations, 1300-1800. LC 68-20238. 1972. reprint ed. 23.95 (*0-405-08775-6*) Ayer.

— A Primer of Wordsworth. LC 72-3170. (Studies in Wordsworth: No. 29). 1972. reprint ed. lib. bdg. 75.00 (*0-8383-1519-4*) M S G Haskell Hse.

Magnus, Laury. The Track of the Repetend: Syntactic & Lexical Repetition in Modern Poetry. LC 86-47850. (Ars Poetica Ser.: No. 4). 1989. 37.50 (*0-404-62504-5*) AMS Pr.

Magnus, Laury, tr. see Goncharov, Ivan A.

Magnus, Leonard A., ed. The Tale of the Armament of Igor, A.D. 1185, A Russian Historical Epic. 1977. lib. bdg. 59.95 (*0-8490-2727-6*) Gordon Pr.

Magnus, Magus. Little Puddles. (Poetry I Ser.). (Illus.). 96p. (Orig.). 1994. pap. 10.00 (*0-9638061-0-6*) M DeLeon Bksmith.

Magnus, Margaret. Gods of the Word: Archetypes in the Consonants. LC 99-14507. 158p. 1999. 25.00 (*0-943549-52-3*) Truman St Univ.

Magnus, Pseudo-Albertus. Quaestiones Alberti de Modis Significandi: A Critical Edition. (Studies in the History of Language Sciences: No. 15). xxxvii, 191p. 1977. 59.00 (*90-272-4510-X*) J Benjamins Pubng Co.

Magnus, R. Body Posture. (C). 1988. 47.50 (*81-205-0061-X*, Pub. by Oxford IBH) S Asia.

Magnus, Ralph. Afghan Alternatives: Issues, Options & Policies. LC 74-165170. 229p. 1985. pap. 21.95 (*0-913750-08-5*) Transaction Pubs.

Magnus, Ralph A. & Collins-Magnus, Bab. A Family of Enemies. LC 97-70488. 224p. (Orig.). 1997. pap. 10.00 (*0-9657028-0-4*) IAS Mktging.

Magnus, Ralph H. Afghan Alternatives: Issues, Options & Policies. 229p. (C). 1985. 44.95 (*0-88738-050-6*) Transaction Pubs.

Magnus, Ralph H., ed. Documents on the Middle East. LC 75-93191. 239p. reprint ed. pap. 74.10 (*0-8357-4465-5*, 203730900008) Bks Demand.

Magnus, Ralph H. & Naby, Eden. Afghanistan: Marx, Mullah & Mujahid. LC 97-19041. 288p. 1997. text 33.00 (*0-86531-513-2*, Pub. by Westview) HarpC.

*__Magnus, Ralph H. & Naby, Eden.__ Afghanistan: Mullah, Marx & Mujahid. LC 99-89977. (Nations of the Modern World Ser). 304p. 2000. pap. write for info. (*0-8133-3798-4*) Westview.

Magnus, S. W., ed. Butterworths Company Forms Manual. 1988. pap. 110.00 (*0-406-01630-5*, UK, MICHIE) LEXIS Pub.

*__Magnus, Shirl.__ Triumph: Never Give Up. 136p. 2000. pap. 13.95 (*1-55306-093-8*, Guardian Bks) Essence Publ.

Magnus, Shulamit S. Jewish Emancipation in a German City: Cologne, 1798-1871. LC 96-25758. (Stanford Studies in Jewish History & Culture). 1997. write for info. (*0-8047-2644-2*) Stanford U Pr.

Magnus, W., jt. auth. see Grossman, I.

Magnus, Wilhelm. Collected Papers. Chandler, B. & Baumslag, Gilbert, eds. (Illus.). 735p. 1983. 105.95 (*0-387-90879-X*) Spr-Verlag.

Magnus, Wilhelm, et al. Combinational Group Theory: Presentations of Groups in Terms of Generators & Relations. 444p. 1976. reprint ed. pap. text 12.95 (*0-486-63281-4*) Dover.

Magnus, Wilhelm, jt. auth. see Chandler, B.

Magnusen, Carmina M. Encounter with the Triune God: An Introduction to the Theology of Edward J. Kilmartin, S. J. LC 97-46147. (Illus.). 150p. 1998. 74.95 (*1-57309-254-1*); pap. 54.95 (*1-57309-253-3*) Intl Scholars.

Magnuson, Ann, et al, texts. Kenny Scharf: When Worlds Collide. (Illus.). 128p. (Orig.). 1996. pap. 29.95 (*0-945558-26-0*, 620731) ISU Univ Galls.

Magnuson, Carl R., jt. auth. see Chinn, Jennie A.

Magnuson, Carol, ed. see Ann, Nicky.

*__Magnuson, Carole.__ The Barbour Collection of Connecticut Town Vital Records Vol. 27: Middletown - Part II, K-Z & No Surname 1651-1854. White, Lorraine C., ed. 360p. 2000. pap. 38.50 (*0-8063-1604-7*) Genealog Pub.

Magnuson, Diana L. Animal Lore & Legend - Rabbit: American Indian Legends. LC 94-46600. (J). 1996. 4.95 (*0-590-22490-5*) Scholastic Inc.

— Animal Lore & Legend-Bear: American Indian Legends. LC 94-47935. (J). 1996. 4.95 (*0-590-22491-3*) Scholastic Inc.

— Animal Lore & Legend-Buffalo: American Indian Legends. LC 94-44267. (J). (ps-3). 1995. 4.95 (*0-590-22489-1*) Scholastic Inc.

— Animal Lore & Legend-Owl. LC 94-43935. 32p. (J). (ps-3). 1995. pap. 4.95 (*0-590-22488-3*) Scholastic Inc.

Magnuson, Douglas, jt. ed. see Beker, Jerome.

Magnuson, James. Windfall. LC 98-33750. 352p. 1999. 23.95 (*0-375-50210-6*) Villard Books.

*__Magnuson, John W.__ Exit Strategies for Real Estate Managers. 1998. pap. 24.95 (*1-57203-059-3*) Inst Real Estate.

Magnuson, M. A., jt. ed. see Matschinsky, F. M.

Magnuson, Mike. The Fire Gospels: A Novel. 272p. 1999. pap. 13.00 (*0-06-093010-1*) HarpC.

— Lummox. 2000. 24.00 (*0-06-019372-7*); pap. 13.00 (*0-06-093188-4*) HarpC.

— The Right Man for the Job: A Novel. 304p. 1998. pap. 13.00 (*0-06-092895-6*, HarperFlamingo) HarpC.

Magnuson, Norris A. & Travis, William G. American Evangelicalism Vol. II: First Bibliographical Supplement, 1990-1996. LC 90-33989. (C). 1997. lib. bdg. 40.00 (*0-933951-68-X*) Locust Hill Pr.

Magnuson, Paul. Coleridge & Wordsworth: A Lyrical Dialogue. LC 87-26341. 345p. reprint ed. pap. 107.00 (*0-608-06389-4*, 206675000008) Bks Demand.

— Coleridge's Nightmare Poetry. LC 74-4422. 151p. reprint ed. pap. 46.90 (*0-608-17538-2*, 203068000069) Bks Demand.

— Reading Public Romanticism. LC 97-33387. 264p. 1998. text 39.50 (*0-691-05794-X*, Pub. by Princeton U Pr) Cal Prin Full Svc.

Magnuson, Roger. Education in New France. 240p. 1992. 60.00 (*0-7735-0907-0*, Pub. by McG-Queens Univ Pr) CUP Services.

— Shareholder Litigation, 1984-1990, 3 vols. LC 81-6078. 350.00 (*0-685-09306-9*) West Group.

Magnuson, Ted. Oregon Trivia. LC 98-15449. 192p. 1998. pap. 6.95 (*1-55853-601-9*) Rutledge Hill Pr.

Magnussen, F., ed. see International Congress of Psychotherapy Staff.

Magnusson, A. L. & McGee, C. E., eds. The Elizabethan Theatre Vol. XI: Papers Given at the International Conference on Elizabethan Theatre Held at the University of Waterloo, Ontario, in July 1985, Vol. XI. (Illus.). 249p. 1990. 38.00 (*0-88835-028-7*) P D Meany.

Magnusson, Ake. Mocambique. 38p. 1969. write for info. (*91-7106-003-0*, Pub. by Nordic Africa) Transaction Pubs.

— Sverige-Sydafrika: En Studie au en Ekonomisk Relation. 174p. 1974. write for info. (*91-7106-072-3*, Pub. by Nordic Africa) Transaction Pubs.

— Swedish Investments in South Africa. (Research Report Ser.: No. 23). 57p. 1974. write for info. (*91-7106-078-2*, Pub. by Nordic Africa) Transaction Pubs.

— Sydafrika i Varlden. 312p. 1979. write for info. (*91-7106-149-5*, Pub. by Nordic Africa) Transaction Pubs.

— The Voice of South Africa. (Research Report Ser.: No. 35). 55p. 1976. write for info. (*91-7106-106-1*, Pub. by Nordic Africa) Transaction Pubs.

*__Magnusson, Bob.__ The Art of Walking Bass: A Method for Acoustic Or Electric Bass. 64p. 1999. pap. 17.95 incl. audio compact disk (*0-7935-8042-0*) H Leonard.

Magnusson, Boris, ed. System Configuration Management: Proceedings of the ECOOP'98 SCM-8, Symposium, Brussels, Belgium, July 20-21, 1998. LC 98-29080. (Lecture Notes in Computer Science Ser.: Vol. 1439). x, 207p. 1998. pap. 46.00 (*3-540-64733-3*) Spr-Verlag.

Magnusson, D., jt. ed. see Gustafson, S. B.

Magnusson, David, ed. Individual Development from an Interactional Perspective: A Longitudinal Study. (Paths Through Life Ser.). 248p. 1988. text 39.95 (*0-89859-707-2*) L Erlbaum Assocs.

— Toward a Psychology of Situations: An Interactional Perspective. 480p. 1981. text 89.95 (*0-89859-061-2*) L Erlbaum Assocs.

Magnusson, David, et al, eds. The Lifespan Development of Individuals: Behavioral, Neurobiological, & Psychosocial Perspectives: A Synthesis. (Illus.). 546p. (C). 1996. text 105.00 (*0-521-47023-4*) Cambridge U Pr.

— The Lifespan Development of Individuals: Behavioral, Neurobiological & Psychosocial Perspectives: A Synthesis. (Illus.). 546p. 1997. pap. text 47.95 (*0-521-62896-2*) Cambridge U Pr.

— Problems & Methods in Longitudinal Research: Stability & Change, Vol. 5. (European Network on Longitudinal Studies on Individual Development). (Illus.). 367p. (C). 1994. pap. text 42.95 (*0-521-46732-2*) Cambridge U Pr.

Magnusson, David & Bergman, Lars R., eds. Data Quality in Longitudinal Research. (Illus.). 297p. (C). 1990. text 69.95 (*0-521-38091-X*) Cambridge U Pr.

Magnusson, David & Casaer, Paul, eds. Longitudinal Research on Individual Development: Present Status & Future Prospectives. LC 93-18120. (European Network on Longitudinal Studies on Individual Development: Vol. 7). (Illus.). 267p. (C). 1993. text 95.00 (*0-521-43478-5*) Cambridge U Pr.

Magnusson, David & Endler, Norman S. Personality at the Crossroads. LC 77-4190. 464p. (C). 1977. text 79.95 (*0-89859-293-3*) L Erlbaum Assocs.

Magnusson, David, jt. auth. see Gustafson, Sigrid B.

Magnusson, David, jt. ed. see Stattin, Haken.

Magnusson, Denis. Canadian Constitutional Dilemmas Revisited. LC 98-136815. 216p. 1997. text 55.00 (*0-88911-595-8*, Pub. by McG-Queens Univ Pr); pap. text 19.95 (*0-88911-593-1*, Pub. by McG-Queens Univ Pr) CUP Services.

Magnusson, Finnur. The Hidden Class: Culture & Class in a Maritime Setting: Iceland 1880-1942. (North Atlantic Studies: No. 1). (Illus.). 156p. (C). 1990. text 36.00 (*87-7288-279-4*, Pub. by Aarhus Univ Pr) David Brown.

Magnusson, Jim, jt. auth. see Maxey, Lisa.

Magnusson, L., jt. auth. see Emmi, P. C.

Magnusson, Lars. The Contest for Control: Metal Industries in Sheffield, Solingen, Remscheid, & Eskilstuna During Industrialization. (Illus.). 224p. 1994. 47.50 (*0-85496-952-7*) Berg Pubs.

***Magnusson, Lars.** An Economic History of Sweden. LC 99-39725. (Explorations in Economic History Ser.). 304p. 2000. 110.00 (*0-415-18167-4*) Routledge.

— Free Trade & Protection in America, 1822-1890. LC 98-45036. 1999. 700.00 (*0-415-18121-6*) Routledge.

Magnusson, Lars, ed. Evolutionary & Neo-Schumpeterian Approaches to Economics. LC 93-5059. (Recent Economic Thought Ser.). 344p. (C). 1994. lib. bdg. 141.00 (*0-7923-9385-6*) Kluwer Academic.

— Free Trade: 1793-1886. LC 96-5497. (Early Sources in Economics Ser.). 1256p. (C). 1997. 650.00 (*0-415-13316-5*) Routledge.

— Mercantilism, 4 vols., Set. LC 94-33823. 1384p. (C). (gr. 13). 1996. text, boxed set 660.00 (*0-415-11600-7*) Routledge.

— Mercantilist Economics. LC 93-1423. (Recent Economic Thought Ser.). 288p. (C). 1993. lib. bdg. 127.00 (*0-7923-9359-7*) Kluwer Academic.

Magnusson, Lars & Ottosson, Jan, eds. Evolutionary Economics & Path Dependence. LC 96-38309. 240p. 1997. 85.00 (*1-85898-213-8*) E Elgar.

Magnusson, lars, jt. auth. see Isacson, Naths.

Magnusson, Lynne. Shakespeare & Social Dialogue: Dramatic Language & Elizabethan Letters. 2nd ed. LC 98-35821. (History of the Book in Britain Ser.). 260p. (C). 1999. text 59.95 (*0-521-64191-8*) Cambridge U Pr.

Magnusson, M. Eirikr. Thomas Saga Erkibyskups: A Life of Archbishop Thomas Becket, in Icelandic, with English Translation, Notes & Glossary, 2 vols. (Rolls Ser.: No. 65). 1974. reprint ed. 140.00 (*0-8115-1133-2*) Periodicals Srv.

Magnusson, Magnus. Laxdaela Saga. (Classics Ser.). 272p. (Orig.). 1969. pap. 12.95 (*0-14-044218-9*, Penguin Classics) Viking Penguin.

— Njal's Saga. (Classics Ser.). 384p. (Orig.). 1960. pap. 19.99 (*0-14-044103-4*, Penguin Classics) Viking Penguin.

***Magnusson, Magnus.** Rum Natures Island. 2000. pap. 14.95 (*0-946487-32-4*) Luath Pr Ltd.

Magnusson, Magnus. Tutankhamun & the Discovery of the Tomb. 1992. 39.00 (*1-56696-002-9*) Jackdaw.

Magnusson, Magnus & Palsson, Hermann, trs. The Vinland Sagas: The Norse Discovery of America. 139th ed. Incl. Eirik's Saga. 1965. pap. Graenlendinga Saga. 1965. pap. (Classics Ser.). 126p. (Orig.). 1965. Set pap. 15.99 (*0-14-044154-9*, Penguin Classics) Viking Penguin.

Magnusson, Magnus & White, Graham. The Nature of Scotland: Landscape, Wildlife & People. (Illus.). 280p. 1998. pap. 25.00 (*0-86241-674-4*, Pub. by Canongate Books) Interlink Pub.

Magnusson, Magnus, jt. auth. see Morris, William.

Magnusson, Magnus, tr. see Sturluson, Snorri.

Magnusson, Michael. Latin Glory: Airline Color Schemes of South America. LC 96-139551. (Illus.). 112p. 1995. pap. 21.95 (*0-7603-0024-0*) MBI Pubg.

***Magnusson, Philip C.** Transmission Lines & Wave Propagation. 4th ed. 1999. pap. text 89.95 (*0-8493-0269-2*) CRC Pr.

Magnusson, Phillip C. & Alexa. Transmission Lines & Wave Propagation. 3rd ed. 480p. 1991. boxed set 89.95 (*0-8493-4279-1*, TK3221) CRC Pr.

Magnusson, Sally. The Flying Scotsman. (Illus.). 191p. 1982. pap. 5.95 (*0-7043-3379-1*, Pub. by Quartet) Charles River Bks.

— A Shout in the Street: The Story of Church House in Bridgeton. (C). 1992. pap. 35.00 (*0-86153-150-7*, Pub. by St Andrew) St Mut.

Magnusson, Tomas, jt. auth. see Carlsson, Gunnar E.

Magnusson, Ulf & Persson, Gunnar. Facets, Phases & Foci: Studies in Lexical Relations in English. (Umea Studies in the Humanities: No. 75). 308p. (Orig.). 1986. pap. text 40.00 (*91-7174-253-0*) Coronet Bks.

Magnusson, Ulla, jt. auth. see Roderick, Hilliard.

Magnusson, Warren. The Search for Political Space: Globalization, Social Movements, & the Urban Political Experience. (Studies in Comparative Political Economy & Public Policy Ser.). 400p. 1996. pap. text 19.95 (*0-8020-6889-8*) U of Toronto Pr.

— The Search for Political Space: Globalization, Social Movements & the Urban Political Experience. (Studies in Comparative Political Economy & Public Policy.). 400p. 1996. text 60.00 (*0-8020-5959-7*) U of Toronto Pr.

Magnusson, Warren & Sancton, Andrew, eds. City Politics in Canada. LC 83-196724. 346p. reprint ed. pap. 107.30 (*0-8357-3782-9*, 203651200003) Bks Demand.

***Magnus, pseud.** Methodology & Tacit Knowledge. LC 98-47539. 426p. (C). 1999. 121.50 (*0-471-98297-0*) Wiley.

Magny, jt. auth. see Hurtaut.

Magny, Claude-Edmonde. L' Age du Roman Americain. (BCL1-PS American Literature Ser.). 252p. 1993. reprint ed. lib. bdg. 79.00 (*0-7812-6592-4*) Rprt Serv.

Magnyickij, A. V., jt. auth. see Pume, N. D.

Magoc, Christopher J., jt. auth. see Forlag, Albert B.

Magocsi, Paul R. Carpatho-Rusyn Studies: An Annotated Bibliography, 1985-1994, Vol. 2. LC 87-29288. (East European Monographs: No. 522). 420p. 1999. 71.00 (*0-88033-420-7*, 522, Pub. by East Eur Monographs) Col U Pr.

— Historical Atlas of East Central Europe. (Illus.). 232p. 1996. text 85.00 (*0-8020-0607-8*); pap. text 45.00 (*0-8020-7789-7*) U of Toronto Pr.

— A History of the Ukraine. (Illus.). 700p. 1996. pap. text 40.00 (*0-295-97580-6*) U of Wash Pr.

— A History of Ukraine. (Illus.). 880p. 1996. text 90.00 (*0-8020-0830-5*); pap. text 45.00 (*0-8020-7820-6*) U of Wash Pr.

***Magocsi, Paul R.** Of the Making of Nationalities: There Is No End, 2 vols. 2000. 140.00 (*0-88033-438-X*, 540, Pub. by East Eur Monographs) Col U Pr.

Magocsi, Paul R. The Russian Americans. Stotsky, Sandra, ed. LC 95-12599. 120p. (YA). (gr. 5 up). 1995. lib. bdg. 19.95 (*0-7910-3367-8*) Chelsea Hse.

— The Rusyns of Slovakia: An Historical Survey. LC 93-71875. 185p. 1994. 31.50 (*0-88033-278-6*, 381, Pub. by East Eur Monographs) Col U Pr.

— Ukraine: A Historical Atlas. 64p. 1985. text 50.00 (*0-8020-3428-4*) U of Toronto Pr.

— Ukraine: A Historical Atlas. 64p. 1986. pap. 27.50 (*0-8020-3429-2*) U of Toronto Pr.

Magocsi, Paul R., ed. Encyclopedia of Canada's Peoples. LC 99-226153. (Illus.). 1300p. 1998. text 200.00 (*0-8020-2938-8*) U of Toronto Pr.

— A New Slavic Language Is Born: The Rusyn Literary Language of Slovakia. LC 95-61203. (East European Monographs: No. CDXXXIV). 68p. 1996. 28.00 (*0-88033-331-6*, 434, Pub. by East Eur Monographs) Col U Pr.

— The Persistence of Regional Cultures: Rusyns & Ukrainians in Their Carpathian Homeland & Abroad. 220p. 1993. 46.50 (*0-88033-262-X*, 365, Pub. by East Eur Monographs) Col U Pr.

— Texts of the Ukraine "Peace" with Maps. (Revolution & Nationalism in the Modern World Ser.: No. 3). 184p. 1981. reprint ed. pap. 28.00 (*0-939738-02-3*) Zubal Inc.

— The Ukrainian Experience in the United States: A Symposium. LC 78-59968. (Sources & Documents Ser.). 1979. pap. text 7.50 (*0-916458-04-0*) Harvard Ukrainian.

Magocsi, Paul R., jt. auth. see Hrushevsky, Michaelo.

Magoffin, Susan S. Down the Santa Fe Trail & into Mexico: The Diary of Susan Shelby Magoffin, 1846-1847. Drumm, Stella M., ed. LC 82-2722. (Illus.). xxxvi, 304p. 1982. reprint ed. pap. 14.00 (*0-8032-8116-1*, Bison Books) U of Nebr Pr.

Magolda, Marcia B. Knowing & Reasoning in College: Gender Related Patterns in Students' Intellectual Development. LC 92-9889. 472p. (C). 1992. text 38.95 (*1-55542-467-8*) Jossey-Bass.

***Magolda, Marcia B. Baxter.** Creating Contexts for Learning & Self-Authorship: Constructive-Developmental Pedagogy. LC 99-6497. (Issues in Higher Education Ser.). 320p. (C). 1999. 49.95 (*0-8265-1343-3*) Vanderbilt U Pr.

Magoldi, Mary & Russell, Bruce. Daily Close-Ups for Fall. 96p. (J). (gr. k-6). 1984. student ed. 9.95 (*0-86653-254-4*, GA 561) Good Apple.

Magomedbekov, E. P., et al. Interaction of Hydrogen Isotopes with Transition-Metals & Intermetallic Compounds. Hohler, G. et al, eds. (Springer Tracts in Modern Physics Ser.: Vol. 132). (Illus.). 112p. 1996. 99.00 (*0-387-58369-6*) Spr-Verlag.

Magomedov, D. M. The Art of Daghestan: Decorative Applied Art, Paintings, Scultpture & Graphics. 200p. 1981. 125.00 (*0-7855-0691-8*) St Mut.

Magon, Ricardo F. Land & Liberty: Anarchist Influences in the Mexican Revolution. Poole, Dave, ed. (Orig.). 1979. pap. 5.50 (*0-932366-04-X*) Black Thorn Bks.

— Mexico: Land & Liberty. (Illus.). 156p. 1977. 41.99 (*0-919618-29-4*, Pub. by Black Rose); pap. 12.99 (*0-919618-30-8*, Pub. by Black Rose) Consort Bk Sales.

Magona, Sindiwe. Forced to Grow. LC 97-17848. 232p. 1998. pap. 12.95 (*1-56656-265-1*) Interlink Pub.

— Living, Loving & Lying Awake at Night. LC 94-4357. (Emerging Voices: New International Fiction Ser.). 208p. 1994. 24.95 (*1-56656-147-7*); pap. 11.95 (*1-56656-141-8*) Interlink Pub.

***Magona, Sindiwe.** Mother to Mother. LC 99-26023. 216p. 1999. 20.00 (*0-8070-0948-2*) Beacon Pr.

— Mother to Mother. 224p. 2000. pap. 14.00 (*0-8070-0949-0*) Beacon Pr.

Magona, Sindiwe. To My Children's Children. LC 94-4358. 256p. 1994. 24.95 (*1-56656-163-9*) Interlink Pub.

— To My Children's Children. 2nd ed. LC 94-4358. 200p. 1998. pap. 11.95 (*1-56656-294-5*) Interlink Pub.

Magone, Jose M. The Changing Architecture of Iberian Politics (1974-1992) An Investigation on the Structuring of Democratic Political Systemic Culture in Semiperipheral Southern European Societies. LC 95-31270. 680p. 1996. text 129.95 (*0-7734-2256-0*) E Mellen.

Magonet, Jonathan. The Explorer's Guide to Judaism. 340p. 1999. mass mkt. 15.95 (*0-340-70984-7*) Hodder & Stought Ltd.

— Form & Meaning: Studies in Literary Techniques in the Book of Jonah. 2nd ed. (Bible & Literature Ser.: No. 8). 184p. 1983. pap. 23.75 (*0-907459-25-0*, Pub. by Sheffield Acad) CUP Services.

Magonet, Jonathan. Subversive Bible. 1997. pap. 23.00 (*0-334-02671-7*) TPI PA.

Magonet, Jonathan, ed. Jewish Explorations of Sexuality. LC 95-17237. (European Judaism Ser.: Vol. 1). 270p. (C). 1995. 55.00 (*1-57181-868-5*); pap. 25.00 (*1-57181-029-3*) Berghahn Bks.

— Returning. LC 78-68143. 1978. pap. 3.95 (*0-8197-0468-7*) Bloch.

Magonet, Philip. Practical Hypnotism. 1976. pap. 3.00 (*0-87980-123-9*) Wilshire.

Magonov, Sergei N. & Whangbo, Myung-Hwan. Surface Analysis with STM & AFM: Experimental & Theoretical Aspects of Image Analysis. (Illus.). 323p. 1996. 175.00 (*3-527-29313-2*, Wiley-VCH) Wiley.

***Magoo, Biz.** Pajama Sam Out to Lunch! LC 00-105052. (Humongous Ser.). (Illus.). (J). (ps-1). 2001. 5.99 (*1-58668-065-X*) Lyrick Studios.

— Pajama Sam's Amazing TV Adventure! LC 00-105049. (Humongous Ser.). (Illus.). 24p. (J). (ps-1). 2001. 3.99 (*1-58668-062-5*) Lyrick Studios.

Magoon, Charles E. Photos at the Archives. 274p. (Orig.). 1981. pap. write for info. (*0-318-54244-7*) Macmillan.

— Reports of the Law of Civil Government in Territory Subject to Military Occupation by the Military Forces of the United States. 3rd ed. Kavass, Igor I. & Sprudzs, Adolf, eds. LC 72-75029. (International Military Law & History Ser.: Vol. 2). 808p. 1972. reprint ed. lib. bdg. 60.00 (*0-930342-39-9*, 300920) W S Hein.

— The Way It Was--the Produce Industry in the Early Years, 1890 to 1930. LC 97-92168. (Illus.). 350p. 1997. 39.00 (*0-9659233-0-4*) Particularly Prod.

Magoon, E. L. Orators of the American Revolution. 2nd ed. 456p. 1993. reprint ed. 47.50 (*0-8377-2442-2*, Rothman) W S Hein.

Magoon, Eaton B., Jr., et al. Numbah One Day of Christmas: The Hawaii Version of the 12 Days. LC 94-77955. (Illus.). 20p. 1994. 9.95 (*1-880188-91-0*) Bess Pr.

Magoon, Leslie B. & Claypool, George E., eds. Alaska North Slope Oil-Rock Correlation Study: Analysis of North Slope Crude. LC 86-1207. (AAPG Studies in Geology: No. 20). (Illus.). 696p. 1985. reprint ed. pap. 200.00 (*0-608-02749-9*, 206341400006) Bks Demand.

Magoon, Leslie B. & Dow, Wallace G., eds. The Petroleum System: From Source to Trap. LC 94-240285. (AAPG Memoir Ser.: No. 60). (Illus.). 655p. 1994. 114.00 (*0-89181-338-1*, 588) AAPG.

Magoon, Orville T., et al, eds. California & the World Ocean '97: Taking a Look at California's Ocean Resources: An Agenda for the Future: Conference Proceedings, 2 vols. LC 97-48327. (Illus.). 1816p. 1998. pap. text 149.00 (*0-7844-0297-3*, 40297) Am Soc Civil Eng.

— Coastal Zone, 1989, 5 vols. 5240p. 1989. pap. text 520.00 (*0-87262-705-5*, 705) Am Soc Civil Eng.

— Coastal Zone, 1991, 4 vols., Set. LC 91-19398. 3800p. 1991. pap. text 37.00 (*0-87262-809-4*) Am Soc Civil Eng.

— Coastal Zone, 1993: Proceedings of the Eighth Symposium & Ocean Management, July 19-23, 1993. New Orleans Louisiana. LC 93-2242. 3624p. 1993. 270.00 (*0-87262-918-X*) Am Soc Civil Eng.

Magoon, Orville T. & Baird, W. F., eds. Durability of Stone for Rubble Mound Breakwaters. LC 91-39609. 288p. 1992. pap. text 31.00 (*0-87262-863-9*) Am Soc Civil Eng.

Magoon, Orville T. & Davidson, D. D., eds. Case Histories of the Design, Construction, & Maintenance of Rubble Mound Structures: Derived from a Seminar Held at the Eureka Inn in Eureka, California, U. S. A., May 26-27, 1994. LC 95-33644. 296p. 1995. 31.00 (*0-7844-0127-6*) Am Soc Civil Eng.

Magoon, Orville T. & Fabbri, Paolo, eds. Coastlines of Italy. 192p. 1989. pap. text 5.00 (*0-87262-706-3*, 706) Am Soc Civil Eng.

Magoon, Orville T. & Hemsley, J. Michael, eds. Ocean Wave Measurement & Analysis: Proceedings of the Second International Symposium, Honoring Robert L. Wiegel, New Orleans, Louisiana, July 25-28, 1993. LC 94-7190. 1064p. 1994. 86.00 (*0-87262-922-8*) Am Soc Civil Eng.

Magoon, Orville T. & Neves, Claudio, eds. Coastlines of Brazil. 304p. 1989. pap. text 6.00 (*0-87262-707-1*, 707) Am Soc Civil Eng.

Magoon, Orville T., jt. ed. see Bolton, H. Suzanne.

Magoon, Orville T., jt. ed. see Cambers, Gillian.

Magoon, Orville T., jt. ed. see Cofer-Shabica, Stephen V.

Magoon, Orville T., jt. ed. see Davidson, D. D.

Magoon, Orville T., jt. ed. see Nagao, Yoshimi.

Magor, John. Pagans in My Blood. 120p. 1992. pap. 14.95 (*0-88839-291-5*) Hancock House.

Magor, Thomasin. African Warriors: The Samburu. LC 93-47465. (Illus.). 256p. 1994. 65.00 (*0-8109-1943-5*, Pub. by Abrams) Time Warner.

Magorian, James. Aardvarks on a Holiday. LC 96-84470. (Illus.). 18p. (Orig.). (J). (gr. 2-4). 1996. pap. 6.00 (*0-930674-46-4*) Black Oak.

— All the Wild Witches, Those Most Noble Ladies. LC 95-77975. (Illus.). 22p. (Orig.). (J). (gr. 2-5). 1995. pap. 6.00 (*0-930674-44-8*) Black Oak.

— America First. LC 92-70840. 156p. (Orig.). 1992. pap. 6.00 (*0-930674-37-5*) Black Oak.

— At the City Limits. LC 86-72766. (Illus.). 34p. 1987. pap. 3.00 (*0-930674-22-7*) Black Oak.

— The Beautiful Music. LC 88-71142. (Illus.). 12p. (J). (gr. 2-5). 1988. pap. 3.00 (*0-930674-25-1*) Black Oak.

— The Bonkly Dribblefink Fables. LC 87-70706. (Illus.). 16p. (J). (gr. 1-4). 1987. pap. 3.00 (*0-930674-24-3*) Black Oak.

— Borderlands. LC 91-75480. 36p. (Orig.). 1992. pap. 6.00 (*0-930674-36-7*) Black Oak.

— Catalpa Blossoms. 42p. 1994. 15.00 (*0-930674-39-1*) Black Oak.

— Dragon Bones. LC 98-74826. 54p. 1999. 20.00 (*0-930674-53-7*) Black Oak.

— The Emily Dickinson Jogging Book. LC 84-71315. 60p. 1984. pap. 5.00 (*0-930674-13-8*) Black Oak.

— Fimperings & Torples. LC 81-69872. (Illus.). 44p. (J). (gr. 4-6). 1981. pap. 3.00 (*0-930674-06-5*) Black Oak.

— The Great Injun Carnival. LC 81-69873. 48p. 1982. pap. 5.00 (*0-930674-07-3*) Black Oak.

— Griddlemort & the Beanstalk. LC 85-73615. (Illus.). 64p. 1986. pap. 5.00 (*0-930674-21-9*) Black Oak.

— Griddlemort Loses His Birthday. LC 88-71604. (Illus.). 32p. (J). (gr. 1-4). 1988. pap. 3.00 (*0-930674-29-4*) Black Oak.

— Haymarket Square. LC 97-70402. 74p. 1998. 20.00 (*0-930674-47-2*) Black Oak.

— Hearts of Gold. LC 95-40021. 230p. 1996. 18.95 (*0-9629880-1-4*) ACME Pr.

— The Hideout of the Sigmund Freud Gang. LC 84-71316. 974p. 1987. pap. 10.00 (*0-930674-16-2*) Black Oak.

— The Hippopotamus. LC 97-78359. (Illus.). 19p. (J). (gr. 2-5). 1998. pap. 6.00 (*0-930674-49-9*) Black Oak.

— Ideas for a Bridal Shower. LC 79-53858. 196p. 1980. pap. 5.00 (*0-930674-02-2*) Black Oak.

— Imaginary Radishes. LC 79-53857. (Illus.). 32p. (J). (gr. 3-5). 1980. 5.00 (*0-930674-03-0*) Black Oak.

— The Invention of the Afternoon Nap. LC 89-62222. (Illus.). 20p. (J). (gr. 2-5). 1989. pap. 3.00 (*0-930674-32-4*) Black Oak.

— The Island of Frequent Foolishness. LC 96-83376. (Illus.). 22p. (J). (gr. 2-4). 1997. pap. 6.00 (*0-930674-45-6*) Black Oak.

— Karl Marx & the Development of International Communism. LC 85-72861. 44p. 1986. pap. 5.00 (*0-930674-18-9*) Black Oak.

— Keeper of Fire. (Indian Culture Ser.). (Illus.). 78p. (Orig.). (J). (gr. 4-12). 1984. pap. 6.95 (*0-89992-088-8*) Coun India Ed.

— The Kingdom of Junk Bonds. LC 88-71143. (Illus.). 24p. (J). (gr. 5-9). 1988. pap. 3.00 (*0-930674-27-8*) Black Oak.

— The Magic Pretzel. LC 88-71603. (Illus.). 32p. (J). (gr. 2-5). 1988. pap. 3.00 (*0-930674-28-6*) Black Oak.

— The Man Who Wore Layers of Clothing in the Winter. LC 94-71880. 121p. (Orig.). 1994. pap. 6.00 (*0-930674-40-5*) Black Oak.

***Magorian, James.** Millennial Journal. LC 00-90544. 64p. 2000. pap. 12.00 (*0-930674-54-5*) Black Oak.

Magorian, James. Mountain Man. LC 88-71606. 40p. 1989. pap. 6.00 (*0-930674-31-6*) Black Oak.

— Mud Pies. LC 91-70218. (Illus.). 24p. (Orig.). (J). (gr. 4-6). 1991. pap. 3.00 (*0-930674-35-9*) Black Oak.

— The Palace of Water. LC 90-81003. (Illus.). 16p. (J). (gr. 2-5). 1990. pap. 3.00 (*0-930674-33-2*) Black Oak.

— Phases of the Moon. LC 77-82560. (Illus.). 40p. 1978. 6.00 (*0-930674-01-4*) Black Oak.

— Plucked Chickens. LC 80-68263. (Illus.). 32p. (J). (gr. 4-6). 1981. 5.00 (*0-930674-04-9*) Black Oak.

— Souvenir Pillows from Mars. unabridged ed. LC 94-79911. 118p. 1996. 25.00 (*0-930674-42-1*) Black Oak.

— Spiritual Rodeo. LC 80-18372. 17p. (Orig.). 1980. pap. 6.00 (*0-915124-37-8*) Coffee Hse.

— Spoonproof Jello & Other Poems. LC 90-81004. (Illus.). 16p. (J). (gr. 2-5). 1990. pap. 3.00 (*0-930674-34-0*) Black Oak.

— Squall Line. LC 85-73614. 52p. 1986. pap. 3.00 (*0-930674-19-7*) Black Oak.

— The Three Diminutive Pigs. LC 88-71605. (Illus.). 20p. (J). (gr. 1-4). 1988. pap. 3.00 (*0-930674-30-8*) Black Oak.

— The Tooth Fairy. LC 93-73338. (Illus.). 22p. (Orig.). (J). (gr. 1-3). 1993. pap. 3.00 (*0-930674-38-3*) Black Oak.

— The Walden Pond Caper. LC 83-71263. 148p. 1983. pap. 6.00 (*0-930674-11-1*) Black Oak.

— The Witches' Olympics. LC 83-71262. 44p. (J). (gr. 4-7). 1983. pap. 5.00 (*0-930674-10-3*) Black Oak.

Magorian, Michelle. Back Home. LC 84-47629. (Charlotte Zolotow Bk.). 384p. (J). (gr. 4-7). 1992. pap. 6.95 (*0-06-440411-0*, HarpTrophy) HarpC Child Bks.

— Back Home. 1992. 11.05 (*0-606-01083-1*, Pub. by Turtleback) Demco.

— Good Night, Mr. Tom. LC 80-8444. 336p. (YA). (gr. 7 up). 1982. 13.95 (*0-06-024078-4*); lib. bdg. 16.89 (*0-06-024079-2*) HarpC Child Bks.

— Good Night, Mr. Tom. LC 80-8444. (Trophy Bk.). 336p. (YA). (gr. 7-12). 1986. mass mkt. 4.95 (*0-06-440174-X*, HarpTrophy) HarpC Child Bks.

— Good Night, Mr. Tom. (J). 1986. 10.05 (*0-606-03224-X*, Pub. by Turtleback) Demco.

— Not a Swan. LC 91-19507. (Laura Geringer Bks.). 416p. (YA). (gr. 7 up). 1992. lib. bdg. 17.89 (*0-06-024215-9*) HarpC Child Bks.

— Who's Going to Take Care of Me? LC 89-26741. (Illus.). 32p. (J). (ps-1). 1990. 13.95 (*0-06-024105-5*) HarpC Child Bks.

Magos, Adam L., jt. ed. see Lewis, B. Victor.

Magos, Alice H. & Small Office/Home Office Editorial Group Staff, eds. Small Business Financing: How & Where to Get It. LC 99-180454. (Business Owner's Toolkit Ser.). (Illus.). x, 210p. 1998. pap. 17.95 (*0-8080-0239-2*) CCH INC.

Magos, Alicia P. The Enduring Ma-Aram Tradition: An Ethnography of a Knaray-a Village in Antique. (Illus.). 147p. 1993. pap. 13.75 (*971-10-0506-9*, Pub. by New Day Pub) Cellar.

Magosi, Paul R., ed. see Pekar, Athanasius.

Magoteaux, Cheryl. IPRA Media Guide. (Illus.). 256p. 1984. pap. 9.95 (*0-318-03395-X*) Intl Rodeo.

Magoulias, Harry J., tr. & anno. see Ducas.

Magoulias, Michael. Shakespeare for Students, Bk. II. 2nd ed. 550p. 1996. text 70.00 (*0-7876-0157-8*) Gale.

— Shakespearean Criticism, Vol. 28. 450p. 1995. text 155.00 (*0-8103-8948-7*) Gale.

— Shakespearean Criticism, Vol. 29. 400p. 1995. text 155.00 (*0-8103-9278-X*) Gale.

M

— Shakespearean Criticism, Vol. 30. 400p. 1996. text 155.00 (0-8103-9279-8) Gale.
— Shakespearean Criticism, Vol. 31. 400p. 1996. text 155.00 (0-8103-9280-1) Gale.
Magoulias, Michael, ed. Shakespearean Criticism, Vol. 2. 422p. 1995. text 155.00 (0-8103-8946-0) Gale.
— Shakespearean Criticism, Vol. 27. 500p. 1995. text 155.00 (0-8103-8947-9, 001349) Gale.
Magoun, F. A. & Hodgins, Eric. History of Aircraft. LC 70-169431. (Literature & History of Aviation Ser.). 1972. reprint ed. 40.95 (0-405-03774-0) Ayer.
Magoun, F. Alexander. The Frigate Constitution & Other Historic Ships. (Illus.). 256p. 1987. reprint ed. pap. 12.95 (0-486-25524-7) Dover.
Magoun, Francis P. A Chaucer Gazetteer. LC 61-11293. 173p. reprint ed. pap. 53.70 (0-608-16151-9, 202405800035) Bks Demand.
Magoun, Francis P. & Lhonnrot, Elias. The Old Kalevala, & Certain Antecedents. LC 74-78520. 331p. reprint ed. pap. 102.70 (0-7837-4119-7, 205794200011) Bks Demand.
Magoun, Francis P., Jr., tr. see Lonnrot, Elias, ed.
Magoun, Horace W., jt. auth. see Marshall, Louise H.
Magowan, B. Churchill's Pocketbook of Obstetrics & Gynaecology. (Illus.). 241p. 1996. pap. write for info. (0-443-05483-5) Church.
Magowan, Brian. Churchill's Pocketbook of Obstetrics & Gynaecology. LC 96-5330. 1996. write for info. (0-463-05483-0) Church.
***Magowan, Brian.** Churchill's Pocketbook of Obstetrics & Gynaecology. 2nd ed. LC 99-89414. 2000. write for info. (0-443-06424-5) Harcrt Hlth Sci Grp.
Magowan, Robin. Lilac Cigarette in a Wish Cathedral: Poems by Robin Magowan. Howard, Richard, ed. LC 97-45433. (Poetry Ser.). 90p. 1998. pap. 9.95 (1-57003-270-X); lib. bdg. 15.95 (1-57003-269-6) U of SC Pr.
— Looking for Binoculars. 50p. 1976. pap. 10.00 (0-87711-062-X) Story Line.
— Memoirs of a Minotaur: From Charles Merrill to Patty Hearst to Poetry by Robin Magowan. 273p. 1999. pap. 16.95 (1-885266-79-0, Pub. by Story Line) Consort Bk Sales.
— Tour de France: The 75th Anniversary Bicycle Race. LC 96-5519. (Illus.). 208p. 1996. 19.95 (1-884737-13-7) VeloPress.
Magrab, E. B. Computer Integrated Experimentation. (Environmental & Energetics Ser.). (Illus.). 272p. 1991. 79.95 (0-387-53291-9) Spr-Verlag.
— Vibrations of Elastic Structural Members, No. 3. (Mechanics of Structural Systems Ser.). 404p. 1980. text 195.50 (90-286-0207-0) Kluwer Academic.
***Magrab, Edward B.** MATLAB in Mechanical Engineering. 512p. 2000. pap. 81.00 (0-13-011335-2) P-H.
Magrab, Edward B., ed. see ASME DED Vibrations Conference Staf, DED Vibrations Conference Staf.
Magrab, Phyllis R., ed. Psychological & Behavioral Assessment: Impact on Pediatric Care. 384p. 1984. 70.00 (0-306-41697-2, Plenum Trade) Perseus Pubng.
Magrab, Phyllis R. & Wohlford, Paul, eds. Improving Psychological Services for Children & Adolescents with Severe Mental Disorders: Clinical Training in Psychology. LC 89-82575. 200p. 1990. pap. text 19.95 (1-55798-080-2) Am Psychol.
Magrab, Phyllis R., jt. auth. see Roberts, Richard N.
Magrabi, Frances M., et al. The Economics of Household Consumption. LC 91-20302. 296p. 1991. 75.00 (0-275-93406-3, C3406, Praeger Pubs); pap. 24.95 (0-275-94113-2, B4113, Praeger Pubs) Greenwood.
Magrah, Edward B. Integrated Product & Process Design & Development. LC 97-15254. 320p. 1997. boxed set 74.95 (0-8493-8483-4) CRC Pr.
Magrass, Yale. Thus Spake the Moguls. 274p. 1981. text 22.95 (0-87073-578-0); pap. text 15.95 (0-87073-579-9) Schenkman Bks Inc.
Magrassi, Mariano. Praying the Bible: An Introduction to Lectio Divina. Hagman, Edward, tr. LC 97-52992. 144p. 1998. pap. 11.95 (0-8146-2446-4) Liturgical Pr.
Magrassi, P., jt. ed. see Bounhoure, J. P.
Magrath. Pianists Guide to Standard Literature. 1995. pap. 29.95 (0-88284-655-8) Alfred Pub.
Magrath, Allan J. How to Achieve Zero-Defect Marketing. 192p. 1993. 22.95 (0-8144-5123-3) AMACOM.
—Marketing Strategies for Growth in Uncertain Times. Knudsen, Anne, ed. LC 94-20721. (Illus.). 192p. 1995. 29.95 (0-8442-3323-4, NTC Business Bks) NTC Contemp Pub Co.
— Marketing Strategies for Growth in Uncertain Times. (Illus.). 192p. 1996. pap. 17.95 (0-8442-3314-5, NTC Business Bks) NTC Contemp Pub Co.
— The 6 Imperatives of Marketing: Lessons from the World's Best Companies. 208p. 1992. 22.95 (0-8144-5042-3) AMACOM.
Magrath, C. Peter. Yazoo: Law & Politics in the New Republic: The Case of Fletcher v. Peck. LC 66-19584. 259p. reprint ed. pap. 80.30 (0-608-18419-5, 203002600067) Bks Demand.
Magrath, C. Peter, et al. Strengthening Teacher Education: The Challenges to College & University Leaders. LC 86-46336. (Jossey-Bass Higher Education Ser.). 206p. reprint ed. pap. 63.90 (0-7837-2524-8, 204268300006) Bks Demand.
Magrath, D. Guide to Poliovirus Isolation & Serological Techniques for Poliomyelitis Surveillance. (WHO Offset Publications: No. 45). 26p. 1979. 4.00 (92-4-170046-7) World Health.
Magrath, Derek. Norton: The Complete History. (Illus.). 160p. 1997. pap. 24.95 (1-86126-062-8, Pub. by Crolwood) Motorbooks Intl.
Magrath, Ian, jt. ed. see Huber, Brian E.
Magrath, Ian T., ed. New Directions in Cancer Treatment. (Illus.). 610p. 1989. pap. 104.00 (0-387-19063-5) Spr-Verlag.
— Non-Hodgkin's Lymphomas. 2nd ed. 1108p. 1997. text 225.00 (0-340-55793-1, Pub. by E A) OUP.
Magrath, Ian T., et al, eds. Pathogenesis of Leukemias & Lymphomas: Environmental Influences. LC 82-42584. (Progress in Cancer Research & Therapy Ser.: Vol. 27). 429p. 1984. reprint ed. pap. 133.00 (0-608-00402-2, 206111600007) Bks Demand.
Magrath, Jane. Masterwork Technical Skills Level 3. 32p. 1992. pap. 6.50 (0-7390-0494-8, 6584) Alfred Pub.
***Magrath, Jane, ed.** Copeland - The Cat & the Mouse. 2000. pap. 2.95 (0-7390-0794-7, 16736) Alfred Pub.
— Encore!, Bk. 3. 88p. 1990. pap. 9.95 (0-7390-0642-8, 307) Alfred Pub.
— Masterpieces with Flair, Bk. 2. 72p. 1993. pap. 8.95 (0-7390-0440-9, 6667) Alfred Pub.
— Masterworks Classics, Level 4. 48p. 1988. pap. 7.50 (0-7390-0754-8, 168) Alfred Pub.
— Modern Masterworks, Vol. 1. 32p. 1999. pap. 7.95 (0-7390-0892-7, 18751) Alfred Pub.
— Sonatina Masterworks, Bk. 1. 40p. 1997. pap. 6.50 (0-7390-0603-7, 17391) Alfred Pub.
— Sonatina Masterworks, Bk. 3. 72p. 1997. pap. 8.95 (0-7390-0384-4, 17393) Alfred Pub.
Magrath, Myler. The Book of Irish Limericks. 40p. 1997. pap. 4.95 (0-85342-741-0, Pub. by Mercier Pr) Irish Amer Bk.
Magrath, P. Methodologies for Studying Agricultural Markets in Developing Countries. 1992. pap. 40.00 (0-85954-310-2, Pub. by Nat Res Inst) St Mut.
Magrath, P., et al, eds. Rice Marketing in Indonesia: Methodology, Results & Implications of a Research Study. 1992. pap. 30.00 (0-85954-311-0, Pub. by Nat Res Inst) St Mut.
Magraw, Daniel B., ed. International Law & Pollution. LC 90-19454. 384p. (C). 1991. text 45.00 (0-8122-3052-3) U of Pa Pr.
Magraw, Trisha. Cowgirl Megan. (Magic Attic Club Ser.). (Illus.). 72p. (J). (gr. 2-6). 1995. 12.95 (1-57513-012-2); pap. 5.95 (1-57513-013-0) Magic Attic.
— Cowgirl Megan. (Magic Attic Club Ser.). (J). (gr. 2-6). 1995. 11.15 (0-606-08509-2, Pub. by Turtleback) Demco.
— Downhill Megan. (Magic Attic Club Ser.). (Illus.). 80p. (J). (gr. 2-6). 1996. 12.95 (1-57513-022-X); pap. 5.95 (1-57513-023-8) Magic Attic.
— Megan's Masquerade. (Magic Attic Club Ser.). (Illus.). 80p. (J). (gr. 2-6). 1996. 12.95 (1-57513-071-8); pap. 5.95 (1-57513-072-6) Magic Attic.
— Princess Megan. (Magic Attic Club Ser.). (Illus.). 72p. (J). (gr. 2-6). 1995. 12.95 (1-57513-004-1); pap. 5.95 (1-57513-005-X) Magic Attic.
Magraw, Trisha. Princess Megan. (Magic Attic Club Ser.). (J). (gr. 2-6). 1995. 11.15 (0-606-08590-4, Pub. by Turtleback) Demco.
Magraw, Trisha & Sinykin, Sheri Cooper. Magic Attic Club Series Boxed Set: Alison on the Trail; Keisha the Fairy Queen; Cowgirl Megan; Heather, Belle of the Ball, 4 vols., Set. (Magic Attic Club Ser.). (Illus.). (J). (gr. 2-6). 1995. boxed set 22.95 (1-57513-030-0) Magic Attic.
— Magic Attic Club Series Boxed Set: Alison Saves the Wedding; Heather Takes the Reins; Keisha Leads the Way; Downhill Megan, 4 vols., Set. (Magic Attic Club Ser.). (Illus.). (J). (gr. 2-6). 1996. boxed set 22.95 (1-57513-033-5) Magic Attic.
— Magic Attic Club Series Boxed Set: The Secret of the Attic; Three Cheers for Keisha; Alison Goes for the Gold; Princess Megan; Heather at the Barre, 5 vols., Set. (Magic Attic Club Ser.). (Illus.). (J). (gr. 2-6). 1995. pap., boxed set 22.95 (1-57513-029-7) Magic Attic.
Magray, Mary P. The Transforming Power of the Nuns: Women, Religion & Cutlural Change in Ireland, 1750-1900. LC 97-8446. (Illus.). 208p. 1998. text 45.00 (0-19-511299-7) OUP.
Magre, Maurice, tr. see Merton, Reginald.
Magrelli, Valerio. The Contagion of Matter: New & Selected Poems. 100p. 2000. 30.00 (0-8419-1399-4) Holmes & Meier.
***Magrelli, Valerio.** The Contagion of Matter: New & Selected Poems. Molino, Tony, tr. from ITA. 100p. 2000. pap. 14.95 (0-8419-1400-1) Holmes & Meier.
***Magretta, Joan, ed.** Managing in the New Economy. LC 99-24214. 304p. 1999. 29.95 (1-57851-186-0, HBS Pr) Harvard Busn.
Magri, Gennaro, et al. Theoretical & Practical Treatise on Dancing. (Illus.). 280p. 1980. text 65.00 (0-903102-99-4, Pub. by Dance Bks) Princeton Bk Co.
Magri, Iole F., tr. see Cancogni, Manlio.
Magri, Iole F., tr. see Fargion, Maria L.
Magriel, Paul, ed. Bibliography of Dancing. LC 65-16242. (Illus.). 1972. 20.95 (0-405-08776-4) Ayer.
— Chronicles of the American Dance. LC 77-25865. (Series in Dance). (Illus.). 1978. reprint ed. lib. bdg. 35.00 (0-306-77566-2) Da Capo.
— Chronicles of the American Dance: From the Shakers to Martha Graham. LC 78-9067. (Quality Paperbacks Ser.). (Illus.). 1978. reprint ed. pap. 7.95 (0-306-80082-9) Da Capo.
— Nijinsky, Pavlova, Duncan: Three Lives in Dance. (Series in Dance). 1977. reprint ed. lib. bdg. 35.00 (0-306-70845-0) Da Capo.
— Nijinsky, Pavlova, Duncan: Three Lives in Dance. (Series in Dance). (Illus.). 288p. 1977. reprint ed. pap. 14.95 (0-306-80035-7) Da Capo.
Magriel, Paul, ed. see Mendoza, Daniel.
Magris, C. Different Sea. pap. 11.00 (1-86046-052-6, Pub. by Harvill Press) HarpC.
Magris, Claudio. Danube: A Sentimental Journey from the Source to the Black Sea. Creagh, Patrick, tr. (Illus.). 416p. 1999. pap. 15.00 (1-86046-633-8) Harvill Press.
— Inferences from a Sabre. 1993. pap. 12.95 (0-7486-6036-4, Pub. by Edinburgh U Pr) Col U Pr.
***Magris, Claudio.** Microcosms. 2000. 25.00 (1-86046-787-3) Harvill Press.
Magriso, Yitzchok. Torah Anthology: Avoth. Barocas, David N., tr. (Torah Anthology - Meam Loez Ser.). 400p. 1990. 20.00 (0-940118-22-X) Moznaim.
Magritte, Rene, et al. Rene Magritte, 1898-1967. LC 99-166762. 335 p. 1998. write for info. (90-5544-132-5) Dist Art Pubs.
Magritte, Rene, jt. auth. see Robbe-Grillet, Alain.
Magrizi, Ahmad ibn Ali. Macrizi's Geschichte der Copten. (GER.). 142p. 1979. reprint ed. write for info. (3-487-06763-3) G Olms Pubs.
Magro, A., et al, eds. Central & Peripheral Mechanisms of Cardiovascular Regulation. LC 86-15101. (NATO ASI Series A, Life Sciences: Vol. 109). 554p. 1986. 125.00 (0-306-42360-X, Plenum Trade) Perseus Pubng.
Magrs, Paul. Scarlet Empress. 1998. pap. 5.95 (0-563-40595-3) BBC.
***Magrs, Paul.** Verdigris. (Doctor Who Ser.). 288p. 2000. mass mkt. 6.95 (0-563-55592-0) BBC Bks.
Magruder, Allan B. John Marshall. Morse, John T., Jr., ed. LC 73-128974. (American Statesmen Ser.: No. 10). reprint ed. 45.00 (0-404-50860-X) AMS Pr.
Magruder, Carter Bowie. Recurring Logistic Problems As I Have Observed Them. 134p. (C). 1994. pap. text 45.00 (0-7881-1310-0) DIANE Pub.
— Recurring Logistic Problems As I Have Observed Them. 148p. 1991. per. 7.00 (0-16-021126-3) USGPO.
Magruder, Clark, ed. see Torres, Eliseo, et al.
Magruder, Dudley B., Jr. The Two-Dollar Boat: Boat Stories & Other Lies. LC 91-24247. (Illus.). 208p. 1992. 18.95 (1-56474-000-5) Fithian Pr.
Magruder, G. Brock & Gilbert, Walter R., Jr. The Book on Cataracts. Curley & Pynn Public Relations Management, Inc. St, ed. (Illus.). (Orig.). (C). 1988. pap. text 4.95 (0-9622095-2-X) G B Magruder.
Magruder, J. Scott. CARP: User's Guide & Introduction to Authoring Tutorials. 119p. 1991. pap. text 50.00 (0-933179-07-3) Bus Account Pubns.
Magruder, James, tr. see Mariuaux.
Magruder, James, tr. & intro. see Coleman, C. B., ed.
Magruder, James M., Jr. Index to Maryland Colonial Wills, 1634-1777: In the Hall of Records, Annapolis, Maryland. 543p. 1999. 35.00 (0-8063-0233-X, 3660) Genealog Pub.
Magruder, Julia. Miss Ayr of Virginia & Other Stories. LC 77-110207. (Short Story Index Reprint Ser.). 1977. 23.95 (0-8369-3358-3) Ayer.
***Magruder, Owen.** The Strange Case of Mr. Nobody. LC 00-34118. 2000. pap. write for info. (1-892059-01-0) Edmonston Publ.
Magruder, Scott. Using a Computer Simulation to Teach General Equilibrium Concepts. 63p. 1989. pap. text 26.50 (0-931179-03-8) Bus Account Pubns.
Magruder, Trula, ed. Bright Ideas: From Girls, for Girls. LC 97-19933. (American Girl Library Ser.). (Illus.). 63p. (Orig.). (J). (gr. 3-7). 1997. pap. text 5.95 (1-56247-527-4, Amer Girl Library) Pleasant Co.
Magruder, Trula, jt. ed. see Watkins, Michelle.
Magryta, Leslie. Introduction to Paralegal Studies: A Skills Approach. LC 92-28396. 350p. (C). 1992. text 29.00 (0-256-12390-X, Irwn McGrw-H) McGrw-H Hghr Educ.
***Magsamen, Sandra.** And They Lived Happily Ever After. (Illus.). 32p. 2000. 12.95 (1-58479-007-5) Stewart Tabori & Chang.
— Babies Are Born with Hearts of Gold. 32p. 2000. 12.95 (1-58479-004-0) Stewart Tabori & Chang.
Magsamen, Sandra. Espresso Yourself. 96p. 1999. 8.95 (1-55670-899-8) Stewart Tabori & Chang.
***Magsamen, Sandra.** Happy Birthday to You. (Illus.). 32p. 2000. 12.95 (1-58479-005-9) Stewart Tabori & Chang.
— Let Your Dreams Take Flight. 96p. 1999. text 8.95 (1-55670-898-X) Stewart Tabori & Chang.
— Thanks a Bunch. (Illus.). 32p. 2000. 12.95 (1-58479-006-7) Stewart Tabori & Chang.
Magsamen, Sandra. Dear Mom: Thank You with All of My Heart. 32p. 1999. text 12.95 (1-55670-896-3) Stewart Tabori & Chang.
— Things to Do. 32p. 1999. text 12.95 (1-55670-897-1) Stewart Tabori & Chang.
Magsino, Romula, jt. ed. see Miranda, Evelina O.
Magson, Mal, jt. auth. see Utley, Chris.
Magstadt. Thumbs Understanding Politics. 1998. pap. text, teacher ed. 10.00 (0-312-19631-8) St Martin.
— Understanding Politics. 5th ed. LC 98-84992. xxiii, 598 p. 1998. pap. text 56.95 (0-312-18449-2) St Martin.
— Understanding Politics. 5th ed. 2000. pap. text, teacher ed. write for info. (0-312-19137-5) St Martin.
Magstadt, Thomas M. Nations & Governments. 2nd ed. 1994. pap. text, teacher ed. 5.00 (0-312-09557-0) St Martin.
— Nations & Governments. 3rd ed. LC 97-65173. 608p. 1997. pap. text 56.95 (0-312-15396-1) St Martin.
— Understanding Politics. 3rd ed. 1992. pap. text 1.17 (0-312-08077-8) St Martin.
Magubane, Bernard M. African Sociology - Towards a Critical Perspective: The Collected Essays of Bernard Makhosezwe Magubane. LC 98-52239. 600p. 1998. 89.95 (0-86543-660-6); pap. 24.95 (0-86543-661-4) Africa World.
— The Making of a Racist State: British Imperialism & the Union of South Africa. 474p. 1995. pap. text 19.95 (0-86543-241-4) Africa World.
— The Making of a Racist State: British Imperialism & the Union of South Africa, 1875-1910. 474p. 1995. 69.95 (0-86543-240-6) Africa World.
— Political Economy of Race & Class in South Africa. LC 78-13917. 364p. 1980. pap. 18.00 (0-85345-506-6, Pub. by Monthly Rev) NYU Pr.
— South Africa: From Soweto to Uitenhage: The Political Economy of the South African Revolution. LC 86-73223. 225p. (C). 1989. 35.00 (0-86543-050-0); pap. 11.95 (0-86543-051-9) Africa World.
— The Ties That Bind: African American Consciousness of Africa. 2nd ed. LC 86-70980. 250p. (C). 1990. 35.00 (0-86543-036-5); pap. 12.95 (0-86543-037-3) Africa World.
Magubane, Bernard M. & Mandaza, Ibbo, eds. Whither South Africa? LC 86-73224. 250p. (C). 1988. 29.95 (0-86543-048-9); pap. 9.95 (0-86543-049-7) Africa World.
Magubane, Peter. Soweto: Portrait of a City. (Illus.). 156p. 1992. 39.95 (1-56757-007-0) Appleton Comms.
— Soweto: The Fruit of Fear: A School Children's Revolt That Ignited a Nation. LC 86-71992. 125p. (C). 1987. 29.95 (0-86543-041-1); pap. 14.95 (0-86543-040-3) Africa World.
Magubane, Peter, photos by. Vanishing Cultures of South Africa: Changing Customs in a Changing World. LC 97-46829. (Illus.). 168p. 1998. pap. 40.00 (0-8478-2097-1, Pub. by Rizzoli Intl) St Martin.
Maguet, P., tr. see Pauwels, F.
Maguglin, Robert O. Howard Hughes: His Achievements & Legacy. LC 85-50968. (Illus.). 120p. 1988. pap. 10.95 (0-917859-22-7) Sunrise SBCA.
— The Queen Mary: The Official Pictorial History. LC 85-50967. (Illus.). 120p. 1988. pap. 10.95 (0-917859-21-9) Sunrise SBCA.
Maguin, Jean-Marie, jt. ed. see Klein, Holger.
Maguin, Jean-Marie, jt. ed. see Willems, Michele M.
Maguiness, David. MacWorld Guide to Microsoft Excel 4. (Illus.). 432p. 1992. 22.95 (1-878058-40-1) IDG Bks.
Maguiness, David, jt. auth. see Nelson, Stephen L.
Maguiness, David, jt. auth. see Van Buren, Christopher.
Maguiness, David, jt. auth. see Walkenbach, John.
Maguiness, Nancy. Giving Back the Elements. 80p. (Orig.). 1993. pap. text 10.00 (1-879260-19-0) Evanston Pub.
Maguinness, W. S., ed. Virgil: Aeneid XII. (Bristol Latin Texts Ser.). (LAT.). 160p. 1992. pap. 20.95 (1-85399-244-5, Pub. by Brist Class Pr) Focus Pub-R Pullins.
Maguire. Dry Land Tourist. 1995. per. write for info. (0-920813-67-4) Sister Vis Pr.
— Engineering Drawing. 192p. 1998. pap. 44.95 (0-470-32365-5) Wiley.
— Going Native: The Unmaking of a Liberal. 1994. 21.95 (0-02-919741-4) S&S Trade.
Maguire, Aisling. Breaking Out. LC 96-151270. 194p. 1997. pap. 13.95 (0-85640-574-4, Pub. by Blackstaff Pr) Dufour.
Maguire, Anne. For Brian's Sake: The Story of the Keenan Sisters. 144p. (Orig.). 1991. pap. 13.95 (0-85640-481-0, Pub. by Blackstaff Pr) Dufour.
Maguire, Anne, et al. Miscarriage of Justice: An Irish Family's Story of Wrongful Conviction As IRA Terrorists. rev. ed. (Illus.). 188p. 1994. pap. 10.95 (1-57098-006-3) Roberts Rinehart.
Maguire, Arlene. Dinosaur Pop-Up ABC. (Illus.). (J). 1995. 14.95 (0-671-89076-X) Litle Simon.
— Life's Changes. LC 91-9353. (Illus.). 32p. (Orig.). (J). (ps-5). 1991. 6.95 (0-941992-26-8) Los Arboles Pub.
— Special People, Special Ways. Carpenter, Christina D., ed. LC 98-87351. (Illus.). 32p. (J). (gr. k-4). 1999. 14.95 (1-886440-00-X) Portunus Pubng.
— We're All Special. (Illus.). 164p. (J). (ps up). 1995. 12.00 (0-9641330-3-2) Portunus Pubng.
Maguire, Bassett. The Botany of the Guayana Highland, Pt. XI. LC 78-9099. (Memoirs Ser.: Vol. 32). (Illus.). 391p. 1981. pap. 40.00 (0-89327-229-9) NY Botanical.
Maguire, Bassett, et al. The Botany of the Guayana Highland, Pt. XIII. LC 78-9099. (Memoirs Ser.: No. 51). (Illus.). 127p. 1989. pap. text 28.75 (0-89327-331-7) NY Botanical.
Maguire, Bernadette. Immigration: Public Legislation & Private Bills. LC 97-24848. 578p. 1997. 58.00 (0-7618-0791-8) U Pr of Amer.
Maguire, Byron W. Cabinetmaking: From Design to Finish. 2nd ed. 416p. 1990. reprint ed. pap. 22.00 (0-934041-62-8) Craftsman.
— Carpentry in Commercial Construction. 272p. 1988. reprint ed. pap. 19.00 (0-934041-33-4) Craftsman.
— Deskbook of Building Construction: Charts, Tables, & Forms. (Illus.). 256p. (C). 1985. pap. text 36.00 (0-13-202037-8) P-H.
— European Cabinet & Furniture Making. 1990. pap. 19.95 (0-13-292053-0) P-H.
Maguire, Cecilia. Excelling: The Nutritional Way to Good Health. (Excelling Ser.). 109p. (gr. 7-12). 1985. 10.97 (0-8239-0635-3) Rosen Group.
Maguire, Charles, jt. ed. see Umali-Deininger, Dina.
Maguire, Chris. Southcentral Alaska Fishing Guide 1997. 1997. pap. text 5.00 (1-57833-011-4) Todd Commns.
Maguire, D. P., ed. Appropriate Development for Basic Needs. 360p. 1991. text 76.00 (0-7277-1618-2, Pub. by T Telford) RCH.
Maguire, Daniel C. The Moral Choice. 1984. reprint ed. 12.95 (0-86683-771-X, AY8112) Harper SF.
— The Moral Core of Judaism & Christianity: Reclaiming the Revolution. LC 92-39136. 256p. 1993. pap. 18.00 (0-8006-2689-3, 1-2689) Augsburg Fortress.
— Reflections of a Catholic Theologian on Visiting an Abortion Clinic. 11p. 1985. pap. 3.00 (0-915365-10-3) Cath Free Choice.
Maguire, Daniel C. & Maguire, Marjorie R. Aborto: Una Guia para Tomar Decisiones Eticas. 2nd ed. Inda, Caridad & Newberry, Sara, eds. Alvarez, Elena &

An Asterisk (*) at the beginning of an entry indicates that the title is appearing for the first time.

M

Maguire, Sarah, ed. Civil & Criminal Procedure. 265p. (C). 1991. 90.00 (*1-85352-864-1*, Pub. by HLT Pubns) St Mut.

Maguire, Steve. Debugging the Development Process. LC 94-22182. (Code Ser.). 216p. 1994. pap. 24.95 (*1-55615-650-2*) Microsoft.

— Software Engineering Classics. 712p. 1998. boxed set 69.99 (*0-7356-0597-1*) Microsoft.

— Writing Solid Code. (Code Ser.). 288p. 1993. pap. 24.95 (*1-55615-551-4*) Microsoft.

***Maguire, Steve, ed.** Complexity & Management: Where are We? 208p. 1999. pap. 35.00 (*0-8058-9774-7*) L Erlbaum Assocs.

Maguire, Susan. We Are the Miracle: Seeking Blessings, Asking Guidance, Finding Help. LC 96-38334. 208p. (Orig.). 1997. pap. 14.95 (*0-915556-30-8*) Great Ocean.

***Maguire, Susie.** Something Wicked: New Scottish Crime Fiction. 2000. pap. 16.95 (*0-7486-6253-7*, Pub. by Edinburgh U Pr) Col U Pr.

Maguire, Susie, ed. Scottish Love Stories. 288p. (Orig.). 1995. pap. 18.95 (*0-7486-6202-2*, Pub. by Polygon) Subterranean Co.

Maguire, Susie & Young, David J., eds. Hoots! An Anthology of Scottish Comic Writing. 256p. (Orig.). 1997. pap. 19.95 (*0-7486-6229-4*, Pub. by Polygon) Subterranean Co.

Maguire, Timothy E., jt. auth. see Kautrowitz, R. Marc.

Maguire, Tom. An Irish Whistle Book. 40p. 1996. pap. 8.95 (*0-946005-90-7*, Pub. by Ossian) Dufour.

— An Irish Whistle Tune Book. 40p. 1996. pap. 8.95 (*0-946005-91-5*, Pub. by Ossian) Dufour.

Maguire, W. A. Kings in Conflict: Revolutionary War in Ireland & Its Aftermath. 224p. 1990. 29.95 (*0-85640-435-7*, Pub. by Blackstaff Pr) Dufour.

Maguire, W. B. All You Need to Know about Joint Replacement. (C). 1990. pap. 30.00 (*0-86439-101-3*, Pub. by Boolarong Pubns) St Mut.

Maguire, Wilhelmina. AKIA Spa Cookbook. 71p. (Orig.). 1992. pap. 13.50 (*0-9639039-0-X*) AKIA.

Magun, Carol. Circling Eden. 200p. 1995. 19.95 (*0-89733-412-4*) Academy Chi Pubs.

Magun-Jackson, et al. Bridges: A Guide to Academic Success at the University of Memphis. 2nd ed. 214p. (C). 1997. per. 18.95 (*0-7872-4369-8*, 41436901) Kendall-Hunt.

Magun-Jackson, Susan. Bridges Guide Academic Success. 160p. (C). 1996. pap. text, per. 14.95 (*0-7872-1227-X*) Kendall-Hunt.

Magura, Stephen & Moses, Beth Silverman. Child Well-Being Scales & Rating Form. 1987. pap. 10.00 (*0-87868-306-2*) Child Welfare.

— Outcome Measures for Child Welfare Services: Theory & Applications. 252p. 1986. pap. 34.95 (*0-87868-224-4*) Child Welfare.

Magura, Stephen & Rosenblum, Andrew, eds. Experimental Therapeutics in Addiction Medicine. LC 94-43278. (Journal of Addictive Diseases). (Illus.). 256p. 1995. lib. bdg. 49.95 (*1-56024-699-5*) Haworth Pr.

Magurn, Bruce A., ed. Reviews in K-Theory, 1940-1984. LC 85-7481. 811p. 1985. pap. 321.00 (*0-8218-0088-4*, REVKC) Am Math.

Magurran, Anne E. & May, Robert M., eds. Evolution of Biological Diversity: From Population Differentiation to Speciation. LC 98-47315. (Illus.). 344p. 1999. text 98.00 (*0-19-850305-9*); pap. text 45.00 (*0-19-850304-0*) OUP.

***Magurussa, Tiffani, et al.** Back to School Grades K-3, Vol. 3353. Hults, Alaska B., ed. 128p. 2000. pap., teacher ed. write for info. (*1-57471-685-9*) Creat Teach Pr.

Magwood, Chris, jt. auth. see Mack, Peter.

Magy, Ronna. U. S. Citizens Package. (Illus.). 110p. (J). 1996. pap. 17.95 incl. audio (*0-8384-6750-4*) Heinle & Heinle.

— U. S. Citizenship-Yes! LC 96-150138. (Global ESL/ELT Ser.). (Illus.). 110p. (J). 1996. pap. 14.95 (*0-8384-6714-8*) Heinle & Heinle.

— Working It Out: Interactive English for the Workplace. 1998. 18.50 incl. audio (*0-8384-7792-5*) Heinle & Heinle.

Magy, Tamas. English-Hungarian Dictionary of Technology & Science, 2 vols. (ENG & HUN.). 1993. 250.00 (*0-7859-8884-X*) Fr & Eur.

***Magyar, George.** A Radical Voice in the Science of Science. 194p. 1999. pap. 14.00 (*963-9132-19-5*, Pub. by Akade Kiado) Intl Spec Bk.

Magyar, I. Differential Diagnosis of Internal Diseases: In Russian, 2 vols., Set. (RUS.). 1154p. (C). 1987. 300.00 (*963-05-4233-1*) St Mut.

Magyar, Judith, ed. see Domjan, Evelyn.

Magyar, Karl P. Challenge & Response: Anticipating U. S. Military Security Concern. LC 94-18448. 444p. 1994. pap. 27.00 (*1-58566-053-1*) Air Univ.

— Challenge & Response: Anticipating United States Military Security Concerns. 443p. 1994. per. 31.00 (*0-16-061361-2*) USGPO.

— Global Security Concerns: Anticipating the Twenty-First Century. (Illus.). 336p. 1996. pap. 20.00 (*1-58566-006-X*) Air Univ.

— Prolonged Wars: A Post-Nuclear Challenge. Danopo, Constantine P., ed. LC 94-32131. 475p. pap. 27.00 (*1-58566-056-6*) Air Univ.

***Magyar, Karl P.** United States Interests & Policies in Africa: Transition to A New Era. LC 99-15387. 1999. text 59.95 (*0-312-22388-9*) St Martin.

Magyar, Laszlo. Reisen in Sud-Afrika in den Jahren, 1849-1857. (B. E. Ser.: No. 155). (GER.). 1859. 50.00 (*0-8115-3073-6*) Periodicals Srv.

Magyar, P., ed. see Czaki, F., et al.

Magyar, Zoltan. The Lebesgue Integral. LC 97-202930. 106p. 1997. pap. 75.00 (*963-05-7346-6*, Pub. by Akade Kiado) St Mut.

Magyari, E., jt. auth. see Constantinescu, F.

***Mah, Adeline Yen.** Chinese Cinderella. (YA). 2001. mass mkt. 5.99 (*0-440-22865-4*) BDD Bks Young Read.

Mah, Anmarie J., jt. auth. see Tomascik, Tomas.

Mah, Stuart. Fundamentals of Course Design for Dog Agility. Percival, Monica et al, eds. (Illus.). 124p. 1997. spiral bd. 26.95 (*0-9653994-4-3*) Clean Run Prods.

Mah, Stuart, jt. auth. see Houston, Bud.

Mahabir, Cynthia. Crime & Nation Building in the Caribbean: The Legacy of Legal Barriers. LC 84-5304. 280p. (Orig.). 1985. 24.95 (*0-87073-601-9*); pap. 18.95 (*0-87073-602-7*) Schenkman Bks Inc.

Mahadev, N. V. & Peled, U. N. Threshold Graphs & Related Topics. LC 95-24781. (Annals of Discrete Mathematics Ser.: Vol. 56). 558p. 1995. 158.50 (*0-444-89287-7*) Elsevier.

Mahadeva, A. & Rangacharya, K., eds. The Taitiriya Samhita of the Black Yajurveda, 10 vols. (C). 1986. reprint ed. 185.00 (*81-208-0228-4*, Pub. by Motilal Bnarsidass) S Asia.

Mahadevan, jt. ed. see Ramachandran.

Mahadevan, A. Biochemical Aspects of Plant Disease Resistance: Preformed Inhibitory Substance 'Prohibitions', Pt. 1. (International Bioscience Monographs: No. 11). (Illus.). xiv, 400p. 1989. reprint ed. 59.00 (*0-88065-225-X*, Pub. by Today Tomorrow) Scholarly Pubns.

— Biochemical Aspects of Plant Disease Resistance Vol. 2: Post Infectional Defence Mechanisms. (Illus.). 800p. 1991. 95.00 (*1-55528-231-8*, Pub. by Today Tomorrow) Scholarly Pubns.

Mahadevan, A., jt. auth. see Gnanamanickam, S. S.

Mahadevan, Kuttan. Population Dynamics in Indian States. 1989. 38.50 (*81-7099-178-1*, Pub. by Mittal Pubs Dist) S Asia.

— Sociology of Fertility: Determinants of Fertility Differentials in South India. 1978. 11.00 (*0-8364-0293-6*) S Asia.

Mahadevan, Kuttan, ed. Ecology, Development & Population Problem: Perspectives from India, China & Australia. (C). 1992. 48.00 (*81-7018-735-4*, Pub. by BR Pub) S Asia.

— Fertility Policies of Asian Countries. 288p. (C). 1989. text 27.50 (*0-8039-9570-9*) Sage.

— Women & Population Dynamics: Perspectives from Asia. 320p. (C). 1990. text 25.00 (*0-8039-9615-2*) Sage.

Mahadevan, Kuttan, et al, eds. Differential Development & Demographic Dilemma: Perspectives from China & India. (C). 1994. 44.00 (*81-7018-816-4*, Pub. by BR Pub) S Asia.

— Society & Development in China & India. (C). 1994. 48.00 (*81-7018-812-1*, Pub. by BR Pub) S Asia.

Mahadevan, Kuttan & Aiyappan, A. Population & Social Change in an Indian Village. (C). 1988. 40.00 (*81-7099-073-4*, Pub. by Mittal Pubs Dist) S Asia.

Mahadevan, Kuttan & Krishnan, Parameswara, eds. Methodology for Population Studies & Development. LC 92-15028. (Illus.). 428p. (C). 1993. text 42.00 (*0-8039-9431-1*, Pub. by Sage India Pvt) Sage.

Mahadevan, Kuttan & Sumangala, M. Social Development, Cultural Change, & Fertility Decline: A Study of Fertility Change in Kerala. 160p. (C). 1989. text 17.95 (*0-8039-9536-9*) Sage.

— Welfare Model of Development & Demographic Transition: Successful Programmes on Health, Nutrition, Family Planning & Development. LC 97-913700. x, 334 p. 1997. write for info. (*81-7018-946-2*) BR Pub.

Mahadevan, Sankaran, jt. auth. see Haldar, Achintya.

Mahadevan, Sridhar, jt. ed. see Connell, Jonathan H.

Mahadevan, T. M. The Hymns of Sankara. 188p. 1986. reprint ed. 15.00 (*81-208-0094-X*, Pub. by Motilal Bnarsidass); reprint ed. pap. 11.00 (*81-208-0097-4*, Pub. by Motilal Bnarsidass) S Asia.

— Invitation to Indian Philosophy. (Orig.). (C). 1979. pap. 7.50 (*0-89684-090-5*, Pub. by Arnold-Heinemann Pubs) Humanities.

— Sankaracharya. 119p. 1968. 3.95 (*0-318-37165-0*) Asia Bk Corp.

Mahadevan, T. M. & Saroja, G. V. Contemporary Indian Philosophy. 282p. 1983. 34.95 (*0-940500-51-5*, Pub. by Sterling) Asia Bk Corp.

***Mahadevan, T. M. P.** Upanisads: The Selections from 108 Upanisads. 240p. 1998. pap. 100.00 (*81-208-1611-0*, Pub. by Motilal Bnarsidass) St Mut.

Mahady. Foreign Exchange Market. 1994. text 50.00 (*0-13-325382-1*) S&S Trade.

Mahaffey, Foyne, jt. auth. see Burns-Wolfe, Marty.

Mahaffey, George & Kleiman, Evan. Country Inn: The Best of Casual Country Cooking. LC 97-3606. (Casual Cuisines of the World Ser.). 128p. 1997. 19.95 (*0-376-02042-3*) Sunset Books.

Mahaffey, J. A., jt. ed. see Thompson, R. C.

Mahaffey, Joy, jt. auth. see Peel, Kathy.

Mahaffey, Maryann & Hanks, John W., eds. Practical Politics: Social Work & Political Responsibility. LC 82-80273. 260p. (C). 1982. 23.95 (*0-87101-099-2*) Natl Assn Soc Wkrs.

Mahaffey, Redge. A Higher Education. 250p. 1989. pap. 7.95 (*0-9622546-0-6*) Ramsgate MD.

— Me, Myself & I. (Illus.). 54p. (Orig.). 1990. pap. 3.95 (*0-9622546-1-4*) Ramsgate MD.

Mahaffey, Robert, ed. Safe Schools: A Handbook for Practitioners. (Illus.). 200p. (Orig.). 1995. pap. 125.00 (*0-88210-304-0*) Natl Assn Principals.

Mahaffey, Vicki. Reauthorizing Joyce. LC 94-34181. (Florida James Joyce Ser.). 248p. (C). 1995. pap. 19.95 (*0-8130-1344-5*) U Press Fla.

— States of Desire: Wilde, Yeats, Joyce, & the Irish Experiment. (Illus.). 288p. 1998. text 45.00 (*0-19-511592-9*) OUP.

Mahaffie, Charles D., Jr. A Land of Discord Always: Acadia from Its Beginnings to the Expulsion of Its People, 1604-1755. LC 95-8904. (Illus.). 328p. 1997. pap. 16.95 (*0-89272-375-0*) Down East.

Mahaffie, John B., jt. auth. see Coates, Joseph F.

Mahaffy, Carcus & Beck, Lewis W. Prolegomena to Any Future Metaphysics: Kant. (C). 1950. pap. text 8.60 (*0-02-319330-1*, Pub. by P-H) S&S Trade.

Mahaffy, Ellen. Nothing Was Ever Said. (Illus.). 116p. 1993. 25.00 (*0-89822-109-9*) Visual Studies.

Mahaffy, J. P. Alexander's Empire. 323p. 1981. 25.00 (*0-89005-391-X*) Ares.

Mahaffy, John D. Never Stop Dancing. 184p. 1996. 19.95 (*0-9634828-2-3*) Pan Pr NY.

Mahaffy, John P. Descartes. LC 71-94277. (Select Bibliographies Reprint Ser.). 1977. 21.95 (*0-8369-5051-8*) Ayer.

— Greek Life & Thought from the Age of Alexander to the Roman Conquest. LC 75-13278. (History of Ideas in Ancient Greece Ser.). 1976. reprint ed. 55.95 (*0-405-07318-6*) Ayer.

— Problems in Greek History. Date not set. 22.95 (*0-518-10186-X*) Ayer.

— Rambles & Studies in Greece. 1982. 24.95 (*0-8434-0137-0*) McGrath NH.

Mahafza, Bassem R. Introduction to Radar Analysis. LC 98-15595. 352p. 1998. boxed set 89.95 (*0-8493-1879-3*) CRC Pr.

***Mahafza, Bassem R.** Radar Systems Analysis & Design Using Matlab. LC 00-26914. (Illus.). 552p. (C). 2000. boxed set 94.95 (*1-58488-182-8*, Chap & Hall CRC) CRC Pr.

Mahajan. Educational Administration in Sikkim: Structures, Processes & Future Prospects. 1995. 20.00 (*0-7069-9466-3*, Pub. by Vikas) S Asia.

— New Millennium Fullfills Ancient Prophecies. LC 99-931139. ix, 93 p. 1999. write for info. (*81-208-1644-7*, Pub. by Motilal Bnarsidass) S Asia.

Mahajan & Baldev, B. Educational Administration in Andaman & Nicobar Islands: Structures, Processes & Future Prospects. 1995. 24.00 (*0-7069-9981-9*, Pub. by Vikas) S Asia.

— Educational Administration in Chandigarh: Structures, Processes & Future Prospects. 1995. pap. 14.00 (*0-7069-9706-9*, Pub. by Vikas) S Asia.

— Educational Administration in Goa: Structures, Processes & Future Prospects. 1994. 22.00 (*0-7069-7890-0*, Pub. by Vikas) S Asia.

— Educational Administration in Lakshadweep: Structures, Processes & Future Prospects. 1995. 16.00 (*0-7069-9695-X*, Pub. by Vikas) S Asia.

— Educational Administration in Mizoram: Structures, Processes & Future Prospects. 1994. 20.00 (*0-7069-7889-7*, Pub. by Vikas) S Asia.

Mahajan, A. Indian Police-Women. 189p. 1982. 27.95 (*0-318-37063-8*) Asia Bk Corp.

Mahajan, Amar J. & Luthra, Nirupamja. Family & Television. (C). 1993. 16.00 (*81-212-0435-6*, Pub. by Gian Publng Hse) S Asia.

Mahajan, Amarjit & Madhurima. Family Violence & Abuse in India. (C). 1995. 22.00 (*81-7100-712-0*, Pub. by Deep & Deep Pubns) S Asia.

Mahajan, Anupam. The Ragas in Indian Classical Music. (Illus.). xi, 138p. 1989. 20.00 (*81-212-0269-8*, Pub. by Gyan Publishing Hse) Nataraj Bks.

Mahajan, Baldev & Goyal, J. C. Educational Administration in Karnataka: Structures, Processes & Future Prospects. 1994. 26.00 (*0-7069-9056-0*, Pub. by Vikas) S Asia.

Mahajan, Baldev & Tyagi, R. S. Educational Administration in Haryana: Structures, Processes & Future Prospects. 1994. 20.00 (*0-7069-7891-9*, Pub. by Vikas) S Asia.

— Educational Administration in Madhya Pradesh: Structures, Processes & Future Prospects. 1995. 24.00 (*0-7069-9055-2*, Pub. by Vikas) S Asia.

Mahajan, G. Evaluation & Development of Ground Water. (C). 1989. 50.00 (*81-7024-241-X*, Pub. by Ashish Pub Hse) S Asia.

Mahajan, Gurpreet. Explanation & Understanding in the Human Sciences. 2nd ed. LC 99-208407. (Oxford India Paperbacks Ser.). 168p. 1998. pap. text 9.95 (*0-19-564396-8*) OUP.

— Identities & Rights: Aspects of Liberal Democracy in India. LC 98-909286. 190p. 1998. text 23.95 (*0-19-564417-4*) OUP.

Mahajan, Gurpreet, ed. Democracy, Difference & Social Justice. LC 98-907625. 598p. 1998. text 42.00 (*0-19-564152-3*) OUP.

Mahajan, Gurpreet & Sheth, D. L., eds. Minority Identities & the Nation State. LC 99-939173. 344p. 2000. text 29.95 (*0-19-564541-3*) OUP.

Mahajan, J. P. Principles of Office Management. 306p. 1996. pap. 50.00 (*81-209-0391-9*, Pub. by Pitambar Pub) St Mut.

Mahajan, J. P., jt. auth. see Vardharajan, B.

Mahajan, Kanti K. Design of Process Equipment: Selected Topics. 3rd ed. (Illus.). 1990. 78.00 (*0-914458-15-9*) Pressure Vessel.

Mahajan, Mehr C., ed. Looking Back: Autobiography of Mehr Chand Mahajan. (C). 1994. 28.00 (*81-241-0194-9*, Pub. by Har-Anand Pubns) S Asia.

Mahajan, R. L., ed. Proceedings of the 1995 National Heat Transfer Conference: August 6-9, 1995, Portland, Oregon, Vol. 4. 264p. 1995. 112.00 (*0-7918-1705-9*, H00987) ASME.

***Mahajan, R. P.** Mass Determination. 562p. 2000. 185.00 (*3-527-29614-X*) Wiley.

Mahajan, R. P., jt. auth. see Crossley, A. W.

Mahajan, S. Imperialist Strategy & Moderate Politics: Indian Legislature at Work, 1909-1920. 1983. 24.00 (*0-8364-0979-5*, Pub. by Chanakya) S Asia.

Mahajan, S., ed. Materials, Properties & Preparation, 2 vols. enl. rev. ed. LC 93-732. (Handbook on Semiconductors Ser.: Vol. 3). 2398p. 1994. 771.75 (*0-444-88835-7*, North Holland) Elsevier.

Mahajan, S. & Kimerling, L. C., eds. Concise Encyclopedia of Semiconducting Materials & Related Technologies. (Advances in Materials Science & Engineering Ser.: No. 8). 600p. 1992. 247.00 (*0-08-034724-X*, Pergamon Pr) Elsevier.

Mahajan, S., ed. see Symposium on III-V Opto-Electronics Epitaxy & Devi.

Mahajan, Satinder N. Political Authority: A Comparative Study. 113p. 1986. 12.00 (*1-881338-72-X*) Nataraj Bks.

Mahajan, Subhash & Sreeharsha, K. S. Principles of Growth & Processing of Semiconductors. LC 98-3385. 528p. 1998. 91.56 (*0-07-039605-1*) McGraw.

Mahajan, T. T. Aspects of Agrarian & Urban History of the Marathas. (C). 1991. 21.00 (*81-7169-162-5*, Pub. by Commonwealth) S Asia.

— Courts & Administration of Justice under Chhatrapati Shivaji. (C). 1992. 18.00 (*81-7169-198-6*, Commonwealth) S Asia.

— Shivaji & His Diplomats. (C). 1991. 16.00 (*81-7169-110-2*, Pub. by Commonwealth) S Asia.

Mahajan, V. D. Chief Justice Mehr Chand Mahajan. (C). 1989. 30.00 (*0-89771-766-X*, Pub. by Eastern Book) St Mut.

— Constitutional Law of India. 600p. 1984. 165.00 (*0-7855-1298-5*) St Mut.

— Constitutional Law of India. (C). 1991. text 140.00 (*0-89771-486-5*) St Mut.

— A History of India, Set. 1100p. 1990. 310.00 (*0-7855-1191-1*) St Mut.

— History of Modern India, 2 vols., I:1919-74. 1220p. 1987. 117.00 (*0-7855-1192-X*) St Mut.

— History of Modern India, 2 vols., II:1974-82. 1220p. 1987. write for info. (*0-7855-2555-6*) St Mut.

— History of Modern India Nineteen Nineteen to Nineteen Eighty-Two, 2 vols., Set. 1983. text 77.50 (*0-685-14075-X*) Coronet Bks.

— Jurisprudence & Legal Theory. 5th ed. (C). 1987. 75.00 (*0-7855-3494-6*) St Mut.

Mahajan, V. D., ed. Constitutional Law of India. 7th ed. (C). 1991. 125.00 (*0-7855-5622-2*) St Mut.

— General Clauses Acts (Central & States) 1600p. (C). 1990. 175.00 (*0-7855-5242-1*); text 350.00 (*0-89771-487-3*) St Mut.

— General Clauses Acts (Central & States) 6th ed. (C). 1990. 350.00 (*0-7855-5549-8*) St Mut.

***Mahajan, V. S.** Agriculture, Rural Development & Panchayati Raj, 2 vols. 862p. 1998. pap. 550.00 (*81-7100-778-3*, Pub. by Print Hse) St Mut.

Mahajan, V. S. Growth of Agriculture & Industry in India. 1985. 13.50 (*0-8364-1443-8*, Pub. by Deep & Deep Pubns) S Asia.

— Manmohan's India & Other Current Writings. (C). 1994. text 29.00 (*81-7100-640-X*, Pub. by Deep & Deep Pubns) S Asia.

Mahajan, Vijay & Pegels, C. Carl, eds. Systems Analysis in Health Care. LC 78-19461. 504p. 1979. 79.50 (*0-275-90384-2*, C0384, Praeger Pubs) Greenwood.

Mahajan, Vijay & Peterson, Robert A. Models for Innovation Diffusion. (Quantitative Applications in the Social Sciences Ser.: Vol. 48). 1985. 10.95 (*0-8039-2136-5*) Sage.

Mahajan, Vijay & Wind, Yoram, eds. Innovation Diffusion Models of New Product Acceptance. LC 85-23300. 336p. 1986. text 34.95 (*0-88730-076-6*, HarpBusn) HarpInfo.

***Mahajan, Vijay, et al.** New Product Diffusion Models. LC 00-24639. (International Series in Quantitative Marketing). 2000. write for info. (*0-7923-7751-6*) Kluwer Academic.

Mahajan, Vijay, jt. auth. see Wind, Jerry.

Mahajan, Virendra N. Optical Imaging & Propagation with Emphasis on Aberration Theory. LC 97-7721. 469p. 1997. write for info. (*0-8194-2515-X*) SPIE.

Mahajan, Virendra N., ed. Aberration Theory Made Simple. (Tutorial Texts in Optical Engineering Ser.: Vol. TT 6). 157p. 1991. 38.00 (*0-8194-0536-1*) SPIE.

— Selected Papers on Effects of Aberrations in Optical Imaging. LC 92-46455. (Milestone Ser.: Vol. MS 74). 1993. 55.00 (*0-8194-1215-5*, MS74/HC) SPIE.

— Selected Papers on Effects of Aberrations in Optical Imaging. LC 92-46455. (Milestone Ser.: Vol. MS74). 1993. pap. 45.00 (*0-8194-1214-7*) SPIE.

Mahajan, Yogi. The Ascent. (C). 1993. text 7.00 (*81-208-1182-8*, Pub. by Motilal Bnarsidass) S Asia.

— Geeta Enlightened. xi, 177p. 1986. 14.00 (*81-208-0066-4*, Pub. by Motilal Bnarsidass); pap. 10.95 (*81-208-0156-3*, Pub. by Motilal Bnarsidass) S Asia.

Mahak, Francine T., tr. see Martinez, Eliseo R. & Martinez, Irma C.

Mahak, Francine T., tr. see Taraqqi, Goli.

Mahal, Susan & McIntire, Molly, contrib. by. Felicity's Cookbook: A Peek at Dining in the Past with Meals You Can Cook Today. LC 94-19194. (American Girls Collection). (Illus.). 44p. (J). (gr. 3-7). 1994. pap. text 5.95 (*1-56247-120-1*) Pleasant Co.

Mahal, Taj. Taj Mahal: Autobiography Of A Bluesman. 2000. 25.00 (*1-86074-247-5*) Sanctuary.

Mahalanobis, P. C. Rabindranath Tagore's Visit to Canada. LC 76-52432. (Studies in Asiatic Literature: No. 57). 1977. lib. bdg. 75.00 (*0-8383-2130-5*) M S G Haskell Hse.

Mahalanobis, Surojit. What They All Said: Manifestos of Major Political Parties of India. (C). 1997. 42.00 (*81-7488-526-9*, Pub. by Anmol) S Asia.

Mahalick. Diagnosis & Rehabilitation of Pediatric Head Injuries. 1998. 36.75 (*1-56593-175-0*) Thomson Learn.

Mahalingam, Indira, jt. auth. see Carr, Brian.

An Asterisk (*) at the beginning of an entry indicates that the title is appearing for the first time.

Mahalingam, Indira, jt. ed. see Carr, Brian.

Mahalingam, N., ed. see Sekkizhaar.

***Mahalingam, Ram & McCarthy, Cameron.** Multicultural Curriculum: New Directions for Social Theory, Practice & Policy. LC 99-42140. 320p. (C). 2000. text 65.99 (*0-415-92013-2*) Routledge.

— Multicultural Curriculum: New Directions for Social Theory, Practice & Policy. LC 99-42140. 320p. 2000. pap. 21.99 (*0-415-92014-0*) Routledge.

Mahalingam, S. Institutional Finance for Development of Tribal Economy. 1995. 36.00 (*0-7069-8759-4*, Pub. by Vikas) S Asia.

Mahalingam, S. Tribal Cooperative System: A Study of North-East India. (C). 1992. text 21.00 (*81-7033-169-2*, Pub. by Rawat Pubns) S Asia.

***Mahalingam, Sundara.** Air Traffic Control: Past, Present & Future. LC 98-917419. 142 p. 1999. write for info. (*81-7479-021-7*) S Asia.

Mahalingam, T. V., ed. Inscriptions of the Pallavas. 1988. 120.00 (*0-8364-2300-3*, Pub. by Agam) S Asia.

Mahalinjam, N., ed. see Tirumulav.

Mahall, K. Quality Assessment of Textiles. 1993. 107.00 (*0-614-20937-4*) Spr-Verlag.

Mahall, Karl. Quality Assessment of Textiles: Damage Detection by Microscopy. LC 93-42572. (Illus.). 322p. 1993. 141.95 (*0-387-57390-9*) Spr-Verlag.

Mahan. Krause's Food, Nutrition, Diet. 10th ed. LC 99-16752. (C). 1999. text 70.00 (*0-7216-7904-8*, W B Saunders Co) Harcrt Hlth Sci Grp.

— Physical Vapor Deposition of Thin Films. LC 99-21926. 312p. 2000. 84.95 (*0-471-33001-9*) Wiley.

— State Dependent. (Human Performance & Productivity Ser.: Vol. 7, No. 2). 1994. 20.00 (*0-8058-9978-2*) L Erlbaum Assocs.

— State Dependent. (Human Performance & Productivity Ser.: Vol. 7, No. 3). 1994. 20.00 (*0-8058-9967-7*) L Erlbaum Assocs.

— With New Testament Eyes, Vol. 2. 1995. pap. 8.99 (*0-85234-330-2*, Pub. by Evangelical Pr) P & R Pubng.

Mahan, Alfred Thayer. Admiral Farragut. LC 68-26360. (American Biography Ser.: No. 32). 1969. reprint ed. lib. bdg. 75.00 (*0-8383-0268-8*) M S G Haskell Hse.

— Admiral Farragut. (History - United States Ser.). 333p. 1992. reprint ed. lib. bdg. 89.00 (*0-7812-6177-5*) Rprt Serv.

— Admiral Farragut. (Notable American Authors Ser.). 1999. reprint ed. lib. bdg. 125.00 (*0-7812-3917-6*) Rprt Serv.

— Admiral Farragut. LC 74-108509. 1970. reprint ed. 14.00 (*0-403-00217-6*) Scholarly.

— Armaments & Arbitration. (Notable American Authors Ser.). 1999. reprint ed. lib. bdg. 125.00 (*0-7812-3931-1*) Rprt Serv.

— From Sail to Steam: Recollections of Naval Life. (American Biography Ser.). 458p. 1991. reprint ed. lib. bdg. 89.00 (*0-7812-8261-6*) Rprt Serv.

— From Sail to Steam: Recollections of Naval Life. (Notable American Authors Ser.). 1999. reprint ed. lib. bdg. 125.00 (*0-7812-3926-5*) Rprt Serv.

— The Gulf & Inland Waters: The Navy in the Civil War. LC 74-140367. (Select Bibliographies Reprint Ser.). 1977. reprint ed. 23.95 (*0-8369-5610-9*) Ayer.

— The Gulf & Inland Waters (The Navy in the Civil War) (Notable American Authors Ser.). 1999. reprint ed. lib. bdg. 125.00 (*0-7812-3914-1*) Rprt Serv.

— The Harvest Within. (Notable American Authors Ser.). 1999. reprint ed. lib. bdg. 125.00 (*0-7812-3928-1*) Rprt Serv.

— The Influence of Sea Power upon History, 1660-1783. (Illus.). 1970. 24.95 (*0-316-54382-9*) Little.

— The Influence of Sea Power upon History, 1660-1783. (Illus.). 640p. 1987. reprint ed. pap. 12.95 (*0-486-25509-3*) Dover.

— The Influence of Sea Power upon History, 1660-1783. (Notable American Authors Ser.). 1999. reprint ed. lib. bdg. 125.00 (*0-7812-3915-X*) Rprt Serv.

— Influence of Sea Power upon the French Revolution & Empire, 2 vols. 1970. 33.00 (*0-403-00193-5*) Scholarly.

— The Influence of Sea Power upon the French Revolution & Empire. (Notable American Authors Ser.). 1999. reprint ed. lib. bdg. 125.00 (*0-7812-3916-8*) Rprt Serv.

— The Interest of America in International Conditions. (Notable American Authors Ser.). 1999. reprint ed. lib. bdg. 125.00 (*0-7812-3929-X*) Rprt Serv.

— The Interest of America in Sea Power: Present & Future. (Notable American Authors Ser.). 1999. reprint ed. lib. bdg. 125.00 (*0-7812-3918-4*) Rprt Serv.

— The Interest of America in Sea Power, Present & Future. LC 75-137382. (Select Bibliographies Reprint Ser.). 1977. reprint ed. 23.95 (*0-8369-5583-8*) Ayer.

— Lesson of the Spanish War. (Notable American Authors Ser.). 1999. reprint ed. lib. bdg. 125.00 (*0-7812-3921-4*) Rprt Serv.

— Lessons of the War with Spain. LC 79-133526. (Select Bibliographies Reprint Ser.). 1977. reprint ed. 23.95 (*0-8369-5558-7*) Ayer.

— The Life of Nelson. (Notable American Authors Ser.). 1999. reprint ed. lib. bdg. 125.00 (*0-7812-3920-6*) Rprt Serv.

— The Life of Nelson: The Embodiment of the Sea Power of Great Britain, 2 vols. in 1. 1999. 26.00 (*0-403-00076-9*) Scholarly.

***Mahan, Alfred Thayer.** The Life of Nelson: The Embodiment of the Sea Power of Great Britain. fac. ed. (Illus.). 792p. 2000. 84.95 (*0-9674826-2-3*) Regatta Pr.

Mahan, Alfred Thayer. The Life of Nelson: The Embodiment of the Sea Power of Great Britain, 2 Vols. LC 68-26361. (English Biography Ser.: No. 31). 1969. reprint ed. lib. bdg. 99.95 (*0-8383-0182-7*) M S G Haskell Hse.

— Mahan on Naval Warfare: Selections from the Writings of Rear Admiral Alfred T. Mahan. LC 99-30216. 416p. 1999. pap. text 13.95 (*0-486-40729-2*) Dover.

— The Major Operations of the Navies in the War American Independence. (Notable American Authors Ser.). 1999. reprint ed. lib. bdg. 125.00 (*0-7812-3932-X*) Rprt Serv.

— The Major Operations of the Navies in the War of American Independence. LC 69-10128. (Illus.). 280p. 1969. reprint ed. lib. bdg. 35.00 (*0-8371-1002-5*, MAWI, Greenwood Pr) Greenwood.

— The Major Operations of the Navies in the War of American Independence. (BCL1 - U. S. History Ser.). 280p. 1991. reprint ed. lib. bdg. 79.00 (*0-7812-6119-8*) Rprt Serv.

— Naval Administration & Warfare. (Notable American Authors Ser.). 1999. reprint ed. lib. bdg. 125.00 (*0-7812-3927-3*) Rprt Serv.

— Naval Strategy. LC 74-14359. (Illus.). 475p. 1975. reprint ed. lib. bdg. 99.75 (*0-8371-7802-9*, MANS, Greenwood Pr) Greenwood.

— Naval Strategy. (Notable American Authors Ser.). 1999. reprint ed. lib. bdg. 125.00 (*0-7812-3930-3*) Rprt Serv.

— The Problem of Asia. (Notable American Authors Ser.). 1999. reprint ed. lib. bdg. 125.00 (*0-7812-3922-2*) Rprt Serv.

— Retrospect & Prospect. (Notable American Authors Ser.). 1999. reprint ed. lib. bdg. 125.00 (*0-7812-3924-9*) Rprt Serv.

— Sea Power in Its Relation to the War of 1812, 2 vols., Set. 1993. reprint ed. lib. bdg. 150.00 (*0-7812-5190-7*) Rprt Serv.

— Sea Power in Its Relations to the War of 1812, 2 Vols. LC 68-26362. (World History Ser.: No. 48). 1969. reprint ed. lib. bdg. 150.00 (*0-8383-0181-9*) M S G Haskell Hse.

— Sea Power in Its Relations to the War of 1812. (Notable American Authors Ser.). 1999. reprint ed. lib. bdg. 125.00 (*0-7812-3925-7*) Rprt Serv.

— Types of Naval Officers. (Notable American Authors Ser.). 1999. reprint ed. lib. bdg. 125.00 (*0-7812-3923-0*) Rprt Serv.

— Types of Naval Officers: Drawn from the History of the British Navy. LC 77-84323. (Essay Index Reprint Ser.). 1977. 25.95 (*0-8369-1093-1*) Ayer.

— Types of Naval Officers: Drawn from the History of the British Navy. LC 77-84323. (Essay Index Reprint Ser.). 500p. reprint ed. lib. bdg. 21.75 (*0-8290-0473-4*) Irvington.

Mahan, Ann, jt. auth. see Mahan, John.

Mahan, Asa. Autobiography: Intellectual, Moral, & Spiritual. (American Biography Ser.). 458p. 1991. reprint ed. lib. bdg. 99.00 (*0-7812-8262-4*) Rprt Serv.

— Autobiography - Intellectual, Moral & Spiritual. LC 75-3269. reprint ed. 45.00 (*0-404-59257-0*) AMS Pr.

— Doctrine of the Will. LC 75-3270. reprint ed. 42.00 (*0-404-59258-9*) AMS Pr.

Mahan, Asa. Misunderstood Texts of Scripture Expounded & Explained: The Doctrine of the Higher Life Thereby Verified. 181p. 1996. pap. 9.99 (*0-88019-358-1*) Schmul Pub Co.

Mahan, Asa. The Science of Natural Theology. LC 75-3273. reprint ed. 37.50 (*0-404-59261-9*) AMS Pr.

Mahan, Asa, intro. The Science of Logic: or An Analysis of the Laws of Thought. 1986. reprint ed. pap. 38.95 (*0-935005-84-6*) Lincoln-Rembrandt.

Mahan, Ben. God's World Colors & Shapes. 1999. pap. text 2.49 (*0-7847-0758-8*) Standard Pub.

— God's World Letters & Numbers. 1999. pap. text 2.49 (*0-7847-0757-X*) Standard Pub.

Mahan, Ben. Kitty's Busy Valentine. 7p. (J). (ps-k). 1998. 7.95 (*0-694-01095-2*) HarpC.

Mahan, Benton. Goldilocks & the Three Bears. LC 80-27631. 32p. (J). (gr. k-2). 1997. pap. 3.95 (*0-89375-471-4*) Troll Communs.

***Mahan, Benton.** Rain, Rain, Go Away. large type ed. (Getting Ready to Read with Mother Goose). 8p. (J). 1999. 39.00 (*0-8215-6976-7*) Sadlier.

— Rain, Rain, Go Away. large type ed. (Getting Ready to Read with Mother Goose). 8p. (J). (gr. k). 1999. 18.89 (*0-8215-6961-9*) Sadlier.

Mahan, Brian & Richesin, L. Dale, eds. The Challenge of Liberation Theology: A First-World Response. LC 81-9527. 160p. reprint ed. pap. 49.60 (*0-8357-2683-5*, 20402190015) Bks Demand.

Mahan, Bruce M. University Chemistry. 3rd ed. LC 74-19696. (C). 1975. text. write for info. (*0-201-04405-6*) Addison-Wesley.

— University Chemistry. 4th ed. (C). 1987. pap. text 55.33 (*0-201-05846-4*) Addison-Wesley.

Mahan, Bruce M. & Myers, Rollie J. S/M Restr Univ Chem. 4th ed. LC 86-14063. (Chemistry Ser.). (Illus.). 1076p. (C). 1987. pap. text 15.00 (*0-201-05838-3*) Benjamin-Cummings.

— University Chemistry. 4th ed. LC 86-14063. (Chemistry Ser.). (Illus.). 1076p. (C). 1987. text 51.95 (*0-201-05833-2*) Addison-Wesley.

— University Chemistry. 4th ed. LC 86-14063. (Chemistry Ser.). (Illus.). 1076p. (C). 1987. student ed. 17.25 (*0-201-05835-9*) Benjamin-Cummings.

Mahan, Charles, jt. auth. see Young, Diony.

***Mahan, David G.** That Hunger Bunch. 2000. mass mkt. 9.99 (*1-55279-005-3*) Picasso Publ.

Mahan, Dennis H. Complete Treatise on Field Fortification. LC 68-54797. 268p. 1969. reprint ed. lib. bdg. 35.00 (*0-8371-0557-9*, MAFF, Greenwood Pr) Greenwood.

Mahan, G. D. Many-Particle Physics. 2nd ed. (Physics of Solids & Liquids Ser.). (Illus.). 1046p. (C). 1990. text 145.00 (*0-306-43423-7*, Kluwer Plenum) Kluwer Academic.

Mahan, G. D. & Subbaswamy, K. R. Local Density Theory of Polarization. LC 90-42552. (Physics of Solids & Liquids Ser.). (Illus.). 260p. (C). 1990. 75.00 (*0-306-43685-X*, Kluwer Plenum) Kluwer Academic.

Mahan, Gary P. The Demand for Residential Telephone Service. LC 79-620020. (MSU Public Utilities Papers: Vol. 1979). 224p. reprint ed. pap. 69.50 (*0-608-20497-8*, 207174900002) Bks Demand.

***Mahan, Gerald D.** Many-Particle Physics. 3rd ed. LC 00-39101. (Physics of Solids & Liquids Ser.). (Illus.). 2000. write for info. (*0-306-46338-5*, Kluwer Plenum) Kluwer Academic.

Mahan, Harold E. Benson J. Lossing & Historical Writing in the United States, 4. LC 95-35713. (Studies in Historiography: No. 4). 160p. 1996. 57.95 (*0-313-28806-2*, Greenwood Pr) Greenwood.

Mahan, Henry T. Bible Class Commentaries, 6 vols., Set. Incl. 1st & 2nd Corinthians. 1984. mass mkt. 5.00 (*0-85234-194-6*); 1st & 2nd Thessalonians: 1st & 2nd Timothy. 1984. mass mkt. 5.00 (*0-85234-185-7*); Galatians. 1983. mass mkt. 2.00 (*1-56186-510-9*); Galatians Thru Colossians. 1984. mass mkt. 5.00 (*0-85234-210-1*); Hebrews & James. 1984. mass mkt. 5.00 (*0-85234-187-3*); Romans. 1984. mass mkt. 5.00 (*0-85234-184-9*); Titus, Philemon, & 1st & 2nd Peter Thru Jude. 1984. mass mkt. 5.00 (*0-85234-211-X*); 1984. Set pap. 30.00 (*0-85234-215-2*) Pilgrim Pubns.

— Gospel of John. 1987. pap. 4.99 (*0-85234-238-1*, Pub. by Evangelical Pr) P & R Pubng.

— With New Testament Eyes. 1993. pap. 8.99 (*0-85234-304-3*, Pub. by Evangelical Pr) P & R Pubng.

Mahan, J. Alex. Vienna: Yesterday & Today. 1976. lib. bdg. 59.95 (*0-8490-2797-7*) Gordon Pr.

Mahan, Jeffrey H. A Long Way from Solving That One: Psycho-Social & Ethical Implications of Ross Macdonald's Lew Archer Tales. 166p. (C). 1990. lib. bdg. 37.50 (*0-8191-7710-5*) U Pr of Amer.

Mahan, Jeffrey H., et al. Shared Wisdom: A Guide to Case Study Reflection in Ministry. LC 93-4458. 144p. (Orig.). 1993. pap. 12.95 (*0-687-38335-8*) Abingdon.

Mahan, Jeffrey H., jt. ed. see Forbes, Bruce D.

Mahan, John & Mahan, Ann. Lake Superior: Story & Spirit. LC 96-35972. 1997. write for info. (*1-883755-11-5*) Lost Riv Pr.

— Lake Superior, Story & Spirit. LC 97-92359. (Illus.). 260p. 1998. 56.00 (*0-9659189-0-4*) Sweetwater Vis.

Mahan, Joseph B. North American Sun Kings: Keepers of the Flame. 300p. 1992. 30.00 (*1-880820-03-X*) ISAC Pr.

Mahan, Kathleen, jt. auth. see Krause, Marie V.

Mahan, L. Kathleen & Escott-Stump, Sylvia, eds. Krause's Food, Nutrition, & Diet Therapy. 9th ed. (Illus.). 1996. teacher ed. write for info. (*0-7216-5836-9*, W B Saunders Co) Harcrt Hlth Sci Grp.

Mahan, Lois. Willits Scrapbook: The Way It Was, 1958-1974. LC 78-108189. 1975. 3.00 (*0-932820-00-X*) M P Pubs.

Mahan, Margaret, ed. see Suoboda, Robert E.

Mahan, Nancie S., ed. see Mobley, Chuck & Mobley, Andrea.

Mahan, Nancie S., ed. see Taylor, Richard C.

Mahan, Rajan, jt. ed. see Jain, Pratibha.

Mahan, Sue. Crack Cocaine, Crime, & Women: Legal, Social, & Treatment Issues. (Drugs, Health, & Social Policy Ser.: Vol. 4). 136p. 1996. 45.00 (*0-7619-0141-8*); pap. 18.95 (*0-7619-0142-6*) Sage.

***Mahan, Sue.** Yummy. Wise, Noreen, ed. (Lemonade Collection). 96p. (YA). (gr. 4 up). 2000. pap. 6.95 (*1-58584-266-4*) Huckleberry CT.

Mahan, Sue & O'Neil, Katherine. Organized Crime in the Americas: Beyond the Mafia. LC 98-19692. 257p. 1998. write for info. (*0-7619-1358-0*); pap. write for info. (*0-7619-1359-9*) Sage.

Mahan, Wayne W. The New Testament: A Manual for College Students. 111p. (Orig.). 1997. pap. text 11.95 (*0-87563-722-1*) Stipes.

Mahan, William Dennes, ed. The Acts of Pilate. 215p. (Orig.). 1997. pap. 9.95 (*0-89228-127-8*) Impact Christian.

Mahanama, jt. auth. see Bullis, Douglas.

Mahaney, Astrid Witte, jt. auth. see Mahaney, Casey.

Mahaney, C. J., jt. auth. see Boisvert, Robin.

Mahaney, C. J., jt. auth. see Loftness, John.

Mahaney, C. J., jt. ed. see Somerville, Greg.

Mahaney, Casey. Hawaiian Reef Fish: The Identification Book. (Illus.). pap. 19.95 (*0-9636252-0-9*) Planet Ocean.

***Mahaney, Casey & Mahaney, Astrid Witte.** Diving & Snorkeling Hawaii: Top Dives in Oahu, the Big Island, Maui County, Kauai, Niihau & Midway. (Pisces Bks.). (Illus.). 144p. 2000. pap. text 17.95 (*1-86450-090-5*) Lonely Planet.

Mahaney, Casey & Witte, Astrid. The Essential Guide to Live Aboard Dive Travel. LC 96-84464. 162p. 1996. pap. 14.95 (*0-941332-54-3*, D852) Best Pub Co.

Mahaney, Casey, jt. auth. see Witte, Astrid.

Mahaney, Michael C., ed. see Rounds, Joseph B.

Mahaney, N., jt. auth. see Harris, Joshua.

Mahaney, Teri. Change Your Mind: How to Create Your Own Subliminal Tapes. rev. ed. LC 89-51990. 1990. pap. 19.95 (*0-9624140-1-8*) Supertraining Pr.

Mahaney, Teri. Change Your Mind - life: Self Empowerment Series Scripts. 24p. 1992. pap. 5.00 (*1-893158-11-X*) Supertraining Pr.

— Change Your Mind - Life: The Spirituality Series Scripts. 32p. 1998. pap. 5.00 (*1-893158-23-3*) Supertraining Pr.

***Mahaney, Teri D.** Change Your Mind/Life: Loving Relationship Series Scripts. 2000. 5.00 (*1-893158-36-5*) Supertraining Pr.

Mahaney, W. C., ed. Quaternary & Environmental Research on East African Mountains. 400p. (C). 1989. text 136.00 (*90-6191-794-8*, Pub. by A A Balkema) Ashgate Pub Co.

Mahaney, William C. Ice on the Equator: Quaternary Geology of Mount Kenya, East Africa. LC 90-41212. (Illus.). xii, 386p. 1990. 65.00 (*0-940473-19-4*) Wm Caxton.

Mahaney, William E. WKBK CURRENT ENGLISH 4E. 4th ed. (C). 1989. 19.13 (*0-673-38585-X*, Scott Frsmn) Addson-Wesley Educ.

— Workbook of Current English. 3rd ed. (C). 1985. 12.33 (*0-673-15959-0*, Scott Frsmn) Addson-Wesley Educ.

Mahang, Lois, jt. auth. see Burton, Eric.

Mahanjan, Ashok. Goan Vignettes & Other Poems. 64p. 1986. pap. 3.95 (*0-19-561912-9*) OUP.

***Mahant, Edelgard & Mount, Graeme S.** Invisible & Inaudible in Washington: American Policies Toward Canada. 265p. 2000. pap. 23.95 (*0-87013-525-2*) Mich St U Pr.

Mahant Krsna Balaram Swami. Srimad Bhagavatam: The Beautiful Narrations of the Supreme Lord, Vol. 2. 350p. 1995. write for info. (*0-9631403-1-0*) H H K B S.

— Srimad Bhagavatam: The Beautiful Narrations of the Supreme Lord, Vol. 3. 350p. 1995. write for info. (*0-9631403-2-9*) H H K B S.

Mahanta, Jogeshwar. Sex, Crime & Society. viii, 112p. (C). 1993. 15.00 (*81-7024-548-6*, Pub. by Ashish Pub Hse) Nataraj Bks.

Mahanthappa, K. T., jt. ed. see Freund, P. G.

Mahanti, Neeti. Tribal Issues: A Non-Conventional Approach. LC 94-900505. (C). 1994. 14.00 (*81-210-0332-6*, Pub. by Inter-India Pubns) S Asia.

Mahanti, S. D. & Jena, P., eds. Local Order in Condensed Matter Physics. (Illus.). 287p. (C). 1995. lib. bdg. 165.00 (*1-56072-220-7*) Nova Sci Pubs.

Mahanti, S. D., jt. auth. see Kaplan, T. A.

Mahanty, D. K. Indian Political Tradition: From Manu to Ambedkar. 1998. 32.00 (*81-7488-791-1*) Anmol.

Mahanty, J. & Das, M. P., eds. Condensed Matter Physics. 440p. (C). 1989. text 123.00 (*9971-5-0886-9*) World Scientific Pub.

Mahanty, J., jt. auth. see Das, M. P.

Mahanty, Shukla, jt. auth. see Singh, Bhagawan P.

***Mahany, Patricia Shely.** Hurry up, Noah. Derico, Laura, ed. (Illus.). 24p. (J). (ps-k). 2000. pap. 1.99 (*0-7847-1062-7*, 04335) Standard Pub.

Mahany, Christine Michal, et al. Roman Alcester Southern Extramural Area, 1964-1966 Excavations. LC 95-150844. 1994. write for info. (*1-872414-42-7*) Council for British Archeology.

Mahany, Patricia S. Baby Moses in a Basket. (Happy Day Bks.). (Illus.). 24p. (J). 1996. pap. 1.99 (*0-7847-0446-5*, \) Standard Pub.

— Hurry up, Noah. Beegle, Shirley, ed. (Happy Day Bks.). (Illus.). 24p. (J). (ps-k). 1994. reprint ed. pap. 1.99 (*0-7847-0257-8*, 04207) Standard Pub.

***Mahapatra, Anil Baran Singha.** Essentials of Medical Physiology. 550p. 1999. pap. (*81-86793-36-4*) Current Bks Intl.

Mahapatra, Anuradha. Another Spring, Darkness: Selected Poems of Anuradha Mahapatra. Wright, Carolyne et al, trs. from BEN. 112p. (Orig.). 1996. 23.95 (*0-934971-52-8*); pap. 12.95 (*0-934971-51-X*) Calyx Bks.

Mahapatra, Jayanta. Burden of Waves & Fruit. 59p. 1988. 18.00 (*1-57889-070-5*) Passeggiata.

— Life Signs. (Three Crowns Bks.). (Illus.). 1984. pap. 5.95 (*0-19-561585-9*) OUP.

— Selected Poems. 80p. 1989. pap. 8.95 (*0-19-562051-8*) OUP.

Mahapatra, L. K. Tribal Development in India: Myth & Reality. (C). 1994. 15.00 (*0-7069-7351-8*, Pub. by Vikas) S Asia.

Mahapatra, L. K., jt. auth. see Das, K. B.

Mahapatra, P.R. Aviation Weather Surveillance Systems: Advanced Radar & Surface Sensors for Flight Safety & Air Traffic Management. (Radar, Sonar, Navigation & Avionics Ser.: No. 8). 416p. 1999. 98.00 (*0-85296-937-6*, RA008) INSPEC Inc.

Mahapatra, Sitakant. Beyond the Word: The Multiple Gestures of Tradition. (C). 1993. 14.00 (*81-208-1108-9*, Pub. by Motilal Bnarsidass) S Asia.

— Role of Tradition in Literature. LC 97-901657. (C). 1997. 17.50 (*81-259-0246-5*, Pub. by Vikas) S Asia.

— Unending Rhythms: Oral Poetry of Indian Tribes. (Tribal Studies of India Series T: No. T 145). (C). 1992. 32.00 (*81-210-0277-X*, Pub. by Inter-India Pubns) S Asia.

Mahapatra, Sitakanta. Modernization & Ritual: Identity & Social Change in Santal Society. (Illus.). 180p. 1987. 29.95 (*0-19-561794-0*) OUP.

Mahapatra, Sitakanta, ed. The Realm of the Sacred: Verbal Symbolism & Ritual Structures. (Illus.). 228p. 1993. text 32.00 (*0-19-562610-9*) OUP.

Mahapatra, Sthapaka N. Silparatnakosa: Glossary of Orissan Temple Architecture. (C). 1994. 38.00 (*0-614-96185-8*, Pub. by Motilal Bnarsidass) S Asia.

Mahapatro, P. C. Economics of Cotton Handloom Industry in India. 1986. 31.00 (*81-7024-060-3*, Pub. by Ashish Pub Hse) S Asia.

***Mahapragya.** Jainism: Ethics & Morality. 2000. 26.00 (*81-261-0587-9*, Pub. by Anmol) S Asia.

— Jainism & Its Philosophical Foundations. 2000. 26.00 (*81-261-0586-0*, Pub. by Anmol) S Asia.

Mahaprajna, Yuvacharya. Mysteries of Mind. 225p. 1982. 11.00 (*0-88065-223-3*, Pub. by Today Tomorrow) Scholarly Pubns.

Mahar, Danny. Aramaic Made EZ, One. (Illus.). 114p. spiral bd. 39.95 (*0-9675989-1-5*) Aramaic Bible.

— Enlightenment from the Aramaic: Words & Phrases in Estrangel Script, One. rev. abr. ed. Orig. Title: Enlightenment from the Aramiac. (Illus.). 57p. 1974. spiral bd. 29.95 (*0-9675989-2-3*) Aramaic Bible.

M

An Asterisk (*) at the beginning of an entry indicates that the title is appearing for the first time.

Mahar, Dennis J. Frontier Development Policy in Brazil: A Study of Amazonia. LC 78-19750. (Praeger Special Studies). 182p. 1979. 47.95 (*0-275-90385-0*, C0385, Praeger Pubs) Greenwood.

Mahar, J. Michael, ed. The Untouchables in Contemporary India. LC 79-152039. (Illus.). 528p. reprint ed. pap. 163.70 (*0-608-15586-1*, 202965400062) Bks Demand.

Mahar-Keplinger, Lisa. Grain Elevators. LC 92-29683. (Illus.). 88p. (Orig.). 1993. pap. 19.95 (*1-878271-35-0*) Princeton Arch.

Mahar, Paul, et al. Teach Yourself IntraBuilder in 21 Days. LC 96-70714. 800p. 1997. 39.99 (*1-57521-224-2*) Sams.

Mahar, William J. Behind the Burnt Cork Mask: Early Blackface Minstrelsy & Antebellum American Popular Culture. LC 97-33851. (Music in American Life Ser). (Illus.). 512p. 1998. 60.00 (*0-252-02396-X*); pap. 24.95 (*0-252-06696-0*) U of Ill Pr.

Maharaj, B., jt. auth. see Charran, R.

Maharaj, Clement. The Dispossessed. (Caribbean Writers Ser.). 128p. (C). 1992. pap. 9.95 (*0-435-98928-6*, 98928) Heinemann.

Maharaj, Niala & Dorren, Gaston. The Game of the Rose: The Third World in the Global Flower Trade. 112p. (Orig.). 1996. pap. 17.50 (*90-6224-981-7*, Pub. by Uitgeverij Arkel) LPC InBook.

Maharaj, Nisargadatta. Consciousness & the Absolute: The Final Talks of Sri Nisargadatta Maharaj. Dunn, Jean, ed. (Illus.). vii, 119p. (Orig.). 1998. reprint ed. pap. 11.95 (*0-89386-041-7*) Acorn NC.

— I Am That: Talks with Sri Nisargadatta Maharaj. Dikshit, Sudhaker S., ed. Frydman, Maurice, tr. from MAR. LC 81-66800. (Illus.). xx, 550p. 1997. reprint ed. pap. 24.95 (*0-89386-022-0*) Acorn NC.

— Prior to Consciousness: Talks with Sri Nisargadatta Maharaj. Dunn, Jean, ed. LC 89-81145. xi, 157p. 1997. reprint ed. pap. 13.95 (*0-89386-024-7*) Acorn NC.

— Seeds of Consciousness: The Wisdom of Sri Nisargadatta Maharaj. Dunn, Jean, ed. LC 89-81146. 215p. 1997. reprint ed. pap. 14.95 (*0-89386-025-5*) Acorn NC.

Maharaj, Rabindranath. Homer in Flight. LC 97-169810. 323p. 1998. pap. 15.95 (*0-86492-220-5*, Pub. by Goose Ln Edits) Genl Dist Srvs.

— The Interloper. LC 95-182122. 181p. 1995. pap. 12.95 (*0-86492-155-1*, Pub. by Goose Ln Edits) Genl Dist Srvs.

Maharaj, Rabindranath R. & Hunt, Dave. Death of a Guru. rev. ed. LC 84-81212. 208p. 1986. reprint ed. pap. 9.99 (*0-89081-434-1*) Harvest Hse.

Maharaj, Ratnachandraji, jt. auth. see Shri, Shatavadhani J.

Maharaj, Saraswati J., jt. auth. see Devanand, Swami Guru.

Maharaj, Saraswati J., jt. auth. see Swami Guru Devanand.

Maharaj, Saraswati J., jt. auth. see Swami Guru Devanand Staff.

Maharaj, Yogeshwaranand S. Science of Divine Sound: Divya Shabad Vijnana: A Latest Research on Self & God Realization with the Medium of Sound. Ji, Muktanand S., tr. xi, 160p. 1984. 12.00 (*0-614-06354-X*, Pub. by Yoga Niketan) Nataraj Bks.

— Science of Soul: A Practical Exposition of Ancient Method of Visualisation of Soul. Atma-Vijnana. 2nd ed. xx, 280p. 1987. 18.00 (*0-614-06349-3*, Pub. by Yoga Niketan) Nataraj Bks.

— Science of Vital Force: A New Research of Self & God-Realisation by the Medium of Prana. Saraswati, Muktanand, tr. v, 143p. 1980. 12.00 (*0-614-06352-3*, Pub. by Yoga Niketan) Nataraj Bks.

***Maharaja, B. B. Tirtha.** Chaitanya Vol. 1: His Life & Associates. 300p. 2000. 24.95 (*1-886069-28-X*) Mandala Pub Grp.

Maharaja, Bhakti. The Art of Sadhana: A Practical Guide to Daily Devotion, 2 vols., No. 1. (Illus.). 144p. 1999. 19.95 (*1-886069-02-6*, Pub. by Mandala Pub Grp); pap. 14.95 (*1-886069-03-4*, Pub. by Mandala Pub Grp) Bookpeople.

Maharaja, Jagadguru S. Vedic Mathematics: Sixteen Simple Mathematical Formulae from the Vedas. Agrawala, V. S., ed. 367p. (C). 1992. pap. 14.00 (*81-208-0164-4*, Pub. by Motilal Bnarsidass) S Asia.

Maharaja, Krsna Tirthaji, jt. auth. see Bharati, Jahadhuru Swami Sri.

Maharaja Yogiraja, ed. see Maitriya.

Maharajah of Cooch Behar. Big Game Shooting in Cooch Behar, the Duars & Assam. 1993. reprint ed. 118.00 (*1-879356-23-6*) Wolfe Pub Co.

Maharajan, M. Economic Thought of Mahatma Gandhi. 124p. 1998. 22.00 (*81-7141-415-X*, Pub. by Discovery Pub Hse) Nataraj Bks.

— Gandhian Thought: As Study of Tradition & Modernity. 176p. (C). 1996. write for info. (*81-207-1336-2*) Sterling Pubs.

Maharam, Lewis. A Healthy Back, Vol. 1. LC 97-43020. 192p. 1998. pap. 12.95 (*0-8050-3541-9*, Owl) H Holt & Co.

Maharam, Lewis G. Backs in Motion: The Only Back-Care Program for Everybody. (Illus.). 88p. 1995. 25.00 (*0-8050-3540-0*) H Holt & Co.

Maharana, J., et al, eds. Physics at the Planck Scale: Proceedings of the Workshop, Puri, India 12 - 21 December 1994. 500p. 1997. text 112.00 (*981-02-2470-2*, PhMaPma-P2941) World Scientific Pub.

Maharary, George S., ed. see Westervelt, William B.

Maharatna, Arup. The Demography of Famines: An Indian Historical Perspective. LC 96-900514. (Illus.). 336p. (C). 1996. text 32.00 (*0-19-563711-9*) OUP.

Maharg, James. Call to Authenticity: The Essays of Ezequiel Martinez Estrada. LC 77-7175. (Romance Monographs: No. 26). 1977. 26.00 (*84-399-7352-7*) Romance.

Maharg, Lois, jt. auth. see Burton, Eric.

Maharidge, Dale. The Coming White Minority: California, Multiculturalism & America. LC 99-204463. 1999. pap. 14.00 (*0-679-75008-8*) Vin Bks.

Maharidge, Dale & Williamson, Michael. Journey to Nowhere. rev. ed. LC 96-38872. (Illus.). 224p. (J). 1996. pap. 17.45 (*0-7868-8204-2*, Pub. by Hyperion) Time Warner.

— The Last Great American Hobo. LC 92-40480. (Illus.). 288p. 1993. 24.95 (*1-55958-299-5*) Prima Pub.

Maharidge, Dale, jt. auth. see Mather, Jay.

Maharishi Mahesh Yogi. Bhagavad - Gita: A New Translation & Commentary, Chapters 1-6. 373p. 1967. 18.95 (*0-89186-000-2*); 5.00 (*0-89186-002-9*) Age Enlight Pr.

— Life Supported by Natural Law: Lectures by His Holiness Maharishi Mahesh Yogi to the World Assembly on Vedic Science, July 9-17, 1975, Washington, D.C. LC 86-14204. (Illus.). 210p. 1986. pap. 12.00 (*0-89186-051-7*) Age Enlight Pr.

— Love & God. 56p. 1973. 9.00 (*0-89186-003-7*) Age Enlight Pr.

— Science of Being & Art of Living. rev. ed. 335p. 1966. 18.95 (*0-89186-001-0*) Age Enlight Pr.

— Transcendental Meditation: Science of Being & Art of Living. (New Age Ser.). 320p. 1988. pap. 4.95 (*0-317-67301-7*, Sig) NAL.

Maharriyum, Thaemas A. Love Communings: Soul Embracings with the Spirit of the Unborn Child. (Illus.). 68p. (Orig.). 1985. write for info. (*0-912323-02-7*); pap. write for info. (*0-912323-01-9*) Apollo Phonic.

Maharshi, Ramana. The Spiritual Teaching of Ramana Maharshi. (Dragon Editions Ser.). 133p. (Orig.). 1989. pap. 14.00 (*0-87773-024-5*, Pub. by Shambhala Pubns) Random.

***Maharshi, Ramana.** Talks with Ramana Maharshi: On Realizing Abiding Peace & Happiness. LC 99-95497. 552p. 2000. pap. 26.95 (*1-878019-00-7*) Inner Drctns.

Mahasattva, D., ed. see Osho & Sambuddha, D.

Mahasattva Geet Govind, ed. see Osho.

Mahasattva, K., ed. see Osho.

Mahathera, A. P. Concise Pali-English Dictionary. (ENG & PLI.). 1992. reprint ed. 39.95 (*0-8288-8462-5*) Fr & Eur.

— English Pali Dictionary. (ENG & PLI.). 1992. reprint ed. 49.95 (*0-8288-8463-3*, F46280) Fr & Eur.

Mahathera, Narada. The Buddha & His Teachings. 412p. (Orig.). 1997. 21.60 (*955-24-0025-2*, Pub. by Buddhist Pub Soc) Vipassana Res Pubns.

Mahathera, Nyanatiloka. Buddhist Dictionary: A Manual of Buddhist Terms & Doctrines. 272p. (C). 1997. 14.40 (*955-24-0019-8*, Pub. by Buddhist Pub Soc) Vipassana Res Pubns.

— Guide Through the Abhidhamma Pitaka. Date not set. write for info. (*955-24-0133-X*, Pub. by Buddhist Pub Soc) Vipassana Res Pubns.

Mahatme, Anand. Concepts & Procedures in Indian Census. (C). 1988. 21.00 (*0-8364-2455-7*) S Asia.

Mahboubi, Soroosh. Pediatric Bone Imaging: A Practical Approach. 1989. 120.00 (*0-316-54381-0*, Little Brwn Med Div) Lppncott W & W.

Mahboubian, Houshang. The Art of Ancient Iran: Copper & Bronze. (Illus.). 368p. 1998. 190.00 (*0-85667-483-4*, Pub. by P Wilson) Antique Collect.

***Mahdavi.** For God, Man & Country. LC 99-27937. 286p. 2000. pap. 55.00 (*0-8133-3642-2*, Pub. by Westview) HarpC.

Mahdavieh, Y. & Gonzalez, R. C., eds. Advances in Image Analysis. LC 92-25969. 1992. pap. 30.00 (*0-8194-1047-0*, PM08) SPIE.

Mahdev, P. D., ed. Contributions to Indian Geography Vol. 7: Urban Geography. 1986. 44.00 (*0-8364-1600-7*, Pub. by Heritage IA) S Asia.

***Mahdi, Kamil A., ed.** Warer in the Arabian Peninsula. 252p. 2000. 62.00 (*0-86372-246-6*, Pub. by Garnet-Ithaca) LPC InBook.

Mahdi, Louise C., et al, eds. Betwixt & Between: Patterns of Masculine & Feminine Initiation. LC 86-31271. (Reality of the Psyche Ser.). 528p. 1987. pap. 19.95 (*0-8126-9048-6*) Open Court.

— Betwixt & Between: Patterns of Masculine & Feminine Initiation. LC 86-31271. (Reality of the Psyche Ser.). 528p. (C). 1987. 39.95 (*0-8126-9047-8*) Open Court.

— Crossroads: The Quest for Contemporary Rites of Passage. 478p. (Orig.). 1996. pap. 22.95 (*0-8126-9190-3*) Open Court.

Mahdi, Muhsin. Studies in the Philosophy of Ibn Khaldun. 1998. pap. 17.00 (*1-883058-35-X*, Nur) Global Pubns.

— The Thousand & One Nights. LC 95-3212. 1995. pap. 36.50 (*90-04-10204-3*) Brill Academic Pubs.

— The Thousand & One Nights. 278p. 1996. pap. 19.95 (*0-614-21658-3*, 1362) Kazi Pubns.

Mahdi, Muhsin, ed. The Thousand & One Nights (Alf Layla Wa-Layla) From Earliest Known Sources, Vol. 3. (ARA & ENG.). 396p. 1994. 143.00 (*90-04-10106-3*) Brill Academic Pubs.

Mahdi, Muhsin, jt. ed. see Lerner, Ralph.

Mahdi, Mushin. Arabian Nights: The Thousand & One Nights. 1992. 20.00 (*0-679-41338-3*) Everymns Lib.

Mahdi Xan. Sanglax, a Persian Guide to the Turkish Language. (Gibb Memorial New Ser.: Vol. 20). 1992. 30.00 (*0-906094-31-3*, Pub. by Aris & Phillips) David Brown.

***Mahdy, Christine.** Tutankhamen. (Illus.). 352p. 2000. text 24.95 (*0-312-26241-8*) St Martin.

Mahdy, Christine El, see El Mahdy, Christine.

Mahe, John A., II, et al, eds. Encyclopaedia of New Orleans Artists, 1718-1918. LC 87-80477. xxii, 466p. 1987. 39.95 (*0-917860-23-3*) Historic New Orleans.

Mahecha, Alberto, ed. see Pollock, Algernon J.

Mahedy, William & Bernardi, Janet. A Generation Alone: Xers Making a Place in the World. LC 94-18634. 182p. (Orig.). 1994. pap. 11.99 (*0-8308-1696-8*, 1696) InterVarsity.

Mahedy, William P. Out of the Night: The Spiritual Journey of Vietnam Veterans. rev. ed. 256p. 1996. pap. 16.95 (*1-884189-00-8*, 101) StressCare Pr.

Mahel, Michal & Buday, Tibor, eds. Regional Geology of Czechoslovakia Pt. II: The West Carpathians. (Illus.). 723p. 1968. 42.00 (*3-510-99066-8*, Pub. by E Schweizerbartsche) Balogh.

Mahendra, B. Dementia. 2nd ed. 1987. text 119.00 (*0-7462-0044-7*) Kluwer Academic.

— Depression. 1987. text 176.50 (*0-85200-983-6*) Kluwer Academic.

***Mahendrarajah, S. & McAleer, M. J.** Modelling Change in Integrated Economic & Environmental Systems. Jakeman, A. J., ed. LC 98-55968. 412p. 1999. 140.00 (*0-471-98544-9*) Wiley.

Maher. Managerial Accounting. 6th ed. 1997. teacher ed. 246.00 (*0-03-018197-6*, Pub. by Harcourt Coll Pubs) Harcourt.

— Study Guide to Accompany Mangerial Accounting. 6th ed. (C). 1997. pap. text, student ed. 31.00 (*0-03-018207-7*) Harcourt Coll Pubs.

Maher, jt. auth. see Della Rocca.

Maher, Alan, ed. see Dewazien, Karl.

Maher, Alan E. Complete Soccer Handbook. LC 83-2278. 216p. 1983. 19.95 (*0-13-163386-4*, Parker Publishing Co) P-H.

Maher, Ali, et al. Soil Improvement for Big Digs: Proceedings of Sessions Sponsored by the Geotechnical Engineering Division of the American Society of Civil Engineers in Conjunction with the Asce National Convention in Boston, Massachusetts, October 18-21, 1998. LC 98-39144. (Geotechnical Special Publication). 352p. 1998. 49.00 (*0-7844-0388-0*) Am Soc Civil Eng.

Maher, Ann B., et al. Orthopaedic Nursing. 2nd ed. LC 97-37502. (Illus.). 944p. 1998. text 99.00 (*0-7216-6952-2*, W B Saunders Co) Harcrt Hlth Sci Grp.

Maher, Barbara. Ultimate Cake. LC 96-4222. (DK Living Ser.). 160p. 1998. pap. 13.95 (*0-7894-3760-0*) DK Pub Inc.

— Ultimate Cake: The New Illustrated Guide to Baking Luscious Cakes. LC 96-4222. 160p. 1996. 24.95 (*0-7894-0441-9*) DK Pub Inc.

Maher, Barbara & Thompson, Roy, eds. Quaternary Climates, Environments & Magnetism. LC 99-11967. (Illus.). 335p. (C). 1999. 115.00 (*0-521-62417-7*) Cambridge U Pr.

***Maher, Barry.** Filling the Glass: How to Succeed at Business Without Selling Out. 2001. pap. 19.95 (*0-7931-3865-5*) Dearborn.

Maher, Barry. Getting the Most from Your Yellow Pages Advertising: Maximum Profits at Minimum Cost. 2nd rev. ed. LC 97-73918. (Illus.). 304p. (Orig.). 1997. pap. 19.95 (*1-890154-05-9*) Aegis Pub Grp.

Maher, Barry & Garber, Bernard J. Legend: A Novel. LC 83-83169. 304p. (Orig.). 1987. pap. 12.95 (*0-8334-0024-X*, Spir Lit Lib) Garber Comm.

Maher, Beth. Focus on Reading & Writing: Basic Level. LC 97-43273. 216p. 1998. pap. text 23.33 (*0-201-69423-9*) Addison-Wesley.

Maher, Bill. Does Anybody Have a Problem with That? The Best of Politically Incorrect. 1997. pap. 10.00 (*0-345-41281-8*) Ballantine Pub Grp.

— Does Anyone Have a Problem. 1996. pap. write for info. (*0-679-77354-1*) Villard Books.

— Politically Incorrect's Greatest Hits. 1996. 12.95 (*0-614-96847-X*) Villard Books.

***Maher, Bill.** True Story. LC 00-25217. (Illus.). 304p. 2000. 22.50 (*0-684-87360-5*) S&S Trade.

Maher, Bill. True Story: A Comedy Novel. 224p. 1994. pap. 12.00 (*0-679-75337-0*) Random.

Maher, Bradford, ed. see Traister, John E.

Maher, Brendan, tr. see From, Franz.

Maher, Brendan A. A Passage to Sword Beach: Minesweeping in the Royal Navy. LC 95-24424. (Illus.). 270p. 1996. 29.95 (*1-55750-572-1*) Naval Inst Pr.

Maher, Brendan A. & Spitzer, Manfred, eds. Philosophy & Psychopathology. xii, 247p. 1990. 63.95 (*0-387-97303-6*) Spr-Verlag.

Maher, Brendan A., jt. ed. see Oltmanns, Thomas F.

Maher, Carolyn A. Math Two. 1981. 20.00 (*0-07-039595-0*) McGraw.

Maher, Charles A., ed. Advances in Psychology & Education, Vol. 1. Date not set. 78.50 (*0-89232-842-8*) Jai Pr.

Maher, Charles A. & Bennett, Randy E. Planning & Evaluating Special Education Services. (Illus.). 288p. (C). 1984. text 21.75 (*0-13-679481-5*) P-H.

Maher, Charles A. & Forman, Susan G., eds. A Behavioral Approach to Education of Children & Youth. (Kratochwill-Yesseldyke School Psychology Ser.). 344p. 1987. text 69.95 (*0-89859-634-3*) L Erlbaum Assocs.

Maher, Charles A., jt. auth. see Bollettieri, Nick.

Maher, Charles A., jt. ed. see Bennett, Randy E.

Maher, Charles A., jt. ed. see Schwebel, Milton.

Maher, Daniel P., ed. The Bishop & the Future of Catholic Health Care: Challenges & Opportunities: Proceedings of the 16th Workshop for Bishops. LC 97-36565. 230p. 1997. pap. 19.95 (*0-935372-41-5*) NCBC.

Maher, E. R., jt. auth. see Hodgson, S. V.

Maher, Eamonn R., jt. auth. see Hodgson, Shirley V.

Maher, Edward R. Pilot's Avionics Survival Guide. (Illus.). 224p. 1994. pap. 19.95 (*0-07-039622-1*) McGraw.

— Pilot's Avionics Survival Guide. LC 93-8051. 1993. pap. 18.95 (*0-8306-4204-8*) McGraw-Hill Prof.

Maher, F. K. & Waller, P. L. Derham, Maher & Waller: An Introduction to Law. 6th ed. xi, 238p. 1991. 45.00 (*0-455-21015-2*, Pub. by LawBk Co); pap. 29.00 (*0-455-21016-0*, Pub. by LawBk Co) Gaunt.

Maher, G. & Cusine, D. J. Law & Practice of Diligence. 500p. 1990. boxed set 108.00 (*0-406-11121-9*, U.K., MICHIE) LEXIS Pub.

Maher, Gerry, jt. auth. see McLean, Sheila A.

Maher, J. Peter. Papers on Language Theory & History I: Creation & Tradition in Language. (Current Issues in Linguistic Theory Ser.: No. 3). xx, 171p. 1979. 48.00 (*90-272-0904-9*) J Benjamins Pubng Co.

Maher, J. Peter, et al, eds. Papers from the Third International Conference on Historical Linguistics, Hamburg, August 22-26, 1977. (Current Issues in Linguistic Theory Ser.: No. 13). xvi, 434p. 1982. 81.00 (*90-272-3505-8*) J Benjamins Pubng Co.

Maher, Jacqueline, et al. The Small Business Guide to Hazardous Materials Management. 200p. 1988. ring bd. 48.00 (*0-9621718-0-8*) WSOS Cmnt Action Com.

Maher, James P. Index to Marriages & Deaths in the New York Herald, 1835-1855. 560p. 35.00 (*0-8063-1184-3*, 3670) Clearfield Co.

Maher, Jane. Mina P. Shaughnessy: Her Life & Work. LC 96-37306. (Illus.). 331p. (Orig.). 1997. pap. 25.95 (*0-8141-5029-2*) NCTE.

— One Step More: The Life & Work of Father Joseph C. Martin. (Illus.). 272p. 1998. 35.00 (*0-9661760-0-6*); pap. 20.00 (*0-9661760-1-4*) Ashley Press.

— Seeing Language in Sign: The Work of William C. Stokoe. LC 95-46906. 216p. 1996. 24.95 (*1-56368-053-X*) Gallaudet Univ Pr.

Maher, Jim. Harry Boland: A Biography. LC 99-197410. 1999. pap. 15.95 (*1-85635-236-6*) Mercier Pr.

Maher, John. Introducing Chomsky. LC 96-61111. 1997. pap. 10.95 (*1-874166-42-0*, Pub. by Totem Bks) Natl Bk Netwk.

— Introducing Chomsky. 1997. pap. 10.95 (*0-614-27594-6*) Totem Pubns.

Maher, John, ed. Music U. S. A., 1998: Statistical Review of the Music Products Industry. (Illus.). 72p. 1998. pap. text 45.00 (*0-9641677-4-3*) Natl Music Merchants.

***Maher, John, ed.** Music U. S. A., 1999: Statistical Review of the Music Products Industry. (Illus.). 48p. 1999. pap. text 45.00 (*0-9641677-5-1*) Natl Music Merchants.

— Music USA 2000: Statistical Review of the Music Products Industry. (Illus.). 48p. 2000. pap. text 45.00 (*0-9641677-6-X*) Natl Music Merchants.

Maher, John & Briggs, Dennie, eds. An Open Life: Joseph Campbell in Conversation with Michael Toms. LC 88-51185. (Illus.). 144p. (Orig.). 1988. pap. 9.95 (*0-943914-47-7*) Larson Pubns.

Maher, John, jt. auth. see Hoy, Mark.

Maher, John C. International Medical Communication. LC 91-36916. 200p. (C). 1992. pap. text 16.95 (*0-472-08174-8*, 08174) U of Mich Pr.

Maher, John C. & Macdonald, Gaynor, eds. Diversity in Japanese Culture & Language. LC 94-44932. (Japanese Studies). 240p. 1995. 76.50 (*0-7103-0477-3*) Routledge.

Maher, John C. & Yashiro, Kyoko, eds. Multilingual Japan. 180p. 1995. 59.00 (*1-85359-287-0*, Pub. by Multilingual Matters) Taylor & Francis.

Maher, John E. Thinker, Sailor, Brother, Spy. 330p. (Orig.). 1995. pap. 10.00 (*0-9643121-0-7*) Maher & Maher.

Maher, John F., ed. Replacement of Renal Function by Dialysis: A Textbook of Dialysis. 3rd enl. ed. (C). 1989. text 420.50 (*0-89838-414-1*) Kluwer Academic.

Maher, John T., et al. Maritime Litigation. LC 94-34469. 1994. ring bd. 100.00 (*0-250-40734-5*, MICHIE) LEXIS Pub.

Maher, Karen J., jt. auth. see Lord, Robert G.

Maher, Kathleen M., jt. auth. see Healy, Phyllis F.

Maher, Larry. The Mulligan's Complete Golf Etiquette Handbook. Bicknell, Robert, ed. LC 95-194865. (Illus.). 64p. 1995. pap. 8.95 (*0-9646234-0-4*) Happy Ft Creat.

Maher, Lisa. Sexed Work: Gender, Race & Resistance in a Brooklyn Drug Market. LC 97-8002. (Clarendon Studies in Criminology). 294p. (C). 1997. text 55.00 (*0-19-826495-X*, Clarendon Pr) OUP.

***Maher, Lisa.** Sexed Work: Gender, Race, & Resistance in a Brooklyn Drug Market. (Clarendon Studies in Criminology). 294p. 2000. pap. 19.95 (*0-19-829931-1*) OUP.

Maher, Lisa, jt. ed. see Daly, Kathleen.

Maher, M., et al, eds. Principles & Practice of Constraint Programming, CP98: 4th International Conference, CP98, Pisa, Italy, October 26-30, 1998, Proceedings. LC 98-44829. (Lecture Notes in Computer Science Ser.: Vol. 1520). 482p. 1998. pap. 69.00 (*3-540-65224-8*) Spr-Verlag.

Maher, Marie B. Flight for Life. Silvestro, Denise, ed. (Illus.). 232p. (Orig.). 1993. mass mkt. 5.99 (*0-671-74464-X*) PB.

Maher, Mary & Cruise-O'Brien, Kate, eds. In Sunshine or in Shadow: Stories by Irish Women. 336p. 1999. pap. 12.95 (*0-385-33335-8*) Dell.

Maher, Mary D. To Bind up the Wounds: Catholic Sister Nurses in the U. S. Civil War. LC 99-33889. (Illus.). 200p. 1999. pap. 14.95 (*0-8071-2439-7*) La State U Pr.

— To Bind up the Wounds: Catholic Sister Nurses in the U. S. Civil War, 107. LC 89-2217. (Contributions in Women's Studies: No. 107). 188p. 1989. 45.00 (*0-313-26458-9*, MRM/, Greenwood Pr) Greenwood.

Maher, Mary L., ed. Expert Systems for Civil Engineers: Technology & Application. 170p. 1987. 28.00 (*0-87262-617-2*) Am Soc Civil Eng.

Maher, Mary L. & Pu, Pearl, eds. Issues & Applications of Case Based Reasoning to Design. LC 96-49426. 376p. 1997. 79.95 (*0-8058-2312-3*); pap. 39.95 (*0-8058-2313-1*) L Erlbaum Assocs.

An Asterisk (*) at the beginning of an entry indicates that the title is appearing for the first time.

Maher, Mary L., et al. Case-Based Reasoning in Design. 256p. 1995. text 59.95 (*0-8058-1831-6*); pap. text 29.95 (*0-8058-1832-4*) L Erlbaum Assocs.

Maher, Mary L., jt. ed. see Gero, John S.

Maher, Mary L., jt. ed. see Kostem, Celal N.

Maher, Mary L., jt. ed. see Mohan, Satish.

***Maher, Mary Lou, et al.** Understanding Virtual Design Studios. LC 99-31322. (Computer Supported Cooperative Work Ser.). (Illus.). 245p. 1999. 54.00 (*1-85233-154-2*) Spr-Verlag.

Maher, Mary M. The Places We Save: Wisconsin Chapter of the Nature Conservancy. (Illus.). 88p. (Orig.). 1988. pap. text 11.95 (*0-9619854-0-2*) Nat Conserv WI.

Maher, Mary Z. Modern Hamlets & Their Soliloquies. LC 92-12900. (Studies in Theatre History & Culture). (Illus.). 258p. 1992. pap. 14.95 (*0-87745-504-X*) U of Iowa Pr.

— Modern Hamlets & Their Soliloquies. LC 92-12900. (Studies in Theatre History & Culture). (Illus.). 258p. 1992. 32.95 (*0-87745-380-2*) U of Iowa Pr.

Maher, Michael. Cost Accounting. 4th ed. 1993. pap. text, teacher ed. 52.50 (*0-256-12422-1*) McGraw.

— Cost Accounting. 5th ed. (C). 1996. text 94.00 (*0-256-26720-0*) McGraw.

— Cost Accounting. 5th ed. (C). 1997. pap., student ed. 31.25 (*0-256-17002-9*) McGraw.

— Cost Accounting. 5th ed. 1997. pap. text, teacher ed. write for info. (*0-256-17004-5*) McGraw.

— Lieutenants: The Evolution of Political Style. LC 90-39105. 208p. 1990. 55.00 (*0-275-93461-6*, C3461, Praeger Pubs) Greenwood.

— The Targum Pseudo - Jonathan: Genesis. (Aramaic Bible Ser.: No. 1B). 256p. (Orig.). 1992. 65.00 (*0-8146-5492-4*) Liturgical Pr.

Maher, Michael, ed. Logic Programming: Proceedings of the 13th 1996 Joint International Conference & Symposium on Logic Programming, September 2-6, 1996, Bonn, Germany. (Logic Programming Ser.). (Illus.). 576p. 1996. pap. text 85.00 (*0-262-63173-3*) MIT Pr.

Maher, Michael, jt. ed. see Cathcart, Kevin J.

Maher, Michael J., ed. Science & Cultivation of Edible Fungi: Proceedings of the Thirteenth International Congress, Dublin, 1-6 September 1991, 2 vols. (Illus.). 880p. 1991. text 181.00 (*90-5410-021-4*, Pub. by A A Balkema) Ashgate Pub Co.

Maher, Michael W. Cost Accounting. 5th ed. LC 96-44028. 896p. (C). 1996. text 71.50 (*0-256-17001-0*, Irwn McGrw-H) McGrw-H Hghr Educ.

— Cost Accounting Ready Notes. 5th ed. (C). 1997. text 22.50 (*0-256-24429-4*, Irwn McGrw-H) McGrw-H Hghr Educ.

— Managerial Accounting. 6th ed. LC 96-85709. (C). 1996. text 94.50 (*0-03-018193-3*, Pub. by Harcourt Coll Pubs) Harcourt.

— Managerial Accounting. 6th ed. (C). 1997. pap. text, teacher ed. 42.00 (*0-03-018194-1*) Harcourt Coll Pubs.

Maher, Michael W. & Deakin, Edward. Cost Accounting. 4th ed. 1016p. (C). 1993. text 71.50 (*0-256-11657-1*, Irwn McGrw-H) McGrw-H Hghr Educ.

— Cost Accounting, International. 3rd ed. (C). 1991. text, student ed. 30.95 (*0-256-11407-2*, Irwn McGrw-H) McGrw-H Hghr Educ.

Maher, Michael W. & Deakin, Edward B. Cost Accounting. 4th ed. 304p. (C). 1994. text 28.75 (*0-256-12416-7*, Irwn McGrw-H) McGrw-H Hghr Educ.

— Cost Accounting. 4th ed. (C). 1996. text 48.50 (*0-256-25711-6*, Irwn McGrw-H) McGrw-H Hghr Educ.

Maher, Michael W., jt. ed. see Donnelly, John P.

Maher Mooney, Bernice. Salt of the Earth: The History of the Catholic Church in Utah, 1776- 1987. 2nd rev. ed. (Illus.). 546p. 1992. 15.00 (*0-9619627-1-2*) Catholic Diocese SLC.

Maher, Patrick. Betting on Theories. LC 92-13817. (Studies in Probability, Induction & Decision Theory). 323p. (C). 1993. text 74.95 (*0-521-41850-X*) Cambridge U Pr.

Maher, Patrick T. Assessor Training Manual for Public Sector Assessment Centers. 2nd ed. LC 93-84900. 225p. (C). 1993. text 99.95 (*0-943865-00-X*); pap. text 59.95 (*0-943865-01-8*) Persnl & Org Dev.

— Designing Emergency Scene Simulations for Police & Fire Promotional Examinations. 65p. (C). 1993. pap. text 14.95 (*0-943865-02-6*) Persnl & Org Dev.

Maher, Patrick T. & Michelson, Richard S. Preparing for Fire Service Assessment Centers. 115p. 1992. 21.95 (*0-941943-04-6*, 35597) Fire Pubns.

***Maher, Paul A., Jr.** The Seeds of Galloway: Jack Kerouac's Lowell. (Illus.). 32p. 1999. pap. 4.95 (*1-888213-43-4*) Eastern National.

Maher, Peter J., jt. auth. see Danielsen, Niels.

Maher, Richard. Roald Dahl Quiz Book, Over 300 Questions to Challenge Dahl Fans Everywhere. (J). 1997. 9.09 (*0-606-11802-0*, Pub. by Turtleback) Demco.

Maher, Richard & Bond, Sylvia. Roald Dahl Quiz Book: Over 300 Questions to Challenge Dahl Fans Everywhere. (Illus.). 128p. 1997. pap. 3.99 (*0-14-038477-4*, PuffinBks) Peng Put Young Read.

***Maher, Robert A. & Wise, James E.** Sailors' Journey into War. LC 97-30538. (Illus.). 210p. 1998. 30.00 (*0-87338-583-7*) Kent St U Pr.

Maher, Susan M. An Overview of Solutions to Breastfeeding & Sucking Problems. 32p. 1988. pap. 6.50 (*0-912500-31-X*) La Leche.

Maher, Thomas K. The Jarvie Shop: The Candlesticks & Metalwork of Robert R. Jarvie. Gray, Stephen, ed. (Illus.). (Orig.). 1997. pap. 17.50 (*0-940326-20-5*) Turn of Cent.

Maher, Thomas K., jt. auth. see Rudolf, David S.

Maher, Tod & Gill, Bob, eds. Pro Football Encyclopedia: The Complete & Definitive Record of Professional Football. 1467p. 1997. 44.95 (*0-02-861989-7*) Macmillan.

Maher, Vanessa A., ed. The Anthropology of Breast-Feeding: Natural Law or Social Construct. 224p. 1992. pap. 16.00 (*0-85496-814-8*, Pub. by Berg Pubs) NYU Pr.

Maher, William J. The Management of College & University Archives. LC 92-11667. (Society of American Archivists Ser.). (Illus.). 430p. 1992. 52.00 (*0-8108-2568-6*) Scarecrow.

Maher, William L. A Shepherd in Combat Boots: Chaplain Emil Kapaun of the 1st Cavalry Division. LC 97-19800. 199p. 1997. 24.95 (*1-57249-069-1*, Burd St Pr) White Mane Pub.

Maher, Winifred B., jt. auth. see Appley, Mortimer H.

Mahesh. Microsoft MS-DOS & Windows. (DF-Computer Applications Ser.). 1996. mass mkt., wbk. ed. 12.75 (*0-314-09340-0*) S-W Pub.

Mahesh, Kavi, ed. Natural Language Processing for the World Wide Web: Papers from the 1997 Spring Symposium. (Technical Reports). (Illus.). 158p. 1997. spiral bd. 25.00 (*1-57735-025-1*) AAAI Pr.

Mahesh, Virendra B., et al, eds. Regulation of Ovarian & Testicular Function. LC 87-22073. (Advances in Experimental Medicine & Biology Ser.: Vol. 219). (Illus.). 774p. 1987. 135.00 (*0-306-42676-5*, Plenum Trade) Perseus Pubng.

Mahesh, Virendra B., jt. ed. see Brann, Darrell W.

Maheshri, Jagdish C. It's All in Timing. LC 97-65522. 112p. 1997. 17.95 (*1-56167-353-6*) Noble Hse MD.

Maheshsvari. My Body Is My Planet: Surfing the Cosmic Wave. Cline, Jeff & Cline, C., eds. LC 97-92812. (Illus.). 200p. 1998. pap. 19.95 (*1-892009-00-5*) Maheshsvari Pub.

Maheshwar, ed. see Aurobindo, Sri.

Maheshwari, Anil. Crescent over Kashmir: Politics of Mullaism. (C). 1993. 19.50 (*81-7167-157-8*, Pub. by Rupa) S Asia.

Maheshwari, Anil, ed. see Husain, Zakir.

Maheshwari, B. B. India & Sri Lanka: Economic Relations. 1987. 26.00 (*0-8364-2245-7*, Pub. by Agam) S Asia.

Maheshwari, J. K. Ethnobotany in South Asia. 1996. pap. 300.00 (*81-7233-143-6*, Pub. by Scientific Pubs) St Mut.

— Orchids in India. 1995. pap. 240.00 (*81-7233-330-7*, Pub. by Scientific Pubs) St Mut.

***Maheshwari, Naresh & Sapatnekar, Stachin.** Timing Analysis & Optimization of Sequential Circuits. LC 98-42471. 13p. 1998. 98.00 (*0-7923-8321-4*) Kluwer Academic.

Maheshwari, Naresh K., jt. auth. see Sharma, R. S.

Maheshwari, R. P. A Complete Course in ISC Commerce, Vol. 1. 240p. 1997. pap. 50.00 (*81-209-0447-8*, Pub. by Pitambar Pub) St Mut.

— A Complete Course in ISC Commerce, Vol. 2. 196p. 1997. pap. 70.00 (*81-209-0643-8*, Pub. by Pitambar Pub) St Mut.

— Principles of Business Studies, Vol. 1. 448p. 1997. pap. 61.50 (*81-209-0188-6*, Pub. by Pitambar Pub) St Mut.

— Principles of Business Studies, Vol. 2. 256p. 1997. pap. 40.00 (*81-209-0189-4*, Pub. by Pitambar Pub) St Mut.

— Principles of Functional Management. 284p. 1997. pap. 55.00 (*81-209-0448-6*, Pub. by Pitambar Pub) St Mut.

Maheshwari, R. P. & Singh, B. Principles & Practice of Auditing. 624p. 1988. 70.00 (*81-209-0002-2*, Pub. by Pitambar Pub) St Mut.

Maheshwari, S. N. Advanced Accountancy, Vol. 1. 1995. 40.00 (*0-7069-8987-2*, Pub. by Vikas); pap. 18.00 (*0-7069-9767-0*, Pub. by Vikas) S Asia.

— Advanced Accountancy, Vol. 2. 1995. 40.00 (*0-7069-8988-0*, Pub. by Vikas); pap. 18.00 (*0-7069-9911-8*, Pub. by Vikas) S Asia.

Maheshwari, S. N., ed. Foundations of Software Technology & Theoretical Computer Science. (Lecture Notes in Computer Science Ser.: Vol. 206). ix, 522p. 1985. 49.00 (*0-387-16042-6*) Spr-Verlag.

Maheshwari, S. R. Mandal Commision & Mandalisation: A Critique. (C). 1990. text 21.00 (*81-7022-338-5*, Pub. by Concept) S Asia.

Maheshwari, Shriman. The Higher Civil Service in France. (C). 1991. 17.50 (*81-7023-289-9*, Pub. by Allied Pubs) S Asia.

— President's Rule in India. 1977. 12.50 (*0-88386-985-3*) S Asia.

Maheshwari, Shriram. Rural Development in India: A Public Policy Approach. 2nd ed. LC 94-34877. 280p. 1995. text 24.95 (*0-8039-9209-2*) Sage.

Maheshwary, Sharda, jt. auth. see Gupta, Virendra K.

Mahesvarananda, Paramhansa Syami. Meetings with a Yogi. (C). 1994. 16.00 (*81-7018-795-8*, Pub. by BR Pub) S Asia.

Maheswar, Neg. Early History of the Vaisnava Faith & Movement in Assam: Sankaradeva & His Times. xx, 400p. 1986. 38.00 (*81-208-0007-9*, Pub. by Motilal Bnarsidass) S Asia.

Maheswari, C. S. Uma, see Uma Maheswari, C. S.

Maheu, Louis. Social Movements & Social Classes. 272p. 1995. text 75.00 (*0-8039-7952-5*) Sage.

Maheu, Louis, ed. Social Movements & Social Classes: The Future of Collective Action. (Studies in International Sociology: Vol. 46). 296p. 1995. pap. 26.95 (*0-8039-7953-3*) Sage.

Maheux, Anne F. Degas Pastels. (Illus.). 96p. 1988. pap. 19.95 (*0-88884-547-2*, Pub. by Natl Gallery) U Ch Pr.

Maheux, R., jt. ed. see Lemay, A.

***Mahew, Bradley, et al.** Lonely Planet Indian Himalaya. 2nd ed. (Illus.). 496p. 2000. pap. 19.95 (*0-86442-688-7*) Lonely Planet.

Mahfood, Phillip E. The Customer Crisis: Turning an Unhappy Customer into a Life-Long Client. 200p. 1993. text 24.95 (*1-55738-421-5*, Irwn Prfssnl) McGraw-Hill Prof.

Mahfouz, Afaf M., jt. ed. see Serageldin, Ismail.

Mahfouz, Afaf M., jt. ed. see Smith, Joseph H.

Mahfouz, Naguib. Adrift on the Nile. 176p. 1993. 13.99 (*0-385-40336-4*) Doubleday.

— Adrift on the Nile. 176p. 1994. pap. 7.99 (*0-385-40473-5*) Doubleday.

***Mahfouz, Naguib.** Akhenaten: Dweller in Truth. 1999. 19.95 (*977-424-470-2*, Pub. by Am Univ Cairo Pr) Col U Pr.

Mahfouz, Naguib. Al Tareeq: The Road. (ARA.). 150p. pap. 8.95 (*0-86685-152-6*, LDL533, Pub. by Librairie du Liban) Intl Bk Ctr.

— Arabian Nights & Days. 240p. 1995. 15.99 (*0-385-40451-4*) Doubleday.

— Arabian Nights & Days. (ARA.). 240p. 1995. reprint ed. pap. 12.95 (*0-385-46901-2*, Anchor NY) Doubleday.

— Assamman wal Khareef: Autumn Quail. (ARA.). 246p. pap. 8.95 (*0-86685-162-3*, LDL541, Pub. by Librairie du Liban) Intl Bk Ctr.

— The Beggar: Al Shahad. (ARA.). 1985. pap. 8.95 (*0-86685-151-8*) Intl Bk Ctr.

— The Beginning & the End. 416p. 1989. pap. 11.95 (*0-385-26458-5*) Doubleday.

— Bidaya Bila Nihaya: Beginning Without End. (ARA.). pap. 8.95 (*0-86685-155-0*, LDL545, Pub. by Librairie du Liban) Intl Bk Ctr.

— Bidayah Wal Nahayah: Beginning & the End. (ARA.). 200p. pap. 8.95 (*0-86685-153-4*, LDL534, Pub. by Librairie du Liban) Intl Bk Ctr.

— Children of Gebelaawi. 3rd rev. ed. Stewart, Philip, tr. from ARA. LC 94-45586. 403p. 1997. reprint ed. pap. 16.00 (*1-57889-038-1*) Passeggiata.

— Children of the Alley. Theroux, Peter, tr.Tr. of Awlad al-Haratina. 464p. 1996. pap. 14.00 (*0-385-26473-9*, Anchor NY) Doubleday.

— Collection of His Famous Works, Vol. I. (ARA.). 880p. 1990. 39.95 (*0-86685-424-X*, LDL727X, Pub. by Librairie du Liban) Intl Bk Ctr.

— Collection of His Famous Works, Vol. II. (ARA.). 880p. 1990. 39.95 (*0-86685-725-7*, LDL727Y, Pub. by Librairie du Liban) Intl Bk Ctr.

— Collection of His Famous Works, Vol. III. (ARA.). 880p. 1993. 39.95 (*0-86685-739-7*, LDL727Z, Pub. by Librairie du Liban) Intl Bk Ctr.

— Collection of His Famous Works, Vol. IV. (ARA.). 880p. 1994. 39.95 (*0-86685-328-6*, LDL727W, Pub. by Librairie du Liban) Intl Bk Ctr.

Mahfouz, Naguib. Collection of Naguib Mahfouz, Vol. 4. (ARA.). 880p. 39.95 (*0-86685-740-0*) Intl Bk Ctr.

Mahfouz, Naguib. The Crime: Al Jar'imah. (ARA.). 1985. pap. 9.95 (*0-86685-147-X*) Intl Bk Ctr.

***Mahfouz, Naguib.** Day the Leader Was Killed. 1999. 14.95 (*977-424-454-0*, Pub. by Am Univ Cairo Pr) Col U Pr.

— Day the Leader Was Killed. LC 00-24572. 112p. 2000. pap. 11.00 (*0-385-49922-1*, Anchor NY) Doubleday.

Mahfouz, Naguib. Echoes of an Autobiography. Johnson-Davies, Denys, tr. 144p. 1997. pap. 12.00 (*0-385-48556-5*, Anchor NY) Doubleday.

— Fountain & Tomb. Kenneson, James et al, trs. LC 86-51004.Tr. of Hakayat Haretna. (Illus.). 120p. (C). 1988. reprint ed. pap. 12.00 (*0-89410-581-7*, Three Contnts) L Rienner.

— God's World: An Anthology of Short Stories. Abadir, Akef & Allen, Roger, trs. LC 73-79201. (Studies in Middle Eastern Literatures: No. 2). 1973. pap. 16.00 (*0-88297-044-5*) Bibliotheca.

— The Harafish. Orig. Title: Malhamat al-Harafish. 416p. 1995. pap. 9.99 (*0-385-40583-9*) Doubleday.

— The Harafish. Cobham, Catherine, tr. from ARA. LC 94-38311. Orig. Title: Malhamat al-Harafish. 416p. 1997. pap. 14.00 (*0-385-42335-7*, Anchor NY) Doubleday.

— Harafish. 416p. 1994. 15.99 (*0-385-40362-3*) Doubleday.

— Kamart Quet Kaswaa: Tales of the Black Cat Tavern. (ARA.). 165p. pap. 7.95 (*0-86685-157-7*, LDL536, Pub. by Librairie du Liban) Intl Bk Ctr.

— Khan el Khalili: Novel in Arabic. 1987. pap. 8.95 (*0-86685-177-1*) Intl Bk Ctr.

— Love in the Rain: Hebeh Tahtal Matar. (ARA.). pap. 9.95 (*0-86685-154-2*) Intl Bk Ctr.

— Midaq Alley. 304p. 1991. pap. 12.95 (*0-385-26476-3*, Anchor NY) Doubleday.

— Midaq Alley. 304p. 1992. pap. 7.99 (*0-385-26940-4*) Doubleday.

— Miramar. 2nd enl. ed. Moussa-Mahmoud, Fatma, tr. LC 89-20627. (ARA.). 156p. 1996. reprint ed. pap. 12.00 (*1-57889-037-3*) Passeggiata.

— Miramar: U. K. Edition. 192p. 1993. pap. 7.99 (*0-385-26941-2*) Doubleday.

— Mirrors. Allen, Roger, tr. LC 76-47306. 1977. pap. 16.00 (*0-88297-016-X*) Bibliotheca.

— Palace of Desire. (Cairo Trilogy Ser.: 2). 432p. 1991. pap. 12.95 (*0-385-26468-2*, Anchor NY) Doubleday.

— Palace of Desire. 432p. 1992. pap. 8.95 (*0-385-40208-2*) Doubleday.

— Palace Walk. (Cairo Trilogy Ser.: 1). 512p. 1990. pap. 14.00 (*0-385-26466-6*, Anchor NY) Doubleday.

— Shahre Assal: The Honeymoon. (ARA.). pap. 8.95 (*0-86685-161-5*, LDL540, Pub. by Librairie du Liban) Intl Bk Ctr.

— Stories of the Neighborhood (Hekayat Haretna) (Novel in Arabic) (ARA.). 1982. pap. 9.95 (*0-86685-156-9*) Intl Bk Ctr.

— Sugar Street. 320p. 1993. pap. 8.99 (*0-385-40306-2*, Anchor NY) Doubleday.

— Sugar Street, Vol. III. Hutchins, William M., tr. LC 92-25362. (Cairo Trilogy Ser.: Vol. 3). 320p. 1992. pap. 12.95 (*0-385-26470-4*, Anchor NY) Doubleday.

— Tales of New Cairo: Qahira Al Jadida. pap. 8.95 (*0-86685-150-X*) Intl Bk Ctr.

— The Thief & the Dogs: Les Wil Kelab. (ARA.). 1976. pap. 9.95 (*0-86685-158-5*) Intl Bk Ctr.

***Mahfouz, Naguib.** Three by Mahfouz, Vol. 2. 2001. pap. 15.00 (*0-385-49836-5*, Pub. by Doubleday) Random House.

— Three by Mahfouz: The Beggar, the Thief & the Dogs, Autumn Quail. 480p. 2000. pap. 16.00 (*0-385-49835-7*) Doubleday.

Mahfouz, Naguib. Time & the Place. 192p. 1991. pap. 14.99 (*0-385-26938-2*) Doubleday.

— Whisperings on the Nile (Saraarah Fouk el Nil) Arabic Novel. (ARA.). 1976. 8.95 (*0-86685-160-7*) Intl Bk Ctr.

— Zaqaq al Madak: Madaq Alley. (ARA.). 246p. pap. 8.95 (*0-86685-163-1*, LDL542, Pub. by Librairie du Liban) Intl Bk Ctr.

***Mahfouz, Naguib, et al.** Akhenaten: Dweller in Truth. LC 99-56659. 192p. 2000. pap. 12.00 (*0-385-49909-4*, Anchor NY) Doubleday.

***Mahfuz, Najib.** Las Noches de Las Mil y una Noches. (SPA.). 1998. pap. 6.95 (*84-01-42746-0*, Pub. by Plaza) Lectorum Pubns.

Mahgary, Y. El, see Karkainnen, S. & El Mahgary, Y.

Mahi. A Dream: Once upon a Quiet Mind. Poole, Denise, ed. LC 98-60182. 75p. 1998. 10.95 (*1-887472-50-9*) Sunstar Pubng.

— Rediscovering Our Heart. Poole, Denise, ed. LC 98-60180. (Illus.). 200p. 1998. pap. 17.95 (*1-887472-51-7*) Sunstar Pubng.

Mahi Pal. Capital Formation & Employment Generation in Rural India: A Case Study of Saharanpur District (U. P.) LC 99-932590. xiv, 203 p. 1999. write for info. (*81-7099-712-7*, Pub. by Mittal Pubns) S Asia.

M

Mahiau, Louis J. The Plumber's Toolbox Manual. (On-the-Job Reference Ser.). 352p. 1992. pap. text 10.00 (*0-13-683806-5*) P-H.

Mahidhara, R. K., et al, eds. Design & Reliability of Solders & Solder Interconnections. (Illus.). 372p. 1997. 102.00 (*0-87339-354-6*, 3546) Minerals Metals.

— Recent Advancements in Fracture. (Illus.). 300p. 1997. 74.00 (*0-87339-364-3*, 3643) Minerals Metals.

Mahidhara, Rao K., jt. ed. see Taleff, Eric M.

Mahieu, Vincent. The Hunt for the Heart: Selected Tales from the Dutch East Indies. Alibasah, Margaret M., tr. (Oxford in Asia Paperbacks Ser.). 222p. 1996. pap. text 28.00 (*967-65-3098-0*) OUP.

Mahin, Andrew. Grasshoppers & Bushcrickets. (Natural History Ser.: No. 25). (Illus.). 24p. 1988. pap. 5.25 (*0-85263-946-5*, Pub. by Shire Pubns) Parkwest Pubns.

Mahin, Dean B. Olive Branch & Sword: The United States & Mexico, 1845-1848. LC 96-29655. (Illus.). 239p. 1997. lib. bdg. 39.95 (*0-7864-0258-X*) McFarland & Co.

— One War at a Time: The International Dimensions of the American Civil War. LC 99-29912. 1999. write for info. (*1-57488-209-0*) Brasseys.

***Mahin, Dean B.** One War at a Time: The International Dimensions of the American Civil War. 2000. reprint ed. pap. 21.95 (*1-57488-301-1*) Brasseys.

Mahin, Sierra M. Hawaii's Favorite Fish. pap. 4.95 (*0-930492-49-8*) Hawaiian Serv.

Mahinda, Deegalle, jt. ed. see Hoffman, Frank.

Mahindra, Indira. The End Play. LC 94-36001. (Emerging Voices: New International Fiction Ser.). 192p. 1994. 24.95 (*1-56656-175-2*); pap. 11.95 (*1-56656-166-3*) Interlink Pub.

***Mahinto.** Wind Wolf Woman: Road of a Shamian. 590p. 2000. write for info. (*0-9677461-0-8*) S Senness.

Mahipati. Life of Tukaram. Abbott, Justin E., tr. from MAR. 346p. 1986. reprint ed. 12.95 (*81-208-0169-5*, Pub. by Motilal Bnarsidass); reprint ed. pap. 9.50 (*81-208-0170-9*, Pub. by Motilal Bnarsidass) S Asia.

Mahiri, Jabari. The Day They Stole the Letter J. (Illus.). 30p. (Orig.). (J). (gr. 3-5). 1981. pap. 3.95 (*0-88378-084-4*) Third World.

— Shooting for Excellence: What African American Sports Discourse Offers to Discourse in Schools. (C). (gr. 13). 1999. 55.00 (*0-415-90855-8*) Routledge.

***Mahizhnan, Arun & Lee, Tsao Yuan.** Singapore Re-engineering Success. LC 98-837251. 1998. write for info. (*0-19-588479-5*); write for info. (*0-19-588507-4*) OUP.

Mahjan, Bakhtaver S. New Biology & Inherited Diseases. (Illus.). 148p. 1999. pap. text 22.95 (*0-19-564769-6*) OUP.

Mahjoub, Azzam, ed. Adjustment or Delinking? The African Experience. Berrett, A. M., tr. from FRE. LC 89-9027. (UNU Studies in African Political Economy). (Illus.). 272p. (C). 1990. text 62.50 (*0-86232-842-X*, Pub. by St Martin) St Martin.

Mahjoub, Jamal. In the Hour of Signs. (African Writers Ser.). 1996. pap. 13.95 (*0-435-90922-3*, 90922) Heinemann.

— Navigation of a Rainmaker: An Apocalyptic Vision of War-Torn Africa. (African Writers Ser.). 184p. (Orig.). (C). 1989. pap. 9.95 (*0-435-90560-0*) Heinemann.

— Wings of Dust. (African Writers Ser.). 224p. 1994. pap. 9.95 (*0-435-90984-3*, 90984) Heinemann.

Mahjoub, Mohammad-Ja'far, ed. Obayd Zakani: Collected Works. (Persian Text Ser.: No. 2). 544p. 1999. text 48.00 (*0-933273-30-4*, Pub. by Bibliotheca Persica) Eisenbrauns.

Mahl, Alan R., ed. Interpretive Centers for More Effective Education: Proceedings of the Natural Science Center Conference 1971-Saint Paul, Minnesota. (Illus.). (Orig.). 1972. 5.00 (*0-916544-01-X*) Natural Sci Youth.

— Leadership to Meet Our Environmental Crisis: Proceedings of the Natural Science Center Conference 1970 - Dayton Ohio. (NCS Conference Proceedings Ser.). (Illus.). (Orig.). 1971. 5.00 (*0-916544-00-1*) Natural Sci Youth.

Mahl, George. Explorations in Nonverbal & Vocal Behavior. 440p. 1987. 89.95 (*0-89859-757-9*) L Erlbaum Assocs.

An Asterisk (*) at the beginning of an entry indicates that the title is appearing for the first time.

Mahl, Mary R. & Koon, Helene W., eds. The Female Spectator: English Women Writers before 1800. LC 76-26430. 310p. reprint ed. pap. 96.10 (*0-608-13202-0*, 205604600044) Bks Demand.

***Mahl, Thomas E.** Desperate Deception: British Convert Operations in the United States, 1939-1944. 1999. pap. 18.95 (*1-57488-223-6*) Brasseys.

Mahl, Thomas E. Desperate Deception: British Covert Operations in the United States, 1939-44. LC 97-19550. (Intelligence & National Security Library). (Illus.). 257p. 1998. 26.95 (*1-57488-080-2*) Brasseys.

Mahlangu-Ngcobo, Mankekolo. To God Be the Glory: A Celebration of the Life of Bishop Frederick Calhoun James. LC 96-75560. 82p. 1996. 15.95 (*0-9652001-1-6*) Mahlangu-Ngcobo.

Mahlck, jt. auth. see Ross.

Mahlck, Lars O., jt. ed. see Chapman, David W.

Mahle, Benj. Power Teaching. 1989. pap. 9.99 (*0-8224-5192-1*) Fearon Teacher Aids.

Mahlendorf, tr. see Bienek, Horst.

Mahlendorf, Ursula R. The Wellsprings of Literary Creation: An Analysis of Male & Female "Artist Stories" from the German Romantics to the Present. LC 84-72198. (GERM Ser.: Vol. 18). (Illus.). 292p. 1985. 35.00 (*0-938100-34-3*) Camden Hse.

Mahlendorf, Ursula R., jt. auth. see Lerner, Arthur.

Mahler. Annual Edition: Canadian Politics 90/91. (C). 1989. per. write for info. (*0-87967-816-X*) Brown & Benchmark.

***Mahler.** Comparative Politics. 3rd ed. LC 98-51169. 383p. 1999. pap. text 38.67 (*0-13-649195-2*) P-H.

Mahler. History of Modern Jewry. Date not set. 37.50 (*0-85303-041-3*, Pub. by M Vallentine & Co) Intl Spec Bk.

Mahler, Annie, tr. see Antelme, Robert.

Mahler, Daniel. The Public Relations Activities of German Companies in the United States. (ENG & GER.). 1996. 25.00 (*0-86640-056-7*) German Am Chamber.

Mahler, Donald A. Dyspnea. LC 97-42473. (Lung Biology in Health & Disease Ser.) (Illus.). 432p. 1997. text 180.00 (*0-8247-9814-7*) Dekker.

Mahler, Donald A., ed. Pulmonary Disease in the Elderly Patient. LC 92-49321. (Lung Biology in Health & Disease Ser.: Vol. 63). (Illus.). 528p. 1992. text 210.00 (*0-8247-8752-8*) Dekker.

Mahler, Donald A. & American College of Sports Medicine Staff. ACSM's Guidelines for Exercise Testing & Prescription: American College of Sports Medicine. 5th ed. LC 94-40330. (Illus.). 384p. 1995. 25.95 (*0-683-00023-3*) Lppncott W & W.

Mahler, F., et al, eds. Methoden der Klinischen Kapillarmikroskopie. (Illus.). 168p. 1986. pap. 68.75 (*3-8055-4409-X*) S Karger.

— Techniques in Clinical Capillary Microscopy. (Mikrozirkulation in Forschung und Klinik; Progress in Applied Microcirculation Ser.: Vol. 11). (Illus.). xii, 152p. 1986. pap. 68.78 (*3-8055-4327-1*) S Karger.

***Mahler, Ferd.** Under the Painted Eyes: A Story of Nepal. LC 99-936926. 426p. 1999. pap. 175.00 (*81-208-1683-8*, Pub. by Motilal Bnarsidass) St Mut.

Mahler, G. Quantum Networks. (Illus.). 390p. 1995. 79.95 (*3-540-58850-7*) Spr-Verlag.

Mahler, Gregory S. The Knesset: Parliament in the Israeli Political System. LC 80-67633. 256p. 1982. 35.00 (*0-8386-3071-5*) Fairleigh Dickinson.

— New Dimensions of Canadian Federalism. LC 85-46013. 192p. 1987. 36.50 (*0-8386-3289-0*) Fairleigh Dickinson.

Mahler, Gregory S., compiled by. Contemporary Canadian Politics: An Annotated Bibliography, 1970-1987. 10. LC 88-21357. (Bibliographies & Indexes in Law & Political Science Ser.: No. 10). 414p. 1988. lib. bdg. 65.00 (*0-313-25510-5*, MCF/, Greenwood Pr) Greenwood.

Mahler, Gregory S., compiled by. Contemporary Canadian Politics, 1988-1994: An Annotated Bibliography, Vol. 23. LC 95-31621. (Bibliographies Ser.). 232p. 1995. lib. bdg. 75.00 (*0-313-28924-7*, Greenwood Pr) Greenwood.

Mahler, Gregory S., ed. Israel. LC 99-26978. (International Library of Politics & Comparative Government). 480p. 2000. text 157.95 (*1-84014-069-0*, Pub. by Ashgate Pub) Ashgate Pub Co.

— Israel in the Post-Begin Era. (WVSS on Africs & the Middle East Ser.). (C). 1996. text 32.50 (*0-8133-7647-5*) Westview.

— Readings on the Israeli Political System: Structures & Processes. LC 81-40031. 450p. (Orig.). 1982. pap. text 37.00 (*0-8191-2118-5*) U Pr of Amer.

Mahler, Gregory S. & Karsh, Efraim, eds. Israel at the Crossroads. 256p. 1994. text 59.50 (*1-85043-731-9*, Pub. by I B T) St Martin.

Mahler, Gregory S. & March, Roman R. Canadian Politics, 98-99. 4th ed. (Annual Ser.). (Illus.). 240p. 1998. pap. text 12.25 (*0-07-292513-2*, Dshkn McG-Hill) McGrw-H Hghr Educ.

Mahler, Gregory S., jt. auth. see Lazin, Frederick A.

Mahler, Gunter, et al, eds. Molecular Electronics: Properties, Dynamics & Applications. (Illus.). 424p. 1996. text 175.00 (*0-8247-9526-1*) Dekker.

Mahler, Gunter & Weberrub, V. A. Quantum Networks: Dynamics of Open Nanostructures. 2nd enl. rev. ed. LC 98-12039. (Illus.). xviii, 411p. 1998. 59.95 (*3-540-63668-4*) Spr-Verlag.

***Mahler, Gustav.** Des Knaben Wunderhorn & the Ruckert Lieder for Voice & Piano. 1999. pap. text 14.95 (*0-486-40634-2*) Dover.

Mahler, Gustav. Das Lied von der Erde in Full Score. 160p. 1988. pap. 9.95 (*0-486-25657-X*) Dover.

— Songs of a Wayfarer & Kindertotenlieder in Full Score. 160p. 1990. pap. 9.95 (*0-486-26318-5*) Dover.

— Symphonies Nos. 5 & 6 in Full Score. 512p. 1992. pap. 21.95 (*0-486-26888-8*) Dover.

— Symphonies Nos. 1 & 2 in Full Score. 384p. 1987. pap. 14.95 (*0-486-25473-9*) Dover.

— Symphonies Nos. 3 & 4 in Full Score. 368p. 1990. pap. 16.95 (*0-486-26166-2*) Dover.

— Symphony No. 8 in Full Score. 272p. 1989. pap. 12.95 (*0-486-26022-4*) Dover.

— Symphony No. 5 in C-Sharp Minor. 256p. Date not set. 4.95 (*0-486-40115-4*) Dover.

— Symphony No. 9 in Full Score. 192p. 1993. pap. 9.95 (*0-486-27492-6*) Dover.

— Symphony No. 7 in Full Score. (GER.). 272p. 1992. pap. 13.95 (*0-486-27339-3*) Dover.

***Mahler, Gustav.** Symphony No. 4 in G Major for Soprano & Orchestra. 2000. pap. 4.95 (*0-486-41170-2*) Dover.

— Symphony Number 2 in C Minor. 1998. 4.95 (*0-486-29952-X*, 741737Q) Dover.

Mahler, Gustav. Three Song Cycles in Vocal Score: Songs of a Wayfarer, Kindertotemieder & das Lied von der Erde. 160p. 1992. pap. 10.95 (*0-486-26954-X*) Dover.

Mahler, Gustav & Strauss, Richard. Gustav Mahler-Richard Strauss: Correspondence, 1887-1911. Blaukopf, Herta, ed. (Illus.). 172p. (C). 1996. reprint ed. pap. text 14.95 (*0-226-05768-2*) U Ch Pr.

Mahler, Gustav, jt. auth. see Brahms.

Mahler, Henry. Legendary America. LC 95-60855. (YA). (gr. 7-12). 1995. 10.00 (*0-9638455-2-7*) Warwick Hse.

Mahler, Julianne. Agency Learning. (Theoretical Lenses on Public Policy Ser.). 256p. 1999. 60.00 (*0-8133-6683-6*); pap. 23.00 (*0-8133-6684-4*) Westview.

Mahler, Margaret S. Infantile Psychosis & Early Contribution Vol. 1: The Selected Papers of Margaret S. Mahler. LC 79-51915. 334p. 1995. pap. text 55.00 (*1-56821-421-9*) Aronson.

***Mahler, Margaret S.** Psychological Birth of the Human Infant: Symbiosis & Individuation. (Illus.). 2000. pap. 27.50 (*0-465-09554-2*, Pub. by Basic) HarpC.

Mahler, Margaret S. Separation-Individuation Vol. 2: The Selected Papers of Margaret S. Mahler, Vol. 2. LC 94-70014. 272p. 1995. reprint ed. pap. 50.00 (*1-56821-224-0*) Aronson.

Mahler, Margaret S. & Furer, Manuel. On Human Symbiosis & the Vicissitudes of Individuation Vol. 1: Infantile Psychoses. LC 68-24453. 271p. 1968. 45.00 (*0-8236-3780-8*) Intl Univs Pr.

Mahler, Margaret S., et al. The Psychological Birth of the Human Infant. LC 74-77255. 320p. 1975. pap. 37.50 (*0-465-06659-3*, Pub. by Basic) HarpC.

Mahler, Michael D. Dictionary of Spanish Slang. (SPA & ENG.). 304p. 1999. pap. 8.95 (*0-7641-0619-8*) Barron.

— Ringed in Steel. 256p. 1987. mass mkt. 4.99 (*0-515-09074-3*, Jove) Berkley Pub.

— Ringed in Steel: Armored Cavalry, Vietnam, 1967-68. 224p. 1998. pap. 15.95 (*0-89141-674-9*, Pub. by Presidio Pr) Natl Bk Netwk.

— United States Civil War Revenue Stamp Taxes. LC 88-72215. (C. & S. Revenue Ser.). (Illus.). 384p. 1988. 49.95 (*0-9603498-3-9*) Castenholz Sons.

Mahler, Paul. Building Distributed System. 300p. (C). 2001. pap. 24.95 (*0-13-230590-9*) P-H.

Mahler, Philip H. & Wesner, Terry H. Intermediate Algebra with Early Graphing & Functions. 4th alternate ed. 160p. (C). 1996. student ed., per. write for info. (*0-697-25733-9*, WCB McGr Hill) McGrw-H Hghr Educ.

Mahler, Philip H., et al. Intermediate Algebra with Early Graphing & Functions. 4th ed. 688p. (C). 1995. text. write for info. (*0-697-24938-7*, WCB McGr Hill) McGrw-H Hghr Educ.

— Precalculus with Applications. 608p. (C). 1995. text 30.00 (*0-697-11656-5*, WCB McGr Hill) McGrw-H Hghr Educ.

Mahler, Richard. Adventures in Nature: Belize. 2nd rev. ed. LC 99-18072. (Adventures in Nature Ser.). (Illus.). 408p. 1999. pap. 18.95 (*1-56261-431-2*) Avalon Travel.

— Adventures in Nature: Guatemala. 2nd rev. ed. LC 99-18064. (Adventures in Nature Ser.). (Illus.). 408p. 1999. pap. 18.95 (*1-56261-430-4*) Avalon Travel.

— New Mexico's Best. (Illus.). 240p. 1996. pap. 15.95 (*1-55591-232-X*) Fulcrum Pub.

Mahler, Richard, jt. auth. see Goldman, Connie.

Mahler, Richard, jt. contrib. by see Goldman, Connie.

Mahler, Roger, jt. auth. see Nasr, Jimmy.

Mahler, Roland. Verantwortung der Freiheit: Eine Hermeneutische Untersuchung Zum Problem Theologischen Umganges Mit Wirklichkeit. (Europaische Hochschulschriften Ser.: Reihe 23, Bd. 474). (GER.). 248p. 1993. 38.80 (*3-906750-67-1*, Pub. by P Lang) P Lang Pubng.

Mahler, Sarah J. American Dreaming: Immigrant Life on the Margins. LC 95-13473. 256p. 1995. text 49.50 (*0-691-03783-3*, Pub. by Princeton U Pr); pap. text 16.95 (*0-691-03782-5*, Pub. by Princeton U Pr) Cal Prin Full Svc.

— Salvadorans in Suburbia: Symbiosis & Conflict. Foner, Nancy, ed. LC 96-170288. (New Immigrants Ser.). 100p. (C). 1996. pap. 20.00 (*0-205-16737-3*) Allyn.

Mahler, Vincent A. Dependency Approaches to International Political Economy: A Cross-National Study. LC 79-26200. 1980. text 52.50 (*0-231-04836-X*) Col U Pr.

Mahler, Walter R. Diversified Company: An Endangered Species. 1992. 24.95 (*0-914431-03-X*) Mahler Pub Co.

Mahler, Walter R. & Drotter, Stephen J. Succession Planning Handbook for the Chief Executive. 300p. 1986. 45.00 (*0-914431-01-3*) Mahler Pub Co.

Mahler, Walter R. & Moss, Robert. The Highly Diversified Company. 360p. 1989. write for info. (*0-318-65383-4*) Mahler Pub Co.

***Mahler-Werfel, Alma.** Diaries, 1898-1902. (Illus.). 494p. 2000. pap. text 20.00 (*0-8014-8664-5*) Cornell U Pr.

Mahler-Werfel, Alma. The Diaries, 1898-1902. Beaumont, Antony & Rode-Breymann, Susanne, eds. Beaumont, Anthony, tr. LC 98-42165. (Illus.). 1999. 35.00 (*0-8014-3654-0*) Cornell U Pr.

Mahley, Mary J. & McCoy, Toni. The Rock Beneath Vol. 1: 100 Years Ago in Webster Groves. LC 96-86511. (Illus.). 195p. (Orig.). 1996. pap. 29.95 (*0-9654641-0-5*) Century Registry.

Mahlke, G. & Goessing, P. Fiber Optic Cables: Fundamentals, Cable Engineering, Systems Planning. 3rd ed. LC TA1800.L5313 1997. 276p. 1997. 99.95 (*3-89578-068-5*) Wiley.

Mahlknecht, Brigitte, jt. auth. see Kelly, Robert.

Mahlmann, John J. & Boston, Bruce O. Fighting the Good Fight. 4p. 1994. pap. 6.75 (*1-56545-063-9*, 4012) MENC.

Mahlmann, John J., jt. intro. see Down, A. Graham.

Mahlmann, Lewis & Jones, David C. Plays for Young Puppeteers. LC 92-38529. 328p. (Orig.). (J). (gr. 1-6). 1993. pap. text 14.95 (*0-8238-0298-1*) Kalmbach.

Mahlmeiste. Perinatal Nursing: Legal Dimensions. pap. text. write for info. (*0-7216-5919-5*, W B Saunders Co) Harcrt Hlth Sci Grp.

Mahlmeister, Laura R., jt. auth. see May, Kathryn A.

Mahlo, Edwin K. Home by Christmas: Memories of a German P. O. W. Giorgi, Josephine, ed. (Memories...Ser.: Vol. 2). (Illus.). xx, 380p. 1996. 24.95 (*0-9655013-2-9*) Condor Literary.

— Paid in Full: War Memories of a German Lieutenant. unabridged ed. Poersch, Eric, ed. (Memories...Ser.: Vol. 1). (Illus.). 225p. 1995. 24.95 (*0-9655013-0-2*) Condor Literary.

— Twenty-Seven Dollars: Memories of a German Immigrant. (Memories...Ser.: Vol. 3). (Illus.). 1997. 24.95 (*0-9655013-4-5*) Condor Literary.

Mahlstedt, Susanne. Zweisprachigkeitserziehung in Gemischtsprachigen Familien: Eine Analyse der Erfolgsbedingenden Merkmale. (GER.). 233p. 1996. 44.95 (*3-631-30762-4*) P Lang Pubng.

Mahlum, D. Dennis, et al, eds. Coal Conversion & the Environment: Chemical, Biomedical, & Ecological Considerations. LC 81-607088. (DOE Symposium Ser.: Proceedings). 622p. 1981. pap. 24.75 (*0-87079-128-1*, CONF-801039); fiche 9.00 (*0-87079-401-9*, CONF-801039) DOE.

Mahlum, D. Dennis & Sikov, M. R., eds. Developmental Toxicology of Energy-Related Pollutants: Proceedings. LC 78-606139. (DOE Symposium Ser.). 661p. 1978. pap. 24.50 (*0-87079-113-3*, CONF-771017); fiche 9.00 (*0-87079-178-8*, CONF-771017) DOE.

Mahlum, D. Dennis, jt. ed. see Sikov, Melvin R.

Mahmood, Arshud. Site Investigation, Remediation, & Closure: A Simplified Guide for Environmental & Real Estate Professionals. LC 98-16429. 178p. 1998. pap. text 59.00 (*0-86587-623-1*, 623) Gov Insts.

Mahmood, Atiya, ed. see Edelman, Gary.

Mahmood, Cynthia K. Fighting for Faith & Nation: Dialogues with Sikh Militants. LC 96-34959. (Contemporary Ethnography Ser.). (Illus.). 314p. 1996. text 39.95 (*0-8122-3361-1*); pap. text 18.95 (*0-8122-1592-3*) U of Pa Pr.

Mahmood, Farida, jt. ed. see Maramorosch, Karl.

***Mahmood, Hikmat F., ed.** Crashworthiness, Occupant Protection & Biomechanics in Transportation Systems, 1999. (AMD - BED Ser.: Vol. 237, Vol. 45). 343p. 1999. 90.00 (*0-7918-1655-9*) ASME Pr.

Mahmood, Hikmat F., et al, eds. Crashworthiness & Occupant Protection in Transportation Systems, 1996: Proceedings: ASME International Mechanical Engineering Congress & Exposition (1996: Atlanta, Georgia) LC 96-79039. (AMD Ser.: Vol. 218). 191p. pap. 60.00 (*0-7918-1554-4*) ASME.

— Crashworthiness & Occupant Protection in Transportation Systems, 1998: Proceedings ASME International Mechanical Engineering Congress & Exposition, Anaheim, CA. LC 99-182512. (AMD - BED Ser.: Vol. 230, Vol. 41). 281p. 1998. 120.00 (*0-7918-1604-4*) ASME.

— Crashworthiness, Occupant Protection & Biomechanics in Transportation Systems, 1997: Proceedings, ASME International Mechanical Engineering Congress & Exposition, Dallas, TX, 1997. LC 97-77358. (AMD - BED Ser.: Vols. 225 & 38). 353p. 1997. pap. 140.00 (*0-7918-1851-9*, TA656) ASME Pr.

Mahmood, K., et al, eds. Mechanics of Alluvial Channels. LC 87-51101. 536p. 1988. 60.00 (*0-918334-63-2*) WRP.

Mahmood, K., et al. Alluvial Channel Data on PC. 1989. 350.00 incl. disk (*0-318-41785-5*) WRP.

Mahmood, Mo A. & Szewczak, Edward J., eds. Measuring Information Technology Investment Payoff: Contemporary Approaches. LC 98-42507. (Series in Information Technology Management). (Illus.). 568p. 1998. 139.95 (*1-878289-42-X*) Idea Group Pub.

Mahmood, Rohana, ed. Peace in the Making. 108p. 1992. 56.50 (*0-7103-0419-6*, A7252) Routledge.

***Mahmood, Safdar.** Pakistan: Political Roots & Development 1947-1999. 500p. 2000. text 24.95 (*0-19-579373-0*) OUP.

Mahmood, Safdar. Pakistan Divided. 1993. 35.00 (*1-56744-178-5*) Kazi Pubns.

Mahmood, Zia. Bridge for Beginners: Your Complete Coursef from a Top Coach. 1998. pap. text 17.95 (*0-7134-8359-8*, Pub. by B T B) Branford.

— Bridge My Way. 264p. 1994. pap. 12.95 (*0-9634715-2-X*) L Cohen NJ.

Mahmoody, Betty & Hoffer, William. Not Without My Daughter. 1991. reprint ed. mass mkt. 6.99 (*0-312-92588-3*) St Martin.

Mahmoud, A., ed. Schistosomiasis. (Tropical Medicine Ser.). 550p. 1999. 96.00 (*1-86094-146-X*, Pub. by Imperial College) World Scientific Pub.

Mahmoud, Adel A. Parasitic Lung Diseases. LC 96-39908. (Lung Biology in Health & Disease Ser.: Vol. 101). (Illus.). 256p. 1997. text 145.00 (*0-8247-9722-1*) Dekker.

Mahmoud, Adel A., jt. auth. see Warren, K. S.

Mahmoud, Adel A., jt. ed. see Warren, Kenneth S.

Mahmoud, Adel A. F., ed. Tropical & Geographical Medicine: Companion Handbook. 2nd ed. (Companion Handbook Ser.). (Illus.). 464p. 1993. 32.00 (*0-07-039625-6*) McGraw-Hill HPD.

Mahmoud, Ben, jt. auth. see Dunning, William V.

Mahmoud, Hosam M. Evolution of Random Search Trees. LC 91-16041. (Interscience Series in Discrete Mathematics: No. 1484). 336p. 1991. 135.00 (*0-471-53228-2*) Wiley.

***Mahmoud, Hosam M.** Sorting: A Distribution Theory. LC 99-86783. 416p. 2000. text 84.95 (*0-471-32710-7*) Wiley.

Mahmoud, Magdi S. Computer-Operated Systems Control. (Electrical Engineering & Electronics Ser.: Vol. 70). (Illus.). 680p. 1991. text 215.00 (*0-8247-8092-2*) Dekker.

***Mahmoud, Magdi S.** Robust Control & Filtering for Time-delay Systems. LC 99-54346. (Control Engineering Ser.: Vol. 5). 427p. 2000. 165.00 (*0-8247-0327-8*) Dekker.

Mahmoud, Magdi S., et al. Large Scale Control Systems: Theories & Techniques. (Electrical Engineering & Electronics Ser.: Vol. 26). (Illus.). 384p. 1985. text 165.00 (*0-8247-7289-X*) Dekker.

Mahmoud, Magdi S., jt. auth. see Bahnasawi, A. A.

Mahmoud, Parvine. Zarathushtra. 80p. 1998. 10.00 (*0-8059-4306-4*) Dorrance.

Mahmoud, Qusay. Distributed Programming with Java. LC 99-27785. 300p. 1999. pap. 43.95 (*1-884777-65-1*) Manning Pubns.

Mahmoud, Zaki N. The Land & People of Egypt. rev. ed. LC 71-37247. (Portraits of the Nations Ser.). (Illus.). (J). (gr. 6 up). 1972. lib. bdg. 12.89 (*0-397-31259-8*, Lippncott) Lppncott W & W.

Mahmoudi, Abdelrashid. Taha Husein's Education: From Al Azhar to the Sorbonne. LC 99-182871. 260p. 1998. 65.00 (*0-7007-1027-2*, Pub. by Curzon Pr Ltd) Paul & Co Pubs.

Mahmoudi, Kooros. Sociological Inquiry. 6th ed. 176p. (C). 1997. pap. text, per. 29.95 (*0-7872-3319-6*, 41331901) Kendall-Hunt.

Mahmoudi, Said. The Law of Deep Sea-Bed Mining: A Study of the Progressive Development of International Law Concerning the Management of the Polymetallic Nodules of the Deep Sea-Bed. 362p. 1987. text 121.00 (*91-22-01156-0*) Coronet Bks.

Mahmoudian, Morteza. Modern Theories of Language: The Empirical Challenge. LC 92-13538. (Sound & Meaning: The Roman Jakobson Series in Linguistics & Poetics). (Illus.). 256p. 1993. text 42.95 (*0-8223-1278-6*) Duke.

Mahmoudov, Alexei. The Soviet Oil & Natural Gas Industries: Problems of Reserve Estimation. Williams, John, ed. 95p. (Orig.). 1986. pap. text 75.00 (*1-55831-029-0*) Delphic Associates.

Mahmoudov, Vadim, tr. see Kozhina, Elena.

Mahmud Ahmad Ghazanfar. Talim Ul-Hajj. 94p. (Orig.). 1985. pap. 5.99 (*1-56744-399-0*) Kazi Pubns.

Mahmud-i-Zarqani. Mahmud's Diary: The Diary of Mirza Mahmud-i-Zarqani - Chronicling Abdu'l-Baha's Journey to America. Sobhani, Mohi & Macias, Shirley, trs. from PER. (Illus.). 600p. 1998. 39.95 (*0-85398-418-2*) G Ronald Pub.

Mahmud, Ibrahim. Al-Hijrah ila al-Islam: Hawl al-'Alam al-Fikri li-Jawdat Sa'id: Hiwar, Dirasat, Ta'qib. 352p. Date not set. pap. 11.95 (*1-57547-203-1*) Dar Al-Fikr.

Mahmud, Jafar S. Buddhism: Religion & Meditation. 386p. 1998. 40.00 (*81-7024-949-X*, Pub. by APH Pubng) Nataraj Bks.

Mahmud, S. Jafar. Science Technology & Development since Independence. 1997. 34.00 (*81-7488-793-8*, Pub. by Anmol) S Asia.

Mahmud, Sakah S. State, Class & Underdevelopment in Nigeria & Early Meiji Japan. 176p. 1996. text 59.95 (*0-312-15932-3*) St Martin.

Mahmud, Sayed J. Pillars on Modern India, 1757-1947. 140p. 1994. 16.00 (*81-7024-586-9*, Pub. by Ashish Pub Hse) Nataraj Bks.

Mahmud, Sayyid F. A Concise History of Indo Pakistan. (Illus.). 336p. 1989. pap. 11.95 (*0-19-577385-3*) OUP.

— Indo-Pakistan: A Concise History. 315p. 1996. pap. 10.50 (*0-614-21693-1*, 499) Kazi Pubns.

— Junior History of Indo-Pakistan. 72p. (J). 1996. pap. 5.95 (*0-614-21022-4*, 683) Kazi Pubns.

— A Short History of Islam. rev. ed. (Illus.). 442p. 1989. pap. 19.95 (*0-19-577384-5*) OUP.

Mahmud, Shabana. Urdu Language & Literature: A Bibliography of Sources in European Languages. 352p. 1992. text 120.00 (*0-7201-2143-4*) Continuum.

Mahmud, Simeen, jt. auth. see Van Koppen, Barbara.

Mahmud, Syed J. Lecture Notes on 16 & 32 Bit Microprocssors. 2nd ed. 340p. (C). 1995. text 42.00 (*0-536-59023-0*) Pearson Custom.

Mahmud, Zafer, ed. see Adams, J. F.

***Mahmutcehajic, Rusmir.** Bosnia the Good: Tolerance & Tradition. 260p. (C). 2000. 44.95 (*963-9116-86-6*); pap. 21.95 (*963-9116-87-4*) Ctrl Europ Univ.

— The Denial of Bosnia. LC 99-56307. (Post-Communist Cultural Studies). 184p. 2000. 24.95 (*0-271-02030-X*) Pa St U Pr.

Mahn, Patrick, jt. auth. see Valentine, Tom.

Mahncke, Dieter. Nukleare Mitwirkung: Die Bundesrepublik Deutschland in der atlantischen Allianz 1954-1970. (Beitraege zur Auswaertigen und Internationalen Politik Ser.: Vol. 6). xvi, 274p. (C). 1972. 79.25 (*3-11-001820-9*) De Gruyter.

An Asterisk (*) at the beginning of an entry indicates that the title is appearing for the first time.

Mahner, M. & Bunge, Mario. Foundations of Biophilosophy. LC 97-11448. 420p. 1997. 54.00 (*3-540-61838-4*) Spr-Verlag.

Mahnke, Dan. Antique Roads of America: Bicycle Guide for Route 66. (Illus.). 102p. (Orig.). 1992. pap. 9.95 (*0-9633853-0-5*, TX 3 345 672) D Mahnke.

— Mahnke Grammar. Date not set. pap. text 13.77 (*0-395-94523-2*); pap. text 13.77 (*0-395-94525-9*) HM.

— Mahnke Grammar: Level 1. Date not set. pap. text 23.67 incl. audio (*0-395-94520-8*) HM.

— Mahnke Grammar Links. Date not set. pap. text 19.77 (*0-395-82884-8*); pap. text 9.87 (*0-395-82885-6*); pap. text 9.87 (*0-395-82886-4*) HM.

Mahnke, Doug, jt. auth. see Arcudi, John.

Mahnke, Frank H. Color, Environment, & Human Response. 1996. 59.95 (*0-614-95684-6*, VNR) Wiley.

Mahnke, Frank H. & Mahnke, Rudolf H. Color & Light in Man-Made Environments. 152p. 1993. pap. 49.95 (*0-471-28527-7*, VNR) Wiley.

— Color & Light in Man-Made Environments. 140p. 1996. pap. text 46.95 (*0-442-01322-1*, VNR) Wiley.

— Color & Light in Man-Made Environments: An Interdisciplinary Understanding of Color & Its Use As a Beneficial Element in the Design of the Architectural Environment. (Interior Design Ser.). (Illus.). 140p. 1996. text 59.95 (*0-442-01935-1*, VNR) Wiley.

Mahnke, Frank H. & Mahnke, Rudolf H. Color, Environment, & Human Response: An Interdisciplinary Understanding of Color & Its Use As a Beneficial Element in the Design of the Architectural Environment. (Interior Design Ser.). 234p. 1996. 69.95 (*0-471-28667-2*, VNR) Wiley.

***Mahnke, M. Kathleen & O'Dowd, Elizabeth M.** Grammar Links 2: A Theme-Based Course for Reference & Practice LC 98-72232. xv, 436 p. 1999. write for info. (*0-395-82888-0*) HM.

Mahnke, R. Theory & Computer Simulation of Aggregation Phenomena in Complex Systems. LC 99-191627. 476p. 1999. 199.00 (*3-527-29354-X*) Wiley.

Mahnke, Rudolf H., jt. auth. see Mahnke, Frank H.

Mahnke, Volker, jt. ed. see Foss, Nicolai J.

Mahnken, Jan. The Backyard Bird-Lover's Guide: Attracting, Nesting, Feeding. Steege, Gwen, ed. (Illus.). 312p. (Orig.). 1996. pap. 24.95 (*0-88266-927-3*, 927-3, Storey Pub) Storey Bks.

— Hosting the Birds: How to Attract Birds to Nest in Your Yard. Mason, Jill, ed. LC 88-45487. (Illus.). 216p. 1989. 21.95 (*0-88266-534-0*, Garden Way Pub); pap. 10.95 (*0-88266-525-1*, Garden Way Pub) Storey Bks.

Mahnkey, Mary E. Marigold Gold: Verses of the Ozarks. Gray Massey, Ellen, ed. LC 99-73189. 158p. 1999. pap. 9.95 (*0-934426-90-2*) NAPSAC Reprods.

Mahoe, Noelani K., jt. compiled by see Elbert, Samuel H.

Mahomet, Dean. The Travels of Dean Mahomet: An Eighteenth-Century Journey Through India. Fisher, Michael H., ed. LC 96-19700. (Illus.). 214p. 1997. 48.00 (*0-520-20716-5*, Pub. by U CA Pr); pap. 16.95 (*0-520-20717-3*, Pub. by U CA Pr) Cal Prin Full Svc.

Mahon. Introduction to Clinical Lab Science: International Edition. (C). 1998. pap. text 22.00 (*0-8089-2063-4*, Grune & Strat) Harcrt Hlth Sci Grp.

— Text Book of Diagonostic Microbiology. 1995. 575.00 (*0-7216-4216-0*) Harcourt.

***Mahon, Cathal J.** Charting Complexity: Analysing How Strategy Emerges in Organisations. 117p. 1999. 20.00 (*87-16-13506-7*, Pub. by Copenhagen Busn Schl) Bks Intl VA.

Mahon, Annette. Above the Rainbow. LC 95-94895. 192p. 1995. 18.95 (*0-8034-9142-5*, Avalon Bks) Bouregy.

— Chase Your Dream. LC 97-93727. 192p. 1997. 18.95 (*0-8034-9245-6*, Avalon Bks) Bouregy.

— Just Friends. LC 98-96337. 192p. 1998. lib. bdg. 18.95 (*0-8034-9317-7*, Avalon Bks) Bouregy.

— Lei of Love. LC 95-96218. 192p. 1996. 18.95 (*0-8034-9165-4*, Avalon Bks) Bouregy.

— Maui Rose. LC 96-97003. 192p. 1996. 18.95 (*0-8034-9182-4*, Avalon Bks) Bouregy.

Mahon, Brbid. While Green Grass Grows: Memoirs of a Folklorist. LC 98-132158. 208p. 1998. write for info. (*1-85635-206-4*) Mercier Pr.

Mahon, Brid. Land of Milk & Honey: The Story of Traditional Irish Food & Drink. LC 99-194148. 160p. (Orig.). 1998. 12.95 (*1-85635-210-2*, Pub. by Mercier Pr) Irish Amer Bk.

— Land of Milk & Honey: The Story of Traditional Irish Food & Drink. (Illus.). 176p. (Orig.). 1992. pap. 17.95 (*1-85371-142-X*, Pub. by Poolbeg Pr) Dufour.

— A Time to Love. 484p. 1992. pap. 13.95 (*1-85371-221-3*, Pub. by Poolbeg Pr) Dufour.

Mahon, Connie. Diagnostic Microbiology. 1995. pap. text, lab manual ed. 22.00 (*0-7216-4029-X*, W B Saunders Co) Harcrt Hlth Sci Grp.

— An Introduction to Clinical Laboratory Science. LC 97-36630. (C). 1998. pap. text 29.95 (*0-7216-4990-4*, W B Saunders Co) Harcrt Hlth Sci Grp.

Mahon, Connie, et al, eds. Textbook of Diagnostic Microbiology. LC 94-21550. (Illus.). 1152p. 1995. text 68.00 (*0-7216-4028-1*, W B Saunders Co) Harcrt Hlth Sci Grp.

Mahon, Connie & Manuselis, George. Textbook of Diagnostic Microbiology. 2nd ed. (Illus.). 895p. Date not set. text. write for info. (*0-7216-7917-X*, W B Saunders Co) Harcrt Hlth Sci Grp.

Mahon, Denis. Studies in Seicento Art & Theory, Vol. 16. LC 73-114544. (Illus.). 351p. 1971. reprint ed. lib. bdg. 35.00 (*0-8371-4743-3*, MAST, Greenwood Pr) Greenwood.

Mahon, Derek. The Bacchae: After Euripides. 62p. 1991. pap. 12.95 (*1-85235-067-9*) Dufour.

— The Chimeras: Translations from de Nerval. 20p. 1982. pap. 10.95 (*0-904011-32-1*) Dufour.

***Mahon, Derek.** Collected Poems. 288p. 2000. 49.95 (*1-85235-256-6*, Pub. by Gallery Pr); pap. 27.95 (*1-85235-255-8*, Pub. by Gallery Pr) Dufour.

Mahon, Derek. High Time: A Comedy in One Act Based on Moliere's The School for Husbands. 58p. 1985. pap. 12.95 (*0-904011-80-1*, Pub. by Gallery Pr) Dufour.

— The Hudson Letter. LC 95-62043. 64p. (Orig.). 1996. 14.95 (*0-916390-71-3*); pap. 8.95 (*0-916390-70-5*) Wake Forest.

— The Hunt by Night. rev. ed. LC 82-50938. 63p. 1983. pap. 6.95 (*0-916390-17-9*) Wake Forest.

— Journalism: Selected Prose. LC 97-117556. 242p. 1997. pap. 19.95 (*1-85235-178-0*) Dufour.

— Journalism: Selected Prose, 1970-1995. LC 97-117556. 242p. 1997. 42.00 (*1-85235-179-9*) Dufour.

— The School for Wives: After Moliere. 76p. 1986. pap. 12.95 (*1-85235-004-0*) Dufour.

— The Yellow Book. 1998. 15.95 (*0-916390-82-9*); pap. 9.95 (*0-916390-81-0*) Wake Forest.

Mahon, Derek, jt. ed. see Fallon, Peter.

Mahon, Derek, tr. see Jaccottet, Philippe.

Mahon, Derek, tr. see Racine, Jean.

Mahon, George, compiled by. A Policies & Procedures Handbook for Induction & Foundation Training. 1991. pap. 21.00 (*0-7855-2689-7*, Pub. by Natl Inst Soc Work) St Mut.

Mahon, Gigi. The Last Days of the New Yorker. 1989. pap. 9.95 (*0-317-02698-4*, Plume) Dutton Plume.

Mahon, Harold P., et al. Efficient Energy Management. (Illus.). 496p. (C). 1983. 29.95 (*0-13-791434-2*) P-H.

Mahon, James E. Mobile Capital & the Structure of Development in Latin America. LC 95-17440. 232p. 1996. 48.50 (*0-271-01525-X*); pap. 18.95 (*0-271-01526-8*) Pa St U Pr.

Mahon, Jana. Coupon & Refund Guide. (Illus.). 52p. (Orig.). 1989. pap. 4.00 (*0-685-25744-4*) J L Mahon.

Mahon, John & Pendleton, Thomas A., eds. Fanned & Winnowed Opinions: Shakespearean Essays Presented to Harold Jenkins. 320p. 1988. pap. 67.50 (*0-416-00422-9*) Routledge.

Mahon, John F. Industry As a Player in the Political & Social Arena: Defining the Competitive Environment. LC 96-2213. 232p. 1996. 59.95 (*0-89930-978-X*, Quorum Bks) Greenwood.

Mahon, John K. The American Militia: Decade of Decision, 1789-1800. LC 60-63132. (University of Florida Monographs: Vol. 6). 78p. 1960. reprint ed. pap. 30.00 (*0-608-04497-0*, 206524200001) Bks Demand.

— History of the Second Seminole War, 1835-1842. rev. ed. LC 85-16443. (Illus.). 401p. 1991. pap. 16.95 (*0-8130-1097-7*) U Press Fla.

— The War of 1812. (Quality Paperbacks Ser.). (Illus.). xii, 476p. 1991. reprint ed. pap. 15.95 (*0-306-80429-8*) Da Capo.

Mahon, K. L. Just One Tear. LC 93-80198. (YA). (gr. 5 up). 1994. 14.00 (*0-688-13519-6*) Lothrop.

Mahon, L. L. Diesel Generator Handbook. (Illus.). 416p. 1992. text 260.00 (*0-7506-1147-2*) Buttrwrth-Heinemann.

***Mahon, Leo T.** Jesus & His Message: An Introduction to the Good News. LC 99-97623. 110p. 2000. pap. 6.95 (*0-87946-211-6*) ACTA Pubns.

Mahon, Lord, ed. see Chesterfield, Philip Dormer Stanhope.

Mahon, Michael. Foucault's Nietzschean Genealogy: Truth, Power, & the Subject. LC 91-35092. (SUNY Series in Contemporary Continental Philosophy). 255p. (C). 1992. text 21.50 (*0-7914-1149-4*) State U NY Pr.

Mahon, Michael, jt. auth. see Bullock, Charles.

***Mahon, Michael G.** Shenandoah Valley, 1861-1865: The Destruction of the Granary of the Confederacy. LC 99-41087. (Illus.). 192p. 1999. 22.95 (*0-8117-1540-X*) Stackpole.

Mahon, Rianne. The Politics of Industrial Restructuring: Canadian Textiles. (State & Economic Life Ser.: No. 7). xii, 204p. 1984. pap. 13.95 (*0-8020-6546-5*); text 30.00 (*0-8020-2538-2*) U of Toronto Pr.

Mahon, Rianne, jt. ed. see Jenson, Jane.

Mahon, William J., jt. ed. see Jefferiss, Paul.

Mahone-Lonesome, Robyn. Charles Drew: Physician. Huggins, Nathan I., ed. (Black Americans of Achievement Ser.). (Illus.). (YA). (gr. 5 up). 1990. lib. bdg. 19.95 (*1-55546-581-1*) Chelsea Hse.

Mahone, Sydne, intro. Moon Marked & Touched by Sun: Plays by African-American Women. LC 93-11831. 448p. 1994. reprint ed. pap. 15.95 (*1-55936-065-8*) Theatre Comm.

Mahoney. Human Sexuality. LC 97-75316. (C). Date not set. pap. text 16.36 (*0-395-90255-X*) HM.

— The Longevity Strategy. 272p. 1999. pap. 14.95 (*0-471-32794-8*) Wiley.

— Students Guide Intro Sociology. 4th ed. 1998. pap. 10.50 (*0-07-234369-9*) McGraw.

Mahoney & Price. Philosophy. (Philosophy Ser.). 2000. pap. text 35.00 (*0-534-55857-7*) Thomson Learn.

Mahoney, Anne R. Juvenile Justice in Context. 224p. 1987. text 45.00 (*1-55553-011-7*) NE U Pr.

Mahoney, Anne R., et al. Ruts: Gender Roles & Realities. 160p. (Orig.). 1996. pap. text 15.95 (*0-9630149-1-9*) Red Mesa.

Mahoney, Barbara, jt. ed. see Jones, Iris C.

Mahoney, Barry, et al. How to Use Structured Fines (Day Fines) As an Intermediate Sanction. (Illus.). 81p. (C). 1999. reprint ed. pap. text 25.00 (*0-7881-7578-5*) DIANE Pub.

Mahoney, Bateman & Mahoney, Bill. Macho: Is This What I Really Want? (J). 1986. pap. 6.00 (*0-87738-024-4*) Youth Ed.

Mahoney, Beverly S. & Olsen, Larry K., eds. Health Education Teacher Resource Handbook: A Practical Guide for K-12 Health Education. (Teacher Resource Handbook Ser.). (Illus.). 448p. 1993. pap. 34.95 (*0-8039-6371-8*) Corwin Pr.

Mahoney, Bill, jt. auth. see Mahoney, Bateman.

Mahoney-Briscoe, Charlotte, jt. auth. see Briscoe, David.

Mahoney, Connie, jt. auth. see Pardini, Alan.

Mahoney, Dan. Black & White. LC 99-21853. 368p. 1999. text 24.95 (*0-312-20278-4*) St Martin.

***Mahoney, Dan.** Black & White. LC 99-21853. 528p. 2000. mass mkt. 6.99 (*0-312-97149-4*) St Martin.

— Ciscos Saga. 2000. text. write for info. (*0-312-26134-9*) St Martin.

Mahoney, Dan. Detective First Grade. LC 93-555. 1994. mass mkt. 6.99 (*0-312-95313-5*) St Martin.

— The Edge of the City. 1996. mass mkt. 6.99 (*0-312-95788-2*) St Martin.

— Hyde. 560p. 1997. mass mkt. 6.99 (*0-312-96392-0*, St Martins Paperbacks) St Martin.

— Once in, Never Out. LC 97-40422. 352p. 1998. text 24.95 (*0-312-18228-7*) St Martin.

— Once in, Never Out. 480p. Date not set. pap. 6.99 (*0-312-96676-8*, Pub. by Tor Bks) St Martin.

Mahoney, Dan, et al, eds. Early Modern Skepticism & the Origins of Toleration. LC 98-47858. (Applications of Political Theory Ser.). 266p. 1999. 60.00 (*0-7391-0023-8*) Lxngtn Bks.

Mahoney, Daniel J. De Gaulle: Statesmanship, Grandeur, & Modern Democracy. LC 95-50530. 208p. 1996. 59.95 (*0-275-94922-2*, Praeger Pubs) Greenwood.

***Mahoney, Daniel J.** De Gaulle: Statesmanship, Grandeur & Modern Democracy. LC 00-23489. 200p. 2000. pap. 24.95 (*0-7658-0689-4*) Transaction Pubs.

Mahoney, Daniel J. The Liberal Political Science of Raymond Aron: A Critical Introduction. 192p. 1991. pap. text 15.95 (*0-8476-7716-8*) Rowman.

— The Liberal Political Science of Raymond Aron: A Critical Introduction. 192p. (C). 1991. text 58.00 (*0-8476-7715-X*) Rowman.

Mahoney, Daniel J., ed. In Defense of Political Reason: Essays by Raymond Aron. 200p. (C). 1994. pap. text 21.95 (*0-8476-7878-4*); lib. bdg. 56.50 (*0-8476-7877-6*) Rowman.

— Waterpower, '97: Proceedings of the International Conference on Hydropower, Atlanta, GA, August 5-8, 3 vols. 2392p. 1997. 190.00 (*0-7844-0266-3*) Am Soc Civil Eng.

Mahoney, Daniel J., ed. see Kolnai, Aurel.

Mahoney, Daniel J., ed. & tr. see Manent, Pierre.

Mahoney, Daniela. Outstanding Oregon Recipes. (Illus.). 120p. 1992. reprint ed. spiral bd. 6.95 (*0-941016-87-0*) Penfield.

Mahoney, David & Restak, Richard. The Longevity Strategy: How to Live to 100 Using the Brain-Body Connection. LC 97-50639. 272p. 1998. 22.95 (*0-471-24867-3*) Wiley.

***Mahoney, Debbie.** Innocence Lost: Protecting Your Child from the Trauma of Abuse. LC 99-57498. 1999. pap. 16.95 (*1-890613-09-6*) West Coast Media.

Mahoney, Denis. Black Pig Bk. 1: In Red Ochre. 1994. pap. 7.00 (*0-614-04109-0*) Hozomeen Pr.

Mahoney, Dennis F. Critical Fortunes of a Romantic Novel: Novalis's Heinrich von Ofterdingen. LC 94-11094. (LCGERM Ser.). xiv, 160p. 1994. 55.00 (*1-879751-58-5*) Camden Hse.

Mahoney, Dennis J., jt. auth. see Levy, Leonard W.

Mahoney, Dennis J., jt. ed. see Levy, Leonard W.

Mahoney, Des. Trees of Somalia: Oxfam Research Discussion Papers. (Oxfam Research Papers). 196p. (C). 1990. 15.95 (*0-85598-109-1*, Pub. by Oxfam Pub) Stylus Pub VA.

Mahoney, Dhira. Rhetoric of Medieval Prefaces. (Literature Reference Ser.). 200p. Date not set. text 29.00 (*0-8240-2946-1*) Garland.

Mahoney, Dhira, ed. The Grail: A Casebook. LC 99-34171. (Arthurian Characters & Themes Ser.: Vol. 5). (Illus.). 616p. 1999. text 70.00 (*0-8153-0648-2*, H1510) Garland.

Mahoney, Dino. Yo-Yo. (Oberon Bks.). 74p. 1997. pap. 12.95 (*1-870259-50-5*) Theatre Comm.

Mahoney, Donna T. Touching the Face of God: Intimacy & Celibacy in the Priesthood. LC 91-76864. 233p. 1991. pap. 12.95 (*0-9631517-0-3*) Jeremiah Pr.

Mahoney, E. F. & Dwiggins, B. H. Automotive Electricity & Electronics: Concepts & Applications. LC 95-15895. 285p. (C). 1995. pap. text 74.00 (*0-13-359233-2*) P-H.

Mahoney, Edward. Electricity for Air Conditioning & Refrigeration Technicians. 5th ed. LC 99-35431. (Illus.). 444p. 1999. pap. 69.00 (*0-13-010572-4*) P-H.

Mahoney, Edward F., jt. auth. see Dwiggins, Boyce H.

***Mahoney, Ellen K., et al.** Management of Challenging Behaviors in Dementia. 288p. 2000. pap. 34.00 (*1-878812-46-7*, 2467) Hlth Prof Pr.

Mahoney, Ellen V. Now You've Got Your Period. rev. ed. Rosen, Roger, ed. (Coping Ser.). (YA). (gr. 7-12). 1993. lib. bdg. 17.95 (*0-8239-1662-6*) Rosen Group.

Mahoney, Ellen V. & Wilcox, Leah. Ready, Set, Read: Best Books to Prepare Preschoolers. LC 83-27087. 1985. 34.50 (*0-8108-1684-9*) Scarecrow.

Mahoney, Eugene J. There's a Light in the Gardibee House & Other Stories. 117p. (Orig.). 1985. pap. 2.95 (*0-9615994-0-5*) E J Mahoney.

Mahoney, Francis X. & Thor, Carl G. The TQM Trilogy: Using ISO 9000, the Deming Prize, & the Baldrige Award to Establish a System for Total Quality Management. 224p. 1994. 29.95 (*0-8144-5105-5*) AMACOM.

Mahoney, Gene. Effective Supervisory Practices Study Guide. 112p. (Orig.). 1987. pap. 11.95 (*0-945250-00-2*) Davis Pub Co.

— Fire Department Oral Interviews: Practices & Procedures. 350p. (C). 1988. pap. text 27.95 (*0-87814-911-2*) Fire Eng.

— Introduction to Fire Apparatus & Equipment. 2nd ed. LC 85-82103. (Illus.). 524p. (C). 1986. text 28.50 (*0-912212-12-8*); student ed. 12.95 (*0-87814-901-5*) Fire Eng.

Mahoney, Harry T. & Mahoney, Marjorie L. Biographic Dictionary of Espionage. LC 97-3108. 462p. 1998. 79.95 (*1-57292-065-3*) Austin & Winfield.

— Espionage in Mexico: The 20th Century. LC 96-47999. 320p. 1997. 69.95 (*1-57292-057-2*) Austin & Winfield.

— Espionage in Mexico: The 20th Century. LC 96-47999. 290p. 1997. pap. 49.95 (*1-57292-056-4*) Intl Scholars.

— Espionage in the American Revolutionary War, 1775-1783: A Reference Primer to People & Events. (Illus.). 350p. 1998. 74.95 (*1-57292-126-9*); pap. 54.95 (*1-57292-125-0*) Austin & Winfield.

***Mahoney, Harry T. & Mahoney, Marjorie L.** Gallantry in Action: A Biographic Dictionary of Espionage in the American Revolutionary War LC 99-33534. 1999. write for info. (*0-7618-1479-5*) U Pr of Amer.

Mahoney, Harry T. & Mahoney, Marjorie L. Mexico & the Confederacy, 1860-1867. LC 96-53879. (Illus.). 286p. 1997. pap. 49.95 (*1-57292-066-1*) Austin & Winfield.

Mahoney, Harry Thayer & Mahoney, Marjorie Locke. Biographic Dictionary of Espionage. LC 97-3108. 900p. 1998. pap. 60.00 (*1-57292-064-5*) Austin & Winfield.

***Mahoney, Harry Thayer & Mahoney, Marjorie Locke.** Ireland Defined: Espionage Through the Ages. LC 00-37436. (Illus.). 2000. pap. write for info. (*0-7618-1723-9*) U Pr of Amer.

Mahoney, Harry Thayer & Mahoney, Marjorie Locke. Mexico & the Confederacy, 1860-1867. LC 96-53879. (Illus.). 240p. 1997. 69.95 (*1-57292-067-X*) Intl Scholars.

— The Saga of Leon Trotsky: His Clandestine Operations & His Assassination. LC 98-8299. (Illus.). 450p. 1998. 74.95 (*1-57292-124-2*) Austin & Winfield.

Mahoney, Haynes R. Yarmouth's Proud Packets: The Commodore Hull Didn't Sail So Dull. (Illus.). 46p. 1986. pap. 4.00 (*0-9625068-1-8*) Hist Soc Yarmouth.

Mahoney, Irene, ed. A Company of Women: Journeys Through the Feminine Experience of Faith. LC 96-18407. 240p. (Orig.). 1996. pap. 14.00 (*0-89243-923-8*, Liguori Triumph) Liguori Pubns.

— Marie of the Incarnation: Selected Writings. (Sources of American Spirituality Ser.). 1989. 24.95 (*0-8091-0428-8*) Paulist Pr.

Mahoney, Ivan. Trout Flies & Flowers. (Illus.). 70p. 1998. 19.95 (*1-55821-724-X*) Lyons Pr.

Mahoney, J. Seeking the Spirit. 1990. 70.00 (*0-7220-7923-0*); pap. 30.00 (*0-7220-7929-X*) St Mut.

Mahoney, J. J. Inlets for Supersonic Missiles. (Educ Ser.). (Illus.). 237p. 1991. 57.95 (*0-930403-79-7*, 79-7) AIAA.

Mahoney, Jack. The Golf History of New England: Centennial Edition. 256p. 1995. 35.00 (*0-9647426-0-8*) J Mahoney.

— Teaching Business Ethics in the U. K., U. S. A. & Europe: A Comparative Study. LC 90-635. 224p. (C). 1990. text 49.95 (*0-485-11399-6*, Pub. by Athlone Pr) Humanities.

— Virginia Broderick: Artist Extraordinary. 1983. pap. 1.00 (*0-915866-13-7*) Am Cath Pr.

Mahoney, Jack & Vallance, Elizabeth, eds. Business Ethics in a New Europe. LC 92-26437. (Issues in Business Ethics Ser.: Vol. 3). 244p. (C). 1992. lib. bdg. 104.50 (*0-7923-1931-1*, Pub. by Kluwer Academic) Kluwer Academic.

Mahoney, James. Saving Molly: A Research Veterinarian's Choice. LC 98-11596. 252p. 1998. 21.95 (*1-56512-173-2*) Algonquin Bks.

Mahoney, James R. The Learning Edge: Advanced Technological Education at Community Colleges. 120p. 2000. pap. 24.00 (*0-87117-326-3*, 1437) Comm Coll Pr Am Assn Comm Coll.

Mahoney, James R., ed. Improving Science, Mathematics, Engineering, & Technology Instruction: Strategies for the Community College. 114p. 1997. pap. 15.00 (*0-87117-301-8*, 1397) Comm Coll Pr Am Assn Comm Coll.

Mahoney, James R. & Barnett, Lynn, eds. Developing Technicians: Successful International Systems. (Illus.). 175p. 1998. pap. 25.00 (*0-87117-319-0*, 1431) Comm Coll Pr Am Assn Comm Coll.

Mahoney, James R. & Sakamoto, Clyde, eds. International Trade Education: Issues & Programs. LC 85-216111. (AACJC Issues Ser.: No. 2). 97p. reprint ed. pap. 30.10 (*0-7837-2483-7*, 204264000005) Bks Demand.

Mahoney, James R., jt. ed. see Kee, Arnold M.

Mahoney, Jane & Euhardy, Reenie. Coping with Impaired Mobility. LC 93-40443. (Coping with Aging Ser.). 272p. 1994. pap. 18.95 (*1-879105-65-9*, 0329) Thomson Learn.

Mahoney, Jean & Rao, Peggy L. At Home with Japanese Design: Accents, Structure & Spirit. (Illus.). 184p. 1990. 34.95 (*4-07-975061-7*, Pub. by Shufunomoto Co Ltd) Tuttle Pubng.

Mahoney, Jean, jt. auth. see Rao, Peggy L.

Mahoney, John. The Making of Moral Theology: A Study of the Roman Catholic Tradition (Martin D'Arcy Memorial Lectures 1981-1982) (Illus.). 382p. 1989. pap. text 23.00 (*0-19-826730-4*) OUP.

— Wordsworth & the Critics. (Studies in English & American Literature). 2000. 55.00 (*1-57113-090-X*) Camden Hse.

Mahoney, John, ed. Bioethics & Belief. 128p. 1990. pap. 24.00 (*0-7220-1319-1*, Pub. by Sheed Ward Ltd) St Mut.

Mahoney, John, ed. see Hungness, Carl.

Mahoney, John F. Tao of the Jump Shot: An Eastern Approach to Life & Basketball. LC 99-24740. 128p. 1999. 16.00 (*1-56975-186-2*) Ulysses Pr.

M

***Mahoney, John F.** Tao of the Jump Shot: An Eastern Approach to Life & Basketball. 128p. 2000. pap. 9.95 (*1-56975-228-1*) Ulysses Pr.

Mahoney, John J. & Coffin, Millard F., eds. Large Igneous Provinces: Continental, Oceanic, & Planetary Flood Volcanism, Vol. 100. LC 97-43026. (Geophysical Monograph Ser.). 1997. 65.00 (*0-87590-082-8*) Am Geophysical.

***Mahoney, John K., ed.** Advances in the Productivity & Use of Steel with Improved Internal Cleanliness. LC 99-13369. (STP Ser.: Vol. 1361). (Illus.). 15p. 1999. pap. text 44.00 (*0-8031-2605-0*, STP1361) ASTM.

Mahoney, John L. The Logic of Passion: The Literary Criticism of William Hazlitt. rev. ed. LC 81-67501. 135p. reprint ed. pap. 41.90 (*0-7837-5879-0*, 204559900006) Bks Demand.

— The Whole Internal Universe: Imitation & the New Defense of Poetry in British Criticism, 1660-1830. LC 85-80479. 176p. reprint ed. pap. 54.60 (*0-7837-5878-2*, 204559800006) Bks Demand.

— Wiliam Wordsworth: A Poetic Life. LC 96-39355. (Illus.). xxviii, 301p. 1996. 32.00 (*0-8232-1715-9*); pap. 17.00 (*0-8232-1716-7*) Fordham.

Mahoney, John L., ed. The English Romantics: Major Poetry & Critical Theory. 828p. (C). 1997. reprint ed. pap. text 55.95 (*0-88133-957-1*) Waveland Pr.

***Mahoney, John L., ed.** The Enlightenment & English Literature: Prose & Poetry of the 18th Century. 625p. (C). 1999. pap. 43.95 (*1-57766-081-1*) Waveland Pr.

Mahoney, John L., ed. Seeing into the Life of Things: Essays on Religion in Literature. LC 97-45736. Vol. 1. xx, 364p. (C). 1997. 35.00 (*0-8232-1732-9*) Fordham.

— Seeing into the Life of Things: Essays on Religion in Literature. LC 97-45736. Vol. 1. xx, 364p. 1997. pap. 17.00 (*0-8232-1733-7*) Fordham.

Mahoney, John L., jt. auth. see Dryden, John.

Mahoney, John L., jt. ed. see Barth, J. Robert.

Mahoney, John L., ed. see Dryden, John.

Mahoney, John P. & Keckler, Linda S. The Complete Guide to Contracts Management for Facilities Services. LC 96-10826. 1996. pap. text 18.95 (*0-945456-26-3*) PT Pubns.

Mahoney, Joseph F. & Wosh, Peter J., eds. The Diocesan Journal of Michael Augustine Corrigan, Bishope of Newark, 1872-1880, Vol. XXII. (Collections of the New Jersey Historical Society). 443p. 1987. 35.00 (*0-911020-17-9*) NJ Hist Soc.

Mahoney, Judith. Dolly Parton. LC 97-42467. 1998. 19.98 (*1-56799-557-8*, Friedman-Fairfax) M Friedman Pub Grp Inc.

Mahoney, Judy. Sing with Me in French: A Teach Me Tapes Songbook. (FRE., Illus.). 20p. (J). (ps-6). 1994. pap. 7.95 (*0-934633-91-6*) Teach Me.

Mahoney, Judy. Sing with Me in Spanish: A Teach Me Tapes Songbook. (SPA., Illus.). 20p. (J). (ps-6). 1994. pap. 7.95 (*0-934633-92-4*) Teach Me.

Mahoney, Judy. Teach Me... Chinese: A Musical Journey Through the Day. (Teach Me... Ser.). (CHI & ENG., Illus.). 20p. (J). (ps-7). 1996. pap. 13.95 incl. audio (*0-934633-84-3*, 119, Pub. by Teach Me) Penton Overseas.

— Teach Me... Chinese: A Musical Journey Through the Day. (Teach Me... Ser.). (CHI & ENG., Illus.). 20p. (J). (ps-6). 1998. pap. 15.95 incl. audio compact disk (*0-934633-82-7*, Pub. by Teach Me) Penton Overseas.

— Teach Me English: Teaching Guide. (Illus.), 31p. 1993. pap., teacher ed. 6.95 (*0-934633-25-8*) Teach Me.

— Teach Me... English/ESL: A Musical Journey Through the Day. (Teach Me... Ser.). (Illus.). 20p. (J). (ps-7). 1993. pap. 13.95 incl. audio (*0-934633-60-6*, Pub. by Teach Me) Penton Overseas.

***Mahoney, Judy.** Teach Me... English/ESL: A Musical Journey Through the Day. (Teach Me... Ser.). (Illus.). 20p. (J). (ps-6). 1999. pap. 15.95 incl. audio compact disk (*0-934633-58-4*, Pub. by Teach Me) Penton Overseas.

Mahoney, Judy. Teach Me Even More... French: Twenty-One Songs to Sing & a Story about Pen Pals. (Teach Me Even More... Ser.). (ENG & FRE., Illus.). 24p. (J). (ps-7). 1996. pap. 13.95 incl. audio (*0-934633-72-X*, Pub. by Teach Me) Penton Overseas.

— Teach Me Even More... French: Twenty-One Songs to Sing & a Story about Pen Pals. (Teach Me Even More... Ser.). (ENG & FRE., Illus.). 24p. (J). (ps-7). 1996. pap. 16.95 incl. audio compact disk (*0-934633-98-3*, Pub. by Teach Me) Penton Overseas.

Mahoney, Judy. Teach Me Even More... French: Twenty-One Songs to Sing & a Story about Pen Pals. gif. ed. (Teach Me Even More...Ser.). (FRE & ENG., Illus.). 24p. (J). (ps-6). 1996. pap. 17.95 incl. audio compact disk (*0-934633-99-1*, Pub. by Teach Me) Penton Overseas.

Mahoney, Judy. Teach Me Even More... Spanish: Twenty-One Songs to Sing & a Story about Pen Pals. (Teach Me Even More... Ser.). (ENG & SPA., Illus.). 24p. (J). (ps-7). 1995. pap. 13.95 incl. audio (*0-934633-69-X*, Pub. by Teach Me) Penton Overseas.

— Teach Me Even More... Spanish: Twenty-One Songs to Sing & a Story about Pen Pals. (Teach Me Even More... Ser.). (ENG & SPA., Illus.). 24p. (J). (ps-7). 1996. pap., boxed set 15.95 incl. audio compact disk (*0-934633-97-5*, Pub. by Teach Me) Penton Overseas.

— Teach Me Even More... Spanish: Twenty-One Songs to Sing & a Story about Pen Pals. gif. ed. (Teach Me Even More... Ser.). (ENG & SPA., Illus.). 24p. (J). (ps-7). 1995. pap., boxed set 14.95 incl. audio (*0-934633-67-3*, 172, Pub. by Teach Me) Penton Overseas.

Mahoney, Judy. Teach Me Even More... Spanish: Twenty-One Songs to Sing & a Story about Pen Pals. gif. ed. (Teach Me Even More... Ser.). (ENG & SPA., Illus.). 24p. (J). (gr. 2-8). 1996. pap., boxed set 17.95 incl. audio compact disk (*0-934633-89-4*, 172, Pub. by Teach Me) Penton Overseas.

— Teach Me Even More Spanish Book Box: Twenty-One Songs to Sing & a Story about Pen Pals. (Foreign Language Ser.). (SPA.). (J). Price not set. incl. audio NewSound.

— Teach Me... French, gif. ed. (Teach Me... Ser.). (ENG & FRE., Illus.). 20p. (J). (ps-6). 1994. pap., boxed set 14.95 incl. audio (*0-934633-00-2*, Pub. by Teach Me) Penton Overseas.

Mahoney, Judy. Teach Me... French: A Musical Journey Through the Day. rev. ed. (Teach Me... Ser.). (ENG & FRE., Illus.). 20p. (YA). (ps-7). 1989. pap. 13.95 incl. audio (*0-934633-02-9*, Pub. by Teach Me) Penton Overseas.

— Teach Me French: Teaching Guide. rev. ed. (FRE.). 32p. 1994. pap., teacher ed. 6.95 (*0-934633-26-6*) Teach Me.

— Teach Me... German: A Musical Journey Through the Day, rev. ed. (Teach Me... Ser.). (ENG & GER., Illus.). 20p. (J). (ps-6). 1986. pap. 13.95 incl. audio (*0-934633-07-X*, Pub. by Teach Me) Penton Overseas.

— Teach Me German: Teaching Guide. rev. ed. 31p. 1996. pap., teacher ed. 6.95 (*0-934633-27-4*) Teach Me.

***Mahoney, Judy.** Teach Me Hebrew: A Musical Journey Through the Day. (Teach Me... Ser.). (HEB & ENG., Illus.). 20p. (J). (ps-6). 1999. pap. 15.95 incl. audio compact disk (*0-934633-52-5*, Pub. by Teach Me) Penton Overseas.

Mahoney, Judy. Teach Me... Hebrew: A Musical Journey Through the Day. Horowitz, Shelly, tr. (Teach Me... Ser.). (ENG & HEB., Illus.). 20p. (J). (ps-7). 1991. pap. 13.95 incl. audio (*0-934633-54-1*, Pub. by Teach Me) Penton Overseas.

— Teach Me Hebrew: Teaching Guide. 18p. 1991. pap., teacher ed. 6.95 (*0-934633-28-2*) Teach Me.

— Teach Me... Italian: A Musical Journey Through the Day. Grifoni, Maria C., tr. LC 95-787641. (Teach Me... Ser.). (ENG & ITA., Illus.). 20p. (J). (ps-7). 1992. pap. 13.95 incl. audio (*0-934633-57-6*, Pub. by Teach Me) Penton Overseas.

***Mahoney, Judy.** Teach Me... Italian: A Musical Journey Through the Day. Grifoni, Maria C., tr. (Teach Me... Ser.). (ITA & ENG., Illus.). 20p. (J). (ps-6). 1999. pap. 15.95 incl. audio compact disk (*0-934633-55-X*, Pub. by Teach Me) Penton Overseas.

Mahoney, Judy. Teach Me Italian: Teaching Guide. (Illus.). 20p. 1992. pap., teacher ed. 6.95 (*0-934633-29-0*) Teach Me.

Mahoney, Judy. Teach Me... Japanese: A Musical Journey Through the Day. (Teach Me... Ser.). (ENG & JPN., Illus.). 20p. (J). (ps-6). 1990. pap. 13.95 incl. audio (*0-934633-17-7*, Pub. by Teach Me) Penton Overseas.

Mahoney, Judy. Teach Me... Japanese: A Musical Journey Through the Day. (Teach Me... Ser.). (ENG & JPN., Illus.). 20p. (J). (ps-6). 1998. pap. 15.95 incl. audio compact disk (*0-934633-15-0*, Pub. by Teach Me) Penton Overseas.

— Teach Me Japanese: Teaching Guide. rev. ed. (Illus.). 29p. 1996. pap., teacher ed. 6.95 (*0-934633-30-4*) Teach Me.

— Teach Me More... Chinese: A Musical Journey Through the Year. Wang, Amy, tr. (Teach Me More... Ser.). (CHI & ENG., Illus.). 20p. (J). (ps-7). 1997. pap. 13.95 incl. audio (*0-934633-48-7*, Pub. by Teach Me) Penton Overseas.

***Mahoney, Judy.** Teach Me More... Chinese: A Musical Journey Through the Year. Wang, Amy, tr. (Teach Me More... Ser.). (CHI & ENG., Illus.). 20p. (J). (ps-7). 1998. pap. 15.95 incl. audio compact disk (*0-934633-47-9*, Pub. by Teach Me) Penton Overseas.

— Teach Me More Chinese: Teaching Guide. 34p. 1999. pap., teacher ed. 6.95 (*0-934633-42-8*, Pub. by Teach Me) Penton Overseas.

Mahoney, Judy. Teach Me More English: Teaching Guide. (Illus.). 37p. 1994. pap. text, teacher ed. 6.95 (*0-934633-38-X*) Teach Me.

— Teach Me More... English/ESL: A Musical Journey Through the Year. (Teach Me More... Ser.). (Illus.). 20p. (J). (ps-7). 1994. pap. 13.95 incl. audio (*0-934633-66-5*, Pub. by Teach Me) Penton Overseas.

***Mahoney, Judy.** Teach Me More... English/ESL: A Musical Journey Through the Year. (Teach Me More... Ser.). (Illus.). 20p. (J). (ps-6). 1999. pap. 15.95 incl. audio compact disk (*0-934633-64-9*, Pub. by Teach Me) Penton Overseas.

Mahoney, Judy. Teach Me More... French. gif. ed. (Teach Me More... Ser.). (ENG & FRE., Illus.). 20p. (J). (ps-6). 1995. pap., boxed set 14.95 incl. audio (*0-934633-10-X*, Pub. by Teach Me) Penton Overseas.

— Teach Me More... French. gif. ed. (Teach Me More... Ser.). (ENG & FRE., Illus.). 20p. (J). (ps-7). 1996. pap., boxed set 17.95 incl. audio compact disk (*0-934633-88-6*, Pub. by Teach Me) Penton Overseas.

— Teach Me More... French: A Musical Journey Through the Year. (Teach Me More... Ser.). (ENG & FRE., Illus.). 20p. (YA). (ps-7). 1989. pap. 13.95 incl. audio (*0-934633-11-8*, Pub. by Teach Me) Penton Overseas.

— Teach Me More French: Teaching Guide. rev. ed. 35p. 1994. pap., teacher ed. 6.95 (*0-934633-33-9*) Teach Me.

— Teach Me More... German: A Musical Journey Through the Year. (Teach Me More... Ser.). (ENG & GER., Illus.). 20p. (J). (ps-7). 1990. pap. 13.95 incl. audio (*0-934633-23-1*, Pub. by Teach Me) Penton Overseas.

***Mahoney, Judy.** Teach Me More... German: A Musical Journey Through the Year. (Teach Me More... Ser.). (GER & ENG., Illus.). 20p. (J). (ps-6). 1999. pap. 15.95 incl. audio compact disk (*0-934633-21-5*, Pub. by Teach Me) Penton Overseas.

Mahoney, Judy. Teach Me More German: Teaching Guide. rev. ed. (GER.). 36p. 1994. pap., teacher ed. 6.95 (*0-934633-34-7*) Teach Me.

— Teach Me More... Italian: A Musical Journey Through the Year. Grifoni, Maria C., tr. (Teach Me More... Ser.). (ENG & ITA., Illus.). 20p. (J). (ps-7). 1993. pap. 13.95 incl. audio (*0-934633-63-0*, Pub. by Teach Me) Penton Overseas.

***Mahoney, Judy.** Teach Me More... Italian: A Musical Journey Through the Year. Grifoni, Maria C., tr. (Teach Me More... Ser.). (ITA & ENG., Illus.). 20p. (J). (ps-6). 1999. pap. 15.95 incl. audio compact disk (*0-934633-61-4*, Pub. by Teach Me) Penton Overseas.

Mahoney, Judy. Teach Me More Italian: Teaching Guide. 31p. 1993. pap., teacher ed. 6.95 (*0-934633-35-5*) Teach Me.

— Teach Me More... Japanese: A Musical Journey Through the Year. Satoh, Naomi, tr. (Teach Me More... Ser.). (ENG & JPN., Illus.). 20p. (J). (ps-7). 1991. pap. 13.95 incl. audio (*0-934633-20-7*, Pub. by Teach Me) Penton Overseas.

***Mahoney, Judy.** Teach Me More... Japanese: A Musical Journey Through the Year. Satoh, Naomi, tr. (Teach Me More... Ser.). (ENG & JPN., Illus.). 20p. (J). (ps-7). 1998. pap. 15.95 incl. audio compact disk (*0-934633-18-5*, Pub. by Teach Me) Penton Overseas.

Mahoney, Judy. Teach Me More Japanese: Teaching Guide. rev. ed. (JPN.). 35p. 1994. pap., teacher ed. 6.95 (*0-934633-36-3*) Teach Me.

— Teach Me More... Russian: A Musical Journey Through the Year. (Teach Me More... Ser.). (RUS & ENG., Illus.). 20p. (J). (ps-7). 1997. pap. 13.95 incl. audio (*0-934633-78-9*, 126, Pub. by Teach Me) Penton Overseas.

***Mahoney, Judy.** Teach Me More... Russian: A Musical Journey Through the Year. (Teach Me More... Ser.). (RUS & ENG., Illus.). 20p. (J). (ps-6). 1999. pap. 15.95 incl. audio compact disk (*0-934633-76-2*, Pub. by Teach Me) Penton Overseas.

Mahoney, Judy. Teach Me More Russian: Teaching Guide. 35p. 1997. pap., teacher ed. 6.95 (*0-934633-39-8*) Teach Me.

Mahoney, Judy. Teach Me More... Spanish. gif. ed. (Teach Me More... Ser.). (ENG & SPA., Illus.). 20p. (J). (ps-7). 1995. pap., boxed set 14.95 incl. audio (*0-934633-13-4*, Pub. by Teach Me) Penton Overseas.

Mahoney, Judy. Teach Me More... Spanish. gif. ed. (Teach Me More... Ser.). (ENG & SPA., Illus.). 20p. (J). (ps-7). 1996. pap., boxed set 17.95 incl. audio compact disk (*0-934633-87-8*, Pub. by Teach Me) Penton Overseas.

— Teach Me More... Spanish: A Musical Journey Through the Year. (Teach Me More... Ser.). (SPA & ENG., Illus.). 20p. (J). (ps-7). 1989. pap. 13.95 incl. audio (*0-934633-14-2*, Pub. by Teach Me) Penton Overseas.

— Teach Me More... Spanish: A Musical Journey Through the Year. (Teach Me More... Ser.). (ENG & SPA., Illus.). 20p. (J). (ps-7). 1996. pap. 15.95 incl. audio compact disk (*0-934633-95-9*, Pub. by Teach Me) Penton Overseas.

— Teach Me More Spanish: Teaching Guide. rev. ed. 35p. 1996. pap., teacher ed. 6.95 (*0-934633-37-1*) Teach Me.

— Teach Me... Russian: A Musical Journey Through the Day. Gybin, Sasha, tr. (Teach Me... Ser.). (ENG & RUS.). 20p. (J). (ps-7). 1991. pap. 13.95 incl. audio (*0-934633-51-7*, Pub. by Teach Me) Penton Overseas.

***Mahoney, Judy.** Teach Me... Russian: A Musical Journey Through the Day. (Teach Me... Ser.). (RUS & ENG., Illus.). 20p. (J). (ps-6). 1999. pap. 15.95 incl. audio compact disk (*0-934633-24-X*, Pub. by Teach Me) Penton Overseas.

Mahoney, Judy. Teach Me Russian: Teaching Guide. 22p. 1991. pap., teacher ed. 6.95 (*0-934633-31-2*) Teach Me.

— Teach Me... Spanish. gif. ed. (Teach Me... Ser.). (ENG & SPA., Illus.). 20p. (J). (ps-6). 1994. pap., boxed set 14.95 incl. audio (*0-934633-03-7*, Pub. by Teach Me) Penton Overseas.

— Teach Me... Spanish. gif. ed. (Teach Me... Ser.). (ENG & SPA., Illus.). 20p. (J). (ps-7). 1996. pap., boxed set 17.95 incl. audio compact disk (*0-934633-85-1*, Pub. by Teach Me) Penton Overseas.

— Teach Me... Spanish: A Musical Journey Through the Day. rev. ed. (Teach Me... Ser.). (SPA & ENG., Illus.). 20p. (J). (ps-6). 1989. pap. 13.95 incl. audio (*0-934633-05-3*, Pub. by Teach Me) Penton Overseas.

— Teach Me Spanish: Teaching Guide. rev. ed. (Teach Me . . . Ser.). 32p. 1994. pap., teacher ed. 6.95 (*0-934633-32-0*) Teach Me.

— Teach Me...French. gif. ed. (Teach Me... Ser.). (ENG & FRE., Illus.). 20p. (J). (ps-7). 1996. pap., boxed set 17.95 incl. audio compact disk (*0-934633-86-X*, Pub. by Teach Me) Penton Overseas.

Mahoney, Judy, compiled by. Sing with Me in English: A Teach Me Tapes Songbook. (Illus.). 20p. (J). (ps-6). 1994. pap. 7.95 (*0-934633-90-8*) Teach Me.

Mahoney, Judy & Cronan, Mary. Teach Me... French: A Musical Journey Through the Day, rev. ed. (Teach Me... Ser.). (ENG & FRE., Illus.). 20p. (J). (ps-7). 1996. pap. 15.95 incl. audio compact disk (*0-934633-94-0*, Pub. by Teach Me) Penton Overseas.

— Teach Me More... French: A Musical Journey Through the Year. (Teach Me More... Ser.). (ENG & FRE., Illus.). 20p. (J). (ps-7). 1996. pap. 15.95 incl. audio compact disk (*0-934633-96-7*, Pub. by Teach Me) Penton Overseas.

— Teach Me... Spanish: A Musical Journey Through the Day. rev. ed. (Teach Me... Ser.). (ENG & SPA., Illus.). 20p. (J). (ps-7). 1996. pap. 15.95 incl. audio compact disk (*0-934633-93-2*, Pub. by Teach Me) Penton Overseas.

Mahoney, Judy, et al. Teach Me... German: A Musical Journey Through the Day. rev. ed. (Teach Me... Ser.). (GER., Illus.). 16p. (J). (ps-5). 1986. pap. 14.95 incl. audio compact disk (*0-934633-06-1*, Pub. by Teach Me) Penton Overseas.

Mahoney, Kate, jt. auth. see Burmeister, George.

Mahoney, Katherine A. & Murakami, Linda K. Farewell to Arms: Cleaning up Nuclear Weapons Facilities. 70p. 1993. 15.00 (*1-55516-497-8*, 4639) Natl Conf State Legis.

Mahoney, Katherine A., jt. auth. see Reed, James B.

Mahoney, Kathleen. Gothic Style: Architecture & Interiors from the Eighteenth Century to the Present. LC 94-32731. (Illus.). 264p. 1995. 60.00 (*0-8109-3381-0*, Pub. by Abrams) Time Warner.

— Simple Wisdom: Shaker Sayings, Poems, & Songs. LC 92-50729. (Illus.). 96p. 1993. 13.95 (*0-670-84808-5*, Viking Studio) Studio Bks.

— Wisdom from a Shaker Garden. LC 97-48442. 96p. 1998. 14.95 (*0-670-87365-9*) Viking Penguin.

Mahoney, Kathleen E. & Mahoney, Paul, eds. Human Rights in the Twenty-First Century: A Global Challenge. LC 92-15848. 1993. lib. bdg. 266.00 (*0-7923-1810-2*) Kluwer Academic.

Mahoney, Kevin, ed. In Pursuit of Justice: Examining the Evidence of the Holocaust. unabridged ed. LC 96-61170. (Illus.). 259p. 1996. pap. 25.95 (*0-89604-702-4*, Holocaust Library) US Holocaust.

Mahoney, Kevin, ed. Liberation, 1945. 1995. pap. 24.95 (*0-89604-701-6*, Holocaust Library) US Holocaust.

— 1945 Year of Liberation. 1995. pap. 19.95 (*0-89604-700-8*, Holocaust Library) US Holocaust.

Mahoney, Laura. Agricultural Drainages. McClurg, Sue, ed. (Layperson's Guide Ser.). (Illus.). 20p. 1996. pap. 5.00 (*1-893246-54-X*) Water Educ.

Mahoney, M. H. Women in Espionage: A Biographical Dictionary. LC 93-36559. 253p. 1993. lib. bdg. 65.00 (*0-87436-743-3*) ABC-CLIO.

Mahoney, M. J. & Freeman, A. Cognition & Psychotherapy. LC 85-3370. (Illus.). 370p. (C). 1985. 84.00 (*0-306-41858-4*, Plenum Trade) Perseus Pubng.

Mahoney, Marci. Strategic Resumes: Writing for Results. Manber, Beverly, ed. LC 91-76255. (Fifty-Minute Ser.). (Illus.). 151p. (Orig.). 1993. pap. 10.95 (*1-56052-129-5*) Crisp Pubns.

Mahoney, Margaret M. Stepfamilies & the Law. 256p. 1994. text 49.50 (*0-472-10519-1*, 10519) U of Mich Pr.

Mahoney, Mari, et al. Will It Ever Close? 200p. (Orig.). 1995. pap. 6.95 (*0-9649346-0-4*) BWB Ent.

Mahoney, Maria F. Meaning in Dreams & Dreaming. 1966. reprint ed. pap. 9.95 (*0-8065-0095-6*, Citadel Pr) Carol Pub Group.

— What Do Dreams Mean? LC 97-5628. 256p. 1997. pap. 12.95 (*0-8065-1867-7*, Citadel Pr) Carol Pub Group.

Mahoney, Marie M. Reflections on Mary's Help Hospital & Seton Medical Center, 1893-1985. 180p. 1986. 25.00 (*0-9616516-0-1*) Seton Med Ctr.

Mahoney, Marjorie L., jt. auth. see Mahoney, Harry T.

Mahoney, Marjorie Locke, jt. auth. see Mahoney, Harry Thayer.

Mahoney, Mary C., ed. see Forte, Imogene.

Mahoney, Maureen R., jt. auth. see Frenay, Clare A.

Mahoney, Michael, jt. ed. see Arnold, Christopher.

Mahoney, Michael J., ed. Cognitive & Constructive Psychotherapies: Theory, Research, & Practice. (Illus.). 232p. 1994. 38.95 (*0-8261-8610-6*) Springer Pub.

Mahoney, Michael J., jt. ed. see Neimeyer, Robert A.

Mahoney, Michael S. The Mathematical Career of Pierre de Fermat, 1601-1665. 438p. (C). 1994. pap. text 19.95 (*0-691-03666-7*, Pub. by Princeton U Pr) Cal Prin Full Svc.

— The Mathematical Career of Pierre de Fermat, 1601-1665. LC 72-733. 439p. reprint ed. pap. 136.10 (*0-608-30734-3*, 201601700006) Bks Demand.

Mahoney, Michael S., tr. see Descartes, Rene.

***Mahoney, Mick.** Sacred Heart. 1999. pap. 10.95 (*1-84002-106-3*, Pub. by Theatre Comm) Consort Bk Sales.

Mahoney, Mick & Murray, Melissa. The Verity Bargate Award Plays, 1984. Keefe, Barrie, ed. (Methuen New Theatrescripts Ser.). 64p. (C). 1988. pap. write for info. (*0-413-58930-7*, A0305, Methuen Drama) Methn.

***Mahoney, Myra.** Really Useful Guinea Pig Guide. (Illus.). 1999. 6.95 (*1-85279-127-6*) TFH Pubns.

Mahoney-Norris, Kathleen, jt. ed. see Campbell, Patricia J.

Mahoney, Olivia. Go West! Chicago & American Expasion. LC 98-53941. 1999. pap. 19.95 (*0-913820-22-9*) Chicago Hist.

Mahoney, Olivia, jt. auth. see Foner, Eric.

Mahoney Pasternak, Judith. Oprah. LC 99-13865. (Illus.). 120p. 1999. 19.98 (*1-56799-749-X*) M Friedman Pub Grp Inc.

Mahoney, Patrick, jt. auth. see Chanda, Linda J.

Mahoney, Paul. Difficulties with Rosary Meditation. (Queen of Apostles Ser.: Vol. VIII). 11p. 1990. 0.65 (*0-911988-98-X*, 49739) AMI Pr.

Mahoney, Paul, jt. ed. see Mahoney, Kathleen E.

Mahoney, Paul F., et al. Historical Atlas of Colorado. LC 93-21919. (Illus.). 192p. 1994. pap. 19.95 (*0-8061-2591-8*) U of Okla Pr.

Mahoney, Paul T. Narcotics Investigation Techniques. (Illus.). 406p. (C). 1992. pap. 49.95 (*0-398-06263-3*); text 72.95 (*0-398-05803-2*) C C Thomas.

Mahoney, R. C. Animal Behavior: Index of New Information with Authors, Subjects & Bibliography. rev. ed. 1994. 47.50 (*0-7883-0170-5*); pap. 44.50 (*0-7883-0171-3*) ABBE Pubs Assn.

An Asterisk (*) at the beginning of an entry indicates that the title is appearing for the first time.

Mahoney, R. Michael. High-Mix, Low-Volume Manufacturing: Techniques for World Class Competition. LC 97-1613. 222p. (C). 1997. 74.00 (*0-13-255688-X*) P-H.

Mahoney, Richard D. Sons & Brothers: The Days of Jack & Bobby Kennedy. LC 99-25681. 512p. 1999. 27.95 (*1-55970-480-2*, Pub. by Arcade Pub Inc) Time Warner.

***Mahoney, Richard D.** Sons & Brothers: The Days of Jack & Bobby Kennedy. (Illus.). 2000. pap. 14.95 (*1-55970-534-5*, Pub. by Arcade Pub Inc) Time Warner.

Mahoney, Richard O. Petalos. (Illus.). (Orig.). Date not set. pap. write for info. (*1-880708-03-5*) U Phoenix Pr.

Mahoney, Robert. Bruce Helander. LC 93-80843. (Illus.). 112p. 1994. 50.00 (*0-9628514-6-9*) Grassfield Pr.

Mahoney, Rose M. Understanding Medical Terminology. 8th ed. 640p. (C). 1990. text. write for info. (*0-697-14056-3*, WCB McGr Hill) McGrw-H Hghr Educ.

Mahoney, Rose M., jt. auth. see Frenay, Agnes C.

Mahoney, Rosemary. A Likely Story: One Summer with Lillian Hellman. LC 98-22116. 288p. 1998. 23.95 (*0-385-47793-7*) Doubleday.

***Mahoney, Rosemary.** A Likely Story: One Summer with Lillian Hellman. 288p. 1999. pap. 14.00 (*0-385-47931-X*, Anchor NY) Doubleday.

Mahoney, Rosemary. Whoredom in Kimmage: The Private Lives of Irish Women. LC 94-11848. 336p. 1994. pap. 14.95 (*0-385-47450-4*, Anchor NY) Doubleday.

Mahoney, Ruth C. Animal Communications: Index of New Information with Authors, Subjects & Bibliography. 180p. 1993. 47.50 (*1-55914-792-X*); pap. 44.50 (*1-55914-793-8*) ABBE Pubs Assn.

— Animal Testing Alternatives in Health Sciences: Index of New Information with Authors, Subjects & Bibliography. rev. ed. 147p. 1994. 47.50 (*0-7883-0368-6*); pap. 44.50 (*0-7883-0369-4*) ABBE Pubs Assn.

Mahoney, Sheila, ed. see Goode, Erica T., et al.

Mahoney, Sheila, ed. see Rosenbaum, Ernest H.

Mahoney, Sheila, ed. see Rosenbaum, Ernest H., et al.

Mahoney, Sheila, ed. see Wheat, Mary E. & Rosenbaum, Ernest H.

Mahoney, Stephen J. Reason & Write: A Step-by-Step Approach for Success on Written Exams. 160p. 1995. teacher ed. 13.99 (*1-56417-637-1*, GA1546) Good Apple.

Mahoney, T. J., jt. ed. see Beckman, J. E.

Mahoney, Thomas. Law Enforcement Career Planning. (Illus.). 92p. 1989. 29.95 (*0-398-05589-0*); pap. 20.95 (*0-398-06264-1*) C C Thomas.

Mahoney, Thomas H., ed. see Burke, Edmund.

Mahoney, Timothy R. Provincial Lives: Middle-Class Experience in the Antebellum Middle West. LC 98-35800. (Publications of the German Historical Institute, Washington, D. C.). (Illus.). 384p. (C). 1999. text 54.95 (*0-521-64092-X*) Cambridge U Pr.

— River Towns in the Great West: The Structure of Provincial Urbanization in the American Midwest, 1820-1870. (Illus.). 331p. (C). 1990. text 57.95 (*0-521-36130-3*) Cambridge U Pr.

Mahoney, Timothy R., et al. America's History: Instructor's Resource Manual, Vol. 1. 3rd ed. 1997. teacher ed., ring bd. write for info. (*1-57259-217-6*); teacher ed., ring bd. write for info. (*1-57259-362-8*) Worth.

— America's History: Instructor's Resource Manual, Vol. 2. 3rd ed. 1997. teacher ed., ring bd. write for info. (*1-57259-218-4*) Worth.

Mahoney, Tom. Merchants of Life: An Account of the American Pharmaceutical Industry. LC 77-167381. (Essay Index Reprint Ser.). 1977. reprint ed. 20.95 (*0-8369-2608-0*) Ayer.

Mahoney Valley Historical Society Staff. Historical Collections of the Mahoney Valley - (Ohio), Vol. I. 524p. 1993. reprint ed. lib. bdg. 55.00 (*0-8328-3225-1*) Higginson Bk Co.

Mahoney, William F. CFROI Portfolio Management: Buy - Sell - Hold . . . How Many Managers Use CFROI to Help Decide . . . 2000. text 79.95 (*0-7506-4013-8*) Buttrwrth-Heinemann.

Mahoni, William. Polynesian Cultural Center - English. 50p. 1995. pap. write for info. (*0-9644640-0-4*) Polynesian Cult.

Mahony, Ann. Handwriting & Personality: How Graphology Reveals What Makes People Tick. 368p. 1990. mass mkt. 6.99 (*0-8041-0575-8*) Ivy Books.

Mahony, Bertha E., intro. MECH '91 Australia: Engineering for a Competitive World, Conference 6: Maintenance Engineering: Emerging Technologies & a New Professionalism. (Illus.). 105p. (Orig.). 1991. pap. 38.50 (*0-85825-530-8*, Pub. by Inst Engrs Aust-EA Bks) Accents Pubns.

Mahony, Christina Hunt. Contemporary Irish Literature: Transforming Tradition. LC 98-26784. 320p. 1998. text 55.00 (*0-312-15871-8*) St Martin.

— Contemporary Irish Literature: Transforming Tradition. LC 93-26784. 336p. 1999. pap. 18.95 (*0-312-21901-6*) St Martin.

Mahony, J. H., jt. ed. see Stokes, G. S.

Mahony, Jacqueline, jt. auth. see Waller, Diane.

Mahony, John J., jt. ed. see Fowkes, N. D.

Mahony, Liam & Eguren, Luis E. Unarmed Bodyguards: International Accompaniment for the Protection of Human Rights. LC 96-37848. (Illus.). xii, 290p. 1997. 46.00 (*1-56549-069-X*); pap. 21.95 (*1-56549-068-1*) Kumarian Pr.

***Mahony, Margaret A.** Saving the Soul of Medicine. Jacobs, Pamela D., ed. LC 99-67841. (Illus.). 350p. 2000. 21.95 (*1-885003-35-8*, Pub. by R D Reed Pubs) Midpt Trade.

***Mahony, Mary.** There's an "S" on My Back, "S" Is for Scoliosis. (Illus.). 196p. (YA). (gr. 5-8). 1999. pap. 14.95 (*0-9658879-1-X*) Redding Pr.

Mahony, Mary. What Can I Give You? Pasternack, Susan, ed. LC 97-91901. (Illus.). 180p. (Orig.). 1997. per. 12.95 (*0-9658879-0-1*) Redding Pr.

***Mahony, Pat & Hextall, Ian.** Reconstructing Teaching: Standards, Performance & Accountability. LC 00-32302. 2000. pap. write for info. (*0-415-23097-7*) Routledge.

Mahony, Pat & Zmroczek, Christine. Women & Social Class: International Feminist Perspectives. LC 99-17710. 1999. write for info. (*0-8153-3414-1*) Garland.

Mahony, Pat, jt. ed. see Frith, Ruth.

Mahony, Patrick. Psychoanalysis & Discourse. Tuckett, David, ed. (New Library of Psychoanalysis). 250p. (C). 1987. pap. 12.95 (*0-422-61720-2*, Pub. by Tavistock); lib. bdg. 42.50 (*0-422-61030-5*, Pub. by Tavistock) Routldge.

Mahony, Patrick, et al, eds. Behind the Scenes: Freud in Correspondence. 432p. 1997. text 37.00 (*82-00-12706-0*) Scandnvan Univ Pr.

Mahony, Patrick F. Barbed Wit & Malicious Humor. 1985. 20.00 (*0-941694-12-7*) Inst Study Man.

— Escape into the Psychic Kingdom. 1985. 20.00 (*0-941694-18-6*) Inst Study Man.

— It's Better in America. 1985. 20.00 (*0-941694-11-9*) Inst Study Man.

— Maurice Maeterlinck. 1985. 20.00 (*0-941694-22-4*) Inst Study Man.

— Out of the Silence. 1985. 20.00 (*0-941694-17-8*) Inst Study Man.

— You Can Find a Way. 1985. 20.00 (*0-941694-10-0*) Inst Study Man.

Mahony, Patrick J. Freud As a Writer. LC 81-14306. 227p. 1981. 35.00 (*0-8236-2018-2*) Intl Univs Pr.

— Freud's Dora: A Psychoanalytic, Historical, & Textual Study. LC 96-10372. 192p. 1996. 27.00 (*0-300-06622-8*) Yale U Pr.

Mahony, Philip, ed. From Both Sides Now: The Poetry of the Vietnam War & Its Aftermath. LC 98-16628. (ENG & VIE.). 320p. 1998. 29.50 (*0-684-84946-1*); per. 16.00 (*0-684-84947-X*) Scribner.

Mahony, Phillip. Catching Bodies. 80p. 1984. pap. 7.95 (*0-938190-55-5*); text 20.00 (*0-938190-56-3*) North Atlantic.

— Supreme. 80p. 1989. pap. 7.95 (*1-55643-053-1*) North Atlantic.

Mahony, Rhona. Kidding Ourselves: Breadwinning, Babies, & Bargaining Power. 224p. 1996. pap. 15.00 (*0-465-08594-6*, Pub. by Basic) HarpC.

Mahony, Robert. Jonathan Swift's Irish Identity. LC 95-18352. 1995. 35.00 (*0-300-06374-1*) Yale U Pr.

Mahony, Robert, jt. ed. see Rizzo, Betty.

Mahony, Stephan. Mastering Government Securities: A Step-by-Step Guide to the Products, Applications & Risks. 256p. (Orig.). 1996. pap. text 45.00 (*0-273-62416-4*) F T P-H.

Mahony, Stephen. Eurobonds. 1998. wbk. ed. 107.00 (*1-873446-33-0*, Pub. by IFR Pub) Am Educ Systs.

— The Financial Times A-Z of International Finance: The Essential Guide to Tools, Terms & Techniques. LC 99-182104. (Illus.). 280p. (Orig.). 1997. 30.00 (*0-273-62552-7*) F T P-H.

***Mahony, Terry.** Principled Headship: A Headteacher's Guide to the Galaxy. 1999. pap. 14.95 (*1-899836-40-3*, Pub. by Crown Hse) LPC Group.

Mahony, William K. The Artful Universe: An Introduction to the Vedic Religious Imagination. LC 97-9205. (SUNY Series in Hindu Studies). 325p. (C). 1997. text 65.50 (*0-7914-3579-2*); pap. text 21.95 (*0-7914-3580-6*) State U NY Pr.

— The Guru. LC 97-68977. 80p. 1997. pap. 4.75 (*0-911307-59-1*) SYDA Found.

***Mahony, William K., frwd.** Refresh Your Resolution. Smile at Your Destiny: A Book of Contemplations. LC 98-60033. 88p. 1998. pap. text 4.75 (*0-911307-68-0*) SYDA Found.

Mahony, William K., frwd. Blaze the Trail of Equipoise: A Book of Contemplations. 96p. (Orig.). 1995. pap. 4.75 (*0-911307-40-0*) SYDA Found.

MaHood, James, ed. see Mosher, Clelia D.

Mahood, Jan. Adopting a Dog: A Complete & Authoritative Guide. (Illus.). 64p. 1997. 12.95 (*0-7938-0235-0*, WW069) TFH Pubns.

— The Perfect Children's Dogs: A Complete Authoritative Guide. 64p. 1998. 12.95 (*0-7938-0236-9*, WW-070) TFH Pubns.

Mahood, Linda, jt. ed. see Schissel, Bernard.

Mahood, Marie. A Bunch of Strays: A Novel of the Outback. LC 97-159020. 247p. 1996. pap. 16.95 (*1-875998-10-1*, Pub. by Central Queensland) Accents Pubns.

— Icing on the Damper. LC 96-147917. (Illus.). iii, 210p. 1995. reprint ed. pap. 19.95 (*1-875998-03-9*, Pub. by Central Queensland) Accents Pubns.

— Nut Milk Chocolate Gang. (Illus.). 92p. 1997. pap. 15.95 (*1-875998-23-3*, Pub. by Central Queensland) Accents Pubns.

Mahood, Marie. Still Bleating about the Bush. 1997. pap. 14.95 (*1-875998-43-8*, Pub. by Central Queensland) Accents Pubns.

Mahood, Molly M. Poetry & Humanism. (C). 1970. reprint ed. pap. 3.00 (*0-393-00533-X*) Norton.

Mahood, Molly M., ed. see Shakespeare, William.

***Mahood, Shirley A.** Making Our Lives Work: Strategies to Lessen Stress & Build Self-Esteem. 2nd rev. ed. LC 99-72942. xiv, 146p. 1999. pap. 12.95 (*1-887322-14-0*) Emprise NY.

Mahood, Wayne. Written in Blood: A History of the 126th New York Regiment in the Civil War. LC 98-114027. (Illus.). 540p. 1997. 40.00 (*0-944413-33-1*, NB 133) Longstreet Hse.

Mahood, Wayne, et al. Teaching Social Studies in the Middle & Senior High School. 416p. (C). 1990. text 52.60 (*0-675-21253-7*, Merrill Coll) P-H.

Mahootian, Shahrzad. Persian. (Descriptive Grammars Ser.). 408p. (C). 1997. 185.00 (*0-415-02311-4*) Routledge.

Mahota, William J. Russian Motion Verbs for Intermediate Students. LC 95-48780. (RUS.). 139p. (C). 1996. pap. 18.00 (*0-300-06413-6*) Yale U Pr.

Mahover, Mosheh, jt. auth. see Felsenthal, Dan S.

***Mahovlich, Ted.** The Big M: The Frank Mahovlich Story. 244p. 2000. 30.00 (*0-00-200010-5*) HarpC.

Mahovlich, Ted. The Big M: The Frank Mahovlich Story. (Illus.). 256p. 1999. 24.95 (*1-58382-029-9*, Pub. by Sports Masters) Partners-West.

***Mahowald.** Genetics in the Clinic. 2001. pap. text. write for info. (*0-323-01203-5*) Mosby Inc.

Mahowald. Women & Children in Healthcare: An Unequal Majority. (Illus.). 304p. (C). 1996. pap. text 19.95 (*0-19-510870-1*) OUP.

Mahowald, Mark & Priddy, Stewart, eds. Homotopy Theory via Algebraic Geometry & Group Representations: Proceedings of a Conference on Homotopy Theory, March 23-27, 1997, Northwestern University. LC 98-27238. (Contemporary Mathematics Ser.: Vol. 220). 379p. 1998. pap. 74.00 (*0-8218-0805-2*) Am Math.

Mahowald, Mark E. The Metastable Homotopy of S-to-the-N. LC 52-42839. (Memoirs Ser.: No. 1/72). 81p. 1967. pap. 16.00 (*0-8218-1272-6*, MEMO/1/72) Am Math.

Mahowald, Mark E. & Priddy, Stewart. Algebraic Topology: (Proceedings of the International Conference) LC 89-15023. (CONM Ser.: Vol. 96). 350p. 1989. pap. 49.00 (*0-8218-5102-0*, CONM/96) Am Math.

Mahowald, Mark E., jt. ed. see Friedlander, Eric M.

Mahowald, Mary B., ed. Philosophy of Woman: An Anthology of Classic to Current Concepts. 3rd ed. LC 94-25616. 544p. (C). 1994. pap. text 16.95 (*0-87220-261-5*); lib. bdg. 39.95 (*0-87220-262-3*) Hackett Pub.

Mahowald, Mary Briody. Genes, Women, Equality. LC 99-14296. (Illus.). 336p. 1999. text 39.95 (*0-19-512110-4*) OUP.

Mahowald, Misha. An Analog VLSI System for Stereoscopic Vision. LC 93-49498. (International Series in Engineering & Computer Science, VLSI, Computer Architecture, & Digital Screen Processing). 232p. (C). 1994. text 133.50 (*0-7923-9444-5*) Kluwer Academic.

Mahowald, Stephen C. Beyond the Bars: A Journey of Faith in the Modern World. 128p. (Orig.). 1989. pap. 6.95 (*0-685-25936-6*) Goals Unlimited.

Mahr, D., jt. auth. see Boyd, T. J.

Mahr, Daniel, jt. ed. see Boyd, Thomas J.

Mahr, Daniel L. & Ridgway, Nino M. Biological Control of Insects & Mites: An Introduction to Beneficial Natural Enemies & Their Use in Pest Management. (Illus.). 91p. 1998. pap. text 25.00 (*0-7881-7147-X*) DIANE Pub.

***Mahr, Juli.** Mama Tiger, Baba Tiger. LC 99-53519. (Share-a-Story Ser.). (Illus.). (J). 2000. write for info. (*0-7894-5615-X*) DK Pub Inc.

Mahr, Mark. Between Ourselves: The Photographs of Mari Mahr. LC 97-81168. (Illus.). 128p. 1998. pap. 30.00 (*1-85242-550-4*) Serpents Tail.

Mahrad, Ahmad, ed. Jahrbuch des Verbandes Iranischer Akademiker in der Bundesrepublik Deutschland und Berlin-West, Heft 1. 118p. 1981. write for info. (*3-487-07329-3*) G Olms Pubs.

— Jahrbuch des Verbandes Iranischer Akademiker in der Bundesrepublik Deutschland und Berlin-West, Heft 2. 144p. 1982. write for info. (*3-487-07369-2*) G Olms Pubs.

— Jahrbuch des Verbandes Iranischer Akademiker in der Bundesrepublik Deutschland und Berlin-West, Heft 3. 246p. 1983. write for info. (*3-487-07666-7*) G Olms Pubs.

Mahrer, Alvin R. The Complete Guide to Experiential Psychotherapy. LC 95-7302. 412p. 1995. 90.00 (*0-471-12438-9*) Wiley.

— Dream Work in Psychotherapy & Self-Change. 1990. 34.95 (*0-393-70089-5*) Norton.

— Integrations of Psychotherapies: A Guide for Practicing Therapists. LC 87-26091. 208p. 1989. 38.95 (*0-89885-412-1*, Kluwer Acad Hman Sci) Kluwer Academic.

Mahrer, Debi & Levy, Ruth. Being Torah Teacher's Guide. 116p. 1987. pap. 12.95 (*0-933873-37-9*) Torah Aura.

Mahrer, Lawrence N. & Rowe, Debi Mahrer. A Guide to Small Congregation Religious Schools. 1996. pap. text 10.00 (*0-8074-0556-6*, 241852) UAHC.

Mahrous, Haroun, et al. The Electric Power Calculations Handbook. 2nd ed. (Illus.). 496p. 1996. 64.95 (*0-07-057048-5*) McGraw.

Mahry, DiAnna. Muttsey, an Unforgettable Mutt. 1991. 7.95 (*0-924663-16-2*) Alaskan Viewpoint.

***Mahshie, Shawn.** Enhancing Communication Skills of the Deaf & Hard of Hearing Children in Mainstream. 2001. pap. 36.00 (*0-7693-0099-5*) Singular Publishing.

Mahshie, Shawn. A First Language: Whose Choice Is It? (Sharing Ideas Ser.). 30p. 1997. pap. text 2.00 (*0-88095-208-3*) Gallaudet U Pre Coll.

Mahshie, Shawn, ed. see Fisher, Sandi.

Mahshie, Shawn, ed. see Nussbaum, Debra.

Mahshie, Shawn, ed. see Peyton, Joy K. & French, Martha.

Mahshie, Shawn, ed. see Welsh-Charrier, C.

Mahshie, Shawn N. Educating Deaf Children Bilingually: With Insights & Applications from Sweden & Denmark. LC 94-73127. (Illus.). 262p. (J). 1995. pap. text, teacher ed. 19.95 (*0-88095-201-6*) Gallaudet U Pre Coll.

Mahshie, Shawn N., ed. Family Communication Folio: A Folio of Articles from Perspectives in Education & Deafness. 62p. 1997. pap. text 10.95 (*0-88095-215-6*) Gallaudet U Pre Coll.

Mahshie, Shawn N., ed. see Edmonston, Nellie K. & Thane, Nancy L.

Mahshie, Shawn N., ed. see Erting, Lynne & Pfau, Judy.

Mahshie, Shawn N., ed. see Fernandes, Jane K.

Mahshie, Shawn N., ed. see Graney, Sharon.

Mahshie, Shawn N., ed. see Lee, James.

Mahshie, Shawn N., ed. see Sass-Lehrer, Marilyn, et al.

Mahshie, Shawn N., ed. see Schleper, David R.

Mahsun, Carol A. Pop Art & the Critics. Kuspit, Donald, ed. LC 87-6032. (Studies in the Fine Arts: Criticism: No. 23). (Illus.). 156p. reprint ed. pap. 48.40 (*0-8357-1960-X*, 207067200016) Bks Demand.

Mahsun, Carol A., ed. Pop Art: The Critical Dialogue. LC 88-39868. (Studies in the Fine Arts: Criticism: No. 29). Orig. Title: Pop Art: The Critical Dialogue. 258p. reprint ed. 80.00 (*0-8357-1922-7*, 207073500004) Bks Demand.

Mahta, Tarla. Sanskrit Play Production in Ancient India. LC 95-901716. (C). 1995. 38.00 (*81-208-1057-0*, Pub. by Motilal Bnarsidass) S Asia.

Mahtab, M. Ashraf & Grasso, Piergiorgo. Geomechanics Principles in the Design of Tunnels & Caverns in Rocks. LC 92-32794. (Developments in Geotechnical Engineering Ser.: No. 72). 250p. 1992. 190.25 (*0-444-88308-8*) Elsevier.

Mahtani, Aruna, jt. auth. see D'Ardennes, Patricia.

Mahtowin. Columbus: Sinking the Myth/Colon: Ahundir el Mito. 26p. 1992. pap. 2.50 (*0-89567-110-7*) World View Forum.

***Mahugh, Nona Lee Henriksen.** Bacon, Pills & $5 Nills: The Story of Frank & Helen Henriksen. (Illus.). 224p. 2000. pap. 14.95 (*0-9653074-5-X*) Eagle Riv.

Mahunka, S., ed. Natural History of the National Parks of Hungary Vol. 1: The Fauna of the Hortobgay National Park. 415p. 1981. 155.00 (*963-05-2519-4*, Pub. by Akade Kiado) St Mut.

— Natural History of the National Parks of Hungary Vol. 4: The Fauna of the Kisjunsag National Park. 490p. 1986. 150.00 (*963-05-3875-X*, Pub. by Akade Kiado) St Mut.

— Natural History of the National Parks of Hungary Vol. 5: The Fauna of the Kisjunsag National Park. 479p. 1987. 165.00 (*963-05-4352-4*, Pub. by Akade Kiado) St Mut.

Mahunka, S. & Zombort, L., eds. Natural History of the National Parks of Hungary Vol. 2: The Fauna of the Hortobagy National Park. 489p. 1983. 155.00 (*963-05-3198-4*, Pub. by Akade Kiado) St Mut.

Mahurin, Matt. Matt Mahurin: Japan & America. Ishiwata, Maya & Luisotti, Theresa, eds. (ENG & JPN., Illus.). 48p. 1993. 49.95 (*4-947671-01-7*) RAM Publications.

Mahurin, Matt, photos by. Matt Mahurin: Photographs. (Illus.). 96p. 1998. 60.00 (*0-944092-60-8*) Twin Palms Pub.

— Matt Mahurin: Photographs. limited ed. (Illus.). 96p. 1998. 750.00 (*0-944092-61-6*) Twin Palms Pub.

Mahurin, Tim. Jeremy Kooloo. 32p. 1999. pap. 5.99 (*0-14-055749-0*) Viking Penguin.

— Little Petey & Big. 1999. 14.99 (*0-525-45447-0*) NAL.

Mahurin, Walker M. "Bud". Hitler's Fall Guys: An Examination of the Luftwaffe by One of America's Most Famous Aces. (Illus.). 200p. 1999. 29.95 (*0-7643-0871-8*) Schiffer.

Mahut, Helen, ed. see Walesa, Lech.

Mahuzier, Brigitte, et al. Yale French Studies, 90: Same Sex/Different Text? Gay & Lesbian Writing in French. 1996. pap. 18.00 (*0-300-06955-3*) Yale U Pr.

Mahy, Brian W., ed. A Dictionary of Virology. 2nd ed. (Illus.). 368p. 1996. text 49.95 (*0-12-465325-1*) Morgan Kaufmann.

Mahy, Brian W., et al, eds. Molecular Biology of Positive Strand RNA Viruses. (Fems Symposia Ser.). 334p. 1987. text 104.00 (*0-12-599930-5*) Acad Pr.

Mahy, Brian W. & Kangro, Hillar O., eds. Virology Methods Manual. (Illus.). 384p. 1996. pap. text 69.95 (*0-12-465330-8*) Acad Pr.

Mahy, Brian W. & Lvov, Dmitri K., eds. Current Concepts in Virology: From Ivanofsky to the Present. LC 93-3449. 350p. 1993. text 120.00 (*3-7186-0568-6*) Gordon & Breach.

Mahy, Brian W. & Rowson, K. E. Lactic Dehydrogenase Virus. LC 74-34231. (Virology Monographs: Vol. 13). (Illus.). iv, 121p. 1975. 47.00 (*0-387-81270-9*) Spr-Verlag.

Mahy, Brian W.J. & Compans, Richard W., eds. Immunology & Pathogenicity of Persistent Virus Infections. 292p. 1996. text 42.00 (*3-7186-0607-0*, Harwood Acad Pubs) Gordon & Breach.

Mahy, Brian W.J. & Cpmpans, Richard W., eds. Immunology & Pathogenicity of Persistent Virus Infections. 292p. 1996. pap. text 20.00 (*3-7186-0622-4*, Harwood Acad Pubs) Gordon & Breach.

Mahy, Margaret. Aliens in the Family. 192p. (J). (gr. 6-9). 1991. pap. 3.25 (*0-590-44898-6*, Apple Paperbacks) Scholastic Inc.

— Aliens in the Family. 1985. 8.35 (*0-606-06171-1*, Pub. by Turtleback) Demco.

***Mahy, Margaret.** Beaten by a Balloon. (J). 2000. pap. 5.99 (*0-14-056666-X*, PuffinBks) Peng Put Young Read.

Mahy, Margaret. The Blood-&-Thunder Adventure on Hurricane Peak. LC 89-8098. (Illus.). (J). (gr. 4-7). 1989. 13.95 (*0-689-50488-8*) McElderry Bks.

— Boom, Baby, Boom, Boom! LC 96-60725. 32p. (J). 1997. 15.99 (*0-670-87314-4*, Viking) Viking Penguin.

— Bubble Trouble: And Other Poems & Stories. LC 92-3540. (Illus.). 80p. (J). (gr. 3-7). 1992. lib. bdg. 13.95 (*0-689-50557-4*) McElderry Bks.

Mahy, Margaret. A Busy Day for a Good Grandmother. LC 93-77331. (Illus.). 32p. (J). (gr. k-3). 1993. text 14.95 (*0-689-50595-7*) McElderry Bks.

Mahy, Margaret. Catalogue of the Universe. (J). 1987. mass mkt. 2.75 (*0-590-42318-5*) Scholastic Inc.
— The Changeover: A Supernatural Romance. LC 83-83446. 224p. (YA). (gr. 7 up). 1984. 16.00 (*0-689-50303-2*) McElderry Bks.
Mahy, Margaret. The Changeover: A Supernatural Romance. (YA). 1994. 10.09 (*0-606-05784-6*, Pub. by Turtleback) Demco.
Mahy, Margaret. The Chewing-Gum Rescue & Other Stories. (Illus.). 142p. (J). (gr. 3-7). 1991. 12.95 (*0-87951-424-8*, Pub. by Overlook Pr) Penguin Putnam.
— Christmas Tree Tangle. LC 93-80959. (Illus.). 32p. (J). (gr. k-3). 1994. mass mkt. 16.00 (*0-689-50616-3*) McElderry Bks.
— Clancy's Cabin. LC 94-46278. (Illus.). 96p. (J). (gr. 3-5). 1995. 14.95 (*0-87951-592-9*, Pub. by Overlook Pr) Penguin Putnam.
***Mahy, Margaret.** A Dissolving Ghost: Essays & More. 160p. 2000. pap. 22.50 (*0-86473-347-X*, Pub. by Victoria Univ Pr) Paul & Co Pubs.
Mahy, Margaret. 5 Sisters. LC 97-150997. (Illus.). 80p. 1997. 14.99 (*0-670-87042-0*) Viking Penguin.
— Five Sisters. LC 98-49696. (Puffin Chapters Ser.). 80p. (gr. 2-5). 1999. pap. 3.99 (*0-14-130334-4*, PuffinBks) Peng Put Young Read.
— The Five Sisters: A Herculeah Jones Mystery. (Illus.). (J). (gr. 3-7). 1997. 13.99 (*0-614-29143-7*) Viking Penguin.
— Fortunate Name. (Cousins Quartet Ser.). (J). 1995. 8.70 (*0-606-07532-1*) Turtleback.
— Great Ghost Chase. (Illus.). 128p. (YA). (gr. 4-7). 1998. 14.99 (*0-670-87490-6*) Viking Penguin.
— The Great White Man-Eating Shark. (Illus.). 32p. (J). (ps-3). 1996. pap. 5.99 (*0-14-055745-8*, PuffinBks) Peng Put Young Read.
— The Great White Man-Eating Shark: A Cautionary Tale. (J). 1996. 10.19 (*0-606-08757-5*, Pub. by Turtleback) Demco.
— The Greatest Show Off Earth. LC 94-20287. 1996. 10.09 (*0-606-11421-1*, Pub. by Turtleback) Demco.
— The Horrendous Hullabaloo. 32p. 1999. pap. write for info. (*0-14-054533-6*) NAL.
— The Horribly Haunted School. large type ed. (Illus.). (J). 1998. pap. 16.95 (*0-7540-6032-2*, Galaxy Child Lrg Print) Chivers N Amer.
— A Lion in the Meadow. (Illus.). 32p. (J). (ps-3). 1992. 13.95 (*0-87951-446-9*, Pub. by Overlook Pr) Penguin Putnam.
— Making Friends. LC 89-13246. (Illus.). 32p. (J). (gr. k-3). 1990. 13.95 (*0-689-50498-5*) McElderry Bks.
— Memory. (Illus.). 272p. (gr. 7). 1999. 8.00 (*0-689-82911-6*) Aladdin.
— My Mysterious World. LC 95-1291. (Meet the Author Ser.). (Illus.). 32p. (J). (gr. 2-5). 1995. 14.95 (*1-878450-58-1*, 710) R Owen Pubs.
Mahy, Margaret. The Other Side of Silence. 1997. 10.09 (*0-606-13010-1*, Pub. by Turtleback) Demco.
Mahy, Margaret. The Other Side of Silence. LC 95-8615. 192p. (J). 1995. 14.99 (*0-670-86455-2*, Viking) Viking Penguin.
— The Pirate Uncle. (Illus.). 128p. (J). (gr. 3-7). 1994. 14.95 (*0-87951-555-4*, Pub. by Overlook Pr) Penguin Putnam.
— Raging Robots & Unruly Uncles. (Illus.). 94p. (J). (gr. 3-7). 1993. 13.95 (*0-87951-469-8*, Pub. by Overlook Pr) Penguin Putnam.
— The Rattlebang Picnic. (J). 1999. pap. write for info. (*0-241-13477-3*, Sig) NAL.
— Rattlebang Picnic. (Picture Puffin Ser.). (Illus.). 32p. (J). (gr. k-2). 1998. pap. 5.99 (*0-14-055579-X*, PuffinBks) Peng Put Young Read.
— Rattlebang Picnic. (Picture Puffin Ser.). (J). 1998. 11.19 (*0-606-13728-9*, Pub. by Turtleback) Demco.
— The Seven Chinese Brothers. 40p. (J). (ps-3). 1992. pap. 4.99 (*0-590-42057-7*) Scholastic Inc.
— The Seven Chinese Brothers. (SPA., Illus.). 40p. (J). (ps-3). 1994. pap. 3.95 (*0-590-25211-9*) Scholastic Inc.
— Seven Chinese Brothers. (Blue Ribbon Bks.). (J). 1989. 10.19 (*0-606-01945-6*, Pub. by Turtleback) Demco.
— Seventeen Kings & Forty-Two Elephants. LC 87-5311. (Illus.). 32p. (J). (ps-3). 1987. 16.99 (*0-8037-0458-5*, Dial Yng Read) Peng Put Young Read.
— Los Siete Hermanos Chinos - The Seven Chinese Brothers. 40p. (J). (ps-3). 1994. pap. 5.95 (*0-590-48131-2*) Scholastic Inc.
***Mahy, Margaret.** Simply Delicious! LC 98-46185. (Illus.). 32p. (J). (gr. k-4). 1999. 15.95 (*0-531-30181-8*) Orchard Books.
— Summery Saturday Morning. (Picture Puffin Ser.). (Illus.). 32p. (J). (ps-3). 2000. pap. 5.99 (*0-14-056720-8*, PuffinBks) Peng Put Young Read.
Mahy, Margaret. Summery Saturday Morning. (Illus.). 32p. (J). (ps-4). 1998. 15.99 (*0-670-87943-6*) Viking Penguin.
— A Tall Story & Other Tales. LC 91-62222. (Illus.). 96p. (J). (gr. 3-7). 1992. 15.95 (*0-689-50547-7*) McElderry Bks.
— Tangled Fortunes. LC 93-32202. (Cousins Quartet Ser.: Bk. 4). (Illus.). 112p. (J). (gr. 3-6). 1994. 14.95 (*0-385-32066-3*) Delacorte.
— Tangled Fortunes. 1995. 18.95 (*0-385-30979-1*) Doubleday.
— Three Legged Cat. (J). 1995. 10.19 (*0-606-08302-2*, Pub. by Turtleback) Demco.
— Tick Tock Tales. (Illus.). 96p. (J). (gr. k-4). 1994. mass mkt. 16.95 (*0-689-50604-X*) McElderry Bks.
— Tingleberries, Tuckertubs & Telephones. 1998. 9.70 (*0-606-13052-7*, Pub. by Turtleback) Demco.
— Tingleberries, Tuckertubs & Telephones. (Illus.). 96p. (YA). (gr. 3-7). 1998. pap. 4.50 (*0-14-038973-3*) Viking Penguin.
***Mahy, Margaret.** The Tricksters. (Illus.). 272p. (J). 1999. per. 8.00 (*0-689-82910-8*) Aladdin.
— Twenty-Four Hours. LC 99-58947. (Illus.). (J). 2000. write for info. (*0-689-83884-0*) McElderry Bks.
— A Villain's Night Out. large type ed. (Illus.). (J). 1999. pap. write for info. (*0-7540-6083-7*, Galaxy Child Lrg Print) Chivers N Amer.
Mahy, Margaret. When the King Rides By. LC 95-5424. (Illus.). 16p. (Orig.). (J). (ps-2). 1995. pap. 4.95 (*1-57255-002-3*) Mondo Pubng.
***Mahy, Margaret & MacCarthy, Patricia.** Down the Dragon's Tongue. LC 99-50070. (Illus.). 32p. (J). (gr. k-2). 2000. 15.95 (*0-531-30272-5*) Orchard Bks Watts.
Mahy, Margaret, et al. Don't Read This! And Other Tales of the Unnatural. LC 98-3215. (Illus.). 180p. (YA). (gr. 5 up). 2000. 15.95 (*1-886910-22-7*, Pub. by Front Str) Publishers Group.
Mai-Aru & Anisson du Perron, J. Dictionnaire Francais-Tahitien et Tahitien-Francais.Tr. of Tahitian-French-Tahitian Dictionary. (FRE.). 380p. 1973. 39.95 (*0-8288-6267-2*, M-6383) Fr & Eur.
Mai, Bill. Best in Tent Camping: Northern California. LC 97-21675. (Best in Tent Camping Ser.). 200p. (Orig.). 1997. pap. 13.95 (*0-89732-249-5*) Menasha Ridge.
— Best in Tent Camping: Southern California. LC 96-17945. 220p. 1996. pap. 13.95 (*0-89732-216-9*) Menasha Ridge.
Mai, Charles F. Secrets of Major Gift Fund Raising. LC 87-25568. 170p. 1987. 25.95 (*0-914756-39-7*) Taft Group.
***Mai, Gerald.** Die Rechtliche Zulassigkeit der Embryonalen Gewebe- Und Zellentnahme Zum Zwecke der Entwicklung Einer Neuartigen Therapiestrategie Gegen die Parkinsonsche Krankheit. XVI, 140p. 1999. 37.95 (*3-631-34289-6*) P Lang Pubng.
Mai, Hoang D. Tinh-Yeu Trong Doi Thuong. 104p. pap. text 7.50 (*1-885550-03-0*) Du-Sinh St Joseph.
Mai, Juergen K., et al, eds. Atlas of the Human Brain. LC 97-10171. (Illus.). 328p. 1997. pap. text 89.95 (*0-12-465361-8*) Morgan Kaufmann.
Mai, Jurgen K. Atlas of the Human Brain. 1998. pap. text 109.95 (*0-12-465362-6*) Acad Pr.
Mai, Jurgen K., et al, eds. Atlas of the Human Brain. LC 97-10171. (Illus.). 328p. 1997. text 135.00 (*0-12-465360-X*) Morgan Kaufmann.
Mai, Ludwig H. Men & Ideas in Economics: A Dictionary of World Economists Past & Present. (Quality Paperbacks Ser.: No. 284). 270p. (Orig.). 1977. reprint ed. pap. 9.95 (*0-8226-0284-9*) Rowman.
Mai, Nguyen T. The Rubber Tree: Memoir of a Vietnamese Woman Who Was an Anti-French Guerrilla, a Publisher & a Peace Activist. Senderowicz, Monique, ed. LC 94-2055. (Illus.). 272p. 1994. lib. bdg. 29.95 (*0-89950-954-1*) McFarland & Co.
Mai, Robert P. & McAdams, Jerry L. Learning Partnerships: How Leading American Companies Implement Organizational Learning. LC 95-21265. 240p. 1995. 29.95 (*0-7863-0388-3*, Irwn Prfssnl) McGraw-Hill Prof.
Mai, Y. W., jt. auth. see Atkins, Anthony G.
Mai, Y. W., jt. auth. see Kim, Jang-Kyo.
Mai, Y. W., jt. ed. see Ye, L.
Mai, Yiv-Wing & Cotterell, Brian. Fracture Mechanics of Cementitious Materials. (Illus.). 320p. 1996. text 124.95 (*0-7514-0036-X*, Pub. by B Acad & Prof) Routldge.
Maia. Peptides 1994. 1000p. 1995. text 349.50 (*90-72199-21-9*) Kluwer Academic.
Maia & Rektorys, Karel. Survey of Applicable, Vol. II. 1994. lib. bdg. write for info. (*0-7923-0681-3*) Kluwer Academic.
Maia, Fred, jt. auth. see West, Gordon.
Maia, Marcello. Prometheus. LC 96-44344. (Illus.). 96p. 1997. 13.00 (*0-312-15166-7*, Stonewall Inn) St Martin.
Maia Neto, Jose R. Machado de Assis, the Brazilian Pyrrhonian. LC 94-3008. (Studies in Romance Literatures: Vol. 5). 248p. 1994. 42.95 (*1-55753-051-3*) Purdue U Pr.
***Maia, Nuno Manuel Mendes & Montalvdao e Silva, J. M.** Modal Analysis & Testing. LC 99-26683. (NATO Science Ser.). 1999. write for info. (*0-7923-5893-7*) Kluwer Academic.
Maia, Ronaldo & Otis, Denise. More Decorating with Flowers. (Illus.). 208p. 1991. 60.00 (*0-8109-3622-4*) Abrams.
Maiakovskii, V. V. Chelovek, Sobytiia Vremiia. 184p. 1984. 75.00 (*0-7855-2921-7*) St Mut.
Maiani, L., et al, eds. 3 K Cosmology: EC-TMR Conference. (Conference Proceedings Ser.: Vol. 476). 13p. 1999. 110.00 (*1-56396-847-9*) Am Inst Physics.
Maib, Donald E., Jr. & Tindall, James A. Speed-Strength Training for Martial Artists: Mind-Body Link. unabridged ed. (Illus.). (Orig.). 1997. pap. 49.95 incl. VHS (*1-890540-00-5*) Taylor Sports.
Maib, Karen M., et al, eds. Tree Fruit Physiology: Growth & Development: A Comprehensive Manual for Deciduous Tree Fruit Growth & Development Needs. LC 96-46960. 216p. (Orig.). 1996. pap. 17.00 (*0-9630659-6-3*) Good Fruit Grow.
Maibach, Edward & Parrot, Roxanne L. Designing Health Messages: Public Health Practice & Communication Theory. 250p. 1995. text 48.00 (*0-8039-5397-6*); pap. text 22.95 (*0-8039-5398-4*) Sage.
Maibach, H. I., jt. auth. see Shah, V. P.
Maibach, Howard, jt. auth. see Aly, Raza.
Maibach, Howard I., ed. Animal Models in Dermatology, Relevance to Human Dermatopharmacology & Dermatotoxicology: Proceedings of a Symposium, University of California Medical School, San Francisco. LC 75-16283. 288p. reprint ed. pap. 89.30 (*0-8357-5489-8*, 205632700059) Bks Demand.
— Dermatologic Research Techniques. (CRC Press Dermatology). 288p. 1995. boxed set 119.95 (*0-8493-8373-0*, 8373) CRC Pr.
Maibach, Howard I., et al, eds. Cutaneous Infection & Therapy. LC 97-5560. (Clinical Dermatology Ser.: Vol. 14). (Illus.). 512p. 1997. text 165.00 (*0-8247-9826-0*) Dekker.
— Prevention of Contact Dermatitis. LC 96-20543. (Current Problems in Dermatology Ser.: Vol. 25, 1996). (Illus.). x, 226p. 1996. text 240.00 (*3-8055-6311-6*) S Karger.
Maibach, Howard I. & Boisits, Edward K. Neonatal Skin: Structure & Function. (Dermatology Ser.: Vol. 1). (Illus.). 296p. 1982. text 135.00 (*0-8247-1860-7*) Dekker.
Maibach, Howard I. & Bronaugh, Robert L. Percutaneous Absorption: Mechanisms - Methodology - Drug Delivery. 2nd ed. (Illus.). 632p. 1989. text 215.00 (*0-8247-8036-1*) Dekker.
Maibach, Howard I. & Elsner, P., eds. Irritant Dermatitis: New Clinical & Experimental Aspects. (Current Problems in Dermatology Ser.: Vol. 23). (Illus.). x, 302p. 1995. 259.25 (*3-8055-6083-4*) S Karger.
Maibach, Howard I. & Lowe, N. J., eds. Dermatology. (Models in Dermatology Ser.: No. 1). (Illus.). x, 374p. 1984. 217.50 (*3-8055-3945-2*) S Karger.
— Dermatopharmacology & Toxicology. (Models in Dermatology Ser.: No. 2). (Illus.). x, 370p. 1984. 217.50 (*3-8055-3947-9*) S Karger.
— Models in Dermatology, Vol. 4. x, 298p. 1989. 321.75 (*3-8055-4761-7*) S Karger.
— Models in Dermatology, 1987, Vol. 3. xvi, 204p. 1987. 217.50 (*3-8055-4239-9*) S Karger.
Maibach, Howard I. & Smith, Eric W., eds. Percutaneous Penetration Enhancers. LC 95-7119. 512p. 1995. boxed set 159.95 (*0-8493-2605-2*, 2605) CRC Pr.
Maibach, Howard I. & Surber, C., eds. Topical Corticosteroids. (Illus.). viii, 518p. 1991. 275.75 (*3-8055-5332-3*) S Karger.
Maibach, Howard I., et al. Handbook of Contact Dermatitis. 350p. 1995. 69.95 (*0-8493-7351-4*) CRC Pr.
***Maibach, Howard I., et al.** Pesticide Dermatosis. 500p. 1999. 89.95 (*1-56670-293-3*) Lewis Pubs.
Maibach, Howard I., jt. auth. see Avalos, Javier.
Maibach, Howard I., jt. auth. see Baran, Robert.
Maibach, Howard I., jt. auth. see Bronaugh, Robert L.
Maibach, Howard I., jt. auth. see Elsner, Peter.
Maibach, Howard I., jt. auth. see Loden, Marie.
Maibach, Howard I., jt. auth. see Menne, Torkil.
Maibach, Howard I., jt. auth. see Orkin, Milton.
Maibach, Howard I., jt. auth. see Reeves, John R.
Maibach, Howard I., jt. auth. see Roenigk, Henry H.
Maibach, Howard I., jt. auth. see Schwindt, Doris A.
Maibach, Howard I., jt. auth. see Steigleder, G. K.
Maibach, Howard I., jt. ed. see Andersen, K. E.
Maibach, Howard I., jt. ed. see Korting, H. C.
Maibach, Howard I., jt. ed. see Marzulli, Francis N.
Maibach, Howard I., jt. ed. see Menne, Torkil.
Maibach, Howard I., jt. ed. see Van Der Valk, Pieter.
Maiback, Howard I., ed. Nickel & the Skin. 232p. 1989. boxed set 166.95 (*0-8493-6976-2*, RL803) CRC Pr.
Maibaum, Thomas S. E., ed. see FASE 2000 Staff.
Maiben, Dina, jt. auth. see Zlotowitz, Bernard M.
Maiboroda, Tanya. School. (Hidden Pictures Coloring Bks.). (Illus.). 48p. (J). 1994. pap. 3.95 (*1-56565-179-0*, 01790W, Pub. by Lowell Hse) NTC Contemp Pub Co.
— Zoo. (Hidden Pictures Coloring Bks.). (Illus.). 48p. (Orig.). (J). (gr. k-2). 1987. pap. 3.99 (*0-8431-1879-2*, Price Stern) Peng Put Young Read.
Maid, Amy. Communication As a Second Language, 5 pts. Incl. Pt. 1. Language. 1978. pap. 10.95 (*0-916250-28-8*); Pt. 2. Ideas. 1978. pap. 10.95 (*0-916250-29-6*); Pt. 3. Mass Communication. 1978. pap. 10.95 (*0-916250-30-X*); Pt. 4. Print. 1978. pap. 10.95 (*0-916250-31-8*); Pt. 5. Airwaves & Beyond. 1978. pap. 10.95 (*0-916250-32-6*); (Mandala Series in Education). (Illus.). write for info. (*0-318-53705-2*) Irvington.
— Mindscapes. LC 82-9904. 67p. (J). (gr. 3-8). 1983. pap. 11.95 (*0-8290-1001-7*) Irvington.
— Write from the Beginning. (Illus.). 94p. (Orig.). (J). (gr. k-5). 1987. pap. 19.95 (*0-8290-0993-0*) Irvington.
Maid, Amy & Timmekmann, Tim. Something for 10:30: Involvement Cards for Social Skills. rev. ed. LC 77-92392. (Illus.). 158p. (YA). (gr. 7-12). 1987. pap. 29.95 (*0-8290-0353-3*) Irvington.
Maida, Carl A., et al. The Crisis of Competence: Transitional Stress & the Displaced Worker. LC 89-15825. (Psychosocial Stress Ser.: No. 16). 224p. 1990. text 33.95 (*0-87630-559-1*) Brunner-Mazel.
Maida, Pamela. Freedom of Information Act Guide & Privacy Act Overview 1996. 711p. 1996. per. 36.00 (*0-16-048853-2*) USGPO.
— Freedom of Information Act Guide & Privacy Act Overview 1997. 757p. 1997. boxed set 39.00 (*0-16-049273-4*) USGPO.
***Maida, Pamela, ed.** Freedom of Information Act Guide & Privacy Act Overview. 755p. (Orig.). 1999. reprint ed. pap. text 65.00 (*0-7881-7245-X*) DIANE Pub.
Maida, Pamela, ed. Freedom of Information Act Guide & Privacy Act Overview, 1998. 809p. 1998. pap. 39.00 (*0-16-049784-1*) USGPO.
— Freedom of Information Case List, 1998. 524p. 1998. pap. 26.00 (*0-16-049785-X*) USGPO.
Maida, Patricia D. Mother of Detective Fiction: The Life & Works of Anna Katharine Green. 120p. 1989. 24.95 (*0-87972-445-5*) Bowling Green Univ Popular Press.
Maida, Patricia D. & Spornick, Nicholas B. Murder She Wrote: A Study of Agatha Christie's Detective Fiction. 199p. 1982. 16.95 (*0-87972-215-0*) Bowling Green Univ Popular Press.
Maida, Shuichi. The Evil Person: Essays on Shin Buddhism. Haneda, Nobuo, tr. from JPN. & intro. by. LC 88-84034. 101p. (Orig.). (C). 1989. pap. 8.00 (*0-9622047-0-6*) HHNATC.
— Heard by Me: Essays on My Buddhist Teacher. Haneda, Nobuo, ed. & tr. by. LC 90-82529. 242p. (Orig.). 1992. pap. 15.00 (*0-9627231-0-X*) Frog Pr.
Maiden, Anne H. & Farwell, Edie. The Tibetan Art of Parenting: From Before Conception Through Early Childhood. LC 97-17055. (Illus.). 224p. 1997. pap. 16.95 (*0-86171-129-7*) Wisdom MA.
***Maiden, Jennifer.** Mines. 104p. 1999. pap. text 15.95 (*90-5704-046-8*) Gordon & Breach.
Maiden, Martin. A Linguistic History of Italian. LC 93-46832. (Longman Linguistics Library). 1994. write for info. (*0-582-05929-1*, Pub. by Addison-Wesley) Longman.
Maiden, Martin & Parry, Mair, eds. Dialects of Italy. 496p. (C). 1997. 150.00 (*0-415-11104-8*) Routledge.
***Maiden, Martin & Robustelli, Cecelia.** A Reference Grammar of Modern Italian. LC 99-47884. 544p. 2000. pap. 30.31 (*0-658-00430-1*, 004301) NTC Contemp Pub Co.
Maiden, Martin, jt. ed. see Smith, John C.
Maiden, Mike. The Joshua Generation: God's Conquering Manifesto. Walker, Jeff E., ed. 193p. (Orig.). (C). 1990. pap. text 7.95 (*0-9626327-1-6*) Victory Chris Ctr.
Maiden, Neil, jt. ed. see Walton, Paul.
Maiden, Nell. Reflections in a Clockshop. (Illus.). 48p. 1996. pap. 8.00 (*1-885912-06-4*) Sows Ear Pr.
Maiden, Peter. Take My Plastic: Christian Giving & Stewardship for Today. 90p. 1997. reprint ed. pap. text 6.99 (*1-85078-263-6*, Pub. by O M Pubng) OM Literature.
Maiden, R. Paul, ed. Employee Assistance Programs in South Africa. LC 92-12236. (Employee Assistance Quarterly Ser.: Vol. 7, No. 3). (Illus.). 145p. 1992. text 39.95 (*1-56024-302-3*) Haworth Pr.
— Employee Assistance Services in the New South Africa. LC 99-11631. 115p. 1999. 49.95 (*0-7890-0681-2*) Haworth Pr.
Maiden, Robert J., jt. auth. see Peterson, Steven A.
Maidens, Marion & Marks, Mel. Jewish Heroes of the Wild West. LC 96-6602. (J). 1997. pap. 10.95 (*0-8197-0623-X*) Bloch.
Maidens, Melinda, ed. American Technology: Are We Falling Behind? LC 82-15603. 191p. reprint ed. pap. 59.30 (*0-8357-3493-5*, 203975200013) Bks Demand.
— Immigration: New Americans, Old Questions. LC 81-9914. 198p. reprint ed. pap. 61.40 (*0-608-16448-8*, 202722000054) Bks Demand.
— Life, Death & the Government. fac. ed. LC 80-29094. (Illus.). 200p. 1980. reprint ed. pap. 62.00 (*0-7837-8143-1*, 204795100008) Bks Demand.
— Religion, Morality & the "New Right" LC 82-2333. (Illus.). 224p. reprint ed. pap. 69.50 (*0-8357-4242-3*, 203703000007) Bks Demand.
Maidens, Melinda, jt. ed. see Burr, Jeanne.
Maidin, Uinseann O., tr. The Celtic Monk: Rules & Writings of Early Irish Monks. 1997. pap. 18.95 (*0-87907-662-3*) Cistercian Pubns.
— The Celtic Monk: Rules & Writings of Early Irish Monks. (Cistercian Studies: No. 162). 1997. 38.95 (*0-87907-562-7*) Cistercian Pubns.
Maidique, Modesto A., jt. auth. see Burgelman, Robert A.
Maidman, Frank. Child Welfare: A Source Book of Knowledge & Practice. 454p. 1984. pap. 32.95 (*0-87868-236-8*) Child Welfare.
***Maidman Joshua, Janice & DiMenna, Donna.** Read Two Books & Let's Talk Next Week: Using Bibliotherapy in Clinical Practice. LC 99-89721. 415p. 2000. pap. text 39.95 (*0-471-37565-9*) Wiley.
Maidman, M. P. Two Hundred Nuzi Texts from the Oriental Institute of the University of Chicago, Pt. I. (Studies on the Civilization & Culture of Nuzi & the Hurrians: Vol. 6). 449p. (C). 1994. 50.00 (*1-883053-05-6*) CDL Pr.
Maidman, Maynard P., jt. auth. see Lacheman, Ernest R.
Maidment. Annual Editions: Human Resources, 97-98. 7th ed. 256p. (C). 1997. text. write for info. (*0-697-37291-X*) Brown & Benchmark.
— Annual Editions: International Business, 97-98. 6th ed. 256p. (C). 1997. text. write for info. (*0-697-37301-0*, WCB McGr Hill) McGrw-H Hghr Educ.
***Maidment.** Business in Government & Society. LC 99-45118. (Illus.). 378p. (C). 1999. 53.00 (*0-13-769217-X*, Macmillan Coll) P-H.
Maidment. Human Resources. 4th ed. 1993. 12.74 (*1-56134-204-1*) McGraw.
— Human Resources. 5th ed. 1995. 12.74 (*1-56134-338-2*) McGraw.
— Human Resources 1999-2000 Edition. 9th ed. 1998. pap., student ed. 16.56 (*0-07-041355-X*) McGraw.
— Human Resources 1996/97. 6th annot. ed. 1996. teacher ed. 13.12 (*0-697-31541-X*, WCB McGr Hill) McGrw-H Hghr Educ.
— International Business. 3rd ed. 1994. 12.74 (*1-56134-280-7*) McGraw.
— International Business. 4th ed. 1995. 12.74 (*1-56134-361-7*) McGraw.
— International Business 1996/97. 5th annot. ed. 1995. teacher ed. 13.12 (*0-697-31087-6*, WCB McGr Hill) McGrw-H Hghr Educ.
— Internationl Business 1999-2000 Edition. 8th ed. 1998. pap., student ed. 16.56 (*0-07-040337-6*) McGraw.
— Management. 3rd ed. 1994. 12.74 (*1-56134-281-5*) McGraw.
Maidment, jt. auth. see Cateora.
Maidment, Brian, ed. The Poorhouse Fugitives: Self-Taught Poets & Poetry in Victorian Britain. pap. write for info. (*0-85635-970-X*, Pub. by Carcanet Pr) Paul & Co Pubs.
Maidment, David R. Handbook of Hydrology. 1424p. 1993. 135.00 (*0-07-039732-5*) McGraw.
Maidment, Derek, jt. ed. see Owen, Fred.

An Asterisk (*) at the beginning of an entry indicates that the title is appearing for the first time.

Maidment, Fred H. Annual Editions: International Business, 96-97. 5th ed. 256p. (C). 1995. text. write for info. (*0-697-31088-4*) Brown & Benchmark.
— Annual Editions: Management, 96-97. 4th ed. 288p. (C). 1995. per. (*1-56134-433-8*) Brown & Benchmark.
— Annual Editions: Management, 97-98. 5th ed. 256p. (C). 1997. per. write for info. (*0-697-37306-1*) Brown & Benchmark.
— Human Resources: 1996-1997. annuals 6th ed. 256p. (C). 1996. text. write for info. (*0-697-31540-1*) Brown & Benchmark.
— Human Resources, 98-99. 8th ed. (Annual Ser.). (Illus.). 240p. 1998. pap. text 12.25 (*0-697-39184-1*, Dshkn McG-Hill) McGrw-H Hghr Educ.
***Maidment, Fred H.** Human Resources 2000-2001. (Annual Editions Ser.). 240p. (C). 1999. pap. 16.56 (*0-07-236414-9*) McGrw-H Hghr Educ.
Maidment, Fred H. International Business, 98-99. 7th ed. (Annual Ser.). (Illus.). 240p. 1998. pap. text 12.25 (*0-697-39182-5*, Dshkn McG-Hill) McGrw-H Hghr Educ.
***Maidment, Fred H.** International Business 2000-2001. 9th ed. (Annual Editions Ser.). 240p. (C). 1999. pap. 16.56 (*0-07-236406-8*) McGrw-H Hghr Educ.
Maidment, Fred H. Key Documents: United States in the Twentieth Century. 1995. text 14.95 (*0-340-60988-5*, Pub. by E A) St Martin.
— Management, 98-99. 6th ed. (Annual Ser.). (Illus.). 240p. 1998. pap. text 12.25 (*0-697-39181-7*, Dshkn McG-Hill) McGrw-H Hghr Educ.
***Maidment, Fred H.** Management 2000-2001. 8th ed. (Annual Editions Ser.). 240p. (C). 1999. pap. 16.56 (*0-07-236402-5*) McGrw-H Hghr Educ.
— Organization Behavior 2000-2001. (Annual Editions Ser.). 240p. (C). 1999. pap. 16.56 (*0-07-233376-6*) McGrw-H Hghr Educ.
Maidment, Fred H. Popular Prints, 1790-1870: Reading Popular Graphic Images. LC 95-43364. (Illus.). 240p. (C). 1997. text 69.95 (*0-7190-3370-5*, Pub. by Manchester Univ Pr) St Martin.
Maidment, James. Chronicle of Perth. LC 72-1038. (Maitland Club, Glasgow. Publications: No. 10). reprint ed. 27.50 (*0-404-52939-9*) AMS Pr.
— Notices Relative to the Bannatyne Club. LC 70-172715. (Bannatyne Club, Edinburgh. Publications). reprint ed. 37.50 (*0-404-52887-2*) AMS Pr.
— Scottish Ballads & Songs, Historical & Traditionary, 2 vols. LC 78-144497. reprint ed. 67.50 (*0-404-08670-5*) AMS Pr.
Maidment, James, ed. see Cokain, Aston.
Maidment, James, ed. see Crowne, John.
Maidment, James, ed. see Lacy, John.
Maidment, James, ed. see Marmion, Shakerley.
Maidment, James, ed. see Tatham, John.
Maidment, James, ed. see Wilson, John.
Maidment, John A., jt. auth. see Lecumberri, M. Luisa Garcia.
Maidment, K. J., tr. Minor Attic Orators, Vol. 1. Incl. Antiphon & Andocides. (Loeb Classical Library: No. 308). 15.50 (*0-674-99340-3*) HUP.
Maidment, Liz. Art Embroidery. (Illus.). 80p. 1996. pap. 19.95 (*0-233-98949-8*, Pub. by Andre Deutsch) Trafalgar.
Maidment, Margaret. A Manual of Hand-Made Bobbin Lace Work. (Illus.). 1983. 22.50 (*0-7134-3855-X*) Robin & Russ.
Maidment, Patricia. How to Build & Furnish a Dollhouse for 100 Dollars or Less. LC 82-17778. 224p. 1983. pap. 10.95 (*0-672-52745-6*) Macmillan.
Maidment, Richard & Goldblatt, David, eds. Governance in the Asia Pacific. LC 98-226793. (The Open University Pacific Studies Course: Vol. 4). (Illus.). 320p. (C). 1998. 75.00 (*0-415-17275-6*); pap. 24.99 (*0-415-17276-4*) Routledge.
Maidment, Richard & Mackerras, Colin, eds. Culture & Society in the Asia Pacific. LC 98-196110. (The Open University Pacific Studies Course: Vol. 3). (Illus.). 3p. (C). 1998. 75.00 (*0-415-17277-2*); pap. 24.99 (*0-415-17278-0*) Routledge.
Maidment, Richard A., ed. Democracy. (The U. S. in the Twentieth Century Ser.). 288p. 1995. text 14.95 (*0-340-59686-4*, Pub. by E A) St Martin.
Maidment, Richard A. & Dawson, Michael, eds. Key Documents. 288p. 1995. text 14.95 (*0-340-59689-9*, Pub. by E A) St Martin.
Maidment, Richard A. & Tappin, Michael. American Politics Today. 3rd ed. (Politics Today Ser.). 200p. 1989. text 14.95 (*0-7190-3081-1*) Manchester Univ Pr.
Maidment, Richard A. & Thompson, Grahame. Managing the United Kingdom: An Introduction to Its Political Economy & Public Policy. (Illus.). 288p. (C). 1993. text 59.95 (*0-8039-8850-8*); pap. text 21.95 (*0-8039-8851-6*) Sage.
Maidment, Robert. Decisions: Perspectives for the School Administrator. 48p. 1986. pap. 8.00 (*0-88210-192-7*) Natl Assn Principals.
— Robert's Rules of Disorder: A Guide to Mismanagement. (Illus.). 114p. 1994. pap. 8.95 (*1-56554-111-1*) Pelican.
Maidment, Robert & Bullock, William. Meetings, Meetings, Meetings: Accomplishing More with Better & Fewer. George, Patricia L., ed. 48p. (Orig.). 1984. pap. 6.00 (*0-88210-162-5*) Natl Assn Principals.
Maidment, Stella. A Brave Knight to the Rescue! LC 97-12349. (Gamebook Preschool Puzzler Ser.). (Illus.). 32p. (J). (gr. k-3). 1998. pap. 5.99 (*0-7636-0325-2*) Candlewick Pr.
— Sir Roland Saves Lion Castle. Reader's Digest Editors, ed. (Playmobil Play Towers Ser.: Vol. 1). (Illus.). 12p. (J). (gr. k-3). 1998. boxed set 10.99 (*1-57584-238-6*, Pub. by Rdrs Digest) Random.
— Stampede at Fort Glory. Reader's Digest Editors, ed. (Playmobil Play Towers Ser.: Vol. 2). (Illus.). 12p. (J). (gr. k-3). 1998. boxed set 10.99 (*1-57584-239-4*, Pub. by Rdrs Digest) Random.
Maidment, William. Triple Play. 160p. (Orig.). 1993. pap. 4.95 (*0-9619930-9-X*) Moonfall Pr VA.
Maidoff, Ilka. Let's Explore the Shore. (Illus.). (J). (gr. 5 up). 1962. 9.95 (*0-8392-3017-6*) Astor-Honor.
Maiello, Anthony, jt. auth. see Bullock, Jack.
Maienschein, Jane. One Hundred Years Exploring Life, 1888-1988, the Marine Biological Laboratory at Woods Hole. 208p. 1989. pap. 24.95 (*0-86720-120-7*) Jones & Bartlett.
— Transforming Traditions in American Biology, 1880-1915. LC 90-15623. (Illus.). 288p. 1991. text 48.00 (*0-8018-4126-7*) Johns Hopkins.
Maienschein, Jane, ed. Defining Biology: Lectures from the 1890's. LC 86-307. (Illus.). 352p. 1986. 41.00 (*0-674-19615-5*) HUP.
Maienschein, Jane & Ruse, Michael, eds. Biology & the Foundation of Ethics. LC 98-30711. (Studies in Philosophy & Biology). (Illus.). 350p. (C). 1999. text 64.95 (*0-521-55100-5*); pap. text 19.95 (*0-521-55923-5*) Cambridge U Pr.
Maienschein, Jane, jt. ed. see Creath, Richard.
***Maier.** Passing of the Territorial Age. 2000. 30.00 (*0-465-04319-4*, Pub. by Basic); pap. 15.00 (*0-465-04320-8*, Pub. by Basic) HarpC.
Maier, A. English in the Cockpit. (ENG & GER.). 400p. 1986. lib. bdg. 85.00 (*0-8288-3400-8*, F41073) Fr & Eur.
Maier, Albert M. Friendly Concern. 14p. (Orig.). 1994. pap. write for info. (*1-885206-13-5*, Iliad Pr) Cader Pubng.
Maier, Alexandra. Audiovisuelle Vernehmung Kindlicher Opfer von Straftaten Gegen die Sexuelle Selbstbestimmung Im Strafverfahren. 227p. 1997. 51.95 (*3-631-32289-5*) P Lang Pubng.
Maier, Ann H. Elderly Care Source Book: Comprehensive Guide to Long Term Care Facilities in Connecticut. 532p. (Orig.). 1996. pap. 85.00 (*0-9626513-1-1*) Maier Pubns.
— Elderly Care Source Book: Comprehensive Guide to Long Term Care Facilities in New York State. 536p. (Orig.). 1997. pap. 85.00 (*0-9626513-3-8*) Maier Pubns.
Maier, Anne M. Mother Love, Deadly Love: The Texas Cheerleader Murder Plot. (Illus.). 256p. 1992. 18.95 (*1-55972-137-5*, Birch Ln Pr) Carol Pub Group.
Maier, Arlee S., jt. auth. see Guerin, Gilbert R.
Maier, Art, jt. auth. see Alberta, Eric.
Maier, B., jt. auth. see Suck, J. B.
Maier, Beatrice R., tr. see Graf, Max.
Maier, C. Integrated Management of Tentiform Leafminers, Phyllonorycter Spp. (Lepidoptera: Gracillariidae), in North American Apple Orchards. (Thomas Say Publications in Entomology). 82p. 1994. pap. 16.50 (*0-938522-48-5*, ESATSPS) Entomol Soc.
Maier, Camelia, jt. auth. see Smith, Don.
Maier, Carol & Salper, Roberta L., eds. Ramon Maria del Valle-Inclan: Questions of Gender. LC 93-42561. 1994. 42.50 (*0-8387-5261-6*) Bucknell U Pr.
Maier, Carol, jt. ed. see Dingwaney, Anuradha.
Maier, Carol, jt. ed. see Valis, Noel.
Maier, Carol, tr. see Armand, Octavio.
Maier, Carol, tr. see Sarduy, Severo.
Maier, Carol, tr. see Zambrano, Maria.
Maier, Carol, tr. & afterword by see Chacel, Rosa.
***Maier, Carolina M. & Steinberg, Gary K., eds.** Hypothermia & Cerebral Ischemia. 350p. 2000. 145.00 (*0-89603-660-X*) Humana.
Maier, Charles. Dissolution: The Crisis of Communism & the End of East Germany. LC 96-39995. 376p. 1997. 29.95 (*0-691-07879-3*, Pub. by Princeton U Pr) Cal Prin Full Svc.
Maier, Charles S. Changing Boundaries of the Political: Essays on the Evolving Balance Between the State & Society, Public & Private in Europe. (Cambridge Studies in Modern Political Economies). (Illus.). 432p. 1987. text 69.95 (*0-521-34366-6*); pap. text 19.95 (*0-521-34847-1*) Cambridge U Pr.
— The Cold War in Europe: Era of a Divided Continent. 3rd rev. ed. LC 96-30536. 420p. 1997. pap. 22.95 (*1-55876-133-0*) Wiener Pubs Inc.
— Dissolution. 1999. pap. 19.95 (*0-691-00746-2*, Pub. by Princeton U Pr) Cal Prin Full Svc.
— Dissolution: The Crisis of Communism & the End of East Germany. 1997. 29.95 (*0-614-27831-7*) Princeton U Pr.
— In Search of Stability: Explorations in Historical Political Economy. (Studies in Modern Political Economies). 304p. 1988. text 69.95 (*0-521-23001-2*) Cambridge U Pr.
— The Unmasterable Past: History, Holocaust, & German National Identity. LC 88-11690. 240p. 1988. 38.50 (*0-674-92975-6*) HUP.
— Unmasterable Past: History, Holocaust & German National Identity. 256p. 1998. pap. text 14.00 (*0-674-92977-2*) HUP.
— The Unmasterable Past: History, Holocaust & German National Identity. 240p. 1988. pap. text 12.00 (*0-674-92976-4*) HUP.
Maier, Charles S., jt. auth. see Kistiakowsky, George B.
Maier, Charles S., jt. ed. see Lindberg, Leon N.
Maier, Christian, jt. auth. see Wildi, Robert H.
Maier, Christl. Die Fremde Frau in Proverbien 1-9: Eine Exegetische und Sozialgeschichtliche Studie. (Orbis Biblicus et Orientalis Ser.: Vol. 144). (GER.). 296p. 1995. text 61.75 (*3-7278-1017-3*, Pub. by Presses Univ Fribourg) Eisenbrauns.
***Maier, Christoph T.** Crusade Propaganda & Ideology: Model Sermons for the Preaching of the Cross. 288p. 2000. 59.95 (*0-521-59061-2*) Cambridge U Pr.
Maier, Christoph T. Preaching the Crusades: Mendicant Friars & the Cross in the Thirteenth Century. LC 93-32162. (Cambridge Studies in Medieval Life & Thought: No. 28). 210p. (C). 1994. text 54.95 (*0-521-45246-5*) Cambridge U Pr.
— Preaching the Crusades: Mendicant Friars & the Cross in the Thirteenth Century. (Cambridge Studies in Medieval Life & Thought: No. 28). 212p. (C). 1998. reprint ed. pap. text 19.95 (*0-521-63873-9*) Cambridge U Pr.
Maier, Clive. Mold Shrinkage & Warpage Handbook. LC 99-63216. 400p. 1999. 285.00 (*1-884207-72-3*) William Andrew.
Maier, Clive, ed. Polypropylene: The Definitive User's Guide. LC 97-76233. (PDL Handbook Ser.). 425p. 1998. 285.00 (*1-884207-58-8*) William Andrew.
Maier, David. The Theory of Relational Databases. LC 82-2518. 653p. 1983. reprint ed. pap. 200.00 (*0-608-03561-0*, AU0048000009) Bks Demand.
Maier, David & Warren, David. Computing with Logic. 475p. (C). 1988. pap. text 64.00 (*0-8053-6681-4*) Benjamin-Cummings.
Maier, Donna J. Priests & Power: The Case of the Dente Shrine in Nineteenth-Century Ghana. LC 82-48582. (Illus.). 271p. reprint ed. pap. 84.10 (*0-7837-3717-3*, 205789500009) Bks Demand.
Maier, E. A., jt. auth. see Lightfoot, N. F.
Maier, E. A., jt. auth. see Quevauviller, P.
Maier, E. A., jt. ed. see Lightfoot, N. F.
Maier, Elaine C. How to Prepare a Legal Citation. 192p. 1986. pap. 13.95 (*0-8120-2960-7*) Barron.
Maier, Elisabeth, et al. Dialogue Processing in Spoken Language Systems: ECAI '96 Workshop, Budapest, Hungary, August 13, 1996: Revised Papers, No. 3. LC 97-22249. (Lecture Notes in Artificial Intelligence Ser.: Vol. 123). 1997. pap. write for info. (*3-540-63175-5*) Spr-Verlag.
Maier, Ernest. Cases in Business to Business Relationship Selling. 4th ed. LC 95-5112. 160p. (C). 1995. pap. text 23.20 (*0-13-340290-8*) P-H.
Maier, Ernest, et al, eds. Business Library & How to Use It. 330p. 1996. lib. bdg. 56.00 (*0-7808-0026-5*) Omnigraphics Inc.
Maier, Eugene. Opening Eyes to Mathematics: Sketching Solutions to Algebraic Equations. unabridged ed. (Illus.). 57p. 1997. ring bd. 20.00 incl. VHS (*1-886131-43-0*, ME13) Math Lrning.
Maier, Eugene & Nelson, L. Ted. Modeling Real & Complex Numbers, Unit XII. (Math & the Mind's Eye Ser.). (Illus.). 91p. 1996. ring bd. 10.00 (*1-886131-41-4*, ME12) Math Lrning.
Maier, Eugene & Shaughnessy, Michael. Graphing Algebraic Relationships: Unit XI. (Math & the Mind's Eye Ser.). (Illus.). 76p. (C). 1996. teacher ed. 14.50 (*1-886131-39-2*, ME11) Math Lrning.
Maier, Eugene, jt. auth. see Arcidiacono, Michael J.
Maier, Franz G., ed. see Muller, Urs.
Maier, Frith. Trekking in Russia & Central Asia, a Traveler's Guide: Urals, Pamirs, Caucasus, Siberia, Lake Baikal, Crimean Peninsula, Kamchatka Peninsula. (Illus.). 320p. 1994. pap. 16.95 (*0-89886-355-4*) Mountaineers.
Maier, G. Spatial Search Structure, Complexity, & Implications. Bos, D. et al, eds. (Studies in Contemporary Economics). (Illus.). viii, 254p. 1995. pap. 71.00 (*3-7908-0874-1*) Spr-Verlag.
Maier, G., ed. Case Histories in Offshore Engineering. (CISM International Centre for Mechanical Sciences Ser.: Vol. 283). (Illus.). ix, 365p. 1985. 64.95 (*0-387-81817-0*) Spr-Verlag.
Maier, G., jt. ed. see Brebbia, Carlos A.
Maier, Hans J., jt. auth. see Sehitoglu, Huseyin.
Maier, Harold G., jt. auth. see Buergenthal, Thomas.
Maier, Heinrich. Die Syllogistik Des Aristoteles, 2 vols. in 3. xxiv, 1195p. 1969. reprint ed. write for info. (*0-318-70973-2*) G Olms Pubs.
Maier, Hendrik M. In the Center of Authority: The Malay Hikayat Merong Mahawangsa. LC 89-157454. (Studies on Southeast Asia). 210p. (Orig.). 1988. pap. 65.10 (*0-7837-8497-X*, 204930400010) Bks Demand.
Maier, Henry W. Developmental Group Care of Children & Youth: Concepts & Practice. 225p. 1988. pap. 19.95 (*0-86656-834-4*) Haworth Pr.
— The Mayor Who Made Milwaukee Famous: An Autobiography. LC 92-30042. 304p. 1993. 24.95 (*0-8191-8621-X*) Madison Bks UPA.
Maier, Henry W., et al. Developmental Group Care of Children & Youth: Concepts & Practice. LC 87-7421. (Child & Youth Services Ser.: Vol. 9, No. 2). 233p. 1987. text 49.95 (*0-86656-655-4*) Haworth Pr.
Maier, Hermann N., jt. auth. see Demell, Reinhardt.
Maier, Hermann N., jt. auth. see Demoll, Reinhard.
Maier, Isaac. Esoteric Freemasonry. 117p. 1996. reprint ed. pap. 18.95 (*1-56459-986-8*) Kessinger Pub.
Maier, Johann. Geschichte der Juedischen Religion: Von der Zeit Alexanders des Grossen bis zur Aufklaerung. Mit einem Ausblick auf das 19.-20. Jahrhundert. LC 72-77437. (GER.). xx, 641p. (C). 1972. 60.00 (*3-11-002448-9*) De Gruyter.
Maier, Johann, ed. see Oegema, Gerbern S.
Maier, Johann E. Gnade Und Asthetik: Von der Wiedergeburt Zur Gnadenpoetik. 446p. 1998. 56.95 (*3-631-49585-4*) P Lang Pubng.
Maier, John. Desert Songs: Western Images of Morocco & Moroccan Images of the West. LC 96-4822. (SUNY Series, the Margins of Literature). (Illus.). 354p. (C). 1996. text 65.50 (*0-7914-3017-0*); pap. text 21.95 (*0-7914-3018-9*) State U NY Pr.
— Gilgamesh: A Reader. LC 97-708. (Illus.). 528p. 1997. 70.00 (*0-86516-349-9*) Bolchazy-Carducci.
Maier, John, ed. A Gilgamesh Reader. LC 97-708. 600p. 1997. pap. 30.00 (*0-86516-339-1*) Bolchazy-Carducci.
Maier, John, jt. ed. see Tollers, Vincent L.
Maier, John M. Participant Directed Investment Answer Book, 1. 2nd ed. LC 98-193419. (Panel Answer Book Ser.). 680p. 1998. boxed set. write for info. (*1-56706-898-7*) Panel Pubs.
Maier, John R., jt. tr. see Gardner, John.
Maier, Josef. On Hegel's Critique of Kant. LC 39-31564. reprint ed. 20.00 (*0-404-04168-X*) AMS Pr.
Maier, Joseph B., et al, eds. German Jewry: Its History & Sociology: Selected Essays of Werner J. Cahnman. 250p. 1989. 44.95 (*0-88738-253-3*) Transaction Pubs.
Maier, Joseph B. & Waxman, Chaim I., eds. Ethnicity, Identity & History: Essays in Memory of Werner J. Cahnman. LC 82-6928. (Illus.). 350p. 1983. 44.95 (*0-87855-461-0*) Transaction Pubs.
Maier, Jul J., ed. see Oeglin, Erhart.
Maier, Karl. Angola: Promises & Lies. 224p. Date not set. pap. 19.95 (*1-897959-22-2*, Pub. by Serif) IPG Chicago.
— Into the House of the Ancestors: Inside the New Africa. LC 97-26809. 278p. 1997. 24.95 (*0-471-13547-X*) Wiley.
***Maier, Karl.** Into the House of the Ancestors: Inside the New Africa. 288p. 1999. reprint ed. pap. 14.95 (*0-471-29583-3*) Wiley.
— This House Has Fallen: A Journey Through Nigeria's Heart of Darkness. 240p. 2000. 26.00 (*1-891620-60-6*, Pub. by PublicAffairs NY) HarpC.
***Maier, Karyn Siegel.** 50 Simple Ways to Pamper Your Baby. LC 99-86760. (Illus.). 144p. 2000. pap. 9.95 (*1-58017-257-1*) Storey Bks.
***Maier, Klaus A.** SEE: Adult Entertainment. 2000. pap. 42.00 (*3-931126-40-4*) Die Gestalten.
Maier, Klaus A., et al. Germany & the Second World War Vol. 2: Germany's Initial Conquests in Europe. McMurry, Dean S. & Osers, Ewald, trs. (Illus.). 460p. 1991. text 115.00 (*0-19-822885-6*, 12188) OUP.
***Maier, Kurt Salomon.** The Library of Congress: A Tour in Words & Pictures. LC 00-38654. (Illus.). 160p. 2000. pap. 8.99 (*0-517-16249-0*) Gramrcy Bks.
Maier, Larry B. Rough & Regular: A History of the 119th Regiment of Pennsylvania Volunteer Infantry... LC 97-25357. 359p. 1997. 30.00 (*1-57249-082-9*, Burd St Pr) White Mane Pub.
Maier, Leo. The Costs & Benefits of U. S. Agricultural Policies with Imperfect Competition in Food Manufacturing. LC 92-36023. (Government & the Economy Ser.). 328p. 1993. text 10.00 (*0-8153-1233-4*) Garland.
Maier, Leo & Steenblik, Ronald. The Environmental Effects of Reforming Agricultural Policies. LC 98-144303. 132p. 1998. pap. 22.00 (*92-64-16041-8*, 51 98 04 1 P, Pub. by Org for Econ) OECD.
Maier, Linda S. Borges & the European Avant-Garde. LC 91-29511. (American University Studies Series II: Romance Languages & Literatures: Vol. 183). XIII, 186p. (C). 1996. text 38.95 (*0-8204-1702-5*) P Lang Pubng.
Maier, Lory, jt. auth. see Sieglou, Magdalene.
Maier, Louis. In Lieu of Flowers: In Memory of the Jews of Malsch, a Village in Southern Germany. LC 95-19563. (Illus.). vi, 194p. 1995. pap. 17.00 (*0-86663-213-1*) Ide Hse.
***Maier, Mark & Rechtin, Eberhardt.** The Art of Systems Architecting. 2nd ed. LC 00-39848. 2000. write for info. (*0-8493-0440-7*) CRC Pr.
Maier, Mark H. The Data Game: Controversies in Social Science Statistics. LC 90-39658. 264p. (C). (gr. 13). 1991. 79.95 (*0-87332-588-5*) M E Sharpe.
Maier, Mark H. The Data Game: Controversies in Social Science Statistics. LC 90-39658. 264p. (C). (gr. 13). 1991. pap. 34.95 (*0-87332-768-3*) M E Sharpe.
Maier, Mark H. The Data Game: Controversies in Social Science Statistics. 2nd rev. ed. LC 94-47648. (Illus.). 312p. (C). (gr. 13). 1995. text 77.95 (*1-56324-481-0*); pap. text 32.95 (*1-56324-482-9*) M E Sharpe.
— The Data Game: Controversies in Social Science Statistics. 3rd rev. ed. LC 98-55371. (Illus.). 350p. 1999. pap. text 26.95 (*0-7656-0376-4*) M E Sharpe.
— The Data Game: Controversies in Social Science Statistics. 3rd rev. ed. LC 98-55371. (Illus.). 350p. (gr. 13). 1999. text 63.95 (*0-7656-0375-6*) M E Sharpe.
***Maier, Mary Anne & Isom, Joan Shaddox, eds.** The Leap Years: Women Reflect on Change, Loss & Love. 2nd ed. LC 99-27395. 256p. 1999. pap. 16.00 (*0-8070-6515-3*) Beacon Pr.
Maier, Michael. Laws of the Fraternity of the Rosie Crosse (Themis Aurea) (Illus.). 136p. 1999. 15.50 (*0-89314-402-9*) Philos Res.
— The Secrets of Alchemy. 1984. reprint ed. pap. 4.95 (*0-916411-17-6*) Holmes Pub.
Maier, Michael, et al. A Rosicrucian Primer: Ancient Landmarks of the Rosicrucians. 128p. (Orig.). 1994. pap. 12.95 (*1-55818-277-2*) Holmes Pub.
Maier, Norman R. Frustration: The Study of Behavior Without a Goal. LC BF0181.M25. (Ann Arbor Paperbacks Ser.: Vol. 48). 264p. reprint ed. pap. 81.90 (*0-608-30767-X*, 205562800029) Bks Demand.
— The Natural Goodness of Man: The Study of Behavior Without a Goal. LC 81-20092. (Illus.). 264p. 1982. reprint ed. lib. bdg. 65.00 (*0-313-23340-3*, MAFRU, Greenwood Pr) Greenwood.
Maier, Norman R. & Verser, Trudy G. Psychology in Industrial Organizations, 5 vols. 5th ed. LC 81-81702. (Illus.). 672p. (C). 1982. text 75.96 (*0-395-31740-1*) HM.
Maier, P. E., jt. auth. see Bakker-Arkema, F.
Maier, Pat, et al. Using Technology in Teaching & Learning. 144p. 1998. pap. 24.95 (*0-7494-2516-4*, Kogan Pg Educ) Stylus Pub VA.
***Maier, Paul.** Discover the Joy of the Very First Easter. 32p. 2000. 16.99 (*0-570-07053-8*) Concordia.

M

An Asterisk (*) at the beginning of an entry indicates that the title is appearing for the first time.

Maier, Paul L. Eusebio (Eusebius) Historia Eclesiastica (The Church History) (SPA.). 416p. 1998. 22.99 (*0-8254-1221-8*, Edit Portavoz) Kregel.

— Eusebius: The Church History. LC 98-13442.Tr. of Ecclesiastical History. (Illus.). 416p. 1999. 24.99 (*0-8254-3328-2*) Kregel.

— The Flames of Rome: A Novel. 456p. 1995. pap. 12.99 (*0-8254-3297-9*) Kregel.

— The Flames of Rome: A Novel. LC 90-28622. 456p. 1991. reprint ed. 20.99 (*0-8254-3262-6*) Kregel.

— In the Fullness of Time: A Historian Looks at Christmas, Easter, & the Early Church. LC 97-49892. (Illus.). 388p. 1997. 20.99 (*0-8254-3329-0*) Kregel.

— Josefo: Las Obras Esenciales (Full-Color Edition) (SPA., Illus.). 416p. 1995. 24.99 (*0-8254-1457-1*, Edit Portavoz) Kregel.

— Josefo: Los Escritos Esenciales. Orig. Title: Josephus: The Essential Writings. (SPA.). 400p. 1992. pap. 14.99 (*0-8254-1456-3*, Edit Portavoz) Kregel.

— Pontius Pilate: A Biographical Novel. 384p. 1995. pap. 12.99 (*0-8254-3296-0*) Kregel.

— A Skeleton in God Closet. 360p. 1996. mass mkt. 5.99 (*0-7852-7537-1*) Nelson.

— A Skeleton in God's Closet. LC 93-28203. 1993. pap. 14.99 (*0-8407-3424-7*) Nelson.

— The Very First Christmas. LC 98-23475. (Illus.). 32p. (J). (gr. k-5). 1998. 14.99 (*0-570-05064-2*) Concordia.

Maier, Paul L., ed. see Cornfeld.

Maier, Paul L., ed. & tr. see Josephus, Flavius.

Maier, Pauline. American Scripture: Making the Declaration of Independence. LC 97-2769. 1997. 27.50 (*0-679-45492-6*) Knopf.

— American Scripture: Making the Declaration of Independence. 336p. 1998. pap. 14.00 (*0-679-77908-6*) Vin Bks.

— From Resistance to Revolution: Colonial Radicals & the Development of American Opposition to Britain, 1765-1776. 360p. 1992. pap. 14.95 (*0-393-30825-1*) Norton.

Maier, Pauline, intro. The Declaration of Independence & the Constitution of the United States. LC 98-210524. 112p. 1998. mass mkt. 2.95 (*0-553-21482-9*) Bantam.

Maier, Phyllis C. & Wood, Mary M., eds. Lower Merion: A History. 120p. 1988. text 20.00 (*0-9649368-1-X*) Lower Merion.

— Lower Merion: A History. rev. ed. (Illus.). 128p. 1992. text 20.00 (*0-9649368-2-8*) Lower Merion.

Maier, Richard A. Comparative Animal Behavior. LC 97-27885. 640p. 1997. 75.00 (*0-205-19985-2*) Allyn.

Maier, Robert. Location Scouting & Management Handbook: Television, Film & Still Photography. (Illus.). 192p. 1994. pap. 29.95 (*0-240-80152-0*, Focal) Buttrwrth-Heinemann.

Maier, Robert, ed. Norms in Argumentation. (Studies of Argumentation in Pragmatic & Discourse Analysis). 218p. (Orig.). (C). 1989. pap. 67.70 (*90-6765-423-X*) Mouton.

Maier, Robert, jt. ed. see De Graaf, Willibrord.

Maier, Robert Von, see Von Maier, Robert.

Maier, S. F., jt. ed. see Watkins, L. R.

Maier, Sarah, ed. see Hardy, Thomas.

Maier, Steven F., jt. auth. see Watkins, Linda R.

Maier, Thomas. Dr. Spock: An American Life. LC 97-32632. (Illus.). 528p. (C). 1998. 30.00 (*0-15-100203-7*) Harcourt Coll Pubs.

Maier, Wolfgang. Fremdsprachen in der Grundschule: Fremdsprachen-Unterricht in Theorie und Praxis. (GER.). 256p. 1996. 26.25 (*3-468-49442-4*) Langenscheidt.

— Spielfilmsynchronisation. (Forum Anglicum Ser.: No. 23). (GER.). 151p. 1997. 35.95 (*3-631-31303-9*) P Lang Pubng.

Maier, Zita, jt. auth. see Britz, Andrew.

Maierbacher, Ilse. Stenciling: 140 Historical Patterns for Room Decoration. (Schiffer Design Bks.). (Illus.). 128p. 1997. pap. 24.95 (*0-7643-0376-7*) Schiffer.

Maiers, Wolfgang, jt. ed. see Tolman, Charles W.

Maifair, Linda L. Batter Up, Bailey Benson! LC 96-45170. (Winners! Ser.). 64p. (Orig.). (J). (gr. 2-5). 1997. pap. 3.99 (*0-310-20705-3*) Zondervan.

— The Case of the Angry Actress. (Darcy J. Doyle, Daring Detective Ser.: Vol. 7). 64p. (J). (gr. 2-5). 1994. 3.99 (*0-310-43301-0*) Zondervan.

— The Case of the Bashed-Up Bicycle, Bk. 11. LC 96-18373. (Darcy J. Doyle, Daring Detective Ser.: 11). 64p. (J). (gr. 2-5). 1996. pap. 3.99 (*0-310-20736-3*) Zondervan.

— The Case of the Bashful Bully. (Darcy J. Doyle, Daring Detective Ser.: Vol. 6). 64p. (J). (gr. 2-5). 1994. pap. 3.99 (*0-310-43281-2*) Zondervan.

— The Case of the Creepy Campout. (Darcy J. Doyle, Daring Detective Ser.: Vol. 5). 64p. (J). (gr. 2-5). 1994. pap. 3.99 (*0-310-43271-5*) Zondervan.

— The Case of the Missing Max. (Darcy J. Doyle, Daring Detective Ser.: Vol. 8). 64p. (J). (gr. 2-5). 1994. pap. 3.99 (*0-310-43311-8*) Zondervan.

— The Case of the Near-Sighted Neighbor, Bk. 12. LC 96-18369. (Darcy J. Doyle, Daring Detective Ser.: 12). 64p. (J). (gr. 2-5). 1996. pap. 3.99 (*0-310-20737-1*) Zondervan.

— The Case of the Sweet-Toothed Shoplifter, Bk. 10. LC 96-15102. (Darcy J. Doyle, Daring Detective Ser.: 10). 64p. (J). (gr. 2-5). 1996. pap. 3.99 (*0-310-20735-5*) Zondervan.

— The Case of the Troublesome Treasure, Bk. 9. (Darcy J. Doyle, Daring Detective Ser.: 9). 64p. (J). (gr. 2-5). 1996. pap. 3.99 (*0-310-20734-7*) Zondervan.

— Go Figure, Gabriella Grant! LC 96-49098. (Winners! Ser.). 64p. (Orig.). (J). (gr. 2-5). 1997. pap. 3.99 (*0-310-20702-9*) Zondervan.

— Little House on the Prairie. (Literature Unit Ser.). (Illus.). 48p. 1995. pap., teacher ed. 7.95 (*1-55734-539-2*) Tchr Create Mat.

— Use Your Head, Molly Malone! LC 96-37828. (Winners! Ser.). 64p. (Orig.). (J). (gr. 2-5). 1997. pap. 3.99 (*0-310-20704-5*) Zondervan.

— Whoa There, Wanda Wilson! LC 99-184967. (Winners! Ser.). 64p. (Orig.). (J). (gr. 2-5). 1997. pap. 3.99 (*0-310-20703-7*) Zondervan.

Maifair, Linda L., jt. auth. see Sussman, Ellen.

Maiga, Fatima, tr. see Kamava, Connie H.

Maigne, Robert. Diagnosis & Treatment of Pain of Vertebral Origin: A Manual Medicine Approach. Nieves, Walter L., ed. & tr. by. from FRE. LC 94-29321. Orig. Title: Diagnostic et Traitement des Douleurs Commones d'Origine Rachidienne. (Illus.). 464p. 1996. 95.00 (*0-683-05376-0*) Lppncott W & W.

Maiguashca, Raffaella, jt. auth. see Karumanchiri, Luisa P.

Maiguashea, Raffaella, et al. Schede di Lavoro, No. 1. 1985. mass mkt., teacher ed. 5.00 (*0-8020-6599-6*) U of Toronto Pr.

— Schede di Lavoro, No. 2. 1985. pap. text, teacher ed. 5.00 (*0-8020-6601-1*) U of Toronto Pr.

— Schede di Lavoro, Pt. 1. 276p. 1985. pap. text, student ed. 23.95 (*0-8020-6598-8*) U of Toronto Pr.

— Schede di Lavoro, Pt. 2. 200p. 1985. pap. text, student ed. 21.95 (*0-8020-6600-3*) U of Toronto Pr.

Maihafer, Harry J. Brave Decisions: Moral Courage from the Revolutionary War to Desert Storm. (Association of the U. S. Army Book Ser.). 283p. 1995. 24.95 (*0-02-881108-9*) Brasseys.

***Maihafer, Harry J.** Brave Decisions: Moral Courage from the Revolutionary War to Desert Storm. (Illus.). 263p. 2000. text 24.00 (*0-7881-9065-2*) DIANE Pub.

Maihafer, Harry J. Brave Decisions: Profiles In Courage & Character from American Military History. 1999. pap. text 16.95 (*1-57488-207-4*) Brasseys.

— From the Hudson to the Yalu: West Point '49 in the Korean War. LC 93-12948. (Military History Ser.: No. 31). (Illus.). 296p. 1993. 29.50 (*0-89096-554-4*) Tex A&M Univ Pr.

— The General & the Journalists: Ulysses S. Grant, Horace Greeley, & Charles Dana. LC 98-19351. (Association of the U. S. Army Book Ser.: Vol. 3). (Illus.). 336p. 1998. 29.95 (*1-57488-105-1*) Brasseys.

— Oblivion: The Mystery of West Point Cadet Richard Cox. LC 96-25098. 256p. 1996. 24.95 (*1-57488-043-8*) Brasseys.

***Maihafer, Harry J.** Oblivion: The Mystery of West Point Cadet Richard Cox. 1999. pap. 16.95 (*1-57488-224-4*) Brasseys.

Maihafer, Harry J., jt. auth. see Goldstein, Donald M.

Maijala, K., ed. Genetic Resources of Pig, Sheep & Goat. (World Animal Science Ser.: Vol. B8). 556p. 1991. 308.75 (*0-444-88279-0*) Elsevier.

Maik, Thomas A. The Masses Magazine, 1911-1917: Odyssey of an Era. LC 93-43979. (Modern American History Ser.). 272p. 1994. text 30.00 (*0-8153-1642-9*) Garland.

— A Reexamination of Mark Twain's 'Joan of Arc' LC 92-5601. 168p. 1992. lib. bdg. 79.95 (*0-88946-164-3*) E Mellen.

***Maik, Thomas A., ed.** Fiction by Nineteenth-Century Women Writers: A New England Sampler. LC 99-29224. (Gender & Genre in Literature Ser.: Vol. 10). 332p. 1999. 68.00 (*0-8153-3189-4*, H2112) Garland.

Maik, W., jt. ed. see Carter, F. W.

Maika, Patricia. Virginia Woolf's "Between the Acts" & Jane Harrison's Con-spiracy. Litz, A. Walton, ed. LC 87-13897. (Studies in Modern Literature: No. 78). 102p. 1987. reprint ed. 31.70 (*0-8357-1818-2*, 207073600004) Bks Demand.

Maiken, Peter T. Night Trains: The Pullman System in the Golden Years of American Rail Travel. LC 92-12586. (Illus.). 416p. 1992. pap. 24.95 (*0-8018-4503-3*) Johns Hopkins.

— Night Trains: The Pullman System in the Golden Years of American Rail Travel. (Illus.). 416p. (C). 1989. boxed set 49.95 (*0-9621480-0-8*) Lakme Pr.

Maikmeat. How to Build a Doh. 1986. 10.95 (*0-02-579370-5*) Macmillan.

***Maikovich, Andrew J. & Brown, Michele D.** Sports Quotations: Maxims, Quips & Pronouncements for Writers & Fans. 2nd ed. LC 99-59281. (Illus.). 245p. 2000. 29.95 (*0-7864-0817-0*) McFarland & Co.

Mail, Patricia, jt. ed. see Martin, Susan E.

Mail, Patricia D. & McDonald, David R. Tulapai to Tokay: A Bibliography of Alcohol Use & Abuse Among Native Americans of North America. LC 80-81243. (Bibliographies Ser.). 372p. 1981. 20.00 (*0-87536-253-2*) HRAFP.

Mailafiya, Obed. Europe & Economic Reform in Africa: Structural Adjustment & Economic Diplomacy. LC 96-22557. (Routledge Studies in Development Economics). 368p. (C). 1997. 100.00 (*0-415-14825-1*) Routledge.

***Mailand, Harold F. & Alig, Dorothy Stites.** Preserving Textiles: A Guide for the Nonspecialist. LC 99-16496. 96p. 1999. pap. 15.00 (*0-936260-71-8*) Ind Mus Art.

Mailart, Ella. The Land of the Sherpas. 1998. pap. 42.00 (*0-7855-7425-5*, Pub. by Ratna Pustak Bhandar) St Mut.

Maile. Principles to Apply & Remember. 111p. 1994. pap. 11.95 (*0-929385-59-4*) Light Tech Pubng.

Maile. Stakeholding in a New International Order. 59.95 (*1-84014-153-0*) Ashgate Pub Co.

Maile, jt. auth. see Wren.

***Maile, Roger, ed.** Best of Friends: The Yearbook of Creative Monochrome. annuals 6th ed. (Illus.). 144p. 1999. pap. write for info. (*1-873319-35-5*, Pub. by Creative Monochrome) Vine Hse Dist.

Mailer, Adele. The Last Party: Stories from My Life with Norman Mailer. LC 96-47445. (Illus.). 400p. 1997. 25.00 (*1-56980-098-7*) Barricade Bks.

Mailer, Carol. Jumping Problems Solved. (Illus.). 176p. 1998. pap. 21.95 (*0-7063-7694-3*, Pub. by WrLock) Sterling.

Mailer, F. Josef Strauss: Genius Against His Will. Povey, P., tr. (Illus.). 117p. 1985. text 34.00 (*0-08-026765-3*, Pub. by PPL) Elsevier.

Mailer, Norman. Advertisements for Myself. 532p. 1992. reprint ed. pap. text 15.95 (*0-674-00590-2*) HUP.

— An American Dream. LC 97-6684. 288p. 1999. pap. 13.00 (*0-375-70070-6*) Vin Bks.

— Ancient Evenings. 864p. 1988. mass mkt. 7.99 (*0-446-35769-3*, Pub. by Warner Bks) Little.

— The Armies of the Night: History As a Novel - The Novel As History. 304p. 1995. pap. 13.95 (*0-452-27279-3*, Plume) Dutton Plume.

— Barbary Shore. LC 97-6683. 1997. pap. 13.00 (*0-375-70039-0*) Vin Bks.

— The Deer Park. LC 97-8274. 375p. 1997. pap. 13.00 (*0-375-70040-4*) Vin Bks.

— The Executioner's Song. 1104p. 1993. 22.00 (*0-679-42471-7*) Modern Lib NY.

— The Executioner's Song. LC 98-60167. 1072p. 1998. pap. 15.00 (*0-375-70081-1*) Vin Bks.

— The Fight. LC 97-11107. 1997. pap. 12.00 (*0-375-70038-2*) Vin Bks.

— The Gospel According to the Son. 1998. mass mkt. 6.99 (*0-345-42132-9*) Ballantine Pub Grp.

***Mailer, Norman.** The Gospel According to the Son. 256p. 1999. pap. 12.00 (*0-345-43408-0*, Ballantine) Ballantine Pub Grp.

Mailer, Norman. The Gospel According to the Son. LC 97-44469. 1997. 25.95 (*1-56895-510-3*, Compass) Wheeler Pub.

— Harlot's Ghost. 1992. mass mkt. 6.99 (*0-345-37755-9*) Ballantine Pub Grp.

— Harlot's Ghost: A Novel. 1200p. 1992. pap. 12.50 (*0-345-37965-9*) Ballantine Pub Grp.

— How the Wimp Won the War. deluxe ed. 36p. 1991. 75.00 (*0-935716-57-2*) Lord John.

— The Naked & the Dead. 1994. lib. bdg. 65.00 (*1-56849-421-1*) Buccaneer Bks.

— The Naked & the Dead. LC 80-25751. 740p. 1995. pap. 14.95 (*0-8050-0521-8*, Owl) H Holt & Co.

— The Naked & the Dead. 721p. 1998. 30.00 (*0-8050-6018-9*); pap. 16.00 (*0-8050-6017-0*, Owl) H Holt & Co.

***Mailer, Norman.** The Naked & the Dead. 752p. 2000. pap. 16.00 (*0-312-26505-0*) St Martin.

Mailer, Norman. The Naked & the Dead. limited ed. (Classics Ser.). 736p. 1995. 30.00 (*0-8050-1273-7*) H Holt & Co.

— Of a Small & Modest Malignancy, Wicked & Bristling with Dots. deluxe limited ed. 120p. 1980. 200.00 (*0-935716-05-X*) Lord John.

— Pablo & Fernande: Portrait of Picasso As a Young Man: an Interpretive Biography. LC 93-2332. 1994. 40.00 (*0-385-47272-2*, N A Talese) Doubleday.

Mailer, Norman. Pieces & Pontifications LC 84-203538. x, 208p. 1983. write for info. (*0-450-06030-6*, Pub. by New Eng Lib) Trafalgar.

Mailer, Norman. Portrait of Picasso as a Young Man: An Interpretive Biography. (Illus.). 400p. 1999. reprint ed. text 35.00 (*0-7881-6112-1*) DIANE Pub.

— Potrait of Picasso As a Young Man: An Interpretive Biography. (Illus.). 464p. 1996. mass mkt. 19.99 (*0-446-67266-1*, Pub. by Warner Bks) Little.

— Rivage de Barbarie. (FRE.). 1977. pap. 11.95 (*0-7859-4084-7*) Fr & Eur.

— Un Sueno Americano. 1998. pap. 9.95 (*84-08-01417-X*) Planeta.

— The Time of Our Time. 1312p. 1999. pap. 24.95 (*0-375-75491-1*) Modern Lib NY.

— The Time of Our Time. LC 97-44879. 1216p. 1998. 39.50 (*0-375-50097-9*) Random.

— Tough Guys Don't Dance. 288p. 1985. mass mkt. 6.99 (*0-345-32321-1*) Ballantine Pub Grp.

— A Transit to Narcissus: A Facsimile of the Original Typescript. LC 77-24755. xiv, 848p. 1978. lib. bdg. 49.50 (*0-86527-315-4*) Fertig.

***Mailer, Norman.** Why Are We in Vietnam? 224p. 2000. pap. 13.00 (*0-312-26506-9*) St Martin.

Mailer, Norman. Why Are We in Vietnam? A Novel. 216p. 1995. pap. 9.95 (*0-8050-1880-8*, Owl) H Holt & Co.

Mailer, Norman & Lennon, Michael J. Pontifications: Interviews. LC 82-82201. xv, 192 p. 1982. write for info. (*0-316-54419-1*) Little.

Mailer, Norman, et al. Black Messiah: Tribute to Henry Miller. 1981. 20.00 (*0-912824-25-5*); pap. 9.00 (*0-912824-26-3*) Vagabond Pr.

***Mailer, Norris Church.** Windchill Summer. LC 99-43649. 448p. 2000. 24.95 (*0-375-50319-6*) Random.

Mailer, Phil. Portugal: The Impossible Revolution. 400p. 1977. 41.99 (*0-919618-34-0*, Pub. by Black Rose); pap. 12.99 (*0-919618-33-2*, Pub. by Black Rose) Consort Bk Sales.

Mailer, Stan. The Green Bay & Western: The First 111 Years. Hundman, Robert L. & Lee, Cathy H., eds. LC 88-81184. (Illus.). 350p. 1989. 47.95 (*0-945434-01-4*) Hundman Pub.

Mailes, Kim, jt. auth. see Torres, Luis.

Mailhebiau, Philippe. Portraits in Oils. pap. 23.95 (*0-8464-4484-4*) Beekman Pubs.

— Portraits in Oils: The Personality of Aromatherapy Oils & Their Link with Human Temperament. 304p. pap. 19.95 (*0-85207-237-6*, Pub. by C W Daniel) Natl Bk Netwk.

Mailho, John S., jt. auth. see Fagg, Gary.

Mailhol, Philippe D. Dictionnaire Historique et Heraldique de la Noblesse Francaise. 2 vols., Set. (FRE.). vii, 1452p. reprint ed. write for info. (*0-318-71375-6*) G Olms Pubs.

***Mailhot, Claire, et al.** Surgery: A Patient's Guide from Diagnosis to Recovery. 254p. 1999. pap. 20.00 (*0-943671-19-1*) UCSF Schl Nursing.

Mailhot, Ernie, et al. The Eastern Airlines Strike: Accomplishments of the Rank-&-File Machinists & Gains for the Labor Movement. LC 91-60839. (Illus.). 191p. (C). 1991. pap. 9.95 (*0-87348-626-9*); lib. bdg. 35.00 (*0-87348-635-8*) Pathfinder NY.

Mailick, Mildred D. & Caroff, Phyllis, eds. Professional Social Work Education & Health Care: Challenges for the Future. LC 96-30654. (Social Work in Health Care Ser.: Vol. 24, Nos. 1/2). 158p. (C). 1996. 39.95 (*0-7890-0010-5*) Haworth Pr.

Mailick, Mildred D., jt. ed. see Rehr, Helen.

Mailick, Sidney, et al, eds. The Practice of Management Development. LC 88-2398. 226p. 1988. 59.95 (*0-275-92357-6*, C2357, Praeger Pubs) Greenwood.

Mailick, Sidney, jt. auth. see Hoberman, Solomon.

Mailick, Sidney, jt. auth. see Reymond, Henri.

Mailick, Sidney, jt. ed. see Hoberman, Solomon.

Mailick, Sidney A., et al. Learning Theory in the Practice of Management Development: Evolution & Applications. LC 97-32993. 184p. 1998. 55.00 (*1-56720-052-4*, Quorum Bks) Greenwood.

Maillard, Antoine S. Grammar of the Mikmaque Language of Nova Scotia. Bellenger, Joseph M., ed. LC 11-29307. (Library of American Linguistics: Vol. 9). reprint ed. 42.75 (*0-404-50989-4*) AMS Pr.

Maillard, Claude, jt. auth. see Gordon, Coco.

Maillard, Jean. Jean Maillard: Modolorum Ioannis Maillardi: The Four-Part Motets. Rosenstock, Raymond H., ed. (Recent Researches in Music of the Renaissance Ser.: Vol. RRR73). (Illus.). xxi, 117p. 1987. pap. 45.00 (*0-89579-218-4*, RRR73) A-R Eds.

— Jean Maillard: Modulorum Ioannis Maillardi - The Five-, Six-, & Seven-Part Motets. Rosenstock, Raymond H., ed. (Recent Researches in Music of the Renaissance Ser.: Vol. RRR95). (Illus.). xxiv, 140p. 1993. pap. 50.00 (*0-89579-353-9*) A-R Eds.

— Jean Maillard: Modulorum Ionnis Maillardi - The Five-, Six-, & Seven-Part Motets. Rosenstock, Raymond H., ed. (Recent Researches in Music of the Renaissance Ser.: Vol. RRR96). (Illus.). 1993. pap. 50.00 (*0-89579-354-7*) A-R Eds.

— The Masses. Rosenstock, R., ed. (Collected Works: Vol. XVI, Pt. 1). (ENG, FRE & LAT.). 282p. 1997. 70.00 (*1-896926-07-X*) Inst Mediaeval Mus.

***Maillard, Keith.** Gloria. 660p. (J). 2000. pap. 27.00 (*0-00-648175-2*) HarpC Child Bks.

— Gloria. LC 00-26548. 680p. 2000. 27.00 (*1-56947-206-8*) Soho Press.

Maillbaum, T. S., jt. ed. see Abramsky, S.

Maillefer, Francois-Elie & D'Auge, Bernard. John Baptist de la Salle: Two Early Biographies. Mouton, Donald & Grass, Paul, eds. Quinn, William, tr. from FRE. LC 96-83015. (Lasallian Resources: Vol. 1). (Illus.). x, 384p. 1997. 28.00 (*0-944808-15-8*); pap. 23.00 (*0-944808-16-6*) Lasallian Pubns.

***Maillefer, Jean M.** Chevaliers et Princes Allemands en Suede et En Finlande a l'Epoque des Folkungar (1250-1363) Le Premier Etablissement d'Une Noblesse Allemande sur la Rive Septentrionale de la Baltique. (Illus.). 444p. 1999. 67.95 (*3-631-34524-0*) P Lang Pubng.

Maillelle, H., jt. auth. see Jerue, A.

Mailler, Carolyn D., ed. Parenting from the Heart Vol. 1: Selected Articles from Motherwear's Magazine for Nurturing Families. LC 95-81645. (Illus.). 240p. (Orig.). 1996. pap. 14.95 (*0-9649867-0-1*) Motherwear.

Mailles, Jacques De, see De Mailles, Jacques.

Maillet, Antonine. The Devil Is Loose! 310p. 1987. 16.95 (*0-8027-0958-3*) Walker & Co.

— Pelagie-la-Charrette. 1987. pap. 11.95 (*0-7145-3966-X*) Riverrun NY.

— Tale of Don l'Orginal. 107p. 1978. 3.95 (*0-7720-1216-4*) Genl Dist Srvs.

— The Tales of Don L'Orignal. 107p. 1989. pap. 5.95 (*0-7736-7234-6*) Genl Dist Srvs.

***Maillet, Denis.** Thermal Quadrupoles: Solving the Heat Equation Through Integral Transforms. LC 00-39931. 2000. write for info. (*0-471-98320-9*) Wiley.

Maillet, Dominique. Lexique de l'Informatique. 205p. 1993. pap. 32.00 (*0-7859-5575-5*, 2010200519) Fr & Eur.

Maillet, Julie O. Ethical Issues & Decision in Feeding. 30p. 1989. student ed. 10.25 (*0-88091-051-8*, 1219) Am Dietetic Assn.

Maillet, Lynda L. Commercial & Investment Law: Uzbekistan. LC 94-30392. 1994. write for info. (*1-56425-045-8*) Juris Pubng.

Maillet, M. Dictionnaire Abreviations en Biologie. (FRE.). 248p. 1996. 95.00 (*0-320-00660-3*) Fr & Eur.

Mailliard, Daniel, jt. auth. see Stein, Elissa.

***Maillit, Stephane M.** Binary Digital Image Processing: A Discrete Approach. LC 99-64631. 251p. 1999. 74.95 (*0-12-470505-7*) Acad Pr.

Maillol, Aristide. Maillol Nudes: Thirty-Five Lithographs by Aristide Maillol. (Dover Art Library). Orig. Title: The Dialogues of the Courtesans. (Illus.). 32p. 1980. pap. 4.95 (*0-486-24000-2*) Dover.

Maillot, Antoine L. La Musique au Theatre. LC 80-2288. 1981. reprint ed. 44.00 (*0-404-18856-7*) AMS Pr.

Maillot, J. La Traduction Scientifique et Technique. 2nd ed. (FRE.). 280p. 1981. 49.95 (*0-8288-2105-4*, M14402) Fr & Eur.

Mailloux. Rhetoric of Reception, Vol. 1. Date not set. pap. text. write for info. (*0-312-09219-9*) St Martin.

Mailloux, Peter. A Hesitation Before Birth: The Life of Franz Kafka. LC 87-40268. (Illus.). 624p. 1988. 50.00 (*0-87413-331-9*) U Delaware Pr.

Mailloux, Robert, jt. auth. see De Vosjoli, Philippe.

Mailloux, Robert J. Phased Array Antenna Handbook. (Antenna Ser.). 534p. 1993. text 137.00 (*0-89006-502-0*) Artech Hse.

Mailloux, Steven. Interpretive Conventions: The Reader in the Study of American Fiction. LC 81-70712. 232p. 1982. pap. text 15.95 (*0-8014-9285-8*) Cornell U Pr.

— Reception Histories: Rhetoric, Pragmatism, & American Cultural Politics. LC 98-10513. 224p. 1998. pap. write for info. (*0-8014-8506-1*) Cornell U Pr.

— Reception Histories: Rhetoric, Pragmatism, & American Cultural Politics. LC 98-10513. (Illus.). 224p. 1998. text 42.50 (*0-8014-3505-6*) Cornell U Pr.

— Rhetorical Power. LC 89-42878. 208p. 1989. text 37.50 (*0-8014-2245-0*); pap. text 14.95 (*0-8014-9602-0*) Cornell U Pr.

Mailloux, Steven, ed. Rhetoric, Sophistry, Pragmatism. (Literature, Culture, Theory Ser.: No. 15). 263p. (C). 1995. text 64.95 (*0-521-46225-8*); pap. text 19.95 (*0-521-46780-2*) Cambridge U Pr.

Mailloux, Steven & Levinson, Sanford, eds. Interpreting Law & Literature: A Hermeneutic Reader. 502p. (C). 1988. 62.95 (*0-8101-0770-8*); pap. 29.95 (*0-8101-0793-7*) Northwestern U Pr.

Mailloux, Zoe. Sensory Integrative Approaches in Occupational Therapy. LC 87-2878. (Occupational Therapy in Health Care Ser.: Vol. 4, No. 2). 179p. 1987. 49.95 (*0-86656-665-1*) Haworth Pr.

Mailly Nesle, Solange De, see De Mailly Nesle, Solange.

Mailman, Harriet. Activity Centers. Whitfield, Jennifer, ed. (Thinking Skills Library). (Illus.). 108p. (Orig.). (J). (gr. 2-5). 1997. pap., teacher ed. 9.95 (*1-56784-709-9*) Newbridge Educ.

Mailman, Leo. The Kid Comes Home. LC 76-29868. (Illus.). 1976. pap. 2.00 (*0-685-01523-8*) Duck Down.

— The Kid Comes Home. 1976. 3.00 (*0-685-03276-0*) Maelstrom.

Mails, Thomas. The Pueblo Children of the Earth Mother, Vol. 2. LC 98-27441. (Illus.). 544p. 1998. reprint ed. pap. 27.50 (*1-56924-669-6*) Marlowe & Co.

Mails, Thomas E. The Cherokee People. LC 96-76535. (Illus.). 368p. 1996. pap. 29.95 (*1-56924-762-5*, Pub. by Marlowe & Co) Publishers Group.

— The Cherokee People: The Story of the Cherokees from Earliest Origins to Contemporary Times. LC 91-73541. (Illus.). 368p. 1996. 49.95 (*0-933031-45-9*) Coun Oak Bks.

— The Cherokee People: The Story of the Cherokees from Earliest Origins to Contemporary Times. limited ed. LC 91-73541. (Illus.). 368p. 1996. 250.00 (*0-933031-46-7*) Coun Oak Bks.

— Creators of the Plains. Meisel, Anthony, ed. LC 97-12699. (Library of Native Peoples). (Illus.). 96p. (Orig.). (YA). 1997. pap. 10.95 (*1-57178-047-5*) Coun Oak Bks.

— Dancing in the Paths of the Ancestors, 2. (Pueblo Children of the Earth Mother Series). (Illus.). 544p. 1999. pap. 29.95 (*1-56924-689-0*) Marlowe & Co.

— Dog Soldier Societies of the Plains. LC 98-65594. (Illus.). 384p. 1998. pap. text 29.95 (*1-56924-673-4*) Marlowe & Co.

— Dog Soldiers. 1976. 22.95 (*0-8488-1089-9*) Amereon Ltd.

— Fools Crow: Wisdom & Power. 1976. 19.95 (*0-8488-1090-2*) Amereon Ltd.

— Fools Crow: Wisdom & Power. LC 90-85350. (Illus.). 204p. 1995. pap. 16.95 (*0-933031-35-1*) Coun Oak Bks.

— Fools Crow: Wisdom & Power. LC 90-33803. (Illus.). v, 294p. 1990. reprint ed. pap. 13.00 (*0-8032-8174-9*, Bison Books) U of Nebr Pr.

— Hopi Survival Kit. LC 96-61237. 384p. 1997. pap. 11.95 (*0-14-019545-9*) Viking Penguin.

— Hopi Survival Kit. 376p. 1999. reprint ed. 18.95 (*1-56649-067-7*) Welcome Rain.

— Mystic Warriors of the Plains. 1976. 22.95 (*0-8488-1091-0*) Amereon Ltd.

— The Mystic Warriors of the Plains: The Culture, Arts, Crafts, & Religion of the Plains Indians. (Illus.). 618p. 1995. pap. 29.95 (*1-56924-843-5*) Marlowe & Co.

— Peoples of the Plains. Meisel, Anthony, ed. LC 97-12698. (Library of Native Peoples). (Illus.). 96p. (Orig.). (YA). 1997. pap. 10.95 (*1-57178-046-7*) Coun Oak Bks.

— Secret Native American Pathways: A Guide to Inner Peace. LC 88-70084. (Illus.). 312p. 1995. pap. 17.95 (*0-933031-15-7*) Coun Oak Bks.

— Spirits of the Plains. Meisel, Anthony, ed. LC 97-12697. (Library of Native Peoples). (Illus.). 96p. (Orig.). (YA). 1997. pap. 10.95 (*1-57178-044-0*) Coun Oak Bks.

— Sundancing: The Great Sioux Piercing Ceremony. (Illus.). 338p. (C). 1997. pap. 32.95 (*1-57178-062-9*) Coun Oak Bks.

— Warriors of the Plains. Meisel, Anthony, ed. LC 97-12696. (Library of Native Peoples). (Illus.). 96p. (Orig.). (YA). 1997. pap. 10.95 (*1-57178-045-9*) Coun Oak Bks.

Mails, Thomas E. & Evehema, Dan. Hotevilla: Hopi Shrine of the Covenant/Microcosm of the World. (Illus.). 577p. 1996. 40.00 (*1-56924-835-4*); pap. 25.00 (*1-56924-810-9*) Marlowe & Co.

Mailvaganam, N. P. Repair & Protection of Concrete Structures. 496p. 1991. lib. bdg. 225.00 (*0-8493-4993-1*, TA681) CRC Pr.

Mailvaganam, N. P., jt. auth. see Rixom, M. R.

Mailvaganam, Noel P. & Swamy, R. Narayan. Repair, Rehabilitation & Protection of Concrete Structures. 2nd ed. 2000. 89.95 (*0-8493-1869-6*) CRC Pr.

Maiman, Jaye. Baby, It's Cold: A Robin Miller Mystery. LC 96-8544. 288p. 1996. 19.95 (*1-56280-141-4*) Naiad Pr.

— Crazy for Loving. LC 92-21680. (Robin Miller Mystery Ser.: No. 2). 320p. 1992. pap. 11.95 (*1-56280-025-6*) Naiad Pr.

***Maiman, Jaye.** Every Time We Say Goodbye. LC 98-48234. (Robin Miller Mystery Ser.: No. 7). 272p. 1999. pap. 11.95 (*1-56280-248-8*) Naiad Pr.

Maiman, Jaye. Old Black Magic: A Robin Miller Mystery. LC 97-10004. Vol. 6. 288p. (Orig.). 1997. pap. 11.95 (*1-56280-175-9*) Naiad Pr.

— Someone to Watch. LC 94-43988. Vol. 4. 288p. 1995. pap. 10.95 (*1-56280-095-7*) Naiad Pr.

— Under My Skin. LC 93-24909. (Robin Miller Mystery Ser.: No. 3). 336p. 1993. pap. 11.95 (*1-56280-049-3*) Naiad Pr.

Maiman, Judith C. Poems of a Manic Depressive. (Illus.). 96p. (Orig.). 1992. pap. 10.95 (*0-9627860-4-7*) Lone Oak MN.

Maiman, Richard J., jt. auth. see Steamer, Robert J.

Maime, Jane H., jt. auth. see Youngman, Joan M.

***Maimistov, A. I. & Basharov, A. M.** Nonlinear Optical Waves LC 99-27060. (Fundamental Theories of Physics Ser.). 1999. write for info. (*0-7923-5752-3*) Kluwer Academic.

Maimo, A. O. I Am Vindicated. rev. ed. (B. E. Ser.: No. 67). 1959. 25.00 (*0-8115-3017-5*) Periodicals Srv.

Maimon. WAC Handbook. 2001. 14.95 (*0-07-040055-5*) McGraw.

Maimon, Albert S., ed. see Maimon, Sam B.

Maimon, Moses Ben, see Ben Maimon, Moses.

Maimon, Oded Z., et al. Optimal Flow Control in Manufacturing Systems: Production Planning & Scheduling. LC 98-21517. (Applied Optimization Ser.). 346p. 1998. write for info. (*0-7923-5106-1*) Kluwer Academic.

Maimon, Oded Z., jt. auth. see Braha, Dan.

Maimon, Salomon. Gesammelte Werke, 7 vols. 1250.00 (*3-487-00882-3*) Adlers Foreign Bks.

Maimon, Sam B. The Beauty of Sephardic Life: Scholarly, Humorous & Personal Reflections. Maimon, Albert S. & Normand, Eugene, eds. 254p. (Orig.). 1993. pap. 15.00 (*0-9636764-0-7*) Marmon Ideas.

Maimone, Donella, ed. see Balzatti, James D.

Maimonides. Code of Maimonides, Bk. 3, Treatise 8, Sanctification Of The New Moon. Gandz, Solomon, tr. (Judaica Ser.: No. 11). 1956. 35.00 (*0-300-00476-1*) Yale U Pr.

Maimonides. Code of Maimonides Bk. 3: The Book of Seasons. Gandz, Solomon & Klein, Hyman, trs. (Judaica Ser.: No. 14). 1961. 80.00 (*0-300-00475-3*) Yale U Pr.

— The Commandments of Maimonides, 2 vols. 802p. 1967. 39.95 (*0-900689-71-4*) Soncino Pr.

— Commentary to Mishnah Aboth. David, Arthur, tr. LC 68-27871. 1968. 12.95 (*0-8197-0154-8*) Bloch.

— Ethical Writings of Maimonides. (Philosophy & Religion Ser.). 192p. (Orig.). 1983. pap. 6.95 (*0-486-24522-5*) Dover.

— A Guide for the Perplexed. Friedlander, M., tr. 473p. 1956. pap. 9.95 (*0-486-20351-4*) Dover.

— Guide for the Perplexed: A Fifteenth Century Spanish Translation by Pedro de Toledo. Dilligan, Robert, ed. Lazar, Moshe, ed. & tr. by. LC 89-85092. (Sephardic Classical Library: No. 2). (LAD., Illus.). 370p. (C). 1989. lib. bdg. 75.00 (*0-911437-49-5*) Labyrinthos.

— A Guide for the Perplexed: Morah Nevochim. Alcharizi, Yehuda & Friedlander, M., trs. 42.50 (*0-87559-079-9*) Shalom.

— The Guide of the Perplexed. Rabin, Chaim, tr. 256p. (C). 1995. reprint ed. pap. text 8.95 (*0-87220-324-7*); reprint ed. lib. bdg. 34.95 (*0-87220-325-5*) Hackett Pub.

— The Guide of the Perplexed, 1. Pines, Shlomo, tr. & intro. by. Strauss, Leo, intro. LC 62-18113. 365p. 1974. reprint ed. pap. 25.00 (*0-226-50230-9*, P609) U Ch Pr.

— The Guide of the Perplexed, 2 vols., 2. Pines, Shlomo, tr. LC 62-18113. 1994. lib. bdg. 25.00 (*0-226-50233-3*) U Ch Pr.

— The Guide of the Perplexed, 2. Pines, Shlomo, tr. & intro. by. Strauss, Leo, intro. LC 62-18113. 431p. 1974. reprint ed. pap. 27.00 (*0-226-50231-7*, P610) U Ch Pr.

— Mishne Torah Hilchot Avodat Kochavim (The Laws of Star Worship & Statues) Touger, Eliyahu, tr. & comment by. (Mishneh Torah Ser.: 3). 239p. 1990. 20.00 (*0-940118-67-X*) Moznaim.

— Mishne Torah Hilchot Berachot - Hilchot Milah Laws of Blessings Laws of Circumcision. Touger, Eliyahu, tr. & comment by. (Mishneh Torah Ser.: 8). 256p. 1991. 20.00 (*0-940118-69-6*) Moznaim.

— Mishne Torah Hilchot Eruvin, Hilchot Sh'vitat Asor Hilchot Sh'vitat Yom Tov: Laws of Eruvin, Laws of Resting on the 10th of Tishrie, Laws of Resting on Yom Tov. (Mishneh Torah Ser.: Vol. 11). (Illus.). 316p. 1993. 20.00 (*0-940118-93-9*) Moznaim.

— Mishne Torah Hilchot Gittin Vol. 17: Laws of Divorce. Touger, Eliyahu, tr. from HEB. (Mishneh Torah Ser.). (Illus.). 247p. 1995. 20.00 (*1-885220-02-2*) Moznaim.

— Mishne Torah Hilchot Ishut: Laws Pertaining to Marriage. Touger, Eliyahu, ed. & tr. by. (Mishneh Torah Ser.: Vol. 16). (HEB.). 337p. 1994. 20.00 (*1-885220-01-4*) Moznaim.

— Mishne Torah Hilchot Shabbat Pt. 1: Laws of Shabbat. Touger, Eliyahu, tr. & comment by. (Mishneh Torah Ser.: 9). 296p. 1992. 20.00 (*0-940118-71-8*) Moznaim.

— Mishne Torah Hilchot Shabbat Pt. 2: Laws of Shabbat. (Mishneh Torah Ser.). 358p. 1993. 20.00 (*0-940118-81-5*) Moznaim.

— Mishne Torah Hilchot Ta'aniot Hilchot Megillah & Chanukah: Laws of Fasts, Laws of Reading the Megillah & of Chanukah. Touger, Eliyahu, tr. & comment by. (Mishneh Torah Ser.: 15). 189p. 1991. 20.00 (*0-940118-70-X*) Moznaim.

— Mishne Torah Hilchot Tefilah Pt. 2: Laws of Prayer & Priestly Blessings. Touger, Eliyahu, tr. from HEB. (Mishneh Torah Ser.: 6). 232p. 1989. 20.00 (*0-940118-30-0*) Moznaim.

— Mishne Torah Hilchot Tefillin U'Mezuza Lu'Sefer Torah: Hilchot Tzizit Laws of Tefillin, Mezuza & Torah Scrolls, Laws of Tzitzit. Touger, Eliyahu, tr. & comment by. (Mishneh Torah Ser.: 7). 139p. 1990. 20.00 (*0-940118-68-8*) Moznaim.

— Mishne Torah Hilchot Yesodei HaTorah: The Laws (Which Are the) Foundations of the Torah. Touger, Eliyahu, tr. from HEB. & comment by. (Mishneh Torah Ser.: 1). 300p. 1989. 20.00 (*0-940118-41-6*) Moznaim.

— Mishne Torah Hilchot Yibbum Va'chalitza, Hilchot Na'Arahmh Betula, Hilchot Sotah: Laws of Yibbum Va'chalitza, Laws of a Virgin Maiden, Laws Pertaining to a Sotah. (Mishneh Torah Ser.: No. 18). (Illus.). 237p. 1995. 20.00 (*1-885220-04-9*) Moznaim.

— Mishne Torah Seder Nezikin: Book of Damages. Touser, Eliyahu, tr. 607p. 1997. 32.00 (*1-885220-18-9*) Moznaim.

— Mishneh Torah Hilchos Chametz U'Matzah: Laws of Chametz & Matzah. Touger, Eliyahu, tr. from HEB. & comment by. (Mishneh Torah Ser.: 12). 198p. 1988. 20.00 (*0-940118-21-1*) Moznaim.

— Mishneh Torah Hilchos Melachim V'Milchomoteihem: Laws of Kings & Their Wars. Touger, Eliyahu, tr. from HEB. & comment by. (Mishneh Torah Ser.). 263p. 1987. 20.00 (*0-940118-34-3*) Moznaim.

— Mishneh Torah Hilchot Bais Habechira: Laws of (God's) Chosen House. Touger, Eliyahu, tr. from HEB. & comment by. (Mishneh Torah Ser.). 223p. 1986. 20.00 (*0-940118-19-X*) Moznaim.

— Mishneh Torah Hilchot De'ot - Hilchot Talmud Torah: Laws of De'ot - Personality Development Laws of Torah Study. Touger, Eliyahu, tr. from HEB. & comment by. (Mishneh Torah Ser.: 2). 304p. 1989. 20.00 (*0-940118-23-8*) Moznaim.

— Mishneh Torah Hilchot Kriat Shema Hilchot Tefilah Pt. 1: Laws of Kriat Shema & Laws of Prayer. Kaplan, Boruch, tr. from HEB. & comment by. (Mishneh Torah Ser.: 5). 224p. 1989. 20.00 (*0-940118-24-6*) Moznaim.

— Mishneh Torah Hilchot Shofar, Sukkah, VE Lulav: Laws of the Shofar Sukah & Lulav. Touger, Eliyahu, tr. from HEB. & comment by. (Mishneh Torah Ser.: 13). 231p. 1988. 20.00 (*0-940118-42-4*) Moznaim.

— Mishneh Torah Hilchot Teshuvah: Laws of Repentance. Touger, Eliyahu, tr. from HEB. & comment by. (Mishneh Torah Ser.: 4). 241p. 1987. 20.00 (*0-940118-20-3*) Moznaim.

— The Mishneh Torah Series, 25 vols., Set. Touger, Eliyahu, tr. 1989. 510.00 (*0-940118-18-1*) Moznaim.

— Pirkie Avot - Shemona Perakim/Thirteen Principles of Faith. Touger, Eliyahu, tr. from HEB. (Mishneh Torah Ser.). 184p. 1994. 20.00 (*0-940118-98-X*) Moznaim.

— The Reason of the Laws of Moses. Townley, James, ed. LC 78-97294. 451p. 1970. reprint ed. lib. bdg. 35.00 (*0-8371-2618-5*, MARL, Greenwood Pr) Greenwood.

— Sein Leben, Seine Werke und Sein Einfluss, Bd. 2 in 1. (GER.). xvi, 839p. 1971. reprint ed. write for info. (*3-487-04099-9*) G Olms Pubs.

Maimonides & Klein, Isaac. The Book of Agriculture. LC 49-9495. (Yale Judaica Ser.: No. 7). 1979. 75.00 (*0-300-02223-9*) Yale U Pr.

— The Book of Women: The Code of Maimonides, Bk. 4. LC 49-9495. (Judaica Ser.: No. 19). 592p. 1972. 65.00 (*0-300-01438-4*) Yale U Pr.

Maimonides & Twersky, Isadore. Introduction to the Code of Maimonides (Mishneh Torah) LC 79-10347. (Yale Judaica Ser.: No. XXII). 1980. pap. 25.00 (*0-300-02846-6*) Yale U Pr.

Maimonides, jt. auth. see Lerner, Ralph.

***Maimonides, Moses.** Medical Aphorishms, Bks. 1-5. Bos, Gerrit, ed. (Graeco-Arabic Sciences Ser.). (ARA & ENG.). 320p. 2000. 29.95 (*0-8425-2474-6*) Brigham.

— On Asthma. Bos, Gerrit & McVaugh, Machael, eds. (Graeco-Arabic Sciences Ser.). (ARA & ENG.). 350p. 2000. 29.95 (*0-8425-2475-4*) Brigham.

Maimonides, Obadyah. The Treatise of the Pool: Al-Mawala al Hawdiyya. Fenton, Paul, tr. LC 83-164852. 30p. 1981. 23.00 (*0-900860-87-1*, Pub. by Octagon Pr) ISHK.

Main. Creating the Successful 21st Century Enterprise. 1997. 25.00 (*0-02-874079-3*) Free Pr.

— Quality Wars. 1994. text 29.95 (*0-13-440744-X*) S&S Trade.

— The U. S. S. R. & the Defeat of Nazi Germany, 1941-1945. (C). 1997. pap. text. write for info. (*0-582-29211-5*) Addison-Wesley.

Main, ed. Better Writing. (C). 2000. pap. text Price not set. (*0-321-01580-0*) Addison-Wesley.

Main, Alayne. Sailing Promise: Around the World on a Catamaran. 296p. 1999. pap. 17.95 (*0-9684544-0-2*) Base Camp Bks.

Main, Barbara Y., jt. ed. see Choate, Alec.

***Main, Brian G. M. & Peacock, Alan.** What Price Civil Justice? 96p. 2000. 18.95 (*0-255-36429-6*, Pub. by Inst Economic Affairs) Coronet Bks.

Main, C. J., jt. auth. see Spanswick, C. C.

Main, Cecil, jt. auth. see Althouse, Rosemary.

Main, Chris J., et al, eds. Clinical Psychology & Medicine: A Behavioral Perspective. LC 81-19978. 384p. 1981. 65.00 (*0-306-40900-3*, Plenum Trade) Perseus Pubng.

***Main, Darren J.** Spiritual Journeys along the Yellow Brick Road. LC 99-67786. 144p. 2000. pap. 12.95 (*1-899171-23-1*, Pub. by Findhorn Pr) Words Distrib.

Main, Elizabeth C. Richer by Far. LC 97-97212. 192p. 1998. 18.95 (*0-8034-9282-0*, Avalon Bks) Bouregy.

Main, Ernest. Palestine at the Crossroads. LC 71-180359. reprint ed. 42.50 (*0-404-56291-4*) AMS Pr.

Main, Gail. Michigan: Savor Its Flavors. 1996. pap. 8.95 (*0-9629554-0-X*) Mainly Food.

Main, Gregg. Every Trace. LC 98-25153. 336p. 1999. 24.00 (*0-06-019178-3*) HarpC.

— Every Trace. 400p. 2000. mass mkt. 6.99 (*0-06-109707-1*) HarpC.

Main, Hamish & Williams, Stephen Wynn, eds. Environmental Housing Third Wo. 282p. 1994. 110.00 (*0-471-94831-4*) Wiley.

Main, Iain G. Vibrations & Waves in Physics. 3rd ed. LC 92-33323. (Illus.). 377p. (C). 1993. pap. text 32.95 (*0-521-44701-1*) Cambridge U Pr.

Main, Jackie H., ed. see Henderson, Cary S. & Andrews, Nancy.

Main, Jackson T. Inherited or Achieved? The Social Origins of the World's Leaders, 2000 BC to AD 1850. 400p. 1998. 49.95 (*1-881089-14-2*) Brandywine Press.

— Political Parties Before the Constitution. LC 71-184228. 501p. reprint ed. pap. 155.40 (*0-7837-0291-4*, 204061200018) Bks Demand.

— Political Parties Before the Constitution. Vol. 718. (Illus.). 512p. (C). 1974. reprint ed. pap. 5.75 (*0-393-00718-9*) Norton.

— The Social Structure of Revolutionary America. LC 65-17146. 340p. reprint ed. pap. 105.40 (*0-608-30959-1*, 201196900080) Bks Demand.

— Society & Economy in Colonial Connecticut. LC 84-42892. (Illus.). 412p. reprint ed. pap. 127.80 (*0-608-06304-5*, 206666600008) Bks Demand.

— The Upper House in Revolutionary America, 1763-1788. LC 67-20753. 323p. reprint ed. pap. 100.20 (*0-608-30098-5*, 200497400048) Bks Demand.

Main, James, jt. ed. see Gorman, Gala.

Main, Jan. The Lactose-Free Family Cookbook. (Illus.). 218p. (Orig.). 1996. pap. 17.95 (*1-896503-24-1*, Pub. by R Rose Inc) Firefly Bks Ltd.

Main, Jane M. Living on the Stem of Hope: An Uplifting Personal Account of One Person's Quest for Wellness Filled with Faith, Humor & Encouragement. large type ed. (Illus.). 56p. (Orig.). 1997. pap. 9.95 (*0-9656720-0-X*) J M Main.

Main, Jeremy. Quality Wars: The Triumphs & Defeats of American Business. LC 93-41905. 256p. 1994. 32.95 (*0-02-916684-5*) Free Pr.

Main, Jeremy, jt. auth. see Wind, Jerry Y.

Main, Jody S., jt. auth. see Portugal, Nancy.

Main, John. Awakening. 1997. pap. 7.95 (*0-85305-424-X*, 6307, Pub. by Arthur James) Morehouse Pub.

— Christian Meditation: The Gethsemani Talks. 1999. pap. 7.95 (*0-9666941-0-4*, Pub. by Medio Media) Continuum.

— Community of Love. LC 96-37251. 208p. 1999. pap. 14.95 (*0-8264-1180-0*) Continuum.

— The Heart of Creation. Freeman, Laurence, ed. LC 71-149478. 96p. 1998. reprint ed. pap. 10.95 (*0-8264-1122-3*) Continuum.

— John Main. Hallward, Clare, ed. (Modern Spirituality Ser.). 96p. 1988. pap. 4.95 (*0-87243-166-5*) Templegate.

— Moment of Christ: The Path of Meditation. LC 62-9684. 128p. 1998. reprint ed. pap. 10.95 (*0-8264-1123-1*) Continuum.

— Silence & Stillness in Every Season. Harris, Paul, ed. LC 62-19082. 378p. 1998. 16.95 (*0-8264-1075-8*) Continuum.

— Word into Silence. LC 98-24983. 96p. 1998. reprint ed. pap. 9.95 (*0-8264-1124-X*) Continuum.

— Word Made Flesh. Freeman, Laurence, ed. 80p. 1998. reprint ed. pap. 9.95 (*0-8264-1125-8*) Continuum.

Main, John, jt. ed. see Archer, Clive.

Main, June & Eggen, Paul D. Developing Critical Thinking through Science Book 1. 136p. (J). (gr. 1-4). 1991. pap. 22.95 (*0-89455-424-7*) Crit Think Bks.

Main, June, jt. auth. see Eggen, Paul D.

Main, Katy. Baby Animals of the North. LC 91-78180. (Illus.). 40p. (J). (ps-k). 1994. 10.95 (*0-88240-395-8*, Alaska NW Bks) Gr Arts Ctr Pub.

Main, Kevan L., jt. auth. see Brock, James A.

Main, Kevan L., jt. ed. see Fulks, Wendy.

Main, Laurence. A Bristol Countryway. (C). 1988. pap. 40.00 (*0-904110-80-X*, Pub. by Thornhill Pr) St Mut.

— King Alfred's Way. (C). 1988. pap. 29.00 (*0-904110-82-6*, Pub. by Thornhill Pr) St Mut.

— A South Coast Way. (C). 1988. pap. 29.00 (*0-904110-86-9*, Pub. by Thornhill Pr) St Mut.

— A South Wessex Way. (C). 1988. pap. 29.00 (*0-904110-81-8*, Pub. by Thornhill Pr) St Mut.

— A Wiltshire Way. (C). 1988. pap. 40.00 (*0-904110-85-0*, Pub. by Thornhill Pr) St Mut.

Main, Lawrence. A Somerset Way. (C). 1988. pap. text 29.00 (*0-904110-79-6*, Pub. by Thornhill Pr) St Mut.

Main, Linda & Whitaker, Char. Automating Literacy: A Challenge for Libraries, 24. LC 90-47285. (New Directions in Information Management Ser.: No. 24). 144p. 1991. 47.95 (*0-313-27528-9*, MLX/, Greenwood Pr) Greenwood.

***Main, M. & Savitch, Walter J.** Data Structures & Other Objects Using C++ 2nd ed. LC 00-26255. 800p. 2000. pap. 67.00 (*0-201-70297-5*) Addison-Wesley.

Main, Mary. Deadliest of Friends. (J). 1997. pap. 3.95 (*0-8167-4311-8*) Troll Communs.

— Tower of Evil. 160p. (YA). 1996. pap. 2.95 (*0-8167-3533-6*) Troll Communs.

Main, Michael. Data Structures & Other Objects Using Java. LC 98-36207. 784p. (C). 1998. pap. text 68.00 (*0-201-35744-5*) Addison-Wesley.

Main, Michael G. & Savitch, Walter J. Data Structures & Other Objects Using C++ A Second Course in Computer Science. Wernholm, Karen, ed. LC 96-34045. 800p. (C). 1996. pap. text 68.00 (*0-8053-7470-1*) Addison-Wesley.

Main, Michael G., et al. Mathematical Foundations of Programming Semantics. (Lecture Notes in Computer Science Ser.: Vol. 802). 648p. 1994. 93.95 (*0-387-58027-1*) Spr-Verlag.

Main, Michael G., jt. auth. see Savitch, Walter J.

Main, Mike. Visitors' Guide to Botswana. 220p. pap. 17.95 (*1-86812-657-9*) Menasha Ridge.

M

An Asterisk (*) at the beginning of an entry indicates that the title is appearing for the first time.

Main, Norman. Muirfield: Home of the Honourable Company (1744-1994) (Illus.). 160p. 1995. 45.00 (*1-85158-617-2*, Pub. by Mainstream Pubng) Trafalgar.

Main, Roderick. Jung on Synchronicity & the Paranormal. 192p. (C). 1998. pap. 18.95 (*0-415-15509-6*) Routledge.

Main, Roderick, ed. Jung on Synchronicity & the Paranormal. 192p. (C). 1998. text 69.95 (*0-415-15508-8*) Routledge.

Main, Ron, jt. auth. see Mann, David.

Main, Ronald C. & Zervas, Judy. Keep Your Kids Straight: What Parents Need to Know about Drugs & Alcohol. 126p. 1991. pap. 7.95 (*0-8306-7681-3*, 3681) Sulzburger & Graham Pub.

Main, Shalt M. Towards the Close of the Century of Counter-Revolutions. unabridged ed. 186p. 1999. pap. 13.95 (*0-9658580-0-6*) Engger.

Main Street Staff. Birthdays: A Celebration of the Journey Through Life. (Main Street Editions Ser.). (Illus.). 40p. 1996. 6.95 (*0-8362-1063-8*) Andrews & McMeel.

— A Book of Ireland. LC 97-147947. (Main Street Editions Ser.). (Illus.). 40p. 1996. 6.95 (*0-8362-1066-2*) Andrews & McMeel.

— With Thanks: A Book of Gratitude & Friendship. (Main Street Editions Ser.). (Illus.). 48p. 1996. 6.95 (*0-8362-1064-6*) Andrews & McMeel.

— A Woman Is . . . (Main Street Editions Ser.). (Illus.). 48p. 1996. 6.95 (*0-8362-1061-1*) Andrews & McMeel.

Main, Thomas J., jt. auth. see Hill, M. A.

Main, Tucker W. Selling Solutions: Redefining Value Instead of Negotiating Price. (Illus.). 128p. 1997. pap. 14.95 (*1-891356-03-8*) B Main & Assocs.

Main, Tucker W. & Geshekter, Barbara. Signature Solutions: A Retail Grocer's Guide to HMR. (Illus.). 85p. 1998. pap. 60.00 (*1-891356-04-6*) B Main & Assocs.

Main, Wynell F. An Investigation of Angels. 1992. pap. 7.75 (*0-89137-462-0*) Quality Pubns.

Maina, J. N. The Gas Exchangers: Structure, Function, & Evolution of the Respiratory Processes. Bradshaw, S. D. et al, eds. LC 98-4125. (Zoophysiology Ser.: Vol. 37). (Illus.). 420p. 1998. 250.00 (*3-540-62511-9*) Spr-Verlag.

Mainar, Luis M. Narrative & Stylistic Patterns in the Films of Stanley Kubrick. Nischik, Reingard, ed. LC 98-32423. (European Studies in the Humanities). (Illus.). 190p. 1999. 55.00 (*1-57113-264-3*) Camden Hse.

Mainard, Christopher. Why Are Pineapples Prickly? (Why Bks.). (J). (ps up). 1997. 9.95 (*0-614-28704-9*) DK Pub Inc.

— Why Are There Waves? (Why Bks.). (J). (ps up). 1997. 9.95 (*0-614-28705-7*) DK Pub Inc.

— Why Do Seasons Change? (Why Bks.). (J). (ps up). 1997. 9.95 (*0-614-28703-0*) DK Pub Inc.

— Why Do Volcanoes Erupt? (Why Bks.). (J). (ps up). 1997. 9.95 (*0-614-28706-5*) DK Pub Inc.

Mainardi, F., jt. ed. see Carpinteri, A.

Mainardi, Patricia. Art & Politics of the Second Empire: The Universal Expositions of 1855 & 1867. LC 87-6262. (Illus.). 248p. 1987. 60.00 (*0-300-03871-2*) Yale U Pr.

— Art & Politics of the Second Empire: The Universal Expositions of 1855 & 1867. 248p. (C). 1990. reprint ed. pap. 25.00 (*0-300-04747-9*) Yale U Pr.

— The End of the Salon: Art & the State in the Early Third Republic. (Cambridge Studies in New Art History & Criticism). (Illus.). 224p. (C). 1994. pap. text 22.95 (*0-521-46921-X*) Cambridge U Pr.

— Quilts: The Great American Art. xix, 57p. 1985. reprint ed. 8.95 (*0-936810-06-8*); reprint ed. pap. 3.95 (*0-936810-24-6*) M & M.

Mainardi, Patricia, et al. The Persistence of Classicism. LC 95-5958. (Illus.). 68p. (Orig.). 1995. pap. 4.50 (*0-931102-36-7*) S & F Clark Art.

Maine Appalachian Trail Club Staff. A Guide to Log Lean-To Construction. (Illus.). 68p. 1992. pap. 4.95 (*0-917953-47-9*, 524) Appalachian Trail.

Maine Attorney General. Maine Consumer Law Guide. 2nd ed. 445p. 1998. pap. text, per. 19.95 (*1-881758-41-9*) Tower Pub ME.

Maine, Barry, ed. American Novelists: John Dos Passos. (Critical Heritage Ser.). 304p. (C). 1997. 125.00 (*0-415-15935-0*) Routledge.

— Dos Pasos. (Critical Heritage Ser.). 320p. (C). 1988. text 49.50 (*0-415-00229-X*) Routledge.

Maine, Basil. Elgar: His Life & Works, 2 vols., Set. LC 74-26065. reprint ed. 42.50 (*0-404-13005-4*) AMS Pr.

Maine Board of Overseers of the Bar Staff. Maine Manual on Professional Responsibility. rev. ed. 300p. 1994. ring bd. 65.00 (*0-89442-082-8*, MICHIE) LEXIS Pub.

— Maine Manual on Professional Responsibility, Vol. 2. rev. ed. 370p. 1994. ring bd. 65.00 (*1-56257-301-2*, MICHIE) LEXIS Pub.

Maine Board of Overseers Staff. Maine Manual on Professional Responsibility. 2nd rev. ed. 500p. 1997. pap. 125.00 (*1-881758-37-0*) Tower Pub ME.

Maine, Cathleen M., jt. auth. see Nalls, Patricia.

Maine Commissioners Staff. Maine at Gettysburg: Report of the Maine Monuments Commission. (Illus.). 602p. 1994. 45.00 (*1-879664-23-2*) Stan Clark Military.

Maine De Biran, Pierre. Influence of Habit on the Faculty of Thinking. Boehm, Margaret D., tr. LC 79-98854. 227p. 1970. reprint ed. lib. bdg. 35.00 (*0-8371-3124-3*, MBTH, Greenwood Pr) Greenwood.

Maine, Diana, ed. Science. LC 92-54482. (Picturepedia Ser.). (Illus.). (J). 1993. write for info. (*1-56458-248-5*) DK Pub Inc.

Maine, Edward L., jt. auth. see Adams, David M.

Maine, Henry J. Ancient Law: Its Connection with the Early History of Society & Its Relation to Modern Ideas. Reams, Bernard D., Jr., ed. LC 30-21428. (Historical Reprints in Jurisprudence & Classical Legal Literature Ser.). xxiv, 426p. 1983. reprint ed. lib. bdg. 72.50 (*0-89941-249-1*, 303180) W S Hein.

Maine, Henry S. Ancient Law. LC 86-6929. (Classics of Anthropology Ser.). 400p. 1986. reprint ed. pap. 22.50 (*0-8165-1006-7*) U of Ariz Pr.

— Ancient Law: Its Connection with the Early History of Society, & its Relation to Modern Ideas. 7th ed. ix, 415p. 1998. reprint ed. 128.00 (*1-56169-421-5*) Gaunt.

— Dissertations on Early Law & Custom Chiefly Selected from Lectures Delivered at Oxford. LC 74-25768. (European Sociology Ser.). 414p. 1975. reprint ed. 30.95 (*0-405-06522-1*) Ayer.

— International Law: A Series of Lectures Delivered Before the University of Cambridge 1887. LC 97-74170. 234p. 1997. reprint ed. 72.00 (*1-56169-325-1*, 14645) Gaunt.

— Lectures on the Early History of Institutions. ix, 412p. 1998. reprint ed. 127.50 (*1-56169-438-X*) Gaunt.

— Lectures on the Early History of Institutions. 4th ed. ix, 412p. 1998. reprint ed. 127.50 (*1-56169-428-2*) Gaunt.

***Maine, Henry S.** Lectures on the Early History of Institutions. 5th ed. viii, 412p. 1999. reprint ed. 127.50 (*1-56169-473-8*) Gaunt.

— Lectures on the Early History of Institutions. 6th ed. viii, 812p. 1999. reprint ed. 125.00 (*1-56169-474-6*) Gaunt.

Maine, Henry S. Lectures on the Early History of Institutions: A Sequel to Ancient Law. LC 87-81276. 1987. reprint ed. lib. bdg. 52.00 (*0-89941-562-8*, 305200) W S Hein.

— Popular Government. LC 76-26329. 1977. reprint ed. 8.50 (*0-913966-14-2*) Liberty Fund.

— Village-Communities in the East & West. LC 73-14169. (Perspectives in Social Inquiry Ser.). 430p. 1974. reprint ed. 25.95 (*0-405-05513-7*) Ayer.

— Village Communities in the East & West. 2nd ed. Mersky, Roy M. & Jacobstein, J. Myron, eds. (Classics in Legal History Reprint Ser.: Vol. 15). 444p. 1972. reprint ed. lib. bdg. 45.00 (*0-89941-014-6*, 302780) W S Hein.

Maine Historical Society Staff. Collections of the Maine Historical Society, 10 vols., Set. reprint ed. 345.00 (*0-404-11059-2*) AMS Pr.

— Collections of the Maine Historical Society, Vol. IV. (Illus.). 433p. 1995. pap. text 28.00 (*0-7884-0172-6*) Heritage Bk.

— The Maine Bicentennial Atlas: An Historical Survey. (Illus.). 1976. pap. 10.00 (*0-685-03278-7*); pap. write for info. (*0-915592-23-1*) Maine Hist.

Maine Joint Special Committee. Report of the Joint Special Committee on Investigation of the Affairs of the Maine State Prison: Made to the Fifty-Third Legislature. LC 74-3832. (Criminal Justice in America Ser.). 1974. reprint ed. 15.95 (*0-405-06152-8*) Ayer.

Maine Literature Project Staff, ed. Maine Speaks: An Anthology of Maine Literature. LC 89-60344. (Illus.). 466p. (gr. 7-12). 1989. 29.95 (*0-9618592-1-0*); pap. 19.95 (*0-9618592-2-9*) Maine Writers.

Maine, Margo. Body Wars: Making Peace with Women's Bodies. 224p. 1999. pap. 14.95 (*0-936077-34-4*) Gurze Bks.

— Father Hunger: Fathers, Daughters & Food. 272p. 1991. pap. 13.95 (*0-936077-09-3*) Gurze Bks.

Maine, R. A., et al. Participatory Analysis, Monitoring & Evaluation for Fishing Communities: A Manual. (Fisheries Technical Papers: No. 364). 142p. 1997. pap. 19.00 (*92-5-103919-4*, F39194, Pub. by FAO) Bernan Associates.

Maine, Sandy. Big Mamma Buffalo & the Gift of the Great Mystery. (Illus.). 24p. (Orig.). (J). (gr. k-12). 1995. pap. 6.50 (*0-9649620-0-4*) Mntn Tree Commty Schl.

— Creating an Herbal Bodycare Business. LC 98-30916. (Making a Living Naturally Ser.). 1999. pap. 16.95 (*1-58017-094-3*) Storey Bks.

— Herbal Homekeeping: Simple Recipes for a Naturally Clean Home. LC 99-10975. 1999. pap. 12.95 (*1-883010-55-1*) Interweave.

— The Soap Book: Simple Herbal Recipes. LC 95-4865. (Illus.). 96p. 1995. pap. 9.95 (*1-883010-14-4*) Interweave.

— Soothing Soaps: For Healthy Skin. LC 97-36761. (Illus.). 96p. 1997. pap. text 9.95 (*1-883010-36-5*) Interweave.

Maine State Bar Association Staff. Maine Media Law Guide. (State Law Ser.). 140p. (Orig.). 1993. pap. text 14.95 (*0-913507-42-3*) New Forums.

Maine Trial Lawyers Association Staff. Maine Jury Instructions Manual. 2nd ed. 1996. ring bd. write for info. (*1-894421-08-6*, 81655-10, MICHIE) LEXIS Pub.

— Maine Jury Instructions Manual, Issue 1. 3rd ed. 1997. ring bd. 45.00 (*1-55834-352-0*, 81657-12, MICHIE) LEXIS Pub.

Mainella, Eleanor M., jt. auth. see Baskette, Michael.

Mainelli, Helen K. Numbers. (Bible Commentary - Old Testament Ser.). 136p. 1985. pap. 4.95 (*0-8146-1373-X*) Liturgical Pr.

Mainer, Jose C., ed. see Fernandez Florez, Wenceslao.

Maines, David R., ed. Social Organization & Social Process: Essays in Honor of Anselm Strauss. (Communication & Social Order Ser.). 408p. 1991. lib. bdg. 67.95 (*0-202-30390-X*) Aldine de Gruyter.

Maines, David R., ed. see Blumer, Herbert.

Maines, David R., ed. see Couch, Carl J.

Maines, David R., jt. ed. see Lopata, Helena Z.

Maines, Leah. Looking to the East with Western Eyes. LC 99-187912. (New Women's Voices Ser.: Vol. 1). 25p. 1998. pap. 7.00 (*0-9664324-0-1*) Finishng Line.

Maines, Leah, jt. ed. see Larkin, Elle.

Maines, Leah, ed. see Watson, Denise Brennan.

Maines, Mahin D. Heme Oxygenase: Clinical Applications & Functions. 288p. 1992. lib. bdg. 225.00 (*0-8493-5408-0*, QP603) CRC Pr.

***Maines, Mahin D., et al.** JNL Current Protocols in Toxicology. LC 98-46552. 700p. 1999. pap. text 395.00 (*0-471-24106-7*) Wiley.

Maines, Mahin D., jt. ed. see Conn, P. Michael.

Maines, Patrick D., jt. auth. see Kaplar, Richard T.

Maines, Patrick T., jt. auth. see Kaplar, Richard T.

Maines, Rachel P. The Technology of Orgasm: "Hysteria," the Vibrator, & Women's Sexual Satisfaction. LC 98-20213. (Johns Hopkins Studies in the History of Technology: Vol. 24). (Illus.). 196p. 1998. 22.00 (*0-8018-5941-7*) Johns Hopkins.

Mainfort, Robert, ed. Middle Woodland Settlement & Ceremonialism in the Mid-South & Lower Mississippi Valley: Proceedings of the 1984 Mid-South Archaeological Conference. LC 89-60071. (Archaeological Report Ser.: No. 22). (Illus.). (Orig.). 1989. pap. text 10.00 (*0-938896-55-5*) Mississippi Archives.

***Mainfort, Robert C. & Jeter, Marvin D., eds.** Arkansas Archaeology: Essays in Honor of Dan & Phyllis Morse. LC 99-30696. (Illus.). 344p. 1999. pap. 22.00 (*1-55728-571-3*) U of Ark Pr.

Mainfort, Robert C., Jr. & Sullivan, Lynne P., eds. Ancient Earthen Enclosures of the Eastern Woodlands. LC 98-5507. (Ripley P. Bullen Ser.). (Illus.). 336p. 1998. 49.95 (*0-8130-1592-8*) U Press Fla.

Mainfort, Robert C. & Walling, Richard, eds. Mounds, Embankments, & Ceremonialism in the Midsouth. LC 96-38731. (Arkansas Archaeological Survey Research Ser.). (Illus.). 98p. (Orig.). 1996. pap. 15.00 (*1-56349-077-3*, RS46) AR Archaeol.

***Mainfort, Robert C., Jr., et al.** Archeological Data Recovery at the Skaggs, Madison County, Arkansas. (Arkansas Archeological Survey Research Report Ser.: Vol. 28). (Illus.). 124p. 2000. pap. write for info. (*1-56349-087-0*) AR Archaeol.

Maingon, Charles, jt. auth. see Cova, J. L.

Maingot, Anthony P., ed. Trends in U. S.-Caribbean Relations. LC 93-85876. (Annals of the American Academy of Political & Social Science Ser.: Vol. 533). 1994. 28.00 (*0-8039-5588-X*); pap. 18.00 (*0-8039-5589-8*) Am Acad Pol Soc Sci.

Maingot, Joseph P. Parliamentary Privilege in Canada. 2nd ed. LC 98-223747. 432p. 1997. text 65.00 (*0-7735-1718-9*, Pub. by McG-Queens Univ Pr) CUP Services.

Maingot, Rodney & Zinner, Michael J. Maingot's Abdominal Operations, Vol. I. 10th ed. LC 96-28893. (C). 1998. pap. text 175.00 (*0-8385-6104-7*, A-6104-2, Apple Lange Med) McGraw.

— Maingot's Abdominal Operations, Vol. II. 10th ed. LC 96-28893. (C). 1998. pap. text 175.00 (*0-8385-6105-5*, A6105-9, Apple Lange Med) McGraw.

— Maingot's Abdominal Operations, 2 vols., Vols. I & II. 10th ed. LC 96-28893. 2150p. (C). 1997. 325.00 (*0-8385-6106-3*, A6106-7, Apple Lange Med) McGraw.

Mainguet, M. Desertification: Natural Background & Human Mismanagement. (Physical Environment Ser.: Vol. 9). (Illus.). xvi, 306p. 1991. 159.00 (*0-387-52519-X*) Spr-Verlag.

Mainguet, Monique. Desertification: Natural Background & Human Mismanagement. LC 94-14998. 1994. 79.95 (*0-387-57746-7*) Spr-Verlag.

Mainhardt, Ricia, jt. auth. see Varley, John.

Mainhardt, Ricia, ed. see Matheson, Richard.

Maini, Darshan S. Henry James: The Indirect Vision. 2nd enl. rev. ed. Litz, A. Walton, ed. LC 87-24871. (Studies in Modern Literature: No. 83). 258p. reprint ed. 80.00 (*0-8357-1838-7*, 207073700004) Bks Demand.

***Maini, Philip K. & Othmer, H. G.** Mathematical Models for Biological Pattern Formulation: Frontiers in Biological Mathematics. LC 00-44018. (IMA Volumes in Mathematics & Its Applications Ser.). 2000. write for info. (*0-387-95103-2*) Spr-Verlag.

Maini, R. N. Manual of Biological Markers of Disease. Van Venrooij, W. J., ed. LC 96-31174. 744p. (C). 1997. lib. bdg. 330.00 (*0-7923-4242-9*) Kluwer Academic.

Maini, S. M., et al. Barrier Fabrics for Protection Against Aerosols. (Textile Progress Ser.: Vol. 26, No. 1). 1995. pap. 36.00 (*1-870812-74-3*, Pub. by Textile Inst) St Mut.

Mainiero, Lina, ed. American Women Writers: A Critical Reference Guide, Vol. 3, Li-R. LC 78-20945. 600p. 1981. 95.00 (*0-8044-3153-1*) F Ungar Bks.

Mainiero, Lisa A. & Tromley, Cheryl L. Developing Managerial Skills in Organizational Behavior: Exercises, Cases & Readings. 2nd ed. LC 93-5071. 491p. (C). 1993. pap. text 49.60 (*0-13-208190-3*) P-H.

Mainiero, Lisa A., jt. auth. see Brindle, Margaret A.

Mainkar, T. G. The Making of Vedant. 170p. 1980. 15.95 (*0-318-37172-3*) Asia Bk Corp.

Mainlaender, Philipp. Schriften: Die Letzten Hohenstaufen. Mueller-Seyfarth, Winfried H., ed. (GER.). 668p. 1997. write for info. (*3-487-10551-9*) G Olms Pubs.

Mainland, Pauline. A Yoga Parade of Animals: A First Fun Picture Book on Yoga. (Illus.). 32p. (J). (gr. 2-6). 1998. 15.95 (*1-901881-65-2*, Pub. by Element MA) Penguin Putnam.

— Yoga Parade of Animals: A First Fun Picture Book on Yoga. (Illus.). 32p. (J). 1999. pap. 6.95 (*1-901881-89-X*, Pub. by Element MA) Penguin Putnam.

Mainland, W. F., ed. Hoffman: Der Goldene Topf ein Marchen aus der Neuen Zeit. (Bristol German Texts Ser.). (GER.). 128p. 1942. pap. 16.95 (*0-631-01310-5*) Blackwell Pubs.

Mainland, William F., tr. see Schiller, Friedrich.

Mainlander, Philipp. Die Philosophie der Erlosung Band I: Erster Band. Berlin 1876. (GER.). xi, 632p. 1996. reprint ed. 178.00 (*3-487-09556-4*) G Olms Pubs.

— Die Philosophie der Erlosung Band II: Zweiter Band. Zwolf Philosophische Essays. (GER.). ix, 668p. 1996. reprint ed. 178.00 (*3-487-09557-2*) G Olms Pubs.

— Schriften Bd. III: Die Letzten Hohenstaufen. Muller-Seyfarth, W., ed. 668p. 1997. reprint ed. 160.00 (*3-487-09558-0*) G Olms Pubs.

Maino, Charles A. Old Times: San Luis Obispo CA Memoirs. Maino, Jeannette G., ed. 50p. (Orig.). 1990. write for info. (*0-318-66925-0*) Dry Creeks Bks.

Maino, Evelyn, jt. auth. see McMinn, Howard E.

Maino, Giuseppe, et al, eds. Nonlinear Phenomena in Physics of Fluids & Plasmas - Proceedings of the ENEA Workshops on Nonlinear Dynamics, Bologna, Italy, October 30-31, 1989. (ENEA Workshop on Nonlinear Dynamics Ser.: Vol. 2). 208p. 1991. text 89.00 (*981-02-0363-2*) World Scientific Pub.

Maino, Giuseppe & Carmignani, C., eds. Nonlinear Problems in Engineering: Proceedings of the ENEA Workshop on Nonlinear Dynamics, Rome, Italy, 6-7 May 1991. (ENEA Workshop on Nonlinear Dynamics Ser.: Vol. 4). 400p. 1991. text 104.00 (*981-02-0832-4*) World Scientific Pub.

Maino, Giuseppe & Ottaviani, Maurizio. Dynamics of Transport in Plasmas & Changed Beams. 300p. 1996. text 93.00 (*981-02-2154-1*) World Scientific Pub.

Maino, Giuseppe, et al. Dynamical Symmetries & Chaotic Behavior in Physical Systems: ENEA Workshop on Nonlinear Dynamics, Vol. 1. Fronzoni, L., ed. 288p. (C). 1990. text 101.00 (*981-02-0296-2*) World Scientific Pub.

— Nuclear Level Densities: Proceedings of the OECD Meeting. 350p. 1992. text 95.00 (*981-02-1077-9*) World Scientific Pub.

— Simulation of Nonlinear Systems in Physics: ENEA Workshop on Nonlinear Dynamics, Vol. 3. 250p. 1991. text 84.00 (*981-02-0402-7*) World Scientific Pub.

Maino, Jeannette G. Places, Paths & Passes. 80p. (Orig.). 1991. write for info. (*0-941885-07-0*) Dry Creeks Bks.

— Speeding into Lost Landscapes. (Orig.). 1982. pap. 5.50 (*0-941885-00-3*) Dry Creeks Bks.

Maino, Jeannette G., ed. see Maino, Charles A.

Maino, Joseph H., jt. auth. see Ashton, Sheree J.

Mainone, Robert F. An American Naturalist's Haiku Poems. 3rd ed. Mohrhardt, David, ed. (Haiku Series: Vol. 1). (Illus.). 32p. 1964. pap. 7.00 (*1-888693-01-0*) Wnderlnd MI.

— Haiku: The Collected Works of Robert F. Mainone, 10 vols., Set. Mohrhardt, David, ed. (Illus.). 492p. 1989. pap. 73.00 (*1-888693-00-2*) Wnderlnd MI.

— High on the Wind. 2nd ed. (Haiku Series: Vol. 7). (Illus.). 48p. 1975. pap. 7.00 (*1-888693-07-X*) Wnderlnd MI.

— The Journey North. (Haiku Series: Vol. 9). (Illus.). 60p. 1984. pap. 7.00 (*1-888693-09-6*) Wnderlnd MI.

— Moonlight. (Haiku Series: Vol. 8). (Illus.). 52p. 1979. pap. 7.00 (*1-888693-08-8*) Wnderlnd MI.

— Parnassus Flowers. 3rd rev. ed. Mohrhardt, David, ed. (Haiku Series: Vol. 2). (Illus.). 32p. 1982. pap. 7.00 (*1-888693-02-9*) Wnderlnd MI.

— Shadows. (Haiku Series: Vol. 5). (Illus.). 52p. (Orig.). 1971. pap. 7.00 (*1-888693-05-3*) Wnderlnd MI.

— The Spring Within. (Haiku Series: Vol. 10). (Illus.). 52p. 1989. pap. 10.00 (*1-888693-10-X*) Wnderlnd MI.

— This Boundless Mist. (Haiku Series: Vol. 4). (Illus.). 60p. (Orig.). 1984. pap. 7.00 (*1-888693-04-5*) Wnderlnd MI.

— Where Waves Were. 3rd rev. ed. (Haiku Series: Vol. 3). (Illus.). 60p. 1986. pap. 7.00 (*1-888693-03-7*) Wnderlnd MI.

— Young Leaves. (Haiku Series: Vol. 6). (Illus.). 44p. 1974. pap. 7.00 (*1-888693-06-1*) Wnderlnd MI.

***Mainor, Prudence J.** Commodity Trading: A Story of the White Slave Trade. LC 99-74158. 176p. 1999. pap. 9.95 (*0-9672432-0-3*) Prime Time Bks.

***Mainous, Arch G., III & Pomeroy, Claire, eds.** Management of Antimicrobials in Infectious Diseases: Impact of Antibiotic Resistance. (Infectious Disease Ser.). 353p. 2000. 99.50 (*0-89603-821-1*) Humana.

Mainous, Frank D., jt. auth. see Ottman.

Mainous, Frank D., jt. auth. see Ottman, Robert W.

Mainprize, Virginia. The Sanctuary: Preparing the Church for Worship. 96p. 1996. pap. 10.95 (*1-55126-096-4*) Forward Movement.

Mainprize, Virginia, ed. Women in Profile, 6 vols. (Illus.). 1998. pap. 65.70 (*0-7787-0022-4*) Crabtree Pub Co.

— Women in Profile, 6 vols. (Illus.). (J). (gr. 4-11). 1998. lib. bdg. 143.70 (*0-7787-0000-3*) Crabtree Pub Co.

***Mainquet, M.** Aridity: Droughts & Human Development. Reimer, T. O., tr. from FRE. LC 98-30231. (Illus.). ix, 302p. 1998. 89.95 (*3-540-63342-1*) Spr-Verlag.

Mains, A. A. Field Security-Very Ordinary Intelligence. 181p. 1990. pap. 39.00 (*0-948251-57-3*, Pub. by Picton) St Mut.

— Soldiers with Railways. 200p. 1990. pap. 51.00 (*0-948251-70-0*, Pub. by Picton) St Mut.

***Mains, David.** Celebrate Jesus! Adult Journal. (Celebrate Jesus! Ser.). 80p. 1999. 7.00 (*1-57849-171-1*) Mainstay Church.

— Celebrate Jesus! Large Print Adult Journal. large type ed. (Celebrate Jesus! Ser.). 96p. 1999. 7.00 (*1-57849-173-8*) Mainstay Church.

— Tales of the Kingdom. 128p. 2000. pap. text 6.99 (*0-7814-3288-X*) Chariot Victor.

— Tales of the Resistance. LC 99-89170. (Kingdom Tales Ser.). 128p. 2000. pap. 6.99 (*0-7814-3287-1*) Chariot Victor.

— Tales of the Restoration. LC 99-87659. (Kingdom Tales Ser.). 128p. 2000. pap. text 6.99 (*0-7814-3289-8*) Chariot Victor.

Mains, David, ed. Promises Worth Keeping. (Nineteen Ninety-Nine 50-Day Spiritual Adventure Ser.). (Illus.). 80p. 1998. pap. 7.00 (*1-57849-104-5*) Mainstay Church.

***Mains, David, ed.** Promises Worth Keeping: Large Print Adult Journal. large type ed. (Illus.). 128p. 1998. 7.00 (*1-57849-105-3*) Mainstay Church.

An Asterisk (*) at the beginning of an entry indicates that the title is appearing for the first time.

Mains, David R. Healing the Dysfunctional Church Family. 168p. (Orig.). 1992. pap. 2.20 (*0-89693-050-5*, 6-1050) Chariot Victor.
— The Sunday Search Pamphlet. (Nineteen Ninety-Seven 50-Day Spiritual Adventure Ser.). 1996. pap. 6.00 (*1-57849-020-0*) Chapel of Air.
— The Truth about the Lie. 128p. 1987. pap. 7.95 (*0-310-34831-5*, 12750P) Zondervan.
— When the Troops Are Tired: Guidebook. Gruben, Nancy, ed. LC 98-149846. (Nineteen Ninety-Eight Fifty-Day Spiritual Adventure Ser.). 157p. Date not set. wbk. ed. 6.00 (*1-57849-044-8*) Mainstay Church.
Mains, David R. & Bell, Steve. Two Are Better Than One: A Guide to Prayer Partnerships That Work. 144p. 1995. reprint ed. pap. 4.99 (*1-879050-78-1*) Chapel of Air.
Mains, David R. & Mains, Karen B. Tales of the Kingdom. (Illus.). 112p. (J). (gr. 1 up). 1983. 16.99 (*0-89191-560-5*) Chariot Victor.
Mains, David R. & Mains, Laurie. When Life Becomes a Maze: Discovering Christ's Resources for Times of Confusion. LC 96-132484. (Nineteen Ninety-Six 50-Day Spiritual Adventure Ser.). 192p. (Orig.). 1995. pap. 6.00 (*1-879050-77-3*) Chapel of Air.
Mains, David R. & Timberlake, Melissa M. Getting Beyond "How Are You?" LC 92-23325. 112p. 1992. pap. 4.99 (*1-56476-035-9*, 6-3035, Victor Bks) Chariot Victor.
Mains, Karen. Comforting One Another. LC 97-2280. 256p. 1997. 14.99 (*0-7852-7566-5*) Nelson.
— Open Heart, Open Home. rev. ed. Mains, Laurie, ed. LC 98-100598. 208p. 1997. reprint ed. wbk. ed. 11.00 (*1-57849-036-7*) Mainstay Church.
Mains, Karen & Calhoun, Adele. Opening Our Hearts & Homes Group Study Guide. Mains, Laurie, ed. (Illus.). 96p. 1998. pap. 7.99 (*1-57849-100-2*) Mainstay Church.
Mains, Karen B. You Are What You Say: Diagnosis & Cure for the Troublesome Tongue. 256p. 1988. pap. 7.99 (*0-310-34211-2*, 12767P) Zondervan.
Mains, Karen B. & Hancock, Maxine. Child Sexual Abuse: A Hope for Healing. 2nd rev. ed. 250p. (Orig.). 1997. pap. 11.99 (*0-87788-162-6*, H Shaw Pubs) Waterbrook Pr.
Mains, Karen B., jt. auth. see Mains, David R.
Mains, Kristine M., jt. auth. see Strumpf, Lori.
Mains, Laura L., compiled by. Wisdom from Proverbs: Time-Tested Principles for Living. (Pocketpac Bks.). 112p. (Orig.). 1993. pap. text 2.99 (*0-87788-845-0*, H Shaw Pubs) Waterbrook Pr.
***Mains, Laurie.** Advent Calendar. (Ninety Eight Seasonal Advent Celebration Ser.). (Illus.). 96p. 1998. 11.00 (*1-57849-092-8*) Mainstay Church.
— Advent Calendar - A Season of Wonder: Opening Your Heart's Door to Christmas & Beyond. (Illus.). 112p. 2000. 11.00 (*1-57849-155-X*) Mainstay Church.
Mains, Laurie, ed. Advent Church Resource Manual. (Ninety Eight Seasonal Advent Celebration Ser.). 1998. 50.00 (*1-57849-093-6*) Mainstay Church.
Mains, Laurie, jt. auth. see Mains, David R.
Mains, Laurie, ed. see Asimakoupoulos, Greg.
Mains, Laurie, ed. see Lupton, Dan.
Mains, Laurie, ed. see Mains, Karen.
Mains, Laurie, ed. see Mains, Karen & Calhoun, Adele.
Mains, Ray, photos by. Capturing Hawai'i Maui. (Capturing Hawai'i Ser.). (Illus.). 32p. 1998. pap. 7.95 (*1-56647-210-5*) Mutual Pub HI.
Mainstay Church Resources Staff. Untapped Miracles for Tapped-Out Christians: Adult Journal. Oliver, Marian, ed. (Nineteen Ninety-Eight Fifty-Day Spiritual Adventure Ser.). (Illus.). 80p. 1997. wbk. ed. 6.00 (*1-57849-038-3*) Mainstay Church.
Mainstone, Rowland. Developments in Structural Form. 2nd ed. LC 99-166307. (Illus.). 384p. 1998. text 99.95 (*0-7506-2893-6*, Butterwrth Archit) Buttrwrth-Heinemann.
Mainstone, Rowland J. Hagia Sophia: Architecture, Structure, & Liturgy of Justinian's Great Church. LC 86-50969. (Illus.). 288p. 1997. pap. 39.95 (*0-500-27945-4*, Pub. by Thames Hudson) Norton.
— Structure in Architecture: The History of Design & Innovation. LC 99-26181. (Collected Studies Ser.: No. 659). (Illus.). 423p. 1999. text 110.95 (*0-86078-763-X*, Pub. by Variorum) Ashgate Pub Co.
Maintenance Council Staff, ed. Preventive Maintenance Inspection Guidelines: Dry-Van Trailers. 1996. pap. 49.95 (*0-88711-327-3*) Am Trucking Assns.
Mainwaring, Bill. Government, Oregon-Style, 1997-99: Classroom Edition. LC 97-61772. (Illus.). 88p. 1997. pap. text 8.00 (*0-918832-04-7*) Westridge.
Mainwaring, Douglas S., ed. see Bevan, Carol S.
Mainwaring, G. B. & Grunwedel, A. Dictionary of the Lepcha Language. (C). 1979. 130.00 (*0-89771-111-4*, Pub. by Ratna Pustak Bhandar) St Mut.
Mainwaring, Lynn. Dynamics of Uneven Development: An Analysis of the Global Accumulation of Capital. 256p. 1990. text 90.00 (*1-85278-319-2*) E Elgar.
Mainwaring, Marion. Mysteries of Paris: The Quest for Morton Fullerton. (Illus.). 384p. 2000. 30.00 (*1-58465-008-7*) U Pr of New Eng.
Mainwaring, Marion, jt. auth. see Wharton, Edith.
Mainwaring, Marion, ed. see Wharton, Edith.
Mainwaring, S. Learning Through Sewing & Pattern Design. 35p. (J). (gr. k-3). 1976. pap. 8.95 (*1-57379-064-8*, E1006) High-Scope.
Mainwaring, S. & Shouse, C. Learning Through Construction. 43p. (J). (gr. k-3). 1983. pap. 8.95 (*1-57379-063-X*, E1007) High-Scope.
Mainwaring, Scott. The Catholic Church & Politics in Brazil, 1916-1985. LC 86-1272. 343p. 1986. reprint ed. pap. 30.00 (*0-608-02958-0*, 206342300006) Bks Demand.
— Rethinking Party Systems in the Third Wave of Democratization: The Case of Brazil. LC 98-39078. 8p. 1999. write for info. (*0-8047-3057-1*); 22.95 (*0-8047-3059-8*) Stanford U Pr.
Mainwaring, Scott, et al, eds. Issues in Democratic Consolidation: The New South American Democracies in Comparative Perspective. LC 91-50566. (From the Helen Kellogg Institute for International Studies). (C). 1992. text 49.50 (*0-268-01210-5*) U of Notre Dame Pr.
— Issues in Democratic Consolidation: The New South American Democracies in Comparative Perspective. LC 91-50566. (From the Helen Kellogg Institute for International Studies). (C). 1992. pap. text 23.00 (*0-268-01211-3*) U of Notre Dame Pr.
Mainwaring, Scott & Scully, Timothy R., eds. Building Democratic Instutitions: Party Systems in Latin America. 600p. 1995. 65.00 (*0-8047-2307-9*) Stanford U Pr.
— Building Democratic Instutitions: Party Systems in Latin America. LC 93-46528. 600p. 1995. pap. 24.95 (*0-8047-2305-2*) Stanford U Pr.
Mainwaring, Scott & Shugart, Matthew S., eds. Presidentialism & Democracy in Latin America. LC 96-26086. (Cambridge Studies in Comparative Politics). 502p. 1997. text 74.95 (*0-521-57266-5*); pap. text 29.95 (*0-521-57614-8*) Cambridge U Pr.
Mainwaring, William L. Exploring the Mt. Hood Loop. LC 92-96979. (Illus.). 64p. (Orig.). 1992. pap. 9.95 (*0-918832-00-4*) Westridge.
— Exploring the Oregon Coast. 5th ed. LC 77-77250. (Illus.). 64p. 1994. pap. 7.95 (*0-918832-01-2*) Westridge.
Mainwarsng, C. B. & Grunwedel, A. Dictionary of the Lepcha Language. 1979. 90.00 (*0-7855-0267-X*, Pub. by Ratna Pustak Bhandar) St Mut.
Mainwarsng, M. & Grunwedel, G. Dictionary of the Lepcha Language. 1979. 80.00 (*0-7855-0310-2*, Pub. by Ratna Pustak Bhandar) St Mut.
Mainwood, Alison. Defects in Solids: An Introduction. 250p. 1999. 34.00 (*981-02-3770-7*) World Scientific Pub.
Mainx, Felix. Foundations of Biology. (Foundations of the Unity of Science Ser.: Vol. 1, No. 9). 1993. pap. text 2.25 (*0-226-57584-5*) U Ch Pr.
***Mainz, Valerie & Pollock, Griselda.** Work & the Image, 2 vols. LC 00-40610. 2000. pap. write for info. (*0-7546-0233-8*, Pub. by Ashgate Pub) Ashgate Pub Co.
Mainzer, Klaus. Computer - Neue Fluegel des Geistes? Die Evolution Computergestuetzter Techik, Wissenschaft, Kultur & Philosophie. (Philosophie & Wissenschaft - Transdisziplinaere Studien: Bd. 9). (GER.). xii, 882p. (Orig.). (C). 1995. pap. text 60.00 (*3-11-014808-0*) De Gruyter.
— Computer - Neue Fluegel des Geistes? Die Evolution Computergestuetzter Technick, Wissenschaft, Kultur & Philosophie. (GER., Illus.). xii, 882p. (C). 1994. lib. bdg. 344.65 (*3-11-014004-7*) De Gruyter.
— Symmetries of Nature: A Handbook for Philosophy of Nature & Science. LC 95-50834. (Illus.). 681p. (C). 1996. 218.00 (*3-11-012990-6*, Q172) De Gruyter.
— Thinking in Complexity. (Illus.). 329p. 1995. 34.50 (*0-387-57597-9*) Spr-Verlag.
— Thinking in Complexity: The Complex Dynamics of Matter, Mind & Mankind. 2nd enl. rev. ed. LC 95-53966. (Illus.). xii, 350p. 1996. 39.95 (*3-540-60637-8*) Spr-Verlag.
— Thinking in Complexity: The Complex Dynamics of Matter, Mind, & Mankind. 3rd ed. LC 97-656. 355p. 1997. 39.95 (*3-540-62555-0*) Spr-Verlag.
Maio, Barbara & Lewis, Sue. Borders Clip Art, Vol. 2345. (Illus.). 95p. 1998. pap. 18.98 (*1-57471-370-1*) Creat Teach Pr.
— Primary Themes Clip Art, Vol. 2344. (Illus.). 56p. 1998. pap. 18.98 (*1-57471-369-8*) Creat Teach Pr.
— Seasons & Holidays Clip Art, Vol. 2343. (Illus.). 52p. 1998. pap. 18.98 (*1-57471-368-X*) Creat Teach Pr.
Maio, Eugene, tr. see Pearson, D'Orsay W., ed.
Maio, Gerald De, see Kushner, Harvey W. & De Maio, Gerald.
Maio, Gregory R. & Olson, James M. Why We Evaluate: Functions of Attitudes LC 99-28185. 1999. write for info. (*0-8058-2770-6*) L Erlbaum Assocs.
Maio, Samuel. The Burning of Los Angeles: Poems. LC 96-38810. 92p. 1997. 20.00 (*0-943549-45-0*); pap. 10.00 (*0-943549-44-2*) Truman St Univ.
— Creating Another Self: Voice in Modern American Personal Poetry. LC 95-6311. 286p. (C). 1995. lib. bdg. 40.00 (*0-943549-33-7*) Truman St Univ.
Maio-sin Wu, Samuel, jt. auth. see Johnston, Daniel.
Maio, Vincent J. Di, see Di Maio, Vincent J.
Maiocco, Joseph F. Signs of the Times: A Time of Shaking, a Time of Building. 64p. 1999. pap. 6.95 (*0-9670713-0-5*) Mavbooks.
Maiolo, John R., jt. ed. see Vasoli, Robert H.
Maiolo, Joseph A. The Royal Navy & Nazi Germany, 1933-39: A Study in Appeasement & the Origins of the Second World War LC 98-12708. (Studies in Military & Strategic History). xii, 259p. 1998. write for info. (*0-333-72007-5*) Macmillan.
***Maione, Dennis.** MCDBA Training Guide: 5-in-1. 3000p. 1999. pap. 199.99 incl. cd-rom (*0-7357-0943-2*) New Riders Pub.
Maione, Dennis. MCSE Training Guide: WIndows NT Server $ 2nd ed. 1998. 49.99 (*1-56205-916-5*) New Riders Pub.
— MCSE Training Guide: Windows NT Workstation. 2nd ed. (Training Guides). 1998. 49.99 (*1-56205-918-1*) New Riders Pub.
— MCSE Training Guides: Core Exams. 2nd ed. (Training Guides). 1998. 149.99 (*1-56205-926-2*) New Riders Pub.
Maione, Michael. Tooty's Corner. LC 98-67425. 96p. (Orig.). 1999. pap. 10.95 (*1-57197-131-9*) Pentland Pr.
Maioni, Antonia. Divergent Pasts, Converging Futures? The Politics of Health Care Reform in Canada & the United States LC 96-227551. (Public Policy Ser.). 34 p. 1994. write for info. (*1-882582-06-3*) Canadian-Amer Ctr.
Maioni, Antonia. Parting at the Crossroads: The Emergence of Health Insurance in the United States & Canada. LC 97-43548. 216p. 1998. text 37.50 (*0-691-05796-6*, Pub. by Princeton U Pr) Cal Prin Full Svc.
Maior, Plinius. C. Plinii Secundi Naturalis Historia, 6 vols. in 3. (GER.). 1784p. 1992. reprint ed. write for info. (*0-318-70543-5*); reprint ed. write for info. (*0-318-70544-3*); reprint ed. write for info. (*0-318-70545-1*) G Olms Pubs.
— C. Plinii Secundi Naturalis Historia, 6 vols. in 3, Set. (GER.). 1784p. 1992. reprint ed. write for info. (*3-487-09678-1*) G Olms Pubs.
Maiorana, Sal. Relentless: The Hard-Hitting History of Buffalo Bills Football. (Illus.). 480p. 1994. 39.50 (*1-885758-00-6*) Quality Sports.
***Maiorana, Sal.** Relentless II: The Hard-Hitting History of Buffalo Bills Football, Vol. II. (Illus.). 1999. 39.50 (*1-885758-17-0*) Quality Sports.
Maiorana, Sal. Thank You Sabres: Memories of the 1972-73 Season. (Illus.). 208p. 1997. 24.50 (*1-885758-10-3*) Quality Sports.
— Through the Green: The Mind & Art of a Professional Golfer. (Illus.). 272p. 1993. text 21.95 (*0-312-09363-2*) St Martin.
Maiorana, Victor P. The Analytic College Student: Introduction to Cognitive-Analytic Strategies & Techniques (Cogetics) (Student Learn & Study Bks.: Vol. 4). 175p. (C). (gr. 6-8). 1997. pap. text 28.95 (*1-879611-11-2*) Rosebrooke.
— The Analytic Elementary School Student: Introduction to Cognitive-Analytic Strategies & Techniques (Cogetics) (Student Learn & Study Bks.: Vol. 1). 100p. (J). (gr. 3-5). 1997. pap. text 17.95 (*1-879611-20-1*) Rosebrooke.
— The Analytic High School Student: Introduction to Cognitive-Analytic Strategies & Techniques (Cogetics) (Student Learn & Study Bks.: Vol. 3). 120p. (YA). (gr. 9-12). 1997. pap. text 23.95 (*1-879611-10-4*) Rosebrooke.
— The Analytic Middle School Student: Introduction to Cognitive-Analytic Strategies & Techniques (Cogetics) (Student Learn & Study Bks.: Vol. 2). 105p. (J). (gr. 6-8). 1997. pap. text 18.95 (*1-879611-19-8*) Rosebrooke.
— The Analytic Teacher. 2nd ed. (Teacher Preparation, Inservice, & Professional Development Bks.: Vol. 1). 290p. (YA). 1997. pap. text 32.95 (*1-879611-06-6*) Rosebrooke.
— The Analytical Student: Whole Learning for the High School & College Student. LC 94-13031. 1994. 16.95 (*0-927516-59-4*) ERIC-REC.
— The Analytical Teacher: Whole Teaching, Whole Learning for the High School & College Teacher. LC 94-13030. 1994. 16.95 (*0-927516-58-6*) ERIC-REC.
— Critical Thinking Across the Curriculum: Building the Analytical Classroom. LC 92-20683. 180p. (Orig.). (C). 1992. pap. text 14.95 (*0-927516-35-7*) ERIC-REC.
— Subject Matter Frameworks. (Teacher Preparation, Inservice, & Professional Development Bks.: Vol. 2). 140p. (YA). 1997. pap. text 25.95 (*1-879611-17-1*) Rosebrooke.
— Teacher's Resource for the Analytic Classroom. (Teacher Preparation, Inservice, & Professional Development Bks.: Vol. 3). 300p. (YA). 1997. pap. text 33.95 (*1-879611-05-8*) Rosebrooke.
— Teacher's Taxonomy for the Analytic Classroom. (Teacher Preparation, Inservice, & Professional Development Bks.: Vol. 4). 91p. (YA). 1993. pap. text 27.95 (*1-879611-08-2*) Rosebrooke.
— Teacher's Workbook for the Analytic Classroom. (Teacher Preparation, Inservice, & Professional Development Bks.). 125p. (YA). 1997. pap. 23.95 (*1-879611-07-4*) Rosebrooke.
Maiorano, Robert & Brooks, Valerie. Balanchine's Mozartiana: The Making of a Masterpiece. (Illus.). 192p. 1985. 17.95 (*0-88191-013-9*) Freundlich.
Maiorino, Giancarlo. Portrait of Eccentricity: Arcimboldo & the Mannerist Grotesque. (Illus.). 160p. 1991. 35.00 (*0-271-00727-3*) Pa St U Pr.
Maiorino, Giancarlo. Adam, "New Born & Perfect" The Renaissance Promise of Eternity. LC 86-46144. (Illus.). 167p. 1987. reprint ed. pap. 51.80 (*0-7837-9659-5*, 205929200005) Bks Demand.
— The Cornucopian Mind & the Baroque Unity of the Arts. LC 89-3894. (Illus.). 224p. 1990. lib. bdg. 35.00 (*0-271-00679-X*) Pa St U Pr.
— Leonardo da Vinci: The Daedalian Myth-Maker. (Illus.). 320p. 1992. text 40.00 (*0-271-00817-2*) Pa St U Pr.
Maiorino, Giancarlo, ed. The Picaresque: Tradition & Displacement. (Hispanic Issues Ser.: Vol. 12). 1996. pap. 21.95 (*0-8166-2723-1*); text 54.95 (*0-8166-2722-3*) U of Minn Pr.
Maiping, Chen, tr. see Anyi, Wang.
Mair. Equine Medicine: Surgery & Repair. 1997. text 89.00 (*0-7020-1725-6*, W B Saunders Co) Harcrt Hlth Sci Grp.
Mair, A. W., tr. see Mair, G. R.
Mair, Andrew. Honda's Global Local Corporation: Japanization the Honda Way. LC 93-31246. 1993. text 69.95 (*0-312-10668-8*) St Martin.
Mair, Craig. Mercat Cross & Tolbooth: Understanding Scotland's Old Burghs. 238p. (C). 1996. pap. 23.00 (*0-85976-196-7*, Pub. by J Donald) St Mut.
— Stirling: The Royal Burgh. 220p. 1996. pap. 30.00 (*0-85976-420-6*, Pub. by J Donald) St Mut.
Mair, Denis C., jt. auth. see Feng, Youlan.
Mair, Denis C., tr. see Chen-hua.
Mair, Denis C., tr. see Feng, Youlan.
Mair, Denis C., tr. see Pu, Songling.
Mair, Denis C., tr. see Wang, Meng.
Mair, Denis C., tr. see Yan Jiaqi.
Mair, Douglas, ed. The Scottish Contribution to Modern Economic Thought. 1990. text 39.00 (*0-08-037723-8*, Pub. by Aberdeen U Pr) Macmillan.
Mair, Douglas, jt. auth. see Laramie, Anthony J.
Mair, G. R. Hymns & Epigrams: Poems. Mair, A. W., tr. (Loeb Classical Library: No. 129). 15.50 (*0-674-99143-5*) HUP.
Mair, Gary. Directory of Public Companies: Stockbrokers Bible. 400p. 1993. 49.95 (*1-884821-00-6*) Wall St Finan.
***Mair, George.** Barry Diller Story: The Life & Times of America's Entertainment Mogul. 348p. 1998. pap. 14.95 (*0-471-29948-0*) Wiley.
Mair, George. The Barry Diller Story: The Life & Times of America's Greatest Entertainment Mogul. LC 96-49770. (Illus.). 352p. 1997. 24.95 (*0-471-13082-6*) Wiley.
— Bette: An Intimate Biography of Bette Midler. (Illus.). 368p. 1995. 22.50 (*1-55972-272-X*, Birch Ln Pr) Carol Pub Group.
— Bette: An Intimate Biography of Bette Midler. rev. ed. LC 96-26426. (Illus.). 320p. 1996. mass mkt. 6.99 (*0-8065-8006-2*, Citadel Stars) Carol Pub Group.
— The Complete Idiot's Guide to Retiring in Comfort & Security. 350p. 1995. 16.95 (*1-56761-601-1*, Alpha Ref) Macmillan Gen Ref.
— Family Money. 352p. 1994. mass mkt. 4.99 (*0-7860-0010-4*, Pinncle Kensgtn) Kensgtn Pub Corp.
— Frank Sinatra: An American Legend. abr. ed. Fenster, Julie, ed. 1995. 16.95 incl. audio (*1-882071-61-1*) B&B Audio.
— The Judds: The True Story of Naomi, Wynonna & Ashley. LC 98-3943. (Illus.). 256p. 1998. 21.95 (*1-55972-459-5*, Birch Ln Pr) Carol Pub Group.
***Mair, George.** Judds The True Story of Naomi, Wynonna & Ashley. 1999. pap. text 14.95 (*0-8065-2120-1*) Carol Pub Group.
Mair, George. Natural Born Winner. LC 97-97155. 1998. mass mkt. 5.99 (*0-345-42419-0*) Ballantine Pub Grp.
— Oprah Winfrey: The Real Story. LC 94-18112. (Illus.). 352p. 1994. 21.95 (*1-55972-250-9*, Birch Ln Pr) Carol Pub Group.
Mair, George. Oprah Winfrey: The Real Story. abr. ed. 1995. 16.95 incl. audio (*1-882071-56-5*) B&B Audio.
Mair, George. Oprah Winfrey: The Real Story. rev. ed. (Citadel Stars Ser.). (Illus.). 404p. 1996. mass mkt. 5.99 (*0-8065-8003-8*, Citadel Pr) Carol Pub Group.
— Oprah Winfrey: The Real Story. rev. ed. (Illus.). 416p. 1998. mass mkt. 6.99 (*0-8065-8017-8*, Citadel Pr) Carol Pub Group.
— Rosie O'Donnell: Her True Story. LC 97-178. (Illus.). 288p. 1997. 22.50 (*1-55972-416-1*, Birch Ln Pr) Carol Pub Group.
— Rosie O'Donnell: Her True Story. (Illus.). 272p. 1998. mass mkt. 6.99 (*0-8065-8014-3*, Citadel Pr) Carol Pub Group.
— Star Stalkers. 352p. 1995. pap. 4.99 (*0-7860-0138-0*, Pinncle Kensgtn); pap. 4.99 (*0-7860-0162-3*) Kensgtn Pub Corp.
Mair, George, ed. Evaluating the Effectiveness of Community Penalties. LC 96-79949. (Evaluative Studies in Social Work). 208p. 1997. 69.95 (*1-85972-025-0*, Pub. by Avebry) Ashgate Pub Co.
Mair, George, jt. auth. see Karn, Richard.
Mair, George, jt. auth. see Phillips, Patricia.
Mair, J. Pictorial History of Darvel. (C). 1989. pap. 50.00 (*0-907526-40-3*, Pub. by Alloway Pub) St Mut.
— Pictorial History of Galston. (C). 1988. pap. 50.00 (*0-907526-37-3*, Pub. by Alloway Pub) St Mut.
— Pictorial History of Newmilns. (C). 1988. pap. 50.00 (*0-907526-34-9*, Pub. by Alloway Pub) St Mut.
Mair, Johannes & Puschendorf, Bernd. Myocardial Injury: Laboratory Diagnosis. LC 96-27642. (Medical Intelligence Unit Ser.). 204p. 1996. 89.95 (*1-57059-303-5*) Landes Bioscience.
Mair, John. Book-Keeping Moderniz'd: Or, Merchant-Accounts by Double Entry, According to the Italian Form. Brief, Richard P., ed. LC 77-87276. (Development of Contemporary Accounting Thought Ser.). 1978. reprint ed. lib. bdg. 52.95 (*0-405-10904-0*) Ayer.
— Fourth Forger: William Ireland & the Shakespeare Papers. LC 70-146864. (Select Bibliographies Reprint Ser.). 1977. reprint ed. 21.95 (*0-8369-5631-1*) Ayer.
Mair, Lucy P. Anthropology & Social Change. (London School of Economics Monographs on Social Anthropology: No. 38). 206p. (C). 1971. pap. 14.95 (*0-485-19638-7*, Pub. by Athlone Pr) Humanities.
— An Introduction to Social Anthropology. 2nd ed. (C). 1972. pap. text 14.95 (*0-19-874011-5*) OUP.
— An Introduction to Social Anthropology. 2nd ed. LC 85-19895. 317p. 1985. reprint ed. lib. bdg. 57.75 (*0-313-24977-6*, MISA, Greenwood Pr) Greenwood.
— New Nations. LC 63-20197. (Nature of Human Society Ser.). 1993. lib. bdg. 19.00 (*0-226-50275-9*) U Ch Pr.
— New Nations. LC 63-20917. (Nature of Human Society Ser.). 235p. reprint ed. pap. 72.90 (*0-608-09018-2*, 206965300005) Bks Demand.
Mair, Miller. Between Psychology & Psychotherapy: A Poetics of Experience. 272p. 1989. 49.95 (*0-415-00021-1*, A3317) Routledge.
Mair, Nancy. Grace: Freeing the Swan Within for a Beautiful Life. 272p. 56.85 (*0-87596-544-X*) Rodale Pr Inc.
***Mair, Nancy.** Intimate Vegetarian: Delicious Practical Recipes for Singles & Couples. (Illus.). 224p. 2000. pap. 17.95 (*1-58063-167-3*) Renaissance.
Mair, Nancy. Simply Vegetarian! (Orig.). 1993. mass mkt. 4.99 (*0-425-13993-X*) Berkley Pub.
Mair, Nancy & Rinzler, Susan. Simply Vegetarian! Easy-to-Prepare Recipes for the Vegetarian Gourmet. rev. ed. LC 90-131641. (Illus.). 256p. 1985. pap. 11.95 (*0-916124-53-3*, DES1) Crystal Clarity.

M

An Asterisk (*) at the beginning of an entry indicates that the title is appearing for the first time.

Mair, Peter. Party System Change: Approaches & Interpretation. LC 97-174372. (Illus.). 264p. 1997. text 69.00 (*0-19-829235-X*) OUP.

— Party System Change: Approaches & Interpretations. (Illus.). 260p. 1999. pap. text 29.95 (*0-19-829549-9*) OUP.

Mair, Peter, ed. The West European Party System. (Oxford Readings in Politics & Government Ser.). 376p. 1990. pap. text 19.95 (*0-19-827583-8*) OUP.

Mair, Peter & Smith, Gordon, eds. Understanding Party System Change in Western Europe. 191p. 1990. text 37.50 (*0-7146-3381-X*, Pub. by F Cass Pubs) Intl Spec Bk.

Mair, Peter, jt. auth. see Cranston, Maurice W.

Mair, Peter, jt. auth. see Katz, Richard S.

Mair, Peter, jt. ed. see Bartolini, Stefano.

Mair, Peter, jt. ed. see Daalder, Hans.

Mair, R. J. & Taylor, R. N., eds. Geotechnical Aspects of Underground Construction in Soft Ground: Proceedings of the International Symposium, London, U. K. 15-17 April 1996. (Illus.). 804p. (C). 1996. text 181.00 (*90-5410-856-8*, Pub. by A A Balkema) Ashgate Pub Co.

Mair, Rafe. The Last Cast: Fishing Reminiscences. (Illus.). 160p. 1995. 12.95 (*0-88839-346-6*) Hancock House.

— The Last Cast: Fishing Reminiscences. 128p. 1996. pap. 12.95 (*0-88839-384-9*) Hancock House.

Mair, Thomas A. Batavia Revisited. (Illus.). 227p. (Orig.). 1990. pap. 12.00 (*0-9628268-0-4*) Benson Mair & Gosselin.

Mair, Tim S. Self-Assessment Color Review of Equine Internal Medicine. (Illus.). 192p. 1997. pap. text 34.95 (*0-8138-2864-3*) Iowa St U Pr.

Mair, Victor, et al. Four Introspective Poets: A Concordance to Selected Poems. LC 86-71604. (Arizona State University Center for Asian Studies Monograph Ser.: No. 20). xiii, 243p. (Orig.). 1987. pap. 10.00 (*0-317-58260-7*) ASU Ctr Asian.

Mair, Victor H. The Bronze Age & Early Iron Age Peoples of Eastern Central Asia, 2 vols. LC 98-70337. (Journal of Indo-European Studies Monograph Ser.: No. 26). (Illus.). 912p. (C). 1998. lib. bdg. 165.00 (*0-941694-63-1*) Inst Study Man.

— Painting & Performance: Chinese Picture Recitation & Its Indian Genesis. (Illus.). 302p. 1997. pap. text 19.00 (*0-8248-1915-2*) UH Pr.

***Mair, Victor H.** The Shorter Columbia Anthology of Traditional Chinese Literature. LC 00-35878. (Translations from the Asian Classics Ser.). 2000. 25.00 (*0-231-11999-2*) Col U Pr.

Mair, Victor H. T'ang Transformation Texts: A Study of the Buddhist Contribution to the Rise of Vernacular Fiction & Drama in China. LC 88-37893. (Harvard-Yenching Institute Monographs: No. 28). 150p. 1989. 30.00 (*0-674-86815-3*) HUP.

Mair, Victor H., ed. The Columbia Anthology of Traditional Chinese Literature. LC 93-48174. (Translations from the Asian Classics Ser.). 1,350p. 1995. 76.00 (*0-231-07428-X*) Col U Pr.

— The Columbia Anthology of Traditional Chinese Literature. 1368p. 1996. pap. 30.00 (*0-231-07429-8*) Col U Pr.

— Experimental Essays on Chuang-TZU. LC 83-3615. (Asian Studies at Hawaii: No. 29). 196p. 1983. reprint ed. pap. text 12.00 (*0-8248-0836-3*) UH Pr.

***Mair, Victor H., ed.** The Shorter Columbia Anthology of Traditional Chinese Literature. 704p. 2000. text 60.00 (*0-231-11998-4*) Col U Pr.

Mair, Victor H. & Liu, Yongquan, eds. Characters & Computers. 200p. (gr. 12). 1991. 65.00 (*90-5199-061-8*, Pub. by IOS Pr) IOS Press.

***Mair, Victor H., et al.** The Bronze Age & Early Iron Age Peoples of Eastern Central Asia. (Journal of Indo-European Studies Monographs: Vol. 26). (Illus.). 912p. (C). 1999. pap. 165.00 (*0-941694-66-6*) Inst Study Man.

Mair, Victor H., jt. auth. see Mallory, J. P.

Mair, Victor H., tr. see Chuang Tzu.

Mair, Victor H., tr. see Mei Cherng & Wang Bor.

Mair, Victor H., tr. see Pu, Songling.

Mair, W. Austyn & Birdsall, David L. Aircraft Performance. (Cambridge Aerospace Ser.: No. 5). (Illus.). 320p. 1996. pap. text 38.95 (*0-521-56836-6*) Cambridge U Pr.

Maira, Arun, jt. auth. see Scott-Morgan, Peter B.

Maira, Sunaina & Srikanth, Rajini, eds. Contours of the Heart: South Asians Map North America. LC 96-78960. (Illus.). 480p. (Orig.). 1996. pap. 19.95 (*1-889876-00-3*) Asian Am Writers.

Mairal-Usbon, Ricardo, jt. auth. see Faber, Pamela B.

Mairants, Ivor. The Flamenco Guitar: A Complete Method for Playing Flamenco. (Illus.). 200p. 1958. 16.95 (*0-686-09074-8*, 60481-910); lp 9.95 (*0-686-09075-6*, 61609-960) Peermusic Classical.

Mairants, Ivor. Jazz Sonatas for Solo Guitar. 88p. 1997. pap. 19.95 incl. audio compact disk (*0-7866-1376-9*, 95634BCD) Mel Bay.

Maire, Albert. Materials Used to Write upon Before the Invention of Printing. fac. ed. (Shorey Lost Arts Ser.). (Illus.). 44p. 1904. reprint ed. pap. 10.00 (*0-8466-6006-7*, U-6) Shoreys Bkstore.

Maire, J. C., jt. auth. see Waegell, B.

Mairead, Dunne, jt. auth. see Cooper, Barry.

Mairesse, Jacques, jt. ed. see Griliches, Zvi.

Mairet, Philip, tr. see Eliade, Mircea.

Mairet, Philip, tr. see Mounier, Emmanuel.

Mairet, Philip, tr. see Wendel, Francois.

Mairinger, Franz. Horses Are Made to Be Horses. LC 85-27027. (Illus.). 168p. 1999. 16.95 (*0-87605-855-1*) Howell Bks.

— Horses are Made to Be Horses. 1996. 16.95 (*0-87605-717-2*) Howell Bks.

Mairota, Paola & Thornes, John B., eds. Atlas of Mediterranean Environments in Europe: The Desertification Context. LC 95-48761. 224p. 1997. 600.00 (*0-471-96092-6*) Wiley.

***Mairowitz, David Z.** Introducing Kafka. 2000. pap. 11.95 (*1-84046-122-5*) Totem Bks.

Mairowitz, David Z. Kafka. (Illus.). 176p. 1996. 19.95 (*0-87816-466-9*) Kitchen Sink.

— Reich for Beginners. (Writers & Readers Documentary Comic Bks.). 176p. 1986. pap. 6.95 (*0-86316-031-X*) Writers & Readers.

Mairs. Plaintext. LC 85-27043. 154p. 1992. reprint ed. pap. 14.95 (*0-8165-1337-6*) U of Ariz Pr.

Mairs & Hoerauf. The Puget Sound Region: A Portfolio of Computer Maps. (Occasional Papers: No. 3). 1986. pap. 2.95 (*0-318-23323-1*) WWU CPNS.

Mairs, Nancy. Carnal Acts: Essays. 2nd ed. LC 96-15131. 176p. 1996. pap. 11.00 (*0-8070-7085-8*) Beacon Pr.

— In All the Rooms of the Yellow House. 1984. 14.95 (*0-933188-26-9*) Blue Moon Pr.

— Ordinary Time: Cycles in Marriage, Faith, & Renewal. 256p. 1994. pap. 15.00 (*0-8070-7057-2*) Beacon Pr.

— Remembering the Bone House: An Erotics of Place & Space. LC 94-41563. 288p. 1995. pap. 12.95 (*0-8070-7069-6*) Beacon Pr.

— Voice Lessons: On Becoming a (Woman) Writer. 176p. 1997. pap. 11.00 (*0-8070-6007-0*) Beacon Pr.

— Waist High in the World. large type ed. LC 97-1498. 1997. 22.95 (*0-7838-8099-5*) Thorndike Pr.

— Waist-High in the World: A Life among the Nondisabled. LC 96-21819. 224p. 1998. pap. 12.00 (*0-8070-7087-4*) Beacon Pr.

— Waist-High in the World: A Life among the Nondisabled. 212p. 1999. text 20.00 (*0-7881-5998-4*) DIANE Pub.

Mais, D. E., jt. ed. see Halushka, P. V.

Mais, Roger. Brother Man. (Caribbean Writers Ser.). 191p. (C). 1974. pap. 8.95 (*0-435-98585-X*) Heinemann.

Mais, Roger. The Hills Were Joyful Together. (Caribbean Writers Ser.). 288p. (C). 1981. pap. 9.95 (*0-435-98586-8*, 98586) Heinemann.

Mais, Stuart P. Books & Their Writers. LC 68-54359. (Essay Index Reprint Ser.). 1977. 21.95 (*0-8369-0667-5*) Ayer.

— From Shakespeare to O. Henry: Studies in Literature. rev. ed. LC 68-16952. (Essay Index Reprint Ser.). 1977. 20.95 (*0-8369-0668-3*) Ayer.

— Some Modern Authors. LC 73-128276. (Essay Index Reprint Ser.). 1977. 23.95 (*0-8369-1836-3*) Ayer.

— Why We Should Read. LC 67-26760. (Essay Index Reprint Ser.). 1977. 20.95 (*0-8369-0669-1*) Ayer.

Maisch, Ingrid. Mary Magdalene: The Image of a Woman Through the Centuries. Maloney, Linda M., tr. from ENG. LC 98-5542. 1998. 19.95 (*0-8146-2471-5*) Liturgical Pr.

Maisch, J. M. A Manual of Organic Materia Medica: Drugs from Natural Sources. (Alternative Medicine Ser.). 1992. lib. bdg. 275.95 (*0-8490-5441-9*) Gordon Pr.

Maisch, Maire, jt. auth. see Winter, Richard.

Maisch, Rob. Confessions of a Cereal Eater. LC 95-71765. (Illus.). 64p. 1996. 17.95 (*1-56163-141-8*, Comics Lit) NBM.

— Confessions of a Cereal Eater. limited ed. LC 95-71765. (Illus.). 64p. 1996. 50.00 (*1-56163-142-6*, Comics Lit) NBM.

Maisel. Real Estate Finance. 2nd ed. (C). 1992. pap. text, teacher ed. 4.50 (*0-15-575853-5*) Harcourt Coll Pubs.

Maisel, Albert Q. Miracles of Military Medicine. LC 70-167382. (Essay Index Reprint Ser.). 1977. reprint ed. 23.95 (*0-8369-2561-0*) Ayer.

Maisel, Carolyn. Witnessing. LC 78-60979. 59p. 1978. per. 3.75 (*0-934332-07-X*) LEpervier Pr.

Maisel, David, tr. see Coquery-Vidrovitch, Catherine.

Maisel, David, tr. see Knohl, Israel.

Maisel, David, tr. see Neher, Andre.

Maisel, David, tr. see Sternhell, Zeev.

Maisel, David, tr. see Sternhell, Zeev, et al.

Maisel, David, tr. see Ye'or, Bat.

Maisel, Edward. The Alexander Technique. 1989. pap. 9.95 (*0-8065-1118-4*, Citadel Pr) Carol Pub Group.

— Charles T. Griffes: The Life of an American Composer. (Music Book Index Ser.). 347p. 1992. reprint ed. lib. bdg. 89.00 (*0-7812-9464-9*) Rprt Serv.

— Tai Chi for Health. LC 97-51964. 1998. 14.95 (*0-8348-0420-4*) Weatherhill.

Maisel, Edward, intro. The Alexander Technique. 256p. 1989. pap. 9.95 (*0-8184-0506-6*, L Stuart) Carol Pub Group.

Maisel, Ephraim. The Foreign Office & Foreign Policy, 1919-1926. 352p. 1994. pap. 29.95 (*1-898723-43-5*, Pub. by Sussex Acad Pr) Intl Spec Bk.

— The Foreign Office & Foreign Policy, 1919-1926. LC 95-138352. 352p. 1997. 54.95 (*1-898723-04-4*, Pub. by Sussex Acad Pr) Intl Spec Bk.

Maisel, Eric. Affirmations for Artists. 188p. (Orig.). 1996. pap. 12.95 (*0-87477-839-5*, Tarcher Putnam) Putnam Pub Group.

— The Blackbirds of Mulhouse. LC 83-60319. 287p. (Orig.). 1984. pap. 7.95 (*0-910997-01-2*) Maya Pr.

***Maisel, Eric.** The Creativity Book: A Year's Worth of Creativity & Guidance. 256p. 2000. pap. 13.95 (*1-58542-029-8*, Tarcher Putnam) Putnam Pub Group.

Maisel, Eric. Deep Writing: 7 Principles That Bring Ideas to Life. LC 98-36116. 176p. 1999. pap. 12.95 (*0-87477-947-2*, Tarcher Putnam) Putnam Pub Group.

— Dismay. LC 82-61850. 211p. (Orig.). 1983. pap. 7.95 (*0-910997-00-4*) Maya Pr.

— Fearless Creating: A Step-by-Step Guide to Starting & Completing Your Work of Art. LC 95-10427. (An Innerwork Book). 272p. (Orig.). 1995. pap. 15.95 (*0-87477-805-0*, Tarcher Putnam) Putnam Pub Group.

— Fearless Presenting: A Self-Help Guide for Anyone Who Speaks, Sells, or Performs in Public. LC 97-7930. 176p. 1997. pap. text 16.95 (*0-8230-8834-0*) Watsn-Guptill.

— A Life in the Arts: Practical Guidance & Inspiration for Creative & Performing Artists. LC 93-21257. (Inner Work Bks.). 272p. 1994. pap., student ed. 15.95 (*0-87477-766-6*, Tarcher Putnam) Putnam Pub Group.

— Living the Writer's Life: A Complete Self-Made Guide. LC 99-41976. 192p. 1999. pap. 16.95 (*0-8230-8848-0*) Watsn-Guptill.

***Maisel, Eric.** Sleep Thinking: The Revolutionary Program That Helps You Solve Problems, Reduce Stress & Increase Creativity While You Sleep. 240p. 2000. 10.95 (*1-58062-445-6*) Adams Media.

— 20 Communication Tips for Families Vol. 2: A 30-Minute Guide to a Better Family Relationship. LC 99-86447. (20 Communication Tips Ser.). 128p. 2000. pap. 8.95 (*1-57731-166-3*, Pub. by New Wrld Lib) Publishers Group.

Maisel, Hary, ed. The Ocular Lens: Structure, Function, & Pathology. 496p. 1985. text 190.00 (*0-8247-7297-0*) Dekker.

***Maisel, Jay, photos by.** Jay Maisel's New York. (Illus.). 192p. 2000. 40.00 (*1-55209-496-0*) Firefly Bks Ltd.

Maisel, Jay, tr. see Stewart, J. David.

***Maisel, John.** Can I Really Know for Sure? 79p. 2000. pap. 4.50 (*1-56582-140-8*) Christ Renew Min.

— Does God Really Care about Me? 16p. 2000. pap. 1.00 (*1-56582-139-4*) Christ Renew Min.

Maisel, John. Is Jesus God? Regular Script - Chinese Edition. Lee, Margaret, tr. from ENG. (CHI.). 76p. 1993. pap. 2.00 (*1-56582-016-9*) Christ Renew Min.

— Is Jesus God? Simplified Script - Chinese Edition. Lee, Margaret, tr. (CHI.). 76p. 1993. pap. 2.00 (*1-56582-017-7*) Christ Renew Min.

Maisel, L. Sandy. Parties & Elections in America: The Electoral Process. 3rd ed. LC 99-28825. 616p. 1999. pap. text 35.00 (*0-8476-8549-7*) Rowman.

Maisel, L. Sandy, ed. The Parties Respond: Changes in American Parties & Campaigns. 3rd ed. LC 97-32510. (Transforming American Politics Ser.). 432p. (C). 1997. pap. text 31.00 (*0-8133-9960-2*, Pub. by Westview) HarpC.

Maisel, L. Sandy & Bibby, John F. Two Parties - Or More? The American Party System. LC 98-10672. (Dilemmas in American Politics Ser.). 160p. (C). 1998. pap. text 17.00 (*0-8133-9993-9*, Pub. by Westview) HarpC.

Maisel, Louis S. From Obscurity to Oblivion: Running in the Congressional Primary. rev. ed. LC 81-21994. 208p. 1986. pap. text 15.00 (*0-87049-348-5*) U of Tenn Pr.

— Parties & Elections in America: The Electoral Process. 2nd ed. LC 92-37941. 384p. (C). 1992. pap. 49.06 (*0-07-039738-4*) McGraw.

Maisel, Louis S., ed. Political Parties & Elections in the United States: An Encyclopedia, 2 vols., Set. LC 91-6940. 1367p. 1991. text 75.00 (*0-8240-7975-2*, SS498) Garland.

Maisel, Louis S., jt. ed. see Cooper, Joseph.

***Maisel, Martin D.** History of XV-15 Tilt Rotor Research Aircraft: From Concept to Flight. 216p. 2000. per. 21.00 (*0-16-050276-4*) USGPO.

Maisel, Merry, ed. see Trotsky, Leon.

Maisel, Richard & Persell, Caroline H. How Sampling Works. LC 94-47987. (Research Methods & Statistics Ser.). 264p. (Orig.). (C). 1995. pap. 21.95 incl. disk (*0-8039-9061-8*) Pine Forge.

Maisel, Sally J. Cruising Solo: The Single Person's Guide to Adventure on the High Seas. (Illus.). 400p. (Orig.). 1993. pap. 14.95 (*0-934377-14-6*) Marin Pubns.

Maisel, Sandy L. & Shade, William G., eds. Parties & Politics in American History: A Reader. LC 94-8022. 296p. 1994. text 15.00 (*0-8153-1690-9*, H1724) Garland.

Maisel, Sherman J. Managing the Dollar. (Illus.). 1973. 10.95 (*0-393-05494-2*) Norton.

— Real Estate & Finance. 2nd ed. 570p. (C). 1992. text 86.50 (*0-15-575852-7*) Dryden Pr.

Maisel, Sherman J., ed. Risk & Capital Adequacy in Commercial Banks. LC 81-3324. (National Bureau of Economic Research Monographs). x, 436p. 1994. pap. text 35.00 (*0-226-50282-1*, Midway Reprint) U Ch Pr.

— Risk & Capital Adequacy in Commercial Banks. LC 81-3324. (National Bureau of Economic Research Monograph Ser.). (Illus.). 446p. reprint ed. pap. 138.30 (*0-608-09477-3*, 205427700005) Bks Demand.

Maisello, Antonio. Variational Methods in Lorentzian Geometry. LC 94-7089. 1994. pap. 84.95 (*0-582-23799-8*, Pub. by Addison-Wesley) Longman.

Maisels, Charles. Early Civilizations of the Old World: Formative Histories of Egypt the Levant Mesopotamia India & China. LC 99-220327. (Illus.). 480p. (C). 1999. 60.00 (*0-415-10975-2*) Routledge.

Maisels, Charles K. The Emergence of Civilization: From Hunting & Gathering to Agriculture, Cities & the State in the Near East. (Illus.). 480p. 1990. 82.50 (*0-415-00168-4*, A4138) Routledge.

— The Emergence of Civilization: From Hunting & Gathering to Agriculture, Cities & the State in the Near East. LC 93-7453. (Illus.). 416p. (C). 1993. pap. 27.99 (*0-415-09659-6*) Routledge.

— Near East: Archaeology in the 'Cradle of Civilization' (Experience of Archaeology Ser.). (Illus.). 256p. (C). 1998. pap. 27.99 (*0-415-18607-2*) Routledge.

***Maisey.** Discovering Fossil Fishes. (Illus.). 224p. 2000. pap. 25.00 (*0-8133-3807-7*, Pub. by Westview) HarpC.

Maisey, John, et al. The Hall of Vertebrate Origins: A Guide to Fish, Amphibians, Turtles, Lizards, Crocodiles, & Pterosaurs with an Introduction to the Miriam & Ira D. Wallach Orientation Center. Maestro, Vittorio, ed. (Illus.). 100p. (Orig.). 1996. pap. 7.95 (*0-913424-17-X*) Am Mus Natl Hist.

Maisey, John G. Santana Formation Fossils. 460p. 1991. 200.00 (*0-86622-549-8*, H-1108) TFH Pubns.

Maisey, M. N., et al, eds. Clinical Nuclear Medicine. 3rd ed. (Illus.). 784p. 1999. text 195.00 (*0-412-75180-1*, Pub. by E A) OUP.

Maisey, M. N., ed. see Maisey, Michael.

Maisey, Michael. Clinical Nuclear Medicine. 2nd ed. Maisey, M. N. et al, eds. LC RC0078.7.R4. (Illus.). 693p. 1991. reprint ed. pap. 200.00 (*0-608-05762-2*, 205972600007) Bks Demand.

Maisey, Michael N. Clinical Nuclear Medicine. 1983. 97.50 (*0-7020-1243-2*, W B Saunders Co) Harcrt Hlth Sci Grp.

Maisey, Michael N., et al. Atlas of Clinical Positron Emission Tomography. (An Arnold Publication). (Illus.). 360p. 1999. text 125.00 (*0-340-74098-1*, Pub. by E A) OUP.

— Clinical Nuclear Medicine. (Illus.). 525p. 1983. text 142.00 (*0-7216-1087-0*, W B Saunders Co) Harcrt Hlth Sci Grp.

— New Developments in Myocardial Imaging: Technetium 99m Tc Sestamibi. 1993. 120.00 (*1-85317-112-3*, M Dunitz) Scovill Paterson.

Maislin, Sam. New York Criminal Law Designed for Criminal Justice (Paralegal Students) 3rd ed. 240p. 1990. per. 39.95 (*0-8403-6105-X*) Kendall-Hunt.

Maisner, Heather. Find Mouse in the House. LC 93-3638. (Illus.). 20p. (J). (ps up). 1994. 9.95 (*1-56402-351-6*) Candlewick Pr.

— Find Mouse in the Yard. LC 93-12825. (Illus.). 20p. (J). (ps up). 1994. 9.95 (*1-56402-350-8*) Candlewick Pr.

— The Magic Crystal. LC 95-39346. (Candlewick Gamebook Ser.). (Illus.). 32p. (J). (gr. 3-6). 1997. reprint ed. pap. 7.99 (*0-7636-0140-3*) Candlewick Pr.

— The Magic Crystal: A Wildlife Adventure Game. LC 95-39346. (Illus.). 32p. (J). (gr. 4-7). 1996. pap. 14.99 (*1-56402-867-4*) Candlewick Pr.

— The Magic Globe: An Around-the-World Adventure Gamebook. LC 94-15164. (Illus.). (J). (gr. 3-6). 1995. 12.95 (*1-56402-445-8*) Candlewick Pr.

— The Magic Globe: An Around-the-World Adventure Gamebook. LC 94-15164. (Candlewick Gamebks.). (Illus.). 32p. (J). (gr. 4-7). 1996. reprint ed. pap. 7.99 (*1-56402-853-4*) Candlewick Pr.

— The Magic Hourglass: A Time-Travel Adventure Gamebook. LC 94-10404. (Candlewick Gamebks.). (Illus.). 32p. (J). (gr. 2-5). 1996. reprint ed. pap. 7.99 (*1-56402-854-2*) Candlewick Pr.

— The Magic Stopwatch. LC 97-6311. (Illus.). 32p. (J). (gr. 3-6). 1997. 14.99 (*0-7636-0302-3*) Candlewick Pr.

— Planet Monster. LC 95-47979. (Illus.). (J). 1996. write for info. (*1-56402-864-X*) Candlewick Pr.

— Planet Monster: A Math-Fun Gamebook. LC 95-47979. (Gamebks.). (Illus.). 32p. (J). (gr. 1-3). 1997. reprint ed. pap. 5.99 (*0-7636-0292-2*) Candlewick Pr.

— Planet Monster: A Number Puzzle Adventure. LC 95-47979. (Illus.). 32p. (J). (ps-3). 1996. 12.99 (*0-7636-0057-1*) Candlewick Pr.

— Save Brave Ted. (Illus.). 32p. (J). (ps-1). 1996. 14.99 (*1-56402-878-X*) Candlewick Pr.

— Save Brave Ted. (Candlewick Gamebook Ser.). (Illus.). 32p. (J). (gr. k-2). 1997. reprint ed. pap. 5.99 (*0-7636-0136-5*) Candlewick Pr.

Maisner, Larry. Practical Soccer Tactics. LC 78-64382. (Illus.). 144p. 1979. pap. 4.95 (*0-89037-157-1*) Anderson World.

Maisner, Larry, jt. auth. see Mason, Bill.

Maison de la Revelation Staff, ed. see Potay, Michel.

Maison, Jeffrey. I Love to Tell the Story: Storytelling in Children's Sermons. LC 97-45699. 144p. 1998. pap. 14.99 (*0-8272-1617-3*) Chalice Pr.

Maison, K. E. Honore Daumier Catalogue Raisonne of the Paintings, Watercolours & Drawings: Catalogue Raisonne of the Paintings, Watercolours & Drawings, 2 vols., Set, Vols. 1-2. (Illus.). 1066p. 1995. reprint ed. 350.00 (*1-55660-251-0*) A Wofsy Fine Arts.

***Maison, Karen M.** The Maison System Bk. I: Games. (J). (gr. k). 1999. write for info. (*0-9671421-3-X*) K M Maison.

Maison, Karen M. The Maison System Bk. I: Music Fundamentals for Beginners, 3 vols. (Illus.). 60p. (J). (gr. k-6). 1996. spiral bd. write for info. (*0-9671421-0-5*) K M Maison.

***Maison, Karen M.** The Maison System Bk. II: Games. (J). (gr. k-6). 1999. write for info. (*0-9671421-4-8*) K M Maison.

Maison, Karen M. The Maison System Bk. II: Music Fundamentals for Beginners, 3 vols. (Illus.). 60p. (J). (gr. k-6). 1996. spiral bd. write for info. (*0-9671421-1-3*) K M Maison.

***Maison, Karen M.** The Maison System Bk. III: Games. (J). (gr. k-6). 1999. write for info. (*0-9671421-5-6*) K M Maison.

Maison, Karen M. The Maison System Bk. III: Music Fundamentals for Beginners, 3 vols. (Illus.). 64p. (J). (gr. k-6). 1996. spiral bd. write for info. (*0-9671421-2-1*) K M Maison.

Maison, Mary Beth. Easy Quilts...by Jupiter! (Illus.). 75p. 1996. pap. text 7.95 (*0-486-29470-6*) Dover.

Maisse, G., jt. auth. see Bagliniaere, Jean-Luc.

Maissel, Leon I. & Francombre, Maurice H. Introduction to Thin Films. viii, 300p. 1973. text 288.00 (*0-677-02840-7*) Gordon & Breach.

Maissin, Eugene. French in Mexico & Texas, 1838-1839. Sheppherd, J. L., tr. (Illus.). 1961. 65.00 (*0-685-05002-5*) A Jones.

Maister, David H. Managing the Professional Service Firm. 448p. 1993. 45.00 (*0-02-919782-1*) Free Pr.

— Managing the Professional Service Firm. 1997. per. 25.00 (*0-684-83431-6*) Free Pr.

— True Professionalism. LC 96-51994. 192p. 1997. 23.50 (*0-684-83466-9*) Free Pr.

An Asterisk (*) at the beginning of an entry indicates that the title is appearing for the first time.

***Maister, David H.** True Professionalism: The Courage to Care about Your People, Your Clients & Your Career. 224p. 2000. per. 15.00 (0-684-84004-9) S&S Trade.

***Maister, David H., et al.** The Trusted Advisor. 2000. 25.00 (0-7432-0414-X) Free Pr.

Maister, Philippa. The Insider's Atlanta. (Illus.). 252p. (Orig.). 1982. pap. 7.95 (0-9608596-0-8) Good Hope GA.

Maister, Robert. Ipswich: Town on the Orwell. 112p. 1994. pap. 21.00 (0-7855-2641-2) St Mut.

Maisto. Drug Use & Abuse. 3rd ed. LC 98-85987. (C). 1998. pap. 43.00 (0-15-508356-2, Pub. by Harcourt Coll Pubs) Harcourt.

— Drug Use & Abuse: Instructor's Manual & Test Bank. 3rd ed. (C). 1998. pap. text, teacher ed. 30.00 (0-15-507148-3) Harcourt Coll Pubs.

Maisto, Albert, jt. auth. see Morris, Charles G.

Maisto, Albert A., jt. auth. see Morris, Charles G.

Maisto, G., ed. Tax Treatment of Cost-Contribution Arrangements. 324p. 1988. lib. bdg. 124.50 (90-6544-352-5) Kluwer Academic.

Maisto, S. A., jt. auth. see Galizio, M.

Maisto, Stephen A. Drug Use & Abuse. 2nd ed. (C). 1994. pap. text, teacher ed. 49.75 (0-15-502524-4) Harcourt Coll Pubs.

Maisto, Stephen A., jt. auth. see Nirenberg, Ted D.

Maistre, Christopher Le, see Le Maistre, Christopher.

Maistre, Joseph. Considerations on France. Lebrun, Richard A., tr. (Cambridge Texts in the History of Political Thought Ser.). 176p. (C). 1995. text 59.95 (0-521-46076-X); pap. text 19.95 (0-521-46628-8) Cambridge U Pr.

Maistre, Joseph De, see De Maistre, Joseph.

Maistre, Joseph M. de. Essay on the Generative Principle of Political Constitutions. LC 77-24972. 176p. 1977. reprint ed. 50.00 (0-8201-1294-1) Schol Facsimiles.

Maistre, Joseph M. De, see De Maistre, Joseph M., tr.

Maistre, Le, see Le Maistre.

Maistrellis, Nicholas, jt. ed. see Zeiderman, Howard.

Maistrellis, Nicholas, tr. & intro. see Comber, Geoffrey & Zeiderman, Howard, eds.

Maisy, John. Discovering Fossil Fishes: Your Guide to the Wonders of Prehistoric Ocean Life. (Illus.). 224p. 1995. 40.00 (0-8050-4366-7) H Holt & Co.

Maital, Sharone, jt. ed. see Maital, Shlomo.

Maital, Shlomo. Executive Economics: Ten Essential Tools for Business Decision Managers. 1994. 27.95 (0-02-919785-6) Free Pr.

Maital, Shlomo & Maital, Sharone, eds. Economics & Psychology. (International Library of Critical Writings in Economics: Vol. 26). 616p. 1993. 225.00 (1-85278-693-0) E Elgar.

***Maitam, Jean J.** A House Divided - Viet Nam. LC 00-21673. 2000. write for info. (0-936389-76-1) Tudor Pubs.

Maitax, Virginnia. Maternidades. 1999. pap. text 9.95 (84-08-02429-9) Planeta.

Maitha, J. K., jt. auth. see Senga, W. M.

***Maithghon, Donncuan M.** Gods & Goddesses of Druid Ireland. (Illus.). ii, xvi, 175p. 1999. pap. 16.95 (1-929608-00-4) Mac Maithghon.

Maiti & Goswami, G. Clinical Electro-Cardiography. (C). 1989. 40.00 (0-89771-373-7, Pub. by Current Dist) St Mut.

Maiti, R. K. Pearl Millet Science. (Illus.). 246p. 1997. 58.00 (1-886106-96-7, 6967) Science Pubs.

— Phaseolus SPP. Bean Science. (Illus.). 554p. (C). 1997. 79.00 (1-57808-007-X, V07X) Science Pubs.

— Sorghum Science. 2nd rev. ed. (Illus.). 300p. 1996. lib. bdg. 69.00 (1-886106-68-1) Science Pubs.

— World Fibre Crops. (Illus.). 220p. (C). 1997. 59.50 (1-886106-91-6) Science Pubs.

Maiti, R. K. & Wesche-Ebeling, Pedro. Maize Science. (Illus.). 542p. 1998. 85.00 (1 57808 019 3) Science Pubs.

Maitino, John R. & Peck, David R., eds. Teaching American Ethnic Literatures: Nineteen Essays. 384p. (Orig.). (C). 1996. pap. 22.50 (0-8263-1686-7) U of NM Pr.

Maitland. The Business Environment. 300p. Date not set. pap. text 19.95 (0-7506-0954-0) Buttrwrth-Heinemann.

— Business Planning Made Simple. 200p. Date not set. pap. text 19.95 (0-7506-2762-X) Buttrwrth-Heinemann.

Maitland. Maitlands Vertibal Manipulation. 400p. Date not set. pap. 80.00 (0-7506-2447-7) Buttrwrth-Heinemann.

Maitland. Select Essays in Anglo-American Legal History, 1907-1909, 3 vols. Association of American Law Schools Staff, ed. LC 91-77977. 2532p. 1992. reprint ed. 195.00 (0-9630106-1-1) Lawbk Exchange.

Maitland, jt. auth. see Corrigan.

Maitland, A. & Sibbett, W. QE8 - 8th National Quantum Electronics Conference: Special Issue - Journal of Modern Optics, Vol. 35 No. 3. 320p. 1988. pap. 66.00 (0-85066-899-9) Taylor & Francis.

Maitland, Alan, selected by. Favourite Sea Stories from Seaside Al. (Illus.). 322p. 1996. text. write for info. (0-670-86538-9) Viking Penguin.

Maitland, Antony. Stories from Shakespeare. 128p. (YA). (gr. 7). 1995. per. 19.95 (0-689-80037-1) McElderry Bks.

***Maitland, Arnaud.** Masterwork: Master of Time. 217p. 2000. pap. 15.95 (0-89800-309-1) Dharma Pub.

Maitland, Arthur & Dunn, M. H. Laser Physics. LC 76-97205. 425p. reprint ed. pap. 131.80 (0-608-10150-8, 205161200097) Bks Demand.

Maitland, Barbara. The Bear Who Didn't Like Honey. LC 96-15458. (Illus.). 32p. (J). (ps-1). 1997. 14.95 (0-531-09546-0) Orchard Bks Watts.

— The Bookstore Ghost. (Puffin Easy-to-Read Program Ser.). 32p. (J). (gr. k-3). 1998. pap. 3.99 (0-14-130084-1, PuffinBks) Peng Put Young Read.

— The Bookstore Ghost. LC 98-13809. (Illus.). 29p. (J). (gr. k-2). 1998. 13.89 (0-525-46049-7, Dutton Child) Peng Put Young Read.

— Moo in the Morning. LC 97-17354. (Illus.). 32p. (J). 2000. 15.00 (0-374-35038-8) FS&G.

— My Bear & Me. LC 97-75775. (Illus.). 32p. (J). (ps-2). 1999. 16.00 (0-689-82085-2) McElderry Bks.

***Maitland, Barry.** The Malcontenta. 2000. 24.95 (1-55970-527-2, Pub. by Arcade Pub Inc) Time Warner.

— Marx Sisters. (Kathy & Brock Mysteries Ser.). 2000. pap. 6.99 (0-14-029176-8) Viking Penguin.

Maitland, Barry. The Marx Sisters: A Kathy Kolla & David Brock Mystery. LC 99-72640. 288p. 1999. 23.95 (1-55970-474-8, Pub. by Arcade Pub Inc) Time Warner.

Maitland, Barry, jt. auth. see Gosling, David.

Maitland Club Staff. Catalogue of the Works Printed for the Maitland Club. LC 72-1043. (Maitland Club, Glasgow. Publications: No. 38). reprint ed. 27.50 (0-404-53011-7) AMS Pr.

— Miscellany of the Maitland Club, 4 vols. Macdonald, Alexander et al, eds. LC 72-982. (Maitland Club, Glasgow. Publications: No. 25). reprint ed. 165.00 (0-404-52971-2) AMS Pr.

— Publications of the Maitland Club, Nos. 1-75. reprint ed. write for info. (0-404-52920-8) AMS Pr.

— Registrum Metellanum, I. LC 72-967. (Maitland Club, Glasgow. Publications: No. 11). reprint ed. 27.50 (0-404-52941-0) AMS Pr.

Maitland, Derek. Hong Kong 98-99. 3rd ed. (Traveler's Companion Ser.). (Illus.). 240p. 1998. pap. text 22.95 (0-7627-0238-9) Globe Pequot.

— Vietnam, Laos & Cambodia. (Insider's Guides Ser.). (Illus.). 224p. (Orig.). 1994. pap. 15.95 (1-55650-625-2) Hunter NJ.

Maitland, Derek & Gotcher, Jill. Traveler's Companion: Vietnam, Laos, & Cambodia. (Illus.). 1998. pap. 22.95 (0-7627-0365-2) Globe Pequot.

Maitland, Derek & Taylor, Chris. Traveler's Companion: China, 1998-99. 2nd ed. (Traveler's Companion Ser.). (Illus.). 272p. 1998. pap. 23.95 (0-7627-0249-4) Globe Pequot.

Maitland, Donald. Diverse Times, Sundry Places. LC 97-160226. 320p. 1996. 45.00 (1-898595-17-8, Pub. by Sussex Acad Pr) Intl Spec Bk.

Maitland, Edward. By & By: An Historical Romance of the Future. 460p. 1977. reprint ed. 60.00 (0-8398-2379-7) Ultramarine Pub.

— The Higher Law: A Romance, 3 vols., 2 bks., Set. LC 79-8165. reprint ed. 84.50 (0-404-62184-8) AMS Pr.

Maitland, Edward, jt. auth. see Kingsford, Anna B.

Maitland, Edward, tr. see Trismegistus, Hermes M.

Maitland, F. W. English Law & the Renaissance: The Rede Lecture for 1901 with Some Notes. 98p. 1985. reprint ed. 30.00 (0-8377-0822-2, Rothman) W S Hein.

— Equity, Also the Forms of Action at Common Law: Two Courses of Lectures. 1984. reprint ed. 52.00 (0-8377-0824-9, Rothman) W S Hein.

Maitland, F. W., ed. Bracton's Note Book: A Collection of Cases, 3 Vols. LC 98-88550. 1999. reprint ed. 225.00 (1-57588-488-7, 322260) W S Hein.

Maitland, Francis. Chile: Its Land & People. 1976. lib. bdg. 59.95 (0-8490-1604-5) Gordon Pr.

Maitland, Frederic W. The Constitutional History of England: A Course of Lectures Delivered. LC 92-75950. 578p. 1993. reprint ed. 120.00 (1-56169-026-0) Gaunt.

— Domesday Book & Beyond: Three Essays in the Early History of England. 556p. 1988. pap. text 37.95 (0-521-34918-4) Cambridge U Pr.

— Domesday Book & Beyond: Three Essays in the Early History of England. LC 71-114032. (Classics in Legal History Ser.: Vol. 3). xiv, 528p. 1994. 45.00 (1-57588-248-5, 308890) W S Hein.

***Maitland, Frederic W.** English Law & the Renaissance: With Some Notes. LC 99-41674. 2000. write for info. (1-58477-034-1) Lawbk Exchange.

Maitland, Frederic W. Forms of Action at Common Law. 92p. (C). 1936. pap. text 17.95 (0-521-09185-3) Cambridge U Pr.

— Justice & Police. LC 77-38669. reprint ed. 29.50 (0-404-09179-2) AMS Pr.

— Roman Canon Law in the Church of England: Six Essays, 1898. LC 98-22357. 1998. 65.00 (1-886363-57-9) Lawbk Exchange.

— Selected Essays. Hazeltine, H. D. et al, eds. LC 68-20316. (Essay Index Reprint Ser.). 1977. 20.95 (0-8369-0670-5) Ayer.

— Selected Historical Essays of F. W. Maitland. LC 85-12552. 278p. 1985. reprint ed. lib. bdg. 65.00 (0-313-24954-7, MSHE, Greenwood Pr) Greenwood.

— A Sketch of English Legal History. LC 75-41185. 1976. reprint ed. 34.50 (0-404-14684-8) AMS Pr.

Maitland, Frederic W., ed. Memoranda de Parliamento: Records of the Parliament Holden at Westminster, 28th February, in the 33rd Year of the Reign of Edward I (1305) (Rolls Ser.: No. 98). 1969. reprint ed. 70.00 (0-8115-1177-4) Periodicals Srv.

Maitland, Frederic W., et al. A Sketch of English Legal History, 1915. LC 98-11337. 1998. 50.00 (1-886363-50-1) Lawbk Exchange.

Maitland, Frederic W., jt. auth. see Pollock, Frederick.

Maitland, Frederic W., tr. & intro. see Gierke, Otto.

***Maitland, Frederic William.** A Historical Sketch of Liberty & Equality. LC 00-27491. 2001. write for info. (0-86597-293-1) Liberty Fund.

Maitland, G. D. Peripheral Manipulation. 3rd ed. (Illus.). 336p. 1991. pap. text 60.00 (0-7506-1031-X) Buttrwrth-Heinemann.

— Vertebral Manipulation. 5th ed. (Illus.). 400p. 1986. pap. text 60.00 (0-7506-1333-5) Buttrwrth-Heinemann.

Maitland, G. D., jt. auth. see Banks, Kevin.

Maitland, G. D., jt. auth. see Corrigan, Brian.

Maitland, Iain. Budgeting for Non-Financial Managers. 2nd ed. (Financial Solutions Ser.). 216p. 1997. pap. 48.50 (0-273-62681-7, Pub. by Pitman Pub) Trans-Atl Phila.

— Getting a Result. 98p. (C). 1994. pap. 18.00 (0-85292-551-4, Pub. by IPM Hse) St Mut.

— How to Organize a Conference. 256p. 1996. 59.95 (0-566-07552-0, Pub. by Gower) Ashgate Pub Co.

— How to Plan Direct Mail. (How to Guides Ser.). (Illus.). 160p. 1996. pap. 25.95 (0-304-33430-8) Continuum.

— How to Plan Exhibitions. LC 97-204034. (How to Guides Ser.). (Illus.). 160p. 1996. pap. 25.95 (0-304-33431-6) Continuum.

— How to Plan Press Advertising. (How to Guides Ser.). (Illus.). 160p. 1996. pap. 25.95 (0-304-33432-4) Continuum.

— How to Plan Radio Advertising. (How to Guides Ser.). (Illus.). 160p. 1996. pap. 25.95 (0-304-33429-4) Continuum.

— How to Recruit. 200p. 1991. text 56.95 (0-566-02968-5, Pub. by Gower) Ashgate Pub Co.

— Managing Staff: A Guide for First Time Managers. 160p. 1998. pap. 24.95 (0-304-33470-7) Continuum.

***Maitland, Iain.** Managing Your Time. 96p. 2000. pap. 17.95 (0-8464-5119-0) Beekman Pubs.

— Motivating People. 96p. 2000. pap. 17.95 (0-8464-5121-2) Beekman Pubs.

Maitland, Iain. Perfect Pr. LC 99-187872. (ITBP PROFESSIONAL). 256p. 1998. pap. 24.95 (1-86152-221-5) Thomson Learn.

***Maitland, Iain.** Profitable Direct Marketing. LC 98-149379. (Bus Press-New). 256p. 1998. pap. 24.95 (1-86152-145-6) Thomson Learn.

Maitland, Iain. Recruiting: How to Do It. LC 97-202661. (Illus.). 224p. 1996. pap. 25.95 (0-304-33315-8) Continuum.

— Small Business Advertising Handbook. LC 99-218192. 1998. pap. text 32.95 (0-304-70419-9) Continuum.

— Write That Letter! Winning Tactics for 101 Difficult Business Letters. (Personal Development Ser.). 1996. pap. 14.95 (0-7494-1910-5) Kogan Page Ltd.

***Maitland, Ian.** Budgeting for Non-Financial Managers: How to Master & Maintain Effective Budgets. rev. ed. 206p. 2000. pap. 22.50 (0-273-64494-7, Pub. by S Thornes Pubs) Trans-Atl Phila.

***Maitland, Jeffery.** Spinal Manipulation Made Simple: A Manual of Soft Tissue Techniques. (Illus.). 175p. (C). 2000. pap. 20.00 (1-55643-352-2) North Atlantic.

Maitland, Jeffrey. Spacious Body: Explorations in Somatic Ontology. LC 95-8725. 250p. 1995. pap. 12.95 (1-55643-188-0) North Atlantic.

Maitland, John A. & Squire, W. Barclay. Fitzwilliam Virginal Book 2 Vols, Vol. 1. 1963. pap. 16.95 (0-486-21068-5) Dover.

— Fitzwilliam Virginal Book 2 Vols, Vol. 2. 1963. pap. 17.95 (0-486-21069-3) Dover.

Maitland, Katherine. Ashes for Gold: A Tale from Mexico. LC 94-14349. (Mondo Folktales ser.). (Illus.). 24p. (Orig.). (J). (gr. k-4). 1994. pap. 4.95 (1-879531-22-4) Mondo Pubng.

Maitland, Leslie & Taylor, Louis. Historical Sketches of Ottawa. 160p. 1990. 24.95 (0-921149-67-0) Broadview Pr.

Maitland, Leslie, et al. A Guide to Canadian Architectural Styles. 320p. 1992. pap. 19.95 (1-55111-002-4) Broadview Pr.

Maitland, P. S., et al, eds. The Fresh Waters of Scotland: A National Resource of International Significance. 654p. 1994. text 160.00 (0-471-94462-9) Wiley.

Maitland, Peter S. Conservation Management of Freshwater Habitats: Lakes, Rivers & Wetlands. LC 96-72121. 1997. 95.00 (0-412-59410-2) Chapman & Hall.

Maitland, Peter S. The Ecology of Scotland's Largest Lochs. (Monographiae Biologicae: No. 44). 304p. 1981. text 191.50 (90-6193-097-9) Kluwer Academic.

— A Key to British Freshwater Fishes. 1972. 60.00 (0-900386-18-5) St Mut.

Maitland, Richard. History of the House of Seytoun to the Year 1559. LC 74-172716. reprint ed. 37.50 (0-404-52921-6) AMS Pr.

— Poems of Sir Richard Maitland, Knight of Lethingtoun. Bain, Joseph, ed. LC 77-144427. reprint ed. 41.50 (0-404-52927-5) AMS Pr.

Maitland, Sandra M. The Cedar Glen Secret. (Illus.). 24p. (J). (ps-8). 1983. pap. 6.95 (0-920806-44-9, Pub. by Penumbra Pr) U of Toronto Pr.

Maitland, Sara. Angel & Me. LC 97-17347. 160p. (Orig.). 1997. pap. 12.95 (0-8192-1692-5) Morehouse Pub.

— Angel Maker: The Collected Short Stories of Sara Maitland. LC 95-33667. 88p. 1995. 25.00 (0-8050-4412-4, J Macrae Bks) H Holt & Co.

— Angel Maker: The Short Stories of Sara Maitland. 288p. 1998. pap. 12.00 (0-8050-5529-0) H Holt & Co.

— A Big-Enough God: A Feminist's Search for a Joyful Theology. 88p. 1995. 22.50 (0-8050-4183-4) H Holt & Co.

— Daughter of Jerusalem: A Novel. LC 95-971. 88p. 1995. pap. write for info. (0-8050-3810-8, Owl) H Holt & Co.

— A Map of the New Country: Women & Christianity. LC 82-13142. 280p. 1984. pap. 13.95 (0-7100-9301-2, Routledge Thoemms) Routledge.

Maitland, Sara & Appignanesi, Lisa, eds. The Rushdie File. (Contemporary Issues in the Middle East Ser.). (Illus.). 256p. 1990. pap. 17.95 (0-8156-0248-0) Syracuse U Pr.

***Maitland, Sara & Matthews, Peter.** Gardens of Illusion. 2000. 29.95 (0-304-35434-1, Pub. by Cassell) Sterling.

Maitland, Sara & Mulford, Wendy. Virtuous Magic: Women Saints & Their Meanings. LC 97-35579. (Illus.). 400p. 1998. 29.95 (0-8264-1074-X) Continuum.

***Maitland, Terrence & McInerney, Peter.** A Contagion of War (1965-1967) The Vietnam Experience. Manning, Robert, ed. (Illus.). 192p. 2000. reprint ed. 25.00 (0-7881-9445-3) DIANE Pub.

Maitland, Terrence, jt. auth. see Fulghum, David.

Maitland, Thomas, ed. see Dalgarno, George.

Maitland, Thomas, ed. see Drummond, William.

Maitland-Walker, Julian. EC Banking Directives. Date not set. ring bd. 160.00 (1-85044-577-X) LLP.

Maitland-Walker, Julian & Russell, Charles. EC Insurance Directives. rev. ed. ring bd. 305.00 (1-85044-392-0) LLP.

Maitland, William J. Beginning Weight Training for Young Athletes. (Illus.). 84p. (YA). (gr. 7 up). 1987. pap. 9.95 (0-936759-00-3) Maitland Enter.

— Weight Training for Gifted Athletes. LC 89-90833. (Illus.). 147p. (Orig.). (YA). (gr. 8 up). 1990. pap. 17.95 (0-936759-01-1) Maitland Enter.

— Young Ball Player's Guide to Safe Pitching: Ages Eight Thru Adult with Conditioning, Strengthening. (Illus.). 140p. (YA). (gr. 3 up). 1994. pap. 14.95 (0-936759-14-3) Maitland Enter.

Maitlen, Bonnie, jt. auth. see Ludden, LaVerne L.

Maitman, ed. see Shakespeare, William.

Maitra, A. P. & Sudderth, William D. Discrete Gambling & Stochastic Games. Balakrishnan, A. V. et al, eds. (Applications of Mathematics Ser.: Vol. 32). 256p. 1996. 60.95 (0-387-94628-4) Spr-Verlag.

M

Maitra, Amit. Managing a Corporate Internet Strategy. 1996. 29.95 (0-614-14507-4, VNR) Wiley.

Maitra, Amit K. Building a Corporate Internet Strategy. LC 96-19588. (Communications Ser.). 300p. 1996. pap. 30.95 (0-442-02246-8, VNR) Wiley.

Maitra, Amit K. Building a Corporate Internet Strategy: The IT Manager's Guide. 256p. 1996. pap. 30.95 (0-471-28757-1, VNR) Wiley.

Maitra, Amit K. Internet Solutions for Project Managers. LC 99-29529. (Wiley Operations Management for Professionals Ser.). 217p. 1999. 60.00 (0-471-33027-2) Wiley.

Maitra, Apurba. We Cried Together. 1983. 11.00 (0-8364-0952-3, Pub. by Mukhopadhyaya) S Asia.

Maitra, Ashok P. & Sudderth, William D. Discrete Gambling & Stochastic Games. LC 95-44636. (Applications of Mathematics Ser.: Vol. 32). 256p. 1996. 49.95 (0-614-09507-7) Spr-Verlag.

Maitra, Kiran S. Roy, Comintern & Marxism in India. (C). 1991. 22.00 (81-85169-24-1, Pub. by Naya Prokash) S Asia.

Maitra, Kiranshankar. Nagas Rebel & Insurgency in the North-East. LC 98-901176. 1998. 30.00 (81-259-0447-6, Pub. by Vikas) S Asia.

Maitra, M. K. Groundwater Management: An Application. (C). 1992. 58.00 (81-7024-466-8, Pub. by Ashish Pub Hse) S Asia.

Maitra, P., jt. ed. see Tisdell, Clement A.

Maitra, Priyatosh. The Globalization of Capitalism & Its Impact on Third World: India as a Case Study. LC 95-7549. 256p. 1996. 65.00 (0-275-95159-6, Praeger Pubs) Greenwood.

— Indian Economic Development. (C). 1991. 28.00 (81-7024-387-4, Pub. by Ashish Pub Hse) S Asia.

Maitra, S. K. An Introduction to the Philosophy of Sri Aurobindo. 2nd ed. 73p. 1993. pap. 2.00 (81-7058-346-2, Pub. by SAA) E-W Cultural Ctr.

— Sriaravindopanishad. 3rd ed. 31p. 1996. pap. 15.95 (81-7058-078-1, Pub. by SAA) E-W Cultural Ctr.

Maitra-Sinha, Anjana. Women in a Changing Society. xii, 166p. 1993. 15.95 (1-881338-35-5) Nataraj Bks.

Maitre, H. & Zinn-Justin, J., eds. Les Progres du Traitement des Images (Progress in Picture Processing) LC 96-17001. 376p. 1996. 207.00 (0-444-82407-3) Elsevier.

Maitre, H. Joachim, jt. ed. see Hahn, Walter.

Maitre, Luce-Claude. Introduction to the Thought of Iqbal. 1975. 14.50 (1-56744-297-8) Kazi Pubns.

— Introduction to the Thought of Iqbal. 55p. 1996. 14.50 (0-614-21405-X, 516) Kazi Pubns.

***Maitre, Pascal.** Mon Afrique: Photographs of Sub-Saharan Africa. (Illus.). 176p. 2000. 50.00 (0-89381-916-6) Aperture.

Maitreya, Ananda. The Dhammapada: The Path of Truth. Kramer, Rose, tr. 110p. (Orig.). 1995. pap. 7.50 (0-938077-87-2) Parallax Pr.

Maitreya, Arya, et al. Buddha Nature: The Mahayana Uttaratantra Shastra with Commentary. Fuchs, Rosemarie, tr. 320p. 2000. pap. 19.95 (1-55939-128-6) Snow Lion Pubns.

Maitreya, Aryasanga. Uttaratantra, or Ratnagotravibhaga: Sublime Science of the Great Vehicle to Salvation. Obermiller, E., tr. from TIB. 225p. 1984. reprint ed. lib. bdg. 27.50 (0-88181-001-0) Canon Pubns.

***Maitri, Sandra.** The Spiritual Dimension of the Enneagram: Nine Faces of the Soul. LC 99-49664. (Illus.). 336p. 2000. 24.95 (1-58542-017-4, Tarcher Putnam) Putnam Pub Group.

Maitri, Sandra, ed. see Almaas, A. H.

Maitriya. The Buddha Mimansa: Maharaja Yogiraja, ed. LC 78-70098. reprint ed. 23.50 (0-404-17347-0) AMS Pr.

Maitron, Jean. Dictionnaire Biographique du Mouvement Ouvrier Francais, 8 vols., Set. (FRE.). 295.00 (0-7859-0939-7, M-6384) Fr & Eur.

— Dictionnaire Biographique du Movement Ouvrier Francais: De la Revolution Francaise a la Fondation de la Premiere Internationale (1789-1864, 3 tomes. Incl. Tome I. De A a C. 16.95 Tome II. De D a L. 19.95 Tome III. De M a Z. (FRE.). 19.95 write for info. (0-318-51979-8) Fr & Eur.

Maity, Bimal. Bengali Phrasebook. (BEN., Illus.). 160p. 1996. pap. 5.95 (0-86442-312-8) Lonely Planet.

Maity, M. & Ghosh, G. K. Integral Calculus (Analysis) (C). 1989. 60.00 (*0-89771-395-8*, Pub. by Current Dist) St Mut.
— Vector Analysis (Vect. Alg. & Vect. Calculus) (C). 1989. 85.00 (*0-89771-392-3*, Pub. by Current Dist) St Mut.

Maity, M., jt. auth. see Ghosh, G. K.

Maity, P. K. Folk Ritual of Eastern India. 1988. 21.00 (*81-7017-235-7*, Pub. by Abhinav) S Asia.
— Human Fertility Cults & Rituals of Bengal. (C). 1989. 37.50 (*81-7017-263-2*, Pub. by Abhinav) S Asia.

Maity, S. K., ed. Indological Studies. (C). 1987. 49.00 (*81-7017-220-9*, Pub. by Abhinav) S Asia.

Maitzen, H. M., jt. ed. see Van Paradijs, Jan.

Maitzen, Rohan A. Gender, Genre & Victorian Historical Writing. Mitchell, Sally, ed. LC 98-29566. (Literature & Society in Victorian Britain Ser.: Vol. 5). 248p. 1998. 60.00 (*0-8153-2897-4*) Garland.

Maiullari-Pontois, Maria Teresa, jt. auth. see Bergeron, Louis.

Maiuro, Roland D., jt. auth. see O'Leary, K. Daniel.

***Maiwald, Klaus.** Literarisierung ALS Aneignung Von Alteritat. 425p. 1999. 56.95 (*3-631-34609-3*) P Lang Pubng.

Maiwald, Manfred, ed. see Fontaine, Ulrike.

Maiwald, Sue. Exposed! How to Become a Model Without Getting Scammed. (Orig.). (YA). (gr. 7-12). 1994. pap. 4.95 (*0-9644526-0-X*) Maiwald Prod.

Maiworm, Friedhelm & Teichler, Ulrich. Study Abroad & Early Careers: Experience of Former ERASMUS Students. 112p. 1996. pap. 34.95 (*1-85302-378-7*, Pub. by Jessica Kingsley) Taylor & Francis.

Maiworm, Friedhelm, et al. Learning in Europe: The Erasmus Experience: A Survey of the 1988-89 Erasmus Students. (Higher Education Policy Ser.). 160p. 1991. 45.00 (*1-85302-527-5*) Taylor & Francis.

Maiworm, Friedhelm, jt. auth. see Teichler, Ulrich.

Maixner, Paul. Robert Louis Stevenson: The Critical Heritage. (Critical Heritage Ser.). 556p. 1981. 53.00 (*0-7100-0505-9*, Routledge Thoemms) Routledge.

Maiz, Ramon, jt. ed. see Safran, William.

Maiz, Ramon, ed. & tr. see Sieyes, Enmanuel J.

Maiza, Maria Sainz De La, see Foster, C. Stephen & Sainz De La Maiza, Maria.

Maize. Cutaneous Pathology. LC 98-16468. (C). 1998. text 129.00 (*0-443-08717-2*, W B Saunders Co) Harcrt Hlth Sci Grp.

Maizel, Abby L., ed. see Symposium on Fundamental Cancer Research Staff.

Maizel, Bruno. Food & Beverage Cost Controls. LC 77-142501. 1971. write for info. (*0-672-96079-6*); text 13.98 (*0-672-96077-X*) Macmillan.
— Food & Beverage Purchasing. LC 77-142502. 1971. write for info. (*0-672-96073-7*); text. write for info. (*0-672-96071-0*) Macmillan.

Maizel, Harry. The Golden Links Between Young & Old. LC 98-90443. 1998. pap. 10.00 (*0-533-12804-8*) Vantage.

Maizelis, I., jt. auth. see Averbakh, Yuri.

Maizell, Robert, et al. Abstracting Scientific & Technical Literature. LC 78-9756. 316p. 1979. reprint ed. 31.50 (*0-88275-703-2*) Krieger.

Maizell, Robert E. How to Find Chemical Information: A Guide for Practicing Chemists, Educators, & Students. 3rd ed. LC 97-29120. 544p. 1998. 69.95 (*0-471-12579-2*, Wiley-Interscience) Wiley.

Maizels, Alfred, et al. Commodity Supply Management by Producing Countries: A Case-Study of the Tropical Beverage Crops. LC 96-52502. (UNU-WIDER Studies in Development Economics). (Illus.). 254p. 1997. text 78.00 (*0-19-823338-8*) OUP.

***Maizels, Jennie.** Journey to Jigsaw Town. (J). 1999. 10.95 (*1-86233-073-5*) Levinson Bks.
— Picnic at Jigsaw Farm. 14p. (J). 1999. 10.95 (*1-86233-068-9*) Levinson Bks.

Maizels, Jennie & Petty, Kate. The Amazing Pop-Up Grammar Book. LC 96-217876. (Illus.). (J). (gr. 2 up). 1996. 18.99 (*0-525-45580-9*) NAL.

***Maizels, John.** Raw Creation: Outsider Art & Beyond. (Illus.). 2000. pap. 29.95 (*0-7148-4009-2*) Phaidon Pr.

Maizels, John. Raw Creation: Outsider Art & Beyond. LC 96-198389. (Illus.). 240p. 1996. 69.95 (*0-7148-3149-2*, Pub. by Phaidon Press) Phaidon Pr.

Maizels, Judith K. & Caseldine, Chris, eds. Environmental Change in Iceland: Past & Present. (C). 1991. lib. bdg. 141.50 (*0-7923-1209-0*) Kluwer Academic.

Maizels, Max, et al. Getting to Dry: How to Help Your Child Overcome Bedwetting. LC 97-36913. (Illus.). xxix, 240 p. 1999. 19.95 (*1-55832-130-6*); pap. 14.95 (*1-55832-131-4*) Harvard Common Pr.

Maizels, R. M., et al. Parasite Antigens, Parasite Genes: A Laboratory Manual for Molecular Parasitology. (Illus.). 234p. (C). 1992. spiral bd. 74.95 (*0-521-41927-1*) Cambridge U Pr.

Maizey, James & Williams, Claire. The Orphan Swaggy: Australian Lifestyle in the 1930's. LC 97-106290. (Illus.). 179p. 1996. pap. 16.95 (*1-875998-12-8*, Pub. by Central Queensland) Accents Pubns.

Maizlich, Stephen E. & Kushma, John J., eds. Essays on American Antebellum Politics, 1840-1860. LC 82-40314. (Walter Prescott Webb Memorial Lectures: No. 16). 240p. 1982. 20.95 (*0-89096-136-0*) Tex A&M Univ Pr.

Maizlish, Lisa. The Ring. LC 95-20768. 24p. (J). (ps-3). 1996. 15.00 (*0-688-14217-6*, Grenwillow Bks) HarpC Child Bks.

***Maizlish, Neil A.** Workplace Health Surveillance: An Action-Oriented Approach. (Illus.). 384p. 2000. text 75.00 (*0-19-512888-5*) OUP.

Maizlish, Stephen E. The Triumph of Sectionalism: The Transformation of Ohio Politics, 1844-1856. LC 83-11255. 325p. reprint ed. pap. 100.80 (*0-7837-1353-3*, 204150100020) Bks Demand.

Maizlish, Stephen E., jt. ed. see Reinhartz, Dennis.

Maizys, Donald J. Life in the Passionate Lane. LC 89-91457. 1990. 10.95 (*0-87212-230-1*) Libra.

Maj. Depressive Disorders. LC 99-14217. 506p. 1999. 150.00 (*0-471-99905-9*) Wiley.
— Obsessive-Compulsive Disorder. Date not set. text. write for info. (*0-471-87163-X*) Wiley.

***Maj.** Schizophrenia , Vol. 2. LC 99-14218. 508p. 1999. 150.00 (*0-471-99906-7*) Wiley.

Maj, S. P. The Use of Computers for Laboratory Automation. 380p. 1993. 63.00 (*0-85186-744-8*, R6744) CRC Pr.

Maja-Pearce, Adewale. A Mask Dancing: Nigerian Novelists of the Eighties. (New Perspectives on African Literature Ser.: No. 4). 216p. 1992. lib. bdg. 85.00 (*0-905450-92-2*, Pub. by H Zell Pubs) Seven Hills Bk.
— Who's Afraid of Wole Soyinka? Essays on Censorship. (Studies in African Literature). 128p. (C). 1991. pap. 17.50 (*0-435-90977-0*, 90977) Heinemann.
— Wole Soyinka: An Appraisal. 160p. 1994. pap. 17.50 (*0-435-91151-1*, 91151) Heinemann.

Maja-Pearce, Adewale, ed. The Heinemann Book of African Poetry in English. (African Writers Ser.). 224p. (C). 1990. pap. 9.95 (*0-435-91323-9*, 91323) Heinemann.

Majaj, Lisa Suhair, jt. ed. see Amireh, Amal.

Majam-Majumdar, R. C. Classical Accounts of India: Rome, Greek. reprint ed. 18.50 (*0-8364-0704-0*, Pub. by Mukhopadhyaya) S Asia.

Majapuria, M. Yeti: The Abominable Snowman of the Silent Snows of the Himalayas. (C). 1993. 45.00 (*0-7855-0223-8*, Pub. by Ratna Pustak Bhandar) St Mut.

Majapuria, M. & Roberts, R. Kumari: Her Worship, Fate of Ex-Kumaries & Sceptical Views. (C). 1993. 65.00 (*0-7855-0188-6*, Pub. by Ratna Pustak Bhandar) St Mut.

Majaraja, Dasa D. Vrndavana Dhama Kijaya. 1992. 19.95 (*0-945475-00-4*, Pub. by Mandala Pub Grp) Words Distrib.

Majaro, Simon, et al. Strategy: A Guide to Marketing for Senior Executives. (Gower Business Enterprise Ser.). 191p. 1989. text 28.95 (*0-7045-0618-1*, Pub. by Gower) Ashgate Pub Co.

Majarro, Tomas. Bramadero (Roaring Place) (SPA.). 1995. reprint ed. 7.99 (*968-16-1420-8*, Pub. by Fondo) Continental Bk.

***Majchrowski, Andrzej & Zielinski, Jerzy, eds.** Single Crystal Growth, Characterization & Applications. 384p. 1999. pap. text 84.00 (*0-8194-3198-2*) SPIE.

Majchrzak, Ann. The Human Side of Factory Automation: Managerial & Human Resource Strategies for Making Automation Succeed. LC 87-45505. (Management Ser.). 408p. 1988. text 43.95 (*1-55542-050-8*) Jossey-Bass.
— Methods for Policy Research. 10th ed. (Applied Social Research Methods Ser.: Vol. 3). 112p. 1984. 42.00 (*0-8039-2059-8*) Sage.

Majda, A. J. Compressible Fluid Flow & Systems of Conservation Laws in Several Space Variables. (Applied Mathematical Sciences Ser.: Vol. 53). 160p. 1984. 54.95 (*0-387-96037-6*) Spr-Verlag.

Majda, A. J., jt. ed. see Chorin, A.J.

Majda, Andrew. The Existence of Multi-Dimensional Shock Fronts. LC 83-3725. (Memoirs of the American Mathematical Society Ser.: No. 43/281). 92p. 1983. pap. 18.00 (*0-8218-2281-0*, MEMO/43/281) Am Math.
— The Stability of Multi-Dimensional Shock Fronts. LC 82-20636. (Memoirs Ser.: No. 41/275). 95p. 1982. pap. 16.00 (*0-8218-2275-6*, MEMO/41/275) Am Math.

***Majdalany, Fred.** Cassino: Portrait of a Battle. 2000. pap. 9.95 (*0-304-35232-2*) Continuum.

Majdalany, Jeanne & Wicks, Edith M. The Early Settlements of Stamford, Connecticut, 1641-1700: Including Genealogies of the Stamford Families of the Seventeenth Century. (Illus.). xiv, 211p. (Orig.). 1991. pap. 17.50 (*1-55613-394-4*) Heritage Bk.

Majdi, Sam. Lovers Paradise: 222 Love Quotations. LC 96-95509. 72p. 1997. pap. 9.95 (*0-9658378-0-7*) Saman Publ.

Majeed, Javed. Ungoverned Imaginings: James Mill's the History of British India & Orientalism. (Oxford English Monographs). 234p. 1992. text 65.00 (*0-19-811786-8*) OUP.

Majeed, Javed, jt. ed. see Shackle, Christopher.

Majeed, Muhammad, et al. Turmeric & the Healing Curcuminoids: Their Amazing Antioxidant Properties & Protective Powers. (Good Health Guides Ser.). 48p. (Orig.). 1997. pap. 3.95 (*0-87983-768-3*, 37683K, Keats Publng) NTC Contemp Pub Co.

***Majeed, Muhammed.** Bioperine: Nature's Own Thermonutrient & Natural Bioavailability Enhancer. 82p. (Orig.). 1999. pap. write for info. (*0-9647856-6-8*) Nutrisci Pubs.

Majeed, Muhammed. Boswellin: The Anti-Inflammatory Phytonutrient. (Illus.). 80p. (Orig.). 1996. pap. text. write for info. (*0-9647856-1-7*) Nutrisci Pubs.
— Bronchial Asthma: Its Etiology & Control with Traditional Herbal Extracts. 1998. pap. text 2.00 (*0-9647856-5-X*) Nutrisci Pubs.
— Capsaicin: The Anti-Arthritic Phytochemical. (Illus.). 84p. 1997. pap. write for info. (*0-9647856-2-5*) Nutrisci Pubs.
— Diabetes: Its Etiology & Control with Ayurvedic Herbs. 1998. pap. text. write for info. (*0-9647856-3-3*) Nutrisci Pubs.

***Majeed, Muhammed & Prakash, Lakshmi.** Lactospheres: Lactic Acid Bacillus Lactobacillus Sporogenes. (Illus.). 56p. 1998. pap. write for info. (*0-9647856-4-1*) Nutrisci Pubs.

Majeed, Muhammed, et al. Curcuminoids: Antioxidant Phytonutrients. (Illus.). 80p. (Orig.). 1995. pap. text. write for info. (*0-9647856-0-9*) Nutrisci Pubs.

Majer, David Ben, see Ben Majer, David.

Majer, J. R. The Mass Spectrometer. (Wykeham Science Ser.: No. 44). 160p. 1977. pap. 18.00 (*0-85109-550-X*) Taylor & Francis.

Majer, J. R. & Berry, M. The Mass Spectrometer. LC 77-15307. (Wykeham Science Ser.: No. 44). 159p. (C). 1977. 18.00 (*0-8448-1171-8*, Crane Russak) Taylor & Francis.

Majer, M. & Plotkin, S. A., eds. Strains of Human Viruses. 160p. 1972. 85.25 (*3-8055-1401-8*) S Karger.

Majer, U. & Schmidt, H. J., eds. Reflections on Spacetime: Foundations, Philosophy, History. LC 95-37544. 1995. text 55.50 (*0-7923-3712-3*) Kluwer Academic.

Majer, Vladimir & Svoboda. Enthalpies of Vaporization of Organic Compounds. 1991. 55.00 (*0-632-01529-2*) CRC Pr.

Majerus, Marianne, jt. auth. see Cooper, Nicholas.

Majerus, Michael. Evolution: Four Billion. (C). 1996. pap. text 41.25 (*0-582-21569-2*, Pub. by Addison-Wesley) Longman.

Majerus, Michael E. N. Melanism: Evolution in Action. LC 97-28434. (Illus.). 352p. 1998. text 105.00 (*0-19-854983-0*); pap. text 45.00 (*0-19-854982-2*) OUP.

Majerus, Rick. My Life on a Napkin: Pillow Mints, Playground Dreams & Coaching the Runnin' Utes. LC 99-190566. (Illus.). 256p. 1999. 22.95 (*0-7868-6527-X*, Pub. by Hyperion) Time Warner.

Majeska, George P. Russian Travelers to Constantinople in the Fourteenth & Fifteenth Centuries. LC 82-24255. (Dumbarton Oaks Studies: Vol. 19). (Illus.). 464p. 1984. 35.00 (*0-88402-101-7*) Dumbarton Oaks.

Majeske, Christopher, jt. auth. see Collins, H. Thomas.

Majeski, Bill. Doubletalk: 50 Comedy Duets for Actors. Zapel, Arthur L., ed. LC 90-52981. 208p. (Orig.). (YA). (gr. 9 up). 1990. pap. 12.95 (*0-916260-66-6*, B186) Meriwether Pub.

Majeski, Bill. Easy Skits, Blackouts, & Pantomimes. 84p. 1981. pap. 5.50 (*0-87129-805-8*, E10) Dramatic Pub.

Majeski, Bill. 50 Great Monologs for Student Actors: A Workbook of Comedy Characterizations for Students. Zapel, Arthur L., ed. LC 87-14103. 144p. (YA). (gr. 10 up). 1987. pap. 12.95 (*0-916260-43-7*, B197) Meriwether Pub.
— Gross Encounters of the Worst Kind. 1978. pap. 3.50 (*0-87129-076-6*, G30) Dramatic Pub.
— Oh, Mr. President. (Orig.). 1985. pap. 6.00 (*0-88734-206-X*) Players Pr.

Majeski, Bill, jt. auth. see Sheridan, Don.

Majeski, Shloma. The Chassidic Approach to Joy. LC 95-237463. 128p. 1995. 14.00 (*1-881400-12-3*) S I E.

Majetschak, Stefan, jt. ed. see Hoffmann, Thomas S.

Majette, Baji, ed. see Allums, Charles.

Majewski, Arthur J. Moneta Polska. LC 88-92614.Tr. of Polish Coin. (Illus.). 216p. 1991. 19.50 (*0-9617557-1-7*) Maryt Pub.

Majewski, Arthur J. When Hamtramck & I Were Young. LC 86-62351. 120p. 1987. 11.00 (*0-9617557-0-9*) Maryt Pub.

Majewski, Henry F. Paradigm & Parody: Images of Creativity in French Romanticism - Vigny, Hugo, Balzac, Gautier, Musset. LC 88-15419. 192p. 1989. text 35.00 (*0-8139-1177-X*) U Pr of Va.

Majewski, Henry F., jt. ed. see Schor, Naomi.

***Majewski, John.** A House Dividing: Economic Development in Pennsylvania & Virginia, 1800-1860. LC 99-28146. (Studies in Economic History & Policy). (Illus.). 240p. (C). 2000. 49.95 (*0-521-59023-X*) Cambridge U Pr.

***Majewski, Martin.** Rational Homotopical Models & Uniqueness. LC 99-49715. (Memoirs of the American Mathematical Society Ser.). 2000. write for info. (*0-8218-1920-8*) Am Math.

Majewski, Michael S. & Capel, Paul D. Pesticides in the Atmosphere: Distribution, Trends & Governing Factors. Gilliom, Robert J., ed. LC 95-34078. (Pesticides in the Hydrologic System Ser.). 215p. (C). 1996. ring bd. 69.95 (*1-57504-004-2*) CRC Pr.

Majewski, S. R., ed. Galaxy Evolution: The Milky Way Perspective. (ASP Conference Series Proceedings: Vol. 49). 256p. 1993. 34.00 (*0-937707-68-6*) Astron Soc Pacific.

Majewski, Stephen. Great Linebackers. LC 97-9044. (Illus.). 80p. (J). 1997. 14.98 (*1-56799-484-9*, MetroBooks) M Friedman Pub Grp Inc.
— Sports Great Jerome Bettis. LC 96-25400. (Sports Great Bks.). (Illus.). 64p. (J). (gr. 4-10). 1997. lib. bdg. 17.95 (*0-89490-872-3*) Enslow Pubs.

***Majewski, Stephen.** Terrell Davis: Star Running Back. LC 99-41012. (Sports Reports Ser.). (Illus.). 104p. (gr. 4-10). 2000. lib. bdg. 20.95 (*0-7660-1331-6*) Enslow Pubs.

Majewski, T. & O'Brien, M. J. An Analysis of Historical Ceramics from the Central Salt River Valley of Northeast Missouri. (Illus.). viii, 121p. 1984. 15.00 (*0-917111-02-8*) Mus Anthro MO.

Majewski, Teresita, jt. auth. see Vanderpot, Rein.

***Maji, Arup & American Society of Civil Engineers Staff.** Advances in Composite Materials & Mechanics. LC 99-45695. 1999. write for info. (*0-7844-0456-9*) Am Soc Civil Eng.

Maji, Jessica. The Place of Gentle Waters. (Heartbeats Ser.). 112p. (YA). (gr. 7 up). 1994. pap. 5.95 (*0-7910-2933-6*) Chelsea Hse.

Majia. Spanish 004. 98p. (C). 1998. pap. text, suppl. ed. 15.75 (*0-536-01341-1*) Pearson Custom.

Majid al Najjar, Abdul. Dawr Hurriyat al Ra'y fi al Wahdah al Fikriyah Bayna al Muslimin: (The Role of Freedom of Opinion in the Intellectual Unity Amongst Muslims) LC 91-44549. (Silsilat Abhath 'Ilmiyah: No. 6). (ARA.). 88p. (Orig.). 1992. pap. 5.00 (*1-56564-024-1*) IIIT VA.

Majid Ali Khan, tr. see Maulana Muhammad Kandhlawi.

Majid, Amir A. Legal Status of International Institutions: SITA, INMARSAT & Eurocontrol Examined. (Illus.). 276p. 1996. text 82.95 (*1-85521-761-9*, Pub. by Dartmth Pub) Ashgate Pub Co.

Majid, Anouar. Si Youssef. 160p. 1993. 19.95 (*0-7043-7032-8*, Pub. by Quartet) Interlink Pub.

***Majid, Anouar.** Unveiling Traditions: Postcolonial Islam in a Polycentric World. LC 00-37553. 304p. 2000. pap. 18.95 (*0-8223-2623-X*); lib. bdg. 54.95 (*0-8223-2629-9*) Duke.

***Majid, Arshad, ed.** Review Questions for the USMLE Step 3 Examination. (Review Questions Ser.). (Illus.). 175p. 2001. pap. 35.95 (*1-85070-063-X*) Prthnon Pub.

Majid, Mimi K. Dangerous Drugs Laws in Malaysia. write for info. (*0-614-05482-6*, MICHIE) LEXIS Pub.

Majid, Shahn. Foundations of Quantum Group Theory. (Illus.). 627p. (C). 1996. text 115.00 (*0-521-46032-8*) Cambridge U Pr.
— Foundations of Quantum Group Theory. (Illus.). 627p. (C). 2000. pap. text 49.95 (*0-521-64868-8*) Cambridge U Pr.

Majidimehr, Amir H. One Thousand Questions & Answers about UNIX Systems. 2001. pap. text 30.00 (*0-13-119884-X*) P-H.
— Optimizing Unix for Performance. LC 95-40312. 352p. (C). 1995. pap. 47.00 (*0-13-111551-0*) P-H.

Majied, Atiyah, ed. The Teachings of Both Bible & Holy Qur'an As Taught by, The Most Honorable Elijah Muhammad Messenger of Allah (God) Master Fard Muhammad, Bk. I. (Illus.). 359p. 1995. pap. 16.00 (*1-56411-078-8*) Untd Bros & Sis.

Majiid Ali Khan, tr. see Maulana, Muhammad K.

Majima, H. Asymptotic Analysis for Integrable Connections with Irregular Singular Points. (Lecture Notes in Mathematics Ser.: Vol. 1075). ix, 159p. 1984. 34.95 (*0-387-13375-5*) Spr-Verlag.

Majima, Ryuichi. Bulletins of American Paleontology Vol. 96: Cenozoic Fossil Naticidae (Mollusca: Gastropoda) in Japan, Vol. 331. 159p. 1989. 30.00 (*0-87710-412-3*) Paleo Res.

Majithia, M., ed. see Kazansky, V. I.

Majka, Chris & Hunt, Sheilagh. Prudence Valiant: Aviatrix Extraordinaire. (Illus.). 124p. (J). 1991. bds. 16.95 (*0-88780-083-1*, Pub. by Formac Publ Co) Formac Dist Ltd.

Majka, Chris & Hunt, Sheilagh. Prudence Valiant: Aviatrix Extraordinaire. (Illus.). 124p. (J). 1991. mass mkt. 6.95 (*0-88780-082-3*, Pub. by Formac Publ Co) Formac Dist Ltd.

Majka, Genevieve W. Kazimiera & Jan. LC 97-91225. 1998. pap. 8.95 (*0-533-12594-4*) Vantage.

Majka, Linda C., jt. ed. see Voydanoff, Patricia.

Majka, Theo J., jt. auth. see Mooney, Patrick H.

Majkowski, J. Epilepsy. (Monographs in Neural Sciences: Vol. 5). (Illus.). xvi, 304p. 1981. pap. 81.75 (*3-8055-0635-X*) S Karger.

Majkowski, J., et al. Interactions of Pacific Tuna Fisheries: Papers on Biology & Fish, Vol. 2. (Fisheries Technical Papers: 336-2). 450p. 1994. pap. 48.00 (*92-5-103454-0*, F34540) Bernan Associates.

Majkowski, Wladyslaw. People's Poland: Patterns of Social Inequality & Conflict, 55. LC 84-15689. (Contributions in Sociology Ser.). (Illus.). 234p. 1985. 59.95 (*0-313-24614-9*, MJP/, Greenwood Pr) Greenwood.

Majkut, Paul. Asterion, the Minotaur: A Book of Suspicion, Resentment, Confusion, Regret, Poor Memory, Tales, Poetry, & Conversation. LC 93-16136. 1993. write for info. (*0-9632702-3-0*) Lightning.

***Majlis, Norberto.** Quantam Theory of Magnetism. 2000. pap. 41.00 (*981-02-4018-X*) World Scientific Pub.

Majluf, Nicholas S., jt. auth. see Hax, Arnoldo C.

Majmudar, Amit. Entrance. 1997. pap. 4.99 (*0-9658704-9-9*) Ohm Pub.

Majnaric, Niko. Greek-Serbocroatian Dictionary: Grcko-Hrvatski ili Srpski Rjecnik. (CRO, GRE & SER.). 468p. 1983. 29.95 (*0-8288-1054-0*, F79182) Fr & Eur.

Majno, Guido. Cell Tissues. (C). text. write for info. (*0-7167-7035-0*) W H Freeman.
— The Healing Hand: Man & Wound in the Ancient World. (Commonwealth Fund Publications). (Illus.). 616p. (C). 1991. pap. text 19.95 (*0-674-38331-1*) HUP.

Majno, Guido & Joris, Isabelle. Cells, Tissues & Disease. (Illus.). 832p. 1996. text 95.00 (*0-86542-372-5*) Blackwell Sci.

Majo, Gian F. De, see De Majo, Gian F.

Majok, Aggrey A. & Schwabe, Calvin W. Development among Africa's Migratory Pastoralists. LC 96-10374. 304p. 1996. 69.50 (*0-89789-477-4*, Bergin & Garvey) Greenwood.

Majone, Giandomenico. Evidence, Argument, & Persuasion in the Policy Progress. 224p. (C). 1992. reprint ed. pap. 15.00 (*0-300-05259-6*) Yale U Pr.

Majone, Giandomenico, ed. Deregulation or Re-Regulation? Regulatory Reform in Europe & the United States. 272p. 1992. pap. text 24.50 (*1-85567-067-4*, Pub. by P P Pubs) Cassell & Continuum.
— Regulating Europe. LC 96-7015. (European Public Policy Ser.). 336p. (C). 1996. 90.00 (*0-415-14295-4*); pap. 29.99 (*0-415-14296-2*) Routledge.

Majone, Giandomenico, et al, eds. Guidance, Control & Evaluation in the Public Sector: The Bielefeld Interdisciplinary Project. (Studies in Organization: No. 4). (Illus.). xiv, 830p. 1986. 169.25 (*3-11-009707-9*) De Gruyter.

***Majoor, Mireille.** Inside the Hindenburg. (Illus.). 24p. (J). 2000. 18.85 (*0-316-12386-2*) Little.

Major. Bath Science Materials. (UK - Science Ser.). 1993. text 13.95 (*0-17-438433-5*) S-W Pub.
— End of the World. 1988. 2.98 (*0-7710-5472-6*) McCland & Stewart.

An Asterisk (*) at the beginning of an entry indicates that the title is appearing for the first time.

— Saint-Exupery: L'Ecriture et la Pensee. 28.90 (*0-685-37091-7*) Fr & Eur.

Major, jt. ed. see Poland.

Major, A. Dynamics in Civil Engineering Vol. 3: Foundations for High-Speed Machinery, Steam & Nuclear Power Plants, Structural Details. 292p. (C). 1983. 100.00 (*0-7855-2649-8*, Pub. by Akade Kiado) St Mut.

— Dynamics in Civil Engineering Analysis & Design, 4 vols., Set. (C). 1983. 324.00 (*963-05-3162-3*) St Mut.

— Dynamics in Civil Engineering Analysis & Design: Fundamentals in Vibration Theory & Practice Including Machine Foundations, Soil Dynamics, Instrumentation, Vibrations, Soil Dynamics, Vol. 1. 320p. (C). 1983. 81.00 (*963-05-3163-1*, Pub. by Akade Kiado) St Mut.

— Dynamics in Civil Engineering Analysis & Design Vol. 2: Foundations for Hammers, Reciprocating Engines, & Other Machines, Vibration Isolation & Damping, Vol. 2. 302p. (C). 1983. 81.00 (*963-05-3164-X*, Pub. by Akade Kiado) St Mut.

— Dynamics in Civil Engineering Analysis & Design Vol. 3: Foundations for High Speed Machinery, Steram & Nuclear Power Plants, Structural Details. 292p. 1983. 81.00 (*963-05-3165-8*, Pub. by Akade Kiado) St Mut.

— Dynamics in Civil Engineering Analysis & Design Vol. 4: Vibrations in Buildings & Industrial Structures & Bridges, Vol. 4. 306p. (C). 1983. 100.00 (*963-05-3166-6*, Pub. by Akade Kiado) St Mut.

***Major, A. & Rayner, Ann.** Access in Mind: Towards the Inclusive Museum. 140p. 1999. pap. 19.95 (*1-901663-18-3*) Natl Mus Scotland.

Major, A. Jayne & Supancic, Ronald M. Winning the Custody War: Without Casualties. (Illus.). 168p. 1996. 98.95 (*0-9655939-0-8*) MSR Pub.

***Major, Alice.** Tales for an Urban Sky. 96p. 1999. pap. 10.50 (*1-896647-11-1*) Genl Dist Srvs.

Major, Ann. The Accidental Bodyguard. large type ed. 285p. 1998. 21.95 (*0-373-59934-X*, Harlequin) Harlequin Bks.

— The Accidental Bodyguard: Man of the Month. (Desire Ser.). 1996. per. 3.50 (*0-373-76003-5*, 1-76003-2) Silhouette.

— The Accidental Bridegroom. 1994. per. 2.99 (*0-373-05889-6*, 1-05889-0) Harlequin Bks.

— A Cowboy Christmas. 1995. per. 3.25 (*0-373-05967-1*, 1-05967-4) Silhouette.

— Dazzled! Dazzle, Meant to Be, Beyond Love, 3 bks. in 1. (By Request Ser.). 1999. per. 6.99 (*0-373-20165-6*, 1-20165-6) Harlequin Bks.

— Destiny's Child. LC 96-2785. (Western Lovers Ser.). 251p. 1995. per. 3.99 (*0-373-88548-2*, 1-88548-2) Harlequin Bks.

— Dream Come True. (Men Made in America Ser.). 1994. mass mkt. 3.59 (*0-373-45159-8*, 1-45159-0) Silhouette.

— The Fairy Tale Girl. (Western Lovers Ser.). 1995. per. 3.99 (*0-373-88521-0*, 1-88521-9) Harlequin Bks.

— Guardaespaldas a la Fuerza. Vol. 86. (SPA.). 1997. per. 3.50 (*0-373-35186-0*, 1-35186-5) Harlequin Bks.

***Major, Ann.** Inseparable. 2000. mass mkt. 5.99 (*1-55166-548-4*, 1-66548-8, Mira Bks) Harlequin Bks.

Major, Ann. Love Me Again. (Family Continuity Program Ser.: No. 22). 1999. per. 4.50 (*0-373-82170-0*, 1-82170-1) Harlequin Bks.

— Love Me True: Man of the Month/ Anniversary. anniversary ed. (Desire Ser.: No. 1213). 1999. per. 3.75 (*0-373-76213-5*, 1-76213-7) Silhouette.

— Married to the Enemy. (Desire Ser.: No. 716). 1992. per. 2.89 (*0-373-05716-4*, 5-05716-1) Harlequin Bks.

— El Mejor Regalo: A Cowboy Christmas. (Deseo Ser.). (SPA.). 1996. per. 3.50 (*0-373-35164-X*, 1-35164-2) Harlequin Bks.

***Major, Ann.** Midnight Fantasy. (Desire Ser.: Bk. 1304). 2000. mass mkt. 3.99 (*0-373-76304-2*, 1-76304-4) Silhouette.

Major, Ann. Nobody's Child. 1997. per. 3.50 (*0-373-76105-8*, 1-76105-5) Silhouette.

***Major, Ann.** Quiereme (Love Me) Love Me True. (Deseo Ser.: No. 188). 1999. per. 3.50 (*0-373-35318-9*, 1-35318-4) Harlequin Bks.

Major, Ann. The Secret Child. (Silhouette Promo Ser.). 1998. per. 5.99 (*0-373-48356-2*, 1-48356-9) Harlequin Bks.

— La Sirene et l'Aventurier. (Rouge Passion Ser.). (FRE.). 1994. pap. 3.50 (*0-373-37291-4*, 1-37291-1) Harlequin Bks.

— Traicion Inocente (Wild Innocence) (Deseo Ser.). (SPA.). 1997. per. 3.50 (*0-373-35171-2*, 1-351717) Harlequin Bks.

***Major, Ann.** Wild Enough for Willa. 2000. mass mkt. 5.99 (*1-55166-623-5*, 1-66623-9, Mira Bks) Harlequin Bks.

Major, Ann. Wild Honey: Man of the Month, Something Wild. (Desire Ser.). 1993. mass mkt. 2.99 (*0-373-05805-5*, 5-05805-2) Silhouette.

— Wild Innocence: (Man of the Month, Something Wild) (Desire Ser.). 1994. per. 2.99 (*0-373-05835-7*, 5-05835-9) Silhouette.

— Wild Midnight: Something Wild. (Desire Ser.). 1993. per. 2.99 (*0-373-05819-5*, 5-05819-3) Silhouette.

— The Wrong Man. (Men in America Ser.). 1995. mass mkt. 3.59 (*0-373-45188-1*, 1-45188-9) Harlequin Bks.

Major, Ann, et al. The Man She Married: Wilderness Child, The Wedding, Mystery Wife, 3 bks. in 1. (By Request Ser.). 1999. per. 6.99 (*0-373-20161-3*, 1-20161-5) Harlequin Bks.

Major, Ann, jt. auth. see Browning, Dixie.

Major, Ann, jt. auth. see Parker, Laura.

Major, Ann M., jt. auth. see Atwood, L. Erwin.

Major, Beverly. Over Back. LC 91-19696. (Illus.). 32p. (J). (gr. k-4). 1993. 15.00 (*0-06-020286-6*); lib. bdg. 14.89 (*0-06-020287-4*) HarpC Child Bks.

Major, Charles. The Bears of Blue River. LC 83-49522. (Library of Indiana Classics). (Illus.). 288p. 1984. 20.00 (*0-253-10590-0*); pap. 10.95 (*0-253-20330-9*, MB-330) Ind U Pr.

— Bears of Blue River. reprint ed. lib. bdg. 23.95 (*0-88411-094-X*) Amereon Ltd.

— The Bears of Blue River. 1998. reprint ed. 35.95 (*1-56849-716-4*) Buccaneer Bks.

— Uncle Tom Andy Bill. 350p. 1992. reprint ed. lib. bdg. 26.95 (*0-89966-914-X*) Buccaneer Bks.

— Uncle Tom Andy Bill: A Story of Bears & Indian Treasure. LC 93-22086. (Library of Indiana Classics). 352p. (C). 1993. 17.95 (*0-253-33653-8*); pap. 10.95 (*0-253-33654-6*) Ind U Pr.

— When Knighthood Was in Flower. LC 70-126656. reprint ed. 45.00 (*0-404-04169-8*) AMS Pr.

— When Knighthood Was in Flower. reprint ed. lib. bdg. 23.95 (*0-88411-095-8*) Amereon Ltd.

— When Knighthood Was in Flower. (BCL1-PS American Literature Ser.). 295p. 1992. reprint ed. lib. bdg. 79.00 (*0-7812-6792-7*) Rprt Serv.

***Major, Cherie, et al.** Teaching to Teach. LC 99-48680. 1999. write for info. (*0-8106-2083-9*) NEA.

***Major, Clarence.** All-Night Visitors. abr. ed. (Library of Black Literature). 256p. 2000. pap. text 15.95 (*1-55553-428-7*) NE U Pr.

Major, Clarence. All-Night Visitors. unexpurgated ed. LC 98-33492. (Northeastern Library of Black Literature). 288p. 1998. text 37.50 (*1-55553-367-1*) NE U Pr.

— Configurations: New & Selected Poems, 1958-1998. LC 98-40085. 322p. 1999. pap. 17.00 (*1-55659-090-3*, Pub. by Copper Canyon) Consort Bk Sales.

— The Dark & Feeling. LC 73-83162. 196p. 1974. 19.95 (*0-89388-118-X*) Okpaku Communications.

— The Dark & the Feeling. LC 73-83162. 12.95 (*0-89388-119-8*) Okpaku Communications.

— Dirty Bird Blues. 1997. mass mkt. 6.99 (*0-614-27726-4*); mass mkt. 6.99 (*0-425-15903-5*) Berkley Pub.

— Dirty Bird Blues: A Novel. LC 96-13310. 224p. 1996. 22.95 (*1-56279-083-8*) Mercury Hse Inc.

— Emergency Exit. LC 79-52031. (Illus.). 1979. 15.95 (*0-914590-58-8*); pap. 6.95 (*0-914590-59-6*) Fiction Coll.

— Fun & Games: Short Fictions. LC 88-45370. 144p. 1990. 15.95 (*0-930100-34-4*) Holy Cow.

— The Garden Thrives: Twentieth-Century African-American Poetry. 400th ed. LC 95-49137. 512p. 1996. pap. 20.00 (*0-06-095121-4*) HarpC.

— Painted Turtle: Woman with Guitar. (Sun & Moon Classics Ser.: No. 73). 64p. 1996. pap. 11.95 (*1-55713-085-X*) Sun & Moon CA.

— Reflex & Bone Structure. LC 96-11532. 144p. 1996. reprint ed. pap. 12.95 (*1-56279-084-6*) Mercury Hse Inc.

— Some Observations of a Stranger at Zuni in the Latter Part of the Century. (New American Poetry Ser.: No. 2). 79p. 1990. pap. 9.95 (*1-55713-020-5*) Sun & Moon CA.

— Surfaces & Masks. LC 88-23673. 128p. (Orig.). 1988. pap. 8.95 (*0-918273-43-9*) Coffee Hse.

Major, Clarence, ed. Calling the Wind: Twentieth Century African-American Short Stories. 368th ed. LC 92-52620. 656p. 1993. pap. 17.00 (*0-06-098201-2*, Perennial) HarperTrade.

Major, David. A Long Way from Zero. 246p. (Orig.). (J). (gr. 6-10). 1996. pap. 12.95 (*0-9655533-0-2*) Davdsn Pubng VA.

Major, David C. Multiobjective Water Resource Planning. (Water Resources Monograph Ser.: Vol. 4). (Illus.). 81p. 1977. 10.00 (*0-87590-305-3*) Am Geophysical.

Major, David C. & Schwarz, Harry E. Large-Scale Regional Water Resources Planning: The North Atlantic Regional Study. (C). 1990. text 124.00 (*0-7923-0711-9*) Kluwer Academic.

Major, Devorah. An Open Weave. LC 95-14834. 176p. (Orig.). 1995. pap. 20.95 (*1-878067-66-4*) Seal Pr WA.

— An Open Weave. 256p. (Orig.). 1997. reprint ed. mass mkt. 6.99 (*0-425-15665-6*) Berkley Pub.

— Street Smarts. 56p. (Orig.). 1996. pap. 10.95 (*1-880684-27-6*) Curbstone.

Major, Devorah, jt. auth. see Adisa, Opal P.

Major, Devorah, ed. see Norrise, Bobbe.

Major, Diana. The Acquisition of Modal Auxiliaries in the Language of Children. (Janua Linguarum, Series Minor: No. 195). 1974. pap. text 49.25 (*90-279-2664-6*) Mouton.

Major, Eugene O., et al, eds. Technical Advances in AIDS Research in the Human Nervous System: Proceedings of a NIH Workshop Held in Washington, D. C., October 4-5, 1993. (Illus.). 352p. (C). 1995. text 110.00 (*0-306-45000-3*, Kluwer Plenum) Kluwer Academic.

Major, Fouad G. The Quantum Beat: The Physical Principles of Atomic Clocks. LC 97-24027. (Illus.). 336p. (C). 1998. 49.95 (*0-387-98301-5*) Spr-Verlag.

Major, Geri. Black Society. LC 75-39546. 1977. 25.00 (*0-87485-075-4*) Johnson Chicago.

Major, Grace. Take Charge! How to Manage Your Customer Relationships. LC 92-60371. (Executive Edition Ser.). 266p. (Orig.). 1992. teacher ed. 149.00 (*0-9632406-2-5*); text 27.95 (*0-9632406-1-7*); pap. text 27.95 (*0-9632406-0-9*) Sigma Bks.

Major, H. D., ed. see Rashdall, Hastings.

Major, Henry D. Civilization & Religious Values. LC 77-27137. (Hibbert Lectures: 1946). reprint ed. 30.00 (*0-404-60431-5*) AMS Pr.

Major, Howard. Domestic Architecture of the Early American Republic. 236p. 1993. reprint ed. lib. bdg. 79.00 (*0-7812-5299-7*) Rprt Serv.

Major, Ivan. Privatization in Eastern Europe: A Critical Approach. (Studies of Communism in Transition). (Illus.). 176p. 1993. 85.00 (*1-85278-887-9*) E Elgar.

***Major, Ivan, ed.** Privatization & Economic Performance in Central & Eastern Europe: Lessons to Be Learnt from Western Europe. LC 99-14859. (European Association for Comparative Economic Studies Ser.). 448p. 1999. 115.00 (*1-84064-119-3*) E Elgar.

Major, J. Kenneth. Animal Powered Machines. (C). 1989. pap. 25.00 (*0-85263-710-1*, Pub. by Shire Pubns) St Mut.

Major, J. Russell. From Renaissance Monarchy to Absolute Monarchy: French Kings, Nobles, & Estates. 444p. 1997. reprint ed. text 18.95 (*0-8018-5631-0*) Johns Hopkins.

***Major, J. Russell.** The Memoirs of an Artillery Forward Observer, 1944-1945. (Illus.). 184p. 1999. pap. 18.95 (*0-89745-229-1*) Sunflower U Pr.

Major, J. Russell. The Monarchy, the Estates & the Aristocracy in Renaissance France. (Collected Studies: No. CS279). 298p. (C). 1988. reprint ed. text 101.95 (*0-86078-227-1*, Pub. by Variorum) Ashgate Pub Co.

— Representative Government in Early Modern France. LC 79-14711. 752p. 1980. 67.00 (*0-300-02300-6*) Yale U Pr.

Major, Jack, jt. ed. see Barbour, Michael G.

Major, James. Dulcimer Chord Encyclopedia. 140p. 1982. spiral bd. 10.95 (*0-87166-613-8*, 93858) Mel Bay.

— Mandolin Chord Book. 1984. pap. 5.95 (*0-8256-2296-4*, AM34729) Music Sales.

Major, James & Smith, Doug. World Cup Ski Technique 2. (World Cup Ski Technique Ser.). (Illus.). 384p. (Orig.). 1990. 33.00 (*0-935240-08-X*) Poudre Pr.

Major, James, jt. auth. see Larsson, Olle.

Major, James, tr. see Joubert, Georges.

Major, James R. Representative Institutions in Renaissance France, 1421-1559. LC 82-25305. 182p. (C). 1983. reprint ed. lib. bdg. 65.00 (*0-313-23569-4*, MAJR, Greenwood Pr) Greenwood.

Major, Jill C., jt. auth. see Chapman, Eugenia.

Major, John. Prize Possession: The United States & the Panama Canal, 1903-1979. LC 92-32406. (Illus.). 454p. (C). 1993. text 57.95 (*0-521-43306-1*) Cambridge U Pr.

Major, John, jt. ed. see Love, Robert W., Jr.

Major, John B. & Pan, Fung-Shine, eds. Contemporary Real Estate Finance: Selected Readings. LC 95-23701. 406p. 1995. pap. text 62.00 (*0-13-356791-5*) P-H.

Major, John M. Sir Thomas Elyot & Renaissance Humanism. LC 64-11351. 292p. reprint ed. pap. 90.60 (*0-7837-6020-5*, 204583200008) Bks Demand.

Major, John S. Heaven & Earth in Early Han Thought: Chapters Three, Four, & Five of the Huainanzi. LC 92-27071. (SUNY Series in Chinese Philosophy & Culture). 388p. (C). 1993. text 74.50 (*0-7914-1585-6*); pap. text 24.95 (*0-7914-1586-4*) State U NY Pr.

— The Land & People of China. LC 88-23427. (Portraits of the Nations Ser.). (Illus.). 288p. (J). (gr. 6 up). 1989. 19.00 (*0-397-32336-0*) HarpC Child Bks.

— The Land & People of Mongolia. LC 89-37790. (Portraits of the Nations Ser.). (Illus.). 224p. (J). (gr. 6 up). 1990. 15.95 (*0-397-32386-7*); lib. bdg. 15.89 (*0-397-32387-5*) HarpC Child Bks.

— The Silk Route: 7,000 Miles of History. (J). 1995. 11.15 (*0-606-09855-0*, Pub. by Turtleback) Demco.

— The Silk Route: 7,000 Miles of History. 97th ed. LC 92-38169. (Trophy Picture Bk.). (Illus.). 32p. (J). (ps-3). 1996. pap. 6.95 (*0-06-443468-0*, HarpTrophy) HarpC Child Bks.

Major, John S., jt. auth. see Fadiman, Clifton.

Major, John S., jt. auth. see Steele, Valerie.

Major, John S., ed. see Blakeley, Barry B.

Major, Judith K. To Live in the New World: A. J. Downing & American Landscape Gardening. LC 96-36407. (Illus.). 232p. 1997. pap. text 40.00 (*0-262-13331-8*) MIT Pr.

Major, Kevin. Blood Red Ochre. 160p. 1996. mass mkt. 4.99 (*0-7704-2717-0*) Bantam.

— Blood Red Ochre. 160p. 1994. pap. 10.95 (*0-385-25465-2*) Doubleday.

— Dear Bruce Springsteen. 144p. (YA). 1994. pap. 10.95 (*0-385-25459-8*) Doubleday.

— Diana: My Autobiography. 144p. (J). 1993. pap. 12.95 (*0-385-25413-X*) Doubleday.

— Diana: My Autobiography. 144p. (J). 1995. reprint ed. pap. 4.99 (*0-7704-2702-2*) Bantam.

— Eating Between the Lines. 144p. (YA). (gr. 8 up). 1991. pap. 13.50 (*0-385-25293-5*) Doubleday.

— Eating Between the Lines. 144p. 1995. reprint ed. mass mkt. 4.99 (*0-7704-2705-7*) Bantam.

— Far from Shore. unabridged ed. LC 99-175038. 192p. (YA). (gr. 8 up). 1980. pap. 5.99 (*0-7736-7439-X*) STDK.

— Gaffer. LC 98-108293. 202p. 1997. pap. 24.95 (*0-385-25667-1*) Bantam.

— Gaffer. 208p. 1998. pap. 14.95 (*0-385-25729-5*) Bantam.

— Hold Fast. unabridged ed. 172p. (YA). (gr. 7 up). 1991. mass mkt. 4.95 (*0-7736-7438-1*) STDK.

— No Man's Land. 272p. 1995. 22.95 (*0-385-25503-9*) Doubleday.

***Major, Kevin.** The Story of the House of Wooden Santas: An Advent Read-Along in 24 Chapters. rev. ed. LC 98-16810. (Illus.). 96p. (gr. 4-7). 1998. 12.98 (*0-7651-0829-1*) Smithmark.

Major, Kevin. Thirty-Six Exposures. 1994. pap. 10.95 (*0-385-25464-4*) Doubleday.

Major League Baseball Properties, Inc. Staff & Baseball Encyclopedia Editors. The Official Major League Baseball Stat Book, 1992. (Illus.). 480p. 1992. pap. 14.95 (*0-02-079646-3*) Macmillan.

***Major League Baseball Staff.** Official Rules of Major League Baseball: 2000. LC 95-29374. 208p. 1999. pap. 9.95 (*1-57243-332-9*) Triumph Bks.

Major League Baseball Training Staff & Lowenfish, Lee. The Professional Baseball Trainers' Fitness Book. (Orig.). 1988. mass mkt. 12.95 (*0-446-38751-7*, Pub. by Warner Bks) Little.

Major, Mabel. Southwest Heritage: Literary History with Bibliography. (BCL1-PS American Literature Ser.). 199p. 1993. reprint ed. lib. bdg. 69.00 (*0-7812-6581-9*) Rprt Serv.

Major, Mabel, ed. see Duval, John C.

***Major, Marcus.** Good Peoples: A Novel. LC 99-45734. 272p. 2000. 22.95 (*0-525-94535-0*, Dutt) Dutton Plume.

Major, Mark T., jt. auth. see Ward, Leo L.

Major, Mike & Patzer, Nancy. A Light in the Sky: A Biography of Warren G. Grimes & a History of Aviation Lighting. (Illus.). 130p. 1996. 35.00 (*0-9641149-8-4*) Main Graphics.

Major, Norma. Chequers: The Prime Minister's Country House & Its History. LC 97-204951. (Illus.). 272p. 1997. 50.00 (*0-7892-0319-7*, Cross Riv Pr) Abbeville Pr.

Major, Patrick. The Death of KPD: Communism & Anti-Communism in West Germany, 1945-1956. (Oxford Historical Monographs). (Illus.). 370p. (C). 1998. text 85.00 (*0-19-820693-3*) OUP.

Major-Poetzl, Pamela. Michel Foucault's Archaeology of Western Culture: Toward a New Science of History. LC 81-19689. 295p. reprint ed. pap. 91.50 (*0-7837-0308-2*, 204063000018) Bks Demand.

Major, Ralph H. Classic Descriptions of Disease: With Biographical Sketches of the Authors. 3rd ed. (Illus.). 712p. 1978. pap. 84.95 (*0-398-06265-X*) C C Thomas.

Major, Ralph H. Classic Descriptions of Disease: With Biographical Sketches of the Authors. 3rd ed. (Illus.). 712p. 1978. 110.95 (*0-398-01202-4*) C C Thomas.

Major, Reginald. Justice in the Round: The Trial of Angela Davis. LC 72-84108. 256p. 1973. 35.00 (*0-89388-052-3*) Okpaku Communications.

***Major, Reginald.** A Panther Is a Black Cat: A Study in Depth of the Black Panther Party--Its Origins, Its Goals, Its Struggle for Survival. 308p. 2000. reprint ed. pap. write for info. (*1-58073-027-2*) BCP Bks.

Major, Richard. Developing a Dynamic Drama Ministry. Caldwell, Lise, ed. LC 98-31323. 208p. 1999. pap. 19.99 (*0-7847-0915-7*, 03391) Standard Pub.

Major, Richard H. India in the Fifteenth Century Being a Collection of Narratives & Voyages to India in the Century Preceeding the Portuguese Discovery of Good Hope from Latin, Persian, Russian & Italian Sources. (C). 1992. reprint ed. 19.00 (*81-206-0768-6*, Pub. by Asian Educ Servs) S Asia.

— Life of Prince Henry of Portugal. 487p. 1967. reprint ed. 49.50 (*0-7146-1045-3*, Pub. by F Cass Pubs) Intl Spec Bk.

Major, Richard H., ed. Christopher Columbus: Four Voyages to the New World. (Illus.). 240p. 1992. pap. 9.95 (*0-8065-1337-3*, Citadel Pr) Carol Pub Group.

Major, Richard H., ed. & tr. see Columbus, Christopher.

Major, Robert. The American Dream in 19th Century Quebec: Ideologies & Utopia in Gerin-Lajoie's "Jean Rivard" LC 96-208765. (Theory/Culture Ser.). 272p. 1996. text 60.00 (*0-8020-0766-X*) U of Toronto Pr.

Major, Robert & Porad, Francine. Sunlight Through Rain: A Northwest Haiku Year. (Illus.). 58p. (Orig.). 1996. pap. 9.25 (*1-887381-03-1*) Vandina Pr.

Major, Robert L. Discipline: The Most Important Subject We Teach. 142p. (Orig.). (C). 1990. pap. text 17.50 (*0-8191-7745-8*) U Pr of Amer.

Major, S. Architectural Woodwork. 1995. pap. 52.95 (*0-442-01402-3*, VNR) Wiley.

Major, Stephen P. Architectural Woodwork: Details for Construction. (Architecture Ser.). 240p. 1995. pap. 59.95 (*0-471-28551-X*, VNR) Wiley.

Major, Teresa L. A Time to Plant: 52 Children's Sermons. LC 97-28493. 116p. 1998. pap. 10.95 (*0-7880-1163-4*) CSS OH.

— Time to Plant: 52 Children's Sermons. 1998. 10.95 incl. disk (*0-7880-1164-2*) CSS OH.

Major-Tingey, Susan. More Than 70 Native American Art Projects. LC 95-223049. 1995. pap. 18.95 (*0-590-25635-1*) Scholastic Inc.

***Major, Wade.** Jackie Chan. LC 99-12335. 1999. 12.98 (*1-56799-863-1*) M Friedman Pub Grp Inc.

Major, Walter & Hoagland, David. Counseling: Offering a Needed Touch in Times of Trouble, a Guide for Personal Care-Giving. Spear, Cindy G. & Johnson, Tamara, eds. 144p. (Orig.). 1993. pap. 10.95 (*0-941005-91-7*) Chrch Grwth VA.

Major, Wayne, ed. see Percival, Lloyd.

Major, Wilfred, jt. auth. see O'Brien, Joan.

***Major, William D., et al.** William P. Major: A Bergenfield Life. LC 99-76414. (Illus.). iii, 108p. 1999. 18.00 (*0-9674554-3-X*) Bergenfield Museum.

Majoral, Roser, jt. ed. see Singh, R. B.

Majorano, Sabatino. Blessed Are the Poor in Spirit, Vol. 10. (Reflections on the Commandments Ser.). 120p. 1995. pap. 2.95 (*0-8198-1147-5*) Pauline Bks.

Majorbanks, Kevin, jt. auth. see Keeves, John P.

***Majoribanks, Timothy.** News Corporation, Technology & the Workplace: Global Strategies, Local Change. (Illus.). 240p. (C). 2000. 54.95 (*0-521-77280-X*); pap. 19.95 (*0-521-77535-3*) Cambridge U Pr.

Majorin, Matti P., jt. auth. see Walker, Steve L.

Majorin, Matti P., jt. auth. see Walker, Steven L.

Majors, Alexander. Seventy Years on the Frontier: Alexander Majors' Memoirs of a Lifetime on the Border. abr. ed. Ingraham, Prentiss, ed. (American Biography Ser.). 325p. (J). (gr. 2). 1991. lib. bdg. 79.00 (*0-7812-8263-2*) Rprt Serv.

— Seventy Years on the Frontier: Alexander Majors'

M

Memoirs of a Lifetime on the Border. Ingraham, Prentiss, ed. LC 88-31597. (Illus.). 325p. 1989. reprint ed. pap. 100.80 (0-608-02731-6, 206339600004) Bks Demand.

Majors, E. B. Nightmare Trail. large type ed. LC 98-41737. 1998. 21.95 (0-7838-0387-7, G K Hall Lrg Type) Mac Lib Ref.

Majors, E.B. Slaughter & Son. large type ed. LC 98-5793. (Paperback Ser.). 259p. 1998. pap. 21.95 (0-7838-0132-7) Thorndike Pr.

Majors, Ellen M. Community-Acquired Infections & Diseases: Index of New Information with Authors, Subjects & References. 150p. 1996. 47.50 (0-7883-1262-6); pap. 44.50 (0-7883-1263-4) ABBE Pubs Assn.

— Community Health Services: Index of New Information with Authors, Subjects & References. 2nd ed. 150p. 1996. 47.50 (0-7883-1260-X); pap. 44.50 (0-7883-1261-8) ABBE Pubs Assn.

***Majors, Inman.** Swimming in Sky. 2000. 19.95 (0-87074-455-0) SMU Press.

Majors, Jack H. Communicating the Joy, Pain & Everything. 2nd ed. 176p. (C). 1976. pap. 6.00 (0-937104-00-0) Programs Comm.

Majors, Judith S. Sugar Free: Goodies. LC 87-70318. pap. 6.95 (0-941905-00-4) Apple Pr.

— Sugar Free: Hawaiian Cookery. LC 87-70229. pap. 6.95 (0-9602238-9-4) Apple Pr.

— Sugar Free: Kids Cookery. LC 79-66220. 1979. pap. 6.95 (0-9602238-1-9) Apple Pr.

— Sugar Free . . . Good & Easy. LC 85-72597. 1985. pap. 5.95 (0-9602238-8-6) Apple Pr.

— Sugar Free . . . Microwavery. LC 80-67167. pap. 6.95 (0-9602238-3-5) Apple Pr.

— Sugar Free . . . Sweets & Treats. LC 82-73049. 1982. pap. 6.95 (0-9602238-6-X) Apple Pr.

— Sugar Free . . . That's Me. LC 78-74029. (Illus.). 1978. pap. 6.95 (0-9602238-0-0) Apple Pr.

Majors, Ken & MacTague, Bendan. MCSE Windows NT Server 4 for Dummies. LC QA76.3.M324 1998. (For Dummies Ser.). 512p. 1998. 29.99 incl. cd-rom (0-7645-0400-2) IDG Bks.

***Majors, Kenneth & Ferris, Jeffrey E.** MCSE Windows Networking Server 4 in the Enterprise for Dummies. 2nd ed. (For Dummies Ser.). (Illus.). 540p. 1999. pap. 29.99 incl. cd-rom (0-7645-0615-3) IDG Bks.

Majors, Lance. Tropical Seed. LC 99-62037. 365p. 1999. 25.00 (0-7388-0388-X); pap. 15.00 (0-7388-0389-8) Xlibris Corp.

Majors, Monroe A. Noted Negro Women. LC 73-138341. (Black Heritage Library Collection). 1977. 29.95 (0-8369-8733-0) Ayer.

— Noted Negro Women. 1972. 99.95 (0-8490-0737-2) Gordon Pr.

Majors, Randall E. & Yamasaki, Joan M. "Is This Going to Be on the Test?" & Ten Other Questions that Can Save Your Company. 3rd ed. 224p. (C). 1997. pap. text 18.40 (0-13-776741-2) P-H.

Majors, Richard G. The Black Education Revolution. 232p. 1999. pap. 23.95 (0-7507-0964-2, Falmer Pr) Taylor & Francis.

Majors, Richard G. & Billson, Janet M. Cool Pose: The Dilemma of Black Manhood in America. 160p. 1993. per. 11.00 (0-671-86572-2) S&S Trade Pap.

— Cool Pose: The Dilemmas of Black Manhood in America. 144p. 1992. 22.95 (0-669-24523-2) Lxngtn Bks.

Majors, Richard G. & Joliffe, Jo. The Black Education Revolution. 232p. 1999. 79.95 (0-7507-0965-0, Falmer Pr) Taylor & Francis.

Majors, Stanley. Celestial Home: A Book of Poems. 1998. pap. write for info. (1-57553-780-X) Watermrk Pr.

— Moody Millenium. 1998. pap. write for info. (1-58235-091-4) Watermrk Pr.

***Majors, Stanley.** Sandstone Poems. 2000. write for info. (1-58235-486-3) Watermrk Pr.

Majors, Susan. Child at Work Vol. 2: Colors. (Illus.). (Orig.). 1988. pap. 5.95 (0-937104-06-X) Programs Comm.

— Quackers, an Idea Book for Preschool Teachers. rev. ed. 288p. 1986. pap. text 24.95 (0-937104-03-5) Programs Comm.

Majors, William R. Change & Continuity: Tennessee Politics since the Civil War. LC 86-12523. 144p. (Orig.). (C). 1986. pap. text 8.95 (0-86554-209-0, MUP\P025) Mercer Univ Pr.

— Volunteer Trails: A Program of Visual Aids for the Study of Tennessee. (Illus.). 80p. 1980. 20.00 (0-939710-06-4) Meridional Pubns.

Majors-Williams, Michelle L. Gardens & Seeds: Early Childhood Theme Teaching Collection. Mitchell, Judy, ed. (Illus.). 64p. (J). (ps-2). 1998. pap., teacher ed. 7.95 (1-57310-105-2) Teachng & Lrning Co.

***Majot, Tulla.** Coudersport Glass, 1900-1904. (Illus.). 128p. 1999. 34.95 (1-57080-068-5); pap. 24.95 (1-57080-067-7) Antique Pubns.

Majoza, Estella C. Libation. (Illus.). 105p. (Orig.). 1996. pap. 12.00 (0-86316-024-7) Writers & Readers.

Majozo, Estella C. Jiva Telling Rites: An Initiation. (Orig.). 1989. pap. text 8.00 (0-88378-138-7) Third World.

— Libation. 106p. (Orig.). 1992. 24.00 (0-86316-303-3) Writers & Readers.

***Majozo, Estella Conwill.** Come Out the Wilderness: Memoir of a Black Woman Artist. 2000. pap. 14.95 (1-55861-207-6); pap. 14.95 (1-55861-242-4, Pub. by Feminist Pr) Consort Bk Sales.

— Come Out the Wilderness: Memoir of a Black Woman Artist. unabridged ed. LC 98-44371. (Cross-Cultural Memoir Ser.). (Illus.). 256p. 1999. 21.95 (1-55861-206-8, Pub. by Feminist Pr) Consort Bk Sales.

Majua, Margaret & Weingarten, David. Souvenir Buildings & Miniature Monuments: From the Collection of Ace Architects. LC 96-10852. (Illus.). 128p. 1996. 19.95 (0-8109-4470-7, Pub. by Abrams) Time Warner.

Majua, Margaret, jt. auth. see Weingarten, David.

Majul, Cesar A. The Contemporary Muslim Movement in the Philippines. LC 85-21519. 158p. (Orig.). (C). 1985. 15.95 (0-933782-16-0); pap. 8.95 (0-933782-17-9) Mizan Pr.

— Contemporary Muslim Movement in the Philippines. 84p. 1996. pap. 8.95 (0-614-21481-5, 170) Kazi Pubns.

***Majul, Cesar Adib.** Muslims in the Philippines. (Illus.). 488p. 1999. pap. text 40.00 (971-542-188-1, Pub. by U of Philippines Pr) UH Pr.

— The Political & Constitutional Ideas of the Philippine Revolution. (Illus.). 252p. 1999. pap. text 23.00 (971-542-115-6, Pub. by U of Philippines Pr) UH Pr.

Majumader, Robin & McLaurin, Allen, eds. Virginia Woolf: The Critical Heritage. (Critical Heritage Ser.). 1975. 69.50 (0-7100-8138-3, Routledge Thoemms) Routledge.

Majumdar. Althusser & the End of Leninism? LC 95-3741. 6p. (C). 69.95 (0-7453-0888-0, Pub. by Pluto GBR); pap. 22.95 (0-7453-0887-2, Pub. by Pluto GBR) Stylus Pub VA.

Majumdar, A. K. & Singh, Bhanwar, eds. Ambedkar & Social Justice. (C). 1997. 42.00 (81-7487-095-4, Pub. by Manohar) S Asia.

***Majumdar, Amiya Bhushan.** Rajnagar. Bardhan, Kalpana, tr. from BEN. LC 98-904474. 1998. 16.00 (81-260-0392-8, Pub. by Rabindra Bhawn) S Asia.

Majumdar, Asoke K. Concise History of Ancient India, 3 vols., Set. 1931p. 1983. text 100.00 (0-685-13637-X) Coronet Bks.

Majumdar, B. S., et al, eds. Constitutive Behavior of High-Temperature Composites. (MD Ser.: Vol. 40). 184p. 1992. 50.00 (0-7918-1117-4, G00761) ASME.

Majumdar, Biman B. History of Indian Social & Political Ideas. 1996. 54.00 (81-7102-038-0, Pub. by Firma KLM) S Asia.

Majumdar, D. N. Social Contours of an Industrial City. LC 72-13863. (Illus.). 247p. 1975. reprint ed. lib. bdg. 65.00 (0-8371-6762-0, MASD, Greenwood Pr) Greenwood.

***Majumdar, Debu.** From the Ganges to the Snake River: An East Indian in the American West. LC 00-20777. (Illus.). xii, 244p. 2000. pap. 14.95 (0-87004-397-8, 039780) Caxton.

Majumdar, Dipika. Ramendrasundar Trivedi: A Study of His Social & Political Ideas. (C). 1988. 40.00 (81-85195-13-7, Pub. by Minerva) S Asia.

Majumdar, Gopa. In the Same Boat: Golden Tales from Bengal. LC 94-901126. (C). 1994. text 8.50 (81-86112-09-X, Pub. by UBS Pubs Dist) S Asia.

Majumdar, Gopa, jt. auth. see Debi, Asapurna.

Majumdar, Gopa, jt. auth. see Ray, Satyajit.

Majumdar, Ila, jt. auth. see Majumdar, P. S.

Majumdar, J. K., ed. Indian Speeches & Documents on British Rule, 1821-1918. 1987. 34.95 (0-318-37217-7) Asia Bk Corp.

Majumdar, Jatindra K., jt. auth. see Chanda, Ram P.

Majumdar, K. A Comprehensive Handbook for the Practitioner. (C). 1984. 30.00 (0-89771-354-0, Pub. by Current Dist) St Mut.

— Handbook of Practical Medicine & Treatment. (C). 1989. 75.00 (0-89771-353-2, Pub. by Current Dist) St Mut.

— A Medical Handbook for Medical. (C). 1989. 65.00 (0-89771-355-9, Pub. by Current Dist) St Mut.

Majumdar, M. A Comprehensive Medical Handbook. (C). 1984. 45.00 (0-7855-4665-0, Pub. by Current Dist) St Mut.

***Majumdar, M., et al, eds.** Optimization & Chaos. (Studies in Economic Theory: Vol. 11). (Illus.). x, 454p. 2000. 79.00 (3-540-67030-0) Spr-Verlag.

Majumdar, M. C., et al, eds. Artificial Intelligence & Other Innovative Computer Applications in the Nuclear Industry. LC 88-9396. (Illus.). 928p. 1988. 150.00 (0-306-42902-0, Plenum Trade) Perseus Pubng.

Majumdar, Mukul, ed. Organizations with Incomplete Information: Essays in Economic Analysis Tribute to Roy Radner. LC 98-226794. (Illus.). 356p. (C). 1998. text 64.95 (0-521-55300-8) Cambridge U Pr.

Majumdar, P. S. & Majumdar, Ila. Rural Migrants in an Urban Setting. 176p. (C). 1978. text 32.95 (0-87855-330-4) Transaction Pubs.

Majumdar, R. C. Champa: History & Culture of an Indian Colonial Kingdom in the Far East 2nd Century A.D. (C). 1985. 36.00 (0-8364-2802-1, Pub. by Gian Publng Hse) S Asia.

— Hindu Colonies in the Far East. (C). 1991. reprint ed. 32.00 (0-8364-2740-8, Pub. by Firma KLM) S Asia.

— History of the Freedom Movement in India, Vol. I. (C). 1988. reprint ed. 17.00 (0-8364-2374-7, Pub. by Firma KLM) S Asia.

— History of the Freedom Movement in India, Vol. II. (C). 1988. reprint ed. 17.00 (0-8364-2375-5, Pub. by Firma KLM) S Asia.

— History of the Freedom Movement in India, Vol. III. (C). 1988. reprint ed. 32.50 (0-8364-2376-3, Pub. by Firma KLM) S Asia.

— Suvarnadvipa Ancient Indian Colonies in the Far East, 2 vols., Set. (C). 1986. 110.00 (81-212-0040-7) S Asia.

Majumdar, R. C. & Altekar, A. S. The Vakataka - Gupta Age Circa 200-550 A.D. 515p. 1986. reprint ed. 17.50 (81-208-0026-5, Pub. by Motilal Bnarsidass) S Asia.

Majumdar, Ramesh, jt. ed. see Madhavananda, Swami.

Majumdar, Robin & McLauren, Aden, eds. Virginia Woolf. (Critical Heritage Ser.). 484p. (C). 1997. 140.00 (0-415-15914-8) Routledge.

***Majumdar, S.** Assessment of Current Understanding of Mechanisms of Initiation, Arrest & Reinitiation of Stress Corrosion Cracks in Power Steam Generator Tubing. 131p. 2000. per. 13.00 (0-16-059087-6) USGPO.

— Failure Behavior of Internally Pressurized Flawed & Unflawed Steam Generator Tubing at High Temperatures: Experiments & Comparison with Model Predictions. 99p. 1998. per. 8.00 (0-16-062901-2) USGPO.

Majumdar, S. K., et al, eds. Ecology of Wetlands & Associated Systems. LC 97-75667. (Illus.). 685p. 1998. 50.00 (0-945809-14-X) Penn Science.

— The Era of Materials. LC 97-76325. (Illus.). 510p. 1998. 50.00 (0-945809-15-8) Penn Science.

***Majumdar, S. K., et al, eds.** Ethics in Academia. LC 99-80093. (Illus.). 349p. 2000. 50.00 (0-945809-16-6) Penn Science.

Majumdar, S. R. Pneumatic Systems: Principles & Maintenance. 282p. 1995. 65.00 (0-07-460231-4) McGraw.

Majumdar, Shyamal K., ed. Energy, Environment & the Economy. LC 81-82465. xxi, 228p. 1981. 20.00 (0-9606670-0-8) Penn Science.

Majumdar, Shyamal K., et al, eds. Air Pollution: Environmental Issues & Health Effects. LC 91-61996. (Illus.). x, 496p. (C). 1991. text 45.00 (0-945809-05-0) Penn Science.

— Conservation & Resource Management. LC 93-71958. (Illus.). x, 444p. (C). 1993. 45.00 (0-945809-08-5) Penn Science.

— Contaminant Problems & Management of Living Chesapeake Bay Resources. LC 87-62940. xii, 573p. (C). 1987. 40.00 (0-9606670-7-5) Penn Science.

— Ecology & Restoration of the Delaware River Basin. LC 88-60133. (Illus.). xiv, 431p. (C). 1988. text 40.00 (0-9606670-8-3) Penn Science.

— Endangered & Threatened Species Programs in Pennsylvania & Other States: Causes, Issues & Management. LC 86-61186. (Illus.). xix, 519p. 1986. 40.00 (0-9606670-5-9) Penn Science.

— Environmental Consequences of Energy Production: Problems & Prospects. LC 87-61248. (Illus.). 531p. 1987. 40.00 (0-9606670-6-7) Penn Science.

— Environmental Radon: Occurrence, Control, & Health Hazards. LC 90-61965. (Illus.). xi, 436p. 1990. text 45.00 (0-945809-03-4) Penn Science.

— Global Climate Change: Implications, Challenges & Mitigation Measures. LC 92-85374. (Illus.). xiv, 566p. (C). 1992. text 45.00 (0-945809-07-7) Penn Science.

— Management of Hazardous Materials & Wastes: Treatment, Minimization & Environmental Impacts. LC 89-60201. (Illus.). xviii, 474p. (C). 1989. text 45.00 (0-9606670-9-1) Penn Science.

— Natural & Technological Disasters: Causes, Effects & Preventive Measures. (Illus.). x, 561p. (C). 1992. 45.00 (0-945809-06-9) Penn Science.

— The Oceans: Physical-Chemical Dynamics & Human Impact. LC 94-67523. (Illus.). x, 498p. (C). 1994. 45.00 (0-945809-10-7) Penn Science.

— Science Education in the United States: Issues, Crises, Priorities. LC 91-60096. (Illus.). 550p. 1991. text 45.00 (0-945809-04-2) Penn Science.

— Water Resources in Pennsylvania: Availability, Quality & Management. LC 89-63978. (Illus.). xiii, 580p. (C). 1990. text 45.00 (0-945809-02-6) Penn Science.

— Wetlands Conservation: Emphasis in Pennsylvania. LC 89-61084. (Illus.). xiv, 395p. (C). 1989. text 45.00 (0-945809-01-8) Penn Science.

Majumdar, Shyamal K. & Miller, E. Willard. Biological Diversity: Problems & Challenges. LC 93-87463. (Illus.). x, 461p. (C). 1994. 45.00 (0-945809-09-3) Penn Science.

— Environmental Contaminants, Ecosystems & Human Health. LC 95-74813. (Illus.). 507p. 1995. 40.00 (0-945809-12-3) Penn Science.

— Forests: A Global Perspective. LC 96-68259. (Illus.). 513p. 1996. 40.00 (0-945809-13-1) Penn Science.

Majumdar, Shyamal K. & Miller, E. Willard, eds. Hazardous & Toxic Wastes: Technology Management & Health Effects. LC 83-8317. (Illus.). xxii, 442p. 1984. 35.00 (0-9606670-2-4) Penn Science.

— Management of Radioactive Materials & Wastes: Issues & Progress. LC 85-61443. (Illus.). 405p. 1985. 35.00 (0-9606670-4-0) Penn Science.

— Pennsylvania Coal: Resources, Technology & Utilization. LC 82-62857. (Illus.). xxvi, 594p. 1983. 25.00 (0-9606670-1-6) Penn Science.

— Solid & Liquid Wastes: Management, Methods & Socioeconomic Considerations. LC 84-61472. (Illus.). xxii, 412p. 1984. 35.00 (0-9606670-3-2) Penn Science.

Majumdar, Shyamal K. & Nash, David B. Medicine & Health Care into the Twenty-First Century. LC 95-67144. (Illus.). xii, 613p. 1995. 50.00 (0-945809-11-5) Penn Science.

Majumdar, Somendu. Regulation Requirements for Hazardous Materials. LC 92-32345. 524p. 1991. 70.00 (0-07-039761-9) McGraw.

Majumdar, Tapas. The Measurement of Utility. LC 74-14113. (Illus.). 149p. 1975. reprint ed. lib. bdg. 35.00 (0-8371-7785-5, MAMUT, Greenwood Pr) Greenwood.

Majumdar, Tapas, et al, eds. Nature, Man & the Indian Economy. (Illus.). 430p. 1994. text 39.95 (0-19-562915-9) OUP.

Majumder, Khaletum, jt. auth. see Dey-Bergmoser, Olga.

Majumder, Kiganta, ed. see Needle, Sheldon & Hollander, Nathan.

Majumder, M. Medical Handbook for the Medical Representative. 7th ed. (C). 1989. 40.00 (0-7855-4666-9, Pub. by Current Dist) St Mut.

Majumder, P. P. Human Population Genetics: A Centennial Tribute to J. B. S. Haldane. LC 93-32262. (Illus.). 358p. (C). 1993. text 110.00 (0-306-44572-7, Kluwer Plenum) Kluwer Academic.

Majundar, M. K. Microbiology & Immunology - An Encyclopedic Approach. (C). 1989. 90.00 (0-89771-367-2, Pub. by Current Dist) St Mut.

Majupuria. Wildlife, National Park & Reserve of Nepal. 1997. pap. 174.00 (0-7855-7507-3, Pub. by Ratna Pustak Bhandar) St Mut.

Majupuria, T. L. & Kumar, Rohit, eds. Gods & Goddesses: An Illustrated Account of Hindu, Buddhist, Tantric, Hybrid & Tibetan Deities. (Illus.). 1994. pap. 95.00 (0-7855-0448-6, Pub. by Ratna Pustak Bhandar) St Mut.

Majupuria, Trilok C. Glimpses of Nepal. (Illus.). 327p. 1980. pap. 19.95 (0-686-92276-X); pap. text 21.95 (0-686-98496-X) Asia Bk Corp.

Majupuria, Trilok C. & Gupta, S. P. Nepal: The Land of Festivals (Religious, Cultural, Social & Historical Festivals) (Illus.). 152p. 1981. 14.95 (0-940500-83-3) Asia Bk Corp.

Majure, Dave. Direct Hit: Real-World Insights & Common Sense Advice from a Direct Marketing Pro. 250p. 1994. text 22.95 (1-55738-821-0, Irwn Prfssnl) McGraw-Hill Prof.

Majure, Janet. AIDS. LC 97-44139. (Diseases & People Ser.). 128p. (YA). (gr. 6 up). 1998. lib. bdg. 20.95 (0-7660-1182-8) Enslow Pubs.

***Majure, Janet.** Breast Cancer. LC 99-32153. (Diseases & People Ser.). (Illus.). 128p. (gr. 6 up). 2000. lib. bdg. 20.95 (0-7660-1312-X) Enslow Pubs.

Majure, Janet. Elections. LC 95-52154. (Overview Ser.). (Illus.). (J). 1996. lib. bdg. 22.45 (1-56006-174-X) Lucent Bks.

— Recipes Worth Sharing. (Illus.). 192p. (Orig.). 1997. pap. 14.95 (0-9656695-0-5) Breadbasket Pub.

Majus, J. & Spaniol, Otto, eds. Data Networks with Satellites. (Informatik-Fachberechte Ser.: Vol. 67). 251p. 1983. pap. 32.00 (0-387-12311-3) Spr-Verlag.

Majzels, Robert. City of Forgetting: A Novel. LC 98-138692. 168p. 1998. pap. text 16.95 (1-55128-045-0, Pub. by Mercury Bk) LPC InBook.

Majzels, Robert, tr. see Daigle, France.

Majzlik, Linda. Party Food for Vegetarians. 1994. pap. 10.95 (1-897766-04-1, Pub. by Jon Carpenter) Paul & Co Pubs.

***Majzlik, Linda.** Vegan Barbecues & Buffets. 96p. 2000. pap. 9.95 (1-897766-55-6, Pub. by Jon Carpenter) Paul & Co Pubs.

— Vegan Dinner Parties. (Illus.). 96p. 1999. pap. 9.95 (1-897766-46-7, Pub. by Jon Carpenter) Paul & Co Pubs.

Mak. Gene Knockout Factsbook. LC 98-86602. 424p. 1998. pap. text. write for info. (0-12-466045-2) Acad Pr.

Mak, jt. auth. see Sheldon.

Mak, Dayton & Kennedy, Charles S. American Ambassadors in a Troubled World: Interviews with Senior Diplomats, 303. LC 92-7398. (Contributions in Political Science Ser.: No. 303). 248p. 1992. 59.95 (0-313-28558-6, MKR, Greenwood Pr) Greenwood.

Mak, Felice L. & Nadelson, Carol C., eds. The International Review of Psychiatry, Vol. 2. LC 96-13648. 494p. 1996. text 59.95 (0-88048-992-8, 8992) Am Psychiatric.

***Mak, Geert.** Amsterdam. LC 00-39707. (Illus.). 304p. 2000. 29.95 (0-674-00331-4) HUP.

Mak, Grace C. & Beauchamp, Edward R., eds. Women, Education, & Development in Asia: Cross-National Perspectives. LC 96-16773. (Reference Books in International Education: Vol. 33). (Illus.). 288p. 1996. text 56.00 (0-8153-0795-0, H825) Garland.

Mak, Grace C., jt. auth. see Postiglione, Gerard A.

Mak, J. N., jt. ed. see Gill, Bates.

Mak, James, et al, eds. Japan: Why It Works, Why It Doesn't: Economics in Everyday Life. LC 97-21306. (Illus.). 240p. 1997. pap. text 20.00 (0-8248-1967-5) UH Pr.

Mak, Kam. Chinatown. 32p. (gr. k-3). 15.95 (0-06-029190-7); pap. 5.95 (0-06-443732-9); lib. bdg. 15.89 (0-06-029191-5) HarpC.

Mak, Ricardo K. The Future of the Non-Western World in the Social Sciences of 19th Century England. LC 98-51085. (European University Studies: No. 815). 236p. 1998. pap. text 39.95 (0-8204-3619-4) P Lang Pubng.

***Mak, Ricardo K. S. & Paau, Danny S. L., eds.** Sino-German Relations Since 1800: Multidisciplinary Explorations. 298p. 2000. pap. text 47.95 (0-8204-4373-5) P Lang Pubng.

***Mak, Ricardo King Sang.** The Future of the Non-Western World in the Social Sciences of 19th Century England. (European University Studies: Vol. 815). 236p. 1999. pap. 39.95 (3-631-33697-7) P Lang Pubng.

Mak, Ronald L. Writing Compilers & Interpreters: An Applied Approach Using C++ 2nd ed. LC 96-5938. 864p. 1996. pap. 59.99 (0-471-11353-0) Wiley.

Mak, T. W. The T-Cell Receptors. LC 87-38495. (Illus.). 254p. (C). 1988. text 79.50 (0-306-42708-7, Kluwer Plenum) Kluwer Academic.

***Mak, Tak W.** Gene Knockout Factsbook. LC 98-86602. (Factsbook Ser.). 1998. pap. text 69.95 (0-12-466044-4) Acad Pr.

— The Gene Knockout Factsbook. LC 98-86602. (Illus.). 1998. write for info. (0-12-466046-0) Acad Pr.

Mak, Tak W. Handbook of Immune Response Genes. LC 97-48244. (Illus.). 408p. (C). 1998. text 95.00 (0-306-45647-8, Kluwer Plenum) Kluwer Academic.

Mak, Thomas C. & Zhou, Gong-Du. Crystallography in Modern Chemistry: A Resource Book of Crystal Structures. LC 91-23395. 1323p. 1992. 240.00 (0-471-54702-6) Wiley.

An Asterisk (*) at the beginning of an entry indicates that the title is appearing for the first time.

Mak, Thomas C. & Zhou, Gong-Du. Crystallography in Modern Chemistry: A Resource Book of Crystal Structures. LC 91-23395. 1323p. 1997. pap. 89.95 (*0-471-18438-1*, Wiley-Interscience) Wiley.

***Maka, Gwen.** Riding with Ghosts. 272p. 2000. pap. 14.95 (*1-903070-00-7*, Pub. by Travellerseye Ltd) Midpt Trade.

Makabe, Tomoko. The Canadian Sansei. LC 98-167183. (Illus.). 224p. 1998. text 45.00 (*0-8020-4179-5*); pap. text 19.95 (*0-8020-8038-3*) U of Toronto Pr.

— Japanese Picture Brides: Japanese Women in Canada. Merken, Kathleen, tr. (Illus.). 200p. 1995. pap. 24.95 (*0-919045-68-5*) U of Toronto Pr.

Makadon, Harvey, jt. ed. see Libman, Howard.

Makaev, E. A. The Language of the Oldest Runic Inscriptions: A Linguistic & Historical-Philological Analysis. Meredig, John & Antonsen, Elmer H., trs. from RUS. (Filologisk-Filosofiska Ser.: Vol. 21). 137p. (Orig.). 1996. pap. 39.50 (*91-7402-259-8*) Coronet Bks.

Makaira, Robert. The Institute. LC 82-16393. 1989. pap. 14.95 (*0-87949-231-7*) Ashley Bks.

Makanin, Vladimir. Baize-Covered Table with Decanter. Tait, Arch, tr. from RUS. 128p. (Orig.). 1996. pap. 10.95 (*0-930523-66-0*) Readers Intl.

— Escape Hatch & The Long Road Ahead: Two Novellas. Szporluk, Mary A., tr. from RUS. LC 94-7869. 1996. 24.00 (*0-87501-110-1*) Ardis Pubs.

— The Loss: A Novella & Two Short Stories. Lindsey, Byron, tr. from ENG. LC 98-15526. (Writings from an Unbound Europe Ser.). 136p. 1998. text 44.95 (*0-8101-1639-1*); pap. text 14.95 (*0-8101-1640-5*, Marlboro) Northwestern U Pr.

Makankov, V., et al. Nonlinear Evolution Equations. 504p. 1993. text 121.00 (*981-02-1448-0*) World Scientific Pub.

Makanna, Philip. Ghosts of the Skies: Aviation in the Second World War. (Illus.). 160p. 1995. 40.00 (*0-8118-0742-8*) Chronicle Bks.

Makansi, Jason, ed. Managing Steam: An Engineering Guide to Industrial, Commercial, & Utility Systems. 224p. 1986. 60.95 (*0-89116-462-6*) Hemisp Pub.

Makapela, Alven. The Problem of Africanity in the Seventh-Day Adventist Church. LC 96-17514. (African Studies: Vol. 42). 448p. 1996. text 109.95 (*0-7734-8969-X*) E Mellen.

Makar-Limanov, S., tr. see Sadovskii, L. E. & Sadovskii, A. L.

Makar, Ragai N. & Bloyer, Christen T. Modern Arabic Literature: A Bibliography. LC 98-22136. (Scarecrow Area Bibliographies Ser.: No. 17). 352p. 1998. 75.00 (*0-8108-3539-8*) Scarecrow.

Makara, jt. auth. see Koike.

Makarczyk. Theory of International Law at the Threshold of the 21st Century. LC 96-54220. 1997. 327.00 (*90-411-0296-5*) Kluwer Law Intl.

Makarczyk, Jerzy. Principles of a New International Economic Order: A Study of International Law in the Making. (C). 1988. lib. bdg. 150.50 (*90-247-3746-X*) Kluwer Academic.

Makarczyk, Jerzy, ed. Essays in International Law in Honour of Judge Manfred Lachs. 1984. lib. bdg. 270.00 (*90-247-3071-6*) Kluwer Academic.

Makarenko, A. S. Collective Family: A Handbook for Russian Parents. Orig. Title: Book for Parents. 1990. 16.50 (*0-8446-2515-9*) Peter Smith.

Makarets, M. V. & Reshetnyak. Ordinary Differential Equations & Calculus of Variations. 384p. 1995. text 86.00 (*981-02-2191-6*) World Scientific Pub.

Makarim, Sami N. Druze Faith. LC 73-19819. 168p. 1974. 25.00 (*0-88206-003-1*) Caravan Bks.

Makarim, Sami N., tr. see Ya'qub, Abu A.

Makarinus, Jorg. Ernst Schroeder 1928-1989: Leben und Werk. (GER., Illus.). 328p. 1996. text 113.00 (*90-5705-034-X*, Verlag Kunst) Gordon & Breach.

Makarius, Theodore F. Operation of the Offset Press. (Illus.). 327p. (C). 1993. pap. 29.50 (*0-911126-07-4*) Perfect Graphic.

Makaroff, Dmitri, jt. auth. see Duff, Charles.

Makaroskaia, Galina. Museum of History & Art in Zagorsk. (Illus.). 200p. (C). 1986. text 100.00 (*0-7855-5852-7*, Pub. by Collets) St Mut.

Makarov, A., et al. The Russian Gas Industry. (Illus.). 121p. (C). 1998. pap. text 35.00 (*0-7881-7404-5*) DIANE Pub.

Makarov, B. M., et al. Selected Problems in Real Analysis. LC 92-15594. (Translations of Mathematical Monographs, 0065-9282: Vol. 107). 370p. 1992. text 49.00 (*0-8218-4559-4*, MMONO/107) Am Math.

Makarov, Evgeniis S. Crystal Chemistry of Simple Compounds of Uranium, Thorium, Plutonium, Neptunium. Uvarov, E. B., tr. from RUS. LC 59-14486. 153p. reprint ed. pap. 47.50 (*0-608-10074-9*, 200336600021) Bks Demand.

Makarov, I. & Vinogradskaia, T. Theory of Choice & Decision Making. 328p. (C). 1987. 80.00 (*0-685-46646-9*, Pub. by Collets) St Mut.

Makarov, I. M. Engineering Artificial Intelligence. 1990. 130.00 (*0-89116-963-6*) Hemisp Pub.

Modelling Robotic & Flexible Manufacturing Systems. 1990. 109.00 (*0-89116-964-4*) Hemisp Pub.

Makarov, S. O. Discussions of Questions in Naval Tactics. Hattendorf, John B. & Huges, Wayne P., eds. Bernadou, J. B., tr. LC 90-6279. (Classics of Sea Power Ser.). 320p. 1990. 34.95 (*0-87021-779-8*) Naval Inst Pr.

Makarov, V. & Matveeva, N., eds. Dictionary of Lexical Difficulties Encountered in Literary Texts. 368p. (C). 1989. 60.00 (*0-7855-6674-0*, Pub. by Collets) St Mut.

Makarov, Valery L., et al. Mathematical Economic Theory: Pure & Mixed Types of Economic Mechanisms. LC 94-33657. (Advanced Textbooks in Economics Ser.: Vol. 33). 632p. 1994. 95.00 (*0-444-89443-8*) Elsevier.

Makarova, A. A. Energy Reviews Vol. 5, Pt. 3: Characteristics of Energy Systems Development - Formulating & Implementing an Energy Strategy: Economic Estimates, Vol. 5. (Soviet Technology Reviews Ser.: Section A). 72p. 1991. pap. text 71.00 (*3-7186-5164-5*, Harwood Acad Pubs) Gordon & Breach.

Makarova, A. S. Energy Reviews Vol. 5, Pt. 2: Systems for Management of Energy Development in the U. S. S. R. - Methods for Assessment of Future Energy Development in the U. S. S. R., Vol. 5. (Soviet Technology Reviews Ser.: Section A). iii, 81p. 1991. pap. text 110.00 (*3-7186-5163-7*, Harwood Acad Pubs) Gordon & Breach.

— Energy Reviews Vol. 5, Pt. 5: The Concept of Hierarchy in the Energy Industry, Vol. 5. (Soviet Technology Reviews Ser.: Section A). 85p. 1992. pap. text 112.00 (*3-7186-5217-X*, Harwood Acad Pubs) Gordon & Breach.

Makarova, Lena, ed. see Chapin, Melissa C.

Makarowski, Lou. How to Keep Your C.O.O.L. with Your Kids: Learning to Be Better Parents by Controlling Our Own Lives. LC 95-23049. 224p. (Orig.). 1996. pap. 12.00 (*0-399-51991-2*, Perigee Bks) Berkley Pub.

Makaryk, Irena R., ed. Encyclopedia of Contemporary Literary Theory: Approaches, Scholars, Terms. 576p. 1993. text 150.00 (*0-8020-5914-7*); pap. text 39.95 (*0-8020-6860-X*) U of Toronto Pr.

Makas, E. The Development of the MIDS-AI/AN: The American Indian - Alaska Native Version of the Modified Issues in Disability Scale. 38p. 1995. pap. text. write for info. (*1-888557-50-8*) No Ariz Univ.

Makasheva, R. K. The Pea. Sharma, B. R., tr. from RUS. 275p. (C). 1984. text 97.00 (*90-6191-431-0*, Pub. by A A Balkema) Ashgate Pub Co.

Makau, Josina M. & Arnett, Ronald C., eds. Communication Ethics in an Age of Diversity. 240p. 1996. text 29.95 (*0-252-02269-6*); pap. text 14.95 (*0-252-06571-9*) U of Ill Pr.

Makay. Management. 5th ed. (C). Date not set. write for info. (*0-395-77771-2*) HM.

Makay, John. Public Speaking: Theory into Practice. 3rd ed. 500p. 1997. 36.95 (*0-7872-3247-5*) Kendall-Hunt.

Makay, John J. Public Speaking: Theory & Practice. 2nd ed. (C). 1995. pap. text, teacher ed. 47.75 (*0-15-503062-0*) Harcourt Coll Pubs.

— Public Speaking for Analysis. (C). 1995. pap. text 30.00 (*0-15-503304-2*) Harcourt Coll Pubs.

— Public Speeches for Analysis I. 2nd ed. (C). 1995. 139.00 (*0-15-502117-6*) Harcourt Coll Pubs.

Makay, John J., ed. Free Speech Yearbook, Vol. 34. Vol. 34. 208p. 1997. 49.95 (*0-8093-2151-3*); pap. 19.95 (*0-8093-2152-1*) S Ill U Pr.

— Free Speech Yearbook, 1995. 208p. (C). 1996. pap. 19.95 (*0-8093-2049-5*) S Ill U Pr.

— Free Speech Yearbook, 1995, Vol. 33. 208p. (C). 1996. 49.95 (*0-8093-2048-7*) S Ill U Pr.

Makay, Leigh. Communicating Today: A Student Workbook. 2nd ed. 346p. (C). 1997. pap. text 20.95 (*0-7872-3463-X*, 41346301) Kendall-Hunt.

— Practicing Public Speaking: A Student Coursebook. 288p. (C). 1994. per. 18.36 (*0-8403-9368-7*) Kendall-Hunt.

— Public Speaking: Theory into Practice, a Coursebook. 256p. (C). 1995. pap. text, per. 33.95 (*0-7872-1780-8*) Kendall-Hunt.

***Makboul, R.** Bartending in One Day: An Exceptional Method for Becoming an Exceptional Bartender. deluxe ed. Jerrick, Nancy, ed. (Illus.). 192p. 1999. 119.95 (*0-9671284-0-4*) Makboul Pubg.

Makdisi. Beirut Fragments: A War Memoir. 1999. pap. 13.95 (*0-89255-245-X*, Pub. by Persea Bks) Norton.

Makdisi, ed. see Qudamas, Ibn.

Makdisi, George. History & Politics in Eleventh-Century Baghdad. (Collected Studies: No. CS 336). (ENG & FRE.). 320p. 1991. text 113.95 (*0-86078-289-1*, Pub. by Variorum) Ashgate Pub Co.

— Ibn 'Aqil: Religion & Culture in Classical Islam. LC 98-172873. 288p. 1998. 60.00 (*0-7486-0960-1*, Pub. by Edinburgh U Pr) Col U Pr.

— Religion, Law & Learning in Classical Islam. (Collected Studies: No. CS 347). 336p. 1991. text 99.95 (*0-86078-301-4*, Pub. by Variorum) Ashgate Pub Co.

— The Rise of Colleges: Institutions of Learning in Islam & the West. 377p. 1982. 85.00 (*0-85224-375-8*, Pub. by Edinburgh U Pr) Col U Pr.

— The Rise of Humanism in Classical Islam & the Christian West. 448p. 1990. 85.00 (*0-85224-630-7*, Pub. by Edinburgh U Pr) Col U Pr.

— The Rise of Humanism in Classical Islam & the Christian West. 450p. 1996. 49.50 (*0-614-21238-3*, 1083) Kazi Pubns.

Makdisi, Jean S. Beirut Fragments: A War Memoir. LC 89-26533. 256p. 1990. 19.95 (*0-89255-150-X*) Persea Bks.

— Beirut Fragments: A War Memoir. LC 89-26533. 256p. 1991. reprint ed. pap. 9.95 (*0-89255-164-X*) Persea Bks.

***Makdisi, John.** Estates in Land & Future Interests: Problems & Answers. 3rd ed. LC 98-47779. 224p. 1999. pap. text 26.95 (*0-7355-0035-5*) Panel Pubs.

Makdisi, John. Introduction to the Study of Law: Cases & Materials. LC 90-512. 325p. 1990. pap. 29.00 (*0-87084-551-9*) Anderson Pub Co.

***Makdisi, John.** Introduction to the Study of Law: Cases & Materials. 2nd ed. (C). 2000. pap. write for info. (*1-58360-756-0*) Anderson Pub Co.

Makdisi, Saree. Romantic Imperialism: Universal Empire & the Culture of Modernity. LC 97-20599. (Studies in Romanticism: Vol. 27). 266p. (C). 1998. pap. text 18.95 (*0-521-58604-6*) Cambridge U Pr.

Makdisi, Saree & Casarino, Cesare. Marxism Beyond Marxism. 290p. (C). 1995. pap. 21.99 (*0-415-91443-4*) Routledge.

Makdisi, Saree & Casarino, Cesare, eds. Marxism Beyond Marxism. 290p. (C). (gr. 13). 1996. 75.00 (*0-415-91442-6*) Routledge.

***Makdisi, Ussama S.** The Culture of Sectarianism. LC 99-47861. 302p. 2000. pap. 22.00 (*0-520-21846-9*, Pub. by U CA Pr) Cal Prin Full Svc.

Makechnie, George K. Seventy Stories about Boston University, 1923-1993: A Memoir. LC 93-4005. 1993. write for info. (*0-87270-104-2*) U Pr of Amer.

Makedon, F. & Rebelsky, Samuel A., eds. Electronic Multimedia Publishing: Enabling Technologies & Authoring Issues. LC 97-52233. 632p. 1998. 94.00 (*0-7923-8108-4*) Kluwer Academic.

Makedon, F., jt. auth. see Owen, Charles B.

Makedon, Fillia, jt. ed. see Gloor, Peter A.

Makeeev, Boris N., jt. auth. see Meconis, Charles A.

***Makeen, Makeen Fouad.** Copyright in a Global Information Society: The Scope of Copyright Protection under International, U. S., U. K. & French Law. LC 00-25062. (Studies in Law). 2000. write for info. (*90-411-9786-9*) Kluwer Law Intl.

Makeham, jt. auth. see Abbott.

Makeham, J. P. & Malcolm, L. R. The Farming Game Now. 2nd ed. (Illus.). 411p. (C). 1993. text 85.00 (*0-521-40452-5*); pap. text 30.95 (*0-521-42679-0*) Cambridge U Pr.

Makeham, John. Name & Actuality in Early Chinese Thought. LC 93-31922. (SUNY Series in Chinese Philosophy & Culture). 286p. (C). 1994. pap. text 19.95 (*0-7914-1984-3*) State U NY Pr.

— Name & Actuality in Early Chinese Thought. LC 93-31922. (SUNY Series in Chinese Philosophy & Culture). 286p. (C). 1994. text 59.50 (*0-7914-1983-5*) State U NY Pr.

Makek, M. Clinical Pathology of Fibro-Osteo-Cemental Lesions in the Cranio-Facial & Jaw Bones. (Illus.). x, 230p. 1983. 138.50 (*3-8055-3704-2*) S Karger.

Makela, Benjamin R., jt. ed. see Haskins, Mark.

***Makela, Casey.** Making Natural Milk Soap. LC 99-34998. 1999. pap. 3.95 (*1-58017-220-2*) Random.

Makela, Casey. Milk-Based Soaps: Making Natural, Skin-Nourishing Soap. Balmuth, Deborah, ed. LC 97-30670. (Herbal Body Ser.). (Illus.). 96p. 1997. pap. 12.95 (*0-88266-984-2*, Storey Pub) Storey Bks.

Makela, Casey & Booth, Nancy M. Perfumes, Spashes & Colognes: Discovering & Crafting Your Personal Fragrances. Balmuth, Deborah, ed. LC 97-26374. (Herbal Body Ser.). (Illus.). 171p. 1997. pap. 14.95 (*0-88266-985-0*, Storey Pub) Storey Bks.

Makela, Chuck. After You've Tried Everything Else: A "More Excellent Way" to Freedom from Addictions. 32p. (Orig.). 1987. pap. 1.00 (*0-9618532-0-4*) Just Pub Hse.

Makela, Constance E. Iron Mining Fun Book for Children: Featuring Orville Ore. (Illus.). 44p. (Orig.). (J). (gr. k-6). 1982. pap. 2.00 (*0-9608686-0-7*) Happy Thoughts & Rainbow.

Makela, JoAnne. Sidedoor, Vol. 6. (Northfield Women Poets Chapbook Ser.). 24p. 1992. 4.00 (*0-9614314-6-6*) Heywood Pr.

Makela, Klaus, et al. Alcoholics Anonymous As a Mutual-Help Movement: A Study in Eight Societies. LC 95-42146. 322p. 1996. 46.00 (*0-299-15000-3*); pap. 19.95 (*0-299-15004-6*) U of Wis Pr.

Makela, Laurie, jt. auth. see Makela, Scott.

Makela, M. M., et al. Evolutionary Algorithms in Engineering & Computer Science. LC 99-24638. 483p. 1999. 125.00 (*0-471-99902-4*) Wiley.

Makela, M. M., jt. auth. see Neittaanmaki, Pekka.

Makela, Scott & Makela, Laurie. Whereishere: A Real & Virtual Book. Blackwell, Lewis, ed. (Illus.). 192p. 1998. pap. 39.95 (*3-927258-87-3*) Gingko Press.

Makely, Sherry. Health Care Worker's Primer on Professionalism. 2nd ed. LC 99-17379. (Illus.). 170p. 1999. pap. text 26.60 (*0-8359-5483-8*, Prentice Hall) P-H.

— Multiskilled Health Care Workers: Issues & Approaches to Cross-Training. Christian, Lana, ed. 288p. 1997. pap. 34.95 (*0-9652954-3-5*) Pine Ridge Publns.

Makely, Sherry & Christian, Lana. Exploring the Jungle: A Teacher's Guide to Preparing for Health Careers. (Illus.). 38p. 1996. pap. 12.95 (*0-9652954-2-7*) Pine Ridge Publns.

— It's a Jungle Out There! An Insider's Outlook on Jobs in Health Care. (Illus.). 55p. 1996. spiral bd. 14.95 (*0-9652954-0-0*) Pine Ridge Publns.

Makely, Sherry, jt. auth. see Christian, Lana.

Makem, Tommy. Tommy Makems Secret Ireland. LC 97-7601. 1997. text 21.95 (*0-312-15675-8*) St Martin.

Maken, Neil. Hand-Cranked Phonographs: It All Started with Edison. (Illus.). 87p. 1993. pap. 15.95 (*0-9640687-1-0*); lib. bdg. 25.95 (*0-9640687-0-2*) Promar Pubng.

Makens, James C. The Marketing Plan Workbook. 240p. (C). 1988. pap. text 24.95 (*0-13-558537-6*) P-H.

***Makepeace.** Cps Family Violence Rdr V1. 1998. pap. 42.81 (*0-07-233304-9*) McGraw.

Makepeace. Family Violence, 2. 2nd ed. 1999. pap. 40.94 (*0-07-234887-9*) McGraw.

— Family Violence. . .Readings in the Social Sciences & Professions. (C). 1995. pap. text 52.00 (*0-07-039774-0*) McGraw.

Makepeace, C. Manchester. LC 97-130405. (Best of Britain in Old Photographs Ser.). (Illus.). 128p. 1998. pap. 15.95 (*0-7509-1204-9*, Pub. by Sutton Pub Ltd) Intl Pubs Mktg.

Makepeace, Chris. Ephemera. 1985. text 59.95 (*0-566-03439-5*, Pub. by Gower) Ashgate Pub Co.

Makepeace, Joanna. The Baron's Bride. large type ed. (Mills & Boon Large Print Ser.). 350p. 1998. 24.99 (*0-263-15529-3*, Pub. by Mills & Boon) Ulverscroft.

— Crown Hostage. large type ed. 350p. 1995. 23.99 (*0-263-14189-6*, Pub. by Mills & Boon) Ulverscroft.

— Daughter of Isis. large type ed. LC 96-45046. 236p. 1997. pap. write for info. (*0-7838-2017-8*, G K Hall Lrg Type) Mac Lib Ref.

— The Devil's Mark. large type ed. 350p. 1995. 23.99 (*0-263-14427-5*, Pub. by Mills & Boon) Ulverscroft.

— Divine Son of Ra. large type ed. LC 96-45130. 1997. pap. 21.95 (*0-7838-2016-X*, G K Hall Lrg Type) Mac Lib Ref.

Makepeace, Joanna. Dragon's Court. large type ed. 1994. 25.99 (*0-263-15996-5*, Pub. by Mills & Boon) Ulverscroft.

Makepeace, Joanna. King's Pawn. large type ed. (Mills & Boon Large Print Ser.). 350p. 1997. 23.99 (*0-263-14899-8*) Ulverscroft.

— Love's Raging Fires. large type ed. LC 94-19598. 597p. 1995. pap. 19.95 (*0-7862-0300-5*) Thorndike Pr.

— My Lord Enemy. large type ed. (Large Print Ser.). 512p. 1997. 27.99 (*0-7089-3670-9*) Ulverscroft.

— Stolen Heiress. large type ed. (Mills & Boon Large Print Ser.). 350p. 1997. 23.99 (*0-263-15092-5*) Ulverscroft.

Makepeace, Margaret, ed. Trade on the Guinea Coast, 1657-1666: The Correspondence of the English East India Company. LC 91-34443. (African Primary Texts Ser.: No. 5). 158p. (Orig.). 1991. pap. 26.00 (*0-942615-11-5*) U Wis African Stud.

Makepeace, Margaret, jt. auth. see Baladouni, Vahe.

Makepeace-Warne, Antony. Brassey's Companion to the British Army. (Illus.). 416p. 1995. 39.95 (*1-85753-175-2*, Pub. by Brasseys) Brasseys.

— Brassey's Companion to the British Army. 1998. pap. text 34.95 (*1-85753-287-2*, Pub. by Brasseys) Brasseys.

Maker. College Reading with the Active Critical Thinking Method: Book 1. 5th ed. LC 99-42551. (Developmental Study/Stdy Skill). 1999. pap. 31.50 (*0-534-51850-8*) Wadsworth Pub.

— College Reading with the Active Critical Thinking Method: Book 2. 6th ed. LC 99-25013. (Developmental Study/Stdy Skill). 1999. pap. 32.25 (*0-534-51851-6*) Wadsworth Pub.

Maker, C. June, ed. Critical Issues in Gifted Education Vol. I: Defensible Programs for the Gifted. LC 86-17345. (Critical Issues in Gifted Education Ser.). 357p. 1986. text 39.00 (*0-89079-194-5*, 2069) PRO-ED.

— Critical Issues in Gifted Education Vol. III: Programs for the Gifted in Regular Classroom, Vol. III. LC 92-39. (Critical Issues in Gifted Education Ser.). 480p. (C). 1993. text 41.00 (*0-89079-549-5*, 2071) PRO-ED.

Maker, C. June & Nielson, Aleene B. Curriculum Development & Teaching Strategies for Gifted Learners. 2nd rev. ed. LC 95-9020. 345p. (C). 1996. text 39.00 (*0-89079-631-9*, 7321) PRO-ED.

— Teaching Models in Education of the Gifted. 2nd ed. (C). 1995. text 41.00 (*0-89079-609-2*, 6802) PRO-ED.

Maker, C. June & Schiever, Shirley W., eds. Critical Issues in Gifted Education, Vol. II: Defensible Programs for Cultural & Ethnic Minorities. LC 88-992. (Critical Issues in Gifted Education Ser.). 368p. 1989. text 39.00 (*0-89079-184-8*, 2072) PRO-ED.

Maker, C. June, et al. Nurturing Giftedness in Young Children. LC 96-20045. 58p. 1996. pap. text 15.00 (*0-86586-282-6*, P5156) Coun Exc Child.

Maker, Janet. Academic Reading with Academic Critical Thinking. (Developmental Study/Study Skills Ser.). 1995. pap., student ed. 13.50 (*0-534-22023-1*) Wadsworth Pub.

Maker, Janet & Lenier, Minnette. Academic Reading with Active Critical Thinking. 310p. (C). 1995. pap. 27.50 (*0-534-22020-7*) Wadsworth Pub.

— College Reading, Bk. 2. 4th ed. 471p. (C). 1992. pap. 23.75 (*0-534-17082-X*) Wadsworth Pub.

— College Reading with Active Critical Thinking, Bk. 1. 4th ed. (C). 1997. pap. text 24.95 (*0-317-32174-9*) Wadsworth Pub.

— College Reading with Active Critical Thinking, Bk. 2. 5th ed. LC 96-8419. (Developmental Study/Study Skills Ser.: Bk. II). (C). 1996. pap. 28.50 (*0-534-51599-1*) Wadsworth Pub.

— Keys to a Powerful Vocabulary, Level 1. 3rd ed. LC 93-10922. 278p. (C). 1993. pap. text 41.00 (*0-13-668948-5*) Prntice Hall Bks.

Maker, Janet, jt. auth. see Chesneylind.

Maker, Janet, jt. auth. see Lenier, Minnette.

***Maker, Lenier.** College Reading with Active Critical Thinking Method, Bk. 3. 2nd ed. (Developmental Study/Stdy Skill). 2000. 31.00 (*0-534-51878-8*) Wadsworth Pub.

Maker, William. Philosophy Without Foundations: Rethinking Hegel. LC 93-42703. (SUNY Series in Hegelian Studies). 298p. (C). 1994. text 59.50 (*0-7914-2099-X*); pap. text 19.95 (*0-7914-2100-7*) State U NY Pr.

Maker, William, ed. Hegel & Aesthetics. LC 00-27467. (C). 2000. text 59.50 (*0-7914-4551-8*); pap. text 19.95 (*0-7914-4552-6*) State U NY Pr.

Makey, Miller S., et al. How to Fly a Kite: A Kiteflier's Manual. (Illus.). 66p. (Orig.). 1992. pap. 3.00 (*0-9631175-9-9*) Am Kite MD.

Makgill, Jacques & Bellenden, Jean. Discours Particulier D'Escosse. Thomson, Thomas, ed. LC 72-172710. (Bannatyne Club, Edinburgh. Publications: No. 5). reprint ed. 27.50 (*0-404-52706-X*) AMS Pr.

***Makhan, Rosemary.** Floral Abundance: Projects N Applique. (Illus.). 80p. 2000. pap. 22.95 (*1-56477-325-6*) Martingale & Co.

— Rose Sampler Supreme. LC 99-51339. (Illus.). 80p. 1999. pap. 22.95 (*1-56477-316-7*, B451, Pub. by Martingale & Co) F & W Pubns Inc.

M

Makhankov, Vladimir G. Soliton Phenomenology. (Mathematics & Its Applications, Soviet Ser.). 464p. (C). 1990. text 268.50 (90-277-2830-5) Kluwer Academic.

Makhankov, Vladimir G., et al, eds. Solitons & Applications. 450p. (C). 1990. text 130.00 (981-02-0130-3) World Scientific Pub.

Makhankov, Vladimir G. & Pashaev, O. K., eds. Nonlinear Evolution Equations & Dynamical Systems, '90. (Research Reports in Physics). (Illus.). 240p. 1991. 75.95 (0-387-53294-3) Spr-Verlag.

Makhankov, Vladimir G., et al. The Skyrme Model: Fundamentals, Methods, Applications. LC 92-28266. (Series in Nuclear & Particle Physics). 1993. 107.95 (0-387-54905-6) Spr-Verlag.

Makharita, R. M., jt. ed. see El-Baz, Farouk.

Makheeja, R. D., jt. auth. see Bhandari, M. C.

Makhija, Anju, et al. Freedom & Fissures: An Anthology of Sindhi Partition Poetry LC 98-908546. xxi, 75 p. 1998. write for info. (81-260-0588-2, Pub. by Rabindra Bhawn) S Asia.

Makhijani, Annie, jt. auth. see Makhijani, Arjun.

Makhijani, Arjun. From Global Capitalism to Economic Justice: An Inquiry into the Elimination of Systemic Poverty, Violence & Environmental Destruction in the World Economy. LC 91-36571. 192p. (Orig.). 1992. pap. 14.95 (0-945257-41-4) Apex Pr.

M

Makhijani, Arjun, et al, eds. Nuclear Wastelands: A Global Guide to Nuclear Weapons Production & Its Health & Environmental Effects. LC 95-945. 666p. 1995. 65.00 (0-262-13307-5) MIT Pr.

***Makhijani, Arjun, et al, eds.** Nuclear Wastelands: A Global Guide to Nuclear Weapons Production & Its Health & Environmental Effects. (Illus.). 696p. (C). 2000. reprint ed. pap. 42.00 (0-262-63204-7) MIT Pr.

Makhijani, Arjun & Gurney, Kevin R. Mending the Ozone Hole: Science, Technology & Policy. (Illus.). 360p. 1995. 44.00 (0-262-13308-3) MIT Pr.

Makhijani, Arjun & Makhijani, Annie. Fissile Materials in a Glass, Darkly: Technical & Policy Aspects of the Disposition of Plutonium & High Enriched Uranium. 2nd ed. LC 95-75104. (Illus.). 126p. (Orig.). 1995. pap. write for info. (0-9645168-0-2) IEER.

— Yaderny Materialy Skvoz' Tuskoe Steklo? Tekhnicheskie i Politicheskie Aspekty Utilizatsii Plutonia i Vysokoobogaschennogo Urana. (RUS., Illus.). 132p. (Orig.). 1996. pap. write for info. (0-9645168-1-0) IEER.

Makhijani, Arjun & Saleska, Scott. High-Level Dollars, Low-Level Sense: A Critique of Present Policy for the Management of Long-Lived Radioactive Wastes & Discussion of an Alternative Approach. 144p. (Orig.). 1992. pap. 12.95 (0-945257-42-2) Apex Pr.

— The Nuclear Power Deception: U. S. Nuclear Mythology from Electricity "Too Cheap to Meter" to "Inherently Safe" Reactors. LC 98-36673. (Illus.). 240p. 1999. 38.50 (0-945257-75-9); pap. 17.50 (0-945257-92-9) Apex Pr.

Makhlouf, Gabriel M. & Schultz, Stanley G., eds. Handbook of Physiology Sect. 6, Vol. II: The Gastrointestinal System: Neural & Endocrine Biology. (American Physiological Society Book). (Illus.). 736p. 1989. text 195.00 (0-19-520795-5) OUP.

Makhno, Nestor. The Struggle Against the State & Other Essays. Skirda, Alexandre, tr. from RUS. 128p. (Orig.). 1996. pap. 9.95 (1-873176-78-3, AK Pr San Fran) AK Pr Dist.

Makhoul, John, jt. auth. see Kazimi, Mujid S.

Makhult, Mihaly. Machine Support Design Based on Vibration Calculus. 136p. 1977. 60.00 (963-05-1150-9, Pub. by Akade Kiado) St Mut.

Makhviladze, T. M., ed. Lithography in Microelectronics. (Proceedings of the Institute of General Physics of the Academy of Sciences of the U. S. S. R. Ser.: Vol. 8). 207p. 1989. text 165.00 (0-941743-30-6) Nova Sci Pubs.

Makhzoumi, Jala & Pungetti, Gloria. Ecological Landscape Design & Planning: The Mediterranean Context. LC 98-39233. 1999. pap. 60.00 (0-419-23250-8, E & FN Spon) Routledge.

Maki. Finite Mathematics. 3rd ed. 1989. text, teacher ed. 47.18 (0-07-039752-X) McGraw.

— Writing in Organizations. 1986. teacher ed. 21.56 (0-07-030362-2) McGraw.

Maki, A., jt. auth. see Dickson, K.

***Maki, Alan.** A Choice to Cherish. 160p. 2000. 14.99 (0-8054-2338-9) Broadman.

Maki, Alan, jt. auth. see Smith, Gary.

Maki, Alan, jt. auth. see Smith, Gary R.

Maki, Arthur G. & Wells, Joseph S. New Wavenumber Calibration Tables from Heterodyne Frequency Measurements. (Illus.). 62p. (Orig.). (C). 1992. pap. text 30.00 (1-56806-136-6) DIANE Pub.

— Wavenumber Calibration Tables from Heterodynes Frequency Measurements. (Illus.). 654p. (C). 1997. reprint ed. pap. text 65.00 (0-7881-3784-0) DIANE Pub.

Maki, Daniel & Thompson, Maynard. Finite Mathematics. 4th ed. (C). 1995. pap. text, student ed. 26.25 (0-07-039767-8) McGraw.

***Maki, Daniel P.** Finite Mathematics. 4th ed. (Illus.). 1999. pap. 52.08 (0-07-228866-3) McGraw.

Maki, Daniel P. Finite Mathematics. 5th ed. 2001. 49.50 (0-07-232572-0) McGraw.

Maki, Daniel P. & Thompson, Maynard. Finite Mathematics. 3rd ed. (C). 1989. text 55.25 (0-07-039751-1) McGraw.

— Finite Mathematics. 4th ed. LC 94-48013. 656p. (C). 1995. 69.06 (0-07-039763-5) McGraw.

Maki, Dennis R. & Riggar, T. F., eds. Rehabilitation Counseling: Profession & Practice. LC 96-46426. (Springer Rehabilitation Ser.: Vol. 11). (Illus.). 392p. 1997. 46.95 (0-8261-9510-5) Springer Pub.

Maki, Fumihiko, et al. Fumihiko Maki: Selected Buildings & Projects. LC 97-3063. (Illus.). 288p. 1997. 60.00 (1-56898-108-2); pap. 40.00 (1-56898-109-0) Princeton Arch.

Maki, Fumihiko, jt. auth. see Bognar, Botond.

Maki, John M., ed. Japan's Commission on the Constitution: The Final Report. LC 80-50869. (Asian Law Ser.: No. 7). 424p. 1980. 40.00 (0-295-95767-0) U of Wash Pr.

Maki, Ken. Macintosh Revelations. 2nd ed. LC 97-37449. 640p. 1998. pap., pap. text 44.99 incl. cd-rom (0-471-19563-4) Wiley.

Maki, Masao. Dr. Fritz Phenomenon: In Search of Brazil's Quantum Surgeon. (Illus.). 160p. 1998. pap. 15.95 (1-56931-297-4, Cadence Bks) Viz Commns Inc.

— Spiritual Adventures of a Sushi Chef. (Illus.). 150p. 1997. pap. 12.95 (1-56931-218-4, Cadence Bks) Viz Commns Inc.

Maki, Mitchell T. & Berthold, S. Megan. Achieving the Impossible Dream: How Japanese Americans Obtained Redress. LC 98-58016. (Asian American Experience Ser.). (Illus.). 309p. 1999. pap. 22.50 (0-252-06764-9) U of Ill Pr.

Maki, Mitchell T., et al. Achieving the Impossible Dream: How Japanese Americans Obtained Redress. LC 98-58016. (Asian American Experience Ser.). 352p. 1999. 49.95 (0-252-02458-3) U of Ill Pr.

Maki, P. & Schilling, C. Writing in Organizations: Purposes, Strategies & Processes. 416p. (C). 1987. pap. text 37.74 (0-07-030361-4) McGraw.

Maki, Uskali, et al, eds. Rationality, Institutions, & Economic Methodology. LC 93-6926. (Economics as Social Theory Ser.). 320p. (C). 1993. pap. 32.99 (0-415-09208-6, B0145) Routledge.

***Maki, Wilbur R. & Lichty, Richard W.** Urban Regional Economics: Concepts, Tools, Applications. LC 99-59767. (Illus.). 494p. 2000. 54.95 (0-8138-2679-9) Iowa St U Pr.

Maki, Wilbur R., et al. Alabama's Forest Products Industry: Performance & Contribution to the State's Economy, 1970 to 1980. (Illus.). 28p. 1997. reprint ed. pap. 4.00 (0-89904-767-X, Ecosytems Resrch) Crumb Elbow Pub.

— Oklahoma's Forest Products Industry: Performance & Contribution to the State's Economy, 1970 to 1980. (Illus.). 30p. 1988. reprint ed. pap. 4.00 (0-89904-933-8, Ecosytems Resrch) Crumb Elbow Pub.

Maki, Wilbur R., jt. auth. see Schallau, Con H.

Maki, William S., jt. ed. see Zentall, Thomas R.

Makielski, Kathleen H., jt. auth. see Larrabee, Wayne F., Jr.

Makiko, Nakano, tr. from JPN. Makiko's Diary: A Merchant Wife in 1910 Kyoto. LC 94-39864.Tr. of Meiji Yonjusannen Kyoto. (ENG & JPN., Illus.). 304p. 1995. 45.00 (0-8047-2440-7); pap. 14.95 (0-8047-2441-5) Stanford U Pr.

Makil, Perla Q., jt. ed. see Yengoyan, Aram A.

Makimaa, Julie & Reardon, David. Give Us Love, Not Abortions: Voices of Sexual Assault Victims & Their Children. 108p. (Orig.). 1999. pap. 9.95 (0-9648957-3-0) Acorn Books.

***Makimoto, M. & Yamashita, S.** Microwave Resonators & Filters for Wireless Communication: Theory, Design & Application. LC 00-41924. (Series in Advanced Microelectronics). (Illus.). 2000. write for info. (3-540-67535-3) Spr-Verlag.

Makimoto, Tsugio & Manners, David. Digital Nomad. LC 97-20247. 256p. 1997. pap. 39.95 (0-471-97499-4) Wiley.

***Makin, A. J.** Global Finance & the Macroeconomy. LC 99-54939. 2000. text 65.00 (0-312-23128-8) St Martin.

Makin, Bathsua, jt. auth. see Teague, Frances N.

Makin, Ena, ed. see Puccini, Giacomo.

Makin, Hugh L. J. & Trafford, David James Hamilton. Mass Spectra & GC Data of Steroids: Androgens & Estrogens. (Lopkowski/Ross). 806p. 1999. 690.00 (3-527-29644-1) Wiley.

Makin, Jock. The Big Run. 193p. 1992. 85.00 (1-86302-228-7, Pub. by Natl Bk Dist) St Mut.

Makin, Michael & Toman, Jindrich, eds. On Karel Capek: A Michigan Slavic Colloquium. LC 92-20812. (Materials Ser.: No. 34). 1992. pap. 15.00 (0-930042-71-9) Mich Slavic Pubns.

Makin, Peter. Bunting: The Shaping of His Verse. (Illus.). 390p. 1992. text 100.00 (0-19-811254-8) OUP.

— Pound's Cantos. Rawson, Claude, ed. (Unwin Critical Library). 368p. 1985. pap. text 18.95 (0-04-811002-7) Routledge.

— Pound's Cantos. 352p. 1992. reprint ed. pap. text 15.95 (0-8018-4371-5) Johns Hopkins.

— Provence & Pound. LC 77-76186. 442p. reprint ed. pap. 137.10 (0-7837-4694-6, 204444100003) Bks Demand.

Makin, Peter, et al. Organizations & the Psychological Contract: Managing People at Work. LC 96-7011. 416p. 1996. 75.00 (1-56720-091-5, Quorum Bks) Greenwood.

Makin, Peter, jt. auth. see Bunting, Basil.

Makin, Peter J., et al. Managing People at Work. LC 89-8475. 221p. 1989. 57.95 (0-89930-505-9, MKW/, Quorum Bks) Greenwood.

— Organizations & the Psychological Contract: Managing People at Work. LC 96-7011. 416p. 1996. pap. 32.95 (0-275-95685-7, Praeger Pubs) Greenwood.

Makin, Royce E. You Are the Christ? Nine One-Act Plays. LC 93-12109. 152p. (Orig.). 1993. pap. 10.99 (0-8272-4404-5) Chalice Pr.

Makin, Stephen. Indifference Arguments. LC 93-9799. (Issues in Ancient Philosophy Ser.). (Illus.). 248p. 1993. 64.95 (0-631-17838-4) Blackwell Pubs.

Makin, Susan R. A Consumer's Guide to Art Therapy: For Prospective Employers, Clients & Students. 112p. (C). 1994. pap. 18.95 (0-398-06511-X); text 31.95 (0-398-05917-9) C C Thomas.

— Poetic Wisdom: Poetic Wisdom: Revealing & Healing. LC 98-16987. 246p. 1998. text 50.95 (0-398-06878-X); pap. text 37.95 (0-398-06879-8) C C Thomas.

Makin, Wendy, jt. auth. see Hoskin, Peter.

Makinde, M. Akin. African Philosophy, Culture & Traditional Medicine. LC 88-15680. (Monographs in International Studies, Africa: No. 53). 172p. 1988. pap. text 16.00 (0-89680-152-7) Ohio U Pr.

***Makine, Andrei.** Au Temps du Fleuve Nori, Vol. 1. 4th ed. (FRE.). 1998. pap. text 11.95 (2-07-040062-X) CFR Pubns.

— Confessions of a Fallen Standard-Bearer. Strachan, Geoffrey, tr. 2000. 22.95 (1-55970-529-9, Pub. by Arcade Pub Inc) Time Warner.

— The Crime of Olga Arbyelina. Strachan, Geoffrey, tr. from FRE. LC 99-26987. 224p. 1999. 24.95 (1-55970-494-2, Pub. by Arcade Pub Inc) Time Warner.

Makine, Andrei. Dreams of My Russian Summers. Strachan, Geoffrey, tr. from FRE. LC 97-2720. 320p. 1997. 23.45 (1-55970-383-0, Pub. by Arcade Pub Inc) Time Warner.

— Dreams of My Russian Summers. Strachan, Geoffrey, tr. from FRE. LC 98-16347. 256p. 1998. per. 12.00 (0-684-85268-3) S&S Trade.

— Once upon the River Love. Strachan, Geoffrey, tr. from FRE. LC 98-22706. 224p. 1998. 23.95 (1-55970-438-1, Pub. by Arcade Pub Inc) Time Warner.

— Once upon the River Love. 224p. 1999. pap. 12.95 (0-14-028362-5) Viking Penguin.

— Le Testament Francais. (FRE.). 1995. pap. 34.95 (2-7152-1936-9) Schoenhof.

Makinen, Ilkka H. On Suicide in European Countries: Some Theoretical, Legal & Historical Views on Suicide Mortality & Its Concomitants. LC 97-165184. (Stockholm Studies in Sociology: Vol. 5). 140p. 1997. pap. 47.50 (91-22-01753-4, Pub. by Almqvist Wiksell) Coronet Bks.

Makinen, M. Joyce Cary: A Descriptive Bibliography. 264p. 1989. text 110.00 (0-7201-1985-5) Continuum.

Makinen, Merja, jt. auth. see Gamman, Lorraine.

Makinen, Paul, tr. see Barenblatt, G. I.

Makinen, Paul, tr. see Kuz'min, A. D., ed.

Makinen, Paul, tr. see Plotnikov, A. F., ed.

Making, Anne E. Guardian Accounts of Princess Anne County, Virginia. LC 97-222709. vi, 270p. 1997. pap. text 17.50 (0-7884-0734-1, M043) Heritage Bk.

Makino. Nakama, Vol. 1. (C). Date not set. pap., teacher ed. 11.96 (0-669-27584-0) HM.

— Nakama, Vol. 1. (C). 1998. pap. text, student ed. 32.36 (0-669-27585-9) HM.

— Nakama, Vol. 1. (C). 1998. pap. text 52.36 (0-669-27583-2) HM.

Makino, Erika B. Six of Cups: A Circle of Stories. LC 92-70849. (Illus.). 160p. (Orig.). 1992. pap. 8.50 (0-929151-05-4) Earth Bks.

Makino, Junichiro & Taiji, Makoto. Scientific Simulations with Special-Purpose Computers: The Grape Systems. LC 97-44584. 248p. 1998. 150.00 (0-471-96946-X) Wiley.

Makino, Noboru. Total Forecast Japan: The 1990's. 352p. 1993. text 130.00 (0-304-32717-4) Continuum.

***Makino, S., et al, eds.** Asthma Prevention Management Guidelines: 1998, Japan (JGL 1998) (International Archives of Allergy & Immunology Ser.: Vol. 121, Suppl. 1). (Illus.). viii, 78p. 2000. pap. 34.00 (3-8055-7074-0) S Karger.

— Eosinophils in Allergy & Related Diseases: Workshop, Tokyo, June 1998: Proceedings. (International Archives of Allergy & Immunology Ser.: Vol. 120, Suppl. 1). (Illus.). iv, 106p. 1999. pap. 34.00 (3-8055-6992-0) S Karger.

Makino, S. & Ishikawa, Takeru H., eds. Eosinophils in Allergy. (Journal: International Archives of Allergy & Immunology Ser.: Vol. 108, Suppl. 1, 1995). (Illus.). 56p. 1995. pap. 26.25 (3-8055-6216-0) S Karger.

Makino, S., jt. ed. see Ishikawa, Takeru H.

***Makino, Seiichi.** Kodansha Basic English-Japanese Dictionary. (JPN & ENG., Illus.). 1508p. 2000. pap. 45.00 (4-7700-2628-5) Kodansha Intl.

Makino, Seiichi. Kodansha's Daily English-Japanese Dictionary. 1999. pap. 40.00 (4-7700-2135-6) Kodansha.

***Makino, Seiichi, et al.** Basic English-Japanese Dictionary. (ENG & JPN.). 1999. pap. 45.00 (4-7700-2471-1, Pub. by Kodansha Intl) Kodansha.

Makino, Sohei, et al, eds. Eosinophils in Allergy & Related Diseases: Proceedings of a Workshop, Tokyo, June 1995. (Journal Ser.: Vol. 111, Supplement 1, 1996). (Illus.). iv, 70p. 1996. pap. 32.25 (3-8055-6397-3) S Karger.

— Eosinophils in Allergy & Related Diseases: Proceedings of a Workshop, Tokyo, June 1996. (International Archives of Allergy & Immunology Ser.: Vol. 114, Suppl. 1). (Illus.). iv, 90p. 1997. pap. 41.00 (3-8055-6580-1) S Karger.

Makino, Sohei & Fukuda, Takeshi, eds. Eosinophils: Biological & Clinical Aspects. 464p. 1992. 256.00 (0-8493-6822-7, RB145, CRC Reprint) Franklin.

Makino, Yasuko. Japan Through Children's Literature: An Annotated Bibliography. 2nd ed. LC 85-21941. 144p. 1985. lib. bdg. 49.95 (0-313-24611-4, MJA/, Greenwood Pr) Greenwood.

Makino, Yasuko & Miki, Mihoko, compiled by. Japan & the Japanese: A Bibliographic Guide to Reference Sources, 1. LC 96-12377. (Bibliographies & Indexes in Asian Studies Ser.: Vol. 1). 168p. 1996. lib. bdg. 65.00 (0-313-26311-6, Greenwood Pr) Greenwood.

Makino, Yasuko & Saito, Masaei. A Student Guide to Japanese Sources in the Humanities. LC 93-34031. (Michigan Papers in Japanese Studies: No. 24). ix, 155p. (C). 1994. pap. 17.95 (0-939512-64-5) U MI Japan.

Makinodan, Takashi & Kay, Marguerite M., eds. Handbook of Immunology of Aging. LC 80-24315. (Series in Aging). 328p. 1981. 181.00 (0-8493-3144-7, QP86, CRC Reprint) Franklin.

Makinodan, Takashi, et al. Aging & the Immune Function. 227p. 1974. text 31.50 (0-8422-7228-3) Irvington.

Makinouchi, Akifumi, ed. Database Systems for Advanced Applications '91: Proceedings of the Second International Symposium on Database Systems for Advanced Applications, April 2-4, 1991, Tokyo, Japan. LC 92-19671. (Advanced Database Research & Development Ser.: Vol. 2). 568p. 1992. text 121.00 (981-02-1055-8) World Scientific Pub.

Makins, Christopher J. The Study of Europe in the United States. (Illus.). 80p. 1999. pap. text 20.00 (0-7881-8048-7) DIANE Pub.

Makins, Geoffrey E. Waymarks: An Artist's Attempt at a Natural Religion. (C). 1988. 51.00 (1-85072-026-6, Pub. by W Sessions) St Mut.

Makins, Virginia. The Invisible Children: Nipping Failure in the Bud. LC 97-195781. 80p. 1997. pap. 22.95 (1-85346-492-9, Pub. by David Fulton) Taylor & Francis.

Makinson, K. Rachel. Shrinkproofing of Wool. LC 79-17661. (Fiber Science Ser.: Vol. 8). (Illus.). 391p. reprint ed. pap. 121.30 (0-608-08953-2, 206958800005) Bks Demand.

Makinson, Kellie S. Prematurely Yours, Jessica. 144p. 2000. pap. 15.95 (1-58244-021-2) Rutledge Bks.

Makinson, Larry. The Big Picture: Money Follows Power Shift on Capitol Hill. (Illus.). 80p. 1998. pap. text 20.00 (0-7881-7231-X) DIANE Pub.

— Follow the Money Handbook. (Illus.). 172p. 1994. pap. 10.00 (0-939715-20-1) Ctr Politics.

***Makinson, Larry.** Follow the Money Handbook. 2nd rev. ed. 175p. 2000. pap. 10.00 (0-939715-26-0) Ctr Politics.

Makinson, Larry. Open Secrets: Congressional Money & Politics. 2nd ed. LC 92-5802. 1400p. 1992. 169.95 (0-87187-689-2) Congr Quarterly.

— The Price of Admission: Campaign Spending in the 1990 Elections. (Illus.). 160p. 1992. pap. text 19.95 (0-939715-16-3) Ctr Politics.

— The Price of Admission: Campaign Spending in the 1994 Elections. 250p. 1995. pap. 19.95 (0-939715-25-2) Ctr Politics.

***Makinson, Larry.** Secrets of Modern Slot Playing. 2nd ed. (Illus.). 1998. pap. 9.00 (0-9664592-0-2) L&M Pubns.

***Makinson, Larry, ed.** Who[0012]s Paying for This Election? A Special Report on Fundraising in the 1998 Elections. (Illus.). 55p. 2000. reprint ed. pap. text 20.00 (0-7881-8419-9) DIANE Pub.

Makinson, Larry & Goldstein, Joshua F. The Cash Constituents of Congress, 1992 Elections. LC 94-31799. 385p. (YA). (gr. 11 up). 1994. pap. text 36.95 (1-56802-010-4) Congr Quarterly.

— Open Secrets: The Encyclopedia of Congressional Money & Politics. 3rd ed. 1362p. 1994. 179.95 (1-56802-026-0) Congr Quarterly.

Makinson, R. B. Songwriters & Lyricists Handbook. 50p. 1996. pap. 15.00 (0-9654228-2-8) R Makinson.

Makinson, R. O., jt. auth. see McGillivray, D. J.

Makinson, Randall L., jt. auth. see McCoy, Esther.

Makinson, Randell L. Greene & Greene: Architecture As a Fine Art, Vol. 1. LC 76-57792. (Illus.). 288p. 1977. 34.95 (0-87905-023-3) Gibbs Smith Pub.

— Greene & Greene: Furniture & Related Designs, Vol. 2. LC 97-6061. (Illus.). 190p. 1977. 39.95 (0-87905-060-8) Gibbs Smith Pub.

— Greene & Greene: Furniture & Related Designs, Vol. 2. LC 76-57792. (Illus.). 190p. 1983. pap. 29.95 (0-87905-125-6) Gibbs Smith Pub.

— Greene & Greene: The Passion & the Legacy. LC 97-43568. (Illus.). 240p. 1998. 75.00 (0-87905-847-1) Gibbs Smith Pub.

— Greene & Greene Vol. 2: Architecture As a Fine Art. LC 76-57792. (Illus.). 288p. 1977. pap. 27.95 (0-87905-126-4) Gibbs Smith Pub.

***Makinson, Randell L., et al.** Greene & Greene: The Blacker House. LC 99-89918. (Illus.). 144p. 2000. 49.95 (0-87905-949-4) Gibbs Smith Pub.

Makinson, Robert, jt. auth. see Page, Roberta.

Makinster, Genie. Ravensloch: Gothic Mystery. LC 83-26303. (Illus.). 141p. (Orig.). 1982. pap. 1.95 (0-9608742-0-8) Gemak Pub.

Makintosh, Allan, jt. auth. see Jensen, Jens.

Makita, Akira, et al, eds. Membrane Alterations in Cancer. (GANN Monographs on Cancer Research: No. 29). 312p. 1983. 85.00 (0-306-41565-8, Plenum Trade) Perseus Pubng.

Makiuchi, Reiko, jt. auth. see Shelley, Rex.

Makiya, Hind & Rogers, Margaret. Design & Technology in the Primary School: Case Studies for Teachers. LC 91-48095. (Illus.). 160p. (C). (gr. 13). 1993. 80.00 (0-415-08089-4, A7629) Routledge.

Makiya, Kanan. Cruelty & Silence: War, Tyranny, Uprising, & the Arab World. 1994. pap. 10.95 (0-393-31141-4) Norton.

— Republic of Fear: The Politics of Modern Iraq. LC 97-50620. 346p. 1998. pap. text 17.95 (0-520-21439-0, Pub. by U CA Pr) Cal Prin Full Svc.

Makiya, Kanan. The Rock. 1999. write for info. (0-375-40087-7) Pantheon.

***Makiya, Kanan.** The Rock. 2000. pap. write for info. (0-375-70078-1) Vin Bks.

Makiyama, Thomas. Keijutsukai Aikido: Japanese Art of Self Defense. LC 83-61559. (Japanese Arts Ser.). (Illus.). (Orig.). 1983. pap. 15.95 (0-89750-092-X, 428) Ohara Pubns.

***Makiyama, Thomas.** Keijutsukai Aikido: Japanese Art of Self-Defense. 1999. pap. text 40.95 (1-58133-139-8) Black Belt Mag.

An Asterisk (*) at the beginning of an entry indicates that the title is appearing for the first time.

Makkai & Pare. Accessible Categories: The Foundations of Categorical Model Theory. LC 89-18125. (CONM Ser.: Vol. 104). 176p. 1990. reprint ed. pap. 34.00 (0-8218-5111-X, CONM/104) Am Math.

Makkai, Adam. A Dictionary of American Idioms. 3rd ed. 1995. pap. 12.95 (0-8120-1248-8) Barron.

— A Dictionary of Space English. LC 73-171582. (Illus.). viii, 72p. (Orig.). 1973. pap. 20.00 (0-933104-23-5) Jupiter Pr.

— Ecolinguistics: Toward a New Paradigm for the Science of Language. 600p. 1993. text 89.00 (1-85567-018-6, Pub. by P P Pubs) Cassell & Continuum.

— Idiom Structure in English. LC 76-144014. (Janua Linguarum, Ser. Major: No. 48). (Illus.). 371p. 1972. text 78.50 (90-279-2105-9) Mouton.

— In Quest of the Miracle Stag: The Poetry of Hungary. 1997. pap. text 39.95 (0-9642093-1-4) Arts Guild.

— K-Square Equals Thirteen: K A Negyzeten Tizenharommal. (Illus.). 112p. 1970. 29.00 (0-933104-18-9) Jupiter Pr.

— Languages for Peace: A Tribute to Kenneth L. Pike. (Languages for Peace Ser.: No. 1). (Illus.). 32p. (Orig.). 1983. pap. 10.00 (0-933104-14-6) Jupiter Pr.

Makkai, Adam, ed. Toward a Theory of Context in Linguistics & Literature: Proceedings of a Conference of the Kelemen Mikes Hungarian Cultural Society, Maastricht, September 21-25, 1971. (De Proprietatibus Litterarum, Ser. Minor: No. 18). pap. 40.00 (90-279-3273-5) Mouton.

Makkai, Adam, et al, eds. Linguistics at the Crossroads. LC 79-312499. viii, 502p. (Orig.). (C). 1977. pap. 48.00 (0-933104-02-2) Jupiter Pr.

Makkai, Adam & Lockwood, David G., eds. Readings in Stratificational Linguistics. viii, 331p. 1973. 48.00 (0-933104-24-3) Jupiter Pr.

Makkai, Adam & Melby, Alan K., eds. Linguistics & Philosophy: Festschrift For Rulon S. Wells. LC 85-20099. (Current Issues in Linguistic Theory Ser.: No. 42). xviii, 472p. 1986. 94.00 (90-272-3536-8) J Benjamins Pubng Co.

Makkai, Adam, et al. Handbook of Commonly Used American Idioms. 3rd ed. 320p. 1995. pap. 7.95 (0-8120-9239-2) Barron.

Makkai, Adam, tr. see Alexander, Michael.

Makkai, Michael. Duality & Definability in First Order Logic. LC 93-4868. (Memoirs Ser.: No. 503). 106p. 1993. pap. 30.00 (0-8218-2565-8, MEMO/105/503) Am Math.

***Makkai, Toni.** Drug Use Monitoring in Australia. 1999. pap. 75.00 (0-642-24136-8, Pub. by Aust Inst Criminology) St Mut.

Makkai, Valerie B., ed. Phonological Theory: Evolution & Current Practice. LC 76-138654. xii, 711p. (C). 1978. reprint ed. pap. 35.00 (0-933104-05-7) Jupiter Pr.

Makkar, G. C. Three Number Author Tables. 200p. 1974. 6.00 (0-88065-153-9) Scholarly Pubns.

Makkar, S. P., ed. Law of Culpable Homicide, Murder & Punishment in India. (C). 1990. 125.00 (0-89771-180-7) St Mut.

Makkar, S. P. & Hamid, Abdul, eds. Constitutional Law, a Miscellany. (C). 1990. 150.00 (0-89771-203-X) St Mut.

Makkay, Janos. Early Stamp Seals in South-East Europe. 3rd ed. 124p. (C). 1984. pap. 60.00 (963-05-3424-X, Pub. by Akade Kiado) St Mut.

— Tarantella: Avagy Utazasok a Pokhalon (Egy Pszichoanalizis Tortenete) 63p. (Orig.). 1985. pap. 15.00 (0-933104-21-9) Jupiter Pr.

— The Tiszaszolos Treasure: In Search of a Copper Age Prince. (Studia Archaeologica Ser.: Vol. 10). (Illus.). 186p. (C). 1989. pap. 102.00 (963-05-4726-0, Pub. by Akade Kiado) St Mut.

Makker, Sudesh P., jt. ed. see Kher, Kanwal K.

Makki, M. S. Medina, Saudi Arabia: A Geographic Analysis of the City & Region. 242p. 1982. text 46.25 (0-86127-301-X) Ashgate Pub Co.

Makkink, Henri J. Philip Massinger & John Fletcher: A Comparison. LC 68-1145. (Studies in Drama: No. 39). 1969. reprint ed. lib. bdg. 75.00 (0-8383-0669-1) M S G Haskell Hse.

Makkonen, L. Ice & Construction. (Illus.). 112p. (C). 1994. 120.00 (0-419-20020-7, E & FN Spon) Routledge.

Makkreel, Rudolf A. Dilthey Foundation. 49.50 (0-691-07309-0, Pub. by Princeton U Pr) Cal Prin Full Svc.

— Dilthey Problems. 0.00 (0-691-07308-2) Princeton U Pr.

Makkreel, Rudolf A. Imagination & Interpretation in Kant: The Hermeneutical Import of the Critique of Judgment. xii, 200p. 1994. pap. text 12.95 (0-226-50277-5) U Ch Pr.

— Imagination & Interpretation in Kant: The Hermeneutical Import of the Critique of Judgment. LC 89-39715. 200p. 1996. 29.95 (0-226-50276-7) U Ch Pr.

Makkreel, Rudolf A. & Scanlon, John, eds. Dilthey & Phenomenology. LC 87-8102. (Current Continental Research Ser.: No. 006). 182p. (Orig.). (C). 1987. lib. bdg. 46.00 (0-8191-6305-8) U Pr of Amer.

Makkreel, Rudolf A., ed. see Dilthey, Wilhelm.

Makky, Wagih H., ed. Aviation Security Problem & Related Technologies: Proceedings of a Conference Held 19-20 July 1992, San Diego, California. LC 92-17417. (Critical Reviews of Optical Science & Technology Ser.: Vol. CR42). 1992. 30.00 (0-8194-0954-5); pap. 30.00 (0-8194-0955-3) SPIE.

Maklad, Nabil F., ed. Ultrasound in Perinatology. fac. ed. LC 85-29139. (Clinics in Diagnostic Ultrasound Ser.: No. 19). (Illus.). 238p. 1986. reprint ed. pap. 73.80 (0-7837-7892-9, 204764800008) Bks Demand.

Maklan, David M. The Four-Day Work Week: Blue Collar Adjustment to a Nonconventional Arrangement of Work & Leisure Time. LC 77-14308. (Special Studies). 204p. 1977. 52.95 (0-275-90270-6, C0270, Praeger Pubs) Greenwood.

Maklan, Stan & Knox, Simon. Competing on Value: Bridging the Gap Between Brand & Customer Value. (Illus.). 288p. 1998. 27.95 (0-273-63105-5, Pub. by F T P-H) Natl Bk Netwk.

Maklansky, Steven. Cameraderie: A Relational Interpretation of Photographic History. LC 97-66184. (Illus.). 72p. 1997. pap. 9.95 (0-89494-056-2) New Orleans Mus Art.

***Maklar, Andra.** Teaching for Justice in the Social Studies Classroom: Millions of Intricate Moves. 2000. pap. text 24.00 (0-325-00264-9) Heinemann.

***Maklebust, JoAnn & Sieggreen, Mary.** Pressure Ulcers: Guidelines for Prevention & Management. 3rd ed. LC 00-44625. P. :p. 2000. write for info. (1-58255-035-2) Springhouse Corp.

Maklebust, JoAnn & Sieggreen, Mary. Pressure Ulcers: Guidelines for Prevention & Nursing Management. 2nd ed. 320p. 1995. pap. 34.95 (0-87434-836-6) Springhouse Corp.

Makley, Michael J. The Apprentice Twain. LC 93-91080. 172p. (Orig.). 1994. pap. 6.25 (0-9636608-1-0) Estrn Sierra.

— The Hanging of Lucky Bill. 145p. 1993. pap. 9.95 (0-9636608-0-2) Estrn Sierra.

Makman, Maynard H. & Stefano, George B., eds. Neuroregulatory Mechanisms in Aging. LC 93-21169. (Studies in Neuroscience). 212p. 1993. 160.50 (0-08-041989-5, Pergamon Pr) Elsevier.

***Mako, Ed.** Does the Water Remember? LC 99-13116. 448p. 1999. 24.95 (1-880090-74-0) Galde Pr.

Mako, William P. U. S. Ground Forces & the Defense of Central Europe. LC 83-2817. (Studies in Defense Policy). 137p. 1983. 26.95 (0-8157-5444-2); pap. 9.95 (0-8157-5443-4) Brookings.

Makoba, J. Wagona. Government Policy & Public Enterprise Performance in Sub-Saharan Africa: The Case Studies of Tanzania & Zambia, 1964-1984. LC 97-51486. 568p. 1998. text 119.95 (0-7734-2229-3) E Mellen.

Makoff & Duncan Staff. Display for All Seasons: A Thematic Approach to Teaching with Children from Five to Nine. (Kids' Stuff Ser.). (Illus.). 1995. pap. 15.95 (0-947882-04-9) Belair Pubns Ltd.

Makofske, Mary. Disappearance of Gargoyles. 64p. (Orig.). 1988. pap. 5.95 (0-939395-10-X) Thorntree Pr.

— Eating Nasturtiums. 28p. 1998. pap. 7.00 (1-886226-04-0) Flume Pr.

Makofske, William J. & Edelstein, Michael R., eds. Radon & the Environment. LC 87-35242. (Illus.). 465p. 1988. 39.00 (0-8155-1161-2) Noyes.

Makofske, William J., jt. auth. see Edelstein, Michael R.

Makogon, Yuri F. Hydrates of Hydrocarbons. LC 96-51830. 1997. 129.00 (0-87814-718-7) PennWell Bks.

***Makolkin, Anna.** The Genealogy of Our Present Moral Disarray: An Essay in Comparative Philosophy. LC 99-88232. (Problems in Contemporary Philosophy Ser.). 2000. write for info. (0-7734-7800-0) E Mellen.

Makolkin, Anna. Name, Hero, Icon: Semiotics of Nationalism Through Heroic Biography. LC 91-48252. (Approaches to Semiotics Ser.: No. 105). xvi, 264p. (C). 1992. lib. bdg. 113.85 (3-11-013012-2) Mouton.

— Semiotics of Misogyny Through the Humor of Chekhov & Maugham. LC 92-18419. 260p. 1992. text 89.95 (0-7734-9570-3) E Mellen.

Makoondekwa, Joao, jt. auth. see Carter, Hazel.

Makos, Christopher. Makos. LC 96-47566. (Illus.). 96p. 1997. text 13.00 (0-312-15291-4, Stonewall Inn) St Martin.

Makos, Christopher, photos by. Makos Men - Sewn Photos. (Illus.). 96p. 1996. pap. 35.00 (0-9642009-3-7) Pohlmann Pr.

Makos, Marc L. Interviewing & the Smart Job Search. LC 93-28985. 117p. 1994. pap. 10.95 (0-9630394-5-8) HD Pub.

— Resumes for the Smart Job Search: The Ultimate Guide to Writing Resumes in the 90s. LC 92-47008. 160p. 1993. pap. 14.95 (0-9630394-9-0) HD Pub.

— The Smart Job Search: A Guide to Proven Methods for Finding a Great Job. LC 91-31232. 297p. 1991. pap. 18.95 (0-9630394-8-2) HD Pub.

Makoshi, K., jt. auth. see Ilisca, E.

Makoshi, K., ed. see Kasai, H.

Makoski, Ellen H. Scenic Parks & Landscape Value. LC 90-39467. (Environment: Problems & Solutions Ser.: Vol. 15). 283p. 1990. text 25.00 (0-8240-0470-1) Garland.

Makosky, Veronica. Susan Glaspell's Century of American Women: A Critical Interpretation of Her Work. LC 92-23329. 184p. 1993. text 52.00 (0-19-507866-7) OUP.

Makosky, Vivian P., et al, eds. Activities Handbook for the Teaching of Psychology, Vol. 2. LC 81-1648. Vol. 2. 345p. 1988. pap. 24.95 (1-55798-030-6, 4280050) Am Psychol.

— Activities Handbook for the Teaching of Psychology, Vol. 3. LC 81-1648. Vol. 3. (Illus.). 372p. (C). 1981. 24.95 (1-55798-081-0) Am Psychol.

Makosza, Mieczyslaw. Vicarious Nucleophilic Substitution & Related Processes in Organic Synthesis. (Organic & Bio-Organic Chemistry Ser.). Date not set. 75.00 (0-8493-7864-8, 7864) CRC Pr.

Makoto, Ooka. Beneath the Restless Turning of the Planets: Selected Poems, 1972-1989. Fitzsimmons, Thomas, ed. Beichman, Janine, tr. from JPN. LC 95-41648. (Asian Poetry in Translation Ser.: No. 17). (Illus.). 178p. (C). 1996. pap. text 19.95 (0-942668-46-4) Katydid Bks.

— The Colors of Poetry: Essays on Classic Japanese Verse. Fitzsimmons, Thomas, ed. Lento, Takako & Lento, Thomas, trs. from JPN. (Reflections Ser.: No. 1). 144p. (C). 1991. 30.00 (0-942668-28-6); pap. 20.00 (0-942668-27-8) Katydid Bks.

— Elegy & Benediction: Selected Poems, 1947-1989. Elliott, William I. & Kazuo, Kawamura, trs. from JPN. 96p. 1991. pap. 15.00 (0-942668-32-4); text 20.00 (0-942668-31-6) Katydid Bks.

— A String Around Autumn: Selected Poems, 1952-1980. Fitzsimmons, Thomas, ed. & tr. by. from JPN. LC 82-80672. (Asian Poetry in Translation: Japan Ser.: No. 3). 94p. (Orig.). 1982. pap. 9.50 (0-942668-01-4) Katydid Bks.

Makoto, Ooka, jt. ed. see Fitzsimmons, Thomas.

Makov, Susan. The Hormone of Desire: The Truth about Testosterone, Sexuality & Menopause. LC 98-44342. 144p. 1999. pap. 12.00 (0-609-80386-7) Harmony Bks.

Makov, Susan, jt. auth. see Eddington, Patrick.

Makover, Michael E. Mismanaged Care: How Corporate Medicine Jeopardizes Your Health. LC 98-38860. 296p. 1998. 26.00 (1-57392-248-X) Prometheus Bks.

Makover, Richard B. Treatment Planning for Psychotherapists. 256p. 1996. text 37.00 (0-88048-743-7, 8743) Am Psychiatric.

Makovsky, Andre, ed. see Cisco, Bob.

Makovsky, David. Making Peace with the PLO: The Rabin's Government Road to the Oslo Accord. LC 95-39631. 239p. 1995. pap. 8.00 (0-944029-60-4) Wash Inst NEP.

Makower. Elizabeth Longford. 1997. 40.00 (0-340-64311-0, Pub. by Hodder & Stought Ltd) Trafalgar.

Makower, F. Elizabeth Longford. mass mkt. 15.95 (0-340-69472-6, Pub. by Hodder & Stought Ltd) Trafalgar.

Makower, Frances, ed. Call & Response: Jesuit Journeys in Faith. 174p. 1996. pap. 12.95 (0-8294-0868-1, Jesuit Way) Loyola Pr.

***Makower, Katharine.** The Coming of the Rain: The LIfe of Dr. Joe Church - A Personal Account of Revival in Rwanda. xvi, 228p. 1999. reprint ed. pap. 16.99 (0-85364-968-5, Pub. by Paternoster Pub) OM Literature.

Makower, Stanley V. & Blackwell, Basil H., eds. Book of English Essays: Sixteen Hundred to Nineteen Hundred. LC 73-37845. (Essay Index Reprint Ser.). 1977. reprint ed. 29.95 (0-8369-2609-9) Ayer.

Makowicki, Jim. Making Heirloom Toys. LC 96-17860. 160p. 1996. pap. 19.95 (1-56158-112-7) Taunton.

***Makowicki, Jim.** Marvelous Transforming Toys: With Complete Instructions & Plans. (Illus.). 2000. pap. 24.95 (1-56158-381-2) Taunton.

Makowka, Leonard, ed. Handbook of Animal Models in Transplantation Research. 368p. 1993. boxed set 250.95 (0-8493-3629-5, RD120) CRC Pr.

Makowka, Leonard, jt. ed. see Sher, Linda S.

Makowski, Colleen L. Charles Burchfield: An Annotated Bibliography. LC 95-26776. 320p. 1996. 47.50 (0-8108-3131-7) Scarecrow.

— Quilting, 1915-1983: An Annotated Bibliography. LC 85-2497. (Illus.). 165p. 1985. pap. text 21.00 (0-8108-1813-2) Scarecrow.

Makowski, Elizabeth M. Canon Law & Cloistered Women: Periculoso & Its Commentators 1298-1545. LC 96-43744. (Studies in Medieval & Early Modern Canon Law: Vol. 5). 149p. (C). 1998. text 46.95 (0-8132-0884-X) Cath U Pr.

— Canon Law & Cloistered Women: Periculoso & its Commentators, 1298-1545. 1999. pap. text 14.95 (0-8132-0949-8) Cath U Pr.

Makowski, Elizabeth M., jt. ed. see Wilson, Katharina M.

Makowski, Francois. French Made Easy - Beginners. LC 95-75594. (FRE.). 320p. 1995. 19.95 incl. audio (0-8120-8350-4) Barron.

Makowski, Lee J. Horace Bushnell on Christian Character Development. LC 99-14680. 1p. 1999. 52.00 (0-7618-1400-0); pap. 31.50 (0-7618-1401-9) U Pr of Amer.

Makowski, Nancy, ed. see Ayad, Graciela & Panzer, Richard.

Makowski, Silk. Serious about Series: Evaluations & Annotations of Teen Fiction in Paperback Series. Broderick, Dorothy M., ed. LC 97-48913. 272p. 1998. pap. 26.50 (0-8108-3304-2) Scarecrow.

Makowsky, Johanna A., ed. see Association of Symbolic Logic Staff.

Makowsky, Michael. Minstrel of Love: A Biography of Satguru Sant Keshavadas. (Illus.). 334p. (Orig.). 1980. pap. 12.00 (0-942508-20-3) Vishwa.

Makowsky, Michael, jt. auth. see Collins, Randall.

Makowsky, Veronica A., ed. see Blackmur, R. P.

Makowsky, Veronica A., ed. see Blackmur, Richard P.

Makrakis, Apostolos. The Bible & the World & Triluminal Science. Orthodox Christian Educational Society Staff, ed. Cummings, Denver, tr. 531p. 1950. 24.95 (0-938366-18-1) Orthodox Chr.

— Catechesis of the Orthodox Church. rev. ed. Orthodox Christian Educational Society Staff, ed. 239p. 1969. reprint ed. 14.95 (0-614-23213-9); reprint ed. pap. text 9.95 (0-938366-14-9) Orthodox Chr.

— The City of Zion-The Human Society in Christ, i.e., the Church Built upon a Rock. Orthodox Christian Educational Society Staff, ed. Cummings, Denver, tr. 109p. (C). 1958. pap. 9.95 (0-938366-16-5) Orthodox Chr.

— Commentary on the Psalms of David. Orthodox Christian Educational Society Staff, ed. Cummings, Denver, tr. 990p. 1950. 34.95 (0-938366-19-X) Orthodox Chr.

— Concerning Our Duties to God. Orthodox Christian Educational Society Staff, ed. 170p. 1958. pap. text 8.95 (0-938366-13-0) Orthodox Chr.

— Divine & Sacred Catechism. Orthodox Christian Educational Society Staff, ed. 224p. (C). 1946. 9.95 (0-938366-15-7); 14.95 (0-614-23214-7) Orthodox Chr.

— The Foundation of Philosophy - A Refutation of Skepticism, the True Jesus Christ, the Science of God & Man: The God of the Christians. Orthodox Christian Educational Society Staff, ed. Lekatsos, Anthony & Cummings, Denver, trs. from FRE. 395p. 1955. 14.96 (0-938366-07-6) Orthodox Chr.

— Freemasonry Known by the Masonic Diploma. Cummings, Denver, tr. 135p. (Orig.). 1956. reprint ed. pap. 8.95 (0-938366-42-4) Orthodox Chr.

— Hellenism & the Unfinished Revolution. Orthodox Christian Educational Society Staff, ed. 191p. (Orig.). 1968. pap. 10.95 (0-938366-26-2) Orthodox Chr.

— The Holy Orthodox Church. Orthodox Christian Educational Society Staff, ed. Lisney, M. I. & Krick, L., trs. 290p. (Orig.). 1980. pap. 14.95 (0-938366-34-3) Orthodox Chr.

— The Human Nature of Christ: Growth & Perfection. Orthodox Christian Educational Society Staff, ed. Cummings, D., tr. 52p. (Orig.). 1965. pap. 4.95 (0-938366-28-9) Orthodox Chr.

— The Innovations of the Roman Church. 82p. (Orig.). 1966. reprint ed. pap. 4.95 (0-938366-39-4) Orthodox Chr.

— Interpretation of the Book of Revelation. Orthodox Christian Educational Society Staff, ed. Alexander, A. G., tr. 564p. 1972. 24.95 (0-938366-12-2) Orthodox Chr.

— Interpretation of the Entire New Testament (Revelation Not Incl.), 2 vols., Set. Orthodox Christian Educational Society Staff, ed. Alexander, Albert G., tr. 2052p. (C). 1949. 49.95 (0-938366-08-4) Orthodox Chr.

— The Interpretation of the Gospel Law. Orthodox Christian Educational Society Staff, ed. Cummings, Denver, tr. 453p. 1955. 15.95 (0-938366-10-6) Orthodox Chr.

— Kyriakodromion (Sunday Sermonary) Orthodox Christian Educational Society Staff, ed. Cummings, D., tr. 637p. 1951. 21.95 (0-938366-20-3) Orthodox Chr.

— Logic: An Orthodox Christian Approach. Orthodox Christian Educational Society Staff, ed. Cummings, Denver, tr. (Logos & Holy Spirit in the Unity of Christian Thought Ser.: Vol. 3). 200p. 1977. reprint ed. pap. 6.95 (0-938366-04-1) Orthodox Chr.

— Memoir of the Nature of the Church of Christ. Orthodox Christian Educational Society Staff, ed. Cummings, Denver, tr. 175p. 1947. 8.95 (0-938366-21-1); 12.00 (0-614-23215-5) Orthodox Chr.

— A New Philosophy & the Philosophical Sciences, 2 vols., Set. Orthodox Christian Educational Society Staff & Cummings, Denver, eds. Incl. Vol. 1. Introduction to Philosophy, Psychology, Logic, & Theology. 888p. 1940. Vol. 2. Introduction to Ethics. 745p. 1940. 1940. reprint ed. 44.95 (0-938366-01-7) Orthodox Chr.

— The Orthodox Approach to Philosophy. Orthodox Christian Educational Society Staff, ed. Cummings, Denver, tr. (Logos & Holy Spirit in the Unity of Christian Thought Ser.: Vol. 1). 82p. 1977. reprint ed. pap. 5.00 (0-938366-06-8) Orthodox Chr.

— Orthodox Christian Meditations: Spiritual Discourses for the Orthodox Christians. Orthodox Christian Educational Society Staff, ed. Cummings, Denver, tr. 143p. (Orig.). 1965. pap. 3.95 (0-938366-22-X) Orthodox Chr.

— The Orthodox Definition of Political Science. Orthodox Christian Educational Society Staff, ed. Cummings, Denver, tr. 163p. 1968. reprint ed. pap. 4.95 (0-938366-31-9) Orthodox Chr.

— An Orthodox-Protestant Debate. Cummings, Denver, tr. 101p. 1949. reprint ed. pap. 5.95 (0-938366-37-8) Orthodox Chr.

— The Paramount Doctrines of Orthodoxy-the Tricompositeness of Man, Apology of A. Makrakis & the Trial of A. Makrakis. Orthodox Christian Educational Society Staff, ed. Cummings, Denver, tr. 904p. 1954. 19.95 (0-938366-17-3) Orthodox Chr.

— Philosophy: An Orthodox Christian Understanding. Orthodox Christian Educational Society Staff, ed. Cummings, Denver, tr. (Logos & Holy Spirit in the Unity of Christian Thought Ser.: Vol. 5). 279p. 1977. reprint ed. pap. 5.00 (0-938366-02-5) Orthodox Chr.

— The Political Philosophy of the Orthodox Church. Orthodox Christian Educational Society Staff, ed. Cummings, Denver, tr. Orig. Title: The Orthodox Definition of Political Science. 163p. (Orig.). (C). 1965. pap. 4.95 (0-938366-11-4) Orthodox Chr.

— Psychology: An Orthodox Christian Perspective. Orthodox Christian Educational Society Staff, ed. Cummings, Denver, tr. (Logos & Holy Spirit in the Unity of Christian Thought Ser.: Vol. 2). 151p. 1977. reprint ed. pap. 5.00 (0-938366-05-X) Orthodox Chr.

— A Revelation of Treasure Hid--Concerning Freedom, Concerning the Motherland, Concerning Justice, Apostolical Canons Respecting Baptism. Orthodox Christian Educational Society Staff, ed. Cummings, Denver, tr. 80p. (Orig.). 1952. pap. 3.95 (0-938366-23-8) Orthodox Chr.

— A Scriptural Refutation of the Pope's Primacy. Cummings, Denver, tr. 171p. (Orig.). 1952. reprint ed. pap. 4.95 (0-938366-40-8) Orthodox Chr.

— Theology: An Orthodox Standpoint. Orthodox Christian Educational Society Staff, ed. Cummings, Denver, tr. (Logos & Holy Spirit in the Unity of Christian Thought Ser.: Vol. 4). 216p. 1977. reprint ed. pap. 5.00 (0-938366-03-3) Orthodox Chr.

— Three Great Friday Sermons & Other Theological Discourses. Orthodox Christian Educational Society Staff, ed. Cummings, Denver, tr. 107p. (Orig.). 1952. pap. 6.95 (0-938366-48-3) Orthodox Chr.

— The Two Contrariant Schools, Concerning the Establishment of a Christian University. Orthodox Christian Educational Society Staff, ed. Cummings, Denver, tr. 87p. (Orig.). 1949. pap. 2.95 (0-938366-27-0) Orthodox Chr.

Makrakis, Apostolos & Philaretos, Soterios. Christocracy: A Christ-Like Government of People. Eliopoulos, Nicholas C., tr. from GRE. 103p. 1985. pap. 10.00 (1-893760-07-3) Eliopoulos.

Makrakis, Apostolos, jt. auth. see Stratman, Chrysostomos H.

M

An Asterisk (*) at the beginning of an entry indicates that the title is appearing for the first time.

Makrakis, Apostolos, ed. see Agapius, et al.

Makram-Ebeid, S. & Tuck, B., eds. Semi-Insulating Three-Four Materials: Evian, 1982. 420p. 1980. 62.95 (*0-906812-22-4*) Birkhauser.

Makranczy, Judit. We Have to Escape. 185p. (J). (gr. 4-6). 1999. pap. 9.99 (*0-88092-373-3*, 3733) Royal Fireworks.

Makransky, John, jt. ed. see Jackson, Roger.

Makransky, John J. Buddhahood Embodied: Sources of Controversy in India & Tibet. LC 97-2682. (SUNY Series in Buddhist Studies). 454p. (C). 1997. text 73.50 (*0-7914-3431-1*); pap. text 24.95 (*0-7914-3432-X*) State U NY Pr.

Makreel, Rudolf A. Wilhelm Dilthey's Selected Works: Poetry & Experience, Vol. 5. 416p. 1985. pap. text 24.95 (*0-691-02928-8*, Pub. by Princeton U Pr) Cal Prin Full Svc.

Makridakis, Spyros, et al. Forecasting: Methods & Applications. 3rd ed. LC 97-44416. 656p. 1997. text 97.95 (*0-471-53233-9*) Wiley.

***Makridakis, Spyros, et al.** Forecasting: Methods & Applications. 3rd ed. 656p. 1998. 153.90 incl. disk (*0-471-34627-6*) Wiley.

Makridakis, Spyros G. Forecasting, Planning, & Strategy for the 21st Century. 293p. 1990. 40.00 (*0-02-919781-3*) Free Pr.

Makridakis, Spyros G. & Wheelright, Steven C. Interactive Forcasting: Univariate & Multivariate Methods. 2nd ed. LC 77-27396. 1978. teacher ed. 6.95 (*0-8162-5426-5*); text 42.00 (*0-8162-5416-8*) Holden-Day.

Makrides, Vasilios. Die Religiose Kritik Am Kopernikanischen Weltbild in Griechenland Zwischen 1794 und 1821: Aspekte Griechisch-Orthodoxer Apologetik Angesichts Naturwissenschaftlicher Fortschritte. (Tubinger Beitrage Zur Religionswissenschaft Ser.: Bd. 2). (GER.). 664p. 1995. 85.95 (*3-631-45846-0*) P Lang Pubng.

Makrinenko, Leonid I. & Bradley, John S., eds. Acoustics of Auditoriums in Public Buildings. 2nd ed. Ratner, R. S., tr. LC 94-16573. 172p. 1994. reprint ed. 46.00 (*1-56396-360-4*) Am Inst Physics.

Makris, Barbara L. & Davis-Debeuneure, Linda. Parenting: A Curriculum for the Single Working Mother. 22p. 1983. pap. text 15.00 (*0-934966-10-9*) Wider Oppor Women.

Makris, Barbara L., jt. auth. see Thomas, Melissa L.

***Makris, G. P.** Changing Masters: Spirit Possession & Identity Construction Among the Descendants of Slaves in. 2000. 75.00 (*0-8101-1698-7*) Northwestern U Pr.

Makris, Kallistos. The God-Inspired Orthodox Julian Calendar vs. the False Gregorian Papal Calendar. Vlesmas, Jerry, tr. 118p. (Orig.). 1971. reprint ed. pap. 6.95 (*0-938366-36-X*) Orthodox Chr.

Makris, Kathryn. Almost Sisters: The Sisters Scheme. 144p. (Orig.). (YA). 1991. pap. 2.99 (*0-380-76035-5*, Avon Bks) Morrow Avon.

— Almost Sisters: The Sisters Team. 176p. (Orig.). (J). (gr. 5 up). 1992. pap. 3.50 (*0-380-76056-8*, Avon Bks) Morrow Avon.

— Almost Sisters, No. 2: The Sisters War. 160p. (Orig.). (YA). 1991. pap. 3.50 (*0-380-76055-X*, Avon Bks) Morrow Avon.

— The Clean-up Crew. (Eco-Kids Ser.: No. 2). 160p. (Orig.). (J). (gr. 5 up). 1994. pap. 3.50 (*0-380-77050-4*, Avon Bks) Morrow Avon.

— Crosstown. 176p. (Orig.). (YA). 1993. pap. 3.50 (*0-380-76226-9*, Avon Bks) Morrow Avon.

— A Different Way. 192p. (J). 1989. pap. 2.95 (*0-380-75728-1*, Avon Bks) Morrow Avon.

— The Five Cat Club. (Eco-Kids Ser.: No. 1). 176p. (Orig.). (J). (gr. 5 up). 1994. pap. 3.50 (*0-380-77049-0*, Avon Bks) Morrow Avon.

— The Green Team. (Eco-Kids Ser.: No. 3). 160p. (Orig.). (J). (gr. 5 up). 1994. pap. 3.50 (*0-380-77051-2*, Avon Bks) Morrow Avon.

Makros, Jan, jt. auth. see Wright, Tracey.

Maksad, Ali K. Dream-World. 1997. pap. 56.95 (*1-57553-669-2*) Watermrk Pr.

Maksad, Ali k. Meditations Day by Day. 1998. pap. write for info. (*1-57553-776-1*) Watermrk Pr.

Maksen, Sue, ed. see Izzo, John B. & Klein, Eric.

Maksen, Sue, ed. see Murphy, Donna M.

Maksen, Tammy, ed. see Clark, Robin A.

Maksic, Azonimir B. Modelling of Structure & Properties of Molecules. 390p. 1987. text 75.95 (*0-470-21010-9*) P-H.

Maksic, Z. B., ed. The Concept of the Chemical Bond, Pt. 2. (Theoretical Models of Chemical Bonding Ser.). (Illus.). 664p. 1990. 411.95 (*0-387-51553-4*) Spr-Verlag.

— Molecular Spectroscopy, Electronic Structure & Intramolecular Interactions, Pt. 3. (Illus.). x, 638p. 1991. 244.00 (*0-387-52252-2*) Spr-Verlag.

— Theoretical Treatment of Large Molecules & Their Interactions, Pt. 4. (Illus.). x, 458p. 1991. 244.00 (*0-387-52253-0*) Spr-Verlag.

Maksic, Z. B. & Orville-Thomas, W. J. Pauling's Legacy. LC 99-10936. (Theoretical & Computational Chemistry Ser.: Vol. 6). 782p. 1999. 360.50 (*0-444-82508-8*) Elsevier.

Maksimov, Vladimir. A Man Survives. Hollo, Anselm, tr. from RUS. LC 75-15657. 106p. 1975. reprint ed. lib. bdg. 49.50 (*0-8371-8217-4*, MAMSU, Greenwood Pr) Greenwood.

Maksimov, Ye A., jt. auth. see Stradomskii, M. V.

Maksimov, Yu P., ed. The Strategic Rocket Forces: A Military Historical Work. (Illus.). 246p. (Orig.). 2000. pap. 29.95 (*0-614-14022-6*) East View Pubns.

Maksimovic-Ambodik, N. M. Emvlevy i Simvoly Seventeen Eighty-Eight, the First Russian Emblem Book. Hippisley, Anthony, ed. LC 89-850. (Symbola et Emblemata Ser.: Vol. 1). 368p. 1989. reprint ed. text 186.00 (*90-04-08992-6*) Brill Academic Pubs.

Maksimovic, C. Urban Drainage Modelling--Urban Drainage Catchments. 1986. 150.00 (*0-08-034333-3*, Pergamon Pr) Elsevier.

Maksimovic, C., ed. New Technologies in Urban Drainage: UDT 91. (Illus.). 540p. (C). (gr. 13). 1991. text 200.00 (*1-85166-650-8*) Elsevier Applied Sci.

Maksimovic, C., et al. Water Supply Systems: New Technologies. LC 96-32374. (NATO ASI Ser.: Environment: Vol. 15). 615p. 1996. 219.50 (*3-540-61533-4*) Spr-Verlag.

Maksimovic, C., jt. ed. see Butler, D.

Maksimovic, Ljubomir. The Byzantine Provincal Administration under the Palaiologoi. viii, 308p. 1988. pap. 90.00 (*90-256-0968-6*, Pub. by AM Hakkert) BookLink Distributors.

Maksimowicz, Michelle. Focus on Authentic Learning & Assessment in the Middle School. Romano, Louis G., ed. 20p. 1993. pap. text. write for info. (*0-318-72648-3*) MI Middle Educ.

Maksoudian, Krikor, ed. see Draskhanakertetsi, Hovhannes.

Maksoudian, Krikor, ed. see Koriun.

Maksoudian, Krikor, tr. see Petrosian, Levon T.

Maksoudian, Krikor H., tr. see Ayvazian, Argam.

Maksy, Mostafa M., jt. auth. see Bernstein, Leopold A.

Maksymiuk, Stephan. The Court Magician in Medieval German Romance. Harms, Wolfgang, ed. LC 96-167043. (Mikrokosmos Ser.: Bd. 44). IX, 185p. 1996. pap. 42.95 (*0-8204-3176-1*) P Lang Pubng.

— The Court Magician in Medieval German Romance. Harms, Wolfgang, ed. LC 96-167043. (Mikrokosmos Ser.: Bd. 44). ix, 185p. 1996. 42.95 (*3-631-30099-9*) P Lang Pubng.

Maktin, Jamie, et al, eds. The Bahamas Index & Yearbook 1998. 1999. text 100.00 (*0-932265-53-7*); pap. text 49.95 (*0-932265-54-5*) White Sound.

Makuch, Jack & Rodgers, June S. Chattanooga: River City Renaissance. LC 98-37335. (Urban Tapestry Ser.). (Illus.). 1998. 49.95 (*1-881096-59-9*) Towery Pub.

Makuch, Joe & Emment, Bonnie, eds. Agricultural Perspectives on Water Resource Management in the Americas: Bibliography. 54p. 1993. pap. text 30.00 (*1-57979-150-6*) DIANE Pub.

Makuch, Joe & Emmert, Bonnie. Irrigating Efficiently: January 1988-February 1994: A Bibliography. 62p. (Orig.). (C). 1995. pap. text 25.00 (*0-7881-1839-0*) DIANE Pub.

Makuch, Joe & Emmert, Bonnie, eds. Agricultural Perspectives on Water Resource Management in the America's: Bibliography, January 1985-July 1993. 49p. (Orig.). (C). 1995. pap. text 25.00 (*0-7881-2164-2*) DIANE Pub.

— Bioassessment of Water Resources: Bibliography: 1985-June 1993. 31p. (Orig.). (C). 1995. pap. text 25.00 (*0-7881-2163-4*) DIANE Pub.

— Risk Assessment & Communication Related to Water Resources: Bibliography January 1985-December 1993. 30p. (Orig.). (C). 1995. pap. text 25.00 (*0-7881-2199-5*) DIANE Pub.

Makuch, Joe, jt. auth. see Emmert, Bonnie.

Makuch, Joe, jt. auth. see Holloway, David.

Makuch, Joe, jt. ed. see Emert, Bonnie.

Makuck, Peter. Against Distance. LC 96-80094. (American Poets Continuum Ser.: No. 42). 75p. 1997. 20.00 (*1-880238-44-6*); pap. 12.50 (*1-880238-45-4*) BOA Edns.

— Breaking & Entering. Stories. LC 81-3406. (Illinois Short Fiction Ser.). 172p. 1981. 9.95 (*0-252-00925-8*); text 14.95 (*0-252-00898-7*) U of Ill Pr.

— Where We Live. (New Poets of America Ser.: Vol. 8). 80p. (C). 1982. 14.00 (*0-918526-40-X*); pap. 7.00 (*0-918526-41-8*) BOA Edns.

Makuck, Peter, jt. ed. see England, Eugene.

***Makujin, John.** Measuring the Music: Another Look at the Contemporary Christian Music Debate. 304p. 2000. pap. 14.99 (*0-88019-403-0*) Schmul Pub Co.

Makus, Eric J. Los Angeles Town Compass: Vital Telephone Numbers Conveniently Organized to Save You Time, Money & Aggravation. ix, 138p. (Orig.). 1996. pap. 14.95 (*0-9654237-0-0*) Town Compass.

— Seattle & Puget Sound Town Compass: Vital Telephone Numbers Conveniently Organized to Save You Time, Money & Aggravation. (Illus.). ix, 158p. 1998. pap. 14.95 (*0-9654237-1-9*) Town Compass.

***Makus, Eric J. & Usibelli, Robert L.** Town Compass Global Internet Directory: 300 Travel Websites for the Urban Astronaut. deluxe ed. 22p. 1999. 4.95 (*0-9654237-4-3*) Town Compass.

— Town Compass Pocket Travel Directory: 300 Travel Telephone Numbers for the Urban Astronaut. deluxe ed. 22p. 1999. 4.95 (*0-9654237-3-5*) Town Compass.

— Town Compass Seattle Internet Directory: 300 Websites for the Urban Astronaut. deluxe ed. 22p. 1999. 4.95 (*0-9654237-6-X*) Town Compass.

— Town Compass Seattle Telephone Directory: 300 Telephone Numbers for the Urban Astronaut. deluxe ed. 22p. 1999. 4.95 (*0-9654237-5-1*) Town Compass.

Makus, Horst. Adrien Dalpayrat (1844-1910) French Ceramics of Art Nouveau. 1998. 75.00 (*3-925369-56-2*, Pub. by Arnoldsche Art Pubs) Antique Collect.

— Day to Day of Modernism: Ceramics in the Fifties. 1998. 75.00 (*3-925369-69-4*, Pub. by Arnoldsche Art Pubs) Antique Collect.

Makus, Ingrid. Women, Politics & Reproduction: The Liberal Legacy. LC 96-223098. vi, 274p. 1996. pap. text 17.75 (*0-8020-7663-7*) U of Toronto Pr.

Makwana, Kashmira, jt. ed. see Carneal, Garry.

Makward, Christiane. Dictionnaire Litteraire des Femmes de la Langue Francaise de Marie de France a Marie Ndiaye. (FRE.). 639p. 1996. pap. 85.00 (*0-7859-9511-0*) Fr & Eur.

Makward, Christiane P. & Miller, Judith G., eds. Plays by French & Francophone Women: A Critical Anthology. (Illus.). 320p. (C). 1994. pap. text 19.95 (*0-472-08258-2*, 08258) U of Mich Pr.

— Plays by French & Francophone Women: A Critical Anthology. LC 95-20373. (Illus.). 320p. (C). 1995. text 49.50 (*0-472-10263-X*, 10263) U of Mich Pr.

Makward, Edris & Ravell-Pinto, Thelma, eds. The Growth of African Literature: Twenty-Five Years after Dakar & Fourah Bay. (Annual Selected Papers of the ALA Ser.). (Illus.). 328p. 1998. 69.95 (*0-86543-658-4*) Africa Wrld Bks.

Makward, Edris, ed. see African Literature Association Staff.

***Mal, Ajit K., ed.** Nondestructive Evaluation of Aging Aircraft, Airports & Aerospace Hardware III. LC 99-226052. 364p. 1999. pap. text 92.00 (*0-8194-3056-0*) SPIE.

Mal, Mary. Where Are We in God's Timing? Examining the Evidence. Date not set. spiral bd. write for info. incl. audio (*0-9659430-3-8*) M Mal.

— Yes, Let's Have a Bible Study, Especially with a Jehovah's Witness, 2 vols. Incl. Vol. I. iii, 152p. 1997. spiral bd. 18.00 (*0-9659430-0-3*); Vol. II. 1997. spiral bd. (*0-9659430-1-1*); 35.00 (*0-9659430-2-X*) M Mal.

Malabe, Frank & Weiner, Bob. Afro-Cuban Rhythms for Drum Set. (Drummers Collective Ser.). (Illus.). 64p. (Orig.). 1990. pap. text 26.95 (*0-89724-574-1*, MMBK0001CD) Wrner Bros.

Malabre. Lost Prophets. 1995. pap. 14.95 (*0-07-103641-5*) McGraw.

Malabre, Alfred L., Jr. Lost Prophets: An Insider's History of the Modern Economists. 272p. 1995. pap. 14.95 (*0-87584-644-0*) Harvard Busn.

Malacara, ed. Interferogram Analysis for Optical Testing. LC 98-24471. (Illus.). 456p. 1998. text 175.00 (*0-8247-9940-2*) Dekker.

Malacara, D., ed. Selected Papers on Optical Shop Metrology. 720p. 1990. pap. 50.00 (*0-8194-0479-9*, VOL. MS18) SPIE.

Malacara, Daniel. Optical Shop Testing. 2nd ed. LC 91-16856. (Series In Pure & Applied Optics: No. 1349). 792p. 1992. 150.00 (*0-471-52232-5*) Wiley.

***Malacara, Daniel.** Optical Testing. 568p. 1999. 105.00 (*0-8194-3216-4*) SPIE.

Malacara, Daniel. Telescopios y Estrellas. (Ciencia para Todos Ser.). (SPA.). pap. 6.99 (*968-16-2862-4*, Pub. by Fondo) Continental Bk.

Malacara, Daniel & Malacara, Zacarias. Handbook of Lens Design. LC 94-18940. (Optical Engineering Ser.: Vol. 44). (Illus.). 672p. 1994. text 150.00 (*0-8247-9225-4*) Dekker.

Malacara, Daniel & Thompson, B. J. Handbook of Optical Engineering. (Optical Engineering Ser.). Date not set. write for info. (*0-8247-9960-7*) Dekker.

Malacara, Daniel, jt. ed. see Hariharan, P.

Malacara, Zacarias, jt. auth. see Malacara, Daniel.

***Malach, Atara.** You Owe It to Yourself: Effective Keys to a Happier Marriage. Birnhack, Sarah, ed. 301p. 1999. 21.95 (*0-9654702-1-0*, Pub. by M Birnhack) Feldheim Pubs.

Malachosky, Tim & Greene, James. Mae West. deluxe limited ed. (Illus.). 350p. 1993. 85.00 (*0-9637169-4-8*) Empire Pub CA.

Malachow, et al. Noise & Diffusion in Bistable Nonequilibrium Systems. 168p. (C). 1985. 80.00 (*0-685-46638-8*, Pub. by Collets) St Mut.

Malachowski, Alan, ed. Reading Rorty: Critical Response to Philosophy & the Mirror of Nature. 288p. 1990. pap. 28.95 (*0-631-16149-X*) Blackwell Pubs.

Malachowski, Cindy, jt. auth. see Quinn, Dawn.

Malachowski, Michael J. & Goldberg, Arleen F. Health Effects of Toxic Substances. 2nd ed. LC 98-32315. 292p. 1999. pap. 69.00 (*0-86587-649-5*) Gov Insts.

Malacinski, George. Essentials of Molecular Biology. 3rd ed. (Life Science Ser.). 1998. pap., student ed. 17.50 (*0-7637-0417-2*) Jones & Bartlett.

— Essentials of Molecular Biology. 3rd ed. LC 97-44023. (Life Science Ser.). 532p. 1998. pap. 57.50 (*0-86720-860-0*) Jones & Bartlett.

Malacinski, George M. Essentials of Molecular Biology. 2nd ed. (Life Science Ser.). 336p. Date not set. pap., student ed. 17.50 (*0-86720-898-8*) Jones & Bartlett.

Malacinski, George M., et al. Molecular Genetics of Mammalian Cells. 1986. text 58.50 (*0-07-039755-4*) McGraw.

Malacinski, George M., jt. ed. see Armstrong, John.

Malafosse. Idiopathic Generalized Epilepsies. 560p. 96.00 (*0-86196-436-5*, Pub. by J Libbey Med) Bks Intl VA.

Malafronie, Victor A. The Complete Book of Frisbee: The History of the Sport & the First Official Price Guide. Johnson, F. Davis, ed. LC 98-167454. (Illus.). 288p. 1998. pap. 19.95 (*0-9663855-2-7*) Amer Trends.

Malaga, Ernie, et al. AS/400 Primer: Fundamental Concepts & Training for Programmers, Administrators, & System Operations. 3rd ed. (Illus.). 560p. 2000. pap. 99.00 (*1-883884-59-4*) Midrange Comput.

— Complete CL: The Definitive Control Language Programming Guide. 3rd ed. (Illus.). 496p. 1999. pap. 79.00 (*1-883884-58-6*) Midrange Comput.

Malaga, Ernie, jt. auth. see Holt, Ted.

Malaga, S., jt. ed. see Santos, F.

Malagon, Joseph. Cinderella Suicide. LC 83-62348. (Illus.). 70p. (Orig.). 1984. pap. 6.00 (*0-318-00451-8*) Metropol Press.

Malagon Ortuondo, J. M. Nautical Dictionary Spanish-English - English-Spanish. (ENG & SPA.). 523p. 1996. pap. 50.00 (*84-283-2254-6*, Pub. by Edit Paraninfon) IBD Ltd.

Malahoff, Alexander, jt. auth. see Chave, E. H.

Malaika, Susan, jt. ed. see Cheng, Josephine.

Malaise, Joseph, ed. see Groote, Gerard.

Malaisse, F. & Brooks, R. R. The Heavy Metal Tolerant Flora of Southcentral Africa: A Multidisciplinary Approach. 206p. (C). 1985. text 136.00 (*90-6191-543-0*, Pub. by A A Balkema) Ashgate Pub Co.

Malaiyandi, M. & Suffet, Irwin H., eds. Organic Pollutants in Water. LC 86-22218. (Advances in Chemistry Ser.: No. 214). (Illus.). xv, 797p. 1986. 99.95 (*0-8412-0951-0*, Pub. by Am Chemical) OUP.

Malaiyandi, Murugan & Suffet, Irwin H., eds. Organic Pollutants in Water: Sampling, Analysis, & Toxicity Testing. LC 86-22218. (Advances in Chemistry Ser.: Vol. 214). 816p. 1987. reprint ed. pap. 200.00 (*0-608-03893-8*, 206434000008) Bks Demand.

Malak, Annabel. L' Alchimiste.Tr. of Alchemist. (FRE.). pap., boxed set 19.95 incl. audio compact disk (*2-921997-33-9*, Pub. by Coffragants) Penton Overseas.

Malak, Annabel. L'Alchimiste.Tr. of Alchemist. (FRE., Illus.). boxed set 14.95 incl. audio (*2-921997-29-0*, Pub. by Coffragants) Penton Overseas.

Malak, Annabel. Cinderella. (Pocketaudio Ser.). (J). (ps-2). 9.95 incl. audio (*2-921997-75-4*, Pub. by Coffragants) Penton Overseas.

— Goldilocks & the Three Bears. (Pocketaudio Ser.). (J). 9.95 incl. audio (*2-921997-84-3*, Pub. by Coffragants) Penton Overseas.

— The Little Match Girl. (Pocketaudio Ser.). (J). (ps-2). 2000. 9.95 incl. audio (*2-921997-88-6*, Pub. by Coffragants) Penton Overseas.

— Puss 'n' Boots. (Pocketaudio Ser.). 2000. 9.95 incl. audio (*2-921997-85-1*, Pub. by Coffragants) Penton Overseas.

— Sleeping Beauty. (Pocketaudio Ser.). (J). (ps-2). 2000. 9.95 incl. audio (*2-921997-74-6*, Pub. by Coffragants) Penton Overseas.

— Three Little Pigs. (Pocketaudio Ser.). (J). (ps-2). 2000. 9.95 incl. audio (*2-921997-73-8*, Pub. by Coffragants) Penton Overseas.

Malaka, Tan. From Jail to Jail, 3 vols. Jarvis, Helen, tr. LC 90-47586. (Monographs in International Studies, Southeast Asia Ser.: No. 83). 1209p. (Orig.). 1991. pap. text 55.00 (*0-89680-150-0*) Ohio U Pr.

***Malakellis, Michael.** Integrated Macro-Micro-Modelling under Rational Expectations: With an Application to Tariff Reform in Australia. Muller, W. A. & Bihn, M., eds. LC 00-21175. (Contributions to Economics Ser.). xiv, 279p. 2000. pap. (*3-7908-1274-9*) Spr-Verlag.

Malaker, Kamal, jt. auth. see Bump, Edward A.

Malaker, Kristin S., jt. auth. see Anderson, Philip C.

Malakhov, A. Mystery of the Earth's Mantle. (Illus.). 204p. 1975. 14.95 (*0-8464-0664-0*) Beekman Pubs.

Malakhov, Mikhail, jt. auth. see Weber, Richard.

Malakhov, N. Fedoskino. (Illus.). 168p. (C). 1984. text 225.00 (*0-7855-5880-2*, Pub. by Collets) St Mut.

Malakhovski, L. V. A Dictionary of English Homonyms & Homoforms: (English to Russian) (ENG & RUS.). 624p. (C). 1995. 27.95 (*0-8285-5229-0*) Firebird NY.

Malaki, Akhil. Development Patterns in the Commonwealth Caribbean: Jamaica & Trinidad & Tobago. (Institute of Latin American Studies: Vol. 30). (Illus.). 141p. 1996. pap. 69.50 (*91-85894-44-3*, Pub. by Almqvist Wiksell) Coronet Bks.

Malaki, Akhil, jt. ed. see Behar, Jaime.

Malaki, Akhil, jt. ed. see Karlsson, Weine.

Malakoff, Edward & Malakoff, Sheila. Pairpoint Lamps. LC 90-63190. (Illus.). 160p. 1990. 95.00 (*0-88740-281-X*) Schiffer.

Malakoff, Laura Z. Housing Options for the Elderly: The Innovation Process in Community Settings. rev. ed. LC 91-30753. (Studies on the Elderly in America). 152p. 1991. text 25.00 (*0-8153-0525-7*) Garland.

Malakoff, Sheila, jt. auth. see Malakoff, Edward.

Malalas, Ioannes. Chronographia. 690p. 1997. text 311.00 (*3-11-008800-2*) De Gruyter.

Malalasekera, George P. Dictionary of Pali Proper Names, 2 vols. (PLI.). 1983. 250.00 (*0-8288-1721-9*, F 27380) Fr & Eur.

Malalasekera, George P. & Jayatilleke, K. N. Buddhism & the Race Question. LC 77-18853. (Race Question in Modern Thought). 73p. 1978. reprint ed. lib. bdg. 55.00 (*0-313-20208-7*, MABU, Greenwood Pr) Greenwood.

Malam, John. Airport: Explore the Building Room by Room. LC 99-14504. (Building Works). 32p. 1999. 16.95 (*0-87226-586-2*, 65862B, P Bedrick Books) NTC Contemp Pub Co.

— Ancient Egypt. (Remains to Be Seen Ser.). (Illus.). 48p. (J). (gr. 5-8). 1998. 19.95 (*0-237-51839-2*) EVN1 UK.

***Malam, John.** Ancient Egypt. (Art & Civilization Ser.). (Illus.). 40p. (J). 2000. 16.95 (*0-87226-617-6*, 66176B, P Bedrick Books) NTC Contemp Pub Co.

— Ancient Greece. (Art & Civilization Ser.). (Illus.). 40p. (J). 2000. 16.95 (*0-87226-616-8*, 66176B, P Bedrick Books) NTC Contemp Pub Co.

— The Ancient Greeks. LC 99-32523. (History Starts Here Ser.). 32p. (J). 2000. lib. bdg. 22.83 (*0-7398-1350-1*) Raintree Steck-V.

— Ancient Greeks. (History Starts Here Ser.). (J). 2000. pap. 8.95 (*0-7398-1823-6*) Raintree Steck-V.

Malam, John. Ancient Greeks at a Glance. LC 98-11862. (At a Glance Ser.). (Illus.). 32p. (YA). (gr. 3 up). 1998. 14.95 (*0-87226-557-9*, 65579B, P Bedrick Books) NTC Contemp Pub Co.

— Beatrix Potter. LC 97-30608. (Tell Me About Ser.). (Illus.). (J). (gr. k-5). 1997. 19.93 (*1-57505-275-X*, Carolrhoda) Lerner Pub.

— Claude Monet. LC 97-6618. (Tell Me about Ser.). (Illus.). 24p. (J). (gr. 2-4). 1998. lib. bdg. 19.93 (*1-57505-250-4*, Carolrhoda) Lerner Pub.

***Malam, John.** Cleaning the House. (Everyday History Ser.). (Illus.). (J). 2000. pap. 6.95 (*0-531-15411-4*) Watts.

An Asterisk (*) at the beginning of an entry indicates that the title is appearing for the first time.

— Exploring Ancient Greece. (Remains to Be Seen Ser.). (Illus.). 47p. (YA). 1999. 19.95 (*0-237-51994-1*) EVN1 UK.

Malam, John. Gods & Goddesses. LC 99-11849. (Ancient Greece Ser.). 48p. (J). 1999. 18.95 (*0-87226-598-6*, 65986B, P Bedrick Books) NTC Contemp Pub Co.

— Greek Town. LC 98-41945. (Metropolis Ser.). (Illus.). 45p. (J). (gr. 4-6). 1999. lib. bdg. 25.00 (*0-531-14529-8*) Watts.

***Malam, John.** Greek Town. (Metropolis Ser.). (Illus.). (J). 2000. pap. 8.95 (*0-531-15379-7*) Watts.

Malam, John. Highest, Longest, Deepest. LC 96-69702. (Extraordinary World Ser.). (Illus.). 44p. (J). (gr. 4-7). 1996. 16.95 (*0-689-80951-4*) S&S Childrens.

— Hospital. LC 99-24757. (Building Works Ser.). 32p. 1999. 16.95 (*0-87226-585-4*, 65854B, P Bedrick Books) NTC Contemp Pub Co.

— How It Works, No. 3. LC 97-67970. (Illus.). 32p. (J). 1998. 14.00 (*0-689-81188-8*) S&S Childrens.

— How It Works, No. 4. LC 97-67988. (Illus.). (J). 1998. 14.00 (*0-689-81189-6*) S&S Childrens.

— Indiana Jones Explores Ancient Greece. (Illus.). 47p. (J). (gr. 5-8). 1996. write for info. (*0-237-51221-1*) EVN1 UK.

— Indiana Jones Explores Ancient Rome. (Illus.). 47p. (J). (gr. 5-8). 1996. write for info. (*0-237-51223-8*) EVN1 UK.

Malam, John. Indiana Jones Explores the Incas. (Indiana Jones Explores Ser.). (Illus.). 48p. (J). (gr. 3-7). 1993. 14.45 (*1-55970-199-4*, Pub. by Arcade Pub Inc) Time Warner.

Malam, John. Indiana Jones Explores the Vikings. (Illus.). 47p. (J). (gr. 5-8). 1996. write for info. (*0-237-51222-X*) EVN1 UK.

***Malam, John.** John Cabot. LC 98-8488. (Tell Me about Ser.). (Illus.). 24p. (J). (ps-3). 1999. 19.93 (*1-57505-365-9*, Carolrhoda) Lerner Pub.

Malam, John. Leonardo da Vinci. LC 98-8489. (Tell Me about Ser.). 24p. (J). (gr. k-3). 1999. 19.93 (*1-57505-367-5*, Carolrhoda) Lerner Pub.

***Malam, John.** Library. LC 99-57835. (Building Works Ser.). 32p. 2000. 16.95 (*0-87226-587-0*, 65870B, P Bedrick Books) NTC Contemp Pub Co.

Malam, John. Myths & Civilization of the Ancient Romans. (Myths & Civilization Ser.). 48p. (J). 1999. lib. bdg. 16.95 (*0-87226-590-0*, 65900B, P Bedrick Books) NTC Contemp Pub Co.

— Pieter Breughel. LC 98-8486. (Tell Me about Ser.). (Illus.). 24p. (J). (ps-3). 1999. 19.93 (*1-57505-366-7*, Carolrhoda) Lerner Pub.

***Malam, John.** Song & Dance. (Everyday History Ser.). (Illus.). (YA). 2000. pap. 6.95 (*0-531-15984-1*) Watts.

— Super Structures. (Fast Forward Ser.). (Illus.). (J). 2000. write for info. (*0-531-11875-4*); pap. 9.95 (*0-531-16441-1*) Watts.

— Theater. (Building Works Ser.). 32p. 2000. 16.95 (*0-87226-588-9*, 65889B, P Bedrick Books) NTC Contemp Pub Co.

— Thor Heyerdahl. LC 98-8487. (Tell Me about Ser.). 24p. (J). (gr. k-3). 1999. 19.93 (*1-57505-364-0*, Carolrhoda) Lerner Pub.

Malam, John. The Traveler's Guide to Ancient Rome. LC 98-7365. (Illus.). (J). 1999. write for info. (*0-590-11763-7*) Scholastic Inc.

— Vincent Van Gogh. LC 97-8066. (Tell Me about Ser.). (Illus.). 24p. (J). (gr. k-5). 1998. 19.93 (*1-57505-249-0*, Carolrhoda) Lerner Pub.

— Wolfgang Amadeus Mozart. LC 97-9246. (Tell Me about Ser.). (Illus.). 24p. (J). (gr. 2-4). 1998. 19.93 (*1-57505-247-4*, Carolrhoda) Lerner Pub.

***Malam, John.** You Wouldn't Want to Be a Roman Gladiator: Gory Things You'd Rather Not Know! LC 00-24728. (Illus.). (J). 2000. write for info. (*0-531-14598-0*) Watts.

Malam, John & Hincks, Gary. Extraordinary World: Highest, Longest, Deepest - An Exploration of the World's Most Fantastic Features. (Illus.). 44p. (J). 19.99 (*0-590-24956-8*) Scholastic Inc.

Malamah-Thomas, Ann. Classroom Interaction. Widdowson, H. G. & Candlin, C. N., eds. (Illus.). 160p. 1987. pap. text 14.95 (*0-19-437131-X*) OUP.

Malamat, Abraham. Mari & the Bible. LC 97-18282. (Studies in the History & Culture of the Ancient Near East). viii, 270p. 1998. 84.50 (*90-04-10863-7*) Brill Academic Pubs.

— Mari & the Early Israelite Experience: The Schweich Lectures, 1984. (Schweich Lectures on Biblical Archaeology, British Academy Ser.). (Illus.). 174p. 1992. reprint ed. pap. text 28.00 (*0-19-726117-5*) OUP.

Malamat, Abraham, jt. auth. see Brown University Staff.

Malamed, Stanley F. Handbook of Local Anesthesia. 4th ed. (Illus.). 352p. (C). (gr. 13). 1996. pap. text 48.00 (*0-8151-6423-8*, 26260) Mosby Inc.

— Medical Emergencies in the Dental Office. 4th rev. ed. LC 92-49542. (Illus.). 480p. (C). (gr. 13). 1992. pap. text 52.00 (*0-8016-6386-5*, 06386) Mosby Inc.

***Malamed, Stanley F.** Medical Emergencies in the Dental Office. 5th ed. LC 99-40660. 1999. write for info. (*1-55664-420-5*) Mosby Inc.

Malamed, Stanley F. Sedation: A Guide to Patient Management. 3rd ed. LC 94-32507. (Illus.). 656p. (C). (gr. 13). 1994. pap. text 54.00 (*0-8151-5736-3*, 24148) Mosby Inc.

Malamet, Elliott. The World Remade: Graham Greene & the Art of Detection. (American University Studies IV: Vol. 183). 150p. (C). 1998. text 34.95 (*0-8204-3304-7*) P Lang Pubng.

Malami, Alhaji S. Sir Siddiq Abubakar III, 17th Sultan of Sokoto: Seventeenth Sultan of Sokoto. (Kenya People Ser.). (Illus.). 240p. 1991. write for info. (*0-237-51196-7*) EVN1 UK.

Malami, Chris. The Purple Palace. LC 95-5817. 76p. 1995. 11.95 (*1-883911-05-2*) Brandylane.

Malami, Shehu. Sir Siddiq Abubakar III, 17th Sultan of Sokoto: The Sokoto Caliphate in Perspective. LC 89-584. 1989. write for info. (*0-7146-3173-6*, Pub. by F Cass Pubs); pap. write for info. (*0-7146-4068-9*, Pub. by F Cass Pubs) Intl Spec Bk.

Malamud, Bernard. The Assistant. 272p. 1980. mass mkt. 6.99 (*0-380-51474-5*, Avon Bks) Morrow Avon.

— The Assistant. 304p. 1993. pap. 10.00 (*0-380-72085-X*, Avon Bks) Morrow Avon.

— The Assistant. LC 57-7397. 1957. 11.09 (*0-606-03718-7*, Pub. by Turtleback) Demco.

***Malamud, Bernard.** Assistant. (Perennial Classics Ser.). 2000. pap. 13.00 (*0-06-095830-8*) HarpC.

Malamud, Bernard. The Assistant. large type ed. LC 98-33788. 1998. 24.95 (*0-7838-0364-8*, G K Hall Lrg Type) Mac Lib Ref.

— The Complete Stories of Bernard Malamud. LC 97-12394. 1997. 35.00 (*0-374-12639-9*) FS&G.

— The Complete Stories of Bernard Malamud. 656p. 1998. pap. 16.00 (*0-374-52575-7*) FS&G.

— The Fixer. 316p. Date not set. 24.95 (*0-8488-2360-5*) Amereon Ltd.

— The Fixer. 1989. pap. 3.95 (*0-685-53965-2*, WSP) PB.

— The Fixer. 304p. 1994. pap. 12.95 (*0-14-018515-1*, Penguin Classics) Viking Penguin.

— The Fixer. large type ed. LC 98-54108. 395p. 1999. 27.95 (*1-56000-484-3*) Transaction Pubs.

— God's Grace. (Twentieth-Century Classics Ser.). 208p. 1995. pap. 11.95 (*0-14-018491-0*, Penguin Classics) Viking Penguin.

— Long Work, Short Life. (Chapbooks in Literature Ser.). (Illus.). 1985. 5.00 (*0-9614940-1-8*) Bennington Coll.

***Malamud, Bernard.** The Magic Barrel. 224p. 1999. pap. 12.00 (*0-374-52586-2*) FS&G.

— The Magic Barrel. large type ed. LC 00-24297. 267p. 2000. 27.95 (*0-7838-9010-9*, G K Hall Lrg Type) Mac Lib Ref.

Malamud, Bernard. The Natural. 336p. (YA). (gr. 8 up). 1999. pap. 13.50 (*0-380-72084-1*, Avon Bks) Morrow Avon.

— The Natural. 1995. 8.95 (*0-606-01688-0*, Pub. by Turtleback) Demco.

***Malamud, Bernard.** Natural. (Perennial Classics Ser.). 2000. pap. 13.00 (*0-06-095829-4*) HarpC.

Malamud, Bernard. Natural M. 217p. 1980. mass mkt. 6.99 (*0-380-50609-2*, Avon Bks) Morrow Avon.

— A New Life. 208p. 1995. pap. 12.95 (*0-14-018681-6*, Penguin Classics) Viking Penguin.

— The People: And Other Uncollected Fiction. 1989. 18.95 (*0-374-23067-6*) FS&G.

— Talking Horse: Bernard Malamud on Life & Work. Cheuse, Alan & Delbance, Nicholas, eds. LC 95-25957. 246p. 1996. pap. 37.00 (*0-231-10184-8*) Col U Pr.

— Talking Horse: Bernard Malamud on Life & Work. 220p. 1997. pap. 16.50 (*0-231-10185-6*) Col U Pr.

Malamud, Bernard & Kinsella, W. P. The Natural & Shoeless Joe: Curriculum Unit. (Novel Ser.). 79p. (YA). (gr. 9-12). 1992. spiral bd. 18.95 (*1-56077-236-0*) Ctr Learning.

Malamud, Bernard, jt. auth. see Center for Learning Network Staff.

Malamud, Carl. A World's Fair for the Global Village. LC 97-11146. (Illus.). 304p. 1997. 44.00 (*0-262-13338-5*) MIT Pr.

Malamud-Goti, Jaime E. Game Without End: State Terror & the Politics of Justice. LC 96-20117. 256p. 1996. 24.95 (*0-8061-2826-7*) U of Okla Pr.

Malamud, Martha A. A Poetics of Transformation: Prudentius & Classical Mythology. LC 88-43290. (Cornell Studies in Classical Philology). 224p. 1989. 35.00 (*0-8014-2249-3*) Cornell U Pr.

— A Poetics of Transformation: Prudentius & Classical Mythology. LC 88-43290. (Cornell Studies in Classical Philology: Vol. 49). 208p. reprint ed. pap. 64.50 (*0-608-20920-1*, 207201900003) Bks Demand.

Malamud, Randy. The Language of Modernism. Litz, A. Walton, ed. LC 89-20134. (Studies in Modern Literature: No. 108). 208p. reprint ed. 64.50 (*0-8357-2030-6*, 207073800004) Bks Demand.

— Reading Zoos: Representations of Animals & Captivity. LC 97-38182. 320p. 1998. text 55.00 (*0-8147-5602-6*); pap. text 18.50 (*0-8147-5603-4*) NYU Pr.

— T. S. Eliot's Drama: A Research & Production Sourcebook, 2. LC 91-46960. (Modern Dramatists Research & Production Sourcebooks Ser.: No. 2). 328p. 1992. lib. bdg. 59.95 (*0-313-27813-X*, MTK, Greenwood Pr) Greenwood.

— Where the Words Are Valid: T. S. Eliot's Communities of Drama, 58. LC 94-22018. (Contributions in Drama & Theatre Studies: Vol. 58). 224p. 1994. 55.00 (*0-313-27818-0*, Greenwood Pr) Greenwood.

Malamud Rikles, Carlos D., et al. Historia de Espana Vol. 2, No. 31: La Epoca de la Ilustracion: Las Indias y la Politica Exterior. 904p. 1992. 189.50 (*84-239-4979-6*) Elliots Bks.

Malamuth, Charles, tr. see Kataev, Valentin.

Malamuth, Neil M. & Donnerstein, Edward. Pornography & Sexual Aggression. 1984. text 84.93 (*0-12-466280-3*) Acad Pr.

— Pornography & Sexual Aggression. 1986. pap. text 55.00 (*0-12-466281-1*) Acad Pr.

Malamuth, Neil M., jt. auth. see Linz, Daniel.

Malamuth, Neil M., jt. ed. see Buss, David M.

Malan. Anorexia, Murder & Suicide. 256p. 2000. text 46.50 (*0-7506-3003-5*) Buttrwrth-Heinemann.

Malan, Allan R. & Malan, Deanna E. The Friendly Spinning Wheel. LC 97-66107. (Michigan Pioneer Farmer Ser.: Vol. 1). (Illus.). 304p. (J). (gr. 4-6). 1997. 19.95 (*0-9657503-0-2*) Scribes.

Malan, Cesar. The Cross - Where All Roads Meet. 1994. pap. 7.99 (*0-85234-316-7*, Pub. by Evangelical Pr) P & R Pubng.

Malan, D. H. The Frontier of Brief Psychotherapy: An Example of the Convergence of Research & Clinical Practice. LC 76-9646. (Topics in General Psychiatry Ser.). (Illus.). 388p. (C). 1976. 49.50 (*0-306-30895-9*, Plenum Trade) Perseus Pubng.

— A Study of Brief Psychotherapy. LC 75-30916. 326p. 1976. pap. 27.50 (*0-306-20019-8*, Plenum Trade) Perseus Pubng.

— Toward the Validation of Dynamic Psychotherapy: A Replication. LC 76-10182. 308p. 1976. 59.50 (*0-306-30896-7*, Plenum Trade) Perseus Pubng.

Malan, Dan. Angels: 100 Engravings by Gustave Dore. (Illus.). 112p. 1996. pap. 14.95 (*0-9631135-9-3*) MCE Publ Co.

— The Complete Guide to Classics Illustrated. (U. S. Ser.: Vol. 1). (Illus.). 112p. 1994. reprint ed. pap. 24.95 (*0-9631135-0-X*) MCE Publ Co.

— The Complete Guide to Classics Illustrated. (Foreign Ser.: Vol. 2). (Illus.). 116p. 1994. reprint ed. pap. 24.95 (*0-9631135-1-8*) MCE Publ Co.

— Gustave Dore, a Biography. 208p. 1996. per. 19.95 (*1-888957-02-6*) MCE Publ Co.

Malan, David H. Individual Psychotherapy & the Science of Psychodynamics. 2nd ed. (Illus.). 288p. 1995. pap. text 45.00 (*0-7506-2387-X*) Buttrwrth-Heinemann.

Malan, Deanna E., jt. auth. see Malan, Allan R.

Malan, F. R. Bills of Exchange, Cheques & Promissory Notes in South African Law. 441p. 1983. pap. 100.00 (*0-409-04074-6*, SA, MICHIE) LEXIS Pub.

— Butterworths Selection of Statutes: Persons & Family Law. 192p. 1990. pap. 41.00 (*0-409-01504-0*, SA, MICHIE) LEXIS Pub.

— Provisional Sentence on Bills of Exchange, Cheques & Promissory Notes. 269p. 1986. pap. 92.00 (*0-409-04086-X*, SA, MICHIE) LEXIS Pub.

Malan, F. R. & Labuschagne, E. Butterworths Wetbundel: Persone- en Familiereg. 3rd ed. (AFR.). 208p. 1994. pap. write for info. (*0-409-01490-7*, MICHIE) LEXIS Pub.

Malan, F. R. & Oelofse, A. N. South African Banking Legislation. 400p. 1991. ring bd. write for info. (*0-7021-2572-5*, Pub. by Juta & Co) Gaunt.

Malan, F. R. & Pretorius, J. T. Malan on Bills of Exchange, Cheques, & Promissory Notes in South African Law. 3rd ed. LC 98-189422. 573p. 1997. write for info. (*0-409-04106-8*) Buttrwrth-Heinemann.

Malan, F. R., et al. Malan on Bills of Exchange, Cheques & Promissory Notes in South African Law. 2nd rev. ed. 570p. 1995. pap. write for info. (*0-409-04105-X*, MICHIE) LEXIS Pub.

Malan, F. R., jt. ed. see Van Der Walt, J. C.

Malan, Michael, jt. ed. see Sears, Peter.

Malan, Rian. My Traitor's Heart. LC 90-50145. (Vintage International Ser.). 432p. 1991. pap. 14.00 (*0-679-73215-2*) Vin Bks.

***Malan, Rian.** My Traitor's Heart: A South African Exile Returns to Face His Country, His Tribe & His Conscience. 368p. 2000. reprint ed. pap. 13.00 (*0-8021-3684-2*, Pub. by Grove-Atltc) Publishers Group.

***Malan, Robin.** No Place Like: And Other Stories. LC 00-38950. 2000. pap. write for info. (*0-86543-862-5*) Africa World.

***Malana, D.** Critical Technologies & Competitiveness. 247p. 2000. lib. bdg. 59.00 (*1-56072-795-0*) Nova Sci Pubs.

Malana, D., ed. Critical Technologies & Economic Competitiveness. 227p. (C). 1994. lib. bdg. 125.00 (*1-56072-091-3*) Nova Sci Pubs.

Malanchuk, Maureen. Inforelief: Stay Afloat in the InfoFlood. (Warren Bennis Executive Briefing Ser.). (Illus.). 125p. 1996. 22.50 (*0-7879-0347-7*, Pfiff & Co) Jossey-Bass.

Malanczuk, Peter. Akehurst's Modern Introduction to International Law. 7th ed. LC 97-2294. 472p. (C). 1997. pap. 29.99 (*0-415-11120-X*) Routledge.

Malanczuk, Peter & Akehurst, Michael B. Akehurst's Modern Introduction to International Law. 7th ed. LC 97-2294. 472p. (C). 1997. 125.00 (*0-415-16553-9*) Routledge.

Maland, Charles J. American Visions, the Films of Chaplin, Ford, Capra & Welles, 1936-1941. 1977. 36.95 (*0-405-09892-8*, 11487) Ayer.

— Chaplin & American Culture: The Evolution of a Star Image. (Illus.). 464p. 1989. pap. text 19.95 (*0-691-02860-5*, Pub. by Princeton U Pr) Cal Prin Full Svc.

— Frank Capra. (Twayne's Filmmakers Ser.). 1995. pap. 20.00 (*0-8057-4501-7*, Twyne) Mac Lib Ref.

Maland, David. Europe in the Seventeenth Century. 1969. pap. text 11.50 (*0-312-26775-4*) St Martin.

Malandain & Verdol. Methode Orange, Bk 1. (Methode Orange Ser.). (Illus.). (gr. 7-12). 1979. text 6.25 (*0-88345-407-6*) Prentice ESL.

Malandra, Geri H. Unfolding a Mandala: The Buddhist Cave Temples at Ellora. (C). 1997. 68.00 (*81-7030-517-9*, Pub. by Sri Satguru Pubns) S Asia.

— Unfolding a Mandala: The Buddhist Cave Temples at Ellora. LC 92-8142. (SUNY Series in Buddhist Studies). (Illus.). 348p. (C). 1993. text 89.50 (*0-7914-1355-1*); pap. text 29.95 (*0-7914-1356-X*) State U NY Pr.

Malandra, William W., ed. An Introduction to Ancient Iranian Religion: Readings from the "Avesta" & "Achaemenid" Inscriptions. LC 82-21784. (Minnesota Publications in the Humanities: No. 2). 208p. 1983. reprint ed. pap. 64.50 (*0-608-00837-0*, 206162800010) Bks Demand.

Malandro, Loretta A., et al. Nonverbal Communication. 2nd ed. 352p. (C). 1988. pap. 45.94 (*0-07-555059-8*) McGraw.

Malandro, Loretta A., jt. auth. see Smith, Lawrence J.

Malanga, Gerard. Chic Death. 131p. 1971. 12.50 (*0-913219-14-2*) Pym-Rand Pr.

— Chic Death. deluxe ed. 131p. 1971. 22.50 (*0-913219-16-9*) Pym-Rand Pr.

— Equal Time. deluxe ed. 1979. pap. 10.00 (*0-317-42210-3*) Bellevue Pr.

— Mythologies of the Heart. LC 95-53182. (Illus.). 179p. (Orig.). (C). 1996. 25.00 (*0-87685-994-5*); pap. 13.50 (*0-87685-993-7*) Black Sparrow.

— Mythologies of the Heart, signed ed. deluxe ed. LC 95-53182. (Illus.). 179p. (Orig.). (C). 1996. 35.00 (*0-87685-995-3*) Black Sparrow.

— Rosebud. deluxe ed. (Illus.). 40p. 1975. 25.00 (*0-915778-15-7*) Penmaen Pr.

— Screen Tests, Portraits, Nudes, 1964-1996. (Illus.). 200p. 1998. 44.95 (*3-88243-577-1*) Steidl.

— Three Diamonds. LC 91-23551. (Illus.). 220p. 1991. 20.00 (*0-87685-838-8*) Black Sparrow.

— Three Diamonds. LC 91-23551. (Illus.). 220p. 1991. pap. 12.50 (*0-87685-837-X*) Black Sparrow.

Malanga, Gerard, photos by. Gerard Malanga: Resistance to Memory. (Illus.). 120p. 1998. 65.00 (*0-9657280-6-4*, 810171) Arena Editions.

Malanga, Gerard, et al, texts. Andy Warhol: Thirty Are Better Than One. (Illus.). 51p. 1998. pap. 35.00 (*1-891475-07-X*, 810951) T Shafrazi.

Malanga, Gerard, jt. auth. see Bockris, Victor.

***Malanga, Tara.** Sleepy Angel Gift Set. (Illus.). 32p. (ps-2). 2000. 29.95 (*0-8091-6681-X*) Paulist Pr.

***Malanga, Tara & Okeefe, Susan Heyboer.** Sleepy Angel's First Bedtime Story. 32p. (J). 2000. 9.95 (*0-8091-6670-4*) Paulist Pr.

***Malanga, Tara, et al.** Sleepy Angel's First Bedtime Story. LC 99-48050. (Illus.). (J). 1999. pap. write for info. (*0-8091-6671-2*) Paulist Pr.

Malangoni, Mark A. Critical Issues in Operating Room Management. LC 96-15605. 288p. 1996. text 76.00 (*0-397-51636-3*) Lppncott W & W.

Malangoni, Mark A., ed. Critical Issues in Operating Room Management. LC 96-15605. 1997. write for info. (*0-397-51796-3*) Lppncott W & W.

Malani, I., jt. auth. see Phadnis, U.

Malania, Leo, ed. Ministry to the Sick. 192p. 1988. 10.95 (*0-89869-205-9*) Church Pub Inc.

***Malano, Hector M. & Hofwegen, Paul J. M.** Management of Irrigation & Drainage Systems: A Service Approach. (Illus.). 160p. (C). 1999. text 65.00 (*90-5410-482-1*, Pub. by A A Balkema); pap. text 38.00 (*90-5410-483-X*, Pub. by A A Balkema) Ashgate Pub Co.

Malanotte-Rizzoli, P., ed. Modern Approaches to Data Assimilation in Ocean Modeling. (Oceanography Ser.: Vol. 61). 468p. 1996. pap. text 55.75 (*0-444-82484-7*) Elsevier.

— Modern Approaches to Data Assimilation in Ocean Modeling. LC 96-3901. (Oceanography Ser.: No. 61). 468p. 1996. text 154.50 (*0-444-82079-5*) Elsevier.

Malanotte-Rizzoli, Paola & Eremeev, Valery N. The Eastern Mediterranenan as a Laboratory Basin for the Assessment of Contrasting Ecosystems. LC 99-10161. (NATO Science Ser.). 16p. 1999. write for info. (*0-7923-5585-7*) Kluwer Academic.

Malanotte-Rizzoli, Paola & Robinson, Allan R., eds. Ocean Processes in Climate Dynamics - Global & Mediterranean Examples: Proceedings of the NATO Advanced Study Institute, Erice, Italy, January 20-February 2, 1993. LC 93-38824. (NATO Advanced Study Institutes Series C, Mathematical & Physical Sciences). 460p. (C). 1995. text 259.00 (*0-7923-2624-5*) Kluwer Academic.

Malanowski, Jamie. Mr. Stupid Goes to Washington: A Political Satire. LC 92-15474. 224p. 1992. 16.95 (*1-55972-132-4*, Birch Ln Pr) Carol Pub Group.

Malanowski, K. Stability of Solutions to Convex Problems of Optimization. (Lecture Notes in Control & Information Sciences: Vol. 93). ix, 137p. 1987. 31.95 (*0-387-17589-X*) Spr-Verlag.

Malanowski, K. & Mizukami, K., eds. Analysis & Algorithms of Optimization Problems. (Lecture Notes in Control & Information Sciences: Vol. 82). viii, 240p. 1986. 35.95 (*0-387-16660-2*) Spr-Verlag.

Malanowski, Stanislaw. Thermodynamics of Fluids: Measurement & Correlation. Anderko, Andrzej, ed. 524p. (C). 1990. text 113.00 (*981-02-0169-9*) World Scientific Pub.

Malanowski, Stanislaw & Anderko, Andrzej. Modelling Phase Equilibria: Thermodynamic Background & Practical Tools. (Series in Chemical Engineering: No. 1793). 328p. 1992. 79.95 (*0-471-57103-2*) Wiley.

Malanson, George P. Riparian Landscapes. LC 92-30617. (Studies in Ecology). (Illus.). 306p. (C). 1993. text 64.95 (*0-521-38431-1*) Cambridge U Pr.

Malanson, George P. Riparian Landscapes. (Cambridge Studies in Ecology). (Illus.). 306p. 1996. pap. text 30.95 (*0-521-56683-5*) Cambridge U Pr.

Malanson, George P., ed. Natural Areas Facing Climate Change. (Illus.). viii, 92p. 1989. pap. 30.00 (*90-5103-030-4*, Pub. by SPB Acad Pub) Balogh.

Malantschuk, Gregor. Kierkegaard's Thought. Hong, Howard V. & Hong, Edna H., eds. & trs. by. LC 77-155000. 398p. reprint ed. pap. 123.40 (*0-8357-3236-3*, 205713000011) Bks Demand.

Malapanis, Argiris, ed. see Waters, Mary-Alice, et al.

Malaparte, Curzio. Kaputt. Foligno, Cesare, tr. from ITA. LC 95-36162. (European Classics Ser.). (Illus.). 407p. (C). 1995. pap. 10.95 (*0-8101-1341-4*, Marlboro) Northwestern U Pr.

— La Peau. (FRE.). 1982. pap. 13.95 (*0-7859-4021-9*) Fr & Eur.

M

— The Skin. Moore, David, tr. LC 97-29545. (European Classics Ser.). 274p. 1997. pap. 16.95 (0-8101-1572-7) Northwestern U Pr.

Malapetsas, Tasos. The Industrial Sensor Business. LC 98-120886. (Report Ser.: No. GB-200). 144p. 1997. 2950.00 (1-56965-459-X) BCC.

Malaquais, Dominique. The Kingdom of Benin. LC 97-37373. (First Bks.). (J). 1998. 22.50 (0-531-20279-8) Watts.

Malar, Ryan, jt. auth. see Eliason, Alan.

Malarek, Victor. Hey Malarek. 241p. 1984. mass mkt. 5.95 (0-88780-140-4, Pub. by Formac Publ Co) Formac Dist Ltd.

Malarkey, Joe. It's Not the Fall That Kills You: Laughing All the Way to That Sudden Stop at the End. LC 98-86050. 147p. 1998. pap. 12.95 (1-892447-09-6) Laten Print.

Malarkey, John J., 3rd, ed. Term Papers & Reports: The Wilmington College Style Guide. LC 93-5797. 120p. (Orig.). (C). 1993. pap. text 4.95 (0-9636944-0-5) Wilmington Coll.

Malarkey, Louise, jt. auth. see McMorrow, Mary E.

Malarkey, Louise M. & McMorrow, Mary E. Nurse's Manual of Laboratory Test & Diagnostic Procedures. 2nd ed. Eoyang, Thomas, ed. LC 99-11885. (Illus.). 895p. 1999. pap. text. write for info. (0-7216-7812-2, W B Saunders Co) Harcrt Hlth Sci Grp.

— Nurse's Manual of Laboratory Tests & Diagnostic Procedures. Eoyang, Ton, ed. LC 95-17715. (Illus.). 1005p. 1996. pap. text 31.50 (0-7216-3774-4, W B Saunders Co) Harcrt Hlth Sci Grp.

Malarkey, Ryan, jt. auth. see Eliason, Alan.

***Malarkey, Tucker.** An Obvious Enchantment. LC 99-55334. 224p. 2000. 23.95 (0-375-50409-5) Random.

Malarkey, William B. Take Control of Your Aging. LC 99-32910. 256p. 1999. 23.95 (1-888683-60-0) Wooster Bk.

Malaro, Marie C. A Legal Primer on Managing Museum Collections. LC 84-23497. 366p. 1987. pap. text 19.95 (0-87474-697-3, MALPP) Smithsonian.

— A Legal Primer on Managing Museum Collections. 2nd ed. LC 97-11780. 544p. 1998. text 55.00 (1-56098-762-6); pap. text 29.95 (1-56098-787-1) Smithsonian.

— Museum Governance: Mission, Ethics, Policy. LC 93-49384. 208p. (Orig.). 1994. pap. text 16.95 (1-56098-363-9) Smithsonian.

Malas, J. C., jt. ed. see Gunasekera, J. S.

Malasekera, G. P. Dictionary of Pali Proper Names, 2 vols. (C). 1938. 79.50 (0-86013-269-2, Pub. by Pali Text) Elsevier.

Malashenko, Alexei & Gordon-Polonskaya, Ludmilla. Islam in Central Asia. 171p. 1996. pap. 19.95 (0-614-21625-7, 581) Kazi Pubns.

Malaski, Christine, jt. auth. see Anderson, Laura.

Malaspina, Ann. Children's Rights. LC 97-35064. (Overview Ser.). (Illus.). 112p. (YA). (gr. 7 up). 1997. lib. bdg. 22.45 (1-56006-175-8) Lucent Bks.

***Malaspina, Ann.** Mahatma Gandhi & India's Independence in World History. LC 99-50570. (In World History Ser.). (Illus.). 128p. (YA). (gr. 5 up). 2000. lib. bdg. 20.95 (0-7660-1398-7) Enslow Pubs.

Malaspina, Anna. Saving the American Wilderness. LC 98-31959. (Overview Ser.). (Illus.). 128p. (YA). (gr. 4-12). 1999. lib. bdg. 23.70 (1-56006-505-2) Lucent Bks.

Malaspina, Margaret A. Don't Die Broke: How to Turn Your Retirement Savings into Lasting Income. LC 99-14869. 256p. 1999. 21.95 (1-57660-068-8, Pub. by Bloomberg NJ) Norton.

Malaspina, Margaret A. Don't Die Broke: Taking Money Out of Your IRA, 401k, or Other Savings Plan & Creating Lasting Retirement Income. pap. 15.95 (1-57660-040-8, Pub. by Bloomberg NJ) Norton.

Malaspina, Mark, et al. What Works Report No. 1: Air Pollution Solutions. (What Works Ser.). (Illus.). 113p. (Orig.). (C). 1992. pap. text 17.00 (0-9638613-0-1) Environ Exchange.

Malat, Joe. Surf Fishing. 40p. (Orig.). 1993. pap. 3.80 (0-940844-75-3) Wellspring.

Malat, Randy. Passport Mexico: Your Pocket Guide to Mexican Business, Customs & Etiquette. Szerlip, Barbara, ed. LC 96-25689. (Passport to the World Ser.). (Illus.). 96p. (Orig.). 1996. pap. 6.95 (1-885073-30-5) Wrld Trade Pr.

Malatesha, Rattihalli N. Neuropsychology & Cognition. 1987. lib. bdg. 375.00 (90-247-2752-9) Kluwer Academic.

Malatesha, Rattihalli N. & Whitaker, Harry A., eds. Dyslexia: A Global Issue. (NATO Advanced Study Institutes Series D: Behavioural & Social Sciences). 1983. text 306.00 (90-247-2909-2) Kluwer Academic.

Malatesta, Carol Z. & Izard, Carroll E., eds. Emotion in Adult Development. LC 84-1937. (Illus.). 343p. reprint ed. pap. 106.40 (0-8357-8494-0, 203476900091) Bks Demand.

Malatesta, Carol Z., et al. The Development of Emotion Expression during the First Two Years of Life. (Child Development Monographs: No. 219 54: 1-2). 146p. 1989. pap. text 15.00 (0-226-50285-6) U Ch Pr.

Malatesta, Edward J., ed. see Ricci, Matteo.

Malatesta, Errico. Malatesta: Life & Ideas. Richards, Vernon, ed. 309p. 1965. pap. 10.00 (0-900384-15-8) Left Bank.

Malatesta, Louise. The Lost Breeches: A Tale of Adventure, True Love- & Discipline! (Illus.). 144p. 39.95 (1-899861-15-7, Pub. by AKS Bks) Xclusiv Distrib.

Malatesta, Maria, ed. Society & the Professions in Italy, 1860-1914. (Studies in Italian History & Culture). 348p. (C). 1996. text 59.95 (0-521-46536-2) Cambridge U Pr.

Malati, Mournir A., jt. auth. see Barrett, Jack.

Malatich, John M. & Tucker, Wayne C. Tricks of the Trade for Divers. LC 85-47839. (Illus.). 255p. (Orig.). 1986. reprint ed. pap. 79.10 (0-7837-9072-4, 204982100003) Bks Demand.

Malatinsky, Joseph P. Slovak Handy Extra Dictionary: Hippocrene Handy Dictionary. (ENG & SLO.). 200p. 1996. pap. 12.95 (0-7818-0101-X) Hippocrene Bks.

***Malatrait, Solveig.** Die Amor-Motive: Ihre Rezeption, Gestaltung und Funktion in der Franzosischen Renaissancelyrik: Eine Motivische Untersuchung Aus der Perspektive der Diskursanalyse. (Europaische Hochschulschriften Franzosische Sprache und Literatur Ser.). 248p. 1999. 37.95 (3-631-35368-5) P Lang Pubng.

Malaurie, Jean. The Last Kings of Thule. Foulke, Adrienne, tr. LC 85-8765. (Illus.). xx, 490p. 1994. pap. 17.50 (0-226-50284-8) U Ch Pr.

Malavbe, Efraibn Rodriquez. Medicina Natural: Retorno a Nuestra Esencia. LC 98-50215. 1999. write for info. (0-8477-0365-7) U of PR Pr.

Malave, Lilliam & Duquette, George S., eds. Language, Culture, & Cognition: A Collection of Studies in First & Second Language Acquisition. (Multilingual Matters Ser.: No. 69). 300p. 1991. 99.00 (1-85359-103-3, Pub. by Multilingual Matters); pap. 39.95 (1-85359-102-5, Pub. by Multilingual Matters) Taylor & Francis.

Malavis, Nicholas G. Bless the Pure & Humble: Texas Lawyers & Oil Regulation, 1919-1936. LC 96-19245. (Kenneth E. Montague Series in Oil & Business History: No. 8). (Illus.). 350p. 1996. 44.95 (0-89096-714-8) Tex A&M Univ Pr.

— Man of Amazing Grace: In Memoriam, Frank H. Wardlaw, 1913-1989. (Illus.). 46p. 1990. pap. 12.50 (0-89096-456-4) Tex A&M Univ Pr.

Malawar, Martin, jt. auth. see Sugarbaker, Paul.

Malawar, Stuart S., ed. Federal Regulation of International Business Vols. 1-4: Annotated Source Book of Legislation, Regulations & Treaties, 10 bks. in 4. LC 80-69834. 1986. reprint ed. 995.00 (0-89941-654-3, 303840) W S Hein.

Malay, Paula C., tr. see Alvarez, Santiago V.

Malayan Law Journal Editors. Malayan Law Journal: Consolidated Subject Index, General Index & Table of Cases Reported, 1932-1991, 1992-1994, 3 vols. 1995. write for info. (0-409-99660-2, MICHIE) LEXIS Pub.

Malayan Law Journal Staff, ed. Mallal's Digest, 1993. 1994. write for info. (0-409-99694-7, ASIA, MICHIE) LEXIS Pub.

Malaysian Coastal Resources Study Team Staff & Ministry of Science, Technology & the Environ. Sta. The Coastal Resources Management Plan for South Johore, Malaysia. (ICLARM Technical Reports: No. 33). 291p. 1992. per. write for info. (971-8709-19-3, Pub. by ICLARM) Intl Spec Bk.

Malayter, Shawn, et al. Find a Way: Valpo's "Sweet" Dream. LC 98-43645. (Illus.). 1999. 22.95 (1-888698-23-3) Diamond Communications.

Malbert, Roger, jt. auth. see Hyman, Timothy.

Malbin, Michael J., ed. Money & Politics in the United States: Financing Elections in the 1980s. LC 84-2900. 336p. reprint ed. pap. 104.20 (0-8357-4828-6, 203776500009) Bks Demand.

Malbin, Michael J., jt. auth. see Benjamin, Gerald.

Malbin, Michael J., jt. auth. see Gais, Thomas L.

***Malbon, Ben.** Clubbing: Clubbing & Experience. LC 99-12888. 256p. (C). 1999. text. write for info. (0-415-20213-2) Routledge.

— Clubbing: Clubbing Culture & Experience. LC 99-12888. 256p. (C). 1999. pap. write for info. (0-415-20214-0) Routledge.

Malbon, Elizabeth S. & McKnight, Edgar V., eds. The New Literary Criticism & the New Testament. (Journal for the Study of the New Testament, Supplement Ser.: Vol. 109). 276p. 1994. 80.00 (1-85075-510-8, Pub. by Sheffield Acad) CUP Services.

Malbon, Elizabeth S., jt. auth. see McKnight, Edgar V.

***Malbon, Elizabeth Struthers.** In the Company of Jesus: Characters in Mark's Gospel. 184p. 2000. pap. 21.95 (0-664-22255-2) Westminster John Knox.

Malbon, Elizabeth Struthers. Narrative Space & Mythic Meaning in Mark. (Biblical Seminar Ser.: No. 13). (Illus.). 212p. (C). 1991. pap. 23.75 (1-85075-711-9, Pub. by Sheffield Acad) CUP Services.

Malbon, Justin, jt. auth. see Hossain, Moazzem.

Malbrough, Ray T. Charms, Spells & Formulas for the Making & Use of Gris-Gris Bags, Herb Candles, Doll Magick, Incenses, Oils & Powders...to Gain Love, Protection, Prosperity, Luck & Prophetic Dreams. LC 85-45286. (Practical Magick Ser.). (Illus.). 192p. 1986. pap. 7.95 (0-87542-501-1) Llewellyn Pubns.

— Hechizos y Conjuros. 2nd rev. ed. Rojas, Edgar, ed. & tr. by. from ENG.Tr. of Charms, Spells & Formulas. (SPA., Illus.). 176p. 1999. pap. 6.95 (1-56718-455-3) Llewellyn Pubns.

— The Magical Power of the Saints: Evocations & Candle Rituals. LC 98-19622. (Illus.). 240p. 1998. pap. 7.95 (1-56718-456-1) Llewellyn Pubns.

— El Poder Magico de los Santos (The Magical Power of the Saints) (SPA., Illus.). 240p. 1999. pap. 7.95 (1-56718-453-7) Llewellyn Pubns.

Malburg, Christopher R. Accounting for the New Business. 304p. 1996. pap. 9.95 (1-55850-759-0) Adams Media.

— All-in-One Business Planner. 304p. 1995. pap. 9.95 (1-55850-757-4) Adams Media.

— Controller's & Treasurer's Desk Reference. 415p. 1992. 69.95 (0-07-911604-3) McGraw.

— How to Write a Knock-Em-Dead Book Proposal: Structuring, Packaging & Presenting Book Ideas That Sell. 200p. (Orig.). 1994. pap. 29.95 (0-9640035-0-3) Writers Res Grp.

Malburg, Christopher R., jt. auth. see Tylczak, Lynn.

Malby, Dave. How to Market Your Crafts to Retail Stores: A Complete Guide from Product Evaluation to Product Distribution. (Illus.). 122p. (Orig.). 1995. reprint ed. pap. 19.95 (0-9648128-0-0) TPS Pubng.

Malby, Dave, jt. auth. see Benbow, Ann.

Malca, Leon A., ed. see Marshall, Richard.

Malcara, Daniel. Optica Tradicional y Moderna. (Ciencia para Todos Ser.). (SPA.). pap. 6.99 (968-16-3240-0, Pub. by Fondo) Continental Bk.

Malcata, F. Xavier, ed. Engineering of/with Lipases: Proceedings of the NATO Advanced Study Institute, Povoa de Varzim, Portugal, May 22-June 2, 1995. (NATO ASI Ser.: Series E, Vol. 317). 636p. (C). 1996. text 331.50 (0-7923-4003-5) Kluwer Academic.

Mal'Cev, A. A., jt. ed. see Fadeev, L. D.

Mal'cev, A. I. Algebraic Systems. Seckler, B. D. & Doohovskoy, A. P., trs. from RUS. (Grundlehren der Mathematischen Wissenschaften Ser.: Vol. 192). 320p. 1973. 86.95 (0-387-05792-7) Spr-Verlag.

Malchaire, Jacques. Heat Stress Evaluation, Version 2.0. 69p. 1993. lib. bdg. 139.00 (0-87371-847-X, L847) Lewis Pubs.

Malchiodi, Cathy. The Art Therapy Sourcebook: Art Making for Personal Growth, Insight & Transformation. LC 98-44494. (Illus.). 288p. 1998. pap. 18.00 (1-56565-884-1, 08841W, Pub. by Lowell Hse) NTC Contemp Pub Co.

***Malchiodi, Cathy, ed.** Medical Art Therapy with Adults. 240p. 1999. text 69.95 (1-85302-678-6, Pub. by Jessica Kingsley) Taylor & Francis.

Malchiodi, Cathy A. Breaking the Silence: Art Therapy with Children from Violent Homes. LC 90-1466. (Illus.). 230p. 1990. text 30.95 (0-87630-578-8) Brunner-Mazel.

— Breaking the Silence: Art Therapy with Children from Violent Homes. 2nd rev. ed. LC 97-14098. (Illus.). 208p. 1997. 31.95 (0-87630-824-8) Brunner-Mazel.

***Malchiodi, Cathy A.** Medical Art Therapy With Adults. 1999. pap. text 29.95 (1-85302-679-4) ITCP.

— Medical Art Therapy with Children. (Illus.). 1998. pap. 25.95 (1-85302-677-8) Jessica Kingsley.

Malchiodi, Cathy A. Medical Art Therapy with Children. 1998. 69.95 (1-85302-676-X) Taylor & Francis.

— Understanding Children's Drawings. LC 98-17311. 252p. 1998. pap. text 23.00 (1-57230-372-7); lib. bdg. 41.95 (1-57230-351-4) Guilford Pubns.

Malchiodi, Cathy A., ed. Art Therapy. (Journal of the American Art Therapy Association Ser.: Vol. 10, No. 4). (Illus.). (C). pap. 18.00 (1-882147-45-6) Am Art Therapy.

— Art Therapy. (Journal of the American Art Therapy Association Ser.: Vol. 9, No. 1). (Illus.). 60p. (C). 1992. 16.00 (1-882147-00-6) Am Art Therapy.

— Art Therapy. (Journal of the American Art Therapy Association Ser.: Vol. 9, No. 2). 51p. (C). 1992. 16.00 (1-882147-01-4) Am Art Therapy.

— Art Therapy. (Journal of the American Art Therapy Association Ser.: Vol. 9, No. 3). (Illus.). 52p. (C). 1992. 16.00 (1-882147-02-2) Am Art Therapy.

— Art Therapy. (Journal of the American Art Therapy Association Ser.: Vol. 9, No. 4). (Illus.). 56p. (C). 1992. pap. 18.00 (1-882147-15-4) Am Art Therapy.

— Art Therapy. (Journal of the American Art Therapy Association Ser.: Vol. 10, No. 1). (Illus.). 64p. (C). 1993. 16.00 (1-882147-17-0) Am Art Therapy.

— Art Therapy. (Journal of the American Art Therapy Association Ser.: Vol. 10, No. 2). (Illus.). 55p. (C). 1993. 16.00 (1-882147-18-9) Am Art Therapy.

Malchiodi, Cathy A. & Riley, Shirley. Supervision & Related Issues: A Handbook for Professionals. 250p. 1996. pap. 28.95 (0-9613309-7-X) Magnolia St Pub.

Malchiodi, Cathy A., jt. auth. see Riley, Shirley.

Malchiodi, Kathy A., ed. Art Therapy. (Journal of the American Art Therapy Association Ser.: Vol. 10, No. 3). 66p. (C). 1993. pap. 18.00 (1-882147-19-7) Am Art Therapy.

Malchiodi, Kathy A. & Saqvage, Karen D., eds. Art Therapy. (Journal of the American Art Therapy Association Ser.: Vol. 12, No. 4). write for info. (0-614-97089-X) Am Art Therapy.

Malchow, Bruce V. Social Justice in the Hebrew Bible: What Is New & What Is Old. LC 95-37823. 104p. (Orig.). 1996. pap. text 8.95 (0-8146-5523-8, M Glazier) Liturgical Pr.

Malchow, H. L. Gentlemen Capitalists: The Social & Political World of the Victorian Businessman. LC 89-64241. (Illus.). 450p. 1991. 52.50 (0-8047-1807-5) Stanford U Pr.

— Gothic Images of Race in Nineteenth-Century Britain. 1996. pap. 18.95 (0-8047-2793-7) Stanford U Pr.

— Gothic Images of Race in Nineteenth-Century Britain. LC 95-25870. 1996. 55.00 (0-8047-2664-7) Stanford U Pr.

Malchow, Howard L. Population Pressures: Emigration & Government in Late Nineteenth-Century Britain. LC 79-64166. (Illus.). 335p. 1979. 18.00 (0-930664-02-7) SPOSS.

Malcioln, Jose V. The African Origin of Modern Judaism: From Hebrews to Jews. LC 96-33719. 533p. 1996. 69.95 (0-86543-371-2); pap. 21.95 (0-86543-372-0) Africa World.

Malcles. Les Sources du Travail Bibliographique, 3 tomes. Incl. Set. Bibliographies Specialisees: Sciences Humaines., 2 pts. 46.50 Tome I. Bibliographies Generales. 22.50 Tome III. Bibliographies Specialisees: Sciences Exactes et Techniques. 22.50 write for info. (0-318-52266-7) Fr & Eur.

Malcolm. Diagnostic Histopathology. 1999. text. write for info. (0-443-04086-9, W B Saunders Co) Harcrt Hlth Sci Grp.

— Fundamentals of Electronics. 2nd ed. (Electronics Technology Ser.). 1987. mass mkt. 64.25 (0-8273-3885-6) Delmar.

— Fundamentals of Electronics. 3rd ed. (Electronics Technology Ser.). 1997. teacher ed. 18.00 (0-8273-6157-2) Delmar.

— Tolley's Health & Safety at Work Handbook, 1995. 900p. (C). 1994. 175.00 (0-85459-945-2, Pub. by Tolley Pubng) St Mut.

Malcolm, Alan D., ed. Molecular Medicine, Vol. 2. 140p. 1987. pap. text 45.00 (0-947946-58-6) OUP.

Malcolm, Alexander. Treatise of Musick, Speculative, Practical & Historical. LC 69-16676. (Music Ser.). 1970. reprint ed. lib. bdg. 75.00 (0-306-71099-4) Da Capo.

Malcolm, Alix. Falcon's Lure. large type ed. 1991. 27.99 (0-7089-2371-2) Ulverscroft.

Malcolm, Andrew. Fury: Inside the Life of Theoren Fleury. LC 99-172163. (Illus.). 288p. 1998. 23.95 (0-7710-5655-9) McCland & Stewart.

— Fury: Inside the Life of Theoren Fleury. (Illus.). 288p. 1998. pap. 15.95 (0-7710-5656-7) McCland & Stewart.

— The Tyranny of the Group. (Quality Paperback Ser.: No. 294). 190p. (Orig.). 1975. reprint ed. pap. 8.00 (0-8226-0294-6) Littlefield.

Malcolm, Andrew H. The Canadians. (Illus.). 416p. 1991. pap. 16.95 (0-312-06921-9) St Martin.

Malcolm, Anthea. An Improper Proposal. 400p. 1992. mass mkt. 4.50 (0-8217-3858-5, Zebra Kensgtn) Kensgtn Pub Corp.

— The Widow's Gambit. 256p. 1988. pap. 2.95 (0-8217-2357-X, Zebra Kensgtn) Kensgtn Pub Corp.

— The Widow's Gambit. 352p. 1993. mass mkt. 3.99 (0-8217-4075-X, Zebra Kensgtn) Kensgtn Pub Corp.

***Malcolm, Bill & Malcolm, Nancy.** Mosses & Other Bryophytes: An Illustrated Glossary. (Illus.). 226p. 2000. 39.95 (0-473-06730-7) Timber.

Malcolm, Bill & Malcolm, Nancy. New Zealand's Alpine Plants Inside & Out. (Illus.). 136p. 1996. pap. 14.95 (0-908802-04-8, Pub. by C Potton Pubng) Timber.

Malcolm, C. A. The Piper in Peace & War. (Illus.). 300p. 1993. boxed set 29.95 (0-9521580-0-0) Lancer.

Malcolm, Cheryl A. Jean Rhys. 1996. 29.00 (0-8057-0855-3) Macmillan.

Malcolm, Clark & Houseman, William, eds. Everybody's Business: A Fund of Retrievable Ideas for Humanizing Life in the Office. LC 85-5872. (Illus.). 112p. 1985. text 30.00 (0-936658-19-3) H Miller Res.

Malcolm, Clark, ed. see Grant, Christin N. & Meima, Karla L.

Malcolm, Davis W., tr. see Vernadskii, Georgii.

Malcolm, Don, et al. The 1998 Big Bad Baseball Annual: The Book Baseball Deserves. (Illus.). 428p. 1998. pap. 19.95 (1-57028-201-3, Mstrs Pr) NTC Contemp Pub Co.

— The 1999 Big Bad Baseball Annual: The Book Baseball Deserves. (Illus.). 428p. 1999. pap. 19.95 (0-8092-2655-3) NTC Contemp Pub Co.

***Malcolm, Don, et al.** 2000 Big Bad Baseball Annual 2000 Edition: The Book Baseball Deserves. (Illus.). 432p. 2000. pap. text 19.95 (0-8092-9889-9, 988990, Contemporary Bks) NTC Contemp Pub Co.

Malcolm, Douglas R., Jr. Fundamentals of Electronics. (Electronics Technology Ser.). 1997. text 61.95 (0-8273-6063-0) Delmar.

Malcolm, Douglas R. Robotics: An Introduction. 2nd ed. (Electronics Technology Ser.). (C). 1988. mass mkt. 58.75 (0-8273-3913-5) Delmar.

— Robotics: An Introduction. 2nd ed. 1988. 50.25 (0-534-91474-8) PWS Pubs.

Malcolm, Elizabeth. Ireland Sober, Ireland Free: Drink & Temperance in Nineteenth-Century Ireland. LC HV5450.3.M3. (Irish Studies). 377p. 1986. reprint ed. pap. 116.90 (0-608-06960-4, 206716800009) Bks Demand.

Malcolm, Elizabeth, jt. ed. see Jones, Greta.

Malcolm, George A. The Commonwealth of the Philippines. Philippines Commonwealth Constitution 1972 Staff, ed. 1977. 40.95 (0-8369-6982-0, 7860) Ayer.

— First Malayan Republic: Story of the Philippines. LC 75-161776. reprint ed. 41.50 (0-404-09032-X) AMS Pr.

Malcolm, Grant, jt. auth. see Goguen, Joseph A.

Malcolm, H. Historical Documents Relating to the Bahama Islands. 1976. lib. bdg. 59.95 (0-8490-1958-3) Gordon Pr.

Malcolm, Ian Z. Pursuits of Leisure & Other Essays. LC 68-20317. (Essay Index Reprint Ser.). 1977. reprint ed. 17.95 (0-8369-0671-3) Ayer.

— Vacant Thrones: A Volume of Political Portraits. LC 67-28760. (Essay Index Reprint Ser.). 1977. 20.95 (0-8369-0672-1) Ayer.

Malcolm, J. Cooper. The Tau: Its Origin & Symbolic Use in Royal Arch Masonry. 1990. pap. 7.95 (1-55818-173-3, Sure Fire) Holmes Pub.

Malcolm, Jack. Bottom-Line Selling: The Sales Professional's Guide to Improving Customer Profits. LC 98-22489. 240p. 1999. 34.95 (0-8092-2852-1, 285210, Contemporary Bks) NTC Contemp Pub Co.

***Malcolm, Jack.** Bottom-Line Selling: The Sales Professionals Guide to Improving Customer Profits. 256p. 2000. pap. 17.95 (0-8092-2854-8, 285480, Contemporary Bks) NTC Contemp Pub Co.

***Malcolm, Jahnna N.** Battle of the Bunheads. (Bad News Ballet Ser.: Vol. 2).Tr. of Le fantome d'Ivan Scapinsky. 160p. (J). (gr. 4-6). 2000. pap. 3.95 (0-9700164-1-7, Pub. by Starcatcher) Publishers Group.

Malcolm, Jahnna N. The Clue in the Shadows. (Clue Ser.: No. 8). 96p. (J). (gr. 3-6). 1995. pap. 3.50 (0-590-48934-8) Scholastic Inc.

— The Clue in the Shadows. (Clue Ser.: No. 8). (J). (gr. 3-6). 1995. 8.95 (0-606-09154-8, Pub. by Turtleback) Demco.

— The Diamond Princess & the Magic Ball. (Jewel Kingdom Ser.: No. 8). (J). (gr. 1-3). 1998. pap. 3.99 (0-590-11739-4, Little Apple) Scholastic Inc.

An Asterisk (*) at the beginning of an entry indicates that the title is appearing for the first time.

— The Diamond Princess Saves the Day. (Jewel Kingdom Ser.: No. 4). (Illus.). (J). (gr. 1-4). 1997. mass mkt. 3.99 (*0-590-21289-3*) Scholastic Inc.
— The Diamond Princess Steps Through the Mirror, 12. (Jewel Kingdom Ser.: No. 12). 80p. (J). (gr. 1-4). 1999. pap. 3.99 (*0-590-97880-2*) Scholastic Inc.
*__Malcolm, Jahnna N.__ Drat! We're Rats! (Bad News Ballet Ser.). Orig. Title: The Terrible Tryouts. 160p. (J). (gr. 4-6). 2000. pap. 3.95 (*0-9700164-0-9*, Pub. by Starcatcher) Publishers Group.
Malcolm, Jahnna N. The Emerald Princess Finds a Fairy. (Jewel Kingdom Ser.: No. 7). (Illus.). 66p. (J). (gr. 1-4). 1998. pap. 3.99 (*0-590-11738-6*, Little Apple) Scholastic Inc.
— The Emerald Princess Follows a Unicorn, Vol. 11. (Jewel Kingdom Ser.: No. 11). (Illus.). 80p. (J). (gr. 1-4). 1999. pap. 3.99 (*0-590-97879-9*) Scholastic Inc.
— The Emerald Princess Plays a Trick. (Jewel Kingdom Ser.: No. 3). (Illus.). 80p. (J). (gr. 1-4). 1997. mass mkt. 3.99 (*0-590-21287-7*) Scholastic Inc.
— The Jewel Princess & the Missing Crown. (Jewel Kingdom Super Special Ser.). (J). (gr. 1-4). 1998. pap. 4.99 (*0-590-37705-1*, Little Apple) Scholastic Inc.
— The Picture-Perfect Crime. (Clue Ser.: No. 7). 112p. (J). (gr. 3-6). 1994. pap. 3.25 (*0-590-48735-3*) Scholastic Inc.
— The Picture-Perfect Crime. (Clue Ser.: No. 7). (J). (gr. 3-6). 1994. 9.09 (*0-606-09748-1*, Pub. by Turtleback) Demco.
— Ride of Courage, Vol. 2. (Treasured Horses Ser.: No. 2). (Illus.). (J). (gr. 3-9). 1997. pap. 3.99 (*0-590-06865-2*) Scholastic Inc.
— The Ruby Princess & the Baby Dragon. (Jewel Kingdom Ser.: No. 9). (J). (gr. 1-3). 1998. pap. 3.99 (*0-590-97877-2*) Scholastic Inc.
— The Ruby Princess Runs Away. (Jewel Kingdom Ser.: No. 1). (Illus.). 64p. (J). (gr. 1-4). 1997. pap. text 3.99 (*0-590-21283-4*) Scholastic Inc.
— The Ruby Princess Sees a Ghost, Vol. 5. (Jewel Kingdom Ser.: No. 5). (Illus.). (J). (gr. 1-4). 1997. pap. 3.99 (*0-590-11713-0*, Apple Classics) Scholastic Inc.
— The Sapphire Princess Helps a Mermaid, Vol. 10. (Jewel Kingdom Ser.). (Illus.). 80p. (J). (gr. 1-3). 1999. pap. 3.99 (*0-590-97878-0*) Scholastic Inc.
— The Sapphire Princess Hunts for Treasure. (Jewel Kingdom Ser.: No. 6). (J). (gr. 1-4). 1998. pap. text 3.99 (*0-590-11714-9*) Scholastic Inc.
— The Sapphire Princess Meets a Monster. (Jewel Kingdom Ser.: No. 1). (Illus.). 64p. (J). (gr. 1-4). 1997. mass mkt. 3.99 (*0-590-21284-2*) Scholastic Inc.
— Scared Stiff. 128p. (J). (gr. 3-7). 1995. pap. 3.50 (*0-590-44996-6*, Apple Paperbacks) Scholastic Inc.
— Scared Stiff. (J). 1991. 8.60 (*0-606-08136-4*, Pub. by Turtleback) Demco.
— Scared to Death. 144p. (J). 1992. pap. 2.95 (*0-590-44995-8*, Apple Paperbacks) Scholastic Inc.
— Scared to Death. 144p. (J). (gr. 4-7). 1995. pap. 3.50 (*0-590-55217-1*) Scholastic Inc.
— Spirit of the West. (Treasured Horses Ser.). 1997. 9.09 (*0-606-13056-X*, Pub. by Turtleback) Demco.
— Spirit of the West, Vol. 1. (Treasured Horses Ser.: No. 1). (Illus.). (J). (gr. 3-7). 1997. pap. 3.99 (*0-590-06866-0*) Scholastic Inc.
Malcolm, Jan. Fortunes. Orig. Title: Roulette. 304p. 1989. reprint ed. pap. 3.95 (*0-380-75492-4*, Avon Bks) Morrow Avon.
Malcolm, Janet. Collected Essays. 1992. write for info. (*0-679-74046-5*) McKay.
— The Crime of Sheila McGough. LC 98-48635. 176p. 1999. 22.00 (*0-375-40508-9*) Knopf.
*__Malcolm, Janet.__ The Crime of Sheila McGough. 2000. pap. 12.00 (*0-375-70459-0*) Vin Bks.
Malcolm, Janet. Diana & Nikon: Essays on Photography. 240p. 1997. pap. 24.95 (*0-89381-737-6*) Aperture.
— Diana & Nikon: Essays on Photography. (Illus.). 224p. 1997. 29.95 (*0-89381-727-9*) Aperture.
— In the Freud Archives. 165p. 1998. pap. text 5.00 (*0-7881-5310-2*) DIANE Pub.
— The Journalist & the Murderer. LC 90-50156. 192p. 1990. pap. 12.00 (*0-679-73183-0*) Vin Bks.
— Psychoanalysis: The Impossible Profession. LC 94-72518. 184p. 1994. 30.00 (*1-56821-342-5*) Aronson.
— Psychoanalysis: The Impossible Profession. LC 82-40036. 192p. 1982. pap. 13.00 (*0-394-71034-7*) Vin Bks.
— The Purloined Clinic: Selected Writings. LC 93-7859. 382p. 1993. reprint ed. pap. 13.00 (*0-679-74810-5*) Vin Bks.
— The Silent Woman: Sylvia Plath & Ted Hughes. LC 93-33848. 1994. 23.00 (*0-685-70236-7*) Knopf.
— Silent Woman: Sylvia Plath & Ted Hughes. 1995. pap. 12.00 (*0-679-75140-8*) Vin Bks.
Malcolm, Jean. Table de la Bibliographie de Voltaire par Bengesco: Geneva, 1953, Vol. 1. 1974. 30.00 (*0-8115-0898-6*) Periodicals Srv.
Malcolm, John. A Deceptive Appearance. large type ed. LC 93-9001. (Nightingale Ser.). 318p. 1993. lib. bdg. 15.95 (*0-8161-5780-4*, G K Hall Lrg Type) Mac Lib Ref.
— Into the Vortex, Vol. 1. LC 97-5853. Vol. 1. 240p. 1997. text 21.95 (*0-312-15555-7*) St Martin.
— Plato on the Self-Predication of Forms: Early & Middle Dialogues. 238p. 1991. text 70.00 (*0-19-823906-8*) OUP.
— Sheep, Goats & Soap: A Tim Simpson Mystery. large type ed. 275p. 1992. pap. 14.95 (*0-8161-5475-9*, G K Hall Lrg Type) Mac Lib Ref.
*__Malcolm, Jonathan, et al.__ The Amazing, Colossal Book of Horror Trivia: Everything You Always Wanted to Know about Scary Movies. LC 99-61495. (Illus.). 224p. 1999. pap. 12.95 (*1-58182-045-3*, Cumberland Hearthside) Cumberland Hse.
Malcolm, Joyce L. The Struggle for Sovereignty: Seventeenth-Century English Political Tracts, 2 vols. LC 97-28248. 1999. 35.00 (*0-86597-152-8*) Liberty Fund.
— To Keep & Bear Arms: The Origins of an Anglo-American Right. LC 93-26710. 248p. 1994. 36.95 (*0-674-89306-9*) HUP.
— To Keep & Bear Arms: The Origins of an Anglo-American Right. 256p. 1996. pap. 18.95 (*0-674-89307-7*) HUP.
*__Malcolm, Joyce Lee, ed.__ Struggle For Sovereignty Seventeenth Century English Political Tracts: Restoration Through the Glorious Revolution, 2. 1999. 20.00 (*0-86597-186-2*) Liberty Fund.
Malcolm, Kari T. Women at the Crossroads: A Path Beyond Feminism & Traditionalism. LC 82-7228. 215p. (Orig.). 1982. pap. 12.99 (*0-87784-379-1*, 379) InterVarsity.
Malcolm, L. Diccionario Tecnico Frances-Espanol.Tr. of French - Spanish Technical Dictionary. (FRE & SPA.). 544p. 1973. 39.95 (*0-8288-6242-7*, S-31563) Fr & Eur.
Malcolm, L. R., jt. auth. see Makeham, J. P.
Malcolm, Lyle R., et al. Agriculture in Australia: An Introduction, Vol. 1. LC 97-179484. (Illus.). 512p. 1997. pap. text 80.00 (*0-19-553695-9*) OUP.
Malcolm, M. C. Making Sense of Metric. 64p. (Orig.). 1989. pap. 9.95 (*0-8464-1390-6*) Beekman Pubs.
Malcolm, Nancy, jt. auth. see Malcolm, Bill.
Malcolm, Neil, ed. Russia & Europe: An End to Confrontation? LC 93-27883. 1994. 49.00 (*1-85567-161-1*) St Martin.
Malcolm, Neil, et al. Internal Factors in Russian Foreign Policy. (Illus.). 366p. 1996. text 79.00 (*0-19-828011-4*) OUP.
Malcolm, Noel. Bosnia: A Short History. (Illus.). 340p. (C). 1994. text 40.00 (*0-8147-5520-8*) NYU Pr.
— Bosnia: A Short History. 360p. (C). 1996. pap. 18.95 (*0-8147-5561-5*) NYU Pr.
— Kosovo: A Short History. 544p. (YA). (gr. 9-12). 1999. pap. 16.00 (*0-06-097775-2*) HarpC.
Malcolm, Noel. Kosovo: A Short History. text 35.00 (*0-8147-5642-5*) NYU Pr.
Malcolm, Noel. Kosovo: A Short History. LC 97-27456. 544p. 1998. 28.95 (*0-8147-5598-4*) NYU Pr.
*__Malcolm, Noel.__ Origins of English Nonsense. 1998. pap. 13.95 (*0-00-638844-2*, Pub. by HarpC) Trafalgar.
Malcolm, Noel, ed. see Hobbes, Thomas.
Malcolm, Norman. Wittgenstein: A Religious Point of View? Winch, Peter, ed. LC 93-25808. 152p. 1994. text 35.00 (*0-8014-2978-1*) Cornell U Pr.
— Wittgenstein: A Religious Point of View? Winch, Peter, ed. 152p. 1995. pap. text 11.95 (*0-8014-8266-6*) Cornell U Pr.
— Wittgensteinian Themes: Essays 1978-1989. Von Wright, George H., ed. 256p. 1995. text 39.95 (*0-8014-3042-9*) Cornell U Pr.
— Wittgensteinian Themes: Essays 1978-1989. Von Wright, George H., ed. 232p. 1996. pap. text 15.95 (*0-8014-8381-6*) Cornell U Pr.
Malcolm, R. E., jt. ed. see Vaughan, D.
Malcolm, S., jt. ed. see Humphries, S. E.
Malcolm, Sue, jt. auth. see Emery, Alan E.
*__Malcolm, Trisha.__ Vogue Knitting Socks: Knitting on the Go. (Vogue Knitting on the Go Ser.). (Illus.). 96p. 1999. 12.95 (*1-57389-008-1*, Pub. by Butterick Co) Sterling.
*__Malcolm, Trisha, contrib. by.__ Vogue Knitting Mittens & Gloves: Vogue Knitting on the Go. LC 99-32428. (Illus.). 79p. 1999. pap. 12.95 (*1-57389-013-8*) Butterick Co.
Malcolm, Trisha, ed. Designer Knits: Vogue Knitting. (Illus.). 160p. 1999. 29.95 (*1-57389-009-X*, Pub. by Butterick Co) Sterling.
*__Malcolm, Trisha, ed.__ Vogue Knitting: American Collection. (Illus.). 160p. 2000. 29.95 (*1-57389-020-0*, Pub. by Butterick Co) Sterling.
— Vogue Knitting Baby Blankets. (Vogue Knitting on the Go Ser.). (Illus.). 96p. 2000. 12.95 (*1-57389-019-7*, Pub. by Butterick Co) Sterling.
Malcolm, Trisha, ed. Vogue Knitting Baby Knits: Knitting on the Go. (Vogue Knitting on the Go Ser.). (Illus.). 96p. 1999. 12.95 (*1-57389-011-1*, Pub. by Butterick Co) Sterling.
— Vogue Knitting Caps & Hats: Knitting on the Go. LC 97-77518. (Vogue Knitting on the Go Ser.). (Illus.). 96p. 1999. 12.95 (*1-57389-010-3*, Pub. by Butterick Co) Sterling.
*__Malcolm, Trisha, ed.__ Vogue Knitting Pillows: Knitting on the Go. (Vogue Knitting on the Go Ser.). (Illus.). 96p. 1999. 12.95 (*1-57389-007-3*, Pub. by Butterick Co) Sterling.
— Vogue Knitting Scarves: Vogue Knitting on the Go. LC 99-32427. (Vogue Knitting on the Go Ser.). (Illus.). 96p. 1999. pap. 12.95 (*1-57389-014-6*) Butterick Co.
Malcolm, Trisha, ed. see Vogue Magazine Editors & Butterick Patterns Editors.
Malcolm, W. K., ed. A Blasphemer & Reformer: A Study of James Leslie Mitchell-Lewis Grassic Gibbon. 224p. 1984. text 27.90 (*0-08-030373-0*, Pergamon Pr) Elsevier.
Malcolm X. The Autobiography of Malcolm X. (Black History Titles Ser.). 466p. 1987. mass mkt. 6.99 (*0-345-35068-5*) Ballantine Pub Grp.
— The Autobiography of Malcolm X. 1987. 11.09 (*0-606-00367-3*, Pub. by Turtleback) Demco.
— The Autobiography of Malcolm X. 1976. 27.95 (*0-89190-216-3*) Amereon Ltd.
— The Autobiography of Malcolm X. 527p. 1992. pap. 14.00 (*0-345-37671-4*) Ballantine Pub Grp.
— The Autobiography of Malcolm X. LC 92-52659. 500p. 1992. 25.00 (*0-345-37975-6*, Ballantine) Ballantine Pub Grp.
— The Black Book: The True Political Philosophy of Malcolm X. Kly, Y. N., ed. LC 86-72174. 104p. (Orig.). 1986. pap. 9.95 (*0-932863-03-5*) Clarity Pr.
— By Any Means Necessary. rev. ed. LC 92-64456. (Illus.). 191p. 1970. reprint ed. lib. bdg. 45.00 (*0-87348-759-1*) Pathfinder NY.
— By Any Means Necessary. 2nd rev. ed. LC 92-64456. (Illus.). 191p. 1970. reprint ed. pap. 15.95 (*0-87348-754-0*) Pathfinder NY.
— The End of White World Supremacy. 1994. pap. 12.95 incl. audio (*1-55970-271-0*, Pub. by Arcade Pub Inc) Little.
— The End of White World Supremacy: Four Speeches by Malcolm X. 160p. 1989. reprint ed. pap. 9.70 (*1-55970-006-8*, Pub. by Arcade Pub Inc) Time Warner.
— The End of White World Supremacy: Two Speeches. Karim, Imam B., ed. 1992. 16.95 incl. audio (*1-55970-205-2*, Pub. by Arcade Pub Inc) Time Warner.
— February, 1965: The Final Speeches. Clark, Steve, ed. LC 92-62259. (Illus.). 293p. (C). 1992. 50.00 (*0-87348-753-2*); pap. 18.95 (*0-87348-749-4*) Pathfinder NY.
— Habla Malcolm X. Koppel, Martin, ed. LC 92-83753. (SPA., Illus.). 233p. 1993. pap. 17.95 (*0-87348-733-8*); lib. bdg. 50.00 (*0-87348-764-8*) Pathfinder NY.
— King, Malcolm, Baldwin: Three Interviews. rev. ed. LC 83-23490. Orig. Title: Negro Protest. (Illus.). 75p. 1985. pap. 9.95 (*0-8195-6090-1*, Wesleyan Univ Pr) U Pr of New Eng.
— Malcolm X: The Last Speeches. Perry, Bruce, ed. LC 89-61591. (Illus.). 188p. (Orig.). (C). 1989. reprint ed. pap. 16.95 (*0-87348-543-2*) Pathfinder NY.
— Malcolm X on Afro-American History. 3rd ed. LC 72-103696. (Illus.). 92p. 1990. pap. 10.95 (*0-87348-592-0*) Pathfinder NY.
— Malcolm X Speaks. 2nd ed. LC 90-64058. (Illus.). 233p. 1989. reprint ed. lib. bdg. 17.95 (*0-87348-546-7*) Pathfinder NY.
— Malcolm X Speaks: Selected Speeches & Statements. Breitman, George, ed. LC 90-300551. (Illus.). 240p. 1990. pap. 9.95 (*0-8021-3213-8*, Grove) Grove-Atltic.
— Malcolm X Talks to Young People. LC 90-64197. (Illus.). 110p. (Orig.). 1990. reprint ed. pap. 10.95 (*0-87348-628-5*) Pathfinder NY.
— Malcolm X Talks to Young People. LC 90-64197. (Illus.). 110p. (Orig.). 1991. reprint ed. lib. bdg. 35.00 (*0-87348-631-5*) Pathfinder NY.
— Two Speeches by Malcolm X. 3rd ed. 46p. (Orig.). 1990. reprint ed. pap. 5.00 (*0-87348-591-2*) Pathfinder NY.
Malcolm X & Haley, Alex. The Autobiography of Malcolm X. 1999. 20.00 (*0-345-91536-4*) Ballantine Pub Grp.
Malcolm X, jt. auth. see Haley, Alex.
Malcolme-Lawes, D. J. Microcomputers & Laboratory Instrumentation. 2nd ed. LC 88-5794. (Illus.). 284p. (C). 1988. text 55.00 (*0-306-42903-9*, Kluwer Plenum) Kluwer Academic.
— Programming--fortran. LC 78-109582. v, 122p. 1970. write for info. (*0-08-015508-1*, Pergamon Pr) Elsevier.
*__Malcolmson, Christina.__ Renaissance Poetry. LC 98-17501. (Critical Readers Ser.). 304p. (C). 1998. 74.00 (*0-582-05093-6*) Longman.
*__Malcolmson, Cristina.__ Heart-Work: George Herbert & the Protestant Ethic. LC 99-39448. 1999. 45.00 (*0-8047-2988-3*) Stanford U Pr.
Malcolmson, Patricia E. English Laundresses: A Social History, 1850-1930. LC 85-24599. (Working Class in European History Ser.). (Illus.). 236p. 1986. text 26.95 (*0-252-01293-3*) U of Ill Pr.
Malcolmson, Patrick & Myers, Richard. The Canadian Regime. LC 96-932229. 270p. (C). 1997. pap. 22.95 (*1-55111-112-8*) Broadview Pr.
Malcolmson, Patrick, et al. Liberal Education & Value Relativism: A Guide to Today's B. A. 111p. 1996. pap. text 19.95 (*0-7618-0337-8*) U Pr of Amer.
— Liberal Education & Value Relativism: A Guide to Today's B. A. LC 96-13032. 111p. 1996. lib. bdg. 39.00 (*0-7618-0336-X*) U Pr of Amer.
Malcolmson, Robert, jt. ed. see Rule, John.
Malcolmson, Robert W. Beyond Nuclear Thinking. 160p. (C). 1990. text 60.00 (*0-7735-0784-1*, Pub. by McG-Queens Univ Pr); pap. text 24.95 (*0-7735-0802-3*, Pub. by McG-Queens Univ Pr) CUP Services.
— Nuclear Fallacies: How We Have Been Misguided since Hiroshima. 128p. 1985. pap. 24.95 (*0-7735-0586-5*, Pub. by McG-Queens Univ Pr) CUP Services.
— Nuclear Fallacies: How We Have Been Misguided since Hiroshima. 128p. 1985. 60.00 (*0-7735-0585-7*, Pub. by McG-Queens Univ Pr) CUP Services.
Malcolmson, Robert W. & Mastoris, Stephanos. The English Pig: A History. LC 98-35352. 1998. 45.00 (*1-85285-174-0*) Hambledon Press.
Malcolmson, Scott. Empire's Edge: Travels in South-Eastern Europe, Turkey & Central Asia. 256p. 1995. pap. 16.00 (*1-85984-098-1*, Pub. by Verso) Norton.
Malcom, et al. Big Bad Baseball Annual 2000. pap. 21.95 (*0-9625846-2-2*, 932-001, Pub. by Mad Aztec Pr) BookWorld.
Malcom, Ben S. & Martz, Ron. White Tigers: My Secret War in North Korea. (Association of the U. S. Army Book Ser.). (Illus.). 265p. 1996. 24.95 (*1-57488-016-0*) Brasseys.
— White Tigers: My Secret War in North Korea. (Association of the U. S. Army Book Ser.). (Illus.). 265p. 1999. pap. 19.95 (*1-57488-198-1*) Brasseys.
Malcom, H. Rooney. Elements of Urban Stormwater Design. LC 89-82034. (Illus.). 134p. (Orig.). (C). 1990. pap. text 30.00 (*1-56049-016-0*) NCSU CE IES.
Malcom, Joyce L. The Struggle for Sovereignty: Seventeenth-Century English Political Tracts, 2 vols. LC 97-28248. 1999. pap. 18.00 (*0-86597-153-6*) Liberty Fund.
Malcom, Paul J., jt. auth. see Fitch, Margaret E.
Malcom, Shirley, et al, eds. The Effect of the Changing Policy Climate on Science, Mathematics, & Engineering Diversity. 138p. 1996. pap. write for info. (*0-87168-589-2*) AAAS.
Malcom, Shirley M., jt. auth. see Matyas, Marsha L.
Malcom, Shirley M., jt. ed. see Kulm, Gerald.
Malcom, Shirley M., jt. ed. see Sosa, Maria.
Malcomson, R. M. Daisy Ashford: Her Life. LC 84-187230. 110p. 1984. write for info. (*0-7011-2787-2*) Chatto & Windus.
Malcomson, Robert. Lords of the Lake: The Naval War on Lake Ontario, 1812-1814. LC 98-67770. (Illus.). 432p. 1999. 36.95 (*1-55750-532-2*) Naval Inst Pr.
Malcomson, Robert, ed. Sailors of 1812: Memoirs & Letters of Naval Officers on Lake Ontario. (Illus.). 96p. 1997. pap. 7.95 (*0-941967-19-0*) Old Fort Niagara Assn.
*__Malcomson, Scott L.__ One Drop of Blood: The American Misadventure of Race. LC 00-24487. 544p. 2000. 30.00 (*0-374-24079-5*) FS&G.
Malcor, Linda A., jt. auth. see Littleton, C. Scott.
Malcovati, ed. Ciceronis, M. Tulli Fascicule 4: Brutus. (LAT.). 1970. 21.95 (*3-322-00187-3*, T1172, Pub. by B G Teubner) U of Mich Pr.
Malczewski, Jacek. GIS & Multicriteria Decision Analysis. LC 98-31452. 408p. (C). 1999. 79.00 (*0-471-32944-4*) Wiley.
— The Spatial Planning of Health Services Vol. 33: Case Studies in Warsaw, Poland. (Progress in Planning Ser.: No. 2). (Illus.). 63p. 1990. pap. 41.50 (*0-08-040171-6*, Pergamon Pr) Elsevier.
Maldague, Xavier P. Non Destructive Evaluation of Materials by Infrared Thermography. LC 92-33616. 1993. 238.95 (*0-387-19769-9*) Spr-Verlag.
Maldague, Xavier P., ed. Advances in Signal Processing for Nondestructive Evaluation of Materials: Proceedings of the NATO Advanced Research Workshop, Quebec City, Quebec, Canada, August 17-20, 1993. LC 94-6394. (NATO Advanced Study Institutes Series E, Applied Sciences: Vol. 262). 504p. (C). 1994. text 298.50 (*0-7923-2765-9*) Kluwer Academic.
— Infrared Methodology & Technology. LC 92-43489. (Nondestructive Testing Monographs & Tracts: Vol. 7). 320p. 1993. pap. text 140.00 (*2-88124-590-0*) Gordon & Breach.
Malde, Harold E. Guidelines for Reviewers of Geological Manuscripts. 36p. 1986. pap. 7.50 (*0-913312-82-7*) Am Geol.
Maldeghem, H. Van, see Van Maldeghem, H.
Malden, Carla, jt. auth. see Malden, Karl.
*__Malden Historical Society Staff.__ Malden: Massachusetts. LC 99-69233. (Images of America Ser.). (Illus.). 128p. 2000. pap. 18.99 (*0-7385-0405-X*) Arcadia Publng.
Malden, John. Register of York Freemen, 1680-1986. 1200p. 1999. pap. 21.00 (*1-85072-054-1*, Pub. by W Sessions) St Mut.
Malden, Karl, mem. When Do I Start? A Memoir. LC 97-18104. (Illus.). 352p. 1997. 24.50 (*0-684-84309-9*) Simon & Schuster.
Malden, Karl & Malden, Carla. When Do I Start? A Memoir. LC 98-33839. (Illus.). 352p. 1998. reprint ed. pap. 18.95 (*0-87910-272-1*) Limelight Edns.
Maldere, Pierre V. Pierre Van Maldere: 6 Symphonies a Pie Strumenti, Opus 4. Lister, Craig, ed. (Recent Researches in Music of the Classic Era Ser.: Vol. RRC35-36). (Illus.). xxvii, 174p. 1990. pap. 60.00 (*0-89579-248-6*) A-R Eds.
*__Malderen, Luc van.__ American Architecture: A Vintage Postcard Collection. (Illus.). 200p. 2000. 49.95 (*1-86470-078-5*, Pub. by Images) Antique Collect.
Malderez, Angi & Bodoczky, Caroline. Mentor Courses: A Resource Book for Trainer-Trainers. LC 98-44352. (Teacher Training & Development Ser.). (Illus.). 232p. (C). 1999. 59.95 (*0-521-56204-X*); pap. 22.95 (*0-521-56690-8*) Cambridge U Pr.
Maldifassi, Jose O. & Abetti, Pier A. Defense Industries in Latin American Countries: Argentina, Brazil, & Chile. LC 93-43070. 280p. 1994. 65.00 (*0-275-94729-7*, Praeger Pubs) Greenwood.
Maldon. Battle of Maldon & Short Poems from the Saxon Chronicle. Sedgefield, Walter J., ed. LC 70-144444. (Belles Lettres Ser., Section I: No. 9). reprint ed. 27.50 (*0-404-53610-7*) AMS Pr.
Maldonado. American Landscape. (Sociology-Upper Level). 2001. mass mkt. 28.00 (*0-534-56817-3*) Wadsworth Pub.
Maldonado, jt. auth. see Garcia.
Maldonado, A. W. Teodoro Moscoso & Puerto Rico's Operation Bootstrap. LC 96-49822. (Illus.). 280p. 1997. 49.95 (*0-8130-1501-4*) U Press Fla.
Maldonado-Bear, Rita & Bear, Larry A. Free Markets, Finance, Ethics & Law. LC 93-18901. 434p. (C). 1993. pap. text 33.00 (*0-13-457896-1*) P-H.
Maldonado, C., ed. see International Labour Office Staff.
Maldonado-Capriles, Jenaro & Medina-Gaud, Silverio. Insectos Daninos y Beneficiosos de Puerto Rico: Manual de Laboratorio. 200p. (C). 1987. pap. text 24.95 (*1-881375-16-1*) Libreria Univ.
Maldonado, Carlos E. Human Right, Solidarity & Subsidiarity: Essays on Social Ontology. LC 97-26586. (Cultural Heritage & Contemporary Change Series V). 1997. pap. 17.50 (*1-56518-110-7*) Coun Res Values.
*__Maldonado, Carlos S.__ Colegio Cesar Chavez, 1973-1983: A Chicano Struggle for Educational Self-Determination. LC 00-27245. (Latino Communities Ser.). 2000. write for info. (*0-8153-3631-4*) Garland.
Maldonado, David, Jr. Protestantes/Protestants: Hispanic Christianity Within Mainline Traditions. LC 98-31142. 400p. 1999. pap. 24.95 (*0-687-05509-1*) Abingdon.
Maldonado, David, jt. ed. see Barton, Paul.
Maldonado de Ortiz, Candida. Antonio S. Pedreira: Vida y Obra. 192p. (C). 1974. 5.00 (*0-8477-0512-9*); pap. 4.00 (*0-8477-0513-7*) U of PR Pr.

M

An Asterisk (*) at the beginning of an entry indicates that the title is appearing for the first time.

Maldonado-Denis, Manuel. The Emigration Dialectic: Puerto Rico & the U. S. A. LC 80-16640. (Illus.). 168p. (C). 1980. pap. 3.25 (0-7178-0563-8) Intl Pubs Co.

Maldonado, Denise & Quinn, Campion. A Case Manager's Study Guide: Preparing for Certification. LC 99-12292. 346p. 1999. student ed. 99.00 (0-8342-1368-0) Aspen Pub.

Maldonado, J. R., jt. ed. see Celler, G. K.

Maldonado, Jesus M. Esta Era una Vez: Once upon a Time. LC 94-71028. (ENG & SPA., Illus.). 48p. (J). (gr. 2-6). 1994. lib. bdg. 14.95 (0-9636912-1-X) J M Maldonado.

— In the Still of My Heart. 112p. (Orig.). (C). 1993. pap. text 9.98 (0-9636912-0-1) J M Maldonado.

Maldonado, Jorge E. Aun en las Mejores Familias. (SPA.). 93p. pap. 9.00 (1-55883-401-X, 6792-0011C) Libros Desafio.

Maldonado, Kirk F. Golden Parachute Payments. 40p. (Orig.). 1995. pap. text 34.95 (0-7811-0121-2) Res Inst Am.

Maldonado Lopez, Celia, see Lopez, Celia Maldonado.

Maldonado, Luis & Power, David, eds. Symbol & Art in Worship. (Concilium Ser.: Vol. 132). 128p. (Orig.). 1980. 6.95 (0-8164-2274-5) Harper SF.

Maldonado, Manuel. Eugenio Maria de Hostos. (SPA.). 186p. 1992. pap. 12.99 (968-16-3871-9, Pub. by Fondo) Continental Bk.

Maldonado, Premier. Conceptualizing. 147p. 1995. pap. text. write for info. (1-56758-041-6) Edit Cultl.

Maldonado, Rafael & Stinus, Luis. Neurobiological Mechanisms of Opiate Withdrawal. LC 96-8139. (Neuroscience Intelligence Unit Ser.). 196p. 1996. 99.00 (1-57059-347-7) Landes Bioscience.

Maldonado, Raul. Poetry for the Common Man. 96p. 1998. pap. 10.00 (0-8059-4377-3) Dorrance.

Maldonado, Sigrid R. Estonian Experience & Roots: Ethnic Estonian Genealogy with Historical Perspective, Social Influences & Possible Family History Resources. LC 96-85886. (Illus.). vi, 120p. 1996. 24.00 (0-9653936-0-7) As Was Pub.

Maldre, Mati & Kruty, Paul. Walter Burley Griffin in America. LC 95-11632. (Illus.). 192p. 1996. 49.95 (0-252-02193-2) U of Ill Pr.

Male. Advanced Immunology. 3rd ed. 1996. mass mkt. 54.00 (0-7234-2059-9) Wolfe Pubng AZ.

— L' Art Religieux en France, 3 tomes. Incl. Tome III. De la Fin du Moyen Age. 75.00 (0-8288-9914-2, F22172); (FRE.). write for info. (0-318-51926-7) Fr & Eur.

— Immunology: Illustrated Outline. 5th ed. 1997. pap. text 17.95 (0-7234-2617-1) Mosby Inc.

Male, Belkis C. Woman on the Front Lines. Carmell, Pamella, tr. from SPA. & intro. by. 88p. 1987. 17.50 (0-87775-202-8); pap. 9.95 (0-87775-203-6) Unicorn Pr.

Male, Belkis C., ed. see Diaz-Rodriguez, Ernesto.

***Male, Carolyn.** 100 Heirloom Tomatoes for the American Garden. LC 99-17665. (Smith & Hawken Ser.). (Illus.). 246p. 1999. pap. 17.95 (0-7611-1400-9) Workman Pub.

Male Chauvinist Pigs of America, Staff. The Male Chauvinist Pigs' Guide to Women: Every Day is Halloween. LC 95-81190. (Illus.). 104p. (Orig.). 1996. pap. 9.95 (0-9648853-1-X) Male Chauvinist.

Male, Emile. Gothic Image. Nussey, Dora, tr. from FRE. (Icon Editions Ser.). (Illus.). 440p. 1973. reprint ed. pap. 40.00 (0-06-430032-3, IN-32, Icon Edns) HarpC.

Male, Emile. Religious Art from the Twelfth to the Eighteenth Century. LC 82-47903. (Illus.). 256p. 1982. pap. text 19.95 (0-691-00347-5, Pub. by Princeton U Pr) Cal Prin Full Svc.

— Religious Art in France: The Late Middle Ages: A Study of Medieval Iconography & Its Sources. Bober, Harry, ed. Mathews, Marthiel, tr. (Bollingen Ser.: Vol. XC, No. 3). 600p. 1986. text 99.50 (0-691-09914-6, Pub. by Princeton U Pr) Cal Prin Full Svc.

— Religious Art in France: The Twelfth Century. LC 72-14029. (Bollingen Ser.: Vol. I, No. 90). 664p. 1978. text 145.00 (0-691-09912-X, Pub. by Princeton U Pr) Cal Prin Full Svc.

***Male, Emile.** Religious Art in France of the Thirteenth Century. (Illus.). 2000. pap. 12.95 (0-486-41061-7) Dover.

Male, Emile. Religious Art in France, the Twelfth Century: A Study of the Origins of Medieval Iconography. LC 72-14029. (Bollingen Ser.: No. 1). 607p. 1978. reprint ed. pap. 188.20 (0-608-02552-6, 206319600004) Bks Demand.

Male, George A. Issues in the Education of Minorities: England & the United States. LC 88-38808. 110p. 1989. 22.50 (0-89341-552-9, Longwood Academic); pap. 15.00 (0-89341-553-7, Longwood Academic) Hollowbrook.

Male, James W. & Walski, Thomas M. Water Distribution Systems: A Troubleshooting Manual. (Illus.). 128p. 1990. lib. bdg. 95.00 (0-87371-232-3, L232) Lewis Pubs.

Male, Mary. Technology for Inclusion. 3rd ed. LC 96-41904. 208p. 1996. pap. text 57.00 (0-205-19654-3) Allyn.

Male, Steven, jt. auth. see Kelly, John.

Malebranche, Nicolas. Entretiens sur la Metaphysique et sur la Religion. Doney, Willis, tr. LC 77-86229. (Janus Ser.).Tr. of Dialogue on Metaphysics. (FRE.). 359p. 1980. lib. bdg. 25.00 (0-913870-57-9) Abaris Bks.

Malebranche, Nicolas. Oeuvres: De la Recherche de la Verite, Conversations Chretiennes, Vol. 1. write for info. (0-318-52179-2) Fr & Eur.

— Oeuvres Completes. (FRE.). 1978. lib. bdg. 105.00 (0-8288-3550-0, M5422) Fr & Eur.

Malebranche, Nicolas. Philosophical Selections: From the Search after Truth, Dialogue on Metaphysics, Treatise on Nature & Grace. Nadler, Steven, ed. Lennon, Thomas M. et al, trs. from FRE. LC 92-19801. 288p. (C). 1992. 37.95 (0-87220-153-8); pap. text 14.95 (0-87220-152-X) Hackett Pub.

— The Search after Truth & Elucidations of the Search after Truth: Translated from the French. LC 79-23881. (Illus.). 893p. reprint ed. pap. 200.00 (0-608-09853-1, 206981800006) Bks Demand.

— Treatise on Ethics (1684) Walton, Craig, tr. & intro. by. LC 92-13823. (International Archives of the History of Ideas Ser.: Vol. 133). 240p. 1992. lib. bdg. 155.50 (0-7923-1763-7, Pub. by Kluwer Academic) Kluwer Academic.

— Treatise on Nature & Grace. Riley, Patrick, tr. & intro. by. 244p. 1992. text 65.00 (0-19-824832-6) OUP.

Malec, Glenn. The Azure Scroll. 257p. (Orig.). 1991. pap. write for info. (0-9630657-1-8) Godolphin Hse.

— International Horoscopes, 2 vols., Vol. 1. LC 82-72573. 176p. 1982. 19.00 (0-86690-043-8, M2643-014) Am Fed Astrologers.

— International Horoscopes, 2 vols., Vol. 2. LC 82-72573. 130p. 1985. 18.00 (0-86690-271-6, 2530-01) Am Fed Astrologers.

Malec, Henry A. Benchmarking Purchasing in the Semiconductor Industry with Sigma Barometers. Ketchum, Carol L., ed. 22p. (Orig.). (C). 1991. pap. text 20.00 (0-945968-09-4) Ctr Advanced Purchasing.

Malec, Michael A., ed. Social Role of Sport in Caribbean Societies, Vol. 9. (Caribbean Studies). 256p. 1995. text 50.00 (2-88449-134-1) Gordon & Breach.

— Social Role of Sport in Caribbean Societies, Vol. 9. (Caribbean Studies). 256p. 1995. pap. text 21.00 (2-88449-135-X) Gordon & Breach.

***Malec, Pam.** Guide to Sea Kayaking in North Carolina: The Best Trips from Knotts Island to Cape Fear. (Guide to Sea Kayaking Ser.). (Illus.). 2000. pap. 14.95 (0-7627-0817-4) Globe Pequot.

Malecha, Scarlet, jt. auth. see Hoyt, Doris.

Malecki, Donald S. & Filtner, Arthur L. Commercial Liability Insurance & Risk Management, 2 vols. 4th ed. LC 98-71631. 344p. (C). 1998. 41.00 (0-89463-082-2, 402) Am Inst FCPCU.

***Malecki, Donald S., et al.** The Additional Insured Book. 4th rev. ed. 458p. 2000. pap. 49.98 (1-886813-49-3) Intl Risk Mgt.

Malecki, Donald S., jt. auth. see Hamilton, Karen L.

Malecki, Donald S., jt. auth. see Wiening, Eric A.

Malecki, Edward J. Technology & Economic Development. 2nd ed. LC 98-146562. (C). 1997. pap. text 26.25 (0-582-27723-X, Pub. by Addison-Wesley) Longman.

***Malecki, Edward J. & Oinas, Paivi, eds.** Making Connections: Technological Learning & Regional Economic Change. LC 98-45773. (Organization of Industrial Space Ser.). 298p. 1999. text 69.95 (1-84014-550-1, Pub. by Ashgate Pub) Ashgate Pub Co.

Malecki, I. & Bellert, I. Physical Foundations of Technical Acoustics. LC 64-17267. 1969. 332.00 (0-08-011097-5, Pub. by Pergamon Repr) Franklin.

Malecki, Joseph. Achieving Customer Satisfaction. Hankinson, Mari-Lynn, ed. (AT&T Quality Library). (Illus.). 126p. (Orig.). 1990. pap. 24.95 (0-932764-21-5, 500-443) AT&T Customer Info.

Malecki, Joseph & Lee, Janet. Great Performances: The Best in Customer Satisfaction & Customer Service. Hankinson, Mari-Lynn, ed. (AT&T Quality Library). (Illus.). 176p. (Orig.). 1991. pap. 24.95 (0-932764-28-2, 500-450) AT&T Customer Info.

Malecki, M. & Roomans, G. M. The Science of Biological Specimen Preparation for Microscopy Vol. 10: Scanning Microscopy Supplement. (Illus.). 476p. 1998. 95.00 (0-931288-49-5) Scanning Microscopy.

Malecot, Andre. Contribution a L'etude de la Force D'articulation En Francais. 1977. 21.15 (90-279-3176-3) Mouton.

— Eye on the Western Stars: A Novel. 176p. (Orig.). 1995. pap. 10.95 (1-56474-113-3) Fithian Pr.

— Frogs Out of Water: Stories. LC 98-6692. (Illus.). 144p. 1998. pap. 10.95 (1-56474-274-1) Fithian Pr.

— Fundamental French: Language & Culture. LC 63-10567. (Illus.). 1963. 30.50 (0-89197-184-X); pap. text 19.95 (0-89197-766-X) Irvington.

— Introduction a la Phonetique Francaise. (Janua Linguarum, Ser.: No. 15). 1977. pap. 21.55 (90-279-3395-2) Mouton.

Malee, Noi D. Hot Thai Cooking. 128p. 1996. 27.50 (0-572-02188-7, Pub. by W Foulsham) Trans-Atl Phila.

Maleh, Ghassan & Sirhan, Samir, eds. World Encyclopedia of Contemporary Theatre Vol. 4: The Arab World. (Illus.). 352p. (C). 1999. 160.00 (0-415-05932-1, B0388) Routledge.

Malehorn, Merlin K. & Davenport, Tim. United States Sales Tax Tokens & Stamps: A History & Catalog. LC 93-79632. (Illus.). 403p. 1993. text 49.95 (0-942596-05-6) Jade Hse Pubns.

Maleiko, Nancy E. Business Documents That Work: Five Steps to Writing Effective Reports, Manuals & Other Business Publications. LC 97-91677. (Illus.). 104p. (Orig.). 1997. pap. 15.00 (0-9657369-0-3) Rusty Rock.

Malek. Theban Necropolis Vol. 1: Private Tombs. 2nd ed. (Topographical Bibliography of Ancient Egyptian Hieroglyphic Texts Ser.: Reliefs & Paintings, Vol. 1-1). 520p. 1994. reprint ed. 91.50 (0-900416-10-6, Pub. by Aris & Phillips) David Brown.

— Theban Temples. (Topographical Bibliography of Ancient Egyptian Hieroglyphic Texts Ser.: Reliefs & Paintings, Vol. 2). 1972. 99.00 (0-900416-18-1, Pub. by Aris & Phillips) David Brown.

— Topographical Bibliography (Gr) No. 8i: Objects of Unknown Provenance, Statues. write for info. (0-900416-29-7, Pub. by Aris & Phillips) David Brown.

Malek, Abbas, ed. News Media & Foreign Relations: A Multifaceted Perspective. (Communication, Culture & Information Studies Ser.). 268p. 1996. pap. 39.50 (1-56750-273-3); text 78.50 (1-56750-272-5) Ablx Pub.

***Malek, Abbas & Kavoori, Anandam P.** The Global Dynamics of News: Studies in International News Coverage & News Agenda. LC 99-29339. (Contemporary Studies in International Political Communication). 350p. 1999. 49.38 (1-56750-463-9) Ablx Pub.

Malek, Doreen O. Above the Law. (Desire Ser.). 1994. per. 2.99 (0-373-05869-1, 1-05869-2) Silhouette.

— Big Sky Drifter. 1997. per. 3.50 (0-373-76097-3, 1-76097-4) Silhouette.

— Boda Frustrada-The Harder They Fall. 1996. per. 3.50 (0-373-35138-0) Harlequin Bks.

— Clash by Night. 448p. 1988. per. 4.50 (0-373-97059-5) Harlequin Bks.

— Daddy's Choice. (Desire Ser.). 1996. per. 3.50 (0-373-05983-3, 1-05983-1) Silhouette.

— Fair Game. 352p. (Orig.). 1989. mass mkt. 3.95 (0-445-20920-8, Pub. by Warner Bks) Little.

— Una Flecha en la Nieve: Arrow in the Snow. (Deseo Ser.). (SPA.). 1997. per. 3.50 (0-373-35213-1, 1-35213-7) Harlequin Bks.

— The Harder They Fall. (Desire Ser.). 1993. pap. 2.89 (0-373-05778-4, 5-05778-1) Silhouette.

— The Lion & the Lark. 1996. mass mkt. 4.99 (0-8217-5291-X, Zebra Kensgtn) Kensgtn Pub Corp.

— Luchando por el Amor: Daddy's Choice. (Deseo Ser.). (SPA.). 1996. per. 3.50 (0-373-35157-7, 1-35157-6) Harlequin Bks.

— Marriage in Name Only. (Intimate Moments Ser.). 1995. per. 3.75 (0-373-07620-7, 1-07620-7) Silhouette.

— An Officer & a Gentle Woman: Men in Blue. (Intimate Moments Ser.: No. 958). 1999. per. 4.25 (0-373-07958-3, 1-07958-1) Silhouette.

— Panther's Prey. 432p. (Orig.). 1996. mass mkt. 5.99 (0-8439-4015-8) Dorchester Pub Co.

***Malek, Doreen Owens.** Made for Each Other. (Intimate Moments Ser.: Bk. 1041). 2000. mass mkt. 4.50 (0-373-27111-5, 1-27111-3) Silhouette.

Malek, Edith M. American Clematis Society's Guide to Growing Clematis in the United States. (Illus.). 59p. (Orig.). 1999. pap. 19.99 (0-9670538-0-3) Am Clematis.

Malek, Eliza & Uniwersytet Lodzki, Zaklad Literatury Rosyjskiej. Proza Rosyjska Epoki Obswiecenia: Nowe Odkrycia I Interpretacje : Tezy Referatbow Miqedzynarodowej Konferencji Naukowej, !bodbz, 19-21 Pabzdziernika, 1995 R. / LC 96-216194. 50 p. 1995. write for info. (83-7016-871-X) Lodzki Univ Pr.

Malek, Emile A. Snail Hosts of Schistosomiasis & Other: A Manual. (Scientific Publications: Vol. 478). 334p. 1985. 12.00 (92-75-11478-1) PAHO.

Malek, Emile A. Snail Transmitted Parasitic Diseases, 2 vols., Vol. 1. 352p. 1980. 193.00 (0-8493-5269-X, RC119, CRC Reprint) Franklin.

— Snail Transmitted Parasitic Diseases, 2 vols., Vol. 2. 344p. 1980. 188.00 (0-8493-5270-3, CRC Reprint) Franklin.

Malek, J., et al, eds. Advanced Topics in Theoretical Fluid Mechanics. (Pitman Research Notes in Mathematics Ser.: No. 392). 224p. 1998. pap. 46.50 (0-582-36803-0, LM0616, Chap & Hall CRC) Addison-Wesley.

***Malek, J., et al.** Advanced Topics in Theoretical Fluid Mechanics, Vol. 392. (C&H/CRC Research Notes in Mathematics Series). 224p. 1998. ring bd. 54.95 (0-8493-0616-7) CRC Pr.

Malek, James S. The Arts Compared: An Aspect of Eighteenth-Century British Aesthetics. LC 74-11088. 176p. reprint ed. pap. 54.60 (0-7837-3602-9, 204346700009) Bks Demand.

Malek, Jaromir. The ABC of Hieroglyphs - Ancient Egyptian Writing. (Illus.). 48p. 1995. pap. 8.95 (1-85444-052-7, 0527, Pub. by Ashmolean Mus) A Schwartz & Co.

— The Cat in Ancient Egypt. LC 97-14191. (C). (gr. 13). 1997. pap. 17.95 (0-8122-1632-6) U of Pa Pr.

— Egypt. LC 92-50718. (Cradles of Civilization Ser.: Vol. 1). (Illus.). 186p. 1993. 34.95 (0-8061-2526-8) U of Okla Pr.

— Egyptian Art. 448p. 1999. pap. 24.95 (0-7148-3627-3, Pub. by Phaidon Press) Phaidon Pr.

— In the Shadow of the Pyramids: Egypt During the Old Kingdom. LC 86-40188. (Illus.). 128p. 1992. pap. 19.95 (0-8061-2027-4) U of Okla Pr.

— Lower & Middle Egypt. (Topographical Bibliography of Ancient Egyptian Hieroglyphic Texts Ser.: Reliefs & Paintings, Vol. 4). 35.00 incl. fiche (0-900416-20-3, Pub. by Aris & Phillips) David Brown.

***Malek, Jaromir.** Objects of Provenance Not Known: Index to Parts I & 2, 3 vols. (Topographical Bibliography of Ancient Egyptian Hieroglyphic Ser.: Vol. VIII). 100p. (C). 2000. pap. 350.00 (0-900416-70-X, Pub. by Griffith Inst) David Brown.

***Malek, Jaromir, et al.** Objects of Provenance Not Known: Private Statues (Dynasty XVIII to the Roman Period) - Deities, 3 vols. (Topographical Bibliography of Ancient Egyptian Hieroglyphic Ser.: Vol. VIII). 700p. (C). 2000. 350.00 (0-900416-69-6, Pub. by Griffith Inst) David Brown.

— Objects of Provenance Not Known: Royal Statues. Private Statues, 3 vols. (Predynastic to Dynasty Ser.: Vol. XVII, Pt. 1). 500p. 2000. 350.00 (0-900416-67-X, Pub. by Griffith Inst) David Brown.

— Objects of Provenance Not Known: Royal Statues, Private Statues (Predynastic to Dynasty XVII) (Topographical Bibliography of Ancient Egyptian Hieroglyphic Ser.: Vol. VIII). 500p. (C). 2000. 350.00 (0-900416-68-8, Pub. by Griffith Inst) David Brown.

Malek, Jaromir, et al. The Theban Necropolis Vol. Iii: Royal Tombs & Smaller Cemeteries, 2 vols., Set. 2nd ed. (Topographical Bibliography of Ancient Egyptian Hieroglyphic Ser.). 440p. (C). 2000. reprint ed. 115.00 (0-900416-15-7, Pub. by Griffith Inst) David Brown.

Malek, Jaromir, jt. auth. see Baines, John.

Malek, M. International Mediation & the Gulf War. 250p. (C). 1991. 175.00 (0-7855-6800-X, Pub. by Royston Ltd) St Mut.

Malek, M., ed. see Rasquinha, J.

Malek, M. M. The Political Economy of Iran under the Shah. 288p. 1987. 42.00 (0-7099-3519-6, Pub. by C Helm) Routldge.

***Malek, M. Mike.** Knee Surgery: Complications, Pitfalls & Salvage. LC 99-40673. 512p. 2000. (0-387-98294-9) Spr-Verlag.

MALEK-MADANI. Instructor's Solution Manual. (C). 1997. pap. text. write for info. (0-201-59882-5) Addison-Wesley.

Malek-Madani, Reza. Advanced Engineering Mathematics, Vol. 2. LC 97-22716. Vol. 2. 576p. (C). 1998. 66.00 (0-201-32549-7) Addison-Wesley.

— Advanced Engineering Mathematics: With Mathematica & Matlab. Guardino, Karen, ed. LC 97-22716. Vol. 1. (Illus.). 1008p. (C). 1997. pap. 65.00 (0-201-59881-7) Addison-Wesley.

Malek, Mhemooda. Making Home-School Work. 54p. 1997. spiral bd. 15.00 (1-874579-96-2, Pub. by Natl Childrens Bur) Paul & Co Pubs.

Malek, Miroslaw. High-Performance Computing in Europe. 46p. (Orig.). (C). 1993. pap. text 40.00 (1-56806-305-9) DIANE Pub.

— Responsive Computing. LC 94-31249. 120p. (C). 1994. text 98.50 (0-7923-9511-5) Kluwer Academic.

Malek, Miroslaw, ed. see Fussell, Donald.

Malek, Mo, ed. Setting Priorities in Health Care. 348p. 1994. 196.50 (0-471-94394-0) Wiley.

Malek, Mo, et al, eds. Strategic Issues in Health Care Management. 298p. 1993. 181.95 (0-471-93964-1) Wiley.

***Malek, Rene.** Cleft Lip & Palate: Examination, Surgery & Rehabilitation. (Illus.). 360p. 2000. 175.00 (1-85317-491-2, Pub. by Martin Dunitz) Thieme Med Pubs.

Malek-Zavarei, M., jt. auth. see Jamshidi, Mohammad.

Malek-Zavarei, Manu. Network Management. 1999. audio compact disk 250.00 (0-7803-5309-9) IEEE Standards.

Malek-Zavarei, Manu, jt. auth. see Jamshidi, Mohammad.

Malekian, Farhad. The Concept of Islamic International Criminal Law: A Comparative Study. 232p. 1994. lib. bdg. 107.50 (1-85966-085-1, Pub. by Graham & Trotman) Kluwer Academic.

— Condemning the Use of Force in the Gulf Crisis. 116p. (Orig.). 1992. pap. 78.00 (91-630-1251-0) Coronet Bks.

— International Criminal Law: The Legal & Critical Analysis of International Crimes, 2 vols., Set. 1121p. 1991. 795.00 (91-630-0244-2) Coronet Bks.

— The Monopolization of International Criminal Law in the United Nations: A Jurisprudential Approach. 2nd ed. 240p. (Orig.). 1995. pap. 122.50 (91-630-3196-5) Coronet Bks.

Malekin, Peter. Literature, Spirituality & the Theater. LC 96-44006. 200p. 1997. text 49.95 (0-312-16015-1) St Martin.

Malekoff, Andrew. Group Work with Adolescents: Principles & Practice. LC 96-47770. (Social Work Practice with Children & Families Ser.). 336p. 1997. lib. bdg. 39.95 (1-57230-209-7) Guilford Pubns.

— Group Work with Adolescents: Principles & Practice. (Social Work Practice with Children & Families Ser.). 336p. 1999. pap. text 21.00 (1-57230-465-0) Guilford Pubns.

— Night Crawlers: After Hours at the ER. LC 97-32928. (Illus.). 56p. 1998. pap. 7.95 (0-9646450-7-6) DeeMar Commun.

Malekoff, Andrew, ed. Group Work with Suburbia's Children: Difference, Acceptance & Belonging. (Social Work with Groups Ser.). 127p. 1991. text 39.95 (1-56024-100-4) Haworth Pr.

Malekzadeh, Ali R., jt. auth. see Nahavandi, Afsaneh.

Malen, Betty, jt. ed. see Fuhrman, Susan H.

Malen, Betty, jt. ed. see Theobald, Neil D.

Malen, Lenore. Images from Dante. LC 91-62103. (Books by Artists - Poetry Ser.). (Illus.). 32p. (Orig.). 1991. pap. text 14.00 (1-877675-08-3) Midmarch Arts.

Malena, Anne. The Negotiated Self: The Dynamics of Identity in Francophone Caribbean Narrative. LC 97-26600. (Francophone Cultures & Literatures Ser.: Vol. 24). X, 192p. (C). 1999. text 47.95 (0-8204-3887-1) P Lang Pubng.

Malena, C. Gender Issues in Integrated Pest Management in African Agriculture. 1994. pap. 40.00 (0-85954-377-3, Pub. by Nat Res Inst) St Mut.

Malenda, John W. Being. 35p. (Orig.). 1995. pap. 3.50 (1-886482-01-2) Guiding Lght.

— Destinations. 180p. 1995. pap. 10.95 (1-886482-00-4) Guiding Lght.

Malensek, Kristina, ed. see Hardin, Valerie.

Malenter Symposion Staff, et al. Economies in Transition & Globalized Markets: The Challenge to International Economic Organizations; Proceedings from the XI Malente Symposium LC 99-168854. (Drhager Foundation Ser.). 179p. 1997. write for info. (3-7890-4970-0, Pub. by Nomos Verlags) Intl Bk Import.

Maleparampil, Joseph. The Trinitarian Formulae in St. Paul: An Exegetical Investigation in the Meaning & Function of Those Pauline Sayings Which Compositely Make Mention of God, Christ & the Holy Spirit. (European University Studies: Series 23, Vol. 546). 299p. 1995. pap. 57.95 (3-631-49431-9) P Lang Pubng.

— The Trinitarian Formulae in St. Paul: An Exegetical Investigation into the Meaning & Function of Those Pauline Sayings Which Compositely Make Mention of God, Christ & the Holy Spirit. LC 95-39185. (Illus.). 299p. 1995. pap. 57.95 (0-8204-2943-0) P Lang Pubng.

An Asterisk (*) at the beginning of an entry indicates that the title is appearing for the first time.

Maler, Anselm, ed. Literatur und Regionalitat. (Studien Zur Neuren Literatur: Bd. 4). (Illus.). 228p. 1997. pap. 40.95 (*3-631-32067-1*) P Lang Pubng.

Maler, Anselm, et al. Europaische Aspekte der Aufklarung: (Deutschland, England, Frankreich, Italien, Spanien) (Studien Zur Neuren Literatur: Bd. 6). (GER.). 112p. 1998. 26.95 (*3-631-32648-3*) P Lang Pubng.

Maler, Anselm, ed. see Sun, Ying.

Maler, Elvira, tr. see Potter, Beatrix & Pomaska, Anna.

Maler, Eve. Developing SGML Document Type Definitions. 560p. 1995. 66.00 (*0-13-309881-8*) P-H.

Maler, Karl-Goran. Economic Sciences, 1981-1990: The Sveriges Riksbank (Bank of Sweden) Prize in Economic Sciences in Memory of Alfred Nobel. LC 92-37996. (Nobel Lectures, Including Presentation Speeches & Laureates' Biographies Ser.). 400p. 1994. text 86.00 (*981-02-0835-9*); pap. text 46.00 (*981-02-0836-7*) World Scientific Pub.

— Environmental Economics: A Theoretical Inquiry. LC 73-19347. (Illus.). 286p. reprint ed. pap. 88.70 (*0-8357-4678-X*, 203762500008) Bks Demand.

Maler, Karl-Goran, jt. ed. see Dasgupta, Partha.

Maler, O. Hybrid & Real-Time Systems: International Workshop, HART '97, Grenoble, France, March 26-28, 1997: Proceedings. LC 97-6971. (Lecture Notes in Computer Sciences Ser.: Vol. 120). 1997. pap. 67.00 (*3-540-62600-X*) Spr-Verlag.

Maler, T. Researches in the Central Portion of the Usumatsintla Valley. (HU PMM Ser.). 1974. reprint ed. 50.00 (*0-527-01156-8*) Periodicals Srv.

— Researches in the Usumatsintla Valley, Pt. 2. (HU PMM Ser.). 1974. reprint ed. 80.00 (*0-527-01157-6*) Periodicals Srv.

Malerba, Diana. The BubbleBuds Coloring & Activity Book. (Illus.). 24p. (Orig.). (J). (ps-1). 1996. pap. 1.99 (*1-889914-01-0*) Bubblebud Bks.

— The BubbleBuds Rainbow Adventure. Kelly, Grace, ed. (Illus.). 24p. (Orig.). (J). (ps-2). 1996. pap. 4.99 (*1-889914-00-2*) Bubblebud Bks.

Malerba, Franco, jt. ed. see Gambardella, Alfonso.

Malerba, L., ed. Italian Cinema, 1945-51. 1976. lib. bdg. 69.95 (*0-8490-2084-0*) Gordon Pr.

Malerba, Luigi. La Historia y la Gloria y Otros Relatos (History & Glory & Other Tales) Morabito, Fabio, tr. (SPA., Illus.). 52p. (J). (gr. 5-6). 1992. pap. 5.99 (*968-16-3767-4*, Pub. by Fondo) Continental Bk.

— Pinocho Con Botas (Pinocchio with Boots) Morabito, Fabio, tr. (SPA., Illus.). 68p. (J). (gr. 5-6). 1992. pap. 5.99 (*968-16-3913-8*, Pub. by Fondo) Continental Bk.

Malerich, Charles, jt. auth. see Scharf, Walter.

Malerstein, Abraham J. The Conscious Mind: A Developmental Theory. 163p. (C). 1993. text 22.50 (*0-9644089-1-0*) Cole Valley Pr.

Malerstein, Abraham J. & Ahern, Mary. A Piagetian Model of Character Structure. 252p. (C). 1993. text 22.50 (*0-9644089-0-2*) Cole Valley Pr.

Malerstein, Abraham J., jt. auth. see Ahern, Mary.

***Males, Carolyn, et al.** Wish You Were Here! A Guide to Baltimore City for Natives & Newcomers. LC 98-55255. (Illus.). 480p. 1999. pap. 19.95 (*1-891521-05-5*) Woodholme Hse.

Males, Mike. The Scapegoat Generation: America's War Against Adolescents. 300p. (Orig.). 1996. pap. 17.95 (*1-56751-080-9*) Common Courage.

— The Scapegoat Generation: America's War Against Adolescents. 300p. (Orig.). 1996. lib. bdg. 29.95 (*1-56751-081-7*) Common Courage.

Males, Mike A. Framing Youth: Ten Myths about the Next Generation. LC 98-49506. 224p. 1998. pap. 18.95 (*1-56751-148-1*); lib. bdg. 29.95 (*1-56751-149-X*) Common Courage.

***Males, Mike A.** Juvenile Injustice: America's "Youth Violence" Hoax. (Read & Resist Ser.). 200p. 2000. pap. 12.00 (*1-56751-198-8*, Pub. by Common Courage); lib. bdg. 29.95 (*1-56751-199-6*, Pub. by Common Courage) Login Brothers Bk Co.

Males, Mike A. Smoked: Why Joe Camel Is Still Smiling. LC 99-41103. 1999. 29.95 (*1-56751-173-2*); pap. 7.50 (*1-56751-172-4*) Common Courage.

Males, R., jt. ed. see Barrett, Peter.

Males, Richard M., et al. Use of Expert Systems in a Water Utility. (Illus.). 120p. (Orig.). (C). 1994. pap. text 40.00 (*0-7881-0277-X*) DIANE Pub.

Malesani, M. G., jt. auth. see Valenti, R.

Malesis, C. H. Where the Trilliums Bloom. 192p. 1991. pap. 11.95 (*0-9631266-0-1*) Poon Crick Pub.

Maleska, Eugene. New York Times Crossword Puzzle Omnibus, Vol. 9. 1997. pap. 11.00 (*0-8129-2951-9*, Times Bks) Crown Pub Group.

***Maleska, Eugene.** New York Times Daily Crossword Puzzles, Vol. 24. 2000. pap. 9.95 (*0-8129-3288-9*) Random.

Maleska, Eugene. New York Times Daily Crossword. 1998. pap. 9.00 (*0-8129-3073-8*, Times Bks) Crown Pub Group.

— The New York Times Sunday Crosword Puzzles, 5. 10th ed. Vol. 10. 64p. 1999. pap. 9.00 (*0-8129-3105-X*, Times Bks) Crown Pub Group.

— NY Times Sunday Crossword Puzzles, 9. Vol. 9. 64p. 1998. pap. 9.00 (*0-8129-3087-8*, Times Bks) Crown Pub Group.

— New York Times Toughest Crossword Puzzles, Vol. 6. 6th ed. 1998. pap. 10.00 (*0-8129-2805-9*, Times Bks) Crown Pub Group.

— Simon & Schuster Crossword Treasury. 96p. 1999. per. 9.00 (*0-684-84366-8*) Free Pr.

Maleska, Eugene T. Children's Word Games & Crossword Puzzles, Vol. 2. (J). (gr. 2-4). 1988. pap. 8.00 (*0-8129-1692-1*) Random.

— Children's Word Games & Crossword Puzzles, Vol. 3. Vol. 3. (J). (ps up). 1992. pap. 8.50 (*0-8129-1980-7*, Times Bks) Crown Pub Group.

— Crossword Series, Vol. 161. 1991. pap. 6.95 (*0-671-74047-4*, Fireside) S&S Trade Pap.

***Maleska, Eugene T.** Crossword Treasury, Vol. 3. large type ed. (Illus.). 144p. 1999. per. 9.00 (*0-684-84367-6*) S&S Trade.

— New York Times Daily Crossword Puzzles, Vol. 27. 64p. 2000. pap. 9.95 (*0-8129-3363-X*, Times Bks) Crown Pub Group.

Maleska, Eugene T. The New York Times Daily Crossword Puzzles, Vol. 27. 27th ed. 1990. pap. 7.50 (*0-8129-1879-7*, Times Bks) Crown Pub Group.

— New York Times Daily Crossword Puzzles, Vol. 28. 28th ed. Vol. 28. 1991. pap. 7.00 (*0-8129-1899-1*, Times Bks) Crown Pub Group.

***Maleska, Eugene T.** New York Times Daily Crossword Puzzles, Vol. 30. 2000. pap. 9.95 (*0-8129-3380-X*, Times Bks) Crown Pub Group.

— New York Times Daily Crossword Puzzles, Vol. 31. 2000. pap. 9.95 (*0-8129-3383-4*, Times Bks) Crown Pub Group.

Maleska, Eugene T. New York Times Daily Crossword Puzzles, Vol. 31. 31st ed. 1992. pap. 8.00 (*0-8129-2043-0*, Times Bks) Crown Pub Group.

***Maleska, Eugene T.** New York Times Daily Crossword Puzzles, Vol. 32. 2000. pap. 9.95 (*0-8129-3385-0*, Times Bks) Crown Pub Group.

— New York Times Daily Crossword Puzzles, Vol. 33. 2000. pap. 9.95 (*0-8129-3388-5*, Times Bks) Crown Pub Group.

Maleska, Eugene T. New York Times Daily Crossword Puzzles, Vol. 33. 33rd ed. Vol. 33. 1993. pap. 8.50 (*0-8129-2183-6*, Times Bks) Crown Pub Group.

— New York Times Daily Crossword Puzzles, Vol. 34. 34th ed. Vol. 34. 1993. pap. 8.00 (*0-8129-2209-3*, Times Bks) Crown Pub Group.

— The New York Times Daily Crossword Puzzles, Vol. 39. Vol. 39. 1995. pap. 9.95 (*0-8129-2481-9*, Times Bks) Crown Pub Group.

— New York Times Daily Crossword Puzzles Friday, Skill Level 5, Vol. 1. 1997. mass mkt. 2.99 (*0-8041-1583-4*) Ivy Books.

— The New York Times Daily Crossword Puzzles (Monday), Vol. I. Vol. 1. 1997. mass mkt. 2.99 (*0-8041-1579-6*) Ivy Books.

— New York Times Daily Crossword Puzzles Saturday, Skill Level 6, Vol. 1. 1997. mass mkt. 2.99 (*0-8041-1584-2*) Ivy Books.

— The New York Times Daily Crossword Puzzles (Thursday), Vol. 2. 1997. mass mkt. 2.99 (*0-8041-1582-6*) Ivy Books.

— The New York Times Daily Crossword Puzzles (Tuesday), Vol. I. 1997. mass mkt. 2.99 (*0-8041-1580-X*) Ivy Books.

— The New York Times Daily Crossword Puzzles, Vol. 35, Vol. 26. 1990. pap. 6.95 (*0-8129-1860-6*) Random.

— The New York Times Daily Crossword Puzzles, Vol. 35, Vol. 35. Vol. 35. 1993. pap. 8.50 (*0-8129-2270-0*, Times Bks) Crown Pub Group.

— The New York Times Daily Crossword Puzzles (Wednesday), Vol. I. 1997. mass mkt. 2.99 (*0-8041-1581-8*) Ivy Books.

— The New York Times Sunday Crossword Puzzles, Vol. 15. 1989. pap. 9.00 (*0-8129-1781-2*, Times Bks) Crown Pub Group.

— The New York Times Sunday Crossword Puzzles, Vol. 16. 1990. pap. 9.00 (*0-8129-1839-8*, Times Bks) Crown Pub Group.

— The New York Times Sunday Crossword Puzzles, Vol. 17. 1990. pap. 9.00 (*0-8129-1878-9*, Times Bks) Crown Pub Group.

— The New York Times Sunday Crossword Puzzles, Vol. 18. 1994. pap. 9.95 (*0-8129-2268-9*, Times Bks) Crown Pub Group.

— New York Times Sunday Crossword Puzzles, Vol. 19. Vol. 19. 1992. pap. 9.00 (*0-8129-2083-X*, Times Bks) Crown Pub Group.

— The New York Times Sunday Crossword Puzzles, Vol. 21. Vol. 21. 64p. 1995. pap. 9.00 (*0-8129-2615-3*, Times Bks) Crown Pub Group.

— The New York Times Sunday Crossword Puzzles, Vol. 22. 22nd ed. Vol. 22. 64p. 1996. pap. 9.00 (*0-8129-2803-2*, Times Bks) Crown Pub Group.

— The New York Times Sunday Crossword Puzzles, Vol. 23. 23rd ed. 1997. pap. 9.00 (*0-8129-2939-X*, Times Bks) Crown Pub Group.

— The New York Times Sunday Crosswords Omnibus, Vol. 4. 1995. pap. 11.00 (*0-8129-2480-0*, Times Bks) Crown Pub Group.

***Maleska, Eugene T.** New York Times Toughest Crossword Puzzle Megaomnibus. 336p. (Orig.). 1999. pap. 13.50 (*0-8129-3166-1*, Times Bks) Crown Pub Group.

Maleska, Eugene T. The New York Times Toughest Crossword Puzzles, Vol. 1. 1988. pap. 9.00 (*0-8129-1694-8*, Times Bks) Crown Pub Group.

— The New York Times Toughest Crossword Puzzles, Vol. 2. 1989. pap. 9.00 (*0-8129-1828-2*, Times Bks) Crown Pub Group.

— New York Times Toughest Crossword Puzzles, Vol. 3. Vol. 3. 1991. pap. 10.00 (*0-8129-1912-2*, Times Bks) Crown Pub Group.

— New York Times Toughest Crossword Puzzles, Vol. 4. 4th ed. Vol. 4. 1993. pap. 9.00 (*0-8129-2178-X*, Times Bks) Crown Pub Group.

— New York Times Toughest Crossword Puzzles, Vol. 5. Vol. 5. 64p. 1995. pap. 9.00 (*0-8129-2618-8*, Times Bks) Crown Pub Group.

— S&S Crosswords. 64p. 1994. pap. 7.50 (*0-671-87197-8*, No. 178, Fireside) S&S Trade Pap.

— Simon & Schuster Crossword Treasury, No. 38. 96p. 1995. per. 8.00 (*0-684-81393-9*) S&S Trade Pap.

— Simon & Schuster Large Type Crossword Treasury, No. 1. large type ed. 144p. 1995. per. 9.00 (*0-684-81187-1*, Fireside) S&S Trade Pap.

— Simon & Schuster Super Crossword, Bk. 9. 256p. 1996. pap. 9.00 (*0-684-82964-9*) S&S Trade.

— Simon & Schuster's Crossword Puzzle Book Series, No. 168. Vol. 168. 64p. 1992. per. 6.99 (*0-671-77850-1*) S&S Trade.

— Simon & Schuster's Super Crossword Book, No. 7. 256p. 1992. per. 9.00 (*0-671-79232-6*) S&S Trade.

***Maleska, Eugene T.** A Super Crossword Book: The Biggest & the Best, Bk. 10. (Simon & Schuster Crossword Puzzle Bks.). 256p. 1998. per. 10.00 (*0-684-84365-X*) S&S Trade.

Maleska, Eugene T., ed. Children's Word Games & Crossword Puzzles, Vol. 1. LC 86-888. 80p. 1986. pap. 9.00 (*0-8129-1243-8*, Times Bks) Crown Pub Group.

— Children's Word Games & Crossword Puzzles: Ages 9 & up. 2nd ed. LC 86-886. 80p. (J). (gr. 3 up). 1986. pap. 9.00 (*0-8129-1308-6*) Random.

— New York Times Crossword Puzzles, Vol. 34. 1993. write for info. (*0-8129-2264-6*) Random.

— New York Times Crossword Puzzles, Vol. 37. 1994. pap. 8.50 (*0-8129-2358-8*) Random.

— The New York Times Daily Crossword Puzzles, Vol. 29. 29th ed. 64p. 1991. pap. 7.00 (*0-8129-1937-8*, Times Bks) Crown Pub Group.

— New York Times Daily Crossword Puzzles, Vol. 38. Vol. 38. 64p. 1994. pap. 9.00 (*0-8129-2450-9*, Times Bks) Crown Pub Group.

— The New York Times Daily Crossword Puzzles, Vol. 35, Vol. 30. 1992. pap. 7.50 (*0-8129-1997-1*) Random.

— The New York Times Daily Crossword Puzzles, Vol. 35, Vol. 35. 1994. pap. 8.50 (*0-8129-2340-5*) Random.

— The New York Times Large Print Crossword Puzzle Omnibus, Vol. 1. large type ed. 1994. pap. 13.00 (*0-679-75144-0*) Random Hse Lrg Prnt.

— New York Times Large Print Crossword Puzzles, Vol. 7. large type ed. 1992. pap. 10.00 (*0-679-74118-6*) Random Hse Lrg Prnt.

— NY Times Omnibus, 2. large type ed. 1998. pap. 13.00 (*0-8129-3069-X*, Times Bks) Crown Pub Group.

— The New York Times Sunday Crossword Puzzles, Vol. II. Vol. II. 1985. pap. 9.00 (*0-8129-1115-6*, Times Bks) Crown Pub Group.

Maleska, Eugene T., ed. The New York Times Sunday Crossword Puzzles, Vol. 10. Vol. 10. 64p. 1984. pap., spiral bd. 9.00 (*0-8129-1083-4*, Times Bks) Crown Pub Group.

Maleska, Eugene T., ed. The New York Times Sunday Crossword Puzzles, Vol. 12. Vol. 12. 64p. 1985. pap. 9.00 (*0-8129-1166-0*, Times Bks) Crown Pub Group.

— The New York Times Sunday Crossword Puzzles, Vol. 13. Vol. 13. 64p. 1986. pap. 9.00 (*0-8129-1191-1*, Times Bks) Crown Pub Group.

— The New York Times Sunday Crossword Puzzles, Vol. 14. 64p. 1988. pap. 9.00 (*0-8129-1681-6*, Times Bks) Crown Pub Group.

— New York Times Sunday Crossword Puzzles, Vol. 20. Vol. 20. 64p. 1995. pap. 9.00 (*0-8129-2451-7*, Times Bks) Crown Pub Group.

— The New York Times Sunday Omnibus, Vol. 3. 3rd ed. Vol. 3. 240p. 1991. pap. 11.00 (*0-8129-1936-X*, Times Bks) Crown Pub Group.

— S&S Crossword, No. 180. 64p. 1994. per. 8.00 (*0-671-89268-1*) S&S Trade Pap.

— Simon & Schuster Crossword, No. 175. 1993. pap. 7.50 (*0-671-87194-3*, Fireside) S&S Trade Pap.

— Simon & Schuster Super Crossword, Bk. 8. 256p. 1994. per. 9.00 (*0-671-89709-8*, Fireside) S&S Trade Pap.

— Simon & Schuster's Crossword Book Of Quotations, No. 13. 1981. pap. 4.95 (*0-686-73805-5*, Fireside) S&S Trade Pap.

***Maleska, Eugene T. & Newman, Stanley, eds.** The New York Times Daily Crossword Puzzles, Vol. 28. 64p. 2000. pap. 9.95 (*0-8129-3361-3*, Times Bks) Crown Pub Group.

Maleska, Eugene T. & Samson, John M. Simon & Schuster Crossword Puzzle Book, No. 152. 1989. pap. 6.95 (*0-671-67988-0*, Fireside) S&S Trade Pap.

Maleska, Eugene T. & Samson, John M., eds. Simon & Schuster Crossword Puzzle Book. 1995. pap. 9.00 (*0-671-51131-9*) S&S Trade.

Maleska, Eugene T. & Samson, John M., eds. Simon & Schuster's Crossword Puzzle Book, No. 18. Vol. 183. 64p. 1995. pap. 8.00 (*0-671-51056-8*, Fireside) S&S Trade Pap.

— Simon & Schuster's Crossword Puzzle Book, No. 171. 64p. 1993. per. 9.00 (*0-671-79787-5*) S&S Trade.

— Simon & Schuster's Large Type Crosswords, No. 18. 96p. 1995. pap. 8.00 (*0-671-51134-3*, Fireside) S&S Trade Pap.

Maleska, Eugene T., et al. Simon & Schuster's Crossword Puzzle Book, No. 173. Vol. 173. 1993. pap. 7.50 (*0-671-86408-4*, Fireside) S&S Trade Pap.

Maleska, Eugene T., jt. auth. see Samson, John M.

Maleska, Eugene T., jt. ed. see Farrar, Margaret P.

Maleska, Eugene T., ed. see New York Times Staff.

Maleske, Robert T. Foundations for Gathering & Interpreting Behavioral Data. 1994. mass mkt., teacher ed. write for info. (*0-534-23743-6*) Brooks-Cole.

— Foundations for Gathering & Interpreting Behavioral Data. LC 94-15947. (Illus.). 464p. 1994. mass mkt. 56.25 (*0-534-23742-8*) Brooks-Cole.

***Maleskey, Gale, et al.** Get Well, Stay Well: Holding the Line Against Disease. LC 00-36603. 2000. write for info. (*1-57954-239-5*) Rodale Pr Inc.

Maleskey, Gale, jt. auth. see Bricklin, Mark.

Maleski, Mary A., ed. A Fine Tuning: Studies of the Religious Poetry of Herbert & Milton. (Medieval & Renaissance Texts & Studies: Vol. 64). 336p. 1989. 32.00 (*0-86698-048-2*, MR64) MRTS.

Malesky, Gale. Take This Book to the Gynecologist with You. 1991. pap. 9.95 (*0-201-52379-5*) Addison-Wesley.

Malesky, Gale & Kaufman, Brian P. Home Remedies: What Works. 512p. 1996. pap. 14.95 (*0-87596-407-9*) St Martin.

Malesky, Gale, et al. Nature's Medicines: From Asthma to Weight Gain, from Colds to High Cholesterol-The Most Powerful All-Natural Cures. LC 99-15694. 704p. 1999. 29.95 (*1-57954-028-7*) Rodale Pr Inc.

Malesky, Gaynelle. The Mouse Hunter. 112p. 1994. 16.50 (*0-87012-515-X*) McClain.
THE MOUSE HUNTER is a loving & poignant reminiscence of the joys & sometimes sorrows of growing up as the youngest of eleven children on a farm in Marion County, West Virginia. It captures the simple pleasures in life in a simpler time such as picking greens, cracking hickory nuts & making apple butter in October. THE MOUSE HUNTER shares remembrances of the author as a newly-graduated school teacher who faces tragedy & a love & marriage that has lasted over fifty-eight years. *Publisher Paid Annotation.*

Malesn, S., jt. auth. see Spencer, J.

Maleson, Sandra, jt. auth. see Spencer, Janet.

Malet, Hugh. Voyage in a Bowler Hat. 272p. (C). 1989. 60.00 (*0-947712-02-X*, Pub. by S A Baldwin) St Mut.

Malet, Lucas, pseud. The History of Sir Richard Calmady: A Romance, 2 vols., 1 bk. LC 79-8424. reprint ed. 44.50 (*0-404-62015-9*) AMS Pr.

Malet, Marianne D. Violet: or The Danseuse: A Portraiture of the Human Passions & Character, 2 vols., 1 bk. LC 79-8167. reprint ed. 44.50 (*0-404-62018-3*) AMS Pr.

Malet, R. Maria, et al. Surrealismo en Cataluna. (SPA., Illus.). 208p. 1993. 150.00 (*84-343-0546-1*) Elliots Bks.

Malet, Rosa M. Joan Miro. LC 83-62002. (Illus.). 128p. 1993. 27.50 (*0-8478-0524-7*, Pub. by Rizzoli Intl) St Martin.

***Malet, Rosa Maria.** Joan Miro Foundation Guidebook, Vol. 1. 1999. pap. text 12.95 (*84-7254-764-7*) Skirball Cultural.

***Malet, Rosa Maria, ed.** Joan Miro Foundation Guidebook. (Illus.). 128p. 1999. 12.95 (*88-8118-764-7*, Pub. by Skira IT) Abbeville Pr.

Malet-Veale, Decima. Putting on the Polish: A Guide to Image Enhancement for Men & Women. (Illus.). 488p. 1993. pap. 21.95 (*1-55059-074-X*) Temeron Bks.

***Maleti, Gabriella.** Bitter Asylum. Wood, Sharon, tr. 160p. 2000. pap. 19.95 (*1-85754-436-6*, Pub. by Carcanet Pr) Paul & Co Pubs.

Maletic, Vera. Body Space Expressions: The Development of Rudolf Laban's Movement & Dance Concepts. (Approaches to Semiotics Ser.: No. 75). (Illus.). xvi, 268p. 1987. lib. bdg. 90.80 (*0-89925-141-2*) Mouton.

Maletis, Margaret, jt. auth. see Patton, Sally J.

Maletsky, jt. auth. see Sobel.

Maletsky, Evan M., ed. Teaching with "Student Math Notes", Vol. 2. (Illus.). 128p. 1993. pap. text 17.50 (*0-87353-369-0*) NCTM.

Maletsky, Evan M. & Hirsch, Christian R., eds. Activities from the "Mathematics Teacher" LC 81-4028. (Illus.). 140p. (YA). (gr. 7 up). 1981. pap. 12.95 (*0-87353-173-6*) NCTM.

Maletsky, Evan M., jt. auth. see Sobel, Max A.

Maletta, Gabe J. & Pirozzolo, Francis J., eds. Assessment & Treatment of the Elderly Neuropsychiatric Patient, 4. LC 86-9507. (Advances in Neurogerontology Ser.: Vol. 4). 291p. 1986. 65.00 (*0-275-92112-3*, C2112, Praeger Pubs) Greenwood.

Malette, Louise, jt. ed. see Chalouh.

Maletz, M. Analytical Determination of the Form Factor in the Beam Formula for a Tooth. (Technical Papers: Vol. P221). (Illus.). 45p. 1994. pap. text 30.00 (*1-55589-267-1*) AGMA.

— Combined Static Stresses in Teeth of Spur Gears - A New Approach. (Technical Papers: Vol. P247). (Illus.). 24p. 1944. pap. text 30.00 (*1-55589-295-7*) AGMA.

Maletz, Mark C. Creating the New Corporate Culture: A Handbook of Transformational Change. 1999. 35.00 (*1-84112-029-4*) Capstone Pr.

Maletzky, Barry M. Multiple Monitores Electro-Convulsive Therapy. LC 80-23111. 256p. 1981. 143.00 (*0-8493-5940-6*, RC485, CRC Reprint) Franklin.

— Treating the Sexual Offender. 320p. (C). 1990. text 49.95 (*0-8039-3662-1*); pap. text 23.50 (*0-8039-3663-X*) Sage.

Maleuvre, Didier. Museum Memories: History, Technology, Art. LC 98-35055. (Cultural Memory in the Present Ser.). 1999. 49.50 (*0-8047-3202-7*); pap. 19.95 (*0-8047-3604-9*) Stanford U Pr.

Malewicki, Douglas J. How to Build the One Hundred Fifty-Five MPG at 55 MPH California Commuter. 2nd ed. (Illus.). 50p. 1982. reprint ed. pap. 15.00 (*0-941730-00-X*); reprint ed. pap. text 15.00 (*0-941730-01-8*) Aero Vis.

— New Unified Performance Graphs & Comparisons for Streamlined Human Powered Vehicles. 20p. 1983. 3.50 (*0-912468-29-7*) CA Rocketry.

— One Hundred Fifty-Five Mile per Gallon California Commuter. 8p. 1984. 3.00 (*0-912468-30-0*) CA Rocketry.

Malewicki, Douglas J. & Schwenn, Donald C. Model Rockets from Design to Launch. 1976. teacher ed. 9.95 (*0-912468-15-7*, MRDTL-T); student ed. 9.95 (*0-912468-16-5*, MRDTL-S) CA Rocketry.

An Asterisk (*) at the beginning of an entry indicates that the title is appearing for the first time.

Maley. Dans le Vent. 4th ed. (C). 1998. pap. text 42.00 (0-03-025113-3, Pub. by Harcourt Coll Pubs) Harcourt.
Maley, Alan. Oxford Supplementary Skills: Elementary Writing. (Illus.). 64p. 1992. pap. text 6.95 (0-19-453404-9) OUP.
— Oxford Supplementary Skills: Upper-Intermediate Reading. (Illus.). 96p. 1992. pap. text 6.95 (0-19-453402-2) OUP.
— The Victorian Lady. LC 98-3264. (Illus.). 84p. 1998. 15.99 (1-56507-865-9) Harvest Hse.
— Writing Intermediate. (Illus.). 72p. 1992. pap. text 6.95 (0-19-453405-7) OUP.
Maley, Alan, ed. Advanced Writing. (Illus.). 128p. 1992. pap. text 6.95 (0-19-453407-3) OUP.
— Listening. (Illus.). 154p. 1998. pap. text 13.95 (0-19-437216-2) OUP.
— Oxford Supplementary Skills: Elementary Reading. (Illus.). 64p. 1992. pap. text 6.95 (0-19-453400-6) OUP.
— Oxford Supplementary Skills: Upper-Intermediate Writing. (Illus.). 96p. 1992. pap. text 6.95 (0-19-453406-5) OUP.
— Reading Advanced. (Illus.). 144p. 1992. pap. text 6.95 (0-19-453403-0) OUP.
— Reading Intermediate. (Illus.). 64p. 1992. pap. text 6.95 (0-19-453401-4) OUP.
Maley, Alan & Duff, Alan. Drama Techniques in Language Learning: A Resource Book of Communication Activities for Language Teachers. (Cambridge Handbooks for Language Teachers Ser.). (Illus.). 240p. 1983. pap. text 19.95 (0-521-28868-1) Cambridge U Pr.
— Sounds Intriguing: Resource Material for Teachers. 80p. 1979. pap. text 14.95 (0-521-22138-2) Cambridge U Pr.
Maley, Alan, et al. The Mind's Eye: Using Pictures Creatively in Language Learning. 64p. 1981. pap. text, teacher ed. 14.95 (0-521-23333-X) Cambridge U Pr.
Maley, Alan, jt. auth. see Duff, Alan.
Maley, Alan, ed. see Campbell, Colin & Kryszewska, Hanna.
Maley, Alan, ed. see Dufeu, Bernard.
Maley, Alan, ed. see Duff, Alan.
Maley, Alan, ed. see Greenwood, Jean.
Maley, Alan, ed. see Grundy, Peter.
Maley, Alan, ed. see Hadfield, Jill.
Maley, Alan, ed. see Hardisty, David & Windeatt, Scott.
Maley, Alan, ed. see Nolasco, Rob & Arthur, Lois.
Maley, Alan, ed. see Phillips, Sarah.
Maley, Alan, ed. see Rinvolucri, Mario & Morgan, John.
Maley, Alan, ed. see Sheerin, Susan.
Maley, Alan, ed. see Stevick, Earl W.
Maley, Alan, ed. see Tomalin, Barry & Stempleski, Susan.
Maley, Alan, ed. see Wajnryb, Ruth.
Maley, Alan, ed. see Wessels, Charlyn.
Maley, Alan, ed. see Wright, Andrew.
Maley, Anne, jt. auth. see Simons, Sandra M.
Maley, Catherine A. Dans Le Vent. 1998. pap. text 51.00 (0-03-025606-2) Holt R&W.
— Dans le Vent. 3rd ed. (FRE.). 224p. (C). 1990. pap. text 48.50 (0-03-012663-0) Harcourt Coll Pubs.
— The Pronouns of Address in Modern Standard French. LC 74-17218. (Romance Monographs: No. 10). 1974. 22.00 (84-399-2792-4) Romance.
Maley, Catherine A., jt. ed. see King, Larry D.
Maley, Dale C. Index Mutual Funds: How to Simplify Your Financial Life & Beat the Pro's. LC 98-96634. (Illus.). 192p. 1999. pap. 19.95 (0-9667052-0-3) Artephius.
Maley, F. Miller. Single-Layer Wire Routing & Compaction: Foundations of Computing. 424p. 1989. 45.00 (0-262-13250-8) MIT Pr.
Maley, John. Appellate Handbook for Indiana Lawyers. 2nd ed. 1997. text 120.00 (0-327-00968-3, 68740-11, MICHIE) LEXIS Pub.
Maley, John & DeBonis, Anthony. Appellate Handbook for Indiana Lawyers. 2nd ed. LC 87-82288. Date not set. text 110.00 (0-318-33004-0, 68740-11, MICHIE) LEXIS Pub.
Maley, John R. Appellate Handbook for Indiana Lawyers: 1998 Cumulative Supplement. 41p. 1998. pap. 120.00 (0-327-00570-X, 6874511) LEXIS Pub.
*Maley, John R. Appellate Handbook for Indiana Lawyers, 1999 Cumulative Supplement: Pocketpart. 2nd ed. 100p. 1999. suppl. ed. write for info. (0-327-01712-0, 6874512) LEXIS Pub.
Maley, Michael J. Living in the Question: An Exploration of Formlessness, Change, & Healing. (Illus.). (Orig.). 1995. pap. 13.95 (0-9649741-0-X) Bodysmart Pubns.
Maley, Saundra R. Solitary Apprenticeship: James Wright & German Poetry. LC 96-22211. 718p. 1996. text 139.95 (0-7734-2257-9) E Mellen.
Maley, Saundra R., jt. auth. see Burkle-Young, Francis A.
Maley, Terry S. Field Geology Illustrated. LC 94-75576. (Illus.). 316p. (Orig.). (C). 1994. pap. text 15.95 (0-940949-03-2) Mineral Pubns.
— Mineral Law. rev. ed. (Illus.). 936p. 1996. pap. 65.00 (0-940949-04-0) Mineral Pubns.
Maley, Terry S., ed. see Horowitz, Asher.
Maley, Terry S., jt. ed. see Horowitz, Asher.
Maley, V. Carlton, Jr. The Theory of Beats & Combination Tones, 1700-1863. LC 90-3350. (Harvard Dissertations in the History of Science Ser.). 184p. 1990. text 15.00 (0-8240-0040-4) Garland.
Maley, William, ed. Fundamentalism Reborn? LC 97-52616. 253p. 1998. text 50.00 (0-8147-5585-2); pap. text 19.50 (0-8147-5586-0) NYU Pr.
Maley, William & Saikal, Fazel H. Political Order in Post-Communist Afghanistan. LC 92-32723. (Internaational Peace Academy Occasional Papers). 80p. 1992. pap. text 7.95 (1-55587-361-8) L Rienner.
Maley, William, jt. ed. see Saikal, Amin.
Maley, Willy. A Spenser Chronology. LC 93-2455. 164p. (C). 1994. lib. bdg. 44.00 (0-389-21010-2) B&N Imports.
Maley, Willy, ed. see Spenser, Edmund.

Malezi, Kwasi. Alaska Room & Board Employment Guide: Your One Step Guide to Alaska Employment Opportunities. 50p. 1998. lib. bdg. 19.95 (0-9667753-0-9) Malezi Pub.
Malezieux, E., jt. auth. see Malezieux, J.
Malezieux, J. & Malezieux, E. Travaux Publics des Etats - Unis Amerique en 1870 Souvenirs d'une Mission. (Industrial Antiquities Ser.). (FRE., Illus.). 256p. 1998. reprint ed. pap. 240.00 (1-85297-014-6, Pub. by Archival Facs) St Mut.
*Malfatti, Patrizia. Look Inside an Airplane. (Poke & Look Learning Bks.). (Illus.). 16p. (J). (ps-3). 2000. 9.99 (0-448-42401-0, Planet Dexter) Peng Put Young Read.
Malfatti, Patrizia. Look Inside the Ocean. LC 99-202338. (Poke & Look Learning Ser.). (Illus.). 16p. (J). (ps-3). 1998. mass mkt. 9.99 (0-448-41891-6, G & D) Peng Put Young Read.
Malfatti, Patrizia, tr. Look Inside an Airplane. LC 93-77479. (Poke & Look Learning Ser.). (Illus.). 16p. (J). (ps-3). 1994. spiral bd., bds. 12.95 (0-448-40543-1, G & D) Peng Put Young Read.
Malfertheiner, P., et al, eds. Diagnostic Procedures in Pancreatic Disease. LC 97-5281. (Illus.). 400p. 1997. 68.00 (3-540-61821-X) Spr-Verlag.
Malfetti, James L. & Eidlitz, Elizabeth, eds. Perspectives on Sexuality: A Literary Collection. LC 78-144052. (Illus.). 611p. 1972. pap. text 9.95 (0-03-082826-0) Irvington.
Malfetti, James L., jt. auth. see Stewart, Ernest.
Malfeyt, Norma de Waal, jt. auth. see Vanderwall, Howard.
Malfliet, Katlijn, jt. ed. see Casier, Tom.
Malfliet, W., jt. auth. see Callebaut, D. K.
Malgady, Robert G. & Rodriguez, Orlando, eds. Theoretical & Conceptual Issues in Hispanic Mental Health. LC 93-38655. 274p. 1994. 39.50 (0-89464-839-X) Krieger.
Malgavkar, P. D. Biotechnology: Business Possibilities & Prospects. (C). 1988. 12.00 (81-204-0287-1, Pub. by Oxford IBH) S Asia.
— Industrial Policy & Prospects 2001 A.D. (C). 1988. 15.00 (81-204-0282-0, Pub. by Oxford IBH) S Asia.
— Population & Development. 1982. 18.50 (0-8364-0923-X, Pub. by Somaiya) S Asia.
— Technologies for Economic Development. (C). 1987. 18.00 (81-204-0158-1, Pub. by Oxford IBH) S Asia.
Malgieri, Nick. Chocolate: From Simple Cookies to Extravagant Showstoppers. LC 97-53168. 480p. 1998. 40.00 (0-06-018711-5) HarpC.
*Malgieri, Nick. Cookies Unlimited: Nick Malgieri. LC 99-87185. (Illus.). 384p. 2000. 35.00 (0-06-019285-2) HarpC.
Malgieri, Nick. Great Italian Desserts. 276p. (gr. 8). 1990. 26.95 (0-316-54519-8) Little.
— How to Bake: Complete Guide to Perfect Cakes, Cookies, Pies, Tarts, Breads, Pizzas, Muffins. LC 95-32231. (Illus.). 480p. 1995. 37.50 (0-06-016819-6) HarperTrade.
*Malgieri, Nick. Nick Malgieri's Perfect Pastry: Create Fantastic Desserts by Mastering the Basic Techniques. 352p. 1998. pap. text 19.95 (0-02-862335-5, Pub. by Macmillan) S&S Trade.
Malgo, Wim. How to Walk with God. 1980. pap. 1.95 (0-937422-02-9) Midnight Call.
— Seven Signs of a Born Again Person. 1996. reprint ed. pap. 1.45 (0-937422-14-2) Midnight Call.
Malgonkar, Manohar, jt. auth. see Scindia, Vijaya R.
Malgorn, Guy. Diccionario Tecnico Espanol-Ingles. 5th ed. (ENG & SPA.). 576p. 1990. pap. write for info. (0-7859-4906-2) Fr & Eur.
— Diccionario Tecnico Frances-Espanol: Technical Dictionary French-Spanish. deluxe ed. (FRE & SPA.). 544p. 1973. 59.95 (0-8288-4782-7, S50241) Fr & Eur.
— Diccionario Tecnico Ingles-Espanol. 7th ed. (SPA.). 632p. 1991. pap. 34.95 (0-7859-3715-3, 842830923X) Fr & Eur.
— Dictionaire Technique Francais-Espagnol. 2nd ed. (FRE & SPA.). 544p. 1974. 69.95 (0-8288-6000-9, M6387) Fr & Eur.
— Dictionnaire Technique Anglais-Francais. (ENG & FRE.). 495p. 1976. 89.95 (0-8288-5657-5, M6385) Fr & Eur.
— English-Spanish Technical Dictionary. Rodriguez, M. R. & Armisen, P., trs. (ENG & SPA.). 606p. 1991. 41.00 (84-283-0923-X, Pub. by Paraninfo) IBD Ltd.
— Spanish-English Technical Dictionary. 4th ed. (ENG & SPA.). 1990. 39.00 (0-7859-8966-8) Fr & Eur.
— Spanish-English Technical Dictionary. 4th ed. Rodriguez, M. R. & Armisen, P., trs. (ENG & SPA.). 570p. 1990. 41.00 (84-283-1354-7, Pub. by Paraninfo) IBD Ltd.
Malgorna, Guy. Dictionnaire Technique Francais-Anglais (French-English Technical Dictionary) (ENG & FRE.). 475p. 1972. 105.00 (0-7859-4831-7) Fr & Eur.
Malgrange, B. Equations Differentielles a Coefficients Polynomiaux. (Progress in Mathematics Ser.: Vol. 96). (FRE.). viii, 232p. 1991. 60.50 (0-8176-3556-4) Birkhauser.
Malhan, S. Indian Cookery. 143p. 1977. 7.95 (0-318-36292-9) Asia Bk Corp.
Malherbe. Oeuvres. 1128p. 35.95 (0-686-56536-3) Fr & Eur.
— Oeuvres: Poesies - Lettres. (FRE.). 1971. lib. bdg. 89.95 (0-8288-3551-9, F39530) Fr & Eur.
Malherbe & Sall. Parlons Wolof & Lexique Wolof/Francais/Wolof. 181p. 1989. 39.95 (0-320-00830-4) Fr & Eur.
Malherbe, Abraham J. The Cynic Epistles: A Study Edition. LC 77-21619. (Society for Biblical Literature. Sources for Biblical Study Ser.: No. 12). 342p. reprint ed. pap. 106.10 (0-7837-5447-7, 204521200005) Bks Demand.
*Malherbe, Abraham J. The Letters to the Thessalonians. LC 00-21363. (Anchor Bible Ser.). 2000. 50.00 (0-385-18460-3) Doubleday.

— Paul & the Thessalonians. 130p. 2000. reprint ed. pap. 14.00 (1-888961-13-9) Sigler Pr.
Malherbe, Abraham J. The World of the New Testament. LC 68-5578. 1984. 12.95 (0-915547-16-3) Abilene Christ U.
Malherbe, Abraham J. & Ferguson, Everett, trs. Gregory of Nyssa: The Life of Moses. LC 78-56352. (Classics of Western Spirituality Ser.). (Illus.). 1988. pap. 19.95 (0-8091-2112-3) Paulist Pr.
Malherbe, Ernest G. The Bilingual School. Cordasco, Francesco, ed. LC 77-90547. (Bilingual-Bicultural Education in the U. S. Ser.). 1978. reprint ed. lib. bdg. 19.95 (0-405-11086-3) Ayer.
Malherbe, H. H. Viral Cytopathology. 112p. 1980. 98.95 (0-8493-5567-2, RC114) CRC Pr.
Malherbe, J. A. Microwave Transmission Line Couplers. LC 88-19338. (Artech House Microwave Library). 231p. reprint ed. pap. 71.70 (0-7837-3018-7, 204292200006) Bks Demand.
Malherber, J. A. Microwave Transmission Line Filters. LC 78-31243. (Illus.). 352p. reprint ed. pap. 109.20 (0-8357-5589-4, 203522000093) Bks Demand.
*Malhi, Gin S. MCQS for the MRCPsych Pt. II: Basic Sciences Examination. LC 99-58726. 181p. 2000. pap. text 40.00 (0-7506-4089-8) Buttrwrth-Heinemann.
*Malhi, Gin S. & Mitchell, Alexander. Examination Notes in Psychiatry. LC 99-37335. 265p. 1999. pap. text 40.00 (0-7506-4088-X) Buttrwrth-Heinemann.
*Malhi, Gin S., et al. Neurology for Psychiatrists. 120p. 2000. pap. 39.95 (1-85317-922-1, Pub. by Martin Dunitz) Blackwell Sci.
Malhortra, Ashok, jt. auth. see Hollander, Dave.
Malhos, Georges, ed. see Voltaire.
Malhotra. Applied Marketing Resrch: An Applied Orientation. 3rd ed. LC 98-38880. (Illus.). 1008p. 1999. 97.00 (0-13-083044-5) P-H.
Malhotra, A. Auditory Evoked Responses in Clinical Responses. xviii, 278p. 1997. 99.00 (3-540-63405-3) Spr-Verlag.
Malhotra, Anil K. A Survey of Asia's Energy Prices. LC 94-16612. (Technical Papers: Vol. 248). 194p. 1994. pap. 22.00 (0-8213-2860-3, 12860) World Bank.
Malhotra, Ashok. Culture & Self: Philosophical & Religious Perspectives, East & West. Allen, Douglas, ed. LC 97-8093. (C). 1997. pap. text 25.00 (0-8133-2674-5, Pub. by Westview) HarpC.
Malhotra, Ashok, jt. auth. see Shrader, Douglas W.
Malhotra, Ashok K. Jean-Paul Sartre's Existentialism in Literature & Philosophy. (Oneonta Philosophy Studies). 149p. (Orig.). (C). 1995. pap. 12.00 (1-883058-14-7, Oneonta Philosophy) Global Pubns.
— Mysticism & the Hindu Tradition. 42p. 1993. 3.00 (1-883058-04-X, Oneonta Philosophy) Global Pubns.
— On Hindu Philosophies of Experience: Cults, Mysticism & Meditations. 59p. 1993. 3.00 (1-883058-03-1, Oneonta Philosophy) Global Pubns.
— Transcreation Bhagavd Gita. LC 98-9468. (Library of Liberal Arts). 86p. 1998. pap. text 12.60 (0-02-374921-0) P-H.
Malhotra, Deepak. Flotation Plants: Are They Optimized? fac. ed. LC 92-62902. (Illus.). 185p. 1993. reprint ed. pap. 57.40 (0-7837-7870-8, 204762700007) Bks Demand.
Malhotra, Deepak & Riggs, William F., eds. Chemical Reagents in the Mineral Processing Industry. LC 86-63354. 320p. reprint ed. pap. 99.20 (0-8357-3484-6, 203974300013) Bks Demand.
Malhotra, I. J. Hindu Vivah Adhiniyam.Tr. of Hindu Marriage Act. 303p. 1984. 90.00 (0-7855-7568-5) St Mut.
Malhotra, I. J. Hindu Vivah Adhiniyam: (Hindu Marriage Act in Hindi) 2nd ed. (HIN.). (C). 1991. 95.00 (0-7855-5489-0) St Mut.
— Madhyastham Adhiniyam Arbitration Act. (HIN.). (C). 1990. text 70.00 (0-89771-488-1) St Mut.
Malhotra, I. J., ed. Hindu Vivah Adhiniyam (Hindu Marriage Act in Hindi) (C). 1991. 85.00 (0-89771-784-8, Pub. by Eastern Book) St Mut.
Malhotra, M., jt. auth. see Arora, A.
Malhotra, M. M. & Subramaninian, R. Textbook in Applied Mechanics. 1994. write for info. (81-224-0645-9, Pub. by Wiley Estn) Franklin.
Malhotra, Naresh K., ed. see Conference of the Academy of Marketing Science.
Malhotra, O. P. The Law of Industrial Disputes. (C). 1985. 650.00 (0-7855-3528-4) St Mut.
Malhotra, R. The Indian Islanders: An Anthropological Perspective. (C). 1989. 17.50 (81-7099-148-X, Pub. by Mittal Pubs Dist) S Asia.
Malhotra, R., ed. Anthropology of Development: Commemoration Volume in Honour of Professor I. P. Singh. (C). 1992. text 37.50 (81-7099-328-8, Pub. by Mittal Pubs Dist) S Asia.
Malhotra, R. K. Encyclopaedia of Hotel Management & Tourism, 10 vols. 1997. 4500.00 (81-7488-488-2, Pub. by Print Hse) St Mut.
Malhotra, R. K., et al. Encyclopaedia of Modern Management, 10 vols. 1996. 2750.00 (81-7488-167-0, Pub. by Print Hse) St Mut.
Malhotra, Ramen & Easty, David. Revision in Sciences Basic to Ophthalmology. LC 97-9710. (An Arnold Publication). 256p. 1997. pap. text 29.95 (0-340-67678-7, Pub. by E A) OUP.
Malhotra, Ripudaman, jt. auth. see Olah, George A.
Malhotra, S. Bharat Dictionary of Physics. 176p. 1995. pap. 75.00 (81-86378-08-1, Pub. by Pitambar Pub) St Mut.
Malhotra, S. L., jt. auth. see Sharma, S. K.
Malhotra, Sharan. Divine Darshan. (C). 1994. 20.00 (81-224-0677-7) S Asia.
Malhotra, Sudarshan, ed. Advances in Neural Science, Vol. 2. 256p. 1995. 128.50 (1-55938-625-8) Jai Pr.

— Advances in Neural Science, Vol. 3. Date not set. 128.50 (0-7623-0087-6) Jai Pr.
— Advances in Structural Biology, Vol. 1. 368p. 1992. 128.50 (1-55938-292-9) Jai Pr.
— Advances in Structural Biology, Vol. 2. 352p. 1993. 109.50 (1-55938-584-7) Jai Pr.
— Advances in Structural Biology, Vol. 3. 328p. 1994. 128.50 (1-55938-627-4) Jai Pr.
— Advances in Structural Biology, Vol. 4. 1996. 128.50 (1-55938-967-2) Jai Pr.
Malhotra, Sudarshan & Das, G. D., eds. Advances in Neural Science, Vol. 1. 240p. 1993. 128.50 (1-55938-356-9) Jai Pr.
Malhotra, V. M. Pozzolanic & Cementitious Materials. (Advances in Concrete Technology Ser). 136p. 1996. pap. text 27.00 (2-88449-211-9) Gordon & Breach.
Malhotra, V. M., ed. Developments in the Use of Super-Plasticizers. LC 81-65667. (American Concrete Institute Ser.: SP-68). 570p. 1981. reprint ed. pap. 176.70 (0-608-04606-X, 206537600003) Bks Demand.
— Fly Ash, Silica Fume, Slag & Other Mineral by-Products in Concrete. LC 83-70390. (American Concrete Institute Publication: Vol. 1, No. SP-79). (Illus.). 631p. 1983. reprint ed. pap. 195.70 (0-608-07957-X, 206793000001) Bks Demand.
— Fly Ash, Silica Fume, Slag & Other Mineral by-Products in Concrete. LC 83-70390. (American Concrete Institute Publication: Vol. 2, No. SP-79). (Illus.). 566p. 1983. reprint ed. pap. 175.50 (0-608-07958-8, 206793000002) Bks Demand.
— In Situ - Nondestructive Testing of Concrete. LC 84-71537. (American Concrete Institute, Publication: No. SP-82). (Illus.). 839p. 1984. reprint ed. pap. 200.00 (0-7837-9998-5, 206072500006) Bks Demand.
Malhotra, V. M. & Carino, Nicholas J. Handbook of Nondestructive Testing of Concrete. (Illus.). 360p. 1990. boxed set 236.95 (0-8493-2984-1, TA440) CRC Pr.
Malhotra, V. M., jt. auth. see Mehta, P. Kumar.
Malhotra, V. M., ed. see ACI International Conference Staff.
Malhotra, V. M., ed. see International Conference on Performance of Concret.
Malhotra, V. M., ed. see International Conference on the Use of Fly Ash, Si.
Malhotra, Veena. Kenya under Kenyatta. 1990. 16.00 (81-85163-16-2, Pub. by Kalinga) S Asia.
Malhotra, Vinay K. Clinton Administration & South Asia, 1993-1997. LC 97-904892. (C). 1997. 25.00 (81-7003-207-5, Pub. by S Asia Pubs) S Asia.
— Contemporary Socialist Thought: A Critical Study. 1990. 54.00 (81-7041-235-8, Pub. by Anmol) S Asia.
Malhotra, Vinay K., ed. Indo-U. S. Relations in Nineties. (C). 1995. 16.00 (81-7488-043-7, Pub. by Anmol) S Asia.
Malhotra, Vinod, ed. Anesthesia for Renal & Genito-Urologic Surgery. LC 95-36418. (Illus.). 320p. 1995. text 62.00 (0-07-039877-1) McGraw-Hill HPD.
*Malhotra, Yogesh, ed. Knowledge Management & Virtual Organizations. LC 00-24902. (Illus.). 350p. (C). 2000. pap. 149.95 (1-878289-73-X) Idea Group Pub.
Mali, Anya. Mystic in the New World: Marie de l'Incarnation, 1599-1672. LC 96-32576. (Studies in the History of Christian Thought). 1996. 87.00 (90-04-10606-5) Brill Academic Pubs.
Mali, J. W., ed. Current Problems in Dermatology, Vol. 3. 1970. 72.25 (3-8055-0484-5) S Karger.
— Current Problems in Dermatology, Vol. 4. 1972. 83.50 (3-8055-1248-1) S Karger.
— Current Problems in Dermatology, Vol. 5. 1973. 77.50 (3-8055-1380-1) S Karger.
— Keratinization & Growth Regulation. (Current Problems in Dermatology Ser.: Vol. 6). (Illus.). 250p. 1976. 85.25 (3-8055-2294-0) S Karger.
— Some Fundamental Approaches in Skin Research. (Current Problems in Dermatology Ser.: Vol. 9). (Illus.). viii, 152p. 1981. pap. 85.25 (3-8055-3080-3) S Karger.
Mali, J. W., ed. see Oholo Biological Conference Staff.
Mali, Jane L., jt. auth. see Herzig, Alison C.
Mali, Millicent S. French Faience: Fantaisie et Populaire of the Nineteenth & Twentieth Centuries. (Illus.). 136p. (Orig.). 1986. pap. 25.00 (0-9603824-2-9) M S Mali.
— Madame Campan: Educator of Women, Confidante of Queens. LC 78-65428. 1978. pap. text 23.00 (0-8191-0662-3) U Pr of Amer.
Malia, Elizabeth, jt. auth. see Milton, Suzanne.
Malia, Joe H., jt. auth. see Carbajal, Xavier J.
Malia, Martin. Russia under Western Eyes: From the Bronze Horseman to the Lenin Mausoleum. LC 98-39769. 528p. 1999. 35.00 (0-674-78120-1) HUP.
*Malia, Martin. Russia under Western Eyes: From the Bronze Horseman to the Lenin Mausoleum. 2000. pap. 17.95 (0-674-00210-5) HUP.
Malia, Martin E. The Soviet Tragedy. 1996. pap. 18.00 (0-02-874120-X) Free Pr.
— The Soviet Tragedy: A History of Socialism in Russia 1917-1991. 500p. 1994. 24.95 (0-02-919795-3) Free Pr.
— The Soviet Tragedy: A History of Socialism in Russia 1917-1991. 576p. 1995. pap. 18.00 (0-684-82313-6) Free Pr.
Malick, Javed. Toward a Theater of the Oppressed: The Dramaturgy of John Arden. LC 95-17397. (Theater: Theory - Text - Performance Ser.). 224p. 1995. text 42.50 (0-472-10587-6, 10587) U of Mich Pr.
Malick, Jeffrey B., et al, eds. Anxiolytics: Neurochemical, Behavioral, & Clinical Perspectives. LC 81-40758. (Central Nervous System Pharmacology Ser.: Vol. 2). 232p. 1983. reprint ed. pap. 72.00 (0-608-00445-6, 206116000007) Bks Demand.

 An Asterisk (*) at the beginning of an entry indicates that the title is appearing for the first time.

Malick, Jeffrey B. & Bell, Robert M., eds. Endorphins: Chemistry, Physiology, Pharmacology & Clinical Relevance. LC 81-22214. (Modern Pharmacology-Toxicology Ser.: No. 20). 314p. 1982. reprint ed. pap. 97.40 (*0-608-01288-2*, 206203400001) Bks Demand.

Malick, Jeffrey B., jt. ed. see Williams, Michael.

Malicki, Lawrence E. & Malicki, Michael L. Card Collection - Diary Log Book: The Collector. (Illus.). 250p. 1993. pap. 28.95 (*1-893976-02-5*) Tri-Cun Industries.

— Card Collection - Diary Log Book - Gift Pack: The Collector. (Illus.). 250p. 1993. pap. 35.00 (*1-893976-03-3*) Tri-Cun Industries.

— The Collector: The Avid Collector - Senior Edition. (Illus.). 1999. pap. write for info. (*1-893976-04-1*) Tri-Cun Industries.

— The Collector: The Avid Collector - Senior Edition - Gift Pack. (Illus.). 1999. pap. write for info. (*1-893976-05-X*) Tri-Cun Industries.

— The Collector: The Collector Record Log Book. (Illus.). 240p. 1993. pap. 24.95 (*1-893976-00-9*) Tri-Cun Industries.

— The Collector: The Collector Record Log Book - Gift Pack. (Illus.). 240p. 1993. pap. 32.95 (*1-893976-01-7*) Tri-Cun Industries.

Malicki, Michael L., jt. auth. see Malicki, Lawrence E.

Malicky, Hans, ed. Verhandlungen des Sechsten Internationalen Symposiums uber Entonomofaunistik in Mitteleuropa. 1977. pap. text 155.50 (*90-6193-559-8*) Kluwer Academic.

Malicoat, Galen. Small, Honest Hollows. 32p. (Orig.). 1992. pap. 10.00 (*0-911623-11-6*) I Klang.

Malicoat, Myrna, jt. auth. see Ashcraft, Martha.

Maliepaard, Marc. Mitosenes & Related Antitumor Drugs: Rational Drug Design of Cytostatic Agents. (Medical Intelligence Unit Ser.). 139p. 1995. 99.00 (*1-57059-335-3*) Landes Bioscience.

Malier, Y., ed. High Performance Concrete: From Material to Structure. (Illus.). 542p. (C). 1992. 125.00 (*0-419-17600-4*, E & FN Spon) Routledge.

Malies, Harold. A Short History of the English Microscope, Vol. 11. LC 80-83457. (Illus.). 1981. 20.00 (*0-904962-09-1*) Microscope Pubns.

Maliga, P., et al, eds. Methods in Plant Molecular Biology: A Laboratory Course Manual. (Illus.). 250p. (C). 1994. pap. text 75.00 (*0-87969-386-X*) Cold Spring Harbor.

Maliga, P., et al. Methods in Plant Molecular Biology: A Laboratory Course Manual. LC 94-36570. 1995. write for info. (*0-87969-450-5*) Cold Spring Harbor.

Malignon, Jean. Dictionnaire des Ecrivains Francais, 2 vols. (FRE.). 709p. 1995. 55.00 (*0-7859-9912-4*) Fr & Eur.

— Dictionnaire des Ecrivains Francais: Dictionary of French Writers. (FRE.). 576p. 1971. 39.95 (*0-8288-6445-4*, M-6388) Fr & Eur.

— Petit Dictionnaire Rameau. (FRE.). 280p. 1983. pap. 26.95 (*0-7859-7912-3*, 2700703146) Fr & Eur.

Maligo, Pedro. Land of Metaphorical Desires: The Representation of Amazonia in Brazilian Literature. LC 97-32321. (Wor(l)ds of Change Ser.: Vol. 21). IX, 192p. (C). 1998. 44.95 (*0-8204-3005-6*) P Lang Pubng.

***Malik.** Islam Nationalism & the West. LC 98-53898. 1999. text 65.00 (*0-312-22060-X*) St Martin.

— Sword of the Khalsa: Sikh Peoples War, 1699-1768. 1999. 20.00 (*81-7304-294-2*, Pub. by Manohar) S Asia.

Malik, A. India Watching: The Media Game. 149p. 1977. 14.95 (*0-318-37277-0*) Asia Bk Corp.

Malik, Afshan, et al. Safar, Gulp & Happiness: New Welsh Drama. Teare, Jeff, ed. & intro. by. LC 99-206610. 300p. 1998. pap. 15.95 (*0-9521558-7-7*, Pub. by Parthian Bks) Dufour.

Malik, Ajmer S. Concept & Strategy of Rural Industrial Development. 206p. 1995. pap. 125.00 (*0-7855-2724-9*, Pub. by Print Hse) St Mut.

Malik, Ajmer Singh, see Singh Malik, Ajmer.

Malik, Anjali. Merchants & Merchandise in Northern India, Ad 600-1000. LC 98-909705. 189 p. 1998. write for info. (*81-7304-228-4*) Manohar.

Malik, B. Survey Search & Seizure. (C). 1988. 375.00 (*0-7855-3523-3*) St Mut.

Malik, C. P., ed. Pollen Physiology & Biotechnology. (Advances in Pollen-Spore Research Ser.: Vol. XIX). (Illus.). 196p. 1992. 65.00 (*1-55528-267-9*, Pub. by Today Tomorrow) Scholarly Pubns.

— Recent Researches in Palynology: Hensferdinand Linskens Commemoration Volume. (Illus.). 295p. 1984. 50.00 (*1-55528-071-4*, Pub. by Today Tomorrow) Scholarly Pubns.

Malik, Charles, ed. God & Man in Contemporary Christian Thought. (C). 1970. 24.95 (*0-8156-6091-X*, Pub. by Am U Beirut) Syracuse U Pr.

— God & Man in Contemporary Islamic Thought. (C). 1972. 24.95 (*0-8156-6035-9*) Syracuse U Pr.

Malik, D. S., et al. Fundamentals of Abstract Algebra. LC 96-33312. (International Series in Pure & Applied Mathematics). 656p. (C). 1996. 72.81 (*0-07-040035-0*) McGraw.

Malik, F. B., ed. Condensed Matter Theories, Vol. 1. LC 86-9400. 354p. 1986. 125.00 (*0-306-42284-0*, Plenum Trade) Perseus Pubng.

Malik, F. B., jt. auth. see Blum, L.

Malik, F. B., jt. auth. see de Providencia, Joao.

Malik, Ghulam. Muhammad: An Islamic Perspective. LC 96-33730. 194p. 1996. lib. bdg. 36.50 (*0-7618-0307-6*) U Pr of Amer.

Malik, Habib C. Between Damascus & Jerusalem: Lebanon & the Middle East Peace Process. LC 97-10910. (Policy Papers: No. 45). 130p. 1997. pap. 19.95 (*0-944029-70-1*) Wash Inst NEP.

— Receiving Soren Kierkegaard: The Early Impact & Transmission of His Thought. LC 96-23905. 437p. (C). 1997. text 59.95 (*0-8132-0878-5*) Cath U Pr.

Malik, Hafeez. Central Asia: Its Strategic Importance & Future Prospects. 337p. 1996. pap. 19.95 (*0-312-16452-1*) St Martin.

***Malik, Hafeez.** Russian-American Relations: Islamic & Turkic Dimensions. 2000. text 65.00 (*0-312-23168-7*) St Martin.

Malik, Hafeez, ed. International Security in Southwest Asia. LC 83-24637. 240p. 1984. 45.00 (*0-275-91222-1*, C1222, Praeger Pubs) Greenwood.

— Iqbal: Poet-Philosopher of Pakistan. LC 75-135475. (Studies in Oriental Culture: No. 7). 460p. reprint ed. pap. 142.60 (*0-608-14243-3*, 202205800024) Bks Demand.

— Roles of the United States, Russia, & China in the New World. LC 96-2607. 350p. 1997. text 59.95 (*0-312-12896-7*) St Martin.

Malik, Hyacinth. A Practical Guide to Equal Opportunities. 128p. 1998. pap. 26.00 (*0-7487-3652-2*, Pub. by S Thornes Pubs) Trans-Atl Phila.

Malik, Iftikhar H. Pakistanis in Michigan: A Study of Third Culture & Acculturation. LC 88-84006. (Immigrant Communities & Ethnic Minorities in the U. S. & Canada Ser.: No. 59). 1989. 42.50 (*0-404-19469-9*) AMS Pr.

Malik, Imam & Din, M. R. Muwata. 1991. 25.50 (*1-56744-162-9*) Kazi Pubns.

Malik, J. Mohan. Peace & Security Bk. Three. (Asian Defense Policies Ser.: Bk. 3). 96p. (C). 1995. pap. 40.00 (*0-7300-1811-3*, Pub. by Deakin Univ) St Mut.

— Regional Conflicts & Security Issues. (Asian Defense Policies Ser.: Bk. 2). 263p. (C). 1995. pap. 72.00 (*0-7300-1720-6*, Pub. by Deakin Univ) St Mut.

***Malik, J. Mohan, ed.** Australia's Security in the 21st Century. (Illus.). 304p. 1999. pap. 29.95 (*1-86448-603-1*, Pub. by Allen & Unwin Pty) Paul & Co Pubs.

Malik, Jamal, Colonization of Islam. LC 96-903921. (C). 1996. 38.00 (*81-7304-148-2*, Pub. by Manohar) S Asia.

— Islamische Gelehrtenkultur in Nordindien: Entwicklungsgeschichte und Tendenzen am Beispiel von Lucknow. LC 97-19312. (Islamic History & Culture Ser.: No. 19). (GER., Illus.). 624p. 1997. 181.50 (*90-04-10703-7*) Brill Academic Pubs.

***Malik, Jamal.** Perspectives of Mutual Encounters in South Asian History, 1750-1850. LC 00-29732. 492p. 2000. 140.00 (*90-04-11802-0*) Brill Academic Pubs.

Malik, Justice. Land Acquisition Act. (C). 1990. 70.00 (*0-89771-301-X*) St Mut.

Malik, K. K. Supreme Court Rules, 1966. 119p. 1984. 110.00 (*0-7855-1455-4*) St Mut.

Malik, K. N. India & the United Kingdom: Change & Continuity in the 1980s. LC 97-14482. 280p. 1997. 36.00 (*0-8039-9380-3*) Sage.

Malik, Kauser A., et al, eds. Nitrogen Fixation with Non-Legumes. LC 97-43109. (Developments in Plant & Soil Sciences Ser.). 360p. 1998. lib. bdg. 169.00 (*0-7923-4873-7*) Kluwer Academic.

Malik, Kenan. The Meaning of Race. (C). 1996. text 55.00 (*0-8147-5552-6*); pap. text 19.00 (*0-8147-5553-4*) NYU Pr.

Malik, Keshav. Between Nobodies & Stars: Stories Portraits. 1985. 11.50 (*0-8364-1490-X*, Pub. by Abhinav) S Asia.

Malik, Keshav, jt. auth. see Waisler, Lee.

Malik, M. Limitation Act. (C). 1990. 50.00 (*0-89771-250-1*) St Mut.

Malik, M. A. Solar Distillation. 1982. 22.00 (*0-08-028700-X*, Pergamon Pr) Elsevier.

Malik, M. A., et al. Solar Distillation. 1982. 89.00 (*0-08-028679-8*, Pub. by Pergamon Repr) Franklin.

***Malik, M. Aslam.** Allama Mashraqi: A Political Biography. (Illus.). 288p. 2000. text 19.95 (*0-19-579158-4*) OUP.

Malik, Marek. Clinical Guide to Cardiac Autonomic Tests. LC 98-27478. (Developments in Cardiovascular Medicine Ser.). 423p. 1998. write for info. (*0-7923-5178-9*) Kluwer Academic.

***Malik, Marek & Batchvarov, Velislav.** QT Dispersion. (Clinical Approaches to Tachyarrhythmias Ser.: Vol. 12). (Illus.). 160p. 2000. pap. 24.50 (*0-87993-456-5*) Futura Pub.

Malik, Marek & Camm, A. John, eds. Heart Rate Variability. LC 94-45665. (Illus.). 400p. 1995. 98.00 (*0-87993-607-X*) Futura Pub.

Malik, Miroslav, jt. auth. see Bresky, Dushan.

Malik Mueen Azhar. Bibliography of Articles on Iqbal. 64p. (Orig.). 1985. pap. 7.95 (*1-56744-233-1*) Kazi Pubns.

Malik, Muhammad Farooq-i-Azam. English Translation of the Meaning of Al-Quran: The Guidance for Mankind. LC 97-70435. 1997. write for info. (*0-911119-77-9*) Igram Pr.

Malik, N. H., et al. Electrical Insulation in Power Systems. LC 97-34427. (Power Engineering Ser.: Vol. 3). (Illus.). 408p. 1997. text 145.00 (*0-8247-0106-2*) Dekker.

Malik, Norbert R. Electronic Circuits: Analysis, Simulation & Design. LC 94-26013. 1008p. (C). 1995. 75.00 (*0-02-374910-5*, Macmillan Coll) P-H.

Malik, P. L. Arms Act, Nineteen Fifty-Nine with Rules, 1962. annot. ed. 160p. 1984. 60.00 (*0-7855-1454-6*) St Mut.

— Arms Act, 1959: With Rules, 1962. 6th ed. (C). 1990. 45.00 (*0-7855-5644-3*) St Mut.

— Arms Act, 1959, with Rules, 1962 (Annotated) (C). 1992. 75.00 (*0-89771-775-9*, Pub. by Eastern Book) St Mut.

— Central Acts & Ordinances, 1975. 518p. 1976. 180.00 (*0-7855-1453-8*) St Mut.

— Commentaries on the Opium Act, 1878. 175p. 1984. 90.00 (*0-7855-1452-X*) St Mut.

— Criminal Court Handbook: Three Major Acts. 808p. 1982. 270.00 (*0-7855-1451-1*) St Mut.

— Criminal Court Handbook: (Three Major Acts) 15th ed. (C). 1991. 95.00 (*0-7855-5602-8*) St Mut.

— Criminal Court Handbook (Minor Acts), 4 vols., Set. (C). 1991. 150.00 (*0-7855-5603-6*) St Mut.

— Criminal Court Handbook (Three Major Acts) 18th ed. (C). 1992. 150.00 (*81-7012-489-1*, Pub. by Eastern Book) St Mut.

— The Customs Act 1962. 649p. 1982. 255.00 (*0-7855-1450-3*) St Mut.

— Customs Act, 1962. (C). 1990. 60.00 (*0-7855-5344-4*) St Mut.

— Employees Provident Funds & Miscellaneous Provisions Act, 1952. (C). 1992. 60.00 (*0-89771-786-4*, Pub. by Eastern Book) St Mut.

— Employees Provident Funds & Miscellaneous Provisions Act, 1990. (C). 1990. reprint ed. 50.00 (*0-7855-5576-5*) St Mut.

— Employees Provident Funds & Miscellaneous Provisions Act, 1990: With Supplement. (C). 1990. reprint ed. 50.00 (*0-7855-6516-7*) St Mut.

— Guide to Foreign Exchange Regulations. 336p. 1981. 135.00 (*0-7855-1449-X*) St Mut.

— Handbook of Electricity Laws. (C). 1992. 100.00 (*0-89771-781-3*, Pub. by Eastern Book) St Mut.

***Malik, P. L.** Handbook of Labour & Industrial Law. 2000. pap. 150.00 (*0-7855-7667-3*, Pub. by Eastern Book) St Mut.

Malik, P. L. Handbook of Labour & Industrial Law. 1985. 65.00 (*0-7855-1471-6*) St Mut.

— Handbook of Labour & Industrial Law. 4th ed. (C). 1990. 120.00 (*0-7855-5513-7*) St Mut.

— Handbook of Labour & Industrial Laws. (C). 1993. 200.00 (*0-7855-0171-1*, Pub. by Eastern Book) St Mut.

— Handbook of Labour & Industrial Laws. 5th ed. (C). 1993. 100.00 (*81-7012-502-2*, Pub. by Eastern Book) St Mut.

— Indian Stamp Act (As Applicable in the State of Uttar Pradesh) Alongwith Registration Act (As Applicable in the State of Uttar Pradesh) 3rd ed. (C). 1993. 50.00 (*81-7012-521-9*, Pub. by Eastern Book) St Mut.

— Indian Stamp Act, 1899 & Indian Registration Act, 1908: (As Applicable in Uttar Pradesh) (C). 1988. 165.00 (*0-7855-6025-4*) St Mut.

— Indian Stamp Act, 1899 (As Applicable to U. P.) With Supplement, 1990. (C). 1990. 55.00 (*0-7855-5415-7*) St Mut.

— Indian Stamp Act, 1899 (As Applicable to U. P.), 1988. (C). 1990. 55.00 (*0-7855-5414-9*) St Mut.

— Industrial Law. (C). 1992. 480.00 (*0-7855-0168-1*, Pub. by Eastern Book) St Mut.

— Industrial Law. 1774p. 1985. 675.00 (*0-7855-1448-1*) St Mut.

— Industrial Law. (C). 1990. 400.00 (*0-7855-5122-0*); 200.00 (*0-89771-325-7*); text 400.00 (*0-89771-489-X*) St Mut.

— Industrial Law. 15th ed. (C). 1990. reprint ed. 400.00 (*0-7855-5512-9*) St Mut.

***Malik, P. L.** Industrial Law: An Encyclopaedia of All Central Labour Acts (with State Amendments), Rules, Regulations, Notifications & Orders, 2 vols. 1999. pap. 430.00 (*81-7012-665-7*, Pub. by Eastern Book) St Mut.

Malik, P. L. Industrial Law, 1989. 15th ed. (C). 1990. 400.00 (*0-7855-5531-5*) St Mut.

— Industries Development & Regulation Act, 1951. 1985. 65.00 (*0-7855-1472-4*) St Mut.

— Industries Development & Regulation Act, 1951. (C). 1991. 95.00 (*0-7855-5530-7*) St Mut.

— Intermediate Education Act, 1921: Together with Amending Acts Regulations & Notifications. 173p. 1982. 75.00 (*0-7855-1447-3*) St Mut.

— Labour Laws in U. P. 3rd ed. (C). 1985. 330.00 (*0-7855-5518-8*) St Mut.

— Law of Motor Vehicles in U. P. 820p. 1984. 300.00 (*0-7855-3002-9*) St Mut.

— The Law Relating to Forests in Uttar Pradesh. 206p. 1984. 110.00 (*0-7855-1446-5*) St Mut.

— Law Relating to Weights & Measures. (C). 1991. 125.00 (*0-89771-794-5*, Pub. by Eastern Book) St Mut.

— Law Relating to Weights & Measures. 1996. pap. 70.00 (*81-7012-575-8*, Pub. by Eastern Book) St Mut.

***Malik, P. L.** Law Relating to Weights & Measures. 2000. pap. 125.00 (*81-7012-660-6*, Pub. by Eastern Book) St Mut.

Malik, P. L. Minimum Wages Act. 1985. 150.00 (*0-7855-1445-7*) St Mut.

— U. P. Excise Act, 1910: Together with Rules & Notifications. 4th ed. (C). 1991. 95.00 (*0-7855-5562-5*) St Mut.

— U. P. Police Regulations. 4th ed. (C). 1991. 95.00 (*0-7855-5449-1*) St Mut.

— U. P. Sales Tax Act, 1948, Together with Rules & Notifications. 8th ed. (C). 1989. 50.00 (*0-7855-5270-7*) St Mut.

— U. P. Sales Tax Act, 1948: Together with Rules & Notifications. 220p. 1985. 120.00 (*0-7855-1444-9*) St Mut.

— U. P. Sales Tax Act, 1948: Together with Rules & Notifications with Supplement. 8th ed. (C). 1990. 65.00 (*0-7855-5429-7*) St Mut.

Malik, P. L., ed. Commentaries on Opium Act, 1878: With U. P. Opium Rules, 1961, U. P. Poppy-Head Rules, 1961 & U. P. Opium Smoking Act & Rules. (C). 1984. 40.00 (*0-7855-5462-9*) St Mut.

— Customs Act, 1962. 3rd ed. (C). 1990. 105.00 (*0-7855-5595-1*) St Mut.

— Employees Provident Funds & Miscellaneous Provisions Act, 1952. (C). 1989. 60.00 (*0-7855-5263-4*) St Mut.

— Guide to Foreign Exchange Regulations. 2nd ed. (C). 1991. 95.00 (*0-7855-5556-0*) St Mut.

— Handbook of Electricity Laws along with Guidelines for Electricity: Generation, Supply, & Distribution by Private Sector. 1995. pap. 45.00 (*81-7012-561-8*, Pub. by Eastern Book) St Mut.

— Industrial Law. 15th ed. (C). 1989. 400.00 (*0-7855-4719-3*) St Mut.

— Intermediate Education Act, 1921: Together with Amending Acts, Regulation & Notifications, 1982 with Supplement. (C). 1988. 30.00 (*0-7855-5579-X*) St Mut.

— Law of Electricity in U. P. 3rd ed. (C). 1991. 110.00 (*0-7855-5577-3*) St Mut.

— Minimum Wages Act with Central & U. P. Rules & Notification Fixing Minimum Wages in Various Industries & Establishments. 7th ed. (C). 1991. 95.00 (*0-7855-5483-1*) St Mut.

— Minimum Wages Act with Central & U. P. Rules & Notifications Fixing Minimum Wages in Various Industries & Establishments. (C). 1987. 50.00 (*0-7855-5264-2*) St Mut.

— U. P. Industrial Disputes Act, 1947: With Rules & Notifications. (C). 1991. 95.00 (*0-7855-5511-0*) St Mut.

Malik, P. L. & Nath, Bholeshwar. Cases & Materials on Code of Criminal Procedure, 1973. (C). 1987. 260.00 (*0-7855-3512-8*) St Mut.

Malik, P. L., jt. auth. see Nath, Bholeshwar.

Malik, P. L., jt. auth. see Saxena, R. P.

Malik, P. O. Handbook of Labour & Industrial Law. 1996. pap. 130.00 (*81-7012-583-9*, Pub. by Eastern Book) St Mut.

Malik, Rashid. Chinese Entrepreneurs in the Economic Development of China. LC 97-1918. 248p. 1997. 67.95 (*0-275-95848-5*, Praeger Pubs) Greenwood.

Malik, S. Comparative Tables of Supreme Court Cases, 1950-1985. 1986. 65.00 (*0-7855-1474-0*) St Mut.

— The Complete Digest of Supreme Court Cases (1950 to Date), 16 vols. (C). 1989. 2100.00 (*0-7855-3655-8*) St Mut.

Malik, S., ed. The Complete Supreme Court Criminal Digest, 1950 to June 1987, 7 vols. (C). 1989. 660.00 (*0-7855-3656-6*) St Mut.

— Supreme Court Labour & Services Digest, 1950-1986, 4 vols. (C). 1989. 415.00 (*0-7855-3657-4*) St Mut.

Malik, S. B. & Mehra, R. K. Principles & Digest of the Arbitration Law. (C). 1990. 120.00 (*0-89771-249-8*) St Mut.

Malik, S. C. Indian Civilization: The Formative Period: A Study of Archaeology & the Anthropology. 204p. (C). 1987. reprint ed. 14.00 (*81-208-0328-0*) S Asia.

— Indian Movements: Some Aspects of Dissent Protest & Reform. 296p. 1978. 14.95 (*0-940500-67-1*, Pub. by Indian Inst Comm) Asia Bk Corp.

— Modern Civilization: A Crisis of Fragmentation. (C). 1989. 22.50 (*81-7017-255-1*, Pub. by Abhinav) S Asia.

— Reconceptualising the Sciences & the Humanities: An Integral Approach. 1995. 26.00 (*81-7304-113-X*, Pub. by Manohar) S Asia.

Malik, S. C., ed. Determinants of Social Status in India. xi, 192p. 1986. 22.00 (*81-208-0073-7*, Pub. by Motilal Bnarsidass) S Asia.

Malik, S. C. & Indira Gandhi National Centre for the Arts Staff. Dhvani: Nature & Culture of Sound. LC 98-917370. 175 p. 1999. write for info. (*81-246-0111-9*) S Asia.

Malik, S. C., ed. see Freidman, Maurice.

Malik, S. K. The Quranic Concept of War. 195p. (C). 1986. 110.00 (*81-7002-020-4*, Pub. by Himalayan Bks) St Mut.

Malik, S. K. & Shah, S. S., eds. Physical & Material Properties of High Temperature Superconductors. (Illus.). 711p. (C). 1994. lib. bdg. 195.00 (*1-56072-114-6*) Nova Sci Pubs.

Malik, S. K., jt. auth. see Graham, G. A.

Malik, S. K., jt. ed. see Gupta, L. C.

Malik, S. Surendra. Supreme Court on Preventive Detention from 1950 to Present. 478p. 1985. 270.00 (*0-7855-7566-9*) St Mut.

Malik, Shahin P., jt. auth. see Evans, Graham.

Malik, Shahin P., jt. ed. see Hill, Stephen M.

Malik, Sharad, jt. auth. see Ehrenberg, Benjamin.

Malik, Sharad, jt. ed. see Meng, Teresa H.

Malik, Surendra. Central Administrative Tribunal Digest 1986-1994. 1996. 160.00 (*81-7012-577-4*, Pub. by Eastern Book) St Mut.

— Commentaries of U. P. Nagar Mahapalika Act, 1959. 818p. 1985. 345.00 (*0-7855-1432-5*) St Mut.

— Commentaries on U. P. Municipalities Act, 1916. 866p. 1984. 360.00 (*0-7855-1431-7*) St Mut.

— Commentaries on U. P. Municipalities Act, 1916. (C). 1989. 205.00 (*0-7855-5478-5*) St Mut.

— Commentaries on U. P. Nagar Mahapalika Adhiniyam, 1959. 5th ed. (C). 1989. 135.00 (*0-7855-5473-4*) St Mut.

— Commentaries on U. P. Panchayar Raj Act, 1948. 2nd ed. (C). 1991. 100.00 (*0-7855-5461-0*) St Mut.

— The Complete Digest of Supreme Court Cases, 16 vols. (C). 1991. 135.00 (*0-7855-2626-9*) St Mut.

— The Complete Digest of Supreme Court Cases, 16 vols., 15. (C). 1991. 165.00 (*0-7855-6716-X*) St Mut.

— The Complete Digest of Supreme Court Cases, 16 vols., 16. (C). 1991. 175.00 (*0-89771-692-2*) St Mut.

— The Complete Digest of Supreme Court Cases, 13 vols., Set. 9100p. (C). 1987. 1235.00 (*0-7855-3506-3*) St Mut.

— The Complete Digest of Supreme Court Cases, Vol. XVI. (C). 1991. text 180.00 (*0-7855-6597-3*) St Mut.

The Complete Digest of Supreme Court Cases (Since 1950), Vol. XV. (C). 1991. 150.00 (*0-7855-5591-9*) St Mut.

— The Complete Digest of Supreme Court Cases, 1950 to Present, Vol. XIV. 700p. 1987. 125.00 (*0-7855-1443-0*) St Mut.

Malik, Surendra. The Complete Supreme Court Criminal Digest. LC 94-904782. lxxv, 380 p. 1993. write for info. (*81-7012-526-X*) St Mut.

Malik, Surendra. The Complete Supreme Court Criminal Digest - Second Cumulative Supplement (July 1987 to Dec. 1990) (C). 1991. text 125.00 (*0-89771-494-6*) St Mut.

M

— The Complete Supreme Court Criminal Digest, 1950 to Present, 8 vols., Set. 800p. 1991. 595.00 (*0-7855-1442-2*) St Mut.

— The Complete Supreme Court Criminal Digest, 1950 up to Date, Set, Vols. I, II, III-A, III-B, IV & V. (C). 1987. 660.00 (*0-7855-5110-7*) St Mut.

— The Complete Supreme Court Criminal Digest, 1950 up to 1990 with 1st & 2nd Supplements, Set. (C). 1991. text 1000.00 (*0-89771-493-8*) St Mut.

— The Complete Supreme Court Labour & Services Digest, 4 vols., Set. (C). 1987. 360.00 (*0-7855-3507-1*) St Mut.

Malik, Surendra. Fundamental Rights Case, 1951-1973. 1078p. 1973. 145.00 (*0-7855-7567-7*) St Mut.

Malik, Surendra. Laws of Preventive Detention - Past & Present. (C). 1988. 70.00 (*0-7855-3325-7*) St Mut.

— Supreme Court Decennial Digest, 1981-1990, Set. 1995. text 600.00 (*81-7012-506-5*) St Mut.

— Supreme Court Decennial Digest 1981-1990, Vol. I. (C). 1993. 180.00 (*81-7012-505-7*, Pub. by Eastern Book) St Mut.

— Supreme Court Decennial Digest 1981-1990, Vol. II. (C). 1993. 180.00 (*81-7012-515-4*, Pub. by Eastern Book) St Mut.

— Supreme Court Decennial Digest 1981-1990, Vol. III. (C). 1993. 180.00 (*81-7012-519-7*, Pub. by Eastern Book) St Mut.

— Supreme Court Judgement on Prime Minister's Election Case. 283p. 1975. 75.00 (*0-7855-1434-1*) St Mut.

— Supreme Court Labour & Services Digest, Vol. V. (C). 1991. 110.00 (*0-7855-5517-X*) St Mut.

— Supreme Court Labour & Services Digest, 1950-1982, 3 vols. 1532p. 1983. 750.00 (*0-7855-1439-2*) St Mut.

— Supreme Court Labour & Services Digest, 1950-1989, 5 vols., Set, Vols. I-IV. (C). 1991. 400.00 (*0-7855-5504-8*) St Mut.

— Supreme Court Labour & Services Digest, 1950-1993, Vols. I-VI. 1996. text 190.00 (*81-7012-545-6*, Pub. by Eastern Book) St Mut.

— Supreme Court Labour & Services Digest, 1987-1990. (C). 1991. 200.00 (*0-89771-700-7*) St Mut.

— Supreme Court Mandal Commission Case, 1992. (C). 1993. 70.00 (*81-7012-498-0*, Pub. by Eastern Book) St Mut.

— Supreme Court on Essential Commodities Act, 1955. 161p. 1984. 120.00 (*0-7855-1436-8*) St Mut.

— Supreme Court on Hindu Law. 247p. 1977. 115.00 (*0-7855-1438-4*) St Mut.

— Supreme Court on Interpretation of Statutes. (C). 1977. 35.00 (*0-7855-5527-7*) St Mut.

— Supreme Court on Law of Limitation, 1950-1979. 226p. 1981. 75.00 (*0-7855-1437-6*) St Mut.

— Supreme Court on Law of Limitation, 1950-1979. (C). 1981. 40.00 (*0-7855-5491-2*) St Mut.

— Supreme Court on Preventive Detention (1950 up to Date) (C). 1991. 95.00 (*0-7855-5584-6*) St Mut.

— Supreme Court on Preventive Detention, 1950- (C). 1991. 95.00 (*0-7855-5444-0*) St Mut.

— Supreme Court on Rent Control & Eviction. (C). 1992. 200.00 (*0-89771-792-9*, Pub. by Eastern Book); 100.00 (*81-7012-471-9*, Pub. by Eastern Book) St Mut.

— Supreme Court on Words & Phrases. (C). 1993. 140.00 (*81-7012-510-3*, Pub. by Eastern Book) St Mut.

— Supreme Court Yearly Digest for 1986. (C). 1987. 100.00 (*0-7855-5586-2*) St Mut.

— Supreme Court Yearly Digest for 1985. (C). 1986. 100.00 (*0-7855-5588-9*) St Mut.

— Supreme Court Yearly Digest for 1982. (C). 1983. 55.00 (*0-7855-5589-7*) St Mut.

— Supreme Court Yearly Digest for 1991. (C). 1992. 320.00 (*0-89771-780-5*, Pub. by Eastern Book) St Mut.

— Supreme Court Yearly Digest for 1992. (C). 1993. 200.00 (*81-7012-500-6*, Pub. by Eastern Book) St Mut.

— Supreme Court Yearly Digest, 1989. (C). 1990. 195.00 (*0-7855-4715-0*) St Mut.

— Supreme Court Yearly Digest, 1990. (C). 1990. 110.00 (*0-89771-329-X*) St Mut.

— Supreme Court Yearly Digest, 1990. (C). 1991. text 220.00 (*0-89771-491-1*) St Mut.

— U. P. Consolidation of Holdings Act. 250p. 1980. 82.50 (*0-7855-1430-9*) St Mut.

— U. P. Consolidation of Holdings Act, 1953: Together with Exhaustive Commentaries, Notifications & Rules. (C). 1991. 95.00 (*0-7855-5625-7*) St Mut.

— Yearly Digest of Supreme Court Criminal Cases. 1988. 80.00 (*0-7855-1433-3*) St Mut.

Malik, Surendra, ed. The Complete Digest of Supreme Court Cases (Since 1950), Vol. XVI. (C). 1991. 110.00 (*0-7855-5590-0*) St Mut.

— The Complete Digest of Supreme Court Cases (Since 1950), Vols. I-XIV. (C). 1991. 135.00 (*0-7855-7065-9*) St Mut.

— The Complete Supreme Court Criminal Digest, 1950 up to Date: With Supplement, 1987 Vol., 6 vols., Set, Vols. I, II, III-A, III-B, IV & V. (C). 1990. 660.00 (*0-7855-5585-4*) St Mut.

— Supreme Court Labour & Services Digest, 1950-1989, 5 vols., Set. (C). 1989. 200.00 (*0-7855-5250-2*) St Mut.

— Supreme Court Labour & Services Digest, 1950-1989, 5 vols., V. (C). 1989. write for info. (*0-7855-2612-9*) St Mut.

— Supreme Court Labour & Services Digest, 1950-1989, 5 vols., Vol. III, 1979-1982. (C). 1989. 40.00 (*0-7855-5248-0*) St Mut.

— Supreme Court Labour & Services Digest, 1950-1989, 5 vols., Vol. IV, 1983-1986. (C). 1989. 40.00 (*0-7855-5249-9*) St Mut.

— Supreme Court Labour & Services Digest, 1950-1989, 5 vols., Vols. I & II, 1950-1978. (C). 1989. 130.00 (*0-7855-5247-2*) St Mut.

— Supreme Court Labour & Services Digest, 1987-1990, Vol. V. (C). 1991. text 160.00 (*0-89771-490-3*) St Mut.

— Supreme Court on Essential Commodities Act, 1984: With Supplement. (C). 1987. reprint ed. 50.00 (*0-7855-5569-2*) St Mut.

— Supreme Court on Tenancy & Land Laws, 1950-1990. (C). 1991. 135.00 (*0-89771-682-5*) St Mut.

— Supreme Court Yearly Digest for 1988. (C). 1989. 140.00 (*0-7855-5587-0*) St Mut.

Malik, Syed A. Tale of a Nomadic Soul. (C). 1990. text 19.50 (*81-7018-584-X*, Pub. by BR Pub) S Asia.

Malik, Tarun, jt. auth. see Collins, Galen.

Malik, V. Drugs & Cosmetics Act, 1940. 1996. 100.00 (*0-7855-2842-3*, Pub. by Eastern Book) St Mut.

Malik, Vedpal S. & Lillehoj, Erik P., eds. Antibody Techniques: A Guide for Nonimmunologists. (Illus.). 353p. 1994. pap. 53.00 (*0-12-466460-1*) Acad Pr.

Malik, Vedpal S. & Sridhar, P. Industrial Biotechnology. 633p. 1992. text 98.00 (*1-881570-04-5*) Science Pubs.

Malik, Vijay. The Banking Regulation Act Nineteen Forty-Nine. 163p. 1984. 110.00 (*0-7855-1429-5*) St Mut.

— Criminal Manual. 550p. 1983. 140.00 (*0-7855-1314-0*) St Mut.

— Dand Vidhi Nirdeshika. 561p. 1985. 90.00 (*0-7855-1311-6*) St Mut.

— Dand Vidhi Nirdeshika: (Three Major Acts in Hindi) Pocket Edition. (HIN.). (C). 1990. 42.00 (*0-7855-5599-4*) St Mut.

— Dand Vidhi Nirdeshika (Three Major Acts in Hindi) (C). 1992. 55.00 (*0-89771-777-5*, Pub. by Eastern Book) St Mut.

— Dandniya Manual: (Three Major Acts, Cr.P.C., I.P.C. & Evidence in Hindi) (HIN.). (C). 1990. 90.00 (*0-7855-5600-1*) St Mut.

— Dandniya Manual: Three Major Acts in Hindi. 550p. 1983. 135.00 (*0-7855-1312-4*) St Mut.

— Drugs & Cosmetics Act, Nineteen Forty. 447p. 1984. 195.00 (*0-7855-1309-4*) St Mut.

***Malik, Vijay.** Drugs & Cosmetics Act, 1940. 1999. pap. 100.00 (*81-7012-664-9*, Pub. by Eastern Book) St Mut.

Malik, Vijay. Drugs & Cosmetics Act, 1940 Together with Drugs & Cosmetics Rules, 1945, Drugs (Price Control) Order, 1987. (C). 1993. 100.00 (*81-7012-514-6*, Pub. by Eastern Book) St Mut.

— Drugs & Cosmetics Act, 1940 with Drugs & Cosmetics Rules, 1945, Drugs, Prices Control Order, 1987 & Notifications & Short Notes. (C). 1990. 63.00 (*0-89771-321-4*) St Mut.

— Handbook on Environment & Pollution Control Law. 2nd ed. (C). 1991. 95.00 (*0-7855-5446-7*) St Mut.

— Handbook on Environment & Pollution Control Laws. 2nd ed. (C). 1991. 95.00 (*0-7855-5573-0*) St Mut.

— The Indian Explosives Act, 1884 & Explosive Rules, 1983. 255p. 1984. 120.00 (*0-7855-1306-X*) St Mut.

— The Indian Explosives Act, Eighteen Eighty-Four & Explosive Rules, 1983 Together with Explosive Substances Act, 1908, Gas Cylinders Rules, 1981 & Static & Mobile Pressure Vessels (Unfired) Rules, 1981. 5th ed. (C). 1989. 60.00 (*0-7855-5109-3*) St Mut.

— Law for Cinemas & Videos. (C). 1990. 45.00 (*0-7855-5243-X*); text 95.00 (*0-89771-495-4*) St Mut.

— Law Relating to Banking & Financial Institutions. (C). 1989. 135.00 (*0-7855-5641-9*) St Mut.

— Muslim Law of Marriage, Divorce & Maintenance. 2nd ed. (C). 1988. 60.00 (*0-7855-5474-2*) St Mut.

— National Security Act, 1980. (C). 1991. 110.00 (*0-89771-688-4*) St Mut.

— National Security Act, 1980 along with Other Laws on Preventive Detention - Past & Present. (C). 1991. text 110.00 (*0-89771-496-2*) St Mut.

— Tax on Luxuries in Hotels in U. P. 40p. 1975. 60.00 (*0-7855-1303-5*) St Mut.

— Tax on Luxuries in Hotels in U. P. 2nd ed. (C). 1991. 95.00 (*0-7855-5490-4*) St Mut.

— U. P. Land Records Manual. 138p. 1975. 50.00 (*0-7855-1302-7*) St Mut.

— Water (Prevention & Control of Pollution) Act, 1974. 2nd ed. (C). 1991. 95.00 (*0-7855-5390-8*) St Mut.

Malik, Vijay, ed. Criminal Manual: (Three Major Acts, CRP.C., I.P.C. & Evidence in English) (C). 1990. 90.00 (*0-7855-5601-X*) St Mut.

— Indian Explosives Act, 1884 & Explosives Rules, 1983: Together with Explosive Substances Act, 1908, Gas Cylinders Rules, 1981 & Static & Mobile Pressure Vessels (Unfired) Rules, 1981. 5th ed. (C). 1990. 60.00 (*0-7855-5561-7*) St Mut.

— Indian Explosives Act, 1984. 1993. 60.00 (*81-7012-520-0*) St Mut.

— Railway Property (Unlawful Possession) Act, 1966: Together with R. P. F. Act & Rules. 2nd ed. (C). 1991. 90.00 (*0-89771-687-6*) St Mut.

Malik, Vijay, tr. see Shukla, V. M.

Malik, Vijay, tr. see Shukla, V. M., ed.

Malik, Waleed Haider, jt. ed. see Sureda, Andres Rigo.

Malik, Yogendra. South Asian Intellectuals & Social Change. 1982. 15.00 (*0-686-81181-X*) S Asia.

Malik, Yogendra, ed. Boeings & Bullock Carts Vol. 1: Studies in Change & Continuity in Indian Civilization: Essays in Honour of K. Ishwaran: India Culture & Society. 1990. 42.00 (*81-7001-063-2*, Pub. by Chanakya) S Asia.

Malik, Yogendra & Marquette, Jesse. Political Mercenaries & Citizen Soldiers: A Profile of North Indian Party Activists. 1990. 24.50 (*81-7001-081-0*, Pub. by Chanakya) S Asia.

Malik, Yogendra, jt. ed. see Vajpeyi, Dhirendra K.

Malik, Yogendra K. & Kapoor, Ashok. India: Fifty Years of Democracy & Development. LC 98-902298. xli, 489p. 1998. 66.00 (*81-7024-929-5*, Pub. by APH Pubng) Nataraj Bks.

Malikow, Max, jt. auth. see Grollman, Earl A.

Malik's Chief Justice. The Art of Lawyer. (C). 1988. 65.00 (*0-7855-3554-3*) St Mut.

Malim. Cognative Processes. 1997. pap. 14.95 (*0-333-58811-8*) St Martin.

Malin, ed. Converting Psychotherapy to Psychoanalysis. (Psychoanalytic Inquiry Ser.: Vol. 10, No. 1). 1990. 20.00 (*0-88163-955-9*) Analytic Pr.

Malin, Jennifer. As You Wish. (Time Passages Ser.). 299p. 1999. mass mkt. 5.99 (*0-515-12433-8*, Jove) Berkley Pub.

Malin, David. The Invisible Universe. (Illus.). 130p. 1999. 60.00 (*0-8212-2628-2*, Pub. by Bulfinch Pr) Little.

— A View of the Universe. LC 92-46469. (Illus.). 284p. (C). 1993. 39.95 (*0-521-44477-2*) Cambridge U Pr.

— A View of the Universe. (Illus.). 292p. 1993. 39.95 (*0-933346-66-2*) Sky Pub.

Malin, David & Frew, David J. Hartung's Astronomical Objects for Southern Telescopes: A Handbook for Amateur Observers. 2nd ed. (Illus.). 448p. (C). 1995. text 74.95 (*0-521-55491-8*) Cambridge U Pr.

Malin, Edward. Northwest Coast Indian Painting: House Fronts & Interior Screens. LC 98-39230. (Illus.). 288p. 1999. 39.95 (*0-88192-471-7*) Timber.

— Totem Poles of the Pacific Northwest Coast. (Illus.). 195p. 1994. pap. 19.95 (*0-88192-295-1*) Timber.

— A World of Faces: Masks of the Northwest Coast Indians. LC 77-26786. (Illus.). 160p. 1994. pap. 17.95 (*0-917304-05-5*) Timber.

Malin, Edyth L. & Tunick, Michael H., eds. Chemistry of Structure-Function Relationships in Cheese: Proceedings of ACS Symposium Held in Chicago, Illinois, August 23-25, 1993. (Advances in Experimental Medicine & Biology Ser.: Vol. 367). (Illus.). 408p. 1995. 120.00 (*0-306-44982-X*, Kluwer Plenum) Kluwer Academic.

Malin, Eleanor. Earthquake & Disaster Preparedness: Surviving the Next Great Disaster. 32p. (Orig.). 1995. pap. 9.95 (*1-884958-10-9*) Am Prods.

Malin, Ian. Mud, Blood & Money: English Rugby Union Goes Professional. (Illus.). 192p. 1998. 35.00 (*1-85158-938-4*, Pub. by Mainstream Pubng) Trafalgar.

Malin, Irving. William Faulkner: An Interpretation. LC 76-165664. 109p. 1972. reprint ed. 40.00 (*0-87752-154-9*) Gordian.

Malin, Irving, jt. auth. see Horvath, Brooke.

Malin, Irving, jt. auth. see Kellman, Steven G.

Malin, Irving, jt. ed. see Horvath, Brooke.

Malin, Irving, jt. ed. see Kellman, Steven G.

Malin, James. John Brown & the Legend of Fifty-Six, 2 vols., Set. LC 70-117588. (Studies in History & Culture: No. 54). 1970. reprint ed. lib. bdg. 150.00 (*0-8383-1021-4*) M S G Haskell Hse.

Malin, James C. Doctors, Devils & the Woman: Fort Scott, Kansas 1870-1890. 122p. 1975. 8.50 (*0-87291-074-1*) Coronado Pr.

— History & Ecology: Studies of the Grassland. Swierenga, Robert P., ed. LC 83-16951. xxx, 376p. 1984. pap. text 14.95 (*0-8032-8125-0*, Bison Books) U of Nebr Pr.

— Ironquil-Paint Creek Essays. 183p. 1972. 7.50 (*0-87291-025-3*) Coronado Pr.

— The United States after the World War. LC 77-37897. (Select Bibliographies Reprint Ser.). 1977. reprint ed. 31.95 (*0-8369-6735-6*) Ayer.

***Malin, Joanne.** The Voice of the Mother: Embedded Maternal Narratives in Twentieth-Century Women's Autobiographies LC 99-16863. 2000. 32.95 (*0-8093-2266-8*) S Ill U Pr.

Malin, Karl S. & Valentich, John D., eds. Functional Epithelial Cells in Culture. (Modern Cell Biology Ser.: Vol. 8). 300p. 1989. 295.00 (*0-471-50810-1*) Wiley.

Malin, Margot E., jt. auth. see Northrup, Herbert R.

Malin, Martin H. Individual Rights Within the Union. 740p. 1987. trans. 88.00 (*0-87179-537-X*, 0537) BNA Books.

Malin, N. Community Care Nurses & Caring. LC 98-40515. (Social Science for Nurses & the Caring Professions Ser.). 1999. pap. 26.95 (*0-335-19670-5*); pap. 85.00 (*0-335-19671-3*) OpUniv Pr.

***Malin, Nigel.** Professionalism Boundaries & Workplace. LC 99-17035. 2000. pap. write for info. (*0-415-19263-3*) Routledge.

***Malin, Nigel, ed.** Professionalism Boundaries & the Workplace. LC 99-17035. 288p. (C). 2000. text. write for info. (*0-415-19262-5*) Routledge.

Malin, Nigel A. Services for People with Learning Disabilities. LC 94-5049. 256p. (C). 1994. pap. 27.99 (*0-415-09938-2*, B4669) Routledge.

— Services for People with Learning Disabilities. LC 94-5049. 256p. (C). (gr. 13). 1994. 90.00 (*0-415-09937-4*, B4665) Routledge.

Malin, Nigel A., ed. Implementing Community Care. LC 93-42337. (C). 1994. pap. 37.95 (*0-335-15738-6*) OpUniv Pr.

— Reassessing Community Care. (C). 1987. 57.50 (*0-7099-1738-4*, Pub. by C Helm) Routldge.

Malin, S., jt. auth. see Carmeli, Moshe.

Malin, Shimon, jt. auth. see Carmeli, Moshe.

Malin, Stuart. The Greenwich Guide to Stars, Galaxies & Nebulae. (Greenwich Guides to Astronomy Ser.). (Illus.). 96p. (C). 1990. pap. 11.95 (*0-521-37777-3*) Cambridge U Pr.

— Story of the Earth. LC 90-11019. (Exploring the Universe Ser.). (Illus.). 32p. (J). (gr. 4-6). 1991. lib. bdg. 18.60 (*0-8167-2134-3*) Troll Communs.

— Story of the Earth. LC 90-11019. (Exploring the Universe Ser.). (Illus.). 32p. (J). (gr. 4-6). 1996. pap. 4.95 (*0-8167-2135-1*) Troll Communs.

***Malina, Bruce J.** The New Jerusalem in the Revelation of John: The City As Symbol of Life with God. 112p. 2000. pap. 11.95 (*0-8146-5938-1*) Liturgical Pr.

Malina, Bruce J. The New Testament World: Insights from Cultural Anthropology. rev. ed. 224p. 1993. pap. 19.95 (*0-664-25456-X*) Westminster John Knox.

— On the Genre & Message of Revelation: Star Visions & Sky Journeys. 350p. 1995. 24.95 (*1-56563-040-8*) Hendrickson MA.

— Social-Science Commentary on the Gospel on John. LC 98-24813. 1998. pap. text 20.00 (*0-8006-2992-2*, 1-2992, Fortress Pr) Augsburg Fortress.

— The Social World of Jesus & the Gospels. LC 96-12602. 272p. (C). 1996. pap. 25.99 (*0-415-14629-1*) Routledge.

— Windows on the World of Jesus: Time Travel to Ancient Judea. LC 93-10360. 208p. (Orig.). 1993. pap. 19.95 (*0-664-25457-8*) Westminster John Knox.

Malina, Bruce J. & Neyrey, Jerome H. Portraits of Paul: An Archaeology of Ancient Personality. LC 96-18497. 272p. (Orig.). 1996. pap. 29.95 (*0-664-25681-3*) Westminster John Knox.

***Malina, Bruce J. & Pilch, John J.** Social-Science Commentary on the Book of Revelation. (Illus.). 272p. 2000. pap. 20.00 (*0-8006-3227-3*, Fortress Pr) Augsburg Fortress.

Malina, Bruce J. & Rohrbaugh, Richard L. Social-Science Commentary on the Synoptic Gospels. LC 92-359. 432p. 1993. pap. 28.00 (*0-8006-2562-5*, 1-2562, Fortress Pr) Augsburg Fortress.

Malina, Bruce J., jt. auth. see Pilch, John J.

Malina, Danusia. Surviving the Academy: Feminist Perspectives. 1998. pap. text 39.95 (*0-7507-0924-3*) Taylor & Francis.

Malina, Frank J., ed. Visual Art, Mathematics & Computers: Selections from the Journal Leonardo. 1979. 151.00 (*0-08-021854-7*, Pub. by Pergamon Repr) Franklin.

Malina, Joseph F., Jr., ed. Environmental Engineering. 936p. 1989. pap. text 87.00 (*0-87262-711-X*, 711) Am Soc Civil Eng.

Malina, Joseph F., Jr. & Pohland, Frederick G., eds. Design of Anaerobic Processes for the Treatment of Industrial & Municipal Wastes. LC 92-53523. (Water Quality Management Library: Vol. 7). 200p. 1992. text 99.95 (*0-87762-942-0*) Technomic.

Malina, Joshua. Nutshell Classics: The Haunted House. 1988. pap. text 80.00 (*0-938735-99-3*) Classic Theatre Schl.

— Nutshell Classics: The Importance of Being Earnest. 1988. pap. text 55.00 (*0-938735-51-9*) Classic Theatre Schl.

Malina, Judith, tr. from GER. Antigone: In a Version by Bertolt Brecht. (Illus.). 96p. 1990. pap. 7.95 (*0-936839-25-2*) Applause Theatre Bk Pubs.

Malina, Robert, ed. Michigan PACE: Program for Athletic Coaches' Education. (Illus.). 490p. (C). 1995. pap. text, spiral bd. 30.00 (*1-884125-49-2*) Cooper Pubng.

— Wisconsin PACE: Program for Athletic Coaches' Education. (Illus.). 425p. (C). 1995. pap. text, spiral bd. 30.00 (*1-884125-48-4*) Cooper Pubng.

Malina, Robert M. & Bouchard, Claude. Growth, Maturation, & Physical Activity. LC 90-25553. (Illus.). 520p. (Orig.). (C). 1991. text 55.00 (*0-87322-321-7*, BMAL0321) Human Kinetics.

Malina, Robert M., ed. see Child & Sport Conference (1984, Urbino, Italy) Staff.

Malina, Robert M., ed. see Olympic Scientific Congress (1984, Eugene, OR) Staff.

Malina, Robert M., ed. see Olympic Scientific Congress (1984: Eugene, OR) Sta.

Malina, Robert M., jt. ed. see Roche, Alex F.

Malina, Roger F., ed. Proceedings of the Extreme Ultraviolet Astronomy Colloquium. (Illus.). 208p. 1991. 80.00 (*0-08-037303-8*, Pergamon Pr) Elsevier.

Malina, Roger F., jt. ed. see Bowyer, Stuart.

Malinchak, James. From College to the Real World: Street-Smart Strategies for Landing Your Dream Job & Creating a Successful Future! Ashe-Dudley, Suzanne & Simmons, Gay, eds. LC 95-71837. 128p. (Orig.). (C). 1995. pap. 11.95 (*0-9646924-0-6*) Positive Pub.

Malinconico, L. L., Jr. & Lillie, R. J., eds. Tectonics of the Western Himalayas. (Special Papers: No. 232). (Illus.). 300p. 1989. pap. 20.00 (*0-8137-2232-2*) Geol Soc.

Maline, Karen F., et al, eds. Criminal Justice Issues in the States: 1996 Directory. 13th ed. 110p. (C). 1999. reprint ed. pap. text 30.00 (*0-7881-7904-7*) DIANE Pub.

***Maline, Sarah, et al.** Polyalterity: New Cyberworks by Ron Hutt, Joseph Nechvatal & Jan Piribeck. (Illus.). 24p. 2000. pap. write for info. (*0-9677432-0-6*) UMF Art Gallery.

***Malinen, Anita.** Towards the Essence of Adult Experiental Learning: A Reading of the Theories of Knowles, Mezirow, Revans & Schon. 174p. 2000. pap. 24.95 (*951-39-0661-2*, Pub. by SoPhi Academic) Intl Spec Bk.

Maling, Anne E. Princess Anne County, Virginia, Land & Probate Records Abstracted from Deed Books One to Eighteen 1691-1783. 243p. (Orig.). 1995. pap. text 19.00 (*0-7884-0175-0*) Heritage Bk.

— Princess Anne County, Virginia, Land & Probate Records Abstracted from Deed Books 1-7. 118p. (Orig.). 1992. pap. 14.50 (*1-55613-620-X*) Heritage Bk.

— Princess Anne County, Virginia, Wills, 1783-1871. 255p. (Orig.). 1994. pap. 22.50 (*1-55613-966-7*) Heritage Bk.

Maling, Arthur. The Koberg Link. large type ed. 406p. 1981. 27.99 (*0-7089-0674-5*) Ulverscroft.

— A Taste of Treason. large type ed. 416p. 1985. 27.99 (*0-7089-1338-5*) Ulverscroft.

Maling, George C., Jr., ed. Transportation Noise Control: NOISE-CON 77. (Noise-Con Ser.). ix, 502p. pap. 35.00 (*0-614-25015-3*) Noise Control.

Maling, George C., Jr., ed. see International Conference on Noise Control Engineer.

Maling, John E., ed. see Briles, Judith.

Malingrey, A. M., ed. see Chrysostomus.

Malingue, Maurice, ed. see Gauguin, Paul.

Malinin, M. V. Mpabga o Npabax Zeaobeka (Pravda o Pravah Cheloveka) (RUS.). 8p. 1995. write for info. (*1-887869-50-6*) ASOFSPP.

Malino, Frances. A Jew in the French Revolution: The Life of Zalkind Hourwitz. LC 95-49997. (Jewish Society & Culture Ser.). 304p. (C). 1996. text 55.95 (*1-55786-193-5*) Blackwell Pubs.

Malino, Frances & Albert, Phyllis C., eds. Essays in Modern Jewish History: A Tribute to Ben Halpern. LC 80-70585. 500p. 1982. 36.50 (*0-8386-3095-2*) Fairleigh Dickinson.

Malino, Frances & Sorkin, David J. Profiles in Diversity: Jews in a Changing Europe, 1750-1870. LC 97-37514. 352p. 1997. pap. 18.95 (*0-8143-2715-X*) Wayne St U Pr.

Malinoff, Lauren M. A How-To Guide for Downtown Rehab, Rescue & Repair. (Illus.). 36p. 1998. spiral bd. write for info. (*0-9668274-0-6*) State of NC.

Malinoski, Robert R. A Golden Decade of Trains: The 1950's in Color. LC 91-62001. (Illus.). 128p. 1991. 45.00 (*1-878887-06-8*) Morning NJ.

Malinova, Libuse. Czech-English Technical Dictionary: Cesko-Anglicky Technicky Slovnik. 4th ed. (CZE & ENG.). 945p. 1986. 95.00 (*0-8288-0679-9*, F42070) Fr & Eur.

— Czech-English/English-Czech Dictionary of Electrical Engineering. (CZE & ENG.). 924p. 1992. 48.00 (*0-7859-9574-9*) Fr & Eur.

— English-Czech, Czech-English, Electrotechnic & Electronic Dictionary. (CZE & ENG.). 1985. 49.95 (*0-8288-7202-3*, M1362) Fr & Eur.

Malinovich, Alisa, jt. auth. see Miedzian, Myriam.

Malinow, Wendy W. The Nutcracker: With Nutcracker CD. LC 99-181954. (BookNotes Ser.). 56p. 1998. 13.99 incl. cd-rom (*0-88088-406-1*) Peter Pauper.

Malinowitz, Harriet. Textual Orientations: Lesbian & Gay Students & the Making of Discourse Communities. LC 94-36734. 294p. 1995. pap. text 25.00 (*0-86709-353-6*, 0353, Pub. by Boynton Cook Pubs) Heinemann.

Malinowska, Barbara. Dynamics of Being, Space, & Time in the Poetry of Czeslaw Milosz & John Ashbery. LC 96-9588. (Studies in Modern Poetry: Vol. 8). 192p. (C). 2000. text 46.95 (*0-8204-3464-7*) P Lang Pubng.

Malinowski, Bronislaw. Argonauts of the Western Pacific. (Illus.). 527p. (C). 1984. reprint ed. pap. text 16.95 (*0-88133-084-1*) Waveland Pr.

— Crime & Custom in Savage Society. LC 84-19807. (Illus.). 132p. 1984. reprint ed. lib. bdg. 45.00 (*0-313-24686-6*, MCRC, Greenwood Pr) Greenwood.

— Crime & Custom in Savage Society. (Quality Paperback Ser.: No. 210). 1976. reprint ed. pap. 19.00 (*0-8226-0210-5*) Littlefield.

— A Diary in the Strict Sense of the Term. 360p. 1989. 47.50 (*0-8047-1706-0*); pap. 18.95 (*0-8047-1707-9*) Stanford U Pr.

— The Dynamics of Culture Change. Kaberry, Phyllis M., ed. LC 75-14599. 171p. 1976. reprint ed. lib. bdg. 55.00 (*0-8371-8216-6*, MADCC, Greenwood Pr) Greenwood.

— Freedom & Civilization. LC 76-40226. 338p. 1977. reprint ed. lib. bdg. 35.00 (*0-8371-9277-3*, MAFA, Greenwood Pr) Greenwood.

— Magic, Science & Religion & Other Essays. LC 84-19290. 274p. 1984. reprint ed. lib. bdg. 65.00 (*0-313-24687-4*, MMSR, Greenwood Pr) Greenwood.

— Magic, Science & Religion & Other Essays. (Illus.). 274p. (C). 1992. reprint ed. pap. text 12.95 (*0-88133-657-2*) Waveland Pr.

— Malinowski among the Magi: The Natives of Mailu. Young, Michael, ed. 250p. (C). 1988. lib. bdg. 57.50 (*0-415-00249-4*) Routledge.

— A Scientific Theory of Culture. LC 44-8385. x, 228p. (C). 1990. reprint ed. pap. 14.95 (*0-8078-4283-4*) U of NC Pr.

— A Scientific Theory of Culture, & Other Essays by Bronislaw Malinowski with a Preface by Huntington Cairns. LC 44-8385. 238p. 1944. pap. 73.80 (*0-608-05213-2*, 206575000001) Bks Demand.

— Sex & Repression in Savage Society. LC 85-971. xii, 300p. 1996. pap. text 16.00 (*0-226-50287-2*) U Ch Pr.

— The Sexual Life of Savages. LC 86-47760. (Illus.). 650p. 1987. reprint ed. pap. 22.00 (*0-8070-4607-8*, BP 740) Beacon Pr.

— The Sexual Life of Savages in North-Western Melanesia. 700p. 1982. pap. text 22.50 (*0-7100-6659-7*, Routledge Thoemms) Routledge.

Malinowski, Bronislaw & De La Fuente, Julio. Malinowski in Mexico: The Economics of a Mexican Market System. Drucker-Brown, Susan, ed. (International Library of Anthropology). 246p. 1985. pap. 13.95 (*0-7102-0584-8*, Routledge Thoemms) Routledge.

Malinowski, Bronislaw, jt. auth. see Briffault, Robert.

Malinowski, Edmund R. Factor Analysis in Chemistry. 2nd ed. LC 90-24193. 368p. 1991. 99.95 (*0-471-53009-3*) Wiley.

Malinowski, Edmund R. & Howery, Darryl G. Factor Analysis in Chemistry. LC 88-13742. 264p. (C). 1989. reprint ed. lib. bdg. 47.50 (*0-89464-343-6*) Krieger.

Malinowski, Gregory P. & Jahani, Mohammad. An Information Systems Guide for Community Action Agencies. (Illus.). 250p. 1981. 15.00 (*0-936130-04-0*) Intl Sci Tech.

Malinowski, Grzegorz. Many-Valued Logics. LC 93-36413. (Oxford Logic Guides Ser.: No. 25). 138p. (C). 1994. text 45.00 (*0-19-853787-5*, Clarendon Pr) OUP.

Malinowski, James H., jt. auth. see Miller, Robert H.

Malinowski, Janet S. Nursing Care During the Labor Process. 3rd ed. LC 88-30981. (Illus.). 433p. (C). 1989. pap. text 26.95 (*0-8036-5803-6*) Davis Co.

Malinowski, Judy & Malinowski, Mel. Snorkel Hawaii: Maui & Lana'i Guide to the Underwater World. LC 96-95140. (Illus.). 160p. (Orig.). 1996. pap. 14.95 (*0-9646680-1-7*) Indigo CA.

— Snorkel Hawaii the Big Island: Guide to the Underwater World. LC 96-94357. 128p. 1996. pap. 14.95 (*0-9646680-0-9*) Indigo CA.

***Malinowski, Judy & Malinowski, Mel.** Snorkel Maui & Lanai: Guide to the Underwater World of Hawaii. 2nd ed. (Illus.). 192p. 2000. pap. 19.95 (*0-9646680-3-3*) Indigo CA.

Malinowski, K., jt. auth. see Brdys, M. A.

***Malinowski, MaryEllen.** The Sacred Light. 56p. 1999. 45.00 (*0-9676907-0-6*) Infrared Lgt Gallery.

Malinowski, Mel, jt. auth. see Malinowski, Judy.

Malinowski, Michael J. & Arnold, Beth E. Biotechnology: Law, Business & Regulation. LC 99-20598. 1999. ring bd. 225.00 (*0-7355-0309-5*) Panel Pubs.

Malinowski, Michal, jt. ed. see Wolinski, Wieslaw.

Malinowski, Sharon, ed. Gay & Lesbian Literature, Vol. 1. LC 93-47362. 488p. 1993. 99.00 (*1-55862-174-1*) St James Pr.

***Malinowski, Sharon, et al, eds.** Encyclopedia of Native American Tribes, Vol. 3. LC 98-54353. 832p. (J). 1999. text 35.00 (*0-7876-2841-7*, GML00299-112401, UXL) Gale.

— Encyclopedia of Native American Tribes, Vol. 4. LC 98-54353. 832p. (J). 1999. text 35.00 (*0-7876-2842-5*, GML00299-112402, UXL) Gale.

— Native North American Tribes, 4 vols. LC 98-54353. (J). 1998. text 99.00 (*0-7876-2838-7*, 00158642, UXL) Gale.

— U-X-L Encyclopedia of Native American Tribes, Vol. 1. LC 98-54353. 832p. (J). 1999. text 35.00 (*0-7876-2839-5*, GML00299-112399, UXL) Gale.

— U-X-L Encyclopedia of Native American Tribes, Vol. 2. LC 98-54353. 832p. (J). 1999. text 35.00 (*0-7876-2840-9*, GML00299-112400, UXL) Gale.

Malinowski, Sharon & Abrams, George H. J., eds. Notable Native Americans. 2nd ed. LC 94-36202. 492p. 1994. 80.00 (*0-8103-9638-6*) Gale.

Malinowski, Sharon, jt. auth. see Glickman, Simon.

Malinowski, Stanley B. & Melodia, Thomas V. The Easter Bunny Comes to Forgottenville. 48p. (J). (ps-3). 1988. 11.95 (*0-941316-02-5*) TSM Books.

Malinowski, Walt. More Decisive Than Bastogne, Hitler's "Bulge" Dream for Dunkirk II Exploded Green GI's & Vets on Elsenborn Ridge & N. Shoulder Did It! Green GI's & Vets on Elsenborn Ridge & N. Shoulder Did It! (Illus.). 42p. (Orig.). (C). pap. write for info. (*0-935648-47-X*) Halldin Pub.

Malinowsky, H. Robert, ed. Best Science & Technology Reference Books for Young People. LC 90-48595. 232p. 1991. pap. 24.95 (*0-89774-580-9*) Oryx Pr.

— Reference Sources in Science, Engineering, Medicine, & Agriculture. LC 94-16133. 368p. 1994. pap. 39.95 (*0-89774-745-3*) Oryx Pr.

Malins & Numan. Gary Numan. LC 99-199918. text 29.95 (*0-233-99205-7*, Pub. by Andre Deutsch) Trafalgar.

Malins, Dana H. How to Write Twice As Fast with the New Word-Shortening System. 53p. 1990. pap. 19.95 (*0-9628032-0-0*) Peninsu MA.

Malins, Donald C. & Ostrander, Gary K., eds. Aquatic Toxicology: Molecular, Biochemical, & Cellular Perspectives. 560p. 1994. lib. bdg. 75.00 (*0-87371-545-4*, L545) Lewis Pubs.

Malins, Edward. Preface Yeates Edition. 2nd rev. ed. LC 93-39017. (Preface Bks.). 280p. (C). 1994. pap. text 33.25 (*0-582-09093-8*, Pub. by Addison-Wesley) Longman.

Malins, Geoffrey H. How I Filmed the War. (Great War Ser.: No. 25). (Illus.). 347p. reprint ed. 34.95 (*0-89839-183-0*) Battery Pr.

Malins, John. The Pruner's Handbook: Practical Pruning Advice for Healthy. (Illus.). 192p. 1996. pap. 19.95 (*0-7153-0399-6*, Pub. by D & C Pub) Sterling.

***Malins, S.** Depeche Mode: Stripped. 1999. text 29.95 (*0-233-99425-4*, Pub. by Andre Deutsch) Trafalgar.

Malins, S. Radiohead. 1998. pap. text 16.95 (*0-7535-0125-2*) London Brdge.

Malins, Steve. Paul Weller: The Unauthorized Biography. (Illus.). 256p. (Orig.). 1997. pap. text 14.95 (*0-7535-0087-6*, Pub. by Virgin Bks) London Brdge.

Malinski, Violet M. Explorations on Martha Rogers' Science of Unitary Human Beings. 240p. (C). 1986. pap. text 38.95 (*0-8385-2493-1*, A2493-3) Appleton & Lange.

Malinski, Violet M. & Barrett, Elizabeth A., eds. Martha E. Rogers: Her Life & Her Work. LC 94-6137. (Illus.). 366p. 1994. 50.00 (*0-8036-5807-9*) Davis Co.

Malinvaud, A. Statistical Methods in Econometrics. 3rd rev. ed. (Studies in Mathematical & Managerial Economics: Vol. 6). 770p. 1980. 132.25 (*0-444-85473-8*, North Holland) Elsevier.

Malinvaud, Edmond. Diagnosing Unemployment. (Caffe Lectures Ser.: No. 1). 168p. (C). 1994. text 36.95 (*0-521-44533-7*) Cambridge U Pr.

— Lectures on Microeconomic Theory. rev. ed. Silvey, A., tr. (Advanced Textbooks in Economics Ser.: Vol. 2). 386p. 1985. 79.50 (*0-444-87650-2*, North Holland) Elsevier.

— Macroeconomic Theory: A Textbook on Macroeconomic Knowledge & Analysis. LC 98-15139. (Advanced Textbooks in Economics). 1998. write for info. (*0-444-82862-1*); pap. 95.00 (*0-444-82863-X*) Elsevier.

Malinvaud, Edmond, et al. Development Strategy & Management of the Market Economy, Vol. 1. LC 98-134893. (Illus.). 316p. 1998. text 45.00 (*0-19-829212-0*) OUP.

Malis, Carol. Michigan, the Great Lakes State: Celebrating a Century of Success. LC 98-71770. (Illus.). 414p. 1999. 39.95 (*1-882933-23-0*) Cherbo Pub Grp.

Malis, Carolyn. Juicing. 224p. (Orig.). 1993. mass mkt. 4.99 (*0-380-77185-3*, Avon Bks) Morrow Avon.

Malis, G. Research on the Etiology of Schizophrenia. LC 61-11828. (International Behavioral Sciences Ser.). (Illus.). 207p. reprint ed. pap. 64.20 (*0-608-11184-8*, 202065700018) Bks Demand.

Malis, Leonard I. Acoustic Neuroma. 152p. 1998. 212.50 (*0-444-82976-8*) Elsevier.

Malisani, Eduardo A. Diccionario de Fisica. (SPA.). 320p. 1987. pap. 55.00 (*0-7859-6402-9*, 8486592402) Fr & Eur.

***Malise.** Scots on the Rocks: The First Wee Books of Worst Vessel Jokes & Puns. LC 00-131121. (Illus.). 120p. 2000. pap. 10.50 (*1-58597-032-8*) Leathers Pub.

Malison, Andrew F. Semiconductors: Industry & Trade Summary. (Illus.). 53p. (Orig.). (C). 1994. pap. text 30.00 (*0-7881-0320-2*) DIANE Pub.

Malisova, Nataliya, ed. see Averbach, Lera.

Malisova, Nataliya, ed. see Silver, Raisa.

Malisova, Nataliya, ed. see Tarlova, Lina.

Malisova, Nataliya, ed. see Ochildiev, David.

Malisow, Betty. Recipes from Minnesota: With Love. (Illus.). 199p. 1981. spiral bd. 13.95 (*0-913703-00-1*, MN29) Strawberry Pt.

Maliszewska-Kordybach, B., jt. auth. see Wilson, M. J.

Maliszewski, James, jt. auth. see Ford, John M.

Maliszewski, Michael. Great Traditions of the Martial Arts. (Frontiers of Consciousness Ser.). (Illus.). 300p. 1994. write for info. (*0-8290-2632-0*) Irvington.

— Spiritual Dimensions of the Martial Arts. LC 96-60594. (Illus.). 224p. 1996. pap. 16.95 (*0-8048-2048-1*) Tuttle Pubng.

Maliszewski, Michael, jt. ed. see Diamond, Seymour.

Maliszewski-Pickart, Margaret. Architecture & Ornament: An Illustrated Dictionary. LC 97-33112. (Illus.). 208p. 1997. boxed set 35.00 (*0-7864-0383-7*) McFarland & Co.

Malits, Elena, jt. auth. see Burrell, David.

Malitz, Gerald. Technology @ Your Fingertips: A Guide to Implementing Technology Solutions for Education Agencies & Institutions. (Illus.). 102p. (C). 1999. pap. text 25.00 (*0-7881-7762-1*) DIANE Pub.

Malitz, J. Introduction to Mathematical Logic: Set Theory-Computable Functions-Model Theory. (Undergraduate Texts in Mathematics Ser.). (Illus.). 1987. 47.95 (*0-387-90346-1*) Spr-Verlag.

Malitz, Jerome. Plants for the Future: A Gardener's Wishbook. (Illus.). 270p. 1996. 34.95 (*0-88192-349-4*) Timber.

— Rocky Mountain National Park Dayhiker's Guide: A Scenic Guide to 33 Favorite Hikes Including Longs Peak. LC 92-42538. (Illus.). 144p. (Orig.). 1993. pap. 15.95 (*1-55566-110-6*) Johnson Bks.

Malitz, Jerome & Malitz, Seth. Reflecting Nature: Garden Designs for Wild Landscapes. LC 97-48266. (Illus.). 267p. 1998. 39.95 (*0-88192-455-5*) Timber.

Malitz, Maxwell, et al. Zero-Resistance Selling: Achieve Extraordinary Sales Results Using the World-Renowned Techniques of Psycho-Cybernetics. 224p. 1998. pap. text 13.00 (*0-7352-0039-4*) PH Pr.

Malitz, Seth, jt. auth. see Malitz, Jerome.

Malitz, Sidney. L-Dopa & Behavior. fac. ed. LC 75-181306. (Illus.). 144p. pap. 44.70 (*0-7837-7194-0*, 204710500005) Bks Demand.

Maliushitskii, Iurii N. The Centrifugal Model Testing of Waste-Heap Embankments. Schofield, A. N., ed. LC 78-67431. 218p. reprint ed. pap. 62.20 (*0-608-15749-X*, 2031686) Bks Demand.

Maliwal, G. L. Salt Tolerance of Crops & Plant Metabolism in Saline Substrate: An Annotated Bibliography, 1940-1980. 1981. 75.00 (*0-7855-3113-0*, Pub. by Intl Bk Distr) St Mut.

— Salt Tolerance of Crops & Plants Metabolism in Saline Substrate: An Annotated Bibliography. (C). 1989. text 135.00 (*0-89771-581-0*, Pub. by Intl Bk Distr) St Mut.

Maliyamkono, T. L. & Bagachwa, Mboya S. The Second Economy in Tanzania. LC 89-27398. 216p. 1990. lib. bdg. 29.95 (*0-8214-0949-2*) Ohio U Pr.

Maliyamkono, T. L., et al. Training & Productivity in Eastern Africa. (Eastern African Universities Research Project Ser.). 400p. (C). 1982. text 60.00 (*0-435-89582-6*, 89582) Heinemann.

Malizia, Emil E. & Feser, Edward J. Understanding Local Economic Development. LC 98-44999. 314p. (C). 1999. 24.95 (*0-88285-163-2*) Ctr Urban Pol Res.

Malizio, Andrew G., jt. auth. see Berkner, Lutz.

Maljkovic-Petkovic, Djero, ed. see Mraovitch, Sima.

Maljkovic-Petkovic, Djuro, ed. see Rajacic, Roy.

Maljugin, Vitaly, et al. The Revolutionary Guide to Assembly Language. 1000p. 1993. pap. 44.95 incl. disk (*1-874416-12-5*) Wrox Pr Inc.

Malka, Eli S. Jacob's Children in the Land of the Mahdi: Jews of the Sudan. LC 96-72628. (Illus.). 232p. 1997. text 34.95 (*0-8156-8122-4*) Syracuse U Pr.

Malka, Lucy. Fun with Hats. LC 95-17750. (Illus.). 8p. (J). (ps-1). 1995. pap. 2.95 (*1-57255-043-0*) Mondo Pubng.

Malka, Sol. Visions Revealed: A Review of the Visions Edition of Magic: The Gathering. LC 97-34122. 152p. 1997. pap. 12.95 (*1-55622-563-6*) Wordware Pub.

Malkan, Matthew A., jt. ed. see Zuckerman, Ben.

Malkani, K., tr. see Chauvet, Gilbert A.

***Malkani, Sheila V. & Walsh, Francis, eds.** The Insider's Guide to Law Firms. 5th ed. 650p. (Orig.). 1999. pap. 32.95 (*0-9637970-8-5*) Mobius Pr CO.

Malkani, Sheila V. & Walsh, Michael F., eds. The Insider's Guide to Law Firms. 3rd ed. 734p. (Orig.). 1997. pap. 32.95 (*0-9637970-6-9*) Mobius Pr CO.

— The Insider's Guide to Law Firms. 4th ed. 550p. (Orig.). 1998. pap. 32.95 (*0-9637970-7-7*) Mobius Pr CO.

Malkasian, C. A. The Big Cry Quandary. 1991. text. write for info. (*0-9631541-0-9*) W Dewey.

Malkasian, Mark. Gha-Ra-Bagh! The Emergence of the National Democratic Movement in Armenia. LC 96-20808. (Illus.). 250p. 1996. 34.95 (*0-8143-2604-8*) Wayne St U Pr.

— "Gha-Ra-Bagh!" The Emergence of the National Democratic Movement in Armenia. LC 96-20808. Date not set. 18.50 (*0-8143-2605-6*) Wayne St U Pr.

***Malkasian, Mark Charles.** Star-Crossed Voyager: The Teck Naums Chronicles. LC 99-91010. 1999. 25.00 (*0-7388-0560-2*); pap. 18.00 (*0-7388-0561-0*) Xlibris Corp.

Malkeiwicz, Kris. Cinematography. 214p. 1989. per. 22.00 (*0-671-76220-6*) S&S Trade.

Malkemes, Fred & Pires, Deborah S. Looking at English, Bk. 3. (Illus.). 288p. (C). 1983. pap. text 14.00 (*0-13-540435-5*) P-H.

Malkevich, M. S., jt. auth. see Feigelson, E. M.

Malkevitch, Joseph. Properties of Planar Graphs with Uniform Vertex & Face Structure. LC 52-42839. (Memoirs Ser.: No. 1/99). 116p. 1970. pap. 16.00 (*0-8218-1299-8*, MEMO/1/99) Am Math.

— Properties of Planar Graphs with Uniform Vertex & Face Structure. LC 52-42839. (American Mathematical Society Ser.: Vol. 99). (Illus.). 120p. reprint ed. pap. 37.20 (*0-608-09607-5*, 205276500007) Bks Demand.

Malkevitch, Joseph, ed. Geometry's Future. (Illus.). 122p. 1991. pap. 5.99 (*0-912843-21-7*) COMAP Inc.

Malkevitch, Joseph & Froelich, G. Loads of Codes. (Hi Map Ser.: No. 22). 208p. pap. text 11.99 (*0-614-05307-2*, HM 5622) COMAP Inc.

Malkevitch, Joseph, ed. see Guy, Richard K.

Malkevitch, Joseph, ed. see Meyer, Rochelle W. & Meyer, Walter J.

Malkiel, Burton Gordon. Random Walk. 6th ed. (Illus.). 528p. 1996. pap. 15.95 (*0-393-31529-0*) Norton.

***Malkiel, Burton Gordon.** A Random Walk down Wall Street. 7th rev. ed. (Illus.). 464p. 2000. pap. 16.95 (*0-393-32040-5*) Norton.

— A Random Walk down Wall Street: The Best Investment Advice for the New Century. 7th rev. ed. LC 98-50671. (Illus.). 416p. 1999. text 29.95 (*0-393-04781-4*) Norton.

Malkiel, Burton Gordon. The Term Structure of Interest Rates: Expectations & Behavior Patterns. LC 66-21836. (Illus.). 293p. reprint ed. pap. 90.90 (*0-608-30989-3*, 205194400015) Bks Demand.

Malkiel, Burton Gordon & Mei, J. P. Global Bargain Hunting: The Investor's Guide to Big Profits in Emerging Markets. LC 97-29744. 256p. 1998. 24.50 (*0-684-83518-5*) Free Pr.

— Global Bargain Hunting: The Investors Guide to Profits in Emerging Markets. (Illus.). 240p. 1999. pap. 14.00 (*0-684-84808-2*, Touchstone) S&S Trade Pap.

Malkiel, Burton Gordon, jt. auth. see Cragg, John G.

Malkiel, Burton Gordon, jt. auth. see Evans, Richard E.

Malkiel, Theresa S. Diary of a Shirtwaist Striker. (Literature of American Labor Ser.). 224p. 1990. pap. text 13.95 (*0-87546-168-9*, ILR Press) Cornell U Pr.

Malkiel, Yakov. Diachronic Problems in Phonosymbolism: Edita & Inedita, 1979-1988, Vol. 1. LC 89-17827. vii, 274p. 1990. 89.00 (*90-272-2066-2*) J Benjamins Pubng Co.

— Diachronic Studies in Lexicology, Affixation, & Phonology Vol. II: Edita & Inedita, 1979-1988. LC 91-48116. vi, 312p. 1992. 83.00 (*90-272-2072-7*) J Benjamins Pubng Co.

— From Particular to General Linguistics: Selected Essays 1965-1978. (Studies in Language Companion Ser.: No. 3). xxii, 659p. 1983. 127.00 (*90-272-3002-1*) J Benjamins Pubng Co.

— Linguistics & Philology in Spanish America: A Survey (1925-1970) (Janua Linguarum, Ser. Minor: No. 97). 179p. (Orig.). 1972. pap. text 36.95 (*90-279-2313-2*) Mouton.

— Patterns of Derivational Affixation in the Cabraniego Dialect of East-Central Asturian. LC 70-627777. (U. C. Publ. in Linguistics Ser.: Vol. 64). 203p. reprint ed. 63.00 (*0-8357-9637-X*, 201510300092) Bks Demand.

— Theory & Practice of Romance Etymology: Studies in Language, Culture & History. (Collected Studies: No. CS288). 348p. (C). 1989. lib. bdg. 119.95 (*0-86078-236-0*, Pub. by Variorum) Ashgate Pub Co.

Malkiel, Yakov, jt. ed. see Lehmann, Winfred P.

Malkiewicz, Kris. Film Lighting. 208p. 1986. pap. 20.00 (*0-671-76634-1*, Fireside) S&S Trade Pap.

Malkin, A. Y. Photophysical & Photochemical Properties: Aromatic Compounds. 448p. 1992. lib. bdg. 245.00 (*0-8493-6802-2*) CRC Pr.

Malkin, Benjamin H. A Father's Memoirs of His Child, 1806. LC 97-6476. (Revolution & Romanticism, 1789-1834 Ser.). (Illus.). 230p. 1997. 85.00 (*1-85477-210-4*) Continuum.

Malkin, Carole. The Journeys of David Toback: As Retold by His Granddaughter. large type ed. 288p. 1992. pap. 15.95 (*0-8027-2665-8*) Walker & Co.

Malkin, David. Cancer: Inherited Tumors. 1997. pap. text 39.00 (*3-540-19975-6*) Spr-Verlag.

Malkin, Harold M. Out of the Mist: The Foundation of Modern Pathology & Medicine During the Nineteenth Century. (Illus.). 422p. 1993. pap. text 35.00 (*0-9637689-1-3*) Vesalius Bks.

— Out of the Mist: The Foundation of Modern Pathology & Medicine During the Nineteenth Century. (Illus.). 422p. 1995. reprint ed. 80.00 (*0-9637689-0-5*) Vesalius Bks.

Malkin, Irad. Myth & Territory in the Spartan Mediterranean. LC 93-30357. (Illus.). 296p. (C). 1994. text 74.95 (*0-521-41183-1*) Cambridge U Pr.

Malkin, Irad, ed. La France et la Mediterranee: Vingt-Sept Siecles d'Interdependance. LC 89-7177. (FRE.). x, 423p. 1990. 142.00 (*90-04-08930-6*) Brill Academic Pubs.

Malkin, Jain. Hospital Interior Architecture: Creating Healing Environments for Special Patient Populations. 478p. 1992. 190.00 (*0-471-28976-0*, VNR) Wiley.

Malkin, Jain. Medical & Dental Space Planning for the 1990s. 2nd ed. 512p. 1989. 125.00 (*0-471-28944-2*, VNR) Wiley.

— Medical & Dental Space Planning for the 1990s. 2nd ed. (Illus.). 144p. 1989. text 92.95 (*0-442-26485-2*, VNR) Wiley.

M

An Asterisk (*) at the beginning of an entry indicates that the title is appearing for the first time.

Malkin, Jeanette. Verbal Violence in Contemporary Drama: From Handke to Shepard. 255p. (C). 1992. text 69.95 (*0-521-38335-8*) Cambridge U Pr.

Malkin, Jeanette R. Memory - Theater & Postmodern Drama. LC 99-6220. (Theater: Theory - Text - Performance Ser.). 272p. 1999. text 49.50 (*0-472-11037-3*, 11037) U of Mich Pr.

Malkin, John. Sir Alexander Fleming: Man of Penicillin. 92p. 1985. 40.00 (*0-907526-06-3*, Pub. by Alloway Pub) St Mut.

Malkin, Marjorie & Howe, Christine Z., eds. Research in Therapeutic Recreation: Concepts & Methods. LC 92-63340. 354p. (C). 1993. boxed set 31.95 (*0-910251-53-3*) Venture Pub PA.

Malkin, Marsha, jt. auth. see Anschell, Helen.

Malkin, Martin, ed. see Anschell, Helen & Malkin, Marsha.

Malkin, Mort. Aerobic Walking, the Weight-Loss Exercise: A Complete Program to Reduce Weight, Stress & Hypertension. LC 94-40817. 240p. 1995. pap. 15.95 (*0-471-55672-6*) Wiley.

Malkin, Peter Z. & Stein, Harry. Eichmann in My Hands. 1990. 22.95 (*0-446-51418-7*) Warner Bks.

Malkin, R., jt. ed. see Barber, J.

Malkin, Stephen. Grinding Technology: Theory & Applications of Machining with Abrasives. 1989. text 59.95 (*0-470-21325-6*) P-H.

— Grinding Technology: Theory & Applications of Machining with Abrasives. LC 89-11182. (Illus.). 275p. 1996. 104.00 (*0-87263-480-9*, 2521) SME.

***Malkin, Stephen.** Jewish Mother's Guide to Worrying. 142p. 1999. 15.00 (*0-942540-20-4*) Breakthru Pub.

***Malkin, Stuart.** Fifty Years at the Craps Tables. 96p. 2000. pap. 11.95 (*0-9678178-0-3*) Desert Mktg.

Malkina-Pykh, I. G., jt. ed. see Pykh, Yuri A.

***Malkind, Samuel.** Opportunities in Options. (Illus.). 40p. 2000. 10.00 (*0-8059-4844-9*) Dorrance.

Malkind, Samuel. Option Strategies for Beginners. (Illus.). 32p. 1997. 10.00 (*0-8059-4186-X*) Dorrance.

Malkind, Samuel N. Back to the Futures! LC 96-90793. (Illus.). 49p. 1997. 13.95 (*0-533-12181-7*) Vantage.

— Commodities for Kids of All Ages. 1993. 10.95 (*0-533-10334-7*) Vantage.

— Options Are Easy to Understand. 1995. 11.95 (*0-533-11500-0*) Vantage.

Malkinson, Ruth, et al, eds. Traumatic & Nontraumatic Loss & Bereavement: Clinical Theory & Practice. 275p. 2000. 55.00 (*1-887841-30-X*, 66627, Psychosocial) Intl Univs Pr.

Malkki, Liisa H. Purity & Exile: Violence, Memory, & National Cosmology Among Hutu Refugees in Tanzania. LC 94-37099. 374p. 1995. pap. text 21.50 (*0-226-50272-4*) U Ch Pr.

— Purity & Exile: Violence, Memory, & National Cosmology Among Hutu Refugees in Tanzania. LC 94-37099. 374p. 1995. lib. bdg. 60.00 (*0-226-50271-6*) U Ch Pr.

Malkmus, George H. God's Way to Ultimate Health: A Common Sense Guide for the Elimination of Sickness Through Nutrition. 3rd large type ed. LC 94-96534. (Illus.). 282p. 1995. pap. 18.95 (*0-929619-02-1*, 202) Hallelujah Acres.

— Why Christians Get Sick. 154p. (Orig.). 1995. pap. 9.99 (*1-56043-849-5*, Treasure Hse) Destiny Image.

Malkmus, Rhonda J. Recipes for Life . . . From God's Garden. LC 97-95318. (Illus.). 344p. lib. bdg. 24.95 (*0-929619-03-X*) Hallelujah Acres.

Malko, J. Robert, jt. auth. see Faruqui, Ahmad.

Malko, J. Robert, jt. ed. see Enholm, Gregory B.

Malkoc, Anna M. Easy Plays in English. rev. ed. LC 93-16407. 112p. (C). 1993. pap. text 15.13 (*0-13-061698-2*) P-H.

Malkoff, Karl. Muriel Spark. LC 68-54456. (Columbia Essays on Modern Writers Ser.: No. 36). 48p. (Orig.). 1968. pap. text 12.00 (*0-231-03063-0*) Col U Pr.

Malkoff, Michael. The Every Day Gourmet: Quick & Healthy Recipes from Around the World. LC 98-41646. 192p. 1998. pap. 16.00 (*0-89281-785-2*, Heal Arts VT) Inner Tradit.

Malkoskie, Mariana, ed. see Murphy, Lee.

***Malkovsky, Bradley J., ed.** New Perspectives on Advaita Vedanta: Essays in Commemoration of Professor Richard De Smet, S. J. 184p. 2000. 73.00 (*90-04-11666-4*) Brill Academic Pubs.

Malks, Josh. How to Maintain & Enjoy Your Collector Car. LC 95-38151. (Illus.). 160p. 1995. pap. 19.95 (*0-7603-0056-9*) MBI Pubg.

Malks, Josh B. Cord 810-812: The Timeless Classic. LC 95-77313. (Illus.). 272p. 1995. 34.95 (*0-87341-396-2*, CORD) Krause Pubns.

Malks, Josh B., jt. auth. see Beck, Lee.

Mall, C. J. From Shelley to the Absurd: Collected Essays. LC 96-28640. 128p. 1996. text 69.95 (*0-7734-4226-X*) E Mellen.

Mall, David. In Good Conscience: Abortion & Moral Necessity. LC 82-9918. xii, 212p. 1982. 20.00 (*0-9608410-1-6*); pap. 10.00 (*0-9608410-0-8*) Kairos Bks.

Mall, David, ed. When Life & Choice Collide: Essays on Rhetoric & Abortion To Set the Dawn Free, Vol. 1. LC 93-20573. (Words in Conflict Ser.). (Illus.). 368p. 1994. 30.00 (*0-9608410-3-2*); pap. 15.00 (*0-9608410-2-4*) Kairos Bks.

Mall, David & Watts, Walter F., eds. Psychological Aspects of Abortion. LC 79-88679. 156p. 1979. pap. 19.95 (*0-313-27053-8*, P7053, Greenwood Pr) Greenwood.

Mall, David, jt. ed. see Horan, Dennis J.

Mall, E. Jane. How to Become Wealthy Publishing a Newsletter. 9th ed. 110p. 1998. pap. 17.50 (*1-56150-216-2*) Intl Wealth.

— How to Become Wealthy Publishing a Newsletter. 10th ed. 110p. 1999. pap. 17.50 (*1-56150-267-7*) Intl Wealth.

***Mall, E. Jane.** How to Become Wealthy Publishing a Newsletter. 11th ed. 110p. 2000. pap. 17.50 (*1-56150-327-4*) Intl Wealth.

Mall, E. Jane. Kitty, My Rib. LC 59-10977. 173p. 1970. reprint ed. pap. 8.99 (*0-570-03113-3*, 12-2347) Concordia.

Mall, E. Jane, jt. auth. see Powers, Betty.

Mall-Haefeli, Marianne, ed. Hormonale Kontrazeption: Eine Standortbestimmung. (Illus.). viii, 148p. 1983. 51.50 (*3-8055-3767-0*) S Karger.

Mall, Julian. Poetics. 74p. pap. write for info. (*3-7052-0939-6*, Pub. by Poetry Salzburg) Intl Spec Bk.

Mall, Laurence. Origines & Retraites dans La Nouvelle Heloise. LC 96-22117. (Eighteenth-Century French Intellectual History Ser.: No. 5). (FRE.). 211p. (C). 1997. text 45.95 (*0-8204-3349-7*) P Lang Pubng.

Mall, R. A. Experience & Reason: The Phenomenology of Husserl & Its Relation to Hume's Philosophy. 163p. 1973. pap. text 78.00 (*90-247-1494-X*) Kluwer Academic.

***Mall, Ram A.** Intercultural Philosophy. LC 99-37921. 160p. 1999. pap. 16.95 (*0-8476-9279-5*); text 62.00 (*0-8476-9278-7*) Rowman.

Mall, S., jt. ed. see Nagar, A.

Mall, Shankar & Nicholas, Theodore, eds. Titanium Matrix Composites: Mechanical Behavior. LC 97-61635. 480p. 1997. 169.95 (*1-56676-567-6*) Technomic.

***Malla.** Trees in Indian Art Mythology & Folklore. 2000. 88.00 (*81-7305-179-8*, Pub. by Aryan Bks Intl) S Asia.

Malla, Bansi L. Vaisnava Art & Iconography of Kashmir. (C). 1996. 38.00 (*81-7017-305-1*, Pub. by Abhinav) S Asia.

Malla, Bansilal. Sculptures of Kashmir. 1990. 73.00 (*0-8364-2521-9*, Pub. by Agam Kala Prakashan) S Asia.

Malla, Jean. Trout with Flair & Taste. (Illus.). 44p. 1997. pap. 8.95 (*0-9587143-3-9*) F Amato Pubns.

Malla, Kamal P. English in Nepalese Education. 1977. 35.00 (*0-7855-0272-6*, Pub. by Ratna Pustak Bhandar) St Mut.

— English in Nepalese Education. (C). 1977. 35.00 (*0-89771-074-6*, Pub. by Ratna Pustak Bhandar) St Mut.

Malla, Ramesh B., ed. Dynamic Response & Progressive Failure of Special Structures: Proceedings of the Technical Sessions on Response of Truss & Truss-Type Structures During Progressive Failure & Dynamic Loading & Analysis of Structures. LC 93-40323. 164p. 1993. 22.00 (*0-87262-946-5*) Am Soc Civil Eng.

Malla, Samal B., jt. ed. see Ohba, Hideaki.

Malla, Sarah B., jt. auth. see Ohba, Hideaki.

Mallabarman, Adwaita. A River Called Titash. Bardhan, Kalpana, tr. & afterword by by. LC 92-46698. 1993. pap. 16.95 (*0-520-08050-5*, Pub. by U CA Pr) Cal Prin Full Svc.

Mallaby, Sebastian. After Apartheid: The Future of South Africa. LC 91-50190. (Illus.). 275p. 1992. 22.00 (*0-8129-1938-6*, Times Bks) Crown Pub Group.

Mallac, Guy De, see De Mallac, Guy.

Mallach, Alan. Inclusionary Housing Programs: Policies & Practices. LC 84-7055. 288p. 1984. text 24.95 (*0-88285-100-4*) Transaction Pubs.

Mallach, Efrem G. Decision Support & Data Warehouse Systems. LC 99-54014. write for info. (*0-07-289981-6*) McGrw-H Hghr Educ.

Mallach, Efrem G. Parallel Supercomputing in SIMD Architectures. 404p. (C). 1990. text 51.50 (*0-07-413090-0*, Irwn McGrw-H) McGrw-H Hghr Educ.

Mallach, Efrem G., ed. see Sondak, Norman E.

Mallach, Stanley, jt. auth. see Curtis, Verna P.

Mallada, Victor F., tr. see Pineda y Ramirez, Antonio de.

Mallakh, Dorothea E., ed. Energy Watchers No. 2: Phoenix Like OPEC: Changing Structures, Markets, & Future Stability & the Oil-Gas Relationship. LC 90-81130. (Illus.). 189p. 1991. 24.00 (*0-918714-26-5*) Intl Res Ctr Energy.

— Energy Watchers Five: Energy & Development Revisited: Twenty Years & Beyond & the United States & North America: International Implications for Supply & Demand. (Illus.). 189p. 1994. pap. 24.00 (*0-918714-40-0*) Intl Res Ctr Energy.

Mallakh, Ragaei E. The Middle East, Pacific Basin, & the United States: Refining & Petrochemicals. LC 86-81024. (Illus.). 180p. 1986. pap. 36.00 (*0-918714-10-9*) Intl Res Ctr Energy.

— Qatar: Energy & Development. LC 84-29317. (Illus.). 184p. 1985. 21.00 (*0-7099-0955-1*, Pub. by C Helm) Routldge.

— U. S. & World Energy Resources: Prospects & Priorities. LC 77-88785. (Illus.). 1977. 12.50 (*0-918714-03-6*) Intl Res Ctr Energy.

Mallakh, Ragaei E., et al. Implications of Regional Development in the Middle East for U. S. Trade, Capital Flows, & Balance of Payments. LC 77-73035. 1977. pap. 5.00 (*0-918714-01-X*) Intl Res Ctr Energy.

Mallalieu, H. L. The Dictionary of British Watercolour Artists up to 1920, Vol. 3. (Illus.). 288p. 1991. 69.50 (*1-85149-111-2*) Antique Collect.

— The Dictionary of British Watercolour Artists up to 1920 Vol. II: The Plates. (Illus.). 284p. 1979. 69.50 (*0-902028-63-4*) Antique Collect.

— Understanding Watercolours. (Understanding Ser.). (Illus.). 224p. 1985. 49.50 (*0-907462-39-1*) Antique Collect.

Mallalieu, Huon. Illustrated History of Antiques The Essential Reference for All Antique Lovers & Collectors. 1999. 24.98 (*0-7624-0647-X*) Running Pr.

Mallalieu, J. P. W. Very Ordinary Seaman. 253p. 1984. pap. 7.00 (*0-583-12808-4*) Academy Chi Pubs.

Mallalieu, Jonathan. The Prince of Wales & Stories. 272p. 1993. pap. (*1-897580-11-8*) Phoenix Hse.

Mallalieu, Robin, jt. auth. see Brady, Angela.

Mallam, R. Clark. Indian Creek Memories: A Sense of Place. LC 87-60995. (Illus.). 200p. (Orig.). 1987. 13.00 (*0-9618412-1-4*); pap. 6.00 (*0-9618412-0-6*) Prairie Song Pr.

Mallam, R. Clark, jt. auth. see Alex, Lynn M.

Mallamace, F. & Stanley, H. E., eds. The Physics of Complex Systems. LC 97-75045. (International School of Physics Enrico Fermi Ser.: Vol. 134). 750p. Date not set. 145.00 (*90-5199-351-X*, 351-X) IOS Press.

Mallamace, F., jt. ed. see Corti, M.

Mallampally, Padma, jt. ed. see Sauvant, Karl P.

Mallan, Chicki. Moon Handbooks: Cancun: Mexico's Caribbean Coast. 5th rev. ed. (Illus.). 240p. 1998. pap. 14.95 (*1-56691-121-4*, Moon Handbks) Avalon Travel.

— Moon Handbooks: Yucatan Peninsula: Including Yucatan, Campeche, Chiapas, Tabasco, Quintana Roo. 6th rev. ed. LC 98-657779. Vol. 6. (Illus.). 400p. 1998. pap. 16.95 (*1-56691-122-2*, Moon Handbks) Avalon Travel.

Mallan, Chicki & Lange, Patti. Moon Handbooks: Belize. 4th rev. ed. (Illus.). 360p. 1998. pap. 15.95 (*1-56691-137-0*, Moon Handbks) Avalon Travel.

Mallan, Chicki & Mallan, Oz. Moon Handbooks: Colonial Mexico: A Traveler's Guide to Distinctive Lodging, Dining & Shopping in Historic Districts & Artisans' Communities Throughout Mexico. (Illus.). 400p. 1998. pap. 18.95 (*1-56691-109-5*, Moon Handbks) Avalon Travel.

Mallan, Chicki, jt. auth. see Cummings, Joe.

Mallan, John T., jt. auth. see Welton, David A.

Mallan, Kerry. Children as Storytellers LC 93-218308. 88 p. 1991. write for info. (*0-909955-97-2*) Primary English.

Mallan, Kerry. Children as Storytellers. LC 92-20527. 87p. (C). 1992. pap. text 16.00 (*0-435-08779-7*, 08779) Heinemann.

Mallan, Oz, jt. auth. see Mallan, Chicki.

Mallan, Sandra. Caring in Emergencies. (Skills for Caring Ser.). (Illus.). 48p. (Orig.). 1992. pap. text 9.95 (*0-443-04622-0*) Church.

Mallander, J. O., jt. auth. see Sangharakshita.

Mallard, Ann. Bear. 1998. 10.99 (*0-7858-0829-9*) Bk Sales Inc.

— Century of Style & Fashion: 1900-1999, 1. 1999. 24.95 (*1-885440-53-7*) First Glance.

Mallard, Catherine O., jt. auth. see Barnum, Barbara S.

Mallard, Colin D. Mr. President: A Spiritual Journey. rev. ed. LC 95-90227. 336p. (Orig.). 1996. pap. 16.95 (*0-9646040-5-1*) Wild Duck Pubng.

Mallard, Colin D., ed. Like a Large Immovable Rock: A Festschrift. LC 95-90814. 204p. (Orig.). 1996. pap. 15.00 (*0-9646040-1-9*) Wild Duck Pubng.

Mallard, Paula M. Don't Step on the Diaper. 122p. (YA). (gr. 8-12). 1999. per. 12.00 (*1-886623-04-X*) Canal Side Pubs.

Mallard, Philip, et al, eds. The Naturalists Directory & Almanac (International) 48th ed. (Naturalist Directory & Almanac Ser.). (Illus.). 500p. Date not set. pap. 32.50 (*1-889130-01-X*) Naturalists Dir.

Mallard, Robert Q. Montevideo-Maybank: Some Memoirs of a Southern Christian. 1977. text 21.95 (*0-8369-9230-X*, 9084) Ayer.

Mallard, S. New Wine: A Commentary on Religion & the Bible. LC 94-72833. 232p. 1995. pap. 24.95 (*0-9643891-9-3*) AMI Bk Bldrs.

Mallard, William. Language & Love: Introduction to Augustine's Religious Thought Through the Confessions Story. LC 93-9070. 1994. 40.00 (*0-271-01037-1*); pap. 17.95 (*0-271-01038-X*) Pa St U Pr.

Mallarme, Stephane. Collected Poems of Stephane Mallarme. Weinfield, Henry, tr. & comment by. LC 94-26794. 1994. 45.00 (*0-520-08188-9*, Pub. by U CA Pr) Cal Prin Full Svc.

— Collected Poems of Stephane Mallarme. Weinfield, Henry, tr. & comment by. 300p. 1996. pap. 22.50 (*0-520-20711-4*, Pub. by U CA Pr) Cal Prin Full Svc.

— Correspondance, 3 tomes. Mondor, ed. Incl. Tome III. 1886-1889. 19.95 (*0-7859-0024-1*, F67222); Vol. I. 1862-1871. (FRE.). 15.95 (*0-7859-0022-5*, F67220); Vol. II. 1871-1885. (FRE.). 15.95 (*0-7859-0023-3*, F67221); (FRE.). write for info. (*0-318-51969-0*) Fr & Eur.

— Correspondence, 1890-1891, Vol. 4. (FRE.). 1973. pap. 65.00 (*0-7859-3969-5*) Fr & Eur.

— Correspondence, 1893-1894, Vol. 6. (FRE.). 1981. pap. 55.00 (*0-7859-3959-8*) Fr & Eur.

— Correspondence, 1894-1895, Vol. 7. (FRE.). 1982. pap. 75.00 (*0-7859-3965-2*) Fr & Eur.

— Correspondence, 1896, Vol. 8. (FRE.). 1983. pap. 65.00 (*0-685-68103-3*) Fr & Eur.

— Correspondence, 1897, Vol. 9. (FRE.). 1983. pap. 75.00 (*0-7859-3966-0*) Fr & Eur.

— Herodias. Mills, Clark, tr. LC 77-10277. reprint ed. 27.50 (*0-404-16329-7*) AMS Pr.

— Igitur, Divagations, Un Coup de Des. (Poesie Ser.). (FRE.). 443p. (Orig.). 1976. pap. 13.95 (*2-07-032157-6*) Schoenhof.

— Igitur, Divagations, un Coup de Des. (FRE.). 1976. pap. 10.95 (*0-8288-3864-X*, M2440) Fr & Eur.

***Mallarme, Stephane.** Mallarme in Prose. Caws, Mary Ann, ed. & tr. by. from FRE. Anderson, Jill, et al, trs. from FRE. 2001. pap. 14.95 (*0-8112-1451-6*, Pub. by New Directions) Norton.

Mallarme, Stephane. The Meaning of Mllarme: A Bilingual Edition of His Poesie & Un Coup de Des. 256p. 1990. pap. 30.00 (*1-898218-29-3*) St Mut.

— Oeuvres Completes. deluxe ed. Mondor & Jean-Aubry, Georges, eds. (Pleiade Ser.). (FRE.). 1945. 77.95 (*2-07-010326-9*) Schoenhof.

— Poems. Fry, Roger, tr. from ENG. LC 77-10279. 320p. reprint ed. 32.00 (*0-404-16330-0*) AMS Pr.

— Poesies. unabridged ed. (FRE.). pap. 5.95 (*2-87714-162-4*, Pub. by Bookking Intl) Distribks Inc.

— Poesies: Poesies Choix de Vers de Circonstance. (FRE.). 1966. pap. 10.95 (*0-8288-3865-8*, F67270) Fr & Eur.

— Poesies: (Poesies Choix de vers de Circonstance; Poemes d'Enfance et de Jeunesse) (Poesie Ser.). (FRE.). pap. 11.95 (*2-07-032716-7*) Schoenhof.

— Selected Letters of Stephane Mallarme. Lloyd, Rosemary, ed. & tr. by. 262p. 1988. 33.00 (*0-226-48841-1*) U Ch Pr.

— Selected Poems. MacIntyre, C. F., tr. (C). 1957. pap. 12.95 (*0-520-00801-4*, Pub. by U CA Pr) Cal Prin Full Svc.

— Selected Poetry & Prose. Caws, Mary A., ed. & intro. by. LC 81-18899. 128p. 1982. pap. 10.95 (*0-8112-0823-0*, NDP529, Pub. by New Directions) Norton.

— To Purify the Words of the Tribe: The Major Verse Poems of Stephane Mallarme. Aldan, Daisy, tr. from FRE. & reader by. LC 98-61790. 207p. 1999. pap. 19.95 incl. audio (*0-9652364-3-9*) Sky Blue Pr.

— Villiers de l'Isle Adam. Raitt, Jill, ed. (Exeter French Texts Ser.: No. 78). (FRE.). 84p. Date not set. pap. text 19.95 (*0-85989-360-X*, Pub. by Univ Exeter Pr) Northwestern U Pr.

***Mallarme, Stephane & Hirschman, Jack.** To Marry the Notion.Tr. of Epouser la Notion. 40p. 2000. pap. 4.95 (*0-9647373-8-8*) Marimbo Commun.

Mallarme, Stephane, et al. Le Tombeau de Charles Baudelaire. LC 77-11490. reprint ed. 64.50 (*0-404-16350-5*) AMS Pr.

Mallarme, Stephane, jt. auth. see Baudelaire, Charles.

Mallarme, Stephane, jt. auth. see Woolley, Grange.

Mallarme, Stephane, tr. see Poe, Edgar Allan.

Mallary, R. DeWitt. Lenox (Mass.) & the Berkshire Highlands. (Illus.). 363p. 1995. reprint ed. lib. bdg. 42.50 (*0-8328-4465-9*) Higginson Bk Co.

Mallasz, Gitta, tr. Talking with Angels. LC 81-40465. 443p. 1995. pap. 17.95 (*3-85630-505-X*, Pub. by Daimon Pubs) Cassell & Continuum.

Mallat, Chibli. Middle East into the Twenty-First Century: Studies on the Arab-Israeli Conflict, the Gulf Crisis. 1998. pap. text 19.95 (*0-86372-224-5*, Pub. by Garnet-Ithaca) LPC InBook.

Mallat, Chibli, ed. Islam & Public Law. (Arab & Islamic Laws Ser.). (C). 1993. lib. bdg. 107.50 (*1-85333-768-4*) Kluwer Academic.

Mallat, Chibli, jt. ed. see Allan, J. A.

Mallat, Chibli, jt. ed. see Cotran, Eugene.

***Mallat, Kathy.** Brave Bear. LC 98-53873. (Illus.). 24p. (J). 1999. 14.95 (*0-8027-8704-5*) Walker & Co.

— Brave Bear. LC 98-53873. (Illus.). 24p. (J). (ps-k). 1999. lib. bdg. 15.85 (*0-8027-8705-3*) Walker & Co.

Mallat, Kathy. Seven Stars More! LC 98-6497. (Illus.). 24p. (J). (ps-1). 1998. 14.95 (*0-8027-8675-8*); lib. bdg. 15.85 (*0-8027-8676-6*) Walker & Co.

Mallat, Kathy, jt. auth. see McMillan, Bruce.

***Mallatt, Johnny.** Coaching Football's Wing-Bone Offense. (Illus.). 120p. 1999. pap. 22.95 (*1-57167-369-5*) Coaches Choice.

Mallatt, Jon, jt. auth. see Marieb, Elaine N.

***Malle, Gunter & Matzat, B. Heinrich.** Inverse Galois Theory. LC 99-41790. (Monographs in Mathematics). (Illus.). xvi, 436p. 1999. 59.95 (*3-540-62890-8*) Spr-Verlag.

Malle, Louis. Au Revoir les Enfants. Hollo, Anselm, tr. LC 87-34656. (FRE., Illus.). 96p. 1988. pap. 9.95 (*0-8021-3114-X*, Grove) Grove-Atltic.

— Au Revoir les Enfants. (Gallimard Ser.). (FRE.). 132p. 1987. pap. 27.95 (*2-07-071187-0*) Schoenhof.

Mallea, Eduardo. Las Aguilas. (SPA.). 12.95 (*0-7859-0128-0*, S2130) Fr & Eur.

— History of an Argentine Passion. Miller, Yvette E., ed. Lichtblau, Myron I., tr. from SPA. & anno. by. LC 82-20816. (Explorations Ser.). 184p. 1983. pap. 13.95 (*0-935480-10-2*) Lat Am Lit Rev Pr.

Mallea, John R. Schooling in a Plural Canada. 120p. 1989. 69.00 (*1-85359-030-4*, Pub. by Multilingual Matters); pap. 24.95 (*1-85359-029-0*, Pub. by Multilingual Matters) Taylor & Francis.

Mallea, John R. & Shea, Edward C. Multiculturalism & Education: A Select Bibliography. LC 80-481969. (Ontario Institute for Studies in Education, Symposium Ser.: No. 9). 300p. reprint ed. pap. 93.00 (*0-608-17710-5*, 203010300067) Bks Demand.

***Mallea-Olaetxe, J.** Speaking Through the Aspens: Basque Tree Carvings in Nevada & California. LC 00-8553. (Basque Ser.). 248p. 2000. 39.95 (*0-87417-358-2*) U of Nev Pr.

***Mallek, Henry.** The New Logevity Dier. 224p. 2001. 23.95 (*0-399-14628-8*) Putnam Pub Group.

Mallek, Henry. Women's Advantage Diet. 1990. mass mkt. 4.95 (*0-671-67676-8*) PB.

Mallemont, A., jt. auth. see Campbell, Mark.

Mallen, Ronald E. & Smith, Jeffrey M. Legal Malpractice, Vol. 1. 4th ed. LC 95-5502. 700p. (C). 1995. text. write for info. (*0-314-05492-8*) West Pub.

— Legal Malpractice, Vol. 2. 4th ed. LC 95-5502. 700p. (C). 1995. text. write for info. (*0-314-05493-6*) West Pub.

— Legal Malpractice, Vol. 3. 4th ed. LC 95-5502. 700p. (C). 1995. text. write for info. (*0-314-05494-4*) West Pub.

Mallen, Ronald E., jt. auth. see Smith, Jeffrey M.

Mallen, Terry. Taking Charge of Your Child's Education: Nine Steps to Becoming a Learning Ally. LC 94-72481. (Illus.). 200p. (Orig.). 1995. pap. 14.95 (*0-9642369-9-0*) Acumen Pr.

M

An Asterisk (*) at the beginning of an entry indicates that the title is appearing for the first time.

Mallender, Paul & Rayson, Jane. How to Make Applications in the Family Proceedings Court. (C). 1992. pap. 38.00 (*1-85431-201-4*, Pub. by Blackstone Pr) Gaunt.

Maller, Dick & Feinman, Jeffrey. Twenty-One Days to a Trained Dog. 144p. 1979. per. 9.00 (*0-671-25193-7*, Fireside) S&S Trade Pap.

Maller, J. The Therapeutic Community with Chronic Mental Patients. (Bibliotheca Psychiatrica Ser.: No. 146). 1971. pap. 38.50 (*3-8055-1157-4*) S Karger.

Maller, Julius B. Cooperation & Competition: An Experimental Study in Motivation. LC 74-177049. (Columbia University. Teachers College. Contributions to Education Ser.: No. 384). reprint ed. 37.50 (*0-404-55384-2*) AMS Pr.

Maller, R. A. Survival Analysis with Long-Term Survivors. LC 96-26979. (Wiley Probability & Mathematics Ser.). 304p. 1996. 110.00 (*0-471-96201-5*) Wiley.

Maller, R. A., jt. auth. see Pakes, Anthony G.

Malleret, Thierry. Conversion of the Defense Industry in the Former Soviet Union. LC 92-11692. (Occasional Papers: Vol. 23). 1992. 12.85 (*0-913449-30-X*) Inst EW Stud.

Mallerich, Dallas J., III. Greenberg's American Toy Trains. (Illus.). 288p. (Orig.). 1990. pap. 17.95 (*0-89778-171-6*, 10-7385, Greenberg Books) Kalmbach.

Mallernee, Nora, tr. see Hood, Christine.

Mallernee, Nora, tr. see Jordano, Kimberly.

Mallernee, Nora, tr. see Nunn, Tamara.

Mallernee, Nora, tr. see Williams, Rozanne L.

Malleron, J. L., et al. Handbook of Paaladium Catalysed Organic Reactions. (Illus.). 320p. 1997. boxed set 75.00 (*0-12-466615-9*) Morgan Kaufmann.

Mallery. Integrated Curriculum. LC 99-18205. 184p. 1999. pap. text 29.33 (*0-205-28671-2*) Allyn.

Mallery, Dick. Dick E. Bird's Birdfeeding 101. LC 96-54742. 208p. 1997. pap. 12.95 (*0-385-48700-2*, Main St Bks) Doubleday.

Mallery, G., et al. The Sioux Indians: A Socio-Ethnological History. (Illus.). 1897. 24.50 (*0-914074-06-7*, J M C & Co) Amereon Ltd.

***Mallery, Garrick.** Israelite & Indain: A Parallel in Planes of Culture. (LC History-America-E). 47p. 1999. reprint ed. lib. bdg. 69.00 (*0-7812-4264-9*) Rprt Serv.

Mallery, Garrick. Picture-Writing of the American Indians. 1972. 79.95 (*0-8490-0836-0*) Gordon Pr.

— Picture-Writing of the American Indians, 2 vols., 1. (Illus.). 822p. 1972. reprint ed. pap. 14.95 (*0-486-22842-8*) Dover.

— Picture-Writing of the American Indians, 2 vols., 2. (Illus.). 822p. 1972. reprint ed. pap. 12.95 (*0-486-22843-6*) Dover.

***Mallery, Joyce.** Funtastic Math! Multiplication & Division: Great Skill-Building Activities, Games & Reproductions. (Illus.). (J). 1998. mass mkt. 9.95 (*0-590-37366-8*) Scholastic Inc.

Mallery, Otto T. Economic Union & Durable Peace. LC 76-142663. (Essay Index Reprint Ser.). 1977. reprint ed. 18.95 (*0-8369-2778-8*) Ayer.

Mallery, Paul. Bridge & Trestle Handbook. (Illus.). 160p. 1992. pap. 18.95 (*0-911868-79-8*, C79) Carstens Pubns.

— Electrical Handbook for Model Railroads. 3rd rev. ed. (Illus.). 68p. 1998. pap. 10.95 (*0-911868-92-5*) Carstens Pubns.

— Electrical Handbook for Model Railroads Vol. 2: Advanced. 4th rev. ed. (Illus.). 1997. pap. 14.95 (*0-911868-89-5*) Carstens Pubns.

— Operation Handbook for Model Railroads. (Illus.). 200p. 1991. pap. 12.95 (*0-911868-74-7*, C74) Carstens Pubns.

— Trackwork for Model Railroaders. (Hobby Bks.: No. C86). (Illus.). 116p. 1997. 13.95 (*0-911868-90-9*, C86) Carstens Pubns.

Mallery, Paul, jt. auth. see George, Darren.

Mallery, Richard D., ed. Masterworks of Autobiography. LC 70-111848. (Essay Index Reprint Ser.). 1977. 40.95 (*0-8369-1760-X*) Ayer.

— Masterworks of Travel & Exploration. LC 73-111849. (Essay Index Reprint Ser.). 1977. 34.95 (*0-8369-1761-8*) Ayer.

***Mallery, Richard E.** Nuts about Squirrels: A Guide to Coexisting with - And Even Appreciating - Your Bushy-Tailed Friends. LC 99-86730. 192p. 2000. pap. 11.95 (*0-446-67576-8*) Warner Bks.

Mallery, Susan. The Best Bride. (Special Edition Ser.). 1995. per. 3.50 (*0-373-09933-9*, 1-09933-2) Silhouette.

— The Best Bride. large type ed. (Silhouette Romance Ser.). 1996. lib. bdg. 19.95 (*0-373-59739-8*) Mac Lib Ref.

— Beth & the Bachelor. (Special Edition Ser.: No. 1263). 1999. per. 4.25 (*0-373-24263-8*, 1-24263-5) Silhouette.

— The Bodyguard & Ms. Jones. 1996. per. 3.75 (*0-373-24008-2*, 1-24008-4) Silhouette.

***Mallery, Susan.** Cinderella for a Night. (Intimate Moments Ser.: Vol. 1029). 2000. mass mkt. 4.50 (*0-373-27099-2*, 1-27099-0) Harlequin Bks.

Mallery, Susan. Cowboy Daddy. 1994. per. 3.50 (*0-373-09898-7*, 1-09898-7) Harlequin Bks.

— A Dad for Billie. (Special Edition Ser.). 1993. mass mkt. 3.50 (*0-373-09834-0*, 5-09834-8) Silhouette.

— Dream Bride (That Special Woman!/Brides of the Bradley House) (Special Edition Ser.: No. 1231). 1999. per. 4.25 (*0-373-24231-X*, 1-24231-2) Harlequin Bks.

— Dream Groom: Brides of Bradley House. (Special Edition Ser.: No. 1244). 1999. per. 4.25 (*0-373-24244-1*, 1-24244-5) Silhouette.

— Father in Training. (Special Edition Ser.). 1995. per. 3.75 (*0-373-09969-X*, 1-09969-6) Silhouette.

— Father in Training. large type ed. (Silhouette Romance Ser.). 1997. 20.95 (*0-373-59770-3*) Mac Lib Ref.

— Full-Time Father. (Special Edition Ser.: No. 1042). 1996. per. 3.99 (*0-373-24042-2*, 1-24042-3) Silhouette.

— Full Time Father. large type ed. 1999. 21.95 (*0-373-59552-2*) Harlequin Bks.

— The Girl of His Dreams. 1997. per. 3.99 (*0-373-24118-6*, 1-24118-1) Silhouette.

— Holly & Mistletoe. 1996. per. 3.99 (*0-373-24071-6*, 1-24071-2) Silhouette.

***Mallery, Susan.** Holly & Mistletoe. large type ed. 287p. 1999. 21.95 (*0-373-59654-5*) Harlequin Bks.

Mallery, Susan. Husband by the Hour. (That Special Woman!/Hometown Heart Breakers Ser.). 1997. per. 3.99 (*0-373-24099-6*, 1-24099-3) Silhouette.

***Mallery, Susan.** Husband by the Hour. large type ed. (Romance Ser.). 2000. 22.95 (*0-373-59698-7*) Silhouette.

Mallery, Susan. Justin's Bride. LC 95-13552. (Historical Ser.). 299p. 1995. per. 4.50 (*0-373-28870-0*, 1-28870-3) Harlequin Bks.

— Lone Star Millionaire. (World's Most Eligible Ser.: No. 10). 1999. per. 4.50 (*0-373-65027-2*, 1-65027-4, Harlequin) Harlequin Bks.

— Marriage on Demand. (Special Edition Ser.). 1995. per. 3.75 (*0-373-09939-8*, 1-09939-9) Silhouette.

— Marriage on Demand. large type ed. (Silhouette Romance Ser.). 1996. lib. bdg. 19.95 (*0-373-59745-2*, G K Hall Lrg Type) Mac Lib Ref.

— The Millionaire Bachelor. 1998. per. 4.25 (*0-373-24220-4*, 1-24220-5, Mira Bks) Harlequin Bks.

— More Than Friends. (Men at Work Ser.: Vol. 28). 1998. mass mkt. 4.50 (*0-373-81040-7*, 1-81040-7) Harlequin Bks.

— More Than Friends. 1993. mass mkt. 3.39 (*0-373-09802-2*, 5-09802-5) Silhouette.

— The Mysterious Stranger. 1997. per. 3.99 (*0-373-24130-5*, 1-24130-6) Silhouette.

— The Only Way Out. (Intimate Moments Ser.). 1995. per. 3.75 (*0-373-07646-0*, 1-07646-2) Silhouette.

— The Only Way Out. large type ed. (Silhouette Romance Ser.). 1997. 20.95 (*0-373-59813-0*) Mac Lib Ref.

— Part-Time Wife. 1998. 21.95 (*0-373-59933-1*) Harlequin Bks.

— Part-Time Wife. (That Special Woman, Hometown Heartbreakers Ser.). 1996. per. 3.99 (*0-373-24027-9*, 1-24027-4) Silhouette.

— Prince Charming, M. D. Prescription: Marriage. 1998. per. 4.25 (*0-373-24209-3*, 1-24209-8) Silhouette.

***Mallery, Susan.** The Rancher Next Door. (Special Edition Ser.: Bk. 1358). 2000. mass mkt. 4.50 (*0-373-24358-8*, 1-24358-3) Silhouette.

Mallery, Susan. The Rander & the Runaway Bride. (Thirty-Six Hours Ser.). 1997. per. 4.50 (*0-373-65012-4*) Harlequin Bks.

***Mallery, Susan.** A Royal Baby on the Way: Royally Wed. (Special Edition Ser.: No. 1281). 1999. per. 4.25 (*0-373-24281-6*, 1-24281-7) Silhouette.

Mallery, Susan. The Secret Wife. 1997. per. 3.99 (*0-373-24123-2*, 1-24123-1) Silhouette.

***Mallery, Susan.** The Sheik's Arranged Marriage. Vol. 1324. 2000. mass mkt. 4.50 (*0-373-24324-3*) Harlequin Bks.

— The Sheik's Secret Bride: Desert Rogues. (Special Edition Ser.: Bk. 1331). 2000. per. 4.50 (*0-373-24331-6*, 1-24331-0) Silhouette.

Mallery, Susan. Surprise Delivery: That's My Baby. (Special Edition Ser.: No. 1273). 1999. per. 4.25 (*0-373-24273-5*, 1-24273-4) Silhouette.

— Surrender in Silk. (Intimate Moments Ser.). 1997. per. 3.99 (*0-373-07770-X*, 1-07770-0) Silhouette.

— Tempting Faith. (Intimate Moments Ser.). 1994. per. 3.50 (*0-373-07554-5*, 5-07554-4) Silhouette.

***Mallery, Susan.** Their Little Princess: (Prescription: Marriage) (Special Edition Ser.: No. 1298). 2000. per. 4.50 (*0-373-24298-0*, 1-24298-1) Harlequin Bks.

Mallery, Susan. The Wedding Ring Promise. (Special Edition Ser.). 1998. per. 4.25 (*0-373-24190-9*, 1-24190-0) Silhouette.

— Wild West Wife: Montana Mavericks: Return to Whitehorn. (Historical Ser.: Vol. 419). 1998. per. 4.99 (*0-373-29019-5*, 1-29019-6) Harlequin Bks.

***Mallery, Susan & Hughes, Karen.** A Montana Mavericks Christmas: Married in Whitehorn; Born in Whitehorn, No. 128. 1999. mass mkt. 4.25 (*0-373-24286-7*) Silhouette.

Malleson, George B. Battlefields of Germany, from the Outbreak of the Thirty-Years' War. LC 68-54798. 360p. 1971. reprint ed. lib. bdg. 38.50 (*0-8371-5017-5*, MABG, Greenwood Pr) Greenwood.

Malleson, George B., ed. see Kaye, John W.

Malleson, Kate. The New Judiciary: The Effects of Expansion & Activism. LC 98-37427. 260p. 1999. text 78.95 (*1-84014-077-1*, Pub. by Ashgate Pub) Ashgate Pub Co.

***Mallesons Stephen Jaques Staff.** Australian Finance Law. 4th ed. Allan, David, ed. 926p. 1999. pap. 69.50 (*0-455-21668-1*, Pub. by LBC Info Servs) Gaunt.

Malless, Stan & McQain, Jeff. The Elements of English: A Glossary of Basic Terms for Literature, Composition, & Grammar. 86p. 1988. pap. 6.95 (*0-8191-6803-3*) U Pr of Amer.

Malless, Stan & McQuain, Jeff. A Handlist to English: Basic Terms for Literature, Composition, & Grammar. LC 86-9176. 48p. (Orig.). (C). 1986. pap. text 10.50 (*0-8191-5408-3*) U Pr of Amer.

Malless, Stanley, jt. auth. see McQuain, Jeffrey.

Mallet, jt. auth. see Cotran.

Mallet, Chibli. Islamic Family Law. 1991. lib. bdg. 88.50 (*1-85333-301-8*) Kluwer Academic.

Mallet, D., ed. Viscount Henry St. John Bolingbroke: The Works, 5 vols. (Anglistica & Americana Ser.: No. 13). 1968. reprint ed. 637.00 (*0-685-66435-X*, 05102021) G Olms Pubs.

Mallet, David. Works of David Mallet, 3 vols. LC 74-144567. reprint ed. 165.00 (*0-404-08580-6*) AMS Pr.

Mallet Du Pan, Jacques. Considerations on the Nature of the French Revolution & on the Causes Which Prolong Its Duration. LC 74-13491. xxii, 114p. 1975. reprint ed. 35.00 (*0-86527-032-5*) Fertig.

***Mallet, Eleanor.** The Nation of Family. LC 99-32222. (Illus.). 80p. 2000. 18.00 (*1-882203-57-7*) Orange Frazer.

Mallet, Francoise. The Illusionist. Briffault, Herma, tr. from FRE. LC 75-12335. (Homosexuality Ser.). (ENG.). 1975. reprint ed. 15.95 (*0-405-07383-6*) Ayer.

Mallet, Jacques, jt. auth. see Weisinger, Gary.

***Mallet, Joanna.** Love & Laments. vi, 26p. (C). 2000. pap. 5.95 (*0-9700740-0-X*) Athena Press NY.

Mallet-Joris, Francoise. Adriana Sposa. (FRE.). 1991. pap. 12.95 (*0-7859-3284-4*, 2277230626) Fr & Eur.

— Allegra. 416p. 1976. 25.00 (*0-686-56296-8*) Fr & Eur.

— Un Chagrin d'Amour et d'Ailleurs. (FRE.). 1983. pap. 6.95 (*0-7859-3111-2*) Fr & Eur.

— La Chambre Rouge. (FRE.). 284p. 1955. 9.95 (*0-8288-9836-7*, F110720) Fr & Eur.

— Le Clin d'Oeil de l'Ange. (FRE.). 1985. pap. 12.95 (*0-7859-2909-6*) Fr & Eur.

— Cordelia. (FRE.). 300p. 1956. 8.95 (*0-8288-9837-5*, F110730) Fr & Eur.

— Dickie-Roi. (FRE.). 1982. pap. 12.95 (*0-7859-3106-6*) Fr & Eur.

— Divine. (FRE.). 1992. pap. 12.95 (*0-7859-3438-3*) Fr & Eur.

— L' Empire Celeste. (FRE.). 400p. 1973. 13.95 (*0-8288-9838-3*, F110740) Fr & Eur.

— J'Aurais Voulu Jouer de L'Accordeon. 128p. 1976. 9.95 (*0-686-56302-6*) Fr & Eur.

— Le Jeu du Souterrain. (FRE.). 288p. 1973. pap. 10.95 (*0-7859-1467-6*, 2253011592); pap. 3.95 (*0-685-73293-2*) Fr & Eur.

— Lettre a Moi-Meme. (FRE.). 304p. 1970. 6.95 (*0-8288-9839-1*, F110761) Fr & Eur.

— La Maison de Papier. (FRE.). 272p. 1970. 10.95 (*0-8288-9910-X*, F140728); pap. 3.95 (*0-686-56308-5*) Fr & Eur.

— Les Mensonges. (FRE.). 1956. 6.95 (*0-8288-9840-5*, F110780) Fr & Eur.

— Les Personnages. (FRE.). 462p. 1973. 13.95 (*0-8288-9841-3*, F110790); pap. 3.95 (*0-686-56311-5*) Fr & Eur.

— Le Rempart des Beguines. 1951. 8.95 (*0-686-56312-3*); 10.95 (*0-8288-9842-1*, F110801) Fr & Eur.

— Le Rire de Laura. (FRE.). 1987. pap. 12.95 (*0-7859-3392-1*) Fr & Eur.

— Les Signes et les Prodiges. (FRE.). 416p. 1966. pap. 10.95 (*0-8288-9843-X*, F110821); pap. 3.95 (*0-686-56316-6*) Fr & Eur.

— Trilingual Psychological Dictionary Vol. 3: German-English-French. 592p. 1978. pap. 55.00 (*0-7859-0061-6*, M12024) Fr & Eur.

— La Tristesse de la Cerf-Volant. (FRE.). 1989. pap. 12.95 (*0-7859-3279-8*, 2277225967) Fr & Eur.

— Trois Ages de la Nuit. (FRE.). 1992. pap. 13.95 (*0-7859-4774-4*) Fr & Eur.

Mallet, M. Dominique. Les Rapports des Grecs avec l'Egypte. 218p. 1980. 30.00 (*0-89005-299-9*) Ares.

Mallet, Marla. Woven Structures: A Guide to Oriental Rug & Textile Analysis. LC 98-72134. (Illus.). 188p. 1998. pap. 39.00 (*0-9663057-3-6*) Christoph Pubns.

Mallet, Paul H. Northern Antiquities. LC 68-57868. (Bohn's Antiquarian Library). reprint ed. 56.00 (*0-404-50020-X*) AMS Pr.

Mallet, Reginald. Journeying with Jesus: A Lenten Study for Adults. 48p. 1996. pap. 3.50 (*0-687-03538-4*) Abingdon.

Mallet, Robert, ed. see Gide, Andre.

Mallet, Serge. Essays on the New Working Class. Howard, Dick, ed. & tr. by. from FRE. Savage, Dean, ed. LC 75-34904. 240p. (Orig.). (C). 1975. 25.00 (*0-914386-13-1*); pap. 15.00 (*0-914386-14-X*) Telos Pr.

Mallet, Serge, ed. The New Working Class. Shepherd, Andree, tr. from FRE. 210p. 1975. 25.00 (*0-85124-131-X*, Pub. by Spkesman) Coronet Bks.

Mallet, Todd. Raining Cats & Dogs. 72p. 1994. pap. 10.50 (*1-56770-304-6*) S Scheewe Pubns.

Mallett, A. S. Mallet: John Mallet, the Huguenot, & His Descendants, 1694-1894. 342p. 1992. reprint ed. pap. 43.00 (*0-8328-2208-6*); reprint ed. lib. bdg. 53.00 (*0-8328-2207-8*) Higginson Bk Co.

— The Union-Castle Line. 1990. 59.00 (*0-9516038-1-7*, Pub. by Ship Pictorial Pubng) St Mut.

Mallett, A. S. & Bell, A. M. The Pirrie Kylsant Motorships, 1915-1932. 1990. 50.00 (*0-9509453-0-7*, Pub. by Ship Pictorial Pubng) St Mut.

Mallett, Annette Y., jt. auth. see Mallett, Daryl F.

Mallett, Ashley. Clarrie Grimmett: The Bradman of Spin. 1993. pap. 17.95 (*0-7022-2531-2*, Pub. by Univ Queensland Pr) Intl Spec Bk.

Mallett, D. T. Index of Artists, International: Biographical. 1990. 29.00 (*0-8446-1297-9*) Peter Smith.

— Supplement to Index of Artists. 1990. 29.00 (*0-8446-1298-7*) Peter Smith.

Mallett, Daryl F. & Mallett, Annette Y. The Work of Elizabeth Chater: An Annotated Bibliography & Guide. Clarke, Boden, ed. LC 93-333. (Bibliographies of Modern Authors Ser.: No. 27). 80p. 1994. pap. 13.00 (*0-89370-490-3*) Millefleurs.

Mallett, Daryl F. & Reginald, Robert. Reginald's Science Fiction & Fantasy Awards: A Comprehensive Guide to the Awards & Their Winners. 3rd enl. rev. ed. LC 92-24445. (Borgo Literary Guides Ser.: No. 1). 248p. 1993. pap. 23.00 (*0-8095-1200-9*) Millefleurs.

Mallett, Daryl F., jt. auth. see Hewett, Jerry.

Mallett, Daryl F., ed. see Bamberger, W. C.

Mallett, Daryl F., ed. see Goehlert, Robert & Stamatoplos, Anthony C.

Mallett, Daryl F., jt. ed. see Hewett, Jerry.

Mallett, Daryl F., ed. see Indick, Ben P.

Mallett, Daryl F., ed. see Wood, Martine.

Mallett, David. Inch by Inch: The Garden Song. LC 93-38352. (Illus.). 32p. (J). (ps-1). 1995. 14.95 (*0-06-024303-1*) HarpC Child Bks.

— Inch by Inch: The Garden Song. LC 93-38352. (Trophy Picture Bk.). (Illus.). 32p. (J). (ps-1). 1997. pap. 5.95 (*0-06-443481-8*, HarpTrophy) HarpC Child Bks.

Mallett, David. Inch by Inch the Garden Song. (J). 1997. 11.15 (*0-606-11507-2*, Pub. by Turtleback) Demco.

Mallett, G. P. Repair of Concrete Bridges: State-of-the-Art Review. LC 95-117819. 206p. 1994. 87.00 (*0-7277-2007-4*) Am Soc Civil Eng.

Mallett, Gavin, ed. see Conference on Applications of X-Ray Analysis.

Mallett, Jane & Bailey, Christopher. The Royal Marsden NHS Trust Manual of Clinical Nursing Procedures. 4th ed. LC 96-19076. 662p. 1996. pap. 34.95 (*0-632-04068-8*) Blackwell Sci.

***Mallett, Jane, et al.** The Royal Marsden Hospital Manual of Clinical Nursing Procedures. 5th ed. LC 00-23642. (Illus.). 2000. pap. write for info. (*0-632-05235-X*) Blackwell Sci.

Mallett, Jerry J. Library Skills Activities Kit: Puzzles, Games, Bulletin Boards & Other Interest-Rousers for the Elementary School Library. 1981. pap. text 24.95 (*0-87628-535-3*) Ctr Appl Res.

— Reading Bulletin Boards Activities Kit. 288p. (C). 1998. pap. 21.95 (*0-87628-138-2*) P-H.

— Reading Bulletin Boards & Displays Kit. 288p. 1987. pap. 19.95 (*0-318-32867-4*, Busn) P-H.

Mallett, Jerry J. & Bartch, Marian R. Elementary School Library Resource Kit. (Illus.). 251p. 1983. pap. text 27.95 (*0-87628-301-6*) Ctr Appl Res.

Mallett, Jerry J. & Ervin, Timothy. Fold & Cut Stories. 56p. 1992. pap. text 11.95 (*0-913853-26-7*, 32538, Alleyside) Highsmith Pr.

— Sound & Action Stories. 48p. 1992. pap. text 11.95 (*0-913853-23-2*, 32534, Alleyside) Highsmith Pr.

Mallett, Jerry J. & Ervin, Timothy S. Elevator. (Illus.). 24p. (J). (ps-2). 1992. lib. bdg. 10.05 (*0-7804-3989-9*, 088542) Perma-Bound.

— Elevator: Paper Big Book. (Illus.). 24p. (Orig.). (J). (ps-2). 1992. pap. 22.00 (*0-7804-3988-0*, 088544) Perma-Bound.

— Elevator: Perma Big Book. (Illus.). 23p. (J). (ps-2). 1992. lib. bdg. 47.50 (*0-7804-3987-2*, 088543) Perma-Bound.

— Good Day, Blue Goose. (Illus.). 28p. (J). (ps-2). 1942. lib. bdg. 10.05 (*0-7804-3992-9*, 120051) Perma-Bound.

— Good Day, Blue Goose: Paper Big Book. (Illus.). 28p. (Orig.). (J). (ps-2). 1992. pap. 22.00 (*0-7804-3990-2*, 120052) Perma-Bound.

— Good Day, Blue Goose: Perma Big Book. (Illus.). 28p. (J). (ps-2). 1992. lib. bdg. 47.50 (*0-7804-3991-0*, 120053) Perma-Bound.

Mallett, Jerry J. & Polette, Keith. World Folktales Vol. 1: A Multicultural Approach to Whole Language, K-2. LC 94-21691. 70p. (J). (gr. k-2). 1994. pap. 14.95 (*0-917846-43-5*, Alleyside) Highsmith Pr.

— World Folktales Vol. 2: A Multicultural Approach to Whole Language, 3-5. LC 94-21691. 70p. (J). (gr. 3-5). 1994. pap. 14.95 (*0-917846-44-3*, Alleyside) Highsmith Pr.

— World Folktales Vol. 3: A Multicultural Approach to Whole Language, 6-8. LC 94-21691. 70p. (J). (gr. 6-8). 1994. pap. 14.95 (*0-917846-45-1*, Alleyside) Highsmith Pr.

***Mallett, Keith.** Three Women with Baby. (Illus.). 1999. 9.00 (*1-57977-958-1*) Havoc Pub.

Mallett, Margaret. Making Facts Matter: Reading Non-Fiction 5-11. 160p. 1992. pap. 27.00 (*1-85396-165-5*, Pub. by P Chapman) Taylor & Francis.

— Young Researchers: Informational Reading & Writing in the Early & Primary Years. LC 99-13532. 1999. pap. write for info. (*0-415-17951-3*) Routledge.

Mallett, Marshall. Handbook of Anatomy & Physiology for Students of Medical Radiation Technology. 3rd ed. (Illus.). 280p. (C). 1995. reprint ed. text 30.00 (*0-916973-00-X*) Burnell Co.

Mallett, Michael. The Borgias: The Rise & Fall of the Most Infamous Family in History. (Illus.). 368p. 1987. reprint ed. pap. 10.00 (*0-89733-238-5*) Academy Chi Pubs.

***Mallett, Phillip.** The Achievement of Thomas Hardy. LC 00-36900. 2000. write for info. (*0-312-23536-4*) St Martin.

Mallett, R. H., et al, eds. Effects of Piping Restraints on Piping Integrity: Pressure Vessels & Piping Conference, 1980, San Francisco, CA. LC 80-66028. (PVP Ser.: No. 40). 323p. pap. 100.20 (*0-608-15565-9*, 205639400064) Bks Demand.

Mallett, Reginald. The Cradle & the Star. 48p. (J). (ps-3). 1996. 3.25 (*0-687-02128-6*) Abingdon.

— God's Coming in Christ: An Advent Study for Adults. LC 95-11871. 1995. 3.25 (*0-687-00574-4*) Abingdon.

Mallett, Robert. The Italian Navy & Fascist Expansionism, 1935-1940. LC 98-22477. (Naval Policy & History Ser.: No. 7). (Illus.). 256p. 1998. 57.50 (*0-7146-4878-7*, Pub. by F Cass Pubs); pap. 26.50 (*0-7146-4432-3*, Pub. by F Cass Pubs) Intl Spec Bk.

Mallett, Sherri, jt. auth. see Smith, Gail.

Mallett, Sherri, jt. auth. see Smith, Gail I.

Mallett, Sherri A. ICD-9-CM: Beyond the Basics. rev. ed. 128p. 1999. pap. text 50.00 (*1-58426-021-1*, AC400799) Am Hlth Info.

Mallette, Bruce I. & Howard, Richard P., eds. Monitoring & Assessing Intercollegiate Athletics. LC 85-645339. (New Directions for Institutional Research Ser.: No. IR 74). 100p. 1992. pap. 22.00 (*1-55542-756-1*) Jossey-Bass.

Mallette, Gloria. When We Practice to Deceive. 224p. 1995. mass mkt. 4.95 (*0-87067-865-5*) Holloway.

M

***Mallette, Gloria A.** Shades of Jade. unabridged ed. LC 00-90040. 285p. 2000. pap. 16.00 (*0-9678789-0-X*) Gemini NY.

Mallette, Kathleen & Tomlinson, Joann. Benchmarking: Focus on World-Class Practices. Serritella, Susan, ed. (AT&T Quality Library). (Illus.). 126p. (Orig.). 1992. pap. 24.95 (*0-932764-24-X*, 500-454) AT&T Customer Info.

Mallette, Richard. The Mystery Colossians 1:25-27. LC 99-175353. 330 p. 1998. write for info. (*1-878146-09-2*) A C Design NY.

— Spenser, Milton, & Renaissance Pastoral. LC 78-73154. 224p. 1980. 32.50 (*0-8387-2412-4*) Bucknell U Pr.

Mallette, Vincent P., jt. auth. see Watkins, Christopher D.

Mallevialle, J. & Suf. Influence & Removal - Organics in Drinking Water Treatment. 368p. 1992. lib. bdg. 120.00 (*0-87371-386-9*, L386) Lewis Pubs.

Malley. Clinical Blood Gases: Invasive & Noninvasive Techniques & Applications. (Illus.). 400p. 1990. text 52.00 (*0-7216-5861-X*, W B Saunders Co) Harcrt Hlth Sci Grp.

Malley, B., tr. see Pradera, Victor.

Malley, Barbara & Allen, Frances. Poetry with a Purpose. (Illus.). 128p. (J). (gr. 4-7). 1987. pap. 12.99 (*0-86653-415-6*, GA 1018) Good Apple.

Malley, Barbara B. Rhyme Time. 1992. pap. 10.99 (*0-86653-968-9*) Fearon Teacher Aids.

Malley, E. Louise. Treasury of Animal Stories. 1994. 10.98 (*0-7858-0213-4*) Bk Sales Inc.

Malley, Elaine, tr. see Seara Vazquez, M.

Malley, Ian. Censorship & Libraries. LC 89-60255. (Viewpoints in Library & Information Science: Vol. 5). 43p. 1990. reprint ed. pap. 30.00 (*0-608-02478-3*, 206312200004) Bks Demand.

Malley, James D. Optimal Unbiased Estimation of Variance Components. (Lecture Notes in Statistics Ser.: Vol. 39). ix, 146p. 1986. 47.95 (*0-387-96449-5*) Spr-Verlag.

— Statistical Applications of Jordan Algebras. LC 94-28225. (Lecture Notes in Statistics Ser.: Vol. 91). 1994. 39.95 (*0-387-94341-2*) Spr-Verlag.

Malley, James O. & Shea, Gail H., eds. Erzincan, Turkey, Earthquake of March 13, 1992, Reconnaissance Report. (Illus.). 210p. 1993. pap. 15.00 (*0-943198-74-7*, 93-01) Earthquake Eng.

Malley, James P., Jr., et al. Evaluation of the By-Products Produced by the Treatment of Groundwaters with Ultraviolet Irradiation (UV) LC 96-136843. (Illus.). 115p. 1996. pap. 75.00 (*0-89867-842-0*, 90685) Am Water Wks Assn.

Malley, Patrick B. Legal & Ethical Dimensions for Mental Health Professionals. LC 98-31545. 367p. 1999. pap. 29.95 (*1-56032-687-5*) Hemisp Pub.

Malley, Richard C. In Their Hours of Ocean Leisure: Scrimshaw in the Cold Spring Harbor Whaling Museum. 96p. 1993. 19.50 (*0-9636361-0-3*) Whaling Mus.

Malley, Robert. The Call from Algeria: Third Worldism, Revolution, & the Turn to Islam. LC 95-36054. 310p. (C). 1996. 48.00 (*0-520-20300-3*, Pub. by U CA Pr); pap. 19.95 (*0-520-20301-1*, Pub. by U CA Pr) Cal Prin Full Svc.

Malley, Sarah H., jt. auth. see Lightbody, Nancy K.

Malley, Stephen, ed. The Kid's Guide to the 1996 Summer Olympics. (Illus.). 80p. (Orig.). 1996. pap. 5.95 (*1-886749-04-3*) SI For Kids.

Mallgrave, Harry F. Gottfried Semper: Architect of the Nineteenth Century: A Personal & Intellectual Biography. LC 95-47561. 433p. (C). 1996. 52.50 (*0-300-06624-4*) Yale U Pr.

Mallgrave, Harry F., ed. Otto Wagner: Reflections on the Raiment of Modernity. LC 93-3808. (Issues & Debates Ser.). (Illus.). 436p. 1993. 55.00 (*0-89236-258-8*, Pub. by J P Getty Trust); pap. 29.95 (*0-89236-257-X*, Pub. by J P Getty Trust) OUP.

Mallgrave, Harry F., et al, trs. Empathy, Form, & Space: Problems in German Aesthetics, 1873-1893. LC 93-20722. (Texts & Documents Ser.). (Illus.). 342p. 1994. pap. 24.95 (*0-89236-259-6*, Pub. by J P Getty Trust) OUP.

— Empathy, Form, & Space: Problems in German Aesthetics, 1873-1893. LC 93-20722. (Texts & Documents Ser.). (Illus.). 342p. 1996. 49.95 (*0-89236-260-X*, Pub. by J P Getty Trust) OUP.

Mallgrave, Harry F., tr. see Behrendt, Walter C.

Mallgrave, Harry F., tr. see Wagner, Otto.

Mallgrave, Harry P. Northern European Books: Sixteenth to Early Nineteenth Centuries, Vol. 3. 1999. 90.00 (*0-8076-1459-9*) Braziller.

Malli, G. L. Relativistic & Electron Correlation Effects in Molecules & Solids. (NATO ASI Ser.: Vol. 318). (Illus.). 484p. (C). 1994. text 139.50 (*0-306-44625-1*, Kluwer Plenum) Kluwer Academic.

***Mallia, Carmel.** Marionetoj. (ESP.). 62p. 1999. pap. 5.50 (*1-882251-28-8*) Eldonejo Bero.

— Rheumaderm: Current Issues in Rheumatology & Dermatology. LC 98-31757. (Advances in Experimental Medicine & Biology Ser.). 562p. 1999. text. write for info. (*0-306-46047-5*, Kluwer Plenum) Kluwer Academic.

Mallia, Marianne, ed. Twenty-Five Years of Excellence: A History of the Texas Heart Institute. (Illus.). 300p. (C). 1989. 35.00 (*0-317-91336-0*) TX Heart Inst Found.

Malliani, A., et al, eds. Neural Mechanisms & Cardiovascular Disease: Proceedings of the International Symposium Held in S. Margherita Ligure, Italy, in May 1985. (FIDIA Research Ser.). 650p. 1987. 196.00 (*0-387-96454-1*) Spr-Verlag.

***Malliani, Alberto.** Colon Cancer Prevention - Dietary Modulation Of Cellular And Molecular Mechanisms. 170p. 2000. 95.00 (*0-306-46207-9*, Kluwer Plenum) Kluwer Academic.

— Principles of Cardiovascular Neural Regulation in Health. 240p. 2000. 160.00 (*0-7923-7775-3*) Kluwer Academic.

***Malliaris, A. G.** Foundations of Futures Markets: Selected Essays of A. G. Malliaris. LC 99-41671. (Financial Economists of the Twentieth Century Ser.). 360p. 2000. 100.00 (*1-85898-836-5*) E Elgar.

Malliaris, A. G., ed. Futures Markets, 3 vols. LC 96-24637. (International Library of Critical Writings in Economics Ser.: No. 2). 1456p. 1997. 510.00 (*1-85898-070-4*) E Elgar.

Malliaris, A. G., jt. auth. see Brock, W. A.

Malliaris, T. G. Stochastic Methods in Economics & Finance. LC 99-29824. (Advanced Textbooks in Economics Ser.: Vol. 17). 304p. 1982. 65.00 (*0-444-86201-3*, North Holland) Elsevier.

Malliavin, M. P. Seminaire d'Algebre Paul Dubreil et Marie-Paule Malliavin. (Lecture Notes in Mathematics Ser.: Vol. 1146). (ENG & FRE.). iv, 420p. 1985. 54.95 (*0-387-15686-0*) Spr-Verlag.

Malliavin, M. P., ed. Seminaire d'Algebre Paul Dubreil et Marie-Paule Malliavin. (Lecture Notes in Mathematics Ser.: Vol. 1029). 339p. 1983. 42.95 (*0-387-12699-6*) Spr-Verlag.

— Seminaire d'Algebre Paule Dubreil et Marie-Paul Malliavin. Vol. 1404. ix, 410p. 1989. pap. 51.30 (*0-387-51812-6*) Spr-Verlag.

Malliavin, P. Stochastic Analysis, Vol. XI. (Grundlehren der Mathematischen Wissenschaften Ser.: Vol. 313). 370p. 1997. 125.00 (*0-387-57024-1*) Spr-Verlag.

Malliavin, P., ed. see Leray, Jean.

Malliavin, Paul. Stochastic Analysis. LC 97-6419. (Grundlehren der Mathematischen Wissenschaften Ser.: Vol. 313). 370p. 1997. 125.00 (*3-540-57024-1*) Spr-Verlag.

Malliavin, Paul, et al. Integration & Probability. (Graduate Texts in Mathematics Ser.: Vol. 157). 360p. 1995. 49.95 (*0-387-94409-5*) Spr-Verlag.

Mallick. Bayesian Nonparametric Regression text. write for info. (*0-471-49036-9*) Wiley.

***Mallick, B. N. & Inoue, S., eds.** Rapid Eye Movement Sleep. 419p. 1999. 145.00 (*0-8247-0322-7*) Dekker.

Mallick, B. S. Money, Banking & Trade in Mughal India. (C). 1991. 22.50 (*0-685-59783-0*, Pub. by Rawat Pubns) S Asia.

Mallick, David. How Tall Is This Ghost, John? (Illus.). 124p. 1998. pap. text 12.50 (*0-909955-50-6*, 955506) Calendar Islands.

Mallick, Joan. The Health Professionals Guide to the Internet: A Reference Guide to Health & Medical Web Sites. 42p. 1997. pap. 5.00 (*1-893549-09-7*) Biomed Genl.

Mallick, Kanka, jt. ed. see Bagley, Christopher.

Mallick, M. R. Bail-Law & Practice. (C). 1990. 110.00 (*0-89771-175-0*) St Mut.

Mallick, P. K. Composites Engineering Handbook. LC 97-4058. (Materials Engineering Ser.: Vol. 11). (Illus.). 1264p. 1997. text 275.00 (*0-8247-9304-8*) Dekker.

— Fiber-Reinforced Composites: Materials, Manufacturing & Designs. 2nd ed. (Mechanical Engineering Ser.: Vol. 83). (Illus.). 584p. 1993. text 185.00 (*0-8247-9031-6*) Dekker.

Mallick, P. K. & Newman, S. Composite Materials Technology: Processes & Properties. 400p. (C). 1991. 89.95 (*1-56990-056-6*) Hanser-Gardner.

Mallick, Ross. Development, Ethnicity & Human Rights in South Asia. LC 97-45134. 375p. 1998. write for info. (*0-7619-9227-8*); pap. write for info. (*0-7619-9228-6*) Sage.

Mallick, S., jt. auth. see Francon, Maurice.

***Mallick, Sushanta K.** Modelling Macroeconomic Adjustment with Growth in Developing Economies. 218p. 2000. text 65.95 (*0-7546-1180-9*, Pub. by Ashgate Pub) Ashgate Pub Co.

Mallier, Tony, jt. auth. see Shafto, Tony.

Mallige, G. R. Quest for Harmoncy in Romen Basu Novels. 134p. 1998. 19.95 (*0-932377-71-8*) Facet Bks.

Mallik, A. K., jt. auth. see Ghosh, A.

Mallik, Asok K., et al. Kinematic Analysis & Synthesis of Mechanisms. LC 93-37108. 688p. 1994. boxed set 104.95 (*0-8493-9121-0*, No. 9121) CRC Pr.

Mallik, C. C. A Short Textbook of Medical Jurisprudence. 850p. 1993. pap. (*0-7855-7516-2*) Current Bks Intl.

Mallik, C. C. A Short Textbook of Medical Jurisprudence. 1985. 100.00 (*0-7855-0749-3*, Pub. by Current Dist) St Mut.

Mallik, G. N. Philosophy of Vaisnava Religion. 1972. 59.95 (*0-8490-0829-8*) Gordon Pr.

Mallik, Maggie. Nursing Knowledge & Practice: A Decision-Making Approach. 1997. pap. text 39.95 (*0-7020-1991-7*, Pub. by W B Saunders) Saunders.

***Mallin, Barri Cae.** Intimate Moments with the Hebrew Names of God. (Illus.). 2000. pap. 10.99 (*0-88270-801-5*) Bridge-Logos.

Mallin, Eric S. Inscribing the Time: Shakespeare & the End of Elizabethan England. LC 94-28943. (New Historicism Ser.: Vol. 33). 288p. 1995. 45.00 (*0-520-08623-6*, Pub. by U CA Pr) Cal Prin Full Svc.

Mallin, Gail. Marry in Haste. large type ed. 350p. 1996. 23.99 (*0-263-14689-8*, Pub. by Mills & Boon) Ulverscroft.

Mallin, Jay, Sr. Adventures in Journalism. LC 98-91461. 270p. 1998. pap. 15.00 (*1-57502-806-9*, PO2222) Morris Pubng.

— Covering Castro. 200p. (C). 1994. 34.95 (*1-56000-156-9*) Transaction Pubs.

— Covering Castro: Rise & Decline of Cuba's Communist Dictator. LC 93-46178. 1994. 25.00 (*1-884750-00-1*) U S Cuba Pr.

Mallin, Jay. Covering Castro: The Rise & Fall of Cuba's Communist Dictator. 250p. 1992. 21.95 (*0-944273-09-2*) U S Cuba Pr.

Mallin, Jay, ed. Strategy for Conquest: Communist Documents on Guerrilla Warfare. LC 71-102688. 1970. 24.95 (*0-87024-144-3*) U of Miami Pr.

— Terror & Urban Guerillas: A Study of Tactics & Documents. LC 79-163842. 1983. 19.95 (*0-87024-223-7*) U of Miami Pr.

Mallin, Ken, jt. auth. see Mann, Steve.

Mallin, Samuel B. Art Line Thought. LC 95-36284. (Contributions to Phenomenology Ser.: Vol. 21). 512p. (C). 1995. text 220.50 (*0-7923-3774-3*) Kluwer Academic.

Mallinckrodt, Anita, ed. from GER. A History of Augusta, MO & Its Area (II), 1870s... Vol. II: As Reported in the "St. Charles Demokrat" LC 98-225302. 229p. 1998. pap. 19.95 (*0-931227-12-7*) Mallinckrodt Comm.

***Mallinckrodt, Anita, ed. from GER.** A History of Augusta, MO & Its Area (III) 1880s/1890s No. III: As Reported in the "St. Charles Demokrat" 257p. 1999. pap. 19.95 (*0-931227-13-5*) Mallinckrodt Comm.

Mallinckrodt, Anita M. A Dream Left High & Dry: Town of Dortmund. (Illus.). 20p. (Orig.). 1992. pap. text 4.00 (*0-931227-05-4*) Mallinckrodt Comm.

***Mallinckrodt, Anita M.** Freed Slaves - Ex-Slaves & Augusta: Missouri's Germans During & after the Civil War. (Missouri Research Roundtable Papers: No. 1). 20p. 1999. pap. 4.00 (*0-931227-14-3*) Mallinckrodt Comm.

Mallinckrodt, Anita M. From Knights to Pioneers: One German Family in Westphalia & Missouri. LC 93-16891. (Illus.). 560p. (C). 1994. 46.95 (*0-8093-1917-9*) S Ill U Pr.

— Historic Augusta: Its Buildings & People, 1820-1900. rev. ed. (Illus.). 104p. (Orig.). 1996. pap. 9.50 (*0-931227-06-2*) Mallinckrodt Comm.

— Historical Highlights - Augusta, Missouri: From Town Board Records, 1855-1903. (Illus.). 28p. (Orig.). 1990. pap. text 5.00 (*0-931227-04-6*) Mallinckrodt Comm.

— How They Came: German Immigration from Prussia to Missouri. (Illus.). 50p. (Orig.). 1989. pap. 6.25 (*0-931227-02-X*) Mallinckrodt Comm.

— Justice's Docket: For Femme Osage Township, St. Charles County, Missouri 1866-1878. (Illus.). 180p. (Orig.). 1996. pap. 12.00 (*0-931227-10-0*) Mallinckrodt Comm.

***Mallinckrodt, Anita M.** To Fence, or Not to Fence: St. Charles County's Long Road to Laws Putting Farm Animals Behind Fences & off City Streets. (Missouri Research Roundtable Papers: No. 4). (Illus.). 20p. 1999. pap. 4.00 (*0-931227-52-6*) Mallinckrodt Comm.

Mallinckrodt, Anita M. What They Thought Vol. II: Missouri's German Immigrants Assess Their World 1860s. 32p. 1995. 5.00 (*0-931227-08-9*) Mallinckrodt Comm.

— Why They Left: German Immigration from Prussia to Missouri. rev. ed. (Illus.). 34p. 1989. reprint ed. pap. 5.25 (*0-931227-03-8*) Mallinckrodt Comm.

Mallinckrodt, Anita M., ed. What They Thought Vol. I: Missouri's German Immigrants Assess Their World, 1850s. 44p. 1995. 6.00 (*0-931227-07-0*) Mallinckrodt Comm.

Mallinckrodt, Anita M., ed. from GER. A History of Augusta, MO & Its Area (I), 1870s... Vol. I: As Reported in the "St. Charles Demokrat", 3 vols. LC 98-225302. 204p. (J). (ps-12). 1998. pap. 19.95 (*0-931227-11-9*) Mallinckrodt Comm.

***Mallinckrodt, Anita M. & Gregory, Ralph.** Wine-Making in "Duden Country" 1800s History & Customs. (Illus.). 26p. 1999. pap. 7.00 (*0-931227-15-1*) Mallinckrodt Comm.

Mallinger, Allan & Dewyze, Jeannette. Too Perfect. 224p. 1993. pap. 10.00 (*0-449-90800-3*, Columbine) Fawcett.

Mallinson. Applications for Word Processing. 1988. pap. text, teacher ed. 12.00 (*0-15-309011-1*) Holt R&W.

Mallinson, et al. H'mong Batik: A Textile Technique from Laos. LC 88-90587. (Illus.). 96p. (Orig.). 1997. pap. 14.95 (*0-295-97054-5*) U of Wash Pr.

***Mallinson, Allan.** A Close Run Thing. 320p. 2000. pap. 13.95 (*0-553-38043-5*, Spectra) Bantam.

Mallinson, Allan. A Close Run Thing: A Novel of Wellington's Army of 1815. LC 98-52512. 320p. 1999. 23.95 (*0-553-11114-0*) Bantam.

***Mallinson, Allan.** Honorable Company: A Novel of India Before the Raj. LC 00-39737. 2000. 23.95 (*0-553-11134-5*) Bantam.

Mallinson, Bill. Public Lies & Private Truths: An Introduction to PR. (Illus.). 176p. 1997. 79.50 (*0-304-33832-X*); pap. 32.50 (*0-304-33833-8*) Continuum.

Mallinson, G. Moliere: Le Misanthrope. (French Texts Ser.). (FRE.). 168p. 1996. pap. 18.95 (*1-85399-392-1*, Pub. by Brist Class Pr) Focus Pub-R Pullins.

Mallinson, Graham. Rumanian. (Descriptive Grammars Ser.). 384p. 1986. 72.50 (*0-7099-3537-4*, Pub. by C Helm) Routldge.

Mallinson, Ian. Care Planning in Residential Care for Older People in Scotland: A Research Study. LC 96-85553. 174p. 1996. text 63.95 (*1-85972-440-X*, Pub. by Avebry) Ashgate Pub Co.

— Keyworking: An Examination of a Method of Individualizing Care for Older People in Residential Establishments. 160p. 1995. 66.95 (*1-85972-179-6*, Pub. by Avebry) Ashgate Pub Co.

— Keyworking in Social Care: A Structured Approach to Provision. 1995. 70.00 (*1-871177-06-5*, Pub. by Whiting & Birch); pap. 32.95 (*1-871177-12-X*, Pub. by Whiting & Birch) Paul & Co Pubs.

Mallinson, J. D. Composition of a European City. 66p. pap. write for info. (*3-7052-0291-X*, Pub. by Poetry Salzburg) Intl Spec Bk.

Mallinson, Jane, et al. H'mong Batik: A Textile Technique from Laos. LC 88-90587. (Illus.). 87p. (Orig.). 1988. pap. 12.50 (*0-9620278-0-4*) Mallinson Info Servs.

Mallinson, John C. The Foundations of Magnetic Recording. 2nd ed. LC 92-43462. (Illus.). 217p. 1993. text 48.00 (*0-12-466626-4*) Acad Pr.

— Magneto-Resistive Heads: Fundamentals & Applications. (Electromagnetism Ser.). (Illus.). 133p. 1995. text 49.95 (*0-12-466630-2*) Acad Pr.

Mallinson, Linda. Office Guide. LC 97-23630. 155p. (C). 1997. spiral bd. 9.20 (*0-13-861402-4*) P-H.

Mallinson, Vernon. None Can Be Called Deformed. Phillips, William R. & Rosenberg, Janet, eds. LC 79-6917. (Physically Handicapped in Society Ser.). 1980. reprint ed. lib. bdg. 24.95 (*0-405-13124-0*) Ayer.

Mallion, ed. see Sand, George.

Mallios, Anastasios. Geometry of Vector Sheaves: An Axiomatic Approach to Differential Geometry. (Mathematics & Its Applications Ser.: 439). 441p. 1998. 195.00 (*0-7923-5004-9*) Kluwer Academic.

— Geometry of Vector Sheaves: An Axiomatic Approach to Differential Geometry. LC 98-9440. (Mathematics & Its Applications Ser.). 1998. write for info. (*0-7923-5006-5*) Kluwer Academic.

— Geometry of Vector Sheaves: An Axiomatic Approach to Differential Geometry, 2. (Mathematics & Its Applications Ser.: 439). 436p. 1998. 195.00 (*0-7923-5005-7*) Kluwer Academic.

Mallios, William S. Statistical Modeling: Applications in Contemporary Issues. LC 89-31303. (Illus.). 248p. (C). 1989. text 52.95 (*0-8138-0307-1*) Iowa St U Pr.

Mallis, Arnold. Handbook of Pest Control. 8th ed. LC 97-93097. (Illus.). 1500p. 1997. 135.00 (*1-890561-00-2*) Mallis Handbk.

Mallis, George, jt. auth. see VanAllen, Leory C.

Mallis, Jackie. Diamonds in the Dust: Discover & Develop Your Child's Gifts. 2nd ed. 448p. (Orig.). 1992. pap. 15.95 (*0-86617-056-1*) Multi Media TX.

— Earn Cash Creating Word Puzzles. (Illus.). 160p. (Orig.). 1993. 17.95 (*0-86617-055-3*) Multi Media TX.

— Effective Composition: A Problem-Solving Process. 100p. 1988. pap. 17.95 (*0-86617-040-5*) Multi Media TX.

— Making the Connection Between Grammar & Composition - With Forbidden Words. rev. ed. 244p. 1997. pap., per. 25.00 (*0-86617-057-X*) Multi Media TX.

— Mosaics. (Pathways to Poetry Ser.). 95p. 1984. pap. 17.95 (*0-86617-030-8*) Multi Media TX.

Mallis, Jackie, ed. Fantasies: Short Story Masterpieces, Vol. 1-10, set. unabridged ed. (J). (gr. 5 up). 1984. 156.74 incl. audio (*0-86617-052-9*) Multi Media TX.

Mallis, Jackie, ed. Ideas for Teaching Gifted Students, 8 bks., Set. Incl. Language Arts. 203p. 1980. pap. 29.95 (*0-86617-021-9*); Music. 206p. 1980. pap. 29.95 (*0-86617-028-6*); Science. 245p. 1980. pap. 29.95 (*0-86617-026-X*); Social Studies: Elementary. 200p. 1982. pap. 29.95 (*0-86617-023-5*); 1980. Set pap. text 215.64 (*0-86617-029-4*) Multi Media TX.

— Visual Arts. (Ideas for Teaching Gifted Students Ser.). (Illus.). 1980. pap. 29.95 (*0-86617-016-2*) Multi Media TX.

Mallison, Arthur, ed. see Sullivan, Joseph R. & Leafgren, Fred.

Mallison, Francoise, jt. ed. see Eck, Diana L.

Mallison, Francoise, jt. ed. see Entwistle, Alan W.

Mallison, Fred M. The Civil War on the Outer Banks: A History of the Late Rebellion along the Coast of North Carolina from Carteret to Currituck, with Comments on Prewar Conditions & an Account of Postwar Recovery. LC 97-40304. (Illus.). 251p. 1997. boxed set 37.50 (*0-7864-0417-5*) McFarland & Co.

***Mallison, Fred M.** To Ocracoke! Boyhood Summers on the Outer Banks. (Carolina Childhood Ser.). 216p. 2000. pap. 13.95 (*0-9643396-3-3*) Sweet Bay Tree.

Mallison, George. Color at Home & Abroad. LC 72-132388. reprint ed. 39.50 (*0-404-00198-X*) AMS Pr.

Mallison, J. D. Evidence of Time. 1997. pap. 12.95 (*3-7052-0094-1*) Intl Spec Bk.

Mallison, Sally V. & Mallison, Thomas W. Settlements & the Law: A Juridicial Analysis of the Israeli Settlements in the Occupied Territories. (Illus.). 1982. pap. 1.00 (*0-318-01027-5*) Am Educ Trust.

Mallison, Sally V. & Mallison, W. Thomas. Armed Conflict in Lebanon, 1982: Humanitarian Law in a Real World Setting. (Illus.). 86p. 1985. pap. 8.95 (*0-318-01034-8*) Am Educ Trust.

Mallison, Thomas W., jt. auth. see Mallison, Sally V.

Mallison, W. Thomas, Jr. The Balfour Declaration: An Apprai in International Law. (Information Papers: No. 4). 52p. 1971. pap. text 1.00 (*0-937694-20-7*) Assn Arab-Amer U Grads.

Mallison, W. Thomas, jt. auth. see Mallison, Sally V.

Mallmann, Jacob E. Shelter Island & Presbyterian Church. 1976. 25.95 (*0-8488-0874-6*) Amereon Ltd.

Mallmann, Joanne, jt. auth. see Dittl, Barbara.

Malloc. The Mature Traveler's Book of Deals. 3rd rev. ed. 144p. 1998. pap. 7.95 (*0-9629034-9-3*) GEM Pub Group.

Malloch, Christian A., tr. see Wieser, Friedrich von.

Malloch, D. Macleod, jt. auth. see Morton, George A.

Malloch, David. Moulds: Their Isolation, Cultivation & Identification. LC 81-195429. (Illus.). 107p. reprint ed. pap. 33.20 (*0-8357-3996-1*, 203669600005) Bks Demand.

Malloch, David, jt. auth. see Ker, John.

***Malloch, Per.** How to Play Japanese Imports Without Knowing a Word of Japanese. (Illus.). 64p. 1999. pap. 12.95 (*0-9677088-0-X*) Gamethought Prods.

Malloch, Theodore R. Beyond Reductionism. 290p. 1983. text 29.50 (*0-8290-1292-3*) Irvington.

— Issues in International Trade & Development Policy. LC 87-11697. 187p. 1987. 55.00 (*0-275-92356-8*, C2356, Praeger Pubs) Greenwood.

Malloch, Theodore R., jt. auth. see Norris, Donald M.

An Asterisk (*) at the beginning of an entry indicates that the title is appearing for the first time.

Mallock, William H. The New Republic: Or, Culture, Faith & Philosophy in an English Country House. LC 75-30033. 376p. reprint ed. 47.50 (*0-404-14036-X*) AMS Pr.

— Studies of Contemporary Superstition. LC 72-333. (Essay Index Reprint Ser.). 1977. reprint ed. 23.95 (*0-8369-2804-0*) Ayer.

Mallon, A. The Religion of Egypt. (African Heritage Classical Research Studies). pap. 10.00 (*0-938818-37-6*) ECA Assoc.

— The Religion of Egypt. (African Studies). reprint ed. 10.00 (*0-685-56712-5*) ECA Assoc.

Mallon, Bill. The Golf Doctor. 220p. 1996. 14.95 (*0-02-860853-4*) Macmillan.

— The 1904 Olympic Games: Complete Results for All Competitors in All Events, with Commentary. LC 98-30989. 287p. 1999. lib. bdg. 39.50 (*0-7864-0550-3*) McFarland & Co.

— The 1900 Olympic Games. LC 97-36094. 351p. 1997. lib. bdg. 39.50 (*0-7864-0378-0*) McFarland & Co.

— The 1906 Olympic Games: Complete Results for All Competitors in All Events, with Commentary. LC 98-46197. 250p. 1999. lib. bdg. 39.50 (*0-7864-0551-1*) McFarland & Co.

***Mallon, Bill.** Total Olympics: The Complete Record of Every Event in Every Olympics. 1000p. 2001. 49.95 (*1-892129-30-2*) Total Sprts.

Mallon, Bill & Buchanan, Ian. The 1908 Olympic Games: Results for All Competitors in All Events, with Commentary. LC 99-57985. (Illus.). 516p. 2000. lib. bdg. 49.50 (*0-7864-0598-8*) McFarland & Co.

Mallon, Bill & Widland, Ture. The 1896 Olympic Games. LC 97-26356. 168p. 1997. lib. bdg. 32.50 (*0-7864-0379-9*) McFarland & Co.

Mallon, Bill, et al. Quest for Gold: The Encyclopedia of American Olympians. LC 84-966. (Illus.). 496p. 1984. reprint ed. pap. 153.80 (*0-608-07084-X*, 206731300009) Bks Demand.

Mallon, Bill, jt. auth. see Buchanan, Ian.

Mallon, Brenda. Creative Visualization with Color: Healing Your Life with the Power of Color. LC 99-21497. 160p. 1999. pap. 12.95 (*1-86204-448-1*, Pub. by Element MA) Penguin Putnam.

— Helping Children Manage Loss. LC 98-204421. 184p. 1998. pap. 26.95 (*1-85302-605-0*, Pub. by Jessica Kingsley) Taylor & Francis.

Mallon, Elias. Neighbors: Muslims in North America. 104p. 1996. pap. 6.50 (*0-614-21713-X*, 893) Kazi Pubns.

Mallon, Florencia E. The Defense of Community in Peru's Central Highlands: Peasant Struggle & Capitalist Transition, 1860-1940. LC 83-42565. 399p. 1983. reprint ed. pap. 123.70 (*0-608-04588-8*, 206535800003) Bks Demand.

— Peasant & Nation: The Making of Postcolonial Mexico & Peru. LC 93-34677. 1994. pap. 24.95 (*0-520-08505-1*, Pub. by U CA Pr) Cal Prin Full Svc.

— Peasant & Nation: The Making of Postcolonial Mexico & Peru. LC 93-34677. 1995. 55.00 (*0-520-08504-3*, Pub. by U CA Pr) Cal Prin Full Svc.

Mallon, G. W. Bankers Versus Consumers. 1972. 59.95 (*0-87968-703-7*) Gordon Pr.

***Mallon, Gareth.** Focus on Electrocardiograph. (Illus.). 100p. 2000. pap. text 14.95 (*1-873413-04-1*) Merit Pub Intl.

Mallon, Gerald. We Don't Exactly Get the Welcome Wagon: The Experiences of Gay & Lesbian Adolescents in Child Welfare Systems. LC 97-45545. 208p. 1998. pap. 23.50 (*0-231-10455-3*) Col U Pr.

— We Don't Exactly Get the Welcome Wagon: The Experiences of Gay & Lesbian Adolescents in Child Welfare Systems. LC 97-45545. 208p. 1998. 52.00 (*0-231-10454-5*) Col U Pr.

***Mallon, Gerald P.** Let's Get This Straight: A Gay & Lesbian Affirming Approach to Child Welfare. 2000. 49.50 (*0-231-11136-3*) Col U Pr.

— Let's Get This Straight: A Gay & Lesbian Affirming Approach to Child Welfare. 2000. pap. text 22.00 (*0-231-11137-1*) Col U Pr.

Mallon, Gerald P., ed. Foundations of Social Work Practice with Lesbian & Gay Persons. LC 97-13382. 298p. 1997. 49.95 (*0-7890-0348-1*, Harrington Park); pap. 24.95 (*1-56023-101-7*, Harrington Park); pap. 24.95 (*2-9802310-1-0*) Haworth Pr.

***Mallon, Gerald P., ed.** Social Services with Transgendered Youth. LC 99-58923. 163p. 2000. 39.95 (*1-56023-135-1*) Harrington Pk.

— Social Services with Transgendered Youth. LC 99-58923. 163p. 2000. pap. text 19.95 (*1-56023-136-X*) Harrington Pk.

Mallon, Gerald P., jt. auth. see Levinson, Boris M.

***Mallon, James.** Magazine. LC 99-70723. 256p. 2000. 22.95 (*1-57197-181-5*) Pentland Pr.

Mallon, James M. No Toads in Heaven. (Gene Florian in the Caribbean Ser.). 262p. (Orig.). 1996. pap. 13.00 (*1-886163-05-7*) SoloZone.

Mallon, Maurus E. Ex Novo Mundo: Ten Tales of the Americas. LC 91-60949. 126p. (Orig.). 1991. pap. write for info. (*0-88100-074-4*) Natl Writ Pr.

— A Matter of Conscience. LC 89-64249. 112p. (Orig.). (C). 1990. pap. 6.95 (*0-88100-067-1*) Natl Writ Pr.

***Mallon, Richard D.** New Missionaries: Memoirs of a Foreign Advisor in Less-Developed Countries. 128p. 2000. pap. 14.95 (*0-674-00348-9*) HUP.

Mallon, Richard D. & Sourrouille, Juan V. Economic Policymaking in a Conflict Society: The Argentine Case. LC 74-21227. (Center for International Affairs Ser.). 288p. 1975. 37.95 (*0-674-22930-4*) HUP.

Mallon, Sarah R., ed. see Handy, Isaac W.

Mallon, Thomas. Aurora, No. 7. 246p. 1992. pap. 8.95 (*0-393-30848-0*) Norton.

— Book of One's Own: People & Their Diaries. LC 95-79538. 314p. 1995. reprint ed. pap. 14.00 (*1-886913-02-1*) Ruminator Bks.

— Dewey Defeats Truman. LC 96-26812. 355p. 1997. 24.00 (*0-679-44425-4*) Pantheon.

— Dewey Defeats Truman. LC 97-33390. 368p. 1997. pap. 14.00 (*0-312-18086-1*) St Martin.

— Henry & Clara: A Novel. 5th ed. LC 95-23938. 368p. 1995. pap. 13.00 (*0-312-13508-4*, Picador USA) St Martin.

— Rockets & Rodeos: And Other American Spectacles. 290p. Date not set. reprint ed. text 15.00 (*0-7881-5211-4*) DIANE Pub.

— Stolen Words: Forays into the Origins & Ravages of Plagiarism. 288p. 1989. 18.45 (*0-89919-393-5*, Pub. by Ticknor & Fields) HM.

***Mallon, Thomas.** Two Moons. LC 99-34235. 303p. 2000. 24.00 (*0-375-40025-7*) Pantheon.

Mallon, William J., et al. Orthopaedics for the House Officer. (Illus.). 200p. 1990. 21.95 (*0-683-05420-1*) Lppncott W & W.

Mallonee, Barbara C., et al. Minute by Minute: A History of the Baltimore Monthly Meetings of Friends, Homewood & Stony Run. (Illus.). 308p. (Orig.). 1992. pap. 17.00 (*0-9635053-1-9*) Baltimore Monthly.

Mallonee, David. Foolproof Finances. 167p. pap. 14.97 incl. audio (*1-883906-11-3*) Kingdom Prods.

Mallonee, Dennis. The Coming of Aphrodite. (Illus.). 32p. (Orig.). 1992. pap. 3.95 (*0-929729-00-5*) Heroic Pub CA.

— Eternity Smith, Bk. 1. (Illus.). 64p. (Orig.). 1988. pap. 7.95 (*0-317-91226-7*) Heroic Pub CA.

— Flare, Bk. 1. (Illus.). 64p. (Orig.). 1988. pap. 7.95 (*0-317-91227-5*) Heroic Pub CA.

— League of Champions, Bk. 1. (Illus.). 160p. (Orig.). 1990. pap. 9.95 (*0-929729-01-3*) Heroic Pub CA.

Mallonee, Sue, ed. see Azeredo, Ruth.

Mallor. Business Law & Regulatory Environment. 10th ed. 344p. 1997. pap. 30.00 (*0-256-27148-8*) McGraw.

— Business Law & the Regulatory Environment. 11th ed. 2001. 71.25 (*0-07-231407-9*) McGraw.

Mallor, Jane & Barnes, A. James. Business Law & the Regulatory Environment: Concepts & Cases. 10th ed. LC 97-25762. 1248p. (C). 1997. text 101.25 (*0-256-19716-4*, Irwn McGrw-H) McGrw-H Hghr Educ.

Mallor, Jane, et al. CPS - Business Law & the Regulatory Environment Select Material. 9th ed. 628p. (C). 1995. text 36.95 (*0-256-20360-1*, Irwn McGrw-H) McGrw-H Hghr Educ.

Mallorca, Jacqueline. Breads. Williams, Chuck, ed. LC 95-47664. (Williams-Sonoma Kitchen Library). (Illus.). 108p. (J). (gr. 11). 1999. 18.95 (*0-7835-0316-4*) Time-Life.

— Cooking Basics. Williams, Chuck, ed. LC 95-47663. (Williams-Sonoma Kitchen Library). (Illus.). 108p. (gr. 11). 1999. 18.95 (*0-7835-0318-0*) Time-Life.

— The Perfect Dinner: Fine Food Cooked with Foil. LC 98-73198. (Illus.). 127p. 1999. 22.95 (*0-9658811-8-0*, 99PD) Fairoaks Pr.

Mallord, Lauri A. No More Black Days: Complete Freedom from Depression, Eating Disorders & Other Compulsive Behaviors. 128p. (Orig.). 1992. pap. 5.95 (*0-9630069-0-8*, 1000) Whi Stone.

***Mallore, Eugene F.** Fire from Ice: Searching for the Truth Behind the Cold Fusion Furor. (Illus.). 340p. 1999. reprint ed. pap. 25.95 (*1-892925-02-8*) Cold Fusion Tech.

Mallory, A. W. Guidelines for Centrifugal Blast Cleaning. (Illus.). 1984. pap. text 15.00 (*0-938477-09-9*) SSPC.

Mallory, Bob F., jt. auth. see Cargo, David N.

Mallory, Bruce & New, Rebecca. Diversity & Developmentally Appropriate Practice in Early Childhood Education: Challenges for Early Childhood Education. (Early Childhood Education Ser.). 304p. (C). 1993. text 41.00 (*0-8077-3300-8*); pap. text 18.95 (*0-8077-3299-0*) Tchrs Coll.

Mallory, Charles. Direct Mail Magic: A Practice Guide to Effective Direct Mail Advertising. Brett, Elaine, ed. LC 90-83478. (Fifty-Minute Ser.). (Illus.). 73p. (Orig.). 1991. pap. 10.95 (*1-56052-075-2*) Crisp Pubns.

— How to Get Everything Done (& Still Have a Life) Miller, Karen M., ed. LC 97-70153. (How-to Book Ser.). 104p. (Orig.). 1997. pap. 12.95 (*1-884926-73-8*, DONOW) Amer Media.

— It's a Jungle Out There! Dealing with Difficult Behavior in the Workplace. Miller, Karen M., ed. LC 98-70376. (How-To Book Ser.). 100p. 1998. pap. 12.95 (*1-884926-86-X*, JUNGL) Amer Media.

— Publicity Power: A Practical Guide to Effective Promotion. Crisp, Michael G., ed. LC 88-92737. (Fifty-Minute Ser.). (Illus.). 70p. (Orig.). 1989. pap. 10.95 (*0-931961-82-3*) Crisp Pubns.

Mallory, Charles. Workhealing: The Healing Process for You & Your Job. 128p. (Orig.). 1993. pap. 8.95 (*0-87516-664-4*) DeVorss.

Mallory, Claire. The Snowman's Song. (Illus.). 24p. (J). (ps-k). 1998. 1.99 (*0-679-87010-5*, Pub. by Random Bks Yng Read) Random.

Mallory, Clare. Snowman's Song. (J). 1998. lib. bdg. 7.99 (*0-679-97010-X*, Pub. by Random Bks Yng Read) Random.

Mallory, Daniel, jt. auth. see Clay, Henry.

Mallory, Doug. Football Drill Book. (Illus.). 240p. (Orig.). 1993. pap. 14.95 (*0-940279-72-X*, 7972XH, Mstrs Pr) NTC Contemp Pub Co.

Mallory, Eva L. Riding the Right Roads. (Illus.). 640p. 1989. ring bd. 25.00 (*0-685-28999-0*) Right Roads Pubns.

Mallory, F. R. 18: First Taking. Blake, Lynn M., ed. 280p. 1998. 11.95 (*1-893006-22-0*) Unbound Bks.

***Mallory, F. R.** 18: First Taking. Blake, Lynn M., ed. 280p. 1998. lthr. 65.95 (*1-893006-20-4*) Unbound Bks.

Mallory, F. R. Extreme Space: The Domination & Submission Handbook. Blake, Lynn M., ed. 278p. 1998. 21.95 (*1-893006-24-7*) Unbound Bks.

— Rhapsody: To Touch the Face of the Goddess. Blake, Lynn M., ed. 230p. 1998. 11.95 (*1-893006-23-9*) Unbound Bks.

Mallory, Franklin B. Serial Numbers of U. S. Martial Arms. LC 82-63083. 112p. 1983. pap. 15.00 (*0-9603306-1-5*) Springfield Res Serv.

— Serial Numbers of U. S. Martial Arms. 208p. 1990. pap. 20.00 (*0-9603306-4-X*) Springfield Res Serv.

— Serial Numbers of U. S. Martial Arms. 320p. 1995. pap. 30.00 (*0-9603306-5-8*) Springfield Res Serv.

— Serial Numbers of U. S. Martial Arms, Vol. 2. 209p. 1986. pap. 20.00 (*0-9603306-3-1*) Springfield Res Serv.

Mallory, Geoffrey R., jt. auth. see Cray, David.

Mallory, Glenn O. & Hajdu, Juan B., eds. Electroless Plating: Fundamentals & Applications. 539p. 1990. 95.00 (*0-936569-07-7*) Noyes.

Mallory, J. P. In Search of the Indo-Europeans: Language, Archaeology & Myth. 1991. pap. 19.95 (*0-500-27616-1*, Pub. by Thames Hudson) Norton.

***Mallory, J. P. & Mair, Victor H.** The Tarim Mummies: Ancient China & the Mysteries of the Earliest Peoples from the West. LC 99-66166. (Illus.). 352p. 2000. 50.00 (*0-500-05101-1*, Pub. by Thames Hudson) Norton.

Mallory, J. P., et al. The Indo-Europeanization of Northern Europe. LC 96-76203. (Journal of Indo-European Studies: No. 17). (Illus.). 376p. 1996. pap. 48.00 (*0-941694-53-4*) Inst Study Man.

— The Indo-Europeanization of Northern Europe. LC 96-76203. (Journal of Indo-European Studies: No. 17). (Illus.). 376p. (C). 1996. 56.00 (*0-941694-52-6*) Inst Study Man.

Mallory, J. P., jt. auth. see Telegin, D. Ya.

***Mallory, James.** Merlin Pt. I: The Old Magic. 273p. 1999. mass mkt. 6.99 (*0-446-60766-5*, Pub. by Warner Bks) Little.

— Merlin Pt. I: The Old Magic. large type ed. LC 99-40366. 1999. 23.95 (*0-7838-8772-8*, G K Hall Lrg Type) Mac Lib Ref.

Mallory, James. Merlin Pt. 2: The King's Wizard. 304p. 1999. mass mkt. 6.99 (*0-446-60791-6*, Pub. by Warner Bks) Little.

***Mallory, James.** Merlin Pt. 3: The End of Magic. 304p. 2000. mass mkt. 6.99 (*0-446-60792-4*, Pub. by Warner Bks) Little.

Mallory, James & Adams, D. Q., eds. Encyclopedia of Indo-European Culture. LC 98-101334. 1000p. 1997. lib. bdg. 135.00 (*1-884964-98-2*) Fitzroy Dearborn.

Mallory, James D., Jr. Battles of the Sexes: How Both Sides Can Win with Honor. LC 94-36449. 224p. 1996. pap. 12.99 (*0-89107-812-6*) Crossway Bks.

Mallory, James D., Jr., jt. auth. see Kubetin, Cynthia A.

Mallory, Kenneth. Families of the Deep Blue Sea. LC 95-7039. (Illus.). 32p. (J). (ps-3). 1995. 14.95 (*0-88106-886-1*); pap. 6.95 (*0-88106-885-3*) Charlesbridge Pub.

— Families of the Deep Blue Sea. LC 95-7039. 1995. 12.15 (*0-606-09258-7*, Pub. by Turtleback) Demco.

— Home by the Sea. 1998. 27.12 (*0-8172-5766-7*) Raintree Steck-V.

— A Home by the Sea: Protecting Coastal Wildlife. LC 97-38020. (Illus.). 64p. (J). (gr. 4-7). 1998. 18.00 (*0-15-200043-7*); pap. 9.00 (*0-15-201802-6*) Harcourt.

***Mallory, Kenneth.** Home by the Sea: Protecting Coastal Wildlife. (Illus.). (J). 1998. 14.45 (*0-606-18175-X*) Turtleback.

Mallory, Kenneth, jt. ed. see Kaufman, Les.

Mallory, L. Leading Self-Help Groups: A Guide for Training Facilitators. LC 83-48659. 72p. 1984. pap. 7.95 (*0-87304-206-9*) Manticore Pubs.

Mallory, Lee. Full Moon, Empty Hands. Harrell, John C., ed. (Illus.). 69p. 1994. pap. 12.95 (*0-9632702-7-3*) Lightning.

Mallory, Lee, ed. see Edelman, Bart.

Mallory, Lee, ed. see Harrell, John C.

Mallory, Nina A., et al. Painting in Spain, 1650-1700. Guicherneau, June, ed. (Illus.). 182p. (C). 1982. text 55.00 (*0-691-03992-5*, Pub. by Princeton U Pr) Cal Prin Full Svc.

Mallory, Nina A., jt. auth. see Sullivan, Edward J.

Mallory, Norman. Profitable No-Load Mutual Fund Trading Techniques: For the Individual Investor. (Illus.). 153p. 1988. pap. 37.95 (*0-930233-11-5*, Pub. by Windsor) Natl Bk Netwk.

Mallory, Perry M., ed. see Tetsola, John.

Mallory, Randy & Lastage, Donna. Tyler, Texas. (Illus.). 150p. 1997. 34.95 (*1-890291-01-3*) Platinum Pubng.

***Mallory, S. B. & Treadwell, P. A.** Handbook of Pediatric Dermatology. 2nd ed. (Illus.). 200p. 2001. 60.00 (*1-85070-753-7*) Prthnon Pub.

Mallory, Steven R. Software Quality Assurance SOPs for Healthcare Manufacturers. LC 97-6739. 425p. 1997. 189.00 (*1-57491-038-8*) Interpharm.

Mallory, Steven R., ed. Software Development & Quality Assurance for the Healthcare Manufacturing Industries. 2nd ed. LC 97-5731. (Illus.). 340p. 1997. 189.00 (*1-57491-052-3*) Interpharm.

Mallory, Susan B. & Leal-Khouri, Susana. An Illustrated Dictionary of Dermatologic Syndromes. LC 94-15125. (Illus.). 258p. 1994. 54.95 (*1-85070-458-9*) Prthnon Pub.

***Mallory, Tess.** To Touch the Stars. 320p. 1998. mass mkt. 4.99 (*0-505-52253-5*, Love Spell) Dorchester Pub Co.

Mallory, Virgil S. Lower Tertiary Biostratigraphy of the California Coast Ranges. LC 59-1390. 460p. reprint ed. pap. 142.60 (*0-608-13923-8*, 202374500033) Bks Demand.

***Mallory, W. Z.** Surreal Song of Reno. 119p. 2000. 9.95 (*0-9672387-1-4*) Rhinestone Bks.

Mallory, Walter H. China: Land of Famine. LC 76-39655. (Select Bibliographies Reprint Ser.). 1977. reprint ed. 23.95 (*0-8369-9940-1*) Ayer.

Mallory, William & Simpson-Housley, Paul, eds. Geography & Literature: A Meeting of the Disciplines. LC 86-22968. (Illus.). 192p. 1989. pap. text 16.95 (*0-8156-2464-6*) Syracuse U Pr.

Mallos, Tess. The Complete Mediterranean Cookbook. (Illus.). 304p. 1996. 34.95 (*0-8048-3090-8*) Tuttle Pubng.

— The Complete Middle East Cookbook. (Illus.). 500p. 1993. 34.95 (*0-8048-1982-3*) Tuttle Pubng.

***Mallot, Hanspeter A.** Computational Vision: Information Processing in Perception & Visual Behavior. (Computational Neuroscience Ser.). (Illus.). 290p. 2000. 50.00 (*0-262-13381-4*, Bradford Bks) MIT Pr.

Mallouk & Mills. Getting Productive with Microsoft Excel. 1997. pap. 23.95 (*0-87393-534-9*) Dame Pubns.

Mallouk, Brenda M. Accounting: The Basis for Business Decisions: Problem Supplement II Solutions Manual. (C). 1990. pap. text. write for info. (*0-07-551001-4*) McG-H Ryerson.

— Adders 'N Keyes: One Month in the Life of a Sole Proprietorship. 2nd ed. (C). 1991. pap. text. write for info. (*0-07-551221-1*) McG-H Ryerson.

— Problems Plus Solutions in Financial Accounting. Smythe, Kelly, ed. 124p. (C). 1991. pap. text. write for info. (*0-07-551340-4*) McG-H Ryerson.

— Problems, Problems & More Problems in Accounting. Smythe, Kelly, ed. (C). 1991. reprint ed. pap. text. write for info. (*0-07-551331-5*) McG-H Ryerson.

***Mallouk, Mark.** "One in a Million" A Book for Future Jayhawks. LC 98-75251. (Illus.). (J). (gr. 1-3). 1998. pap. 9.95 (*1-890622-52-4*) Leathers Pub.

Mallouk, Peter. Kissing in Kansas City. LC 97-51143. (Illus.). 144p. 1998. 12.95 (*1-886110-47-6*) Addax Pubng.

Mallouk, Thomas E., ed. Advances in the Synthesis & Reactivity of Solids, Vol. 1. 276p. 1991. 109.50 (*1-55938-182-5*) Jai Pr.

— Advances in the Synthesis & Reactivity of Solids, Vol. 2. 283p. 1994. 109.50 (*1-55938-330-5*) Jai Pr.

— Advances in the Synthesis & Reactivity of Solids, Vol. 3. Date not set. 109.50 (*1-55938-795-5*) Jai Pr.

Mallouk, Thomas E. & Harrison, D. Jed, eds. Interfacial Design & Chemical Sensing. LC 94-19957. (Symposium Ser.: Vol. 561). 352p. 1994. text 105.00 (*0-8412-2931-7*, Pub. by Am Chemical) OUP.

Mallove, Eugene, ed. see Mizuno, Tadahiko.

Mallove, Eugene F. & Matloff, Gregory L. The Starflight Handbook: A Pioneer's Guide to Interstellar Travel. LC 88-31933. (Wiley Science Editions Ser.). 288p. 1989. 29.95 (*0-471-61912-4*) Wiley.

Mallow, David. True Vipers: Biology & Toxinology. 2000. 50.00 (*0-89464-877-2*) Krieger.

***Mallow, Frances & Patterson, Leslie, eds.** Framing Literacy: Teaching/Learning in K-8 Classrooms. 288p. 2000. pap. text, teacher ed. 41.95 (*0-926842-90-0*, 312) CG Pubs Inc.

Mallow, Jeffry V. Science Anxiety. Hackworth, Robert & Howland, Joseph W., eds. (Illus.). 200p. (Orig.). 1986. 12.95 (*0-943202-18-3*) H & H Pub.

Mallow, Judy M. Pine Needle Basketry: From Forest Floor to Finished Project. Rich, Chris, ed. LC 96-26504. (Illus.). 120p. 1997. 18.95 (*1-887374-14-0*) Lark Books.

Mallowe, Mike, jt. auth. see McCarthy, Bill.

Mallows, Michael, jt. auth. see Sinclair, Joseph.

Malloy. Bank Law. 2nd ed. LC 93-80968. 1994. 165.00 (*0-316-54541-4*, Aspen Law & Bus) Aspen Pub.

— Bank Law, Vol. 2. LC 93-80968. 1994. 165.00 (*0-316-54573-2*, Aspen Law & Bus) Aspen Pub.

— Bank Law, Vol. 3. 2nd ed. LC 93-80968. 1994. 165.00 (*0-316-54764-6*, Aspen Law & Bus) Aspen Pub.

— Landmarks in Liberty. (C). 1993. pap. text 20.50 (*0-07-039823-2*) McGraw.

Malloy, jt. auth. see Ross.

Malloy, tr. see Gallegos, Romulo.

Malloy, Alex G. American Games: Comprehensive Collector's Guide. large type ed. LC 99-68105. (Illus.). 352p. 2000. pap. 26.95 (*0-930625-60-9*, AT5609) Krause Pubns.

— Comic Book Artists. (Illus.). 352p. 1993. pap. 14.95 (*0-87069-707-2*, Wllce-Homestd) Krause Pubns.

***Malloy, Alex G.** Comics Values Annual 2000: The Comic Books Price Guide. annuals (Illus.). 776p. 2000. pap. 16.95 (*1-58221-020-9*, Antique Trader) Krause Pubns.

— Official Guide to Artifacts of Ancient Civilizations. 256p. 1997. pap. 19.95 (*0-676-60079-4*) Random.

Malloy, Alex G. Price Guide to Medieval Coins in the Christian J. Thomsen Collection, Vol. 1. 1993. 9.50 (*0-915018-46-2*) Attic Bks.

Malloy, Alex G. & Wells, Stuart W., III. Comics Collectibles & Their Values. LC 96-155384. (Illus.). 352p. 1996. pap. 17.95 (*0-87069-724-2*, Wllce-Homestd) Krause Pubns.

Malloy, Alex G., jt. auth. see Sydenham, Edward A.

***Malloy, Barbara.** Newport. (Images of America Ser.). 128p. 1999. pap. 18.99 (*0-7385-0298-7*) Arcadia Publng.

Malloy, Carol E. & Brader-Araje, Laura, eds. Challenges in the Mathematics Education of African American Children: Proceedings of the Benjamin Banneker Association Leadership Conference. LC 98-54410. 85 p. 1998. pap. 11.95 (*0-87353-458-1*) NCTM.

Malloy, Catharine & Carey, Phyllis, eds. Seamus Heaney: The Shaping Spirit. LC 95-33643. (Illus.). 200p. 1996. 24.50 (*0-87413-581-8*) U Delaware Pr.

M

An Asterisk (*) at the beginning of an entry indicates that the title is appearing for the first time.

M

Malloy, Catheric & Hartshorn, Edward A. Acute Care Nursing in the Home: A Holistic Approach. (Illus.). 606p. 1988. text 36.50 (*0-397-54661-0*) Lppncott W & W.

Malloy, Charles. The Poems of Emerson: Selected Criticism from the Coming Age & the Arena, 1899-1905. LC 80-2539. 1981. 55.00 (*0-404-19265-3*) AMS Pr.

***Malloy, David C., et al.** Sport Ethics: Concepts & Cases in Sport & Recreation. 192p. 1999. pap. 19.95 (*1-55077-107-8*) Thompson Educ.

Malloy, Dick, jt. auth. see Ott, John S.

Malloy, E. Michael. Malloy's GMDSS: A Technical Approach. Johnson, Jane, ed. (Illus.). 300p. 1995. spiral bd. write for info. (*0-9673944-0-6*) Malloy Comm.

Malloy, Edward A. Monk's Reflections: A View From the Dome. LC 99-21803. 256p. 1999. 19.95 (*0-7407-0116-9*) Andrews & McMeel.

Malloy, Ione. Southie Won't Go: A Teacher's Diary of the Desegregation of South Boston High School. LC 86-16563. (Illus.). 304p. 1986. text 29.95 (*0-252-01276-3*) U of Ill Pr.

Malloy, James M. Bolivia: The Uncompleted Revolution. LC 77-101486. (Pitt Latin American Ser.). 406p. reprint ed. 125.90 (*0-8357-9751-1*, 201544900094) Bks Demand.

Malloy, James M., ed. Authoritarianism & Corporatism in Latin America. LC 76-6669. (Latin American Ser.). 552p. (C). 1976. pap. 19.95 (*0-8229-5275-0*) U of Pittsburgh Pr.

Malloy, James M. & Gamarra, Eduardo A. Revolution & Reaction: Bolivia, 1964-1985. 256p. 1987. 29.95 (*0-88738-159-6*) Transaction Pubs.

— Revolution & Reaction: Bolivia, 1964-1992. 2nd ed. 1992. 32.95 (*1-56000-032-5*) Transaction Pubs.

Malloy, James M. & Gamarra, Eduardo A., eds. Latin America & Caribbean Contemporary Record, 1987-1988, VII. 1000p. 1990. 380.00 (*0-8419-1237-8*) Holmes & Meier.

— Latin America & Caribbean Contemporary Record, 1988-1989, Vol. VIII. x, 1100p. 1996. 390.00 (*0-8419-1290-4*) Holmes & Meier.

Malloy, James M. & Seligson, Mitchell A., eds. Authoritarians & Democrats: Regime Transition in Latin America. LC 86-25035. (Latin American Ser.). (Illus.). 288p. (C). 1987. pap. 15.95 (*0-8229-5387-0*); text 49.95 (*0-8229-3551-1*) U of Pittsburgh Pr.

Malloy, James M., jt. auth. see Conaghan, Catherine M.

Malloy, James M., jt. auth. see Von Mettenheim, Kurt.

Malloy, John B. What Are Stocks Really Worth? The Smartvalue Formula for Buying Low & Selling High LC 98-96295. xxi, 313 p. 1998. 29.95 (*0-9664208-0-2*) Analytical Bks.

— Winning Investment Strategies. 1991. 49.95 (*0-8306-6741-5*) McGraw-Hill Prof.

— Winning Investment Strategies: Using Security Analysis to Build Wealth. 1990. 22.95 (*0-8306-3509-2*) McGraw-Hill Prof.

Malloy, John F., jt. auth. see Turner, William C.

Malloy, Joseph L., ed. Catechism for Inquirers. 4th ed. 1984. pap. 4.95 (*0-8091-5012-3*) Paulist Pr.

Malloy, Joseph T., tr. see Diez, Klemens, pseud.

Malloy, Kevin, ed. see Stefaniak, Norbert J.

Malloy, Lawrence J. Quick Works: Introduction to Microsoft Window 3.0 122p. (C). 1994. text 25.00 (*0-536-58567-9*) Pearson Custom.

Malloy, Mary. African Americans in the Maritime Trades: A Guide to Resources in New England. Frank, Stuart M., ed. (Kendall Whaling Museum Monograph: No. 6). (Illus.). 26p. 1990. pap. text 8.50 (*0-937854-30-1*) Kendall Whaling.

— Boston Men on the Northwest Coast: The American Maritime Fur Trade, 1788-1844. (Alaska History Ser.: No. 47). 232p. 1998. 28.00 (*1-895901-18-9*) Limestone.

Malloy, Mary, ed. see Sturgis, William.

Malloy, Mary G. & Jacobs, Marion. Genealogical Abstracts Montgomery County Sentinel, 1855-1899. 1987. 24.00 (*0-317-68194-X*) Montgomery Co Hist.

Malloy, Maureen A. Things in Small Quantities Have Lasting Appeal. Soeder, Robert F., ed. (Illus.). 114p. (Orig.). 1996. pap. 12.95 (*0-9655355-0-9*) Academy Prods.

Malloy, Merrit. Great Rock & Roll Quote Book. (Illus.). 96p. 1995. pap. 6.95 (*0-312-13504-1*) St Martin.

— Irish American Funny Quotes. LC 94-26206. (Illus.). 128p. 1994. pap. 6.95 (*0-8069-0753-3*) Sterling.

— The People Who Didn't Say Goodbye. LC 82-45932. 144p. 1985. pap. 11.95 (*0-385-18784-X*) Doubleday.

— Semi-Deep Thoughts. 1996. mass mkt. 5.99 (*0-7860-0278-6*, Pinncle Kensgtn) Kensgtn Pub Corp.

Malloy, Michael P. Banking & Financial Services: Cases, Materials, & Problems. LC 98-48221. 720p. 1999. 90.00 (*0-89089-823-5*) Carolina Acad Pr.

— Banking Law & Regulation, 3 vols. 1600p. 1998. ring bd. 440.00 (*0-316-54461-2*, 44612) Aspen Law.

— The Corporate Law of Banks: Regulation of Corporate & Securities Activities of Depository Institutions, 2 vols., Set. 1800p. 1987. 160.00 (*0-316-54462-0*, Aspen Law & Bus) Aspen Pub.

— Economic Sanctions. 176p. 1995. 20.95 (*0-316-54357-8*, Aspen Law & Bus) Aspen Pub.

— Economic Sanctions & U. S. Trade. annuals 777p. 1990. boxed set 175.00 (*0-316-54538-4*, 45384) Aspen Law.

— Economic Sanctions & U. S. Trade. 1990. 175.00 (*0-316-54515-5*, Aspen Law & Bus) Aspen Pub.

— Economic Sanctions in U. S. International Trade. 1989. write for info. (*0-318-63269-1*, Aspen Law & Bus) Aspen Pub.

— Economic Sanctions, 1994. 1994. suppl. ed. 100.00 (*0-316-54804-9*, Aspen Law & Bus) Aspen Pub.

— Economic Sanctions, 1995. 1996. 110.00 (*0-316-54936-3*) Little.

— Fundamentals of Banking Regulation. LC 98-27605. 1998. ring bd. 185.00 (*1-56706-675-5*) Aspen Law.

— International Banking. LC 98-39696. 480p. 1998. boxed set 80.00 (*0-89089-851-0*) Carolina Acad Pr.

Malloy, Mike. Lee Van Cleef: A Biographical, Film & Television Reference. LC 98-13033. 204p. 1998. lib. bdg. 35.00 (*0-7864-0437-X*) McFarland & Co.

Malloy, Nancy. European Art since 1850. Turner, C. M., ed. LC 97-165193. (International Encyclopedia of Art Ser.). 64p. 1997. 19.95 (*0-8160-3334-X*) Facts on File.

Malloy, Robert A. Plastic Part Design for Injection Molding: An Introduction. 450p. (C). 1994. 79.50 (*1-56990-129-5*) Hanser-Gardner.

Malloy, Robet, contrib. by. Cast down Your Bucket Where You Are Vol. 10: Black Americans on Immigration. 31p. (Orig.). 1996. pap. 7.00 (*1-881290-12-3*) Ctr Immigrat.

Malloy, Robin P. Law & Economics: A Comparative Approach to Theory & Practice. 166p. (C). 1990. pap. text 17.50 (*0-314-72586-5*) West Pub.

— Planning for Serfdom: Legal Economic Discourse & Downtown Development. LC 90-29188. 208p. (C). 1991. text 32.50 (*0-8122-3055-8*) U of Pa Pr.

Malloy, Robin P. & Braun, Christopher K., eds. Law & Economics: New & Critical Perspectives. (Critic of Institutions Ser.: Vol. 4). 460p. (C). 1995. pap. text 29.95 (*0-8204-2627-X*) P Lang Pubng.

Malloy, Robin P. & Evensky, Jerry, eds. Adam Smith & the Philosophy of Law & Economics. (Law & Philosophy Library: No. 20). 235p. 1995. pap. text 50.50 (*0-7923-3425-6*) Kluwer Academic.

***Malloy, Robin P. & Smith, James C.** Real Estate: Aspen RoadMap Law Course Outline. LC 99-86975. 300p. 2000. pap. text 21.95 (*0-7355-1249-3*, Aspen Law & Bus) Aspen Pub.

Malloy, Robin P. & Smith, James C. Real Estate Transactions: Problems, Cases & Materials. LC 98-9719. 1408p. 1998. boxed set 60.00 (*1-56706-644-5*) Aspen Pub.

***Malloy, Robin Paul.** Law & Market Economy: Reinterpreting the Values of Law & Economics. 200p. (C). 2000. text Price not set. (*0-521-78214-7*); pap. text Price not set. (*0-521-78731-9*) Cambridge U Pr.

Malloy, Roderick A. Malloy's Sports Collectibles Value Guide. LC 92-50673. (Illus.). 448p. 1993. pap. 17.95 (*0-87069-689-0*, Wllce-Homestd) Krause Pubns.

***Malloy, Ruth L.** China Guide. 10th ed. 800p. 1999. pap. text 21.95 (*1-892975-01-7*) Open Rd Pub.

***Malloy, Terry & Monaco, Robert.** Creatine & Other Natural Muscle Enhancers. 224p. 1999. mass mkt. 5.99 (*0-440-23555-3*) Dell.

Malloy, Terry, jt. auth. see Whitehead, E. Douglas.

Malloy, William M. Senate Documents, Treaties, Conventions, International Acts, Protocols, & Agreements Between the United States of America & Other Powers, 4 vols., Set. reprint ed. lib. bdg. 395.00 (*0-403-00246-X*) Scholarly.

Malloy, William M. Treaties, Conventions, International Acts, Protocols & Agreements, 2 vols. 2518p. 1996. reprint ed. 395.00 (*1-56169-225-5*) Gaunt.

Mallozzi, F., et al. Amici: A Text for Beginners in Italian, Vol. I. (ITA., Illus.). 116p. (J). (gr. 7-9). 1993. reprint ed. wbk. ed. 10.00 (*0-9637279-1-5*); reprint ed. text 32.50 (*0-9637279-0-7*) MVM Pubs.

— Amici: An Intermediate Text for Italian, Vol. II. (Illus.). 304p. (YA). (gr. 10-12). 1995. text 37.50 (*0-9637279-2-3*) MVM Pubs.

Mallozzi, Fernando, et al. Amici Vol. 2: An Intermediate Text for Italian. (ENG & ITA., Illus.). 200p. (YA). (gr. 10-12). 1997. pap. text, wbk. ed. 14.50 (*0-9637279-3-1*) MVM Pubs.

***Mallozzi, Fernando, et al.** AMILI Vol. 1: A Text for Beginners in Italian. 2nd rev. ed. (Illus.). 321p. (YA). (gr. 7-8). 1999. 34.00 (*0-9637279-4-X*) MVM Pubs.

Mallozzi, John S. & DeLillo, Nicholas J. Computability with Pascal. LC 83-24450. (Illus.). 193p. (C). 1984. text 26.95 (*0-685-07560-5*) P-H.

Mallozzi, Vincent M. Basketball: The Legends & the Game. (Illus.). 350p. 1998. text 35.00 (*1-55209-247-X*) Firefly Bks Ltd.

— Hoop Drills: The Coach's Guide. (Illus.). 128p. 1998. pap. 14.95 (*1-55209-197-X*) Firefly Bks Ltd.

Malluche, H. H., ed. Bone Disease in Renal Failure. (Mineral & Electrolyte Metabolism Ser.: Vol. 17, No. 4). (Illus.). 92p. 1992. pap. 59.25 (*3-8055-5506-7*) S Karger.

Malluche, H. H. & Faugere, Marie-Claude. Atlas of Mineralized Bone Histology. (Illus.). xiii, 136p. 1986. 208.00 (*3-8055-4201-1*) S Karger.

Mallwitz, Alfred, jt. auth. see Heyder, Wolfgang.

Mally, E. Logische Schriften: Grosses Logikfragment, Grundgesetze des Sollens. LC 73-135106. (Synthese Historical Library: No. 3). (GER.). 357p. 1971. text 141.50 (*90-277-0174-1*, D Reidel) Kluwer Academic.

Mally, E. Louise. A Treasury of Animal Stories. 1976. 25.95 (*0-8488-0764-2*) Amereon Ltd.

Mally, Lynn. Culture of the Future: The Proletkult Movement in Revolutionary Russia. 1989. 50.00 (*0-520-06577-8*, Pub. by U CA Pr) Cal Prin Full Svc.

***Mally, Lynn.** Revolutionary Acts: Amateur Theater & the Soviet State, 1917-1938. LC 00-9282. (Illus.). 2000. write for info. (*0-8014-3769-5*) Cornell U Pr.

Malm, Gerhard A. Bridles & Bits: An Encyclopedia. LC 96-94493. (Illus.). ix, 550p. 1996. lib. bdg. 65.00 (*0-9652818-0-9*) Grasshpper Pub.

Malm, Karen. Behavior Management in K-6 Classrooms. 128p. 1992. pap. 11.95 (*0-8106-0365-9*) NEA.

***Malm, Kiyoko.** Irasshai Explorer Japanese in the Middle: A Multimedia Exploratory Course for Middle Schools. Rieken, Elizabeth & Duncan, Gregory, eds. (Illus.). 144p. (gr. 6-8). 1998. pap. text, student ed. 24.95 incl. VHS (*1-892720-02-7*) GA Public Brdcstng.

Malm, Kiyoko. Irasshai Explorer Japanese in the Middle: Teacher Resource Guide. Rieken, Elizabeth & Duncan, Gregory, eds. (Illus.). 370p. 1998. teacher ed., ring bd. 100.00 incl. VHS (*1-892720-01-9*) GA Public Brdcstng.

Malm, Richard. Perfected Praise. 96p. (Orig.). 1988. pap. 8.99 (*0-914903-62-4*) Destiny Image.

Malm, Rita. NASD Series 6. LC 97-62218. 250p. (Orig.). 1999. pap. text 26.95 (*1-884803-08-3*) Werbel Pub.

— NASD Series 63. LC 97-62219. 65p. (Orig.). 1999. pap. 12.95 (*1-884803-09-1*) Werbel Pub.

Malm, Rita & Sadowsky, Donald. Dying on Wall Street. 66p. 1993. pap. text 12.00 (*1-884803-06-7*) Werbel Pub.

Malm, Rita P. NASD Series 7. 300p. 1999. pap. text 32.95 (*1-884803-16-4*) Werbel Pub.

Malm, Suzanne, jt. auth. see Leggett, John C.

Malm, William P. Music Cultures of the Pacific, the Near East & Asia. 3rd ed. LC 94-48578. (History of Music Ser.). 278p. (C). 1995. pap. text 48.00 (*0-13-182387-6*) P-H.

— Nagauta: The Heart of Kabuki Music. LC 73-6260. (Illus.). 344p. 1973. reprint ed. lib. bdg. 49.75 (*0-8371-6900-3*, Greenwood Pr) Greenwood.

***Malm, William P.** Traditional Japanese Music & Musical Instruments. (Illus.). 2001. 35.00 (*4-7700-2395-2*) Kodansha.

Malman, Laurie. Federal Income Taxation: Problems, Cases & Materials. Solomon, Lewis D. & Hesck, Jerome H., eds. (American Casebook Ser.). 440p. 1994. pap. text. write for info. (*0-314-04150-8*) West Pub.

Malman, Laurie L., et al. Federal Income Taxation: Problems, Cases & Materials. 2nd ed. LC 94-4266. (American Casebook Ser.). 991p. (C). 1994. 60.00 (*0-314-03503-6*) West Pub.

Malmat, Bonnie. Abstracts of the Washington County Reporter 1808-1814. 323p. 1990. per. 19.95 (*1-55856-041-6*, 109) Closson Pr.

— Through the Window of the Past Abstracts of the Washington Reporter: August 1, 1814-December 30, 1816. 222p. 1993. pap. text 19.95 (*1-55856-151-X*, 111) Closson Pr.

Malmaud, Roslyn. Work & Marriage: The Two-Profession Couple. LC 84-104. (Research in Clinical Psychology Ser.: No. 10). 299p. reprint ed. pap. 92.70 (*0-8357-1543-4*, 207040300088) Bks Demand.

Malmberg, Bertil. Linguistique Generale et Romane: Etudes en Allemand, Anglais, Espagnol et Francais. (Janua Linguarum, Series Major: No. 66). 1973. 112.35 (*90-279-2429-5*) Mouton.

Malmberg, Bertil, ed. Readings in Modern Linguistics: An Anthology. 384p. (Orig.). 1972. pap. text 70.80 (*90-279-2100-8*) Mouton.

Malmberg, Carl, tr. see Kristensen, Tom.

Malmberg, Carl, tr. see Paludan, Jacob.

Malmberg, Gunnar. Metropolitan Growth & Migration in Peru. (University of Umea Geographical Reports: No. 9). (Illus.). 266p. (Orig.). 1988. pap. 87.50 (*91-7174-329-4*, Pub. by Umea U Bibl) Coronet Bks.

Malmberg, Lars, tr. see Bergfeldt, Inga.

***Malmberg, Melody.** The Making of Disney's Animal Kingdom Theme Park. LC 98-200587. 160p. (J). 1998. 24.95 (*0-7868-6402-8*, Pub. by Hyperion) Time Warner.

Malmberg, Torsten. Human Territoriality. (New Babylon Studies in the Social Sciences). 352p. 1980. 57.70 (*3-10-800346-1*) Mouton.

— Human Territoriality: A Survey on the Behavioral Territories of Man with Preliminary Analysis & Discussion of Meaning. 1979. pap. 23.10 (*3-10-800384-4*) Mouton.

Malmendier, C. L., et al, eds. Hypercholesterolemia, Hypocholesterolemia & Hypertriglyceridemia in Vivo Kinetics. LC 91-2557. (Advances in Experimental Medicine & Biology Ser.: Vol. 285). (Illus.). 454p. (C). 1991. text 150.00 (*0-306-43814-3*, Kluwer Plenum) Kluwer Academic.

Malmendier, C. L. & Alaupovic, P., eds. Eicosanoids, Apolipoproteins, Lipoprotein Particles, & Atherosclerosis. LC 88-28929. (Advances in Experimental Medicine & Biology Ser.: Vol. 243). (Illus.). 372p. 1988. 89.50 (*0-306-43037-1*, Plenum Trade) Perseus Pubng.

— Lipoproteins & Atherosclerosis. LC 87-2345. (Advances in Experimental Medicine & Biology Ser.: Vol. 210). 266p. 1987. 69.50 (*0-306-42487-8*, Plenum Trade) Perseus Pubng.

Malmesbury, James H. Diaries & Correspondence of the Earl of Malmesbury, 4 vols. 2nd ed. LC 73-121023. reprint ed. 265.00 (*0-404-04170-1*) AMS Pr.

Malmgreen, Gail, jt. ed. see Lebowitz, Arieh.

Malmgren, Carl D. Fictional Space in the Modernist & Postmodernist American Novel. 240p. 1985. 36.50 (*0-8387-5067-2*) Bucknell U Pr.

— Worlds Apart: Narratology of Science Fiction. LC 90-25045. 222p. 1991. 9.95 (*0-253-33645-7*) Ind U Pr.

***Malmgren, H., et al, eds.** Artificial Neural Networks in Medicine & Biology. (Perspectives in Neural Computing Ser.). 335p. 2000. pap. 79.95 (*1-85233-289-1*) Spr-Verlag.

Malmgren, Robert. The Equine Arena Handbook: Developing a User-Friendly Facility. LC 99-26226. (Illus.). 136p. 1999. pap. 13.95 (*1-57779-016-2*) Alpine Pubns.

Malmgren, Ulf. When the Leaves Begin to Fall. Tate, Joan, tr. from SWE. LC 78-24819. 128p. (J). (gr. 5 up). 1979. 9.95 (*0-06-024046-6*) HarpC Child Bks.

***Malmin, Glenda.** Journey of a Mother's Heart: Encouragement for Moms. LC 99-52689. 2000. pap. 9.99 (*0-8307-2538-5*, Regal Bks) Gospel Lght.

Malmin, Glenda. Woman You Are Called & Anointed. 237p. 1998. pap. 12.95 (*1-886849-17-X*) City Bible Pub.

Malmin, Jack. El Otro Lado (The Other Side) The True Story of Marcus Hooks--Smuggler. LC 90-70919. (Illus.). 1991. 19.95 (*0-9627198-0-3*) Trailblazer Pub.

Malmin, Ken & Conner, Kevin. New Testament Survey. 35p. 1975. pap. 5.99 (*0-914936-22-0*) City Bible Pub.

— Old Testament Survey. 47p. 1974. pap. 5.99 (*0-914936-21-2*) City Bible Pub.

Malmin, Ken, jt. auth. see Conner, Kevin J.

Malmin, Kenneth P. Bible Research - Revised. (Illus.). 202p. 1990. pap. 14.99 (*0-914936-71-9*) City Bible Pub.

Malmin, Kenneth P., jt. auth. see Conner, Kevin J.

Malmivuo, Jaakko & Plonsey, Robert. Bioelectromagnetism: Principles & Applications of Bioelectric & Biomagnetic Fields. (Illus.). 512p. 1995. text 98.00 (*0-19-505823-2*) OUP.

Malmkjaer, Kirsten, ed. The Linguistics Encyclopedia. (Illus.). 592p. (C). (gr. 13). 1991. 125.00 (*0-415-02942-2*, A6266) Routledge.

— The Linguistics Encyclopedia. (Illus.). 592p. (C). (gr. 13). 1995. pap. 29.99 (*0-415-12566-9*, C0435) Routledge.

Malmkjaer, Kirsten, jt. auth. see Knowles, Murray.

Malmkjaer, Kirsten, jt. ed. see Bush, Peter.

***Malmkjr, Kirsten, et al.** Context in Language Learning & Language Understanding. LC 98-39986. 1998. write for info. (*0-521-63337-0*); write for info. (*0-521-63355-9*) Cambridge U Pr.

Malmn, Y. & Rouhiainen, Veikko, eds. Reliability & Safety of Processes & Manufacturing Systems: Proc. of the Twelfth Annual Symp. of the Society of Reliability Engineers, Scandinavian Chapter, 1-3 October 1991, Tampere, Finland. 384p. 1991. ring bd. 165.00 (*1-85166-710-5*, Chap & Hall CRC) CRC Pr.

***Malmont, Valerie S.** Death, Guns & Sticky Buns. 320p. 2000. mass mkt. 5.99 (*0-440-23598-7*) Bantam Dell.

Malmont, Valerie S. Death, Lies & Apple Pies. (Tori Miracle Mysteries Ser.). 272p. 1998. mass mkt. 5.99 (*0-440-22634-1*) Dell.

— Death, Lies & Apple Pies. LC 97-359. 208p. 1997. 21.50 (*0-684-80189-2*) S&S Trade.

— Death Pays the Rose Rent: A Tori Miracle Mystery. (Tori Miracle Mysteries Ser.). 352p. 1999. mass mkt. 6.50 (*0-440-22633-3*) Dell.

— Death Pays the Rose Rent: A Tori Miracle Mystery. LC 93-42075. 1994. 20.00 (*0-671-86967-1*) S&S Trade.

***Malmont, Valerie S.** Death, Snow, & Mistletoe. 2000. mass mkt. 5.99 (*0-440-23601-0*) Dell.

Malmouth, Charles, tr. see Ilf, Ilya & Petrov, Eugene.

Malmquist, Carl P. Homicide: A Psychiatric Perspective. 268p. 1996. 49.50 (*0-88048-690-2*, 8690) Am Psychiatric.

Malmquist, Lisa & Deines, Bradley W. Flight Maneuvers for the Private & Commercial Pilot: Step by Step Procedures Plus Profiles. 2nd rev. ed. LC 94-73794. (Illus.). 134p. 1995. pap. text 18.95 (*1-886474-02-8*, Pub. by Aero Tech AZ) BookMasters.

Malmquist, O. N. The First Hundred Years: A History of the Salt Lake Tribune, 1871-1971. LC 74-158989. (Illus.). 496p. 1971. 8.00 (*0-913738-21-2*) Utah St Hist Soc.

Malmqvist, Bjorn, jt. auth. see Giller, Paul S.

Malmqvist, N. G. D., jt. auth. see Yeh, Michelle Mi-Hsi.

Malmros, Mark K. The Hand-Crafted Folding Knife: Making a Lockback Knife with Simple Hand Tools. (Illus.). 128p. (Orig.). 1996. pap. 14.95 (*0-9639950-1-4*) Tamarax Pr.

Malmsheimer, Richard. Doctors Only: The Evolving Image of the American Physician, 25. LC 88-5685. (Contributions in Medical Studies: No. 25). 185p. 1988. 57.95 (*0-313-23465-5*, MAD/, Greenwood Pr) Greenwood.

Malmstad, John E. Andrey Bely: Spirit of Symbolism. (Illus.). 352p. 1987. pap. 25.00 (*0-8014-9445-1*); text 55.00 (*0-8014-1984-0*) Cornell U Pr.

Malmstad, John E. & Bogomolov, N. A. Mikhail Kuzmin: A Life in Art. LC 98-44379. xvi, 463p. 1999. 49.95 (*0-674-53087-X*) HUP.

Malmstad, John E., ed. see Khodasevich, Vladislav F.

Malmstad, John E., ed. & afterword by see Bely, Andrey.

Malmstad, John E., tr. see Bely, Andrei.

Malmstadt, Howard V., et al. Addbook One: Experiements in Digital & Analog Electronics. (Addbook Ser.: Bk. 1). 1977. pap. text 17.00 (*0-89704-019-8*) E&L Instru.

— Microcomputers & Electronic Instrumentation: Making the Right Connections. LC 94-1407. 1994. 75.00 (*0-8412-2861-2*) Am Chemical.

Malmstadt, Susan & Freier, Marilynn. How to Teach Exercise to Senior Adults. rev. ed. 56p. 1993. 7.95 (*1-877673-10-2*, EXG) Cottonwood Pr.

Malmsteen, J. J. Malmsteen: Transcribed Solos. 80p. 1991. pap. 16.95 (*0-7935-0256-X*, 00660090) H Leonard.

Malmsteen, Yngwie. Marching Out. 104p. 1987. per. 19.95 (*0-88188-765-X*) H Leonard.

— Rising Force. 144p. 1987. per. 19.95 (*0-88188-622-X*) H Leonard.

Malmsten, ed. Biopolymers at Interfaces. LC 98-29984. (Illus.). 680p. 1998. text 235.00 (*0-8247-0201-8*) Dekker.

Malmsten, D. M., ed. see Timmermann Sisters.

Malmstrom, Bo G. Nobel Lectures in Chemistry 1981-1990. 800p. 1993. text 122.00 (*981-02-0788-3*) World Scientific Pub.

Malmstrom, Bo G. Nobel Lectures in Chemistry 1981-1990. 800p. 1993. pap. text 61.00 (*981-02-0789-1*) World Scientific Pub.

— Nobel Lectures in Chemistry, 1991-1995. LC 97-178966. 296p. 1997. pap. text 26.00 (*981-02-2680-2*) World Scientific Pub.

Malmstrom, Bo G. Nobel Lectures in Chemistry, 1991-1995. LC 97-178966. 1997. 54.00 (*981-02-2679-9*) World Scientific Pub.

Malmstrom, Christer, jt. auth. see Jeppsson-McClintock, Annika.

***Malmstrom, Dan.** Introduccion a la Musica Mexicana del Siglo XX. 252p. 1999. pap. 5.99 (*968-16-4061-6*) Fondo CA.

An Asterisk (*) at the beginning of an entry indicates that the title is appearing for the first time.

Malmstrom, Jean, et al. Webster's Third on Nonstandard Usage; Social Aspects of Bilingualism in San Antonio, Texas; Names in Gardening; Needed Research in American English (1943); Needed Research in American English (1963) (Publications of the American Dialect Society). 69p. 1966. pap. text 7.05 (*0-8173-0641-2*) U of Ala Pr.

Malmstrom, Karin & Nash, Nancy. The Man with the Key Is Not Here: A Key to What They Really Mean in China. Davies, Shann, ed. (Illus.). (Orig.). 1990. pap. text 5.95 (*0-9626164-0-0*) Pacific Venture.

Malmstrom, Margit. Terrocotta. (Illus.). 160p. 1996. pap. text 19.95 (*0-8230-5321-0*) Watsn-Guptill.

Malmstrom, Margit, jt. auth. see Etter, Howard.

Malmstrom, Marilyn. My Tongue Is the Pen: How Audiocassettes Can Serve the Nonreading World. LC 91-66074. 224p. (Orig.). 1991. pap. 17.00 (*0-88312-812-8*) S I L Intl.

Malmstrom, Patricia M. & Poland, Janet. The Art of Parenting Twins: The Unique Joys & Challenges of Raising Twins & Other Multiples. LC 99-28672. 1999. pap. 14.95 (*0-345-42267-8*) Ballantine Pub Grp.

Malmstrom, S. Bonnier's Swedish Dictionary: Bonniers Svenska Ordbok. (SWE.). 744p. 1986. 150.00 (*0-8288-2072-4*, F60694) Fr & Eur.

Malmstrom, Vincent H. Cycles of the Sun, Mysteries of the Moon: The Calendar in Mesoamerican Civilization. LC 96-11638. 1997. 40.00 (*0-292-75196-6*); pap. 17.95 (*0-292-75197-4*) U of Tex Pr.

Malmuth, Mason. Blackjack Essays. 4th ed. Loomis, Lynne, ed. 236p. 1996. pap. 19.95 (*1-880685-05-1*) Two Plus NV.

— Gambling Theory & Other Topics. 5th ed. Loomis, Lynne, ed. LC 94-228308. 355p. 1999. pap. text 29.95 (*1-880685-03-5*) Two Plus NV.

— Poker Essays. 2nd ed. Loomis, Lynne, ed. 262p. 1996. pap. text 24.95 (*1-880685-09-4*) Two Plus NV.

— Poker Essays, Vol. II. Cizmar, Paula, ed. (Illus.). 286p. 1996. pap. 24.95 (*1-880685-15-9*) Two Plus NV.

— Winning Concepts in Draw & Lowball. 2nd ed. Levis, Bob, ed. 378p. 1993. pap. text 24.95 (*1-880685-07-8*) Two Plus NV.

Malmuth, Mason & Loomis, Lynne. Fundamentals of Craps. (Illus.). 70p. 1995. pap. 3.95 (*1-880685-14-0*) Two Plus NV.

***Malmuth, Mason & Loomis, Lynne.** Fundamentals of Poker. 3rd rev. ed. (Illus.). 72p. 2000. pap. 5.95 (*1-880685-24-8*, Pub. by Two Plus NV) Herveys Bklink.

Malmuth, Mason & Loomis, Lynne. Fundamentals of "Twenty-One" 2nd ed. (Illus.). 70p. 1995. pap. 3.95 (*1-880685-13-2*) Two Plus NV.

— Fundamentals of Video Poker. 2nd ed. (Illus.). 70p. (Orig.). 1995. pap. 3.95 (*1-880685-12-4*) Two Plus NV.

Malmuth, Mason, jt. auth. see Sklansky, David.

Malnar, Joy M. & Vodvarka, Frank. The Interior Dimension: A Theoretical Approach to Enclosed Space. 384p. 1991. 80.00 (*0-471-28902-7*, VNR) Wiley.

— The Interior Dimension: A Theoretical Approach to Enclosed Space. LC 91-6291. (Illus.). 464p. 1992. text 62.95 (*0-442-23739-1*, VNR) Wiley.

Malnassy, Phillip G. Laboratory Investigations into the World of Plants. 104p. 1996. spiral bd. 18.95 (*0-8403-7085-7*) Kendall-Hunt.

Malnati, Peggy, ed. see Trantina, Gerry & Nimmer, Ron.

Malnati, Richard, jt. auth. see Donigian, Jeremiah.

Malnes, Raino. National Interests, Morality & International Law. 156p. (C). 1994. 20.00 (*82-00-21968-2*, Pub. by Scand Univ Pr) IBD Ltd.

— Valuing the Environment. (Issues in Environmental Politics Ser.). 160p. 1996. text 79.95 (*0-7190-4485-5*, Pub. by Manchester Univ Pr); text 27.95 (*0-7190-4486-3*, Pub. by Manchester Univ Pr) St Martin.

Malnev, V. & Sitenko, A. G. Plasma Physics Theory. LC 94-71831. (Applied Mathematics & Mathematical Computation Ser.: No. 10). 403p. 1994. lib. bdg. 99.95 (*0-412-56790-3*) ASME Pr.

Malnic, Jutta, jt. auth. see Mowaljarlai, David.

Malnic, Nicola, jt. auth. see Ashurst, John.

Malnig, Anita. Where the Waves Break: Life at the Edge of the Sea. LC 84-9614. (Nature Watch Bks.). (Illus.). 48p. (J). (gr. 2-5). 1985. lib. bdg. 14.95 (*0-87614-226-9*, Carolrhoda) Lerner Pub.

— Where the Waves Break: Life at the Edge of the Sea. (Nature Watch Bks.). (Illus.). 48p. (J). (gr. 2-5). 1987. reprint ed. pap. 6.95 (*0-87614-477-6*, First Ave Edns) Lerner Pub.

Malnig, Anita, jt. auth. see Malnig, Lawrence R.

Malnig, Julie. Dancing Till Dawn: A Century of Exhibition Ballroom Dance. LC 94-45361. (Illus.). 174p. (C). 1995. pap. text 18.50 (*0-8147-5528-3*) NYU Pr.

— Dancing Till Dawn: A Century of Exhibition Ballroom Dance, 25. LC 91-33482. (Contributions to the Study of Music & Dance Ser.: No. 25). 192p. 1992. 49.95 (*0-313-27647-1*, MND, Greenwood Pr) Greenwood.

Malnig, Lawrence R. & Malnig, Anita. What Can I Do with a Major In...? How to Choose & Use Your College Major. LC 83-73269. (Illus.). 250p. 1984. 26.95 (*0-9612678-1-X*) Abbott Pr.

Malnor, Bruce. Teacher's Guide to Lifetimes. Malnor, Carol, ed. 48p. 1997. pap. 7.95 (*1-883220-60-2*) Dawn CA.

Malnor, Bruce & Malnor, Carol. Teacher's Guide to a Drop Around the World. (Sharing Nature with Children Book Ser.). (Illus.). 48p. 1998. pap. 7.95 (*1-883220-77-7*) Dawn CA.

— Teacher's Guide to a Fly in the Sky. (Sharing Nature with Children Book Ser.). (Illus.). 48p. 1998. pap. 7.95 (*1-883220-76-9*) Dawn CA.

— Teacher's Guide to a Swim Through the Sea. (Sharing Nature with Children Book Ser.). (Illus.). 48p. 1998. pap. 7.95 (*1-883220-75-0*) Dawn CA.

— Teacher's Guide to a Walk in the Rainforest. (Sharing Nature with Children Book Ser.). (Illus.). 48p. 1998. pap. 7.95 (*1-883220-74-2*) Dawn CA.

***Malnor, Carol.** Teacher's Guide to Endangered Peoples. (Sharing Nature with Children Book Ser.). (Illus.). 64p. 1998. 8.95 (*1-883220-88-2*) Dawn CA.

Malnor, Carol, jt. auth. see Malnor, Bruce.

Malnor, Carol, ed. see Malnor, Bruce.

Malo, Anthony. The Lady Killer: A Tale of Horror & the Erotic. LC 96-85490. 205p. (Orig.). 1998. pap. 12.95 (*0-9640963-3-1*) Artemis Creat.

Malo, David. Hawaiian Antiquities. 4th ed. (Special Publications: No. 2). (Illus.). 278p. (C). 1987. reprint ed. pap. 19.95 (*0-910240-15-9*) Bishop Mus.

— Ka Mo'olelo Hawaii (Hawaiian Antiquities) Chun, Malcolm N., ed. (HAW., Illus.). 178p. (Orig.). 1987. pap. 12.95 (*0-938603-01-9*) Folk Press.

Malo de Molina, Jose L., et al. Monetary Policy & Inflation in Spain. LC 97-38847. 256p. 1998. text 79.95 (*0-312-21295-X*) St Martin.

Malo, Jean-Jacques & Williams, Tony, eds. Vietnam War Films: Over 600 Feature, Made-for-TV, Pilot & Short Movies, 1939-1992, from the United States, Vietnam, France, Belgium, Australia, Hong Kong, South Africa, Great Britain & Other Countries. LC 92-56662. (Illus.). 592p. 1994. lib. bdg. 85.00 (*0-89950-781-6*) McFarland & Co.

Malo, John. Basic Canoeing. Gattis, Lou S., ed. (Illus.). (Orig.). 1987. pap., teacher ed. 9.95 (*0-936241-17-9*) Cheetah Pub.

Maloba, Wunyabari O. Mau Mau & Kenya: An Analysis of a Peasant Revolt. LC 92-31421. (Blacks in the Diaspora Ser.). (Illus.). 244p. (C). 1998. pap. 11.95 (*0-253-21166-2*); text 36.95 (*0-253-33664-3*) Ind U Pr.

Maloch, David T. Marketing Guide for Small Business. 62p. (Orig.). 1989. pap. 7.95 (*0-9623457-0-9*) Perfidia Pr.

Malocsay, Zoltan. More Trails: In Pikes Peak Country. (Illus.). 1994. pap. 9.99 (*0-9629250-2-0*) Squeezy Pr.

— Opening Forbidden Lakes: Fishing Colorado's Watersheds - Without Getting Arrested. (Illus.). 144p. 1992. pap. write for info. (*0-9629250-1-2*) Squeezy Pr.

***Malocsay, Zoltan.** Trails Guide to Front Range Colorado-Denver to Pikes Peak. 6th rev. ed. (Illus.). 368p. 1999. pap. 19.99 (*0-9629250-4-7*) Squeezy Pr.

Malocsay, Zoltan & Topo Maps U. S. Staff. Trails Guide to Pikes Peak County. 5th ed. (Illus.). 1991. pap. write for info. (*0-9629250-3-9*) Squeezy Pr.

Malof, Joseph. A Manual of English Meters. LC 77-823. 236p. 1978. reprint ed. lib. bdg. 59.50 (*0-313-20293-1*, MAMEM, Greenwood Pr) Greenwood.

Maloff, Chalda & Wood, Susan M. Business & Social Etiquette with Disabled People: A Guide to Getting along with Persons Who Have Impairments of Mobility, Vision, Hearing or Speech. 162p. 1988. pap. 28.95 (*0-398-06266-8*) C C Thomas.

— Business & Social Etiquette with Disabled People: A Guide to Getting along with Persons Who Have Impairments of Mobility, Vision, Hearing or Speech. 162p. (C). 1988. text 41.95 (*0-398-05463-0*) C C Thomas.

Maloff, Chalda & Zears, Russell W. Computers in Nutrition. LC 79-4339. (Illus.). 368p. reprint ed. pap. 114.10 (*0-8357-5587-8*, 203521800093) Bks Demand.

Maloff, Debbie, ed. see Paulsen & Associates Staff.

Maloff, Deborah, ed. see Paulsen & Associates Staff.

Maloff, Joel. 1994-1995 Internet Access Providers Marketplace Analysis. (Illus.). 159p. 1995. pap. text 200.00 (*1-57074-258-8*) Greyden Pr.

Maloine Staff. Dictionnaire Medical Illustre De Semiologie Patronymique. (FRE.). 1979. 49.95 (*0-8288-4798-3*, M6149) Fr & Eur.

— Nouvelle Encyclopedie du Cheval. (FRE.). 784p. 1992. 225.00 (*0-8288-9443-4*) Fr & Eur.

Maloiy, G. M., jt. ed. see Jewell, P. A.

Malok, jt. auth. see Porter, Bern.

Malon, Diana L. Rainbows in the Darkness. (Illus.). 45p. (Orig.). 1998. pap. 12.95 (*0-9663526-0-2*) Reflect Blue.

Malon, P., jt. ed. see Blaha, K.

Malone. Basic Concepts of Chemistry. 5th ed. 360p. 1996. pap., student ed. 34.95 (*0-471-16032-6*) Wiley.

Malone. Chemistry 4th ed. 1996. text, lab manual ed. 79.00 (*0-471-18334-2*) Wiley.

Malone. Drug Information: Guide for the Pharmacist. 416p. (C). 1996. pap. text 39.95 (*0-8385-8065-3*, Apple Lange Med) McGraw.

— Orthopedic & Sports Physical Therapy. 3rd ed. Mcpoil, Thomas G., ed. (Illus.). 656p. (C). (gr. 13). 1996. text 64.00 (*0-8151-5886-6*, 24514) Mosby Inc.

— Quilting Basics. Date not set. write for info. (*0-8069-0474-7*) Sterling.

Malone & Mosdell. Drug Information. 2nd ed. 1999. pap. text 38.95 (*0-8385-1577-0*) Appleton & Lange.

Malone, et al. Montana: History of 2 Centuries. rev. ed. LC 91-21742. (Illus.). 480p. 1991. pap. 22.50 (*0-295-97129-0*) U of Wash Pr.

Malone, jt. auth. see Gordon Staff.

Malone, jt. auth. see Moore, Wesley S.

Malone, jt. auth. see Pitre.

Malone, jt. auth. see Sherry.

Malone, jt. auth. see Tabb.

Malone, Dan. The Arming of America. text. write for info. (*0-374-10584-7*) FS&G.

Malone, Dan & Swindle, Howard. America's Condemned: Death Row Inmates in Their Own Words. LC 99-19522. 1999. pap. 12.95 (*0-8362-8198-5*) Andrews & McMeel.

Malone, Alicia. What God Can't Do Just Can't Be Done. LC 97-72117. (Illus.). 66p. (YA). (gr. 9 up). 1998. pap. 9.95 (*1-884242-82-0*) Multicult Pubns.

Malone, Andrew E. The Irish Drama. LC 65-16243. 351p. 1972. 30.95 (*0-405-08777-2*, Pub. by Blom Pubns) Ayer.

Malone, Ann P. Sweet Chariot: Slave Family & Household Structure in Nineteenth-Century Louisiana. LC 91-50787. (Fred W. Morrison Series in Southern Studies). (Illus.). xvi, 369p. (C). 1992. 55.00 (*0-8078-2026-1*) U of NC Pr.

— Sweet Chariot: Slave Family & Household Structure in Nineteenth-Century Louisiana. LC 91-50787. (Fred W. Morrison Series in Southern Studies). (Illus.). 383p. (C). 1996. pap. text 19.95 (*0-8078-4590-6*) U of NC Pr.

Malone, Anne-Frisbie. Santa's Workshop: A Punch-Out Village & Characters. (Illus.). (J). (gr. 4-7). 1993. pap. 4.95 (*0-486-27622-8*) Dover.

Malone, Avon, jt. auth. see Malone, David.

Malone, Barbara. Florida Seafood. 36p. (Orig.). 1982. pap. 3.25 (*0-940844-09-5*) Wellspring.

Malone, Bartlett Y. Whipt 'Em Everytime: The Diary of Bartlett Yancey Malone Co H 6th North Carolina Regiment. Pierson, William W., Jr. & Wiley, Bell I., eds. (Illus.). 131p. 1992. reprint ed. 25.00 (*0-916107-37-X*) Broadfoot.

Malone, Bill, et al. 1001 Internet Tips. (Illus.). 750p. 2000. pap. 54.95 incl. cd-rom (*1-884133-67-3*, Jamsa Press) Gulf Pub.

Malone, Bill C. Country Music, U. S. A. rev. ed. LC 84-21896. (Illus.). 576p. 1985. pap. 22.95 (*0-292-71096-8*) U of Tex Pr.

— Singing Cowboys & Musical Mountaineers: Southern Culture & the Roots of Country Music. LC 92-12430. (Mercer University Lamar Memorial Lectures: No. 34). 160p. 1993. 24.95 (*0-8203-1483-8*) U of Ga Pr.

— Singing Cowboys & Musical Mountaineers: Southern Culture & the Roots of Country Music. LC 92-12430. (Brown Thrasher Bks.). 168p. 1994. pap. 13.95 (*0-8203-1679-2*) U of Ga Pr.

Malone, Bill C. & McCulloh, Judith, eds. Stars of Country Music. (Quality Paperbacks Ser.). (Illus.). 476p. 1991. reprint ed. pap. 14.95 (*0-306-80444-1*) Da Capo.

— Stars of Country Music: Uncle Dave Macon to Johnny Rodriguez. LC 75-15848. (Music in American Life Ser.). 488p. 1975. 29.95 (*0-252-00527-9*) U of Ill Pr.

Malone, Bobbie. Another Look: Wisconsin Photographs Past & Present. 1998. pap. text 11.95 (*0-87020-297-9*) State Hist Soc Wis.

— Celebrating Everyday Life in Wisconsin History: A Classroom Exhibit Resource & Planning Guide. (Illus.). 60p. (Orig.). 1997. pap. text 9.95 (*0-87020-300-2*) U of Wis Pr.

— Learning from the Land: Wisconsin Land Use. (New Badger History Ser.). (Illus.). 80p. (Orig.). 1998. pap. text 7.95 (*0-87020-294-4*) U of Wis Pr.

— Learning from the Land: Wisconsin Land Use. (New Badger History Ser.). (Illus.). 62p. (Orig.). (J). (gr. 1-12). 1998. pap. text, teacher ed., student ed. 20.00 (*0-87020-295-2*) U of Wis Pr.

— Rabbi Max Heller: Reformer, Zionist, Southerner, 1860-1929. LC 96-48359. (Judaic Studies). 240p. 1997. text 34.95 (*0-8173-0875-X*) U of Ala Pr.

— Wisconsin's Built Environment, 1. 1998. pap. 11.95 (*0-87020-308-8*) State Hist Soc Wis.

***Malone, Bobbie & Wisconsin Cartographers Guild Staff.** Mapping Wisconsin History: Teacher's Guide & Student Materials. LC 00-30122. (Illus.). 2000. pap. write for info. (*0-87020-318-5*) State Hist Soc Wis.

Malone, Bobbie, jt. auth. see Holliday, Diane Y.

Malone, C. B., jt. auth. see Bowler, N. P.

Malone, Carlos. Hidden in His Hands: Held by His Heart. 140p. (Orig.). 1996. pap. 9.99 (*1-56043-274-8*, Treasure Hse) Destiny Image.

***Malone, Caroline.** Neolithic Britain. (Illus.). 176p. 2000. pap. 24.99 (*0-7524-1442-9*, Pub. by Tempus Pubng) Arcadia Publng.

Malone, Caroline, et al. The Memory Bird: Survivors of Sexual Abuse. LC 96-35173. 256p. 1997. 59.95 (*1-56639-525-9*) Temple U Pr.

— The Memory Bird: Survivors of Sexual Abuse. LC 96-35173. (Illus.). 256p. 1997. pap. 16.95 (*1-56639-526-7*) Temple U Pr.

Malone, Caroline, jt. ed. see Stoddart, Simon.

Malone, Carolyn. Availability to Ticketing. (Illus.). 135p. (C). 1985. pap. text 21.95 (*0-917063-07-4*) Travel Text.

Malone, Dandridge M. Small Unit Leadership: A Commonsense Approach. (Illus.). 180p. 1983. pap. 17.95 (*0-89141-173-9*, Pub. by Presidio Pr) Natl Bk Netwk.

Malone, Dave. Poems to Love & the Body. LC 98-93926. 56p. 1999. pap. 7.95 (*0-9667744-0-X*) Bliss Sta.

***Malone, Dave.** 23 Sonnets. 32p. 1999. write for info. (*0-9667744-2-6*) Bliss Sta.

***Malone, David & Malone, Avon.** Drawn in Christ. unabridged ed. (Illus.). 1998. pap. 6.00 (*0-89137-152-4*, 71524) Quality Pubns.

— Drawn to Christ. unabridged ed. (Illus.). 102p. 1998. pap. 6.00 (*0-89137-151-6*, 71516) Quality Pubns.

Malone, David M. Decision-Making in the U. N. Security Council: The Case of Haiti. LC 98-30962. 334p. 1999. text 85.00 (*0-19-829483-2*) OUP.

— Deposition Rules: The Pocket Guide to Who, What, When, Where, Why & How. 2nd ed. LC 99-162712. 94 p. 1998. 14.95 (*1-55681-627-8*) Natl Inst Trial Ad.

***Malone, David M.** Expert Rules: 100 & More Points You Need to Know about Expert Witnesses. LC 99-209399. 119p. 1999. write for info. (*1-55681-649-9*) Natl Inst Trial Ad.

— Expert Rules: 100 & More Points You Need to Know about Expert Witnesses. 119p. 2000. 14.95 (*1-55681-673-1*) Natl Inst Trial Ad.

Malone, David M. & Hoffman, Peter T. The Effective Deposition: Techniques & Strategies That Work. 2nd ed. LC 97-221667. 318p. 1996. 44.95 (*1-55681-504-2*) Natl Inst Trial Ad.

***Malone, David M. & Zwier, Paul J.** Effective Expert Testimony. (Practical Guide Ser.). 2000. pap. 44.95 (*1-55681-564-6*) Natl Inst Trial Ad.

Malone, David M., jt. ed. see Berdal, Mats.

***Malone, Debbie.** The Stormy Journey. 2000. write for info. (*0-9674268-1-2*) S B G Pubg.

Malone, Dumas. Jefferson , 6 Vols., Set. 1995. Price not set. (*0-316-54898-7*) Little.

— Jefferson & His Time. (History - United States Ser.). 1993. reprint ed. lib. bdg. 90.00 (*0-7812-4885-X*) Rprt Serv.

— Jefferson & His Time: The Sage of Monticello, Vol. 6. (Illus.). 551p. (gr. 8). 1981. 29.95 (*0-316-54463-9*) Little.

— Jefferson & His Time: The Sage of Monticello, Vol. 6. (Illus.). 551p. 1982. pap. 17.95 (*0-316-54478-7*) Little.

— Jefferson & the Ordeal of Liberty, Vol. 3. (Jefferson & His Time Ser.). 545p. (gr. 8). 1962. 29.95 (*0-316-54475-2*) Little.

— Jefferson & the Rights of Man, Vol. 2. (Jefferson & His Time Ser.). (Illus.). 523p. 1951. 29.95 (*0-316-54473-6*) Little.

— Jefferson & the Rights of Man, Vol. 2. (Illus.). 523p. 1968. pap. 15.95 (*0-316-54470-1*, Back Bay) Little.

— Jefferson the President: First Term, 1801-1805, Vol. 4. LC 48-5972. (Illus.). 539p. 1970. 29.95 (*0-316-54467-1*) Little.

— Jefferson the President: First Term, 1801-1805, Vol. 4. LC 48-5972. (Jefferson & His Time Ser.). (Illus.). 542p. 1971. pap. 15.95 (*0-316-54466-3*, Back Bay) Little.

— Jefferson the President: Second Term, 1805-1809, Vol. 5. (Jefferson & His Time Ser.). 704p. 1974. 29.95 (*0-316-54465-5*) Little.

— Jefferson the President: Second Term, 1805-1809, Vol. 5. 704p. 1975. pap. 15.95 (*0-316-54464-7*, Back Bay) Little.

— Jefferson the Virginian, Vol. 1. (Jefferson & His Time Ser.). (Illus.). 484p. 1948. 29.95 (*0-316-54474-4*, Aspen Law & Bus) Aspen Pub.

— Jefferson the Virginian, Vol. 1. (Illus.). 484p. 1967. pap. 17.95 (*0-316-54472-8*, LB78, Back Bay) Little.

— Mr. Jefferson's Private Life. 8p. 1974. pap. 3.00 (*0-944026-85-0*) Am Antiquarian.

— The Public Life of Thomas Cooper, 1783-1839. LC 75-3122. reprint ed. 46.00 (*0-404-59117-5*) AMS Pr.

— Saints in Action. LC 70-142664. (Essay Index Reprint Ser.). 1977. 18.95 (*0-8369-2062-7*) Ayer.

— Thomas Jefferson: A Brief Biography. (Monticello Monographs). (Illus.). 48p. (Orig.). 1993. reprint ed. pap. 4.95 (*1-882886-00-3*) T J Mem Fnd.

— Thomas Jefferson As Political Leader. LC 78-21568. 75p. 1979. reprint ed. lib. bdg. 35.00 (*0-313-20730-5*, MATJ, Greenwood Pr) Greenwood.

Malone, Dumas, ed. see Jefferson, Thomas.

Malone, E. E. Malone: Jeremiah Dumas Malone, a Genealogical Outline. (Illus.). 159p. 1993. reprint ed. pap. 25.00 (*0-8328-3714-8*); reprint ed. lib. bdg. 35.00 (*0-8328-3713-X*) Higginson Bk Co.

Malone, E. T., Jr. The View from Wrightsville Beach. (Illus.). (Orig.). 1988. pap. 8.95 (*0-9621668-0-4*) Lit Lantern.

Malone, E. T., Jr., jt. auth. see Walser, Richard.

Malone, Edgar W., jt. auth. see Hart, William C.

Malone, Edmond. Cursory Observations on the Poems Attributed to Thomas Rowley: The Second Edition, Revised & Augmented. 2nd rev. ed. LC 92-2372. (Augustan Reprints Ser.: No. 123). 1966. reprint ed. 14.50 (*0-404-70123-X*, PR3344) AMS Pr.

— 18th Century Shakespeare, Vol. 22. 440p. 1970. reprint ed. 32.50 (*0-7146-2514-0*, Pub. by F Cass Pubs) Intl Spec Bk.

Malone, Edmond, jt. auth. see Reynolds, Joshua.

Malone, Edmond, jt. auth. see Ritson, Joseph.

Malone, Edmond, ed. see Shakespeare, William.

Malone, Edmund. An Inquiry into the Authenticity of Certain Miscellaneous Papers & Legal Instruments. LC 73-96356. (Eighteenth Century Shakespeare Ser.: No. 22). vii, 424p. 1970. reprint ed. lib. bdg. 30.00 (*0-678-05123-2*) Kelley.

Malone, Eileen. The Complete Guide to Writers' Groups & Workshops: Where to Find Them & How to Get the Most Out of Them. 304p. 1995. pap. 12.95 (*0-8065-1642-9*, Citadel Pr) Carol Pub Group.

— The Complete Guide to Writer's Groups, Conferences, & Workshops. LC 96-14684. 245p. 1996. pap. 14.95 (*0-471-14217-4*) Wiley.

Malone, Elizabeth, jt. ed. see Raynor, Steve.

Malone, Eloise F., jt. auth. see Cochran, Charles L.

Malone, Fred. Bees Don't Get Arthritis. (Illus.). 179p. 1992. pap. 13.95 (*0-914960-60-1*) Academy Bks.

Malone, Fred A. A String of Pearls Unstrung: A Theological Journey into Believers' Baptism. LC 99-164917. 56p. 1998. pap. 4.50 (*0-9654955-2-3*) Founders Pr.

Malone, G. Kimba. (Illus.). (J). mass mkt. 8.95 (*0-340-71585-5*, Pub. by Hodder & Stought Ltd) Trafalgar.

— Torn Ear. mass mkt. 8.95 (*0-340-68295-7*, Pub. by Hodder & Stought Ltd) Trafalgar.

Malone, Gifford D. Political Advocacy & Cultural Communication: Organizing the Nation's Public Diplomacy. (Exxon Education Foundation Series on Rhetoric & Political Discourse: Vol. 11). 178p. (Orig.). (C). 1988. pap. text 20.00 (*0-8191-6620-0*) U Pr of Amer.

— Political Advocacy & Cultural Communication: Organizing the Nation's Public Diplomacy. (Exxon Education Foundation Series on Rhetoric & Political Discourse: Vol. 11). 178p. (Orig.). (C). 1988. lib. bdg. 41.00 (*0-8191-6619-7*, Pub. by White Miller Center) U Pr of Amer.

***Malone, Guy.** Come Sail Away: UFO Phenomenon & the Bible. 138p. 1999. pap. 7.95 *(1-893788-00-8)* Seekyel.

Malone, Hank. Experiencing New Mexico: Lyrical & Critical Essays. 54p. (Orig.). 1998. pap. 9.95 *(1-888923-04-0)* Poetic License.

***Malone, Hank.** James Dickey: On the Eve of the New Millennium. 8p. 1999. pap. write for info. *(1-888923-06-7)* Poetic License.

Malone, Hank. New Mexico Haiku. rev. ed. viii, 100p. (Orig.). 1998. pap. 6.95 *(1-888923-05-9)* Poetic License.

Malone, Harold J. The Democracy That Nearly Was. LC 97-90838. 1998. pap. 8.95 *(0-533-12491-3)* Vantage.

Malone, J. B. The Complete Wicklow Way: A Step-by-Step Guide. rev. ed. (Illus.). 128p. 1997. pap. 10.95 *(0-86278-158-2,* Pub. by OBrien Pr) Irish Amer Bk.

Malone, J. L. Poets at Play. 1990. pap. text. write for info. *(0-582-86818-1,* Pub. by Addison-Wesley) Longman.

Malone, Jacqui. Steppin' on the Blues: The Visible Rhythms of African American Dance. LC 95-4413. (Illus.). 296p. 1996. 18.95 *(0-252-06508-5)*; text 44.95 *(0-252-02211-4)* U of Ill Pr.

Malone, James H. No-Job Dad. LC 92-15873. (Illus.). 30p. (J). (gr. 1-2). 1992. pap. 13.95 *(1-878217-06-2)* Victory Press.

Malone, Jeanette. Wild Adventures: A Guidebook of Activities for Building Connections. (Illus.). 188p. 1998. spiral bd. 22.95 *(0-536-01782-4)* Pearson Custom.

Malone, Joanne. Stencilling. 1997. write for info. *(0-8069-6139-2)* Sterling.

— Stencilling: A Practical & Inspirational Guide to Decorative Ideas for Interiors, Furnishings, Clothing, Stationery & More. LC 92-38336. (Illus.). 132p. 1993. pap. 14.95 *(0-8069-0360-0)* Sterling.

— Wearable & Decorative Stencilling. (Illus.). 144p. 1998. 14.95 *(0-8069-9447-9)* Sterling.

— Wearable & Decorative Stencilling: Patterns, Projects & Possibilities. LC 96-38700. (Illus.). 144p. 1997. 27.95 *(0-8069-9446-0)* Sterling.

Malone, John. The Civil War Quiz Book. (Quill Quiz Bk.). (Illus.). 224p. 1992. pap. 10.00 *(0-688-11269-2,* Quil) HarperTrade.

***Malone, John.** The 125 Most Asked Questions about Cats: (And the Answers) 160p. 1999. 5.98 *(1-56731-338-8,* MJF Bks) Fine Comms.

Malone, John. Predicting the Future: From Jules Verne to Bill Gates. LC 97-21360. 194p. 1997. 19.95 *(0-87131-830-X)* M Evans.

***Malone, John.** 21st Century Gay. 320p. 2000. 19.95 *(0-87131-911-X)* M Evans.

Malone, John A., et al, eds. Research & Supervision in Mathematics & Science Education. LC 98-26310. 400p. 1998. write for info. *(0-8058-2968-7)*; pap. 39.95 *(0-8058-2969-5)* L Erlbaum Assocs.

Malone, John C. Theories of Learning: A Historical Approach, Test Items. 1991. mass mkt. write for info. *(0-534-05761-6)* Brooks-Cole.

Malone, John S. Look Whats Cooking at Spanish Point Lodge: Chef John Irish/American Cookbook. (Illus.). 7p. (Orig.). 1997. pap. 10.00 *(0-9657105-0-5)* J S Malone.

— The Malone's of Glendine, County Clare Ireland Cookbook. 1999. pap. 25.00 *(0-9657105-2-1)* J S Malone.

— The Stowell Family Windham Cook Book. 1997. pap. 12.50 *(0-9657105-1-3)* J S Malone.

Malone, John W. The Encyclopedia of Figure Skating. LC 97-46360. (Illus.). 272p. 35.00 *(0-8160-3226-2)* Facts on File.

— The Encyclopedia of Figure Skating. LC 97-46360. 272p. 1998. pap. 18.95 *(0-8160-3796-5)* Facts on File.

Malone, Johnita P. Land Records of Sussex County, Delaware, 1722-1731: Deed Book F, No. 6. viii, 124p. 1997. pap. text 11.50 *(0-7884-0775-9,* MO45) Heritage Bk.

Malone, Joseph J. Pine Trees & Politics. Bruchey, Stuart, ed. LC 78-53552. (Development of Public Land Law in the U. S. Ser.). 1979. reprint ed. lib. bdg. 19.95 *(0-405-11380-3)* Ayer.

Malone, Joseph L. The Science of Linguistics in the Art of Translation: Some Tools from Linguistics for the Analysis & Practice of Translation. LC 87-13888. (SUNY Series in Linguistics). 241p. (C). 1988. text 89.50 *(0-88706-653-4)*; pap. text 29.95 *(0-88706-654-2)* State U NY Pr.

— Tiberian Hebrew Phonology. LC 92-43400. (American Schools of Oriental Research Dissertation Ser.). x, 204p. 1993. 55.00 *(0-931464-75-7)* Eisenbrauns.

***Malone, Kareen R. & Friedlander, Stephen R., eds.** The Subject of Lacan: A Lacanian Reader for Psychologists. LC 99-48450. (C). 2000. text 73.50 *(0-7914-4623-9)*; pap. text 24.95 *(0-7914-4624-7)* State U NY Pr.

Malone, Kemp. Chapters on Chaucer. LC 79-4628. 240p. 1979. reprint ed. lib. bdg. 38.50 *(0-313-21260-0,* MACHC, Greenwood Pr) Greenwood.

— Literary History of Hamlet. LC 65-15886. (Studies in Shakespeare: No. 24). 1969. reprint ed. lib. bdg. 75.00 *(0-8383-0593-8)* M S G Haskell Hse.

Malone, Kemp, ed. Deor. (Old English Ser.). 1966. pap. text 9.95 *(0-89197-566-7)* Irvington.

Malone, Kemp, et al, eds. Early English Manuscripts in Facsimile. Incl. Aelfric's First Series of Catholic Homilies. Eliason, Norman & Clemoes, Peter, eds. 468p. 1966. 390.00 *(0-8018-0445-0)*; Aelfric's First Series of Catholic Homilies. Eliason, Norman & Clemoes, Peter, eds. 468p. 1966. pap. 320.50 *(0-8018-0444-2)*; British Museum Cotton Nero A. Loyn, H, intro. 1972. 380.00 *(0-8018-1341-7)*; British Museum Cotton Nero A. Loyn, H, intro. 1972. pap. 320.00 *(0-8018-1340-9)*; Durham Gospels. Verey, Christopher D., ed. 362p. 1981. 1040.00 *(0-8018-2315-3)*; Durham Gospels. Verey, Christopher D., ed. 362p. 1981. pap. 975.00 Durham Ritual. Brown, T. J., ed. 1970. 445.00 *(0-8018-1107-4)*; Durham Ritual. Brown, T. J., ed. 1970. pap. 380.00 *(0-8018-1106-6)*; Eleventh-Century Anglo-Saxon Illustrated Miscelleny. McGurk, P., ed. 294p. 1983. 595.00 *(0-8018-3211-X)*; Eleventh-Century Anglo-Saxon Illustrated Miscelleny. McGurk, P., ed. 294p. 1983. pap. 555.00 *(0-8018-3212-8)*; Nowell Codex. 236p. 1963. 300.00 *(0-8018-0443-4)*; Nowell Codex. 236p. 1963. pap. 235.00 *(0-8018-0442-6)*; Old English Illustrated Hexateuch. Dodwell, C. R. & Clemoes, Peter, intros. 1974. 540.00 *(0-8018-1339-5)*; Old English Illustrated Hexateuch. Dodwell, C. R. & Clemoes, Peter, intros. 1974. pap. 465.00 *(0-8018-1338-7)*; Rule of Saint Benedict. 157p. (Orig.). 1968. 275.00 *(0-8018-0449-3,* Pub. by Gra1cewing); Rule of Saint Benedict. 157p. (Orig.). 1968. pap. 215.00 *(0-8018-0448-5)*; Vercelli Book. Sisam, Celia, ed. 210p. 1977. 540.00 *(0-8018-1976-8)*; Vercelli Book. Sisam, Celia, ed. 210p. 1977. pap. 465.00 *(0-8018-1977-6)*; Vespasion Psalter. Wright, David H. & Campbell, Alastair, eds. 425p. 1967. 500.00 *(0-8018-0447-7)*; Vespasion Psalter. Wright, David H. & Campbell, Alastair, eds. 425p. 1967. pap. 425.00 *(0-8018-0446-9)*; Pt. 2. Textus Roffensis. Sawyer, Peter, ed. 278p. 1962. pap. 180.00 *(0-8018-0440-X)*; write for info. *(0-318-53778-8)* Johns Hopkins.

Malone Kennedy, Dana. Front Porch Embraces. LC 98-67018. 96p. 1998. pap. 12.95 *(1-892616-00-9)* Post Oak Pubns.

Malone, Kitty. Girl Power: A Smart Woman's Handbook. 1998. mass mkt. 6.95 *(1-84024-021-0,* Pub. by Summers) Howell Pr VA.

***Malone, Kobutsu.** Prison Chaplaincy Guidelines for Zen Buddhism: A Source Book for Prison Chaplains, Administrators & Security Personnel. (EZF Monographs Ser.). (Illus.). 85p. 2000. pap. 9.95 *(0-9677775-0-X)* Engaged Zen Fndt.

Malone, Laurence J. Opening the West: Federal Internal Improvements Before 1860. 196. LC 97-43932. (Contributions in Economics & Economic History Ser.: Vol. 196). 176p. 1998. 59.95 *(0-313-30671-0,* Greenwood Pr) Greenwood.

Malone, Lawrence. Coordinated Urban Economic Development: A Case Study Analysis. Linger, Juyne, ed. 269p. (Orig.). 1978. pap. 17.50 *(0-317-04920-8)* Natl Coun Econ Dev.

Malone, Lawrence J., ed. see Smith, Adam.

Malone, Lee, jt. auth. see Malone, Paul.

Malone-Lee, James G. & Wagg, Adrian, eds. Urinary Incontinence. (Greenwich Medical Media Ser.). (Illus.). 256p. 2000. pap. text 59.50 *(1-900151-16-2)* OUP.

Malone, Leo J. The Basic Concepts of Chemistry. 5th ed. LC 96-38353. 608p. 1996. text 90.95 *(0-471-14878-4)* Wiley.

***Malone, Leo J.** Basic Concepts of Chemistry. 6th ed. 589p. (C). 2000. write for info. incl. cd-rom *(0-471-32247-4)* Wiley.

Malone, Linda. International Law. 2nd rev. ed. (Professor Ser.). 271p. 1997. pap. text 16.95 *(1-56542-168-X)* E Pub Corp.

Malone, Linda A. Environmental Law. (Professor Ser.). (Orig.). 1997. pap. text *(1-56542-171-X)* E Pub Corp.

— Environmental Regulation of Land Use. LC 90-267. (Environmental Law Ser.). 1990. ring bd. 145.00 *(0-87632-739-0)* West Group.

Malone, Linda A., et al. Stanford Environmental Law Journal, Vol. 12. 220p. (C). 1993. pap. 15.00 *(0-942007-36-0)* Stanford Enviro.

Malone, Linda C., jt. auth. see Ostle, Bernard.

Malone, Maggie. Christmas Scrapcrafts. (Illus.). 136p. (J). (gr. 5-10). 1992. pap. 12.95 *(0-8069-6805-2)* Sterling.

— Treasury of Applique Quilt Pattern. (Illus.). 144p. 1998. 14.95 *(0-8069-0747-9)* Sterling.

— Treasury of Applique Quilt Patterns. LC 95-40526. (Illus.). 144p. 1996. 24.95 *(0-8069-0746-0)* Sterling.

Malone, Maggie, jt. auth. see Cornwell, Neil.

***Malone, Marian.** No Angel. (Sapphire Ser.). 1999. pap. text 9.95 *(0-352-33462-2)* London Brdge.

Malone, Martin. Worlds of Talk: The Presentation of Self in Everyday Conversation. 224p. 1997. pap. text 25.95 *(0-7456-1897-9)* Blackwell Pubs.

Malone, Martin J., jt. auth. see Levinson, David.

Malone, Mary. Andrew Johnson. LC 98-29560. (United States Presidents Ser.). 128p. (YA). (gr. 5 up). 1999. lib. bdg. 20.95 *(0-7660-1034-1)* Enslow Pubs.

— James Madison. LC 96-39133. (United States Presidents Ser.). (Illus.). 128p. (YA). (gr. 5 up). 1997. lib. bdg. 20.95 *(0-89490-834-0)* Enslow Pubs.

— Maya Lin: Architect & Artist. LC 94-5333. (People to Know Ser.). (Illus.). 112p. (YA). (gr. 6 up). 1995. lib. bdg. 20.95 *(0-89490-499-X)* Enslow Pubs.

— Will Rogers: Cowboy Philosopher. LC 95-32149. (People to Know Ser.). (Illus.). 128p. (YA). (gr. 6 up). 1996. lib. bdg. 20.95 *(0-89490-695-X)* Enslow Pubs.

Malone, Mary A. The Disobedient Angel: A Christmas Story. (Poetry Ser.). 42p. 1995. pap. 9.95 *(1-887888-02-0)* Marigold Ent.

— The Whole Heart: Poems about Abraham Lincoln. (Marigold Poetry Ser.). 50p. 1995. pap. 9.95 *(1-887888-00-4)* Marigold Ent.

Malone, Mary Huddleston, jt. auth. see Brinkley, Velma Howell.

Malone, Michael. Dingley Falls. 1989. mass mkt. 4.95 *(0-671-67180-4)* PB.

— Dingley Falls. LC 93-5836. 672p. 1994. per. 10.00 *(0-671-87529-9,* WSP) PB.

— Foolscap. Rosenman, Jane, ed. LC 92-42591. 400p. 1993. reprint ed. per. 10.00 *(0-671-78857-4,* WSP) PB.

— Guatemalan Family. (Illus.). 56p. (J). (gr. 3-6). 1996. pap. text 8.95 *(0-8225-9742-X)* Lerner Pub.

— Handling Sin. Rosenman, Jane, ed. 672p. 1993. per. 14.00 *(0-671-87526-4,* WSP) PB.

— A Nicaraguan Family. LC 97-13827. (Journey Between Two Worlds Ser.). 1998. lib. bdg. write for info. *(0-8225-9779-9)* Lerner Pub.

— A Nicaraguan Family. LC 97-13827. (Journey Between Two Worlds Ser.). (J). 1998. lib. bdg. 22.60 *(0-8225-3412-6)* Lerner Pub.

— The Only Begotten. unabridged ed. 455p. 1999. pap. 39.95 *(1-885692-06-4)* Cath Treas.

— Scott U. S. First Day Cover Catalog: 1996 Edition. 1995. pap. text 6.95 *(0-89487-217-6)* Scott Pub Co.

— Time's Witness. Rosenman, Jane, ed. 562p. 1994. pap. 10.00 *(0-671-87527-2,* WSP) PB.

— Times Witness. Peters, Sally, ed. 592p. 1991. reprint ed. mass mkt. 5.95 *(0-671-70318-8)* PB.

— Uncivil Seasons. Rosenman, Jane, ed. 320p. 1993. pap. 12.00 *(0-671-87528-0,* WSP) PB.

Malone, Michael, ed. Apostolic Digest. abr. ed. 190p. 1995. reprint ed. pap. 9.95 *(1-885692-00-5)* Cath Treas.

***Malone, Michael F., et al.** Fifth International Conference on Foundations of Computer-Aided Process Design. LC 00-42050. (Symposium Ser.). 2000. write for info. *(0-8169-0826-5)* Am Inst Chem Eng.

Malone, Michael P. The Battle for Butte: Mining & Politics on the Northern Frontier, 1864-1906. LC 95-14591. (Illus.). 281p. (C). 1995. reprint ed. pap. 18.95 *(0-917298-34-9)* MT Hist Soc.

— C. Ben Ross & the New Deal in Idaho. LC 69-14207. (Illus.). 217p. 1970. 20.00 *(0-295-95060-9)* U of Wash Pr.

— James J. Hill: Empire Builder of the Northwest. LC 95-36518. (Oklahoma Western Biographies Ser.: Vol. 12). (Illus.). 322p. 1997. pap. 14.95 *(0-8061-2860-7)* U of Okla Pr.

— Montana: A Contemporary Profile. 200p. 1996. pap. 14.95 *(1-56037-109-9)* Am Wrld Geog.

***Malone, Michael P.** Montana Century: 100 Years in Pictures & Words. LC 99-27502. 307p. 1999. 50.00 *(1-56044-827-X,* Two Dot) Falcon Pub Inc.

Malone, Michael P., ed. Historians & the American West. LC 82-17550. 461p. 1983. reprint ed. pap. 143.00 *(0-608-02782-0,* 206384900007) Bks Demand.

Malone, Michael P. & Etulain, Richard W. The American West: A Twentieth-Century History. LC 88-26840. (Illus.). xii, 347p. 1989. pap. text 18.00 *(0-8032-8167-6,* Bison Books) U of Nebr Pr.

Malone, Michael S. Infinite Loop: How Apple, the World's Most Insanely Great Computer Company, Went Insane. LC 98-19288. 608p. 1999. 27.50 *(0-385-48684-7)* Doubleday.

— The Microprocessor: A Biography. (TELOS - the Electronic Library of Science). (Illus.). 333p. 1995. 32.95 incl. cd-rom *(0-387-94342-0)* Spr-Verlag.

Malone, Michael S., jt. auth. see Davidow, William H.

Malone, Michael S., jt. auth. see Siebel, Thomas M.

Malone, Mike. The Guide to Silicon Valley Careers, Vol. 2. 2nd ed. Hillan, Peter, ed. (Illus.). 560p. 1997. pap. 24.95 *(0-9653207-0-7)* San Jose Mercury.

Malone, Myrtle D., ed. MGM Grand Hotel, Inc. Hotel-Casino-Theme Park: Grand Opening Commemorative. (Illus.). 135p. 1993. 20.00 *(1-881547-17-5)* Pioneer Pubns.

Malone, Myrtle D., ed. see Black, Geoff & Colson, Brett.

Malone, Myrtle D., ed. see Sheehan, Jack.

***Malone, Niamh.** Mothers: Memories from Famous Daughters & Sons. LC 99-490355. 160p. 1999. write for info. *(0-86278-605-3,* Pub. by OBrien Pr) Irish Amer Bk.

Malone, P. M. Into the High Branches. (Deep Woods Trilogy Ser.: Bk. II). (Illus.). 196p. (Orig.). (J). (gr. 1-8). 1992. pap. text 11.95 *(0-9631957-1-9)* Raspberry Hill.

— Out of the Nest. (Deep Woods Trilogy Ser.: Bk. I). (Illus.). 198p. (Orig.). (J). (gr. 1-8). 1991. pap. text 11.95 *(0-9631957-0-0)* Raspberry Hill.

— To Find a Way Home. (Deep Woods Trilogy Ser.: Bk. III). (Illus.). 200p. (Orig.). (J). (gr. 1-8). 1993. pap. text 11.95 *(0-9631957-2-7)* Raspberry Hill.

Malone, Patricia. Julia Bk. 1: The Proposal. Edwards, Ellen, ed. (Kingston Chronicles Ser.). (Illus.). 128p. 1998. pap. 3.50 *(1-57513-131-5)* Magic Attic.

Malone, Patrick, ed. City, Capital, & Water. LC 95-52400. (Illus.). 288p. (C). 1997. 85.00 *(0-415-09942-0)* Routledge.

Malone, Patrick M. Canals & Industry: Engineering in Lowell, 1821-1880. (Illus.). 27p. (Orig.). 1983. pap. 2.50 *(0-942472-07-1)* Lowell Museum.

— The Skulking Way of War. 1991. 29.95 *(0-8191-8067-X)* Madison Bks UPA.

— The Skulking Way of War: Technology & Tactics among the New England Indians. LC 92-22740. (Illus.). 160p. 1993. reprint ed. pap. 13.95 *(0-8018-4554-8)* Johns Hopkins.

***Malone, Patrick M.** The Skulking Way of War: Technology & Tactics among the New England Indians. 144p. 2000. reprint ed. pap. 18.95 *(1-56833-165-7,* Pub. by Madison Bks UPA) Natl Bk Netwk.

Malone, Patrick M., jt. auth. see Gordon, Robert B.

Malone, Paul. Garden District. (Majesty Architecture Ser.). (Illus.). 160p. 1998. pap. text 16.95 *(1-56554-378-5)* Pelican.

— Louisiana Plantation Homes: A Return to Splendor. LC 84-25369. (Illus.). 160p. 1986. 39.95 *(0-88289-403-X)* Pelican.

***Malone, Paul.** Louisiana Plantation Homes Postcard Book. 1999. pap. 9.95 *(1-56554-641-5)* Pelican.

— Majesty of the Garden District Postcard Book. 1999. pap. 9.95 *(1-56554-640-7)* Pelican.

Malone, Paul. New Orleans. (Majesty Architecture Ser.). (Illus.). 112p. 1998. pap. text 14.95 *(1-56554-377-7)* Pelican.

— Pipeline. (Agents Bks.: No. 02). 1991. per. 3.50 *(0-373-63802-7)* Harlequin Bks.

— Shakedown. (Agents Bks.: No. 03). 1992. per. 3.50 *(0-373-63803-5)* Harlequin Bks.

— Trigger Pull. (Agents Bks.: No. 1). 1991. per. 3.50 *(0-373-63801-9)* Harlequin Bks.

Malone, Paul & Malone, Lee. The Majesty of the Felicianas. LC 88-29072. (Illus.). 96p. 1989. 15.95 *(0-88289-712-8)* Pelican.

— Majesty of the River Road. LC 87-31160. (Illus.). 96p. 1988. 15.95 *(0-88289-674-1)* Pelican.

Malone, Paul B., III. Abuse 'Em & Lose 'Em: Eighteen Leadership Styles That Were Made in Hell. LC 90-70734. (Illus.). 240p. (Orig.). 1990. pap. 11.95 *(0-9616548-2-1)* Synergy Pr.

— Love 'Em & Lead 'Em. LC 86-60237. (Illus.). 192p. (Orig.). 1986. 18.95 *(0-9616548-1-3)*; pap. 10.95 *(0-9616548-0-5)* Synergy Pr.

— Total Hip Replacement (THR) Surgery & You Vol. 1: Absolute Must Reading for Those Involved in THR Surgery. (Illus.). 176p. 1998. pap. 14.95 *(0-9616548-3-X)* Synergy Pr.

Malone, Paul S. In an Arid Land: Thirteen Stories of Texas. LC 94-16972. 232p. 1995. 21.50 *(0-87565-140-2)* Tex Christian.

***Malone, Paul Scott.** Memorial Day & Other Stories. LC 99-48286. 184p. 2000. pap. 15.95 *(0-87565-219-0,* Pub. by Tex Christian) Tex A&M Univ Pr.

***Malone, Peter.** The Drowsy Hours. 2000. write for info. *(0-688-16603-2)* Lothrop.

Malone, Peter. Star Shapes. LC 95-38256. (Illus.). 40p. (J). 1997. 15.95 *(0-8118-0726-6)* Chronicle Bks.

Malone, Peter. The Adventures of Odysseus. LC 96-28365. 72p. (J). (gr. 3 up). 1997. 17.95 *(0-531-30000-5)* Orchard Bks Watts.

Malone, Peter, jt. auth. see Biriotti, Sophie.

Malone, Peter, jt. auth. see French, Vivian.

Malone, Peter, jt. auth. see Tobias, Tobi.

Malone, Raven. Introducing Willie. Cameron, Darrell L., ed. (Wheeling Willie Ser.). (Illus.). 24p. (J). (gr. k-2). 1995. 4.95 *(1-887886-00-1)*; pap. 2.95 *(1-887886-01-X)* Charity Publns.

Malone, Rick L. Violet of a Deeper Blue. 1999. pap. 14.00 *(0-9663926-0-4)* Azure Pub MN.

Malone, Robeert L., jt. auth. see Eckhardt, Jason C.

Malone, Ross. Old Times There Are Not Forgotten: Tales from Sowega. 136p. 1995. text 14.95 *(0-941072-16-9)* Southern Herit.

Malone, Roy, jt. auth. see Rose, Louis J.

***Malone, Samuel.** Learning Skills for Managers. 180p. 2000. pap. 16.95 *(1-86076-170-4,* Pub. by Oak Tr) Midpt Trade.

Malone, Samuel A. How to Set up & Manage an Open Learning Centre. LC 96-15514. 200p. 1996. 65.95 *(0-566-07818-X,* Pub. by Gower) Ashgate Pub Co.

— Mind Skills for Managers. LC 96-15513. 240p. 1997. 51.95 *(0-566-07817-1,* Pub. by Gower) Ashgate Pub Co.

Malone, Shelley B. & Strunk, Phyllis B. Postcards of Old Key West. (Illus.). 64p. (Orig.). 1989. pap. write for info. *(0-318-65765-1)* S B Malone & P B Strunk.

Malone, Susan, jt. auth. see Weisbeck, Chuck.

Malone, Susan M. By the Book. LC 92-74829. 247p. 1993. 18.00 *(1-880909-00-6)* Baskerville.

Malone, Susan M., ed. see Morrison, Mary B.

Malone, Sylvester L. Dr. Edward McGlynn. 1978. 19.95 *(0-405-10841-9,* 11847) Ayer.

***Malone, Ted.** Windows 2000 Automated Deployment Guide. (Illus.). 400p. 2000. 39.99 *(0-7897-1749-2)* Que.

Malone, Thomas C., ed. Ecosystems at the Land-Sea Margin: Drainage Basin to Coastal Sea. LC 98-49007. (Coastal & Estuarine Studies). 378p. 1999. 62.00 *(0-87590-269-3)* Am Geophysical.

Malone, Thomas E., jt. ed. see Porter, Roger J.

Malone, Thomas F. International Networks for Addressing Issues of Global Change. (Illus.). 244p. 1994. pap. 2.00 *(0-914446-06-1)* Sigma Xi.

Malone, Thomas P., jt. auth. see Whitaker, Carl A.

***Malone, Tom.** For Men Only. 15p. 1999. pap. write for info. *(0-87398-287-8)* Sword of the Lord.

Malone, Vernon, jt. auth. see Dodge, Steve.

Malone, W. Henry. A Treatise on Real Property Trials: Showing the Difference . . . 788p. 1998. reprint ed. 205.00 *(1-56169-419-3)* Gaunt.

Malone, Walter. From Holy Power to Holy Profits. rev. ed. 132p. 1994. pap. 10.95 *(0-913543-38-1)* African Am Imag.

Malone, Wex S. Essays on Torts. LC 85-82407. 400p. 1986. lib. bdg. 50.00 *(0-940448-13-0)* LSU Law Pubns.

Malone, William F. & Koth, David L. Tylman's Theory & Practice of Fixed Prosthodontics. 8th ed. 461p. 1989. 59.50 *(0-912791-48-9,* Ishiyaku EuroAmerica) Med Dent Media.

Malone, Willie. Your New Beginning: Step Two. 64p. (Orig.). 1983. pap. 2.50 *(0-88144-008-6)* Christian Pub.

Malone, Willie J. Buck Van Huss: The Legend. 160p. 1989. 15.00 *(0-317-93444-9)*; pap. 6.95 *(0-317-93445-7)* Willane Pub.

Maloney. Electricity: Fundamentals & Applications. (Electronics Technology Ser.). 1992. pap., teacher ed. 28.50 *(0-8273-5040-6)* Delmar.

Maloney. WFT Corp. '97: Student Notetaking Guide. 14th ed. (SWC-Taxation Ser.). 1996. pap. 12.50 *(0-314-20250-1)* Sth-Wstrn College.

Maloney, jt. auth. see Harris.

Maloney, jt. auth. see Titone.

Maloney, tr. see Ryokan.

Maloney, William C. Pioneering Hematology: The Research & Treatment of Malignant Blood Disorders. LC 98-126281. xv, 196p. 1997. 24.95 *(0-88135-195-4,* Sci Hist) Watson Pub Intl.

Maloney, Bernard K., ed. Human Activities & the Tropical Rain Forest Past, Present & Possible Future. LC 97-45512. 224p. 1998. lib. bdg. 130.50 *(0-7923-4858-3)* Kluwer Academic.

***Maloney, Beth.** Equine Physiology. 1999. 90.00 (*0-85131-735-9*, Pub. by J A Allen) Trafalgar.

Maloney, Beth. Nutrition & the Feeding of Horses. (Illus.). 216p. 1998. pap. 32.95 (*1-85310-744-1*, Pub. by Swan Hill Pr) Voyageur Pr.

Maloney, Betty, jt. auth. see Blombery, Alec M.

Maloney, Betty, jt. auth. see Thompson, Patricia.

Maloney, Betty, jt. auth. see Thompson, Patricia A.

Maloney, Betty, jt. auth. see Thomson, Patricia.

Maloney, Clarence. Dimensions of Morning Sky. 1964. pap. 10.00 (*0-685-62611-3*) Atlantis Edns.

Maloney, Clarence & Raju, K. V. Managing Irrigation Together: Practice & Policy in India. LC 94-7771. 340p. 1994. 36.00 (*0-8039-9175-4*) Sage.

Maloney, David J., Jr. Maloney's Antiques & Collectibles Resource Directory. 5th ed. 672p. 1999. pap. 29.95 (*1-58221-016-0*) Krause Pubns.

Maloney, David J., et al. West's Federal Taxation: Comprehensive Volume, 1995. Fenton, ed. 1200p. (C). 1994. text 71.25 (*0-314-03349-1*) West Pub.

***Maloney, Dayle.** Last Call for Help: Changing North America One Teen at a Time. 1999. pap. 14.95 (*0-9664118-5-4*) D L Maloney.

Maloney, Dayle & Prokop, Lori. I Could Have Quit $7,000,000 Ago! 1998. pap. 14.95 (*0-9664118-2-X*) D L Maloney.

Maloney, Dennis. Lost in Language: Translations from the Japanese & Spanish. 24p. (Orig.). 1989. pap. text 2.00 (*1-877800-00-7*) Springhse Editions.

— Selected Poems. 100p. 1990. 17.50 (*0-87775-232-X*); pap. 7.95 (*0-87775-231-1*) Unicorn Pr.

— Sitting in Circles. Keida, Yusuke, tr. (ENG & JPN.). 112p. 1987. pap. 8.00 (*0-934834-87-3*) White Pine.

Maloney, Dennis, ed. see Neruda, Pablo.

Maloney, Dennis, jt. ed. see Seaton, J. P.

Maloney, Dennis, ed. & tr. see Neruda, Pablo.

Maloney, Dennis, tr. see Akiko, Yosano.

Maloney, Dennis, tr. see Jimenez, Juan Ramon.

Maloney, Dennis, tr. see Machado, Antonio.

Maloney, Dennis M. Protection of Human Research Subjects: A Practical Guide to Federal Laws & Regulations. LC 84-4873. (Illus.). 442p. 1984. 107.00 (*0-306-41522-4*, Kluwer Plenum) Kluwer Academic.

Maloney, E. Using 1-2-3 for Windows 95. (Illus.). 416p. 1995. 21.99 (*0-7897-0142-1*) Que.

Maloney, Eddie. Tough Guy. 416p. 1997. mass mkt. 5.99 (*0-7860-0535-1*, Pinncle Kensgtn) Kensgtn Pub Corp.

Maloney, Eddie & Hoffman, William. Tough Guy. 384p. 1995. mass mkt. 4.99 (*0-7860-0168-2*, Pinncle Kensgtn) Kensgtn Pub Corp.

Maloney, Edward T. Northrop Flying Wings. (Illus.). 55p. 1975. pap. 19.95 (*0-915464-00-4*, WW II Pubns) Aviation.

***Maloney, Elberrt S.** Chapman Piloting: Seamanship & Small Boat Handling. 63rd ed. 656p. 1999. 45.00 (*0-688-16890-6*, Wm Morrow) Morrow Avon.

Maloney, Elbert S. Chapman Piloting: Seamanship & Small Boat Handling. 61st deluxe ed. 1993. 50.00 (*0-688-11684-1*, Wm Morrow) Morrow Avon.

— Chapman Piloting, Seamanship & Small Boat Handling. 60th ed. (Illus.). 652p. 1991. 32.50 (*0-688-10425-8*, Wm Morrow) Morrow Avon.

— Dutton's Navigation & Piloting. 14th ed. (Illus.). 664p. 1985. 75.00 (*0-87021-157-9*) Naval Inst Pr.

— Problems & Answers in Navigation & Piloting. 2nd ed. 83p. 1985. pap. 6.95 (*0-87021-150-1*) Naval Inst Pr.

Maloney, Eric & Nossiter, Joshua C. Using Word 97. LC 96-71428. 523p. 1996. 24.99 (*0-7897-0956-2*) Que.

Maloney, Florence & Burns, Lois. Basic Transcription. (Medical Assisting Ser.). (Illus.). 336p. (C). 1996. text, mass mkt. 43.95 incl. disk (*0-8273-6374-5*) Delmar.

Maloney, Florence C. & Burns, Lois M. Basic Transcription. (Medical Assisting Ser.). 64p. 1996. pap., teacher ed. 15.95 (*0-8273-6375-3*) Delmar.

Maloney, Gary, ed. see American Political Network, Inc. Staff & LTV Corporation Staff.

Maloney, Gene. Fire Department Lieutenant Captain Battalion Chief: Score High on Firefighter Promotion Exams. LC 89-277. 256p. 1990. per. 14.95 (*0-13-318361-0*, Arc) IDG Bks.

***Maloney, George A.** Called to Be Free: Reflections on the Meaning of Christian Freedom. 150p. (YA). 2000. pap. 8.95 (*0-8189-0837-8*, Saint Pauls) Alba.

Maloney, George A. Called to Intimacy. LC 83-3782. 164p. 1983. pap. 6.95 (*0-8189-0452-6*) Alba.

— Death: Where Is Your Sting? LC 84-9216. 155p. (Orig.). 1984. pap. 6.95 (*0-8189-0470-4*) Alba.

— Entering into the Heart of Jesus: Meditations on the Indwelling Trinity in St. John's Gospel. LC 87-30659. 170p. 1988. pap. 8.95 (*0-8189-0527-1*) Alba.

— God's Community of Love: Living in the Indwelling Trinity. 2nd ed. 144p. (Orig.). 1993. reprint ed. pap. 9.95 (*1-56548-042-2*) New City.

— God's Incredible Mercy. LC 88-30108. 183p. (Orig.). 1989. pap. 9.95 (*0-8189-0544-1*) Alba.

— Inward Stillness. 1974. pap. 14.95 (*0-87193-062-5*) Dimension Bks.

— The Mystery of Christ in You: The Mystical Vision of Saint Paul. LC 97-27145. 112p. 1998. pap. 8.95 (*0-8189-0802-5*) Alba.

— On the Road to Perfection: Christian Humility in Modern Society. 144p. 1995. pap. 9.95 (*1-56548-035-X*) New City.

— The Spirit Broods over the World. LC 92-40239. 210p. 1993. pap. 9.95 (*0-8189-0633-2*) Alba.

— That Your Joy May Be Complete: The Secret of Becoming a Joyful Person. 3rd ed. LC 93-47943. 144p. 1994. 9.95 (*1-56548-062-7*) New City.

— Your Sins Are Forgiven You: Rediscovering the Sacrament of Reconciliation. LC 93-43836. 142p. 1994. pap. 7.95 (*0-8189-0691-X*) Alba.

Maloney, George A., ed. from RUS. Nil Sorsky: The Complete Writings. (Classics of Western Spirituality Ser.). 192p. 2000. 24.95 (*0-8091-0497-0*); pap. 18.95 (*0-8091-3810-7*) Paulist Pr.

Maloney, George A., tr. Pseudo-Macarius: The Fifty Spiritual Homilies & the Great Letter. LC 92-4736. (Classics of Western Spirituality Ser.). 320p. 1992. 24.95 (*0-8091-0455-5*); pap. 17.95 (*0-8091-3312-1*) Paulist Pr.

Maloney, George S. A Theology of Uncreated Energies of God. LC 78-55049. (Pere Marquette Lectures). 1978. 15.00 (*0-87462-516-5*) Marquette.

Maloney, Gilles & Frohn, Winnie, eds. Hippocrates - Concordantia in Corpus Hippocraticum, 6 vols., Set. (Alpha Omega, Reihe A Ser.: No. LXXV). (GER.). xxiii, 4869p. 1986. lib. bdg. 1025.70 (*3-487-07740-X*) G Olms Pubs.

— Hippocrates - Concordantia in Corpus Hippocraticum, 6 vols., Vol. 6. (Alpha Omega, Reihe A Ser.: No. LXXV). (GER.). vi, 487p. 1986. lib. bdg. write for info. (*3-487-09130-5*) G Olms Pubs.

Maloney, J. Christopher. The Mundane Matter of the Mental Language. (Cambridge Studies in Philosophy). (Illus.). 304p. (C). 1989. text 80.00 (*0-521-37031-0*) Cambridge U Pr.

Maloney, J. J. Beyond the Wall. 1973. per. 3.00 (*0-912678-05-4*, Greenfld Rev Pr) Greenfld Rev Lit.

— The Pariah's Handbook. LC 92-32968. 1992. write for info. (*0-9617499-3-8*) Woods Colt Pr.

Maloney, James C. A Critical Edition of Mira De Amescua's "La Fe De Hungria" & "El Monte De la Piedad", Vol. 7. 149p. 1975. pap. 7.00 (*0-912788-06-2*) Tulane Romance Lang.

***Maloney, James M.** The Stump Man, 1. 250p. 2000. pap. 9.95 (*1-892614-29-4*) Briarwood VA.

***Maloney, Jim.** Distributed COM Application Development Using Visual Basic 6.0. LC 99-42022. 414p. 1999. pap. text 49.99 (*0-13-084874-3*) P-H.

— Visual Basic 7 Distributed Com+ Developer's Guide. 825p. 2000. pap. 49.99 (*0-13-028209-X*) P-H.

Maloney, John. The Professionalization of Economics: Alfred Marshall & the Dominance of Orthodoxy. 248p. (C). 1990. pap. 24.95 (*0-88738-345-9*) Transaction Pubs.

— Proposal. LC 98-54307. 112p. 1999. pap. 13.00 (*1-58195-004-7*, Pub. by Zoland Bks) Consort Bk Sales.

Maloney, John, ed. Debt & Deficits: An Historical Perspective. LC 97-27155. 160p. 1998. 70.00 (*1-85898-479-3*) E Elgar.

Maloney, John C., ed. see Attitude Research Conference Staff.

Maloney, Karen B. Infant Food & Nutrition of Newborn: Medical Subject Analysis with Reference Bibliography. LC 85-48104. 150p. 1997. 47.50 (*0-88164-480-3*); pap. 44.50 (*0-88164-481-1*) ABBE Pubs Assn.

Maloney, Karen L., jt. auth. see Phagan-Schostok, Patricia A.

Maloney, Kerry A., jt. ed. see Barry, William A.

Maloney, L., tr. see Buhler, Walther.

Maloney, Laura & Hughes, Catherine, eds. Case Studies in Museum, Zoo & Aquarium Theater. (Professional Practice Ser.). (Illus.). 129p. 1999. pap. 30.50 (*0-931201-60-8*, 810) Am Assn Mus.

Maloney, Laurence T., ed. see Gaylord, Richard J. & Pavel, Misha.

Maloney, Linda, tr. see Schroer, Silvia.

Maloney, Linda M. All That God Hath Done with Them: The Narration of the Works of God in the Early Christian Community as Described in the Acts of the Apostles. LC 90-40424. (American University Studies: Theology & Religion: Ser. VII, Vol. 91). XIII, 238p. (C). 1991. text 42.95 (*0-8204-1410-7*) P Lang Pubng.

Maloney, Linda M., tr. see Aristide, Jean-Bertrand & Wargny, Christophe.

Maloney, Linda M., tr. see Braun, Josef.

Maloney, Linda M., tr. see Domen, Christoph.

Maloney, Linda M., tr. see Eisen, Ute E.

Maloney, Linda M., tr. see Emminghaus, Johannes.

Maloney, Linda M., tr. see Haussling, Angelus A., et al, eds.

Maloney, Linda M., tr. see Hildegard of Bingen.

Maloney, Linda M., tr. see Lohfink, Gerhard.

Maloney, Linda M., tr. see Lohfink, Norbert.

Maloney, Linda M., tr. see Maisch, Ingrid.

Maloney, Linda M., tr. see Raphael, Pierre.

Maloney, Linda M., tr. see Reimer, Ivoni R.

Maloney, Linda M., tr. see Reiser, Marius.

Maloney, Linda M., tr. see Richter, Klemens.

Maloney, Linda M., tr. see Strecker, Georg.

Maloney, Linda M., tr. see Ulrich, Ingeborg.

Maloney, Linda M., tr. see Vorgrimler, Herbert.

Maloney, Mack. Chopper Ops. 1999. mass mkt. 5.99 (*0-425-17116-7*) Berkley Pub.

— The Circle War. (Wingman Ser.: 2). 416p. 1996. mass mkt. 4.99 (*0-7860-0346-4*, Pinncle Kensgtn) Kensgtn Pub Corp.

— The Death Orbit. (Wingman Ser.: No. 13). 416p. 1997. mass mkt. 4.99 (*0-7860-0357-X*, Pinncle Kensgtn) Kensgtn Pub Corp.

— The Final Storm. (Wingman Ser.: No. 6). 1998. pap. 4.99 (*0 7860 0505-X*, Pinncle Kensgtn) Kensgtn Pub Corp.

— Freedmon Express. (Wingman Ser.: No. 7). 1990. mass mkt. 3.99 (*0-8217-4022-9*, Zebra Kensgtn) Kensgtn Pub Corp.

— Freedom Express. (Wingman Ser.: No. 7). 384p. 1998. pap. 4.99 (*0-7860-0548-3*, Pinncle Kensgtn) Kensgtn Pub Corp.

— The Ghost War. 448p. 1993. mass mkt. 4.50 (*0-8217-4223-X*, Zebra Kensgtn) Kensgtn Pub Corp.

— The Lucifer Crusade. (Wingman Ser.: No. 3). 432p. 1987. mass mkt. 3.95 (*0-8217-2232-8*, Zebra Kensgtn) Kensgtn Pub Corp.

— The Lucifer Crusade. (Wingman Ser.: No. 3). 416p. 1997. mass mkt. 4.99 (*0-7860-0388-X*, Pinncle Kensgtn) Kensgtn Pub Corp.

— Return from the Inferno. (Wingman Ser.: No. 9). 1991. mass mkt. 3.95 (*0-8217-3510-1*, Zebra Kensgtn) Kensgtn Pub Corp.

— Return from the Inferno. (Wingman Ser.: No. 9). 1999. mass mkt. 4.99 (*0-7860-0645-5*) Kensgtn Pub Corp.

— Return of Sky Ghost. (Wingman Ser.: No. 15). 352p. 1998. pap. 4.99 (*0-7860-0510-6*, Pinncle Kensgtn) Kensgtn Pub Corp.

— The Sky Ghost. (Wingman Ser.: No. 14). 384p. 1997. mass mkt. 4.99 (*0-7860-0452-5*, Pinncle Kensgtn) Kensgtn Pub Corp.

— Skyfire. (Wingman Ser.: No. 8). (gr. k). 1990. mass mkt. 3.95 (*0-8217-3121-1*, Zebra Kensgtn) Kensgtn Pub Corp.

— Skyfire. (Wingman Ser.: No. 8). 352p. 1998. mass mkt. 4.99 (*0-7860-0605-6*, Pinncle Kensgtn) Kensgtn Pub Corp.

— Target: Point Zero. (Wingman Ser.). 384p. 1996. mass mkt. 4.99 (*0-7860-0299-9*, Pinncle Kensgtn) Kensgtn Pub Corp.

— Thunder Alley. 432p. 1988. mass mkt. 3.95 (*0-8217-2405-3*, Zebra Kensgtn) Kensgtn Pub Corp.

— Thunder in the East. (Wingman Ser.: No. 4). 432p. 1988. mass mkt. 3.95 (*0-8217-2453-3*, Zebra Kensgtn) Kensgtn Pub Corp.

— Thunder in the East. (Wingman Ser.: No. 4). 432p. 1997. mass mkt. 4.99 (*0-7860-0428-2*) Kensgtn Pub Corp.

— Twisted Cross. (Wingman Ser.: No. 5). 400p. 1989. mass mkt. 3.95 (*0-8217-2553-X*, Zebra Kensgtn) Kensgtn Pub Corp.

— The Twisted Cross. (Wingman Ser.: No. 5). 1997. mass mkt. 4.99 (*0-7860-0467-3*, Pinncle Kensgtn) Kensgtn Pub Corp.

— War Heaven. 432p. 1991. mass mkt. 4.95 (*0-8217-3414-8*, Zebra Kensgtn) Kensgtn Pub Corp.

— War of the Sun. (Wingman Ser.: No. 10). 448p. 1999. mass mkt. 4.99 (*0-7860-0665-X*) Kensgtn Pub Corp.

***Maloney, Mack.** War of the Sun. (Wingman Ser.). 441p. 1999. mass mkt. 4.99 (*0-7860-1033-9*) Pinnacle Books.

Maloney, Mack. Wingman. (Wingman Ser.: No. 1). 464p. 1996. mass mkt. 4.99 (*0-7860-0310-3*, Pinncle Kensgtn) Kensgtn Pub Corp.

— Wingman No. 2: The Circle War. 1987. mass mkt. 3.95 (*0-8217-2120-8*, Zebra Kensgtn) Kensgtn Pub Corp.

— Wingman No. 6: The Final Storm. 1989. mass mkt. 3.95 (*0-8217-2655-2*, Zebra Kensgtn) Kensgtn Pub Corp.

***Maloney, Mack.** Zero Red. (Chopper Ops Ser.: Vol. 2). 2000. mass mkt. 5.99 (*0-425-17370-4*) Berkley Pub.

Maloney, Margaret. Goodman of Ballangiech. (Illus.). 32p. (J). (gr. k-3). 1991. pap. write for info. (*0-614-17731-6*) Stoddart Publ.

— The Goodman of Ballengiech. 1996. pap. 8.95 (*0-7736-7349-0*) Stoddart Publ.

— The Little Mermaid. (Illus.). 32p. (J). (gr. k-3). 1983. write for info. (*0-458-95110-2*) Stoddart Publ.

Maloney, Margret VanOrden. Memories from Harbor View Pathway. LC 97-66205. (Illus.). 1997. write for info. (*0-89725-300-0*) Picton Pr.

Maloney, Mark. Wingman. 464p. 1987. mass mkt. 3.95 (*0-8217-2015-5*, Zebra Kensgtn) Kensgtn Pub Corp.

Maloney, Martin. Conversation Pieces. (Illus.). 48p. 1999. pap. 16.95 (*88-8158-198-1*, Pub. by Charta) Dist Art Pubs.

Maloney, Martin J., jt. auth. see Rubenstein, Paul M.

Maloney, Mary E. Dermatologic Surgical Suite: Design & Materials. (Practical Manuals in Dermatologic Surgery Ser.). (Illus.). 105p. 1990. pap. text 39.95 (*0-443-08688-5*) Church.

Maloney, Mary E., et al, eds. Surgical Dermatopathology. LC 98-33478. (Illus.). xi, 506p. 1999. 160.00 (*0-86542-299-0*) Blackwell Sci.

Maloney, Mary E., jt. auth. see Miller, Stanley J.

Maloney, Michael. Teach Your Children Well: A Solution to North America's Educational Problems. LC 98-37879. 1998. pap. 16.95 (*1-881317-06-4*) Cambdge Ctr Behav.

Maloney, Michael & Kranz, Rachel. Straight Talk about Eating Disorders. (Straight Talk Ser.). 128p. (YA). (gr. 6-12). 1991. 19.95 (*0-8160-2414-6*) Facts on File.

Maloney, Michael C., et al. Pocket Guide to Fly Casting. (Illus.). 28p. 1995. spiral bd. 12.95 (*1-886127-10-7*) Greycliff Pub.

Maloney, Michael P. & Ward, Michael P. Psychological Assessment: A Conceptual Approach. (Illus.). 422p. 1976. text 41.95 (*0-19-502027-8*) OUP.

Maloney, Michael W., jt. auth. see Czerniawski, Richard D.

Maloney, Mike. Flash! Splash! Crash! All at Sea with Cap'n Bob: My Astonishing Adventures With Robert Maxwell. LC 97-131975. (Illus.). 224p. 1998. 29.95 (*1-85158-853-1*, Pub. by Mainstream Pubng) Trafalgar.

Maloney, Pat. Give Me Your Tired - Your Poor. 260p. 1999. pap. write for info. (*0-7392-0055-0*, No. P02870) Morris Pubng.

***Maloney, Pat, Sr.** Give Me Your Tired, Your Poor. 2nd rev. ed. 1999. pap. 14.99 (*0-9672979-0-7*) Presidio Pub.

Maloney, Patricia L. Practical Guidance for Parents of the Visually Handicapped Preschooler. (Illus.). 88p. 1981. pap., spiral bd. 23.95 (*0-398-04583-6*) C C Thomas.

***Maloney, Peter.** Belly Button Boy. (Illus.). 40p. (J). (ps-3). 2000. 15.99 (*0-8037-2542-6*, Dial Yng Read) Peng Put Young Read.

Maloney, Peter. Redbird at Rockefeller Center. LC 96-45728. (Illus.). (J). 1997. 14.89 (*0-8037-2257-5*, Dial Yng Read) Peng Put Young Read.

Maloney, Peter & Zekauskas, Felicia. The Magic Hockey Stick. Arico, Diane, ed. LC 99-17201. (Illus.). 40p. (J). (ps-3). 1999. 12.99 (*0-8037-2476-4*, Dial Yng Read) Peng Put Young Read.

Maloney, Queen. Trail Wanderings: A Folk History of Bay Bulls, Newfoundland. (Illus.). 1994. pap. 9.55 (*1-895387-46-9*) Creative Bk Pub.

Maloney, R. Kay, ed. Personnel Development in Libraries. (Issues in Library & Information Sciences Ser.: No. 3). 1977. pap. text 15.00 (*0-8135-0843-6*) Rutgers U SICLS.

Maloney, Ralph. Twenty-Four Hour Drink Book. (Illus.). 1962. 10.95 (*0-8392-1121-X*) Astor-Honor.

Maloney, Robert M. Your Guide to Medical Schools & Residency Programs: The Information You Need to Know, You Should Know, You Must Know. DeVito, Richard A., ed. (Illus.). 250p. (Orig.). 1996. pap. 189.95 (*0-932834-25-6*) Prime Natl Pub.

Maloney, Robert P. He Hears the Cry of the Poor: On the Spirituality of Vincent de Paul. 2nd ed. LC 95-9621. 160p. 1995. pap. 9.95 (*1-56548-034-1*) New City.

— Seasons in Spirituality: Reflections on Vincentian Spirituality in Today's World. LC 97-30872. 184p. 1997. pap. 9.95 (*1-56548-095-3*) New City.

***Maloney, Roy T.** Celestial Navigation Quick & Easy... In Your Head Calculations of Latitude & Longitude. (Illus.). 128p. 2000. pap. 15.95 (*0-913257-11-7*) Dropzone Pr.

Maloney, Roy T. Real Estate Quick & Easy: Concepts of Real Estate Clearly Illustrated. 15th ed. (Illus.). 384p. 1999. pap. 29.50 (*0-913257-14-1*) Dropzone Pr.

Maloney, Sean M. Securing Command of the Sea: NATO Naval Planning, 1948-1954. (Illus.). 256p. 1994. 45.00 (*1-55750-562-4*) Naval Inst Pr.

Maloney, Shane. The Brush-Off: An Arcade Mystery. LC 98-5405. 320p. 1998. 23.45 (*1-55970-440-3*, Pub. by Arcade Pub Inc) Time Warner.

***Maloney, Shane.** Nice Try: A Murray Whelan Mystery. LC 99-59581. 272p. 2000. 23.95 (*1-55970-513-2*, Pub. by Arcade Pub Inc) Time Warner.

Maloney, Shane. Stiff. LC 98-50762. 240p. 1999. 23.95 (*1-55970-481-0*, Pub. by Arcade Pub Inc) Time Warner.

Maloney, Stephen R. Speaker's Portable Answer Book. LC 93-8251. 304p. (C). 1993. text 29.95 (*0-13-501016-0*) P-H.

Maloney, Susan, jt. ed. see Tate, Suzanne.

Maloney, Thomas M. Modern Particleboard & Dry-Process Fiberboard Manufacturing. LC 76-47094. (Forest Industries Book). (Illus.). 688p. 1993. 59.00 (*0-87930-288-7*) Miller Freeman.

Maloney, Thomas R., jt. auth. see Milligan, Robert A.

Maloney, Thomas S., tr. Roger Bacon, Three Treatments of Universals: A Translation With Introduction & Notes. (Medieval & Renaissance Texts & Studies: Vol. 66). 176p. 1989. 24.00 (*0-86698-075-X*, MR66) MRTS.

Maloney, Tim. Benefit Reforms & Labour Market Behaviour in New Zealand. LC 98-150327. (Illus.). 1997. write for info. (*0-908935-16-1*) Vict U Well IPS.

***Maloney, Tim & Victoria University of Wellington. Institute of Policy Studies.** Five Years after: The New Zealand Labour Market & the Employment Contracts Act. LC 99-195733. (Illus.). 1998. 30.00 (*0-908935-29-3*) Vict U Well IPS.

Maloney, Timothy. Electricity: Fundamental Concepts & Applications. 1991. pap., teacher ed. 28.00 (*0-8273-4677-8*) Delmar.

Maloney, Timothy J. Electric Circuits: Principles & Applications. (Illus.). 896p. (C). 1984. 32.15 (*0-685-07187-1*) P-H.

— Electric Circuits: Principles & Applications. 2nd ed. 864p. 1988. boxed set 41.00 (*0-13-247735-1*) P-H.

— Electricity: Fundamental Concepts & Applications. 448p. 1992. pap. 80.95 (*0-8273-4675-1*) Delmar.

— Laboratory Projects Manual for Solid-State Electronics. 83p. 1994. pap. text 9.25 (*0-9639857-7-9*) Dirk Pubng.

— Modern Industrial Electronics. 3rd ed. 864p. (C). 1995. 106.00 (*0-13-457516-4*) P-H.

— Solid-State Electronics: Principles & Applications. 535p. (C). 1994. pap. text 33.50 (*0-9639857-4-4*) Dirk Pubng.

Maloney, Timothy J., jt. auth. see Dabral, Sanjay.

Maloney, W. A. & Richardson, J. J. Managing Policy Change in Britain: The Politics of Water. LC 96-162489. 176p. 1996. 69.50 (*0-7486-0669-6*, Pub. by Edinburgh U Pr) Col U Pr.

Maloney, Walter C. A Sketch of the History of Key West, Florida. Peters, Thelma B., ed. & intro. by. LC 68-21658. (Floridiana Facsimile & Reprint Ser.). xxi, 85p. 1968. reprint ed. 16.95 (*0-8130-0157-9*) U Press Fla.

Maloney, William & Grindle, Lincoln. Textbook of Phacoemulsification. LC 87-28607. (Illus.). 1988. 68.00 (*0-918916-06-2*) Lasenda.

Maloney, William, et al. Consumer Guide to Modern Cataract Surgery. LC 85-80392. (Illus.). 1986. pap. 12.95 (*0-918916-05-4*) Lasenda.

Maloney, William A., jt. auth. see Jordan, Grant.

Maloney, William A., jt. auth. see McLaughlin, Andrew M.

Maloni, Ruby. European Merchant Capital & the Indian Economy: A Historical Reconstruction Based on Surat Factory Records 1630-1668. (C). 1992. 30.00 (*81-85425-50-7*, Pub. by Manohar) S Asia.

Maloni, Ruby, jt. auth. see Dossal, Mariam.

***Malonis, Jane A.** Encyclopedia of Business, 2 vols. 2nd ed. LC 99-47471. 1999. write for info. (*0-7876-2440-3*) Gale.

Malony, H. Newton. Church Organization Development: Perspectives & Resources. LC 86-81285. (Orig.). 1986. pap. 16.95 (*0-9609928-2-0*) Integ Pr.

— Integration Musings: Thoughts on Being A Christian Professional. LC 86-81512. (Orig.). 1986. pap. 16.33 (*0-9609928-3-9*) Integ Pr.

— Living with Paradox: Religious Leadership & the Genius of Double Vision. LC 97-48677. (Religion in Practice Ser.). 160p. 1998. 22.00 (*0-7879-4057-7*) Jossey-Bass.

M

— Psychology & the Cross: A Christian Approach to Psychology. (Illus.). 284p. (Orig.). 1996. pap. 15.00 (*0-9650740-0-5*) Fuller Theolog.

— The Psychology of Religion for Ministry. LC 94-41661. (Integration Bks.). 144p. 1994. pap. 12.95 (*0-8091-3483-7*) Paulist Pr.

Malony, H. Newton, ed. Is There a Shrink in the Lord's House? How Psychologists Can Help the Church. LC 86-81513. (Orig.). 1986. pap. 12.95 (*0-9609928-4-7*) Integ Pr.

— Spirit-Centered Wholeness: Beyond the Psychology of Self. LC 87-23028. (Studies in the Psychology of Religion: Vol. 2). 256p. 1987. lib. bdg. 89.95 (*0-88946-246-1*) E Mellen.

Malony, H. Newton & Southard, Samuel, eds. Handbook of Religious Conversion. 314p. (Orig.). 1992. 34.95 (*0-89135-086-1*) Religious Educ.

Malony, H. Newton & Spilka, Bernard, eds. Religion in Psychodynamic Perspective: The Contributions of Paul W. Pruyser. 254p. 1991. text 55.00 (*0-19-506234-5*) OUP.

Malony, H. Newton, jt. ed. see Rosik, Christopher H.

Maloof. Finite Mathematics. (C). 1991. pap. text, student ed. 26.50 (*0-15-527547-X*) Harcourt Coll Pubs.

Maloof & Morris. Finite Mathematics. (C). 1991. pap. text, teacher ed. 21.00 (*0-15-527549-6*) Harcourt Coll Pubs.

Maloof, Alfreda W. Recollections from My Time in the Indian Service, 1935-1942: Maria Martinez Makes Pottery. LC 98-189021. (Illus.). 72p. (Orig.). 1997. pap. 15.00 (*0-9651377-1-6*) Liv Gold Pr.

Maloof, Catherine, jt. auth. see Maloof, Maureen.

Maloof, Judy. Over Her Dead Body: The Construction of Male Subjectivity in Onetti. LC 93-44115. (American University Studies, Series XXII: Vol. 24). 189p. (C). 1995. text 41.95 (*0-8204-2450-1*) P Lang Pubng.

Maloof, Judy, ed. from SPA. Voices of Resistance: Testimonies of Cuban & Chilean Women. LC 98-21801. (Illus.). 240p. 1999. 27.95 (*0-8131-2079-9*) U Pr of Ky.

Maloof, Karen. For My Grandchild: An Album of Memories from Grandparent to Grandchild. 56p. 1992. 17.95 (*0-8249-8545-1*, Ideals Child) Hambleton-Hill.

Maloof, Maureen & Maloof, Catherine. Healthy Eating One Bite at a Time. 109p. 1998. pap. 9.95 (*1-891361-01-5*, 27253) Maloof Enter.

— Renew Your Heart One Beat at a Time. 127p. 1998. pap. 9.95 (*1-891361-00-7*, 27252) Maloof Enter.

Maloof, Rich. Joe Satriani Riff by Riff. 91p. pap. 17.95 (*0-89524-851-4*, 02506314, Pub. by Cherry Lane) H Leonard.

Maloof, Sam. Sam Maloof: Woodworker. (Illus.). 228p. 1989. pap. 50.00 (*0-87011-910-9*) Kodansha.

Malor, J., et al, eds. Annotations to the Acts & Regulations of the Australian Parliament. 490.00 (*0-409-49007-5*, MICHIE) LEXIS Pub.

Maloratsky, Leo G. Passive RF & Microwave Integrated Circuits. 300p. 1999. 69.95 (*0-7803-1191-4*, PC5661-QOE) Inst Electrical.

Malory, Thomas. Arthur & the Sword. LC 95-9968. (Illus.). 32p. (J). (gr. 1-4). 1995. 16.00 (*0-689-31987-8*) Atheneum Yung Read.

— King Arthur & His Knights. Vinaver, Eugene, ed. (Illus.). 254p. 1975. pap. 11.95 (*0-19-501905-9*) OUP.

— Malory Works. 2nd ed. Vinaver, Eugene, ed. (Oxford Standard Authors Ser.). 828p. 1977. pap. text 25.95 (*0-19-281217-3*) OUP.

— Le Morte d' Arthur: The Winchester Manuscript. Cooper, Helen, ed. & intro. by. (The World's Classics Ser.). 610p. 1998. pap. 16.95 (*0-19-282420-1*) OUP.

Malory, Thomas. Le Morte D'Arthur. 432p. 28.95 (*0-8488-2616-7*) Amereon Ltd.

Malory, Thomas. Le Morte D'Arthur. 976p. 1994. 22.00 (*0-679-60099-X*) Modern Lib NY.

— Le Morte D'Arthur. LC 98-31432. 976p. 1999. pap. 12.95 (*0-375-75322-2*) Modern Lib NY.

— Le Morte D'Arthur. 1962. mass mkt. 7.99 (*0-451-62567-6*, Ment) NAL.

— Le Morte D'Arthur. Brewer, Derek S., ed. LC 68-22420. (York Medieval Texts Ser.). 166p. (C). 1968. pap. 17.95 (*0-8101-0031-2*) Northwestern U Pr.

— Le Morte D'Arthur. (Classics of World Literature Ser.). 1997. pap. 5.95 (*1-85326-463-6*, 4636WW, Pub. by Wrdsworth Edits) NTC Contemp Pub Co.

— Le Morte D'Arthur. abr. ed. Sanders, C. R. & Ward, C. E., eds. 1979. reprint ed. pap. text 13.95 (*0-89197-308-7*) Irvington.

— Le Morte D'Arthur, 3 vols. in 2. Sommer, H. Oskar, ed. LC 78-172839. reprint ed. 185.00 (*0-404-04175-2*) AMS Pr.

— Le Morte D'Arthur. (BCL1-PR English Literature Ser.). 148p. 1992. reprint ed. lib. bdg. 69.00 (*0-7812-7189-4*) Rprt Serv.

— Le Morte D'Arthur, 2 vols., 2. Cowen, Janet, ed. (English Library). 554p. 1970. pap. 11.95 (*0-14-043044-X*, Penguin Classics) Viking Penguin.

— Le Morte D'Arthur, 2 vols., Vol. 1. Cowen, Janet, ed. (English Library). 494p. 1970. pap. 10.95 (*0-14-043043-1*, Penguin Classics) Viking Penguin.

— Sir Thomas Malory: Views & Re-Views. Hanks, D., Jr., ed. LC 91-11928. (Studies in the Middle Ages: No. 19). 1991. 39.50 (*0-404-61449-3*) AMS Pr.

— Tales of King Arthur. 1981. 24.95 (*0-8052-3779-8*) Schocken.

Malory, Thomas & Center for Learning Network Staff. Le Morte D'Arthur: Curriculum Unit. (Novel Ser.). 89p. (YA). (gr. 9-12). 1995. spiral bd. 18.95 (*1-56077-341-3*) Ctr Learning.

Malory, Thomas, jt. auth. see Lister, Robin.

Malory, Thomas, ed. see Lanier, Sidney.

Malos, Ellen, ed. The Politics of Housework. 256p. 1995. 45.00 (*1-873797-19-2*); pap. 19.95 (*1-873797-18-4*) Paul & Co Pubs.

Malos, Ellen, jt. auth. see Hague, Gill.

Malossi, Giannino. Style Engine. LC 97-76232. 224p. 1998. 45.00 (*1-885254-95-4*, Pub. by Monacelli Pr) Penguin Putnam.

***Malossi, Giannino, ed.** Material Man: Masculinity, Sexuality, Style. LC 99-67946. (Illus.). 208p. 2000. pap. 39.95 (*0-8109-2709-8*, Pub. by Abrams) Time Warner.

Malossi, Giannino, ed. Volare: The Icon of Italy in Global Pop Culture. LC 98-68731. (Illus.). 224p. 1999. pap. 49.95 (*1-58093-039-5*, Pub. by Monacelli Pr) Penguin Putnam.

Malot, F. Sans Famille. unabridged ed. (FRE.). pap. 7.95 (*2-87714-288-4*, Pub. by Bookking Intl) Distribks Inc.

Malot, Hector. En Famille, Tome 1. (Folio - Junior Ser.: No. 131). (FRE., Illus.). 220p. (J). (gr. 5-10). 1980. pap. 9.95 (*2-07-033131-8*) Schoenhof.

— En Famille, Tome 2. (Folio - Junior Ser.: No. 132). (FRE., Illus.). 221p. (J). (gr. 5-10). 1980. pap. 9.95 (*2-07-033132-6*) Schoenhof.

— Sans Famille, Tome 1. (Folio - Junior Ser.: No. 612). (FRE., Illus.). 351p. (J). (gr. 5-10). 1990. pap. 10.95 (*2-07-033612-3*) Schoenhof.

— Sans Famille, Tome 2. (Folio - Junior Ser.: No. 617). (FRE., Illus.). 417p. (J). (gr. 5-10). 1991. pap. 10.95 (*2-07-033617-4*) Schoenhof.

Malot, Hector H. Nobody's Boy. 301p. 1991. reprint ed. lib. bdg. 35.95 (*0-89966-760-0*) Buccaneer Bks.

Malot, Hector H. Nobody's Girl. 301p. 1991. reprint ed. 31.95 (*0-89966-759-7*) Buccaneer Bks.

Malotki, Ekkehart. Hopi Time: A Linguistic Analysis of the Temporal Concepts in the Hopi Language. (Trends in Linguistics, Studies & Monographs: No. 20). xxii, 677p. 1983. 169.25 (*90-279-3349-9*) Mouton.

***Malotki, Ekkehart.** Kokopelli: The Making of an Icon. LC 99-88276. (Illus.). 200p. 2000. 35.00 (*0-8032-3213-6*, Bison Books) U of Nebr Pr.

Malotki, Ekkehart, ed. Hopi Animal Tales. LC 97-48996. (ENG & NAI., Illus.). xxxiii, 524p. 1998. text 45.00 (*0-8032-3199-7*) U of Nebr Pr.

Malotki, Ekkehart, photos by. Tapamveni: The Rock Art Galleries of Petrified Forest & Beyond. LC 94-17796. (Illus.). 194p. 1994. pap. 29.95 (*0-945695-05-5*) Petrified Forest Mus Assn.

Malotki, Ekkehart, tr. The Bedbugs' Night Dance & Other Hopi Tales of Sexual Encounter. LC 97-10431. (Illus.). xxiii, 389p. 1997. pap. 16.95 (*0-8032-8239-7*, Bison Books) U of Nebr Pr.

— The Magic Hummingbird: A Hopi Folktale. LC 95-80961. (Illus.). 40p. (J). (gr. k-7). 1996. 15.95 (*1-885772-04-1*) Kiva Pubng.

***Malotki, Ekkehart & Gary, Ken.** Hopi Stories of Witchcraft, Shamanism & Magic. (Illus.). 2001. 29.95 (*0-8032-3217-9*) U of Nebr Pr.

Malotki, Ekkehart & Lomatuway'ma, Michael. Hopi Coyote Tales: Istutuwutsi. LC 83-23412. (Illus.). viii, 343p. 1984. pap. 15.00 (*0-8032-8123-4*, Bison Books) U of Nebr Pr.

— Maasaw: Profile of a Hopi God. LC 87-163. (American Tribal Religions Ser.: No. 11). 283p. 1987. reprint ed. pap. 87.80 (*0-608-01407-9*, 206217000002) Bks Demand.

— Stories of Maasaw: A Hopi God. LC 87-164. (American Tribal Religions Ser.: Vol. 10). (Illus.). 357p. 1987. reprint ed. pap. 110.70 (*0-7837-8895-9*, 204960600001) Bks Demand.

Malotki, Ekkehart, ed. & tr. see Lomatuway'ma, Michael, et al.

Malotky, Lyle O. & Pennella, John J., eds. Physics-Based Technologies for the Detection of Contraband, Vol. 2936. LC 96-69886. 238p. 1997. 56.00 (*0-8194-2338-6*) SPIE.

Malott, Jack C. & Fodor, Joseph, III. The Art & Science of Medical Radiography. 7th ed. LC 92-49306. (Illus.). 320p. (gr. 13). 1993. pap. text 45.95 (*0-8016-6321-0*, 06321) Mosby Inc.

Malott, Richard W., et al. Elementary Principles of Behavior. 3rd ed. LC 96-21581. 1996. pap. text 61.00 (*0-13-533571-X*) P-H.

— Elementary Principles of Behavior. 4th ed. LC 99-22635. 500p. 1999. pap. 59.00 (*0-13-083706-7*) P-H.

Malott, Valerie J., jt. auth. see Doughman, Paula.

Malotte, A. The Lord's Prayer: For 2 or 3 Octave Handbells. 4p. 1989. 3.50 (*0-7935-5540-X*, 50488973) H Leonard.

— The Lord's Prayer: High E Flat Voice & Piano. 8p. 1986. pap. 3.95 (*0-7935-5331-8*, 50279830) H Leonard.

— The Lord's Prayer: Low in G with Voice & Organ. 6p. 1986. pap. 3.95 (*0-7935-5355-5*, 50284400) H Leonard.

— The Lord's Prayer: Low Voice & Piano in G. 6p. 1986. pap. 3.95 (*0-7935-5329-6*, 50284370) H Leonard.

— The Lord's Prayer: Medium High in D Flat. 8p. 1986. pap. 3.95 (*0-7935-5327-X*, 50279710) H Leonard.

— The Lord's Prayer: Medium in C Voice & Piano. 8p. 1986. pap. 3.95 (*0-7935-5317-2*, 50281100) H Leonard.

— The Lord's Prayer: Medium Low Voice & Piano. 8p. 1986. pap. 3.95 (*0-7935-5322-9*, 50279720) H Leonard.

Malotte, Stan, ed. The Painless Path to Proper Punctuation: or Who Killed Albert the Crook? (Illus.). 161p. 1998. reprint ed. pap. text 9.00 (*0-7881-5191-6*) DIANE Pub.

Malou, Job. The Dinka Vowel System. LC 88-60939. (Publications in Linguistics: No. 82). (Illus.). 100p. 1988. pap. 20.00 (*0-88312-008-9*) S I L Intl.

Malouf, David. Child's Play. LC 98-52931. 224p. 1998. pap. 12.00 (*0-375-70141-9*) Vin Bks.

— Conversations at Curlow Creek. LC 96-31641. 233p. 1997. 23.00 (*0-679-44266-9*) Pantheon.

— Conversations at Curlow Creek. 1998. pap. 12.00 (*0-679-77905-1*) Vin Bks.

— The Conversations at Curlow Creek. large type ed. LC 97-15406. (Basic Ser.). 314p. 1997. lib. bdg. 23.95 (*0-7862-1149-0*, G K Hall Lrg Type) Mac Lib Ref.

***Malouf, David.** Dream Stuff. LC 99-88859. 192p. 2000. 22.00 (*0-375-42053-3*) Pantheon.

Malouf, David. First Things Last. 58p. 1981. text 16.95 (*0-7022-1564-3*, Pub. by Univ Queensland Pr) Intl Spec Bk.

— Fly Away Peter. LC 98-11054. 1998. pap. 11.00 (*0-679-77670-2*) Vin Bks.

— The Great World: A Novel. LC 93-15510. 330p. 1993. pap. 14.00 (*0-679-74836-9*) Vin Bks.

— Harland's Half Acre. 1997. pap. 12.00 (*0-679-77647-8*) Random.

— An Imaginary Life. 1996. pap. 11.00 (*0-679-76793-2*) Random.

— Johnno. LC 97-40710. 170p. 1998. pap. 13.50 (*0-8076-1429-7*) Braziller.

— Johnno. 50th anniversary ed. 1998. reprint ed. 19.95 (*0-7022-3015-4*, Pub. by Univ Queensland Pr) Intl Spec Bk.

— Neighbours in a Thicket. 2nd ed. 1980. pap. 12.95 (*0-7022-1547-3*, Pub. by Univ Queensland Pr) Intl Spec Bk.

— Remembering Babylon. 1994. pap. 12.00 (*0-679-74951-9*) Vin Bks.

***Malouf, David.** Untold Tales. 64p. 1999. text 25.00 (*90-5704-016-6*) Gordon & Breach.

Malouf, David, jt. auth. see Jay, Charlotte.

Malouf, Dian L. Cattle Kings of Texas. LC 91-73402. (Illus.). 176p. 1991. 39.95 (*0-941831-69-8*) Beyond Words Pub.

— Cattle Kings of Texas. limited ed. 156p. 1992. 1000.00 (*1-885223-03-X*) Beyond Words Pub.

Malouf, Diana L. Unveiling the Hidden Words: The Norms Used by Shoghi Effendi in His Translation of the Hidden Words. LC 97-100920. (Baha'i Studies: No. 2). 240p. (Orig.). 1997. pap. 18.95 (*0-85398-414-X*) G Ronald Pub.

Malouf, Doug. How to Be the Best Speaker in Town. (Illus.). 156p. 1999. pap. 19.95 (*1-875680-25-X*) Woodslane.

***Malouf, Doug.** How to Teach Adults in a Fun & Exciting Way. 217p. 1999. pap. 24.95 (*1-875680-09-8*) Woodslane.

Malouf, Doug. Sold on Selling: Skills & Techniques. LC 96-84567. (How-to Book Ser.). 86p. (Orig.). 1996. pap. 12.95 (*1-884926-54-1*, SOLDS) Amer Media.

Malouf, George H. Maloof: The Ghassani Legacy. (Illus.). 608p. 1992. text 150.00 (*0-9632681-0-4*) Malouf Prods.

Malouf, John L., jt. auth. see Haas, Leonard J.

***Malouf, Lena.** Behind the Scenes at Special Events: Flowers, Props, & Design. LC 98-17815. 224p. 1998. 80.00 (*0-471-25491-6*) Wiley.

Malouf, Melissa. It Had to Be You: The Joan & Ernest Story. LC 97-2125. 176p. 1997. 25.00 (*1-888105-19-4*) Avisson Pr.

Malouf, Renee, jt. auth. see Orton, Diane.

Malouf, Renee B., jt. auth. see Orton, Diane B.

Malouf, Waldy & Finn, Molly. The Hudson River Valley Cookbook: A Leading American Chef Savors the Region's Bounty. 409p. 1995. 27.50 (*0-201-62253-X*) Addison-Wesley.

— The Hudson River Valley Cookbook: A Leading American Chef Savors the Region's Bounty. LC 98-29724. 336p. 1998. reprint ed. pap. 16.95 (*1-55832-143-8*, Pub. by Harvard Common Pr) Natl Bk Netwk.

Malouff, John & Schutte, Nicola S. Games to Enhance Social & Emotional Skills: Games That Teach Children, Adolescents, & Adults Skills Critical to Success in Life. LC 97-41232. (Illus.). 218p. 1998. spiral bd. 33.95 (*0-398-06836-4*) C C Thomas.

Malouff, John M., jt. auth. see Schutte, Nicola S.

Maloux, M. Dictionnaire des Proverbes, Sentences, Maximes. (FRE.). 1998. 59.95 (*0-320-00251-9*) Fr & Eur.

Maloux, Maurice. Dictionnaire de l'Humour et du Libertinage. (FRE.). 360p. 1983. 34.95 (*0-7859-7835-6*, 2226017674) Fr & Eur.

— Dictionnaire des Proverbs, Sentences, et Maximes. (FRE.). 628p. 1994. pap. 32.40 (*0-7859-8887-4*) Fr & Eur.

— Dictionnaire des Proverbes, Sentences, et Maximes. 2nd ed. (FRE.). 628p. 1990. pap. write for info. (*0-7859-4738-8*) Fr & Eur.

— Larousse Dictionnaire des Proverbes, Sentences et Maximes. (FRE.). 1992. 59.95 (*0-7859-7648-5*, 2033409066) Fr & Eur.

Malovitzki, Sinai. Parshas Lech. (Bible in Yiddish Ser.). (YID., Illus.). 160p. (YA). 1987. teacher ed. 15.00 (*0-944704-03-4*) Sinai Heritage.

— Parshas Nitzuvim. (Bible in Yiddish Ser.). (YID., Illus.). 150p. (J). 1988. pap. 7.00 (*0-944704-61-1*) Sinai Heritage.

— Parshas Yisroy. (Bible in Yiddish Ser.). (YID., Illus.). 400p. (J). 1988. lib. bdg. 35.00 (*0-944704-19-0*) Sinai Heritage.

— Parshaw Va'Yeilech. (Bible in Yiddish Ser.). (YID., Illus.). 95p. (YA). 1988. pap. 5.00 (*0-944704-62-X*) Sinai Heritage.

— Zochor Veshomor. (Bible in Yiddish Ser.). (YID., Illus.). 200p. (C). 1987. reprint ed. pap. text 16.00 (*0-944704-67-0*) Sinai Heritage.

Malowicki, Sinai. An Illustrated Guide to the Korbanos & Menachos. Fruchter, Yaakov, ed. (Illus.). 136p. (Orig.). 1991. pap. text 8.00 (*0-914131-99-0*) Torah Umesorah.

Malowicki, Sinai, ed. & illus. see Teitelbaum, Eli.

***Maloy, Bernard P. & Higgins, Charles R.** No Excuses Risk Management. 150p. 2000. pap. text 25.00 (*1-884125-77-8*) Cooper Pubng.

Maloy, Delores J. Memoirs & Memories. LC 98-72114. 48p. 1998. pap. 8.95 (*1-56167-435-4*) Am Literary Pr.

Maloy, Jacqueline. Teeth. (Real Readers Ser.: Level Blue). (Illus.). 32p. (J). (ps-3). 1989. lib. bdg. 21.40 (*0-8172-3520-5*) Raintree Steck-V.

— Teeth. (Real Readers Ser.: Level Blue). (Illus.). 32p. (J). (gr. 1-4). 1989. pap. 4.95 (*0-8114-6722-8*) Raintree Steck-V.

Maloy, Kate. Toward a New Science of Instruction. 73p. (Orig.). (C). 1994. pap. text 20.00 (*0-7881-0595-7*) DIANE Pub.

Maloy, Otis C. Plant Disease Control: Principles & Practice. 2nd ed. 360p. 1993. 110.00 (*0-471-57317-5*) Wiley.

Maloy, Richard H. & Bird, David D. Bankruptcy Practice Deskbook, 3 vols., 3. 2400p. 1991. 100.00 (*0-88063-730-7*, MICHIE) LEXIS Pub.

— Bankruptcy Practice Deskbook, 3 vols., Set. 2400p. 1994. ring bd. 285.00 (*0-88063-779-X*, MICHIE) LEXIS Pub.

— Bankruptcy Practice Deskbook, 3 vols., Vols. 1 & 2. 2400p. 1991. 205.00 (*0-88063-729-3*, MICHIE) LEXIS Pub.

Maloy, Robert W. & Seidman, Irving. The Essential Career Guide to Becoming a Middle & High School Teacher. LC 98-44207. 256p. 1999. 45.00 (*0-89789-559-2*, H559, Bergin & Garvey) Greenwood.

Maloy, Robert W., jt. auth. see Jones, Byrd L.

Maloy, Stanley R. Experimental Techniques in Bacterial Genetics. 196p. (Orig.). 1989. spiral bd. 41.25 (*0-86720-118-5*) Jones & Bartlett.

***Maloy, Stanley R. & Cronan, John.** Microbial Genetics. 3rd ed. (Illus.). 544p. (C). 2000. text 67.50 (*0-7637-1059-8*) Jones & Bartlett.

Maloy, Stanley R., et al. Genetic Analysis of Pathogenic Bacteria. 1996. 170.00 (*0-87969-452-1*); spiral bd., lab manual ed. 65.00 (*0-87969-453-X*) Cold Spring Harbor.

— Microbial Genetics. 2nd ed. (Life Science Ser.). 512p. 1994. 66.25 (*0-86720-248-3*) Jones & Bartlett.

Maloy, Timothy K. The Internet Research Guide. rev. ed. LC 98-72763. 224p. (Orig.). 1999. pap. 18.95 (*1-58115-012-1*) Allworth Pr.

— The Internet Research Guide: A Concise, Friendly & Practical Handbook for Anyone Researching in the Wide World of Cyberspace. LC 95-83010. 208p. 1996. pap. 18.95 (*1-880559-45-5*) Allworth Pr.

— The Writer's Internet Handbook. LC 96-84656. (Illus.). 208p. (Orig.). 1997. pap. 18.95 (*1-880559-80-3*) Allworth Pr.

Malpa, Alfred P., jt. auth. see Fenn, Patricia.

Malpas & Abbs. The Music Box. Date not set. pap. text, write for info. (*0-582-25597-X*, Pub. by Addison-Wesley) Longman.

Malpas, Emeline H. Run Away to War. 288p. (Orig.). 1997. pap. 12.95 (*1-884570-72-0*) Research Triangle.

Malpas, J. E. Place & Experience: A Philosophical Topography. LC 98-39069. 232p. (C). 1999. 54.95 (*0-521-64217-5*) Cambridge U Pr.

Malpas, J. E. & Solomon, Robert C. Death & Philosophy. LC 98-21615. 240p. (C). 1998. 75.00 (*0-415-19143-2*); pap. 24.99 (*0-415-19144-0*) Routledge.

Malpas, J. E., ed. see Donagan, Alan.

Malpas, James. Realism. (Movements in Modern Art Ser.). (Illus.). 80p. (C). 1998. pap. 13.95 (*0-521-62757-5*) Cambridge U Pr.

Malpas, James, et al, eds. Myeloma: Biology & Management. 2nd ed. LC 97-18025. (Illus.). 686p. 1998. text 175.00 (*0-19-262882-8*) OUP.

Malpas, Jeff, jt. ed. see Wrathall, Mark.

Malpas, Phillip A. True Messiah. 160p. 1989. pap. 12.95 (*0-913004-67-7*, 352) Point Loma Pub.

Malpas, Simon, ed. see Cowper, William.

***Malpass, Brian.** The Bluffer's Guide to Science: Bluff Your Way in Science. rev. ed. (Bluffer's Guides Ser.). 64p. 2000. pap. 5.95 (*1-902825-58-6*) Oval Bks.

Malpass, Eric. The Long Long Dances. large type ed. 354p. 1982. 27.99 (*0-7089-0825-X*) Ulverscroft.

— Oh, My Darling Daughter. large type ed. 384p. 1982. 27.99 (*0-7089-0881-0*) Ulverscroft.

— Summer Awakening. large type ed. 336p. 1983. 27.99 (*0-7089-0961-2*) Ulverscroft.

Malpass, Kenneth, et al. Workshop on Protecting & Assuring Critical National Infrastructure. 58p. 1997. pap. 7.50 (*0-935371-47-8*) CFISAC.

Malpass, Michael A. Daily Life in the Inca Empire. LC 95-44689. (Daily Life Through History Ser.). 200p. 1996. 45.00 (*0-313-29390-2*, Greenwood Pr) Greenwood.

Malpass, Michael A., ed. Provincial Inca: Archaeological & Ethnohistorical Assessment of the Impact of the Inca State. LC 93-30296. (Illus.). 290p. 1993. pap. text 25.95 (*0-87745-426-4*) U of Iowa Pr.

***Malpass, Peter.** Housing Associations & Housing Policy: A Historical Perspective. LC 99-50210. 2000. text 65.00 (*0-312-23095-8*) St Martin.

Malpass, Peter & Means, Robin, eds. Implementing Housing Policy. LC 92-23835. 208p. 1993. 118.00 (*0-335-15751-3*); pap. 34.95 (*0-335-15750-5*) OpUniv Pr.

Malpass, Roy S., jt. ed. see Lonner, Walter J.

Malpezzi, Frances M. & Clements, William M. Italian-American Folklore. 304p. 1998. pap. 14.95 (*0-87483-533-X*) August Hse.

Malphrus, Benjamin K. The History of Radio Astronomy & the National Radio Astronomy Observatory: Evolution Toward Big Science. 210p. (C). 1996. 49.50 (*0-89464-841-1*) Krieger.

Malphurs, Aubrey. Advanced Strategic Planning: A New Model for Church & Ministry Leaders. LC BV652.M3563 1999. (Illus.). 288p. 1999. pap. 16.99 (*0-8010-9068-7*) Baker Bks.

— Developing a Dynamic Mission for Your Ministry: Finding Direction & Making an Impact As a Church Leader. LC 98-10292. 144p. 1998. pap. 9.99 (*0-8254-3189-1*) Kregel.

— Developing a Vision for Ministry in the Twenty-First Century. 2nd rev. ed. LC 99-22034. 240p. 1999. pap. 15.99 (*0-8010-9087-3*) Baker Bks.

An Asterisk (*) at the beginning of an entry indicates that the title is appearing for the first time.

***Malphurs, Aubrey.** Doing Church: A Biblical Guide for Leading Ministries Through Change. LC 99-36575. 112p. 1999. pap. 8.99 (0-8254-3187-5) Kregel.

Malphurs, Aubrey. Dynamics of Church Leadership. Wiergbe, Warren W., ed. LC 99-38440. (Ministry Dynamics for a New Century Ser.). 160p. 1999. pap. 10.99 (0-8010-9090-3) Baker Bks.

— Maximizing Your Effectiveness: How to Discover & Develop Your Divine Design. LC 94-40064. (Illus.). 256p. 1995. pap. 14.99 (0-8010-6317-5) Baker Bks.

— Ministry Nuts & Bolts: What They Don't Teach Pastors in Seminary. LC 97-41092. 192p. 1997. pap. 11.99 (0-8254-3190-5) Kregel.

— Planting Growing Churches for the Twenty-First Century: Comprehensive Guide for New Churches & Those Desiring Renewal. 2nd rev. ed. LC 98-24675. 432p. 1998. pap. 22.99 (0-8010-9053-9) Baker Bks.

— Pouring New Wine into Old Wineskins: How to Change a Church Without Destroying It. LC 93-10368. 224p. 1993. pap. 12.99 (0-8010-6301-9) Baker Bks.

— Strategy 2000: Churches Making Disciples for the Next Millennium. LC 96-30480. 224p. 1996. pap. 11.99 (0-8254-3196-4) Kregel.

— Values Driven Leadership: Discovering & Developing Your Core Values for Ministry. LC 95-47524. 208p. 1996. pap. 16.99 (0-8010-9015-6) Baker Bks.

Malphurs, Aubrey & Malphurs, Susan. Biblical Manhood & Womanhood: Understanding Masculinity & Femininity from God's Perspective. LC 96-31497. 160p. 1996. pap. 10.99 (0-8254-3195-6) Kregel.

Malphurs, J. G. Amusement for Your Bible Hour. 1961. pap. 0.60 (0-88027-100-0) Firm Foun Pub.

— Let's Do Something. 1958. pap. 0.60 (0-88027-099-3) Firm Foun Pub.

— My Hand in His. 1961. 5.00 (0-88027-012-8) Firm Foun Pub.

Malphurs, Susan, jt. auth. see Malphurs, Aubrey.

Malpighi, Marcello. Opera Omnia, Figuris Elegantissimis in Aesincisis Illustrata. (GER.). 1997. reprint ed. 298.00 (3-487-05639-9) G Olms Pubs.

Malpighi, Stefania, tr. see Eggenberger, David, ed.

Malraux, Andre. Antimemoires. (Folio Ser.: No. 23). (FRE.). 1972. pap. 14.50 (2-07-036023-7) Schoenhof.

— Les Chenes Qu'on Abat. (FRE.). 1970. pap. 10.95 (0-8288-3709-0, M3706) Fr & Eur.

— Condition Humaine. (Folio Ser.: No. 1). (FRE.). 1933. pap. 10.50 (2-07-036001-6) Schoenhof.

— La Condition Humaine. (FRE.). 1972. pap. 11.95 (0-8288-3710-4, F110891) Fr & Eur.

— Les Conquerants. (FRE.). 256p. 1954. 10.95 (0-8288-9844-8, F110901); 3.95 (0-686-56321-2) Fr & Eur.

— The Conquerors. Becker, Stephen, tr. LC 72-91594. 212p. 1991. pap. text 16.00 (0-226-50290-2) U Ch Pr.

— La Corde et les Souris: Avec Les Hotes de Passage, Les Chenes Qu'On Abat (Version Difinitive), La Tete d'Obsidienne (Version Definitive), Lazare. 1976. 4.95 (0-686-56322-0) Fr & Eur.

— L' Espoir. (FRE.). 1972. pap. 15.95 (0-8288-3711-2, F110911) Fr & Eur.

— L' Espoir. (Folio Ser.: No. 20). (FRE.). 1937. pap. 12.50 (2-07-036020-2) Schoenhof.

— L' Homme Precaire et la Litterature. (FRE.). 330p. 1977. pap. 19.95 (0-7859-1349-1, 2070295559) Fr & Eur.

— Les Hotes de Passage: Comprend les 3 Premiers Chapitres du Tome 2 de Le Memoir des Limbes. (FRE.). 240p. 1975. 17.95 (0-7859-0106-X, M3708) Fr & Eur.

— Man's Fate. 360p. (C). 1965. 8.44 (0-07-553654-4) McGraw.

— Man's Fate. Chevalier, Haakon M., tr. 1965. pap. 4.50 (0-685-06615-0) Modern Lib NY.

— Man's Fate. 1990. pap. 13.00 (0-679-72574-1) Vin Bks.

— La Metamorphose des Dieux: L'Intemporel. (FRE., Illus.). 424p. 1976. 125.00 (0-7859-1282-7, 2070108619) Fr & Eur.

— La Metamorphose des Dieux: L'Surnaturel, Vol. 1. (FRE., Illus.). 386p. 1977. 125.00 (0-7859-1283-5, 2070109070) Fr & Eur.

— Le Miroir des Limbes: La Corde et les Souris, Tome 2. (Folio Ser.: No. 731). (FRE.). 1986. pap. 13.95 (2-07-036731-2) Schoenhof.

— Le Miroir des Limbes: La Corde et les Souris, Vol. 2. (FRE.). 1986. pap. 16.95 (0-8288-3713-9, M11056) Fr & Eur.

— Le Miroir des Limbes Vol. 1: Antimemoires. (FRE.). 1972. pap. 17.95 (0-8288-3712-0, F110871) Fr & Eur.

— Oraisons Funebres: Discours Prononces par l'Auteur, 1958-1965. (Coll. Soleil). 13.50 (0-685-34270-0) Fr & Eur.

— Picasso's Mask. annot. ed. Guicharnaud, June, tr. from FRE. & anno. by. LC 94-34604.Tr. of Tete d'Obsidienne. (Illus.). 285p. 1995. pap. 13.95 (0-306-80629-0) Da Capo.

— Romans. Incl. Condition Humaine. 1947. Conquerants. 1947. Espoir. (FRE.). 1947. 1947. write for info. (0-318-63592-5) Fr & Eur.

— Romans. deluxe ed. (FRE.). 864p. 1978. 110.00 (0-7859-1621-0, 2070103293) Fr & Eur.

— Scenes Choisies. 8.50 (0-685-34268-9) Fr & Eur.

— The Temptation of the West. Hollander, Robert, tr. 136p. 1998. pap. 12.95 (0-226-50291-0) U Ch Pr.

— La Tentation de L'Occident. pap. 6.95 (0-685-34271-9) Fr & Eur.

— La Tentation de L'Occident. (FRE.). 1972. pap. 10.95 (0-7859-3096-5) Fr & Eur.

— Le Triangle Noir: Laclos, Goysa, Saint-Just. 13.15 (0-685-34272-7) Fr & Eur.

— The Voices of Silence. Gilbert, Stuart, tr. from FRE. LC 77-92101. (Bollingen Ser.: Vol. XXIV: A). (Illus.). 661p. 1978. reprint ed. pap. text 32.50 (0-691-01821-9, Pub. by Princeton U Pr) Cal Prin Full Svc.

— Voie Royale. (Coll. Soleil). 1954. 12.50 (0-7859-0612-6) Fr & Eur.

— The Walnut Trees of Altenburg. Fielding, A. W., tr. from FRE. LC 88-37363. 224p. 1989. lib. bdg. 35.00 (0-86527-392-8) Fertig.

— The Walnut Trees of Altenburg. Fielding, A. W., tr. LC 88-37363. 226p. 1992. pap. 13.95 (0-226-50289-9) U Ch Pr.

Malraux, La, see La Malraux.

***Malrieu, Jean P.** Evaluative Semantics: Cognition Language & Ideology. LC 98-33200. 1999. text. write for info. (0-415-19761-9) Routledge.

Malroux, Claire. Edge. Hacker, Marilyn, tr. from FRE. LC 96-60024. 90p. (Orig.). 1996. pap. 9.95 (0-916390-74-8) Wake Forest.

***Malroux, Claire.** A Long Gone Sun: Bilingual Edition. Hacker, Marilyn, tr. from FRE. Orig. Title: Soleil de Jadis. 260p. 2000. pap. 15.95 (1-878818-87-2, Pub. by Sheep Meadow) U Pr of New Eng.

Malsam, Margaret A. Camping Circus. LC 85-62593. (Illus.). 120p. 1986. pap. 7.95 (0-9616108-0-8) Beaumont Bks.

— Meditations for Today's Married Christians: Profiles of Married Saints for Troubled Times. LC 94-70558. 64p. (Orig.). 1994. pap. 5.99 (0-9616108-8-3) Beaumont Bks.

Malsam, Margaret A., ed. see Sadow, Sue.

Malsam, Margaret A., ed. see Weyer, Ruth C.

Malsbary, Gerald, tr. see Messori, Vittorio.

Malsbary, Gerald, tr. see Pieper, Josef.

Malsbary, Gerald, tr. see Rhonheimer, Martin.

Malsberg, Edward, jt. auth. see Adler, Bill, Jr.

***Malsberger, Brian M., et al.** Employee Duty of Loyalty: A State-by-State Survey. 2nd ed. LC 99-30188. 1999. 115.00 (1-57018-211-6) BNA Books.

Malsberger, Brian M., ed. Covenants Not to Compete: A State-by-State Survey with 1999 Supplement. 2nd ed. LC 96-18836. 1275p. 1998. 395.00 (1-57018-030-X, 1079) BNA Books.

***Malsberger, Brian M., et al, eds.** Employee Duty of Loyalty: A State-by-State Survey. 2nd ed. LC 99-30188. 2016p. 1999. 295.00 (1-57018-182-9) BNA Books.

Malsberger, Brian M., ed. see Employee Rights & Responsibilities Committee of the American Bar Association Staff.

Malsberger, Brian M., ed. see Employee Rights & Responsibilities Committee of the American Bar Association Staff & American Rights & Responsibilities Committee of the American Bar Association Staff.

***Malsberger, John W.** From Obstruction to Moderation: The Transformation of Senate Conservatism, 1938-1952. LC 99-40422. 320p. 2000. 47.50 (1-57591-026-8) Susquehanna U Pr.

Malsburg, C. Von Der, see Eckmiller, Rolf & Von Der Malsburg, C., eds.

Malsch, Brownson. Indianola: The Mother of Western Texas. LC 88-8557. (Illus.). 363p. 1995. pap. 17.95 (1-880510-30-8) State House Pr.

— "Lone Wolf" Gonzaullas, Texas Ranger. LC 98-6495. (Illus.). 240p. 1998. pap. 13.95 (0-8061-3016-4) U of Okla Pr.

Malseva, F. Alexei Savrasov. 407p. 1977. 60.00 (0-7855-0687-X) St Mut.

Malshe, Milind S. Literary Classification. 200p. 1993. text 35.00 (81-85218-35-8, Pub. by Prestige) Advent Bks Div.

Malsin, Peter. The Eyes of the Sun: Astrology in Light of Psychology. 352p. (Orig.). 1997. pap. 16.95 (1-56184-099-8) New Falcon Pubns.

Malson, Helen. The Thin Woman: Feminism, Post-Structuralism & the Social Psychology of Anorexia Nervosa. LC 96-39930. (Women & Psychology Ser.). 256p. (C). 1997. pap. 21.99 (0-415-16333-1) Routledge.

Malson, Micheline R., et al, eds. Black Women in America: Social Science Perspectives. 352p. 1990. pap. 19.50 (0-226-50296-1) U Ch Pr.

— Black Women in America: Social Science Perspectives. 348p. 1992. lib. bdg. 34.95 (0-226-50295-3) U Ch Pr.

— Feminist Theory in Practice & Process. 376p. 1989. pap. 19.50 (0-226-50294-5); lib. bdg. 36.00 (0-226-50293-7) U Ch Pr.

Malster, Robert. Ipswich: Town on the Orwell. 112p. (C). 1990. 35.00 (0-900963-92-1, Pub. by T Dalton) St Mut.

— Lowestoft: East Coast Port. 128p. 1994. pap. 21.00 (0-86138-013-4, Pub. by T Dalton) St Mut.

— Saved from the Sea: The Story of Life-Saving Services on the East Anglian Coast. 296p. 1990. 42.00 (0-900963-32-8, Pub. by T Dalton) St Mut.

— Suffolk at Work: Trades & Industries. LC 97-121755. (Britain in Old Photographs Ser.). (Illus.). 126p. 1995. write for info. (0-7509-1304-5) Sutton Pub Ltd.

— Wherries & Waterways. 176p. 1994. 36.00 (0-86138-042-8, Pub. by T Dalton) St Mut.

Malstrom. Manufacturing Cost Engineering Handbook. (Cost Engineering Ser.: Vol. 5). (Illus.). 472p. 1984. text 175.00 (0-8247-7126-5) Dekker.

— WEESKA Manufacturing Cost Estimating. (What Every Engineer Should Know Ser.: Vol. 6). (Illus.). 208p. 1981. text 59.75 (0-8247-1511-X) Dekker.

***Malstrom, C. D. Bud.** Warriorship - Life Lesson of a Martial Artist. (Illus.). 200p. 2000. pap. 12.50 (1-892614-31-6) Briarwood VA.

Malstrom, Stan. Own Your Own Body. LC 76-58968. 414p. 1980. reprint ed. pap. 5.95 (0-87983-215-0, Keats Publng) NTC Contemp Pub Co.

Malt, Ronald A. On Call in Anesthesia & Surgery. (Illus.). 248p. 1994. pap. text 40.00 (0-7216-3884-8, W B Saunders Co) Harcrt Hlth Sci Grp.

— The Practice of Surgery. LC 92-22929. (Illus.). 512p. 1993. text 240.00 (0-7216-1811-1, W B Saunders Co) Harcrt Hlth Sci Grp.

Malt, Ronald A., et al. Complex Operations at Massachusetts General Hospital. (Illus.). 272p. 1983. text 135.00 (0-7216-6008-8, W B Saunders Co) Harcrt Hlth Sci Grp.

Malt, Ronald A., jt. ed. see Morris, Peter J.

Malta, Victor G. Espejos Negros y los Caminos del Silencio. (SPA.). 90p. (Orig.). 1992. pap. 8.00 (0-9623552-4-0) Ed Arcas.

— Huellas de Arena/Salome. (SPA.). 124p. 1998. pap. 10.00 (1-882573-12-9, Zinnia Bks) Serena Bay.

Maltagliati, Raoul. How to Dream Your Lucky Lotto Numbers: Manual & Dictionary for Forecasting the Future & Lotto Numbers Through the Interpretation of Dreams. 2nd ed. LC 90-35093. (How-to Ser.). (Illus.). 208p. (Orig.). 1994. pap. 3.95 (0-87542-483-X) Llewellyn Pubns.

***Maltaite, Willy.** Robinsonia. Johnson, Joe, tr. from FRE. 56p. 2000. pap. 11.95 (1-56163-255-4, Eurotica) NBM.

Maltbaek, J. C. Dynamics in Engineering: Classical Yet Modern, General Yet Comprehensive, Original in Approach. 1988. text 51.95 (0-470-21125-3) P-H.

Maltbie, Cynthis, jt. auth. see Mays, Bruce.

***Maltbie, Karen.** I Am the Leader of My Own Parade. 36p. (J). (gr. k-5). 2000. 15.00 (0-9670934-1-4) Magic Shoes Pr.

— Just for Being Me. (Illus.). 30p. (J). (ps-3). 2000. 15.00 (0-9670934-0-6) Magic Shoes Pr.

Maltbie, Milo R. English Local Government of To-Day: A Study of the Relations of Central & Local Government. LC 74-76664. (Columbia University. Studies in the Social Sciences: No. 23). reprint ed. 27.50 (0-404-51023-X) AMS Pr.

***Maltbie, Roger.** Range Rats: How to Get Your Swing from the Practice Range to the Golf Course. 1999. pap. 16.95 (0-942627-58-X) Woodford Pubng.

Maltby. Educational Psychology. 734p. write for info. (0-471-33614-9) Wiley.

Maltby. Sayers' Manual for Classifications. (C). 1977. text 29.50 (0-233-96603-X) Westview.

Maltby, Arthur & McKenna, Brian. Irish Official Publications: A Guide to Republic of Ireland Papers, with a Breviate of Reports 1922-1972. LC 80-40873. (Guides to Official Publications: Vol. 7). 388p. 1980. 170.00 (0-08-023703-7, Pub. by Pergamon Repr) Franklin.

Maltby, Arthur, jt. ed. see Marcella, Rita.

Maltby, Edward, ed. see IUCN Commission on Ecosystem Managment Staff & Tropical Peatland Expert Group Staff.

***Maltby, Gordon.** Porsche 356 & RS Spyders. (Illus.). 160p. 2000. pap. 24.95 (0-7603-0903-5, 130530AP, Pub. by MBI Pubg) Motorbooks Intl.

Maltby, Gregory P., jt. ed. see Cooper, Lloyd G.

Maltby, J. D. Short Parliamentary Diary of Sir Thomas Aston, 1640. (Camden Fourth Ser.). 27.00 (0-86193-116-5) David Brown.

Maltby, Josephine. Cases in Auditing. 2nd ed. 176p. 1996. pap. 21.95 (1-85396-312-7, Pub. by P Chapman) Taylor & Francis.

Maltby, Judith. Prayer Book & People in Elizabethan & Early Stuart England. LC 97-15776. (Cambridge Studies in Early Modern British History). (Illus.). 328p. (C). 1998. text 64.95 (0-521-45313-5) Cambridge U Pr.

***Maltby, Judith.** Prayer Book & People in Elizabethan & Early Stuart England. (Cambridge Studies in Early Modern British History). (Illus.). 331p. 2000. pap. write for info. (0-521-79387-4) Cambridge U Pr.

Maltby, L. & Calow, P. Methods in Ecotoxicology. 224p. 1997. pap. 42.95 (0-632-03549-8, Pub. by Blckwll Scitfc UK) Blackwell Sci.

Maltby, Marc S. The Origins & Development of Professional Football, 1890-1920. rev. ed. LC 97-10251. (Studies in American Popular History & Culture). 256p. 1997. text 54.00 (0-8153-2797-8) Garland.

Maltby, Paul. Dissident Postmodernists: Barthelme, Coover, Pynchon. LC 91-25115. (Pennsylvania Studies in Contemporary American Fiction). 232p. (C). 1992. text 31.50 (0-8122-3064-7) U of Pa Pr.

Maltby, R., ed. Latin Love Elegy. 151p. 1980. pap. 16.95 (0-906515-01-7, Pub. by Brist Class Pr) Focus Pub-R Pullins.

— Latin Love Elegy. vi, 143p. 1991. reprint ed. 14.00 (0-86516-061-9) Bolchazy-Carducci.

Maltby, Ralph D. The Complete Golf Club Fitting Plan. (Illus.). 400p. 1986. pap. 38.50 (0-9606792-7-8) R Maltby.

— Golf Club Assembly Manual: Basic & Advanced Techniques. (Illus.). 36p. 1981. pap. 9.95 (0-927956-02-0) R Maltby.

— Golf Club Design, Fitting, Alteration & Repair. rev. ed. (Illus.). 890p. 1995. 39.95 (0-927956-05-5) R Maltby.

Maltby, Ralph D., jt. auth. see Wilson, Mark.

Maltby, Richard. Harmless Entertainment: Hollywood & the Ideology of Consensus. LC 82-10244. 425p. 1983. 40.00 (0-8108-1548-6) Scarecrow.

***Maltby, Richard.** Identifying Hollywood Audiences: Cultural Identity & the Movies. 1999. pap. text 27.95 (0-85170-739-4) Ind U Pr.

Maltby, Richard & Craven, Ian. Hollywood Cinema: An Introduction. LC 94-3794. 1995. pap. 36.95 (0-631-15732-8) Blackwell Pubs.

Maltby, Richard, Jr., jt. auth. see Galli, E. R.

Maltby, Richard, jt. auth. see Stokes, Melvyn.

Maltby, Richard, ed. see Barnes, John.

Maltby, Richard, jt. ed. see Higson, Andrew.

Maltby, Richard, ed. see Ramphal.

Maltby, Richard, ed. & intro. see Barnes, John.

Maltby, Sally. The ABC of Gardening. (Illus.). 64p. 1998. 13.95 (1-85626-269-3, Pub. by Cathie Kyle) Trafalgar.

— The Perverse Person's ABC. (Illus.). 64p. 1998. 15.95 (1-85626-270-7, Pub. by Cathie Kyle) Trafalgar.

Maltby, T. J. Practical Handbook of the Oriya Language. (ENG & ORI.). 214p. 1986. 39.95 (0-8288-8464-1) Fr & Eur.

Maltby, Tony. Women & Pensions in Britain & Hungary: A Cross-National & Comparative Case Study of Social Dependency. 260p. 1994. 72.95 (1-85628-630-4, Pub. by Avebry) Ashgate Pub Co.

Maltby, Tony & Great Britain, Equal Opportunities Commission. Women & Men in Britain: A Statistical Profile. LC 88-111918. 68 p. 1987. write for info. (0-11-701336-6) Statnry Office.

Maltby, Tony, jt. auth. see Walker, Alan.

Maltby, William S. The Black Legend in England: The Development of Anti-Spanish Sentiment, 1558-1660. LC 78-161356. (Duke Historical Publications). 188p. reprint ed. pap. 58.30 (0-8357-7291-8, 202376400033) Bks Demand.

Maltby, William S., jt. auth. see Hause, Steven C.

Maltenfort, George G. Corrugated Shipping Containers: An Engineering Approach. rev. ed. LC 96-14604. (Illus.). 291p. 1996. 98.50 (1-885067-06-2) Jelmar Pub.

— Performance & Evaluation of Shipping Containers. LC 89-63845. (Illus.). 488p. 1990. reprint ed. 97.50 (0-9616302-3-X) Jelmar Pub.

— Understanding Statistics. LC 92-28704. 128p. 1993. 62.00 (0-9616302-8-0) Jelmar Pub.

Malter, Alan J., jt. auth. see Jensen, Merle H.

Malter, Heinrich, ed. see Steinschneider, Moritz.

Malter, Rick & Malter, Rosalie. Shrinking the Judge: Freeing the Inner Child. McCullough, Virginia, ed. (Illus.). 1998. pap. 14.95 (0-9660415-1-8) Educ & Health.

Malter, Rosalie, jt. auth. see Malter, Rick.

***Malter, Valerie F. & Kaye, Stuart P.** How to Be a Growth Investor. (McGraw-Hill Mastering the Market Ser.). (Illus.). 179p. 1999. pap. 16.95 (0-07-040068-7) McGraw.

Malterre, Elona. The Last Wolf of Ireland. 144p. (J). (gr. 4-9). 1990. 15.00 (0-395-54381-9, Clarion Bks) HM.

Maltese, ed. Plethonis, Georgii Gemisti: Contra Scholarii Pro Aristotele Obiectiones. (GRE.). 1988. 22.95 (3-322-00460-0, T1589, Pub. by B G Teubner) U of Mich Pr.

— Plethonis, Georgii Gemisti: Opuscula de Historia Graeca. (GRE.). 1989. 22.95 (3-322-00674-3, T1590, Pub. by B G Teubner) U of Mich Pr.

Maltese, G. I., ed. The U. S. Federal Budget Process: An Overview & Glossary of Terms. 137p. (C). 1995. lib. bdg. 75.00 (1-56072-192-8) Nova Sci Pubs.

***Maltese, G. I., ed.** The U. S. Federal Budget Process: An Overview & Glossary of Terms. 177p. 2000. lib. bdg. 65.00 (1-56072-791-8) Nova Sci Pubs.

Maltese, John A. The Selling of Supreme Court Nominees. LC 95-3536. (Interpreting American Politics Ser.). 232p. 1995. 26.95 (0-8018-5102-5) Johns Hopkins.

— The Selling of Supreme Court Nominees. (Interpreting American Politics Ser.). 232p. 1998. reprint ed. pap. text 15.95 (0-8018-5883-6) Johns Hopkins.

— Spin Control: The White House Office of Communications & the Management of Presidential News. 2nd rev. ed. LC 93-29368. (Illus.). xii, 323p. (C). 1994. pap. 19.95 (0-8078-4452-7) U of NC Pr.

Maltese, Phillip J. Sons of Babylon: One Financial Step for Man One Monetary Leap for Mankind. (Illus.). 120p. 1996. write for info. (0-9649478-0-3) B J Mud.

— Sons of Babylon: One Financial Step for Man One Monetary Leap for Mankind. (Illus.). 120p. 1996. pap. write for info. (0-9649478-1-1) B J Mud.

Maltese, William. California Creamin' And Other Stories. 1999. pap. text 11.95 (1-902644-04-2) Prowler Pr.

***Maltese, William.** A Slip To Die For: A Stud Draqual Mystery. iv, 211p. 1999. pap. 11.95 (0-9672420-0-2) Lambert III Lib.

— Summer Sweaters. (Orig.). 1999. pap. 11.95 (1-902644-10-7) Prowler Pr.

Malteste, Louis, et al. The Art of Discipline: A Pictorial History of the Smacked Bottom. 210p. 1997. 59.95 (1-899861-09-2, Pub. by AKS Bks) Xclusiv Distrib.

Maltezou, S., et al. Hazardous Waste Management. 364p. 1989. text 90.00 (1-85148-027-7, Tycooly Pub) Weidner & Sons.

***Malthez, Edmond A., ed.** Earth Inside & Out. 2000. pap. 19.95 (1-56584-595-1, Pub. by New Press NY) Norton.

Malthouse, Becci & Tan, Sang. Snowboarding. LC 98-19787. (Extreme Sports Ser.). (Illus.). 32p. (J). (gr. 5-9). 1998. pap. 6.95 (0-7641-0794-1) Barron.

Malthus. Environmental Remote Sensing. text. write for info. (0-471-49095-4); pap. text 28.00 (0-471-98566-X) Wiley.

Malthus, Cecil. Musset et Shakespeare: Etude Analytique de l'Influence de Shakespeare sur le Theatre d'Alfred de Musset. Barrell, Rex A., ed. (American University Studies: Romance Languages & Literature: Ser. II, Vol. 62). XIV, 449p. (C). 1988. text 56.50 (0-8204-0490-X) P Lang Pubng.

Malthus, Daniel, tr. see Goethe, Johann Wolfgang Von.

Malthus, Thomas Robert. Definitions in Political Economy: Preceded by an Inquiry into the Rules Which Ought to Guide Political Economists in the Definition & Use of Their Terms. LC 86-7468. (Reprints of Economic Classics Ser.). xvi, 261p. 1986. reprint ed. 39.50 (0-678-00018-2) Kelley.

— An Essay on the Principle of Population, 2 vols. James, Patricia, ed. 1159p. 1990. text 160.00 (0-521-32361-4) Cambridge U Pr.

— An Essay on the Principle of Population. Winch, Donald, ed. (Cambridge Texts in the History of Political Thought Ser.). 426p. (C). 1992. text 44.95 (0-521-41954-9); pap. text 13.95 (0-521-42972-2) Cambridge U Pr.

— An Essay on the Principle of Population. Appleman, Philip, ed. (Critical Editions in the History of Ideas Ser.). 256p. (C). 1976. pap. text 12.50 (0-393-09202-X) Norton.

— An Essay on the Principle of Population. Flew, Antony G., ed. (English Library). 304p. 1983. pap. 10.95 (0-14-043206-X, Penguin Classics) Viking Penguin.

*Malthus, Thomas Robert. Essay on the Principle of Population. (Oxford World Classics Ser.). 208p. 1999. pap. text 9.95 (0-19-283747-8) OUP.

Malthus, Thomas Robert. An Essay on the Principle of Population. (Great Minds Ser.). 400p. 1998. reprint ed. pap. 14.95 (1-57392-255-2) Prometheus Bks.

— An Essay on the Principle of Population or a View of Its Past & Present Effects on Human Happiness. 7th ed. LC 86-7453. (Reprints of Economic Classics Ser.). xv, 551p. 1986. reprint ed. lib. bdg. 49.50 (0-678-00838-8) Kelley.

— The Measure of Value Stated & Illuminated. LC 87-17246. (Reprints of Economic Classics Ser.). v, 81p. 1989. reprint ed. 25.00 (0-678-00603-2) Kelley.

— The Pamphlets of Thomas Robert Malthus, 1800-1817. LC 77-117389. (Reprints of Economic Classics Ser.). v, 320p. 1970. reprint ed. lib. bdg. 45.00 (0-678-00646-6) Kelley.

— Population: The First Essay. 160p. 1959. pap. text 13.95 (0-472-06031-7, 06031, Ann Arbor Bks) U of Mich Pr.

— Principles of Political Economy: Considered with a View to Their Practical Application. 2nd ed. LC 86-10606. (Reprints of Economic Classics Ser.). liv, 460p. 1986. reprint ed. 49.50 (0-678-00038-7) Kelley.

— Principles of Political Economy: Variorum Edition, 2 vols., Set. Pullen, John, ed. 1147p. 1990. 150.00 (0-521-24775-6) Cambridge U Pr.

Malthus, Thomas Robert, et al. The Malthus Library Catalogue: The Personal Collection of Thomas Robert Malthus at Jesus College, Cambridge University. 150p. 1983. 46.00 (0-08-029386-7, Pergamon Pr) Elsevier.

Malti-Douglas, F. Structures of Avarice. (Studies in Arabic Literature: Vol. 11). 183p. 1985. 46.00 (90-04-07485-6) Brill Academic Pubs.

Malti-Douglas, Fedwa. Blindness & Autobiography: Al-Ayyam of Taha Husayn. LC 87-29095. 214p. reprint ed. pap. 66.40 (0-608-06322-3, 206668400008) Bks Demand.

— Hisland: Adventures in Ac-Ac-Ademe. LC 97-1207. (Series, the Margins of Literature). 192p. (C). 1997. text 29.50 (0-7914-3603-9) State U NY Pr.

— Hisland: Adventures in Ac-Ac-ademe. LC 97-1207. (SUNY Series, the Margins of Literature). 192p. (C). 1999. pap. text 19.95 (0-7914-3604-7) State U NY Pr.

*Malti-Douglas, Fedwa. Medicines of the Soul: Female Bodies & Sacred Geographies in a Transnational Islam. LC 00-21550. (Illus.). 2001. write for info. (0-520-22284-9) U CA Pr.

Malti-Douglas, Fedwa. Men, Women, & God(s) Nawal El Saadawi & Arab Feminist Poetics. LC 94-44255. (Centennial Bk.). 277p. 1995. 50.00 (0-520-20071-3, Pub. by U CA Pr); pap. 18.95 (0-520-20072-1, Pub. by U CA Pr) Cal Prin Full Svc.

*Malti-Douglas, Fedwa. The Starr Report Disrobed. 2000. 39.50 (0-231-11931-3) Col U Pr.

— The Starr Report Disrobed. LC 99-44094. 2000. pap. 16.00 (0-231-11933-X) Col U Pr.

— The Starr Report Disrobed. LC 99-44094. 2000. 39.50 (0-231-11932-1) Col U Pr.

Malti-Douglas, Fedwa. Woman's Body, Woman's Word: Gender & Discourse in Arabo-Islamic Writing. LC 91-12804. 216p. reprint ed. pap. 67.00 (0-608-09572-9, 2054374); reprint ed. pap. 67.60 (0-608-20159-6, 205444000011) Bks Demand.

Malti-Douglas, Fedwa, jt. auth. see Douglas, Allen.

Maltin, Leonard. The Art of the Cinematographer: A Survey & Interviews with Five Masters. (Illus.). 144p. 1978. reprint ed. pap. 12.95 (0-486-23686-2) Dover.

— The Disney Films. 3rd ed. LC 84-12667. (Illus.). 400p. (J). 1995. pap. 16.95 (0-7868-8137-2, Pub. by Hyperion) Time Warner.

— The Disney Films. 4th ed. (Illus.). 432p. (J). 2000. pap. 19.95 (0-7868-8527-0, Pub. by Disney Pr) Time Warner.

— The Great American Broadcast: A Celebration of Radio's Golden Age. LC 97-11490. 384p. 1997. 36.95 (0-525-94183-5) NAL.

— Leonard Maltin's Family Film Guide. LC 99-219505. 653p. 1999. mass mkt. 6.99 (0-451-19714-3, Sig) NAL.

— Leonard Maltin's Movie & Video Guide 2000: 2000 Edition. 1999. mass mkt. 7.99 (0-451-19837-9, Sig) NAL.

*Maltin, Leonard. Leonard Maltin's Movie & Video Guide 2000. 1999. pap. 19.95 (0-452-28123-7, Plume) Dutton Plume.

— Leonard Maltin's Movie & Video Guide 2001. 2000. pap. 20.00 (0-452-28187-3, Plume) Dutton Plume.

— Leonard Maltin's Movie & Video Guide 2001. (Leonard Maltin's Movie & Video Guide Ser.). (Illus.). 2000. mass mkt. 8.99 (0-451-20107-8) Signet.

Maltin, Leonard. Leonard Maltin's Movie Encyclopedia: Career Profiles of More Than 2,000 Actors & Filmmakers, Past & Present. 992p. 1995. pap. 21.95 (0-452-27058-8, Plume) Dutton Plume.

— Leonard Maltin's 1999 Movie-a-Day Calendar. 1998. pap. 10.95 (0-525-94360-9) NAL.

— Leonard Maltin's 1999 Movie & Video Guide. rev. ed. 1998. pap. 19.95 (0-452-27992-5, Plume) Dutton Plume.

— Of Mice & Magic: A History of American Animated Cartoons. LC 87-20234. 1987. pap. 26.95 (0-452-25993-2, Plume) Dutton Plume.

Maltin, Leonard, ed. Leonard Maltin's Movie & Video Guide, 1998. 1632p. 1997. pap. 19.95 (0-452-27914-3) NAL.

Maltin, Leonard & Bann, Richard W. The Little Rascals: The Life & Times of Our Gang. enl. ed. LC 92-16724. 1992. pap. 20.00 (0-517-58325-9, Crown) Crown Pub Group.

Maltitz, Ian Von, see Von Maltitz, Ian.

*Maltman, Alex. Geological Maps. 2nd ed. 272p. 1998. pap. 54.95 (0-471-97696-2) Wiley.

Maltman, Kim. Technologies/Installations. 92p. 1990. pap. 9.95 (0-919626-46-7, Pub. by Brick Bks) Genl Dist Srvs.

Maltman, Kim, jt. auth. see Borson, Roo.

*Malton, H. Mel. Cue the Dead Guy: A Polly Deacon Murder Mystery. (Rendezvous Crime Ser.). 288p. 1999. pap. 8.95 (0-929141-66-0) Napoleon Publ.

Malton, H. Mel. Down in the Dumps: A Polly Deacon Murder Mystery. (Illus.). 288p. 1999. pap. text 8.95 (0-929141-62-8) Napoleon Publ.

Malton, James. Georgian Dublin. 64p. 1996. pap. 9.95 (0-85105-425-0, Pub. by Smyth) Dufour.

Maltoni, Cesare, et al, eds. Experimental Research on Trichloroethylene Carcinogenesis. LC 86-61069. (Archives of Research on Industrial Carcinogenesis Ser.: Vol. 5). (Illus.). 393p. 1986. 220.00 (0-911131-40-X) Specialist Journals.

— Experimental Research on Vinyl Chloride Carcinogenesis. LC 84-60231. (Archives of Research on Industrial Carcinogenesis Ser.). (Illus.). 250p. 1984. text 220.00 (0-911131-36-1) Specialist Journals.

— Experimental Research on Vinylidene Chloride Carcinogenesis. LC 85-61066. (Archives of Research on Industrial Carcinogenesis Ser.: Vol. 3). (Illus.). 229p. 1985. 180.00 (0-911131-38-8) Specialist Journals.

Maltoni, Cesare, et al. Experimental Research on Acrylonitrile Carcinogenesis. LC 86-62753. (Archives of Research on Industrial Carcinogenesis Ser.: Vol. 6). (Illus.). 348p. 1987. 220.00 (0-911131-41-8) Specialist Journals.

— Experimental Research on Methylene Chloride Carcinogenesis. LC 86-61069. (Archives of Research on Industrial Carcinogenesis Ser.: Vol. 4). (Illus.). 244p. 1987. 180.00 (0-911131-39-6) Specialist Journals.

— The Scientific Bases of Cancer Chemoprevention: Proceedings of the International Forum on the Scientific Bases of Cancer Chemoprevention, 31 March-2 April 1996. LC 96-36161. (International Congress Ser.). 310p. 1996. 184.50 (0-444-82453-7) Elsevier.

Maltsberger, John T. Essential Papers on Suicide. (C). 1996. pap. text 27.50 (0-8147-5550-X) NYU Pr.

— Essential Papers on Suicide. (C). 1996. text 75.00 (0-8147-5549-6) NYU Pr.

Maltseff, Michele. Draw Science: Horses & Ponies. 64p. (J). Date not set. pap. 7.95 (1-56565-655-5) NTC Contemp Pub Co.

Maltseff, Michele, jt. auth. see Kidd, Nina.

Maltsev, Yuri N. Requiem for Marx. 301p. (Orig.). 1993. pap. text 17.95 (0-945466-13-7) Ludwig von Mises.

Maltz, Alan S. Celebrities of Nature: Endangered & Selected Species of Florida. (Post Card Pictorial Ser.). 50p. 1991. pap. 12.95 (0-9626677-1-4) Light Key West.

— Key West Color. (Illus.). 192p. 1995. 50.00 (0-9626677-2-2) Light Key West.

— Key West Sunsets: A Postcard Pictorial. 2nd ed. (Illus.). 1990. pap. 12.95 (0-9626677-0-6) Light Key West.

— Miami: City of Dreams. LC 96-33441. (Illus.). 204p. 1997. 60.00 (0-9626677-3-0) Light Key West.

Maltz, Albert. Afternoon in the Jungle: The Selected Short Stories of Albert Maltz. 1971. pap. 2.75 (0-87140-256-4, Pub. by Liveright) Norton.

Maltz, Albert, jt. auth. see Wald, Malvin.

Maltz, Arnold. The Changing Role of Warehousing. Coleman, Rita, ed. (Illus.). 46p. 1998. pap. 30.00 (1-892663-14-7) WERC.

Maltz, Arnold, jt. auth. see Ellram, Lisa.

*Maltz, Earl M. Chief Justiceship of Warren Burger, 1969-1986: A Provocative Interpretation of the Burger Court. (Chief Justiceships of the United States Supreme Court Ser.). 350p. 2000. 39.95 (1-57003-335-8) U of SC Pr.

Maltz, Earl M. Civil Rights, the Constitution & Congress, 1863-1869. LC 90-32818. xii, 196p. 1990. 29.95 (0-7006-0467-7) U Pr of KS.

— Rethinking Constitutional Law: Originalism, Interventionism, & the Politics of Judicial Review. LC 93-30266. 158p. 1994. 29.95 (0-7006-0653-X) U Pr of KS.

*Maltz, Fran. Keeping Faith in the Dust. LC 98-22134. (Illus.). 72p. (J). (gr. 4-7). 1999. pap. 7.95 (1-881283-25-9) Alef Design.

Maltz, M. D., et al. Mapping Crime in Its Community Setting: Event Geography Analysis. (Illus.). 152p. 1990. 82.95 (0-387-97381-8) Spr-Verlag.

Maltz, Maxwell. Five Minutes to Happiness. 1962. 10.95 (0-8392-1033-7) Astor-Honor.

— Magic Power of Self-Image. 1989. mass mkt. 5.99 (0-671-70461-3) PB.

— Psycho-Cybernetics. 1973. pap. 10.00 (0-87980-127-1) Wilshire.

— Psycho Cybernetics. 1989. per. 6.99 (0-671-70075-8) PB.

— Zero-Resistance Selling. LC 97-28993. (C). 1997. text 19.95 (0-13-609074-5) P-H.

*Maltz, Michael D. Bridging Gaps in Police Crime Data. (Illus.). 71p. 2000. pap. text 20.00 (0-7881-8796-1) DIANE Pub.

Maltz, Michael D. Measuring the Effectiveness of Organized Crime Control Efforts. 132p. 1990. pap. 11.95 (0-942511-38-7) OICJ.

Maltz, Wendy. The Sexual Healing Journey: A Guide for Survivors of Sexual Abuse. LC 90-55934. (Illus.). 368p. 1992. reprint ed. pap. 14.00 (0-06-092155-2, Perennial) HarperTrade.

Maltz, Wendy, ed. Passionate Hearts: The Poetry of Sexual Love. LC 96-31046. 224p. 1996. 17.00 (1-57731-007-1, Pub. by New Wrld Lib) Publishers Group.

*Maltz, Wendy, ed. Passionate Hearts: The Poetry of Sexual Love. 2nd ed. LC 96-31046. 224p. 2000. pap. 14.00 (1-57731-122-1, Pub. by New Wrld Lib) Publishers Group.

Maltz, Wendy & Holman, Beverly. Incest & Sexuality: A Guide to Understanding & Healing. 166p. 1997. pap. 14.95 (0-669-14085-6) Lxngtn Bks.

Maltzahn, Kraft E. Von, see von Maltzahn, Kraft E.

Maltzahn, Nicholas Von, see Von Maltzahn, Nicholas.

Maltzahn, Wendelin V. Deutscher Bucherschatz des 16, 17 und 18, Bis um die Mitte des 19 Jahrhunderts. x, 627p. 1966. reprint ed. write for info. (0-318-71842-1) G Olms Pubs.

Maltzan, Heinrich F. Reise Nach Sudarabien. (Illus.). 422p. reprint ed. write for info. (0-318-71530-9) G Olms Pubs.

Maltzan, Heinrich F. Von, see Von Maltzan, Heinrich F.

Maltzman, Forrest. Competing Principals: Committees, Parties, & the Organization of Congress. 216p. 1998. pap. text 18.95 (0-472-08581-6, 08581) U of Mich Pr.

Maltzman, Forrest & American Political Science Association Staff. Competing Principals: Committees, Parties, & the Organization of Congress. LC 96-51494. 216p. (C). 1997. text 42.50 (0-472-10781-X, 10781) U of Mich Pr.

*Maltzman, Forrest, et al. Crafting Law on the Supreme Court: The Collegial Game. LC 99-47720. (Illus.). 179p. (C). 2000. write for info. (0-521-78010-1); pap. write for info. (0-521-78394-1) Cambridge U Pr.

*Maltzman, Irving. Alcoholism: A Review of Its Characteristics, Etiology, Treatments & Controversies. 400p. 1999. 125.00 (0-7923-8656-6) Kluwer Academic.

Maltzman, Jeffrey. Jobs in Paradise Revised Edition. rev. ed. LC 92-53297. 448p. 1993. pap. 16.00 (0-06-273186-6, Harper Ref) HarpC.

Maltzman, Stanley. Drawing Nature. (Illus.). 144p. 1998. pap. 19.99 (0-89134-933-2, North Lght Bks) F & W Pubns Inc.

*Maltzman, Stanley. Drawing Trees Step by Step. LC 99-26559. (Illus.). 128p. 1999. pap. 24.99 (0-89134-885-9, 31439, North Lght Bks) F & W Pubns Inc.

Maltzman, Steve. Remodelers Cost of Doing Business. 3rd ed. LC 97-70029. (Illus.). 74p. (Orig.). 1997. pap. 26.95 (0-86718-430-2) Home Builder.

Maltzman, Steve, jt. auth. see Needle, Sheldon.

Maltzoff, Nicholas. Basic Structure Practice in Russian. (RUS & ENG., Illus.). 80p. 1992. pap. 12.95 (0-8442-4260-8, 42608, Passprt Bks) NTC Contemp Pub Co.

— Essentials of Russian Grammar. LC 84-138632. (RUS & ENG., Illus.). 352p. 1994. pap. 17.95 (0-8442-4244-6, 42446, Natl Textbk Co) NTC Contemp Pub Co.

— Everyday Conversations in Russian. (RUS.). 64p. 1993. pap. 8.40 (0-8442-4241-1, Natl Textbk Co) NTC Contemp Pub Co.

*Malucci, Terri. Menopause Pink: Mid-Life Reflections of Wisdom & Humor. LC 99-63720. (Illus.). 112p. 1999. pap. 9.95 (0-9673744-4-8) Creativa Pr.

Maluccio, Anthony N., et al, eds. Preparing Adolescents for Life After Foster Care: The Central Role of Foster Parents. 1990. pap. 24.95 (0-87868-433-6, 3526) Child Welfare.

Maluccio, Anthony N., et al. Permanency Planning for Children: Concepts & Methods. 350p. 1986. text 32.50 (0-422-78840-6, 4074, Pub. by Tavistock) Routldge.

Maluccio, John, jt. auth. see Thomas, Duncan.

Maludzinska, G. Dictionary of Analytical Chemistry in English, German, French, Polish & Russian. (ENG, FRE, GER & POL.). 392p. 1990. 225.00 (0-8288-9226-1) Fr & Eur.

Maludzinska, G., ed. Dictionary of Analytical Chemistry in English, German, French, Polish & Russian. (ENG, FRE, GER, POL & RUS.). 404p. 1991. 170.50 (0-444-98729-0) Elsevier.

Maluf, Leonard, tr. see Lafont, Ghislain.

*Maluf, Nadim. Introduction to Microelectromechanical Systems Engineering. LC 99-52406. (Illus.). 265p. 1999. 79.00 (0-89006-581-0) Artech Hse.

Maluf, Ramez, jt. auth. see Gavin, Angus.

Maluka, Zulfikar K. The Myth of Constitutionalism in Pakistan. 374p. 1996. text 42.00 (0-19-577572-4) OUP.

Malul, Meir. Studies in Mesopotamian Legal Symbolism. (Alter Orient und Altes Testament Ser.: Vol. 221). xii, 512p. 1988. text 69.50 (3-7887-1299-6) NeukirchenerV.

Maluso, Diane, jt. ed. see Lott, Bernice.

Maluszynski, Jan, ed. Logic Programming: Proceedings of the 1997 International Symposium. (Logic Programming/Research Reports & Notes Ser.). (Illus.). 443p. 1997. pap. text 85.00 (0-262-63180-6) MIT Pr.

Maluszynski, Jan, et al, eds. Programming Language Implementation & Logic Programming: 3rd International Symposium, PLILP '91, Passau, Germany, August 26-28, 1991 Proceedings. (Lecture Notes in Computer Science Ser.: Vol. 528). xi, 433p. 1991. 44.95 (0-387-54444-5) Spr-Verlag.

Maluszynski, Jan, jt. auth. see Deransert, Pierre.

Maluszynski, M., ed. Current Options for Cereal Improvement: Doubled Haploids, Mutants & Heterosis. (Advances in Agricultural Biotechnology Ser.). (C). 1988. text 107.50 (0-7923-0064-5) Kluwer Academic.

*Maluwa, Tiyanjana. International Law in Post-Colonial Africa. LC 99-31848. (Studies & Materials on the Settlement of International Disputes). 1999. 129.00 (90-411-1089-5) Kluwer Law Intl.

Malvadkar, C. B., tr. see Gyachev, L. V., ed.

Malval, Fritz J. Dictionary Catalog of the George Foster Peabody Collection of Negro Literature & History, 2 vols., Set. 1972. lib. bdg. 315.00 (0-8371-6065-0, HIL/, Greenwood Pr) Greenwood.

— A Guide to the Archives of Hampton Institute, 5. LC 85-5599. (Bibliographies & Indexes in Afro-American & African Studies: No. 5). 599p. 1985. lib. bdg. 135.00 (0-313-24968-7, MGH/, Greenwood Pr) Greenwood.

Malvaney, Sam. At the Beach. LC 85-62693. (Illus.). 104p. 1985. boxed set 12.95 (0-935180-17-6) Mutual Pub HI.

Malvano. Malvano Immunoenzymatic Essay. 1980. lib. bdg. 141.50 (90-247-2314-0, Pub. by M Nijhoff) Kluwer Academic.

Malvar, Henrique S. Digital Signal Compression. (C). 2000. 55.00 (0-13-605882-5) P-H.

— Signal Processing with Lapped Transforms. LC 91-35984. (Artech House Telecommunications Library). (Illus.). 379p. 1992. reprint ed. pap. 117.50 (0-608-02497-X, 206314100004) Bks Demand.

Malvasi, Mark G. Unregenerate South: The Agrarian Thought of John Crowe Ransom, Allen Tate, & Donald Davidson. LC 97-10950. (Southern Literary Studies). 296p. 1997. text 35.00 (0-8071-2143-6) La State U Pr.

Malvasia, Carlo C. The Life of Guido Reni. Enggass, Catherine & Enggass, Robert, trs. from ITA. LC 80-11650. (Illus.). 150p. 1981. 28.50 (0-271-00264-6) Pa St U Pr.

*Malvasia, Carlo C. & Summerscale, Anne. Malvasia's Life of the Carracci: Commentary & Translation. LC 99-36322. 2000. 85.00 (0-271-01899-2) Pa St U Pr.

Malvavkar, C. B., tr. see Zelenin, A. N., et al, eds.

Malveau, Raphael C., jt. auth. see Mowbray, Thomas J.

Malveau, Raphael C., jt. auth. see Mowbray, Tom.

Malveaux, Julianne. Wall Street, Main Street & the Side Street: A Mad Economist Takes a Stroll. LC 98-50213. 250p. 1999. pap. 15.95 (1-890194-22-0) Pines One.

Malveaux, Julianne M. Sex, Lies & Stereotypes: Perspectives of a Mad Economist. LC 94-235716. 350p. (Orig.). 1994. pap. 14.95 (0-9636952-5-8) Pines One.

Malveaux, Julianne M., jt. ed. see Simms, Margaret C.

Malven, Paul V. Mammalian Neuroendocrinology. 272p. (C). 1993. boxed set 89.95 (0-8493-8757-4, QP356) CRC Pr.

Malvern, Lawrence E. Introduction to the Mechanics of a Continuous Medium. (C). 1977. text 82.60 (0-13-487603-2) P-H.

Malvern, Lawrence E., ed. see Midwestern Mechanics Conference.

Malvey, Mari. Simple Systems, Complex Environments: Hospital Financial Information Systems. LC 80-29597. (Managing Information Ser.: No. 2). 188p. 1981. reprint ed. pap. 58.30 (0-608-01473-7, 205951700001) Bks Demand.

Malvey, Victoria. Enchanted. 1999. mass mkt. 6.50 (0-671-02071-4) S&S Trade.

*Malvey, Victoria. Fortune's Bride. 2000. 6.50 (0-7434-0334-7, Sonnet Bks) PB.

— A Merry Chase. 312p. 2000. per. 6.50 (0-671-77525-1, Sonnet Bks) PB.

Malvey, Victoria. Portrait Dreams. 1998. mass mkt. 6.50 (0-671-02070-6) S&S Trade.

— Temptress. 1999. per. 6.50 (0-671-02072-2) S&S Trade.

Malvezzi, Cristofano, et al. Cristofano Malvezzi, Jacopo Peri & Annibale Padovano: Ensemble Ricercars. Swenson, Milton A., ed. (Recent Researches in Music of the Renaissance Ser.: Vol. RRR27). (Illus.). xxxi, 75p. 1978. pap. 35.00 (0-89579-089-0) A-R Eds.

Malvezzi, Virgilio. Historia de los Primeros Anos del Reinado de Felipe IV. Shaw, D. L., ed. (Textos B Ser.: Vol. VII). (SPA., Illus.). 206p. (Orig.). (C). 1968. pap. 51.00 (0-900411-01-5, Pub. by Tamesis Bks Ltd) Boydell & Brewer.

Malville, J. McKim & Putnam, Claudia. Prehistoric Astronomy in the Southwest. rev. ed. LC 93-17712. (Illus.). 112p. 1993. pap. 9.95 (1-55566-116-5) Johnson Bks.

Malvin, Richard L., et al. Concepts Human Physiology. LC 96-32232. 450p. (C). 1997. 90.00 (0-673-98562-8) Addson-Wesley Educ.

Malvino. Digital Computer Elonics. 3rd ed. 44.95 (0-02-800594-5) Glencoe.

Malvino, Albert P. AC Circuits: A Whole-Brain Learning System. (APPLE II Ser.: No. 2). (Illus.). 224p. (Orig.). (C). 1987. pap. text 19.95 incl. disk (1-56048-102-1, 102) Malvino Inc.

— Basic Semiconductors: A Whole-Brain Learning System. (APPLE II Ser.: No. 3). (Illus.). 288p. (Orig.). (C). 1987. pap. text 19.95 incl. disk (1-56048-103-X, 103) Malvino Inc.

— DC Circuits: A Whole-Brain Learning System. (APPLE II Ser.: No. 1). (Illus.). 224p. (Orig.). (C). 1986. text, pap. text 19.95 incl. disk (1-56048-101-3, 101E) Malvino Inc.

— Electronic Principles. LC 92-36587. 1992. write for info. (0-02-808845-X) Glencoe.

— Electronic Principles. 3rd ed. 1984. text 76.44 (0-07-039912-3) McGraw.

— Electronic Principles. 4th ed. 992p. 1989. text 93.24 (0-07-039957-3) McGraw.

— Electronic Principles. 5th ed. 1992. 44.95 (0-02-800845-6) Macmillan.

*Malvino, Albert P. Electronic Principles. 6th ed. 1998. teacher ed. 15.00 (0-02-802841-4) Glencoe.

Malvino, Albert P. Electronic Principles. 6th ed. LC 97-50343. 1998. 61.50 (0-02-802833-3) Glencoe.

*Malvino, Albert P. Electronic Principles. 6th annot. ed. 1998. teacher ed. 78.25 (0-02-802838-4) Glencoe.

Malvino, Albert P. Quick-Lab II for AC Circuits: Conventional-Flow Edition. (CGA, Hercules, EGA - VGA Graphics Ser.). (Illus.). 188p. (Orig.). (C). 1991. pap., student ed. 18.45 (1-56048-986-3, 982C) Malvino Inc.

M

An Asterisk (*) at the beginning of an entry indicates that the title is appearing for the first time.

— Quik-Lab for Basic Electronics - Electron-Flow Version: A Whole-Brain Learning System. (IBM (MS-DOS) Ser.: No. 3). (Illus.). 240p. (C). 1988. wbk. ed. 16.45 incl. disk (*1-56048-803-4*, 803E) Malvino Inc.

— Quik-Lab II for Advanced Electronics. (IBM PC Series, CGA, Hercules, EGA - VGA Graphics). (Illus.). 164p. (C). 1991. student ed. 18.45 (*1-56048-984-7*, 984); disk. write for info. (*0-318-68964-2*) Malvino Inc.

— Quik-Lab II for Basic Electronics: Electron-Flow Edition. (IBM PC Series, CGA, Hercules, EGA - VGA Graphics). (Illus.). 192p. (Orig.). (C). 1991. student ed. 18.45 (*1-56048-983-9*, 983) Malvino Inc.

— Quik-Lab II for AC Circuits: Electron-Flow Edition. (EGA - VGA - Hercules Graphics Ser.). (Illus.). 188p. (C). 1991. student ed. 18.45 (*1-56048-982-0*, 982) Malvino Inc.

— Quik-Lab II for DC Circuits: Conventional-Flow Edition. (CGA, Hercules, EGA - VGA Graphics Ser.). (Illus.). 176p. (C). 1990. student ed. 18.45 (*1-56048-985-5*, 981C) Malvino Inc.

— Quik-Lab II for DC Circuits: Electron-Flow Edition. (EGA - VGA - Hercules Graphics Ser.). (Illus.). 176p. (C). 1990. student ed. 18.45 (*1-56048-981-2*, 981) Malvino Inc.

— Semiconductor Circuit Approximations: An Introduction to Transistors & Integrated Circuits; Experiments for Semiconductor Circuit Approximations. 4th ed. 128p. 1985. text 86.95 (*0-07-039898-4*) McGraw.

— Theory of AC Circuits. (Illus.). 304p. (Orig.). (C). 1989. pap. text 16.95 (*1-56048-302-4*, 302) Malvino Inc.

— Theory of AC Circuits - Quik-Lab for AC Circuits: Conventional-Flow Version, 2 bks., Bks. 1 & 2. (IBM Package Ser.: No. 2). (Illus.). (Orig.). (C). 1989. pap. text 24.95 incl. disk (*1-56048-383-0*, 3802C) Malvino Inc.

— Theory of AC Circuits - Quik-Lab for AC Circuits: Electron-Flow Version, 2 bks., Bks. 1 & 2. (IBM Package Ser.: No. 2). (Illus.). (Orig.). (C). 1989. pap. text 24.95 incl. disk (*1-56048-382-2*, 3802E) Malvino Inc.

— Theory of AC Circuits - Quik-Lab II for AC Circuits Package: Conventional-Flow Edition, 2 bks. (CGA, Hercules, EGA - VGA Graphics Ser.). (Illus.). 492p. (Orig.). (C). 1991. pap. text 26.95 (*1-56048-397-0*, 3982C) Malvino Inc.

— Theory of AC Circuits - Quik-Lab Two for AC Circuits: Electron-Flow Edition Package, 2 vols. (EGA - VGA - Hercules Graphics Ser.). (Illus.). 480p. (Orig.). (C). pap. text 26.95 (*1-56048-399-7*, 3982); write for info. (*0-318-68173-0*); write for info. (*0-318-68174-9*) Malvino Inc.

— Theory of DC Circuits: Conventional-Flow Edition. (Illus.). 272p. (Orig.). (C). 1989. pap. text 16.95 (*1-56048-301-6*, 301C) Malvino Inc.

— Theory of DC Circuits - Quik-Lab II for DC Circuits Package: Convention-Flow Edition, 2 bks. (CGA, Hercules, EGA - VGA Graphics Ser.). (Illus.). 448p. (Orig.). (C). 1990. pap. text 26.95 (*1-56048-396-2*, 3981C) Malvino Inc.

— Theory of DC Circuits - Quik-Lab Two for DC Circuits: Electron-Flow Edition Package, 2 vols. (EGA - VGA - Hercules Graphics Ser.). (Illus.). 448p. (Orig.). (C). pap. text 26.95 (*1-56048-398-9*, 3981); write for info. (*0-318-68171-4*); write for info. (*0-318-68172-2*) Malvino Inc.

— 3.Quik-Lab for AC Circuits - Conventional-Flow Version: A Whole-Brain Learning System. (IBM (MS-DOS) Ser.: No. 2). (Illus.). 224p. (C). 1989. wbk. ed. 16.45 incl. disk (*1-56048-812-3*, 802C) Malvino Inc.

— Troubleshooting for Electronics. (IBM PC Ser.). (Illus.). 82p. (C). 1990. student ed. 12.50 (*1-56048-901-4*, 904) Malvino Inc.

Malvino, Albert P. & Malvino, Joanna M. Quik-Lab for AC Circuits - Electron-Flow Version: A Whole-Brain Learning System. (IBM (MS-DOS) Ser.: No. 2). (Illus.). 224p. (C). 1989. wbk. ed. 16.45 incl. disk (*1-56048-802-6*, 802E) Malvino Inc.

— Quik-Lab for Basic Electronics - Conventional-Flow Version: A Whole-Brain Learning System. (IBM (MS-DOS) Ser.: No. 3). (Illus.). 240p. (C). 1988. wbk. ed. 16.45 incl. disk (*1-56048-813-1*, 803C) Malvino Inc.

— Quik-Lab II for Basic Electronics: Conventional-Flow Edition. (CGA, Hercules, EGA - VGA Graphics Ser.). (Illus.). 192p. (Orig.). (C). 1991. pap., student ed. 18.45 (*1-56048-987-1*, 983C) Malvino Inc.

— Theory of DC Circuits: Electron-Flow Edition. (Illus.). 272p. (Orig.). (C). 1989. pap. text 16.95 (*1-56048-300-8*, 301E) Malvino Inc.

Malvino, Albert P., jt. auth. see Leach, Donald P.

Malvino, Joanna M., jt. auth. see Malvino, Albert P.

Malvitz. Oral Health Promotion & Disease Prevention: Disease Prevention. 1996. pap. write for info. (*0-7216-4008-7*, W B Saunders Co) Harcrt Hlth Sci Grp.

Malviya, A. K. Management of Exports Marketing in India. (C). 1990. 94.00 (*0-8364-2641-X*, Pub. by Chugh Pubns) S Asia.

Malviya, Achla, jt. auth. see Rani, Seema.

Malvy, Claude, et al. Triple Helix Forming Oligonucleotides. LC 98-50990. 1999. write for info. (*0-7923-8418-0*) Kluwer Academic.

Malvy, Claude, jt. auth. see Couvreur, Patrick.

***Malwatkar, S. G.** Integrated Textbook of Anatomy for Undergraduates: Gross Anatomy, Embryology, Histology. (Illus.). 640p. 2000. text 45.00 (*0-19-564872-2*) OUP.

Maly, Bonnie C., ed. see Curl, Cathleen M., et al.

Maly, Bonnie C., ed. see Flaig, Robert B., et al.

Maly, Bonnie C., ed. see Hansen, Charles A. & Cambray, Joan M.

Maly, Bonnie C., ed. see Javor, Ronald S., et al.

Maly, Bonnie C., ed. see Judge, John A., et al.

Maly, Bonnie C., ed. see Moskovitz, Myron, et al.

Maly, Bonnie C., ed. see Weir, William J. A., et al.

Maly, Jan Y. & Ziemer, William P. Fine Regularity of Solutions of Elliptic Partial Differential Equations. LC 97-11982. (Mathematical Surveys & Monographs: Vol. 51). 291p. 1997. text 75.00 (*0-8218-0335-2*) Am Math.

Maly, Kenneth, ed. The Path of Archaic Thinking: Unfolding the Work of John Sallis. LC 94-11959. (SUNY Series in Contemporary Continental Philosophy). 316p. (C). 1995. text 64.50 (*0-7914-2355-7*); pap. text 21.95 (*0-7914-2356-5*) State U NY Pr.

Maly, Kenneth, tr. see Heidegger, Martin.

Maly, Kenneth, tr. see Petzet, Heinrich W.

Maly, M. Wojciech. Romans. 1989. pap. 21.00 (*0-86217-009-5*, Pub. by Veritas Pubns) St Mut.

Maly, W., jt. ed. see Director, S. W.

Maly, Wojciech, jt. auth. see Khare, Jitendra B.

Malyaskaya, Great R., tr. see Idelchik, I. E.

Malyavskaya, Greta R. & Shveyeva, Natalia K. Russian-english Dictionary of Scientific & Engineering Terms: A Guide to Usage LC 99-13566. (ENG.). 6p. 1999. write for info. (*1-56700-128-9*) Begell Hse.

Malygin, E. G., et al. Physicochemical Biology: Restriction-Modification Enzymes; Cell-Model Membrane Interactions, Vol. 9. Skulachev, V. P., ed. (Soviet Scientific Reviews Ser.: Vol. 9, Pt. 2). 196p. 1989. text 87.00 (*3-7186-4917-9*) Gordon & Breach.

Malyn-Smith, Joyce, et al. Project Smart: Work-Based Learning in the Manufacturing Firm. 125p. 1997. pap. 19.95 (*0-89292-285-0*) Educ Dev Ctr.

Malynes, Gerard. A Treatise of the Canker of Englands Common Wealth. LC 77-7412. (English Experience Ser.: No. 880). 1977. reprint ed. lib. bdg. 15.00 (*90-221-0880-5*) Walter J Johnson.

Malynes, Gerard, jt. auth. see Hamilton, Katie F.

Malyon, Carol. Lovers & Other Strangers. 176p. 1996. pap. text. write for info. (*0-88984-169-1*) Porcup Quill.

Malyshev, Anna. Russian for Tourists: Teach Yourself Russian the Quick & Easy Way. LC 97-80460. (ENG & RUS.). 240p. 1998. pap. 17.95 incl. cd-rom (*0-9660648-8-7*) Cyrillica Pub.

Malyshev, D. V., tr. see Sharkovsky, A. N., et al.

Malyshev, Peter V., tr. see Berezanskii, I. Makarovich, et al.

Malyshev, V. A. & Minlos, R. A. Gibbs Random Fields: Cluster Expansions. (C). 1991. text 185.50 (*0-7923-0232-X*) Kluwer Academic.

— Linear Infinite Particle Operators. LC 94-42578. (Translations of Mathematical Monographs: Vol. 143).Tr. of Lineinye Operatory v Beskonechnochastichnykh Sistemakh. (ENG & RUS.). 298p. 1995. text 125.00 (*0-8218-0283-6*, MMONO/143) Am Math.

Malyshev, V. A., et al. Random Walks in the Quarter Plane: Algebraic Methods, Boundary Value Problems & Applications. LC 98-52367. (Applications of Mathematics Ser.). xvi, 160p. 1999. 89.95 (*3-540-65047-4*) Spr-Verlag.

Malyshev, V. V., et al. Optimization of Observation & Control Processes. (Educ Ser.). (Illus.). 349p. 1992. 69.95 (*1-56347-040-3*, 40-3) AIAA.

***Malyshkin, V. E., et al, eds.** Parallel Computing Technologies: 5th International Conference, PaCT-99, St. Petersburg, Russia, September 6-10, 1999. LC 99-41063. (Lecture Notes in Computer Science Ser.: Vol. 1662). xix, 510p. 1999. pap. 79.00 (*3-540-66363-0*) Spr-Verlag.

Malyshkin, V. E., ed. see Conference on Parallel Computing Technologies Staf.

Malyshkin, Victor, et al, eds. Parallel Computing Technologies: Third International Conference, PaCT-95, St. Petersburg, Russia, September 12-15, 1995, Proceedings, Vol. XII. LC 95-36460. (Lecture Notes in Computer Science Ser.: Vol. 964). 497p. 1995. 81.00 (*3-540-60222-4*) Spr-Verlag.

Malyurek, Victoria J. The ABCs, God's Creatures & Me Book. (Illus.). iii, 52p. (Orig.). (J). (gr. k-1). 1996. pap. write for info. (*1-889294-00-4*) Victorias Pub.

— Around the World with Queenee the Bee. (Illus.). (J). (gr. k-5). 1996. 2.95 (*1-889294-07-1*) Victorias Pub.

— The Berrees from Planet Cherree. (Illus.). ii, 16p. (Orig.). (J). (ps-3). 1996. pap. write for info. (*1-889294-01-2*) Victorias Pub.

— The Colors, God's Country & Me Book. (Illus.). vi, 50p. (Orig.). (J). (gr. 1-4). 1996. pap. write for info. (*1-889294-02-0*) Victorias Pub.

— Hearts & Souls. iii, 37p. (Orig.). 1996. pap. write for info. (*1-889294-03-9*) Victorias Pub.

— Memento's The "Wonder" Years Scrapbook. i, 33p. (Orig.). (J). (gr. k-12). 1995. pap. 5.95 (*1-889294-05-5*) Victorias Pub.

— The Nutt Family Tree. (Illus.). ii, 10p. (Orig.). (J). (ps-3). 1996. pap. write for info. (*1-889294-06-3*) Victorias Pub.

— Rai 'n' Bo Heart Meet Sunny, the Funny Weather Bunny. (Illus.). 12p. (J). (gr. 1-7). 1997. pap. 3.95 (*1-889294-09-8*) Victorias Pub.

Malyusz, E. Kaiser Sigismund in Ungarn, 1387-1437. 422p. 1990. 105.00 (*963-05-4978-6*, Pub. by Akade Kiado) St Mut.

***Malz, Betty.** Angels Watching over Me. 128p. (gr. 13 up). 2000. mass mkt. 4.99 (*0-8007-8678-5*, Spire) Revell.

Malz, Betty. Heaven a Bright & Glorious Place. LC 89-9879. 144p. (gr. 11). 1988. 11.99 (*0-8007-9145-2*) Chosen Bks.

— Making Your Husband Feel Loved. LC 97-48824. (Orig.). 1998. pap. 12.99 (*0-88419-534-1*) Creation House.

— My Glimpse of Eternity. LC 77-22671. 128p. (gr. 10). 1979. mass mkt. 4.99 (*0-8007-8363-8*, Spire) Revell.

Malz, Russell E. Catalysis of Organic Reactions. LC 96-25976. (Chemical Industries Ser.: Vol. 68). (Illus.). 536p. 1996. text 215.00 (*0-8247-9807-4*) Dekker.

Malzac, R. P. Dictionnaire Francais-Malgache. (FRE.). 861p. 1953. pap. 59.95 (*0-8288-6876-X*, M-6390) Fr & Eur.

Malzan, Jerry G., jt. auth. see Djokovic, D. Z.

Malzberg, Barry. Galaxies. 128p. 1989. pap. 2.95 (*0-88184-491-8*) Carroll & Graf.

Malzberg, Barry N. The Passage of the Light: The Recursive Science Fiction of Barry N. Malzberg. Resnick, Mike & Lewis, Anthony R., eds. LC 94-65656. x, 281p. 1994. pap. 14.00 (*0-915368-59-5*) New Eng SF Assoc.

— Underlay. 256p. 1986. pap. 4.95 (*0-930330-41-2*) Intl Polygonics.

Malzberg, Barry N. & Greenberg, Martin H., eds. The Science Fiction of Mark Clifton. LC 80-20977. (Alternatives Ser.). 318p. 1980. 21.95 (*0-8093-0985-8*) S Ill U Pr.

Malzberg, Barry N., ed. see Neville, Kris.

Malzberg, Benjamin. Social & Biological Aspects of Mental Disease. Grob, Gerald N., ed. LC 78-22573. (Historical Issues in Mental Health Ser.). (Illus.). 1980. reprint ed. lib. bdg. 28.95 (*0-405-11926-7*) Ayer.

Mama, Amina. Beyond the Masks: Race, Gender & Subjectivity. LC 95-8479. (Critical Psychology Ser.). 240p. (C). 1995. pap. 25.99 (*0-415-03544-9*) Routledge.

— Beyond the Masks: Race, Gender & Subjectivity. LC 95-8479. (Critical Psychology Ser.). 224p. (C). (gr. 13). 1995. 80.00 (*0-415-03543-0*) Routledge.

— Domestic Violence & Multi-Agency Working: New Opportunities, Old Challenges? 300p. 1996. pap. 28.95 (*1-86177-003-0*, Pub. by Whiting & Birch) Paul & Co Pubs.

Mama, Amina, et al, eds. Engendering African Social Sciences. 470p. 1997. pap. 38.00 (*2-86978-063-X*, Pub. by African Bks Collective) Women Ink.

Mama, Raouf. The Barefoot Book of Tropical Tales. (Illus.). 64p. (J). (gr. 3-6). 2000. 19.95 (*1-902283-21-X*) Barefoot Bks NY.

Mamaev, B. M. & Krivosheina, N. P. The Larvae of the Gall Midges (Diptera & Cecidomyiidae) Roskam, J. C., ed. Wieffering, J. H., tr. (Illus.). 304p. (C). 1991. text 123.00 (*90-6191-787-5*, Pub. by A A Balkema) Ashgate Pub Co.

Mamak, Alexander F. Colour, Culture & Conflict: A Study of Pluralism in Fiji. (Illus.). 1979. pap. text 21.00 (*0-08-023353-8*, Pergamon Pr) Elsevier.

Mamak, Alexander F., ed. see Young Nations Conference, Sidney, 1976 Staff.

Mamalakis, Markos J. The Growth & Structure of the Chilean Economy: From Independence to Allende. LC 74-29729. (Economic Growth Center, Yale University Publication Ser.). 412p. 1976. reprint ed. pap. 127.80 (*0-8357-8158-5*, 203381100087) Bks Demand.

— Historical Statistics of Chile: Banking, & Financial Services, Vol. 5. LC 78-66721. (Illus.). 532p. 1985. lib. bdg. 195.00 (*0-313-25136-3*, MHC/5, Greenwood Pr) Greenwood.

— Historical Statistics of Chile: Forestry & Related Activities, Vol. 3. LC 78-66721. (Illus.). 443p. 1982. lib. bdg. 175.00 (*0-313-20855-7*, MHC/3, Greenwood Pr) Greenwood.

Mamalakis, Markos J., compiled by. Historical Statistics of Chile: Demography & Labor Force, Vol. 2. LC 79-54051. (Illus.). 420p. 1980. lib. bdg. 175.00 (*0-313-20854-9*, MHC/2, Greenwood Pr) Greenwood.

— Historical Statistics of Chile: Government Services & Public Sector & a Theory of Services, Vol. 6. LC 78-66721. 976p. 1989. lib. bdg. 235.00 (*0-313-26563-1*, MHC/6, Greenwood Pr) Greenwood.

— Historical Statistics of Chile: Money, Prices, & Credit Services, Vol. 4. LC 78-66721. (Illus.). 510p. 1983. lib. bdg. 175.00 (*0-313-20856-5*, MHC/4, Greenwood Pr) Greenwood.

— Historical Statistics of Chile: National Accounts. LC 78-66721. 262p. 1978. lib. bdg. 175.00 (*0-313-20619-8*, MHC/1, Greenwood Pr) Greenwood.

Mamaliga, Emil, jt. auth. see Dowell, Linus J.

***Mamalis, A. G., et al.** Innovative Systems for Seismic Repair & Rehabilitation of Structure: Processing of High-Temperature Superconductors at High Strain Rates. LC 00-102582. 280p. 2000. text 149.95 (*1-56676-878-0*) Technomic.

Mamalis, Athanasios G., et al. Crashworthiness of Composite Thin-Walled Structural Components. LC 97-62362. 250p. 1998. pap. text 149.95 (*1-56676-635-4*) Technomic.

Mamalis, George J. Isle of Deliverance. 323p. (Orig.). 1998. pap. 17.95 (*1-892896-12-5*) Buy Books.

***Maman, Marie.** Sigrid Undset in America: An Annotated Bibliography & Research Guide. annot. ed. LC 00-44059. 2000. write for info. (*0-8108-3738-2*) Scarecrow.

Maman, Marie & Tate, Thelma H. Women in Agriculture: A Guide to Research. LC 95-41230. (Women's History & Culture Ser.: Vol. 11). 308p. 1996. text 62.00 (*0-8153-1354-3*, SS908) Garland.

Mamantov, Gleb, ed. Molten Salts: Characterization & Analysis. LC 75-88481. (Illus.). 627p. reprint ed. pap. 194.40 (*0-608-30544-8*, 205500700007) Bks Demand.

Mamantov, Gleb & Marassi, Roberto, eds. Molten Salt Chemistry: An Introduction & Selected Applications. (C). 1987. text 234.00 (*90-277-2483-0*) Kluwer Academic.

Mamantov, Gleb & Popov, Alexander. Chemistry of Nonaqueous Solutions. LC 93-40038. 1994. 125.00 (*1-56081-546-9*, Wiley-VCH) Wiley.

Mamantov, Gleb & Popov, Alexander. Chemistry of Nonaqueous Solutions: Current Progress. 377p. 1994. 185.00 (*0-471-18569-8*) Wiley.

Mamantov, Gleb, ed. see International Symposium on Molten Salts Staff.

Mamantov, Ilya A., ed. see Altman, Moses S.

Mamaril, Marie, ed. S. W. A. P. - "Sent with a Prayer" Expressions of Life. (Illus.). 92p. (Orig.). 1996. pap. text. write for info. (*1-889534-05-6*) Jay St Pubs.

Mamaril, Marie, ed. see Pursifull, Carmen M.

Mamary, Anne J., jt. ed. see James Gonzalez, Gertrude M.

Mamas, Michael. Angels, Einstein & You: A Healer's Journey. LC 99-72257. (Illus.). 304p. 1999. pap. 15.95 (*1-58151-035-7*) BookPartners.

Mamatas, Emanuel. The No Hair-Loss Hair Care Book: With Hair Replacement Solutions & Treatments. 1988. pap. 14.95 (*0-13-623018-0*) P-H.

Mamatey, Victor S. Rise of the Habsburg Empire. 192p. 1994. pap. 11.50 (*0-89464-920-5*) Krieger.

Mamay, Carl O., photos by. Opinions Six: Philatelic Expertizing - An Inside View. (Opinions Ser.). (Illus.). ii, 226p. 1992. text 32.50 (*0-911989-25-0*) Philatelic Found.

Mambert, W. A. The Elements of Effective Communication. LC 71-141366. 180p. 1971. 19.95 (*0-941822-04-4*); pap. 14.95 (*0-941822-06-0*) C E R I Pr.

— The Human Touch Vol. 1: Readings for Thinking & Caring Managers. 70p. 1997. pap. 9.95 (*0-941822-03-6*) C E R I Pr.

— On Becoming an Educated Person: A Practical Handbook for Developing Your Basic Thinking, Problem Solving & Communicating Skills. LC 80-81014. 1982. pap. text 18.95 (*0-941822-00-1*) C E R I Pr.

— Presenting Technical Ideas: A Guide to Audience Communication. LC 67-28335. (Wiley Series on Human Communication). (Illus.). 229p. reprint ed. pap. 71.00 (*0-608-11433-2*, 20551750001l) Bks Demand.

— A Trip into Your Unconscious. LC 72-12393. (Illus.). 279p. 1973. 19.95 (*0-941822-05-2*); pap. 14.95 (*0-941822-07-9*) C E R I Pr.

— Untrapped in the Organization: Surviving & Thriving in the Corporate World. pap. 14.95 (*0-941822-02-8*) C E R I Pr.

***Mambo, Masahiro & Zheng, Yuliang, eds.** Information Security: Proceedings of the Second International Workshop, ISW'99, Kuala Lumpur, Malaysia, November 6-7, 1999. rev. ed. LC 99-52052. (Lecture Notes in Computer Science Ser.: Vol. 1729). ix, 277p. 1999. pap. 52.00 (*3-540-66695-8*) Spr-Verlag.

Mambretti, Catherine. CD-ROM Technology: A Manual for Librarians & Educators. LC 98-10321. (Illus.). 310p. 1998. pap. 39.95 (*0-7864-0501-5*) McFarland & Co.

***Mambretti, Catherine.** Internet Technology for Schools. LC 99-17284. (Illus.). 315p. 1999. 39.95 (*0-7864-0727-1*) McFarland & Co.

Mambretti, Joel J. & Schmidt, Andrew. Internet 2: Building the Next Generation Internet. LC 99-30832. 324p. 1999. pap. 44.99 (*0-471-32762-X*) Wiley.

Mambuca, Annette, ed. Free at Last: Daily Meditations by & for Inmates. LC 93-84893. 375p. (Orig.). 1993. pap. 10.00 (*1-56838-070-4*) Hazelden.

Mamchak, P. Susan & Mamchak, Steven R. Complete Communications Manual for Coaches & Athletic Directors. LC 88-19521. 288p. (C). 1988. pap. text 37.95 (*0-13-159229-7*, Busn) P-H.

***Mamchak, P. Susan & Mamchak, Steven R.** Educator's Lifetime Encyclopedia of Letters. LC 98-9492. 256p. (C). 1998. 37.95 (*0-13-795436-0*) P-H.

Mamchak, P. Susan & Mamchak, Steven R. Elementary Principal's Portfolio of Model Speeches for All Occasions. 320p. (C). 1996. text 37.95 (*0-13-340449-8*) P-H.

— Encyclopedia of School Humor: Icebreakers, Classics, Stories, Puns, & Roasts for All Occasions. 256p. 1986. text 29.95 (*0-13-276346-X*) P-H.

— School Administrator's Encyclopedia. LC 81-22492. 414p. 1982. text 27.95 (*0-13-792390-2*, Parker Publishing Co) P-H.

— Teacher's Time Management Survival Kit: Ready-to-Use Techniques & Materials. LC 93-3737. 256p. (C). 1993. pap. text 27.95 (*0-13-014374-X*) P-H.

Mamchak, Steven R., jt. auth. see Mamchak, P. Susan.

Mamchak, Steven R., jt. auth. see Mamchak, Susan.

Mamchak, Susan & Mamchak, Steven R. The New Encyclopedia of School Letters. LC 89-48884. 420p. (C). 1990. pap. text 29.95 (*0-13-612656-1*) P-H.

Mamchur, Carolyn. The Popcorn Tree. LC 99-162384. (Illus.). 32p. (J). (ps-3). 1998. 15.95 (*0-7737-2896-1*) STDK.

— A Teacher's Guide to Cognitive Type Theory & Learning Style. LC 96-45842. (Illus.). 132p. 1996. pap. 18.95 (*0-87120-278-6*, 196275) ASCD.

***Mamdani, Mahmood.** Beyond Culture Talk & Rights Talk: Comparative Essays on the Politics of Rights & Culture. LC 00-27821. 2000. pap. write for info. (*0-312-23498-8*) St Martin.

Mamdani, Mahmood. Citizen & Subject: Contemporary Africa & the Legacy of Late Colonialism. 344p. 1996. pap. text 19.95 (*0-691-02793-5*, Pub. by Princeton U Pr) Cal Prin Full Svc.

— Imperialism & Fascism in Uganda. ix, 125p. (Orig.). 1984. 29.95 (*0-86543-028-4*); pap. 6.95 (*0-86543-029-2*) Africa World.

— The Making of Citizen & Subject in Contemporary Africa. LC 95-25318. (Princeton Studies in Culture, Power & History). 344p. 1996. text 57.50 (*0-691-01107-9*, Pub. by Princeton U Pr) Cal Prin Full Svc.

— The Myth of Population Control: Family, Caste & Class in an Indian Village. LC 72-81761. (Illus.). 176p. 1973. pap. 15.00 (*0-85345-284-9*, Pub. by Monthly Rev) NYU Pr.

Mamdani, Mahmood, jt. auth. see Leys, Colin.

Mamdani, Shelby. Traditions from India. LC 98-23308. (Cultural Journeys Ser.). (J). 1999. 25.69 (*0-8172-5385-8*) Raintree Steck-V.

Mame & Plon. Catechisme de l'Eglise Catholique. (FRE.). 1992. pap. 59.95 (*0-7859-1006-9*, 2728905495) Fr & Eur.

M

An Asterisk (*) at the beginning of an entry indicates that the title is appearing for the first time.

M

Mamede, Nuno J. & Pinto-Ferreira, Carlos, eds. Applications of Artificial Intelligence: Expert Sytems, Robots & Vision Systems, Fuzzy Logic & Neural Networks. (Advanced Manufacturing Forum: Vol. 1). (Illus.). 304p. 1996. text 91.00 (3-908450-17-9, Pub. by Scitec Pubns) Enfield Pubs NH.

Mamede, Nuno J., et al. Progress in Artificial Intelligence: 7th Portuguese Conference on Artificial Intelligence, EPIA '95, Funchal, Madeira Island, Portugal, October 3-6, 1995 - Proceedings. (Lecture Notes in Computer Science Subseries: Lecture Notes in Artificial Intelligence: Vol. 990). xiv, 487p. 1995. pap. 81.00 (3-540-60428-6) Spr-Verlag.

Mamedov, Seville. English-Azerbaijani - Azerbaijani-English Concise Dictionary. (Concise Dictionaries Ser.). (AZE & ENG.). 144p. (Orig.). 1994. pap. 14.95 (0-7818-0244-X) Hippocrene Bks.

Mamen, Moojan. Studies in the Babi & Baha'i Religions Vol. 5: Studies in Honor of the Late H. M. Balyuzi. 1989. pap. 24.95 (0-933770-44-8) Kalimat.

— Studies in the Babi & Baha'i Religions, Vol. 5: Studies in Honor of the Late H. M. Balyuzi, Vol. 5. 293p. 1989. 32.50 (0-933770-72-3) Kalimat.

Mamer. Film Production Technique: Creating the Accomplished Image. 2nd ed. LC 99-25660. (Radio/Tv/Film Ser.). 1999. pap. 64.95 (0-534-56205-1) Wadsworth Pub.

Mamer, Bruce. Film Production Technique: Creating the Accomplished Image. LC 95-14856. 492p. (C). 1995. 40.75 (0-534-20568-2) Wadsworth Pub.

Mamertinus, Claudius. Die Neujahrsrede des Konsuls Claudius Mamertinus Vor Dem Kaiser Julian. (Basler Beitrage Zur Geschichtswissenschaft Ser.: No. 10). 254p. 1980. write for info. (3-487-07045-6) G Olms Pubs.

Mamet, David. American Buffalo. LC 77-78079. 128p. 1977. pap. 11.00 (0-8021-5057-8, Grove) Grove-Atltic.

— American Buffalo. limited ed. (Illus.). 118p. 1992. 350.00 (0-910457-24-7) Arion Pr.

— Bar Mitzvah. 48p. (gr. 8). 1999. 26.95 (0-8212-2546-4) Little.

***Mamet, David.** Boston Marriage. LC 99-56575. 112p. 2000. pap. 11.00 (0-375-70665-8) Vin Bks.

Mamet, David. The Cabin: Reminiscence & Diversions. LC 93-10493. 1993. pap. 11.00 (0-679-74720-6) Vin Bks.

— The Chinaman. LC 98-31821. 144p. 1999. text 19.95 (0-87951-897-9, Pub. by Overlook Pr) Penguin Putnam.

Mamet, David. A Collection of Dramatic Sketches & Monologues. LC 86-118976. 144 p. 1985. write for info. (0-573-68908-3) S French Trade.

Mamet, David. The Cryptogram. LC 95-237699. 1995. pap. 5.25 (0-8222-1495-4) Dramatists Play.

— Cryptogram & Other Plays. 1995. pap. 11.00 (0-679-74653-6) Random.

— Duck & the Goat. LC 96-21761. (Illus.). 32p. 1996. 16.95 (0-312-14817-8) St Martin.

— Five Television Plays: A Waitress in Yellowstone; Bradford; The Museum of Science & Industry Story; A Wasted Weekend; We Will Take You There. LC 89-25661. 224p. 1990. pap. 12.95 (0-8021-3171-9, Grove) Grove-Atltic.

— Glengarry Glenn Ross. LC 83-49380. 112p. 1984. pap. 12.00 (0-8021-3091-7, Grove) Grove-Atltic.

— Goldberg Street: Short Plays & Monologues. LC 84-7310. 208p. 1985. pap. 12.00 (0-8021-5104-3, Grove) Grove-Atltic.

***Mamet, David.** Henrietta. LC 99-15171. (Illus.). 32p. 1999. 16.00 (0-618-00416-5) HM.

Mamet, David. Homicide: A Screenplay. LC 91-33891. 126p. 1992. pap. 9.95 (0-8021-3308-8, Grove) Grove-Atltic.

— House of Games. LC 86-32013. (Illus.). 104p. 1987. pap. 11.00 (0-8021-3028-3, Grove) Grove-Atltic.

— Jaffsie & John Henry: Essays. LC 98-49040. (Illus.). 192p. 1999. 22.00 (0-684-84120-7) S&S Trade.

— A Life in the Theatre. LC 77-91884. 96p. 1978. pap. 10.95 (0-8021-5067-5, Grove) Grove-Atltic.

— No One Will Be Immune: And Other Plays & Pieces. LC 95-118215. 1994. pap. 5.25 (0-8222-1321-4) Dramatists Play.

— The Old Neighborhood. LC 97-32224. 96p. 1998. pap. 10.00 (0-679-74652-8) Vin Bks.

— The Old Religion: A Novel. LC 97-17854. 288p. 1997. 23.50 (0-684-84119-3) Free Pr.

— Oleanna. 1993. pap. 5.25 (0-8222-1343-5) Dramatists Play.

— Oleanna. LC 92-50638. 1993. pap. 11.00 (0-679-74536-X) Vin Bks.

— On Acting. 1999. pap. write for info. (0-14-010104-7, Viking) Viking Penguin.

— On Directing Film. 128p. 1992. pap. 12.95 (0-14-012722-4, Penguin Bks) Viking Penguin.

— Passover. LC 95-26035. (Illus.). 64p. 1995. text 14.95 (0-312-13141-0) St Martin.

— Reunion & Dark Pony: Two Plays. LC 79-2319. 64p. 1990. pap. 8.95 (0-8021-5171-X, Grove) Grove-Atltic.

— The Revenge of the Space Pandas. 1978. 5.50 (0-87129-532-6, R26) Dramatic Pub.

— Sexual Perversity in Chicago & the Duck Variations. LC 77-91885. 128p. 1978. pap. 11.00 (0-8021-5011-X, Grove) Grove-Atltic.

— The Shawl & Prairie du Chien. LC 85-14884. 96p. 1985. pap. 9.95 (0-8021-5172-8, Grove) Grove-Atltic.

— Short Plays & Monologues. 1981. pap. 5.25 (0-8222-0720-6) Dramatists Play.

***Mamet, David.** Spanish Prisoner & the Winslow Boy: Two Screenplays. LC 99-12286. 224p. 1999. pap. 12.00 (0-375-70664-X) Vin Bks.

Mamet, David. Speed-the-Plow. LC 87-37252. 96p. 1988. pap. 10.00 (0-8021-3046-1, Grove) Grove-Atltic.

— Speed-the-Plow. 1995. reprint ed. lib. bdg. 21.95 (1-56849-630-3) Buccaneer Bks.

— Three Children's Plays: The Poet & the Rent; The Frog Prince; The Revenge of the Space Pandas or Binky Rudich & the Two-Speed Clock. LC 86-45245. 144p. (J). (gr. 3-7). 1986. pap. 8.95 (0-8021-5173-6, Grove) Grove-Atltic.

— Three Uses of the Knife. 96p. 2000. pap. 10.00 (0-375-70423-X) Vin Bks.

— Three Uses of the Knife: On the Nature & Purpose of Drama. LC 97-23606. 96p. 1998. 21.95 (0-231-11088-X) Col U Pr.

— True & False: Heresy & Common Sense for the Author. 1999. pap. 11.00 (0-679-77264-2) McKay.

***Mamet, David.** The Village. 1998. pap. 11.95 (0-316-19100-0, Back Bay) Little.

Mamet, David. We're No Angels. LC 59-25204. 144p. 1990. pap. 7.95 (0-8021-3202-2, Grove) Grove-Atltic.

— The Woods, Lakeboat, Edmond. LC 86-33489. 304p. 1987. pap. 13.00 (0-8021-5109-4, Grove) Grove-Atltic.

— Writing in Restaurants. 176p. 1987. pap. 11.95 (0-14-008981-0, Penguin Bks) Viking Penguin.

Mamet, David & Silverstein, Shel. Things Change. (Illus.). 64p. 1988. pap. 7.95 (0-8021-3047-X, Grove) Grove-Atltic.

Mamet, David, et al. The Ensemble Studio Theatre Marathon '84. 94p. (Orig.). 1985. pap. 6.95 (0-88145-030-8) Broadway Play.

Mamet, David, jt. auth. see Madoff, Steven H.

***Mamgain, Vaishali.** Productivity Growth in Developing Countries: The Role of Efficiency. LC 99-44756. (Studies on Industrial Productivity). 1999. write for info. (0-8153-3551-2) Garland.

Mamin-Sibiryak, D. N. Grey Neck. LC 88-2100. (Illus.). 32p. (J). (gr. k-3). 1988. 13.95 (0-88045-068-1) Stemmer Hse.

***Mamis, Justin.** Nature of Risk: Stock Market Survival & the Meaning of Life. 2nd ed. LC 91-14143. 241p. 1999. reprint ed. pap. 18.00 (0-87034-132-4) Fraser Pub Co.

— When to Sell: Inside Strategies for Stock Market Profits. 3rd rev. ed. 335p. 1999. pap. 22.00 (0-87034-134-0) Fraser Pub Co.

Mamiya, Christin J. Pop Art & Consumer Culture: American Super Market. LC 91-18892. (American Studies Ser.). (Illus.). 230p. 1992. pap. 71.30 (0-608-05105-5, 206566600005) Bks Demand.

Mamiya, Lawrence, jt. auth. see Lincoln, C. Eric.

Mamleev, Jurii. Vzglid 12 Nichto: Rasskazy. LC 88-83825. (RUS., Illus.). 328p. 1989. 32.00 (0-911971-42-4); pap. 25.00 (0-911971-43-2) Effect Pub.

Mamlouk. Materials for Civil & Construction Engineers. 400p. (C). 1998. 95.00 (0-673-98187-8, Prentice Hall) P-H.

Mammana, Carmelo, ed. Perspectives on the Teaching of Geometry for the 21st Century. (ICMI Studies). 364p. 1998. pap. 65.00 (0-7923-4991-1) Kluwer Academic.

Mammana, Carmelo & Villani, Vinicio. Perspectives on the Teaching of Geometry for the 21st Century. LC 98-9444. (ICMI Studies). 353p. 1998. 129.00 (0-7923-4990-3) Kluwer Academic.

Mammana, Dennis L. The Backyard Astronomer. LC 96-1337. 80p. 1996. 11.98 (1-56799-343-5, MetroBooks) M Friedman Pub Grp Inc.

Mammano, Julie. Rhinos Who Skateboard. LC 98-36201. (Illus.). 32p. (J). (gr. k-1). 1999. 12.95 (0-8118-2356-3) Chronicle Bks.

— Rhinos Who Snowboard. LC 97-1349. (Illus.). 32p. (J). 1997. 11.95 (0-8118-1715-6) Chronicle Bks.

— Rhinos Who Surf. (Illus.). 32p. (J). 1996. 12.95 (0-8118-1000-3) Chronicle Bks.

Mammem, Lori. TAAS Master Social Studies, Grade 4. (TAAS Master Ser.). (Illus.). 144p. 1993. pap. text 20.95 (0-944459-92-7) ECS Lrn Systs.

Mammen, Eberhard F., et al, eds. Treatment of Bleeding Disorders with Blood Components. (Reviews of Hematology: Vol. I). 1980. 49.95 (0-915340-01-1) PJD Pubns.

Mammen, Lori. Bright Blue Thinking Book, Bk. 1. Durst, Shirley J., ed. (Illus.). 114p. (J). (gr. 1-2). 1997. pap., wbk. ed. 8.95 (1-57011-110-3, ECS1103) ECS Lrn Systs.

— Bright Blue Thinking Book, Bk. 2. Durst, Shirley J., ed. (Illus.). 114p. (J). (gr. 3-4). 1997. pap. 8.95 (1-57022-111-1, ECS1111) ECS Lrn Systs.

— Bright Blue Thinking Book, Bk. 3. Durst, Shirley J., ed. (Illus.). 114p. (J). (gr. 5-7). 1997. pap., wbk. ed. 8.95 (1-57022-112-X, ECS112X) ECS Lrn Systs.

— Bright Blue Thinking Books, 3 vols. Durst, Shirley J., ed. (Illus.). (J). (gr. 1-7). pap., wbk. ed. 26.85 (1-57022-131-6, ECS-BBTB-SET-03) ECS Lrn Systs.

***Mammen, Lori.** Harry Potter & the Sorcerer's Stone Student Packet. Robbins, Dawn Michelle, ed. (J). 1999. student ed. 11.95 (1-58130-607-2); student ed. 9.95 (1-58130-606-7) Novel Units.

Mammen, Lori. Home Study Collection, Reading & More, 6 bks. 60p. (J). (gr. 1-6). 1995. 29.70 (1-57022-184-7) ECS Lrn Systs.

— Language Arts & More: Home Study Collection, 6 bks. 56p. (J). (gr. 1-6). 1995. 29.70 (1-57022-185-5) ECS Lrn Systs.

— Little Red Writing Book 1. Day, Nancy S., ed. (Illus.). 114p. (J). (gr. 1-2). 1997. pap., wbk. ed. 8.95 (1-57022-107-3, ECS1073) ECS Lrn Systs.

— Little Red Writing Book 3. Day, Nancy S., ed. (Illus.). 114p. (J). (gr. 5-7). 1997. pap., wbk. ed. 8.95 (1-57022-109-X, ECS109X) ECS Lrn Systs.

— Little Red Writing Book 2. Day, Nancy S., ed. (Illus.). 114p. 1997. pap., wbk. ed. 8.95 (1-57022-108-1, ECS1081) ECS Lrn Systs.

— Little Red Writing Books, 3 vols. Day, Nancy, ed. (Illus.). (J). (gr. 1-7). pap., wbk. ed. 26.85 (1-57022-130-8, ECS-LRWB-SET-03) ECS Lrn Systs.

— Math & More: Home Study Collection, 6 bks. 56p. (J). (gr. 1-6). 1995. 29.70 (1-57022-186-3) ECS Lrn Systs.

***Mammen, Lori.** On the Chalkboard Reading & Writing Grade 1. 2000. write for info. (1-57022-230-4) ECS Lrn Systs.

— On the Chalkboard Reading & Writing Grade 2. 2000. write for info. (1-57022-231-2) ECS Lrn Systs.

— On the Chalkboard Reading & Writing Grade 3. 2000. write for info. (1-57022-232-0) ECS Lrn Systs.

— On the Chalkboard Reading & Writing Grade 4. 2000. write for info. (1-57022-233-9) ECS Lrn Systs.

— On the Chalkboard Reading & Writing Grade 5. 2000. write for info. (1-57022-234-7) ECS Lrn Systs.

— On the Chalkboard Reading & Writing Grade 6. 2000. write for info. (1-57022-235-5) ECS Lrn Systs.

Mammen, Lori. Passageways: Vocabulary Activities to Build Writing Skills. 96p. 1992. pap. text 12.95 (0-944459-62-5) ECS Lrn Systs.

— Springboards for Reading, Grades 7-12: 38 Strategic Reading Lessons. (ECS Activity Book for Language Arts Ser.). 80p. 1993. pap. text 10.95 (0-944459-70-6) ECS Lrn Systs.

— Springboards for Reading, Grades 3-6: 48 Strategic Reading Lessons. (ECS Activity Book for Language Arts Ser.). 96p. 1993. pap. text 11.95 (0-944459-69-2) ECS Lrn Systs.

— TAAS Master Social Studies, Grade 8. (TAAS Master Ser.). (Illus.). 144p. 1993. pap. 20.95 (0-944459-91-9) ECS Lrn Systs.

— TAAS Master Writing, Grade 10/Exit Level: Teacher's Handbook for Texas Assessment of Academic Skills. 112p. 1990. pap. text, teacher ed. 14.95 (0-944459-13-7) ECS Lrn Systs.

— TAAS Master Writing, Grades 4-5: Teacher's Handbook for Texas Assessment of Academic Skills. (Illus.). 128p. (Orig.). 1990. pap. text 15.95 (0-944459-10-2) ECS Lrn Systs.

— TAAS Quick Review Writing, Grade 9. 64p. 1991. pap. text 9.95 (0-944459-29-3) ECS Lrn Systs.

— TAAS Quick Review Writing, Grade 7. 64p. 1991. pap. text 9.95 (0-944459-28-5) ECS Lrn Systs.

***Mammen, Lori.** TestSMART for Reading Skills & Comprehension - Grade 3: Help for Basic Reading Skills, State Competency Tests, Achievement Tests. Sullivan, Jennifer, ed. (Illus.). 128p. (J). (gr. 3). 1999. pap., wbk. ed. 16.95 (1-57022-198-7, ECS1987) ECS Lrn Systs.

— TestSMART for Reading Skills & Comprehension - Grade 4: Help for Basic Reading Skills, State Competency Tests, Achievement Tests. Sullivan, Jennifer, ed. (Illus.). 128p. (J). (gr. 4). 1999. pap., wbk. ed. 16.95 (1-57022-199-5, ECS1995) ECS Lrn Systs.

— TestSMART for Reading Skills & Comprehension - Grade 5: Help for Basic Reading Skills, State Competency Tests, Achievement Tests. Sullivan, Jennifer, ed. (Illus.). 128p. (J). (gr. 5). 1999. pap., wbk. ed. 16.95 (1-57022-200-2, ECS2002) ECS Lrn Systs.

— TestSMART for Reading Skills & Comprehension - Grade 6: Help for Basic Reading Skills, State Competency Tests, Achievement Tests. Sullivan, Jennifer, ed. (Illus.). 128p. (J). (gr. 6). 1999. pap., wbk. ed. 16.95 (1-57022-201-0, ECS2010) ECS Lrn Systs.

— TestSMART for Reading Skills & Comprehension - Grade 7: Help for Basic Reading Skills, State Competency Tests, Achievement Tests. Sullivan, Jennifer, ed. (Illus.). 128p. (YA). (gr. 7). 1999. pap., wbk. ed. 16.95 (1-57022-202-9, ECS2029) ECS Lrn Systs.

— TestSMART for Reading Skills & Comprehension - Grade 8: Help for Basic Reading Skills, State Competency Tests, Achievement Tests. Sullivan, Jennifer, ed. (Illus.). 128p. (J). (gr. 8). 1999. pap., wbk. ed. 16.95 (1-57022-203-7, ECS2037) ECS Lrn Systs.

— TestSMART MATH - Concepts, Grade 5. 2000. write for info. (1-57022-244-4) ECS Lrn Systs.

— TestSMART MATH - Concepts, Grade 4. 2000. write for info. (1-57022-242-8) ECS Lrn Systs.

— TestSMART MATH - Concepts, Grade 3. 2000. write for info. (1-57022-240-1) ECS Lrn Systs.

— TestSMART MATH - Operations & Problem Solving, Grade 3. 2000. write for info. (1-57022-241-X) ECS Lrn Systs.

— TestSMART MATH - Operations & Problem Solving, Grade 4. 2000. write for info. (1-57022-243-6) ECS Lrn Systs.

— TestSMART MATH - Operations & Problem Solving, Grade 5. 2000. write for info. (1-57022-245-2) ECS Lrn Systs.

— TestSMART Reading Grade 2. 2000. write for info. (1-57022-236-3) ECS Lrn Systs.

— Watsons Go to Birmingham, 1963. (J). 1999. 11.95 (1-58130-611-3); 9.95 (1-58130-610-5) Novel Units.

Mammen, Lori. Writing Warm-Ups. 80p. (J). (gr. k-6). 1989. pap. text 10.95 (0-944459-07-2) ECS Lrn Systs.

— Writing Warm-Ups. 80p. (YA). (gr. 7-12). 1989. pap. text 10.95 (0-944459-08-0) ECS Lrn Systs.

— Writing Warm-Ups Two K-6: Quick, Creative, & Challenging Writing Exercises. 80p. (J). (gr. k-6). 1992. pap. text 10.95 (0-944459-45-5) ECS Lrn Systs.

— Writing Warm-Ups Two 7-12: Quick, Creative, & Challenging Writing Exercises. 80p. (YA). (gr. 7-12). 1992. pap. text 10.95 (0-944459-46-3) ECS Lrn Systs.

Mammen, Lori, ed. TAAS Master Student Practice Book: Math, Exit Level. (Illus.). 144p. 1996. pap. text 20.95 (1-57022-093-X) ECS Lrn Systs.

— TAAS Master Student Practice Book: Math, Grade 3. (Illus.). 144p. 1996. pap. text 20.95 (1-57022-079-4, ECS0794) ECS Lrn Systs.

— TAAS Master Student Practice Book: Math, Grade 4. (Illus.). 128p. 1996. pap. text 19.95 (1-57022-081-6, ECS0816) ECS Lrn Systs.

— TAAS Master Student Practice Book: Math, Grade 5. (Illus.). 160p. 1996. pap. text 21.95 (1-57022-084-0, ECS0840) ECS Lrn Systs.

— TAAS Master Student Practice Book: Math, Grade 6. (Illus.). 144p. 1996. pap. text 20.95 (1-57022-086-7, ECS0867) ECS Lrn Systs.

— TAAS Master Student Practice Book: Math, Grade 7. (Illus.). 144p. 1996. pap. text 20.95 (1-57022-088-3, ECS0883) ECS Lrn Systs.

— TAAS Master Student Practice Book: Math, Grade 8. (Illus.). 144p. 1996. pap. text 20.95 (1-57022-090-5, ECS0905) ECS Lrn Systs.

— TAAS Master Student Practice Book: Reading, Exit Level. (Illus.). 96p. 1996. pap. text 17.95 (1-57022-094-8, ECS0948) ECS Lrn Systs.

— TAAS Master Student Practice Book: Reading, Grade 3. (Illus.). 96p. 1996. pap. text 17.95 (1-57022-080-8, ECS0808) ECS Lrn Systs.

— TAAS Master Student Practice Book: Reading, Grade 4. (Illus.). 96p. 1996. pap. text 17.95 (1-57022-082-4, ECS0824) ECS Lrn Systs.

— TAAS Master Student Practice Book: Reading, Grade 5. (Illus.). 96p. 1996. pap. text 17.95 (1-57022-085-9, ECS0859) ECS Lrn Systs.

— TAAS Master Student Practice Book: Reading, Grade 6. (Illus.). 96p. 1996. pap. text 17.95 (1-57022-087-5, ECS0875) ECS Lrn Systs.

— TAAS Master Student Practice Book: Reading, Grade 7. (Illus.). 96p. 1996. pap. text 17.95 (1-57022-089-1, ECS0891) ECS Lrn Systs.

— TAAS Master Student Practice Book: Reading, Grade 8. (Illus.). 96p. 1996. pap. text 17.95 (1-57022-091-3, ECS0913) ECS Lrn Systs.

— TAAS Master Student Practice Book: Writing, Exit Level. (Illus.). 112p. 1996. pap. text 18.95 (1-57022-095-6, ECS0956) ECS Lrn Systs.

— TAAS Master Student Practice Book: Writing, Grade 4. (Illus.). 112p. 1996. pap. text 18.95 (1-57022-083-2, ECS0832) ECS Lrn Systs.

— TAAS Master Student Practice Book: Writing, Grade 8. (Illus.). 112p. 1996. pap. text 18.95 (1-57022-092-1, ECS0921) ECS Lrn Systs.

Mammen, Lori, et al. TAAS Master Reading, Exit Level: Teacher's Handbook for Texas Assessment of Academic Skills. (Illus.). 112p. (Orig.). 1990. pap. text 14.95 (0-944459-23-4) ECS Lrn Systs.

Mammen, Lori, jt. auth. see Parker, Violette.

Mammen, Lori, ed. see Graft, Janine & McNamee, Daniel.

Mammen, Lori, ed. see McNamee, Daniel & Graft, Janine.

Mammen, Lori, ed. see Watson, Pat.

Mammen, P. M. Gandhian Utopia: Its Relevance & Justification. 1988. 12.50 (81-85195-09-9, Pub. by Minerva) S Asia.

Mammen, Sarah N., ed. see Coltman, Debbie.

Mammen, Suzanne K., jt. auth. see Watson, Pat.

Mammen, Thampy. India's Economic Prospects: A Macroeconomic & Econometric Analysis. (Economic Ideas Leading to the 21st Century Ser.: Vol. 4). 350p. 1998. 48.00 (981-02-3233-0) World Scientific Pub.

Mammerickx, Jacqueline, jt. auth. see Langseth, Marcus G.

Mammerickx, M., jt. ed. see Burny, A.

Mammitzsch, Ulrich H. Evolution of the Garbhadhatu Mandala. (C). 1991. 64.00 (81-85179-70-0, Pub. by Aditya Prakashan) S Asia.

Mammitzsch, Ulrich H., tr. see Huizinga, Johan.

Mammitzsch, Ulrich H., tr. see Seckel, Dietrich.

Mammitzsch, Volker & Schneeweiss, Hans, eds. Symposia Gausina Conference B: Statistical Sciences: Proceedings of the 2nd Gauss Symposium, Munich, Germany, August 2-7, 1993. (Symposia Gaussiana Ser.). x, 342p. (C). 1995. lib. bdg. 152.95 (3-11-014412-3) De Gruyter.

Mammo, Tirfe. The Paradox of Africa's Poverty. LC 97-46979. 321p. 1997. pap. 18.95 (1-56902-049-3) Red Sea Pr.

— The Paradox of Africa's Poverty: The Role of Indigenous Knowledge, Traditional Practices & Local Institutions - the Case of Ethiopia. LC 97-46979. 321p. 1997. 59.95 (1-56902-048-5) Red Sea Pr.

Mammone, Lisa E. & Moore, Jack. The Real Estate Inspection Book: A Guide to Self Home Inspection. (Illus.). 49p. (Orig.). 1995. pap. 6.95 (0-9648713-0-0) Kooba.

Mammone, Richard J. Computational Methods of Signal Recovery & Recognition. LC 91-31951. (Series in Telecommunications: No. 1794). 448p. 1992. 170.00 incl. disk (0-471-85384-4) Wiley.

Mammone, Richard J., ed. Artificial Neural Networks for Speech & Vision. LC 93-32966. 1993. mass mkt. 84.95 (0-412-54850-X, Chap & Hall NY) Chapman & Hall.

Mammone, Richard J., jt. ed. see Ramachandran, Ravi P.

Mamola, Claire Z. Japanese Women Writers in English Translation Vol. 2: An Annotated Bibliography. LC 89-1319. 480p. 1992. text 35.00 (0-8240-7077-1, H1317) Garland.

— Japanese Women's Fiction. (Literature Reference Ser.). 300p. Date not set. text 43.00 (0-8240-5168-8) Garland.

***Mamola, Karl C., ed.** Apparatus for Teaching Physics. 247p. 1998. pap. 34.00 (0-917853-90-3, OP-65) Am Assn Physics.

Mamone, Robert A., jt. auth. see Lee, William W.

Mamonova, Tatyana. Russian Women's Studies: Essays on Sexism in Soviet Culture. (Athene Ser.). (Illus.). 198p. 1988. text 45.00 (0-08-036482-9, Pergamon Pr); pap. text 17.95 (0-08-036481-0, Pergamon Pr) Elsevier.

An Asterisk (*) at the beginning of an entry indicates that the title is appearing for the first time.

— Russian Women's Studies: Essays on Sexism in the Soviet Culture. (Athene Ser.). 198p. (C). 1988. pap. text 18.95 (*0-8077-6210-5*) Tchrs Coll.

Mamonova, Tatyana, ed. Women & Russia: Feminist Writings from the Soviet Union. Park, Rebecca & Fitzpatrick, Catherine A., trs. LC 82-73963. 297p. reprint ed. pap. 92.10 (*0-7837-1386-X*, 204156200021) Bks Demand.

Mamonova, Tatyana & Folsom, Chandra N., contrib. by. Women's Glasnost Vs. Naglost: Stopping Russian Backlash. LC 93-15181. 208p. 1993. 57.95 (*0-89789-339-5*, H339, Bergin & Garvey); pap. 19.95 (*0-89789-340-9*, G340, Bergin & Garvey) Greenwood.

Mamoon, Muntassir & Ray, Jayanta K. Civil Society in Bangladesh: Resilience & Retreat. LC 96-901190. (C). 1996. 32.00 (*81-7102-047-X*, Pub. by Firma KLM) S Asia.

Mamorsky, Jeffrey D. Employee Benefits Handbook. 3rd ed. 1992. 129.00 (*0-7913-1069-8*) Warren Gorham & Lamont.

— Employee Benefits Law: Erisa & Beyond, 2 vols. 1100p. 1986. reprint ed. ring bd. 135.00 (*0-318-21430-X*, 00557) NY Law Pub.

— Health Care Benefits Handbook, 1. LC 97-209327. 600p. 1997. ring bd. 245.00 (*1-56706-408-6*, 642) Panel Pubs.

Mamorsky, Jeffrey D., ed. Employee Benefits Handbook. 3rd ed. 1991. text 142.00 (*0-685-69669-3*, EBH) Warren Gorham & Lamont.

— Journal of Compensation & Benefits. 137.00 (*0-685-69672-3*, JCB) Warren Gorham & Lamont.

Mamorsky, Jeffrey D., jt. ed. see Duva, Joseph W.

Mamourian, Arsene, tr. see Khrakhouni, Zareh.

Mamourian, Arsene, tr. see Mavian, Vahram.

***Mamula, Mark.** Immunology. 1999. pap. text 19.95 (*1-889325-40-6*) Fence Crk Pubng.

Mamulyan, A. English-Russian Comprehensive Law Dictionary. (ENG & RUS.). 389p. 1993. 95.00 (*0-614-00407-1*, 5874650016) Fr & Eur.

Mamut, Eden, jt. auth. see Bejan, Adrian.

Mamzic, Charles L., ed. Statistical Process Control. LC 94-9020. (Practical Guides for Measurement & Control Ser.). 325p. 1994. 145.00 (*1-55617-511-6*) ISA.

Man. From Manchuria to Tibet. LC 98-50150. 1998. 49.95 (*962-217-098-6*) Norton.

***Man, Kathy.** Chinese. 96p. 1999. pap. 12.95 (*0-7548-0261-2*) Anness Pub.

— Healthy Life: Low Fat Chinese. 96p. 2000. 12.95 (*1-84215-088-X*) Anness Pub.

Man, Abu B. Che, see Che Man, Abu B.

Man, Adrianus P. De, see Van Den Bosch, F. A. & De Man, Adrianus P.

Man, Ana, ed. see Freire, Paulo.

Man at Arms Magazine Staff. Man at Arms, 15-Year Index, 1979-1993. LC 94-78248. (Illus.). 117p. 1994. pap. 20.00 (*0-917218-66-3*) A Mowbray.

***Man, C. M. D. & Jones, Adrian.** Shelf-Life Evaluation of Foods. 2nd ed. LC 00-23883. 2000. write for info. (*0-8342-1782-1*) Aspen Pub.

Man-Cheong, Iona, tr. see Dao, Bei.

Man, Chik H. & Yuk, Ng L., eds. Chinese-English Dictionary. (Illus.). 624p. (C). pap. text 23.00 (*962-201-922-6*, Pub. by Chinese Univ) U of Mich Pr.

Man-ch'ing, Cheng. Cheng Man-ch'ing: Essays on Man & His Culture. Hennessy, Mark, tr. from CHI. LC 95-3877. 200p. (Orig.). (C). 1997. pap. 16.95 (*1-883319-26-9*) Frog Ltd CA.

— Cheng Man-ch'ing: Master of Five Excellences. Hennessy, Mark, tr. from CHI. LC 94-46661. (Illus.). 200p. 1995. pap. 16.95 (*1-883319-03-X*) Frog Ltd CA.

— Cheng Man-ch'ings Advanced T'ai-chi Form Instructions. 7th ed. Wile, Douglas, tr. from CHI. (Illus.). 162p. (Orig.). 1985. pap. 10.95 (*0-912059-03-6*) Sweet Ch I Pr.

— Lao Tzu: My Words Are Very Easy to Understand. 2nd ed. Gibbs, Tam & Huang, Juh-Hua, trs. (CHI & ENG.). 256p. 1981. pap. 16.95 (*0-913028-91-6*) North Atlantic.

— Master Cheng's New Method of T'ai Chi Self-Cultivation. Hennessy, Mark, tr. from CHI. LC 99-11813. 100p. 1999. pap. 11.95 (*1-883319-92-7*) Frog Ltd CA.

— T'ai Chi Ch'uan: A Simplified Method of Calisthenics for Health & Self Defense. T'seng, Beauson, tr. from CHI. (Illus.). 160p. (Orig.). 1981. pap. 11.95 (*0-913028-85-1*) North Atlantic.

Man-ch'ing, Cheng, et al. Cheng-Tzu's Thirteen Treatises on T'ai Chi Ch'uan. Inn, Martin & Jeng Lo, Benjamin P., trs. from CHI. LC 85-15218. (Illus.). 226p. 1985. 22.50 (*0-938190-45-8*) North Atlantic.

Man Chong Fung, tr. Be Perfect. 2nd ed. (CHI.). 160p. 1982. pap. write for info. (*0-941598-03-9*) Living Spring Pubns.

Man-Chung Han & Chu-Wan Kim. Sectional Human Anatomy: Correlated with CT & MRI. 3rd ed. (Illus.). 336p. 1995. 95.00 (*0-89640-279-7*) Igaku-Shoin.

Man, Daniel & Faye, L. C. The Art of Man: Faces of Plastic Surgery. rev. ed. (Illus.). 247p. 1998. pap. 29.95 (*0-9666345-1-9*) BeautyArt Pr.

Man, Dianne L., jt. auth. see Yap, Melaine.

Man, Eagle, jt. auth. see McGaa, Ed.

Man, Edward H. The Nicobar Islands & Their People. LC 77-86996. (Royal Anthropological Institute of Great Britain & Ireland. Publication Ser.). reprint ed. 55.00 (*0-404-16767-5*) AMS Pr.

Man, E.H. Nicobarase Vocabulary. 1858. 19.95 (*0-7859-9825-X*) Fr & Eur.

Man, Felix H. Graham Sutherland: The Graphic Work, 1922-1970. 234p. 1970. 125.00 (*1-55660-107-7*) A Wofsy Fine Arts.

Man Fong, C. F. Chan, see Chan Man Fong, C. F.

Man, Glenn. Radical Visions: American Film Renaissance, 1967-1976, 41. LC 94-3049. (Contributions in the Study of Popular Culture Ser.: No. 41). 232p. 1994. 57.95 (*0-313-29306-6*, Greenwood Pr) Greenwood.

Man-Jo, Kim, et al. The Kim Chee Cookbook. Rector, Gary, tr. (Illus.). 144p. 1999. 29.95 (*962-593-506-1*) Tuttle Pubng.

Man, John. Atlas of the Year 1000. 1999. 26.00 (*0-674-54187-1*) HUP.

— Battlefields Then & Now. LC 97-15920. 144p. 1997. 29.95 (*0-02-861986-2*) Macmillan.

Man, John. Berlin Blockade. LC 73-174218. (Illustrated History of the Violent Century. Politics in Action Ser.). (Illus.). 156p. 1973. write for info. (*0-345-03315-9*, Ballantine) Ballantine Pub Grp.

— The Birth of Our Planet. Douglas-Cooper, Helen & Reader's Digest Editors, eds. LC 99-13280. 1999. write for info. (*0-7621-0139-3*); write for info. (*0-276-42228-7*, Pub. by RD Assn) RD Assn.

Man, John. D-Day Atlas. 144p. 1994. 26.95 (*0-8160-3137-1*) Facts on File.

— Dinosaurs. 1988. 4.98 (*0-671-06145-3*) S&S Trade.

***Man, John.** Gobi: Tracking the Desert. LC 99-26761. (Illus.). 232p. 1999. 24.95 (*0-300-07609-6*) Yale U Pr.

***Man, John & Newark, Tim.** Battlefields: Then & Now. (Illus.). 144p. 1999. reprint ed. text 30.00 (*0-7881-6576-3*) DIANE Pub.

Man, John, et al. The Traveler's Atlas: A Global Guide to the Places You Must See in a Lifetime. Rodgers, Nigel, ed. LC 98-5885. (Illus.). 224p. 1998. 29.95 (*0-7641-5121-5*) Barron.

Man, John, ed. see Defoe, Daniel.

Man-jung Mignon Chan. Industrial Policy in the PRC: Changing Patterns of Production & Distribution. 208p. (C). 1989. pap. text. write for info. (*0-8133-7707-2*) Westview.

Man, K. F., et al. Genetic Algorithms: Concepts & Designs. 2nd ed. Grimble, M. & Johnson, M., eds. LC 98-53817. (Advanced Textbooks in Control & Signal Processing Ser.). 350p. 1999. pap. 54.95 (*1-85233-072-4*) Spr-Verlag.

— Genetic Algorithms for Control & Signal Processing, Vol. XX. LC 96-37094. (Advances in Industrial Control Ser.). (Illus.). 211p. 1996. 69.95 (*3-540-76101-2*) Spr-Verlag.

Man, K. W. Contact Mechanics Using Boundary Elements. LC 94-72216. (Topics in Engineering Ser.: Vol. 22). 200p. 1994. 95.00 (*1-56252-258-2*, 334X) Computational Mech MA.

Man-Kit, Dominic, jt. ed. see Shapley, Robert.

Man-Kong, Mary. Emily Cleans Up. 1999. 4.99 (*0-375-80165-0*) Random.

***Man-Kong, Mary.** Hooray for Thomas! (Jellybean Books Just for Preschoolers). (Illus.). 24p. (J). (ps). 2000. 2.99 (*0-375-80275-4*, Pub. by Random Bks Yng Read) Random.

— Theodore & the Scary Cove. LC 99-35231. (Early Step into Reading Ser.). (Illus.). 32p. (J). (ps-k). 2000. pap. 3.99 (*0-375-80508-7*, Pub. by Random Bks Yng Read) Random.

— Theodore & the Scary Cove. (Early Step into Reading Ser.). (Illus.). 32p. (J). (ps-1). 2000. lib. bdg. 11.99 (*0-375-90508-1*, Pub. by Random Bks Yng Read) Random.

Man-Kong, Mary. Theodore & the Treasure Hunt. (Let's Go Lift & Peek Bks.). (Illus.). 7p. (J). (ps). 1999. 4.99 (*0-375-80086-7*, Pub. by Random Bks Yng Read) Random.

— Theodore & the Whale. LC 98-35243. (Pictureback Ser.). (J). 1998. pap. 3.25 (*0-679-89421-7*, Pub. by Random Bks Yng Read) Random.

— Theodore Jellybean: Theodore's Best Friend. (t). (J). 1999. lib. bdg. 7.99 (*0-679-99409-2*, Pub. by Random Bks Yng Read) Random.

***Man-Kong, Mary.** Theodore to the Rescue. (Illus.). 24p. (J). (ps). 2000. 2.99 (*0-375-80325-4*, Pub. by Random Bks Yng Read) Random.

Man-Kong, Mary. Theodore's Best Friend. 24p. (J). 1999. 1.99 (*0-679-89409-8*, Pub. by Random Bks Yng Read) Random.

— Theodore's Splash. 10p. (J). 1999. 4.99 (*0-679-89410-1*, Pub. by Random Bks Yng Read) Random.

***Man-Kong, Mary, ed.** Thomas' Busy Day. (Illus.). 6p. (J). (ps). 2000. bds. 2.99 (*0-375-80239-8*, Pub. by Random Bks Yng Read) Random.

Man, Nguyen-Khoa, et al. Long-Term Hemodialysis. LC 95-14248. 148p. (C). 1995. text 81.00 (*0-7923-3477-9*) Kluwer Academic.

Man-Sik, Chae. Peace under Heaven: A Modern Korean Novel. Kyung-Ja, Chun, tr. from KOR. LC 92-31807. 272p. (C). 1993. pap. text 24.95 (*1-56324-172-2*, East Gate Bk) M E Sharpe.

Man-Tu Lee, Anthony. The Japanese Tea Ceremony: Explore the Mysteries & Traditions of the Ancient Japanese Tea Ceremony. (Illus.). 96p. 1999. text 29.95 (*1-86204-590-9*, Pub. by Element MA) Penguin Putnam.

Mana. Biopsychology. 4th ed. 1999. pap. text, student ed. 16.00 (*0-205-28993-2*) Allyn.

***Manaay, Sol M.** The Elfin Princess. (J). (gr. k-2). 2000. pap. 5.95 (*0-533-13492-7*) Vantage.

Manabe, Johji. Appleseed Data Book, Bk. 1. (Illus.). 128p. 1995. pap. 12.95 (*1-56971-103-8*) Dark Horse Comics.

— Caravan Kidd, 1. (Caravan Kidd Ser.). 1997. pap. 19.95 (*1-56971-260-3*) Dark Horse Comics.

— Outlanders, Bk. 4. (Illus.). 168p. 1995. pap. 12.95 (*1-56971-069-4*) Dark Horse Comics.

— Outlanders, Vol. 3. (Illus.). 160p. 1994. pap. 13.95 (*1-56971-011-2*) Dark Horse Comics.

— Outlanders, Vol. 5. (Illus.). 1998. pap. 14.95 (*1-56971-275-1*) Dark Horse Comics.

***Manabe, Von Johji.** Drakuun. 1999. 12.95 (*1-56971-302-2*) Dark Horse Comics.

Manach, Jorge. La Crisis de la Alta Cultura en Cuba: Indagacion del Choteo. (Coleccion Cuba y sus Jueces). (SPA.). 96p. 1991. reprint ed. pap. 9.95 (*0-89729-606-0*) Ediciones.

— Marti: Apostle of Freedom. (Illus.). 9.50 (*0-8159-6201-0*) Devin.

— Marti el Apostol. (SPA.). 248p. 1998. reprint ed. pap. 12.00 (*84-239-0252-8*, Pub. by Espasa Calpe) IBD Ltd.

— Teoria de la Frontera. 171p. 1970. 3.00 (*0-8477-2412-3*) U of PR Pr.

Manachino, Albert J. Dark Bible. (Willie Button Stories Ser.). 12p. (Orig.). 1985. pap. 2.50 (*0-9634181-1-4*) Argo Pr.

— Noctet: Tales of Madonna-Moloch. (Illus.). 200p. (Orig.). 1997. pap. 14.95 (*0-9634181-3-0*) Argo Pr.

Manachino, Albert J., jt. auth. see Ambrose, Michael.

Managaro, Gabriele. Cellular Neural Networks. LC 98-45460. 1998. 74.95 (*3-540-65202-7*) Spr-Verlag.

Management Accounting Practices Committee. Accounting for Software Used Internally. (Issues Paper). 24p. 1985. pap. 20.00 (*0-86641-122-4*, 85178) Inst Mgmt Account.

***Management Advisory Service Consulting Staff.** How to Prepare Service Level Agreements for Application Service Provisioning. Kuong, J. F., ed. (Information Technologies Management, Control & Security Ser.). (Illus.). 110p. 2000. ring bd. 175.00 (*0-940706-45-8*) Management Advisory Pubns.

Management Analysis Center, Inc. Staff. Implementing Strategy: Making Strategy Happen. Stonich, Paul J., ed. LC 82-1667. 200p. 1985. pap. 18.95 (*0-88730-062-6*, HarpBusn) HarpInfo.

Management Development Centre of Hong Kong. Hong Kong Management Cases in Hotel Management. LC 97-160900. 123p. 1996. 26.95 (*962-201-734-7*, Pub. by Chinese Univ) U of Mich Pr.

***Management Development Centre of Hong Kong Staff, ed.** Business English & Communication. 140p. 1999. pap. 24.95 (*962-201-842-4*, Pub. by Chinese Univ) U of Mich Pr.

Management Development Centre of Hong Kong Staff, ed. Hong Kong Management Cases in Human Resources Management. LC 98-180623. 120p. 1998. pap. text 24.95 (*962-201-740-1*, Pub. by Chinese Univ) U of Mich Pr.

Management Development Centre Staff, ed. Hong Kong Management Cases in Information Systems Management. LC 97-154181. 1997. pap. text 26.95 (*962-201-756-8*, Pub. by Chinese Univ) U of Mich Pr.

— Hong Kong Management Cases in Marketing. LC 97-160896. 1997. pap. text 26.95 (*962-201-724-X*, Pub. by Chinese Univ) U of Mich Pr.

Management Information Systems Staff. Management Information Systems in Higher Education: The State of the Art. Johnson, Charles B. & Katzenmeyer, William G., eds. LC 74-109171. 215p. reprint ed. pap. 66.70 (*0-608-15072-X*, 202620600048) Bks Demand.

Management of an Accounting Practice Committee, Am. Human Resources. LC 94-17000. (Management Ser.). 1994. 17.00 (*0-87051-151-3*) Am Inst CPA.

Management Resources Staff. Company Policy Manual Binder: A Complete Guide to Legal & Effective Company Policies. 1990. 79.95 (*0-88730-475-3*, HarpBusn) HarpInfo.

Management Roundtable, Inc. Staff. CAD-CAM Manager's Complete Anthology. (Illus.). 176p. (Orig.). 1987. per. 75.00 (*0-932007-11-2*, B54) Mgmt Roundtable.

Management Roundtable, Inc. Staff, ed. CAD-CAM Databases: Implementation & Planning Strategies. (Illus.). 350p. 1986. spiral bd. 295.00 (*0-932007-08-2*, B00045) Mgmt Roundtable.

Management Sciences for Health Staff. Managing Drug Supply: The Selection, Procurement, Distribution, & Use of Pharmaceuticals. 2nd expanded rev. ed. LC 96-42268. (Books on International Development). (Illus.). 832p. 1997. pap. 84.95 (*1-56549-047-9*) Kumarian Pr.

Management Studies Program Staff. Alternative Structures for the United States Trustee Program. 120p. (Orig.). 1995. pap. 15.00 (*0-9646874-8-8*) Nat Acad Public Admin.

***Managers Edge Editors.** Moving Up: A Blueprint for Planning Your Entry into the Executive Suite. 8p. 1999. pap. 5.00 (*1-878604-31-7*) Briefings Pub Grp.

— The Successful Managers Guide Giving & Receiving Feedback. 32p. 1999. pap. 12.50 (*1-878604-30-9*) Briefings Pub Grp.

Managing Automation Group Staff. 1996 MES Directory Vols. 1 & 2: Manufacturing Execution Systems. 2nd ed. Greene, Alice H., ed. (Illus.). 1500p. 1996. 125.00 incl. cd-rom (*1-882554-05-1*) Thomas Pub NY.

Manahan. General Applied Chemistry. (Chemistry Ser.). Date not set. 20.75 (*0-87150-723-4*) PWS Pubs.

Manahan, Liala, jt. auth. see Lawless, Richard.

Manahan, Michael P., jt. auth. see Siewert, T. A.

Manahan, Nancy, jt. auth. see Curb, Rosemary.

Manahan, Stanley E. Environmental Chemistry. 5th ed. 600p. 1991. lib. bdg. 65.00 (*0-87371-425-3*, L425) Lewis Pubs.

— Environmental Chemistry. 6th ed. 832p. (C). 1994. boxed set 75.00 (*1-56670-088-4*, L1088) Lewis Pubs.

— Environmental Chemistry. 6th ed. 101p. 1995. lib. bdg., lab manual ed. write for info. (*1-56670-187-2*) Lewis Pubs.

***Manahan, Stanley E.** Environmental Chemistry. 7th ed. LC 99-47521. 1999. 79.95 (*1-56670-492-8*) Lewis Pubs.

Manahan, Stanley E. Environmental Science & Technology. LC 97-306. 576p. 1997. lib. bdg. 55.00 (*1-56670-213-5*) Lewis Pubs.

— Fundamentals of Environmental Chemistry. 864p. 1993. lib. bdg. 65.00 (*0-87371-587-X*, L587) Lewis Pubs.

***Manahan, Stanley E.** Fundamentals of Environmental Chemistry. 2nd ed. LC 00-42128. 2000. write for info. (*1-56670-491-X*) Lewis Pubs.

Manahan, Stanley E. Hazardous Waste Chemistry: Toxicology & Treatment. 392p. 1990. lib. bdg. 99.95 (*0-87371-209-9*, L209) Lewis Pubs.

***Manahan, Stanley E.** Industrial Ecology. LC 98-49415. 325p. 1999. 69.95 (*1-56670-381-6*) Lewis Pubs.

Manahan, Stanley E. Toxicological Chemistry: A Guide to Toxic Substances in Chemistry. (Illus.). 310p. 1988. lib. bdg. 76.00 (*0-87371-149-1*, RA1219) Lewis Pubs.

— Toxicological Chemistry: A Guide to Toxic Substances in Chemistry. 2nd ed. (Illus.). 464p. 1992. lib. bdg. 79.95 (*0-87371-621-3*, L621) Lewis Pubs.

Manahan, Stanley E., jt. auth. see Martin, R. Scott.

Manak, Frank C. American Freedom: The Fight for People's Rights from Colonia Petitions to Modern Courtrooms. Brooke, Cheryl, ed. LC 95-60858. (Illus.). 960p. 1998. 39.95 (*0-9666508-0-8*) QuidPro Pubg.

Manaka, Yoshio. Chinese Massage: Quick & Easy. 7.95 (*0-685-70676-1*) Wehman.

Manaka, Yoshio, et al. Chasing the Dragon's Tail: Theory & Practice of Acupuncture in the Work of Yoshio Manaka. LC 95-10827. 453p. 1995. text 53.00 (*0-912111-32-1*) Paradigm Publns.

— Chasing the Dragon's Tail: Theory & Practice of Acupuncture in the Work of Yoshio Manaka. 453p. 1996. text 60.00 (*0-912111-53-4*) Paradigm Publns.

— The Layman's Guide to Acupuncture. LC 72-78590. (Illus.). 144p. 1972. 12.50 (*0-8348-0072-1*); pap. 10.95 (*0-8348-0107-8*) Weatherhill.

Manakee, Harold R. Indians of Early Maryland. 1998. pap. 6.00 (*0-938420-40-2*) MD Hist.

Manaker, George H. Interior Plantscapes. 3rd ed. 352p. (C). 1996. 95.00 (*0-13-238494-9*) P-H.

Manaktala. Smart Practice Development. LC 95-231677. 192p. 1995. pap. 27.00 (*0-8080-0058-6*) CCH INC.

***Manalansan, Martin F., IV, ed.** Cultural Compass: Ethnographic Explorations of Asian America. (Asian American History & Culture Ser.). (Illus.). 272p. 2000. 69.50 (*1-56639-772-3*); pap. 22.95 (*1-56639-773-1*) Temple U Pr.

***Manalo, Ricky.** Beyond the Days: Choral Book. 125p. 1998. pap. 8.95 (*1-57992-022-5*) OR Catholic.

Manamon, James, jt. ed. see Kiemen, Mathias C.

Manamura, Robert. Asian Roots, Western Soil: Japanese Influences in American Culture. Schildgen, Robert D., ed. (Illus.). 32p. (Orig.). 1993. pap. 5.99 (*0-942744-02-0*) Berkeley Art.

***Manandhar, N. P.** Public Enterprise & Privatization. 1998. pap. 25.00 (*0-7855-7627-4*) St Mut.

Manandhar, N. P., ed. Medicinal Plants of Nepal Himalaya. 87p. (C). 1980. 75.00 (*0-89771-096-7*, Pub. by Ratna Pustak Bhandar) St Mut.

Manandise, Esmeralda. Evidence from Basque for a New Theory of Grammar. (Linguistics Ser.). 384p. 1988. text 15.00 (*0-8240-5191-2*) Garland.

Mananzan, Mary J., et al, eds. Women Resisting Violence: Spirituality for Life. LC 96-22683. 192p. (Orig.). 1996. pap. 16.00 (*1-57075-080-7*) Orbis Bks.

Manara, Milo. Art of Spanking. Bell, Elisabeth, tr. from FRE. 96p. 1993. pap. 17.95 (*1-56163-090-X*, Eurotica) NBM.

— Butterscotch, Vol. 1. 64p. (Orig.). 1994. pap. 12.95 (*1-56163-109-4*, Eurotica) NBM.

— Butterscotch, Vol. 2. (Illus.). 48p. (Orig.). 1996. pap. 10.95 (*1-56163-158-2*, Eurotica) NBM.

— Click, Vol. 3. LC 99-169795. (Illus.). 72p. 1998. pap. 12.95 (*1-56163-210-4*) NBM.

— Click One. Leighton, Tom, tr. from ITA. 48p. 1993. pap. 10.95 (*1-56163-084-5*, Eurotica) NBM.

— Click Two. Huntley, Michael, tr. from ITA. 72p. 1993. pap. 12.95 (*1-56163-062-4*, Eurotica) NBM.

— Gullivera. (Illus.). 72p. 1996. pap. 13.95 (*1-56163-170-1*, Eurotica) NBM.

— Hidden Camera. 48p. (Orig.). 1994. pap. 10.95 (*1-56163-114-0*, Eurotica) NBM.

— Manara's Kama Sutra. Johnson, Joe, tr. from FRE. LC 98-193978. (Illus.). 67p. 1998. pap. 12.95 (*1-56163-206-6*, Eurotica) NBM.

— To See the Stars. Johnson, Joe, tr. from FRE. LC 99-169538. (Illus.). 64p. 1998. pap. 13.95 (*1-56163-203-1*, Eurotica) NBM.

***Manara, Milo.** Women of Manara. (Illus.). 1998. 16.95 (*1-882931-42-4*) Heavy Metal Magazine.

— WWW. (Illus.). 48p. 1999. pap. 10.95 (*1-56163-249-X*, Eurotica) NBM.

Manara, Milo & Pratt, Hugo. Indian Summer. 152p. 1994. pap. 21.95 (*1-56163-107-8*, Comics Lit) NBM.

Manarchy, Dennis. En Passant: Black & White Photographs by Dennis Manarchy. (Illus.). 120p. 1998. text. write for info. (*0-9664545-0-2*) Physiognomy Pr.

Manard, Barbara & Perone, Christopher. Hospice Care: An Introduction & Review of the Evidence. 40p. 1994. 10.50 (*0-931207-23-1*) Natl Hospice.

Manari, Hiroshi, jt. auth. see Marsh, Robert M.

Manarin, Louis H. Fifteenth Virginia Infantry. (Virginia Regimental Histories Ser.). (Illus.). 125p. 1990. 19.95 (*0-930919-95-5*) H E Howard.

Manarin, Louis H., ed. Confederate Veteran Index, 3 vols. Set. 1990. 300.00 (*0-916107-15-9*) Broadfoot.

Manarin, Louis H. & Dowdey, Clifford. The History of Henrico County. LC 84-7323. (Illus.). 581p. reprint ed. pap. 180.20 (*0-7837-1924-8*, 204213900001) Bks Demand.

Manarin, Louis H. & Wallace, Lee A., Jr. Richmond Volunteers: The Volunteer Companies of the City of Richmond & Henrico County, Virginia, 1861-1865. LC 72-100103. 312p. reprint ed. pap. 96.80 (*0-8357-9815-1*, 201463200093) Bks Demand.

Manarin, Louis H., jt. ed. see Dowdey, Clifford.

M

An Asterisk (*) at the beginning of an entry indicates that the title is appearing for the first time.

***Manary, Adria.** Mommy Magic: 450 Ways to Nurture Your Child. LC 99-96512. 221p. 2000. pap. 12.95 (*0-9665830-2-7*, Pub. by Angel Power Pr) ACCESS Pubs Network.

Manary, Adria H., jt. auth. see Burnett, Catherine M.

Manas-Zloczower, Ica & Tadmor, Zehev, eds. Mixing & Compounding of Polymers: Theory & Practice. LC 93-33468. (Progress in Polymer Processing Ser.). 982p. 1993. 179.00 (*1-56990-156-2*) Hanser-Gardner.

Manasek, F. J. Uncommon Values: A Rare Book Dealer's World. 148p. 1995. 20.00 (*1-883817-02-1*) Anglers & Scholars.

Manasek, Francis J. Collecting Old Maps. (Illus.). 328p. 1998. 65.00 (*0-9649000-6-8*, T Nova Pr) G.B Manasek.

Manasevit, Leigh, et al. Opportunities & Challenges: An Administrator's Guide to the New IDEA. O'Neil, Ginger R., ed. LC 97-74687. 205p. 1997. pap. 39.95 (*0-87652-230-4*, 760) Am Assn Sch Admin.

Manasevit, Leigh M. & Cowan, Kristen T. Great Expectations: Understanding the New Title I. 195p. 1995. 35.95 (*0-87652-218-5*, 021-0503) Am Assn Sch Admin.

Manasi, Mark, et al. Inside MS-DOS 6.22. 3rd ed. LC 94-35118. (Illus.). 1632p. (Orig.). 1994. pap. 39.99 (*1-56205-414-7*) New Riders Pub.

Manasian, N. English-Russian Frequency Glossary of Quantum Generators. 272p. (C). 1983. 90.00 (*0-7855-6460-8*, Pub. by Collets) St Mut.

Manasreh, M. O. Semiconductor Quantum Wells & Superlattices for Long-Wavelength Infrared Detectors. LC 92-32246. (Materials Ser.). 265p. (C). 1992. text 10.00 (*0-89006-603-5*) Artech Hse.

Manasreh, M. O., ed. Antimonide-Related Strained-Layer Heterostructures. (Optoelectronic Properties of Semiconducter Ser.: Vol. 3). 501p. 1997. text 81.00 (*90-5699-544-8*) Gordon & Breach.

— Strained-Layer Quantum Wells & Their Applications. (Optoelectronic Properties of Semiconducter Ser.: Vol. 4). 578p. 1997. text 91.00 (*90-5699-567-7*) Gordon & Breach.

Manasreh, M. O., et al, eds. Infrared Applications of Semiconductors--Materials, Processing & Devices. LC 97-3671. (Materials Research Society Symposium Proceedings Ser.: No. 450). 485p. 1997. text 75.00 (*1-55899-354-1*) Materials Res.

Manassas Museum Systems Staff, jt. auth. see Mulvaney, Kathleen.

Manasse, A. Lorri & Schoeppler, Claire. A Banker's Guide to Better Service, Bigger Profits. 1989. pap. 49.95 (*1-55840-053-2*) Exec Ent Pubns.

Manassen-Mori, Charlotte. Sayonara My Friend Love Annie. (Illus.). 247p. 1994. 22.50 (*0-85572-239-8*) Seven Hills Bk.

Manassewitsch. Frequency Synthesizers: Theory & Design. 3rd ed. 624p. 1997. text 110.00 (*0-471-13793-6*) Wiley.

Manassewitsch, Vadim. Frequency Synthesizers: Theory & Design. 3rd ed. LC 86-18968. 624p. 1987. 155.00 (*0-471-01116-9*) Wiley.

***Manassiev, N. & Whitehead, M.** Female Reproductive Health. (Illus.). 300p. 2001. 79.00 (*1-85070-491-0*) Prthnon Pub.

Manassis, Katharine. Keys to Parenting Your Anxious Child. LC 95-40440. (Parenting Keys Ser.). 180'p. 1996. pap. 6.95 (*0-8120-9605-3*) Barron.

***Manaster.** Musculoskeletl Imaging: The Requisite. 2nd ed. 2001. text. write for info. (*0-323-01189-6*) Mosby Inc.

Manaster & Selmi, Daniel P. CA Environmental Law, 6 vols., Set. 1989. 620.00 (*0-8205-1102-1*) Bender.

Manaster, Benjamin. Skyla, Caso, Adolfo, ed. LC 94-43023. 246p. 1995. 21.95 (*0-8283-2002-0*) Branden Bks.

Manaster, Guy J. & Corsini, Raymond J. Individual Psychology: Theory & Practice. LC 81-82887. 322p. 1982. pap. 19.95 (*0-87581-274-0*) Adler Sch Prof Psy.

Manaster, Jane. Horned Lizards. LC 96-25203. (Corrie Herring Hooks Ser.). (Illus.). 101p. 1997. 17.95 (*0-292-75177-X*) U of Tex Pr.

— The Pecan Tree. LC 93-49563. (Corrie Herring Hooks Ser.: No. 27). (Illus.). 112p. 1994. 17.95 (*0-292-75153-2*) U of Tex Pr.

***Manaster, Kenneth A.** Environmental Protection & Justice. 2nd ed. (C). 2000. pap. text. write for info. (*1-58360-762-5*) Anderson Pub Co.

Manaster, Kenneth A. Environmental Protection & Justice: Readings & Commentary on Environmental Law & Practice. LC 95-7757. 239p. 1995. pap. 29.00 (*0-87084-253-6*) Anderson Pub Co.

Manaster, Kenneth A., jt. auth. see Selmi, Daniel P.

Manaster-Ramer, Alexis, ed. Mathematics of Language: Proceedings of a Conference Held at the University of Michigan, Ann Arbor, October, 1984. LC 87-9183. ix, 401p. (C). 1988. 83.00 (*1-55619-032-8*) J Benjamins Pubng Co.

Manaster, Robert A., ed. see Daldorph, Brian.

Manat, G. P., ed. Guide to Books on Black Americans. (Illus.). 454p. 1994. text 145.00 (*1-56072-174-X*) Nova Sci Pubs.

— Politics & Economics of the Soviet Union: An Annotated Bibliography. 82p. (C). 1992. pap. text 95.00 (*1-56072-048-4*) Nova Sci Pubs.

Manatt. GED Social Studies Exercise Book. (YA - Adult Education Ser.). 1995. pap. 6.95 (*0-538-71136-1*) S-W Pub.

Manatt, Katherine K. Before the Baby Boomers: A Southwest Family's Story. (Illus.). 141p. (Orig.). 1997. pap. 10.95 (*0-9648638-3-9*) T Berryhill.

Manatt, Kathleen G., jt. auth. see Salit, Vivian L.

Manatt, Marsha. Parents, Peers, & Pot II: Parents in Action. 160p. (Orig.). 1996. reprint ed. pap. text 25.00 (*0-7881-3091-9*) DIANE Pub.

Manatt, Richard. When Right Is Wrong: Fundamentalists & the Public Schools. LC 94-61497. 150p. 1994. pap. text 24.95 (*1-56676-222-7*) Scarecrow.

Manaugh, Melanie, ed. see Kiefer, Joseph & Kemple, Martin.

Manber, Beverly, ed. see Antonini, Orlando.

Manber, Beverly, ed. see Bivins, Betty.

Manber, Beverly, ed. see Brock, Susan L.

Manber, Beverly, ed. see Brounstein, Marty.

Manber, Beverly, ed. see Chapman, Elwood N.

Manber, Beverly, ed. see Davidson, E.

Manber, Beverly, ed. see Dickey, Terry.

Manber, Beverly, ed. see Gerson, Richard F.

Manber, Beverly, ed. see Gill, J.

Manber, Beverly, ed. see Goman, Carol K.

Manber, Beverly, ed. see Harrison, L.

Manber, Beverly, ed. see Karlson, David.

Manber, Beverly, ed. see Lickson, Charles P.

Manber, Beverly, ed. see Liljenstolpe, Carl & Burke, Mary A.

Manber, Beverly, ed. see Mahoney, Marci.

Manber, Beverly, ed. see McArdle, Geri.

Manber, Beverly, ed. see Scott, Dru.

Manber, Beverly, ed. see Sitterly, Connie.

Manber, Beverly, ed. see Visconti, R.

Manber, David. Zachary of the Wings. 88p. (YA). (gr. 9-12). 1993. lib. bdg. 10.95 (*1-879567-27-X*) Wonder Well.

Manber, Udi. Introduction to Algorithms: A Creative Approach. (Illus.). 478p. (C). 1989. 51.00 (*0-201-12037-2*) Addison-Wesley.

Manber, Udi & Baeza-Yates, Ricardo A., eds. Computer Science: Research & Applications. (Illus.). 498p. (C). 1992. 156.00 (*0-306-44223-X*, Plenum Trade) Perseus Pubng.

Manby, Thomas. Journal of the Voyages of the H. M. S. Discovery & Chatham. 230p. 1998. 32.50 (*0-87770-459-7*) Ye Galleon.

Manca, Alessandra, jt. ed. see Manca, Luigi.

Manca, John & Cosgrove, Vincent. Tin for Sale. 320p. 1993. reprint ed. mass mkt. 4.99 (*0-380-71034-X*, Avon Bks) Morrow Avon.

***Manca, Joseph.** Cosme Tura: The Life & Art of a Painter in Estense Ferrara. (Illus.). 288p. 2000. 125.00 (*0-19-817424-1*) OUP.

Manca, Joseph, ed. Titian 500. 1994. 70.00 (*0-300-07712-2*) Yale U Pr.

Manca, Luigi & Manca, Alessandra, eds. Gender & Utopia in Advertising: A Critical Reader. 1995. 16.95 (*0-8156-8119-4*) Syracuse U Pr.

Mancall, ed. Envisioning America: English Plans for the Colonization of North America, 1580-1640. (Illus.). 208p. 1995. text 45.00 (*0-312-12252-7*) St Martin.

Mancall, Elliott L., et al, eds. Computer-Based Examinations for Board Certification. LC 96-86080. (Illus.). 212p. 1996. 44.95 (*0-934277-22-2*) Am Bd Med Spec.

Mancall, Elliott L. & Bashook, Philip G., eds. Assessing Clinical Reasoning: The Oral Examination & Alternative Methods. LC 95-79294. 224p. 1995. lib. bdg. 44.95 (*0-934277-21-4*) Am Bd Med Spec.

— Recertification: New Evaluation Methods & Strategies. LC 94-70217. 195p. 1994. lib. bdg. 44.95 (*0-934277-19-2*) Am Bd Med Spec.

Mancall, Mark. Russia & China: Their Diplomatic Relations to 1728. LC 74-85077. (Harvard East Asian Ser.: No. 61). 412p. reprint ed. pap. 127.80 (*0-608-17493-9*, 202999300067) Bks Demand.

Mancall, Peter C. Deadly Medicine: Indians & Alcohol in Early America. (Illus.). 296p. 1995. text 37.50 (*0-8014-2762-2*) Cornell U Pr.

— Deadly Medicine: Indians & Alcohol in Early America. (Illus.). 296p. 1996. pap. text 15.95 (*0-8014-8044-2*) Cornell U Pr.

— Envisioning America: English Plans for Colonies in North America 1580-1640. 192p. 1995. pap. 12.95 (*0-312-09670-4*) St Martin.

— Valley of Opportunity: Economic Culture along the Upper Susquhanna, 1700-1800. LC 90-55719. (Illus.). 253p. 1991. text 35.00 (*0-8014-2503-4*) Cornell U Pr.

Mancall, Peter C., ed. Land of Rivers: American in Word & Image. (Illus.). 224p. 1996. text 35.00 (*0-8014-3105-0*) Cornell U Pr.

***Mancall, Peter C. & Merrell, James H., eds.** American Encounters: Natives & Newcomers from European Contact to Indian Removal, 1500-1850. LC 99-28708. 646p. 1999. pap. 24.99 (*0-415-92375-1*) Routledge.

***Mancall, Peter C. & Merrell, James Hart, eds.** American Encounters: Natives & Newcomers from European Contact to Indian Removal, 1500-1850. LC 99-28708. 646p. 1999. text 80.00 (*0-415-92374-3*) Routledge.

***Mancarello, Wendy Black.** His Sister, Her Brother. (Illus.). 16p. (J). (ps). 1999. 5.95 (*1-891846-08-6*) Busn Word.

Mance, Azell. How to Buy a Car Without Getting Cheated. LC 92-60561. (Illus.). 208p. (Orig.). 1993. pap. 29.95 (*0-9633258-0-9*) Share The Know.

Mance, Brett. Cruise Ship Employment Guide. Mance, Eric, ed. (Illus.). 28p. (Orig.). 1996. pap. 14.95 (*1-880836-13-0*) Pine Isl Pr.

— Cruise Ship Employment Guide. 4th rev. ed. Mance, Eric, ed. 88p. (Orig.). 1997. pap. 14.95 (*0-9657172-0-8*) Tropical Dest.

— Cruise Ship Employment Guide. 5th ed. Mance, Eric, ed. (Illus.). (Orig.). 1999. pap. 14.95 (*0-9657172-1-6*) Tropical Dest.

Mance, Eric, ed. see Mance, Brett.

Mance, Ginger. I Say a Prayer for You Black Men. LC 95-95129. 50p. 1996. pap. 7.00 (*0-88378-163-8*) Third World.

Mance, Lora S. La, see Stowe, A. A. & La Mance, Lora S.

Mancebo, Manuel R. El Domino Azul. LC 80-66398. (Coleccion Caniqui). (SPA.). 146p. (Orig.). 1982. pap. 7.95 (*0-89729-259-6*) Ediciones.

Mancebo, pseud. Cecil, the Nearsighted Dragon. (Illus.). 32p. (J). (ps-3). 1998. pap. 14.95 (*0-9626993-4-9*) Armadillo Niche.

— Villa Sara. LC 90-62235. 240p. (Orig.). 1990. 16.95 (*0-9626993-1-4*) Armadillo Niche.

Mancer, Clifford J. Guide to New Zealand Estate Planning & Tax. 297p. 1994. pap. 30.00 (*0-455-21263-5*, Pub. by LawBk Co) Gaunt.

— Taxation Questions. vii, 122p. 1990. pap. 21.00 (*0-455-21005-5*, Pub. by LawBk Co) Gaunt.

Manceron, Anne. Revolution Francais Dictionnaire General. (FRE.). 385p. 1989. 75.00 (*0-7859-8189-6*, 2877420329) Fr & Eur.

Manceron, Claude. The Age of the French Revolution Vol. 1: Twilight of the Old Order (1774-1778) 1989. 14.95 (*0-318-41868-1*, Touchstone) S&S Trade Pap.

— Revolution Francaise, Dictionnaire Biographique. (FRE.). 571p. 1989. 95.00 (*0-7859-8188-8*, 2877420086) Fr & Eur.

Manch, Susan G., jt. auth. see Pennington Shannon, Marcia.

Manchanda, S. C., jt. auth. see Shabbir, Mahammod.

Manchao, Cheng. The Origin of Chinese Deities. 240p. 1995. 9.95 (*7-119-00030-6*, Pub. by Foreign Lang) China Bks.

***Manchee, William.** Second Chair: A Stan Turner Mystery. (Stan Turner Mysteries Ser.: Vol. 3). 451p. 2000. 14.95 (*0-9666366-9-4*, Pub. by Top Pubns) Herveys Bklink.

— Twice Tempted. LC 99-65462. 247p. 1999. pap. 17.95 (*0-9666366-5-1*) iUniversecom.

Manchee, William L. Brash Endeavor. 288p. 1998. pap. 12.95 (*1-884570-89-5*) Research Triangle.

***Manchee, William L.** Death Pact: A Romantic Mystery. 277p. 1999. 19.95 (*0-9666366-3-5*, Pub. by Top Pubns) Herveys Bklink.

Manchel, Frank. Film Study: A Resource Guide. LC 72-3262. 422p. 1973. 27.50 (*0-8386-1225-3*) Fairleigh Dickinson.

— Film Study Vol. 1: An Analytical Bibliography, 4 vols. enl. rev. ed. LC 85-45026. (Illus.). 976p. 1990. 65.00 (*0-8386-3186-X*) Fairleigh Dickinson.

— Film Study Vol. 1: An Analytical Bibliography, 4 vols., 2. enl. rev. ed. LC 85-45026. (Illus.). 976p. 1990. 65.00 (*0-8386-3412-5*) Fairleigh Dickinson.

— Film Study Vol. 1: An Analytical Bibliography, 4 vols., 3. enl. rev. ed. LC 85-45026. (Illus.). 976p. 1991. 65.00 (*0-8386-3413-3*) Fairleigh Dickinson.

— Film Study Vol. 1: An Analytical Bibliography, 4 vols., 4. enl. rev. ed. LC 85-45026. (Illus.). 976p. 1991. 65.00 (*0-8386-3414-1*) Fairleigh Dickinson.

Manchester & Bradford. Review of Textile Progress. 538p. 1972. 75.00 (*0-7855-7225-2*) St Mut.

Manchester, A. H. A Modern Legal History of England & Wales, 1750-1950. 1980. pap. 63.00 (*0-406-62264-7*, UK, MICHIE); boxed set 76.00 (*0-406-62263-9*, UK, MICHIE) LEXIS Pub.

— Sources of English Legal History, 1750-1950. 1984. 102.00 (*0-406-51659-6*, U.K., MICHIE) LEXIS Pub.

Manchester, A. H., jt. ed. see Ives, E. W.

Manchester, Caroel. French Tea. LC 92-45129. (Illus.). 144p. 1993. 17.00 (*0-688-11355-9*, Hearst) Hearst Commns.

Manchester, Carole. Tea in the East: Tea Habits Along the Tea Route. LC 95-47841. 176p. 1996. 23.00 (*0-688-13243-X*, Wm Morrow) Morrow Avon.

Manchester, Colin. Sex Shops & the Law. 200p. 1986. text 87.95 (*0-566-05232-6*, Pub. by Dartmth Pub) Ashgate Pub Co.

Manchester, Colin, jt. auth. see Leng, Roger.

Manchester, Diana, ed. Germany Philatelic Society Fortieth Anniversary Anthology. (Illus.). (Orig.). 1989. pap. write for info. (*0-318-65953-0*) D Manchester.

Manchester, Frederick, ed. see Babbitt, Irving.

Manchester, Frederick, jt. tr. see Prabhavananda, Swami.

Manchester, Herbert. Four Centuries of Sport in America. LC 68-21221. (Illus.). 1972. reprint ed. 55.95 (*0-405-08778-0*, Pub. by Blom Pubns) Ayer.

— Four Centuries of Sport in America. 2nd ed. (Fifty Greatest Bks.). (Illus.). 245p. 1992. reprint ed. 60.00 (*1-56416-031-9*) Derrydale Pr.

Manchester, Irving E. History of Colebrook, Connecticut, & Other Papers. (Illus.). 208p. 1997. reprint ed. lib. bdg. 29.00 (*0-8328-7050-1*) Higginson Bk Co.

Manchester, Jason H., ed. see Barnette, David W.

Manchester, Joe. Balloon Shot. 1968. pap. 3.25 (*0-8222-0093-7*) Dramatists Play.

— Run, Thief Run! 1964. pap. 3.00 (*0-8222-0977-2*) Dramatists Play.

Manchester, Kate, jt. auth. see Weinstock, Sylvia.

Manchester, Keith, jt. auth. see Roberts, Charlotte.

Manchester, Lydia & Bogart, Geoffrey S. Contracting & Volunteerism in Local Government. (Special Reports). 224p. (Orig.). 1988. pap. text 30.00 (*0-87326-933-0*) Intl City-Cnty Mgt.

Manchester, Lydia & Valente, Carl. Service Delivery in the '90s: Alternative Approaches for Local Governments. Farr, Cheryl A., ed. 189p. (Orig.). 1989. pap. text 38.00 (*0-87326-926-8*) Intl City-Cnty Mgt.

Manchester, Marsha L. Vintage White Linen. LC 97-19734. 240p. 1997. 39.95 (*0-7643-0363-5*) Schiffer.

Manchester, Martin L. The Philosophical Foundations of Humboldt's Linguistic Doctrines. LC 85-9209. (Studies in the History of the Language Sciences: No. 32). xii, 216p. 1985. 48.00 (*90-272-4514-2*) J Benjamins Pubng Co.

***Manchester, Richard.** Grab a Pencil Book of Seek-a-Word. 2nd ed. (Illus.). 2000. pap. 6.95 (*0-88486-263-1*, Bristol Park Bks) Arrowood Pr.

Manchester, Richard. New Mammoth Book of Crossword Puzzles. 1997. pap. text 12.95 (*0-88486-173-2*, Bristol Park Bks) Arrowood Pr.

***Manchester, Richard.** New Mammoth Book of Seek-A-Word. 2nd ed. 416p. 2000. pap. 13.95 (*0-88486-279-8*, Bristol Park Bks) Arrowood Pr.

Manchester, Richard. New Mammoth Book of Word Games. 1997. pap. text 12.95 (*0-88486-174-0*, Bristol Park Bks) Arrowood Pr.

***Manchester, Richard.** New Mammoth Book of Word Games. 2nd ed. 416p. 2000. pap. 13.95 (*0-88486-278-X*, Bristol Park Bks) Arrowood Pr.

Manchester, Richard. New Pencil Pastime's Book of Word Games. 1998. pap. 9.95 (*0-88486-189-9*, Bristol Park Bks) Arrowood Pr.

***Manchester, Richard.** The 2nd New Pencil Pastimes Book of Word Games. (New Pencil Pastimes Ser.). (Illus.). 256p. 2000. pap. text 9.95 (*0-88486-264-X*, Pub. by Arrowood Pr) Publishers Group.

Manchester, Richard, ed. The New Pencil Pastimes Book of Crosswords. 256p. 1999. pap. 9.95 (*0-88486-244-5*, Bristol Park Bks) Arrowood Pr.

— The New Pencil Pastimes Book of Seek-a-Word. 256p. 1999. pap. 9.95 (*0-88486-245-3*, Bristol Park Bks) Arrowood Pr.

Manchester, Richard B. Incredible Facts. 352p. 1990. pap. 9.95 (*0-88486-036-1*) Arrowood Pr.

— Incredible Facts: The Indispensable Collection of True Life Facts & Oddities. 1994. 7.98 (*0-88365-708-2*) Galahad Bks.

— Mammoth Book of Crossword Puzzles. 416p. 1989. pap. 12.95 (*0-88486-030-2*) Arrowood Pr.

— Mammoth Book of Fun & Games. 416p. 1991. pap. 12.95 (*0-88486-044-2*) Arrowood Pr.

— Mammoth Book of Seek-a-Word Puzzles. 400p. 1996. pap. text 12.95 (*0-88486-146-5*, Bristol Park Bks) Arrowood Pr.

— Mammoth Book of Word Games. 416p. 1990. pap. 12.95 (*0-88486-031-0*) Arrowood Pr.

— New Grab a Pencil Book of Crosswords. 1998. pap. text 6.95 (*0-88486-227-5*, Bristol Park Bks) Arrowood Pr.

— New Grab a Pencil Book of Word Games. 1998. pap. text 6.95 (*0-88486-228-3*, Bristol Park Bks) Arrowood Pr.

— New Mammoth Book of Seek-a-Word. 416p. 1998. pap. 12.95 (*0-88486-210-0*, Bristol Park Bks) Arrowood Pr.

— The Pencil Pastimes Book of Fun & Games. (Illus.). 256p. 1994. pap. 8.95 (*0-88486-098-1*, Bristol Park Bks) Arrowood Pr.

— The Pencil Pastimes Book of Seek-a-Word. (Pencil Pastimes Ser.). 256p. 1992. pap. 6.95 (*0-88486-055-8*) Arrowood Pr.

— Pencil Pastimes Book of Word Games. (Pencil Pastimes Ser.). 256p. 1992. pap. 8.95 (*0-88486-056-6*) Arrowood Pr.

***Manchester, Steven R.** The Unexpected Storm: The Gulf War Legacy. 230p. 2000. 18.95 (*1-55571-542-7*, Pub. by PSI Resch) Midpt Trade.

Manchester, Steven R., jt. auth. see Meyer, Herbert W.

Manchester, William. American Caesar: Douglas MacArthur, 1880-1964. 960p. 1983. mass mkt. 8.50 (*0-440-30424-5*, LE) Dell.

— Death of a President. 736p. 1996. 14.98 (*0-88365-956-5*) Galahad Bks.

— The Glory & the Dream: A Narrative History of America, 1932-1972. 1408p. 1984. pap. 29.95 (*0-553-34589-3*) Bantam.

— Goodbye Darkness: A Memoir of the Pacific War. 464p. 1987. mass mkt. 7.99 (*0-440-32907-8*, LE) Dell.

— In Our Time: The World As Seen by Magnum Photographers. 456p. 1994. pap. 49.95 (*0-393-31129-5*) Norton.

— The Last Lion. 1996. write for info. (*0-316-54770-0*) Little.

— The Last Lion: Biography of Winston Churchill, 1932-40. (Illus.). 800p. (gr. 8). 1988. 45.00 (*0-316-54512-0*) Little.

— The Last Lion: Visions of Glory: Winston Spencer Churchill. 992p. 1984. pap. 19.95 (*0-385-31348-9*, Delta Trade) Dell.

— The Last Lion: Winston Spencer Churchill Visions of Glory, 1874-1932. LC 82-24972. (Illus.). 973p. (gr. 8). 1983. 45.00 (*0-316-54503-1*) Little.

— The Last Lion - Winston Spencer Churchill: Alone, 1932-1940. 800p. 1989. pap. 19.95 (*0-385-31331-4*, Delta Trade) Dell.

— One Brief Shining Moment: Remembering Kennedy. (Illus.). 280p. 1988. pap. 16.95 (*0-316-54511-2*) Little.

— A World Lit Only by Fire: The Medieval Mind & the Renaissance - Portrait of an Age. (Illus.). 318p. (gr. 8). 1992. 25.95 (*0-316-54531-7*) Little.

— A World Lit Only by Fire: The Medieval Mind & the Renaissance - Portrait of an Age. (Illus.). 322p. 1993. pap. 16.00 (*0-316-54556-2*, Back Bay) Little.

Manchette, Jean-Patrick. L' Affaire N'Gustro. (FRE.). 224p. 1987. pap. 10.95 (*0-7859-4270-X*, 2070378543) Fr & Eur.

— Fatale. (FRE.). 1983. pap. 8.95 (*0-7859-4192-4*) Fr & Eur.

Manchise, Louis J., jt. auth. see Lobel, Ira B.

Mancho Duque, Maria J., ed. see De Jesus, Teresa.

Mancho, Maria J. The Text & Concordance of the Tratado de la Generacion de la Criatura: I-51 Biblioteca Nacional, Madrid. (Spanish Medical Texts Ser.: No. 11). 12p. 1987. 10.00 incl. fiche (*0-940639-07-6*) Hispanic Seminary.

Manchot, C. The Cutaneous Arteries of the Human Body. (Illus.). 149p. 1983. 145.00 (*0-387-90792-0*) Spr-Verlag.

Manchuelle, Francois. Willing Migrants: Soninke Labor Diasporas, 1848-1960. LC 97-27492. 391p. 1997. text 44.95 (*0-8214-1201-9*); pap. text 24.95 (*0-8214-1202-7*) Ohio U Pr.

Manchur, Gail, ed. see Collins, Max Allan.

Manchur, Gail, ed. see Martin, Rick & Martin, Charlotte.

Manchur, Gail, ed. see Stevens, Ben.

Manchur, Gail, ed. see Steward, Nicholas.

Mancia, G., jt. auth. see Zanchetti, A.

Mancia, Giuseppe, jt. auth. see Zanchetti, Alberto.

Mancia, Mauro. From Oedipus to Dream. LC 98-150915. (Illus.). 192p. 1996. pap. 15.00 (*1-85575-133-X*, Pub. by H Karnac Bks Ltd) Other Pr LLC.

Mancia, Mauro. In the Gaze of Narcissus: Memory, Affects & Creativity. 220p. 1993. pap. text 15.00 (*1-85575-042-2*, Pub. by H Karnac Bks Ltd) Other Pr LLC.

Mancia, Mauro & Marini, Gabriella, eds. The Diencephalon & Sleep. LC 90-8524. 418p. reprint ed. 129.60 (*0-608-03429-0*, 206412900008) Bks Demand.

Manciaux, M., ed. Handicaps in Childhood. (Child Health & Development Ser.: Vol. 1). (Illus.). x, 182p. 1981. 72.25 (*3-8055-2935-X*) S Karger.

Manciaux, M. & Romer, C. J., eds. Accidents in Childhood & Adolescence: The Role of Research. (ENG & FRE.). xiii, 217p. 1991. pap. text 35.00 (*92-4-156119-X*, 1150313) World Health.

Manciaux, M., et al. Sante de la Mere et de l'Enfant: Nouveaux Concepts en Pediatrie Sociale. 2nd ed. (Illus.). 504p. 1984. lib. bdg. 35.00 (*0-318-04482-X*) S M P F Inc.

Manciaux, M., jt. auth. see Senault, R.

***Mancil, Tony.** Linux Routers: A Primer for Network Administrators. 350p. 2000. 44.99 (*0-13-086113-8*) P-H.

Mancinelli, Fabrizio. The Sistine Chapel. (Illus.). 111p. 1997. pap. 25.00 (*88-86921-01-2*) Treasures Inc.

Mancing, Howard. The Golden Age Comedia: Text, Theory & Performance. Ganelin, Charles, ed. LC 93-1959. 414p. 1994. pap. 34.95 (*1-55753-086-6*) Purdue U Pr.

Mancini. Conducting Tours. 2nd ed. (Hospitality, Travel & Tourism Ser.). 72p. 1996. text, teacher ed. 12.00 (*0-8273-7472-0*) Delmar.

— Conducting Tours. 3rd ed. 2000. pap. 40.95 (*0-7668-1419-X*) Delmar.

— Conducting Tours: A Practical Guide. (Hospitality, Travel & Tourism Ser.). 1990. pap. 32.95 (*0-538-70159-5*) S-W Pub.

— Cruising: Guide to the Cruise Lines Industry. LC 99-33793. (Hospitality, Travel & Tourism Ser.). (C). 1999. pap. 46.95 (*0-7668-0971-4*) Delmar.

— Selling Destinations: Geography. 3rd rev. abr. ed. LC 98-49624. 576p. (C). 1999. pap. text 72.95 (*0-7668-0848-3*) Delmar.

— Selling Destinations: Geography Travel. (Hospitality, Travel & Tourism Ser.). 1992. teacher ed. 54.95 (*0-538-70403-9*); pap. 35.95 (*0-538-70402-0*) S-W Pub.

Mancini, ed. Upper Cretaceous & Paleogene Biostratigraphy & Lithostratigraphy of the Eastern Gulf Coastal Plain, No. T372. (IGC Field Trip Guidebooks Ser.). 128p. 1989. 21.00 (*0-87590-561-7*) Am Geophysical.

Mancini, A. M., et al, eds. Advances in Crystal Growth. (Materials Science Forum Ser.: Vol. 203). (Illus.). 336p. 1996. text 116.00 (*0-87849-718-8*, Pub. by Trans T Pub) Enfield Pubs NH.

Mancini, Daniel D. From Time to Time: An Historical Misadventure. LC 96-33666. (J). 1996. 14.95 (*0-944957-84-6*) Rivercross Pub.

Mancini, Dario, et al, eds. New Trends in Fuzzy Systems: Proceedings of the International Joint Workshop on Current Issues on Fuzzy Technologies & Methods & Environments for Planning & Programming CIFT/MEPP '96 Aversa, Italy 10 October, 1996 Napoli, Italy 11 October, 1996. 300p. 1997. 78.00 (*981-02-3245-4*) World Scientific Pub.

Mancini, Elaine. Struggles of the Italian Film Industry During Fascism, 1930-1935. LC 85-1069. (Studies in Cinema: No. 34). (Illus.). 310p. reprint ed. pap. 96.10 (*0-8357-1655-4*, 207050600097) Bks Demand.

Mancini, Ferdinando, ed. Lectures in the Physics of Highly Correlated Electron Systems. LC 98-71903. (Conference Proceedings Ser.: Vol. 438). (Illus.). 208p. 1998. 62.00 (*1-56396-789-8*) Spr-Verlag.

***Mancini, Ferdinando, ed.** Lectures on the Physics of Highly Correlated Electron Systems: Fourth Training Course in the Physics of Correlated Electron Systems. LC 00-104877. (AIP Conference Proceedings Ser.: Vol. 527). (Illus.). vii, 381p. 2000. 125.00 (*1-56396-950-5*) Am Inst Physics.

Mancini, G. B., ed. Clinical Applications of Cardiac Digital Angiography. LC 86-42505. (Illus.). 358p. 1998. reprint ed. pap. 111.00 (*0-608-05783-5*, 205974800007) Bks Demand.

***Mancini, G. F.** Constitutionalism & Democracy in the European Union. 280p. 2000. 60.00 (*1-84113-114-8*, Pub. by Hart Pub) Intl Spec Bk.

Mancini, Genevieve. Uncaring Eyes Can Never See. 1979. 2.95 (*0-9604328-0-9*) G Mancini.

Mancini, George. Instant Keyboard: Starter Pack. (Illus.). 48p. pap. 17.95 (*0-7119-1514-8*, AM71424) Music Sales.

Mancini, Giambattista. Practical Reflections on Figured Song. rev. ed. Foreman, Edward V., tr. from ITA. (Masterworks on Singing Ser.: Vol. VII). 1996. reprint ed. pap. 15.00 (*1-887117-04-0*) Pro musica pr.

Mancini, Henry. Sounds & Scores. 1995. pap. text 29.95 incl. audio (*0-89898-666-4*, P0732SMXAT); pap. text 32.95 incl. cd-rom (*0-89898-667-2*, P0732SMXCD) Wrner Bros.

Mancini, Henry & Mathis, Johnny. The Hollywood Musicals. 1987. pap. 13.95 (*0-89898-506-4*, P0769SMX) Wrner Bros.

Mancini, Henry, jt. auth. see Galway, James.

Mancini, Janet K. Strategic Styles: Coping in the Inner City. LC 79-56773. 349p. reprint ed. pap. 108.20 (*0-8357-6519-9*, 203589000097) Bks Demand.

Mancini, John, ed. Credit Reports & Insurance Underwriting. 138p. (Orig.). (C). 1997. pap. 25.00 (*0-89382-493-3*, CRU-OM) Nat Assn Insurance.

— Final Report of the Insurance Availability & Affordability Task Force. 380p. 1998. ring bd. 55.00i (*0-89382-536-0*, IAA-PB) Nat Assn Insurance.

— Sales & Marketing Practices, Auditing & Accounting Procedures & Products of Insurers Utilizing the Home Service System. 90p. 1998. pap. 40.00i (*0-89382-579-4*, HSR-PB) Nat Assn Insurance.

***Mancini, John F.** Will's Christmas List. 140p. 2000. pap. 9.95 (*0-595-08869-4*, Writers Showcase) iUniversecom.

Mancini, Kitty. Goatina Goes to New York. LC 99-228021. (Illus.). 72p. (J). (gr. k-3). 1999. pap. 10.00 (*0-9648010-7-8*) Hypertext Pub.

Mancini, Laura Drake, ed. see Bertolino, Angela & Lewis, Carla.

Mancini, M., et al. Treatment of Severe Hypercholesterolemia in the Prevention of Coronary Heart Disease - 2. Gotto, A. M., Jr. et al, eds. viii, 274p. 1990. 68.75 (*3-8055-5085-5*) S Karger.

Mancini, Marc. Conducting Tours. 2nd ed. LC 95-10906. 272p. (C). 1995. pap. 48.95 (*0-8273-7471-2*) Delmar.

Mancini, Marc. Selling Destinations: Geography for the Travel Professional. 2nd ed. LC 94-13909. 1994. pap. 47.75 (*0-538-63450-2*) S-W Pub.

— Selling Destinations: Geography for the Travel Professional. 2nd ed. 512p. 1995. pap., teacher ed. write for info. (*0-538-63451-0*) S-W Pub.

— Time Management. LC 93-3443. (Business Skills Express Ser.). 176p. 1993. pap. 10.00 (*1-55623-888-6*, Irwn Prfssnl) McGraw-Hill Prof.

Mancini, Marie. La Verite dans Son Jour. LC 98-18680. (Scholars' Facsimiles & Reprints Ser.: Vol. 510). (Illus.). 110p. 1998. reprint ed. 50.00 (*0-8201-1510-X*) Schol Facsimiles.

Mancini, Mario, jt. ed. see Stokes, Joseph, III.

***Mancini, Mark.** Using Space Advertising As Effective Direct Marketing. (Illus.). 72p. 1999. pap. 12.95 (*1-879644-12-6*) Direct Mktg.

Mancini, Mark & McVey, Michael. The Aaronville Midnight Parade. 40p. (J). (gr. k-8). 1997. 14.95 (*0-9672482-0-5*) Mancini Creat.

Mancini, Matthew. Alexis de Tocqueville. (Twayne's World Authors Ser.). 184p. 1993. 32.00 (*0-8057-4305-7*, Twyne) Mac Lib Ref.

Mancini, Matthew J. One Dies, Get Another: Convict Leasing in the American South, 1866-1928. LC 95-50208. (Illus.). 290p. 1996. text 34.95 (*1-57003-083-9*) U of SC Pr.

Mancini, Paolo, jt. ed. see Swanson, David L.

Mancini, Richard. Everything You Need to Know about Living with a Single Parent. rev. ed. (Need to Know Library). (Illus.). 64p. (YA). (gr. 7-12). 1995. lib. bdg. 17.95 (*0-8239-2118-2*) Rosen Group.

Mancini, Richard E. Indians of the Southeast. (First Americans Ser.). (Illus.). 96p. (J). (gr. 5-9). 1992. lib. bdg. 23.95 (*0-8160-2390-5*) Facts on File.

Mancini, Rob, jt. auth. see O'Byrne, John.

***Mancino, Doug, et al.** Navigating Your Way Through the Federal Physician Self-Referral Law. 3rd rev. ed. 1998. pap. 169.00 (*0-929156-45-5*) Atlantic Info Services Inc.

Mancino, Douglas M. Taxation of Hospitals & Health Care Organizations. 1200p. 1995. 345.00 (*0-7913-2512-1*) Warren Gorham & Lamont.

Mancke, Richard B. Mexican Oil & Natural Gas: Political, Strategic & Economic Implications. LC 78-27095. 163p. 1979. 49.95 (*0-275-90386-9*, C0386, Praeger Pubs) Greenwood.

Mancl, Karen, et al. Private Drinking Water Supplies: Quality, Testing & Options for Problem Waters. (Illus.). 60p. 1991. pap. 8.00 (*0-935817-22-0*, 47) NRAES.

Manclark, C. R. & Hennessen, W., eds. Pertussis. (Developments in Biological Standardization Ser.: Vol. 61). (Illus.). xii, 600p. 1986. pap. 61.00 (*3-8055-4210-0*) S Karger.

Manco-Johnson, Michael L., et al. Diagnostic Ultrasound Test & Syllabus, Vol. 23. (Professional Self-Evaluation & Continuing Education Program Ser.). (Illus.). 700p. 1988. 165.00 (*1-55903-023-2*) Am Coll Radiology.

Manco, Joseph. The Nerves of Some Hangovers. LC 97-66422. 310p. (Orig.). 1997. pap. 12.95 (*1-890279-00-5*) Rising Star MD.

Mancoff, Debra N. Burne-Jones. LC 97-43406. (Illus.). 128p. 1998. pap. 30.00 (*0-7649-0615-1*) Pomegranate Calif.

***Mancoff, Debra N.** Jane Morris: The Pre-Raphaelite Model of Beauty. LC 00-29335. (Illus.). 128p. 2000. pap. 30.00 (*0-7649-1337-9*) Pomegranate Calif.

Mancoff, Debra N. Mary Cassatt: Reflections of Women's Lives. 96p. 1998. 24.95 (*1-55670-852-1*) Stewart Tabori & Chang.

***Mancoff, Debra N.** Treasures from the Art Institute of Chicago. 336p. 2000. 75.00 (*0-86559-182-2*, Pub. by Art Inst Chi) Hudson Hills.

— Van Gogh Fields & Flowers. LC 99-58901. (Illus.). 96p. 1999. 18.95 (*0-8118-2569-8*) Chronicle Bks.

Mancoff, Debra N., ed. The Arthurian Revival: Essays on Form, Tradition, & Transformation. LC 92-8108. (Illus.). 360p. 1992. text 10.00 (*0-8153-0060-3*, H1419) Garland.

— King Arthur's Modern Return. LC 98-16203. (Literature-Reference Ser.). (Illus.). 252p. 1998. 55.00 (*0-8153-2500-2*, H2022) Garland.

Mancoff, Debra N., et al, eds. Victorian Urban Settings: Essays on the Nineteenth-Century City & Its Contexts. LC 96-12754. (Literature & Society in Victorian Britain Ser.: Vol. 1). (Illus.). 288p. 1996. text 60.00 (*0-8153-1949-5*, H1889) Garland.

***Mancoff, Debra N. & Roberts, David.** David Roberts: Travels in Egypt & the Holy Land. LC 99-26457. (Illus.). 128p. 1999. pap. 30.00 (*0-7649-1029-9*) Pomegranate Calif.

Mancoff, Neal A. & Weiner, David M. Nonqualified Deferred Compensation Arrangements. 1990. 145.00 (*0-685-24500-4*) West Group.

Mancoff, Neil & Steinberg, Allen T. Qualified Deferred Compensation Plans: Forms. LC 83-23222. 798p. 1990. 135.00 (*0-317-11358-5*) West Group.

Mancoske, Ronald J., jt. ed. see Smith, James D.

Mancosu, Paolo. Philosophy of Mathematics & Mathematical Practices in the Seventeenth Century. (Illus.). 288p. 1996. text 70.00 (*0-19-508463-2*) OUP.

— Philosophy of Mathematics & Mathematical Practices in the Seventeenth Century. (Illus.). 288p. 1999. pap. 19.95 (*0-19-513244-0*) OUP.

Mancosu, Paolo, ed. From Brouwer to Hilbert: The Debate on the Foundations of Mathematics in the 1920's. LC 96-32918. (Illus.). 352p. (C). 1997. text 70.00 (*0-19-509631-2*); pap. text 32.95 (*0-19-509632-0*) OUP.

Mancour, T. L. Spartacus. Stern, Dave, ed. (Star Trek: The Next Generation Ser.: No. 20). 288p. (Orig.). 1992. mass mkt. 5.50 (*0-671-76051-3*) PB.

Mancrief, C. K. Scott, tr. see Proust, Marcel.

Mancusi-Ungaro, Carol, jt. auth. see Anfam, David.

Mancusi-Ungaro, Donna. Dante & the Empire. (American University Studies: Romance Languages & Literature: Ser. II, Vol. 49). XIV, 201p. 1990. text 73.95 (*0-8204-0337-7*) P Lang Pubng.

Mancusi-Ungaro, Harold R., Jr. Michelangelo: The Bruges Madonna & the Piccolomini Altar. LC 70-151582. (College Ser.: No. 11). (Illus.). 240p. reprint ed. 74.40 (*0-8357-9387-7*, 201319200085) Bks Demand.

Mancuso, Anthony. California Incorporator 2.0. 2nd ed. 336p. 1997. pap., student ed. 79.95 incl. disk (*0-87337-331-6*) Nolo com.

***Mancuso, Anthony.** The California Nonprofit Corporation Handbook. 8th ed. LC 98-39121. 352p. 1999. pap. 34.95 (*0-87337-503-3*) Nolo com.

Mancuso, Anthony. The California Nonprofit Corporation Kit. 2nd ed. LC 98-25569. 368p. 1999. 49.95 (*0-87337-488-6*) Nolo com.

— The California Professional Corporation Handbook. 6th ed. LC 93-40930. 352p. 1999. pap. 34.95 (*0-87337-234-4*) Nolo com.

— Corporate & LLC Minute Book: How to Hold & Document Essential Meetings. 2nd ed. LC 97-52271. 1998. pap. text 34.95 (*0-87337-453-3*) Nolo com.

— Corporate Minutes Book: A Legal Guide to Taking Care of Corporate Business. LC 98-24913. 1998. pap. 69.95 incl. disk (*0-87337-479-7*) Nolo com.

— Form Your Own Limited Liability Company. 2nd ed. LC 97-29739. 1996. pap. 44.95 (*0-87337-419-3*) Nolo com.

***Mancuso, Anthony.** Form Your Own Limited Liability Company. 3rd ed. LC 99-40306. 2000. pap. write for info. (*0-87337-552-1*) Nolo com.

Mancuso, Anthony. How to Form a California Professional Corporation. 6th ed. LC 98-35443. (Illus.). 1999. pap. 49.95 (*0-87337-496-7*) Nolo com.

— How to Form a Nonprofit Corporation. 3rd ed. LC 95-53709. (Illus.). 368p. 1997. reprint ed. pap. 39.95 (*0-87337-333-2*) Nolo com.

— How to Form a Nonprofit Corporation. 4th ed. LC 97-34980. (Illus.). 368p. 1997. pap. 39.95 (*0-87337-451-7*) Nolo com.

— How to Form Your Own California Corporation. 9th ed. LC 97-35425. 1998. 34.95 (*0-87337-455-X*) Nolo com.

— How to Form Your Own California Corporation: With Corporate Records Binder & Disk. 288p. 1996. pap. 39.95 (*0-87337-248-4*) Nolo com.

— How to Form Your Own California Corporation: With Corporate Records Binder & Disk. 2nd ed. LC 97-35424. 304p. 1998. 39.95 (*0-87337-456-8*) Nolo com.

— How to Form Your Own California Corporation 8.2. 8th ed. LC 94-30164. (Illus.). 304p. 1996. reprint ed. pap. 29.95 (*0-87337-271-9*) Nolo com.

***Mancuso, Anthony.** How to Form Your Own Florida Corporation. 4th ed. LC KFF213.5.Z9M36 1999. 1999. write for info. (*0-87337-550-5*) Nolo com.

Mancuso, Anthony. How to Form Your Own New York Corporation. 3rd ed. LC 94-24780. 304p. 1994. pap. 39.95 incl. disk (*0-87337-277-8*) Nolo com.

— How to Form Your Own New York Corporation. 4th rev. ed. LC 97-28824. (Illus.). 304p. 1998. pap. 39.95 incl. disk (*0-87337-422-3*) Nolo com.

***Mancuso, Anthony.** How to Form Your Own Texas Corporation. 5th ed. LC KFT1415.C55M36 2000. 2000. pap. 44.95 (*0-87337-559-9*) Nolo com.

Mancuso, Anthony. How to Form Your Own Texas Corporation, Set incl. Disk. 4th ed. 272p. 1996. pap. 39.95 incl. disk (*0-87337-255-7*) Nolo com.

— LLC Maker: Form Your Own Limited Liability Company. LC 97-38253. 1997. write for info. (*0-87337-387-1*) Nolo com.

— Nolo's California Quick Corp: Incorporate Your Business Without a Lawyer, 1. LC 99-12534. (Quick & Legal Ser.). (Illus.). 250p. 1999. pap. text 19.95 (*0-87337-477-0*) Nolo com.

***Mancuso, Anthony.** Nolo's Quick LLC. LC 00-20580. (Quick & Legal Ser.). (Illus.). 200p. 2000. pap. 29.95 (*0-87337-573-4*) Nolo com.

Mancuso, Anthony. Taking Care of Your Corporation Vol. 2: Key Corporate Decisions Made Easy. 320p. 1995. pap. 39.95 incl. disk (*0-87337-276-X*) Nolo com.

— Your Limited Liability Company: An Operating Manual. LC 99-24828. 400p. 1999. pap. 49.95 incl. disk (*0-87337-510-6*) Nolo com.

Mancuso, Anthony & Laurence, Bethany K. How to Create a Buy-Sell Agreement & Control the Destiny of Your Small Business. LC 98-19262. 250p. 1999. pap. 49.95 incl. disk (*0-87337-464-9*) Nolo com.

Mancuso, Anthony, et al. Computed Tomography & Magnetic Resonance Imaging of the Head & Neck. 2nd ed. (Illus.). 504p. 1985. 99.95 (*0-683-05476-7*) Lppncott W & W.

Mancuso, Anthony A. Workbook for MRI & CT of the Head & Neck. 2nd ed. (Illus.). 236p. 1988. 60.00 (*0-683-05478-3*) Lppncott W & W.

Mancuso, Anthony A. & Quisling, Ronald G. Head & Neck: A Teaching File. (Illus.). 400p. 1998. write for info. (*0-683-30144-6*) Lppncott W & W.

Mancuso, J. R. Coupling & Joints: Design, Selection & Applications. 2nd expanded rev. ed. LC 99-22028. (Mechanical Engineering Ser.). (Illus.). 592p. 1999. text 195.00 (*0-8247-9950-X*, 9950-X) Dekker.

Mancuso, James C. & Shaw, Mildred L., eds. Cognition & Personal Structure: Computer Access & Analysis. LC 87-13770. 348p. 1988. 69.50 (*0-275-92606-0*, C2606, Praeger Pubs) Greenwood.

Mancuso, James C., ed. see Adams-Webber, Jack R.

Mancuso, Janice T. Herbed Wine Cuisine. LC 97-9076. (Orig.). 1997. pap. 21.95 (*0-88266-967-2*) Storey Bks.

Mancuso, Janice T., jt. auth. see Herget, J. B.

***Mancuso, Janics, compiled by.** North Carolina Cookbook. (Cooking Across America Ser.). (Illus.). 94p. 1999. pap. 6.95 (*1-885590-42-3*) Golden West Pub.

Mancuso, Joan, jt. auth. see Fetridge, Keith R.

Mancuso, John H. & Kopek, Richard A. Bank Regulatory Update: Beyond Consumer Issues. 1995. 210.00 (*0-7913-2487-7*) Warren Gorham & Lamont.

Mancuso, Jon R., jt. ed. see South, David W.

Mancuso, Joseph C. Mastering Technical Writing. 1990. pap. 29.95 (*0-201-52350-7*) Addison-Wesley.

— Mastering Technical Writing. 1995. reprint ed. pap. text 29.95 (*0-9643750-1-X*) Training Edge.

— Memos in Minutes. 88p. (Orig.). 1995. pap. text 14.95 (*0-9643750-2-8*) Training Edge.

— Technical Editing. 208p. (C). 1991. text 33.00 (*0-13-898503-0*, 640704) P-H.

— Technical Editing. 191p. 1994. 39.95 (*0-9643750-0-1*) Training Edge.

Mancuso, Joseph R. The Entrepreneur's Handbook, 2 vols., 1. LC 74-82601. 253p. 1974. reprint ed. pap. 78.50 (*0-608-08212-0*, 202505500001) Bks Demand.

— The Entrepreneur's Handbook, 2 vols., 2. LC 74-82601. 247p. reprint ed. pap. 76.60 (*0-608-08213-9*, 202505500002) Bks Demand.

— How to Get a Business Loan. 288p. 1990. pap. 13.00 (*0-671-76345-8*, Fireside) S&S Trade Pap.

— How to Prepare & Present a Business Plan. 320p. 1990. per. 15.00 (*0-671-76354-7*) S&S Trade.

— How to Start, Finance, & Manage Your Own Small Business. 400p. 1990. pap. 17.00 (*0-671-76356-3*) P-H.

— How to Write a Winning Business Plan. 352p. 1992. pap. 15.00 (*0-671-76358-X*) S&S Trade.

— Managing Technology Products, Vol. 1. LC 74-82598. (Modern Frontiers in Applied Science Ser.). 184p. reprint ed. pap. 57.10 (*0-608-16257-4*, 202716100001) Bks Demand.

— Mancuso's Small Business Basics: Start, Buy or Franchise Your Way to a Successful Business. 2nd rev. ed. LC 97-50090. 224p. 1997. pap. 12.95 (*1-57071-212-3*) Sourcebks.

— Mancuso's Small Business Resource Guide. rev. ed. LC 95-36910. (Small Business Sourcebooks Ser.). 208p. 1995. pap. 9.95 (*1-57071-066-X*) Sourcebks.

Mancuso, Joseph R., ed. Marketing Technology Products. LC 77-352039. (Technology Products Ser.: No. 2). (Illus.). 205p. reprint ed. pap. 63.60 (*0-8357-4182-6*, 203696000006) Bks Demand.

Mancuso, Joseph R. & Boroian, Donald. How to Buy & Manage a Franchise. 288p. 1993. pap. 11.00 (*0-671-76775-5*, Fireside) S&S Trade Pap.

***Mancuso, Kevin.** The Mane Thing. LC 98-49591. (Illus.). 144p. (gr. 8). 1999. 25.00 (*0-316-16614-6*) Little.

Mancuso, Laurence, tr. from GRE. Troparia & Kondakia: Hymns for Saints & Feastdays. 452p. 1984. 49.50 (*0-9607924-7-3*) Monks of New Skete.

Mancuso, Laurence, ed. see Monks of New Skete.

Mancuso, Laurence, ed. & tr. see Monk of New Skete Staff.

Mancuso, Laurence, ed. & tr. see Monks of New Skete.

Mancuso, Laurence, ed. & tr. see Monks of New Skete Staff.

Mancuso, Laurence, tr. see Monks of New Skete.

Mancuso, Laurence, tr. see Monks of New Skete Staff.

Mancuso, Luke. The Strange Sad War Revolving: Walt Whitman, Reconstruction, & the Emergence of Black Citizenship. LC 97-3940. (ENG Ser.). x, 160p. 1997. 55.00 (*1-57113-125-6*) Camden Hse.

Mancuso, Maureen. The Ethical World of British MP's. LC 96-128108. 248p. 1995. 60.00 (*0-7735-1261-6*, Pub. by McG-Queens Univ Pr) CUP Services.

Mancuso, Maureen, et al, eds. Leaders & Leadership in Canada. 288p. 1994. pap. text 32.00 (*0-19-540922-1*) OUP.

Mancuso, Olga, tr. see Martino, James.

Mancuso, Rob. Assuming the Position: A Family Business Survival Guide. (Illus.). 96p. (Orig.). 1997. pap. 9.95 (*0-9658462-0-2*) Houndstooth Pr.

Mancuso, S., ed. Achievements in Gynecology. (Contributions to Gynecology & Obstetrics Ser.: Vol. 17). (Illus.). vi, 130p. 1989. 85.25 (*3-8055-4825-7*) S Karger.

— Achievements in Gynecology 1989-90. (Contributions to Gynecology & Obstetrics Ser.: Vol. 18). (Illus.). x, 186p. (C). 1991. 156.75 (*3-8055-5122-3*) S Karger.

— Current Status of Fetal Medicine & Its Future, 1989: Journal: Fetal Therapy, Vol. 4, Suppl. 1. (Illus.). vi, 134p. 1990. pap. 42.75 (*3-8055-5284-X*) S Karger.

Mancuso, Ted & Hill, Frank. Kung Fu for Young People. LC 82-80287. (Specialties Ser.). (Illus.). 96p. (Orig.). (J). (ps-7). 1982. reprint ed. pap. 9.95 (*0-89750-079-2*, 416) Ohara Pubns.

Mancuso, Ted, jt. auth. see Lam, Kwong W.

Mancuso, Tony. Taking Care of Your Corporation Vol. 1: Director & Shareholder Meetings Made Easy. 304p. 1994. pap. 29.95 (0-87337-223-9) Nolo com.

Mancy. Environmental Health Sciences. Date not set. 69.95 (0-87371-028-2) Lewis Pubs.

***Mand, Martin G.** Partnering for Performance: Harnessing the Power of Finance in the New Organization. LC 00-29964. 224p. 2000. 27.95 (0-8144-0556-8) AMACOM.

Mandabach, Frederick A., jt. auth. see Adams, Stephen.

Mandabach, Frederick A., jt. auth. see Samuels, M. Dee.

***Mandahar, C. L.** Molecular Biology of Plant Viruses. LC 99-28569. 1999. write for info. (0-7923-8547-0, Kluwer Plenum) Kluwer Academic.

Mandahar, C. L., ed. Plant Viruses: Structure & Replication. (Illus.). 368p. 1989. lib. bdg. 289.00 (0-8493-6947-9, QR351) CRC Pr.

— Plant Viruses Vol. 2: Pathology. (Illus.). 368p. 1990. lib. bdg. 289.00 (0-8493-6948-7, QR351) CRC Pr.

Mandal, Anil K. Assessment of Urinary Sediment by Electron Microscopy: Applications in Renal Disease. LC 87-14153. (Illus.). 284p. (C). 1987. text 90.00 (0-306-42521-1, Kluwer Plenum) Kluwer Academic.

Mandal, Anil K. & Bohman, Sven-Olof, eds. The Renal Papilla & Hypertension. LC 80-15989. (Illus.). 297p. 1980. reprint ed. pap. 92.10 (0-608-05430-5, 206589900006) Bks Demand.

Mandal, Anil K. & Jennette, J. Charles, eds. Diagnosis & Management of Renal Disease & Hypertension. LC 87-29884. 556p. reprint ed. pap. 172.40 (0-7837-2850-6, 205762200006) Bks Demand.

— Diagnosis & Management of Renal Disease & Hypertension. 2nd ed. LC 93-73562. (Illus.). 548p. (C). 1994. boxed set 98.50 (0-89089-557-0) Carolina Acad Pr.

Mandal, Anil K. & Nahman, N. Stanley, eds. Kidney Disease in Primary Care. LC 97-37957. 297p. 1997. write for info. (0-683-30057-1) Lppncott W & W.

Mandal, Ashis K., jt. auth. see Thadepalli, Haragopal.

Mandal, B. N. Advances in Dual Integral Equations. LC 98-54685. (Chapman & Hall/CRC Research Notes in Mat). 232p. 1999. 79.95 (0-8493-0617-5) CRC Pr.

— Integral Expansions Related to Mehler-Fock Type Transforms. 1997. pap. 47.95 (0-582-30816-X, Pub. by Addison-Wesley) Longman.

Mandal, B. N., ed. Mathematical Techniques for Water Waves. LC 96-83306. (Advances in Fluid Mechanics Ser.: Vol. 8). 368p. 1997. 168.00 (1-85312-413-3, 4133) Computational Mech MA.

Mandal, Bankim C. Srikanthacarita: A Mahakavya of Mankhaka. (C). 1992. 24.00 (0-8364-2798-X, Pub. by Sanskrit Pustake) S Asia.

Mandal, Bibhat K., et al. The Infectious Diseases. 5th ed. LC 95-8411. (Lecture Notes Ser.). (Illus.). 264p. 1996. pap. 29.95 (0-632-03351-7) Blackwell Sci.

***Mandal, Birendra N. & Chakrabarti, Aloknath.** Water Wave Scattering by Barriers. 408p. 2000. 197.00 (1-85312-623-3, 6233, Pub. by WIT Pr) Computational Mech MA.

Mandal, Debabrata, ed. Social Structure & Cultural Change in the Saharia Tribe. LC 98-901496. 165p. 1998. pap. 80.00 (81-7533-071-6, Pub. by Print Hse) St Mut.

Mandal, Gobinda C. Rural Development: Retrospect & Prospect. (C). 1992. text 16.00 (81-7022-396-2, Pub. by Concept) S Asia.

Mandal, H., jt. ed. see Thompson, D. P.

Mandal, J. N. Geosynthetics World. 1994. write for info. (81-224-0622-X, Pub. by Wiley Estrn) Franklin.

Mandal, J. N., ed. First Indian Geotextiles Conference on Reinforced Soil & Teotextiles: Proceedings. (C). 1988. 44.00 (81-204-0377-0, Pub. by Oxford IBH) S Asia.

Mandal, J. N. & Divshikar, D. G. Soil Testing in Civil Engineering. LC 99-225804. (Illus.). 256p. 1995. 85.00 (90-5410-233-0) Ashgate Pub Co.

Mandal, R. Privatisation in the Third World. (C). 1994. 22.50 (0-7069-7318-6, Pub. by Vikas) S Asia.

Mandal, Rathindranath, jt. auth. see Naskar, Kumudranjan.

Mandal, Satya. Projective Modules & Complete Intersections, Vol. 167. Dold, A. & Takens, F., eds. LC 97-37176. (Lecture Notes in Mathematics Ser.: Vol. 1672). viii, 114p. 1997. pap. text 27.00 (3-540-63564-5) Spr-Verlag.

Mandal, Tirtha. Women Revolutionaries of Bengal, 1905-1939. (C). 1991. text 14.00 (81-85195-41-2, Pub. by Minerva) S Asia.

Mandala, Elias C. Work & Control in a Peasant Economy: A History of the Lower Tchiri Valley in Malawi, 1859-1960. LC 90-50093. 480p. (Orig.). (C). 1990. text 52.95 (0-299-12490-8); pap. text 24.95 (0-299-12494-0) U of Wis Pr.

***Mandalakas, Anna, et al.** Helping the Children: A Practical Handbook for Complex Humanitarian Emergencies. LC 99-52162. 1999. write for info. (0-9602790-7-5) Hlth Frontiers.

Mandali, Monique. Everyone's Mandala Coloring Book, Vol. 2. (Illus.). 48p. (Orig.). 1994. pap. 8.95 (1-56044-295-6) Falcon Pub Inc.

— Everyone's Mandala Coloring Book, Vol. 3. (Illus.). 48p. (Orig.). 1997. pap. 8.95 (1-56044-585-8, Skyhse) Falcon Pub Inc.

Mandali, Monique. Everyone's Mandala Coloring Book, Vol. 1. 48p. (Orig.). 1991. pap. 8.95 (1-56044-014-7) Falcon Pub Inc.

Mandalios, John. Civilization & the Human Subject. LC 99-14831. 224p. 1999. 65.00 (0-8476-9176-4); pap. 24.95 (0-8476-9177-2) Rowman.

***Mandanis, Greg.** Software Project Management for Dummies. (For Dummies Ser.). 384p. 2000. pap. 24.99 incl. cd-rom (0-7645-0634-X) IDG Bks.

Mandarino, Joseph A. & Anderson, Violet. Monteregian Treasures: The Minerals of Mont Saint-Hilaire, Quebec. (Illus.). 302p. 1989. text 110.00 (0-521-32632-X) Cambridge U Pr.

Mandat-Grancey, Edmond. Cow-boys & Colonels: Narrative of a Journey Across the Prairie & over the Black Hills of Dakota. LC 83-23583. (Illus.). 378p. reprint ed. pap. 117.20 (0-7837-1840-3, 204203600001) Bks Demand.

Mandava. Business Math. 2nd ed. (Trade/Tech Math Ser.). 1989. pap. 104.95 incl. trans. (0-8273-3500-8) Delmar.

— Business Math. 3rd ed. (General Business & Business Education Ser.). 1994. mass mkt., teacher ed. 36.95 (0-8273-6415-6) Delmar.

— Business Math. 3rd ed. (General Business & Business Education Ser.). 1994. trans. 2.95 (0-8273-6413-X) Delmar.

— Business Mathematics. 3rd ed. 1994. text 60.95 (0-8273-6012-6) S-W Pub.

— The Collector's Garden. 1996. 30.00 (0-671-88997-4) S&S Trade.

— Practical Problems in Mathematics for Business & Marketing. (C). 1996. pap. text 14.95 (0-8273-6769-4); pap. text, teacher ed. 12.00 (0-8273-6770-8) Delmar.

Mandava & Cahill. Key into Literacy. 1991. pap. text. write for info. (0-582-87136-0, Pub. by Addison-Wesley) Longman.

— Key into Picture Books. 1992. pap. text. write for info. (0-582-87678-8, Pub. by Addison-Wesley) Longman.

Mandava, et al. Special Education for All Teachers. 2001. 46.50 (0-07-229940-1) McGraw.

Mandava, jt. auth. see Cronly.

Mandava, jt. auth. see Sherwood.

Mandava, Bhargavi C. Where the Oceans Meet: A 2 Novel. LC 96-34887. (Illus.). 288p. (Orig.). 1998. pap. 12.00 (1-58005-000-X) Seal Pr WA.

Mandava, N. Bhushan. Countercurrent Chromatography: Theory & Practice. Ito, Yoihciro, ed. (Chromatographic Science Ser.: Vol. 44). (Illus.). 752p. 1988. text 250.00 (0-8247-7815-4) Dekker.

— Handbook of Natural Pesticides: Insects, Vol. IIIA. 216p. 1988. lib. bdg. 219.00 (0-8493-3654-6) CRC Pr.

— Handbook of Natural Pesticides: Insects, Vol. IIIB. 200p. 1988. lib. bdg. 219.00 (0-8493-3655-4) CRC Pr.

Mandava, N. Bhushan, ed. Handbook of Natural Pesticides: Methods, 2 vols., Vol. I: Theory, Practice, & Detection. 552p. 1985. lib. bdg. 239.00 (0-8493-3651-1, SB951, CRC Reprint) Franklin.

— Handbook of Natural Pesticides: Methods, 2 vols., Vol. II: Isolation & Identification. 576p. 1985. lib. bdg. 220.00 (0-8493-3652-X, SB957, CRC Reprint) Franklin.

— Plant Growth Substances. LC 79-18933. (ACS Symposium Ser.: No. 111). 1979. 43.95 (0-8412-0518-3) Am Chemical.

— Plant Growth Substances. LC 79-18933. (ACS Symposium Ser.: Vol. 111). 320p. 1979. reprint ed. pap. 99.20 (0-608-03051-1, 206350400007) Bks Demand.

Mandava, N. Bhushan & Morgan, E. David, eds. Handbook of Natural Pesticides: Pheromones, 2 pts., Pt. A: Insect Olfaction & Molecular Structure. 224p. 1988. lib. bdg. 225.00 (0-8493-3657-0, SB951) CRC Pr.

— Handbook of Natural Pesticides: Pheromones, 2 pts., Pt. B: Pheromones of Diptera. 368p. 1988. lib. bdg. 239.00 (0-8493-3658-9, SB951) CRC Pr.

Mandava, N. Bhushan, et al. Natural Toxins: Toxicology, Chemistry, & Safety. 370p. (C). 1992. pap. text 79.15 (1-880293-01-3) Alaken.

Mandava, Suresh, et al. Color Atlas of Ophthalmology. LC 98-25048. (Illus.). 640p. 1998. pap. 59.00 (0-86577-685-7) Thieme Med Pubs.

— Meeth Pocket Atlas of Ophthalmology. LC 98-25048. 1998. 9.00 (3-13-107941-X) Thieme Med Pubs.

Mandavdhare, S. M. Caste & Land Relations in India. 1989. 46.00 (81-85024-50-2, Pub. by Uppal Pub Hse) S Asia.

Mandaville, James P. The Flora of Eastern Saudi Arabia. (Illus.). 600p. 1990. 125.00 (0-7103-0371-8, A4186) Routledge.

Mandaza, Ibbo, jt. auth. see Agere, Sam.

Mandaza, Ibbo, jt. ed. see Magubane, Bernard M.

Mande, Pierre. The Broken E String: A Collection of Short Stories. (Illus.). 67p. 1988. 7.95 (0-935087-17-6) Wright Pub Co.

***Mandel.** Crash. 2000. pap. 15.00 (0-465-04359-3, Pub. by Basic) HarpC.

— Feminist Issues. 3rd ed. 2000. pap. 53.27 (0-13-017019-4) P-H.

Mandel, Abby. Food Processor. LC 97-28573. (William-Sonoma Cookware Ser.). 1998. write for info. (1-887451-12-9) Wldon Owen Ref.

***Mandel, Abby.** Williams-Sonoma Food Processor Cookbook. rev. ed. (Williams-Sonoma Cookware Ser.). (Illus.). 95p. 1998. pap. 12.95 (1-892374-08-0) Weldon Owen.

Mandel, Adrienne S., ed. see Marivaux, Pierre Carlet de Chamblain de.

Mandel, Adrienne S., tr. see Marivaux, Pierre Carlet de Chamblain de.

Mandel, Alan. The S. E. X. Blackjack System. LC 86-70882. (Illus.). 224p. (Orig.). 1987. pap. 12.95 (0-9616765-0-7) Bronx Bks.

Mandel, Allan. Community Indicators: Improving Community Management. (Policy Research Project Report Ser.: No. 6). 149p. 1974. pap. 3.00 (0-89940-504-5) LBJ Sch Pub Aff.

Mandel, B. J. & Laessig, Robert E. Statistics for Management: A Practical Introduction to Statistics. 6th rev. ed. LC 95-83928. 538p. 1996. text 49.50 (0-910484-00-7) Dangary Pub.

Mandel, Birgit. Wunschbilder Werden Wahr Gemacht: Aneignung von Urlaubswelt durch Fotosouvenirs am Beispiel Deutscher Italientouristen der 50er und 60er Jahre. (GER., Illus.). 312p. 1996. 57.95 (3-631-30095-6) P Lang Pubng.

Mandel, Bob. Heart over Heels: 50 Ways Not to Leave Your Lover. LC 88-31159. 272p. (Orig.). 1995. pap. 9.95 (0-89087-541-3) Celestial Arts.

— Open Heart Therapy. LC 84-45360. 160p. (Orig.). 1995. pap. 8.95 (0-89087-408-5) Celestial Arts.

— Wake Up to Wealth. LC 93-38528. 192p. 1995. pap. 9.95 (0-89087-709-2) Celestial Arts.

Mandel, Bob, jt. auth. see Ray, Sondra.

Mandel, Brett. Minor Players, Major Dreams. LC 96-32437. (Illus.). xvi, 243p. 1997. pap. 16.95 (0-8032-8232-X, A Bison Orig) U of Nebr Pr.

Mandel, C. E., Jr. Environmental Stress Screening - A Tutorial. rev. ed. 125p. 1991. pap. 115.00 (1-877862-09-6) IEST.

Mandel, C. E., Jr. & Livesay, Billy R. Defect Induced Failure Mechanisms Accelerated by Environmental Stress Screening. rev. ed. LC 62-38584. 200p. 1990. pap. 115.00 (1-877862-04-5) IEST.

Mandel, Charlotte. A Disc of Clear Water. LC 80-25317. (Illus.). 66p. (Orig.). 1981. pap. 5.00 (0-938158-00-7) Saturday Pr.

— Doll. (Illus.). 24p. 1986. pap. 4.00 (0-938535-74-9) Salt-Works Pr.

— Keeping Him Alive. Little, Geraldine C., ed. 32p. (Orig.). 1990. pap. 4.50 (0-943710-04-9); pap. text 4.50 (0-685-46214-5) Silver App Pr.

— The Life of Mary: A Poem-Novella. unabridged ed. LC 87-28677. (Listen to the Poet Ser.). (Illus.). 72p. 1988. pap. 7.00 (0-938158-10-4) Saturday Pr.

— The Life of Mary: A Poem-Novella. unabridged ed. LC 87-28677. (Listen to the Poet Ser.). 1993. audio 9.00 (0-938158-14-7) Saturday Pr.

— The Marriages of Jacob: A Poem Novella. LC 91-10855. 110p. (Orig.). 1991. pap. 10.00 (0-916288-32-3) Micah Pubns.

— Sight Lines. LC 97-75904. (Poetry Ser.). (Illus.). 108p. 1998. pap. 12.00 (1-877675-27-X) Midmarch Arts.

Mandel, Charlotte, et al, eds. Saturday's Women. LC 82-10278. (Eileen W. Barnes Award Ser.). 102p. (Orig.). 1982. pap. 6.50 (0-938158-02-3) Saturday Pr.

Mandel, David. Former "State Socialist" World: Views from the Left. LC 95-79355. 215p. 1996. 48.99 (1-55164-037-6, Pub. by Black Rose); pap. 19.99 (1-55164-036-8, Pub. by Black Rose) Consort Bk Sales.

— Looking East Leftwards, Vol. 2. (Former "State Socialist" World Ser.). 250p. 1997. 53.99 (1-55164-099-6, Pub. by Black Rose); pap. text 24.99 (1-55164-098-8, Pub. by Black Rose) Consort Bk Sales.

— Perestroika & the Soviet People. LC 91-72984. 207p. 1991. 45.99 (1-895431-15-8, Pub. by Black Rose); pap. 16.99 (1-895431-14-X, Pub. by Black Rose) Consort Bk Sales.

— Rabotyagi: Perestroika & after Viewed from Below. 288p. (C). 1993. text 30.00 (0-85345-879-0, Pub. by Monthly Rev) NYU Pr.

— Rabotyagi: Perestroika & after Viewed from Below. 288p. (C). 1994. pap. text 19.00 (0-85345-878-2, Pub. by Monthly Rev) NYU Pr.

Mandel, David, jt. auth. see Fenichel, Allen.

Mandel, Deborah, et al. Lifestyle Redesign: Implementing the Well Elderly Program. LC 99-219954. (Illus.). 1999. pap. 32.00 (1-56900-120-0) Am Occup Therapy.

Mandel, Dorothy. Uncommon Eloquence: A Biography of Angna Enters. LC 86-17386. (Illus.). 368p. (Orig.). 1986. 24.50 (0-912869-07-0) Arden Pr.

Mandel, Edmund. The Right Path: The Autobiography of a Survivor. LC 94-6632. 1994. 35.00 (0-88125-498-3) Ktav.

Mandel, Eli. Contexts of Canadian Criticism. LC 78-143280. (Patterns of Literary Criticism Ser.). 1993. lib. bdg. 21.00 (0-226-50298-8) U Ch Pr.

— Eight More Canadian Poets. LC 73-167974. (Aspects of English Ser.). 88 p. 1972. write for info. (0-03-923376-6) Holt R&W.

Mandel, Eli & Bentley, Thomas Roy. Five Modern Canadian Poets. LC 73-167350. (Aspects of English Ser.). 88p. 1970. write for info. (0-03-923375-8) Holt R&W.

Mandel, Elias, jt. auth. see Meilach, Dona Z.

Mandel, Ellen, jt. auth. see Lydon, Michael.

Mandel, Eric R. & Wagoner, Michael D. Atlas of Corneal Disease. 160p. 1989. text 189.00 (0-7216-2160-0, W B Saunders Co) Harcrt Hlth Sci Grp.

Mandel, Ernest. Introduction to Marxist Economic Theory. 2nd ed. LC 73-82169. 78p. 1973. reprint ed. pap. 10.95 (0-87348-315-4) Pathfinder NY.

— Introduction to Marxist Economic Theory. 2nd ed. Pathfinder Press Staff, ed. LC 73-82169. 78p. 1973. reprint ed. lib. bdg. 30.00 (0-87348-314-6) Pathfinder NY.

— The Long Waves of Capitalist Development: A Marxist Interpretation. 2nd rev. ed. LC 95-3101. 174p. (C). 1995. pap. 23.00 (1-85984-037-X, C0480, Pub. by Verso) Norton.

— Marxist Economic Theory, 2 vols., 2. Pearce, Brian, tr. LC 68-13658. 417p. reprint ed. pap. 129.30 (0-8357-6204-1, 203433600002) Bks Demand.

— Marxist Economic Theory, 2 vols., Vol. 1. Pearce, Brian, tr. LC 68-13658. 383p. reprint ed. pap. 118.80 (0-8357-6203-3, 203433600001) Bks Demand.

— The Place of Marxism in History. LC 93-12067. (Revolutionary Studies). 112p. (C). 1994. pap. 10.95 (0-391-03814-1) Humanities.

— The Place of Marxism in History. LC 98-54283. 104p. 1999. pap. 14.95 (1-57392-331-1, Humanity Bks) Prometheus Bks.

— The Second Slump: A Marxist Analysis of Recession in the Seventies. 226p. 1985. pap. 15.95 (0-86091-728-2) Routledge.

Mandel, Ernest & Novack, George. The Marxist Theory of Alienation. 2nd rev. ed. LC 72-96599. (Illus.). 94p. 1973. reprint ed. pap. 10.95 (0-87348-230-1); reprint ed. lib. bdg. 30.00 (0-87348-229-8) Pathfinder NY.

Mandel, Ernst. Late Capitalism. 2nd ed. 640p. 1998. pap. 20.00 (1-85984-202-X, Pub. by Verso) Norton.

— Trotsky As Alternative. LC 94-48402. 186p. (C). 1995. pap. 19.00 (1-85984-085-X, C051, Pub. by Verso) Norton.

Mandel, Evelyn. The Art of Aging. Frost, Miriam, ed. Orig. Title: The Gray Matter. (Illus.). 176p. (Orig.). 1982. 8.95 (0-86683-752-3) Harper SF.

Mandel, Geoffrey, ed. see Chijiiwa, Hideaki.

Mandel, Gerry, jt. ed. see Rubel, William.

Mandel Glazer, Susan. Assessment Is Instruction: Reading, Writing, Spelling & Phonics for All Learners. LC 98-71294. (Illus.). 368p. 1998. pap. text 38.95 (0-926842-77-3) CG Pubs Inc.

— Phonics Spelling & Word Study: A Sensible Approach. 98p. 1999. pap. text 15.95 (0-926842-82-X) CG Pubs Inc.

Mandel, Hal W., jt. auth. see Bleich, Ronald L.

Mandel, Harvey P. Conduct Disorder & Underachievement: Risk Factors, Assessment, Treatment & Prevention. LC 96-23333. 304p. 1997. 69.95 (0-471-13147-4) Wiley.

— "Could Do Better" Why Children Underachieve & What to Do about It. LC 95-21521. 291p. 1996. pap. 14.95 (0-471-15847-X) Wiley.

— Short-Term Psychotherapy & Brief Treatment Techniques: An Annotated Bibliography, 1920-1980. LC 81-221. 704p. 1981. 95.00 (0-306-40658-6, Plenum Trade) Perseus Pubng.

Mandel, Harvey P. & Marcus, Sander I. The Psychology of Underachievement: Differential Diagnosis & Differential Treatment. LC 87-37127. (Personality Processes Ser.). 397p. 1988. 165.00 (0-471-84855-7) Wiley.

— Why Children Underachieve & What to Do about It: Could Do Better. 291p. 1998. text 26.00 (0-7881-5357-9) DIANE Pub.

Mandel, Harvey P., et al. "Could Do Better" Why Children Underachieve & What to Do about It. LC 95-21521. 1995. 22.95 (0-471-13361-2) Wiley.

Mandel, Hedi M., jt. auth. see Mandel, Linda.

Mandel, Jan, et al, eds. Domain Decomposition Methods 10: The 10th International Conference on Domain Decomposition Methods, August 10-14, 1997, Boulder, Colorado, U. S. A. LC 98-15580. (Contemporary Mathematics Ser.: Vol. 218). 554p. 1998. pap. 110.00 (0-8218-0988-1) Am Math.

Mandel, Jan & McCormick, S., eds. Proceedings of the Fourth Copper Mountain Conference on Multigrid Methods. LC 89-48783. (Proceedings in Applied Mathematics Ser.: No. 41). xii, 438p. 1989. pap. 44.50 (0-89871-248-3) Soc Indus-Appl Math.

Mandel, Jenna, jt. auth. see Da Costa Nunez, Ralph.

Mandel, Jerome. Geoffrey Chaucer: Building the Fragments of the Canterbury Tales. LC 91-55041. 256p. (C). 1992. 39.50 (0-8386-3454-0) Fairleigh Dickinson.

Mandel, Jerome, jt. ed. see Stevens, Martin.

Mandel, John. Analysis of Two-Way Layouts. 144p. (gr. 13). 1994. ring bd. 62.95 (0-412-98611-6, Chap & Hall CRC) CRC Pr.

— Analysis of Two-Way Layouts. LC 93-48326. 1994. 69.95 (0-442-01212-8) Chapman & Hall.

— Evaluation & Control of Measurements. LC 91-14138. (Quality & Reliability Ser.: No. 26). (Illus.). 267p. reprint ed. pap. 82.80 (0-608-20209-6, 207147100012) Bks Demand.

— The Statistical Analysis of Experimental Data. LC 83-20599. (Mathematics Ser.). 448p. 1984. reprint ed. pap. 12.95 (0-486-64666-1) Dover.

Mandel, Josh. SWAT 2: The Official Strategy Guide. LC 97-69341. (Secrets of the Game Ser.). 272p. 1998. per. 19.99 (0-7615-1116-4) Prima Pub.

Mandel, L. & Wolf, E., eds. Coherence & Quantum Optics, Five. LC 83-23067. 1280p. 1984. 195.00 (0-306-41517-8, Plenum Trade) Perseus Pubng.

Mandel, L. & Wolf, E., eds. Selected Papers on Coherence & Fluctuations of Light (1850-1966), MS19. 976p. 1990. pap. 35.00 (0-8194-0440-3) SPIE.

Mandel, L., ed. see Rochester Conference on Coherence & Quantum Optics.

Mandel, Lazaro J., jt. ed. see Eaton, Douglas C.

Mandel, Leonard & Wolf, Emil. Optical Coherence & Quantum Optics. (Illus.). 1192p. (C). 1995. text 54.95 (0-521-41711-2) Cambridge U Pr.

Mandel, Linda & Mandel, Hedi M. The Treasure of Trash: A Recycling Story. LC 92-41222. (Illus.). 48p. (J). (gr. 4 up). 12.95 (0-89529-575-X, Avery) Penguin Putnam.

Mandel-Maczko, Linda. Hanging Out with Thermoforming: A Puffee - Stretch Adventure. (Illus.). 48p. (J). (gr. 1-6). 1998. pap. 9.95 (0-9639432-4-3) Cardinal FL.

Mandel, Margaret. Teddy Bears & Steiff Animals, Second Series, Vol. 2. 2nd ed. (Illus.). 200p. 1996. pap. 19.95 (0-89145-356-3, 1817) Collector Bks.

— Teddy Bears, Annalee Animals. 3rd ed. 1996. 19.95 (0-89145-419-5, 2084) Collector Bks.

Mandel, Margaret F. Teddy Bears & Steiff Animals, Vol. 1. (Illus.). 288p. 1993. pap. 9.95 (0-89145-267-2, 1513) Collector Bks.

Mandel, Martin M. Diabetes: Don't Fear It. Beat It!: My Story, My Message, My Mission. large type ed. (Illus.). 175p. (Orig.). 1997. pap. 19.95 (0-9657143-0-6) Neuro Diabetic.

An Asterisk (*) at the beginning of an entry indicates that the title is appearing for the first time.

Mandel, Mary A. Religion & Sex: Index of New Information & Bibliography. 150p. 1997. 47.50 (*0-7883-1010-0*); pap. 44.50 (*0-7883-1011-9*) ABBE Pubs Assn.

***Mandel, Michael J.** The Coming Internet Depression: Why the High-Tech Boom Will Go Bust, Why the Crash Will Be Worse Than You Think, & How to Prosper Afterward. 2000. 27.00 (*0-465-04358-5*, Pub. by Basic) HarpC.

Mandel, Mike, photos by. Mike Mandel: Making Good Time. 72p. (Orig.). 1992. 27.50 (*0-918290-00-7*) Eighteen Pubns.

Mandel, Mike & Sultan, Larry. The Turk & the Jew. LC 97-97222. (Illus.). 32p. 1977. pap. 25.00 (*0-918290-01-5*) Eighteen Pubns.

Mandel, Mimi. Teen Resources on the Web: A Guide for Librarians, Parents & Teachers. 120p. 2000. pap. 17.95 (*1-57950-042-0*) Highsmith Pr.

Mandel, Miriam. Reading Hemingway: The Facts in the Fictions. LC 94-14481. 609p. 1995. 76.50 (*0-8108-2870-7*) Scarecrow.

Mandel, Morris. Stories for Public Speakers. abr. rev. ed. LC 96-3750. Orig. Title: A Complete Treasury of Stories for Public Speakers. x, 300 p. 1996. 19.95 (*0-8246-0389-3*) Jonathan David.

Mandel, Muriel. Simple Experiments in Time with Everyday Materials. LC 97-992. (Illus.). 96p. (J). 1997. 14.95 (*0-8069-3803-X*) Sterling.

Mandel, Neville. The Arabs & Zionism Before World War One. LC 73-78545. 1977. pap. 13.95 (*0-520-03940-8*, Pub. by U CA Pr) Cal Prin Full Svc.

Mandel, Oscar. The Book of Elaborations. LC 85-114320. 320p. 1985. 17.95 (*0-8112-0962-8*, Pub. by New Directions) Norton.

— The Book of Elaborations. LC 85-114320. 320p. 1987. pap. 12.95 (*0-8112-1023-5*, NDP643, Pub. by New Directions) Norton.

— Collected Lyrics & Epigrams. LC 81-410. 104p. 1982. 9.50 (*0-89807-025-2*) Spectrum Prods.

— Collected Plays, 2 vols. LC 70-134738. 1971. 24.00 (*0-914502-04-2*); pap. 16.00 (*0-914502-05-0*) Spectrum Prods.

— Five Comedies of Medieval France. LC 71-20643. (Illus.). 158p. 1970. reprint ed. pap. 45.10 (*0-608-04421-0*, AU00482) Bks Demand.

— The Kukkurrik Fables: 43 Mini-Plays for All Media. LC 86-63083. (Illus.). 116p. (Orig.). 1987. pap. 4.25 (*0-914502-06-9*) Spectrum Prods.

— Philoctetes & the Fall of Troy: Plays, Documents, Iconography, Interpretations. LC 80-28524. (Illus.). 287p. 1981. reprint ed. pap. 81.80 (*0-7837-6021-3*, 2045833) Bks Demand.

— Sigismund, Prince of Poland: A Baroque Entertainment. LC 88-204. (Illus.). 72p. (Orig.). (C). 1988. pap. text 13.50 (*0-8191-6931-5*); lib. bdg. 25.50 (*0-8191-6930-7*) U Pr of Amer.

— Simplicities: Poems. LC 74-79131. 64p. 1974. pap. 4.00 (*0-914502-01-8*) Spectrum Prods.

— The Virgin & the Unicorn: Four Plays by Oscar Mandel. LC 93-83430. (Orig.). 1993. pap. 15.95 (*0-914502-10-7*) Spectrum Prods.

Mandel, Oscar, ed. The Theatre of Don Juan: A Collection of Plays & Views, 1630-1963. LC 86-1491. (Illus.). x, 731p. 1986. pap. text 35.00 (*0-8032-8137-4*, Bison Books) U of Nebr Pr.

Mandel, Oscar, jt. auth. see Merimee, Prosper.

Mandel, Oscar, jt. auth. see Sutherland, John.

Mandel, Oscar, ed. see Marivaux, Pierre Carlet de Chamblain de.

Mandel, Oscar, ed. & tr. see Marivaux, Pierre Carlet de Chamblain de.

Mandel, Oscar, tr. see Corneille, Thomas.

Mandel, Oscar, tr. see Moliere.

Mandel, Oscar, tr. see Tieck, Ludwig.

Mandel, Patricia C. Fair Wilderness: American Paintings in the Collection of the Adirondack Museum. Gilborn, Alice W. et al, eds. (Illus.). 176p. 1990. pap. 39.95 (*0-910020-40-X*) Adirondack Mus.

Mandel, Patricia C., jt. auth. see O'Brien, Maureen C.

Mandel, Paul. Theoretical Problems in Cavity Nonlinear Optics. LC 96-15181. (Cambridge Studies in Modern Optics: No. 21). (Illus.). 198p. (C). 1997. text 64.95 (*0-521-55385-7*) Cambridge U Pr.

Mandel, Paul & DeFeudis, Francis V., eds. CNS Receptors: From Molecular Pharmacology to Behavior. LC 83-11175. (Advances in Biochemical Psychopharmacology Ser.: Vol. 37). (Illus.). 527p. reprint ed. pap. 163.40 (*0-7837-9571-8*, 206032000005) Bks Demand.

Mandel, Peter. Esogetics: The Sense & Nonsense of Sickness & Pain. Kristen, S. & Allanach, J., trs. from GER. (Illus.). 182p. (Orig.). 1993. pap. text 25.00 (*3-925806-71-7*) Medicina Bio.

— My Ocean Liner: Across the North Atlantic on the Great Ship Normandie. (Illus.). 48p. (J). (gr. 3-6). 2000. 16.95 (*0-88045-149-1*) Stemmer Hse.

— The Official Dog I. Q. Test. (Illus.). 47p. 1995. pap. 6.95 (*1-56625-015-3*) Bonus Books.

— Practical Compendium of Colorpuncture. Baker, Christopher, tr. from GER. (Illus.). 269p. 1986. text 98.00 (*3-925806-08-3*) Medicina Bio.

— Red Cat, White Cat. (J). 1995. 14.95 (*0-8050-2929-X*) H Holt & Co.

— Say Hey! LC 99-34441. 32p. (J). 2000. 15.99 (*0-7868-0480-7*, Pub. by Hyprn Child) Time Warner.

— Say Hey! 786th ed. LC 99-34441. 32p. (J). (ps-3). 2000. lib. bdg. 16.01 (*0-7868-2417-4*, Pub. by Hyprn Child) Time Warner.

Mandel, Ralph, tr. see Hirsch, Moshe, et al.

Mandel, Richard D. Weavings from Nahuala: A Mayan Tradition. Cilella, Salvatore G., ed. McRae, Patricia B., tr. (SPA., Illus.). 28p. (C). 1992. write for info. (*0-9627858-1-4*) Columbia Mus Art.

Mandel, Robert. The Changing Face of National Security, 156. LC 94-17982. (Contributions in Military Studies Ser.: No. 156). 176p. 1994. 55.00 (*0-313-28519-5*, Greenwood Pr) Greenwood.

— Conflict over the World's Resources: Background, Trends, Case Studies, & Considerations for the Future, 225. LC 88-15489. (Contributions in Political Science Ser.: No. 225). 156p. 1988. 47.95 (*0-313-26129-6*, MCQ/) Greenwood.

— Deadly Transfers & the Global Playground: Transnational Security Threats in a Disorderly World. LC 98-46794. 160p. 1999. 55.00 (*0-275-96228-8*, Praeger Pubs) Greenwood.

— Irrationality in International Confrontation, 185. LC 87-7588. (Contributions in Political Science Ser.: No. 185). 162p. 1987. 49.95 (*0-313-25950-X*, MIY/, Greenwood Pr) Greenwood.

***Mandel, Rolfe D., ed.** Geoarchaeology in the Great Plains. (Illus.). 336p. 2001. pap. 29.95 (*0-8061-3261-2*) U of Okla Pr.

***Mandel, Sally.** Out of the Blue. LC 99-42026. 304p. 2000. 23.00 (*0-345-42890-0*, Ballantine Epiphany) Ballantine Pub Grp.

— Out of the Blue. large type ed. LC 00-27767. 478p. 2000. 26.95 (*0-7862-2551-3*) Thorndike Pr.

***Mandel, Scott.** Wired into Judaism: The Internet & Jewish Education. LC 00-101925. 150p. 2000. pap. write for info. (*0-86705-049-7*) A R E Pub.

***Mandel, Scott M.** Virtual Field Trips in the Cyberage: A Content Mapping Approach. 172p. 1999. 32.95 (*1-57517-159-7*) SkyLght.

***Mandel, Scott M. & Kinsman, Amy.** Social Studies in the Cyberage. LC 98-61239. ix, 162p. 1998. write for info. (*1-57517-122-8*) SkyLght.

Mandel, Siegfried. Nietzsche & the Jews: Exaltation & Denigration. LC 98-21368. 350p. 1998. 49.95 (*1-57392-223-4*) Prometheus Bks.

Mandel, Steve. Effective Presentation Skills: A Practical Guide to Better Speaking. 4th rev. ed. LC 99-69618. (Illus.). 104p. 1999. pap. 12.95 (*1-56052-526-6*) Crisp Pubns.

— Effective Presentation Skills: A Practice Guide for Better Speaking. 2nd rev. ed. Crisp, Michael, ed. LC 92-75722. (Fifty-Minute Ser.). 85p. 1993. pap. 10.95 (*1-56052-202-X*) Crisp Pubns.

— Presentation Power! 85p. 1995. pap. 149.00 incl. audio, VHS (*1-56052-370-0*) Crisp Pubns.

Mandel, Steve. Presentation Power! 1995. pap. 24.95 incl. audio (*1-56052-371-9*) Crisp Pubns.

Mandel, Steve. Technical Presentation Skills: A Practical Guide for Better Speaking. rev. ed. Gerould, Philip, ed. LC 93-74052. (Fifty-Minute Ser.). (Illus.). 94p. (Orig.). 1994. pap. 10.95 (*1-56052-263-1*) Crisp Pubns.

Mandel, Steven, et al, eds. Minor Head Trauma. LC 92-49619. (Illus.). 347p. 1993. 139.00 (*0-387-97943-3*) Spr-Verlag.

***Mandel, Steven & Willis, Jeanean D., eds.** Handbook of Lower Extremity Neurology. LC 98-53549. (Illus.). 256p. 1999. pap. write for info. (*0-443-07548-4*, W B Saunders Co) Harcrt Hlth Sci Grp.

Mandel, Theo. The Elements of User Interface Design. LC 96-45973. 464p. 1997. pap. 44.99 (*0-471-16267-1*) Wiley.

Mandel, Thomas & Van Der Leun, Gerard. Rules of the Net: How to Live & Thrive in Cyberspace Once You've Finally Arrived. 288p. (J). 1996. pap. 11.50 (*0-7868-8135-6*, Pub. by Hyperion) Time Warner.

Mandel, Thomas E., jt. ed. see Green, Marjorie K.

Mandel, Tom. Erat: Poems. deluxe limited ed. (Burning Deck Poetry Ser.). 24p. 1981. pap. 15.00 (*0-930900-99-5*) Burning Deck.

— Four Strange Books. 128p. (Orig.). (C). 1990. pap. 12.00 (*0-9623399-1-1*) Gaz NJ.

— Letters of the Law. LC 94-4020. (New American Poetry Ser.: No. 15). 128p. (Orig.). 1994. pap. 10.95 (*1-55713-164-3*) Sun & Moon CA.

— Prospect of Release. 64p. (Orig.). 1996. pap. 11.00 (*0-925904-16-3*) Chax Pr.

— Prospect of Release. LC 96-13879. (Orig.). 1996. write for info. (*0-925904-11-2*) Chax Pr.

— Ready to Go. LC 81-4904. 69p. (Orig.). 1981. pap. 4.00 (*0-87886-113-0*, Greenfld Rev Pr) Greenfld Rev Lit.

— Realism. (Burning Deck Poetry Ser.). 80p. (Orig.). 1991. pap. 8.00 (*0-930901-70-3*) Burning Deck.

— Realism. limited ed. (Burning Deck Poetry Ser.). 80p. (Orig.). 1991. pap. 15.00 (*0-930901-71-1*) Burning Deck.

Mandel, Tom & Davidson, Daniel. Absence Sensorium. 135p. 1997. pap. 14.00 (*0-937013-64-1*) Potes Poets.

***Mandel, William.** Saying No to Power. LC 99-63842. (Illus.). 550p. 1999. pap. 18.50 (*0-88739-286-5*) Creat Arts Bk.

Mandel, William. The Soviet Far East & Central Asia. LC 75-30111. (Institute of Pacific Relations Ser.). reprint ed. 32.50 (*0-404-59545-6*) AMS Pr.

Mandel, William J. Cardiac Arrhythmias. 3rd ed. 860p. 1995. text 180.00 (*0-397-51185-X*) Lppncott W & W.

Mandel-Yehuda, Sarah, ed. see Brioschi, Antonio.

Mandela, Nelson. Long Walk to Freedom: The Autobiography of Nelson Mandela. (Illus.). 608p. 1995. pap. 14.95 (*0-316-54818-9*) Little.

— Mandela: An Illustrated Autobiography. LC 96-77497. (Illus.). 208p. (gr. 8). 1996. 29.95 (*0-316-55038-8*) Little.

— Nelson Mandela: Intensifiquemos la Lucha: Discursos en Africa, Europa y Norteamerica. Madrid, Luis, ed. & intro. by. McCattan, Greg, intro. LC 90-63059. (SPA., Illus.). 108p. (Orig.). 1990. pap. 13.95 (*0-87348-597-1*); lib. bdg. 35.00 (*0-87348-598-X*) Pathfinder NY.

— Nelson Mandela Speaks: Forging a Democratic, Nonracial South Africa. Clark, Steve, ed. LC 93-85689. (Illus.). 96p. (Orig.). 1993. pap. 18.95 (*0-87348-774-5*); lib. bdg. 50.00 (*0-87348-775-3*) Pathfinder NY.

— Nelson Mandela Speeches, 1990: 'Intensify the Struggle to Abolish Apartheid' (Illus.). 74p. (Orig.). (C). 1990. pap. 6.00 (*0-87348-595-5*) Pathfinder NY.

— No Easy Walk to Freedom. pap. 8.95 (*0-7493-0504-5*, AO452) Heinemann.

— No Easy Walk to Freedom. (African Writers Ser.). (Illus.). 189p. (C). 1986. pap. 8.95 (*0-435-90782-4*, 90782) Heinemann.

— The Struggle Is My Life. 2nd ed. LC 90-63060. (Illus.). 281p. 1990. pap. 15.95 (*0-87348-593-9*); lib. bdg. 50.00 (*0-87348-594-7*) Pathfinder NY.

Mandela, Nelson, frwd. Housing Generator: Competition Results & Context. LC 98-120905. (Illus.). 120p. 1998. pap. 30.00 (*90-5662-070-3*, 810771, Pub. by NAi Uitgevers) Dist Art Pubs.

Mandela, Nelson, intro. My Wish for Tomorrow: Words & Pictures From Children Around the World: In Celebration of the Fiftieth Anniversary of the United Nations. (Illus.). 48p. (J). (ps up). 1995. lib. bdg. 15.93 (*0-688-14456-X*, Wm Morrow) Morrow Avon.

Mandela, Nelson & Castro, Fidel. How Far We Slaves Have Come! LC 91-66760. (Illus.). 83p. (Orig.). (C). 1991. pap. 8.95 (*0-87348-729-X*); lib. bdg. 30.00 (*0-87348-497-5*) Pathfinder NY.

— Que Lejos Hemos Llegado los Esclavos! Sudafrica y Cuba En el Mundo de Hoy. LC 91-66761. (SPA., Illus.). 83p. (Orig.). 1991. pap. 10.95 (*0-87348-732-X*) Pathfinder NY.

Mandela, Winnie. A Part of My Soul Went with Him. Benjamin, Anne & Benson, Mary, eds. LC 85-21632. (Illus.). 164p. 1985. pap. 6.95 (*0-393-30290-3*) Norton.

***Mandelaris, William M.** A Clash of Values: Are the Media & other Outside Influences Underminding Our Family Principles? LC 99-90245. 240p. 1999. 24.95 (*1-893160-00-9*) Desert Sky Pubg.

Mandelaro, Jim & Pitoniak, Scott. Silver Seasons: The Story of the Rochester Red Wings. LC 95-50078. (Illus.). (C). 1996. pap. 19.95 (*0-8156-0379-7*, MASSP); text 42.95 (*0-8156-2703-3*, MASS) Syracuse U Pr.

Mandelbaum. From Homer to Dante. 2001. pap. write for info. (*0-15-600220-5*) Harcourt.

***Mandelbaum, Adam.** The Psychic Battlefield: A History of the Military-Occult Complex. LC 99-55025. 336p. 2000. text 26.95 (*0-312-20955-X*) St Martin.

Mandelbaum, Alexander Aryeh. Simchah - the Spark of Life. 190p. 1995. 16.95 (*0-87306-732-0*) Feldheim.

Mandelbaum, Allen. Lectura Dantis: Inferno. LC 98-34223. 490p. 1998. 45.00 (*0-520-21249-5*, Pub. by U CA Pr); pap. 19.95 (*0-520-21270-3*, Pub. by U CA Pr) Cal Prin Full Svc.

— The Metamorphoses of Ovid. 576p. 1995. pap. 17.00 (*0-15-600126-8*) Harcourt.

— The Odyssey of Homer: A New Verse Translation. (Illus.). 1990. 48.00 (*0-520-07021-6*, Pub. by U CA Pr) Cal Prin Full Svc.

— The Savantasse of Montparnasse. (Illus.). 203p. 1987. pap. 16.95 (*0-935296-71-9*, Pub. by Sheep Meadow); text 27.50 (*0-935296-70-0*, Pub. by Sheep Meadow) U Pr of New Eng.

Mandelbaum, Allen, tr. from ITA. The Divine Comedy. LC 92-553. 484p. 1995. 0.23 (*0-679-43313-9*) Everymns Lib.

— The Metamorphoses of Ovid. LC 93-8118. 1993. 40.00 (*0-15-170529-1*) Harcourt.

Mandelbaum, Allen & Richardson, Robert D., eds. Three Centuries of American Poetry. LC 98-31408. 768p. 1999. pap. 20.00 (*0-553-37518-0*) Bantam.

— Three Centuries of American Poetry, 1623-1923. LC 98-31408. 912p. 1999. 35.00 (*0-553-10250-8*) Bantam.

Mandelbaum, Allen, tr. see Dante Alighieri.

Mandelbaum, Allen, tr. see Virgil.

Mandelbaum, Allen, tr. & intro. see Dante Alighieri.

***Mandelbaum, Ann, photos by.** Ann Mandelbaum - New York. (Illus.). 1999. 45.00 (*3-908161-59-2*) Abbeville Pr.

Mandelbaum, Bernard. Choose Life. 1972. pap. 9.95 (*0-8197-0006-1*) Bloch.

— Tales of the Fathers of the Conservative Movement. LC 89-63758. (Illus.). 80p. 1990. pap. 9.95 (*0-88400-140-7*, Shengold Bks) Schreiber Pub.

— Wisdom of Solomon Schechter. 1963. pap. 2.50 (*0-8381-3103-4*) USCJE.

Mandelbaum, David G. The Plains Cree, Vol. 37, Pt. 2. LC 76-43772. reprint ed. 42.00 (*0-404-15626-6*) AMS Pr.

— Society in India Vol. I: Continuity & Change. 392p. 1972. pap. 17.95 (*0-520-01893-1*, Pub. by U CA Pr) Cal Prin Full Svc.

— Society in India Vol. II: Change & Continuity. 408p. 1972. pap. 17.95 (*0-520-01895-8*, Pub. by U CA Pr) Cal Prin Full Svc.

— Women's Seclusion & Men's Honor: Sex Roles in North India, Bangladesh, & Pakistan. LC 87-36547. (Illus.). 153p. 1993. reprint ed. pap. text 16.95 (*0-8165-1400-3*) U of Ariz Pr.

Mandelbaum, David G., ed. see Sapir, Edward.

Mandelbaum, Ellen. The Divine Comedy. (Critical Editions Ser.). (C). Date not set. pap. write for info. (*0-393-96796-4*, Norton Paperbks) Norton.

Mandelbaum, Irving J., ed. The Talmud of the Land of Israel, a Preliminary Translation & Explanation, Vol. 4: Kilayim. LC 90-10979. (Chicago Studies in the History of Judaism). (Illus.). 450p. 1990. lib. bdg. 90.00 (*0-226-57661-2*) U Ch Pr.

Mandelbaum, Jane. Small Project Automation for Libraries & Information Centers. (Supplement to Small Computers in Libraries Ser.: No. 28). 350p. 1992. lib. bdg. 42.50 (*0-88736-731-3*) Mecklermedia.

Mandelbaum, Jonathan, tr. see Furet, Francois.

Mandelbaum, Jonathan, tr. see Pera, Marcello.

Mandelbaum, Jonathan, tr. see Plessis, Alain.

Mandelbaum, Jonna L. The Missionary As a Cultural Interpreter. (American University Studies: Series 7, Vol. 46). 220p. 1989. 34.00 (*0-8204-0692-9*) P Lang Pubng.

Mandelbaum, Ken. Not since Carrie: Forty Years of Broadway Musical Flops. (Illus.). 384p. 1992. pap. 14.95 (*0-312-08273-8*) St Martin.

Mandelbaum, Lyn. Consider Yourself Lucky. LC 79-91629. (Illus.). 52p. (Orig.). 1979. pap. 6.00 (*0-935694-00-5*) St Edns.

— Consider Yourself Lucky. deluxe ed. LC 79-91629. (Illus.). 52p. (Orig.). 1979. pap. 12.00 (*0-686-31786-6*) St Edns.

— Say! deluxe limited ed. (Illus.). 1982. pap. 10.00 (*0-935694-02-1*) St Edns.

Mandelbaum, Maurice. The Phenomenology of Moral Experience. LC 72-13895. (Johns Hopkins Paperbacks Ser.: No. 65). 336p. reprint ed. pap. 104.20 (*0-8357-6745-0*, 203540000095) Bks Demand.

— Philosophy, Science, & Sense Perception: Historical & Critical Studies. LC 64-16312. 276p. reprint ed. pap. 85.60 (*0-608-06124-7*, 206645700008) Bks Demand.

— Purpose & Necessity in Social Theory. LC 86-46283. 208p. 1987. reprint ed. pap. 64.50 (*0-608-06711-3*, 206690800009) Bks Demand.

Mandelbaum, Maurice, jt. ed. see Lee, Edward N.

Mandelbaum, Maurice H. The Anatomy of Historical Knowledge. LC 76-46945. 240p. reprint ed. pap. 74.40 (*0-8357-5463-4*, 202413300035) Bks Demand.

— History, Man & Reason: A Study in Nineteenth-Century Thought. LC 75-150042. 565p. reprint ed. pap. 175.20 (*0-608-30622-3*, 201994600015) Bks Demand.

— The Problem of Historical Knowledge: An Answer to Relativism. LC 74-152993. (Select Bibliographies Reprint Ser.). 1977. reprint ed. 24.95 (*0-8369-5745-8*) Ayer.

Mandelbaum, Michael. The Dawn of Peace in Europe. LC 96-21875. 207p. 1996. 19.95 (*0-87078-396-3*) Century Foundation.

— The Fate of Nations: The Search for National Security in the Nineteenth & Twentieth Centuries. (Illus.). 384p. 1988. 17.95 (*0-521-35527-3*); pap. text 21.95 (*0-521-35790-X*) Cambridge U Pr.

***Mandelbaum, Michael.** The New European Diasporas. 2000. pap. 19.95 (*0-87609-257-1*) Coun Foreign.

Mandelbaum, Michael. The Nuclear Future. LC 82-74068. (Cornell Studies in Security Affairs). 131p. 1983. pap. 12.95 (*0-8014-9254-8*) Cornell U Pr.

Mandelbaum, Michael, ed. America's Defense. LC 87-35705. 360p. 1989. 45.00 (*0-8419-1156-8*); pap. 24.95 (*0-8419-1157-6*) Holmes & Meier.

— The Other Side of the Table: The Soviet Approach to Arms Control. LC 89-22239. 215p. 1990. reprint ed. pap. 66.70 (*0-608-02004-4*, 206266000003) Bks Demand.

— The Rise of Nations in the Soviet Union: American Foreign Policy & the Disintegration of the U. S. S. R. LC 91-418. 128p. 1991. reprint ed. pap. 39.70 (*0-608-02002-8*, 206265800003) Bks Demand.

Mandelbaum, Michael, jt. ed. see Kapstein, Ethan.

Mandelbaum, Michael, ed. see Treverton, Gregory F., et al.

Mandelbaum, Miriam, jt. auth. see Lee, Jennifer B.

***Mandelbaum, Paul, ed.** First Words: Earliest Writing from Favorite Contemporary Authors. rev. ed. LC 99-86208. (Illus.). 288p. 2000. pap. 16.95 (*1-56512-272-0*, 72272) Algonquin Bks.

Mandelbaum, Pili. You Be Me, I'll Be You.Tr. of Noire Comme le Cafe, Blanc Comme la Lune. (Illus.). 40p. (J). (ps-3). 1993. reprint ed. pap. 6.95 (*0-916291-47-2*) Kane-Miller Bk.

Mandelbaum, R., jt. ed. see Harper, J.

Mandelbaum, Seymour J. Boss Tweed's New York. Cantor, Norman F., ed. LC 81-13368. (New Dimensions in History Ser.: Historical Cities). (Illus.). 196p. 1982. reprint ed. lib. bdg. 49.75 (*0-313-23259-8*, MATY, Greenwood Pr) Greenwood.

***Mandelbaum, Seymour J.** Open Moral Communities. LC 99-43445. 415p. 2000. 35.00 (*0-262-13365-2*) MIT Pr.

Mandelbaum, Seymour J., et al, eds. Explorations in Planning Theory. LC 95-20379. 566p. (C). 1996. text 44.95 (*0-88285-153-5*); pap. text 21.95 (*0-88285-154-3*) Ctr Urban Pol Res.

Mandelbaum, Yitta H., ed. Holy Brother: Inspiring Stories & Enchanted Tales about Rabbi Shlomo Carlebach. LC 96-33144. 240p. 1997. 30.00 (*0-7657-5959-4*) Aronson.

Mandelblatt, Abe & Mandelblatt, Malka. Abe & Malka's One Hundred Guitar Accompaniment Patterns. (Illus.). 200p. 1974. pap. 21.95 (*0-8256-2812-1*, AM41369) Music Sales.

Mandelblatt, Malka, jt. auth. see Mandelblatt, Abe.

Mandelbrojt, S. Principles & Methods. LC 75-170339. (Dirichlet Ser.). 166p. 1971. text 139.00 (*90-277-0214-4*) Kluwer Academic.

Mandelbrojt-Sweeney, Mireille. Anglais Medical: Medical English. (ENG & FRE.). 168p. 1992. 49.95 (*0-8288-6918-9*, 2225827028) Fr & Eur.

Mandelbrot, B. Multifractals & 1/f Noise. (Illus.). 400p. 1998. 42.95 (*0-387-98539-5*) Spr-Verlag.

Mandelbrot, Benoit, ed. Fractals & Scaling in Finance: Discontinuity, Concentration, & Risk. LC 97-37930. (Illus.). 551p. 39.95 (*0-387-98363-5*) Spr-Verlag.

Mandelbrot, Benoit B. The Fractal Geometry of Nature. LC 81-15085. (Illus.). 460p. (C). 1982. text 39.95 (*0-7167-1186-9*) W H Freeman.

M

M

***Mandelbrot, Benoit B.** Gaussian Self-Affinity & Fractals: Globality, the Earth, 1/F Noise, R/S. (Illus.). 400p. 2000. 42.95 (*0-387-98993-5*) Spr-Verlag.

Mandelbrot, Benoit B. & Hirst, Bill. Fractal Landscapes from the Real World. (Illus.). 86p. 1995. 45.00 (*0-948797-24-X*) Dist Art Pubs.

Mandelbrot, Benoit B. & Scholz, Christopher H. Fractals in Geophysics. 350p. 1990. 34.50 (*0-8176-2206-3*) Birkhauser.

Mandelbrot Set International, Ltd. Staff. Advanced Microsoft Visual Basics. 2nd ed. 896p. 59.99 incl. cd-rom (*1-57231-893-7*) Microsoft.

Mandelbrote, Giles, et al, eds. The Book Trade & Its Customers: 1450-1990. LC 97-8786. (Illus.). 334p. 1997. 75.00 (*1-884718-34-5*) Oak Knoll.

***Mandeles, Mark D.** The Development of the B-52 & Jet Propulsion: A Case Study for Organizational Innovation. LC 98-14703. (Illus.). 208p. 1998. pap. 13.00 (*1-58566-036-1*) Air Univ.

Mandeles, Mark D. & Hone, Thomas C. Managing "Command & Control" in the Persian Gulf War. LC 95-46157. 192p. 1996. 57.95 (*0-275-95261-4*, Praeger Pubs) Greenwood.

Mandelglatt, James L., jt. auth. see Langess, Robert S.

***Mandelis, Andreas.** Semiconductors & Electronic Materials, Vol. 4. 1999. pap. text 58.00 (*0-8194-3506-6*) SPIE.

Mandelis, Andreas, ed. Photoacoustic & Thermal Wave Phenomena in Semiconductors. 480p. 1987. 91.00 (*0-444-01226-5*) P-H.

— Principles & Perspectives of Photothermal & Photoacoustic Phenomena. 1991. 110.00 (*0-444-01641-4*) P-H.

Mandelis, Andreas & Christofides, Constantinos. Physics, Chemistry, & Technology of Solid State Gas Sensor Devices. (Chemical Analysis Ser.: Vol. 125). 352p. 1993. 98.95 (*0-471-55885-0*) Wiley.

Mandelis, Andreas & Hess, P. Life & Earth Sciences. LC 96-48001. (Progress in Photothermal & Photoacoustic Science & Technology Ser.). 454p. 1996. 80.00 (*0-8194-2450-1*) SPIE.

***Mandelker.** Land Use Law, 1999 Supplement: Pocketpart. 4th ed. 80p. 1999. suppl. ed. write for info. (*0-327-01759-7*, 6458315) LEXIS Pub.

Mandelker & Cunningham. Planning & Controlling Land Development, 1995. 4th ed. LC 95-80658. 957p. 1995. text 54.00 (*1-55834-279-6*, 12209-11, MICHIE) LEXIS Pub.

Mandelker, et al. State & Local Government in the Federal System, 1983. 4th ed. 1982. text 52.00 (*0-87215-663-X*, 12277-10, MICHIE) LEXIS Pub.

Mandelker, Amy. Bakhtin in Contexts: Across the Disciplines. LC 95-23880. (Rethinking Theory Ser.). vii, 218p. (C). 1995. pap. text 16.95 (*0-8101-1269-8*) Northwestern U Pr.

— Framing Anna Karenina: Tolstoy, the Woman Question & the Victorian Novel. LC 93-5570. (Theory & Interpretation of Narrative Ser.). 241p. 1994. text 45.00 (*0-8142-0613-1*) Ohio St U Pr.

Mandelker, Amy, ed. Bakhtin in Contexts: Across the Disciplines. LC 95-23880. (Rethinking Theory Ser.). 200p. 1995. text 69.95 (*0-8101-1268-X*) Northwestern U Pr.

Mandelker, Amy & Powers, Elizabeth, eds. Pilgrim Souls: A Collection of Spiritual Autobiographies. LC 98-40813. 544p. 1999. per. 17.00 (*0-684-84311-0*) S&S Trade.

Mandelker, Daniel. Land Use Law, 1997. 4th ed. LC 97-75493. 734p. 1997. text 105.00 (*1-55834-701-1*, 64584-11, MICHIE) LEXIS Pub.

Mandelker, Daniel R. Land Use Law. 3rd ed. 632p. 1993. 85.00 (*1-55834-126-9*, MICHIE) LEXIS Pub.

— NEPA Law & Litigation. LC 92-24290. 1992. ring bd. 145.00 (*0-87632-904-0*) West Group.

Mandelker, Daniel R. & Ewald, William R., Jr. Street Graphics & the Law. 3rd ed. LC 87-71118. (Illus.). 207p. 1988. pap. 35.95 (*0-918286-50-6*, Planners Press) Am Plan Assn.

Mandelker, Daniel R. & Montgomery. Housing in America: Problems & Perspectives. LC 73-7689. 1973. pap. 19.95 (*0-672-61346-8*, Bobbs) Macmillan.

Mandelker, Daniel R. & Netsch, Dawn Clark. State & Local Government in a Federal System. 3rd ed. (Contemporary Legal Education Ser.). 828p. 1992. suppl. ed. 6.00 (*0-685-57756-2*, MICHIE) LEXIS Pub.

Mandelker, Daniel R., et al. Federal Land Use Law: Limitations, Procedures, Remedies. LC 86-17099. (Real Property - Zoning Ser.). 1986. ring bd. 145.00 (*0-87632-516-9*) West Group.

— Intergovernmental Decisionmaking for Environmental Protection & Public Works. (Illus.). 85p. (Orig.). (C). 1994. pap. text 25.00 (*0-7881-1516-2*) DIANE Pub.

Mandelker, Daniel R., jt. auth. see Ewald, William.

Mandelker, Ira L. Religion, Society, & Utopia in Nineteenth-Century America. LC 84-47. 200p. 1984. lib. bdg. 30.00 (*0-87023-436-6*) U of Mass Pr.

Mandelker, Lester, jt. ed. see Glasofer, Seymour.

***Mandelker, Scott.** Universal Vision: Soul Evolution & the Cosmic Plan. 3p. 2000. pap. 18.00 (*0-9701985-0-7*) U V Way.

— Universal Vision: Soul-Evolution & the Cosmic Plan. rev. ed. 326p. 1999. reprint ed. pap. 14.95 (*1-891850-14-8*) Med Bear.

Mandelkern, Leo. An Introduction to Macromolecules. 2nd ed. 180p. 1983. 44.95 (*0-387-90796-3*) Spr-Verlag.

Mandelkern, Mark. Constructive Continuity. LC 82-24358. (Memoirs of the American Mathematical Society Ser.: No. 42/277). 117p. 1983. pap. 17.00 (*0-8218-2277-2*, MEMO 42/277) Am Math.

Mandelkern, Nicholas D. & Weber, Vicki L. The Jewish Holiday Home Companion: A Parent's Guide to Family Celebration. LC 94-231812. (Illus.). 96p. pap. 5.95 (*0-87441-566-7*) Behrman.

Mandelkern, Nicholas D., ed. see Bamberger, David.

Mandelkern, Nicholas D., ed. see Fishman, Priscilla, et al.

Mandelkern, S. Heichal Hakodesh Concordance to the Old Testament, 1 vol. (ENG & HEB.). 1532p. 95.00 (*0-87559-163-9*) Shalom.

Mandelkorn, Philip, ed. To Know Your Self: The Essential Teachings of Swami Satchidananda. LC 77-80901. 264p. 1988. pap. 9.95 (*0-932040-34-9*) Integral Yoga Pubns.

Mandell. Advanced Placement-Computer Science with Pascal. 2nd ed. 1989. mass mkt., wbk. ed. 25.25 (*0-314-51399-X*) West Pub.

— Computers & Information Processing. 7th ed. (Computer Applications Ser.). 1998. pap., student ed. 29.95 (*0-538-68277-9*) S-W Pub.

— Computers & Information Processing: Conce. 7th ed. (Computer Applications Ser.). 1998. pap. 51.95 (*0-538-68276-0*) S-W Pub.

— Terrapin, Bk. A. Date not set. pap. text, teacher ed. 37.95 (*0-314-87128-4*) West Pub.

— Terrapin Logo. Date not set. pap. text, teacher ed. 25.95 (*0-314-90685-1*) West Pub.

— Terrapin Logo Time. Date not set. pap. text 27.25 (*0-314-90684-3*) West Pub.

— Working with Appleworks: A Complete Guide. (DF - Computer Applications Ser.). 1988. mass mkt., wbk. ed. 18.00 (*0-314-47165-0*) S-W Pub.

— Working with Appleworks: A Complete Guide. (DF - Computer Applications Ser.). 1988. mass mkt. 37.25 (*0-314-35874-9*) S-W Pub.

— Working with Application Software: Microsoft Works for Macintosh. (DF - Computer Applications Ser.). 1991. 38.75 (*0-314-91028-X*) West Pub.

Mandell & Baumann. Working with Aplications MS Works for Mac. (Computer Applications). 1993. pap., wbk. ed. 21.25 (*0-314-00094-1*) West Pub.

Mandell, jt. auth. see Kirszner.

Mandell, Allan, jt. auth. see Ashmun, Barbara Blossom.

Mandell, Arnold J., ed. Neurobiological Mechanisms of Adaptation & Behavior. fac. ed. LC 74-14475. (Advances in Biochemical Psychopharmacology Ser.: No. 13). (Illus.). 314p. pap. 97.40 (*0-7837-7189-4*, 204711000005) Bks Demand.

Mandell, Arnold J., et al, eds. Dynamic Patterns in Complex Systems: Proceedings of the Conference in Honor of Hermann Haken's 60th Birthday. 432p. (C). 1988. text 117.00 (*9971-5-0485-5*) World Scientific Pub.

Mandell, Arnold J., ed. see Usdin, Earl.

Mandell, Barbara. Spain: Costa Brava. (Visitor's Guides Ser.). (Illus.). 256p. (Orig.). 1991. pap. 13.95 (*1-55650-470-5*) Hunter NJ.

Mandell, Betty R., jt. auth. see Schram, Barbara A.

Mandell, Betty Reid, jt. auth. see Schram, Barbara.

Mandell, Brain F., ed. Acute Rheumatic & Immunological Disease: Management of the Critically Ill Patient. (Inflammatory Disease & Therapy Ser.). (Illus.). 640p. 1994. text 250.00 (*0-8247-9125-8*) Dekker.

Mandell, Charles H., jt. auth. see Mandell, David B.

Mandell, Charlotte & McCabe, Allyssa. The Problem of Meaning: Behavioral & Cognitive Perspectives. LC 97-25320. (Advances in Psychology Ser.: Vol. 122). 1997. write for info. (*0-444-82479-0*) Elsevier.

Mandell, Charlotte, tr. see Blanchot, Maurice.

Mandell, Charmaine. Remember Tomorrow. 1998. pap. text 20.00 (*0-89716-822-4*, Peanut Btr Pubng) Elton-Wolf Pub.

Mandell, Colleen J., jt. auth. see Fiscus, Edward D.

Mandell, Daniel R. Behind the Frontier: Indians in Eighteenth-Century Eastern Massachusetts. LC 95-20900. (Illus.). xi, 257p. 1996. text 50.00 (*0-8032-3179-2*) U of Nebr Pr.

***Mandell, Daniel R.** Behind the Frontier: Indians in Eighteenth-Century Eastern Massachusetts. LC 95-20900. (Illus.). 257p. 2000. pap. 19.95 (*0-8032-8249-4*, Bison Books) U of Nebr Pr.

Mandell, David B. The Doctors' Forum: Wealth-Protecting Strategies. 1996. 9.95 incl. audio (*1-890415-03-0*) Guardian Pub.

Mandell, David B. For Dentists Only: How to Protect Your Practice, Property & Savings from Lawsuits & Other Creditor Risks. LC 99-210164. (Illus.). 305p. 1997. ring bd. write for info. (*1-890415-06-5*) Guardian Pub.

— For Doctors Only: How to Protect Your Practice, Property & Savings from Lawsuits & Other Creditor Threats. LC 97-90452. (Illus.). 297p. (Orig.). 1996. pap., spiral bd. write for info. (*1-890415-00-6*) Guardian Pub.

***Mandell, David B. & Goldstein, Arnold.** Offshore Solutions: An Asset Protection Seminar. 1999. 9.95 incl. audio (*1-890415-17-0*) Guardian Pub.

Mandell, David B. & Mandell, Charles H. Risk Management for the Practicing Physician. (Illus.). 65p. 1998. 49.95 (*1-890415-10-3*) Guardian Pub.

***Mandell, David B., et al.** The Doctor's Health Protection Guide. (Illus.). 315p. 1999. pap. 35.00 (*1-890415-11-1*) Guardian Pub.

Mandell, G. L., et al, eds. Pentoxifylline & Analogues: Effects on Leukocyte Function. (Illus.). x, 232p. 1990. 170.50 (*3-8055-5302-1*) S Karger.

Mandell, G. L., et al. Principles & Practice of Infectious Diseases: Antimicrobial Therapy 1996/1997. 200p. 1996. pap. write for info. (*0-443-07844-0*) Church.

Mandell, Gail P. Madeleva: A Biography. LC 96-36300. (Illus.). 303p. (C). 1997. text 54.50 (*0-7914-3439-7*); pap. text 19.95 (*0-7914-3440-0*) State U NY Pr.

— Madeleva, 1994: One Woman's Life. LC 94-5932. (Madeleva Lectures). 64p. (Orig.). 1994. pap. 4.95 (*0-8091-3499-3*) Paulist Pr.

— The Phoenix Paradox: A Study of Renewal Through Change in the "Collected Poems" & "Last Poems" of D. H. Lawrence. LC 83-10563. 288p. 1984. 26.95 (*0-8093-1121-6*) S Ill U Pr.

Mandell, Gerald L. Atlas of Infectious Diseases: Pediatric Infections, Vol. 11. (C). 1999. audio compact disk 195.00 (*0-443-06528-4*) Harcourt.

— Atlas of Infectious Diseases: Pediatric Infections, Vol. 11. (C). 1999. text 135.00 (*0-443-06526-8*) Harcourt.

Mandell, Gerald L., et al, eds. Anti-Infective Therapy. LC 85-3135. 536p. reprint ed. pap. 166.20 (*0-7837-1615-X*, 204190700024) Bks Demand.

— Principles & Practice of Infectious Diseases. 2nd ed. LC 84-13076. (Illus.). 1800p. 1988. pap. 200.00 (*0-8357-6554-7*, 203591900097) Bks Demand.

— Principles & Practice of Infectious Diseases. 3rd ed. (Illus.). 2340p. 1990. text 225.00 (*0-443-08686-9*) Church.

— Principles & Practice of Infectious Diseases, 2 vols. 4th ed. 1994. text 295.00 (*0-443-08935-3*) Church.

— Principles & Practice of Infectious Diseases, Vol. 1. 3rd ed. LC 89-15734. (Illus.). 1304p. reprint ed. pap. 200.00 (*0-7837-8713-8*, 204956100001) Bks Demand.

— Principles & Practice of Infectious Diseases, Vol. 2. 3rd ed. LC 89-15734. (Illus.). 1307p. reprint ed. pap. 200.00 (*0-7837-8737-5*, 204956100002) Bks Demand.

Mandell, Gerald L. & Bleck, Thomas P. Essential Atlas of Infectious Diseases for Primary Care. LC 96-45957. 1997. text 135.00 (*0-443-07961-7*) Church.

Mandell, Gerald L. & Bleck, Thomas P., eds. Central Nervous System & Eye Infections. LC 94-41262. (Atlas of Infectious Diseases Ser.: Vol. 3). (Illus.). 264p. 1995. text 135.00 (*0-443-07700-2*) Current Med.

Mandell, Gerald L. & Brook, Itzhak, eds. Upper Respiratory & Head & Neck Infections. LC 95-1977. (Atlas of Infectious Diseases Ser.: Vol. 4). 1995. text 135.00 (*0-443-07710-X*) Current Med.

Mandell, Gerald L. & Korzeniowski, Oksana M. Cardiovascular Infections, Vol. 10. LC 97-15076. (Atlas of Infectious Diseases Ser.). 1997. text 135.00 (*0-443-07750-9*) Current Med.

Mandell, Gerald L. & Lorber, Bennett, eds. Intra-Abdominal Infections, Hepatitis & Gastroenteritis. LC 96-13984. (Atlas of Infectious Diseases Ser.: Vol. 7). 1996. text 135.00 (*0-443-07730-4*) Current Med.

Mandell, Gerald L. & Mildvan, Donna. AIDS. 2nd ed. LC 96-38725. (Atlas of Infectious Diseases Ser.). 1997. text 135.00 (*0-443-07946-3*) Church.

Mandell, Gerald L. & Rein, Michael F., eds. Atlas of Infectious Diseases Vol. 5: Sexually Transmitted Diseases, Vol. 5. LC 95-32207. (Illus.). 304p. 1995. text 125.00 (*0-443-07720-7*) Church.

Mandell, Gerald L. & Sobel, Jack D., eds. Atlas of Infectious Disease Vol. 9: Urinary Tract Infections & Infections of the Female Pelvis, Vol. 9. LC 96-24706. (Atlas of Infectious Diseases Ser.). (Illus.). 216p. 1996. text 135.00 (*0-443-07770-3*) Church.

***Mandell, Gerald L., et al.** Mandell, Douglas & Bennett's Principles & Practice of Infectious Diseases, 2 vols. 5th ed. LC 99-16736. 1999. text. write for info. (*0-443-07593-X*, W B Saunders Co) Harcrt Hlth Sci Grp.

Mandell, Gerald L., et al. Principles & Practice of Infectious Diseases: Antimicrobial Therapy, 1992. LC 91-36236. 184p. reprint ed. pap. 57.10 (*0-7837-6255-0*, 204596700010) Bks Demand.

— Principles & Practice of Infectious Diseases: Antimicrobial Therapy, 1993-1994. LC 93-194225. 191p. 1993. reprint ed. pap. 59.30 (*0-7837-9616-1*, 206037300005) Bks Demand.

— Principles & Practice of Infectious Diseases: Handbook of Antimicrobial Therapy. 166p. (Orig.). 1992. 19.95 (*0-443-08818-7*) Church.

Mandell, Gerald L., jt. ed. see Fekety, Robert.

Mandell, Gerald L., jt. ed. see Simberkoff, Michael.

Mandell, Harvey & Spiro, Howard, eds. When Doctors Get Sick. LC 87-14104. (Illus.). 484p. 1987. 35.00 (*0-306-42653-6*, Kluwer Plenum) Kluwer Academic.

Mandell, Howard. Future Jazz. LC 98-30134. 256p. 1999. 26.00 (*0-19-506378-3*) OUP.

***Mandell, Howard.** Future Jazz. 256p. 2000. pap. 13.95 (*0-19-514121-0*) OUP.

Mandell, Jack. Workers' Compensation. (Illus.). 93p. 1992. pap. 35.00 (*0-317-57854-5*) NJ Inst CLE.

Mandell, Jeffery. Pension Administration: Forms System LC 99-202101. 1998. ring bd. 185.00 (*0-7355-0066-5*) Panel Pubs.

Mandell, Jim. The Studio Business Book. 2nd expanded rev. ed. Jewett, Andy, ed. LC 94-73192. (Illus.). 288p. 1995. pap. 34.95 (*0-918371-04-X*, MixBooks) Intertec Pub.

Mandell, Joan G. & Damon, Linda. Group Treatment for Sexually Abused Children. LC 89-7462. 170p. 1989. pap. text 27.95 (*0-89862-515-5*) Guilford Pubns.

Mandell, Judy. Book Editors Talk to Writers. LC 94-41641. 240p. 1995. pap. 14.95 (*0-471-00391-3*) Wiley.

— Magazine Editors Talk to Writers. LC 95-52686. 208p. 1996. pap. 14.95 (*0-471-11991-1*) Wiley.

— The Writer's Guide to Magazine Editors & Publishers, 1997-98: Who They Are! What They Want! & How to Win Them Over! 416p. 1996. per. 23.00 (*0-7615-0409-5*) Prima Pub.

Mandell, Judy, ed. Fiction Writers Guidelines: Over 260 Periodical Editors' Instructions Reproduced & Indexed. 2nd ed. LC 92-53504. 349p. (Orig.). 1992. pap. 35.00 (*0-89950-673-9*) McFarland & Co.

Mandell, L., jt. auth. see Menger, F. M.

Mandell, Laura C. Misogynous Economies. LC 99-17695. (Illus.). 256p. 1999. 42.00 (*0-8131-2116-7*) U Pr of Ky.

Mandell, Lewis. The Credit Card Industry: A History. (Twayne's Evolution of American Business Ser.: No. 4). 200p. (C). 1990. 26.95 (*0-8057-9810-2*, Twyne); pap. 14.95 (*0-8057-9816-1*, Twyne) Mac Lib Ref.

— Credit Card Use in the United States. LC 72-86124. (Illus.). 121p. reprint ed. pap. 37.60 (*0-7837-5275-X*, 204501300005) Bks Demand.

— The Demand for Money in Israel, 1955-1967. LC 75-192. (Business Economics & Finance Ser.: No. 3). 132p. reprint ed. pap. 41.00 (*0-7837-0785-1*, 204109900019) Bks Demand.

— Our Vulnerable Youth: The Financial Literacy of American 12th Graders. LC 98-67337. 117p. 1998. pap. 14.95 (*0-9666010-0-9*) JumpStart Coalition.

***Mandell, Lionel A.** First International Moxifloxacin Symposium - Berlin 1999. LC 99-45431. (Illus.). xiii, 191p. 1999. 59.00 (*3-540-66476-9*) Spr-Verlag.

***Mandell, Lionel A. & Wiederman, Richard.** Sheffield Dawson Guide to Prognosis & Management of CAP & HAP. 90p. 1999. pap. 29.95 (*0-9668202-4-X*) S Dawson Pubs.

Mandell, Margery. Self-Made Americans: Interviews with Dreamers, Visionaries & Entrepreneurs. Dorszynski, Alexia, ed. (Illus.). 310p. 1996. 24.00 (*0-9634249-9-8*) Gift Future Two Thous.

Mandell, Mark & Johnson, Les. Tube Flies: A Tying, Fishing & Historical Guide. (Illus.). 95p. 1995. 45.00 (*1-57188-037-2*); pap. 29.95 (*1-57188-036-4*) F Amato Pubns.

Mandell, Muriel. Fantastic Book of Logic Puzzles. LC 86-5980. (Illus.). 128p. 1986. pap. 5.95 (*0-8069-4756-X*) Sterling.

— Physics Experiments for Children. LC 68-9308. Orig. Title: Science for Children. (Illus.). 96p. (J). (gr. 3-10). 1968. reprint ed. pap. 3.50 (*0-486-22033-8*) Dover.

— Simple Experiments in Time. (Illus.). 96p. (J). 1998. 4.95 (*0-8069-4298-3*) Sterling.

— Simple Kitchen Experiments: Learning Science with Everyday Foods. (Illus.). 128p. (J). 1994. pap. 4.95 (*0-8069-8415-5*) Sterling.

— Simple Science Experiments with Everyday Materials. LC 88-31201. (Illus.). 128p. (YA). (gr. 4-10). 1990. pap. 4.95 (*0-8069-5764-6*) Sterling.

— Simple Weather Experiments with Everyday Materials. LC 90-37915. (Illus.). 128p. (J). (gr. 4 up). 1991. pap. 5.95 (*0-8069-7295-5*) Sterling.

Mandell, Myrna P., jt. ed. see Gage, Robert W.

Mandell, Nancy, ed. Sociological Studies of Children, Vol. 1. 303p. 1986. 73.25 (*0-89232-565-8*) Jai Pr.

— Sociological Studies of Children, Vol. 2. 244p. 1987. 73.25 (*0-89232-760-X*) Jai Pr.

— Sociological Studies of Children, Vol. 3. 264p. 1990. 73.25 (*0-89232-903-3*) Jai Pr.

— Sociological Studies of Children, Vol. 4: Perspectives on & of Children. 248p. 1991. 73.25 (*1-55938-195-7*) Jai Pr.

— Sociological Studies of Children, Vol. 5. 252p. 1993. 73.25 (*1-55938-480-8*) Jai Pr.

— Sociological Studies of Children, Vol. 6: Macro-Micro Connections in the Pathways to. 219p. 1994. 73.25 (*1-55938-746-7*) Jai Pr.

— Sociological Studies of Children, Vol. 7. 268p. 1995. 73.25 (*1-55938-900-1*) Jai Pr.

— Sociological Studies of Children, Vol. 8. Date not set. 73.25 (*0-7623-0051-5*) Jai Pr.

Mandell, Patricia. Hidden Boston & Cape Cod. 4th rev. ed. (Hidden Travel Ser.). (Illus.). 264p. 1999. pap. 13.95 (*1-56975-178-1*) Ulysses Pr.

Mandell, Patricia, jt. auth. see Vollmer, Ryan.

Mandell, Richard. The Bats. LC 80-83027. 170p. (Orig.). 1981. pap. 4.50 (*0-9605008-0-4*) Hermes Hse Pr.

Mandell, Richard, ed. see Jean, Raymond.

Mandell, Richard D. The Nazi Olympics. LC 86-19347. (Sport & Society Ser.). (Illus.). 344p. 1987. pap. text 16.95 (*0-252-01325-5*) U of Ill Pr.

— The Olympics of 1972: A Munich Diary. LC 90-23544. 223p. reprint ed. pap. 69.20 (*0-7837-5239-3*, 204497300005) Bks Demand.

Mandell, Robert B. Contact Lens Practice. 4th ed. (Illus.). 1040p. (C). 1988. text 91.95 (*0-398-05509-2*) C C Thomas.

Mandell, Sandy, jt. ed. see More, Phyllis K.

Mandell, Sara R., jt. auth. see Hayes, John H.

Mandell, Stephen R. & Kirszner, Laurie G. The Blair Reader. 3rd ed. LC 98-2805. 838p. (C). 1998. pap. text 37.00 (*0-13-080140-2*) P-H.

Mandell, Stephen R., jt. auth. see Kirszner, Laurie G.

Mandell, Steven. Busy Lawyer's Guide to On-Line Services. LC 95-25304. 100p. 1996. pap. text. write for info. (*0-314-07626-3*) West Pub.

Mandell, Steven L. Applied Software Manual. 1992. mass mkt. 17.25 (*0-314-01064-5*) West Pub.

— BASIC Program Instructor Manual. 2nd ed. 349p. 1989. pap. text 13.95 (*0-314-57501-4*) West Pub.

— BASIC Programming Today: A Structured Approach. 2nd ed. (DG - Computer Programming Ser.). (Orig.). (C). 1989. mass mkt. 51.75 (*0-314-47155-3*) West Pub.

— Beginning BASIC for the Commodore 64. (Illus.). 160p. (Orig.). 1985. pap. text 36.50 (*0-314-85264-6*) West Pub.

— Building Computer Awareness. 1985. mass mkt. 29.50 (*0-314-87698-7*) West Pub.

— Building LOGO Skills: Terrapin Book B. 376p. (gr. 4-6). 1986. pap. text 31.50 (*0-314-89685-6*); pap. text, teacher ed. 37.95 (*0-314-88708-3*) West Pub.

— The Commodore 64 Guidebook. (Illus.). 170p. (Orig.). 1985. pap. text 34.25 (*0-314-85261-1*) West Pub.

— Complete Basic Programming High School Edition. 2nd ed. (DG - Computer Programming Ser.). (C). 1986. mass mkt. 42.00 (*0-314-32147-0*) West Pub.

— Computer Awareness. Date not set. pap. text, teacher ed. 37.95 (*0-314-88517-X*) West Pub.

— Computer Fun. 1986. mass mkt. 22.75 (*0-314-85268-9*) West Pub.

— Computer Information Processing 6. 6th ed. 1992. mass mkt., student ed. 20.00 (*0-314-00699-0*) West Pub.

— Computer Science with Pascal. 2nd ed. (DF - Computer Applications Ser.). (C). 1989. mass mkt. 42.00 (*0-314-40275-6*) West Pub.
— Computer Time. Date not set. pap. text, teacher ed. 24.95 (*0-314-87257-4*) West Pub.
— Computers & Data Processing: Concepts & Applications. 3rd ed. (Illus.). 512p. (C). 1984. text 33.00 (*0-314-85262-X*) West Pub.
— Computers & Data Processing: Concepts & Applications with BASIC. 3rd ed. (Illus.). 292p. (C). 1984. text 35.00 (*0-314-87560-3*) West Pub.
— Computers & Data Processing Today with BASIC. 2nd ed. (Illus.). 472p. (C). 1985. pap. text 35.50 (*0-314-96079-1*) West Pub.
— Computers in Education Today. Date not set. pap. text 52.00 (*0-314-85275-1*) West Pub.
— Computers in Our World. Date not set. text 43.75 (*0-314-85271-9*) West Pub.
— Computers Today. Date not set. write for info. (*0-314-07223-3*) West Pub.
— Computing Today. 2nd ed. LC 97-123356. 350p. 1996. mass mkt. 48.95 (*0-314-09873-9*) West Pub.
— DCM Works Software. (C). 1997. write for info. (*0-314-07224-1*) West Pub.
— Exploring Computers. Date not set. text 43.75 (*0-314-85272-7*) West Pub.
— Fundamental BASIC Programming. Date not set. pap. text, teacher ed. 43.95 (*0-314-87134-9*) West Pub.
— Instructor Manual to Computer Basics. 499p. 1991. pap. text. write for info. (*0-314-82969-5*) West Pub.
— Introduction to BASIC Programming. 3rd ed. 248p. (C). 1987. mass mkt. 32.00 (*0-314-34731-3*) West Pub.
— Introduction to Business. Date not set. pap. text, teacher ed. write for info. (*0-8299-0444-1*) West Pub.
— Introduction to Computers Using the Apple II. Perlee, Clyde, ed. (Illus.). 539p. (C). 1985. pap. text 55.50 (*0-314-85265-4*) West Pub.
— Introduction to Computers Using the IBM & MS DOS PCs: Popular Commercial Software Version. 3rd ed. Perlee, Clyde, ed. 674p. (C). 1991. mass mkt. 50.00 (*0-314-79211-2*) West Pub.
— Introduction to Computers Using the IBM & MS DOS PCs: West 2.5 Version. 127p. 1987. pap. text, teacher ed. write for info. (*0-314-35263-5*) West Pub.
— Introduction to Computers Using the IBM & MS DOS PCs: West 2.5 Version. 2nd ed. 439p. 1987. mass mkt. 47.00 (*0-314-32170-5*) West Pub.
— Introduction to Computers Using the IBM PC. Perlee, Clyde, ed. 547p. (C). pap. text 38.00 (*0-314-85267-0*) West Pub.
— Introduction to Computers Using the TRS 80 Model III. (Illus.). 535p. (C). 1986. pap. text 55.50 (*0-314-85266-2*) West Pub.
— Mac with Basic: Testbank. Date not set. pap. text, teacher ed. write for info. (*0-314-00706-7*) West Pub.
— Microcomputers Today. LC 95-31207. 260p. (C). 1996. mass mkt. 40.95 (*0-314-04624-0*) West Pub.
— Pascal Programming Today. LC 86-24610. (Illus.). 550p. (Orig.). (C). 1987. pap. text 55.50 (*0-314-33935-3*); pap. text, teacher ed. 21.95 (*0-314-97186-6*) West Pub.
— Personal Computer Desk Reference. 608p. 1993. 32.95 (*0-9637426-0-4*); pap. 23.95 (*0-9637426-1-2*) Rawhide Pr.
— Turbo Pascal Programming High School Edition. (DG - Computer Programming Ser.). (C). 1987. mass mkt. 42.00 (*0-314-34629-5*) West Pub.
— Turbo Pascal Programming Today. (Illus.). 561p. (Orig.). (C). 1987. pap. text 52.75 (*0-314-34628-7*); pap. text, teacher ed. 21.95 (*0-314-35260-0*) West Pub.
— Understanding Computers. 1991. mass mkt. 11.50 (*0-314-87930-7*) West Pub.
— Understanding Pascal. Date not set. pap. text, teacher ed. 21.95 (*0-314-87254-X*) West Pub.
— Understanding Pascal. 1985. mass mkt. 38.50 (*0-314-89691-0*) West Pub.
— Working with Application Software - IBM-PC. (Illus.). 253p. (C). 1986. text 45.25 (*0-314-96495-9*) West Pub.
— Working with Application Software - TRS-80. (Illus.). 242p. (C). 1986. text 45.25 (*0-314-96493-2*) West Pub.
Mandell, Steven L. & Brenan. Introduction to Computers & Basic Programming. 3rd ed. (DC - Introduction to Computing Ser.). (C). 1992. mass mkt., wbk. ed. 42.00 (*0-314-00335-5*) West Pub.
Mandell, Steven L., et al. Introduction to Business Concepts & Applications: Test Bank. 93p. (C). 1980. pap. text. write for info. (*0-8299-0527-8*) West Pub.
— Word Processing for Legal Professionals Using WordPerfect 5.1. LC 95-2009. 633p. (C). 1995. mass mkt. 29.75 (*0-314-05250-X*) West Pub.
Mandell, Steven L., jt. auth. see Baumann, Susan K.
Mandell, Steven L., jt. auth. see Brenan, Kathleen M.
Mandell, Steven L., jt. auth. see Clark, Ann L.
Mandell, Steven L., jt. auth. see Flyn, Meredith.
Mandell, Steven L., jt. auth. see Hopper, Grace M.
Mandell, Susan. A Historical Survey of Transit Buses in the United States. 96p. 1990. pap. 19.00 (*1-56091-090-9*, SP-842) Soc Auto Engineers.
***Mandell, Ted.** Heartstoppers & Hail Marys: 100 of the Greatest College Football Finishes (1970-1999) 2000. 39.95 (*1-888698-32-2*) Diamond Communications.
Mandell, Terri. Power Schmoozing: The New Etiquette for Social & Business Success. (First Books for Business Ser.). 173p. 1996. pap. 14.95 (*0-07-039887-9*) McGraw.
Mandella, Keith A. Drugged Cannons Whisper. 1998. pap. write for info. (*1-57553-983-7*) Watermrk Pr.
Mandelsberg, Rose G. Cult Killers. 1991. mass mkt. 4.95 (*1-55817-528-8*, Pinncle Kensgtn) Kensgtn Pub Corp.
— From the Files of True Detective: Crimes of Passion. (Illus.). 448p. 1993. mass mkt. 4.99 (*1-55817-684-5*, Pinncle Kensgtn) Kensgtn Pub Corp.
— Medical Murderers: From the Files of True Detective. 1992. mass mkt. 4.99 (*1-55817-582-2*, Pinncle Kensgtn) Kensgtn Pub Corp.
— Torture Killers. 1991. mass mkt. 4.95 (*1-55817-506-7*, Pinncle Kensgtn) Kensgtn Pub Corp.
Mandelsberg, Rose G., ed. From the Files of True Detective: Bizarre Murders II. (Illus.). 448p. 1993. mass mkt. 4.99 (*1-55817-760-4*, Pinncle Kensgtn) Kensgtn Pub Corp.
— From the Files of True Detective: Greed Killers. (Illus.). 448p. 1994. mass mkt. 4.99 (*1-55817-888-0*, Pinncle Kensgtn) Kensgtn Pub Corp.
— From the Files of True Detective: Mass Murderers. (Illus.). 448p. 1993. mass mkt. 4.99 (*1-55817-777-9*, Pinncle Kensgtn) Kensgtn Pub Corp.
— From the Files of True Detective: Spouse Killers. (Illus.). 448p. 1994. mass mkt. 4.99 (*1-55817-785-X*, Pinncle Kensgtn) Kensgtn Pub Corp.
— From the Files of True Detective: The Crimes of the Rich & Famous. (Illus.). 448p. 1992. mass mkt. 4.99 (*1-55817-630-6*, Pinncle Kensgtn) Kensgtn Pub Corp.
— From the Files of True Detective: The Mutilators. (Illus.). 448p. 1993. mass mkt. 4.99 (*1-55817-768-X*, Pinncle Kensgtn) Kensgtn Pub Corp.
— From the Files of True Detective: Torture Killers II. (Illus.). 448p. 1994. mass mkt. 4.99 (*1-55817-793-0*, Pinncle Kensgtn) Kensgtn Pub Corp.
— From the Files of True Detective Magazine: Cop Killers. LC 93-122811. (Illus.). 448p. 1992. mass mkt. 4.99 (*1-55817-603-9*, Pinncle Kensgtn) Kensgtn Pub Corp.
— Hitmen. (True Detective Ser.). 448p. 1994. mass mkt. 4.99 (*0-7860-0048-1*, Pinncle Kensgtn) Kensgtn Pub Corp.
— Killer Teens. 448p. 1994. mass mkt. 4.99 (*1-55817-895-3*, Pinncle Kensgtn) Kensgtn Pub Corp.
— Stranglers. 448p. 1994. mass mkt. 4.99 (*0-7860-0015-5*, Pinncle Kensgtn) Kensgtn Pub Corp.
Mandelshtam, Osip. Fifty Poems. Meares, Bernard, tr. from RUS. LC 76-52274. 120p. (Orig.). 1977. pap. 11.95 (*0-89255-006-6*) Persea Bks.
— Moscow Notebooks. McKane, Richard & McKane, Elizabeth, trs. from RUS. 80p. (Orig.). 1991. pap. 14.95 (*1-85224-126-8*, Pub. by Bloodaxe Bks) Dufour.
— Osip Mandelstam's Stone. LC 80-7545. (Lockert Library of Poetry in Translation). 268p. reprint ed. pap. 83.10 (*0-8357-6930-5*, 203798900009) Bks Demand.
— Quarterly Review of Literature: The 1960s, Special Issue, Vol. XI, No. 4. 1960. pap. 35.00 (*1-888545-26-7*) Quarterly Rev.
— Selected Poems. Green, James, tr. 144p. 1992. pap. 12.95 (*0-14-018474-0*, Penguin Classics) Viking Penguin.
— The Voronezh Notebooks: Poems, 1935-1937. McKane, Richard & McKane, Elizabeth, trs. LC 93-247633. 128p. 1996. pap. 16.95 (*1-85224-205-1*, Pub. by Bloodaxe Bks) Dufour.
Mandelshtam, Osip, et al. Quarterly Review of Literature: The 1970s, Prose, Vol. XVIII, Nos. 3-4. 1970. pap. 15.00 (*1-888545-16-X*) Quarterly Rev.
Mandelssohn. Trio in C Minor Opus 66: Violin-Violoncello-Piano. 72p. 1986. pap. 16.95 (*0-7935-4990-6*, 50259390) H Leonard.
Mandelstam, Dorothy, ed. Incontinence & Its Management. 2nd ed. LC 85-27001. 288p. 1986. pap. 25.00 (*0-7099-3580-3*, Pub. by C Helm) Routldge.
Mandelstam, Michael. An A-Z of Community Care Law. LC 98-101772. 128p. 1997. pap. 19.95 (*1-85302-560-7*, Pub. by Jessica Kingsley) Taylor & Francis.
— Community Care Practice & the Law. 2nd ed. LC 98-37066. 1998. pap. 49.95 (*1-85302-647-6*) Jessica Kingsley.
— Equipment for Older or Disabled People & the Law. LC 97-135389. 200p. 1996. pap. 32.95 (*1-85302-352-3*, Pub. by Jessica Kingsley) Taylor & Francis.
— How to Get Equipment for Disability. 3rd ed. 528p. 1993. pap. 55.00 (*1-85302-190-3*) Taylor & Francis.
Mandelstam, Michael & Schwehr, Belinda. Community Care Practice & the Law. LC 95-5881. 450p. 1995. pap. 39.95 (*1-85302-273-X*) Taylor & Francis.
Mandelstam, Nadezhda. Hope Against Hope. LC 87-19333. 448p. (C). 1976. pap. 13.95 (*0-689-70530-1*, 218, Pub. by Ctrl Bur voor Schimmel) Macmillan.
— Hope Against Hope. LC 98-47833. 1999. pap. 13.95 (*0-375-75316-8*) Modern Lib NY.
Mandelstam, P. Stone. 1993. pap. 13.00 (*1-86046-223-5*) Harvill Press.
Mandelstam, S. L., ed. Spectrochemical Analysis in the U. S. S. R. 112p. 1982. pap. 19.25 (*0-08-028747-6*, Pergamon Pr) Elsevier.
Mandelstam, Stanley, jt. auth. see Yourgrau, Wolfgang.
Mander, David. Images of Hertfordshire. (Best of Britain in Old Photographs Ser.). (Illus.). 160p. 1998. 29.95 (*0-7509-1662-1*, Pub. by Sutton Pub Ltd) Intl Pubs Mktg.
Mander, Jerry. Four Arguments Elimi. LC 77-12558. 371p. 1978. pap. 12.00 (*0-688-08274-2*, Quil) HarperTrade.
— In the Absence of the Sacred. 1998. 25.50 (*0-8446-6951-2*) Peter Smith.
— In the Absence of the Sacred: The Failure of Technology & the Survival of the Indian Nations. LC 91-13869. 464p. 1992. reprint ed. pap. 14.00 (*0-87156-509-9*, Pub. by Sierra) Random.
***Mander, Jerry.** Wizard of "IS" The Short, Ugly Story of the Impeachment of Billy Jeff Clinton & His Trailor Park Presidency. 1999. pap. 14.00 (*0-9675425-0-2*) J Mander Pr.
Mander, Jerry & Goldsmith, Edward, eds. The Case Against the Global Economy. 560p. 1997. pap. 16.00 (*0-87156-865-9*, Pub. by Sierra) Random.
— The Case Against the Global Economy: And for a Turn Toward the Local. LC 96-20149. 600p. 1996. 28.00 (*0-87156-352-5*, Pub. by Sierra) Random.
Mander, John. Berlin: Hostage for the West. LC 79-9953. (Illus.). 124p. 1979. reprint ed. lib. bdg. 55.00 (*0-313-20996-0*, MABE, Greenwood Pr) Greenwood.
— The Writer & Commitment. LC 75-18402. 215p. 1975. reprint ed. lib. bdg. 65.00 (*0-8371-8332-4*, MAWCO, Greenwood Pr) Greenwood.
Mander-Jones, Phyllis. Catalogue of the Manuscripts in the Library of the Royal Geographical Society of Australasia (South Australian Branch) Inc. (C). 1981. 95.00 (*0-7855-0333-1*, Pub. by Royal Geograp Soc) St Mut.
Mander, Linden. Some Dependent Peoples of the South Pacific. LC 75-30071. (Institute of Pacific Relations Ser.). reprint ed. 84.50 (*0-404-59544-8*) AMS Pr.
Mander, Mary S., ed. Communications in Transition: Issues & Debates in Current Research. LC 83-13985. 327p. 1983. 42.95 (*0-275-91040-7*, C1040, Praeger Pubs) Greenwood.
— Framing Friction: Media & Social Conflict. LC 98-9006. 304p. 1999. text 49.95 (*0-252-02426-5*); text 19.95 (*0-252-06733-9*) U of Ill Pr.
Mander, Matthias. The Cassowary. Mitchell, Michael, tr. & afterword by by. (Studies in Austrian Literature, Culture, & Thought. Translation Ser.). 340p. 1994. pap. 23.95 (*0-929497-73-2*) Ariadne CA.
Mander, Raymond & Mitchenson, Joe. The Theatres of London. LC 78-11868. 292p. 1979. reprint ed. lib. bdg. 65.00 (*0-313-21227-9*, MATL, Greenwood Pr) Greenwood.
***Mander, Raymond & Mitchenson, Joe.** Theatrical Companion to Coward. (Illus.). 400p. 1999. 65.00 (*1-84002-054-7*, Pub. by Theatre Comm) Consort Bk Sales.
Mander, Raymond & Mitchinson, J. Hamlet Through the Ages: A Pictorial Record from 1709. Marshall, H., ed. 1977. lib. bdg. 150.00 (*0-8490-1929-X*) Gordon Pr.
Mander, Robert R. Sales: Building Lifetime Skills for Success. (Illus.). 168p. 1999. pap. 14.95 (*0-9669696-0-X*) Ryan Pubs.
Mander, Rosemary. Care of the Mother Grieving a Baby Relinquished for Adoption. 240p. 1995. 72.95 (*1-85628-597-9*, Pub. by Avebry) Ashgate Pub Co.
— Loss & Bereavement in Childbearing. LC 94-13658. (Illus.). 240p. 1994. pap. 24.95 (*0-632-03826-8*, Pub. by Blckwll Scitfc UK) Blackwell Sci.
— Pain in Childbearing & Its Control. LC 98-15544. xii, 252p. 1998. pap. 29.95 (*0-632-04097-1*) Blackwell Sci.
***Mander, U. & Jongman, R. H. G., eds.** Consequences of Land Use Changes. (Advances in Ecological Sciences Ser.). 328p. 2000. 157.00 (*1-85312-650-0*, 6500, Pub. by WIT Pr) Computational Mech MA.
— Landscape Perspectives of Land Use Changes. (Advances in Ecological Sciences Ser.: Vol. 6). 240p. 2000. 126.00 (*1-85312-848-1*, Pub. by WIT Pr) Computational Mech MA.
***Mander, W. J.** Anglo-American Idealism, 1865-1927, Vol. 74. LC 99-33831. (Contributions in Philosophy Ser.). 240p. 2000. 59.95 (*0-313-31152-8*) Greenwood.
Mander, W. J. An Introduction to Bradley's Metaphysics. 184p. 1994. text 45.00 (*0-19-824090-2*) OUP.
Mander, W. J., ed. Perspectives on the Logic & Metaphysics of F. H. Bradley. (Idealism Ser.: No. 2). 310p. 1996. 72.00 (*1-85506-433-2*); pap. 24.00 (*1-85506-432-4*) Bks Intl VA.
Mandera, Franklin R. An Inquiry into the Effects of Bilingualism on Native & Non-Native Americans: Viewed in Sociopsychologic & Cultural Terms. Cordasco, Francesco, ed. LC 77-90548. (Bilingual-Bicultural Education in the U. S. Ser.). 1978. lib. bdg. 24.95 (*0-405-11087-1*) Ayer.
Manderick, Bernard, jt. ed. see Manner, Reinhard.
Manderino, John. The Man Who Once Played Catch with Nellie Fox. LC 98-2824. 280p. 1998. 22.50 (*0-89733-448-5*) Academy Chi Pubs.
— Sam & His Brother Len. LC 94-9992. 248p. 1994. 19.95 (*0-89733-407-8*) Academy Chi Pubs.
Manderino, Ned. Actor As Artist. 176p. (Orig.). 1991. pap. 10.95 (*0-9601194-7-7*) Manderino Bks.
— All about Method Acting. 192p. (Orig.). 1985. pap. 10.95 (*0-9601194-3-4*) Manderino Bks.
— The Transpersonal Actor: Reinterpreting Stanislavski. rev. ed. 240p. (Orig.). 1989. pap. 14.95 (*0-9601194-5-0*) Manderino Bks.
Manders, Andre J.C., jt. ed. see van der Linden, Joep T.J.M.
Manderscheid, Ronald W. Mental Health, United States, 1996. 261p. 1997. pap. text 22.00 (*0-16-048884-2*) USGPO.
— Mental Health United States, 1998. 302p. 1999. pap. text 25.00 (*0-16-049883-X*) USGPO.
***Manderscheid, Ronald W. & Henderson, Marilyn J., eds.** Mental Health, United States, 1998. 8th ed. (Illus.). 292p. 1999. pap. text 45.00 (*0-7881-7999-3*) DIANE Pub.
Manderscheid, Ronald W. & Sonnenschein, Mary A., eds. Mental Health, United States, 1996, 2 vols. (Illus.). 260p. 1996. pap. text 45.00 (*1-57979-154-9*) DIANE Pub.
— Mental Health, United States, 1996. (Illus.). 249p. (C). 1998. pap. text 45.00 (*0-7881-4889-3*) DIANE Pub.
— Mental Health, United States, 1994. (Illus.). 192p. (Orig.). (C). 1995. pap. text 45.00 (*0-7881-1833-1*) DIANE Pub.
Manderson, jt. auth. see Bhamidimarri, R.
Manderson, Desmond. Courting Death: The Legal Constitution of Mortality. LC 99-19593. (Law & Social Theory Ser.). 224p. 1999. 59.95 (*0-7453-1366-3*, Pub. by Pluto GBR) Stylus Pub VA.
***Manderson, Desmond.** Songs Without Music. LC 99-38447. (Philosophy, Social Theory & the Rule of Law Ser.: Vol. 7). 355p. 2000. 55.00 (*0-520-21688-1*, Pub. by U CA Pr) Cal Prin Full Svc.
***Manderson, Desmond, ed.** Courting Death: The Legal Constitution of Mortality. 224p. 1999. pap. 22.50 (*0-7453-1361-2*, Pub. by Pluto GBR) Stylus Pub VA.
Manderson, Lenore. Sickness & the State: Health & Illness in Colonial Malaya, 1870-1940. LC 95-42786. (Illus.). 335p. (C). 1996. text 69.95 (*0-521-56008-X*) Cambridge U Pr.
— Women, Politics, & Change: The Kaum Ibu UMNO Malaysia, 1945-1972. (East Asian Social Science Monographs). (Illus.). 1981. 45.00 (*0-19-580437-6*) OUP.
Manderson, Lenore, ed. Australian Women's Health: Innovations in Social Science & Community Research. LC 98-51297. 163p. 1998. 49.95 (*0-7890-0668-5*) Haworth Pr.
Manderson, Lenore & Jolly, Margaret. Sites of Desire, Economies of Pleasure: Sexualities in Asia & the Pacific. LC 96-40938. (Chicago Series on Sexuality, History, & Society). 1997. pap. text 19.95 (*0-226-50304-6*); lib. bdg. 54.00 (*0-226-50303-8*) U Ch Pr.
Manderson, Lenore, jt. auth. see Crouch, Mira.
Manderson, Lenore, jt. auth. see Rice, Pranee L.
Manderson, Lenore, jt. ed. see Whiteford, Linda M.
Mandery, Evan J. The Campaign: Rudy Giuliani, Ruth Messinger, Al Sharpton & the Race to Be Mayor of New York City. LC JS1238.3.M36 1999. 416p. 1999. 27.00 (*0-8133-6698-4*, Pub. by Westview) HarpC.
Mandes, Ric. Life with Granny. 144p. 1997. 12.95 (*0-9652800-3-9*) Mandes Pub.
Mandes, Ric. Mind Me & Love the Lord: Life with Granny. 160p. 1996. write for info. (*0-9652800-1-2*) Mandes Pub.
— Off Stage. 144p. 1997. 12.95 (*0-9652800-2-0*) Mandes Pub.
Mandesson, A. English-Greek Dictionary, with a Complete & Accurate System for the Pronunciation of the Words. (ENG & GRE.). 1102p. 1961. 36.00 (*0-88431-125-2*, Pub. by U Politecnica) IBD Ltd.
— Greek-English, with a Complete & Accurate System for the Pronunciation of the Words. (ENG & GRE.). 1380p. 1961. 36.00 (*0-88431-922-9*, Pub. by U Politecnica) IBD Ltd.
Mandetta, Anne & Gustaveson, Patricia. Abortion to Zoophilia: A Sourcebook of Sexual Facts. LC 75-31909. (Illus.). 1975. pap. text 3.00 (*0-89055-114-6*) Carolina Pop Ctr.
Mandeville, A. Glenn. Barbie Doll Collector's Handbook. LC 97-167777. 96p. 1997. pap. 12.95 (*0-87588-480-6*, 5301) Hobby Hse.
— Ginny "America's Sweetheart" LC 98-188406. (Illus.). 160p. 1998. pap. 14.95 (*0-87588-512-8*, H5455) Hobby Hse.
***Mandeville, A. Glenn.** A Glenn Mandevilles's Madame Alexander Dolls: Collector's Price Guide, Vol. 3. 3rd ed. (Illus.). 128p. 2000. pap. 11.95 (*0-87588-560-8*) Hobby Hse.
Mandeville, A. Glenn. The Golden Age of Collectible Dolls: With Price Guide. (Illus.). 144p. 1990. 25.00 (*0-87588-350-8*) Hobby Hse.
— Sensational '60s: Doll Album with Price Guide. LC 97-148420. (Illus.). 112p. 1996. 29.95 (*0-87588-469-5*, 5233) Hobby Hse.
— 6th Doll Fashion Anthology & PG. 6th ed. LC 97-643170. (Illus.). 220p. 1998. pap. 14.95 (*0-87588-510-1*, H5453) Hobby Hse.
Mandeville, Amy. How to Chat-Up Men. 1998. pap. 7.95 (*1-84024-022-9*, Pub. by Summers) Howell Pr VA.
***Mandeville, Amy.** The Rituals of Love. (Whispers Ser.). (Illus.). 72p. 2000. mass mkt. 5.99 (*1-903222-09-5*, Pub. by Wimbledon Publishing Co) Anthem.
Mandeville, Bernard. Collected Works Vol. II: A Treatise of the Hypochondriack & Hysterick Passions, Vulgarly Call'd the Hypo in Men an Vapours in Women. xxiv, 288p. 1981. reprint ed. write for info. incl. 3.5 hd (*3-487-07037-5*) G Olms Pubs.
— Collected Works Vol. III: The Fable of the Bees: or, Private Vices Publick Benefits. 404p. 1983. reprint ed. write for info. incl. 3.5 hd (*3-487-07177-0*) G Olms Pubs.
— Collected Works Vol. IV: The Fable of the Bees, Pt. II. 456p. 1980. reprint ed. write for info. incl. 3.5 hd (*3-487-07038-3*) G Olms Pubs.
— Collected Works Vol. V: Free Thoughts on Religion, the Church, & National Happiness. xxii, 364p. 1987. reprint ed. write for info. incl. 3.5 hd (*3-487-07782-5*) G Olms Pubs.
— Collected Works Vol. VI: An Enquiry into the Origin of Honour, & the Usefulness of Christianity in War. xi, 240p. 1990. reprint ed. write for info. incl. 3.5 hd (*3-487-09315-4*) G Olms Pubs.
— The Fable of the Bees. LC 02-15833. 13p. 1987. reprint ed. pap. 2.00 (*0-942153-19-7*) Entropy Conserv.
— The Fable of the Bees, 2 vols., Set. LC 88-646. 1988. 30.00 (*0-86597-072-6*); pap. 15.00 (*0-86597-075-0*) Liberty Fund.
— The Fable of the Bees & Other Writings. Hundert, E. J., ed. LC 97-29593. (Classics Ser.). 260p. (C). 1997. pap. 9.95 (*0-87220-374-3*); lib. bdg. 34.95 (*0-87220-375-1*) Hackett Pub.
***Mandeville, Bernard.** Free Thoughts on Religion, the Church & National Happiness. 2000. 49.95 (*0-7658-0029-2*) Transaction Pubs.
Mandeville, Bernard. Free Thoughts on Religion, the Church, & National Happiness. LC 77-17171. 416p. 1981. reprint ed. lib. bdg. 60.00 (*0-8201-1300-X*) Schol Facsimiles.
— The Mischiefs That Ought Justly to Be Apprehended from a Whig-Government. LC 92-544. (Augustan Reprints Ser.: No. 174). 1975. reprint ed. 14.50 (*0-404-70174-4*, DA503) AMS Pr.
— A Modest Defence of Publick Stews: or An Essay upon

M

Whoring, As It Is Now Practis'd in These Kingdoms. LC 92-23890. (Augustan Reprints Ser.: No. 162). 1973. reprint ed. 14.50 (*0-404-70162-0*, HQ185) AMS Pr.
— A Modest Defense of Publick Stews. 1972. 95.95 (*0-8490-0656-2*) Gordon Pr.
— Open Minora II & Doubtful Works. (GER.). 271p. 1999. reprint ed. write for info. (*3-487-10525-X*) G Olms Pubs.
— A Treatise of the Hypochondriack & Hysterick Diseases. LC 76-45623. 432p. 1976. reprint ed. 60.00 (*0-8201-1277-1*) Schol Facsimiles.
— The Virgin Unmask'd. LC 75-14288. 256p. 1975. reprint ed. lib. bdg. 50.00 (*0-8201-1155-4*) Schol Facsimiles.
Mandeville, Bernard & Aesop. Aesop Dress'd or A Collection of Fables Writ in Familiar Verse. LC 92-23720. (Augustan Reprints Ser.: No. 120). 1966. reprint ed. 14.50 (*0-404-70120-5*, PR3545) AMS Pr.
Mandeville, Bernard De, see De Mandeville, Bernard.
Mandeville, D. C., jt. ed. see Holmyard, E. J.
Mandeville, D. C., tr. see Avicennae.
Mandeville, Ernest W. The Story of Middletown, the Oldest Settlement in New Jersey. (Illus.). 143p. 1997. reprint ed. pap. 21.00 (*0-8328-6057-3*) Higginson Bk Co.
Mandeville, Francine. Midnight in Paris. (Lucky in Love Ser.: No. 9). 320p. 1992. mass mkt. 3.99 (*0-8217-3865-8*, Zebra Kensgtn) Kensgtn Pub Corp.
Mandeville, G. Henry. Flushing, Past & Present: A Historical Sketch. (Illus.). 180p. 1997. reprint ed. lib. bdg. 25.00 (*0-8328-6140-5*) Higginson Bk Co.
Mandeville, Glenn A. Glenn Mandeville's Madame Alexander Dolls Value Guide. 128p. 1993. pap. 9.95 (*0-87588-406-7*, 4532) Hobby Hse.
Mandeville, John. The Danish Version of Mandeville's Travels in Sixteenth-Century Epitome. Bradley, S. A., ed. University of Sussex Staff, S. A. J., tr. from DAN. LC 98-31509. (Scandinavian Studies: Vol. 4). 140p. 1998. 69.95 (*0-7734-8261-X*) E Mellen.
— Mandeville's Travels from the French, Pt. 1. Hamelius, P., ed. (EETS, OS Ser.: No. 153). 1916. 45.00 (*0-527-00150-3*) Periodicals Srv.
— The Travels of Sir Johb Mandeville. Moseley, Charles, tr. & intro. by. (Classics Ser.). 208p. 1984. pap. 12.95 (*0-14-044435-1*, Penguin Classics) Viking Penguin.
*__Mandeville, John.__ Turkey. 2nd ed. (Globetrotter Travel Guides Ser.). (Illus.). 128p. 2000. pap. 10.95 (*1-85974-376-5*) New5 Holland.
Mandeville, Joyce. Careful Mistakes: A Novel. LC 97-120580. 432p. 1997. 21.95 (*0-316-87999-1*) Little.
Mandeville, Joyce C. & Foster, Susen. Historic Inns of California's Gold Country Cookbook & Guide. (Illus.). 112p. (Orig.). 1993. pap. 12.95 (*0-9637112-0-2*) Greater Success.
Mandeville, Lisa K. & Troiano, Nan H. High Risk & Critical Care: Intrapartum Nursing. 2nd ed. LC 98-21938. 352p. 1998. pap. text 41.95 (*0-397-55467-2*) Lppncott W & W.
— High Risk Intrapartum Care. (Illus.). 352p. 1992. pap. text 39.95 (*0-397-54811-7*) Lppncott W & W.
Mandeville, M., et al. Solar Alcohol: The Fuel Revolution. rev. ed. (Illus.). 128p. 1980. pap. 8.95 (*0-940828-00-6*) D Youra Studios.
Mandeville, Mildred S., ed. The Used Book Price Guide: Five Year Edition, 2 vols., Set. Incl. A-K May 1967 to May 1972. 376p. 1977. L-Z, May 1968 to May 1973. 368p. 1977. reprint ed. (*0-911182-72-1*); 1977. 59.00 (*0-911182-73-X*) Price Guide.
— The Used Book Price Guide: Five Year Edition, 1977 Supplement. 479p. 1977. 49.00 (*0-911182-76-4*) Price Guide.
— The Used Book Price Guide: Five Year, 1983 Edition. 536p. 1983. 79.00 (*0-685-05650-3*) Price Guide.
Mandeville, Thomas. Understanding Novelty: Information, Technological Change, & the Patent System. Dervin, Brenda, ed. LC 91-27948. (Communication & Information Science Ser.). 144p. (C). 1995. text 73.25 (*0-89391-632-3*) Ablx Pub.
Mandfield Historical Society Staff, ed. The History of Mansfield, Texas. LC 96-225080. (Illus.). 405p. 1996. reprint ed. text 60.00 (*0-88107-266-4*) Curtis Media.
Mandi, Peter. Education & Economic Growth in the Developing Countries. 224p. (C). 1981. 60.00 (*963-05-2781-2*, Pub. by Akade Kiado) St Mut.
— Education & Economic Growth in the Developing Countries. 226p. 1981. 67.50 (*0-569-08693-0*) St Mut.
Mandia, M. Structures of the Level One Standard Modules for the Affine Lie Algebra. LC 86-28797. (Memoirs of the American Mathematical Society Ser.: Vol. 66/362). 146p. 1987. pap. 25.00 (*0-8218-2423-6*, MEMO/66/362) Am Math.
Mandiargue, Andre Pieyre De, see Pieyre de Mandiargue, Andre.
Mandiargues, Andre Pieyre De, see De Mandiargues, Andre Pieyre.
Mandiberg, Susan F. & Smith, Susan L. Crimes Against the Environment. 838p. 105.00 (*0-327-01955-7*) LEXIS Pub.
Mandiberg, Susan F. & Smith, Susan L. Crimes Against the Environment. LC 97-71237. 800p. 1997. text 105.00 (*1-55834-484-5*, 60920-10, MICHIE) LEXIS Pub.
*__Mandiberg, Susan F. & Smith, Susan L.__ Crimes Against the Environment, 1999 Cumulative Supplement: Pocketpart. 110p. 1999. write for info. (*0-327-01527-6*, 6092111) LEXIS Pub.
Mandich, D. R. & Placek, Joseph A. Russian Heraldry & Nobility. (Illus.). 700p. 1992. 135.00 (*0-9633063-9-1*) Dramco Pubs.
Mandiela. Guyana Betrayal. 280p. 1994. per. write for info. (*0-920813-80-1*) Sister Vis Pr.
— Speshal Rikwes. 70p. pap. write for info. (*0-920813-00-3*) Sister Vis Pr.
Mandiela, Andri Zhina. Dark Diaspora. 64p. Date not set. pap. write for info. (*0-920813-79-8*) Sister Vis Pr.
Mandilaras, Basil G. The Verb in the Greek Non-Literary Papyri. 493p. 1973. 84.00 (*0-685-47544-1*, Pub. by AM Hakkert) BookLink Distributors.
Mandilk, Fred & Gangloff, Marv. Training Dogs: For Protection Work. (Illus.). 160p. 1999. 35.00 (*0-85131-736-7*, Pub. by J A Allen) Trafalgar.
Mandiloff, Velerie, jt. auth. see Vail, Ann.
Mandinach, Ellen B. & Cline, Hugh F. Classroom Dynamics: Implementing a Technology-Based Learning Environment. 224p. 1994. text 49.95 (*0-8058-0555-9*) L Erlbaum Assocs.
Mandino, O. Greatest Salesman in the World. 1996. mass mkt. 7.99 (*0-553-85157-8*) Bantam.
Mandino, Og. A Better Way to Live: For the First Time, Og Mandino Shares His Personal Success Story. 144p. 1990. mass mkt. 6.99 (*0-553-28674-9*) Bantam.
— The Choice. 176p. 1986. mass mkt. 6.99 (*0-553-24576-7*) Bantam.
— The Christ Commission. 272p. 1983. mass mkt. 6.99 (*0-553-27742-1*) Bantam.
Mandino, Og. El Angel Numero Doce. Orig. Title: El Angel Numero Doce. (SPA.). 184p. (Orig.). 1997. pap. text 15.98 (*968-13-2465-X*) Edit Diana.
Mandino, Og. The God Memorandum. rev. ed. (Illus.). 96p. 1996. text 12.95 (*0-8119-0657-4*) F Fell Pubs Inc.
— The Greatest Gift in the World. 128p. 1998. pap. 12.95 (*0-8119-0915-8*) F Fell Pubs Inc.
Mandino, Og. The Greatest Miracle in the World. 128p. 1977. mass mkt. 6.99 (*0-553-27972-6*) Bantam.
Mandino, Og. The Greatest Miracle in the World. 1996. mass mkt. 7.99 (*0-553-85139-X*) Bantam.
— The Greatest Miracle in the World. large type ed. 128p. 1988. pap. 9.95 (*0-8027-2605-4*) Walker & Co.
— The Greatest Miracle in the World. 1993. reprint ed. lib. bdg. 16.95 (*1-56849-089-5*) Buccaneer Bks.
— The Greatest Miracle in the World. LC 75-12823. 128p. 1975. reprint ed. text 14.95 (*0-8119-0255-2*) F Fell Pubs Inc.
— The Greatest Mystery in the World. LC 96-48010. 1997. 18.00 (*0-449-91261-2*) Fawcett.
— The Greatest Mystery in the World. 1998. mass mkt. 5.99 (*0-449-22503-8*) Fawcett.
— Greatest Salesman. 1996. mass mkt. 7.99 (*0-553-85133-0*) Bantam.
— The Greatest Salesman in the World.Tr. of Vendedor Mas Grande del Mundo. 128p. 1983. mass mkt. 6.99 (*0-553-27757-X*) Bantam.
— Greatest Salesman in the World. 1996. mass mkt. 7.99 (*0-553-85154-3*) Bantam.
— The Greatest Salesman in the World. deluxe ed. LC 68-10798.Tr. of Vendedor Mas Grande del Mundo. 108p. (YA). (gr. 9 up). 1968. text 14.95 (*0-8119-0067-3*) F Fell Pubs Inc.
— The Greatest Salesman in the World.Tr. of Vendedor Mas Grande del Mundo. 1993. reprint ed. lib. bdg. 16.95 (*1-56849-090-9*) Buccaneer Bks.
— The Greatest Salesman in the World Pt. 2: The End of the Story. 134p. 1989. mass mkt. 6.99 (*0-553-27699-9*) Bantam.
— Greatest Salest Salesman in the World, Pt. 2. 1996. mass mkt. 7.99 (*0-553-85136-5*) Bantam.
— The Greatest Secret in the World. 176p. 1997. mass mkt. 6.99 (*0-553-28038-4*) Bantam.
— The Greatest Secret in the World. deluxe ed. LC 79-175423. 186p. 1972. text 14.95 (*0-8119-0212-9*) F Fell Pubs Inc.
— The Greatest Success in the World. 112p. 1983. mass mkt. 6.99 (*0-553-27825-8*) Bantam.
— Mission Success! 176p. (Orig.). 1987. mass mkt. 6.99 (*0-553-26500-8*) Bantam.
— Og Mandino's Great Trilogy: The Greatest Salesman in the World, the Greatest Secret in the World, the Greatest Miracle in the World. 419p. 1996. 14.98 (*0-8119-0852-6*) F Fell Pubs Inc.
— The Return of the Ragpicker. 160p. 1993. mass mkt. 6.99 (*0-553-29993-X*) Bantam.
— The Secrets of Success & Happiness. 1996. mass mkt. 5.99 (*0-449-14799-1*) Fawcett.
— The Ten Ancient Scrolls for Success: From the Greatest Salesman in the World. LC 97-8558. 108p. 1997. 9.95 (*0-8119-0856-9*) F Fell Pubs Inc.
— The Twelfth Angel. (YA). 1996. pap. 10.00 (*0-449-91150-0*) Fawcett.
Mandino Og. Universidad Del Exito. (SPA.). 1997. pap. text 27.98 (*968-13-1440-9*) Libros Fronteras.
Mandino, Og. University of Success. 544p. 1983. pap. 16.95 (*0-553-34535-4*) Bantam.
Mandino, Og & Kaye, Buddy. Gift of Acabar. 128p. 1983. mass mkt. 6.50 (*0-553-26084-7*) Bantam.
Mandl, Dave & Wilson, Peter L., eds. Wild Children: A Zine for Kids. 64p. Date not set. 5.00 (*0-936756-83-7*) Autonomedia.
Mandl, Dave, jt. ed. see Strauss, Neil.
Mandl, Franz. Quantum Mechanics. LC 91-24255. (Manchester Physics Ser.: No. 1173). 314p. 1992. pap. 85.00 (*0-471-93155-1*) Wiley.
Mandl, Franz. Quantum Mechanics. fac. ed. LC 91-24255. (The Manchester Physics Ser.). 314p. 1992. reprint ed. pap. 97.40 (*0-7837-8284-5*, 204906600009) Bks Demand.
— Statistical Physics. 2nd ed. LC 87-8283. (Manchester Physics Ser.). 402p. 1988. pap. 69.95 (*0-471-91533-5*) Wiley.
— Statistical Physics. 2nd ed. LC 87-8283. (Manchester Physics Ser.). (Illus.). 406p. reprint ed. pap. 125.90 (*0-8357-3091-3*, 203934800012) Bks Demand.
Mandl, Franz, jt. auth. see Shaw, G.
*__Mandl, G.__ Faulting in Brittle Rocks: An Introduction to the Mechanics of Tectonic Faults. LC 99-45432. (Illus.). x, 430p. 1999. 105.00 (*3-540-66436-X*) Spr-Verlag.
Mandl, G. Mechanics of Tectonic Faulting: Models & Basic Concepts. (Developments in Structural Geology Ser.: No. 1). 408p. 1988. 171.00 (*0-444-42946-8*) Elsevier.
Mandl, Heinz, et al, eds. Learning & Comprehension of Text. LC 83-14050. (Illus.). 470p. reprint ed. pap. 145.70 (*0-8357-4211-3*, 203698800003) Bks Demand.
Mandl, Heinz & Lesgold, Alan M., eds. Learning Issues for Intelligent Tutoring Systems. (Cognitive Science Ser.). (Illus.). 225p. 1988. 58.95 (*0-387-96616-1*) Spr-Verlag.
Mandl, Heinz, jt. ed. see Jonassen, David H.
Mandl, Heinz, jt. ed. see Tiberghien, Andree.
Mandl, Matthew. Basics of Electricity & Electronics. (Illus.). 448p. 1975. 42.00 (*0-13-060228-0*) P-H.
— Repairing & Maintaining Your Own Stereo System. (Illus.). 176p. 1983. text 45.00 (*0-13-773515-4*) P-H.
— Unusual Mathematical Puzzles, Tricks, & Oddities. (Illus.). 128p. 1984. 19.95 (*0-13-938150-3*); pap. 15.95 (*0-13-938101-5*) P-H.
Mandl, P. Analytical Treatment of One-Dimensional Markov Processes. LC 68-59694. (Grundlehren der Mathematischen Wissenschaften Ser.: Vol. 151). 1969. 69.95 (*0-387-04142-7*) Spr-Verlag.
— Asymptotic Statistics. 1996. 125.00 (*3-7908-0770-2*) Spr-Verlag.
Mandl, P. & Huskova, M., eds. Asymptotic Statistics: Proceedings of the Fifth Prague Symposium, Held from September 4-9, 1993. (Contributions to Statistics Ser.). x, 474p. 1994. 93.95 (*0-387-91488-9*) Spr-Verlag.
Mandle, Jay R. Not Slave, Not Free: The African American Economic Experience since the Civil War. LC 91-27995. (Illus.). 152p. 1992. pap. text 17.95 (*0-8223-1220-4*) Duke.
— Patterns of Caribbean Development: An Interpretive Essay on Economic Change. (Caribbean Studies: Vol. 2). 168p. 1982. text 39.00 (*0-677-06000-9*) Gordon & Breach.
— Persistent Underdevelopment: Change & Economic Modernization in the West Indies, Vol. 10. (Caribbean Studies). 200p. 1996. pap. text 14.00 (*2-88449-194-5*) Gordon & Breach.
— Persistent Underdevelopment: Change & Economic Modernization in the West Indies, Vol. 10. (Caribbean Studies). 200p. 1996. text 35.00 (*2-88449-193-7*) Gordon & Breach.
Mandle, Jay R. & Mandle, Joan D. Caribbean Hoops: The Development of West Indian Basketball. LC 94-4491. (Caribbean Studies: Vol. 8). 152p. 1994. text 38.00 (*2-88449-106-6*); pap. text 20.00 (*2-88449-107-4*) Gordon & Breach.
Mandle, Jay R., jt. auth. see Ferleger, Louis A.
*__Mandle, Joan.__ Can We Wear Our Pearls & Still Be Feminists? Memoirs of a Campus Struggle. LC 00-29923. 280p. (Orig.). 2000. pap. 19.95 (*0-8262-1289-1*) U of Mo Pr.
Mandle, Joan D., jt. auth. see Mandle, Jay R.
*__Mandle, Jon.__ What's Left of Liberalism? An Interpretation & Defense of Justice As Fairness. 336p. 2000. 77.00 (*0-7391-0103-X*, Pub. by Lxngtn Bks); pap. write for info. (*0-7391-0104-8*, Pub. by Lxngtn Bks) Rowman.
Mandle, Julia B. & Rothschild, Deborah M. Sites of Recollection: Four Altars & a Rap Opera. LC 92-50560. (Illus.). 112p. (Orig.). 1993. pap. 22.95 (*0-913697-15-X*) U of Pa Pr.
*__Mandleberg, Hilary.__ Dried Flowers: Home Decorating Workbooks with 20 Step-By-Step Projects on Fold-Out Pages. 112p. 1999. pap., wbk. ed. 19.95 (*0-8230-2328-1*) Watsn-Guptill.
— Essence of Blue. LC 99-36730. 2000. 15.00 (*0-688-17431-0*, Hearst) Hearst Commns.
— Essence of Stone. 2000. 15.00 (*0-688-17434-5*, HarpRes) HarpInfo.
— Essence of White. LC 99-37354. (Illus.). 64p. 2000. 15.00 (*0-688-17432-9*, Wm Morrow) Morrow Avon.
— Essence of Wood. 2000. 15.00 (*0-688-17433-7*, HarpRes) HarpInfo.
Mandleco, Barbara L. Dimensions Characteristics & Roles in Client Care. (C). 1998. pap. text. write for info. (*0-8053-7190-7*) Addison-Wesley.
Mandler, George. Cognitive Psychology: An Essay in Cognitive Science. 144p. (C). 1985. pap. 6.95 (*0-89859-659-9*); text 29.95 (*0-89859-537-1*) L Erlbaum Assocs.
— Human Nature Explored. LC 97-22045. 224p. 1997. 24.95 (*0-19-511223-7*) OUP.
Mandler, George, jt. auth. see Mandler, Jean M.
Mandler, Jean M. Stories, Scripts, & Scenes: Aspects of Schema Theory. 144p. (C). 1984. text 39.95 (*0-89859-446-4*) L Erlbaum Assocs.
Mandler, Jean M. & Mandler, George. Thinking: From Association to Gestalt. LC 81-13347. (Perspectives in Psychology Ser.). 300p. 1982. reprint ed. lib. bdg. 59.75 (*0-313-23261-X*, MATK, Greenwood Pr) Greenwood.
Mandler, Michael. Dilemmas in Economic Theory: Persisting Foundational Problems in Microeconomics. LC 98-5437. (Illus.). 224p. 1999. text 35.00 (*0-19-510087-5*) OUP.
Mandler, Peter. Aristocratic Government in the Age of Reform: Whigs & Liberals, 1830-1852. (Illus.). 320p. 1990. text 75.00 (*0-19-821781-1*) OUP.
— The Fall & Rise of the Stately Home. LC 96-24203. (Illus.). 544p. 1997. 45.00 (*0-300-06703-8*) Yale U Pr.
— The Fall & Rise of the Stately Home. LC 96-24203. (Illus.). 523p. 1999. pap. text 19.95 (*0-300-07869-2*) Yale U Pr.
Mandler, Peter, ed. The Uses of Charity: The Poor on Relief in the Nineteenth-Century Metropolis. LC 90-30496. (Shelby Cullom Davis Center Ser.). (Illus.). 264p. (C). 1990. text 36.50 (*0-8122-8214-0*) U of Pa Pr.
Mandler, Peter & Pedersen, Susan, eds. After the Victorians: Private Conscience & Public Duty in Modern Britain. LC 93-17693. 256p. (C). (gr. 13). 1994. 80.00 (*0-415-07056-2*) Routledge.
Mandlowitz, Lynda. Como Conseguir el Empleo Que Usted Desea. (Careers in Depth Ser.). (Illus.). 128p. 1987. lib. bdg. 7.97 (*0-8239-0517-9*) Rosen Group.
Mandolesi, N. & Vittorio, N., eds. The Cosmic Microwave Background: Twenty-Five Years Later. (C). 1990. lib. bdg. 145.00 (*0-7923-0849-2*) Kluwer Academic.
*__Mandolini, Luigi.__ Calixarenes in Action. 2000. 56.00 (*1-86094-194-X*) World Scientific Pub.
Mandos, George. The Everything Casino Gambling Book: From Poker, to Roulette, to Slots - The Rules, Strategies & Secrets You Need to Beat the Odds. LC 97-32779. (Everything Ser.). (Illus.). 288p. 1998. pap. 12.95 (*1-55850-762-0*) Adams Media.
Mandouvalos, N. Scattering Operator, Eisenstein Series, Inner Product Formula & "Maass-Selberg" Relations for Kleinian Groups. LC 89-180. (Memoirs Ser.: Vol. 78/400). 87p. 1989. pap. 16.00 (*0-8218-2463-5*, MEMO/78/400) Am Math.
Mandover, Joan. Because I Care. large type ed. (Linford Romance Library). 1990. pap. 16.99 (*0-7089-6823-6*) Ulverscroft.
— My Love Has Wings. large type ed. (Linford Romance Library). 224p. 1989. pap. 16.99 (*0-7089-6688-8*, Linford) Ulverscroft.
Mandowsky, E., ed. see Ripa, Cesare.
*__Mandraachi.__ Podiatric Radiology. 2001. text. write for info. (*0-7216-9123-4*) Harcrt Hlth Sci Grp.
Mandrak, Nicholas E. & Crossman, E. J. A Checklist of Ontario Freshwater Fishes: Annotated with Distribution Maps. (Illus.). 1994. pap. write for info. (*0-88854-402-2*) Royal Ontario.
Mandrekar, V. R. & Masani, Pesi R. Proceedings of the Norbert Wiener Centenary Congress, 1994: Michigan State University, November 27-December 3, 1994. LC 96-43346. (Proceedings of Symposia in Applied Mathematics Ser.: Vol. 52). 566p. 1996. text 99.00 (*0-8218-0452-9*, PSAPM/52) Am Math.
Mandrell, Barbara. Get to the Heart: My Story. 464p. 1991. mass mkt. 6.99 (*0-553-29243-9*) Bantam.
Mandrell, James. Don Juan & the Point of Honor: Seduction, Patriarchal Society, & Literary Tradition. (Illus.). 336p. 1992. text 40.00 (*0-271-00781-8*) Pa St U Pr.
Mandrell, Louise. Peril in Evans Woods: A Story about the Meaning of Easter. 1993. 12.95 (*1-56530-053-X*) Summit TX.
Mandrell, Regina M. Our Family: Facts & Fancies: The Crary & Related Families. Coker, William S. et al, eds. (Southern History & Genealogy Ser.). (Illus.). 276p. 1993. pap. text 27.50 (*1-882695-05-4*) Patagonia Pr.
Mandrik, M. Amara Vivovojo. (ESP.). 79p. 1997. pap. 8.40 (*1-882251-21-0*) Eldonejo Bero.
Mandrioli, Dino & Ghezzi, Carlo. Theoretical Foundations of Computer Sciences. 504p. (C). 1992. reprint ed. lib. bdg. 59.95 (*0-89464-798-9*) Krieger.
Mandrou, Robert. From Humanism to Science, 1480-1700. LC 92-29506. (Classics in the History & Philosophy of Science Ser.: Vol. 11). 1992. pap. write for info. (*2-88124-568-4*) Gordon & Breach.
Mandruzzato, G. P., ed. The Risk at Delivery. (Contributions to Gynecology & Obstetrics Ser.: Vol. 3). (Illus.). 1977. 42.75 (*3-8055-2421-8*) S Karger.
Mandruzzato, G. P., jt. auth. see Carrera, J. M.
Mandt, Jinger, jt. ed. see Lange, Marie A.
Manduca, Joseph. The Meccano Magazine, 1916-1981. (Hornby Companion Ser.: Vol. 7). 484p. 1992. 60.00 (*0-904568-37-7*) Pincushion Pr.
Mandunu, Joseph Kufulu, see Kufulu Mandunu, Joseph.
*__Mandy, Ivan.__ Fabulya's Wives & Other Stories. 192p. 1999. pap. 22.00 (*963-13-4817-2*, Pub. by Corvina Bks) St Mut.
Mandy, W. J., jt. ed. see Inman, F. P.
Mandych, A. F. Enclosed Seas & Large Lakes of Eastern Europe & Middle Asia. (Illus.). 273p. 1995. 110.00 (*90-5103-110-6*, Pub. by SPB Acad Pub) Balogh.
Mandyczewski, Eusebius, ed. see Brahms, Johannes.
Mandyczewski, Euseblus, ed. see Schubert, Franz.
Mandyczewski, Eusibius, ed. see Schubert, Franz.
Mandziuk, Roseann M., jt. auth. see Fitch, Suzanne P.
Mane, Perrine, jt. auth. see Piponnier, Fran C.
Mane, Perrine, jt. auth. see Piponnier, Francoise.
Mane, R. Ergodic Theory & Differentiable Dynamics. (Ergebnisse der Mathematik und Ihrer Grenzgebiete Ser.: Vol. 8). (Illus.). 330p. 1987. 135.95 (*0-387-15278-4*) Spr-Verlag.
Mane, Robert. Henry Adams on the Road to Chartres. LC 74-154502. 300p. reprint ed. pap. 93.00 (*0-7837-2295-8*, 205738300004) Bks Demand.
Manea, Norman. The Black Envelope. Camiller, Patrick, tr. LC 94-39253.Tr. of Plicul Negru. (ENG & RUM.). 336p. 1995. text 25.00 (*0-374-11397-1*) FS&G.
— The Black Envelope. Camiller, Patrick, tr.Tr. of Plicul Negru. 329p. 1996. pap. 16.95 (*0-8101-1377-5*, Hydra Bks) Northwestern U Pr.
— Compulsory Happiness. Coverdale, Linda, tr. LC 92-38608.Tr. of Le Bonheur Obligatoire. (FRE & ROM.). 1993. 22.00 (*0-374-12785-9*) FS&G.
— Compulsory Happiness. Coverdale, Linda, tr. from ROM. LC 94-17021. (Writings from an Unbound Europe).Tr. of Le Bonheur Obligatoire. 264p. 1994. pap. 13.95 (*0-8101-1190-X*) Northwestern U Pr.
— October, Eight O'Clock: Stories. LC 91-36377. 224p. 1993. pap. 12.00 (*0-8021-3371-1*, Grove) Grove-Atltic.
— On Clowns: The Dictator & the Artist - Essays. LC 91-23866. 192p. 1993. pap. 12.00 (*0-8021-3375-4*, Grove) Grove-Atltic.
Manea, Norman. Variations to a Self Portrait. text (*0-374-28256-0*) FS&G.

M

An Asterisk (*) at the beginning of an entry indicates that the title is appearing for the first time.

Manedov, Russell. Soviet Military Medicine: Research Subject Index with Bibliography. LC 88-47621. 150p. 1988. 47.50 (0-88164-722-5); pap. 44.50 (0-88164-723-3) ABBE Pubs Assn.

Manees, Raynetta. All for Love. 224p. 1996. mass mkt. 4.99 (0-7860-0309-X, Pinncle Kensgtn) Kensgtn Pub Corp.

— Fantasy. (Arabesque Ser.). 1999. mass mkt. 4.99 (1-58314-030-1) BET Bks.

— Follow Your Heart. 256p. 1998. pap. 4.99 (0-7860-0560-2) Kensgtn Pub Corp.

— Wishing on a Star. 256p. 1997. mass mkt. 4.99 (0-7860-0423-1, Pinncle Kensgtn) Kensgtn Pub Corp.

Maneesha, Ma P., ed. see Osho.

Maneesha, Sambodhi M., ed. see Osho.

Manegold, Catherine S. In Glory's Shadow: Shannon Faulkner, the Citadel & a Changing America. LC 99-18919. (Illus.). 352p. 2000. 26.95 (0-679-44635-4) Knopf.

***Manegold, J.** Intermediate Accounting. 1999. 37.50 (0-07-040037-7) McGraw.

Manekeller, Wolfgang. Hundert Briefe Deutsch fuer Export & Import. 160p. 1983. pap. 15.95 (3-468-41111-1) Langenscheidt.

— So Bewirbt Man Sich. (GER.). 160p. 1980. pap. 8.95 (3-581-66255-8) Langenscheidt.

— So Schreibt Man Geschaeftsbriefe. (GER.). 160p. 1982. pap. 8.95 (3-581-66229-9) Langenscheidt.

Maneker, Jerry S. Applied Sociology: Sociological Understanding & Its Application. 70p. (Orig.). (C). 1994. pap. text 14.50 (0-8191-9777-7) U Pr of Amer.

Manekin, Charles H. The Logic of Gersonides: A Translation of Sefer Ha-Heqqesh Ha-Yashar (The Book of the Correct Syllogism) of Rabbi Levi ben Gershom with Introduction, Commentary, & Analytical Glossary. (New Synthese Historical Library). 364p. (C). 1991. lib. bdg. 175.00 (0-7923-1513-8, Pub. by Kluwer Academic) Kluwer Academic.

Manekin, Charles H. & Kellner, Menachem M., eds. Freedom & Moral Responsibility: General & Jewish Perspectives. LC 97-11286. (Studies & Texts in Jewish History & Culture: Vol. 2). viii, 273p. 1997. 35.00 (1-883053-29-3) Univ Pr MD.

Manela. Principal Communication Systems. 2nd ed. 1986. student ed. 34.68 (0-07-062956-0) McGraw.

Manela, Roger, jt. auth. see Ferman, Louis A.

Manela, Stewart S., et al, eds. Employee Duty of Loyalty: A State-by-State Survey: Includes the 1999 Cumulative Supplement, 2 vols. 1779p. 1998. suppl. ed. 285.00 (0-87179-853-0, 9134) BNA Books.

Manelfe, Claude, ed. Imaging of the Spine & Spinal Cord. rev. ed. 928p. 1992. text 204.00 (0-88167-863-5) Lppncott W & W.

Maneli, Mieczyslaw. Perelman's New Rhetoric As Philosophy & Methodology for the Next Century. LC 93-18161. (Library of Rhetorics: Vol. 1). 151p. (C). 1994. text 115.00 (0-7923-2166-9) Kluwer Academic.

Manelis, G. B. Chemistry Reviews Vol. 15, Pt. 5.2: Effect of Mechanical Stresses on Kinetics of Solid State Chemical Reactions, Vol. 15. (Soviet Scientific Reviews Ser.: Section B). 101p. 1991. pap. text 85.00 (3-7186-5118-1, Harwood Acad Pubs) Gordon & Breach.

Manelis, G. B., et al. Chemistry Reviews: Pulsed NMR Study of Molecular Motion in Solids, Vol. 14. Vol'pin, M. E., ed. (Soviet Scientific Reviews Ser.: Vol. 14, Pt. 2). ii, 92p. 1989. pap. text 75.00 (3-7186-4959-4) Gordon & Breach.

Manelis, Judith, ed. see Epilepsy International Symposium Staff.

Manelli, Nino. And You Ask Me Why I Drink. 304p. 1997. 21.00 (0-671-55160-4, PB Hardcover) PB.

Manen, Hans P. Van, see Van Manen, Hans P.

Manen, Lucie. Bel Canto: The Teaching of the Classical Italian Song-Schools, Its Decline & Restoration. (Illus.). 86p. 1987. pap. text 24.95 (0-19-317109-0) OUP.

Manenc, J. Structural Thermodynamics of Alloys. Corcoran, N., tr. from FRE. LC 73-83564. Orig. Title: Thermodynamique Structurale Des Alliages. (Illus.). 1973. text 96.00 (90-277-0346-9) Kluwer Academic.

Manenkov, A. A., ed. Laser Techniques for Investigation of Defects in Semiconductors & Dielectrics. (Proceedings of the Institute of General Physics of the Academy of Sciences of the U. S. S. R. Ser.: Vol. 4). 204p. (C). 1988. text 165.00 (0-941743-15-2) Nova Sci Pubs.

Manent, Pierre. The City of Man. LC 97-42953. 225p. 1998. text 24.95 (0-691-01144-3, Pub. by Princeton U Pr) Cal Prin Full Svc.

***Manent, Pierre.** City of Man. LC 97-42953. (New French Thought Ser.). 225p. 2000. pap. text 16.95 (0-691-05025-2, Pub. by Princeton U Pr) Cal Prin Full Svc.

Manent, Pierre. An Intellectual History of Liberalism.Tr. of Histoire Intellectuelle du Liberalisme. 142p. 1994. pap. text 12.95 (0-691-02911-3, Pub. by Princeton U Pr) Cal Prin Full Svc.

— An Intellectual History of Liberalism. Balinski, Rebecca, tr. from FRE. LC 94-3110. (New French Thought Ser.).Tr. of Histoire Intellectuelle du Liberalisme. 144p. 1994. text 29.50 (0-691-03437-0, Pub. by Princeton U Pr) Cal Prin Full Svc.

— Modern Liberty & Its Discontents by Pierre Manent. Mahoney, Daniel J. & Seaton, Paul, eds. & trs. by. LC 98-4323. 248p. 1998. 58.00 (0-8476-9087-3); pap. 22.95 (0-8476-9088-1) Rowman.

— Tocqueville & the Nature of Democracy. Waggoner, John, tr. LC 95-38604. 166p. (C). 1995. pap. text 21.95 (0-8476-8116-5); lib. bdg. 44.50 (0-8476-8115-7) Rowman.

***Maner, Martin.** The Research Process: A Complete Guide & Reference for Writers. 2nd ed. LC 99-30605. xx, 386p. 2000. pap. text 21.95 (0-7674-1139-0, 1139-0) Mayfield Pub.

Manera, Anthony. A Dream Betrayed: The Battle for the CBC. LC 97-137480. (Illus.). 224p. 1996. 27.95 (0-7737-2980-1) Stoddart Publ.

Manera, Elizabeth S., ed. Substitute Teaching: Planning for Success. LC 96-26437. (Illus.). 162p. 1996. pap. 20.00 (0-912099-06-2, 506) Kappa Delta Pi.

Manera, Nancy & Donoghue, Simon J. Mixed Nuts. 1983. 5.50 (0-87129-576-8, M59) Dramatic Pub.

Manero, Juan R., jt. auth. see Atienza, Manuel.

Manes, Christopher. Other Creations. 1910. mass mkt. 14.95 (0-385-48368-6) Doubleday.

Manes, Ernest G. Predicate Transformer Semantics. (Cambridge Tracts in Theoretical Computer Science Ser.: No. 33). 233p. (C). 1992. text 49.95 (0-521-42036-9) Cambridge U Pr.

Manes, Ernest G. & Arbib, Michael A. Algebraic Approaches to Program Semantics. (Texts & Monographs in Computer Science). (Illus.). 355p. 1986. 109.95 (0-387-96324-3) Spr-Verlag.

Manes, Joan, jt. ed. see Wolfson, Nessa.

Manes, L., ed. Actinides: Chemistry & Physical Properties. (Structure & Bonding Ser.: Vol. 59-60). (Illus.). 250p. 1985. 131.95 (0-387-13752-1) Spr-Verlag.

Manes, Rene P. The Effects of United States Oil Import Policy on the Petroleum Industry. Bruchey, Stuart, ed. LC 78-22696. (Energy in the American Economy Ser.). (Illus.). 1979. lib. bdg. 35.95 (0-405-11999-2) Ayer.

Manes, Rene P. & Cheng, C. S. Agnes. The Marginal Approach to Joint Cost Allocation: Theory & Application. (Studies in Accounting Research: No. 29). 219p. 1988. 20.00 (0-86539-068-1) Am Accounting.

Manes, Rose T. Prima Vera: Springtime. Costa, Gwen, ed. LC 90-21706. 1991. pap. 13.95 (0-87949-330-5) Ashley Bks.

Manes, Stephen. An Almost Perfect Game. LC 94-18192. 176p. (J). (gr. 4-7). 1995. 14.95 (0-590-44432-8) Scholastic Inc.

— Almost Perfect Game. (J). 1997. mass mkt. 3.99 (0-590-44433-6) Scholastic Inc.

Manes, Stephen. Almost Perfect Game. 1997. 9.09 (0-606-11031-3, Pub. by Turtleback) Demco.

Manes, Stephen. Be a Perfect Person in Just Three Days! (Illus.). 76p. (J). (gr. 3-7). 1996. pap. 4.50 (0-440-41349-4, YB BDD) BDD Bks Young Read.

— Be a Perfect Person in Just Three Days! (Illus.). (J). 1996. pap. 3.99 (0-440-23314-3) BDD Bks Young Read.

— Be a Perfect Person in Just Three Days! LC 81-10275. (Illus.). 64p. (J). (gr. 4-7). 1982. 16.00 (0-89919-064-2, Clarion Bks) HM.

— The Boy Who Turned into a TV Set. (Illus.). 32p. (Orig.). (J). (gr. 2-5). 1983. pap. 2.50 (0-380-62000-6, Avon Bks) Morrow Avon.

— Chocolate-Covered Ants. 112p. (J). (gr. 4-7). 1993. pap. 2.95 (0-590-40961-1) Scholastic Inc.

— Comedy High. 176p. (YA). (gr. 7 up). 1992. 13.95 (0-590-44436-0, Scholastic Hardcover) Scholastic Inc.

— Comedy High. 224p. (YA). (gr. 7-9). 1994. pap. 3.50 (0-590-44437-9) Scholastic Inc.

— The Great Gerbil Roundup. LC 88-2266. (Illus.). 105p. (J). (gr. 3-7). 1988. 13.95 (0-15-232490-9, Harcourt Child Bks) Harcourt.

— The Hooples' Haunted House. (Illus.). 112p. (J). (gr. 3-7). 1983. pap. 2.25 (0-440-43794-6, YB BDD) BDD Bks Young Read.

— The Hooples' Horrible Holiday. 128p. (Orig.). (J). (gr. 3-7). 1986. pap. 2.50 (0-380-89740-7, Avon Bks) Morrow Avon.

— Hooples on the Highway. 96p. 1985. pap. 2.50 (0-380-69989-3, Avon Bks) Morrow Avon.

Manes, Stephen. How to be a Perfect Person in Just Three Days! 1996. 9.19 (0-606-03058-1, Pub. by Turtleback) Demco.

Manes, Stephen. Make Four Million Dollars by Next Thursday! (Illus.). 96p. (J). 1996. pap. 4.50 (0-440-41370-2) BDD Bks Young Read.

— Make Four Million Dollars by Next Thursday! 1996. 9.19 (0-606-00584-6, Pub. by Turtleback) Demco.

Manes, Stephen & Andrews, Paul. Gates: How Microsoft Mogul Reinvented an Industry & Made Himself the Richest Man in America. 560p. 1994. per. 14.00 (0-671-88074-8, Touchstone) S&S Trade Pap.

***Manes, Virginia & Frohlich, Mary, eds.** The Lay Contemplative: Testimonies, Perspectives, Resources. 216p. 2000. pap. text 10.95 (0-86716-370-4) St Anthony Mess Pr.

Manes, Virginia, ed. see Walters, Kerry.

Maneschi, Andrea. Comparative Advantage in International Trade: A Historical Perspective. LC 98-6258. 272p. 1998. 85.00 (1-85898-300-2) E Elgar.

Manese, Wilfredo R. Employment Testing, Validation & the Law: A Primer. 213p. 1979. 25.00 (0-9604586-0-3) EGM Ent.

— Fair & Effective Employment Testing: Administrative, Psychometric, & Legal Issues for the Human Resources Professional. LC 85-27151. (Illus.). 157p. 1986. 55.00 (0-89930-171-1, MFE/, Quorum Bks) Greenwood.

— Occupational Job Evalution: A Research-Based Approach to Job Classification. LC 87-32280. 177p. 1988. 55.00 (0-89930-261-0, MOL/, Quorum Bks) Greenwood.

Manesiotis, Joy. They Sing to Her Bones. 64p. Date not set. 22.00 (0-932826-86-5) WMU Poetry & Prose.

— They Sing to Her Bones. 64p. 2000. pap. 12.00 (0-932826-87-3) WMU Poetry & Prose.

Manesis, John. The Journey of Andrew Burke. LC 99-201490. 25p. 1998. pap. write for info. (0-9668175-0-8) J Manesis.

Maness, Larry. Strangler: A Jake Eaton Mystery. LC 97-40722. 192p. 1998. 19.95 (0-89141-568-8) Presidio Pr.

Maness, Malia. Curious Kimo. LC 93-86143. (Illus.). 32p. (J). (ps-3). 1993. 9.95 (0-9633493-0-9) Pacific Greetings.

— The Toad That Taught Flying. LC 93-86144. (Illus.). 32p. (J). (ps-3). 1993. 9.95 (0-9633493-1-7) Pacific Greetings.

Maness, Roger, et al. The Playbook: A Resource for Games & Other Group Related Activities. (Illus.). 144p. 1995. spiral bd. 17.95 (0-9658328-0-5) Playbook Pubs.

Maness, Terry S. Path Telecourse. 1996. pap., student ed. 14.50 (0-314-09707-4) West Pub.

— Short Term: Testbank. Date not set. pap. text, teacher ed., suppl. ed. write for info. (0-314-02002-0) West Pub.

Maness, Terry S. & Zietlow, John T. Short-Term Financial Management. LC 97-66402. 656p. (C). 1997. text 90.00 (0-15-503971-7) Dryden Pr.

— Short-Term Financial Management: Text, Cases, & Readings. Burvikovs, ed. LC 92-32830. 550p. (C). 1992. 69.25 (0-314-01268-0) West Pub.

***Maness, William H.** Dear William: The Yeast Is There. LC 99-91953. 2000. 25.00 (0-7388-1408-3); pap. 18.00 (0-7388-1409-1) Xlibris Corp.

Manesse, Rosalyn F. Easy Kosher Cooking. LC 96-5189. 328p. 1996. 35.00 (1-56821-903-2) Aronson.

Manet, Eduardo, et al. Playwrights of Exile: An International Anthology. Kourilsky, Francoise, ed. Vogel, Stephen J. et al, trs. from FRE. 456p. 1997. pap. 19.95 (0-913745-48-0) Ubu Repertory.

***Manetsch, S. M.** Theodore Beza & the Quest for Peace in France, 1572-1598. (Studies in Medieval & Reformation Thought). 2000. 122.00 (90-04-11101-8) Brill Academic Pubs.

Manetti, Larry & Silverman, Chip. Aloha Magnum: Larry Manetti's Magnum, P. I. Memories. LC 98-39327. (Illus.). 272p. 1998. pap. 14.95 (1-58063-052-9, Pub. by Renaissance) St Martin.

Manetti, Antonio. The Fat Woodworker. Martone, Valerie, tr. from ITA. LC 90-55850. (Illus.). 88p. (Orig.). 1991. pap. 10.00 (0-934977-23-2) Italica Pr.

Manetti, Giovanni. Theories of the Sign in Classical Antiquity. Richardson, Christine, tr. LC 92-28924. (Advances in Semiotics Ser.). (ENG & ITA.). 220p. 1993. 15.00 (0-253-33684-8) Ind U Pr.

Manevich, Eleanor D. Such Were the Times: A Personal View of the Lysenko Era in the U. S. S. R. LC 89-64119. 100p. 1990. pap. 9.95 (0-938875-22-1) Pittenbruach Pr.

***Manevich, Leonard.** O, How Much Heavenly Music Is Heard! (RUS.). 16p. 1999. pap. 12.99 (0-9679201-0-8) Kolobok.

Maney, A. S. A Faith for Living. 1999. pap. 21.00 (1-85072-112-2, Pub. by W Sessions) St Mut.

Maney, Ann & Wells, Susan, eds. Professional Responsibilities in Protecting Children: A Public Health Approach to Child Sexual Abuse, 9. LC 87-32798. 237p. 1988. 55.00 (0-275-92966-3, C2966, Praeger Pubs) Greenwood.

Maney, Ardith L. Still Hungry after All These Years: Food Assistance Policy from Kennedy to Reagan, 11. LC 88-7711. (Studies in Social Welfare Policies & Programs). 203p. 1989. 52.95 (0-313-26327-2, MSY, Greenwood Pr) Greenwood.

Maney, Ardith L. & Bykerk, Loree. Consumer Politics: Protecting Public Interests on Capitol Hill, 343. LC 93-30980. (Contributions in Political Science Ser.: No. 343). 200p. 1994. 57.95 (0-313-26428-7, Greenwood Pr) Greenwood.

— U. S. Consumer Interest Groups: Institutional Profiles. LC 94-27949. 296p. 1995. lib. bdg. 75.00 (0-313-26429-5, Greenwood Pr) Greenwood.

Maney, J. P. & Hazuka, Tom. A Celestial Omnibus: Short Fiction on Faith. Hooks, Tisha, ed. 1998. pap. 15.00 (0-8070-8335-6) Beacon Pr.

Maney, Jill M. Emily Dickinson in Amherst: A Guide. (Famous Footsteps Ser.). (Illus.). (Orig.). 1989. pap. 4.95 (0-929709-05-5) Computer Lab.

Maney, Kevin. Megamedia Shakeout: The Inside Story of the Leaders & the Losers in the Exploding Communications Industry. LC 94-43311. 358p. 1995. 24.95 (0-471-10719-0) Wiley.

Maney, Mabel. The Case of the Good-for-Nothing Girlfriend. 2nd ed. 300p. 1998. pap. 14.95 (1-57344-075-2) Cleis Pr.

— The Case of the Not-So-Nice Nurse. LC 93-11846. 160p. 1993. pap. 9.95 (0-939416-76-X) Cleis Pr.

***Maney, Mabel.** A Ghost in the Closet. 2nd ed. LaBonte, Richard, ed. (Nancy Clue & the Hardly Boys Ser.: No. 3). 180p. 1999. pap. 14.95 (1-57344-095-7, Pub. by Cleis Pr) Publishers Group.

Maney, Patrick J. Franklin D. Roosevelt. (Twentieth Century American Biography Ser.). 272p. 1992. pap. 16.95 (0-8057-7786-5) Macmillan.

— The Roosevelt Presence: A Biography of F. D. R. (Twayne's Twentieth-Century American Biography Ser.). 250p. (C). 1992. pap. 14.95 (0-8057-9825-0, Twyne) Mac Lib Ref.

— The Roosevelt Presence: A Biography of F. D. R. (Twayne's Twentieth-Century American Biography Ser.). 250p. (C). 1993. 26.95 (0-8057-7758-X, Twyne) Mac Lib Ref.

— The Roosevelt Presence: The Life & Legacy of FDR. LC 98-16354. 270p. 1998. 17.95 (0-520-21637-7, Pub. by U CA Pr) Cal Prin Full Svc.

Maney, Susan. The Smart Approach to Bath Design. Robitz, Kathie, ed. LC 97-75267. (Illus.). 176p. 1998. pap. 19.95 (1-58011-009-6) Creative Homeowner.

— Smart Approach to Kitchen Design. Robitz, Kathie & Elliott, Lynn, eds. LC 98-84953. (Illus.). 176p. 1998. pap. 19.95 (1-58011-024-X) Creative Homeowner.

Manford, Alan, ed. see Hardy, Thomas.

Manford, Alan, ed. & intro. see Hardy, Thomas.

Manford, Toby, jt. auth. see Appleyard, Reginald T.

Manfre, Karen, jt. auth. see Van Ost, Lynn.

Manfred, Frederick, pseud. Conquering Horse. LC 83-5826. xvi, 355p. 1983. reprint ed. pap. 11.95 (0-8032-8119-6, Bison Books) U of Nebr Pr.

— Duke's Mixture. (Prairie Plains Ser.). 260p. (YA). (gr. 8). 1994. pap. 15.95 (0-931170-55-9) Ctr Western Studies.

— Flowers of Desire. LC 89-23569. 248p. 1989. 19.95 (0-9624298-0-5); pap. 10.95 (0-9624298-1-3) Dancing Badger.

— The Frederick Manfred Reader. Rezmerski, John C., ed. & intro. by. (Illus.). 556p. 1996. pap. 21.95 (0-930100-67-0) Holy Cow.

— The Golden Bowl: Golden Anniversary Edition. LC 92-5627. 250p. 1992. pap. 9.95 (0-9632157-0-1) SD Human Fnd.

— Lord Grizzly. 1994. mass mkt. 4.50 (0-451-18413-0, Sig) NAL.

— No Fun on Sunday. LC 89-40738. 296p. 1990. 24.95 (0-8061-2273-0) U of Okla Pr.

— Of Lizards & Angels: A Saga of Siouxland. LC 91-50865. 626p. (C). 1993. pap. 14.95 (0-8061-2514-4) U of Okla Pr.

— The Selected Letters of Frederick Manfred, 1932-1954. Huseboe, Arthur R. & Nelson, Nancy O., eds. LC 88-4798. (Illus.). viii, 421p. 1989. text 40.00 (0-8032-2344-7) U of Nebr Pr.

— The Selected Letters of Frederick Manfred, 1932-1954. Huseboe, Arthur R. & Nelson, Nancy O., eds. LC 88-4798. 429p. reprint ed. pap. 133.00 (0-608-08694-0, 206921700003) Bks Demand.

— Winter Count. deluxe limited ed. 1966. 100.00 (0-911506-05-5) Thueson.

— Winter Count II, Bk. I. 1987. 40.00 (0-911506-20-9) Thueson.

Manfred, Freya. American Roads. LC 79-51029. 96p. 1984. pap. 8.95 (0-87951-958-4, Pub. by Overlook Pr) Penguin Putnam.

— American Roads: A Book of Poems. LC 79-51029. 96p. 1980. 14.95 (0-87951-100-1, Pub. by Overlook Pr); 50.00 (0-87951-103-6, Pub. by Overlook Pr) Penguin Putnam.

— Frederick Manfred: A Daughter Remembers. LC 98-54633. (Midwest Reflections Ser.). 224p. 1999. 24.95 (0-87351-371-1, Borealis Book); pap. 15.95 (0-87351-372-X, Borealis Book) Minn Hist.

— A Goldenrod Will Grow. 1971. pap. 6.95 (0-911506-10-1) Thueson.

Manfred, Griehl. Fighters over Russia. LC 96-39872. (Luftwaffe at War Ser.). 1997. 13.95 (1-85367-270-X) Stackpole.

Manfred, Hofer, jt. auth. see Eckel, Denis.

Manfred, Madge, jt. auth. see Strenski, Ellen.

Manfred, Riedel, jt. ed. see Mittelstrass, Juergen.

Manfred, Victor & Glutchison, John. Current Approaches to African Linguistics, Vol. 7. (Publications in African Languages & Linguistics: No. 11). 235p. 1990. pap. 83.10 (90-6765-498-1) Mouton.

***Manfredi, Christopher P.** Judicial Power & the Charter: Canada & the Paradox of Liberal Constitutionalism. 2nd ed. 320p. 2000. pap. 29.95 (0-19-541504-3) OUP.

Manfredi, Christopher P. Judicial Power & the Charter of Rights & Freedoms: Canada & the Paradox of Liberal Constitutionalism. LC 92-50725. 1993. pap. 21.95 (0-8061-2527-6) U of Okla Pr.

— The Supreme Court & Juvenile Justice. LC 97-18993. 272p. 1997. 35.00 (0-7006-0851-6) U Pr of KS.

***Manfredi, Christopher P.** Supreme Court & Juvenile Justice. xvi, 256p. 2000. pap. text 15.95 (0-7006-1028-6) U Pr of KS.

Manfredi, John. The Social Limits of Art. LC 82-8661. (Illus.). 208p. 1982. lib. bdg. 30.00 (0-87023-372-6) U of Mass Pr.

Manfredi, Michael A., jt. auth. see Weiss, Marion.

Manfredi-Petitt, Lynn A., jt. auth. see Baker, Amy C.

Manfredi, Renee. Where Love Leaves Us. LC 93-28456. (Iowa Short Fiction Award Ser.). 158p. 1994. 11.50 (0-87745-444-2) U of Iowa Pr.

Manfredi-Romanini, Maria G. & Bolognani-Fantin, Anna M. Polysaccharides & Glycoconjugates in Invertebrates & Polysaccharides & Glycoconjugates in Non-Mammalian Vertebrates. (Handbook of Histochemistry, Poly-Saccharides Ser.: Vol. 11, Pt. 5). (Illus.). 450p. 1991. text 255.00 (1-56081-324-5, Pub. by Gustav Fischer) Balogh.

Manfredi, Stephen J. AIDS: Answers for Everyone. 96p. (Orig.). (YA). (gr. 6-12). 1989. pap. text 9.95 (0-929496-01-9) Treehaus Comns.

***Manfredini, Lou.** Mr. Fix-It: 101 Answers to the Most Commonly Asked Questions about Repairing Your Home. Neumeyer, Kathy, ed. LC 99-69007. (Illus.). 156p. 2000. pap. 14.99 (1-892866-22-6) Rare Air.

Manfredini, Vincenzo. Regole Armoniche. fac. ed. (Monuments of Music & Music Literature in Facsimile, II Ser.: Vol. 10). (Illus.). 1966. lib. bdg. 40.00 (0-8450-2210-5) Broude.

Manfredo, Michael J. Influencing Human Behavior: Theory & Applications in Recreation & Tourism & Natural Resources Management. LC 91-67445. 400p. (C). 1992. text 15.00 (0-915611-35-X) Sagamore Pub.

Manfredo, Ralph P. Electronic Transformers & Inductors - U.S. Markets & Opportunities: 1993-1998 Analysis & Forecasts. 370p. 1994. pap. text 1900.00 (1-878218-48-4) World Info Tech.

Manfredonia, Salvatore J. Twenty Eight Styles for Student Practice. (SPA.). 1984. 10.95 (0-87350-149-7) Milady Pub.

— Twenty-Eight Styles for Student Practice. Healy, Mary, ed. (Illus.). 62p. 1984. pap. 15.95 (0-87350-400-3) Milady Pub.

***Manfridi, Giuseppe.** Cuckoos. 72p. 2000. pap. 14.95 (1-84002-151-9) Theatre Comm.

Manfull, et al. The Stage in Action. 2nd ed. LC 99-159112. 688p. (C). 1998. per. 59.95 (*0-7872-5456-8*) Kendall-Hunt.

Manfull, Helen. In Other Words: Women Directors Speak. LC 96-42077. (Illus.). 192p. 1997. pap. 19.95 (*1-57525-102-7*) Smith & Kraus.

— The Stage in Action. 672p. 1996. per. 34.95 (*0-8403-7624-3*) Kendall-Hunt.

Mang, Christa. Zaire. (Bradt Country Guides Ser.). (Illus.). 224p. (Orig.). 1994. pap. 15.95 (*1-56440-557-5*, Pub. by Bradt Pubns) Globe Pequot.

Mang, H., jt. auth. see Kuhn, G.

Mang, Herbert J., Jr., jt. auth. see Palmisano, Donald J.

***Mang, Theo.** Lubricants & Lubrications. 528p. 2000. text 184.95 (*3-527-29536-4*) Wiley.

Manga, Ekema T. The African Economic Dilemma: The Case of Cameroon. LC 97-45623. 280p. (C). 1997. text 46.00 (*0-7618-0991-0*) U Pr of Amer.

Manga, Janos. Hungarian Folk Songs & Folk Instruments. (Hungarian Folk Art Ser.). 114p. 1999. 25.00 (*963-13-7443-2*, Pub. by Corvina Bks) St Mut.

Mangabhai, R. J., ed. Calcium Aluminate Cements: Proceedings of a Symposium Dedicated to H. G. Midgley, London, July 1990. (Illus.). 400p. (C). 1990. 115.00 (*0-419-15200-8*, E & FN Spon) Routledge.

***Mangahas, Federico & Mangahas, Ruby K.** Maybe: Incidentally: The Satire of Federico Mangahas: Essays LC 98-947832. xxxi, 653p. 1998. write for info. (*971-542-189-X*, Pub. by U of Philippines Pr) UH Pr.

Mangahas, Ruby K., jt. auth. see Mangahas, Federico.

Mangajin Magazine Editorss. Basic Japanese Through Comics, Vol. 2. (JPN., Illus.). 160p. (Orig.). 1998. pap. 14.95 (*0-9634335-4-7*) Mangajin.

Mangal, Roshni. The Shine Around the Moon. (Illus.). 32p. (J). (ps-3). 1997. pap. 14.95 (*0-9644695-2-9*) Image Maker Pub.

— The Stray Bullet. (Illus.). 48p. (J). (ps-3). 1999. pap. 17.95 (*0-9644695-3-7*) Image Maker Pub.

Mangalam, S. J. Historical Geography & Toponomy of Andhra Pradesh. 260p. (C). 1987. 38.50 (*81-85055-99-8*, Pub. by Sundeep Prak) S Asia.

Mangaliso, Mzamo P. & Weiner, Joan, eds. Proceedings of the Eastern Academy of Management. 1995. write for info. (*0-916958-13-2*) Eastrn Acad Mgmt.

Mangaliso, Nomazengele A. The South African Mosaic: A Sociological Analysis of Post-Apartheid Conflict. 144p. (Orig.). 1994. pap. text 29.50 (*0-8191-9506-5*); lib. bdg. 46.00 (*0-8191-9505-7*) U Pr of Amer.

Mangalwadi, Ruth, et al. William Carey & the Regeneration of India. 3rd ed. 160p. 1997. reprint ed. pap. 11.95 (*81-86701-01-X*) Nivedit Good Bks.

Mangalwadi, Ruth, jt. auth. see Mangalwadi, Vishal.

Mangalwadi, Vishal. India: The Grand Experiment. LC 98-110023. 384p. 1997. 13.95 (*0-9513089-5-5*) Rann Pippa Bks.

***Mangalwadi, Vishal.** Missionary Conspiracy: Letters to a Postmodern Hindu. 320p. 1998. reprint ed. pap. 16.99 (*1-85078-327-6*, Pub. by O M Pubng) OM Literature.

Mangalwadi, Vishal. The World of Gurus. 1987. 12.00 (*0-8364-2046-2*, Pub. by Usha) S Asia.

Mangalwadi, Vishal, intro. Missionary Conspiracy: Letters to a Postmodern Hindu. 2nd rev. ed. LC 96-903508. 488p. 1996. 23.50 (*81-86701-00-1*, Pub. by Nivedit Good Bks) MacLaurin Inst.

Mangalwadi, Vishal & Mangalwadi, Ruth. Carey, Christ & Cultural Transformation: The Life & Influence of William Carey. LC 98-110146. 142p. 1997. reprint ed. pap. 10.99 (*1-85078-258-X*, Pub. by O M Pubng) OM Literature.

Mangalwadi, Vishal & Mangalwadi, Ruth. The Legacy of William Carey: A Model for the Transformation of a Culture. LC 99-25218. 160p. 1999. reprint ed. pap. 10.99 (*1-58134-112-1*) Crossway Bks.

Mangalwadi, Vishal, jt. auth. see Schaeffer, Francis A.

Mangan, Anne. The Smallest Bear. LC 97-29669. (Illus.). 32p. (J). (ps-k). 1998. 14.95 (*1-56656-266-X*, Crocodile Bks) Interlink Pub.

Mangan, Celine, et al. The Targums of Job, Proverbs, & Qohelet. (Aramaic Bible Ser.: No. 15). 256p. 1991. text 65.00 (*0-8146-5490-8*) Liturgical Pr.

Mangan, Charles, ed. see John Paul, II, pseud.

Mangan, Frank. El Paso in Pictures. LC 70-184833. (Illus.). 174p. 1971. 39.95 (*0-930208-02-1*) Mangan Books TX.

Mangan, Frank & Mangan, Judy. Ruidoso Country. LC 94-20105. (Illus.). 192p. 1994. 39.95 (*0-930208-33-1*) Mangan Books TX.

Mangan, Frank, ed. see Metz, Leon C.

Mangan, Gerald. Waiting for the Storm. 64p. (Orig.). 1990. pap. 15.95 (*1-85224-110-1*, Pub. by Bloodaxe Bks) Dufour.

Mangan, Gordon L. Review of Published Research on the Relationship of Some Personality Variables to ESP Scoring Level. (Parapsychological Monographs: No. 1). 1958. pap. 5.00 (*0-912328-03-7*) Parapsych Foun.

Mangan, I., jt. auth. see Keogh, S.

***Mangan, J. A.** Athleticism in the Victorian & Edwardian Public School: The Emergence & Consolidation of an Educational Ideology. 380p. 2000. pap. 32.50 (*0-7146-8043-5*) F Cass Pubs.

Mangan, J. A. The Games Ethic & Imperialism: Aspects of the Diffusion of an Ideal. 2nd ed. LC 97-43854. (Sport in the Global Society Ser.). 240p. (C). 1998. pap. text 27.50 (*0-7146-4399-8*, Pub. by F Cass Pubs) Intl Spec Bk.

***Mangan, J. A., ed.** Shaping the Superman: Fascist Body As Political Icon: Aryan Fascism. LC 99-25234. (Sport in the Global Society Ser.: No. 14). (Illus.). 176p. 1999. 45.00 (*0-7146-4954-6*, Pub. by F Cass Pubs); pap. 24.50 (*0-7146-8013-3*, Pub. by F Cass Pubs) Intl Spec Bk.

Mangan, J. A., ed. Sport in Europe: Politics, Class, Gender. (European Sports History Review Ser.: Vol. 1). (Illus.). 4p. 1999. 65.00 (*0-7146-4946-5*, Pub. by F Cass Pubs); pap. 35.00 (*0-7146-8005-2*, Pub. by F Cass Pubs) Intl Spec Bk.

***Mangan, J. A., ed.** Superman Supreme: Fascist Body as Political Icon - Global Fascism. (Sport in the Global Society Ser.: No. 15). 224p. 2000. pap. 24.50 (*0-7146-8014-1*, Pub. by F Cass Pubs) Intl Spec Bk.

— Superman Supreme: Fascist Body as Political Icon - Global Fascism. (Sport in the Global Society Ser.: No. 15). (Illus.). 224p. 2000. 57.50 (*0-7146-4955-4*, Pub. by F Cass Pubs) Intl Spec Bk.

***Mangan, J. A. & Nauright, John.** The Australasian World: Sport in Society. LC 00-43188. (Sport in the Global Society Ser.). (Illus.). 2000. write for info. (*0-7146-8112-1*, Pub. by F Cass Pubs) Intl Spec Bk.

Mangan, James A. Cultural Bond: Sport, Empire, Society. LC 91-10190. 1992. 45.00 (*0-7146-3398-4*, Pub. by F Cass Pubs) Intl Spec Bk.

Mangan, James A., ed. Pleasure, Profit, Proselytism: British Culture & Sport at Home & Abroad, 1700-1914. 250p. 1986. 45.00 (*0-7146-3289-9*, Pub. by F Cass Pubs); pap. 22.50 (*0-7146-4050-6*, Pub. by F Cass Pubs) Intl Spec Bk.

— A Significant Social Revolution: Cross-Cultural Aspects of the Evolution of Compulsory Education. 232p. 1994. 37.50 (*0-7130-0189-5*, Pub. by Woburn Pr) Intl Spec Bk.

— Tribal Identities: Historical Perspectives on Nationalism, Europe, & Sport. (International Journal of the History of Sport Ser.). 260p. (C). 1996. 49.50 (*0-7146-4666-0*, Pub. by F Cass Pubs); pap. 22.50 (*0-7146-4201-0*, Pub. by F Cass Pubs) Intl Spec Bk.

Mangan, James A., jt. ed. see Baker, William J.

Mangan, James A., jt. ed. see Park, Roberta J.

Mangan, James A., jt. ed. see Staudohar, Paul D.

Mangan, James C. The Prose Writings of James Clarence Mangan. O'Donoghue, David J., ed. LC 75-28826. reprint ed. 49.50 (*0-404-13818-7*) AMS Pr.

Mangan, James C., tr. Poets & Poetry of Munster: A Selection of Irish Songs by the Poets of the Last Century. 5th ed. LC 75-28824. reprint ed. 34.50 (*0-404-13816-0*) AMS Pr.

Mangan, James Clarence, tr. Poets & Poetry of Munster. LC 96-23326. (Hibernia Ser.). 1996. 75.00 (*1-85477-217-1*) Continuum.

Mangan, James M. To the Four Winds. LC 90-83585. 96p. 1990. 34.95 (*0-938021-98-2*) Turner Pub KY.

***Mangan, John.** Workers Without Traditional Employment: An International Study of Non-Standard Work. LC 00-44258. 2000. write for info. (*1-84064-267-X*) E Elgar.

Mangan, John J. Life, Character & Influence of Desiderius Erasmus of Rotterdam, 2 vols. LC 73-147113. reprint ed. 78.50 (*0-404-04178-7*) AMS Pr.

Mangan, Joseph F. & Harrison, Connor M. Advanced Underwriting Techniques. LC 95-81904. (Illus.). 233p. (Orig.). (C). 1995. pap. text 41.00 (*0-89462-096-7*, AU66) IIA.

— Underwriting Commercial Liability. LC 95-81905. (Illus.). 347p. (C). 1995. pap. text 41.00 (*0-89462-095-9*, 6602) IIA.

***Mangan, Joseph F. & Harrison, Connor M.** Underwriting Commercial Liability. LC 99-76143. 361p. 2000. 41.00 (*0-89462-134-3*, 6602) IIA.

Mangan, Joseph F. & Harrison, Connor M. Underwriting Commercial Property. 2nd ed. LC 97-77729. (Illus.). 347p. (Orig.). (C). 1997. pap. text 41.00 (*0-89462-120-3*, 6503) IIA.

— Underwriting Principles. LC 95-81452. (Illus.). 201p. (Orig.). (C). 1995. pap. text 41.00 (*0-89462-094-0*, 6502) IIA.

Mangan, Judy, jt. auth. see Mangan, Frank.

Mangan, Judy, ed. see Metz, Leon C.

Mangan, Kathy. Above the Tree Line. LC 94-70462. (Poetry Ser.). 64p. 1995. pap. 11.95 (*0-88748-191-4*) Carnegie-Mellon.

Mangan, Mark, jt. auth. see Wallace, Jonathan.

Mangan, Pat. The Harness. LC 97-61429. (Stahlecker Ser.). 64p. 1998. pap. 12.95 (*1-884800-15-7*) Four Way Bks.

Mangan, Sherry. Blackness of a White Night: Stories & Poems. Brooks, Marshall, ed. LC 86-20666. 64p. 1987. 13.50 (*0-933292-16-3*); pap. 6.50 (*0-933292-17-1*) Arts End.

Mangan, Terry W. Colorado on Glass: First 50 Years of Glass-Plate Photography in Colorado. (Illus.). 416p. 1976. 59.00 (*0-913582-13-1*) Sundance.

Mangan, Velda B., ed. see Bair, Elmer O.

Manganaro, Marc, ed. Modernist Anthropology: From Fieldwork to Text. 340p. (C). 1990. pap. text 17.95 (*0-691-01480-9*, Pub. by Princeton U Pr) Cal Prin Full Svc.

Manganelli, Giorgio. All the Errors. Martin, Henry, tr. from ITA. LC 90-5489. 158p. 1990. 20.00 (*0-929701-07-0*); pap. 10.00 (*0-929701-06-2*) McPherson & Co.

Manganelli, Raymond L. & Klein, Mark M. The Reengineering Handbook: A Step-by-Step Guide to Business Transformation. LC 94-26609. 288p. 1994. 29.95 (*0-8144-0236-4*) AMACOM.

— The Reengineering Handbook: A Step-by-Step Guide to Business Transformation. 320p. 1996. pap. 17.95 (*0-8144-7923-5*) AMACOM.

Manganese Bronze, Ltd. Staff. Complex Aluminum Bronze Alloys with Improved Mechanical Corrosion-Resistance Properties. 79p. 1970. 11.85 (*0-317-34500-1*, 56) Intl Copper.

Mangano, Christina. Ace's Exambusters Even More Sign Language Study, 3 parts, Part 3. Burchard, Elizabeth, ed. & photos by by. (Exambusters Ser.). (Illus.). 210p. 2000. reprint ed. pap. 10.95 (*1-881374-76-9*) Ace Acad.

— Ace's Exambusters Sign Language Study, 3 parts, Part 1. 2nd ed. (Exambusters Ser.). (Illus.). 250p. (YA). (gr. 7 up). 2000. reprint ed. pap. 10.95 (*1-881374-95-5*, Exambusters) Ace Acad.

— American Sign Language: Giant Alphabet Study. Burchard, Elizabeth, ed. & photos by by. (Exambusters Ser.). (Illus.). 26p. 1998. pap. 18.95 (*1-881374-75-0*) Ace Acad.

Mangano, Christina, tr. see Burchard, Elizabeth R., ed.

Mangano, Dennis T. Preoperative Cardiac Assessment: A Society of Cardiovascular Anesthesiologists Mono. (Illus.). 200p. 1990. text 38.00 (*0-397-51089-6*) Lppncott W & W.

Mangano, Joseph & Karaffa, Melani C., eds. Health Information Management. 260p. 1993. 49.95 (*1-878487-54-X*, ME051) Practice Mgmt Info.

Mangano, Joseph J. Living Legacy: How Nineteen Sixty-Four Changed America. LC 93-26725. 228p. (Orig.). (C). 1993. pap. text 24.50 (*0-8191-9270-8*) U Pr of Amer.

***Mangano, Joseph J.** Low Level Radiation & Immune System Damage: An Atomic Era Legacy. LC 98-18138. 1998. lib. bdg. 49.95 (*1-56670-334-4*, L1334) Lewis Pubs.

Manganyi, N. C. Mashangu's Reverie. LC 78-386905. 106 p. 1977. write for info. (*0-86975-068-2*) Ohio U Pr.

Manganyi, N. Chabani. Treachery & Innocence: Psychology & Racial Difference in South Africa. 164p. 1992. 50.00 (*1-873836-05-8*, Pub. by H Zell Pubs) Seven Hills Bk.

Manganyi, Noel C. Alienation & the Body in Racist Society: A Study of the Society That Invented Sow. LC 74-81854. 1977. text 13.95 (*0-88357-053-X*) NOK Pubs.

***Mangarella, Charles.** ISO 9000 ABC's: The Small Company Guide to Successful Registration LC 99-25815. 352p. 1999. boxed set 59.95 (*1-57444-265-1*) St Lucie Pr.

Mangarella, Gina I., ed. see Mangarella, Michael A.

Mangarella, Michael A. The Art of Dealing Poker, Vol. II. Mangarella, Gina I., ed. (Illus.). 208p. (Orig.). (C). 1991. pap. 9.95 (*1-877725-12-9*) Video One Prodns.

Mangas, Brian. Carrot Delight. (J). 1990. pap. 5.95 (*0-671-67886-8*) S&S Bks Yung.

— Follow that Puppy. LC 90-33877. 40p. (J). 1991. pap. 12.95 (*0-671-70780-9*) Litle Simon.

— Sshaboom! LC 91-24764. (Illus.). 40p. (J). (ps-1). 1993. pap. 14.00 (*0-671-75538-2*) S&S Bks Yung.

— You Don't Get a Carrot Unless You're a Bunny. (Illus.). (J). 1989. pap. 5.95 (*0-671-67201-0*) Litle Simon.

Mangas Manjarres, Julio, et al. Historia de Espana Vol. 2, No. 2: Espana Romana: La Sociedad, el Derecho y la Cultura. 764p. 1992. 189.50 (*84-239-4984-2*) Elliots Bks.

Mangasarian, Leon, ed. see Jafarian, Boghos.

Mangasarian, Olvi L. Nonlinear Programming. LC 94-36844. (Classics in Applied Mathematics Ser.: Vol. 10). xv, 220p. 1994. pap. 33.00 (*0-89871-341-2*) Soc Indus-Appl Math.

***Mangasarian, Olvi L. & Pang, Jong-Shi.** Computational Optimization: A Tribute to Olvi Mangasarian LC 99-13159. 1999. write for info. (*0-7923-8413-X*) Kluwer Academic.

Mangat, Devinder S., jt. auth. see Krause, Charles J.

Mangat, Naurang S., jt. auth. see Singh, Ravindra.

Mangat, S. S. Policeman's Guide to Crime & Criminal Investigation. (C). 1979. 160.00 (*0-7855-5451-3*) St Mut.

Mangay-Maglacas, A. & Pizurki, H. Traditional Birth Attendant in Seven Countries: The Case Studies in Utilization & Training. (Public Health Papers: No. 75). 211p. 1981. pap. text 15.00 (*92-4-130075-2*, 1110075) World Health.

Mange, Alyce E. The Near Eastern Policy of the Emperor Napoleon III, Vol. XXV, Nos. 1$2.-- LC 74-12762. (Illinois Studies in the Social Sciences). 150p. 1975. reprint ed. lib. bdg. 55.00 (*0-8371-7742-1*, MAEN, Greenwood Pr) Greenwood.

Mange, Arthur P., jt. auth. see Mange, Elaine J.

Mange, D. Microprogrammed Systems. (ITCP-UK Computer Science Ser.). (C). 1992. mass mkt. 62.95 (*0-412-40800-7*) Chapman & Hall.

— Microprogrammed Systems: An Introduction to Firmware Theory. 400p. 1992. pap. 49.95 (*0-442-31551-1*) Chapman & Hall.

Mange, Elaine J. & Mange, Arthur P. Basic Human Genetics. 2nd rev. ed. LC 98-40485. (Illus.). 530p. (C). 1998. pap. text 74.95 incl. cd-rom (*0-87893-497-9*) Sinauer Assocs.

Mange, Maria A. & Maurer, Heinz F. Heavy Minerals in Colour. (Illus.). 128p. 1989. 90.00 (*0-04-445564-X*) Routledge.

Mangel, Gary D. Corporate's Struggle with Ethics (The Lures & the Lies) A Guide to Climbing the Corporate Ladder. LC 95-75256. 152p. (Orig.). 1995. pap. 12.95 (*1-887057-13-7*) A M Publ IA.

Mangel, M., ed. Sex Allocation & Sex Change: Experiments & Models. LC 90-45411. (LLSCI Ser.: Vol. 22). 205p. 1990. pap. 43.00 (*0-8218-1172-X*, LLSCI/22) Am Math.

Mangel, M., et al, eds. Pest Control: Operations & Systems Analysis in Fruit Fly Management. (NATO ASI Series G Ecological Sciences: No. 11). xii, 465p. 1986. 158.95 (*0-387-16088-4*) Spr-Verlag.

Mangel, Marc, jt. auth. see Clark, Colin W.

Mangel, Marc, jt. auth. see Hilborn, Ray.

Mangel, Nissen, tr. see Danzinger, Eliezer Y., ed.

Mangel, Nissen, tr. see Zalman, Schneur.

***Mangels, Andy.** From Scream to Dawson's Creek to Wasteland: The Phenomenal Career of Kevin Williamson. (Illus.). 320p. 2000. pap. text 16.95 (*1-58063-122-3*) Renaissance.

Mangels, Andy. Star Wars: The Essential Guide to Characters. 224p. 1995. pap. 18.95 (*0-345-39535-2*) Ballantine Pub Grp.

Mangels, George. Franks World. LC 97-20255. 240p. 1997. pap. 12.95 (*0-312-16846-2*) St Martin.

— Frank's World: The Odyssey of a Fleshy Lump. LC 94-44487. 1995. 22.95 (*0-312-11791-4*) St Martin.

Mangels, James I., et al, eds. Alba's Medical Technology Board Examination Questions & Answers on IBM Disk: Questions & Answers Interactive with Volume I: 1996 Edition, Interactive, 1996. 12th ed. LC 72-172446. (Illus.). 1996. 3.5 hd 38.00 (*0-910224-21-8*) Berkeley Sci.

— Alba's Medical Technology Board Examination Questions & Answers on Mac Disk: Questions & Answers Interactive with Volume I, Interactive, 1996. 12th ed. LC 72-172446. (Illus.). 1996. mac hd 38.00 (*0-910224-22-6*) Berkeley Sci.

— Alba's Medical Technology Board Examination Review Vol. 1: Complete Clinical Laboratory Text. 12th rev. ed. LC 72-172446. (Illus.). 747p. 1996. text 42.00 (*0-910224-18-8*) Berkeley Sci.

— Medical Technology Board Examination Review Vol. 2: Questions & Answers. 8th rev. ed. (Illus.). 550p. 1996. text 38.00 (*0-910224-19-6*) Berkeley Sci.

Mangels, Reed, jt. auth. see Waserman, Debra.

Mangels, Reed, jt. auth. see Wasserman, Debra.

Mangels, Reed, ed. see Wasserman, Debra.

Mangels, Reed, jt. ed. see Wasserman, Debra.

Mangels, William F. Outdoor Amusement Industry. lib. bdg. 20.95 (*0-8488-2002-9*) Amereon Ltd.

Mangelsdorf. Your Choice. 1996. pap. text 5.00 (*0-312-11154-1*) St Martin.

— Your Choice. 2nd ed. 2000. pap. text 32.95 (*0-312-20113-3*) St Martin.

— Your Choice: Basic Writing Guide. LC 95-73184. 576p. 1996. pap. 32.95 (*0-312-11153-3*) St Martin.

— Your Choice & Pocket Style. 2nd ed. 1997. pap. text 26.65 (*0-312-17141-2*) St Martin.

Mangelsdorf, Guenter. Die Ortswuestungen des Havellandes: Historisch-Archaeologische Beitraege Zur Wuestungkunde der Mark Brandenburg. Bd. 86. (GER.). 338p. (C). 1994. lib. bdg. 110.80 (*3-11-014086-1*) De Gruyter.

Mangelsdorf, Gunter, ed. Tradition und Fortschritt Archaeologischer Forschung in Greifswald. (Greifswalder Mitteilungen - Beitraege zur Ur- und Fruehgeschichte und Mittelalterarchaeologie Ser.: Band 2). (GER., Illus.). 273p. 1997. 54.95 (*3-631-31272-5*) P Lang Pubng.

Mangelsdorf, J., et al. River Morphology: A Guide for Geoscientists & Engineers. (Springer Series in Physical Environement: Vol. 7). (Illus.). 264p. 1990. 150.95 (*0-387-51108-3*) Spr-Verlag.

Mangelsdorf, Martha, ed. 101 Great Ideas for Managing People: From America's Most Innovative Small Companies. 2nd ed. 192p. 1999. pap. 14.95 (*1-880394-93-6*) Thomson Learn.

Mangelsdorf, Paul C. Corn: Its Origin, Evolution & Development. LC 72-95454. (Illus.). 288p. 1974. 35.95 (*0-674-17175-6*) HUP.

Mangelsdorf, Tom. History of Steinbeck's Cannery Row. LC 86-50500. (Illus.). 216p. 1991. pap. 14.95 (*0-934136-35-1*) Good Life.

Mangelsdorff, A. David, ed. Military Cohesion: A Special Issue of Military Psychology. 128p. 1998. pap. 24.50 (*0-8058-9809-3*) L Erlbaum Assocs.

Mangelsdorff, David, jt. ed. see Gal, Reuven.

Mangelsdorff, Rich. Selected Essays. (American Dust Ser.: No. 8). 1977. pap. 2.95 (*0-913218-50-2*) Dustbooks.

Mangelsen, Mary A., ed. see Cayten, C. Gene, et al.

***Mangelsen, Thomas D.** Spirit of the Rockies: The Mountain Lions of Jackson Hole. (Illus.). 2000. 19.95 (*1-890310-19-0*) Thomas D Mangelsen Inc Images.

Mangelsen, Thomas D., photos by. Polar Dance: Born of the North Wind. LC 97-71666. (Illus.). 264p. 1997. 65.00 (*1-890310-03-4*) Thomas D Mangelsen Inc Images.

Mangelsen, Thomas D. & Bruemmer, Fred. Polar Dance: Born of the North Wind. deluxe ed. (Illus.). 264p. 1997. 65.00 (*0-9633080-8-4*) Thomas D Mangelsen Inc Images.

Mangelsen, Thomas D., tr. see Hirschi, Ron.

Mangen, David J., et al, eds. The Measurement of Intergenerational Relations. LC 87-28466. (Sage Focus Editions Ser.: No. 92). 253p. reprint ed. pap. 78.50 (*0-7837-6579-7*, 204614400011) Bks Demand.

Mangen, Stephen, ed. see Hantrais, Linda.

***Manger, B. J.** Documentation Requirements for Non-Acute Care Facilities & Organizations. 220p. 2001. 38.00 (*1-84214-001-9*) Prthnon Pub.

Manger, Jason J. The Essential Java: Developing Interactive Applications to the World Wide Web. (Illus.). 352p. 1996. pap., pap. text 39.95 incl. cd-rom (*0-07-709292-9*) McGraw.

— Java: The Complete Development Kit. 1996. pap. text 39.95 incl. cd-rom (*0-07-709332-1*) McGraw.

— JavaScript Essentials: Creating Interactive Web Applications. LC 97-107171. 448p. 1996. pap. text 32.95 (*0-07-882234-3*) Osborne-McGraw.

Manger, Leif. Muslim Diversity: Local Islam in Global Contexts. 288p. 1998. 75.00 (*0-7007-1104-X*, Pub. by Curzon Pr Ltd) Paul & Co Pubs.

Manger, Leif, jt. ed. see Bovin, Mette.

Manger, Leif O. From the Mountains to the Plains: The Integration of the Lafofa Nuba into Sudanese Society. (Scandinavian Institute of African Studies). 173p. (Orig.). 1994. pap. 37.50 (*91-7106-336-6*) Coronet Bks.

M

An Asterisk (*) at the beginning of an entry indicates that the title is appearing for the first time.

— The Sand Swallows Our Land. (Bergen Studies in Social Anthropology: No. 24). 137p. (Orig.). 1985. pap. text 11.95 (*0-936508-60-4*, Pub. by Bergen Univ Dept Social Anthro) MBIPubg.

Manger, Leif O., ed. Communal Labour in the Sudan. (Bergen Studies in Social Anthropology: No. 41). 150p. 1988. pap. 13.95 (*0-936508-71-X*) Barber Pr.

Manger, Leif O., et al, eds. Survival on Meagre Resources: Hadendowa Pastoralism in the Red Sea Hills. 244p. (Orig.). 1996. pap. 52.50 (*91-7106-386-2*) Coronet Bks.

Manger, William M. Catecholamines in Normal & Abnormal Cardiac Function. (Advances in Cardiology Ser.: Vol. 30). (Illus.). xxiv, 152p. 1982. 85.25 (*3-8055-3516-3*) S Karger.

Manger, William M., ed. Pheochromocytoma: A Clinical & Experimental Overview. 2nd ed. 700p. (C). 1995. write for info. (*0-393-71028-9*) Norton.

Manger, William M. & Gifford, Ray. Clinical & Experimental Pheochromocytoma. 2nd ed. (Illus.). 400p. 1996. text 135.00 (*0-86542-494-2*) Blackwell Sci.

***Manger, William M. & Gifford, Ray W., Jr.** 100 Questions & Answers about Hypertension. (Illus.). 191p. 2000. pap. 14.95 (*0-632-04481-0*) Blackwell Sci.

Manget, J. Jacob. Bibliotheca Chemica Curiosa, 2 vols., Set. write for info. (*0-318-71843-X*) G Olms Pubs.

Mangham, Iain L. Interactions & Interventions in Organizations. LC 78-2602. (Wiley Series on Individuals, Groups & Organizations). (Illus.). 166p. reprint ed. pap. 51.50 (*0-608-18146-3*, 203283300081) Bks Demand.

— The Politics of Organizational Change, 26. LC 79-23. (Contributions in Economics & Economic History Ser.: No. 26). 221p. 1979. 55.00 (*0-313-20981-2*, MPC/, Greenwood Pr) Greenwood.

Mangham, Iain L., ed. Organization Analysis & Development: A Social Construction of Organizational Behaviour. LC 86-26713. (Industrial Psychology & Organization Behaviour Ser.). 283p. reprint ed. pap. 87.80 (*0-7837-6162-7*, 204588400009) Bks Demand.

Mangham, Iain L. & Overington, Michael A. Organizations As Theatre: A Social Psychology of Dramatic Appearances. LC 86-19199. 224p. reprint ed. pap. 69.50 (*0-7837-6163-5*, 204588500009) Bks Demand.

Mangham, Iain L., jt. auth. see Bate, Paul.

Manghezi, Alpheus. Class, Elite & Community in African Development. 118p. 1976. write for info. (*91-7106-099-5*, Pub. by Nordic Africa) Transaction Pubs.

Manghi, F., jt. auth. see Reatto, L.

Manghnani, M. H. & Yagi, Takehiko, eds. Properties of Earth & Planetary Materials at High Pressure & Temperature. LC 97-46529. (Geophysical Monograph Ser.: Vol. 101). 1997. pap. 90.00 (*0-87590-084-4*) Am Geophysical.

— Properties of Earth & Planetary Materials at High Pressure & Temperature, Vol. 101. LC 97-46529. (Geophysical Monograph Ser.). 1997. 90.00 (*0-87590-083-6*) Am Geophysical.

Manghnani, Murli H. & Syono, Yasuhiko, eds. High Pressure Research in Mineral Physics: The Akimoto Volume. (Mineral Physics Ser.: Vol. 39). (Illus.). 486p. 1987. 60.00 (*0-87590-066-6*) Am Geophysical.

Manghnani, Murli H., jt. auth. see Akimoto, S.

Manghnani, Murli H., jt. auth. see Syono, Yasuhiko.

Mangiafico, Luciano. Contemporary American Immigrants: Patterns of Filipino, Korean, & Chinese Settlement in the United States. LC 87-17752. 229p. 1988. 49.95 (*0-275-92726-1*, C2726, Praeger Pubs) Greenwood.

Mangiapane, E. H. & Salter, A. M. Diet, Lipoproteins & Coronary Heart Disease: A Biochemical Perspective. 180p. 1999. pap. 100.00 (*1-897676-81-6*, Pub. by Nottingham Univ Pr) St Mut.

Mangiaracina, Greg & Payne, R. E. How to Market a Home Inspection Business. large type ed. (Illus.). 75p. 1997. pap. text 49.95 (*1-885308-05-1*) Sr Polit Action.

— How to Operate a Home Inspection Business. large type ed. (Illus.). 75p. 1997. pap. text 49.95 (*1-885308-06-X*) Sr Polit Action.

Mangiarotti, L. Gauge Mechanics. 1998. 58.00 (*981-02-3603-4*) World Scientific Pub.

Mangiarotti, L. & Sardanashvily, Gennadi A. New Lagrangian & Hamiltonian Methods in Field Theory. LC 98-196719. 300p. 1997. text 71.00 (*981-02-1587-8*) World Scientific Pub.

Mangieri, John N., ed. Excellence in Education. LC 85-50539. 248p. 1985. 25.00 (*0-87565-020-1*) Tex Christian.

Mangieri, John N. & Collins, Cathy, eds. Teaching Thinking: An Agenda for the 21st Century. 352p. (C). 1992. text 79.95 (*0-8058-0867-1*) L Erlbaum Assocs.

Mangieri, John N., jt. auth. see Block, Cathy C.

Mangieri, Nick. Broken Badge: The Silencing of a Federal Agent. LC 98-73814. 421p. 1998. pap. 19.50 (*0-9665364-0-1*) Integrity Pubg.

— The Frozen Shield: Alaska Cover-Up. (Illus.). 400p. 2000. pap. 19.50 (*0-9665364-2-8*) Integrity Pubg.

Mangin, jt. auth. see Linkow, Leonard I.

Mangin, P. & Ludes, B. Acta Medicinae Legalis 1994: Proceedings of the XVIIth Congress of the International Academy of Legal Medicine. 560p. 1996. pap. 159.00 (*3-540-58847-7*) Spr-Verlag.

Mangin, Patrice J., ed. see Technical Association of the Pulp & Paper Industry.

Mangina. Correction Key. 1994. write for info. (*0-8058-1759-X*) L Erlbaum Assocs.

— Manual. 1994. write for info. (*0-8058-1760-3*) L Erlbaum Assocs.

— Manual & Correction Key. 1994. 19.75 (*0-8058-1758-1*) L Erlbaum Assocs.

Mangine, Robert E., ed. Physical Therapy of the Knee. LC 87-24284. (Clinics in Physical Therapy Ser.: Vol. 19). (Illus.). 264p. reprint ed. pap. 81.90 (*0-7837-1611-7*, 204190300024) Bks Demand.

— Physical Therapy of the Knee. 2nd ed. LC 95-12053. (Clinics in Physical Therapy Ser.). 1995. pap. text 44.00 (*0-443-08916-7*) Church.

Manginello, Frank P. Your Premature Baby: Everything You Need to know about the Childbirth, Treatment, & Parenting of Premature Infants. 2nd rev. ed. LC 97-31835. 336p. 1998. pap. 17.95 (*0-471-23996-8*) Wiley.

Manginello, Frank P. & DiGeronimo, Theresa F. Your Premature Baby: Everything You Need to Know about the Childbirth Treatment & Parenting of Premature Infants. LC 91-10572. 304p. 1991. pap. 16.95 (*0-471-53587-7*) Wiley.

Mangini, A., et al. Summary of Some of My Research on Organosulphur Compounds: Rotational Isomerism of Vinyl Ethers & Sulfides: The Effect of Organic Sulphur Compounds on Oxidation Processes of Hydrocarbon Fuels, Vol. 7. Senning, Alexander, ed. (Sulfer Reports: Vol. 7, No. 5). 83p. 1987. pap. text 105.00 (*3-7186-4804-0*) Gordon & Breach.

Mangini-Gonzalez, Shirley. Memories of Resistance: Women's Voices from the Spanish Civil War. LC 94-29752. 226p. 1995. 30.00 (*0-300-05816-0*) Yale U Pr.

Mangiola, Leslie, jt. auth. see Heath, Shirley B.

Mangiona, Mary, jt. auth. see Iacono, Jeanne M.

Mangione, Jerre. The Dream & the Deal: The Federal Writers Project 1935-1943. LC 96-31893. 416p. 1996. reprint ed. pap. 19.95 (*0-8156-0415-7*, MADDP) Syracuse U Pr.

— A Passion for Sicillians: The World Around Danilo Dolici. 320p. (C). 1985. pap. 24.95 (*0-88738-606-7*) Transaction Pubs.

Mangione, Jerre & Morreale, Ben. La Storia: Five Centuries of the Italian American Experience. LC 92-52553. (Illus.). 560p. 1993. reprint ed. pap. 18.00 (*0-06-092441-1*, Perennial) HarperTrade.

Mangione, Jerre G. Mount Allegro: A Memoir of Italian American Life. LC 97-50547. (New York Classics Ser.). 1998. pap. 19.95 (*0-8156-0429-7*) Syracuse U Pr.

Mangione, S., jt. auth. see Gerace, P.

Mangione, Salvatore, ed. Physical Diagnosis Secrets. LC 98-43417. (Secrets Ser.). (Illus.). 350p. (Orig.). 1999. pap. text 38.00 (*1-56053-164-9*) Hanley & Belfus.

Mangione, Thomas W. Mail Surveys. (Applied Social Research Methods Ser.: Vol. 40). 132p. 1995. 42.00 (*0-8039-4662-7*); pap. 18.95 (*0-8039-4663-5*) Sage.

Mangione, Thomas W., jt. auth. see Fowler, Floyd J., Jr.

Mangir, Metin S., ed. Nonlinear Optical Engineering, Vol. 3263. 184p. 1998. 69.00 (*0-8194-2702-0*) SPIE.

Mangjin's Staff. Basic Japanese Through Comics. (Illus.). 160p. (Orig.). 1998. pap. 14.95 (*0-8348-0452-2*) Weatherhill.

Manglano-Ovalle, Inigo, et al. Inigo Manglano-Ovalle: The Garden Of Delights Artist & the Community Southeastern Center for Contemporary Art, July 18-September 30, 1998. LC 98-61506. 40p. 1998. write for info. (*1-888826-07-X*) SEC Contemp Art.

Manglapus, Raul S. Philippines, the Silenced Democracy. LC 75-3342. 221p. reprint ed. pap. 68.60 (*0-8357-8982-9*, 203352300086) Bks Demand.

— Will of the People: Original Democracy in Non-Western Societies, 4. LC 86-29594. (Studies in Freedom: No. 4). 194p. 1987. 52.95 (*0-313-25837-6*, MWG/, Greenwood Pr) Greenwood.

Mangles, Andy. Beyond Mulder & Scully: The Mysterious Characters of the X-Files. LC 97-47084. (Illus.). 256p. 1997. pap. text 16.95 (*0-8065-1933-9*, Citadel Pr) Carol Pub Group.

Mangles, J., jt. auth. see Irby, C.

***Manglik, R. M. & Sunden, B., eds.** Thermal-Hydraulic Analysis of Plate & Frame Heat Exchangers. (Developments in Heat Transfer Ser.). 350p. 2000. 180.00 (*1-85312-737-X*, 737X, Pub. by WIT Pr) Computational Mech MA.

***Mango, Andrew.** Ataturk: The Biography of the Founder of Modern Turkey. LC 99-86845. (Illus.). 666p. 2000. 40.00 (*1-58567-011-1*, Pub. by Overlook Pr) Penguin Putnam.

Mango, Andrew. Turkey: The Challenge of a New Role, 163. LC 94-10581. (Washington Papers). 160p. 1994. 49.95 (*0-275-94985-0*, Praeger Pubs); pap. 15.95 (*0-275-94986-9*, Praeger Pubs) Greenwood.

Mango, Cyril, tr. see Theophanes.

Mango, Cyril A. Byzantine Architecture. LC 85-62749. (History of World Architecture Ser.). (Illus.). 224p. 1991. pap. 29.95 (*0-8478-0615-4*, Pub. by Rizzoli Intl) St Martin.

— Byzantium & Its Image: History & Culture of the Byzantine Empire & Its Heritage. (Collected Studies: CS191). (Illus.). 360p. (C). 1984. reprint ed. lib. bdg. 124.95 (*0-86078-139-9*, Pub. by Variorum) Ashgate Pub Co.

— Studies on Constantinople. (Collected Studies: No. 394). 288p. 1993. 113.95 (*0-86078-372-3*, Pub. by Variorum) Ashgate Pub Co.

Mango, Cyril A., ed. The Art of the Byzantine Empire, 312-1453: Sources & Documents. (Medieval Academy Reprints for Teaching Ser.). 272p. 1986. reprint ed. pap. text 14.95 (*0-8020-6627-5*) U of Toronto Pr.

Mango, Cyril A., tr. Nikephoros, Patriarch of Constantinople, Short History. LC 89-17058. (Dumbarton Oaks Texts: Vol. 10). (Illus.). 264p. 1990. 30.00 (*0-88402-184-X*, MANI, Dumbarton Rsch Lib) Dumbarton Oaks.

Mango, Cyril A. & Greatrex, Geoffrey, eds. Constantinople & Its Hinterland: Papers from the Twenty-Seventh Spring Symposium of Byzantine Studies, Oxford, April 1993. (Society for the Promotion of Byzantine Studies: No. 3). (Illus.). 448p. 1995. 86.95 (*0-86078-487-8*, Pub. by Variorum) Ashgate Pub Co.

Mango, Cyril A., tr. see Ignatios & Efthymiadis, Stephanos.

Mango, Karin M. Just for the Summer. LC 89-36568. (Charlotte Zolotow Bk.). 208p. (YA). (gr. 7 up). 1990. 13.95 (*0-06-024038-5*) HarpC Child Bks.

Mango, Karin N. Portrait of Miranda. LC 92-8191. (Charlotte Zolotow Bk.). 240p. (YA). (gr. 7 up). 1993. 16.00 (*0-06-021777-4*); lib. bdg. 15.89 (*0-06-021778-2*) HarpC Child Bks.

Mango, Marlia M. & Bennett, Anna. The Sevso Treasure: Art Historical Description & Inscriptions; Methods of Manufacture & Scientific Analyses. (JRA Supplementary Ser.: No. 12, Pt. 1). (Illus.). 480p. 1994. 198.00 (*1-887829-12-1*) Jour Roman Arch.

Mango, Marlia M., jt. ed. see Boyd, Susan A.

Mango, Wanda P. Grandma's Home Kitchen: Where Lessons & Life Were Mixed with Love: Family Recipes & Traditions of Grandma's Swedish Bakery, Door County. LC 94-90145. (Illus.). 128p. 1994. pap. 12.95 (*0-942495-38-1*) Palmer Pubns Inc.

Mangold. Duden Woerterbuch Vol. 6: Aussptache. (GER.). 794p. 1990. 49.95 (*0-614-00369-5*, 341120916X) Fr & Eur.

Mangold, George B. Labor Argument in the American Protective Tariff Discussion. LC 73-156433. (American Labor Ser., No. 2). 1971. reprint ed. 15.95 (*0-405-02931-4*) Ayer.

***Mangold, Hal.** Half-Damned: Dhampyri. (Kindred of the East Ser.). 2000. pap. 13.95 (*1-56504-247-6*) White Wolf.

Mangold, Helmut K., ed. Handbook of Chromatography: Lipids, 2 vols., Vol. I. LC 82-25510. (Series in Chromatography). 624p. 1984. lib. bdg. 335.00 (*0-8493-3037-8*, QD305, CRC Reprint) Franklin.

— Handbook of Chromatography: Lipids, 2 vols., Vol. II. LC 82-25510. (Series in Chromatography). 368p. 1984. lib. bdg. 202.00 (*0-8493-3038-6*, QD305, CRC Reprint) Franklin.

***Mangold, James.** Copland & Heavy. (Screenplays Ser.). (Illus.). 352p. 1999. pap. 17.00 (*0-571-19425-7*) Faber & Faber.

— Girl, Interrupted. (Screenplays Ser.). (Illus.). 144p. 1999. pap. 13.00 (*0-571-20211-X*) Faber & Faber.

Mangold, Lori & Mangold, Scott. The Professional Pet Sitter: Your Guide to Starting & Operating a Successful Service. 108p. 1994. pap. 29.95 (*0-9635442-1-7*) Paws-itive Pr.

Mangold, Margaret M., ed. La Causa Chicana: The Movement for Justice. LC 72-92083. 236p. reprint ed. pap. 73.20 (*0-608-18323-7*, 203159700075) Bks Demand.

***Mangold, Mark.** The New Faith: A "How-To" Guide to Create the Life You Really Want. LC 99-93940. 1999. pap. 7.95 (*0-533-13203-7*) Vantage.

Mangold, Max & Duden Editorial Staff. Aussprachewoerterbuch. (Duden Ser.: Vol. 6). 794p. 1993. 33.50 (*3-411-20916-X*, Pub. by Bibliogr Inst Brockhaus) Langenscheidt.

Mangold, Nancy R. Changing Auditors & the Effect on Earnings, Auditors' Opinions & Stock Prices. Farmer, Richard, ed. LC 87-19128. (Research for Business Decisions Ser.: No. 93). 175p. 1988. reprint ed. pap. 54.30 (*0-8357-1786-0*, 207040400088) Bks Demand.

Mangold, Paul, jt. auth. see Gipson, Morrell.

Mangold, Sally, ed. A Teacher's Guide to the Special Educational Needs of Blind & Visually Handicapped Children. LC 82-4025. 164p. 1982. pap. 27.95 (*0-89128-108-8*) Am Foun Blind.

Mangold, Sally S., jt. auth. see Olson, Myrna R.

Mangold, Sarah. Blood Substitutes. 45p. (C). 1998. 7.00 (*0-937013-77-3*) Potes Poets.

Mangold, Scott, jt. auth. see Mangold, Lori.

Mangold, Tom & Goldberg, Jeff. Plague Wars: The Terrifying Reality of Biological Warfare. LC 99-17022. (Illus.). 336p. 2000. text 27.95 (*0-312-20353-5*) St Martin.

Mangold, Tom & Penycate, John. The Tunnels of Cu Chi. 320p. 1986. mass mkt. 6.99 (*0-425-08951-7*) Berkley Pub.

Mangone, Gerard J. Concise Marine Almanac. 1990. 85.00 (*0-8448-1674-4*) Taylor & Francis.

— The Idea & Practice of World Government. LC 74-3620. 278p. 1975. reprint ed. lib. bdg. 65.00 (*0-8371-7453-8*, MAPW, Greenwood Pr) Greenwood.

— United States Admiralty Law. LC 97-18831. 328p. 1997. 195.00 (*90-411-0417-8*) Kluwer Law Intl.

Mangone, Gerard J., ed. International Straits. (Special Issue of Ocean Development & International Law Ser.: Vol. 18, No. 4). 106p. 1987. pap. 22.00 (*0-8448-1534-9*) Taylor & Francis.

Mangonon, P. L. The Principles of Materials Selection for Engineering Design. LC 97-39039. 824p. 1998. 105.00 (*0-13-242595-5*) P-H.

Mangonon, P. L., ed. see Metallurgical Society of AIME Staff.

Mangore, Augustin B. La Catedral. Stover, Richard, ed. (SPA.). 16p. (C). 1985. pap. text 6.95 (*0-7692-1280-8*, S100154) Wrner Bros.

— Vals, Op. 8, No. 3. Stover, Richard, ed. 12p. (Orig.). (C). 1985. pap. text 6.50 (*0-7692-1279-4*, S100153) Wrner Bros.

Mangoubi, R. S. Robust Estimation & Failure Detection: A Concise Treatment. LC 98-4616. (Advances in Industrial Control Ser.). (Illus.). xviii, 222p. 1998. 79.95 (*3-540-76251-5*) Spr-Verlag.

Mangravite, Andrew, ed. & tr. see De Gourmont, Remy.

***Mangraviti, James J., Jr. & Babitsky, Steven J.** How to Excel During Depositions: Techniques for Experts That Work. 284p. 1999. 59.95 (*1-892904-00-4*) SEAK.

— The Successful Physician Negotiator: How to Get What You Deserve. 284p. 1998. 59.95 (*0-9652197-7-1*) SEAK.

***Mangraviti, James J., Jr., et al.** The Comprehensive Forensic Services Manual: The Essential Resources for All Experts. 621p. 2000. 124.99 (*1-892904-07-1*) SEAK.

Mangraviti, James J., Jr., jt. auth. see Babitsky, Steven J.

Mangravito, Artie. How Well Do You Know Jerry...& His Friends? 16p. 1997. pap. 6.00 (*0-8059-4177-0*) Dorrance.

Mangru, Basdeo. A History of East Indian Resistance on the Guyana Sugar Estates, 1869-1948. LC 95-46918. (Caribbean Studies: Vol. 4). 384p. 1996. 99.95 (*0-7734-8790-5*) E Mellen.

— Indians in Guyana: A Concise History from Their Arrival to the Present. (Illus.). 110p. 1999. pap. text 6.95 (*0-9670093-0-8*) B Mangru.

Mangrum, Charles & Strichart, Stephen. Colleges with Programs for Students with Learning Disabilities or Attention Deficit Disorders 1998. 5th ed. Latimer, Jon, ed. 688p. 1997. pap. 32.95 (*1-56079-853-X*) Petersons.

Mangrum, Charles T. & Strichart, Stephen S. Peterson's Guide to Colleges with Programs for Students with Learning Disabilities. 4th ed. LC 94-4760. 684p. (C). 1994. 32.95 (*1-56079-400-3*) Petersons.

***Mangrum, Charles T., II & Strichart, Stephen S., eds.** Colleges with Programs for Students with Learning Disabilities or Attention Deficit Disorders. 6th ed. 672p. 2000. pap. 29.95 (*0-7689-0455-2*) Petersons.

Mangrum, Charles T., et al. Study Skills & Strategies for Grades 4-8 in the Information Age. LC 97-13470. 206p. (C). 1997. pap. text 29.00 (*0-205-19879-1*) Allyn.

Mangrum, Charles T., jt. auth. see Strichart, Stephen S.

Mangrum, Grace S. From Mourning into Morning. LC 89-92263. (Illus.). (Orig.). 1989. pap. 8.50 (*0-9624524-0-8*) G S Mangrum.

Mangrum, Joe. Carnival. (AD&D Accessory Ser.). 1999. 13.95 (*0-7869-1382-7*, Pub. by TSR Inc) Random.

Mangrum, R. Collin, jt. auth. see Firmage, Edwin B.

Mangrum, R. Edward. The New Testament & the Christian Church. LC 98-90075. 1998. pap. 14.95 (*0-533-12701-7*) Vantage.

Mangrum, Robert G. Route Step March: Edwin M. Stanton's Special Military Units & the Prosecution of the War, 1862-1865. 237p. 1980. 37.95 (*0-89126-091-9*) MA-AH Pub.

Mangrum, Roger. Waves of Passion: Inspirations for Love. Howard, Kathy, ed. (Illus.). 128p. 1999. per. 13.95 (*1-892783-05-3*) AVerzADay Write.

Mangrum, Terrie & Thomas, Pamala. Terrie Mangrum's Hog Pit Barbecue Cookbook. 2000. write for info. (*0-316-16651-0*) Little.

Mangubhai, Francis & Everingham, Joanne. English on Cue: Developing Skills in English Language: Listening, Level 3. 129p. 1997. pap. 24.95 (*0-949414-71-9*, Pub. by U Sthn Queenslnd) Accents Pubns.

Manguel, A. Dictionnaire des Lieux Imaginaires. (FRE.). 1998. 75.00 (*0-320-00174-1*) Fr & Eur.

***Manguel, Alberto.** Dictionary of Imaginary Places. (Illus.). 776p. (J). 2000. pap. 22.50 (*0-15-600872-6*, Harcourt Child Bks) Harcourt.

Manguel, Alberto. Fathers & Sons: An Anthology. LC 97-32271. 291p. 1998. 15.95 (*0-8118-1630-3*) Chronicle Bks.

— A History of Reading. 1997. pap. 14.95 (*0-14-016654-8*) Viking Penguin.

***Manguel, Alberto.** Into the Looking-Glass Wood: Essays on Books, Reading & the World. LC 99-55234. (Harvest Original Ser.). 2000. pap. 13.00 (*0-15-601265-0*) Harcourt.

Manguel, Alberto. Mothers & Daughters: An Anthology. LC 97-32273. 352p. 1998. 15.95 (*0-8118-1629-X*) Chronicle Bks.

— The Second Gates of Paradise. LC 97-170097. 704p. 1994. pap. 19.50 (*0-921912-77-3*) MW&R.

Manguel, Alberto, ed. By the Light of the Glow-Worm Lamp: Three Centuries of Reflections on Nature. LC 98-26198. (Illus.). 384p. (C). 1998. pap. 19.95 (*0-306-45992-2*, Plenum Trade) Perseus Pubng.

***Manguel, Alberto, ed.** By the Light of the Glow-Worm Lamp: Three Centuries of Reflections on Nature. LC 98-26198. (Illus.). 384p. (C). 1998. 32.50 (*0-306-45991-4*, Plenum Trade) Perseus Pubng.

Manguel, Alberto & Guadalupi, Gianni. The Dictionary of Imaginary Places. LC 99-46994. 776p. (C). 1999. 40.00 (*0-15-100541-9*) Harcourt.

Manguel, Alberto, tr. see Andahazi, Federico.

Manguel, Alberto, tr. see Maalouf, Amin.

Manguel, Alberto, tr. see Yourcenar, Marguerite.

Manguel, Albertro. Bride of Frankenstein. LC 97-216106. 1997. pap. text 10.95 (*0-85170-608-8*) U of Ill Pr.

Manguerra Brainard, Cecilia, ed. Contemporary Fiction by Filipinos in America. 254p. 1997. pap. 19.95 (*971-27-0701-6*, Pub. by Anvil Pub Inc) Phil Amer Lit.

Mangum, jt. auth. see Robbins, Dennis A.

***Mangum, Brad.** Jacob's Blood: With Family on the Line-To Whom, Where & to What Does Your Loyalty Lie? 2000. 16.95 (*1-55517-478-7*) CFI Dist.

***Mangum, Charles S.** The Legal Status of the Negro, 1940. fac. ed. LC 99-88240. 2000. 85.00 (*1-58477-081-3*) Lawbk Exchange.

***Mangum, Eric.** Dod Presents 100 Superstars Guitar Sounds on a Stompbox Budget. (Guitar Presents Ser.). 2000. pap. text 19.95 (*1-57560-342-X*, Pub. by Cherry Lane) H Leonard.

Mangum, Eric & Stubbs, Dean. 87 Superstar Guitar Sounds on a Stompbox Budget. LC 96-139923. (Illus.). 112p. (Orig.). 1995. pap. text 14.95 (*0-89524-883-2*, Pub. by Cherry Lane) H Leonard.

Mangum, Garth L. The Operating Engineers: The Economic History of a Trade Union. LC 63-19144. (Publications in Industrial Relations). 366p. reprint ed. pap. 113.50 (*0-608-15242-0*, 202917100059) Bks Demand.

Mangum, Garth L. & Glenn, Lowell M. Employing the Disadvantaged in the Federal Civil Service. LC 79-626166. (Policy Papers in Human Resources & Industrial Relations Ser.: No. 13). (Orig.). 1969. pap. 5.00 (*0-87736-113-4*) U of Mich Inst Labor.

Mangum, Garth L. & Mangum, Stephen, eds. Of Heart & Mind: Social Policy Essays in Honor of Sar Levitan. 350p. 1996. 40.00 (*0-88099-172-0*); pap. 22.00 (*0-88099-171-2*) W E Upjohn.

Mangum, Garth L. & Philips, Peter, eds. Three Worlds of Labor Economics. LC 87-26423. 392p. (C). (gr. 13). 1988. text 74.95 (*0-87332-455-2*) M E Sharpe.

Mangum, Garth L. & Philips, Peter, eds. Three Worlds of Labor Economics. LC 87-26423. 392p. (C). (gr. 13). 1988. pap. text 40.95 (*0-87332-456-0*) M E Sharpe.

Mangum, Garth L. & Seninger, Stephen F. Coming of Age in the Ghetto: A Dilemma of Youth Unemployment: A Report to the Ford Foundation. LC 78-8422. (Policy Studies in Employment & Welfare: Vol. 33). 128p. 1978. reprint ed. pap. 39.70 (*0-608-03667-6*, 206449300009) Bks Demand.

Mangum, Garth L. & Walsh, John. Labor Struggle in the Post Office: From Selective Lobbying to Collective Bargaining. LC 91-43910. (Labor & Human Resources). 293p. (C). (gr. 13). 1992. text 70.95 (*1-56324-028-9*) M E Sharpe.

— Union Resilience in Troubled Times: The Story of the Operating Engineers, AFL-CIO, 1960-1993. LC 94-10047. (Labor & Human Resources Ser.). (Illus.). 294p. (gr. 13). 1994. text 74.95 (*1-56324-452-7*); pap. text 35.95 (*1-56324-453-5*) M E Sharpe.

Mangum, Garth L., et al. On Being Poor in Utah. LC 97-40575. 384p. 1998. 24.95 (*0-87480-554-6*) U of Utah Pr.

— Portable Pension Plans for Casual Labor Markets: Lessons from the Operating Engineers' Central Pension Fund. LC 95-7960. 216p. 1995. 67.95 (*0-89930-995-X*, Quorum Bks) Greenwood.

Mangum, Garth L., et al. The Rise, Fall & Replacement of Industry-Wide Bargaining in the Basic Steel. LC 96-41492. (Labor & Humana Resources Ser.). 228p. (C). (gr. 13). 1996. text 74.95 (*1-56324-982-0*) M E Sharpe.

— The Rise, Fall & Replacement of Industry-Wide Bargaining in the Basic Steel Industry. LC 96-41492. (Labor & Human Resources Ser.). 228p. (C). (gr. 13). 1996. pap. text 30.95 (*1-56324-983-9*) M E Sharpe.

Mangum, Garth L., et al. Transnational Marriages in the Steel Industry: Experience & Lessons for Global Business. LC 95-45964. 216p. 1996. 62.95 (*1-56720-040-0*, Quorum Bks) Greenwood.

Mangum, Garth L., jt. auth. see Hildebrand, George H.

Mangum, Garth L., jt. auth. see Levitan, Sar A.

Mangum, Garth L., jt. auth. see Nemore, Arnold L.

Mangum, Garth L., jt. auth. see Walsh, John.

Mangum, Garth L., ed. see Levitan, Sar A.

Mangum, Garth L., jt. ed. see Levitan, Sar A.

Mangum, Harold, jt. auth. see Ross, Nola Mae.

Mangum, Karen. Vegetarian Pleasures: Healthy Cooking for Sharing & Celebration. (Illus.). 192p. (Orig.). 1997. pap. text 19.95 (*1-883214-18-1*) Bon Vivant Pr.

Mangum, Kim, et al. Voter Purging: The Perils & the Promise. 50p. 1990. 15.00 (*0-685-56594-7*) CPA Washington.

Mangum, Neil C. Battle of the Rosebud: Prelude to the Little Bighorn. 3rd ed. LC 87-50694. (Montana & the West Ser.: Vol. 5). (Illus.). 200p. (C). 1996. 35.00 (*0-912783-11-7*) Upton & Sons.

***Mangum, Richard K.** Sedona Hikes: 135 Day Hikes & 5 Vortex Sites Around Sedona, AZ. 5th rev. ed. Orig. Title: Sedona Hikes & Mountain Bike Rides. (Illus.). 256p. 2000. pap. 14.95 (*1-891517-02-3*) Hexagon Pr.

Mangum, Richard K. & Mangum, Sherry G. Flagstaff Hikes: 146 Day Hikes Around Flagstaff, Arizona. 4th rev. ed. (Illus.). 288p. 1997. pap. 15.95 (*0-9632265-9-2*) Hexagon Pr.

— Flagstaff Historic Walk: A Stroll Through Old Downtown. (Illus.). 64p. (Orig.). 1993. pap. 6.95 (*0-9632265-3-3*) Hexagon Pr.

***Mangum, Richard K. & Mangum, Sherry G.** Grand Canyon-Flagstaff Stagecoach Line: A History & Exploration Guide. (Illus.). 100p. 1999. pap. 14.95 (*1-891517-01-5*) Hexagon Pr.

Mangum, Richard K. & Mangum, Sherry G. Sedona Hikes: 135 Day Hikes & 5 Vortex Sites Around Sedona, AZ. 4th rev. ed. LC 99-165488. Orig. Title: Sedona Hikes & Mountain Bike Rides. (Illus.). 264p. 1998. pap. 14.95 (*1-891517-00-7*) Hexagon Pr.

— Williams Guidebook: What to Do & See Around Williams, Arizona. (Illus.). 128p. 1998. pap. 9.95 (*0-9632265-5-X*) Hexagon Pr.

Mangum, Sarita. Zephyr the Zebra. (Illus.). 26p. (Orig.). (J). (gr. k-5). 1995. pap. text 6.00 (*0-9649870-0-7*) Purpose Publ.

Mangum, Sherry G., jt. auth. see Mangum, Richard K.

Mangum, Stephen, jt. ed. see Mangum, Garth L.

Mangum, Stephen L., jt. auth. see Hsieh, Ching-Yao.

Mangum, Stephen L., ed. see Levitan, Sar A.

Mangum, Teresa. Married, Middle-Brow, & Militant: Sarah Grand & the New Woman Novel. LC 98-40079. (Illus.). 304p. 1998. text 47.50 (*0-472-10977-4*, 10977) U of Mich Pr.

***Mangum, Tianika L.** Teardrops from My Soul. LC 99-97757. 54p. 2000. pap. 9.95 (*0-9678394-2-4*) Tyger Eye.

Mangum, William P. A Kingdom for a Horse: The Legacy of R. A. Alexander & Woodburn Farms. LC 97-39671. 1998. 24.99 (*1-56469-037-7*) Harmony Hse Pub.

Mangum, William T. Job Search Workbook: A Companion to the Book "99 Minutes to Your Ideal Job" 116p. (Orig.). 1995. pap., student ed. 12.95 (*1-881474-04-6*) TMI Pubng.

— 99 Minutes to Your Ideal Job. 219p. 1995. pap. 12.95 (*0-471-11126-0*) Wiley.

Mangun, Kenneth G., jt. auth. see Hahn, Fred E.

Mangun, Vesta. The Best of Vesta Mangun. (Illus.). 180p. (Orig.). 1987. pap. write for info. (*0-9619753-0-X*) Pentecostals Alexandria.

— Vesta Mangun Continues. 87p. (Orig.). 1990. pap. 6.00 (*0-9619753-1-8*) Pentecostals Alexandria.

Mangun, William R., ed. American Fish & Wildlife Policy: The Human Dimension. LC 91-47741. (Illus.). 288p. (C). 1992. 31.95 (*0-8093-1821-0*) S Ill U Pr.

— Public Policy Issues in Wildlife Management, 286. LC 91-20774. (Contributions in Political Science Ser.: No. 286). 208p. 1991. 57.95 (*0-313-28010-X*, MIW, Greenwood Pr) Greenwood.

— Wildlife Conservation & Public Policy. (Orig.). 1991. pap. 15.00 (*0-944285-22-8*) Pol Studies.

Mangun, William R & Henning, Daniel H. Managing the Environmental Crisis: Incorporating Competing Values in Natural Resource Administration 2nd ed. LC 99-26267. 1999. 21.95 (*0-8223-2413-X*) Duke.

***Mangun, William R. & Henning, Daniel H.** Managing the Environmental Crisis: Incorporating Competing Values in Natural Resource Administration. 2nd ed. LC 99-26267. 416p. 1999. 64.95 (*0-8223-2379-6*) Duke.

Mangun, William R., jt. auth. see Henning, Daniel H.

***Mangurian, Robert.** Wrapper: Faces Looking for the Future from the Past: 40 Possible City Surfaces for the Museum of Jurassic Technology. (Illus.). 96p. 1999. 25.00 (*0-9651144-9-X*, Pub. by W K Stout) RAM Publications.

Mangurian, Robert & Ray, Mary-Ann. Wrapper: Faces Looking for the Future from the Past: 40 Possible City Surfaces for the Museum of Jurassic Technology. (Illus.). 108p. 1997. pap. write for info. (*1-889629-02-2*) Form Zero.

Mangus, jt. auth. see Pfeiffer.

Mangus, A. L. Changing Aspects of Rural Relief. LC 74-165685. (Research Monographs: Vol. 14). 1971. reprint ed. lib. bdg. 29.50 (*0-306-70346-7*) Da Capo.

Mangus, A. R., jt. auth. see Asch, Berta.

Mangus, Brent, jt. auth. see Pfeiffer, Ron.

Mangus, Brent, jt. auth. see Pfeiffer, Ronald.

Mangus, Brent, jt. auth. see Pfeiffer, Ronald P.

Mangus, Brent C., jt. auth. see Pfeiffer, Ronald P.

Mangus, Donald J. Chizuru, 1945. (JPN., Illus.). 96p. (Orig.). Date not set. pap. write for info. (*1-887733-00-0*) Serenissima.

— Chizuru, 1945. Heidelberg Press Staff, ed. Ota, Masako, tr. (JPN., Illus.). 96p. (Orig.). 1995. pap. write for info. (*1-887733-01-9*) Serenissima.

Mangus, Jim. Banks: Identification & Values. (Collector's Guide to Ser.). 1998. pap. text 19.95 (*1-57432-035-1*, 5032) Collector Bks.

— Shawnee Pottery: An Identification & Value Guide. 1996. 24.95 (*0-89145-574-4*, 3738) Collector Bks.

***Mangus, Jon L. & Chin, Llewellyn P.** Handling Real Property Sales Transactions Pts. 1 & 2: Spring 1998 Action Guide. Chapin, John K., ed. 128p. 1998. pap. 58.00 (*0-7626-0217-1*, RE-11345) Cont Ed Bar-CA.

Mangus, Ron, jt. auth. see Taylor, Don.

***Manhard, Stephen J.** Goof-Proofer: How to Avoid the 41 Most Embarrassing Errors in Your Speaking & Writing. 1999. per. 5.95 (*0-684-83826-5*) S&S Trade.

Manhart Barrett, Elizabeth A., jt. ed. see Madrid, Mary.

Manhart, Marcia Y. Objects & Drawings from the Sanford M. & Diane Besser Collection. 94p. 1992. pap. 20.00 (*1-884240-01-1*) Arkansas Art Ctr.

Manhart, Paul, jt. auth. see Buechel, Eugene.

Manhart, Warren. Apples for the Twenty-First Century. (Illus.). 286p. 1995. 39.95 (*0-9648417-0-3*, SB354) N Amer Tree.

Manhas, J. S., jt. auth. see Singh, R. K.

Manhas, Maghar S. & Bose, Ajay K. Synthesis of Penicillin, Cephalosporin C, & Analogs. LC 69-13151. (New Directions in Organic Chemistry Ser.). 132p. reprint ed. pap. 41.00 (*0-608-16945-5*, 202710100054) Bks Demand.

Manhattan, Avro. Catholic Imperialism & World Freedom. LC 73-161336. (Atheist Viewpoint Ser.). 528p. 1972. reprint ed. 31.95 (*0-405-03810-0*) Ayer.

Manheim, Camryn. Wake up, I'm Fat! LC 99-10954. (Illus.). 289p. 1999. 23.00 (*0-7679-0362-5*) Broadway BDD.

***Manheim, Camryn.** Wake up, I'm Fat! (Illus.). 304p. 2000. pap. 14.00 (*0-7679-0363-3*) Broadway BDD.

Manheim, Carol J. The Myofascial Release Manual. 2nd ed. LC 94-13677. (Illus.). 214p. (C). 1994. pap. 39.00 (*1-55642-241-5*) SLACK Inc.

***Manheim, Carol J.** The Myofascial Release Manual. 3rd ed. 214p. (C). 2000. pap. text 40.00 (*1-55642-452-3*) SLACK Inc.

Manheim, Carol J. & Lavett, Diane K. The Self-Healing Body: Craniosacral Therapy & Somato-Emotional Release. LC 89-42578. (Illus.). 250p. 1994. pap. 32.00 (*1-55642-250-4*) SLACK Inc.

Manheim, Ivan & Winter, Dave. Jordan, Syria & Lebanon Handbook. LC 97-78487. (Footprint Handbooks Ser.). 572p. 1998. 21.95 (*0-8442-4869-X*, 4869X, Natl Textbk Co) NTC Contemp Pub Co.

Manheim, Jarol B. All of the People, All the Time: Strategic Communication & American Politics. LC 90-39657. 272p. (gr. 13). 1991. text 53.95 (*0-87332-796-9*) M E Sharpe.

— The Corporate Campaign: Origins, Strategy & Tactics of the Contemporary Attach on the Corporation. 264p. 2000. write for info. (*0-8058-3831-7*) L Erlbaum Assocs.

Manheim, Jarol B. Empirical Political Analysis: Research Methods in Political Science. 5th ed. (C). 1998. pap. text. write for info. (*0-8013-1849-1*) Addison-Wesley.

— Empirical Political Analysis: Research Methods in Political Science. 5th ed. (C). 2000. text. write for info. (*0-8013-1848-3*) Longman.

— Stragtegic Public Diplomacy & American Foreign Policy: The Evolution of Influence. (Illus.). 224p. (C). 1994. pap. text 21.95 (*0-19-508738-0*) OUP.

— Strategic Public Diplomacy & American Foreign Policy: The Evolution of Influence. (Illus.). 224p. (C). 1994. text 60.00 (*0-19-508737-2*) OUP.

Manheim, Jarol B. & Rich, Richard C. Empirical Political Analysis. 3rd ed. 399p. (C). 1991. text 48.95 (*0-8013-0407-5*, 78216) Longman.

Manheim, Michael. Eugene O'Neill's New Language of Kinship. LC 82-3190. 252p. 1982. reprint ed. pap. 78.20 (*0-608-07615-5*, 205993000010) Bks Demand.

Manheim, Michael, ed. The Cambridge Companion to Eugene O'Neill. LC 97-42228. (Cambridge Companions to Literature Ser.). (Illus.). 320p. (C). 1998. text 59.95 (*0-521-55389-X*); pap. text 18.95 (*0-521-55645-7*) Cambridge U Pr.

Manheim, R., tr. see Corbin, Henry.

Manheim, R., tr. see Jacobi, Jolande.

Manheim, R., tr. see Kerenyi, Carl.

Manheim, Ralph, tr. Hesse, Hermann: Hesse As Painter (with 20 Full-Page Watercolors) (Illus.). 46p. 1980. 15.00 (*3-518-03176-7*, Pub. by Suhr Verlag) Intl Bk Import.

Manheim, Ralph, ed. see Brecht, Bertolt.

Manheim, Ralph, ed. & tr. see Brecht, Bertolt.

Manheim, Ralph, tr. see Andersch, Alfred.

Manheim, Ralph, tr. see Auerbach, Erich.

Manheim, Ralph, tr. see Babinger, Franz.

Manheim, Ralph, tr. see Brecht, Bertolt.

Manheim, Ralph, tr. see Buber-Neumann, Margarete.

Manheim, Ralph, tr. see Buch, Hans C.

Manheim, Ralph, tr. see Campbell, Joseph & Hull, R. F. C., eds.

Manheim, Ralph, tr. see Cassirer, Ernst.

Manheim, Ralph, tr. see Celine, Louis-Ferdinand.

Manheim, Ralph, tr. see Corbin, Henry.

Manheim, Ralph, tr. see Ende, Michael.

Manheim, Ralph, tr. see Freud, Sigmund.

Manheim, Ralph, tr. see Freud, Sigmund & Jung, C. G.

Manheim, Ralph, tr. see Gary, Romain.

Manheim, Ralph, tr. see Grass, Gunter.

Manheim, Ralph, tr. see Grimm, Jacob W. & Grimm, Wilhelm K.

Manheim, Ralph, tr. see Grimm, Wilhelm K.

Manheim, Ralph, tr. see Handke, Peter.

Manheim, Ralph, tr. see Heidegger, Martin.

Manheim, Ralph, tr. see Hesse, Hermann.

Manheim, Ralph, tr. see Hitler, Adolf.

Manheim, Ralph, tr. see Hoffmann, E. T. A.

Manheim, Ralph, tr. see Jacobi, Jolande.

Manheim, Ralph, tr. see Jaspers, Karl.

Manheim, Ralph, tr. see Jung, C. G.

Manheim, Ralph, tr. see Kerenyi, Carl.

Manheim, Ralph, tr. see Kis, Danilo.

Manheim, Ralph, tr. see Mrozek, Slawomir.

Manheim, Ralph, tr. see Neumann, Erich.

Manheim, Ralph, tr. see Proust, Marcel.

Manheim, Ralph, tr. see Raddatz, Fritz.

Manheim, Ralph, tr. see Reich, Wilhelm.

Manheim, Ralph, tr. see Rouaud, Jean.

Manheim, Ralph, tr. see Scholem, Gershom.

Manheim, Ralph, tr. see Tournier, Michel.

Manheim, Ralph, tr. see Valery, Paul.

Manheim, Theodore, et al. Sources in Educational Research: A Selected & Annotated Bibliography, Vol. 1. LC 68-64690. 319p. reprint ed. pap. 98.90 (*0-608-18699-6*, 202760100001) Bks Demand.

Manheimer, Martha L. Style Manual: A Guide for the Preparation of Reports & Dissertations. LC 73-82623. (Books in Library & Information Science: Vol. 5). (Illus.). 173p. reprint ed. pap. 53.70 (*0-608-08954-0*, 206958900005) Bks Demand.

Manheimer, Martha L., jt. ed. see Williams, James G.

Manheimer, Ronald J. Map to the End of Time: Wayfarings with Friends & Philosophers. LC 98-33336. 332p. 1999. 24.95 (*0-393-04725-3*) Norton.

Manheimer, Ronald J., et al. Older Adult Education: A Guide to Research, Programs, & Policies. LC 95-10277. 264p. 1995. lib. bdg. 69.50 (*0-313-28878-X*, Greenwood Pr) Greenwood.

Manheimer, Wallace, et al. Plasma Science & the Environment. LC 96-27719. 1996. 75.00 (*1-56396-377-9*) Spr-Verlag.

Manheimer, Wallace M. An Introduction to Trapped-Particle Instability in Tokamaks. LC 77-8530. (ERDA Critical Review Ser.: Advances in Fusion Science & Engineering). 104p. 1977. pap. 10.50 (*0-87079-105-2*, TID-27157); fiche 9.00 (*0-87079-251-2*, TID-27157) DOE.

Manheimer, Wallace M. & Lashmore-Davies, C. N. MHD & Microinstabilities in Confined Plasma. (Plasma Physics Ser.). (Illus.). 300p. 1989. 208.00 (*0-85274-282-7*) IOP Pub.

Manheimteel, Karen, jt. auth. see Covington, Martin V.

Manhein, Mary H. The Bone Lady: Life as a Forensic Anthropologist. LC 99-17244. (Illus.). 224p. 1999. 24.95 (*0-8071-2404-4*) La State U Pr.

***Manhein, Mary H.** Bone Lady: Life as a Forensic Anthropologist. 2000. pap. 11.95 (*0-14-029192-X*) Viking Penguin.

Manhire, Bill. Mutes & Earthquakes: Bill Manhire's Creative Writing Course at Victoria. LC 98-103421. 333p. 1997. write for info. (*0-86473-318-6*) Victoria Univ Pr.

— South Pacific. LC 94-202665. 239p. 1995. 27.95 (*1-85754-046-8*, Pub. by Carcanet Pr) Paul & Co Pubs.

Manhire, Bill, jt. auth. see McLeod, Marion.

Manhire, Bill, jt. ed. see McLeod, Marion.

Manhire, Wilson. The Examination Candidate's Guide to Scale & Arpeggio Piano Playing. 66p. 1991. reprint ed. text 59.00 (*0-7812-9320-0*) Rprt Serv.

***Manhoff.** Emt: Infants/Children. 1998. text 6.96 (*0-323-00774-0*) Harcourt.

Manhoff, David H. Mosby's Outdoor Emergency Medical Guide. 1996. spiral bd. 12.95 (*0-916363-14-7*) Mosby Inc.

Manhoff, David H., jt. auth. see Vogel, Stephen.

Mani. Chronic Wound Healing: Clinical Measurement & Basic Science. (C). text 69.00 (*0-7020-2206-3*) W B Saunders.

Mani, B. N. Laws of Dharmasastra. (C). 1989. 58.00 (*81-7013-025-5*) S Asia.

Mani, B. R. Delhi Threshold of the Orient: Studies in Archeological Investigations. LC 98-900525. (C). 1997. 120.00 (*81-7305-128-3*, Pub. by Aryan Bks Intl) S Asia.

Mani, Dinesh, jt. auth. see Misra, S. G.

Mani, Dinesh, jt. ed. see Misra, S. G.

Mani, G. S., ed. Evolutionary Dynamics of Genetic Diversity: Proceedings of a Symposium Held in Manchester, England, March 29-30, 1983. (Lecture Notes in Biomathematics Ser.: Vol. 53). vii, 312p. 1984. 44.95 (*0-387-12903-0*) Spr-Verlag.

Mani, Gomathi. Adult Learning. (C). 1994. write for info. (*81-207-1608-6*) Sterling Pubs.

Mani, H. S., jt. ed. see Ramachandran, R.

***Mani, Inderjeet & Maybury, Mark T., eds.** Advances in Automatic Text Summarization. LC 99-22688. 300p. 1999. 45.00 (*0-262-13359-8*) MIT Pr.

Mani, J. C. & Dornand, J., eds. Lymphocyte Activation & Differentiation: Fundamental & Clinical Aspects. 960p. (C). 1988. lib. bdg. 276.95 (*3-11-010760-0*) De Gruyter.

Mani, Lata. Contentious Traditions: The Debate on Sati in Colonial India. LC 98-21003. (Illus.). 259p. 1998. 47.00 (*0-520-21406-4*, Pub. by U CA Pr); pap. 18.00 (*0-520-21407-2*, Pub. by U CA Pr) Cal Prin Full Svc.

Mani, M. N. Techniques of Teaching Blind Children. 1998. pap. write for info. (*81-207-1453-9*) Sterling Pubs.

Mani, M. S. Butterflies of the Himalaya. 1986. text 188.50 (*90-6193-545-8*) Kluwer Academic.

— Fundamentals of High Altitude Biology. rev. ed. 1990. 28.00 (*81-204-0493-9*, Pub. by Oxford IBH) S Asia.

— Himalayan Flowers. 1994. pap. 45.00 (*0-7855-0451-6*, Pub. by Ratna Pustak Bhandar) St Mut.

***Mani, M. S.** Plant Galls of India. 2nd ed. (Illus.). 400p. 2000. text 112.00 (*1-57808-131-9*) Science Pubs.

Mani, M. S. Pollination Ecology & Evolution in Composite (Astereceae) LC 99-23855. (Illus.). 166p. 1999. text 49.50 (*1-57808-058-4*) Science Pubs.

Mani, M. S. & Giddings, L. E. Ecology of Highlands. (Monographiae Biologicae: No. 40). (Illus.). 236p. 1980. text 171.00 (*90-6193-093-6*) Kluwer Academic.

Mani, Nicholas. Collection of Poetry & Prose. 88p. 1999. pap. 10.00 (*0-8059-4703-5*) Dorrance.

Mani, R. S., jt. auth. see Gadre, Dhananjay.

Mani, V. V., ed. Fats, Oleochemicals & Surfactants: Challenges in the 21st Century. (Illus.). 326p. 1998. 75.00 (*1-57808-026-6*) Science Pubs.

Mani, Vettam. Puranic Encyclopaedia: A Comprehensive Work with Special Reference to the Epic & Puranic Literature. 992p. (C). 1996. reprint ed. 68.00 (*81-208-0597-6*, Pub. by Motilal Bnarsidass) S Asia.

Mania, Cathy. A Forest's Life: From Meadow to Mature Woodland. (First Bks.). (J). 1998. pap. 6.95 (*0-531-15878-0*) Watts.

***Mania, Cathy.** Woodpecker in the Backyard. (Illus.). (J). 2000. 22.50 (*0-531-11799-5*) Watts.

Mania, Cathy & Mania, Robert. A Forest's Life: From Meadow to Mature Woodland. LC 96-37286. (First Bks.). (J). (gr. 4-6). 1997. lib. bdg. 22.00 (*0-531-20319-0*) Watts.

Mania, Robert, jt. auth. see Mania, Cathy.

Maniacci, Michael P., jt. auth. see Mosak, Harold H.

Maniak, Angela J. Audit Report Writing Manual. 196p. 1989. per. 49.00 (*1-55520-132-6*, Irwn Prfssnl) McGraw-Hill Prof.

— Maximizing the Value of Your Audit Reports: Managing Quality & Timeliness. 100p. 1991. text 95.00 (*0-9629337-0-8*) A J Maniak.

Manian. The Curbside Consult: Infectious Diseases. LC 97-39640. (Illus.). 256p. (C). (gr. 13). 1997. pap. text 29.95 (*0-8151-2345-0*, 27220) Mosby Inc.

Manian, Padma. Straddling Two Cultures: Asian Indian Children in America. Link, Terry & Beggs, Marjorie, eds. (Illus.). 24p. 1997. pap. 5.00 (*1-888956-01-1*) SF Study Ctr.

Manias, Paul & May, Fiona. The Americas. (Family Library of World Travel). (Illus.). 64p. 1985. pap. 4.95 (*0-933521-14-6*) AGT Pub.

Maniates, Christian, ed. Chicago Prop Finders Handbook. 596p. 1990. write for info. (*0-9625639-0-0*) Print Grp.

— Chicago Prop Finders Handbook: 1991. 3rd ed. 600p. 1991. write for info. (*0-9625639-1-9*) Print Grp.

Maniates, Maria R. Music Discourse from Classical to Early Modern Times: Editing & Translating Texts. (Illus.). 158p. 1998. text 40.00 (*0-8020-0972-7*) U of Toronto Pr.

Maniates, Maria R., ed. see Dufay, Guillaume, et al.

Maniates, Maria R., tr. & intro. see Vincentino, Nicola.

Maniatis, T., et al. Molecular Cloning: A Laboratory Manual. LC 81-68891. 555p. reprint ed. pap. 172.10 (*0-7837-1892-6*, 204209600001) Bks Demand.

An Asterisk (*) at the beginning of an entry indicates that the title is appearing for the first time.

Maniatty, Taramesha. Glory Trail. Thatch, Nancy R., ed. LC 95-8701. (Books for Students by Students). (Illus.). 29p. (J). (gr. 5-8). 1995. lib. bdg. 15.95 (*0-933849-59-1*) Landmark Edns.

Manibhai, ed. see Aurobindo, Sri.

Manibhai, ed. see Aurobindo, Sri & Mother.

Manicas. Social Process in Hawaii: A Reader. (C). 1993. pap. text. write for info. (*0-07-040029-6*) McGraw.

***Manickam, R. N.** Security, Espionage & Counter Intelligence. 2000. 28.50 (*81-7049-104-5*, Pub. by Manas Pubns) S Asia.

Manickam, V. S. Ecological Studies on the Fern Flora of the Palni Hills (S. India) (International Bioscience Ser.: No. 5). 76p. 1984. 19.00 (*1-55528-103-6*) Scholarly Pubns.

— Fern Flora of the Palni Hills (S. India) (International Bioscience Ser.: No. 11). 200p. 1986. 27.00 (*1-55528-072-2*) Scholarly Pubns.

Manickam, V. S. & Irudayaraj, V. Cytology of Ferns of the Western Ghats South India. (Illus.). 109p. 1988. 35.00 (*1-55528-099-4*, Pub. by Today Tomorrow) Scholarly Pubns.

Manicom, D. Older Graces. LC 97-203868. 80p. 1997. pap. text 12.95 (*0-88982-164-X*, Pub. by Oolichan Bks) Genl Dist Srvs.

***Manicom, D.** Progeny of Ghosts. LC 98-199377. 252p. 1998. text 34.95 (*0-88982-170-4*, Pub. by Oolichan Bks); pap. text 19.95 (*0-88982-168-2*, Pub. by Oolichan Bks) Genl Dist Srvs.

Manicom, David. Theology of Swallows. 1991. pap. text 10.95 (*0-88982-109-7*, Pub. by Oolichan Bks) Genl Dist Srvs.

Manicom, Linzi, jt. ed. see Walters, Shirley.

Manier, Edward. The Young Darwin & His Cultural Circle. (Studies in the History of Modern Science: No. 2). 254p. 1978. lib. bdg. 88.00 (*90-277-0856-8*, D Reidel) Kluwer Academic.

— The Young Darwin & His Cultural Circle. (Studies in the History of Modern Science: No. 2). 254p. 1978. pap. text 51.50 (*90-277-0857-6*, D Reidel) Kluwer Academic.

Manier, Edward, et al, eds. Abortion: New Directions for Policy Studies. LC 76-51617. 198p. reprint ed. pap. 61.40 (*0-8357-5017-5*, 202436300036) Bks Demand.

Maniere, Jacques. Cuisine a la Vapeur: The Art of Cooking with Steam. Lyness, Stephanie, tr. (FRE., Illus.). 318p. 1998. text 25.00 (*0-7881-5263-7*) DIANE Pub.

Manies, Barbara A. The Sarzan Method of Ear Care for Pets. (Sarzan How to Bks.: No. 1). (Illus.). 48p. (Orig.). (J). (gr. 5 up). 1983. pap. 5.00 (*0-911935-00-2*) Edwards Pub Co.

Maniet, Albert, ed. Plautus: Plaute, Lexique Inverse, Listes Grammaticales, Releves Divers. viii, 201p. 1969. write for info. (*0-318-71975-4*) G Olms Pubs.

— Plautus - Plaute, Asinaria: Index Verborum, Lexiques Inverses, Releves Lexicaux et Grammaticaus. write for info. (*0-318-71978-9*) G Olms Pubs.

— Plautus - Plaute, Lexique Inverse: Listes Grammaticales. Releves Divers. viii, 201p. 1969. write for info. (*0-318-70660-1*) G Olms Pubs.

Maniet, Albert & Paquot, Annette, eds. Plautus - Plaute, Amphitryon: Index Verborum, Lexiques Inverses, Releves Lexicaus et Grammaticaux. vii, 217p. 1970. write for info. (*0-318-71976-2*) G Olms Pubs.

— Plautus - Plaute, Amphitryon: Index Verborum, Lexiques Inverses, Releves Lexicaux et Grammaticaux. vii, 217p. 1970. write for info. (*0-318-70661-X*) G Olms Pubs.

Maniet, Albert, ed. see Denooz, Laurence.

Maniet, Albert, ed. see Plautus.

Maniet, Monique. CatMinder. 100p. 1991. 19.95 (*0-914783-52-1*) Charles.

— DogMinder. 98p. 1991. 19.95 (*0-914783-53-X*) Charles.

Manifold, George O. Calculating with Fortran. LC 70-174575. x, 190 p. 1972. write for info. (*0-675-09181-0*) Mrrill.

Manifold, Diane L. Japanese Corporate Activities in Asia: Implications for U. S.-Japan Relations. 87p. (C). 1998. pap. text 25.00 (*0-7881-7187-9*) DIANE Pub.

Manifold, Gay. George Sand's Gabriel, 49. LC 92-15368. (Contributions in Drama & Theatre Studies: No. 49). 164p. 1992. 47.95 (*0-313-28390-7*, MOX, Greenwood Pr) Greenwood.

— George Sand's Theatre Career. LC 84-28098. (Theater & Dramatic Studies: No. 28). (Illus.). 206p. reprint ed. pap. 63.90 (*0-8357-1653-8*, 207059600004) Bks Demand.

Manifold, John S. The Music in English Drama. 1988. reprint ed. lib. bdg. 75.00 (*0-7812-0242-6*) Rprt Serv.

— The Music in English Drama from Shakespeare to Purcell. LC 70-181207. 208p. 1956. reprint ed. 49.00 (*0-403-01617-7*) Scholarly.

Manigart, P. Future Roles, Missions & Structures of Armed Forces in the New World Order: The Public View. 173p. 1996. 115.00 (*1-56072-262-2*) Nova Sci Pubs.

Manigat, Leslie F., jt. ed. see Heine, Jorge.

Manigault, Sandra. The Book for Math Empowerment: Rethinking the Subject of Mathematics. LC 97-72334. (Illus.). 128p. (Orig.). (C). 1997. pap. 12.95 (*0-9658541-0-8*) Godosan Pubns.

***Manigault, Sandra.** Fragments of a Woman's Life: A Memoir. 96p. 2000. pap. 12.95 (*0-9658541-1-6*) Godosan Pubns.

Maniglia, Anthony J., et al. Surgical Reconstruction of the Face: Nose, Midface & Anterior Skull Base. Donley, Stephanie et al, eds. LC 98-25699. (Illus.). 335p. 1999. text. write for info. (*0-7216-6993-X*, W B Saunders Co) Harcrt Hlth Sci Grp.

***Manigualt, Faye S.** Glorious Reflections of Strength. 82p. 1999. pap. 10.95 (*0-9655253-4-1*) Merging Worlds Publishers.

Maniguet, Xavier. Survival: How to Prevail in Hostile Environments. Roberts, Ivanka, tr. from ENG. LC 93-16118.Tr. of Survivre. (ENG & FRE.). 464p. 1994. 35.00 (*0-8160-2518-5*) Facts on File.

Manikas, Athanassios N. Principles of Spread Spectrum Theory & Systems. 300p. 1998. 38.00 (*1-86094-043-9*); pap. 20.00 (*1-86094-044-7*) World Scientific Pub.

Manikowski, John. Wild Fish & Game Cookbook. LC 97-16187. (Illus.). 192p. 1997. 35.00 (*1-885183-50-X*) Artisan.

Manikyamba, P. Women in Panchayti Raj Structures. 180p. 1989. 22.50 (*81-212-0286-8*, Pub. by Gian Publng Hse) S Asia.

Manikyanandi. Pariksamukham: With Prameya-ratnamala by Anantavirya. Ghoshal, Sarat C., tr. LC 73-3845. (Sacred Books of the Jainas Ser.: No. 11). 1995. reprint ed. 57.50 (*0-404-57711-3*) AMS Pr.

Manilal, K. S., ed. Botany & History of Hortus Malabaricus. 245p. (C). 1980. text 70.00 (*90-6191-071-4*, Pub. by A A Balkema) Ashgate Pub Co.

Manilius. Five Books of Manilius. 190p. 1953. 10.00 (*0-86690-128-0*, E1096-014) Am Fed Astrologers.

Manilius, M. Five Books of M. Manilius. 194p. 1998. reprint ed. pap. 17.95 (*0-7661-0644-6*) Kessinger Pub.

Manilius, Marcus. Astronomica. (Loeb Classical Library: No. 469). 510p. (C). 1978. text 19.95 (*0-674-99516-3*) HUP.

— Astronomica, 5 vols. in 2, Set. cxcvii, 627p. 1972. reprint ed. write for info. (*3-487-04271-1*) G Olms Pubs.

Maniloff, Jack, et al, eds. Mycoplasmas: Molecular Biology & Pathogenesis. LC 92-49746. (Illus.). 609p. 1992. 109.00 (*1-55581-050-0*) ASM Pr.

Manimala, Mathew J. Entrepreneurial Policies & Strategies: The Innovator's Choice. LC 99-11081. 1999. write for info. (*0-7619-9327-4*) Sage.

Manimala, Matthew J. Entrepreneurial Policies & Strategies: The Innovator's Choice. LC 99-11081. 1999. write for info. (*0-7619-9328-2*) Sage.

Manimaran, G., jt. auth. see Murthy, C. Silva Ram.

Manin, Bernard. The Principles of Representative Government. (Themes in the Social Sciences Ser.). 252p. 1997. pap. text 16.95 (*0-521-45891-9*) Cambridge U Pr.

— The Principles of Representative Government. (Themes in the Social Sciences Ser.). 252p. 1997. text 54.95 (*0-521-45258-9*) Cambridge U Pr.

Manin, Ju. I., et al. Seven Papers on Algebra, Algebraic Geometry & Algebraic Topology. LC 51-5559. (Translations Ser.: Series 2, Vol. 63). 279p. 1967. 50.00 (*0-8218-1763-9*, TRANS2/63) Am Math.

Manin, kIIU. I. Frobenius Manifolds, Quantum Cohomology, & Moduli Spaces. LC 99-18035. (American Mathematical Society. Colloquium Publications). 1999. write for info. (*0-8218-1917-8*) Am Math.

Manin, Mark B. Flexible Benefits Answer Books: Special Supplement Forms & Checklists, 1. LC 99-173363. (Flexible Benefits Answer Books). 832p. 1998. pap. text 96.00 (*1-56706-967-3*) Panel Pubs.

Manin, Mark B., et al. Flexible Benefits Answer Book. annuals 528p. boxed set 118.00 (*1-56706-422-1*, 64221) Panel Pubs.

— Flexible Benefits Answer Book. annuals 528p. 1994. 118.00 (*1-56706-063-3*, S156) Panel Pubs.

Manin, Y. J., jt. auth. see Gelfand, S. J.

Manin, Y. J., jt. auth. see Gelfand, Sergei I.

Manin, Yu I. A Course in Mathematical Logic. Ewing, J. H. et al, eds. Koblitz, Neal, tr. from RUS. (Graduate Tests in Mathematics Ser.: Vol. 53). xiii, 286p. 1991. reprint ed. 59.95 (*0-387-90243-0*) Spr-Verlag.

— Cubic Forms: Algebra, Geometry, Arithmetic. rev. ed. (North-Holland Mathematical Library: Vol. 4). 326p. 1986. 162.00 (*0-444-87823-8*, North Holland) Elsevier.

— Gauge Field Theory & Complex Geometry. (Grundlehren Ser.: Vol. 289). x, 297p. 1988. 135.95 (*0-387-18275-6*) Spr-Verlag.

— K-Theory, Arithmetic & Geometry. (Lecture Notes in Mathematics Ser.: Vol. 1289). v, 399p. 1987. 54.40 (*0-387-18571-2*) Spr-Verlag.

— Selected Papers of Yu. I. Manin. LC 96-18705. (World Scientific Series in 20th Century Mathematics). 612p. 1996. write for info. (*981-02-2498-2*) World Scientific Pub.

Manin, Yu I. & Kobzarev, I. Yu. Elementary Particles: Mathematics, Physics & Philosophy. (C). 1989. text 182.50 (*0-7923-0098-X*) Kluwer Academic.

Manin, Yu I. & Kostrikin, Alexei I. Linear Algebra & Geometry, Vol. 1. x, 310p. 1989. text 240.00 (*2-88124-683-4*) Gordon & Breach.

Manin, Yu I., jt. auth. see Kostrikin, A. I.

Manin, Yu I., tr. see Kostrikin, Alexei I. & Shararevich, I. R., eds.

Manin, Yuri I. Gauge Field Theory & Complex Geometry, Vol. X. 2nd ed. King, J. R. & Koblitz, N., trs. from RUS. LC 96-35228. (Grundelehren der Mathematischen Wissenschaften Ser.: Vol. 289). 335p. 1997. 129.00 (*3-540-61378-1*) Spr-Verlag.

— Topics in Noncommutative Geometry. 163p. 1991. text 45.00 (*0-691-08588-9*, Pub. by Princeton U Pr) Cal Prin Full Svc.

Manion, C. L., jt. ed. see Taylor, J. G.

Manion, Christopher, jt. auth. see Stone, Deborah J.

Manion, Ian Gregory & Wilson, Susan K. An Examination of the Association Between Histories of Maltreatment & Adolescent Risk Behaviours LC 96-181879. 37p. 1995. write for info. (*0-662-23798-6*) Intl Spec Bk.

Manion, Jerry. Friedel-Craft Alkylation: Kinetic Versus Thermodynamic Control. Jeffers, J., ed. (Modular Laboratory Program in Chemistry Ser.). 12p. (C). 1998. pap. text 1.75 (*0-87540-724-2*, SYNT 724) Chem Educ Res.

— Friedel-Crafts Acylation: Synthesis of 4-Methoxyacetophenone. Jeffers, J., ed. (Modular Laboratory Program in Chemistry Ser.). 12p. (C). 1998. pap. text 1.75 (*0-87540-723-4*, SYNT 723) Chem Educ Res.

***Manion, Jerry.** Molecular Rearrangement Reactions: Azobenzene & Benzilic Acid. Jeffers, Joe, ed. (Modular Laboratory in Chemistry Ser.). 8p. (C). 1999. pap. text 1.75 (*0-87540-734-X*, REAC 734-X) Chem Educ Res.

Manion, Jerry. Separating Acids & Neutral Compounds by Solvent Extraction. Jeffers, J., ed. (Modular Laboratory Program in Chemistry Ser.). 16p. (C). 1997. pap. text 1.75 (*0-87540-705-6*) Chem Educ Res.

— Separating Cyclohexane & Toluene by Distillation. Jeffers, J., ed. (Modular Laboratory Program in Chemistry Ser.). 16p. (C). 1997. pap. text 1.75 (*0-87540-704-8*) Chem Educ Res.

— Studying Sn1 & Sn2 Reaction: Nucleophilic Substitution at a Saturated Carbon. Jeffers, J., ed. (Modular Laboratory Program in Chemistry Ser.). 16p. (C). 1998. pap. text 1.75 (*0-87540-714-5*, REAC 714) Chem Educ Res.

***Manion, Jerry.** Two Methods for the Synthesis of Phenacetin. Jeffers, Joe, ed. (Modular Laboratory in Chemistry Ser.). 16p. (C). 1999. pap. text 1.75 (*0-87540-726-9*, SYNT 726-9) Chem Educ Res.

Manion, Jo, et al. Team-Based Health Care Organizations: Blueprint for Success. LC 96-19770. 380p. 1996. 49.00 (*0-8342-0782-6*) Aspen Pub.

***Manion, John.** General Terry's Last Statement to Custer. LC 99-61575. (Echoes of the Little Big Horn Ser.: Vol. 5). (Illus.). 182p. 2000. 37.50 (*0-912783-33-8*) Upton & Sons.

Manion, Judith, et al. Research Guide to Congress: How to Make Congress Work for You. 2nd ed. 204p. 1991. text 75.00 (*1-880955-00-8*) Legi-Slate.

Manion, Lawrence, jt. auth. see Cohen, Louis.

Manion, Margaret M. & Muir, Bernard J., eds. The Art of the Book: Its Place in Medieval Worship. 240p. 1998. text 80.00 (*0-85989-566-1*, Pub. by Univ Exeter Pr) Northwestern U Pr.

— Medieval Texts & Images. LC 91-8868. xx, 224p. 1991. text 55.00 (*3-7186-5133-5*, Z6) Gordon & Breach.

— Medieval Texts & Images: Studies of Manuscripts from the Middle Ages. (Illus.). 224p. 50.00 (*976-8097-17-5*, Pub. by Craftsman House) Gordon & Breach.

Manion, Margaret M., et al. Medieval & Renaissance Manuscripts in New Zealand. LC 88-51139. (Illus.). 1989. 45.00 (*0-500-23544-9*, Pub. by Thames Hudson) Norton.

Manion, Martha L. Writings about Henry Cowell: An Annotated Bibliography. LC 82-81925. (I.S.A.M. Monographs: No. 16). (Illus.). 368p. (Orig.). 1982. pap. 15.00 (*0-914678-17-5*) Inst Am Music.

Manion, Melanie. Retirement of Revolutionaries in China: Public Policies, Social Norms, Private Interests. LC 92-32031. (Illus.). 224p. (C). 1993. text 39.50 (*0-691-08653-2*, Pub. by Princeton U Pr) Cal Prin Full Svc.

Manion, Paul D. Scleroderris Canker in Conifers. (Forestry Sciences Ser.). 1984. text 147.50 (*90-247-2912-2*) Kluwer Academic.

— Tree Disease Concepts. 2nd rev. ed. (C). 1990. text 67.51 (*0-13-929423-6*, 510101) P-H.

Manion, Paul D. & Lachance, Denis, eds. Forest Decline Concepts. LC 92-73742. (Illus.). vi, 250p. 1992. pap. 44.00 (*0-89054-143-4*) Am Phytopathol Soc.

Manion, Ron. American Military Collectibles Price Guide. LC 94-79665. (Illus.). 288p. 1995. pap. 16.95 (*0-930625-47-1*) Krause Pubns.

— American Military Collectibles Price Guide: Collector Items of Historical Interest from the United States of America. Johansson, Eric J., ed. (Illus.). 288p. 1998. reprint ed. pap. text 17.00 (*0-7881-5143-6*) DIANE Pub.

— German Military Collectibles Price Guide. LC 94-73111. (Illus.). 316p. 1995. pap. 16.95 (*0-930625-44-7*) Krause Pubns.

— Japanese & Other Foreign Military Collectibles Price Guide. LC 94-73110. (Illus.). 248p. 1996. pap. 16.95 (*0-930625-43-9*, Antique Trader) Krause Pubns.

Maniosainis, Jeannie, ed. see Jackson, John C.

Maniotes, John, jt. auth. see Quasney, James S.

Maniquis, Robert M. & Donato, Clorinda, eds. The Encyclopedie & the Age of Revolution. (Illus.). 232p. (C). 1992. 75.00 (*0-8161-0527-8*, G K Hall & Co) Mac Lib Ref.

Maniruzzaman, Talukder. Group Interests & Political Changes. 271p. 1982. 29.95 (*0-318-37236-3*) Asia Bk Corp.

— Group Interests & Political Changes: Studies of Pakistan & Bangladesh. 1982. 24.00 (*0-8364-0892-6*) S Asia.

— Military Withdrawal from Politics: A Comparative Study. LC 86-28741. (Wilson Center Series on International Security Studies). 272p. 1987. text 34.95 (*0-88730-147-9*, HarpBusn) HarpInfo.

***Manis, Andrew M.** A Fire You Can't Put Out: The Civil Rights Life of Birmingham's Reverend Fred Shuttlesworth LC 99-6033. (Religion & American Culture Ser.). 1999. 29.95 (*0-8173-0968-3*) U of Ala Pr.

Manis, Andrew M., jt. ed. see White, Marjorie L.

Manis, Laura G. Assertion Training Workshop. LC 83-83316. 32p. 1998. pap., student ed. 7.45 (*1-55691-144-0*, 440) Learning Pubns.

— Assertion Training Workshop: Leader Guide. 2nd ed. LC 83-83316. 144p. 1998. pap., teacher ed. 21.50 (*1-55691-140-8*, 408) Learning Pubns.

— Womanpower: A Manual for Workshops in Personal Effectiveness. LC 76-54156. 1977. pap. text 6.75 (*0-910328-10-2*) Sulzburger & Graham Pub.

***Manis, Robert.** The Marriage & Family Workbook: An Interactive Reader. 208p. 2000. wbk. ed. 20.00 (*0-205-30931-3*) Allyn.

Manis, Rod. UNIX Relational Database Management: Application Development in the UNIX Environment. (C). 1988. pap. text 75.00 (*0-13-938622-X*) P-H.

Manis, Rod, et al. Relational Database Management in the UNIX Environment. (Illus.). 576p. (C). 1988. pap. text 28.00 (*0-13-771833-0*) P-H.

Manis, Vincent C. & Little, James J. The Schematics of Computation. LC 94-21432. 608p. 1995. 64.00 (*0-13-834284-9*) P-H.

Manis, Vincent C., jt. auth. see Little.

Maniscalco, E. F., tr. see Lemche, Niels P.

Maniscalco, Joe. Old Barn: Springtime. 32p. (J). (gr. 2-4). 1988. pap. 3.99 (*0-8280-0423-4*) Review & Herald.

Maniscalco, Ruth A. The Root of All Good - Essene Reflections: The Link of Basic Health, Religion, Spirituality in Ancient, Traditional & Modern Beliefs. LC 97-60776. 168p. (Orig.). 1997. pap. 19.95 (*0-9658581-9-7*) Essene Found.

Maniscalco, Steve, jt. auth. see Korwin, Alan.

***Manistre, Hugh.** Beginners Guide to Crop Circles. (Guides for Beginners Ser.). (Illus.). 96p. 1999. mass mkt. 11.95 (*0-340-74753-6*, Pub. by Headway) Trafalgar.

***Manitara, Olivier.** The Essenes: From Jesus to Our Time. 80p. 1998. pap. 8.95 (*1-894341-00-7*) Telesma-Evida.

— Peace: New Method, New Light.Tr. of Paix - Nouvelle Methode, Nouvelle Lumiere. (Illus.). 232p. (Orig.). 1999. pap. 0.00 (*1-894341-01-5*) Telesma-Evida.

— The Rose & Cross: A Rosicrucian Insight into Contemporary Inner Development. 234p. 1999. pap. 15.95 (*1-894341-02-3*) Telesma-Evida.

Manitius, ed. Gemini: Elementa Astronomiae. (GER & GRE.). 1974. reprint ed. 49.50 (*3-519-01386-X*, T1386, Pub. by B G Teubner) U of Mich Pr.

— Procli Diadochi. (GER & GRE.). 1974. reprint ed. 53.50 (*3-519-01732-6*, T1732, Pub. by B G Teubner) U of Mich Pr.

Manitonquat (Medicine Story). Return to Creation: A Survival Manual for Native & Natural People. (Illus.). 188p. (Orig.). (YA). (gr. 7 up). 1991. pap. 9.95 (*0-943404-20-7*) Bear Tribe.

***Manitz, Herbert.** Bibliography of the Flora of Cuba: A Survey of Systematic & Phytogeographical Literature Concerning the Vascular Plants in Cuba & the Caribbean Region. 1008p. 1999. 297.00 (*3-904144-13-8*, Pub. by Gantner) Lubrecht & Cramer.

Manitz, Hermann, et al, eds. Flora de la Republica de Cuba: Araceae, Aristolochiaceae, Bombacaceae, Droseraceae, Linaceae. (Plantas Vasculares Ser.: Seris A). (SPA., Illus.). 150p. 1998. pap. text 45.00 (*3-87429-407-2*, Pub. by Koeltz Sci Bks) Lubrecht & Cramer.

Manivannan, Gurusamy, jt. ed. see Lessard, Roger A.

Manivannan, Gurusamy, jt. ed. see Sawan, Samuel P.

Manjarres, J. M., ed. see Menendez Pidal, Ramon.

***Manji, Husseini K., et al.** Bipolar Medications: Mechanisms of Action. LC 99-26052. 2000. 58.50 (*0-88048-927-8*) Am Psychiatric.

Manjikian, Hagon, et al. Houshamatian of Arf-Dashnaktsutium Album - Atlas, Vol. I: Diutsaznamart. 1992. 45.00 (*0-9635278-0-0*) ARF Central.

Manjon, Maite, jt. auth. see Read, Jan.

Manjounes, George. Good Morning, Morning Glory: When the Flower of Your Life Dies. 200p. 1996. 20.00 (*1-879384-30-2*) Cypress Hse.

Manju, jt. auth. see Pandeya, Ram C.

Manjusri, jt. auth. see Sadhvi, Jaina.

***Mank, Gregory.** The Invisible Man Vol. 3: Original Shooting Script (1932) Conforti, John, ed. (Universal Filmscript Ser.: Vol. 3). (Illus.). 2000. pap. 19.95 (*1-882127-18-8*) Magicimage Filmbooks.

Mank, Gregory W. Hollywood Cauldron: Thirteen Horror Films from the Genre's Golden Age. LC 92-56663. (Illus.). 428p. 1994. lib. bdg. 42.50 (*0-89950-865-0*) McFarland & Co.

— The Hollywood Hissables. LC 88-28163. (Illus.). 530p. 1989. 55.00 (*0-8108-2134-6*) Scarecrow.

— Karloff & Lugosi: The Story of a Haunting Collaboration, with a Complete Filmography of Their Films Together. LC 90-42734. (Illus.). 384p. 1990. lib. bdg. 42.50 (*0-89950-437-X*) McFarland & Co.

— Mummys Curse: Universal Filmscripts Classic Horror Films, Vol. 11. 2000. pap. 19.95 (*1-882127-35-8*) Magicimage Filmbooks.

***Mank, Gregory W.** Women in Horror Films, 2 vols. Set. Incl. Vol. 1. Women in Horror Films: 1930s. LC 98-17188. (Illus.). 415p. 1999. boxed set 45.00 (*0-7864-0553-8*); Vol. 2. Women in Horror Films: 1940s. LC 98-21544. (Illus.). 405p. 1999. boxed set 45.00 (*0-7864-0464-7*); (Illus.). 820p. 1999. Set boxed set 75.00 (*0-7864-0580-5*) McFarland & Co.

Mank, Gregory W., jt. auth. see Riley, Philip J.

Manka, R., jt. auth. see Zralek, M.

Manka, R., jt. ed. see Zralek, M.

Mankad, Mohammad. Zankhana (Gujerati) large type ed. (Charnwood Large Print Ser.). 1990. 27.99 (*0-7089-2268-6*, Charnwood) Ulverscroft.

Mankad, N. R. Citrus in India. 1994. write for info. (*81-7236-096-7*, Pub. by Wiley Estrn) Franklin.

Mankad, Vipul N. & Moore, Blaine R., eds. Sickle Cell Disease: Pathophysiology, Diagnosis, & Management. LC 91-32168. 432p. 1992. 89.50 (*0-275-92503-X*, C2503, Praeger Pubs) Greenwood.

***Mankamo, T.** Action Requirements for AFW System Failures: Analysis for Four Nuclear Power Plants. 179p. 1998. per. 15.00 (*0-16-062940-3*) USGPO.

Mankbadi, Reda R. Transition, Turbulence & Noise, 287. LC 94-21221. (International Engineering & Computer Science, VLSI, Computer Architecture, & Digital Screen Processing Ser.). 400p. (C). 1994. text 176.50 (*0-7923-9481-X*) Kluwer Academic.

M

Mankbadi, Reda R., et al, eds. Computational Aero- & Hydro-Acoustics 1993. LC 93-71634. (FED Ser.: Vol. 147). 131p. 1993. pap. 35.00 (*0-7918-0955-2*, H00787) ASME.

— Computational Aeroacoustics. LC 95-79138. (1995 ASME/JSME Fluids Engineering Conference Ser.: FED-Vol. 219). 120p. 1995. 76.00 (*0-7918-1474-2*, G00969) ASME.

Manke. Diversity in Democracy. 322p. 1998. pap. text 34.44 (*0-536-01516-3*) Pearson Custom.

***Manke, Elisabeth.** Cactus: The Most Beautiful Species & Their Care. LC 99-47359. (Illus.). 160p. 2000. 14.95 (*0-7641-1226-0*) Barron.

Manke, Mary P. Classroom Power Relations: Understanding Student-Teacher Interaction. LC 97-12619. 192p. 1997. pap. text 22.00 (*0-8058-2496-0*) L Erlbaum Assocs.

Mankekar, D. R. One Way Free Flow. 171p. 1978. 11.95 (*0-318-37286-X*) Asia Bk Corp.

— The Press vs. the Government. 187p. 1978. 14.95 (*0-318-37288-6*) Asia Bk Corp.

— Sheer Anecdotages Leaves from a Reporter's Diary. 1984. 12.50 (*0-8364-1167-6*, Pub. by Allied Pubs) S Asia.

***Mankekar, Purnima.** Screening Culture, Viewing Politics: An Ethnography of Television, Womanhood, & Nation in Post-Colonial India. LC 99-21159. (Illus.). 432p. 1999. 59.95 (*0-8223-2357-5*) Duke.

Mankekar, Purnima. Screening Culture, Viewing Politics: An Ethnography of Television, Womanhood & Nation Postcolonial India. LC 99-21159. (Illus.). 432p. 1999. pap. 19.95 (*0-8223-2390-7*) Duke.

Mankell, Henning. Faceless Killers. Murray, Steven T., tr. from SWE. LC 96-26260. 1997. 23.00 (*1-56584-341-X*, Pub. by New Press NY) Norton.

***Mankell, Henning.** Faceless Killers: A Kurt Wallander Mystery. 2000. pap. 14.95 (*1-56584-605-2*, Pub. by New Press NY) Norton.

— The Fifth Woman: A Kurt Wallander Mystery. 2000. 24.95 (*1-56584-547-1*, Pub. by New Press NY) Norton.

Mankell, Henning. Nelio. Nunnally, Tiina, tr. from SWE. Orig. Title: Comedia Infantil. 272p. 1999. pap. 14.00 (*0-940242-72-9*) Fjord Pr.

— Pig Tales: A Novel of Lust & Transformation. Thompson, Laurie, tr. from SWE. 1998. pap. 10.95 (*1-56584-442-4*, Pub. by New Press NY) Norton.

— Sidetracked. Murray, Steven T., tr. from SWE. LC 98-43980. 352p. 1999. 25.00 (*1-56584-507-2*, Pub. by New Press NY) Norton.

***Mankell, Henning.** Sidetracked: A Kurt Wallander Mystery. 2000. pap. 14.95 (*1-56584-611-7*, Pub. by New Press NY) Norton.

Mankell, Henning. The White Lioness (Den Vita Lejoninnan) Thompson, Laurie, tr. from SWE. LC 97-49699. (Kurt Wallander Ser.: Vol. II). 432p. 1998. 25.00 (*1-56584-424-6*, Pub. by New Press NY) Norton.

Manker, Dayton A. Invasion from Heaven. pap. 5.99 (*0-88019-073-6*) Schmul Pub Co.

Mankey Calasibetta, Charlotte. Fairchild's Dictionary of Fashion. 2nd rev. ed. Tortora, Phyllis G., ed. LC 88-80198. (Illus.). 749p. 1998. pap. 45.00 (*1-56367-169-7*) Fairchild.

Mankiewicz, Rene H. The Liability Regime of the International Air Carrier. 288p. 1981. 104.00 (*90-268-1170-5*) Kluwer Law Intl.

Mankiller, Wilma, et al, eds. The Reader's Companion to U. S. Women's History. LC 97-39923. (Illus.). 696p. (YA). (gr. 7 up). 1998. 45.00 (*0-395-67173-6*) HM.

***Mankiller, Wilma, et al, eds.** The Reader's Companion to U. S. Women's History. (Illus.). 720p. 1999. pap. 20.00 (*0-618-00182-4*) HM.

Mankiller, Wilma P., jt. auth. see Wallis, Michael.

Mankin, Allison, ed. see Bradner, Scott O.

Mankin, David. Epodes. (Cambridge Greek & Latin Classics Ser.). 329p. (C). 1995. pap. text 24.95 (*0-521-39774-X*) Cambridge U Pr.

Mankin, David, ed. see Horace.

Mankin, Don, et al. Teams & Technology: Fulfilling the Promise of the New Organization. LC 95-35767. 320p. (C). 1996. 29.95 (*0-87584-399-9*) Harvard Busn.

Mankin, Donald A. Toward a Post-Industrial Psychology: Emerging Perspectives on Technology, Work, Education, & Leisure. LC 78-5302. 227p. reprint ed. pap. 70.40 (*0-608-13354-X*, 205577300037) Bks Demand.

Mankin, Ian. Natural Fabrics: Simple & Stylish Soft Furnishings. (Illus.). 128p. 1998. 27.50 (*0-09-182020-0*, Pub. by Ebury Pr) Trafalgar.

***Mankin, Ian & Moore.** Natural Fabrics: Simple & Stylish Soft Furnishings. (Illus.). 128p. 1999. reprint ed. pap. 22.95 (*0-09-186891-2*, Pub. by Ebury Pr) Trafalgar.

Mankin, Paul A. Precious Irony: The Theatre of Jean Giraudoux. LC 78-165146. (Studies in French Literature: No. 19). 195p. (Orig.). 1971. pap. text 40.00 (*90-279-1918-6*) Mouton.

Mankiw. Macroeconomics. 4th ed. LC 99-22254. 1999. text. write for info. (*1-57259-644-9*) Worth.

***Mankiw.** Macroeconomics. 4th ed. 1999. pap. text, student ed. 22.95 (*1-57259-645-7*) Worth.

Mankiw. Principles of Economics. (C). 1998. pap. text 157.50 (*0-03-024777-2*, Pub. by Harcourt Coll Pubs) Harcourt.

***Mankiw.** Principles of Macro Brief. 2nd ed. (C). 2000. pap. text. write for info. (*0-03-028336-1*, Pub. by Harcourt Coll Pubs) Harcourt.

Mankiw. Principles of Macroeconomics. 1997. pap. text 82.00 (*0-03-025233-4*) Harcourt.

— Principles of Macroeconomics. (C). 1997. pap. text. write for info. (*0-03-024779-9*) Harcourt Coll Pubs.

— Principles of Macroeconomics - Beta Version. (C). 1997. pap. text 14.00 (*0-03-020643-X*) Harcourt Coll Pubs.

— Principles of Micro & Macroeconomics. (C). 1997. text 132.50 (*0-03-024288-6*) Harcourt.

— Principles of Microeconomics. (C). 1997. pap. text. write for info. (*0-03-024778-0*) Harcourt Coll Pubs.

Mankiw & Scarth. Macroeconomics. 2nd ed. 1994. text 68.95 (*1-57259-001-7*) Worth.

Mankiw, Dorothy. Lesson Plans for the Van Dean Manual. Rubenstein, Israel, ed. 1977. ring bd., vinyl bd. 51.00 (*0-87350-074-1*) Milady Pub.

Mankiw, Gregory. Monetary Policy, Vol. 29. (NBER Studies in Business Cycle). 1997. pap. text 18.00 (*0-226-50309-7*) U Ch Pr.

— Principles of Economics. LC 96-71397. 688p. (C). 1997. text 85.00 (*0-03-098238-3*, Pub. by Harcourt Coll Pubs) Harcourt.

Mankiw, N. Gregory. Introduction to Economics. (C). 1997. pap. text, teacher ed. 23.75 (*0-03-020178-0*) Harcourt Coll Pubs.

— Introduction to Economics. 656p. (C). 1997. pap. text, student ed. 26.50 (*0-03-020192-6*, Pub. by Harcourt Coll Pubs) Harcourt.

— Introduction to Macroeconomics. 456p. (C). 1997. pap. text, student ed. 24.00 (*0-03-020193-4*, Pub. by Harcourt Coll Pubs) Harcourt.

— Introduction to Macroeconomics. (C). 1998. pap. text 110.50 (*0-03-020184-5*, Pub. by Harcourt Coll Pubs) Harcourt.

— Introduction to Microeconomics. (C). 1997. pap. text, teacher ed. 23.75 (*0-03-020177-2*) Harcourt Coll Pubs.

— Introduction to Microeconomics. 384p. (C). 1997. pap. text, student ed. 24.00 (*0-03-020194-2*, Pub. by Harcourt Coll Pubs) Harcourt.

— Introduction to Microeconomics. (C). 1998. pap. text 110.50 (*0-03-020183-7*, Pub. by Harcourt Coll Pubs) Harcourt.

— Macroeconomics. (C). 1997. pap. text, teacher ed. 23.75 (*0-03-020189-6*) Harcourt Coll Pubs.

— Macroeconomics. 3rd ed. LC 96-60597. 532p. 1996. text 51.80 (*1-57259-141-2*) Worth.

— Macroeconomics. 3rd ed. 339p. 1996. pap. text, student ed. 13.20 (*1-57259-233-8*) Worth.

— Macroeconomics: Casebook. 514p. (C). 1991. text 54.95 (*0-87901-502-0*) Worth.

— Macroeconomics: Casebook. 514p. (C). 1991. pap., student ed. 10.95 (*0-87901-503-9*) Worth.

— Macroeconomics: Casebook. 121p. (C). 1992. pap. text 8.95 (*0-87901-597-7*) Worth.

— Principles of Macroeconomics. (C). 1997. pap. text 60.50 (*0-03-024501-X*, Pub. by Harcourt Coll Pubs) Harcourt.

— Principles of Microeconomics. 528p. (C). 1997. pap. text 73.00 (*0-03-024502-8*) Dryden Pr.

Mankiw, N. Gregory, ed. Monetary Policy. (Illus.). 356p. 1996. lib. bdg. 50.00 (*0-226-50308-9*) U Ch Pr.

Mankiw, N. Gregory & Romer, David, eds. New Keynesian Economics Vol. 1: Imperfect Competition & Sticky Prices. (Illus.). 444p. 1991. pap. text 25.00 (*0-262-63133-4*) MIT Pr.

— New Keynesian Economics Vol. 2: Coordination Failures & Real Rigidities. (Illus.). 340p. 1991. pap. text 25.00 (*0-262-63134-2*) MIT Pr.

Mankiw, N. Gregory & Weil, David. Macroeconomics, Macrobytes Software 3.0 Windows. 3rd ed. 1996. disk 14.80 (*1-57259-309-1*) Worth.

Manko. Solders & Soldering. 2nd ed. 1998. pap. 65.00 (*0-07-134687-2*) McGraw.

— Solders & Soldering. 4th ed. 2000. 75.00 (*0-07-134417-9*) McGraw.

Manko, David J. A General Model of Legged Locomotion on Natural Terrain. LC 92-13547. (International Series in Engineering & Computer Science, VLSI, Computer Architecture, & Digital Screen Processing). 128p. (C). 1992. text 109.00 (*0-7923-9247-7*) Kluwer Academic.

Manko, Howard M. Soldering Handbook for Printed Circuits & Surface Mounting. 1986. text 74.95 (*0-442-26423-2*, VNR) Wiley.

Man'ko, V. I. & Markov, M. A., eds. Research in Quantum Field Theory: Proceedings of the Lebedev Physics Institute, Vol. 214. 217p. (C). 1995. lib. bdg. 165.00 (*1-56072-221-5*) Nova Sci Pubs.

— Theory of Interaction of Multilevel Systems with Quantized Fields. (Proceedings of P. N. Lebedev Physics Institute Ser.: Vol. 209). 237p. (C). 1996. lib. bdg. 165.00 (*1-56072-297-5*) Nova Sci Pubs.

Man'ko, V. I., jt. ed. see Dodonov, V. V.

Mankodi, K. Queen's Stepwell at Patan. (C). 1992. 120.00 (*81-900184-0-X*, Pub. by Franco-Indian) S Asia.

Mankoff, Al. Sacramento's Shining Rails: A History of Trolley Transportation in California's Capital. Date not set. pap. 19.95 (*0-912113-44-8*) Railhead Pubns.

***Mankoff, Bob, ed.** The New Yorker Book of Literary Cartoons. 112p. 2000. 19.95 (*0-671-03557-6*) PB.

***Mankoff, Bob, ed.** New Yorker 75th Anniversary Cartoon Collection. rev. ed. (Illus.). 304p. 1999. 40.00 (*0-671-03555-X*, PB Hardcover) PB.

Mankoff, Curt. Complete In-Home Investing Seminar. (Illus.). 1998. 59.95 (*0-9655827-0-1*) Mankoff Intl.

***Mankoff, Robert.** New Yorker: Book of Political Cartoons. (Illus.). 128p. 2000. 21.95 (*1-57660-080-7*) Bloomberg NJ.

— The New Yorker Book of Technology Cartoons. LC 00-30390. (Illus.). 2000. 24.95 (*1-57660-075-0*, Pub. by Bloomberg NJ) Norton.

Mankoff, Robert, ed. The New Yorker Book of Business Cartoons from the New Yorker. (Illus.). pap. 12.00 (*1-57660-042-4*, Pub. by Bloomberg NJ) Norton.

Mankoff, Robert, ed. The New Yorker Book of Business Cartoons from the New Yorker. LC 98-33461. (Illus.). 128p. 1998. 21.95 (*1-57660-056-4*, Pub. by Bloomberg NJ) Norton.

***Mankoff, Robert, ed.** The New Yorker Book of Money Cartoons. LC 99-36941. (Illus.). 128p. 1999. text 21.95 (*1-57660-033-5*, Pub. by Bloomberg NJ) Norton.

Mankowitz, Ann. Change of Life. 128p. 1995. pap. 16.00 (*0-919123-15-5*, Pub. by Inner City Bks) BookWorld.

***Mankowski, Paul V.** Akkadian Loanwords in Biblical Hebrew. LC 00-26490. (Harvard Semitic Studies). 2000. write for info. (*1-57506-900-8*) Eisenbrauns.

Manktelo, James. Mind Tools: Powerful Techniques For Improving Your Creativity & Think Skills. 1999. pap. 17.95 (*0-7494-2537-7*) Kogan Page Ltd.

***Manktelow, K. I.** Reasoning & Thinking. 272p. 1999. 49.95 (*0-86377-708-2*, Pub. by Psychol Pr) Taylor & Francis.

Manktelow, R. T. Microvascular Reconstruction. (Illus.). 245p. 1986. 427.00 (*0-387-15271-7*) Spr-Verlag.

***Manktelow, R. T.** Reasoning & Thinking. (Cognitive Psychology Ser.). 272p. 1999. pap. 24.95 (*0-86377-709-0*) L Erlbaum Assocs.

Manktelow, Roger. Routes to Hospital: A Sociological Analysis of the Paths to Psychiatric Hospitalization. LC 94-9576. 1994. 61.95 (*1-85628-492-1*, Pub. by Avebry) Ashgate Pub Co.

Manktelow, Roger, jt. ed. see Campbell, Jim.

Manley. Basketball Heaven 1989. pap. text 12.95 (*0-944877-01-X*) Facts Publishing Co.

Manley. Horizons Instructor's Resource Manual, Vol. 1. (College Spanish Ser.). (C). 1998. pap., teacher ed. 15.00 (*0-8384-8019-5*) Heinle & Heinle.

— Poverty & Nations. 122p. (C). 44.95 (*0-7453-0314-5*, Pub. by Pluto GBR); pap. 14.95 (*0-7453-0449-4*, Pub. by Pluto GBR) Stylus Pub VA.

Manley & Smith. Horizons-Workbook. (College French Ser.). (C). 1998. text, lab manual ed. 30.25 (*0-8384-7947-2*) Heinle & Heinle.

Manley, Albert E. A Legacy Continues: The Manley Years at Spelman College, 1953-1976. (Illus.). 246p. (C). 1995. lib. bdg. 39.00 (*0-8191-9880-3*) U Pr of Amer.

Manley, Anita & O'Neill, Cecily. Dreamseekers: Creative Approaches to the African American Heritage. LC 97-30128. 1997. pap. text 24.50 (*0-435-07045-2*) Heinemann.

Manley, Atwood. Rushton & His Times in American Canoeing. (Illus.). 224p. 1968. pap. 17.95 (*0-8156-0141-7*) Syracuse U Pr.

Manley, Audrey F. Physical Activity & Health: A Report of the Surgeon General. (Illus.). 278p. (Orig.). (C). 1996. pap. text 40.00 (*0-7881-3496-5*) DIANE Pub.

Manley, Beatrice. My Breath in Art: Acting from Within. LC 97-19329. 320p. 1998. pap. text 16.95 (*1-55783-281-1*) Applause Theatre Bk Pubs.

Manley, Belinda. Through Streets Broad & Narrow: A Woman Pacifist's 17-Year Sojourn in the Bruderhof Communities. Huntington, Gertrude E., ed. LC 96-83706. (Women from Utopia Ser.). (Illus.). 270p. (Orig.). 1996. pap. 17.00 (*1-882260-05-8*) Carrier Pigeon.

Manley, Bill. Penguin Historical Atlas of Ancient Egypt. 1997. pap. 16.95 (*0-14-051331-0*) Viking Penguin.

Manley, Bob N. The World War I Letters of Private Milford Manley. McKee, Elaine M., ed. LC 95-83258. (Illus.). 144p. (Orig.). 1995. pap. 14.95 (*1-886225-06-0*) Dageforde Pub.

Manley, Brent, jt. auth. see Hamman, Bob.

Manley-Casimir, Michael E. & Luke, Carmen, eds. Children & Television: A Challenge for Education. LC 87-2469. 334p. 1987. 65.00 (*0-275-92355-X*, C2355, Praeger Pubs) Greenwood.

Manley-Casimir, Michael E., jt. ed. see Cochrane, Donald B.

Manley, Charles H., jt. ed. see Ho, Chi-Tang.

***Manley, Claudia.** Everything You Need to Know about Custody. LC 00-9966. 2000. write for info. (*0-8239-3328-8*) Rosen Group.

***Manley, D. J. R.** Technology of Biscuits, Crackers & Cookies. 3rd ed. LC 00-31247. (Illus.). 2000. write for info. (*0-8493-0895-X*) CRC Pr.

Manley, David, ed. see Reilly, Hugh J. & Hyland, Terry L.

Manley, David E. A Root of Jesse. LC 93-26072. (Illus.). 288p. (Orig.). 1997. pap. 14.95 (*0-89407-090-8*) Strawberry Hill.

Manley, Dean V., ed. see Ashcam, Roger & Ford, Horace.

***Manley, Delarivier.** The Adventures of Rivella. Zelinsky, Katherine, ed. (Literary Texts Ser.). 1999. text 24.95 (*1-55111-316-3*) Broadview.

— The Adventures of Rivella. Zelinsky, Katherine, ed. (Literary Texts Ser.). 280p. 1999. pap. 12.95 (*1-55111-121-7*) Broadview Pr.

Manley, Delarivier. The New Atalantis. Ballaster, Rosalind, ed. (Women's Classics Ser.). 600p. (C). 1992. text 55.00 (*0-8147-5478-3*) NYU Pr.

Manley, Delariviere. Lucius, the First Christian King of Britain: A Tragedy. LC 92-24018. (Augustan Reprints Ser.: Nos. 253-254). 1989. reprint ed. 21.50 (*0-404-70253-8*) AMS Pr.

Manley, Duncan, Jr. Baking & Cooling of Biscuits. (Biscuit, Cookie & Cracker Manufacturing Training Manuals Ser.). 96p. 1998. pap. 54.00 (*1-85573-295-5*, Pub. by Woodhead Pubng) Am Educ Systs.

— Biscuit Dough Piece Forming. (Biscuit, Cookie & Cracker Manufacturing Training Manuals Ser.). 96p. 1998. pap. 54.00 (*1-85573-294-7*, Pub. by Woodhead Pubng) Am Educ Systs.

— Biscuit Doughs. (Biscuit, Cookie & Cracker Manufacturing Training Manuals Ser.). 80p. 1998. pap. 54.00 (*1-85573-293-9*, Pub. by Woodhead Pubng) Am Educ Systs.

— Biscuit Packaging & Storage. (Biscuit, Cookie & Cracker Manufacturing Training Manuals Ser.). 80p. 1998. pap. 54.00 (*1-85573-297-1*, Pub. by Woodhead Pubng) Am Educ Systs.

— Ingredients: Most Important Ingredients Used to Make Biscuits. (Biscuit, Cookie & Cracker Manufacturing Training Manuals Ser.). 96p. 1998. pap. 54.00 (*1-85573-292-0*, Pub. by Woodhead Pubng) Am Educ Systs.

— Secondary Processing in Biscuit Manufacturing. (Biscuit, Cookie & Cracker Manufacturing Training Manuals Ser.). 96p. 1998. pap. 54.00 (*1-85573-296-3*, Pub. by Woodhead Pubng) Am Educ Systs.

***Manley, Duncan.** Technology of Biscuits, Cookies & Crackers. 600p. 2000. 243.00 (*1-85573-532-6*, Pub. by Woodhead Pubng) Am Educ Systs.

Manley, Duncan. Technology of Biscuits, Crackers & Cookies. 2nd ed. 476p. 1996. text 229.95 (*1-85573-280-7*) Technomic.

— Technology of Biscuits, Crackers & Cookies. 2nd ed. 500p. 1991. pap. 170.50 (*0-442-31400-0*) Thomson Learn.

Manley, Francis, ed. see Pace, Richard.

Manley, Frank. Among Prisoners. LC 99-35307. 169p. 2000. pap. 14.95 (*1-56689-089-6*, Pub. by Coffee Hse) SPD-Small Pr Dist.

— The Cockfighter. LC 97-43198. 224p. 1998. 19.95 (*1-56689-073-X*) Coffee Hse.

— The Cockfighter. LC 98-48920. 208p. 1999. pap. 11.95 (*0-385-49420-3*) Doubleday.

— Two Masters: Prior Engagements. LC 87-24619. (Illus.). 176p. (Orig.). 1987. pap. 8.95 (*0-932419-14-3*) Cherokee.

Manley, Frank, ed. see Chapman, George.

Manley, Frank, ed. see More, Thomas.

Manley, Frank, ed. & intro. see More, Thomas.

Manley, G. A., et al. Advances in Hearing Research: Proceedings of the 10th International Symposium on Hearing. 580p. 1995. text 147.00 (*981-02-2260-2*) World Scientific Pub.

***Manley, Gary V.** Arise Jerusalem! 154p. 2000. pap. 10.97 (*0-9672519-1-5*, 1952) Omega House Pubg.

— Thread of Blue: Discerning Healing. 200p. 1999. pap. 10.97 (*0-9672519-0-7*, 1951) Omega House Pubg.

***Manley, Geoffrey A., ed.** Auditory Worlds: Sensory Analysis & Perception in Animals & Man Final Report. 376p. 2000. 120.00 (*3-527-27587-8*) Wiley.

Manley, Inza. Effects of the Germanic Invasions on Gaul, 234-284 A. D. LC 34-2822. (University of California Publications in Social Welfare: Vol. 17, No. 2). 124p. reprint ed. pap. 38.50 (*0-608-13921-1*, 202144900021) Bks Demand.

Manley, J., et al, eds. Proceedings of the Third European Conference on Mathematics in Industry. (C). 1990. text 226.50 (*0-7923-0807-7*) Kluwer Academic.

Manley, Jane E., ed. see Dailey, John F.

Manley, Joan B. She Flew No Flags. LC 94-27623. 272p. (J). (gr. 5-9). 1995. 16.00 (*0-395-71130-4*) HM.

Manley, Joan H., et al. Horizons. 2nd ed. LC 97-49590. (ENG & FRE.). (C). 1998. pap. 52.95 (*0-8384-7060-2*) Heinle & Heinle.

— Qu'Est-Ce Qu'On Dit? LC 93-43695. (ENG & FRE.). (C). 1994. mass mkt., student ed. 56.95 (*0-8384-4487-3*) Heinle & Heinle.

— Qu'Est-Ce Qu'On Dit? LC 93-43695. (ENG & FRE.). (C). 1994. text, wbk. ed. 19.95 (*0-8384-4489-X*) Heinle & Heinle.

Manley, Joan H., jt. auth. see Smith.

Manley, Johanna. The Lament of Eve. 160p. (Orig.). (C). 1993. pap. 6.68 (*0-9622536-2-6*) Monastery Bks.

Manley, Johanna, compiled by. The Bible & the Holy Fathers for Orthodox: Daily Scripture Readings & Commentary. LC 89-90759. (Illus.). 1136p. 1990. 45.00 (*0-9622536-0-X*) Monastery Bks.

— Grace for Grace: The Psalter & the Holy Fathers. LC 92-80344. (Illus.). 768p. 1992. 32.00 (*0-9622536-1-8*) Monastery Bks.

Manley, Johanna, ed. Isaiah Through the Ages. LC 95-3251. 1094p. 1995. 40.00 (*0-9622536-3-4*) Monastery Bks.

— Wisdom, Let Us Attend: Job, the Fathers & the Old Testament. LC 97-22532. 920p. 1997. 34.00 (*0-9622536-4-2*) Monastery Bks.

Manley, Johanna, tr. see Velimirovich, Nikolai.

Manley, John F. & Dolbeare, Kenneth M., eds. The Case Against the Constitution: From the Antifederalists to the Present. LC 87-4640. 216p. (gr. 13). 1987. pap. text 35.95 (*0-87332-433-1*) M E Sharpe.

Manley, K. & Bellman, L., eds. Surgical Nursing. (Illus.). 544p. 1998. pap. write for info. (*0-443-05421-5*) Church.

Manley, Lawrence. Convention, Fifteen Hundred to Seventeen Fifty. LC 79-27773. 365p. 1980. 43.50 (*0-674-17015-6*) HUP.

— Literature & Culture in Early Modern London. LC 93-51069. (Illus.). 619p. (C). 1995. text 80.00 (*0-521-46161-8*) Cambridge U Pr.

— London in the Age of Shakespeare. LC 86-20476. 372p. 1986. 35.00 (*0-271-00445-2*) Pa St U Pr.

Manley, Lawrence. London in the Age of Shakespeare: An Anthology LC 88-672399. 372p. 1986. write for info. (*0-7099-3560-9*, Pub. by C Helm) Routldge.

Manley, Marc W., jt. auth. see Glynn, Thomas J.

Manley, Mary. Memoirs of the Life of Mrs. Manley, Author of the Atalantis. 3rd ed. LC 71-37701. reprint ed. 29.00 (*0-404-56765-7*) AMS Pr.

Manley, Mary D. Novels, 1705 to 1714, 7 Vols. in Two, Set. LC 75-161934. 1816p. 1971. 200.00 (*0-8201-1094-9*) Schol Facsimiles.

Manley, Michael. The Case of the Bleeding Limo. LC 96-27930. (Clooz Calahan Mystery Ser.). (J). 1996. write for info. (*0-382-39689-8*); pap. write for info. (*0-382-39690-1*) Silver Burdett Pr.

— The Case of the Creepy Convertible. LC 96-27932. (Clooz Calahan Mystery Ser.). (J). 1996. write for info. (*0-382-39687-1*); pap. write for info. (*0-382-39688-X*) Silver Burdett Pr.

An Asterisk (*) at the beginning of an entry indicates that the title is appearing for the first time.

— The Case of the Missing Ghost. LC 95-33366. (J). 1996. pap. 4.95 (*0-382-39256-6*); lib. bdg. 12.95 (*0-382-39255-8*) Silver Burdett Pr.
— History of West Indies Cricket. rev. ed. (Illus.). 704p. 1996. pap. 34.95 (*0-233-98937-4*, Pub. by Andre Deutsch) Trafalgar.
— Jamaica: Struggle in the Periphery. (Illus.). 259p. 1982. 15.95 (*0-906495-97-0*); pap. 7.95 (*0-906495-98-9*) Writers & Readers.
— The Politics of Change: A Jamaican Testament. rev. ed. 1990. pap. 15.95 (*0-88258-029-9*) Howard U Pr.
— Up the down Escalator: Development & the Economy, a Jamaican Case Study. (Illus.). 320p. 1987. 27.50 (*0-88258-112-0*) Howard U Pr.
— A Voice At the Workplace: Reflections on Colonialism & the Jamaican Worker. 1991. pap. 16.95 (*0-88258-068-X*) Howard U Pr.

Manley, Michael T., jt. ed. see Geesink, Rudolph G.

Manley, Micheal. A Voice At the Workplace: Reflections on Colonialism & the Jamaican Worker. 1991. 29.95 (*0-88258-067-1*) Howard U Pr.

Manley, Mike, jt. auth. see Stradley, Randy.

Manley, Mychal-Jerome. The Emeritus Vol. 1: Who Will Rule. LC 97-90010. 334p. 1996. text 14.95 (*0-533-12269-4*) Vantage.
— Parlay. LC 96-90050. 221p. (Orig.). 1996. reprint ed. pap. text 12.95 (*0-533-11863-8*) Vantage.

Manley, Myrna. GED Math Problem Solver. 1992. pap. 11.93 (*0-8092-4050-5*) NTC Contemp Pub Co.

Manley, Myrna, ed. GED Math Problem Solving. 1992. pap., teacher ed. 8.95 (*0-8092-4049-1*) NTC Contemp Pub Co.

Manley, Norris C. First Love. 149p. (Orig.). 1993. pap. 10.00 (*1-880365-44-8*) Prof Pr NC.

Manley, Pamela J. Ortho's Complete Guide to Vegetables. Allen, Ben, ed. LC 96-67631. (Illus.). 320p. 1997. 29.95 (*0-89721-317-3*, Ortho Bks) Meredith Bks.
— Ortho's Complete Guide to Vegetables. LC 96-67631. (Illus.). 320p. 1993. pap. 24.95 (*0-89721-314-9*) Meredith Bks.

Manley, Patricia L., jt. ed. see Manley, Thomas O.

Manley, Robert. Notes on Nebraska. LC 91-66158. 80p. 1997. reprint ed. pap. 7.99 (*1-886225-24-9*, 500) Dageforde Pub.

Manley, Robert, adapted by. I Am Bound for California: The Overland Diary of Edgar Reynolds. 208p. 1991. pap. 10.00 (*1-886225-12-5*) Dageforde Pub.

Manley, Robert H. Guyana Emergent: The Post Independence Struggle for Nondependent Development. 180p. 1982. 18.95 (*0-87073-375-3*); pap. text 11.95 (*0-87073-349-4*) Schenkman Bks Inc.

Manley, Roger. Signs & Wonders: Outsider Art Inside North Carolina. LC 89-60598. (Illus.). 152p. 1989. pap. 19.95 (*0-88259-957-7*) NCMA.

Manley, Roger, et al, texts. The End Is Near! Visions of Apocalypse, Millennium & Utopia. LC 98-71882. (Illus.). 191p. 1998. 55.00 (*0-9664272-6-2*) Dilettante Pr.
— The End is Near! Visions of Apocalypse, Millennium & Utopia. LC 98-71882. (Illus.). 192p. 1998. pap. 49.95 (*0-9664272-7-0*) Dilettante Pr.

Manley, Roger, et al. Self-Made Worlds: Visionary Folk Art Environments. LC 97-70519. (Illus.). 128p. 1997. 60.00 (*0-89381-732-5*) Aperture.

Manley, Rosie, jt. auth. see Brackett, Karen.

Manley, Sally R. Mr. Crispy's Story of the First Candy Canes, Vol. 1. 2nd rev. ed. LC TXU775-417. (Illus.). 32p. (J). (gr. k-4). 1997. 16.95 (*0-9655303-0-2*) Sunny Lane.

Manley, Scott, ed. see Whiteneck, Gale G., et al.

Manley, Stephen. Feast at Your Fingertips: The Ultimate Catalog of Fabulous Foods by Mail. (Illus.). 192p. 1992. pap. 9.95 (*0-8065-1379-9*, Citadel Pr) Carol Pub Group.

***Manley, Thomas O. & Manley, Patricia L., eds.** Lake Champlain in Transition: From Research Toward Restoration. (Water Science & Application Ser.: Vol. 1). 451p. 1999. 50.00 (*0-87590-350-9*) Am Geophysical.

Manley-Tucker, Audrie. Champagne Girl. large type ed. (Dales Large Print Ser.). 372p. 1996. pap. 18.99 (*1-85389-693-4*, Dales) Ulverscroft.
— A Rainbow in My Hand. large type ed. (Dales Large Print Ser.). 350p. 1997. pap. 18.99 (*1-85389-691-8*) Ulverscroft.
— Two for Joy. large type ed. (Dales Large Print Ser.). 336p. 1998. pap. 19.99 (*1-85389-810-4*, Dales) Ulverscroft.

Manley, Walter, II. Handbook Good Business Practice. (Bus Press-Previous Routledge). 288p. (C). 1995. mass mkt. 49.95 (*0-415-06232-2*, B0183) Routledge.

Manley, Walter, II & Shrode, William A. Critical Issues in Business Conduct: Legal, Ethical, & Social Challenges for the 1990s. LC 90-30009. 336p. 1990. 59.95 (*0-89930-570-9*, MCZ/, Quorum Bks) Greenwood.

Manley, Walter W., II, et al, eds. The Supreme Court of Florida & Its Predecessor Courts, 1821-1917. LC 97-40291. 472p. 1998. 49.95 (*0-8130-1540-5*) U Press Fla.

Manley, Will. For Library Directors Only: Talking about Trustees & for Library Trustees Only, Living with Your Director. LC 92-50942. (Illus.). 236p. 1993. pap. 32.50 (*0-89950-826-X*) McFarland & Co.
— For Library Trustees Only: Living with Your Director. LC 92-50942. (Illus.), 122p. 1993. pap. 28.00 (*0-89950-827-8*) McFarland & Co.
— The Manley Art of Librarianship. LC 92-56664. (Illus.). 248p. 1993. lib. bdg. 32.50 (*0-89950-866-9*) McFarland & Co.
— The Truth about Catalogers. LC 95-14828. (Illus.). 142p. 1995. pap. 28.50 (*0-7864-0103-6*) McFarland & Co.
— The Truth about Reference Librarians. LC 96-1461. (Illus.). 164p. 1996. pap. 28.50 (*0-7864-0220-2*) McFarland & Co.
— Uncensored Thoughts: Pot Shots from a Public Librarian. LC 94-20155. (Illus.). 173p. 1994. lib. bdg. 30.00 (*0-89950-992-4*) McFarland & Co.
— Unintellectual Freedoms: Opinions of a Public Librarian. LC 90-53505. (Illus.). 174p. 1991. lib. bdg. 30.00 (*0-89950-575-9*) McFarland & Co.
— Unprofessional Behavior: Confessions of a Public Librarian. LC 91-40350. (Illus.). 208p. 1992. lib. bdg. 30.00 (*0-89950-690-9*) McFarland & Co.
— Unsolicited Advice: Observations of a Public Librarian. LC 92-50311. (Illus.). 208p. 1992. lib. bdg. 30.00 (*0-89950-745-X*) McFarland & Co.

***Manley, Yvonne.** You've Got a Friend: New Life after Breast Cancer. 184p. 2000. pap. 14.95 (*1-57826-056-6*, Pub. by Hatherleigh) Norton.

Manlove, Colin. An Anthology of Scottish Fantasy Literature. 256p. 1996. pap. 17.95 (*0-7486-6213-8*, Pub. by Polygon) Subterranean Co.

Manlove, Colin. Fantasy Literature of England. LC 98-46271. 220p. 1999. text 49.95 (*0-312-21987-3*) St Martin.

Manlove, Colin N. Christian Fantasy: From Twelve Hundred to the Present. LC 91-47494. (C). 1992. text 38.00 (*0-268-00790-X*) U of Notre Dame Pr.
— The Chronicles of Narnia: The Patterning of a Fantastic World. (Masterwork Studies). 160p. 1993. 29.00 (*0-8057-8800-X*); pap. 18.00 (*0-8057-8801-8*, Twayne) Mac Lib Ref.
— Critical Thinking: A Guide to Interpreting Literary Texts. LC 89-30824. 180p. 1989. text 35.00 (*0-312-03166-1*) St Martin.
— The Impulse of Fantasy Literature. LC 82-15335. 188p. reprint ed. pap. 58.30 (*0-7837-0570-0*, 204091400019) Bks Demand.
— Modern Fantasy: Five Studies. LC 74-31798. 316p. reprint ed. pap. 90.10 (*0-608-16456-9*, 2026346) Bks Demand.
— Science Fiction: Ten Explorations. LC 85-14738. 224p. 1986. 22.50 (*0-87338-326-5*) Kent St U Pr.

Manlove, Donald C., ed. see Riley, James Whitcomb.

Manlowe, Jennifer L. Faith Born of Seduction: Sexual Trauma, Body Image & Religion. 230p. (C). 1995. text 45.00 (*0-8147-5517-8*); pap. text 18.50 (*0-8147-5529-1*) NYU Pr.

Manlowe, Jennifer L., jt. ed. see Goldstein, Nancy.

Manly. American Decades, 1910-1919, Vol. 5. 2nd ed. 500p. 1996. 90.00 (*0-8103-5723-2*) Gale.
— American Decades, 1930-1939, Vol. 7. 4th ed. 500p. 1995. 90.00 (*0-8103-5725-9*) Gale.
— American Decades, 1920-1929, Vol. 6. 3rd ed. 500p. 1995. 90.00 (*0-8103-5724-0*) Gale.
— American Decades, 1900-1909, Vol. 4. Tompkins, Vincent, ed. 500p. 1996. 90.00 (*0-8103-5722-4*) Gale.

Manly, Basil, Jr. The Bible Doctrine of Inspiration, Vol. 1. George, Denise & George, Timothy F., eds. LC 95-35293. (Library of Baptist Classics). 288p. 1995. 14.99 (*0-8054-1251-4*, 4212-51) Broadman.

Manly, Basil, Sr. Southern Baptist Sermons on Sovereignty & Responsibility. 1992. 12.99 (*0-87377-935-5*) GAM Pubns.

Manly, Bryan. Randomization, Bootstrap & Monte Carlo Methods in Biology. 2nd rev. ed. (Texts in Statistical Science Ser.). 356p. (C). (gr. 13). 1997. 64.95 (*0-412-36710-6*, A5017) Chapman & Hall.

Manly, Bryan F. The Design & Analysis of Research Studies. (Illus.). 369p. (C). 1992. pap. text 39.95 (*0-521-42580-8*) Cambridge U Pr.

Manly, Bryan F., Jr. Multivariate Statistical Methods: A Primer. 2nd ed. 232p. 1994. per. 41.95 (*0-412-60300-4*, Chap & Hall CRC) CRC Pr.

Manly, Bryan F. Stage-Structured Populations: Sampling, Analysis & Simulation. (Population & Community Biology Ser.). (Illus.). 160p. 1990. 49.95 (*0-412-35060-2*, A4128) Chapman & Hall.
— The Statistics of Natural Selection. 500p. 1987. pap. text 37.50 (*0-412-30700-6*) Chapman & Hall.

Manly, Howard, jt. auth. see Turnbull, Walter.

Manly, Isaac. Slaying the Dragon Evolution. (Small Group Studies). 90p. 1999. pap. 5.99 (*0-89900-831-3*) College Pr Pub.

Manly, Isaac V. God Made: A Medical Doctor Looks at the Reality of Creation. LC 93-74576. 209p. 1994. pap. 9.99 (*0-89900-676-0*) College Pr Pub.

Manly, John M. Manly Anniversary Studies in Language & Literature. LC 68-22110. (Essay Index Reprint Ser.). 1977. reprint ed. 24.95 (*0-8369-0673-X*) Ayer.
— Specimens of Pre-Shakespearean Drama. (BCL1-PR English Literature Ser.). 1992. reprint ed. lib. bdg. 75.00 (*0-7812-7152-5*) Rprt Serv.
— Specimens of the Pre-Shakespearean Drama, 2 Vols, Set. LC 67-18432. 1997. 50.00 (*0-8196-0200-0*) Biblo.

Manly, John M. & Rickert, Edith. Contemporary American Literature. LC 74-4436. (American Literature Ser.: No. 49). 1974. lib. bdg. 75.00 (*0-8383-2048-1*) M S G Haskell Hse.
— Contemporary American Literature, Bibliographies & Study Outlines. (BCL1-PS American Literature Ser.). 378p. 1992. reprint ed. lib. bdg. 89.00 (*0-7812-6620-3*) Rprt Serv.
— Contemporary British Literature. LC 73-21795. (English Literature Ser.: No. 33). 1974. lib. bdg. 75.00 (*0-8383-1827-4*) M S G Haskell Hse.

Manly, Louise. Manly Family: Account of the Descendants of Captain Basil Manly of the Revolution, & Related Families. (Illus.). 351p. 1994. reprint ed. pap. 54.50 (*0-8328-4030-0*); reprint ed. lib. bdg. 64.50 (*0-8328-4029-7*) Higginson Bk Co.

Manly, Myrna. The Math Problem Solver: Reasoning Skills for Application. LC 92-38293. 1993. pap. 11.93 (*0-8092-3764-4*) NTC Contemp Pub Co.

Manly, Myrna, ed. The Math Problem Solver. 1993. pap., teacher ed. 8.95 (*0-8092-3763-6*) NTC Contemp Pub Co.

Manly, Peter L. The 20-cm Schmidt-Cassegrain Telescope: A Practical Observing Guide. (Illus.). 283p. 1999. pap. 18.95 (*0-521-64441-0*) Cambridge U Pr.

***Manly, Stanley.** Raiders of Low Forehead. 160p. 1999. pap. 10.95 (*1-84068-031-8*, Pub. by Creation Books) Last Gasp.

Manly, William L. Death Valley Crossing. Hunter, Paul, ed. (Illus.). 72p. 1998. pap. 18.00 (*1-890654-14-0*) Wood Work.
— Death Valley Crossing. limited ed. Hunter, Paul, ed. (Illus.). 72p. 1998. 40.00 (*1-890654-15-9*) Wood Work.
— Death Valley in '49. LC 77-2273. 1977. reprint ed. pap. 30.95 (*0-912494-23-9*) Commun Print.
— Death Valley in '49. 1992. reprint ed. lib. bdg. 75.00 (*0-7812-5063-3*) Rprt Serv.

Mann. Business Law & the Regulations of Business. 5th ed. (Swc-Business Law Ser.). 1996. pap., student ed. 21.50 (*0-314-06512-1*) West Pub.

***Mann.** Business Statistics. 1999. text, student ed. 65.00 (*0-471-37799-6*) Wiley.
— Funeral Sites. 1989. mass mkt. write for info. (*0-8125-0663-4*) Tor Bks.

Mann. Instructors Manual to Accompany Introductory Statistics. 520p. 1991. pap. text 37.50 (*0-471-55023-X*) Wiley.

Mann. Introductory Statistics. 3rd ed. 336p. 1997. pap. 34.95 (*0-471-19164-7*) Wiley.
— Introductory Statistics: Student Solutions Manual. 3rd ed. 264p. 1998. pap. text, student ed. 36.95 (*0-471-19158-2*) Wiley.

Mann. Madrigals Michelangelo Rossi. 1998. lib. bdg. 150.00 (*0-226-50338-0*) U Ch Pr.
— Meridians of Acupuncture. 174p. 1964. text 50.00 (*0-433-20303-X*) Buttrwrth-Heinemann.
— Practical Organic Chemistry. 1979. pap. 34.95 (*0-582-44407-1*, Pub. by Addison-Wesley) Longman.

***Mann.** Silent Trumpets. 2000. pap. 15.00 (*0-465-04370-4*, Pub. by Basic) HarpC.

Mann. Statistics: Selected Chapters. 3rd ed. (C). 1998. pap. text 42.00 (*0-471-32195-8*) Wiley.
— Der Tod in Venedig. (GER.). (C). 1954. 16.95 (*0-8442-2767-6*, X2767-6) NTC Contemp Pub Co.
— Tonio Kroger. (GER.). (C). 1988. 14.95 (*0-8442-2769-2*, X2769-2) NTC Contemp Pub Co.

***Mann.** Wulfsyarn: A Mosaic. 2000. 22.00 (*0-380-97211-5*) Morrow Avon.

Mann & Lazier, Audrey. Dynamics of Marine Ecosystems. (Illus.). 350p. 1991. pap. 59.95 (*0-86542-082-3*) Blackwell Sci.

***Mann & Roberts.** Business Law & the Regulation of Business. 7th ed. 2001. pap. 77.00 (*0-324-06196-X*) Sth-Wstn College.

Mann & Roberts. Smith & Robersons Business Law. 11th ed. LC 99-23199. (SWC-Business Law Ser.). 1999. pap. 18.50 (*0-324-00673-X*) Thomson Learn.

Mann, jt. auth. see Gell.

***Mann, Bill.** I Want My MP3: How to Download, Rip & Play Digital Music. (Illus.). 356p. 1999. pap. 19.99 (*0-07-212290-0*) McGraw.

Mann, Bill, jt. auth. see Mann, Patti.

Mann, Patti & Mann, Bill. Welcome Home! Aol's Guide for Families. LC 98-48710. 1998. write for info. (*1-891556-54-1*) Amer Online.

Mann, A. & Revzen, M., eds. The Dilemma of Einstein, Podolsky, & Rosen, 60 Years Later: Proceedings, International Symposium the Dilemma of Einstein, Podolsky, & Rosen, Haifa, 1995. (Annals of the Israel Physical Society Ser.: Vol. 12). 314p. 1996. 135.00 (*0-7503-0394-8*, QC174) IOP Pub.

Mann, A. T. Elements of Reincarnation. (Elements of...Ser.). 144p. (Orig.). 1997. pap. 9.95 (*1-86204-141-5*, Pub. by Element MA) Penguin Putnam.

***Mann, A. T.** Tarot: Intro Guide to Unlocking the Secrets of the Tarot. (New Perspectives Ser.). (Illus.). 2000. pap. 9.95 (*1-86204-673-5*, Pub. by Element MA) Penguin Putnam.

Mann, A. Tad. Elements of Tarot. (Elements of...Ser.). 1997. pap. 9.95 (*1-86204-041-9*, Pub. by Element MA) Penguin Putnam.
— Life Time Astrology: From Conception to Transcendance. 288p. 1991. pap. 15.95 (*1-85230-234-8*, Pub. by Element MA) Penguin Putnam.
— Millennium Prophecies. 1995. pap. 7.95 (*1-85230-685-8*, Pub. by Element MA) Penguin Putnam.
— Sacred Architecture. 1993. pap. 24.95 (*1-85230-391-3*, Pub. by Element MA) Penguin Putnam.
— Sacred Sexuality. (Sacred Arts). (Illus.). 192p. 1995. pap. 24.95 (*1-85230-658-0*, Pub. by Element MA) Penguin Putnam.

Mann, Abby. A Child Is Waiting. 18.95 (*0-89190-629-0*) Amereon Ltd.

Mann, Alan. The A-Z of Buddy Holly. (Illus.). 192p. (Orig.). 1996. pap. 12.95 (*1-85410-433-0*, Pub. by Aurum Pr) London Brdge.

Mann, Alan E. Human Biology & Behavior. 6th ed. Weiss, Mark L., ed. (C). 1998. text. write for info. (*0-321-01223-2*) Addson-Wesley Educ.

Mann, Alan E., jt. auth. see Weiss, Mark L.

Mann, Albert W. Civil War Militia, History of the 45th Regiment, M. V. M., "The Cadet Regiment" (Illus.). 562p. 1995. reprint ed. lib. bdg. 62.00 (*0-8328-4626-0*) Higginson Bk Co.

Mann, Alex von, see Von Mann, Alex.

Mann, Alfred. Bach & Handel: Choral Performance Practice. 124p. 1993. pap. 16.95 (*0-937276-15-4*, HMB184) Hinshaw Mus.
— The Great Composer As Teacher & Student: Theory & Practice of Composition. unabridged ed. LC 94-28795. (Illus.). 176p. 1994. pap. text 10.95 (*0-486-28316-X*) Dover.
— Handel's Orchestral Music: Orchestral Concertos, Organ Concertos, Water Music, & Music for the Royal Fireworks. (Monuments of Western Music Ser.). (Illus.). 1995. 36.00 (*0-02-871382-6*, Schirmer Books) Mac Lib Ref.
— Randall Thompson: A Choral Legacy. 1983. pap. 13.75 (*0-911318-12-7*) E C Schirmer.
— The Study of Fugue. 352p. 1987. reprint ed. pap. 10.95 (*0-486-25439-9*) Dover.
— The Study of Fugue. LC 81-4183. (Illus.). 341p. 1981. reprint ed. lib. bdg. 69.50 (*0-313-22623-7*, MASF, Greenwood Pr) Greenwood.

Mann, Alfred, pref. Modern Music Librarianship: Essays in Honor of Ruth Watanabe. LC 89-30559. (Festschrift Ser.: No. 8). (Illus.). 200p. 1989. lib. bdg. 54.00 (*0-918728-93-2*) Pendragon NY.

Mann, Alfred, ed. see Meek, Harold A.

***Mann, Alfred K.** For Better or for Worse: The Marriage of Science & Government in the United States. 2001. 27.50 (*0-231-11706-X*) Col U Pr.

Mann, Alfred K. Neutrino Interactions with Electrons & Protons. LC 93-23103. (Key Papers in Physics). 160p. 1993. text 54.95 (*1-56396-228-4*, AIP Pr) Spr-Verlag.
— Shadow of a Star: The Neutrino Story of Supernova 1987A. LC 96-29967. (Illus.). 192p. 1997. pap. text 22.95 (*0-7167-3097-9*) W H Freeman.

Mann, Alfred K. & Cline, David B., eds. Discovery of Weak Neutral Currents: The Weak Interaction Before & After. LC 94-70515. (AIP Conference Proceeding Ser.: Vol. 300). 676p. 1994. 145.00 (*1-56396-306-X*) Am Inst Physics.

Mann, Alice. The In-Between Church: Navigating Size Transitions in Congregations. 1998. pap. 11.25 (*1-56699-207-9*, AL197) Alban Inst.

Mann, Alicja, jt. auth. see Mills, Earl, Sr.

Mann, Alicja, ed. & des. see Ingham, Merton.

Mann, Alicja, ed. & des. see Mullen, Lisa.

Mann, Alison. The Politics of Breast Cancer Screening. (Developments in Nursing & Health Care Ser.: Vol. 8). 176p. 1996. 63.95 (*1-85972-323-3*, Pub. by Avebry) Ashgate Pub Co.

***Mann, Allen.** Infrared Optics & Zoom Lenses. LC 99-51577. (Tutorial Texts in Optical Engineering Ser.). 140p. 1999. pap. 44.00 (*0-8194-3510-4*) SPIE.

Mann, Allen, ed. Selected Papers on Zoom Lenses. LC 93-32573. (Milestone Ser.: Vol. MS 85). 1993. pap. 45.00 (*0-8194-1388-7*) SPIE.
— Selected Papers on Zoom Lenses. LC 93-32573. (Milestone Ser.: Vol. MS 85/HC). 1993. 55.00 (*0-8194-1389-5*) SPIE.

Mann, Anna A. The Wild Gold Beauty. 32p. (J). 1998. pap. 7.00 (*0-8059-4136-3*) Dorrance.

Mann, Anthony. Microsoft SQL Server 7 for Dummies. LC QA76.9.D3.M3374 1998. (For Dummies Ser.). 384p. 1998. pap. text 29.99 incl. cd-rom (*0-7645-0416-9*) IDG Bks.

Mann, Anthony T. Real World Programming with Visual Basic 4. 2nd ed. (Illus.). 1184p. 1995. 49.99 (*0-672-30779-0*) Sams.
— Visual Basic 5 Developer's Guide. LC 96-72078. 1032p. 1997. 49.99 (*0-672-31048-1*) Sams.

Mann, Arthur. LaGuardia Comes to Power, 1933. 1969. pap. text 1.95 (*0-226-50331-3*, P331) U Ch Pr.
— LaGuardia Comes to Power, 1933. LC 81-4124. (Illus.). 199p. 1981. reprint ed. lib. bdg. 55.00 (*0-313-22787-X*, MALC, Greenwood Pr) Greenwood.
— The One & the Many: Reflections on the American Identity. LC 78-27849. 1993. 12.95 (*0-226-50337-2*) U Ch Pr.

Mann, Arthur, ed. see Kantowicz, Edward.

Mann, Arthur R., jt. intro. see Hamilton, William H.

Mann, Audrey. Recent Glass Sculpture: A Union of Ideas. LC 97-73989. 39p. 1997. pap. 12.00 (*0-944110-57-6*) Milwauk Art Mus.

Mann, Barry. Sigmund Freud. LC 92-42548. (Pioneers Ser.). 112p. (YA). 1993. lib. bdg. 25.27 (*0-86625-491-9*) Rourke Pubns.

Mann, Betsy. By Request: The Most Wanted Recipes from Arizona's Favorite Restaurants. LC 98-3982. 160p. 1998. pap. 9.95 (*0-87358-730-8*) Northland AZ.

Mann, Bill. On-Line Games: In-Depth Strategies & Secrets. 1995. pap. text 19.95 (*0-7615-0076-6*) Prima Pub.

***Mann, Bob.** ASE L1 Preparation Guide. (Illus.). 2000. pap. 99.00 (*1-930717-27-X*) Advantg Busn.

Mann, Bob. Bob Mann's Automatic Golf Complete. (Illus.). 128p. (Orig.). 1992. pap. 9.99 (*0-671-74049-0*, Fireside) S&S Trade Pap.

***Mann, Bob.** Emissions Guide. 2000. write for info. (*1-930717-26-1*) Advantg Busn.

Mann, Bob. Hot Dog Skiing. 1977. pap. 3.95 (*0-393-08690-9*) Norton.
— How to Make a Metal-Bending Machine. (Workshop Equipment Manual Ser.: No. 10). 20p. 1987. pap. 10.00 (*0-903031-29-9*, Pub. by Intermed Tech) Stylus Pub VA.

***Mann, Bob.** Sensor Guide. (Illus.). 2000. pap. write for info. (*1-930717-25-3*) Advantg Busn.

Mann, Bob, jt. auth. see Mayfield, Rich.

Mann, Bob R., jt. auth. see Townsend, Bryan.

Mann, Bond. Mother Goose & Others in Wall Street. LC 68-21700. 1968. reprint ed. pap. 5.00 (*0-87034-032-8*) Fraser Pub Co.

Mann Borgese, Elisabeth, et al, eds. Ocean Yearbook, Vol. 14. 1999. lib. bdg. 77.00 (*0-226-06617-7*) U Ch Pr.

***Mann, Brenda.** Who's New at the Zoo? LC 97-143864. (Oke Children's Classics Ser.). 152p. (J). (gr. 3 up). 1998. pap. 5.99 (*0-934998-55-8*) Bethany Hse.

Mann, Brenda J., jt. auth. see Spradley, James P.

M

M

Mann, Brian. The Secular Madrigals of Filippo Di Monte, 1521-1603. LC 83-1061. (Studies in Musicology: No. 64). 497p. reprint ed. pap. 154.10 (*0-8357-1402-0*, 207048300096) Bks Demand.

Mann, Brian, ed. Paolo Quagliati: Recercate, et Canzone, Libro Primo a Quattro Voci, Rome, 1601. LC 94-1961. (Italian Instrumental Music of the Sixteenth & Early Seventeenth Centuries Ser.: Vol. 15). 168p. 1994. text 77.00 (*0-8240-4514-9*) Garland.

Mann, Brian E. & Akitt, James W. NMR & Chemistry. 4th rev. ed. (Illus.). 288p. 2000. pap. (*0-7487-4344-8*) S Thornes Pubs.

Mann, Bruce A., et al. California Corporate Practice & Forms: The Morrison & Foerster Manual. LC 99-34129. 1506p. 1999. ring bd. 275.00 (*1-57400-046-2*) Data Trace Pubng.

Mann, Bruce H. Neighbors & Strangers: Law & Community in Early Connecticut. LC 87-6001. (Studies in Legal History). 216p. reprint ed. pap. 67.00 (*0-7837-6858-3*, 204668700003) Bks Demand.

Mann, C., jt. auth. see Hughes, Matthew.

Mann, C. S. Mark: A New Translation with Introduction & Commentary. LC 85-4433. (Anchor Bible Ser.: Vol. 27). (Illus.). 752p. 1986. 44.95 (*0-385-03253-6*, Anchor NY) Doubleday.

Mann, C. S., jt. ed. see Albright, William F.

Mann, C. V. & Glass, R. E. Surgical Treatment of Anal Incontinence. (Illus.). xiii, 160p. 1991. 232.00 (*0-387-19640-4*) Spr-Verlag.

Mann, C. V., et al. Bailey & Love's Short Practice of Surgery. 22nd ed. (Illus.). 1056p. 1995. text 75.00 (*0-412-49490-6*, Pub. by E A) OUP.

Mann, Cameron. Concordance to the English Poems of George Herbert. 277p. reprint ed. lib. bdg. 79.00 (*0-7812-0251-5*) Rprt Serv.

— Concordance to the English Poems of George Herbert. 1971. reprint ed. 49.00 (*0-403-01089-6*) Scholarly.

Mann, Carleton H. How Schools Use Their Time: Time Allotment Practice in 444 Cities. LC 72-177051. (Columbia University. Teachers College. Contributions to Education Ser.: No. 333). reprint ed. 37.50 (*0-404-55333-8*) AMS Pr.

Mann, Carlos G. Panamanian Militarism: A Historical Interpretation. LC 95-40747. (Monographs in International Studies, Latin America Ser.: No. 25). (Illus.). 243p. (Orig.). (C). 1996. pap. text 23.00 (*0-89680-189-6*) Ohio U Pr.

Mann, Carol. Modigliani. (World of Art Ser.). 1985. 19.95 (*0-500-18176-4*, Pub. by Thames Hudson) Norton.

— Modigliani. LC 90-72012. (World of Art Ser.). (Illus.). 216p. 1991. pap. 14.95 (*0-500-20176-5*, Pub. by Thames Hudson) Norton.

Mann, Catherine L. International Lender of Last Resort? 1999. LC-99-31295. write for info. (*0-88132-265-2*) Inst Intl Eco.

"An International Lender of Last Resort? starts from the perspective of national lender of last resort functions & supporting institutional structures to discuss whether the IMF has & can perform the job of an international lender of last resort. It also uses this framework to address difficulties that the European System of Central Banks may face should a financial crisis engulf Europe. *Publisher Paid Annotation.*

Mann, Catherine L. Is the U. S. Trade Deficit Sustainable? LC 99-31295. 200p. (C). 1999. pap. 20.00 (*0-88132-264-4*) Inst Intl Eco.

This study presents salient facts on the magnitude & characteristics of US economic relations with the rest of the world in both trade & finance. It also answers some of the perennial questions about external balance. These questions include: Why, if US exporters are so intensely competitive, has the external deficit persisted? Does the external deficit represent protectionism abroad; will it lead to protectionism at home? Is a chronic & widening external deficit sustainable? The United States trade deficit has hit record levels & continues to rise. Is a chronic & widening deficit sustainable or will the dollar crash, perhaps taking the economy with it? If the problem was one of "twin deficits," why has the external deficit continued to worsen even as the budget deficit narrowed to zero? If US companies are so intensively competitive, why does the external deficit persist? Does the external deficit represent protectionism abroad; will it lead to protectionism at hone? This study seeks to answer these perennial questions about the trade deficit. Each chapter presents simple analytical frameworks as a basis for concise succinct & clear statements on each major issue. The last section of the book provides an outlook for the deficit & suggests alternative policy courses for dealing with it. Is the US Trade Deficit Sustainable? is designed for the policymaker & general public who are interested in the US role in the world economy, but who need not be experts in economics. It is also suited for courses in international economics, business & international affairs. *Publisher Paid Annotation.*

***Mann, Catherine L., et al.** Global Electronic Commerce: A Policy Primer. 200p. 2000. pap. 20.00 (*0-88132-274-1*) Inst Intl Eco.

Mann, Catherine L., jt. auth. see Hooper, Peter.

Mann, Charles C. & Freedman, David H. At Large: The Strange Case of the World's Biggest Internet Invasion. LC 97-960. 315p. 1997. 24.00 (*0-684-82464-7*) S&S Trade.

Mann, Charles C., jt. auth. see Crease, Robert P.

Mann, Charles E., ed. see Hutchinson, John Wallace.

Mann, Charles F. Madeleine Delbrel: A Life Beyond Boundaries. LC 95-67111. 208p. 1996. pap. 12.95 (*0-9645600-9-7*) New Wrld Pr.

— Madeleine Delbrel: A Life Beyond Boundaries. 2nd expanded rev. ed. LC 97-75546. (Illus.). 232p. 1998. pap. 12.95 (*0-9645600-6-2*, 0-9645600) New Wrld Pr.

Mann, Charles K., et al, eds. Seeking Solutions: Case Leader's Guide. fac. ed. LC 90-35169. (Kumarian Press Library of Management for Development). 199p. 1990. pap. 61.70 (*0-7837-7583-0*, 204733600007) Bks Demand.

Mann, Charles K. & Huddleston, Barbara, eds. Food Policy, Frameworks for Analysis & Action. LC 85-42526. 254p. 1986. pap. 78.80 (*0-608-05031-8*, 205969200004) Bks Demand.

Mann, Charles V. & Glass, Richard. Surgical Treatment of Anal Incontinence. 2nd ed. LC 96-36555. 1996. 149.00 (*3-540-76061-X*) Spr-Verlag.

Mann, Charlie. Built Hard. LC 97-15311. (Illus.). 280p. (Orig.). 1997. pap. 19.95 (*0-88011-696-X*, PMAN0696) Human Kinetics.

Mann, Chester. D. L. Moody Soulwinner. 2nd ed. 128p. 1997. pap. 10.99 (*1-84030-007-8*) Emerald House Group Inc.

Mann, Chris. Chris Mann on Grammar. LC 90-61818. 90p. 1990. pap. 10.95 (*0-939044-30-7*) Lingua Pr.

— Come & Knock on Our Door: A Hers & Hers & His Guide to "Three's Company" LC 97-23628. (Illus.). 288p. 1998. pap. 17.95 (*0-312-16803-9*) St Martin.

— South Africans: A Series of Portrait Poems. 80p. 1996. pap. 17.00 (*0-86980-922-9*, Pub. by Univ Natal Pr) Intl Spec Bk.

— Working Hypothesis. LC 98-27144. 105p. 1998. pap. 15.00 (*1-58177-050-2*, Pub. by Barrytown Ltd) Consort Bk Sales.

***Mann, Chris & Griffiths, Terry.** Beginners Guide to Flytying. (Illus.). 76p. 1999. 15.95 (*1-57188-184-0*, BFTH) F Amato Pubns.

Mann, Chris, jt. auth. see Hughes, Matthew.

Mann, Coramae R. Female Crime & Delinquency. LC 82-16052. (Illus.). 347p. reprint ed. pap. 107.60 (*0-608-09230-4*, 205273400005) Bks Demand.

— Unequal Justice: A Question of Color. LC 92-25110. (Blacks in the Diaspora Ser.). 320p. (C). 1993. pap. 15.95 (*0-253-20783-5*) Ind U Pr.

— When Women Kill. LC 95-15374. (SUNY Series in Violence). 215p. (C). 1996. pap. text 19.95 (*0-7914-2812-5*) State U NY Pr.

Mann, Coramae Richey & Zatz, Marjorie S., eds. Images of Color, Images of Crime: Readings. LC 97-23659. (Illus.). 270p. (C). 1998. pap. text. write for info. (*0-935732-97-7*) Roxbury Pub Co.

***Mann, Coramae Richey & Zatz, Marjorie S., eds.** Images of Color, Images of Crime: Readings. 2nd ed. 270p. (C). 2001. pap. text. write for info. (*1-891487-58-2*) Roxbury Pub Co.

Mann, Cuthbert. Hitler's Three Struggles. 336p. (Orig.). 1995. pap. 19.95 (*1-886094-16-0*) Chicago Spectrum.

***Mann, D.** Automotive Plastics & Composites. 2nd ed. 250p. 1999. 2878.00 (*1-85617-349-6*) Elsevier.

Mann, D. M. Sense & Senility: The Neuropathy of the Aged Human Brain. LC 96-29707. (Neuroscience Intelligence Unit Ser.). 206p. 1997. 99.00 (*1-57059-422-8*) Landes Bioscience.

Mann, Dale, ed. Making Change Happen? fac. ed. LC 78-21849. (Policy Analysis & Education Ser.). 363p. 1978. reprint ed. pap. 112.60 (*0-7837-8645-X*, 204794300009) Bks Demand.

Mann, Dale & Skinulis, Richard. The Complete Log House Book. (Illus.). (Orig.). 1979. pap. text 12.95 (*0-07-082817-2*) McGraw.

Mann, David. Clinical Approaches to the Erotic Transference & Countertransference. LC 98-30535. 1999. 85.00 (*0-415-18452-5*); pap. 27.99 (*0-415-18453-3*) Routledge.

— Psychotherapy, an Erotic Relationship: Transference & Countertransference Passions. LC 96-27225. 224p. (C). 1997. 80.00 (*0-415-14851-0*); pap. 25.99 (*0-415-14852-9*) Routledge.

Mann, David & Main, Ron. Races, Chases & Crashes: A Complete Guide to Car Movies & Biker Flicks. (Illus.). 144p. 1994. pap. text 14.95 (*0-87938-859-5*) MBI Pubg.

Mann, David D., compiled by. A Concordance to the Plays & Poems of Sir George Etherege. LC 84-27917. 445p. 1985. lib. bdg. 135.00 (*0-313-20976-6*, MPO/, Greenwood Pr) Greenwood.

Mann, David D., ed. see Congreve, William.

Mann, David D., ed. see Mann, Susan G., et al.

Mann, David K. The 1972 Invasion of Military Region 1: Fall of Quang Tri & Defense of Hue. 93p. 1993. reprint ed. pap. 11.50 (*0-923135-62-6*) Dalley Bk Service.

Mann, David M., et al. A Color Atlas & Text of Adult Dementias. LC 94-43604. 1994. 65.00 (*0-7234-1784-9*) Wolfe Pub.

Mann, David S., jt. ed. see Carter, Luther F.

Mann, Dean E., ed. Environmental Policy. (Orig.). 1980. pap. 15.00 (*0-918592-43-7*) Pol Studies.

Mann, Dean E., et al, eds. Water Resources & Public Policy. 304p. (Orig.). 1985. pap. 15.00 (*0-918592-79-8*) Pol Studies.

Mann, Dean E., jt. auth. see Ingram, Helen M.

Mann, Dean E., jt. auth. see Wyner, Alan J.

Mann, Dean E., jt. ed. see Feldman, David.

Mann, Dean E., jt. ed. see Ingram, Helen M.

Mann, Delbert. Looking Back... At Live Television & Other Matters. Skutch, Ira, ed. LC 98-74095. (Illus.). 383p. 1999. 44.95 (*1-882766-05-9*); pap. 32.95 (*1-882766-06-7*) Dirs Guild Am.

Mann, Denise, jt. ed. see Spigel, Lynn.

***Mann, Don & Schaad, Kara.** The Complete Guide to Adventure Racing. (Illus.). 160p. 2001. pap. 19.95 (*1-57826-064-7*, Pub. by Hatherleigh) Norton.

Mann, Don, jt. auth. see Carter, W. Horace.

Mann, E. A. Boundaries & Identities: Muslims, Work & Status in Aligarh. LC 92-3334. (Illus.). 212p. (C). 1992. text 39.95 (*0-8039-9422-2*) Sage.

Mann, E. B. Brett Randall, Gambler. large type ed. (Linford Western Library). 352p. 1988. pap. 16.99 (*0-7089-6527-X*, Linford) Ulverscroft.

Mann, Edward C., III. Thunder & Lightning Vol. 2: Desert Storm & the Airpower Debates. (Illus.). 240p. 1995. pap. 14.00 (*1-58566-001-9*) Air Univ.

Mann, Edward S. The Things That Count. 160p. 1983. kivar 8.99 (*0-8341-0830-5*) Nazarene.

Mann, Edwin J. The Deaf & Dumb. 1972. 59.95 (*0-8490-0002-5*) Gordon Pr.

Mann, Eleanor, jt. auth. see Thomsen, Thomas C.

Mann, Eleanor, ed. see Thomsen, Thomas C.

Mann, Elizabeth. The Great Wall: The Story of Thousands of Miles of Earth & Stone that Turned a Nation into a Fortress. LC 97-21246. (Wonders of the World Ser.). (Illus.). 48p. (J). (gr. 4 up). 1997. 18.95 (*0-9650493-2-9*, Pub. by Mikaya Pr) Firefly Bks Ltd.

***Mann, Elizabeth.** Machu Picchu: The Story of the Amazing Incas & Their City in the Clouds. LC 99-55172. (Wonders of the World Bks.: Vol. 6). (Illus.). 48p. (J). (gr. 3-6). 2000. 19.95 (*0-9650493-9-6*, Pub. by Mikaya Pr) Firefly Bks Ltd.

Mann, Elizabeth. The Panama Canal: The Story of How a Jungle Was Conquered & the World Made Smaller. LC 98-22457. (Wonders of the World Book Ser.). (Illus.). 48p. (YA). (gr. 4 up). 1998. 19.95 (*0-9650493-4-5*, Pub. by Mikaya Pr) Firefly Bks Ltd.

— The Roman Colosseum: The Story of the World's Most Famous Stadium & Its Deadly Games. LC 98-20060. (Wonders of the World Ser.). (Illus.). 48p. (YA). (gr. 4 up). 1998. 19.95 (*0-9650493-3-7*, Pub. by Mikaya Pr) Firefly Bks Ltd.

Mann, Elizabeth B. The Brooklyn Bridge: The Story of the World's Most Famous Bridge & the Remarkable Family That Built It. LC 96-14752. (Wonders of the World Bks.). (Illus.). 48p. (J). (gr. 5-7). 1996. 19.95 (*0-9650493-0-2*, Pub. by Mikaya Pr) Firefly Bks Ltd.

— The Great Pyramid: The Story of the Farmers, the God-King & the Most Astounding Structure Ever Built. (Wonders of the World Bks.). (Illus.). 48p. (J). (gr. 3 up). 1996. 19.95 (*0-9650493-1-0*, Pub. by Mikaya Pr) Firefly Bks Ltd.

***Mann, Elizabeth Mudge.** Freddie Rides a Moose. (J). (gr. 5-7). 2000. pap. 5.95 (*0-533-13545-1*) Vantage.

Mann, Emily. The Cherry Orchard. Date not set. pap. 5.95 (*0-8222-1779-1*) Dramatists Play.

Mann, Emily. Still Life. 1981. pap. 5.25 (*0-8222-1081-9*) Dramatists Play.

— Testimonies: Four Plays. LC 96-7092. 268p. 1996. pap. text 15.95 (*1-55936-117-4*) Theatre Comm.

Mann, Eric. Taking on General Motors: A Case Study of the UAW Campaign to Keep GM Van Nuys Open. (Illus.). 408p. (Orig.). (C). 1987. pap. 20.00 (*0-89215-141-2*) U Cal LA Indus Rel.

Mann, Eric, et al. PC Week Guide to Lotus Notes & Domino. 1997. pap. 49.99 (*0-614-28489-9*, Ziff-Davis Pr) Que.

Mann, Erika. Last Year of Thomas Mann. Graves, Richard, tr. LC 72-126323. (Biography Index Reprint Ser.). 1977. 17.95 (*0-8369-8029-8*) Ayer.

Mann, Ernest. Free I Got. 3269p. (Orig.). (C). 1993. pap. 8.95 (*0-9620301-1-2*) Little Free.

— I Was Robot: (Utopia Now Possible) 320p. (C). 1990. pap. 7.95 (*0-9620301-0-4*) Little Free.

Mann, F. A. The Legal Aspect of Money. 5th ed. 662p. 1992. text 195.00 (*0-19-825650-7*) OUP.

— Notes & Comments on Cases in International Law, Commercial Law, & Arbitration. LC 92-15318. 304p. (C). 1993. text 75.00 (*0-19-825798-8*, Clarendon Pr) OUP.

Mann, Felix. Acupuncture. rev. ed. (Illus.). 192p. 1973. pap. 9.00 (*0-394-71727-9*) Vin Bks.

— Acupuncture: Cure of Many Diseases. 2nd ed. (Illus.). 140p. 1992. pap. text 36.50 (*0-7506-0700-9*) Buttrwrth-Heinemann.

— Acupuncture, the Ancient Chinese Art of Healing. (Illus.). 1990. 21.00 (*0-8446-4583-4*) Peter Smith.

— Atlas of Acupuncture. 1993. pap. text 69.50 (*0-7506-1678-4*) Buttrwrth-Heinemann.

— Reinventing Acupuncture: A New Concept of Ancient Medicine. LC 92-27735. 1993. pap. text 42.50 (*0-7506-0844-7*) Buttrwrth-Heinemann.

***Mann, Felix.** Reinventing Acupuncture: A New Concept of Ancient Medicine. 2nd ed. LC 00-41433. 2000. write for info. (*0-7506-4857-0*) Buttrwrth-Heinemann.

Mann, Felix. Textbook of Acupuncture. (Illus.). 640p. 1987. text 105.00 (*0-7506-1895-7*) Buttrwrth-Heinemann.

Mann, Floyd C. & Hoffman, L. Richard. Automation & the Worker: A Study of Social Change in Power Plants. LC 83-12978. (Illus.). 272p. 1983. reprint ed. lib. bdg. 65.00 (*0-313-24222-4*, MAUW, Greenwood Pr) Greenwood.

Mann, Frederick G. & Saunders, Bernard C. Introduction to Practical Organic Chemistry. 2nd ed. LC 66-84573. 219p. reprint ed. pap. 67.90 (*0-608-10088-9*, 200364700038) Bks Demand.

***Mann, Friedhelm, ed.** Lexicon Gregorianum, 2. (GER & GRE.). 600p. 1999. text 500.00 (*90-04-11450-5*) Brill Academic Pubs.

Mann, Friedhelm, et al, eds. Gregorii Nysseni Sermones, Pars II. LC 64-42055. (Gregorius Nyssenus Opera Ser.: Vol. X, Tomus 1). (LAT., Illus.). cclxiii, 176p. 1990. 137.00 (*90-04-08123-2*) Brill Academic Pubs.

Mann, Friedhelm & Rhein, Ernestus, eds. Sermones Pars Iii, VOL. 2. Vol. 2. (GRE., Illus.). Lx, 377p. 1996. text (*90-04-10442-9*) Brill Academic Pubs.

Mann, Fritz A. Foreign Affairs in English Courts. 300p. 1986. 65.00 (*0-19-825564-0*) OUP.

Mann, G., ed. Internationale Bibliographie Zur Geschichte der Medzin, 1875-1901. 589p. 1971. write for info. (*0-318-71806-5*) G Olms Pubs.

Mann, G. B. Low-Hanging Fruit. LC 96-94783. 128p. 1997. 18.95 (*0-9655117-0-7*, LHF001) GrapeVinePress.

Mann, G. C., et al, eds. Applied Radionuclide Metrology: Proceedings of the International Committee for Radionuclide Metrology Seminar, Geel, Belgium, 16-17 May 1983. (International Journal of Applied Radiation & Isotopes Ser.: Vol. 34, No. 8). 286p. 1984. pap. 28.00 (*0-08-030271-8*, Pergamon Pr) Elsevier.

Mann, George. Theatre Lethbridge: A History of Theatrical Production in Lethbridge, Alberta (1885-1988) (Illus.). 440p. (Orig.). 1993. pap. 29.95 (*1-55059-055-3*) Temeron Bks.

Mann, George W. The Handbook for Women Drivers: The Road to Understanding What Every Woman Who Drives Needs to Know. large type ed. Murphy, Thomas, ed. (Illus.). 178p. (Orig.). 1996. pap. 11.95 (*0-9652593-0-7*) Documnt Maintenance.

Mann, Gerald. Book of Wisecracks: Windows of Wisdom for Living Well. 1998. 15.95 (*0-9647272-1-8*) Riverbend Pr.

— Common Sense Religion: Renewing Your Christian Values. 166p. (Orig.). reprint ed. pap. text 9.95 (*0-9647272-0-X*) Riverbend Pr.

***Mann, Gerald.** The Search for Inner Peace. 125p. 2000. pap. write for info. (*0-9678502-0-7*) G Mann Min.

Mann, Gerald. When One Day at a Time Is Too Long: Practical Answers to 42 of Life's Toughest Questions. LC 94-1589. 1994. pap. text 11.95 (*0-9647272-2-6*) Riverbend Pr.

— When the Bad Times Are over for Good: Transforming Trouble into Triumph. 1997. pap. 9.95 (*0-9647272-3-4*) Riverbend Pr.

***Mann, Gerald.** You Can Begin Again. 96p. 2000. pap. write for info. (*0-9678502-1-5*) G Mann Min.

Mann, Gerhard. Holstein Horses. (Breed Ser.). 1977. pap. 4.95 (*0-88376-017-7*) Dreenan Pr.

Mann, Gil. How to Get More Out of Being Jewish Even If: A. You're Not Sure You Believe in God, B. You Think Going to the Synagogue Is a Waste of Time, C. You Think Keeping Kosher Is Stupid, D. You Hated Hebrew School, Or, E. All of the Above! LC 96-75728. 158p. 1996. pap. 14.95 (*0-965709-0-X*) Leo & Sons Pub.

Mann, Giovanni, et al, eds. European Pancreatic Club Meeting (EPC) 29th Meeting, London, July 1997: Abstracts & Papers of the Young Researcher's Corner. (Digestion Ser.: Vol. 58, Suppl. 2, 1997). (Illus.). iv, 98p. 1997. pap. 44.50 (*3-8055-6552-6*) S Karger.

Mann, Glennis A., jt. auth. see Pray, Bobbie A.

***Mann, Gloria, ed.** The Heritage of Montgomery County, Alabama. (Heritage of Alabama Ser.: Vol. 51). 320p. 2001. 50.00 (*1-891647-61-X*) Herit Pub Consult.

Mann, Golo, ed. see Nitschke, A.

Mann, Graham, et al. Conceptual Structures: Knowledge Representation as Interlingua: Fourth International Conference on Conceptual Structures, ICCS '96, Sydney, Australia, August 19-22, 1996: Proceedings, Vol. 111. Eklund, Peter W. & Ellis, Gerard, eds. LC 96-32200. (Lecture Notes in Artificial Intelligence). 321p. 1996. pap. 56.00 (*3-540-61534-2*) Spr-Verlag.

***Mann, Gurinder S.** Buddhists, Hindus & Sikhs. (Illus.). 2000. pap. 0.00 (*0-19-512442-1*) OUP.

Mann, Gurinder S. The Goindval Pothis: The Earliest Extant Source of the Sikh Canon. (Illus.). 233p. 1997. 35.00 (*0-674-35618-7*) HUP.

Mann, Gurinder S., jt. ed. see Hawley, John S.

Mann, H., jt. ed. see Sieberth, H. G.

Mann, H. Allan. Affected with the Public Interest. 172p. 1994. 30.00 (*0-614-06940-8*) NARUC.

Mann, H. H. Fodder Crops of Western India. (C). 1991. 125.00 (*81-7136-028-9*, Pub. by Periodical Expert) St Mut.

Mann, H. K. Radiation Sterilization of Plastic Medical Devices: Seminar under the Auspices of the University of Lowell, Mass., March 1979. 128p. 1980. pap. 25.00 (*0-08-025067-X*, Pergamon Pr) Elsevier.

Mann, H. S. Arid Zone Research & Development. 531p. 1980. 300.00 (*0-7855-1864-9*, Pub. by Scientific) St Mut.

Mann, H. S., jt. auth. see Spooner, B.

Mann, Harold H. The Social Framework of Agriculture. Thorner, Daniel, ed. (Illus.). 501p. 1968. 37.50 (*0-7146-2333-4*, Pub. by F Cass Pubs) Intl Spec Bk.

— The Social Framework of Agriculture. LC 67-29802. xxx, 501p. 1967. 49.50 (*0-678-08007-0*) Kelley.

Mann, Heinrich. Henry King of France. LC 84-22682. 800p. 1987. 25.00 (*0-87951-999-1*, Pub. by Overlook Pr); pap. 19.95 (*0-87951-224-5*, Pub. by Overlook Pr) Penguin Putnam.

— The Loyal Subject. Peitsch, Helmut, ed. LC 97-22094. (The German Library). 348p. 1997. pap. 24.00 (*0-8264-0955-5*) Continuum.

— Man of Straw. 304p. 1992. pap. 11.95 (*0-14-018137-7*, Penguin Classics) Viking Penguin.

An Asterisk (*) at the beginning of an entry indicates that the title is appearing for the first time.

— Young Henry of Navarre. Sutton, Eric, tr. from GER. LC 84-42673. 585p. 1986. reprint ed. pap. 19.95 (*0-87951-206-7*, Pub. by Overlook Pr) Penguin Putnam.

— Young Henry of Navarre. Sutton, Eric, tr. from GER. LC 84-42673. 585p. 1994. reprint ed. 25.00 (*0-87951-981-9*, Pub. by Overlook Pr) Penguin Putnam.

Mann, Heinrich, ed. see Mann, Thomas, et al.

Mann, Helen R. Crawford's Horn Winding: A Biographical Novel about Ethan Allen Crawford & His Wife, Lucy, of Crawford Notch. 390p. 1997. 25.00 (*0-914339-63-X*, Pub. by P E Randall Pub) U Pr of New Eng.

Mann, Helen S. Charles Ezra Sprague. Brief, Richard P., ed. LC 77-87277. (Development of Contemporary Accounting Thought Ser.). 1978. reprint ed. lib. bdg. 19.95 (*0-405-10905-9*) Ayer.

Mann, Henrietta. Cheyenne-Arapaho Education, 1871-1982. LC 97-21814. 1997. 34.95 (*0-87081-462-1*) Univ Pr Colo.

Mann, Henry B. Addition Theorems: The Addition Theorems of Group Theory & Number Theory. LC 76-16766. 124p. 1976. reprint ed. text 15.50 (*0-88275-418-1*) Krieger.

Mann, Herman. The Female Review: Life of Deborah Sampson, the Female Soldier in the War of the Revolution. LC 72-2603. (American Women Ser.: Images & Realities). 276p. 1978. reprint ed. 21.95 (*0-405-04476-3*) Ayer.

— The Female Review: or Memoirs of an American Young Lady. LC 78-64079. reprint ed. 37.50 (*0-404-17069-2*) AMS Pr.

— Historical Annals of Dedham, from Its Settlement in 1635 to 1847. 136p. 1995. reprint ed. pap. 22.50 (*0-8328-4663-5*) Higginson Bk Co.

Mann, Hiram & Phears, Bill. Forever Dreaming: One Is Young, Only Once. LC 98-70691. 192p. 1998. 24.95 (*1-878398-41-5*, Blue Note Bks) Blue Note Pubns.

Mann, Horace. A Few Thoughts for a Young Man. (Notable American Authors Ser.). 1999. reprint ed. lib. bdg. 125.00 (*0-7812-3935-4*) Rprt Serv.

— Lectures on Education. LC 70-89197. (American Education: Its Men, Institutions, & Ideas. Series 1). 1978. reprint ed. 19.95 (*0-405-01437-6*) Ayer.

— Lectures on Education. (Notable American Authors Ser.). 1999. reprint ed. lib. bdg. 125.00 (*0-7812-3934-6*) Rprt Serv.

— On the Art of Teaching. 31p. 1990. 9.95 (*1-55709-129-3*) Applewood.

— Powers & Duties of Women. (Notable American Authors Ser.). 1999. reprint ed. lib. bdg. 125.00 (*0-7812-3938-9*) Rprt Serv.

— Sermons. (Notable American Authors Ser.). 1999. reprint ed. lib. bdg. 125.00 (*0-7812-3939-7*) Rprt Serv.

— Slavery: Letters & Speeches. LC 79-81126. (Black Heritage Library Collection). 1977. 32.95 (*0-8369-8623-7*) Ayer.

— Slavery, Letters & Speeches. LC 70-82205. (Anti-Slavery Crusade in America Ser.). 1970. reprint ed. 32.95 (*0-405-00643-8*) Ayer.

— Slavery Letters & Speeches. (Notable American Authors Ser.). 1999. reprint ed. lib. bdg. 125.00 (*0-7812-3936-2*) Rprt Serv.

— Twelve Annual Reports. (Notable American Authors Ser.). 1999. reprint ed. lib. bdg. 125.00 (*0-7812-3933-8*) Rprt Serv.

Mann, Hugh. Hugh Mann Writes. 106p. (Orig.). 1993. pap. 15.00 (*0-9623892-0-X*) Hugh Mann.

Mann, J. Natural Products. (C). 1994. pap. text 44.50 (*0-582-06009-5*, Pub. by Addison-Wesley) Longman.

— Second Metabolism. 2nd ed. 390p. 1987. pap. 39.95 (*0-19-855529-6*) OUP.

Mann, J. A. Cotton Trade of Great Britain: Its Rise, Progress & Present Extent. (Illus.). 134p. 1968. reprint ed. 29.50 (*0-7146-1405-X*, Pub. by F Cass Pubs) Intl Spec Bk.

Mann, J. C. Britain & the Roman Empire. (Collected Studies: No. CS545). 300p. 1996. 115.95 (*0-86078-580-7*, Pub. by Variorum) Ashgate Pub Co.

— Staindrop Quaker Meeting House. 1999. pap. 21.00 (*1-85072-118-1*, Pub. by W Sessions) St Mut.

Mann, J. G. The Wallace Collection Catalogue of European Arms & Armour, 2 vols., Set. (Illus.). pap. 50.00 (*0-614-11688-0*, Pub. by Wallace Collect) Antique Collect.

— The Wallace Collection Catalogue of Sculpture, 2 vols., Set. (Illus.). 258p. 1931. pap. 19.95 (*0-900785-02-0*, Pub. by Wallace Collect) Antique Collect.

Mann, J. J. Models of Depressive Disorders: Psychological, Biological & Genetic Perspectives. (Depressive Illness Ser.: Vol. 2). (Illus.). 198p. (C). 1989. text 49.50 (*0-306-43277-3*, Kluwer Plenum) Kluwer Academic.

Mann, J. J. & Kuper, David J., eds. Biology of Depressive Disorders, Set, Pts. A & B. (Depressive Illness Ser.: Vols. 3 & 4). (Illus.). 1993. 79.50 (*0-685-67873-3*, Plenum Trade) Perseus Pubng.

Mann, J. J. & Kupfer, D. J. Biology of Depressive Disorders Pt. A: A Systems Perspective. (Depressive Illness Ser.: Vol. 3). (Illus.). 286p. (C). 1993. text 59.50 (*0-306-44295-7*, Kluwer Plenum) Kluwer Academic.

— Biology of Depressive Disorders Pt. B: Subtypes of Depression & Comobid Disorders. (Depressive Illness Ser.: Vol. 4). (Illus.). 196p. (C). 1993. text 52.50 (*0-306-44296-5*, Kluwer Plenum) Kluwer Academic.

Mann, J. John, ed. The Phenomenology of Depressive Illness. (Depressive Illness Ser.: Vol. 1). 263p. 1988. 42.95 (*0-89885-369-9*, Kluwer Plenum) Kluwer Academic.

Mann, J. John, jt. ed. see Stoff, David M.

Mann, J. Johnston. The Art of Dapping. 1989. 30.00 (*0-7223-2094-9*, Pub. by A H S Ltd) St Mut.

— Fishing for Fun. 90p. (C). 1989. 50.00 (*0-7223-2181-3*, Pub. by A H S Ltd) St Mut.

Mann, Jack. Gees' First Case. 1970. 6.50 (*0-685-33435-X*) Bookfinger.

— Glass Too Many. 1973. 6.50 (*0-685-33436-8*) Bookfinger.

— Grey Shapes. 1970. 6.50 (*0-685-26775-X*) Bookfinger.

— Her Ways Are Death. 287p. 1981. 6.50 (*0-686-73102-6*) Bookfinger.

— Maker of Shadows. 1977. 6.50 (*0-685-88837-1*) Bookfinger.

— Nightmare Farm. 1975. 6.50 (*0-685-54480-X*) Bookfinger.

— The Ninth Life. 1970. 6.50 (*0-685-26776-8*) Bookfinger.

Mann, Jacob. The Responsa of the Babylonian Geonim As a Source of Jewish History. LC 73-2215. (Jewish People; History, Religion, Literature Ser.). 1973. reprint ed. 25.95 (*0-405-05279-0*) Ayer.

Mann, James. Time-Limited Psychotherapy. LC 72-96631. (Commonwealth Fund Publications). 212p. 1973. pap. 19.95 (*0-674-89191-0*) HUP.

Mann, James, ed. see Smith, Cordwainer.

Mann, James A., ed. see Boucher, Anthony.

Mann, James A., ed. see Smith, Cordwainer.

Mann, James E., Jr., jt. auth. see Simmonds, James G.

Mann, James G. Industrial Water Reuse & Wastewater Minimization. LC 99-29588. (Professional Engineering Ser.). 450p. 1999. 99.95 (*0-07-134855-7*) McGraw.

Mann, James H. About Face: A History of America's Curious Relationship with China, from Nixon to Clinton. LC 98-6285. 432p. 1998. 30.00 (*0-679-45053-X*) Knopf.

— About Face: A History of America's Curious Relationship with China, from Nixon to Clinton. 1999. pap. 16.00 (*0-679-76861-0*) Vin Bks.

Mann, Janet. Cetacean Societies: Field Studies of Dolphins & Whales. 400p. 2000. lib. bdg. 85.00 (*0-226-50340-2*) U Ch Pr.

Mann, Jeff. Bliss: Latest Winner: Stonewall Chapbook Competition. unabridged ed. (Stonewall Ser.: No. 4). 42p. (Orig.). 1998. pap. 8.00 (*0-932616-60-7*, STON4) Brick Hse Bks.

Mann, Jeff, jt. ed. see Cranston, Meg.

Mann, Jeffrey. Client/Server Development with Uniface. 1996. mass mkt. 29.95 (*1-85032-284-8*) ITCP.

Mann, Jessica. Captive Audience. 1997. 19.50 (*0-7451-8700-5*, Black Dagger) Chivers N Amer.

***Mann, Jessica.** The Eighth Deadly Sin. unabridged large type ed. 2000. 25.95 (*0-7531-5990-2*, 159902, Pub. by ISIS Lrg Prnt) ISIS Pub.

— Hanging Fire. large type unabridged ed. 290p. 1999. 26.95 (*0-7531-5890-6*, 158906, Pub. by ISIS Lrg Prnt) ISIS Pub.

Mann, Jessica. A Private Inquiry. large type unabridged ed. 294p. 1998. 24.95 (*0-7531-5557-5*, 155575) ISIS Pub.

Mann, Jill. Langland & Allegory. (Morton W. Bloomfield Lectures on Medieval English Literature Ser.: Vol. II). (C). 1992. pap. 5.00 (*1-879288-15-X*) Medieval Inst.

Mann, Jill, jt. ed. see Boitani, Piero.

Mann, Jim. Beijing Jeep: A Case Study of Western Business in China. LC 96-51810. 352p. (C). 1997. pap. text 30.00 (*0-8133-3327-X*, Pub. by Westview) HarpC.

— Tomorrow's Global Community: How the Information Deluge is Transforming Business & Government. LC 98-29812. 390p. 1998. 24.95 (*1-891696-06-8*) BainBridgeBooks.

Mann, Jim, ed. NESFA Index to Short Science Fiction for 1988. viii, 136p. 1990. 12.00 (*0-915368-43-9*) New Eng SF Assoc.

— NESFA Index to Short Science Fiction for 1989. viii, 164p. 1992. 12.00 (*0-915368-48-X*) New Eng SF Assoc.

— NESFA Index to Short Science Fiction, 1987. (Index Ser.). vi, 42p. 1989. pap. 12.00 (*0-915368-41-2*) New Eng SF Assoc.

— NESFA Index to the Science Fiction Magazines & Original Anthologies, 1986. (Index Ser.). vi, 82p. 1988. pap. 12.00 (*0-915368-32-3*) New Eng SF Assoc.

Mann, Jim & Trusell, A. Stewart, eds. Essentials of Human Nutrition. (Illus.). 658p. 1998. pap. text 59.95 (*0-19-262756-2*) OUP.

Mann, Jim, jt. auth. see Ball, Madaleine.

Mann, John. Chemical Aspects of Biosynthesis. (Chemistry Primers Ser.: No. 20). (Illus.). 96p. (C). 1995. pap. text 12.95 (*0-19-855676-4*) OUP.

— The Elusive Magic Bullet: The Search for the Perfect Drug. LC 98-50251. (Illus.). 220p. 1999. 29.95 (*0-19-850093-9*) OUP.

— Murder, Magic, & Medicine. (Illus.). 240p. 1994. reprint ed. pap. text 24.50 (*0-19-855854-6*) OUP.

— Rudi: Fourteen Years with My Teacher. iv, 243p. 1987. pap. 14.95 (*0-915801-04-3*) Rudra Pr.

Mann, John & Crabbe, James C. Bacteria & Anitbacterial Agents. LC 95-7004. (Biochemical & Medicinal Chemistry Ser.). (Illus.). 88p. (C). 1998. pap. text 21.95 (*0-7167-4508-9*) OUP.

Mann, John & Short, Lar. The Body of Light: History & Practical Techniques for Awakening Your Subtle Body. (Illus.). 192p. (Orig.). 1993. reprint ed. 14.95 (*0-8048-1992-0*) Tuttle Pubng.

Mann, John C., jt. auth. see Pomeroy, John N.

Mann, John E. Southampton Past & Present. 96p. 1987. 30.00 (*0-905392-53-1*) St Mut.

— Southampton People Eminent Sotonians & Assorted Characters. (C). 1989. 39.00 (*1-85455-021-7*, Pub. by Ensign Pubns & Print) St Mut.

Mann, John M. Understanding & Investigating Lost Wage Claims. 48p. 1999. pap. 14.95 (*1-883726-40-9*) Bradford Pub.

Mann, Jonathan, et al, eds. AIDS in the World, 1992. (Illus.). 800p. 1992. text 57.00 (*0-674-01265-8*); pap. text 25.95 (*0-674-01266-6*) HUP.

Mann, Jonathan & Tarantola, Daniel J., eds. AIDS in the World II. 2nd ed. LC 96-20008. (Illus.). 648p. 1996. pap. text 34.50 (*0-19-509097-7*) OUP.

Mann, Jonathan M. Health & Human Rights: A Reader. LC 98-20899. 448p. (C). 1999. 80.00 (*0-415-92101-5*) Routledge.

Mann, Jonathan M., et al, eds. Health & Human Rights: A Reader. LC 98-20899. 448p. 1999. pap. 28.00 (*0-415-92102-3*, D5779) Routledge.

Mann, Josiah S. Before the Wedding Bell Rings: A Marriage Preparation Manual. 96p. 1986. pap. 5.95 (*0-937673-02-1*) Peacock Ent LA.

Mann, Joy H. Voices from the Other Side of the Moon. 40p. 1998. pap. 5.00 (*0-934776-12-1*) Bard Pr.

Mann, Judy. The Difference: Discovering the Hidden Ways We Silence Girls: Finding Alternatives That Can Give Them a Voice. 336p. 1994. 22.95 (*0-446-51707-0*) Warner Bks.

— The Difference: Discovering the Hidden Ways We Silence Girls: Finding Alternatives That Can Give Them a Voice. 336p. 1996. mass mkt. 13.95 (*0-446-67118-5*, Pub. by Warner Bks) Little.

Mann, Jules. Get Naked And. Mycue, Edward, ed. (Took Modern Poetry in English Ser.: Vol. 5). (Illus.). 28p. (Orig.). 1991. pap. 4.00 (*0-9625855-8-0*) Norton Coker Pr.

Mann, Jules, et al. Triad. (Took Modern Poetry in English Ser.: No. 48). (Illus.). 64p. 1997. pap. 12.00 (*1-879457-55-5*) Norton Coker Pr.

Mann, Jules, ed. see Hirshkowitz, Lois.

Mann, K. Tribal Women in Changing Society. 178p. 1987. 21.00 (*0-8364-2034-9*, Pub. by Mittal Pubs Dist) S Asia.

Mann, K., et al. Cultures of the Past: Group 4. (Illus.). 80p. (YA). (gr. 5 up). lib. bdg. 114.00 (*0-7614-0300-0*) Marshall Cavendish.

Mann, K., jt. auth. see Russell, G. L.

Mann, K. H., jt. auth. see Elliott, J. M.

Mann, K. H., jt. ed. see Barnes, R. S.

Mann, Kalman Jacob. Kalman Jacob Mann - Reflections on a Life in Health Care. 334p. 1994. 26.00 (*965-09-0126-4*, 66800, Pub. by R Mass Ltd) Lambda Pubs.

Mann, Kamlesh. Tribal Women: On the Threshold of Twenty-First Century. 174p. 1996. pap. 150.00 (*81-85880-88-3*, Pub. by Print Hse) St Mut.

Mann, Karen B. The Language That Makes George Eliot's Fiction. LC 83-257. 240p. reprint ed. pap. 74.40 (*0-8357-6621-7*, 203526600094) Bks Demand.

Mann, Keith O. & Lane, H. Richard, eds. Graphic Correlation. (SEPM Special Publications: No. 53). (Illus.). 268p. 1995. 89.00 (*1-56576-023-9*) SEPM.

Mann, Kelly M., jt. auth. see Chase-Dunn, Christopher K.

***Mann, Ken.** Ecology of Coastal Waters with Implications for Management. 2nd ed. LC 00-23630. (Illus.). 448p. 2000. pap. 49.95 (*0-86542-550-7*) Blackwell Sci.

Mann, Ken. Implementing Gigabit Networks. (Computer Communications Ser.). 400p. 1998. pap. 49.95 (*0-07-040067-9*) McGraw.

Mann, Kenneth H. & Lazier, John R. Dynamics of Marine Ecosystems: Biological-Physical Interactions in the Oceans. 2nd ed. LC 97-16736. (Illus.). 475p. 1996. pap. text 61.95 (*0-86542-539-6*) Blackwell Sci.

Mann, Kenny. The Ancient Hebrews. LC 97-6551. (Cultures of the Past Ser.). (J). 1998. lib. bdg. 28.50 (*0-7614-0302-7*, Benchmark NY) Marshall Cavendish.

— Egypt, Kush, Aksum: Northeast Africa. LC 96-16440. (African Kingdoms of the Past Ser.). (J). (gr. 4 up). 1996. lib. bdg. 15.95 (*0-87518-655-6*) Silver Burdett Pr.

— Egypt, Kush, Aksum: Northeast Africa. LC 96-16440. (African Kingdoms of the Past Ser.). (Illus.). 128p. (J). (gr. 4 up). 1996. pap. 7.95 (*0-382-39657-X*, Dillon Silver Burdett) Silver Burdett Pr.

— The Guinea Coast: Oyo, Benin, Ashanti. LC 95-16060. (African Kingdoms of the Past Ser.). 128p. (J). (gr. 5-10). 1995. 15.95 (*0-87518-657-2*, Dillon Silver Burdett) Silver Burdett Pr.

— The Guinea Coast: Oyo, Benin, Ashanti. LC 95-16060. (African Kingdoms of the Past Ser.). (Illus.). 128p. (YA). (gr. 5 up). 1995. pap. 7.95 (*0-382-39177-2*) Silver Burdett Pr.

— I Am Not Afraid! Based on a Masai Tale. LC 92-13811. (Illus.). 32p. (J). 1993. pap. 4.50 (*0-553-37108-8*, Litl Rooster) BDD Bks Young Read.

— Kongo Ndongo: West Central Africa. (African Kingdoms of the Past Ser.). (J). (gr. 5). 1996. 15.95 (*0-87518-658-0*, Dillon Silver Burdett); pap. 7.95 (*0-382-39298-1*, Dillon Silver Burdett) Silver Burdett Pr.

— Monomotapa, Great Zimbabwe, Zululand, Lesotho: Southern Africa. LC 95-45536. (African Kingdoms of the Past Ser.). (Illus.). 128p. (J). (gr. 5 up). 1996. pap. 7.95 (*0-382-39300-7*) Silver Burdett Pr.

— Monomotapa, Great Zimbabwe, Zululand, Lesotho: Southern Africa. LC 95-45536. (African Kingdoms of the Past Ser.). (Illus.). 128p. (YA). (gr. 5 up). 1996. lib. bdg. 15.95 (*0-87518-659-9*, Dillon Silver Burdett) Silver Burdett Pr.

— The Western Sudan: Ghana, Mali, Songhay. 128p. 1995. 15.95 (*0-87518-656-4*, Dillon Silver Burdett) Silver Burdett Pr.

— The Western Sudan: Ghana, Mali, Songhay. (African Kingdoms of the Past Ser.). (Illus.). 128p. (YA). (gr. 5 up). 1995. pap. 7.95 (*0-382-39176-4*) Silver Burdett Pr.

— Yellow Dog Dreaming. (Illus.). 74p. 1996. pap. 15.00 (*1-887478-06-X*, WiseAcre) Red Sea NY.

— Yellow Dog Dreaming. 2nd ed. (Illus.). 73p. 1995. reprint ed. 15.00 (*0-9657999-0-5*) raflki Bks.

— Zenj, Buganda: East Africa. (African Kingdoms of the Past Ser.). 1996. 15.95 (*0-87518-660-2*, Dillon Silver Burdett) Silver Burdett Pr.

— Zenj, Buganda: East Africa. LC 96-10618. (African Kingdoms of the Past Ser.). (Illus.). 128p. (J). 1996. pap. 7.95 (*0-382-39658-8*, Dillon Silver Burdett) Silver Burdett Pr.

Mann, Kenton, jt. auth. see Farrell, Isabel.

Mann, Kirk. If Dogs Could Talk & Other Animal Poems. Lanz, Lucille, ed. (Illus.). 128p. (J). (gr. 2-4). 1998. pap. text 12.95 (*1-892517-00-0*) Flying Snail.

— The Making of an English 'Underclass'? The Social Divisions of Welfare & Labour. 192p. 1991. pap. 34.95 (*0-335-09718-9*) OpUniv Pr.

Mann, Klaus. Mephisto. Smyth, Robyn, tr. 272p. 1995. pap. 13.95 (*0-14-018918-1*, Penguin Classics) Viking Penguin.

— Pathetic Symphony: A Biographical Novel about Tchaikovsky. LC 85-50532. (Illus.). 380p. 1985. reprint ed. pap. 9.95 (*0-910129-24-X*) Wiener Pubs Inc.

— The Turning Point: The Autobiography of Klaus Mann. LC 83-27414. 420p. 1984. reprint ed. 18.95 (*0-910129-13-4*); reprint ed. pap. 9.95 (*0-910129-14-2*) Wiener Pubs Inc.

Mann, Kristin & Roberts, Richard. Law in Colonial Africa. LC 90-25784. (Social History of Africa Ser.). 264p. (C). 1991. pap. 22.95 (*0-435-08055-5*, 08055); text 45.00 (*0-435-08053-9*, 08053) Heinemann.

Mann, Laurie, ed. The Noreascon 3 Memory Book. (Illus.). 64p. 1991. 3.00 (*0-9603146-7-9*) MA Convent Fandom.

Mann, Leon, jt. auth. see Janis, Irving L.

Mann, Leonard W. A Bird in the Hand: And the Stories Behind 250 Other Common Expressions. 272p. 1994. pap. 12.00 (*0-671-88994-X*) Prntice Hall Bks.

— Is Anything Too Wonderful for the Lord? Sermons for Sundays after Pentecost, First Third. LC 98-9387. (First Lessons Ser.). 88p. 1998. pap. 8.50 (*0-7880-1233-9*) CSS OH.

— Life-Size Living. Sherer, Michael L., ed. (Orig.). 1986. pap. 6.55 (*0-89536-820-X*, 6829) CSS OH.

Mann, Lester, jt. auth. see Reynolds, Cecil R.

Mann, Lester, jt. ed. see Reynolds, Cecil R.

Mann, Lisa H., jt. ed. see Dutton, Thomas A.

Mann, Lori. A Guide to Better Reading: A Reading Lab Manual. 128p. (C). 1997. ring bd., lab manual ed. 50.95 (*0-7872-3683-7*, 41368301) Kendall-Hunt.

Mann, Marek. Annie's City Adventures. Max, Jill, ed. Verlag, Mangold, tr. from GER. LC 91-21302. (Magic Mountain Fables Ser.). (Illus.). 24p. (J). (gr. k-3). 1991. lib. bdg. 14.60 (*1-56074-031-0*) Garrett Ed Corp.

— Annie's High Sea Adventure. Max, Jill & Bradford, Elizabeth, eds. Verlag, Mangold, tr. from GER. LC 91-21305. (Magic Mountain Fables Ser.). (Illus.). 24p. (J). (gr. k-3). 1991. lib. bdg. 14.60 (*1-56074-027-2*) Garrett Ed Corp.

— Dino, the Star Keeper. Max, Jill, ed. Verlag, Mangold, tr. from GER. LC 91-21304. (Magic Mountain Fables Ser.). (Illus.). 24p. (J). (gr. k-3). 1991. lib. bdg. 14.60 (*1-56074-028-0*) Garrett Ed Corp.

Mann, Maria A. La Mere dans la Litterature Francaise, 1678-1831. (American University Studies: Romance Languages & Literature: Ser. II, Vol. 92). 299p. (C). 1989. text 40.10 (*0-8204-0878-6*) P Lang Pubng.

Mann, Mark. Astrology for the Absolute Beginner: How to Interpret Your Own Birth Chart. LC 95-79881. (Breakthrough Astrology Ser.). (Illus.). 217p. 1997. 21.95 (*0-9648470-0-0*, M3648-014) Am Fed Astrologers.

— The Gringo Trail. 288p. 1999. pap. 12.95 (*1-84024-094-6*, Pub. by Summers) Seven Hills Bk.

— I Had to Drive, I Was Too Drunk to Walk. LC 98-88289. 325p. 1998. 25.00 (*0-7388-0139-9*); pap. 15.00 (*0-7388-0140-2*) Xlibris Corp.

Mann, Martan. Improvising Blues Piano. 1997. pap. text 16.95 (*0-8256-1624-7*, AM945142) Music Sales.

— Jazz Improvisation for the Classical Pianist. (Illus.). 221p. (Orig.). 1989. pap. 29.95 (*0-8256-1229-2*, AM83841) Music Sales.

***Mann, Martin.** China: Library of Nations. rev. ed. (Illus.). 160p. 2000. 25.00 (*0-7881-9444-5*) DIANE Pub.

Mann, Mary J., jt. auth. see Carl, Elsie.

***Mann, Mary Peabody.** Juanita: A Romance of Real Life in Cuba Fifty Years Ago. Ard, Patricia M., ed. & intro. by. LC 99-88124. 304p. 2000. 55.00 (*0-8139-1955-X*); pap. 18.50 (*0-8139-1956-8*) U Pr of Va.

Mann, Mary T. Life of Horace Mann. LC 73-89396. (Black Heritage Library Collection). 1977. 28.95 (*0-8369-8624-5*) Ayer.

Mann, Mary T., tr. see Sarmiento, Domingo Faustino.

Mann, Maybelle. The American Art Union. rev. ed. LC 87-70145. (Illus.). 128p. (C). 1987. pap. 14.95 (*0-9618779-0-1*) ALM Assocs.

— Art in Florida, 1564-1940. LC 98-40884. (Illus.). 208p. 1999. 44.95 (*1-56164-171-5*) Pineapple Pr.

— Walter Launt Palmer. LC 84-50506. (Illus.). 192p. 1989. 35.00 (*0-88740-001-9*) Schiffer.

Mann, Melvin, ed. see Hobson, Vincent H.

***Mann, Michael.** British Rule on Indian Soil: North India in the First Half of the Nineteenth Century. Baron, tr. from GER. LC 99-940402. 1999. 32.00 (*81-7304-271-3*, Pub. by Manohar) S Asia.

Mann, Michael. The Sources of Social Power Vol. 1: A History of Power from the Beginning to AD 1760. (Illus.). 559p. 1986. text 105.00 (*0-521-30851-8*); pap. text 34.95 (*0-521-31349-X*) Cambridge U Pr.

— The Sources of Social Power Vol. 2: The Rise of Classes & Nation States, 1760-1914. (Illus.). 838p. (C). 1993. text 90.00 (*0-521-44015-7*) Cambridge U Pr.

Mann, Michael, jt. auth. see Crompton, Rosemary.

Mann, Michael, ed. see Jacobs, Alan.

Mann, Michael J., et al. Innovative Site Remediation Technology Vol. 3: Soil Washing - Soil Flushing. Anderson, William C., ed. LC 93-20786. (Illus.). 160p. 1994. 79.95 (*1-883767-03-2*) Am Acad Environ.

Mann, N. H. & Carr, N. G. Photosynthetic Prokaryotes. (Biotechnology Handbooks Ser.: Vol. 6). (Illus.). 296p. (C). 1991. text 95.00 (*0-306-43879-8*, Kluwer Plenum) Kluwer Academic.

M

Mann, Nancy R. The Keys to Excellence: The Story of the Deming Philosophy. 3rd ed. 196p. 1989. text 19.00 (*0-9614986-0-9*) Quality Enhance.

Mann, Nicholas. Isle of Avalon: Sacred Mysteries of Arthur & Glastonbury Tor. LC 95-51433. (Illus.). 240p. 1996. pap. 14.95 (*1-56718-459-6*) Llewellyn Pubns.

Mann, Nicholas E. & Olsen, Birger M. Medieval & Renaissance Scholarship: Proceedings of the Second European Science Foundation Workshop on the Classical Tradition in the Middle Ages & the Renaissance (London, Warburg Institute, 27-28 November 1992) LC 96-9830. (Mittellateinische Studien und Texte). 1996. 101.50 (*90-04-10508-5*) Brill Academic Pubs.

Mann, Nicholas R. Dark God: A Personal Journey Through the Underworld. LC 96-50189. 240p. 1997. pap. 14.95 (*1-56718-460-X*) Llewellyn Pubns.

— His Story: Masculinity in the Post-Patriarchal World. LC 95-12264. (Male Mysteries Ser.). (Illus.). 336p. 1999. pap. 16.95 (*1-56718-458-8*) Llewellyn Pubns.

Mann, Nicholas R., jt. auth. see Sutton, Maya Magee.

***Mann, P., ed.** Caribbean Basins: Sedimentary Basins of the World 4. (Sedimentary Basins of the World Ser.). 736p. 1999. 353.00 (*0-444-82649-1*) Elsevier.

Mann, Pamela. Current Issues in Advising Nonprofit Organizations. LC 98-230524. (New York Practice Skills Course Handbook Ser.). 264 p. 1998. 129.00 (*0-87224-528-4*) PLI.

Mann, Patricia S. Micro-Politics: Agency in a Postfeminist Era. LC 93-28965. 264p. 1994. pap. 18.95 (*0-8166-2049-0*) U of Minn Pr.

Mann, Patrick C., ed. see Michigan State University, Institute of Public Utilities Staff.

Mann, Paul. The Burning Ghats. (George Sansi Mystery Ser.). 1997. mass mkt. 5.99 (*0-8041-1550-8*) Ivy Books.

— Masocriticism. LC 98-13738. (SUNY Series in Postmodern Culture). 224p. (C). 1998. text 59.50 (*0-7914-4031-1*); pap. text 19.95 (*0-7914-4032-X*) State U NY Pr.

— Season of the Monsoon. 1995. mass mkt. 5.99 (*0-8041-1259-2*) Ivy Books.

— The Theory - Death of the Avant-Garde. LC 90-49768. (Illus.). 154p. reprint ed. pap. 47.80 (*0-608-09349-1*, 205409500002) Bks Demand.

Mann, Paul, ed. Geologic & Tectonic Development of the Caribbean Plate Boundary in Southern Central America. LC 94-41170. (Special Papers: Vol. 295). 1995. pap. 100.00 (*0-8137-2295-0*) Geol Soc.

Mann, Paul, et al, eds. Geologic & Tectonic Development of the North American-Caribbean Plate Boundary in Hispaniola. (Special Papers: No. 262). (Illus.). 1992. pap. 49.38 (*0-8137-2262-4*) Geol Soc.

Mann, Paul, jt. auth. see Dolan, James F.

***Mann, Paul Z.** I Can Jump Higher. (Fisher-Price All-Star Readers Ser.). (Illus.). 32p. (J). (gr. 1-2). 2000. pap. 3.99 (*1-57584-658-6*, Pub. by Rdrs Digest) S&S Trade.

Mann, Paul Z. Meet My Monster, Level 2. LC 99-19688. (Fisher-Price All-Star Readers Ser.). (Illus.). 32p. (J). (gr. k-3). 1999. pap. 3.99 (*1-57584-308-0*) Rdrs Digest.

Mann, Paul Z. & Doty, Eldon. Kiss Me, I'm a Prince. (Funny Faces Ser.). (J). 2000. bds. 5.99 (*1-57584-415-X*) Rdrs Digest.

***Mann, Paul Z. & Doty, Eldon.** This Little Piggy. (Funny Faces Ser.). (Illus.). 7p. 2000. bds. 5.99 (*1-57584-414-1*) Rdrs Digest.

Mann, Peggy. La Historia de Maria Wanna: O Como te Dana la Marihuana. Ramirez, Gloria & Gatti, Maria N., trs. from ENG. (SPA., Illus.). 44p. (Orig.). (J). (gr. 1-6). 1990. pap. text 3.95 (*0-942493-15-X*) Woodmere Press.

— The Mary Wanna Teacher's Guide. 20p. (gr. 3-6). 1989. pap. 4.50 (*0-318-50074-4*) Woodmere Press.

— Pot Safari: A Visit to the Top Marijuana Researchers. rev. ed. LC 82-91050. 133p. (Orig.). (YA). (gr. 9-12). 1987. pap. 6.95 (*0-942493-01-X*) Woodmere Press.

— The Sad Story of Mary Wanna: or How Marijuana Harms You. rev. ed. 40p. (J). (gr. 1-6). 1990. pap. 3.95 (*0-318-50073-6*) Woodmere Press.

— Twelve Is Too Old. 140p. (YA). (gr. 6-9). 1987. pap. 6.95 (*0-942493-00-1*) Woodmere Press.

Mann, Peggy, jt. auth. see Moran, Bill.

Mann, Penny J. Best Friends. (Miss Penny's Adventures Ser.: No. 1). 48p. 1993. pap. 5.00 (*0-9638742-0-9*) Good News Express.

— Center Lane... Turn Only. (Miss Penny's Adventures Ser.: No. 2). 64p. pap. write for info. (*0-318-72210-0*) Good News Express.

— Don't Die, Marvin. No. 3. 80p. pap. write for info. (*0-318-72211-9*) Good News Express.

Mann, Pete, jt. ed. see Jones, Merrick.

Mann, Pete M., jt. auth. see Mann, Rebecca C.

***Mann, Peter.** The Simpsons. 2000. pap. 5.95 (*1-903047-09-9*, Pub. by Pocket Essentials) Trafalgar.

— The Slayer Files: A Completely & Utterly Unauthorised Guide to Buffy the Vampire Slayer. 96p. 2000. pap. 5.95 (*1-903047-02-1*, Pub. by Pocket Essentials) Trafalgar.

— Stephen King. 2000. pap. 5.95 (*1-903047-16-1*, Pub. by Pocket Essentials) Trafalgar.

Mann, Peter & Lewis, Candace. Annotated Insurance Contracts Act. 300p. 1994. pap. 65.00 (*0-455-21255-4*, Pub. by LawBk Co) Gaunt.

***Mann, Peter & Lewis, Candace.** Annotated Insurance Contracts Act. 3rd ed. 1999. pap. 53.00 (*0-455-21640-1*, 18161, Pub. by LBC Info Servs) Gaunt.

Mann, Philip, jt. ed. see Crompton, Rob.

Mann, Philip H. Guide for Educating Mainstreamed Students. 4th ed. LC 91-4162. 588p. 1991. pap. text 63.00 (*0-205-13225-1*, Longwood Div) Allyn.

Mann, Phillip. Wulfsyarn: A Mosaic. 368p. 1993. mass mkt. 4.99 (*0-380-71717-4*, Avon Bks) Morrow Avon.

Mann, Prem S. Introductory Statistics. 2nd ed. 1995. pap. text 25.00 (*0-471-11743-9*) Wiley.

Mann, Prem S. Introductory Statistics. 3rd ed. LC 97-11033. 816p. 1997. text 93.95 (*0-471-16546-8*) Wiley.

***Mann, Prem S.** Introductory Statistics. 4th ed. 832p. (C). 2000. write for info. (*0-471-37353-2*) Wiley.

— Introductory Statistics: Graphing Calculator Manual. 3rd ed. 144p. 1997. pap. 28.95 (*0-471-19855-2*) Wiley.

Mann, Prem S. Statistics for Business & Economics. 912p. 1994. text 95.95 (*0-471-58969-1*) Wiley.

Mann, Prem S. Statistics for Business & Economics. 360p. 1995. pap. text, student ed. 31.95 (*0-471-11678-5*) Wiley.

— Statistics for Business & Economics. 1995. pap. text 25.00 (*0-471-11745-5*) Wiley.

Mann, Prem S. & Minitab, Inc. Staff. Statistics for Business & Economics & the Student Edition of Minitab for Windows. 1080p. 1996. 89.95 incl. disk (*0-471-17446-7*) Wiley.

Mann, R., et al, eds. Gravitation: A BANFF Summer Institute: BANFF Center, Alberta, Canada, 12-25 August 1990. 650p. (C). 1991. text 130.00 (*981-02-0751-4*) World Scientific Pub.

Mann, R. B. & Mclenaghan, R. G. General Relativity & Relativistic Astrophysics-Proceedings of the 5th Canadian Conference. 500p. 1994. text 118.00 (*981-02-1916-4*) World Scientific Pub.

Mann, R. D., ed. The History of the Management of Pain: From Early Principles to Present Practice. (History of Medicine Ser.). (Illus.). 204p. 1988. 58.00 (*1-85070-183-0*) Prthnon Pub.

— Oral Contraceptives & Breast Cancer: The Implications of the Present Findings for Informed Consent & Informed Choice. (Illus.). 406p. 1990. 65.00 (*1-85070-282-9*) Prthnon Pub.

Mann, R. D., et al. William Withering & the Foxglove. 1986. text 330.00 (*0-85200-950-X*) Kluwer Academic.

Mann, R. D., jt. ed. see Costello, J. F.

Mann, R. J. Our Miss Brooks - Musical. 182p. 1962. pap. 5.95 (*0-87129-708-6*, O03) Dramatic Pub.

— Our Miss Brooks - Straight. rev. ed. 1978. pap. 5.95 (*0-87129-253-X*, O25) Dramatic Pub.

— Our Miss Brooks & the Christmas Carol. 1954. pap. 3.50 (*0-87129-209-2*, O26) Dramatic Pub.

Mann, R. K. Tribal Cultures & Change. (C). 1989. 42.00 (*0-685-32674-8*, Pub. by Mittal Pubs Dist) S Asia.

Mann, R. S. Culture & Integration of Indian Tribes. 193p. (C). 1993. pap. 125.00 (*81-85880-03-4*, Pub. by Print Hse) St Mut.

Mann, R. S., ed. Tribes of India: Ongoing Challenges. LC 96-900898. 411p. 1996. pap. 325.00 (*81-7533-007-4*, Pub. by Print Hse) St Mut.

Mann, Ralph. After the Gold Rush: Society in Grass Valley & Nevada City, California, 1849-1870. LC 81-52825. (Illus.). 320p. 1982. 39.50 (*0-8047-1136-4*) Stanford U Pr.

Mann, Ralph & Griffin, Fred. Swing Like a Pro: Breakthrough Scientific Method of Perfecting Your Golf Swing. LC 98-23534. (Illus.). 256p. 1998. 27.50 (*0-7679-0236-X*) Broadway BDD.

Mann, Randy, jt. auth. see Loffman, Tom.

Mann, Randy, ed. & illus. see Loffman, Tom.

Mann, Rebecca C. & Mann, Pete M. Essay Writing: Methods & Models. 416p. (C). 1989. 27.50 (*0-534-12168-3*) Wadsworth Pub.

Mann, Richard A. Business Law. 9th ed. Date not set. pap. text, teacher ed. write for info. (*0-314-03383-1*) West Pub.

— Business Law: Chap. 1-19, Chapters 1-19. 8th ed. Date not set. pap. text 38.50 (*0-314-90598-7*) West Pub.

— Business Law Ucc 9e Classic Cases Supp. 10th ed. (Paralegal). (C). 1993. pap. 14.75 (*0-314-03579-6*) West Pub.

— Contemporary Business Law. Date not set. pap. text, teacher ed. write for info. (*0-314-06368-4*) West Pub.

— Smith & Roberson's Business Law. 10th ed. (LA - Business Law Ser). (C). 1997. mass mkt. 67.95 (*0-314-14080-8*) Wadsworth Pub.

Mann, Richard A. & Roberts, Barry S. Bus Law & The Regulation Of Business.5/e. 5th ed. LC 95-44763. (SWC-Business Law). 1000p. (C). 1995. pap. 74.00 (*0-314-06460-5*) West Pub.

— Business Law & the Regulation of Business. 6th ed. LC 98-7411. 1998. write for info. (*0-324-00286-6*); pap. 109.95 (*0-538-88482-7*) Sth-Wstrn College.

— Business Law For Ucc 9e. 9th ed. Bruckner, ed. LC 93-21510. (SWC-Business Law). 1250p. (C). 1993. text 71.25 (*0-314-02712-2*) West Pub.

Mann, Richard A. & Roberts, Barry S. Essentials of B-law & The Legal Environment. 5th ed. LC 94-28022. (SWC-Business Law). 1226p. (C). 1994. mass mkt. 58.25 (*0-314-04529-5*) West Pub.

Mann, Richard A. & Roberts, Barry S. Essentials of Business Law & the Legal Environment. 6th ed. LC 97-21395. 1997. 104.95 (*0-538-87876-2*) S-W Pub.

Mann, Richard A., et al. Smith & Roberson's Business Law. 10th ed. LC 96-38398. 1996. write for info. (*0-314-20227-7*) West Pub.

Mann, Richard A., jt. auth. see Smith.

Mann, Richard D. The Light of Consciousness: Explorations in Transpersonal Psychology. LC 83-18088. 177p. (C). 1984. pap. text 14.95 (*0-87395-906-X*) State U NY Pr.

Mann, Richard G. El Greco & His Patrons: Three Major Projects. (Cambridge Studies in the History of Art). (Illus.). 184p. 1989. pap. text 28.95 (*0-521-38943-7*) Cambridge U Pr.

Mann, Richard I. Travel Guide Indonesia. (Holiday Sports of Tomorrow Ser.). (Illus.). 200p. 1991. pap. 14.95 (*981-00-2393-6*) Intl Spec Bk.

Mann, Rink. Backyard Sugarin' 3rd rev. ed. LC 91-38399. (Illus.). 96p. 1978. pap. 9.50 (*0-88150-216-2*, Pub. by Countryman) Norton.

Mann, Rip & Mann, Tammi. Hewing Contemporary Bowls. LC 94-24311. (Schiffer Book for Woodcarvers Ser.). (Illus.). 64p. (Orig.). 1995. pap. 12.95 (*0-88740-710-2*) Schiffer.

— Sculpting Traditional Bowls. LC 94-66374. (Illus.). 48p. (Orig.). 1994. pap. 12.95 (*0-88740-698-X*) Schiffer.

Mann, Robert. Andrei Bely's Petersburg & the Cult of Dionysus. (Illus.). 124p. (C). 1987. 15.00 (*0-87291-170-5*) Coronado Pr.

— The Dionysian Art of Isaac Babel. (Illus.). 134p. (Orig.). (C). 1994. pap. 12.50 (*0-936041-08-0*) Barbary Coast Bks.

***Mann, Robert.** A Grand Delusion: America's Descent into Vietnam. 2000. 35.00 (*0-465-04369-0*, Pub. by Basic) HarpC.

Mann, Robert. Lances Sing: A Study of the Igor Tale. 231p. (Orig.). 1990. pap. 21.95 (*0-89357-208-X*) Slavica.

— Russian Apocalypse: Songs & Tales about the Coming of Christianity to Russia. 151p. (C). 1987. 12.95 (*0-87291-172-1*) Coronado Pr.

— The Walls of Jericho: Lyndon Johnson, Hubert Humphrey, Richard Russell, & the Struggle for Civil Rights. 624p. 1997. pap. 15.00 (*0-15-600501-8*); pap. 15.00 (*0-614-27376-5*, Harvest Bks) Harcourt.

Mann, Robert W. & Murphy, Sean P. Regional Atlas of Bone Disease: A Guide to Pathologic & Normal Variation in the Human Skeleton. (Illus.). 224p. 1990. pap. 34.95 (*0-398-06267-6*) C C Thomas.

— Regional Atlas of Bone Disease: A Guide to Pathologic & Normal Variation in the Human Skeleton. (Illus.). 224p. (C). 1990. text 47.95 (*0-398-05675-7*) C C Thomas.

Mann, Robert W., ed. see McCullough, Christopher J.

***Mann, Roberts.** Essentials of Business Law & the Legal Environment. 7th ed. (SWC-General Business Ser.). 2000. pap. 105.95 (*0-324-04052-0*) Thomson Learn.

— Smith & Roberson's Business Law. 11th ed. LC 99-27528. (SWC-Business Law Ser.). 1142p. 1999. pap. 109.95 (*0-324-00195-9*) Thomson Learn.

Mann, Roger. Antimarket Economics: Blind Logic, Better Science, & the Diversity of Economic Competition. LC 96-16272. 208p. 1996. 57.95 (*0-275-95466-8*, Praeger Pubs) Greenwood.

Mann, Roger, jt. ed. see Rosenfield, Aaron.

Mann, Ronald D. Hormone Replacement Therapy & Breast Cancer Risk. (Illus.). 321p. 1992. 78.00 (*1-85070-399-X*) Prthnon Pub.

— Modern Drug Use. 1984. text 242.50 (*0-85200-717-5*) Kluwer Academic.

Mann, Ronald D., ed. Patient Information in Medicine. (Illus.). 199p. 1991. text 35.00 (*1-85070-367-1*) Prthnon Pub.

Mann, Ronald J. Cases, Materials & Problems on Payment Systems & Other Financial Transactions LC 98-48313. 1999. boxed set 48.00 (*0-7355-0342-7*) Panel Pubs.

— Infections of the Hand. LC 87-21434. 204p. reprint ed. pap. 63.30 (*0-7837-2726-7*, 204310600006) Bks Demand.

***Mann, Ronald J.** Payment Systems & Other Financial Transactions: With Teacher's Manual. (Casebook Ser.). 650p. 1999. teacher ed. write for info. (*0-7355-0014-2*, 00142) Panel Pubs.

Mann, Ronald L. Personal Relationship Inventory (PRI) Manual for Scoring & Interpretation. 91p. (Orig.). 1994. pap. 18.00 (*1-879858-03-7*) Behaviordyne.

— Sacred Healing: Integrating Spirituality with Psychotherapy. LC 97-48821. 256p. (Orig.). 1997. 14.95 (*1-57733-016-1*) B Dolphin Pub.

— Sacred Healing: Integrating Spirituality with Psychotherapy. LC 97-48821. 272p. (Orig.). 1998. pap. 19.95 incl. cd-rom (*1-57733-028-5*) B Dolphin Pub.

Mann, Russell A. USL Journalism Manual of Style & Format. LC 86-90665. 115p. (Orig.). 1986. pap. 9.95 (*0-940205-00-9*) Journalism Style.

Mann, Ruth, jt. auth. see Horowitz, Estelle.

Mann, Sally. Immediate Family. (Illus.). 88p. 1992. 68.00 (*0-89381-518-7*) Aperture.

— Immediate Family. 1994. pap. 37.95 (*0-89381-523-3*) Aperture.

— Still Time. (Illus.). 80p. 1994. pap. 44.95 (*0-89381-593-4*) Aperture.

Mann, Sally, photos by. At Twelve. (Illus.). 56p. 1991. reprint ed. pap. 37.95 (*0-89381-330-3*) Aperture.

***Mann, Samuel.** Healing Hypertension: A Revolutional New Approach. LC 99-57436. 244p. 1999. pap. 14.95 (*0-471-37643-4*) Wiley.

***Mann, Samuel J.** A Revolutionary New Approach: Uncovering the Secret Power of Your Hidden Emotions. LC 98-17434. 256p. 1998. 24.95 (*0-471-17547-1*) Wiley.

Mann, Sandi. Hiding What We Feel, Faking What We Don't: Understanding the Role of Your Emotions at Work. LC 99-13981. 224p. 1999. pap. 19.95 (*1-86204-464-3*, Pub. by Element MA) Penguin Putnam.

Mann, Scott. Heart of a Heartless World: Religion As Ideology. 400p. 1998. 53.99 (*1-55164-127-5*, Pub. by Black Rose); pap. 24.99 (*1-55164-126-7*, Pub. by Black Rose) Consort Bk Sales.

***Mann, Scott.** Linux System Security: The Administrator's Guide to Open Source Security Tools. LC 99-59100. 604p. 1999. 48.99 (*0-13-015807-0*) P-H.

Mann, Scott. Psychoanalysis & Society: An Introduction. 290p. 1994. pap. 27.95 (*0-614-13110-3*, Pub. by New South Wales Univ Pr) Intl Spec Bk.

***Mann, Sheilah & Karpowicz, Polly Leonard, eds.** Earning a PhD in Political Science. 3rd rev. ed. 16p. (C). 1999. pap. 4.00 (*1-878147-44-7*) Am Political.

Mann, Stanley. Triggers: A New Approach to Self-Motivation. 226p. (C). 1986. text 25.95 (*0-13-930793-1*) P-H.

Mann, Stephen, ed. Biomimetic Materials Chemistry. 400p. 1995. 165.00 (*0-471-18597-3*) Wiley.

Mann, Stephen, ed. Biomimetic Materials Chemistry. (Illus.). xvi, 384p. 1995. 125.00 (*1-56081-669-4*, Wiley-VCH) Wiley.

Mann, Steve. Programming Applications with the Wireless Application Protocol: The Complete Developer's Guide. LC 99-42181. 256p. 1999. 49.99 incl. cd-rom (*0-471-32754-9*) Wiley.

— The Smalltalk Resource Guide. 3rd ed. 300p. 1995. pap. write for info. (*0-9642181-1-9*) Creat Digital.

Mann, Steve & Mallin, Ken. The Mann-Mallin Fantasy Baseball Guide - 1992. (Illus.). 184p. 1998. reprint ed. pap. text 5.00 (*0-7881-5152-5*) DIANE Pub.

***Mann, Steve & Rischpater, Ray.** Advanced Palm Programming: Professional Developer's Guide. 2000. pap. 49.99 incl. cd-rom (*0-471-39087-9*) Wiley.

***Mann, Steve & Sbihli, Scott.** The Wireless Application Protocol (WAP) A Wiley Tech Brief. 208p. 2000. pap. 29.99 (*0-471-39992-2*) Wiley.

Mann, Steven. Being Ill: Personal & Social Meanings. 204p. 1982. text 29.50 (*0-8290-0720-2*) Irvington.

— Being Ill: Personal & Social Meanings. 204p. 1985. reprint ed. pap. text 12.95 (*0-8290-1661-9*) Irvington.

***Mann, Steven.** The Firefly: A Novel. 2000. pap. 18.00 (*0-7388-2203-5*) Xlibris Corp.

Mann, Stuart H., jt. auth. see Johnson, Edward R.

***Mann, Susan.** East Asia (China, Japan, Korea) LC 99-57347. (Women's & Gender History in Global Perspective Ser.). (Illus.). (C). 1999. pap. 8.00 (*0-87229-116-2*) Am Hist Assn.

Mann, Susan. Local Merchants & the Chinese Bureaucracy, 1750-1950. LC 86-14403. (Illus.). 296p. 1987. 42.50 (*0-8047-1341-3*) Stanford U Pr.

— Precious Records: Women in China's Long Eighteenth Century. LC 96-25757. 1997. write for info. (*0-8047-2743-0*); pap. 19.95 (*0-8047-2744-9*) Stanford U Pr.

Mann, Susan A. Agrarian Capitalism in Theory & Practice. LC 89-22656. (Illus.). xvi, 212p. (C). 1990. 39.95 (*0-8078-1885-2*) U of NC Pr.

Mann, Susan G., et al. Women Playwrights in England, Ireland, & Scotland, 1660-1823. Mann, David D., ed. LC 95-78939. 432p. (C). 1996. text 69.95 (*0-253-33087-4*) Ind U Pr.

Mann, T. Spermatophores: Development, Structure, Biochemical Attributes & Role in the Transfer of Spermatozoa. (Zoophysiology Ser.: Vol. 15). (Illus.). 240p. 1984. 114.95 (*0-387-13583-9*) Spr-Verlag.

Mann, T. & Lutwak-Mann, C. Male Reproductive Function & Semen. (Illus.). 498p. 1981. 142.00 (*0-387-10383-X*) Spr-Verlag.

Mann, Tammi, jt. auth. see Mann, Rip.

***Mann, Tanny McCarthy.** I Wish Someone Had Told Me - For Women Vol. 1: I Wish I Had Listened. 380p. 1999. pap. 10.95 (*0-9656667-3-5*) Sales Networks.

Mann, Tanny McCarthy. Life's Wake-Up Calls. (Illus.). 368p. 1997. pap. 24.95 (*0-9656667-0-0*) Sales Networks.

Mann, Thomas. The Black Swan. Trask, Willard R., tr. 155p. 1990. 30.00 (*0-520-07008-9*, Pub. by U CA Pr); pap. 14.95 (*0-520-07009-7*, Pub. by U CA Pr) Cal Prin Full Svc.

Mann, Thomas. Black Swan. 158p. 18.95 (*0-8488-2490-3*) Amereon Ltd.

Mann, Thomas. Buddenbrooks: The Decline of a Family. Woods, John E., tr. from GER. LC 92-18990. 1993. 35.00 (*0-679-41994-2*) Knopf.

— Buddenbrooks: The Decline of a Family. Woods, John E., tr. LC 92-52929. 640p. 1994. 20.00 (*0-679-41737-0*) Knopf.

— Buddenbrooks: The Decline of a Family. Woods, John E., tr. 848p. 1994. pap. 16.00 (*0-679-75260-9*) Random.

— Children & Fools. Scheffauer, Herman G., tr. LC 71-142268. (Short Story Index Reprint Ser.). 1977. 18.95 (*0-8369-3752-X*) Ayer.

— Confessions of Felix Krull, Confidence Man. 1993. 28.50 (*0-8446-6715-3*) Peter Smith.

— Confessions of Felix Krull, Confidence Man: The Early Years. Lindley, Denver, tr. 1992. pap. 14.00 (*0-679-73904-1*) Vin Bks.

— Death in Venice. annot. ed. Appelbaum, Stanley, tr. & comment by. LC 95-2967. (Thrift Editions Ser.). 96p. (Orig.). 1995. pap. text 1.00 (*0-486-28714-9*) Dover.

— Death in Venice: A Case Study in Contemporary Criticism, Vol. 1. Ritter, Naomi, ed. (Case Studies in Contemporary Criticism). 288p. 1998. pap. text 12.95 (*0-312-12002-8*) St Martin.

— Death in Venice: And Seven Other Stories. Lowe-Porter, Helen T., tr. (International Ser.). 404p. (Orig.). 1989. pap. 10.00 (*0-679-72206-8*) Vin Bks.

— Death in Venice & Other Stories. Luke, David, tr. & intro. by. 320p. 1988. mass mkt. 5.95 (*0-553-21333-4*) Bantam.

— Death in Venice & Other Tales. 1976. 13.95 (*0-8488-0574-7*) Amereon Ltd.

— Death in Venice & Other Tales. Heller, Erich, tr. (Modern Library College Editions). 436p. (C). 1970. 8.44 (*0-07-553669-2*, T99) McGraw.

— Death in Venice & Other Tales. Chase, Jefferson S., tr. from GER. LC 98-50734. 320p. 1999. mass mkt. 5.95 (*0-451-52609-0*, Sig Classics) NAL.

— Death in Venice & Other Tales. Kolb, Clayton, ed. & tr. by. (Critical Editions Ser.). (C). 1994. pap. 10.50 (*0-393-96013-7*) Norton.

— Death in Venice & Other Tales. 1999. pap. 9.95 (*0-14-118173-7*) Viking Penguin.

— Death in Venice & Other Tales. 451p. 1983. reprint ed. lib. bdg. 16.95 (*0-89966-455-5*) Buccaneer Bks.

— Death in Venice, Tonio Kroger & Other Writings. Lubich, Frederick A., ed. LC 98-53761. (German Library: Vol. 63). 324p. 1999. 39.50 (*0-8264-0970-9*) Continuum.

— Doctor Faustus. 1992. 20.00 (*0-679-41328-6*) Everymns Lib.

An Asterisk (*) at the beginning of an entry indicates that the title is appearing for the first time.

— Doctor Faustus. Lowe-Porter, H. T., tr. 1992. 20.00 (*0-679-40996-3*) Everymns Lib.

— Doctor Faustus: The Life of a German Composer, Adrian Leverkukn, As Told a Friend. Lowe-Porter, H. T., tr. 1992. pap. 14.00 (*0-679-73905-X*) Vin Bks.

— A Guide to Library Research Methods. LC 87-1565. (Illus.). 224p. 1987. text 30.00 (*0-19-504943-8*) OUP.

— A Guide to Library Research Methods. LC 87-1565. (Illus.). 224p. 1990. pap. text 12.95 (*0-19-504944-6*) OUP.

— The Holy Sinner. Lowe-Porter, Helen T., tr. 1992. 30.00 (*0-520-07672-9*, Pub. by U CA Pr); pap. 16.95 (*0-520-07671-0*, Pub. by U CA Pr) Cal Prin Full Svc.

— The Letters of Thomas Mann, 1889-1955. Winston, Richard & Winston, Clara, eds. & trs. by. 1990. 50.00 (*0-520-07004-6*, Pub. by U CA Pr); pap. 15.95 (*0-520-06968-4*, Pub. by U CA Pr) Cal Prin Full Svc.

— Letters to Paul Amann, 1915-1952. Wegener, Herbert, ed. Winston, Richard & Winston, Clara, trs. LC 60-7258. 196p. reprint ed. pap. 60.80 (*0-608-30825-0*, 200195500011) Bks Demand.

— Library Research Models: A Guide to Classifications, Catalogs & Computers. LC 92-34311. (Illus.). 264p. 1993. text 30.00 (*0-19-508190-0*) OUP.

— Library Research Models: A Guide to Classifications, Catalogs & Computers. (Illus.). 268p. (C). 1994. reprint ed. pap. 17.95 (*0-19-509395-X*) OUP.

— Lotte in Weimar: The Beloved Returns. Lowe-Porter, Helen T., tr. 475p. 1990. 30.00 (*0-520-07006-2*, Pub. by U CA Pr); pap. 17.95 (*0-520-07007-0*, Pub. by U CA Pr) Cal Prin Full Svc.

— The Magic Mountain. 1976. 33.95 (*0-8488-0576-3*) Amereon Ltd.

— The Magic Mountain. Lowe-Porter, Helen T., tr. (C). 1967. pap. text 6.75 (*0-07-553665-X*, 30993) McGraw.

— The Magic Mountain. 1996. pap. 17.00 (*0-679-77287-1*) McKay.

— The Magic Mountain. 340p. 1983. reprint ed. lib. bdg. 28.95 (*0-89966-454-7*) Buccaneer Bks.

— The Magic Mountain. Woods, John E., tr. 700p. 1995. reprint ed. 50.00 (*0-679-44183-2*) Knopf.

— Mario the Magician. 1991. reprint ed. lib. bdg. 19.95 (*1-56849-035-6*) Buccaneer Bks.

— La Montana Magica. 1998. pap. 10.95 (*84-01-42611-1*) Lectorum Pubns.

— Nocturnes. LC 79-140336. (Short Story Index Reprint Ser.). 1977. 11.95 (*0-8369-3728-7*) Ayer.

— On Myself & Other Princeton Lectures. 2nd rev. ed. LC 98-12586. (European University Studies: Vol. 36). 201p. (C). 1998. pap. text 37.95 (*0-8204-3522-8*) P Lang Pubng.

— On Myself & Other Princeton Lectures: An Annotated Edition by James N. Bade Based on Mann's Lecture Typescripts. 2nd ed. Kraft, Herbert, ed. (Historisch-kritische Arbeiten zur Deutschen Literatur Ser.: Bd. 18). 166p. 1997. 35.95 (*3-631-32403-0*) P Lang Pubng.

— Order of the Day: Political Speeches of Two Decades. LC 79-80389. (Essay Index Reprint Ser.). 1977. 31.95 (*0-8369-1060-5*) Ayer.

— The Oxford Guide to Library Research. (Illus.). 336p. 1998. 35.00 (*0-19-512312-3*); pap. 14.95 (*0-19-512313-1*) OUP.

— Past Masters & Other Papers. Lowe-Porter, Helen T., tr. LC 68-25605. (Essay Index Reprint Ser.). 1977. 17.95 (*0-8369-0674-8*) Ayer.

— Pro & Contra Wagner/Thomas Mann. Blunden, Allan, tr. LC 85-20819. (GER.). 240p. 1992. lib. bdg. 25.00 (*0-226-50334-8*) U Ch Pr.

— Royal Highness. Curtis, A. Cecil, tr. 360p. 1992. 30.00 (*0-520-07674-5*, Pub. by U CA Pr); pap. 16.95 (*0-520-07673-7*, Pub. by U CA Pr) Cal Prin Full Svc.

— Six Early Stories. Pike, Burton, ed. Constantine, Peter, tr. from GER. (Classics Ser.: No. 109). 136p. 1997. 22.95 (*1-55713-298-4*) Sun & Moon CA.

— Six Early Stories. 136p. 1999. pap. 11.95 (*1-55713-385-9*, Pub. by Sun & Moon CA) SPD-Small Pr Dist.

— Tagebuecher, 1953-1952. Jens, Inge, ed. (GER.). 978p. 1995. 115.25 (*3-10-048214-X*, Pub. by S Fischer) Intl Bk Import.

— Thomas Mann - Felix Bertaux: Correspondence, 1923-1948. Cap, Biruta, ed. LC 93-26886. (Studies in Modern German Literature: Vol. 49). XVII, 216p. (C). 1994. text 49.95 (*0-8204-1842-0*) P Lang Pubng.

— Thomas Mann's "Goethe & Tolstoy" Notes & Sources. Koelb, Clayton, ed. & tr. by. Scott, Alcyone, tr. LC 82-13497. 267p. 1984. pap. 82.80 (*0-7837-8388-4*, 205919900009) Bks Demand.

— Der Tod in Venedig und andere Erzaehlungen. (GER.). 330p. 1995. pap. 13.50 (*3-596-20054-7*, Pub. by Fischer Tasch) Intl Bk Import.

— Tonio Kroeger/Mario und der Zauberer. (GER.). 128p. 1996. pap. 10.00 (*3-596-21381-9*, Pub. by Fischer Tasch) Intl Bk Import.

— Tonio Kroger. (GER.). 126p. (C). 1992. reprint ed. pap. text 8.50 (*0-88133-655-6*) Waveland Pr.

— Transposed Heads. 1959. pap. 10.00 (*0-394-70086-4*) Vin Bks.

— Unordnung und fruehes Leid: Erzaehlungen, 1910-1930. (GER.). 240p. 1991. pap. 13.50 (*3-596-29441-X*, Pub. by Fischer Tasch) Intl Bk Import.

— Der Zauberberg: Roman. (GER.). 1008p. 1991. pap. 22.50 (*3-596-29433-9*, Pub. by Fischer Tasch) Intl Bk Import.

***Mann, Thomas & Woods, John E.** Doctor Faustus: Life of German Composer A. Leverkuhn as Told by a Frienc. 544p. 1999. pap. 16.00 (*0-375-70116-8*) Vin Bks.

Mann, Thomas, et al. Letters of Heinrich & Thomas Mann, 1900-1949. Mann, Heinrich & Wysling, Hans, eds. Winston, Richard & Winston, Clara, trs. from GER. LC 96-38461. (Weimar & Now Ser.). (Illus.). 700p. 1997. 50.00 (*0-520-07278-2*, Pub. by U CA Pr) Cal Prin Full Svc.

Mann, Thomas, jt. auth. see Amoia, Alba della Fazia.

Mann, Thomas, jt. auth. see Swales, Martin.

Mann, Thomas E. Intensive Care: How Congress Shapes Health Policy. Ornstein, Norman J., ed. LC 95-4436. 316p. 1995. pap. text 18.95 (*0-8157-5463-9*) Brookings.

Mann, Thomas E., ed. A Question of Balance: The President, the Congress, & Foreign Policy. 265p. 1989. pap. 16.95 (*0-8157-5453-1*) Brookings.

— A Question of Balance: The President, the Congress, & Foreign Policy. 265p. 1990. 36.95 (*0-8157-5454-X*) Brookings.

Mann, Thomas E. & Ornstein, Norman J. Congress, the Press, & the Public. 212p. (C). 1994. 38.95 (*0-8157-5462-0*) Brookings.

— Congress, the Press, & the Public. 212p. (C). 1994. pap. 16.95 (*0-8157-5461-2*) Brookings.

— Renewing Congress: A Second Report. 86p. (C). 1993. pap. 9.95 (*0-8157-5459-0*) Brookings.

Mann, Thomas E. & Ornstein, Norman J., eds. The American Elections of 1982. LC 83-11843. (AEI Studies: No. 389). (Illus.). 223p. reprint ed. pap. 69.20 (*0-7837-1079-8*, 204160900021) Bks Demand.

— Intensive Care: How Congress Shapes Health Policy. LC 95-4436. (Renewing Congress Ser.). 316p. (C). 1995. 42.95 (*0-8157-5464-7*) Brookings.

Mann, Thomas E. & Orren, Gary R., eds. Media Polls in American Politics. 172p. (C). 1992. 34.95 (*0-8157-5456-6*); pap. 14.95 (*0-8157-5455-8*) Brookings.

Mann, Thomas E. & Orstein, Norman J. Renewing Congress: A First Report. 76p. (C). 1992. pap. 9.95 (*0-8157-5457-4*) Brookings.

Mann, Thomas E., jt. ed. see Jennings, M. Kent.

Mann, Thomas E., jt. ed. see Ornstein, Norman J.

***Mann, Thomas H. & Hennessy, John J., eds.** Fighting with the Eighteenth Massachusetts: The Civil War Memoir of Thomas H. Mann. LC 00-8371. (Illus.). 288p. 2000. 34.95 (*0-8071-2577-6*) La State U Pr.

Mann, Thomas W. The Book of the Torah. LC 87-25079. 1988. pap. 19.95 (*0-8042-0085-8*) Westminster John Knox.

— Deuteronomy. Bartlett, David L. & Miller, Patrick D., eds. (Westminster Bible Companion Ser.). 196p. 1995. pap. 16.00 (*0-664-25266-4*) Westminster John Knox.

Mann, Thomas W., Jr. Financing Information Services: Problems Changing Approaches & New Opportunities for Academic & Research Libraries, 6. Spyers-Duran, Peter, ed. LC 84-15729. (New Directions in Librarianship Ser.: No. 6). (Illus.). 197p. 1985. 49.95 (*0-313-24644-0*, SPY/) Greenwood.

Mann, Thomas W., Jr., jt. ed. see Spyers-Duran, Peter.

Mann, Thorbjoern. Building Economics for Architects. 199p. 1992. 54.95 (*0-471-28403-3*, VNR) Wiley.

— Building Economics for Architects. (Illus.). 224p. 1992. text 42.95 (*0-442-00389-7*, VNR) Wiley.

Mann, Tom. Speak Now or Forever Rest in Peace: The Very Real Dangers of HMOs - & What You Can Do about Them. LC 99-173185. (Illus.). iv, 110 p. 1997. 7.99 (*0-9659594-0-6*) G Miller.

Mann, Traci, jt. ed. see Kato, Pamela M.

***Mann, U.** Synthetic Oils for Worm Gear Lubrication. (Technical Papers: Vol. 99FTM17). 9p. 1999. pap. 30.00 (*1-55589-755-X*) AGMA.

Mann, Uzi. Principles of Chemical Reactor Analysis & Design: New Tools for Industrial Chemical Reactor Operations. 450p. 1999. 89.00 (*0-9673761-0-6*) Plains.

Mann, V. The Seeds That Grew to Be a Hundred. Matthew 13:1-17. LC 59-1209. (Arch Bks.). (Illus.). 24p. 1973. pap. 1.99 (*0-570-06091-5*, 59-1209) Concordia.

Mann, Vivian, et al, eds. Convivencia: Jews, Muslims, & Christians in Medieval Spain. LC 92-10069. (Illus.). 272p. (Orig.). 1992. pap. 25.00 (*0-8076-1286-3*) Braziller.

— Convivencia: Jews, Muslims & Christians in Medieval Spain. LC 92-10069. (Illus.). 272p. (Orig.). 1992. 50.00 (*0-8076-1283-9*) Braziller.

***Mann, Vivian B.** Jewish Texts on the Visual Arts. LC 99-14938. (Illus.). 272p. (C). 2000. 70.00 (*0-521-65217-0*) Cambridge U Pr.

Mann, Vivian B., ed. Gardens & Ghettos: The Art of Jewish Life in Italy. (Illus.). 250p. 1989. pap. 50.00 (*0-520-06825-4*, Pub. by U CA Pr) Cal Prin Full Svc.

Mann, Vivian B. & Cohen, Richard I. From Court Jews to the Rothschilds, 1600-1800: Art, Patronage, Power. LC 97-115581. (Illus.). 252p. 1996. 65.00 (*3-7913-1624-9*, Pub. by Prestel) te Neues.

Mann, Vivian B. & Kleeblatt, Norman L. Treasures of the Jewish Museum. LC 85-28913. (Illus.). 216p. 1986. pap. 19.95 (*0-87663-890-6*, Pub. by Universe); text 35.00 (*0-87663-493-5*, Pub. by Universe) St Martin.

Mann, Vivian B. & Tucker, Gordon, eds. The Seminar on Jewish Art: Proceedings. 37p. (Orig.). 1985. pap. 6.00 (*0-87334-029-9*) Jewish Sem.

Mann, Vivian B., et al. The Jewish Museum. (Illus.). 128p. 1993. 30.00 (*1-85759-015-5*) Scala Books.

***Mann, Vivian B., et al.** Morocco: Jews & Art in a Muslim Land. (Illus.). 192p. 2000. 50.00 (*1-85894-110-5*, Pub. by Merrell Holberton) Rizzoli Intl.

Mann, Vivian B., ed. see Grafman, Rafi.

Mann, W. B., et al, eds. Radioactivity & Its Measurement. 2nd ed. LC 79-40881. (Illus.). 1980. text 135.00 (*0-08-025028-9*, Pub. by Aberdeen U Pr) Macmillan.

— Radioactivity Measurements: Principles & Practice. (International Journal of Applied Radiation & Isotopes Ser.: No. ARI 228 JARI 39). Orig. Title: Applied Radiation & Isotopes, Vol. 39, No. 8. 220p. 1991. pap. text 30.00 (*0-08-037239-2*, Pergamon Pr) Elsevier.

Mann, W. B., jt. auth. see Debertin, K.

Mann, W. B., jt. ed. see Hutchinson, J. M.

Mann, W. Edward & Hoffman, Edward. Wilhelm Reich: The Man Who Dreamed of Tomorrow. (Orig.). 1991. 14.95 (*1-85274-087-6*, Pub. by Aqrn Pr) Harper SF.

Mann, W. Edward & Mottman, Edward. Wilhelm Reich: The Man Who Dreamed of Tomorrow. 295p. (Orig.). (C). Date not set. reprint ed. pap. 14.95 (*0-9637902-4-2*) Four Worlds.

Mann, W. Robert, jt. auth. see Taylor, Angus E.

Mann, Wayne M. Obliquely Wild. Hammack, Susan M. & Hammack, Edie, eds. (Illus.). 476p. 1982. pap. 9.95 (*0-9608904-0-8*) Mann Found.

Mann, William. Ant Hill Odyssey. (American Autobiography Ser.). 338p. 1995. reprint ed. lib. bdg. 89.00 (*0-7812-8585-2*) Rprt Serv.

***Mann, William.** Labyrinth of the Grail. LC 99-33317. (Illus.). 350p. 1999. pap. 24.95 (*0-9659701-8-3*) Laughing Owl.

Mann, William & Backa, Bruce. Microsoft Exchange 5TM Sourcebook. LC 97-5930. 612p. 1997. pap. text 49.95 incl. cd-rom (*0-471-17841-1*) Wiley.

Mann, William, ed. see De La Salle, John B.

Mann, William, tr. see Schwinger, Wolfram.

Mann, William A. Landscape Architecture: An Illustrated History in Timelines, Site Plans, & Biography. 480p. (Orig.). 1993. pap. 64.95 (*0-471-59465-2*) Wiley.

Mann, William C. & Lane, Joseph P. Assistive Technology for Persons with Disabilities: The Role of Occupational Therapy. 2nd ed. 400p. (C). 1995. pap. text 58.00 (*1-56900-028-X*) Am Occup Therapy.

Mann, William C. & Thompson, Sandra A., eds. Discourse Description: Diverse Linguistic Analysis of a Fund-Raising Text. LC 91-46957. (Pragmatics & Beyond New Ser.: No. 16). xiii, 409p. 1992. 118.00 (*1-55619-282-7*) J Benjamins Pubng Co.

Mann, William D. Fads & Fancies of Representative Americans at the Beginning of the Twentieth Century... LC 75-1857. (Leisure Class in America Ser.). (Illus.). 1978. reprint ed. 150.95 (*0-405-06923-5*) Ayer.

***Mann, William J.** The Biograph Girl. 448p. 2000. 23.00 (*1-57566-559-X*) Kensgtn Pub Corp.

Mann, William J. The Men from the Boys. 448p. 1998. pap. 12.95 (*0-452-27856-2*, Plume) Dutton Plume.

— The Men from the Boys. 1997. 22.95 (*0-614-27940-2*) NAL.

— Wisecracker: The Life & Times of William Haines, Hollywood's First Openly Gay Star. LC 97-39665. (Illus.). 320p. 1998. 29.95 (*0-670-87155-9*) Viking Penguin.

— Wisecracker: The Life & Times of William Haines, Hollywood's First Openly Gay Star. (Illus.). 480p. 1999. pap. 14.95 (*0-14-027568-1*) Viking Penguin.

Mann, William J., ed. Grave Passions. (Orig.). 1997. mass mkt. 6.50 (*1-56333-405-4*, Badboy) Masquerade.

Mann, William J. & Stovall, Thomas G., eds. Gynecologic Surgery. LC 96-17726. 884p. 1996. text 135.00 (*0-443-08958-2*) Church.

Mann, Wolf, jt. ed. see Thumfart, Walter F.

Mann, Woody. The Anthology of Blues Guitar. (Library Of...). (Illus.). 158p. 1996. pap. 21.95 (*0-8256-0315-3*, OK 64973, Oak) Music Sales.

— The Blues Fakebook. LC 95-751062. (Library Of...). 176p. 1997. pap. 24.95 (*0-8256-1417-1*, OK 64983) Omnibus NY.

— Bottleneck Blues Guitar. 125p. 1997. pap. 19.95 (*0-8256-0317-X*, OK 64984) Music Sales.

— The Complete Robert Johnson. (Illus.). 96p. 1992. pap. 16.95 (*0-8256-0314-5*, OK64965, Oak) Music Sales.

— The Gig Bag Book of Alternate Tunings. (Gig Bag Bks.). (Illus.). 111p. 1997. pap. text 12.95 (*0-8256-1490-2*, AM931271, Amsco Music) Music Sales.

— Six Early Blues Guitarists. (Illus.). 112p. 1973. pap. 17.95 (*0-8256-0135-5*, OK62703, Oak) Music Sales.

Mann, Woody, jt. auth. see Grossman, Stefan.

Manna, Anthony L. & Mitakidou, Christodoula. Mr. Semolina Semolinus. LC 96-1924. (Illus.). 40p. (J). (ps up). 1997. 15.00 (*0-689-81093-8*) S&S Childrens.

Manna, Anthony L. & Symons, Cynthia W. Children's Literature for Health Awareness. LC 92-29737. (Illus.). 629p. 1992. 58.00 (*0-8108-2582-1*) Scarecrow.

Manna, Anthony L., ed. see Virginia Hamilton Conference Staff.

Manna, Anthony L. Conference Staff & Brodie, Carolyn S. Art & Story: The Role of Illustration in Multicultural Literature for Youth: The Virginia Hamilton Conference. LC 97-11112. (Illus.). 216p. 1997. pap. 30.00 (*0-917846-77-X*) Highsmith Pr.

***Manna, Giovanni.** Someone I Like: Poems about People. 40p. (J). (gr. 1-5). 2000. 16.95 (*1-84148-004-5*) Barefoot Bks NY.

Manna, Gunomoy. The Shal Forest. (C). 1990. text 18.00 (*81-7017-268-3*, Pub. by Abhinav) S Asia.

Manna, M., jt. auth. see Ghosh, G.

Manna, M., jt. auth. see Ghosh, G. K.

Manna, Philip, jt. auth. see McCarthy, Mary.

Manna, Sibendu. Mother Goddess Candi: (Its Socio Ritual Impact on the Folk Life) 1993. 36.00 (*81-85094-60-8*, Pub. by Punthi Pus) S Asia.

Manna, Zohar. Lectures on the Logic of Computer Programming. LC 79-93153. (CBMS-NSF Regional Conference Ser.: No. 31). iv, 49p. 1980. pap. text 19.00 (*0-89871-164-9*) Soc Indus-Appl Math.

Manna, Zohar & Pnueli, A. The Temporal Logic of Reactive & Concurrent Systems , Vol. 1. LC 91-28181. 1992. write for info. (*3-540-97664-7*) Spr-Verlag.

Manna, Zohar & Pnueli, Amir. The Temporal Logic of Reactive Systems Vol. 1: Specification. (Illus.). 392p. 1991. 65.95 (*0-387-97664-7*) Spr-Verlag.

— Temporal Verification of Reactive Systems: Safety. LC 95-5442. (Illus.). 464p. 1995. 72.95 (*0-387-94459-1*) Spr-Verlag.

Manna, Zohar & Waldinger, Richard. The Logical Basis for Computer Programming: Combined Volume. (Computer Science Ser.). (Illus.). 736p. (C). 1999. 55.95 (*0-201-54886-0*) Addison-Wesley.

— The Logical Basis for Computer Programming Vol. I: Informal Reasoning. 632p. (C). 1985. 49.95 (*0-201-18260-2*) Addison-Wesley.

Mannack, Thomas. Summary Guide to Corpus Vasorum Antiquorum. 2nd ed. 90p. 2000. pap. text 17.95 (*0-19-726203-1*) OUP.

Mannaioni, P. F. Clinical Pharmacology of Drug Dependence. 282p. 1984. pap. text 32.00 (*1-57235-060-1*) Piccin Nuova.

Mannan, Abdul, tr. see Nooruddin, Allamah.

Mannan, M. A. Growth & Development of Small Enterprises: The Case of a Developing Economy. 120p. 1993. 72.95 (*1-85628-544-8*, Pub. by Avebry) Ashgate Pub Co.

Mannan, M. M. Islamic Economics in Theory & Practice. 1989. 16.95 (*1-56744-092-4*) Kazi Pubns.

***Mannarino, Melanie.** Seventeen: The Boyfriend Clinic: The Final Word on Flirting, Dating, Guys, & Love. (Seventeen Ser.). (Illus.). 128p. (YA). (gr. 7-12). 2000. mass mkt. 6.95 (*0-06-447235-3*, HarpTrophy) HarpC Child Bks.

***Mannato, Franco.** OECD Steel Outlook 1999/2000: 1999 Edition. 60p. 1999. pap. 32.00 (*92-64-17139-8*, 58 1999 03 1 P, Pub. by Org for Econ) OECD.

Mannckе, K. Minimal Access Thoracic Surgery. (Illus.). 296p. 1999. text 110.00 (*0-412-81600-8*, Pub. by E A) OUP.

Manne, Alan & Richels, Richard. Buying Greenhouse Insurance: The Economic Costs of CO2 Emission Limits. (Illus.). 192p. 1992. 32.00 (*0-262-13280-X*) MIT Pr.

***Manne, Alan S., et al.** Climate Change Policy: Practical Strategies to Promote Economic Growth & Environmental Quality. (Monograph Series on Tax, Trade & Environmental Policies). (Illus.). 208p. 1999. pap. 25.00 (*1-884032-09-5*) Am Coun Capital.

Manne, Henry G. & Miller, Roger L., eds. Auto Safety Regulation: The Cure or the Problem? LC 76-1676. 1976. 15.95 (*0-913878-09-X*) T Horton & Dghts.

Manne, Henry G. & Wallich, Henry C. The Modern Corporation & Social Responsibility. LC 72-91865. (Rational Debate Ser.: No. 6). 120p. reprint ed. pap. 37.20 (*0-8357-4511-2*, 203736800008) Bks Demand.

Manne, Henry G., ed. see Dorn, James A.

Manne, Joy. Soul Therapy. LC 97-15002. 178p. (Orig.). 1997. pap. 13.95 (*1-55643-255-0*) North Atlantic.

Manne, Srinivas, jt. auth. see Warr, Gregory G.

Mannel, Bob. Mustang & Ford Small Block V8, 1962-1969. LC 98-91185. (Illus.). 736p. 1998. pap. 49.95 (*0-9662741-0-5*) RPM Press.

Mannell, Roger C. & Kleiber, Douglas A. A Social Psychology of Leisure. LC 97-60787. 450p. 1997. text 37.95 (*0-910251-88-6*, PSY92) Venture Pub PA.

Mannello, Tim. A CQI System for Healthcare: How the Williamsport Hospital Brings Quality to Life. LC 94-46508. 318p. 1995. 39.95 (*0-527-76290-3*) Productivity Inc.

Mannenberg, Denny van. Effective Retail Security: Protecting the Bottom Line. LC 96-161359. 200p. 1995. pap. 44.95 (*0-7506-8923-4*) Buttrwrth-Heinemann.

Manner, A. English - Tulu Dictionary. 660p. 1987. 79.95 (*0-8288-8465-X*) Fr & Eur.

English Tulu Dictionary. (C). 1987. reprint ed. 35.00 (*0-8364-2404-2*, Pub. by Asian Educ Servs) S Asia.

— Tulu English Dictionary. 696p. 1983. 79.95 (*0-8288-8466-8*) Fr & Eur.

Manner, Eeva L. Fog Horses. Barkan, Stanley H., ed. Poom, Rilva, tr. (Review Chapbook Ser.: No. 19: Finnish Poetry).Tr. of Finnish & Eng.. 48p. 1988. 15.00 (*0-89304-820-8*, CCC185); pap. 5.00 (*0-89304-821-6*) Cross-Cultrl NY.

Manner, Kim, jt. auth. see Sorby, Sherly S.

Manner, Reinhard & Manderick, Bernard, eds. Parallel Problem Solving from Nature, 2: Proceedings of the Second Conference on Parallel Problem Solving from Nature, Brussels, Belgium, 28-30 September, 1992. LC 92-23499. 618p. 1992. 228.50 (*0-444-89730-5*, North Holland) Elsevier.

Manner, Reinhard, jt. ed. see Schwefel, H. P.

Mannering, Dennis D. & Mannering, Wendy K. Attitudes Are Contagious... Are Yours Worth Catching? LC 99-64005. 104p. 1999. reprint ed. pap. 10.99 (*0-945890-00-1*) Options Unltd.

Mannering, Dennis E. Everyday Heroes. Mannering, Wendy K. & Mason, Virginia, eds. 91p. 1992. 10.00 (*0-945890-02-8*) Options Unltd.

Mannering, Dennis E. & Wilde, Kevin. How Good Managers Become Great Leaders. Mason, Virginia, ed. 163p. 1989. 72.00 (*0-945890-01-X*) Options Unltd.

Mannering, Derek. Mario Lanza: A Biography. (Illus.). 176p. pap. 14.95 (*0-7090-5052-6*, Pub. by R Hale Ltd) Seven Hills Bk.

Mannering, Fred L. & Kilareski, Walter P. Principles of Highway Engineering & Traffic Analysis. 2nd ed. LC 97-3077. 352p. 1997. pap. 64.95 (*0-471-13085-0*) Wiley.

***Mannering, Karen.** Managing Difficult People: Proven Strategies to Deal with Awkwardness in Business Situations. (Business Management Ser.). (Illus.). 144p. 2000. pap. 19.95 (*1-85703-573-9*, Pub. by How To Bks) Midpt Trade.

M

An Asterisk (*) at the beginning of an entry indicates that the title is appearing for the first time.

Mannering, Karen. Staying Ahead at Work: How to Develop a Winning Portfolio of Work Skills & Attitudes. 144p. 1998. pap. 19.95 (*1-85703-298-5*, Pub. by How To Bks) Trans-Atl Phila.

Mannering, Wendy K., jt. auth. see Mannering, Dennis D.

Mannering, Wendy K., ed. see Mannering, Dennis E.

Manners. Hitchiker's Guide to Electronics in 90's. 1990. pap. text 39.95 (*1-85384-020-3*) Buttrwrth-Heinemann.

Manners, David, jt. auth. see Makimoto, Tsugio.

Manners, Gerald. The Changing World Market for Iron Ore, 1950-1980: An Economic Geography. LC 70-146734. 400p. reprint ed. pap. 124.00 (*0-608-12541-5*, 202380600034) Bks Demand.

— Regional Development in Britain 2nd ed. LC 79-42901. xiv, 432p. 1980. write for info. (*0-471-27635-9*) Wiley.

Manners, Gerald, et al. Regional Development in Britain. 2nd ed. LC 79-42901. (Illus.). 440p. reprint ed. pap. 136.40 (*0-608-17549-8*, 203052900069) Bks Demand.

Manners, Gerald, jt. auth. see McDivitt, James M.

Manners, Hazel K. A Framework for Physical Education in the Early Years. LC 94-45068. 1995. pap. 27.95 (*0-7507-0417-9*, Falmer Pr) Taylor & Francis.

Manners, Hazel K., jt. auth. see Carroll, M. E.

Manners, Hazel K., jt. ed. see Carroll, M. E.

Manners, L. J. An Acre of England. 160p. 1980. pap. 35.00 (*0-905418-06-9*, Pub. by Gresham Bks) St Mut.

Manners, Robert, jt. auth. see Kaplan, David.

Manners, Robert A., jt. auth. see Kaplan, David.

Manners, Ruth A. & Manners, William. The Quick & Easy Vegetarian Cookbook. LC 93-28789. 240p. 1993. pap. 12.95 (*0-87131-738-9*) M Evans.

Manners, Terry. Deadlier Than the Male: Stories of Female Serial Killers. (Illus.). 372p. 1997. pap. 9.95 (*0-330-33711-4*, Pub. by Pan) Trafalgar.

Manners, William, jt. auth. see Manners, Ruth A.

Mannes, Philip. Tables of Bullet Performance. Wolfe, Dave, ed. 407p. (Orig.). 1980. text 17.50 (*0-935632-06-9*); pap. text 17.50 (*0-935632-05-0*) Wolfe Pub Co.

Mannes, Willibald. Techniques of Staircase Construction. (Illus.). 112p. (C). (gr. 13). 1986. text 67.95 (*0-442-26086-5*) Chapman & Hall.

Mannetje, L. & Jones, R. M., eds. Forages. (PROSEA Ser.: No. 4). (Illus.). 300p. 1992. 183.00 (*90-220-1032-5*, Pub. by Backhuys Pubs); pap. 57.00 (*979-8316-04-5*, Pub. by Backhuys Pubs) Balogh.

Mannetje, L. T., ed. Measurement of Grassland Vegetation. 260p. (Orig.). 1978. pap. text 40.00 (*0-85198-404-5*) OUP.

Mannetje, L. T. & Jones, R. M. PROSEA Vol. IV: (Forages) PUDOC Staff, ed. 250p. (C). 1991. text 500.00 (*0-89771-636-1*, Pub. by Intl Bk Distr) St Mut.

Mannett, Luana, ed. see Morrall, June.

Mannetter, Terrance A., ed. Text & Concordance of the Leyes de Estilo, MS5764: Biblioteca Nacional, Madrid. (Spanish Legal Texts Ser.: No. 6). (SPA.). 8p. 1989. 10.00 incl. fiche (*0-940639-43-2*) Hispanic Seminary.

Mannetter, Terrence A., et al, eds. Text & Concordance of the Leyes del Estilo, MS. Z.III.11, Escorial. (Spanish Legal Texts Ser.: No. 8). 6p. 1990. 10.00 incl. fiche (*0-940639-47-5*) Hispanic Seminary.

Mannetti, William. Dinosaurs in Your Backyard. LC 81-7998. (Illus.). 160p. (J). (gr. 4-7). 1982. 15.00 (*0-689-30906-6*) Atheneum Yung Read.

Manneville, P., et al, eds. Cellular Automata & Modeling of Complex Physical Systems. (Proceedings in Physics Ser.: Vol. 46). (Illus.). 350p. 1990. 72.00 (*0-387-51933-5*, 3776) Spr-Verlag.

Manneville, Paul, jt. ed. see Godreche, Claude.

Manney, Gerald, jt. auth. see De Santis, Richard.

Manney, James, ed. How I Pray Now. LC 96-70438. 120p. 1977. pap. 9.95 (*0-87973-855-3*) Our Sunday Visitor.

Manney, James, jt. auth. see Scanlan, Michael.

Manney, Linda Joyce. Middle Voice in Modern Greek: Meaning & Function of an Inflectional Category. LC 98-44715. (Studies in Language Companion Ser.: Vol. 48). xiii, 262p. 2000. 94.00 (*1-55619-934-1*) J Benjamins Pubng Co.

Mannhardt, Karl-Heinz. Dictionary of Energy Science: Nuclear & Non-Nuclear Energy. (ENG & GER.). 166p. 1981. 110.00 (*0-8288-0700-0*, M 15045); 75.00 (*0-8288-2292-1*, M15046); 110.00 (*0-8288-2293-X*, M 15047) Fr & Eur.

Mannhardt, Werner G., tr. see Muller, Herbert W.

Mannhardt, Wilhelm. Mythologische Forschungen Aus Dem Nachlasse, 2 vols. Bolle, Kees W., ed. LC 77-79142. (Mythology Ser.). (GER.). 1978. reprint ed. lib. bdg. 42.95 (*0-405-10551-7*) Ayer.

Mannheim. Regeln und Sprache Des Sports, 2 vols. (GER.). 55.00 (*3-411-01362-1*, M-7601) Fr & Eur.

Mannheim, Bruce. The Language of the Inka since the European Invasion. (Illus.). 346p. 1991. text 25.00 (*0-292-74663-6*) U of Tex Pr.

Mannheim, Bruce, jt. ed. see Huizer, Gerrit.

Mannheim, Bruce, jt. ed. see Tedlock, Dennis.

Mannheim Centre Staff, jt. auth. see Caramani, Daniele.

Mannheim, Hermann. Group Problems in Crime & Punishment. 2nd enl. ed. LC 73-108234. (Criminology, Law Enforcement, & Social Problems Ser.: No. 117). 1972. 25.00 (*0-87585-117-7*) Patterson Smith.

— Juvenile Delinquency in an English Middletown. LC 73-108226. (Criminology, Law Enforcement, & Social Problems Ser.: No. 109). (Illus.). 144p. 1970. reprint ed. 22.00 (*0-87585-109-6*) Patterson Smith.

— Pioneers in Criminology. enl. ed. LC 78-108238. (Criminology, Law Enforcement, & Social Problems Ser.: No. 121). (C). 1972. pap. 20.00 (*0-87585-902-X*) Patterson Smith.

— Pioneers in Criminology. 2nd enl. ed. LC 78-108238. (Criminology, Law Enforcement, & Social Problems Ser.: No. 121). (C). 1972. 31.50 (*0-87585-121-5*) Patterson Smith.

Mannheim, Ivan, jt. auth. see Winter, David.

Mannheim, Karl. Conservatism: A Contribution to the Sociology of Knowledge. Kettler, David et al, eds. King, Elizabeth, tr. from GER. (International Library of Sociology Ser.). 256p. (C). 1986. text 49.95 (*0-7102-0338-1*, Routledge Thoemms) Routledge.

— Diagnosis of Our Time: Wartime Essays of a Sociologist. LC 86-22787. (International Library of Sociology & Social Reconstruction). 190p. 1987. reprint ed. lib. bdg. 59.50 (*0-313-25165-7*, MDIA) Greenwood.

— Essays on the Sociology of Culture. 2nd ed. (Classics in Sociology Ser.). 288p. (C). (gr. 13). 1992. 110.00 (*0-415-07553-X*, A6974) Routledge.

— Ideology & Utopia: An Introduction to the Sociology of Knowledge. LC 68-77694. 384p. 1955. pap. 15.00 (*0-15-643955-7*, Harvest Bks) Harcourt.

— Introduction to the Sociology of Education: Karl Mannheim Collected English Writings, Vol. 9. (Routledge Classics in Sociology Ser.). (C). 1998. 100.00 (*0-415-15085-X*) Routledge.

— Structures of Thinking. Kettler, David et al, eds. (International Library of Sociology Ser.). 240p. 1985. pap. 15.95 (*0-7102-0730-1*, Routledge Thoemms) Routledge.

— Systematic Sociology: An Introduction to the Study of Society. Eros, J. S. & Stewart, W. A., eds. LC 83-22743. (International Library of Sociology & Social Reconstruction). 169p. 1984. reprint ed. lib. bdg. 55.00 (*0-313-24378-6*, MASY) Greenwood.

Mannheim, Karl, tr. see Jaspers, Karl.

Mannheim, Linda. Harvesting Our History: A Botanical & Cultural Guide to Queens' Chinese, Korean, & Latin American Communities. (Illus.). 96p. 1998. pap. 4.95 (*0-9665474-0-3*) Queens Botanical.

Mannheim, Linda, jt. ed. see Yolen, Jane.

Mannheimer, Monica. The Generations in Meredith's Novels. (Gothenburg Studies in English: No. 23). 199p. (Orig.). 1972. pap. 40.00 (*0-317-65793-3*) Coronet Bks.

Mannheimer, Steve. Pacer Power: The 1994 Wonder Season of the Indiana Pacers. LC 94-77613. 210p. 1994. pap. 9.95 (*1-878208-48-9*) Guild Pr IN.

Manni, Alessandra & Sollins, Susan. Eternal Metaphors: New Art from Italy. LC 89-85331. 72p. 1989. 20.00 (*0-916365-28-X*) Ind Curators.

Manni, Andrea. Endocrinology of Breast Cancer. LC 98-33989. (Contemporary Endocrinology Ser.: Vol. 11). (Illus.). 408p. 1999. 145.00 (*0-89603-591-3*) Humana.

Manni, Andrea, jt. auth. see Santen, Richard J.

Manniche, Lise. An Ancient Egyptian Herbal. (Illus.). 176p. (Orig.). 1989. pap. 19.95 (*0-292-70415-1*) U of Tex Pr.

— City of the Dead: Thebes in Egypt. LC 87-5022. (British Museum Publications). (Illus.). x, 160p. (C). 1987. 27.50 (*0-226-50339-9*) U Ch Pr.

— Musical Instruments from the Tomb of Tutankhamun. (Tutankhamuns Tomb Ser.: Vol. 6). 48p. 1976. 30.00 (*0-900416-05-X*, Pub. by Aris & Phillips) David Brown.

***Manniche, Lise.** Sacred Luxuries: Fragrance, Aromatherapy, & Cosmetics in Ancient Egypt. LC 99-27112. (Illus.). 160p. 1999. 39.95 (*0-8014-3720-2*) Cornell U Pr.

Manniche, Lise. Sexual Life in Ancient Egypt. LC 96-16781. (Illus.). 130p. 1996. pap. 42.50 (*0-7103-0551-6*, Pub. by Kegan Paul Intl) Col U Pr.

— Sexual Life in Ancient Egypt. (Illus.). 127p. 1987. 35.00 (*0-7103-0202-9*) Routledge.

— The Wall Decoration of Three Theban Tombs. (Illus.). 31p. (Orig.). 1988. pap. 87.50 (*87-7289-036-3*) Coronet Bks.

Manniche, Lise, tr. How Djadja-Em-Ankh Saved the Day: A Tale from Ancient Egypt. LC 76-26919. 19p. (J). (gr. 4-6). 1942. 11.95 (*0-690-01280-2*) HarpC Child Bks.

Manniche, Peter. Living Democracy in Denmark. LC 73-98779. 237p. 1970. reprint ed. lib. bdg. 65.00 (*0-8371-3985-6*, MADD, Greenwood Pr) Greenwood.

***Mannik, Lolita.** Excel 2000 Introduction. rev. ed. (Illus.). 250p. 2000. pap. 20.00 (*1-58264-109-9*) ActiveEd.

Mannikka, Eleanor. Angkor Wat: Time, Space, & Kingship. LC 96-4368. (Illus.). 360p. 1996. text 55.00 (*0-8248-1720-6*) UH Pr.

— Selected Topics in Cataloging Asian Art. 1989. 20.00 (*0-685-46055-X*) Visual Resources Assn.

Mannin, Ethel. The Saga of Sammy-Cat. (Illus.). (J). (gr. 1-3). 1969. reprint ed. 2.59 (*0-08-013397-5*, Pergamon Pr) Elsevier.

— Women & the Revolution. 1976. lib. bdg. 59.95 (*0-8490-2834-5*) Gordon Pr.

Mannin, Mike. Pushing Back The Boundaries: The European Union & Central & Eastern Europe. (Illus.). 352p. 1999. pap. text 29.95 (*0-7190-5215-7*, Pub. by Manchester Univ Pr) St Martin.

Mannin, Mike, ed. Pushing Back The Boundaries: The European Union & Central & Eastern Europe. 352p. 1999. 69.95 (*0-7190-5214-9*, Pub. by Manchester Univ Pr) St Martin.

Manninen, J., jt. ed. see Tuomela, Raimo.

Manninen, Juha, ed. see Kaitaro, Timo.

Manninen, Julia, ed. see Patokorpi, Erkki.

***Manninen, Mary Jean.** Living the Christian Story: The Good News in Worship & Daily Life. LC BV4501.2.M3375 2000. 128p. 2000. pap. 12.00 (*0-8028-4706-4*) Eerdmans.

Manninen, Mika, jt. auth. see Lumme, Helena.

Manninen, V., ed. see Paavo Nurmi Symposium Staff.

Manninezhath, Thomas. Harmony of Religions: Vedanta Siddhanta Samarasam of Tayumanavar. (C). 1993. text 22.50 (*81-208-1001-5*, Pub. by Motilal Bnarsidass) S Asia.

Manning. Asia's Coming Energy Wars 1999. text 29.95 (*0-312-22437-0*) St Martin.

— Business Entity. LC 95-81327. 1995. 125.00 (*0-316-54827-8*) Little.

— Cardiac Magnetic Resonance. 1999. text 99.00 (*0-443-07519-0*, W B Saunders Co) Harcrt Hlth Sci Grp.

— Communicational Theory of Politics. 1990. lib. bdg. 34.95 (*0-226-50351-8*) U Ch Pr.

— Corporate Buying & Selling. LC 95-76611. 1995. 125.00 (*0-316-54337-3*, Aspen Law & Bus) Aspen Pub.

***Manning.** Helping Yourself with Esp. 2000. pap. 13.00 (*0-13-030950-8*) P-H.

Manning. Helping Yourslf with ESP. 2nd ed. 1999. pap. 13.00 (*0-7352-0123-4*) PH Pr.

***Manning.** My 1st Baby Games. 14p. (J). 2001. 5.95 (*0-694-01435-4*) HarpC Child Bks.

Manning. Partnership & Selling. 125p. 1994. pap. text 25.80 (*0-205-15990-7*) P-H.

Manning. Social Problems & Welfare Ideology. 1985. pap. 35.95 (*0-566-05067-6*) Ashgate Pub Co.

— Teaching in the Middle School. LC 99-86514. 368p. 2000. pap. 41.00 (*0-13-950420-6*) P-H.

Manning. Understanding Landscape Design. (Illus.). 224p. (Orig.). 1997. pap. text 34.50 (*0-419-20260-9*, E & FN Spon) Routledge.

***Manning & Baruth, Leroy G.** Multicultural Education of Children & Adolescents. 3rd ed. LC 99-29162. 382p. 1999. pap. text 54.00 (*0-205-29760-9*) Allyn.

***Manning & Weber.** Radiographic Pathology. (C). 2001. pap., wbk. ed. 14.50 (*0-7668-1282-0*) Delmar.

Manning, et al. Social & Employment Policy in Russia. 74.95 (*1-84014-530-7*) Ashgate Pub Co.

Manning, A. D. Supposition Error: A Novel. (Illus.). 313p. (Orig.). 1996. pap. 12.95 (*0-9644636-3-6*) Parlay Enter.

Manning, Adrian. April Adventure. (YA). 1999. pap. 17.95 (*0-9667883-5-4*) Ravensyard.

Manning, Al G. Ayudese con la Magia Blanca. (SPA.). 1997. pap. text 19.98 (*968-13-0744-5*) Edit Diana.

Manning, Al G. Eye of Newt in My Martini: A Certified Public Accountant Turned Occultist Tells Why & How. LC 81-84169. (Illus.). 1981. 12.95 (*0-941698-00-9*); pap. 6.95 (*0-941698-01-7*) Pan Ishtar.

***Manning, Al G.** Helping Yourself with E.S.P. Tap the Power of Extra-Sensory Perception & Make It Work for You. LC 99-34453. 240p. 1999. pap. 13.00 (*0-7352-0124-2*) PH Pr.

Manning, Al G. Helping Yourself with Psycho-Cosmic Power. LC 68-12433. 1983. pap. 6.95 (*0-941698-06-8*) Pan Ishtar.

— Helping Yourself with Real Spirit Contact. LC 89-92375. 180p. (Orig.). 1990. pap. 9.95 (*0-941698-18-1*) Pan Ishtar.

— Helping Yourself with the Magick of the White Unicorn. LC 97-92520. (Illus.). 180p. 1998. pap. 9.95 (*0-941698-21-1*) Pan Ishtar.

— Helping Yourself with the Power of Gnostic Magic. LC 79-13447. 1984. reprint ed. pap. 9.95 (*0-941698-11-4*) Pan Ishtar.

— Helping Yourself with White Witchcraft. 225p. (C). 1974. pap. text 9.95 (*0-13-386573-8*, Reward) P-H.

— How to Get the Most Out of Life: A Novel Approach That Works Because It's Fun. LC 88-90687. 180p. (Orig.). 1988. pap. 7.95 (*0-941698-17-3*) Pan Ishtar.

— Life after Death? Sex? Dinner? The Lighter Side of the Occult. LC 83-60386. 144p. (Orig.). 1983. pap. 6.95 (*0-941698-07-6*) Pan Ishtar.

— The Magic of New Ishtar Power. LC 77-4502. 229p. 1986. reprint ed. pap. 9.95 (*0-941698-13-0*) Pan Ishtar.

— Mighty Maverick Magick: The Essence of Victorious Living. 180p. 1983. 12.95 (*0-941698-08-4*); pap. 6.95 (*0-941698-09-2*) Pan Ishtar.

— Miracle Spiritology. LC 75-19350. 1975. 13.95 (*0-13-585745-7*) Pan Ishtar.

— The Miraculous Laws of Universal Dynamics. 1964. pap. 6.95 (*0-317-46046-3*) Pan Ishtar.

— Moon Lore & Moon Magic. 1980. 14.95 (*0-13-600668-X*) Pan Ishtar.

— Rainbows Falling on My Head: The Magic of the Great God Pan. LC 82-90133. (Illus.). 1982. 12.95 (*0-941698-02-5*); pap. 6.95 (*0-941698-03-3*) Pan Ishtar.

Manning, Al G. Real Ritual Magick: For People Ready to Enjoy Life Now. LC 86-63701. 180p. (Orig.). 1987. pap. 9.95 (*0-941698-15-7*) Pan Ishtar.

Manning, Al G. Your Golden Key to Success: A Self Help Odyssey. LC 82-60767. (Illus.). 1982. 12.95 (*0-941698-04-1*); pap. 6.95 (*0-941698-05-X*) Pan Ishtar.

Manning, Al G. & Manning, Rachel L. Faerie Tales Are True-Get Your Share. LC 85-80465. 180p. (Orig.). 1986. pap. 7.95 (*0-941698-12-2*) Pan Ishtar.

— You're Beautiful: Quick Reference Self Help Program for All Situations. LC 87-62127. 1987. pap. 7.95 (*0-941698-16-5*) Pan Ishtar.

Manning, Al G., jt. auth. see Manning, Rachel L.

Manning, Alice H. Meadow City Milestones: A Collection of Historical Sketches. (Illus.). 94p. (Orig.). 1987. pap. 4.95 (*0-9618052-1-8*) Daily Hampshire.

Manning, Ambrose N., jt. auth. see Higgs, Robert.

Manning, Anabel, tr. see Royo, Luis.

Manning, Anita S. Shattered Dreams. 62p. 1991. pap. 3.00 (*0-9630309-0-6*) Anita S Buchanan.

Manning, Anne. The Maiden & Married Life of Mary Powell, Afterwards Mistress Milton, 2 vols., 1 bk. LC 79-8166. reprint ed. 44.50 (*0-404-62021-3*) AMS Pr.

***Manning, Anne.** Ripples. LC 99-36366. (Romances Ser.). 1999. 24.95 (*0-7862-2149-6*) Five Star.

Manning, Anne. Valentine Duval: An Autobiography. (Art, History & the Connoisseur Ser.). (Illus.). 142p. (C). 1990. reprint ed. 19.95 (*1-879080-00-1*) Clios Cabinet.

Manning, Aubrey. Introduction to Animal Behaviour. 3rd ed. 1979. pap. 15.95 (*0-201-04446-3*) Addison-Wesley.

Manning, Aubrey & Dawkins, Marian S. An Introduction to Animal Behaviour. 5th ed. LC 97-46775. (Illus.). 460p. (C). 1998. text 80.00 (*0-521-57024-7*); pap. text 29.95 (*0-521-57891-4*) Cambridge U Pr.

Manning, Barbara. Genealogical Abstracts from Newspapers of the German Reformed Church, 1840-1843. 344p. (Orig.). 1995. pap. text 25.00 (*0-7884-0177-7*) Heritage Bk.

Manning, Bayless & Hanks, James J., Jr. Legal Capital. 3rd ed. (University Textbook Ser.). 213p. 1990. pap. text 17.95 (*0-88277-799-8*) Foundation Pr.

Manning, Bernard L. The Hymns of Wesley & Watts. 1987. pap. 6.99 (*0-88019-220-8*) Schmul Pub Co.

Manning, Bertina S. Chrysler Art Museum of Provincetown, Inaugural Exhibition. (Illus.). 115p. 1958. pap. 7.50 (*0-940744-00-7*) Chrysler Museum.

Manning, Beverley. Index to American Women Speakers, Eighteen Twenty-Eight to Nineteen Seventy-Eight. LC 79-26928. viii, 672p. 1980. lib. bdg. 45.00 (*0-8108-1282-7*) Scarecrow.

— We Shall Be Heard: An Index to Speeches by American Women, 1978-1985. LC 88-6644. 626p. 1988. 66.00 (*0-8108-2122-2*) Scarecrow.

Manning, Bill. Beacon Small Group Bible Studies, Joel-Jonah. 76p. (Orig.). 1987. pap. 4.99 (*0-8341-1207-8*) Beacon Hill.

Manning, Brenda, jt. auth. see Richlin, Laurie.

Manning, Brenda H. Cognitive Self-Instruction (CSI) for Classroom Processes. LC 90-32701. 370p. (C). 1991. text 29.50 (*0-7914-0479-X*) State U NY Pr.

Manning, Brenda H. & Payne, Beverly D. Self-Talk for Teachers & Students: Metacognitive Strategies for Personal & Classroom Use. LC 95-32106. 256p. 1996. pap. text 33.00 (*0-205-15948-6*) Allyn.

Manning, Brennan. Abba's Child. LC 94-14008. 192p. (Orig.). 1994. pap. 12.00 (*0-89109-826-7*) NavPress.

— Lion & Lamb. LC 86-15409. 192p. (gr. 10). 1986. pap. 9.99 (*0-8007-9083-9*) Chosen Bks.

***Manning, Brennan.** Ragamuffin Gospel. 227p. 2000. pap. 10.99 (*1-57673-716-0*) Multnomah Pubs.

Manning, Brennan. The Ragamuffin Gospel: Embracing the Unconditional Love of God. 227p. 1990. pap. 10.99 (*0-88070-631-7*, Multnomah Bks) Multnomah Pubs.

— Reflections for Ragamuffins: Daily Devotions from the Writings of Brennan Manning. LC 97-46167. 384p. 1998. pap. 13.00 (*0-06-065457-0*) HarpC.

***Manning, Brennan.** Ruthless Trust: The Way of the Ragamuffin. 256p. 2000. 22.00 (*0-06-251709-0*) Harper SF.

Manning, Brennan. The Signature of Jesus. LC 96-143422. 210p. 1996. pap. 10.99 (*0-88070-859-X*, Multnomah Bks) Multnomah Pubs.

— Stranger to Self-Hatred. 1981. pap. 14.95 (*0-87193-156-7*) Dimension Bks.

— The Wisdom of Accepted Tenderness. 1979. pap. 14.95 (*0-87193-110-9*) Dimension Bks.

Manning, Brent. Welfare Became My Stepping Stone. 28p. 1997. pap. 12.00 (*0-9659315-0-1*) Inspir Pubns.

Manning, Brian. Aristocrats, Plebeians & Revolution in England, 1640-1660. LC 95-38686. (Socialist History of Britain Ser.). 128p. 1996. 45.00 (*0-7453-0940-2*, Pub. by Pluto GBR); pap. 14.95 (*0-7453-0939-9*, Pub. by Pluto GBR) Stylus Pub VA.

Manning, Carol S. Female Tradition in Southern Literature: Essays on Southern Women. 296p. 1994. pap. text 13.95 (*0-252-06444-5*) U of Ill Pr.

— With Ears Opening Like Morning Glories: Eudora Welty & the Love of Storytelling, 58. LC 85-921. (Contributions in Women's Studies: No. 58). 221p. 1985. 57.95 (*0-313-24776-5*, MWE/, Greenwood Pr) Greenwood.

Manning, Caroline. Immigrant Woman & Her Job. LC 73-129407. (American Immigration Collection. Series 2). (Illus.). 1975. reprint ed. 14.95 (*0-405-00560-1*) Ayer.

Manning, Catherine. Fortunes a Faire: The French in Asian Trade, 1719-48. 304p. 1996. text 83.95 (*0-86078-552-1*, Pub. by Variorum) Ashgate Pub Co.

Manning, Charles A. Toughlove for Education: How Accreditation Has Hurt Our Schools & What to Do about It. 120p. 1997. pap. 16.95 (*1-880153-88-2*) AmericaWORKS.

Manning, Charles W. Colorado Policy Guide to Higher Education Governance. 14p. 1989. pap. text 8.00 (*1-57655-120-2*) Independ Inst.

Manning, Chris. Indonesian Labour in Transition: An East Asian Success Story. LC 97-6562. (Trade & Development Ser.). 336p. (C). 1998. text 59.95 (*0-521-59412-X*) Cambridge U Pr.

Manning, Chris, jt. auth. see Athukorala, Prema-Chandra.

Manning, Christel J. God Gave Us the Right: Conservative Catholic, Evangelical Protestant & Orthodox Jewish Women Grapple with Feminism. LC 98-8500. 256p. (C). 1999. text 50.00 (*0-8135-2598-5*); pap. text 20.00 (*0-8135-2599-3*) Rutgers U Pr.

Manning, Christopher D. Ergativity: Argument Structure & Grammatical Relations. (Dissertations in Linguistics Ser.). 240p. (C). 1996. 64.95 (*1-57586-037-6*); pap. 22.95 (*1-57586-036-8*) CSLI.

***Manning, Christopher D. & Schutze, Hinrich.** Foundations of Statistical Natural Language Programming. LC 99-21137. (Illus.). 1041p. 1999. 60.00 (*0-262-13360-1*) MIT Pr.

Manning, Christopher D., jt. auth. see Andrews, Avery D.

Manning, Clarence A. Ukrainian Literature: Studies of the Leading Authors. LC 70-86771. (Essay Index Reprint Ser.). 1977. reprint ed. 20.95 (*0-8369-2244-1*) Ayer.

Manning, Clarence A., tr. see Korolenko, Vladimir G.

Manning, Clark, jt. auth. see Vanrenen, Louis J.

Manning, Conleth. Early Irish Monasteries. (Irish Treasures Ser.). (Illus.). 48p. (Orig.). 1995. pap. 8.95 (*0-946172-48-X*, Pub. by Town Hse) Roberts Rinehart.

Manning, Connie. I Know Someone Who Died: Coloring Book. (Illus.). 32p. (J). (ps-3). 1998. mass mkt. 6.95 (*1-892785-05-6*) In-Sight Bks Inc.

An Asterisk (*) at the beginning of an entry indicates that the title is appearing for the first time.

Manning, Conrad. Sandbox: A Study in the Optimal Lifestyle. 175p. (Orig.). pap. 14.95 (0-9618479-0-5) Sandbox Inc.

Manning, Constance. Measurement of Image Accuracy. (C). 1991. pap. text 11.11 (0-913412-58-9) Brandon Hse.

Manning, D. J. Liberalism. LC 76-15053. (Modern Ideologies Ser.). (C). 1976. pap. text 9.00 (0-312-48335-X) St Martin.

Manning, Dale, jt. auth. see Davidson, Edward.

***Manning, Dan.** Little Dictators. LC 99-93681. 1999. 21.95 (0-533-13120-0) Vantage.

Manning, David. Exotic Pets Handbook. LC 98-20367. (Illus.). 128p. 1998. pap. 11.95 (0-7641-0653-8) Barron.

***Manning, David.** Negotiating Physics. 32p. 1999. pap. text 7.95 (1-884778-59-3) Old Mountain.

Manning, David J. The Mind of Jeremy Bentham. LC 84-6551. 118p. 1984. reprint ed. lib. bdg. 39.75 (0-313-22579-6, MAMJ, Greenwood Pr) Greenwood.

Manning, David L., jt. ed. see Rapley, Ralph.

Manning, David R. G Proteins Techniques of Analysis. LC 98-49670. (Methods In Life Sciences - Signal Transduction Ser.). 320p. 1999. boxed set 79.95 (0-8493-3381-4) CRC Pr.

Manning, Diane K. & Ritchie, Donald A. Hill Country Schoolteacher: Memories from the One-Room School & Beyond. (Twayne's Oral History Ser.: No. 3). 224p. (C). 1990. 22.95 (0-8057-9102-7) Macmillan.

Manning, Doug. Aging Is a Family Affair: Planning the Care of Aging Loved Ones. 120p. 1999. pap. 8.95 (1-892785-27-7) In-Sight Bks Inc.

— Building Memories: A Guide for Families. 32p. 1998. reprint ed. spiral bd. 4.95 (1-892785-03-X) In-Sight Bks Inc.

— Comforting Those Who Grieve: A Guide for Helping Others. 71p. 1999. reprint ed. pap. text 12.00 (0-7881-6213-6) DIANE Pub.

Manning, Doug. Don't Take My Grief Away: What to Do When You Lose a Loved One. LC 84-47730. 144p. 1984. pap. 14.00 (0-06-065417-1, RD 522, Pub. by Harper SF) HarpC.

Manning, Doug. Don't Take My Grief Away from Me. 9th ed. 129p. 1980. reprint ed. pap. 8.95 (1-892785-04-8) In-Sight Bks Inc.

— The Gift of Significance: Walking People Through a Loss. 9th ed. 90p. 1995. reprint ed. pap. 8.95 (1-892785-01-3) In-Sight Bks Inc.

— Lean on Me Gently: Helping the Grieving Child. 56p. 1998. pap. 5.95 (1-892785-06-4) In-Sight Bks Inc.

— Parenting Our Parents. 6th ed. 14p. 1989. reprint ed. pap. 1.50 (1-892785-08-0) In-Sight Bks Inc.

— Planning a Meaningful Cremation Funeral. 32p. 1998. spiral bd. 4.95 (1-892785-11-0) In-Sight Bks Inc.

— The Riffraff Chronicles: Featuring Ray. LC 95-94992. 104p. 1995. pap. 6.95 (0-9648690-1-2) Lowdown Bros.

— Searching for Normal Feelings. 6th ed. 14p. 1989. reprint ed. pap. 1.50 (1-892785-07-2) In-Sight Bks Inc.

— Share My Lonesome Valley: The Slow Grief of Long-Term Care. 120p. 1999. pap. 8.95 (1-892785-33-1) In-Sight Bks Inc.

— Socks - How to Solve Problems. 6th ed. 14p. 1989. reprint ed. pap. 1.50 (1-892785-09-9) In-Sight Bks Inc.

— The Special Care Series. 6th ed. 32p. 1994. reprint ed. pap. 10.95 (1-892785-02-1) In-Sight Bks Inc.

***Manning, Doug.** Thoughts for the Lonely Night: A Conversation about Grief. 135p. 2000. spiral bd. 17.95 (1-892785-36-6) In-Sight Bks Inc.

Manning, Doug. Visiting in a Nursing Home. 6th ed. 14p. 1989. reprint ed. pap. 1.50 (1-892785-10-2) In-Sight Bks Inc.

— When Love Gets Tough. LC 85-42783. 1990. pap. 11.00 (0-06-250561-0, Pub. by Harper SF) HarpC.

— When Love Gets Tough: Making the Nursing Home Decision. 9th ed. 90p. 1983. reprint ed. pap. 6.95 (1-892785-00-5) In-Sight Bks Inc.

Manning, Edward W. Big Sky & Beyond. (Illus.). 104p. (Orig.). 1998. pap. 10.00 (1-892773-00-7) Vagabond Bks.

***Manning, Elizabeth J. B. & Collins, Michael T., eds.** Paratuberculosis: Proceedings International Colloguium on Paratuberculosis, 6th, Melbourne, Australia, 1999. LC 99-48113. 720p. 1999. 225.00 (0-9633043-4-8) Intl Assn Paratuber.

Manning, Ellis L., jt. ed. see Reynolds, Neil B.

Manning, Eugenia. DeSoto Parish History. 1994. 50.00 (0-9644415-0-0) DeSoto Hist & Geneal.

Manning, Francis S. Oilfield Processing Vol. 2: Crude Oil. Thompson, Richard E., ed. 400p. 1995. 99.95 (0-87814-354-8) PennWell Bks.

Manning, Francis S. & Thompson, Richard. Oilfield Processing Vol. 1: Natural Gas. 420p. 1991. 99.95 (0-87814-343-2) PennWell Bks.

Manning, Francis S., jt. auth. see Canjar, Lawrence N.

Manning, Francis V., tr. see Bernard, Pierre R.

Manning, Frank. Creative Chip Carving. rev. ed. (Illus.). 48p. 1984. pap. 3.95 (0-486-23735-4) Dover.

Manning, Frank & Philibert, J. M., eds. Customs in Conflict: The Anthropology of a Changing World. 320p. 1990. pap. text 21.95 (0-921149-34-4) Broadview Pr.

Manning, Frank A. Fetal Medicine: Principles & Practice. LC 94-44480. 596p. (C). 1995. pap. text 135.00 (0-8385-2572-5, A2572-4, Apple Lange Med) McGraw.

Manning, Frank E. The Celebration of Society: Perspectives on Contemporary Cultural Performance. LC 83-72059. 208p. 1983. pap. 10.95 (0-87972-246-0) Bowling Green Univ Popular Press.

Manning, Frank E., ed. see Association for the Anthropological Study of Play, Meeting (7th, Fort Worth, TX) Staff.

Manning, Frank E., ed. see Association for the Anthropological Study of Play Staff.

Manning, Frank E., jt. ed. see Flaherty, David H.

***Manning, Frederic.** Her Privates We. 1999. pap. 14.00 (1-85242-717-5, Pub. by Serpents Tail) Consort Bk Sales.

Manning, Frederic. The Vigil of Brunhild: A Narrative Poem. LC 90-26796. 76p. 1990. reprint ed. lib. bdg. 49.95 (0-7734-9986-5) E Mellen.

Manning, Frederick, ed. see Institute of Medicine Staff.

Manning, Frederick J., et al, eds. Changing Health Care Systems & Rheumatic Disease. LC 97-116822. 256p. (Orig.). 1997. pap. 30.00 (0-309-05683-7, Joseph Henry Pr) Natl Acad Pr.

Manning, Frederick J., ed. see Institute of Medicine, Committee on Biomedical Iso.

Manning, Gary L., et al. Theme Immersion: Inquiry-Based Curriculum in Elementary & Middle Schools. LC 93-43027. (Illus.). 192p. (YA). 1994. pap. text 25.00 (0-435-08806-8, 08806) Heinemann.

Manning, Gary L., jt. auth. see Murphy Manning, Maryann.

Manning, Gary L., jt. ed. see Manning, Maryann M.

Manning, George. Building Community: The Human Side of Work. (GC - Principles of Management Ser.). 350p. (C). 1995. pap. 41.95 (0-538-83586-9) S-W Pub.

Manning, George. Stress: Living & Working in a Changing World. LC 98-40160. xxviii, 507p. 1999. pap. text 29.95 (1-57025-176-2) Whole Person.

Manning, George & Curtis, Kent. Ethics at Work: Fire in a Dark World. (Human Side of Work Ser.). 265p. (C). 1988. pap. 21.25 (0-538-21254-3, U254) S-W Pub.

***Manning, George A.** Financial Investigation & Forensic Accounting. LC 99-21263. 488p. 1999. boxed set 69.95 (0-8493-0435-0) CRC Pr.

— Solutions Manual Financial Investigations & Forensic Accounting Instructor's Manual. 314p. (C). 1999. teacher ed., ring bd. 1.00 (0-8493-0046-0) CRC Pr.

Manning, Gerald L. & Reece, Barry L. Selling Today: A Personal Approach. 4th ed. 570p. 1989. text 48.00 (0-205-12102-0, H21025) Allyn.

— Selling Today: A Personal Approach. 4th ed. 570p. 1989. teacher ed. write for info. (0-318-66325-2, H27253); write for info. (0-318-66326-0, H21041); VHS. write for info. (0-318-66327-9, H21066) P-H.

— Selling Today: Building Quality Partnerships. 7th ed. LC 97-11434. 525p. 1997. 90.67 (0-13-613837-3) P-H.

***Manning, Gerald L. & Reece, Barry L.** Selling Today: Building Quality Partnerships. 8th ed. LC 00-23065. 566p. 2000. 84.00 (0-13-027477-1) P-H.

***Manning, Gerry.** Airliners of the 1960s. (Illus.). 112p. 2000. pap. 24.95 (0-7603-0944-2, 130680AP, Pub. by MBI Pubg) Motorbooks Intl.

Manning, Gerry. 1000 Airlines in Color. LC 98-25176. (Illus.). 144p. 1998. pap. 22.95 (0-89658-410-0) Voyageur Pr.

— Workhorse Props. LC 96-143031. (Illus.). 112p. 1995. pap. 21.95 (0-7603-0189-1) MBI Pubg.

***Manning, Gillian.** Libertine Plays of the Restoration, Vol. 1. 2000. pap. 12.50 (0-460-87745-3, Everyman's Classic Lib) Tuttle Pubng.

Manning, Gordon P. Life in the Colchester Reef Lighthouse. (Illus.). (Orig.). 1958. pap. 4.00 (0-939384-01-9) Shelburne.

Manning, Harvey. Backpacking, One Step at a Time. rev. ed. 1986. pap. 15.00 (0-394-72939-0) Vin Bks.

— Hiking the Mountains to Sound Greenway. LC 93-6011. (Illus.). 224p. 1993. pap. 12.95 (0-89886-369-4) Mountaineers.

Manning, Harvey & Manning, Penny. Walks & Hikes in the Foothills & Lowlands Around Puget Sound. (Illus.). 288p. 1995. pap. 14.95 (0-89886-431-3) Mountaineers.

— Walks & Hikes on the Beaches Around Puget Sound. (Illus.). 288p. 1995. pap. 14.95 (0-89886-411-9) Mountaineers.

Manning, Harvey, jt. auth. see Spring, Ira.

Manning, Henry. The Fourth Dimension Simply Explained. 1990. 16.50 (0-8446-5276-8) Peter Smith.

Manning, Hiram. Manning on Decoupage. (Illus.). 254p. 1980. reprint ed. pap. 9.95 (0-486-24028-2) Dover.

Manning, Ian. With a Gun in Good Country. limited ed. LC 95-61226. (Illus.). 295p. 1995. 85.00 (1-882458-07-9) Trophy Rm Bks.

Manning, J. Rives, Jr. Headstones of Halifax Vol. 2: Sunset Hill, Littleton. LC 96-181402. 60p. 1998. pap. 15.00 (0-9652273-1-6) J R Manning.

Manning, Jackie. Silver Hearts. (Historical Ser.: No. 454). 1999. per. 4.99 (0-373-29054-3, 1-29054-3) Harlequin Bks.

— A Wish for Nicholas. (Historical Ser.: No. 398). 1998. per. 4.99 (0-373-28998-7, 1-28998-2) Harlequin Bks.

Manning, James. Prophecies for the New Millennium: Psychics, Seers, & Oracles Tell You What to Expect from the Next 1000 Years. LC 97-10762. 128p. 1997. 15.00 (0-06-270211-4) HarpC.

Manning, Jane. My First Songs. LC 97-73142. 24p. (J). (ps up). 1998. 9.95 (0-694-00983-0) HarpC Child Bks.

— New Vocal Repertory, Vol. 2. (Illus.). 336p. 1999. text 55.00 (0-19-879018-X); pap. text 19.95 (0-19-879019-8) OUP.

— New Vocal Repertory: An Introduction. LC 93-30975. (Illus.). 290p. 1994. pap. text 27.95 (0-19-816413-0) OUP.

Manning, Jane. This Little Piggy. 10p. (J). (ps up). 1997. 7.95 (0-694-01000-6, HarpFestival) HarpC Child Bks.

Manning, Janet. Cetacean Societies: Field Studies of Dolphins & Whales. 400p. 2000. pap. text 35.00 (0-226-50341-0) U Ch Pr.

Manning, Jason. Falconer's Law. (Falconer Saga Ser.: No. 01). 352p. 1996. pap., mass mkt. 5.50 (0-451-18645-1, Sig) NAL.

— Gun Justice. 240p. 1999. mass mkt. 5.99 (0-312-97191-5, St Martins Paperbacks) St Martin.

— Gunsmoke on the Sierra Line. 1989. mass mkt. 2.95 (0-8217-2632-3, Zebra Kensgtn) Kensgtn Pub Corp.

— High Country. 352p. (Orig.). 1993. mass mkt. 4.50 (0-451-17680-4, Sig) NAL.

— Mountain Massacre, 1 vol. 320p. 1999. mass mkt. 5.99 (0-451-19689-9) NAL.

— Mountain Passage: The Life of a Mountain Man/The Story of America. 1998. mass mkt. 5.99 (0-451-19569-8, Sig) NAL.

***Manning, Jason.** The Outlaw Trail. 240p. 2000. mass mkt. 5.99 (0-312-97569-4) St Martin.

Manning, Jason. Revenge in Little Texas. 1990. mass mkt. 2.95 (0-8217-2898-9, Zebra Kensgtn) Kensgtn Pub Corp.

— Showdown at Seven Springs. 224p. 1992. mass mkt. 3.50 (0-8217-3999-9, Zebra Kensgtn) Kensgtn Pub Corp.

— Texas Blood Kill. 1991. mass mkt. 3.50 (0-8217-3577-2, Zebra Kensgtn) Kensgtn Pub Corp.

— Texas Gundown. 1990. mass mkt. 2.95 (0-8217-2970-5, Zebra Kensgtn) Kensgtn Pub Corp.

— Texas Helltown. 1990. mass mkt. 2.95 (0-8217-3218-8, Zebra Kensgtn) Kensgtn Pub Corp.

***Manning, Jeane.** Beyond Tide & Time. 1999. pap. write for info. (1-58235-094-9) Watermrk Pr.

Manning, Jeane. The Coming Energy Revolution: The Search for Free Energy. (Illus.). 243p. Date not set. pap. 12.95 (0-89529-713-2, Avery) Penguin Putnam.

Manning, Jeff. Got Milk? The Story of an Ad Campaign. LC 99-30813. Orig. Title: Got Milk? The Story of an Ad Campaign. (Illus.). 224p. 1999. 27.95 (0-7615-1801-0) Prima Pub.

Manning, Jerome A. Estate Planning. 4th ed. 746p. 1991. text 110.00 (0-685-54556-3, D1-0160) PLI.

— Estate Planning: How to Preserve Your Estate for Your Loved Ones. 312p. 1992. pap. 14.95 (0-614-17128-8, K1-1100) PLI.

— Estate Planning - with Supplement. 3rd ed. 661p. 1982. 125.00 (0-685-69426-7) PLI.

— Estate Planning & 1989 Supplement. 3rd ed. LC 87-63222. 735p. 1988. 95.00 (0-685-69427-5) PLI.

Manning, Jerome A., et al. Manning on Estate Planning. 5th ed. 720p. 1995. ring bd. 145.00 (0-614-17124-5, D1-0165) PLI.

Manning, Jo. The Reluctant Guardian. 258p. 1999. 19.95 (1-929085-07-9); lib. bdg. 17.95 (1-929085-08-7); mass mkt. 4.95 (1-929085-06-0) Rgncy Pr.

— The Reluctant Guardian. large type ed. 356p. 1999. lib. bdg. 23.95 (1-929085-09-5); per. 19.95 (1-929085-10-9) Rgncy Pr.

***Manning, Joanna.** Is the Pope Catholic? A Woman Confronts Her Church. 264p. 2000. pap. 18.95 (0-8245-1869-1, Pub. by Crossroad NY) Natl Bk Netwk.

Manning, Joe. Steeples: Sketches of North Adams. 2nd rev. ed. LC 98-93268. (Illus.). 264p. 1998. pap. 19.95 (0-9658684-8-6) Flatiron Pr.

Manning, John, ed. Abraham Fraunce, Symbolicae Philosophiae Liber. Haan, Estelle, tr. LC 89-45845. (Studies in the Emblem: No. 7). 1991. 63.00 (0-404-63707-8) AMS Pr.

— The Emblems of Thomas Palmer: Two Hundred Poosees. LC 87-45812. (Studies in the Emblem: No. 2). 1988. 72.45 (0-404-63702-7) AMS Pr.

***Manning, John & Hudson, Robert.** North Brevard County. (Images of America Ser.). (Illus.). 128p. 1999. pap. 18.99 (0-7385-0241-3) Arcadia Publng.

Manning, John, jt. auth. see Burnett, Mark T.

Manning, John, jt. auth. see Daly, Peter M.

Manning, John, jt. auth. see Goldblatt, Peter.

Manning, John, jt. auth. see Thornton, Mark.

Manning, John, ed. see Alciato, Andrea.

Manning, John C. Applied Principles of Hydrology. 3rd ed. LC 96-17796. 276p. (C). 1996. pap. text 48.00 (0-13-565532-3, Pub. by P-H) S&S Trade.

— In Defense of Human Endeavor: The Environmental Consequences of the Rise of the Human Species. (Illus.). 272p. 1999. pap. 19.95 (0-9649679-9-5) Hawks Cry.

Manning, John J. John Hayward's The Life & Raigne of King Henrie III. (Camden Fourth Ser.: No. 42). 272p. (C). 35.00 (0-86193-129-7) David Brown.

Manning, John R. Diffusion Kinetics for Atoms in Crystals. LC 68-20921. 274p. reprint ed. pap. 85.00 (0-608-10295-4, 200579000060) Bks Demand.

Manning, Joseph F. The Miracle of Agape Love. 160p. 1977. mass mkt. 5.99 (0-88368-079-3) Whitaker Hse.

Manning, Justice A. Control Techniques for Fugitive VOC Emissions from Chemical Process Facilities. (Illus.). 163p. (C). 1997. reprint ed. pap. text 40.00 (0-7881-4159-7) DIANE Pub.

Manning, Karen. AIDS: Can This Epidemic Be Stopped? LC 95-19443. (Issues of Our Time Ser.). (Illus.). 96p. (J). (gr. 5-8). 1995. lib. bdg. 18.90 (0-8050-4240-7) TFC Bks NY.

***Manning, Kathleen.** Ritual, Ceremonies & Cultural Meaning in Higher Education. LC 99-55887. (Critical Studies in Education & Culture Ser.). 184p. 2000. 49.95 (0-89789-504-5, H504, Bergin & Garvey) Greenwood.

Manning, Kathleen, ed. Giving Voice to Critical Campus Issues: Qualitative Research in Student Affairs. LC 98-32256. 160p. 1999. 43.00 (1-883485-13-4) Am Coll Personnel.

***Manning, Kathleen, ed.** Giving Voice to Critical Campus Issues: Qualitative Research in Student Affairs. LC 98-32256. 160p. 1999. pap. 24.50 (1-883485-14-2) Am Coll Personnel.

Manning, Kathleen, jt. auth. see Stage, Frances K.

***Manning, Kay S.** Little Indian & Whiney Gator. 36p. (J). 2001. 22.95 (1-57532-291-9) Press-Tige Pub.

Manning, Kenneth R. Black Apollo of Science: The Life of Ernest Everett Just. (Illus.). 416p. 1985. pap. 15.95 (0-19-503498-8) OUP.

Manning, Kenneth V., jt. auth. see White, Marsh W.

Manning, Kristy, jt. auth. see Beatley, Timothy.

Manning, Laura L. The Dispute Processing Model of Public Policy Evolution: The Case of Endangered Species Policy Changes from 1973 to 1983. LC 90-39465. (Environment: Problems & Solutions Ser.: Vol. 14). 490p. 1990. text 30.00 (0-8240-2520-2) Garland.

Manning, Laurie, ed. see Huang, Yu C.

Manning, Laurie, ed. see Huang, Yu Cheng.

Manning, Laurie, ed. see Yu Cheng Huang.

Manning, Lee M., jt. auth. see Baruth, Leroy G.

Manning, Linda. Animal Hours. (Illus.). 32p. (J). (gr. k-3). 1992. pap. write for info. (0-614-17733-2) Stoddart Publ.

— Animal Hours. unabridged ed. (Illus.). 32p. (J). (gr. k up). 1984. pap. 6.95 (0-19-540844-6) STDK.

— Dinosaur Days. LC 93-28443. (Illus.). 32p. (J). (ps-2). 1996. 12.95 (0-8167-3315-5) BrdgeWater.

— Dinosaur Days. LC 93-28443. (Illus.). 32p. (J). (ps-2). 1995. pap. 3.95 (0-8167-3316-3, Troll Medallion) Troll Communs.

— Dinosaur Days. 1993. 9.15 (0-606-07434-1, Pub. by Turtleback) Demco.

Manning, Liz R. The New Wallpaper: Creative Ideas for Decorating Walls, Ceilings & Home Accessories. (Illus.). 160p. 1999. pap. 24.99 (1-56496-544-9) Rockport Vitae Pub.

Manning, Lloyd R. Appraisal of a Fast Food Restaurant. 44p. (Orig.). 1995. pap. 25.00 (0-614-23695-9) Todd Pub.

— What It's Worth: A Guide to Valuing a Small Business. 320p. 2000. pap. text 22.95 (1-55571-504-4) PSI Resch.

Manning, Loretta, jt. auth. see Rayfield, Sylvia.

Manning, M. Drama School. 1999. pap. 9.95 (0-7534-5178-6) LKC.

Manning, M. C., jt. auth. see Ahern, T. J.

Manning, M. Lee. Celebrating Diversity: Multicultural Education in Middle Level Schools. 142p. (C). 1994. pap. text 22.00 (1-56090-089-X) Natl Middle Schl.

— Developmentally Appropriate Middle Level Schools. LC 93-34185. 1993. 15.00 (0-87173-132-0) ACEI.

Manning, M. Lee & Baruth, Leroy G. Students at Risk. LC 93-50125. 368p. 1994. 52.00 (0-205-15464-6) Allyn.

Manning, M. Lee, jt. auth. see Baruth, Leroy G.

Manning, M. Lee, jt. auth. see Butler, Deborah A.

Manning, Mari C. For Women Only: A Guide to Healthy Living. 68p. 1992. pap. text 5.95 (0-9617800-5-3) Zebra Run Pr.

Manning, Marilyn. Leadership Skills for Women: Achieving Impact As a Manager. rev. ed. LC 94-80009. (Fifty-Minutes Ser.). 66p. 1995. pap. 10.95 (1-56052-325-5) Crisp Pubns.

Manning, Marilyn & Barnes, Carolyn. Professional Excellence for Secretaries: Practical Proven Techniques for Professional Development. Crisp, Michael G., ed. LC 87-73561. (Fifty-Minute Ser.). (Illus.). 71p. 1988. pap. 10.95 (0-931961-52-1) Crisp Pubns.

Manning, Marilyn, jt. auth. see Haddock, Patricia.

Manning, Marilyn, jt. auth. see Rietz, Helen L.

***Manning, Mark.** Crucify Me Again. 2000. pap. 14.50 (1-899598-14-6) Codex.

— Get Your Cock Out. 160p. 2000. pap. 10.95 (1-84068-034-2, Pub. by Creation Books) Last Gasp.

***Manning, Martha.** All Seasons Pass: Grieving a Miscarriage. LC 99-67516. 64p. 2000. pap. 9.95 (1-893732-08-8) SORIN BKS.

Manning, Martha. Chasing Grace: Reflections of a Catholic Girl, Grown Up. LC 96-6773. 240p. 1997. pap. 11.00 (0-06-251312-5, Pub. by Harper SF) HarpC.

— Undercurrents: A Therapist's Reckoning with Depression. LC 94-33043. 208p. 1995. pap. 13.00 (0-06-251184-X, Pub. by Harper SF) HarpC.

— Undercurrents: A Therapist's Reckoning with Her Own Depression. 197p. 1998. text 20.00 (0-7881-5241-6) DIANE Pub.

***Manning, Martin.** From Barbie to the Wild West: An Encyclopedia of U.S. Cultural Influence. 2001. lib. bdg. 60.00 (0-87436-981-9) ABC-CLIO.

***Manning, Maryann, et al.** The Theme Immersion Resource Guide for Teaching Science. 2000. pap. write for info. (0-325-00285-1) Heinemann.

Manning, Maryann M. & Manning, Gary L., eds. Whole Language: Beliefs & Practices, K-8. 240p. 1989. pap. 16.95 (0-8106-1482-0) NEA.

Manning, Maryann M., et al. Reading & Writing in the Middle Grades: A Whole-Language View. 1990. pap. 8.95 (0-8106-3071-0) NEA.

— Reading & Writing in the Primary Grades. 80p. 1987. pap. 9.95 (0-8106-1697-1) NEA.

— The Theme Immersion Compendium for Social Studies Teaching. LC 96-53523. 1997. pap. text 25.00 (0-435-08884-X) Heinemann.

— The Theme Immersion Compendium for Social Studies Teaching: How to Effect Large-Scale Change in the Reporting Process. LC 97-22906. 1997. pap. text 21.00 (0-435-07238-2) Heinemann.

Manning, Matthew. Link: Extraordinary Gifts of a Teenage Psychic. (Illus.). 176p. 1987. reprint ed. pap. 10.95 (0-86140-283-9, Pub. by Smyth) Dufour.

***Manning, Matthew.** One Foot in the Stars: Story of the World's Most Extraordinary Healer. 2000. 29.95 (1-86204-591-7, Pub. by Element MA) Penguin Putnam.

Manning, Matthew. The Strangers. 176p. 1996. pap. 13.95 (0-86140-387-8, Pub. by Smyth) Dufour.

Manning, Maurice. The Blueshirts. 2nd ed. (Illus.). 276p. 1987. reprint ed. pap. 23.95 (0-7171-1515-1, Pub. by Gill & MacMill) Irish Bks Media.

Manning, Michael. Cathexis. (Illus.). 104p. 1997. pap. 12.95 (1-56163-174-4, Amerotica) NBM.

— Hydrophidian. (Illus.). 64p. 1996. pap. 10.95 (1-56163-167-1, Amerotica) NBM.

M

— Lumenagerie. (Illus.). 72p. 1996. pap. 11.95 (*1-56163-151-5*, Amerotica) NBM.

— The Spider Garden. 96p. 1995. pap. 11.95 (*1-56163-117-5*, Amerotica) NBM.

Manning, Michael, contrib. by. Euthanasia & Physician-Assisted Suicide, Killing or Caring. LC 98-17655. 96p. 1998. pap. 8.95 (*0-8091-3804-2*, 3804-2) Paulist Pr.

Manning, Michael & Conlon, Patrick. Tranceptor Vol. 1: The Way Station. (Illus.). 64p. 1998. pap. 10.95 (*1-56163-211-2*) NBM.

Manning, Michael R., jt. ed. see Jackson, Conrad N.

Manning, Michael V. Safety Is a People Business: A Practical Guide to the Human Side of Safety. LC 97-37710. 225p. 1997. pap. 49.00 (*0-86587-597-9*, 597) Gov Insts.

— So You're the Safety Director: An Introduction to Loss Control & Safety Management. 2nd rev. ed. 220p. 1998. pap. text 59.00 (*0-86587-617-7*, 617) Gov Insts.

Manning, Michelle. Borland's Official Non-Nonsense Guide to Delphi 2. (Illus.). 416p. 1996. 25.00 (*0-672-30871-1*) Sams.

Manning, Michelle M. Teach Yourself JBuilder 2 in 21 Days. (Teach Yourself Ser.). 1998. pap. 39.99 (*0-672-31318-9*) Sams.

Manning, Mick. A Ruined House. LC 93-21295. (Read & Wonder Ser.). 1996. 11.19 (*0-606-10296-5*, Pub. by Turtleback) Demco.

Manning, Mick. A Ruined House. LC 93-21295. (Illus.). 32p. (J). (gr. k-4). 1996. reprint ed. pap. 5.99 (*1-56402-936-0*) Candlewick Pr.

***Manning, Mick & Granstrhom, Brita.** What a Viking! LC 00-24193. (Illus.). 32p. (J). (gr. k-3). 2000. 15.00 (*91-29-64883-1*) R&S Bks SW.

Manning, Mick & Granstrom, Brita. Art School. (Illus.). 48p. (J). (gr. 1-4). 1996. pap. 9.95 (*0-7534-5000-3*, Kingfisher) LKC.

— Honk! Honk! A Story of Migration. LC 97-1427. 32p. (J). (ps-2). 1997. 14.95 (*0-7534-5103-4*, Kingfisher) LKC.

— Nature Watch. LC 96-30162. (Illus.). 48p. (J). (gr. 1-4). 1997. 9.95 (*0-7534-5063-1*, Kingfisher) LKC.

***Manning, Mick & Granstrom, Brita.** Science School. LC 97-51598. 47p. (YA). (gr. 1-6). 1998. 9.95 (*0-7534-5097-6*) LKC.

Manning, Mick & Granstrom, Brita. Yum-Yum! LC 97-10726. 32p. (J). (ps-3). 1997. pap. 6.95 (*0-531-15322-3*) Watts.

— Yum-Yum! LC 97-10726. (Illus.). 32p. (J). (gr. k-3). 1997. lib. bdg. 22.00 (*0-531-14484-4*) Watts.

Manning, Mick & Granstrom Om, Brita. My Body, Your Body. LC 97-10727. (Wonderwise Ser.). (J). 1997. pap. write for info. (*0-531-15324-X*) Watts.

— My Body, Your Body. LC 97-10727. (Wonderwise Ser.). 32p. (J). (ps-2). 1997. lib. bdg. 20.00 (*0-531-14486-0*) Watts.

Manning, Mick & Om, Brita G. Splish, Splash, Splosh! A Book about Water. LC 97-16325. (Wonderwise Ser.). (J). 1997. pap. 6.95 (*0-531-15326-6*) Watts.

— Splish, Splash, Splosh! A Book about Water. LC 97-16325. (Wonderwise). 27p. (J). (ps-1). 1997. lib. bdg. 22.00 (*0-531-14488-7*) Watts.

— What's under the Bed? LC 97-16326. (Wonderwise Ser.). 1997. pap. 6.95 (*0-531-15327-4*) Watts.

— What's under the Bed? LC 97-16326. (Wonderwise Ser.). (Illus.). (J). 1997. lib. bdg. 22.00 (*0-531-14489-5*) Watts.

— What's Up? LC 97-14014. (Wonderwise Ser.). (J). 1997. pap. 6.95 (*0-531-15323-1*); lib. bdg. 22.00 (*0-531-14485-2*) Watts.

Manning-Miller, Carmen L., jt. auth. see Berry, Venise T.

Manning, Ned. Close to the Bone. 64p. (C). 1994. pap. 16.95 (*0-86819-389-5*, Pub. by Currency Pr) Accents Pubns.

Manning, Nick P. The Therapeutic Community Movement: Charisma & Routinisation. (Therapeutic Communities Section, International Library of Group Psychotherapy & Group Processes). 256p. 1989. 49.50 (*0-415-02913-9*) Routledge.

— The Therapeutic Community Movement: Charisma & Routinization. LC 88-32436. (International Library of Group Psychotherapy & Group Process). (Illus.). 256p. reprint ed. pap. 79.40 (*0-608-20360-2*, 207161300002) Bks Demand.

***Manning, Nick P., et al.** Strategic Decisionmaking in Cabinet Government: Institutional Underpinnings & Obstacles. LC 99-56442. (Sector Study Ser.). 56p. 1999. 22.00 (*0-8213-4627-X*, 14627) World Bank.

Manning, P., jt. ed. see Wagner, J.

Manning, P. R. & DeBakey, L., eds. Medicine: Preserving the Passion. (Illus.). 315p. 1988. 62.00 (*0-387-96361-8*) Spr-Verlag.

Manning, Patrick. Francophone Sub-Saharan Africa, 1880-1995. 2nd ed. LC 98-38091. (Illus.). 248p. (C). 1999. text 69.95 (*0-521-64255-8*); pap. text 19.95 (*0-521-64519-0*) Cambridge U Pr.

Manning, Patrick. Slavery & African Life: Occidental, Oriental & African Slave Trades. (African Studies: No. 67). (Illus.). 247p. (C). 1990. pap. text 20.95 (*0-521-34867-6*) Cambridge U Pr.

Manning, Patrick, ed. Slave Trades, 1500-1800: Globalization of Forces Labour. LC 96-3760. (Expanding World Ser.: Vol. 15). 400p. 1996. text 128.95 (*0-86078-512-2*, Pub. by Variorum) Ashgate Pub Co.

Manning, Patrick J., et al, eds. The Biology of the Laboratory Rabbit. 2nd ed. LC 93-39577. (American College of Laboratory Animal Medicine Ser.). (Illus.). 483p. 1994. text 132.00 (*0-12-469235-4*) Acad Pr.

Manning, Patrick J., jt. ed. see Wagner, Joseph E.

Manning, Patrick L. In Search of the Senior Tour. 1994. 16.95 (*0-533-11133-1*) Vantage.

Manning, Paul. Martin Bormann: Nazi in Exile. (Illus.). 320p. (C). 1981. 14.95 (*0-8184-0309-8*) Carol Pub Group.

— Spinning for Labour: Trade Unions & the New Media Environment. LC 97-78314. (Illus.). 401p. 1998. text 76.95 (*1-84014-339-8*, Pub. by Ashgate Pub) Ashgate Pub Co.

Manning, Pauline, ed. see Potter, Neal & Christy, Francis T.

Manning, Penny, jt. auth. see Manning, Harvey.

Manning, Peter. Electronic & Computer Music. 2nd ed. (Illus.). 408p. 1994. pap. text 26.00 (*0-19-816329-0*) OUP.

Manning, Peter J. Byron & His Fictions. LC 78-7943. 297p. reprint ed. pap. 92.10 (*0-7837-3667-3*, 204354000009) Bks Demand.

Manning, Peter K. Organizational Communication. (Communication & Social Order Ser.). 260p. 1992. pap. text 25.95 (*0-202-30402-7*); lib. bdg. 49.95 (*0-202-30401-9*) Aldine de Gruyter.

— Police Work: The Social Organization of Policing. 2nd rev. ed. LC 98-115517. (Illus.). 372p. (C). 1997. pap. text 22.95 (*0-88133-953-9*) Waveland Pr.

— Semiotics & Fieldwork. (Qualitative Research Methods Ser.: Vol. 7). 96p. (C). 1987. text 24.00 (*0-8039-2761-4*); pap. text 10.50 (*0-8039-2640-5*) Sage.

— Symbolic Communication: Signifying Calls & Police Response. (Organization Studies: No. 9). 290p. 1989. 44.00 (*0-262-13234-6*) MIT Pr.

Manning, Peter K. & Zucker, Martine. The Sociology of Mental Health & Illness. LC 76-16067. (Studies in Sociology). (C). 1976. pap. text. write for info. (*0-672-61265-8*, Bobbs) Macmillan.

Manning, Peter K., jt. auth. see Cullum-Swan, Betsy.

Manning, Peter K., jt. auth. see Forst, Brian.

Manning, Peyton. Manning. 2000. mass mkt. 6.99 (*0-06-102024-9*) HarpC.

***Manning, Peyton, et al.** Manning: A Father, His Sons & a Football Legacy. (Illus.). 256p. 2000. 24.00 (*0-06-105136-5*, HarpEntertain) Morrow Avon.

Manning, Philip. Erving Goffman & Modern Sociology. (Key Contemporary Thinkers Ser.). vi, 202p. 1992. 45.50 (*0-8047-2025-8*); pap. 16.95 (*0-8047-2026-6*) Stanford U Pr.

Manning, Phillip. Afoot in the South: Walks in the Natural Areas of North Carolina. LC 92-46868. (Afoot in the South Ser.). (Illus.). 256p. (Orig.). 1996. pap. 12.95 (*0-89587-099-1*) Blair.

— Islands of Hope: Lessons from North America's Great Wildlife Sanctuaries. LC 99-32139. (Illus.). 208p. 1999. 15.95 (*0-89587-183-1*) Blair.

— Orange Blossom Trails: Walks in the Natural Areas of Florida. LC 97-25696. (Afoot in the South Ser.). (Illus.). (Orig.). 1997. pap. 13.95 (*0-89587-201-3*) Blair.

— Palmetto Journal: Walks in the Natural Areas of South Carolina. LC 94-49584. (Illus.). 238p. (Orig.). 1995. pap. 13.95 (*0-89587-124-6*) Blair.

Manning Publications Staff, jt. auth. see Fritz, Jeffrey N.

Manning Publications Staff, jt. auth. see Richardson, Ronny.

Manning Publications Staff, jt. auth. see Rosen, Evan.

Manning, Rachel L. Your Spirit Guides Are Thoroughbreds: A Self Help Manual for Mule Headed People. LC 86-62341. 160p. (Orig.). 1988. pap. 7.95 (*0-941698-14-9*) Pan Ishtar.

Manning, Rachel L. & Manning, Al G. Puck'em All: We've Got the Magick. 150p. (Orig.). 1985. pap. 7.95 (*0-941698-10-6*) Pan Ishtar.

Manning, Rachel L., jt. auth. see Manning, Al G.

Manning, Raymond B. & Chace, Fenner A. Decapod & Stomatopod Crustacea from Ascension Island, South Atlantic Ocean. LC 90-10365. (Smithsonian Contributions to Zoology Ser.: No. 503). 97p. reprint ed. pap. 30.10 (*0-8357-2752-1*, 203986800013) Bks Demand.

Manning, Reed. Earthly Pleasures: Erotic Science Fiction Stories by Reed Manning. 144p. (Orig.). 1996. pap. 9.95 (*1-885865-07-4*) Circlet Pr.

Manning, Renfro C. Schools for All Learners: Beyond the Bell Curve. LC 94-34139. 200p. 1994. 29.95 (*1-883001-06-4*) Eye On Educ.

— The Teacher Evaluation Handbook. 208p. (C). 1988. text 29.95 (*0-13-888389-0*) P-H.

Manning, Rich. Vinny's Wide World of Sports. LC 95-94690. 104p. 1995. pap. 6.95 (*0-9648690-0-4*) Lowdown Bros.

***Manning, Richard.** Food's Frontier: The Next Green Revolution. 240p. 2000. 24.00 (*0-86547-593-8*) N Point Pr.

Manning, Richard. Grassland. 1995. 23.95 (*0-614-15502-9*, Viking) Viking Penguin.

— Grassland. 320p. 1997. pap. 13.95 (*0-14-023388-1*) Viking Penguin.

***Manning, Richard.** Inside Passage: A Journey Beyond Borders. (Illus.). 250p. 2000. 25.00 (*1-55963-655-6*, Shearwater Bks) Island Pr.

Manning, Richard. One Round River: The Curse of Gold & the Fight for the Big Blackfoot. LC 97-27537. 222p. 1998. 25.00 (*0-8050-4792-1*) H Holt & Co.

— A River's Life. 1996. pap. 14.95 (*0-8050-4793-X*) H Holt & Co.

Manning, Richard W., jt. auth. see Jones, J. Knox, Jr.

Manning, Rita C. Speaking from the Heart: A Feminist Perspective on Ethics. 224p. (C). 1992. text 49.00 (*0-8476-7733-8*) Rowman.

Manning, Rita C. & Trujillo, Rene. Social Justice in a Diverse Society. LC 95-34562. 553p. 1996. pap. text 43.95 (*1-55934-411-3*, 1411) Mayfield Pub.

Manning, Robert, ed. The Aftermath: The Legacy of War, 1975-1985. (Vietnam Experience Ser.). (Illus.). 192p. 1986. 16.30 (*0-201-11273-6*) Addison-Wesley.

— Combat Photographer: Vietnam Through G.I. Lenses. (Vietnam Experience Ser.). (Illus.). 192p. 1984. 16.30 (*0-201-11266-3*) Addison-Wesley.

— The False Peace: The Beginning of the End, 1972-1974. (Vietnam Experience Ser.). (Illus.). 192p. 1986. 16.30 (*0-201-11272-8*) Addison-Wesley.

— Fighting for Time: The War Changes Time, 1969-1970. (Vietnam Experience Ser.). (Illus.). 192p. 1984. 16.30 (*0-201-11267-1*) Addison-Wesley.

— A Nation Divided: The War at Home, 1945-1972. (Vietnam Experience Ser.). (Illus.). 192p. 1984. 16.30 (*0-201-11263-9*) Addison-Wesley.

— South Vietnam on Trial: The Test of Vietnamization, 1970-1973. (Vietnam Experience Ser.). (Illus.). 192p. 1984. 16.30 (*0-201-11264-7*) Addison-Wesley.

— Thunder from Above: The War in the Air Through 1968. (Vietnam Experience Ser.). (Illus.). 192p. 1984. 16.30 (*0-201-11265-5*) Addison-Wesley.

— The Vietnam Experience: The Fall of the South, the False Peace. write for info. (*0-318-60206-7*) Addison-Wesley.

— Words of War. (Vietnam Experience Ser.). (Illus.). 192p. 1988. 16.30 (*0-201-11943-9*) Addison-Wesley.

Manning, Robert & Williams, Brett. Credit Card Nation: America's Dangerous Addiction to Consumer Debt. 304p. 1996. 25.00 (*0-465-01552-2*) Basic.

Manning, Robert, ed. see Doyle, Edward G. & Lipsman, Samuel L.

Manning, Robert, ed. see Fulghum, David & Maitland, Terrence.

Manning, Robert, ed. see Maitland, Terrence & McInerney, Peter.

Manning, Robert A. Asian Policy: The New Soviet Challenge in the Pacific - A Twentieth Century Fund Paper. 150p. 1988. 18.95 (*0-87078-245-2*); pap. 8.95 (*0-87078-244-4*) Century Foundation.

Manning, Robert A., jt. ed. see Geipel, Gary L.

***Manning, Robert D.** Credit Card Nation: The Consequences of America's Addiction to Credit. 2000. 26.00 (*0-465-04366-6*, Pub. by Basic) HarpC.

Manning, Robert E. Studies in Outdoor Recreation: Search & Research for Satisfaction. 2nd ed. (Illus.). 374p. 1999. pap. 24.95 (*0-87071-463-5*) Oreg St U Pr.

Manning, Robert J. Interpreting Otherwise Than Heidegger: Emmanuel Levinas's Ethics As First Philosophy. LC 92-45191. 268p. 1993. text 38.95 (*0-8207-0246-3*); pap. text 21.95 (*0-8207-0253-6*) Duquesne.

Manning, Roberta T. The Crisis of the Old Order in Russia: Gentry & Government. LC 81-47933. (Studies of the Russian Institute, Columbia University & Harvard Series in Ukrainian Studies). 571p. 1982. reprint ed. pap. 177.10 (*0-7837-9378-2*, 206012200004) Bks Demand.

Manning, Roger. Fuck You Have A Nice Day: The Selected Works of Roger Manning. 88p. 1997. pap. 8.00 (*1-887128-23-9*) Soft Skull Pr.

Manning, Roger B. Hunters & Poachers: A Cultural & Social History of Unlawful Hunting in England 1485-1640. (Illus.). 280p. 1993. text 55.00 (*0-19-820324-1*) OUP.

— Village Revolts: Social Protest & Popular Disturbances in England, 1509-1640. (Illus.). 368p. 1988. 85.00 (*0-19-820116-8*) OUP.

Manning, Rosemary. The Chinese Garden. LC 99-56679. 208p. 2000. 29.00 (*1-55861-215-7*, Pub. by Feminist Pr) Consort Bk Sales.

— The Chinese Garden. LC 99-56679. 192p. 2000. pap. 12.95 (*1-55861-216-5*, Pub. by Feminist Pr) Consort Bk Sales.

— Heraldry. (Junior Reference Ser.). (Illus.). (J). (gr. 7 up). 1975. 14.95 (*0-7136-0108-6*) Dufour.

— A Time & A Time: An Autobiography. LC 71-596230. 158p. 1971. write for info. (*0-7145-0706-7*) M Boyars Pubs.

***Manning-Ross, L.** Businessplan.com: How to Write a Ecommerce Business Plan. 2nd ed. 200p. 2000. pap. 19.95 (*1-55571-531-1*, Pub. by PSI Resch) Midpt Trade.

Manning, Roy. Redneck Rhymer Strikes. 44p. Date not set. pap. 7.95 (*0-932662-56-0*) St Andrews NC.

Manning, Russ. Exploring the Big South Fork: A Handbook to the National River & Recreation Area. (Illus.). 252p. (Orig.). 1994. pap. 15.95 (*0-9625122-6-5*) Mtn Laurel Pl.

***Manning, Russ.** 40 Hikes in Tennessee's South Cumberland. 3rd ed. LC 99-50630. (100 Hikes in Ser.). (Illus.). 112p. 2000. pap. 12.95 (*0-89886-637-5*) Mountaineers.

Manning, Russ. The Historic Cumberland Plateau: An Explorer's Guide. 2nd ed. LC 98-40194. (Outdoor Tennessee Ser.). (Illus.). 376p. 1999. pap. 18.95 (*1-57233-044-9*) U of Tenn Pr.

— 100 Hikes in the Great Smoky Mountains National Park. 2nd ed. LC 99-6456. 1999. pap. 14.95 (*0-89886-636-7*) Mountaineers.

***Manning, Russ.** 100 Trails of the Big South Fork: Tennessee & Kentucky Hiking, Mountain Biking, Horseback Riding. 4th ed. LC 99-50715. (100 Hikes in Ser.). (Illus.). 208p. 2000. pap. 14.95 (*0-89886-638-3*) Mountaineers.

— An Outdoor Guide to the Big South Fork: National River & Recreation Area. 2nd ed. LC 00-9435. (Illus.). 240p. 2000. pap. 16.95 (*0-89886-639-1*) Mountaineers.

— 75 Hikes in Virginia's Shenandoah National Park. 2nd ed. LC 99-50638. (100 Hikes in Ser.). (Illus.). 192p. 2000. pap. 12.95 (*0-89886-635-9*) Mountaineers.

Manning, Russ & Burroughs, Edgar Rice. Tarzan: The Land That Time Forgot. unabridged ed. (Illus.). 112p. (Orig.). (YA). (gr. 9 up). 1996. pap. 12.95 (*1-56971-151-8*) Dark Horse Comics.

Manning, Russ & Jamieson, Sondra. The Best of Shenandoah National Park: A Guide to Trails & the Skyline Drive. LC 97-204866. (Tag-Along Bks.). (Illus.). 224p. (Orig.). 1997. pap. 12.95 (*0-9625122-8-1*) Mtn Laurel Pl.

— The Best of the Great Smoky Mountains National Park: A Hikers Guide to Trails & Attractions. (Tag-Along Bks.). (Illus.). 256p. (Orig.). 1991. pap. 12.95 (*0-9625122-2-2*) Mtn Laurel Pl.

— Historic Knoxville & Knox County Bicentennial Edition: A Walking & Touring Guide. (Tag-Along Bks.). (Illus.). 256p. (Orig.). 1990. pap. 8.95 (*0-9625122-3-0*) Mtn Laurel Pl.

— Tennessee's South Cumberland: A Hiker's Guide to Trails & Attractions. 2nd ed. (Tag-along Bks.). Orig. Title: The South Cumberland & Fall Creek Falls. (Illus.). 144p. 1994. pap. 8.95 (*0-9625122-7-3*) Mtn Laurel Pl.

— Trails of the Big South Fork National River & Recreation Area: A Guide for Hikers, Bikers, & Horse Riders. 3rd ed. (Tag-Along Bks.). (Illus.). 256p. 1995. pap. 12.95 (*0-9625122-5-7*) Mtn Laurel Pl.

Manning, Sam, jt. auth. see Greenhill, Basil.

***Manning, Sara.** Love Money. 1998. pap. 6.95 (*0-09-926376-9*, Pub. by Random) Trafalgar.

Manning, Scott, jt. auth. see Cook, Peter.

Manning, Shirley, ed. see Young, Ronald D.

Manning, Shirley, ed. see Young, Ronald D. & Fennell, Robert A.

Manning, Sturt W. The Absolute Chronology of the Aegean Early Bronze Age: Archaeology, Radiocarbon & History. (Monographs in Mediterranean Archaeology). (Illus.). 370p. 1995. 85.00 (*1-85075-336-9*, Pub. by Sheffield Acad) CUP Services.

***Manning, Sturt W.** A Test of Time: The Volcano of Thera & the Chronology & History of Aegean & East Mediterranean in the Mid Second Millennium B. C. (Illus.). 494p. (C). 2000. pap. 45.00 (*1-900188-99-6*, Pub. by Oxbow Bks) David Brown.

Manning, Susan, ed. The Works of Henry Mackenzie. 3141p. (C). 1997. 1155.00 (*0-415-13744-6*) Routledge.

Manning, Susan, ed. see Irving, Washington.

Manning, Susan, ed. & intro. see St. John de Crevecoeur, J. Hector.

Manning, Susan A. Ecstasy & the Demon: Feminism & Nationalism in the Dances of Mary Wigman. LC 92-32232. (C). 1993. 34.95 (*0-520-08193-5*, Pub. by U CA Pr) Cal Prin Full Svc.

— The Puritan-Provincial Vision: Scottish & American Literature in the Nineteenth Century. (Cambridge Studies in American Literature & Culture: No. 41). 253p. (C). 1990. text 69.95 (*0-521-37237-2*) Cambridge U Pr.

Manning, Sylvia B. Hard Times: An Annotated Bibliography LC 99-24624. 1999. write for info. (*0-404-62472-3*) AMS Pr.

Manning, Thomas G. United States Coast Survey vs. Naval Hydrographic Office: A 19th Century Rivalry in Science & Politics. LC 87-25524. (History of American Science & Technology Ser.). 216p. reprint ed. pap. 67.00 (*0-608-09231-2*, 205273500005) Bks Demand.

Manning, Tom, tr. see Chodkiewicz, Michel.

Manning, Tony. World Class! Strategies for Winning with Your Customer. 2nd rev. ed. (Illus.). 418p. 1991. text 50.30 (*0-7021-2663-2*, Pub. by Juta & Co) Intl Spec Bk.

Manning, Tony, ed. Trends Transforming South Africa: Insights, Information & Ideas. 188p. (C). 1991. pap. text 26.00 (*0-7021-2682-9*, Pub. by Juta & Co) Intl Spec Bk.

***Manning, Trevor.** Microwave Radio Transmission Design Guide. LC 99-41774. (Microwave Library). 231p. 1999. 79.00 (*1-58053-031-1*) Artech Hse.

Manning, W. H. The Genealogical & Biographical History of the Manning Family of New England & Descendants from Settlement in America to Present Time. (Illus.). 865p. 1989. reprint ed. pap. 130.00 (*0-8328-0851-2*); reprint ed. lib. bdg. 140.00 (*0-8328-0850-4*) Higginson Bk Co.

— The Roman Small Finds Vol.3: Report on the Excavations at USK, 1965-1976. 353p. 1995. 98.00 (*0-7083-1302-7*, Pub. by Univ Wales Pr) Paul & Co Pubs.

Manning, Walter H. Clinical Decision Making in the Diagnosis & Treatment of Fluency Disorders. (Home Care Aide Ser.). 300p. (C). 1996. mass mkt. 55.95 (*0-8273-6396-6*) Delmar.

Manning-Weber, Claudia & Kovanda, Beverly. Multiskilling: Radiology for Healthcare Providers. LC 99-17639. 150p. 1999. pap. 19.95 (*0-7668-0906-4*) Delmar.

Manning-Weber, Claudia, jt. auth. see Linville, Dorothy.

Manning, Willard G., et al. The Costs of Poor Health Habits. (Illus.). 256p. (C). 1991. 40.50 (*0-674-17485-2*) HUP.

— Health Insurance: The Trade-off Between Risk Pooling & Moral Hazard. LC 89-24276. xiii, 60p. 1989. pap. 7.50 (*0-8330-1016-6*) Rand Corp.

Manning, William, et al. Building Rural Hospital Networks: Lessons in Providing Care to Underserved Populations. LC 95-174. 244p. 1995. pap. 19.50 (*1-56793-028-X*, 0958) Health Admin Pr.

Manning, William R. Early Diplomatic Relations Between the United States & Mexico. LC 77-158857. reprint ed. 37.50 (*0-404-04181-7*) AMS Pr.

— Early Diplomatic Relations Between the United States & Mexico. (BCL1 - U. S. History Ser.). 406p. 1991. reprint ed. lib. bdg. 99.00 (*0-7812-6075-2*) Rprt Serv.

— The Nootka Sound Controversy. LC 65-27195. 1969. reprint ed. 22.95 (*0-405-03678-7*) Ayer.

Manningham, John. The Diary of John Manningham. Bruce, John, ed. LC 17-1264. (Camden Society, London. Publications, First Ser.: No. 99). reprint ed. 49.50 (*0-404-50199-0*) AMS Pr.

— The Diary of John Manningham of the Middle Temple, 1602-1603: Newly Edited in Complete & Unexpurgated Form from the Original Manuscript in the British Museum. LC 74-22553. 485p. reprint ed. pap. 150.40 (*0-8357-6520-2*, 203589100097) Bks Demand.

An Asterisk (*) at the beginning of an entry indicates that the title is appearing for the first time.

***Mannings, David & Postle, Martin.** Sir Joshua Reynolds: A Complete Catalogue of His Paintings, 2 vols. Set. (Illus.). 1200p. 2000. 250.00 (*0-300-08533-8*) Yale U Pr.

***Mannings, Vincent.** Protostars & Planets IV. LC 99-50922. (Space Science Ser.). (Illus.). 1700p. 2000. 95.00 (*0-8165-2059-3*) U of Ariz Pr.

Mannino. Human Biology. 1995. (*0-8151-5980-3*) Mosby Inc.

Mannino, Angelica L., jt. auth. see Mannino, Marc P.

Mannino, Edward F. Business & Commercial Litigation: A Trial Lawyer's Handbook. LC 95-75153. 469p. 1995. 110.00 (*1-55834-213-3*, 64587-10, MICHIE) LEXIS Pub.

— The Civil RICO Primer. LC 96-33856. 1996. write for info. (*0-614-13963-5*) LRP Pubns.

— Lender Liability & Banking Litigation. 700p. 1989. ring bd. 98.00 (*0-317-05405-8*, 00611) NY Law Pub.

Mannino, Fortune V. Practice of Mental Health Consultation. 1975. 24.95 (*0-89876-082-8*) Gardner Pr.

Mannino, Fortune V., ed. Mental Health & Social Change: Fifty Years of Orthopsychiatry, No. 7. LC 74-26634. (Studies in Modern Society: Political & Social Issues). 34.50 (*0-404-11277-3*) AMS Pr.

Mannino, J. Davis. Grieving Days, Healing Days. LC 97-133974. 264p. 1996. pap. text 31.00 (*0-205-19983-6*) Allyn.

— The Moon ups & the Sun Downs. (Illus.). 150p. (C). 1995. 20.00 (*0-9647388-0-5*) Teddy-Bear Pub.

***Mannino, J. Davis.** Sexually Speaking. (C). 1998. pap. 31.25 (*0-07-289347-8*) McGrw-H Hghr Educ.

Mannino, Joseph & Oelerich, Randall W. Human Biology. 272p. (C). 1995. text. write for info. (*0-8151-8710-6*, WCB McGr Hill) McGrw-H Hghr Educ.

Mannino, Joseph & Thurman. Human Biology. 136p. (C). 1995. text, student ed. write for info. (*0-8151-6353-3*, WCB McGr Hill) McGrw-H Hghr Educ.

Mannino, Marc P. & Mannino, Angelica L. Marjorie's Magical Tail. LC 93-86041. (Illus.). 32p. (Orig.). (J). (ps-5). 1993. pap. 7.95 (*0-9638340-0-2*) Sugar Sand.

***Mannino, Michael.** Database Application Development & Design. LC 00-44784. 2001. write for info. (*0-07-303345-6*) McGraw.

Mannino, Philip. ABCs of Audio-Visual Equipment & the School Projectionist Manual. 2nd ed. pap. 4.00 (*0-911328-01-7*) Sch Proj Club.

— Organizing a School Projectionist Club. pap. 0.75 (*0-685-48118-2*) Sch Proj Club.

Mannino, Ronald, ed. see Haber, Lindsey, et al.

Mannion, et al. Companion Practice Book. 1989. pap. text, student ed. write for info. (*0-582-05149-5*, Drumbeat) Longman.

Mannion, A. M. Global Environmantal Change. 2nd ed. (Illus.). 1p. (C). 1998. pap. text 28.13 (*0-582-27722-1*, Pub. by Addison-Wesley) Longman.

Mannion, A. M. & Bowlby, S. R. Environmental Issues in the 1990s. LC 91-36821. 366p. 1992. pap. 75.00 (*0-471-93326-0*) Wiley.

Mannion, Antoinette M. Natural Environmental Change. LC 98-25877. (Introductions to Environment Ser.). 1999. 65.00 (*0-415-13932-5*); pap. 20.99 (*0-415-13933-3*) Routledge.

Mannion, C. L., jt. ed. see Taylor, J. G.

Mannion, James. Nurture Me, Baby: Poems by James Mannion. 36p. (Orig.). 1995. pap. 5.00 (*1-887775-06-4*) Cryptic NY.

Mannion, James & Nigro, Nicholas J. I'm Kirk, He's Stubing: Classic Television on the Couch. LC 95-71614. (Illus.). 128p. (Orig.). 1996. pap. 12.95 (*1-887775-02-1*) Cryptic NY.

Mannion, James, jt. auth. see Nigro, Nicholas J.

Mannion, James, ed. see Nigro, Nicholas J.

Mannion, John, jt. auth. see Harris, Kate, pseud.

Mannion, John B., jt. auth. see Westerhoff, Garret P.

Mannion, John J. Irish Settlements in Eastern Canada: A Study of Cultural Transfer & Adaptation. LC 73-84354. (University of Toronto, Department of Geography Research Publications: No. 12). (Illus.). 231p. reprint ed. pap. 71.70 (*0-8357-6387-0*, 203574200096) Bks Demand.

***Mannion, Michael.** Frankenstein Foods: Genetically Modified Foods & Your Health. 2000. pap. 12.95 (*1-56649-167-3*) Welcome Rain.

Mannion, Michael. How to Help Your Teenager Stop Smoking. LC 99-39378. 208p. 2000. 25.00 (*1-56649-348-X*) Welcome Rain.

***Mannion, Michael.** How to Help Your Teenager Stop Smoking: First Complete Guide of Its Kind, 1. LC 99-39378. 2000. pap. 12.95 (*1-56649-029-4*) Welcome Rain.

— Project Mindshift: The Re-Education of the American Public Concerning Extraterrestrial Life 1947-1997. LC 98-6510. 256p. 1998. 19.95 (*0-87131-856-3*) M Evans.

***Mannion, Michael.** Project Mindshift: The Re-Education of the American Public Concerning Extraterrestrial Life 1947-1997. (Illus.). 304p. 2000. pap. 14.95 (*0-87131-907-1*) M Evans.

Mannion, Michael, jt. auth. see Garrison, Robert.

Mannion, Michael T. Abortion & Healing: A Cry to Be Whole. 2nd ed. LC 86-60382. (Illus.). 96p. (Orig.). 1986. pap. 6.95 (*0-934134-35-9*) Sheed & Ward WI.

Mannion, Michael T. Embracing Life. 32p. pap. 2.25 (*0-7648-0445-6*) Liguori Pubns.

Mannion, Michael T. Post-Abortion Aftermath: A Comprehensive Consideration. LC 94-21556. 190p. (Orig.). 1994. pap. 12.95 (*1-55612-708-1*) Sheed & Ward WI.

— Spiritual Reflections of a Pro-Life Pilgrim. LC 86-63590. (Illus.). 60p. (Orig.). 1987. pap. 3.50 (*1-55612-060-5*) Sheed & Ward WI.

Mannion, Michael T., jt. auth. see Crawford, Douglas R.

Mannion, Paris. Create Your Indoor Fountain: Expressions of the Self. 2nd ed. LC 98-96635. (Illus.). 176p. 1999. pap. text 17.99 (*0-9667102-0-7*) FountainBk.

Mannion, R., et al. Direct Payments from Income Support. (DSS Research Report Ser.). 1994. 35.00 (*0-11-762290-7*, Pub. by Statnry Office) Bernan Associates.

Mannion, Roger J. The Duchess: Stainer's Masterpiece. (Illus.). 192p. 1996. pap. 31.95 (*0-7509-0903-X*, Pub. by Sutton Pub Ltd) Intl Pubs Mktg.

Mannis, Barbara & Lewis, Catherine. The Incredible Little Book of 10,001 Names for Horses. Evers, June V., ed. 1999. pap. 8.95 (*0-9638814-3-4*, Pub. by Horse Hollow) IPG Chicago.

***Mannis, George B.** The Third Patient. LC 99-65199. 348p. 1999. pap. 17.95 (*1-58244-056-5*) Rutledge Bks.

Mannis, Mark J., et al, eds. Eye & Skin Disease. LC 95-14343. (Illus.). 705p. 1995. text 175.00 (*0-7817-0269-0*) Lppncott W & W.

Mannis, Mark J. & Smith, Morton E. Case Studies in Ophthalmology for Medical Students. 1989. teacher ed. 15.00 (*0-317-94086-4*); student ed. 10.00 (*0-317-94085-6*) Am Acad Ophthal.

Mannison, D. S., et al, eds. Environmental Philosophy. (Monograph Ser.: No. 2). vi, 386p. (C). 1980. pap. text 21.00 (*0-909596-39-5*) Ridgeview.

Mannison, Mary & Morris, June. Teaching Adolescents about Contraception. 1991. pap. 110.00 (*0-86431-081-1*, Pub. by Aust Council Educ Res) St Mut.

***Mannix.** Academic & Practical Living Skills Activities. 2000. pap. 4.95 (*0-13-089284-X*) P-H.

— Vocational, Lifestyle & Problem-solving Skills Activities. 2000. pap. 4.95 (*0-13-028121-2*) P-H.

Mannix, Daniel P. Freaks: We Who Are Not As Others. 124p. 1999. pap. text 15.99 (*0-9651042-5-7*, Pub. by Juno Bks) Consort Bk Sales.

— Memoirs of a Sword Swallower: Formerly Step Right Up. Orig. Title: Step Right Up. (Illus.). 128p. (Orig.). 1996. pap. 15.99 (*0-9650469-5-8*) RE Search.

Mannix, Darlene. Be a Better Student: Lessons & Worksheets for Teaching Behavior Management in Grades 4-9. 248p. 1989. pap. text 24.95 (*0-87628-009-2*) Ctr Appl Res.

— Life Skills Activities for Secondary Students with Special Needs. LC 95-12270. (Illus.). 510p. 1995. spiral bd. 29.95 (*0-87628-541-8*) Ctr Appl Res.

— Life Skills Activities for Special Children. 368p. 1991. pap. text 27.95 (*0-87628-547-7*) Ctr Appl Res.

— 100 Everyday Words to Read, Write, & Understand: A Guide for Teaching the Instant Usage of High Frequency Words. (C). 1996. pap. text 29.00 (*0-89079-645-9*) PRO-ED.

— Oral Language Activities for Special Children. 280p. (C). 1986. pap. text 29.95 (*0-87628-637-6*) P-H.

— Ready-to-Use Self-Esteem Activities for Secondary Students with Special Needs. LC 96-9694. 352p. 1996. pap. text 29.95 (*0-87628-758-5*) Ctr Appl Res.

— Ready-to-Use Self-Esteem Activities for Secondary Students with Special Needs. LC 96-9694. 352p. 1996. pap. text 29.50 (*0-87628-887-5*) Ctr Appl Res.

— Social Skills Activities for Secondary Learners with Special Needs. LC 97-30725. 1997. spiral bd. 29.95 (*0-87628-896-4*) Ctr Appl Res.

— Social Skills Activities for Special Children. LC 93-12222. (Illus.). 416p. 1993. pap. text 29.95 (*0-87628-868-9*) Ctr Appl Res.

Mannix, E., jt. auth. see Neale, Margaret.

***Mannix, Iain.** Autocross to Win. (Illus.). 160p. 2000. pap. 15.95 (*0-7603-0693-1*, 129818AP, Pub. by MBI Pubg) Motorbooks Intl.

Mannix, Patrick. The Rhetoric of Antinuclear Fiction: Persuasive Strategies in Novels & Films. LC 91-55466. 192p. 1992. 36.50 (*0-8387-5218-7*) Bucknell U Pr.

Mannle. Fundamentals of Criminology. 2nd ed. (C). 1999. write for info. (*0-13-332560-1*, Macmillan Coll) P-H.

Mannle, Henry W. & Hirschel, David. Fundamental of Criminology. (Illus.). 512p. 1988. text 28.00 (*0-317-62576-4*) P-H.

Manno. Thermal Engineering: An Integrated Approach. 304p. (C). 1994. 55.00 (*0-02-375762-0*, Macmillan Coll) P-H.

Manno, Bruno. Outcome Based Education. (Issue Paper #3-96 Ser.). 30p. 1996. pap. write for info. (*1-57655-147-4*) Independ Inst.

Manno, Bruno V. Outcome Based Education: Miracle Cure or Plague? (Illus.). 24p. (Orig.). 1995. pap. 5.00 (*0-9647703-1-8*, S95-06) Mackinac Ctr Public Pol.

Manno, Christopher E. & Gartner, Steven J. Doing Business in Europe: Before & after 1992. Merritt, Raymond W. & Ennico, Clifford M., eds. (Corporate Counseling Monograph). 113p. (Orig.). 1991. pap. 27.00 (*0-942954-46-7*) NYS Bar.

***Manno, Istvan.** Introduction to the Monte-Carlo Method. 164p. 1999. pap. 36.00 (*963-05-7615-5*, Pub. by Akade Kiado) Intl Spec Bk.

***Manno, Jack P.** Commoditization & Its Impact on Environment & Society. LC 99-43469. (Ecological Economics Ser.). 280p. 1999. boxed set 49.95 (*1-56670-390-5*) Lewis Pubs.

Manno, Rosemary, tr. Camourade: Selected Poems of Paul Laraque. LC 87-71704. 124p. 1988. pap. 9.95 (*0-915306-71-9*) Curbstone.

Manno, V. & Ring, J., eds. Infrared Detection Techniques for Space Research: Proceedings-E S L A B-E S R I N Symposium, 5th, Noordwijk, The Netherlands, 1971. LC 70-179894. (Astrophysics & Space Science Library: No. 30). 344p. 1972. lib. bdg. 129.50 (*90-277-0226-8*) Kluwer Academic.

Manno, V., ed. see ESLAB-ESRIN Symposium Staff.

Manno, Vittorio, jt. auth. see Bonnet, Roger M.

Mannocci, Lino. The Etchings of Claude Lorrain. (Illus.). 256p. (C). 1988. 90.00 (*0-300-04222-1*) Yale U Pr.

Mannoia, Kevin W. Church Planting: The Next Generation: Introducing the Century 21 Church Planting System. (C). 1995. wbk. ed. 85.00 (*0-89367-234-3*); lab manual ed. 250.00 (*0-89367-235-1*) Light & Life Comm.

— Church Planting: The Next Generation: Introducing the Century 21 Church Planting System. 2nd ed. (C). 1995. pap. text 8.99 (*0-89367-183-5*) Light & Life Comm.

— The Integrity Factor: A Journey in Leadership Formation. 147p. 1997. reprint ed. pap. 9.99 (*0-89367-217-3*) Light & Life Comm.

***Mannoia, Richard J.** Knock up to 6 Strokes Off Your Golf Game... Guaranteed! The 1st Really Great Golf Book. large type ed. Yudkin, Mel, ed. LC 00-91051. 144p. 2000. pap. 19.95 (*0-9679992-0-0*) Paradise NY.

***Mannoia, V. James, Jr.** Christian Liberal Arts: An Education That Goes Beyond. 240p. 2000. 58.00 (*0-8476-9958-7*); pap. 22.95 (*0-8476-9959-5*) Rowman.

Mannoia, V. James, Jr. What Is Science? An Introduction to the Structure & Methodology of Science. LC 79-47988. (Illus.). 149p. 1980. pap. text 15.00 (*0-8191-0989-4*) U Pr of Amer.

Mannon, James. Measuring Up: The Performance Ethic in American Culture. LC 97-16789. 176p. (C). 1997. pap. text 18.00 (*0-8133-3297-4*, Pub. by Westview) HarpC.

Mannon, James M. Caring for the Burned: Life & Death in a Hospital Burn Center. 274p. (C). 1985. 47.95 (*0-398-05089-9*) C C Thomas.

— Emergency Encounters. 1992. pap. 27.50 (*0-86720-189-4*) Jones & Bartlett.

Mannon, Melissa. Waltham. LC 98-85876. (Images of America Ser.). (Illus.). 128p. 1998. pap. 16.99 (*0-7524-0963-8*) Arcadia Publng.

Mannone, F., ed. Lexicon Gregorianum. 1999. 291.00 (*90-04-11228-6*) Brill Academic Pubs.

— Safety in Tritium Handling Technology: Based on the Lectures Given During the Eurocourse on 'Safety in Tritium Handling Technology' Held at the Joint Research Centre Ispra, Italy, April 28-30, 1993. LC 93-30126. (Eurocourses: Nuclear Science & Technology Ser.). 248p. (C). 1993. text 134.50 (*0-7923-2511-7*) Kluwer Academic.

Mannoni, Edith. Classic French Paperweights. Selman, Lawrence H. & Jokelson, Paul, eds. LC 84-61013. (Illus.). 60p. 1984. 35.00 (*0-933756-06-2*) Paperwght Pr.

Mannoni, Laurent, et al. Light & Movement: Incunabula of the Motion Picture, 1420-1896. (Distributed for the British Film Institute Ser.). 400p. 1996. text 95.00 (*88-86155-05-0*, Pub. by British Film Inst) Ind U Pr.

Mannoni, Luciana & Mannoni, Tiziano. Marble: The History of a Culture. LC 86-160034. (Illus.). 284p. reprint ed. pap. 88.10 (*0-8357-4254-7*, 203704300007) Bks Demand.

Mannoni, Maud. The Child, His "Illness," & the Others. 292p. 1990. reprint ed. pap. text 36.50 (*0-946439-39-7*, Pub. by H Karnac Bks Ltd) Brunner-Mazel.

— Separation & Creativity: Refinding the Lost Language of Childhood. LC 98-50475. (Lacanian Clinical Field Ser.).Tr. of Amour, Haine, Separation, Renoueravee la Langue Perdue l'Enfance. 196p. 1999. pap. 17.95 (*1-892746-20-4*, 46204) Other Pr LLC.

Mannoni, Octave. Prospero & Caliban: The Psychology of Colonization. 224p. 1990. text 49.50 (*0-472-09430-0*, 09430); pap. text 18.95 (*0-472-06430-4*, 06430) U of Mich Pr.

Mannoni, Tiziano, jt. auth. see Mannoni, Luciana.

Mannroberts, Robert. Smith & Roberson's Business Law. 10th ed. (LA - Business Law Ser.). (C). 1997. mass mkt., student ed. 22.95 (*0-314-22062-3*) Wadsworth Pub.

Manns, James. Aesthetics. LC 97-21723. (Explorations in Philosophy Ser.). 195p. (C). (gr. 13). 1997. text 66.95 (*1-56324-953-7*) M E Sharpe.

Manns, James. Aesthetics. LC 97-21723. (Explorations in Philosophy Ser.). 195p. (C). (gr. 13). 1997. pap. text 24.95 (*1-56324-954-5*) M E Sharpe.

Manns, James W. Reid & His French Disciples: Aesthetics & Metaphysics. (Brill's Studies in Intellectual History: Vol. 45). ix, 225p. 1994. 86.00 (*90-04-09942-5*, NLG110) Brill Academic Pubs.

Manns, M. P., et al, eds. Cholestatic Liver Diseases. (Falk Symposium Ser.). 320p. 1998. 173.00 (*0-7923-8746-5*) Kluwer Academic.

Manns, M. P., ed. see Chapman, R. W., et al.

Manns, William, et al. Painted Ponies: American Carousel Art. Riley, Dru, ed. LC 86-51050. (Illus.). 256p. 1986. 40.00 (*0-939549-01-8*) ZON Intl Pub.

Mannucci, P. M., ed. Current Therapy of Von Willebrand's Disease. (Journal: Haemostasis: Vol. 24, No. 5, 1994). (Illus.). 64p. 1994. pap. 46.25 (*3-8055-6078-8*) S Karger.

Mannucci, P. M., et al, eds. Viral Safety of Plasma-Derived Replacement Factors for Hemophilia: How Safe Is Safe? (Journal: Vox Sanguinis: Vol. 67, Supplement 4, 1994). (Illus.). iv, 28p. 1994. pap. 14.00 (*3-8055-6066-4*) S Karger.

Mannucci, P. M., jt. auth. see Mariani, G.

Mannweiler, Ulrich, ed. Light Metals, 1994. LC 94-75197. (Illus.). 1100p. 1994. 164.00 (*0-87339-264-7*, 2647) Minerals Metals.

Mannyng, Robert. Robert of Brunne's Handlyng Synne, Pts. 1-2. Furnivall, Frederic J., ed. (EETS, OS Ser.: No. 119, 123). 1974. reprint ed. 70.00 (*0-527-00117-1*) Periodicals Srv.

Mano, D. Keith. The Fergus Dialogues: A Meditation on the Gender of Christ. LC 98-7756. 190p. 1998. 74.95 (*1-57309-299-1*) Intl Scholars.

***Mano, D. Keith.** The Fergus Dialogues: A Meditation on the Gender of Christ. LC 98-7756. 190p. 1998. pap. 54.95 (*1-57309-298-3*) Intl Scholars.

Mano, D. Keith. Take Five. LC 98-8065. 583p. 1998. reprint ed. pap. 14.95 (*1-56478-193-3*) Dalkey Arch.

Mano, M. Morris. Computer Engineering. LC 87-29282. (Illus.). 464p. (C). 1988. 100.00 (*0-13-162926-3*) P-H.

— Computer System Architecture. 3rd ed. LC 92-12094. 524p. (C). 1992. 95.00 (*0-13-175563-3*) P-H.

— Digital Design. 2nd ed. LC 90-37650. 592p. 1995. 100.00 (*0-13-212937-X*) P-H.

***Mano, Morris M.** Logic & Computer Design Fundamentals. 2nd ed. LC 99-48790. (Illus.). 652p. 1999. 100.00 incl. cd-rom (*0-13-012468-0*) P-H.

Mano, Sadako. Painting Baby Animals. (How to Draw & Paint Ser.). (Illus.). 32p. 1989. pap. 6.95 (*0-929261-86-0*, HT189) W Foster Pub.

Mano, Sandra, jt. auth. see Rico.

Mano, Sandra, jt. auth. see Rico, Barbara R.

Manocchi, Vincent & Wagner, Rob L. Toy Tractors. (Enthusiast Color Ser.). (Illus.). 96p. 1996. pap. 13.95 (*0-7603-0167-0*) MBI Pubg.

Manocchi, Vincent, jt. auth. see Browne, Tom.

Manocchio, Anthony J. & Dunn, Jimmy. The Time Game: Two Views of a Prison. LC 77-85238. 272p. 1989. pap. 84.40 (*0-608-05072-5*, 206562700005) Bks Demand.

— The Time Game: Two Views of a Prison. 1970. pap. 19.95 (*0-8039-0920-9*) Sage.

Manocha, Dinesh N. Algebra & Its Applications. Srivastava, J. B., ed. (Lecture Notes in Pure & Applied Mathematics Ser.: Vol. 91). (Illus.). 416p. 1984. pap. text 165.00 (*0-8247-7165-6*) Dekker.

— Applications of Computational Algebraic Geometry: American Mathematical Society Short Course, January 6-7, 1997. Cox, David A. & Sturmfels, Bernd, eds. LC 97-29117. (Proceedings of Symposia in Applied Mathematics Ser.: Vol. 53). 173p. 1997. text 35.00 (*0-8218-0750-1*) Am Math.

Manocha, Dinesh N., jt. auth. see Lin, Ming C.

Manocha, L. M., jt. auth. see Fitzer, Erich.

Manoff. Family Medical Emergency Library. (C). (gr. 13). 1996. pap. 12.04 (*0-8151-2503-8*, 31238) Mosby Inc.

Manoff. Music Living Language. 2nd ed. pap. text 0.00 (*0-393-96072-2*); pap. text, teacher ed. 0.00 (*0-393-96073-0*) Norton.

Manoff, Richard K. Have We Become Surrogates for Failure? Proposing a New Nutrition Education. LC 93-27281. (Martin J. Forman Memorial Lectures: Vol. 6). (Illus.). 32p. (Orig.). 1993. pap. 7.50 (*0-915173-25-5*) Helen Keller Intl.

Manoff, Robert K., ed. The Buck Starts Here: Enterprise & the Arts. 165p. 1984. 11.95 (*0-917103-00-9*) Vol Lawyers Arts.

Manoff, Robert K. & Schudson, Michael, eds. Reading the News. LC 86-72639. 256p. 1986. pap. 11.16 (*0-394-74649-X*) Pantheon.

Manoff, Tom. Music: A Living Language. (Illus.). 350p. (C). 1982. write for info. (*0-393-95228-2*); pap. text 36.25 (*0-393-95194-4*) Norton.

— Music: A Living Language. (Illus.). 350p. (C). 1982. pap. text, teacher ed. write for info. (*0-393-95220-7*) Norton.

— The Music Kit. 2nd ed. (C). Date not set. pap. write for info. (*0-393-95988-0*) Norton.

— The Music Kit. 3rd ed. (C). Date not set. pap. write for info. (*0-393-99945-9*) Norton.

— The Music Kit. 3rd ed. (C). 1994. pap. text, teacher ed. write for info. (*0-393-96326-8*) Norton.

— The Music Kit: Rhythm Reader. 3rd ed. (C). Date not set. pap. write for info. (*0-393-99203-9*) Norton.

— The Music Kit: Wkbk., Rhythm Reader, Scorebook. 3rd ed. 391p. (C). 1994. pap. text 37.50 incl. digital audio (*0-393-96325-X*) Norton.

— The Music Kit: Workbook. 3rd ed. (C). Date not set. pap. write for info. (*0-393-99199-7*) Norton.

Manoff, Tom & Miller, John. The Music Kit: Computer - Assisted Instruction. 3rd ed. (C). 1994. pap. 44.00 (*0-393-96330-6*); pap. text. write for info. (*0-393-96327-6*) Norton.

Manogaran, Chelvadurai. Ethnic Conflict & Reconciliation in Sri Lanka. LC 87-16247. (Illus.). 248p. 1987. reprint ed. pap. 76.90 (*0-608-04382-6*, 206516300001) Bks Demand.

***Manohar, Aneesh V. & Wise, Mark B.** Heavy Quark Physics. LC 99-38167. (Cambridge Monographs on Particle Physics, Nuclear Physics & Cosmology: No. 10). (Illus.). 230p. (C). 2000. 64.95 (*0-521-64241-8*) Cambridge U Pr.

Manohar, Murli. The Art of Conveyancing & Pleading. 290p. 1974. 45.00 (*0-7855-1294-2*) St Mut.

— Art of Conveyancing & Pleading. (C). 1990. 35.00 (*0-7855-5612-5*) St Mut.

— Dand Prakriya Vyakhyan (Code of Criminal Procedure in Hindi) 212p. 1981. 45.00 (*0-7855-1295-0*) St Mut.

Manohar, Murli, ed. The Art of Conveyancing & Pleadings. (C). 1989. reprint ed. 65.00 (*0-7855-5146-8*) St Mut.

— Pralekhan aur Abhivechan. 2nd ed. (HIN.). (C). 1991. 95.00 (*0-7855-5609-5*) St Mut.

Manoharan, S., jt. auth. see Singh, K. S.

Manoil, Mark L. Arizona Property Tax Liens: Guide to Profit, Protection & Prosecution. 2nd ed. LC 98-97017. (Illus.). 1999. pap. 59.95 (*0-9669711-0-8*) Cap West.

Manoilov, P., et al. Elsevier's Dictionary of Computer Graphics. 2000. write for info. (*0-444-50027-8*) Elsevier.

Manoilov, P., jt. auth. see Delijska, B.

Manoj Kumar Srivastava. Succession to Rule under Dehli Sultan. 1990. 24.00 (*81-7169-053-X*, Commonwealth) S Asia.

Manokaran, N., jt. ed. see Dransfield, J.

Manolache, Mircea. Romanian-English/English-Romanian Dictionary. (ENG & RUM.). 752p. 1997. 39.95 (*0-7859-9620-6*) Fr & Eur.

Manolagas, Stavros C. & Olefsky, Jerrold M., eds. Metabolic Bone & Mineral Disorders. fac. ed. LC 88-22864. (Contemporary Issues in Endocrinology & Metabolism Ser.: No. 5). (Illus.). 266p. 1988. reprint ed. pap. 82.50 (*0-7837-7877-5*, 204763400007) Bks Demand.

Manolakis, Dimitris G., jt. auth. see Proakis, John G.

Manolakis, Ingle K. Stat & Adaptive Signal Process. LC 99-30380. 816p. 1999. 102.19 (*0-07-040051-2*) McGraw.

***Manoleas, Peter.** The Cross-Cultural Practice of Clinical Case Management in Mental Health. LC 94-47017. 232p. 2000. pap. 24.95 (*1-56024-875-0*) Haworth Pr.

Manoleas, Peter, ed. The Cross-Cultural Practice of Clinical Case Management in Mental Health. LC 94-47017. 232p. (C). 1995. lib. bdg. 69.95 (*1-56024-874-2*) Haworth Pr.

Manolis, Argie, ed. The Doll Sourcebook. (Illus.). 352p. (Orig.). 1996. pap. 22.99 (*1-55870-431-0*, Betrwy Bks) F & W Pubns Inc.

Manolis, Charlie, jt. auth. see Webb, Grahame.

Manolis, G. D. Boundary Element Techniques in Geomechanics. 1993. 224.00 (*1-85861-024-9*) Elsevier.

Manolis, G. D., et al, eds. Earthquake Resistant Engineering Structures: Proceedings of the First International Conference on Earthquake Resistant Engineering Structures. LC 96-83654. (Advances in Earthquake Engineering Ser.: Vol. 2). 752p. 1996. 297.00 (*1-85312-456-7*, 4567, Pub. by WIT Pr) Computational Mech MA.

Manolis, G. D. & Davies, T., eds. Boundary Element Techniques in Geomechanics. LC 93-72574. (Computational Engineering Ser.). 548p. 1993. 245.00 (*1-56252-183-7*) Computational Mech MA.

***Manolis, G. D. & Koliopoulos, P. K.** Stochastic Structural Dynamics: With Applications in Earthquake Engineering. 300p. 2000. 145.00 (*1-85312-851-1*, Pub. by WIT Pr) Computational Mech MA.

Manolis, G. D., jt. ed. see Kausel, E.

***Manoliu, I., et al, eds.** Geotechinical Engineering Education & Training: Proceedings of the First International Conference, Sinaia, Romania, 12-14 June 2000. (Illus.). 500p. 2000. 105.00 (*90-5809-154-6*, Pub. by A A Balkema) Ashgate Pub Co.

Manoliu-Manea, Maria. Discourse & Pragmatic Constraints on Grammatical Choices: A Grammar of Surprises. Price, Glanville, ed. LC 94-39160. (Linguistic Ser.: Vol. 57). 440p. 1994. 149.50 (*0-444-82043-4*, North Holland) Elsevier.

Manoloff, Dennis. Omar Vizquel: The Man with the Golden Glove. Rains, Rob, ed. (Super Star Ser.). (Illus.). 96p. (J). (gr. 4-7). 1999. pap. 4.95 (*1-58261-045-2*) Sprts Pubng.

Manolopoulos, D. E., jt. auth. see Fowler, P. W.

Manolson, Gila. The Magic Touch. 1992. pap. 11.95 (*1-56871-185-9*) Feldheim.

Manolson, Gila. Outside, Inside: A Fresh Look at Tzniut. 100p. 1997. pap. 11.95 (*1-56871-123-9*, Pub. by Targum Pr) Feldheim.

Manolukas, Nick, jt. auth. see Neale, Heidi.

Manon, Melvin & H, Jose I. Operacion Estrella: Con Caamano, la Resistencia y la Inteligencia Cubana. (SPA., Illus.). iii, 178p. (Orig.). 1989. pap. 15.00 (*0-89729-524-2*) Ediciones.

***Manoo-Rahming, Lelawattee.** Curry Flavour. 120p. 2000. 14.95 (*1-900715-35-X*, Pub. by Peepal Tree Pr) Paul & Co Pubs.

Manoogian, Sam, jt. auth. see Kirkland, Karen.

Manooja, D. C. Adoption Law & Practice. (C). 1993. 32.00 (*81-7100-581-0*, Pub. by Deep & Deep Pubns) S Asia.

Manor, Gloria, ed. The Bible in Dance, Vol. 2, Part 3. 100p. 1992. text 15.00 (*3-7186-5296-X*, Harwood Acad Pubs) Gordon & Breach.

Manor Healthcare Corporation Staff & Switkes, Betty. Armchair Fitness. (Illus.). 64p. 1984. write for info. (*0-917025-00-8*) Manor Health.

Manor, James. Political Change in an Indian State, Mysore, 1917-1955. 1978. 12.50 (*0-8364-0069-0*) S Asia.

— The Political Economy of Democratic Decentralization. LC 99-11245. (Directions in Development Ser.). 144p. 1999. pap. 22.00 (*0-8213-4470-6*) World Bank.

— Power, Poverty, & Poison: Disaster & Response in an Indian City. LC 92-40655. (Illus.). 200p. 1993. 28.50 (*0-8039-9466-4*) Sage.

Manor, James, ed. Rethink Third World Politics. 352p. (C). 1991. pap. text 30.75 (*0-582-07458-4*, 78937) Longman.

— Rethink Third World Politics. 352p. (C). 1992. text 60.95 (*0-582-07459-2*, 78936) Longman.

Manor, James, jt. auth. see Crook, Richard C.

Manor, James, jt. ed. see Colclough, Christopher.

Manor, Yohanan. To Right a Wrong: The Revocation of UN General Assembly Resolution 3379 Defaming Zionism. (Illus.). 279p. 1996. 25.00 (*0-88400-189-X*, Pub. by Schreiber Pub) Natl Bk Netwk.

***Manore, Jean L.** Cross-Currents: Hydroelectricity & the Engineering of Northern Ontario. (Illus.). 224p. 1999. text 48.95 (*0-88920-317-2*, HD9685) W Laurier U Pr.

***Manore, Melinda & Thompson, Janice L.** Sport Nutrition for Health & Performance. LC 00-23158. 2000. write for info. (*0-87322-939-8*) Human Kinetics.

Manos. Plasma Materials. 2nd ed. 500p. 1997. write for info. (*0-12-469365-2*) Acad Pr.

***Manos.** Writng Smarter: Over 100 Step-by-Step Lessons with Reproducible Activity Sheets to Build Writing Proficiency. LC 98-33700. (Illus.). 416p. (YA). (gr. 7-12). 1998. pap. text 32.95 (*0-87628-435-7*) Ctr Appl Res.

***Manos, Constantine.** Greek Portfolio. 128p. 1999. 50.00 (*0-393-04683-4*) Norton.

Manos, Constantine, photos by. American Color. (Illus.). 96p. 1996. 29.95 (*0-393-03912-9*) Norton.

Manos, Dennis M. & Flamm, Daniel L., eds. Plasma Etching: An Introduction. (Plasma Materials Interactions Ser.). 476p. 1989. text 100.00 (*0-12-469370-9*) Acad Pr.

Manos, Fran. Beautiful Hands & Nails Naturally: Achieving & Maintaining Youthful, Radiantly Healthy Hands. LC 98-154517. (Illus.). 224p. 1998. pap. text 9.95 (*0-89529-838-4*, Avery) Penguin Putnam.

***Manos, James, Jr.** Little Ellie Claus. 256p. 2000. 15.95 (*0-7434-0624-9*) PB.

***Manos-Jones, Maraleen.** The Spirit of Butterflies: Myth, Magic & Art. (Illus.). 136p. 2000. 34.95 (*0-8109-4115-5*, Pub. by Abrams) Time Warner.

Manos, Keith T. Wrestling Coach's Survival Guide: Practical Techniques & Materials for Building an Effective Program & a Winning Team. (Illus.). 256p. (C). 1995. spiral bd. 32.95 (*0-13-458951-3*, Parker Publishing Co) P-H.

— Wrestling Coach's Survival Guide: Practical Techniques & Materials for Building an Effective Program & a Winning Team. 256p. (C). 1996. pap. text 32.50 (*0-13-490392-7*, Parker Publishing Co) P-H.

Manos, Nikki L. & Rochelson, Meri-Jane, eds. Transforming Genres: New Approaches to British Fiction of the 1890s. LC 94-9855. 1994. text 45.00 (*0-312-12154-7*) St Martin.

Manos, Paris. Collectible Action Figures. 2nd ed. 160p. 1995. pap. 17.95 (*0-89145-668-6*, 4559) Collector Bks.

Manos, Paris & Manos, Susan. The Wonder of Barbie. (Illus.). 136p. 1995. pap. 9.95 (*0-89145-336-9*, 1808) Collector Bks.

— The World of Barbie Dolls. (Illus.). 144p. 1994. pap. 9.95 (*0-89145-229-X*) Collector Bks.

Manos, Susan, jt. auth. see Manos, Paris.

Manouca, Mia, jt. auth. see Cabral, Len.

Manougian, Manoug. All You Need to Know about the Lottery: Play to Win. LC 91-3240. (Illus.). 114p. 1991. 12.95 (*0-931541-23-9*); pap. 5.95 (*0-931541-24-7*) Mancorp Pub.

— Precalculus Algebra & Trigonometry. 2nd ed. LC 86-34332. 1987. 34.50 (*0-931541-07-7*) Mancorp Pub.

Manoukian, Edward B. Mathematical Nonparametric Statistics. xvi, 326p. 1986. text 252.00 (*2-88124-093-3*) Gordon & Breach.

— Modern Concepts & Theorems of Mathematical Statistics. (Series in Statistics). 175p. 1985. 62.95 (*0-387-96186-0*) Spr-Verlag.

Manousakes, Efstratios. Lectures on Statistical Mechanics. 1999. write for info. (*0-201-32827-5*) Addison-Wesley.

Manousakis, Efstratios. Physical Phenomena at High Magnetic Fields: Proceedings. (C). 1991. 64.00 (*0-201-57869-7*) Addison-Wesley.

***Manousakis, Efstratios.** Statisical Mechanics: A Course for Physics Students. (Frontiers in Physics Ser.). 2000. pap. 55.00 (*0-7382-0178-2*) Perseus Pubng.

Manousos, Anthony. Spiritual Linkage with Russians. LC 91-68220. 32p. (Orig.). 1992. pap. 1.00 (*0-87574-301-3*, PHP 301) Pendle Hill.

***Manovich, Lev.** The Language of New Media. (Illus.). 352p. 2000. 34.95 (*0-262-13374-1*, A Leonardo Bk) MIT Pr.

Manovich, Lev, jt. ed. see Efimova, Alla.

Manovrier, Lynne. Animal Farm: A Study Guide. (Novel-Ties Ser.). (J). (gr. 6-10). 1983. pap. text, teacher ed., student ed. 15.95 (*0-88122-021-3*) Lrn Links.

Manrai, Ajay K. Global Perspectives in Cross-Cultural & Cross-National Consumer Research. Manrai, Lalita A., ed. LC 95-47013. (Journal of International Consumer Marketing: Vol. 8, Nos. 3 & 4). 242p. 1996. 49.95 (*1-56024-737-1*, Intl Busn Pr) Haworth Pr.

Manrai, Lalita A., ed. see Manrai, Ajay K.

Manraj, A. Shakoor & Haines, Paul D. The Law on Speeding & Radar. 2nd ed. 168p. 1991. boxed set 45.00 (*0-409-90376-0*, MICHIE) LEXIS Pub.

***Manresa, Kim, photos by.** The Day Kadi Lost Part of Her Life. (Illus.). 50p. 1999. 14.95 (*1-875559-74-4*) SpiniFex Pr.

Manring, M. M. Slave in a Box: The Strange Career of Aunt Jemima. (American South Ser.). 221p. 1998. pap. 14.95 (*0-8139-1811-1*) U Pr of Va.

Manrique, Angel. Poesia. unabridged ed. (SPA.). pap. 5.95 (*84-410-0011-5*, Pub. by Bookking Intl) Distribks Inc.

***Manrique, Cecilia G. & Manrique, Gabriel G.** The Multicultural or Immigrant Faculty in American Society. LC 99-21899. (Studies in Education: Vol. 43). 198p. 1999. text 79.95 (*0-7734-8027-7*) E Mellen.

Manrique, Gabriel G., jt. auth. see Manrique, Cecilia G.

Manrique, Jaime. Besame Mucho: An Anthology of Gay Latino Fiction. LC 98-50721. 1999. pap. text 15.00 (*1-891305-06-9*) Painted Leaf.

— Columbian Gold: A Thriller. 1998. pap. text 14.95 (*1-891305-01-8*) Painted Leaf.

— Eminent Maricones: Arenas, Lorca, Puig & Me. LC 98-49022. (Living Out Ser.). 1999. 19.95 (*0-299-16180-3*) U of Wis Pr.

— Latin Moon in Manhattan. LC 92-40802. 1993. pap. 9.95 (*0-312-08835-3*) St Martin.

— My Night with Federico Garcia Lorca - Mi Noche Con Federico Garcia Lorca. Grossman, Edith & Richie, Eugene, trs. LC 96-48543. (ENG & SPA.). 127p. 1997. pap. 12.00 (*0-9651558-3-8*) Painted Leaf.

Manrique, Jaime, jt. tr. see Larkin, Joan.

Manrique, Jorge. Poesias Completas. Perez Priego, Miguel A., ed. (Nueva Austral Ser.: Vol. 152). (SPA.). 1991. pap. text 24.95 (*84-239-1952-8*) Elliots Bks.

Manroe, Candace. Uncluttered: Storage Room by Room. LC 97-24986. 128p. 1997. 27.50 (*1-56799-428-8*, Friedman-Fairfax) M Friedman Pub Grp Inc.

Manroe, Candace O. The Book of Upholstery: A Complete Reference. LC 96-34238. 1996. write for info. (*1-56799-140-8*, Friedman-Fairfax) M Friedman Pub Grp Inc.

— Designing with Collectibles. LC 92-30120. (Illus.). 144p. 1993. 25.00 (*0-671-76103-X*) S&S Trade.

— The Home Office. LC 97-9763. 1997. 22.95 (*0-89577-974-9*, Pub. by RD Assn) Penguin Putnam.

— Window Treatment Styles. LC 96-67109. (Illus.). 192p. 1997. write for info. (*0-7853-1306-0*) Pubns Intl Ltd.

Manross, William W. Episcopal Church in the United States, 1800-1840: A Study in Church Life. LC 38-38020. (Columbia University. Studies in the Social Sciences: No. 441). reprint ed. 27.50 (*0-404-51441-3*) AMS Pr.

Manross, William W., ed. S. P. G. Papers in the Lambeth Palace Library: Calendar & Indexes. 239p. 1974. 37.00 (*0-19-920065-3*) OUP.

***Manrseurei, Riszea & Brandenberger, Robert H.** Large Scale Structure Formation. LC 00-33082. (Astrophysics & Space Science Library). 2000. write for info. (*0-7923-6411-2*) Kluwer Academic.

Manry, Douglas. The Land the Cleves Built. Sloan, Stephen, ed. (Illus.). 32p. (J). (gr. 2-5). 1989. write for info. (*0-9622316-0-6*) Sloan Manry Pubs.

Mans, Charles C. & Simms, Henry P. Super Leadership. 1990. pap. 12.00 (*0-425-12356-1*) Berkley Pub.

Mans, Lorenzo. The Mango Grove. 41p. 1993. pap. text 3.95 (*1-885901-11-9*) Presbyters Peartree.

Mans, Lorenzo, tr. see Arrabal, Fernando.

Mansaray, Alasan. A Haunting Heritage: An African Saga in America. LC 93-87204. 320p. 1994. 21.95 (*0-9639497-5-6*) Sahara Pubng.

Mansbach. Global Politics. 1999. pap. text 26.07 (*0-395-84970-5*) HM.

— Global Puzzle. (C). 1994. pap., teacher ed. 5.96 (*0-395-69696-8*) HM.

— The Global Puzzle. LC 93-78639. (C). 1994. pap. text 44.76 (*0-395-52580-2*) HM.

— Global Puzzle, 2 vols. 2nd ed. LC 96-76928. (C). 1996. pap. text 44.76 (*0-395-77090-4*) HM.

— Global Puzzle: Testbank, 2 vols. (C). 1996. pap., teacher ed. 11.96 (*0-395-77091-2*) HM.

***Mansbach, Charles M., et al.** Intestinal Lipid Metabolism. LC 00-28732. 2000. write for info. (*0-306-46241-9*, Kluwer Plenum) Kluwer Academic.

Mansbach, Richard W. & Vasquez, John A. In Search of Theory: A New Paradigm for Global Politics. LC 80-19365. 544p. 1981. text 72.50 (*0-231-05060-7*) Col U Pr.

Mansbach, Richard W., jt. auth. see Ferguson, Yale H.

Mansbach, S. A. Modern Art in Eastern Europe: From the Baltic to the Balkans, CA. 1890-1939. LC 97-42894. (Illus.). 400p. (C). 1999. text 65.00 (*0-521-45085-3*) Cambridge U Pr.

Mansbach, Steven A., ed. Standing in the Tempest: Painters of the Hungarian Avante-Garde, 1908-1930. (Illus.). 240p. 1991. 47.50 (*0-262-13274-5*) MIT Pr.

Mansberg, Ruth, jt. auth. see Carlin, Vivian F.

Mansberger, Floyd R. & Fever River Research Staff. Early Industrialized Pottery Production in Illinois: Archaeological Investigations at White & Company's Gooselake Stoneware Manufactory & Tile Works, Rural Grundy County, Illinois. LC 98-179444. (Reports of Investigations). xv, 112p. 1997. write for info. (*0-89792-154-2*) Ill St Museum.

Mansbridge, Albert. Fellow Men. LC 73-117329. (Biography Index Reprint Ser.). 1977. 23.95 (*0-8369-8021-2*) Ayer.

Mansbridge, Beth, ed. see Syman, Alice B.

Mansbridge, Francis. Irving Layton: God's Recording Angel. LC 95-193413. (Illus.). 150p. 1995. pap. 14.95 (*1-55022-216-3*, Pub. by ECW) Genl Dist Srvs.

Mansbridge, Jane, jt. ed. see Okin, Susan M.

Mansbridge, Jane J. Beyond Adversary Democracy. xiv, 412p. 1983. pap. text 19.95 (*0-226-50355-0*) U Ch Pr.

— Why We Lost the E. R. A. LC 86-6954. (Illus.). xii, 336p. 1986. pap. text 18.00 (*0-226-50358-5*) U Ch Pr.

— Why We Lost the E. R. A. LC 86-6954. (Illus.). xii, 336p. 1999. lib. bdg. 42.00 (*0-226-50357-7*) U Ch Pr.

Mansbridge, Jane J., ed. Beyond Self-Interest. LC 89-38629. 416p. 1990. pap. text 17.95 (*0-226-50360-7*) U Ch Pr.

— Beyond Self-Interest. LC 89-38629. 332p. 1998. lib. bdg. 55.00 (*0-226-50359-3*) U Ch Pr.

Mansbridge, John. Graphic History of Architecture. LC 98-49277. (Illus.). 192p. 1999. reprint ed. pap. 39.95 (*0-940512-15-7*) Hennessey.

Mansbridge, Michael. John Nash: A Complete Catalogue. (Illus.). 336p. 1991. 75.00 (*0-7148-2678-2*) Chronicle Bks.

Mansch, Larry D. Rube Marquard: The Life & Times of a Baseball Hall of Famer. LC 98-17876. (Illus.). 262p. 1998. pap. 29.95 (*0-7864-0497-3*) McFarland & Co.

***Manschke, Doris.** Genese und Funktion Von Autobiographie in der Westafrikanischen Englischsprachigen Literatur: Eine Gattungsgeschichte. 192p. 1999. 37.95 (*3-631-34988-2*) P Lang Pubng.

Manschreck, Clyde L. A History of Christianity in the World: From Persecution to Uncertainty. 2nd ed. (Illus.). 352p. (C). 1984. text 47.20 (*0-13-389354-5*) P-H.

— Melanchthon: The Quiet Reformer. LC 73-21263. (Illus.). 350p. 1975. reprint ed. lib. bdg. 38.50 (*0-8371-6131-2*, MAMQ, Greenwood Pr) Greenwood.

Mansdoerfer, Caroline B. I Plead the Fifth: The Story of Alpha One Trek America. LC 93-93634. (Illus.). 125p. (Orig.). 1993. pap. 12.95 (*0-9638663-0-3*) Alpha One Crusades.

Mansdorf, S. Z., jt. auth. see Forsberg, Krister.

Mansdorf, S. Z., jt. auth. see Frosberg, Krister.

Mansdorf, S. Z., jt. auth. see Roseman, Theodore J.

Mansdorf, S. Z., jt. ed. see Johnson, James S.

Mansdorf, Zack, jt. auth. see Stern, Martin B.

Mansel, Henry L. The Gnostic Heresies of the First & Second Centuries. Lightfoot, J. B., ed. LC 78-63170. (Heresies of the Early Christian & Medieval Era Ser.: Second Ser.). reprint ed. 47.50 (*0-404-16185-5*) AMS Pr.

— Limits of Religious Thought Examined. LC 72-172840. reprint ed. 45.00 (*0-404-04182-5*) AMS Pr.

Mansel, Philip. Constantinople: City of the World's Desire, 1453-1924, Vol. 1. LC 96-19951. 544p. 1996. text 35.00 (*0-312-14574-8*) St Martin.

— The Court of France, 1789-1830. (Illus.). 355p. (C). 1991. pap. text 24.95 (*0-521-42398-8*) Cambridge U Pr.

— Louis XVIII. 1999. pap. text 24.95 (*0-7509-2217-6*) Sutton Pub Ltd.

— Witnesses: Meditations on the Way of the Cross. (Illus.). 1994. pap. 21.00 (*0-86012-231-X*, Pub. by Srch Pr) St Mut.

Mansel, Philip, jt. auth. see Carpenter, Kristy.

Mansel, Phillip. Constantinople, 1453-1924. LC 98-14329. 1998. pap. 19.95 (*0-312-18708-4*) St Martin.

Mansel, R. E. Recent Developments in the Study of Benign Breast Disease. 4th ed. (Illus.). 233p. 1992. 68.00 (*1-85070-386-8*) Prthnon Pub.

Mansel, R. E., ed. Recent Developments in the Study of Benign Breast Disease: The Proceedings of the 5th International Symposium on Benign Breast Disease. 5th ed. LC 93-41022. (Illus.). 280p. (C). 1994. pap. text 45.00 (*1-85070-532-1*) Prthnon Pub.

— Recent Developments in the Study of Benign Breast Disease: The Proceedings of the 6th International Symposium on Benign Breast Disease. LC 97-3902. (Illus.). 158p. 1997. pap. text 58.00 (*1-85070-775-8*) Prthnon Pub.

Mansel, Robert E. A Color Atlas of Breast Diseases. (Illus.). 128p. (C). (gr. 13). 1994. text 29.95 (*0-8151-5756-8*, 21951) Mosby Inc.

Mansel, Robert E. & Bundred, Nigel J. A Color Atlas of Breast Diseases. LC 94-44123. (Illus.). 1994. text 37.50 (*0-7234-1721-0*) Mosby Inc.

Mansell. If Dinosaurs Came. (Illus.). 64p. (J). (gr. 3). 1998. pap. 7.95 (*0-316-57021-4*) Little.

— Key Guide to Information Sources on World Religions. 1991. 65.00 (*0-8161-7394-X*, G K Hall & Co) Mac Lib Ref.

Mansell, Chris. Redshift - Blueshift. 64p. (C). 1990. 45.00 (*0-9587972-1-8*, Pub. by Pascoe Pub) St Mut.

Mansell, Colette. A Collector's Guide to British Dolls since 1920. (Illus.). 390p. 1983. 45.00 (*0-7091-9380-7*, Pub. by R Hale Ltd) Antique Collect.

— History of Sindy: Britain's Top Teenage Doll 1962-1992. (Illus.). 296p. 1995. 49.95 (*0-904568-64-4*, Pub. by New Cavendish) Pincushion Pr.

Mansell, Dom. If Dinosaurs Came to Town. (Illus.). 32p. (J). (gr. k-3). 1998. pap. 5.95 (*0-316-67028-6*) Little.

— If Dinosaurs Came to Town. (J). 1998. 11.15 (*0-606-13513-8*, Pub. by Turtleback) Demco.

— My Old Teddy. LC 91-71830. (Illus.). 32p. (J). (ps). 1992. 12.95 (*1-56402-035-5*) Candlewick Pr.

***Mansell, Donald E.** Adventists & Armageddon: Have We Misinterpreted Prophecy? Robinson, Glen, ed. LC 98-40667. 143p. 1999. pap. 10.99 (*0-8163-1684-8*) Pacific Pr Pub Assn.

Mansell, Donald E. The Shape of the Coming Crisis: A Sequence of Endtime Events Based on the Writings of Ellen G. White. LC 97-18424. 1998. pap. 12.99 (*0-8163-1402-0*) Pacific Pr Pub Assn.

Mansell, Donald E. & Mansell, Vesta W. Sure As the Dawn. LC 93-3782. 1993. 10.99 (*0-8280-0723-3*) Review & Herald.

***Mansell, Donald Ernest & Mansell, Vesta West.** Angels & the Unseen Conflict: The Role of God's Messengers from Eternity to Eternity Based on Scripture & the Writings of Ellen G. White. Holt, B. Russell, ed. LC 00-27042. 255p. 2000. pap. 13.99 (*0-8163-1794-1*) Pacific Pr Pub Assn.

Mansell, J. Perfect Timing. 1997. text 28.00 (*0-7472-2019-0*, Pub. by Headline Bk Pub) Trafalgar.

— Perfect Timing. 1999. pap. 11.00 (*0-7472-5783-3*, Pub. by Headline Bk Pub) Trafalgar.

Mansell, J. & Ericsson, K. Deinstitutionalization & Community Living: Intellectual Disability Services in Britain, Scandinavia, & the U. S. A. (Illus.). 240p. 1996. 127.50 (*1-56593-315-X*, 0451) Singular Publishing.

Mansell, Joanna. Haunted Summer. (Presents Ser.: No. 436). 1992. pap. 2.79 (*0-373-11436-2*, 1-11436-2) Harlequin Bks.

— Istanbul Affair. 1994. per. 2.99 (*0-373-11662-4*, 1-11662-3) Harlequin Bks.

— A Kiss by Candlelight. large type ed. (Magna Large Print Ser.). 261p. 1996. 27.99 (*0-7505-0965-1*, Pub. by Mgna Lrg Print) Ulverscroft.

— A Perfect Seduction. large type ed. 1994. 18.95 (*0-263-13931-X*) Thorndike Pr.

— The Touch of Aphrodite. (Presents Ser.). 1994. per. 2.99 (*0-373-11684-5*, 1-11684-7) Harlequin Bks.

Mansell, John & Parker, Allene. Voices Crying in the Wilderness: Scripture-Based Dramas for Church Life & Worship. 106p. 1997. pap. 12.95 (*1-57438-022-2*) Ed Ministries.

Mansell, John S. The Funeral: A Pastor's Handbook. Ratcliff, Bob, ed. LC 98-21180. 96p. 1998. pap. 12.95 (*0-687-06790-1*) Abingdon.

Mansell, Lilene, ed. see Skinner, Edith.

***Mansell, Lisa, ed.** Bimini Twist. (Illus.). 280p. (YA). 1999. 22.50 (*0-9676853-0-3*) Bimini Twist Adventures.

Mansell, Mary, ed. see Birnholz, Mary B., et al.

Mansell, Maureen E. By the Power of Their Dreams: Songs, Prayers, & Sacred Shields of the Plains Indians. LC 93-8148. (Illus.). 96p. 1994. 16.95 (*0-8118-0460-7*) Chronicle Bks.

Mansell, Nigel. Nigel Mansell's Autobiography. 1996. pap. 11.95 (*0-00-218703-5*, Pub. by HarpC) Trafalgar.

An Asterisk (*) at the beginning of an entry indicates that the title is appearing for the first time.

Mansell, Robin & Silverstone, Roger, eds. Communication by Design: The Politics of Information & Communication Technologies. (Illus.). 292p. 1998. reprint ed. pap. text 32.00 (*0-19-829400-X*) OUP.

***Mansell, Robin & Steinmueller, W. Edward.** Mobilizing the Information Society: A View from Europe. (Illus.). 600p. 2000. text 105.00 (*0-19-829556-1*) OUP.

Mansell, Robin & Wehn, Uta, eds. Knowledge Societies: Information Technology for Sustainable Development. LC 97-48482. (Illus.). 330p. 1998. pap. text 29.95 (*0-19-829410-7*) OUP.

Mansell, Robin, jt. auth. see Crede, Andreas.

Mansell, Robin E. The New Telecommunications: A Political Economy of Network Evolution. (C). 1994. text 65.00 (*0-8039-8535-5*); pap. text 24.95 (*0-8039-8536-3*) Sage.

Mansell, Susan. How to Give Your Child an Excellent Public School Education. LC 98-39567. 224p. 1998. pap. text 12.95 (*0-8065-1999-1*, Citadel Pr) Carol Pub Group.

Mansell, Vesta W., jt. auth. see Mansell, Donald E.

Mansell, Vesta West, jt. auth. see Mansell, Donald Ernest.

Mansell, Wade, et al. A Critical Introduction to Law. 177p. 1995. pap. 22.00 (*1-85941-139-8*, Pub. by Cavendish Pubng) Gaunt.

Mansella, Elizabeth. Desastres. 310p. 1996. pap. 20.00 (*1-85339-282-0*, Pub. by Intermed Tech) Stylus Pub VA.

Manselli, Raoul. St. Francis of Assisi. Duggan, Paul, tr. 363p. 1988. 24.95 (*0-8199-0880-0*, Frncscn Herld) Franciscan Pr.

Mansen, Cynthia, et al, eds. Women of Mystery. 336p. (Orig.). 1993. mass mkt. 5.99 (*0-425-13747-3*) Berkley Pub.

Mansen, Darrel. The Novels of Jane Austen: An Interpretation. LC 73-166540. xiv, 226p. 1973. write for info. (*0-333-14661-1*) Macmillan.

Manser. Dictionary of Synonyms & Antonyms. (Reference Library). 256p. 1998. pap. 6.95 (*1-85326-757-0*, 7570WW, Pub. by Wrdsworth Edits) NTC Contemp Pub Co.

Manser, jt. auth. see TNP Staff.

Manser, A. G. & Keeling, Alan A. Practical Handbook of Processing & Recycling of Municipal Waste. 560p. 1996. lib. bdg. 85.00 (*1-56670-164-3*, L1164) Lewis Pubs.

Manser, Anthony R. Sartre: A Philosophic Study. LC 81-765. 280p. 1981. reprint ed. lib. bdg. 35.00 (*0-313-22827-2*, MASPS, Greenwood Pr) Greenwood.

Manser, J.E. Economics: A Foundation Course for the Built Environment. 290p. 1994. mass mkt. 28.95 (*0-419-18260-8*) Wiley.

Manser, Martin. The Macmillan Dictionary of English Spelling. 512p. 1997. pap. 19.95 (*0-333-65777-2*, Pub. by Macmillan) Trans-Atl Phila.

Manser, Martin H. A Closer Walk with God: Daily Readings from Matthew Henry. 368p. 1989. 12.95 (*0-310-51700-1*) Zondervan.

— Dictionary of Eponyms. (Reference Library). 224p. 1998. pap. 6.95 (*1-85326-373-7*, 3737WW, Pub. by Wrdsworth Edits) NTC Contemp Pub Co.

— Dictionary of Slang. (Reference Library). 992p. 1998. pap. 6.95 (*1-85326-396-6*, 3966WW, Pub. by Wrdsworth Edits) NTC Contemp Pub Co.

— Get to the Roots: A Dictionary of Word & Phrase Origins. 272p. (Orig.). 1992. pap. 10.00 (*0-380-71473-6*, Avon Bks) Morrow Avon.

— Melba Toast, Bowie's Knife & Caesar's Wife: A Dictionary of Eponyms. 256p. 1990. pap. 7.95 (*0-380-70877-9*, Avon Bks) Morrow Avon.

***Manser, Martin H.** Zondervan Dictiony of Bible Themes. LC 99-47974. 1246p. 1999. 39.99 (*0-310-20668-5*) Zondervan.

Manser, Martin H. & McQuain, Jeffrey, eds. The World Almanac Guide to Good Word Usage. 288p. 1991. reprint ed. pap. 8.95 (*0 380 71449-3*, Avon Bks) Morrow Avon.

Manser, Roger. Failed Transitions: The Eastern European Economy Since the Fall of Communism. LC 93-26990. 1994. 22.95 (*1-56584-119-0*, Pub. by New Press NY) Norton.

Manser, Thomas & Kurz, Rolf. Bizjets: Executive Jets in Color. LC 99-30753. (Illus.). 112p. 1999. pap. 24.95 (*0-7603-0787-3*, Pub. by MBI Pubg) Motorbooks Intl.

Manser, W. A. P. Britain in Balance. LC 78-860633. x, 213 p. 1971. write for info. (*0-582-50029-X*) Longman.

Manser, William, jt. auth. see Bannock, Graham.

Mansergh, Diana, ed. see Mansergh, Nicholas.

Mansergh, Ian & Broome, Linda. The Mountain Pygmy-Possum of the Australian Alps. (Natural History Ser.). (Illus.). 116p. 1996. reprint ed. pap. 21.95 (*0-86840-085-8*, Pub. by New South Wales Univ Pr) Intl Spec Bk.

Mansergh, Nicholas. The Commonwealth Experience, 2 vols. rev. ed. Incl. Vol. 1. Commonwealth Experience., 2 vols. rev. ed. 1982. pap. 12.95 (*0-8020-6515-5*); Vol. 2. Commonwealth Experience., 2 vols. rev. ed. 1982. pap. 12.95 (*0-8020-6516-3*); Vol. 2. From British to Multiracial Commonwealth. 1982. text 27.50 (*0-8020-2492-0*); 1982. Set boxed set 25.00 (*0-8020-6497-3*) U of Toronto Pr.

— The Commonwealth Experience, 2 vols., Set. rev. ed. Incl. Vol. 1. Commonwealth Experience., 2 vols. rev. ed. 1982. pap. 12.95 (*0-8020-6515-5*); Vol. 2. Commonwealth Experience., 2 vols. rev. ed. 1982. pap. 12.95 (*0-8020-6516-3*); Vol. 2. From British to Multiracial Commonwealth. 1982. text 27.50 (*0-8020-2492-0*); 1982. Set boxed set 50.00 (*0-8020-2477-7*) U of Toronto Pr.

— Independence Years: The Selected Indian & Commonwealth Papers of Nicholas Mansergh. Mansergh, Diana, ed. 290p. 2000. text 29.95 (*0-19-564847-1*) OUP.

— The Irish Question, 1840-1921: A Commentary on Anglo-Irish Relations & on Social & Political Forces in Ireland in the Age of Reform & Revolution. 3rd ed. LC DA0951.M3. 341p. reprint ed. pap. 105.80 (*0-608-15410-5*, 202933800060) Bks Demand.

— Nationalism & Independence: Selected Essays on Modern Irish History. LC 97-146037. 320p. 1997. 64.95 (*1-85918-105-8*, Pub. by Cork Univ); pap. 24.95 (*1-85918-106-6*, Pub. by Cork Univ) Intl Spec Bk.

— Survey of British Commonwealth Affairs: Problems of Wartime Cooperation & Post-War Change, 1939-1952. 470p. 1968. reprint ed. 47.50 (*0-7146-1496-3*, Pub. by F Cass Pubs) Intl Spec Bk.

— The Unresolved Question: The Anglo-Irish Settlement & Its Undoing, 1912-72. 384p. (C). 1991. 45.00 (*0-300-05069-0*) Yale U Pr.

Mansergh, Nicholas, ed. Commonwealth Perspectives. LC 58-11381. (Duke University Commonwealth Studies Center: No. 8). 224p. reprint ed. 69.50 (*0-8357-9100-9*, 201791100010) Bks Demand.

Mansfield, F., ed. see Symposia on Corrosion Effects of Acid Deposition &.

Mansfield, Florian. Corrosion Mechanisms. (Chemical Industries Ser.: Vol. 28). (Illus.). 472p. 1986. text 215.00 (*0-8247-7627-5*) Dekker.

Mansfield, Florian & Latanision, R. M. H. H. Uhlig Memorial Symposium. (Proceedings Ser.: Vol. 94-26). 330p. 1995. pap. 58.00 (*1-56677-085-8*) Electrochem Soc.

Mansfield, Florian, ed. see Electrochemical Society Staff.

Mansfield, Guenter. Die Fibeln der Heuneburg, 1950-1970: Ein Beitrag zur Geschichte der Spaethallstattfibel Heuneburgstudien II. LC 72-75868. (Roemisch-Germanische Forschungen Ser.: Vol. 33). (Illus.). xii, 299p. (C). 1973. 200.00 (*3-11-003769-6*) De Gruyter.

Mansfield, J. J. & Runia, David T. Aetiana: The Method & Intellectual Context of a Doxographer, Vol. I. LC 96-42463. (Philosophia Antiqua Ser.: Vol. 73). 416p. 1996. text 134.50 (*90-04-10580-8*, NLG225) Brill Academic Pubs.

Mansfield, Jaap. Heresiography in Context: Hippolytus' Elenchos As a Source for Greek Philosophy. LC 92-6285. (Philosophia Antiqua Ser.: Vol. 56). xviii, 394p. 1992. 134.00 (*90-04-09616-7*) Brill Academic Pubs.

— Prolegomena: Questions to Be Settled before the Study of an Author or a Text. LC 94-16216. (Philosophia Antiqua Ser.: Vol. 61). vii, 246p. 1994. 75.00 (*90-04-10084-9*) Brill Academic Pubs.

— Prolegomena Mathematica: From Apollonius of Perga to Late Neoplatonism: With an Appendix on Pappus & the History of Platonism. LC 98-38382. (Philosphia Antiqua). viii, 182p. 1998. 68.00 (*90-04-11267-7*) Brill Academic Pubs.

— Studies in Later Greek Philosophy & Gnosticism. (Collected Studies: No. CS292). 334p. (C). 1989. lib. bdg. 115.95 (*0-86078-240-9*, Pub. by Variorum) Ashgate Pub Co.

Mansfield, Jaap, jt. ed. see Inwood, Brad.

Mansfield, Y. Tourism: Towards a Behavioural Approach. (Progress in Planning Ser.: Vol. 38). 1992. 66.00 (*0-08-042039-7*, Pergamon Pr) Elsevier.

Mansfield, Yoel, jt. ed. see Pizam, Abraham.

Mansfield. Economics. 7th ed. 1993. write for info. (*0-393-96434-5*) Norton.

***Mansfield.** Excel for Busy People. 298p. 1999. pap. 19.99 (*0-07-211988-8*) McGraw.

Mansfield. Management Economics. 4th ed. Date not set. pap. text. write for info. (*0-393-97316-6*) Norton.

— Management Economics: Study Guide & Casebook. 4th ed. 1998. pap., student ed. write for info. (*0-393-97314-X*) Norton.

— Management Economics: Theory, Applications, & Cases. 4th ed. LC 98-18812. 1998. 91.75 (*0-393-97315-8*) Norton.

Mansfield. Problem Sets in Economics. pap. text 0.00 (*0-393-09393-X*) Norton.

Mansfield. Therapeutic Radiology. 3rd ed. 1999. pap. text 97.00 (*0-8385-8949-9*, Medical Exam) Appleton & Lange.

— Understanding Physics. 154p. (C). 2000. pap., student ed. 19.95 (*0-471-98614-3*) Wiley.

— Windows '95 for Busy People. 2nd ed. 1997. 24.99 (*0-07-882324-2*) McGraw.

Mansfield & Behravesh, Mohamad M. Economy of the USA. 5th ed. 1998. pap. text, student ed. write for info. (*0-393-97205-4*) Norton.

Mansfield, et al. Management Economics with Thinking Strategies. 4th ed. 1999. text. write for info. (*0-393-99030-3*) Norton.

Mansfield, Arlene F. Descendants of Conrad Bower, Martin Easterday Sr., John Hoover Sr., & Gabriel Swinehart Sr. Families: From Colonial Maryland to Ohio in the Early 1800's. 490p. 1993. 32.50 (*0-9635981-0-4*) Coyote Tales.

Mansfield, Bob & Mitchell, Lindsay. Towards a Competent Workforce. 175p. 1996. text 96.95 (*0-566-07699-3*, Pub. by Gower) Ashgate Pub Co.

Mansfield, Bobby, et al. Vision Therapist Vol. 36 2: Vision Screenings. (Illus.). 90p. (Orig.). 1994. pap. text 18.00 (*0-943599-69-5*) OEPF.

Mansfield, Bruce. Interpretations of Erasmus c1750-1920: Man on His Own. (Erasmus Studies: No. 11). 480p. 1992. text 75.00 (*0-8020-5950-3*) U of Toronto Pr.

Mansfield, C. M. Early Breast Cancer: Its History & Results of Treatment. Wolsky, A., ed. (Experimental Biology & Medicine Ser.: Vol. 5). (Illus.). 120p. 1976. 42.75 (*3-8055-2300-9*) S Karger.

Mansfield, Carmella E. Writing Business Letters & Reports. 2nd ed. 1986. pap. 24.61 (*0-02-682970-3*) Macmillan.

Mansfield, Carmella E. & Bahniuk, Margaret H. Writing Business Letters & Reports. 1981. teacher ed. write for info. (*0-672-97375-8*); pap. write for info. (*0-672-97374-X*) Macmillan.

Mansfield, Charles B. Paraguay, Brazil, & the Plate. LC 79-128414. reprint ed. 55.00 (*0-404-04183-3*) AMS Pr.

Mansfield, Clay B. & Cunningham, Timothy W. Pension Funds: A Commonsense Guide to a Common Goal. LC 92-12182. 190p. 1992. text 37.50 (*1-55623-810-X*, Irwn Prfssnl) McGraw-Hill Prof.

Mansfield, Clay B., jt. auth. see Cunningham, Timothy W.

Mansfield, Creina. My Nasty Neighbours. (J). 1997. pap. 6.95 (*0-86278-462-X*, Pub. by OBrien Pr) Irish Amer Bk.

Mansfield, D. L. History of Dummerston - from Vermont Historical Gazetteer, Vol. V. (Illus.). 216p. 1995. reprint ed. lib. bdg. 32.50 (*0-8328-4656-2*) Higginson Bk Co.

Mansfield, D. L. & Benford, R. L. Harmonic Drive - A Factor in the Gear Industry: Part I - Principles & ApplicationsPart II - Harmonic Drive Compared with Gearing. (Technical Papers: Vol. P109.12). (Illus.). 48p. 1962. pap. text 30.00 (*1-55589-441-0*) AGMA.

Mansfield, Danielle F. Good-Bye, Baby Venus. LC 92-44490. 1993. 43.00 (*0-8191-9028-4*) U Pr of Amer.

Mansfield, Dick. Central New York Mountain Biking: The 30 Best Back Road & Trail Rides in Upstate New York. LC 94-2715. 176p. 1994. pap. 12.95 (*0-937921-50-5*) Acorn Pub.

— Runners Guide to Cross Country-Skiing. 2nd ed. LC 89-17754. (Illus.). 160p. 1990. pap. 10.95 (*0-937921-49-1*) Acorn Pub.

— Vermont Mountain Biking: The Best Back Road & Trail Rides in Southern Vermont. LC 88-355596. (Illus.). 176p. 1989. pap. 10.95 (*0-937921-48-3*) Acorn Pub.

Mansfield, Dick, jt. auth. see Heed, Peter.

Mansfield, Donald H. Flora of Steens Mountain. LC 99-57160. (Illus.). 424p. 1999. pap. 29.95 (*0-87071-471-6*) Oreg St U Pr.

Mansfield, E. D., jt. auth. see Abbott, Evelyn.

Mansfield, E. H. The Bending & Stretching of Plates. 2nd ed. (Illus.). 240p. (C). 1989. text 85.00 (*0-521-33304-0*) Cambridge U Pr.

Mansfield, Edward D. The Legal Rights, Liabilities & Duties of Women. LC 78-72352. (Free Love in America Ser.). reprint ed. 45.00 (*0-404-60951-1*) AMS Pr.

— Memoirs of the Life & Services of Daniel Drake, M. D. 1993. reprint ed. lib. bdg. 89.00 (*0-7812-5386-1*) Rprt Serv.

— Memoirs of the Life & Services of Daniel Drake, M. D., Physician, Professor, & Author. LC 75-108. (Mid-American Frontier Ser.). 1975. reprint ed. 34.95 (*0-405-06875-1*) Ayer.

— Personal Memories: Social, Political, & Literary. LC 72-133527. (Select Bibliographies Reprint Ser.). 1977. reprint ed. 23.95 (*0-8369-5559-5*) Ayer.

— Personal Memories, Social, Political & Literary. LC 74-125707. (American Journalists Ser.). 1971. reprint ed. 35.95 (*0-405-01688-3*) Ayer.

— Personal Memories, Social, Political & Literary, with Sketches of Many Noted People. (American Biography Ser.). 348p. 1991. reprint ed. lib. bdg. 79.00 (*0-7812-8264-0*) Rprt Serv.

— Power, Trade, & War. LC 93-13700. 300p. 1994. text 45.00 (*0-691-03288-2*, Pub. by Princeton U Pr) Cal Prin Full Svc.

Mansfield, Edward D. & Milner, Helen V. The Political Economy of Regionalism. LC 96-54832. (New Directions in World Politics Ser.). 1997. 47.50 (*0-231-10662-9*); pap. 19.50 (*0-231-10663-7*) Col U Pr.

Mansfield, Edwin. Applied Microeconomics. 2nd ed. LC 96-8232. (C). 1997. 65.00 (*0-393-97032-9*) Norton.

— Basic Statistics: With Applications. (C). 1986. pap. text, teacher ed. write for info. (*0-393-95402-1*) Norton.

Mansfield, Edwin. Basic Statistics. With Applications. (C). 1986. text 62.50 (*0-393-95393-9*); pap. text, student ed. 21.00 (*0-393-95396-3*) Norton.

Mansfield, Edwin. Economics: Principles, Problems, Decisions. 7th ed. (C). 1992. 78.50 (*0-393-96138-9*); pap. 75.00 (*0-393-96230-X*) Norton.

— Economics: Principles, Problems, Decisions. 7th ed. (C). 1992. pap. text 25.00 (*0-393-96172-9*) Norton.

Mansfield, Edwin. Economics USA. 6th ed. (C). pap. text. write for info. (*0-393-97621-1*) Norton.

Mansfield, Edwin. Essential Macroeconomics: Principles, Cases, & Problems. LC 97-46627. 1998. pap. text. write for info. (*0-393-97041-8*) Norton.

— Essential Microeconomics: Principles, Cases, Problems. LC 96-16023. (C). 1998. pap. text. write for info. (*0-393-97040-X*) Norton.

— Essentials of the Mac. 1998. pap. text. write for info. (*0-393-95869-8*) Norton.

— Innovation, Technology & the Economy: The Selected Essays of Edwin Mansfield, 2 vols. LC 95-5533. (Economists of the Twentieth Century Ser.). 696p. 1995. 185.00 (*1-85898-035-6*) E Elgar.

— Intellectual Property Protection, Direct Investment, & Technology Transfer: Germany, Japan, & the United States. LC 95-36687. (IFC Discussion Papers: No. 27). 42p. 1995. pap. 22.00 (*0-8213-3442-5*) World Bank.

Mansfield, Edwin. Manual with IBM 3.5 Disk/Pkged with Text. 1994. pap. 67.00 (*0-393-96538-4*) Norton.

Mansfield, Edwin. Micro Problems: Case Studies & Exercises for Review. 9th ed. LC 97-120789. 1996. pap. write for info. (*0-393-97036-1*) Norton.

— Microeconomics: Theory & Applications. 5th ed. (C). 1985. pap. text 18.25 (*0-393-95403-X*) Norton.

***Mansfield, Edwin.** Microeconomics: Theory & Applications. 10th ed. LC 99-32766. (Illus.). 646p. (C). 2000. text 65.00 (*0-393-97466-9*) Norton.

— Pkged with MansfieldTutor Macintosh. 1993. pap. 57.00 (*0-393-96438-8*) Norton.

Mansfield, Edwin. Principles of Macroeconomics. 7th ed. (Illus.). (C). 1992. pap. text 58.50 (*0-393-96173-7*) Norton.

— Principles of Macroeconomics. 7th ed. (C). 1993. pap. text, student ed. 42.00 (*0-393-96524-4*) Norton.

— Principles of Macroeconomics: Reading Issues & Cases. 4th ed. (C). 1983. pap. text 8.50 (*0-393-95340-8*) Norton.

— Principles of Macroeconomics: Study Guide. 7th ed. (Illus.). (C). 1992. pap. 21.00 (*0-393-96174-5*) Norton.

— Principles of Microeconomics. (Illus.). (C). 1992. student ed. write for info. (*0-393-96179-6*) Norton.

— Principles of Microeconomics. (Illus.). (C). 1992. pap. text, student ed. write for info. (*0-393-96178-8*) Norton.

— Principles of Microeconomics. 7th ed. (Illus.). (C). 1992. pap. text 58.50 (*0-393-96175-3*) Norton.

— Principles of Microeconomics. 7th ed. (C). 1993. pap. text, student ed. 42.00 (*0-393-96525-2*) Norton.

— Principles of Microeconomics: Readings, Issues & Cases. 4th ed. (C). 1983. pap. text 8.50 (*0-393-95331-9*) Norton.

— Principles of Microeconomics: Study Guide. 7th ed. (Illus.). (C). 1992. pap., student ed. 21.00 (*0-393-96176-1*) Norton.

— Statistics for Business & Economics: Methods & Applications. 5th ed. LC 93-7702. (C). 1994. 89.00 (*0-393-96460-4*) Norton.

— Statistics for Business & Economics: Problems. 5th ed. (C). 1994. pap. 69.00 (*0-393-96655-0*) Norton.

— Statistics for Business & Economics: Problems, Exercises, & Case Studies. 5th ed. LC 93-22745. (C). 1994. pap. 25.00 (*0-393-96488-4*) Norton.

Mansfield, Edwin. Study Guide & Case Book. pap. 16.00 (*0-393-97033-7*) Norton.

— Text Review Guide for Economics USA. 1997. pap. 14.50 (*0-393-97206-2*) Norton.

— With MansfieldTutor Macintosh. 1993. pap. 43.00 (*0-393-96443-4*) Norton.

Mansfield, Edwin, contrib. by. Leading Economic Controversies of 1998. LC 98-125268. (Illus.). (C). 1997. pap. text (*0-393-97225-9*) Norton.

Mansfield, Edwin, ed. Managerial Economics & Operations Research: Techniques, Applications, Cases. 5th ed. 500p. (C). 1987. pap. text 21.00 (*0-393-95590-7*) Norton.

Mansfield, Edwin & Behravesh, Nariman. Economics U $ A. 5th ed. (Illus.). 600p. (C). 1998. pap. 64.00 (*0-393-97159-7*) Norton.

Mansfield, Edwin & Mansfield, Elizabeth, eds. The Economics of Technical Change. (International Library of Critical Writings in Economics: Vol. 31). (Illus.). 516p. 1993. 230.00 (*1-85278-783-X*) E Elgar.

Mansfield, Edwin D., jt. auth. see Abbott, Evelyn.

Mansfield, Elisabeth. Lady Lu. large type ed. LC 90-44228. 302p. 1990. reprint ed. lib. bdg. 18.95 (*1-56054-050-8*) Thorndike Pr.

Mansfield, Elizabeth. The Bartered Bride. 224p. 1994. mass mkt. 4.50 (*0-515-11521-5*, Jove) Berkley Pub.

— A Brilliant Mismatch. 224p. 1991. mass mkt. 4.50 (*0-515-10545-7*, Jove) Berkley Pub.

— Christmas Kiss. 1990. mass mkt. 4.99 (*0-515-10520-1*, Jove) Berkley Pub.

— Duel of Hearts. 224p. 1997. mass mkt. 4.99 (*0-515-08846-3*, Jove) Berkley Pub.

— The Fifth Kiss. large type ed. LC 94-28138. 341p. 1994. pap. 19.95 (*0-8161-7471-7*, G K Hall Lrg Type) Mac Lib Ref.

— Her Man of Affairs. 224p. 1996. mass mkt. 4.99 (*0-614-17456-2*, Jove) Berkley Pub.

***Mansfield, Elizabeth.** Her Man of Affairs, Set. unabridged ed. (C). 1999. 35.95 incl. audio (*1-55685-610-5*) Audio Bk Con.

Mansfield, Elizabeth. The Magnificent Masquerade. large type ed. LC 90-35643. 393p. 1990. reprint ed. lib. bdg. 18.95 (*1-56054-009-5*) Thorndike Pr.

— Matched Pairs. 224p. (Orig.). 1996. mass mkt. 4.99 (*0-515-11785-4*, Jove) Berkley Pub.

***Mansfield, Elizabeth.** Miscalculations. 304p. 2000. mass mkt. 5.99 (*0-515-12834-1*, Jove) Berkley Pub.

Mansfield, Elizabeth. Mother's Choice. 208p. (Orig.). 1994. mass mkt. 3.99 (*0-515-11386-7*, Jove) Berkley Pub.

— My Lord Murderer. 256p. 1986. mass mkt. 4.50 (*0-515-08743-2*, Jove) Berkley Pub.

— Poor Caroline. 224p. (Orig.). 1995. mass mkt. 4.50 (*0-515-11659-9*, Jove) Berkley Pub.

— A Prior Engagement. 240p. 1990. pap. text 4.50 (*0-515-10398-5*, Jove) Berkley Pub.

— Regency Sting. 240p. 1996. mass mkt. 4.99 (*0-515-08773-4*, Jove) Berkley Pub.

— A Very Dutiful Daughter. 256p. (Orig.). 1986. mass mkt. 4.50 (*0-515-08740-8*, Jove) Berkley Pub.

— Winter Wonderland. 1993. mass mkt. 3.99 (*0-515-11234-8*, Jove) Berkley Pub.

Mansfield, Elizabeth, ed. see Lawrence, D. H.

Mansfield, Elizabeth, jt. ed. see Mansfield, Edwin.

Mansfield, F. & Bertocci, U., eds. Electrochemical Corrosion Testing - STP 727. 411p. 1984. 36.00 (*0-8031-0704-8*, STP727) ASTM.

Mansfield, F., jt. auth. see Wilson, F.

Mansfield, Felicity, jt. auth. see Wilson, Francis.

Mansfield, Francis, tr. see Muller, Karl, et al, eds.

Mansfield, H. O. Norfolk Churches: Their Foundations, Architecture & Furnishings. 208p. 1994. 30.00 (*0-900963-57-3*, Pub. by T Dalton) St Mut.

Mansfield, H. P. Key to Understanding the Scriptures. 1989. pap. 4.95 (*0-317-02705-0*, Pub. by Logos Pubns) Intl Spec Bk.

M

An Asterisk (*) at the beginning of an entry indicates that the title is appearing for the first time.

Mansfield, Harold. Billion Dollar Battle: The Story Behind the "Impossible" 727 Project. Gilbert, James B., ed. LC 79-7283. (Flight: Its First Seventy-Five Years Ser.). (Illus.). 1980. reprint ed. lib. bdg. 19.95 (*0-405-12192-X*) Ayer.

— Vision: A Saga of the Sky. Gilbert, James B., ed. LC 79-7284. (Flight: Its First Seventy-Five Years Ser.). (Illus.). 1980. reprint ed. lib. bdg. 37.95 (*0-405-12193-8*) Ayer.

Mansfield, Harvey C. America's Constitutional Soul. LC 90-19210. (Series in Constitutional Thought). 224p. 1991. 39.95 (*0-8018-4114-3*) Johns Hopkins.

Mansfield, Harvey C., Jr. America's Constitutional Soul. (Series in Constitutional Thought). 224p. 1993. reprint ed. pap. 15.95 (*0-8018-4634-X*) Johns Hopkins.

Mansfield, Harvey C., Sr. Illustrations of Presidential Management: Johnson's Cost Reduction & Tax Increase Campaigns. (Administrative History of the Johnson Presidency Ser.). 75p. 1988. pap. 6.00 (*0-89940-307-7*) LBJ Sch Pub Aff.

Mansfield, Harvey C. Lake Cargo Coal Rate Controversy. LC 73-76629. (Columbia University. Studies in the Social Sciences: No. 373). reprint ed. 32.50 (*0-404-51373-5*) AMS Pr.

— Machiavelli's Virtue. LC 95-24115. 388p. 1996. 29.95 (*0-226-50368-2*) U Ch Pr.

— Machiavelli's Virtue. 372p. 1998. pap. 15.00 (*0-226-50369-0*) U Ch Pr.

— Responsible Citizenship: Ancient & Modern. LC 94-41697. (Kritikos Professorship in the Humanities Ser.). 1994. 5.00 (*0-87114-228-7*) U of Oreg Bks.

— The Spirit of Liberalism. LC 78-7809. 144p. reprint ed. pap. 44.70 (*0-7837-5936-3*, 204573500007) Bks Demand.

***Mansfield, Harvey C., Jr.** A Student's Guide to Political Theory. LC 00-101237. 75p. (C). 2000. text 5.95 (*1-882926-43-9*) ISI Books.

Mansfield, Harvey C., Jr. Taming the Prince: The Ambivalence of Modern Executive Power. 310p. 1989. 32.95 (*0-02-919980-8*) Free Pr.

— Taming the Prince: The Ambivalence of Modern Executive Power. LC 92-31982. 384p. 1993. reprint ed. pap. 17.95 (*0-8018-4589-0*) Johns Hopkins.

Mansfield, Harvey C., jt. auth. see Lowenthal, David.

Mansfield, Harvey C., Jr., ed. see Burke, Edmund.

Mansfield, Harvey C., Jr., ed. see Jefferson, Thomas.

Mansfield, Harvey C., Jr., ed. & tr. see Rousseau, Jean-Jacques.

Mansfield, Harvey C., Jr., tr. see Machiavelli, Niccolo.

***Mansfield, Harvey Claflin, et al.** Machiavellianism & Its Alternatives: Essays in Honor of Harvey Mansfield. LC 00-37283. 2000. write for info. (*0-7425-0827-7*) Rowman.

Mansfield, Helen, et al, eds. Mathematics for Tomorrow's Young Children: International Perspectives on Curriculum. LC 96-10933. (Mathematics Education Library: Vol. 16). 1996. lib. bdg. 128.00 (*0-7923-3998-3*) Kluwer Academic.

Mansfield, Howard. In the Memory House. 288p. 1993. 19.95 (*1-55591-162-5*) Fulcrum Pub.

— In the Memory House. 288p. 1995. pap. 12.95 (*1-55591-247-8*) Fulcrum Pub.

***Mansfield, Howard.** The Same Ax, Twice: Restoration & Renewal in a Throw-Away Age. LC 99-56170. 288p. 2000. 26.00 (*1-58465-028-1*) U Pr of New Eng.

Mansfield, Howard. Skylark: The Life, Lies, & Inventions of Harry Atwood. LC 98-38960. (Illus.). 248p. 1999. 24.95 (*0-87451-891-1*) U Pr of New Eng.

Mansfield, J. A Collector's Guide to Modern Australian Ceramics. (Illus.). 128p. 1989. text 35.00 (*0-947131-09-4*) Gordon & Breach.

Mansfield, J., tr. see Stone, M. E., et al.

Mansfield, Janet. Salt Glaze Ceramics: An International Perspective. (Illus.). 144p. 1991. text. write for info. (*976-8097-11-6*) Gordon & Breach.

Mansfield, John. Asthma Epidemic. 1998. pap. 13.00 (*0-7225-3388-8*) Genl Dist Srvs.

Mansfield, John G., Jr. Cruisers for Breakfast: War Patrols of U. S. S. Darter & U. S. S. Dace. 302p. 1997. text 25.00 (*0-9660938-0-1*) Media Ctr Pub.

Mansfield, John M., ed. Parasitic Diseases: Immunology, Vol. 1. LC 81-9741. 335p. 1981. reprint ed. pap. 103.90 (*0-608-01299-8*, 206204500001) Bks Demand.

— Parasitic Diseases Vol. 2: Chemotherapy. LC 81-9741. 247p. 1981. reprint ed. pap. 76.60 (*0-608-01300-5*, 206204500002) Bks Demand.

Mansfield, Katherine. Bliss, & Other Short Stories. 1977. 36.01 (*0-8369-4240-X*, 6051) Ayer.

— Bliss & Other Stories. (Classics Library). 1998. pap. 3.95 (*1-85326-731-7*, 7317WW, Pub. by Wrdsworth Edits) NTC Contemp Pub Co.

***Mansfield, Katherine.** Bliss, Feuille d'Album. (Short Stories Ser.). 22p. 2000. pap. 3.95 (*1-86092-005-5*, Pub. by Travelman Pub) IPG Chicago.

Mansfield, Katherine. The Collected Letters of Katherine Mansfield, Vol. II: 1918 - September 1919. O'Sullivan, Vincent & Scott, Margaret, eds. (Illus.). 382p. 1987. text 34.00 (*0-19-812614-X*) OUP.

— The Collected Letters of Katherine Mansfield Vol. III: 1919-1920. O'Sullivan, Vincent & Scott, Margaret, eds. 328p. 1993. 59.00 (*0-19-812615-8*) OUP.

— Garden Party. large type ed. 1989. 19.95 (*1-85290-007-5*, G K Hall Lrg Type) Mac Lib Ref.

— The Garden Party & Other Stories. LC 98-171278. (Penguin Twentieth-Century Classics Ser.). 288p. 1998. reprint ed. pap. 10.95 (*0-14-018880-0*, Penguin Bks) Viking Penguin.

— In a German Pension: 13 Stories. unabridged ed. LC 95-1144. (Thrift Editions Ser.). 112p. 1995. reprint ed. pap. text 1.50 (*0-486-28719-X*) Dover.

— Journal. (FRE.). 1983. pap. 19.95 (*0-7859-4193-2*) Fr & Eur.

— Journal of Katherine Mansfield. LC 82-11541. (Illus.). 255p. 1983. reprint ed. pap. 6.95 (*0-88001-023-1*) HarpC.

— Katherine Mansfield: Selected Letters. O'Sullivan, Vincent, ed. (Illus.). 352p. 1989. text 45.00 (*0-19-818592-8*) OUP.

— Katherine Mansfield: Selected Stories. (World's Classics Ser.). 386p. 1981. pap. write for info. (*0-19-281561-X*) OUP.

— Katherine Mansfield: The New Zealand Stories. LC 99-210739. 302p. 1999. pap. 18.95 (*0-19-558404-X*) OUP.

Mansfield, Katherine. Katherine Mansfield Stories. 239p. 21.95 (*0-8488-2588-8*) Amereon Ltd.

Mansfield, Katherine. Letters Between Katherine Mansfield & John Middleton Murry. Hankin, Cherry A., ed. 425p. (Orig.). 1990. pap. 16.95 (*0-941533-76-X*, NAB) I R Dee.

— The New Zealand Stories. O'Sullivan, Vincent, ed. 302p. 1998. text 35.00 (*0-19-558364-7*) OUP.

— Novels & Novelists. reprint ed. 49.00 (*0-403-02290-8*) Somerset Pub.

***Mansfield, Katherine.** Something Childish & Other Stories. Raitt, Suzanne, ed. (Penguin Twentieth Century Classics). 172p. 2000. pap. 13.00 (*0-14-018897-5*, Pub. by Pnguin Bks Ltd) Trafalgar.

Mansfield, Katherine. Stories. LC 90-50474. 384p. 1991. pap. 13.00 (*0-679-73374-4*) Vin Bks.

Mansfield, Katherine, tr. see Gorky, Maxim.

***Mansfield, Ken.** The Beatles, the Bible, & Bodega Bay: My Long & Winding Road. (Illus.). 368p. 2000. 24.99 (*0-8054-2289-7*) Broadman.

Mansfield, Kenneth. Coarse Fishing for Beginners. (Illus.). 160p. (Orig.). 1974. pap. 14.95 (*0-572-01176-8*) Trans-Atl Phila.

Mansfield, Kenneth, jt. auth. see Antonakos, James L.

Mansfield, Kenneth C. & Antonakos, James L. Introduction to Programming Using C++ LC 96-11369. 641p. 1996. pap. text 85.00 (*0-13-254921-2*) P-H.

Mansfield, Kenneth C., jt. auth. see Antonakos, James L.

***Mansfield, Leslie.** Appetizers: Recipes from the Vineyards of Northern California. LC 99-70629. (Illus.). 122p. 1999. pap. 9.95 (*0-89087-890-0*) Celestial Arts.

Mansfield, Leslie. The Mauna Loa Macadamia Cookbook. LC 98-72530. 96p. 1998. pap. 4.95 (*0-89087-879-X*) Celestial Arts.

— The Mauna Loa Macadamia Cooking Treasury. LC 98-16925. (Illus.). 188p. 1998. 29.95 (*0-89087-885-4*); pap. 19.95 (*0-89087-880-3*) Celestial Arts.

— Recipes from the Vineyards of Northern California: Asian Pasta. 128p. 1999. pap. 9.95 (*0-89087-938-9*) Celestial Arts.

***Mansfield, Leslie.** Recipes from the Vineyards of Northern California: Barbecue Dishes. (Illus.). 128p. 2000. pap. 9.95 (*0-89087-958-3*) Celestial Arts.

Mansfield, Leslie. Recipes from the Vineyards of Northern California: Desserts. 128p. 1999. pap. 9.95 (*0-89087-892-7*) Celestial Arts.

— Recipes from the Vineyards of Northern California: Main Courses. 128p. 1999. pap. 9.95 (*0-89087-891-9*) Celestial Arts.

— Recipes from the Vineyards of Northern California: Pasta with Red Wine. 128p. 1999. pap. 9.95 (*0-89087-936-2*) Celestial Arts.

— Recipes from the Vineyards of Northern California: Pasta with White Wine. 128p. Date not set. pap. 9.95 (*0-89087-937-0*) Celestial Arts.

***Mansfield, Leslie.** Recipes from the Vineyards of Northern California: Picnics. (Illus.). 128p. 2000. pap. 9.95 (*0-89087-960-5*) Celestial Arts.

— Recipes from the Vineyards of Northern California: Vegetarian Dishes. 128p. 2000. pap. 9.95 (*0-89087-959-1*) Celestial Arts.

Mansfield, Leslie J. Oregon Coast Aquarium Seafood Cookbook. 144p. 1997. pap. 14.95 (*0-89288-262-X*) Maverick.

Mansfield, Lucile. Micro Problems. 10th ed. (C). pap. text. write for info. (*0-393-97597-5*) Norton.

Mansfield, Luther S., ed. see Melville, Herman.

Mansfield, Lynda & Waldmann, Christopher H. Don't Touch My Heart: Helping Parents Deal with the Pain of an Unattached Child. LC 94-5508. (Illus.). 121p. (Orig.). 1994. pap. 10.00 (*0-89109-820-8*) Pinon Press.

Mansfield, Lyndon E. Primer of Immunology. 1991. 25.00 (*0-07-039919-0*) McGraw.

Mansfield, M., tr. see Di Coppo, Giovanni.

Mansfield, Margaret. Black Like Me Notes. (Cliffs Notes Ser.). 80p. 1971. pap. 4.95 (*0-8220-0245-0*, Cliff) IDG Bks.

Mansfield, Margaret A., jt. auth. see Breeton, John.

Mansfield, Margaret A., jt. auth. see Brereton, John C.

Mansfield, Marilynn. A Change of Destiny. Nesbitt, Marilyn, ed. (Illus.). 1998. pap. 7.00 (*0-9667995-5-0*) DiskUs Publishing.

Mansfield, Mary C. The Humiliation of Sinners: Public Penance in Thirteenth-Century France. (Illus.). 336p. 1994. text 42.50 (*0-8014-2939-0*) Cornell U Pr.

Mansfield, Michael W., jt. ed. see Nimmo, Dan.

***Mansfield, Mike & O'Sullivan, Colm.** Understanding Physics. 776p. 1998. pap. 65.95 (*0-471-97554-0*) Wiley.

Mansfield, Mike & O'Sullivan, Colm. Understanding Physics. 776p. 1998. 160.00 (*0-471-97553-2*) Wiley.

Mansfield, Mike, et al. Japan: A Living Portrait. (Illus.). 80p. 1994. 28.00 (*4-7700-1863-0*) Kodansha.

Mansfield, Murry, jt. ed. see Murry, J. M.

Mansfield, Niall. Joy of X: An Overview of X Window System. 384p. (C). 1992. pap. text 34.95 (*0-201-56512-9*) Addison-Wesley.

— Window System: A User's Guide. 2nd ed. (C). 1995. pap. text 10.00 (*0-201-54438-5*) Addison-Wesley.

Mansfield, Nick. Masochism: The Art of Power. LC 96-26279. 128p. 1997. 52.95 (*0-275-95702-0*) Greenwood.

***Mansfield, Nick.** Subjectivity: Theories of the Self from Freud to Haraway. LC 00-38023. 2000. pap. write for info. (*0-8147-5651-4*) NYU Pr.

Mansfield, Nick, jt. auth. see Fuery, Patrick.

Mansfield, Patti G. As by a New Pentecost. 179p. 1992. pap. 9.95 (*0-940535-44-0*, UP144) Franciscan U Pr.

— More of God. 220p. 1990. pap. 3.75 (*0-940535-32-7*, UP132) Franciscan U Pr.

— Proclaim His Marvelous Deeds: How to Give a Personal Testimony. 93p. (Orig.). 1987. pap. 3.75 (*0-940535-06-8*, UP107) Franciscan U Pr.

Mansfield, Peter. The Arabs. 560p. 1996. pap. 12.00 (*0-614-21504-8*, 67) Kazi Pubns.

— The Bates Method. (Alternative Health Ser.). (Illus.). 166p. (Orig.). 1994. pap. 12.95 (*0-8048-3003-7*) Tuttle Pubng.

— The Bates Method: A Complete Guide to Improving Eyesight Naturally. (Illus.). 178p. 1997. pap. 13.95 (*0-09-181281-X*, Pub. by Random) Trafalgar.

— Flower Remedies. (Tuttle Alternative Health Ser.). (Illus.). 120p. (Orig.). 1995. pap. 14.95 (*0-8048-3005-3*) Tuttle Pubng.

— A History of the Middle East. 374p. 1996. pap. 13.00 (*0-614-21151-4*, 450) Kazi Pubns.

— History of the Middle East. 1992. pap. 14.95 (*0-14-012538-8*) Viking Penguin.

Mansfield, Peter, ed. MRI in Medicine: The Nottingham Conference. LC 95-31244. 333p. 1995. pap. 109.95 (*0-412-07391-9*, Chap & Hall NY) Chapman & Hall.

Mansfield, Philip, ed. Extending EMDR: A Casebook of Innovative Applications. LC 97-51868. 304p. 1998. 37.00 (*0-393-70266-9*) Norton.

Mansfield, Phyllis K. Pregnancy for Older Women: Assessing the Medical Risks. LC 86-9440. 230p. 1986. 59.95 (*0-275-92184-0*, C2184, Praeger Pubs) Greenwood.

Mansfield, Richard. Studio Basics: What You Should Know Before Entering the Recording Studio. LC 97-46341. 164p. 1998. 16.95 (*0-8230-8488-4*, Billboard Bks) Watsn-Guptill.

***Mansfield, Richard.** Visual Basic 6 Weekend Crash Course. LC 99-59505. (Illus.). 432p. 2000. pap. 19.99 (*0-7645-4679-1*) IDG Bks.

— Visual Basic 6 Database Programming for Dummies. (For Dummies Ser.). 384p. 1999. pap. 24.99 (*0-7645-0625-0*) IDG Bks.

Mansfield, Richard. WordPerfect 5 Solutions. 126p. (Orig.). 1989. pap. 14.95 (*0-929307-04-6*) GP Pubns.

Mansfield, Richard & Revette, Debbie. Visual InterDev 6 Bible. LC TK5105.8885.M55M36. (Bible Ser.). (Illus.). 768p. 1998. pap. 49.99 incl. cd-rom (*0-7645-3135-2*) IDG Bks.

Mansfield, Richard H. Progress of the Breed: A History of U. S. Holsteins. Hastings, Robert H., ed. LC 85-60730. 350p. 1985. 34.95 (*0-9614711-0-7*) Holstein-Friesian.

Mansfield, Richard S., jt. auth. see Cripe, Edward J.

***Mansfield-Richardson, Virginia.** Asian Americans & the Mass Media: A Content Analysis of 20 United States' Newspapers & a Survey of Asian American Journalists. LC 99-46174. 1999. write for info. (*0-8153-3476-1*) Garland.

Mansfield, Roger, ed. Frontiers of Management: Research & Practice. 240p. 1990. 67.50 (*0-415-04455-3*, A4013) Routledge.

Mansfield, Ron. Excel for Windows 95 for Busy People, No. 3. (Busy People Bks.). (Illus.). 304p. 1995. pap. text 22.95 (*0-07-882111-8*) McGraw.

— Excel 97 for Busy People. LC 97-138984. 1997. pap. text 24.99 (*0-07-882279-3*) Osborne-McGraw.

— PowerPoint for Windows 95 for Busy People. (Busy People Bks.). 304p. 1996. pap. text 22.95 (*0-07-882204-1*) McGraw.

Mansfield, Ron. Windows 98 for Busy People. 2nd ed. pap. 19.99 (*0-07-212203-X*) Osborne Bks.

Mansfield, Ron. Windows 95 for Busy People. 2nd ed. 304p. 1997. pap. text 24.99 (*0-07-882287-4*) Osborne-McGraw.

— Windows 95 for Busy People, No. 1. (Busy People Bks.). (Illus.). 304p. 1995. pap. text 22.95 (*0-07-882110-X*) Osborne-McGraw.

— Word 97. 4th ed. LC 96-70745. 1120p. 1996. pap. text 34.99 (*0-7821-1926-3*) Sybex.

— Working in Microsoft Office. LC 96-161595. 1008p. 1995. pap. text 34.95 (*0-07-882164-9*) McGraw.

Mansfield, Ron & Olsen, J. W. Mastering Word 2000: Premium Edition. LC 98-88913. (Mastering Ser.). 1088p. 1999. pap. text 39.99 incl. cd-rom (*0-7821-2314-7*) Sybex.

Mansfield, Sally, jt. auth. see Barker, Alex.

Mansfield, Sandra & Groover, Judy. Once in a Long While: The Romancing of a Contemporary Cowboy. 192p. 1996. 24.95 (*0-9630463-8-1*) S & D.

Mansfield, Scott. Engineering Design for Process Facilities. 369p. 1993. 48.00 (*0-07-040010-5*) McGraw.

Mansfield, Stephanie. The Richest Girl in the World. 480p. 1994. mass mkt. 4.99 (*1-55817-792-2*, Pinncle Kensgtn) Kensgtn Pub Corp.

— Richest Girl in the World. 1999. mass mkt. 6.99 (*0-7860-1027-4*) Kensgtn Pub Corp.

***Mansfield, Stephen.** China - Yunnan Province: The Bradt Travel Guide. (Illus.). 7p. 2000. pap. 18.95 (*1-84162-002-5*, Pub. by Bradt Pubns) Globe Pequot.

Mansfield, Stephen. Culture Shock! Laos. LC 96-77211. (Culture Shock Ser.). 1997. pap. 12.95 (*1-55868-301-1*) Gr Arts Ctr Pub.

— Laos: A Portrait. (Illus.). 200p. Date not set. 45.00 (*962-7787-03-5*, Pub. by O&A Edits) Weatherhill.

— Never Give In: The Extraordinary Character of Winston Churchill. LC 96-32251. (Leaders in Action Ser.). 208p. 1996. 14.95 (*1-888952-19-9*) Cumberland Hse.

— Then Darkness Fled: The Liberating Work of Booker T. Washington. LC 99-46972. 320p. 1999. 14.95 (*1-58182-053-4*, Cumberland Hearthside) Cumberland Hse.

Mansfield, Stephen & Bradt, Hilary. Guide to the Philippines. LC 96-53437. (Bradt Guides Ser.). (Illus.). 304p. (Orig.). Date not set. pap. 18.95 (*1-898323-58-5*, Pub. by Bradt Pubns) Globe Pequot.

Mansfield, Stephen & Grant, George. Faithful Volunteers: The History of Religion in Tennessee. LC 97-2287. (Illus.). 288p. (Orig.). 1997. pap. 16.95 (*1-888952-14-8*) Cumberland Hse.

Mansfield, Steve. Photographing Airplanes. LC 91-70476. (Illus.). 160p. 1991. pap. 24.95 (*0-943231-43-4*) Howell Pr VA.

Mansfield, Sue, ed. see Mill, John Stuart.

Mansfield, T. A., jt. ed. see Jarvis, P. G.

Mansfield, Tasha E. When God Talks Back Vol. 1: Madness or Mysticism. unabridged ed. Jenny, Cythia L., ed. (Illus.). 166p. 1998. pap. 18.50 (*1-893083-00-4*) Centauro Pub.

Mansfield, Victor. Synchronicity, Science, & Soulmaking. 270p. 1995. pap. 18.95 (*0-8126-9304-3*) Open Court.

Mansfield, Yoel, jt. auth. see Pizam, Abraham.

Manshard, W. Die Staedte des Tropischen Afrika. (Urbanisierung der Erde Ser.: Vol. 1). (GER., Illus.). 258p. 1977. lib. bdg. 68.60 (*3-443-39070-6*) Lubrecht & Cramer.

Manshard, W. & Fischnich, O. E. Man & Environment. 108p. (C). 1975. pap. 23.00 (*0-08-019673-X*, Pergamon Pr) Elsevier.

Manshard, W. & Ruddle, Kenneth. Renewable Natural Resources & the Environment: Pressing Problems in the Developing World, Vol. 2. (Natural Resources & the Environment Ser.). (Illus.). 410p. 1981. pap. 65.00 (*0-907567-06-1*, Tycooly Pub); text 105.00 (*0-907567-01-0*, Tycooly Pub) Weidner & Sons.

Mansheim, Gerald, jt. auth. see Gebhard, David.

Manshel, Lisa. Nap Time: The True Story of Sexual Abuse at a Suburban Day Care Center. 1991. mass mkt. 4.95 (*0-8217-3262-5*, Zebra Kensgtn) Kensgtn Pub Corp.

Manship, Henry. History of Great Yarmouth, 2 vols., Set. Palmer, Charles J., ed. (Illus.). 823p. 1995. reprint ed. lib. bdg. 92.50 (*0-8328-4650-3*) Higginson Bk Co.

Mansilla, Lucio V. An Expedition to the Ranquel Indians. McCaffrey, Mark, tr. from SPA. LC 96-39454. (Texas Pan American Ser.). (Illus.). 400p. 1997. 50.00 (*0-292-75192-3*); pap. 19.95 (*0-292-75203-2*) U of Tex Pr.

— A Visit to the Ranquel Indians (Una Excursion a los Indios Ranqueles) Gillies, Eva, tr. from SPA. LC 96-49173.Tr. of Una Excursi on a los Indios Ranqueles. (Illus.). xl, 467p. 1997. text 55.00 (*0-8032-3183-0*) U of Nebr Pr.

— A Visit to the Ranquel Indians(Una Excursion a los Indios Ranqueles) Gillies, Eva, tr. LC 96-49173.Tr. of Una Excursi on a los Indios Ranqueles. (Illus.). xl, 467p. 1997. pap. text 25.00 (*0-8032-8235-4*) U of Nebr Pr.

Mansingh, Surjit. Historical Dictionary of India. LC 95-43616. (Asian Historical Dictionaries Ser.: No. 20). 552p. 1996. 78.00 (*0-8108-3078-7*) Scarecrow.

— India's Search for Power: Indira Gandhi's Foreign Policy, 1966-82. 1984. 29.95 (*0-8039-9475-3*) Sage.

Mansinha, L., ed. see NATO Advanced Study Institute Staff.

Mansion, Jean E. French Reference Grammar for Schools & Colleges. LC 72-98855. 247p. 1971. reprint ed. lib. bdg. 65.00 (*0-8371-3125-1*, MAFG, Greenwood Pr) Greenwood.

— Harrap's New College French & English Dictionary. (ENG & FRE.). 39.95 (*0-317-45640-7*) Fr & Eur.

— Harrap's New Standard French & English Dictionary, Pt. 1: French to English, 2 vols. (ENG & FRE.). 125.00 (*0-317-45641-5*) Fr & Eur.

— Harrap's New Standard French & English Dictionary, Pt. 2: English to French, 2 vols. (ENG & FRE.). 125.00 (*0-317-45642-3*) Fr & Eur.

Mansir, A. Richard. Build a Wells Fargo Stagecoach. (Building America Ser.). (Illus.). 24p. (ps-3). 1999. pap. 6.95 (*1-57091-950-X*) Charlesbridge Pub.

— Stagecoach: The Ride of a Century. LC 98-36315. (Building America Ser.). 32p. (J). (ps-3). 1999. pap. 6.95 (*1-57091-955-0*) Charlesbridge Pub.

— Stagecoach: The Ride of a Century. LC 98-36315. (Building America Ser.). (Illus.). 32p. (J). (ps-3). 1999. 15.95 (*1-57091-960-7*) Charlesbridge Pub.

Manskar, Steve. Accountable Discipleship: Living in God's Household. LC 98-88816. 128p. 2001. pap. 13.95 (*0-88177-271-2*, DR271) Discipleship Res.

Manske, Fred A., Jr. Secrets of Effective Leadership: A Practical Guide to Success. 2nd rev. ed. (Illus.). 210p. 1990. 19.95 (*0-943703-03-4*) Leader Educ Dev.

— Secrets of Effective Leadership: A Practical Guide to Success, 1. 3rd ed. LC 98-89401. 263p. 1999. 24.95 (*0-943703-04-2*); pap. text 15.95 (*0-943703-05-0*) Leader Educ Dev.

Manske, Laura, ed. Family Travel: The Farther You Go, the Closer You Get. LC 99-13111. (Travelers' Tales Ser.). 347p. 1999. pap. 17.95 (*1-885211-33-3*) Trvlers Tale.

Manske, Ron. A Polish Love Story. LC 79-84322. (Illus.). 144p. 1979. pap. 2.50 (*0-89221-060-5*) New Leaf.

Manski, Charles F. Analog Estimation Methods in Econometrics. 250p. (gr. 13). 1988. pap. text 36.95 (*0-412-01141-7*, 9961, Chap & Hall CRC) CRC Pr.

An Asterisk (*) at the beginning of an entry indicates that the title is appearing for the first time.

— Identification Problems in the Social Sciences. LC 94-29313. (Illus.). 184p. (C). 1995. text 32.50 (*0-674-44283-0*, MANIDE) HUP.

— Identification Problems in the Social Sciences. 1999. pap. text 17.95 (*0-674-44284-9*) HUP.

Manski, Charles F. & Garfinkel, Irwin, eds. Evaluating Welfare & Training Programs. (Illus.). 368p. (C). 1992. 49.95 (*0-674-27017-7*) HUP.

Manski, Charles F. & Wise, David A. College Choice in America. (Illus.). 240p. 1983. 37.95 (*0-674-14125-3*) HUP.

Manski, Charles F., ed. see National Research Council Staff.

Mansley, Edward H. An Introduction to Christianity for Adults. 120p. 1999. pap. write for info. (*0-7392-0110-7*, PO3006) Morris Pubng.

Mansmann, Patricia A. & Neuhausel, Patricia A. Life after Survival: A Therapeutic Approach for Adult Children of Alcoholics. (Illus.). 56p. 1986. pap. text 6.95 (*0-940967-00-6*) Genesis Pub PA.

— Life after Survival: A Therapeutic Approach for Adult Children of Alcoholics. 2nd rev. ed. (Illus.). 88p. 1989. pap. text 6.95 (*0-940967-01-4*) Genesis Pub PA.

Mansmann, Richard A. Instructions for Equine Clients. (Illus.). 352p. (C). (gr. 13). 1995. text 80.00 (*0-8151-6455-6*, 26582) Mosby Inc.

Mansmann, Richard A., jt. auth. see King, Christine.

Mansmann, Vinzenz. Overcoming Burnout Naturally. LC 99-36726. 1999. pap. text 11.95 (*0-8069-2029-7*) Sterling.

Manso, Gilbert, jt. auth. see Whalen, Freda.

Manso, Peter. Brando: The Biography. (Illus.). 1160p. (J). 1995. pap. 15.95 (*0-7868-8128-3*, Pub. by Hyperion) Time Warner.

Manson. Interest Rate Risk Management. 1992. lib. bdg. 211.50 (*1-85333-765-X*) Kluwer Academic.

Manson, jt. auth. see Biernat.

Manson, Ainslie. Baboo: The Story of Sir John A. MacDonald's Daughter. (Illus.). 32p. (J). (ps-4). 1998. bds. write for info. (*0-88899-329-3*, Pub. by Gro1undwood-Douglas) Publishers Group.

*__Manson, Ainslie.__ Ballerinas Don't Wear Glasses. (Illus.). 32p. (J). 2000. 15.95 (*1-55143-158-0*) Orca Bk Pubs.

Manson, Ainslie. A Dog Came, Too: A True Story. LC 91-44891. (Illus.). 32p. (J). (gr. 1-5). 1993. 13.95 (*0-689-50567-1*) McElderry Bks.

— Just Like New. (Illus.). 32p. (J). (ps-3). 1996. 14.95 (*0-88899-228-9*) Publishers Group.

*__Manson, B. M. & Eley, J. D.__ Outline of Peridontics. (Illus.). 405p. 1999. pap. text 60.00 (*0-7236-1070-3*) Buttrwrth-Heinemann.

Manson, Beverly, ed. see Gerson, Richard F.

*__Manson, Bonita J.__ Downsizing Issues. LC 99-44622. (Studies on Industrial Productivity). 1999. 50.00 (*0-8153-3525-3*) Garland.

Manson, Christopher. Maze: A Riddle in Words & Pictures. (Illus.). 96p. 1995. pap. 8.95 (*0-8050-1088-2*, Owl) H Holt & Co.

— Prospero's Palace. Date not set. pap. write for info. (*0-8050-4865-0*) H Holt & Co.

*__Manson, Christopher.__ Good King Wenceslas. LC 94-17443. 32p. (J). (gr. k-3). 1999. pap. 6.95 (*0-7358-1200-4*, Pub. by North-South Bks NYC) Chronicle Bks.

Manson, Christopher. The Tree in the Wood: An Old Nursery Song. LC 92-23524. 32p. (J). (gr. k-3). 1993. 14.95 (*1-55858-192-8*, Pub. by North-South Bks NYC); lib. bdg. 14.88 (*1-55858-193-6*, Pub. by North-South Bks NYC) Chronicle Bks.

Manson, Connie J. & Gordon, Ian D., compiled by. Directory of Geoscience Libraries: North America, 1997. 113p. 1997. 35.00 (*0-934485-25-9*) Geosci Info.

Manson, Cynthia. Murder by the Book. 1996. mass mkt. 5.99 (*0-425-15516-1*) Berkley Pub.

— Murder Intercontinental. 1 vol. 1999. mass mkt. 6.99 (*0-425-17123-X*) Berkley Pub.

— Murder to Music. 1998. mass mkt. 5.99 (*0-425-16383-0*, Prime Crime) Berkley Pub.

— Senior Sleuths. 288p. (Orig.). 1996. mass mkt. 5.99 (*0-425-15258-8*) Berkley Pub.

— Win, Lose or Die. (Dead Letter Mysteries Ser.). 1997. mass mkt. 5.99 (*0-312-96092-1*) St Martin.

— Women of Mystery II. 1995. mass mkt. 5.99 (*0-425-15054-2*) Berkley Pub.

Manson, Cynthia, ed. Canine Crimes II. 224p. 1997. mass mkt. 5.99 (*0-425-16038-6*, Prime Crime) Berkley Pub.

— Death on the Verandah. 304p. 1995. mass mkt. 5.50 (*0-425-14836-X*, Prime Crime) Berkley Pub.

— Law & Order. 272p. 1997. mass mkt. 5.99 (*0-425-15781-4*, Prime Crime) Berkley Pub.

— Murder by the Book: Literary Mysteries from Alfred Hitchcock Mystery Magazine & Ellery Queen's Mystery Magazine. LC 96-156448. 304p. 1995. 21.95 (*0-7867-0250-8*) Carroll & Graf.

Manson, Cynthia & Manson, Kathleen, eds. Murder to Music: Musical Mysteries from Ellery Queen's Mystery Magazine & Alfred Hitchcock's Mystery Magazine. LC 97-517. 272p. 1997. 22.00 (*0-7867-0406-3*) Carroll & Graf.

Manson, Cynthia & Scarborough, Constance, eds. The Haunted Hour. 256p. (Orig.). 1995. mass mkt. 4.99 (*0-425-15010-0*, Prime Crime) Berkley Pub.

Manson, Cynthia, jt. ed. see Jordan, Cathleen.

Manson, Cynthia, jt. ed. see Sullivan, Eleanor.

Manson, Cynthia, jt. selected by see Williams, Sheila.

Manson, Dan W., ed. Alkaline Papermaking: A TAPPI Press Anthology of Published Papers 1993-1994. 176p. 1995. pap. 72.00 (*0-89852-292-7*, 0101R247) TAPPI.

Manson, Dan W., ed. see Technical Associaton of the Pulp & Paper Industry.

Manson, Edward, jt. ed. see MacDonell, John.

*__Manson, Florine S.__ When My Heart Speaks: A Collection of Unforgettable Thoughts. iv, 55p. 2000. pap. 7.95 (*0-9700627-0-2*) Carmenita Bks.

Manson, Frank A., jt. auth. see Cagle, Malcolm W.

Manson, G., jt. auth. see Cherryholmes, Cleo H.

Manson, Grant. Frank Lloyd Wright to 1910: The First Golden Age. 1958. pap. 39.95 (*0-442-26130-6*, VNR) Wiley.

Manson, Grant C. Frank Lloyd Wright to 1910: The First Golden Age. 256p. 1979. pap. 44.95 (*0-471-28940-X*, VNR) Wiley.

Manson-Hing, Lincoln R. Fundamentals of Dental Radiography. 3rd ed. LC 89-7971. (Illus.). 269p. 1989. pap. text 39.50 (*0-8121-1253-9*) Lppncott W & W.

Manson, J. D. & Eley, B. M. An Outline of Periodontics. 3rd ed. LC 95-7449. 320p. 1995. pap. text 60.00 (*0-7236-1018-5*) Buttrwrth-Heinemann.

Manson, Jane. Tales from the Cryptkeeper. (Illus.). 48p. (J). (ps-3). 1995. pap. 3.50 (*0-590-25088-4*) Scholastic Inc.

Manson, Janet M. Diplomatic Ramifications of Unrestricted Submarine Warfare, 1939-1941, 104. LC 90-34130. (Contributions in Military Studies Ser.: No. 104). 232p. 1990. 62.95 (*0-313-26894-0*, MGC, Greenwood Pr) Greenwood.

Manson, Janet M., jt. ed. see Chapman, Wayne K.

Manson, Joann E., et al, eds. Prevention of Myocardial Infraction. (Illus.). 584p. 1996. text 65.00 (*0-19-508582-5*) OUP.

Manson, Kathleen, jt. ed. see Manson, Cynthia.

Manson, Lionel A., jt. ed. see Kates, Morris.

Manson, M. P. Guns, Mortars & Rockets. LC 96-33619. (Land Warfare: Brassey's New Battlefield Weapons & Technology Ser.). (Illus.). 160p. 1996. 32.95 (*1-85753-172-8*, Pub. by Brasseys) Brasseys.

Manson, Marilyn. The Long Hard Road Out of Hell. LC ML420.M233A3 1998. 288p. 1998. 24.00 (*0-06-039258-4*) HarpC.

Manson, Marilyn & Strauss, Neil. The Long Hard Road Out of Hell. (Illus.). 288p. 1999. pap. 15.00 (*0-06-098746-4*, ReganBks) HarperTrade.

Manson, Nancy J. Sisters Together: Lessons Learned That Have Anchored Our Souls. 1998. pap. 14.95 (*0-9660306-5-6*) Nivek & Gould.

Manson-Perry, Hanna. Strung with Care: Timeless. 77p. 1996. pap. 17.50 (*0-9643885-3-7*) Personal Profiles.

Manson, R. Hunter, jt. auth. see Biernat, Len.

Manson, S., jt. auth. see Gray, I. H.

Manson, Spero M., et al, eds. Psychosocial Research on American Indian & Alaska Native Youth: An Indexed Guide to Recent Dissertations, 1. LC 84-6583. (Bibliographies & Indexes in Psychology Ser.: No. 1). (Illus.). 228p. 1984. lib. bdg. 65.00 (*0-313-23991-6*, MPY/) Greenwood.

Manson, Stuart, jt. auth. see Sheffield, Iain G.

Manson, Tony, jt. auth. see Duhon, Gwendolyn M.

Manson, Tony, jt. ed. see Duhon, Gwendolyn M.

Manson, William. Riddles of Eros: Exploring, Sex, Psyche & Culture. LC 93-38164. 128p. (Orig.). (C). 1994. pap. text 21.00 (*0-8191-9370-4*); lib. bdg. 42.00 (*0-8191-9369-0*) U Pr of Amer.

Manson, William C. The Psychodynamics of Culture: Abram Kardiner & Neo-Freudian Anthropology, 3. LC 88-17778. (Contributions to the Study of Anthropology Ser.: No. 3). 162p. 1988. 55.00 (*0-313-26267-5*, MDY/, Greenwood Pr) Greenwood.

Manson, William R. Bay. (YA). (gr. 6-12). 1997. pap. 8.00 (*0-9660099-0-8*) C C Publs.

— The Family Fun Book of Riddles & Problems: Knock Knock Jokes from A-Z. 51p. 1998. pap. 3.95 (*0-9660099-4-0*) C C Publs.

— Handbook of African American History. (J). (gr. 1-12). 1997. pap. 4.00 (*0-9660099-1-6*) C C Publs.

— Short Stories: For Children of All Ages. (Illus.). 58p. 1998. pap. 3.95 (*0-9660099-2-4*) C C Publs.

Manson, William R. & Peale, C. George, eds. El Conde Don Pero Velez y Don Sancho el Deseado. (SPA.). 241p. 1997. pap. text 17.95 (*1-879853-46-9*) CA St Full Pr.

— Don Pedro Miago. (SPA.). 206p. 1997. pap. text 17.95 (*1-879853-45-0*) CA St Full Pr.

— El Espejo del Mundo. (SPA.). 234p. 1997. pap. text 17.95 (*1-879853-44-2*) CA St Full Pr.

— La Serrana de la Vera. (SPA.). 252p. 1997. pap. text 17.95 (*1-879853-49-3*) CA St Full Pr.

Mansoor, Ali M., jt. auth. see Hemming, Richard.

Mansoor, Menaham. Key to Biblical Hebrew Step by Step, Vol. 2. 64p. 1985. pap. 7.99 (*0-8010-6182-2*) Baker Bks.

Mansoor, Menahem. Biblical Hebrew Step by Step, 1. 2nd ed. 260p. 1978. pap. 22.99 (*0-8010-6041-9*) Baker Bks.

— Biblical Hebrew Step by Step: Readings from the Book of Genesis, 2. 3rd ed. 192p. 1984. pap. 19.99 (*0-8010-6151-2*) Baker Bks.

— Contemporary Hebrew. LC 75-1813. 1976. pap. text 15.95 (*0-87441-251-X*) Behrman.

— Easy Hebrew Phrase Book: Over 770 Basic Phrases for Every Day Use. LC 94-43467. 80p. 1995. pap. text 1.50 (*0-486-28556-1*) Dover.

— Jewish History & Thought: An Introduction. 591p. 1992. 39.50 (*0-88125-403-7*, 91-34985); pap. 19.95 (*0-88125-404-5*) Ktav.

— Key to Biblical Hebrew Step by Step. Vol. 1. 82p. (gr. 13). 1986. pap. 10.99 (*0-8010-6100-8*) Baker Bks.

*__Mansoor, Peter R.__ The GI Offensive in Europe: The Triumph of American Infantry Divisions, 1941-1945. LC 98-55249. (Modern War Studies). (Illus.). 360p. 1999. 35.00 (*0-7006-0958-X*) U Pr of KS.

Mansoori, G. Ali. Thermodynamics: The Application of Classical & Statistical Thermodynamics to the Prediction of Equilibrium Properties. (Advances in Thermodynamics Ser.: Vol. 8). 300p. 1991. 41.00 (*0-8448-1681-7*, Crane Russak) Taylor & Francis.

Mansoori, G. Ali & Chorn, Larry, eds. C Seven Plus Fraction Characterization. (Advances in Thermodynamics Ser.). (Illus.). 240p. (C). 1989. text 115.00 (*0-8448-1565-9*) Taylor & Francis.

Mansoori, G. Ali & Matteoli, Enrico, eds. Fluctuation Theory of Mixtures. (Advances in Thermodynamics Ser.: Vol. 2). 350p. 1990. 115.00 (*0-8448-1630-2*, Crane Russak) Taylor & Francis.

Mansoori, G. Ali, jt. ed. see Haile, J. M.

Mansor, Scott, jt. auth. see Long, David.

Mansour, jt. auth. see Dezilwa.

Mansour, Antoine & Mansour, Claire. Our Lady of Soufanieh: And Other Phenomena. 101p. 1991. pap. 8.00 (*1-890137-24-3*) One Hund-One Fnd.

Mansour, Awad & Rumman, Ali. A Journey to the World of Computers: A Computer Reader for Kids. Dabbour, Mohammed M., tr. from ARA. LC 94-71602. (Illus.). 48p. (J). (gr. 2-6). 1995. 14.95 (*1-884187-06-4*) AMICA Pub Hse.

Mansour, Camille. Beyond Alliance: Israel in U. S. Foreign Policy. LC 93-28046. 1994. 46.00 (*0-231-08492-7*) Col U Pr.

Mansour, Claire, jt. auth. see Mansour, Antoine.

*__Mansour, D.__ The Facts of Contraception. 2001. 35.00 (*1-84214-007-8*) Prthnon Pub.

Mansour, Fawzy. The Arab World: Nation, State & Democracy. Wolfers, Michael, tr. LC 90-47485. (Studies in African Political Economy). 176p. (C). 1992. pap. 19.95 (*0-86232-885-3*, Pub. by St Martin); text 55.00 (*0-86232-884-5*, Pub. by St Martin) St Martin.

Mansour, Gerda. Multilingualism & Nation Building. LC 92-31458. (Multilingual Matters Ser.: No. 91). 1993. 74.95 (*1-85359-175-0*, Pub. by Multilingual Matters); pap. 29.95 (*1-85359-174-2*, Pub. by Multilingual Matters) Taylor & Francis.

Mansour, Jane A., ed. see Nature Conservancy Staff.

Mansour, Jane A., jt. ed. see Redford, Kent H.

Mansour, Joyce. Screams. Gavronsky, Serge, tr. from FRE. & intro. by. 100p. (Orig.). 1995. pap. 10.00 (*0-942996-25-9*) Post Apollo Pr.

— Torn Apart - Dechirures LC 98-74576. 96p. 1999. write for info. (*0-9664358-0-X*) Bitter Oleander.

Mansour, M., et al, eds. Robustness of Dynamic Systems with Parameter Uncertainties. LC 92-27728. (Monte Verita Ser.). ix, 315p. 1992. 87.00 (*0-8176-2791-X*) Birkhauser.

Mansour, M., jt. auth. see Jeltsch, Rolf.

Mansour, M., jt. ed. see Jeltsch, Rolf.

Mansour, M., jt. ed. see Schweitzer, G. E.

Mansour, Mansour H. The Maliki School of Law: Spread & Domination in North & West Africa, 8th-14th Centuries. 197p. 1995. 64.95 (*1-880921-81-2*); pap. 44.95 (*1-880921-80-4*) Austin & Winfield.

Mansour, Mohammed. Pesticide Prediction in Soils, Plants, & Aquatic Systems. 304p. 1993. lib. bdg. 110.00 (*0-87371-616-7*, L616) Lewis Pubs.

Mansour, Monica, tr. see Cazarre, Lourenco.

Mansour, Monica, tr. see Cost, Marco T.

Mansour, Monica, tr. see Doherty, Berlie.

Mansour, Monica, tr. see Kelly, Chris.

Mansour, Monica, tr. see Leeson, Robert.

Mansour, Monica, tr. see Machado, Ana M.

Mansouri, F. & Scanio, J. J. Quantum Gravity & Beyond: Essays in Honor of Louis Witten on His Retirement. 392p. 1993. text 116.00 (*981-02-1290-9*) World Scientific Pub.

Mansouri, Lofti & Layton, Aviva. Lotfi Mansouri: An Operatic Life. (Illus.). 140p. 1994. 19.95 (*0-88962-179-9*) Mosaic.

Mansourov, Alexandre, jt. auth. see Moltz, James C.

Mansourov, Alexandre, jt. ed. see Moltz, James.

Manspeaker, Nancy. Jonathan Edwards: Bibliographical Synopses. LC 81-9491. (Studies in American Religion: Vol. 3). (Illus.). xviii, 278p. 1981. lib. bdg. 89.95 (*0-88946-907-5*) E Mellen.

Manspeizer, W., ed. Triassic-Jurassic Rifting: Continental Breakup & the Origin of the Atlantic Passive Margins, 2 vols. (Developments in Geotectonics Ser.: No. 22). 998p. 1989. 519.75 (*0-444-42903-4*) Elsevier.

Mansson, Sven-Axel. Cultural Conflict & the Swedish Sexual Myth: The Male Immigrant's Encounter with Swedish Sexual & Cohabitation Culture, 107. LC 93-10324. (Contributions in Sociology Ser.: No. 107). 248p. 1993. 65.00 (*0-313-28920-4*, GM8920, Greenwood Pr) Greenwood.

Manstavicius, E. & Schweiger, F., eds. Analytic & Probabilistic Methods in Number Theory. (New Trends in Probability & Statistics Ser.: No. 2). 400p. 1992. 225.00 (*90-6764-094-8*) Coronet Bks.

Manstead, Anthony S., ed. see Ajzen, Icek.

Manstead, Anthony S., ed. see Coupland, N. & Giles, Howard.

Manstead, Anthony S., ed. see Duck, Steve.

Manstead, Anthony S., ed. see Eiser, J. Richard.

Manstead, Anthony S., ed. see Geen, Russell G.

Manstead, Anthony S., jt. ed. see Hewstone, Miles.

Manstead, Anthony S., ed. see Miller, Norman & Brewer, Marilynn B.

Manstead, Anthony S., ed. see Miller, Norman, et al.

Manstead, Anthony S., ed. see Pruitt, Dean G. & Carnevale, Peter J.

Manstead, Anthony S., ed. see Stroebe, Wolfgang & Stroebe, Margaret.

Manstead, Anthony S., ed. see Turner, John C.

Manstead, Anthony S., jt. ed. see Wagner, Hugh L.

Manstead, Anthony S., ed. see Zebrowitz, Leslie.

Manston, Peter B. Manston's Flea Markets, Antique Fairs & Auctions of France. LC 86-30909. (Manston's Travel Key Guide Ser.). (Illus.). 196p. 1987. 9.95 (*0-931367-06-9*) Travel Keys.

— Manston's Flea Markets, Antique Fairs & Auctions of Germany. LC 86-30908. (Illus.). 224p. 1987. pap. 9.95 (*0-931367-08-5*) Travel Keys.

— Manston's Italy. (Illus.). 352p. 1990. pap. 10.95 (*0-931367-12-3*) Travel Keys.

— Manston's Travel Key Britain. LC 89-4488. (Illus.). 384p. (Orig.). 1996. pap. 9.95 (*0-931367-11-5*) Travel Keys.

Mansueto, Anthony E., Jr. Towards Synergism: The Cosmic Significance of the Human Civilizational Project. 552p. (Orig.). (C). Date not set. lib. bdg. 67.50 (*0-7618-0083-2*) U Pr of Amer.

— Towards Synergism: The Cosmic Significance of the Human Civilizational Project. 552p. (Orig.). (C). 1995. pap. text 39.50 (*0-7618-0084-0*) U Pr of Amer.

Mansuetti, Leland & Weidkamp, Keith. Granite Bay Jet Ski, Inc. A Computerized Business Simulation. 3rd ed. 1997. pap. 29.75 (*0-07-561062-0*, Irwn McGrw-H) McGrw-H Hghr Educ.

— Thunder Mountain Snowmobile. (C). 1994. text 28.50 incl. 3.5 hd (*0-256-17251-X*, Irwn McGrw-H) McGrw-H Hghr Educ.

— Thunder Mountain Snowmobile. 2nd ed. 96p. (C). 1995. text, student ed. 29.75 incl. 3.5 ld (*0-256-17809-7*, Irwn McGrw-H) McGrw-H Hghr Educ.

Mansuetti-Weidk. Granite Bay Jet Ski 1. 2nd ed. 1993. pap. 30.94 incl. disk (*0-256-15772-3*) McGraw-Hill Prof.

— Granite Bay Jet Ski 2. 2nd ed. 1995. pap. 30.94 incl. disk (*0-256-15892-4*, Irwn Prfssnl) McGraw-Hill Prof.

Mansukhani, Gobind S., jt. auth. see Dogra, Ramesh C.

Mansum, C. J. Elsevier's Dictionary of Building Construction. (DUT, ENG, FRE & GER.). 472p. 1985. reprint ed. 250.00 (*0-8288-9297-0*, M7920) Fr & Eur.

Mansum, C. J. Van, see Van Mansum, C. J.

Mansur. Moot Corporation. 332p. 1996. pap. text, per. 34.95 (*0-7872-2761-7*) Kendall-Hunt.

*__Mansur, Ahsan S. & Treichel, Volker.__ Oman Beyond the Oil Horizon: Policies Toward Sustainable Growth. LC 99-52694. (Occasional Paper Ser.). 1999. write for info. (*1-55775-833-6*) Intl Monetary.

Mansur, C. W. What May Be Expected from Non-Metallic Gears? (Technical Papers: Vol. P109). (Illus.). 16p. 1931. pap. text 30.00 (*1-55589-323-6*) AGMA.

Mansur, Salim, jt. auth. see Choudhry, Nanda K.

Mansur, Yusuf M. Fuzzy Sets & Economics: Applications of Fuzzy Mathematics to Non-Cooperative Oligopoly. LC 94-34104. 208p. 1995. 80.00 (*1-85898-206-5*) E Elgar.

Mansuri, L. A., jt. auth. see Jhala, C. I.

Mansuripur, Masud. The Physical Principles of Magneto-Optical Recording. LC 93-48553. (Illus.). 776p. (C). 1995. text 115.00 (*0-521-46124-3*) Cambridge U Pr.

— The Physical Principles of Magneto-Optical Recording. (Illus.). 776p. (C). 1998. pap. text 54.95 (*0-521-63418-0*) Cambridge U Pr.

Mansurov, Z. A., jt. ed. see Akovali, G.

Mansuy, Neil. Water Well Rehabilitation: A Practical Guide to Understanding Well Problems & Solutions. LC 98-44337. (Sustainable Wells Ser.). 174p. 1999. 59.95 (*1-56670-387-5*) Lewis Pubs.

Mansvelt-Beck, B. J. The Treatises of Later Han: Their Author, Sources, Contents & Place in Chinese Historiography. LC 90-2156. (Sinica Leidensia Ser.: Vol. 21). xii, 296p. 1990. pap. 80.00 (*90-04-08895-4*) Brill Academic Pubs.

*__Mant.__ Quality Use of Medicines. (Illus.). 160p. 1999. 34.95 (*0-07-470769-8*, McGrw-H College) McGrw-H Hghr Educ.

Mant, C. T., jt. auth. see Hodges, R. S.

Mant, Gilbert, ed. Soldier Boy: The Letters & Memoirs of Gunner W. J. Duffell 1915-1918. 192p. 1993. 24.95 (*0-86417-429-2*, Pub. by Kangaroo Pr); pap. 14.95 (*0-86417-418-7*, Pub. by Kangaroo Pr) Seven Hills Bk.

Mant, Gilblert. Massacre at Parit Sulong. 1996. pap. text 16.95 (*0-86417-732-1*, Pub. by Kangaroo Pr) Seven Hills Bk.

Mant, Joan. All Muck, No Medals: Personal Accounts of Life in the Women's Land Army During WWII. large type ed. (Reminiscence Ser.). 22.95 (*1-85695-069-7*, Pub. by ISIS Lrg Prnt) Transaction Pubs.

Mant, Richard. The Simpliciad, 1808. LC 91-3947. (Revolution & Romanticism Ser.). 62p. 1991. reprint ed. 35.00 (*1-85477-076-4*) Continuum.

Manta, Joseph, jt. auth. see West, Gordon.

Mantabel, P. A 1 Photography: Practical Set. 2nd ed. 1992. pap. text 33.60 (*0-13-014754-0*) S&S Trade.

Mantai, Kenneth E. A Field Guide to the Aquatic Life of Chautauqua County. (Marginal Media Bioguide Ser.: No. 5). (Illus.). 48p. 1983. pap. 3.00 (*0-942788-10-9*) Iris Visual.

Mantaras, Ramon L. De, see De Mantaras, Ramon L.

Mantaras, Ramon Lopez de, see Lopez de Mantaras, Ramon.

Mantas, J., ed. Advances in Health Telematics Education: A Nightingale Perspective. (Studies in Health Technology & Informatics: Vol. 51). 257p. 1998. 70.00 (*90-5199-389-7*, Pub. by IOS Pr) IOS Press.

Manteau-Bonamy, H. M. Immaculate Conception & the Holy Spirit: The Marian Teachings of Father Kolbe. 2nd ed. Geiger, Bernard M., ed. Arnandez, Richard, tr. from FRE. LC 77-93104.Tr. of Doctrine mariale du Pere Kolbe, Esprit-Saint et Conception Immaculee. (Illus.). 172p. 1992. reprint ed. pap. 6.00 (*0-913382-00-0*, 101-20) Marytown Pr.

Mantegazza, Giovanna. The Hippopotamus. LC 91-73871. (Illus.). 12p. (J). (ps-1). 1992. bds. 6.95 (*1-56397-033-3*) Boyds Mills Pr.

Mantegazzini. The Environmental Risks from Biotechnology. 1992. text 47.50 (*0-86187-658-X*, Pub. by P P Pubs) Cassell & Continuum.

M

Mantegna, Gian F. & High, Steven. Oneiric Threshold: An Installation by Alastair Noble. 1993. 5.00 (*0-935519-16-5*) Anderson Gal.

Mantegna, Rosario M. & Stanley, H. Eugene. An Introduction to Econophysics: Correlations & Complexity in Finance. LC 99-28047. (Illus.). 180p. (C). 1999. 34.95 (*0-521-62008-2*) Cambridge U Pr.

Manteiga, Robert C. The Poetry of Rafael Alberti: A Visual Approach. (Monografias A Ser.: Vol. LXXV). 130p. (C). 1978. 51.00 (*0-7293-0069-2*, Pub. by Tamesis Bks Ltd) Boydell & Brewer.

Manteiga, Roberto C., et al, eds. Feminine Concerns in Contemporary Spanish Fiction by Women. 186p. 35.00 (*0-916379-49-3*) Scripta.

Mantel, Chana. Lidingo. 243p. 1998. 19.95 (*0-87306-880-7*) Feldheim.

Mantel, Gerhard. Cello Technique: Principles & Forms of Movement. Thiem, Barbara H., tr. LC 75-313279. 256p. 1995. pap. 16.95 (*0-253-21005-4*) Ind U Pr.

Mantel, Herman & Mantel, Hugo. Mantel's Folks Redner: Mantel's Sermons & Address in Yiddish Language for All Jewish Holidays & Many Other Occasions. (ENG & YID.). 320p. 27.50 (*0-87559-148-5*) Shalom.

Mantel, Hilary. A Change of Climate. 354p. 1994. 22.00 (*0-689-12201-2*) Atheneum Yung Read.

— A Change of Climate. LC 96-39843. 320p. 1997. pap. 12.00 (*0-8050-5205-4*, Owl) H Holt & Co.

— Every Day Is Mother's Day. LC 99-33537. 225p. (Orig.). 2000. pap. 13.00 (*0-8050-6272-6*, Owl) H Holt & Co.

— An Experiment in Love. LC 95-33666. 88p. 1995. 23.00 (*0-8050-4427-2*) H Holt & Co.

— An Experiment in Love. 256p. 1997. pap. 12.00 (*0-8050-5202-X*, Owl) H Holt & Co.

***Mantel, Hilary.** Fludd: A Novel. LC 99-49485. 181p. 2000. pap. 13.00 (*0-8050-6273-4*) H Holt & Co.

Mantel, Hilary. The Giant, O'Brien: A Novel. 192p. 1999. pap. text 12.00 (*0-8050-6295-5*, Owl) H Holt & Co.

— The Giant, O'Brien: A Novel. LC 98-10701. 192p. 1998. text 22.00 (*0-8050-4428-0*) St Martin.

— The Giant, O'Brien: A Novel. large type ed. 1999. 28.95 (*0-7862-1797-9*) Mac Lib Ref.

— A Place of Greater Safety. LC 98-26688. 768p. 1998. pap. 15.00 (*0-8050-5204-6*) St Martin.

***Mantel, Hilary.** Vacant Possession. LC 99-33536. 242p. (Orig.). 2000. pap. 13.00 (*0-8050-6271-8*, Owl) H Holt & Co.

Mantel, Hugo. Studies in the History of the Sanhedrin. LC 61-7391. (Harvard Semitic Studies: No. 17). 392p. 1961. reprint ed. pap. 121.60 (*0-7837-4121-9*, 205794400011) Bks Demand.

Mantel, Hugo, jt. auth. see Mantel, Herman.

Mantel, Linda H., jt. ed. see Bliss, Dorothy E.

***Mantel, O. C.** Mesoscopic Charge Density Wave Wires. (Illus.). 118p. 1999. pap. 39.50 (*90-407-1888-1*, Pub. by Delft U Pr) Coronet Bks.

Mantel, Samuel J., jt. auth. see Meredith, Jack R.

Mantell, Charles L. Solid Wastes: Origin, Collection, Processing, & Disposal. LC 74-26930. (Illus.). 1145p. reprint ed. pap. 200.00 (*0-608-18198-6*, 205660200078) Bks Demand.

— Tin: Its Mining, Production, Technology, & Applications. 2nd ed. LC 29-22211. (ACS Monograph: No. 51). 1949. 47.95 (*0-8412-0257-5*) Am Chemical.

Mantell, Charles L., jt. auth. see Galanti, Anthony V.

Mantell, David M. True Americanism: Green Berets & War Resisters; a Study of Commitment. LC 74-2230. (Foresight Books in Psychology). (Illus.). 293p. 1974. reprint ed. pap. 90.90 (*0-7837-8947-5*, 204965800002) Bks Demand.

Mantell, Gideon A. The Medals of Creation: Or, First Lessons in Geology & the Study of Organic Remains, 2 vols., Set. 2nd rev. ed. Gould, Stephen Jay, ed. LC 79-8334. (History of Paleontology Ser.). (Illus.). 1980. reprint ed. lib. bdg. 88.95 (*0-405-12716-2*) Ayer.

— The Medals of Creation: Or, First Lessons in Geology & the Study of Organic Remains, 2 vols., Vol. 1. 2nd rev. ed. Gould, Stephen Jay, ed. LC 79-8334. (History of Paleontology Ser.). (Illus.). 1980. reprint ed. lib. bdg. 44.95 (*0-405-12717-0*) Ayer.

— The Medals of Creation: Or, First Lessons in Geology & the Study of Organic Remains, 2 vols., Vol. 2. 2nd rev. ed. Gould, Stephen Jay, ed. LC 79-8334. (History of Paleontology Ser.). (Illus.). 1980. reprint ed. lib. bdg. 44.95 (*0-405-12718-9*) Ayer.

Mantell, Joanne E., et al. Evaluating HIV Prevention Interventions. LC 96-53003. (Volume in AIDS Prevention & Mental Health Ser.). (Illus.). 310p. (C). 1997. text 45.00 (*0-306-45476-9*, Kluwer Plenum) Kluwer Academic.

Mantell, Laurie. Murder & Chips. large type ed. 368p. 1989. 27.99 (*0-7089-2028-4*) Ulverscroft.

— Murder in Vain. large type ed. 357p. 1989. 27.99 (*0-7089-1978-2*) Ulverscroft.

— Murder to Burn. large type ed. (Linford Romance Library). 368p. 1987. pap. 16.99 (*0-7089-6391-9*, Linford) Ulverscroft.

Mantell, Matthew E., jt. auth. see Maffetone, Philip.

Mantell, Michael. Ticking Bombs: Defusing Violence in the Workplace. LC 93-44770. 300p. 1994. text 27.00 (*0-7863-0189-9*, Irwn Prfssnl) McGraw-Hill Prof.

Mantell, Michael A., ed. Managing National Park System Resources: A Handbook on Legal Duties, Opportunities & Tools. LC 89-20993. 286p. 1990. reprint ed. pap. 88.70 (*0-608-04186-6*, 206492100011) Bks Demand.

Mantell, Michael A. & Harper, Stephen. Creating Successful Communities: A Guidebook to Growth Management Strategies. LC 89-15473. (Illus.). 230p. (Orig.). 1989. pap. text 29.95 (*1-55963-014-0*) Island Pr.

***Mantell, Paul.** The Man in the Iron Mask. (Bullseye Step into Classics Ser.). (J). 1998. 9.09 (*0-606-13965-6*, Pub. by Turtleback) Demco.

Mantell, Paul, jt. auth. see Hart, Avery.

Mantell, Paul, jt. auth. see Tk.

Mantell, Susan C., jt. ed. see Ciriscioli, Peter R.

Mantell, Suzanne. Vermont: The Spirit of America State-by-State. Landau, Diana, ed. LC 98-3999. (Art of the State Ser.). (Illus.). 96p. 1998. 12.95 (*0-8109-5556-3*, Pub. by Abrams) Time Warner.

Mantellini, Rafael, tr. see D'Annunzio, Gabriele.

Mantello, F., ed. see Grosseteste, Robert.

Mantello, F. A. & Rigg, A. G., eds. Medieval Latin: An Introduction & Bibliographical Guide. LC 95-11339. 774p. 1996. pap. 44.95 (*0-8132-0842-4*) Cath U Pr.

Manten, A. A. Symposia & Symposium Publications: A Guide for Organisers, Lecturers, & Editors of Scientific Meetings. LC 76-837. (Illus.). 176p. reprint ed. pap. 54.60 (*0-608-10770-0*, 205167700002) Bks Demand.

Manten, A. A., jt. auth. see Hulshof, O.

***Manterfield, Richard J.** Telecommunications Signalling. (IEE Telecommunications Ser.: No. 43). 448p. 1999. boxed set 89.00 (*0-85296-761-6*) INSPEC Inc.

Manternach, Janaan & Pfeifer, Carl. Creative Catechist. rev. ed. LC 91-90951. 160p. 1991. pap. 14.95 (*0-89622-490-2*) Twenty-Third.

Manternach, Janaan & Pfeifer, Carl J. How to Be a Better Catechist: Answers to Questions Catechists Ask Most. LC 89-61927. 112p. (Orig.). 1989. pap. 5.95 (*1-55612-268-3*) Sheed & Ward WI.

Manternach, Janaan, et al. The Living Light Vol. 33, No. 2, Winter 1996: Curriculum & Content in Catechesis. 96p. (Orig.). (C). 1996. pap. 8.95 (*1-57455-096-9*) US Catholic.

Manternach, Janaan, jt. auth. see Pfeifer, Carl J.

Mantero, Manuel & Craige, Betty J. Manuel Mantero: New Songs for the Ruins of Spain. LC 84-46101. 120p. 1986. 29.50 (*0-8387-5094-X*) Bucknell U Pr.

Manteuffel, Tadeusz. The Formation of the Polish State: The Period of Ducal Rule. LC 81-11583. 173p. reprint ed. pap. 53.70 (*0-608-16048-2*, 203317800084) Bks Demand.

Mantey, J. R., jt. auth. see Dana, H. E.

Mantha, John, jt. auth. see Hancock, Pat.

Manthe, George L. Inside Dope. (Illus.). 177p. 1984. 15.95 (*0-911603-00-X*); pap. 9.95 (*0-911603-01-8*) Rube Pubns.

Manthei, George. A Gourmet's Fables & Fare. Taylor, Vernon, ed. (Illus.). 140p. 1994. pap. 9.95 (*1-878816-00-4*) Schildge Pub.

— Wild & Famous Fish & Game Cookbook. Taylor, Vernon, ed. (Illus.). 140p. 1992. spiral bd. 9.95 (*1-878816-01-2*) Schildge Pub.

Manthei, R. J. Counselling: The Skills of Finding Solutions to Problems. 2nd ed. LC 97-30747. 192p. (C). 1997. pap. write for info. (*0-415-16206-8*) Routledge.

Manthey, Cynthia M. Pre-K Math: Concepts from Global Sources. LC 95-51841. (Illus.). 162p. (Orig.). 1996. lib. bdg. 29.95 (*0-89334-246-7*, 2477054, Humanics Lrng) Humanics Ltd.

— With Respect for Others: Activities for a Global Neighborhood. LC 95-21242. (Illus.). 160p. (Orig.). 1995. lib. bdg. 28.95 (*0-89334-247-5*, 2475054) Humanics Ltd.

— With Respect, Vol. 1P: Successful Primary Theme Activities. 100p. (J). (ps-1). 1992. pap. text 11.95 (*0-9634651-0-4*); audio 9.95 (*0-9634651-1-2*) Qual Instruct.

Manthey, F. Die Sprachphilosophie des Hl. Thomas Von Aquin. (Philosophy Reprints Ser.). (GER.). reprint ed. lib. bdg. 48.00 (*0-697-00042-7*) Irvington.

Manthey, John. Chemistry & Biochemistry of Plant Nutrition. 384p. 1994. lib. bdg. 120.00 (*0-87371-942-5*, L942) Lewis Pubs.

Manthey, John & Buslig, Bela, eds. Flavonoids in the Living System: Proceedings of an American Chemical Society Symposium Held in Orlando, Florida, August 28-29. LC 98-8317. (Advances in Experimental Medicine & Biology Ser.: Vol. 439). (Illus.). 286p. 1998. 95.00 (*0-306-45905-1*, Kluwer Plenum) Kluwer Academic.

Manthey, Marie. The Practice of Primary Nursing. LC 79-92975. 96p. 1980. 10.00 (*1-886624-10-0*, B240) Creative Nursing.

Manthey, R. & Wolfengagen, V., eds. Advances in Databases & Information Systems: Proceedings of the 1st East-European Symposium on Advances in Databases & Information Systems (ADBIS '97), St. Petersburg, 2-5 September, 1997: Online Version. (Electronic Workshops in Computing Ser.). viii, 24p. 1998. 49.95 (*3-540-76227-2*) Spr-Verlag.

Manthey-Zorn, Otto, tr. see Kant, Immanuel.

Manthorne, Jackie. Final Take: A Harriet Hubbley Mystery. 192p. 1996. pap. 10.95 (*0-921881-41-X*, Pub. by Gynergy-Ragweed) U of Toronto Pr.

— Last Resort: A Harriet Hubbley Mystery, Vol. 3. LC 96-121518. 192p. 1995. per. 10.95 (*0-921881-34-7*, Pub. by Gynergy-Ragweed) U of Toronto Pr.

— Sudden Death. LC 97-180260. 92p. 1997. pap. text 10.95 (*0-921881-43-6*, Pub. by Gynergy-Ragweed) U of Toronto Pr.

Manthorne, Katherine E. The Landscapes of Louis Remy Mignot: A Southern Painter Abroad. (Illus.). 256p. 1996. 55.00 (*1-56098-701-4*) Smithsonian.

Manthorpe, Jill. Social Policy: Nurses & Patients. 224p. (C). (gr. 13). 1999. 75.00 (*0-415-16158-4*, D6313) Routledge.

— Social Policy in a Changing Society. 2nd ed. 224p. (C). 1998. pap. 24.99 (*0-415-16541-5*) Routledge.

Manthorpe, Jill & Atherton, Celia. Grandparent's Rights. (C). 1989. 35.00 (*0-86242-079-2*, Pub. by Age Concern Eng) St Mut.

Manthorpe, Jill, et al. Social Policy: Nurses & Patients. (Illus.). 224p. (C). (gr. 13). 1999. pap. 24.99 (*0-415-16159-2*, D6317) Routledge.

Manthorpe, Victoria. Children of the Empire: The Victorian Haggards. (Illus.). 224p. 1996. 45.00 (*0-575-06311-4*, Pub. by V Gollancz) Trafalgar.

Manthorpe, Victoria, ed. see Smith, Richard G.

Manthy, Robert S. Natural Resource Commodities: A Century of Statistics, Prices, Output, Consumption, Foreign Trade & Employment in the U. S., 1870-1973. LC 78-8429. (Resources for the Future Ser.). 1978. text 25.00 (*0-8018-2142-8*) Johns Hopkins.

— Natural Resource Commodities: A Century of Statistics: Prices, Output, Consumption, Foreign Trade, & Employment in the United States, 1870-1973. Tron, Joan R., ed. LC 78-8429. 254p. reprint ed. pap. 78.80 (*0-8357-4682-8*, 203762900008) Bks Demand.

Mantia, F. P. La, see La Mantia, F. P., ed.

Mantice, Jim. Bug Off! Fifty Simple Ways to Protect Yourself from Burglars, Thieves, Muggers, Con-Artists, & Other Lowlifes. (Illus.). 96p. (Orig.). 1992. pap. 5.95 (*0-9631380-0-6*) Walnut Grove Pubs.

Mantin, Peter. The Islamic World: Beliefs & Civilization, 600-1600. (J). 1996. pap. 9.95 (*0-614-21019-4*, 1440) Kazi Pubns.

Mantin, Peter & Mantin, Ruth. The Islamic World: Beliefs & Civilization, 600-1600. (Cambridge History Programme Ser.). (Illus.). 64p. (C). 1993. pap. 13.95 (*0-521-40609-9*) Cambridge U Pr.

Mantin, Peter & Pulley, R. Investigation Sources. (Hutchinson History Ser.). 96p. (C). 1989. pap. 12.95 (*0-09-182339-0*) Dufour.

Mantin, Peter & Pulley, Richard. Medicine Through the Ages. 2nd ed. (Key History for GCSE Ser.). (Illus.). 112p. 1996. pap. 19.95 (*0-7487-3026-5*, Pub. by S Thornes Pubs) Trans-Atl Phila.

— The Roman World: From Republic to Empire. (Cambridge History Programme Ser.). (Illus.). 80p. (YA). (gr. 6 up). 1993. pap. 14.95 (*0-521-40608-0*) Cambridge U Pr.

Mantin, Ruth, jt. auth. see Mantin, Peter.

Mantinband, James H. Dictionary of Greek Literature. (Quality Paperback Ser.: No. 145). 409p. 1966. reprint ed. pap. 12.95 (*0-8226-0145-1*) Littlefield.

— Dictionary of Latin Literature. (Quality Paperback Ser.: No. 152). 303p. 1964. reprint ed. pap. 9.95 (*0-8226-0152-4*) Littlefield.

Mantione, Denise A. Chatty Hats & Other Props. (Illus.). 148p. 1990. teacher ed. 22.95 (*0-937857-17-3*, 1581) Speech Bin.

— Speech-Language In-Services for Colleagues in Education (SLICE) 112p. 1992. 24.95 (*0-937857-33-5*, 1510) Speech Bin.

***Mantis, C. M.** The World According to Dad: A Manual for the Good Life. LC 99-95479. 152p. 1999. 16.95 (*0-9672875-1-0*); pap. 10.95 (*0-9672875-0-2*) Lindos Bks.

Mantis, Hillary J. Careers in Law Companion. 1997. pap. 15.00 (*0-679-77870-5*) Random.

Mantis, Hillary J & Brady, Kathleen. Jobs for Lawyers: Effective Techniques for Getting Hired in Today's Legal Marketplace. 208p. 1996. pap. 14.95 (*1-57023-054-4*) Impact VA.

Mantis, William C. The $50, 5 Hour Canoe Sail Rig: A Complete Builder/User/Experimenter/Historical Guide & Phi. Trost, Christine, ed. (Illus.). 106p. 1999. pap. 9.95 (*0-9673233-0-4*) Meditrean Ave Pr.

Mantissa Computer Based Training Staff. Trade Tutor: Import Export. 80p. 1997. pap. 695.00 incl. disk (*1-901506-01-0*) Thomson Learn.

Mantius, Peter. Shell Game: A True Story of Banking, Spies, Lies, Politics - And the Arming of Saddam Hussein. (Illus.). 288p. 1999. text 24.00 (*0-7881-6167-9*) DIANE Pub.

— Shell Game: A True Story of Banking, Spies, Lies, Politics - And the Arming of Saddam Hussein. LC 95-8564. 304p. 1995. 23.95 (*0-312-13169-0*, Picador USA) St Martin.

Mantle, Burns, ed. The Best Plays of 1919-1920. LC 75-19860. (Best Plays Series). 1978. 30.95 (*0-405-09168-0*) Ayer.

— The Best Plays of 1928-1929. LC 75-19860. (Best Plays Series). 1976. 30.95 (*0-405-09169-9*) Ayer.

— The Best Plays of 1929-1930. LC 75-19860. (Best Plays Series). 1975. 30.95 (*0-405-09170-2*) Ayer.

— The Best Plays of 1930-1931. LC 75-19860. (Best Plays Series). 1977. 30.95 (*0-405-09171-0*) Ayer.

— The Best Plays of 1938-1939. LC 75-19860. (Best Plays Series). 1977. 30.95 (*0-405-09174-5*) Ayer.

Mantle, Gregory & Baer, Mervin J. The Way of the Cross. 128p. 1993. 63.95 (*0-7399-0219-9*, 2460) Rod & Staff.

***Mantle, Jill & Polden, Margaret.** BH Mars Physiotherapy in Obstetrics & Gynaecology. (Illus.). 2000. pap. text 220.00 (*0-7506-4291-2*) Buttrwrth-Heinemann.

Mantle, Jonathan. Car Wars: Fifty Years of Greed, Treachery & Skulduggery in the Global Marketplace. (Illus.). 256p. 1996. 24.45 (*1-55970-333-4*, Pub. by Arcade Pub Inc) Time Warner.

— Car Wars: Fifty Years of Greed, Treachery & Skulduggery in the Global Marketplace. LC 95-53184. (Illus.). 272p. 1997. pap. 13.45 (*1-55970-400-4*, Pub. by Arcade Pub Inc) Time Warner.

Mantle, Margaret. Some Just Clap Their Hands: Raising a Handicapped Child. LC 85-15026. 264p. 1985. 16.95 (*0-915361-24-8*, 097331) Lambda Pubs.

Mantle, Mickey & Creamer, Robert W. The Quality of Courage: Heroes in & Out of Baseball. LC 98-31558. 185p. 1999. pap. 9.95 (*0-8032-8259-1*, Bison Books) U of Nebr Pr.

Mantle, Mickey & Gluck, Herb. The Mick. 288p. 1986. mass mkt. 5.99 (*0-515-08599-5*, Jove) Berkley Pub.

Mantle, Mickey, jt. auth. see Early, Lewis.

Mantle, Philip & Nagaitis, Carl. Without Consent: A Comprehensive Survey of Missing-Time & Abduction Phenomena. LC 98-43990. 1999. pap. text 12.95 (*1-56924-720-X*) Marlowe & Co.

Mantle, Philip, jt. auth. see Hesemann, Michael.

***Mantle, Raymond A., et al.** Intellectual Property Law of China. 1999. ring bd. write for info. (*1-57823-069-1*) Juris Pubng.

***Mantle, Stacy.** The Odyssey-Literatute Unit. 48p. 2000. pap. 7.95 (*1-57690-633-7*) Tchr Create Mat.

Mantlemann, Lee. Mantlemann's Imaging Guide. 34.95 (*0-936648-67-8*) Telecom Bks.

***Mantley, John.** Cyclops Awakes: A Newspaperman Fights Back after a Massive Stroke. Phelps, Janice, ed. 288p. 2000. 24.95 (*0-9676050-2-4*) Lucky Pr.

Mantley, Ulrich & Schuster, Norbert. Agamid Lizards. (Illus.). 188p. 1997. 22.95 (*0-7938-0128-1*, LR-103) TFH Pubns.

***Mantlo, Bill.** Contest of Champions. (Illus.). 160p. 1999. reprint ed. pap. 17.95 (*0-7851-0726-6*, Pub. by Marvel Entrprs) LPC Group.

Manto, Mike, jt. auth. see Dawson, Mike.

***Manto, Saadat Hasan & Hasan, Khalid.** Stars from Another Sky: The Bombay Film World in the 1940s. LC 98-905092. (Illus.). 1998. write for info. (*0-14-027596-7*) Penguin Books.

Mantoani, Tim. Photographic Global Notes, 2 vols., Vol. I & II. (Illus.). 308p. (C). 1998. pap. 29.95 (*1-883403-23-5*, H 707, Silver Pixel Pr) Saunders Photo.

Manton. Temptation of Christ. 1996. pap. 9.99 (*1-85792-226-3*, Pub. by Christian Focus) Spring Arbor Dist.

Manton, Catherine. Fed Up: Women & Food in America. LC 98-19215. 184p. 1999. 55.00 (*0-89789-448-0*, Bergin & Garvey); pap. 17.95 (*0-89789-629-7*, Bergin & Garvey) Greenwood.

Manton, Charlotte. The Community of Lincoln. Stanley, Karen & Bornemeier, Pam, eds. (Illus.). 116p. (J). (gr. 3-6). pap. text 10.50 (*0-9671920-0-5*) Lincoln Schools.

Manton, Edgar J., et al. Texas Real Estate Principles. LC 85-22668. 432p. 1986. pap. text 34.50 (*0-471-82301-5*) P-H.

Manton, Jo, jt. auth. see Gittings, Robert.

Manton, Kenneth G., et al, eds. Forecasting the Health of Elderly Populations. LC 92-48819. (Series in Statistics in the Health Sciences). (Illus.). 371p. 1993. 84.95 (*0-387-97953-0*) Spr-Verlag.

Manton, Kenneth G. & Stallard, Eric. Chronic Disease Modelling: Measurement & Evaluation of the Risks of Chronic Disease Processes. (Charles Griffin Series-Mathematics in Medicine: No. 2). (Illus.). 288p. 1988. text 69.00 (*0-19-520617-7*) OUP.

Manton, Kenneth G., et al. Statistical Applications Using Fuzzy Sets. (Probability & Mathematical Statistics Ser.). 312p. 1994. 104.95 (*0-471-54561-9*) Wiley.

Manton, M. Dictionary of Theological Terms. 1996. pap. 7.99 (*0-946462-40-2*, Pub. by Evangelical Pr) P & R Pubng.

Manton, Michael, jt. auth. see Webb, Barbara.

Manton, Richard. Aphrodizzia. 192p. 1999. mass mkt. 7.95 (*1-56201-124-3*) Blue Moon Bks.

— Bombay Bound. 190p. (Orig.). 1993. mass mkt. 7.95 (*1-56201-002-6*) Blue Moon Bks.

— The Captive V: The Soundproof Scream. 224p. 1998. mass mkt. 7.95 (*1-56201-106-5*, Pub. by Blue Moon Bks) Publishers Group.

***Manton, Richard.** Captive IV: The Eyes Behind the Mask. 2000. mass mkt. 7.95 (*1-56201-212-6*) Blue Moon Bks.

Manton, Richard. The Captive II. 192p. 1999. mass mkt. 7.95 (*1-56201-113-8*) Blue Moon Bks.

— Days of Floraville. 1998. mass mkt. 6.95 (*1-56333-691-X*) Masquerade.

— Deep South. 284p. (Orig.). 1993. mass mkt. 7.95 (*1-56201-061-1*) Blue Moon Bks.

— Dream Boat. 256p. 1996. mass mkt. 7.95 (*0-929654-59-5*) Blue Moon Bks.

***Manton, Richard.** Dream Boat. 1999. mass mkt. 7.95 (*1-56201-170-7*) Blue Moon Bks.

Manton, Richard. Fancy Girl. 192p. 1999. mass mkt. 7.95 (*1-56201-120-0*) Blue Moon Bks.

— Gardens of the Night. 1998. mass mkt. 6.95 (*1-56333-678-2*) Masquerade.

***Manton, Richard.** Jeremy. 192p. 1999. mass mkt. 7.95 (*1-56201-146-4*, Pub. by Blue Moon Bks) Publishers Group.

Manton, Richard. Max. 192p. 1999. mass mkt. 7.95 (*1-56201-121-9*) Blue Moon Bks.

— Noreen. 1992. mass mkt. 5.95 (*0-929654-89-7*, 110) Blue Moon Bks.

— Noreen. 192p. 1999. mass mkt. 7.95 (*1-56201-129-4*) Blue Moon Bks.

***Manton, Richard.** The Odalisque. 256p. 2000. pap. 7.95 (*1-56201-177-4*, Pub. by Blue Moon Bks) Publishers Group.

Manton, Richard. Tropic of Venus. (Victorian Era Ser.). (Orig.). 1990. mass mkt. 5.95 (*0-929654-69-2*, 86) Blue Moon Bks.

***Manton, Richard.** Vicky. 224p. 1999. mass mkt. 7.95 (*1-56201-138-3*) Blue Moon Bks.

Manton, Richard. Villa Rosa. (Orig.). 1989. mass mkt. 4.50 (*0-929654-13-7*, 47) Blue Moon Bks.

***Manton, Thomas.** By Faith: Sermons on Hebrew 11. 698p. 2000. 33.99 (*0-85151-782-X*) Banner of Truth.

Manton, Thomas. Commentary on Jude. 376p. (C). 1989. reprint ed. 17.99 (*0-85151-553-3*) Banner of Truth.

— Commentary on Jude. LC 88-12127. 384p. 1988. reprint ed. pap. 14.99 (*0-8254-3239-1*, Kregel Class) Kregel.

— The Complete Works of Thomas Manton, 22 vols. 508p. 1999. reprint ed. lib. bdg. 995.00 (*0-9651791-3-3*) Tanski Publns.

An Asterisk (*) at the beginning of an entry indicates that the title is appearing for the first time.

— James. (Geneva Commentaries Ser.). 1983. 24.99 (*0-85151-074-4*) Banner of Truth.

— James. abr. ed. LC 94-47149. (Classic Commentaries Ser.). 224p. 1995. pap. 19.99 (*0-89107-832-0*) Crossway Bks.

— Jude. abr. ed. LC 99-29575. (Classic Commentaries). 224p. 1999. pap. 15.99 (*1-58134-120-2*) Crossway Bks.

— Psalm 119, 3 vols. 580p. 1990. 79.99 (*0-85151-576-2*) Banner of Truth.

— The Works of Thomas Manton, 22 vols. LC 76-172841. reprint ed. 465.00 (*0-404-04200-7*) AMS Pr.

— The Works of Thomas Manton, 3 vols., Vol. 1. 500p. 1993. 25.99 (*0-85151-648-3*) Banner of Truth.

— The Works of Thomas Manton, 3 vols., Vol. 2. 500p. 1993. 25.99 (*0-85151-649-1*) Banner of Truth.

— The Works of Thomas Manton, 3 vols., Vol. 3. 500p. 1993. 25.99 (*0-85151-650-5*) Banner of Truth.

Mantooth, C., jt. auth. see Gettner, R.

Mantooth, Carol, ed. see Geffner, Robert.

Mantooth, Carol, jt. ed. see Geffner, Robert.

Mantooth, F. For Beginning C Instruments - Patterns for Improvisation. 48p. 1996. pap. 9.95 (*0-7935-6854-4*) H Leonard.

— Movin on to Blues B Flat Patterns for Improvisation. 32p. 1997. audio compact disk 9.95 (*0-7935-6859-5*) H Leonard.

— Movin on to Blues Bass Clef Patterns for Improvisation. 32p. 1997. pap. 9.95 (*0-7935-6861-7*) H Leonard.

— Movin on to Blues C Book Patterns for Improvisation. 32p. 1997. pap. 9.95 (*0-7935-6858-7*) H Leonard.

— Movin on to Blues E Flat Patterns for Improvisation. 32p. 1997. pap. 9.95 incl. audio compact disk (*0-7935-6860-9*) H Leonard.

Mantooth, Frank. Best Chord Changes for the Most Requested Standards. (Keyboards-Guitar Ser.). 216p. (C). 1990. spiral bd. 24.95 (*0-88188-853-2*, 00359125) H Leonard.

— Best Chord Changes for the World's Greatest Standards. 216p. 1989. spiral bd. 24.95 (*0-88188-852-4*, HL 00359124) H Leonard.

Mantooth, H. Alan. Modeling with an Analog Hardware Description Language. (International Series in Engineering & Computer Science, Natural Language Processing & Machine Translation). 296p. (C). 1994. text 139.00 (*0-7923-9516-6*) Kluwer Academic.

Mantooth, James. Teen Angst. (Tanbark Ser.). 24p. (Orig.). 1997. pap. 6.00 (*1-887853-13-8*) Radiolarian.

Mantooth, Tonya, jt. auth. see Kayser, Thomas A.

Mantoura, R. F. & Martin, J. M., eds. Neurodegenerative Disorders: Mechanisms & Prospects for Therapy. LC 91-15349. (Dahlem Workshop Reports - Physical, Chemical, Earth Sciences). 320p. 1991. 314.50 (*0-471-92979-4*) Wiley.

Mantoux, Etienne. The Carthaginian Peace: or The Economic Consequences of Mr. Keynes. 240p. 1999. pap. 19.95 (*1-897959-37-0*, Pub. by Serif) IPG Chicago.

— The Carthaginian Peace or the Economic Consequences of Mr. Keynes. Wilkins, Mira, ed. LC 78-3936. (International Finance Ser.). 1979. reprint ed. lib. bdg. 23.95 (*0-405-11237-8*) Ayer.

***Mantoux, Marie-Laure & Crestin-Billet, Frederique.** Halloween. (Illus.). 88p. 2000. pap. 12.95 (*0-7641-1625-8*) Barron.

Mantoux, Paul. Alexis de Tocqueville Livre du Centenaire (1859-1959) 8.95 (*0-8288-6094-7*, F74630) Fr & Eur.

— The Industrial Revolution in the Eighteenth Century: An Outline of the Beginnings of the Modern Factory System in England. LC 82-20219. iv, 528p. 1992. pap. text 17.95 (*0-226-50384-4*) U Ch Pr.

Mantovani, Alberto, ed. Chemokines. 2nd ed. (Chemical Immunology Ser.: Vol. 72). (Illus.). xii, 180p. 1999. 170.50 (*3-8055-6861-4*) S Karger.

***Mantovani, Alberto, et al.** Pharmacology of Cytokines. (Illus.). 336p. 2000. text 110.00 (*0-19-850043-2*); pap. text 50.00 (*0-19-850042-4*) OUP.

Mantovani, Franco, jt. auth. see Marcolongo, Bruno.

Mantovani, Giuseppe. New Communication Environments: From Everyday to Virtual. 224p. 1996. 79.95 (*0-7484-0395-7*); pap. 34.95 (*0-7484-0396-5*) Taylor & Francis.

***Mantovani, Giuseppe.** Understanding Culture & Psychology: Exploring Borders, Acknowledging Differences. LC 99-87219. 2000. write for info. (*0-415-23100-0*) Routledge.

Mantovani, Roberto, jt. auth. see Diemberger, Kurt.

Mantran, contrib. by. L' Empire Ottoman du XVIe au XVIIIe Siecle: Administration, Economie, Societe. (Collected Studies: No. CS202). (FRE., Illus.). 340p. (C). 1984. reprint ed. lib. bdg. 112.95 (*0-86078-150-X*, Pub. by Variorum) Ashgate Pub Co.

***Mantran, Robert.** Great Dates in Islamic History. 418p. 1999. 37.95 (*0-7351-0206-6*) Replica Bks.

Mantran, Robert, ed. Great Dates in Islamic History. LC 95-12883. 416p. 1996. 29.95 (*0-8160-2935-0*) Facts on File.

Mantreswara. Phala Deepika. Kapoor, Gouri S., tr. (C). 1991. 17.00 (*0-8364-2769-6*, Pub. by Ranjan Pubs) S Asia.

Mantross, David H., et al. Career Coaching Your Kids: Guiding Your Child Through the Process of Career Discovery. LC 96-40264. 224p. 1997. pap. 16.95 (*0-89106-100-2*, 7755, Davies-Black Pub) Consulting Psychol.

Mantsch, Henry H. & Chapman, Dennis, eds. Infrared Spectroscopy of Biomolecules. LC 95-24309. 359p. 1996. 129.95 (*0-471-02184-9*) Wiley.

Mantsch, Henry H. & Jackson, Michael, eds. Infrared Spectroscopy Vol. 3257: New Tool in Medicine. LC 98-233144. 330p. 1998. 80.00 (*0-8194-2696-2*) SPIE.

Mantsch, Pat S. & Whitney, Jane, eds. Gifts from the Earth: A Basketmakers Field Guide to Midwest Botanicals. LC 88-50438. (Illus.). 50p. (Orig.). 1988. pap. 14.95 (*0-9614795-1-5*) Wild Willow.

Mantsch, Pat S., ed. see TerBeest, Char.

Mantsios, Gregory & Georgakas, Dan, eds. A New Labor Movement for the New Century. LC 98-4474. (Labor in America Ser.: Vol. 5). 406p. 1998. 80.00 (*0-8153-2473-1*, SS1126) Garland.

Mantsios, Gregory & Queens College Staff (New York, N.Y.). A New Labor Movement for the New Century: A Collection of Essays from the Labor Resource Center, Queens College, City University of New York. LC 98-17905. 1998. 24.00 (*0-85345-937-1*, Pub. by Monthly Rev) NYU Pr.

Mantuanus, Baptista. Adulescentia: The Ecologues of Mantuan. Piepho, Lee, tr. from LAT. LC 89-16967. (World Literature in Translation Ser.: Vol. 14). 206p. 1989. text 20.00 (*0-8240-3309-4*) Garland.

Mantus, Roberta. Design Guidelines for Desktop Publishing. 128p. 1992. pap. 16.95 (*0-8273-5075-9*) Delmar.

— Design Guidelines for Desktop Publishing: Instructor's Guide. 1992. 12.00 (*0-8273-5076-7*) Delmar.

Mantus, Roberta & Moore, Roberta. Telephone Communication in the Information Age. LC 95-37276. 168p. 1995. mass mkt. 26.95 (*0-538-71514-6*) S-W Pub.

Mantyla, Karen. Consultative Sales Power: Achieving Continuous Success. Henry, Carol, ed. LC 94-68200. (Fifty-Minute Ser.). (Illus.). 116p. (Orig.). 1995. pap. 10.95 (*1-56052-304-2*) Crisp Pubns.

***Mantyla, Karen.** Interactive Distance Learning Exercises That Really Work! LC 99-73474. 192p. 1999. pap. 30.00 (*1-56286-128-X*) Am Soc Train & Devel.

***Mantyla, Karen, ed.** The 2000 ASTD Distance Learning Yearbook. (Illus.). 300p. 1999. 79.95 (*0-07-135296-1*) McGraw.

Mantyla, Martti, jt. auth. see Shah, Jami J.

Mantz, Ruth E. & Murry, John M. Life of Katherine Mansfield. LC 75-42109. (English Literature Ser.: No. 33). 1974. lib. bdg. 75.00 (*0-8383-1882-7*) M S G Haskell Hse.

Mantzarides, Giorgios I. Orthodox Spiritual Life. LC 94-13034. 1994. pap. text 12.95 (*0-916586-69-3*, Pub. by Holy Cross Orthodox) BookWorld.

Mantzaridis, Georgios I. The Deification of Man: St. Gregory Palamas & the Orthodox Tradition. Sherrard, Liadain, tr. from GRE. (Contemporary Greek Theologians Ser.: No. 2). 137p. (Orig.). 1984. pap. 9.95 (*0-88141-027-6*) St Vladimirs.

— Time & Man. Vulliamy, Julian, tr. from GRE. LC 96-11015. 1996. write for info. (*1-878997-54-8*) St Tikhons Pr.

Mantzius, Karl. History of Theatrical Art in Ancient & Modern Times, 6 Vols, Set. (Illus.). 1990. 87.00 (*0-8446-0786-X*) Peter Smith.

Manu, Moke. Hawaiian Fishing Traditions. 2nd rev. ed. Kawaharada, Dennis, ed. & intro. by. LC 91-60467. (Illus.). 96p. (C). 1994. pap. 7.95 (*0-9623102-3-9*) Kalamaku Pr.

***Manu, Peter.** The Pharmacotherapy of Common Functional Syndromes: Evidence-Based Guidelines for Primary Care Practice. LC 00-20078. (Illus.). 308 p. 2000. pap. text 39.95 (*0-7890-0589-1*, Hawrth Medical); lib. bdg. 69.95 (*0-7890-0588-3*, Hawrth Medical) Haworth Pr.

Manu, Peter, ed. Functional Somatic Syndromes: Etiology, Diagnosis & Treatment. LC 98-24733. (Illus.). 314p. (C). 1999. text 105.00 (*0-521-59130-9*); pap. text 44.95 (*0-521-63491-1*) Cambridge U Pr.

Manual De Bernardo Ares, Jose. Historiology, Research & Didactics: Elaboration & Transmission of Historical Knowledge. (Iberian Studies in History, Literature & Culture). (SPA.). 159p. 1997. pap. 49.95 (*1-883255-86-4*) Intl Scholars.

Manual Review Committee, jt. auth. see Foundation for Cross-Connection Control & Hydrauli.

Manual Work Team of the Cognitive Research Program. Mediated Learning in & Out of the Classroom, Vol. 1. LC 96-77677. (Illus.). 186p. (Orig.). 1996. pap. 32.95 (*1-57517-059-0*, 1446) SkyLght.

Manucci, Niccolao. Storia Do Mogor: or Mogul India, 1653-1708, 4 vols., Set. Irvine, William, tr. reprint ed. text 125.00 (*0-685-13412-1*) Coronet Bks.

Manucharov, A. A., ed. see Murashkevich, A. M. & Novichkov, N. N.

Manucy, Albert. Artillery Through the Ages: A Short Illustrated History of Cannon, Emphasizing Types Used in America. 96p. (Orig.). 1949. pap. 92.00 (*0-16-003504-X*) USGPO.

Manucy, Albert. Artillery Through the Ages: A Short Illustrated History of Cannon, Emphasizing Types Used in America. (Illus.). 96p. (Orig.). 1985. reprint ed. pap. 4.00 (*0-16-003405-1*, S/N 024-005-00159-0) USGPO.

— Menendez: Pedro Menendez de Aviles: Captain General of the Ocean Sea. LC 92-5128. (Illus.). 112p. 1992. 14.95 (*1-56164-015-8*); pap. 7.95 (*1-56164-016-6*) Pineapple Pr.

Manucy, Albert C. Artillery Through the Ages: A Short Illustrated History of Cannon, Emphasizing Types Used in America. (Illus.). 92p. (Orig.). (C). 1994. pap. text 30.00 (*0-7881-0745-3*) DIANE Pub.

Manucy, Albert C. The Houses of St. Augustine, 1565-1821. (Florida Sand Dollar Bk.). (Illus.). 184p. (C). 1992. reprint ed. pap. 12.95 (*0-8130-1103-5*) U Press Fla.

— Pages from the Past: A Pictorial History of Fort Jefferson. (Illus.). 32p. 1999. pap. 7.95 (*0-945142-06-4*) FL Natl Parks.

— Sixteenth-Century St. Augustine: The People & Their Homes. LC 96-31964. (Illus.). 136p. 1997. 24.95 (*0-8130-1484-0*) U Press Fla.

Manucy, Albert C. & Torres-Reyes, Ricardo. The Forts of Old San Juan. LC 73-83358. (Illus.). 96p. 1989. pap. 16.95 (*0-85699-085-X*) Chatham Pr.

Manuel. El Conde Lucanor: Level C Books. text 8.95 (*0-88436-917-X*) EMC-Paradigm.

Manuel, David. Bosnia: Hope in the Ashes. LC 96-45544. 180p. 1996. pap. 12.95 (*1-55725-171-1*) Paraclete MA.

— Like a Mighty River. LC 77-90948. (Illus.). 220p. 1977. 5.95 (*0-932260-02-0*) Rock Harbor.

***Manuel, David.** A Matter of Diamonds. (Faith Abbey Mystery Ser.: Vol. 2). 350p. 2000. 23.00 (*1-55725-258-0*, 930-059, Pub. by Paraclete MA) BookWorld.

Manuel, David. A Matter of Roses. LC 99-39525. 330p. 1999. 23.00 (*1-55725-234-3*, 930-006, Pub. by Paraclete MA) BookWorld.

— Medjugorje under Siege. LC 92-80352. 182p. 1992. pap. 8.95 (*1-55725-052-9*) Paraclete MA.

Manuel, David, jt. auth. see Marshall, Peter.

Manuel, David, ed. see Ford, Camie & Hale, Sunny.

Manuel De Prada, Jaun, see De Prada, Jaun Manuel.

Manuel Di Bella, Jose. Nailed to the Wound. Polkinhorn, Harry, tr. from SPA. (Baja California Literature in Translation Ser.). 162p. 1993. pap. 12.50 (*1-879691-14-0*) SDSU Press.

Manuel, Don J. El Conde Lucanor. (SPA.). 9.95 (*84-241-5615-3*) E Torres & Sons.

Manuel, Don Juan, see Juan Manuel, Don.

Manuel, Earthlyn M. Shoke Cards - The Black Angels Vol. 1: A Healing Tool for African American Women. (Illus.). i, 90p. (Orig.). (J). 1996. pap. 29.95 (*0-9654420-0-4*) LeaderSpirit.

Manuel, Earthlyn Marselean. Black Angel Cards: A Soul Revival Guide for Black Women. LC BF1879.T2M34 1999. 192p. 1999. pap. 18.00 (*0-06-251612-4*, Pub. by Harper SF) HarpC.

Manuel, Elisabeth. Cette Ombre Familiere - Dark Companion. Suther, Judith, tr. from FRE. (ENG & FRE.). 230p. (Orig.). 1995. pap. 18.00 (*0-9645677-0-9*) Starbks.

Manuel, Elisabeth, tr. see Sage, Kay.

Manuel, Frank E. The Broken Staff: Judaism Through Christian Eyes. (Illus.). 384p. (C). 1992. 46.50 (*0-674-08370-9*) HUP.

— The Changing of the Gods. LC 82-40475. 216p. 1983. reprint ed. pap. 67.00 (*0-608-02307-8*, 206294800004) Bks Demand.

— The Realities of American-Palestine Relations. LC 72-596. 378p. 1975. reprint ed. lib. bdg. 75.00 (*0-8371-5999-7*, MARA, Greenwood Pr) Greenwood.

— A Requiem for Karl Marx. LC 94-48452. (Illus.). 272p. (C). 1995. 24.95 (*0-674-76326-2*) HUP.

— A Requiem for Karl Marx. (Illus.). 288p. 1997. reprint ed. pap. 16.50 (*0-674-76327-0*) HUP.

***Manuel, Frank E.** Scenes from the End: The Last Days of World War II in Europe. LC 99-43516. (Illus.). 135p. 2000. 20.00 (*1-883642-55-8*) Steerforth Pr.

Manuel, Frank E. Shapes of Philosophical History. (Modern Revivals in Philosophy Ser.). 176p. 1993. 56.95 (*0-7512-0210-X*, Pub. by Gregg Revivals) Ashgate Pub Co.

— Shapes of Philosophical History. LC 65-13111. (Harry Camp Lectures at Stanford University). 176p. 1965. reprint ed. pap. 30.00 (*0-7837-4069-7*, 204402500011) Bks Demand.

Manuel, Frank E., ed. The Age of Reason. (Paperbook Series in History). (Illus.). 64p. (C). 1993. reprint ed. pap. text 2.25 (*1-877891-11-8*) Paperbook Pr Inc.

Manuel, Frank E. & Manuel, Fritzie P. Utopian Thought in the Western World. LC 79-12382. 902p. 1979. 50.00 (*0-674-93185-8*) Belknap Pr.

— Utopian Thought in the Western World. LC 79-12382. 902p. 1982. pap. 23.50 (*0-674-93186-6*) Belknap Pr.

Manuel, Fritzie P., jt. auth. see Manuel, Frank E.

Manuel, Infant V. Juan, see Juan Manuel, Infant V.

Manuel, Juan. Cinco Tratados. Ayerbe-Chaux, Reinaldo, ed. (Spanish Ser.: No. 51). lxiv, 270p. 1989. 25.00 (*0-940639-36-X*) Hispanic Seminary.

— Count Lucanor: A Collection of Medieval Spanish Stories. England, John, ed. (Hispanic Classics Ser.). 1987. 59.95 (*0-85668-325-6*, Pub. by Aris & Phillips) David Brown.

— Count Lucanor: A Collection of Medieval Spanish Stories. England, ed. (Hispanic Classics Ser.). 1987. pap. 28.00 (*0-85668-326-4*, Pub. by Aris & Phillips) David Brown.

— Ordenamjentos Dados a la Villa de Penafiel, 10 de Abril de 1345. Kinkade, Richard P., tr. & intro. by. (Spanish Ser.: No. 112). xii, 143p. 1996. 25.00 (*1-56954-052-7*) Hispanic Seminary.

Manuel, Juan, et al. The Book of Count Lucanor & Patronio: A Translation of Don Juan Manuel's El Conde Lucanor. LC 76-24342. (Studies in Romance Languages: No. 16). 207p. reprint ed. pap. 64.20 (*0-7837-5812-X*, 204547900006) Bks Demand.

Manuel, Lynn. The Cherry Pit Princess. (Illus.). 160p. (J). (gr. 1-3). 1997. pap. 5.95 (*1-55050-118-6*, Pub. by Coteau) Genl Dist Srvs.

— Fifty-Five Grandmas & a Llama. LC 96-29473. (Illus.). 32p. (J). (ps-3). 1997. 15.95 (*0-87905-785-8*) Gibbs Smith Pub.

— Lucy Maud & the Cavendish Cat. (Illus.). 32p. (J). (gr. 1-3). 1997. 15.95 (*0-88776-397-9*) Tundra Bks.

— The Night the Moon Blew Kisses. LC 95-24391. (Illus.). 32p. (J). (ps-3). 1996. 14.95 (*0-395-73979-9*) HM.

Manuel, Madelynne. The Epiphany: Sequel to The Interlopers I. 401p. (Orig.). 1993. pap. 6.99 (*0-9635714-1-9*) M Manuel Prods.

— The Interlopers I. Henson, Mari, ed. (Illus.). 290p. (Orig.). 1992. pap. 6.99 (*0-9635714-0-0*) M Manuel Prods.

Manuel, Mark. A Geography of South Australia. LC 93-33370. 1995. pap. 19.95 (*0-521-42330-9*) Cambridge U Pr.

Manuel, Matthew. Macromedia Director Design Guide. 400p. (Orig.). 2000. pap. 34.99 (*0-7897-2146-5*) S&S Trade.

Manuel, Paul C. The Challenges of Democratic Consolidation in Portugal: Political, Economic, & Military Issues, 1976-1991. LC 95-43762. 128p. 1996. 49.95 (*0-275-94849-8*, Praeger Pubs) Greenwood.

— Uncertain Outcome: The Politics of the Portuguese Transition to Democracy. 214p. (C). 1994. lib. bdg. write for info. (*0-8191-9651-7*) U Pr of Amer.

Manuel, Paul C. & Cammisa, Anne M. Checks & Balances? How a Parliamentary System Could Change American Politics. LC 98-27075. (Dilemmas in American Politics Ser.). 240p. 1998. text 65.00 (*0-8133-3026-2*, Pub. by Westview); pap. text 17.00 (*0-8133-3027-0*, Pub. by Westview) HarpC.

Manuel, Peter. Cassette Culture: Popular Music & Technology in North India. LC 92-27626. (Chicago Studies in Ethnomusicology). 322p. (C). 1993. pap. text 22.00 (*0-226-50401-8*) U Ch Pr.

— Cassette Culture: Popular Music & Technology in North India. LC 92-27626. (Chicago Studies in Ethnomusicology). 322p. (C). 1996. lib. bdg. 52.00 (*0-226-50399-2*) U Ch Pr.

***Manuel, Peter.** East Indian Music in the West Indies: Tan-Singing, Chutney & the Making of Indo-Caribbean Culture. LC ML3565.M37 2000. (Studies in Latin American & Caribbean Music). (Illus.). 288p. 2000. 89.50 (*1-56639-762-6*); pap. 29.95 (*1-56639-763-4*) Temple U Pr.

Manuel, Peter. Essays on Cuban Music: North American & Cuban Perspectives. 348p. (C). 1992. lib. bdg. 54.00 (*0-8191-8430-6*) U Pr of Amer.

— Popular Musics of the Non-Western World: An Introductory Survey. (Illus.). 314p. 1990. reprint ed. pap. text 19.95 (*0-19-506334-1*) OUP.

— Thumri in Historical & Stylistic Perspectives. 1989. 47.50 (*81-208-0673-5*, Pub. by Motilal Bnarsidass) S Asia.

Manuel, Peter, et al. Caribbean Currents: Caribbean Music from Rumba to Reggae. LC 95-3152. (Illus.). 272p. (C). 1995. pap. 22.95 (*1-56639-339-6*) Temple U Pr.

***Manuel, Prada Juan.** La Tempestad. (Coleccion Autores Espanoles E Hispanoame Ser.). 1998. 23.95 (*84-08-02294-6*) Planeta Edit.

Manuel, Roland. Maurice Ravel: Music Book Index. 152p. 1993. reprint ed. lib. bdg. 69.00 (*0-7812-9616-1*) Rprt Serv.

Manuel, Ron C., ed. Minority Aging: Sociological & Social Psychological Issues, 8. LC 82-930. (Contributions in Ethnic Studies: No. 8). 285p. 1982. 55.00 (*0-313-22541-9*, MAG/, Greenwood Pr) Greenwood.

Manuel, Sherry W., et al. The Marler Family History. (Illus.). 431p. (Orig.). 1996. pap. 35.00 (*1-887745-06-8*) Dogwood TX.

Manuel, Ted. Five-Hundred-One Types of People Who Can Cause You to Have a Bad Hair Day. Ramirez, Doreen, ed. 100p. (Orig.). 1995. write for info. (*0-9628011-5-1*) Desert Palm Pub.

— Jerks Who Are They? & From Where Do They Come? Ramirez, Doreen, ed. (Illus.). 100p. 1995. write for info. (*0-9628011-3-5*) Desert Palm Pub.

— The PMS-Prudent Mans Survival Cookbook. Ramirez, Doreen, ed. 100p. (Orig.). 1995. write for info. (*0-9628011-4-3*) Desert Palm Pub.

Manuel, Ted & Ramirez, Doreen. The PMS Handbook for Men. rev. ed. (Illus.). 56p. (Orig.). 1994. write for info. (*0-9628011-1-9*) Desert Palm Pub.

Manuel, Ted, et al. Five-Hundred-One Things to Do When Your Computer Crashes!! 100p. (Orig.). 1995. write for info. (*0-9628011-2-7*) Desert Palm Pub.

Manuel Villalpando, Cesar Jose. Amores Mexicanos. 1999. pap. text 19.95 (*968-406-772-0*) F Planeta.

Manuele, Fred A. Essays on the Practice of Safety. LC 92-32859. 1993. text 48.95 (*0-442-01401-5*, VNR) Wiley.

— On the Practice of Safety. 2nd ed. 304p. 1997. 74.95 (*0-471-29213-3*, VNR) Wiley.

Manuele, Fred A. On the Practice of Safety. 2nd ed. LC 97-26554. (Occupational Health & Safety Ser.). (Illus.). 268p. 1997. 54.95 (*0-442-02423-1*, VNR) Wiley.

Manuele, Fred A., jt. auth. see Christensen, Fred A.

Manuele, Fred A., jt. ed. see Christensen, Wayne C.

Manuelian, Jack. Nostradamus: Predictions of World War III. 2nd rev. ed. (Illus.). 192p. (Orig.). 1996. pap. 14.95 (*0-938294-52-0*) Inner Light.

Manuelian, Lucy Der, see Der Manuelian, Lucy.

Manuelian, P. M., tr. from ARM. Proverbs from the Armenian. LC 80-13387. (Illus.). 150p. 1980. 8.95 (*0-933706-20-0*) Ararat Pr.

Manuelian, P. M., ed. see Papazian, K. S.

Manuelian, Peter D. Ancient Egypt: A Fact-Filled Coloring Book. (Start Exploring Ser.). (Illus.). 128p. (ps up). 1997. pap. 8.95 (*0-7624-0002-1*) Running Pr.

Manuelian, Peter Der, see Der Manuelian, Peter.

Manuelli, Rodolfo E. & Sargent, Thomas J. Exercises in Dynamic Macroeconomic Theory. LC 86-25767. (Illus.). 224p. (C). 1987. pap. 29.95 (*0-674-27476-8*) HUP.

Manufactured Housing Institute Staff, jt. auth. see Sanders, Welford.

Manufacturers Group Staff. OnRamp: The Traveler's Radio & Entertainment Guide. (Western Edition Ser.). 169p. (Orig.). 1991. pap. 4.95 (*1-880126-00-1*); pap. 4.95 (*1-880126-02-8*); pap. 4.95 (*1-880126-01-X*) Pacif Pr.

Manuila, Alexandre. Dictionnaire Medical. 6th ed. (FRE.). 544p. 1994. 49.95 (*0-7859-9279-0*) Fr & Eur.

— French Dictionary of Medicine & Biology: Dictionnaire Francais de Medicine et de Biologie, 20 vols. (FRE.). 1981. 450.00 (*0-8288-1817-7*, M15579) Fr & Eur.

— Petit Dictionnaire Medical. 4th ed. (FRE.). 566p. 1985. pap. 49.95 (*0-7859-4942-9*) Fr & Eur.

Manuila, Alexandre, ed. EMRO: Partner in Health in the Eastern Mediterranean 1949-1989. (Illus.). xx, 570p. 1991. pap. text 30.00 (*92-9021-140-7*, 1460009) World Health.
— Progress in Medical Terminology. (Illus.). xii, 116p. 1981. pap. 68.75 (*3-8055-2112-X*) S Karger.
Manuila, Ludmila. Dictionnaire Medical. 5th ed. (FRE.). 504p. 1991. pap. 39.95 (*0-7859-7833-X*, 2225827958) Fr & Eur.
Manuila, Ludmila, et al. Dictionnaire Medical de Poche. (FRE.). 1994. write for info. (*0-7859-7862-3*, 2-253-08521-9) Fr & Eur.
Manuilov, V., ed. Encyclopaedia of Lermontov. (RUS.). 784p. (C). 1981. 150.00 (*0-7855-6479-9*, Pub. by Collets) St Mut.
Manukin, A. B., jt. auth. see Braginsky, Vladimir B.
Manuli, Margery. Radiology. (Illus.). 456p. 1999. pap. 40.00 (*0-07-039999-9*) McGraw-Hill HPD.
Manus Associates Staff. Compass Managerial Practices Survey: Facilitator's Guide. 1998. ring bd. 149.95 (*0-7879-3890-4*, Pfffr & Co) Jossey-Bass.
— Compass Managerial Practices Survey: Observer Instrument. 1998. pap. text 3.95 (*0-7879-3892-0*, Pfffr & Co) Jossey-Bass.
— Compass Managerial Practices Survey: Participant's Workbook. 1998. ring bd., wbk. ed. 9.95 (*0-7879-3891-2*) Jossey-Bass.
Manus, Gerald B. & Manus, Muriel R. Phonic Foolers: A Creative Arts Dictionary of Homophones. LC 97-65995. 238p. 1998. pap. 14.95 (*0-88739-154-0*) Creat Arts Bk.
Manus, Iris, jt. auth. see Manus, Morton.
***Manus, Leslie Michele.** Yiddish for Everyone. unabridged ed. Fife, Bruce, ed. LC 98-44250. (Illus.). 96p. 1999. pap. 10.00 (*0-941599-44-2*, Pub. by Piccadilly Bks) Empire Pub Srvs.
Manus, Marton, et al. Alfred's Basic Piano Lesson Book, Level 1B: Italian Edition. (Alfred's Basic Piano Library Ser.). (ITA.). 48p. 1999. pap. 9.05 (*0-7390-0090-X*, 14573) Alfred Pub.
Manus, Morton. Alfred's Pre-Band Instrument Method: An Introduction to Instrumental Music Using the Flutophone, Recorder, Song Flute. 32p. 1981. pap. 5.50 (*0-7390-0695-9*, 1986) Alfred Pub.
Manus, Morton. Guitar Chord Dictionary. 40p. 1975. 6.50 (*0-88284-153-X*, 377) Alfred Pub.
— How to Play Guitar Chords & Strums. (Alfred Handy Guide Ser.). 48p. 1980. pap. text 5.50 (*0-88284-231-5*, 1890) Alfred Pub.
Manus, Morton. How to Play Mandolin. (Handy Guide Ser.). 48p. 1980. pap. 4.95 (*0-7390-0870-6*, 1887) Alfred Pub.
Manus, Morton. How to Play the Banjo. (Alfred Handy Guide Ser.). 1980. pap. 4.95 (*0-88284-201-3*) Alfred Pub.
— How to Play the Guitar. (Alfred Handy Guide Ser.). 48p. 1980. 4.95 (*0-88284-152-1*, 1888) Alfred Pub.
— How to Play the Recorder. (Alfred Handy Guide Ser.). 48p. 1979. pap. 4.95 (*0-88284-200-5*, 298) Alfred Pub.
— Organ Chord Dictionary. (Alfred Handy Guide Ser.). 48p. 1978. 4.95 (*0-88284-156-4*, 283) Alfred Pub.
— Piano Chord Dictionary. (Alfred Handy Guide Ser.). 48p. 1978. 5.50 (*0-88284-154-8*, 285) Alfred Pub.
Manus, Morton & Manus, Iris. Alfred's Basic Guitar Method, Bk. 1. 1995. pap. 9.95 incl. audio compact disk (*0-88284-903-4*, 14046) Alfred Pub.
— Alfred's Basic Guitar Method, Bk. 3. 1997. pap. 16.90 incl. audio compact disk (*0-88284-905-0*, 14962) Alfred Pub.
Manus, Morton & Manus, Ron. Basix TAB Guitar Method, Bk. 2. (Basix Ser.: Vol. 2). 1998. pap. 8.95 incl. audio compact disk (*0-88284-860-7*, 17864) Alfred Pub.
Manus, Morton & Manus, Ron. Teach Yourself to Play Banjo. 64p. 1996. pap. 9.95 (*0-7390-0903-6*, 14884) Alfred Pub.
Manus, Morton, et al. Alfred's Basic Adult All-in-One Course, Level 2, Vol. 2. (Alfred's Basic Adult Piano Library). 1996. pap. 25.95 incl. audio compact disk (*0-88284-994-8*, 14534) Alfred Pub.
— Alfred's Basic Adult All-in-One Course, Level 3. (Alfred's Basic Adult Piano Course Ser.). 1996. pap. 14.95 (*0-7390-0068-3*, 14540) Alfred Pub.
— Alfred's Basic Adult All-in-One, Level 1. (Alfred's Basic Adult Piano Course Ser.). 1994. pap. 25.95 incl. audio compact disk (*0-88284-931-X*, 5756) Alfred Pub.
Manus, Morton, et al. Alfred's Basic Piano Lesson Book, Level 2. (Basic Adult Piano Library). 96p. 1984. pap. text 8.95 (*0-88284-634-5*, 2461) Alfred Pub.
— Alfred's Basic Piano Lesson Book, Level 3. (Basic Adult Piano Library). 96p. 1987. pap. text 8.95 (*0-88284-636-1*, 2263) Alfred Pub.
— Alfred's Basic Piano Theory Book, Level 3: Italian Edition. (Alfred's Basic Piano Library Ser.). (ITA.). 32p. 1999. pap. 7.95 (*0-7390-0091-8*, 14596) Alfred Pub.
— Alfred's Basic Piano Theory Book, Level 1. (Basic Adult Piano Library). 64p. 1984. pap. text 8.95 (*0-88284-635-3*, 2462) Alfred Pub.
— Alfred's Basic Piano Theory Book, Level 2. (Basic Adult Piano Library). 48p. 1985. pap. text 6.95 (*0-88284-637-X*, 2118) Alfred Pub.
— Teach Yourself to Play Bass. (Teach Yourself to Play Ser.). 1996. pap. 20.90 incl. audio compact disk (*0-7390-0062-4*, 14876) Alfred Pub.
Manus, Morton, jt. auth. see D'Auberge, Alfred.
Manus, Morton, jt. auth. see Palmer, Willard A.
Manus, Morton, jt. auth. see Surmani, Andrew.
Manus, Morty. Basix Recorder Method. 1997. pap. 8.95 (*0-88284-758-9*); pap. 10.95 incl. audio compact disk (*0-88284-759-7*) Alfred Pub.
— Teach Yourself to Play Recorder. 1993. pap. 9.95 (*0-88284-669-8*) Alfred Pub.
— Teach Yourself to Play Recorder. 1996. pap. 19.95 incl. audio compact disk (*0-88284-668-X*) Alfred Pub.
Manus, Morty & Manus, Ron. Teach Yourself Guitar. (Alfred's Handy Guide Ser.). 1995. pap. 9.95 (*0-88284-693-0*); pap. 19.90 incl. audio compact disk (*0-88284-694-9*) Alfred Pub.
— Teach Yourself to Play Bass Guitar. 1992. pap. 9.95 (*0-88284-686-8*) Alfred Pub.
— Teach Yourself to Play Guitar. 1991. pap. 9.95 (*0-88284-675-2*) Alfred Pub.
— Teach Yourself to Play Guitar. 1994. pap. 19.90 incl. audio compact disk (*0-88284-679-5*) Alfred Pub.
— Teach Yourself to Play Ukulele. 1995. pap. 9.95 (*0-88284-687-6*) Alfred Pub.
Manus, Morty, jt. auth. see Manus, Ron.
Manus, Muriel R., jt. auth. see Manus, Gerald B.
Manus, Ron. Hanon for Guitar in TAB. (In TAB Ser.). 32p. 1993. pap. 6.95 (*0-7390-0249-X*, 4469) Alfred Pub.
***Manus, Ron & Harnsberger, L. C.** From Liverpool to Abbey Road: A Beginning Guitar Method Featuring 33 Songs of Lennon & McCartney. 120p. 1999. pap. 24.95 incl. audio compact disk (*0-7390-0251-1*, 19322); pap. 14.95 (*0-7390-0250-3*, 19321) Alfred Pub.
Manus, Ron & Manus, Morty. Basix Bass Guitar Method: German Edition. (GER.). 1996. pap. 11.50 incl. audio compact disk (*0-88284-736-8*) Alfred Pub.
— Basix Bass Method. 1996. pap. 9.50 (*0-88284-703-1*); pap. 11.50 incl. audio compact disk (*0-88284-704-X*) Alfred Pub.
— Basix Guitar Chord Dictionary. 1996. pap. 11.95 incl. audio compact disk (*0-88284-706-6*) Alfred Pub.
— Basix Guitar Method, Bk. 1. 1996. pap. 5.50 (*0-88284-709-0*); pap. 7.95 incl. audio compact disk (*0-88284-710-4*) Alfred Pub.
— Basix Guitar Method, Bk. 2. 1996. pap. 6.50 (*0-88284-707-4*); pap. 8.95 incl. audio compact disk (*0-88284-708-2*) Alfred Pub.
— Basix Guitar Method, Bk. 3. 1997. pap. 7.95 (*0-88284-746-5*); pap. 9.95 incl. audio compact disk (*0-88284-747-3*) Alfred Pub.
— Basix Guitar Method, Bk. 4. 1997. pap. 7.95 (*0-88284-748-1*); pap. 9.95 incl. audio compact disk (*0-88284-749-X*) Alfred Pub.
— Basix Guitar Method: German Edition, Bk. 1. (GER.). 1996. pap. 6.50 incl. audio compact disk (*0-88284-735-X*) Alfred Pub.
— Basix Guitar Theory. 1996. pap. 7.50 (*0-88284-711-2*); pap. 9.50 incl. audio compact disk (*0-88284-712-0*) Alfred Pub.
— Basix TAB Guitar Method, Bk. 1. 1997. pap. 6.95 (*0-88284-750-3*); pap. 8.95 incl. audio compact disk (*0-88284-751-1*) Alfred Pub.
Manus, Ron & Manus, Steve. Basix Harmonica Method. 1996. pap. 8.50 (*0-88284-713-9*); pap. 10.50 incl. audio compact disk (*0-88284-714-7*) Alfred Pub.
Manus, Ron, jt. auth. see Hall, Steve.
Manus, Ron, jt. auth. see Manus, Morton.
Manus, Ron, jt. auth. see Manus, Morty.
Manus, Ron, jt. auth. see Manus, Steve.
Manus, Rosanne M. The Skillful Teacher's Handbook: Effectively Teaching Regular & Special Education Students. (Illus.). 416p. (C). 1990. pap., spiral bd. 59.95 (*0-398-05702-8*) C C Thomas.
Manus, Steve & Manus, Ron. Teach Yourself Harmonica. 1994. pap. 8.95 (*0-88284-689-2*) Alfred Pub.
— Teach Yourself Harmonica. (Alfred's Handy Guide Ser.). 1994. pap. 9.95 (*0-88284-696-5*) Alfred Pub.
— Teach Yourself Harmonica, Incl. harmonica. 1994. pap. 14.95 (*0-88284-690-6*) Alfred Pub.
— Teach Yourself Harmonica, Incl. harmonica. (Alfred's Handy Guide Ser.). 1994. pap. 14.95 (*0-88284-697-3*) Alfred Pub.
Manus, Steve, jt. auth. see Manus, Ron.
Manus, Steven. How to Play the Harmonica. (Alfred Handy Guide Ser.). 48p. 1978. 4.95 (*0-88284-157-2*, 284) Alfred Pub.
Manus, Ukachukwu C. Christ, the African King: New Testament Christology. LC 93-10526. (Illus.). 280p. 1993. 50.00 (*3-631-45211-X*) P Lang Pubng.
Manus, Willard. Connubial Bliss. 1989. pap. 9.95 (*0-915572-82-6*) Panjandrum.
— The Fighting Men. 192p. 1982. 14.95 (*0-915572-55-9*); pap. 6.95 (*0-915572-54-0*) Panjandrum.
— Other Women, Other Men. 1988. pap. 9.95 (*0-915572-38-9*) Panjandrum.
Manus, Willard. The Pigskin Rabbi. 304p. 1999. 23.00 (*1-891369-07-5*, Pub. by Breakaway Bks) Consort Bk Sales.
***Manus, Willard.** The Pigskin Rabbi. 304p. 2000. pap. 15.00 (*1-891369-23-7*, Pub. by Breakaway Bks) Consort Bk Sales.
Manuscriptors Guild Members. Around the Corner: Tenth Anniversary Anthology. Fowler, Dot & Price, Pat, eds. (Illus.). 150p. (Orig.). pap. text 12.50 (*0-9637150-1-1*) Talent By Lb.
Manuscripts International Staff, ed. see Mounts, Willard.
Manuselis, George, jt. auth. see Mahon, Connie.
Manushina, T., ed. Early Russian Embroidery in the Zagorsk Museum Collection. (ENG & RUS.). 294p. 1983. 56.00 (*0-7855-1602-6*) St Mut.
Manushkin, Fran. Buster Loves Buttons! LC 84-48332. (I Can Read Bks.). (Illus.). 64p. (J). (ps-3). 1985. 11.95 (*0-06-024107-1*) HarpC Child Bks.
***Manushkin, Fran.** Come, Let Us Be Joyful: The Story of Hava Nagila. (Illus.). (J). 2000. 12.95 (*0-8074-0731-3*) UAHC.
Manushkin, Fran. Hocus & Pocus at the Circus. LC 82-47704. (I Can Read Bks.). (Illus.). 64p. (J). (ps-3). 1983. 11.95 (*0-06-024091-1*) HarpC Child Bks.
— Joys of the Sabbath. (J). 1995. 14.00 (*0-671-88333-X*) S&S Bks Yung.
— Latkes & Applesauce: A Hannukah Story. (Illus.). 32p. (J). (gr. k-3). 1992. pap. 4.99 (*0-590-42265-0*, Blue Ribbon Bks) Scholastic Inc.
Manushkin, Fran. Latkes & Applesauce: A Hanukkah Story. (Blue Ribbon Bks.). 1992. 10.15 (*0-606-01890-5*, Pub. by Turtleback) Demco.
Manushkin, Fran. Let's Go Riding in Our Strollers. LC 92-72935. (Illus.). 32p. (J). (ps-k). 1993. lib. bdg. 13.89 (*1-56282-391-4*, Pub. by Hyprn Child) Little.
— Let's Go Riding in Our Strollers. LC 92-72935. (Illus.). 32p. (J). (ps-k). 1995. pap. 4.95 (*0-7868-1038-6*, Pub. by Hyprn Ppbks) Little.
— The Matzah That Papa Brought Home. LC 94-9952. (Illus.). 32p. (J). (ps-2). 1995. 14.95 (*0-590-47146-5*) Scholastic Inc.
— Miriam's Cup: A Passover Story. LC 96-2480. (Illus.). 32p. (J). (gr. k-4). 1998. 15.95 (*0-590-67720-9*) Scholastic Inc.
— 101 Dalmatians Counting Book & Puppy, Set. (Illus.). 32p. (J). (ps-1). 1993. pap. 16.95 (*1-56282-572-0*, Pub. by Disney Pr) Little.
— The Perfect Christmas Picture. LC 79-2678. (I Can Read Bks.). (Illus.). 64p. (J). (gr. k-3). 1980. 11.95 (*0-06-024068-7*) HarpC Child Bks.
— Walt Disney-One Hundred One Dalmatas: Un Libro para Contar. Santacruz, Daniel m., tr. from ENG. LC 93-70677. (Libros Buena Vista Ser.). (SPA., Illus.). 32p. (J). 1994. lib. bdg. 13.89 (*1-56282-697-2*, Pub. by Disney Pr) Little.
— Walt Disney's One Hundred One Dalmatians: A Counting Book. LC 90-85426. (Illus.). 32p. (J). (ps-k). 1991. 9.95 (*1-56282-012-5*, Pub. by Disney Pr); lib. bdg. 9.89 (*1-56282-032-X*, Pub. by Disney Pr) Little.
Manuso, James S. Occupational Clinical Psychology. LC 82-19065. 336p. 1983. 67.95 (*0-275-91041-5*, C1041, Praeger Pubs) Greenwood.
Manusov, Eugene V. & Wald, Mike. Character Steins: A Collector's Guide. LC 84-45009. (Illus.). 272p. 1987. 45.00 (*0-8453-4784-5*, Cornwall Bks) Assoc Univ Prs.
Manusov, Eugene V., jt. auth. see Manusov, Patricia L.
Manusov, Patricia L. & Manusov, Eugene V. A Collectors Guide to Diesinger Steins. (Illus.). 96p. (Orig.). 1991. pap. 24.95 (*0-9629458-0-3*) Bristol Pr.
***Manusov, Valerie & Harvey, John H., eds.** Attribution, Communication Behavior & Close Relationships. (Advances in Personal Relationships Ser.). (Illus.). 368p. (C). 2001. Price not set. (*0-521-77089-0*) Cambridge U Pr.
Manutoli, Sophie. Mer'em Ayuqucia.Tr. of Water in All Forms. (ESK., Illus.). 12p. (J). (gr. k-3). 1998. pap. text 6.00 (*1-58084-044-2*) Lower Kuskokwim.
— Uksuq Wallu-qaa Kiak?Tr. of Winter or Summer?. (ESK., Illus.). 20p. (J). (gr. k-3). 1998. pap. text 8.00 (*1-58084-042-6*) Lower Kuskokwim.
Manutoli, Sophie, et al. Ella (Air) (ESK., Illus.). 20p. (J). (gr. k-3). 1998. pap. text 8.00 (*1-58084-049-3*) Lower Kuskokwim.
Manutoli, Sophie, jt. auth. see Coolidge, Nellie.
Manutoli, Sophie, tr. see MacDiarmid, Jim.
Manuz, Roger, ed. Contemporary Literacy Criticism Vol. 59: Yearbook 1989: The Year in Fiction, Poetry, Drama & World Literature & the Year's New Authors, Prizewinners, Obituaries, & Outstanding Literary Events, Vol. 59. (Illus.). 525p. 1990. text 150.00 (*0-8103-4433-5*) Gale.
Manvell, Roger. Elizabeth Inchbald: England's Principal Woman Dramatist & Independent Woman of Letters in 18th Century London. LC 87-21247. (Biography Study). (Illus.). 232p. (Orig.). (C). 1988. lib. bdg. 50.00 (*0-8191-6633-2*) U Pr of Amer.
— Ingmar Bergman: An Appreciation. LC 79-6697. (Dissertations on Film, 1980 Ser.). 1980. lib. bdg. 20.95 (*0-405-12936-X*) Ayer.
Manvell, Roger, ed. Experiment in the Film. LC 73-124017. (Literature of Cinema Ser.). 1975. reprint ed. 20.95 (*0-405-01623-9*) Ayer.
Manvell, Roger, intro. Selected Comedies: Elizabeth Inchbald. (Illus.). 372p. (Orig.). (C). 1988. lib. bdg. 49.00 (*0-8191-6635-9*) U Pr of Amer.
Manvell, Roger & Jowett, Garth S., eds. The Cinema, 1950. LC 77-11380. (Aspects of Film Ser.). (Illus.). 1978. reprint ed. lib. bdg. 18.95 (*0-405-11139-8*) Ayer.
— The Cinema, 1951. LC 77-18644. (Aspects of Film Ser.). (Illus.). 1978. reprint ed. lib. bdg. 18.95 (*0-405-11145-2*) Ayer.
— The Cinema, 1952. LC 77-18645. (Aspects of Film Ser.). (Illus.). 1978. reprint ed. lib. bdg. 18.95 (*0-405-11146-0*) Ayer.
Manvell, Roger, jt. auth. see Fleming, Michael.
Manvell, Roger, ed. see Dickinson, Thorold & De La Roche, Catherine.
Manvell, Roger, ed. see Hardy, Forsyth.
Manvell, Roger, ed. see Jarratt, Vernon.
Manvell, Roger, ed. see Sadoul, Georges.
Manvell, Roger, ed. see Wollenberg, H. H.
Manville, Daniel E., jt. auth. see Boston, John.
Manville, Douglas, ed. see Oliver, George.
Manville, Philip Brook. The Origins of Citizenship in Ancient Athens. 279p. 1990. pap. text 17.95 (*0-691-01593-7*, Pub. by Princeton U Pr) Cal Prin Full Svc.
Manwani, S. N. Evolution of Art & Architecture in Central India: With Special Reference to the Kalachuris of Ratanpur. (C). 1988. 70.00 (*0-8364-2338-0*, Pub. by Agam Kala Prakashan) S Asia.
Manwaring, A., ed. Marathi Proverbs. (C). 1991. reprint ed. 15.00 (*81-206-0704-X*, Pub. by Asian Educ Servs) S Asia.
Manwaring, Charles W., compiled by. Hartford Digest of the Early Connecticut Probate Records: Hartford District, Connecticut, 3 vols. 2174p. 1997. reprint ed. lib. bdg. 220.00 (*0-8328-5656-8*) Higginson Bk Co.
Manwaring, Charles William. A Digest of the Early Connecticut Probate Records, 3 Vols., Set. LC 94-74584. 2224p. 1995. reprint ed. 150.00 (*0-8063-1472-9*) Genealog Pub.
Manwaring, George E., jt. auth. see Dobree, Bonamy.
Manwaring, Kim H. & Crone, Kerry R. Neuroendoscopy. 121p. 1991. 40.00 (*0-913113-57-3*) M Liebert.
***Manwaring, Max G.** Security & Civil-Military Relations in the New World Disorder: The Use of Armed Forces in the Americas. 91p. 1999. pap. write for info. (*1-58487-005-2*) SSI US Army.
Manwaring, Max G. & Fishel, John T., eds. Toward Responsibility in the New World Disorder: Challenges & Lessons of Peace Operations. LC 99-165135. 215p. 1998. 45.00 (*0-7146-4901-5*, Pub. by F Cass Pubs); pap. 22.50 (*0-7146-4456-0*, Pub. by F Cass Pubs) Intl Spec Bk.
***Manwaring, Max G. & Joes, Anthony James.** Beyond Declaring Victory & Coming Home: The Challenges of Peace & Stability Operations. LC 99-55878. 280p. 2000. 69.95 (*0-275-96768-9*, Praeger Pubs) Greenwood.
Manwaring, Max G. & Prisk, Court, eds. El Salvador at War: An Oral History of Conflict from the 1979 Insurrection to the Present. 500p. (C). 1995. reprint ed. pap. text 50.00 (*0-7881-2161-8*) DIANE Pub.
Manwaring, Max G. & Sabrosky, Alan N. Defending Europe: The Iberian Connection. 144p. (C). 1999. pap. 17.00 (*0-8133-7183-X*) Westview.
Manwaring, Randle. A Study of Hymn-Writing & Hymn-Singing in the Christian Church. LC 90-47020. (Texts & Studies in Religion: Vol. 50). 188p. 1990. lib. bdg. 79.95 (*0-88946-798-6*) E Mellen.
Manweller, Richard L., Sr. Funding High Tech Ventures. LC 97-35132. (Illus.). 148p. 1997. pap. 21.95 (*1-55571-405-6*, Oasis Pr) PSI Resch.
Manwood, John. A Treatise of the Laws of the Forest. LC 76-57398. (English Experience Ser.: No. 814). 1977. reprint ed. lib. bdg. 60.00 (*90-221-0814-7*) Walter J Johnson.
Manx Gaelic Society. Manx, a Course in the Spoken Language. 1974. pap. 12.50 (*0-89979-025-9*) British Am Bks.
***Many, Joyce.** Handbook of Instructional Practices for Literacy Teacher Educators: Examples & Reflections from the Teaching Lives of Literacy Scholars. LC 00-29365. 2000. pap. write for info. (*0-8058-3110-X*) L Erlbaum Assocs.
Many, Joyce & Cox, Carole, eds. Reader Stance & Literary Understanding: Exploring the Theories, Research, & Practice. LC 92-17318. 288p. 1992. pap. 39.50 (*0-89391-916-0*); text 73.25 (*0-89391-874-1*) Ablx Pub.
***Many, Paul.** My Life, Take Two. LC 99-55396. 204p. (YA). (gr. 7-12). 2000. 16.95 (*0-8027-8708-8*) Walker & Co.
Many, Paul. These Are the Rules. (J). 1998. 10.09 (*0-606-13843-9*, Pub. by Turtleback) Demco.
— These Are the Rules. LC 96-46324. 192p. (YA). (gr. 7 up). 1997. 15.95 (*0-8027-8619-7*) Walker & Co.
Many Voices Readers Staff. Poems to Our Therapists. W., Lynn, ed. (Illus.). 120p. (Orig.). 1996. pap. 10.00 (*0-9637277-1-0*) Many Voices Pr.
Many, Wesley A. & Friker, Walter. Building Computer Literacy: Levels A thru I. (Illus.). 1985. teacher ed. 9.50 (*0-932957-01-3*); pap. 6.75 (*0-932957-00-5*) Natl School.
Manya, K'Omalowete A. Djonga, see Djonga Manya, K'Omalowete A.
Manyak, Anne, jt. ed. see Almquist, Alan J.
Manyan, Gladys. Recipes & Escapades from a Countrywoman's Journal. LC 87-71572. (Illus.). 248p. 1987. pap. 5.95 (*0-941216-38-1*) Cay-Bel.
Manyarrows, Victoria L. Songs from the Native Lands. LC 95-67634. 96p. 1995. pap. 9.95 (*0-9645234-1-8*) Nopal Pr.
Manye i Marti, Lourdes, ed. see Marti i Pol, Miguel.
Manyon, L. A., tr. see Bloch, Marc.
***Manyonda, I. T. & Hay, F. C.** The Immunology of Obstetrics & Gynecology. (Illus.). 350p. 2000. 88.00 (*1-85070-791-X*) Prthnon Pub.
Manyoni, Angelika. Consistence of Phenotype: A Study of Gottfried Benn's Views on Lyrical Poetry. LC 83-5462. (American University Studies: Germanic Languages & Literature: Ser. I, Vol. 698). 346p. (Orig.). (C). 1983. pap. text 36.30 (*0-8204-0011-4*) P Lang Pubng.
Man'yoshu, English. The Ten Thousand Leaves: A Translation of the Man'yoshu, Japan's Premier Anthology of Classical Poetry, Vol. 1. LC 80-8561. (Princeton Library of Asian Translations). (Illus.). 418p. 1987. reprint ed. pap. 129.60 (*0-7837-8176-8*, 204788100001) Bks Demand.
Manypenny, George W. Our Indian Wards. LC 68-54844. (American Scene Ser.). 1972. reprint ed. lib. bdg. 35.00 (*0-306-71140-0*) Da Capo.
Manz, A. & Becker, H., eds. Microsystem Technology in Chemistry & Life Science. LC 99-13179. (Desktop Editions in Chemistry Ser.). 265p. 1999. pap. 54.95 (*3-540-65555-7*) Spr-Verlag.
Manz, A., jt. ed. see Becker, H.
Manz, Beatrice F., ed. Central Asia in Historical Perspective. 245p. (C). 1994. pap. 75.00 (*0-8133-8801-5*, Pub. by Westview) HarpC.
Manz, Beatrice F., ed. see Fletcher, Joseph F., Jr.
Manz, Beatrice Forbes. The Rise & Rule of Tamerlane. LC 99-225791. (Canto Book Ser.). (Illus.). 240p. (C). 1999. pap. 12.95 (*0-521-63384-2*) Cambridge U Pr.

An Asterisk (*) at the beginning of an entry indicates that the title is appearing for the first time.

Manz, Beatriz. Refugees of a Hidden War: The Aftermath of Counterinsurgency in Guatemala. LC 87-10169. (SUNY Series in Anthropological Studies of Contemporary Issues). (Illus.). 283p. (C). 1988. text 24.50 (*0-88706-675-5*) State U NY Pr.

***Manz, Bruno.** A Mind in Prison: The Memoir of a Son & Soldier in the Third Reich. LC 99-86468. (Illus.). 288p. 2000. 24.95 (*1-57488-242-2*) Brasseys.

Manz, Charles C. The Leadership Wisdom of Jesus: Practical Lessons for Today. 188p. 1999. reprint ed. pap. 14.00 (*1-57675-066-3*) Berrett-Koehler.

— Mastering Self-Leadership: Empowering Yourself for Personal Excellence. 168p. (C). 1991. pap. text 15.95 (*0-13-560863-5*) P-H.

***Manz, Charles C. & Neck, Christopher P.** Mastering Self Leadership: Empowering Yourself for Personal Excellence. 2nd ed. LC 98-34044. 132p. (C). 1998. pap. text 21.00 (*0-13-011087-6*) P-H.

Manz, Charles C. & Sims, Henry P. Business Without Bosses: How Self-Managing Teams Are Building High-Performing Companies. 256p. 1995. pap. 16.95 (*0-471-12725-6*) Wiley.

Manz, Charles C., et al. For Team Members Only: Making Your Workplace Team Productive & Hassle-Free. LC 97-7127. 176p. (Orig.). 1997. pap. 16.95 (*0-8144-7946-4*) AMACOM.

Manz, Charles C., jt. auth. see Sims, Henry P.

Manz, Charles C., jt. auth. see Sims, Henry P., Jr.

Manz, David, jt. auth. see Gehlhar, Philip.

Manz-Davies, Birgit, tr. see Fritz, Volkmar.

Manz, Elizabeth. Scare Tactics. 1996. mass mkt. 5.99 (*0-312-95792-0*) St Martin.

— Wasted Space, Vol. 1. 1996. mass mkt. 5.99 (*0-312-95981-8*) St Martin.

Manz, Jorn & Woste, Ludger, eds. Femtosecond Chemistry, 2 vols., Set. LC 94-43743. 916p. 1995. 475.00 (*3-527-29062-1*, Wiley-VCH) Wiley.

Manz, Kenneth W. The Challenge of Recycling Refrigerants. Turpin, Joanna & Checket-Hanks, B. A., eds. LC 94-34530. (Illus.). 200p. 1995. 29.95 (*1-885863-00-4*) Busn News.

Manz, Olaf & Wolf, Thomas R. Representations of Solvable Groups. (London Mathematical Society Lecture Note Ser.: No. 185). 314p. (C). 1993. pap. text 49.95 (*0-521-39739-1*) Cambridge U Pr.

Manz Simon, Mary. Goodnight Angel. (Illus.). 13p. (J). (ps-1). pap. 9.99 incl. audio (*0-570-04966-0*, 56-1839) Concordia.

— Miriam Watches Baby Moses: A Story of Faith & Loyalty. LC 98-38567. (Prince of Egypt Ser.). 32p. (J). (ps-3). 1998. 8.99 (*0-8499-5851-2*) Tommy Nelson.

— Moses & the Burning Bush: A Story about Faith & Obedience. LC 98-38569. (Prince of Egypt Ser.). 32p. (J). (ps-3). 1998. 8.99 (*0-8499-5853-9*) Tommy Nelson.

— Moses Crosses the Red Sea: A Story of Faith & Courage. LC 98-38568. (Prince of Egypt Ser.). (Illus.). 32p. (J). (ps-3). 1998. 8.99 (*0-8499-5852-0*) Tommy Nelson.

***Manz, William H.** Federal Copyright Law: The Legislative Histories of the Major Enactments of the 105th Congress, 5 vols. LC 99-63566. 5200+p. 1999. lib. bdg. 595.00 (*1-57588-530-1*, 323540) W S Hein.

— Foreign Sovereign Immunities Act of 1976 with Amendments: A Legislative History of Pub. L. No. 94-583. LC 00-25262. 2000. write for info. (*1-57588-628-6*) W S Hein.

Manz, William H., ed. Records & Briefs of Landmark Benjamin Cardozo Opinions, 3 vols. LC 98-87788. 1999. 350.00 (*1-57588-238-8*, 308990) W S Hein.

Manz, William H., jt. auth. see Ciampi, Maria L.

Manz, William H., jt. auth. see Reams, Bernard D., Jr.

Manz, William H., jt. ed. see Reams, Bernard D., Jr.

Manza, G. & Newman, F. One to One. pap. 18.95 (*0-87477-948-0*, Tarcher Putnam) Putnam Pub Group.

***Manza, Jeff & Brooks, Clem.** Social Cleavages & Political Change: Voter Alignment & U.S. Party Coalitions. LC 99-15986. 360p. 1999. text 55.00 (*0-19-829492-1*) OUP.

Manzaloui, Mahmoud, ed. Arabic Short Stories Nineteen Forty-Five to Nineteen Sixty-Five. 1986. pap. 20.00 (*977-424-121-5*, Pub. by Am Univ Cairo Pr) Col U Pr.

— Arabic Writing Today: Drama. Vol. 2. 643p. (Orig.). 1977. pap. 12.50 (*0-936770-00-7*, Pub. by Amer Res Ctr Egypt) Eisenbrauns.

Manzanares, Cesar. Lo Que Usted Necesita Saber Sobre la Nueva Era. (Serie Guia de Bolsillo - Pocket Guides Ser.).Tr. of What You Need to Know about the New Age. (SPA.). 101p. 1991. pap. 2.79 (*1-56063-163-5*, 498071) Editorial Unilit.

Manzanares, Cesar V. En las Raices de la Nueva Era.Tr. of Roots of the New Age. (SPA.). 160p. 1996. 8.99 (*0-89922-575-6*, C082-5756) Caribe Betania.

— Ovnis: Cual Es la Verdad?Tr. of UFO: What Is the Truth?. (SPA.). 63p. 1991. pap. 3.99 (*1-56063-178-3*, 490264) Editorial Unilit.

Manzanares, Cesar Vidal. Como Presentar el Evangelio a los Mormones.Tr. of How to Present the Gospel to Mormons. (SPA.). 64p. 1997. pap. 3.50 (*0-311-13861-6*, Edit Mundo) Casa Bautista.

Manzanares, Cesar Vidal. Como Presentar el Evangelio a los Testigos de Jehova. 3rd ed.Tr. of How to Present the Gospel to the Jehovah's Witnesses. (SPA.). 64p. 1997. reprint ed. pap. text 5.50 (*0-311-13859-4*) Casa Bautista.

Manzanilla, L. Emergence & Change in Early Urban Societies. (Fundamental Issues in Archaeology Ser.). (Illus.). 316p. (C). 1996. 59.00 (*0-306-45494-7*, Kluwer Plenum) Kluwer Academic.

Manzanilla, Linda. Akapana: Una Piramide en el Centro del Mundo. 116p. 1992. pap. 11.50 (*968-36-2261-5*, UN013) UPLAAP.

— La Arqueologia: Una Vision Cientifica. (Ciencia para Todos Ser.). (SPA.). pap. 6.99 (*968-16-4374-7*, Pub. by Fondo) Continental Bk.

— La Constitucion de la Sociedad Urbana en Mesopotamia. 402p. 1986. pap. 9.14 (*968-837-955-7*, UN36) UPLAAP.

Manzanilla, Linda, ed. Anatomia de un Conjunto Residencial Teotihuacano en Oztoyahualco, 2 vols., Set. 1993. pap. 37.00 (*968-36-2930-X*, UN014) UPLAAP.

— Coba, Quintana Roo: Analisis de Dos Unidades Habitacionales Mayas del Horizonte Clasico. 438p. 1987. pap. 11.43 (*968-837-957-3*, UN012) UPLAAP.

— Coloquio V. Gordon Childe: Estudios Sobre la Revolucion Neolitica y la Revolucion Urbana. 412p. 1988. pap. 14.00 (*968-36-0693-8*, UN031) UPLAAP.

— Unidades Habitacionales Mesoamericanas y Sus Areas de Actividad. 470p. 1986. pap. 9.14 (*968-837-585-3*, UN011) UPLAAP.

Manzanilla, Linda & Lopez, Leonardo, eds. Historia Antigua de Mexico, 3 vols., Set. 1190p. 1995. write for info. (*968-842-393-9*) UPLAAP.

— Historia Antigua de Mexico Vol. I: El Mexico Antiguo, Sus Areas Culturales, los Origenes y el Horizonte Preclasico. 360p. 1994. pap. 16.00 (*968-842-394-7*, IN046) UPLAAP.

— Historia Antigua de Mexico Vol. II: El Horizonte Clasico. 302p. 1995. pap. 15.00 (*968-842-395-5*, IN047) UPLAAP.

— Historia Antigua de Mexico Vol. III: El Horizonte Posclasico y Algunos Aspectos Intelectuales de las Culturas Mesoamericanas. 528p. 1995. pap. 24.00 (*968-842-396-3*, IN048) UPLAAP.

Manzanilla, Linda, jt. auth. see Feinman, Gary M.

Manzano, Juan F. The Autobiography of a Slave: A Bilingual Edition. Schulman, Ivan A., ed. Garfield, Evelyn P., tr. from SPA. (Latin American Literature & Culture Ser.). 136p. (C). 1996. 34.95 (*0-8143-2537-8*); pap. 17.95 (*0-8143-2538-6*) Wayne St U Pr.

Manzano, Juan F. & De La Concepcion Valdes, Gabriel. Two Cuban Poets, 2 vols. in 1. (B. E. Ser.: No. 54). 1937. 45.00 (*0-8115-3005-1*) Periodicals Srv.

***Manzano, Linda.** Child Development: Student Handbook. 1999. pap. text, student ed. 10.95 (*1-56870-358-9*) RonJon Pub.

Manzano, M. Extensions of First-Order Logic. (Cambridge Tracts in Theoretical Computer Science Ser.: No. 19). 410p. (C). 1996. text 69.95 (*0-521-35435-8*) Cambridge U Pr.

***Manzano, Maria.** Model Theory. de Queiroz, Ruy J. G. B., tr. (Oxford Logic Guides Ser.: No. 37). (Illus.). 263p. 1999. text 75.00 (*0-19-853851-0*) OUP.

Manzano, Mariano O. Dictionary of Synonyms & Antonyms: Diccionario de Sinonimos y Antonimos. 3rd ed. (ENG & SPA.). 368p. 1990. write for info. (*0-7859-4956-9*) Fr & Eur.

Manzano, R. Whitney, jt. auth. see Cho, David Y.

Manzano, R. Whitney, jt. auth. see Cho, Paul Y.

Manzano, Roy R. Pelly's Exciting Adventures. (Illus.). (J). 1993. 9.95 (*0-533-10526-9*) Vantage.

Manzardo, Lorie M. Current Techniques in Neurosurgery. 240p. 1995. text 174.95 (*1-878132-01-6*) Current Med.

Manzarek, Ray. The Bright Midnight: The Doors. LC 98-6303. (Illus.). 368p. 1998. 26.95 (*0-399-14399-8*, G P Putnam) Peng Put Young Read.

— Light My Fire: My Life with the Doors. 1999. reprint ed. pap. 14.95 (*0-425-17045-4*) Berkley Pub.

Manzella, Giuseppe M. R., ed. see Spezie, Giancarlo.

Manzella, John L. The Businessman's Guide to Free Trade. (Illus.). 90p. (C). 1989. pap. 9.95 (*0-926566-00-8*) Manzella Trade.

— Mexico & NAFTA: The Real Impact. 1994. 35.00 (*0-926566-03-2*) Manzella Trade.

Manzella, John L. & Walker, Tony. Opportunity in Mexico: A Small Business Guide. (Illus.). 1992. write for info. (*0-926566-02-4*) Manzella Trade.

Manzer, Alison. The Bank Act Annotated. 624p. 1993. boxed set 80.00 (*0-409-89901-1*, CN, MICHIE) LEXIS Pub.

Manzer, Ronald A. Public Policies & Political Development in Canada. 256p. 1985. pap. text 19.95 (*0-8020-6559-7*) U of Toronto Pr.

— Public Policies & Political Development in Canada. LC 86-110537. (Illus.). 250p. reprint ed. pap. 77.50 (*0-7837-0527-1*, 204085300019) Bks Demand.

— State Education in Canada: Public Policy & Public Philosophy. 367p. 1994. text 50.00 (*0-8020-0604-3*); pap. text 19.95 (*0-8020-7209-7*) U of Toronto Pr.

Manzetti, Luigi. The International Monetary Fund & Economic Stabilization: The Argentine Case. LC 90-24565. 256p. 1991. 65.00 (*0-275-93397-0*, C3397, Praeger Pubs) Greenwood.

— Privatization South American Style. LC 99-28124. 392p. 2000. text 74.00 (*0-19-829466-2*) OUP.

***Manzetti, Luigi, ed.** Regulatory Policy in Latin America: Post-Privatization Realities. LC 00-89250. 301p. 2000. lib. bdg. 55.00 (*1-57454-073-4*, Pub. by U Miami N-S Ctr) L Rienner.

Manzetti, Luigi, jt. auth. see Snow, Peter G.

Manzheli, V. G. Structure & Thermodynamic Properties of Cryocrystals: Handbook. LC 98-7871. 1998. write for info. (*1-56700-119-X*) Begell Hse.

Manzhelii, V. G. Handbook of Binary Solutions of Cryocrystals. LC 96-34049. 1996. write for info. (*1-56700-070-3*) Begell Hse.

Manzhelii, Vadim G. & Freiman, Yuri A., eds. Physics of Cryocrystals. LC 96-34042. (Illus.). 765p. 1996. text 135.00 (*1-56396-537-2*) Spr-Verlag.

***Manzi, Carolyn.** Coloring Your Prayers: An Inspirational Coloring Book for Making Dreams Come True. LC 99-88979. (Illus.). 192p. 2000. 17.95 (*0-609-60621-2*) Harmony Bks.

Manzi, J. J. & Castagna, M., eds. Clam Mariculture in North America. (Developments in Aquaculture & Fisheries Science Ser.: No. 19). 462p. 1989. 186.00 (*0-444-87300-7*) Elsevier.

***Manzi, Lou & Gunod, Nat.** Intermediate Fingerstyle for Guitar. 96p. 1998. pap. 9.95 (*0-7390-0594-4*, 17823) Alfred Pub.

— Intermediate Fingerstyle for Guitar. 1998. pap. 20.90 incl. audio compact disk (*0-7390-0595-2*, 17825) Alfred Pub.

Manzi, Nina, jt. auth. see Baker, Karen.

Manzi, Raffaele. Christian Multi-Media Catalogue for Multi-Lingual Ministries. Ulrich, Sharon S., ed. LC BR67.2.M36 1994. 384p. (Orig.). 1994. pap. 125.00 (*0-9644029-1-2*) Means GA.

***Manzi, Raffaele.** Christian Multimedia Cataloque for Multi-Lingual: Ministries with World Wide Web. 2nd rev. ed. Ulrich-Manzi, Sharon, ed. LC BR67.2.M36-1999. 368p. 1999. pap. text 125.00 (*1-929551-00-2*) Means GA.

Manzi, Raffaele. Una Esplorazione Biblica Sul Concetto di "Leadership" (SPA., Illus.). 105p. (Orig.). (C). 1996. pap. text 25.00 (*0-9644029-3-9*) Means GA.

— Italian-American Experience in Georgia. rev. ed. LC 98-150011. (Illus.). 156p. (Orig.). (C). 1997. pap. text 25.00 (*0-9644029-4-7*) Means GA.

— The Keepers of the Gate: Immigration, Immigrants & Citizenship in the State of Georgia. Ulrich-Manzi, Sharon, ed. LC 98-206113. (Illus.). 97p. (C). 1998. pap. text 25.00 (*0-9644029-9-8*) Means GA.

— Surviving in Losses. Manzi, Sharon, ed. 454p. (Orig.). (C). 1996. pap. text 25.00 (*0-9644029-2-0*) Means GA.

Manzi, Sharon, ed. see Manzi, Raffaele.

Manzi, Sharon U. Is Joy Vertical or Horizontal? A Woman's Perspective. (Women of Action Ser.: Bk. II). (Illus.). 58p. 1997. pap. text 10.00 (*0-9644029-5-5*) Means GA.

Manzi, Sharon U., ed. see Marakovitz, Alice.

Manzini, Ezio. The Material of Invention: Materials & Design. 250p. (C). 1989. text 150.00 (*0-85072-247-0*) St Mut.

Manzini, Maria R. Locality: A Theory & Some of Its Empirical Consequences. (Linguistic Inquiry Monographs: No. 19). (Illus.). 255p. 1992. 40.00 (*0-262-13279-6*); pap. text 20.00 (*0-262-63140-7*) MIT Pr.

Manzione, Carol K. Christ's Hospital of London, 1552-1598: Passing Deed of Pity. LC 94-16865. 232p. 1995. 37.50 (*0-945636-71-7*) Susquehanna U Pr.

Manzione, Joseph. I Am Looking to the North for My Life: Sitting Bull, 1876-1881. (Publications in the American West: Vol. 25). (Illus.). 300p. 1994. reprint ed. pap. 14.95 (*0-87480-461-2*) U of Utah Pr.

Manzke, Bill. The Encyclopedia of Corgi Toys. (Schiffer Book for Collectors Ser.). (Illus.). 256p. 1997. pap. 34.95 (*0-7643-0308-2*) Schiffer.

Manzo. Content Literacy 2nd ed. 320p. 1997. pap. 56.95 (*0-471-36556-4*) Wiley.

Manzo, jt. auth. see Blum.

Manzo, Anthony V. Teaching Children to Be Leaders. (C). 1994. pap. text, teacher ed. 33.75 (*0-15-502399-3*) Harcourt Coll Pubs.

Manzo, Anthony V. & Manzo, Ula C. Literacy Disorders: Holistic Diagnosis & Remediation. 512p. (C). 1993. pap. text 4.00 (*0-03-097349-X*, Pub. by Harcourt Coll Pubs); lib. bdg. write for info. (*0-03-072566-6*) Harcourt Coll Pubs.

— Teaching Children to Be Literate: A Reflective Approach. (Illus.). 640p. (C). 1994. text 73.00 (*0-15-300560-2*, Pub. by Harcourt Coll Pubs) Harcourt.

***Manzo, Anthony V., et al.** Content Area Literacy: Fusing Curriculum, Culture & Community in the Wired Class. 320p. (C). 2000. pap. write for info. (*0-471-36561-0*) Wiley.

Manzo, Anthony V., et al. Informal Reading-Thinking Inventory (IR-TI) An Informal Reading Inventory (IRI) with Options for Assessing Additional Elements of Higher-Order Literacy. 224p. (C). 1994. pap. text 50.00 (*0-15-500956-7*, Pub. by Harcourt Coll Pubs) Harcourt.

Manzo, Anthony V., jt. auth. see Manzo, Ula C.

Manzo, Bettina. The Animal Rights Movement in the U. S., 1975-1990: An Annotated Bibliography. LC 94-19622. 306p. 1994. text 45.00 (*0-8108-2732-8*) Scarecrow.

Manzo, Jean-Paul & Ferrari, Luciano. Rome. (Great Cities Ser.). (Illus.). 96p. 1999. 20.00 (*1-85995-550-9*) Parkstone Pr.

Manzo, Jean Q. Surviving Without a Secretary: A Guide to Productivity. Paris, Janis, ed. LC 96-83619. (Fifty Minute Ser.). 99p. 1996. pap. 10.95 (*1-56052-393-X*) Crisp Pubns.

Manzo, John F., jt. auth. see Travers, Max.

Manzo, Kate & McHenry, Dean E., Jr. Limited Choices: The Political Struggle for Socialism in Tanzania. LC 94-14623. 5253p. 1998. pap. 18.95 (*1-55587-556-4*) L Rienner.

Manzo, Kathryn A. Creating Boundaries: The Politics of Race & Nation. 253p. 1998. pap. 19.95 (*1-55587-564-5*) L Rienner.

— Domination, Resistance & Social Change in South Africa: The Local Effects of Global Power. LC 92-9116. 304p. 1992. 62.95 (*0-275-94364-X*, C4364, Praeger Pubs) Greenwood.

Manzo, Luigi, jt. auth. see Costa, Lucio G.

Manzo, Norberto T., et al. Hospital Plans in Case of Disaster: For Latin America & the Caribbean Countries. (Illus.). 124p. (Orig.). (C). 1996. pap. text 35.00 (*0-7881-3377-2*) DIANE Pub.

Manzo, Tom, tr. see Yun, Hsing.

Manzo, Ula C. & Manzo, Anthony V. Literary Disorders: Holistic Diagnosis & Remediation. (Illus.). 515p. (C). 1993. text 81.00 (*0-03-072633-6*, Pub. by Harcourt Coll Pubs) Harcourt.

Manzo, Ula C., jt. auth. see Manzo, Anthony V.

***Manzocchi.** Foreign Capital in Developing. LC 99-18736. 1999. text 69.95 (*0-312-22238-6*) St Martin.

Manzolini, Eleonora, jt. auth. see Haas, Elson M.

Manzoni, Alessandro. The Betrothed: (I Promessi Sposi) Penman, Bruce, tr. & intro. by. (Classics Ser.). 720p. 1984. pap. 14.95 (*0-14-044274-X*, Penguin Classics) Viking Penguin.

— On the Historical Novel. Bermann, Sandra, tr. LC 83-10583. x, 134p. 1984. pap. text 12.00 (*0-8032-8226-5*, Bison Books) U of Nebr Pr.

Manzoni, Francesca, jt. auth. see Savona, Ernesto.

Manzoni, J. F., jt. auth. see Dutta, Soumitra.

Manzoor, M. Heat Flow Through Extended Surface Heat Exchangers. (Lecture Notes in Engineering Ser.: Vol. 5). 277p. 1983. 37.00 (*0-387-13047-0*) Spr-Verlag.

***Manzullo, Donald A.** Why Exports Matter: Congressional Hearing. 169p. 2000. reprint ed. pap. text 30.00 (*0-7881-8861-5*) DIANE Pub.

Manzullo, Donald A., jt. ed. see Torkildsen, Peter G.

Manzur, Ibn. Lisan al Arab, 5 vols., Set.Tr. of Arabic Language. (ARA & ENG.). 600p. 1979. 295.00 (*0-86685-541-6*, LDL349, Pub. by Librairie du Liban) Intl Bk Ctr.

Mao, Ashikho D. Nagas: Problems & Politics. (C). 1992. 24.00 (*81-7024-486-2*, Pub. by Ashish Pub Hse) S Asia.

— Nagas: Problems & Politics. x, 206p. 1992. 19.95 (*1-881338-30-4*) Nataraj Bks.

Mao, Cindy. Sing Chinese! Popular Children's Songs & Lullabies. (CHI & ENG.). 64p. (J). 1996. spiral bd. 19.95 incl. audio (*0-8351-2588-2*) China Bks.

Mao, Cindy & Ma Baolin. Sing Chinese! Popular Children's Songs & Lullabies. 1996. audio 7.95 (*0-8351-2589-0*) China Bks.

— Sing Chinese! Popular Children's Songs & Lullabies. (CHI & ENG.). 64p. (J). 1996. spiral bd. 14.95 incl. audio (*0-8351-2587-4*) China Bks.

Mao, Cindy, jt. auth. see Baolin, Ma.

Mao, Douglas. Solid Objects: Modernism & the Test of Production. LC 98-11863. 312p. 1998. text 45.00 (*0-691-05926-8*, Pub. by Princeton U Pr) Cal Prin Full Svc.

Mao Dun. Rainbow. Zelin, Madeleine, tr. from CHI. LC 91-31273. (Voices from Asia Ser.: No. 4). 255p. 1992. pap. 15.95 (*0-520-07328-2*, Pub. by U CA Pr) Cal Prin Full Svc.

Mao, Li, ed. Ancient Way to Keep Fit. Luzeng, Song et al, trs. LC 92-81013. 1992. 20.00 (*0-679-74371-5*) Random.

Mao, Lina, tr. see Wittet, Scott & Wong, Debbie.

Mao Minghua, et al, eds. Selected Papers of Engineering Chemistry & Metallurgy (China), 1995. 159p. 1996. 29.50 (*7-03-005098-3*, Pub. by Sci Pr) Lubrecht & Cramer.

Mao Minghua & Xia Guang, eds. Selected Papers of Engineering Chemistry & Metallurgy (China), 1993, Vol. 4. 178p. 1996. 25.00 (*7-03-004366-9*, Pub. by Sci Pr) Lubrecht & Cramer.

— Selected Papers of Engineering Chemistry & Metallurgy (China), 1994, Vol. 6. 170p. 1996. 30.00 (*7-03-004563-7*, Pub. by Sci Pr) Lubrecht & Cramer.

Mao, Nathan K., tr. see Ch'ien, Chung-Shu.

Mao, Sophie Le, see Fallon, Steve & Le Mao, Sophie.

Mao Tun. Spring Silkworms & Other Stories. 2nd ed. 1980. 9.95 (*0-8351-0615-2*) China Bks.

Mao Tun, Dun. Spring Silkworms & Other Stories. 2nd ed. Shapiro, Sidney, tr. from CHI. 240p. (C). 1979. 9.95 (*0-917056-90-6*, Pub. by Foreign Lang Pr) Cheng & Tsui.

Mao, Xuerong. Exponential Stability of Stochastic Differential Equations. LC 94-6019. (Pure & Applied Mathematics Ser.: Vol. 182). (Illus.). 328p. 1994. text 135.00 (*0-8247-9080-4*) Dekker.

— Stochastic Differential Equations & Applications. LC 98-106168. 360p. 1998. 55.00 (*1-898563-26-8*, Pub. by Horwood Pub) Paul & Co Pubs.

Mao, Y., jt. auth. see Sekine, M.

Mao, Yong, jt. auth. see Fink, Thomas.

Maokley, Maureen, ed. Party Realignment & State Politics. LC 91-40730. (Illus.). 319p. reprint ed. pap. 98.90 (*0-608-09858-2*, 206982300006) Bks Demand.

Maola. Family Law for Paralegals. (Paralegal Ser.). (C). pap. 26.25 (*0-7668-0725-8*) Delmar.

Maolain, Ciaran O. The Radical Right: An International Dictionary. 500p. 1980. lib. bdg. 50.00 (*0-87436-514-7*) ABC-CLIO.

Maor, Eli. E: The Story of a Number. 232p. 1993. pap. 14.95 (*0-691-05854-7*, Pub. by Princeton U Pr) Cal Prin Full Svc.

— E: The Story of a Number. (Illus.). 232p. 1993. text 35.00 (*0-691-03390-0*, Pub. by Princeton U Pr) Cal Prin Full Svc.

***Maor, Eli.** June 8, 2004: Venus in Transit. LC 99-16546. 165p. 2000. 22.95 (*0-691-04874-6*, Pub. by Princeton U Pr) Cal Prin Full Svc.

Maor, Eli. To Infinity & Beyond: A Cultural History of the Infinite. (Illus.). 284p. 1991. 49.50 (*0-8176-3325-1*) Birkhauser.

— To Infinity & Beyond: A Cultural History of the Institute. (Illus.). 294p. 1991. pap. text 17.95 (*0-691-02511-8*, Pub. by Princeton U Pr) Cal Prin Full Svc.

— Trigonometric Delights. LC 97-18001. 248p. 1998. 24.95 (*0-691-05754-0*, Pub. by Princeton U Pr) Cal Prin Full Svc.

Maor, Moshe. Parties, Conflicts & Coalitions in Western Europe: Organizational Determinants of Coalition Bargaining. LC 97-14940. 216p. (C). 1997. 90.00 (*0-415-11602-3*) Routledge.

— Political Parties in Britain. LC 96-36203. 296p. (C). 1997. 85.00 (*0-415-08284-6*); pap. 25.99 (*0-415-08285-4*) Routledge.

M

***Maor, Moshe & Hazan, Reuven Y., eds.** Parties, Elections & Cleavages: Israel in Comparative & Theoretical Perspective. (Israeli History, Politics & Society Ser.). 224p. 2000. 59.50 (*0-7146-5076-5*, Pub. by F Cass Pubs); pap. 26.50 (*0-7146-8123-7*, Pub. by F Cass Pubs) Intl Spec Bk.

Maori Language Commission. Te Matatiki: Contemporary Maori Words. LC 96-196671. 302p. 1996. pap. 21.00 (*0-19-558341-8*) OUP.

Maori, Yeshayahu. The Peshitta Version of the Pentateuch & Early Jewish Exegesis. (HEB.). 403p. 1995. text 24.00 (*965-223-874-0*, Pub. by Magnes Pr) Eisenbrauns.

Maoshing Ni. Chinese Herbology Made Easy. (Illus.). 150p. 1986. pap. text 18.95 (*0-937064-12-2*) SevenStar Comm.

— The Eight Treasures: Energy Enhancement Exercises. LC 94-30068. (Illus.). 176p. (Orig.). 1996. pap. 17.95 (*0-937064-74-2*) SevenStar Comm.

Maoshing Ni & Daoshing Ni. Golden Message: A Guide to Spiritual Life with Self-Study Program for Learning the Integral Way. LC 90-61067. 1993. pap. 11.95 (*0-937064-36-X*) SevenStar Comm.

Maoxin Chen, tr. see Xiaoping Ji.

Maoz, Benjamin, et al. Doctors & Their Feelings: A Pharmacology of Medical Caring. LC 91-29032. 168p. 1992. 57.95 (*0-275-93990-1*, C3990, Praeger Pubs) Greenwood.

***Maoz, Moshe.** Middle Eastern Minorities: Between Integration & Conflict. LC 99-48682. (Policy Papers Ser.: No. 50). 111p. 1999. pap. 19.95 (*0-944029-33-7*) Wash Inst NEP.

Ma'oz, Moshe. Palestinian Leadership on the West Bank: The Changing Role of the Arab Mayors under Jordan & Israel. (Illus.). 232p. 1984. 49.50 (*0-7146-3234-1*, Pub. by F Cass Pubs) Intl Spec Bk.

— Syria & Israel: From War to Peacemaking. 292p. 1995. text 55.00 (*0-19-828018-1*) OUP.

Ma'oz, Moshe, ed. Studies on Palestine During the Ottoman Period. 224p. 1979. text 35.00 (*965-223-589-X*, Pub. by Magnes Pr) Eisenbrauns.

Maoz, Moshe & Pappe, Ilan, eds. Middle Eastern Politics & Ideas: A History from Within. LC 95-62316. 256p. 1998. text 59.50 (*1-86064-012-5*, Pub. by I B T) St Martin.

Ma'oz, Moshe, et al. Modern Syria: From Ottoman Rule to Pivotal Role in the Middle East LC 99-29246. 1999. write for info. (*1-902210-32-8*, Pub. by Sussex Acad Pr) Intl Spec Bk.

Maoz, Moshe, jt. auth. see Sela, Avraham.

Maoz, Zeev. Domestic Sources of Global Change. LC 96-9974. 288p. (C). 1996. text 59.50 (*0-472-10629-5*, 10629) U of Mich Pr.

— National Choices & International Processes. (Cambridge Studies in International Relations: No. 8). (Illus.). 627p. (C). 1990. text 85.00 (*0-521-36595-3*) Cambridge U Pr.

— Regional Security in the Middle East: Past, Present & Future. LC 97-22900. 208p. 1997. 47.50 (*0-7146-4808-6*, Pub. by F Cass Pubs); pap. 26.50 (*0-7146-4375-0*, Pub. by F Cass Pubs) Intl Spec Bk.

Maoz, Zeev & Gat, Azar, eds. War in a Changing World. (Illus.). 240p. (C). text 47.50 (*0-472-11185-X*, 11185) U of Mich Pr.

Map & Geography Round Table of the American Librar & Koepp, Donna P., eds. Exploration & Mapping of the American West: Selected Essays. (Occasional Paper: No. 1). 1986. 18.95 (*0-932757-01-4*) Speculum Orbis.

MAP Staff. EDI Management, Security, Audit & Internal Controls Manual (Map-29) (Security, Audit & Control Ser.). 200p. 1994. student ed., ring bd. 295.00 (*0-940706-50-4*) Management Advisory Pubns.

Map, Walter. De Nugis Curialium. James, Montagu R., ed. (Anecdota Oxoniensia Ser.: No. 14). 1988. reprint ed. 71.50 (*0-404-63964-X*) AMS Pr.

— De Nugis Curialium-Courtiers' Trifles. Brooke, C. N. et al, eds. (Oxford Medieval Texts Ser.). (Illus.). 608p. 1983. text 95.00 (*0-19-822236-X*) OUP.

— Gualteri Mapes De Nugis Curialium Distinctiones Quinque. Wright, Thomas, ed. (Camden Society, London. Publications, First Ser.: No. 50). reprint ed. 60.00 (*0-404-50150-8*) AMS Pr.

— Latin Poems Commonly Attributed to Walter Mapes. Wright, Thomas, ed. (Camden Society, London. Publications, First Ser.: No. 16). reprint ed. 95.00 (*0-404-50116-8*) AMS Pr.

Mapa, Araceli C. Escenas: Como de Pelicula Vieja. Davalos, Felipe, ed. LC 97-90419. (SPA., Illus.). 96p. (Orig.). 1997. pap. 10.98 (*0-9657871-0-9*) Tree Hse.

Mapanje, Jack. The Chattering Wagtails of Mikuyu Prison. (African Writers Ser.). 99p. 1993. pap. 9.95 (*0-435-91198-8*, 91198) Heinemann.

— Of Chameleons & Gods. (African Writers Ser.). 80p. (Orig.). (C). 1991. pap. 8.95 (*0-435-91194-5*, 91194) Heinemann.

— Skipping Without Ropes. LC 99-195833. 80p. 1998. pap. 16.95 (*1-85224-412-7*, Pub. by Bloodaxe Bks) Dufour.

Mapel, David. Social Justice Reconsidered: The Problem of Appropriate Precision in a Theory of Justice. LC 88-30131. 184p. 1989. text 24.95 (*0-252-01598-3*) U of Ill Pr.

Mapel, David & Nardin, Terry. International Society: Diverse Ethical Perspectives. LC 97-19756. (Ethikon Series in Comparative Ethics). 288p. 1998. text 35.00 (*0-691-05771-0*, Pub. by Princeton U Pr) Cal Prin Full Svc.

***Mapel, David R.** International Society: Diverse Ethical Perspectives. (Ethikon Series in Comparative Ethics). 2000. pap. text 18.95 (*0-691-04972-6*) Princeton U Pr.

Mapel, David R., jt. ed. see Nardin, Terry.

Mapelli, Dina. Poems for the Holidays. 50p. 1998. pap. 9.95 (*1-892896-38-9*) Buy Books.

Mapes, Bruce E. Child Eyewitness Testimony: Ecological Sexual Abuse Investigations. LC 94-41029. 1995. write for info. (*0-88422-154-7*) Clinical Psych.

— Child Eyewitness Testimony in Sexual Abuse Investigations. 140p. 1996. 69.95 (*0-471-16197-7*) Wiley.

Mapes, Carrie & Gold, Judith. Goldilocks & the Three Bears. (Folktale Theme Ser.: Vol. 2). (Illus.). 64p. (J). (gr. k-2). 1995. pap. text, teacher ed. 6.95 (*1-55799-373-4*, EMC 525) Evan-Moor Edu Pubs.

— Jack & the Beanstalk. (Folktale Theme Ser.: Vol. 1). (Illus.). 64p. (J). (gr. k-2). 1995. pap. text, teacher ed. 6.95 (*1-55799-372-6*, EMC 524) Evan-Moor Edu Pubs.

— The Little Red Hen. (Folktale Theme Ser.: Vol. 5). (Illus.). 64p. (J). (gr. k-2). 1995. pap. text, teacher ed. 6.95 (*1-55799-376-9*, EMC 528) Evan-Moor Edu Pubs.

— Little Red Riding Hood. (Folktale Theme Ser.: Vol. 4). (Illus.). 64p. (J). (gr. k-2). 1995. pap. text, teacher ed. 6.95 (*1-55799-375-0*, EMC 527) Evan-Moor Edu Pubs.

— The Three Little Pigs. (Folktale Theme Ser.: Vol. 3). (Illus.). 64p. (J). (gr. k-2). 1995. pap. text, teacher ed. 6.95 (*1-55799-374-2*, EMC 526) Evan-Moor Edu Pubs.

— The Ugly Duckling. (Folktale Theme Ser.: Vol. 6). (Illus.). 64p. (J). (gr. k-2). 1995. pap. text, teacher ed. 6.95 (*1-55799-377-7*, EMC 529) Evan-Moor Edu Pubs.

Mapes, E. K. Escritos Ineditos de R. Dario. (SPA.). 224p. 3.80 (*0-318-22345-7*) Hispanic Inst.

***Mapes, Katta.** Stop! Think! Choose! Developing Emotional Intelligences for Young People. (Illus.). 192p. 2000. pap. 35.00 (*1-56976-109-4*, 1106) Zephyr Pr AZ.

Mapes, Lynda. Washington, the Spirit of the Land. LC 99-14767. (Illus.). 144p. 1999. 35.00 (*0-89658-415-1*) Voyageur Pr.

Mapes, Martha & Morrill, Jennifer. Whole Grains. 2nd ed. (Illus.). 100p. 1989. reprint ed. teacher ed. 3.75 (*1-57753-034-9*, 399R202) Corn Coop Ext.

Mapes, Mary J. The Art of Fielding Questions with Finesse: A Guide to Handling Difficult People, Sensitive Situations & Tough Questions. rev. ed. 77p. (C). 1994. pap. 15.00 (*0-9641633-0-6*) M J Mapes.

Mapes Monde Staff. Westmoreland Nee Neville. rev. ed. (Illus.). 226p. (Orig.). 1995. pap. 32.00 (*0-7884-0261-7*) Heritage Bk.

Mapes, Olin V. Westmoreland Nee Neville. (Orig.). 1992. pap. 28.50 (*1-55613-615-3*) Heritage Bk.

Mapes, Sarah, ed. see Wright, Robert O.

Mapes, Victor. Duse & the French. LC 68-56485. 1972. reprint ed. 19.95 (*0-405-08779-9*) Ayer.

***Mapes, Victor L. & Mills, Scott A.** The Butchers, the Baker: The World War II Memoir of a United States Army Air Corps Soldier Captured by the Japanese in the Philippines. LC 99-37721. (Illus.). 248p. 2000. lib. bdg. 29.95 (*0-7864-0636-4*) McFarland & Co.

Maple. Superstition. Are You Superstitious? 1979. pap. 2.00 (*0-87980-245-6*) Wilshire.

Maple, Amanda, jt. auth. see Griscom, Richard.

Maple, Frank F. Dynamic Interviewing: An Introduction to Counseling. (Human Services Guides Ser.: Vol. 41). 160p. (C). 1985. pap. text 18.95 (*0-8039-2513-1*) Sage.

— Dynamic Interviewing: An Introduction to Counseling. LC 85-11986. (Sage Human Services Guides Ser.: Vol. 41). 175p. 1985. reprint ed. pap. 54.30 (*0-608-01986-0*, 206264200003) Bks Demand.

— Goal Focused Interviewing. LC 97-21126. (Sage Human Services Guides Ser.). 1997. 42.00 (*0-7619-0180-9*); pap. 18.95 (*0-7619-0181-7*) Sage.

— Shared Decision-Making. LC 77-12109. (Sage Human Services Guides Ser.: No. 4). 135p. 1977. reprint ed. pap. 41.90 (*0-608-01472-9*, 205951600001) Bks Demand.

Maple, Frank F., jt. auth. see Bertcher, Harvey J.

***Maple, Jack & Mitchell, Chris.** The Crime Fighter: How You Can Make Your Community Crime-Free. 272p. 2000. reprint ed. pap. 14.95 (*0-7679-0554-7*) Broadway BDD.

— The Crime Fighter: Putting the Bad Guys Out of Business. LC 99-27145. 272p. 1999. 24.95 (*0-385-49363-0*) Doubleday.

Maple, M. Brian, jt. ed. see Fischer, O.

Maple, Marilyn. On the Wings of a Butterfly: A Story about Life & Death. LC 91-50854. (Illus.). 32p. (Orig.). (J). (gr. 1-6). 1992. 15.95 (*0-943990-69-6*) Parenting Pr.

Maple, Mary A., jt. auth. see Charney, Mitchell A.

Maple, Maude S. Maudie: An Oregon Trail Childhood. Muller, Will, ed. (Illus.). 169p. (Orig.). (YA). 1993. pap. write for info. (*0-9637370-0-7*) Lincoln Sq.

Maple, Steve. Complete Idiot's Guide to Wills & Estates. 312p. 1997. pap. 16.95 (*0-02-861747-9*, Alpha Ref) Macmillan Gen Ref.

Maple, Steven. 10 Minute Guide to Estate Planning. 144p. 1997. pap. text 10.95 (*0-02-861749-5*) Macmillan.

Maple Summer Workshop & Symposium Staff. Mathematical Computation with Maple V - Ideas & Applications: Proceedings of the Maple Summer Workshop & Symposium, University of Michigan, Ann Arbor, June 28-30, 1993. Lee, Thomas, ed. LC 93-21604. viii, 199p. 1993. 39.50 (*0-8176-3724-9*) Birkhauser.

***Maple, Terry L.** Saving the Giant Panda. LC 00-105140. 168p. 2000. 35.00 (*1-56352-615-8*) Longstreet.

Maple, Terry L. & Archibald, Erika. Zoo Man: Inside the Zoo Revolution. LC 91-61926. (Illus.). 224p. 1993. 19.95 (*1-56352-016-8*) Longstreet.

Maples, jt. auth. see Cash.

Maples, Edna H., jt. auth. see Stewart, Patricia A.

***Maples, J. D.** Trojan Steers. unabridged ed. LC 99-91695. 260p. 2000. per. 14.95 (*1-930371-01-2*, JDM 00-01) Lomaland Bks.

***Maples, Marla.** All That Glitters Is Not Gold. 2000. mass mkt. 6.99 (*0-06-103104-6*) HarpC.

— All That Glitters Is Not Gold. 256p. 2000. 24.00 (*0-06-039381-5*, ReganBks) HarperTrade.

Maples, Mary, ed. see Ghazi, Abidullah & Ghazi, Tasneema.

Maples, Philip G., jt. auth. see Lehr, Teresa K.

Maples, Robert E. Petroleum Refinery Process Economics. LC 92-37931. 384p. 1993. 89.95 (*0-87814-384-X*, P4488) PennWell Bks.

***Maples, Robert E.** Petroleum Refinery Process Economics. 2nd ed. LC 00-39188. 2000. pap. write for info. (*0-87814-779-9*) PennWell Bks.

Maples, Steve. Your Ticket to a Better Ticket: A Fan's Guide for the Best Concert Experience. Hand, Erin, ed. (Illus.). 124p. 1996. pap. 14.95 (*0-9653448-2-7*) S Maples.

Maples, W. C. NSUCO Oculomotor Test. Bleything, Willard, ed. (Illus.). 60p. (Orig.). (C). 1994. lib. bdg. 18.00 (*0-943599-74-1*) OEPF.

Maples, Wallace R. Opportunities in Aerospace Careers. (Illus.). 160p. 1991. 13.95 (*0-8442-8650-8*, VGM Career) NTC Contemp Pub Co.

— Opportunities in Aerospace Careers. (Illus.). 160p. 1993. pap. 10.95 (*0-8442-8651-6*, VGM Career) NTC Contemp Pub Co.

— Opportunities in Aerospace Careers. rev. ed. (Opportunities in... Ser.). (Illus.). 160p. 1995. 14.95 (*0-8442-4577-1*, 45771, Natl Textbk Co); pap. 11.95 (*0-8442-4579-8*, 45798, Natl Textbk Co) NTC Contemp Pub Co.

Maples, William R. & Browning, Michael. Dead Men Do Tell Tales: The Strange & Fascinating Cases of a Forensic Anthropologist. (Illus.). 304p. 1995. pap. 13.95 (*0-385-47968-9*, Main St Bks) Doubleday.

Maplet, John. A Greene Forest, or a Naturall Historie. LC 79-84122. (English Experience Ser.: No. 941). 244p. 1979. reprint ed. lib. bdg. 20.00 (*90-221-0941-0*) Walter J Johnson.

Mapleton Teacher-Research Group Staff, jt. auth. see Chandler, Kelly.

Maplin Staff. Audio IC Projects. (Maplin Ser.). (Illus.). 200p. 1995. pap. text 24.95 (*0-7506-2121-4*) Buttrwrth-Heinemann.

— Integrated Circuits Projects. LC 96-116225. (Illus.). 208p. 1995. pap. text 26.95 (*0-7506-2578-3*) Buttrwrth-Heinemann.

— Maplin Home Security Projects: A Collection of Useful Design Ideas for Security Devices around the Home. (Illus.). 208p. 1999. pap. text 26.95 (*0-7506-2603-8*) Buttrwrth-Heinemann.

— Maplin Power Supply Projects. (Maplin Project Ser.). (Illus.). 208p. 1996. pap. text 26.95 (*0-7506-2602-X*) Buttrwrth-Heinemann.

— TV & Video Projects. LC 96-151481. (Maplin Ser.). (Illus.). 208p. 1996. pap. text 24.95 (*0-7506-2297-0*) Buttrwrth-Heinemann.

Mapoko, I. Mbelenge. Cellular Receptors for Human Growth Hormone: Quantitative Aspects & Clinical Applications. No. 9. 137p. (Orig.). 1989. pap. 33.50 (*90-6186-314-7*, Pub. by Leuven Univ) Coronet Bks.

Mapother, William R. Kentucky Collections: Practice Systems Library Manual. LC 79-91144. ring bd. 120.00 (*0-317-03196-1*) West Group.

— Kentucky Collections: Practice Systems Library Manual. LC 79-91144. 1993. suppl. ed. 65.00 (*0-317-04715-9*) West Group.

Mapou, Robert L. & Spector, Jack, eds. Clinical Neuropsychological Assessment: A Cognitive Approach. (Critical Issues in Neuropsychology Ser.: Vol. 1). (Illus.). 380p. (C). 1995. text 75.00 (*0-306-44869-6*, Kluwer Plenum) Kluwer Academic.

Mapp. Harbrace College Workbook. 13th ed. 456p. (C). 1997. 18.50 (*0-15-508149-7*, Pub. by Harcourt Coll Pubs) Harcourt.

Mapp, Alf J., Jr. Frock Coats & Epaulets: The Men Who Led the Confederacy. LC 96-2691. 520p. 1996. reprint ed. pap. 18.95 (*1-56833-060-X*) Madison Bks UPA.

— Thomas Jefferson: A Strange Case of Mistaken Identity. 512p. 1989. 22.95 (*0-8191-5782-1*); pap. 17.95 (*0-8191-7454-8*) Madison Bks UPA.

— Thomas Jefferson: Passionate Pilgrim - the Presidency, the Founding of the University, & the Private Battle. (Illus.). 472p. 1991. 24.95 (*0-8191-8053-X*) Madison Bks UPA.

Mapp, Alf J. Thomas Jefferson - Passionate Pilgrim: The Presidency & the Founding of the University. 1993. pap. 16.95 (*1-56833-020-0*) Madison Bks UPA.

Mapp, Alf J., Jr. Three Golden Ages: Discovering the Creative Secrets of Renaissance Florence, Elizabethan England & America's Founding. LC 98-17124. (Illus.). 648p. 1998. 35.00 (*1-56833-113-4*, Pub. by Madison Bks UPA) Natl Bk Netwk.

Mapp, Barbara A. Just Like Grandma Used to Make. (Illus.). 308p. (Orig.). 1992. pap. 14.95 (*0-9627087-9-8*) Mt Olive Coll Pr.

Mapp, Edward. Directory of Blacks in the Performing Arts. 2nd ed. LC 89-30477. 612p. 1990. 65.50 (*0-8108-2222-9*) Scarecrow.

Mapp, Edward, ed. Puerto Rican Perspectives. LC 73-20175. 179p. 1974. 21.00 (*0-8108-0691-6*) Scarecrow.

Mapp, Edward, jt. auth. see Kisch, John.

Mapp, Larry G. The Harbrace College Workbook, Form 11B. 11th ed. 360p. (C). 1990. pap. text, teacher ed. 8.00 (*0-15-531882-9*, Pub. by Harcourt Coll Pubs) Harcourt.

— Harbrace College Workbook: Form 12A. 12th ed. (C). 1994. pap. text 29.00 (*0-15-501237-1*) Harcourt Coll Pubs.

Mapp, Nigel, jt. ed. see Norris, Christopher.

Mapp, Shannon H. Black Miracles: The Miracles of Black Inventors & Scientists - A Cross Reference Guide. (Illus.). (Orig.). 1998. mass mkt. 10.00 (*0-9649870-1-5*, BM1000) Purpose Publ.

Mapp, Tom, pref. see Letinsky, Laura.

Mappen, Marc. Jerseyana: The Underside of New Jersey History. LC 91-41139. (Illus.). 235p. (C). 1992. text 40.00 (*0-8135-1818-0*) Rutgers U Pr.

— Murder & Spies, Lovers & Lies: Settling the Great Controversies of American History. LC 95-41401. 304p. (Orig.). 1996. pap. 12.50 (*0-380-77514-X*, Avon Bks) Morrow Avon.

Mappen, Marc, ed. Witches & Historians: Interpretations of Salem. 2nd ed. LC 96-7977. 146p. (C). 1996. pap. 12.50 (*0-89464-999-X*) Krieger.

Mappes, Thomas A. Biomedical Ethics. 5th ed. 2000. pap. 31.25 (*0-07-230365-4*) McGraw.

Mappes, Thomas A. & DeGrazia, David, eds. Biomedical Ethics. 4th ed. LC 95-9348. 672p. (C). 1995. 54.38 (*0-07-040141-1*) McGraw.

Mappes, Thomas A. & Zembaty, Jane S. Social Ethics: Morality & Social Policy. 5th ed. LC 96-7924. 544p. (C). 1996. pap. 39.38 (*0-07-040143-8*) McGraw.

Mappin, Don. Mortal Enemies: Sentinels. 150p. (YA). (gr. 10 up). 1999. pap. 15.00 (*0-9641722-2-4*) Black Gate.

Mappin, George. Electroplated Nickel Silver & Old Sheffield Plate Makers' Marks, 1758-1943. 1999. pap. text 15.95 (*0-572-02419-3*) Foulsham UK.

***Mappin, Strephyn.** Kiss of Blood. 184p. 1999. pap. 12.95 (*1-86368-264-3*, Pub. by Fremantle Arts) Intl Spec Bk.

Mapping Delorme. North Dakota Atlas & Gazetteer. LC 99-464315. 1999. pap. text 16.95 (*0-89933-232-3*) DeLorme Map.

Mapping Specialists, Ltd. Staff. Africa on File, 2 Vols. LC 95-23088. (Illus.). 360p. 1995. 185.00 (*0-8160-3288-2*) Facts on File.

Mapple. Part Tulip, Vol. 1. 1998. 30.00 (*0-8212-2526-X*) Little.

Mapplethorpe. Black Book. 2000. pap. 29.95 (*0-312-19444-7*) St Martin.

Mapplethorpe, Robert. Black Book. 128p. 1986. text 50.00 (*0-312-08302-5*) St Martin.

— Black Book. (Illus.). 112p. 1988. pap. 29.95 (*0-312-02166-6*) St Martin.

— The Black Book: Miniature Edition. (Illus.). 112p. 1996. 10.95 (*0-8212-2278-3*, Pub. by Bulfinch Pr) Little.

— Calla Lily, 1988. 1995. 30.00 (*0-8212-2200-7*, Pub. by Bulfinch Pr) Little.

— Calla Lily 1988. 1992. 30.00 (*0-8212-1948-0*, Pub. by Bulfinch Pr) Little.

— Derrick Cross. 1992. 25.00 (*0-8212-1947-2*, Pub. by Bulfinch Pr) Little.

— Double-Jack. 1995. 30.00 (*0-8212-2203-1*, Pub. by Bulfinch Pr) Little.

— Flower in Vase. 1991. 30.00 (*0-8212-1857-3*, Pub. by Bulfinch Pr) Little.

— Flowers. (Illus.). 108p. 1993. pap. 40.00 (*0-8212-2019-5*, Pub. by Bulfinch Pr) Little.

— Flowers Vol. 1, Mini ed. (Illus.). 108p. 1994. 10.95 (*0-8212-2151-5*, Pub. by Bulfinch Pr) Little.

— Irises, 1982. 1990. 30.00 (*0-8212-1806-9*, Pub. by Bulfinch Pr) Little.

— Lady: Lisa Lyon. 1991. pap. 24.95 (*0-312-05290-1*) St Martin.

— Lady: Lisa Lyon: Miniature Edition. (Illus.). 128p. 1996. 10.95 (*0-8212-2277-5*, Pub. by Bulfinch Pr) Little.

— Lydia Cheng '85. 1992. 25.00 (*0-8212-1946-4*, Pub. by Bulfinch Pr) Little.

— Mapplethorpe. LC 92-50154. 1992. 125.00 (*0-679-40804-5*) Random.

— Melody, 1987. 1993. 25.00 (*0-8212-2007-1*, Pub. by Bulfinch Pr) Little.

— Orchids, 1989. 1991. 30.00 (*0-8212-1874-3*, Pub. by Bulfinch Pr) Little.

— Rose, 1989. 1992. 30.00 (*0-8212-1945-6*, Pub. by Bulfinch Pr) Little.

— Roses, 1988. 1993. 30.00 (*0-8212-2011-X*, Pub. by Bulfinch Pr) Little.

— Some Women. (Illus.). 120p. 1992. pap. 35.00 (*0-8212-1937-5*, Pub. by Bulfinch Pr) Little.

— Some Women, Mini ed. (Illus.). 120p. 1995. 10.95 (*0-8212-2197-3*, Pub. by Bulfinch Pr) Little.

***Mapplethorpe, Robert, photos by.** Robert Mapplethorpe: Pictures. (Illus.). 220p. 1999. 75.00 (*1-892041-16-2*, Pub. by Arena Editions) Dist Art Pubs.

Mapplethorpe, Robert, jt. auth. see Marshall, Richard.

Maprayil, Cyriac. The Soviets & Afghanistan. 129p. 1986. 19.95 (*81-85047-07-3*) Asia Bk Corp.

Maps International Staff, ed. Earth Map Book Environmental Atlas. 1998. pap. 9.95 (*1-57262-089-7*) MapQuest.

Maps International Staff & Liber Kartor AB Staff. Earth MapBook: Environmental Atlas. 3rd ed. Interarts, Ltd. Staff, ed. 187p. 1996. 15.95 (*1-879856-32-8*) MapQuest.

Mapsco Inc. Mapsco Street Guide & Directory. 25.95 (*1-56966-541-9*) Mapsco Inc.

Mapsco Inc Staff. Mapsco Ellis & Johnson: A Routing & Delivery System for Ellis & Johnson Counties: with Additional Coverage for Corsicana, Hillsboro & Selected Areas. LC 96-675589. 1995. write for info. (*1-56966-047-6*) Mapsco Inc.

Mapson, J. Wendell, Jr. The Ministry of Music in the Black Church. 1984. pap. 12.00 (*0-8170-1057-2*) Judson.

Mapson, Jo-Ann. Blue Rodeo: A Novel. 336p. 1995. pap. 13.00 (*0-06-092635-X*, Perennial) HarperTrade.

— Blue Rodeo: A Novel. large type ed. LC 94-12999. 536p. 1994. lib. bdg. 22.95 (*0-7862-0280-7*) Thorndike Pr.

— Fault Line. LC 89-62971. 240p. 1989. pap. 12.95 (*0-944870-02-3*) Pacific Writers Pr.

— Hank & Chloe: A Novel. LC 92-53377. 320p. 1994. reprint ed. pap. 13.00 (*0-06-092464-0*, Perennial) HarperTrade.

— Loving Chloe: A Novel. LC 97-20578. 368p. 1999. pap. 13.00 (*0-06-093028-4*) HarpC.

— Loving Chloe: A Novel. LC 98-24006. 1998. write for info. (*1-56895-567-7*) Wheeler Pub.

— Shadow Ranch: A Novel. LC 69-2123. 384p. 1997. pap. 13.00 (*0-06-092843-3*, Perennial) HarperTrade.

An Asterisk (*) at the beginning of an entry indicates that the title is appearing for the first time.

— Shadow Ranch: A Novel. large type ed. LC 98-48129. 1999. 25.95 (*1-57490-176-1*, Beeler LP Bks) T T Beeler.
— The Wilder Sisters: A Novel. LC 98-41175. 384p. (J). 1999. 24.00 (*0-06-019116-3*) HarpC.
— The Wilder Sisters: A Novel. 320p. 2000. pap. 13.00 (*0-06-093107-8*) HarpC.
***Mapson, Jo-Ann.** The Wilder Sisters: A Novel. large type ed. 2000. 25.95 (*1-56895-866-8*) Wheeler Pub.
***Mapstone, Elizabeth.** War of Words. 1998. pap. 22.95 (*0-7011-6667-3*, Pub. by Random) Trafalgar.
Mapstone, Richard. Policing in a Divided Society: A Study of Part-Time Policing in Northern Ireland. 139p. 1994. 61.95 (*1-85628-598-7*, Pub. by Avebry) Ashgate Pub Co.
Mapstone, Sally, jt. ed. see Cooper, Helen.
Maqay, T. & Orszagh, Laszlo, eds. A Concise English-Hungarian Dictionary. 14th ed. (HUN & ENG.). 1056p. 1990. 49.95 (*0-19-864170-2*) OUP.
Maqbool, M. A. & Kerry, Brian. Plant Nematode Problems & Their Control in the Near East Region. (Plant Production & Protection Papers: No. 09005672). 328p. 1998. 25.00 (*92-5-103798-1*, F37981, Pub. by FAO) Bernan Associates.
Maqsood, Ruqaiyyah W. Islam: A Dictionary. (Illus.). 84p. 1996. pap. 11.95 (*0-7487-2560-1*, Pub. by S Thornes Pubs) Trans-Atl Phila.
— Teach Yourself Islam. (Illus.). 224p. 1995. pap. 11.95 (*0-8442-3746-9*, Teach Yrslf) NTC Contemp Pub Co.
— Thinking about God. 140p. 1996. pap. 9.95 (*0-614-21190-5*, 1495) Kazi Pubns.
Maquarre, A. Daily Exercises for Flute - Ejercicios Diarios Para la Flauta. 40p. 1986. pap. 6.95 (*0-7935-5399-7*, 50328200) H Leonard.
Maquerlot, Jean P. Shakespeare & the Mannerist Tradition: A Reading of Five Problem Plays. (Illus.). 209p. (C). 1996. text 69.95 (*0-521-41083-5*) Cambridge U Pr.
Maquet, Charles. Larousse Dictionnaire Analogique. 11th ed. (FRE.). 600p. 1971. 55.00 (*0-7859-7645-0*, 2033402185) Fr & Eur.
Maquet, J. Introduction to Aesthetic Anthropology. (Other Realities Ser.: No. 1). 110p. (C). 1971. pap. text 12.00 (*0-89003-041-3*) Undena Pubns.
Maquet, Jacques P. Civilizations of Black Africa. Rayfield, Joan R., tr. (Illus.). 200p. 1972. text 22.95 (*0-19-501464-2*) OUP.
— The Sociology of Knowledge. Locke, John F., tr. from FRE. LC 70-168963. 318p. 1973. reprint ed. lib. bdg. 65.00 (*0-8371-6236-X*, MASK, Greenwood Pr) Greenwood.
Maquet, Jacques P., ed. see Greenberg, J., et al.
Maquet, Jaques P. The Aesthetic Experience: An Anthropologist Looks at the Visual Arts. LC 85-8232. (Illus.). 277p. 1986. 50.00 (*0-300-03342-7*) Yale U Pr.
— The Aesthetic Experience: An Anthropologist Looks at the Visual Arts. LC 85-8232. (Illus.). 277p. 1988. pap. 25.00 (*0-300-04134-9*) Yale U Pr.
Maquet, Jaques P., ed. see Mintz, S., et al.
Maquet, P. G. Biomechanics of the Hip. (Illus.). 320p. 1984. 199.00 (*0-387-13257-0*) Spr-Verlag.
— Biomechanics of the Knee. 2nd ed. (Illus.). 330p. 1983. 217.00 (*0-387-12489-6*) Spr-Verlag.
Maquet, P. G., tr. see Braune, W. & Fischer.
Maquet, Paul G., et al, eds. Dissertations on the Mechanics of Effervescence & Fermentation & on the Mechanics of the Movement of the Muscles by John Bernoulli. LC 97-8258. (Transactions Ser.: Vol. 87, Pt. 3).Tr. of Dissertatio de Effervescentia et Fermentatione. 160p. 1997. pap. 18.00 (*0-87169-873-0*, T873-map) Am Philos.
Maquiavelo, Nicolas. El Principe. (Biblioteca De Cultura Basica Ser.). 621p. 1991. 11.50 (*0-8477-0727-X*) U of PR Pr.
— El Principe (Commentado por Napolean Bonaparte) Jungl, Eli L., tr. (Nueva Austral Ser.: Vol. 215). (SPA.). 1991. pap. text 24.95 (*84-239-7215-1*) Elliots Bks.
***Maquire, Daniel C.** Sacred Energies: When the World's Religions Sit down to Talk about the Future of Human Life & the Plight of This Planet. 2000. pap. 13.00 (*0-8006-3216-8*, Fortress Pr) Augsburg Fortress.
Maquire, Gregory. The Good Liar. 144p. (gr. 3-7). mass mkt. 4.95 (*0-06-440874-4*) HarpC.
Maquire, Lambert. Understanding Social Networks. LC 83-4489. (Sage Human Services Guides Ser.: No. 32). 119p. 1983. reprint ed. pap. 36.90 (*0-608-01512-1*, 205955600002) Bks Demand.
Maquire, Timothy E., jt. auth. see Kamrowitz, R. Marc.
Maquire, Tom. Tin Whistle Book. 1997. pap. text 7.95 (*0-946005-25-7*) Dufour.
Maquiso, Mechizedek. Institutional Planning & Development: A Primer. x, 172p. 1983. pap. 15.00 (*971-10-0054-7*, Pub. by New Day Pub) Cellar.
Maqutu, W. C. Contemporary Family Law of Lesotho: A Historical & Critical Commentary. xxvi, 389p. 1992. 80.00 (*99911-30-04-7*, Pub. by Nat Univ Lesotho) Gaunt.
Mar, Alexander D. Collected Works. 1972. 500.00 (*0-87968-887-4*) Gordon Pr.
***Mar, Elaine M.** Paper Daughter. large type unabridged ed. 2000. 26.95 (*0-7531-5789-6*, 157896, Pub. by ISIS Lrg Prnt) ISIS Pub.
Mar, Lee Del, see Del Mar, Lee.
Mar-Lena. The Enchantress. 73p. 1992. pap. 10.50 (*0-9634497-0-2*) Leja Pubns.
Mar, M. Elaine. Paper Daughter: A Memoir. LC 99-10589. 304p. 1999. 23.00 (*0-06-018293-8*) HarpC.
***Mar, M. Elaine.** Paper Daughter: A Memoir. 304p. 2000. pap. 13.00 (*0-06-093052-7*, Perennial) HarperTrade.
Mar Martinez Rodriquez, Maria Del, see Del Mar Martinez Rodriquez, Maria, ed.
***Mar-Molinero, Clare.** Politics of Language in Spanish-Speaking World. LC 99-58473. 256p. (C). 2000. pap. write for info. (*0-415-15655-6*); text. write for info. (*0-415-15654-8*) Routledge.
Mar-Molinero, Clare. The Spanish-Speaking World: A Practical Introduction to Sociolinguistic Issues. LC 96-43952. (Routledge Language in Society Ser.). 200p. (C). 1997. pap. 19.99 (*0-415-12983-4*) Routledge.
— The Spanish-Speaking World: A Practical Introduction to Sociolinguistic Issues. LC 96-43952. (Routledge Language in Society Ser.). 200p. (C). 1997. 65.00 (*0-415-12982-6*) Routledge.
Mar-Molinero, Clare & Smith, Angel, eds. Nationalism & the Nation in the Iberian Peninsula: Competing & Conflicting Identities. 256p. 1996. 49.50 (*1-85973-180-5*, Pub. by Berg Pubs); pap. 19.50 (*1-85973-175-9*, Pub. by Berg Pubs) NYU Pr.
Mar, Norman R. Del, see Del Mar, Norman R.
Mar, Richard D. Dark Migrations. 40p. Date not set. pap. 6.95 (*1-879934-00-0*) St Andrews NC.
Mar, Richard De Los, see De los Mar, Richard.

Mar, Ti. Knowledge Within: Travel the Winds Workbook, Vol. 2. 88p. 1999. 12.00 (*0-9651538-1-9*) Trvl the Winds.
The fruition of this workbook Knowledge Within comes from your spoken & unspoken questions. It is our Bezon, Y-Bon, Spacificia, Ruso, Sog & Ti Mar, it is our gift to you. Included is information to help you look ahead to the years 1999 & beyond by adjusting to new energies of change that has been & will be felt more in all worlds, to gradual changed life of plant, animal & humans as earth renews itself. Bezon & the group say to change your energy & take control of your life will bring tremendous improvements for all phases of earth life, for example, many illnesses will not survive in the new energy & some old human problems will fade away or drop off as the body grows stronger. For months we have compiled information for Knowledge Within. Today we have new instructions for your meditation, ways to accessing your memory bank, release emotional ties, breathing energies, new healing energies with hand positions that generate universal energies. Then we touch lightly on foods to watch out for, talk about reincarnation, offer a brief history of your journeys & how creation changed on earth. It's never too early to find the power that is within yourself & make sure your energies & changes reflect improvements. Should you wonder how such improvements are possible in the midst of the chaotic predictions floating around earth, there is no limit with the power of your mind. As you follow the instructions, make mental & physical adjustments to claim your power to stop negative influences. Negative influences simply give your abundance, love, harmony & balance to someone else. There are instructions to tap into your memory bank (your personal record of all times) to help understand yourself. To order: Travel the Winds Workbook, Knowledge Within. Send to: Travel the Winds Publishing, P.O. Box 781628, Wichita, KS 67278-1628. Price $12.00 + $4.00 S/H.
Publisher Paid Annotation.

-Travel the Winds: A Beginning Mystery, Vol. 1. Green, Mary L., ed. (Illus.). 186p. 1996. pap. 19.95 (*0-9651538-0-0*) Trvl the Winds.
There is a need for humans to increase their conscious awareness, gain control over telepathic communications, change energy to stop unwanted encounters & recognize all contacts. With this control will come a knowledge of all life forms. The importance of Light Being communication is understood through energy, earth & human changes. TRAVEL THE WINDS has seventeen portraits of light beings, nine maps of ancient lands & illustrations of a dome, double carrier & outer shell of a UFO. Today Ti Mar is an author, lecturer & artist & remembers many encounters. Ti Mar's work includes intuitive insights into contacts & memory counseling to help people remember encounters. She does psychic readings. Ti Mar is also available for workshops & seminars on UFOs & can be contacted through Travel the Winds Publishing, P.O. Box 781628, Wichita, KS 67278-1628. The topics of gods & life in Space has received so much of man's attention, speculation & conversation that this trend of thought can be traced from the earliest limit of earth time into the present. Even with the imposed limit, all people should know of the presence & location of all other life forms. $19.95 (plus $4.00 shipping & handling), KS residents add $1.18 tax, Visa, MasterCard & Discovery orders please FAX your order: 1-316-683-6021. Please include Card Number, Expiration Date, & the Name on the Card.
Publisher Paid Annotation.

Mar, Walter Del, see Del Mar, Walter.
Mara, Barbara A., jt. auth. see Winton, Mark A.
Mara, D. D., et al, eds. Waste Stabilization Ponds - Technology & Applications: Selected Proceedings of the 3rd IAWQ International Symposium on Waste Stabilization Ponds, Technology & Applications. (Water Science & Technology 33 Ser.). 262p. 1996. pap. text 128.00 (*0-08-042900-9*, Pergamon Pr) Elsevier.
Mara, D. Duncan. Low Cost Urban Sanitation. LC 95-42464. 240p. 1996. pap. 75.00 (*0-471-96163-9*) Wiley.
Mara, D. Duncan, ed. Low-Cost Sewerage. LC 96-15925. 238p. 1996. pap. 70.00 (*0-471-96691-6*) Wiley.
Mara, D. Duncan, jt. auth. see Cairncross, S.
Mara, D. Duncan, jt. auth. see Rachel, M. Ayres.
Mara, David D. Sewage Treatment in Hot Climates. LC 75-23421. 437p. reprint ed. pap. 135.50 (*0-8357-3399-8*, 203965600013) Bks Demand.
***Mara, Ferent.** Looking-Glass Kate. (J). 1999. pap. 21.00 (*963-13-4780-X*, Pub. by Corvina Bks) St Mut.
Mara, Gerald M. Socrates' Discursive Democracy: Logos & Ergon in Platonic Political Philosophy. LC 96-17779. 324p. (C). 1997. pap. text 21.95 (*0-7914-3300-5*) State U NY Pr.
— Socrates' Discursive Democracy: Logos & Ergon in Platonic Political Philosophy. LC 96-17779. 324p. (C). 1997. text 65.50 (*0-7914-3299-8*) State U NY Pr.
Mara, Joseph, jt. auth. see Newman, Betsy.
Mara, Joy. Clear & Simple: Developing Effective Print Materials for Low-Literate Readers. (Illus.). 61p. (Orig.). 1996. pap. text 25.00 (*0-7881-2982-1*) DIANE Pub.
Mara, Mary J. VBScript Sourcebook. LC 97-17967. 608p. 1997. pap., pap. text 34.99 incl. audio compact disk (*0-471-19106-X*) Wiley.
Mara, P., jt. auth. see Stowell, Gordon.
Mara, Pam. El Arca. (Serie Libros de Carton - Board Bks.).Tr. of Ark. (SPA.). (J). 1986. bds. 4.99 (*1-56063-310-7*, 490448) Editorial Unilit.
— The Greeks Pop-Up. (Tarquin Pop-Up Ser.). (Illus.). 32p. (Orig.). (J). (gr. 3 up). 1985. pap. 8.95 (*0-906212-33-2*, Pub. by Tarquin Pubns) Parkwest Pubns.
Mara, Rachna. Of Customs & Excise: Short Fiction. 120p. pap. 14.95 (*0-929005-25-2*, Pub. by Sec Story Pr) LPC InBook.
Mara, Ratu S. The Pacific Way: A Memoir. LC 96-25815. (Illus.). 298p. 1997. pap. text 15.00 (*0-8248-1893-8*) UH Pr.
Mara, Thalia. First Steps in Ballet: Basic Exercises at the Barre. LC 75-37100. (Illus.). 64p. (J). (gr. 2-5). 1987. reprint ed. pap. 6.95 (*0-916622-53-3*) Princeton Bk Co.
— Fourth Steps in Ballet: On Your Toes! Basic Pointe Work. LC 74-181476. (Illus.). 64p. (YA). (gr. 9-12). 1987. reprint ed. pap. 6.95 (*0-916622-56-8*) Princeton Bk Co.
— The Language of Ballet: A Dictionary. LC 78-181477. (Illus.). 120p. 1987. reprint ed. pap. 11.95 (*0-87127-037-4*) Princeton Bk Co.
— Second Steps in Ballet: Basic Center Exercises. LC 75-37101. (Illus.). 64p. (J). (gr. 4-6). 1987. reprint ed. pap. 6.95 (*0-916622-54-1*) Princeton Bk Co.
— Third Steps in Ballet: Basic Allegro Steps. LC 70-181475. (Illus.). 64p. (J). (gr. 6-9). 1987. reprint ed. pap. 6.95 (*0-916622-55-X*) Princeton Bk Co.
Mara, W. P. Anoles. (Exotic Lizards Ser.). (Illus.). 48p. (J). (gr. 3-7). 1996. 19.00 (*0-516-20252-9*) Childrens.
— Chameleons. (Exotic Lizards Ser.). (Illus.). 48p. (J). (gr. 3-7). 1996. lib. bdg. 19.00 (*0-516-20251-0*) Childrens.
— Garter & Ribbon Snakes. (Illus.). 64p. 1995. pap. text 9.95 (*0-7938-0269-5*, RE102) TFH Pubns.
— Geckos. (Exotic Lizards Ser.). (Illus.). 48p. (J). (gr. 3-7). 1996. 19.00 (*0-516-20254-5*) Childrens.
— Green Snakes. (Illus.). 64p. 1996. pap. 9.95 (*0-7938-2073-1*, RE163) TFH Pubns.
— Iguanas. (Exotic Lizards Ser.). (Illus.). 48p. (J). (gr. 3-7). 1996. 19.00 (*0-516-20253-7*) Childrens.
— Map Turtles & Diamond Back Terrapins. (Illus.). 64p. 1997. 9.95 (*0-7938-2068-5*, RE-156) TFH Pubns.
— Milk Snakes. (Illus.). 64p. 1995. pap. text 9.95 (*0-7938-0250-4*, RE107) TFH Pubns.
— Pinesnakes. (Illus.). 48p. 1995. pap. text 9.95 (*0-7938-0262-8*, RE119) TFH Pubns.
— Racers, Whipsnakes & Indigos. (Illus.). 64p. 1996. pap. 9.95 (*0-7938-2062-6*, RE142) TFH Pubns.
— Venomous Snakes of the World. (TS Ser.). (Illus.). 224p. 1993. text 35.95 (*0-86622-522-6*, TS-189) TFH Pubns.
— Water Snakes of North America. (Illus.). 64p. 1995. pap. 9.95 (*0-7938-0288-1*, RE137) TFH Pubns.
Mara, W. P., jt. auth. see Coborn, John.
Mara, William P. Breeding & Keeping Frogs. (Illus.). 160p. 1995. 22.95 (*0-7938-0130-3*, LR105) TFH Pubns.
— Cuba. LC 98-13075. (Countries of the World Ser.). (J). 1998. 14.00 (*0-7368-0068-9*, Bridgestone Bks) Capstone Pr.
— Cubans: The Ultimate Cigars. LC 98 16877. (Illus.). 176p. 1998. 20.00 (*1-55821-644-8*) Lyons Pr.
— Desert Snakes of North America. (Illus.). 64p. 1997. 9.95 (*0-7938-2047-2*, RE-164) TFH Pubns.
— The Fragile Frog. Tucker, Kathy, ed. LC 95-1409. (Illus.). 48p. (J). (gr. 3-7). 1996. lib. bdg. 16.95 (*0-8075-2580-4*) A Whitman.
— Nascar Racing. LC 98-20865. (Motorsports Ser.). (J). 1998. 19.00 (*0-7368-0025-5*, Cpstone High Low) Capstone Pr.
***Mara, William P.** Pro Stock Car Racing. 1999. 19.93 (*0-516-21469-1*) Capstone Pr.
Mara, William P. Snakes: Look & Learn. (Illus.). 64p. 1993. 9.95 (*0-7938-0074-9*, KD003) TFH Pubns.
— Snowmobile Racing. LC 98-17221. (Motorsports Ser.). (J). 1998. 19.00 (*0-7368-0027-1*, Cpstone High Low) Capstone Pr.
***Mara, William P.** Snowmobile Racing. 1999. 19.93 (*0-516-21471-3*) Capstone Pr.
Mara, William P. Turtles As a Hobby. (Illus.). 96p. 1993. 8.95 (*0-86622-324-X*, TT013) TFH Pubns.
Marabell, George P. Frederick Libby & the American Peace Movement, 1921-1941. 1981. 30.95 (*0-405-14094-0*) Ayer.
Marabin, Jean. L' U. R. S. S. un Portrait en Couleurs. (FRE., Illus.). 276p. 1960. lib. bdg. 19.95 (*0-8288-3980-8*) Fr & Eur.
Marable. Race Reform & Rebellion 2. 1997. pap. 17.95 (*0-333-56433-2*) St Martin.
— Souls. 2000. pap. text 10.00 (*0-8133-6668-2*) Westview.
Marable, Manning. Beyond Black & White: Rethinking Race in American Politics & Society. 240p. (C). (gr. 13 up). 1995. 35.00 (*1-85984-924-5*, Pub. by Verso) Norton.
— Beyond Black & White: Rethinking Race in American Politics & Society. LC 95-23358. (C). 1996. pap. 20.00 (*1-85984-049-3*, Pub. by Verso) Norton.
— Black Leadership. LC 97-32969. 1998. pap. write for info. (*0-231-10747-1*) Col U Pr.
— Black Leadership: Four Great American Leaders & the Struggle for Civil Rights. LC 97-32969. 238p. 1999. pap. 13.95 (*0-14-028113-4*) Viking Penguin.
— Black Leadership: Ideology, Politics & Culture in African-American History. LC 97-32969. 238p. 1998. 29.50 (*0-231-10746-3*) Col U Pr.
— Black Liberation in Conservative America. LC 96-48679. 286p. 1997. 40.00 (*0-89608-560-0*); pap. 16.00 (*0-89608-559-7*) South End Pr.
— How Capitalism Underdeveloped Black America: Problems in Race, Political Economy, & Society. 2nd rev. ed. LC 82-61153. (Classics Ser.: Vol. 4). (Illus.). 400p. 1999. 40.00 (*0-89608-580-5*, Pub. by South End Pr); pap. 22.00 (*0-89608-579-1*, Pub. by South End Pr) Consort Bk Sales.
— Race, Reform, & Rebellion: The Second Reconstruction in Black America, 1945-1990. 2nd rev. ed. LC 90-19215. 1991. pap. text 15.95 (*0-87805-493-6*) U Pr of Miss.
***Marable, Manning.** Race, Reform & Rebellion: The Second Reconstruction in Black America, 1945-2000. 3rd rev. ed. 300p. 2001. pap. text 17.00 (*1-57806-154-7*); lib. bdg. 45.00 (*1-57806-153-9*) U Pr of Miss.
Marable, Manning. Speaking Truth to Power: Essays on Race, Resistance & Radicalism. 304p. (C). 1998. pap. text 20.00 (*0-8133-8828-7*, Pub. by Westview) HarpC.
— W. E. B. Du Bois: Black Radical Democrat. (Twentieth Century American Biography Ser.: No. 3). 304p. 1986. 28.95 (*0-8057-7750-4*) Macmillan.
***Marable, Manning, ed.** Dispatches from the Ebony Tower: Intellectuals Confront the African American Experience. LC 99-55525. 2000. 27.50 (*0-231-11476-1*); pap. 18.50 (*0-231-11477-X*) Col U Pr.
Marable, Manning & Mullings, Leith, eds. African-American Thought: Social & Political Perspectives from Slavery to the Present. 384p. (Orig.). 1997. pap. 19.95 (*0-8476-8346-X*) Rowman.
Marable, Manning & Mullings, Leith, eds. Let Nobody Turn Us Around: Voices of Resistance, Reform & Renewal: An African American Anthology. LC 99-49099. 600p. 1999. 35.00 (*0-8476-8345-1*) Rowman.
***Marable, Manning & Mullings, Leith, eds.** Let Nobody Turn Us Around: Voices of Resistance, Reform & Renewal: An African American Anthology. 560p. 1999. 35.00 (*0-8476-9930-7*, Pub. by Rowman) Natl Bk Netwk.
Marable, Manning, ed. see Brecher, Jeremy.
Marable, Manning, ed. see Hooks, Bell.
Marable, Manning, ed. see Surkin, Marvin.
Marabotto, Don C. & St. Catherine of Genoa. The Spiritual Doctrine of St. Catherine of Genoa. LC 88-50267. 328p. 1989. reprint ed. pap. 12.50 (*0-89555-335-X*) TAN Bks Pubs.
Maracle, David K. Mohawk, Let's Speak. unabridged ed. 100p. 1993. pap. text 49.95 incl. audio (*0-88432-706-X*, AFMH10) Audio-Forum.
— Mohawk, One Thousand Useful Words. 158p. 1992. pap. 12.95 (*0-88432-710-8*, AFMH94) Audio-Forum.
Maracle, Lee. Bobbie Lee: Indian Rebel. 242p. pap. 10.95 (*0-88961-148-3*, Pub. by Womens Pr) LPC InBook.
— I Am Woman: A Native Perspective on Sociology & Feminism. rev. ed. 176p. 1996. pap. 14.95 (*0-88974-059-3*, Pub. by Press Gang Pubs) LPC InBook.
— Ravensong. 208p. 1993. pap. 14.95 (*0-88974-044-5*, Pub. by Press Gang Pubs) LPC InBook.
***Maracle, Lee.** Sojourner's & Sundogs: First Nations Fiction. 342p. 1999. pap. text. write for info. (*0-88974-061-5*, Pub. by Press Gang Pubs) LPC InBook.
Maracle, Lee. Sojourner's Truth: First Nations Fiction. 1995. pap. 10.95 (*0-88974-023-2*, Pub. by Press Gang Pubs) LPC InBook.
Maracle, Lee, jt. auth. see Freire.
Maracotta, Lindsay. The Dead Celeb. LC 97-12386. 288p. 1997. 24.00 (*0-688-14499-3*, Wm Morrow) Morrow Avon.
— The Dead Celeb. 272p. 1998. mass mkt. 5.99 (*0-380-72689-0*, Avon Bks) Morrow Avon.
— The Dead Hollywood Moms Society. 1997. mass mkt. 5.99 (*0-614-27704-3*, Avon Bks); mass mkt. 5.99 (*0-380-72688-2*, Avon Bks) Morrow Avon.
— Playing Dead: A Hollywood Mystery. LC 98-27438. 288p. 1999. 24.00 (*0-688-15867-6*, Wm Morrow) Morrow Avon.

M

Maracz, Laszlo K. Hungarian Revival. LC 98-180621. 1998. pap. 32.95 (*90-75323-11-5*) Intl Spec Bk.

Maradona, Remigio M. Cantos Azules: Blue Songs. Barber, Sara, ed. (Illus.). 55p. 1999. pap. 12.95 (*0-9650878-5-9*) Intl Diplomatic News.

— My Inner Self.Tr. of Dentro de Mis Entranas. (Illus.). 76p. (Orig.). 1996. pap. 12.95 (*0-9650878-0-8*) Intl Diplomatic News.

Maradudin, A. A. & Nardelli, G. F., eds. Elementary Excitations in Solids: The Cortina Lectures, July 1966, & Selected Lectures from the Conference on Localized Excitations, Milan, July 25-26, 1966. LC 68-26772. 536p. reprint ed. pap. 166.20 (*0-608-14552-1*, 202471900038) Bks Demand.

Maradudin, A. A., jt. ed. see Horton, G. K.

Maradudin, Alexei A., jt. ed. see Gu, Zu-Han.

Marafiote, Richard A. The Custody of Children: A Behavioral Assessment Model. LC 85-12217. (Illus.). 290p. (C). 1985. 78.00 (*0-306-41874-6*, Plenum Trade) Perseus Pubng.

Marafioti, P. Mario. Caruso's Method of Voice Production: The Scientific Culture of the Voice. (Illus.). 336p. 1981. reprint ed. pap. 8.95 (*0-486-24180-7*) Dover.

Marafotti, Salvatore, jt. auth. see Creti, Antonio.

Marage, P. The Solvay Councils & the Birth of Modern Physics. (Science Networks Historical Studies). 1998. 79.95 (*0-8176-5705-3*) Birkhauser.

M

Marage, P. & Wallenborn, G., eds. The Solvay Councils & the Birth of Modern Physics. (Science Networks: Vol. 22). 250p. 1998. 72.00 (*3-7643-5705-3*) Spr-Verlag.

Maragos, George D., ed. Seminar on Ambulatory Pediatrics: Journal: Paediatrician, Vol. 5, No. 3. (Illus.). 1977. 26.25 (*3-8055-2433-1*) S Karger.

— Seminar on Geographical Pediatrics. (Journal: Paediatrician: Vol. 6, No. 2). (Illus.). 1977. 27.00 (*3-8055-2795-0*) S Karger.

— Seminar on Human Genetics. (Journal: Paediatrician: Vol. 6, No. 6). (Illus.). 1978. 27.00 (*3-8055-2909-0*) S Karger.

— Seminar on Immunological Aspects of Kidney Diseases in Children. (Journal: Paediatrician: Vol. 10, No. 5-6). (Illus.). 164p. 1981. pap. 61.00 (*3-8055-3488-4*) S Karger.

— Seminar on Infectious Diseases in Childhood. (Journal: Paediatrician: Vol. 8, No. 1-2). (Illus.). 1979. pap. 57.50 (*3-8055-3027-7*) S Karger.

— Seminar on Neonatology. (Journal: Paediatrician: Vol. 5, No. 5). (Illus.). 1977. 26.25 (*3-8055-2702-0*) S Karger.

— Seminar on Office Pediatrics, Pt. II. (Journal: Paediatrician: Vol. 8, No. 3). (Illus.). 1979. pap. 28.75 (*3-8055-3074-9*) S Karger.

— Seminar on Pediatric Allergy. (Journal: Paediatrician: Vol. 5, No. 4). (Illus.). 80p. 1977. 26.25 (*3-8055-2648-2*) S Karger.

— Seminar on Pediatric Cardiology. (Journal: Paediatrician: Vol. 7, No. 1-3). (Illus.). 1978. pap. 81.00 (*3-8055-2912-0*) S Karger.

— Seminar on Public Health, Pt. I. (Journal: Paediatrician: Vol. II, No. 1-2, 1982). (Illus.). iv, 120p. 1982. pap. 67.00 (*3-8055-3533-3*) S Karger.

— Seminar on Public Health, Pt. 2. (Journal: Paediatrician: Vol. II, No. 3-4). (Illus.). 126p. 1982. pap. 67.00 (*3-8055-3532-5*) S Karger.

Maragos, James E., et al, eds. Marine & Coastal Biodiversity in the Tropical Island Pacific Region. LC 95-34642. 1996. pap. write for info. (*0-86638-175-9*) EW Ctr HI.

***Maragos, James E. & Dunsmore, Rikki.** Proceedings of Coral Reef Monitoring Workshop June 9-11, 1998. LC 99-17029. 1999. write for info. (*0-86638-191-0*) EW Ctr HI.

Maragos, Petros, et al, eds. Mathematical Morphology & Its Applications to Image & Signal Processing. LC 96-14893. (Computational Imaging & Vision Ser.). 488p. (C). 1996. text 180.50 (*0-7923-9733-9*) Kluwer Academic.

Maragos, Petros, jt. auth. see Schafer, Ronald W.

Maragoudakis, M. E., et al, eds. Angiogenesis: Molecular Biology & Clinical Aspects. (NATO ASI Ser.: Vol. 263). (Illus.). 382p. (C). 1994. text 115.00 (*0-306-44713-4*, Kluwer Plenum) Kluwer Academic.

Maragoudakis, M. E., et al. Angiogenesis in Health & Disease. (NATO ASI Series A, Life Sciences: Vol. 227). (Illus.). 416p. (C). 1992. text 125.00 (*0-306-44196-9*) Plenum.

Maragoudakis, Michael, ed. Molecular, Cellular & Clinical Aspects of Angiogenesis: Proceedings of a NATO ASI Held in Porto Carras, Halkidiki, Greece, June 16-27, 1995, Vol. A285. LC 96-21623. (NATO ASI Series A: Vol. 285). (Illus.). 302p. 1996. 126.00 (*0-306-45315-0*) Plenum.

***Maragoudakis, Michael E.** Angiogenesis: From the Molecular to Integrative Pharmacology. LC 00-22405. (Advances in Experimental Medicine & Biology Ser.). 2000. write for info. (*0-306-46375-X*, Kluwer Plenum) Kluwer Academic.

Maragoudakis, Michael E., ed. Angiogenesis: Models, Modulators & Clinical Applications. LC 98-17558. (NATO ASI Ser.: No. 298). (Illus.). 584p. (C). 1998. text 159.50 (*0-306-45833-0*, Kluwer Plenum) Kluwer Academic.

Marah, John K. African People in the Global Village: An Introduction to Pan African Studies. LC 98-3846. 316p. (C). 1998. 57.00 (*0-7618-1133-8*); pap. 36.50 (*0-7618-1134-6*) U Pr of Amer.

— Pan-African Education: The Last Stage of Educational Developments. LC 88-1696. (Studies in African Education & Social Development: Vol. 2). 336p. 1989. lib. bdg. 99.95 (*0-88946-186-4*) E Mellen.

Marahimin, Ismail. And the War Is Over. McGlynn, John H., tr. LC 86-10625. 173p. 1987. 16.95 (*0-8071-1340-9*) La State U Pr.

***Marai, Sandor.** Embers. 2000. write for info. (*0-375-40756-1*) Knopf.

Marai, Sandor. Memoir of Hungary, 1944-48. Tuzla, Albert, tr. LC 97-119594. 426p. (C). 1996. pap. text 26.95 (*1-85866-064-5*) Ctrl Europ Univ.

Maraini, Dacia. Bagheria. Kitto, Dick & Spottiswood, Elspeth, trs. from ITA. 119p. 1995. 30.00 (*0-7206-0926-7*, Pub. by P Owen Ltd) Dufour.

— Cercando Emma. LC 97-23304. 146p. 1998. 22.00 (*0-226-50430-1*) U Ch Pr.

— Devour Me Too. 79p. pap. 10.00 (*0-919349-88-9*) Guernica Editions.

— Isolina. Williams, Sian, tr. from ITA. 152p. 1994. 30.00 (*0-7206-0897-X*, Pub. by P Owen Ltd) Dufour.

Maraini, Dacia. Mio Marito e l'Altra Famiglia: Level A. pap. text 7.95 (*0-88436-922-6*) EMC-Paradigm.

Maraini, Dacia. Only Prostitutes Marry in May. 378p. 1994. pap. 18.00 (*0-920717-81-0*) Guernica Editions.

***Maraini, Dacia.** The Silent Duchess. Kitto, Dick & Spottiswood, Elspeth, trs. LC 98-22699. 264p. 2000. pap. 14.95 (*1-55861-222-X*) Feminist Pr.

Maraini, Dacia. The Silent Duchess. 236p. 1993. 23.95 (*1-55082-053-2*, Pub. by Quarry Pr) LPC InBook.

— The Silent Dutchess. Kitto, Dick & Spottiswoode, Elspeth, trs. from ITA. 235p. 1992. 30.00 (*0-7206-0859-7*, Pub. by P Owen Ltd) Dufour.

***Maraini, Dacia.** Stowaway on Board. Poletto, Vittoria Offredi & Bellesia, Giovanna, trs. from ITA. LC 99-54441. (Crossings Ser.: Vol 5). 63p. 1999. pap. 8.00 (*1-884419-24-0*, Pub. by Bordighera) SPD-Small Pr Dist.

Maraini, Dacia. Traveling in the Gait of a Fox. Gunn, Genni, tr. 96p. 1993. pap. 12.95 (*1-55082-055-9*, Pub. by Quarry Pr) LPC InBook.

— Voices. Kilto, Dick & Spottiswood, Elspeth, trs. from ITA. LC 96-69699. 257p. (Orig.). (C). 1997. pap. 13.99 (*1-85242-527-X*) Serpents Tail.

— Woman at War. Benetti, Mara & Spottiswood, Elspeth, trs. from ITA. LC 88-81204. Orig. Title: Donna in Guerra. 282p. (Orig.). 1989. pap. 14.50 (*0-934977-12-7*) Italica Pr.

Maraini, Dacia, et al. The Silent Dutchess. Kitto, Dick & Spottiswood, Elspeth, trs. from ENG. LC 98-22699. 264p. 1998. 19.95 (*1-55861-194-0*, Pub. by Feminist Pr) Consort Bk Sales.

***Maraini, Fosco.** Maraini: Acts of Photography, Acts of Love. (Illus.). 160p. 1999. 60.00 (*1-55670-973-0*) Stewart Tabori & Chang.

Maraire, J. Nozipo. Zenzele: A Letter for My Daughter. 208p. 1997. pap. 9.95 (*0-385-31822-7*, Delta Trade) Dell.

***Marais, Anthony.** The Xenophobe's Guide to the Californians. (Xenophobe's Guides Ser.). 64p. 2000. pap. 5.95 (*1-902825-20-9*) Oval Bks.

Marais, Gill. Right over the Mountain: Travels with a Tibetan Medicine Man. (Illus.). 160p. 1993. pap. 13.95 (*1-85230-150-3*, Pub. by Element MA) Penguin Putnam.

***Marais, Hein.** South Africa: Limits to Change the Political Economy of Transition, Vol. 1. 290p. 2000. pap. text 65.00 (*1-85649-543-4*, Pub. by Zed Books) St Martin.

Marais, Jacobs. Representation in Old Testament Narrative Texts. LC 98-27591. (Biblical Interpretation Ser.). x, 196p. 1998. 69.00 (*90-04-11234-0*) Brill Academic Pubs.

Marais, Johan. A Complete Guide to Snakes of South Africa. 284p. 1992. 39.50 (*1-86812-439-8*) Krieger.

— A Complete Guide to the Snakes of Southern Africa. 250p. pap. 16.95 (*1-86812-380-4*) Menasha Ridge.

Marais, Johannes S. Cape Coloured People, Sixteen Fifty-Two to Nineteen Thirty-Seven. LC 74-15065. reprint ed. 44.00 (*0-404-12106-3*) AMS Pr.

— Colonization of New Zealand. LC 77-137258. reprint ed. 37.50 (*0-404-04184-1*) AMS Pr.

Marais, Marin. Marin Marais: Six Suites for Violin Thorough Bass. Kinney, Gordon J., ed. (Recent Researches in Music of the Baroque Era Ser.: Vol. RRB21-22). (Illus.). xxi, 126p. 1976. pap. 55.00 (*0-89579-069-6*, RRB21-22) A-R Eds.

— Pieces a Une et a Deux Violes (1686-1689) (Instrumental Works: Vol. 1). (Illus.). 1980. lib. bdg. 150.00 (*0-8450-7201-3*) Broude.

— Pieces a une et a Trois Violes, Quatrieme Livre (1717) (Instrumental Works Ser.: Vol. 4). 1998. lib. bdg. 150.00 (*0-8450-7204-8*) Broude.

— Pieces de Voile, Second Livre, 1701. (Instrumental Works: Vol. 2). 1987. lib. bdg. 150.00 (*0-8450-7202-1*) Broude.

— Pieces de Voile, Troisieme Livre (1711) (Instrumental Works: Vol. 3). (Illus.). 1995. lib. bdg. 150.00 (*0-8450-7203-X*) Broude.

Maraist, Frank L. Admiralty in a Nutshell. 2nd ed. (Nutshell Ser.). 379p. (C). 1988. reprint ed. pap. text 17.50 (*0-314-64765-1*) West Pub.

Maraist, Frank L. Admiralty in a Nutshell. 3rd ed. (Nutshell Ser.). 400p. (C). 1996. pap. 22.95 (*0-314-06575-X*) West Pub.

Maraist, Frank L. & Galligan, Thomas C., Jr. Louisiana Tort Law. 612p. 105.00 (*1-55834-406-3*) LEXIS Pub.

Maraist, Frank L. & Galligan, Thomas C., Jr. Louisiana Tort Law. 1996. 105.00 (*1-55834-385-7*, 83175, MICHIE) LEXIS Pub.

— Louisiana Tort Law, 1998 Cumulative Supplement. 125p. 1998. suppl. ed. write for info. (*0-327-00343-X*, 8317611) LEXIS Pub.

Maraj, Pandit Bhopaul. On Hinduism: From Darkness to Light. (Illus.). 250p. (Orig.). 1994. pap. write for info. (*0-614-32026-7*) K Maraj.

Marak, Julius L. Garo Customary Laws & Practices: A Sociological Study. 1986. 27.50 (*0-8364-1568-X*) S Asia.

Marakas. Decision Support Systems. LC 98-44574. 506p. 1998. 83.00 (*0-13-744186-X*) P-H.

***Marakas, George M.** Systems Analysis & Design: An Active Approach. LC 00-44115. 2000. write for info. (*0-13-022515-0*) P-H.

***Marakas, Thalia.** If Gumdrops Fell Like Raindrops... A Collection of Poems. Eltringham, Gail & Bennett, Deeny, eds. (Illus.). 96p. 2000. 19.95 (*0-9676258-1-5*) TM Enter.

Marakovitz, Alice. Kwamin: Means First Born. Manzi, Sharon U., ed. (Illus.). 76p. (J). (gr. 5-6). 1997. pap. text 10.00 (*0-9644029-8-X*) Means GA.

Maral, G. VSAT Networks. LC 94-37789. (Series in Communication & Distributed Systems). 304p. 1995. 145.00 (*0-471-95302-4*) Wiley.

***Maral, Gerard.** Satellite Communications Systems: Systems, Techniques & Technology. 3rd ed. 756p. 1998. pap. 89.95 (*0-471-97166-9*) Wiley.

***Maral, Gerard & Bousquet, Michel.** Satellite Communications Systems: Systems, Techniques & Technology. 3rd ed. 756p. 1998. 185.00 (*0-471-97037-9*) Wiley.

Maraldo, John C., jt. ed. see Heisig, James W.

Maraldo, Pamela & People's Medical Society Staff. Women's Health for Dummies. LC 99-61118. 432p. 1999. pap. 19.99 (*0-7645-5119-1*) IDG Bks.

Maralit, Marie, et al. Transforming State Health Agencies to Meet Current & Future Challenges. 86p. 1997. pap. 22.00 (*1-55877-279-0*) Natl Governor.

Maram, Sheldon L., et al. Hispanic Workers in the Garment & Restaurant Industries in Los Angeles County. (Research Reports: No. 12). 123p. (Orig.). (C). 1980. ring bd. 5.00 (*0-935391-11-8*, RR-12) UCSD Ctr US-Mex.

Maram, Sheldon L., jt. auth. see Greenfield, Gerald M.

Maramark, Sheilah, jt. auth. see Richmond, Peggy A.

Marambaud, Pierre. William Byrd of Westover, 1674-1744. LC 70-151251. 307p. reprint ed. pap. 95.20 (*0-608-16739-8*, 202706900053) Bks Demand.

Marambaud, Pierre, jt. auth. see Fontenilles, Alfred.

***Maramorosch, Karl.** Advances in Virus Research, Vol. 54. Vol. 54. 315p. 1999. 109.95 (*0-12-039854-0*) Acad Pr.

Maramorosch, Karl. Forest Trees & Palms: Diseases & Control. Raychaudhuri, S. P., ed. (Illus.). 350p. 1996. lib. bdg. 118.00 (*1-886106-65-7*) Science Pubs.

— Viroids & Satellites: Molecular Parasites at the Frontier of Life. 176p. 1991. lib. bdg. 129.00 (*0-8493-6783-2*, QP552) CRC Pr.

Maramorosch, Karl, ed. Biotechnology for Biological Control of Pests & Vectors. 248p. 1991. lib. bdg. 210.00 (*0-8493-4836-6*, RA639) CRC Pr.

Maramorosch, Karl, et al, eds. Advances in Virus Research. (Illus.). 358p. (C). 1998. boxed set 89.95 (*0-12-039851-6*) Acad Pr.

— Advances in Virus Research, Vol. 44. (Illus.). 473p. 1994. text. write for info. (*0-12-039844-3*) Acad Pr.

— Advances in Virus Research, Vol. 45. (Illus.). 347p. 1995. text 79.00 (*0-12-039845-1*); boxed set 75.00 (*0-614-05260-2*) Acad Pr.

— Advances in Virus Research, Vol. 46. (Illus.). 512p. 1996. text 99.00 (*0-12-039846-X*) Acad Pr.

— Advances in Virus Research, Vol. 47. (Illus.). 435p. 1996. text 99.00 (*0-12-039847-8*) Acad Pr.

— Advances in Virus Research, Vol. 48. (Illus.). 408p. 1997. text 89.95 (*0-12-039848-6*) Morgan Kaufmann.

— Advances in Virus Research, Vol. 50. (Illus.). 455p. 1998. text 89.95 (*0-12-039850-8*) Morgan Kaufmann.

— Advances in Virus Research Vol. 49: Cumulative Index, Volumes 25-47, Vol. 49. (Illus.). 211p. 1997. text 89.95 (*0-12-039849-4*) Morgan Kaufmann.

***Maramorosch, Karl, et al, eds.** Advances in Virus Research Vol. 53. 400p. 1999. 85.00 (*0-12-039853-2*) Acad Pr.

***Maramorosch, Karl & Mahmood, Farida, eds.** Maintenance of Animal/Human & Plant Pathogen Vectors: A Methods Manual. LC 99-48243. 340p. 1999. 85.00 (*1-57808-049-5*) Science Pubs.

Maramorosch, Karl & McIntosh, Arthur H., eds. Insect Cell Biotechnology. LC 93-33795. 200p. 1994. boxed set 189.00 (*0-8493-4597-9*, CRC Reprint) Franklin.

Maramorosch, Karl & Mitsuhashi, Jun, eds. Invertebrate Cell Culture: Novel Directions & Biotechnology Applications. (Illus.). 308p. 1997. text 109.00 (*1-57808-011-8*) Science Pubs.

Maramorosch, Karl & Raychaudhuri, S. P., eds. Mycoplasma Diseases of Crops. (Illus.). 450p. 1987. 208.00 (*0-387-96646-3*) Spr-Verlag.

***Maramorosch, Karl, et al.** Advances in Virus Research, Vol. 52. (Illus.). 475p. 1999. 99.95 (*0-12-039852-4*) Acad Pr.

Maramorosch, Karl, jt. ed. see McIntosh, Arthur H.

Maramorosch, Karl, jt. ed. see Raychaudhuri, S. P.

***Maran.** HTML Visually. (Teach Yourself Ser.). 320p. 1999. 29.99 (*0-7645-3423-8*) IDG Bks.

— Master Office 2000 Visually. LC HF5548.4.M525M368. 704p. 1999. pap. 39.99 (*0-7645-6050-6*) IDG Bks.

— Master Windows 2000 Professional Visually. 700p. 2000. pap. 39.99 (*0-7645-3421-1*) IDG Bks.

— Teach Yourself Excel 97 Visually. LC 98-75599. 336p. 1999. pap. 29.99 (*0-7645-6063-8*) IDG Bks.

Maran. Teach Yourself More Windows 98 Visually. LC QA76.76.O63M36215. 304p. 1998. pap. 29.99 (*0-7645-6044-1*) IDG Bks.

***Maran.** Teach Yourself Powerpoint 97 Visually. LC T385.M3633 1998. 288p. 1999. pap. 29.99 (*0-7645-6062-X*) IDG Bks.

— Teach Yourself Windows NT 4 Visually. LC QA76.76.O63M36217. 352p. 1998. pap. 29.99 (*0-7645-6061-1*) IDG Bks.

***Maran & Marangraphics Staff.** Teach Yourself Microsoft Office 2000 Visually. LC HF5548.4.M525M372. (Teach Yourself Ser.). (Illus.). 416p. 1999. pap. 29.99 (*0-7645-6051-4*) IDG Bks.

Maran Graphics Staff. Computadores Simplificado. (SPA.). 128p. 1996. pap. 27.99 (*0-7645-6012-3*) IDG Bks.

— Computers Simplified. 2nd ed. 224p. 1995. pap. 19.99 (*1-56884-676-2*) IDG Bks.

— Creating Web Pages Simplified: The 3-D Visual Approach to Learning Web Pages. LC 97-128660. (3-D Visual Ser.). 240p. 1997. pap. 24.99 (*0-7645-6007-7*) IDG Bks.

— Excel for Windows 95 Simplified. LC 95-80941. 224p. 1996. pap. 19.99 (*1-56884-682-7*) IDG Bks.

— Excel 4 for Windows. 1994. pap. 6.00 (*1-56884-655-X*) IDG Bks.

— Internet Simplificado. (SPA.). 240p. 1996. pap. 27.99 (*0-7645-6013-1*) IDG Bks.

— Microsoft Office 4.2 Simplificado. (SPA.). 368p. 1996. pap. 31.99 (*0-7645-6014-X*) IDG Bks.

Maran Graphics Staff. More Windows 95 Simplified. 224p. 1996. pap. 19.99 (*1-56884-689-4*) IDG Bks.

Maran Graphics Staff. Office 97 Simplified. LC 97-129182. 384p. 1997. pap. 29.99 (*0-7645-6009-3*) IDG Bks.

— Teach Yourself Office 97 Visually. LC 97-70147. 356p. 1997. pap. 29.99 (*0-7645-6018-2*) IDG Bks.

— 3-D Visual Dictionary of Computing. 224p. 1995. pap. 19.99 (*1-56884-678-9*) IDG Bks.

Maran Graphics Staff. Windows 95 Visual Pocket Guide. 240p. 1995. spiral bd. 14.99 (*1-56884-661-4*) IDG Bks.

Maran Graphics Staff. Word for Windows 95 Simplified. LC 95-80940. 224p. 1995. pap. 19.99 (*1-56884-681-9*) IDG Bks.

Maran Graphics Staff & Maran, Ruth. Excel 5 for Windows Visual Pocket Guide. 256p. 1994. spiral bd. 14.99 (*1-56884-667-3*) IDG Bks.

— Excel 5 Simplified Expanded Version. expanded ed. LC 94-79408. 352p. 1994. pap. 19.99 (*1-56884-664-9*) IDG Bks.

— Lotus 1-2-3 R5 for Windows Visual Pack Guide: Visual Pocket Guide. 256p. 1995. spiral bd. 14.99 (*1-56884-671-1*) IDG Bks.

— Lotus 1-2-3 R5 Simplified. expanded ed. LC 94-79403. 352p. 1994. pap. 19.99 (*1-56884-670-3*) IDG Bks.

— Windows 3.1 Visual Pocket Guide. LC 94-79416. 256p. 1994. spiral bd. 14.99 (*1-56884-650-9*) IDG Bks.

— Windows 3.1 Simplified & Expanded. expanded ed. LC 94-79412. 240p. 1994. pap. 19.99 (*1-56884-654-1*) IDG Bks.

— Windows 3.1 Simplified: Education Edition. 96p. 1995. pap. 14.99 (*1-56884-652-5*) IDG Bks.

Maran Graphics Staff & Maran, Ruth. Windows 95 Simplified & Expanded. 224p. 1995. pap. 19.99 (*1-56884-662-2*) IDG Bks.

Maran Graphics Staff & Maran, Ruth. Word 6 for Windows Simplified. expanded ed. LC 94-79410. 352p. 1994. pap. 19.99 (*1-56884-660-6*) IDG Bks.

Maran Graphics Staff & Muran, Ruth. Word 97 Simplified. LC 97-70364. 224p. 1997. pap. 24.99 (*0-7645-6011-5*) IDG Bks.

***Maran, Irene Juneal.** Laws of Harm. 630p. 2000. write for info. (*0-940214-00-8*) Acting Off Your Weight.

***Maran, Meredith.** Class Dismissed. (Illus.). 256p. 2000. 23.95 (*0-312-26568-9*) St Martin.

Maran, Meredith. Notes from an Incomplete Revolution: Real Life since Feminism. 272p. 1998. pap. 12.95 (*0-553-37489-3*) Bantam.

***Maran, Michael.** After the Divorce: A Do-It-Yourself Guide to Enforcing or Modifying a Divorce Judgment in Michigan. 360p. 2000. pap. 24.95 (*0-936343-12-5*) Grand River.

Maran, Michael. Make Your Own Will: A Guide to Making a Michigan Statutory Will Without a Lawyer. (Illus.). 96p. (Orig.). 1990. pap. 4.95 (*0-936343-04-4*) Grand River.

— The Michigan Divorce Book: A Guide to Doing an Uncontested Divorce Without an Attorney (with Minor Children) 4th rev. ed. (Illus.). 288p. 1998. pap. 29.95 (*0-936343-11-7*) Grand River.

— The Michigan Divorce Book: A Guide to Doing an Uncontested Divorce Without an Attorney (Without Minor Children) 4th rev. ed. (Illus.). 192p. 1998. pap. 24.95 (*0-936343-10-9*) Grand River.

— The Michigan Estate Planning Book: A Complete Do-It-Yourself Guide to Planning an Estate in Michigan. (Illus.). 1997. pap. 29.95 (*0-936343-09-5*) Grand River.

— The Michigan Power of Attorney Book: A Guide to Making Financial, Health Care & Custodial Powers of Attorney Without a Lawyer. (Illus.). 140p. (Orig.). 1991. pap. 5.95 (*0-936343-05-2*) Grand River.

Maran, Rene. Batouala. LC 87-23642. (African Writers Ser.). 149p. (C). 1987. pap. 8.95 (*0-435-90135-4*, 90135) Heinemann.

— Batouala. 1989. reprint ed. lib. bdg. 25.95 (*0-89966-640-X*) Buccaneer Bks.

Maran, Richard & Feistmantl, Eric. Computers Simplified Academic: MaranGraphics Simplified Computer Guide. LC 93-12260. 160p. (J). 1993. pap. text 23.80 (*0-13-095324-5*) Prntice Hall Bks.

Maran, Rita. Torture: The Role of Ideology in the French-Algerian War. LC 88-37478. 230p. 1989. 59.95 (*0-275-93248-6*, C3248, Praeger Pubs) Greenwood.

***Maran, Ruth.** America Online Simplified. 2nd ed. (Illus.). 240p. 2000. pap. text 24.99 (*0-7645-3433-5*) IDG Bks.

Maran, Ruth. Computers: Simplified. 4th rev. ed. LC 98-72283. (3-D Visual Ser.). (Illus.). 240p. 1998. pap. 24.99 (*0-7645-6042-5*) IDG Bks.

***Maran, Ruth.** Creating Web Pages with HTML: Simplified. 2nd ed. 240p. 1999. pap. 24.99 (*0-7645-6067-0*) IDG Bks.

— Excel 97: Simplified. LC 97-70363. 224p. 1997. pap. 24.99 (*0-7645-6022-0*) IDG Bks.

— FrontPage 2000 Simplified. (Illus.). 240p. 2000. pap. text 24.99 (*0-7645-3450-5*) IDG Bks.

— Internet & World Wide Web Simplified. 240p. 1999. pap. 24.99 (*0-7645-3409-2*) IDG Bks.

An Asterisk (*) at the beginning of an entry indicates that the title is appearing for the first time.

— Master Microsoft's Windows Millenium Visually. (Master Visually Ser.). (Illus.). 704p. 2000. pap. 34.99 (*0-7645-3496-3*) IDG Bks.

— Master Windows 98 Visually. LC 98-84747. 736p. 1998. pap. 39.99 (*0-7645-6034-4*) IDG Bks.

— Microsoft Access 2000: Simplified. 240p. 1999. pap. 24.99 (*0-7645-6058-1*) IDG Bks.

— Microsoft Excel 2000 Simplified. LC 99-62445. (... Simplified Ser.). (Illus.). 240p. 1999. pap. 24.99 (*0-7645-6053-0*) IDG Bks.

— Microsoft Office 2000: Simplified. LC 98-75597. (Illus.). 416p. 1999. pap. 29.99 (*0-7645-6052-2*) IDG Bks.

— Microsoft Word 2000 Simplified. LC 99-62446. (... Simplified Ser.). 240p. 1999. pap. 24.99 (*0-7645-6054-9*) IDG Bks.

— Microsoft's Windows Millennium Edition Simplified. (... Simplified Ser.). 240p. 2000. pap. 24.99 (*0-7645-3494-7*) IDG Bks.

Maran, Ruth. Model ESA Report. 70.00 incl. disk (*0-614-05203-3*) ASFE.

***Maran, Ruth.** More Windows 98: Simplified. LC 98-75156. 224p. 1998. pap. 24.99 (*0-7645-6037-9*) IDG Bks.

Maran, Ruth. PC Upgrade & Repair: Simplified. LC 98-72810. (3-D Visual Ser.). (Illus.). 240p. 1998. pap. 24.99 (*0-7645-6049-2*) IDG Bks.

***Maran, Ruth.** Teach Yourself Computers & the Internet Visually. 2nd ed. LC 98-72811. (3-D Visual Ser.). (Illus.). 352p. 1998. pap. 29.99 (*0-7645-6041-7*) IDG Bks.

— Teach Yourself FrontPage 2000 Visually. (Teach Yourself Ser.). (Illus.). 320p. 2000. pap. text 29.99 (*0-7645-3451-3*) IDG Bks.

— Teach Yourself Linux Visually. (Teach Yourself Visually Ser.). (Illus.). 320p. 2000. pap. 29.99 (*0-7645-3430-0*) IDG Bks.

— Teach Yourself Microsoft Access 2000 Visually. (Teach Yourself Visually Ser.). (Illus.). 384p. 1999. pap. 29.99 (*0-7645-6059-X*, CPG Pr) IDG Bks.

— Teach Yourself Microsoft Excel 2000 Visually. (Teach Yourself Visually Ser.). (Illus.). 384p. 1999. pap. 29.99 (*0-7645-6056-5*) IDG Bks.

— Teach Yourself Microsoft PowerPoint 2000 Visually. (Teach Yourself Ser.). 356p. 1999. pap. 29.99 (*0-7645-6060-3*) IDG Bks.

— Teach Yourself Microsoft's Windows Millennium Edition Visually. (Teach Yourself Visually Ser.). 320p. 2000. pap. 29.99 (*0-7645-3495-5*) IDG Bks.

— Teach Yourself the Internet & World Wide Web Visually. 2nd ed. 352p. 1999. pap. 29.99 (*0-7645-3410-6*) IDG Bks.

— Windows 2000 Professional Simplified. (Simplified Ser.). 240p. 2000. pap. text 24.99 (*0-7645-3422-X*) IDG Bks.

Maran, Ruth & Marangraphics Staff. Teach Yourself Windows 95 Visually. LC 96-76723. (Teach Yourself Ser.). (Illus.). 368p. 1996. pap. 29.99 (*0-7645-6001-8*) IDG Bks.

***Maran, Ruth & Marangraphics Staff.** Windows 98: Simplified. 240p. 1998. pap. 24.99 (*0-7645-6030-1*) IDG Bks.

Maran, Ruth, et al. Windows 98 Visual Pocket Guide. 224p. 1998. spiral bd. 16.99 (*0-7645-6035-2*) IDG Bks.

Maran, Ruth, jt. auth. see Maran Graphics Staff.

Maran, Ruth, jt. auth. see Marangraphics Staff.

Maran, Stephen. Astronomy for Dummies. (For Dummies Ser.). (Illus.). 384p. 1999. pap. 19.99 (*0-7645-5155-8*, Dummies Trade Pr) IDG Bks.

Maran, Stephen P. The Astronomy & Astrophysics Encyclopedia. 1002p. 1991. 175.00 (*0-471-28941-8*, VNR) Wiley.

Maran, Stephen P., ed. The Encyclopedia of Astronomy & Astrophysics. (Illus.). 1000p. 1992. text 152.95 (*0-442-26364-3*, VNR) Wiley.

— Picture the Universe Vol. 1: Images from the Hubble Space Telescope. (Illus.). 228p. 1997. 34.95 (*0-9655136-2-9*) ReedDrabick.

Maran, Stephen P., jt. auth. see Mitton, Jacqueline.

Maranatha Church Staff, ed. see Barr, Joan & Barr, Jack.

***Maranatha! Singers.** Celebrate Jesus! Songbook. (Celebrate Jesus! 2000 50-Day Spiritual Adventure Ser.). 1999. 20.00 (*1-57849-209-2*) Mainstay Church.

***Maranatha! Singers, compiled by.** Celebrate Jesus! Worship Leader's Music Package. 1999. 129.00 (*1-57849-182-7*) Mainstay Church.

***Maranda, C.** Coping with Fatigue. 240p. 2000. pap. 12.95 (*1-891929-52-6*) Four Seasons.

Maranda, D. & Daigle, A. Lexique des Ascenceurs et Monte-Charge: Francais-Anglais, Anglais-Francais. (ENG & FRE.). 32p. 1978. pap. 7.95 (*0-8288-5249-9*, M9224) Fr & Eur.

Maranda, Pierre. French Kinship Structure & History. (Janua Linguarum, Series Practica: No. 169). 1974. pap. text 44.65 (*3-10-800096-9*) Mouton.

Maranda, Pierre, ed. Soviet Structural Folkloristics: Texts by Meletinsky, Nekludov, Novik, & Segal, with Tests of the Approach by Jilek & Jilek-Aall, Reid, & Layton, Vol. 1. LC 73-79892. (Approaches to Semiotics Ser.: No. 42). 194p. 1974. 47.70 (*90-279-2683-2*) Mouton.

Maranda, Pierre, jt. ed. see Pouillon, Jean.

Marandel, Jean-Patrice. Francois de Nome: Mysteries of a Seventeenth-Century Neapolitan Painter. (Illus.). 64p. (Orig.). 1992. pap. 14.95 (*0-939594-27-7*, Menil Collection) Menil Found.

— The French Painting Tradition. LC 87-71234. (Illus.). 32p. (Orig.). 1987. pap. 3.50 (*0-918881-18-8*) Columbus Mus Art.

— Manfred Schwartz: The Last Ten Years. LC 73-93335. (Illus.). 1974. pap. 3.00 (*0-911517-27-8*) Mus of Art RI.

Marandel, Jean-Patrice, intro. Gray Is the Color: An Exhibition of Grisaille Painting, 13th-20th Centuries. LC 73-92776. (Illus.). 1974. pap. 9.95 (*0-914412-08-6*, Inst Arts Catalogues) Menil Found.

Marando, Vincent L. & Thomas, Robert D. The Forgotten Governments: County Commissioners As Policy Makers. LC 77-839. 166p. 1977. reprint ed. pap. 51.50 (*0-608-04468-7*, 206521300001) Bks Demand.

Marando, Vincent L., jt. auth. see Florestano, Patricia S.

Marangell, Virginia J. Gianna Mia. 223p. pap. 17.00 (*0-615-11160-2*) V J Marangell.

Marangolo, M. & Fiorentini, G., eds. Small Cell Lung Cancer: Proceedings of the International Conference on Small Cell Lung Cancer, Ravenna, Italy, 27-28 March, 1987. (Advances in the Biosciences Ser.: Vol. 72). (Illus.). 182p. 1988. 92.00 (*0-08-036631-7*, Pergamon Pr) Elsevier.

Marangoni, Roy D., jt. auth. see Beckwith, Thomas G.

Marangos, Paul J., jt. ed. see Lal, H.

Marangrahics Staff. Teach Yourself Networking Visually. 320p. 1998. pap. 29.99 (*0-7645-6023-9*) IDG Bks.

Marangraphics Development Group. Office 97. LC 97-7648. (Glencoe Visual Ser.). 1998. 34.95 (*0-02-803963-7*) Macmillan.

Marangraphics Development Group Staff. Excel 7 for Windows 95. LC 96-11353. (Glencoe Visual Ser.). 1996. write for info. (*0-02-813974-7*) McGraw.

Marangraphics' Development Group Staff. MaranGraphics' Development Group Learn at First Sight Windows 3.1. 1994. write for info. (*0-318-72421-9*) P-H.

Marangraphics Development Group Staff. MS-DOS 6.2. 1993. pap. 12.95 (*0-685-70706-7*) P-H.

— Windows 95. LC 96-23736. (Glencoe Visual Ser.). 1996. write for info. (*0-02-803960-2*); write for info. (*0-02-814046-X*) Glencoe.

Marangraphics Staff. America Online: Simplified. LC 97-81242. 240p. 1998. pap. 24.99 (*0-7645-6033-6*) IDG Bks.

— Canadian - Computers Simplified. 2nd ed. 1995. pap. 24.95 (*1-896283-05-5*, Pub. by MaGr) IDG Bks.

Marangraphics Staff. Excel 7 for Windows 95. Date not set. teacher ed. 26.95 incl. disk (*0-02-813973-9*) Glencoe.

Marangraphics Staff. Lotus 1-2-3 Release 5 for Windows. expanded ed. 1994. text 24.95 (*0-9695666-9-7*, Pub. by MaGr) IDG Bks.

— Master Office 97 Visually. LC HF5548.4.M525M38. 704p. 1998. pap. 39.99 (*0-7645-6036-0*) IDG Bks.

— Microsoft Office 4.2 for Windows. 1995. text 34.95 (*1-896283-04-7*, Pub. by MaGr) IDG Bks.

Marangraphics Staff. Teach Yourself Access 97 Visually. LC 97-72426. (Teach Yourself Ser.). 320p. 1997. pap. 29.99 (*0-7645-6026-3*) IDG Bks.

— Teach Yourself Netscape Navigator 4 Visually. LC 97-222431. (Teach Yourself Ser.). 320p. 1997. pap. 29.99 (*0-7645-6028-X*) IDG Bks.

— Teach Yourself Windows 98 Visually. LC 98-84749. 320p. 1998. pap. 29.99 (*0-7645-6025-5*) IDG Bks.

Marangraphics Staff. Teach Yourself Windows NT 5 Workstation Visually. 352p. 2000. pap. 29.99 (*0-7645-6040-9*) IDG Bks.

Marangraphics Staff. Teach Yourself Word 97 Visually. LC 97-80493. 320p. 1997. pap. 29.99 (*0-7645-6032-8*) IDG Bks.

— Teach Yourself Word 2000 Visually. (Visually Ser.). (Illus.). 384p. 1999. pap. 29.99 (*0-7645-6055-7*) IDG Bks.

Marangraphics Staff. 3-D Computer Dictionary. 1995. text 24.95 (*1-896283-13-6*, Pub. by MaGr) IDG Bks.

Marangraphics Staff. Windows 95. Date not set. teacher ed. 26.95 incl. disk (*0-02-814045-1*) Glencoe.

Marangraphics Staff. Windows 95 Intermediate. 1996. pap. 26.95 (*1-896283-09-8*, Pub. by MaGr) IDG Bks.

— Windows 95 Pocketguide. 1995. text 15.95 (*1-896283-07-1*, Pub. by MaGr) IDG Bks.

— Windows 95 Simplified. 1995. text 24.95 (*1-896283-06-3*, Pub. by MaGr) IDG Bks.

Marangraphics Staff. Word 7 for Windows 95. (Visual Ser.). Date not set. teacher ed. 26.95 incl. disk (*0-02-813943-7*) Glencoe.

Marangraphics Staff. WordPerfect 6.1 for Windows. 1996. text 24.95 (*1-896283-02-0*, Pub. by MaGr) IDG Bks.

Marangraphics Staff & IDG Books Staff. Teach Yourself Netscape Navigator "X" Visual. (Teach Yourself Ser.). 352p. 1998. pap. 29.99 (*0-7645-6039-5*) IDG Bks.

Marangraphics Staff & Maran, Ruth. Master Windows 95 Visually. LC 97-80209. 800p. 1997. pap. 39.99 (*0-7645-6024-7*) IDG Bks.

Marangraphics Staff & Maran, Ruth. Teach Yourself Internet & World Wide Web Visually. LC 97-72367. (Teach Yourself Ser.). 320p. 1997. pap. 29.99 (*0-7645-6020-4*) IDG Bks.

Marangraphics Staff, jt. auth. see Maran.

Marangraphics Staff, jt. auth. see Maran, Ruth.

Maranhao, Tullio. Therapeutic Discourse & Socratic Dialogue: A Cultural Critique. LC 86-40056. (Rhetoric of the Human Sciences Ser.). 256p. 1986. text 24.95 (*0-299-10920-8*) U of Wis Pr.

Maranhao, Tullio, ed. The Interpretation of Dialogue. LC 89-5074. (Illus.). 384p. 1990. pap. text 21.95 (*0-226-50434-4*) U Ch Pr.

— The Interpretation of Dialogue. LC 89-5074. (Illus.). 368p. 1990. lib. bdg. 50.50 (*0-226-50433-6*) U Ch Pr.

Marani, Pietro. Michelangelo: The Genius of the Sculptor in Michelangelo's Work. (Illus.). 527p. 1996. 100.00 (*2-89192-159-3*) McCland & Stewart.

***Maranian, Matt.** Pad: The Guide to Ultra-Living. LC 99-40880. (Illus.). 208p. 2000. 24.95 (*0-8118-2653-8*) Chronicle Bks.

Maranian, Matt & Lovett, Anthony. L. A. Bizzaro! The Insider's Guide to the Obscure, the Absurd & the Perverse in Los Angeles. 5th ed. LC 97-919. 1997. pap. 16.95 (*0-312-15562-X*, Buzz Bks) St Martin.

Maraniello, Mainolfi. Mainolfi Maraniello. (Illus.). 64p. 1999. pap. 24.95 (*88-8158-188-4*, Pub. by Charta) Dist Art Pubs.

Maraninchi, D., jt. ed. see Aapro, M. S.

Maraniss, David. The Clinton Enigma: A Four-&-A-Half Minute Speech Reveals This President's Entire Life. 110p. 1998. 17.00 (*0-684-86296-4*) S&S Trade.

— First in His Class: The Biography of Bill Clinton. (Illus.). 512p. 1995. 25.00 (*0-7628-0948-5*) Alva Pr.

— First in His Class: The Biography of Bill Clinton. (Illus.). 400p. 1995. 25.00 (*0-671-87109-9*) S&S Trade.

— First in His Class: The Biography of Bill Clinton. LC 95-44894. (Illus.). 512p. 1996. pap. 14.00 (*0-684-81890-6*, Touchstone) S&S Trade Pap.

***Maraniss, David.** Prince of Tennessee: How Al Gore Met His Fate. 224p. 2000. 21.50 (*0-7432-0411-5*) S&S Trade.

— When Pride Still Mattered: A Life of Vince Lombardi. LC 99-37859. (Illus.). 544p. 1999. 25.50 (*0-684-84418-4*) S&S Trade.

— When Pride Still Mattered: A Life of Vince Lombardi. (Illus.). 544p. 2000. pap. 16.00 (*0-684-87018-5*, Touchstone) S&S Trade Pap.

— When Pride Still Mattered: A Life of Vince Lombardi. large type ed. LC 99-462231. (Biography Ser.). 1003p. 2000. 29.95 (*0-7862-2482-7*, MML06500-171791) Thorndike Pr.

Maraniss, James, tr. see Benitez-Rojo, Antonio.

Maraniss, James E., tr. see Benitez-Rojo, Antonio.

Maraniss, Linda, ed. see Center for Environmental Education Staff.

Maranjian, Selena. Investment Clubs: Learn the Nuts & Bolts of Starting & Running One the Motley Fool Way. unabridged ed. Bauer, Brian & Tidewell, Deborah, eds. LC 99-165378. (Illus.). 50p. 1998. pap. 15.00 (*1-892547-00-7*) Motley Fool.

Maranjian, Selena & Lewis, Roy A. Motley Fool's Investment Tax Guide, 2000: Smart Tax Strategies for Investors. unabridged ed. 384p. 1999. pap. 15.00 (*1-892547-05-8*) Motley Fool.

Marano, jt. auth. see Kurland.

Marano, Americo. Italian I. (C). pap. text. write for info. (*1-884155-03-0*) Day & Nite Pub.

— Italian II. (C). pap. text. write for info. (*1-884155-02-2*) Day & Nite Pub.

Marano, Hara Estroff. Why Doesn't Anybody Like Me: A Guide To Raising Socially Confident Kids. LC 98-4037. 288p. 1998. pap. 12.00 (*0-688-14960-X*, Wm Morrow) Morrow Avon.

Marano, Katia. Apoll & Marsyas: Ikonologische Studien Zu Einem Mythos in der Italienischen Renaissance. (Kunstgeschichte Ser.: Bd. 324). (GER., Illus.). 222p. 1998. 37.95 (*3-631-32919-9*) P Lang Pubng.

Marano, Lydia C. House Arrest. (Mystery Files of Shelby Woo Ser.: No. 6). 144p. (J). (gr. 3-7). 1998. pap. 3.99 (*0-671-02006-4*) PB.

— Rock 'n' Roll Robbery. (Mystery Files of Shelby Woo Ser.: No. 4). (J). (gr. 4-6). 1997. pap. 3.99 (*0-671-01155-3*, Minstrel Bks) PB.

Marano, Michael. Dawn Song. LC 98-13211. 400p. 1998. text 24.95 (*0-312-86432-9*) St Martin.

***Marano, Michael.** Dawn Song. 1999. mass mkt. 6.99 (*0-8125-4547-8*, Pub. by Tor Bks) St Martin.

Marano, Philomena. Word Sandwiches. 48p. (J). (gr. 1 up). 1994. pap. 1.95 (*0-590-47588-6*) Scholastic Inc.

***Marano, Rosario.** How to Save Your Home from Foreclosure. large type ed. 34p. 1999. pap. 8.95 (*0-9673078-0-5*) RJM Mktg.

Marano, Russell. Pockets of Love. 58p. 1984. 5.00 (*0-318-03893-5*) Back Fork Bks.

— Poems from a Mountain Ghetto. (Illus.). 76p. (Orig.). 1979. pap. 5.00 (*0-686-37048-1*) Back Fork Bks.

Maranon, Gregorio. Amiel. (Nueva Austral Ser.: Vol. 23). (SPA.). 1991. pap. text 24.95 (*84-239-1823-8*) Elliots Bks.

Marans, David, jt. auth. see Pospesel, Howard.

Marans, Jon. Old Wicked Songs. LC 98-178033. 1996. pap. 5.25 (*0-8222-1544-6*) Dramatists Play.

Marans, Nelly, ed. see Varillon, Francois.

Marans, Nelly, tr. see Cochini, Christian.

Marans, R. W. & Stokols, D. Environmental Simulation: Research & Policy Issues. (Illus.). 342p. (C). 1993. 57.50 (*0-306-44388-0*, Plenum Trade) Perseus Pubng.

Marans, Robert W. & Fly, J. Mark. Recreation & the Quality of Urban Life: Recreational Resources, Behaviors, & Evaluations of People in the Detroit Region. LC 81-623446. (Institute for Social Research, Research Report). (Illus.). 240p. (Orig.). reprint ed. pap. 74.40 (*0-7837-5255-5*, 204499200005) Bks Demand.

Marans, Robert W. & Spreckelmeyer, Kent F. Evaluating Built Environments: A Behavioral Approach. LC 81-6709. (Illus.). 250p. reprint ed. pap. 77.50 (*0-7837-5266-0*, 204500400005) Bks Demand.

Marans, Robert W. & Wellman, John D. The Quality of Nonmetropolitan Living: Evaluations, Behaviors, & Expectations of Northern Michigan Residents. LC 78-69913. 279p. reprint ed. pap. 86.50 (*0-7837-5692-5*, 204498300005) Bks Demand.

Marans, Robert W., et al. Perceptions of Life Quality in Rural America: An Analysis of Survey Data from Four Studies. LC 80-50377. (University of Michigan Institute for Social Research Report Ser.). 118p. reprint ed. pap. 36.60 (*0-608-14964-0*, 202596700047) Bks Demand.

— Waterfront Living: A Report on Permanent & Seasonal Residents in Northern Michigan. LC 76-620083. (Illus.). 301p. reprint ed. pap. 93.40 (*0-7837-5252-0*, 204498900005) Bks Demand.

Marans, Robert W., jt. ed. see Moore, Gary T.

Marans, Steven, et al. The Policy Mental Health Partnership: A Community-Based Response to Urban Violence. LC 95-18519. 1995. 22.50 (*0-300-06420-9*) Yale U Pr.

Maranto, Gina. ADA "Questions & Answers" Pamphlet: 1992. 335p. 1992. pap. 5.00 (*0-614-06148-2*, 2033-PP-4040) EPF.

Maranto, Robert. Politics & Bureaucracy in the Modern Presidency: Careerists & Appointees in the Reagan Administration, 311. LC 92-30014. (Contributions in Political Science Ser.: No. 311). 200p. 1993. 55.00 (*0-313-28332-X*, MTR/, Greenwood Pr) Greenwood.

Maranto, Robert, et al. Frontiers of Public Education: Lessons from Arizona Charter Schools. LC 99-15567. 271p. 1999. 55.00 (*0-8133-6600-3*, Pub. by Westview) HarpC.

Maranto, Robert, jt. auth. see Schultz, David A.

Marantz, Alec P. On the Nature of Grammatical Relations. 351p. (Orig.). 1984. 37.50 (*0-262-13193-5*); pap. text 18.50 (*0-262-63090-7*) MIT Pr.

***Marantz, Alec P., et al, eds.** Image, Language, Brain. (Illus.). 400p. (C). 2000. 35.00 (*0-262-13371-7*) MIT Pr.

Marantz, Kenneth & Marantz, Sylvia. Creating Picturebooks: Interviews with Editors, Art Directors, Reviewers, Booksellers, Professors, Librarians & Showcasers. LC 97-31620. 247p. 1997. lib. bdg. 39.95 (*0-7864-0415-9*) McFarland & Co.

Marantz, Kenneth, jt. auth. see Marantz, Sylvia.

Marantz, Kenneth A. & Marantz, Sylvia S. Artists of the Page: Interviews with Children's Book Illustrators. LC 91-50951. (Illus.). 240p. 1992. lib. bdg. 39.95 (*0-89950-701-8*) McFarland & Co.

— Multicultural Picture Books: Art for Understanding Others. LC 93-50811. (Professional Growth Ser.). 150p. 1994. pap. text 34.95 (*0-938865-22-6*) Linworth Pub.

Marantz, Kenneth A., et al. The Picturebook: Source & Resource for Art Education. 85p. (Orig.). 1994. pap. 18.00 (*0-937652-68-7*, 211) Natl Art Ed.

Marantz, Kenneth A., jt. auth. see Marantz, Sylvia S.

Marantz, Ronne, jt. compiled by see Flaig, Bea.

Marantz, Sylvia & Marantz, Kenneth. Multicultural Picture Books: Art for Understanding Others, Vol. 2. (Professional Growth Ser.). (Orig.). 1997. pap. 36.95 (*0-938865-63-3*) Linworth Pub.

Marantz, Sylvia, jt. auth. see Marantz, Kenneth.

Marantz, Sylvia S. Picture Books for Looking & Learning: Awakening Visual Perceptions Through the Art of Children's Books. LC 92-14953. 216p. 1992. pap. 26.50 (*0-89774-716-X*) Oryx Pr.

Marantz, Sylvia S. & Marantz, Kenneth A. The Art of Children's Picture Books: A Selective Reference Guide. 2nd ed. LC 94-16308. 320p. 1995. text 20.00 (*0-8153-0937-6*, H1636) Garland.

Marantz, Sylvia S., jt. auth. see Marantz, Kenneth A.

Maranville, Rabbit. Run, Rabbit, Run: The Hilarious & Mostly True Tales of Rabbit Maranville. 120p. 1991. pap. 9.95 (*1-55643-081-7*) North Atlantic.

— Run, Rabbit, Run: The Hilarious & Mostly True Tales of Rabbit Maranville. 120p. 1991. pap. 9.95 (*0-910137-44-7*) Soc Am Baseball Res.

Maranz, David E. Peace Is Everything: World View of Muslims in the Senegambia. LC 92-83905. (International Museum of Cultures Publications: No. 28). xiv, 314p. 1993. pap. 32.00 (*0-88312-816-0*) S I L Intl.

Maranzana, M. & International Federation of Automatic Control, Tri. Real Time Programming 1997: (WRTP '97): A Proceedings Volume from the IFAC IFIP Workshop, Lyon, France, 15-17 September 1997. LC 98-14546. 131p. 1998. write for info. (*0-08-043045-7*) Elsevier.

Marapodi, Carlos, tr. see Black, Susan E.

Marapodi, Carlos, tr. see Cox, W. Eugene.

Marapodi, Carlos, tr. see Murphy, Dan.

Marapodi, Carlos, tr. see Palmer, John J.

Marapodi, Carlos, tr. see Robinson, Sandra C. & Robinson, George B.

Marapodi, Carlos, tr. see Rudd, Connie.

Maraqten, Mohammed. Die Semitischen Personennamen in Den Alt- und Reichsamaischen Inschriften Aus Vorderasien. (Texte und Studien Zur Orientalistik Ser.: Vol. 5). vi, 250p. 1988. write for info. (*3-487-09042-2*) G Olms Pubs.

Marar, Eve. More Haunted House Stories. (Illus.). 96p. (Orig.). (J). 1988. pap. 1.95 (*0-942025-64-4*) Kidsbks.

Marar, K. Narayana, tr. see Siddheswarananda, Swami.

Maras, Raymond J. Innocent XI, Pope of Christian Unity. LC 80-. (Church & the World Ser.: Vol. 1). 350p. 1980. 22.75 (*0-940121-02-6*, H102) Cross Cultural Pubns.

In this substantial contribution to our knowledge of early modern Europe, Pope Innocent XI now stands out as one of the pivotal figures. Professor Maras, in true scholarly fashion, has lifted this illustrious churchman out of undeserved obscurity. *Publisher Paid Annotation.*

Marasa, Paul, jt. auth. see Rind.

Marasa, Paul, jt. ed. see Rind, Bruce.

Marasanov, V. English-Russian Dictionary of Civil Aviation. 534p. (C). 1989. 135.00 (*0-7855-5041-0*, Pub. by Collets) St Mut.

Marasas, W. F., et al. Toxigenic Fusarium Species: Identity & Mycotoxicology. LC 82-42779. 350p. 1984. 45.00 (*0-271-00348-0*) Pa St U Pr.

Marascalco, Bobbie P., jt. auth. see Ables, Timothy D.

Maraschi, L., et al, eds. BL Lac Objects. (Lecture Notes in Physics Ser.: Vol. 334). xii, 500p. 1989. 82.95 (*0-387-51389-2*, 3453) Spr-Verlag.

Maraschiello, Christopher A. Wallace P. Roudebush: Spirit of the Institution. 100p. (Orig.). 1993. pap. text. write for info. (*0-918761-04-2*) Miami U Pubns.

Marasco, Judith, jt. auth. see Holton, Christine.

Marasco, M. C., ed. The Complete Commodity Futures Directory. rev. ed. 550p. 1998. ring bd. 195.00 (*0-9610033-4-0*) Christopher Res.

Marasco, Robert. Burnt Offerings. 1993. reprint ed. lib. bdg. 18.95 (*0-89968-437-8*, Lghtyr Pr) Buccaneer Bks.

Marasco, Wayne A. Intracellular Antibodies: Research & Disease Applications. LC 97-36323. (Molecular Biology Intelligence Unit Ser.). 172p. 1998. 159.00 (*1-57059-509-7*) Landes Bioscience.

Marasco, Wayne A., ed. Intracellular Antibodies: Research & Disease Applications. LC 97-36323. (Biotechnology Intelligence Unit Ser.). 172p. 1998. 150.00 (*3-540-64151-3*) Spr-Verlag.

Marash, I. Robert, ed. ISO 9000: Quick Guide to Quality Management. 52p. 1996. 9.95 (*1-891578-01-4*) INFORM VA.

Marash, I. Robert, jt. auth. see Block, Marilyn R.

Marashi, Medhi, ed. Persian Studies in North America, Studies in Honor of Mohammad Ali Jazayery. LC 93-12142. (ENG & PER., Illus.). 560p. 1994. lib. bdg., boxed set 60.00 (*0-936347-35-X*) IBEX.

Marashi, Mehdi. Contemporary Spoken Persian, Vol. 1. 136p. (C). 1986. pap. text 185.00 incl. audio (*0-88432-132-0*, AFPE01) Audio-Forum.

— Persian Handwriting. rev. ed. LC 98-84882. (Illus.). 246p. 1998. pap. text. write for info. (*0-9640537-7-2*) Monterey Pubng.

***Marashi, Mehdi.** Persian Handwriting: Book & CD Manual for Persian (Farsi) Handwriting. LC 98-84882. (Illus.). xviii, 240p. 2000. pap. 35.00 incl. cd-rom (*1-58814-000-8*) IBEX.

Marashi, Mehdi & Merashi, Mehdi. Persian, Contemporary Spoken, Vol. 2. 119p. pap. text 185.00 incl. audio (*0-88432-792-2*, AFPE20) Audio-Forum.

Marashinsky, Amy S. & Janto, Hrana. Goddess Oracle: A Way to Wholeness Through the Goddess & Ritual. LC 97-166. (Illus.). 1997. 29.95 (*1-85230-864-8*, Pub. by Element MA) Penguin Putnam.

Marasinghe, E. W., ed. Bimbamana of Gautamiyasastra: As Heard by Sariputra. LC 94-906611. (C). 1994. 14.00 (*81-7030-417-2*, Pub. by Sri Satguru Pubns) S Asia.

Marasinghe, Lakshman. Contract of Sale in International Trade Law. 437p. 1992. 85.00 (*0-409-99628-9*, MICHIE) LEXIS Pub.

Marasnio, Nancy. Writing: A Window to Our Minos. (Writing Teachers at Work Ser.). 172p. 1982. pap. text 6.50 (*1-883920-01-9*) Nat Writing Proj.

Maraspin, Davis G. Eaton, Fox, Newcomb & Seward Ancestry of Geo. Blunt Wendell & Edward Eaton Wendell. 106p. 1997. reprint ed. pap. 17.50 (*0-8328-8422-7*); reprint ed. lib. bdg. 27.50 (*0-8328-8421-9*) Higginson Bk Co.

Maraspini, A. L. Study of an Italian Village. 1968. pap. text 41.55 (*90-279-6039-9*) Mouton.

Marassi, Roberto, jt. ed. see Mamantov, Gleb.

Marastoni, ed. Statii: Silvae. (LAT.). 1970. 24.95 (*3-322-00188-1*, T1820, Pub. by B G Teubner) U of Mich Pr.

Marat, Abniel. Tres Lirios Cala. (Aqui y Ahora Ser.). 120p. 1997. pap. 6.95 (*0-8477-0266-9*) U of PR Pr.

Marat, Dolores, photos by. Edges. (Illus.). 160p. 1996. 55.00 (*1-899235-15-9*, 620391, Pub. by Dewi Lewis) Dist Art Pubs.

Marat, Jean-Paul. Polish Letters, 2 vols. 1972. 200.00 (*0-8490-0871-9*) Gordon Pr.

Marateck, Samuel L. FORTRAN 77. 584p. 1983. 26.00 (*0-685-30163-X*) Harcourt.

— Pascal. 823p. 1991. 1.00 (*0-471-55016-7*) Wiley.

— Turbo Pascal. LC 90-40176. 880p. 1991. pap. 73.95 (*0-471-60547-6*) Wiley.

— Turbo Pascal. 862p. 1991. pap. 1.00 (*0-471-55170-8*); pap. text 1.00 (*0-471-53549-4*); pap. text 1.00 (*0-471-55030-2*) Wiley.

— Turbo Pascal. 102p. 1991. pap. text, teacher ed. 28.00 (*0-471-53551-6*) Wiley.

— Turbo Pascal. 216p. 1991. pap. text, teacher ed. 24.50 (*0-471-53556-7*) Wiley.

— Turbo Pascal. 862p. 1991. pap. text 25.00 (*0-471-55574-6*) Wiley.

***Marathe, Achla.** Studies on the Behavior of Equity Markets. LC 98-46667. (Financial Sector of the American Economy Ser.). 160p. 1998. 45.00 (*0-8153-3329-3*) Garland.

Marathe, K. B., jt. ed. see Fraser, J. Nelson.

Marathe, K. B., tr. see Tukarama.

Marathe, Kishore B. & Martucci, G. The Mathematical Foundations of Gauge Theories. LC 92-18717. (Studies in Mathematical Physics: Vol. 5). xxii, 372p. 1992. 136.00 (*0-444-89708-9*, North Holland) Elsevier.

Marathe, M. P., et al, eds. Studies in Jainism. 267p. 1986. pap. 9.50 (*0-8364-1665-1*, Pub. by Abhinav) S Asia.

***Marathe, S.** Maharashtrian Cuisine. 1998. pap. 50.00 (*81-86982-12-4*, Pub. by Business Pubns) St Mut.

— Temples of India: Circles of Stone. LC 98-909221. (Illus.). 1998. pap. 125.00 (*81-86982-11-6*, Pub. by Business Pubns) St Mut.

Marathe, Sharad S. Regulation & Development: India's Policy Experience of Controls over India. 2nd ed. 340p. (C). 1990. text 16.95 (*0-8039-9628-4*) Sage.

Marathe, Sudhakar. T. S. Elliot's Shakespeare Criticism. 1989. 20.00 (*81-7018-534-3*, Pub. by BR Pub) S Asia.

Marathi, Ashish R., tr. see Alkunchwar, Mehesh.

Marathon Sports Marketing Inc. Staff, ed. World Marathon Guide. (World Marathon Guide Ser.). 1998. pap. 19.95 (*0-9663453-0-4*) Marath Sports.

Maratica, Z. Terminologia, Definiciones y Criterios Diagnostieos en Endoscopia Digestiva. 3rd rev. ed. (SPA.). 124p. 1994. ring bd. 35.00 (*0-926592-13-0*) Normed Verlag.

Maratka, Zdenek. Endoscopic Diagnosis in Gastroenterology: Fourth Extended & Illustrated Edition of Terminology, Definitions, & Diagnostic Criteria in Digestive Endoscopy. 4th expanded ed. (Illus.). 260p. 1999. text 40.00 (*0-926592-20-3*) Normed Verlag.

— Illustrated Terminology, Definitions & Diagnostic Criteria in Digestive Endoscopy: Atlas. rev. ed. (Illus.). 1992. 46.00 (*0-926592-09-2*) Normed Verlag.

Maratka, Zdenek & Ottenjann, R., eds. Inflammation in Gut: Esophagitis, Duodenitis, Segmental Colitis. (Bibliotheca Gastroenterologica Ser.: No. 9). (Illus.). 1970. pap. 51.50 (*3-8055-0043-2*) S Karger.

Maratos, Daniel C. & Hill, Marnesba D. Escritores de la Diaspora Cubano: Manual Bibliografico-A Bibliographic Handbook. LC 85-31756.Tr. of Cuban Exile Writers. (SPA.). vvi, 391p. 1986. 45.00 (*0-8108-1878-7*) Scarecrow.

Maratsos, Michael P. The Use of Definite & Indefinite Reference in Young Children: An Experimental Study of Semantic Acquisition. 158p. reprint ed. pap. 45.10 (*0-608-13040-0*, 2024500) Bks Demand.

Maratsos, Michael P., jt. ed. see Gunnar, Megan R.

Maratta, James. Using a TI Graphing Calculator. 92p. (C). 1995. spiral bd. 15.95 (*0-7872-1654-2*, 41165401) Kendall-Hunt.

Maratta, Katie. Silent Pictures. 128p. 1992. pap. 9.95 (*0-943728-49-5*) Lone Eagle Pub.

***Maraux, Andre.** Everything You Need to Know about Lupus. LC 00-8573. 2000. lib. bdg. write for info. (*0-8239-3288-5*, PowerKids) Rosen Group.

Maravall Casesnoves, Dario. Diccionario de Matematica Moderna. (SPA.). 332p. 1975. pap. 19.95 (*0-8288-5814-4*, S50009) Fr & Eur.

Maravall, Jose A. Utopia & Counterutopia in the "Quixote" Felkel, Robert W., tr. from SPA. LC 90-20768. 256p. 1991. text 29.95 (*0-8143-2294-8*) Wayne St U Pr.

Maravall, Jose M. Regimes, Politics & Markets: Democratization & Economic Change in Southern & Eastern Europe. Byrne, Justin, tr. LC 97-164763. (Oxford Studies in Democratization). (Illus.). 282p. 1997. text 58.00 (*0-19-828083-1*) OUP.

Maravel, jt. auth. see Rossides.

Maravel, Alexandra, jt. auth. see Rossides, Eugene T.

Maravel, William. Southwest Virginia in the Civil War: The Battles for Saltville. (Virginia Civil War Battles & Leaders Ser.). (Illus.). 192p. 1992. 19.95 (*1-56190-026-5*) H E Howard.

Maravelas, Paul, ed. from FRE. Texts Pertaining to the Invention of the Balloon in 1782. Carpenter, Scott, tr. from FRE. (Illus.). 28p. 1985. text 95.00 (*0-318-19997-1*) P Maravelas.

Maraventano, Sally. Festa del Giardino: A Harvest of Recipes & Family Memories. (Illus.). 220p. (Orig.). 1999. pap. 20.00 (*1-893127-99-0*, Pub. by Forum Ital) Wimmer Bks.

Maraviglia, B., ed. Nuclear Magnetic Double Resonance: Proceedings of the International School of Physics "Enrico Fermi," Course CXXIII, 13-21 October, 1992. LC 93-48564. (Enrico Fermi International School of Physics Ser.: Vol. 123). 518p. 1993. 259.25 (*0-444-81823-5*, North Holland) Elsevier.

Marazon, David A., jt. auth. see Marazon, Renee A.

Marazon, David A., ed. see Marazon, Renee A.

Marazon, Renee A. Activity Cards & Target Objectives: Birth to Age 12 - The Marazon Family Child Care System. Marazon, David A., ed. 96p. 1997. pap. text. write for info. (*1-889114-06-5*) Maps for Life.

— Activity Cards & Target Objectives: Birth to Age 12 - The Marazon Home Visitor System. St. Arnaud, Aimee, ed. 96p. 1999. pap. text. write for info. (*1-889114-11-1*) Maps for Life.

— Deliverance Prayer: A Matter of Wisdom, Disceinment & Obedience. Szyperki, Pat et al, eds. Date not set. pap. text 5.00 (*1-889114-10-3*) Maps for Life.

Marazon, Renee A. Family Child Care: Birth to Age 12 - the Maragon System. Marazon, David A. et al, eds. LC 99-190447. (Illus.). 357p. 1997. pap. write for info. (*1-889114-04-9*) Maps for Life.

— 4 Easy Steps to Developmental Planning & Assessment: Birth to Age 12 - The Marazon System. Marazon, David A., Sr. & Phillips, Sylvia, eds. (Illus.). 172p. (Orig.). 1995. pap. text 50.00 (*1-889114-01-4*) Maps for Life.

— Helping Children Grow, Develop & Learn: Birth to Age 12 - The Marazon System. Marazon, David A. & Phillips, Sylvia, eds. (Illus.). 196p. (Orig.). 1995. pap. text 50.00 (*1-889114-00-6*) Maps for Life.

***Marazon, Renee A.** The Home Visitor's Handbook of Child Development. St. Arnaud, Aimee, ed. 369p. 1999. pap. text. write for info. (*1-889114-09-X*) Maps for Life.

— Parent Activity Cards: Birth to Age 12 - The Marazon Classroom System. Marazon, David A., ed. 96p. 1997. pap. text. write for info. (*1-889114-05-7*) Maps for Life.

— Parent Activity Cards: Birth to Age 12 - The Marazon Parent System. Marazon, David A., ed. 96p. 1997. pap. text. write for info. (*1-889114-08-1*) Maps for Life.

— The Parent System: Birth to Age 12. Marazon, David A., ed. 444p. 1997. boxed set 96.00 (*1-889114-07-3*) Maps for Life.

Marazon, Renee A. Parent Teacher Partnerships: Birth to Age 12 - The Marazon System. Marazon, David A. & Phillips, Sylvia, eds. (Illus.). 276p. (Orig.). 1995. pap. text 30.00 (*1-889114-02-2*) Maps for Life.

— The Parent's Handbook of Child Development. Marazon, David A. et al, eds. LC 98-205942. (Illus.). 338p. (Orig.). 1997. pap. 40.00 (*1-889114-03-0*, 2000) Maps for Life.

***Marazon, Renee A. & Marazon, David A.** The Christian Parent's Activity Cards. St. Arnaud, Aimee et al, eds. 102p. 2000. pap. write for info. (*1-889114-13-8*) Maps for Life.

— The Christian Parent's Handbook of Child Development. Bell, Carolyn et al, eds. (Illus.). 357p. 2000. pap. write for info. (*1-889114-12-X*) Maps for Life.

Marazov, Ivan, et al. Ancient Gold: The Wealth of the Thracians: Treasures from the Republic of Bulgaria. LC 97-36226. 1998. pap. write for info. (*1-882507-06-1*) Abrams.

— Ancient Gold: The Wealth of the Thracians: Treasures from the Republic of Bulgaria. LC 97-36226. (Illus.). 256p. 1998. 49.50 (*0-8109-1992-3*, Pub. by Abrams) Time Warner.

Marazzi, Alfio. Algorithms, Routines & S Functions for Robust Statistics: The FORTRAN Library ROBETH with an Interface to S-PLUS. (Illus.). 440p. (C). (gr. 13). 1993. ring bd. 83.95 (*0-412-07991-7*, Chap & Hall CRC) CRC Pr.

Marazzi, Richard & Fiorito, Len. Aaron to Zuverink: Baseball Players of the Fifties. 552p. 1984. mass mkt. 4.50 (*0-380-68445-4*, 68445, Avon Bks) Morrow Avon.

Marbach, Christian M. Evangelische/Singe-Schule. (GER.). 261p. 1991. reprint ed. write for info. (*3-487-09313-8*) G Olms Pubs.

Marbach, Eduard. Mental Representation & Consciousness: Towards a Phenomenological Theory of Representation & Reference. LC 92-42687. (Contributions to Phenomenology Ser.: Vol. 14). 208p. (C). 1993. lib. bdg. 147.00 (*0-7923-2101-4*, Pub. by Kluwer Academic) Kluwer Academic.

Marbach, Eduard, tr. see Husserl, Edmund.

Marback, Richard. Plato's Dream of Sophistry. Benson, Thomas W., ed. LC 97-45431. (Studies in Rhetoric/Communication). 160p. 1999. lib. bdg. 24.95 (*1-57003-240-8*) U of SC Pr.

Marback, Richard, et al. Cities, Cultures, Conversations: A Urban Reader. (C). 1997. pap., teacher ed. write for info. (*0-205-26460-3*, T6460-4) Allyn.

— Cities, Cultures, Conversations: Readings for Writers. LC 97-16287. 468p. 1997. pap. 34.00 (*0-205-18456-1*) Allyn.

Marbaker, Thomas D. History of the Eleventh New Jersey Volunteers. Martin, David G., ed. (Illus.). 490p. (C). 1990. reprint ed. 32.00 (*0-944413-13-7*, 203) Longstreet Hse.

Marban, Edilberto. El Mundo Iberoamer Hombre: Hombres en Su Historia. 390p. (YA). (gr. 10-12). 1974. pap. text 6.95 (*0-88345-066-6*, 18084) Prentice ESL.

— Puerto Rico: Cuna y Forja (Historia de la Isla Desde su Descubriiento en 1493 Hasta el Ultimo Periedo de Munoz en 1965) LC 86-81158. (Coleccion Textos). (SPA., Illus.). 298p. (Orig.). 1987. pap. 19.00 (*0-89729-405-X*) Ediciones.

Marban, Jorge A. La Florida: Cinco Siglos de Historia Hispanica. LC 78-70500. (Coleccion de Estudios Hispanicos - Hispanic Studies Collection). (Illus.). 1979. pap. 6.00 (*0-89729-214-6*) Ediciones.

Marbe, Karl, jt. auth. see Thumb, Albert.

Marbeck, John. Orgies Unlimited. 44.95 (*1-893263-06-1*) Ipso Facto.

***Marbeck, Pilgram, et al.** Later Writings by Pilgram Marpeck & His Circle. 1999. pap. text 20.00 (*0-9683462-6-X*) Pandora Pr.

Marbeck, Pilgrim. The Writings of Pilgrim Marbeck. Klassen, William & Klaassen, Walter, eds. LC 77-87419. (Classics of the Radical Reformation Ser.: No. 2). 614p. 1978. reprint ed. pap. 175.00 (*0-608-06025-9*, 2066354) Bks Demand.

Marber. Educational Administration. (C). 1989. pap. text. write for info. (*0-7730-4750-6*) Addison-Wes.

— Women's Studies Reader. (C). 1997. pap. text. write for info. (*0-7730-4780-8*) Addison-Wesley.

Marber, Ian, jt. auth. see Edgson, Vicki.

Marber, M. & Yellon, Derek M. Ischaemia: Preconditioning & Adaptation. (UCL Molecular Pathology Ser.). (Illus.). 250p. 1996. text 130.00 (*1-85996-160-6*, Pub. by Bios Sci) Bks Intl VA.

Marber, Patrick. Closer. pap. 5.95 (*0-8222-1722-8*) Dramatists Play.

Marber, Patrick. Closer: A Play. LC 99-23870. 120p. 1999. pap. 13.00 (*0-8021-3645-1*, Grove) Grove-Atltic.

— Dealer's Choice. LC 98-138942. 1997. pap. 5.25 (*0-8222-1616-7*) Dramatists Play.

— Dealer's Choice. 1995. pap. 11.95 (*0-413-69210-8*, A0753) Heinemann.

Marber, Peter. From Third World to World Class. LC 98-13834. 1998. 30.00 (*0-7382-0066-2*) Perseus Pubng.

— From Third World to World Class: The Future of Emerging Markets in the Global Economy. LC 98-13834. 272p. 1998. 30.00 (*0-201-77284-1*) Addison-Wesley.

— From Third World to World Class: The Future of Emerging Markets in the Global Economy. 288p. 1999. pap. text 16.00 (*0-7382-0132-4*, Pub. by Perseus Pubng) HarpC.

Marberger, M., ed. Thermal Tissue Ablation. (Journal: European Urology: Vol. 23, Suppl. 1, 1993). (Illus.). iv, 72p. 1993. pap. 40.00 (*3-8055-5799-X*) S Karger.

Marberger, Michael, et al. Stone Surgery. (Practice of Surgery Ser.). (Illus.). 320p. 1991. text 220.00 (*0-443-03522-9*) Church.

Marberry, Craig, jt. auth. see Cunningham, Michael.

Marberry, Sara O. Color in the Office: Design Trends from 1950 to 1990 & Beyond. (Architecture Ser.). 125p. 1993. 75.00 (*0-471-29078-5*, VNR) Wiley.

— Innovations in Healthcare Design. 1995. text 62.95 (*0-442-01867-3*, VNR) Wiley.

Marberry, Sara O., ed. Innovations in Healthcare Design: Selected presentations from the First Five Sympasia on Healthcare Design. (Architecture Ser.). 306p. 1995. pap. 69.95 (*0-471-28637-0*, VNR) Wiley.

Marberry, Sara O. & Zagon, Laurie. The Power of Color: Creating Healthy Interior Spaces. LC 94-23831. (Construction Business & Management Library). 100p. 1995. 64.95 (*0-471-07685-6*) Wiley.

Marbet, U., jt. ed. see Beglinger, C.

Marble, Allan E. Surgeons, Smallpox & the Poor: A History of Medicine & Social Conditions in Nova Scotia, 1749-1799. (Illus.). 376p. 1993. 65.00 (*0-7735-0988-7*, Pub. by McG-Queens Univ Pr) CUP Services.

— Surgeons, Smallpox & the Poor: A History of Medicine & Social Conditions in Nova Scotia, 1749-1799. (Illus.). 376p. 1997. pap. 24.95 (*0-7735-1639-5*, Pub. by McG-Queens Univ Pr) CUP Services.

Marble, Anne D. Guide to Wetland Functional Design. 240p. 1991. boxed set 94.95 (*0-87371-672-8*) CRC Pr.

Marble, Annie R. Heralds of American Literature. LC 67-26761. (Essay Index Reprint Ser.). 1977. 22.95 (*0-8369-0675-6*) Ayer.

— Nobel Prize Winners in Literature, 1901-1931. LC 70-84324. (Essay Index Reprint Ser.). 1977. 30.95 (*0-8369-1185-7*) Ayer.

— Thoreau: His Home, Friends & Books. LC 73-85906. reprint ed. 34.50 (*0-404-04185-X*) AMS Pr.

— Thoreau: His Home, Friends & Books. (BCL1-PS American Literature Ser.). 343p. 1992. reprint ed. lib. bdg. 89.00 (*0-7812-6884-2*) Rprt Serv.

Marble, Duane F. Two Computer Programs for the Analysis of Simple Markov Chains. (Discussion Papers: No. 6). 1964. pap. 10.00 (*1-55869-128-6*) Regional Sci Res Inst.

Marble, Effie M. Beautiful Bristol. (Illus.). 150p. 1988. pap. 7.95 (*0-933704-73-9*) Dawn Pr.

Marble, Robert. Casebook for Systems Analysis & Design. (C). 1991. text 20.00 (*0-07-040190-X*) McGraw.

Marble, Scott & Kalden, Katrin, eds. Abstract 96/97. (Illus.). 160p. Date not set. pap. write for info. (*1-883584-11-6*) CUGSA.

Marbles, Jim. The College of Obscure Knowledge: A Light Hearted Look at an Odd Collection of Trivia. LC 98-213999. 160p. 1997. pap. 5.99 (*1-57757-017-0*) Trade Life.

— The Fictionary Dictionary. 160p. 1996. pap. 6.99 (*1-57757-019-7*) Honor Bks OK.

***Marbly, Corwin B., Jr.** Faith of Our Fathers. LC 99-93984. 1999. pap. 7.95 (*0-533-13208-8*) Vantage.

Marboe, R. C., et al, eds. Proceedings of the ASME Noise Control & Acoustics Division Vol. 21: Proceedings of the ASME International Mechanical Engineering Congress & Exposition, 1995, San Francisco, CA. LC 95-81064. (1995 International Mechanical Engineering Congress & Exposition Ser.: NCA-Vol. 21). 160p. 1995. 72.00 (*0-7918-1757-1*, H01039) ASME.

Marbot, Baron de, see de Marbot, Baron.

Marbrook, John, jt. ed. see Watson, James Dewey.

Marburg, Anna Von, see Von Marburg, Anna.

Marburg, Theodore, ed. see Levasseur, Emile.

Marburger, Daniel R., ed. Stee-Rike Four! What's Wrong with the Business of Baseball? LC 96-44685. 232p. 1997. 55.00 (*0-275-95706-3*, Praeger Pubs) Greenwood.

Marburger, Heinz, jt. ed. see Luck, Kai von.

Marbury, Mary O. Favorite Flies & Their History. 540p. 1989. 17.98 (*1-55521-241-7*) Bk Sales Inc.

Marbut, Curtis F., jt. auth. see Shantz, Homer L.

Marc, Alexandre, ed. African Art: The World Bank Collection. LC 98-2943. 108p. 1998. pap. 22.00 (*0-8213-4195-2*, 14195) World Bank.

Marc, David. Bonfire of the Humanities: Television, Subliteracy, & Long-Term Memory Loss. (Television Ser.). (Illus.). 186p. 1995. 29.95 (*0-8156-0321-5*) Syracuse U Pr.

— Bonfire of the Humanities: Television, Subliteracy, & Long-Term Memory Loss. (Television Ser.). (Illus.). 186p. 1998. pap. 17.95 (*0-8156-0463-7*) Syracuse U Pr.

— Comic Visions: Television Comedy & American Culture. 256p. 1997. pap. text 23.95 (*1-57718-003-8*) Blackwell Pubs.

— Comic Visions: Television Comedy & American Culture. (Media Studies). 224p. 1989. pap. text 14.95 (*0-04-445285-3*) Routledge.

— Demographic Vistas: Television in American Culture. rev. ed. 272p. (Orig.). 1996. pap. text 17.95 (*0-8122-1560-5*) U of Pa Pr.

Marc, David & Thompson, Robert J. Prime Time, Prime Movers: From I Love Lucy to L. A. Law--America's Greatest TV Shows & the People Who Created Them. (Television Ser.). (Illus.). 350p. 1995. pap. 17.95 (*0-8156-0311-8*) Syracuse U Pr.

— Prime Time, Prime Movers: The Inside Story of the Inside People Who Made American Television. (Illus.). 304p. 1992. 22.95 (*0-316-54589-9*) Little.

Marc, Devan. White Boy: A Black Experience. LC 98-93345. 240p. 1999. pap. 19.95 (*0-9664216-0-4*) Devco Ink.

Marc, Franz. Franz Marc: Letters from the War. Lankheit, Klaus & Steffen, Uwe, eds. Dieckmann, Liselotte, tr. from GER. LC 91-23987. (American University Studies: Fine Arts: Ser. XX, Vol. 16). (Illus.). 113p. (C). 1992. text 29.95 (*0-8204-1588-X*) P Lang Pubng.

Marc, Franz, jt. tr. see Kandinsky, Wassily.

Marc, Gideon. The Secret of the Space Scrolls & Cholent. (Illus.). 144p. (Orig.). (J). (gr. 4-7). 1994. pap. 6.95 (*965-483-001-9*) Pitspopany.

Marc, Michel, ed. see Labiche, Eugene.

Marc, R. E., et al. GABA in the Retina & Central Visual System. (Progress in Brain Research Ser.: Vol. 90). 546p. 1992. 274.75 (*0-444-81446-9*) Elsevier.

An Asterisk (*) at the beginning of an entry indicates that the title is appearing for the first time.

MARC Standards Office Staff, prod. US-MARC Code List for Countries, 1993. LC 93-38625. 1993. write for info. (*0-8444-0825-5*) Lib Congress.

MARC Standards Office Staff, jt. auth. see Network Development Staff.

MARC Standards Office Staff, jt. ed. see Network Development Staff.

Marc, Stephen. Urban Notions. LC 84-180996. (Illus.). 70p. 1983. 15.00 (*0-915109-01-8*); pap. 8.00 (*0-915109-02-6*) Ataraxia.

MARC Users' Group, Seminar (1983, London, England). Databases for Books: Their Uses for Selling, Acquiring, & Cataloguing: Proceedings of the Marc Users' Group Seminar, 3 May 1983. LC 85-110728. (LA Conference Proceedings Series in Library Automation: Vol. 4). 62p. 1983. reprint ed. pap. 30.00 (*0-608-02475-9*, 206311900004) Bks Demand.

Marca, David, jt. auth. see Gold-Bernstein, Beth.

Marca, David A. & Bock, Geoffrey E. Groupware: Software for Computer-Supported Cooperative Work. LC 91-37373. (Illus.). 592p. (C). 1992. 70.00 (*0-8186-2637-2*, 2637) IEEE Comp Soc.

Marca, David A. & McGowan, Clement L. IDEFO - SADT Business Process & Enterprise Modelling. 392p. 1993. pap. 65.00 (*0-9638750-0-0*) Eclectic Solns.

***Marcabrun.** Marcabru: A Critical Edition. Gaunt, Simon et al, eds. LC 99-56191. 2000. 162.00 (*0-85991-574-3*, DS Brewer) Boydell & Brewer.

Marcaccio, Michael D. The Hapgoods Three Earnest Brothers. LC 77-5102. (Illus.). 271p. reprint ed. pap. 84.10 (*0-8357-3136-7*, 203939900012) Bks Demand.

Marcade, Bernhard. Pierre et Gilles. (Jumbo Ser.). 1997. 69.69 (*3-8228-8095-7*) Taschen Amer.

Marcais, Georges, jt. auth. see Diehl, Charles.

Marcangelo, Jo. Italian Vegetarian Cooking. 160p. 1989. pap. 9.95 (*0-89281-343-1*) Inner Tradit.

Marcano-Garcia, Pablo. La Criminelidad y la Crisis de las Prisiones en Puerto Rico. (SPA.). 144p. (Orig.). 1985. pap. 9.00 (*0-685-24434-2*) Editorial El Coqui.

Marcantel, David E., jt. auth. see Gelhay, Patrick.

Marcantel, Pamela. An Army of Angels: A Novel of Joan of Arc. 592p. 1998. pap. 15.95 (*0-312-18042-X*) St Martin.

Marcantognini, S. A., et al, eds. Harmonic Analysis & Operator Theory: Proceedings: Conference in Honor of Mischa Cotlar (1994: Caracas, Venezuela) LC 95-23965. (Contemporary Mathematics Ser.: No. 189). 511p. 1995. pap. 75.00 (*0-8218-0304-2*, CONM/189) Am Math.

Marcarius Starets of Optina & Macarius, Staretz. Russian Letters of Spiritual Direction, 1834-1860. De Beausorbe, Iulia, tr. from RUS. LC 75-1064. 115p. (Orig.). 1994. pap. 7.95 (*0-913836-23-0*) St Vladimirs.

Marcarthy, David J. Local Government Law in a Nutshell. 4th ed. (Nutshell Ser.). 472p. (C). 1995. pap. 22.95 (*0-314-07025-7*) West Pub.

Marcati, P. Mathematical Problems in Semiconductor Physics. 1995. pap. 55.00 (*0-582-28704-9*, Pub. by Addison-Wesley) Longman.

Marcaurelle, Roger. Freedom Through Inner Renunciation: Sankara's Philosophy in a New Light. LC 99-20738. (McGill Studies in the History of Religions). 320p. (C). 1999. text 59.50 (*0-7914-4361-2*); pap. text 19.95 (*0-7914-4362-0*) State U NY Pr.

***Marcdante,** My Mother, My Friend: The Ten Most Important Things to Talk about with Your Mother. 208p. 2001. pap. 12.00 (*0-684-86606-4*, Fireside) S&S Trade Pap.

Marceau-Chenkie, Brittany. Naya, the Inuit Cinderella. large type ed. (Illus.). 24p. (J). (ps-3). 1999. pap. 7.95 (*1-894303-05-9*) RRP.

Marceau, Felicien. Les Anneese Courtes. (FRE.). 1973. pap. 10.95 (*0-7859-4016-2*) Fr & Eur.

— Bergere Legere. (FRE.). 288p. 1973. pap. 8.95 (*0-7859-4012-X*, 2070364437) Fr & Eur.

— Chair et Cuir. (FRE.). 1974. pap. 10.95 (*0-7859-4028-6*) Fr & Eur.

— Le Corps de Mon Enemi. (FRE.). 1978. pap. 10.95 (*0-7859-4096-0*) Fr & Eur.

— Creezy. (FRE.). 1972. pap. 10.95 (*0-7859-3995-4*) Fr & Eur.

— Les Elans du Coeur. (FRE.). 1973. pap. 8.95 (*0-7859-4002-2*) Fr & Eur.

— L' Homme du Roi. (FRE.). 1972. pap. 8.95 (*0-7859-3996-2*) Fr & Eur.

— L' Oeuf. (FRE.). 160p. 1980. pap. 8.95 (*0-7859-4138-X*, 2070372383) Fr & Eur.

Marceau, Gabrielle Z. Anti-Dumping & Anti-Trust Issues in Free Trade Areas. 384p. 1995. text 95.00 (*0-19-825920-4*) OUP.

Marceau, Jane. Class & Status in France: Economic Change & Social Immobility, 1945-1975. 1977. 36.00 (*0-19-827217-0*) OUP.

Marceau, Jane, ed. Reworking the World: Organisations, Technologies, & Cultures in Comparative Perspective. LC 92-32150. (Studies in Organization: No. 42). x, 514p. 1992. lib. bdg. 82.95 (*3-11-013158-7*) De Gruyter.

Marceau, Marcel. Pimporello: A Fable for All Ages. 128p. 1991. 25.00 (*0-7206-0813-9*) Dufour.

Marceau, Stephane. Los Cabos, La Paz. (Due South Guide Ser.) (Illus.). 160p. 1999. pap. 10.95 (*2-89464-186-9*, Pub. by Ulysses Travel) Globe Pequot.

Marceau, Stephane G., jt. auth. see Remillard, Francois.

Marceau, William C. The Eucharist in Theodore de Beze & St. Francis de Sales. LC 93-15464. (Toronto Studies in Theology: Vol. 59). (Illus.). 136p. 1993. text 69.95 (*0-7734-9693-9*) E Mellen.

— Henri Bergson et Joseph Malegue: La convergence de Deux Pensees. (Stanford French & Italian Studies: No. 50). (FRE.). 144p. (Orig.). 1988. pap. 56.50 (*0-915838-66-4*) Anma Libri.

— Optimism in the Works of St. Francis De Sales. LC 89-29359. (Toronto Studies in Theology: Vol. 41). 336p. 1989. lib. bdg. 99.95 (*0-88946-990-3*) E Mellen.

— Stoicism & St. Francis de Sales. (Toronto Studies in Theology: Vol. 44). 112p. 1989. write for info. (*0-88946-749-8*) E Mellen.

Marcel, Francine & Fauntleroy, Gussie. Old Paint New: The Image of the Horse in Contemporary Art. Held, Peter, ed. (Illus.). 1999. pap. 5.00 (*1-891695-02-9*) Holter Museum.

Marcel, A. J. & Bisiach, E., eds. Consciousness in Contemporary Science. (Illus.). 416p. 1992. reprint ed. pap. text 45.00 (*0-19-852237-1*) OUP.

Marcel, Gabriel. The Existential Background of Human Dignity. LC 63-13814. (William James Lectures: 1961-1962). 188p. reprint ed. pap. 58.30 (*0-608-10159-1*, 201102200072) Bks Demand.

— Homo Viator: Introduction to a Metaphysic of Hope. Crauford, Emma, tr. 1990. 27.75 (*0-8446-2529-9*) Peter Smith.

— The Mystery of Being, 2 vols., bk. 1. Hague, Rene, tr. from FRE. LC 77-27179. (Gifford Lectures: 1949-50). 432p. reprint ed. 61.50 (*0-404-60504-4*) AMS Pr.

— Philosophy of Existence. Harai, Manya, tr. LC 73-80390. (Essay Index Reprint Ser.). 1977. 18.95 (*0-8369-1094-X*) Ayer.

— The Philosophy of Existentialism. 132p. 1995. pap. 8.95 (*0-8065-0901-5*, 84, Citadel Pr) Carol Pub Group.

— Royce's Metaphysics. LC 56-11854. 200p. reprint ed. pap. 62.00 (*0-608-10683-6*, 205529200013); reprint ed. pap. 57.00 (*0-608-30306-2*, 2055292) Bks Demand.

— Royce's Metaphysics. Ringer, Gordon, tr. from GER. LC 56-11854. 200p. reprint ed. pap. 57.00 (*0-608-30604-5*, 2055292) Bks Demand.

— Royce's Metaphysics. Ringer, Virginia & Ringer, Gordon, trs. from GER. LC 74-33746. 180p. 1975. reprint ed. lib. bdg. 55.00 (*0-8371-7978-5*, MARO, Greenwood Pr) Greenwood.

— Tragic Wisdom & Beyond. Jolin, Stephen & McCormick, Peter, trs. from FRE. LC 72-96700. (Studies in Phenomenology & Existential Philosophy). 256p. (C). 1973. pap. 24.95 (*0-8101-0614-0*) Northwestern U Pr.

Marcel, Gabriel & Hanley, Katharine R. Gabriel Marcel's Perspectives on the Broken World. LC 98-8998. (Studies in Philosophy). 242p. 1998. 25.00 (*0-87462-617-X*) Marquette.

Marcel, Glenn P. Juggling the Truth. LC 89-61781. 200p. 1989. 14.95 (*0-935773-21-5*) Charleston Pr.

Marcel, Latil, et al. Enhanced Oil Recovery. 252p. 1980. 360.00 (*2-7108-0381-X*, Pub. by Edits Technip) Enfield Pubs NH.

Marcel, Mario & Arenas, Alberto. Social Security Reform in Chile. 53p. 1991. pap. text 8.00 (*0-940602-46-6*) IADB.

Marcel, Mario & Arenas, Alberto, eds. Reformas a la Seguridad Social en Chile. 58p. 1991. 8.00 (*0-940602-41-5*) IADB.

Marcel Socias Studio Staff, jt. auth. see Parramon Editorial Team Staff.

Marcelin, M., jt. ed. see Comte, G.

***Marcelis, Nicole.** Home Sanctuary: Practical Ways to Create a Spiritually Fulfilling Environment. LC 00-24043. 2000. (*0-8092-2489-5*, Contemporary Bks) NTC Contemp Pub Co.

Marcell, David W. Progress & Pragmatism: James, Dewey, Beard & the American Idea of Progress, 9. LC 72-818. (Contributions in American Studies: No. 9). 402p. 1974. 79.50 (*0-8371-6387-0*, MPR/, Greenwood Pr) Greenwood.

***Marcell, Jacqueline.** Elder Rage; or Take My Father... Please! How to Survive Caring for Aging Parents. xx, 368p. 2000. pap. 19.95 (*0-9679703-0-X*) Impressive.

Marcell, Raleigh. And Also Much Cattle. 32p. (Orig.). 1994. pap. 3.00 (*1-57514-133-7*, 1110) Encore Perform Pub.

Marcell, Raleigh, Jr. The Infamous Soothing System of Professor Maillard: Dramatization of Edgar Allen Poe's Story. (Illus.). 23p. 1981. pap. 3.00 (*0-88680-093-5*) I E Clark.

— The Middle of Nowhere: A One-Act Play. (Illus.). 28p. 1982. pap. 3.25 (*0-88680-130-3*) I E Clark.

Marcell, Rita & Newton, Robert. A New Manual of Classification. LC 94-172. 304p. 1994. 84.95 (*0-566-07547-4*, Pub. by Gower) Ashgate Pub Co.

Marcella, A. J., Jr., et al. Automated System for Contingency Planning & Disaster Recovery. Campbell, Lee A., ed. (Took Kit Ser.). 88p. 1992. 200.00 (*0-89413-276-8*, A6055) Inst Inter Aud.

Marcella, Albert J. Auditing IBM's Customer Information Control System. 178p. 1991. pap. 20.00 (*0-89413-240-7*, A827) Inst Inter Aud.

— Outsourcing, Downsizing & Reengineering. Campbell, Lee A., ed. LC 95-189683. 352p. 1995. pap. 50.00 (*0-89413-331-4*, A890) Inst Inter Aud.

Marcella, Albert J. & Sampias, William. Assessing Organizational & Individual Ethics. Campbell, Lee A., ed. (CIP Ser.). 1996. pap., teacher ed. 625.00 (*0-89413-355-1*, A6073); pap., wbk. ed. 15.00 (*0-89413-356-X*, A7012) Inst Inter Aud.

***Marcella, Albert J., et al.** Electronic Commerce: Control Issues for Securing Virtual Enterprises. Campbell, Lee A., ed. LC 99-180779. xvii, 269 p. 1998. write for info. (*0-89413-414-0*) Inst Inter Aud.

Marcella, Albert J., et al. The Hunt for Fraud. Campbell, Lee A., ed. (CIP Ser.). 1996. pap., teacher ed. 625.00 (*0-89413-320-9*, A6727); pap., wbk. ed. 15.00 (*0-89413-321-7*, A7680) Inst Inter Aud.

Marcella, Gabriel, ed. Warriors in Peacetime: The Military & Democracy in Latin America, New Directions for U.S. Policy. LC 94-1380. 190p. (C). 1994. 37.50 (*0-7146-4585-0*, Pub. by F Cass Pubs) Intl Spec Bk.

— Warriors in Peacetime: The Military & Democracy in Latin America, New Directions for U.S. Policy. LC 94-1380. (C). 1994. pap. 19.50 (*0-7146-4115-4*) Intl Spec Bk.

***Marcella, Gabriel & Downes, Richard.** Security Cooperation in the Western Hemisphere: Resolving the Ecuador-Peru Conflict. LC 99-25898. 272p. 1999. 45.00 (*1-57454-064-5*, Pub. by U Miami N-S Ctr) L Rienner.

***Marcella, Rita & Maltby, Arthur, eds.** The Future of Classification. LC 99-46030. 144p. 2000. 99.95 (*0-566-07992-5*, Pub. by Gower) Ashgate Pub Co.

Marcelle, Agatha K. Hidden Gems of Quality & Excellence: Original Inspirational Insights. (Illus.). 94p. (Orig.). 1997. pap. 10.00 (*0-9643786-9-8*) Media Pubng.

Marcelle, R., et al, eds. Biological Control of Photosynthesis. (Advances in Agricultural Biotechnology Ser.). 1986. text 145.50 (*90-247-3287-5*) Kluwer Academic.

— Photosynthesis & Plant Development. 1979. text 206.50 (*90-6193-595-4*) Kluwer Academic.

Marcelli, et al. Dejiny Filozofie. (SLO.). 140p. 1996. write for info. (*80-08-00306-5*, Pub. by Slov Pegagog Naklad) IBD Ltd.

Marcelli, A., jt. ed. see Bianconi, A.

***Marcelli, Enrico.** Alienation. 200p. 1999. 60.00 (*0-8133-9030-3*) Westview.

Marcelli, Marcelo P. Ecologia Liquenica Nos Manguezais Do Sul-Sudeste Brasileiro. Wirth, Volkmar et al, eds. (Bibliotheca Lichenologica: Vol. 47). (GER., Illus.). viii, 310p. 1992. pap. 89.00 (*3-443-58026-2*, Pub. by Gebruder Borntraeger) Balogh.

Marcelli, Romolo, ed. Nonlinear Microwave Signal Processing - Towards a New Range of Devices: Proceedings of the NATO Advanced Research Workshop, Rome, Italy, 3-6 October, 1996. LC 96-52195. (NATO ASI Series: Partnership Sub-Series 3). 528p. (C). 1996. text 291.00 (*0-7923-4358-1*) Kluwer Academic.

Marcellini, P., jt. auth. see Dacorogna, Bernard.

Marcellini, Paolo, et al, eds. Partial Differential Equations & Applications: Collected Papers in Honor of Carlo Pucci. LC 95-50251. (Lecture Notes in Pure & Applied Mathematics Ser.: Vol. 177). (Illus.). 392p. 1996. pap. text 175.00 (*0-8247-9698-5*) Dekker.

Marcellini, Paolo, jt. auth. see Dacorogna, Bernard.

Marcellino, Dennis. Sweeping It under the Drug: A Complete Book about Recreational Drugs & How to Create a Great Life Without Them. LC 88-2083. 192p. 1988. pap. 9.95 (*0-945272-04-9*) Lighthouse.

— Why Are We Here? The Scientific Answer to This Age-Old Question. LC 96-9440. 304p. 1997. pap. 14.50 (*0-945272-10-3*) Lighthouse.

Marcellino, Fred. I, Crocodile. LC 99-66181. (Illus.). 32p. (J). (ps-3). 1999. 15.95 (*0-06-205168-7*) HarpC.

— I, Crocodile. LC 99-66181. (Illus.). 32p. (J). (ps-3). 1999. lib. bdg. 15.89 (*0-06-205199-7*) HarpC.

Marcellino, Jerry. Rediscovering the Lost Treasure of Family Worship. 16p. 1996. pap. 2.99 (*0-9652883-0-7*) Audubon Pr.

Marcellinus, Ammianus. The Later Roman Empire. Hamilton, Walter, tr. 512p. 1986. pap. 15.95 (*0-14-044406-8*, Penguin Classics) Viking Penguin.

— Rerum Gestarum Libri Qui Supersunt, Vols. I & II. (GER.). 1963. write for info. (*0-318-70575-3*); write for info. (*3-296-10401-1*); write for info. (*0-318-70576-1*) G Olms Pubs.

Marcello, Patricia Cronin. Jerry Garcia Mini Edition. 1999. 4.95 (*0-8362-7888-7*) Andrews & McMeel.

— Matt Damon. LC 98-85158. (Little Bks.). (Illus.). 80p. (J). (gr. 4-7). 1998. 4.95 (*0-8362-6992-6*) Andrews & McMeel.

— Pope John Paul II. LC 98-85420. (Little Bks.). (Illus.). 80p. 1998. 4.95 (*0-8362-7160-2*) Andrews & McMeel.

Marcello, B. Six Sonatas for Cello or Double Bass & Piano: Score Parts for Both Instruments. 40p. 1986. pap. 10.95 (*0-7935-5180-3*, 50262690) H Leonard.

Marcello, Beth & Bohn, Earl. Passport to Pittsburgh. Hughes, Mary & Turner, James E., eds. LC 93-31594. 320p. 1993. text 45.00 (*0-9630029-6-1*) Community Comm.

Marcello, J J Armas. Asi En la Habana Como En el Cielo. 5th ed. 482p. (Orig.). 1998. pap. text 24.95 (*84-204-8364-8*) Santillana.

Marcello, Leo L. Blackrobe's Love Letters. (Occasional Publications: No. 4). 39p. (Orig.). 1994. pap. 5.95 (*1-883275-02-4*) Xavier Rev.

— Nothing Grows in One Place Forever: Poems of a Sicilian-American. LC 98-11360. 119p. 1998. 22.00 (*1-56809-036-6*); pap. 14.50 (*1-56809-037-4*) Time Being Bks.

— The Secret Proximity of Everywhere. 32p. (C). 1994. pap. 8.00 (*1-884725-01-5*) Blue Heron LA.

— Silent Film. LC 97-34393. 60p. 1997. pap. 14.95 (*0-7734-2844-5*, Mellen Poetry Pr) E Mellen.

Marcello, Leo L., ed. see Scantelbury, Joy, et al.

Marcello, Ronald E., ed. Building the Death Railway: The Ordeal of American POWs in Burma, 1942-1945. LC 92-97641. (Illus.). 300p. 1993. 24.95 (*0-8420-2428-X*) Scholarly Res Inc.

Marcello, Ronald E., jt. ed. see La Forte, Robert S.

Marcellus, Daniel H. Programming Expert Systems in Turbo Prolog. (Illus.). 256p. (C). 1989. text 34.00 (*0-13-295841-4*) P-H.

— Systems Programming for Small Computers. (C). 1984. pap. 23.95 (*0-13-881656-5*) P-H.

Marcellus, Nonius. De Compendiosa Doctrina Libri XX, 3 vols., Set. Lindsay, Wallace M., ed. xlii, 997p. 1971. reprint ed. write for info. incl. 3.5 hd (*0-318-71187-7*) G Olms Pubs.

— Dictionary of Republican Latin. Lindsay, Wallace M., ed. 120p. reprint ed. lib. bdg. 25.87 (*0-685-13739-2*) G Olms Pubs.

— Dictionary of Republican Latin. Lindsay, Wallace M., ed. 120p. 1965. reprint ed. write for info. (*0-318-72058-2*) G Olms Pubs.

Marcellus, Tom. PC World Q & A Bible, Version 4. LC 90-84495. 888p. 1991. pap. 39.95 (*1-878058-03-7*) IDG Bks.

Marcelo, J. J. Ships Afire. Arvio, Sarah, tr. 336p. (Orig.). 1988. pap. 7.95 (*0-380-89741-5*, Avon Bks) Morrow Avon.

Marcenac, L. N. Encyclopedia of Horses: Encyclopedie du Cheval. 4th ed. (FRE.). 2224p. 1981. 150.00 (*0-8288-2342-1*, M6397) Fr & Eur.

Marcet, Jane. Conversations in Natural Philosophy, 1826. (Illus.). 220p. (C). 1998. reprint ed. pap. 35.00 (*0-87556-862-9*) Saifer.

Marcet, Jorge. Colorectal Cancer: A Guide for Patients. Carey, Larry C., ed. (Surgery Ser.). (Illus.). 32p. (Orig.). 1996. pap. 2.95 (*1-885274-25-4*) Health InfoNet Inc.

Marcet, Jorge E. Colorectal Cancer Screening: Early Detection. abr. ed. Carey, Larry, ed. (Surgery Ser.). (Illus.). 16p. 1996. pap. 1.95 (*1-885274-62-9*) Health InfoNet Inc.

— Hemorrhoids: A Guide for Patients. Carey, Larry C., ed. (Surgery Ser.). (Illus.). 24p. (Orig.). 1996. pap. 2.95 (*1-885274-26-2*) Health InfoNet Inc.

Marcey, Marcella, jt. auth. see Davis, Nancy.

March. Aprenda Astrologia. 1997. pap. text 14.95 (*84-270-1344-2*) E Martinez Roca.

March, ed. see Sophocles.

March, A. C. A Glossary of Buddhist Terms. 3rd ed. (Bibliotheca Indo-Buddhica Ser.: No. 25). 99p. (C). 1986. reprint ed. text 6.00 (*81-7030-025-8*) S Asia.

March, Alden. History & Conquest of the Philippines & Our Other Island Possessions. LC 04-111744. (American Imperialism: Viewpoints of United States Foreign Policy, 1898-1941 Ser.). 1970. reprint ed. 25.95 (*0-405-02038-4*) Ayer.

March, Andrew L. & March, Kathryn G. The Mushroom Basket: A Gourmet Introduction to the Best Common Mushrooms of the Southern Rocky Mountains, with Applications Throughout the Northern Hemisphere, & Tidbits of Mushroom Lore from Europe Russia & China. LC 82-90153. (Illus.). 162p. (Orig.). 1982. pap. 11.95 (*0-940206-02-1*) Meridian Hill.

March, Andrew L., jt. auth. see March, Kathryn G.

March, Arthur F., Jr. Franconia & Sugar Hill. (Images of America Ser.). 1999. pap. 16.99 (*0-7524-0845-3*) Arcadia Publng.

— Littleton. (Images of America Ser.). 1995. pap. 16.99 (*0-7524-0222-6*) Arcadia Publng.

March, Ausias. Ausias March: Selected Poems. Terry, Arthur, ed. LC 76-29514. (Edinburgh Bilingual Library). 1977. 20.00 (*0-292-70323-6*) Lib Soc Sci.

March, Caeia. Between the Worlds. 224p. pap. 13.95 (*0-7043-4471-8*, Pub. by Womens Press) Trafalgar.

— Knowing Me. 1998. pap. 17.95 (*0-7043-4539-0*, Pub. by Womens Press) Trafalgar.

March, Caeia. Reflections. LC 96-143375. 250p. 1997. pap. 13.95 (*0-7043-4419-X*, Pub. by Womens Press) Trafalgar.

***March, Caeia.** Spinsters' Rock. 186p. 2000. pap. 13.95 (*0-7043-4541-2*, Pub. by Womens Press) Trafalgar.

March, Candida, jt. auth. see Piza Lopez, Eugenia.

March, Candida, jt. ed. see Wallace, Tina.

March, Chris, jt. auth. see Curwell, Steve.

March, Connie. The Complete Care Manual for Long-Term Care. rev. ed. LC 96-40182. (Illus.). 120p. 1997. spiral bd. 40.95 (*1-55648-184-5*, 130106) AHPI.

March, Connie. Complete Care Plan Manual for Long Term Care. rev. ed. 120p. 1997. spiral bd. 40.95 (*0-7879-5525-6*) Jossey-Bass.

March, Daniel J., ed. British Warplanes of World War II. (Illus.). 256p. 1998. 34.95 (*1-880588-28-5*) AIRtime Pub.

March, Daniel J. & Heathcott, John, eds. Encyclopedia of Air Warfare Vol. 1: 1911-1945. (Illus.). 256p. 1997. 34.95 (*1-880588-25-0*) AIRtime Pub.

March, David. D'Albert S'Expose: Aubrey Beardsley's Drawings for Mademoiselle de Maupin. LC 85-90379. (Illus.). 48p. 1985. pap. 20.00 (*0-9615493-0-0*) D March.

— Priapusa, Manicure & Fardeuse: or the Reine des Ribauds in the Land of the Queen of Love. (Illus.). 32p. (Orig.). 1988. pap. 100.00 (*0-9615493-1-9*) D March.

March, Deborah & Canull, Nancy. Math in a Snap: Super Simple Beginning Math Experiences for Home & School. Britt, Leslie & Hamstra, Diane, eds. (Illus.). 64p. (Orig.). (J). (ps). 1996. pap. text 8.95 (*0-86530-329-0*, IP 329-0) Incentive Pubns.

March, E. A. The Final Enemy. LC 96-68728. 120p. (Orig.). 1996. pap. 11.95 (*0-9652305-5-4*) Pearl Publng.

March, Francis, et al. March's Thesaurus & Dictionary of the English Language. 1324p. 1980. pap. 10.95 (*0-89659-161-1*) Abbeville Pr.

March, Francis A. Athenagoras. (Notable American Authors Ser.). 1999. reprint ed. lib. bdg. 125.00 (*0-7812-3946-X*) Rprt Serv.

— A Comparative Grammar of the Anglo-Saxon Language. 1977. 59.95 (*0-8490-1651-7*) Gordon Pr.

— A Comparative Grammar of the Anglo-Saxon Language. (Notable American Authors Ser.). 1999. reprint ed. lib. bdg. 125.00 (*0-7812-3941-9*) Rprt Serv.

— Eusebius. (Notable American Authors Ser.). 1999. reprint ed. lib. bdg. 125.00 (*0-7812-3944-3*) Rprt Serv.

— Introduction to Anglo-Saxon: An Anglo-Saxon Reader. (Notable American Authors Ser.). 1999. reprint ed. lib. bdg. 125.00 (*0-7812-3942-7*) Rprt Serv.

M

An Asterisk (*) at the beginning of an entry indicates that the title is appearing for the first time.

— Latin Hymns. (Notable American Authors Ser.). 1999. reprint ed. lib. bdg. 125.00 (*0-7812-3943-5*) Rprt Serv.

— Method of Philological Study of the English Language. (Notable American Authors Ser.). 1999. reprint ed. lib. bdg. 125.00 (*0-7812-3940-0*) Rprt Serv.

— The Select Work of Tertullian. (Notable American Authors Ser.). 1999. reprint ed. lib. bdg. 125.00 (*0-7812-3945-1*) Rprt Serv.

— The Spelling Reform. (Notable American Authors Ser.). 1999. reprint ed. lib. bdg. 125.00 (*0-7812-3947-8*) Rprt Serv.

— Thesaurus Dictionary of the English Language. (Illus.). 1994. reprint ed. lib. bdg. 48.00 (*0-7808-0011-7*) Omnigraphics Inc.

March, Frederic. NEPA Effectiveness: Mastering the Process. LC 98-27527. 244p. 1998. pap. text 79.00 (*0-86587-608-8*, 608) Gov Insts.

March, G. Patrick. Eastern Destiny: Russia in Asia & the North Pacific. LC 96-2199. 296p. 1996. 79.50 (*0-275-95566-4*, Praeger Pubs); pap. 30.95 (*0-275-95648-2*, Praeger Pubs); pap. write for info. (*0-275-95647-4*, Praeger Pubs) Greenwood.

March, George P. Cossacks of the Brotherhood: The Zaporog Kosh of the Dniepr River. LC 89-27980. (American University Studies: History: Ser. IX, Vol. 86). (Illus.). XIV, 264p. 1990. text 51.00 (*0-8204-1191-4*) P Lang Pubng.

M

***March, Ivan.** Guide to Compact Discs Yearbook 2000-2001. 2000. pap. 20.00 (*0-14-051382-5*) Penguin Putnam.

— Penguin Guide to Bargain CDs, 1998-1999. 2nd ed. 1408p. 1999. pap. 22.95 (*0-14-051409-0*) Viking Penguin.

***March, Ivan, et al.** The Penguin Guide to Compact Discs: The Guide to Excellence in Recorded Classical Music. 1600p. 1999. pap. 24.95 (*0-14-051379-5*, Penguin Bks) Viking Penguin.

March, J. Problems in Advanced Organic Chemistry. LC 70-176119. 431p. reprint ed. pap. 133.70 (*0-8357-9093-2*, 205504900008) Bks Demand.

March, J., et al. Open Plan Office Acoustical Privacy. (Illus.). 1984. pap. text 39.95 (*0-931673-00-3*) J March Pub Grp.

March, James G. Autonomy As a Factor in Group Organization. Zuckerman, Harriet & Merton, Robert K., eds. LC 79-9012. (Dissertations on Sociology Ser.). 1980. lib. bdg. 34.95 (*0-405-12980-7*) Ayer.

***March, James G.** Dynamics of Rules: Change in Written Organizational Codes. 2000. 49.50 (*0-8047-3744-4*); pap. text 24.95 (*0-8047-3996-X*) Stanford U Pr.

March, James G. A Primer on Decision Making: How Decisions Happen. LC 94-4414. 1994. 35.00 (*0-02-920035-0*) Free Pr.

— The Pursuit of Organizational Intelligence: Decisions & Learning in Organizations. LC 98-36982. 400p. 1999. 69.95 (*0-631-21101-2*); pap. 34.95 (*0-631-21102-0*) Blackwell Pubs.

March, James G. & Olsen, Johan P. Democratic Governance. 256p. 1995. 30.00 (*0-02-874054-8*) Free Pr.

March, James G. & Weissinger-Baylon, Roger. Ambiguity & Command: Organizational Perspectives on Military Decision Making. LC 85-16875. 320p. 1986. pap. text 19.95 (*0-582-98833-0*, HarpBusn) HarpInfo.

March, James G., jt. auth. see Cohen, Michael D.

March, James G., jt. auth. see Lave, Charles A.

March, Jared A. Golf Directory & Travel Guide. (Illus.). 144p. (Orig.). 1996. pap. 7.00 (*0-931673-06-2*) J March Pub Grp.

— Our Old House-Our New Home: A Practical Real Estate Purchasing Guide for Active Adults Planning for Retirement. LC 98-92058. 275p. 1998. pap. 12.95 (*0-931673-11-9*) J March Pub Grp.

March, Jared A., ed. see Ames, Andrew.

***March, Jenny.** Cassell Dictionary of Classical Mythology. LC 99-179459. 416p. 1999. pap. 37.50 (*0-304-34626-8*) Continuum.

March, Jeremy G. Transportation Law in California: A Comprehensive Guide to Federal & State Statutes, Regulations & Guidelines. 2000. pap. 50.00 (*0-923956-55-7*) Solano Pr.

March, Jerry. Advanced Organic Chemistry: Reactions, Mechanisms, & Structure. 4th ed. 1512p. 1992. pap. text 62.50 (*0-471-58148-8*) Wiley.

— Advanced Organic Chemistry: Reactions, Mechanisms, & Structures. 4th ed. LC 92-728. 1512p. 1992. 79.95 (*0-471-60180-2*) Wiley.

March, Jessica. Illusions. 1988. mass mkt. 5.95 (*0-446-35943-2*) Warner Bks.

— Obsessions. 1990. mass mkt. 5.95 (*0-446-35227-6*) Warner Bks.

— Temptations. 1989. mass mkt. 4.95 (*0-446-35226-8*) Warner Bks.

— Visions. 1999. pap. 5.99 (*0-451-40485-8*, Onyx) NAL.

March, John S. Anxiety Disorders in Children & Adolescents. 448p. 1995. lib. bdg. 47.00 (*0-89862-834-2*) Guilford Pubns.

***March, John S. & Mulle, Karen.** OCD in Children & Adolescents: A Cognitive-Behavioral Treatment Manual. LC 98-2637. 298p. 1998. lib. bdg. 35.00 (*1-57230-242-9*) Guilford Pubns.

March, Joseph M. The Wild Party. (Illus.). 112p. 1999. pap. 13.00 (*0-375-70643-7*) Knopf.

— The Wild Party; The Lost Classic. LC 94-11682. (Illus.). 120p. 1994. 22.00 (*0-679-42450-4*) Pantheon.

March, Judith K., jt. auth. see Peters, Karen H.

March, Karen. The Stranger Who Bore Me: Adoptee-Birth Mother Interactions. 192p. 1995. pap. text 17.95 (*0-8020-7235-6*) U of Toronto Pr.

— The Stranger Who Bore Me: Adoptee-Birth Mother Interactions. 160p. 1995. text 45.00 (*0-8020-0447-4*) U of Toronto Pr.

March, Kathleen N. Festa da Palabra: An Anthology of Contemporary Galician Women Poets. (American University Studies: Romance Languages & Literature: Ser. II, Vol. 51). 254p. (C). 1989. text 41.50 (*0-8204-1022-5*) P Lang Pubng.

March, Kathleen N., ed. An Anthology of Galician Short Stories: Asi Vai o Conto. LC 91-25884. (Hispanic Literature Ser.: Vol. 13). 248p. 1991. lib. bdg. 89.95 (*0-7734-9749-8*) E Mellen.

— First Galician Studies Conference, 1985. 375p. (Orig.). 1987. pap. 20.00 (*0-89101-067-X*) U Maine Pr.

March, Kathleen N., tr. from SPA. Daughter of the Sea. XIII, 168p. (C). 1995. pap. text 33.95 (*0-8204-2427-7*) P Lang Pubng.

March, Kathleen N., tr. see Belli, Gioconda.

March, Kathryn G. & March, Andrew L. The Wild Plant Companion: A Fresh Understanding of Herbal Food & Medicine. (Illus.). 200p. (Orig.). 1986. pap. 11.95 (*0-940206-03-X*) Meridian Hill.

— The Wild Taste: Plant & Mushroom Recipes for the Knowledgeable Cook. LC 88-90947. (Illus.). 320p. (Orig.). 1989. pap. 19.95 (*0-940206-04-8*) Meridian Hill.

March, Kathryn G., jt. auth. see March, Andrew L.

March, Keith L., ed. Gene Transfer in the Cardiovascular System: Experimental Approaches & Therapeutic Implications. LC 96-29740. (Developments in Cardiovascular Medicine Ser.). 536p. (C). 1997. text 185.00 (*0-7923-9859-9*) Kluwer Academic.

March, Lionel. Architectonics of Humanism. (Illus.). 160p. 1997. pap. 38.00 (*1-85490-500-7*) Academy Ed UK.

***March, Lionel.** Architectonics of Humanism. LC 99-184699. 296p. 1998. pap. 54.95 (*0-471-97754-3*) Wiley.

March, Lionel. Frank Lloyd Wright: The Phoenix Papers, 2 vols., Set. Zygas, K. Paul & Johnson, Linda N., eds. LC 97-128655. (Illus.). 321p. 1995. 75.00 (*1-884320-08-2*) ASU Herberger Ctr.

March, Lionel & Sheine, Judith, eds. R. M. Schindler: Composition & Construction. (Illus.). 264p. 1995. pap. 38.00 (*1-85490-423-X*, Pub. by Wiley) Wiley.

March, Louise. Gold Dust. 1980. 20.00 (*0-686-33124-9*) Rochester Folk Art.

March, Marion D. The Only Way to Learn Astrology: Basic Principles. 2nd ed. (Only Way Ser.: Vol. 1). 320p. 1997. pap. 14.95 (*0-935127-61-5*) ACS Pubns.

— The Only Way to Learn Astrology: Math & Interpretation Techniques. 2nd ed. (Only Way Ser.: Vol. 2). 288p. 1999. pap. 14.95 (*0-935127-68-2*) ACS Pubns.

March, Marion D. & McEvers, Joan. The Only Way to Learn about Horary & Electrical Astrology. (Only Way Ser.: Vol. VI). 256p. (Orig.). 1995. pap. 14.95 (*0-935127-29-1*) ACS Pubns.

— The Only Way to Learn about Relationships: Synastry Techniques. (Only Way Ser.: Vol. V). 256p. (Orig.). 1994. pap. 14.95 (*0-935127-21-6*) ACS Pubns.

— The Only Way to Learn about Tomorrow: Current Patterns, Progressions, Directions, Solar & Lunar Returns, Transits. (Only Way Ser.: Vol. IV). 240p. (Orig.). 1992. pap. 14.95 (*0-917086-65-1*) ACS Pubns.

— The Only Way to Learn Astrology: Basic Principles. (Only Way Ser.: Vol. I). (Illus.). 320p. 1996. pap. 14.95 (*0-917086-00-7*) ACS Pubns.

— The Only Way to Learn Astrology: Horoscope Analysis. (Only Way Ser.: Vol. 3). 272p. 1980. pap. 14.95 (*0-917086-43-0*) ACS Pubns.

— The Only Way to Learn Astrology: Math & Interpretation Techniques, 2nd rev. ed. (Only Way Ser.: Vol. 2). (Illus.). 264p. 1982. reprint ed. pap. 14.95 (*0-917086-26-0*) ACS Pubns.

March, Mary V. & Rindhart, Carroll A. Zingers & Swingers. (Illus.). 88p. (YA). 1994. pap. text 10.95 (*0-910957-58-4*, BMR05109) Wrner Bros.

March, Meredith. The Rocky Ridge Man. 1999. per. 3.75 (*0-373-25843-7*, No. 1-25843-3) Harlequin Bks.

March, Michael. Guide to Australia. (World Guides Ser.). (Illus.). 32p. (J). (gr. 2-6). 1998. lib. bdg. 21.27 (*1-884756-38-7*) Davidson Titles.

— Guide to China. (World Guides Ser.). (Illus.). 32p. (J). (gr. 2-6). 1998. lib. bdg. 21.27 (*1-884756-41-7*) Davidson Titles.

— Guide to Egypt. (World Guides Ser.). (Illus.). 32p. (J). (gr. 2-6). 1999. lib. bdg. 21.27 (*1-884756-42-5*) Davidson Titles.

— Guide to France. (World Guides Ser.). (Illus.). 32p. (J). (gr. 2-6). 1998. lib. bdg. 21.27 (*1-884756-43-3*) Davidson Titles.

***March, Michael.** Guide to Germany. rev. ed. (World Guides Ser.). (Illus.). 32p. (gr. 2-6). 1999. lib. bdg. 21.27 (*1-884756-44-1*) Davidson Titles.

— Guide to Greece. (World Guides Ser.). 32p. (J). (gr. 2-6). 2000. lib. bdg. 21.27 (*1-884756-69-7*) Davidson Titles.

March, Michael. Guide to Japan. (World Guides Ser.). (Illus.). 32p. (J). (gr. 2-6). 1998. lib. bdg. 21.27 (*1-884756-49-2*) Davidson Titles.

***March, Michael.** Guide to Russia. rev. ed. (World Guides Ser.). (Illus.). 32p. (gr. 2-6). 1999. lib. bdg. 21.27 (*1-884756-53-0*) Davidson Titles.

March, Michael. Guide to South Africa. (World Guides Ser.). (Illus.). 32p. (J). (gr. 2-6). 1999. lib. bdg. 21.27 (*1-884756-54-9*) Davidson Titles.

— Guide to South Korea. (World Guides Ser.). (Illus.). 32p. (J). (gr. 2-6). 1999. lib. bdg. 21.27 (*1-884756-55-7*) Davidson Titles.

***March, Michael.** Guide to Thailand. (World Guides Ser.). (Illus.). 32p. (J). (gr. 2-6). 2000. lib. bdg. 21.27 (*1-884756-70-0*) Davidson Titles.

March, Michael, tr. see Herbert, Zbigniew.

***March, N. H., ed.** Electron Correlations in the Solid State. 450p. 1999. 86.00 (*1-86094-200-8*, Pub. by Imperial College) World Scientific Pub.

March, N. H. & Mucci, J. F. Chemical Physics of Free Molecules. (Illus.). 414p. (C). 1992. text 59.50 (*0-306-44270-1*, Kluwer Plenum) Kluwer Academic.

March, N. H., jt. auth. see Lundqvist, S.

March, Norman H. Atomic Dynamics in Liquids. 337p. 1991. pap. 8.95 (*0-486-66598-4*) Dover.

— Chemical Bonds Outside Metal Surfaces. LC 86-5022. (Physics of Solids & Liquids Ser.). (Illus.). 294p. (C). 1986. text 107.00 (*0-306-42059-7*, Kluwer Plenum) Kluwer Academic.

— Chemical Physics of Liquids. xii, 326p. 1990. text 306.00 (*2-88124-722-9*) Gordon & Breach.

— Electron Correlation in Molecules & Condensed Phases. LC 95-4195. (Physics of Solids & Liquids Ser.). (Illus.). 440p. (C). 1996. text 125.00 (*0-306-44844-0*, Kluwer Plenum) Kluwer Academic.

— Liquid Metals: Concepts & Theory. (Cambridge Monographs on Mathematical Physics). 454p. (C). 1990. text 140.00 (*0-521-30279-X*) Cambridge U Pr.

March, Norman H., et al, eds. Amorphous Solids & the Liquid State. LC 85-12031. (Physics of Solids & Liquids Ser.). (Illus.). 560p. (C). 1985. text 174.00 (*0-306-41947-5*, Kluwer Plenum) Kluwer Academic.

March, Norman H. & Srivastava, S. K. Condensed Matter-Disordered Solids. 450p. 1995. text 106.00 (*981-02-1924-5*) World Scientific Pub.

March, Norman H. & Tosi, Mario P. Coulomb Liquids: Monograph. 1984. text 151.00 (*0-12-470520-0*) Acad Pr.

March, Norman H. & Tosi, Mario P., eds. Polymers, Liquid Crystals & Low-Dimensional Solids. (Physics of Solids & Liquids Ser.). (Illus.). 648p. (C). 1984. text 174.00 (*0-306-41641-7*, Kluwer Plenum) Kluwer Academic.

March, Norman H., et al. The Many-Body Problem in Quantum Mechanics. unabridged ed. 471p. 1995. reprint ed. pap. text 14.95 (*0-486-68754-6*) Dover.

March, Norman H., jt. auth. see Alonso, Julio A.

March, Norman H., jt. auth. see Jones, William.

March of Dimes Birth Defects Foundation Staff. March of Dimes Statbook: Statistics for Monitorins Maternal & Infant Health. LC 97-20539. 1997. write for info. (*0-86525-078-2*) March of Dimes.

March of Dimes Birth Defects Foundation Staff, jt. auth. see Petrini, Joann.

March, P. Confederate Air Force. pap. 10.95 (*1-85532-772-4*, 861844Q, Pub. by Ospry) Stackpole.

March, Peter. Freedom of the Skies: An Illustrated History of Fifty Years of Nato Air Power. 256p. 1999. 40.00 (*0-304-35238-1*) Continuum.

***March, Peter R.** ABC Civil Airliner Recognition. 6th ed. (Illus.). 128p. 2000. pap. 12.95 (*0-7110-2659-9*, 130354AE, Pub. by Ian Allan) Motorbooks Intl.

March, Peter R. Combat Aircraft Recognition. 3rd rev. ed. (ABC Ser.). (Illus.). 144p. 1998. pap. 14.95 (*1-882663-26-8*) Plymouth VT.

— Confederate Air Force: Celebrating 40 Years. (Illus.). 112p. 1997. write for info. (*0-929726-02-2*); pap. write for info. (*0-929726-01-4*) Confederate Air.

— Desert Warpaint. (Osprey Colour Library). (Illus.). 128p. 1992. pap. 15.95 (*1-85532-193-9*, Pub. by Ospry) Motorbooks Intl.

— Light Aircraft Recognition. 3rd ed. (Illus.). 116p. 1997. pap. 11.95 (*1-882663-15-2*) Plymouth VT.

***March, Peter R.** Sabre to Stealth: 50 Years of the United States Air Force 1947-1997. (Illus.). 192p. 1999. 29.95 (*1-899808-95-7*, Pub. by Royal Air Force) Trafalgar.

March, Peyton C. Nation at War. LC 72-109779. 407p. 1970. reprint ed. lib. bdg. 45.00 (*0-8371-4269-5*, MANW, Greenwood Pr) Greenwood.

March, R. G. Synchronous Reluctance Motors. (Technical Papers: Vol. P109.23D). (Illus.). 8p. 1970. pap. text 30.00 (*1-55589-428-3*) AGMA.

March, R. J. Looking for Trouble: And Other Stories. LC 98-52511. 1999. pap. 12.95 (*1-55583-455-8*, Pub. by Alyson Pubns) Consort Bk Sales.

March, Randolph B. Thirty Years of Army Life on the Border. Comprising Descriptions of the Indian Nomads of the Plains, Explorations... (American Biography Ser.). 442p. 1991. reprint ed. lib. bdg. 89.00 (*0-7812-8265-9*) Rprt Serv.

March, Ray A. A Paradise Called Pebble Beach. Peters, Sally, ed. 1992. 40.00 (*0-671-77722-X*) PB.

March, Raymond E. & Todd, John F., eds. Practical Applications of Ion Trap Mass Spectrometry. (Modern Mass Spectrometry Ser.). 448p. 1995. boxed set 159.95 (*0-8493-4452-2*, 4452) CRC Pr.

— Practical Applications of Ion Trap Mass Spectrometry. (Modern Mass Spectrometry Ser.). 544p. 1995. boxed set 129.95 (*0-8493-8251-3*, 8251) CRC Pr.

— Practical Aspects of Ion Trap Mass Spectrometry Vol. II: Ion Trap Instrumentation, Vol. 2. LC 95-14146. (Modern Mass Spectrometry Ser.). 352p. 1995. boxed set 159.95 (*0-8493-8253-X*, 8253) CRC Pr.

March, Raymond E., jt. auth. see Hughes, Richard.

March, Richard. Wisconsin Folklife: A Celebration of Wisconsin Traditions. 1998. pap. text 9.95 (*1-882280-02-4*) WI Acad Sci.

March, Richard & Tambimuttu, M. J., compiled by. T. S. Eliot. LC 68-55850. (Essay Index Reprint Ser.). 1977. 21.95 (*0-8369-0676-4*) Ayer.

March, Rita N., jt. auth. see Shires, H. Bess.

March, Robert H. Physics for Poets. 4th ed. LC 95-18959. 282p. (C). 1995. pap. 41.88 (*0-07-040248-5*) McGraw.

March, Robert M. The Japanese Negotiator: Subtlety & Strategy Beyond Western Logic. 197p. 1991. pap. 11.00 (*4-7700-1462-7*) Kodansha.

— Reading the Japanese Mind: The Realities Behind Their Thoughts & Actions. 208p. 1996. 25.00 (*4-7700-2044-9*) Kodansha.

— Working for a Japanese Company: Insights into the Multicultural Workplace. 256p. 1996. reprint ed. pap. 10.00 (*4-7700-2085-6*) Kodansha.

March, Robert T. The Investment Side of Corporate Cash Management. LC 88-3100. 246p. 1988. 59.95 (*0-89930-333-1*, MHI/, Quorum Bks) Greenwood.

March, Roman R., jt. auth. see Mahler, Gregory S.

March, Sam. A Marxist Defense of the L. A. Rebellion. 1992. pap. 2.50 (*0-89567-106-9*) World View Forum.

March, Sam, jt. auth. see Gutierrez, Teresa.

March, Stephen, jt. ed. see Brinkmeyer, Robert.

March, Sydney. Stealing Mangoes. (Premeri Ser.: Vol. 4). (Illus.). 28p. (Orig.). 1997. pap. 5.00 (*0-9654421-9-5*) Mica Press.

March, Tony. CD a la Guitare Electrique. Lefferts, Michael, ed. (FRE.). 48p. (Orig.). (C). 1997. pap. text 26.95 (*0-7692-1314-6*, 01010317) Wrner Bros.

March, W. Eugene. Israel & the Politics of Land: A Theological Case Study. LC 93-40125. 112p. (Orig.). 1994. pap. 16.95 (*0-664-25121-8*) Westminster John Knox.

March, W. Eugene, jt. auth. see Rhodes, Arnold B.

March, Wayne F. Practical Ophthalmic Problems for Allied Health Professionals. (Allied Health Professions Monograph). 148p. 1984. pap. 12.50 (*0-87527-329-7*) Green.

March, William. The Bad Seed. 1956. pap. 5.25 (*0-8222-0088-0*) Dramatists Play.

— The Bad Seed. 1993. reprint ed. lib. bdg. 35.95 (*1-56849-107-7*) Buccaneer Bks.

— Bad Seed. LC 96-41686. 224p. 1997. reprint ed. pap. 9.95 (*0-88001-540-3*) HarpC.

— Company K. LC 89-38395. (Library of Alabama Classics). 288p. 1989. pap. 14.95 (*0-8173-0480-0*) U of Ala Pr.

— Company K. 20.95 (*0-89190-097-7*) Amereon Ltd.

Marchac, Daniel. Surgery of Basal Cell Carcinoma. (Illus.). 130p. 1987. 150.00 (*0-387-18034-6*) Spr-Verlag.

Marchac, Daniel, ed. Craniofacial Surgery. (Illus.). 540p. 1987. 318.00 (*0-387-16924-5*) Spr-Verlag.

Marchac, Daniel, et al, eds. Male Aesthetic Surgery. (Illus.). 418p. 1996. text 99.95 (*0-7506-9277-4*) Buttrwrth-Heinemann.

Marc'hadour, Germain. The Bible in the Works of Thomas More, 2 vols., Set. 1098p. 1969. text 187.50 (*90-6004-107-0*, Pub. by B De Graaf) Coronet Bks.

Marchaim, Uri. Biogas Processes for Sustainable Development. (Agricultural Services Bulletin Ser.: No. 95). 137p. 1992. pap. 27.00 (*92-5-103126-6*, F31266, Pub. by FAO) Bernan Associates.

Marchais, Pierre. Glossaire de Psychiatrie: Glossary of Psychiatry. (FRE.). 238p. 1970. 79.95 (*0-8288-6537-X*, M-6398) Fr & Eur.

Marchaj, C. Abracadabra Flute & Clarinet Duets: Elementary. 32p. (J). 1998. pap. 8.95 (*0-7136-4374-9*, Pub. by A & C Blk) Midpt Trade.

Marchaj, C. A. Seaworthiness: The Forgotten Factor. (Illus.). 384p. 1996. 39.95 (*1-888671-09-2*) Tiller.

Marchaj, Czeslaw A. 100 Small Boat Rigs. 1996. pap. text 19.95 (*0-07-156806-9*) McGraw.

— Sail Performance: Design & Techniques to Maximize Sail Power. (Illus.). 401p. 1996. 54.95 (*0-07-040250-7*) McGraw.

Marchaj, Konrad R., ed. see Loori, John D.

Marchak, M. Patricia. The Integrated Circus: The New Right & the Restructuring of Global Markets. 336p. 1991. 65.00 (*0-7735-0845-7*, Pub. by McG-Queens Univ Pr) CUP Services.

Marchak, M. Patricia. The Integrated Circus: The New Right & the Restructuring of Global Markets. 336p. 1993. pap. 22.95 (*0-7735-1149-0*, Pub. by McG-Queens Univ Pr) CUP Services.

— Logging the Globe. LC 96-154371. (Illus.). 440p. 1995. 65.00 (*0-7735-1345-0*, Pub. by McG-Queens Univ Pr); pap. 22.95 (*0-7735-1346-9*, Pub. by McG-Queens Univ Pr) CUP Services.

— Racism, Sexism & the University: The Political Science Affair at the University of British Columbia. LC 97-187326. 192p. 1996. 60.00 (*0-7735-1514-3*, Pub. by McG-Queens Univ Pr); pap. 22.95 (*0-7735-1515-1*, Pub. by McG-Queens Univ Pr) CUP Services.

***Marchak, M. Patricia & Marchak, William.** God's Assassins: State Terrorism in Argentina in the 1970s. 393p. 1999. 29.95 (*0-7735-2013-9*) McG-Queens Univ Pr.

Marchak, William, jt. auth. see Marchak, M. Patricia.

Marchal, Alain, jt. auth. see Hardcastel, William J.

***Marchal, Benoit.** XML by Example. LC 99-66449. (By Example Ser.). (Illus.). 505p. 1999. pap. 24.99 (*0-7897-2242-9*) Que.

Marchal, C. The Three-Body Problem. (Studies in Astronautics: Vol. 4). xvi, 576p. 1990. 256.25 (*0-444-87440-2*) Elsevier.

Marchal, Gaston-Louis. Arras et l'Art Au XIX Siecle Dictionnaire des Peintres, Sculpteurs, Graveurs, Architectes: 1800-1919. (FRE.). 310p. 1987. pap. 115.00 (*0-7859-8205-1*, 2900643066) Fr & Eur.

Marchal, Jean-Yves. La Petite Region Dambohimanambola (Sous-Prefecture de Betafo) La Colonisation Agraire au Moyan-Quest Malgache. (Atlas des Structures Agraires au Sud de Sahara Ser.: No. 2). (FRE., Illus.). 122p. 1974. pap. text 55.40 (*90-279-7935-9*) Mouton.

Marchalonis, John J. Antigen - Specific T Cell Receptors & Factors, 2 vols., Set. 336p. 1987. 305.00 (*0-8493-6169-9*, QR185) CRC Pr.

— Antigen-Specific T-Cell Receptors. 168p. 1987. 163.00 (*0-8493-6167-2*, CRC Reprint) Franklin.

— Antigen-Specific T-Cell Receptors, Vol. II. 144p. 1987. 86.00 (*0-8493-6168-0*, CRC Reprint) Franklin.

— The Lymphocyte: Structure & Function. 2nd ed. (Immunology Ser.: Vol. 37). (Illus.). 440p. 1987. text 199.00 (*0-8247-7797-2*) Dekker.

An Asterisk (*) at the beginning of an entry indicates that the title is appearing for the first time.

Marchalonis, John J., ed. Contemporary Topics in Immunobiology Vol. 12: Immunobiology of Parasites & Parasitic Infections. LC 79-179761. 518p. 1984. 95.00 (*0-306-41418-X*, Plenum Trade) Perseus Pubng.

Marchalonis, John J., et al, eds. Cancer Biology Reviews, Vol. 1. LC 80-644712. (Illus.). 368p. 1980. reprint ed. pap. 114.10 (*0-7837-0741-X*, 204106300001) Bks Demand.

— Cancer Biology Reviews, Vol. 2. LC 80-644712. (Illus.). 294p. 1981. reprint ed. pap. 91.20 (*0-7837-0742-8*, 204106300002) Bks Demand.

— Cancer Biology Reviews, Vol. 3. LC 80-644712. (Illus.). 223p. 1982. reprint ed. pap. 69.20 (*0-7837-0743-6*, 204106300003) Bks Demand.

Marchalonis, Shirley. College Girls: A Century of Fiction. LC 94-41573. (Illus.). 225p. 1995. text 45.00 (*0-8135-2175-0*); pap. text 18.00 (*0-8135-2176-9*) Rutgers U Pr.

— Critical Essays on Mary Wilkins Freeman. (Critical Essays on American Literature Ser.). 200p. 1991. 48.00 (*0-8161-7306-0*, Hall Reference) Macmillan.

Marchalonis, Shirley, ed. Patrons & Protegees: Gender, Friendship, & Writing in 19th-Century America. LC 87-42735. 250p. 1988. 40.00 (*0-8135-1270-0*) Rutgers U Pr.

— Patrons & Protegees: Gender, Friendship, & Writing in 19th-Century America. 243p. (C). 1991. pap. text 18.00 (*0-8135-1690-0*) Rutgers U Pr.

Marcham, David, et al. Lehigh Valley Memories: A Tour of the Lehigh Valley Railroad in New York's Finger Lakes Region, 1941-1959. Marcham, John, ed. LC 98-26025. (Illus.). 88p. 1998. pap. 19.95 (*0-942690-40-0*) DeWitt Hist.

Marcham, Frederick G., jt. ed. see Stephenson, Carl.

***Marcham, Frederick George & Marcham, John.** The Photographs of Frederick C. Marcham. LC 00-31497. (Illus.). 112p. 2000. pap. 21.95 (*0-942690-44-3*) DeWitt Hist.

Marcham, John, ed. Sol Goldberg's Ithaca: The Journal Years. LC 96-71112. (Illus.). 96p. (Orig.). 1996. pap. 17.95 (*0-942690-38-9*) DeWitt Hist.

Marcham, John, jt. auth. see Marcham, Frederick George.

Marcham, John, ed. see Babcock, John B.

Marcham, John, ed. see Edmondson, Brad.

Marcham, John, ed. see Marcham, David, et al.

Marcham, William, jt. ed. see Lovell, Percy.

***Marchand.** Competing with Information. 352p. 2000. 32.95 (*0-471-89969-0*) Wiley.

Marchand, A. P., jt. ed. see Juaristi, Eusebio.

Marchand, Alain B. Entre l'Oeil & l'Espace, le Geste & le Cri. LC 85-868511. (L'Astrolabe Ser.: Vol. 5). (FRE.). 104p. 1982. reprint ed. pap. 32.30 (*0-608-01993-3*, 206264900003) Bks Demand.

Marchand, Alan P., ed. see Dodziuk, Helena.

Marchand, Barb & Armstrong, Jeannette C. Neekna & Chemai. (Illus.). 44p. (J). (gr. 1-4). 1991. pap. 8.95 (*0-919441-15-7*, Pub. by Theytus Bks) Orca Bk Pubs.

Marchand, Blaine. Bodily Presence. LC 95-181012. 112p. Date not set. pap. 11.95 (*1-55082-141-5*, Pub. by Quarry Pr) LPC InBook.

Marchand, Bob. Bowhunter's Tip Book, Vol. 1. 2nd large type ed. (Illus.). 128p. 1997. reprint ed. pap. text 9.95 (*0-9680571-2-8*, Pub. by BS Pubns) Partners Pubs Grp.

— Hunters Tip Book, Vol. 1. 2nd large type ed. (Illus.). 128p. 1996. pap. text 9.95 (*0-9680571-0-1*, Pub. by BS Pubns) Partners Pubs Grp.

— Inept Bowhunter, Vol. 1. LC 96-910720. (Illus.). 1997. pap. text 9.95 (*0-9680571-1-X*, Pub. by BS Pubns) Partners Pubs Grp.

Marchand, C. Roland. The American Peace Movement & Social Reform, 1898-1918. LC 70-166382. 461p. 1972. reprint ed. pap. 143.00 (*0-7837-9379-0*, 206012300004) Bks Demand.

Marchand, Clement. Vanishing Villages. (Prose Ser.: No. 19). 234p. 1993. pap. 13.00 (*0-920717-73-X*) Guernica Editions.

***Marchand, Donald A., et al.** Information Orientation: The Link to Business Performance. (Illus.). 250p. 2000. 45.00 (*0-19-924067-1*) OUP.

Marchand, Donald A., jt. auth. see Davenport, Tom.

Marchand, Eckart & Wright, Alison. With & Without Medici: Studies in Tuscan Art & Patronage, 1434-1530. LC 98-29315. (Illus.). 187p. (C). 1998. text 84.95 (*1-85928-423-X*, N6913.W58, Pub. by Scolar Pr) Ashgate Pub Co.

Marchand-Ennery, Rabbin. Dictionnaire de la Bible Hebraique. 3rd ed. (FRE & HEB.). 304p. 1986. pap. 19.95 (*0-7859-8086-5*, 2853320456) Fr & Eur.

— French-Hebrew Dictionary: Dictionnaire Francais-Hebreu. (FRE & HEB.). 302p. 1981. 13.95 (*0-8288-0460-5*, F19230) Fr & Eur.

Marchand, J., jt. ed. see Setzer, M. J.

Marchand, J. P., ed. see NATO Advanced Study Institute Staff.

Marchand, Jacques & Skalny, Jan, eds. Materials Science of Concrete, Special Volume: Sulfate Attack Mechanisms. (Illus.). 200p. 1999. 85.00 (*1-57498-074-2*, MSCUL) Am Ceramic.

Marchand, James W. The Sounds & Phonemes of Wulfila's Gothic. (Janua Linguarum, Series Practica: No. 25). 1973. pap. text 49.25 (*90-279-2432-5*) Mouton.

Marchand, Kay E. Parenting: The Early Years. LC 95-77707. (Spiritual Discovery Ser.). 96p. 1995. pap., teacher ed. 9.95 (*0-88243-206-0*); pap., student ed. 4.95 (*0-88243-106-4*) Gospel Pub.

Marchand, Leslie A. Byron: A Portrait. LC 79-13248. (Illus.). 1992. pap. 7.95 (*0-226-50436-0*, P829) U Ch Pr.

Marchand, Leslie A., ed. Lord Byron: Selected Letters & Journals. LC 82-9720. 408p. 1984. pap. 10.95 (*0-674-53912-5*) Belknap Pr.

Marchand, Leslie A., ed. see Byron, George Gordon.

Marchand, marianne H. & Parpart, Jane L., eds. Feminism/Postmodernism/Development. LC 94-23866. (International Studies of Women & Places). 272p. (Orig.). (C). (gr. 13). 1995. 75.00 (*0-415-10523-4*, B4140) Routledge.

Marchand, Marianne H. & Parpart, Jane L., eds. Feminism/Postmodernism/Development. LC 94-23866. (International Studies of Women & Places). 272p. (Orig.). (C). 1995. pap. 24.99 (*0-415-10524-2*, B4144) Routledge.

***Marchand, Marianne H. & Runyan, Anne S.** Gender & Global Restructuring: Sightings, Sites & Resistances. LC 99-41531. (Ripe Studies in Global Political Economy). 304p. 2000. pap. 29.99 (*0-415-22175-7*) Routledge.

***Marchand, Marianne H. & Runyan, Anne Sisson, eds.** Gender & Global Restructuring: Sightings Sites & Resistances. LC 99-41531. 304p. (C). 2000. text. write for info. (*0-415-22174-9*) Routledge.

Marchand, Patrick. Graphics & GUIs with Matlab. LC 95-45366. (Illus.). 384p. (C). 1996. otabind 44.95 (*0-8493-9487-2*, 9487) CRC Pr.

— Graphics & GUIs with MATLAB. 2nd ed. LC 99-10803. 464p. 1999. per. 39.95 (*0-8493-9001-X*, 9001) CRC Pr.

Marchand, Peter. What Good Is a Cactus? LC 94-65088. (Illus.). 24p. (Orig.). (J). (gr. 3-6). 1994. pap. 7.95 (*1-879373-83-1*) Roberts Rinehart.

***Marchand, Peter J.** Autumn: A Season of Change. LC 99-54701. (Illus.). 224p. 2000. pap. 17.95 (*0-87451-870-9*); text 50.00 (*0-87451-869-5*) U Pr of New Eng.

Marchand, Peter J. Life in the Cold: An Introduction to Winter Ecology. 3rd ed. LC 96-19460. (Illus.). 320p. 1996. pap. 22.00 (*0-87451-785-0*) U Pr of New Eng.

— North Woods: An Inside Look at the Nature of Forests in the Northeast. (Illus.). 160p. 1987. pap. text 10.95 (*0-910146-64-0*) AMC Books.

Marchand, Philip. Marshall McLuhan: The Medium & the Messenger. (Illus.). 352p. 1989. 19.45 (*0-89919-485-0*, Pub. by Ticknor & Fields) HM.

Marchand, Philip. Marshall McLuhan: The Medium & the Messenger. rev. ed. LC 98-65303. 336p. 1998. pap. text 17.50 (*0-262-63186-5*) MIT Pr.

Marchand, Roland. Advertising the American Dream: Making Way for Modernity, 1920-1940. LC 84-28082. 1985. pap. 24.95 (*0-520-05885-2*, Pub. by U CA Pr) Cal Prin Full Svc.

Marchand, Roland. Creating the Corporate Soul: The Rise of Public Relations & Corporate Imagery in American Big Business. LC 97-50098. (Illus.). 470p. 1998. 39.95 (*0-520-08719-4*, Pub. by U CA Pr) Cal Prin Full Svc.

***Marchand, Roland.** Creating the Corporate Soul: The Rise of Public Relations & Corporate Imagery in American Big Business. (Illus.). 470p. 2001. pap. 29.95 (*0-520-22688-7*) U CA Pr.

Marchand, Sidney A. Attempt to Re-Assemble Old Settlers in Family Groups.Tr. of Acadian Sweet Recipes. 1965. 22.50 (*0-87511-079-7*) Claitors.

— The Flight of a Century (1800-1900) in Ascension Parish. (Illus.). 237p. 1995. reprint ed. lib. bdg. 32.50 (*0-8328-5035-7*) Higginson Bk Co.

— The Story of Ascension Parish. (Illus.). 193p. 1995. reprint ed. lib. bdg. 29.50 (*0-8328-5034-9*) Higginson Bk Co.

Marchand, Suzanne L. Down from Olympus: Archaeology & Philhellenism in Germany, 1750-1970. LC 95-53324. 416p. (C). 1996. text 39.50 (*0-691-04393-0*, Pub. by Princeton U Pr) Cal Prin Full Svc.

Marchant, jt. auth. see Cook.

Marchant, Elizabeth A. Critical Acts: Latin American Women & Cultural Criticism. LC 98-47241. 1999. 49.95 (*0-8130-1683-5*) U Press Fla.

Marchant, Alexander N. De Armond, see De Armond Marchant, Alexander N.

***Marchant, Anne.** Introduction to Computing: Exam "Prepare-Ware" (C). 1998. pap. 28.95 (*0-7872-4996-3*) Kendall-Hunt.

Marchant, Brian & Marchant, Heather. A Boy Named Chong. 40p. (J). (gr. k-9). 1993. pap. 11.95 (*1-885298-00-5*) Project Chong.

— Only a Toad: A Bilingual Hmong Folktale. (Illus.). 30p. (Orig.). (J). (ps-7). 1993. pap. 10.50 (*1-885298-02-1*) Project Chong.

— The World Without "F" Chong Learns the Alphabet. (Illus.). 24p. (J). (gr. k-5). 1997. pap. 10.50 (*1-885298-04-8*) Project Chong.

Marchant, C. M. Le, see Johns, Richard A. & Le Marchant, C. M.

Marchant, David. Understanding Shmittah. 1987. 12.95 (*0-87306-425-9*) Feldheim.

Marchant, Douglas J. Breast Disease. Schmitt, William, ed. LC 96-51068. (Illus.). 288p. 1997. text 52.00 (*0-7216-6429-6*, W B Saunders Co) Harcrt Hlth Sci Grp.

Marchant, Dovid, jt. auth. see Israel Meir Staff.

Marchant, E. C. Thucydides, Bk. 1. (Bristol Greek Texts Ser.). (GRE.). 334p. 1982. reprint ed. 27.95 (*0-86292-027-2*, Pub. by Brist Class Pr) Focus Pub-R Pullins.

Marchant, E. C., ed. Opera Omnia, 4 vols. Incl. Vol. 1, Bks. 1-7. Historia Graeca. 2nd ed. 294p. 1922. text 29.95 (*0-19-814552-7*); Vol. 2. Commentarii, Oeconomicus, Convivium, Apologia Socratis. 2nd ed. 292p. 1922. text 29.95 (*0-19-814553-5*); Vol. III. Opera Omnia: Expeditio Cyri. Xenophon. 266p. 1922. text 35.00 (*0-19-814554-3*); Vol. 5. Opuscula. 250p. 1985. text 29.95 (*0-19-814556-X*); (Oxford Classical Texts Ser.). write for info. (*0-318-54866-6*) OUP.

Marchant, E. C. & Wiedmann, T., eds. Thucydides, Bk. 2. (Bristol Greek Texts Ser.). (GRE.). 281p. 1978. pap. 27.95 (*0-906515-20-3*, Pub. by Brist Class Pr) Focus Pub-R Pullins.

***Marchant, Fred.** Full Moon Boat. 72p. 2000. pap. 12.95 (*1-55597-311-6*) Graywolf.

Marchant, Fred. Tipping Point. LC 93-61079. 80p. 1994. per. 10.00 (*0-915380-30-7*) Word Works.

Marchant, Heather, jt. auth. see Marchant, Brian.

Marchant, James. Alfred Russel Wallace: Letters & Reminiscences. LC 74-26273. (History, Philosophy & Sociology of Science Ser.). 1975. reprint ed. 38.95 (*0-405-06601-5*) Ayer.

— Survival (1924) 214p. 1998. reprint ed. pap. 17.95 (*0-7661-0541-5*) Kessinger Pub.

Marchant, James & Jowett, Garth S., eds. The Cinema in Education. LC 77-11381. (Aspects of Film Ser.). (Illus.). 1978. reprint ed. lib. bdg. 13.95 (*0-405-11140-1*) Ayer.

Marchant, James, ed. see Inge, William R.

Marchant, Jessica. Love Beyond Desire. 400p. (Orig.). 1997. mass mkt. 3.99 (*1-85487-925-1*, Pub. by Scarlet Bks) London Brdge.

Marchant, John & Prater, Tony. Shorebirds: An Identification Guide. (Illus.). 416p. 1991. pap. 29.95 (*0-395-60237-8*) HM.

Marchant, Kerena. Id-Ul-Fitr. LC 97-46035. (Festivals Ser.). (Illus.). 32p. (J). 1998. lib. bdg. 20.90 (*0-7613-0963-2*) Millbrook Pr.

Marchant, Mary A. Political Economic Analysis of U. S. Dairy Policies & European Community Dairy Policy Comparisons. LC 92-40968. (Government & the Economy Ser.). 280p. 1993. text 10.00 (*0-8153-1231-8*) Garland.

Marchant, Mary A. & Williamson, Handy, Jr., eds. Achieving Diversity: The Status & Progress of Women & African Americans in the Agricultural Economics Profession. LC 93-39458. (Studies on Industrial Productivity). 248p. 1994. text 15.00 (*0-8153-1537-6*) Garland.

Marchant, Maurice P. Participative Management in Academic Libraries, 16. LC 76-8740. (Contributions in Librarianship & Information Science Ser.: No. 16). 260p. 1977. 45.00 (*0-8371-8935-7*, MPM/, Greenwood Pr) Greenwood.

Marchant, Robert. Principles of Wordsworth's Poetry. (C). 1986. 110.00 (*0-9502723-3-7*, Pub. by Brynmill Pr Ltd) St Mut.

Marchant-Smith, D. J. & Haslem, P. R. Small Arms & Cannons. (Brassey's Battlefield Weapons Systems & Technology Ser.: Vol. 5). 160p. 1982. text 30.00 (*0-08-028330-6*, Pergamon Pr); pap. text 18.95 (*0-08-028331-4*, Pergamon Pr) Elsevier.

Marchant, Sofia, ed. see Ueda, Marie.

Marchant, Stephen & Higgins, P. J., eds. The Handbook of Australian, New Zealand & Antarctic Birds, Vol. 2: Raptors to Lapwings. (Illus.). 984p. 1994. text 295.00 (*0-19-553069-1*) OUP.

Marchant, Stephen & Higgins, Peter, eds. The Handbook of Australian, New Zealand & Antarctic Birds, 2 vols., Set. 2454p. 1994. 590.00 (*0-19-521066-2*) OUP.

Marchant, Stephen & Higgins, Peter M., eds. The Handbook of Australian, New Zealand & Antarctic Birds, Vol. 1, Pts. A & B: Ratites to Ducks. (Illus.). 1406p. 1991. 350.00 (*0-19-553068-3*) OUP.

Marchant, Sylvia Lanford, ed. see David, C. A.

Marchant, Sylvia Lanford, ed. see David, Charles Alexander, et al.

Marchant, Tony. Thick As Thieves. Incl. Dealt With. 1988. London Calling. 1988. 44p. (C). 1988. pap. write for info. (*0-413-51070-0*, A0292, Methuen Drama) Methn.

— Welcome Home, Raspberry & the Lucky Ones. (Methuen Theatrescripts Ser.). 77p. (C). 1988. pap. 7.95 (*0-413-53820-6*, A0313) Heinemann.

Marchant, William. The Privilege of His Company: Noel Coward Remembered LC 73-22683. 276p. 1975. write for info. (*0-672-51973-9*, Bobbs) Macmillan.

Marchant, William. The Privilege of His Company: Nohel Coward Remembered LC 76-367441. 248 p. 1975. write for info. (*0-297-76937-5*, Pub. by Weidenfeld & Nicolson) Trafalgar.

Marchant, William. To Be Continued. 1952. pap. 3.25 (*0-8222-1156-4*) Dramatists Play.

Marchant, William, tr. see Bourget, Paul C.

Marchbank, Jennifer. Politics of Childcare. 1999. pap. text 27.95 (*1-85728-288-4*) UCL Pr Ltd.

***Marchbank, Jennifer.** Women, Power & Policy: Comparative Studies of Childcare. LC 00-42483. 2000. pap. write for info. (*0-415-23905-2*) Routledge.

Marchbank, Pearce, ed. With the Beatles: The Historic Photographs of Dezo Hoffmann. (Illus.). 128p. (Orig.). pap. 19.95 (*0-7119-0111-2*, OP 41961) Omnibus NY.

Marchblank, Pearce, jt. auth. see Farren, Mick.

Marche, Gary E. Murder As a Business Decision: An Economic Analysis of Criminal Phenomena. LC 98-17072. 356p. 1998. 75.00 (*1-57292-120-X*) Austin & Winfield.

Marche, Pierre, jt. ed. see Meyer, Philippe.

Marchegiani, Irene, tr. see Spaziani, Maria L.

Marchek, Connie P. Determination of the Dynamic Gear Meshing Stiffness of an Acetal Copolymer. (Technical Papers: Vol. 95FTMS1). (Illus.). 34p. 1995. pap. text 30.00 (*1-55589-653-7*) AGMA.

Marchel, John. 101 Casino Gambling Tips: Affordable Strategies & Techniques for Maximizing Profits & Reducing Loses. Cunningham, T. Laine, ed. LC 98-96353. (Illus.). 160p. 1998. pap. 14.95 (*0-9665167-0-2*) Four Suits.

Marchello, Joseph M. Control of Air Pollution Sources. LC 74-79923. (Chemical Processing & Engineering Ser.: No. 7). (Illus.). 640p. reprint ed. pap. 198.40 (*0-608-17912-4*, 202900300058) Bks Demand.

Marchello, Joseph M. & Gomezplata, Albert, eds. Gas-Solids Handling in the Process Industries. LC 76-151314. (Chemical Processing & Engineering Ser.: No. 8). (Illus.). 336p. reprint ed. pap. 104.20 (*0-7837-0677-4*, 204101100019) Bks Demand.

Marchello, Joseph M. & Kelly, John J., eds. Gas Cleaning for Air Quality Control: Industrial & Environmental Health & Safety Requirements. LC 73-78559. (Chemical Processing & Engineering Ser.: No. 2). (Illus.). 432p. reprint ed. pap. 134.00 (*0-7837-4306-8*, 204399700012) Bks Demand.

Marchello, Martin, jt. auth. see Gaida, Urban.

Marchenko, E. Masters of World Painting in the Museums of the Soviet Union. (Illus.). 160p. 1975. 59.95 (*0-8464-0617-9*) Beekman Pubs.

Marchenko, G. N. & Petrov, A. A. Transfer Energy of Semi-Transparent Solids. 1990. 75.00 (*0-89116-753-6*) CRC Pr.

Marchenko, G. N., jt. auth. see Tarchevsky, I. A.

Marchenko, Gennady P. Detection of Enzymes on Electrophoretic Gels: A Handbook. 352p. 1994. boxed set 136.95 (*0-8493-8935-6*, 8935) CRC Pr.

Marchenko, V. A., ed. Spectral Operator Theory & Related Topics. (Advances in Soviet Mathematics Ser.: Vol. 19). 286p. 1994. 100.00 (*0-8218-4122-X*, ADVSOV/19C) Am Math.

Marchenko, Vladimir A. Nonlinear Equations & Operator Algebras. (C). 1987. text 144.00 (*90-277-2654-X*) Kluwer Academic.

— Sturm-Liouville Operators & Applications. (Operator Theory Ser.: Vol. 22). 392p. 1986. 150.00 (*0-8176-1794-9*) Birkhauser.

Marchenko, Vladimir A., jt. ed. see De Monvel, Anne B.

Marchenko, Vyacheslav. House of God. Betts, Richard T., tr. from RUS. (Illus.). 32p. (Orig.). (J). (gr. 1-6). 1997. pap. 8.50 (*0-916700-50-X*) Christ Saviour.

Marchesani, Robert A., jt. ed. see Anson, Jack L.

Marchesani, Robert B., jt. auth. see Stern, E. Mark.

Marchesani, Skip. DB2/400: The New AS/400 Database. LC 98-105324. (Illus.). 284p. (Orig.). 1994. pap. 99.00 (*1-883884-12-8*, 514) Midrange Comput.

Marcheschi, Graziano. Wheat & Weeds & the Wolf of Gubbio: Stories & Prayers for People Who Pray & for People Who Don't. LC 94-131082. (Illus.). 140p. (Orig.). 1993. pap. 9.95 (*1-55612-661-1*) Sheed & Ward WI.

Marcheschi, Graziano & Marcheschi, Nancy S. Scripture at Weddings: Choosing & Proclaiming the Word of God. 128p. (Orig.). 1992. pap. 2.00 (*0-929650-62-X*, READ/W) Liturgy Tr Pubns.

Marcheschi, Nancy S., jt. auth. see Marcheschi, Graziano.

Marchese, Angelo. Diccionario de Retorica, Critica y Terminologia Literaria. 3rd ed. (SPA.). 448p. 1991. pap. 45.00 (*0-7859-5927-0*, 8434483866) Fr & Eur.

Marchese, Francis T., ed. Understanding Images: Finding Meaning in Digital Imagery. LC 93-42645. (TELOS - The Electronic Library of Science). 336p. 1995. 54.95 (*0-387-94148-7*) Spr-Verlag.

Marchese, Raymond. Our Turn, Whitey. Costa, Gwen, ed. LC 91-22351. (Orig.). 1992. pap. 13.95 (*0-87949-316-X*) Ashley Bks.

Marchese, Theodore J. The Search Committee Handbook. 56p. 1988. 12.00 (*0-685-45302-2*) Coll & U Personnel.

Marchese, Theodore J. & Lawrence, Jane F. The Search Committee Handbook: A Guide to Recruiting Administrators. 64p. 1988. pap. 8.95 (*1-56377-002-4*, NO8801) Am Assn Higher Ed.

Marchesi, Blanche. Singer's Pilgrimage. Farkas, Andrew, ed. LC 76-29951. (Opera Biographies Ser.). (Illus.). 1977. reprint ed. lib. bdg. 29.95 (*0-405-09692-5*) Ayer.

— Singer's Pilgrimage. LC 77-1941. (Music Reprint Ser.: 1978). (Illus.). 1978. reprint ed. lib. bdg. 37.50 (*0-306-70878-7*) Da Capo.

Marchesi, Carlo, ed. Ambulatory Monitoring: Cardiovascular System & Applied Applications. (Developments in Cardiovascular Medicine Ser.). 1984. text 219.50 (*0-89838-642-X*) Kluwer Academic.

Marchesi, Mathilde. Bel Canto: Theoretical & Practical Vocal Method. 108p. 1970. reprint ed. pap. text 9.95 (*0-486-22315-9*) Dover.

— Marchesi & Music: Passages from the Life of a Famous Singing-Teacher. LC 77-27354. (Music Reprint Ser.: 1978). 1978. reprint ed. lib. bdg. 39.50 (*0-306-77577-8*) Da Capo.

Marchesi, Michele. Object Oriented Programming with Smalltalk. 352p. 1994. pap. 66.00 (*0-13-630294-7*, Prentice Hall) P-H.

Marchesi, Stephen. Don Quixote & Sancho Panza. LC 90-24098. 80p. (YA). (gr. 6 up). 1992. 16.95 (*0-684-19235-7*) Scribner.

Marchesi, Stephen, jt. auth. see Hitchcock, Alfred.

Marchesi, Stephen, jt. auth. see Korman, Susan.

***Marchessault, Janine & Sawchuk, Kim.** Wild Science: Reading Feminism Medicine & the Media. LC 99-55545. (Writing Corporealities Ser.). (Illus.). 304p. 2000. pap. 24.99 (*0-415-20431-3*) Routledge.

***Marchessault, Janine & Sawchuk, Kim, eds.** Wild Science: Reading Feminism, Medicine & the Media. LC 99-55545. (Writing Corporealities Ser.). (Illus.). 304p. (C). 2000. text 85.00 (*0-415-20430-5*) Routledge.

Marchessault, Jovette. Lesbian Triptych. Klein, Yvonne M., tr. 150p. pap. 8.95 (*0-88961-088-6*, Pub. by Womens Pr) LPC InBook.

Marchessault, Jovette. The Magnificent Voyage of Emily Carr. Gaboriau, Linda, tr. 104p. (Orig.). 1992. pap. 11.95 (*0-88922-314-9*, Pub. by Talonbks) Genl Dist Srvs.

Marchessault, Jovette. Mother of the Grass. Klein, tr. 176p. 1989. pap. 13.95 (*0-88922-267-3*, Pub. by Talonbks) Genl Dist Srvs.

— Saga of the Wet Hens. 136p. pap. 12.95 (*0-88922-213-4*, Pub. by Talonbks) Genl Dist Srvs.

Marchessault, Jovette, jt. tr. see Klein, Yvonne M.

Marchessault, R. H. & Skaar, Christen, eds. Surfaces & Coatings Related to Paper & Wood. LC 66-27617. (C). 1967. 39.95 (*0-8156-5017-5*) Syracuse U Pr.

M

An Asterisk (*) at the beginning of an entry indicates that the title is appearing for the first time.

Marchesseau, Daniel. Chagall: The Art of Dreams. LC 98-7307. (Discoveries Ser.). (Illus.). 176p. 1998. pap. 12.95 (*0-8109-2816-7*, Pub. by Abrams) Time Warner.

— The Lalannes. LC 98-60281. (Illus.). 157p. 1998. 35.00 (*2-08-013652-6*, Pub. by Flammarion) Abbeville Pr.

— Marie Laurencin: Catalogue Raisonne of the Graphic Work. (FRE., Illus.). 184p. 1981. pap. 135.00 (*1-55660-064-X*) A Wofsy Fine Arts.

— Marie Laurencin: Catalogue Raisonne of the Paintings. (FRE., Illus.). 554p. 1986. 575.00 (*1-55660-065-8*) A Wofsy Fine Arts.

Marchesseau, Daniel. Marie Laurencin: Paintings 1903-1946. (FRE & JPN., Illus.). 176p. 1980. pap. 95.00 (*0-8150-0028-6*) Wittenborn Art.

Marchesseault, Paul. Publisher 98 Fast & Easy. LC 97-76321. 400p. 1998. per. 19.99 (*0-7615-1513-5*) Prima Pub.

***Marchesseault, Paul.** Publisher 2000 Fast & Easy. LC 99-70008. (Fast & Easy Ser.). (Illus.). 407p. 1999. pap. 16.99 (*0-7615-2033-3*) Random.

***Marchesseault, Paul & Wagner, Lisa.** Microsoft Money 99 Fast & Easy. LC 98-67609. (Fast & Easy Ser.). 350p. 1998. per. 16.99 (*0-7615-1799-5*) Prima Pub.

Marchesseault, Paul, jt. auth. see Koers, Diane.

Marcheteau, M. Economic, Business & Finance Dictionary Fre-Eng/Eng-Fre. Orig. Title: Dictionnaire de l'Anglais Economique, Commercial & Financier. 669p. 1995. pap. 22.50 (*2-266-06882-2*, Pub. by Presses Pocket) IBD Ltd.

Marcheteau, Michael. NTC's French - English Business Dictionary. (ENG & FRE., Illus.). 600p. 1994. 39.95 (*0-8442-1479-5*, 14795, Natl Textbk Co) NTC Contemp Pub Co.

Marcheteau, Michel. Dictionary of Commercial & Economic English: Dictionnaire de L'Anglais Economique et Commercial. 2nd ed. (ENG & SPA.). 620p. 1990. pap. 24.95 (*0-8288-0075-8*, M513) Fr & Eur.

Marchetta, Camille. Lovers & Friends. 480p. 1991. mass mkt. 4.95 (*0-380-70812-4*, Avon Bks) Morrow Avon.

— Lovers & Friends. Grose, William, ed. 480p. 1995. mass mkt. 5.99 (*0-671-86926-4*) PB.

— Wives of Frankie Ferraro. LC 98-5325. 416p. 1998. text 24.95 (*0-312-18226-0*) St Martin.

***Marchetta, Camille.** The Wives of Frankie Ferraro. 528p. 2000. mass mkt. 6.99 (*0-312-97507-4*, St Martins Paperbacks) St Martin.

Marchetta, Carlo, jt. auth. see Martuscelli, Ezio.

Marchetta, Melina. Looking for Alibrandi. LC 98-35804. 256p. (YA). (gr. 9 up). 1999. 16.95 (*0-531-30142-7*); lib. bdg. 17.99 (*0-531-33142-3*) Orchard Bks Watts.

Marchette, Nyven J. Ecological Relationships & Evolution of the Rickettsiae, Vol. I. 176p. 1982. 104.00 (*0-8493-6125-7*, QR353, CRC Reprint) Franklin.

Marchette, Nyven J., ed. Ecological Relationships & Evolution of the Rickettsiae, Vol. II. 192p. 1982. 165.00 (*0-8493-6126-5*, QR353, CRC Reprint) Franklin.

Marchetti, Albert. Common Cures for Common Ailments: A Doctor's Guide to Nonprescription, Over-the-Counter Medicines & His Recommendations for Their Use. LC 77-16114. 368p. 1981. pap. 8.95 (*0-8128-6107-8*, Scrbrough Hse) Madison Bks UPA.

Marchetti, Domenico, Jr. Productivity & the Business Cycle: Three Essays on U. S. & Polish Manufacturing. rev. ed. LC 96-39992. (Studies on Industrial Productivity). (Illus.). 94p. 1997. text 33.00 (*0-8153-2722-6*) Garland.

Marchetti, Donna. Around the Shores of Lake Erie: A Guide to Small Towns, Rural Areas & Natural Attractions. (Illus.). 255p. 1998. pap. 14.95 (*1-881139-22-0*) Glovebox Guidebks.

***Marchetti, Donna.** Lake Michigan: A Guide to Small Towns, Rural Areas & Natural Attractions. 327p. 2000. pap. 16.95 (*1-881139-25-5*) Glovebox Guidebks.

Marchetti, Gina. Romance & the "Yellow Peril" Race, Sex, & Discursive Strategies in Hollywood Fiction. LC 92-10878. 1993. pap. 16.95 (*0-520-08495-0*, Pub. by U CA Pr) Cal Prin Full Svc.

Marchetti, Lauro, jt. auth. see Howard, Esme.

Marchetti, Louis. History of Marathon & Representative Citizens. (Illus.). 984p. 1997. reprint ed. lib. bdg. 98.50 (*0-8328-6972-4*) Higginson Bk Co.

Marchetti, M., et al, eds. Boundary Elements XIX. LC 97-67019. (BEM Ser.: Vol. 19). 856p. 1997. 345.00 (*1-85312-472-9*, 4729) Computational Mech MA.

Marchetti, N., jt. auth. see Rodriguez, F.

Marchetti-Spaccamela, A., et al. Theoretical Computer Science: Proceedings of the 4th Italian Conference. 372p. 1992. text 121.00 (*981-02-1258-5*) World Scientific Pub.

Marchetti, Tony. Automotive Engine Overhaul. Gorham, Kelly, ed. (Automotive Ser.). 23p. (Orig.). 1992. student ed. 7.00 (*0-8064-0009-9*, A35) Bergwall.

— Working Safely in the Auto Shop. 20p. (YA). (gr. 10 up). 1996. pap., wbk. ed. 7.00 (*0-8064-1327-1*, A40) Bergwall.

Marchetto, Ezio. The Catholic Church & the Phenomenon of Migration: An Overview. 50p. 1989. 5.00 (*0-934733-45-7*) CMS.

Marchetto, Michele. Impersonal Ethics: John Niemeyer Findlay's Value-Theory. LC 96-83232. (Avebury Series in Philosophy). 144p. 1996. 63.95 (*1-85972-272-5*, Pub. by Avebury) Ashgate Pub Co.

Marchevsky, Alberto & Bartels, Peter. Image Analysis: A Primer for Pathologists. 368p. 1994. text 114.00 (*0-7817-0170-8*) Lppncott W & W.

Marchevsky, Alberto M. Surgical Pathology. (Lung Biology in Health & Disease Ser.: Vol. 44). (Illus.). 704p. 1990. text 230.00 (*0-8247-8106-6*) Dekker.

Marchevsky, Alberto M. & Kaneko, Mamoru. Surgical Pathology of the Mediastinum. 2nd ed. LC 91-23675. 352p. 1992. reprint ed. pap. 109.20 (*0-608-04705-8*, 206542600004) Bks Demand.

Marchi, A. De, see De Marchi, A., ed.

Marchi, Attilio De, see De Marchi, Attilio.

Marchi, Dudley M. Montaigne among the Moderns: Receptions of the Essais. LC 94-29461. 352p. (C). 1994. text 59.95 (*1-57181-007-2*) Berghahn Bks.

Marchi, Ena, jt. auth. see Galdo, Giovanna.

Marchi, Francesco. I Cinquecentisti: The Cinquecontisti Five-Accounts Theorists. Brief, Richard P., ed. LC 80-1510. (Dimensions of Accounting Theory & Practice Ser.). (ITA.). 1980. reprint ed. lib. bdg. 23.95 (*0-405-13535-1*) Ayer.

Marchi, Jane G., ed. The Foreign Policies of Caribbean & Central American Countries. 298p. (C). 1990. 21.95 (*0-935501-22-3*, LA218, Pub. by U Miami N-S Ctr) L Rienner.

Marchi, John De, see De Marchi, John.

Marchi, Wina. The Poetry of African-American Invention Vol. I: When One Doors Closes, Another Opens, 4 vols., Vol. 1. 114p. (Orig.). (J). (gr. 3 up). 1996. pap. 17.95 (*0-9655039-0-9*) Reklaw Prodns.

Marchiano, Bruce. In the Footsteps of Jesus. 228p. Date not set. pap. 11.99 (*0-7369-0125-6*) Harvest Hse.

— In the Footsteps of Jesus. LC 97-15530. 275p. 1997. 19.99 (*1-56507-790-3*) Harvest Hse.

***Marchiano, Bruce.** Jesus: Yesterday, Today, Forever. LC 99-21981. 112p. 1999. 24.99 (*0-7369-0048-9*) Harvest Hse.

Marchiano, James J., jt. auth. see Raines, Richard C.

Marchildon, Gregory P. Profits & Politics: Beaverbrook & the Gilded Age of Canadian Finance. (Illus.). 352p. 1996. text 39.00 (*0-8020-0740-6*) U of Toronto Pr.

Marchildon, Gregory P., ed. Mergers & Acquisitions. (International Library of Critical Writings in Business History: No. 3). 608p. 1991. text 250.00 (*1-85278-430-X*) E Elgar.

Marchildon, Gregory P. & McDowall, Duncan, eds. Canadian Multinationals & International Finance. LC 92-12975. 185p. 1992. text 42.50 (*0-7146-3481-6*, Pub. by F Cass Pubs) Intl Spec Bk.

***Marchington & Wilkinson.** Core Personnel & Development. 496p. 2000. pap. 59.95 (*0-8464-5019-4*) Beekman Pubs.

— Core Personnel & Development 2000 Update. 496p. 2000. pap. 59.95 (*0-8464-5163-8*) Beekman Pubs.

Marchington, James. Handguns & Sub-Machine Guns. (Modern Military Equipment Ser.). (Illus.). 126p. 1997. 29.95 (*1-85753-163-9*, Pub. by Brasseys) Brasseys.

— Knives: Military Edged Tools & Weapons. LC 97-179511. (Modern Military Equipment Ser.). 153p. 1997. 29.95 (*1-85753-187-6*, Pub. by Brasseys) Brasseys.

Marchington, James, ed. see Gelbart, Marsh.

Marchington, James, ed. see Norris, John.

Marchington, James, ed. see Norris, John A.

Marchington, Mick. Managing the Team: A Guide to Successful Employee Involvement. LC 92-15428. (Human Resource Management in Action Ser.). 1992. pap. 47.95 (*0-631-18677-8*) Blackwell Pubs.

Marchington, Mick & Wilkinson, Adrian. Core Personnel & Development. 352p. 1996. pap. 60.00 (*0-85292-622-7*, Pub. by IPM Hse) St Mut.

Marchington, Mick, jt. ed. see Sparrow, Paul.

***Marchini, Robert.** Laboratory Manual for First Semester Physics. 96p. (C). 1998. spiral bd., lab manual ed. 18.95 (*0-7872-4697-2*) Kendall-Hunt.

Marchini, Ronald L. The Ultimate Martial Art: Renbukai, Vol. I. 128p. (Orig.). (C). 1981. pap. 7.95 (*0-940522-00-4*) ROMARC Inc.

— The Ultimate Martial Art: Renbukai, Vol. II. 144p. (Orig.). 1982. pap. 7.95 (*0-940522-01-2*) ROMARC Inc.

— The Ultimate Martial Art: Renbukai, Vol. III. 152p. (Orig.). 1982. pap. 7.95 (*0-940522-02-0*) ROMARC Inc.

Marchini, Ronald L. & Fong, Leo. Power Training in Kung-Fu & Karate. Cocoran, John & Scurra, John, eds. LC 74-14128. (Specialties Ser.). (Illus.). 1974. pap. text 17.95 (*0-89750-047-4*, 400) Ohara Pubns.

Marchinton, Buck & McKinney, Deena. The Fools Luck: The Way of the Commoner. (Year of the Reckoning Ser.). (Illus.). 1999. pap. 17.95 (*1-56504-715-X*, 7010) White Wolf.

Marchinton, R. Larry & Miller, Karl V. Quality Whitetails: The Why & How of Quality Deer Management. LC 95-18450. (Illus.). 320p. 1995. 29.95 (*0-8117-1387-3*) Stackpole.

Marchionatti, Roberto. Karl Marx: Critical Responses. LC 97-26905. (ENG, FRE & GER.). 1704p. (C). 1998. 700.00 (*0-415-14059-5*) Routledge.

Marchionatti, Roberto, jt. auth. see Cozzi, Terenzio.

***Marchionda, James V.** The Communion of Love. 2000. pap. write for info. (*1-58459-066-1*, 7821) Wrld Lib Pubns.

Marchionda, James V., jt. auth. see Deiss, Lucien.

Marchione, Joanne. Margaret Newman: Health As Expanding Consciousness. (Notes on Nursing Theories Ser.: Vol. 6). (Illus.). 60p. 1992. 22.95 (*0-8039-4796-8*); pap. 9.95 (*0-8039-4797-6*) Sage.

Marchione, Margherita. The Adventurous Life of Philip Mazzei - La Vita Avventurosa di Filippo Mazzei: La Vita Avventurosa di Filippo Mazzei. LC 95-6188.Tr. of La Vita Avventurosa di Filippo Mazzei. (ENG & ITA.). 226p. (Orig.). (C). 1995. pap. 34.00 (*0-8191-9927-3*) U Pr of Amer.

— Americans of Italian Heritage. (Illus.). 246p. (Orig.). (C). 1995. 47.00 (*0-8191-9825-0*); pap. 28.50 (*0-8191-9826-9*) U Pr of Amer.

— From the Land of the Etruscans (Lucy Filippini) Edizioni di Storia e Letteratura. xiv, 268p. 1986. 20.00 (*0-614-10142-5*, 302870) Am Inst Ital Stud.

— L' Imagine Tesa: The Life & Works of Clemente Rebora. enl. ed. 410p. 1974. reprint ed. pap. 10.00 (*0-916322-16-5*) Am Inst Ital Stud.

— Peter & Sally Sammartino: Biographical Notes. (Biographical Notes Ser.). (Illus.). 305p. 1994. 24.95 (*0-8453-4855-8*, Cornwall Bks) Assoc Univ Prs.

— Philip Mazzei: World Citizen (Jefferson's "Zealous Whig") 158p. (C). 1994. 36.50 (*0-8191-9698-3*) U Pr of Amer.

— A Pictorial History of the Saint Lucy Filippini Chapel: Edizioni del Palazzo, Prato. 130p. 1992. 40.00 (*0-614-10146-8*) Am Inst Ital Stud.

***Marchione, Margherita.** Pope Pius XII: Architect for Peace. LC 99-58456. 368p. 2000. pap. 22.95 (*0-8091-3912-X*) Paulist Pr.

Marchione, Margherita. Yours Is a Precious Witness: Memoirs of Jews & Catholics in Wartime Italy. LC 96-35039. (Stimulus Bks.). (Illus.). 261p. 1997. 14.95 (*0-8091-0485-7*) Paulist Pr.

Marchione, Margherita, ed. Giuseppe Prezzolini: Un Secolo di Attivita. 160p. 1982. write for info. (*0-614-10136-0*) Am Inst Ital Stud.

— Lettere Di Clemente Rebora, 1897-1930, Vol. I. 680p. 1976. pap. 20.00 (*0-916322-17-3*) Am Inst Ital Stud.

— Lettere Di Clemente Rebora, 1930-1957, Vol. 2. 410p. 1982. pap. 20.00 (*0-916322-13-0*) Am Inst Ital Stud.

— Philip Mazzei: My Life & Wanderings. unabridged ed. Scalia, S. Eugene, tr. from ITA. LC 80-69637.Tr. of Memorie della vita e delle peregrinazioni del fiorentino Filippo Mazzei. (Illus.). 438p. (Orig.). (C). 1980. 20.00 (*0-916322-03-3*); pap. 10.00 (*0-916322-04-1*) Am Inst Ital Stud.

— Prophet & Witness of Charity, (Tommaso Maria Fusco) LC 74-127109. 170p. 1973. write for info. (*0-614-10144-1*) Am Inst Ital Stud.

Marchione, Margherita, ed. from FRE. Philip Mazzei: Jefferson's "Zealous Whig" LC 75-29945. 352p. 1975. 9.95 (*0-916322-01-7*); pap. 17.50 (*0-916322-02-5*) Am Inst Ital Stud.

Marchione, Margherita, tr. Twentieth Century Italian Poetry: A Bilingual Anthology. LC 72-6634. 302p. 1974. 10.00 (*0-8386-1245-8*) Am Inst Ital Stud.

Marchione, Margherita, ed. see Prezzolini, Giuseppe.

***Marchione, Thomas J., ed.** Scaling up, Scaling down: Overcoming Malnutrition in Developing Countries. 320p. 1999. text 50.00 (*90-5700-547-6*, Harwood Acad Pubs); pap. text 35.00 (*90-5700-548-4*, Harwood Acad Pubs) Gordon & Breach.

Marchione, William P. Allston-Brighton. LC 97-112788. (Images of America Ser.). 1999. pap. 16.99 (*0-7524-0487-3*) Arcadia Publng.

— The Charles: A River Transformed. (Images of America Ser.). (Illus.). 128p. 1998. pap. 14.99 (*0-7524-0827-5*) Arcadia Publng.

***Marchione, William P.** Italians in Greater Boston. (Images of America Ser.). 128p. 1999. pap. 18.99 (*0-7385-0109-3*) Arcadia Publng.

Marchioness of Londonberry Staff & Hyde, H. M., eds. Russian Journals of Martha & Catherine Wilmot. LC 71-115597. (Russia Observed Ser.). (Illus.). 1971. reprint ed. 29.95 (*0-405-03139-4*) Ayer.

Marchionini, Gary. Information Seeking in Electronic Environments. (Cambridge Series in Human-Computer Interaction: No. 9). (Illus.). 236p. 1997. pap. text 19.95 (*0-521-58674-7*) Cambridge U Pr.

Marchiony, William. The New House Buyer Guide. LC 86-70558. (Illus.). 120p. (Orig.). 1986. pap. text, student ed. 18.95 (*0-938411-00-4*) Carefree Living.

Marchiori & McLean. Imaging of the Skeleton, Chest, & Abdomen: Interpretation of Pattern. LC 98-23694. (Illus.). 1120p. (gr. 13). 1998. text 149.00 (*0-8151-8616-9*, 30549) Mosby Inc.

Marchioro, Carlo & Pulvirenti, Mario. Mathematical Theory of Incompressible Non-Viscous Fluids. LC 93-4683. (Applied Mathematical Sciences Ser.: Vol. 96). (Illus.). 312p. 1993. 65.95 (*0-387-94044-8*) Spr-Verlag.

Marchioro, Carlo, et al. Vortex Methods in Two-Dimensional Fluid Dynamics. (Lecture Notes in Physics Ser.: Vol. 203). iii, 137p. 1984. 18.95 (*0-387-13352-6*) Spr-Verlag.

Marchioro, Thomas, jt. auth. see Wood, Doug.

Marchisio, Linda. With a Little of Both. unabridged ed. (Illus.). 19p. (J). (ps-5). 1987. teacher ed. 10.00 incl. audio (*0-9624224-1-X*) Rainbow Bend.

Marchisio, Sergio & DiBlase, Antonietta. The Food & Agriculture Organization (FAO) (International Organization & the Evolution of World Society Ser.). 268p. 1990. lib. bdg. 130.50 (*0-7923-1012-8*) Kluwer Academic.

Marchitello, Howard. Narrative & Meaning in Early Modern England: Browne's Skull & Other Histories. (Cambridge Studies in Renaissance Literature & Culture: Vol. 20). (Illus.). 245p. (C). 1997. text 59.95 (*0-521-58025-0*) Cambridge U Pr.

***Marchitello, Howard.** What Happens to History: The Renewal of Ethics in Contemporary Thought. 2000. 75.00 (*0-415-92561-4*) Routledge.

***Marchitello, Howard, ed.** What Happens to History: The Renewal of Ethics in Contemporary Thought. LC 00-28616. 256p. 2000. pap. 19.99 (*0-415-92562-2*) Routledge.

Marchlewski, J. B. Antysemityzm a Robotnicy. 94p. 1988. reprint ed. 25.00 (*0-318-23360-6*) Szwede Slavic.

Marchlowitz, Birgit. Freikirchlicher Gemeindeaufbau: Geschichtliche und Empirische Untersuchung Baptistischen Gemeindeverstaendnisses. (Arbeiten zur Praktischen Theologie Ser.: Bd. 7). (GER.). 362p. (C). 1994. lib. bdg. 167.70 (*3-11-014371-2*) De Gruyter.

Marchman. Construction Scheduling with Primavera. (Construction & Building Trades Ser.). 32p. 1998. teacher ed. 10.00 (*0-8273-7087-3*) Delmar.

— Scheduling with Suretrak. LC 99-39199. 383p. (C). 2000. mass mkt. 61.95 (*0-7668-0897-1*) Delmar.

Marchman, David A. Construction Scheduling with Primavera. LC 97-10619. (Construction & Building Trades Ser.). 416p. (C). 1997. pap. 74.95 (*0-8273-7086-5*) Delmar.

***Marchman, Jody L.** Blood Horse Kentucky Derby Glasses Price Guide, 1999-2000 Ed. 2000. pap. text 16.95 (*1-58150-042-4*) Blood-Horse.

Marchman, Judy, ed. Blood Horse Kentucky Derby Glasses Price Guide, 1999-2000 Ed. 1999. pap. text 14.95 (*1-58150-020-3*, Pub. by Blood-Horse) IPG Chicago.

Marchmont, Arthur W. By Right of Sword. 1976. lib. bdg. 15.30 (*0-89968-064-X*, Lghtyr Pr) Buccaneer Bks.

— In the Name of a Woman. 1976. lib. bdg. 16.30 (*0-89968-065-8*, Lghtyr Pr) Buccaneer Bks.

— Marlwych Mystery: or Parson Thring's Secret. 1976. lib. bdg. 15.80 (*0-89968-066-6*, Lghtyr Pr) Buccaneer Bks.

— Miser Hoadley's Secret: A Detective Story. 1976. lib. bdg. 14.85 (*0-89968-067-4*, Lghtyr Pr) Buccaneer Bks.

— The Mystery of Mortimore Strange. 1976. lib. bdg. 16.70 (*0-89968-068-2*, Lghtyr Pr) Buccaneer Bks.

Marchmont, Gally. Wild Grapes. 352p. 1997. pap. 17.95 (*0-7528-0490-1*, Pub. by Orion Pubng Grp) Trafalgar.

Marcho, Guy A., ed. see Goss, Glenda D.

Marchok, Janice M. Oh No! Not My Electric Blanket, Too? A Guide to a Healthier Home. DeSimone, Patricia & Conway, Katherine, eds. LC 91-72193. (Illus.). 183p. (Orig.). 1991. pap. 14.95 (*0-9629215-0-5*) Jetmarc Grp.

Marchon-Arnaud, Catherine. A Gallery of Games. LC 93-25053. (Young Artisan Ser.). (Illus.). 60p. (J). (gr. 3 up). 1994. 12.95 (*0-395-68379-3*) Ticknor & Flds Bks Yng Read.

Marchuk, G. I. Mathematical Modelling of Immune Response in Infectious Diseases, Vol. 395. LC 97-12156. (Mathematics & Its Applications Ser.). 1997. text 187.00 (*0-7923-4528-2*) Kluwer Academic.

Marchuk, Gurii I. Adjoint Equations & Analysis of Complex Systems. LC 94-22318. (Mathematics & Its Applications Ser.: 295). 480p. (C). 1995. text 257.50 (*0-7923-3013-7*) Kluwer Academic.

— Computational Processes & Systems. 288p. 1994. boxed set 89.95 (*0-8493-8947-X*, QA297) CRC Pr.

— Differential Equations & Numerical Mathematics: Proceedings of a U. S. S. R. Council of Ministers for Science & Technology, Moscow. LC 81-81912. (Illus.). 176p. 1982. 74.00 (*0-08-026491-3*, D120, Pub. by Pergamon Repr) Franklin.

— Mathematical Models in Immunology. Balakrishnan, A. V., ed. LC 83-8269. (Translations Series in Mathematics & Engineering). (Illus.). 378p. 1983. pap. text 98.00 (*0-911575-01-4*) Optimization Soft.

— Methods of Numerical Mathematics. 2nd ed. (Applications of Mathematics Ser.: Vol. 2). (Illus.). 510p. 1982. 79.95 (*0-387-90614-2*) Spr-Verlag.

— Numerical Methods for Nuclear Reactor Calculations. LC 59-9229. (Soviet Journal of Atomic Energy: Nos. 3-4, 1958). 300p. reprint ed. pap. 93.00 (*0-608-30741-6*, 202065300018) Bks Demand.

Marchuk, Gurii I. & Agoshkov, V. I. Adjoint Equations & Perturbation Algorithms in Nonlinear Problems of Mathematical Physics. LC 96-19090. 288p. 1996. boxed set 84.95 (*0-8493-2871-3*) CRC Pr.

Marchuk, Gurii I. & Kagan, B. A. Dynamics of Ocean Tides. (C). 1989. text 251.00 (*90-277-2552-7*) Kluwer Academic.

— Ocean Tides: Mathematical Models & Numerical Experiments. Cartwright, D. E., tr. LC 82-18898. (Illus.). 240p. 1984. 131.00 (*0-08-026236-8*, Pub. by Pergamon Repr) Franklin.

Marchuk, Gurii I. & Lebedev, V. I. Numerical Methods in the Theory of Neutron Transport. xx, 601p. 1986. text 421.00 (*3-7186-0182-6*); pap. text 75.00 (*3-7186-0210-5*) Gordon & Breach.

Marchuk, Gurii I. & Nisevich, N. I., eds. Mathematical Methods in Clinical Practice. (Illus.). 150p. 1980. 50.00 (*0-08-025493-4*, Pub. by Pergamon Repr) Franklin.

Marchuk, Gurii I. & Shaidurov, V. V. Difference Methods & their Extrapolations. (Applications of Mathematics Ser.: Vol. 19). (Illus.). 334p. 1983. 58.95 (*0-387-90794-7*) Spr-Verlag.

Marchuk, Gurii I., et al. Monte Carlo Methods in Atmospheric Optics. (Optical Sciences Ser.: Vol. 12). (Illus.). 1980. 44.95 (*0-387-09402-4*) Spr-Verlag.

Marchuk, Gurii I., ed. see IFIP Technical Conference Staff.

Marchuk, Margaret, ed. see Le Van, Gerald.

Marchuk, Michael, jt. auth. see Programming Press Staff.

Marchuk, William N. A Life Science Lexicon. 224p. (C). 1991. text. write for info. (*0-697-12133-X*, WCB McGr Hill) McGrw-H Hghr Educ.

Marcia, James E., et al. Ego Identity: A Handbook for Psychosocial Research. LC 93-2919. 1993. 118.95 (*0-387-94033-2*) Spr-Verlag.

— Ego Identity: A Handbook for Psychosocial Research. (Illus.). 400p. 1993. write for info. (*3-540-94033-2*) Spr-Verlag.

Marcial, Gene. Secrets of the Street: The Dark Side of Making Money. 238p. 1996. pap. 10.95 (*0-07-040256-6*) McGraw.

Marcialis, Louis A. Plastic Twilite: A Novelette. LC 97-90081. 83p. 1998. 12.95 (*0-533-12283-X*) Vantage.

***Marciano, David.** The Taimanov Sicilian. 2000. pap. 21.95 (*1-901983-33-1*, Pub. by Gambit) BHB Intl.

Marciano, Francesca. Rules of the Wild. 1999. pap. 12.00 (*0-375-70343-8*) Knopf.

***Marciano, Francesca.** Rules of the Wild. LC 98-10963. 304p. 1998. 23.00 (*0-375-40358-2*) Pantheon.

Marciano, Francesca. Rules of the Wild. LC PR9120.9.M36R8. 1999. pap. text 144.00 (*0-679-78718-6*) Random.

An Asterisk (*) at the beginning of an entry indicates that the title is appearing for the first time.

***Marciano, John Bemelmans.** Bemelmans: The Life & Art of Madeline's Creator. LC 99-25646. (Illus.). 151p. (YA). 1999. 40.00 (0-670-88460-X) Viking Penguin.

Marciano, John D. Civil Illiteracy & Education: Battle for the Hearts & Minds of American Youth. LC 95-31635. (Counterpoints Ser.). 217p. (C). 1997. pap. text 29.95 (0-8204-2879-5) P Lang Pubng.

Marciano, Theresa D. & Sussman, Marvin B., eds. Wider Families: New Traditional Family Forms. LC 91-19686. (Marriage & Family Review Ser.). (Illus.). 182p. 1991. lib. bdg. 5.95 (1-56024-167-5) Haworth Pr.

— Wider Families: New Traditional Family Forms. LC 91-19686. (Marriage & Family Review Ser.). (Illus.). 182p. 1992. pap. 3.95 (1-56024-271-X) Haworth Pr.

Marciano, Theresa D., jt. ed. see Sussman, Marvin B.

Marciari, John & Beinecke Rare Book-Manuscript Library Staff. Grand Tour Diaries & Other Travel Manuscripts in the James Marshall & Marie-Louise Osborn Collection. LC 98-54889. 1999. write for info. (0-8457-3133-5) Yale U Lib.

Marcic. Labor & Employment Relations. (SWC-Business Law Ser.). 1999. write for info. (0-314-04594-5) S-W Pub.

Marcic, Dorothy. Management International. Date not set. pap. text, teacher ed. write for info. (0-314-03386-6) West Pub.

— Managing with the Wisdom of Love: Uncovering Virtue in People & Organizations. LC 97-1668. (Jossey-Bass Business & Management Ser.). 1997. 25.95 (0-7879-0173-3) Jossey-Bass.

***Marcic, Dorothy.** Organizational Behavior. 6th ed. (SWC-General Business Ser.). 2000. pap. 34.00 (0-324-04850-5) Thomson Learn.

Marcic, Dorothy. Organizational Behavior: Experiences & Cases. 4/e. 4th ed. LC 95-140273. (SWC-Management). 459p. (C). 1995. pap. 34.25 (0-314-04596-1) West Pub.

Marcic, Dorothy, jt. auth. see Daft, Richard L.

Marciel, Scot, jt. ed. see Czinkota, Michael R.

Marcil, Eileen. Charley-Man: The History of Wooden Ship Building at Quebec, 1763-1893. (Illus.). 440p. 1997. 47.95 (1-55082-092-3, Pub. by Quarry Pr) LPC InBook.

— The Charley-Man: The History of Wooden Ship Building at Quebec, 1763-1893. (Illus.). 440p. 1997. pap. text 26.95 (1-55082-093-1, Pub. by Quarry Pr) LPC InBook.

Marcil, Eileen R. The Charley-Man: A History of Wooden Shipbuilding at Quebec, 1763-1893. 1996. pap. text 32.95 (0-07-040286-8) McGraw.

Marcil, Eileen R. Tall Ships & Tankers: The History of the Davie Shipbuilders. LC 98-140371. (Illus.). 604p. 1997. 45.00 (0-7710-5666-4) McCland & Stewart.

Marcil, George, tr. Anthony of Padua, Sermones for the Easter Cycle. (Franciscan Sources). 230p. 1994. pap. 15.00 (1-57659-041-0) Franciscan Inst.

Marcil-Lacoste, Louise. Claude Buffier & Thomas Reid: Two Common-Sense Philosophers. (McGill-Queen's Studies in the History of Religion Ser.). 224p. 1982. 65.00 (0-7735-1003-6, Pub. by McG-Queens Univ Pr) CUP Services.

Marcilhac, Felix. Lalique (Rene) The Complete Work in Glass: Catalogue Raisonne. (FRE., Illus.). 1100p. 1989. 375.00 (1-55660-113-1) A Wofsy Fine Arts.

— Orloff (Chana) Catalogue Raisonne of the Sculptures. (FRE., Illus.). 256p. 1991. 150.00 (1-55660-191-3) A Wofsy Fine Arts.

Marcin, Denny & Peterson, James A. Coaching Football's Tilted-Nose Technique. (Art & Science of Coaching Ser.). (Illus.). 105p. (Orig.). 1997. pap. 16.95 (1-57167-090-4) Coaches Choice.

Marcin, Marietta M. The Herbal Tea Garden: Planning, Planting, Harvesting & Brewing. Webb, Sandra, ed. LC 92-54653. (Illus.). 224p. (Orig.). 1999. pap. 12.95 (0-88266-827-7, Garden Way Pub) Storey Bks.

Marcin, Marietta Marshal. Herbal Tea Gardens. LC 98-41280. 192p. 1999. pap. 16.95 (1-58017 106-0, Storey Pub) Storey Bks.

Marcin, Tess. From Another Angle. 231p. 1999. pap. 15.95 (0-7414-0188-6) Buy Books.

— Hey! Remember Me? I'm Back... (Illus.). 43p. 1999. pap. 9.95 (0-7414-0110-X) Buy Books.

***Marcin, Tess.** Make Your Day. 671p. 1999. pap. 25.95 (0-7414-0237-8) Buy Books.

— You Don't Need a Bodhi Tree: To Find the Light. LC 00-190871. 169p. 2000. 25.00 (0-7388-2061-X); pap. 18.00 (0-7388-2062-8) Xlibris Corp.

Marcin, Tessie. Move That Horizon. 237p. 1999. pap. 15.95 (0-7414-0059-6) Buy Books.

Marcinello, Angela, ed. see Peterson, David & Denney, Dick.

Marciniak. Mechanics Sheet Metal Forming. 1993. text 69.50 (0-340-56405-9, VNR) Wiley.

— Software 2nd ed. Date not set. text. write for info. (0-471-37737-6) Wiley.

Marciniak, A. English-Polish Dictionary of Computer-Science. (ENG & POL.). 671p. 1991. 45.00 (0-7859-7515-2, 8301090200) Fr & Eur.

Marciniak, Andrzej. Numerical Solutions of the N-Body Problem. 1985. text 155.50 (90-277-2058-4) Kluwer Academic.

Marciniak, Barbara. Bringers of the Dawn: Teachings from the Pleiadians. Thomas, Tera L., ed. LC 92-12393. 288p. 1992. pap. 14.00 (0-939680-98-X) Bear & Co.

— Earth: Pleiadian Keys to the Living Library. Thomas, Tera, ed. 288p. 1994. pap. 14.00 (1-879181-21-5) Bear & Co.

— Family of Light. LC 98-41356. 288p. 1998. pap. 15.00 (1-879181-47-9) Bear & Co.

Marciniak, Bonita S. Seatwork Relief: Board Activities for Primary Teachers. 122p. 1991. pap. 15.95 (0-9630787-0-4) Scal-Mar.

Marciniak, James & Marciniak, Steven. Beyond the Silvered Pane. (Illus.). 1978. 5.95 (0-940244-08-X) Flying Buffalo.

Marciniak, John J., ed. Encyclopedia of Software Engineering, 2 vols., 1. 760p. 1994. text. write for info. (0-471-54001-3) Wiley.

— Encyclopedia of Software Engineering, 2 vols., Vol. 2. 1520p. 1994. 375.00 (0-471-54004-8) Wiley.

— Encyclopedia of Software Engineering, 2 vols., Vol. 2. 760p. 1994. text. write for info. (0-471-54002-1) Wiley.

Marciniak, John J. & Reifer, Donald J. Software Acquisition Management: Managing the Acquisition of Custom Software Systems. (Wiley Series in Software Engineering Practice). 290p. 1990. 59.95 (0-471-50643-5) Wiley.

Marciniak, John J., jt. auth. see Evans, Michael W.

Marciniak, Steven, jt. auth. see Marciniak, James.

Marciniec. The Complete Handbook to Hydrosilylation. 766p. 1992. 337.75 (0-08-040272-0, Pergamon Pr) Elsevier.

Marciniec, Bogdan, ed. Progress in Organosilicon Chemistry. 560p. 1995. text 121.00 (2-88449-122-8) Gordon & Breach.

Marciniszyn, Alex, jt. auth. see Martin, Vince.

Marciniszyn, Alex, ed. see Balent, Matthew.

Marciniszyn, Alex, ed. see Carella, C. J. & Siembieda, Kevin.

Marciniszyn, Alex, ed. see Carella, C. J., et al.

Marciniszyn, Alex, ed. see Chilson, Adam.

Marciniszyn, Alex, ed. see Christian, D., et al.

Marciniszyn, Alex, ed. see Coffin, Bill & Siembieda, Kevin.

Marciniszyn, Alex, ed. see Greenberg, Daniel & Siembieda, Kevin.

Marciniszyn, Alex, ed. see Hassall, Kevin.

Marciniszyn, Alex, ed. see Hassall, Kevin & Siembieda, Kevin.

Marciniszyn, Alex, ed. see Jacques, Chester & Siembieda, Kevin.

Marciniszyn, Alex, ed. see Lucas, Ben.

Marciniszyn, Alex, ed. see Martin, Joe & Wujcik, Erick.

Marciniszyn, Alex, ed. see Nowak, Patrick, et al.

Marciniszyn, Alex, ed. see Reed, Gary.

Marciniszyn, Alex, ed. see Siembieba, Kevin.

Marciniszyn, Alex, ed. see Siembieda, Kevin.

Marciniszyn, Alex, ed. see Siembieda, Kevin & Balent, Matthew.

Marciniszyn, Alex, ed. see Siembieda, Kevin & Bartold, Thomas.

Marciniszyn, Alex, ed. see Siembieda, Kevin & Breaux, Wayne, Jr.

Marciniszyn, Alex, ed. see Siembieda, Kevin & Carella, C. J.

Marciniszyn, Alex, ed. see Siembieda, Kevin & Henry, Truman.

Marciniszyn, Alex, ed. see Siembieda, Kevin & Kornmann, Chris.

Marciniszyn, Alex, ed. see Siembieda, Kevin & Long, Kevin.

Marciniszyn, Alex, ed. see Siembieda, Kevin & Siembieda, Maryann.

Marciniszyn, Alex, ed. see Siembieda, Kevin & Thompson, Eric.

Marciniszyn, Alex, ed. see Siembieda, Kevin & Zeleznik, John.

Marciniszyn, Alex, ed. see Siembieda, Kevin, et al.

Marciniszyn, Alex, ed. see Sumimoto, Mark & Siembieda, Kevin.

Marciniszyn, Alex, ed. see Trostle, Jape & Siembieda, Kevin.

Marciniszyn, Alex, ed. see Vezina, Marc-Alexandre, et al.

Marciniszyn, Alex, ed. see Wallis, James & Siembieda, Kevin.

Marciniszyn, Alex, ed. see Wallis, James & Sienbieda, Kevin.

Marciniszyn, Alex, ed. see Wujcik, Erick.

Marciniszyn, Alex, ed. see Wujcik, Erick & Balent, Matthew.

Marciniszyn, Alex, ed. see Wujcik, Erick & Siembieda, Kevin.

Marciniszyn, Alex, ed. see Wujcik, Erick, et al.

***Marcinko.** 2001 Financial Planning for Physicians & Healthcare Professionals. 1000p. 2000. pap. 145.00 (0-15-607028-6) Harcourt Legal.

Marcinko, David E. Infections of the Foot: Diagnosis & Management. (Illus.). 288p. (gr. 13). 1997. text 85.00 (0-8016-7018-7, 07018) Mosby Inc.

— Medical & Surgical Therapeutics of the Foot & Ankle. (Illus.). 968p. 1992. 125.00 (0-683-05549-6) Lppncott W & W.

***Marcinko, David Edward.** The Business of Medical Practice: Profit Maximizing Skill for Savvy Doctors. (Illus.). 368p. 2000. 55.95 (0-8261-1311-7) Springer Pub.

Marcinko, Richard. The Leadership Secrets of the Rogue Warrior: A Commando's Guide to Success. 176p. 1997. per. 14.00 (0-671-54514-0, Pocket Books) PB.

***Marcinko, Richard.** The Leadership Secrets of the Rogue Warrior: A Commando's Guide to Success. ed. 1998. per. 20.00 (0-671-03675-0, Pocket Books) PB.

Marcinko, Richard. Rogue Warrior: Designation Gold. (Rogue Warrior Ser.). 1997. mass mkt. 6.99 (0-671-01743-8) PB.

— Rogue Warrior: Task Force Blue. (Rogue Warrior Ser.). (Illus.). 400p. 1997. per. 6.99 (0-671-89672-5) PB.

— Rogue Warrior: The Real Team. (Rogue Warrior Ser.). (Illus.). 256p. 1999. 23.00 (0-671-02464-7, PB Hardcover) PB.

***Marcinko, Richard.** Rogue Warrior: The Real Team. 272p. 2000. reprint ed. per. 6.99 (0-671-02465-5) PB.

— The Rogue Warrior's Strategy for Success: A Commando's Principles of Winning. 208p. 1999. text 20.00 (0-7881-6770-7) DIANE Pub.

Marcinko, Richard. The Rogue Warrior's Strategy for Success: A Commando's Principles of Winning. LC 98-153676. 208p. 1997. 20.00 (0-671-00993-1, PB Hardcover) PB.

— The Rogue Warrior's Strategy for Success: A Commando's Principles of Winning. 224p. 1998. per. 14.00 (0-671-00994-X, Pocket Books) PB.

Marcinko, Richard & Weisman, John. Detachment Zulu: Rogue Warrior 8. Date not set. write for info. (0-671-00075-6) S&S Childrens.

— Echo Platoon. (Rogue Warrior Ser.). 368p. 2000. 24.95 (0-671-00070-5, PB Hardcover) PB.

— Leadership Secrets of the Rogue Warrior: A Commando's Guide to Success. 176p. 1996. 20.00 (0-671-54515-9) PB.

— Option Delta. (Rogue Warrior Ser.). 416p. 2000. reprint ed. per. 6.99 (0-671-00073-X, Pocket Star Bks) PB.

— Rogue Warrior. Regan, Judith & McCarthy, Paul, eds. (Rogue Warrior Ser.). 352p. 1992. 23.00 (0-671-70390-0) PB.

— Rogue Warrior. Regan, Judith & McCarthy, Paul, eds. (Rogue Warrior Ser.). 416p. 1993. per. 6.99 (0-671-79593-7, Pocket Star Bks) PB.

— Rogue Warrior: Designation Gold. LC 96-42436. (Rogue Warrior Ser.). 368p. 1997. 23.00 (0-671-89673-3) PB.

— Rogue Warrior: Designation Gold. (Rogue Warrior Ser.). 1998. per. 6.99 (0-671-89674-1) PB.

— Rogue Warrior: Green Team. (Rogue Warrior Ser.). 1995. 23.00 (0-614-32264-2) PB.

— Rogue Warrior: Green Team. McCarthy, Paul, ed. (Rogue Warrior Ser.). 368p. 1995. 23.00 (0-671-89671-7) PB.

— Rogue Warrior: Green Team. (Rogue Warrior Ser.). 1996. mass mkt. 6.99 (0-671-79959-2, PB Trade Paper) PB.

— Rogue Warrior: Option Delta. LC 99-204503. (Rogue Warrior Ser.). 352p. 1999. 24.00 (0-671-00068-3) S&S Trade.

— Rogue Warrior: Red Cell. (Rogue Warrior Ser.). 1998. mass mkt. 3.99 (0-671-01977-5) PB.

Marcinko, Richard & Weisman, John. Rogue Warrior: Red Cell. abr. ed. 1994. audio 17.00 (0-671-88590-1) S&S Audio.

Marcinko, Richard & Weisman, John. Rogue Warrior: Task Force Blue. McCarthy, Paul, ed. (Rogue Warrior Ser.). 336p. 1996. 23.00 (0-671-79958-4, PB Hardcover) PB.

Marcinko, Richard & Weisman, John. Rogue Warrior II: Red Cell. (Rogue Warrior Ser.). 368p. 1994. 22.00 (0-671-79956-8) PB.

Marcinko, Richard & Weisman, John. Rogue Warrior II: Red Cell. Regan, Judith & McCarthy, Paul, eds. (Rogue Warrior Ser.: No. 2). (Illus.). 416p. 1994. reprint ed. per. 6.99 (0-671-79957-6) PB.

— Seal Force Alpha. (Rogue Warrior Ser.). 400p. 1999. mass mkt. 6.99 (0-671-00072-1, PB Trade Paper) PB.

— Untitled Rogue Warrior 8. Date not set. pap. text. write for info. (0-671-00071-3) S&S Trade.

Marcinkowski, M. J. Unified Theory of the Mechanical Behavior of Matter. LC 78-27799. 275p. reprint ed. pap. 85.30 (0-608-13331-0, 205572200032) Bks Demand.

Marcinkowski, T. & Mrazek, R., eds. Research in Environmental Education, 1981-1990. 408p. 1997. text 23.00 (1-884008-39-9) NAAEE.

Marcinszyn, Alex, ed. see Carella, C. J.

Marcion Of Sinope. The Gospel of the Lord. Hill, James H., tr. LC 78-63171. (Heresies of the Early Christian & Medieval Era Ser.: Second Ser.). reprint ed. 27.50 (0-404-16186-3) AMS Pr.

Marciszewski, Witold. Logic from a Rhetorical Point of View. LC 93-45843. (Grundlagen der Kommunikation & Kognition (Foundations of Communication & Cognition) Ser.). xv, 312p. (C). 1993. lib. bdg. 118.50 (3-11-013683-X) De Gruyter.

Marcius de Alencar Xavier, Yanko. Die EG-Produkthaftungsrichtlinie - ein Mogliches Modell fur den MERCOSUL? (Europaische Hochschulschriften: Reihe 2: Bd. 2073). (GER.). XV, 309p. 1996. pap. 57.95 (3-631-31335-7) P Lang Pubng.

Marck, E. E. Van, see Gigase, P. L. & Van Marck, E. E., eds.

Marck, J. A. & Lasota, J. P., eds. Relativistic Gravitation & Gravitational Radiation. LC 97-1228. (Cambridge Contemporary Astrophysics Ser.). (Illus.). 491p. (C). 1997. text 79.95 (0-521-59065-5) Cambridge U Pr.

Marck, Jan V. Arman Selected Works. LC 74-18537. (Illus.). 48p. 1974. 8.00 (0-686-99820-0) Mus Contemp Art.

Marck, John T. The First Ladies of the United States. (Illus.). 45p. (Orig.). 1995. pap. text 19.95 (1-884604-01-3) Creative Impress.

— Maryland the Seventh State a History. 4th rev. ed. (Illus.). 456p. 1998. 32.95 (1-884604-78-1) Creative Impress.

— The Presidents of the United States. (Illus.). 45p. (Orig.). 1997. pap. text 19.95 (1-884604-00-5) Creative Impress.

Marck, Patricia, jt. ed. see Field, Peggy A.

Marcken, Gail De, see Cary, Bob.

Marcken, Gail De, see Paull, Frankie & Cary, Bob.

Marcken, Gail De, see Cary, Bob.

***Marckini, Fredrick W.** Webmasters Guide to Search Engine Positioning. 1999. pap. 49.95 incl. cd-rom (1-55622-720-5) Wordware Pub.

Marcks, Gerhard. The Letters of Gerhard Marcks & Marguerite Wildenhain, 1970-1981: A Mingling of Souls. LC 90-48292. (Illus.). 285p. 1991. reprint ed. pap. 88.40 (0-608-06874-8, 206708200009) Bks Demand.

Marckwardt, Albert H. & Moore, Samuel. Historical Outlines of English Sounds & Inflections. 1957. pap. 18.00 (0-911586-22-9) Wahr.

Marckwardt, Albert H. & Willibrand, W. A. Principal & Subsidiary Dialect Areas in the North-Central States; English Loan Words in the Low German Dialect of Westphalia, Missouri. (Publications of the American Dialect Society: No. 27). 32p. 1957. pap. 5.50 (0-8173-0627-7) U of Ala Pr.

Marckwardt, Wilhelm, ed. International Guide to MARC Databases & Services: National Magnetic Tape, CD-ROM, & Online Services & Databases. 3rd rev. ed. (UBCIM Publications). 250p. 1993. reprint ed. lib. bdg. 100.00 (3-598-10987-3) K G Saur Verlag.

Marckx, Barbara, jt. auth. see Tagliareni, M. Elaine.

Marco, Carolyn, jt. auth. see Gach, Michael R.

***Marco, Chris.** Termite. LC 98-42672. (Bug Bks.). 32p. (J). 1999. 19.92 (1-57572-800-1) Heinemann Lib.

Marco, Chris, jt. auth. see Hartley, Karen.

***Marco, David.** Building & Managing the Meta Data Repository: A Full Life-Cycle Guide. 416p. 2000. pap. 44.99 (0-471-35523-2) Wiley.

Marco, Donald De, see Bradley, Gerald V. & De Marco, Donald, eds.

Marco, Gayle J. & Lucas, Anthony J. Video Instructor's Manual to Accompany Boone-Kurtz, Contemporary Business. 7th ed. 186p. (C). 1993. pap. text 5.75 (0-03-076343-6) Dryden Pr.

Marco, Gino J., et al, eds. Regulation of Agrochemicals: A Driving Force in Their Evolution. LC 91-19736. (Illus.). 188p. 1991. text 49.95 (0-8412-2089-1, Pub. by Am Chemical); pap. text 38.00 (0-8412-2085-9, Pub. by Am Chemical) OUP.

— Silent Spring Revisited. 195p. 1987. text 48.00 (0-8412-0980-4, Pub. by Am Chemical); pap. text 38.00 (0-8412-0981-2, Pub. by Am Chemical) OUP.

Marco, Guy, jt. ed. see Ping-Robbins, Nancy R.

Marco, Guy A. Checklist of Writings on American Music, 1640-1992, Vols. 1[00ad]3. LC 95-26773. 248p. 1996. 50.00 (0-8108-3133-3) Scarecrow.

Marco, Guy A. Literature of American Music III & Checklist of Writings on American Music, 2 vols. 105.00 (0-8108-3451-0) Scarecrow.

Marco, Guy A. The Literature of American Music in Books & Folk Music Collections, 1983-1993. LC 95-26774. 472p. 1996. 69.50 (0-8108-3132-5) Scarecrow.

***Marco, Guy A.** Opera: A Research & Information Guide. 2nd ed. (Music Research & Information Guides Ser.). (Illus.). 2000. 95.00 (0-8153-3516-4) Garland.

Marco, Guy A. & Fenton, David W. Mozart: A Research Guide. 2nd ed. (Composer Resource Manuals Ser.). 500p. 1998. text 75.00 (0-8153-2386-7) Garland.

Marco, Guy A. & Marvin, Clara. Palestrina: A Research Guide. (Composer Resource Manuals Ser.). 300p. 1998. text 45.00 (0-8153-2351-4) Garland.

Marco, Guy A., jt. auth. see Bryant, Eric T.

Marco, Guy A., ed. see Antokoletz, Elliott.

Marco, Guy A., ed. see Cassaro, James P.

Marco, Guy A., ed. see Clark, Walter A.

Marco, Guy A., ed. see Cramer, Eugene C.

Marco, Guy A., ed. see Fairtile, Linda B.

Marco, Guy A., ed. see Hodgson, Peter J.

Marco, Guy A., ed. see Parker, Robert L.

Marco, Guy A., ed. see Powers, Doris.

Marco, Guy A., ed. see Robertson, Marta.

Marco, Guy A., ed. see Simms, Bryan R.

Marco, Guy A., ed. see Smialek, William.

Marco, Guy A., tr. see Zarlino, Gioseffo.

Marco, Guy De, see De Marco, Guy.

Marco, Joaquin. Literatura Hispanoamericana: Del Modernismo a Nuestros Dias. (Nueva Austral Ser.: Vol. 17). (SPA.). 1991. pap. text 34.95 (84-239-1817-3) Elliots Bks.

***Marco, John.** The Grand Design. LC 99-36358. (Tyrants & Kings Ser.: Vol. 2). 592p. 2000. pap. 14.95 (0 553-38022-2, Spectra) Bantam.

Marco, John. The Jackal of Nar. (Tyrants & Kings Ser.: Vol. 1). 768p. 2000. reprint ed. mass mkt. 6.99 (0-553-57887-1, Spectra) Bantam.

Marco, Juan B., et al, eds. Stochastic Hydrology & Its Use in Water Resources Systems Simulation. LC 93-19300. (NATO Advanced Study Institutes Series E, Applied Sciences: Vol. 237). 1993. text 276.50 (0-7923-2288-6) Kluwer Academic.

Marco, Michael. The Lymphoma Project Report: Current Issues in Research & Treatment of AIDS-Associated Lymphoma. (Illus.). 64p. (Orig.). (C). 1995. pap. text 20.00 (0-7881-1841-2) DIANE Pub.

Marco, Neil de, see de Marco, Neil.

Marco, Pierre W. Canteen Cuisine. (Illus.). 224p. 1999. reprint ed. pap. (0-09-185372-9) Random.

Marco, Tomas. Spanish Music in the Twentieth Century. Franzen, Cola, tr. LC 92-14270. 288p. (C). 1993. 49.95 (0-674-83102-0) HUP.

Marco, Tomas, tr. see Honegger, Marc.

Marcoci, Roxana. Gardens in Bloom. LC 94-32480. (Celebrations in Art Ser.). (Illus.). 72p. 1995. 12.98 (1-56799-163-7, MetroBooks) M Friedman Pub Grp Inc.

— Mothers & Children. LC 94-32474. (Celebrations in Art Ser.). (Illus.). 72p. 1995. 12.98 (1-56799-162-9, MetroBooks) M Friedman Pub Grp Inc.

Marcoci, Roxana, et al. New Art. LC 96-50361. 1997. lib. bdg. write for info. (0-7172-9090-5) Abrams.

— New Art. LC 96-50361. (Illus.). 160p. 1997. pap. 24.95 (0-8109-2674-1, Pub. by Abrams) Time Warner.

Marcolongo, Bruno & Mantovani, Franco. Photogeology: Remote Sensing Applications in Earth Sciences. 200p. (C). 1996. lib. bdg. 45.00 (1-886106-74-6) Science Pubs.

Marcolongo, Bruno, jt. ed. see Filippi, Gian Giuseppe.

***Marcom, Robert F.** A Custom Study Guide to Accompany the Telecourse for U. S. History to 1877. 206p. (C). 1999. per. 28.95 (0-7872-6307-9) Kendall-Hunt.

M

An Asterisk (*) at the beginning of an entry indicates that the title is appearing for the first time.

Marcombe, David. English Small Town Life: Retford, 1520-1642. (Illus.). 320p. 1994. 35.00 (*1-85041-067-4*, Pub. by U of Nottingham); pap. 17.95 (*1-85041-068-2*, Pub. by U of Nottingham) St Mut.

— Newark's Riverside Heritage: Millgate, a Guided Walk. LC 98-138962. (Illus.). 52p. 1997. pap. 5.95 (*1-85041-086-0*, Pub. by U of Nottingham) Intl Spec Bk.

— Nottingham & the Great War. (C). 1984. text 40.00 (*0-7855-3207-2*, Pub. by Univ Nottingham) St Mut.

— Sounding Boards: Oral Testimony & the Local Historian. LC 95-174976. 90p. 1994. pap. 10.00 (*1-85041-075-5*, Pub. by U of Nottingham) St Mut.

— The Victorian Sailor. (Album Ser.: No. 131). (Illus.). 32p. pap. 4.75 (*0-85263-713-6*, Pub. by Shire Pubns) Parkwest Pubns.

Marcombe, David & Knighton, C. S., eds. Close Encounters: English Cathedrals & Society since 1540. 214p. 1991. 52.00 (*1-85041-038-0*) U of Nottingham.

Marcombe, David, jt. auth. see Bourne, Terry.

Marcondes de Souza Filho, Danilo. Language & Action: A Reassessment of Speech Act Theory. LC 84-4055. (Pragmatics & Beyond Ser.: Vol. V:6). x, 165p. 1985. pap. 50.00 (*0-915027-01-1*) J Benjamins Pubng Co.

Marcone, Stephen. The Internship Manual. 16p. (Orig.). (C). 1996. pap. text 7.95 (*0-9651250-1-7*) HiMarks Pubng.

— Managing Your Band: Artist Management: The Ultimate Responsibility. 2nd rev. ed. LC 99-176419. 250p. (Orig.). 1998. pap. text 27.95 (*0-9651250-2-5*) HiMarks Pubng.

Marconi, Catherine L., ed. Handspan of Red Earth: An Anthology of American Farm Poems. LC 90-21163. (Illus.). 197p. 1991. pap. 12.95 (*0-87745-326-8*) U of Iowa Pr.

Marconi, Degna. My Father, Marconi. 2nd rev. ed. (Prose Ser.: No. 40). 282p. (YA). 1996. reprint ed. pap. 13.00 (*1-55071-044-3*) Guernica Editions.

Marconi, Diego. Lexical Competence. LC 96-29014. (Language, Speech & Communication Ser.). (Illus.). 222p. 1997. 27.50 (*0-262-13333-4*, Bradford Bks) MIT Pr.

Marconi, Elettra, jt. auth. see Marconi, Maria C.

Marconi, Gilberto, jt. ed. see O'Collins, Gerald.

Marconi, Joe. Beyond Branding: How Savvy Marketers Use Brand Extension to Create Products & Open New Markets. 225p. 1993. text 32.50 (*1-55738-428-2*, Irwn Prfssnl) McGraw-Hill Prof.

***Marconi, Joe.** The Brand Marketing Book: Creating, Managing & Extending the Value of Your Brand. LC 99-23371. 256p. 1999. 39.95 (*0-8442-2257-7*, 22577, Natl Textbk Co) NTC Contemp Pub Co.

Marconi, Joe. The Complete Guide to Publicity: Maximize Visibility for Your Product, Service or Organization. LC 98-39670. 239p. 1999. 39.95 (*0-8442-0090-5*, NTC Business Bks) NTC Contemp Pub Co.

— The Complete Guide to Publicity: Maximize Visibility for Your Product, Service or Organization. LC 98-39670. 256p. 1999. pap. 19.95 (*0-8442-0091-3*, 00913, NTC Business Bks) NTC Contemp Pub Co.

— Crisis Marketing: When Bad Things Happen to Good Companies. 225p. 1992. 22.95 (*1-55738-246-8*, Irwn Prfssnl) McGraw-Hill Prof.

— Crisis Marketing: When Bad Things Happen to Good Companies. 2nd ed. LC 97-30304. (Illus.). 256p. 1997. 34.95 (*0-8442-3237-8*, NTC Business Bks) NTC Contemp Pub Co.

***Marconi, Joe.** Future Marketing: Targeting Seniors, Boomers & Generations X & Y. 2000. 39.95 (*0-658-00138-8*) NTC Contemp Pub Co.

Marconi, Joe. Getting the Best from Your Ad Agency: Everything Marketers Need to Know about Working with Agencies - from Creative, Media Planning, Budgeting & Market Strategy to Campaign Execution & Evaluation. 200p. 1991. 24.95 (*1-55738-179-8*, Irwn Prfssnl) McGraw-Hill Prof.

— Image Marketing: Using Public Perceptions to Create Awareness & Build Market Share. LC 95-46960. (Illus.). 256p. 1996. 39.95 (*0-8442-3504-0*, NTC Business Bks) NTC Contemp Pub Co.

— Shock Marketing: Advertising, Influence, & Family Values. LC 97-12070. 185p. 1997. 29.95 (*1-56625-081-1*) Bonus Books.

Marconi, Joseph, ed. Indexed Periodicals. LC 76-12242. 1976. 90.00 (*0-87650-005-X*) Pierian.

***Marconi, Maria C. & Marconi, Elettra.** My Beloved Marconi. LC 99-44852. Orig. Title: Mio Marito Guglielmo. (Illus.). 1999. 29.95 (*0-937832-36-7*) Dante U Am.

Marconi, Paolo. Atlas of Rome. (Illus.). 600p. 1992. 250.00 (*0-941419-70-3*) Marsilio Pubs.

Marconis, E. J. The Sanctuary of Memphis: or Hermes-Masonic Rituals. 230p. 1993. reprint ed. pap. 19.95 (*1-56459-311-8*) Kessinger Pub.

Marconnet, P., et al, eds. Muscle Fatigue Mechanisms in Exercise & Training. (Medicine & Sport Science Ser.: Vol. 34). (Illus.). viii, 244p. 1992. 215.75 (*3-8055-5483-4*) S Karger.

Marconnet, P., jt. ed. see Poortmans, J. R.

***Marcopoulos, Ari.** Transitions & Exits. 2000. 45.00 (*1-57687-092-8*) pwerHse Cultrl.

Marcopoulos-Gambarotta, Eleni & Scamp, Jennifer. Just Listen 'n Learn Greek: Beginning Through Intermediate. (ENG & GRE.). 240p. (C). 1998. pap. 17.95 (*0-8442-8475-0*, X8475-0) NTC Contemp Pub Co.

Marcorich, Miroslav. Studies in Graeco-Roman Religions & Gnosticism. ix, 195p. (C). 1988. pap. 56.00 (*90-04-08624-2*) Brill Academic Pubs.

Marcos. Mexico: A Storm & a Prophecy. 4.00 (*1-884519-08-3*) Open Media.

Marcos, Anastasios C., jt. ed. see Draper, Thomas W.

Marcos, Natalio F. Scribes & Translators: Septuagint & Old Latin in the Books. LC 94-9717. (Supplements to Vetus Testamentum Ser.). 1994. 71.00 (*90-04-10043-1*) Brill Academic Pubs.

***Marcos, Natalio Fernandez.** The Septuagint in Context: Introduction to the Greek Version of the Bible. 256p. 2000. 85.00 (*90-04-11574-9*) Brill Academic Pubs.

Marcos, Plinio, et al. Three Contemporary Brazilian Plays in Bilingual Edition. Szoka, Elzbieta, ed. & tr. by. from POR. Bratcher, Joe, ed. Marques, Lydia et al, trs. from POR. (Illus.). 525p. (Orig.). (C). 1988. pap. 20.00 (*0-924047-00-3*) Host Pubns.

Marcos, Rafael, tr. Old Havana Cookbook: Cuban Recipes in Spanish & English. (Bi-Lingual Cookbks.). (ENG & SPA., Illus.). 128p. 1999. 11.95 (*0-7818-0767-0*) Hippocrene Bks.

Marcos, Rafael, tr. see Gatje, Charles T. & Gatje, John F.

Marcos Sanchez, Maria D., ed. see Casona, Alejandro.

Marcos, Subcomandante. The Story of Colors (La Historia de los Colores) A Bilingual Folktale from the Jungles of Chiapas. Din, Anne B., tr. LC 98-43452. (SPA & ENG., Illus.). 40p. 1999. 15.95 (*0-938317-45-8*, Pub. by Cinco Puntos) Consort Bk Sales.

Marcos, Subcomandante & David, Comandante. Ezln Communiques: Navigating the Seas, Dec. 22, 1997-Jan. 29, 1998. Paulson, Joshua, tr. from SPA. (EZLN Communiques Ser.). (Illus.). 68p. 1998. pap. 3.00 (*1-889059-13-7*, Agit Pr) Regent Pr.

Marcos, Subcomandante, et al. EZLN Communiques: Memory from Below. (Fringe Ser.: Vol. 2). (Illus.). 68p. 1998. pap. 3.00 (*1-889059-16-1*) Regent Pr.

***Marcos, Subcomandante Insurgente.** Our Word Is Our Weapon: Selected Writings. Ponce de Leon, Juana, ed. 416p. 2000. 27.95 (*1-58322-036-4*, Pub. by Seven Stories) Publishers Group.

Marcosson, Isaac F. Adventures in Interviewing. LC 80-130996. reprint ed. 29.50 (*0-404-04186-8*) AMS Pr.

— Anaconda. LC 75-41771. (Companies & Men: Business Enterprises in America Ser.). (Illus.). 1976. reprint ed. 40.95 (*0-405-08085-9*) Ayer.

— Marse Henry: A Biography of Henry Watterson. LC 74-156200. (Illus.). 269p. 1971. reprint ed. lib. bdg. 65.00 (*0-8371-6150-9*, MAMH) Greenwood.

— Turbulent Years. LC 71-90661. (Essay Index Reprint Ser.). 1977. 30.95 (*0-8369-1305-1*) Ayer.

— Wherever Men Trade: The Romance of the Cash Register. LC 72-5062. (Technology & Society Ser.). (Illus.). 310p. 1972. reprint ed. 21.95 (*0-405-04713-4*) Ayer.

Marcot, Bruce G. Owls of Old Forests of the World. (Illus.). 64p. (C). 1998. pap. text 20.00 (*0-7881-7348-0*) DIANE Pub.

Marcot, Roy M. Civil War Chief of Sharpshooters, Hiram Berdan, Military Commander & Firearms Inventor. LC 89-92286. (Illus.). 342p. 1992. 59.95 (*0-9611494-1-8*) Northwood Heritage Pr.

— Spencer Repeating Firearms. (Illus.). 317p. 1995. 100.00 (*1-884849-14-8*) R&R Bks.

— Spencer Repeating Firearms. 2nd rev. ed. LC 89-92524. (Illus.). 316p. 1989. reprint ed. 59.95 (*0-9611494-3-4*) Northwood Heritage Pr.

***Marcott, Craig.** Three Minutes of Intimacy: Dance Your Way to a Sensational Social Life. LC 00-90827. 144p. 2000. pap. 12.95 (*0-9678701-2-7*) Sundance Pubng.

Marcotte, Armand & Druffel, Ann. Past Lives, Future Growth. 216p. 1993. pap. 8.95 (*1-878901-79-6*) Hampton Roads Pub Co.

Marcotte, Armand, jt. auth. see Druffel, Ann.

Marcotte, David B., jt. ed. see Nadelson, Carol C.

Marcotte, Frank B. Private Osborne Massachusetts 23rd Volunteers: Burnside Expedition, Roanoke Island, Second Front Against Richmond. (Illus.). 312p. 1999. lib. bdg. 32.50 (*0-7864-0554-6*) McFarland & Co.

Marcotte, J., jt. auth. see Detienne, M. G.

Marcotte, Joe. Martha's Pet. 24p. (J). (ps-5). 1995. pap. 5.95 (*0-9648807-0-9*) Spking With Insight.

— These Are a Few of My Favorite Things. 150p. 1995. pap. 10.95 (*0-9648807-1-7*) Spking With Insight.

***Marcotte, Michael.** Gold in the Shadow. 376p. 2000. pap. 18.95 (*0-595-09414-7*, Writers Club Pr) iUniversecom.

Marcotte, Michael R., jt. auth. see Burstone, Charles J.

Marcotte, Odile, jt. auth. see Hansen, P.

Marcotte, Patrice & Nguyen, Sang. Equilibrium & Advanced Transportation Modelling. LC 98-17625. 1998. 125.00 (*0-7923-8162-9*) Kluwer Academic.

***Marcotte, Rose, ed.** Where to Turn Plus 2000: The Directory of Health & Human Services Seattle/King County. (Illus.). 275p. 1999. pap. 30.00 (*0-9677225-0-0*) Crisis Clinic.

— Where to Turn 2000. (Illus.). 115p. 1999. pap. 8.00 (*0-9677225-1-9*) Crisis Clinic.

Marcotty, M. W. The World of Programming Languages. (Books on Professional Computing). (Illus.). 385p. 1986. 69.95 (*0-387-96440-1*) Spr-Verlag.

Marcotty, Michael. Software Implementation. 300p. (C). 1991. pap. text 41.00 (*0-13-823493-0*) P-H.

Marcou, Diane, jt. auth. see Steiner, Dieter.

Marcou, Diane, ed. see Haimes, Allen N.

Marcou, Diane, ed. see Lenhart, John P.

Marcou, John B., jt. auth. see Marcou, Jules.

Marcou, Jules, Jr. Jules Marcou on the Taconic System in North America: An Original Anthology. Albritton, Claude C., ed. LC 77-6527. (History of Geology Ser.). (Illus.). 1978. lib. bdg. 65.95 (*0-405-10448-0*) Ayer.

Marcou, Jules & Marcou, John B. Mapoteca Geologica Americana: A Catalogue of Geological Maps of America (North & South), 1752-1881. 184p. 1997. reprint ed. 65.00 (*1-891396-02-1*) Pober Pub.

— Mapoteca Geologica Americana: A Catalogue of Geological Maps of America, 1752-1881. 189p. 1997. reprint ed. 60.00 (*1-57898-060-7*) Martino Pubng.

Marcou, Richard. How to Cook...Roadkill: "Gourmet Cooking" (Illus.). 96p. 1993. reprint ed. 9.95 (*0-9637062-0-9*) MCB Pubns.

Marcouiller, David W. Tourism Planning. LC 95-8753. (Bibliographies Ser.: No. 316). 37p. 1995. pap. 10.00 (*0-86602-316-X*, Sage Prdcls Pr) Sage.

Marcouiller, David W., jt. auth. see Jepson, Edward J., Jr.

Marcoulesco, Ileana. Georges Rouault: The Inner Light. (Illus.). 32p. (Orig.). 1996. pap. 9.24 (*0-939594-35-8*, Menil Collection) Menil Found.

Marcoulides, George A., ed. Modern Methods for Business Research. LC 97-31706. (Methodology for Business & Management Ser.). 350p. 1998. write for info. (*0-8058-2677-7*); pap. 49.95 (*0-8058-3093-6*) L Erlbaum Assocs.

Marcoulides, George A. & Hershberger, Scott L. Multivariate Statistical Methods: A First Course. LC 96-46287. 344p. (C). 1997. text 89.95 (*0-8058-2571-1*); pap. text 39.95 (*0-8058-2572-X*) L Erlbaum Assocs.

Marcoulides, George A. & Schumacker, Randall E., eds. Advanced Structural Equation Modeling: Issues & Techniques. 376p. 1996. text 79.95 (*0-8058-1819-7*) L Erlbaum Assocs.

Marcoulides, George A., jt. ed. see Schumacker, Randall E.

***Marcoux, Alex.** Facades. LC 00-41946. 2000. write for info. (*1-56023-205-6*) Haworth Pr.

Marcoux, J. Paul. Guilbert de Pixerecourt: French Melodrama in the Early Nineteenth Century. LC 92-7271. (Studies in French Theatre: Vol. 1). 154p. 1992. 43.95 (*0-8204-1905-2*) P Lang Pubng.

Marcoux, J. Paul, tr. see Feydeau, Georges.

Marcoux, Linda. Nutrition Power Talks: Over 1,000 Nutrition Ideas for Health Professionals. (Illus.). 157p. (Orig.). Date not set. pap. write for info. (*0-9633536-0-8*) Hlth TREND.

Marcoux, Marcene. Cursillo: Anatomy of a Movement. LC 81-20704. 290p. 1995. 50.00 (*0-931186-00-5*) Lambeth Pr.

Marcoux, Phil. ISO 9000 Compatible Electronic Assembly Workmanship Guidelines. 102p. (C). 1993. student ed. 295.00 (*1-884817-01-7*) PPM Assocs.

— Printed Circuit Assembly Design Guidelines. 258p. (C). 1992. student ed. 395.00 (*1-884817-00-9*) PPM Assocs.

— Printed Circuit Assembly Inspection, Rework, & Repair Techniques. 115p. (C). 1993. student ed. 65.00 (*1-884817-02-5*) PPM Assocs.

Marcoux, Tom. You're the Hero Starring Characters from Boatdreams, the Motion Picture. (Illus.). 164p. (Orig.). 1989. pap. 4.95 (*0-685-29064-6*) Marcoux Media.

Marcove, Ralph C. & Arlen. Atlas of Bone Pathology: With Clinical & Radiographic Correlations. (Illus.). 688p. 1992. text 164.00 (*0-397-51077-2*) Lppncott W & W.

Marcove, Ralph C., jt. auth. see Arlen, Myron.

Marcovich, ed. Diogenis Laertii. (GRE.). 1998. 62.50 (*3-8154-1316-8*, T1316, Pub. by B G Teubner) U of Mich Pr.

— Prodromi, Theodori. 9th ed. (GRE.). 1992. 92.50 (*3-8154-1703-1*, T1703, Pub. by B G Teubner) U of Mich Pr.

Marcovich, M., ed. see Diogenes, Laertius.

Marcovich, Miroslav. Prosper of Aquitaine - De Providentia Dei: Text, Translation & Commentary. LC 89-36313. (Supplements to Vigiliae Christianae Ser.: No. X). xii, 137p. 1989. text 54.00 (*90-04-09090-8*) Brill Academic Pubs.

Marcovich, Miroslav, ed. Athenagoras: Legatio Pro Christianis. (Patristische Texte Und Studien: Vol. 31). xii, 158p. (C). 1990. lib. bdg. 90.80 (*3-11-011881-5*) De Gruyter.

— Hoppolytus Refutatio Omnium Haeresium. (Patristische Texte Und Studien: Vol. 25). xvi, 541p. 1986. lib. bdg. 242.35 (*3-11-008751-0*) De Gruyter.

— Iustini Martyris Apologiae Pro Christianis. (Patristische Texte und Studien: Bd. 38). (GRE.). 223p. (C). 1994. lib. bdg. 90.80 (*3-11-014180-9*) De Gruyter.

— Pseudo-Iustinus: Cohortatio ad Graecos - De Monarchia - Oratio ad Graecos. (Patristische Texte Und Studien: Vol. 32). x, 161p. (C). 1990. lib. bdg. 90.80 (*3-11-012135-2*) De Gruyter.

— Tatiani Oratio ad Graecos/Theophili Antiocheni ad Autolycum. (Patristische Texte und Studien: Vols. 43-44). (GRE.). (C). 1995. lib. bdg. 160.00 (*3-11-014406-9*) De Gruyter.

Marcovich, Miroslav, ed. see Justin, et al.

Marcovitz, Hal. Coronado to Escalate: Francisco Coronado & the Exploration of the American Southwest. LC 99-35228. (Explorers of the New World Ser.). (Illus.). 64p. 1999. 16.95 (*0-7910-5515-9*) Chelsea Hse.

— Marco Polo & the Wonders of the East. LC 99-22255. (Explorers of the New World Ser.). (Illus.). 64p. 1999. 16.95 (*0-7910-5511-6*) Chelsea Hse.

***Marcovitz, Hal.** Reaching for the Moon: The Apollo Astronauts. (Explorers of the New Worlds Ser.). 2000. 17.95 (*0-7910-5957-X*) Chelsea Hse.

— Reaching for the Moon: The Apollo Astronauts. (Explorers of the New Worlds Ser.). (Illus.). 2000. pap. 8.95 (*0-7910-6167-1*) Chelsea Hse.

— Robin Williams. LC 00-25813. (Overcoming Adversity Ser.). (Illus.). 128p. (J). 2000. pap. text 9.95 (*0-7910-5309-1*) Chelsea Hse.

— Sacagawea: Guide for the Lewis & Clark Expedition. (Explorers of the New Worlds Ser.). 2000. 17.95 (*0-7910-5959-6*) Chelsea Hse.

— Sacagawea: Guide for the Lewis & Clark Expedition. (Explorers of the New Worlds Ser.). (Illus.). 2000. pap. 8.95 (*0-7910-6169-8*) Chelsea Hse.

Marcoy, Paul. Travels in South America, 2 vols. rev. ed. Incl. Vol. 1. Travels in South America. rev. ed. (Illus.). 536p. 1996. reprint ed. (*1-887954-12-0*); Vol. 2. Travels in South America. rev. ed. (Illus.). 504p. 1996. reprint ed. (*1-887954-13-9*); reprint ed. 24.95 (*1-887954-11-2*) Athena FL.

Marcozzi, Beth A. & Shapiro, Lawrence E. My Best Friend Is Me. (Illus.). 45p. (J). (ps-3). 1995. pap. 10.50 (*1-882732-25-1*) Childswork.

Marcraft, International. A+ Certification Training Guide. LC 98-85227. 1998. 49.99 (*1-56205-896-7*) New Riders Pub.

Marcrander, Meg, jt. auth. see Luetje, Carolyn.

Marcroft, Karen. Fulbert Firefly. LC 85-90463. (Illus.). 48p. (J). (gr. 3-8). 1986. 14.95 (*0-935849-00-9*) Marcroft Prods.

Marcu, E. D. Nationalism in the Sixteenth Century. LC 75-39172. 1975. lib. bdg. 25.00 (*0-913870-08-0*) Abaris Bks.

Marcu, Nichifor. Perle Si Comori. Beattie, Genovieva Sfatcu, ed. (RUM.). 97p. 1995. pap. 5.00 (*1-893179-09-5*) Eastern Europe Aid.

Marcu, Valeriu. Men & Forces of Our Time. LC 68-29231. (Essay Index Reprint Ser.). 1977. reprint ed. 19.95 (*0-8369-0678-0*) Ayer.

Marcucci, Domenico. Rezando el Rosario Con Fray Angelico. Jimenez-Abreu, Dulce M., tr.Tr. of Through the Rosary with Fra Angelico. (SPA., Illus.). 48p. 1991. pap. 2.50 (*0-8189-0620-0*) Alba.

— Through the Rosary with Fra Angelico. Lane, Edmund C., tr. from ITA. (Illus.). 48p. (Orig.). 1989. pap. 2.50 (*0-8189-0557-3*) Alba.

Marcucci, Robert G. & Schoen, Harold L. Beginning Algebra. (C). 1990. 90.36 (*0-395-52954-9*) HM.

Marcucci, Robert G., jt. auth. see Schoen, Harold L.

Marcuccio, Phyllis & Marshall, Sheila, eds. A Strategy for Change. (Illus.). 176p. 1993. pap. text 17.50 (*0-87355-118-4*) Natl Sci Tchrs.

Marcuccio, Phyllis R., ed. Earthquakes: A Teacher's Package for K-6. (Illus.). 200p. (C). 1999. reprint ed. pap. text, teacher ed. 35.00 (*0-7881-8140-8*) DIANE Pub.

Marculescu, Ileana, jt. ed. see Ibish, Yusuf.

Marcum, Betty. The New Cairn Terrier. LC 95-13520. (Illus.). 256p. 1995. per. 25.95 (*0-87605-073-9*) Howell Bks.

Marcum, David. Exploring American Government. 5th ed. 1998. pap. text. write for info. (*0-393-95874-4*) Norton.

Marcum, Deanna B. Good Books in a Country Home: The Public Library as Cultural Force in Hagerstown, Maryland, 79. LC 93-14463. 208p. 1994. 57.95 (*0-313-28626-4*, Greenwood Pr) Greenwood.

— Preservation Education Institute Final Report. 13p. 1990. pap. 10.00 (*1-887334-02-5*) Coun Lib & Info.

Marcum, John A. Angolan Revolution: The Anatomy of an Explosion, 1950-1962, Vol. 1. (Studies in Communism, Revisionism & Revolution). 1969. 49.50 (*0-262-13048-3*) MIT Pr.

Marcum, Richard & Myers, Reyburn W. Message of the Locust. 200p. 1988. 17.95 (*0-940375-06-0*) WindRiver Pub.

Marcum, Robert. Death of a Tsar. LC 94-22709. 383p. 1994. 15.95 (*0-87579-914-0*) Deseret Bk.

— The Orlov Legacy. LC 96-873. 386p. (Orig.). 1996. pap. 13.95 (*1-57345-146-0*) Deseret Bk.

***Marcum, Robert.** White Out. LC 00-20933. 2000. write for info. (*1-57345-652-7*) Deseret Bk.

Marcum, Walt. Go for It: 25 Faith-Building Adventures for Youth Groups. 96p. 1998. pap. 15.95 (*0-687-08728-7*) Abingdon.

— Living in the Light: Leading Youth to Deeper Spirituality. LC 94-12860. (Essentials for Christian Youth Ser.). 112p. (Orig.). 1994. pap. 13.95 (*0-687-39235-7*) Abingdon.

— Sharing Groups in Youth Ministry. 1991. pap. 13.95 (*0-687-38344-7*) Abingdon.

Marcus. America Firsthand, Vol. 1 & 2. 4th ed. 1998. pap. text 40.50 (*0-312-20187-7*) St Martin.

— Auto-Biographical Discourses: Criticism, Theory, Practice. 322p. 1999. pap. 24.95 (*0-7190-5530-X*, Pub. by Manchester Univ Pr) St Martin.

— Celestial Raise. 230p. 1987. 24.95 (*0-9618316-0-X*) ASSK Pub.

— Celestial Raise. (Illus.). 230p. 1987. pap. 21.95 (*0-941131-01-7*) ASSK Pub.

— Corporate Futures. LC 98-173255. 312p. 1998. lib. bdg. 60.00 (*0-226-50453-0*) U Ch Pr.

— Essentials of Psychiatry. LC 97-42379. (C). 1998. pap. text 32.00 (*0-7216-6721-X*, W B Saunders Co) Harcrt Hlth Sci Grp.

— Experimental General Chemistry. 1988. text, teacher ed. 24.37 (*0-07-054434-4*) McGraw.

— Gilbert Civil Procedure. 15th ed. 1994. pap. text 19.95 (*0-15-900272-9*) Harcourt Legal.

— Gilbert Civil Procedure. 15th ed. (C). 1997. pap. text, suppl. ed. 22.95 (*0-15-900379-2*) Harcourt Legal.

— Gilbert Criminal Procedure. 14th ed. 1995. pap. text 18.95 (*0-15-900347-4*) Harcourt Legal.

— Gilbert Criminal Procedure: With Supplement. 14th ed. 1997. pap. text, suppl. ed. 18.95 (*0-15-900376-8*) Harcourt Legal.

— Leerboek Ansi SQL. (C). 1993. pap. text. write for info. (*0-201-54516-0*) Addison-Wesley.

— Louis Brandeis. 1997. 26.95 (*0-8057-7765-2*, Twyne) Mac Lib Ref.

— Paranoia Within Reason. LC 99-188756. 1999. pap. text 25.00 (*0-226-50458-1*); lib. bdg. 75.00 (*0-226-50457-3*) U Ch Pr.

— Technology in America. 2nd ed. LC 98-75283. (C). 1998. pap. text 34.50 (*0-15-505531-3*, Pub. by Harcourt Coll Pubs) Harcourt.

An Asterisk (*) at the beginning of an entry indicates that the title is appearing for the first time.

Marcus & Burner, David. America Firsthand. pap. text. write for info. (*0-312-24598-X*) St Martin.
— America Firsthand, Vols. 2. 5th ed. pap. text. write for info. (*0-312-24597-1*) St Martin.
— America Firsthand. 5th ed. 1995. pap. write for info. (*0-312-24596-3*) St Martin.
Marcus & Marinsky, Jacob A. Ion Exchange & Solvent Extraction, Vol. 7. (Illus.). 312p. 1977. text 215.00 (*0-8247-6571-0*) Dekker.
— Ion Exchange & Solvent Extraction, Vol. 8. (Illus.). 448p. 1981. text 215.00 (*0-8247-1333-8*) Dekker.
Marcus & Plimpton. Guide to Japanese Food & Restaurants. 1996. pap. 26.95 (*4-07-974015-8*) Shufu No.
Marcus, Aaron R. Graphic Design for Electronic Documents & User Interfaces. (ACM Press Tutorial Ser.). (Illus.). 288p. (C). 1991. pap. text 39.95 (*0-201-54364-8*) Addison-Wesley.
***Marcus, Aaron R.** How to Become a Successful Commercial Model: The Complete Commercial Modeling Handbook. (Illus.). 96p. 2000. mass mkt. 39.95 (*0-9653585-1-8*) Marcus Inst.
Marcus, Aaron R. How to Become a Successful Commercial Model: The Complete Commercial Modeling Manual. (Illus.). v, 92p. 1996. ring bd. 59.95 (*0-9653585-0-X*) Marcus Inst.
— Multimedia Interface Design Studio. 1995. pap. 40.00 (*0-679-75999-9*) Random.
Marcus, Aaron R. & Baecker, Ronald M. Human Factors & Typography for More Readable Programs. (Illus.). 350p. (C). 1989. pap. text. write for info. (*0-318-64907-1*) Addison-Wesley.
Marcus, Aaron R., et al. The Computer Image: Applications of Computer Graphics. 1982. 27.95 (*0-201-06192-9*) Addison-Wesley.
Marcus, Abraham. Introduction to Applied Physics. 2nd ed. (Physics Ser.). (C). 1985. mass mkt. 68.00 (*0-8273-3899-6*) Delmar.
— The Middle East on the Eve of Modernity: Aleppo in the Eighteenth-Century. (Study of the Middle East Institute Ser.). 418p. (C). 1992. pap. 20.00 (*0-231-06595-7*) Col U Pr.
— The Middle East on the Eve of Modernity: Culture & Society in Eighteenth-Century Aleppo. (Study of the Middle East Institute Ser.). (Illus.). 1989. text 57.50 (*0-231-06594-9*) Col U Pr.
Marcus, Abraham & Lenk, John D. Computers for Technicians. (Illus.). 400p. 1973. text 40.00 (*0-13-166181-7*) P-H.
Marcus, Abraham & Marcus, W. Basic Electricity. 4th ed. 1973. 34.48 (*0-13-060152-7*) P-H.
Marcus, Abraham & Thomson, Charles M. Electricity for Technicians. 3rd ed. (Illus.). 512p. (C). 1982. text 52.00 (*0-13-248666-0*) P-H.
Marcus, Abraham, jt. auth. see Gritter, W. V.
Marcus, Adrianne. Divided Weather. 64p. (Orig.). 1985. 25.00 (*0-931757-24-X*); pap. 15.00 (*0-931757-25-8*) Pterodactyl Pr.
Marcus, Alan I. Agricultural Science & the Quest for Legitimacy: Farmers, Agricultural Colleges, & Experiment Stations, 1870-1890. LC 85-11761. (Henry A. Wallace Series on Agricultural History & Rural Studies). 279p. 1985. reprint ed. pap. 86.50 (*0-608-00145-7*, 206092600006) Bks Demand.
— Building Western Civilization: From the Advert of Writing to the Age of Steam. LC 96-79890. 400p. (C). 1997. pap. text 47.50 (*0-15-500115-9*, Pub. by Harcourt Coll Pubs) Harcourt.
— Cancer from Beef: The DES Controversy, Federal Food Regulation, & Consumer Confidence in Modern America. LC 93-21505. 1994. text 40.00 (*0-8018-4700-1*) Johns Hopkins.
— Plague of Strangers: Social Groups & the Origins of City Services in Cincinnati, 1819-1870. LC 91-16750. (Urban Life & Urban Landscape Ser.). 311p. reprint ed. pap. 96.50 (*0-608-09854-X*, 206981900006) Bks Demand.
— Technology in America: A Brief History. 1990. pap. 14.95 (*0-15-688255-8*) Harcourt.
Marcus, Alan I. & Cravens, Hamilton, eds. Health Care Policy in Contemporary America. LC 97-13457. (Issues in Policy History Ser.). 156p. 1997. pap. 15.95 (*0-271-01740-6*) Pa St U Pr.
Marcus, Alan I. & Segal, Howard P. Technology in America: A Brief History. 380p. (C). 1989. pap. text 34.00 (*0-15-589762-4*) Harcourt Coll Pubs.
Marcus, Alan R. Relocating Eden: The Image & Politics of Inuit Exile in the Canadian Arctic. LC 95-3420. (Arctic Visions Ser.). (Illus.). 290p. 1995. pap. 22.95 (*0-87451-659-5*) U Pr of New Eng.
Marcus, Alfred A. The Adversary Economy: Business Responses to Changing Government Requirements. LC 83-17674. (Illus.). 255p. 1984. 67.95 (*0-89930-055-3*, MAV/, Quorum Bks) Greenwood.
— Business & Society: Strategy, Ethics, & the Global Economy. 2nd ed. 768p. (C). 1995. text 67.50 (*0-256-16202-6*, Irwn McGrw-H) McGrw-H Hghr Educ.
— Controversial Issues in Energy Policy. (Controversial Issues In Public Policy Ser.: Vol. 2). (Illus.). 200p. (C). 1992. 42.00 (*0-8039-3969-8*) Sage.
— Promise & Performance: Choosing & Implementing an Environmental Policy, 39. LC 79-8290. (Contributions in Political Science Ser.: No. 39). 204p. 1980. 57.95 (*0-313-20707-0*, MPT/, Greenwood Pr) Greenwood.
Marcus, Alfred A., et al, eds. Business Strategy & Public Policy: Perspectives from Industry & Academia. LC 86-30388. 332p. 1987. 79.50 (*0-89930-172-X*, MBS/, Quorum Bks) Greenwood.
Marcus, Alon. Acute Abdominal Syndromes: Their Diagnosis & Treatment According to Combined Chinese-Western Medicine. LC 91-77707. 161p. (Orig.). 1991. pap. text 18.95 (*0-936185-31-7*) Blue Poppy Pr.
***Marcus, Alon.** Musculoskeletal Disorders: Healing Methods from Chinese Medicine & Orthopaedic Medicine. LC 98-34889. 650p. 1999. 85.00 (*1-55643-282-8*) North Atlantic.
Marcus, Amy Dockser. The View from Nebo: How Archeology Is Rewriting the Bible & Reshaping the Middle East. LC 99-87911. 304p. 2000. 25.95 (*0-316-56167-3*) Little.
***Marcus, Andrei.** Representation Theory of Group Graded Algebras. LC 99-52044. 1999. write for info. (*1-56072-750-0*) Nova Sci Pubs.
Marcus, Andy. Wedding Photojournalism: Techniques & Images in Black & White. 128p. 1999. pap. 29.95 (*1-58428-011-5*, Pub. by Amherst Media) IPG Chicago.
Marcus, Anne. Boyzone All Talk. 1999. pap. text 9.95 (*0-7119-6650-8*) Music Sales.
Marcus, Anthony, ed. Anthropology for a Small Planet: Culture & Community in a Global Environment. 200p. (C). 1996. pap. text 14.90 (*1-881089-86-X*) Brandywine Press.
Marcus, Anthony, jt. ed. see Burner, David.
Marcus, Anthony, jt. ed. see Marcus, Robert D.
Marcus, Arlene. Writing Inspirations: A Fundex of Individualized Activities for English Language Practice. Clark, Raymond C., ed. (Illus.). 96p. (Orig.). 1995. pap. text 20.00 (*0-86647-092-1*) Pro Lingua.
Marcus, Audrey F. & Zwerin, Raymond A., eds. The New Jewish Teachers Handbook. LC 94-70560. 480p. (Orig.). 1994. pap. text, teacher ed. 45.00 (*0-86705-033-0*) A R E Pub.
Marcus, Audrey Friedman & Zwerin, Raymond A. Like a Maccabee. (Illus.). (J). (gr. k-3). 1991. 11.95 (*0-8074-0445-4*, 102564) UAHC.
— Shabbat Can Be. (Illus.). (J). (gr. k-3). 1979. 10.95 (*0-8074-0023-8*, 102560) UAHC.
Marcus, B., jt. auth. see Adler, R. L.
Marcus, Ben. The Age of Wire & String. LC 98-23361. 160p. 1998. reprint ed. pap. 11.95 (*1-56478-196-8*) Dalkey Arch.
Marcus, Bernard A. Human Nutrition Quick Review. LC 97-153187. (Cliffs Quick Reviews Ser.). (Illus.). 101p. (Orig.). (C). 1997. pap. text, student ed. 9.95 (*0-8220-5330-6*, Cliff) IDG Bks.
— Laboratory Exercises in Nutrition. 2nd ed. Petersen, Charlotte & Ferruzzi, Donald R., eds. (Illus.). 34p. (Orig.). (C). 1998. pap. text, lab manual ed. 14.95 (*0-9609098-9-3*) Biomat Pub Co.
Marcus, Beth, ed. Paws & Tales, Vol. 1. (Illus.). 163p. (Orig.). 1998. pap. 12.95 (*0-9667491-9-7*) GDI Pub.
Marcus, Brian, jt. auth. see Lind, Douglas.
Marcus, Bruce. Muck Arbour. Ashbery, John, ed. LC 74-5984. 64p. 1975. 7.95 (*0-87955-500-9*) O'Hara.
Marcus, Bruce W. Competing in the New Capital Markets. 1991. 42.50 (*0-88730-409-5*, HarpBusn) HarpInfo.
Marcus, Bruce W. & Wallace, Sherwood. New Dimensions in Investor Relations: Competing for Capital in the 21st Century. LC 97-3288. 432p. 1997. 69.95 (*0-471-14153-4*) Wiley.
Marcus, Caleb C. The Consistency of Breath. LC 99-171624. 84p. 1999. pap. 7.00 (*0-945298-06-4*) BioMed Intl.
Marcus, Carol E. & Swisher, John D., eds. Working with Youth in High-Risk Environments: Experiences in Prevention. (Illus.). 210p. (Orig.). (C). 1996. reprint ed. pap. text 30.00 (*0-7881-2972-4*) DIANE Pub.
Marcus, Clare C. House As a Mirror of Self: Exploring the Deeper Meaning of Home. (Illus.). 352p. 1995. 24.95 (*0-943233-92-5*) Conari Press.
— House As a Mirror of Self: Exploring the Deeper Meaning of Home. LC 98-149761. (Illus.). 352p. 1997. reprint ed. pap. 16.95 (*1-57324-076-1*) Conari Press.
Marcus, Clare C. & Barnes, Marni. Gardens in Healthcare Facilities: Uses, Therapeutic Benefits & Design Recommendations. (Illus.). 70p. (C). 1995. pap. 27.00 (*0-9638938-2-3*) Ctr for Hlth.
Marcus, Clare C. & Barnes, Marni, eds. Healing Gardens: Therapeutic Benefits & Design Recommendations. LC 98-42154. 624p. 1999. 79.95 (*0-471-19203-1*) Wiley.
Marcus, Clare C. & Francis, Carolyn, eds. People Places: Design Guidelines for Urban Open Space. 2nd ed. 384p. 1997. pap. 49.95 (*0-471-28833-0*, VNR) Wiley.
Marcus, Claudio, jt. auth. see Newberg, Jay.
Marcus, D., jt. auth. see Uliana, E.
***Marcus, Daniel.** The Theory & Practice of Discourse Parsing & Summarization. LC 00-38690. (Illus.). 272p. (C). 2000. 35.00 (*0-262-13372-5*) MIT Pr.
Marcus, Daniel, ed. see Paper Tiger Television Collective Staff.
Marcus, Daniel A. Differential Equations: An Introduction. 656p. (C). 1991. text 56.25 (*0-697-05957-X*, WCB McGr Hill) McGrw-H Hghr Educ.
— Differential Equations: An Introduction. 656p. (C). 1991. text 21.25 (*0-697-11681-6*, WCB McGr Hill) McGrw-H Hghr Educ.
— Number Fields, Vol. VIII. rev. ed. LC 77-21467. 279p. (C). 1997. 39.00 (*0-387-90279-1*) Spr-Verlag.
Marcus, Daniel M. Combinatorics: A Problem Oriented Approach. LC 98-85594. (Classroom Resource Materials Ser.). 156p. 1998. pap. text 28.00 (*0-88385-710-3*) Math Assn.
Marcus, Danny, ed. see Grayson, Stan.
Marcus, David. Jephthah & His Vow. 80p. 1986. 25.00 (*0-89672-136-1*); pap. 15.00 (*0-89672-135-3*) Tex Tech Univ Pr.
— A Manual of Akkadian. LC 78-63068. 1978. pap. text 19.50 (*0-8191-0608-9*) U Pr of Amer.
— A Manual of Babylonian Jewish Aramaic. LC 80-6073. 104p. (Orig.). (C). 1981. pap. text 16.00 (*0-8191-1363-8*) U Pr of Amer.
— The Poolbeg Book of Irish Ghost Stories LC 91-114282. 302 p. 1990. write for info. (*1-85371-112-8*) Poolbeg Pr.
— State Of The Art: Short Stories By The New Irish Writers LC 94-226037. 377p. 1992. write for info. (*0-340-57400-3*) Arnld Pub.
Marcus, David, ed. New Irish Writing. 3.95 (*0-7043-3101-2*, Pub. by Quartet) Charles River Bks.
Marcus, Dora, jt. auth. see Dressel, Paul L.
Marcus, Edward, ed. A New Canaan Private in the Civil War: Letters of Justus M. Silliman, Seventeenth Connecticut Volunteers. (Illus.). 117p. 1984. 7.50 (*0-939958-01-5*) New Canaan.
Marcus, Edward & Marcus, Mildred R. Investment & Development Possibilities in Tropical Africa. Wilkins, Mira, ed. LC 76-29767. (European Business Ser.). 1977. reprint ed. lib. bdg. 25.95 (*0-405-09781-6*) Ayer.
Marcus, Edward, jt. auth. see Marcus, Gerald.
Marcus, Edward, jt. ed. see Schmukler, Nathan.
Marcus, Elliott, et al. An Introduction to the Neurosciences. 2nd ed. LC 93-43196. (Illus.). 750p. 1996. text, student ed. 69.50 (*0-683-05542-9*) Lppncott W & W.
Marcus, Eric. Is It a Choice? Answers to 300 of the Most Frequently Asked Questions about Gays & Lesbians. LC 92-56425. 240p. 1993. pap. 13.00 (*0-06-250664-1*, Pub. by Harper SF) HarpC.
— Is It a Choice - Revised edition: Answers to 300 of the Most Frequently Asked Questions About Gays & Lesbian People. 2nd ed. LC HQ76.3.U5M35 1999. 240p. 1999. pap. 13.00 (*0-06-251623-X*, Pub. by Harper SF) HarpC.
***Marcus, Eric.** Male Couple's Guide: Finding a Man, Making a Home, Building a Life. 3rd ed. LC 98-44944. 320p. 1999. pap. 17.00 (*0-06-095275-X*) HarpC.
Marcus, Eric. Together Forever. LC 98-9743. 368p. 1998. 23.95 (*0-385-48875-0*, Anchor NY) Doubleday.
— Together Forever: Gay & Lesbian Couples Share Their Secrets for Lasting Happiness. (Illus.). 368p. 1999. pap. 14.95 (*0-385-48876-9*) Bantam.
***Marcus, Eric.** What If Someone I Know Is Gay. (Illus.). 128p. (gr. 8-12). 2000. pap. 4.99 (*0-8431-7611-3*, Price Stern) Peng Put Young Read.
— What If Someone I Know Is Gay? 13.89 (*0-8431-7612-1*, Price Stern) Peng Put Young Read.
Marcus, Eric. Why Suicide: Answers to 200 of the Most Frequently Asked Questions about Suicide, Attempted S. LC 95-33431. 256p. 1996. pap. 14.00 (*0-06-251166-1*, Pub. by Harper SF) HarpC.
Marcus, Eric, jt. auth. see Louganis, Greg.
Marcus, Eric R. Psychosis & Near Psychosis: Ego Function, Symbol Structure & Treatment. xviii, 308p. 2000. pap. 29.95 (*0-8236-8264-1*) Intl Univs Pr.
— Psychosis & Near Psychosis: Ego Function, Symbol Structure & Treatment. 328p. 1993. 100.00 (*0-387-97765-1*) Spr-Verlag.
Marcus, Erik. Vegan: The New Ethics of Eating. LC 97-10398. (Illus.). 224p. 1997. pap. 14.95 (*0-935526-35-8*) McBooks Pr.
***Marcus, Erik.** Vegan: The New Ethics of Eating. rev. ed. 228p. 2000. pap. 16.95 (*0-935526-87-0*) McBooks Pr.
***Marcus, Evan & Stern, Hal.** Blueprints for High Availability: Designing Resilient Distributed Systems. LC 99-53030. 344p. 2000. 49.99 (*0-471-35601-8*) Wiley.
Marcus, Francis. People Places: Design Guidelines for Urban Open Space. 2nd ed. LC 97-1233. (Landscape Architecture Ser.). 384p. 1997. pap. 39.95 (*0-442-02546-7*, VNR) Wiley.
Marcus, Fred J., ed. see Hoffman, Marc D. & Hoffman, Leland E.
Marcus, G. J. The Conquest of the North Atlantic. LC 98-150102. (Illus.). 240p. 1998. pap. 24.95 (*0-85115-158-2*, Boydell Pr) Boydell & Brewer.
***Marcus, Gary F.** The Algebraic Mind: Integrating Connectionism & Cognitive Science. (Learning, Development & Conceptual Change Ser.). (Illus.). 225p. (C). 2000. pap. 27.95 (*0-262-13379-2*, Bradford Bks) MIT Pr.
Marcus, Gary F., et al. Overregularization in Language Acquisition. 188p. 1992. pap. text 15.00 (*0-226-50456-5*) U Ch Pr.
Marcus, Geoffrey. The Maiden Voyage. (Illus.). 340p. 1991. reprint ed. lib. bdg. 45.95 (*0-89966-792-9*) Buccaneer Bks.
Marcus, George, et al. Functionalist Design: An Ongoing History. (Illus.). 168p. (Orig.). 1997. pap. 29.95 (*3-7913-1423-8*, Pub. by Prestel) te Neues.
Marcus, George, jt. auth. see Hiesinger, Kathryn.
***Marcus, George E.** Affective Intelligence. 2000. lib. bdg. 42.00 (*0-226-50468-9*) U Ch Pr.
— Anthropology as Cultural Critique: An Experimental Moment in the Human Sciences. 2nd ed. LC 99-12369. 1999. pap. 13.00 (*0-226-50450-6*) U Ch Pr.
Marcus, George E. Connected: Engagements with Media at Century's End. LC 96-162827. (Late Editions Ser.: Vol. 3). (Illus.). 464p. (C). 1996. pap. text 22.50 (*0-226-50442-5*) U Ch Pr.
— Corporate Futures. LC 98-173255. 312p. 1998. pap. text 22.00 (*0-226-50454-9*) U Ch Pr.
***Marcus, George E.** Ethnography Through Thick & Thin. LC 98-21287. (Illus.). 253p. 1999. text 49.50 (*0-691-00252-5*, Pub. by Princeton U Pr); pap. text 14.95 (*0-691-00253-3*, Pub. by Princeton U Pr) Cal Prin Full Svc.
— Zeroing in on the Year 2000: The Final Edition. LC 99-86012. (Late Editions Ser.). 1999. pap. text 22.00 (*0-226-50467-0*) U Ch Pr.
— Zeroing in on Year Two Thousand. 1999. lib. bdg. 50.00 (*0-226-50466-2*) U Ch Pr.
Marcus, George E., ed. Connected: Engagements with Media at Century's End. LC 96-162827. (Late Editions Ser.: Vol. 3). (Illus.). 464p. 1996. lib. bdg. 65.00 (*0-226-50441-7*) U Ch Pr.
— Critical Anthropology Now: Unexpected Contexts, Shifting Constituencies, Changing Agendas. LC 98-41001. (Advanced Seminar Ser.). 370p. 1999. 60.00 (*0-933452-50-0*); pap. 24.95 (*0-933452-51-9*) Schol Am Res.
— Cultural Procedures in Perilous States: Editing Events, Documenting Change. LC 97-118125. (Illus.). 408p. 1996. pap. text 23.50 (*0-226-50440-9*) U Ch Pr.
— Cultural Producers in Perilous States: Editing Events, Documenting Change. LC 97-118125. (Illus.). 408p. 1996. lib. bdg. 65.00 (*0-226-50439-5*) U Ch Pr.
— Perilous States: Conversations on Culture, Politics, & Nation. (Late Editions: Cultural Studies for the End of the Century). (Illus.). 400p. 1993. pap. 20.95 (*0-226-50447-6*) U Ch Pr.
— Perilous States: Conversations on Culture, Politics, & Nation. (Late Editions: Cultural Studies for the End of the Century). (Illus.). 360p. 1995. lib. bdg. 60.50 (*0-226-50446-8*) U Ch Pr.
— Rereading Cultural Anthropology. LC 92-21908. 416p. 1992. text 54.95 (*0-8223-1279-4*); pap. text 17.95 (*0-8223-1297-2*) Duke.
— Technoscientific Imaginaries: Conversations, Profiles, & Memoirs. 570p. 1995. pap. text 22.50 (*0-226-50444-1*); lib. bdg. 65.00 (*0-226-50443-3*) U Ch Pr.
Marcus, George E. & Fischer, Michael M. Anthropology as Cultural Critique: An Experimental Moment in the Human Sciences. LC 85-20686. xiv, 224p. 1986. pap. 11.95 (*0-226-50449-2*); lib. bdg. 22.00 (*0-226-50448-4*) U Ch Pr.

M

Marcus, George E. & Hanson, Russell L., eds. Reconsidering the Democratic Public. LC 92-33653. 464p. 1993. 55.00 (*0-271-00917-9*); pap. 17.95 (*0-271-00927-6*) Pa St U Pr.
Marcus, George E. & Myers, Fred R., eds. The Traffic in Culture: Refiguring Anthropology & Art. LC 94-39487. 1995. 55.00 (*0-520-08846-8*, Pub. by U CA Pr); pap. 19.95 (*0-520-08847-6*, Pub. by U CA Pr) Cal Prin Full Svc.
***Marcus, George E., et al.** Affective Intelligence & Political Judgment. LC 00-8392. 2000. pap. text 15.00 (*0-226-50469-7*) U Ch Pr.
Marcus, George E., et al. With Malice Toward Some: How People Make Civil Liberties Judgments. (Studies in Political Psychology & Public Opinion). (Illus.). 304p. (C). 1995. pap. text 21.95 (*0-521-43997-3*) Cambridge U Pr.
— With Malice Toward Some: How People Make Civil Liberties Judgments. (Cambridge Studies in Political Psychology & Public Opinion). (Illus.). 304p. (C). 1995. text 59.95 (*0-521-43396-7*) Cambridge U Pr.
Marcus, George E., jt. ed. see Clifford, James.
***Marcus, George H.** Le Corbusier: Inside the Machine for Living. (Illus.). 224p. 2000. 50.00 (*1-58093-076-X*, Pub. by Monacelli Pr) Penguin Putnam.
Marcus, George H. Design in the Fifties: When Everyone Went Modern. LC 98-2743. (Illus.). 168p. 1998. pap. 24.95 (*3-7913-1939-6*) te Neues.
Marcus, George H., jt. auth. see Hiesinger, Kathryn B.
Marcus, George H., ed. see Rothschild, Nannette F., et al.
Marcus, Gerald & Marcus, Edward. Optimizing Ocean Current Crossings. 16p. 1993. pap. text 15.00 (*1-882502-18-3*) US Sail Assn.
Marcus, Grania B. Discovering the African-American Experience in Suffolk County, 1620-1860. Date not set. lib. bdg. 14.95 (*0-8488-1720-6*) Amereon Ltd.
Marcus, Gregory, et al. Credit Survival Guide Instructor's Manual. Johnson, Robert W., ed. 162p. (Orig.). 1995. pap., teacher ed. 14.95 (*0-9635779-8-0*) Am Bureau Info.
Marcus, Greil. Dead Elvis: A Chronicle of a Cultural Obsession. 1999. pap. text 17.95 (*0-674-19422-5*) HUP.
***Marcus, Greil.** Double Trouble: Bill Clinton & Elvis Presley in the Land of No Alternatives. LC 00-27814. (Illus.). 272p. 2000. 25.00 (*0-8050-6513-X*) H Holt & Co.
— Double Trouble: Listening to Elvis in the Clinton Years. 2001. pap. write for info. (*0-8050-6514-8*) St Martin.
Marcus, Greil. The Dustbin of History. LC 95-8876. (Illus.). 240p. (C). 1995. 22.95 (*0-674-21857-4*) HUP.
— Dustbin of History. (Illus.). 240p. 1997. pap. text 14.95 (*0-674-21858-2*) HUP.
— In the Fascist Bathroom: Punk in Pop Music, 1977-1992. LC 98-43708. 1999. 15.95 (*0-674-44577-5*) HUP.
— Invisible Republic: Bob Dylan's Basement Tapes. LC 96-50893. 286p. 1995. 22.50 (*0-8050-3393-9*) H Holt & Co.
— Invisible Republic: Bob Dylan's Basement Tapes. 304p. 1998. pap. 13.95 (*0-8050-5842-7*, Owl) H Holt & Co.
— Lipstick Traces: A Secret History of the Twentieth Century. LC 88-24678. (Illus.). 512p. 1989. 37.00 (*0-674-53580-4*) HUP.
— Lipstick Traces: A Secret History of the Twentieth Century. (Illus.). 512p. 1990. pap. text 19.50 (*0-674-53581-2*) HUP.
— Mystery Train. 4th ed. LC 96-53338. 288p. 1997. reprint ed. pap. 15.95 (*0-452-27836-8*, Plume) Dutton Plume.
Marcus, Greil, ed. Stranded: Rock & Roll for a Desert Island. rev. ed. 320p. 1996. pap. 14.95 (*0-306-80682-7*) Da Capo.
Marcus, Greil, et al. Mekons United. (Illus.). 200p. 1996. pap. 47.98 (*0-9649621-1-X*, QS36) Qrterstick Records.
Marcus, Greil, ed. see Bangs, Lester.
Marcus, Hal. The Animal Alphabet Album: By Aunt Alice Alligator. Limbird, Randy, ed. (Aunt Alice Alligator Ser.: Vol. 1). (Illus.). 32p. (Orig.). (J). (gr. k-8). 1996. 16.95 (*0-9652560-0-6*) Paso al Sol.
— The Animal Alphabet Album: By Aunt Alice Alligator. Limbird, Randy, ed. LC 96-85070. (Aunt Alice Alligator Ser.: Vol. 1). (Illus.). 32p. (Orig.). (J). (ps-3). 1996. pap. 10.95 (*0-9652560-1-4*) Paso al Sol.

— The Animal Alphabet Album/Aunt Alice Alligator's Coloring Book. (Illus.). 32p. (J). (ps-8). 1996. pap. 6.95 (0-9652560-2-2) Paso al Sol.

Marcus, Hans, jt. auth. see Beaumont, Ben.

Marcus, Harold G. Haile Sellassie I: The Formative Years, 1892-1936. LC 94-48486. 1995. 49.95 (1-56902-007-8); pap. 16.95 (1-56902-008-6) Red Sea Pr.

— A History of Ethiopia. LC 93-17987. (Illus.). 277p. 1995. pap. 15.95 (0-520-20247-3, Pub. by U CA Pr) Cal Prin Full Svc.

— The Life & Times of Menelik II: Ethiopia 1844-1913. LC 94-48485. 1995. 49.95 (1-56902-009-4); pap. 16.95 (1-56902-010-8) Red Sea Pr.

— The Politics of Empire: Ethiopia, Great Britain & the United States, 1941-1974. LC 94-48479. 1995. 49.95 (1-56902-005-1); pap. 16.95 (1-56902-006-X) Red Sea Pr.

Marcus, Harold G., ed. Ethiopia 94: Papers of the 12th International Conference of Ethiopian Studies Vol. 2: Social Sciences. (New Trends in Ethiopian Studies). 1996. 79.95 (1-56902-014-0); pap. 34.95 (1-56902-015-9) Red Sea Pr.

— Ethiopia 94: Papers of the 12th International Conference of Ethiopian Studies Vol. 1: Humanities & Human Resources. (New Trends in Ethiopian Studies). 1996. 79.95 (1-56902-012-4); pap. 39.95 (1-56902-013-2) Red Sea Pr.

M

Marcus, Hazel Rose, jt. ed. see Kitayama, Shinobu.

Marcus, Henry S. Intermodal Movement of Marine Containers. 15.00 (1-56172-007-0) MIT Sea Grant.

— Marine Transportation Management. LC 86-22188. 323p. 1986. 65.00 (0-86569-158-4, Auburn Hse) Greenwood.

Marcus, Howard. Basketball Basics. 176p. 1991. pap. 12.95 (0-8092-3958-2, 395820, Contemporary Bks) NTC Contemp Pub Co.

Marcus, I. Moshe's Adventures in Brachaland. (YA). 1990. 8.99 (0-89906-990-8) Mesorah Pubns.

Marcus, I. M., et al. An Interdisciplinary Approach to Accident Patterns in Children. (SRCD M Ser.: Vol. 25, No. 2). 1960. pap. 25.00 (0-527-01584-9) Periodicals Srv.

Marcus, Irene W. & Marcus, Paul. Into the Great Forest: A Story for Children Away from Parents for the First Time. LC 91-37636. (Illus.). 32p. (J). (ps-3). 1992. pap. 8.95 (0-945354-40-1) Am Psychol.

— Scary Night Visitors: A Story for Children with Bedtime Fears. LC 90-41919. (Illus.). 32p. (J). (ps-2). 1990. 11.95 (0-945354-26-6) Am Psychol.

Marcus, Irving H. How to Test & Improve Your Wine Judging Ability. 2nd ed. (Illus.). 96p. (C). 1974. pap. 5.00 (0-913840-28-9) Wine Pubns.

Marcus, Irwin M. & Francis, John J., eds. Masturbation: From Infancy to Senescence. LC 73-16855. 634p. 1975. 75.00 (0-8236-3150-8) Intl Univs Pr.

Marcus, Ivan G. Rituals of Childhood: Jewish Acculturation in Medieval Europe. (Illus.). 208p. 1996. pap. 14.00 (0-300-07658-4) Yale U Pr.

Marcus, J. J. Mining Environmental Handbook: Effects of Mining on the Environment & American Environmental Control. 950p. 1997. 168.00 (1-86094-029-3) World Scientific Pub.

Marcus, J. S. The Art of Cartography. 129p. 1997. reprint ed. text 10.00 (0-7881-5048-0) DIANE Pub.

Marcus, Jacob R. The American Jewish Woman: A Documentary History. 1981. 45.00 (0-87068-752-2) Ktav.

— The Colonial American Jew, 1492-1776, Vols. I, II, & III. 1652p. 1994. reprint ed. text 75.00 (0-8143-1403-1) Wayne St U Pr.

— An Index to Articles on American Jewish History. 1971. 25.00 (0-87068-139-7) Ktav.

— The Jew in the Medieval World: A Source Book, 315-1791. LC 71-97295. 504p. 1975. reprint ed. lib. bdg. 35.00 (0-8371-2619-3, MAJM, Greenwood Pr) Greenwood.

***Marcus, Jacob R.** Jew in the Medieval World: A Source Book, 315-1791. rev. ed. 2000. pap. 19.95 (0-8143-2892-X) Wayne St U Pr.

Marcus, Jacob R. The Jew in the Medieval World: A Source Book 315-1791 with an Introduction & Updated Bibliographies by Marc Saperstein. 4th rev. ed. LC 99-28439. 570p. (C). 2000. reprint ed. pap. 19.95 (0-87820-217-X, Pub. by Hebrew Union Coll Pr) Wayne St U Pr.

— This I Believe: Documents of American Jewish Life. LC 90-33814. 304p. 1990. 30.00 (0-87668-782-6) Aronson.

— This I Believe: Documents of American Jewish Life. LC 90-33814. 304p. 1997. pap. 35.00 (1-56821-968-7) Aronson.

— To Count a People: American Jewish Population Data, 1585-1984. LC 89-22458. (Illus.). 274p. (C). 1990. lib. bdg. 52.50 (0-8191-7583-8) U Pr of Amer.

— United States Jewry, 1776-1985 Vol. I: The Sephardic Period. LC 89-5723. (Illus.). 856p. 1989. 49.95 (0-8143-2186-0) Wayne St U Pr.

— United States Jewry, 1776-1985 Vol. II: The Germanic Period, Pt. 1. LC 89-5723. (Illus.). 452p. 1990. text 39.95 (0-8143-2187-9) Wayne St U Pr.

— United States Jewry, 1776-1985 Vol. III: The Germanic Period, Pt. 2. LC 89-5723. (Illus.). 958p. 1993. text 59.95 (0-8143-2188-7) Wayne St U Pr.

— United States Jewry, 1776-1985 Vol. IV: The East European Period, the Emergence of the American Jew, Epilogue. (Illus.). 982p. 1993. 64.95 (0-8143-2189-5) Wayne St U Pr.

Marcus, Jacob R., ed. The American Jewish Woman: 1654-1980. 1981. 19.95 (0-87068-751-4) Ktav.

— The Jew in the American World: A Source Book. LC 95-22271. 664p. 1996. pap. text 24.95 (0-8143-2548-3) Wayne St U Pr.

Marcus, Jacob R. & Daniels, Judith M., eds. The Concise Dictionary of American Jewish Biography. LC 94-20231. 750p. 1994. 200.00 (0-926019-74-0) Carlson Pub.

Marcus, Jacob R. & Peck, Abraham J. The American Rabbinate: A Century of Continuity & Change 1883-1983. 300p. 1985. text 25.00 (0-88125-076-7) Ktav.

Marcus, Jacob R., jt. auth. see Katz, Irving I.

Marcus, James, tr. see Parise, Goffredo.

Marcus, James, tr. see Sciascia, Leonardo.

Marcus, Jamina. Time Will Tell. 384p. (Orig.). 1996. pap. 8.25 (0-9649465-0-5) Humming Wrds.

Marcus, Jane, ed. New Feminist Essays on Virginia Woolf. LC 80-51823. xx, 272p. 1981. text 50.00 (0-8032-3070-2) U of Nebr Pr.

— Virginia Woolf: A Feminist Slant. LC 82-24787. 296p. reprint ed. pap. 91.80 (0-8357-4129-X, 205706400005) Bks Demand.

Marcus, Jane, intro. The Young Rebecca: Writings of Rebecca West, 1911-1917. LC 89-31300. 416p. 1989. pap. 6.95 (0-253-23101-9) Ind U Pr.

Marcus, Jane E. Central America Update: An Update of the 1987 PIER Workshop Report on the Systems & Institutions of Higher Education in Belize, Costa Rica, El Salvador, Guatemala, Honduras, Nicaragua, & Panama: Special Report 1995. LC 95-43818. (PIER World Education Ser.). 1995. 35.00 (0-929851-76-5) Am Assn Coll Registrars.

Marcus, Jay B. The Crime Vaccine: How to End the Crime Epidemic. LC 95-20748. 256p. 1996. 24.95 (0-87511-732-5) Claitors.

— Success from Within: Discovering the Inner State That Creates Personal Fulfillment & Business Success. LC 90-62354. (Illus.). 200p. 1990. pap. 12.00 (0-923569-04-9, G-02) Maharishi U Mgmt Pr.

Marcus, Jerry. Abraham, Isaac, Jacob & Zev. LC 81-70363. 225p. 1982. 13.95 (0-941394-00-X) Brittany Pubns.

— The Last Pope. LC 96-78943. 256p. 1997. 19.95 (0-941394-02-6) Brittany Pubns.

— The Salvation Peddler. LC 87-71614. 235p. 1988. 15.95 (0-941394-01-8) Brittany Pubns.

Marcus, Joel. Mark 1-8: A New Translation with Introduction & Commentary. LC 98-8741. (Anchor Bible Ser.). 592p. 2000. 42.50 (0-385-42349-7) Doubleday.

— The Way of the Lord: Christological Exegesis of Old Testament in the Gospel of Mark. (Studies of the New Testament & Its World Ser.). 248p. 1998. 44.95 (0-567-09637-8, Pub. by T & T Clark) Bks Intl VA.

Marcus, Joel & Soards, Marion L., eds. Apocalyptic & the New Testament: Essays in Honor of J. Louis Martyn. (JSNT Supplement Ser.: No. 24). 351p. 1989. 85.00 (1-85075-175-7, Pub. by Sheffield Acad) CUP Services.

Marcus, John. The Complete Job Interview Handbook. 163p. 7.95 (0-318-41634-4, 216) Am Bartenders.

Marcus, John J. Comp Job Interview H. 3rd ed. LC 93-42353. 208p. 1994. pap. 12.00 (0-06-273266-8, Harper Ref) HarpC.

— The Resume Doctor: How to Transform a Troublesome Work History into a Winning Resume. LC 95-21631. 240p. (Orig.). 1996. pap. 12.95 (0-06-273369-9, Harper Ref) HarpC.

Marcus, John T. Sub Specie Historiae: Essays in the Manifestations of Historical & Moral Consciousness. LC 76-50285. 328p. 1980. 40.00 (0-8386-2057-4) Fairleigh Dickinson.

Marcus, Jon. Boston: A City Life Pictorial Guide. LC 98-6697. (Citylife Pictorial Guide Ser.). (Illus.). 96p. 1998. pap. 16.95 (0-89658-395-3) Voyageur Pr.

— Boston: A City Life Pictorial Guide. LC 98-6697. (Citylife Pictorial Guide Ser.). (Illus.). 96p. 1998. 24.95 (0-89658-362-7) Voyageur Pr.

Marcus, Jonathan. The National Front & French Politics: The Resistible Rise of Jean-Marie Le Pen. LC 95-12259. 212p. (C). 1995. text 50.00 (0-8147-5534-8) NYU Pr.

— The National Front & French Politics: The Resistible Rise of Jean-Marie Le Pen. LC 95-12259. 212p. (C). 1996. pap. text 19.50 (0-8147-5535-6) NYU Pr.

Marcus, Joseph. Social & Political History of the Jews in Poland, 1919-1939. LC 82-22420. (New Babylon Studies in the Social Sciences: No. 37). xviii, 569p. 1983. 115.40 (90-279-3239-5) Mouton.

Marcus, Joseph, ed. Growing up in Groups: The Russian Day Care Center & the Israeli Kibbutz. (Illus.). xxii, 295p. 1972. text 142.00 (0-677-04800-9) Gordon & Breach.

Marcus, Joyce. Emblem & State in the Classic Maya Lowlands: An Epigraphic Approach to Territorial Organization. LC 76-5213. (Illus.). 203p. 1976. 20.00 (0-88402-066-5) Dumbarton Oaks.

— The Inscriptions of Calakmul: The Royal Marriage at a Maya City in Campeche, Mexico. LC 88-621149. (University of Michigan, Museum of Anthropology Memoirs Ser.: Vol. 21). (Illus.). 226p. 1987. reprint ed. pap. 70.10 (0-608-05680-4, 206619600007) Bks Demand.

— Late Intermediate Occupation at Cerro Azul, Peru. (Technical Reports Ser.: No. 20). xvi, 112p. (Orig.). 1987. pap. 8.00 (0-915703-12-2) U Mich Mus Anthro.

— Mesoamerican Writing Systems: Propaganda, Myth, & History in Four Ancient Civilizations. LC 92-9091. (Illus.). 550p. 1992. text 65.00 (0-691-09474-8, Pub. by Princeton U Pr) Cal Prin Full Svc.

— Women's Ritual in Formative Oaxaca: Figurine Making, Divination, Death & the Ancestors. LC 98-54945. (Memoirs of the Museum of Anthropology, University of Michigan Ser.). 1998. 25.00 (0-915703-48-3) U Mich Mus Anthro.

Marcus, Joyce, ed. Debating Oaxaca Archaeology. LC 90-42333. (Anthropological Papers Ser.: No. 84). (Illus.). x, 270p. (Orig.). 1990. pap. 18.00 (0-915703-22-X) U Mich Mus Anthro.

Marcus, Joyce & Flannery, Kent. Zapotec Civilization: How Urban Society Evolved in Mexico's Oaxaca Valley. LC 95-60561. (Illus.). 256p. 1996. 60.00 (0-500-05078-3, Pub. by Thames Hudson) Norton.

Marcus, Joyce & Zeitlin, Judith F., eds. Caciques & Their People: A Volume in Honor of Ronald Spores. LC 94-34805. (Anthropological Papers Ser.: No. 89). 1995. 26.00 (0-915703-37-8) U Mich Mus Anthro.

Marcus, Joyce, jt. auth. see Flannery, Kent V.

Marcus, Joyce, ed. see De Diez Canseco, Maria R.

Marcus, Joyce, jt. ed. see Feinman, Gary M.

Marcus, Joyce, ed. see Hopkins, Joseph W., III.

Marcus, Joyce, ed. see Redmond, Elsa M.

Marcus, Judith. Georg Lukacs & Thomas Mann: A Study in the Sociology of Literature. LC 86-1261. 208p. 1988. lib. bdg. 30.00 (0-87023-486-2) U of Mass Pr.

Marcus, Judith & Tar, Zoltan, eds. Foundations of the Frankfurt School of Social Research. 384p. 1984. pap. 24.95 (0-87855-963-9) Transaction Pubs.

Marcus, Judith & Tarr, Zoltan, eds. Georg Lukacs: Theory, Culture & Politics. 224p. 1989. 44.95 (0-88738-244-4) Transaction Pubs.

Marcus, Judith, ed. & tr. see Lukacs, Georg.

***Marcus, Judith T., ed.** Surviving the Twentieth Century: Social Philosophy from the Frankfurt School to the Columbia Faculty Seminars. LC 99-16173. 498p. 2000. 49.95 (1-56000-352-9) Transaction Pubs.

Marcus, Julie, ed. First in Their Field: Women & Australian Anthropology. 208p. 1993. pap. 24.95 (0-522-84466-9, Pub. by Melbourne Univ Pr) Paul & Co Pubs.

Marcus, K. Melissa, tr. see Mokeddem, Malika.

Marcus, Kenneth K. The National Government & the Natural Gas Industry, 1946-56: A Study in the Making of a National Policy. Bruchey, Stuart, ed. LC 78-22697. (Energy in the American Economy Ser.). (Illus.). 1979. lib. bdg. 91.95 (0-405-12000-1) Ayer.

Marcus, Laura. Auto-Biographical Discourses: Theory, Criticism, Practice. LC 93-47153. 1994. text 89.95 (0-7190-3642-9, Pub. by Manchester Univ Pr) St Martin.

— Sigmund Freud's the Interpretation of Dreams: New Interdisciplinary Essays. LC 98-50272. (Texts in Culture Ser.). 240p. 1999. text 79.95 (0-7190-3973-8) Manchester Univ Pr.

— Virginia Woolf. (Writers & Their Work Ser.). 144p. 1997. pap. 21.00 (0-7463-0726-8, Pub. by Northcote House) U Pr of Miss.

Marcus, Laura & Nead, Lynda, eds. The Actuality of Walter Benjamin. 176p. 1998. pap. 22.50 (0-85315-863-0) Lawrence & Wishart.

Marcus, Laura & Willis, Chris, eds. Twelve Women Detective Stories. LC 98-136146. (Oxford Twelves Ser.). 240p. 1998. pap. 9.95 (0-19-288036-5) OUP.

Marcus, Laura, jt. ed. see Cheyette, Bryan.

Marcus, Laurence R., et al. The Path to Excellence: Quality Assurance in Higher Education. Fife, Jonathan D., ed. LC 83-146405. (ASHE-ERIC Higher Education Reports: No. 83-1). 68p. (Orig.). 1983. pap. 24.00 (0-913317-00-4) GWU Grad Schl E&HD.

Marcus, Laurence R., jt. auth. see Johnson, Janet R.

Marcus, Lawrence R. Fighting Words: The Politics of Hateful Speech. LC 95-26516. 216p. 1996. 39.95 (0-275-95438-2, Praeger Pubs) Greenwood.

Marcus, Leah S. The Politics of Mirth: Jonson, Herrick, Milton, Marvell, & the Defense of Old Holiday Pastimes. LC 86-7133. (Illus.). 330p. (C). 1989. pap. text 19.95 (0-226-50452-2) U Ch Pr.

— The Politics of Mirth: Jonson, Herrick, Milton, Marvell, & the Defense of Old Holiday Pastimes. LC 86-7133. (Illus.). 328p. (C). 1996. 34.95 (0-226-50451-4) U Ch Pr.

— Unediting the Renaissance: Shakespeare, Marlowe, Milton. LC 96-7263. (Illus.). 280p. (C). 1996. 90.00 (0-415-09934-X); pap. 25.99 (0-415-10053-4) Routledge.

Marcus, Leah S., ed. see Elizabeth, et al.

Marcus, Leonard. Petrouchka: A Ballet Cut-Out Book. (Illus.). 16p. (J). (gr. 3-6). 1983. pap. 12.95 (0-87923-469-5) Godine.

— Renegotiating Health Care: Resolving Conflict to Build Collaboration. 480p. 1999. pap. text 35.95 (0-7879-5021-1) Jossey-Bass.

Marcus, Leonard, et al. Renegotiating Health Care: Resolving Conflicts to Build Collaboration. (Health Ser.). 475p. 1995. text 40.95 (0-7879-0151-2) Jossey-Bass.

Marcus, Leonard, tr. see Donoso, Jose.

Marcus, Leonard C. Veterinary Biology & Medicine of Captive Amphibians & Reptiles. LC 80-24859. 251p. reprint ed. pap. 77.90 (0-608-17766-0, 205651800069) Bks Demand.

Marcus, Leonard S. A Caldecott Celebration. LC 98-6616. (J). 1998. lib. bdg. 19.85 (0-8027-8658-8) Walker & Co.

— A Caldecott Celebration: Six Artists Share Their Paths to the Caldecott Medal. LC 98-6616. (Illus.). 48p. (J). (gr. 1-7). 1998. 18.95 (0-8027-8656-1) Walker & Co.

***Marcus, Leonard S.** Dear Genius: The Letters of Ursula Nordstrom. LC 97-18895. (Illus.). 448p. 2000. pap. 16.95 (0-06-446235-8) HarpC.

Marcus, Leonard S. The Making of Goodnight Moon: A 50th Anniversary Retrospective. LC 97-126836. (Trophy Nonfiction Bk.). (Illus.). 32p. (J). 1997. pap. 5.95 (0-06-446192-0, HarpTrophy) HarpC Child Bks.

— Margaret Wise Brown: Awakened by the Moon. LC 99-37202. (Illus.). 352p. 1999. pap. 14.00 (0-688-17188-5, Quil) HarperTrade.

Marcus, Leonard S., ed. The Penguin Book of Classic Children's Characters. LC 97-26295. Orig. Title: The Penguin Complete Children's Classics. (J). 1997. 35.00 (0-525-45826-3, Dutton Child) Peng Put Young Read.

Marcus, Leonard S., intro. Seventy-Five Years of Children Book Week Posters. (Illus.). 96p. (J). (ps up). 1994. 30.00 (0-679-85106-2, Pub. by Knopf Bks Yng Read) Random.

Marcus, Leonard S. & Nordstrom, Ursula. Dear Genius: The Letters of Ursula Nordstrom. LC 97-18895. 448p. (J). 1998. 22.95 (0-06-023625-6) HarpC Child Bks.

Marcus, Leonard S., ed. & compiled by see Blume, Judy, et al.

Marcus, Leslie F., et al, eds. Advances in Morphometrics: Proceedings of the NATO ASI Held in IL Ciocco, Tuscany, Italy, July 18-30,1993, Vol.284. LC 96-18484. (NATO ASI Series A, Life Sciences: No. 284). (Illus.). 588p. (C). 1996. 174.00 (0-306-45301-0, Plenum Trade) Perseus Pubng.

Marcus, Linda & Schram, Ruth E. Faith Hall of Fame: A Children's Musical. Michel, Gwyneth, ed. 48p. 1997. pap. text 5.95 (0-7692-1500-9, BSB9701) Wrner Bros.

— Faith Hall of Fame: Preview Park. Michel, Gwyneth, ed. 48p. (Orig.). (C). 1997. pap. text 9.95 (0-7692-1515-7, BSB9701PP) Wrner Bros.

Marcus, M. E-Radial Processes & Random Fourier Series. LC 87-12569. (Memoirs Ser.: No. 68/368). 181p. 1987. pap. 25.00 (0-8218-2432-5, MEMO/68/368) Am Math.

Marcus, M., ed. see Eberlein, Ernst, et al.

Marcus, M. B. Geometrical & Statistical Aspects of Probability in Banach Spaces. Fernique, X. et al, eds. (Lecture Notes in Mathematics Ser.: Vol. 1193). iv, 128p. 1986. 25.00 (0-387-16487-1) Spr-Verlag.

Marcus, Maeva. The Documentary History of the Supreme Court of the United States, 1789-1800, Vol. 3: The Justices on Circuit, 1795-1800. 1990. text 145.00 (0-231-08870-1) Col U Pr.

— Truman & the Steel Seizure Case: The Limits of Presidential Power. LC 93-43419. (Constitutional Conflicts Ser.). 424p. 1994. pap. text 18.95 (0-8223-1417-7) Duke.

Marcus, Maeva, ed. The Documentary History of the Supreme Court of the United States, 1789-1800, Vol. IV: Organizing the Federal Judiciary Legislation & Commentaries. 832p. 1992. text 145.00 (0-231-08871-X) Col U Pr.

— The Documentary History of the Supreme Court of the United States, 1789-1800: Cases, 1790-1795, Vol. 6. 809p. 1998. 131.50 (0-231-08873-6) Col U Pr.

— Origins of the Federal Judiciary: Essays on the Judiciary Act of 1789. (Illus.). 320p. 1992. text 60.00 (0-19-506721-5, 1528) OUP.

Marcus, Maeva, et al, eds. The Documentary History of the Supreme Court of the United States, 1789-1800 Vol. 5: Suits Against the States. LC 85-3794. 680p. 1995. 154.50 (0-231-08872-8) Col U Pr.

— The Documentary History of the Supreme Court of the United States, 1789-1800, Vol. 2: The Justices on Circuit, 1790-1794. 550p. 1989. text 145.00 (0-231-08869-8) Col U Pr.

Marcus, Maeva & Perry, James R. The Documentary History of the Supreme Court of the United States, 1789-1800, Vol. 1 Pt. 1. LC 85-3794. 1985. lib. bdg. write for info. (0-231-08867-1) Col U Pr.

Marcus, Maeva & Perry, James R., eds. The Documentary History of the Supreme Court of the United States, 1789-1800, Vol. 1. 1986. text 226.00 (0-231-04552-2) Col U Pr.

Marcus, Marcelina A. Arca: The Clear Bear. (Illus.). 16p. (J). (gr. k-2). 1998. pap. 6.00 (0-8059-4357-9) Dorrance.

Marcus, Marne. Two Novels: Ironic Tales: A New Brautigan & Comrades. 64p. 1995. pap. 9.95 (4-88117-419-3) Lowell Print.

Marcus, Marsea & LaBue, Andrea. Don't Diet - Live It! A Journey Book for Healing Food, Weight & Body Issues. unabridged ed. (Illus.). vii, 257p. 1996. 15.00 (0-9655733-1-1) InnerSolutions.

Marcus, Marsea, jt. auth. see LoBue, Andrea.

Marcus, Marvin. Matrices & Matlab: A Tutorial. 736p. (C). 1992. text 53.00 (0-13-562901-2) P-H.

— Paragons of the Ordinary: The Biographical Literature of Mori Ogai. LC 92-26583. (SHAPS Library of Asian Studies). 372p. 1992. text 45.00 (0-8248-1450-9) UH Pr.

— A Survey of Finite Mathematics. LC 92-43550. (Illus.). x, 486p. 1993. reprint ed. pap. 12.95 (0-486-67553-X) Dover.

Marcus, Marvin & Minc, Henryk. Introduction to Linear Algebra. (Illus.). 288p. 1988. reprint ed. pap. text 8.95 (0-486-65695-0) Dover.

— A Survey of Matrix Theory & Matrix Inequalities. xii, 180p. 1992. reprint ed. pap. 8.95 (0-486-67102-X) Dover.

Marcus, Melissa. The Representation of Mesmerism in Honore de Blazac's La Comedie Humaine, Vol. 6. (New Connections Ser.). XI, 111p. (C). 1996. text 38.95 (0-8204-1818-8) P Lang Pubng.

***Marcus, Michael.** Under a Crescent Sun. (Illus.). 48p. 1999. pap. 5.00 (0-9669897-1-6) Gravity Presses.

***Marcus, Michael A. & Culshaw, Brian, eds.** Fiber Optic Sensor Technology & Applications. 1999. pap. text 120.00 (0-8194-3453-1) SPIE.

***Marcus, Michael A. & Wang, Anbo, eds.** Process Monitoring with Optical Fibers & Harsh Sensors, Vol. #353. 1999. 89.00 (0-8194-2999-6) SPIE.

Marcus, Michael B. & Pisier, Gilles. Random Fourier Series with Applications to Harmonic Analysis. LC 81-47145. (Annals of Mathematical Studies: No. 101). 157p. 1981. reprint ed. pap. 48.70 (0-608-06624-9, 206682100009) Bks Demand.

An Asterisk (*) at the beginning of an entry indicates that the title is appearing for the first time.

***Marcus, Michael B. & Rosen, Jay.** Renormalized Self-Intersection Local Times & Wick Power Chaos Processes LC 99-39860. (Memoirs Ser.). 1999. write for info. (*0-8218-1340-4*) Am Math.

Marcus, Michelle I. Emblems of Identity & Prestige: The Seals & Sealings from Hasanlu, Iran. LC 94-15048. (Hansanlu Special Studies: Vol. 84 & III). (Illus.). xxviii, 173p. 1996. 50.00 (*0-924171-26-X*) U Museum Pubns.

Marcus, Mildred R., jt. auth. see Marcus, Edward.

Marcus, Millicent. An Allegory of Form: Literary Self-Consciousness in the "Decameron" (Stanford French & Italian Studies: No. 18). viii, 136p. 1979. pap. 56.50 (*0-915838-21-4*) Anma Libri.

— Filmmaking by the Book: Italian Cinema & Literary Adaptation. (Illus.). 384p. 1993. text 48.50 (*0-8018-4454-1*); pap. text 16.95 (*0-8018-4455-X*) Johns Hopkins.

— Italian Film in the Light of Neorealism. 480p. 1986. pap. text 26.95 (*0-691-10208-2*, Pub. by Princeton U Pr) Cal Prin Full Svc.

Marcus, Mordecai. Emily Dickinson Selected Poem Notes. (Cliffs Notes Ser.). 104p. (Orig.). (C). 1982. pap. text 4.95 (*0-8220-0432-1*, Cliff) IDG Bks.

— Poems of Robert Frost: An Explication. 288p. (C). 1991. 40.00 (*0-8161-7267-6*, Hall Reference) Macmillan.

Marcus, Morton. The Armies Encamped in the Fields Beyond the Unfinished Avenues: Prose Poems. enl. ed. (Illus.). 80p. (C). 1988. reprint ed. pap. 5.95 (*0-9621321-0-1*) Brown Bear.

— Big Winds, Glass Mornings, Shadows Cast by Stars: Poems: 1972-1980. 3rd ed. 80p. 1988. reprint ed. pap. 5.95 (*0-9621321-1-X*) Brown Bear.

— Origins. (Illus.). (Orig.). 1973. pap. 10.00 (*0-87711-045-X*) Story Line.

— Origins. 4th ed. (Illus.). 80p. (Orig.). (C). 1988. reprint ed. pap. 6.95 (*0-9621321-2-8*) Brown Bear.

— Pages from a Scrapbook of Immigrants. LC 88-30234. 144p. (Orig.). (YA). (gr. 10-12). 1988. pap. 8.95 (*0-918273-47-1*) Coffee Hse.

— The Santa Cruz Mountain Poems. 2nd ed. LC 95-30681. (Illus.). 72p. reprint ed. pap. 12.95 (*0-932319-03-3*) Capitola Bk.

— When People Could Fly. LC 97-29674. 1997. 21.00 (*1-882413-45-8*); pap. 13.00 (*1-882413-44-X*) Hanging Loose.

Marcus, Morton J. Tightrope to Tomorrow: Pensions, Productivity, & Public Education. LC 97-60407. 152p. (C). 1997. text 24.98 (*0-7842-0866-2*, 401-BK) Agency Instr Tech.

Marcus, Moshe & Mizel, Victor. Limiting Equations for Problems Involving Long Range Memory. LC 83-3752. (Memoirs of the American Mathematical Society Ser.: No. 43/278). 64p. 1983. pap. 17.00 (*0-8218-2278-0*, MEMO/43/278) Am Math.

Marcus, Nancy H., jt. auth. see Ennis, Christine A.

Marcus, Naomi, tr. see Tamarov, Vladislav.

Marcus, Norman & Klatell, David A. Inside Big Time Sports: A Behind the Scenes Look at Television, Money & the Fans. 220p. 1996. pap. 13.95 (*1-57101-062-9*) MasterMedia Pub.

Marcus, Norman J. & Arbeiter, Jean S. Freedom From Chronic Pain: The Breakthrough Program that Brings Relief to Chronic Sufferers. 240p. 1994. 19.50 (*0-671-79892-8*) S&S Trade.

Marcus, P., et al, eds. Modifications of Passive Films: Papers Presented at the European Symposium on Modifications of Passive Films. (European Federation of Corrosion Publications Ser.: No. 12). 343p. 1994. pap. 140.00 (*0-901716-52-9*, Pub. by Inst Materials) Ashgate Pub Co.

Marcus, P. & Oudar, Jacques L., eds. Corrosion Mechanisms in Theory & Practice. LC 95-7009. (Corrosion Technology Ser.: vol. 8). (Illus.). 656p. 1995. text 199.00 (*0-8247-9592-X*) Dekker.

Marcus, Pamela. Psychiatric Emergencies: Crisis Intervention Booklet, Part 1. 32p. (C). (gr. 13). 1995. pap. text 16.95 (*0-8151-7287-7*, 27739) Mosby Inc.

Marcus, Pamela E. Intoxification, Abreactions, Side Effects. (Psychiatric Emergencies Video Ser.: Module 2). 96p. 1996. write for info. (*0-8151-7289-3*) Mosby Inc.

Marcus, Pamela E. Psychiatric Emergencies, Three-Part Video Series Module 3: Violence, Aggression, Suicide & Post-Traumatic Stress Disorder (PTSD) (Illus.). 20p. (C). (gr. 13). 1995. text 39.95 incl. VHS (*0-8151-7290-7*, 27742) Mosby Inc.

Marcus, Pamela E. Psychiatric Emergencies Video Series, 3 cass.; set. 96p. 1995. write for info. incl. VHS (*0-8151-5699-5*) Mosby Inc.

Marcus, Pamela E. & Hanlon, John J. Psychiatric Emergencies Pt. 1: Crisis Intervention. 1995. write for info. incl. VHS (*0-8151-7286-9*) Mosby Inc.

Marcus, Paul. Autonomy in the Extreme Situation: Bruno Bettelheim, the Nazi Concentration Camps & the Mass Society. LC 98-26657. 232p. 1999. 57.95 (*0-275-94725-4*, Praeger Pubs) Greenwood.

— The Entrapment Defense. 2nd ed. 762p. 1995. 95.00 (*1-55834-256-7*, 64635-11, MICHIE) LEXIS Pub.

— Entrapment Defense: 1990 Supplement. 1989. write for info. (*0-87473-614-5*, 64636-10, MICHIE) LEXIS Pub.

— Entrapment Defense: 1992 Supplement. 62p. 1991. write for info. (*0-87473-833-4*, 64638-10, MICHIE) LEXIS Pub.

— The Entrapment Defense: 1998 Cumulative Supplement. 2nd ed. 70p. 1998. write for info. (*0-327-00238-7*, 64639-15) LEXIS Pub.

***Marcus, Paul.** The Entrapment Defense, 1999 Cumulative Supplement. 2nd ed. 74p. 1999. write for info. (*0-327-01496-2*, 6463916) LEXIS Pub.

Marcus, Paul. Prosecution & Defense of Criminal Conspiracy Cases, 2 vols. 1978. ring bd. 175.00 (*0-8205-1365-2*) Bender.

***Marcus, Paul & Nimmer, Melville B.** Cases & Materials On Copyright & Other Aspects Of Entertainment Litigation Including Unfair Competition, Defamation, Privacy, Fifth Edition, 1998. 1998. text 58.00 (*0-8205-4259-8*) Bender.

Marcus, Paul & Rosenberg, Alan, eds. Healing Their Wounds: Psychotherapy with Holocaust Survivors & Their Families. LC 89-8638. 324p. 1989. 55.00 (*0-275-92948-5*, C2948, Praeger Pubs) Greenwood.

— Psychoanalytic Versions of the Human Condition: Philosophies of Life & Their Impact on Practice. LC 98-6852. 424p. 1998. text 65.00 (*0-8147-5501-1*); pap. text 25.00 (*0-8147-5608-5*) NYU Pr.

Marcus, Paul, jt. see Cook, Joseph G.

Marcus, Paul, jt. auth. see Cook, Joseph G.

Marcus, Paul, jt. auth. see Marcus, Irene W.

Marcus, Paul, jt. ed. see Helmreich, Alan.

Marcus, Phillip A. & Willig, John T., eds. Moving Ahead with ISO 14000: Improving Environmental Management & Advancing Sustainable Development. LC 96-41848. (Wiley Series in Environmental Quality Management). 302p. 1997. 75.00 (*0-471-16877-7*) Wiley.

Marcus, Phillip L. Standish O'Grady. LC 74-124647. (Irish Writers Ser.). 92p. 1975. 8.50 (*0-8387-7751-1*); pap. 1.95 (*0-8387-7660-4*) Bucknell U Pr.

— Yeats & Artistic Power. 320p. (C). 1992. text 45.00 (*0-8147-5471-6*) NYU Pr.

— Yeats & the Beginning of the Irish Renaissance. 2nd ed. LC 86-22969. (Irish Studies). 336p. 1987. reprint ed. pap. text 17.95 (*0-8156-2398-4*) Syracuse U Pr.

Marcus, Phillip L., ed. see Yeats, William Butler.

Marcus, R. D., et al. Pneumatic Conveying of Solids. 528p. (gr. 13). 1990. text 102.95 (*0-412-21490-3*, 6647) Chapman & Hall.

Marcus, R. K. Glow Discharge Spectroscopies. LC 93-10300. (Modern Analytical Chemistry Ser.). (Illus.). 534p. (C). 1993. text 115.00 (*0-306-44396-1*, Kluwer Plenum) Kluwer Academic.

Marcus, Ralph. Jewish Antiquities, 7 & 8. 1998. 19.95 (*0-674-99577-5*) HUP.

— Law in the Apocrypha. LC 29-9822. (Columbia University. Oriental Studies: No. 26). reprint ed. 27.50 (*0-404-50516-3*) AMS Pr.

Marcus, Randall E. Orthopaedics: Problems in Primary Care. Karaffa, Melanie C., ed. (Illus.). 400p. (C). 1991. text 49.95 (*1-878487-33-7*, 5907M) Practice Mgmt Info.

Marcus, Richard, ed. Digital Video 3. rev. ed. (Illus.). 230p. (Orig.). 1982. reprint ed. pap. text 25.00 (*0-940690-04-7*) Soc Motion Pic & TV Engrs.

Marcus, Richard L. Civil Procedure, a Modern Approach, 1994. 200p. 1994. pap. text, suppl. ed. 12.00 (*0-314-04320-9*) West Pub.

— Family & Medical Leave: Policies & Procedures, 1. (Employee Benefits - Human Resources Library). 200p. 1994. boxed set. write for info. (*0-471-04195-5*) Wiley.

Marcus, Richard L. & Sherman, Edward F. Complex Litigation, Cases & Materials on Advanced Civil Procedure. 2nd ed. (American Casebook Ser.). 1026p. (C). 1992. reprint ed. text 53.50 (*0-314-00769-5*) West Pub.

— Complex Litigation, Cases & Materials on Advanced Civil Procedure. 2nd ed. 390p. (C). 1993. reprint ed. pap. text. write for info. (*0-314-01192-7*) West Pub.

— Complex Litigation, Cases & Materials on Advanced Civil Procedure. 3rd ed. LC 98-17915. 1100p. 1998. 65.00 (*0-314-21124-1*) West Pub.

— 1997 Supplement to Complex Litigation, Advanced Civil Procedures. 2nd ed. (American Casebook Ser.). 85p. 1997. pap. text. write for info. (*0-314-22757-1*) West Pub.

Marcus, Richard L., et al. Civil Procedure: A Modern Approach. 2nd ed. LC 95-17813. (American Casebook Ser.). 1181p. (C). 1995. 65.00 (*0-314-06105-3*) West Pub.

— Civil Procedure, a Modern Approach, Teacher's Manual For. 2nd ed. (American Casebook Ser.). 450p. (C). 1995. pap. text. write for info. (*0-314-06902-X*) West Pub.

— Civil Procedure, Cases & Materials. (American Casebook Ser.). 1027p. 1992. reprint ed. text 46.00 (*0-314-49349-2*) West Pub.

— A Modern Approach, Teacher's Manual to Accompany Civil Procedure. (American Casebook Ser.). 342p. 1989. pap. text. write for info. (*0-314-54545-X*) West Pub.

Marcus, Robert. Encyclopedia of Florida: A Reference Guide to the Sunshine State. (Encyclopedia of the United States Ser.). 600p. 1985. reprint ed. lib. bdg. 79.00 (*0-403-09979-X*) Somerset Pub.

Marcus, Robert, ed. Osteoporosis. (Illus.). 352p. 1994. 99.95 (*0-86542-266-4*) Blackwell Sci.

Marcus, Robert, et al, eds. Osteoporosis. (Illus.). 1373p. 1996. text 149.95 (*0-12-470860-9*) Acad Pr.

Marcus, Robert D. America Firsthand. 4th ed. Date not set. pap. text. write for info. (*0-312-15388-0*) St Martin.

— America Firsthand, Vols. 1 & 2. 1996. pap. text 34.20 (*0-312-14776-7*) St Martin.

Marcus, Robert D., ed. American Voices: Readings in History & Literature since 1865, Vol. II. (Illus.). 448p. (C). 1992. reprint ed. pap. 18.50 (*1-881089-05-3*) Brandywine Press.

— American Voices: Readings in History & Literature to 1877, Vol. I. (Illus.). 406p. (C). 1992. reprint ed. pap. 18.50 (*1-881089-04-5*) Brandywine Press.

Marcus, Robert D. & Burner, David. America Firsthand Vol. I: Readings from Settlement to Reconstruction. 4th ed. LC 97-72373. 300p. 1997. pap. text 32.95 (*0-312-15349-X*) St Martin.

— America Firsthand Vol. II: Readings from Reconstruction to the Present. 4th ed. LC 97-72373. 330p. 1997. pap. text 32.95 (*0-312-15348-1*) St Martin.

Marcus, Robert D. & Burner, David, eds. American Scene: Varieties of American History, 2 vols. LC 73-136426. (Orig.). (C). 1971. teacher ed. write for info. (*0-89197-020-7*); pap. text 11.95 (*0-8290-1409-8*); pap. text 9.95 (*0-89197-019-3*); pap. text 11.95 (*0-89197-018-5*) Irvington.

Marcus, Robert D. & Marcus, Anthony, eds. On Trial Vol. I: American History Through Court Proceedings & Hearings. 222p. (C). 1998. pap. text 16.50 (*1-881089-24-X*) Brandywine Press.

— On Trial Vol. II: American History Through Court Proceedings & Hearings. 230p. (C). 1997. pap. text 16.50 (*1-881089-26-6*) Brandywine Press.

Marcus, Robert H., ed. see Stine, Robert J.

Marcus, Robert T., jt. auth. see Pierce, Percy E.

Marcus, Ronald. Stamford, Connecticut - A Bibliography: An Annotated, Indexed Compilation of Books - Pamphlets - Special Editions of Newspapers - Atlas - Articles in Periodicals - Motion Picture Film - Containing Information Relating to the History of Stamford, CT. xxii, 284p. (Orig.). 1995. pap. 49.95 (*1-886054-13-4*) Stamford Hist Soc.

Marcus, Rudolphy A. Theories of Chemical Reactions Rates. (Twentieth Century Chemistry Ser.). 400p. 1997. text 109.00 (*981-02-1505-3*); pap. text 53.00 (*981-02-1506-1*) World Scientific Pub.

Marcus, Rudy, ed. Intersection: Journal of the Guild for Psychological Studies, Vol. I. 160p. (C). 1993. pap. text 10.00 (*0-917479-16-5*) Guild Psy.

Marcus, Russell. English-Lao, Lao-English Dictionary. rev. ed. LC 77-116487. (ENG & LAO.). 416p. 1970. pap. 16.95 (*0-8048-0909-7*) Tuttle Pubng.

— Forms of Man: The Buddhist Vision of Thawan Duchanee. (Illus.). 76p. 1975. pap. 12.00 (*0-916020-01-0*) Books Marcus.

Marcus, Russell, ed. Lao Proverbs. Phengsy, Novanta, tr. from LAO. (Illus.). 56p. 1969. pap. 6.00 (*0-916020-00-2*) Books Marcus.

Marcus, Ruth B. Modalities: Philosophical Essays. 288p. 1995. pap. text 24.95 (*0-19-509657-6*) OUP.

Marcus, Ruth E., ed. see Bauer, Lawrence M., III.

Marcus, Ruth E., ed. see Bodian, Nat G. & Luedtke, Robert.

Marcus, Sander I., jt. auth. see Mandel, Harvey P.

Marcus, Sandra, ed. Knowledge Acquisition: Selected Research & Commentary. (C). 1990. text 83.50 (*0-7923-9062-8*) Kluwer Academic.

Marcus, Scott. What Sucks about South Florida: A Travel-To, Move-To Guide. LC 97-11835. (Illus.). 191p. (Orig.). 1997. pap. 12.95 (*0-9640354-8-0*) Fender Pubng.

Marcus, Scott J. How to Design Wide Area Internetworks: A Practical Guide. LC 99-30060. 416p. (C). 1999. 49.95 (*0-201-69584-7*) Addison-Wesley.

***Marcus, Sharon.** Apartment Stories: City & Home in Nineteenth-Century Paris & London. LC 98-40597. 333p. 1999. 45.00 (*0-520-20852-8*, Pub. by U CA Pr) Cal Prin Full Svc.

— Apartment Stories: City & Home in Nineteenth Century Paris & London. LC 98-40597. 333p. 1999. pap. 16.95 (*0-520-21726-8*, Pub. by U CA Pr) Cal Prin Full Svc.

Marcus, Shirley, jt. auth. see Lee, Kay.

Marcus, Stanley. David Smith: The Sculptor & His Work. LC 83-45148. (Illus.). 208p. 1983. text 45.00 (*0-8014-1510-1*) Cornell U Pr.

— Minding the Store: A Memoir. LC 97-13287. (Illus.). 383p. 1998. 29.95 (*1-57441-039-3*) UNTX Pr.

***Marcus, Stanley.** Stanley Marcus from A to Z Vol. II: Viewpoints. Hazel, Michael V., ed. LC 99-53441. 261p. 2000. 24.95 (*1-57441-073-3*, Pub. by UNTX Pr) Tex A&M Univ Pr.

Marcus, Stanley. The Viewpoints of Stanley Marcus: A Ten-Year Perspective. LC 95-1451. 261p. 1995. 24.95 (*0-929398-86-6*) UNTX Pr.

Marcus, Stanley, jt. ed. see Wilson, Robert A.

Marcus, Steve, jt. auth. see Dornbusch, Rudiger.

Marcus, Steven. Representations: Essays on Literature & Society. 384p. 1990. text 57.50 (*0-231-07400-X*); pap. text 20.50 (*0-231-07401-8*) Col U Pr.

Marcus, Steven, ed. see Hammett, Dashiell.

Marcus, Steven, ed. & intro. see Hammett, Dashiell.

Marcus, Susan A. & McDonald, Penny. Tools for the Cooperative Classroom. (Illus.). 128p. (Orig.). 1990. pap. text 23.95 (*0-932935-27-3*) SkyLght.

Marcus, Sybil. A World of Fiction: Twenty Timeless Short Stories. LC 94-31206. 304p. 1995. pap. text 24.27 (*0-201-82520-1*) Addison-Wesley.

Marcus, Terry. A Feminine Guide to Pro Football. 2nd rev. ed. LC 96-90951. (Illus.). 128p. 1997. pap. write for info. (*0-9648407-1-5*) Terrys Publng.

— A Feminine Guide to Professional Football. LC 95-90762. 56p. 1994. pap. write for info. (*0-9648407-0-7*) Terrys Publng.

Marcus, Tessa. Modernizing Super-Exploitation: Restructuring South African Agriculture. LC 89-5835. 256p. (C). 1989. pap. 19.95 (*0-86232-845-4*, Pub. by Zed Books); text 55.00 (*0-86232-844-6*, Pub. by Zed Books) St Martin.

Marcus, W., jt. auth. see Marcus, Abraham.

Marcus, Warren M. Shalom. LC 93-2551. ix, 275p. 1993. pap. 9.99 (*0-8407-6790-0*) Nelson.

Marcus, Y. The Properties of Solvents. LC 98-18212. (Series in Solution Chemistry). 254p. 1998. 170.00 (*0-471-98369-1*) Wiley.

Marcus, Y., jt. ed. see Kertes, A. S.

Marcus, Yizhak. Introduction to Liquid State Chemistry. LC 76-40230. 375p. reprint ed. pap. 116.30 (*0-608-17550-1*, 203053000069) Bks Demand.

— Ion Properties. LC 97-22067. 272p. 1997. text 135.00 (*0-8247-0011-2*) Dekker.

— Ion Solvation. LC 85-6436. (Illus.). 314p. reprint ed. pap. 97.40 (*0-7837-4392-0*, 204413200012) Bks Demand.

Marcus, Yizhak & Marinsky, Jacob A. Ion Exchange & Solvent Extraction, Vol. 11. (Illus.). 400p. 1993. text 250.00 (*0-8247-8472-3*) Dekker.

— Ion Exchange & Solvent Extraction: A Series of Advances, Vol. 9. (Illus.). 504p. 1985. text 225.00 (*0-8247-7120-6*) Dekker.

— Ion Exchange & Solvent Extraction: A Series of Advances, Vol. 10. (Illus.). 296p. 1987. text 199.00 (*0-8247-7688-7*) Dekker.

— Ion Exchange & Solvent Extraction: A Series of Advances, Vol. 12. (Illus.). 472p. 1995. text 215.00 (*0-8247-9382-X*) Dekker.

Marcus, Yizhak, jt. ed. see Marinsky, Jacob A.

Marcus, Yosef B., ed. see Schneerson, Menachem M.

Marcuse, Aida, tr. see Brown, Margaret Wise.

Marcuse, Aida, tr. see Perrault, Charles.

Marcuse, Aida, tr. see Seuss, Dr., pseud.

Marcuse, Aida, tr. see Zemach, Margot.

Marcuse, Aida E., tr. from ENG. Lizards's Song (Spanish edition) La cancion del lagarto. LC 80-21432. (Books in Spanish). (SPA., Illus.). 32p. (J). (ps-3). 1994. reprint ed. mass mkt. 5.95 (*0-688-13201-4*, Wm Morrow) Morrow Avon.

Marcuse, Aida E., tr. see Brown, Margaret Wise.

Marcuse, Aida E., tr. see Castaneda, Omar S.

Marcuse, Aida E., tr. see Coerr, Eleanor.

Marcuse, Aida E., tr. see Conlon, Laura.

Marcuse, Aida E., tr. see Cowcher, Helen.

Marcuse, Aida E., tr. see Hallinan, P. K.

Marcuse, Aida E., tr. see Hutchins, Pat.

Marcuse, Aida E., tr. see Joyce, Susan.

Marcuse, Aida E., tr. see Kalan, Robert.

Marcuse, Aida E., tr. see Kellogg, Steven.

Marcuse, Aida E., tr. see Maestro, Betsy & Maestro, Giulio.

Marcuse, Aida E., tr. see McCall, Barbara A.

Marcuse, Aida E., tr. see McDermott, Gerald.

Marcuse, Aida E., tr. see Perrault, Charles.

Marcuse, Aida E., tr. see Seuss, Dr., pseud.

Marcuse, Aida E., tr. see Shannon, George.

Marcuse, Aida E., tr. see Singer, Isaac Bashevis.

Marcuse, Aida E., tr. see Singer, Marilyn.

Marcuse, Aida E., tr. see Williams, Vera B.

Marcuse, Aida E., tr. see Zemach, Margot.

Marcuse, Aida R., tr. see Potter, Beatrix.

Marcuse, Dietrich. Principles of Optical Fiber Measurements. 1996. 64.50 (*0-614-18456-8*, B01031) Info Gatekeepers.

Marcuse, Gary, jt. auth. see Whitaker, Reg.

Marcuse, Herbert. The Aesthetic Dimension: Toward a Critique of Marxist Aesthetics. LC 76-9001. 1979. reprint ed. pap. 13.00 (*0-8070-1519-9*) Beacon Pr.

— Counterrevolution & Revolt. LC 79-179150. 140p. 1972. reprint ed. pap. 15.00 (*0-8070-1533-4*) Beacon Pr.

— Eros & Civilization: A Philosophical Inquiry into Freud. LC 66-3219. 320p. 1974. reprint ed. pap. 17.00 (*0-8070-1555-5*) Beacon Pr.

— An Essay on Liberation. LC 69-15591. 1969. reprint ed. pap. 14.00 (*0-8070-0595-9*) Beacon Pr.

— Hegel's Ontology & the Theory of Historicity. 350p. 1989. pap. text 15.95 (*0-262-63125-3*) MIT Pr.

— One-Dimensional Man: Studies in the Ideology of Advanced Industrial Society. LC 91-18246. 320p. 1992. pap. 16.00 (*0-8070-1417-6*) Beacon Pr.

— Reason & Revolution. LC 99-13602. 440p. 1999. pap. 18.95 (*1-57392-718-X*, Humanity Bks) Prometheus Bks.

— Reason & Revolution: Hegel & the Rise of Social Theory. 2nd ed. LC 89-35982. (Humanities Paperback Library). 456p. (C). 1991. reprint ed. pap. 18.50 (*0-391-02999-1*) Humanities.

— Soviet Marxism: A Critical Analysis. LC 57-10943. 271p. 1985. pap. text 21.00 (*0-231-08379-3*) Col U Pr.

Marcuse, Herbert & Kellner, Douglas. Technology, War & Fascism, Vol. 1. LC 97-14885. (Collected Papers of Herbert Marcuse). (Illus.). 296p. (C). 1998. 35.00 (*0-415-13780-2*) Routledge.

Marcuse, Herbert & Popper, Karl R. Revolution or Reform: A Confrontation. LC 75-12192. (Studies in Ethics & Society Ser.: Vol. 2). Orig. Title: Revolution oder Reform. 120p. 1976. 16.95 (*0-89044-020-4*) Transaction Pubs.

***Marcuse, Irene.** The Death of an Amiable Child: An Anita Servi Novel. LC 00-22877. 288p. 2000. 23.95 (*0-8027-3346-8*) Walker & Co.

Marcuse, Michael. Reference Guide for English Studies. 1990. 150.00 (*0-520-05161-0*, Pub. by U CA Pr); pap. 47.50 (*0-520-07992-2*, Pub. by U CA Pr) Cal Prin Full Svc.

Marcuse, Peter & Van Kempen, Ronald, eds. Global Cities: An International & Comparative Perspective. LC 99-43570. (Studies in Urban & Social Change). 256p. 1999. 59.95 (*0-631-21289-2*) Blackwell Pubs.

— Globalizing Cities: A New Spatical Order. LC 99-43570. (Studies in Urban & Social Change). 256p. 2000. pap. 24.95 (*0-631-21290-6*) Blackwell Pubs.

Marcuse, Peter M. Disease: In Search of Remedy. 168p. 1996. 24.95 (*0-252-02215-7*) U of Ill Pr.

Marcuson, Pat. Fishing the Beartooths. 2nd rev. ed. LC 96-39731. (Illus.). 152p. 1997. pap. 14.95 (*1-56044-434-7*) Falcon Pub Inc.

Marcuss, Stanley J. & Marks, Lee R. The Export Administration Act of 1985 & Its Ramification. (Illus.). write for info. (*0-318-61238-0*) Harcourt.

Marcussen, Henrik S., jt. ed. see Van Dijk, Meine P.

Marcussen, Lars. Third World Housing in Social & Spatial Development: The Case of Jakarta Housing in Social & Spatial Development. 205p. 1990. text 82.95 (*1-85628-085-3*, Pub. by Avebry) Ashgate Pub Co.

M

An Asterisk (*) at the beginning of an entry indicates that the title is appearing for the first time.

Marcusson, W. F., et al. Geotechnical Earthquake Engineering in North America: The Last 40 Years. (Illus.). 97p. 1996. pap. text 35.00 (*0-7881-7412-6*) DIANE Pub.

Marcuvitz, N. Waveguide Handbook. (Electromagnetic Waves Ser.: No. 21). 446p. 1986. boxed set 85.00 (*0-86341-058-8*, EW021) INSPEC Inc.

Marcuvitz, Nathan, jt. auth. see Felsen, L. B.

Marcuzzi, G. European Ecosystems. (Biogeographica Ser.: Vol. 15). 1979. text 465.50 (*90-6193-216-5*) Kluwer Academic.

Marcuzzo, Maria C., et al. Monetary Standards & Exchange Rates. LC 96-50052. 320p. (C). 1997. write for info. (*0-415-14297-0*) Routledge.

Marcy, Carl. Presidential Commissions. LC 72-8109. (Studies in American History & Government). 156p. 1973. reprint ed. lib. bdg. 25.00 (*0-306-70532-X*) Da Capo.

Marcy Davis Fawcett Staff. Paralegal Litigation: Forms & Procedures, 1. 2nd ed. 655p. 1995. boxed set 98.00 (*0-7355-1262-0*) Panel Pubs.

Marcy, Jason & Kaposy, Jeremy. Powerwus. Gravelle, Ron, ed. (Illus.). 104p. (YA). 1999. pap. 12.95 (*0-9662984-4-6*) Landwaster Bks.

Marcy, Jean. Cemetery Murders: A Meg Darcy Mystery. LC 96-45120. 200p. 1997. pap. 10.95 (*0-934678-83-9*) New Victoria Pubs.

— Dead & Blonde: A Meg Darcy Mystery. LC 98-26123. (Meg Darcy Mystery Ser.: No. 2). 227p. 1998. pap. 10.95 (*0-934678-98-7*) New Victoria Pubs.

***Marcy, Jean.** Mommy Deadest: A Meg Darcy Mystery. 224p. 2000. pap. 11.95 (*1-892281-12-0*, Pub. by New Victoria Pubs) LPC InBook.

Marcy, Joseph H., jt. ed. see Cook, D. Ryan.

Marcy, Michel, jt. auth. see Nutting, Teresa.

Marcy, Randolph B. The Prairie Traveler. LC 92-38878. 288p. 1988. reprint ed. pap. 10.95 (*0-918222-89-3*) Applewood.

— Scouting & Tracking. (Buckaroos Ser.). (Illus.). 32p. (Orig.). (J). (gr. 2 up). 1996. pap. 1.50 (*1-55709-367-9*) Applewood.

Marcy, Sam. Anatomy of the Economic Crisis. 120p. 1982. pap. 3.25 (*0-89567-077-1*) World View Forum.

— The Bolsheviks & War. 165p. 1985. 4.95 (*0-89567-080-1*) World View Forum.

— Czechoslovakia 1968: The Class Character of the Events. 62p. 1978. pap. 3.00 (*0-89567-002-X*) World View Forum.

— Eurocommunism, New Form of Reformism. 52p. 1978. pap. 3.00 (*0-89567-026-7*) World View Forum.

— Generals over the White House: The Impact of the Military-Industrial Complex. 59p. 1980. pap. 3.00 (*0-89567-042-9*) World View Forum.

— High-Tech, Low Pay. 217p. 1986. pap. 5.95 (*0-89567-083-6*) World View Forum.

— Imperialism & the Crisis in the Socialist Camp. 57p. 1979. pap. 3.50 (*0-89567-030-5*) World View Forum.

— The Klan & the Government: Foes or Allies. 80p. 1983. pap. 2.95 (*0-89567-079-8*) World View Forum.

— Perestroika: A Marxist Critique. 409p. 1990. pap. 12.95 (*0-89567-102-6*) World View Forum.

— Poland: Behind the Crisis. 168p. 1982. pap. 3.95 (*0-89567-076-3*) World View Forum.

— Problems of the Soviet Economic Reforms. 1988. pap. 2.50 (*0-89567-091-7*) World View Forum.

— Reindustrialization: The Menace Behind the Promise. 56p. 1981. pap. 3.50 (*0-89567-045-3*) World View Forum.

— Selected Articles, 1981-82. 89p. 1982. pap. 2.50 (*0-89567-078-X*) World View Forum.

— Soviet Socialism: Utopian or Scientific? 1992. pap. 2.50 (*0-89567-107-7*) World View Forum.

— What the Banks Did to Poland. 26p. 1988. pap. 0.50 (*0-89567-090-9*) World View Forum.

Marcy, Sam, et al. China, the Struggle Within. 2nd ed. 116p. 1972. pap. 4.00 (*0-89567-008-9*) World View Forum.

Marcy, Samuel J. Equal & Distinct Genders: Representation of Women by Women & Men by Men. LC 92-74961. 160p. (Orig.). 1993. pap. 15.00 (*0-9634728-0-1*) EJUT Bks.

Marcy, Willard, ed. Patent Policy: Government, Academic, & Industry Concept. LC 78-9955. (ACS Symposium Ser.: Vol. 81). 183p. 1978. reprint ed. pap. 56.80 (*0-608-03934-9*, 206438100009) Bks Demand.

Marcy, William, ed. Patent Policy: Government, Academic, & Industry Concepts. LC 78-9955. (ACS Symposium Ser.: No. 81). 1978. 27.95 (*0-8412-0454-3*) Am Chemical.

Marczali, Henry. Hungary in the Eighteenth Century. LC 75-135818. (Eastern Europe Collection). 1971. reprint ed. 24.95 (*0-405-02760-5*) Ayer.

Marczely, Bernadette. Personalizing Professional Growth: Staff Development That Works. LC 96-10056. (Illus.). 144p. 1996. 49.95 (*0-8039-6433-1*); pap. 21.95 (*0-8039-6434-X*) Corwin Pr.

— Personalizing Professional Growth: Staff Development That Works. 144p. 1996. 43.95 (*2-8106-6433-1*); pap. 18.95 (*2-8106-6434-X*) NEA.

***Marczely, Bernadette.** Supervision in Education: A Differentiated Approach with Legal Perspectives. LC 00-41609. 2000. write for info. (*0-8342-1778-3*) Aspen Pub.

Marczenko, Z., jt. auth. see Lobinski, R.

Marczenko, Zygmunt. Separation & Spectrophotometric Determination of Elements. 2nd ed. LC 86-2911. (Analytical Chemistry Ser.). 678p. 1986. text 179.00 (*0-470-20334-X*) P-H.

Marczewski, Jan. Inflation & Unemployment in France: A Quantitative Analysis. LC 77-25490. (Praeger Special Studies). 200p. 1978. 57.95 (*0-275-90305-2*, C0305, Praeger Pubs) Greenwood.

Mardaan, Ataullah. Kama Houri/Deva Dasi. (Orig.). 1997. mass mkt. 7.95 (*1-56333-512-3*) Masquerade.

Mardall, Brian. How to Find Out in Biochemistry: A Reference Guide. LC 78-301662. 11p. 1976. 1.00 (*0-904264-08-4*) London Guild Univ.

Mardas, Nikiforos D., jt. auth. see Lovric, Michelle.

***Mardberg, Maria.** Envisioning American Women: The Roads to Communal Identity in Novels by Women of Color. LC 99-158996. (Studia Anglistica Upsaliensia Ser.: Vol. 104). 242p. 1998. pap. 57.50 (*91-554-4317-6*, Pub. by Almqvist Wiksell) Coronet Bks.

Mardell, Ben. From Basketball to the Beatles: In Search of Compelling Early Childhood Curriculum. 190p. 1999. pap. text 18.50 (*0-325-00194-4*) Heinemann.

Marden, Brice. Brice Marden: Paintings, Drawings, Etchings. (Illus.). 48p. 1993. 34.95 (*1-880146-07-X*) M Marks.

Marden, Brice. Brice Marden: Paintings 1985-1993. 1994. pap. text 37.50 (*3-85780-089-5*) Kunsthalle Bern.

Marden, Brice. A Brice Marden Sketchbook. (Illus.). 108p. 1996. pap. 29.95 (*1-881616-49-5*) Dist Art Pubs.

Marden, Brice & Hay, Jonathan, texts. Brice Marden: Chinese Work. (Illus.). 48p. 1998. pap. 49.95 (*1-880146-19-3*, 810892) M Marks.

Marden, C. C., ed. Libro de Apollonio, an Old Spanish Poem, 2 pts. Incl. Vols. 11-12. 1969. reprint ed. pap. 25.00 (*0-527-02615-8*); (SPA.). 1969. Set pap. 25.00 (*0-527-02610-7*) Periodicals Srv.

Marden, Hal. Payofski's Dyscovery. LC 85-45701. 110p. 1986. 6.95 (*0-253-34301-1*) Ind U Pr.

Marden, Luis. The Angler's Bamboo. LC 96-49536. (Illus.). 100p. 1997. 25.00 (*1-55821-535-2*) Lyons Pr.

Marden, Morris. Geometry of Polynomials. rev. ed. LC 66-20882. (Mathematical Surveys & Monographs: Vol. 3). 260p. 1949. pap. 49.00 (*0-8218-1503-2*, SURV/3) Am Math.

Marden, Orison S. Ambition & Success. 75p. 1997. pap. 8.00 (*0-89540-369-2*) Sun Pub.

— Be Good to Yourself. 322p. 1997. pap. 27.00 (*0-89540-364-1*) Sun Pub.

— Character: The Grandest Thing in the World. (Illus.). 55p. 1996. pap. 5.00 (*0-89540-297-1*, SB-297) Sun Pub.

— Cheerfulness As a Life Power. 79p. 1997. pap. 7.50 (*0-89540-363-3*, SB-363) Sun Pub.

— Choosing a Career. 332p. 1998. pap. 30.00 (*0-89540-412-5*, SB-412) Sun Pub.

— The Conquest of Worry. 328p. 1998. pap. 30.00 (*0-89540-396-X*, SB-396) Sun Pub.

— Every Man a King. 1995. reprint ed. lib. bdg. 39.95 (*1-56849-621-4*) Buccaneer Bks.

— Every Man a King or Might in Mind Mastery. 240p. 1997. pap. 22.00 (*0-89540-334-X*, SB-334) Sun Pub.

— Everybody Ahead: or Getting the Most Out of Life. 535p. 1998. pap. 45.00 (*0-89540-409-5*, SB-409) Sun Pub.

— The Exceptional Employee. 202p. 1997. pap. 18.00 (*0-89540-352-8*, SB-352) Sun Pub.

— Getting On. 325p. 1997. pap. 28.00 (*0-89540-370-6*) Sun Pub.

— Good Manners: A Passport to Success. 64p. 1997. pap. 6.00 (*0-89540-366-8*) Sun Pub.

— He Can Who Thinks He Can: And Other Papers on Success in Life. 245p. 1997. pap. 22.00 (*0-89540-346-3*, SB-346) Sun Pub.

— The Hour of Opportunity. (Illus.). 72p. 1997. pap. 7.00 (*0-89540-336-6*, SB-336) Sun Pub.

— How They Succeeded: Life Stories of Successful Men & Women Told by Themselves. 365p. 1997. pap. 33.00 (*0-89540-345-5*, SB-345) Sun Pub.

— How to Get What You Want. 331p. 1997. pap. 30.00 (*0-89540-335-8*, SB-335) Sun Pub.

— How to Succeed or Stepping Stones to Fame & Fortune. 332p. 1997. pap. 30.00 (*0-89540-371-4*) Sun Pub.

— An Iron Will. 52p. 1996. pap. 4.50 (*0-89540-283-1*, SB-283) Sun Pub.

— La Joie de Vivre. 232p. 1986. 18.50 (*2-920083-17-1*) Edns Roseau.

— The Joys of Living or Living Today in the Here & Now. 403p. 1998. pap. 35.00 (*0-89540-389-7*) Sun Pub.

Marden, Orison S. Little Visits with Great Americans, 2 vols. Incl. Vol. I. 352p. 1997. pap. 35.00 (*0-89540-372-2*); Vol. II. 389p. 1997. pap. 35.00 (*0-89540-373-0*); 742p. 50.00 (*0-89540-374-9*) Sun Pub.

Marden, Orison S. Making Life a Masterpiece. 329p. 1998. pap. 28.00 (*0-89540-365-X*) Sun Pub.

— The Making of a Man. 307p. 1998. pap. 26.00 (*0-89540-408-7*, SB-408) Sun Pub.

— Making Yourself. 320p. 1998. pap. 28.00 (*0-89540-413-3*, SB-413) Sun Pub.

— The Miracle of Right Thought. 339p. 1996. pap. 28.00 (*0-89540-311-0*, SB-311) Sun Pub.

— Not the Salary but the Opportunity. 96p. 1998. pap. write for info. (*0-89540-410-9*, SB-410) Sun Pub.

— The Optimistic Life. 316p. 1997. pap. 28.00 (*0-89540-351-X*, SB-351) Sun Pub.

— Peace, Power, & Plenty. 323p. 1997. pap. 28.00 (*0-89540-343-9*, SB-343) Sun Pub.

— The Power of Personality. 86p. 1997. pap. 8.00 (*0-89540-362-5*, SB-362) Sun Pub.

— The Progressive Business Man or How the Right Mental Attitude & Reciprocity Are Revolutionizing Business. 166p. 1997. pap. 15.00 (*0-89540-390-0*) Sun Pub.

— Prosperity, How to Attract It. 325p. 1998. pap. 28.00 (*0-89540-392-7*, SB-392) Sun Pub.

— Pushing to the Front. 1995. reprint ed. lib. bdg. 39.95 (*1-56849-620-6*) Buccaneer Bks.

— Pushing to the Front, 2 vols., Set. 873p. 1997. pap. 65.00 (*0-89540-333-1*, SB-333) Sun Pub.

— Pushing to the Front, Vol. I. 432p. 1997. pap. 40.00 (*0-89540-331-5*, SB-331) Sun Pub.

— Pushing to the Front, Vol. II. 441p. 1997. pap. 40.00 (*0-89540-332-3*, SB-332) Sun Pub.

— Rising in the World or Architects of Fate. 318p. 1997. pap. 27.00 (*0-89540-375-7*) Sun Pub.

— The Secret of Achievement. 301p. 1997. pap. 27.00 (*0-89540-337-4*, SB-337) Sun Pub.

— Self-Investment. 315p. 1997. pap. 27.00 (*0-89540-376-5*) Sun Pub.

— Selling Things. 276p. 1997. pap. 25.00 (*0-89540-339-0*, SB-339) Sun Pub.

— Stories from Life - A Book for Young People. 240p. 1998. pap. 22.00 (*0-89540-411-7*, SB-411) Sun Pub.

— Success: A Book of Ideals, Helps & Examples for All Desiring to Make the Most of Life. 347p. 1997. pap. 32.00 (*0-89540-360-9*, SB-360) Sun Pub.

— Success Fundamentals. 307p. 1998. pap. 26.00 (*0-89540-395-1*, SB-395) Sun Pub.

— Success Nuggets. 76p. 1997. pap. 6.00 (*0-89540-354-4*, SB-354) Sun Pub.

— Talks with Great Workers. 335p. 1998. pap. 30.00 (*0-89540-402-8*, SB-402) Sun Pub.

— Thrift. 92p. 1998. pap. 9.00 (*0-89540-393-5*, SB-393) Sun Pub.

— Training for Efficiency. 360p. 1998. pap. 33.00 (*0-89540-394-3*, SB-394) Sun Pub.

— The Victorious Attitude. 358p. 1997. pap. 32.00 (*0-89540-353-6*, SB-353) Sun Pub.

— Why Grow Old? large type ed. 50p. 1997. pap. 3.50 (*0-89540-340-4*, SB-340) Sun Pub.

— Winning Out: A Book for Young People on Character Building by Habit Forming. 251p. 1997. pap. 22.00 (*0-89540-377-3*) Sun Pub.

— You Can, but Will You? 338p. 1997. pap. 30.00 (*0-89540-342-0*, SB-342) Sun Pub.

— The Young Man Entering Business. 307p. 1998. pap. 26.00 (*0-89540-378-1*) Sun Pub.

Marden, Patricia C. & Barchers, Suzanne I. Cooking up World History: Multicultural Recipes & Resources. (Illus.). xv, 237p. 1994. pap. text 23.50 (*1-56308-116-4*) Teacher Ideas Pr.

Marden, Patricia C., jt. auth. see Barchers, Suzanne I.

Marden, Philip S. Detours (Passable but Unsafe) LC 68-54360. (Essay Index Reprint Ser.). 1977. 19.95 (*0-8369-0677-2*) Ayer.

***Marder.** Condensed Matter Physics. LC 99-36153. 912p. 2000. text 94.95 (*0-471-17779-2*) Wiley.

Marder, et al. The Notre Dame Football Encyclopedia: The Ultimate Guide to America's Favorite College Team. LC 99-20317. (Illus.). 288p. 1999. pap. 19.95 (*0-8065-2108-2*, Citadel Pr) Carol Pub Group.

Marder, A. R., ed. see International Conference on Phase Transformations.

Marder, A. R., ed. see Metallurgical Society of AIME Staff.

Marder, A. R., ed. see Minerals, Metals & Materials Society Staff.

Marder, Amy. Your Healthy Pet: A Practical Guide to Raising Happier, Healthier Dogs & Cats. LC 93-27730. 224p. 1994. pap. 14.95 (*0-87596-185-1*) Rodale Pr Inc.

Marder, Daniel. Arnold Andre Transcripts: A Reconstruction. LC 92-46364. (Illus.). 224p. 1993. 21.00 (*0-912526-59-9*) Lib Res.

— Exiles at Home: A Story of Literature in Nineteenth Century America. LC 84-17303. 382p. (Orig.). 1985. text 55.50 (*0-8191-4284-0*); pap. text 30.00 (*0-8191-4285-9*) U Pr of Amer.

Marder, Daniel, jt. auth. see Guinn, Dorothy.

Marder, Daniel, ed. see Brackenbridge, Hugh H.

Marder, Eric. Laws of Choice. LC 97-7041. 1997. 29.50 (*0-684-83545-2*) S&S Trade.

Marder, Estelle, jt. auth. see Marder, William.

***Marder, Herbert.** The Measure of Life: Virginia Woolf's Last Years. LC 00-20957. (Illus.). 416p. 2000. 35.00 (*0-8014-3729-6*) Cornell U Pr.

Marder, Larry. Larry Marder's Beanworld. (Beanworld Ser.: Bk. 1). Orig. Title: Collection of Tales of the Beanworld Issues #8-11. 128p. 1995. pap. 9.95 (*1-887245-00-6*) Beanworld Pr.

— Larry Marder's Beanworld. (Beanworld Ser.: Bk. 2). Orig. Title: Collection of Tales of the Beanworld Issues #8-11. (Illus.). 104p. 1997. pap. 9.95 (*1-887245-01-4*) Beanworld Pr.

— Larry Marder's Beanworld, Vol. 3. Orig. Title: Collection of Tales of the Beanworld Issues #8-11. (Illus.). 128p. 1998. reprint ed. pap. 11.95 (*1-887245-02-2*) Beanworld Pr.

Marder, Leslie. Calculus of Several Variables. LC 75-318221. (Problem Solvers Ser.: No. 2). 90p. reprint ed. pap. 30.00 (*0-8357-7970-X*, 202326300032) Bks Demand.

Marder, Richard A., jt. auth. see Lian, George J.

Marder, Richard A., jt. auth. see Zarins, Bertram.

Marder, Seth R., et al, eds. Materials for Nonlinear Optics: Chemical Perspectives. LC 90-25768. (ACS Symposium Ser.: No. 455). (Illus.). 740p. 1991. text 140.00 (*0-8412-1939-7*, Pub. by Am Chemical) OUP.

Marder, Stephen. A Supplementary Russian-English Dictionary. (ENG & RUS.). xv, 522p. (Orig.). 1995. reprint ed. pap. 27.95 (*0-89357-253-5*) Slavica.

Marder, Stephen, jt. auth. see Herz, Marvin.

Marder, Sue E. Legal Forms, Contracts & Advice for Horse Owners. 2nd ed. 1997. pap. text 26.50 (*0-914327-69-0*); pap. text 39.95 incl. cd-rom (*0-914327-71-2*) Breakthrgh NY.

Marder, T. A. Bernini & the Art of Architecture. LC 98-17964. (Illus.). 336p. 1998. 95.00 (*0-7892-0115-1*) Abbeville Pr.

— Bernini's Scala Regia at the Vatican Palace. LC 96-3031. (Illus.). 352p. (C). 1997. text 95.00 (*0-521-43198-0*) Cambridge U Pr.

Marder, William. The History & Technique of a New Diffusion Process. 1980. pap. 25.00 (*0-9607480-5-9*) Marder.

Marder, William & Marder, Estelle. Anthony, the Man, the Company, the Cameras. Duncan, Robert G., ed. LC 81-90597. 384p. 1982. 135.00 (*0-9607480-0-8*) Marder.

— Anthony, the Man, the Company, the Cameras. limited ed. Duncan, Robert G., ed. LC 81-90597. 384p. 1982. 200.00 (*0-9607480-2-4*) Marder.

— Pioneers of Photography. 91p. 1991. pap. 28.00 (*0-9607480-3-2*) Marder.

Marderosian, Ara H. Der, see Der Marderosian, Ara H.

***Mardesic, S.** Strong Shape & Homology. LC QA612.7.M353 1999. (Monographs in Mathematics). xiv, 473p. 2000. 96.00 (*3-540-66198-0*) Spr-Verlag.

Mardesic, S., ed. see Segal, J.

Mardh, P. A., et al. Chlamydia. (Illus.). 388p. (C). 1989. text 85.00 (*0-306-42965-9*, Kluwer Plenum) Kluwer Academic.

Mardh, Peter-Anders, jt. ed. see Schleifer, K. H.

Mardia, K. V. Scientific Foundations of Jainism. (C). 1990. reprint ed. 14.00 (*81-208-0658-1*, Pub. by Motilal Bnarsidass) S Asia.

Mardia, K. V., et al. Multivariate Analysis. LC 79-40922. (Probability & Mathematical Statistics Ser.). 1980. pap. text 73.00 (*0-12-471252-5*) Acad Pr.

Mardian, F. Pius. Beyond the Keyhole: An Intimate Journal. LC 97-93694. (Illus.). 179p. 1999. pap. 14.00 (*1-57579-151-X*) Pine Hill Pr.

Mardiguian. Troubleshooting EMI Techniques. LC 99-33555. (Electronics Workbench Circuit Solution Ser.). 300p. 1999. 60.00 (*0-07-134418-7*) McGraw.

Mardiguian, Michael. Grounding & Bonding. LC 88-80528. (Electromagnetic Interference & Compatibility Ser.: Vol. 2). (Illus.). 408p. 1988. 50.00 (*0-944916-02-3*) emf-emi Control.

— How to Control Electrical Noise. 2nd ed. Price, Edward R., ed. LC 81-70305. (Illus.). 87p. 1983. text 29.00 (*0-932263-22-4*) emf-emi Control.

Mardiguian, Michael, jt. auth. see White, Donald R.

***Mardin, P. Serif.** The Genesis of Young Ottoman Thought: A Study in the Modernization of Turkish Political Ideas. LC 00-38779. (Modern Intellectual & Political History of the Middle East Ser.). 2000. pap. 26.95 (*0-8156-2861-7*) Syracuse U Pr.

Mardin, Serif. Religion & Social Change in Modern Turkey: The Case of Bediuzzaman Said Nursi. LC 89-4280. (SUNY Series in Near Eastern Studies). 267p. (C). 1989. text 21.50 (*0-88706-996-7*) State U NY Pr.

***Mardin, Serif.** Religion, Society & Modernity in Turkey. LC 99-36874. 464p. 1999. 75.00 (*0-8156-2810-2*); pap. text 39.95 (*0-8156-2816-1*) Syracuse U Pr.

Mardin, Yusuf. Colloquial Turkish. (Trubner's Colloquial Manuals Ser.). 1976. pap. 14.95 (*0-7100-8415-3*, Routledge Thoemms) Routledge.

Mardiquian, Michael. Electromagnetic Control in Components & Devices. LC 88-80524. (Electromagnetic Interference & Compatibility Ser.: Vol. 5). (Illus.). 492p. 1988. 69.00 (*0-944916-05-8*) emf-emi Control.

— Electrostatic Discharge Understand, Simulate & Fix ESD. Problems. LC 85-80686. (Illus.). 205p. 1985. 65.00 (*0-932263-27-5*) emf-emi Control.

— EMI Control Methodology & Procedures. LC 88-81458. (Electromagnetic Interference & Compatibility Ser.: Vol. 8). (Illus.). 347p. 1988. 165.00 (*0-944916-08-2*) emf-emi Control.

Mardiros, Anthony. William Irvine: The Life of a Prairie Radical. 298p. 1979. 22.95 (*0-88862-238-4*, Pub. by J Lorimer) Formac Dist Ltd.

Mardirosian, Tom. Saved from Obscurity. 1989. pap. 5.25 (*0-8222-0991-8*) Dramatists Play.

— Subfertile. 1991. pap. 5.25 (*0-8222-1092-4*) Dramatists Play.

Mardirossian, F., et al, eds. Clusters & Groups of Galaxies. 704p. 1984. text 309.00 (*90-277-1772-9*) Kluwer Academic.

Mardis, Jas., ed. KenteCloth: Southwest Voices of the African Diaspora. LC 97-44983. 256p. 1998. 25.95 (*1-57441-047-4*); pap. 19.95 (*1-57441-040-7*) UNTX Pr.

Mardis, Lloyd. The Burro & the Basket. LC 97-51131. (Illus.). 32p. (J). 1997. 13.95 (*1-57168-178-7*) Sunbelt Media.

Mardock, Robert W., jt. ed. see Richmond, Robert W.

Mardon, D. K. An Illustrated Catalogue of the Rothschild Collection of Fleas (Siphonaptera) in the British Museum (Natural History) Pygiopsyllidae, Vol. VI. (Illus.). 306p. 1987. 135.00 (*0-318-36425-5*) OUP.

— An Illustrated Catalogue of the Rothschild Collection of Fleas (Siphonaptera) in the British Museum (Natural History) Vol. 6. Pygiopsylliiae. (Illus.). 306p. 1987. 145.00 (*0-565-00820-X*) OUP.

Mardon, J., et al. Stock Quality Factors Affecting Paper Machine Efficiency. 50p. 1972. 10.20 (*1-895288-25-8*) Pulp & Paper.

Mardon, J., et al. The Struggle for Uniformity: The Design & Conduct of a Paper Machine Survey. 75p. 1971. pap. 4.90 (*1-895288-26-6*) Pulp & Paper.

Mardon, Jasper. Headboxes. 100p. 1993. pap. 100.00 (*1-85802-026-3*, Pub. by Pira Internatl) Bks Intl VA.

Mardon, Thomas W. LANs: Applications of IEEE-Ansi 802 Standards. 320p. 1989. pap. 39.95 (*0-471-62049-1*) Wiley.

Mardorf, Judy. When a Drunk Driver Kills: A Widow's Survival. Krumm, LaRue, ed. LC 94-96787. (Illus.). 128p. (Orig.). 1994. pap. 7.95 (*0-9643936-3-8*) Taleteller.

Mardrus, J. C. Thousand Nights & One Night, Vol. 1. 644p. 1986. pap. 18.99 (*0-415-04539-8*) Routledge.

— Thousand Nights & One Night, Vol. 2. 608p. 1986. pap. 18.99 (*0-415-04540-1*) Routledge.

An Asterisk (*) at the beginning of an entry indicates that the title is appearing for the first time.

— Thousand Nights & One Night, Vol. 3. 576p. 1986. pap. 18.99 (*0-415-04541-X*) Routledge.
— Thousand Nights & One Night, Vol. 4. 544p. 1987. pap. 18.99 (*0-415-04542-8*) Routledge.
Mardrus, J. C., jt. ed. see Mathers, E. P.
Mardyks, Raymond. Sedona Starseed: A Galactic Initiation. (Illus.). 144p. 1995. pap. 14.95 (*0-9644180-0-2*) Star Heart.
Mardyks, Raymond & Alana-Leah, Stacia. Maya Calendar: Voice of the Galaxy. (Illus.). 126p. (Orig.). 1999. pap. 13.00 (*0-9644180-2-9*, Pub. by Star Heart) New Leaf Dist.
Mardzhanishvili, K. K., jt. auth. see Bogolyubov, N. N.
Mardzhanishvili, M. A. Analysis of the Spatial Behavior & Size of Modern Buildings for Earthquake-Proof Design. Dhillion, K. S., tr. from RUS. 145p. (C). 1985. 116.00 (*90-6191-595-3*, Pub. by A A Balkema) Ashgate Pub Co.
— Seismic Design of Frame-Panel Buildings & Their Structural Members. Dhillon, K. S., tr. from RUS. 131p. (C). 1984. text 116.00 (*90-6191-424-8*, Pub. by A A Balkema) Ashgate Pub Co.
— Theoretical & Experimental Analysis of Members of Earthquake-Proof Frame Panel Buildings. (C). 1987. 28.50 (*0-8364-2121-3*, Pub. by Oxford IBH) S Asia.
Mardzhanishvilli, L., jt. auth. see Mardzhanishvilli, M. A.
Mardzhanishvilli, M. A. & Mardzhanishvilli, L. Theoretical & Experimental Analysis of Members of Earthquake-Proof Frame Panel Buildings. Dhillon, K., tr. from RUS. 180p. (C). 1986. text 116.00 (*90-6191-472-8*, Pub. by A A Balkema) Ashgate Pub Co.
Mare, jt. auth. see Smith.
Mare, Eric De, see De Mare, Eric.
Mare, G. R. De, see De Mare, G. R.
Mare, Gerhard. Ethnicity & Politics in South Africa. LC 92-33428. 144p. (C). 1993. reprint ed. text 55.00 (*1-85649-207-9*, Pub. by Zed Books); reprint ed. text 19.95 (*1-85649-208-7*, Pub. by Zed Books) St Martin.
Mare, Margaret L. Eduard Morike: The Man & the Poet. LC 72-7860. (Illus.). 275p. 1973. reprint ed. lib. bdg. 19.75 (*0-8371-6538-5*, MEMO, Greenwood Pr) Greenwood.
Mare, Margaret L., tr. see Lichtenberg, Georg C.
Mare, Nancy N., jt. auth. see Smith, Lorraine.
Mare, Nancy N., jt. auth. see Smith, Lorraine C.
Mare Nostrum Enterprises Staff, ed. see Cerisoles, Rene.
Mare, Vladimir. What Is Our Future, America? (Illus.). 1985. 24.95 (*0-933517-00-9*) V & M World Wide.
Mare, Walter De La, see De La Mare, Walter.
Marean, Cameron G., jt. auth. see Werner, Lynne A.
Marecak, Edward. The Art of Edward Marecak. LC 96-14930. (Documents of Colorado Art Ser.). (Illus.). 72p. (Orig.). 1997. pap. 44.95 (*0-938075-60-8*) Ocean View Bks.
Marecek, Mary. Breaking Free from Partner Abuse: Voices of Battered Women Caught in the Cycle of Domestic Violence. LC 98-44933. Orig. Title: Say "No!" to Violence. 1999. 15.95 (*1-885356-57-9*) Morning Glory.
— Breaking Free from Partner Abuse: Voices of Battered Women Caught in the Cycle of Domestic Violence. LC 98-44933. Orig. Title: Say "No!" to Violence. 1999. pap. 8.95 (*1-885356-53-6*) Morning Glory.
— Jane Roberts' a View from the Other Side. 96p. 1998. pap. 14.95 (*0-9663258-0-X*) Pyramid Press FL.
Marechal, Chantal A., ed. In Quest of Marie de France, a Twelfth-Century Poet. LC 92-24244. (Illus.). 308p. 1992. text 99.95 (*0-7734-9586-X*) E Mellen.
Marechal, Ernest, jt. auth. see Kennedy, Joseph P.
Marechal, J. F. Le, see Le Marechal, J. F.
Marechal, Pierre S. Dictionnaire des Athees Anciens et Modernes. 438p. reprint ed. write for info. (*0-318-71376-4*) G Olms Pubs.
Marechal-Ross, Patricia, jt. auth. see Steele, Ross.
Marechaux, Pascal. Impressions of Yemen. Guillaume, Kathleen, tr. from FRE. LC 97-27817. (Illus.). 200p. 1997. 55.00 (*2-08-013647-X*, Pub. by Flammarion) Abbeville Pr.
Marechera, Dambudzo. Black Sunlight. (African Writers Ser.). 117p. (Orig.). (C). 1981. pap. 9.95 (*0-435-90237-7*, 90237) Heinemann.
— House of Hunger. (African Writers Ser.). 154p. (C). 1993. pap. 10.95 (*0-435-90986-X*, 90986) Heinemann.
***Marechera, Dambudzo & Veit-Wild, Flora.** The Black Insider. LC 99-28834. 1999. write for info. (*0-86543-735-1*) Africa World.
Marechera, Dambudzo & Veit-Wild, Flora. Cemetery of Mind. LC 99-28836. 1999. write for info. (*0-86543-733-5*) Africa World.
— Scrapiron Blues. LC 99-15296. 1999. write for info. (*0-86543-731-9*) Africa World.
Marecki, Thomas. Lodown: Graphic Engineering. 192p. 1999. pap. text 39.99 (*3-931126-16-1*, Pub. by Die Gestalten) Consort Bk Sales.
***Marecki, Thomas.** Schizophrenic! More Lodown Graphic Engineering. (Illus.). 2000. pap. text 42.00 (*3-931126-41-2*) Die Gestalten.
Maredia, K. M., jt. ed. see Erbisch, F. H.
Maredia, Karen & Bedford, Bruce. Proceedings of the USAID Latin America Caribbean Region Biosafety Workshop (1993) (Illus.). 39p. (Orig.). (C). 1994. pap. text 25.00 (*0-7881-1504-9*) DIANE Pub.
Maree, Aaron. Dip Me in Chocolate. (Illus.). 256p. 1998. 15.95 (*0-7322-5913-4*) HarpC.
Maree, Kobus. Become an Ace at Math. 1998. pap. text 6.95 (*0-627-01839-4*, Pub. by J L Van Schaik) BHB Intl.
— Kick Start for Math. 1998. pap. text 7.95 (*0-627-01995-1*, Pub. by J L Van Schaik) BHB Intl.
Mareel, Marc M., et al. Mechanisms of Invasion & Metastasis. (Illus.). 608p. 1991. lib. bdg. 251.00 (*0-8493-6254-7*, RC269) CRC Pr.
Mareels, I. & Polderman, Jan W. Adaptive Systems: An Introduction. LC 96-24283. 339p. 1996. 54.50 (*0-8176-3877-6*) Birkhauser.
Mareels, Iven & Polderman, Jan W. Adaptive Systems: An Introduction. LC 96-24283. (Systems & Control Ser.). 1996. write for info. (*3-7643-3877-6*) Birkhauser.
Marefat, Roya, ed. Beyond the Architecture of Death: The Shrine of the Shah-i Zinda in Samarqand. (Islamic Art & Architecture Ser.: No. 7). Date not set. 65.00 (*1-56859-047-4*) Mazda Pubs.
Marei, H. Basic Technical Dictionary: French-English-German-Arabic. (ARA, ENG, FRE & GER.). 363p. 1973. lib. bdg. 125.00 (*0-7859-0804-8*, M-9752) Fr & Eur.
Marei, Sayed A. The World Food Crisis. 2nd ed. LC 77-14527. (Illus.). 144p. reprint ed. pap. 44.70 (*0-608-18743-7*, 203034600068) Bks Demand.
***Mareiner, Michael.** Mittelhochdeutsche Minnereden und Minneallegorien der Prager Handschrift R VI Fc 26. 1999. 52.95 (*3-906763-15-3*, Pub. by P Lang) P Lang Pubng.
Marek, Ann M. & Edelsky, Carole, eds. Reflections & Connections: Essays in Honor of Kenneth Goodman's Influence on Language. 448p. 1998. text 85.00 (*1-57273-157-5*); pap. text 35.00 (*1-57273-158-3*) Hampton Pr NJ.
Marek, Ann M., jt. auth. see Goodman, Yetta M.
***Marek, Annemarie & Berens, Debbie.** Millennium Madness: 2000 Ways to Mark the Moment. 120p. 1999. pap. 17.95 (*0-9674401-0-6*) Marek Company.
Marek, Anthony C., ed. see Marek, Ellie.
Marek, C., et al. Operation Dry Dock: Silent Death Annex Book. (Silent Death - The Next Millennium Ser.). (Illus.). 92p. 1997. pap. 14.00 (*1-55806-292-0*, 7215) Iron Crown Ent Inc.
— Universal Night Watch: Silent Death Forces Book. (Silent Death - The Next Millennium Ser.). (Illus.). 48p. 1997. pap. 14.00 (*1-55806-278-5*, 7214) Iron Crown Ent Inc.
Marek, Charles R., ed. Low-Temperature Properties of Bithuminous Materials & Compacted Bithuminous Paving Mixtures - STP 628. 1977. 11.00 (*0-8031-0194-5*, STP628) ASTM.
Marek, Charles R., jt. ed. see Schreuders, Hans G.
Marek, Claudia Craig, jt. auth. see St. Armand, R. Paul.
Marek, Don. Grand Rapids Art Metalwork: 1902-1918. LC 99-94051. (Illus.). 144p. 1999. 70.00 (*0-9669851-0-9*) Heartwood.
***Marek, Don.** Quaint Furniture Catalog, No. 42. Copeland, Peter A. & Copeland, Janet H., eds. (Illus.). 128p. 1999. pap. 25.00 (*0-9638771-2-7*) Parchment NJ.
Marek, Donna. Creme De Carmel: The Story of the Lively Personalities Who Shaped California's Fabled Coastal Kingdom. LC 94-65083. (Illus.). 160p. 1994. 29.95 (*1-879373-88-2*) D Marek.
Marek, Edmund A. & Lewis, Melanie. Laboratory Investigations for General Science, Part II. (Illus.). 101p. (C). 1982. pap. text 8.95 (*0-89641-078-1*) American Pr.
Marek, Edmund A., et al. Laboratory Investigations for General Science, Pt. I. (Illus.). 89p. 1982. pap. text 9.95 (*0-89641-111-7*) American Pr.
Marek, Edward F. Criminal Federal Rules & Practice. 528p. 1996. ring bd. 69.98 (*0-938065-88-2*) James Pub Santa Ana.
Marek, Ellie. Eating Roses: Bites of Living Humor. unabridged ed. Marek, Anthony C., ed. LC 98-92419. (Illus.). ii, 86p. 1998. pap. 10.95 (*0-9662275-0-6*) Decipher Pub.
Marek, Franz, jt. auth. see Fischer, Ernst.
Marek, George R. A Front Seat at the Opera. 1977. 19.95 (*0-8369-2412-6*) Ayer.
Marek, George R., ed. World Treasury of Grand Opera: Its Triumphs, Trials & Great Personalities. LC 74-167383. (Essay Index Reprint Ser.). 1977. reprint ed. 35.95 (*0-8369-2463-0*) Ayer.
Marek, Jayne. Women Editing Modernism: "Little" Magazines & Literary History. (Illus.). 264p. (C). 1995. pap. 18.00 (*0-8131-0854-3*) U Pr of Ky.
Marek, Jayne, compiled by. Poetry Index, 1912-1997. LC 98-158147. 860p. 1998. lib. bdg. 98.00 (*1-881505-09-X*, Poetry Pr) Modern Poetry.
Marek, Jindrich, jt. auth. see Bauer, Frantisek.
Marek, Lee, et al. Lee Marek's Soakin' Science: Book & Kit. 48p. (J). (gr. 3-7). 1999. pap. 14.99 (*1-58184-029-2*) Somerville Hse.
Marek, Ludwig J. Let Me Show to the World My Eyes (The American Years) LC 98-30724. 68p. 1998. pap. 14.95 (*0-7734-3086-5*, Mellen Poetry Pr) E Mellen.
Marek, M. A., tr. see Glusha, Laura & Muldrew, Karen.
Marek, Michael F. Programming in C. (Introduction to Computing Ser.). 1988. pap. 29.95 (*0-8273-2950-4*) Delmar.
Marek, Michael F., ed. Ciceronis, M. Tulli Fascicule 16: Orationes de Lege Agraria. (LAT.). 1983. 21.95 (*3-322-00190-3*, T1186, Pub. by B G Teubner) U of Mich Pr.
Marek, Michael F. & Cavallo. The Learning Cycle: Elementary School Science Teaching & Beyond. LC 96-52276. 1997. pap. text 32.00 (*0-435-07133-5*, 07133) Heinemann.
Marek, Milos & Schreiber, Igor. Chaotic Behaviour of Deterministic Dissipative Systems. (Illus.). 377p. (C). 1995. pap. text 49.95 (*0-521-43830-6*) Cambridge U Pr.
Marek, Milos, jt. auth. see Kubicek, Milan.
Marek, Pavel, et al. Simulation-Based Reliability Assessment for Structural Engineers. Chen, Wai-Fah, ed. (New Directions in Civil Engineering Ser.). 384p. 1995. lib. bdg. 104.95 incl. disk (*0-8493-8286-6*, 8286) CRC Pr.
Marek, Rosanne J. Opportunities in Social Science. LC 96-47281. (Illus.). 160p. 1997. 14.95 (*0-8442-4573-9*, 45739) NTC Contemp Pub Co.
— Social Science. LC 96-47281. (Opportunities In . . . Ser.). (Illus.). 160p. 1997. pap. 11.95 (*0-8442-4574-7*, 45747, VGM Career) NTC Contemp Pub Co.
Marek, Roseanne J. Opportunities in Social Science Careers. 160p. 1994. pap. 11.95 (*0-8442-8668-0*, VGM Career) NTC Contemp Pub Co.
Marek, Tonia, jt. auth. see Del Rosso, Joy M.
Marek, Wiktor. Elements of Logic & Foundations of Mathematics in Problems. 1983. lib. bdg. 113.50 (*90-277-1084-8*) Kluwer Academic.
Marek, Wiktor, et al, eds. Logic Programming & Non-Monotonic Reasoning: Third International Conference, LPNMR '95, Lexington, KY, USA, June 24-26, 1995: Proceedings. (Lecture Notes in Computer Science Ser.: No. 928). 1995. write for info. (*0-387-59487-6*) Spr-Verlag.
— Logic Programming & Non-Monotonic Reasoning: Third International Conference, LPNMR '95, Lexington, KY, USA, June 24-26, 1995: Proceedings. (Lecture Notes in Computer Science Ser.: No. 928). 415p. 1995. 68.00 (*3-540-59487-6*) Spr-Verlag.
Marek, Wiktor & Onyszkiewicz, Janusz. Elements of Logic & Foundations of Mathematics in Problems. 1985. pap. text 70.50 (*90-277-2131-9*) Kluwer Academic.
Marek, Wiktor & Truszczynski, M. Nonmonotonic Logic: Context-Dependent Reasoning. Loveland, D. W., ed. (Artificial Intelligence Ser.). x, 396p. 1993. 93.95 (*0-387-56448-9*) Spr-Verlag.
Marel, J. Van der, see Van der Marel, J.
MarElia, Beatrice. The Great Mirage. LC 85-15117. 1986. pap. 13.95 (*0-87949-249-X*) Ashley Bks.
***Marelin the Magician Staff.** Merlin's Message: Reawakening & Remembering, 1. LC 97-91214. 123p. 1998. pap. 5.00 (*1-891411-00-4*) Serious Comedy.
— Merlin's Message: Reawakening & Remembering. 2nd rev. ed. 128p. 1998. pap. 7.00 (*1-891411-02-0*) Serious Comedy.
Marelli, Maria E., tr. see Feldman, Cathy, ed.
Marello, Carla, jt. ed. see Fordyce, Rachel.
***Maremaa, John & Stewart, Bill.** QuickTime for Java: A Developer's Reference. (QuickTime Developer Ser.). 600p. 1999. pap. 49.95 incl. cd-rom (*0-12-305440-0*) Morgan Kaufmann.
***Maremaa, Tom.** Filemaker PRO 5 for Dummies. (Illus.). 384p. 1999. pap. 19.99 (*0-7645-0606-4*) IDG Bks.
Maremaa, Tom. FileMaker Pro 4 for Dummies. LC 97-80698. 384p. 1997. pap. 19.99 (*0-7645-0210-7*) IDG Bks.
Mareman, Tom. FileMaker Pro 3 for Macs for Dummies. LC 95-81102. 384p. 1996. pap. 19.99 (*1-56884-906-0*) IDG Bks.
Maremmani, Icro, jt. ed. see Tagliamonte, Alessandro.
Maren, Michael. The Best Intentions. 1996. 25.00 (*0-02-920033-4*) Free Pr.
— The Road to Hell: The Ravaging Effects of Foreing Aid International Charity. LC 96-41168. 320p. 1997. 24.50 (*0-684-82800-6*) Free Pr.
Marenbon, John. Early Medieval Philosophy, 480-1150. 224p. (C). 1988. pap. 27.99 (*0-415-00070-X*) Routledge.
— Later Medieval Philosophy, 1150-1350. 248p. (C). 1987. lib. bdg. 35.00 (*0-685-19266-0*) Routledge.
— Later Medieval Philosophy, 1150-1350: An Introduction. 248p. (C). 1991. pap. 27.99 (*0-415-06807-X*, A6265) Routledge.
— The Philosophy of Peter Abelard. 393p. 1997. text 64.95 (*0-521-55397-0*) Cambridge U Pr.
***Marenbon, John.** The Philosophy of Peter Abelard. 393p. (C). 1999. pap. 24.95 (*0-521-66399-7*) Cambridge U Pr.
Marenbon, John, ed. Medieval Philosophy Vol. 3. LC 97-7483. (Routledge History of Philosophy: Vol. 3). 544p. (C). 1998. 90.00 (*0-415-05377-3*, C0278) Routledge.
Marenco, Ethne K. The Transformation of Sikh Society. 342p. 1976. 24.95 (*0-318-36785-8*) Asia Bk Corp.
— The Transformation of Sikh Society. (Illus.). 342p. 1972. pap. 16.95 (*0-913244-08-2*) Hapi Pr.
Marengo, Franco D. Rules of the Italian Political Game. 144p. 1981. text 55.95 (*0-566-00301-5*, Pub. by Dartmth Pub) Ashgate Pub Co.
Marengo, Silvia. Exchange Rate Policy for Mercosur: Lessons from the European Union. Straubhaar, Thomas, ed. (Schriften zur Wirtschaftstheorie und Wirtschaftspolitik Ser.: Band 9). (Illus.). xvi, 230p. 1998. pap. 45.95 (*3-631-32791-9*) P Lang Pubng.
Marenin, Otwin. Policing Change, Changing Police: International Perspectives. LC 95-37407. (Reference Library of Social Science: Vol. 1025). 1995. write for info. (*0-614-08568-3*) Garland.
Marenin, Otwin, ed. Policing Change, Changing Police: International Perspectives. LC 95-37407. (Current Issues in Criminal Justice Ser.: Vol. 14). (Illus.). 368p. 1996. text 65.00 (*0-8153-1995-9*, SS1025) Garland.
Marenka, Stephen, jt. auth. see Watkins, Christopher.
Marenkov, O. S., ed. Handbook of Partial Attenuation Coefficients of Characteristic X-Ray Radiation. 207p. 1994. lib. bdg. 165.00 (*1-56072-102-2*) Nova Sci Pubs.
Marenkov, O. S. & Komyak, N. I. Handbook of Photon-Interaction Coefficients in Radio Isotope-Excited X-Ray Fluorescence Analysis. 225p. (C). 1990. text 130.00 (*0-941743-79-9*) Nova Sci Pubs.
Marennyi, Ya I. Tunnels with In-Situ Pressed Concrete Lining. Zeidler, Ryszard B., ed. (Illus.). 256p. 1993. text 104.00 (*90-5410-141-5*, Pub. by A A Balkema) Ashgate Pub Co.
Marentes. Joe Vasoconcelos & the Writing of Mexican Revolution. 2000. 32.00 (*0-8057-1646-7*) Mac Lib Ref.
Marentette, Lawrence, jt. auth. see Kellman, Robert M.
Marenzi, Luca. Jean-michel Basquiat. 1999. pap. text 45.00 (*88-8158-239-2*) Charta.
Marenzio, Luca. Il Sesto Libro de' Madrigali a Sei Voci (1595) Myers, Patricia, ed. (Secular Works: Vol. 6). (ITA., Illus.). xxxv, 220p. 1983. pap. 50.00 (*0-8450-7106-8*) Broude.
— Madrigali A Quattro Cinque E Sei Voci, Libro Primo, 1588. Ledbetter, Steven, ed. (Secular Works: Vol. 7). (Illus.). xxvi, 167p. 1977. pap. 50.00 (*0-8450-7107-6*) Broude.
— Madrigali Spirituali a Cinque Voci, Libro Primo, 1584. (Secular Works: Vol. 17). 1991. pap. 50.00 (*0-8450-7117-3*) Broude.
— L' Ottavo Libro de Madrigali a Cinque Voci (1598) (Secular Works: Vol. 15). (Illus.). 1986. pap. 50.00 (*0-8450-7115-7*) Broude.
— Il Settimo Libro de'Madrigali A Cinque Voci (1595) (Secular Works: Vol. 14). (Illus.). 1980. pap. 50.00 (*0-8450-7114-9*) Broude.
— Ten Madrigals for Mixed Voices. Arnold, Denis, ed. 84p. 1985. 17.95 (*0-19-343675-2*) OUP.
Marer, Patrick J. The Safe & Effective Use of Pesticides: Pesticide Application Compendium 1. LC 87-73550. 400p. 1988. pap. 30.00 (*0-931876-83-4*, 3324) ANR Pubns CA.
Marer, Patrick J., ed. Residential, Industrial & Institutional Pest Control: Pesticide Application Compendium 2. (Illus.). 232p. (Orig.). 1991. pap. 25.00 (*0-931876-93-1*, 3334) ANR Pubns CA.
Marer, Patrick J. & Grimes, Mark, eds. Forest & Right-of-Way Pesticide Application: Pesticide Application Compendium 4. 1995. pap. 30.00 (*1-879906-19-8*, 3336) ANR Pubns CA.
Marer, Patrick J., et al. Wood Preservation: Pesticide Application Compendium 3. LC 92-63207. (Illus.). 92p. 1992. pap. 15.00 (*1-879906-05-8*, 3335) ANR Pubns CA.
Marer, Paul. Dollar GNPs of the U .S S.R. & Eastern Europe. LC 85-45101. 256p. reprint ed. pap. 79.40 (*0-7837-4253-8*, 204396500012) Bks Demand.
— U. S. Financing of East-West Trade: The Political Economy of Government Credits & the National Interest. (Studies in East European & Soviet Planning, Development, & Trade: No. 22). (Illus.). 1975. pap. text 5.00 (*0-89249-030-6*) Intl Development.
Marer, Paul & Montias, John M., eds. East European Integration & East-West Trade. LC 79-3181. (Studies in East European & Soviet Planning, Development, & Trade: No. 28). (Illus.). 452p. 1980. reprint ed. pap. 140.20 (*0-608-18467-5*, 205671000081) Bks Demand.
Marer, Paul & Tabaczynski, Eugeniusz, eds. Polish U. S. Industrial Cooperation in the 1980's: Findings of a Joint Research Project. LC 81-47884. (Studies in East European & Soviet Planning, Development, & Trade: No. 30). 438p. 1981. reprint ed. pap. 135.80 (*0-7837-9660-9*, 205929300005) Bks Demand.
Marer, Sharon & Piwonski, Shirley. Sedona, Responding to the Call. (Illus.). 200p. (Orig.). 1994. pap. 12.95 (*1-885782-89-6*) Sources of Light.
Mares, Benny. Executive Protection: A Professional's Guide to Bodyguarding. 112p. 1994. pap. 12.00 (*0-87364-798-X*) Paladin Pr.
Mares, Bill. Fishing with the Presidents. LC 98-21776. xvi, 256 p. 1999. 14.95 (*0-8117-0638-9*) Stackpole.
Mares, Bill & Bryan, Frank. Out of Order: The Very Unofficial Vermont State House Archives. LC 91-66745. (Illus.). 128p. 1991. pap. 9.95 (*0-933050-88-7*) New Eng Pr VT.
Mares, Bill, jt. auth. see Bryan, Frank.
Mares, D. J., jt. ed. see Noda, Kaz.
Mares, David. The Evolution of U. S. - Mexican Agricultural Relations: The Changing Roles of the Mexican State & Mexican Agricultural Producers. (Research Reports: No. 16). 44p. (Orig.). (C). 1981. ring bd. 5.00 (*0-935391-15-0*, RR-16) UCSD Ctr US-Mex.
Mares, David R., ed. Civil-Military Relations: Building Democracy & Regional Cooperation in Latin America, Southern Asia & Central Europe. LC 98-9524. (Latin America in Global Perspective Ser.). 288p. (C). 1998. text 69.00 (*0-8133-2421-1*, Pub. by Westview) HarpC.
Mares, E. A. The Unicorn Poem & Flowers & Songs of Sorrow. 78p. (Orig.). 1992. pap. 8.95 (*0-931122-65-1*) West End.
Mares, E. A., tr. see Lamadrid, Enrique E., ed.
Mares, F. H., ed. see Jonson, Ben.
Mares, F. H., ed. see Shakespeare, William.
***Mares, Frantisek V.** Diachronische Phonologie des Ur - Und Fruhslavischen: Herausgegeben und Redigiert Von Angela Bergermayer und Georg Holzer Mit Zwei Von Hanna Vintr Aus Dem Tschechischen Ubersetzten Sowie Drei Weiteren Aufsatzen. (GER.). 174p. 1999. 38.00 (*3-631-31394-2*) P Lang Pubng.
Mares, George C. The History of the Typewriter Successor to the Pen. LC 85-90315. (Illus.). 320p. 1985. 24.95 (*0-911160-87-6*) Post Group.
Mares, Jeffrey S. Cotton Mather's "Problema Theologicum" An Authoritative Edition. (Illus.). 107p. 1995. pap. 15.00 (*0-944026-65-6*) Am Antiquarian.
Mares, Lorraine M. The Souls Resting Promises. LC 97-61626. 64p. 1998. pap. 8.99 (*1-57921-054-6*, Pub. by WinePress Pub) BookWorld.
***Mares, Michael A.** Encyclopedia of Deserts. LC 98-44437. 1999. 49.95 (*0-8061-3146-2*) U of Okla Pr.
Mares, Michael A. Heritage at Risk: Oklahoma's Hidden Treasure. (Illus.). 73p. (Orig.). 1988. pap. 20.00 (*1-883090-02-4*) OK Museum.
Mares, Michael A. & Schmidly, David J. Latin American Mammalogy: History, Biodiversity, & Conservation. LC 91-10264. (Oklahoma Museum of Natural History Publications). (Illus.). 480p. 1991. 57.50 (*0-8061-2343-5*) U of Okla Pr.
Mares, Michael E., et al. A Guide to Limited Liability Companies, 4 vols. Incl. Vol. 1. 1997. ring bd. 170.00 (*0-7646-0248-9*); Vol. 2. 1997. ring bd. 170.00

M

An Asterisk (*) at the beginning of an entry indicates that the title is appearing for the first time.

(0-7646-0249-7); Vol. 3. 1997. ring bd. 170.00 (0-7646-0250-0); Vol. 4. 1997. ring bd. 170.00 (0-7646-0251-9); LC 97-154311. Set ring bd. 168.00 (0-7646-0058-3); Set ring bd. 168.00 (0-7646-0247-0) Prctnrs Pub Co.

Mares, Milan. Computation Over Fuzzy Quantities. 176p. 1994. boxed set 99.95 (0-8493-7635-1) CRC Pr.

Mares, Penny. In Control: Hel with Incontinence. (C). 1989. 45.00 (0-86242-088-1, Pub. by Age Concern Eng) St Mut.

Mares, Rafael, jt. auth. see Kutner, Laurie A.

Mares, Stanislav. Introduction to Applied Geophysics. 556p. 1984. text 274.00 (90-277-1424-X) Kluwer Academic.

Mares, Stanislav, ed. see Karous, Milos, et al.

Mares, Theun. The Mists of Dragon Lore: The Toltec Teachings. (Toltec Teachings Ser.: Vol. 3). 1998. pap. 16.95 (1-919792-02-3) Lionheart Pub OH.

***Mares, Theun.** The Quest for Maleness. Mitchley, Charles, ed. (Illus.). 232p. 1999. pap. 13.95 (1-919792-07-4) Lionheart Pub OH.

— Return of the Warriors. Mitchley, Charles, ed. (Toltec Teachings Ser.: Vol. 1). (Illus.). 277p. 2000. pap. 16.95 (1-919792-08-2) Lionheart Pub OH.

— Return of the Warriors. 3rd ed. Mitchley, Charles, ed. (Toltec Teachings Ser.: Vol. 1). (Illus.). 2000. 24.95 (1-919792-09-0) Lionheart Pub OH.

— Shadows of Wolf Fire. Mitchley, Charles, ed. (Toltec Teachings Ser.: Vol. 4). (Illus.). 2000. 24.95 (1-919792-05-8); pap. 18.95 (1-919792-04-X) Lionheart Pub OH.

— This Darned Elusive Happiness. Mitchley, Charles, ed. (Illus.). 160p. 1999. pap. 12.95 (1-919792-03-1, Pub. by Lionheart Pub OH) New Leaf Dist.

— Unveil the Mysteries of the Female. Mitchley, Charles, ed. (Illus.). 200p. 1999. pap. 13.95 (1-919792-06-6) Lionheart Pub OH.

Mares, William J. Fishing with the Presidents: An Anecdotal History. LC 98-21776. (Illus.). 160p. 1999. pap. 14.95 (0-8117-2768-8) Stackpole.

— Making Beer. 2nd ed. 208p. 1994. pap. 17.00 (0-679-75502-0) Knopf.

Maresca, Bruno, et al, eds. Molecular Biology & Its Application to Medical Mycology. LC 92-49124. (NATO ASI Ser.: Vol. 69). 1993. write for info. (3-540-54609-X); 211.95 (0-387-54609-X) Spr-Verlag.

Maresca, Bruno & Kobayashi, George S. Molecular Biology of Pathogenic Fungi: A Laboratory Manual. 577p. 1994. spiral bd. 95.00 (0-914386-27-1) Telos Pr.

Maresca, Bruno & Lindquist, S., eds. Heat Shock. (Illus.). 344p. 1991. 109.95 (0-387-54111-X) Spr-Verlag.

Maresca, Frank, jt. ed. see Metcalf, Eugene W.

Maresca, John J. To Helsinki: The Conference on Security & Cooperation in Europe, 1973-75. 2nd ed. LC 87-22261. xv, 315p. (C). 1987. pap. text 22.95 (0-8223-0791-X) Duke.

Maresca, Joseph W., Jr. & Hillger, Robert W. Chemicals Stored in USTs: Characteristics & Leak Detection. (Illus.). 61p. (Orig.). (C). 1992. pap. text 30.00 (1-56806-114-5) DIANE Pub.

Maresca, Joseph W., Jr., et al. Volumetric Leak Detection Methods for Underground Fuel Storage Tanks. LC 89-71008. (Pollution Technology Review Ser.: No. 180). (Illus.). 356p. 1990. 57.00 (0-8155-1230-9) Noyes.

***Maresca, Louis & Maslen, Stuart, eds.** The Banning of Anti-Personnel Landmines: The Work of the International Committee of the Red Cross, 1955-1999. 544p. (C). 2001. Price not set. (0-521-78317-8) Cambridge U Pr.

Maresca, Thomas E. Three English Epics: Studies of Troilus & Criseyde, The Faerie Queen, & Paradise Lost. LC 79-1080. 238p. reprint ed. pap. 73.80 (0-7837-6022-1, 204583400008) Bks Demand.

Maresca, Tom. Mastering Wine: A Learner's Manual. LC 92-8288. 320p. 1992. pap. 14.00 (0-8021-3298-7, Grove) Grove-Atltic.

— The Right Wine. LC 90-43459. 384p. 1992. pap. 14.00 (0-8021-3297-9, Grove) Grove-Atltic.

Maresca, Tom, jt. auth. see Darrow, Diane.

Marescaux, C., et al, eds. Generalized Non-Convulsive Epilepsy: Focus on GABA-B Receptors. LC 92-2422. (Journal of Neural Transmission: Suppl. 35). (Illus.). 160p. 1992. 111.00 (0-387-82340-9) Spr-Verlag.

Maresceau, Marc, ed. Enlarging the European Union: Relations Between the EU & Central & Eastern Europe. xxv, 403p. 1997. 99.00 (0-582-31848-3, 15715) Gaunt.

— The European Community's Commercial Policy after 1992: The Legal Dimension. LC 92-44287. (ENG & FRE.). 488p. (C). 1993. lib. bdg. 123.50 (0-7923-2131-6) Kluwer Academic.

— The Political & Legal Framework of Trade Relations Between the European Community & Eastern Europe. (C). 1989. lib. bdg. 139.00 (0-7923-0046-7) Kluwer Academic.

***Maresceau, Marc & Lannon, Erwan.** The Eu's Enlargement & Mediterranean Strategies: A Comparative Analysis. LC 00-41513. 2000. write for info. (0-333-77281-4) St Martin.

Maresceau, Marc, jt. ed. see Laurent, Pierre-Henri.

Mareschal, M., ed. Microscopic Simulations of Complex Flows. LC 90-46797. (NATO ASI Ser.: Vol. 229). (Illus.). 374p. (C). 1990. text 144.00 (0-306-43687-6, Kluwer Plenum) Kluwer Academic.

Mareschal, M. & Holian, B. L. Microscopic Simulations of Complex Hydrodynamic Phenomena. (NATO ASI Ser.: Vol. 292). (Illus.). 436p. (C). 1992. text 125.00 (0-306-44226-4, Kluwer Plenum) Kluwer Academic.

Maresh, M. Audit in Obstetrics & Gynecology. (Illus.). 288p. 1994. 70.00 (0-632-03352-5) Blackwell Sci.

Maresic, Josip. Phraseological Dictionary of the Serbian & Croatian Languages: Frazeoloski Rjecnik Hrvatskog Ili Srpskog Jezika. 808p. 1982. 49.95 (0-8288-1998-X, F78630) Fr & Eur.

Maresquelle, H. J., jt. auth. see Meyer, Jean.

Marestier, Jean-Baptiste. Memoir on Steamboats of the United States of America, Printed by the Royal Press, Paris, 1824. Withington, Sidney, tr. LC 57-59433. (Marine Historical Association Publication: No. 31). 100p. reprint ed. pap. 31.00 (0-8357-2794-7, 203992000014) Bks Demand.

Maret, Elizabeth. Women of the Range: Women's Roles in the Texas Beef Cattle Industry. LC 92-45787. (Illus.). 176p. 1993. 32.00 (0-89096-532-3); pap. 12.95 (0-89096-541-2) Tex A&M Univ Pr.

Maret, Pierre De, see Childs, S. Terry & De Maret, Pierre.

Maret, Stephen M. The Prenatal Person: Frank Lake's Maternal-Fetal Distress Syndrome. LC 97-3170. 224p. (C). 1997. 39.00 (0-7618-0768-3) U Pr of Amer.

Maret, Susan. Environmental Health & Risk Assessment, 1990-1994. LC 95-39621. (CPL Bibliographies Ser.: No. 325). 114p. 1995. 10.00 (0-86602-325-9, Sage Prdcls Pr) Sage.

Mareth, E. & Kelly, R. Number Skills. 1980. text 8.85 (0-07-040341-4) McGraw.

Maretis, D. K., jt. auth. see Hoffmann, G. R.

Maretski, Thomas, jt. auth. see Chrisman, Noel.

Marett, Allan, ed. Musica Asiatica, No. 6. (Illus.). 144p. (C). 1991. text 69.95 (0-521-39050-8) Cambridge U Pr.

Marett, Paul. Information Law & Practice. 250p. 1991. text 78.95 (0-566-05402-7, Pub. by Gower) Ashgate Pub Co.

Marett, Robert R. Faith, Hope & Charity in Primitive Religion. LC 77-27193. (Gifford Lectures: 1931-32). reprint ed. 29.50 (0-404-60487-0) AMS Pr.

— Faith, Hope & Charity in Primitive Religion. LC 72-80150. 181p. 1972. reprint ed. 24.95 (0-405-08780-2, Pub. by Blom Pubns) Ayer.

— Sacraments of Simple Folk. LC 77-27192. (Gifford Lectures: 1932-33). reprint ed. 36.50 (0-404-60488-9) AMS Pr.

— The Threshold of Religion. LC 76-44755. reprint ed. 34.50 (0-404-15950-8) AMS Pr.

Marett, Robert R., ed. see Spencer, Baldwin.

Marett, Valerie. Immigrants Settling in the City: Ugandan Asians in Leicester. 256p. 1992. 52.00 (0-7185-1283-9, Pub. by Leicester U Pr) Cassell & Continuum.

Maretzek, Max. Crochets & Quavers: Or Revelations of an Opera Manager in America. 2nd ed. LC 65-23397. (Music Ser.). 1966. reprint ed. lib. bdg. 39.50 (0-306-70915-5) Da Capo.

— Crotchets & Quavers: On Revelations of an Opera Manager in America. (American Biography Ser.). 346p. 1991. reprint ed. lib. bdg. 79.00 (0-7812-8266-7) Rprt Serv.

Maretzki, Thomas W., ed. see Kennedy, Raymond.

Mareus, Leonard J., jt. auth. see Dubler, Nancy N.

Marey, Etienne J. Movement. LC 70-169333. (Literature of Cinema, Ser. 2). (Illus.). 344p. 1979. reprint ed. 23.95 (0-405-03900-X) Ayer.

Marezio, M., jt. auth. see Antipov, E. V.

Marfey, Anne & Gayron, Cathy. The Miracle of Learning: How to Inspire Children. (Illus.). 90p. 1998. pap. 17.95 (0-9667733-0-6) Windflower Pub.

Marffin, Kyle. Carmilla - The Return: A Vampire Novel. LC 98-70433. 336p. 1998. pap. 15.95 (1-891946-02-1) Design Image.

***Marffin, Kyle.** Gothique: A Vampire Novel. 448p. 2000. pap. 15.95 (1-891946-06-4) Design Image.

Marfia, Jim. U. S. Open: Ft. Worth, 1984. (Illus.). 98p. (Orig.). 1985. pap. 5.00 (0-931462-40-1) Chess Ent.

— U. S. Open, 1983. (U. S. Tournament Ser.). (Illus.). 100p. (Orig.). 1984. pap. 6.00 (0-931462-29-0) Chess Ent.

Marfia, Jim & Watson, John. U. S. Open: St. Paul, 1982. (Illus.). 83p. (Orig.). 1982. pap. 5.00 (0-931462-21-5) Chess Ent.

Marfia, Jim, jt. auth. see Tejler, Anders.

Marfia, Jim, tr. see Botvinnik, Mikhail.

Marfia, Jim, tr. see Botvinnik, Mikhail M.

Marfia, Jim, tr. see Bronstein, David.

Marfia, Jim, tr. see Cvetkov, Alexander.

Marfia, Jim, tr. see Estrin, Yakov B.

Marfia, Jim, tr. see Kortchnoi, Viktor & Cavallaro, Lenny.

Marfleet, Phil, jt. auth. see Kiely, Ray.

Marfo, Kofi, ed. Early Intervention in Transition: Current Perspectives on Programs for Handicapped Children. LC 91-15312. 368p. 1991. 69.50 (0-275-93470-5, C3470, Praeger Pubs) Greenwood.

— Parent-Child Interaction & Developmental Disabilities: Theory, Research, & Intervention. LC 87-25908. 395p. 1988. 69.50 (0-275-92835-7, C2835, Praeger Pubs) Greenwood.

Marfo, Kofi, et al, eds. Child Disabilities in Developing Countries. LC 85-20871. 1985. 57.95 (0-275-90217-X, C0217, Praeger Pubs) Greenwood.

Marfo, Kofi, jt. ed. see Thornburn, M. J.

Marfori, Mark D. Feng Shui: Discover Money, Health & Love. (Illus.). 192p. (Orig.). 1994. pap. 13.95 (0-9637748-4-0) Dragon Pub.

Marfuggi, Richard. Plastic Surgery: What You Need to Know Before, During, & After. LC 97-15709. 272p. 1998. pap. 15.00 (0-399-52374-X, Perigee Bks) Berkley Pub.

Marfunin, A. S., ed. Advanced Mineralogy Vol. 3: Mineral Matter in Space, Mantle, Ocean Floor, Biosphere, Environmental Management, Jewelry. (Illus.). 490p. 1998. 189.00 (3-540-58245-2) Spr-Verlag.

Marfunin, Arnold S. Composition, Structure & Properties of Mineral Matter: Concepts, Results, & Problems. (Advanced Mineralogy Ser.: Vol. 1). (Illus.). 562p. 1994. 158.95 (0-387-57254-6) Spr-Verlag.

Marfunin, Arnold S., ed. Advanced Mineralogy, Vol. 2. LC 94-13315. 1995. 133.00 (0-387-57255-4) Spr-Verlag.

Marfurt, K. J., jt. ed. see Kelly, K. R.

Marfurt, K. J., jt. ed. see Palaz, Ibrahim.

Marg, Elwyn. Computer-Assisted Eye Examination. (Illus.). 1980. 20.00 (0-911302-40-9) San Francisco Pr.

***Marg, Volkwin, ed.** Hall 8/9: Von Gerkan, Marg + Partners. (Illus.). 64p. 2000. pap. 29.95 (3-7913-2136-6) Prestel.

Marg, Volkwin, ed. Von Gerkan, Marg & Partner - New Leipzig Fair. LC 96-46683. (Illus.). 196p. 1996. 68.00 (3-7643-5429-1) Princeton Arch.

Marg, Walter, jt. auth. see Hirzel, Rudolf.

Margadant, Jo B. Madame le Professeur: Women Educators in the Third Republic. LC 89-70243. 370p. 1990. reprint ed. pap. 114.70 (0-608-02558-5, 206320300004) Bks Demand.

***Margadant, Jo Burr.** The New Biography: Performing Femininity in Nineteenth-century France. LC 99-48288. Vol. 38. (Illus.). 315p. 2001. 48.00 (0-520-22140-0, Pub. by U CA Pr); pap. 17.95 (0-520-22141-9, Pub. by U CA Pr) Cal Prin Full Svc.

Margah, Irish, jt. auth. see Monroe, Elvira.

Margalef, Ramon. Perspectives in Ecological Theory. LC 68-27291. (Illus.). viii, 112p. (C). 1993. pap. text 4.95 (0-226-50506-5, P629) U Ch Pr.

Margalef, Ramon, ed. Limnology Now: Paradigm of Planetary Problems. LC 94-3431. 572p. 1994. 220.50 (0-444-89826-3) Elsevier.

Margalef, Ramon & Treherne, John E. Western Mediterranean. LC 84-10993. (Key Environments Ser.). 275p. 1985. 169.00 (0-08-028870-7, Pub. by Pergamon Repr) Franklin.

Margalef-Roig, J. & Dominguez, E. Outerelo. Differential Topology. LC 92-10918. (North-Holland Mathematics Studies: Vol. 173). 604p. 1992. 180.00 (0-444-88434-3, North Holland) Elsevier.

Margalit, A., ed. Meaning & Use. (Synthese Language Library: No. 3). 319p. 1979. text 160.50 (90-277-0888-6, D Reidel) Kluwer Academic.

Margalit, Avishai. The Decent Society. Goldblum, Naomi, tr. LC 95-42273. 320p. 1996. 39.50 (0-674-19436-5) HUP.

— Decent Society. 320p. 1998. pap. text 16.95 (0-674-19437-3) HUP.

— Views & Reviews: Politics & Culture in the State of the Jews. LC 98-26382. 320p. (gr. 3). 1999. 25.00 (0-374-24941-5) FS&G.

Margalit, Avishai, jt. auth. see Halbertal, Moshe.

Margalit, Avishai, jt. ed. see Ullman-Margalit, Edna.

Margalit, Baruch. A Matter of Life & Death: A Study of the Baal-Mot Epic (CTA 4-5-6) (Alter Orient und Altes Testament Ser.: Vol. 206). vii, 271p. 1980. text 29.50 (3-7887-0608-2) NeukirchenerV.

— The Ugaritic Poem of AQHT: Text - Translation - Commentary. xviii, 534p. (C). 1989. lib. bdg. 161.55 (3-11-011632-4) De Gruyter.

Margalit, M. Effective Technology: Integration for Disabled Children: The Family Perspective. xxii, 226p. 1990. 59.95 (0-387-97256-0) Spr-Verlag.

Margalit, Malka. Loneliness among Children with Special Needs: Theory, Research, Coping, & Intervention. LC 93-32707. 1993. 102.00 (0-387-94158-4) Spr-Verlag.

Margalit, Nehemiah, ed. see Symposium on Power Sources for Biomedical Implanta.

Margalit, Yair. Winery Technology & Operations: A Handbook for Small Wineries. (Illus.). 224p. 29.95 (0-932664-66-0, 6537) Wine Appreciation.

Margalit, Yair & Crum, James, eds. Concepts in Wine Chemistry. (Illus.). 446p. (C). 1997. 79.95 (0-932664-91-1, 6924) Wine Appreciation.

Margalith, Aaron M., jt. auth. see Adler, Cyrus.

***Margalith, Joan L.** Babies Are Landing. (Illus.). 32p. (J). 2000. 9.95 (0-8118-2674-0) Chronicle Bks.

***Margalith, Sanford H.** Captains. Hayden, Gail M., ed. 320p. 2000. 24.95 (0-9657929-8-6) JONA Bks.

***Margam, Kate.** Poor Kevin. LC 98-86425. 1999. pap. 12.99 (1-85242-600-4, Pub. by Serpents Tail) Consort Bk Sales.

Marganne, Marie-Helene. La Chirurgie dans l'Egypte Greco-Romaine d'apres les Papyrus Litteraires Grecs. (Studies in Ancient Medicine: Vol. 17). (Illus.). 256p. 1998. 75.50 (90-04-11134-4) Brill Academic Pubs.

— L' Ophtalmologie dans l'Egypte d'apres les Papyrus Litteraires Grecs. (Studies in Ancient Medicine: No. 8). (FRE.). 272p. 1994. 100.00 (90-04-09907-7, NLG140) Brill Academic Pubs.

Margaral, Brian, jt. illus. see Renzulli, William F.

Margaret, Amy. Fun on the Farm. (Shaped Little Nugget Bks.). 18p. (J). 1998. 4.50 (0-307-13055-X, 13055, Goldn Books) Gldn Bks Pub Co.

***Margaret, Amy.** Jupiter. LC 99-89526. (Library of the Planets). 2000. write for info. (0-8239-5647-4) Rosen Group.

— Mercury. LC 99-40235. (Library of the Planets). 2000. lib. bdg. 15.50 (0-8239-5642-3, PowerKids) Rosen Group.

— Saturn. LC 99-88048. (Library of the Planets). (Illus.). (J). 2000. lib. bdg. 15.50 (0-8239-5646-6) Rosen Group.

— Venus. LC 99-53833. (Library of the Planets). (Illus.). (J). 2001. lib. bdg. write for info. (0-8239-5643-1) Rosen Group.

Margaret, Bunson. Learning Targets: Number Key State 2. 192p. 1998. pap. 45.00 (0-7487-3597-6) St Mut.

— Learning Targets: Phonics & Spelling Key Stage 2. 160p. 1998. pap. 45.00 (0-7487-3598-4) St Mut.

Margaret, Carney. Grandpa's Sugar Bush. (J). 1997. pap. 5.95 (1-55074-671-5) Kids Can Pr.

Margaret, Karla. Spaces. (Illus.). 80p. 1972. per. 14.95 (0-935430-04-0) In Between.

— Witches & Whimsies. 100p. (J). 1975. per. 6.95 (0-935430-02-4) In Between.

Margaret Press Staff. A Scream on the Water. 1997. mass mkt. 5.99 (0-312-96299-1) St Martin.

Margaret Therese of Jesus. The Way Back to Wisdom. (Illus.). 147p. (Orig.). 1988. pap. 10.38 (0-9625008-0-1) Wisdoms Pub Hse.

Margaria, T., et al, eds. Services & Visualization: Towards User-Friendly Design: ACoS'98 Visual'98, AIN'97 Selected Papers. (Lecture Notes in Computer Science: Vol. 1385). xii, 323p. 1998. pap. 55.00 (3-540-64367-2) Spr-Verlag.

Margaria, Tiziana & Steffen, Bernhard, eds. Tools & Algorithms for the Construction & Analysis of Systems: Proceedings, Second International Workshop, TACAS '96, Passau, Germany, March 1996. LC 96-4088. (Lecture Notes in Computer Science Ser.: Vol. 1055). 435p. 1996. pap. 68.00 (3-540-61042-1) Spr-Verlag.

Margaris, Angelo. First Order Mathematical Logic. 212p. 1990. pap. 7.95 (0-486-66269-1) Dover.

Margaris, N. S., et al, eds. Being Alive on Land: Proceedings of the International Symposium on Adaptions to Terrestrial Environment, Held in Halkidiki, Greece, 1982. (Tasks for Vegetation Science Ser.). 334p. 1984. text 225.00 (90-6193-953-4) Kluwer Academic.

Margaris, N. S. & Mooney, Harold A., eds. Components of Productivity of Mediterranean-Climate Regions: Basic & Applied Aspects. (Tasks for Vegetation Science Ser.: No. 4). viii, 280p. 1981. text 162.50 (90-6193-944-5) Kluwer Academic.

Margaris, N. S., jt. ed. see Fantechi, R.

Margarita, Sergio, et al. Neural Networks for Economic & Financial Modelling. (Illus.). 224p. 1995. mass mkt. 45.00 (1-85032-169-8) ITCP.

Margaritondo, G. & Weaver, J. H., eds. Synchrotron Radiation: Selected Reprints. (Reprint Bks.). 128p. 1986. per. 12.00 (0-917853-19-9, RB-46) Am Assn Physics.

Margaritondo, Giorgio. Introduction to Synchrotron Radiation. (Illus.). 296p. 1988. text 60.00 (0-19-504524-6) OUP.

Margaritondo, Giorgio, ed. Electronic Structure of Semiconductor Heterojunctions. (C). 1988. pap. text 104.00 (90-277-2824-0); lib. bdg. 180.50 (90-277-2823-2) Kluwer Academic.

Margaritondo, Giorgio, et al, eds. High-Tc Superconducting Thin Films, Devices & Applications: Proceedings of the Topical Conference of the AVS, Atlanta, GA, October 1988. (AIP Conference Proceedings Ser., American Vacuum Society Ser.: No. 182, 6). (Illus.). 450p. 1989. 70.00 (0-88318-382-X) Am Inst Physics.

Margaritondo, Giorgio, jt. ed. see Capasso, F.

***Margaryan, Alfred.** Ligands & Modifiers in Vitreous Materials: The Spectroscopy of Condensed Systems. LC 99-30374. 160p. 1999. 32.00 (981-02-3899-1) WSC Inst MA Studies.

Margaryan, Alfred, jt. auth. see Piliavin, Michael A.

Margasahayam, R. N., jt. auth. see Drago, Raymond J.

Margasahayam, Ravi N., jt. auth. see Drago, Raymond J.

Margate, Rosaline N., ed. see Thomas, William.

Margavio, Anthony V., et al. Caught in the Net: The Conflict Between Shrimpers & Conservationists. LC 95-37565. (Kenneth E. Montague Series in Oil & Business History: No. 7). (Illus.). 176p. 1996. 32.50 (0-89096-669-9) Tex A&M Univ Pr.

***Margen, Sheldon.** Wellness Encyclopedia of Food & Nutrition. 512p. 1999. pap. 19.95 (0-929661-50-8) Rebus.

Margen, Sheldon. The Wellness Nutrition Counter. 480p. 1998. 34.95 (0-8129-3038-X, Times Bks) Crown Pub Group.

— The Wellness Nutrition Counter: The Essential Guide to Complete Nutritional Information on over 6,000 Foods & Products. LC 97-17959. 1997. 34.95 (0-929661-38-9) Rebus.

Margen, Sheldon, jt. auth. see Swartzberg, John E.

Margen, Sheldon, jt. auth. see Univ. of California at Berkeley Wellness Letter Ed.

Margenau, Eric. Sports Without Pressure: A Guide for Parents & Coaches of Young Athletes. LC 89-16998. 156p. 1992. pap. 12.95 (0-89876-165-4) Brunner-Mazel.

Margenau, Eric, ed. The Encyclopedic Handbook of Private Practice. LC 87-19624. 1050p. 1990. text 120.00 (0-89876-151-4) Gardner Pr.

Margenau, Henry. The Miracle of Existence. LC 83-4972. xii, 143p. 1984. pap. 17.00 (1-881987-03-5) Ox Bow.

— The Nature of Physical Reality: A Philosophy of Modern Physics. LC 77-86356. 1977. reprint ed. 35.00 (0-918024-02-1); reprint ed. pap. 17.00 (0-918024-03-X) Ox Bow.

— Open Vistas. LC 83-60547. x, 256p. 1983. reprint ed. 26.00 (0-918024-27-7); reprint ed. pap. 14.00 (0-918024-28-5) Ox Bow.

— Physics & Philosophy: Selected Essays. (Episteme Ser.: No. 6). 441p. 1978. text 126.50 (90-277-0901-7, D Reidel) Kluwer Academic.

— Thomas & the Physics of 1958: A Confrontation. LC 58-9679. (Aquinas Lectures). 1958. 15.00 (0-87462-123-2) Marquette.

Margenau, Henry, jt. auth. see Lindsay, R. Bruce.

Margeneau, H., ed. Integrative Principles of Modern Thought. (Current Topics of Contemporary Thought Ser.: Vol. 3). x, 522p. (C). 1972. text 228.00 (0-677-14150-5) Gordon & Breach.

Margenot, John B., III, ed. Juan Benet: A Critical Reappraisal of His Fiction. LC 96-51479. (Literary Studies: Vol. 18). 292p. (C). 1997. lib. bdg. 35.00 (0-933951-61-2) Locust Hill Pr.

Marger, Carol, ed. see Gross, Pati M.

Marger, Carol, ed. see Myers Gross, Pati.

Marger, Martin. Race & Ethnic Relations: American Global Perspectives. 5th ed. LC 99-49441. (Sociology-Upper Level). 1999. pap. 80.95 (0-534-51433-2) Wadsworth Pub.

Marger, Martin N. Race & Ethnic Relations. 4th ed. LC 96-18143. (Sociology-Upper Level). (C). 1996. pap. 51.25 (0-534-50563-5) Wadsworth Pub.

An Asterisk (*) at the beginning of an entry indicates that the title is appearing for the first time.

— Race & Ethnic Relations: American & Global Persoectives. 2nd ed. (Sociology - Intro Level Ser.). 1990. pap., teacher ed. write for info. (0-534-13951-5) Wadsworth Pub.

— Race & Ethnic Relations: American & Global Perspectives. 336p. (C). 1984. pap. text. write for info. (0-534-04149-3) Wadsworth Pub.

— Race & Ethnic Relations: American & Global Perspectives. 2nd ed. 591p. (C). 1990. pap. 43.95 (0-534-13950-7) Wadsworth Pub.

— Race & Ethnic Relations: American & Global Perspectives. 3rd ed. 607p. 1993. pap. 44.75 (0-534-20809-6) Wadsworth Pub.

Margeret, Jacques. The Russian Empire & Grand Duchy of Muscovy: A 17th Century French Account. Dunning, Chester S., ed. & tr. by. LC 82-20126. (Russian & East European Studies: No. 5). 251p. 1983. reprint ed. pap. 77.90 (0-608-00909-1, 206170300010) Bks Demand.

Margerie, Bertrand De, see De Margerie, Bertrand.

Margerie, Diane De, see De Margerie, Diane.

Margerison, Charles. Managerial Consulting Skills: A Practical Guide. 256p. 1988. text 65.95 (0-566-02793-3, Pub. by Gower) Ashgate Pub Co.

Margerison, Charles J. Managerial Consulting Skills. 224p. 1996. pap. 33.95 (0-566-07703-5) Ashgate Pub Co.

— Managerial Consulting Skills: A Practical Guide. 2nd ed. LC 00-42964. 2000. write for info. (0-566-08292-6, Pub. by Gower) Ashgate Pub Co.

Margerison, D., jt. auth. see Green, J. R.

Margerison, Kenneth. Pamphlets & Public Opinion: The Campaign for a Union of Orders in the Early French Revolution. LC 97-14474. 296p. 1997. 36.95 (1-55753-109-9) Purdue U Pr.

Margerit, Robert. Mont-Dragon. (FRE.). 1973. pap. 10.95 (0-7859-4018-9) Fr & Eur.

Margesin, Rosa & Schinner, Franz F. Cold Adapted Organisms: Ecology, Physiology, Enzymology & Molecular Biology. LC 99-13852. 416p. 1999. 239.00 (3-540-64973-5) Spr-Verlag.

Margesin, Rosa & Schinner, Franz F., eds. Biotechnological Applications of Cold-Adapted Organisms. LC 98-55124. (Illus.). ix, 338p. 1999. 199.00 (3-540-64972-7) Spr-Verlag.

Margeson, Charles. Experiences of Gold Hunters in Alaska. unabridged ed. (Illus.). 1997. reprint ed. pap. 19.95 (1-877900-09-5) Prince W Sound.

Margeson, Hank, photos by. Quail Plantations of South Georgia & North Florida. LC 91-3054. (Illus.). 120p. 1991. 34.95 (0-8203-1386-6) U of Ga Pr.

Margeson, John, ed. see Shakespeare, William.

***Margeson, Susan M.** Viking. (Eyewitness Books). (Illus.). (J). (gr. 4-7). 2000. 19.99 (0-7894-6599-X) DK Pub Inc.

— Viking. (Eyewitness Books). (J). (gr. 4-8). 2000. 15.95 (0-7894-5894-2) DK Pub Inc.

Marget, Richard & Ludescher, Matt. The Basic Mechanics Book. (Illus.). 181p. 1998. pap. 20.00 (0-9665070-0-2) RM Company.

***Margeton, Stephen G.** Introduction to Academic Law Library Design: A Features Approach. LC 99-54855. 2000. write for info. (0-8377-0870-2) W S Hein.

Margeton, Stephen G. & Meredith, Willis C. Law Library Preservation Issues: Books, Microforms & Electronic Media. (Law Library Information Reports: Vol. 16). 85p. 1994. pap. 50.00 (0-87802-095-0) Glanville.

Margetson, George R. England in the West Indies. 1977. lib. bdg. 59.95 (0-8490-1769-6) Gordon Pr.

— Songs of Life. LC 76-39095. (Black Heritage Library Collection). 1977. reprint ed. 15.95 (0-8369-9033-1) Ayer.

Margetts, Barrie & Nelson, Michael, eds. Design Concepts in Nutritional Epidemiology. 2nd ed. LC 96-43448. (Illus.). 466p. 1997. pap. text 59.95 (0-19-262739-2) OUP.

Margetts, Barrie M., ed. Design Concepts in Nutritional Epidemiology. (Illus.). 432p. 1991. text 69.95 (0-19-261873-3) OUP.

***Margetts, Beth.** Bindi Body Art Kit: Create over 40 Body-Jewel Designs. (Illus.). 64p. 1999. boxed set 24.95 (1-885203-98-5) Jmy Editions.

— Body Painting Pack: Create Sensational Body Designs. 2000. pap. (1-85868-874-4) Carlton Bks Ltd.

Margetts, Helen. Information Technology & Central Government: Britain & America. LC 98-24908. 1999. 85.00 (0-415-17482-1) Routledge.

Margetts, Helen & Smyth, Gareth, eds. Turning Japanese? Britain with a Permanent Party of Government. 224p. (C). 1994. pap. 29.95 (0-85315-785-5, Pub. by Lawrence & Wishart) NYU Pr.

Margetts, Juliet, ed. Who's Who in Business & Industry in the U. K. 1000p. 1991. 250.00 (1-55862-155-5) St James Pr.

Margetts, Martina, jt. contrib. by see Britton, Alison.

Marggraf, Paula, ed. see Mass. Tech. Communications, Inc. Staff.

Margham, J. P., jt. auth. see Hale, W. G.

Margherita, Gayle. The Romance of Origins: Language & Sexual Difference in Middle English Literature. LC 94-12610. 256p. (Orig.). (C). 1994. text 39.95 (0-8122-3217-8); pap. text 15.95 (0-8122-1502-8) U of Pa Pr.

Margherita, Marchione. Clemente Rebora: A Man's Quest for the Absolute. LC 78-7632. (Twayne's World Authors Ser.). 183p. 1979. 12.50 (0-8057-6362-7, Twyne) Mac Lib Ref.

Marghon, Blandine. The Bible: The Greatest Stories. (Illus.). 160p. (J). (ps-3). 1992. 16.95 (0-687-03115-X) Abingdon.

Margic, Joyce D., jt. auth. see Palumbo, P. J.

Margiela, Martin. Martin Margiela. LC 98-141031. (Illus.). 90p. 1997. pap. 40.00 (90-6918-180-0) Dist Art Pubs.

***Margiela, Martin.** Street, 2 vols., set. Vols. 1 & 2. (Illus.). 208p. 2000. pap. 35.00 (2-9512460-1-3, Pub. by Neuf) Dist Art Pubs.

Margin, Alex R., Jr., jt. auth. see Benhart, John E.

Margineanu, D. & Schoffeniels, Ernest. Molecular Basis & Thermodynamics of Bioelectrogenesis. (C). 1990. text 104.00 (0-7923-0975-8) Kluwer Academic.

Marginson, Simon. Educating Australia: Government, Economy & Citizen since 1960. LC 97-26348. (Illus.). 302p. (C). 1997. text 59.95 (0-521-59174-0); pap. text 21.95 (0-521-59830-3) Cambridge U Pr.

— Markets in Education. LC 99-488378. 352p. 1998. pap. 35.00 (1-86448-432-2, Pub. by Allen & Unwin Pty) Paul & Co Pubs.

***Marginson, Simon & Considine, Mark.** The Enterprise University in Australia: Governance, Strategy & Reinvention. (Illus.). 272p. (C). 2000. text Price not set. (0-521-79118-9); pap. text Price not set. (0-521-79448-X) Cambridge U Pr.

Marginter, Peter. The Baron & the Fish. Bangerter, Lowell A., tr. from GER. & afterword by by. LC 91-40593. (Studies in Austrian Literature, Culture, & Thought. Translation Ser.). 311p. (Orig.). 1992. pap. 22.00 (0-929497-46-5) Ariadne CA.

Margioa, Liana. Sumacchedshaya. (RUS., Illus.). text. write for info. (0-9673753-5-5) Gelany.

Margioris, Andrew N. & Chrousos, George P., eds. Adrenal Disorders. (Contemporary Endocrinology Ser.). (Illus.). 400p. 2000. 195.00 (0-89603-411-9) Humana.

Margiotta, Franklin D. Brassey's Encyclopedia of Land Forces & Warfare. (Association of the U. S. Army Book Ser.). (Illus.). 1170p. 1997. 44.95 (1-57488-087-X) Brasseys.

***Margiotta, Franklin D.** Brassey's Encyclopedia of Land Forces & Warfare. 2000. pap. 24.95 (1-57488-250-3) Brasseys.

Margiotta, Franklin D. Brassey's Encyclopedia of Military History & Biography. (Illus.). 1232p. 1994. 46.95 (0-02-881096-1) Brasseys.

***Margiotta, Franklin D.** Brassey's Encyclopedia of Military History & Biography. 2000. pap. 24.95 (1-57488-251-1) Brasseys.

Margiotta, Franklin D., ed. The Changing World of the American Military. LC 78-6765. (Special Studies in Military Affairs). 488p. 1979. text 51.50 (0-89158-331-9); pap. text 14.50 (0-89158-309-2) Westview.

Margiotta, Franklin D., et al. Changing U. S. Military Manpower Realities. LC 82-13372. (Special Studies in Military Affairs). 267p. 1983. pap. text 51.50 (0-89158-935-X) Westview.

***Margis, E. R.** Construction Soul: Let It Grab & Lift You Up. LC 99-96584. 320p. 2000. pap. 17.24 (0-9676050-0-8) Lucky Pr.

Margitay, Tihamer. Theories in Contexts: On the Interpretation of Scientific Theories. LC 98-182634. xi, 190p. 1998. pap. 40.00 (963-05-7474-8) Intl Spec Bk.

Margitic, Milorad R. Essai sur la Mythologie du Cid. LC 76-22508. (Romance Monographs: No. 22). (FRE.). 1976. 30.00 (84-399-5848-X) Romance.

Margitic, Milorad R. & Corneille, Pierre, eds. Le Cid: Tragi-Comedie. LC 89-6655. (Purdue University Monographs in Romance Languages: Vol. 28). (FRE.). lxxxviii, 302p. 1989. 106.00 (1-55619-067-0) J Benjamins Pubng Co.

Margitic, Milorad R., ed. see Corneille, Pierre.

Marglin, Frederique A. & Marglin, Stephen A., eds. Dominating Knowledge: Development, Culture & Resistance. (Illus.). 306p. 1990. text 49.95 (0-19-828694-5) OUP.

— Dominating Knowledge: Development, Culture & Resistance. (WIDER Studies in Development Economics). 312p. 2000. reprint ed. pap. 24.95 (0-19-828838-7) OUP.

Marglin, Stephen A. Growth, Distribution & Prices. LC 83-18569. (Illus.). 584p. 1987. pap. 12.95 (0-674-36416-3) HUP.

— Value & Price in the Labor-Surplus Economy. (Illus.). 260p. 1976. text 49.95 (0-19-828194-3) OUP.

Marglin, Stephen A. & Schor, Juliet B., eds. The Golden Age of Capitalism: Reinterpreting the Postwar Experience. (WIDER Studies in Development Economics). (Illus.). 340p. 1992. pap. text 28.00 (0-19-828741-0) OUP.

Marglin, Stephen A., jt. ed. see Apffel-Marglin, Frederique.

Marglin, Stephen A., jt. ed. see Marglin, Frederique A.

Margo, Adair, jt. ed. see Craver, Rebecca.

Margo Chase Design. Desire Mini-Book. (Illus.). 132p. 1998. pap. 5.95 (0-8118-2010-6) Chronicle Bks.

Margo, Curtis, et al, eds. Diagnostic Problems in Clinical Ophthalmology. LC 92-49132. (Illus.). 896p. 1993. text 102.00 (0-7216-3659-4, W B Saunders Co) Harcrt Hlth Sci Grp.

Margo, Curtis & Grossniklaus. Ocular Histopathology: A Guide to Differential Diagnosis. (Illus.). 352p. 1990. text 130.00 (0-7216-3291-2, W B Saunders Co) Harcrt Hlth Sci Grp.

Margo, Glen, jt. ed. see Krieger, Nancy.

Margo, Robert A. Race & Schooling in the South, 1880-1950: An Economic History. LC 90-11249. (National Bureau of Economic Research Long Term Factors in Economic Development Ser.). (Illus.). 176p. 1990. 29.95 (0-226-50510-3) U Ch Pr.

— Race & Schooling in the South, 1880-1950: An Economic History. (National Bureau of Economic Research Long Term Factors in Economic Development Ser.). (Illus.). x, 174p. 1994. pap. text 12.95 (0-226-50511-1) U Ch Pr.

Margo, Rod D. Margo: Aviation Insurance. 3rd ed. 1997. write for info. (0-406-89101-X, MAIL3, MICHIE) LEXIS Pub.

Margoilin, Philip. Gone but Not Forgotten. 416p. 1994. mass mkt. 7.50 (0-553-56903-1) Bantam.

Margoles, Michael & Weiner, Richard. Chronic Pain: Diagnosis, Assessment, & Management. LC 99-174421. 300p. 1995. lib. bdg. 59.95 (1-57444-103-5, SL1035) St Lucie Pr.

Margolese, Richard G., ed. Breast Cancer. LC 83-10059. (Contemporary Issues in Oncology Ser.: Vol. 1). (Illus.). 318p. reprint ed. pap. 98.60 (0-7837-6240-2, 204595400010) Bks Demand.

Margolf, Charles W. Federal Coal Lease Readjustments: Will Reason Prevail? 120p. (Orig.). (C). 1988. pap. text 15.00 (0-317-91386-7) C W Margolf.

Margolian, Howard. Conduct Unbecoming: The Story of the Murder of Canadian Prisoners of War in Normandy. (Illus.). 336p. 1998. text 34.95 (0-8020-4213-9) U of Toronto Pr.

***Margolian, Howard.** Unauthorized Entry: The Truth about Nazi War Criminals in Canada, 1946-1956. 352p. 2000. 39.95 (0-8020-4277-5) U of Toronto Pr.

***Margolick, David.** Strange Fruit: Billie Holiday, Cafe Society & an Early Cry for Civil Rights. (Illus.). 144p. 2000. 16.95 (0-7624-0677-1) Running Pr.

Margolies. Writing the Revolution: Cultural Criticism from Left Review. LC 97-23977. 1997. 95.95 (0-7453-1161-X, Pub. by Pluto GBR) Stylus Pub VA.

— Writing the Revolution: Cultural Criticism from Left Review. 1998. pap. 28.95 (0-7453-1162-8, Pub. by Pluto GBR) Stylus Pub VA.

Margolies, Alan, ed. see Fitzgerald, F. Scott.

Margolies, Barbara A. Rehema's Journey. (J). 1997. mass mkt. 4.99 (0-590-42847-0) Scholastic Inc.

— Rehema's Journey, a Visit in Tanzania. (J). 1997. 10.19 (0-606-11785-7, Pub. by Turtleback) Demco.

Margolies, David. Novel & Society in Elizabethan England. LC 84-20369. 204p. 1985. 38.50 (0-389-20538-9, BNB-08100) B&N Imports.

Margolies, David & Joannou, Maroula. Heart of the Heartless World: Essays in Cultural Resistance. LC 95-2979. 260p. (C). 1995. 59.95 (0-7453-0981-X, Pub. by Pluto GBR); pap. 22.95 (0-7453-0982-8, Pub. by Pluto GBR) Stylus Pub VA.

Margolies, Edward. Which Way Did He Go? The Private Eye in Dashiell Hammett, Raymond Chandler, Chester Himes, & Ross MacDonald. LC 81-1061. 130p. 1982. 25.00 (0-8419-0436-7) Holmes & Meier.

Margolies, Edward & Fabre, Michael J. Several Lives of Chester Himes. LC 96-39330. 224p. 1997. 28.00 (0-87805-908-3) U Pr of Miss.

Margolies, Eva L. The Best of Friends, the Worst of Enemies. 1987. 4.50 (0-317-61573-4) PB.

Margolies, Jacob. The Negro Leagues: The Story of Black Baseball. (African-American Experience Ser.). (Illus.). 144p. (YA). (gr. 7-12). 1993. lib. bdg. 24.00 (0-531-11130-X) Watts.

— The Negro Leagues: The Story of Black Baseball. (African-American Experience Ser.). (Illus.). 128p. (YA). (gr. 7-12). 1994. pap. 6.95 (0-531-15694-X) Watts.

Margolies, John. Fun along the Road: American Tourist Attractions. LC 97-75127. (Illus.). 128p. 1998. 29.95 (0-8212-2351-8, Pub. by Bulfinch Pr) Little.

— Home Away from Home: Motels in America. LC 95-77074. (Illus.). 128p. 1995. 29.95 (0-8212-2162-0, Pub. by Bulfinch Pr) Little.

— Pump & Circumstance: The Glory Days of the Gas Station. LC 93-12966. (Illus.). 127p. 1993. 29.95 (0-8212-1995-2, Pub. by Bulfinch Pr) Little.

Margolies, John & Eric Baker Design Associates Staff. See the U. S. A. The Art of the American Travel Brochure. LC 99-11752. (Illus.). 132p. 1999. pap. 19.95 (0-8118-2272-9) Chronicle Bks.

Margolies, John & Gwathmey, Emily. Signs of Our Times. LC 92-37283. (Illus.). 96p. 1993. 27.50 (1-55859-209-1) Abbeville Pr.

Margolies, John, jt. auth. see Yorke, Douglas A.

***Margolies, Morris B.** A Gathering of Angels: Angels in Jewish Life & Literature. LC 98-40646. 2000. 30.00 (0-7657-6048-7) Aronson.

Margolies, Morris B. A Gathering of Angels: Angels in Jewish Life & Literature. 288p. 1994. pap. 12.00 (0-345-38104-1) Ballantine Pub Grp.

***Margolies, Morris B.** Twenty/Twenty: Jewish Visionaries Through Two Thousand Years. LC 98-40644. 209p. 2000. 30.00 (0-7657-6057-6) Aronson.

Margolin, David I., ed. Cognitive Neuropsychology in Clinical Practice. (Illus.). 560p. 1992. text 75.00 (0-19-506422-4) OUP.

Margolin, Deb & Hart, Lynda. Of All the Nerve: Deb Margolin Solo. LC 98-31201. 224p. 1999. 70.00 (0-304-70318-4); pap. 18.95 (0-304-70319-2) Continuum.

Margolin, Freddi. Peanuts the Home Collection: Collector's Guide to Identification & Value. LC 99-61592. (Illus.). 352p. 1999. pap. 26.95 (0-930625-82-X, AT2582) Krause Pubns.

Margolin, Gayla, jt. auth. see Jacobson, Neil S.

Margolin, J. B. The Individual's Guide to Grants. LC 83-2252. (Illus.). 314p. 1983. 24.00 (0-306-41309-4, Kluwer Plenum) Kluwer Academic.

Margolin, J. C. & Mesnard, P. Erasmi Opera Omnia, 5 Pts., Pt. 2. Waszink, Jan H., ed. viii,726p. 1971. 593.00 (0-7204-6152-9, North Holland) Elsevier.

Margolin, Jean-Claude. Erasme: Le Prix des Mots et de L'Homme. (Collected Studies: No. CS241). (FRE.). 318p. (C). 1986. reprint ed. text 124.95 (0-86078-189-5, Pub. by Variorum) Ashgate Pub Co.

— Erasme dans son Miroir et dans son Sillage. (Collected Studies: No. CS257). (FRE.). 320p. (C). 1987. reprint ed. text 124.95 (0-86078-205-0, Pub. by Variorum) Ashgate Pub Co.

Margolin, Judith A. Breaking the Silence: Group Therapy for Childhood Sexual Abuse - A Practitioner's Manual. LC 98-39343. (Illus.). 152p. 1998. lib. bdg. 29.95 (0-7890-0200-0) Haworth Pr.

Margolin, Judith B., ed. The Foundation Center's User-Friendly Guide: A Grantseeker's Guide to Resources. 4th ed. 1996. pap. text 14.95 (0-87954-541-0) Foundation Ctr.

— Foundation Fundamentals: A Guide for Grantseekers. 5th ed. 222p. 1994. pap. 24.95 (0-87954-543-7) Foundation Ctr.

Margolin, Leslie. Goodness Personified: The Emergence of Gifted Children. LC 93-47411. (Social Problems & Social Issues Ser.). 204p. 1994. pap. text 21.95 (0-202-30527-9); lib. bdg. 39.95 (0-202-30526-0) Aldine de Gruyter.

***Margolin, Leslie.** Murderess! The Chilling True Story of the Most Infamous Woman Ever Electrocuted. 1999. mass mkt. 6.50 (0-7860-1052-5) Pinal County Schl Office.

Margolin, Leslie. Under the Cover of Kindness: The Invention of Social Work. LC 96-47986. (Knowledge: Disciplinarity & Beyond Ser.). 219p. 1997. 29.95 (0-8139-1713-1) U Pr of Va.

Margolin, Malcolm. The Earth Manual: How to Work on Wild Land Without Taming It. rev. ed. (Illus.). 244p. 1985. reprint ed. pap. 16.00 (0-930588-18-5) Heyday Bks.

— Following the Game: Hunting Traditions of Native California. Date not set. 27.95 (1-890771-06-6) Heyday Bks.

— The Ohlone Way: Indian Life in the San Francisco-Monterey Bay Area. LC 78-56826. (Illus.). 182p. (Orig.). 1994. pap. 12.95 (0-930588-01-0) Heyday Bks.

Margolin, Malcolm, ed. The Way We Lived: California Indian Stories, Songs, & Reminiscences. rev. ed. (Illus.). 260p. (Orig.). 1993. pap. 14.95 (0-930588-55-X) Heyday Bks.

Margolin, Malcolm & Jalbert, Dolores. Following the Game: Hunting Traditions of Native California. (Illus.). 192p. Date not set. pap. 18.00 (1-890771-07-4) Heyday Bks.

Margolin, Malcolm & Montijo, Yolanda. Native Ways: California Indian Stories & Memories. (Illus.). 128p. (J). (gr. 4-6). 1995. pap. 8.95 (0-930588-73-8) Heyday Bks.

Margolin, Malcolm, ed. see Martin, Carol O.

Margolin, Malcolm, ed. see Mayfield, Thomas J.

Margolin, Phillip. After Dark. 384p. 1996. mass mkt. 7.50 (0-553-56908-2) Bantam.

— After Dark. large type ed. LC 95-23557. (Large Print Bks.). 1995. 24.95 (1-56895-240-6) Wheeler Pub.

Margolin, Phillip. The Burning Man. 384p. 1997. mass mkt. 7.50 (0-553-57495-7) Bantam.

Margolin, Phillip. The Burning Man. large type ed. LC 97-3570. (Wheeler Large Print Book Ser.). 1997. 26.95 (1-56895-415-8) Wheeler Pub.

— Heartstone. 416p. 1995. mass mkt. 7.50 (0-553-56978-3) Bantam.

***Margolin, Phillip.** The Last Innocent Man. large type ed. 352p. 1999. 31.99 (0-7089-9071-1) Ulverscroft.

Margolin, Phillip. The Last Innocent Man. 352p. 1995. reprint ed. mass mkt. 7.50 (0-553-56979-1) Bantam.

— The Undertaker's Widow. LC 97-41143. 320p. 1998. 24.95 (0-385-48054-7) Doubleday.

***Margolin, Phillip.** The Undertaker's Widow. large type ed. 392p. 2000. write for info. (0-7089-9146-7) Ulverscroft.

Margolin, Phillip. The Undertaker's Widow. 336p. 1999. reprint ed. mass mkt. 7.50 (0-553-58088-4) Bantam.

***Margolin, Phillip.** Wild Justice. LC 00-24351. 384p. 2000. 26.00 (0-06-019624-6, HarpCollins) HarperTrade.

— Wild Justice. large type ed. 625p. 2000. pap. 26.00 (0-06-019913-X) HarpC.

Margolin, Sylvia. Complete Group Counseling Program for Children of Divorce: Ready-to-Use Plans & Materials. 256p. (C). 1996. pap. text 28.95 (0-87628-124-2) P-H.

Margolin, Tatyana, tr. see Twerski, Abraham J.

***Margolin, Victor.** Design as Culture. 1999. pap. text 16.00 (0-226-50504-9); lib. bdg. 50.00 (0-226-50503-0) U Ch Pr.

Margolin, Victor. Struggle for Utopia: Essays on Rodchenko, Lissitzky & Moholy-Nagy 1917-1946. LC 96-3409. 1997. 39.95 (0-226-50515-4) U Ch Pr.

— The Struggle for Utopia: Rodchenko, Lissitzky, Moholy-Nagy: 1917-1946. LC 96-3409. 262p. 1998. pap. text 19.00 (0-226-50516-2) U Ch Pr.

Margolin, Victor, intro. Design Discourse: History, Theory, Criticism. LC 89-33920. (Illus.). 302p. 1989. pap. text 19.95 (0-226-50514-6) U Ch Pr.

— Design Discourse: History, Theory, Criticism. LC 89-33920. (Illus.). 302p. 1996. lib. bdg. 66.00 (0-226-50513-8) U Ch Pr.

Margolin, Victor & Buchanan, Richard, eds. The Idea of Design. (Design Issues Reader Ser.). (Illus.). 315p. (C). 1996. pap. text 20.00 (0-262-63166-0) MIT Pr.

Margolin, Victor, jt. ed. see Buchanan, Richard.

Margoliouth, David S. Analecta Orientalia Ad Poeticam Aristoteleam. vi, 243p. reprint ed. write for info. (0-318-71531-7) G Olms Pubs.

— Cairo, Jerusalem, & Damascus, Three Chief Cities of the Egyptian Sultans. LC 80-1918. (Illus.). reprint ed. 54.50 (0-404-18980-6) AMS Pr.

— The Early Development of Mohammedanism. LC 77-27156. (Hibbert Lectures: 1913). reprint ed. 34.50 (0-404-60415-3) AMS Pr.

— Mohammed & the Rise of Islam. LC 73-14455. reprint ed. 45.00 (0-404-58273-7) AMS Pr.

— Mohammed & the Rise of Islam. LC 73-38361. (Select Bibliographies Reprint Ser.). 1977. reprint ed. 37.95 (0-8369-6778-X) Ayer.

— The Relations Between Arabs & Israelis Prior to the Rise

M

of Islam. (British Academy, London, Schweich Lectures on Biblical Archaeology Series, 1930). 1974. reprint ed. pap. 25.00 (*0-8115-1263-0*) Periodicals Srv.

Margoliouth, David S., tr. see Miskawayh, Ibn, et al.

Margoliovth, D. S., tr. see Mez, Adam.

Margolis. Elder Law News. 1992. 119.00 (*0-316-54749-2*, Aspen Law & Bus) Aspen Pub.

— Key Elder Law '95. 1995. 49.95 (*0-316-54825-1*, Aspen Law & Bus) Aspen Pub.

***Margolis.** Plastics Calculation Handbook. 2000. 125.00 (*0-07-135172-8*) McGraw.

Margolis. Portfolio, Set. 1468p. 1997. ring bd. 150.00 (*0-316-54742-5*, Aspen Law & Bus) Aspen Pub.

Margolis, Kevin D., jt. auth. see Davis, Todd S.

***Margolis, Sue.** Neurotica. 336p. 2000. reprint ed. mass mkt. 6.50 (*0-553-58106-6*) Bantam.

Margolis, Alan M. & Monahan, Thomas J. United Kingdom: Medical Laboratory Science, Occupational Therapy, Physiotherapy. LC 79-49614. (World Education Ser.). 192p. reprint ed. pap. 59.60 (*0-8357-7534-8*, 203624700001) Bks Demand.

Margolis, Andrew. The Fax Moderm Sourcebook. LC 95-8378. 380p. 1995. pap. 85.00 (*0-471-95072-6*) Wiley.

Margolis, Anne, ed. see Honeywell, Jerry L.

Margolis, Anne T. Henry James & the Problem of Audience: An International Act. LC 84-24073. (Studies in Modern Literature: No. 49). 267p. reprint ed. pap. 82.80 (*0-8357-1624-4*, 207050700097) Bks Demand.

Margolis, Art. Computer Technician's Handbook. 2nd ed. (Illus.). 490p. pap. 19.95 (*0-8306-1939-9*) McGraw-Hill Prof.

— Computer Technician's Handbook. 3rd ed. 580p. 1989. pap. 29.95 (*0-07-157547-2*) McGraw.

— Computer Technician's Handbook. 3rd ed. (Illus.). 512p. 1989. 32.95 (*0-8306-9279-7*); pap. 24.95 (*0-8306-3279-4*) McGraw-Hill Prof.

— Troubleshooting & Repairing Personal Computers. 3rd ed. LC 93-39124. (Glencoe Tech Ser.). 1993. write for info. (*0-02-802003-0*) Macmillan.

— Troubleshooting & Repairing the New Personal Computer. (Illus.). 416p. (Orig.). 1987. 26.95 (*0-8306-0209-7*) McGraw-Hill Prof.

— Troubleshooting & Repairing Your Commodore 128. (Illus.). 400p. 1988. 27.95 (*0-8306-9099-9*, 3099) McGraw-Hill Prof.

— Troubleshooting & Repairing Your Commodore 64. (Illus.). 288p. (Orig.). 1985. 22.95 (*0-8306-0889-3*, 1889) McGraw-Hill Prof.

Margolis, Bernard P., jt. auth. see Bixler, James P.

***Margolis, Bette S.** A Heart Full of Love: With Workshop for Children of Divorce. 80p. (J). (gr. 1-4). 1999. pap. 14.95 (*0-9676360-0-0*) Bettes Bks.

Margolis, Bob, jt. auth. see Weber, Rhoda B.

Margolis, Bob, ed. see Dvorak, Thomas L. & Floyd, Richard L.

Margolis, Bob, ed. see Dvorak, Thomas L., et al.

Margolis, Carmi Z. Clinical Practice Guidelines: Strategies for Effective Implementation. LC 98-19064. 1998. 45.00 (*1-55648-237-X*) AHPI.

Margolis, Char. Questions from Earth, Answers from Heaven: A Psychic Intuitive's Discussion of Life, Death & What Awaits Us Beyond. 2nd ed. LC 99-35896. 272p. 1999. text 23.95 (*0-312-24199-2*) St Martin.

***Margolis, Char & St. George, Victoria.** Questions from Earth, Answers from Heaven: A Psychic Intuitive's Discussion of Life, Death & What Awaits Us Beyond. 320p. 2000. 6.99 (*0-312-97514-7*, St Martins Paperbacks) St Martin.

Margolis, Daniel J. & Schoenberg, Elliot S., eds. Curriculum, Community, Commitment: Views on the American Jewish Day School in Memory of Bennett I. Solomon. LC 93-2812. 1993. 24.95 (*0-87441-545-4*) Behrman.

Margolis, David. Change of Partners. LC 96-23395. 1997. 24.00 (*1-877946-87-7*) Permanent Pr.

— The Stepman. LC 95-22755. 192p. 1996. 22.00 (*1-877946-76-1*) Permanent Pr.

Margolis, Deborah P. Freud & His Mother: Preoedipal Aspects of Freud's Personality. LC 94-44328. 1996. 40.00 (*1-56821-448-0*) Aronson.

Margolis, Diane R. Images of Selves: A Theory of Culture & Emotions. LC 97-34298. 216p. 1998. 30.00 (*0-300-06990-1*) Yale U Pr.

Margolis, Edwin & Moses, Stanley. The Elusive Quest: The Struggle for Equality of Educational Opportunity. LC 87-27076. (Illus.). 170p. (Orig.). 1992. pap. 16.50 (*0-945257-46-5*) Apex Pr.

***Margolis, Eric.** War at the Top of the World: The Struggle for Afghanistan, Kashmir & Tibet. LC 99-56853. 256p. 2000. 26.00 (*0-415-92712-9*) Routledge.

***Margolis, Eric, ed.** Research in Social Policy Vol. 7. 1999. 78.50 (*0-7623-0539-8*) Jai Pr.

Margolis, Eric & Laurence, Stephen, eds. Concepts: Core Readings. LC 98-49117. (Illus.). 557p. 1999. 70.00 (*0-262-13353-9*, Bradford Bks); pap. 37.50 (*0-262-63193-8*, Bradford Bks) MIT Pr.

Margolis, F. L. & Getchell, T. V. Molecular Neurobiology of the Olfactory System: Molecular, Membranous & Cytological Studies. LC 88-14821. (Illus.). 398p. (C). 1988. text 115.00 (*0-306-42858-X*, Kluwer Plenum) Kluwer Academic.

Margolis, Fredric, jt. auth. see Stockard, Oliva.

Margolis, Harold J. Inhibitory Control Theory: A Mind-Body Theory of Sensory Signaling & Stressor Accommodation. 681p. (C). 1991. lib. bdg. 57.00 (*1-879646-04-8*) Silogram.

— Stress: A Mind-Body Approach to Understanding & Overcoming Stress. (Frontiers of Consciousness Ser.). 750p. 1990. text 69.50 (*0-685-26542-0*) Irvington.

***Margolis, Harriet, ed.** Jane Campion's "The Piano" LC 99-21070. (Cambridge Film Handbooks Ser.). (Illus.). 220p. (C). 2000. 54.95 (*0-521-59258-5*); pap. 19.95 (*0-521-59721-8*) Cambridge U Pr.

Margolis, Harry. Elderlaw Forms Manual: Essential Documents for Representing the Older Client. 967p. 1997. ring bd. 150.00 (*0-316-54751-4*, 47514) Aspen Law.

— The Elderlaw Forms System: Document Drafting & Assembly for the Elder Law Attorney. 249.00 incl. disk (*0-316-55032-9*, 50329) Aspen Law.

Margolis, Harry A. Title Fifty-Nine: Tort Claims Against Public Entities, Amendments to May 1, 1984: Comments & Annotations. LC 84-208513. (Illus.). vii, 352p. 1984. pap. 28.00 (*0-933902-10-7*) Gann Law Bks.

Margolis, Harry S. Elderlaw Forms Manual: Essential Documents for Representing the Older Client. 500p. 1992. ring bd. 125.00 (*0-316-54629-1*, Aspen Law & Bus) Aspen Pub.

Margolis, Howard. Dealing with Risk: Why the Public & the Experts Disagree on Environmental Issues. (Illus.). x, 228p. 1997. pap. text 15.95 (*0-226-50529-4*) U Ch Pr.

— Dealing with Risk: Why the Public & the Experts Disagree on Environmental Issues. (Illus.). 200p. (C). 1998. 27.50 (*0-226-50525-1*) U Ch Pr.

— Paradigms & Barriers: How Habits of Mind Govern Scientific Beliefs. LC 92-44650. (Illus.). 288p. (C). 1993. pap. text 15.95 (*0-226-50523-5*); lib. bdg. 40.00 (*0-226-50522-7*) U Ch Pr.

— Patterns, Thinking, & Cognition: A Theory of Judgement. (Illus.). xii, 344p. 1988. pap. text 19.95 (*0-226-50528-6*); lib. bdg. 45.00 (*0-226-50527-8*) U Ch Pr.

— Selfishness, Altruism & Rationality: A Theory of Social Choice. LC 84-2620. xii, 206p. 1984. pap. text 15.00 (*0-226-50524-3*) U Ch Pr.

Margolis, Isidor & Markowitz, Sidney L. Jewish Holidays & Festivals. (Illus.). 132p. (Orig.). 1995. pap. 7.95 (*0-8065-0285-1*, Citadel Pr) Carol Pub Group.

Margolis, James M. Decorating Plastics. 135p. (C). 1986. text 49.00 (*1-56990-058-2*) Hanser-Gardner.

— Engineering Thermoplastics: Properties & Applications. (Plastics Engineering Ser.: Vol. 8). (Illus.). 408p. 1985. text 175.00 (*0-8247-8051-5*) Dekker.

— Medical & Hospital Plastic Products: A Special Report on New Applications & Research. LC 83-15199. (Series of Special Reports: No. 10). 180p. reprint ed. pap. 55.80 (*0-7837-0695-2*, 204102800019) Bks Demand.

Margolis, James M., ed. Conductive Polymers & Plastics. (Illus.). 224p. 1989. 42.50 (*0-412-01431-9*, Chap & Hall NY) Chapman & Hall.

Margolis, James M., et al, eds. Rationality, Relativism & the Human Sciences. 252p. 1986. lib. bdg. 118.50 (*90-247-3271-9*, Pub. by M Nijhoff) Kluwer Academic.

Margolis, Jeffrey A. Teen Crime Wave: A Growing Problem. LC 96-53650. (Issues in Focus Ser.). (Illus.). 112p. (YA). (gr. 6 up). 1997. lib. bdg. 20.95 (*0-89490-910-X*) Enslow Pubs.

— Violence in Sports: Victory at What Price? LC 98-35031. (Issues in Focus Ser.). 128p. (YA). (gr. 6 up). 1999. lib. bdg. 20.95 (*0-89490-961-4*) Enslow Pubs.

Margolis, John D. Joseph Wood Krutch: A Writer's Life. LC 80-182. (Illus.). 272p. reprint ed. pap. 84.40 (*0-608-17427-0*, 202984900066) Bks Demand.

***Margolis, Jon.** The Last Innocent Year: America in 1964. LC 98-48015. (Illus.). 416p. 1999. 25.00 (*0-688-15323-2*, Wm Morrow) Morrow Avon.

— The Last Innocent Year: America in 1964. 432p. 2000. pap. 14.00 (*0-688-17907-X*) Morrow Avon.

Margolis, Jon. The Quotable Bob Dole: Witty, Wise, & Otherwise. LC 95-42230. 224p. (Orig.). 1996. pap. 7.50 (*0-380-78585-4*, Avon Bks) Morrow Avon.

***Margolis, Jonathan.** A Brief History of Tomorrow. (Illus.). 256p. 2000. 24.95 (*1-58234-108-7*) Bloomsbury Pubg.

Margolis, Jonathan. Uri Geller: Magician or Mystic, 1. LC 99-36494. 304p. 1999. 24.95 (*1-56649-025-1*) Welcome Rain.

Margolis, Joseph. Culture & Cultural Entities. LC 83-4635. 183p. 1983. text 112.50 (*90-277-1574-2*, D Reidel) Kluwer Academic.

— The Flux of History & the Flux of Science. LC 93-4134. 1993. 48.00 (*0-520-08319-9*, Pub. by U CA Pr) Cal Prin Full Svc.

— Historied Thought, Constructed World: A Conceptual Primer for the Turn of the Millennium. LC 95-12639. 382p. 1995. 52.00 (*0-520-20113-2*, Pub. by U CA Pr) Cal Prin Full Svc.

— Interpretation Radical but Not Unruly: The New Puzzle of the Arts & History. LC 94-15598. 1995. 48.00 (*0-520-08769-0*, Pub. by U CA Pr) Cal Prin Full Svc.

— Life Without Principles: Reconciling Theory & Practice. LC 95-36405. 256p. (C). 1996. 64.95 (*0-631-17462-1*) Blackwell Pubs.

— Persons & Minds: The Prospects of Nonreductive Materialism. (Synthese Library: No. 121). 314p. 1977. pap. text 55.50 (*90-277-0863-0*, D Reidel); lib. bdg. 88.00 (*90-277-0854-1*, D Reidel) Kluwer Academic.

— Philosophy Looks at the Arts: Contemporary Readings in Aesthetics. 3rd ed. LC 88-12303. 592p. (C). 1987. pap. 27.95 (*0-87722-440-4*) Temple U Pr.

— What, After All, Is a Work of Art? Lectures in the Philosophy of Art. LC 98-41260. 143p. 1999. 35.00 (*0-271-01865-8*); pap. 16.95 (*0-271-01866-6*) Pa St U Pr.

***Margolis, Joseph & Rockmore, Tom, eds.** The Philosophy of Interpretation. (Metaphilosophy Ser.: Vol. 31:1/2). 208p. 2000. pap. 24.95 (*0-631-22047-X*, Pub. by Blackwell Pubs) Blackwell Pubs.

Margolis, Joseph, jt. ed. see Rockmore, Tom.

Margolis, Judy, jt. auth. see English, Sandal.

Margolis, Julius, ed. Analysis of Public Output. (Universities-National Bureau Conference Ser.: No. 23). 425p. 1970. text 111.10 (*0-87014-220-8*) Natl Bur Econ Res.

— The Analysis of Public Output: A Conference of the Universities - National Bureau Committee for Economic Research. LC 78-119997. (Universities-National Bureau Conference Ser.: No. 23). (Illus.). 427p. reprint ed. pap. 132.40 (*0-8357-7565-8*, 205688600096) Bks Demand.

— The Public Economy of Urban Communities: Papers Presented at the 2nd Conference on Urban Public Expenditures, Feb. 21-22, 1964. LC 77-86404. (Resources for the Future, Inc. Publications). 288p. reprint ed. 55.00 (*0-404-60339-4*) AMS Pr.

Margolis, L. & Guoot, C. Pacific Salmon: Life Histories. (Illus.). 608p. 1991. text 95.00 (*0-7748-0359-2*) U of Wash Pr.

Margolis, L., jt. auth. see McDonald, T. E.

Margolis, Lawrence. Executive Agreements & Presidental Power in Foreign Policy. LC 85-12484. 171p. 1985. 49.95 (*0-275-90023-1*, C0023, Praeger Pubs) Greenwood.

***Margolis, Mac.** The Last New World: The Conquest of the Amazon Frontier. (Illus.). 367p. 2000. 23.00 (*0-7881-9395-3*) DIANE Pub.

Margolis, Marianne F., ed. see Stieglitz, Alfred.

Margolis, Matthew. Ultimate Guide to Dog Training: How to Bring Out the Best in Your Pet. LC 98-44300. (Illus.). 288p. 1999. per. 12.00 (*0-684-85646-8*) S&S Trade.

— Woof! 1995. pap. 12.00 (*0-517-88451-8*) Random Hse Value.

Margolis, Matthew & Siegal, Mordecai. Uncle Matty's... Dog Training: The Woof Papers. LC 98-44300. (Illus.). 288p. 1998. 25.00 (*0-684-84556-3*) Simon & Schuster.

Margolis, Matthew & Swan, Catherine. The Dog In Your Life. LC 82-40037. (Illus.). 368p. 1982. pap. 16.00 (*0-394-71174-2*) Vin Bks.

Margolis, Matthew, jt. auth. see Siegal, Mardecai.

Margolis, Matthew, jt. auth. see Siegal, Mordecai.

Margolis, Max L. The Book of Joshua in Greek According to the Critically Restored Text with an Apparatus Containing the Variants of the Principal Recensions & of the Individual Witnesses, Pt. 5: Joshua 19: 39 - 24: 33. LC 91-21422. xxvi, 457p. 1992. pap. 35.00 (*0-900268-66-2*, Ctr Judaic Studies) Eisenbrauns.

Margolis, Maxine L. An Invisible Minority: Brazilians in New York City. Foner, Nancy, ed. LC 97-227966. (New Immigrants Ser.). 141p. (C). 1997. pap. 20.00 (*0-205-26687-8*) Allyn.

— Little Brazil: An Ethnography of Brazilian Immigrants in New York City. LC 93-13699. (Illus.). 328p. 1994. text 55.00 (*0-691-03348-X*, Pub. by Princeton U Pr) Cal Prin Full Svc.

— The Moving Frontier: Social & Economic Change in a Southern Brazilian Community. LC 73-7730. (Latin American Monographs: Ser. 2, No. 11). (Illus.). 292p. reprint ed. pap. 90.60 (*0-7837-5074-9*, 204477200004) Bks Demand.

***Margolis, Maxine L.** True to Her Nature: Changing Advice to American Women. 180p. 2000. pap. 12.95 (*1-57766-127-3*) Waveland Pr.

Margolis, Maxine L. & Murphy, Martin F., eds. The Knight of the Two Swords: A Thirteenth-Century Arthurian Romance. Arthur, Ross G. & Corbett, Noel, trs. LC 95-9219. 224p. (C). 1996. 49.95 (*0-8130-1439-5*) U Press Fla.

Margolis, Maxine L., jt. ed. see Murphy, Martin F.

Margolis, Maxine L., ed. see Watkins, Daniel P.

Margolis, Michael, ed. Free Expression, Public Support, & Censorship: Examining Government's Role in the Arts in Canada & the United States. LC 93-30572. 160p. (Orig.). 1994. text 46.50 (*0-8191-9289-9*); pap. text 21.50 (*0-8191-9290-2*) U Pr of Amer.

***Margolis, Michael & Resnick, David M.** Politics as Usual: The Cyberspace Revolution. LC 99-50650. (Contemporary American Politics Ser.). 2000. write for info. (*0-7619-1331-9*) Sage.

Margolis, Michael, jt. ed. see Green, John C.

Margolis, Nadia. Joan of Arc in History, Literature, & Film: A Select, Annotated Bibliography. LC 90-39611. 432p. 1990. text 10.00 (*0-8240-4638-2*, H1224) Garland.

Margolis, Nadia & Wilson, Katharina. Women in the Middle Ages. 1000p. Date not set. text 100.00 (*0-8240-7272-3*) Garland.

Margolis, Nadia, tr. see De Pizan, Christine.

Margolis, Nancy H., ed. see Adcock, Craig, et al.

Margolis, Nancy H., ed. see Fleming, Jeff.

Margolis, Nancy H., ed. see Fleming, Jeff & Larson, John C.

Margolis, Nancy H., ed. see Fleming, Jeff, et al.

Margolis, Nancy H., ed. see Griffin, Farah J. & Rony, Fatimah T.

Margolis, Nancy H., ed. see Kuspit, Donald, et al.

Margolis, Nancy H., ed. see Rollins, Tim, et al.

Margolis, Nancy H., ed. see Stiles, Kristine & Selz, Peter H.

Margolis, Neal & Harmon, N. Paul. Accounting Essentials. 2nd ed. LC 85-12332. 336p. 1985. pap. 19.95 (*0-471-82721-5*) Wiley.

Margolis, Otto S. Acute Grief: Loss of an Adult Child, 8. LC 87-18315. 201p. 1988. 55.00 (*0-275-91304-X*, C1304, Praeger Pubs) Greenwood.

— Grief & the Meaning of the Funeral. 1979. 17.95 (*0-405-12501-1*) Ayer.

Margolis, Otto S., et al, eds. Loss, Grief, & Bereavement: A Guide for Counseling, 4. LC 85-12260. 176p. 1985. 49.95 (*0-275-90144-0*, C0144, Praeger Pubs) Greenwood.

Margolis, Otto S. & Cherico, Daniel J. Thanatology Abstracts, 1977. 1980. 19.95 (*0-405-12503-8*) Ayer.

— Thanatology Abstracts, 1979. 1981. 18.95 (*0-405-14222-6*, 19702) Ayer.

Margolis, Otto S., jt. auth. see Cherico, Daniel J.

Margolis, Philip E. Random House Webster's Computer & Internet Dictionary. 3rd ed. LC 98-45280. 1998. pap. 15.95 (*0-375-70351-9*) Random Ref & Info.

— Random House Webster's Pocket Computer & Internet Dictionary. 400p. 1999. pap. 8.99 (*0-375-70626-7*) Random.

Margolis, Philip E. & Darnell, P. A. Software Engineering in C. (Books on Professional Computing). (Illus.). 500p. 1989. pap. 32.00 (*0-387-96574-2*) Spr-Verlag.

Margolis, Philip E., jt. auth. see Darnell, P. A.

Margolis, Philip E., jt. auth. see Darnell, Peter A.

Margolis, R. K., jt. auth. see Margolis, R. U.

Margolis, R. U. & Margolis, R. K. Neurobiology of Glycoconjugates. (Illus.). 472p. (C). 1989. text 125.00 (*0-306-43128-9*, Kluwer Plenum) Kluwer Academic.

Margolis, Robert D. & Zweben, Joan E. Treating Patients with Alcohol & Other Drug Problems: An Integrated Approach. LC 97-42378. (Psychologists in Independent Practice Ser.). (Illus.). 358p. 1998. pap. 29.95 (*1-55798-518-9*) Am Psychol.

Margolis, Robert H., et al. Audiology Clinical Protocols. LC 97-1019. 224p. (C). 1997. pap. 54.00 (*0-205-26824-2*) Allyn.

Margolis, Robin, jt. auth. see Goodman-Malmuth, Leslie.

Margolis, Seth, ed. see Hijuelos, Oscar.

Margolis, Seth, ed. see McMurtry, Larry.

Margolis, Seth J. Losing Isaiah. 400p. 1994. reprint ed. mass mkt. 5.99 (*0-515-11539-8*, Jove) Berkley Pub.

— Perfect Angel. large type ed. LC 97-15639. (Cloak & Dagger Ser.). 632p. 1997. 25.95 (*0-7862-1150-4*) Thorndike Pr.

— Perfect Angel. 384p. 1998. reprint ed. mass mkt. 6.99 (*0-380-78748-2*, Avon Bks) Morrow Avon.

Margolis, Simeon. The Johns Hopkins Complete Home Encyclopedia of Drugs: Developed Especially for People over 50. LC 98-20364. 768p. 1999. 39.95 (*0-929661-43-5*) Rebus.

— The Johns Hopkins Complete Home Encyclopedia of Drugs: Developed Especially for People over 50. (Illus.). 768p. 1999. 39.95 (*0-929661-48-6*) Rebus.

***Margolis, Simeon.** The Johns Hopkins Complete Home Encyclopedia of Drugs: Developed Especially for People over 50. LC 00-28044. (Illus.). 2000. pap. write for info. (*0-929661-59-1*) Rebus.

— The Johns Hopkins Medical Handbook: The 100 Major Medical Disorders of People over the Age of 50 : Plus a Directory to the Leading Teaching Hospitals, Research Organizations, Treatment Centers, & Support Groups. LC 99-14516. 1999. write for info. (*0-929661-51-6*) Rebus.

— The Johns Hopkins Medical Handbook: The 100 Major Medical Disorders of People over the Age of 50: Plus a Directory to the Leading Teaching Hospitals, Research Organizations, Treatment Centers & Support.Groups. LC 99-14516. 1999. write for info. (*0-929661-54-0*) Rebus.

— Johns Hopkins Symptoms & Remedies. rev. ed. LC 99-19107. 704p. 1999. 39.95 (*0-929661-49-4*) Rebus.

***Margolis, Simeon & Johns Hopkins Medical Institutions.** Johns Hopkins Symptoms & Remedies: The Complete Home Medical Reference. LC 99-19107. 1999. write for info. (*0-929661-52-4*) Rebus.

Margolis, Stephen E., jt. auth. see Liebowitz, Stanley J.

Margolis, Sue. Neurotica. LC 98-46978. 320p. 1999. 16.95 (*0-553-10984-7*) Bantam.

Margolis, Susanna. Adventuring in the Pacific: The Islands of Polynesia, Melanesia, & Micronesia Including Bora Bora, Fiji, Tahiti, Tonga, Vanuatu, & Hundreds of Others. rev. ed. (Adventure Travel Guide Ser.). (Illus.). 464p. 1996. pap. 16.00 (*0-87156-390-8*, Pub. by Sierra) Random.

Margolis, Victor. The Platespinner: Playing with Time. 300p. (Orig.). 1995. pap. 14.95 (*0-9642973-8-8*) Marik Pubg.

Margolius, F. R. The Secret of Finding Big Winners in the Stock Market. 150p. 1995. text 18.00 (*1-55738-281-6*, Irwn Prfssnl) McGraw-Hill Prof.

Margolius, Harry S., jt. ed. see Greenbaum, Lowell M.

***Margolius, Ivan.** Automobiles by Architects. (Illus.). 160p. 2000. pap. 54.95 (*0-471-60786-X*) Wiley.

Margolius, Ivan. Church of the Sacred Heart: Prague 1922-33: Joze Plecnik. LC 96-139681. (Architecture in Detail Ser.). (Illus.). 60p. (Orig.). (C). 1995. pap. 29.95 (*0-7148-3351-7*, Pub. by Phaidon Press) Phaidon Pr.

— Prague. (Architecture Guides Ser.). (Illus.). 320p. 1997. pap. 5.95 (*3-89508-282-1*, 520191) Konemann.

Margoluis, Richard & Salafsky, Nick. Measures of Success: Designing, Monitoring & Managing Conservation & Development Projects. LC 98-13588. 363p. 1998. pap. text 35.00 (*1-55963-612-2*) Island Pr.

Margolus, Norman, jt. auth. see Toffoli, Tommaso.

Margon, Lester. Construction of American Furniture Treasures. (Illus.). 168p. 1975. reprint ed. pap. 9.95 (*0-486-23056-2*) Dover.

Margoninski, Y., ed. see Israeli Vacuum Congress Staff.

Margopoulos, Richard. Tales of the Black Diamond. (Illus.). 80p. (Orig.). 1993. pap. 8.95 (*0-9623841-9-4*) Fantagor Pr.

Margoshes, Dave. Long Distance Calls. 192p. 1997. pap. 12.95 (*1-55050-104-6*, Pub. by Coteau) Genl Dist Srvs.

Margot, Alain G. The Chinese Community in Vietnam under the French. LC 93-24943. 196p. 1993. pap. 39.95 (*0-7734-1941-1*) E Mellen.

***Margotta, Roberto.** Hamlyn History of Medicine. (Illus.). 2000. pap. 17.95 (*0-600-60092-0*) Hamlyn Publishing Group Ltd.

Margoulith, D. S., tr. see Ibn Ali, Yefet.

An Asterisk (*) at the beginning of an entry indicates that the title is appearing for the first time.

Margraf, Wolfgang. Untersuchungen zur Production und Reingung eines gelben Farbstoffes des Basidiomyceten: Pleurotus ostreatus (Jacq. ex Fr.) Kummer. (Bibliotheca Mycologica Ser.: No. 93). (GER., Illus.). 95p. 1984. 26.00 (*3-7682-1412-5*) Lubrecht & Cramer.

Margraff, Ruth, jt. auth. see Ho, Fred.

Margrave, John L., ed. Modern High Temperature Science. 484p. 1984. 115.00 (*0-89603-072-5*) Humana.

Margrave-Jones, Clive V. Mellows: The Law of Succession. 5th ed. 680p. 1993. pap. text 66.00 (*0-406-02438-3*, UK, MICHIE) LEXIS Pub.

Margrave-Jones, Clive V., et al, eds. Butterworths Wills, Probate & Administration Service, 2 vols. 1990. ring bd. 460.00 (*0-406-12500-7*, U.K., MICHIE) LEXIS Pub.

Margrave-Jones, Clive V., jt. auth. see Rodgers, Christopher P.

Margroff, Robert E., jt. auth. see Anthony, Piers.

Margry, Pierre, ed. Decouvertes et Establissements des francais dans l'ouest et dans le sud de l'Amerique septentrional: 1614-1754, 6 vols., Set. Incl. Vol. 1. Voyages des francais sur les Grands Lacs et Decouverte de l'Ohio et du Mississippi (1614-1684) reprint ed. Vol. 2. Lettres de Cavelier de la Salle et Correspondance Relative a ses Entreprises (1678-1685) reprint ed. Vol. 3. Recherche des Bouches du Mississippi et Voyage a Travers le Continent Depuis les Cotes du Texas jusqu'a Quebec (1669-1698) reprint ed. Vol. 4. Decouverte par mer des bouches du Mississippi et etablissement de Lemoyne d'Iberville sur le golfe du Mexique (1694-1703) reprint ed. Vol. 5. Premiere Formation d'une Chaine de Postes entre le Fleuve Saint-Laurent et le Golfe du Mexique (1683-1724) reprint ed. Vol. 6. Exploration des Affluents du Mississippi et Decouverte des Montagnes Rocheuses (1679-1754) reprint ed. 750.00 (*0-404-04230-9*) AMS Pr.

Margry, Pierre & Cormier, Louis-Philippe. Lettres de Margry a Parkman, 1872-1892. LC 78-377587. (Cahiers du Centre de Recherche en Civilisation Canadienne-Francaise: Vol. 11). (FRE.). 217p. 1977. reprint ed. pap. 67.30 (*0-608-02204-7*, 206287400004) Bks Demand.

Marguardt, Michael & Reynolds, Angus. The Global Learning Organization. LC 93-2391. 336p. 1993. text 32.50 (*1-55623-839-8*, Irwn Prfssnl) McGraw-Hill Prof.

Marguerite d'Angouleme. Correspondance: Annees 1521-1522, Vol. 1. Briconnet, Guillaume et al, eds. (FRE.). 238p. 1975. pap. 49.95 (*0-7859-5530-5*) Fr & Eur.

Marguerite D'Angouleme. L' Heptameron des Nouvelles, 4 vols. (FRE.). 1500p. 1969. 350.00 (*0-7859-5531-3*) Fr & Eur.

— La Navire Ou Consolation du Roi Francois 1er a Sasoeur Marguerite: Edition Critique. Marichal, Robert, ed. (FRE.). 347p. 1956. pap. 115.00 (*0-7859-5533-X*) Fr & Eur.

— Poesies du Roi Francois 1er, de Louise de Savoie, Duchesse D'Angouleme, de Marguerite, Reine de Navarre. (FRE.). 243p. 1970. reprint ed. 75.00 (*0-7859-5529-1*) Fr & Eur.

Marguerite of Angouleme. Theatre Profane: The Seven Plays. Reynolds-Cornell, Regine, tr. 238p. 1992. pap. 8.00 (*1-895537-06-1*, DH90, Pub. by Dovehouse) Sterling.

Marguerite, Yves. Dictionnaires des Reves. (FRE.). 385p. 1990. pap. 38.95 (*0-7859-8639-1*, 226801004x) Fr & Eur.

Margueron, C. Modern Saturn Italian-French, French-Italian Dictionary: Dictionnaire Moderne Saturne Italien-Francais-Italien. (FRE & ITA.). 1600p. 1983. 85.00 (*0-8288-0370-6*, M6833) Fr & Eur.

Margueron, C. & Folena, G. Larousse Apollo French-Italian, Italian-French Dictionary: Dictionnaire Larousse Apollo Francais-Italien-Francais. (FRE & ITA.). 992p. 1980. 22.95 (*0-8288-0369-2*, M14295) Fr & Eur.

Margueron, Claude & Folena, Gianfranco. Dictionnaire General Francais-Italien, Italien-Francais. Larousse Staff, ed. (FRE & ITA.). 1616p. 1994. write for info. (*0-7859-7661-2*, 2034513347) Fr & Eur.

Marguerre, K. Mechanics of Vibrations. Wolfel, H., ed. (Mechanics of Structural Systems Ser.: No. 2). 282p. 1979. text 154.00 (*90-286-0086-8*) Kluwer Academic.

Marguglio, B. W. Environmental Management Systems. (Illus.). 208p. 1991. text 69.75 (*0-8247-8523-1*) Dekker.

Marguglio, B. W., ed. Quality Systems in the Nuclear Industry - STP 616. 700p. 1977. 37.75 (*0-8031-0197-X*, STP616) ASTM.

***Marguiles, Donald.** Dinner with Friends. 112p. 2000. pap. 11.95 (*1-55936-194-8*) Theatre Comm.

Margulies, Alfred. The Empathic Imagination. (C). 1989. 22.95 (*0-393-70076-3*) Norton.

Margulies, Alice. Compassion. (Values Library). (Illus.). 64p. (YA). (gr. 7-12). 1990. lib. bdg. 15.95 (*0-8239-1108-X*) Rosen Group.

Margulies, Donald. Collected Stories. LC 98-164886. 1998. pap. 5.25 (*0-8222-1640-X*) Dramatists Play.

— Collected Stories. LC 98-14965. 112p. 1998. pap. 10.95 (*1-55936-152-2*) Theatre Comm.

***Margulies, Donald.** Dinner with Friends. 2000. pap. 5.95 (*0-8222-1754-6*) Dramatists Play.

Margulies, Donald. Found a Peanut. 1984. pap. 5.25 (*0-8222-0417-7*) Dramatists Play.

— July 7, 1994, Short Plays & Monologues. LC 98-104338. 1997. pap. 5.25 (*0-8222-1568-3*) Dramatists Play.

— The Loman Family Picnic. rev. ed. 1994. pap. 5.25 (*0-8222-0684-6*) Dramatists Play.

— The Model Apartment. 1990. pap. 5.25 (*0-8222-0767-2*) Dramatists Play.

— Pitching to the Star & Other Short Plays. 1993. pap. 5.25 (*0-8222-1358-3*) Dramatists Play.

— Sight Unseen. 1992. pap. 5.25 (*0-8222-1317-6*) Dramatists Play.

— Sight Unseen: And Other Plays. 304p. (Orig.). 1995. pap. 15.95 (*1-55936-103-4*) Theatre Comm.

— What's Wrong with This Picture? 75p. (Orig.). 1988. pap. 6.95 (*0-88145-059-6*) Broadway Play.

Margulies, Donald. What's Wrong with This Picture? (Orig.). Date not set. pap. 5.95 (*0-8222-1769-4*) Dramatists Play.

Margulies, Edwin. Audio Teleconferencing: The Complete Handbook. 436p. 1997. per. 34.95 (*1-57820-015-6*) Telecom Bks.

— Client Server Computer Telephony. 1997. 34.95 (*0-936648-55-4*) Telecom Bks.

— Client Server Computer Telephony. 2nd ed. 552p. 1997. per. 34.95 (*1-57820-004-0*) Telecom Bks.

— SCSA: The Definitive Reference Manual to Using Signal. 2nd ed. 450p. 1996. 34.95 (*0-936648-43-0*, P90063) Telecom Bks.

— SCSA Computer Telephony Building Blocks: The Complete Reference Guide. 2nd ed. 450p. 1996. per. 34.95 (*0-936648-77-5*) Telecom Bks.

— Secrets of Windows Telephony. 688p. 1997. per. 34.95 (*1-57820-002-4*) Telecom Bks.

— 236 Killer Voice Processing Applications. 1997. 34.95 (*0-936648-70-8*) Telecom Bks.

— Understanding Java Telephony. 873p. 1997. per. 34.95 (*1-57820-003-2*) Telecom Bks.

— Understanding the Voice-Enabled Internet. 720p. 1996. per. 34.95 (*0-936648-91-0*, P50003) Telecom Bks.

— Understanding the Voice-Enabled Internet. 2nd ed. 720p. 1998. pap. text 34.95 (*1-57820-022-9*) Telecom Bks.

— The UnPBX: The Complete Guide to the New Breed of Communications Servers. 420p. 1997. per. 34.95 (*1-57820-014-8*) Telecom Bks.

Margulies, Harold & Bloch, Lucille S. Foreign Medical Graduates in the United States. LC 69-18040. (Commonwealth Fund Publications). (Illus.). 186p. 1990. 27.50 (*0-674-30875-1*) HUP.

Margulies, Herbert F. The Decline of the Progressive Movement in Wisconsin, 1890-1920. LC 68-63073. 310p. 1968. 7.50 (*0-87020-060-7*) State Hist Soc Wis.

— The Mild Reservationists & the League of Nations Controversy in the Senate. LC 89-4702. 264p. 1989. text 39.00 (*0-8262-0693-X*) U of Mo Pr.

— Reconciliation & Revival: James R. Mann & the House Republicans in the Wilson Era, 166. LC 95-36434. (Contributions in American History Ser.: No. 166). 264p. 1996. 62.95 (*0-313-29817-3*, Greenwood Pr) Greenwood.

Margulies, Ivone. Nothing Happens: Chantal Akerman's Hyperrealist Everyday. LC 95-30516. (Illus.). 288p. 1996. text 49.95 (*0-8223-1726-5*); pap. text 17.95 (*0-8223-1723-0*) Duke.

Margulies, Jimmy. Hitting Below the Belt: The Best of Jimmy Margulies. LC 98-14474. (Illus.). 160p. 1998. pap. 8.95 (*1-56554-356-4*) Pelican.

Margulies, Joseph. Lumbosacral & Spinopelvic Fixation. LC 93-34226. (Illus.). 976p. 1996. text 209.00 (*0-397-51388-7*) Lppncott W & W.

Margulies, Joseph Y., et al. Revision Spine Surgery. LC 98-36265. (Illus.). 887p. (C). (gr. 13). 1998. text 195.00 (*0-8151-4591-8*, 30029) Mosby Inc.

Margulies, Nancy. Inside Brian's Brain, 5 vols. (Interactive Comics Ser.: Vol. 3). (Illus.). 36p. (YA). (gr. 6-12). 1996. 16.00 (*1-56976-063-2*, 1083-F3) Zephyr Pr AZ.

— Magic 7: Tools for Building Your Multiple Intelligences. (Interactive Comics Ser.: Vol. 2). (Illus.). 36p. 1995. 16.00 (*1-56976-022-5*, 1056-F3) Zephyr Pr AZ.

— Mapping Inner Space: Learning & Teaching Mind Mapping. (Illus.). 128p. (J). (gr. k-12). 1991. 32.00 (*0-913705-56-X*) Zephyr Pr AZ.

— Yes, You Can . . . Draw! Rose, Diana, ed. (Illus.). 75p. (Orig.). 1991. pap. text 39.95 (*0-905553-35-7*, Pub. by Accel Lrn Sys) McClelland & Stewart.

Margulies, Nancy, contrib. by. Map It! Tools for Charting the Vast Territories of Your Mind, 5 bks., Set. (Interactive Comics Ser.). (Illus.). 36p. (Orig.). 1995. pap., teacher ed. 16.00 (*1-56976-008-X*) Zephyr Pr AZ.

Margulies, Sam. Getting Divorced Without Ruining Your Life. 320p. 1992. pap. 12.00 (*0-671-72826-1*, Fireside) S&S Trade Pap.

Margulies, Sheldon & Lasson, Kenneth. Learning Law: The Mastery of Legal Logic. LC 92-71953. 138p. (C). 1992. pap. text 12.50 (*0-89089-494-9*) Carolina Acad Pr.

Margulies, Sylvia R. The Pilgrimage to Russia: The Soviet Union & the Treatment of Foreigners, 1924-1937. LC 68-16062. 302p. 1968. reprint ed. pap. 93.70 (*0-608-01979-8*, 206263400003) Bks Demand.

Margulies, Teddy S. Snow White & the Seven Dwarfs. (Look-Look Bks.). (Illus.). 24p. (J). (ps-3). 1993. pap. 3.29 (*0-307-12686-2*, 12686) Gldn Bks Pub Co.

Margulies, Teddy S., adapted by. Revenge of the Lawn Gnomes. (Goosebumps Presents Ser.: No. 18). (Illus.). 64p. (J). (gr. 2-5). 1998. pap. text 3.99 (*0-590-46441-8*) Scholastic Inc.

— You Can't Scare Me! (Goosebumps Presents Ser.: No. 14). (Illus.). 64p. (J). (gr. 2-5). 1997. pap. text 3.99 (*0-590-30663-4*) Scholastic Inc.

— You Can't Scare Me! (Goosebumps Presents Ser.: No. 14). 1997. 9.19 (*0-606-11408-4*, Pub. by Turtleback) Demco.

Margulies, Timothy S. Scratches. 1998. pap. write for info. (*1-57553-944-6*) Watermrk Pr.

***Margulies, Timothy S.** Selected Collected Poems. 1999. pap. write for info. (*1-58235-301-8*) Watermrk Pr.

Margulis, Alexander & Kholodnaya, Asya, eds. Russian-English Dictionary of Proverbs & Sayings. LC 99-58987. (ENG & RUS.). 495p. 2000. lib. bdg. 55.00 (*0-7864-0703-4*) McFarland & Co.

Margulis, Alexander R. Symbiosis & Evolution. Date not set. 1.20 (*0-7167-9271-0*) W H Freeman.

***Margulis, Alexander R., ed.** Modern Imaging of the Alimentary Tube. (Medical Radiology Ser.). (Illus.). x, 363p. 2000. pap. 75.00 (*3-540-66345-2*) Spr-Verlag.

Margulis, Alexander R., jt. auth. see Eisenberg, Ronald L.

Margulis, Alexander R., ed. see Ando, M.

***Margulis, Dan.** Professional Photoshop 5.0: The Classic Guide to Color Correction. LC 98-39148. 336p. 1998. pap. 64.99 (*0-471-32308-X*) Wiley.

Margulis, Daniel & Schroeder, John. The Literate Typographer. (Illus.). 240p. 1984. pap. 20.00 (*0-938304-03-8*) Cornell Daily.

Margulis, Daniel & Schroeder, John, eds. A Century at Cornell. (Illus.). 232p. 1980. 19.95 (*0-938304-00-3*) Cornell Daily.

Margulis, G. A. Discrete Subgroups of Semisimple Lie Groups. (Ergebnisse der Mathematik und Ihrer Grenzgebiete Ser.: Vol. 17). ix, 338p. 1991. 150.95 (*0-387-12179-X*) Spr-Verlag.

Margulis, Joel, jt. auth. see Benjamin, Gerald A.

Margulis, Lynn. Early Life. (Biology Ser.). (Illus.). 176p. (C). 1982. pap. text 30.00 (*0-86720-005-7*) Jones & Bartlett.

***Margulis, Lynn.** Microcosmos Vol. 1: Sex & Reproduction. (Illus.). 64p. (C). 2000. pap. text 150.00 (*0-7637-1233-7*) Jones & Bartlett.

— Microcosmos Vol. 2: Evolution & Diversity. (Illus.). 64p. (C). 2000. pap. text 150.00 (*0-7637-1234-5*) Jones & Bartlett.

Margulis, Lynn. Protoctista Glossary. 288p. (Orig.). (C). 1993. 53.75 (*0-86720-081-2*) Jones & Bartlett.

— Sharing with Children: New Ideas on the Evolution of Life. (Illus.). 23p. (Orig.). (C). 1985. pap. 3.00 (*0-918374-21-9*) City Coll Wk.

— Slanted Truths: Essays on Gaia, Symbiosis & Evolution. 384p. 1999. pap. text 18.00 (*0-387-98772-X*) Spr-Verlag.

— Symbiosis in Cell Evolution: Microbial Evolution in the Archean & Proterozoic Eons. 2nd ed. LC 92-14565. (C). 1992. pap. 42.95 (*0-7167-7029-6*); pap. text 56.95 (*0-7167-7028-8*) W H Freeman.

— Symbiotic Planet: A New Look at Evolution. (Science Masters Ser.: Vol. 4). 160p. 1998. pap. 12.00 (*0-465-07272-0*, Pub. by Basic) HarpC.

— Symbiotic Planet: A New Look at Evolution. LC 98-38921. (Science Masters Ser.: Vol. 4). 160p. 1998. 23.00 (*0-465-07271-2*, Pub. by Basic) HarpC.

Margulis, Lynn, ed. International Society for Evolutionary Protistology. 1984. text 141.50 (*90-277-1765-6*) Kluwer Academic.

***Margulis, Lynn, et al, eds.** Environmental Evolution: Effects of the Origin & Evolution of Life on Planet Earth. 2nd ed. (Illus.). 324p. 2000. 65.00 (*0-262-13366-0*); pap. 27.95 (*0-262-63197-0*) MIT Pr.

Margulis, Lynn & Fester, Rene, eds. Symbiosis As a Source of Evolutionary Innovation: Speciation & Morphogensis. 408p. 1991. 49.50 (*0-262-13269-9*) MIT Pr.

Margulis, Lynn & Olendzenski, Lorraine, eds. Environmental Evolution: Effects of the Origin & Evolution of Life on Planet Earth. (Illus.). 400p. 1992. 45.00 (*0-262-13273-7*) MIT Pr.

Margulis, Lynn & Sagan, Dorion. Gaia to Microcosm, Vol. I. 120p. (C). 1996. pap. text, per. 93.95 (*0-7872-2067-1*, 41206701) Kendall-Hunt.

— Microcosmos: Four Billion Years of Evolution from Our Microbial Ancestors. LC 96-49685. 304p. 1997. pap. 13.95 (*0-520-21064-6*, Pub. by U CA Pr) Cal Prin Full Svc.

— The Microcosmos Coloring Book. (HBJ-Boston Bk.). 160p. 1988. pap. 14.95 (*0-15-659430-7*) Harcourt.

— Origins of Sex: Three Billion Years of Genetic Recombination. 259p. (Orig.). (C). 1990. pap. 20.00 (*0-300-04619-7*) Yale U Pr.

— Slanted Truths: Essays on Gaia, Symbiosis & Evolution. LC 97-2160. 300p. 1997. 27.00 (*0-387-94927-5*) Spr-Verlag.

***Margulis, Lynn & Sagan, Dorion.** What Is Life? LC 00-25833. (Illus.). 320p. 2000. pap. 29.95 (*0-520-22021-8*, Pub. by U CA Pr) Cal Prin Full Svc.

Margulis, Lynn & Sagan, Dorion. What Is Sex? LC 97-19220. (Illus.). 256p. 1998. 37.50 (*0-684-82691-7*) S&S Trade.

Margulis, Lynn & Schwartz, K. Five Kingdoms: Life on Earth. 1995. 79.00 (*3-540-14500-1*) Spr-Verlag.

— Five Kingdoms: Life on Earth. 1996. cd-rom 79.00 (*3-540-14501-X*) Spr-Verlag.

Margulis, Lynn & Schwartz, Karlene V. Five Kingdoms: An Illustrated Guide to the Phyla of Life on Earth. 3rd ed. LC 97-21338. (C). 1997. pap. 29.95 (*0-7167-3027-8*) W H Freeman.

Margulis, Lynn, et al. Diversity of Life: The Illustrated Guide to the Five Kingdoms LC 99-11879. 248p. 1999. 35.00 (*0-7637-0862-3*) Jones & Bartlett.

— Handbook of Protoctista. (C). 1989. 225.00 (*0-86720-052-9*) Jones & Bartlett.

— Protoctist Glossary. 1995. cd-rom 79.00 (*3-540-14199-5*) Spr-Verlag.

— Protoctist Glossary. 1995. 79.00 (*3-540-14510-9*) Spr-Verlag.

Margulis, Lynn, jt. auth. see Sagan, Dorion.

Margulis, Lynn, jt. ed. see Ponnamperuma, Cyril.

Margulis, Michael. Mountain Biking New York. LC 97-593. (America by Mountain Bike Ser.). (Illus.). 256p. (Orig.). 1997. pap. 14.95 (*1-56044-534-3*) Falcon Pub Inc.

Margulis, Milia A., ed. Sonochemistry & Cavitation. Leib, Garson, tr. 500p. 1995. text 242.00 (*2-88124-849-7*) Gordon & Breach.

Margulis, Rena K. The Complete Guide to Whitewater Rafting Tours: California Edition, 1986. (Complete Guide to Whitewater Rafting Tours Ser.). (Illus.). 304p. (Orig.). 1986. pap. 11.95 (*0-9616150-0-1*) Aquatic Adv Pubns.

— The Complete Guide to Whitewater Rafting Tours: Western States Edition. 2nd rev. ed. (Complete Guide to Whitewater Rafting Tours Ser.). (Illus.). 448p. (Orig.). 1988. pap. 12.95 (*0-9616150-2-8*) Aquatic Adv Pubns.

***Margulus.** Origins of Species. 2000. 28.00 (*0-465-04391-7*, Pub. by Basic); pap. 15.00 (*0-465-04392-5*, Pub. by Basic) HarpC.

Marguth, F., et al, eds. Neurovascular Surgery: Specialized Neurosurgical Techniques. (Advances in Neurosurgery Ser.: Vol. 7). (Illus.). 420p. 1979. 63.95 (*0-387-09675-2*) Spr-Verlag.

Marha, Karel, et al. Electromagnetic Fields & the Life Environment. (Illus.). 1971. 15.00 (*0-614-11703-8*) San Francisco Pr.

Marheine, Allen H. You Belong: A Handbook for Church Members. rev. ed. LC 95-16991. 96p. 1995. pap. 4.95 (*0-8298-1104-4*) Pilgrim OH.

***Marhencke, Ernst-Erich.** Hans Reimer Claussen, 1804-1894: Kampfer Fur Freiheit Und Recht In Zwei Welten Ein Beitrag Zu Herkunft Und Wirken Der .achtundvierziger/ (Kieler Werkstucke Beitrage zur Schleswigholsteinischen und Skandinavischen Geschichte Ser.). 480p. 1999. 63.95 (*3-631-34634-4*) P Lang Pubng.

Marhoefer, Patricia E. Caring for the Developing Child. (Early Childhood Education Ser.). 1988. text 29.95 (*0-8273-2847-8*, VNR) Wiley.

— Caring for the Developing Child. (Early Childhood Education Ser.). 1988. pap., wbk. ed. 12.95 (*0-8273-2849-4*, VNR) Wiley.

— Caring for the Developing Child Workbook. 2nd ed. (C). 1992. pap. 13.00 (*0-8273-4902-5*) Delmar.

Marhoefer, Patricia E. & Vadnais, Lisa A. Caring for the Developing Child. 2nd ed. (C). 1992. pap. 36.95 (*0-8273-4681-6*) Delmar.

— Caring for the Developing Child. 2nd ed. (C). 1992. mass mkt., teacher ed. 13.00 (*0-8273-4682-4*) Delmar.

Marhsall, Alfred. The Correspondence of Alfred Marshall, Economist Vol. 2: At the Summit, 1891-1902, 3 vols. Whitaker, John K., ed. 485p. (C). 1996. text 74.95 (*0-521-55887-5*) Cambridge U Pr.

— The Correspondence of Alfred Marshall, Economist Vol. 3: Towards the Close, 1903-1924, 3 vols. Whitaker, John K., ed. 513p. (C). 1996. text 74.95 (*0-521-55886-7*) Cambridge U Pr.

***Mari, Carlo, photos by.** The Serengeti's Great Migration. (Illus.). 256p. 2000. 65.00 (*0-7892-0669-2*) Abbeville Pr.

***Mari, Carol, photos by.** Pink Flamingos. (Illus.). 208p. 2000. 55.00 (*0-7892-0668-4*) Abbeville Pr.

***Mari, Christopher, ed.** Space Exploration. LC 99-25424. (Reference Shelf Ser.: Vol. 71, No. 2). 157p. 1999. pap. 25.00 (*0-8242-0963-X*) Wilson.

***Mari, J. L.** Geophysics of Reservoir & Civil Engineering. 438p. 1999. 110.00 (*2-7108-0757-2*) Edits Technip.

Mari, J. L., jt. auth. see Boyer, S.

***Mari, Jean Luc.** Signal Processing for Geologists & Geophysicists. Painter, Derrick, tr. (Institut Franpcais du Pbetrole Publications). 458p. 1999. 89.00 (*2-7108-0752-1*) Edits Technip.

Mari, Jean-Luc, et al, eds. Full Waveform Acoustic Data Processing. 1994. 270.00 (*2-7708-0664-5*, Pub. by Edits Technip) Enfield Pubs NH.

Mari, Jean-Luc & Coppens, Francoise. Seismic Well Surveying. 128p. (C). 1991. 255.00 (*2-7108-0605-3*, Pub. by Edits Technip) Enfield Pubs NH.

Mari, Jean-Luc, et al. Full Waveform Acoustic Data Processing. LC 95-175674. (Illus.). 136p. 1994. 270.00 (*2-7108-0664-9*, Pub. by Edits Technip) Enfield Pubs NH.

Mari, Jean-Luc, jt. auth. see Gangleaud, F.

Mari, Jean-Luc, jt. auth. see Glangeaud, Franois.

Mari-Mutt, Jose & Bellinger, Peter F. Catalog of the Neotropical Collembola. LC 89-70038. (Flora & Fauna Handbook Ser.: No. 5). 256p. (Orig.). 1990. lib. bdg. 59.95 (*1-877743-00-3*) Sandhill Crane.

Mar'I, Sami K. Arab Education in Israel. 1978. 45.00 (*0-8156-0145-X*) Syracuse U Pr.

Maria, Audrey E. Di, see Di Maria, Audrey E., ed.

Maria Aurelia Tapia-Ruddy Staff. MCSE Test Success - Exchange Server 5.5. (MCSE Ser.). 432p. 1998. pap. text 24.99 (*0-7821-2250-7*) Sybex.

Maria, Bernard L. Current Management in Child Neurology. LC 99-167190. 387 p. 1999. boxed set 69.95 incl. cd-rom (*1-55009-070-4*) DEKR.

Maria Carrero, Luis. La Ciudad de los Dioses, Level 2. (Leer en Espanol Ser.). (SPA.). (C). 1998. pap. 5.95 (*84-294-3437-2*) Santillana.

— El Secreto de Cristobal Colon, Level 3. (Leer en Espanol Ser.). (SPA.). (C). 1998. pap. 5.95 (*84-294-3492-5*) Santillana.

Maria, Dee. Health Sense: The Cancer Manual - Deal from Strength. 2nd rev. ed. Orig. Title: Back to Health. 60p. 1998. pap. 7.95 (*0-9660414-1-0*) Dee Maria Pub.

Maria, Gerarda & Middendorp, Kooiman-van. The Hero in the Feminine Novel. 174p. (C). 1966. lib. bdg. 75.00 (*0-8383-0576-8*) M S G Haskell Hse.

Maria, Josefina. A Pilgrimage to the Heart of Man Through My Mercy Vol. 1: The Age of Two Hearts. unabridged ed. 274p. 1994. pap. 12.95 (*0-9634307-2-6*) MaxKol Communs.

Maria, Katherine. Reading Comprehension Instruction: Issues & Strategies. LC 90-70057. 306p. (C). 1990. pap. text 30.00 (*0-912752-20-3*) York Pr.

Maria, Lucia, et al. Alexej Jawlensky, 1890-1914 Vol. 1: Catalogue Raisonne of the Oil Paintings. (Illus.). 560p. 1991. 395.00 (*0-85667-398-6*) Sothebys Pubns.

Maria, M. De, see De Maria, M., ed.

Maria Merino, Jose, adapted by. Las Lagrimas del Sol, Level 4. (Leer en Espanol Ser.). (SPA.). (C). 1998. pap. 6.95 (*84-294-3490-9*) Santillana.

M

— El Oro de los Suenos, Level 4. (Leer en Espanol Ser.). (SPA.). (C). 1998. pap. 6.95 (*84-294-3489-5*) Santillana.
— La Tierra del Tiempo Perdido, Level 4. (Leer en Espanol Ser.). (SPA.). (C). 1998. pap. 6.95 (*84-294-3488-7*) Santillana.
Maria of Agreda, tr. The Passion of Our Lord. 284p. 1992. pap. 2.50 (*0-911988-38-6*, 44774) AMI Pr.
Maria, Richard De, see De Maria, Richard.
Maria, Salvatore Di, see Rodini, Robert J.
Maria, Salvatore Di, see Rodini, Robert J. & Di Maria, Salvatore.
Maria, Salvatore Di, see Rodini, Robert J.
Maria, Thomas De Sancta, see De Sancta Maria, Thomas.
Maria Vigil, Jose, jt. auth. see Casaldaliga, Pedro.
Mariabelem. Furtively I Come: A Poetic Journey into Mysticism. 68p. (Orig.). (C). 1994. pap. 6.00 (*0-9626221-4-1*) Vista Pubns FL.
— A Hurtadillas Vengo. (SPA.). 154p. (Orig.). (C). pap. 6.00 (*0-9626221-5-X*) Vista Pubns FL.
Mariage, Thierry. World of Andre LeNotre. LC 98-35185. (Penn Studies in Landscape Architecture). (Illus.). 192p. 1998. 35.00 (*0-8122-3468-5*) U of Pa Pr.
Mariah. The Establishment. LC 97-90679. 1997. pap. 14.95 (*0-533-12450-6*) Vantage.
Mariah, Paul. Personae Non Gratae. 32p. 1977. pap. 1.95 (*0-686-19032-7*) Man-Root.
Mariam, Mesfin W. Rural Vulnerability to Femine in Ethiopia, 1958-77. 208p. (Orig.). 1986. pap. 23.00 (*0-946688-03-6*, Pub. by Intermed Tech) Stylus Pub VA.
Mariama Ba. So Long a Letter. Modupe' Bode'-Thomas, tr. from FRE. (African Writers Ser.). 96p. (Orig.). (C). 1989. pap. 8.95 (*0-435-90555-4*, 90555) Heinemann.
Marian, B. Children's Mass Book. (J). (ps-3). Date not set. pap. 10.95 (*0-88271-081-8*) Regina Pr.
Marian Goodman Gallery Staff, jt. auth. see Deacon, Richard.
Marian Goodman Gallery Staff, ed. see Buch, Benjamin H.
Marian, Jim. Leading Your Students in Worship. 156p. (Orig.). 1993. pap. 9.99 (*1-56476-086-3*, 6-3086, Victor Bks) Chariot Victor.
— Worship Services for Youth Groups: 12 Complete, Thematic & Seasonal Services. LC 96-20118. 144p. 1996. pap. 14.99 (*0-310-20782-7*) Youth Spec.
Marian, Maria. Defeated Optimists. LC 98-66960. 168p. 1998. pap. 12.99 (*0-9623183-7-X*) Moonfall Pr VA.
— Queen of Trouble. Incarcaturilor, Regina, tr. from RUM. LC 98-66961.Tr. of Regina Incarcaturilor. 155p. 1998. pap. 10.99 (*0-9623183-6-1*) Moonfall Pr VA.
***Marian, Maria.** Solomon's Girls. Orig. Title: Fetele Lui Solomon. (EGY.). 1999. pap. 14.99 (*0-9623183-8-8*) Moonfall Pr VA.
Marian, Mary, et al. Geriatric Nutrition Handbook, Vol. 5. LC 97-16251. 175p. 1998. pap. 19.00 (*0-412-13641-4*) Kluwer Academic.
Marian, Susanne. Die Rechtsstellung Des Samenspenders Bei der Insemination / IVF. XXXIV, 260p. 1998. 51.95 (*3-631-33803-1*) P Lang Pubng.
Marian, Thomas W. Cruising Guide to the Northeast's Inland Waterways: Hudson River, New York State Canals... 2nd ed. LC 94-27926. 431p. 1995. 39.95 (*0-07-158011-5*) McGraw.
Marianacci, Dante, ed. see Talbot, G.
Marianetti, Marie C. Religion & Politics in Aristophanes' Clouds. (Altertumswissenschaftliche Texte und Studien: Vol. 24). (GER.). x, 140p. 1992. pap. write for info. (*3-487-09633-1*) G Olms Pubs.
Marianetti, Marie C., tr. Aristophanes: The Clouds- an Annotated Translation. LC 96-43480. 120p. 1996. pap. 23.50 (*0-7618-0588-5*) U Pr of Amer.
Mariani, jt. auth. see Garside, Roger.
Mariani, Cliff. Criminal Law Flash Cards for N. Y. S. Questions/Answer/Explanation Study Aid. 96p. 2000. 6.95 (*0-930137-21-3*) Looseleaf Law.
— Domestic Violence Survival Guide. Sokolich, Patricia, ed. 272p. 1996. pap. 19.95 (*0-930137-99-X*) Looseleaf Law.
— Domestic Violence Survival Guide for NYS. Sokolich, Patricia, ed. 286p. 2000. ring bd. 25.95 (*1-889031-03-8*) Looseleaf Law.
— Police Supervisor's Test Manual Database. 290p. 1996. ring bd. 24.95 (*0-930137-84-1*) Looseleaf Law.
Mariani, E. Advanced Load Dispatch for Power Systems: Principles, Practices & Economics. Grimble, M. J. & Johnson, M. A., eds. LC 97-15159. (Advances in Industrial Control Ser.). (Illus.). xxii, 229p. 1997. 54.95 (*3-540-76167-5*) Spr-Verlag.
Mariani, E. & Murthy, S. S. Control of Modern Integrated Power Systems. Grimble, M. J. & Johnson, M. A., eds. LC 97-15163. (Advances in Industrial Control Ser.). (Illus.). xviii, 260p. 1997. 54.95 (*3-540-76168-3*) Spr-Verlag.
Mariani, G., ed. Activated Prothrombin Complex Concentrates: Managing Hemophilia With Factor VIII Inhibitor. LC 81-23358. 239p. 1982. 67.95 (*0-275-91373-2*, C1373, Praeger Pubs) Greenwood.
Mariani, G. & Brackmann, H. H., eds. Immune Tolerance & the Treatment of Hemophiliacs with an Inhibitor: Proceedings. (Journal Ser.: Vol. 70, Suppl. 1, 1996). (Illus.). iv, 80p. 1996. pap., suppl. ed. 36.50 (*3-8055-6297-7*) S Karger.
Mariani, G. & Mannucci, P. M. Desmopressin in Bleeding Disorders. (NATO ASI Ser.: Vol. 242). (Illus.). 372p. (C). 1993. text 125.00 (*0-306-44414-3*, Kluwer Plenum) Kluwer Academic.
Mariani, G., jt. ed. see Brackmann, H. H.
Mariani, Galina, jt. auth. see Mariani, John.
Mariani, Giorgio. Post-Tribal Epics: The Native American Novel Between Tradition & Modernity. LC 96-31145. (Native American Studies). 280p. 1997. text 89.95 (*0-7734-8936-3*) E Mellen.
— Spectacular Narratives: Representations of Class & War in Stephen Crane & the American 1890s. LC 91-47738. (American University Studies: American Literature: Ser. XXIV, Vol. 37). 184p. 1993. 36.95 (*0-8204-1875-7*) P Lang Pubng.
Mariani, J. A., ed. see Nishinuma, Y. & Espesser, R.
***Mariani, John.** Cracking Boards: Usmle Step 2. 2nd ed. 2000. pap. 29.95 (*0-375-76164-0*) Random.
— Cracking the Boards: USMLE Step 2. 400p. 1999. pap. 29.95 (*0-375-75093-2*, Pub. by PRP NY) Random.
— Cracking the Boards: Usmle Step 3. 2000. pap. 29.95 (*0-375-76165-9*) Random.
***Mariani, John & Mariani, Galina.** The Italian-American Cookbook: A Feast of Food from a Great Cooking Tradition. (Illus.). 400p. 2000. 29.95 (*1-55832-165-9*); pap. 16.95 (*1-55832-166-7*) Harvard Common Pr.
Mariani, John, jt. auth. see Garside, Roger.
Mariani, John, jt. auth. see Rama, Marie.
Mariani, John F. The Dictionary of American Food & Drink. LC 83-4977. 478p. 1985. pap. 11.70 (*0-89919-359-5*, Pub. by Ticknor & Fields) HM.
Mariani, John F. The Dictionary of American Food & Drink. 379p. 1997. reprint ed. pap. text 20.00 (*0-7881-5073-1*) DIANE Pub.
— The Dictionary of Italian Food & Drink: An A-to-Z Guide with 2,300 Authentic Definitions & 50 Classic Recipes. LC 97-29229. (Illus.). 320p. 1998. pap. 17.00 (*0-7679-0129-0*) Broadway BDD.
— The Encyclopedia of American Food & Drink: With More Than 500 Recipes of American Classics. LC 99-23630. 380p. 1999. 29.95 (*0-86730-784-6*) Lebhar Friedman.
***Mariani, John F. & Von Bidder, Alex.** The Four Seasons: A History of America's Premier Restaurant. LC 99-24752. 1999. 19.98 (*0-7651-1709-6*) Smithmark.
Mariani, L., jt. ed. see Cobelli, C.
***Mariani, Luciano, et al, eds.** New Europe: Transformation & Environmental Issues. 424p. 1999. pap. 29.95 (*3-8258-3382-8*) CE24.
Mariani, Luciano, jt. auth. see De Devitiis, Guido.
***Mariani, Matthew.** High-earning Workers Who Don't Have a Bachelor's Degree. 9p. 1999. pap. 2.50 (*0-16-058923-1*) USGPO.
Mariani, Michael M., jt. auth. see Schlesinger, Edward S.
Mariani, Paul. The Broken Tower: A Life of Hart Crane. LC 98-37726. (Illus.). 480p. 1999. 35.00 (*0-393-04726-1*) Norton.
— The Great Wheel. 1997. pap. 11.00 (*0-614-29434-7*) Norton.
— The Great Wheel: Poems. 72p. 1997. pap. 11.00 (*0-393-31702-1*) Norton.
— Lost Puritan: A Life of Robert Lowell. (Illus.). 560p. 1996. pap. 15.00 (*0-393-31374-3*, Norton Paperbks) Norton.
Mariani, Paul J. Salvage Operations: New & Selected Poems. 1991. pap. 9.95 (*0-393-30759-X*) Norton.
— A Usable Past: Essays on Modern & Contemporary Poetry. LC 84-2613. 280p. 1984. lib. bdg. 32.50 (*0-87023-445-5*) U of Mass Pr.
— William Carlos Williams: A New World Naked. 1990. pap. 14.95 (*0-393-30672-0*) Norton.
Mariani, Paul L. Dream Song. (Illus.). 519p. 1994. pap. 16.95 (*1-56924-947-4*) Marlowe & Co.
— Dream Song: The Life of John Berryman. 2nd ed. LC 95-39531. (Illus.). 584p. 1996. pap. 21.95 (*1-55849-017-5*) U of Mass Pr.
— The Great Wheel: Poems. 72p. 1996. 18.95 (*0-393-03921-8*) Norton.
— William Carlos Williams: The Poet & His Critics. LC 75-8645. 285p. reprint ed. pap. 88.40 (*0-608-13297-7*, 202561100044) Bks Demand.
Mariani, Phil, jt. ed. see Kruger, Barbara.
Mariani, Philomena, ed. Critical Fictions: The Politics of Imaginative Writing. (Discussions in Contemporary Culture Ser.: Vol. 7). 304p. (Orig.). 1991. pap. 15.95 (*1-56584-497-1*, Pub. by New Press NY) Norton.
Mariani, Umberto, tr. see Zangrilli, Franco, ed.
Mariani, Umberto, tr. & intro. see Bonaviri, Giuseppe.
Marianna, David, jt. auth. see Hajna, Losonczy.
Mariano. Econometrics: Techniques & Case Studies. (HQ - Econometrics Ser.). 2002. mass mkt. 65.95 (*0-538-86310-2*) S-W Pub.
Mariano, Bernard J. & West, Jill. Espresso Encyclopedia. (Illus.). 208p. (Orig.). 1994. pap. 12.95 (*0-9643222-1-8*) Trendex Intl.
Mariano, Bernard N., et al. Krups Encyclopedia of Coffee & Espresso: From Beans to Brew. 160p. 1995. pap. 9.95 (*0-9643222-2-6*) Trendex Intl.
Mariano, John H. The Italian Contribution to American Democracy. LC 74-17938. (Italian American Experience Ser.). (Illus.). 336p. 1975. reprint ed. 23.95 (*0-405-06409-8*) Ayer.
— The Italian Immigrant & Our Courts. LC 74-17939. (Italian American Experience Ser.). (Illus.). 88p. 1975. reprint ed. pap. 14.95 (*0-405-06410-1*) Ayer.
Mariano, Joseph N., jt. auth. see Brossi, Mario.
Mariano, Nicky. Berenson Archive: An Inventory of Correspondence Compiled on the Centenary of the Birth of Bernard Berenson, 1865-1959. Berenson, Bernard, ed. LC 65-28597. (Illus.). 134p. 1965. 19.00 (*0-674-06750-9*) HUP.
Mariano, Patrick. Advances in Electron Transfer Chemistry, Vol. 6. 1999. 109.50 (*0-7623-0213-5*) Jai Pr.
Mariano, Patrick S., ed. Advances in Electron Transfer Chemistry, Vol. 1. 197p. 1991. 109.50 (*1-55938-167-1*) Jai Pr.
— Advances in Electron Transfer Chemistry, Vol. 2. 286p. 1992. 109.50 (*1-55938-168-X*) Jai Pr.
— Advances in Electron Transfer Chemistry, Vol. 3. 256p. 1994. 109.50 (*1-55938-320-8*) Jai Pr.
— Advances in Electron Transfer Chemistry, Vol. 4. 215p. 1994. 109.50 (*1-55938-506-5*) Jai Pr.
— Advances in Electron Transfer Chemistry, Vol. 5. 1996. 109.50 (*0-7623-0062-0*) Jai Pr.
Mariano, Roberto, et al, eds. Simulation-Based Inference in Econometrics: Methods & Applications. LC 98-35993. (Illus.). 470p. (C). 1998. text 85.00 (*0-521-59112-0*) Cambridge U Pr.
Mariano, Roberto S., ed. Advances in Statistical Analysis & Statistical Computing, Vol. 2. 272p. 1989. 73.25 (*0-89232-826-6*) Jai Pr.
— Advances in Statistical Analysis & Statistical Computing, Vol. 3. Date not set. 73.25 (*1-55938-069-1*) Jai Pr.
Mariano, Roberto S., et al, eds. Asian Capital Markets: Innovations & New Products. LC 96-85148. (Illus.). 227p. 1996. pap. 29.95 (*0-9633012-4-1*) Asian Securit.
Mariano, Roberto S., jt. ed. see Clemente, Lilia C.
Mariano, Thomas. America in Chaos: America's Second Civil War. Huhn, Patricia, ed. 105p. (Orig.). 1994. pap. 5.00 (*1-877637-10-6*) Mariano Pub.
— Essays of an American Peasant. Tate, Laura O., ed. (Illus.). 96p. (Orig.). 1989. pap. text. write for info. (*1-877637-00-9*) Mariano Pub.
— Opinions of an American Peasant. Allison, Carrie C., ed. (Illus.). 256p. (Orig.). 1989. pap. write for info. (*1-877637-01-7*) Mariano Pub.
— Potshot Reviews: Of Southern Colorado Ghostowns. Tate, Laura O., ed. (Illus.). 282p. (Orig.). 1991. pap. 10.00 (*1-877637-04-1*) Mariano Pub.
— Rhymes from the Books of Ham: Mormon Deceptions. Huhn, Patricia, ed. 105p. (Orig.). 1993. pap. 5.00 (*1-877637-09-2*) Mariano Pub.
— Western Tales of Southern Colorado: To Know the West. 2nd ed. (Illus.). 312p. 1991. pap. 13.95 (*1-877637-03-3*) Mariano Pub.
Mariano, Willie. Fan Feast! The Giants Fan Guide to Tailgating. 1999. pap. 14.95 (*1-57243-345-0*) Triumph Bks.
Marians of the Immaculate Conception Staff, ed. Now Is the Time for Mercy: The Message & Devotion to the Divine Mercy. LC 87-62981. 114p. 1988. pap. text 8.00 (*0-944203-05-1*) Marian Pr.
Marianska, Anna, tr. see Koscialkowska, Janina.
Marianska, Anna, tr. see Szereszewska, Helena.
Mariant, Giulian, ed. Pathophysiology of Plasma Protein Metabolism. 416p. 1985. 115.00 (*0-306-41771-5*, Plenum Trade) Perseus Pubng.
Marias Aquilera, Julian. Reason & Life: The Introduction to Philosophy. Reid, Kenneth S. & Sarmiento, Edward, trs. from SPA. LC 74-25891. 413p. 1975. reprint ed. lib. bdg. 79.50 (*0-8371-7866-5*, MARLI, Greenwood Pr) Greenwood.
Marias, Fernando. El Greco in Toledo, 1. 1999. pap. text 25.00 (*1-85759-210-7*) Scala Books.
***Marias, Javier.** All Souls. Costa, Margaret Jull, tr. from SPA. 2000. pap. 13.95 (*0-8112-1453-2*, Pub. by New Directions) Norton.
Marias, Javier. Cuando Fui Mortal. (SPA.). 1996. pap. 14.95 (*0-679-77299-5*) Vin Bks.
***Marias, Javier.** A Heart So White. Costa, Margaret Jull, tr. from SPA. 2000. 24.95 (*0-8112-1452-4*, Pub. by New Directions) Norton.
Marias, Javier. Tomorrow in the Battle Think of Me. Costa, Margaret J., tr. from SPA. LC 97-5841. 1997. 24.00 (*0-15-100276-2*) Harcourt.
***Marias, Javier.** When I Was Mortal. Costa, Margaret Jull, tr. from SPA. LC 99-89177. 176p. 2000. 21.95 (*0-8112-1431-1*, Pub. by New Directions) Norton.
Marias, Julian. Acerca de Ortega. (Nueva Austral Ser.: Vol. 214). (SPA.). 1991. pap. text 24.95 (*84-239-7214-3*) Elliots Bks.
— Gratry's Philosophy. O'Hara, Mary L. & McNamee, Catherine, trs. 136p. 1998. 39.95 (*0-391-04075-8*) Humanities.
— History of Philosophy. 22nd ed. 505p. (YA). (gr. 7-12). 1967. pap. 12.95 (*0-486-21739-6*) Dover.
— Jose Ortega y Gasset: Circumstances & Vocation. Lopez-Morillas, Frances M., tr. LC 71-88141. 490p. reprint ed. pap. 151.90 (*0-8357-9729-5*, 201623900002) Bks Demand.
— Miguel de Unamuno. Lopez-Morillas, Frances M., tr. LC 66-18251. 238p. 1966. reprint ed. pap. 73.80 (*0-7837-2296-6*, 205738400004) Bks Demand.
— Philosophy As Dramatic Theory. Parsons, James, tr. LC 72-84669. 1970. 32.50 (*0-271-00100-3*) Pa St U Pr.
***Marias, Julian.** Sobre el Cristianismo. 1999. 19.95 (*84-08-02289-X*) Planeta Edit.
Marias, Julian. The Structure of Society. Raley, Harold C., tr. LC 84-185. 246p. 1987. pap. 76.30 (*0-608-05145-4*, 206570600005) Bks Demand.
— Understanding Spain. Lopez-Morillas, Frances M., tr. from SPA. 464p. (C). 1992. pap. 29.95 (*0-472-08188-8*, 08188) U of Mich Pr.
Marias, Julian & Michigan University Press Staff. Understanding Spain. LC 89-77991. 462p. 1990. 32.50 (*0-8477-0888-8*) U of PR Pr.
Mariategui, Jose C. The Heroic & Creative Meaning of Socialism: Selected Essays of Jose Carlos Mariategui. Pearlman, Michael, ed. & tr. by. LC 95-30978. 240p. (C). 1996. pap. 17.50 (*0-391-03948-2*); text 49.95 (*0-391-03927-X*) Humanities.
— Textos Basicos. (SPA.). pap. 17.99 (*968-16-4895-1*, Pub. by Fondo) Continental Bk.
Mariau, Dominique. Integrated Pest Management of Tropical Perennial Crops. LC 98-52105. (Illus.). 181p. 1999. pap. 45.00 (*1-57808-042-8*) Science Pubs.
Mariboe, Knud. Encyclopedia of the Celts. (Illus.). 300p. 1997. pap., spiral bd. 24.95 (*0-9661518-0-1*) Celtic Chronicles.
Maric, B., et al, eds. Geotechnical Hazards: Proceedings of the 11th Danube-European Conference, Porec, Croatia, 25-29 May 1998. (Illus.). 892p. (C). 1998. text 116.00 (*90-5410-957-2*, Pub. by A A Balkema) Ashgate Pub Co.
Maric, D. Adapting Working Hours to Modern Needs: The Time Factor in the New Approach to Working Conditions. viii, 50p. 1980. 22.50 (*92-2-101659-5*) Intl Labour Office.
Maric, R. Saint Therese of Lisieux. (Illus.). 30p. (J). (gr. 3-8). 1997. pap. 1.95 (*0-8198-6998-8*) Pauline Bks.
Maric, Svetislav, ed. see Lam, Alex W. & Tantaratana, Sawasd.
***Maric, V.** Regular Variation & Differential Equations. (Lecture Notes in Mathematics Ser.: Vol. 1726). x, 127p. 2000. pap. 29.80 (*3-540-67160-9*) Spr-Verlag.
Mariccino, David. Everything I Know I Learned from Star Trek the Next Generation. 1999. pap. write for info. (*0-671-00998-2*) S&S Trade.
Maricella, tr. see Collins, D'Andre.
Maricevic, Vivienne, photos by. Male to Female: La Cage aux Folles. (Illus.). 140p. 39.95 (*3-905514-86-9*) Dist Art Pubs.
Marich, Stephen, contrib. by. Conference on Railway Engineering, 1995: World Best Practice - the What, Why & How. (National Conference Proceedings 95 Ser.: Vol. 8). (Illus.). 277p. 1995. pap. 60.00 (*0-85825-632-0*, Pub. by Inst Engrs Aust-EA Bks) Accents Pubns.
Marich, Stephen, jt. intro. see O'Rourke, Mike D.
Marichal, Carlos. A Century of Debt Crises in Latin America: From Independence to the Great Depression, 1820-1930. LC 88-17843. (Illus.). 297p. reprint ed. pap. 92.10 (*0-608-06383-5*, 206674400008) Bks Demand.
Marichal, Robert, ed. see D'Angouleme, Marguerite.
Marichal, Robert, ed. see Marguerite D'Angouleme.
Marichev, Oleg I. Handbook of Integral Transforms of Higher Transcendental Functions: Theory & Algorithmic Tables. LC 82-15849. (Mathematics & Its Applications Ser.). 336p. 1983. text 108.00 (*0-470-27364-X*) P-H.
Marick, Brian. Craft of Software Testing. 553p. 1994. text 40.60 (*0-13-177411-5*) P-H.
Mariconda. Sleepy Ted. 32p. (J). 2001. 14.70 (*0-7868-0496-3*, Pub. by Hyperion) Time Warner.
— Sleepy Ted, Vol. 1. 32p. (J). 2001. lib. bdg. 15.49 (*0-7868-2425-5*, Pub. by Hyperion) Little.
***Mariconda, Barbara.** Most Wonderful Writing Lessons Ever: Everything You Need to Know to Teach the Essential Elements. (Illus.). 128p. 1999. pap. 14.95 (*0-590-87304-0*) Scholastic Inc.
— Super Story-Writing Strategies & Activities. (Illus.). 64p. (J). 2000. pap. 10.95 (*0-439-14008-0*) Scholastic Inc.
Mariconda, Barbara. Turn the Cup Around. 1998. 9.09 (*0-606-13878-1*, Pub. by Turtleback) Demco.
— Turn the Cup Around. 160p. (J). (gr. 3-7). 1998. reprint ed. pap. 3.99 (*0-440-41311-7*, YB BDD) BDD Bks Young Read.
— Witch Way to the Beach. LC 96-34400. (Illus.). 48p. (J). 1997. pap. 3.99 (*0-440-41268-4*) BDD Bks Young Read.
— Witch Way to the Beach. (J). 1997. pap. 3.99 (*0-440-91194-X*) BDD Bks Young Read.
— Witch Way to the Country. LC 96-215365. (Illus.). 48p. (J). 1996. pap. 3.99 (*0-440-41100-9*) Dell.
Marie - Queen of Roumania. Story of My Life, 2 vols., Set. LC 73-135820. (Eastern Europe Collection). 1971. reprint ed. 70.95 (*0-405-02793-1*) Ayer.
Marie, Bernard. Prayers for Urgent Occasions. 1990. pap. 5.25 (*0-89942-918-1*, 918/04) Catholic Bk Pub.
Marie, Carol. Milt Larsen's Magical Mystery Tour of Hollywood's Most Amazing Landmark, the Magic Castle. LC 98-72807. 295 p. 1997. write for info. (*0-9661005-0-6*) Brookledge Corp.
Marie, D. Tears for Ashan. LC 88-63766. (Illus.). 32p. (J). (ps-3). 1989. 12.95 (*0-9621681-0-6*) Creative Pr Works.
Marie-Daly, Bernice. Ecofeminism: Sacred Matter - Sacred Mother. (Teilhard Studies: No. 25). 1991. pap. 3.50 (*0-89012-064-1*) Am Teilhard.
Marie, De France. Fables. Spiegel, Harriet, ed. LC 88-148665. (Toronto Medieval Texts & Translations Ser.: No. 5). (ENG & FRE., Illus.). 291p. reprint ed. pap. 90.30 (*0-7837-4287-8*, 204397900012) Bks Demand.
Marie De France. French Medieval Romances from the Lays of Marie De France. Mason, Eugene, tr. from FRE. LC 75-41188. reprint ed. 24.50 (*0-404-14571-X*) AMS Pr.
***Marie, Deana.** A Summer for Boys. LC 98-90535. 1999. 13.95 (*0-533-12838-2*) Vantage.
Marie, Elizabeth, ed. see Everywoman, Catherine.
Marie-Eugene of the Child Jesus. Where the Spirit Breathes: Prayer & Action. Thomas Noble, Mary, tr. from FRE. LC 97-41210. Orig. Title: Au Suffle de l'Esprit. 334p. 1998. mass mkt. 9.95 (*0-8189-0806-8*) Alba.
Marie, Evelyn. The Catbird, the Catfish & the Cat. (Illus.). 32p. (J). (gr. k-3). 1993. pap. 3.50 (*0-9614746-8-8*) Berry Bks.
— Daniel Scott & the Monster. LC 85-13369. (Illus.). 30p. (J). (gr. k-3). 1989. pap. 3.50 (*0-9614746-4-5*) Berry Bks.
— The Halloween Monster Called Lee. (Illus.). 37p. (J). (gr. k-3). 1992. pap. 3.50 (*0-9614746-7-X*) Berry Bks.
— Hugo the Squirrel. 3rd rev. ed. (Illus.). 48p. (J). (gr. 4 up). 1991. pap. 3.50 (*0-9614746-6-1*) Berry Bks.
— My Tree. (Illus.). 24p. (J). (gr. k-2). 1987. pap. 3.50 (*0-9614746-5-3*) Berry Bks.
— Oatmeal. (Illus.). 24p. (J). (gr. k-3). 1997. pap. 3.50 (*1-890579-00-9*) Berry Bks.
— Pick Your Own Strawberries. (Illus.). 32p. (J). (gr. k-3). 1998. reprint ed. pap. 3.50 (*0-9614746-3-7*) Berry Bks.
***Marie, Evelyn.** Sasha, That's Me. (Illus.). 48p. (YA). (gr. 4 up). 1999. pap. 4.75 (*1-890579-01-7*) Berry Bks.
Marie, Evelyn. Sticky Ricky. (Illus.). 30p. (J). (gr. k-3). 1994. pap. 3.50 (*0-9614746-9-6*) Berry Bks.
— That Pup Blueberry. (Illus.). 41p. (J). (gr. 4-6). 1994. 3.50 (*0-9614746-0-2*) Berry Bks.

An Asterisk (*) at the beginning of an entry indicates that the title is appearing for the first time.

Marie, Helena, et al. Womenprints: A Detailed Plan of Action for the New Millennium. LC 97-35916. (Illus.). 244p. 1997. pap. 17.95 (*0-8192-1697-6*) Morehouse Pub.

Marie, J. B. Glossary of Human Rights. (ENG & FRE.). 339p. 1981. pap. 59.95 (*0-8288-1519-4*, M12410) Fr & Eur.

Marie, Jacqueline. Jamaica's Practical Pocket Guide: Your Pocket Full of Gold. Tschetter, Tara et al, eds. (Illus.). 123p. (Orig.). 1995. pap. 14.95 (*0-9649277-0-5*) Jamaicas Pract.

Marie, Jane. Captain Duffy & the Kid Who Threw Eggs: A Story about a Foster Child. (Illus.). 60p. 1984. pap. text 1.00 (*1-57543-033-9*) Mar Co Prods.

***Marie, Julie.** Poems: By Julie Marie. 2000. pap. 6.95 (*0-533-13504-4*) Vantage.

Marie, Lois. Does Your Marriage Suffer from TMS? (Traveling Mate Syndrome) LC 92-93583. 105p. 1993. pap. 9.00 (*0-9635410-0-5*) Beginnings.

Marie, Margurite. Your Interrupted Journey of Evolution Through the Universes from the Beginning to Now & Beyond. 130p. (Orig.). 1997. pap. 7.95 (*0-9656394-0-1*) Margurite Marie.

Marie, Michel, jt. auth. see Mokhtari, Mohand.

***Marie, Montpelier.** Callin' the Children Home. LC 99-93873. 1999. pap. 12.95 (*0-533-13174-X*) Vantage.

Marie Musacchio, Jacqueline. Art & Ritual of Childbirth in Renaissance Italy. LC 98-33417. (Illus.). 224p. 1999. 50.00 (*0-300-07629-0*) Yale U Pr.

Marie, Nancy. The Beckoning Song of Your Soul: A Guidebook for Developing Your Intuition. LC 97-39687. (Illus.). 111p. 1998. pap. 18.00 (*0-9660418-0-1*) Inner Eye.

— Country Christmas. (Jimmy & Sweet Sue's Bks.). (Illus.). 36p. (J). (gr. k-5). 1979. 5.95 (*0-941595-00-5*) Heldreth Pub.

Marie, Raymond, et al, eds. Computer Performance Evaluation Modelling Techniques & Tools: 9th International Conference, St. Malo, France, June 3-6, 1997, Proceedings. LC 97-20661. (Lecture Notes in Computer Science Ser.: No. 1245). viii, 231p. 1997. pap. 43.00 (*3-540-63101-1*) Spr-Verlag.

***Marie, S.** Captiv. LC 99-64125. v, 81p. 1999. pap. 12.95 (*0-9674406-0-2*) Express Press.

Marie, S. Handbook of Sweeteners. 1991. mass mkt. 115.95 (*0-442-31433-7*) Chapman & Hall.

***Marieb.** Human Anatomy & Physiology: Illustration Notebook. 5th ed. 2000. pap. 16.00 (*0-8053-4984-7*) Benjamin-Cummings.

***Marieb, Elaine.** The Anatomy & Physiology Coloring Book. 6th ed. 350p. (C). 1999. pap. text 27.20 (*0-8053-4913-8*) Benjamin-Cummings.

— Essentials of Human Anatomy & Physiology. 6th ed. LC 99-30423. 558p. (C). 1999. pap. text 77.00 (*0-8053-4940-5*) Benjamin-Cummings.

Marieb, Elaine. Essentials of Human Anatomy & Physiology: School Edition. 4th ed. 544p. (C). 1993. text 69.00 (*0-8053-4177-3*) Longman.

— Essentials of Human Anatomy & Physiology: School Version. 5th ed. 560p. 1997. text 49.00 (*0-8053-4195-1*) Addison-Wesley.

— Human Anatomy & Physiology: Cat Manual. 5th ed. (C). 1995. pap. text, spiral bd., lab manual ed. 67.00 incl. disk (*0-8053-4055-6*) Addison-Wesley.

— Interactive Physiology. 1997. text 1919.00 (*0-8053-4112-9*) Addison-Wesley.

***Marieb, Elaine E.** Human Anatomy with Cat Dissection. 3rd ed. 2000. spiral bd., lab manual ed. 52.00 (*0-8053-4968-5*) Benjamin-Cummings.

Marieb, Elaine N. Anatomy & Physiology: Coloring Workbook. 4th rev. ed. 320p. (C). 1993. pap. text 28.00 (*0-8053-4171-4*) Benjamin-Cummings.

— Anatomy & Physiology: Coloring Workbook. 5th ed. 355p. (C). 1996. pap. text 27.20 (*0-8053-4184-6*) Addison-Wesley.

***Marieb, Elaine N.** Essentials of Human Anatomy & Physiology. 384p. 1999. spiral bd., lab manual ed. 25.00 (*0-8053-4943-X*) Benjamin-Cummings.

Marieb, Elaine N. Essentials of Human Anatomy & Physiology. 3rd ed. (Illus.). 464p. (C). 1991. pap. text 17.25 (*0-685-54329-3*) Addison-Wesley.

— Essentials of Human Anatomy & Physiology. 5th ed. LC 96-2396. (Illus.). 544p. (C). 1996. pap. text 77.00 (*0-8053-4185-4*) Benjamin-Cummings.

— Essentials of Human Anatomy & Physiology. 6th ed. 576p. (C). 2000. pap. text 49.00 (*0-8053-4938-3*) Benjamin-Cummings.

— Human Anatomy & Physiology. (Illus.). 384p. (C). 1989. teacher ed. 24.00 (*0-8053-0120-8*); text 62.95 (*0-8053-0122-4*); teacher ed., student ed. 430.25 incl. sl. (*0-8053-0119-4*); trans. 322.75 (*0-8053-0109-7*) Benjamin-Cummings.

— Human Anatomy & Physiology. 2nd ed. Adams, Melinda, ed. 1104p. (C). 1992. disk 268.95 (*0-8053-4125-0*) Addison-Wesley.

— Human Anatomy & Physiology. 2nd ed. Adams, Melinda, ed. 1104p. (C). 1994. teacher ed. 28.33 (*0-8053-4128-5*); 24.00 (*0-8053-4123-4*); trans. 470.33 (*0-8053-4124-2*) Addison-Wesley.

— Human Anatomy & Physiology. 2nd ed. 1985. pap. text 29.25 (*0-8053-6727-6*); pap. text 34.50 (*0-8053-6726-8*) Benjamin-Cummings.

— Human Anatomy & Physiology. 4th ed. 912p. (C). 1997. pap. text, student ed. 27.00 (*0-8053-4369-5*) Addison-Wesley.

— Human Anatomy & Physiology. 4th ed. 1p. (C). 1998. text 86.00 (*0-8053-5117-5*) Benjamin-Cummings.

***Marieb, Elaine N.** Human Anatomy & Physiology. 5th ed. 2000. pap., student ed. 27.00 (*0-8053-4974-X*) Benjamin-Cummings.

— Human Anatomy & Physiology: Instructor's Resource Manual. 4th ed. 18.00 (*0-8053-4397-0*) Benjamin-Cummings.

Marieb, Elaine N. Human Anatomy & Physiology: Lab Manual - Cat Version. 6th ed. LC 98-26986. 804p. 1998. 65.00 incl. cd-rom (*0-8053-4345-8*) Benjamin-Cummings.

— Human Anatomy & Physiology: Lab Manual - Main Version. 5th ed. LC 98-26985. (C). 1999. spiral bd., lab manual ed. 52.50 incl. cd-rom (*0-8053-4347-4*) Benjamin-Cummings.

— Human Anatomy & Physiology: Lab Manual - Pig Version. 3rd ed. (Illus.). 700p. (C). 1989. pap. text 36.75 (*0-8053-0111-9*) Benjamin-Cummings.

— Human Anatomy & Physiology: Lab Manual - Pig Version. 6th ed. LC 98-26984. (C). 1998. spiral bd., lab manual ed. 65.00 incl. cd-rom (*0-8053-4344-X*) Benjamin-Cummings.

— Human Anatomy & Physiology: The Pig Version. 3rd ed. (Illus.). 700p. (C). 1989. teacher ed. write for info. (*0-318-64657-9*); trans. write for info. (*0-318-64658-7*) Benjamin-Cummings.

— Human Anatomy & Physiology Laboratory Manual. 4th ed. LC 97-28664. (Illus.). 1192p. (C). 1997. 107.00 (*0-8053-4196-X*) Benjamin-Cummings.

— Human Anatomy & Physiology Laboratory Manual. 3rd ed. Incl. Human Anatomy & Physiology: Cat Version. 1989. pap. text 24.95 Human Anatomy & Physiology Laboratory Manual: The Pig Version. Mareeib, Elaine N. (Illus.). 700p. 1989. pap. text 24.95 Human Anatomy & Physiology Laboratory Manual: The Pig Version. Mareeib, Elaine N. (Illus.). 700p. 1989. teacher ed. 9.95 Human Anatomy & Physiology Laboratory Manual: The Pig Version. Mareeib, Elaine N. (Illus.). 700p. 1989. trans. (Illus.). 700p. (C). 1989. pap. text. write for info. (*0-318-63301-9*) Benjamin-Cummings.

Marieb, Elaine N. Human Anatomy Laboratory Manual With Cat Dissections. 2nd ed. 512p. (C). 1996. pap. 58.00 (*0-8053-4057-2*) Addison-Wesley.

Marieb, Elaine N. Human Anatomy of Physiology. (C). 1990. text 68.00 (*0-8053-0105-4*) Benjamin-Cummings.

Marieb, Elaine N. Human Musculatr Vid Humn. (Illus.). 1050p. (C). 1989. student ed. 140.25 incl. VHS (*0-8053-0106-2*) Benjamin-Cummings.

Marieb, Elaine N., ed. The A&P Coloring Workbook: A Complete Study Guide. 3rd ed. 350p. (C). 1991. write for info. (*0-318-69059-4*) Addison-Wesley.

Marieb, Elaine N. & Mallatt, Jon. Human Anatomy. 2nd ed. LC 96-7345. 731p. (C). 1996. 107.00 (*0-8053-4068-8*) Benjamin-Cummings.

***Marieb, Elaine Nicpon.** Human Anatomy & Physiology. 5th ed. LC 00-39805. 2000. 90.00 (*0-8053-4950-2*) Benjamin-Cummings.

Marieb, T., et al, eds. Materials Reliability in Microelectronics VIII Vol. 516: Proceedings Materials Research Society Symposium. 365p. 1998. text 79.00 (*1-55899-422-X*) Materials Res.

Mariechild, Diane. Lesbian Sacred Sexuality. LC 94-4125. (Illus.). 144p. (Orig.). 1995. pap. 27.50 (*0-914728-81-4*) Wingbow Pr.

— MotherWit: A Guide to Healing & Psychic Development. rev. ed. (Illus.). 192p. 1989. pap. 14.95 (*0-89594-358-1*) Crossing Pr.

— Open Mind: Women's Daily Inspirations for Becoming Mindful. LC 94-26377. 400p. 1995. pap. 14.00 (*0-06-251093-2*, Pub. by Harper SF) HarpC.

Mariejol, Jean H. Philip II, the First Modern King. 1977. 22.95 (*0-8369-6948-0*, 7829) Ayer.

Mariel, Pierre. Dictionnaire des Societes Secretes en Occident. (FRE.). 1971. pap. 29.95 (*0-8288-6450-0*, M-6642) Fr & Eur.

Marien, Bert. Bibliografica Critica Degli Studi Plotiniani: Con Rassegna Della Loro Recensioni. Cilento, V., ed. (Classical Studies). (ITA.). reprint ed. lib. bdg. 47.00 (*0-697-00043-5*) Irvington.

Marien, Deryk. Practice Using Lotus 1-2-3 R 2.X. LC 93-86101. 1994. wbk. ed. 27.99 (*1-56529-668-0*) Que.

Marien, Edward J. A Guide to Energy Management Opportunities in Warehousing. Bakken, Turina R., ed. 16p. 1992. pap. 10.00 (*1-892663-12-0*) WERC.

Marien, Mary W. Photography & Its Critics: A Cultural History, 1839-1900. (Perspectives on Photography Ser.). (Illus.). 238p. 1997. text 55.00 (*0-521-55043-2*) Cambridge U Pr.

Marien, Matthaeus. Iconum Biblicarum. (Illus.). 320p. 1981. reprint ed. 34.95 (*0-939688-06-9*) Directed Media.

Marien, Michael. Environmental Issues & Sustainable Futures: A Critical Guide to Recent Books, Reports, & Periodicals. LC 96-10658. xii, 170p. (Orig.). 1996. pap. 35.00 (*1-880028-06-9*) Cal Inst Public.

— Environmental Issues & Sustainable Futures: A Critical Guide to Recent Books, Reports, & Periodicals. LC 96-10658. (Future Survey Guidebook Ser.: No. 2). 170p. (Orig.). 1996. pap. 35.00 (*0-930242-51-3*) World Future.

— World Futures & the United Nations: An Annotated Guide to 250 Recent Books & Reports. LC 95-13952. (Future Survey Guidebooks Ser.: Vol. 1). 1995. pap. 25.00 (*0-930242-49-1*) World Future.

Marien, Michael, ed. Future Survey Annual, 1992: A Guide to the Recent Literature of Trends, Forecasts, & Policy Proposals. 192p. (C). 1992. pap. 35.00 (*0-930242-43-2*) World Future.

— Future Survey Annual, 1979: A Guide to Recent Books & Articles Concerning Trends, Forecasts, & Policy Proposals. 280p. 1980. pap. 35.00 (*0-930242-10-6*) World Future.

— Future Survey Annual, 1981-82. 1983. 35.00 (*0-930242-17-3*) World Future.

— Future Survey Annual, 1983: A Guide to the Recent Literature of Trends, Forecasts, & Policy Proposals, Vol. 4. 250p. 1984. pap. 35.00 (*0-930242-23-8*) World Future.

— Future Survey Annual, 1984: A Guide to the Recent Literature of Trends, Forecasts & Policy Proposals. 240p. 1985. pap. 34.95 (*0-930242-26-2*) Transaction Pubs.

— Future Survey Annual, 1985. 208p. 1986. pap. 34.95 (*0-930242-29-7*) Transaction Pubs.

— Future Survey Annual, 1986. 220p. 1987. pap. 34.95 (*0-930242-32-7*) Transaction Pubs.

— Future Survey Annual, 1988-89: A Guide to the Recent Literature of Trends, Forecasts, & Policy Proposal. 212p. 1990. pap. 34.95 (*0-930242-34-3*) Transaction Pubs.

— Future Survey Annual, 1988-89: A Guide to the Recent Literature of Trends, Forecasts & Policy Proposals. 212p. 1989. pap. 35.00 (*0-930242-35-1*) World Future.

— Future Survey Annual, 1990. 196p. 1990. pap. 35.00 (*0-930242-38-6*) World Future.

— Future Survey Annual, 1991. 1991. pap. 35.00 (*0-930242-42-4*) World Future.

— Future Survey Annual, 1993. 1993. pap. 35.00 (*0-930242-44-0*) World Future.

— Future Survey Annual, 1995. 1995. pap. 35.00 (*0-930242-50-5*) World Future.

— Future Survey Annual, 1996. 191p. (Orig.). 1996. pap. 35.00 (*0-930242-54-8*) World Future.

Marien, Michael, et al, eds. Future Survey Annual, 1980-81: A Guide to the Recent Literature of Trends, Forecasts, & Policy Proposals. 280p. (Orig.). 1981. pap. 35.00 (*0-930242-13-0*) World Future.

Marien, Michael & Jennings, Lane, eds. What I Have Learned: Thinking about the Future Then & Now. LC 86-14958. 219p. 1987. 52.95 (*0-313-25071-5*, MWL/, Greenwood Pr) Greenwood.

***Mariengof, Anatoly.** Novel Without Lies. (Glas Ser.: Vol. 23). (Illus.). 192p. 2000. pap. 14.95 (*1-56663-302-8*, Pub. by I R Dee) Natl Bk Netwk.

Marienwerder, Johannes Von, see Von Marienwerder, Johannes.

Marier, Donald & Stoiaken, Larry N., eds. Alternative Sources of Energy. (Orig.). 1988. pap. 5.95 (*0-917328-92-2*) ASEI.

— Alternative Sources of Energy: Cogeneration Wind. (Orig.). 1988. pap. 5.95 (*0-917328-91-4*) ASEI.

— Alternative Sources of Energy: Hydropower. (Orig.). 1988. pap. 5.95 (*0-917328-90-6*) ASEI.

— Alternative Sources of Energy: 1988 Directory, No. 96. (Orig.). 1987. pap. 47.95 (*0-917328-86-8*) ASEI.

— Alternative Sources of Energy No. 97: Hydropower. (Orig.). 1988. pap. 5.95 (*0-917328-87-6*) ASEI.

Marier, Donald, ed. see Wilson & Frumerman.

Marier, Donald, ed. see Wilson, et al.

Marier, Robert L., jt. ed. see Edwards, Janine C.

Marier, Thomas, tr. see Graf, Fritz.

Marietta, Di. Who's on the Throne? The Key to a Victorious Life. Wheeler, Jan, ed. LC 97-92817. (Illus.). 80p. 1997. pap. 7.00 (*0-9660595-0-6*) Di Marietta.

Marietta, Don E., Jr. Introduction to Ancient Philosophy. LC 97-46373. 236p. (C). (gr. 13). 1998. text 66.95 (*0-7656-0215-6*); pap. text 24.95 (*0-7656-0216-4*) M E Sharpe.

— Philosophy of Sexuality. LC 96-16110. 232p. (C). (gr. 13). 1996. text 66.95 (*1-56324-933-2*) M E Sharpe.

Marietta, Don E., Jr Philosophy of Sexuality. LC 96-16110. 232p. (C). (gr. 13). 1996. pap. text 25.95 (*1-56324-934-0*) M E Sharpe.

Marietta, Don E., Jr., jt. ed. see Embree, Lester.

Marietta Rhyne, Chris, tr. see Simonetti, Azra.

Mariette, Auguste E. Abydos (Egyptienne), 3 vols. in 1. vii, 749p. reprint ed. write for info. (*3-487-06719-6*) G Olms Pubs.

— Catalogue General des Monuments D'Abydos Decouverts Pendant les Fouilles De Cette Ville. (FRE.). viii, 596p. reprint ed. write for info. (*0-318-71377-2*) G Olms Pubs.

— Denderah, 6 vols. in 2, Set. vi, 363p. 1980. reprint ed. write for info. (*3-487-07002-2*) G Olms Pubs.

— Karnak. 208p. reprint ed. write for info. (*0-318-71378-0*) G Olms Pubs.

— Les Mastabas de l'Ancien Empire. 592p. 1976. reprint ed. write for info. (*3-487-05987-8*) G Olms Pubs.

Mariette, Nina. Painting Myself In. LC 98-167675. (Illus.). 1997. pap. 19.95 (*1-877133-16-7*, Pub. by Univ Otago Pr) Intl Spec Bk.

Mariger, Randall P. Consumption Behavior & the Effects of Government Fiscal Policies. (Economic Studies: No. 158). (Illus.). 312p. 1986. 32.00 (*0-674-16635-3*) HUP.

Marigny, Jean. Vampires: Restless Creatures of the Night. LC 93-72811. (Discoveries Ser.). (Illus.). 144p. 1994. pap. 12.95 (*0-8109-2869-8*, Pub. by Abrams) Time Warner.

Marigold, Lys, jt. auth. see Popcorn, Faith.

Mariho, Cesare. The Remarkable Story of Carlo Gentile: Italian Photographer of the American & Canadian Frontier. (Illus.). 120p. 1998. 35.00 (*1-887694-14-5*) C Mautz Pubng.

Marija, Landa. English & Serbocroatian Economics Dictionary: Privredno-Poslovni Recnik Englesko-Srpskohrvatski. (ENG & SER.). 358p. 1986. 49.95 (*0-8288-0122-3*, F126828) Fr & Eur.

— Serbocroatian-English Business Dictionary: Privredno-Poslovni Recnik Srpskohrvatsko-Engleski. (ENG & SER.). 260p. 1984. 29.95 (*0-8288-4414-3*, F110100); 24.95 (*0-8288-0121-5*, F18170) Fr & Eur.

***Marijanovic, Stanislav.** A Family Guide to House Monsters II. (Illus.). 32p. (J). (gr. 2-6). 2000. 15.95 (*1-58653-171-9*) Mondo Pubng.

Marijanovic, Stanislav. A Manual of House Monsters. LC 99-20138. 32p. (J). (ps-3). 1999. 15.95 (*1-57255-718-4*) Mondo Pubng.

Marijnissen, J. C. & Gradon, L., eds. Aerosol Inhalation - Recent Research Frontiers: Proceedings of the International Workshop on Aerosol Inhalation, Lung Transport, Deposition & the Relation to the Environment: Recent Research Frontiers. LC 96-17686. 320p. (C). 1996. text 140.00 (*0-7923-4058-2*) Kluwer Academic.

Marijnissen, Roger H. Bosch (Hieronymus) the Complete Works. (Illus.). 516p. 1987. boxed set 250.00 (*1-55660-229-4*) A Wofsy Fine Arts.

Marik, Paul E. The ICU Therapeutics Handbook. (Illus.). 304p. (C). (gr. 13). 1996. pap. text 37.95 (*0-8151-5698-7*, 26662) Mosby Inc.

Marik, Vladimir, et al, eds. Advanced Topics in Artificial Intelligence: Proceedings of the International Summer School, Prague, Czechoslavakia, July 6-17, 1992. LC 92-17999. (Lecture Notes in Artificial Intelligence Ser.: Vol. 617). ix, 484p. 1992. 69.95 (*0-387-55681-8*) Spr-Verlag.

— Artificial Intelligence in Higher Education: CEPES-UNESCO International Symposium, Prague, CSFR, October 23-25, 1989 Proceedings. (Lecture Notes in Computer Science, Lecture Notes in Artificial Intelligence Ser.: Vol. 451). xi, 247p. 1990. 33.00 (*0-387-52952-7*) Spr-Verlag.

— Database & Expert Systems Applications: Fourth International Conference, DEXA '93 Prague, Czech Republic, September 6-8, 1993 Proceedings. (Lecture Notes in Computer Science Ser.: Vol. 720). 768p. 1994. 103.95 (*0-387-57234-1*) Spr-Verlag.

Marikhin, V. A., jt. ed. see Myasnikova, L.

Mariko, Aratani, jt. ed. see Vance-Watkins, Lequita.

Maril, Nadja. American Lighting: 1840-1940. rev. ed. LC 89-84163. (Illus.). 160p. 1995. reprint ed. 39.95 (*0-88740-879-6*) Schiffer.

— Antique Lamp Buyer's Guide: Identifying Late 19th & Early 20th Century American Lighting. LC 97-34938. 160p. 1998. pap. 29.95 (*0-7643-0427-5*) Schiffer.

— Antique Lamp Buyer'S Guide: Identifying Late 19th & Early 20th Century American Lighting. 2nd rev. ed. LC 99-23654. (Illus.). 160p. 1999. pap. 29.95 (*0-7643-0854-8*) Schiffer.

— Me, Molly Midnight, the Artist's Cat. LC 77-22708. (Illus.). 40p. (J). (gr. k up). 1977. 12.95 (*0-916144-15-1*); pap. 5.95 (*0-916144-16-X*) Stemmer Hse.

— Runaway Molly Midnight, the Artist's Cat. LC 80-17097. (Illus.). 40p. (J). (gr. k up). 1980. 12.95 (*0-916144-62-3*) Stemmer Hse.

Maril, Robert L. The Bay Shrimpers of Texas: Rural Fishermen in a Global Economy. LC 95-4191. (Rural America Ser.). (Illus.). 320p. 1995. 35.00 (*0-7006-0703-X*); pap. 17.95 (*0-7006-0704-8*) U Pr of KS.

— Cannibals & Condos: Texans & Texas along the Gulf Coast. LC 86-5759. (Tarleton State University Southwestern Studies in the Humanities: No. 3). 136p. 1986. 27.95 (*0-89096-276-6*) Tex A&M Univ Pr.

— Living on the Edge of America: At Home on the Texas-Mexico Border. LC 91-46457. (Wardlaw Book Ser.). 200p. 1992. 25.95 (*0-89096-505-6*) Tex A&M Univ Pr.

— Texas Shrimpers: Community, Capitalism, & the Sea. LC 82-45897. (Illus.). 256p. 1983. 21.95 (*0-89096-147-6*) Tex A&M Univ Pr.

***Maril, Robert Lee.** Waltzing with the Ghost of Tom Joad: Poverty, Myth & Low-Wage Labor in Oklahoma. LC 00-29936. 192p. 2000. write for info. (*0-8061-3255-8*) U of Okla Pr.

Marill, Alvin H. The Complete Films of Edward G. Robinson. 1990. pap. 15.95 (*0-8065-1181-8*, Citadel Pr) Carol Pub Group.

— The Films of Tommy Lee Jones. LC 95-48051. (Illus.). 240p. 1997. pap. text 21.95 (*0-8065-1952-5*, Citadel Pr) Carol Pub Group.

— Keeping Score: Film & Television Music, 1988-1997. LC 98-28712. 352p. 1998. 45.00 (*0-8108-3416-2*) Scarecrow.

— More Theatre: Stage to Screen to Television, 2 vols. LC 93-4687. 1648p. 1993. 160.00 (*0-8108-2717-4*) Scarecrow.

— The Ultimate John Wayne Trivia Book. LC 95-19765. (Illus.). 128p. 1995. pap. 9.95 (*0-8065-1660-7*, Citadel Pr) Carol Pub Group.

Marill, Alvin H. & Kennedy, Arthur. The Films of Anthony Quinn. (Illus.). 256p. 1975. 12.00 (*0-8065-0470-6*, Citadel Pr); pap. 7.95 (*0-8065-0570-2*, Citadel Pr) Carol Pub Group.

Marilla, A. Bibliography of Henry Vaughan. LC 72-6142. (English Literature Ser.: No. 33). 1972. reprint ed. lib. bdg. 49.00 (*0-8383-1598-4*) M S G Haskell Hse.

Marilla, E. L. The Central Problem of Paradise Lost: The Fall of Man. (Essays & Studies on English Language & Literature: Vol. 15). 1972. reprint ed. pap. 25.00 (*0-8115-0213-9*) Periodicals Srv.

— Three Odes of Keats. (Essays & Studies on English Language & Literature: Vol. 24). (Orig.). 1962. pap. 25.00 (*0-8115-0222-8*) Periodicals Srv.

Marilla, E. L., ed. The Secular Poems of Henry Vaughan. (Essays & Studies on English Language & Literature: Vol. 21). 1974. reprint ed. pap. 40.00 (*0-8115-0219-8*) Periodicals Srv.

Marilley, Suzanne M. Woman Suffrage & the Origins of Liberal Feminism in the United States, 1820-1920. (Illus.). 304p. 1996. 41.50 (*0-674-95465-3*) HUP.

***Marillier, Juliet.** Daughter of the Forest. LC 00-25216. Vol. 1. 384p. 2000. 25.95 (*0-312-84879-X*, Pub. by Tor Bks) St Martin.

Marilue. Bobby Bear & the Friendly Ghost. LC 85-61830. (Bobby Bear Ser.). (Illus.). 32p. (J). (ps-1). 1985. 6.95 (*0-87783-204-8*) Oddo.

— Bobby Bear at the Circus. LC 89-62708. (Bobby Bear Ser.). (Illus.). 32p. (J). (ps-2). 1990. lib. bdg. 12.95 (*0-87783-252-8*) Oddo.

M

— Bobby Bear Meets Cousin Boo. LC 80-82952. (Bobby Bear Ser.). (Illus.). 32p. (J). (ps-1). 1981. lib. bdg. 9.95 (*0-87783-155-6*) Oddo.

— Bobby Bear's Christmas. LC 77-83628. (Illus.). 32p. (J). (ps-1). 1978. lib. bdg. 9.95 (*0-87783-142-4*) Oddo.

— Bobby Bear's Kite Contest. LC 87-62507. (Bobby Bear Ser.). (Illus.). 32p. (J). (ps-1). 1988. lib. bdg. 11.45 (*0-87783-219-6*) Oddo.

— Bobby Bear's Magic Show. LC 89-62707. (Bobby Bear Ser.). (Illus.). 32p. (J). (ps-2). 1990. lib. bdg. 12.95 (*0-87783-253-6*) Oddo.

— Bobby Bear's New Home. LC 78-190265. (Bobby Bear Ser.). (Illus.). 32p. (J). (ps-1). 1973. lib. bdg. 9.95 (*0-87783-054-1*); audio 7.94 (*0-87783-184-X*) Oddo.

— Bobby Bear's Red Raft. LC 71-190266. (Bobby Bear Ser.). (Illus.). 32p. (J). (ps-1). 1973. lib. bdg. 9.95 (*0-87783-055-X*); audio 7.94 (*0-87783-185-8*) Oddo.

— Bobby Bear's Thanksgiving. LC 77-83623. (Bobby Bear Ser.). (Illus.). 32p. (J). (ps-1). 1978. lib. bdg. 9.95 (*0-87783-143-2*) Oddo.

Marimen, Mark. Haunted Indiana. (Illus.). 155p. 1997. pap. 12.95 (*1-882376-38-2*) Thunder Bay Pr.

— Haunted Indiana, Vol. 2. (Tales of the Supernatural Ser.). 144p. 1999. pap. 12.95 (*1-882376-71-4*, Pub. by Thunder Bay Pr) Partners Pubs Grp.

— School Spirits Vol. 1: College Ghost Stories from the East & Midwest. (Illus.). 1998. pap. 12.95 (*1-882376-61-7*) Thunder Bay Pr.

Marimon, Ramon & Scott, Andrew, eds. Computational Methods for the Study of Dynamic Economics. LC 99-219972. (Illus.). 292p. 1999. text 55.00 (*0-19-829497-2*) OUP.

Marimuthu, K. M. & Gopinath, P. M., eds. Recent Trends in Medical Genetics: Proceedings of the Conference on Recent Trends in Medical Genetics, Madras, India, 8-10 December, 1983. (Illus.). 370p. 1986. 114.25 (*0-08-031993-9*, Pergamon Pr) Elsevier.

Marin, Alan. Macroeconomic Policy. 224p. (C). (gr. 13). 1992. text 74.95 (*0-415-08379-6*, A9691) Routledge.

Marin, Alan, jt. ed. see Estrin, Saul.

Marin, Alexis, jt. auth. see Guillou, Lucien.

Marin, Antonio R. Elevation to the Most Blessed Trinity. Parrot, J. Edward, ed. Bolivar Plaza Staff, tr. from SPA. (Illus.). 125p. (C). pap. write for info. (*1-877905-29-1*) Am Soc Defense TFP.

— The Great Unknown: The Holy Ghost & His Gifts. 179p. (Orig.). 1991. pap. 13.50 (*1-881008-00-2*) Am Soc Defense TFP.

Marin, Antonio R., jt. auth. see Saint Louis Grignon de Montfort.

Marin, B. P., ed. Plant Vacuoles: Their Importance in Solute Compartmentation in Cells & Their Applications in Plant Biotechnology. LC 87-14121. (NATO ASI Series A, Life Sciences: Vol. 134). (Illus.). 578p. 1987. 135.00 (*0-306-42613-7*, Plenum Trade) Perseus Pubng.

Marin, Barbara V., jt. auth. see Marin, Gerardo.

Marin, Bayard. Inside Justice: A Comparative Analysis Practices & Procedures for the Determination of Offenses Against Discipline in Prisons of Great Brtain & the United States. LC 81-65465. 416p. 1983. 60.00 (*0-8386-3086-3*) Fairleigh Dickinson.

Marin, Bernd, jt. ed. see Kenis, Patrick.

Marin, Bloc. Votre Livre du Bord, 2 vols., Vol. 1. (C). 1989. 105.00 (*0-7855-7066-7*, Pub. by Laurie Norie & Wilson Ltd) St Mut.

— Votre Livre du Bord, 2 vols., Vol. 2. (C). 1989. 105.00 (*0-7855-7067-5*, Pub. by Laurie Norie & Wilson Ltd) St Mut.

Marin, Catherine, jt. auth. see Blackbourn, Barbara.

Marin Child Care Council Staff. Childhood Emergencies - What to Do: A Quick Reference Guide. 2nd rev. ed. (Illus.). 32p. 1995. 14.95 (*0-923521-33-X*) Bull Pub.

Marin, Christine, jt. ed. see Rios-Bustamante, Antonio.

Marin, Clara, tr. see Ponce de Leon, Carolina & Andreus, Alejanoro.

Marin, Diego. Poesia Paisajistica Espanola, 1940-1970: Estudio Y Antologia. (Monagrafias A Ser.: Vol. LVII). (SPA.). 296p. (C). 1976. 45.00 (*0-7293-0026-9*, Pub. by Tamesis Bks Ltd) Boydell & Brewer.

Marin, Diego & Tayler, Neale H. La Vida Espanola. rev. ed. LC 55-7036. (SPA., Illus.). 1955. reprint ed. pap. text 10.95 (*0-89197-973-5*) Irvington.

Marin, Eileen. Chemotherapy Gives New Meaning to a Bad Hair Day: A Healing Book. (Illus.). 120p. 1996. 11.50 (*1-885676-08-5*) On A Shoestring.

Marin, Estela, ed. see Becker, Greg.

Marin, Eugene A. Cancionero - Songbook 400. (SPA & ENG.). xxiv, 340p. 1999. ring bd. 36.00 (*0-9671195-0-2*) Music Helps Sr.

Marin, Gerald, jt. auth. see Onvural, Raif O.

Marin, Gerardo. Hispanics: Psychosocial Perspectives. 1997. 17.95 (*0-8133-2873-X*) Westview.

Marin, Gerardo & Marin, Barbara V. Research with Hispanic Populations. (Applied Social Research Methods Ser.: Vol. 23). (Illus.). 160p. 1991. 42.00 (*0-8039-3720-2*); pap. 18.95 (*0-8039-3721-0*) Sage.

Marin, Gerardo, et al. Latin American Psychology: A Guide to Research & Training. LC 87-17409. 220p. 1987. pap. 29.95 (*0-912704-84-5*) Am Psychol.

— Latin American Psychology: A Guide to Research & Training. LC 87-17409. 223p. 1987. reprint ed. pap. 69.20 (*0-608-04560-8*, 206529900001) Bks Demand.

Marin, Gustavo A. La Locura de Fidel Castro. LC 96-83521. (Coleccion Cuba y sus Jueces). (SPA., Illus.). 217p. (Orig.). 1996. pap. 16.00 (*0-89729-795-4*) Ediciones.

Marin, Javier-Jose, tr. see Barclay, William.

Marin, John. Letters of John Marin. Seligmann, Herbert J., ed. LC 77-109780. 1971. reprint ed. lib. bdg. 45.00 (*0-8371-4270-9*, MALE, Greenwood Pr) Greenwood.

— The Selected Writings of John Marin. (American Biography Ser.). 241p. 1991. reprint ed. lib. bdg. 69.00 (*0-7812-8267-5*) Rprt Serv.

Marin, John A., jt. auth. see Calabria, Antonio.

Marin, Jose, et al. The Spanish Art Song in the Seventeenth Century. Baron, John H., ed. (Recent Researches in Music of the Baroque Era Ser.: Vol. RRB49). (Illus.). xxxviii, 89p. 1985. pap. 45.00 (*0-89579-203-6*) A-R Eds.

Marin, Louis. Cross-Readings. Todd, Jane M., tr. from FRE. LC 97-15543. (Philosophy & Literary Theory Ser.). 352p. (C). 1997. 70.00 (*0-391-04042-1*) Humanities.

— Food for Thought. Hjort, Mette, tr. (Parallax Ser.). 273p. 1997. reprint ed. pap. text 15.95 (*0-8018-5613-2*) Johns Hopkins.

Marin, Louis. The Power of the Image. (Illus.). (C). text. write for info. (*0-472-09585-4*); pap. text. write for info. (*0-472-06585-8*) U of Mich Pr.

Marin, Louis. The Semiotics of the Passion Narratives. Johnson, Alfred M., Jr., tr. LC 80-18199. (Pittsburgh Theological Monographs: No. 25). 1980. 12.95 (*0-915138-23-9*) Pickwick.

— Sublime Poussin. Porter, Catherine, tr. from FRE. LC 99-11562. (Meridian Crossing Aesthetics Ser.). (Illus.). 267p. 1999. pap. 16.95 (*0-8047-3477-1*) Stanford U Pr.

— To Destroy Painting. Hjort, Mette, tr. (Illus.). 196p. 1994. pap. text 15.95 (*0-226-50535-9*); lib. bdg. 39.95 (*0-226-50534-0*) U Ch Pr.

Marin, Manuela, ed. The Formation of Al-Andalus. LC 98-15270. (Formation of the Classical Islamic World Ser.: Vol. 46). 3p. 1998. text 166.95 (*0-86078-708-7*, DP103.M36, Pub. by Ashgate Pub) Ashgate Pub Co.

Marin, Marguerite V. Social Protest in an Urban Barrio: A Study of the Chicano Movement, 1966-1974. Fisher, Sethard, ed. (Class, Ethnicity, Gender, & the Democratic Nation Ser.). 320p. (C). 1990. lib. bdg. 53.00 (*0-8191-7962-0*) U Pr of Amer.

Marin, Mark. The Island Epicurean. 118p. 1986. 13.95 (*0-317-67969-4*) Antilles Schl.

Marin Martinez, Juan M., ed. see de Vega, Lope.

***Marin, Michael L. & Hollier, Larry H., eds.** Endovascular Grafting: Advanced Treatment for Vascular Disease. LC 00-26470. (Endovascular Intervention Ser.). (Illus.). 200p. 2000. 85.00 (*0-87993-457-3*) Futura Pub.

Marin, Miguel A., et al. El Teatro Cervantes de Alcala de Henares, 1602-1866: Estudio y Documentos. (Fuentes Ser.: No. 18). (Illus.). 390p. (C). 1990. 53.00 (*0-7293-0310-1*, Pub. by Tamesis Bks Ltd) Boydell & Brewer.

Marin, Mindy. Secret to Tender Pie. 1999. pap. write for info. (*0-345-40986-8*) Ballantine Pub Grp.

Marin, Nacho, jt. auth. see Villegas, Benjamin.

Marin, Peter. Freedom & Its Discontents: Reflections on Four Decades of American Moral Experience. LC 94-34344. 260p. 1995. 24.00 (*1-883642-24-8*) Steerforth Pr.

Marin, Ramon. Fiestas Populares de Ponce y la Villa de Ponce. 1994. 12.95 (*0-8477-0189-1*) U of PR Pr.

Marin, Reymundo, jt. auth. see De Marin, Maria V.

Marin, Richard B. Cruise Ship Jobs: The Insider's Guide to Finding & Getting Jobs on Cruise Ships Around the World. LC 98-91297. 144p. 1998. pap. 13.95 (*0-9662857-0-0*) Portofino Pubns.

Marin, S. E. Basic Japanese-English-Japanese Conversation Dictionary. 50th ed. (ENG & JPN.). 1982. pap. 6.95 (*0-8288-1610-7*, M14399) Fr & Eur.

Marin Staff. Diccionario Marin de al Lengua Espanola, Vol. 2. (SPA.). 1668p. 1982. 250.00 (*0-8288-2017-1*, S2556) Fr & Eur.

— Gran Diccionario Infantil Marin, 4 vols., Set. (SPA.). 840p. 1979. 250.00 (*0-8288-4807-6*, S50032) Fr & Eur.

— Gran Mundo Infantil, 3 vols., Set. (SPA.). 1792p. 1979. 375.00 (*0-8288-4808-4*, S50489) Fr & Eur.

— El Mundo de la Cultura: Enciclopedia Formativa Marin, 12 vols., Set. (SPA.). 2400p. 1978. 395.00 (*0-8288-5255-3*, S50488) Fr & Eur.

***Marin, Tobon.** Monitoring & Modelling Hydrological Fluxes in Support of Nutrient Cycling Studies in Amazonian Rain Forest Ecosystems. (Illus.). 174p. 1999. pap. 49.00 (*90-5113-035-X*, TS 17, Pub. by Backhuys Pubs) Balogh.

Marina, R. Fernandez, et al. The Sober Generation: A Topology of Competent Adolescent Coping in Modern Puerto Rico. 798p. 1969. 7.50 (*0-8477-2475-1*); pap. 6.00 (*0-8477-2476-X*) U of PR Pr.

Marina, Sandra, ed. Latin American Media Directory. unabridged ed.Tr. of Guia De Medios Latinoamericanos. 350p. (Orig.). 1997. pap. 77.00 (*0-9656399-0-8*) Fla Internatl Univ.

Marinacci, Alberto A. Applied Electromyography. LC 68-25208. 308p. reprint ed. pap. 95.50 (*0-8357-5676-9*, 200376600033) Bks Demand.

Marinacci, Barbara, ed. Linus Pauling in His Own Words: Selections from Writings Speeches & Interviews. 384p. 1995. 27.50 (*0-684-80749-1*, Touchstone) S&S Trade Pap.

Marinacci, Barbara, jt. auth. see Marinacci, Rudy.

Marinacci, Barbara, jt. auth. see Ray, Eleanor.

Marinacci, Barbara, ed. see Pauling, Linus.

Marinacci, Rudy & Marinacci, Barbara. California Spanish Place - Names. 2nd ed. LC 97-15636. (Illus.). 306p. 1997. pap. 16.95 (*0-88415-842-X*, 5842) Gulf Pub.

Marinaccio, Dave. All the Other Things I Really Need to Know I Learned from Watching Star Trek: The Next Generation. LC 98-203031. 160p. 1998. 20.00 (*0-671-01000-X*) PB.

***Marinakis, Maria M.** Parenting Infants & Toddlers Without Going Nuts. Metellus, Jerry, ed. & photos by by. 129p. 1999. pap. 14.95 (*0-9669558-0-3*) FourKid.

Marinara & Ellington. Writing Outside the Lines. LC 99-39135. 343p. 1999. pap. text 34.00 (*0-205-30510-5*) Allyn.

Marinari, R. M. Why the Righteous Are Afflicted: Job, the Mystery Revealed. 152p. (Orig.). 1996. pap. 8.99 (*1-57502-367-9*, PO1176) Morris Pubng.

Marinaro, M. & Morasso, P. G., eds. ICANN '94. 1488p. 1994. 126.95 (*0-387-19887-3*) Spr-Verlag.

Marinaro, M. & Scarpetta, G. Structure: From Physics to General Systems - Festschrift Volume in Honor of Caianiello's 70th Birthday. 832p. 1993. text 162.00 (*981-02-1291-7*) World Scientific Pub.

Marinaro, M. & Tagliaferri, R. Neural Nets, Wirn Vietri-'96: VIII Italian Workshop on Neural Nets, 23-25 May 1996. (Perspectives in Neural Computing Ser.). (Illus.). 360p. 1996. 89.00 (*3-540-76099-7*) Spr-Verlag.

Marinaro, M. & Tagliaferri, Roberto. Neural Nets, Wirn Vietri-'97: Proceedings of the 9th Italian Workshop On Neural Nets, Vietri Sul Mare, Salerno, 22-24 May 1997. LC 97-26379. (Perspectives in Neural Computing Ser.). 1997. 89.95 (*3-540-76157-8*) Spr-Verlag.

***Marinaro, M. & Tagliaferri, Roberto, eds.** Neural Nets - WIRN Vietri-99: Proceedings of the 11th Italian Workshop on Neural Nets, Vietri Sul Mare, Salerno, Italy, 20-22 May, 1999. LC 99-42437. (Perspectives in Neural Computing Ser.). (Illus.). 440p. 1999. pap. 94.95 (*1-85233-177-1*, Pub. by Spr-Verlag) Spr-Verlag.

Marinaro, M., ed. see Italian Workshop on Neural Nets Staff, et al.

Marinaro, Vincent. A Modern Dry-Fly Code. LC 97-29512. (Illus.). 288p. 1997. reprint ed. 35.00 (*1-55821-413-5*) Lyons Pr.

Marinaro, Vincent C. In the Ring of the Rise. (Illus.). 184p. 1987. reprint ed. 29.95 (*0-941130-59-2*) Lyons Pr.

Marinas, Amante P., Sr. Pananandata Yantok at Daga: Filipino Stick & Dagger. (Illus.). 88p. 1988. pap. 18.00 (*0-87364-447-6*) Paladin Pr.

Marinas, Jeremiah. Colony Wars: Vengeance: Prima's Official Strategy Guide. LC 98-67543. (Games Ser.). 96p. 1998. per. 12.99 (*0-7615-1875-4*) Prima Pub.

— Global Domination: Official Strategy Guide. 1998. pap. text 19.99 (*0-7615-1878-9*) Prima Pub.

— O. D. T. Escape or Die Trying: Prima's Official Strategy Guide. (Games Ser.). 96p. 1998. per. 12.99 (*0-7615-1876-2*) Prima Pub.

Marinatos, Nanno. Minoan Sacrificial Ritual: Cult Practice & Symbolism. (Acta Instituti Rengi Sueciae Ser.: Series 8, IX). (Illus.). 78p. (Orig.). 1986. pap. 34.50 (*91-85086-95-9*, Pub. by P Astroms) Coronet Bks.

Marinatos, Nanno, jt. ed. see Berggreen, Brit.

Marinatos, Nanno, ed. see Hagg, Robin.

Marinatos, Nanno, jt. ed. see Hagg, Robin.

Marinbach, Bernard. Galveston: Ellis Island of the West. LC 82-10609. 288p. (C). 1984. pap. text 24.95 (*0-87395-701-6*) State U NY Pr.

Marinbosch, Miguel. Votes in the U. N. General Assembly. LC 97-47709. (Nijhoff Law Specials Ser.). 256p. 1998. 66.00 (*90-411-0564-6*) Kluwer Academic.

Marincola, John. Authority & Tradition in Ancient Historiography. 378p. (C). 1997. text 69.95 (*0-521-48019-1*) Cambridge U Pr.

Marincola, Paula. ICA Street Sights. LC 80-84550. (Illus.). 1980. pap. 7.00 (*0-88454-056-1*) U of Pa Contemp Art.

— ICA Street Sights 2. (Illus.). 24p. 1982. pap. 7.00 (*0-88454-028-6*) U of Pa Contemp Art.

Marincola, Paula & Crimp, Douglas. Image Scavengers: Photography. 1982. pap. 10.00 (*0-88454-031-6*) U of Pa Contemp Art.

Marincola, Paula, ed. see Rosenthal, Mark, et al.

Marincovich, L. Bulletins of American Paleontology: Vol. 70. Incl. No. 293. Two Foraminiferal Assemblages from the Duplin Marl in Georgia & South Carolina. 43p. 1976. pap. 4.00 (*0-87710-231-7*); 25.00 (*0-87710-299-6*) Paleo Res.

Marincovich, L., Jr. Bulletins of American Paleontology Vol. 84, No. 317: Molluscan Paleontology, Paleoecology, & North Pacific Correlations of the Miocene Tachilni Formation, Alaska Peninsula, Alaska. 97p. 1983. 18.00 (*0-87710-392-5*) Paleo Res.

Marincovich, Michele, et al, eds. The Professional Development of Graduate Teaching Assistants. 300p. 1998. 35.95 (*1-882982-24-X*) Anker Pub.

Marindin, G. E., ed. Encyclopaedia of Classical Mythology & Culture: Including Art, Biography & Ancient Geography, 3 vols. (Illus.). vi, 1020p. 1996. 190.00 (*81-7305-069-4*, Pub. by Aryan Bks Intl) Nataraj Bks.

***Marindin, Hope, ed.** Handbook for Single Adoptive Parents. 88p. 1998. pap. 20.00 (*0-9634045-2-0*) Nat Coun Single.

Marine Accident Investigation Branch, Department of Transport Staff. Marine Accident Investigation Branch Annual Report 1996. (Marine Accident Investigation Branch Reports Ser.). 52p. 1997. 35.00 (*0-11-551934-3*, Pub. by Statnry Office) Balogh.

— Report of the Chief Inspector of Marine Accidents into Explosion on the Motor Tanker Esso Mersey on 4 September Resulting in the Loss of Two Lives. (Marine Accident Investigation Branch Reports Ser.). 45p. 1993. 28.00 (*0-11-551166-0*, Pub. by Statnry Office) Balogh.

— Report of the Chief Inspector of Marine Accidents into the Collision Between Fishing Vessel Wilhelmina J & MV Zulfikar with the Loss of Six Lives on 10 April 1991. (Marine Accident Investigation Branch Reports Ser.). 54p. 1992. 30.00 (*0-11-551140-7*, Pub. by Statnry Office) Balogh.

— Report of the Chief Inspector of Marine Accidents into the Collision Between the Fishing Vessel Antares & HMS Trenchant with the Loss of Four Lives on 22 November 1990. (Marine Accident Investigation Branch Reports Ser.). 46p. 1992. 24.00 (*0-11-551128-8*, Pub. by Statnry Office) Balogh.

— Report of the Chief Inspector of Marine Accidents into the Engine Failure & Subsequent Grounding of the Motor Tanker Braer at Garths Ness, Shetland, on 5 January 1993. 97p. 1994. 60.00 (*0-11-551210-1*, Pub. by Statnry Office) Balogh.

— Report of the Chief Inspector of Marine Accidents into the Failure of the Lifeboat Launching Equipment on MV Norsea on 5 February 1992 with the Loss of 2 Lives. (Marine Accident Investigation Branch Reports Ser.). 62p. 1993. 50.00 (*0-11-551199-7*, Pub. by Statnry Office) Balogh.

Marine Accident Investigation Branch, Department of Transport Staff. Report of the Chief Inspector of Marine Accidents into the Grounding & Subsequent Salvage of the Tanker Sea Empress at Milford Haven Between 15 & 21 February 1996. LC 97-216007. (Marine Accident Investigation Branch Reports Ser.). 192p. 1997. 70.00 (*0-11-551890-8*, Pub. by Statnry Office) Balogh.

Marine Accident Investigation Branch, Department of Transport Staff. Report of the Chief Inspector of Marine Accidents into the Reopened Inquiry into the Explosion on the Motor Tanker Esso Mersey on 4 September 1991 Resulting in the Loss of Two Lives. (Marine Accident Investigation Branch Reports Ser.). 25p. 1996. 25.00 (*0-11-551820-7*, Pub. by Statnry Office) Balogh.

Marine Accident Investigation Branch, Department of Transport Staff. Report of the Inspector & APO's Inquiry into Three Fatalities & Injuries to Six Crew Members on Board FV Atlantic Princess on 25 July 1996 off the Coast of Mauritania, West Africa. (Marine Accident Investigation Branch Reports Ser.: No. 81003062). 44p. 1997. 55.00 (*0-11-552007-4*, HM20074, Pub. by Statnry Office) Balogh.

Marine Accident Investigation Branch, Department of Transport Staff. Report of the Investigation into Fire on Board Ro-Ro Passenger Vessel Sally Star on 25 August 1994. (Marine Accident Investigation Branch Reports Ser.). 50p. 1995. 30.00 (*0-11-551777-4*, Pub. by Statnry Office) Balogh.

— Report of the Investigation into the Collision Between British Trent & Western Winner with the Loss of Nine Lives on 3 June 1993. (Marine Accident Investigation Branch Reports Ser.). 46p. 1995. 35.00 (*0-11-551713-8*, Pub. by Statnry Office) Balogh.

— Report of the Investigation into the Grounding of the Passenger Ro-Ro Ferry Stena Challenger on 19 September 1995, B1<130>Riot-Page, Calais. (Marine Accident Investigation Branch Reports Ser.). 24p. 1996. 30.00 (*0-11-551846-0*, Pub. by Statnry Office) Balogh.

— Report of the Investigation into the Grounding of the Tanker Borga at Milford Haven on 29 October 1995. (Marine Accident Investigation Branch Reports Ser.). 50p. 1996. 45.00 (*0-11-551866-5*, Pub. by Statnry Office) Balogh.

— Report of the Investigation into the Lifeboat Accident on Pride of Hampshire on 25 September 1994. (Marine Accident Investigation Branch Reports Ser.). 46p. 1996. 40.00 (*0-11-551871-1*, Pub. by Statnry Office) Balogh.

— Report of the Investigation into the Loss of the Fishing Vessel Heather Bloom INS 110 with the Loss of One Life on 3 December 1994. (Marine Accident Investigation Branch Reports Ser.). 27p. 1995. 25.00 (*0-11-551789-8*, Pub. by Statnry Office) Balogh.

— Report of the Investigation into the Over-Pressurisation of a Cargo Tank on the Oil Tanker Mobil Petrel at Fawley Oil Terminal on 7 November 1989. (Marine Accident Investigation Branch Reports Ser.). 46p. 1991. 22.00 (*0-11-551085-0*, Pub. by Statnry Office) Balogh.

— Report of the Investigation into the Power Failure on Canberra off the Isle of Wight on 7 December 1994. (Marine Accident Investigation Branch Reports Ser.). 26p. 1996. 40.00 (*0-11-551888-6*, Pub. by Statnry Office) Balogh.

— Report of the Investigation into the Sinking of the Fishing Vessel Grey Flamingo with the Loss of Life of Two Crew Members. (Marine Accident Investigation Branch Reports Ser.). 14p. 1991. 12.00 (*0-11-551037-0*, Pub. by Statnry Office) Balogh.

— RMS "Titanic" Reappraisal of Evidence Relating to SS "Californian" 35p. 1992. 16.00 (*0-11-551111-3*, Pub. by Statnry Office) Balogh.

Marine Biological Association of Hong Kong Staff & Morton, Brian, eds. Asian Marine Biology, Vol. 10. (Illus.). 148p. 1993. pap. 39.95 (*962-209-359-0*, Pub. by HK Univ Pr) Coronet Bks.

— Asian Marine Biology, Vol. 11. (Illus.). 156p. 1994. pap. 39.95 (*962-209-376-0*, Pub. by HK Univ Pr) Coronet Bks.

— Asian Marine Biology, Vol. 12. (Illus.). 156p. 1996. pap. 39.95 (*962-209-408-2*, Pub. by HK Univ Pr) Coronet Bks.

Marine Biological Association of Hong Kong Staff, ed. see Morton, Brian.

Marine Committee. Marine Lighting: RP-12-97. rev. ed. (Recommended Practices Ser.). (Illus.). 25p. 1996. pap. 25.00 (*0-87995-127-3*, RP-12-96) Illum Eng.

Marine Corps Association Staff. Guidebook for Marines. 15th ed. 560p. 1986. pap. 5.00 (*0-940328-07-0*) Marine Corps.

— Leatherneck Laffs. 96p. 1980. reprint ed. 1.50 (*0-686-32444-7*) Marine Corps.

Marine-Dershimer, Greta, jt. ed. see DeBolt, Gary P.

***Marine International Staff.** Tide Tables West Coast of North & South America, Including Hawaiian Islands & the Alaskan Penisula. (Tide Tables Ser.). 2000. pap. 13.95 (*0-07-136463-3*) McGraw.

Marine Law Institute, Staff. North Atlantic Water Dependent Use Study Vol. 3: An Executive Summary. 32p. (Orig.). 1989. pap. 2.00 (*0-9618224-4-9*) Univ S ME Marine Law Inst.

An Asterisk (*) at the beginning of an entry indicates that the title is appearing for the first time.

Marine Law Institute, Staff, ed. North Atlantic Water Dependent Use Study, 3 vols., Vols. I-III. (Orig.). 1989. pap. 20.00 (*0-9618224-0-6*) Univ S ME Marine Law Inst.

Marine Law Institute, Staff & Boston University Institute for Employment Policy,. North Atlantic Water Dependent Use Study Vol. 2: Guidebook to the Economics of Waterfront Planning & Water Dependent Uses. 296p. (Orig.). 1989. pap. 10.00 (*0-9618224-3-0*) Univ S ME Marine Law Inst.

Marine Law Institute, Staff & Robinson & Cole Land Use, Staff. North Atlantic Water Dependent Use Study Vol. 1: Managing the Shoreline for Water Dependent Uses. (Handbook of Legal Tools). (Orig.). 1989. pap. 10.00 (*0-9618224-2-2*) Univ S ME Marine Law Inst.

Marine Libraries Association Staff. Marine Transport: A Guide to Libraries. 76p. 1983. pap. 65.00 (*0-946347-00-X*, Pub. by Witherby & Co) St Mut.

Marine, Rebecca A. Introduction to Early Childhood Education. 174p. (C). 1996. text 15.40 (*0-536-59823-1*) Pearson Custom.

Marine Research Society Staff. The Pirates Own Book: Authentic Narratives of the Most Celebrated Sea Robbers. LC 93-12468. Orig. Title: The Pirates Own Book: or Authentic Narratives of the Lives, Exploits, & Executions of the Most Celebrated Sea Robbers. (Illus.). xv, 479p. 1993. reprint ed. pap. 9.95 (*0-486-27607-4*) Dover.

Marine Safety Agency Staff. The Code of Practice for Safety of Large Commercial Sailing & Motor Vessels. 92p. 1997. pap. 35.00 (*0-11-551911-4*, HM19114, Pub. by Statnry Office) Balogh.

Marine Technology Directorate Staff. Floating Structures: A Guide for Design & Analysis, Delivery Focused Technology, 2 vols. (Illus.). 1100p. 1997. pap. 416.00 (*1-870945-91-3*) Oilfield Publns.

Marine, William M. The British Invasion of Maryland, 1812-1815. LC 98-174815. 519p. 1998. reprint ed. pap. 37.00 (*0-7884-0918-2*, M063) Heritage Bk.

— British Invasion of Maryland, 1812-1815. Dielman, Louis H., ed. (Illus.). 519p. 1997. reprint ed. lib. bdg. 49.50 (*0-8328-5939-7*) Higginson Bk Co.

Marineau, Michele. The Road to Chlifa. Ouriou, Susan, tr. (Northern Lights Young Novels Ser.). 144p. (YA). (gr. 9 up). 1992. pap. 8.95 (*0-88995-129-2*, Pub. by Red Deer) Genl Dist Srvs.

Marinella, Lucrezia. Nobility & Excellence of Women & the Defects & Vices of Men. LC 99-39095. 208p. 2000. pap. text 18.00 (*0-226-50546-4*); lib. bdg. 45.00 (*0-226-50545-6*) U Ch Pr.

Marinelli. Puentes. annot. ed. 1994. text, teacher ed. 49.25 (*0-8384-4296-X*) Thomson Learn.

— Puentes. 2nd ed. (College Spanish Ser.). (C). 1997. pap., wbk. ed. 24.00 (*0-8384-7870-0*) Heinle & Heinle.

Marinelli, Anthony J. Conscience & Catholic Faith: Love & Fidelity. LC 91-27081. 1991. pap. 7.95 (*0-8091-3263-X*) Paulist Pr.

— The Word Made Flesh: An Overview of the Catholic Faith. LC 92-45629. 320p. 1993. pap. 14.95 (*0-8091-3391-1*) Paulist Pr.

Marinelli, David, tr. see Blaukopf, Kurt.

Marinelli, David, tr. see Comte, Hubert.

Marinelli, David, tr. see Gozzano, Guido.

Marinelli, David, fr. see Heller, Karl.

Marinelli, David N., tr. see Maron, Monika.

Marinelli, David N., tr. see Ripellino, Angelo M.

***Marinelli, Deborah A.** Careers in Animal Care & Veterinary Science. LC 00-9720. (Careers Ser.). 2000. lib. bdg. write for info. (*0-8239-3185-4*) Rosen Group.

Marinelli, Donald, ed. Arthur Giron's Edith Stein: A Dramaturgical Sourcebook. LC 93-73515. (Dramaturgical Sourcebook Ser.). (Illus.). 210p. 1994. pap. 15.95 (*0-88748-178-7*) Carnegie-Mellon.

Marinelli, Giovanni. Commentaria in Libros Hippocratis. 280p. reprint ed. write for info. incl. 3.5 hd (*0-318-72047-9*) G Olms Pubs.

Marinelli, Janet. Stalking the Wild Amaranth: Gardening in an Age of Extinction. LC 97-27538. 256p. 1998. text 25.00 (*0-8050-4415-9*) St Martin.

Marinelli, Janet, ed. Brooklyn Botanic Garden Gardener's Desk Reference. LC 98-6314. (Illus.). 800p. 1998. 40.00 (*0-8050-5095-7*) H Holt & Co.

— The Environmental Gardener. (Plants & Gardens Ser.). (Illus.). 1992. pap. 7.95 (*0-945352-70-0*) Bklyn Botanic.

— Going Native: Biodiversity in Our Own Backyards. (21st-Century Gardening Ser.). (Illus.). 112p. 1995. pap. 9.95 (*0-945352-85-9*) Bklyn Botanic.

Marinelli, Janet, jt. ed. see Cutler, Karan D.

Marinelli, Janet, jt. ed. see Hays, Robert M.

Marinelli, Janet, jt. ed. see Randall, John M.

Marinelli, John. Rhyme Time: Original Story Poems for Children of All Ages. 70p. (Orig.). (J). 1996. pap. 6.95 (*1-57502-137-4*) Morris Pubng.

Marinelli, Massimiliano M. Circles of Stories. 20p. (Orig.). 1997. pap. 15.00 (*1-890321-05-2*) Street Co.

Marinelli, Patti J. Puentes. (College Spanish Ser.). (SPA.). (C). 1994. student ed., suppl. ed. 53.95 incl. audio (*0-8384-5409-7*) Heinle & Heinle.

— Puentes. (College Spanish Ser.). (SPA.). (C). 1994. mass mkt., suppl. ed. 31.95 (*0-8384-5411-9*) Heinle & Heinle.

— Puentes. (College Spanish Ser.). (SPA.). (C). 1995. 53.95 incl. cd-rom (*0-8384-5410-0*) Heinle & Heinle.

— Puentes. 2nd ed. (College Spanish Ser.). (C). 1997. pap., teacher ed. 50.95 (*0-8384-7861-1*) Heinle & Heinle.

— Puentes. 2nd ed. LC 97-36718. (College Spanish Ser.). (C). 1997. pap. 50.95 (*0-8384-7834-4*) Wadsworth Pub.

Marinelli, Patti J. Puentes Text. 2nd ed. 1997. pap. 60.95 incl. audio (*0-8384-7825-5*) Heinle & Heinle.

Marinelli, Patti J. & Laughlin, Lizette M. Puentes: Spanish for Intensive & High-Beginner Courses. LC 93-38316. (C). 1994. mass mkt. 53.95 (*0-8384-2163-6*) Heinle & Heinle.

Marinelli, Robert P. & Dell Orto, Arthur E., eds. The Psychological & Social Impact of Disability. 3rd ed. LC 91-4809. 384p. (C). 1991. 39.95 (*0-8261-2212-4*) Springer Pub.

***Marinelli, Robert P. & Dell Orto, Arthur E., eds.** The Psychological & Social Impact of Disability. 4th ed. 384p. 1999. 49.95 (*0-8261-2213-2*) Springer Pub.

Marinelli, William J. Into the Night. Clemente, Vincent, ed. 42p. 1993. pap. 8.00 (*0-925062-15-4*) Writers Ink Pr.

Marinello, Edward A. On the Way: General Patton's Eyes & Ears on the Enemy. LC 98-35928. 1998. 27.95 (*1-56072-605-9*, Nova Kroshka Bks) Nova Sci Pubs.

Marinello, Ginette, jt. ed. see Pierquin, Bernard.

Marinello, Grace. Me, Myself, & I: A Program on Alcoholism & Its Effect on Family for Older Students. LC 93-79192. 16p. (YA). (gr. 6-12). 1993. 1.00 (*1-884063-06-3*) Mar Co Prods.

Mariner Books Staff. Field Guide to Birds. 2nd ed. (Peterson Field Guide Ser.). (Illus.). 384p. 1998. pap. text 19.00 (*0-395-91177-X*, Mariner Bks) HM.

— Field Guide to Eastern Butterflies. 2nd ed. LC 98-13623. (Peterson Field Guide Ser.). (Illus.). 486p. 1998. pap. 20.00 (*0-395-90453-6*, Mariner Bks) HM.

— Field Guide to Eastern Reptiles. 4th ed. LC 98-13622. (Peterson Field Guide Ser.). (Illus.). 616p. 1998. pap. 20.00 (*0-395-90452-8*, Mariner Bks) HM.

— Field Guide to Eastern Trees. 2nd ed. LC 98-13625. (Peterson Field Guide Ser.). (Illus.). 1998. pap. 19.00 (*0-395-90455-2*, Mariner Bks) HM.

— Field Guide to Eastern Wildflowers. 2nd ed. (Peterson Field Guide Ser.). (Illus.). 448p. 1998. pap. 18.00 (*0-395-91172-9*, Mariner Bks) HM.

— Field Guide to Insects. (Peterson Field Guide Ser.). (Illus.). 416p. 1998. pap. 18.00 (*0-395-91170-2*, Mariner Bks) HM.

— Field Guide to Mammals. 3rd ed. (Peterson Field Guide Ser.). (Illus.). 368p. 1998. pap. 18.00 (*0-395-91098-6*, Mariner Bks) HM.

— Field Guide to Mushrooms. 2nd ed. (Peterson Field Guide Ser.). (Illus.). 448p. 1998. pap. 18.00 (*0-395-91090-0*, Mariner Bks) HM.

— Field Guide to Pacific Wildflowers. 2nd ed. (Peterson Field Guide Ser.). (Illus.). 336p. 1998. pap. 18.00 (*0-395-91095-1*, Mariner Bks) HM.

— Field Guide to Stars & Planets. 4th ed. (Peterson Field Guide Ser.). (Illus.). 512p. 1998. 27.00 (*0-395-91100-1*, Mariner Bks); pap. 18.00 (*0-395-91099-4*, Mariner Bks) HM.

— Field Guide to Western Birds. 4th ed. (Peterson Field Guide Ser.). (Illus.). 432p. 1998. 27.00 (*0-395-91174-5*, Mariner Bks) HM.

— Field Guide to Western Birds: A Completely New Guide to Field Marks of All Species Found in North America West of the 100th Meridian. 3rd rev. ed. (Peterson Field Guide Ser.). (Illus.). 431p. 1998. pap. 18.00 (*0-395-91173-7*, Mariner Bks) HM.

— Field Guide to Western Trees. 2nd ed. LC 98-13624. (Peterson Field Guide Ser.). (Illus.). 1998. pap. 19.00 (*0-395-90454-4*, Mariner Bks) HM.

— First Guide to Butterflies. 2nd ed. (First Guide). (Illus.). 128p. (J). 1998. pap. 5.95 (*0-395-90665-2*, Mariner Bks) HM.

— First Guide to Insects. 2nd ed. (First Guide). (Illus.). 128p. (J). 1998. pap. 5.95 (*0-395-90664-4*, Mariner Bks) HM.

— First Guide to Wildflowers. 2nd ed. (First Guide). (Illus.). 128p. (J). 1998. pap. 5.95 (*0-395-90667-9*, Mariner Bks) HM.

— Freshwater Fishes. 2nd ed. (Peterson Field Guide Ser.). (Illus.). 448p. 1998. pap. 18.00 (*0-395-91091-9*, Mariner Bks) HM.

Mariner, C. Sex Files 1: Beyond Limits. 1997. mass mkt. 6.95 (*0-7472-5718-3*, Pub. by Headline Bk Pub) Trafalgar.

Mariner, Elwyn, jt. auth. see Levitan, Donald.

***Mariner, Joanne, et al.** Behind Bars in Brazil. LC 98-89492. xv, 140 p. 1998. write for info. (*1-56432-195-9*) Hum Rts Watch.

***Mariner, Kirk.** God's Island: The History of Tangier. (Illus.). 186p. 1999. pap. 14.95 (*0-9648393-5-0*) Miona Pubns.

Mariner, Kirk. Off 13: The Eastern Shore of Virginia Guidebook. LC 87-70771. (Illus.). 184p. 1994. reprint ed. pap. 14.95 (*0-9648393-1-8*) Miona Pubns.

— Once upon an Island: The History of Chincoteague. LC 96-77369. 224p. 1996. pap. 14.95 (*0-9648393-3-4*) Miona Pubns.

— Revival's Children: A Religious History of Virginia's Eastern Shore. LC 79-64801. (Illus.). 728p. 1979. reprint ed. 22.95 (*0-9648393-0-X*) Miona Pubns.

— Wachapreague, Virginia: Then & Now. (Illus.). 55p. 1995. pap. 5.95 (*0-9648393-2-6*) Miona Pubns.

Mariner, Rodney. The Torah. LC 96-78270. (Illus.). 400p. 1995. 30.00 (*0-8050-4820-0*) H Holt & Co.

— The Torah. 1997. pap. 14.95 (*0-614-19807-0*) H Holt & Co.

Mariner Roxberg, Joan, jt. auth. see Glass Montoya, Candace.

Mariner, Steven A., jt. auth. see Nara, Robert O.

Mariner, Tom. Dillon Press Book of the Earth. 96p. (J). (gr. 5). 1995. pap. 9.95 (*0-382-24729-9*, Dillon Silver Burdett) Silver Burdett Pr.

Mariner, Tom & Ellis, Anyon. The Dillon Press Book of the Earth. LC 94-16855. (J). (gr. 3 up). 1994. text 16.95 (*0-87518-640-8*, Dillon Silver Burdett) Silver Burdett Pr.

Mariner, William. An Account of the Natives of the Tonga Islands in the South Pacific Ocean, 2 vols., Set. LC 75-35204. reprint ed. 124.50 (*0-404-14290-7*) AMS Pr.

Mariners' Museum (Newport News, Va.) Staff, jt. auth. see Benson, Richard.

Mariners Museum Library - Newport News - Virginia. Catalog of Marine Photographs, 5 Vols, Set. 1970. 570.00 (*0-8161-0685-1*, G K Hall & Co) Mac Lib Ref.

— Catalog of Marine Prints & Paintings, 3 Vols, Set. 1970. 345.00 (*0-8161-0684-3*, G K Hall & Co) Mac Lib Ref.

Mariners' Museum Staff. Titanic: Fortune & Fate: Letters, Momentos, & Personal Effects from Those Who Sailed on the Lost Ship. LC 98-36369. (Illus.). 192p. (YA). (gr. 6 up). 1998. 29.50 (*0-684-85710-3*) S&S Trade.

***Mariners Museum Staff, ed.** Monitor Chronicles: One Sailor's Account. LC 00-27158. (Illus.). 272p. 2000. 35.00 (*0-684-86997-7*) Simon & Schuster.

Marinescu, Constantin. Making & Spending Money along the Bosporus: The Lysimachi Coinages Minted by Byzantium & Chalcedon. (Illus.). 300p. Date not set. text 59.50 (*0-472-11052-7*, 11052) U of Mich Pr.

Marinescu, Gheorgha, jt. auth. see Cristescu, Romulus.

Marinescu, Ioan D., et al, eds. Handbook of Ceramics Grinding & Polishing: Properties, Processes, Technology, Tools & Typology. LC 98-17520. (Illus.). 450p. 1998. 145.00 (*0-8155-1424-7*) Noyes.

Marinescu, Ioan D., jt. auth. see Webster, John A.

Marinetti, Filippo Tommaso. Mots en Liberte Futuristes. 1956. pap. 20.00 (*0-87556-216-7*) Saifer.

— Selected Poems & Related Prose. Napier, Elizabeth R. & Studholme, Barbara R., trs. from FRE. LC 96-11140. 1997. 40.00 (*0-300-04103-9*) Yale U Pr.

— The Untameables. Parzen, Jeremy, tr. from ITA. (Sun & Moon Classics Ser.: No. 28). 88p. 1994. pap. 10.95 (*1-55713-064-7*) Sun & Moon CA.

Marinetti, G. V. Disorders of Lipid Metabolism. LC 89-72205. (Illus.). 240p. (C). 1990. text 69.50 (*0-306-43431-8*, Kluwer Plenum) Kluwer Academic.

Marinetti, Guido V., ed. Lipid Chromatographic Analysis, Vol. 1. 2nd ed. LC 75-42515. 351p. reprint ed. pap. 108.90 (*0-7837-0008-3*, 201768900001) Bks Demand.

— Lipid Chromatographic Analysis, Vol. 2. 2nd ed. LC 75-42515. 383p. reprint ed. pap. 118.80 (*0-7837-0009-1*, 201768900002) Bks Demand.

— Lipid Chromatographic Analysis, Vol. 3. LC 75-42515. 300p. reprint ed. pap. 93.00 (*0-8357-9085-1*, 201768900003) Bks Demand.

Marinetto, Michael. Corporate Social Involvement: Social, Political & Environmental Issues in Britain & Italy. LC 98-72804. 244p. 1998. text 63.95 (*1-84014-189-1*, Pub. by Ashgate Pub) Ashgate Pub Co.

— Studies of the Policy Process: A Case Analysis. LC 98-7605. 1998. 55.01 (*0-13-916255-0*) P-H.

Maring, Glady. The Look of Long-Time Lovers. 80p. 1998. pap. 8.00 (*1-57502-817-4*, PO2249) Morris Pubng.

Maring, K. W. & Van Dijk, A. Brikkenaar, eds. Education of the Engineer for Innovative & Entrepreneurial Activity. 470p. (Orig.). 1982. pap. text 42.50 (*90-6275-088-5*, Pub. by Delft U Pr) Coronet Bks.

Maring, Margaret. Louisiana Creole & Cajun. Vol. 7. 64p. 1984. pap., per. 3.95 (*0-942320-14-X*) Am Cooking.

Maring, Norman H. & Hudson, Winthrop S. A Baptist Manual of Polity & Practice. rev. ed. 1991. 24.00 (*0-8170-1171-4*) Judson.

Maring, R. H., jt. auth. see Kaler, S. P.

***Maring, Richard.** Evaluating Business Operations Solutions. (gr. 8). 1999. pap. 39.99 (*0-7356-0725-7*) Little.

Marini, A. Diccionario Enciclopedico Electronica. (SPA.). 376p. 1989. 39.95 (*0-7859-6503-3*) Fr & Eur.

Marini, Alexander. We Win: A Complete Physical Education Program for the Entire Family Without Competition. 1995. pap. text 19.95 (*1-56857-017-1*) Noble Pub Assocs.

Marini-Bettolo, G. B., ed. A Modern Approach to the Protection of the Environment: Proceedings of a Study Week Held in the Vatican, 2-7 November 1987. (Pontifical Academiae Scientiarum Scripta Ser.). (Illus.). 602p. 1990. 94.00 (*0-08-040816-8*, Pergamon Pr) Elsevier.

— Towards a Second Green Revolution: From Chemical to New Biological Tehcnologies in Agriculture in the Tropics. (Developments in Agricultural & Managed-Forest Ecology Ser.: Vol. 19). 530p. 1988. 282.25 (*0-444-98927-7*) Elsevier.

Marini, Enrico, jt. auth. see Dufaux, Jean.

Marini, Enrico, jt. auth. see Smolderen, Thierry.

***Marini, Francis J.** The Power of the Patriarch: Patriarchal Jurisdiction on the Verge of the Third Millennium LC 98-75170. (Maronite Rite Ser.). 413 p. 1998. write for info. (*1-885589-09-3*) St Maron Pubns.

Marini, Gabriella, jt. ed. see Hepp-Reymond, Marie-Claude.

Marini, Gabriella, jt. ed. see Mancia, Mauro.

Marini, John A. The Politics of Budget Control: Congress, the Presidency & Growth of the Administrative State. 300p. 1992. 79.95 (*0-8448-1716-3*, Crane Russak); pap. 32.95 (*0-8448-1717-1*, Crane Russak) Taylor & Francis.

Marini, John J. & Evans, Timothy W., eds. Acute Lung Injury. LC 97-26537. (Update in Intensive Care & Emergency Medicine Ser.: Vol. 30). (Illus.). 400p. 1997. 105.00 (*3-540-62582-8*) Spr-Verlag.

Marini, John J. & Ravenscraft, Sue A. Principles: Practice of Mechanical Ventilation. (Illus.). 544p. 1994. write for info. (*0-683-05556-9*) Lppncott W & W.

Marini, John J. & Slutsky, Arthur S., eds. Physiological Basis of Ventilatory Support. LC 98-4262. (Lung Biology in Health & Disease Ser.). (Illus.). 1480p. 1998. text 295.00 (*0-8247-9861-9*) Dekker.

Marini, John J. & Wheeler, Arthur P. Critical Care Medicine. 344p. (Orig.). 1989. pap. text 35.00 (*0-683-05554-2*) Lppncott W & W.

— Critical Care Medicine: The Essentials. 2nd ed. LC 96-46592. (Illus.). 640p. 1997. pap. 42.95 (*0-683-05555-0*) Lppncott W & W.

Marini, Luis A., ed. Manual de Odontologia Infantil. (SPA.). 463p. (Orig.). (C). 1982. 12.00 (*0-8477-2330-5*) U of PR Pr.

Marini, Marcelle. Jacques Lacan: The French Context. Tomiche, Anne, tr. LC 92-9652. (ENG & FRE.). 310p. (C). 1993. 45.00 (*0-8135-1851-2*); pap. 18.00 (*0-8135-1852-0*) Rutgers U Pr.

Marini, Paola, ed. & intro. see Rearick, W. R., et al.

***Marini, Rose Mary.** Fallen Angel. (Illus.). 1999. pap. 4.95 (*1-929914-04-0*) Megaverse.

Marini, Stephen A. Radical Sects of Revolutionary New England. LC 81-6913. (Illus.). 220p. 1982. 37.95 (*0-674-74625-2*) HUP.

***Marini, Tara & Layton, Carol, eds.** Fifth Grade Skills. (Kelley Wingate Ser.). (Illus.). vi, 128p. (J). 2000. pap. 10.95 (*0-88724-547-1*, CD-3762) Carson-Dellos.

— Fourth Grade Skills. (Kelley Wingate Ser.). (Illus.). vi, 128p. (J). 2000. pap. 10.95 (*0-88724-546-3*, CD-3761) Carson-Dellos.

— Second Grade Skills. (Kelley Wingate Ser.). (Illus.). v, 128p. (J). 2000. pap. 10.95 (*0-88724-544-7*, CD-3759) Carson-Dellos.

— Third Grade Skills. (Kelley Wingate Ser.). (Illus.). vi, 128p. (J). 2000. pap. 10.95 (*0-88724-545-5*, CD-3760) Carson-Dellos.

Mariniello, Silvestra & Bove, Paul A. Gendered Agents: Women & Institutional Knowledge. LC 97-38742. 456p. 1998. 64.95 (*0-8223-2179-3*) Duke.

Mariniello, Silvestra & Bove, Paul A., eds. Gendered Agents: Women & Institutional Knowledge. LC 97-38742. 428p. 1998. pap. 21.95 (*0-8223-2196-3*) Duke.

Marinina. Detective: Novel. Date not set. write for info. (*0-8050-6030-8*) H Holt & Co.

Marinis, Marco De, see De Marinis, Marco.

Marinjnissen, R. H. Paintings - Genuine, Fraud, Fake: Modern Methods of Examining Paintings. (Illus.). 415p. 1987. lib. bdg. 65.00 (*0-313-25874-0*, MPF/, Greenwood Pr) Greenwood.

Marinkas, Paul L., ed. Organic Energetic Compounds. (Illus.). 298p. (C). 1994. lib. bdg. 145.00 (*1-56072-201-0*) Nova Sci Pubs.

Marinker, Marshall, ed. Medical Audit & General Practice. 2nd ed. 250p. 1995. pap. text 12.00 (*0-7279-0908-8*, Pub. by BMJ Pub) Login Brothers Bk Co.

— Sense & Sensibility in Health Care. 296p. (Orig.). (C). Date not set. pap. text 35.00 (*0-7279-1111-2*, Pub. by BMJ Pub) Login Brothers Bk Co.

Marinker, Marshall & Peckham, Michael, eds. Clinical Futures. (Illus.). 219p. 1998. pap. 34.95 (*0-7279-1231-3*) Login Brothers Bk Co.

Marinker, Simon. Beyond the Citadel. LC 99-7. 656p. 1999. pap. 22.72 (*1-55212-238-7*) Trafford Pub.

— Informed Consent to Surgery: Everything You Always Wanted to Know about Your Operaton but Were Afraid to Ask. 114p. (Orig.). 1991. pap. 11.95 (*0-9694811-0-1*) Gordon Soules Bk.

Marinkov, D., tr. see Cardu, Petru.

***Marinkovich, S.** Sectional MRI Anatomy of the Human Body. (Illus.). 540p. 2000. 139.00 (*0-86577-899-X*) Thieme Med Pubs.

Marinkovich, Vincent A., jt. auth. see Zellerbach, Merla.

***Marino & Odum.** Biosphere 2: Research Past & Present. 350p. 1999. text 98.00 (*0-08-043208-5*, Pergamon Pr) Elsevier.

Marino & Richeson. Employment in Florida: Guide to Employment Laws, Regulations & Practices. 1992. ring bd. 89.50 (*0-327-00941-1*, 80856, MICHIE) LEXIS Pub.

Marino & Unkovic. Labor & Employment in Pennsylvania, Issue 6. 151p. 1998. ring bd. write for info. (*0-327-00585-8*, 8231916) LEXIS Pub.

Marino, et al. International Perspectives on Strategic Management. (C). 1993. pap. text 12.25 (*0-07-040442-9*) McGraw.

— Marino, Giovan Battista la Lira a Cura di Ottavio Besomi Janina Hauser, Giovanni Sporanzi. (Archivio Tematico della Lirica Ser.: Vol. 1). (ITA.). 488p. 1991. pap. 102.50 (*0-614-97982-X*) G Olms Pubs.

Marino, jt. auth. see Matthews.

Marino, Adrian. The Biography of "The Idea of Literature" From Antiquity to the Baroque. Stanciu, Virgil & Carlton, Charles M., trs. LC 95-20022. (SUNY Series, the Margins of Literature). 320p. (C). 1996. text 44.50 (*0-7914-2893-1*); pap. text 14.95 (*0-7914-2894-X*) State U NY Pr.

Marino, Al. Making Anything Possible: Excellence in Self-Accountability, Credit & Blame. 176p. 1996. reprint ed. pap. 12.95 (*1-890295-00-0*) Ldrship Resources.

— Platinum Leadership: Above & Beyond Empowerment. 1997. 19.95 (*1-890295-01-9*) Ldrship Resources.

Marino, Andrew A. Modern Bioelectricity. (Illus.). 737p. 1988. text 295.00 (*0-8247-7788-3*) Dekker.

Marino, Andrew A. & Ray, Joel. The Electric Wilderness. 1986. pap. 20.00 (*0-911302-55-7*) San Francisco Pr.

Marino, Andy. A Quiet American: The Secret War of Varian Fry. 2nd ed. LC 99-22064. 288p. 1999. text 26.95 (*0-312-20356-X*) St Martin.

***Marino, Anne N.** Collapsible World. 2000. 22.95 (*0-393-04909-4*) Norton.

Marino, Barbara P. Eric Needs Stitches. LC 84-40753. (Illus.). 32p. (J). (gr. k-3). 1989. lib. bdg. 12.89 (*0-397-32374-3*) HarpC Child Bks.

Marino, Bernard D. Handbook of Capital Expenditure Management. 256p. 1986. text 59.95 (*0-13-372541-3*) P-H.

M

Marino, Bob & D'Alessandro, Joe. Bob & Joe's Smart Seafood Guide. Schneider, Marcia, ed. LC 98-74998. (Illus.). 200p. 1999. mass mkt. 16.95 (*0-965671-2-4*) CATS Pub.

Marino, Bradley, jt. ed. see Fernandopulle, Rushika.

Marino, Brenda. Tourist Death Trap. Holley, Tabatha, ed. (Illus.). 73p. 1999. spiral bd. 14.95 (*0-9672884-0-1*) Brendas Office.

Marino, Bruno & Pueschel, Siegfried M., eds. Heart Disease in Persons with Down Syndrome. LC 95-24884. 1996. 62.00 (*1-55766-224-X*) P H Brookes.

Marino Bustamente. Diccionario de Dudas del Ingles. (ENG & SPA.). 304p. 1995. 49.95 (*0-7859-9773-3*) Fr & Eur.

Marino, C., ed. SuperComputer Applications in Automotive Research & Engineering Development. 452p. 1986. 115.00 (*0-931215-29-3*) Computational Mech MA.

Marino, C., ed. see Horn, Stephen.

Marino, Carlos & Diaz-Guerrero, Rogelio. Diccionario de Terminos Mineralogicos y Cristalograficos. (SPA.). 608p. 1991. 75.00 (*0-7859-5731-6*, 8420652377) Fr & Eur.

Marino, Cesare. The Remarkable Story of Carlo Gentile: Italian Photographer of the American West. (Illus.). 135p. 1998. pap. 24.95 (*1-887694-13-7*) C Mautz Pubng.

Marino, D. & Montresor, M. Proceedings of the 13th International Diatom Symposium. 566p. 1995. 165.00 (*0-948737-35-2*, Pub. by Biopress) Balogh.

Marino, Dan. Marino: On the Record. (Illus.). 1996. pap. 25.00 (*0-614-20473-9*) HarpC.

Marino, Dan & Brown, Greg. First & Goal. LC 96-30008. (Illus.). 40p. (J). (gr. 2-4). 1997. 14.95 (*0-87833-958-2*) Taylor Pub.

Marino, Daniel A. A Whirl Around the World. 180p. pap. 9.95 (*0-9633159-0-0*) Jemet Bks.

Marino, Dorothy. Where Are the Mothers? LC 59-12894. (Illus.). 32p. (J). 1959. lib. bdg. 11.89 (*0-397-31622-4*) HarpC Child Bks.

Marino, Emiliano & Charbonneau, Christine. The Sailmaker's Apprentice: A Guide for the Self-Reliant Sailor. 512p. 1994. 39.95 (*0-07-157980-X*) Intl Marine.

Marino, F. Time Capsules. 1988. 9.95 (*0-7935-1586-6*, 06620615) H Leonard.

Marino, Frank, et al. His Majesty, the Queen: Frank Marino. LC 96-77477. (Illus.). 288p. 1997. 22.00 (*0-9640903-4-1*) Marino Schechter Writings.

Marino, G., et al, eds. Biochemistry of Vitamin B6 & PQQ. 1994. write for info. (*3-7643-5067-9*) Birkhauser.

— Biochemistry of Vitamin B6 & PQQ. LC 94-38750. (Advances in Life Sciences Ser.). (Illus.). 384p. 1994. 99.00 (*0-8176-5067-9*) Birkhauser.

Marino, Gennaro G. Earthquake Damage: Inspection, Evaluation & Repair. LC 97-11357. (Illus.). 404p. 1997. 99.00 (*0-913875-42-2*, 5422-N) Lawyers & Judges.

Marino, Giovan B. La Lira - Archivio Tematico Della Lirica Italiana. (Archivio Tematico Della Lirica Italiana - Atli Ser.: Vol. 1). vii, 488p. 1992. write for info. (*3-487-09526-2*) G Olms Pubs.

Marino, Gordon. Kierkegaard's Anthropology. (Orig.). 1997. write for info. (*0-87462-604-8*) Marquette.

Marino, Gordon, jt. ed. see Hannay, Alastair.

Marino, Jan. The Day That Elvis Came to Town. 208p. (J). (gr. 5). 1993. reprint ed. pap. 3.50 (*0-380-71672-0*, Avon Bks) Morrow Avon.

— Eighty-Eight Steps to September. 160p. (J). (gr. 3-7). 1991. pap. 2.95 (*0-380-71001-3*, Avon Bks) Morrow Avon.

— For the Love of Pete. 208p. (J). (gr. 4 up). 1994. pap. 3.50 (*0-380-72281-X*, Avon Bks) Morrow Avon.

— Letter To My Dad. (J). 1997. write for info. (*0-316-54615-1*) Little.

— Like Some Kind of Hero. 224p. (YA). 1993. pap. 3.50 (*0-380-72010-8*, Avon Bks) Morrow Avon.

*__Marino, Jan.__ The Mona Lisa of Salem Street. 155p. (J). (gr. 3-6). 1999. reprint ed. text 15.00 (*0-7881-6635-2*) DIANE Pub.

Marino, Jan. Searching for Atticus. LC 96-53146. 256p. (J). (gr. 7 up). 1997. per. 16.00 (*0-689-80066-5*) S&S Childrens.

— Write Me a Happy Ending. (J). 1999. pap. 16.00 (*0-689-80067-3*) S&S Trade.

Marino, Jane. Sing Us a Story: Using Music in Preschool & Family Story Times. LC 93-6389. 215p. 1994. 40.00 (*0-8242-0847-1*) Wilson.

Marino, Jane & Houlihan, Dorothy F. Mother Goose Time: Library Programs for Babies & Their Caregivers. 172p. 1992. 30.00 (*0-8242-0850-1*) Wilson.

Marino, John. MVPs. 80p. 1996. 11.98 (*1-56799-243-9*, MetroBooks) M Friedman Pub Grp Inc.

— Pitchers of Perfection. LC 95-23804. 80p. 1996. 11.98 (*1-56799-178-5*, MetroBooks) M Friedman Pub Grp Inc.

— Puerto Rico: Off the Beaten Path: A Guide to Unique Places. LC 99-41721. (Off the Beaten Path Ser.). (Illus.). 256p. 1999. pap. 12.95 (*0-7627-0275-3*) Globe Pequot.

Marino, John A. Pastoral Economics in The Kingdom of Naples. LC 87-9196. (Studies in Historical & Political Science: 106th Series, No. 1). 400p. 1988. text 60.00 (*0-8018-3437-6*) Johns Hopkins.

Marino, Joseph L. Matrimonial & Family Law, MFL: Covering Domestic Relations, General Obligations, Family Court, with Practice Commentaries. Vol. 9A: 10. write for info. (*0-318-58376-3*) West Pub.

Marino, Joseph S., ed. Biblical Themes in Religious Education. LC 83-16124. 294p. (Orig.). 1983. pap. 24.95 (*0-89135-038-1*) Religious Educ.

Marino, Kenneth E. Forcasting Your Company's Sales & Profits: Quickly, Easily & Realistically. (Entrepreneur's Guide Ser.). 1991. per. 22.95 (*1-55738-143-7*, Irwn Prfssnl) McGraw-Hill Prof.

Marino, Kim. Best Resumes for Accountants & Financial Professionals. LC 93-18206. 208p. 1994. 65.00 (*0-471-59542-X*); pap. 17.95 (*0-471-59543-8*) Wiley.

— Just Resumes: Two Hundred Powerful & Proven Successful Resumes to Get the Job. 2nd ed. LC 96-29158. 272p. 1997. pap. 11.95 (*0-471-16567-0*) Wiley.

— Resumes for the Health Care Professional. LC 91-44718. 208p. 1993. pap. 14.95 (*0-471-55862-1*) Wiley.

*__Marino, Kim.__ Resumes for the Health Care Professional. 2nd ed. LC 99-52757. 240p. 2000. pap. 14.95 (*0-471-38073-3*) Wiley.

Marino, Lauren, ed. see Richardson, Cheryl.

*__Marino, Manuel & Boland, John.__ An Integrated Approach to Wastewater Treatment: Deciding Where, When & How Much to Invest. LC 99-12533. (Directions in Development Ser.). 60p. 1999. pap. 22.00 (*0-8213-4467-6*, 14467) World Bank.

Marino, Manuel & Kemper, Karin E., eds. Institutional Frameworks in Successful Water Markets: Brazil, Spain & Colorado, U. S. A. LC 99-12016. (Technical Paper Ser.: Vol. 427). 58p. 1999. pap. 22.00 (*0-8213-4459-5*, 14459) World Bank.

Marino, Maria B., jt. ed. see Rodriguez-Monino, Antonio.

*__Marino, Martha.__ African Journal: Backpacking in Southern Africa. Nett, Del & Baker, Nancy, eds. (Illus.). 114p. 2000. spiral bd. 12.00 (*0-9655142-1-8*) Marino Pr.

Marino, Martha. Asian Adventure: Amusing Tales from Thailand & China. Nett, Del, ed. LC 96-95065. (Illus.). 175p. (YA). (gr. 12 up). 1996. pap. 14.95 (*0-9655142-0-X*) Marino Pr.

Marino, Michael F., III & Richeson, J. David. Employment in Florida: A Guide to Employment Laws, Regulations, & Practices. 132p. 1994. ring bd., suppl. ed. 38.50 (*0-614-03179-6*, MICHIE) LEXIS Pub.

Marino, Michael F. & Richeson, J. David. Employment in Florida: A Guide to Employment Laws, Regulations, & Practices, Issue 5. LC 92-26520. 172p. 1997. ring bd. 89.50 (*0-409-25666-8*, 80856-10, MICHIE) LEXIS Pub.

*__Marino, Michael F. & Richeson, J. David.__ Labor & Employment in Florida, Issue 9. 200p. 1999. ring bd. write for info. (*0-327-01385-0*, 8085815) LEXIS Pub.

Marino, Michael F. & Unkovic. Labor & Employment in Pennsylvania: A Guide to Employment Laws, Regulations, & Practices. 430p. Date not set. ring bd. 95.00 (*0-409-25674-9*, 82318, MICHIE) LEXIS Pub.

Marino, Michael F., et al. The Virginia Employer's Guide to Labor Law. LC 83-171872. (Illus.). 1982. 45.00 (*0-685-08125-7*) VA Chamber Com.

Marino, Michael F., jt. auth. see Liddle, Jeffrey L.

Marino, Miguel A., ed. Subsurface Flow & Contamination: Methods of Analysis & Parameter Uncertainty. LC TC0176.S92. (AWRA Monograph: No. 8). (Illus.). 118p. reprint ed. pap. 36.60 (*0-8357-3170-7*, 203943300012) Bks Demand.

Marino, Nancy. La Serranilla Espanola. 153p. 1990. 29.50 (*0-916379-45-0*) Scripta.

Marino, Nancy F., ed. El Libro Del Conoscimiento de Todos Los Reinos: The Book of Knowledge of All Kingdoms. LC 99-13118. (Medieval & Renaissance Texts & Studies: Vol. 198). (Illus.). 224p. 1999. 24.00 (*0-86698-240-X*, MR198) MRTS.

Marino, Nancy R., jt. auth. see Lallier, Katherine G.

Marino, Norma. Carly, Sweet Angel Child. (J). (gr. k-3). 1999. pap. 6.95 (*0-533-12851-X*) Vantage.

Marino, Paul & Krasner, Jay. The Hemodynamic Expert: Apple Package. 1996. write for info. incl. Apple II (*0-7216-1626-7*, W B Saunders Co) Harcrt Hlth Sci Grp.

— The Hemodynamic Expert: IBM Package. 1996. write for info. incl. disk (*0-7216-1628-3*, W B Saunders Co) Harcrt Hlth Sci Grp.

Marino, Paul L. The ICU Book. LC 90-5622. (Illus.). 713p. 1991. text 49.50 (*0-8121-1306-3*) Lppncott W & W.

— The ICU Book. 2nd ed. LC 96-48756. 800p. 1998. pap. 55.00 (*0-683-05565-8*) Lppncott W & W.

Marino, Ragi. Flying High: The Airplane in Quilts. (Illus.). 72p. (Orig.). 1994. pap. 18.00 (*0-929950-18-6*) ME Pubns.

Marino, Raul, Jr., jt. ed. see Rasmussen, Theodore.

*__Marino, Rick.__ Be Elvis! A Guide to Impersonating the King. LC 00-26582. (Illus.). 2000. write for info. (*1-57071-556-4*) Sourcebks.

*__Marino, Stephen A.__ The Salesman Has a Birthday: Essays Celebrating the Fiftieth Anniversary of Arthur Miller's Death of a Salesman. 160p. 2000. 49.00 (*0-7618-1653-4*); pap. 27.50 (*0-7618-1654-2*) U Pr of Amer.

Marino, T. J. & Sheff, Donald A. Freelance Photographer's Handbook. LC 79-6821. (Illus.). 140p. 1980. pap. write for info. (*0-672-52634-4*) Macmillan.

Marino, Tony. Intergalatic Grudge Match. LC 92-12845. (Widgets Ser.). (J). (gr. 2). 1992. lib. bdg. 13.99 (*1-56239-154-2*) ABDO Pub Co.

— Ratchet Hood. LC 92-12841. (Widgets Ser.). (YA). 1992. lib. bdg. 13.99 (*1-56239-152-6*) ABDO Pub Co.

— Scraboolee Jubilee. LC 92-12840. (Widgets Ser.). (YA). 1992. lib. bdg. 13.99 (*1-56239-153-4*) ABDO Pub Co.

Marino, V. English-Italian Dictionary of Medical Phraseology. 526p. 1985. 184.00 (*88-299-0279-9*) IBD Ltd.

— English-Italian Phraseological Medical Dictionaries. (ENG & ITA.). 526p. 1985. 115.00 (*0-7859-7516-0*, 8828902795) Fr & Eur.

Marino, Vinny. Journey from Hell. 186p. (Orig.). 1996. pap. 12.95 (*0-9651370-0-7*) Habilitat.

Marino, Vito R., jt. auth. see Lonstein, Albert I.

Marinoff, Irene. The Heresy of National Socialism. 1976. lib. bdg. 59.95 (*0-8490-1945-1*) Gordon Pr.

*__Marinoff, Lou.__ Plato, Not Prozac! Applying Eternal Wisdom to Everyday Problems. 320p. 2000. pap. 13.00 (*0-06-093136-1*, Perennial) HarperTrade.

Marinoff, Lou. Plato,Not Prozac! Applying Philosophy to Everyday Problems. LC 99-22650. 320p. 1999. 23.95 (*0-06-019328-X*) HarpC.

Marinone, Nino. All the Greek Verbs. 186p. (C). 1996. reprint ed. pap. text 22.95 (*0-7156-1772-9*, Pub. by G Duckworth) Focus Pub-R Pullins.

Marinone, Nino, ed. All the Greek Verbs. 352p. 1990. pap. text 17.50 (*0-89341-629-0*, Longwood Academic) Hollowbrook.

— Xenophanes - Lessico Di Senofane. (Alpha-Omega, Reihe A Ser.: Bd. XX). 117p. 1972. reprint ed. write for info. (*3-487-04216-9*) G Olms Pubs.

Marinone, Nino & Guala, F. Complete Handbook of Greek Verbs. 353p. 1972. 9.95 (*0-87774-001-1*) Schoenhof.

Marinone, Nino, jt. ed. see Lomanto, Valeria.

Marinos, June. An Odyssey into Greek Cooking. Terzopoulos, Barbara, ed. (Illus.). 168p. 1997. pap. 16.25 (*960-7220-20-X*, Pub. by Terzopoulos) Cosmos.

Marinos, June, jt. auth. see Louis, Diana F.

Marinos Of Neapolis. Life of Proclus & Commentary on the "Dedomena" of Euclid Extant Works. (Ancient Greek & Roman Writers Ser.). xvi, 107p. 1977. pap. 20.00 (*0-89005-218-2*) Ares.

Marinos, P. G., et al, eds. Engineering Geology & the Environment/Geologie de L'Ingenieur et L'Environment: Proceedings of an International Symposium of the IAWG, Athens, 23-27 June 1997, 5 vols. (Illus.). 4000p. (C). 1997. text 449.00 (*90-5410-877-0*, Pub. by A A Balkema) Ashgate Pub Co.

Marinos, Paul G., ed. Engineering Geology of Ancient Works, Monuments & Historical Sites: Proceedings of an International Symposium, Athens, 19-23 September 1988, 4 vols., Set. 2000p. (C). 1989. text 440.00 (*90-6191-793-X*, Pub. by A A Balkema) Ashgate Pub Co.

Marinov. Privatisation In Britain: Results & Implications. 59.95 (*1-84014-358-4*) Ashgate Pub Co.

Marinov, C. A., jt. auth. see Neittaanmaki, Pekka.

*__Marinovich, Greg & Silva, Joao Paulo.__ The Bang Bang Club: Snapshots from a Hidden War. 320p. 2000. 26.00 (*0-465-04412-3*, Pub. by Basic) HarpC.

Marinozzi, V., ed. Ultrastructural Kidney Pathology. (Journal: Applied Pathology: Vol. 2, No. 4, 1984). (Illus.). 52p. 1985. pap. 41.75 (*3-8055-4251-8*) S Karger.

Marinsky, J. A. & Miyajima, T. Charged Polymeric Molecules: Theory & Application. (Studies in Polymer Science: Vol. 14). 1999. write for info. (*0-444-82065-5*) Elsevier.

Marinsky, Jacob A., ed. Ion Exchange, Vol. 1. LC 66-29027. 436p. 1966. reprint ed. pap. 135.20 (*0-608-08289-9*, 202783200001) Bks Demand.

— Ion Exchange, Vol 2. LC 66-29027. 256p. 1969. reprint ed. pap. 79.40 (*0-608-08290-2*, 205505500002) Bks Demand.

Marinsky, Jacob A. & Marcus, Yizhak, eds. Ion Exchange & Solvent Extraction, No. 3. LC 66-29027. 168p. reprint ed. pap. 52.10 (*0-608-16647-2*, 202781300003) Bks Demand.

— Ion Exchange & Solvent Extraction, No. 4. LC 66-29027. 281p. reprint ed. pap. 87.20 (*0-608-16648-0*, 202781300004) Bks Demand.

— Ion Exchange & Solvent Extraction, Vol. 13. (Illus.). 416p. 1997. text 215.00 (*0-8247-9825-2*) Dekker.

— Ion Exchange & Solvent Extraction Vol. 5, 1973: A Series of Advances. LC 73-645531. (Illus.). 307p. reprint ed. pap. 95.20 (*0-608-06204-9*, 202781300005) Bks Demand.

— Ion Exchange & Solvent Extraction Vol. 6: A Series of Advances. LC 73-645531. (Illus.). 315p. reprint ed. pap. 97.70 (*0-7837-4207-X*, 202781300006) Bks Demand.

Marinsky, Jacob A. & Miyajima, T. Charged Polymeric Molecules: Theory & Application. 1996. write for info. (*0-614-17909-2*) Elsevier.

Marinsky, Jacob A., jt. auth. see Marcus.

Marinsky, Jacob A., jt. auth. see Marcus, Yizhak.

Mario, Heidi S. I'd Rather Have an Iguana. LC 97-37049. 32p. (J). 1999. 14.95 (*0-88106-357-6*, Talewinds) Charlesbridge Pub.

Mario, Luis. Ciencia y Arte del Verso Castellano. LC 91-72151. (SPA.). 506p. (Orig.). 1991. pap. 24.95 (*0-89729-607-9*) Ediciones.

*__Mario, Luis.__ Colon Cantado: Discubrimiento de America Como Tema Poetico a Traves de los Tiempos. LC 99-62942. (Coleccion Polymita). (SPA., Illus.). 160p. 1999. pap. 13.00 (*0-89729-902-7*) Ediciones.

Mario, Luis. Cuba en Mis Versos. LC 92-74962. (Coleccion Espejo de Paciencia). (SPA.). 140p. (Orig.). 1993. pap. 12.00 (*0-89729-662-1*) Ediciones.

— Esta Mujer. LC 83-81719. (Coleccion Espejo de Paciencia). (SPA.). 77p. (Orig.). 1984. pap. 6.00 (*0-89729-338-X*) Ediciones.

— La Misma. LC 88-81864. (Coleccion Espejo de Paciencia). (SPA.). 131p. (Orig.). 1990. pap. 9.95 (*0-89729-498-X*) Ediciones.

— Poesia y Poetas. LC 83-81718. (SPA.). 126p. (Orig.). 1984. pap. 8.95 (*0-89729-337-1*) Ediciones.

— Profugo de la Sal. LC 78-56759. 1978. pap. 5.00 (*0-89729-206-5*) Ediciones.

Mariological Society of America, Burlingame, Calif. Marian Studies Vol. 40: Proceedings. 279p. 12.00 (*0-318-50039-6*) Mariological Soc.

Mariological Society of America, East Aurora Conve. Marian Studies Vol. 39: Proceedings. 224p. 12.00 (*0-318-50038-8*) Mariological Soc.

Mariological Society of America. New York City Con. Marian Studies: Proceedings, Vol. 31. 238p. 12.00 (*0-318-14800-5*) Mariological Soc.

Mariological Society of America, Providence, R. I. Marian Studies Vol. 41: Proceedings. 203p. 12.00 (*0-317-04171-1*) Mariological Soc.

Mariological Society of America Staff. Marian Studies - Proceedings Vol. 42: Chicago Convention, 1991. 1991. 12.00 (*0-317-04172-X*) Mariological Soc.

Mariolopoulos, E. Compendium in Astronomy. 1982. text 205.00 (*90-277-1373-1*) Kluwer Academic.

Marion. A Brief View of Astronomy. (C). 1986. pap. text, teacher ed. 28.00 (*0-03-058423-X*) Harcourt Coll Pubs.

— Descartes' Metaphysical Prism. LC 98-35104. 1999. pap. text 25.00 (*0-226-50539-1*) U Ch Pr.

— The Distorted Metaphysics of Descartes. LC 98-35104. 1999. lib. bdg. 55.00 (*0-226-50538-3*) U Ch Pr.

— Guidance of Young Children. 5th ed. LC 98-19194. 319p. (C). 1998. pap. text 40.00 (*0-13-901166-8*) P-H.

— Questions Cartesiennes. LC 98-38335. 1999. lib. bdg. 62.00 (*0-226-50542-1*) U Ch Pr.

Marion & Eames. Fair Wilderness. Date not set. 26.95 (*0-8464-4866-1*) Beekman Pubs.

Marion, A. Introduction to Image Processing. 1991. 54.95 (*0-442-31202-4*) Chapman & Hall.

Marion, Barbara, jt. auth. see Levy, Barbara R.

Marion, Craig A., ed. see Renfro, Nancy & Sullivan, Debbie.

Marion, Cynthia & Hirsh, Carol. Sky: Early Childhood Theme Teaching Collection. Mitchell, Judy, ed. (Illus.). 64p. (J). (ps-2). 1998. pap., teacher ed. 7.95 (*1-57310-107-9*) Teachng & Lrning Co.

Marion, D. Josephine's Catastrophes: Three Great Cat Tales. LC 94-30493. (Illus.). (J). 1995. 14.95 (*0-382-24909-7*); pap. 7.95 (*0-382-24910-0*); lib. bdg. 16.95 (*0-382-24908-9*) Silver Burdett Pr.

Marion, David E. The Jurisprudence of Justice William J. Brennan, Jr. The Law & Politics of "Libertarian Dignity" LC 97-20407. (Studies in American Constitutionalism). 208p. 1997. 55.50 (*0-8476-8566-7*); pap. 23.95 (*0-8476-8567-5*) Rowman.

Marion, Dawn D. The Wizard & the Golden Acorns. Lingard, Tim, ed. (Continuing Adventures of Timothy Glean). (Illus.). 36p. (Orig.). (J). (gr. k-3). 1994. pap. write for info. (*1-885986-00-9*) Glean Pubns.

Marion, Donald J. The Chinese Filmography: The 2485 Feature Films Produced by Studios in the People's Republic of China from 1949 Through 1995. LC 96-49551. (Illus.). 760p. 1997. lib. bdg. 145.00 (*0-7864-0305-5*) McFarland & Co.

Marion, Donald W. Traumatic Brain Injury. LC 98-17720. (Illus.). 320p. 1998. 99.00 (*0-86577-727-6*) Thieme Med Pubs.

Marion, Frances. Valley People. LC 70-144161. (Short Story Index Reprint Ser.). 1977. reprint ed. 20.95 (*0-8369-3776-7*) Ayer.

Marion, Frieda. China Half-Figures Called Pincushion Dolls. LC 74-178257. (Illus.). 1994. reprint ed. pap. 9.50 (*0-89145-058-0*) J Palmer.

Marion, Gina. Creative Hardanger. (Illus.). 80p. 1995. pap. 12.95 (*1-86351-136-9*, Pub. by Sally Milner) Sterling.

— Decorative Designs for Hardanger. (Illus.). 80p. 1998. 12.95 (*1-86351-214-4*, Pub. by Sally Milner) Sterling.

*__Marion Gould Gallagher Law Library Staff.__ Washington State Constitutional Convention 1889: Contemporary Newspaper Articles. LC 99-61655. 1998. reprint ed. 135.00 (*1-57588-527-1*, 322900) W S Hein.

Marion, J., jt. ed. see Heyer, H.

Marion, Jean-Luc. Catesian Questions: Method & Metaphysics. LC 98-38335. 1999. pap. text 25.00 (*0-226-50544-8*) U Ch Pr.

— God Without Being: Hors-Texte. Carlson, Thomas A., tr. 284p. 1995. pap. text 14.00 (*0-226-50541-3*) U Ch Pr.

— God Without Being: Hors-Texte. Carlson, Thomas A., tr. (Religion & Postmodernism Ser.). 284p. 1997. 36.95 (*0-226-50540-5*) U Ch Pr.

— Reduction & Givenness: Investigations of Husserl, Heidegger, & Phenomenology. Carlson, Thomas A., tr. LC 97-52350. (Studies in Phenomenology & Existential Philosophy). 353p. 1997. 79.95 (*0-8101-1216-7*); pap. 24.95 (*0-8101-1235-3*) Northwestern U Pr.

Marion, Jeff D. Lost & Found. (Illus.). 64p. 1994. pap. 9.95 (*1-885912-02-1*) Sows Ear Pr.

— Vigils, Selected Poems. LC 89-17896. 1989. pap. 9.95 (*0-913239-62-3*) Appalach Consortium.

Marion, Jerry B. Classical Dynamics of Particle. 4th ed. (C). 1995. text 100.50 (*0-03-097302-3*, Pub. by Harcourt Coll Pubs); pap. text, student ed. 26.50 (*0-03-097304-X*, Pub. by Harcourt Coll Pubs) Harcourt.

— Classical Dynamics of Particle. 4th ed. (C). 1995. pap. text, teacher ed., suppl. ed. 32.00 (*0-03-097303-1*) Harcourt Coll Pubs.

— Classical Electromagnetic Radiation. 3rd ed. LC 94-67490. (C). 1994. text 100.00 (*0-03-097277-9*) Harcourt Coll Pubs.

— Introduction to Image Processing. (C). 1990. mass mkt. 69.95 (*0-412-37890-6*) Chapman & Hall.

— Physics for Scientists & Engineers, Vol. 2. (C). 1983. pap. text, teacher ed. 27.50 (*0-03-058362-4*) Harcourt Coll Pubs.

— Physics in Modern World. 2nd ed. (C). 1990. pap. text, teacher ed. 34.00 (*0-15-570603-9*) Harcourt Coll Pubs.

Marion, Jerry B. & Thornton, Stephen T. Classical Dynamics of Particles & Systems. 3rd ed. 725p. (C). 1988. teacher ed. 20.00 (*0-15-507641-8*) SCP.

Marion, Jerry B., ed. see International Conference on Fast Neutron Physics S.

*__Marion, Jim.__ Putting on the Mind of Christ: The Inner Work of Christian Spirituality. 2000. 21.95 (*1-57174-173-9*) Hampton Roads Pub Co.

Marion, Joseph. Anti-Aging Manual: The Encyclopedia 2nd rev. ed. 1999. pap. text 49.95 (*0-9644999-1-6*) Info Pioneers.

— Anti-Aging Manual: The Encyclopedia of Natural Health. unabridged ed. LC 94-96784. 1314p. 1996. 89.00 (*0-9644999-0-8*) Info Pioneers.

An Asterisk (*) at the beginning of an entry indicates that the title is appearing for the first time.

— Why the End: Two Millenia of Prophecy & Its Fruitless Attempt to Awaken Humnity. 1999. pap. 29.95 (*0-9644999-2-4*) Info Pioneers.

Marion, Kathryn A. Success in the 'Real World' The Graduate's Complete Guide to Making the Most of Your Career (& Your Life)! LC 95-90069. 64p. (Orig.). 1995. pap. 5.95 (*0-9645391-5-2*) Educ Reality.

Marion, Kenneth P. Volunteer Firefighter. (Illus.). 32p. (J). (ps-2). 1990. pap. 4.00 (*0-945878-00-1*) JK Pub.

Marion Koogler McNay Art Museum Staff, jt. auth. see Udall, Sharyn R.

Marion, Lucy N. & American Nurses Association Staff. Nursing's Vision for Primary Care in the 21st Century. LC 96-10795. 47p. (Orig.). 1996. pap. 23.95 (*1-55810-124-1*, CH-30) Am Nurses Pub.

Marion, M. F. Van, see Van Marion, M. F.

Marion, Marian C. Early Childhood Family Education & Support. (C). 2001. pap. text 37.00 (*0-13-569641-0*, Macmillan Coll) P-H.

Marion, Mathieu. Wittgenstein, Finitism, & the Foundations of Mathematics. (Oxford Philosophical Monographs). 280p. 1999. text 65.00 (*0-19-823516-X*) OUP.

Marion, Mathieu, ed. Marion Quebec Studies in Philosophy of Science Pt. II: Biology, Psychology, Cognitive Science & Economics, Vol. 178. (Boston Studies in the Philosophy of Science). 326p. (C). 1995. lib. bdg. 154.00 (*0-7923-3560-0*, Pub. by Kluwer Academic) Kluwer Academic.

Marion, Mathieu & Cohen, Robert S., eds. Quebec Studies in the Philosophy of Science. LC 95-17467. 336p. (C). 1995. lib. bdg. 180.00 (*0-7923-3559-7*, Pub. by Kluwer Academic) Kluwer Academic.

— Quebec Studies in the Philosophy of Science, Set. LC 95-17467. (Boston Studies in the Philosophy of Science). 326p. (C). 1995. lib. bdg. 275.00 (*0-7923-3561-9*, Pub. by Kluwer Academic) Kluwer Academic.

Marion, Merrick J. College Undercover: What Every Student Needs to Know. LC 93-60309. 117p. (Orig.). 1994. pap. 12.95 (*1-56912-098-6*) Wharton Pub.

Marion, Nancy E. Crime & Criminal Justice in Ohio: Programs & Agencies. LC 98-68007. 280p. 1998. pap. 27.50 (*0-9646524-3-9*) Midwest Pr.

— A History of Federal Crime Control Initiatives, 1960-1993. LC 93-48214. (Criminology & Crime Control Policy Ser.). 288p. 1994. 59.95 (*0-275-94649-5*, Praeger Pubs) Greenwood.

— A Primer in the Politics of Criminal Justice. 120p. (C). 1995. pap. text 21.50 (*0-911577-32-7*, Criminal Justice) Willow Tree NY.

***Marion, Nino.** Math for Welders. LC 00-34077. (Illus.). 2000. write for info. (*1-56637-740-4*) Goodheart.

Marion, Nino. Math for Welders 2-3. LC 95-2199. (Illus.). 224p. (YA). (gr. 9-12). 1995. text 26.00 (*1-56637-194-5*) Goodheart.

Marion, Paul. Hit Singles. 16p. (Orig.). 1995. pap. 7.50 (*0-931507-07-3*) Loom Pr.

Marion, Paul, jt. auth. see Dublin, Thomas.

Marion, Paul, ed. see Ireland, David.

Marion, Paul, ed. see Kerouac, Jack.

Marion, Peller. Crisis-Proof Your Career: Finding Job Security in an Insecure Time. LC 92-39825. 1993. 17.95 (*1-55972-181-2*, Birch Ln Pr) Carol Pub Group.

Marion, Remy. On the Trail of Bears. LC 98-5829. (Nature Travel Guides Ser.). (Illus.). 128p. 1998. pap. 11.95 (*0-7641-0596-5*) Barron.

— Penguins. LC 99-18383. 1999. 21.95 (*0-8069-4232-0*) Sterling.

Marion, Remy, jt. auth. see Dumont, Jean-Michael.

Marion, Robert. The Intern Blues: The Private Ordeals of Three Young Doctors. 384p. 1990. mass mkt. 5.99 (*0-449-21898-8*, Crest) Fawcett.

— Learning to Play God. 1993. mass mkt. 5.99 (*0-449-22192-X*) Fawcett.

— Was George Washington Really the Father of Our Country? A Clinical Geneticist Looks at World History. LC 93-26588. (Illus.). 206p. 1993. 22.95 (*0-201-62255-6*) Addison-Wesley.

Marion, Russ. The Edge of Organization: Chaos & Complexity Theories of Formal Social Systems. LC 98-40063. 336p. 1999. 33.00 (*0-7619-1265-7*); pap. 14.99 (*0-7619-1266-5*) Sage.

Marion, Sheila. Tap Dance (A Dictionary in Labanotation) Cook et al, eds. (Illus.). 60p. (Orig.). 1986. pap. text 20.00 (*0-9602002-5-8*) Ray Cook.

Marion-Wild, E. C. The Prologue of the Gospel of St. John: Esoteric Studies. Roboz, Helga & Roboz, Steven, trs. from GER. 19p. 1984. pap. 3.75 (*0-919924-22-0*) Anthroposophic.

Marion, William, jt. auth. see Simon, Alan R.

Marioni, Tom. Tom Marioni: Sculpture & Installations, 1969-1997. 72p. 1997. pap. 10.00 (*1-891300-09-1*) Crown Point Pr.

Marioni, Tom, ed. Vision Vol. 5: Artists' Photographs. limited ed. (Illus.). 64p. 1981. ring bd. 20.00 (*1-891300-04-0*) Crown Point Pr.

Marioni, Tom & Kantor, Tadeusz. Vision Vol. 2: Eastern Europe. limited ed. (Illus.). 63p. 1976. pap. 20.00 (*1-891300-02-4*) Crown Point Pr.

Marioni, Tom, et al. Vision Vol. 1: California. (Illus.). 66p. 1975. pap. 50.00 (*1-891300-01-6*) Crown Point Pr.

Marioni, Tom, ed. see Close, Chuck.

Mariott, Bernadette M., ed. see Institute of Medicine Staff.

Mariotte, Edme. The Motion of Water & Other Fluids: Being a Treatise of Hydrostaticks. Albritton, Claude C., ed. Desaguliers, J. T., tr. (History of Geology Ser.). (Illus.). 1978. reprint ed. lib. bdg. 30.95 (*0-405-10449-9*) Ayer.

Mariotte, Edme, jt. auth. see Choi.

***Mariotte, Jeff.** Close to the Ground. (Angel Ser.: No. 4). 192p. (YA). (gr. 7 up). 2000. mass mkt. 5.99 (*0-671-04147-9*, Pocket Pulse) PB.

***Mariotte, Jeff, contrib. by.** The Xander Years, Vol. 2. (Buffy the Vampire Slayer Ser.: Vol. 15). (Illus.). 224p. (YA). (gr. 7 up). 2000. per. 4.99 (*0-671-03920-2*, Pocket Pulse) PB.

***Mariotte, Jeff & Cassady, John.** Desperadoes: Epidemic! Layman, John, ed. (Illus.). 48p. 1999. text (*1-56389-554-4*, Pub. by DC Comics) Diamond Comic Distributors Inc.

Mariotti, Arleen S. & Homan, Susan P. Linking Reading Assessment to Instruction: An Application Worktext for Elementary Classroom Teachers. 2nd ed. LC 97-10898. 1997. pap. 23.50 (*0-8058-2651-3*) L Erlbaum Assocs.

Mariotti, Claudio, jt. ed. see Lecomte, Paul.

Mariotti, Federico A., tr. see Hunter, Wayne & Hunter, Emily.

Mariotti, J. M. & Alloin, D. M. Planets Outside the Solar System: Theory & Observations. LC 99-25782. (NATO ASI Series, Series C, Mathematical & Physical Sciences). 1999. write for info. (*0-7923-5708-6*) Kluwer Academic.

Mariotti, Jean-Marie, jt. ed. see Alloin, D. M.

Mariotti, Jean-Marie, jt. ed. see Alloin, Danielle M.

Mariotti, John L. The Power of Partnerships: The Next Step Beyond TQM, Reengineering & Lean Production : A Competitive Cornerstone for the 21st Century. LC 95-1579. 1995. 24.95 (*1-55786-717-8*) Blackwell Pubs.

— The Shape Shifters: Continuous Change for Competitive Advantage. LC 97-33630. (Business Technology Ser.). 320p. 1997. 29.95 (*0-442-02559-9*, VNR) Wiley.

Mariotti, John L. The Shape Shifters: Continuous Change for Competitive Advantage. 276p. 1997. 29.95 (*0-471-29254-0*, VNR) Wiley.

Mariotti, John L. Smart Things to Know About Brands. 1999. pap. text 16.99 (*1-84112-039-1*) Capstone Pub NH.

***Mariotti, John L.** Smart Things to Know about Marketing. (Smart Things to Know about... Ser.). 2000. pap. 16.95 (*1-84112-095-2*) Capstone Pub NH.

Mariotti, Mario. Hand Games. (Illus.). 32p. (J). (ps-4). 1992. 11.95 (*0-916291-43-X*) Kane-Miller Bk.

— Hands Off! (Illus.). 40p. (J). (ps-4). 1990. 10.95 (*0-916291-29-4*) Kane-Miller Bk.

— Hanimations. Orig. Title: Rimani. (Illus.). 40p. (J). (ps-4). 1989. 10.95 (*0-916291-22-7*) Kane-Miller Bk.

— Hanimations. Orig. Title: Rimani. (Illus.). 40p. (J). (ps-4). 1998. pap. 7.95 (*0-916291-84-7*) Kane-Miller Bk.

Mariotti, Richard & Fife, Bruce. How to Be a Literary Agent: An Introductory Guide to Literary Representation. LC 94-15179. 190p. 1994. pap. 16.00 (*0-941599-26-4*, Pub. by Piccadilly Bks) Empire Pub Srvs.

***Mariotti, Steve.** The Young Entrepreneur's Guide to Starting & Running a Business. 272p. (J). 2000. pap. 17.00 (*0-8129-3306-0*, Times Bks) Crown Pub Group.

***Mariotti, Steve & National Federation for Teaching Entrepreneurship.** The Very, Very Rich: How They Got That Way & How You Can Too! LC 00-37878. 192p. 2000. pap. 13.99 (*1-56414-469-0*) Career Pr Inc.

Mariotti, Steve & Towle, Tony. The Young Entrepreneur's Guide to Starting & Running a Business. 256p. 1996. pap. 15.00 (*0-8129-2627-7*, Times Bks) Crown Pub Group.

***Mariotti, Steve, et al.** Entrepreneurs in Profile: "How 20 of the World's Greatest Entrepreneurs Built Their Business Empires... And How You Can Too" LC 00-34289. 2000. pap. write for info. (*1-56414-488-7*) Career Pr Inc.

Maris, Edward. Coins of New Jersey. (Illus.). 1987. reprint ed. pap. 15.00 (*0-685-05536-1*) S J Durst.

Maris, Humphrey J., ed. see International Conference on Phonon Scattering in C.

Maris, Hyllus & Borg, Sonia. Women of the Sun. 234p. 1983. 17.95 (*0-86819-081-0*, Pub. by Currency Pr) Accents Pubns.

Maris, Judy, ed. see Barry, Charles L. & Johnson, Kenneth G.

Maris, Mariann, ed. see Narada Media Staff.

Maris, Michael & Monton, Dennis. Looking Forever Young. (YA). 1995. write for info. (*1-879234-30-0*) Herit Pub TX.

Maris, Ron. Ducks Quack. LC 91-58726. (Illus.). 14p. (J). (ps). 1992. bds. 4.95 (*1-56402-080-0*) Candlewick Pr.

— Frogs Jump. LC 91-58730. (Illus.). 14p. (J). (ps). 1992. 4.95 (*1-56402-081-9*) Candlewick Pr.

— Hold Tight, Bear! 93rd ed. 1993. pap. text 10.25 (*0-15-300309-X*, Harcourt Child Bks) Harcourt.

Maris, Ronald, ed. Biology of Suicide. LC 86-14207. (Illus.). 244p. 1986. reprint ed. pap. 75.70 (*0-608-07814-X*, 205988200010) Bks Demand.

— Understanding & Preventing Suicide, Vol. 18, No. 1. 118p. 1988. lib. bdg. 17.50 (*0-89862-583-1*) Guilford Pubns.

Maris, Ronald W. Pathways to Suicide: A Survey of Self-Destructive Behaviors. LC 80-24520. (Illus.). 399p. 1981. reprint ed. pap. 123.70 (*0-7837-1111-5*, 204164100021) Bks Demand.

Maris, Ronald W., ed. Understanding & Preventing Suicide: Plenary Papers of the First Combined Meeting of the AAS & IASP. LC 88-175957. (Illus.). 142p. reprint ed. pap. 44.10 (*0-7837-1204-9*, 204173600023) Bks Demand.

Maris, Ronald W., et al, eds. Assessment & Prediction of Suicide. LC 91-35408. 697p. 1992. lib. bdg. 75.00 (*0-89862-791-5*) Guilford Pubns.

— Review of Suicidology, 1997. 286p. 1997. lib. bdg. 40.00 (*1-57230-212-7*, 0212) Guilford Pubns.

— Review of Suicidology, 2000. 268p. 2000. lib. bdg. 35.00 (*1-57230-503-7*, C0503) Guilford Pubns.

Maris, Ronald W. & Platt, Stephen D. Suicide & Its Prevention: Role of Attitudes in Suicidal Behavior. LC 87-29976. (Advances in Suicidology Ser.: Vol. I). ix, 371p. (Orig.). 1989. pap. 110.50 (*90-04-08613-7*) Brill Academic Pubs.

***Maris, Ronald W., et al.** Comprehensive Textbook of Suicidology. 610p. 2000. lib. bdg. 75.00 (*1-57230-541-X*, C0541) Guilford Pubns.

Maris, Ronald W., jt. ed. see Battin, Margaret P.

Mariscal, Blanca Lopez de, see Lopez de Mariscal, Blanca.

Mariscal, George. Aztlan & Viet Nam: Chicano & Chicana Experiences of the War. LC 98-39737. (American Crossroads Ser.). 337p. 1999. 50.00 (*0-520-21404-8*, Pub. by U CA Pr); pap. 18.95 (*0-520-21405-6*, Pub. by U CA Pr) Cal Prin Full Svc.

— Contradictory Subjects: Quevedo, Cervantes & Seventeenth-Century Spanish Culture. LC 91-13369. 248p. 1991. text 35.00 (*0-8014-2604-9*) Cornell U Pr.

***Mariscal, Javier.** Implementing & Supporting Microsoft SNA Server 4.0: Exam 70-085. LC 99-27344. (MCSE Ser.). 642p. 1999. pap. text 49.99 (*0-13-011240-2*) P-H.

Marisch, Gerald. The W. D. Gann Method of Trading. 1990. 50.00 (*0-930233-42-5*) Windsor.

Mariscol. Biology of Marine Life. 2nd ed. 1998. 11.74 (*0-07-230246-1*) McGraw.

Mariska, J. T., jt. ed. see Bentley, R. D.

Mariska, John T. The Solar Transition Region. (Cambridge Astrophysics Ser.: No. 23). (Illus.). 290p. (C). 1993. text 74.95 (*0-521-38261-0*) Cambridge U Pr.

Marison, Fiscar, tr. see Agreda, Mary.

Marissen, Michael. Lutheranism, Anti-Judaism, & Bach's St. John's Passion: Witha an Annotated Literal Translation of the Libretto. LC 97-40060. 128p. 1998. 16.95 (*0-19-511471-X*) OUP.

— The Social & Religious Designs of J. S. Bach's Brandenburg Concertos. LC 94-28688. 160p. 1995. text 27.50 (*0-691-03739-6*, Pub. by Princeton U Pr) Cal Prin Full Svc.

***Marissen, Michael.** Social & Religious Designs of J.S. Bach's Brandenburg Concertos. 1999. pap. text 14.95 (*0-691-00686-5*, Pub. by Princeton U Pr) Cal Prin Full Svc.

Marissen, Michael, ed. Bach Perspectives: Creative Responses to Bach from Mozart to Hindemith. (Bach Perspectives Ser.: Vol. 3). (Illus.). x, 160p. 1998. text 65.00 (*0-8032-1048-5*) U of Nebr Pr.

Marissen, Michael, jt. auth. see Melamed, Daniel R.

Marisson, Andrew. Free Trade & Its Reception, 1815-1960: Freedom & Trade, Vol. 1. LC 97-28941. (Routledge Explorations in Economic History Ser.: 8). 336p. (C). 1998. 90.00 (*0-415-15527-4*) Routledge.

Marist Parents' Club Staff, ed. A Touch of Atlanta. (Illus.). 256p. 1990. 16.95 (*0-9626204-0-8*) Marist Parents.

Maristed, Kai. Out after Dark: A Novel. LC 92-34341. 328p. 1993. 22.00 (*1-877946-30-3*) Permanent Pr.

Maritain, Jacques. Approches Sans Entraves. (FRE.). 595p. 1973. 39.95 (*0-7859-5534-8*) Fr & Eur.

— Art & Scholasticism: With Other Essays. Scanlan, J. F., tr. LC 70-152196. (Essay Index Reprint Ser.). 1977. reprint ed. 16.95 (*0-8369-2241-7*) Ayer.

— Art et Scolastique. 4th ed. (FRE.). 280p. 1965. 19.95 (*0-8288-9854-5*, F111960) Fr & Eur.

Maritain, Jacques. Bergsonian Philosophy & Thomism, Vol.1. (The Collected Works of Jacques Maritain Ser.). 288p. Date not set. 35.00 (*0-268-02152-X*, Pub. by U of Notre Dame Pr) Chicago Distribution Ctr.

Maritain, Jacques. Carnet de Notes. 2nd ed. (FRE., Illus.). 424p. 1965. 34.95 (*0-8288-9887-1*, F11670) Fr & Eur.

— A Christian Looks at the Jewish Question. LC 73-2216. (Jewish People; History, Religion, Literature Ser.). 1980. reprint ed. 19.95 (*0-405-05280-4*) Ayer.

— Christianity & Democracy. LC 83-80191. 250p. 1986. pap. 12.95 (*0-89870-030-2*) Ignatius Pr.

— Christianity & Democracy. Anson, Doris C., tr. from FRE. LC 72-6765. (Essay Index Reprint Ser.). 1980. reprint ed. 18.95 (*0-8369-7243-0*) Ayer.

— Court Traite de l'Existence et de l'Existant. (FRE.). 238p. 1964. 11.95 (*0-8288-9846-4*, F111680) Fr & Eur.

— Creative Intuition in Art & Poetry. LC 53-5537. (Bollingen Ser.: No. 35). 517p. 1981. reprint ed. pap. 160.30 (*0-7837-8592-5*, 204940700011) Bks Demand.

— De Bergson a Thomas d'Aquin. (FRE.). 336p. 1944. pap. write for info. (*0-7859-4608-X*) Fr & Eur.

— De la Grace et le l'Humanite de Jesus. 2nd ed. (FRE.). 156p. 1967. 15.95 (*0-8288-9848-0*, F111690) Fr & Eur.

— De l'Eglise du Christ. (FRE.). 430p. 1970. 15.95 (*0-8288-9847-2*, F111685) Fr & Eur.

— Degrees of Knowledge. McInerny, Ralph, ed. Phelan, Gerald B., tr. LC 94-45159. (The Collected Works of Jacques Maritain Ser.: Vol. 7). 528p. 1999. pap. text 25.00 (*0-268-00886-8*, Pub. by U of Notre Dame Pr) Chicago Distribution Ctr.

— Dieu et la Permission du Mal. 3rd ed. (FRE.). 116p. 1963. 13.95 (*0-8288-9849-9*, F111710) Fr & Eur.

— Distinguer Pour Unir: Les Degres du Savoir. 8th ed. (FRE.). 946p. 1959. 59.95 (*0-8288-9850-2*, F111720) Fr & Eur.

— Education at the Crossroads. (Terry Lectures Ser.). 132p. (C). 1943. pap. 13.00 (*0-300-00163-0*, Y15) Yale U Pr.

— Elements de Philosophie: Introduction Generale a la Philosophie. 33rd ed. 240p. 1963. pap. 29.95 (*0-7859-5126-1*, F111730) Fr & Eur.

— Freedom & the Modern World. O'Sullivan, Richard, tr. LC 77-150414. 231p. (C). 1971. reprint ed. 35.00 (*0-87752-147-6*) Gordian.

— L' Homme et l'Etat. 2nd ed. (FRE.). 212p. 1965. 15.95 (*0-8288-9851-0*, F111740) Fr & Eur.

— Humanisme Integral. 320p. 1968. 9.95 (*0-7859-0698-3*) Fr & Eur.

— Integral Humanism, Freedom in the Modern World, & A Letter on Independence. Bird, Otto, ed. O'Sullivan, Richard et al, trs. from FRE. LC 95-50323. (Collected Works of Jacques Maritain: No. 11). 376p. (C). 1996. text 35.00 (*0-268-01177-X*) U of Notre Dame Pr.

— An Introduction to the Basic Problems of Moral Philosophy. Borgerhoff, Cornelia N., tr. from FRE. LC 90-32535.Tr. of Neuf lecons sur les notions premieres de la philosophie Morale. (Illus.). 224p. 1990. 14.95 (*0-87343-052-2*) Magi Bks.

— L' Intuition Creatrice dans l'Art et dans la Poesie. (FRE., Illus.). 424p. 1966. 69.95 (*0-8288-9911-8*, F16910) Fr & Eur.

— Man & the State. LC 51-555. 1995. pap. text 11.95 (*0-226-50552-9*, P5) U Ch Pr.

— Man & the State. LC 97-41522. 224p. 1998. reprint ed. pap. 19.95 (*0-8132-0905-6*) Cath U Pr.

— Maritain-Mounier: Correspondance, 1929-1939. Mounier, Emmanuel, ed. (FRE.). 272p. 1973. 34.95 (*0-7859-0107-8*, M3734) Fr & Eur.

— Le Mystere D'Israel. (FRE.). 302p. 1990. pap. 29.95 (*0-7859-1601-6*, 222003173X) Fr & Eur.

— On the Philosophy of History. LC 73-128059. 180p. 1973. reprint ed. 29.50 (*0-678-02760-9*) Kelley.

— On the Use of Philosophy: Three Essays. LC 81-13338. 71p. 1982. reprint ed. lib. bdg. 42.50 (*0-313-23199-0*, MAUP, Greenwood Pr) Greenwood.

— Paysanne de la Garonne. 405p. 1966. 29.95 (*0-8288-7445-X*) Fr & Eur.

— Le Payson de Garonne: Un Vieux Laic s'Interroge a Propos du Temps Present. 19.95 (*0-685-34274-3*) Fr & Eur.

— Le Peche de l'Ange. De La Trinite & Journet, eds. (FRE.). 248p. 1961. pap. 39.95 (*0-686-56360-3*) Fr & Eur.

— Person & the Common Good. 1966. pap. 7.00 (*0-268-00204-5*) U of Notre Dame Pr.

— La Philosophie Morale: Examen Historique et Critique des Grandes Systemes. (FRE.). 592p. 1960. 39.95 (*0-8288-9852-9*, F111820) Fr & Eur.

— Pour une Philosophie de l'Education. (FRE.). 254p. 1960. 18.95 (*0-8288-9853-7*, F111830) Fr & Eur.

— A Preface to Metaphysics: Seven Lectures on Being. LC 74-157346. (Select Bibliographies Reprint Ser.). 1979. reprint ed. 20.95 (*0-8369-5807-1*) Ayer.

— Ransoming the Time. Binsse, Harry L., tr. LC 70-165665. 322p. 1972. reprint ed. 50.00 (*0-87752-153-0*) Gordian.

— Reflections on America. LC 74-26882. 205p. 1975. reprint ed. 40.00 (*0-87752-166-2*) Gordian.

— Reflexions sur L'Amerique. (FRE.). 224p. 1958. pap. 9.95 (*0-7859-5536-4*) Fr & Eur.

— Religion et Culture. (FRE.). 174p. 1991. pap. 12.95 (*0-7859-1447-1*, 2220031578) Fr & Eur.

— Responsabilite de l'Artiste. 128p. 1961. 9.95 (*0-686-56367-0*) Fr & Eur.

— Responsibility of the Artist. LC 70-150415. 120p. 1972. reprint ed. 40.00 (*0-87752-145-X*) Gordian.

— Rights of Man & Natural Law. LC 74-150416. 120p. 1971. reprint ed. 30.00 (*0-87752-146-8*) Gordian.

— St. Thomas & the Problem of Evil. (Aquinas Lectures). 1942. 15.00 (*0-87462-106-2*) Marquette.

— Scholasticism & Politics. LC 72-353. (Essay Index Reprint Ser.). 1977. reprint ed. 18.95 (*0-8369-2805-9*) Ayer.

— Situation de la Poesie. 2nd ed. (FRE.). 144p. 1964. 10.95 (*0-8288-9912-6*, F16911) Fr & Eur.

— Theonas. LC 74-84325. (Essay Index Reprint Ser.). 1977. 19.95 (*0-8369-1095-8*) Ayer.

— Three Reformers: Luther-Descartes-Rousseau. LC 78-98780. 234p. 1970. reprint ed. lib. bdg. 35.00 (*0-8371-2825-0*, MATR, Greenwood Pr) Greenwood.

— True Humanism. Adamson, M. R., tr. LC 71-114888. (Select Bibliographies Reprint Ser.). 1977. 35.52 (*0-8369-5292-8*) Ayer.

— True Humanism. 3rd ed. Adamson, Margot, tr. LC 71-98781. 304p. 1970. reprint ed. lib. bdg. 41.50 (*0-8371-2902-8*, MAHU, Greenwood Pr) Greenwood.

— Untrammeled Approaches. Doering, Bernard, ed. LC 96-26434. (Collected Works of Jacques Maritain: Vol. 20). Orig. Title: Approches San Entraves. 495p. (C). 1996. text 35.00 (*0-268-04300-0*) U of Notre Dame Pr.

Maritain, Jacques & Maritain, Raissa. Oeuvres Completes, 1952-1959, 15 vols., Vol. X. (FRE.). 1234p. 1985. 79.99 (*2-8271-0302-8*) I B C A.

— Oeuvres Completes, 1906-1920, 15 vols., Vol. 1. 1175p. 1986. 79.00 (*2-8271-0338-9*) I B C A.

— Oeuvres Completes, 1935-1938, 15 vols., Vol. VI. (FRE.). 1317p. 1984. 72.99 (*2-8271-0275-7*, Pub. by Editions Univ) I B C A.

— Oeuvres Completes, 1939-1943 Vol. 7. Allion, J. et al, eds. (FRE.). 1402p. (C). 1988. 87.49 (*2-8271-0388-5*, Pub. by Editions Univ) I B C A.

— Oeuvres Completes, 1932-1935, 15 vols., Vol. V. (FRE.). 1153p. 1982. 72.99 (*2-8271-0224-2*, Pub. by Editions Univ) I B C A.

— Oeuvres Completes, 1924-1929, 15 vols., Vol. III. (FRE.). 1472p. 1985. 79.99 (*2-8271-0287-0*) I B C A.

— Oeuvres Completes, 1929-1932, 15 vols., Vol. IV. (FRE.). 1259p. 1983. 72.99 (*2-8271-0259-5*, Pub. by Editions Univ) I B C A.

Maritain, Raissa, jt. auth. see Maritain, Jacques.

Maritain, Raissa, jt. auth. see Maritan, Jacques.

Maritan, Jacques & Maritain, Raissa. Oeuvres Completes, 1920 to 1923, 15 vols., Vol. 2. Allion, J. et al, eds. 1331p. 1987. 79.99 (*2-8271-0350-8*) I B C A.

Maritato, Luigi, jt. ed. see Cifarelli, Luisa.

Maritato, Nancy, ed. see National Research Council Staff.

***Maritime & Coastguard Agency Staff.** The Carriage of Cargoes Vol. 1: Packaged Cargoes & Cargo Units (Including Containers & Vehicles): Instructions for the Guidance of Surveyors. 64p. 1999. ring bd. 30.00 (*0-11-552113-5*, Pub. by Statnry Office) Balogh.

M

— The Carriage of Cargoes Vol. 2: Solid Bulk Cargoes: Instructions for the Guidance of Surveyors. 40p. 1999. ring bd. 30.00 (*0-11-552127-5*, Pub. by Statnry Office) Balogh.
— Code of Safe Working Practices for Merchant Seamen, Section 4. 63p. 1999. ring bd. 11.00 (*0-11-552041-4*, Pub. by Statnry Office) Balogh.
— Fire Protection Arrangements: Instructions for the Guidance of Surveyors. 145p. 1999. ring bd. 50.00 (*0-11-552000-7*, Pub. by Statnry Office) Balogh.
— International Code of Safety for High Speed Craft: HSC Code: Instructions for the Guidance of Surveyors. 120p. 1999. ring bd. 70.00 (*0-11-552084-8*, Pub. by Statnry Office) Balogh.
— International Safety Management Code for the Safe Operation of Ships & for Pollution Prevention: The ISM Code: Instructions for the Guidance of Surveyors. 34p. 1999. ring bd. 30.00 (*0-11-551810-X*, Pub. by Statnry Office) Balogh.
— Load Line: Instructions for the Guidance of Surveyors. 94p. 1999. ring bd. 50.00 (*0-11-551999-8*, Pub. by Statnry Office) Balogh.
— Merchant Shipping Navigational Equipment: Instructions for the Guidance of Surveyors. 24p. 1999. ring bd. 30.00 (*0-11-552198-4*, Pub. by Statnry Office) Balogh.
— Passenger Ship Construction - Classes I, II & II(A) Instructions for the Guidance of Surveyors. 94p. 1999. ring bd. 50.00 (*0-11-551998-X*, Pub. by Statnry Office) Balogh.
— Passenger Ship Construction Classes III to VI(A) Instructions for the Guidance of Surveyors. 94p. 1999. ring bd. 70.00 (*0-11-552114-3*, Pub. by Statnry Office) Balogh.
— The Prevention of Oil Pollution from Ships: Instructions for the Guidance of Surveyors. 82p. 1999. ring bd. 50.00 (*0-11-552111-9*, Pub. by Statnry Office) Balogh.
— The Prevention of Pollution by Garbage from Ships & the Provision & Use of Port Waste Reception Facilities: Instructions for the Guidance of Surveyors. 22p. 1999. ring bd. 30.00 (*0-11-552107-0*, Pub. by Statnry Office) Balogh.
— Radio Installations on Fishing Vessels: Instructions for the Guidance of Surveyors. 12p. 1999. ring bd. 30.00 (*0-11-552199-2*, Pub. by Statnry Office) Balogh.
— Radio Installations on GMDSS Ships: Instructions to Surveyors. 33p. 1992. write for info. (*0-11-551101-6*, Pub. by Statnry Office) Balogh.
— Radio Installations on GMDSS Ships: Instructions to Surveyors. 33p. 1998. ring bd. 24.00 (*0-11-552010-4*, Pub. by Statnry Office) Balogh.

Maritime & Coastguard Agency Staff. The Ship Captain's Medical Guide. 22nd ed. (Safety Report Ser.). (Illus.). iv, 232p. 1999. 79.95 (*0-11-551658-1*, Pub. by Statnry Office) Balogh.

***Maritime & Coastguard Agency Staff.** Survey of Chemical Tankers: Instructions for the Guidance of Surveyors. 138p. 1999. ring bd. 70.00 (*0-11-552110-0*, Pub. by Statnry Office) Balogh.
— Survey of Crew Accommodation in Merchant Ships: Instructions for the Guidance of Surveyors. 52p. 1999. ring bd. 50.00 (*0-11-552116-X*, Pub. by Statnry Office) Balogh.
— Survey of Gas Carriers: Instructions for the Guidance of Surveyors. 91p. 1999. ring bd. 70.00 (*0-11-552112-7*, Pub. by Statnry Office) Balogh.
— Survey of Life-Saving Appliances Vol. 1: Instructions for the Guidance of Surveyors. 129p. 1999. ring bd. 50.00 (*0-11-552001-5*, Pub. by Statnry Office) Balogh.
— Survey of Life-Saving Appliances Vol. 2: Testing of Life-Saving Appliances: Instructions for the Guidance of Surveyors. 130p. 1999. ring bd. 50.00 (*0-11-552002-3*, Pub. by Statnry Office) Balogh.
— Survey of Lights & Signalling Equipment: Instructions for the Guidance of Surveyors. 30p. 1999. ring bd. 30.00 (*0-11-552173-9*, Pub. by Statnry Office) Balogh.

Maritime Books Staff. A-Z of Ships Badges, 1919-1989, Vol. 1. (C). 1986. text 100.00 (*0-7855-5293-6*, Pub. by Maritime Bks) St Mut.
— A-Z of Ships Badges, 1919-1989, Vol. 2. (C). 1986. text 100.00 (*1-870842-02-2*, Pub. by Maritime Bks) St Mut.
— Aircraft of the Royal Navy since 1945. (C). 1986. 59.00 (*0-907771-06-8*, Pub. by Maritime Bks) St Mut.
— Badges & Battle Honours of HM Ships. (C). 1986. text 290.00 (*0-907771-26-2*, Pub. by Maritime Bks) St Mut.
— British Warships & Auxiliaries, 1990-91. (C). 1986. text 59.00 (*0-907771-44-0*, Pub. by Maritime Bks) St Mut.
— British Warships since Nineteen Forty-Five, Pt. 1. (C). 1986. text 65.00 (*0-9506323-4-1*, Pub. by Maritime Bks) St Mut.
— British Warships since Nineteen Forty-Five, Pt. 4. (C). 1986. text 40.00 (*0-907771-12-2*, Pub. by Maritime Bks) St Mut.
— British Warships since Nineteen Forty-Five, Pt. 5. (C). 1986. text 50.00 (*0-907771-13-0*, Pub. by Maritime Bks) St Mut.
— Channel Sweep. (C). 1986. text 60.00 (*0-907771-40-8*, Pub. by Maritime Bks) St Mut.
— Chatham Dockyard Story. (C). 1986. text 70.00 (*0-948193-30-1*, Pub. by Maritime Bks) St Mut.
— Cruisers of the Royal & Commonwealth Navies. (C). 1986. text 120.00 (*0-907771-35-1*, Pub. by Maritime Bks) St Mut.
— Encyclopaedia of Fleet Air Arm. (C). 1986. text 130.00 (*0-85059-760-9*, Pub. by Maritime Bks) St Mut.
— Encyclopedia of HM Submarines, 1901-55. (C). 1986. text 600.00 (*0-907771-42-4*, Pub. by Maritime Bks) St Mut.
— Falklands Task Force Portfolio, Pt. 1. (C). 1986. text 90.00 (*0-907771-02-5*, Pub. by Maritime Bks) St Mut.
— Falklands Task Force Portfolio, Pt. 2. (C). 1986. text 90.00 (*0-907771-03-3*, Pub. by Maritime Bks) St Mut.
— Fifty Years of Naval Tugs. (C). 1986. text 50.00 (*0-907771-25-4*, Pub. by Maritime Bks) St Mut.
— The Grand Scuttle: The Sinking of the German Fleet at Scapa Flow. (C). 1986. text 40.00 (*0-86228-099-0*, Pub. by Maritime Bks) St Mut.
— Heritage of Ships. (C). 1986. text 95.00 (*0-285-62855-0*, Pub. by Maritime Bks) St Mut.
— HMS Ark Royal - The Ship & Her Men. (C). 1986. text 35.00 (*0-907771-39-4*, Pub. by Maritime Bks) St Mut.
— HMS Bulwark, 1948-84. (C). 1986. text 50.00 (*0-907771-27-0*, Pub. by Maritime Bks) St Mut.
— HMS Ganges - Roll on My Dozen. (C). 1986. text 130.00 (*0-7855-5295-2*, Pub. by Maritime Bks) St Mut.
— HMS Hermes, 1959-84. (C). 1986. text 100.00 (*0-907771-16-5*, Pub. by Maritime Bks); pap. text 50.00 (*0-907771-17-3*, Pub. by Maritime Bks) St Mut.
— HMS Plymouth - Her Story. (C). 1986. pap. text 35.00 (*0-7855-5310-X*, Pub. by Maritime Bks) St Mut.
— Jackspeak RN Slanguage. (C). 1986. text 90.00 (*0-7855-5300-2*, Pub. by Maritime Bks) St Mut.
— Laugh with the Navy Too. (C). 1986. text 50.00 (*0-907771-01-7*, Pub. by Maritime Bks) St Mut.
— Modern Military Techniques Carriers. (C). 1986. pap. text 30.00 (*0-583-31003-6*, Pub. by Maritime Bks) St Mut.
— Modern Military Techniques Combined: OPS. (C). 1986. pap. text 40.00 (*0-583-31004-4*, Pub. by Maritime Bks) St Mut.
— Modern Military Techniques Submarines. (C). 1986. pap. text 40.00 (*0-583-31009-5*, Pub. by Maritime Bks) St Mut.
— Naval Wrecks of Scapa Flow. (C). 1986. text 110.00 (*0-7855-5298-7*, Pub. by Maritime Bks) St Mut.
— Our Falklands War. (C). 1986. text 60.00 (*0-907771-08-4*, Pub. by Maritime Bks) St Mut.
— Portsmouth Built Warships, 1497-1967. (C). 1986. text 50.00 (*0-7855-5294-4*, Pub. by Maritime Bks) St Mut.
— The Royal Navy at Malta Vol. 1: The Victorian Era, 2 vols. (C). 1986. text 190.00 (*0-907771-43-2*, Pub. by Maritime Bks) St Mut.
— The Royal Navy at Portland since 1845. (C). 1986. text 100.00 (*0-907771-29-7*, Pub. by Maritime Bks) St Mut.
— The Royal Navy in Focus, 1950-59. (C). 1986. text 70.00 (*0-907771-22-X*, Pub. by Maritime Bks) St Mut.
— The Royal Navy in Focus, 1940-49. (C). 1986. text 60.00 (*0-907771-11-4*, Pub. by Maritime Bks) St Mut.
— The Royal Navy in Focus, 1960-69. (C). 1986. text 70.00 (*0-907771-33-5*, Pub. by Maritime Bks) St Mut.
— The Royal Navy in Focus, 1930-39. (C). 1986. text 60.00 (*0-907771-04-1*, Pub. by Maritime Bks) St Mut.
— Sea Power in the Falklands. (C). 1986. text 100.00 (*0-03-069534-1*, Pub. by Maritime Bks) St Mut.
— Ships & Aircraft of the Royal Navy. (C). 1986. pap. text 75.00 (*0-907771-23-8*, Pub. by Maritime Bks) St Mut.
— Submarine Versus U Boat. (C). 1986. text 130.00 (*0-7855-5306-1*, Pub. by Maritime Bks) St Mut.
— Warrior - The First & Last. (C). 1986. text 75.00 (*0-907771-34-3*, Pub. by Maritime Bks) St Mut.
— We Joined the Navy (Winton) (C). 1986. text 60.00 (*0-907771-38-6*, Pub. by Maritime Bks) St Mut.
— Wrecks of Scapa Flow. (C). 1986. text 65.00 (*0-7855-5299-5*, Pub. by Maritime Bks) St Mut.

Maritime Books Staff, ed. Chatham Built Warships since Eighteen Eighty. (C). 1986. text 70.00 (*0-907771-07-6*, Pub. by Maritime Bks) St Mut.
— Devonport Dockyard Story. (C). 1986. text 60.00 (*0-907771-14-9*, Pub. by Maritime Bks) St Mut.
— The Ship That Torpedoed Herself. (C). 1986. text 60.00 (*0-7855-5296-0*, Pub. by Maritime Bks) St Mut.
— This Great Harbour Scapa Flow. (C). 1986. text 200.00 (*0-7855-5297-9*, Pub. by Maritime Bks) St Mut.

Mariton, M. Jump Linear Systems in Automatic Control. (Illus.). 320p. 1990. text 175.00 (*0-8247-8200-3*) Dekker.

Maritz, J. S. Distribution-Free Statistical Methods. 2nd ed. 256p. 1995. ring bd. 65.95 (*0-412-55260-4*, Chap & Hall CRC) CRC Pr.

Mariuaux. The Triumph of Love. Magruder, James, tr. from FRE. LC 95-150100. 1994. pap. 5.25 (*0-8222-1415-6*) Dramatists Play.

Marius. College Handbook. 4th ed. 1993. 28.12 (*0-07-040482-8*) McGraw.
— Dutch Painters of the Nineteenth Century. Norman, Geraldine, ed. (Illus.). 328p. 1975. 69.50 (*0-902028-21-9*) Antique Collect.
— A Short Guide to Writing about History. 3rd ed. LC 98-20852. 208p. (C). 1998. pap. 24.20 (*0-321-02387-0*) Addson-Wesley Educ.

Marius, Richard. After the War. LC 94-2927. 640p. (J). 1994. reprint ed. pap. 16.95 (*1-55853-273-0*) Rutledge Hill Pr.
— Bound for the Promised Land. LC 93-18163. 1993. reprint ed. pap. 14.95 (*1-55853-226-9*) Rutledge Hill Pr.
— The Coming of Rain. LC 91-23076. 448p. 1991. reprint ed. pap. 12.95 (*1-55853-142-4*) Rutledge Hill Pr.
— Martin Luther: The Christian Between God & Death. LC 98-36856. (Illus.). 592p. 1999. 35.00 (*0-674-55090-0*) HUP.

***Marius, Richard.** Martin Luther: The Christian Between God & Death. 592p. 2000. pap. 17.95 (*0-674-00387-X*) HUP.

Marius, Richard. Thomas More: A Biography. 592p. 1999. pap. text 18.95 (*0-674-88525-2*) HUP.
— A Writer's Companion. 3rd ed. 288p. (C). 1994. pap. 25.63 (*0-07-040526-3*) McGraw.
— A Writer's Companion. 4th ed. LC 98-7379. 264p. 1998. pap. 25.63 (*0-07-304015-0*) McGraw.

Marius, Richard & Frome, Keith W., eds. The Columbia Book of Civil War Poetry. LC 94-6481. (Illus.). 560p. 1994. 31.50 (*0-231-10002-7*) Col U Pr.

Marius, Richard & Wiener, Harvey S. The McGraw-Hill College Handbook. 4th ed. LC 93-29714. 640p. (C). 1994. 39.06 (*0-07-040481-X*) McGraw.

Marius, Richard C. A Short Guide to Writing about History. (C). 1987. pap. text 7.50 (*0-316-54621-6*) Little.

Mariuzzi, G., jt. ed. see Tosi, Piero.

Marivaux. La Dispute. Wertenbaker, Timberlake, tr. from FRE. 1989. pap. 3.50 (*0-87129-126-6*, L71) Dramatic Pub.
— La Double Inconstance - le Triomphe de l'Amour. unabridged ed. (FRE.). 1996. pap. 5.95 (*2-87714-336-8*, Pub. by Bookking Intl) Distribks Inc.
— False Admissions, Playscript. Wertenbaker, Timberlake, tr. from FRE. 1992. pap. 5.95 (*0-87129-124-X*, F51) Dramatic Pub.
— Successful Strategies. Wertenbaker, Timberlake, tr. from FRE. 1992. pap. 5.95 (*0-87129-125-8*, S82) Dramatic Pub.

Marivaux, A. Oeuvres de Jeunesse. (FRE.). 1972. lib. bdg. 95.00 (*0-8288-3552-7*, F48070) Fr & Eur.
— Romans - Recits, Contes et Nouvelles. (FRE.). 1949. lib. bdg. 85.00 (*0-8288-3553-5*, F48100) Fr & Eur.
— Theatre Complet. (FRE.). 1950. lib. bdg. 110.00 (*0-8288-3554-3*, F48010) Fr & Eur.
— Theatre Complete. deluxe ed. Coulet, Henri & Gilot, Michel, eds. (FRE.). 11376p. 1993. 150.00 (*0-7859-0967-2*, 2070112594) Fr & Eur.
— Three Plays. Wadsworth, Stephen, tr. from FRE. LC 98-38708. 240p. 1999. pap. 19.95 (*1-57525-148-5*) Smith & Kraus.

Marivaux, Pierre Carlet de Chamblain de. Arlequin Poli par L'Amour. (FRE.). 32p. 1951. 7.95 (*0-8288-9602-X*, F48130) Fr & Eur.
— La Double Inconstance. (FRE.). 1987. pap. 10.95 (*0-7859-3136-8*) Fr & Eur.
— L' Ecole des Meres: La Mere Confidente. (FRE.). pap. write for info. (*0-7859-3178-3*, 2253063266) Fr & Eur.
— L' Epreuve. (FRE.). 280p. 1991. pap. 10.95 (*0-7859-1438-2*, 2080706160) Fr & Eur.
— Fausses Confidences. (FRE., Illus.). 208p. 1992. pap. 8.95 (*0-7859-4655-1*) Fr & Eur.
— Le Jeu de l'Amour et du Hasard. (FRE., Illus.). 128p. 1985. pap. 8.95 (*0-7859-4656-X*) Fr & Eur.
— Le Jeu de l'Amour et du Hasard. (FRE.). 1985. pap. 10.95 (*0-7859-3128-7*) Fr & Eur.
— Le Jeu de l'Amour et du Hasard. unabridged ed. (FRE.). pap. 5.95 (*2-87714-168-3*, Pub. by Bookking Intl) Distribks Inc.
— Journaux et Oeuvres Diverses. (FRE.). 832p. 1988. pap. 65.00 (*0-7859-4654-3*) Fr & Eur.
— Marivaux Plays. (Methuen World Dramatists Ser.). (Illus.). 559p. (Orig.). (C). 1988. pap. write for info. (*0-413-18560-5*, A0343, Methuen Drama) Methn.
— Oeuvres de Jeunesse. 1972. 110.00 (*0-8288-9606-2*, F48070) Fr & Eur.
— Paysan Parvenu. (Coll. GF). 1966. pap. 7.95 (*0-8288-9607-0*, M1832) Fr & Eur.
— Le Petit-Maitre Corrige. (FRE.). 206p. 1955. 9.95 (*0-8288-9605-4*, F48050) Fr & Eur.
— Le Prince Travestil l'Ile des Esclaves: Le Triomphe de l'Amour. (FRE.). 1989. pap. 10.95 (*0-7859-2996-7*) Fr & Eur.
— Romans, Recits, Contes et Nouvelles. Arland, Marcel, ed. (Bibliotheque de la Pleiade Ser.). 74.95 (*0-685-34042-2*) Fr & Eur.
— Romans, Recits, Contes et Nouvelles: Avec: La Vie de Marianne. 1192p. 1950. 85.00 (*0-8288-9608-9*, F48100) Fr & Eur.
— Seven Comedies by Marivaux. Mandel, Oscar, ed. & tr. by. from FRE. Mandel, Adrienne S., tr. from FRE. LC 68-16386. 366p. 1968. 19.95 (*0-910278-36-9*) Boulevard.
— Seven Comedies by Marivaux. Mandel, Adrienne S. & Mandel, Oscar, eds. LC 68-16386. (Illus.). 380p. 1968. 42.00 (*0-686-60850-X*) Irvington.
— Seven Comedies by Marivaux. Mandel, Oscar & Mandel, Adrienne S., eds. LC 68-16386. (Illus.). 380p. 1968. pap. text 14.50 (*0-8290-2023-3*) Irvington.
— Seven Comedies of Marivaux. Mandel, Oscar, ed. LC 68-16386. 382p. 1968. reprint ed. pap. 108.90 (*0-608-04422-9*, AU00483) Bks Demand.
— La Surprise de L'Amour: La Second Surprise de L'Amour. (FRE.). 1991. pap. 12.95 (*0-7859-3165-1*, 2253057290) Fr & Eur.
— Theatre Complet. rev. ed. Arland, Marcel, ed. (Bibliotheque de la Pleiade Ser.). (FRE.). 1125p. 1989. pap. 49.95 (*0-685-11591-7*, 2040173455) Fr & Eur.
— Vie de Marianne. (FRE.). 1966. pap. 17.95 (*0-7859-0053-5*, M11000) Fr & Eur.

***Marix-Evans, Martin.** Canals of England. 2000. pap. 16.95 (*0-7538-0533-2*) Phoenix Hse.

Marix-Evans, Martin. The Twelve Days of Christmas. (Charming Petites Ser.). (Illus.). 80p. 1993. 5.95 (*0-88088-780-X*) Peter Pauper.

Marix, Janne, ed. Les Musiciens de la Cour de Bourgogne au XVe Siecle, 1420-1467. LC 76-4478. (Illus.). reprint ed. 55.00 (*0-404-56627-8*) AMS Pr.

Mariz, Cecilia L. Coping with Poverty: Pentecostals & Christian Base Communities in Brazil. LC 93-12511. 224p. (C). 1994. 69.95 (*1-56639-112-1*) Temple U Pr.
— Coping with Poverty: Pentecostals & Christian Base Communities in Brazil. LC 93-12511. 224p. (C). 1994. pap. 22.95 (*1-56639-113-X*) Temple U Pr.

Marj. Into the Silence: Healing the Wounds of Abuse. Hanlon, Judy, ed. 112p. (Orig.). 1992. pap. 9.95 (*0-9630388-1-8*) White Oak NY.

Marjanen, Antti. The Woman Jesus Loved: Mary Magdalene in the Nag Hammadi Library & Related Documents. LC 96-26933. (Nag Hammadi & Manichawan Studies). 1996. 92.00 (*90-04-10658-8*) Brill Academic Pubs.

Marjani, Fathollah, tr. see Shariati, Ali.

Marjara, Harinder S. Contemplations of Created Things: Science in Paradise Lost. 408p. 1992. text 50.00 (*0-8020-2750-4*) U of Toronto Pr.

Marjil de Jesus, Antonio, et al. A Spanish Manuscript Letter on the Lacandones, in the Archives of the Indies at Seville. Tozzer, Alfred M., ed. & tr. by. LC 83-83343. (Illus.). 1984. pap. 10.00 (*0-911437-03-7*) Labyrinthos.

Marjit, Sugata & Raychaudhuri, Ajitava. India's Exports: An Analytical Study. LC 97-914019. (Illus.). 208p. (C). 1998. text 23.00 (*0-19-564235-X*) OUP.

Marjoram, D. T. Further Exercises in Modern Mathematics. 1966. 6.95 (*0-08-011969-7*, Pergamon Pr) Elsevier.
— Modern Mathematics in Secondary Schools. 1964. text 6.95 (*0-08-010719-2*, Pergamon Pr); pap. text 5.40 (*0-08-010718-4*, Pergamon Pr) Elsevier.

Marjoram, Tony, ed. Island Technology. 384p. 1994. pap. 47.50 (*1-85339-223-5*, Pub. by Intermed Tech) Stylus Pub VA.

Marjoribanks, Edward. For the Defence: The Life of Sir Edward Marshall Hall. 490p. 1996. reprint ed. 98.00 (*1-56169-198-4*) Gaunt.

Marjoribanks, Kevin, ed. The Foundations of Students' Learning. LC 90-23256. (Illus.). 359p. reprint ed. pap. 111.30 (*0-608-07421-7*, 206764800009) Bks Demand.

Marjorie Poore Production Staff, ed. From the Recipe Files of the C. I. A. Great Recipes from the Nation's Premier Cooking School. (Illus.). 112p. 1996. pap. 14.95 (*0-9651095-0-X*, Pub. by M Poore Prods) Bristol Pub Ent CA.

***Marjorie Poore Productions Staff.** Cook-Off America: Prize-Winning Recipes from the Public Television Series. Newens, Jennifer, ed. (Illus.). 160p. 1999. pap. 14.95 (*0-9651095-4-2*, Pub. by M Poore Prods) Bristol Pub Ent CA.
— Grilling Maestros. (Illus.). 127p. 1999. pap. 14.95 (*0-9651095-5-0*, Pub. by M Poore Prods) Bristol Pub Ent CA.

Marjorie Poore£roductions Staff, ed. Home Cooking With Amy Coleman, No. 3. (Illus.). 132p. 1997. pap. write for info. (*0-9651095-1-8*) M Poore Prods.
— Home Cooking with Amy Coleman, Vol. 2. (Illus.). 132p. 1998. pap. write for info. (*0-9651095-2-6*) M Poore Prods.

MARK. Aerial Interdiction: Air Power & the Land Battle in Three American Wars. LC 92-13489. 1992. pap. text. write for info. (*0-912799-73-0*) AFH & MP.

Mark. Aerial Interdiction: Air Power & the Land Battle in Three American Wars. (Illus.). 432p. (C). 1995. pap. text 45.00 (*0-7881-1966-4*) DIANE Pub.

***Mark.** Becoming a Professional Pilot. 2nd ed. 304p. 1999. pap. 24.95 (*0-07-134691-0*) McGraw.

Mark. Concise Encyclopedia. 1341p. (C). 1998. pap. 175.00 (*0-471-31856-6*) Wiley.
— Hillingdon Fox. 1995. pap. text. write for info. (*0-582-25985-1*, Pub. by Addison-Wesley) Longman.
— The Inclusive Gospel: Mark. Hays-Lohrey, Steven, tr. from GRE. & intro. by. (Illus.). 89p. (Orig.). 1993. pap. 8.95 (*0-915117-70-3*) Freedom Voices Pubns.

Mark & Junior. Survival Licks & Bar Room Tricks. (Illus.). 76p. 1991. pap. text 8.95 (*0-931759-51-X*) Centerstream Pub.

Mark, et al. Groups: A Manual for Chemical Dependency & Psychotic Treatment. (Illus.). 405p. (Orig.). (C). 1994. pap. text. write for info. (*1-887398-00-7*) CL Prodns.

Mark, A. J., jt. auth. see Heimlich, E. P.

Mark-Age Staff. One Thousand Keys to the Truth: Spiritual Guidelines for Latter Days & Second Coming. LC 75-40976. 156p. 1976. pap. 7.00 (*0-912322-51-9*) Mark-Age.

Mark, Alexandra. Marriage Made in Heaven. LC 89-50407. 256p. 1989. pap. 14.95 (*0-914918-90-7*, Whitford) Schiffer.

***Mark, Alison & Rees-Jones, Deryn.** Contemporary Women's Poetry: Reading, Writing, Practice. LC 00-35394. 2000. write for info. (*0-312-23535-6*) St Martin.

Mark, Amanda, et al. Worldwide Yellow Pages Markets, 1999. (Illus.). 180p. 1999. 7000.00 (*0-88709-095-8*) Simba Info Inc.

Mark, Amanda, jt. auth. see Goddard, David.

Mark, Amanda, ed. see Goddard, David.

***Mark, Andrew.** Falling Bodies. 2000. mass mkt. 6.99 (*0-425-17604-5*) Berkley Pub.

Mark, Andrew. Falling Bodies: Novel. LC 98-33261. 272p. 1999. 21.95 (*0-399-14447-1*, G P Putnam) Peng Put Young Read.

Mark, Ann, ed. Dear Islandman: Ronald Lockley. 250p. 1998. pap. 26.95 (*0-8464-4666-9*) Beekman Pubs.

Mark, Ann, ed. see Lockley, Ronald.

Mark, Arlene M., ed. Words for Worship. LC 95-12504. 240p. 1996. ring bd. 17.99 (*0-8361-9037-8*) Herald Pr.

Mark, Barbara. Hablando con Su Angel de la Guarda-Angelspeake.Tr. of How to Talk with Your Angels. (SPA.). 128p. 1997. per. 7.00 (*0-684-83424-3*) S&S Trade.
— Su Angel de la Guarda Devocionario. 144p. 1997. per. 13.95 (*0-684-84457-5*) S&S Trade.

Mark, Barbara & Griswold, Trudy. AngelSpeake: How to Talk with Your Angels. LC 95-31311. 128p. 1995. 13.95 (*0-684-81547-8*) S&S Trade.
— The Angelspeake Book of Prayer & Healing: How to Work With Your Angels. LC 97-27658. (Illus.). 144p. 1997. 13.95 (*0-684-84336-6*) S&S Trade.

***Mark, Barbara & Griswold, Trudy.** The Angelspeake Storybook: How Angels Work in People's Lives. LC 99-45894. 128p. 2000. 12.95 (*1-58062-250-X*) Adams Media.

Mark, Barbara & Griswold, Trudy. El Devocionario de Su Angel de la Guarda. (Illus.). 176p. 1998. per. 8.00 (*0-684-85260-8*) S&S Trade.

An Asterisk (*) at the beginning of an entry indicates that the title is appearing for the first time.

— Hablando Con Su Angel Be: How to Talk with Your Angels. (SPA.). 128p. 1995. 12.95 (*0-684-81549-4*, Fireside) S&S Trade Pap.

***Mark, Birgitta.** Mysticism & Cognition: The Cognitive Development of John of the Cross As Revealed in His Works. (Studies in Religion: Vol. 1). 256p. 2000. pap. 24.95 (*87-7288-804-0*, Pub. by Aarhus Univ Pr) David Brown.

Mark, Bonnie S. & Incorvaia, James A., eds. The Handbook of Infant, Child & Adolescent Psychotherapy Vol. I: A Guide to Diagnosis & Treatment. LC 94-44248. 464p. 1995. 60.00 (*1-56821-444-8*) Aronson.

— The Handbook of Infant, Child & Adolescent Psychotherapy Vol. 2: New Directions in Integrative Treatment. LC 94-44248. 528p. 1997. 60.00 (*0-7657-0044-1*) Aronson.

Mark, Bonnie S. & Layton, Aviva. I'll Know What to Do: A Kid's Guide to Natural Disasters. 64p. (J). (gr. 3-8). 1997. pap. 9.95 (*1-55798-459-X*) Am Psychol.

Mark, Christopher. Early Benjamin Britten: A Study of Stylistic & Technical Evolution. rev. ed. LC 94-49172. (Outstanding Dissertations in Music from British Universities). (Illus.). 350p. 1995. text 95.00 (*0-8153-1870-7*) Garland.

Mark, Christopher, jt. auth. see van Tartwijk-Novey, Louise B.

Mark, D. Johanna. Timothy's Treasure. (Illus.). 97p. (J). (gr. 1-7). 1997. 14.95 (*0-9656327-0-9*) Marks Pubg IN.

Mark, Dave. Learn C on the Macintosh. 2nd ed. 496p. 1995. pap. text 34.95 (*0-201-48406-4*) Addison-Wesley.

Mark, Dave. Learn C++ on the PC. 448p. 1993. pap. 39.95 incl. disk (*0-201-62622-5*) Addison-Wesley.

— Macintosh Pascal Programming Primer Vol. 1: Inside the Toolbox Using THINK Pascal, Vol. I. 544p. 1990. pap. text 26.95 (*0-201-57084-X*) Addison-Wesley.

— MacIntosh Programming Primer: Inside the Toolbox Using Think C. (C). 1991. pap. text. write for info. (*0-201-55644-8*) Addison-Wesley.

— MacWorld Ultimate Mac Programming: Methods Of. LC 94-72744. 592p. 1995. pap. 39.95 (*1-56884-195-7*) IDG Bks.

Mark, Dave & Reed, Cartwright. Macintosh C Programming Primer Vol. 1: Inside the Toolbox Using THINK C, Vol. I. 2nd ed. 672p. (C). 1992. pap. text 32.95 (*0-201-60838-3*) Addison-Wesley.

Mark, Dave, jt. auth. see Boone, Barry.

Mark, Dave, jt. auth. see Lawrence, David.

Mark, Dave, jt. auth. see Williams, Robin.

Mark, David & Faude, Jeffrey. Psychotherapy of Cocaine Addiction: Entering the Interpersonal World of the Cocaine Addict. LC 97-6518. 288p. 1997. 50.00 (*0-7657-0072-7*) Aronson.

Mark, Deborah, jt. ed. see Brawarsky, Sandee.

Mark, Dennis W. Van De, see Van De Mark, Dennis W.

Mark, Eduard. Aerial Interdiction: Air Power & the Land Battle in Three American Wars. LC 92-13489. 1992. text 25.00 (*0-912799-74-9*) AFH & MP.

— Aerial Interdiction: Air Power & the Land Battle in Three American Wars. 444p. 1994. per. 25.00 (*0-16-036390-X*) USGPO.

Mark, Ference. The Arpads & the Comneni: Political Relations Between Hungary & Byzantium in the 12th Century. 213p. (C). 1989. 90.00 (*963-05-5268-X*, Pub. by Akade Kiado) St Mut.

Mark, Gareth L. Estates Without Wills. (Basics Ser.: Vol. 1). (Illus.). 57p. (Orig.). 1995. 7.95 (*0-9617478-1-1*) Lineages Inc.

— Marriage Bonds of Fleming County, Kentucky, 1798-1825. 184p. 1991. pap. 14.95 (*0-9617478-0-3*) Lineages Inc.

Mark, Gregory, et al. Ethnic Studies Anthology. 480p. (C). 1995. pap. text 57.69 (*0-7872-1695-X*) Kendall-Hunt.

Mark, Grigorii. Graver (Engraver) Stikhotvoreniia (poems) LC 91-71433. (RUS.). 132p. (Orig.). (C). 1991. pap. 12.00 (*0-911971-65-3*) Effect Pub.

— Sredi Veshchei i Golosov. LC 95-2466. (RUS.). 128p. (Orig.). 1995. pap. 9.00 (*1-55779-075-2*) Hermitage Pubs.

Mark H., Walker. Official Heavy Gear II Strategy Guide. LC 98-73573. (Brady Games Strategy Guides Ser.). (Illus.). 223p. 1999. pap. 19.99 (*1-56686-834-3*) Brady Pub.

Mark, Hans. The Space Station: A Personal Journey. LC 86-32892. (Illus.). viii, 264p. 1987. text 32.95 (*0-8223-0727-8*) Duke.

Mark, Hans, jt. auth. see Szebehely, Victor G.

Mark, Harry B., Jr. Water Quality Measurement: The Modern Analytical Techniques. Mattson, James S., ed. LC 81-5408. (Pollution Engineering & Technology Ser.: Vol. 18). 495p. 1981. reprint ed. pap. 153.50 (*0-608-04612-4*, 206538100003) Bks Demand.

Mark, Harry B., Jr., jt. auth. see Mattson, James S.

Mark, Harry B., jt. auth. see Sacks, Richard D.

Mark, Harry H. Optokinetics: A Treatise on the Motions of Lights. LC 81-71626. (Illus.). 150p. 1982. 9.95 (*0-9608152-0-1*) H Mark-Corbett.

Mark, Herman F. Encyclopedia of Polymer Science & Engineering Database, 1985-1990. 2nd ed. Ep. 1990. pap. 230.00 (*0-471-52226-0*) Wiley.

— From Small Organic Molecules to Large: From Small Organic Molecules to Large: A Century of Progress. Seeman, Jeffrey I., ed. LC 92-30099. (Profiles, Pathways, & Dreams Ser.). (Illus.). 148p. 1993. text 36.00 (*0-8412-1776-9*, Pub. by Am Chemical) OUP.

Mark, Herman F., et al, eds. Encyclopedia of Polymer Science & Engineering, 19 vols., Vol. 22. 2nd ed. Incl. Vol. 1, A to Amorphous Polymers. A to Amorphous Polymers. 2nd ed. LC 84-19713. 912p. 1985. 295.00 (*0-471-89540-7*); Vol. 2, Anionic Polymerization to Cationic Polymer. Anionic Polymerization to Cationic Polymerization. 2nd ed. LC 84-19713. 840p. 1985. 325.00 (*0-471-88786-2*); Vol. 3, Cellular Materials to Composites. Cellular Materials to Composites. 2nd ed. LC 84-19713. 848p. 1985. 325.00 (*0-471-88789-7*); Vol. 4, Composites, Fabrication to Die Design. Composites, Fabrication to Die Design. 2nd ed. LC 84-19713. 864p. 1986. 325.00 (*0-471-88099-X*); Vol. 5, Dielectric Heating to Embedding. Dielectric Heating to Embedding. 2nd ed. LC 84-19713. 828p. 1986. 325.00 (*0-471-88098-1*); Vol. 7, Fibers, Optical to Hydrogenation. Encyclopedia of Polymer Science & Engineering: Fibers, Optical to Hydrogenation. 2nd ed. LC 84-19713. 848p. 1987. 325.00 (*0-471-80649-8*); Vol. 8, Identification to Lignin. Encyclopedia of Polymer Science & Engineering: Identification to Lignin. 2nd ed. LC 84-19713. 880p. 1987. 325.00 (*0-471-80937-3*); Vol. 9, Liquid Crystalline Polymers to Mining Appl. Encyclopedia of Polymer Science & Engineering: Liquid Crystalline Polymers to Mining Applications. 2nd ed. LC 84-19713. 840p. 1987. 325.00 (*0-471-80941-1*); Vol. 10, Molecular Weight Determination to Pentadi. Molecular Weight Determination to Pentadiene Polymers: Molecular 2nd ed. LC 84-19713. 896p. 1987. 325.00 (*0-471-80942-X*); Vol. 11 , Peroxy Compounds to Polyelectrolytes. Peroxy Compounds to Polyelectrolytes. 2nd ed. LC 84-19713. 864p. 1988. 325.00 (*0-471-80943-8*); Vol. 12, Polyesters to Polypeptide Synthesis. Polyesters to Polypeptide Synthesis. 2nd ed. LC 84-19713. 858p. 1988. 325.00 (*0-471-80944-6*); Vol. 13, Poly (Phenylene Ether) to Radical Polymer. Encyclopedia of Polymer Science & Engineering, 2E, Vol. 13, Poly (Phenylene Ether) to Radical Polymerization. 2nd ed. LC 84-19713. 867p. 1988. 325.00 (*0-471-80945-4*); Vol. 14, Radiopaque Polymers to Safety. Radiopaque Polymers to Safety. 2nd ed. LC 84-19713. 827p. 1988. 325.00 (*0-471-80946-2*); Vol. 15, Scattering to Structural Foams. Encyclopedia of Polymer Science & Engineering, 2E, Vol. 15, Scattering to Structural Foams. 2nd ed. LC 84-19713. 832p. 1989. 325.00 (*0-471-80947-0*); Vol. 16, Styrene Polymers to Toys. Styrene Polymers to Toys. 2nd ed. LC 84-19713. 968p. 1989. 325.00 (*0-471-81182-3*); Vol. 17, Transitions and Relaxations to Zwitterion. Transitions & Relaxations to Zwitterionic Polymerization. 2nd ed. LC 84-19713. 1072p. 1989. 325.00 (*0-471-81181-5*); Vol. 20. Acid-Base Interactions to Vinyl Chloride Polymers. 2nd ed. LC 84-19713. 889p. 1989. suppl. ed. 325.00 (*0-471-80948-9*); Vol. 21. Encyclopedia of Polymer Science & Engineering Index. 2nd ed. LC 84-19713. 800p. 1990. 325.00 (*0-471-80950-0*); LC 84-19713. 16530p. 1990. 5250.00 (*0-471-86519-2*) Wiley.

Mark, Herman F. & Seymour, Raymond B., eds. Handbook of Organic Coatings. 500p. 1990. 75.00 (*0-444-01519-1*) P-H.

Mark, Herman F., ed. see Alfrey, Turner.

Mark, Herman F., ed. see Menges, George.

Mark, Herman F., jt. ed. see Seymour, Raymond B.

Mark, Howard. Principles & Practice of Spectroscopic Calibration. LC 91-15260. (Chemical Analysis: A Series of Monographs on Analytical Chemistry & Its Applications: No. 1075). 192p. 1991. 115.00 (*0-471-54614-3*) Wiley.

Mark, Howard & Workman, Jerry. Statistics in Spectroscopy. (Illus.). 313p. (C). 1991. text 77.00 (*0-12-472530-9*) Acad Pr.

Mark, Ira S. The Sanctuary of Athena Nike in Athens: Architectural Stages & Chronology. LC 93-37431. (Hesperia Supplement Ser.: No. 26). (Illus.). xv, 160p. 1993. pap. 50.00 (*0-87661-526-4*) Am Sch Athens.

Mark, J. & Williams, G. The Psychological Treatment of Depression: A Guide to Theory & Practice of Cognitive Behavior. 2nd ed. LC 94-44552. 312p. (C). 1995. pap. 24.99 (*0-415-12874-9*, A7433) Routledge.

Mark, J., et al. Food Industries. Maunder, W. F. & Fleming, M. C., eds. 816p. (C). (gr. 13). 1993. ring bd. 278.95 (*0-412-35660-0*, A5607, Chap & Hall CRC) CRC Pr.

Mark, J. E., et al, eds. Computational Methods in Materials Science. (Materials Research Society Symposium Proceedings Ser.: Vol. 278). xiii, 403p. 1992. text 17.50 (*1-55899-173-5*) Materials Res.

Mark, J. E., et al, eds. Hybrid Organic-Inorganic Composites. LC 95-7108. (Symposium Ser.: No. 585). (Illus.). 430p. 1995. text 120.00 (*0-8412-3148-6*, Pub. by Am Chemical) OUP.

Mark, J. E., jt. ed. see Schaefer, D. W.

Mark, James E., ed. Physical Properties of Polymers Handbook. (Polymers & Complex Materials Ser.). (Illus.). 744p. 1996. text 120.00 (*1-56396-295-0*) Spr-Verlag.

— Physical Properties of Polymers Handbook. 1996. text 189.00 (*1-56396-599-2*) Spr-Verlag.

— Polymer Data Handbook. LC 98-46567. (Illus.). 1040p. 1999. text 250.00 (*0-19-510789-6*) OUP.

Mark, James E., et al, eds. Science & Technology of Rubber. 2nd ed. LC 93-8796. (Illus.). 751p. 1994. text 95.00 (*0-12-472525-2*) Acad Pr.

Mark, James E & Erman, Burak. Rubberlike Elasticity: A Molecular Primer. LC 88-5518. 208p. 1988. 125.00 (*0-471-61499-8*) Wiley.

Mark, James E. & Lal, Joginder, eds. Elastomers & Rubber Elasticity. LC 82-11320. (ACS Symposium Ser.: No. 193). 578p. 1982. lib. bdg. 65.95 (*0-8412-0729-1*) Am Chemical.

— Elastomers & Rubber Elasticity: Based on a Symposium. LC 82-11320. (ACS Symposium Ser.: No. 193). (Illus.). 591p. 1982. reprint ed. pap. 183.30 (*0-608-04332-X*, 206511200001) Bks Demand.

Mark, James E., et al. Physical Properties of Polymers. 2nd ed. LC 92-35330. (Illus.). 300p. 1993. text 75.00 (*0-8412-2505-2*, Pub. by Am Chemical) OUP.

— Physical Properties of Polymers. 2nd ed. LC 92-35330. (Illus.). 409p. 1993. pap. 44.95 (*0-8412-2506-0*) Am Chemical.

Mark, James E., jt. auth. see Erman, Burak.

Mark, James E., jt. ed. see Lal, Joginder.

Mark, Jan. Fun with Mrs. Thumb. LC 92-54955. (Illus.). 32p. (J). (ps up). 1993. 9.95 (*1-56402-247-1*) Candlewick Pr.

— Fur. LC 85-45539. (Illus.). 24p. (J). (ps-2). 1986. lib. bdg. 11.89 (*0-397-32170-8*) HarpC Child Bks.

— God's Story: How God Made Humankind. LC 97-18558. (Illus.). 178p. (J). (gr. 3-7). 1998. 17.99 (*0-7636-0376-7*) Candlewick Pr.

***Mark, Jan.** Mr. Dickens Hits Town. (Illus.). 64p. (YA). (gr. 4-7). 1999. 16.95 (*0-88776-468-1*) Tundra Bks.

Mark, Jan. Nothing to Be Afraid Of. LC 81-48064. 128p. (J). (gr. 6 up). 1982. 12.95 (*0-06-024087-3*) HarpC Child Bks.

Mark, Jeffrey P. An Analysis of Usury. 1980. lib. bdg. 250.00 (*0-8490-3085-4*) Gordon Pr.

— The Modern Idolatry: Being an Analysis of Usury & the Pathology of Debt. 1980. lib. bdg. 250.00 (*0-8490-3078-1*) Gordon Pr.

— Saving & Spending. 1980. lib. bdg. 59.95 (*0-8490-3083-8*) Gordon Pr.

Mark, Jeffrey P., jt. auth. see Mark, Vernon H.

***Mark, Jeremy.** S Club 7 in Miami: The Official Scrapbook, 32p. 2000. pap. 8.95 (*0-06-107556-6*) HarpC.

Mark, Joan. The King of the World in the Land of the Pygmies. LC 94-16285. (Illus.). xvi, 292p. 1995. pap. 14.00 (*0-8032-8250-8*, MARKIX) U of Nebr Pr.

— Margaret Mead: Coming of Age in America. Gingerich, Owen, ed. LC 98-18604. (Oxford Portraits in Science Ser.). (Illus.). 112p. (YA). (gr. 6-12). 1999. 22.00 (*0-19-511679-8*) OUP.

Mark, Joan T. Four Anthropologists. LC 80-25414. 1980. 20.00 (*0-88202-190-7*) Watson Pub Intl.

***Mark, Joan T.** The Silver Gringo: William Spratling & Taxco. (Illus.). 160p. 2000. 29.95 (*0-8263-2079-1*) U of NM Pr.

Mark, Joan T., ed. see Gay, E. Jane.

Mark, Jonathan, jt. auth. see Seligman, Ruth.

Mark, Jonathan, jt. auth. see Westheimer, Ruth.

Mark, Jonathan, ed. see Westheimer, Ruth K.

Mark, Jonathan B. Atlas of Cardiovascular Monitoring. LC 97-41359. 1997. text 75.00 (*0-443-08891-8*) Church.

Mark, Joseph. Life: You Are the Dreamer. 20p. 1994. pap. text. write for info. (*1-885206-08-9*, Iliad Pr) Cader Pubng.

Mark, Judith Boyce De, see De Mark, Judith Boyce, ed.

Mark, Kathleen. Meteorite Craters. LC 86-19244. 288p. 1995. pap. 19.95 (*0-8165-1568-9*) U of Ariz Pr.

Mark, Kist Van Der, see Van Der Mark, Kist.

***Mark Krein International Conference on Operator Theory & Applications Staff.** Differential Operators & Related Topics Vol. II: Proceedings of the Mark Krein International Conference on Operator Theory & Applications, Odessa, Ukraine, August 18-22, 1997. Adamyan, V. M. et al, eds. LC 00-23584. (Operator Theory Ser.: Vol. 118). 448p. 2000. 140.00 (*3-7643-6288-X*, Pub. by Birkhauser) Spr-Verlag.

Mark, L. S., et al, eds. Ergonomics & Human Factors. (Recent Research in Psychology Ser.). (Illus.). 291p. 1987. pap. 47.00 (*0-387-96511-4*) Spr-Verlag.

Mark, Laurence. Lonesome Whistle: A Story of Survival. 107p. (Orig.). 1996. pap. 10.95 (*0-9655765-0-7*) L Mark.

Mark, Linda, ed. Reference Sources, 1978. LC 77-79318. 1978. 75.00 (*0-87650-096-3*) Pierian.

— Reference Sources, 1979. LC 77-79318. 1980. 75.00 (*0-87650-117-X*) Pierian.

— Reference Sources, 1977. LC 77-79318. 1977. 75.00 (*0-87650-084-X*) Pierian.

Mark, Lisbeth & Lefrak, Babs. Snow. LC 95-14811. (Illus.). 128p. (Orig.). 1995. pap. 10.00 (*0-399-52166-6*, Perigee Bks) Berkley Pub.

Mark, Lisbeth, jt. auth. see Binswanger, Barbara.

Mark, Lois A. 100 Best Careers in Allied Health. 304p. 1999. 15.95 (*0-02-862520-X*) Macmillan.

Mark, M., ed. see Daitch, Susan, et al.

Mark Map Co. Staff. Captain's Atlas: Jet Route Two Edition. (Illus.). 80p. 1994. pap. 15.95 (*0-916413-24-1*) Aviation.

***Mark, Margaret.** Hero & the Outlaw: Harnessing the Power of Archetypes to Create a Winning Brand. 2001. 24.95 (*0-07-136415-3*) McGraw.

Mark, Margery H., jt. ed. see Sage, Jacob I.

Mark, Mary E. American Odyssey, 1963-1999. LC 99-64609. (Illus.). 151p. 2000. 50.00 (*0-89381-880-1*) Aperture.

— Passport. LC 74-13170. 58p. 1976. pap. 9.95 (*0-912810-14-9*) Lustrum Pr.

Mark, Mary E., photos by. A Cry for Help: Stories of Homelessness & Hope. (Illus.). 104p. 1996. pap. 15.00 (*0-684-82593-7*, Fireside) S&S Trade Pap.

— Portraits: Photographs by Mary Ellen Mark. LC 97-1268. (Illus.). 1997. 24.95 (*1-56098-720-0*) Smithsonian.

***Mark, Melvin.** Evaluation: An Integrated Framework for Understanding, Guiding, & Improving Policies & Programs. 2000. 32.95 (*0-7879-4802-0*) Jossey-Bass.

Mark, Melvin M. & Shotland, R. Lance, eds. Multiple Methods in Program Evaluation. LC 85-644749. (New Directions for Evaluation Ser.: No. PE 35). 1987. pap. 22.00 (*1-55542-943-2*) Jossey-Bass.

Mark, Melvin M., jt. ed. see Shotland, R. Lance.

Mark, Michael, ed. The Music Educator & Community Music: The Best of M. E. J. (Best of MEJ Ser.). (Illus.). 104p. 1992. teacher ed. 20.00 (*1-56545-006-X*, 1612) MENC.

Mark, Michael J. Vander, see Vander Mark, Michael J.

Mark, Michael L. Contemporary Music Education. 2nd ed. 368p. (C). 1985. 30.00 (*0-02-871220-X*, Schirmer Books) Mac Lib Ref.

— Source Readings in Music Education History. rev. ed. 270p. 1986. pap. 29.95 (*1-57171-002-7*) Lincoln-Rembrandt.

Mark, Michael L. & Gary, Charles. A History of American Music Education. 404p. 1991. 42.00 (*0-02-871365-6*, Schirmer Books) Mac Lib Ref.

***Mark, Michael L. & Gary, Charles L.** A History of American Music Education: 2nd Edition. 432p. (Orig.). 1999. pap. 25.00 (*1-56545-115-5*, 1507) MENC.

Mark Mon-Chang Hsieh. The U. S. - Republic of China (Taiwan) Fisheries Negotiations, 1989, No. 4. 84p. 1991. 6.00 (*0-925153-16-8*, 105) Occasional Papers.

Mark, Norman. Chicago: Heart & Soul of America. LC 97-51957. (Urban Tapestry Ser.). (Illus.). 528p. 1998. 44.95 (*1-881096-53-X*) Towery Pub.

Mark Of Ephesus. Encyclical Letter of St. Mark of Ephesus. 1986. pap. 0.50 (*0-89981-021-7*) Eastern Orthodox.

Mark, Peter A. Africans in European Eyes: The Portrayal of Black Africans in Fourteenth & Fifteenth Century Europe. LC 74-25878. (Foreign & Comparative Studies Program, Eastern Africa Ser.: No. 16). 98p. 1975. pap. 3.00 (*0-915984-13-X*) Syracuse U Foreign Comp.

— The Wild Bull & the Sacred Forest: Form, Meaning & Change in Senegambian Initiation Masks of the Diola. (RES Monographs on Anthropology & Aesthetics). (Illus.). 188p. (C). 1992. text 85.00 (*0-521-41346-X*) Cambridge U Pr.

***Mark, R. Seely.** Freedom, Purpose & Personal Meaning. 112p. 1999. pap. 10.85 (*1-886699-27-5*) Five Corners.

Mark, Raymond. Research Made Simple: A Handbook for the Human Services. 411p. 1996. 58.00 (*0-8039-7426-4*); pap. 27.95 (*0-8039-7427-2*) Sage.

Mark, Rebecca. The Dragon's Blood: Feminist Intertextuality in Eudora Welty's 'The Golden Apples' LC 93-29518. 320p. 1994. text 35.00 (*0-87805-661-0*) U Pr of Miss.

Mark, Rebecca, ed. see Stein, Gertrude.

Mark, Richard E. Cell Wall Mechanics of Tracheids. 1967. 100.00 (*0-685-45682-X*) Elliots Bks.

Mark, Richard E. Handbook of Physical & Mechanical Testing of Paper & Paperboard, Vol. 1. (Illus.). 672p. 1983. text 225.00 (*0-8247-1871-2*) Dekker.

Mark, Richard S. Internet BBSs: A Guided Tour. 300p. (C). 1996. pap. text 34.95 incl. disk (*0-13-286998-5*) P-H.

Mark, Richard S. Internet Bbss: A Guided Tour LC 96-30874. xvi, 382 p. 1996. pap. write for info. (*1-884777-30-9*) Manning Pubns.

Mark, Robert. Becoming a Professional Pilot. LC 93-32866. (Illus.). 238p. 1993. pap. 19.95 (*0-07-040486-0*) McGraw-Hill Prof.

— Becoming a Professional Pilot. 1994. pap. 17.95 (*0-8306-4146-7*) McGraw-Hill Prof.

— Experiments in Gothic Structure. (Illus.). 176p. 1984. pap. text 12.95 (*0-262-63095-8*) MIT Pr.

— The Joy of Flying. 3rd ed. LC 93-33783. 192p. 1994. pap. 15.95 (*0-07-040487-9*) McGraw.

— The Joy of Flying. 3rd ed. pap. 15.95 (*0-8306-4432-6*) McGraw-Hill Prof.

— Light, Wind & Structure: The Mystery of the Master Builders. (C). 1990. text 38.25 (*0-07-040403-8*) McGraw.

Mark, Robert, ed. Architectural Technology up to the Scientific Revolution: The Art & Structure of Large-Scale Buildings. (New Liberal Arts Ser.). (Illus.). 272p. 1994. pap. text 25.00 (*0-262-63157-1*) MIT Pr.

Mark, Robert & Portugal, Buddy. Victories of the Heart: The Inside Story of a Pioneer Men's Group. 256p. 1996. pap. 14.95 (*1-85230-800-1*, Pub. by Element MA) Penguin Putnam.

Mark, Sam, tr. see KCRR Staff & Fay, Jennifer.

Mark, Samuel. From Egypt to Mesopotamia: A Study of Predynastic Trade Routes. LC 97-21879. (Studies in Nautical Archaeology: No. 4). (Illus.). 192p. 1997. 27.95 (*0-89096-777-6*) Tex A&M Univ Pr.

Mark, Samuel, ed. Latino Volunteer & Non-Profit Organizations: A Directory. 135p. 1989. pap. text 20.00 (*1-883638-11-9*) Rose Inst.

Mark, Sara, ed. see Time-Life Books Editors.

Mark, Stephen R. In Pictures Crater Lake: The Continuing Story. LC 96-75334. (Illus.). 48p. (Orig.). 1996. pap. 7.95 (*0-88714-109-9*) KC Pubns.

— In Pictures Crater Lake: The Continuing Story. Gregory, Marguerite, tr. LC 96-75334. (FRE., Illus.). 48p. (Orig.). 1996. pap. 8.95 (*0-88714-810-7*) KC Pubns.

— In Pictures Crater Lake: The Continuing Story. Morales, Brigitte, tr. LC 96-75334. (GER., Illus.). 48p. (Orig.). 1996. pap. 8.95 (*0-88714-809-3*) KC Pubns.

— In Pictures Crater Lake: The Continuing Story. Petzinger, Saori, tr. LC 96-75334. (JPN., Illus.). 48p. (Orig.). 1996. pap. 8.95 (*0-88714-811-5*) KC Pubns.

***Mark, Tami.** National Expenditures for Mental Health, Alcohol & Other Drug Abuse Treatment (1996) (Illus.). 75p. (C). 1999. pap. text 20.00 (*0-7881-7901-2*) DIANE Pub.

Mark, Teresa. She Changes: A Goddess Myth for Modern Women. 234p. (Orig.). 1991. pap. 12.95 (*1-878980-03-3*) Delphi IL.

Mark The Deacon. Life of Porphyry, Bishop of Gaza. 1973. pap. 2.95 (*0-89981-041-1*) Eastern Orthodox.

Mark Twain. Tom Sawyer Abroad. 1999. pap. write for info. (*0-14-043383-X*) Viking Penguin.

Mark, V. H., et al, eds. Colloquium on the Use of Embryonic Cell Transplantation for Correction of CNS Disorders. (Journal: Applied Neurophysiology: Vol 47, No. 1-2). (Illus.). 96p. 1984. pap. 30.50 (*3-8055-3952-5*) S Karger.

Mark, Vernon H. Reversing Memory Loss: Medically Proven Methods for Regaining, Strengthening, & Preserving... 256p. 1993. pap. 14.00 (*0-395-65371-1*) HM.

***Mark, Vernon H.** Reversing Memory Loss: Proven Methods for Regaining, Strengthening & Preserving Your Memory. 300p. 2000. pap. 14.00 (*0-395-94452-X*) HM.

M

Mark, Vernon H. & Mark, Jeffrey P. Brain Power: A Neurosurgeon's Complete Program to Maintain & Enhance Brain Fitness Throughout Your Life. 256p. 1991. pap. 14.00 (*0-395-55001-7*) HM.

Mark Williams Company Staff, jt. auth. see Scheetz, Dale.

Mark Wilson & Staff. The Golf Club Identification & Price Guide. 2nd ed. (Illus.). 1989. write for info. (*0-927956-00-4*) R Maltby.

Mark, Yudel, jt. auth. see Efron, S.

Markakis, John. Military Marxist Regimes in Africa. 250p. 1986. 42.50 (*0-7146-3295-3*, Pub. by F Cass Pubs) Intl Spec Bk.

Markakis, John & Ayela, Nega. Class & Revolution in Ethiopia. LC 85-62178. 160p. 1986. 19.95 (*0-932415-04-0*); pap. 7.95 (*0-932415-05-9*) Red Sea Pr.

Markakis, John & Salih, M. A., eds. Ethnicity & the State in Eastern Africa. 215p. 1998. pap. 26.95 (*91-7106-418-4*) Transaction Pubs.

Markakis, John, jt. ed. see Fukui, Katsuyoshi.

Markale, Jean. The Celts: Uncovering the Mythic & Historic Origins of Western Culture. LC 92-47488.Tr. of Celtes et al Civilisation Celtique. (ENG & FRE., Illus.). 320p. 1993. pap. 14.95 (*0-89281-413-6*) Inner Tradit.

***Markale, Jean.** Courtly Love: The Path of Sexual Initiation. 208p. 2000. pap. 16.95 (*0-89281-771-2*) Inner Tradit.

Markale, Jean. The Druids: Celtic Priests of Nature. LC 98-47665. 276p. 1999. pap. 16.95 (*0-89281-703-8*) Inner Tradit.

***Markale, Jean.** The Epics of Celtic Ireland: Ancient Tales of Mystery & Magic. 224p. 2000. pap. 16.95 (*0-89281-815-8*, Inner Trad) Inner Tradit.

Markale, Jean. The Grail: The Celtic Origins of the Sacred Icon. LC 98-55965. 192p. 1999. pap. 14.95 (*0-89281-714-3*) Inner Tradit.

***Markale, Jean.** Great Celtic Epic, 1999. pap. 14.00 (*0-8050-6082-0*) St Martin.

Markale, Jean. The Great Goddess: Reverence of the Divine Feminine from the Paleolithic to the Present. LC 99-40763. 256p. 2000. pap. 16.95 (*0-89281-715-1*) Inner Tradit.

— King of the Celts: Arthurian Legends & Celtic Tradition. LC 93-32512. 320p. (Orig.). 1993. pap. 14.95 (*0-89281-452-7*) Inner Tradit.

— Merlin: Priest of Nature. 230p. 1995. pap. 16.95 (*0-89281-517-5*) Inner Tradit.

— Petit Dictionnaire de Mythologie Celtique. (FRE.). 224p. 1986. pap. 36.95 (*0-7859-7970-0*, 2726600778) Fr & Eur.

— Women of the Celts. 315p. 1986. pap. 14.95 (*0-89281-150-1*) Inner Tradit.

Markan, Kristina & Fischer, Uwe. Untersuchungen Zur Immissionsbelastung der Berliner Forsten: Deposition & Bioindikation. (Dissertationes Botanicae Ser.: Band 170). (GER., Illus.). ii, 258p. 1991. pap. 53.00 (*3-443-64082-6*, Pub. by Gebruder Borntraeger) Balogh.

Markandaya, Kamala. Nectar in a Sieve: A Novel. 190p. (C). 1998. mass mkt. 5.99 (*0-451-16836-4*, AE2291) NAL.

Markandaya, Kamala. Nectar in a Sieve: A Novel. 1982. 11.09 (*0-606-01922-7*, Pub. by Turtleback) Demco.

***Markandya, A. & Murty, M. N.** Cleaning-Up the Ganges: A Cost-Benefit Analysis of the Ganga Action Plan. 352p. 2000. text 24.95 (*0-19-564945-1*) OUP.

Markandya, Anil & Pavan, Marcella. Green Accounting in Europe: Four Case Studies. LC 98-46643. (Economics, Energy & Environment Ser.). 1998. 174.00 (*0-7923-5470-2*) Kluwer Academic.

Markandya, Anil & Richardson, Julie, eds. Environmental Economics: A Reader. LC 92-36048. 288p. 1993. text 49.95 (*0-312-09476-0*) St Martin.

Markarian, Garik, jt. auth. see Honary, Bahram.

Markarian, Herand. Mirrors. (Illus.). 102p. (Orig.). 1996. pap. 10.00 (*0-9654126-0-1*) Hamazkayin Armenian.

Markarian, Margie & Hauss, Deborah, eds. The Incentive Travel Case Study Book. 108p. 1990. pap. text 40.00 (*0-9626880-0-2*) SITE.

Markarian, Yervand, jt. auth. see Walling, Dale.

Markatos, N. C., et al, eds. Numerical Simulation of Fluid Flow & Heat Mass Transfer Processes. (Lecture Notes in Engineering Ser.: Vol. 18). 505p. 1986. 58.95 (*0-387-16377-8*) Spr-Verlag.

Markbreit, Jerry & Steinberg, Alan. Last Call: Memoirs of an NFL Referee. (Illus.). 288p. 1999. 24.95 (*1-58382-030-2*, Pub. by Sports Masters) Partners-West.

Markby, William. Elements of Law: Principles of General Jurisprudence. 4th ed. LC 94-75656. xii,444p. 1994. reprint ed. 98.00 (*1-56169-087-2*) Gaunt.

***Marke, Julius J.** Vignettes of Legal History, 2 vols. 693p. 2000. boxed set 150.00 (*1-898029-45-8*, Pub. by Simmonds & Hill Pubng) Gaunt.

Marke, Julius J. Vignettes of Legal History: Second Series. (Illus.). xiv, 274p. 1977. lib. bdg. 15.00 (*0-8377-0833-8*, Rothman) W S Hein.

Marke, Julius J. & Sloane, Richard. Legal Research & Law Library Management. 750p. 1986. reprint ed. ring bd. 90.00 (*0-318-21438-5*, 00572) NY Law Pub.

Marke, Julius J., jt. auth. see New York University Staff.

Marke, Kay, compiled by. Neal-Schuman Index to Card Games. 125p. (Orig.). 1990. 27.50 (*1-55570-052-7*) Neal-Schuman.

Marke, Richard. The Medieval Stained Glass of Northhamptonshire. LC 99-203412. (Great Britain Summary Catalogue Ser.: No. 4). (Illus.). 432p. 1999. text 175.00 (*0-19-726177-9*) OUP.

***Markee, Dave.** Lost Glory. 2000. pap. 10.99 (*1-85240-257-1*) SOV5.

***Markee, Numa.** Conversation Analysis. LC 99-39744. (SLA Research Ser.). 2000. pap. write for info. (*0-8058-2000-0*) L Erlbaum Assocs.

Markee, Numa. Managing Curricular Innovation. (Cambridge Language Teaching Library). 238p. 1996. text 54.95 (*0-521-55512-4*); pap. text 20.95 (*0-521-55524-8*) Cambridge U Pr.

Markel. Bedside Manner. 1999. pap. text. write for info. (*0-7167-3132-0*) W H Freeman.

***Markel.** Technical Communication. 6th ed. 2000. pap. text. write for info. (*0-312-24890-3*) St Martin.

Markel, jt. auth. see Greenbaum.

Markel, Geraldine & Greenbaum, Judith. Performance Breakthroughs for Adolescents with Learning Disabilities or ADD: How to Help Students Succeed in the Regular Education Classroom. LC 95-73079. 336p. (Orig.). 1995. pap. text 21.95 (*0-87822-349-5*, 4915) Res Press.

Markel, Howard. Quarantine! East European Jewish Immigrants & the New York City Epidemics of 1892. LC 96-43095. (Illus.). 296p. 1997. 29.95 (*0-8018-5512-8*) Johns Hopkins.

Markel, Howard, et al, eds. The Portable Pediatrician. (Illus.). 396p. 1992. pap. text 39.00 (*1-56053-007-3*) Hanley & Belfus.

Markel, Howard & Oski, Frank A. The Practical Pediatrician: The A to Z Guide to Your Child's Health, Behavior, & Safety. (Illus.). 350p. 1996. pap. text 16.95 (*0-7167-2896-6*) W H Freeman.

***Markel, Howard, et al.** The Portable Pediatrician. 2nd ed. LC 99-40835. (Illus.). 450p. 2000. text. write for info. (*1-56053-362-5*, Pub. by Hanley & Belfus) Mosby Inc.

Markel, Lester. Public Opinion & Foreign Policy. (History - United States Ser.). 227p. 1993. reprint ed. lib. bdg. 79.00 (*0-7812-4814-0*) Rprt Serv.

Markel, Lester, ed. Global Challenge to the United States: A Study of the Problems, the Perils & the Proposed Solutions Involved in Washington's Search for a New Role. LC 75-18807. 241p. (C). 1975. 20.00 (*0-8386-1822-7*) Fairleigh Dickinson.

Markel, Lester, et al. Public Opinion & Foreign Policy. LC 78-167404. (Essay Index Reprint Ser.). 1977. reprint ed. 21.95 (*0-8369-7242-2*) Ayer.

***Markel, Michael.** Ethics in Technical Communication: A Critique & Synthesis. Vol. V.14. 2000. write for info. (*1-56750-528-7*) Greenwood.

Markel, Michael. Technical Communication. 5th ed. LC 97-66314. 688p. 1997. pap. text 63.95 (*0-312-17087-4*) St Martin.

Markel, Michael H. Business Writing Essentials. 224p. (C). 1987. teacher ed. write for info. (*0-318-62508-3*); teacher ed. write for info. (*0-318-62509-1*) St Martin.

***Markel, Michael H.** Ethics in Technical Communication: A Critique & Synthesis. LC 00-27629. (ATTW Contemporary Studies in Technical Communication). 2000. pap. write for info. (*1-56750-529-5*) Ablx Pub.

***Markel, Michele.** Dreamer from the Village. 2000. text 15.95 (*0-8050-6373-0*) St Martin.

Markel, Michelle. Gracias, Rosa. LC 94-25979. (Albert Whitman Concept Bks.). (Illus.). (J). (ps-2). 1995. lib. bdg. 14.95 (*0-8075-3024-7*) A Whitman.

***Markel, Michelle.** We Call Them Dolls. LC 99-89789. 2000. 15.00 (*0-618-05487-1*) HM.

Markel, Mike. Writing in the Technical Fields: A Step-by-Step Guide for Engineers, Scientists, & Technicians. LC 93-26817. (Illus.). 296p. 1994. pap. 34.95 (*0-7803-1036-5*, PC3855) Inst Electrical.

— Writing in the Technical Fields: A Step-by-Step Guide for Engineers, Scientists, & Technicians. LC 93-26817. (Illus.). 296p. 1994. 34.95 (*0-7803-1059-4*, PC3855) Inst Electrical.

Markel, Norman. Semiotic Psychology: Speech As an Index of Emotions & Attitudes. LC 95-26227. (Berkeley Insights in Linguistics & Semiotics Ser.: Vol. 26). (Illus.). XXV, 178p. (C). 1998. pap. text 35.95 (*0-8204-3099-4*) P Lang Pubng.

***Markel, Rita J.** Jimi Hendrix. LC 00-8116. (A & E Biography Ser.). 2001. write for info. (*0-8225-4990-5*, Lerner Publctns) Lerner Pub.

Markel, Robert, jt. auth. see Waggoner, Susan.

Markel, Robert J., ed. The Women's Sports Encyclopedia. LC 97-8850. 304p. 1997. 30.00 (*0-8050-4494-9*) H Holt & Co.

Markel, Ronald G. Kingsnakes: Their Care & Breeding. (Illus.). 64p. 1995. pap. 9.95 (*0-7938-0273-3*, RE117) TFH Pubns.

— Kingsnakes & Milk Snakes. (Barron's Pet Owner's Manuals Ser.). 1995. pap. 6.95 (*0-8120-4240-9*) Barron.

— Kingsnakes & Milk Snakes. (Illus.). 144p. 1989. 35.95 (*0-86622-664-8*, TS-125) TFH Pubns.

Markel, Stephen. Origins of the Indian Planetary Deities. LC 93-41911. (Studies in Asian Thought & Religion: Vol. 16). (Illus.). 284p. 1994. text 89.95 (*0-7734-9401-4*) E Mellen.

Markel, Stephen, ed. The World of Jade. 1992. 38.00 (*81-85026-20-3*, Pub. by Marg Publns) Art Media Resources.

Markel, Vadim & George, Thomas, eds. Optics of Nanostructured Materials. 576p. 2000. text 145.00 (*0-471-34968-2*) Wiley.

Markell. Medical Parasitology. 7th ed. 1991. pap. text 54.00 (*0-7216-3411-7*, W B Saunders Co) Harcrt Hlth Sci Grp.

— Medical Parasitology: International Edition. 8th ed. (C). 1998. text 40.00 (*0-8089-2068-5*, Grune & Strat) Harcrt Hlth Sci Grp.

Markell, Edward K., et al. Medical Parasitology. 8th ed. Williams, Adrianne, ed. LC 98-15802. (Illus.). 544p. (C). 1998. text 49.95 (*0-7216-7634-0*, W B Saunders Co) Harcrt Hlth Sci Grp.

Markell, Jeff. Coastal Weather Guide for Southern California & Mexico. 144p. 1997. pap. 17.95 (*1-57785-017-3*) ProStar Pubns.

— Residential Wiring to the 1999 NEC. 4th rev. ed. LC 99-19966. (Illus.). 352p. 1999. pap. 27.00 (*1-57218-073-0*) Craftsman.

— The Sailor's Weather Guide. 1996. pap. text 19.95 (*0-07-040574-3*) McGraw.

— The Sailor's Weather Guide. (Illus.). 285p. 1995. pap. 19.95 (*0-924486-91-0*) Sheridan.

Markels, Bobby. Being Here. (Mendocino Malady Ser.). (Illus.). 68p. Date not set. reprint ed. pap. 6.50 (*1-880991-04-7*) Stone Pub.

— How to Be a Human Bean. (Illus.). 24p. (J). (gr. 3 up). Date not set. reprint ed. pap. 4.50 (*1-880991-01-2*) Stone Pub.

— Lately I've Been Thinking. (Mendocino Malady Ser.). (Illus.). 58p. (Orig.). Date not set. pap. 6.50 (*1-880991-05-5*) Stone Pub.

— Mendocino Malady: On the Eve of My 50th Year. (Mendocino Malady Ser.). 34p. Date not set. pap. 6.50 (*1-880991-03-9*) Stone Pub.

— Popper. (Nonny Ser.). 80p. (Orig.). Date not set. pap. 6.50 (*1-880991-07-1*) Stone Pub.

Markels, Julian. Melville & the Politics of Identity: From King Lear to Moby Dick. LC 92-21497. 176p. 1993. text 29.95 (*0-252-01995-4*); pap. text 13.95 (*0-252-06302-3*) U of Ill Pr.

Markels, Robin B. A New Perspective in Cohesion on Expository Paragraphs. LC 83-14561. (Studies in Writing & Rhetoric). 120p. (Orig.). 1984. pap. text 14.95 (*0-8093-1152-6*) S Ill U Pr.

Marken, Bill. Annuals for Dummies. 1998. pap. 16.99 (*0-676-57290-1*) Random.

***Marken, Bill.** Container Gardening for Dummies. National Gardening Association Editors, ed. (For Dummies Ser.). (Illus.). 384p. 1998. pap. 16.99 (*0-7645-5057-8*) IDG Bks.

Marken, Bill. Container Gardening for Dummies. 1998. pap. 16.99 (*0-676-57291-X*) Random.

Marken, Bill, jt. auth. see National Gardening Association Editors.

Marken, Jack W. American Indian: Language & Literature. LC 76-4624. (Goldentree Bibliographies Series in Language & Literature). (C). 1978. pap. text 14.95 (*0-88295-553-5*) Harlan Davidson.

Marken, Jack W. & Hoover, Herbert T. Bibliography of the Sioux. LC 80-20106. (Native American Bibliography Ser.: No. 1). 388p. 1980. 29.00 (*0-8108-1356-4*) Scarecrow.

Marken, Mitchell W. Pottery from Spanish Shipwrecks, 1500-1800. LC 93-34787. (Illus.). 280p. (C). 1994. 49.95 (*0-8130-1268-6*) U Press Fla.

Markens, Isaac. The Hebrews in America: A Series of Historical & Biographical Sketches. LC 74-29504. (Modern Jewish Experience Ser.). 1975. reprint ed. 33.95 (*0-405-06731-3*) Ayer.

Marker, A. F., jt. ed. see Rai, Hakumat.

Marker, Alexander J., ed. Inorganic Optical Materials. (Proceedings of SPIE Ser.: Vol. 3424). 168p. 1998. 69.00 (*0-8194-2879-5*) SPIE.

Marker, B. R., jt. ed. see McCall, G. J.

Marker, Chris. La Jetee: Cine-Roman. LC 92-14634. (Zone Bks.). (ENG & FRE., Illus.). 256p. 1996. pap. 28.00 (*0-942299-67-1*) Zone Bks.

Marker, D., et al. Model Theory of Fields. (Lecture Notes in Logic Ser.: Vol. 5). 154p. 1996. pap. 39.00 (*3-540-60741-2*) Spr-Verlag.

Marker, F. J. & Innes, Christopher, eds. Modernism in European Drama: Ibsen, Strindberg, Pirandello, Beckett: Essays from Modern Drama. LC 99-170702. 336p. 1998. text 55.00 (*0-8020-4399-2*); pap. text 21.95 (*0-8020-8206-8*) U of Toronto Pr.

Marker, Frederick J. Hans Christian Andersen & the Romantic Theatre: A Study of Stage Practices in the Prenaturalistic Scandinavian Theatre. LC 74-151377. (Illus.). 256p. reprint ed. pap. 79.40 (*0-608-10229-6*, 201435600090) Bks Demand.

Marker, Frederick J. & Marker, Lise-Lone. Edward Gordon Craig & "The Pretenders" A Production Revisited. LC 80-27481. (Special Issues Ser.). (Illus.). 148p. 1981. 21.95 (*0-8093-0966-1*) S Ill U Pr.

— A History of Scandinavian Theatre. LC 96-36241. (Illus.). 399p. (C). 1996. text 69.95 (*0-521-39237-3*) Cambridge U Pr.

Marker, Frederick J., jt. auth. see Marker, Lise-Lone.

Marker, Frederick J., ed. see Bergman, Ingmar.

Marker, Gary. Publishing, Printing, & the Origins of Intellectual Life in Russia, 1700-1800. LC 84-42893. 316p. reprint ed. pap. 98.00 (*0-608-06329-0*, 206669000008) Bks Demand.

Marker, Gary, ed. Reinterpreting Russian History: Readings, 860-1860's. LC 92-46294. (Illus.). 464p. 1994. text 60.00 (*0-19-507857-8*); pap. text 24.95 (*0-19-507858-6*) OUP.

Marker, Gordon A. Internal Migration & Economic Opportunity: France, 1872-1911. Bruchey, Stuart, ed. LC 80-2815. (Dissertations in European Economic History Ser.). (Illus.). 1981. lib. bdg. 30.95 (*0-405-13999-3*) Ayer.

Marker, Lise-Lone. David Belasco: Naturalism in the American Theatre. LC 74-2970. 271p. reprint ed. pap. 84.10 (*0-8357-3421-8*, 203967800013) Bks Demand.

Marker, Lise-Lone & Marker, Frederick J. Ibsen's Lively Art: A Performance Study of the Major Plays. (Illus.). 280p. (C). 1989. text 64.95 (*0-521-26643-2*) Cambridge U Pr.

Marker, Lise-Lone, jt. auth. see Marker, Frederick J.

Marker, Lise-Lone, ed. see Bergman, Ingmar.

Marker, Rita L. Deadly Compassion. 328p. 1995. mass mkt. 5.99 (*0-380-72332-8*, Avon Bks) Morrow Avon.

— Euthanasia: Killing or Caring? (Orig.). (C). 1992. pap. 2.00 (*0-919225-36-5*) Life Cycle Bks.

Marker, Sherry. Plains Indians Wars. Bowman, John, ed. (America at War Ser.). (Illus.). 128p. (J). (gr. 5-12). 1996. 19.95 (*0-8160-3254-8*) Facts on File.

Marker, Willis B. & Helmut, H. Battles of World History. 438p. 1978. 175.00 (*0-7855-1562-3*) St Mut.

Marker, Willis B., jt. auth. see Harrison, Margaret M.

Markert, Bernd. Instrumental Element & Multi-Element Analysis of Plant Samples: Methods & Applications. Haderlie, Brooks, tr. LC 96-5723. 312p. 1996. 205.00 (*0-471-95865-4*) Wiley.

Markert, Bernd, ed. Environmental Sampling for Trace Analysis. 525p. 1994. 275.00 (*3-527-30051-1*, Wiley-VCH) Wiley.

— Plants as Biomonitors: Indicators for Heavy Metals in the Terrestrial Environment. LC 92-34620. 645p. 1993. 236.00 (*3-527-30001-5*, Wiley-VCH) Wiley.

Markert, Bernd, jt. ed. see Schuurmann, Gerrit.

Markert, Christopher. Dan-Tien - Your Secret Energy Center. LC 98-7467. (Illus.). 176p. 1998. pap. 12.95 (*1-57863-043-6*) Weiser.

— The I Ching: Ancient Chinese Wisdom for Modern Decision Making. LC 98-36442. (Illus.). 288p. 1998. pap. 14.95 (*0-8348-0457-3*) Weatherhill.

— I Ching: The No. 1 Success Formula. (Illus.). 282p. (Orig.). 1987. pap. 6.95 (*0-85030-493-8*, Pub. by Aqrn Pr) HarpC.

— Seeing Well Again Without Your Glasses. (Illus.). 128p. 17.95 (*0-8464-4288-4*) Beekman Pubs.

Markert, Clement L., et al. Isozymes: Proceedings of the 7th International Congress. LC 94-37467. 328p. 1994. text 105.00 (*981-02-1449-9*) World Scientific Pub.

Markert, James. The Hell That Is Ice. 320p. 1998. pap. 15.95 (*1-886094-88-8*) Chicago Spectrum.

Markert, Jenny. Arctic Foxes. (Nature Books Ser.). (Illus.). 32p. (J). (gr. 2-6). 1991. lib. bdg. 22.79 (*0-89565-710-4*) Childs World.

— Camels. (Nature Books Ser.). (Illus.). 32p. (J). (gr. 2-6). 1991. lib. bdg. 22.79 (*0-89565-719-8*) Childs World.

— Giraffes. (Nature Books Ser.). (Illus.). 32p. (J). (gr. 2-6). 1991. lib. bdg. 22.79 (*0-89565-723-6*) Childs World.

— Glacier National Park. (Vision Bks.). (Illus.). 32p. (J). (gr. 2-6). 1993. lib. bdg. 22.79 (*0-89565-858-5*) Childs World.

— Glaciers & Icebergs. LC 92-32498. (Vision Bks.). (Illus.). 32p. (J). (gr. 2-6). 1994. lib. bdg. 22.79 (*1-56766-004-5*) Childs World.

— Kangaroos. (Nature Books Ser.). (Illus.). 32p. (J). (gr. 2-6). 1991. lib. bdg. 22.79 (*0-89565-715-5*) Childs World.

— Moose. LC 98-34032. (Illus.). 32p. (J). 1999. lib. bdg. 22.79 (*1-56766-583-7*) Childs World.

— Octopuses. (Nature Books Ser.). (Illus.). 32p. (J). (gr. 2-6). 1992. lib. bdg. 22.79 (*0-89565-836-4*) Childs World.

— Parque Nacional Yellowstone. (Libro Vision Ser.). (SPA., Illus.). 32p. (J). (gr. 2-6). 1993. lib. bdg. 22.79 (*1-56766-031-2*) Childs World.

— Penguins. LC 97-27836. (Illus.). 32p. (J). 1998. lib. bdg. 22.79 (*1-56766-490-3*) Childs World.

— Reptiles. (Nature Books Ser.). (Illus.). 32p. (J). (gr. 2-6). 1993. lib. bdg. 22.79 (*0-89565-850-X*) Childs World.

— Tigers. LC 97-30409. (Nature Books Ser.). 32p. (J). (gr. 2-6). 1997. lib. bdg. 22.79 (*1-56766-397-4*) Childs World.

— Wildcats. (Nature Books Ser.). (Illus.). 32p. (J). (gr. 2-6). 1991. lib. bdg. 22.79 (*0-89565-704-X*) Childs World.

— Yellowstone National Park. (Vision Bks.). (Illus.). 32p. (J). (gr. 2-6). 1993. lib. bdg. 22.79 (*0-89565-859-3*) Childs World.

— Zebras. (Nature Books Ser.). (Illus.). 32p. (J). (gr. 2-6). 1992. lib. bdg. 22.79 (*0-89565-839-9*) Childs World.

Markert, Kathleen O'Donnell & National School Services (Wheeling, Ill.). The Path to Parent Involvement: An Educator's Guide to Building Better Relationships with Parents. LC 98-141687. (Illus.). 1997. write for info. (*0-932957-04-8*) Natl School.

Markert, Lawrence W. Arthur Symons: Critic of the Seven Arts. Kuspit, Donald, ed. LC 87-22802. (Studies in the Fine Arts: Criticism: No. 25). 190p. reprint ed. 58.90 (*0-8357-1845-X*, 207073900004) Bks Demand.

— The Bloomsbury Group: A Reference Guide. 400p. (C). 1989. 50.00 (*0-8161-8936-6*, Hall Reference) Macmillan.

— Riddle & Incest. (New Poets Ser.: Vol. 3). 1974. pap. 1.95 (*0-932616-03-8*) Brick Hse Bks.

Markert, Linda R. Contemporary Technology: Innovations, Issues, & Perspectives. LC 96-22367. 473p. 1997. 35.96 (*1-56637-348-4*) Goodheart.

Markert, Ludwig. Struktur und Bezeichnung des Scheltworts. (Beiheft zur Zeitschrift fuer die Alttestamentliche Wissenschaft Ser.: No. 40). (C). 1977. text 134.60 (*3-11-005813-8*) De Gruyter.

***Markes, Julie.** Good Thing You're Not an Octopus! LC 99-37139. 40p. (J). (ps-1). 2001. pap. 4.95 (*0-06-443586-5*) HarpC Child Bks.

— Good Thing You're Not an Octopus! LC 99-37139. 40p. (J). (ps-1). 2001. 12.95 (*0-06-028465-X*); lib. bdg. 12.89 (*0-06-028466-8*) HarpC Child Bks.

— Sidewalk ABC. 24p. (J). (ps-k). 2001. 8.95 (*0-694-01455-9*, HarpFestival) HarpC Child Bks.

— Sidewalk 123. 12p. (J). (ps-k). bds. 8.95 (*0-694-01500-8*, HarpFestival) HarpC Child Bks.

Markesbery, William R., ed. Neuropathology of Dementing Disorders. (An Arnold Publication). (Illus.). 416p. 1998. text 195.00 (*0-340-59037-8*) OUP.

Markesinis, B. S. Foreign Law & Comparative Methodology: A Subject & a Thesis. LC 97-220060. 500p. 1997. 90.00 (*1-901362-03-5*, Pub. by Hart Pub) Northwestern U Pr.

Markesinis, B. S., et al. The German Law of Obligations. LC 97-27498. (Illus.). write for info. (*0-19-826768-1*); write for info. (*0-19-826767-3*) OUP.

An Asterisk (*) at the beginning of an entry indicates that the title is appearing for the first time.

Markesinis, B. S. The German Law of Obligations: A Comparative Introduction to the Law of Contracts & Restitution. LC 97-27498. 992p. 1997. text 125.00 (*0-19-826053-9*) OUP.

***Markesinis, B. S., ed.** Millennium Lectures: The Coming Together of the Common Law & the Civil Law. 256p. 2000. 54.00 (*1-84113-068-0*, Pub. by Hart Pub) Intl Spec Bk.

***Markesinis, B. S., et al.** Tortious Liability of Statutory Bodies: A Comparative Look at Five Cases. 171p. 1999. 45.00 (*1-84113-124-5*, Pub. by Hart Pub) Intl Spec Bk.

Markesinis, Basil. Tort Law. 4th ed. LC 99-21236. 900p. 1999. pap. text (*0-19-876506-1*) OUP.

— Tort Law. 4th ed. LC 99-21236. 924p. 1999. text 85.00 (*0-19-876507-X*) OUP.

Markesinis, Basil, ed. The Impact of the Bill of Rights on English Law, Vol. 3. (Clifford Chance Lecture Ser.). 200p. 1998. text 65.00 (*0-19-826864-5*) OUP.

***Markesinis, Basil, ed.** Protecting Privacy. (Clifford Chance Lecture Ser.). 260p. 1999. text 80.00 (*0-19-826885-8*) OUP.

Markesinis, Basil S. Law Making, Law Finding & Law Shaping: The Diverse Influences. The Clifford Chance Lectures, Vol. 2. (Clifford Chance Lecture Ser.). 236p. (C). 1998. text 70.00 (*0-19-826497-6*) OUP.

Markesinis, Basil S., ed. The Clifford Chance Lectures Vol. 1: Bridging the Channel. (Clifford Chance Lecture Ser.: Vol. 1). 288p. 1996. text 55.00 (*0-19-826231-0*) OUP.

— The Gradual Convergence: Foreign Influences & English Law on the Eve of the 21st Century. 320p. 1994. text 59.00 (*0-19-825828-3*) OUP.

Markesinis, Basil S. & Deakin, Simon F. Tort Law. 3rd rev. ed. LC 93-43258. (Illus.). 780p. 1994. pap. text. write for info. (*0-19-876293-3*, Clarendon Pr) OUP.

Markesinis, Basil S. & Munday, R. J. An Outline of the Law of Agency. 3rd ed. 338p. 1992. pap. 32.00 (*0-406-00145-6*, UK, MICHIE) LEXIS Pub.

Markeson, Richard. State Employees' Contracts. 9p. 1992. pap. write for info. (*1-58703-003-9*, CRB-92-002) CA St Libry.

***Market & Business Development Staff.** The U. K. Residential Window & Door Market Development. (Illus.). 97p. 1999. pap. text 560.00 (*1-894330-05-6*) AKTRIN.

Market House Books Ltd. Staff. Bantam Medical Dictionary. 1990. 12.09 (*0-606-03045-X*, Pub. by Turtleback) Demco.

***Market House Books Ltd. Staff.** Encyclopedia of World History. LC 99-208428. (Illus.). 784p. (YA). 1999. 30.00 (*0-19-860223-5*) OUP.

Market House Books Staff. Cassell Companion to Theatre. 528p. 1999. pap. 24.95 (*0-304-35317-5*) Continuum.

Market House Books Staff, compiled by. Dictionary of Abbreviations. 2nd ed. (Oxford Paperback Reference Ser.). 424p. 1998. pap. 13.95 (*0-19-280073-6*) OUP.

— A Dictionary of Business. 2nd ed. (Oxford Paperback Reference Ser.). 544p. 1997. pap. 14.95 (*0-19-280047-7*) OUP.

— Dictionary of Finance & Banking. 2nd ed. LC 98-128771. (Oxford Paperback Reference Ser.). 384p. 1998. pap. 14.95 (*0-19-280067-1*) OUP.

Market Intellience Staff. Profiles of U. S. Polymer & Fine Chemical Manufacturers. 372p. 1995. spiral bd. 995.00 (*0-7889-0242-3*, 2803-39) Frost & Sullivan.

Market Intelligence Staff. Abbott Labs: What's Not in the Annual Report. 321p. (Orig.). 1992. 995.00 (*1-56753-378-7*) Frost & Sullivan.

— Acoustic & Vibration Sensors & Test Equipment: Opening of Under-Penetrated Global Markets. 276p. (Orig.). 1992. 1695.00 (*1-56753-054-0*) Frost & Sullivan.

— Agricultural Biotechnology: Staggering Opportunities in World's Largest Market. 323p. (Orig.). 1992. pap. 1895.00 (*1-56753-037-0*) Frost & Sullivan.

— Agricultural Biotechnology Markets. 263p. 1994. 1995.00 (*0-7889-0071-4*) Frost & Sullivan.

— AIDS: Diagnostic, Monitoring & Therapeutic Markets: Technology Assessment & Financial Impact. LC 97-197205. 211p. 1993. 2495.00 (*1-56753-519-4*) Frost & Sullivan.

— Air Emission Monitor & Analyzer Markets: Clean Air Act Opens Windows of Opportunity. 189p. (Orig.). 1992. 1695.00 (*1-56753-040-0*) Frost & Sullivan.

— Air Pollution Control Equipment Markets. 202p. 1993. 2900.00 (*1-56753-543-7*) Frost & Sullivan.

— Alternate Cite Acute Care Equipment & Supply Markets: Quest for Cost Reductions Foster Ambulatory Center Group. 260p. 1993. 1695.00 (*1-56753-495-3*) Frost & Sullivan.

— Alternate Cite Respiratory Therapy Markets. 250p. 1994. 2195.00 (*0-7889-0072-2*) Frost & Sullivan.

— Analytical Instrumentation Markets: Product Sophistication Meets Tough Environmental Regulations & Biotech Research Demands. 255p. (Orig.). 1992. 2295.00 (*1-56753-059-1*) Frost & Sullivan.

— Anesthesia & Gas Monitoring Equipment Markets: Rapid Transition to Multi Parameter Integration & Open Systems. 224p. 1992. 1895.00 (*1-56753-389-2*) Frost & Sullivan.

— Anesthesia Drug Markets: Patent Expirations Have Players Scrambling to Develop Short Duration Drugs. 233p. 1992. 1995.00 (*1-56753-419-8*) Frost & Sullivan.

— Animal Health Products: Who's Hogging the Market? 312p. 1993. 1895.00 (*1-56753-434-1*) Frost & Sullivan.

— Anti-Infective Markets: Manufacturers Build Resistance Against Generic Competition & Evolving Microbials. 229p. 1993. 1995.00 (*1-56753-494-5*) Frost & Sullivan.

— Antisubmarine Warfare Markets. 227p. 1993. 2900.00 (*1-56753-540-2*) Frost & Sullivan.

— Autoimmune Disease Therapeutic Markets: New Therapies Target Causes, Not Symptoms. 320p. 1992. 1895.00 (*1-56753-077-X*) Frost & Sullivan.

— Baxter International: A Strategic Analysis of Success in World Markets. 249p. 1992. 995.00 (*1-56753-285-3*) Frost & Sullivan.

— Biotechnology Food & Nutrition Products Markets: Genetic Engineering Leads Industry into New Era. 196p. (Orig.). 1992. 1895.00 (*1-56753-072-9*) Frost & Sullivan.

— Biotechnology Instrumentation & Software: Pharmaceutical Growth Expands Supplier Markets. 293p. 1993. 1895.00 (*1-56753-468-6*) Frost & Sullivan.

— Bristol-Myers Squibb: World's Largest Pharmaceutical Sales Force in Action. 210p. (Orig.). 1992. 995.00 (*1-56753-047-8*) Frost & Sullivan.

— The Business of Macintosh: Beyond Apple, Achieving Success in the World Market. 1994. 1895.00 (*1-56753-973-4*) Frost & Sullivan.

— Cable & Wire Network Markets. 250p. 1993. 3900.00 (*1-56753-535-6*) Frost & Sullivan.

— Canadian Telecommunication Equipment & Service Markets: Digital Wireless Communications Take Off. 340p. 1994. 2295.00 (*1-56753-989-0*) Frost & Sullivan.

— Cancer Diagnostic Imaging Markets. LC 97-197198. 410p. 1994. 2295.00 (*0-7889-0139-7*) Frost & Sullivan.

— Cardiac Catheters: Forecasts for 22 Products in an Evolving Market. 413p. 1993. 1995.00 (*1-56753-426-0*) Frost & Sullivan.

— Cellular & PCS Telephone Pager & Accessory Markets: Time to Focus on Applications. 600p. (Orig.). 1994. 2295.00 (*0-685-70940-X*) Frost & Sullivan.

— Client/Server in the 1990s: A Strategic Assessment of Market Potential. 342p. 1993. 1495.00 (*1-56753-503-8*) Frost & Sullivan.

— Clinical Laboratory Disposable Markets: Chemistry Tests & Reagents, Toxicology & Pathology Supplies. 416p. 1993. 1895.00 (*1-56753-520-8*) Frost & Sullivan.

— Clinical Laboratory Disposable Markets: Microbiology, Hematology & Immunology. 413p. 1993. 1695.00 (*1-56753-521-6*) Frost & Sullivan.

— Color in the Mainstream Office: Six Complementary Desktop Technologies Paint the Color Market. 249p. (Orig.). 1992. 1495.00 (*1-56753-070-2*) Frost & Sullivan.

— Companion Animal Therapeutic Markets: Profiting from Human Pharmaceutical Research. 276p. (Orig.). 1992. 1895.00 (*1-56753-381-7*) Frost & Sullivan.

— Contraceptive & Fertility Product Markets: Manufacturers Respond to Changing Demographics. 373p. 1993. 2195.00 (*1-56753-529-1*) Frost & Sullivan.

— Contract Manufacturing Services Market: Revenues Quadruple by the Year 2000. 322p. 1993. 1495.00 (*1-56753-441-4*) Frost & Sullivan.

— Corrective & Protective Eyewear Markets: New Technologies Alter Marketing Strategies. 297p. 1993. 1695.00 (*1-56753-481-3*) Frost & Sullivan.

— The Crisis in Healthcare Financing: The Move Toward Universal Access. 246p. (Orig.). 1992. 395.00 (*1-56753-045-1*) Frost & Sullivan.

— Customer Engineering: A Measurement-Based Sales System Designed to Increase Marketing Profitability. 336p. 1993. 95.00 (*1-56753-492-9*) Frost & Sullivan.

— Dental Electronics & Equipment Markets: Dentists Look to Esthetics for New Revenues. 314p. (Orig.). 1992. 1695.00 (*1-56753-031-1*) Frost & Sullivan.

— Desktop Manufacturing Systems: Rapid Prototyping Techniques Take the World by Storm. 231p. (Orig.). 1992. 1895.00 (*1-56753-046-X*) Frost & Sullivan.

— Diabetes Product Markets: Product Penetration Increases with Patient Awareness. 300p. 1992. 1995.00 (*1-56753-404-X*) Frost & Sullivan.

— Diagnostic Electronics & Imaging Equipment Markets: A Detailed Database on a 13 Billion Dollar Market. 370p. 1992. 995.00 (*1-56753-086-9*) Frost & Sullivan.

— Digital Signal Processor, DSP, Markets: Cost Barriers Broken, Hypergrowth Expected Within 18 months. 265p. (Orig.). 1992. 1695.00 (*1-56753-073-7*) Frost & Sullivan.

— Disposable Medical Product Markets: PPE Demand Creates Specialty Products. 299p. 1992. 1495.00 (*1-56753-417-1*) Frost & Sullivan.

— Disposable Medical Product Markets, Vol. Two: Respiratory Disease & Infection Control Dominiate Trends for Growth. 297p. 1993. 1495.00 (*1-56753-474-0*) Frost & Sullivan.

— Distributed Control Systems in Process Industries: End-Users Focus on Smaller, More Modular & Hybrid DCS's. 361p. (Orig.). 1993. 1495.00 (*1-56753-657-3*) Frost & Sullivan.

— Distribution Channel Analysis of Desktops, Portables & Commercial Workstations: Understanding Distribution Patterns Is the Key to Survival. 234p. 1993. 1295.00 (*1-56753-428-7*) Frost & Sullivan.

— Dynamic Growth in World Display Markets: Competition Between Flat Panel Technology & CRT Technology Heats Up. 210p. (Orig.). 1992. 1495.00 (*1-56753-030-3*) Frost & Sullivan.

— EC Market for Fish, Farmed Fish & Products (Europe) 240p. (Orig.). 1992. 3200.00 (*1-56753-651-4*, E1574) Frost & Sullivan.

— Eight Hundred Service Markets: Portability Unleashes Competition. 302p. 1993. 1695.00 (*1-56753-514-3*) Frost & Sullivan.

— Electronic Warfare Outside the U. S. 1993. 3200.00 (*1-56753-479-1*) Frost & Sullivan.

— Electronics Design Automation Software Tools Market: Hot Segments: ASIC, Mixed Signal, MCM. 246p. (Orig.). 1992. 1295.00 (*1-56753-401-5*) Frost & Sullivan.

— Electrostatic Discharge (ESD) Control Product Markets: Industrial Shakeout: Price Wars, Emerging Applications & New Products. 318p. 1993. 1895.00 (*1-56753-467-8*) Frost & Sullivan.

— Eli Lilly: Innovation, Diversification & Globalization. 250p. 1993. 995.00 (*1-56753-432-5*) Frost & Sullivan.

— Emerging & Niche Oriented Auto ID Product Markets: Enormous Growth Potential. 268p. 1993. 1895.00 (*1-56753-523-2*) Frost & Sullivan.

— Endoscope & Peripheral Equipment Markets. 310p. 1994. 1995.00 (*0-7889-0044-7*) Frost & Sullivan.

— Endoscopes & Peripheral Equipment Markets: Technology Pays off - Less Invasive Procedures Benefit Physicians & Patients. 319p. 1992. 1895.00 (*1-56753-175-X*) Frost & Sullivan.

— Endoscopic Accessory Markets: A Fresh Look: New Instruments for New Procedures. 268p. 1993. 1895.00 (*1-56753-449-X*) Frost & Sullivan.

— Entrepreneurial Opportunities in Telecommunications: Shifting Technologies, Regulation, End-User Requirements Drive Opportunities. 209p. (Orig.). 1992. 995.00 (*1-56753-060-5*) Frost & Sullivan.

— Environmental Technology Market Sourcebook. 410p. 1994. 945.00 (*0-7889-0170-2*) Frost & Sullivan.

— Environmental Test Equipment Markets. 360p. 1994. 1695.00 (*0-7889-0045-5*) Frost & Sullivan.

— European Adhesive Label Markets. 334p. (Orig.). 1994. 3800.00 (*0-7889-0115-X*) Frost & Sullivan.

— European Adhesive Tape Markets. 280p. 1994. 3800.00 (*0-7889-0111-7*) Frost & Sullivan.

— European Advanced Building Control System Markets. 279p. 1994. 3950.00 (*0-7889-0040-4*) Frost & Sullivan.

— European Advanced Control Markets. 250p. 1994. 3950.00 (*0-7889-0024-2*) Frost & Sullivan.

— European Advanced Motion Control Markets. 212p. 1994. 3950.00 (*0-7889-0096-X*) Frost & Sullivan.

— European Air Pollution Control Equipment Markets. 305p. 1995. spiral bd. 7500.00 (*0-7889-0233-4*) Frost & Sullivan.

— European Air Pollution Monitoring Equipment Markets. 268p. 1995. 3950.00 (*0-7889-0187-7*, 3119-15) Frost & Sullivan.

— European Anesthetic Product Markets. 1994. 3800.00 (*0-7889-0120-6*) Frost & Sullivan.

— European Animal Feed Markets. 245p. 1994. 3800.00 (*0-7889-0059-5*) Frost & Sullivan.

— European Antihypertensive Drug Markets. LC 98-168740. 338p. 1995. spiral bd. 3800.00 (*0-7889-0254-7*, 3161-45) Frost & Sullivan.

— European Antiviral Drug & Vaccine Markets. 400p. 1994. 3800.00 (*0-7889-0016-1*) Frost & Sullivan.

— European Arthritis Markets. LC 97-213401. 230p. 1994. 3800.00 (*0-7889-0153-2*) Frost & Sullivan.

— European Asthma Treatment Product Markets: Shift in Use of Single-Agent Bronchodialation. 250p. 1994. 3800.00 (*1-56753-941-6*) Frost & Sullivan.

— European Automated Material Handling Markets. 475p. 1994. 3950.00 (*1-56753-980-7*) Frost & Sullivan.

— European Biopesticides & Related Agricultural Biotechnology Markets: New Market Growth Accompanied by Intense Competition. 385p. 1993. 4200.00 (*1-56753-582-8*) Frost & Sullivan.

— European Biotechnology Pharmaceutical Markets: The Lucrative Business of Genetic Engineering. 450p. (Orig.). 1993. 3500.00 (*1-56753-623-9*) Frost & Sullivan.

— European Cardiac Catheter Markets: Healthcare System Differences Require Regional Specific Strategies. 400p. 1994. 3800.00 (*1-56753-940-8*) Frost & Sullivan.

— European Cell Culture Reagents Consumables Markets. 408p. 1995. spiral bd. 3500.00 (*0-7889-0263-6*, 3073-53) Frost & Sullivan.

— European Chemical Industry. 514p. 1994. 3800.00 (*0-7889-0152-4*) Frost & Sullivan.

— European Clinical Diagnostics Industry Manufacturers & Suppliers: Detailed Profiles of 148 Industry Leaders. (Orig.). 1993. 1500.00 (*1-56259-621-7*) Frost & Sullivan.

— European Commercial & Industrial Composite Markets. 225p. 1993. 4300.00 (*1-56753-531-3*) Frost & Sullivan.

— European Commercial-Industrial Security Markets. 273p. 1994. 3300.00 (*1-56753-928-9*) Frost & Sullivan.

— European Commercial Workstation Markets. 308p. 1995. spiral bd. 3800.00 (*0-7889-0173-7*, 3131-71) Frost & Sullivan.

— European Confectionery Equipment Markets: Chocolate Confectionery Production Machinery. 150p. 1993. 1750.00 (*1-56753-560-7*) Frost & Sullivan.

— European Confectionery Equipment Markets: Confectionery Packaging Machinery. 150p. 1993. 1750.00 (*1-56753-562-3*) Frost & Sullivan.

— European Consumer Telephony Markets. 438p. 1993. 3950.00 (*1-56753-541-0*) Frost & Sullivan.

— European Cosmetic & Toiletries Industry Company Profiles. (Orig.). 1992. 495.00 (*1-56753-630-1*, E1582) Frost & Sullivan.

— European Cosmetics & Toiletries Packaging Markets. 299p. 1993. 2900.00 (*1-56753-518-6*) Frost & Sullivan.

— European Datacommunication Services Market. 200p. 1994. 3900.00 (*0-7889-0077-3*) Frost & Sullivan.

— European Dietary Supplement Markets. 266p. 1995. spiral bd. 3800.00 (*0-7889-0188-5*, 3005-88) Frost & Sullivan.

— European Disposable Non-Woven Markets. 275p. 1994. 2100.00 (*0-7889-0069-2*) Frost & Sullivan.

— European Disposal Airway Management Device Markets. 394p. 1995. spiral bd. 3900.00 (*0-7889-0205-9*, 3164-54) Frost & Sullivan.

— European Drug Delivery System Markets. 400p. 1994. 3800.00 (*0-7889-0005-6*) Frost & Sullivan.

— European Durable Non-Woven Markets. 207p. 1994. 2100.00 (*0-7889-0070-6*) Frost & Sullivan.

— European EFT-POS Terminal Markets. 115p. 1993. 1800.00 (*1-56753-883-5*) Frost & Sullivan.

— European Electromagnetic Compatibility Markets: EMC Materials Components. 250p. (Orig.). 1994. 1750.00 (*1-56753-888-6*) Frost & Sullivan.

— European Electromagnetic Compatibility Markets: EMC Test Facilities & Equipment. 250p. (Orig.). 1994. 1750.00 (*1-56753-889-4*) Frost & Sullivan.

— European Electromagnetic Compatibility Markets: EMC Testing & Consultancy Services. 300p. (Orig.). 1994. 1750.00 (*1-56753-890-8*) Frost & Sullivan.

— European Electronic Access Markets. 236p. (Orig.). 1992. 2450.00 (*1-56753-648-4*) Frost & Sullivan.

— European Electronic Data Interchange Markets. 425p. 1994. 3450.00 (*0-7889-0174-5*, 1924-73) Frost & Sullivan.

— European Electronic Image Management System Markets. 265p. 1994. 3900.00 (*1-56753-939-4*) Frost & Sullivan.

— European Electronic Navigation Equipment Markets. 350p. (Orig.). 1993. 3900.00 (*1-56753-884-3*) Frost & Sullivan.

— European Electronic Navigation Equipment Markets: New Opportunities Emerging in Consumer Applications. (Orig.). 1993. 3900.00 (*1-56753-621-2*) Frost & Sullivan.

— European Electronic Switch Markets. 146p. 1993. 1750.00 (*1-56753-537-2*) Frost & Sullivan.

— European EMC Product & Services Supply Markets. 212p. 1994. 975.00 (*0-7889-0060-9*) Frost & Sullivan.

— European Environmental Consultancy Industry. 195p. 1994. 1500.00 (*0-7889-0009-9*) Frost & Sullivan.

— European Environmental Laboratory Testing Markets. 309p. 1994. 3950.00 (*0-7889-0054-4*) Frost & Sullivan.

— European EPOS-EFT POS Terminal Markets: Electronic Funds Transfer at Point of Sale, EFT-POS Markets. 148p. 1993. 1800.00 (*1-56753-567-4*) Frost & Sullivan.

— European EPOS-EFT POS Terminal Markets: Electroonic Point of Sale Markets. 148p. 1993. 1800.00 (*1-56753-566-6*) Frost & Sullivan.

— European EPOS Terminal Markets. 116p. 1993. 1800.00 (*1-56753-882-7*) Frost & Sullivan.

— European Ethical Skin Care Product Markets: Recent Surge in Scientific Interest in Dermatology Promotes Growth. 300p. 1993. 3800.00 (*1-56753-555-0*) Frost & Sullivan.

— European Fabric Washing & Household Care Markets. 234p. 1993. 2400.00 (*1-56753-922-X*) Frost & Sullivan.

— European Fabric Washing & Household Products. 211p. 1993. 2400.00 (*1-56753-921-1*) Frost & Sullivan.

— European Facilities Management Markets. 287p. (Orig.). 1992. 3700.00 (*1-56753-645-X*, E1600) Frost & Sullivan.

— European Facsimilie Scanning & OCR Markets. 475p. 1994. 3700.00 (*0-7889-0039-0*) Frost & Sullivan.

— European Fibre Optic Communications Markets. 164p. 1994. 2400.00 (*1-56753-993-9*) Frost & Sullivan.

— European Fibre Optic Sensor Markets: Growing User Acceptance Generates Competition & Sustains Industry Growth. 416p. 1994. 3800.00 (*1-56753-929-7*) Frost & Sullivan.

— European Flexible Manufacturing System Markets. 206p. (Orig.). 1994. 3800.00 (*0-7889-0114-1*) Frost & Sullivan.

— European Fluid & Drug Delivery Systems Market: Extensive Forecasts Document Country Differences & Usage Trends. 344p. 1992. 1895.00 (*1-56753-078-8*) Frost & Sullivan.

— European Food Aid Markets. 194p. 1994. 3800.00 (*0-7889-0066-8*) Frost & Sullivan.

— European Food & Drink Strategies. (Orig.). 1994. 3800.00 (*0-7889-0117-6*) Frost & Sullivan.

— European Food Processing Equipment Markets. 437p. (Orig.). 1994. 3950.00 (*0-7889-0105-2*) Frost & Sullivan.

— European Fractional Horsepower Motor Markets. 533p. (Orig.). 1994. 3950.00 (*0-7889-0104-4*) Frost & Sullivan.

— European Fragrance & Flavour Markets. 193p. 1994. 1900.00 (*0-7889-0047-1*); 1900.00 (*0-7889-0046-3*) Frost & Sullivan.

— The European Functional Fluids Market. 240p. 1993. 4200.00 (*1-56753-510-0*) Frost & Sullivan.

— European Gas Sensor Markets. 386p. 1994. 3950.00 (*1-56753-983-1*) Frost & Sullivan.

— European General System for Mobile Communications (GSM) A Strategic Report. 233p. 1994. write for info. (*1-56753-896-7*) Frost & Sullivan.

— The European Generic Drugs Market. 207p. 1993. 3900.00 (*1-56753-509-7*) Frost & Sullivan.

— European Heat Exchanger Markets. 370p. 1994. 3950.00 (*0-7889-0172-9*) Frost & Sullivan.

— European Hospital Infection Control Equipment & Supply Market: Governmental Responses to AIDS Stimulate Product Demand. 350p. 1992. 1895.00 (*1-56753-080-X*) Frost & Sullivan.

— European Hospital Information System Markets. 200p. 1994. 3500.00 (*1-56753-977-7*) Frost & Sullivan.

— European Hybrid Circuit Markets. 293p. 1993. 3700.00 (*1-56753-595-X*) Frost & Sullivan.

— European Hydraulic Equipment Markets. 712p. 1995. spiral bd. 3950.00 (*0-7889-0253-9*, 19952-17) Frost & Sullivan.

— European Immunohaematology Reagents & Instruments. (Orig.). 1993. 1500.00 (*0-685-70179-4*) Frost & Sullivan.

— European Immunotherapeutics Markets. 334p. 1994. 3800.00 (*0-7889-0017-X*) Frost & Sullivan.

— European Impact & Non-Impact Printer Markets. 429p. 1995. spiral bd. 3800.00 (*0-7889-0219-9*, 3049-72) Frost & Sullivan.

— European Industrial Battery & Fuel Cell Markets. 257p. 1994. 3900.00 (*0-7889-0010-2*) Frost & Sullivan.

M

— European Industrial Switch Markets. 87p. 1993. 1750.00 (*1-56753-539-9*) Frost & Sullivan.
— European Industrial Vision System Markets. 263p. 1995. spiral bd. 3950.00 (*0-7889-0251-2*, 3086-10) Frost & Sullivan.
— European Industrial Weighing Machinery Markets. 196p. (Orig.). 1994. 3950.00 (*0-7889-0124-9*) Frost & Sullivan.
— European Infectious & Sexually Transmitted Disease Diagnostic Product Markets. 276p. 1994. 3800.00 (*0-685-71264-8*) Frost & Sullivan.
— European Information System Outsourcing Markets. 357p. 1994. 3900.00 (*0-7889-0029-3*) Frost & Sullivan.
— European Integral Horsepower Motor Markets. 470p. 1994. 3950.00 (*0-7889-0042-0*) Frost & Sullivan.
— European Intelligent LAN Hub Markets. 240p. 1994. 2750.00 (*1-56753-978-5*) Frost & Sullivan.
— European Intra-Ocular Lens Markets. 104p. 1994. 1750.00 (*0-7889-0004-8*) Frost & Sullivan.
— European Keyboard - Keyswitches Market. 119p. 1993. 1750.00 (*1-56753-538-0*) Frost & Sullivan.
— European Laboratory Analytical Instrument Markets: Chromatography & LIMS. 209p. 1994. 1950.00 (*1-56753-951-3*) Frost & Sullivan.
— European Laboratory Analytical Instrument Markets: Magnetic Field, Thermal & Other Analysis. 242p. 1994. 1950.00 (*1-56753-953-X*) Frost & Sullivan.
— European Laboratory Analytical Instrument Markets: Spectroscopy & Spectrography. 228p. 1994. 1950.00 (*1-56753-952-1*) Frost & Sullivan.
— European Laminating Material Markets. 240p. 1995. spiral bd. 3800.00 (*0-7889-0182-6*, 3098-21) Frost & Sullivan.
— European LAN Support & Maintenance Markets. 227p. 1994. 3300.00 (*0-7889-0035-8*) Frost & Sullivan.
— European Liquid - Solid & Liquid - Liquid Separations Equipment Markets. 1994. 3800.00 (*1-56753-949-1*) Frost & Sullivan.
— European Lithium Battery Markets. 280p. 1994. 3900.00 (*1-56753-994-7*) Frost & Sullivan.
— European Low Voltage Switch & Fusegear Markets. 395p. (Orig.). 1994. 3950.00 (*0-7889-0118-4*) Frost & Sullivan.
— European Lubricant Addictive Markets. 176p. 1994. 4200.00 (*1-56753-970-X*) Frost & Sullivan.
— European Market for Access Control Lock & Identification Products. 1993. 3450.00 (*1-56753-493-7*) Frost & Sullivan.
— European Market for Automatic Identification Equipment: Need to Improve Productivity & Manufacturing Efficiencies Fuels Increased Implementation. 216p. (Orig.). 1992. 1495.00 (*1-56753-058-3*) Frost & Sullivan.
— The European Market for Computer Maintenance. 1993. 3900.00 (*1-56753-482-1*) Frost & Sullivan.
— The European Market for Digital Telecommunications. 277p. 1993. 3800.00 (*1-56753-526-7*) Frost & Sullivan.
— The European Market for Distributed Control Systems. 295p. 1993. 4200.00 (*1-56753-485-6*) Frost & Sullivan.
— European Market for Fillers & Fibers. 250p. 1993. 4400.00 (*1-56753-585-2*) Frost & Sullivan.
— European Market for Hydrocolloids & Emulsifiers Used in the Food Industry. 238p. 1994. 3800.00 (*1-56753-965-3*) Frost & Sullivan.
— European Market for Industrial Nondestructive Test Equipment & Consumables: Acoustic, Ultrasonic, Eddy Current, Liquid Penetrant & Magnetic Testing & Thermography. 196p. 1993. 2950.00 (*1-56753-583-6*) Frost & Sullivan.
— European Market for Industrial Nondestructive Test Equipment & Consumables: Radiography & Optical Inspection. 240p. 1993. 2950.00 (*1-56753-584-4*) Frost & Sullivan.
— The European Market for Industrial Power Transmissions: Chains, Belts & Mechanical Couplings. 156p. 1993. 1500.00 (*1-56753-513-5*) Frost & Sullivan.
— The European Market for Industrial Power Transmissions: Clutches, Brakes & Hydraulic Couplings. 134p. 1993. 1500.00 (*1-56753-512-7*) Frost & Sullivan.
— The European Market for Industrial Power Transmissions: Gears, Industrial Gearboxes , Geared Motors & Mechanical Variators. 164p. 1993. 1500.00 (*1-56753-511-9*) Frost & Sullivan.
— European Market for Mobile Data Communications. 260p. 1993. 3900.00 (*1-56753-452-X*) Frost & Sullivan.
— European Market for Personal Data-Recorders with Integral Bar Code Scanners Market. 150p. 1993. 1750.00 (*1-56753-470-8*) Frost & Sullivan.
— European Market for Personal Data Recorders with Programmable Portable Data Recorders Market. 150p. 1993. 1750.00 (*1-56753-471-6*) Frost & Sullivan.
— European Market for Personal Data Recorders with Radio Frequency Communications Market. 150p. 1993. 1750.00 (*1-56753-469-4*) Frost & Sullivan.
— European Market for Uninterruptible Power Supplies. 277p. 1993. 3900.00 (*1-56753-893-2*) Frost & Sullivan.
— The European Market for Variable Speed Drives. 216p. 1993. 3900.00 (*1-56753-522-4*) Frost & Sullivan.
— The European Market for X-Ray Diagnostic Images. 1993. 3900.00 (*1-56753-501-1*) Frost & Sullivan.
— European Medical Diagnostic Ultrasound Equipment Markets. 430p. 1995. 3800.00 (*0-7889-0189-3*, 1968-50) Frost & Sullivan.
— European Medical Ventilator Markets. 250p. 1994. 3800.00 (*0-7889-0085-4*) Frost & Sullivan.
— European Membrane Separation System Markets. 581p. 1994. 3950.00 (*0-7889-0176-1*, 1996-10) Frost & Sullivan.
— European Metallic Welding Equipment & Consumables Markets. (Orig.). 1994. 3950.00 (*0-7889-0133-8*) Frost & Sullivan.
— European Minimally Invasive Surgical Equipment Markets. 324p. 1994. 3800.00 (*1-56753-974-2*) Frost & Sullivan.
— European Mobility Aid & Associated Paramedical Product Markets. 385p. 1994. 3800.00 (*1-56753-971-8*) Frost & Sullivan.
— European Multilayer & Flexible Printed Circuit Board Markets. 212p. 1993. 1895.00 (*1-56753-592-5*) Frost & Sullivan.
— European Multilayer & Flexible Printed Circuit Board Markets: Declining Prices Force Shakeout. 230p. 1993. 1895.00 (*1-56753-508-9*) Frost & Sullivan.
— European Multimedia Markets. 439p. 1995. 3700.00 (*0-7889-0179-6*, 3133-73) Frost & Sullivan.
— European Network Systems Integration & Outsourcing: A Strategic Report. 255p. 1993. 3900.00 (*1-56753-596-8*) Frost & Sullivan.
— European Neuroleptic Drug Markets. LC 98-168743. 295p. 1995. spiral bd. 3800.00 (*0-7889-0259-8*, 3075-45) Frost & Sullivan.
— European Non Isotopic Immunoassay Product Markets. 374p. (Orig.). 1994. 3800.00 (*1-56753-891-6*) Frost & Sullivan.
— European Oleochemical Markets. 236p. 1995. spiral bd. 3800.00 (*0-7889-0203-2*, 1911-82) Frost & Sullivan.
— European Ophthalmic Diagnostic Markets. 94p. 1994. 1750.00 (*0-7889-0003-X*) Frost & Sullivan.
— European Ophthalmic Laser Markets. 113p. 1994. 1750.00 (*0-7889-0002-1*) Frost & Sullivan.
— European Original Equipment Market for Automotive Chassis Components. 445p. 1994. 3950.00 (*0-7889-0025-0*) Frost & Sullivan.
— European Orthopaedic Soft Goods & Cast Room Markets. (Orig.). 1994. 3800.00 (*0-7889-0125-7*) Frost & Sullivan.
— European Osteoporosis Treatment Markets. LC 98-168516. 335p. 1995. spiral bd. 4000.00 (*0-7889-0258-X*, 3169-44) Frost & Sullivan.
— European OTC Internal Analgesic Markets. 306p. 1995. spiral bd. 3800.00 (*0-7889-0221-0*, 306344) Frost & Sullivan.
— European over the Counter Cough & Cold Medicine Markets. 392p. 1994. 3800.00 (*0-7889-0141-9*) Frost & Sullivan.
— European Packaging Machinery Markets. 347p. 1994. 3950.00 (*1-56753-999-8*) Frost & Sullivan.
— European Payphone Markets. 265p. 1994. 3800.00 (*0-7889-0108-7*) Frost & Sullivan.
— European Payphone Markets: Radical Shifts in Purchasing Patterns & Technology. 850p. 1992. 1895.00 (*1-56753-335-3*) Frost & Sullivan.
— European PC LAN Market: Highest Growth Rates Found in Germany & Spain. 365p. (Orig.). 1992. 1695.00 (*1-56753-042-7*) Frost & Sullivan.
— European Personal Communications Network Markets. LC 98-168729. 356p. 1995. spiral bd. 3800.00 (*0-7889-0248-2*, 3054-65) Frost & Sullivan.
— European Portable Electric Power Tool Markets. 363p. 1994. 3950.00 (*0-7889-0028-5*) Frost & Sullivan.
— European Position Sensor Markets: New Opportunities Spring from an Ever-Increasing Range of Applications. 219p. 1993. 3950.00 (*1-56753-704-9*) Frost & Sullivan.
— European Positive Displacement (PD) Pump Market. 147p. 1993. 1700.00 (*1-56753-587-9*) Frost & Sullivan.
— European Positive Displacement (PD) Pump Markets. 152p. 1993. 1700.00 (*1-56753-589-5*) Frost & Sullivan.
— European Powder Coating Markets. 360p. 1994. 3800.00 (*0-7889-0101-X*) Frost & Sullivan.
— European Power Supply Manufacturer Profiles. 240p. 1993. 795.00 (*1-56753-586-0*) Frost & Sullivan.
— European Prescription Psychotropic Rheumaceutical Markets. 459p. 1995. spiral bd. 3800.00 (*0-7889-0215-6*, 3066-45) Frost & Sullivan.
— European Printing Ink Markets. 241p. 1995. spiral bd. 3900.00 (*0-7889-0220-2*, 190639) Frost & Sullivan.
— European Private Mobile Radio Markets. LC 98-168935. 473p. 1995. 3800.00 (*0-7889-0255-5*, 3060-65) Frost & Sullivan.
— European Process Analytical Instruments Markets: Complex Process Analysers. 190p. 1993. 1900.00 (*1-56753-571-2*) Frost & Sullivan.
— European Process Analytical Instruments Markets: Process Gas Analysers. 190p. 1993. 1900.00 (*1-56753-569-0*) Frost & Sullivan.
— European Process Control Valve & Actuator Markets. 320p. 1994. 3950.00 (*0-7889-0011-0*) Frost & Sullivan.
— European Professional Lighting Equipment Markets. 327p. 1994. 3950.00 (*0-7889-0056-0*) Frost & Sullivan.
— European Radio Paging Hardware & Service Markets. 257p. 1993. 3895.00 (*1-56753-506-2*) Frost & Sullivan.
— European Rapid Microbiology Markets. 559p. 1994. 3800.00 (*1-56753-979-3*) Frost & Sullivan.
— European Refraction Correction Markets. 103p. 1994. 1750.00 (*0-7889-0001-3*) Frost & Sullivan.
— European Rehabilitation Support Product Markets. 374p. 1995. spiral bd. 3800.00 (*0-7889-0181-8*, 1977-58) Frost & Sullivan.
— European Relay Markets. 408p. (Orig.). 1994. 3400.00 (*0-7889-0086-2*) Frost & Sullivan.
— European Research Biochemical Markets. 280p. 1993. 3800.00 (*1-56753-604-2*) Frost & Sullivan.
— European Research Biochemical Markets: Molecular Biology Stimulates & Rejuvenates the Marketplace. 290p. 1993. 3800.00 (*1-56753-559-3*) Frost & Sullivan.
— European Residential Security Markets. 244p. 1994. 3000.00 (*1-56753-968-8*) Frost & Sullivan.
— European RX to OTC Switching Markets. 154p. 1994. 3800.00 (*0-7889-0102-8*) Frost & Sullivan.
— European Sensor Markets: Old-Line Sensors at Risk, Silicon Micro-Machined Technologies in the Forefront. 414p. (Orig.). 1992. 1495.00 (*1-56753-035-4*) Frost & Sullivan.
— European Septicaemia & Septic Shock Therapy Markets: Increasing Numbers of Patients Paralleled by Decreasing Treatment Costs. 285p. 1993. 3800.00 (*1-56753-558-5*) Frost & Sullivan.
— European Silicon Sensor Markets. 250p. 1993. 2400.00 (*1-56753-536-4*) Frost & Sullivan.
— European Single Layer Printed Circuit Board Markets. 240p. 1993. 1895.00 (*1-56753-591-7*) Frost & Sullivan.
— European Single-Layer Printed Circuit Board Markets: Declining Prices Force Shakeout. 230p. 1993. 1895.00 (*1-56753-507-0*) Frost & Sullivan.
— European Smart Card Markets. 368p. 1994. 3800.00 (*1-56753-990-4*) Frost & Sullivan.
— European Special & Diabetic Food Markets. 260p. 1994. 3800.00 (*0-7889-0058-7*) Frost & Sullivan.
— European Specialty Paper Markets. 1994. 3800.00 (*0-7889-0180-X*, 3091-48) Frost & Sullivan.
— European Stand Alone Bridge & Router Markets: Expanding Communications Needs Prompt Dynamic Changes in Applications & Technology. 237p. 1994. 2750.00 (*1-56753-950-5*) Frost & Sullivan.
— European Stroke Therapy Markets. 240p. 1994. 3800.00 (*0-7889-0051-X*) Frost & Sullivan.
— European Switched Mode Power Supply Markets. 260p. 1994. 3800.00 (*0-7889-0055-2*) Frost & Sullivan.
— European Synthetic Lubricant Markets. 184p. 1994. 3800.00 (*0-7889-0154-0*) Frost & Sullivan.
— European Technical Workstation Markets. 264p. 1994. 3800.00 (*0-7889-0167-2*) Frost & Sullivan.
— European Thrombotic Drug Markets. 280p. 1995. spiral bd. 3800.00 (*0-7889-0216-4*, 3067-45) Frost & Sullivan.
— European Uninterruptible Power Supply & Power Conditioning Markets. 250p. (Orig.). 1993. 3900.00 (*1-56753-885-1*) Frost & Sullivan.
— European Union Chemical Industry & the GATT Agreement. 360p. 1995. spiral bd. 2995.00 (*0-7889-0222-9*, 3090-39) Frost & Sullivan.
— European Value-Added Service Markets. 240p. 1994. 3800.00 (*0-7889-0084-6*) Frost & Sullivan.
— European Videoconferencing Markets. 360p. 1994. 3900.00 (*0-7889-0166-4*) Frost & Sullivan.
— European Waste to Energy Markets. 250p. 1994. 3950.00 (*0-7889-0100-1*) Frost & Sullivan.
— European Water Pollution Monitoring Instrument Markets. 480p. 1995. spiral bd. 3950.00 (*0-7889-0249-0*, 3147-15) Frost & Sullivan.
— European Water Treatment Chemical Markets. 209p. 1993. 4400.00 (*1-56753-530-5*) Frost & Sullivan.
— Far East Variable Speed Drive Market. 250p. 1994. 2295.00 (*0-7889-0023-4*) Frost & Sullivan.
— Fetal, Neonatal & Infant Monitoring Markets. 364p. (Orig.). 1994. 2195.00 (*0-7889-0074-9*) Frost & Sullivan.
— Fiber Optic Communication Application Markets: Fiber in the Loop & Lans Light the Way. 340p. (Orig.). 1992. 1895.00 (*1-56753-402-3*) Frost & Sullivan.
— Field - on Site Wastewater Analytical Instrumentation Markets: Era of Portability Dawns, Regulation Tightens. 231p. 1993. 1495.00 (*1-56753-423-6*) Frost & Sullivan.
— Financial & Marketing Analysis of the World Sensor Industry. 370p. 1993. 1295.00 (*1-56753-445-7*) Frost & Sullivan.
— Fine Chem Source 1994. 292p. 1994. 545.00 (*0-318-72951-2*) Frost & Sullivan.
— Fluid & Drug Delivery System Markets: Patients on the Move: Patches, Ambulatory Packs & Implants. 305p. 1993. 2295.00 (*1-56753-502-X*) Frost & Sullivan.
— Fractional Horsepower Electric Motor Markets: Who's Winning, Who's Losing & Why? 323p. 1993. 2395.00 (*1-56753-505-4*) Frost & Sullivan.
— Generic Prescription Pharmaceutical Markets: Patent Expirations Breathe New Life into Generic Competitors. 314p. 1993. 1995.00 (*1-56753-480-5*) Frost & Sullivan.
— Global Personal Communication System Markets. 460p. 1994. 2995.00 (*0-7889-0146-X*) Frost & Sullivan.
— Global Strategic Assessment of Personal Communications: It's All Here. 609p. 1993. 1695.00 (*1-56753-424-4*) Frost & Sullivan.
— Haematology Reagents & Instruments. (Orig.). 1993. 1500.00 (*0-685-70180-8*) Frost & Sullivan.
— Hazardous Waste Management Equipment & Service Markets: Bright Spot for Defense Contractors to Go Commercial. 185p. (Orig.). 1992. 1895.00 (*1-56753-399-X*) Frost & Sullivan.
— Hazardous Waste Remediation & Management Markets. 308p. 1995. spiral bd. 2295.00 (*0-7889-0195-8*, 5117-15) Frost & Sullivan.
— The Healthcare Compendium: A Demographic & Statistical Analysis Beyond Government Sources. 240p. (Orig.). 1992. 695.00 (*1-56753-052-4*) Frost & Sullivan.
— Healthcare Market Engineering. (Orig.). 1994. 95.00 (*0-7889-0053-6*) Frost & Sullivan.
— Healthcare Scenarios in the Year 2000: A Common Sense Look at Four Alternatives to Get Us There. 279p. 1993. 95.00 (*1-56753-421-X*) Frost & Sullivan.
— Home Diagnostic & Monitoring Markets: FDA & Distribution Issues Characterize a Changing Marketplace. 230p. 1992. 1895.00 (*1-56753-405-8*) Frost & Sullivan.
— Hospital Infection Control Equipment & Supply Markets: Human & Monetary Costs Shape Sterilization & Disinfection Industries. 213p. 1993. 1995.00 (*1-56753-443-0*) Frost & Sullivan.
— Hospital Procedures & Diagnoses Data: 1988-1995 Vol. II: Healthcare Compendium. 1995. spiral bd. 1495.00 (*0-7889-0243-1*, 5232-59) Frost & Sullivan.
— Imitating Human Reasoning: The Viability & Commercialization of Neural Networks & Fuzzy Logic. 227p. (Orig.). 1992. 1895.00 (*1-56753-061-3*) Frost & Sullivan.
— Immunodiagnostic Markets: Long-Term R & D Pays Off. 213p. 1992. 1995.00 (*1-56753-408-2*) Frost & Sullivan.
— Impact & Non-Impact Printer Markets: Marketing Strategies Focus on Applications, Not Technology. 423p. (Orig.). 1992. 1495.00 (*1-56753-034-6*) Frost & Sullivan.
— Incontinence & Ostomy Product Markets: Aggressive Marketers Target Alternate Sites. 340p. 1993. 1695.00 (*1-56753-457-0*) Frost & Sullivan.
— Industrial Automation Market Sourcebook. 310p. 1994. 545.00 (*0-7889-0083-8*) Frost & Sullivan.
— Industrial Bus Interface Board Markets: Higher Performance & Open Systems Stimulate World Growth. 305p. (Orig.). 1992. 1695.00 (*1-56753-029-X*) Frost & Sullivan.
— Industrial Market Engineering. 476p. 1994. 95.00 (*0-7889-0052-8*) Frost & Sullivan.
— Industrial Personal & Occupational Safety Monitor, Device & Accessory Markets: Business Steps up Compliance Efforts. 454p. 1992. 1495.00 (*1-56753-409-0*) Frost & Sullivan.
— Industrial Temperature Measurement & Control in Western Europe: Market for Controllers. 200p. 1993. 1950.00 (*1-56753-581-X*) Frost & Sullivan.
— Industrial Temperature Measurement & Control in Western Europe: Market for Temperature Sensors, Converters & Transmitters. 200p. 1992. 1950.00 (*1-56753-579-8*) Frost & Sullivan.
— Industrial Temperature Measurement & Control in Western Europe: Market for Thermometers, Indicators & Recorders. 200p. 1993. 1950.00 (*1-56753-580-1*) Frost & Sullivan.
— Intelligent Vehicle Highway System Markets. 394p. 1993. 1850.00 (*1-56753-550-X*) Frost & Sullivan.
— International Telecommunications Standards. 307p. 1993. 795.00 (*1-56753-701-4*) Frost & Sullivan.
— The International Telecommunications Standards Service. 225p. 795.00 (*1-56753-597-6*) Frost & Sullivan.
— Johnson & Johnson: Global Expansion in the Face of Intense Competition. 250p. (Orig.). 1993. 1295.00 (*1-56753-624-7*) Frost & Sullivan.
— Laboratory Equipment Markets: A Detailed Database on a 25 Billion Dollar Market. 270p. 1992. 995.00 (*1-56753-082-6*) Frost & Sullivan.
— LAN & WAN Connectivity Markets: Routes, Bridges & Gateways: Are They Obsolete? 287p. 1993. 1695.00 (*1-56753-430-9*) Frost & Sullivan.
— LAN Support Services. 1993. 3200.00 (*1-56753-478-3*) Frost & Sullivan.
— LAN/WAN Network Management Software Service & System Markets: Your First Source about Outsourcing. 198p. 1992. 1695.00 (*1-56753-663-8*) Frost & Sullivan.
— Latin American Telecommunications Service & Equipment Markets: Emphasis on Service Offers Investment Opportunities to Equipment Manufacturers. 375p. 1994. 2695.00 (*1-56753-937-8*) Frost & Sullivan.
— Legal Information System Markets (U. S.) 262p. 1992. 2250.00 (*1-56753-666-2*, A2502) Frost & Sullivan.
— Long Distance & Reseller Markets: Small Players Rise Again. 295p. 1992. 1695.00 (*1-56753-385-X*) Frost & Sullivan.
— Man Made Fibres in the European Community: Proportion of Imports Expected to Exceed 10 Percent of Market by 1997. 248p. 1993. 4500.00 (*1-56753-556-9*) Frost & Sullivan.
— Market for Antifungals. 310p. 1992. 3700.00 (*1-56753-674-3*, A2500) Frost & Sullivan.
— Market for Bathroom Products & Deodorants (Europe) 305p. 1992. 1250.00 (*1-56753-736-7*, E1580) Frost & Sullivan.
— Market for Cellular Communications (Europe) 272p. 1992. 3850.00 (*1-56753-746-4*, E1586) Frost & Sullivan.
— Market for Dairy Products (Europe) Butter Cheese & Fermented Products. 400p. 1992. 1200.00 (*1-56753-726-X*, E1616) Frost & Sullivan.
— Market for Dairy Products (Europe) Milk, Cream & Dairy Drinks. 290p. 1992. 1200.00 (*1-56753-725-1*, E1617) Frost & Sullivan.
— Market for Dairy Products (Europe) Yogurt, Dairy Desserts & Ice Cream. 325p. 1992. 1200.00 (*1-56753-724-3*, E1618) Frost & Sullivan.
— Market for Facsimile Equipment (Europe) 259p. 1992. 3800.00 (*1-56753-711-1*, E1562) Frost & Sullivan.
— Market for Fragrances (Europe) 383p. 1992. 1250.00 (*1-56753-710-3*, E1576) Frost & Sullivan.
— Market for Hair Care (Europe) 397p. 1992. 1250.00 (*1-56753-708-1*, E1579) Frost & Sullivan.
— Market for Hazardous Waste Management (Europe) 412p. 1992. 3900.00 (*1-56753-707-3*, E1590) Frost & Sullivan.
— Market for Heat Exchangers (U. S.) 253p. 1992. 2450.00 (*1-56753-706-5*, A2547) Frost & Sullivan.
— Market for High Power Semiconductors (Europe) 386p. 1992. 2300.00 (*0-685-70257-X*) Frost & Sullivan.
— Market for Information Technology (IT) Security Products & Services (Europe) 415p. 1992. 3400.00 (*1-56753-787-1*, E1513) Frost & Sullivan.
— Market for Intravenous Therapy & Interal Nutrition (Europe) 405p. 1992. 3800.00 (*1-56753-784-7*, E1584) Frost & Sullivan.
— Market for LAN Value Added Resellers (U. S.) 300p. 1992. 2400.00 (*1-56753-781-2*, A2456) Frost & Sullivan.
— Market for Liquid - Solid Separation Equipment (U. S.) 301p. 1992. 2800.00 (*1-56753-780-4*, A2568) Frost & Sullivan.

An Asterisk (*) at the beginning of an entry indicates that the title is appearing for the first time.

— Market for Local Area Network (LAN) Maintenance (Europe) 272p. 1992. 3200.00 (*1-56753-779-0*, E1556) Frost & Sullivan.
— Market for Low Power Semiconductors - Smart Power ICs (Europe) 387p. 1992. 2300.00 (*1-56753-778-2*, E1614) Frost & Sullivan.
— Market for Make-Up (Europe) 394p. 1992. 1250.00 (*1-56753-777-4*, E1577) Frost & Sullivan.
— Market for Manufacturing Systems Integration (U. S.) 250p. 1992. 2400.00 (*1-56753-775-8*, A2551) Frost & Sullivan.
— Market for Meat & Meat Products (Europe) Carcass Meats. 382p. 1994. 1200.00 (*1-56753-774-X*, E1619) Frost & Sullivan.
— Market for Meat & Meat Products (Europe) Comminuted Meat Products. 389p. 1992. 1200.00 (*1-56753-773-1*, E1621) Frost & Sullivan.
— Market for Meat & Meat Products (Europe) Prepared Meat & Associated Products. 411p. 1992. 1200.00 (*1-56753-772-3*, E1620) Frost & Sullivan.
— Market for Metropolitan Area Networks (U. S.) 233p. 1992. 3300.00 (*1-56753-770-7*, A2540) Frost & Sullivan.
— Market for Military Automated Mission Planning (U. S.) 300p. 1992. 2700.00 (*1-56753-769-3*, A2516) Frost & Sullivan.
— Market for Military C3I (Europe) 302p. 1992. 2900.00 (*1-56753-768-5*, E1632) Frost & Sullivan.
— Market for Military Passive Night Vision (U. S.) 250p. 1992. 2450.00 (*1-56753-755-3*, A2495) Frost & Sullivan.
— Market for Military Power Supplies (U. S.) 250p. 1992. 2700.00 (*1-56753-756-1*, A2541) Frost & Sullivan.
— Market for Multichip Modules (MCMs) (U. S.) 215p. 1992. 2200.00 (*1-56753-760-X*, A2530) Frost & Sullivan.
— Market for Multimedia (Europe) 340p. 1992. 3700.00 (*1-56753-762-6*, E1646) Frost & Sullivan.
— Market for North American Video & Audio Post-Production Equipment (U. S.) 200p. 1992. 1450.00 (*1-56753-765-0*) Frost & Sullivan.
— Market for Oral Hygiene Products (Europe) 384p. 1992. 1250.00 (*1-56753-800-2*, E1581) Frost & Sullivan.
— Market for Outsourcing Services (U. S.) 246p. 1992. 2450.00 (*1-56753-802-9*, A2497) Frost & Sullivan.
— Market for Pet Healthcare Products (Europe) 405p. 1992. 3800.00 (*1-56753-823-1*, E1608) Frost & Sullivan.
— Market for Process Control: Flow & Level Instrumentation. 176p. 1993. 1900.00 (*1-56753-490-2*) Frost & Sullivan.
— Market for Process Control: Temperature Instrumentation. 180p. 1993. 1900.00 (*1-56753-489-9*) Frost & Sullivan.
— Market for Process Control Pressure - Differentiation Pressure Instrumentation. 180p. 1993. 1900.00 (*1-56753-491-0*) Frost & Sullivan.
— Market for Professional Studio & Portable Video Equipment in North America (U. S.) 200p. 1992. 1450.00 (*1-56753-805-3*, A2462) Frost & Sullivan.
— Market for Skin Care (Europe) 394p. 1992. 1250.00 (*1-56753-809-6*, E1578) Frost & Sullivan.
— Market for Trunked Radio Equipment for SMRs & Users (U. S.) 225p. 1992. 2900.00 (*1-56753-819-3*, A2510) Frost & Sullivan.
— Market for TV Transmission Systems Technology in North America (U. S.) 397p. 1992. 1850.00 (*1-56753-820-7*, A2461) Frost & Sullivan.
— Market for UNIX (Europe) 350p. 1992. 3900.00 (*1-56753-821-5*, E1593) Frost & Sullivan.
— Market for VANs (Europe) 291p. 1992. 3900.00 (*1-56753-855-X*, E1601) Frost & Sullivan.
— Mechanical Springs Markets. 360p. 1994. 1895.00 (*0-7889-0090-0*) Frost & Sullivan.
— Medical - Surgical Market, '94. 346p. 1994. 595.00 (*1-56753-934-3*) Frost & Sullivan.
— Medical & Dental Suction & Irrigation Equipment Markets: Environment & Infection Control Issues Encourage Innovations. 279p. 1993. 1695.00 (*1-56753-451-1*) Frost & Sullivan.
— Medical Catheter Markets: New Applications, Technologies, & Safety Issues Overcome Cost Containment. 245p. (Orig.). 1992. 1895.00 (*1-56753-057-5*) Frost & Sullivan.
— Medical Device Markets: A Detailed Database on a 41 Billion Dollar Market. 240p. 1992. 995.00 (*1-56753-085-0*) Frost & Sullivan.
— Medical Diagnostic Electronics Products: Market Share Analysis, 1991. 246p. (Orig.). 1992. 1495.00 (*1-56753-064-8*) Frost & Sullivan.
— Medical Disposables Markets: A Detailed Database on a 45 Billion Dollar Market. 340p. 1992. 995.00 (*1-56753-084-2*) Frost & Sullivan.
— Medical Image Management Markets: Telemedicine Is Here: PACS & Teleradiology Lead the Way. 215p. (Orig.). 1992. 1895.00 (*1-56753-079-6*) Frost & Sullivan.
— Medical Monitoring Markets: A Detailed Database on a 6 Billion Dollar Market. 480p. 1992. 995.00 (*1-56753-087-7*) Frost & Sullivan.
— Medical Services Market: Increasing Cost Constraints Put 20 Billion Dollar Business Up for Grabs. 379p. (Orig.). 1992. 1295.00 (*1-56753-036-2*) Frost & Sullivan.
— Medical Waste Management & Disposable Markets: Regulations, Regulations & More Regulations Promote Rapid Technological Innovations. 315p. 1992. 1895.00 (*1-56753-382-5*) Frost & Sullivan.
— Membrane Separation Systems Market (Europe) 387p. 1992. 3600.00 (*1-56753-860-6*, E1594) Frost & Sullivan.
— Microdisk Drives vs. Flash Memory Cards: World Technology Battle over Form, Function, Power, Capacity, Price & Access. 259p. (Orig.). 1992. 1695.00 (*1-56753-056-7*) Frost & Sullivan.
— MIL-SPEC, Ruggedized, & Commercially Rugged Computer Market: Purchasing Shifts Toward Commercial Products Offering Portability. 322p. (Orig.). 1992. 1495.00 (*1-56753-071-0*) Frost & Sullivan.
— Military Electro-Optics Equipment Markets: Despite Peace Dividend, Numerous Segments Still Hot. 174p. (Orig.). 1992. 1695.00 (*1-56753-065-6*) Frost & Sullivan.
— Military Reconnaissance Market (U. S.) 350p. 1992. 2600.00 (*1-56753-865-7*, A2521) Frost & Sullivan.
— Military Simulation & Training Systems Market: Increased Networking Propels Mission Simulation. 251p. 1993. 1695.00 (*1-56753-447-3*) Frost & Sullivan.
— MobilCom '94. 248p. 1994. 595.00 (*1-56753-933-5*) Frost & Sullivan.
— Mobile Communication Service Markets: Enhanced Offerings Expand User-Base. 396p. 1993. 1695.00 (*1-56753-465-1*) Frost & Sullivan.
— Modem Markets: Survival of the Fastest. 265p. 1992. 1495.00 (*1-56753-388-4*) Frost & Sullivan.
— Molecular Probe Markets: Hoffman-La Roche Bids for Dominance. 230p. (Orig.). 1992. 1895.00 (*1-56753-379-5*) Frost & Sullivan.
— Monoclonal Antibody Markets. 320p. 1994. 2295.00 (*0-7889-0057-9*) Frost & Sullivan.
— Monoclonal Antibody Markets: Enormous Potential in Diagnostic & Therapeutic Products, Cancer Leads the Way. 267p. (Orig.). 1992. 1995.00 (*1-56753-048-6*) Frost & Sullivan.
— Motor Control & Accessories Market (U. S.) 284p. 1992. 2400.00 (*1-56753-868-1*, A2494) Frost & Sullivan.
— Motor Control, Feedback Elements & Variable Speed Drive Markets: Technology Advancements & Production Methods Transform Industry. 306p. 1993. 2400.00 (*1-56753-483-X*) Frost & Sullivan.
— Non PCB Mounted Thermal Management Component Markets. 1993. 1750.00 (*1-56753-477-5*) Frost & Sullivan.
— North American Air Pollution Control Equipment: Deadline 1995 - Compliance with CAAA Phase I. 325p. (Orig.). 1992. 1695.00 (*1-56753-336-1*) Frost & Sullivan.
— North American Air Pollution Control Equipment Markets. 455p. 1994. spiral bd. 2395.00 (*0-7889-0149-4*, 5194-15) Frost & Sullivan.
— North American Automotive Sensor Markets: Legislation Guarantees Growth, New Technologies Guarantee Battle Royale. 342p. 1992. 1895.00 (*1-56753-394-9*) Frost & Sullivan.
— North American Industrial Operator Interface Device & Software Markets. 298p. 1994. 2195.00 (*0-7889-0142-7*) Frost & Sullivan.
— North American Power Semiconductor Markets: Who's Got the Power? Vendors Target Portability & Energy Efficiency. 300p. 1994. 1995.00 (*0-7889-0026-9*) Frost & Sullivan.
— North American T1 Equipment Markets: LAN Interconnectivity, Hybrid Networks Accurate Growth. 520p. (Orig.). 1992. 1695.00 (*1-56753-375-2*) Frost & Sullivan.
— Obstetrics & Gynecological Pharmaceutical Markets: New Delivery Systems for Changing Lifestyles. 288p. 1993. 1995.00 (*1-56753-453-8*) Frost & Sullivan.
— Ophthalmic Diagnostic Equipment Markets: Industry Focuses on Automated Equipment & Corneal Topography. 343p. 1992. 1695.00 (*1-56753-414-7*) Frost & Sullivan.
— Ophthalmic Pharmaceuticals: Successful Laboratory Results Equal Market Success. 180p. (Orig.). 1992. 1895.00 (*1-56753-337-X*) Frost & Sullivan.
— Ophthalmic Product Markets: Manufacturers Seek Ways to Penetrate Untapped Markets. 400p. 1993. 1995.00 (*1-56753-572-0*) Frost & Sullivan.
— Ophthalmic Surgical Device Markets: New IDL Technology Improves Reimbursement Outlook. 204p. 1992. 1695.00 (*1-56753-418-X*) Frost & Sullivan.
— Opportunities & Directions in Antisense & Other Oligonucleotide-Based Technologies. 218p. 1993. 1495.00 (*1-56753-603-4*) Frost & Sullivan.
— OptoSource '94. 396p. 1994. 595.00 (*1-56753-959-9*) Frost & Sullivan.
— Pain Management: Expiring Patents Open OTC Markets. 332p. 1993. 1995.00 (*1-56753-488-0*) Frost & Sullivan.
— Patient Monitoring Markets: Integrated Non-Invasive Products Enhance Manufacturer Opportunities. 317p. (Orig.). 1992. 1995.00 (*1-56753-396-5*) Frost & Sullivan.
— PC LAN Markets: Downsizing, Peer to Peer & FDDI-Copper Stir the Pot. 380p. (Orig.). 1992. 1495.00 (*1-56753-380-9*) Frost & Sullivan.
— PCB Mounted Thermal Management Component Markets. 1993. 1750.00 (*1-56753-476-7*) Frost & Sullivan.
— Pen, Palmtop, & Notebook Computer & Peripheral Markets: Applications, Applications, Applications. 364p. (Orig.). 1992. 1495.00 (*1-56753-069-9*) Frost & Sullivan.
— Perfumery, Cosmetic & Toiletry Chemical Markets in the European Community: Perfumery & Cosmetic Chemicals. 189p. 1994. 2750.00 (*1-56753-606-9*) Frost & Sullivan.
— Perfumery, Cosmetic & Toiletry Chemical Markets in the European Community: Toiletry Chemicals. 186p. 1994. 2750.00 (*1-56753-605-0*) Frost & Sullivan.
— Personal Protection Safety Product Markets. 170p. 1994. 1650.00 (*0-7889-0031-5*); 1650.00 (*0-7889-0032-3*) Frost & Sullivan.
— Pharmaceutical Market Outlook. 53p. 1994. 695.00 (*0-7889-0065-X*) Frost & Sullivan.
— Pharmaceutical Markets: A Detailed Database on a 94 Billion Dollar Market. 270p. 1992. 995.00 (*1-56753-083-4*) Frost & Sullivan.
— Pharmasource, '94. 311p. 1994. 595.00 (*1-56753-985-8*) Frost & Sullivan.
— Pickles & Chutney Markets. 263p. 1993. 1200.00 (*1-56753-553-4*) Frost & Sullivan.
— Polymers-Plastics Market 1994. 239p. 1994. 545.00 (*0-7889-0033-1*) Frost & Sullivan.
— Positive Displacement Pumps: European Positive Displacement (PD) Pump Markets. 160p. 1993. 1700.00 (*1-56753-588-7*) Frost & Sullivan.
— Power Transmission Sourcebook. 309p. 1994. 545.00 (*0-7889-0008-0*) Frost & Sullivan.
— Premises Wiring Systems (U. S.) 350p. 1992. 3300.00 (*1-56753-906-8*, A2479) Frost & Sullivan.
— Private-Line Service Markets: High-Capacity T-Services, CAPS to Grow Vigorously. 287p. 1993. 1695.00 (*1-56753-908-4*) Frost & Sullivan.
— Process Control Markets Instrumentation. Hammersley, Milmoth, ed. 230p. 1992. pap. text 995.00 (*1-56753-910-6*) Frost & Sullivan.
— Process Control Source, 1994. 250p. 1994. 545.00 (*0-7889-0041-2*) Frost & Sullivan.
— Profiles of European Clinical Diagnostic Industry. 313p. 1993. 1500.00 (*0-685-71265-6*) Frost & Sullivan.
— Profiles of European Computer Equipment & Service Suppliers. 253p. 1994. 975.00 (*0-7889-0007-2*) Frost & Sullivan.
— Profiles of European Datacommunications Equipment & Service Suppliers. 364p. 1994. 950.00 (*1-56753-995-5*) Frost & Sullivan.
— Profiles of European Electro-Mechanical Component Suppliers. 350p. 1994. 895.00 (*0-685-71483-7*) Frost & Sullivan.
— Profiles of European Electronic Chemical Companies. 305p. 1995. spiral bd. 1500.00 (*0-7889-0246-6*, 3089-39) Frost & Sullivan.
— Profiles of European Electronic Test & Measurement Suppliers. 366p. 1994. 950.00 (*1-56753-984-X*) Frost & Sullivan.
— Profiles of European OTC Pharmaceutical Manufacturers & Suppliers: Continued Growth in a 45 Billion Dollar Industry. 300p. 1993. 1495.00 (*1-56753-557-7*) Frost & Sullivan.
— Profiles of European Pneumatic & Hydraulic Equipment Suppliers. (Orig.). 1994. 950.00 (*0-7889-0116-8*) Frost & Sullivan.
— Profiles of European Printed Circuit Board Manufacturers: A Market Assessment. 225p. 1993. 695.00 (*1-56753-564-X*) Frost & Sullivan.
— Profiles of European Suppliers of Process Control Instrumentation. 364p. 1994. 995.00 (*1-56753-955-6*) Frost & Sullivan.
— Profiles of PCB Manufacturers. 298p. 1994. 995.00 (*0-7889-0140-0*) Frost & Sullivan.
— Profiles of U. S. Test & Measurement Equipment Manufacturers. 308p. 1994. 995.00 (*1-56753-969-6*) Frost & Sullivan.
— RBOC Strategies in Data Communications. 180p. 1993. 2400.00 (*1-56753-547-X*) Frost & Sullivan.
— RBOC Strategies in Information Services. 180p. 1993. 2400.00 (*1-56753-548-8*) Frost & Sullivan.
— Regional Holding Companies Refocus Channel Efforts: Returning to Home Regions & Telecon Products. 341p. (Orig.). 1992. 1295.00 (*1-56753-049-4*) Frost & Sullivan.
— Robot Markets: Increased Plant Automation Translates to 10 Percent Annual Growth. 277p. 1993. 1895.00 (*1-56753-472-4*) Frost & Sullivan.
— Satellite Communications in North American Commercial Systems (U. S.) 200p. 1992. 2900.00 (*1-56753-916-5*, A2473) Frost & Sullivan.
— Sauces & Dressing Markets. 295p. 1993. 1200.00 (*1-56753-551-8*) Frost & Sullivan.
— Scanning & OCR Devices (U. S.) 385p. 1992. 2900.00 (*1-56753-917-3*, A2524) Frost & Sullivan.
— Scanning & OCR Market (Europe) 270p. 1992. 3700.00 (*1-56753-918-1*, E1595) Frost & Sullivan.
— Seasoning & Condiment Markets. 319p. 1993. 1200.00 (*1-56753-552-6*) Frost & Sullivan.
— Sensor Market '94. 244p. 1994. 545.00 (*1-56753-932-7*) Frost & Sullivan.
— Site Cleanup under Superfund, DOD & DOE Markets: High Growth Potential. 268p. 1993. 1495.00 (*1-56753-458-9*) Frost & Sullivan.
— Soft Tissue Implant Markets: Manufacturers Address Regulations & Defend Against Litigation. 221p. 1993. 1895.00 (*1-56753-454-6*) Frost & Sullivan.
— Speech, Image, & Video Data Compression Markets: Chips, Board, & Software Transcend Data Cram Barriers. 208p. (Orig.). 1992. 1895.00 (*1-56753-075-3*) Frost & Sullivan.
— Standalone Facsimile Equipment Market (U. S.) 200p. 1992. 2900.00 (*1-56753-827-4*, A2515) Frost & Sullivan.
— Strategic Analysis of System Integration & Outstanding Markets. 420p. 1993. 1495.00 (*1-56753-464-3*) Frost & Sullivan.
— Strategies for Marketing Cosmetics & Toiletries in Europe: Competitive Positioning in a 33 Billion Dollar Marketplace. 469p. 1993. 3800.00 (*1-56753-565-8*) Frost & Sullivan.
— Survey of Rapid Prototyping End-Users: First Generation a Smashing Success, End-Users Waiting for Next Generation Systems. 425p. (Orig.). 1992. 1695.00 (*1-56753-398-1*) Frost & Sullivan.
— Telecom Distribution Channel Analysis: Complex Issues, Trends & Channel Definitions Clarified. 377p. 1992. 995.00 (*1-56753-415-5*) Frost & Sullivan.
— Telecom Sourcebook, 1993. 1993. 545.00 (*1-56753-594-1*) Frost & Sullivan.
— Telecommunications Market Sourcebook, 1995 Edition. 298p. 1995. spiral bd. 595.00 (*0-7889-0217-2*, 2827-68) Frost & Sullivan.
— Telemanagement Systems, Software, & Services Market: Who's Winning, Who's Losing, & Why. 303p. (Orig.). 1992. 1495.00 (*1-56753-044-3*) Frost & Sullivan.
— Test & Measurement Equipment '94. 298p. 1994. 545.00 (*1-56753-960-2*) Frost & Sullivan.
— Therapeutic & Surgical Equipment Markets: New Technologies Flourish Despite Slow FDA Approval & Reimbursement Issues. 251p. 1993. 1895.00 (*1-56753-427-9*) Frost & Sullivan.
— Therapeutic Surgical & Electronic Device Markets: A Detailed Database on a 13 Billion Dollar Market. 280p. 1992. 995.00 (*1-56753-081-8*) Frost & Sullivan.
— U. S. Absorbable & Erodible Biomaterial Product Markets: Emerging Technologies Create Multi-Billion Dollar Industry. 326p. 1995. spiral bd. 1995.00 (*0-7889-0206-7*, 523954) Frost & Sullivan.
— U. S. Air Emissions Monitor & Analyzer Markets: Multiple Environmental Regulations Continue to Drive Growth. 400p. (Orig.). 1994. 1895.00 (*1-56753-892-4*) Frost & Sullivan.
— U. S. Allergy & Asthma Markets. LC 97-212932. 300p. 1994. 3295.00 (*0-7889-0158-3*) Frost & Sullivan.
— U. S. Allergy & Asthma Treatment Markets: New Approaches in Therapy Promise Major Breakthroughs. 240p. 1993. 2295.00 (*1-56753-544-5*) Frost & Sullivan.
— U. S. Analytical Instruments in Process Control. 1994. 1995.00 (*0-7889-0147-8*) Frost & Sullivan.
— U. S. & International Production Market for T. V. & New Video Technologies (U. S.), 2 vols., Set. 1992. 2450.00 (*1-56753-840-1*, A2258) Frost & Sullivan.
— U. S. Anesthesia & Gas Monitoring Equipment Markets Continuing Development of Integrated & Compact Products. 210p. 1994. 1995.00 (*0-7889-0027-7*) Frost & Sullivan.
— U. S. Antifungal Markets: High Growth Era for Systemic & OTC Products. 340p. (Orig.). 1994. 2495.00 (*1-56753-899-1*) Frost & Sullivan.
— U. S. Autoimmune Disease Markets. LC 97-213049. 370p. 1994. 2395.00 (*0-7889-0138-9*) Frost & Sullivan.
— U. S. Autoimmune Disease Therapeutic Markets: Betaseron & Other New Compounds Advance Through Clinical Trials. 450p. 1993. 1995.00 (*1-56753-545-3*) Frost & Sullivan.
— U. S. Automotive Hard Parts Markets. 460p. 1994. 2395.00 (*0-7889-0063-3*) Frost & Sullivan.
— U. S. Biopharmaceutical Markets: Wall Street Dries Up: Growth Through Alliances. 345p. 1994. 1995.00 (*0-7889-0088-9*) Frost & Sullivan.
— U. S. Cable Television & Associated Technology Product Markets. (Orig.). 1994. 2295.00 (*0-614-00722-4*) Frost & Sullivan.
— U. S. Call Processing Equipment Markets: Popularity of Call Centers & Computer Integration Creates a Dramatic Revolution. 401p. 1993. 2895.00 (*1-56753-703-0*) Frost & Sullivan.
— U. S. Cellular & PCS Telephone, Pager & Accessory Markets: Time to Focus on Applications. 546p. 1993. 2295.00 (*1-56753-705-7*) Frost & Sullivan.
— U. S. Communications Test Equipment Markets. 260p. 1994. 1895.00 (*0-614-00344-X*) Frost & Sullivan.
— U. S. Complex Carbohydrate Therapeutics Markets. 1994. 2195.00 (*0-7889-0135-4*) Frost & Sullivan.
— U. S. Computer Outlet to Laser Disk (Cold) Markets. 256p. 1994. 2495.00 (*0-7889-0095-1*) Frost & Sullivan.
— U. S. Computers in the Banking Industry Markets. (Orig.). 1994. 1995.00 (*0-7889-0137-0*) Frost & Sullivan.
— U. S. Customer Receptions of Diagnostic Imaging Equipment: Users Evaluate Manufacturers. 250p. 1993. 1195.00 (*1-56753-573-9*) Frost & Sullivan.
— U. S. Data Compression Markets: Established Standards Set Stage for Rhenomenal Growth Quarterly. 239p. 1995. spiral bd. 2995.00 (*0-7889-0214-8*, 5179-26) Frost & Sullivan.
— U. S. Data Compression Product Markets: Video Compression Leads Growth Through the 1990s. 207p. (Orig.). 1994. 1895.00 (*1-56753-926-2*) Frost & Sullivan.
— U. S. Desktop Video Markets: The First Definitive Business & Technology Assessment. 450p. 1993. 1895.00 (*1-56753-841-X*) Frost & Sullivan.
— U. S. E-Mail & Voice Mail Markets. 266p. (Orig.). 1992. 2900.00 (*1-56753-656-5*) Frost & Sullivan.
— U. S. Earth Moving Equipment Markets. 313p. 1994. 1995.00 (*0-7889-0143-5*) Frost & Sullivan.
— The U. S. EFT - POS Debit Terminal Market. 279p. 1993. 2900.00 (*1-56753-527-5*) Frost & Sullivan.
— U. S. Electro-Optical Instrument & Inspection System Markets. 336p. 1994. 2195.00 (*0-7889-0144-3*) Frost & Sullivan.
— U. S. Electronic Access Control System Markets Requirements: High Security Promote Biometric Identification. 250p. 1994. 1895.00 (*1-56753-998-X*) Frost & Sullivan.
— U. S. Electronic-Electrical Adhesive, Sealant & Coating Markets: Growth Applications Swing Toward Polyimide. 250p. 1993. 2895.00 (*1-56753-574-7*) Frost & Sullivan.
— U. S. Emergency & Trauma Care Device Markets: New Technologies Focus on Safety & Ease of Use. 342p. (Orig.). 1995. spiral bd. 1895.00 (*0-7889-0119-2*, 5078-54) Frost & Sullivan.
— U. S. Enclosed Geardrive & Gearmotor Markets: Another Traditional Domestic Market under International Pressure. 298p. 1993. 2395.00 (*1-56753-546-1*) Frost & Sullivan.

— U. S. Ethical Nutrition Markets: Manufacturers Target Home Healthcare for Growth. 1994. 1895.00 (*0-7889-0061-7*) Frost & Sullivan.
— U. S. Federal Non-DOD Physical Security Equipment Markets: Government Market Still Provides Lucrative Growth. 325p. (Orig.). 1994. 1995.00 (*0-7889-0113-3*) Frost & Sullivan.
— U. S. Field & On-Site Waste Water Analytical Instrument Markets. 360p. 1995. spiral bd. 1995.00 (*0-7889-0150-8*) Frost & Sullivan.
— U. S. Filtration Product Markets: A Comprehensive Overview of Four Filtration Types: Macro, Micro, Ultra, & Reverse Osmosis. 1994. 1995.00 (*1-56753-996-3*) Frost & Sullivan.
— U. S. Fine & Ultrafine Filtration Product Markets: Capturing Smaller Particles Generates Larger Dollars. 470p. 1994. 1995.00 (*1-56753-966-1*) Frost & Sullivan.
— U. S. Fitness & Exercise Equipment Markets: How Is the Industry Shaping Up? 520p. (Orig.). 1994. 1895.00 (*0-685-71179-X*) Frost & Sullivan.
— U. S. Fluid & Drug Delivery System Markets. (Orig.). 1994. 2295.00 (*0-7889-0097-8*) Frost & Sullivan.
— U. S. Gasket Packaging & Mechanical Sealing Device Markets. 246p. 1993. 2895.00 (*1-56753-577-1*) Frost & Sullivan.

M

— U. S. Genitourological Pharmaceutical & Diagnostic Markets: Competitors Focus on Quality of Life for an Aging Population. 233p. 1995. spiral bd. 2495.00 (*0-7889-0202-4*, 5080-45) Frost & Sullivan.
— U. S. Ground Based & Ship Based Electronic Warfare Markets. 400p. 1992. 2700.00 (*1-56753-692-1*, A2377) Frost & Sullivan.
— U. S. Healthcare Compendium Vol. I: A Demographic & Statistical Analysis. 221p. (Orig.). 1994. 795.00 (*0-7889-0127-3*) Frost & Sullivan.
— U. S. Home Diagnostic & Monitoring Product Markets: Cost Containment Pressures Motivate Self-Testing. 289p. 1994. 1995.00 (*0-7889-0018-8*) Frost & Sullivan.
— U. S. Home Improvement Product Markets: DIY: A Bright Spot in a Mature Construction Industry. 290p. 1993. 2595.00 (*1-56753-629-8*) Frost & Sullivan.
— U. S. Hospital Infection Control Equipment & Supply Markets: New Product Development Substantially Alters Market Share. 360p. 1994. 2295.00 (*1-56753-961-0*) Frost & Sullivan.
— U. S. Hospital Information Systems Market. 388p. 1992. 2600.00 (*1-56753-683-2*, A2546) Frost & Sullivan.
— U. S. Hospital Kit & Tray Markets: Manufacturers Meet User Demands with Customization & Safety Features. 358p. 1994. 1895.00 (*0-7889-0107-9*) Frost & Sullivan.
— U. S. Hospital Respiratory Therapy Markets: Vendors Strategize in the Face of Economic Pressures. 290p. 1994. 1995.00 (*1-56753-945-9*) Frost & Sullivan.
— U. S. Hot Melt Markets: Technology Is Geared for Fast Packaging Applications. 271p. (Orig.). 1994. 2995.00 (*1-56753-895-9*) Frost & Sullivan.
— U. S. Hydraulic Power Component Markets: Applications Open Opportunities As Industry Experiences Resurgance. 350p. 1995. spiral bd. 2495.00 (*0-7889-0250-4*, 5130-17) Frost & Sullivan.
— U. S. Immunodiagnostic Markets: Industry Leader Aggressively Pursues Market Share Through New Instrumentation. 350p. 1994. 2295.00 (*0-7889-0087-0*) Frost & Sullivan.
— U. S. Implantable & Interventional Cardiovascular Device Markets. 328p. (Orig.). 1995. spiral bd. 2295.00 (*0-7889-0130-3*, 5084-54) Frost & Sullivan.
— U. S. Industrial Air Filtration Markets. (Orig.). 1994. 1995.00 (*0-7889-0129-X*) Frost & Sullivan.
— U. S. Industrial & Scientific Laser System Markets Expanding Industrial Sales Lead Resurgence. (Orig.). 1994. 1895.00 (*0-7889-0132-X*) Frost & Sullivan.
— U. S. Industrial Battery Markets. 26p. 1995. spiral bd. 2495.00 (*0-7889-0163-X*, 5125-27) Frost & Sullivan.
— U. S. Industrial Gas Sensor Markets: Migration from Traditional to More Innovative Technologies. 237p. 1994. 1895.00 (*0-7889-0037-4*) Frost & Sullivan.
— U. S. Industrial Scale & Weighing Equipment Markets: Systems Approach Tilts the Balance. 350p. 1993. 2395.00 (*1-56753-515-1*) Frost & Sullivan.
— U. S. Industrial Solvent Markets: New Environmental Legislation Changes Market Dynamics. 260p. 1994. 2295.00 (*0-7889-0078-1*) Frost & Sullivan.
— U. S. Intravenous Equipment & Supply Markets Vol. 1: Intravenous Solutions. 101p. 1993. 1295.00 (*1-56753-532-1*) Frost & Sullivan.
— U. S. Intravenous Equipment & Supply Markets Vol. 2: Vascular Access Devices. 182p. 1993. 1295.00 (*1-56753-533-X*) Frost & Sullivan.
— U. S. Intravenous Equipment & Supply Markets Vol. 3: Infusion Devices. 155p. 1993. 1295.00 (*1-56753-534-8*) Frost & Sullivan.
— U. S. ISDN Customer Premise Equipment (CPE) Markets. 294p. 1994. 3300.00 (*1-56753-927-0*) Frost & Sullivan.
— U. S. Large Cogeneration System Equipment Markets: Competition Intensifies As Industry Matures. 291p. 1995. spiral bd. 2395.00 (*0-7889-0213-X*, 5008-14) Frost & Sullivan.
— U. S. Liquid & Solid Separation Equipment Markets. (Orig.). 1994. 1895.00 (*0-7889-0128-1*) Frost & Sullivan.
— U. S. Long Distance & Reseller Service Markets. 755p. 1994. 1995.00 (*0-7889-0157-5*) Frost & Sullivan.
— U. S. Low End Workstations for the Commercial Marketplace. 261p. 1994. 1995.00 (*0-7889-0177-X*, 2610-70) Frost & Sullivan.
— U. S. Lubricant Additive Markets. 215p. 1993. 2900.00 (*1-56753-599-2*) Frost & Sullivan.
— U. S. Mail Service Pharmacy Markets: Distribution Channel Comes of Age in the Face of Economic Pressures. 450p. 1994. 2995.00 (*1-56753-936-X*) Frost & Sullivan.
— U. S. Manufacturing Systems Integration. 283p. 1994. 2495.00 (*0-7889-0062-5*) Frost & Sullivan.
— The U. S. Market for Centrifugal & Turbine Pumps. 210p. 1993. 2200.00 (*1-56753-487-2*) Frost & Sullivan.
— The U. S. Market for Flat Panel Display: Readout Types. 1993. 1650.00 (*1-56753-497-X*) Frost & Sullivan.
— The U. S. Market for Flat Panel Displays: Display Systems. 1993. 1650.00 (*1-56753-498-8*) Frost & Sullivan.
— The U. S. Market for Flat Panel Displays: Panel Types. 1993. 1650.00 (*1-56753-499-6*) Frost & Sullivan.
— The U. S. Market for Integral Horsepower Adjustable Speed Drives. 147p. 1993. 2800.00 (*1-56753-486-4*) Frost & Sullivan.
— The U. S. Market for Private Satellite Networks. 212p. 1993. 2900.00 (*1-56753-549-6*) Frost & Sullivan.
— U. S. Medical & Pharmaceutical Packaging Markets: Manufacturers Focus on Cost Containment & Waste Reduction. 300p. (Orig.). 1993. 1695.00 (*1-56753-628-X*) Frost & Sullivan.
— U. S. Medical Disposable Product Markets: Specialized Products Show Greatest Growth. 327p. 1995. spiral bd. 1895.00 (*0-7889-0191-5*, 5198-51) Frost & Sullivan.
— U. S. Medical Disposable Product Markets Vol. 3: Needles, Syringes & Related Products. 370p. (Orig.). 1994. 1895.00 (*1-56753-924-6*) Frost & Sullivan.
— U. S. Medical Waste Management & Disposal Markets: Huge Impact on Alternate Cites Due to Stringent Regulation Enforcement. 560p. 1994. 1995.00 (*0-7889-0012-9*) Frost & Sullivan.
— U. S. Men's Personal Care Product Markets: Manufacturers Shift Focus in Response to Changing Attitudes. 371p. 1994. 1895.00 (*0-7889-0019-6*) Frost & Sullivan.
— U. S. Military & Commercial Infrared System Markets: Emerging Materials, Price Reduction Offer Excellent Opportunities. 493p. 1995. spiral bd. 2495.00 (*0-7889-0204-0*, 5216-16) Frost & Sullivan.
— U. S. Military Command Control, Communications, & Intelligence, C3I: Service Markets. 510p. 1993. 2495.00 (*1-56753-590-9*) Frost & Sullivan.
— U. S. Military Display Markets. 324p. 1995. spiral bd. 2195.00 (*0-7889-0156-7*, 5207-16) Frost & Sullivan.
— U. S. Military Electronic Warfare Markets. 600p. 1994. 2950.00 (*0-7889-0022-6*) Frost & Sullivan.
— U. S. Military Non-Mission Avionics Equipment Markets: Aircraft Upgrades, New Technologies Offset Declining Defense Budget. 600p. 1994. 2195.00 (*1-56753-976-9*) Frost & Sullivan.
— U. S. Military Satellite Communications Equipment Markets: Budget Constraints Bring Spending Down to Earth. 364p. 1993. 2295.00 (*1-56753-601-8*) Frost & Sullivan.
— U. S. Military Trainer Markets. (Orig.). 1994. 2900.00 (*0-7889-0126-5*) Frost & Sullivan.
— U. S. Military Trainers & Simulator Markets, Vols. I & II. 806p. 1993. 2900.00 (*1-56753-622-0*) Frost & Sullivan.
— U. S. Military Unmanned Vehicle & Robotics Markets. 200p. 1994. 1995.00 (*0-7889-0000-5*) Frost & Sullivan.
— U. S Modem Markets: Wireless Saves the Day. 350p. 1994. 1995.00 (*1-56753-986-6*) Frost & Sullivan.
— U. S. Network Management System & Service Markets. 272p. 1994. 2800.00 (*1-56753-988-2*) Frost & Sullivan.
— U. S. Network Systems Integration Markets: New Revenue Growth Offers Great Potential to New Entrants. 180p. 1993. 3150.00 (*1-56753-610-7*) Frost & Sullivan.
— U. S. Neurodiagnostic & Neurosurgical Equipment Markets. 1995. 1995.00 (*0-7889-0198-2*, 5197-57) Frost & Sullivan.
— U. S. Neurodiagnostic & Neurosurgical Product Markets. LC 98-168738. 344p. 1995. 1995.00 (*0-7889-0151-6*, 5197-54) Frost & Sullivan.
— U. S. OEM Coating Markets. 256p. 1994. 2395.00 (*0-7889-0145-1*) Frost & Sullivan.
— U. S. On-Premises Telecommunications Equipment Markets. 217p. 1994. 2595.00 (*1-56753-946-7*) Frost & Sullivan.
— U. S. Operator Services & Card Calling Markets. 334p. (Orig.). 1994. 1895.00 (*0-7889-0030-7*) Frost & Sullivan.
— U. S. Ophthalmic Diagnostic Equipment Markets: Manufacturers Visualize High Growth from Emerging Technologies. 320p. 1994. 1895.00 (*0-7889-0050-1*) Frost & Sullivan.
— U. S. Ophthalmic Surgical Device Markets. 288p. (Orig.). 1994. 1895.00 (*0-7889-0103-6*) Frost & Sullivan.
— U. S. Oral OTC Markets: Line Extensions & Rx to OTC Switches Support Self Medication Trends. 360p. 1994. 1995.00 (*1-56753-930-0*) Frost & Sullivan.
— U. S. Organ Transplant & Artificial Organ Product Markets. LC 98-167119. 309p. 1995. spiral bd. 1995.00 (*0-7889-0165-6*, 5081-54) Frost & Sullivan.
— U. S. Orthopedic Prosthetic Device & Ins. 367p. 1994. 2295.00 (*0-7889-0081-1*) Frost & Sullivan.
— U. S. Orthopedic Soft Goods & Cast Room Product Markets. 453p. 1994. 1995.00 (*0-7889-0079-X*) Frost & Sullivan.
— U. S. Osteoporosis Markets. LC 98-167130. 412p. 1994. 2295.00 (*0-7889-0122-2*) Frost & Sullivan.
— U. S. Patient & Mobility Aid Markets. 345p. 1994. 1895.00 (*0-7889-0155-9*) Frost & Sullivan.
— U. S. Patient & Mobility Aid Markets: Niche Markets on the Move. (Orig.). 1994. 1895.00 (*0-7889-0123-0*) Frost & Sullivan.
— U. S. Patient Monitoring Markets. 308p. 1995. spiral bd. 2195.00 (*0-7889-0161-3*, 5196-56) Frost & Sullivan.
— U. S. PC - Workstation Storage Strategies: Technology Tradeoffs: How Big? How Much? 320p. 1994. 1695.00 (*1-56753-991-2*) Frost & Sullivan.
— U. S. Plastic Compounding Industry: Sophisticated Blends & Alloys Replace Engineered Resins. 270p. 1993. 3295.00 (*1-56753-615-8*) Frost & Sullivan.
— U. S. Portable Power Tool Consumable Markets. 286p. 1994. spiral bd. 2295.00 (*0-7889-0159-1*, 5057-87) Frost & Sullivan.
— U. S. Power Supply Manufactures Profiles. 310p. 1994. 975.00 (*0-7889-0112-5*) Frost & Sullivan.
— U. S. Prescription Gastrointestinal Pharmaceutical Markets in a Period of Transition. 1994. 2495.00 (*0-7889-0064-1*) Frost & Sullivan.
— U. S. Prescription Generic Pharmaceutical Markets. (Quarterly Business Planning Ser.). 260p. 1993. 3295.00 (*0-7889-0099-4*) Frost & Sullivan.
— U. S. Prescription Neurological - Psychotherapeutic Pharmaceuticals: R & D Efforts Paying Off. 300p. 1993. 2295.00 (*1-56753-617-4*) Frost & Sullivan.
— U. S. Prescription Respiratory Pharmaceutical Markets: New Asthma Treatment Guidelines Breathe Life into Industry. 300p. 1994. 2295.00 (*1-56753-962-9*) Frost & Sullivan.
— U. S. Pressure Sensitive Adhesive Markets: Recycling Technology & Label Applications Lead the Way. 233p. 1993. 3295.00 (*1-56753-614-X*) Frost & Sullivan.
— U. S. Protein Ingredients Markets. 281p. 1993. 2900.00 (*1-56753-516-X*) Frost & Sullivan.
— U. S. Public Data Service Markets: LAN Interconnection, High Bandwidth Applications Fuel Fast-Packet Surge. 340p. 1994. 2495.00 (*1-56753-964-5*) Frost & Sullivan.
— U. S. Radio Frequency Identification Equipment Markets: Demand Fueled by Transportation Industry. 247p. 1995. spiral bd. 2295.00 (*0-7889-0241-5*, 2717-11) Frost & Sullivan.
— U. S. Radio Paging Equipment & Service Markets: An Economical & Efficient Option for Everyone. 425p. 1994. 2395.00 (*0-7889-0186-9*, 2748-62) Frost & Sullivan.
— U. S. Rehabilitation Product Markets. 300p. 1994. 1895.00 (*0-7889-0048-X*) Frost & Sullivan.
— U. S. Relay Markets: Shift from Conventional to Solid State Technology. 363p. 1994. 1895.00 (*1-56753-967-X*) Frost & Sullivan.
— U. S. Research Biochemical Markets: Cross-Discipline Applications Multiply Commercial Value of Products. 350p. (Orig.). 1994. 2995.00 (*1-56753-898-3*) Frost & Sullivan.
— U. S. Residential Security Markets. 214p. 1994. 2495.00 (*1-56753-938-6*) Frost & Sullivan.
— U. S. Residential Security Product & Service Markets: Increase in Homeowner Investment Promotes Industry Growth. (Orig.). 1993. 2450.00 (*1-56753-640-9*) Frost & Sullivan.
— U. S. Sales Automation Software Markets: Customizing, Implementation, Training & Services Explode. 300p. 1994. 1795.00 (*1-56753-992-0*) Frost & Sullivan.
— U. S. Septecemia & Septic Shock Markets: The Search for Therapy Continues: New Agents & Their Potential. 250p. 1994. 2895.00 (*1-56753-935-1*) Frost & Sullivan.
— U. S. Sexually Transmitted Disease, Diagnostic & Therapeutic Markets. (Orig.). 1994. 2295.00 (*0-7889-0136-2*) Frost & Sullivan.
— U. S. Small Compressor & Vacuum Pump Markets. 328p. 1995. spiral bd. 2295.00 (*0-7889-0160-5*, 5054-12) Frost & Sullivan.
— U. S. Specialty Biocide Markets: EPA Regulations Redefine Industry Focus. 510p. 1994. 1995.00 (*1-56753-997-1*) Frost & Sullivan.
— U. S. Telecommunications Multimedia Markets. 189p. 1994. 2295.00 (*0-7889-0073-0*) Frost & Sullivan.
— U. S. Telecommunications Network Security & Reliability Equipment & Service Markets. 221p. 1995. 2495.00 (*0-7889-0178-8*, 2821-60) Frost & Sullivan.
— U. S. Thrombosis Markets: Anticoagulants, Antithrombotics & Thrombolytics: New Drugs, New Indications Expand Market. LC 97-203018. 290p. 1994. 2495.00 (*1-56753-957-2*) Frost & Sullivan.
— U. S. Two Way Land Mobile Radio Markets: Traditional Markets Being Affected by Evolving Technologies & Regulatory Conditions. 276p. 1993. 2900.00 (*1-56753-568-2*) Frost & Sullivan.
— U. S. Uninterruptible Power Supply Markets. 217p. 1993. 2900.00 (*1-56753-575-5*) Frost & Sullivan.
— U. S. Urology Product Markets: Infection Control in an Aging Population Stimulates Growth. 250p. 1993. 1995.00 (*1-56753-619-0*) Frost & Sullivan.
— U. S. Virtual Reality Hardware, Software, System & Service Markets: Current Applications Show Great Promise. 320p. 1993. 2795.00 (*1-56753-563-1*) Frost & Sullivan.
— U. S. Voc Recovery & Destruction Equipment Markets: Regulations Spark New Acquisition Activity. 210p. 1993. 1895.00 (*1-56753-600-X*) Frost & Sullivan.
— U. S. Voice Messaging Service Markets. 349p. 1994. 1995.00 (*0-7889-0168-0*) Frost & Sullivan.
— U. S. Vxlbus Instrumentation Markets. 207p. 1993. 2900.00 (*1-56753-576-3*) Frost & Sullivan.
— U. S. Water Soluble Polymers: Green Thinking Means Growth Despite Overcapacity. 300p. 1993. 2950.00 (*1-56753-616-6*) Frost & Sullivan.
— U. S. Wire & Cable Markets: Ten Applications & Eight Industries Led by Telecommunications & Consumer Electronics. 488p. 1993. 3900.00 (*1-56753-611-5*) Frost & Sullivan.
— U. S. Wireless Office Equipment Markets: Anytime, Anywhere Communications. 360p. 1994. 2295.00 (*0-7889-0094-3*) Frost & Sullivan.
— U. S. Wound Management Markets: The Quest for Less Damaging, More Active Products. 300p. (Orig.). 1994. 2295.00 (*1-56753-887-8*) Frost & Sullivan.
— U.S. LAN Systems Integration Markets. 240p. 1994. 1995.00 (*0-7889-0014-5*) Frost & Sullivan.
— Virtual Reality Markets: Hardware, Software, Systems & Services. 320p. 2795.00 (*1-56753-593-3*) Frost & Sullivan.
— Voice Messaging Service Markets. 220p. 1993. 1695.00 (*1-56753-431-7*) Frost & Sullivan.
— Voice Recognition, Response & Synthesis Markets: Explosive Growth Across All Segments. 284p. 1992. 1695.00 (*1-56753-410-4*) Frost & Sullivan.
— West European Industrial Enzyme Markets: New Applications Emerge Out of Changing Technology. 248p. (Orig.). 1993. 3800.00 (*1-56753-897-5*) Frost & Sullivan.
— West European Market for Fluorochemicals. 443p. 1993. 4450.00 (*1-56753-554-2*) Frost & Sullivan.
— West European Pulp & Paper Chemical Markets. 322p. 1994. 3800.00 (*1-56753-598-4*) Frost & Sullivan.
— Western European Market for Chiral Reagents & Instrumentation Markets. 196p. 1993. 4200.00 (*1-56753-578-X*) Frost & Sullivan.
— Western European Synthetic Adhesive Markets. 342p. 1994. 3800.00 (*1-56753-975-0*) Frost & Sullivan.
— Western European Thermoplastic Elastomer Markets. 191p. 1993. 4300.00 (*1-56753-517-8*) Frost & Sullivan.
— Western European Water-Soluble Polymer Markets. 237p. 1994. 3800.00 (*1-56753-942-4*) Frost & Sullivan.
— Word Diagnostic Imaging Equipment Markets: A Comprehensive Snapshot on Medical Imaging Modalities & Related Products. 570p. 1994. 2895.00 (*1-56753-987-4*) Frost & Sullivan.
— World Analog & Mix Signal IC Markets. 377p. 1993. 1895.00 (*1-56753-473-2*) Frost & Sullivan.
— World Arthritis Treatment Products: Rx, OTC & Prosthetics: OTC Changes Dynamics of Rx Markets. 280p. 1993. 2295.00 (*1-56753-496-1*) Frost & Sullivan.
— World Audiology Product Markets: Competitors Keep Their Ears to the Ground for Hints of Improving Sales. 310p. 1994. 1695.00 (*0-7889-0106-0*) Frost & Sullivan.
— World Audiology Product Markets: Consumer Advertising Overcoming the Stigma. 349p. 1992. 1495.00 (*1-56753-390-6*) Frost & Sullivan.
— World Barcode Equipment Markets. 410p. 1995. spiral bd. 2995.00 (*0-7889-0162-1*, 5193-11) Frost & Sullivan.
— World Barcode Equipment Markets: Fast Paybacks, Customer Awareness Creates Recession Proof Growth. 262p. 1993. 1895.00 (*1-56753-462-7*) Frost & Sullivan.
— World Biomedical Sensor Markets. 250p. 1994. 1895.00 (*0-7889-0036-6*) Frost & Sullivan.
— World Biomedical Sensor Markets: Cross Contamination & Ease of Use Reshape the Industry. 1992. 1695.00 (*1-56753-416-3*) Frost & Sullivan.
— World Biomedical Sensor Markets: Cross Contamination & Ease of Use Reshape the Industry. 341p. 1992. 1695.00 (*1-56753-422-8*) Frost & Sullivan.
— World Biotech Company Profiles: An In-Depth Look at 100 Leading Industry Innovators. 619p. 1995. spiral bd. 1695.00 (*0-7889-0169-9*, 5085-43) Frost & Sullivan.
— World Blood Banking: A Plasma Product Markets: Patient & Healthcare Professionals Shape Product Development. LC 97-212934. 340p. 1994. 1695.00 (*1-56753-931-9*) Frost & Sullivan.
— World Cancer Therapeutic Markets: Strategic Alliances Globalize the Marketplace. 295p. 1993. 2495.00 (*1-56753-524-0*) Frost & Sullivan.
— World Cancer Therapeutic Markets by Disease Cite: Accelerated R & D Intensifies Race for Cure. 400p. (Orig.). 1994. 2895.00 (*1-56753-886-X*) Frost & Sullivan.
— World Cancer Therapeutic Pharmaceuticals Market: Biotech Becomes Big Business. 258p. (Orig.). 1992. 2295.00 (*1-56753-063-X*) Frost & Sullivan.
— World Cardiovascular Diagnostic & Therapeutic Equipment Markets: Multi-Billion Dollar Battle, Technology Advances vs Cost Constraints. 313p. (Orig.). 1992. 1995.00 (*1-56753-043-5*) Frost & Sullivan.
— World Cardiovascular Drug Markets: Primary Prevention Creates Opportunities. 430p. (Orig.). 1994. 2695.00 (*1-56753-925-4*) Frost & Sullivan.
— World Cell Therapy Markets: Harnessing the Power of the Cell. 444p. 1995. spiral bd. 2895.00 (*0-7889-0193-1*, 5033-43) Frost & Sullivan.
— World Cellular & PCN Telephone, Pager & Accessories Markets: Changes . . . Changes . . . Changes. 630p. 1992. 1695.00 (*1-56753-334-5*) Frost & Sullivan.
— World Clinical Laboratory Instrument Markets: Cost Containment...Consolidation...Point of Care; Report #909-56. 306p. 1994. 2195.00 (*1-56753-702-2*) Frost & Sullivan.
— World Computer Numerical Controller Markets: User Interest Sparked by 32-Bit Architecture & Graphics Capabilities. 221p. 1993. 1695.00 (*1-56753-612-3*) Frost & Sullivan.
— World Computer Numerical Controller Markets: Waking up to Japanese Manufacturing Expertise. 219p. (Orig.). 1992. 1495.00 (*1-56753-039-7*) Frost & Sullivan.
— World Contrast Media Markets: New Dynamics in an Evolving Market. (Orig.). 1994. 2295.00 (*0-7889-0121-4*) Frost & Sullivan.
— World Data Acquisition Boards, Systems & Software: New Entrants Flood the Market. 231p. 1993. 1895.00 (*1-56753-466-X*) Frost & Sullivan.
— World Dental Product Markets: Esthetics Expand Globally. 313p. 1993. 1995.00 (*1-56753-528-3*) Frost & Sullivan.
— World Diagnostic Imaging Company Profiles. 478p. (Orig.). 1994. 1595.00 (*0-7889-0131-1*) Frost & Sullivan.

An Asterisk (*) at the beginning of an entry indicates that the title is appearing for the first time.

— World Diagnostic Imaging Contrast Media: Manufacturers Vie for Japanese Market. 216p. 1993. 1995.00 (*1-56753-439-2*) Frost & Sullivan.
— World Digital Signal Processor (DSP) Markets: Increasing Price - Performance Ratio Generates New Applications. 250p. (Orig.). 1994. 1995.00 (*1-56753-894-0*) Frost & Sullivan.
— World Discrete Electronic Active Device Markets: New Opportunities Arise in Telecommunications & Medical Applications. 245p. 1993. 1495.00 (*1-56753-436-8*) Frost & Sullivan.
— World Discrete Electronic Passive Device Markets: Century-Old Technology Thrives on Leading-Edge Telecommunication Products. 273p. 1992. 1495.00 (*1-56753-406-6*) Frost & Sullivan.
— World Discrete Manufacturing Software Markets: Shop Floor Goes High Tech - 3 Million Dollar Market Doubles. 248p. 1993. 1495.00 (*1-56753-420-1*) Frost & Sullivan.
— World Electronic Cleaning Equipment Markets: Spurred by Regulations, North America Leads "Clean" Revolution. 231p. (Orig.). 1992. 1495.00 (*1-56753-397-3*) Frost & Sullivan.
— World Electronic Data Interchange Market: Countries Trading Partners Press for Cooperation & Standards. 561p. (Orig.). 1992. 1895.00 (*1-56753-848-7*) Frost & Sullivan.
— World Electronic Switch Markets. 289p. (Orig.). 1994. 1995.00 (*0-7889-0093-5*) Frost & Sullivan.
— World Embedded Controller Markets: Industry Goes Mainstream with 386 & Power PC. 370p. 1994. 1995.00 (*0-7889-0038-2*) Frost & Sullivan.
— World Emerging Sensor Technologies: High Growth Markets Uncovered. 317p. 1993. 1495.00 (*1-56753-456-2*) Frost & Sullivan.
— World Fetal, Neonatal & Infant Monitor Markets: Manufacturers Push Hi-Tech Products Through One-Stop Shopping. 433p. (Orig.). 1992. 1995.00 (*1-56753-033-8*) Frost & Sullivan.
— World Fiber Optic Communication Markets: Cable, Transmitters, Connectors, Couplers, Receivers. 244p. 1993. 1695.00 (*1-56753-463-5*) Frost & Sullivan.
— World Fiber Optic Sensor Markets: Phenomenal Growth Across All Segments by Medical Applications. 335p. 1993. 1495.00 (*1-56753-435-X*) Frost & Sullivan.
— World Flow Sensor Markets: Moderate Overall Growth Belies High Growth Opportunities. 466p. 1993. 1695.00 (*1-56753-475-9*) Frost & Sullivan.
— World Frame Relay Markets: Preparing for ATM. 305p. 1993. 1995.00 (*1-56753-542-9*) Frost & Sullivan.
— World Gastrointestinal Drug Markets: Generic Competition Intensified As Block Buster Drugs Lose Patent Protection. 537p. (Orig.). 1992. 2295.00 (*1-56753-400-7*) Frost & Sullivan.
— World Gene Therapy Markets: Gene-Based Services & Products to Provide Numerous Commercial Opportunities. (Illus.). 475p. 1994. 2995.00 (*0-7889-0076-5*) Frost & Sullivan.
— World Geographic Information Systems Software & Service Markets. (Orig.). 1994. 1995.00 (*0-7889-0134-6*) Frost & Sullivan.
— World Growth Factor Markets: Tissue Applications Poised for Commercialization. 300p. (Orig.). 1993. 2495.00 (*1-56753-620-4*) Frost & Sullivan.
— World Human Vaccine Markets: Over 60 Productions: Which Competitors Are Attacking Viruses? 478p. 1993. 2295.00 (*1-56753-460-0*) Frost & Sullivan.
— World Image Processing & Enhancement Equipment: Clinical Applications Open Market to New Entrants. 287p. 1993. 1695.00 (*1-56753-849-5*) Frost & Sullivan.
— World Indoor Air Quality Monitoring & Building Control System Markets: Opportunities for Non-Traditional Suppliers. 326p. 1994. 1895.00 (*0-7889-0034-X*) Frost & Sullivan.
— World Industrial - Broadcast Solid State Camera & System Markets: Picture This . . . Revenues Double. 322p. 1993. 1695.00 (*1-56753-438-4*) Frost & Sullivan.
— World Industrial & Scientific Laser Systems Markets: Rebounding Global Economy Eases Price Wars. 538p. 1993. 1695.00 (*1-56753-446-5*) Frost & Sullivan.
— World Intelligent Materials Handling Markets: Installation of Modular Designs & Integrated Systems on the Rise. 576p. 1993. 1695.00 (*1-56753-459-7*) Frost & Sullivan.
— World Machine Tool Cutting Tool Markets: Expansion Driven by Innovation: New Materials, New Coatings, New Geometries. 283p. 1992. 1495.00 (*1-56753-384-1*) Frost & Sullivan.
— World Machine Vision System, Component & Software Markets: Innovative, Affordable & Reliable Solutions Lead Way to Billion Dollar Industry. 389p. (Orig.). 1992. 1495.00 (*1-56753-376-0*) Frost & Sullivan.
— World Market for Electronic Ceramics: Developments Enable Next Generation Products. 345p. (Orig.). 1992. 1695.00 (*1-56753-066-4*) Frost & Sullivan.
— World Medical Diagnostic Ultrasound Imaging Equipment Markets at the Forefront of Diagnostic. 363p. 1995. spiral bd. 2495.00 (*0-7889-0247-4*, 5230-50) Frost & Sullivan.
— World Medical Image Management Markets: Minipacs & Facility-to-Facility Teleradiology Offer Cost Effective Solutions. 310p. 1994. 2495.00 (*0-7889-0082-X*) Frost & Sullivan.
— World Medical Imaging & Therapeutic Immunoconjugate Markets: Competitors Refocusing R&D & Marketing Strategies. 351p. 1994. 2695.00 (*1-56753-954-8*) Frost & Sullivan.
— World Medical Laser Markets: Manufacturers Focus on Alternate Cites & New Applications. 332p. 1993. 1995.00 (*1-56753-440-6*) Frost & Sullivan.
— World Medical Resonance Imaging Markets: Dedicated Imaging Coils Lead Shift to Lower Field Systems. 250p. (Orig.). 1994. 2495.00 (*0-685-71178-1*) Frost & Sullivan.
— World Memory IC Markets. 286p. 1995. spiral bd. 2195.00 (*0-7889-0164-8*, 5208-26) Frost & Sullivan.
— World Microdisk Drive & PCMC1A Flash Memory Card Markets: Flash Encroaches on Hard Drives Even as Capacities Increase. 250p. 1994. 1995.00 (*1-56753-958-0*) Frost & Sullivan.
— World Micromachine & Microstructure Markets: Technology Qualified: After Sensors, the Real Search for Applications Begins. 1992. 1695.00 (*1-56753-395-7*) Frost & Sullivan.
— World Microscope & Spectrometer Markets: Hyphenate Technologies & Software Enhancements Spawn New Breed of Inspection & Testing Equipment. 427p. 1992. 1895.00 (*1-56753-393-0*) Frost & Sullivan.
— World Military Microwave Component & Assembly Markets. 213p. (Orig.). 1994. 1895.00 (*0-7889-0110-9*) Frost & Sullivan.
— World Mobile Data Communications Markets: Market Emerges, Alliances Follow Quickly. 400p. 1994. 1995.00 (*0-7889-0013-7*) Frost & Sullivan.
— World Multi-Chip Module Markets: From Concept Through Testing Applications Drive the Technology. 288p. (Orig.). 1992. 1695.00 (*1-56753-053-2*) Frost & Sullivan.
— World Multimedia Application Markets. 370p. 1994. 1995.00 (*0-7889-0049-8*) Frost & Sullivan.
— World Multimedia Application Markets: The Complete Market & Sales Targeting Tool. 338p. 1993. 2495.00 (*1-56753-425-2*) Frost & Sullivan.
— World Multimedia Hardware & Software Markets. (Quarterly Business Planning Ser.). 425p. 1994. 2995.00 (*0-7889-0020-X*) Frost & Sullivan.
— World Multimedia Hardware & Software Markets: Finally a Definition. 430p. (Orig.). 1992. 1495.00 (*1-56753-403-1*) Frost & Sullivan.
— World Niche & Specialized Sensor Markets: Growth Potential Lies in Exploring New Applications. 219p. 1993. 1295.00 (*1-56753-411-2*) Frost & Sullivan.
— World Non-Destructive Test Equipment Markets: Increasing Automation & Integration Represent Wave of the Future. 383p. 1992. 1495.00 (*1-56753-407-4*) Frost & Sullivan.
— World Nuclear Medical Imaging, NMI, Market: Radiopharmaceutical Applications Drive Double-Digit Growth Despite Cost-Benefit Concerns. 323p. (Orig.). 1992. 2295.00 (*1-56753-074-5*) Frost & Sullivan.
— World On-Line Transaction Terminal Markets: Communicaiton & Information Technologies Go Retail. 550p. 1993. 1695.00 (*1-56753-876-2*) Frost & Sullivan.
— World Ophthalmic Pharmaceutical Markets. 470p. (Orig.). 1994. 2395.00 (*1-56753-923-8*) Frost & Sullivan.
— World Optical Disk Drive & Media Markets. 496p. 1995. spiral bd. 1995.00 (*0-7889-0190-7*, 5177-72) Frost & Sullivan.
— World Orthopedic & Prosthetic Product Markets: Impact of Lifestyles, Demographics & Biomaterials. 627p. 1992. 1995.00 (*1-56753-386-8*) Frost & Sullivan.
— World OTC Dermatology Pharmaceutical Markets. 411p. 1995. spiral bd. 2295.00 (*0-7889-0196-6*, 0960-45) Frost & Sullivan.
— World PBX & Key System Markets. 553p. 1994. 2295.00 (*0-7889-0021-8*) Frost & Sullivan.
— World PC-Based Instrumentation & Software Markets: Invading the Laboratory & Industrial Environments. 447p. 1992. 1895.00 (*1-56753-076-1*) Frost & Sullivan.
— World PC Card Markets: PCMCIA Standard Opens the Flood Gates. 250p. 1993. 1495.00 (*1-56753-448-1*) Frost & Sullivan.
— World PC Card Markets: Peripheral & Flash Cards Byte into Ram Share. 320p. 1994. 1995.00 (*0-7889-0089-7*) Frost & Sullivan.
— World Pen, Palmtop & Notebook Computer & Peripheral Markets: Solid Profits in Accessories, but Will PDA's Follow? 370p. 1993. 1995.00 (*1-56753-608-5*) Frost & Sullivan.
— World Prescription Dermatology Markets. 380p. 1994. 2695.00 (*0-7889-0043-9*) Frost & Sullivan.
— World Pressure Sensor Markets: Fiber Optic & Silicon Micromachine Technologies Usher in New Era of Growth. 340p. 1994. 1695.00 (*1-56753-982-3*) Frost & Sullivan.
— World Pressure Sensor Markets: Micromachined Applications Rejuvenate Growth. 219p. (Orig.). 1992. 1495.00 (*1-56753-051-6*) Frost & Sullivan.
— World Process Controller Markets: PC-Based Technology Offers New Opportunity in a Highly Competitive Environment. 320p. 1994. 1995.00 (*0-7889-0098-6*) Frost & Sullivan.
— World Process Flow Control Markets: Electronics Revolutionizes Values & Accessories, Pumps & Controllers. 168p. (Orig.). 1992. 1495.00 (*1-56753-050-8*) Frost & Sullivan.
— World Programmable Logic Controller & Software Markets: Downsizing, Eroding Brand Loyalty & New Entrants Challenge Leader. 300p. 1992. 1495.00 (*1-56753-391-4*) Frost & Sullivan.
— World Programmable Logic Controller & Software Markets: Software & Service Become Key Industry Issues. 298p. 1993. 1695.00 (*1-56753-613-1*) Frost & Sullivan.
— World Programmable Logic Controller Markets. 313p. 1994. spiral bd. 2095.00 (*0-7889-0148-6*, 5191-10) Frost & Sullivan.
— World Proximity & Displacement Sensor Markets: Applications Boom with the Advent of Smaller, Smarter & Faster Sensors. 340p. 1993. 1495.00 (*1-56753-433-3*) Frost & Sullivan.
— World Recorder, Datalogger & Indicator Markets: Niche Recorder Segments Counter PC-Based Data Acquisition. 297p. (Orig.). 1992. 1495.00 (*1-56753-038-9*) Frost & Sullivan.
— World Renal & Hemodialysis Equipment & Supply Markets: Cost Containment Pressures Influence World Markets. 347p. 1994. 1995.00 (*0-7889-0015-3*) Frost & Sullivan.
— World Renal & Hemodialysis Equipment & Supply Markets: U. S. Struggles with Cost Constraints While Europe & Japan Expand. 309p. 1992. 1895.00 (*1-56753-383-3*) Frost & Sullivan.
— World Satellite Communications Equipment Markets: VSAT 7 Mobile Applications Unleash SatCom. 394p. 1993. 1695.00 (*1-56753-437-6*) Frost & Sullivan.
— World Satellite Communications in Developing Countries (Wordlwide) 397p. 1992. 3700.00 (*1-56753-877-0*, W1597) Frost & Sullivan.
— World Semiconductor Production Equipment Markets: Increased Productivity Justifies Higher Prices, Industry Profits. 300p. 1994. 1995.00 (*1-56753-948-3*) Frost & Sullivan.
— World SMT Manufacturing Equipment Markets: End-User Demands Prompt Explosive Growth - Test & Inspection Revenues Double. 315p. 1993. 1695.00 (*0-685-66576-3*) Frost & Sullivan.
— World Standard & Special Machine Tool Markets: Competitors Move into New Segments. 444p. 1993. 2395.00 (*1-56753-504-6*) Frost & Sullivan.
— World Switching Power Supply Markets: European Standards, New Technologies & Increased Defense Cuts Redirect the Markets. 349p. 1993. 1895.00 (*1-56753-484-8*) Frost & Sullivan.
— World Telecom & Datacom Test Equipment Markets: Fiber, TIMS, & PC-Based Instrumentation Stimulate Growth. 432p. (Orig.). 1992. 1895.00 (*1-56753-067-2*) Frost & Sullivan.
— World Telecommunications Services Database, 1994. 1994. 595.00 (*1-56753-981-5*) Frost & Sullivan.
— World Teleconferencing System & Service Markets: Look Who's Talking. 410p. 1993. 1695.00 (*1-56753-450-3*) Frost & Sullivan.
— World Test & Measurement Equipment Markets: Multiple Trends Converge to Promote Impressive ATE & Time Growth. 288p. (Orig.). 1992. 1895.00 (*1-56753-032-X*) Frost & Sullivan.
— World Test & Measurement Equipment Markets: The Industry Makes a Comeback As Technology Advances & New Markets Emerge. 630p. 1994. 1695.00 (*1-56753-947-5*) Frost & Sullivan.
— World 3-D Diagnostic Medical Imaging Equipment & Software Markets: Dramatic Global Expansion Led by Clinical Applications & Ultrasound Technology. 250p. 1992. 1995.00 (*1-56753-413-9*) Frost & Sullivan.
— World Transducer-Sensor Technology Assessment: A Qualitative Analysis of the State of the Art Based on More Than 500 Interviews with Industry Experts. 342p. 1992. 1495.00 (*1-56753-392-2*) Frost & Sullivan.
— World Ultrasound Imaging Markets: Manufacturers Focus on Developing Niche Applications. 365p. 1993. 2295.00 (*1-56753-618-2*) Frost & Sullivan.
— World Uninterruptible Power Supply Markets: Increased Awareness of Data & Equipment Protection Sustains Growth. 336p. 1994. 2195.00 (*1-56753-972-6*) Frost & Sullivan.
— World Uninterruptible Power Supply Markets: Mission Critical Applications & Fierce Competition Characterize Markets. 271p. (Orig.). 1992. 1895.00 (*1-56753-028-1*) Frost & Sullivan.
— World Voice Processing Application & End-User Markets: Technologies Merge, Obstacles Recede. 460p. 1994. 1895.00 (*1-56753-963-7*) Frost & Sullivan.
— World Welding Equipment Markets: Automation: The Future Direction. 320p. 1993. 1495.00 (*1-56753-442-2*) Frost & Sullivan.
— World Workstation Markets: Proven Applications, with New Pentium-Power PC Chips, Attract New Users. 306p. 1993. 1995.00 (*1-56753-609-3*) Frost & Sullivan.
— World Wound Closure Products: Staplers Invade Suture Markets. 345p. 1992. 1695.00 (*1-56753-387-6*) Frost & Sullivan.
— World X-Ray & Computed Tomography Equipment Markets: Manufacturers Exploit Niche Opportunities & Polarized Markets. 293p. (Orig.). 1992. 1895.00 (*1-56753-041-9*) Frost & Sullivan.
— Worldwide Telecom Services Markets: Comprehensive Forecast of Basic, Mobile, Private Line, & Value-Added Services by Five Geographic Regions. 305p. (Orig.). 1992. 1495.00 (*1-56753-068-0*) Frost & Sullivan.
— Wound Management Products in Europe. 300p. 1993. 3900.00 (*1-56753-500-3*) Frost & Sullivan.

Market Intelligence Staff, contrib. by. European Laser System Markets. 360p. 1994. 3950.00 (*0-7889-0109-5*) Frost & Sullivan.

Market, M. Frances, tr. see Gruen, Anselm.

Market Share Company Staff, ed. see Shaughnessy, Carol.

Market, Stephen. Pleasure Gardens of the Mind. (Jane Greenough Green Collection of Indian Paintings). (Illus.). 168p. 1997. 50.00 (*0-944142-93-1*) Grantha.

Marketdata Enterprises, Inc. Staff. Child Day Care Services: An Industry Analysis. 28p. 1998. 59.00 (*1-891084-16-X*) Mktdata Ent.
— The Commercial & Residential Cleaning Services Industry. 31p. 1999. 59.00 (*1-891084-23-2*) Mktdata Ent.

Marketdata Enterprises Inc. Staff. The Medical Equipment Leasing Services Industry. rev. ed. 26p. 1999. 59.00 (*1-891084-33-X*) Mktdata Ent.

Marketdata Enterprises, Inc. Staff. The Medical Lab Testing Industry. 25p. 1999. 59.00 (*1-891084-35-6*) Mktdata Ent.
— Rich, Black, & Southern: The Harris Family of Williamsburg (& Boston) LC 98-232304. (Illus.). 59p. 1998. pap. write for info. (*0-9648393-4-2*) Miona Pubns.
— The Temporary Help Services Industry. 30p. 1999. 59.00 (*1-891084-24-0*) Mktdata Ent.
— The U. S. Carpet Cleaning Industry. 18p. 1998. 59.00 (*1-891084-18-6*) Mktdata Ent.

***Marketdata Enterprises, Inc. Staff.** U. S. Check Cashing, Money Transfers Services. 21p. 1999. 59.00 (*1-891084-28-3*) Mktdata Ent.
— U. S. Collection Agencies Industry. 20p. 1997. 59.00 (*1-891084-11-9*) Mktdata Ent.

Marketdata Enterprises, Inc. Staff. The U. S. Dating Services Market. 23p. 1998. 59.00 (*1-891084-21-6*) Mktdata Ent.
— The U. S. Dental Laboratories Industry. 19p. 1998. 59.00 (*1-891084-20-8*) Mktdata Ent.

***Marketdata Enterprises, Inc. Staff.** U. S. Office Machines Leasing Market. 1999. 59.00 (*1-891084-34-8*) Mktdata Ent.

Marketdata Enterprises, Inc. Staff. The U. S. Parking Garages Industry. 17p. 1998. 59.00 (*1-891084-19-4*) Mktdata Ent.

***Marketdata Enterprises, Inc. Staff.** The U. S. Pawn Shops Industry. 24p. 1999. 59.00 (*1-891084-26-7*) Mktdata Ent.
— The U. S. Rent-to-Own Stores Industry. 22p. 1999. 59.00 (*1-891084-27-5*) Mktdata Ent.

Marketdata Enterprises, Inc. Staff. The U. S. Weight Loss & Diet Control Market. 40p. 1998. 59.00 (*1-891084-17-8*) Mktdata Ent.

Marketing Consultants International Inc. Staff. Who, What & Where in Communications Security. Nye, J. Michael, ed. (Illus.). 124p. 1986. pap. 75.00 (*0-937195-25-1*) Mktg Consult Intl.

***Marketing Department, The Kellogg Graduate School of Management, Northwestern University Staff, et al, eds.** Kellogg on Marketing. 400p. 2000. text 29.95 (*0-471-35399-X*) Wiley.

Marketing Graphics Corporation Staff & Lewis, Jan. Using IBM PC Storyboard: The Guide to Applications. 320p. (C). 1988. pap. 24.95 (*0-685-19365-9*) P-H.

Marketing Science Institute Staff, jt. auth. see Deshpande, Rohit.

***Marketing Staff.** Complete MBA Companion in Marketing. (Illus.). 342p. 1999. pap. 39.95 (*0-273-64223-5*, Pub. by F T P-H) Natl Bk Netwk.

Marketos, Joshua. The Java Developer's Toolkit: Techniques & Technologies for Web Programmers. LC 96-35812. 383p. 1996. pap. 29.95 (*0-471-16519-0*) Wiley.

Markevich, A. P. Russian-Ukrainian-Latin Zoological Dictionary. 410p. 1983. 39.95 (*0-8288-2393-6*, M 15541) Fr & Eur.

Markevitch, Dimitry. Cello Story. Seder, Florence, tr. from FRE. (Illus.). 192p. (Orig.). 1984. pap. 13.95 (*0-87487-406-8*) Summy-Birchard.
— The Solo Cello: A Bibliography of the Unaccompanied Violoncello Literature. LC 89-23355. (Reference Books in Music: No. 12). viii, 113p. 1989. pap. 14.95 (*0-914913-11-5*, Fallen Lef Pr) Scarecrow.

Markewich, Reese. Definitive Bibliography of Harmonically Sophisticated Tonal Music. LC 77-104898. 1970. pap. 4.95 (*0-9600160-2-3*) Markewich.
— Inside Outside: Substitute Harmony in Modern Jazz & Pop Music. LC 67-7697. 102p. 1967. pap. 4.95 (*0-9600160-0-7*) Markewich.
— The New Expanded Bibliography of Jazz Compositions Based on the Chord Progressions of Standard Tunes. LC 74-84745. 1974. pap. 4.95 (*0-9600160-5-8*) Markewich.

Markewicz, Debra K. FirstFruits, a Poetic Endeavor. (Orig.). 1997. pap. write for info. (*1-57553-483-5*) Watermrk Pr.
— Offerings of Ambiance. 1998. pap. write for info. (*1-57553-945-4*) Watermrk Pr.

Markey. Criminal Law for Paralegals. 2nd ed. (C). 2000. 30.75 (*0-8273-8462-9*) Delmar.
— Italo Calvino. 1998. 23.95 (*0-8057-4510-6*) Macmillan.

Markey, Barb & Hunt, Tad. Airways: Rising to the Challenge of Managing COPD. Allen, Susan D. & Holloran, Colleen A., eds. (Illus.). 56p. pap. text 3.50 (*0-916999-13-0*) HERC Inc.

Markey, Christian E., jt. auth. see Kirkland, Kathryn.

***Markey, Constance.** Italo Calvino: A Journey Toward Postmodernism. LC 99-42653. 192p. 1999. 49.95 (*0-8130-1722-X*) U Press Fla.

Markey, Daniel J., Jr. & Donnelly, Mary Q. Criminal Law for Paralegals. 266p. (C). 1993. mass mkt., student ed. 46.75 (*0-538-70860-3*) S-W Pub.
— Criminal Law for Paralegals. 266p. 1994. teacher ed. write for info. (*0-538-70863-8*) S-W Pub.

Markey, Frances V. Imaginative Behavior of Preschool Children. LC 75-35075. (Studies in Play & Games). 1976. reprint ed. 15.95 (*0-405-07925-7*) Ayer.

Markey, Janice. A Journey into the Red Eye: The Poetry of Sylvia Plath - A Critique. 216p. 1997. pap. 16.95 (*0-7043-4316-9*, Pub. by Womens Press) Trafalgar.

Markey, Judy. The Daddy Clock. 320p. 1998. reprint ed. mass mkt. 5.99 (*0-553-57743-3*) Bantam.

Markey, Karen. Subject Access to Visual Resources Collections; A Model for the Computer Construction of Thematic Catalogs, 11. LC 86-7658. (New Directions in Information Management Ser.: No. 11). 209p. 1986. 55.00 (*0-313-24031-0*, MSI/) Greenwood.
— Subject Searching in Library Catalogs: Before & After the Introduction of Online Catalogs. LC 84-7226. (Library, Information, & Computer Science Ser.: No. 4). (Illus.). 192p. (Orig.). 1984. pap. 21.00 (*0-933418-54-X*) OCLC Online Comp.

Markey, Penny, ed. see Wilmshurst, Ann.

M

An Asterisk (*) at the beginning of an entry indicates that the title is appearing for the first time.

Markey, Raymond. The Making of the Labor Party in New South Wales, 1880-1990. 328p. 1989. 27.95 (0-86840-370-9, Pub. by New South Wales Univ Pr) Intl Spec Bk.

Markey, Raymond & Monat, Macques, eds. Innovation & Employee Participation Through Works Councils: International Case Studies. LC 96-79849. 480p. 1997. 91.95 (1-85972-434-5, Pub. by Avebry) Ashgate Pub Co.

Markey, T. L., et al. Germanic & Its Dialects: A Grammar of Protogermanic, Vol. 3. 525p. 1977. 100.00 (90-272-0981-2) J Benjamins Pubng Co.

Markey, Thomas L. Frisian. (Contributions to the Sociology of Language Ser.: No. 30). 1979. text 70.80 (90-279-3128-3) Mouton.

Markfield, Wallace. Multiple Orgasms. limited ed. 1977. 35.00 (0-89723-006-X) Bruccoli.

***Markfield, Wallace.** Teitlebaum's Window. LC 99-35092. 400p. 1999. reprint ed. pap. 13.95 (1-56478-219-0, Pub. by Dalkey Arch) Chicago Distribution Ctr.

Markfield, Wallace. To an Early Grave. 1994. lib. bdg. 24.95 (1-56849-402-5) Buccaneer Bks.

***Markfield, Wallace.** To an Early Grave. 255p. 2000. pap. 12.50 (1-56478-261-1) Dalkey Arch.

Markgraf, Carl. J. M. Barrie: An Annotated Secondary Bibliography. LC 89-84405. (British Authors, 1880-1920 Ser.: No. 4). 440p. (C). 1989. lib. bdg. 35.00 (0-944318-03-7) ELT Pr.

Markgraf, Gerry. Douglas Skyshark A2D Turbo-Prop Attack. (Naval Fighters Ser.: No. 43). (Illus.). 80p. 1997. pap. 15.95 (0-942612-43-4, NF43) Naval Fighters.

Markgraf, J. F., ed. Collimators for Thermal Neutron Radiography: An Overview. (C). 1987. text 115.00 (90-277-2568-3) Kluwer Academic.

Markgraf, Richard. Diversions: Fifty Comic Short Stories. LC 95-90221. 128p. (Orig.). 1995. pap. 8.95 (0-9646025-0-4) WMKB Ent.

Markgraf, Vera, jt. ed. see Diaz, Henry F.

Markham. A Consumer's Guide to Social Research. 2nd ed. 178p. (C). 1997. per. 28.95 (0-7872-4290-X, 41429001) Kendall-Hunt.

Markham, Adam. The Environment, Set I. LC 88-5978. (World Issues Ser.). (Illus.). 48p. (J). (gr. 5 up). 1988. lib. bdg. 25.27 (0-86592-286-1) Rourke Enter.

— Potential Impacts of Climate Change on Tropical Forest Ecosystems. LC 98-35416. 1998. 141.00 (0-7923-5124-X) Kluwer Academic.

Markham, Ann. The Cat with a Black Ring. (Illus.). 25p. (J). (gr. 1-3). 1996. 7.95 (0-533-11337-7) Vantage.

***Markham, Ann.** Gray Wolf. (Illus.). 30p. (J). 1999. 9.95 (0-533-13048-4) Vantage.

Markham, Ann. Woody & the Gray Wolf Pup. (Illus.). 24p. (J). (gr. 2-5). 1997. 8.95 (0-533-12084-5) Vantage.

Markham, Annette. Life Online: Researching Real Experience in Virtual Space. LC 98-25339. 248p. (C). 1998. 62.00 (0-7619-9030-5); pap. 21.95 (0-7619-9031-3) AltaMira Pr.

Markham, Beryl. West with the Night. LC 82-62789. 320p. 1982. reprint ed. pap. 13.00 (0-86547-118-5) N Point Pr.

Markham, Bonnie. Sarah & Her Missionary Daughters: Personal Glimpses into the Lives of 32 Missionary Ladies. LC 97-50221. 272p. 1998. pap. 9.99 (1-56722-210-2) Word Aflame.

Markham, Bonnie J. The Nitty-Gritty for Ministers' Wives. LC 88-11750. (Illus.). 208p. (Orig.). 1988. pap. 7.99 (0-932581-34-X) Word Aflame.

***Markham, Calvert.** How to Be Your Own Management Consultant: Tools & Techniques to Improve Your Business Through Internal Consulting. 2000. pap. 32.00 (0-7494-2931-3) Kogan Page Ltd.

Markham, Calvert. Top Consultant: Your Skills for Greater Effectiveness. 3rd ed. 1998. pap. text 30.00 (0-7494-2579-2) Kogan Page Ltd.

Markham, Cecily. Sisters in Rain. 24p. (Orig.). 1996. pap. 6.00 (1-877801-32-1) Still Waters.

***Markham, Chris.** Mississippi Odyssey. (Illus.). 145p. 2000. pap. 11.95 (0-595-09123-7) iUniversecom.

Markham, Clements R. Antarctic Obsession. Holland, Clive, ed. & intro. by. (Illus.). 208p. (C). 1989. pap. 90.00 (0-948285-09-5, Pub. by Erskine Press) St Mut.

— History of Peru. 1976. lib. bdg. 69.95 (0-8490-1983-4) Gordon Pr.

— Incas of Peru. LC 79-84877. (Illus.). reprint ed. 47.50 (0-404-04188-4) AMS Pr.

— Markham in Peru: The Travels of Clements R. Markham, 1852-1853. Blanchard, Peter, ed. (Illus.). 168p. (Orig.). 1991. pap. 10.95 (0-292-75127-3); text 25.00 (0-292-71132-8) U of Tex Pr.

— The War Between Peru & Chile, 1879-1882. 1976. lib. bdg. 59.95 (0-8490-2805-1) Gordon Pr.

Markham, Clements R., ed. Voyages of Sir James Lancaster to the East Indies: With Abstracts of Journals of Voyages to the East Indies, During the 17th Century & the Voyage of Captain John Knight (1606), to Seek the North-West Passage. 1998. 38.00 (81-215-0824-X, Pub. by M Manoharial) Coronet Bks.

Markham, Clements R., ed. see De Gamboa, Pedro S.

***Markham, Clements Robert.** The Land of Silence: A History of Arctic & Antarctic Exploration. (Illus.). 540p. 1998. reprint ed. 75.00 (1-57898-097-6) Martino Pubng.

Markham-David, Sally. Hands & Feet. LC 93-28978. (Voyages Ser.). (Illus.). (J). 1994. 4.25 (0-383-03746-8) SRA McGraw.

— It Takes All Kinds. LC 93-21246. (Voyages Ser.). (Illus.). (J). 1994. 4.25 (0-383-03753-0) SRA McGraw.

— Mouths & Noses. LC 93-29008. (Illus.). (J). 1994. 4.25 (0-383-03764-6) SRA McGraw.

— The Secrets of a Garden. LC 93-29003. (Voyages Ser.). (Illus.). (J). 1994. 4.25 (0-383-03773-5) SRA McGraw.

— Tail Tales. LC 93-6631. (Illus.). (J). 1994. pap. write for info. (0-383-03718-2) SRA McGraw.

Markham, Dewey. 1855: A History of the Bordeaux Classification. LC 97-20015. 560p. 1997. 69.95 (0-471-19421-2) Wiley.

Markham, Dewey, Jr. Wine Basics: A Quick & Easy Guide. LC 92-27315. (Illus.). 208p. 1993. pap. 14.95 (0-471-58258-1) Wiley.

Markham, Donna J. Spiritlinking Leadership. LC 98-49088. 144p. 1999. 16.95 (0-8091-3840-9) Paulist Pr.

Markham, Doug. Boxes, Rockets & Pens: A History of Wildlife Recovery in Tennessee. LC 97-4804. (Outdoor Tennessee Ser.). (Illus.). 176p. (Orig.). 1997. pap. 19.95 (0-87049-993-9) U of Tenn Pr.

Markham, Doyle. Llamas Are the Ultimate: Training, Feeding, Packing, Hunting, Fishing & Care. LC 90-92191. (Illus.). 292p. (Orig.). 1990. pap. 14.95 (0-9628326-0-X) Snake Riv Llamas.

Markham, E. A. Caribbean Short Stories. LC 97-152829. 464p. 1997. pap. 13.95 (0-14-024503-0) Viking Penguin.

— Human Rites. 128p. 1984. pap. 14.95 (0-85646-113-X, Pub. by Anvil Press) Dufour.

— Human Rites: Selected Poems, 1970-1982. 128p. 1984. 22.95 (0-85646-112-1, Pub. by Anvil Press) Dufour.

— Living in Disquise. 118p. 1986. 24.95 (0-85646-172-5, Pub. by Anvil Press); pap. 14.95 (0-85646-173-3, Pub. by Anvil Press) Dufour.

***Markham, E. A.** Marking Time. 264p. 2000. 16.95 (1-900715-29-5, Pub. by Peepal Tree Pr) Paul & Co Pubs.

Markham, E. A. Misapprehensions. 96p. 1995. pap. 17.95 (0-85646-271-3, Pub. by Anvil Press) Dufour.

— A Papua New Guinea Sojourn: More Pleasures in Exile. LC 98-217141. 220p. 1998. 34.95 (1-85754-328-9, Pub. by Carcanet Pr) Paul & Co Pubs.

— Towards the End of the Century. 108p. 1989. pap. 14.95 (0-85646-223-3, Pub. by Anvil Press) Dufour.

Markham, E. A., ed. Hinterland: Afro-Caribbean & Black British Poetry. LC 89-82062. 336p. (Orig.). 1990. 45.00 (1-85224-086-5, Pub. by Bloodaxe Bks); pap. 21.00 (1-85224-087-3, Pub. by Bloodaxe Bks) Dufour.

Markham, Edwin. Songs & Stories, Selected & Annotated. 1977. 31.95 (0-8369-4268-X, 6066) Ayer.

Markham, Edwin, et al. Children in Bondage. LC 76-89753. (American Labor, from Conspiracy to Collective Bargaining Ser., No. 1). 411p. 1974. reprint ed. 25.95 (0-405-02140-2) Ayer.

Markham, Felix M. Napoleon. 1966. mass mkt. 7.99 (0-451-62798-9) NAL.

Markham, Frederick M. My Favorite Works of Poetry. 1998. pap. write for info. (1-57553-757-5) Watermrk Pr.

***Markham, Frederick M.** Testimonies to Freedom: History of the Civil Rights Movement. LC 99-91886. 1999. 25.00 (0-7388-1374-5); pap. 18.00 (0-7388-1375-3) Xlibris Corp.

Markham, George. Guns of the Elite: Special Forces Firearms, 1940 to the Present. (Illus.). 176p. (Orig.). 1996. pap. 19.95 (1-85409-382-7, Pub. by Arms & Armour) Sterling.

— Guns of the Elite: Special Forces Firearms, 1940 to the Present. 2nd ed. (Illus.). 176p. (Orig.). 1999. reprint ed. pap. text 25.00 (0-7881-6122-9) DIANE Pub.

Markham, Gervase. The English Housewife. Best, Michael R., ed. (Illus.). 384p. (C). 1986. text 65.00 (0-7735-0582-2, Pub. by McG-Queens Univ Pr) CUP Services.

— The English Housewife: Containing the Inward & Outward Virtues Which Ought to Be in a Complete Woman. (Illus.). 321p. 1994. pap. 19.95 (0-7735-1103-2, Pub. by McG-Queens Univ Pr) CUP Services.

Markham, Gretchen. Dempsey's Hot Summer: The July Adventures of a Cape Cod Dog. LC 95-76153. (Illus.). 30p. (Orig.). (J). (gr. 1-3). 1995. pap. 9.95 (1-887146-01-6) Ark Works.

— A Gift for Dempsey: The Christmas Adventure of a Cape Cod Dog. LC 95-94230. (Illus.). 30p. (Orig.). (J). (gr. 1-3). 1995. pap. 9.95 (1-887146-00-8) Ark Works.

— The Good-Bye Waltz. 100p. 1996. pap. 5.00 (1-887146-19-9) Ark Works.

— Second Helpings: Timeless Recipes Fondly Remembered. unabridged ed. (Illus.). 100p. (Orig.). 1996. pap. 5.00 (1-887146-18-0) Ark Works.

— Suddenly a Widow. 100p. 1996. pap. 5.00 (1-887146-20-2) Ark Works.

Markham, Ian S. Plurality & Christian Ethics. (New Studies in Christian Ethics: No. 4). 239p. (C). 1994. text 59.95 (0-521-45328-3) Cambridge U Pr.

— Plurality & Christian Ethics. rev. ed. 208p. (C). 1998. pap. text 19.95 (1-889119-06-7) Seven Bridges.

***Markham, Ian S., ed.** A World Religions Reader. 2nd ed. 400p. 1999. pap. 34.95 (0-631-21519-0); text 69.95 (0-631-21518-2) Blackwell Pubs.

Markham, Ian S., ed. A World Religions Reader. (Illus.). 416p. (C). 1996. 60.95 (0-631-18239-X); pap. 33.95 (0-631-18242-X) Blackwell Pubs.

***Markham, Ian S. & Ruperell, Tinu, eds.** Encountering Religion: An Introduction to the Religions of the World. LC 99-85999. (Illus.). 384p. 2000. text 69.95 (0-631-20673-6); pap. text 34.95 (0-631-20674-4) Blackwell Pubs.

Markham, James J., et al. The Claims Environment. LC 93-71086. 423p. (C). 1994. pap. text 44.00 (0-89462-078-9, 3302) IIA.

Markham, James J., ed. see Anderson, Robert G., et al.

Markham, Jerald H. The Botetourt Artillery. (Virginia Regimental Histories Ser.). (Illus.). 95p. 1987. 19.95 (0-318-32502-0) H E Howard.

Markham, Jerry W. Commodities Regulation: Fraud, Manipulation & Other Claims, 2 vols., Set. LC 87-12979. (Securities Law Ser.). 1987. ring bd. 250.00 (0-87632-552-5) West Group.

— The History of Commodity Futures Trading & Its Regulation. 321p. 1986. 75.00 (0-275-92313-4, C2313, Praeger Pubs) Greenwood.

Markham, Jerry W. & Hazen, Thomas L. Broker Dealer Operations Under Securities & Commodities Law: Financial Responsibility, Credit Regulation, & Consumer Protection, 2 vols. LC 95-18931. (Securities Law Ser.). 1995. write for info. (0-87632-392-1) West Group.

Markham, John. Final Class. (C). 1989. text 35.00 (0-948929-38-3) St Mut.

— Friary Families. (C). 1989. text 50.00 (0-948929-03-0) St Mut.

— Hunting Scenes. (C). 1989. text 35.00 (0-948929-20-0) St Mut.

— Keep the Home Fires Burning. (C). 1989. text 45.00 (0-948929-14-6) St Mut.

— The Old Tiger Inn, Beverley. (C). 1989. text 40.00 (0-948929-15-4) St Mut.

— Streets of Hedon. (C). 1989. text 40.00 (0-948929-24-3) St Mut.

— Streets of Hull. (C). 1989. text 35.00 (0-948929-43-X) St Mut.

— Streets of Hull: A History of Their Names. (C). 1989. text 35.00 (0-948929-07-3) St Mut.

— Successful Business Communication. 201p. 1978. pap. 55.00 (0-900886-21-8, Pub. by Witherby & Co) St Mut.

Markham, Judith, jt. auth. see Vander Laan, Raynard.

Markham, K. R. Techniques of Flavonoid Identification. (Biological Techniques Ser.). 1982. text 73.00 (0-12-472680-1) Acad Pr.

Markham, Kathy, ed. see Crews, Paul B.

Markham, Kathy, ed. see Sterner, Doris M.

Markham, Lois. Avi: Meet the Author. (Meet the Author Ser.). 128p. (Orig.). (J). (gr. 3-6). 1996. pap. 6.95 (0-88160-280-9, LW350) Learning Wks.

— Discoveries That Changed Science. (Twenty Events Ser.). (Illus.). 48p. (J). (gr. 5-6). 1994. lib. bdg. 24.26 (0-8114-4936-X) Raintree Steck-V.

— Harvest. LC 98-15096. (World Celebrations & Ceremonies Ser.). (Illus.). 24p. (J). (gr. 3-5). 1998. lib. bdg. 15.95 (1-56711-275-7) Blackbirch.

— Inventions That Changed Modern Life. LC 93-17022. (Twenty Events Ser.). (Illus.). 48p. (J). (gr. 5-7). 1993. lib. bdg. 24.26 (0-8114-4930-0) Raintree Steck-V.

— Jacques-Yves Cousteau: Exploring the Wonders of the Deep. LC 96-19497. (Innovative Minds Ser.). 112p. (J). 1997. lib. bdg. 27.11 (0-8172-4404-2) Raintree Steck-V.

— Lois Lowry. Clark, Kimberly, ed. (Meet the Author Ser.). 128p. (J). (gr. 5-8). 1995. pap. 6.95 (0-88160-278-7, LW348) Learning Wks.

— Theodore Roosevelt. (World Leaders Past & Present Ser.). (Illus.). 120p. (YA). (gr. 5 up). 1985. lib. bdg. 19.95 (0-87754-553-7) Chelsea Hse.

Markham, Lorena, jt. auth. see Markham, Reed.

Markham, M. Roland. Alcar, the Captive Creole. LC 77-170701. (Black Heritage Library Collection). 1977. reprint ed. 21.95 (0-8369-8891-4) Ayer.

Markham, Marcella. Old is...great. 1998. 9.00 (1-86187-105-8) Exley Giftbooks.

Markham, Marion M. The April Fool's Day Mystery. 64p. (J). 1993. pap. 3.50 (0-380-71716-6, Avon Bks) Morrow Avon.

— The Birthday Party Mystery. 64p. (J). (gr. 1-4). 1990. reprint ed. pap. 2.95 (0-380-70968-6, Avon Bks) Morrow Avon.

— The Christmas Present Mystery. (Illus.). 64p. (J). 1990. pap. 2.95 (0-380-70966-X, Avon Bks) Morrow Avon.

— The Halloween Candy Mystery. 64p. (J). (gr. 1-4). 1990. reprint ed. pap. 2.95 (0-380-70965-1, Avon Bks) Morrow Avon.

— The St. Patrick's Day Shamrock Mystery. LC 94-36716. (Illus.). 48p. (J). (gr. 2-5). 1995. 15.00 (0-395-72137-7) HM.

Markham, Marion M. Starlight & Candles: The Joys of the Sabbath. LC 94-20232. (Illus.). 40p. (J). (ps-3). 1995. pap. 15.00 (0-689-80274-9) S&S Childrens.

Markham, Marion M. The Thanksgiving Day Parade Mystery. (Illus.). 64p. (J). 1990. pap. 2.95 (0-380-70967-8, Avon Bks) Morrow Avon.

Markham, Meeler. History of Alto Frio Baptist Encampment: A Seventy-Five Year Story. LC 97-74615. (Illus.). 154p. 1997. pap. 8.00 (1-57502-588-4, PO1682) Morris Pubng.

***Markham, P.** Convict Chains. 240p. 1998. mass mkt. 9.95 (0-352-33300-6) Buccaneer Bks.

MARKHAM, PHILIP. Fair Cop. 203p. 2000. pap. text 10.95 (0-352-33445-2) London Brdge.

***MARKHAM, PHILIP.** Love of Old Egypt. 224p. 1999. pap. 14.99 (0-352-33354-5) Virgin Bks.

Markham, Reed. Leadership 2000: Success Skills for University Students. 212p. (C). 1995. text 37.00 (0-536-59076-1) Pearson Custom.

Markham, Reed & Markham, Lorena. Making Marriage Magnificent: 365 Ways to Happiness. 128p. 1997. pap. 6.98 (0-88290-613-5) Horizon Utah.

***Markham-Smith, Ian & Hodgson, Liz.** Nicolas Cage: The Biography. 2000. 26.00 (1-85782-396-6, Pub. by Blake Publng) Seven Hills Bk.

MARKHAM-SMITHAN. The Outrageous Jerry Springer. 256p. 1999. 26.00 (1-85782-331-1, Pub. by Blake Publng) Seven Hills Bk.

Markham, Sydney F. Climate & the Energy of Nations. LC 77-10234. 248p. reprint ed. 42.50 (0-404-16214-2) AMS Pr.

Markham, Tony. The Jaxon Files. (Illus.). 240p. 1996. pap. 12.95 (1-55978-781-3) R K Bks.

Markham, Tony, ed. see Taylor, Eldon.

Markham, Ursula. Creating a Positive Self-Image: Simple Techniques to Transform Your Life. 1995. pap. 10.95 (1-85230-622-X, Pub. by Element MA) Penguin Putnam.

— Element Guide to Bereavement: Your Questions Answered. LC 95-40210. 144p. 1996. pap. 9.95 (1-85230-774-9, Pub. by Element MA) Penguin Putnam.

— Element Guide to Childhood Trauma: Your Questions Answered. LC 97-38012. 128p. 1998. pap. 9.95 (1-86204-181-4, Pub. by Element MA) Penguin Putnam.

— Elements of Visualization. LC 97-187573. (Elements of...Ser.). 1997. pap. 9.95 (1-86204-078-8, Pub. by Element MA) Penguin Putnam.

— Fortune-Telling by Crystals & Semiprecious Stones. (Illus.). 96p. (Orig.). 1988. pap. 7.95 (0-85030-510-1) Sterling.

***Markham, Ursula.** How to Deal with Difficult People. 160p. 1998. 10.00 (0-7225-2764-0, Pub. by Thorsons MD) Natl Bk Netwk.

Markham, Ursula. Hypnosis. (Alternative Health Ser.). (Illus.). 128p. 1993. pap. 12.95 (0-8048-1835-5) Tuttle Pubng.

— Hypnotherapy: A Guide to Improving Health & Well-Being with Hypnosis. (Illus.). 128p. 1997. pap. 13.95 (0-09-181519-3) Random.

— Managing Stress. LC 99-193526. 1995. pap. 11.95 (1-85230-631-9, Pub. by Element MA) Penguin Putnam.

— Miscarriage: Your Questions Answered. LC 98-29524. (Element Guide Ser.). 128p. 1999. pap. 9.95 (1-86204-297-7, Pub. by Element MA) Penguin Putnam.

— Regression Therapy Using Hypnosis: How Reliving Early Experiences Can Improve Your Life. (Orig.). 1995. pap. text 12.95 (0-7499-1530-7, Pub. by Piatkus Bks) London Brdge.

— Regression Therapy Using Hypnosis: How Reliving Early Experiences Can Improve Your Life. 126p. (Orig.). 1996. pap. text 12.95 (0-7499-1032-1, Pub. by Piatkus Bks) London Brdge.

— Ultimate Stress Handbook for Women. LC 96-51515. 160p. 1997. pap. 10.95 (1-85230-857-5, Pub. by Element MA) Penguin Putnam.

— Women under Pressure: A Practical Guide for Today's Woman. LC 93-16174. (Orig.). 1993. pap. 11.95 (1-85230-138-4, Pub. by Element MA) Penguin Putnam.

— Your Four Point Plan for Life: How to Achieve a Balance Between the Physical, Emotional, Mental & Spiritual Aspects of Ourselves. (Illus.). 144p. 1993. pap. 12.95 (1-85230-212-7, Pub. by Element MA) Penguin Putnam.

Markham, William. Autobiography of William Colfax Markham. (American Autobiography Ser.). 241p. 1995. reprint ed. lib. bdg. 79.00 (0-7812-8586-0) Rprt Serv.

Markham, William T. A Consumer's Guide to Social Research. 128p. 1994. pap. text, per. 18.95 (0-8403-6500-4) Kendall-Hunt.

Markham, William T., jt. auth. see Simerson, Byron K.

Markhaseva, E. L. Copepods: Aetideidae of the World. Expert-Center for Taxonomic Identification (ETI) S, ed. (World Biodiversity Database Ser.). 1997. pap. 127.95 incl. cd-rom (3-540-14622-9) Spr-Verlag.

— Copepods, Aetideidae of the World. Expert-Center for Taxonomic Identification (ETI) S, ed. (World Biodiversity Database Ser.). 1997. 129.95 incl. cd-rom (3-540-14617-2) Spr-Verlag.

Markhoff, Angela & Schneiders, Ulrike. Faszinierende Puppenstuben: Grosse Welt Im Kleinen die Sammlung der Prinzessin Monika von Hannover. (GER., Illus.). 112p. (C). 1995. 67.00 (3-8170-1020-6, Pub. by Knstvrlag Weingrtn) Intl Bk Import.

Markholt, Ottilie. Maritime Solidarity: Pacific Coast Unionism, 1929-1938. LC 98-68428. (Illus.). 461p. 1999. pap. 19.95 (0-9664397-0-8) Pac Coast Maritime.

Markholt, Ottilie, ed. To Live in Dignity: Pierce County Labor, 1883-1989. (Illus.). (Orig.). 1989. pap. 10.00 (0-9624071-0-0) Pierce Cty Labor.

Markhum Who. Strugglin' 2B Free. (Orig.). 1996. pap. 10.95 (0-9647391-9-4) Veracity CA.

Marki, Laszl, jt. ed. see Dlab, Vlastimil.

Markides, Constantinos C. All the Right Moves: A Guide to Crafting Breakthrough Strategy. LC 99-32401. 256p. 1999. 27.50 (0-87584-833-8) Harvard Busn.

— Diversification, Refocusing & Economic Performance. LC 95-22500. 219p. 1996. 39.00 (0-262-13311-3) MIT Pr.

Markides, Kyriacos C. Fire in the Heart: Healers, Sages & Mystics. LC 91-50056. 320p. 1992. pap. 14.95 (0-14-019285-9, Arkana) Viking Penguin.

— Homage to the Sun. 249p. 1988. pap. 12.95 (0-14-019024-4, Penguin Bks) Viking Penguin.

— Magus of Strovolos. 236p. 1989. pap. 13.95 (0-14-019034-1, Penguin Bks) Viking Penguin.

— Riding with the Lion: In Search of Mystical Christianity. 384p. 1996. pap. 13.95 (0-14-019481-9, Arkana) Viking Penguin.

Markides, Kyriacos C., ed. Aging & Health: Perspectives on Gender, Race, Ethnicity, & Class. (Focus Editions Ser.: Vol. 104). 288p. (C). 1989. text 59.95 (0-8039-3206-5); pap. text 26.00 (0-8039-3207-3) Sage.

Markides, Kyriacos C. & Mindel, Charles S. Aging & Ethnicity. LC 86-13910. (Library of Social Research: Vol. 163). 256p. (Orig.). (C). 1987. text 59.95 (0-8039-2728-2); pap. text 26.00 (0-8039-2729-0) Sage.

Markides, Kyriakos S., ed. Aging & Health: Perspectives on Gender, Race, Ethnicity, & Class. LC 88-35932. (Sage Focus Editions Ser.: Vol. 104). 256p. 1989. reprint ed. pap. 79.40 (0-608-01722-1, 206237800003) Bks Demand.

Markides, Kyriakos S. & Cooper, Cary L., eds. Aging, Stress & Health. LC 88-37841. 300p. reprint ed. pap. 93.00 (0-608-20233-9, 207149200012) Bks Demand.

— Retirement in Industrialized Societies: Social, Psychological & Health Factors. LC 86-19016. 343p. reprint ed. pap. 106.40 (0-7837-4766-7, 204452000003) Bks Demand.

Markides, Kyriakos S. & Miranda, Manuel R., eds. Minorities, Aging & Health. LC 97-4841. 384p. 1997. 59.95 (0-8039-5973-7); pap. 28.95 (0-8039-5974-5) Sage.

Markie, David, ed. YAC Protocols. LC 95-20892. (Methods in Molecular Biology Ser.: Vol. 54). (Illus.). 384p. 1995. 84.50 (*0-89603-313-9*) Humana.

Markie, Peter, jt. ed. see Cahn, Steven M.

Markie, Peter J. A Professor's Duties: Ethical Issues in College Teaching. (Issues in Academic Ethics Ser.). 224p. (C). 1994. pap. text 22.95 (*0-8476-7952-7*); lib. bdg. 58.50 (*0-8476-7951-9*) Rowman.

Markiewicz, Dana. The Mexican Revolution & the Limits of Agrarian Reform, 1915-1946. LC 93-12003. 216p. 1993. lib. bdg. 45.00 (*1-55587-321-9*) L Rienner.

Markiewicz, Pete, jt. auth. see Novak, Jeannie.

Markin, Carole. Bad Dates: Celebrities & Other Talented Types Reveal Their Worst Nights Out. 256p. 1990. pap. 9.95 (*0-8065-1158-3*, Citadel Pr) Carol Pub Group.

— More Bad Dates: Tales from the Dark Side of Love. LC 98-14773. 224p. 1998. pap. 10.95 (*1-58063-016-2*) Renaissance.

Markin, Ed & Beloit, Christian. Skidmarks in the Sky: An Irreverent Look at Aviation History. Sload, Pamela, ed. LC 85-807. (Illus.). 152p. (Orig.). 1986. pap. 4.95 (*0-9615223-0-5*) Flaming Hooker Pr.

Markin, Gabe, et al. Fat Free, Flavor Full: Dr. Gabe Mirkin's Guide to Losing Weight & Living Longer. (Illus.). 336p. 1996. pap. 13.95 (*0-316-57473-2*) Little.

Markin, R. E. The Affordable Funeral: Going in Style, Not in Debt. 2nd rev. ed. 104p. 1999. per. 19.95 (*0-9615223-4-8*) Flaming Hooker Pr.

— The Alzheimer's Cope Book: The Complete Care Manual for Patients & Their Families. 1992. pap. 7.95 (*0-8065-1370-5*, Citadel Pr) Carol Pub Group.

— Coping with Alzheimer's: The Complete Care Manual for Patients & Their Families. rev. ed. LC 97-53124. 128p. 1998. pap. text 9.95 (*0-8065-1962-2*, Citadel Pr) Carol Pub Group.

Markin, Roe E. In-Home Alzheimer's Screening Test (I-HAST) large type ed. (Illus.). 40p. 1999. 29.95 (*0-9615223-2-1*) Flaming Hooker Pr.

***Markin, William R.** Visioneering: Creating the Successful Business of the Future. (Illus.). 2000. pap. write for info. (*0-9702229-0-4*) Lauerer Markin.

Marking, L. L. & Kimerke, R. A., eds. Aquatic Toxicology: 2nd Conference- STP 667. 403p. 1979. 37.75 (*0-8031-0279-8*, STP667) ASTM.

Markish, Ester. Stol Dolgoe Vozvrashchenie. LC 84-60572. (RUS., Illus.). 320p. (Orig.). 1989. pap. 22.00 (*0-89830-084-3*) Russica Pubs.

Markish, Heidi. A Special Delivery. (Illus.). 28p. 1998. 8.99 (*1-58050-040-4*, 40-6166) Provo Craft.

Markish, Shimon. Erasmus & the Jews. Olcott, Anthony, tr. from RUS. LC 85-16454. 216p. 1986. lib. bdg. 30.00 (*0-226-50590-1*) U Ch Pr.

Markisz. Principles of MRI: Selected Topics. 2nd ed. 260p. (C). 1998. pap. 45.00 (*0-8385-8152-8*, Apple Lange Med) McGraw.

Markisz, John A. Musculoskeletal Imaging. 1991. 159.95 (*0-316-54613-5*, Little Brwn Med Div) Lppncott W & W.

Markisz, John A. & Kazam, Elias, eds. MRI Atlas of the Abdomen. (Illus.). 256p. 1997. 125.00 (*0-86542-398-9*) Blackwell Sci.

Markisz, John A. & Levine, Martin P. Applied Contemporary Chemistry. 3rd ed. (Illus.). 152p. 1989. student ed. 13.95 (*0-89529-406-0*, Avery) Penguin Putnam.

Markisz, John A., et al. MRI Atlas of the Chest & Neck: Normal Anatomy & Pathology. LC 97-4962. (Illus.). 306p. 1997. 125.00 (*0-86542-391-1*) Blackwell Sci.

— MRI Atlas of the Pelvis: Normal Anatomy & Pathology. LC 92-14015. (Illus.). 248p. 1993. 135.00 (*0-683-05557-7*) Lppncott W & W.

Markisz, John A., jt. auth. see Aquilia, Michael G.

Markisz, John A., jt. auth. see Knowles, James R.

Markisz, John A., jt. auth. see Zirinsky, Kenneth.

Markkanen, Raija & Schroder, Hartmut, eds. Hedging & Discourse: Approaches to the Analysis of a Prgamatic Phenomenon in Academic Texts. LC 97-17338. (Untersuchungen zur Texttheorie Ser.). 280p. 1997. text 125.35 (*3-11-015591-5*) De Gruyter.

Markko, K., et al, eds. Columbia Poetry Review, No. 4. (Orig.). (C). 1991. pap. text 8.00 (*0-932026-25-7*) Columbia College Chi.

Markl, Hermann & Meyer, Dieter. Gerichtskostengesetz. rev. ed. 750p. 1996. write for info. (*3-11-014615-0*) De Gruyter.

Markland, Cecily, ed. see Deaton, Dennis R.

Markland, Francis S., Jr., ed. see Pirkle, Hubert.

Markland, Robert D. Topics in Management Science. 3rd ed. LC 88-33751. 880p. 1989. text 93.95 (*0-471-61786-5*) Wiley.

— Topics in Management Science. 3rd ed. 692p. 1989. pap. text, teacher ed. 75.00 (*0-471-50100-X*) Wiley.

Markland, Robert E. & Sweigart, James R. Quantitative Methods: Applications to Managerial Decision Making. 99th ed. LC 87-2025. 560p. 1987. text 73.95 (*0-471-87885-5*) Wiley.

Markland, Robert E. & Victery. Insights: In Readings OPS Management. (SWC-Management Ser.). Date not set. 57.00 (*0-314-08620-X*) Sth-Wstrn College.

Markland, Robert E., et al. Operations Management: Concepts in Manufacturing & Services. 2nd ed. LC 97-19602. (SWC-Management Ser.). 1997. pap. 86.95 (*0-538-87831-2*); pap. 21.75 (*0-538-87834-7*) Thomson Learn.

— Operations Managemt: Concepts In Manufacturing & Services. LC 94-30524. (SWC-Management). 868p. (C). 1995. pap. 69.75 (*0-314-04398-5*) West Pub.

Markle. Adelie Penguins: Growing up Wild. LC 99-23393. (J). 2000. 16.00 (*0-689-81884-X*) S&S Childrens.

— Criminal Investigations. Date not set. pap. text, teacher ed. write for info. (*0-314-35439-5*) West Pub.

— Gray Wolves: Growing up Wild. LC 99-54145. (J). 2001. 16.00 (*0-689-81886-6*) S&S Childrens.

Markle, Allan, jt. auth. see Rinn, Roger C.

Markle, Donald. Spies & Spymasters of the Civil War. rev. ed. (Illus.). 260p. 1999. pap. 14.95 (*0-7818-0761-1*) Hippocrene Bks.

***Markle, Garold L.** Catalytic Coaching: The End of the Performance Review. LC 99-36599. 336p. 2000. 65.00 (*1-56720-308-6*) Greenwood.

Markle, George B., IV. Beyond Ophir. (Illus.). 195p. 1998. pap. 16.50 (*0-88100-095-7*) Natl Writ Pr.

Markle, George M., et al. Food & Feed Crops of the United States. 2nd rev. ed. (Illus.). xix, 497p. 1998. pap. 34.95 (*1-892829-00-2*) Meister Pub Co.

Markle, Gerald E. Meditations of a Holocaust Traveler. LC 94-42915. 185p. (C). 1995. text 39.50 (*0-7914-2643-2*); pap. text 16.95 (*0-7914-2644-0*) State U NY Pr.

***Markle, Helen M.** History of Prisons - Index of Modern Authors & Subjects with Guide for Rapid Research. rev. ed. LC 90-56266. 119p. 1999. 47.50 (*0-7883-1992-2*); pap. 44.50 (*0-7883-1993-0*) ABBE Pubs Assn.

Markle, Helen M. Prisons: Index of Modern Information. LC 88-47617. 150p. 1988. 47.50 (*0-88164-862-0*); pap. 44.50 (*0-88164-863-9*) ABBE Pubs Assn.

— Sex & Orgasm Research: Index of Modern Information. rev. ed. LC 88-48009. 150p. 1991. 47.50 (*1-55914-478-5*); pap. 44.50 (*1-55914-479-3*) ABBE Pubs Assn.

— Sex & the Biology of Coitus: Index of Modern Authors & Subjects with Guide for Rapid Research. LC 88-47980. 153p. 1991. 47.50 (*1-55914-220-0*); pap. 44.50 (*1-55914-221-9*) ABBE Pubs Assn.

— Sexology Encyclopedia Vol. 7: Sexually Transmitted Diseases: Index & Reference Books of New Information, 25 vols., Set. Bartone, John C., ed. (Illus.). 159p. 1996. 49.95 (*0-7883-0862-9*) ABBE Pubs Assn.

— Sexology Encyclopedia Vol. 25: Orgasm Research: Index & Reference Books of New Information. Bartone, John C., ed. 167p. 1996. 49.95 (*0-7883-0898-X*); pap. 39.95 (*0-7883-0899-8*) ABBE Pubs Assn.

— Sexually Transmitted Diseases & Appearance of Warts & Papillomas: Index of Modern Authors & Subjects with Guide for Rapid Research. LC 90-56248. 190p. 1991. 47.50 (*1-55914-264-2*); pap. 44.50 (*1-55914-265-0*) ABBE Pubs Assn.

Markle, Helen M. & Bartone, John C. Sexology Encyclopedia Vol. 7: Sexually Transmitted Diseases: Index & Reference Books of New Information. (Illus.). 159p. 1996. pap. 39.95 (*0-7883-0863-7*) ABBE Pubs Assn.

***Markle, Sandra.** After the Spill: The Exxon Valdez Diaster Then & Now. LC 98-38550. (Illus.). 32p. (J). (gr. 2-6). 1999. 16.95 (*0-8027-8610-3*) Walker & Co.

— After the Spill: The Exxon Valdez Disaster, Then & Now. LC 98-38550. (Illus.). 32p. (J). (gr. 3-7). 1999. lib. bdg. 17.85 (*0-8027-8611-1*) Walker & Co.

Markle, Sandra. Creepy, Crawly Baby Bugs. LC 95-47178. (J). 1996. 15.95 (*0-8027-8443-7*) Walker & Co.

— Creepy, Crawly Baby Bugs. LC 95-47178. (J). (ps-3). 1996. lib. bdg. 16.85 (*0-8027-8444-5*) Walker & Co.

— Creepy, Spooky Science. LC 95-50780. (Illus.). 80p. (J). (gr. 3-7). 1996. lib. bdg. 15.49 (*0-7868-2178-7*, Pub. by Hyprn Child) Little.

— Creepy, Spooky Science. LC 95-50780. (Illus.). 80p. (J). (gr. 3-7). 1996. pap. 4.95 (*0-7868-1088-2*, Pub. by Hyprn Ppbks) Little.

— Discovering Graph Secrets. LC 96-15435. (Illus.). 40p. (J). (gr. 2-6). 1997. 17.00 (*0-689-31942-8*) Atheneum Yung Read.

***Markle, Sandra.** Down, down, down in the Ocean. LC 99-38607. (Illus.). 32p. (J). (gr. k-3). 1999. lib. bdg. 16.85 (*0-8027-8655-3*) Walker & Co.

— Down, down, down in the Ocean. LC 99-38607. (Illus.). 32p. (J). (gr. 3-5). 1999. 15.95 (*0 8027 8654 5*) Walker & Co.

Markle, Sandra. Exploring Autumn: A Season of Science Activities, Puzzlers, & Games. (Exploring Seasons Ser.: Bk. 4). 160p. (YA). 1993. pap. 3.50 (*0-380-71910-X*, Avon Bks) Morrow Avon.

— Exploring Spring. 128p. (J). (gr. 4-7). 1992. pap. 2.99 (*0-380-71319-5*, Avon Bks) Morrow Avon.

— Exploring Summer. 176p. (J). (gr. 7-8). 1991. reprint ed. pap. 2.95 (*0-380-71320-9*, Avon Bks) Morrow Avon.

— Exploring Winter. 160p. (J). (gr. 7 up). 1992. reprint ed. pap. 2.99 (*0-380-71321-7*, Avon Bks) Morrow Avon.

— Fledglings. LC 98-174939. 178p. (J). 1998. pap. 9.95 (*1-56397-696-X*) Boyds Mills Pr.

— Grizzly Bears: Growing up Wild. LC 98-44693. (Illus.). 32p. (J). (gr. 3). 2000. 16.00 (*0-689-81888-2*) Atheneum Yung Read.

— Icky, Squishy Science. LC 95-46173. (Illus.). 96p. (J). (gr. 3-7). 1996. pap. 3.95 (*0-7868-1087-4*, Pub. by Hyprn Ppbks) Little.

— Icky, Squishy Science. LC 95-46173. 1996. 9.15 (*0-606-09455-5*, Pub. by Turtleback) Demco.

— Icky Squishy Science. (J). 1996. pap. write for info. (*0-7868-1210-9*) Hyprn Child.

— Math Mini-Mysteries. LC 92-11217. (Illus.). 64p. (J). (gr. 3-7). 1993. 14.95 (*0-689-31700-X*) Atheneum Yung Read.

— Measuring Up: Experiments, Puzzles & Games Exploring Measurement. LC 94-19240. (Illus.). 48p. (J). (gr. 3-7). 1995. 17.00 (*0-689-31904-5*) Atheneum Yung Read.

— Outside & Inside Alligators. LC 97-39804. (Illus.). 40p. (J). (gr. 3-6). 1998. 16.00 (*0-689-81457-7*) Atheneum Yung Read.

— Outside & Inside Bats. LC 96-48291. (Illus.). 40p. (J). (gr. 1-5). 1997. 16.00 (*0-689-81165-9*) S&S Childrens.

— Outside & Inside Birds. LC 93-38910. (Illus.). 40p. (J). (ps-3). 1994. mass mkt. 15.95 (*0-02-762312-2*, Mac Bks Young Read) S&S Childrens.

— Outside & Inside Dinosaurs. LC 99-45808. (J). (gr. k-3). 2001. 16.00 (*0-689-82300-2*) Atheneum Yung Read.

— Outside & Inside Kangaroos. LC 98-45354. 40p. (J). (gr. 3-6). 1999. 16.00 (*0-689-81456-9*) Atheneum Yung Read.

— Outside & Inside Sharks. LC 95-30245. (Illus.). 40p. (J). (ps-3). 1996. 16.00 (*0-689-80348-6*) Atheneum Yung Read.

— Outside & Inside Sharks. LC 95-30245. (Illus.). 40p. (ps-3). 1999. pap. 5.99 (*0-689-82683-4*, 076714005990) S&S Childrens.

— Outside & Inside Snakes. LC 94-20647. 40p. (J). 1998. mass mkt. 5.99 (*0-689-81998-6*) Aladdin.

— Outside & Inside Snakes. LC 94-20647. (Illus.). 40p. (J). (ps-3). 1995. lib. bdg. 17.00 (*0-02-762315-7*) Atheneum Yung Read.

***Markle, Sandra.** Outside & Inside Snakes. (Illus.). (J). 1999. pap. 13.40 (*0-613-08505-1*) Econo-Clad Bks.

Markle, Sandra. Outside & Inside Snakes. (Outside & Inside Ser.). 1998. 11.19 (*0-606-13691-6*, Pub. by Turtleback) Demco.

***Markle, Sandra.** Outside & Inside Spiders. LC 92-22643. (Illus.). 40p. (J). (ps-3). 1999. mass mkt. 5.99 (*0-689-83120-X*) Aladdin.

Markle, Sandra. Outside & Inside Spiders. LC 93-22643. (Illus.). 40p. (J). (ps-3). 1994. lib. bdg. 17.00 (*0-02-762314-9*) Atheneum Yung Read.

— Outside & Inside You. (Illus.). (J). 1996. pap. 4.95 (*0-689-71896-9*) Aladdin.

— Outside & Inside You. LC 90-37791. (Illus.). 40p. (J). (ps-3). 1991. 14.95 (*0-02-762311-4*) Atheneum Yung Read.

— Pioneering Frozen Worlds: Polar Region Exploration. LC 95-15971. (Illus.). 48p. (J). (gr. 3-7). 1996. 17.00 (*0-689-31824-3*) Aladdin.

— Pioneering Ocean Depths. LC 93-33555. (Illus.). 40p. (J). (gr. 3-7). 1995. 17.00 (*0-689-31823-5*) Atheneum Yung Read.

— Pioneering Space. LC 91-24936. (Illus.). 40p. (J). (gr. 3-7). 1992. lib. bdg. 14.95 (*0-689-31748-4*) Atheneum Yung Read.

— A Rainy Day. LC 91-17059. (Illus.). 32p. (J). (ps-2). 1993. 15.95 (*0-531-05976-6*); lib. bdg. 16.99 (*0-531-08576-7*) Orchard Bks Watts.

— Science in a Bottle. 64p. (J). (gr. 2-5). 1995. pap. 2.99 (*0-590-47595-9*) Scholastic Inc.

— Science Surprises. (J). (gr. 5-7). 1996. pap. 2.99 (*0-590-48401-X*) Scholastic Inc.

Markle, Sandra. Science Surprises. 1996. 8.19 (*0-606-11818-7*, Pub. by Turtleback) Demco.

Markle, Sandra. Science to the Rescue. LC 92-41096. (Illus.). 48p. (J). (gr. 3-7). 1994. 15.95 (*0-689-31783-2*) Atheneum Yung Read.

— Super Cool Science: South Pole Stations, Past, Present, & Future. LC 97-14890. (Illus.). 32p. (J). (gr. 3-5). 1998. 16.95 (*0-8027-8470-4*); lib. bdg. 17.85 (*0-8027-8471-2*) Walker & Co.

— Super Science Secrets: Exploring Nature Through Games, Puzzles & Activities, 3 vols. LC 96-79798. (Illus.). 48p. (J). (gr. 3-7). 1997. 14.95 (*1-56352-396-5*) Longstreet.

— What Happens Next? LC 95-77257. (Illus.). 48p. (J). (ps-3). 1995. 14.95 (*1-56352-232-2*) Longstreet.

— What Happens Next?, Vol. 2. LC 95-77257. Vol. 2. (Illus.). 2p. (J). (ps-3). 1996. 14.95 (*1-56352-286-1*) Longstreet.

Markle, Sandra & Markle, William. Gone Forever: An Alphabet of Extinct Animals. LC 95-30805. (Illus.). 40p. (J). 1998. 16.00 (*0-689-31961-4*) Atheneum Yung Read.

Markle, Sandras. Science: Just Add Salt. 64p. (J). (gr. 4-7). 1994. pap. 2.99 (*0-590-46537-6*) Scholastic Inc.

Markle, Susan M. Good Frames & Bad: A Grammar of Frame Writing. 2nd ed. LC 71-91153. 324p. reprint ed. pap. 100.50 (*0-608-10817-0*, 201700200006) Bks Demand.

Markle, William, jt. auth. see Markle, Sandra.

Marklew. Felicidades es Una Varon, Regalo.Tr. of Congratulations It's a Boy. (SPA.). 11p. 4.99 (*1-56063-312-3*, 490343) Editorial Unilit.

— Felicidades es Una Nina, Regalo.Tr. of Congratulations It's a Girl. (SPA.). 11p. 4.99 (*1-56063-313-1*, 490344) Editorial Unilit.

Marklew, Victoria. Cash, Crisis & Corporate Governance: The Role of National Finance Systems in Industrial Restructuring. LC 95-8273. 273p. 1995. text 47.50 (*0-472-10504-3*, 10504) U of Mich Pr.

Markley, Deborah. Availability of Capital in Rural America: Problems & Options. (New Alliances for Rural America Ser.). 60p. (Orig.). 1988. pap. text 6.00 (*1-55877-018-6*) Natl Governor.

Markley, Elaine & Bergamot, Stella. Soul Song. LC 98-85448. x, 192p. 1998. 22.95 (*0-9664412-4-9*) Spirit Song CO.

Markley, Elinore, jt. auth. see Crofts, Beatrice.

Markley, J. Gerald. The Life of Lazarillo de Tormes. LC 55-34585. 80p. (C). 1954. pap. text 7.51 (*0-02-376160-1*, LLA37, Macmillan Coll) P-H.

Markley, J. Gerald, tr. Epic of the Cid. LC 61-14564. 1961. pap. 3.95 (*0-672-60259-8*, LLA77, Bobbs) Macmillan.

Markley, John L., et al, eds. High Pressure Effects in Biophysics & Enzymology. (Illus.). 400p. (C). 1996. text 110.00 (*0-19-509722-X*) OUP.

Markley, John L. & Opella, Stanley J., eds. Biological N. M. R. Spectroscopy. (Illus.). 376p. 1997. text 70.00 (*0-19-509468-9*) OUP.

Markley, Klare S. Fatty Acids: Their Chemistry, Properties, Production & Uses, 5 pts., Set. 2nd ed. LC 82-8934. 3888p. (C). 1982. lib. bdg. 450.00 (*0-89874-576-4*) Krieger.

Markley, Merle, jt. ed. see Berryman, Jack H.

Markley, Nelson G. Introduction to Probability. rev. ed. (C). 1991. pap. text 28.40 (*0-536-04960-2*) Pearson Custom.

Markley, Nelson G. Introduction to Probability. 2nd ed. 352p. (C). 1994. pap. 36.20 (*0-536-58737-X*) Pearson Custom.

Markley, Oliver W. & McCuan, Walter R., eds. America Beyond 2001: Opposing Viewpoints. LC 94-46738. (Opposing Viewpoints Ser.). (Illus.). 312p. 1996. pap. text 16.20 (*1-56510-292-4*) Greenhaven.

Markley, Oliver W. & McCuan, Walter R., eds. 21st Century Earth: Opposing Viewpoints. (Opposing Viewpoints Ser.). (Illus.). 312p. (J). (gr. 5-12). 1996. pap. 16.20 (*1-56510-414-5*) Greenhaven.

Markley, Oliver W. & McCuan, Walter R., eds. 21st Century Earth: Opposing Viewpoints. (Opposing Viewpoints Ser.). (Illus.). 288p. (J). (gr. 5-12). 1996. lib. bdg. 26.20 (*1-56510-415-3*) Greenhaven.

Markley, Oliver W. & Wygant, Alice C. Information & the Future: A Handbook of Sources & Strategies Ser. LC 87-36063. 275p. 1988. lib. bdg. 55.00 (*0-313-24813-3*, MIU/, Greenwood Pr) Greenwood.

Markley, R. W. & Sheeler, Willard D. Words, Words, Words, Bk 2. (Words, Words, Words Ser.). 128p. (gr. 9-12). 1987. pap. text. write for info. (*0-13-964289-7*, 18830) Prentice ESL.

Markley, Rayner W. Handwriting Workbook. Evans, A. R., ed. (Welcome to English Ser.). 1977. student ed. 3.45 (*0-89285-043-4*) ELS Educ Servs.

— Spot Drills, Bk. 1. (Illus.). 140p. 1983. pap. text 9.50 (*0-19-434125-9*) OUP.

— Spot Drills, Bk. 2. (Illus.). 96p. 1987. pap. text 9.50 (*0-19-434126-7*) OUP.

— Spot Drills, Bk. 3. (Illus.). 96p. 1987. pap. text 9.50 (*0-19-434127-5*) OUP.

***Markley, Robert.** Encyclopedia of Roses. 240p. 1999. 35.00 (*0-7641-5193-2*) Barron.

Markley, Robert. Fallen Languages: Crises of Representation in Newtonian England, 1660-1740. (Illus.). 288p. 1993. text 42.50 (*0-8014-2588-3*) Cornell U Pr.

— Two Edged Weapons: Style & Ideology in the Comedies of Etherege, Wycherley, & Congreve. 280p. 1988. 69.00 (*0-19-812960-2*) OUP.

Markley, Robert, ed. Virtual Realities & Their Discontents. 197p. 1995. text 38.50 (*0-8018-5225-0*); pap. text 14.95 (*0-8018-5226-9*) Johns Hopkins.

Marklin, Megan. The Summoned. Zion, Claire, ed. 320p. (Orig.). 1993. mass mkt. 4.99 (*0-671-76098-X*) PB.

Markline, Judy. Thinking on Paper. 3rd ed. (C). 1994. pap. text 37.00 (*0-15-501120-0*) Harcourt Coll Pubs.

Markline, Judy. Thinking on Paper. 3rd ed. (C). 1995. pap. text, teacher ed. 33.75 (*0-15-501634-2*) Harcourt Coll Pubs.

— Thinking on Paper. 4th ed. (C). 1997. text, teacher ed. 28.00 (*0-15-505224-1*) Harcourt.

— Thinking on Paper. 4th ed. (C). 1999. text 43.50 (*0-15-505223-3*) Harcourt.

Marklyn, B., jt. auth. see Whitehorn, M.

Marklyn, Bill. Business Intelligence: The IBM Solution. LC 98-32313. xiii, 289p. 1999. pap. 79.95 incl. audio compact disk (*1-85233-085-6*) Spr-Verlag.

— Relational Databases Explained. 1997. pap. text 34.95 (*3-540-76032-6*) Spr-Verlag.

Marklyn, Bill, jt. auth. see Whitehorn, Mark.

Marklyn, Bill, jt. auth. see Whitehorn, Mary.

Markmam, Charles W. Prehispanic Settlement Dynamics in Central Oaxaca, Mexico: A View from the Miahuatlan Valley. (Vanderbilt University Publications in Anthropology: No. 26). (Illus.). 185p. 1981. pap. 11.85 (*0-935462-17-1*) VUPA.

Markman, Arthur. Knowledge Representation. LC 98-19006. 336p. 1998. 69.95 (*0-8058-2440-5*); pap. 36.00 (*0-8058-2441-3*) L Erlbaum Assocs.

Markman, Arthur B., jt. auth. see Hoffman, Robert R.

Markman, Arthur B., jt. ed. see Dietrich, Eric.

Markman, Charles W. & Kreisa, Paul P. Investigations at the Deere Creek Site: Early Woodland Camping Locality in Rock Island County, Illinois. (Northern Illinois University Archaeological Research Ser.: No. 1). (Illus.). 70p. 1984. pap. 4.95 (*0-917039-00-9*) N Ill Anthro.

Markman, Ellen M. Categorization & Naming in Children: Problems of Induction. (Learning, Development & Conceptual Change Ser.). (Illus.). 264p. 1991. reprint ed. pap. text 15.00 (*0-262-63136-9*, Bradford Bks) MIT Pr.

Markman, Ellen M., jt. ed. see Mussen, Paul H.

Markman, Howard, et al. Fighting for Your Marriage: Positive Steps for Preventing Divorce & Preserving a Lasting Love. (Illus.). 331p. 1996. pap. 14.00 (*0-7879-0280-2*) Jossey-Bass.

Markman, Howard, jt. auth. see Halford, W. Kim.

Markman, Howard, ed. see Notarius, Clifford.

***Markman, Jon D.** Online Investing. LC 99-37221. 352p. 1999. pap. text 24.99 (*0-7356-0650-1*) Microsoft.

— Online Investing. 2nd ed. 336p. 2001. 24.99 (*0-7356-1123-8*) Microsoft.

Markman, Marsha, et al, eds. The American Journey: United States History Through Letters & Diaries: Colonial Period Through Reconstruction, Vol. I. (Illus.). 232p. 1995. pap. text 16.50 (*1-881089-36-3*) Brandywine Press.

— The American Journey: United States History Through Letters & Diaries: From Reconstruction to Recent Times, Vol. II. (Illus.). 240p. 1997. pap. text 16.50 (*1-881089-96-7*) Brandywine Press.

***Markman, Marsha, et al, eds.** American Journey Vol. 1: United States History Through Letters & Diaries, 2 vols. rev. ed. (Illus.). 232p. (C). 1998. pap. text 16.50 (*1-881089-50-9*) Brandywine Press.

Markman, Marsha, et al, eds. Writing Women's Lives: American Women's History through Letters & Diaries. (Illus.), 352p. (C). 1999. pap. text 19.50 (*1-881089-32-0*) Brandywine Press.

M

Markman, Maurie. Basic Cancer Medicine. Zorab, Richard, ed. LC 97-706. 128p. 1997. pap. text 35.00 (*0-7216-5824-5*, W B Saunders Co) Harcrt Hlth Sci Grp.
— Handbook of Chemotherapy for Gynecologic Cancers LC 99-14011. 1999. write for info. (*0-944496-62-8*) Precept Pr.
— Handbooks of Chemotherapy Regimens for Gynecologic Cancers: An Indispensable Quick Reference Guide. 1999. pap. text 39.95 (*1-56625-136-2*) Bonus Books.
— Regional Antineoplastic Drug Delivery in the Management of Malignant Disease. LC 90-15596. (Johns Hopkins Series in Contemporary Medicine & Public Health). 159p. reprint ed. pap. 49.30 (*0-608-06170-0*, 206650300008) Bks Demand.
Markman, Maurie, ed. Regional Chemotherapy: Clinical Research & Practice. LC 99-22882. (Current Clinical Oncology Ser.). 376p. 1999. 135.00 (*0-89603-729-0*) Humana.
Markman, Maurie & Belinson, Jerome L., eds. Expert Consultations in Gynecological Cancers. LC 96-43175. (Basic & Clinical Oncology Ser.: Vol. 11). (Illus.). 528p. 1996. text 85.00 (*0-8247-9768-X*) Dekker.
Markman, Maurie & Hoskins, William J., eds. Cancer of the Ovary. LC 92-49712. (Illus.). 457p. 1993. reprint ed. pap. 141.70 (*0-608-05825-4*, 205979000007) Bks Demand.
Markman, Michael. The Path: An Adventure in African History. Gift, Wendy, ed. LC 96-22412. (Illus.). 32p. (J). (gr. 1-5). 1997. 7.95 (*1-881316-19-X*) A&B Bks.
Markman, Michael. The Path: An Adventure in African History. Gift, Wendy, ed. LC 96-22412. (Illus.). 32p. (J). (gr. 2-9). 1997. pap. 8.95 (*1-881316-35-1*) A&B Bks.
Markman, Peter T., jt. auth. see Markman, Roberta H.
***Markman, Robert.** Hazardous to Your Wealth: Extraordinary Popular Delusions & the Madness of Mutual Fund Experts. 154p. 2000. pap. 17.95 (*1-58619-006-7*, Pub. by Elton-Wolf Pub) Midpt Trade.
Markman, Roberta H. & Markman, Peter T. Masks of the Spirit: Image & Metaphor in Mesoamerica. (Illus.). 276p. 1989. 75.00 (*0-520-06418-6*, Pub. by U CA Pr) Cal Prin Full Svc.
— Masks of the Spirit: Image & Metaphor in Mesoamerica. (Illus.). 276p. (C). 1994. pap. 32.50 (*0-520-08654-6*, Pub. by U CA Pr) Cal Prin Full Svc.
Markman, Roberta H. & Waddell, Marie L. Ten Steps in Writing the Research Paper. 5th ed. 160p. (C). 1994. pap. 9.95 (*0-8120-1868-0*) Barron.
***Markman, Roberta H., et al.** 10 Steps in Writing the Research Paper. 6th ed. LC 99-87545. 2001. write for info. (*0-7641-1362-3*) Barron.
Markman, Roger. Classic Aircraft in Aviation Art. (Illus.). 96p. 1994. 49.95 (*0-943231-64-7*) Howell Pr VA.
Markman, Ronald & LaBrecque, Ron. Obsessed: The Anatomy of a Stalker. (Illus.). 304p. 1995. reprint ed. mass mkt. 5.99 (*0-380-76650-7*, Avon Bks) Morrow Avon.
Markman, Sidney D. Architecture & Urbanization in Colonial Chiapas, Mexico. LC 81-68194. (Memoirs Ser.: Vol. 153). 443p. 1984. 50.00 (*0-87169-153-1*, M153-MAS) Am Philos.
— Architecture & Urbanization of Colonial Central America Vol. I: Selected Primary Documentary & Literary Sources. LC 93-21536. (Illus.). 285p. 1994. per. 35.00 (*0-87918-078-1*) ASU Lat Am St.
— Architecture & Urbanization of Colonial Central America Vol. II: A Geographical Gazetteer of Primary Documentary, Literary & Visual Sources. LC 93-21536. (Monographs). (Illus.). 342p. (C). 1995. pap. 50.00 (*0-87918-080-3*) ASU Lat Am St.
— Colonial Architecture of Antigua, Guatemala. LC 66-13634. (American Philosophical Society, Memoirs Ser.: No. 64). 355p. reprint ed. pap. 110.10 (*0-7837-2681-3*, 204305800006) Bks Demand.
— Colonial Central America: A Bibliography. LC 76-23299. 345p. 1977. 15.00 (*0-87918-023-4*) ASU Lat Am St.
— The Horse in Greek Art. LC 72-88057. (Illus.). 1969. reprint ed. 30.00 (*0-8196-0247-7*) Biblo.
Markmann, Charles, tr. see Fanon, Frantz.
Markmann, Charles L., tr. see Lemaitre, Solange.
Marko-Geenen, Suzette & Caillat, Carleen. Preparer & Reussir le TOEFL. (FRE.). 158p. 1993. pap. 49.95 (*0-7859-1003-4*, 2708115367) Fr & Eur.
Marko, H., et al, eds. Processing Structures for Perception & Action. LC 87-34522. 279p. 1988. 145.00 (*3-527-27705-6*) Wiley.
Marko, Katherine M. Pocket Babies. (First Bks.). (Illus.). 64p. (J). (gr. 4-6). 1995. lib. bdg. 22.00 (*0-531-20211-9*) Watts.
***Marko, Paul.** Candlecraft. 1999. pap. text 12.99 (*0-7858-1066-8*) Bk Sales Inc.
Marko, Stephanie K., ed. see Peet, Jennifer.
Markoe, Glen, et al. Ars Longa, Vita Brevis: Ancient Art from the Walter I. Farmer Collection.Tr. of Art Is Long, Life Is Short. (Illus.). 107p. (Orig.). 1996. pap. 30.00 (*0-940784-17-3*) Miami Univ Art.
Markoe, Glenn. Phoenician Bronze & Silver Bowls from Cyprus & the Mediterranean. fac. ed. LC 83-18305. (University of California Publication, Classical Studies: No. 26). (Illus.). 392p. 1985. pap. 121.60 (*0-7837-8612-3*, 205916700008) Bks Demand.
***Markoe, Glenn.** Phoenicians. 350p. 2000. 45.00 (*0-520-22613-5*, Pub. by U CA Pr) Cal Prin Full Svc.
Markoe, Glenn, et al. Mistress of the House, Mistress of Heaven: Women in Ancient Egypt. LC 96-9376. (Illus.). 240p. 1996. 50.00 (*1-55595-129-5*) Hudson Hills.
Markoe, Merrill. The Day My Dogs Became Guys. LC 97-24624. (Illus.). 32p. (J). (ps-3). 1999. 15.99 (*0-670-85344-5*) Viking Penguin.
— Merrill Markoe's Guide to Love. 192p. 1998. pap. 12.00 (*0-87113-706-2*, Atlntc Mnthly) Grove-Atltic.
Markoff, Annabelle M. Quick Cognitive Inventory (QCI) 39p. (Orig.). 1990. pap. text, student ed. 20.00 (*0-87879-643-6*); student ed. 17.00 (*0-87879-644-4*) Acad Therapy.
— Receptive Oral Language Inventory. Martin, Nancy, ed. 64p. 1995. 40.00 (*0-87879-996-6*, 996-6); pap. 17.00 (*0-87879-997-4*, 996-6) Acad Therapy.
— Within Reach: Academic Achievement Through Parent-Teacher Communication. LC 92-17388. 1992. 16.50 (*0-87879-955-9*) Acad Therapy.
Markoff, John. The Abolition of Feudalism: Peasants, Lords, & Legislators in the French Revolution. 1995. 90.00 (*0-271-01538-1*); pap. 25.00 (*0-271-01539-X*) Pa St U Pr.
— Waves of Democracy: Social Movements & Political Change. 1996. pap. 18.95 (*0-8039-9019-7*) Pine Forge.
Markoff, John, jt. auth. see Hafner, Katie.
Markoff, John, jt. auth. see Shimomura, Tsutomu.
Markoff, Mortimer & Platt, Frederic W. The Art of Playing the Piano: Conversations with Mortimer Markoff. Holmes, Merlyn, ed. LC 93-38483. (Illus.). 144p. (Orig.). 1993. pap. 14.95 (*0-9639221-7-3*) London Rd Bks.
Markolin, Caroline. Modern Austrian Writing: A Study Guide for Austrian Literature 1945-1990. (Austrian Culture Ser.). XII, 272p. (C). 1995. pap. text 35.95 (*0-8204-2752-7*) P Lang Pubng.
— Thomas Bernhard & His Grandfather Johannes Freumbichler: Our Grandfathers Are Our Teachers. Hartweg, Petra, tr. LC 92-38175. (Studies in Austrian Literature, Culture, & Thought). 1993. 27.50 (*0-929497-51-1*) Ariadne CA.
Markopoulos, P., et al, eds. Design, Specification & Verification of Interactive Systems '98: Proceedings of the Eurographics Workshop in Abingdon, U. K., June 3-5, 1998. (Eurographics Ser.). (Illus.). ix, 326p. 1998. pap. 79.95 (*3-211-83212-2*) Spr-Verlag.
Markos, Louis, ed. see Boochny, Etty.
Markos, Prudence, jt. auth. see Sullivan, Patricia.
Markotic, Nicole. Yellow Pages: A Catalogue of Intentions. 164p. 1995. pap. 10.95 (*0-88995-132-2*, Pub. by Red Deer) Genl Dist Srvs.
Markov, A. S. Dictionary of Scientific & Technical Terminology: English-French-German-Dutch-Russian. (DUT, ENG, FRE, GER & RUS.). 496p. 1984. 155.00 (*0-7859-7151-3*) Fr & Eur.
Markov, A. S., et al. Dictionary of Scientific & Technical Terminology. 1984. text 196.50 (*90-201-1667-3*) Kluwer Academic.
Markov, Georgi. The Truth That Killed. LC 84-673507. xv, 280p. 1983. write for info. (*0-297-78300-9*) Weidenfeld & Nicolson.
Markov, I. V. Crystal Growth for Beginners - Fundamentals of Nucleation, Crystal Growth & Epitaxy. 300p. 1995. text 67.00 (*981-02-1531-2*); pap. text 32.00 (*981-02-2177-0*) World Scientific Pub.
Markov, Konstantin Z. Advances in Mathematical Modeling of Composite Materials. (Series on Advances in Mathematics). 304p. 1994. text 81.00 (*981-02-1644-0*) World Scientific Pub.
Markov, Konstantin Z., ed. Continuum Models & Discrete Systems: Proceedings of the Eighth International Symposium, Varna, Bulgaria, 11-16 June 1995. LC 95-47204. 680p. 1996. write for info. (*981-02-2552-0*) World Scientific Pub.
***Markov, Konstantin Z. & Preziosi, Luigi, eds.** Heterogeneous Solids: Micromechanics Modeling Methods & Simulations. LC 99-46355. (Modeling & Simulation in Science, Engineering & Technology Ser.). (Illus.). 32p. 1999. 79.95 (*0-8176-4083-5*, Pub. by Birkhauser) Spr-Verlag.
Markov, Konstantine Z., ed. see International Symposium on Continuum Models of Discrete Systems Staff.
Markov, M. A. Electromagnetic Fields & Biomembranes. Blank, Martin, ed. LC 87-29276. 326p. 1988. 85.00 (*0-306-42778-8*, Plenum Trade) Perseus Pubng.
— Quantum Gravity. Beresin, V. & Frolov, V. P., eds. 960p. (C). 1988. text 181.00 (*9971-5-0409-X*) World Scientific Pub.
Markov, M. A., ed. Invariants & the Evolution of Nonstationary. (Proceedings of the Lebedev Physics Institute Ser.: Vol. 183). 370p. 1989. 195.00 (*0-941743-49-7*) Nova Sci Pubs.
— Physical Effects in the Gravitational Field of Black Holes. (Proceedings of the Lebedev Physics Institute Ser.: Vol. 169). 262p. (C). 1987. text 175.00 (*0-941743-04-7*) Nova Sci Pubs.
— Squeezed & Correlated States of Quantum Systems. Dodonov, V. V. et al, trs. LC 93-20853. (Proceedings of the Lebedev Physics Institute Ser.: Vol. 205). 242p. 1993. 165.00 (*1-56072-117-0*) Nova Sci Pubs.
— Theory of Nonstationary Quantum Oscillators: Proceedings of the Lebedev Physics Institute, Vol. 198. (Proceedings of the Lebedev Physics Institute Ser.: Vol. 198). 181p. (C). 1992. lib. bdg. 175.00 (*1-56072-076-X*) Nova Sci Pubs.
Markov, M. A., et al, eds. A. A. Friedmann: Centenary Volume. 370p. (C). 1989. text 123.00 (*9971-5-0899-0*) World Scientific Pub.
— Group Theoretical Methods in Physics: Proceedings of the Second Zvenigorod Seminar on Group Theoretical Methods in Physics, Zvenigorod, USSR, 24-26th November 1982, 3 vols., Vol. 1. xvi, 718p. 1985. text 934.00 (*3-7186-0245-8*) Gordon & Breach.
— Group Theoretical Methods in Physics: Proceedings of the Second Zvenigorod Seminar on Group Theoretical Methods in Physics, Zvenigorod, USSR, 24-26th November 1982, 3 vols., Vol. 2. xii, 458p. 1987. text 489.00 (*3-7186-0246-6*) Gordon & Breach.
— Group Theoretical Methods in Physics: Proceedings of the Second Zvenigorod Seminar on Group Theoretical Methods in Physics, Zvenigorod, USSR, 24-26th November 1982, 2 Vols., Vol. 3. 1615p. 1987. text 1254.00 (*3-7186-0247-4*); text 436.00 (*3-7186-0301-2*) Gordon & Breach.
— Group Theoretical Methods in Physics: Proceedings of the Third Yurmala Seminar, U. S. S. R., May, 1956, 2 vols., Set. 1388p. 1986. lib. bdg. 275.00 (*90-6764-072-7*, Pub. by VSP) Coronet Bks.
— Quantum Gravity: Proceedings of the Third Seminar, Moscow, 1984. 716p. 1985. 130.00 (*9971-978-90-3*) World Scientific Pub.
Markov, M. A., et al. Quantum Gravity: Proceedings of the 5th Seminar. 716p. 1991. text 130.00 (*981-02-0440-X*) World Scientific Pub.
Markov, M. A., jt. ed. see Man'ko, V. I.
Markov, Sergei, jt. auth. see McFaul, Michael.
Markov, Vladimir & Worth, Dean S., eds. From Los Angeles to Kiev: Papers on the Occasion of the Ninth International Congress of Slavists (Kiev 1983) (UCLA Slavic Studies: Vol. 7). 250p. 1983. 24.95 (*0-89357-119-9*) Slavica.
Markov, Vladimir, ed. see Kuzmin, Mikhail A.
Markov, Vladimir B. & Kostyukevitch, Sergey A., eds. International Conference on Optical Holography & Its Application. LC 98-227287. (Proceedings of SPIE Ser.: Vol. 3486). 179p. 1998. 59.00 (*0-8194-2944-9*) SPIE.
Markov, Yuri. Winning with the Slav. (Batsford Chess Library). 1995. pap. 19.95 (*0-8050-3283-5*) H Holt & Co.
Markova, Aelita K. The Teaching & Mastery of Language. Szekely, Beatrice B., ed. Vale, Michel, tr. LC 78-65595. 293p. reprint ed. pap. 90.90 (*0-608-14934-9*, 202612400048) Bks Demand.
***Markova, Dawna.** I will Not Die an Unlived Life: Reclaiming Purpose & Passion. 150p. 2000. pap. 13.95 (*1-57324-101-6*) Conari Press.
Markova, Dawna. No Enemies Within: A Creative Process for Discovering What's Right about What's Wrong. 340p. (Orig.). 1994. pap. 14.95 (*0-943233-64-X*) Conari Press.
— The Open Mind: Exploring the 6 Patterns of Natural Intelligence. rev. ed. (Illus.). 250p. 1996. pap. 14.95 (*1-57324-064-8*) Conari Press.
Markova, Dawna & Bryner, Andy. An Unused Intelligence: Physical Thinking for 21st Century Leadership. (Illus.). 300p. (Orig.). 1996. pap. 18.95 (*0-943233-97-6*) Conari Press.
Markova, Dawna & Powell, Anne R. How Your Child Is Smart: A Life-Changing Approach to Learning. 200p. (Orig.). 1992. pap. 12.95 (*0-943233-38-0*) Conari Press.
— Learning Unlimited: Using Homework to Engage Your Child's Natural Style of Intelligence. LC 98-16484. 300p. 1998. pap. 13.95 (*1-57324-116-4*) Conari Press.
— Your Child Is Smart. 208p. 1997. 6.98 (*1-56731-196-2*, MJF Bks) Fine Comms.
Markova, Elena. Off Nevsky Prospekt: St. Peterburg's Theatre Studios in the 1980s & 1990s. (Russian Theatre Archive Ser.). (Illus.). 125p. 1998. pap. text 22.00 (*90-5702-135-8*, Harwood Acad Pubs) Gordon & Breach.
***Markova, Elena.** Off Nevsky Prospekt: St Petersburg's Theatre Studios in the 1980s & 1990s. (Russian Theatre Archive Ser.: Vol. 16). (Illus.). 125p. 1998. text 67.00 (*90-5702-134-X*, Harwood Acad Pubs) Gordon & Breach.
Markova, Ivana. Paradigms, Thought & Language. LC 81-22022. (Illus.). 241p. reprint ed. pap. 74.80 (*0-8357-3098-0*, 203935500012) Bks Demand.
Markova, Ivana, et al, eds. Mutualities in Dialogue. (Illus.). 300p. (C). 1996. text 59.95 (*0-521-49595-4*); pap. text 19.95 (*0-521-49941-0*) Cambridge U Pr.
Markova, Ivana & Farr, Robert M., eds. Representations of Health, Illness & Handicap. 271p. 1995. pap. text 22.00 (*3-7186-5658-2*, Harwood Acad Pubs) Gordon & Breach.
— Representations of Health, Illness & Handicap. 271p. 1995. text 64.00 (*3-7186-5657-4*, Harwood Acad Pubs) Gordon & Breach.
Markova, Ivana & Foppa, Klaus, eds. The Dynamics of Dialogue. 200p. 1990. 54.00 (*0-387-91388-2*) Spr-Verlag.
Markova, Ivana & Foppa, Klaus, eds. Asymmetries in Dialogue. 300p. (C). 1991. text 69.50 (*0-389-20980-5*) B&N Imports.
Markova, Ivena, ed. The Social Context of Language. LC 77-3861. 251p. reprint ed. pap. 77.90 (*0-608-17591-9*, 203043600069) Bks Demand.
Markova, N., jt. ed. see Kadieva, D.
Markovchick, V., jt. auth. see Pons, Peter T.
Markovchick, Vincent J. & Pons, Peter T. Emergency Medicine Secrets. 2nd rev. ed. LC 98-43419. (Secrets Ser.). (Illus.). 475p. 1998. pap. text 39.00 (*1-56053-253-X*) Hanley & Belfus.
Markovic, D., ed. see Jones, B. J.
Markovic, Mihailo. The Contemporary Marx. 224p. 1986. 40.00 (*0-7855-2940-3*) St Mut.
— Dialectical Theory of Meaning. 444p. 1984. text 252.50 (*90-277-1596-3*, D Reidel) Kluwer Academic.
Markovic, Mihailo & Petrovic, Gajo, eds. Praxis. (Boston Studies in the Philosophy of Science: No. XXXVI; Synthese Library, No. 134). 441p. 1979. pap. text 78.00 (*90-277-0968-8*, D Reidel); lib. bdg. 141.50 (*90-277-0727-8*, D Reidel) Kluwer Academic.
Markovic, Mira. Answer. LC 97-199991. 160p. 1997. pap. 14.95 (*1-55082-169-5*, Pub. by Quarry Pr) LPC InBook.
— Night & Day. LC 97-199993. 240p. 1997. 14.95 (*1-55082-168-7*, Pub. by Quarry Pr) LPC InBook.
Markovic, V., ed. Radiation Processing: Fourth International Meeting on Radiation Processing, Dubrovnik, Yugoslavia, October 1982, 2 vols. 980p. 1984. pap. 155.00 (*0-08-029162-7*, Pergamon Pr) Elsevier.
Markovich, Denise. Effective Asset-Liability Management for the Community Bank. 1991. text 55.00 (*1-55520-047-8*, Irwn Prfssnl) McGraw-Hill Prof.
Markovich, Efimov I. Bremia Dobra: Russkii Pisatel' Kak Vlastitel' Dum. LC 93-15793. (RUS.). 204p. (Orig.). 1993. pap. 14.00 (*1-55779-064-7*) Hermitage Pubs.
Markovits, Andrei S., ed. The Political Economy of West Germany: Modell Deutschland. LC 81-20996. 240p. 1982. 55.00 (*0-275-90854-2*, C0854, Praeger Pubs) Greenwood.
Markovits, Andrei S. & Reich, Simon. The German Predicament: Memory & Power in the New Europe. LC 96-42943. (Illus.). 408p. 1996. text 29.95 (*0-8014-2802-5*) Cornell U Pr.
Markovits, Andrei S. & Sysyn, Frank E., eds. Nationbuilding & the Politics of Nationalism: Essays on Austrian Galicia. LC 80-53800. (Harvard Ukrainian Research Institute Monograph). 345p. 1990. pap. text 18.00 (*0-674-60312-5*) Harvard Ukrainian.
Markovits, Andrei S., jt. auth. see Reich, Simon.
***Markovits, Claude.** The Global World of Indian Merchants, 1750-1947: Traders of Sind from Bukhara to Panama. LC 99-47925. (Illus.). 343p. (C). 2000. text 64.95 (*0-521-62285-9*) Cambridge U Pr.
***MARKOVITS, HAL.** Terrorism. (Crime, Justice & Punishment Ser.). (Illus.). 128p. (YA). 2000. 19.95 (*0-7910-5264-8*) Chelsea Hse.
Markovits, Inge. Imperfect Justice: A German Diary. 216p. 1995. pap. 22.00 (*0-19-825961-1*); text 49.95 (*0-19-825814-3*) OUP.
Markovits, Richard S. Matters of Principle: Legal Argument & Constitutional Interpretation. LC 98-19602. 352p. 1998. text 50.00 (*0-8147-5513-5*) NYU Pr.
Markovitz, Andrei S. & Silverstein, Mark, eds. The Politics of Scandal: Power & Process in Liberal Democracies. LC 88-11045. 288p. (C). 1988. 39.50 (*0-8419-1097-9*); pap. 19.95 (*0-8419-1098-7*) Holmes & Meier.
Markovitz, David C. Becoming the Best! Making Optimization Happen. 64p. 1997. pap. 8.95 (*1-890338-00-1*) Optimization Pr.
Markovitz, David C. & Wulfeck, James A., Jr. GMP Makes Good Business Sense: Prevent Contamination, Mix-Ups, & Errors. 25p. 1997. pap. 3.95 (*1-890338-02-8*) Optimization Pr.
Markovitz, Irving L., ed. Studies in Power & Class in Africa. (Illus.). 415p. (C). 1987. pap. text 23.95 (*0-19-504130-5*) OUP.
Markovitz, Morris J. & Lam, Michael. How to Beat the Street with Plan Z: The New Strategy for Safe & Lucrative Investing in the Money Markets. 272p. 1993. 24.95 (*0-471-58286-7*) Wiley.
Markovitz, Paul, et al. Guidelines for the Evaluation of File Transfer, Access & Management Implementations. (Illus.). 99p. (Orig.). (C). 1994. pap. text 35.00 (*0-7881-0624-4*) DIANE Pub.
Markovitz, Paul, jt. auth. see Garguilo, John J.
Markovski, B. L. & Vinitsky, S. I. Adiabatic Representation in Quantum Theory: Rigorous Results & Applications. 400p. 1995. text 86.00 (*981-02-0847-2*) World Scientific Pub.
Markovski, Venko. Goli Otok-Island of Death: A Diary in Letters. 229p. 1984. text 72.00 (*0-88033-055-4*, Pub. by East Eur Monographs) Col U Pr.
Markovsky, Barry, jt. ed. see Lawler, Edward J.
Markow, Paul. Professional Secrets of Advertising Photography. (Illus.). 128p. 1999. pap. 29.95 (*0-936262-79-6*) Amherst Media.
Markow, Herbert L. Small Boat Law. LC 77-154289. (Illus.). 435p. (Orig.). (C). 1977. pap. 40.00 (*0-934108-00-5*) H L Markow.
— Small Boat Law: 1978 Supplement. LC 79-88475. 144p. (C). 1979. pap. 20.00 (*0-934108-01-3*) H L Markow.
— Small Boat Law: 1981-1983 Supplement. LC 77-154289. 274p. (C). 1984. pap. text 36.00 (*0-934108-03-X*) H L Markow.
Markow, Jack. The Art of Cartooning. (Illus.). 80p. 1990. pap. 9.00 (*0-399-51626-3*, Perigee Bks) Berkley Pub.
Markow, Joseph, jt. auth. see DeVito, Jill.
***Markow, Peter.** Separating & Isolating the Major Components of Milk. (Modular Laboratory in Chemistry Ser.). 12p. (C). 1999. pap. text 1.50 (*0-87540-513-4*, PROP 513-4) Chem Educ Res.
Markow, Peter G. Biochemistry of the Human Body. 80p. (C). 1994. 17.44 (*1-56870-030-X*) RonJon Pub.
— Estimating the Calorie Content of Nuts. Neidig, H. Anthony, ed. (Modular Laboratory Program in Chemistry Ser.). 12p. (C). 1993. pap. text 1.50 (*0-87540-428-6*, THER 428-6) Chem Educ Res.
— Separating & Identifying Food Dyes by Paper Chromatography. Stanitski, C. L., ed. (Modular Laboratory Program in Chemistry Ser.). 16p. (C). 1997. pap. text 1.50 (*0-87540-492-8*) Chem Educ Res.
Markow, Theresa A., ed. Developmental Instability - Its Origins & Evolutionary Implications: Proceedings of the International Conference, Tempe, Arizona, U. S. A., 14-15 June 1993. LC 94-1934. (Contemporary Issues in Genetics & Evolution Ser.: Vol. 2). 436p. (C). 1994. text 298.50 (*0-7923-2678-4*) Kluwer Academic.
Markow-Totevy, Georges. Henry James. Griffiths, John, tr. from FRE. (C). 1969. 16.00 (*0-8464-1164-4*) Beekman Pubs.
Markow-Totevy, Georges, jt. auth. see Bree, Germaine.
Markowe, Laura. Redefining the Self: Coming Out As Lesbian. LC 96-798. 230p. 1996. 54.95 (*0-7456-1128-1*, Pub. by Polity Pr) Blackwell Pubs.
— Redefining the Self: Coming Out As Lesbian. LC 96-798. 230p. 1996. pap. 25.95 (*0-7456-1129-X*, Pub. by Polity Pr) Blackwell Pubs.
***Markowiak, Linda.** And Baby Makes Six: 9 Months Later. (Superromance Ser.: Bk. 920). 2000. per. 4.50 (*0-373-70920-X*, 1-70920-3) Harlequin Bks.

An Asterisk (*) at the beginning of an entry indicates that the title is appearing for the first time.

Markowiak, Linda. A Cop's Good Name. (Superromance Ser.). 1999. per. 4.25 (*0-373-70846-7*, 1-70846-0) Harlequin Bks.
— Courting Valerie. LC 95-6954. (Superromance Ser.). 297p. 1995. per. 3.50 (*0-373-70629-4*, 1-70629-0) Harlequin Bks.
— Firm Commitment. 1996. per. 3.99 (*0-373-70717-7*, 1-70717-3) Harlequin Bks.
— Love, Lies & Alibis: Love the Man. (Love That Man Ser.: No. 819). 1998. per. 4.25 (*0-373-70819-X*, 1-70819-7) Harlequin Bks.
— Motive for Marriage. (Superromance Ser.: No. 755). 1997. per. 3.99 (*0-373-70755-X*, 1-70755-3) Harlequin Bks.
— Reluctant Witness. (Superromance Ser.). (Orig.). 1998. per. 4.25 (*0-373-70785-1*, 1-70785-0) Harlequin Bks.
Markowich, M. Michael. Selling Skills for HR Professionals: How to Obtain Support for Ideas & New Programs. (How to Ser.). (Illus.). 45p. 1997. pap. 19.95 (*1-57963-052-9*, A0601) Am Compensation.
Markowich, P. A. Semiconductor Equations. (Illus.). 250p. 1990. 86.95 (*0-387-82157-0*) Spr-Verlag.
— The Stationary Semiconductor Device Equations. (Computational Microelectronics Ser.). (Illus.). 210p. 1986. 87.95 (*0-387-81892-8*) Spr-Verlag.
Markowicz, Andrzej A., jt. ed. see Van Grieken, Rene E.
Markowicz, Elysa. Living with Green Power: A Gourmet Collection of Living Food Recipes. LC 97-910032. (Illus.). 176p. 1997. 24.95 (*0-920470-11-4*) Alive Bks.
Markowitsch, Hans J. Intellectual Functions & the Brain: An Historical Perspective. LC 92-1482. (Illus.). 240p. 1992. text 78.00 (*0-88937-081-8*) Hogrefe & Huber Pubs.
Markowitsch, Hans J., ed. Information Processing by the Brain: Views & Hypotheses from a Physiological-Cognitive Perspective. LC 87-22542. 272p. 1988. 69.00 (*0-920887-15-5*) Hogrefe & Huber Pubs.
— Transient Global Amnesia & Related Disorders. LC 90-4811. (Illus.). 260p. 1990. text 58.00 (*0-920887-70-8*) Hogrefe & Huber Pubs.
Markowitsch, Hans J. & Nilsson, Lars-Goran. Cognitive Neuroscience of Memory. LC 99-71722. (Illus.). 312p. 1999. 59.00 (*0-88937-213-6*) Hogrefe & Huber Pubs.
Markowitz. Transform Analysis. (Electronics Technology Ser.). 1998. teacher ed. 12.00 (*0-8273-6948-4*); text 68.95 (*0-8273-6947-6*) Delmar.
Markowitz, Elysa. Warming up to Living Foods. LC 98-37160. 1998. pap. text 15.95 (*1-57067-065-X*) Book Pub Co.
Markowitz, Endel. Kid-Ish Yiddish. (Illus.). 44p. (J). 1993. lib. bdg. 16.95 (*0-933910-05-3*) Haymark.
***Markowitz, Fran.** Coming of Age in Post-Soviet Russia. LC 99-6787. 2000. 18.95 (*0-252-06864-5*) U of Ill Pr.
Markowitz, Fran. A Community in Spite of Itself: Soviet Jewish Emigres in New York. LC 92-31989. (Series in Ethnographic Inquiry). 320p. (C). 1993. text 55.00 (*1-56098-200-4*); pap. text 21.95 (*1-56098-225-X*) Smithsonian.
Markowitz, Fran & Ashkenazi, Michael. Sex, Sexuality, & the Anthropologist. LC 98-19727. 248p. 1999. 34.95 (*0-252-02437-0*); pap. 18.95 (*0-252-06747-9*) U of Ill Pr.
Markowitz, Gerald & Rosner, David. Children, Race, & Power: Kenneth & Mamie Clark's Northside Center. (Illus.). 308p. 1996. 29.95 (*0-8139-1687-9*) U Pr of Va.
— Slaves of the Depression: Workers' Letters about Life on the Job. LC 87-6671. 243p. reprint ed. pap. 75.40 (*0-608-20093-X*, 207136500011) Bks Demand.
Markowitz, Gerald, jt. auth. see Cook, Blanche Wiesen.
Markowitz, Gerald, jt. auth. see Rosner, David.
***Markowitz, Gerald E. & Rosner, David.** Children Race & Power: Kenneth & Mamie Clark's Northside Center. LC 99-47634. 328p. (C). 1999. pap. 21.99 (*0-415-92671-8*) Routledge.
Markowitz, Gerald E. & Rosner, David, eds. Slaves of the Depression: Workers' Letters about Life on the Job. LC 87-6671. 272p. 1987. 45.00 (*0-8014-1956-5*) Cornell U Pr.
Markowitz, Gerald E., jt. auth. see Park, Marlene.
***Markowitz, Harry M.** Mean Variance Analysis in Portfolio Choice & Capital Markets. 2000. 65.00 (*1-883249-75-9*) F J Fabozzi.
Markowitz, Harry M. Portfolio Selection: Efficient Diversification of Investments. 1991. 52.95 (*1-55786-108-0*) Blackwell Pubs.
Markowitz, Harvey, jt. auth. see Hoxie, Frederick E.
Markowitz, Harvey, ed. see Salem Press Editors.
Markowitz, Harvey, jt. ed. see Salem Press Staff.
Markowitz, Jamie, jt. auth. see Sprayregen, Richard.
Markowitz, Jerome. Triumphs & Trials of an Organ Builder. (Illus.). 195p. 1989. 20.00 (*0-9624896-0-3*) Vox Humana.
Markowitz, John C. Interpersonal Psychotherapy for Dysthymic Disorder. 176p. 1998. 33.50 (*0-88048-914-6*, 8914) Am Psychiatric.
Markowitz, John C., ed. Interpersonal Psychotherapy. (Review of Psychiatry Ser.). 156p. 1998. pap. text 27.00 (*0-88048-836-0*, 8836) Am Psychiatric.
Markowitz, Linda. Worker Activism after Successful Union Organizing. LC 99-23904. 216p. 1999. text 58.95 (*0-7656-0492-2*) M E Sharpe.
***Markowitz, Linda.** Worker Activism after Successful Union Organizing. 216p. 2000. reprint ed. pap. text 22.95 (*0-7656-0493-0*) M E Sharpe.
Markowitz, Michael W. & Jones-Brown, Delores D., eds. The System in Black & White: Exploring the Connections Between Race, Crime & Justice. LC 98-53399. 312p. 2000. 69.50 (*0-275-95974-0*, Praeger Pubs) Greenwood.
Markowitz, Milton, jt. auth. see Taranta, Angelo.
Markowitz, Ruth J. My Daughter, the Teacher: Jewish Teachers in the New York City Schools. LC 92-37565. 288p. (C). 1993. text 40.00 (*0-8135-1974-8*); pap. text 16.00 (*0-8135-1975-6*) Rutgers U Pr.
Markowitz, Sidney L. What You Should Know about Jewish Religion, History, Ethics & Culture. 240p. 1992. pap. 8.95 (*0-8065-0811-6*, Citadel Pr) Carol Pub Group.
Markowitz, Sidney L., jt. auth. see Margolis, Isidor.
Markowitz, Yvonne, jt. auth. see Curreri-Alibrandi, Gaetano.
Markowski, Benedict. Carissima: A Lyric Drama. rev. ed. LC 81-479565. (Illus.). 140p. 1980. ring bd. 25.00 (*0-9614820-0-1*) Poets Mark.
— Kopernik the Great Humanist. (Illus.). 1973. 1.00 (*0-685-37750-4*) Endurance.
Markowski, Carol & Hoder, Tom. Tomart's Price Guide to Character & Promotional Glasses. 3rd rev. ed. (Illus.). 176p. 1998. pap. 27.95 (*0-914293-35-4*) Tomart Pubns.
Markowski, Marjie, ed. see Drew, Brian & Edwards, John.
Markowski, Marjie, ed. see Fuhrman, John.
Markowski, Marjie, ed. see Rifenbary, Jay.
Markowski, Michael A. Ultralight Flight: The Pilot's Handbook of Ultralight Knowledge. LC 81-71889. (Ultralight Aviation Ser.: No. 3). (Illus.). 206p. (Orig.). 1984. 20.95 (*0-938716-07-7*); pap. 14.95 (*0-938716-06-9*) Markowski Intl.
Markowski, Michael A., ed. see Lambie, Jack.
Markowski, Mike, ed. see Drew, Brian & Edwards, John.
Markowski, Mike, ed. see Fuhrman, John.
Markowski, Mike, ed. see Lambie, Jack.
Markowski, Mike, ed. see Rifenbary, Jay.
Markowski, Mike, ed. see Ross, Don.
Markowsky, George. The DOS Windows Book. 304p. (C). 1995. pap. text, per. 28.95 (*0-8403-9968-5*) Kendall-Hunt.
Markowsky, Judy Kellogg. Shelterwood Teacher's Guide: Discovering the Forest. (Illus.). 80p. 1999. pap., teacher ed. 9.95 (*0-88448-211-1*) Tilbury Hse.
Markowsky, Judy Kellogg, see Mason, Cherie & Kellogg Markowsky, Judy.
Markrich, Mike & Bourke, Bob. Hanauma Bay. (Illus.). (J). pap. 5.95 (*0-9643421-0-3*) Ecology Comics.
Marks. Biochemistry. 2nd ed. (Board Review Ser.). 1994. 19.95 (*0-685-75161-9*) Lppncott W & W.
— Biochemistry. 3rd ed. (National Medical Ser.). 1993. 25.00 (*0-685-75166-X*) Lppncott W & W.
— The Economics of Work & Pay. 6th ed. LC 95-40602. (Illus.). (C). 1996. teacher ed. write for info. (*0-673-55888-6*) Addson-Wesley Educ.
— Economics Work Pay. 6th ed. LC 95-40602. (Illus.). (C). 1996. pap. text, student ed. 27.19 (*0-673-99563-1*) Addson-Wesley Educ.
Marks & Plewig, Gerd. Acne & Related Disorders: International Meeting, Ardiff, Held March, 1988. 1989. 98.00 (*0-948269-94-4*) CRC Pr.
Marks, jt. auth. see Williams.
Marks, A., et al, eds. Impact of Technology on Society: A Documentation of Current Research. 642p. 40.75 (*0-444-85725-7*) Elsevier.
Marks, A. & Tingay, Graham I. The Romans. (Illustrated World History Ser.). (Illus.). 96p. (YA). (gr. 6 up). 1990. pap. 12.95 (*0-7460-0340-4*) EDC.
— The Romans. (Illustrated World History Ser.). (Illus.). 194p. (YA). (gr. 6 up). 1999. lib. bdg. 20.95 (*0-88110-439-6*) EDC.
Marks, Abby. Study Skills: Tools for Active Learning. (C). 1994. pap. 23.75 (*0-8273-5437-1*) Delmar.
Marks, Alan. Nowhere to Be Found. LC 87-32729. (Illus.). 28p. (J). (ps up). 1991. pap. 14.95 (*0-88708-062-6*, Picture Book Studio) S&S Childrens.
— Social Psychology. 208p. 1994. pap. text, student ed. 12.80 (*0-87901-749-X*) Worth.
— Thief's Daughter. LC 93-73031. (Illus.). 48p. (J). (gr. 1-4). 1994. 11.00 (*0-374-37481-3*) FS&G.
— Treasury of Nursery Rhymes. (Illus.). (J). (ps-k). 1998. 25.00 (*0-7358-1008-7*, Pub. by North-South Bks NYC) Chronicle Bks.
Marks, Alan, ed. Over the Hills & Far Away: A Book of Nursery Rhymes. LC 94-10263. 104p. (J). (ps-1). 1994. 19.95 (*1-55858-285-1*, Pub. by North-South Bks NYC) Chronicle Bks.
— Ring-a-Ring O'Roses & a Ding, Dong Bell: A Collection of Nursery Rhymes. LC 91-15222. 96p. (J). (gr. k up). 1991. 19.95 (*0-88708-187-8*, Picture Book Studio) S&S Childrens.
Marks, Alan. Ring-a-Ring O'Roses & a Ding, Dong Bell: A Book of Nursery Rhymes. LC 96-21731. 102p. (J). (ps-1). 1996. 19.95 (*1-55858-363-7*, Pub. by North-South Bks NYC) Chronicle Bks.
***Marks, Alan.** Ring-a-Ring O'Roses & a Ding, Dong Bell. LC 96-21731. 96p. (J). (ps-1). 1999. pap. 12.95 (*1-55858-671-7*, Pub. by North-South Bks NYC) Chronicle Bks.
Marks, Alan M., jt. auth. see Adelman, Phillip J.
Marks, Alfred H., tr. see Ihara, Saikaku.
Marks, Alfred H., tr. see Mishima, Yukio, pseud.
Marks, Aminta. A Pieta for the Dispossessed: The Grace of Palestinians. LC 93-80534. (Illus.). 170p. (Orig.). 1994. pap. 12.00 (*0-9626898-2-3*) Grindstone Pr.
— So It Is: In the Image of God He Created Them (Poems) LC 90-82231. (Illus.). 179p. (Orig.). 1990. pap. 12.00 (*0-9626898-0-7*) Grindstone Pr.
— Sweet Water & Polar: Poems from the Length of a Marriage. LC 92-81196. 177p. (Orig.). 1992. pap. 12.00 (*0-9626898-1-5*) Grindstone Pr.
Marks, Andrew R. The Rabbi & the Poet: Victor Reichert & Robert Frost. LC 93-72556. (Illus.). 64p. (Orig.). 1994. pap. 14.00 (*1-885934-01-7*) Andover Green.
Marks, Anthony. Learn to Play Keyboards. (Learn to Play Ser.). (Illus.). 48p. (J). (gr. 1 up). 1997. lib. bdg. 17.95 (*0-88110-899-5*, Usborne) EDC.
— Learn to Play Keyboards. (Learn to Play Ser.). (Illus.). 48p. (J). (gr. 4-7). 1997. pap. 9.95 (*0-7460-2412-6*, Usborne) EDC.
Marks, Anthony & Balazard, Sylvestre. French Songbook. (Songbooks Ser.). (Illus.). 32p. (J). (ps-3). 1996. pap. 6.95 (*0-7460-2425-8*, Usborne); lib. bdg. 14.95 (*0-88110-819-7*, Usborne) EDC.
Marks, Anthony & Rye, Howard W. Learn to Play Blues. (Learn to Play Ser.). (Illus.). 64p. (J). (gr. 4-7). 1995. lib. bdg. 17.95 (*0-88110-765-4*, Usborne) EDC.
Marks, Anthony E., ed. Prehistory & Paleoenvironments in the Central Negev, Israel Vol. I, Pt. 1: The Avdat-Aqev Area. LC 75-40116. (Institute for the Study of Earth & Man: Reports of Investigations Ser.: No. 1). (Illus.). 392p. 1976. pap. 27.50 (*0-87074-153-5*) SMU Press.
— Prehistory & Paleoenvironments in the Central Negev, Israel Vol. II, Pt. 2: The Avdat-Aqev Area & the Har Harif. LC 75-40116. (Institute for the Study of Earth & Man: Reports of Investigations Ser.: No. 2). (Illus.). x, 368p. 1977. pap. 25.00 (*0-89643-000-6*) SMU Press.
— Prehistory & Paleoenvironments in the Central Negev, Israel Vol. III, Pt. 3: The Advat-Aqev Area. LC 75-40116. (Institute for the Study of Earth & Man: Reports of Investigations Ser.: No. 3). (Illus.). xvi, 368p. 1983. pap. 35.00 (*0-89643-113-4*) SMU Press.
Marks, Anthony E. & Mohammed-Ali, Abbas, eds. Late Prehistory of the Eastern Sahel: The Mesolithic & Neolithic of Shaqadud, Sudan. LC 90-52656. (Illus.). 304p. 1991. pap. text 29.95 (*0-87074-310-4*) SMU Press.
Marks, Anthony E., jt. ed. see Wendorf, Fred.
Marks, Anton. Dancehall. 280p. 1996. 9.95 (*1-874509-19-0*, Pub. by X Pr) LPC InBook.
***Marks, Arnold.** Card Games Properly Explained. 2nd ed. (Illus.). 224p. 2001. pap. 9.95 (*0-7160-2042-4*, Pub. by Elliot RW Bks) Midpt Trade.
Marks, B. & Taubman, eds. Molecular Biology of Cardiovascular Diseases. LC 96-40406. (Fundamental & Clinical Cardiology Ser.: Vol. 30). (Illus.). 560p. 1997. text 210.00 (*0-8247-9405-2*) Dekker.
Marks, Barbara, jt. auth. see Knipe, Judy.
Marks, Barry. The Talmud: Selections. LC 97-60835. (Public Library Ser.). 192p. 1997. pap. 4.95 (*0-87243-230-0*) Templegate.
Marks, Bayly E., ed. see Glenn, William W.
Marks-Beale, Abby. Study Skills Instructor's Guide: The Tools for Active Learning. 84p. 1994. teacher ed. 16.00 (*0-8273-5439-8*) Delmar.
Marks, Ben. Forbidden Entry: Installations by George Geyer, Lilla Locurto, Carol Newborg, Karen Frimkiss Wolff. (Illus.). 24p. (Orig.). 1990. pap. 8.00 (*0-945192-05-3*) USC Fisher Gallery.
Marks, Betty. Light & Easy Diabetes Cuisine. 256p. 1990. pap. 15.95 (*0-89586-640-4*, HP Books) Berkley Pub.
— The Microwave Diabetes Cookbook. LC 90-24555. 200p. (Orig.). 1991. pap. 10.95 (*0-940625-26-1*) Surrey Bks.
Marks, Bill. South to Sillytown. 1997. pap. 14.95 (*1-86368-175-2*, Pub. by Fremantle Arts) Intl Spec Bk.
***Marks, Brendon M.** On Your Marks, Get Set, Laugh. LC 99-91261. 1999. 25.00 (*0-7388-0708-7*); pap. 18.00 (*0-7388-0709-5*) Xlibris Corp.
Marks, Brian & Hannah, Ian. Heat & Light. 80p. 1993. pap. 22.00 (*0-86153-169-8*, Pub. by St Andrew) St Mut.
Marks, Burton. Animals. LC 91-3656. (Read-a-Picture Ser.). (Illus.). 24p. (J). (gr. k-2). 1996. pap. 2.50 (*0-8167-2416-4*) Troll Communs.
— Let's Go. LC 91-9986. (Read-a-Picture Ser.). (Illus.). 24p. (J). (gr. k-2). 1997. pap. 2.50 (*0-8167-2414-8*) Troll Communs.
— Rhymes & Stories. LC 91-3663. (Read-a-Picture Ser.). (Illus.). 24p. (J). (gr. k-2). 1992. pap. 2.95 (*0-8167-2410-5*) Troll Communs.
Marks, Cara G. God Bless You. (Illus.). 1993. 6.95 (*0-8378-5446-6*) Gibson.
— The Handbook of Hebrew Calligraphy. LC 90-728. 208p. 1990. 30.00 (*0-87668-798-2*) Aronson.
— The Handbook of Hebrew Calligraphy. LC 90-728. 208p. 1995. pap. 30.00 (*1-56821-631-9*) Aronson.
Marks, Carol, tr. see Le Clezio, J. M. G.
***Marks, Carole L. & Edkins, Diana.** The Power of Pride: The Man & Women Who Embodied the Spirit of the Harlem Renaissance. LC 98-31259. (Illus.). 272p. 1999. 35.00 (*0-609-60096-6*, Crown) Crown Pub Group.
Marks, Carolyna. Creativity in the Lions Den: Releasing Our Children from Violence - A Peace Empowerment Process for the Artist in Everyone. Alexander, Shoshana, ed. LC 98-96781. (Illus.). 136p. 1998. pap. 17.00 (*0-9667303-0-5*) World Wall Peace.
Marks, Cathy. Dance, Ballerina. LC 93-79213. (Look-Look Bks.). (Illus.). (J). (ps-3). 1995. pap. 3.29 (*0-307-12822-9*, 12822, Goldn Books) Gldn Bks Pub Co.
Marks, Cathy & Marks, Steve. Swing, Dawn of a New Era: The Alternative Lifestyle. LC 94-75819. 320p. 1994. 24.95 (*0-9640903-0-9*) M S W Pubng.
— Swing II, after the Dawn. 320p. 1995. 24.95 (*0-9640903-2-5*) M S W Pubng.
Marks, Cathy, jt. auth. see Marks, Steve.
Marks, Celia. Come into My Kitchen. 1969. spiral bd. 12.95 (*0-9606574-0-1*) Plum Nelly.
***Marks, Charles.** Behind Barbed Wire. LC 99-93820. 1999. 18.95 (*0-533-13154-5*) Vantage.
Marks, Charles, jt. auth. see Marks, Malcolm W.
Marks, Christine. I-75 & The 401: A Traveller's Guide Between Toronto & Miami. (Illus.). 240p. 1999. pap. 13.95 (*1-55046-255-5*, Pub. by Boston Mills) Genl Dist Srvs.
***Marks, Cindy.** Another Summer: If Only There Was. large type ed. LC 96-90887. (Illus.). 56p. (J). (gr. 1-4). 1999. pap. 3.95 (*0-9655425-0-5*, Pub. by TiaraMoon Pub) Bookmen Inc.
Marks, Claude. World Artists, 1950-1980. LC 84-13152. (Illus.). 928p. 1984. 83.00 (*0-8242-0707-6*) Wilson.
***Marks, Clifford S.** The Bull's-Eye Connection: Recognizing & Experiencing the Ultimate Man-Woman Relationship. King, M. A., ed. 120p. 1999. pap. 14.95 (*1-879854-34-1*, Writerservice Pubns) Christian Servs Pub.
Marks, Coleen, jt. ed. see Groth, Patricia C.
Marks, Constant R., ed. Part & Present of Sioux City & Woodbury Co., Iowa. (Illus.). 826p. 1996. reprint ed. lib. bdg. 85.00 (*0-8328-5194-9*) Higginson Bk Co.
Marks, Copeland. Copeland Marks' Indian & Chinese Cooking from the Himalayan Rim. (Illus.). 304p. 1999. text 27.00 (*0-7881-5987-9*) DIANE Pub.
— The Exotic Kitchens of Indonesia: Recipes from the Outer Islands. LC 93-174982. 320p. 1993. pap. 12.95 (*0-87131-737-0*) M Evans.
— The Exotic Kitchens of Malaysia. LC 97-11377. 320p. 1997. 26.95 (*1-55611-526-1*, Pub. by D I Fine) Penguin Putnam.
— The Exotic Kitchens of Peru: The Land of the Inca. (Illus.). 320p. 1999. 27.50 (*0-87131-880-6*, Pub. by M Evans) Natl Bk Netwk.
— The Great Book of Couscous. LC 96-52950. 336p. 1997. pap. 14.95 (*1-55611-524-5*, Pub. by D I Fine) Penguin Putnam.
— The Great Book of Couscous: Classic Cuisines of Morocco, Algeria & Tunisia. LC 94-71117. 384p. 1994. pap. 24.95 (*1-55611-420-6*, Pub. by D I Fine) Penguin Putnam.
***Marks, Copeland.** Indian & Chinese Cooking from the Himalayan Rim. (Illus.). 224p. 1999. pap. 14.95 (*0-87131-885-7*, Pub. by M Evans) Natl Bk Netwk.
Marks, Copeland. The Korean Kitchen: Classic Recipes from the Land of the Morning Calm. (Illus.). 240p. 1999. pap. 12.95 (*0-8118-2233-8*) Chronicle Bks.
— The Varied Kitchens of India: Cuisines of the Anglo-Indians of Calcutta, Bengalis, Jews of Calcutta, Kashmiris, Parsis, & Tibetans of Darjeeling. LC 86-2028. 288p. 1986. 19.95 (*0-87131-476-2*) M Evans.
Marks, Copeland & Soeharjo, Mintari. The Indonesian Kitchen. LC 80-23103. 288p. 1984. pap. 12.95 (*0-689-70667-7*, 309, Pub. by Ctrl Bur voor Schimmel) Macmillan.
Marks, Copeland & Thein, Aung. The Burmese Kitchen: Recipes from the Golden Land. LC 87-22242. 276p. 1994. pap. 12.95 (*0-87131-768-0*) M Evans.
***Marks, Corey.** Renunciation: Poems. (National Poetry Ser.). 80p. 2000. 30.00 (*0-252-02581-4*); pap. 14.95 (*0-252-06898-X*) U of Ill Pr.
Marks, D. J. & Donnelly, J. Introduction to Physical Inorganic Chemistry. LC QD0475.M37. 283p. reprint ed. pap. 87.80 (*0-608-13195-4*, 202524800043) Bks Demand.
Marks, Daniel, ed. Foundations of Empire: Archaeology & Art of the Eurasian Steppes. Zirin, Mary F., tr. from RUS. LC 91-70732. (Illus.). 250p. (Orig.). (C). 1991. pap. 12.00 (*1-878986-02-3*) Ethnographics Pr.
— Rulers from the Steppe: State Formation on the Inner Eurasian Periphery. Zirin, Mary F., tr. LC 90-84794. (Ethnographics Monographs). (Illus.). 328p. (Orig.). (C). 1991. pap. 12.00 (*1-878986-01-5*) Ethnographics Pr.
Marks, Dave. Communication & Interpersonal Relationships: How to Say What You Mean to Say. (YA). 1998. pap. 17.95 (*1-888344-15-6*) National Writing.
— Evaluating Writing. (Writing Strands Ser.). 1999. pap. 19.95 (*1-888344-05-9*) National Writing.
— Gentle Steps Series, 2 vols., Set. 379p. 1996. 30.00 (*0-614-10203-0*) National Writing.
— Gentle Steps to Writing Skill, Bk. I. (Gentle Steps Ser.). 151p. 1994. pap. text 30.00 (*1-888344-04-0*) National Writing.
Marks, Dave. Gentle Steps to Writing Skill, Bk. II. (Gentle Steps Ser.). 228p. 1996. pap. text 30.00 (*1-888344-03-2*) National Writing.
Marks, Dave. Guide to College Writing: What You Need to Know but Didn't Learn in High School. LC 95-71618. 77p. (C). 1995. pap. text 18.95 (*1-888344-11-3*) National Writing.
— Reading Strands: Understanding Fiction. 1998. pap. 22.95 (*1-888344-16-4*) National Writing.
— Writing Exposition. (Writing Strands Ser.). (Illus.). (YA). (gr. 9 up). pap. 22.95 (*1-888344-02-4*) National Writing.
— Writing Strands 5. (Writing Strands Ser.). (J). (gr. 4-11). 1999. pap. 20.95 (*1-888344-08-3*) National Writing.
— Writing Strands 4. (Writing Strands Ser.). 92p. (J). (gr. 4-9). 1998. pap. 18.95 (*1-888344-09-1*) National Writing.
— Writing Strands Series, 2 vols., Set. 265p. 1992. pap. text. write for info. (*1-888344-00-8*) National Writing.
— Writing Strands 7. (Writing Strands Ser.). (YA). (gr. 7 up). 1998. pap. 22.95 (*1-888344-07-5*) National Writing.
— Writing Strands 6. (Writing Strands Ser.). (YA). (gr. 6-12). 1998. pap. 20.95 (*1-888344-06-7*) National Writing.
— Writing Strands 3. (Writing Strands Ser.). 86p. (J). (gr. 3-8). 1998. pap. 18.95 (*1-888344-10-5*) National Writing.
— Writing Strands 2. (Writing Strands Ser.). 77p. (YA). (gr. 1-3). 1998. pap. 18.95 (*1-888344-12-1*) National Writing.
Marks, David. Dragonslaying Is for Dreamers. 261p. (J). (gr. 4-11). 1998. pap. 9.95 (*1-888344-26-1*) National Writing.

M

Marks, David & Kammann, Richard. The Psychology of the Psychic. LC 80-7458. (Science & the Paranormal Ser.). 238p. (C). 1980. 28.95 (*0-87975-121-5*) Prometheus Bks.

— The Psychology of the Psychic. LC 80-7458. (Science & the Paranormal Ser.). (Illus.). 238p. (C). 1980. pap. 21.95 (*0-87975-122-3*) Prometheus Bks.

***Marks, David F.** The Psychology of the Psychic. 305p. 2000. pap. 22.95 (*1-57392-798-8*) Prometheus Bks.

Marks, David F. Theories of Image Formation. 1986. lib. bdg. 45.00 (*0-913412-18-X*) Brandon Hse.

Marks, David M. Testing Very Big Systems. 240p. 1991. 39.95 (*0-8306-2555-0*) McGraw-Hill Prof.

Marks, David M., jt. ed. see Freksa, C.

***Marks, David R. & Marks, Laura.** The Headache Prevention Cookbook. 256p. 2000. pap. 15.00 (*0-395-96716-3*) HM.

Marks, Dawn B. Biochemistry. 3rd ed. LC 98-34102. (Board Review Ser.). 352p. 1998. pap. 22.95 (*0-683-30491-7*) Lppncott W & W.

Marks, Dawn B., et al. Basic Medical Biochemistry: A Clinical Approach. (Illus.). 528p. 1996. pap. 34.00 (*0-683-05595-X*) Lppncott W & W.

***Marks, Deborah.** Disability: Controversial Debates & Psychosocial Perspectives. LC 99-14620. 224p. (C). 1999. text. write for info. (*0-415-16202-5*) Routledge.

— Disability: Controversial Debates & Psychosocial Perspectives. LC 99-14620. 217p. 1999. pap. write for info. (*0-415-16203-3*) Routledge.

Marks, Diana F. Glues, Brews, & Goos: Recipes & Formulas for Almost Any Classroom Project. xvi, 179p. 1996. pap. text 23.00 (*1-56308-362-0*) Teacher Ideas Pr.

— Let's Celebrate Today: Calendars, Events, & Holidays. LC 98-26745. 350p. 1998. pap. 35.00 (*1-56308-558-5*) Teacher Ideas Pr.

Marks, Dorrit K., ed. Women & Grass Roots Democracy in the Americas: Sustaining the Initiative. 2nd ed. LC 96-9677. (University of Miami North-South Center Ser.). 288p. (C). 1996. pap. 25.95 (*1-57454-017-3*, 540173, Pub. by U Miami N-S Ctr) L Rienner.

Marks, Dustin D. Cheating at Blackjack: And Advantage Play. LC 94-76753. (Illus.). 232p. (Orig.). 1994. pap. 19.95 (*1-56866-071-5*) Index Pub Grp.

— Cheating at Blackjack Squared: The Dark Side of Gambling. LC 95-81302. (Illus.). 220p. (Orig.). 1995. pap. 24.95 (*1-56866-073-1*) Index Pub Grp.

Marks, E. S. & Elsdon, K. T. Adults in the Colleges of Further Education. (C). 1991. 45.00 (*1-85041-042-9*, Pub. by Univ Nottingham) St Mut.

Marks, Edith & Montauredes, Rita. Coping with Glaucoma: A Guide to Living with Glaucoma for You & Your Family. 13th ed. LC 97-223069. 320p. 1997. pap. 13.95 (*0-89529-804-X*, Avery) Penguin Putnam.

Marks, Edward, jt. auth. see Lewis, William.

***Marks, Edward B.** For a Better World: Posters from the United Nations. LC 00-28113. (Illus.). 160p. 2000. pap. 35.00 (*0-7649-1340-9*, A547) Pomegranate Calif.

Marks, Edward S. Entry Strategies in School Consultation. LC 94-27760. (School Practitioner Ser.). 287p. 1995. lib. bdg. 35.00 (*0-89862-368-5*, 2368) Guilford Pubns.

Marks, Elaine. Marrano As Metaphor: The Jewish Presence in French Writing. LC 95-9627. (Illus.). 224p. 1996. pap. text 30.50 (*0-231-10308-5*) Col U Pr.

Marks, Elaine, ed. Homosexualities & French Literature: Cultural Contexts Critical Texts. LC 78-25659. 392p. 1990. reprint ed. pap. text 17.95 (*0-8014-9766-3*) Cornell U Pr.

Marks, Ellen L. Case Management in Service Integration: A Concept Paper. 32p. 1994. pap. text 8.00 (*0-926582-13-5*) NCCP.

Marks, Ellen L., jt. auth. see Darling-Hammond, Linda.

Marks, Emerson R. Coleridge on the Language of Verse. LC 80-8562. (Princeton Essays in Literature Ser.). 129p. 1981. reprint ed. pap. 40.00 (*0-7837-9380-4*, 206012400004) Bks Demand.

— Relativist & Absolutist: The Early Neoclassical Debate in England. LC 75-23348. 171p. 1975. reprint ed. lib. bdg. 55.00 (*0-8371-8348-0*, MARAB, Greenwood Pr) Greenwood.

— Taming the Chaos: English Poetic Diction Theory since the Renaissance. LC 97-35272. 432p. (C). 1998. text 39.95 (*0-8143-2698-6*) Wayne St U Pr.

Marks, Emmaline L., ed. see Harris, Patty.

Marks, Esther S., et al, eds. Primary Eyecare in Systemic Disease. LC 94-10704. 706p. (C). 1995. pap. text 115.00 (*0-8385-7997-3*, A7997-8, Apple Lange Med) McGraw.

Marks, Ethel M., jt. auth. see Marks, Stanley J.

Marks, Eugene. Lemonade Gravy. 1994. pap. 4.95 (*0-9644648-0-2*) ideaReserve.

Marks, F., ed. see Furstenberger, G.

Marks, F., Helena. The Sonata. 1977. text 16.95 (*0-8369-8188-X*) Ayer.

— The Sonata, Its Form & Meaning as Exemplified in the Piano Sonatas by Mozart: A Descriptive Analysis. 167p. 1990. reprint ed. lib. bdg. 59.00 (*0-7812-9170-4*) Rprt Serv.

***Marks, Frederick.** A Brief for Belief - A Case for Catholicism. 152p. 1999. pap. 7.95 (*1-57918-114-7*, 3791) Queenship Pub.

Marks, Frederick W., III. A Catholic Handbook for Engaged & Newly Married Couples. LC 94-72069. 126p. (Orig.). 1994. pap. 6.00 (*1-880033-14-3*) Emmaus Road.

— Independence on Trial: Foreign Affairs & the Making of the Constitution. 2nd ed. LC 86-11876. 276p. (Orig.). (C). 1986. 45.00 (*0-8420-2272-4*); pap. text 17.95 (*0-8420-2273-2*) Scholarly Res Inc.

— Power & Peace: The Diplomacy of John Foster Dulles. LC 92-42442. 296p. 1993. 59.95 (*0-275-94497-2*, C4497, Praeger Pubs) Greenwood.

— Power & Peace: The Diplomacy of John Foster Dulles. LC 92-42442. 296p. 1995. pap. 24.95 (*0-275-95232-0*, Praeger Pubs) Greenwood.

Marks, Friedrich, ed. Protein Phosphorylation. (Illus.). 381p. 1996. 145.00 (*3-527-29241-1*, Wiley-VCH) Wiley.

Marks, G. Harrap's Dictionnaire d'Argot: French to English, English to French Slang Dictionary. rev. ed. 879p. 1986. pap. 45.00 (*0-7859-4824-4*, M6308) Fr & Eur.

Marks, G. Warren, ed. The Planning & Engineering Interface with a Modernized Land Data System. LC 80-66123. 269p. 1980. pap. 5.00 (*0-87262-243-6*) Am Soc Civil Eng.

Marks, Gary & Diamond, Larry. Reexamining Democracy. 352p. (C). 1992. text 36.00 (*0-8039-4641-4*) Sage.

Marks, Gary, jt. ed. see Lemke, Christiane.

Marks, Gary H., ed. Mathematics/Science Education & Technology, 1994: Proceedings of the 1994 International Symposium on Mathematics/Science Education & Technology. (Illus.). 254p. (Orig.). 1994. pap. 25.00 (*1-880094-12-6*) Assn Advan Comput Educ.

Marks, Gary W. Unions in Politics: Britain, Germany & the United States in the Nineteenth & Early Twentieth Centuries. LC 88-25054. (Illus.). 294p. 1989. reprint ed. pap. 91.20 (*0-608-02526-7*, 206317000004) Bks Demand.

Marks, Genee. Integration of Children into Regular Schools Each an Individual (ECT 324) 168p. (C). 1989. 66.00 (*0-7300-0706-5*, Pub. by Deakin Univ) St Mut.

Marks, Genee, jt. auth. see Mousley, Judith.

Marks, Geoffry W. Messages from the Universal House of Justice, 1963-1986: The Third Epoch of the Formative Age. LC 96-43430. 1996. 24.95 (*0-87743-239-2*) Bahai.

Marks, Geoffry W., compiled by. Call to Remembrance: Connecting the Heart to Baha'u'llah. limited deluxe ed. (Illus.). 308p. 1992. pap. 12.00 (*0-87743-236-8*) Bahai.

Marks, George P. The Black Press Views American Imperialism (1898-1900) 1973. 24.95 (*0-405-01985-8*, 19466) Ayer.

Marks, George V. & Lall, Bhagirath, eds. Organization & Management of Public Transport Projects: Proceedings of a Conference Sponsored by the Public Transport Committee of the Urban Transportation Division. 32p. 1985. 34.00 (*0-87262-458-7*) Am Soc Civil Eng.

Marks, Gil. The World of Jewish Cooking. 384p. 1996. 30.00 (*0-684-82491-4*) S&S Trade.

— The World of Jewish Cooking: More Than 500 Traditional Recipes from Alsace to Yemen. 416p. 1999. pap. 17.00 (*0-684-83559-2*) S&S Trade.

— The World of Jewish Entertaining: Menus & Recipes for the Sabbath, Holidays, & Other Family Celebrations. LC 98-19913. (Illus.). 416p. 1998. 29.50 (*0-684-84788-4*) S&S Trade.

***Marks, Gringras.** Merging Ecology & Economy. 2000. pap. 60.00 (*0-324-04186-1*) Thomson Learn.

Marks, Guy. This is Egypt. LC 99-488024. 1999. 39.95 (*1-85368-881-9*) New5 Holland.

Marks, Hardy. Pierced Hearts & True Loves: A Century of Drawings for Tattoos. (Illus.). 128p. 1995. pap. 30.00 (*0-942324-09-9*) Drawing Ctr.

Marks, Harry. I Can Jump Oceans: The World of Alan Marshall LC 77-379995. viii, 369 p. 1976. write for info. (*0-17-001977-2*) ITP Nelson.

Marks, Harry M. The Progress of Experiment: Science & Therapeutic Reform in the United States, 1900-1990. LC 96-38997. (Cambridge History of Medicine Ser.). 271p. (C). 1997. text 59.95 (*0-521-58142-7*) Cambridge U Pr.

***Marks, Harry M.** The Progress of Experiment: Science & Therapeutic Reform in the United States, 1900-1990. (Cambridge Studies in the History of Medicine). 271p. 2000. text. write for info. (*0-521-78561-8*) Cambridge U Pr.

Marks, Heather. Stalking the Side Hill Salmon. LC 96-75494. (Illus.). 143p. (Orig.). 1996. pap. 12.95 (*0-614-14404-3*) Great Wave AK.

Marks, Herbert, jt. auth. see Hammond, Gerald.

Marks, Hilary. Food & Farming in Eastern Europe: A Market Report. 2nd ed. (Illus.). 210p. 1994. pap. 445.00 (*1-85573-181-9*, Pub. by Woodhead Pubng) Am Educ Systs.

— Food & Farming in the European Union: A Market Report. 200p. 1995. pap. 445.00 (*1-85573-196-7*, Pub. by Woodhead Pubng) Am Educ Systs.

— Food & Farming in the Fifteen Republics of the Former U. S. S. R. A Market Survey. 2nd ed. 310p. 1994. pap. 445.00 (*1-85573-199-1*, Pub. by Woodhead Pubng) Am Educ Systs.

Marks, Hilary F. A Hundred Years of British Food & Farming: A Statistical Survey. Britton, Denis K., ed. 300p. 1989. 130.00 (*0-85066-452-7*, Pub. by Tay Francis Ltd) Taylor & Francis.

Marks III, Frederick W. Velvet on Iron: The Diplomacy of Theodore Roosevelt. LC 79-1216. 263p. reprint ed. pap. 81.60 (*0-608-01787-6*, AU0045700003) Bks Demand.

Marks, Isaac M. Behavioural Psychotherapy: Maudsley Pocket Book of Clinical Management. (Illus.). 150p. 1986. pap. 22.50 (*0-317-56190-1*) Mosby Inc.

— Fears, Phobias & Rituals: Panic, Anxiety & Their Disorders. (Illus.). 704p. 1987. text 55.00 (*0-19-503927-0*) OUP.

Marks, Isaac M. & Scott, Robert A., eds. Mental Health Care Delivery: Innovations, Impediments & Implementation. (Illus.). 280p. (C). 1990. text 74.95 (*0-521-38494-X*) Cambridge U Pr.

Marks, J. Benzodiazepines, Use, Overuse, Misuse, & Abuse. 2nd ed. 1985. text 73.50 (*0-85200-870-8*) Kluwer Academic.

Marks, J., jt. ed. see Glatt, Max.

Marks, James C. & Deleo. Contact & Occupational Dermatology. 2nd ed. LC 96-47750. (Illus.). 416p. (C). (gr. 13). 1997. text 89.95 (*0-8151-6954-X*, 27226) Mosby Inc.

Marks, James G., jt. auth. see Helm, Klaus F.

Marks, James G., Jr., jt. auth. see Lookingbill, Donald P.

Marks, James R. & Craigie, John D. Sharing the Risk: How the Nation's Businesses, Homes, & Autos Are Insured. 2nd rev. ed. LC 81-65769. 191p. reprint ed. pap. 59.30 (*0-608-18108-0*, 203270700081) Bks Demand.

Marks, Jane. The Hidden Children: The Secret Survivors of the Holocaust. 336p. 1995. pap. 12.00 (*0-449-90686-8*) Fawcett.

Marks, Jason. Around the World in Seventy-Two Days: The Race Between Pulitzer's Nellie Bly & Cosmopolitan's Elizabeth Bisland. LC 92-73586. (Illus.). 261p. (Orig.). 1993. pap. 12.95 (*0-9633696-2-8*) Gemittarius.

— Around the World in 72 Days: The Race Between Pulitzer's Nellie Bly & Cosmopolitan's Elizabeth Bisland. 2nd abr. ed. LC 98-95370. (Illus.). 185p. 1999. reprint ed. pap. 11.95 (*1-56315-103-0*, Pub. by SterlingHse) Natl Bk Netwk.

— Twelve Who Made It Big. LC 81-68767. (Illus.). 112p. (Orig.). 1981. pap. write for info. (*0-9606858-0-4*) Alumni Assn.

Marks, Jeannette A. English Pastoral Drama. LC 76-173175. 240p. 1972. reprint ed. 20.95 (*0-405-08781-0*, Pub. by Blom Pubns) Ayer.

— Through Welsh Doorways. LC 78-167463. (Short Story Index Reprint Ser.). 1977. reprint ed. 20.95 (*0-8369-3989-1*) Ayer.

Marks, Jeffrey. Canine Crimes. 1998. mass mkt. 5.99 (*0-345-42411-5*) Ballantine Pub Grp.

— Lasting Images Price Guide to Adult Entertainment & Fantasy Art Pinup Cards, Vol. 3. (Illus.). 32p. 1997. pap. 19.95 (*0-9641536-5-9*) Lasting Images.

***Marks, Jeffrey.** Magnolias & Mayhem. 2000. 24.50 (*1-57072-112-2*); pap. 15.00 (*1-57072-128-9*) Overmountain Pr.

***Marks, Jeffrey, ed.** A Canine Christmas. 1999. mass mkt. 5.99 (*0-345-43657-1*) Ballantine Pub Grp.

Marks, Jeffrey S. Lasting Images Price Guide to Adult Entertainment & Fantasy Art Pinup Cards. (Illus.). 60p. (Orig.). 1994. 14.95 (*0-9641536-0-2*) Lasting Images.

— Lasting Images Price Guide to Adult Entertainment & Fantasy Art Pinup Cards, Vol. II. (Lasting Images Price Guide Ser.: Vol. 2). (Illus.). 80p. (Orig.). 1995. 18.95 (*0-9641536-1-0*) Lasting Images.

Marks, Jennifer B., jt. auth. see Romaine, Deborah S.

Marks, Joan H., ed. Advocacy in Health Care: The Power of a Silent Constituency. LC 86-283. (Contemporary Issues in Biomedicine, Ethics, & Society Ser.). 160p. 1986. 49.50 (*0-89603-092-X*) Humana.

Marks, Joel, ed. The Ways of Desire: New Essays in Philosophical Psychology on the Concept of Wanting. 1986. 29.95 (*0-913750-44-1*); pap. 14.95 (*0-913750-03-4*) Precednt Pub.

Marks, Joel & Ames, Roger T., eds. Emotions in Asian Thought: A Dialogue in Comparative Philosophy, with a Discussion by Robert C. Solomon. LC 94-2723. 321p. (C). 1994. pap. text 19.95 (*0-7914-2224-0*) State U NY Pr.

— Emotions in Asian Thought: A Dialogue in Comparative Philosophy, with a Discussion by Robert C. Solomon. LC 94-2723. 321p. (C). 1994. text 59.50 (*0-7914-2223-2*) State U NY Pr.

Marks, John. Gilles Deleuze: Vitalism & Multiplicity. 160p. 1998. pap. 17.95 (*0-7453-0874-0*, Pub. by Pluto GBR); text 55.00 (*0-7453-0873-2*, Pub. by Pluto GBR) Stylus Pub VA.

— Lost Quotes. LC 94-60808. (Illus.). 81p. (Orig.). 1994. pap. 5.95 (*0-9642648-0-3*) Toranaga Pr.

— Science & the Making of the Modern World. 507p. (C). 1984. pap. text 35.00 (*0-435-54781-X*, 54781) Heinemann.

— The Wall. LC 98-3717. 384p. 1998. 24.95 (*1-57322-122-8*, Riverhead Books) Putnam Pub Group.

***Marks, John.** The Wall. 1999. reprint ed. pap. 14.00 (*1-57322-757-9*, Riverhrd Trade) Berkley Pub.

Marks, John D. The Search for the "Manchurian Candidate" The CIA & Mind Control. 228p. 1991. pap. 11.95 (*0-393-30794-8*) Norton.

Marks, John H. Visions of One World: Legacy of Alexander. LC 85-4441. (Illus.). iv, 257p. (Orig.). (C). 1985. pap. 16.95 (*0-931500-09-5*); text 25.00 (*0-931500-10-9*) Eisenbrauns.

Marks, John H. & Good, Robert M., eds. Love & Death in the Ancient Near East: Essays in Honor of Marvin H. Pope. LC 86-29441. ix, 258p. 1987. text 39.50 (*0-931500-06-0*) Eisenbrauns.

Marks, John H. & Rogers, Virgil M. A Beginner's Handbook to Biblical Hebrew. LC 58-7434. xiv, 174p. 1958. 19.95 (*0-687-02616-4*) Abingdon.

Marks, Jonathan. Human Biodiversity: Genes, Race, & History. (Evolutionary Foundations of Human Behavior Ser.). 334p. 1995. pap. text 25.95 (*0-202-02033-9*); lib. bdg. 49.95 (*0-202-02032-0*) Aldine de Gruyter.

Marks, Jonathan, tr. see Devillers, Marceau.

Marks, Judy, ed. see Fish, Kathleen D.

Marks, Judy, ed. see Fish, Kathleen D. & Fish, Robert.

Marks, Judy, ed. see McKinstry, Pamela.

Marks, Jym. Flashback. LC 98-74225. 100p. 1999. pap. 12.95 (*0-88739-190-7*) Creat Arts Bk.

Marks, Karen I. Beaded & Sequined Applique Techniques. (Illus.). 12p. 1991. spiral bd. 24.95 (*0-9673569-1-1*) Marks Designs.

— Polynesian Dance Directory: Includes Suppliers & Musicians. 115p. 1998. spiral bd. 59.95 (*0-9673569-0-3*) Marks Designs.

— Polynesian Dance Directory: Includes Suppoiers & Musicians. 210p. 1998. pap. 39.95 (*0-9673569-2-X*) Marks Designs.

Marks, Kate. Circle of Song: Songs, Chants & Dances for Ritual & Celebration. LC 93-73300. (Illus.). 278p. (Orig.). 1994. pap. 17.95 (*0-9637489-0-4*) Full Circle MA.

***Marks, Kate.** Circle of Song, CD Pack: Songs & Chants for Ritual & Celebration. 278p. 1999. 32.95 incl. audio compact disk (*0-9637489-2-0*, Pub. by Full Circle MA) ACCESS Pubs Network.

Marks, Kathy. Faces of Right Wing Extremism. Caso, Adolfo, ed. (Illus.). 240p. 1996. pap. 16.95 (*0-8283-2016-0*) Branden Bks.

— The Littlest Detective. (Harlequin Temptation Ser.: No. 596). 1996. per. 3.50 (*0-373-25696-5*, 1-25696-5) Harlequin Bks.

— Seducing Sydney. (Yours Truly Ser.). 1996. per. 3.50 (*0-373-52018-2*, 1-52018-8) Silhouette.

Marks, Kenneth E. & Nielson, Steven P. Using Windows for Library Administration. LC 96-24956. 140p. 1997. 34.95 (*1-57387-029-3*) Info Today Inc.

Marks, Kristin. Handbook of Server Management & Administration: 1999 Edition. 99th ed. LC 98-34583. 544p. 1998. 180.00 (*0-8493-9959-9*) CRC Pr.

Marks, Kristin, jt. auth. see Bundesen, Lynne.

Marks, Lara V. Model Mothers: Jewish Mothers & Maternity Provision in East London 1870-1939. (Oxford Historical Monographs). (Illus.). 342p. 1994. text 59.00 (*0-19-820454-X*) OUP.

Marks, Lara V. & Worboys, Michael. Migrants, Minorities, & Health: Historical & Contemporary Studies. LC 96-22911. (Studies in the Social History of Medicine Ser.). (Illus.). 264p. (C). 1997. 85.00 (*0-415-11213-3*) Routledge.

Marks, Larry. Unemployment: A State of Mind. (Illus.). 80p. 1994. 29.00 (*1-56216-223-3*); pap. 14.00 (*1-56216-224-1*) Systems Co.

Marks, Laura, jt. auth. see Marks, David R.

***Marks, Laura U.** The Skin of the Film: Intercultural Cinema, Embodiment, & the Senses. LC 99-26487. (Illus.). 304p. 1999. 54.95 (*0-8223-2358-3*) Duke.

Marks, Laura U. The Skin of the Film: Intercultural Cinema, Embodiment & the Senses. LC 99-26487. 304p. 1999. pap. text 18.95 (*0-8223-2391-5*) Duke.

Marks, Lawrence E., ed. see Hammeal, Robin J. & Bornstein, Marc H.

Marks, Lawrence K. New York Pretrial Criminal Procedure. LC 96-60314. (New York Practice Ser.). xxviii, 831p. 1996. pap. 105.00 incl. disk (*0-314-09764-3*) West Pub.

Marks, Lee, jt. ed. see George, Alice Rose.

Marks, Lee A., jt. ed. see Jones, Melinda.

Marks, Lee R., jt. auth. see Brower, Charles N.

Marks, Lee R., jt. auth. see Marcuss, Stanley J.

Marks, Leo. Between Silk & Cyanide: A Codemaker's War, 1941-1945. LC 99-17581. (Illus.). 624p. 1999. 27.50 (*0-684-86422-3*) Free Pr.

***Marks, Leo.** Between Silk & Cyanide: A Codemaker's War, 1941-1945. (Illus.). 624p. 2000. pap. 16.00 (*0-684-86780-X*, Touchstone) S&S Trade Pap.

Marks, Leo. Peeping Tom. (Illus.). 160p. 1998. pap. 14.95 (*0-571-19403-6*) Faber & Faber.

Marks, Leonard. Printed Circuit Assembly Design. (Professional Engineering Ser.). 368p. 2000. 65.00 (*0-07-041107-7*) McGraw.

Marks, Leta W. Time's Tapestry: Four Generations of a New Orleans Family. LC 97-25816. (Illus.). 167p. 1997. 24.95 (*0-8071-2205-X*) La State U Pr.

Marks, Lillian S. On Printing in the Tradition. 24p. 1989. 8.00 (*0-929722-31-0*) CA State Library Fndtn.

— Touch Typing Made Simple. LC 85-4431. (Made Simple Bks.). (Illus.). 192p. 1985. pap. 12.95 (*0-385-19426-9*) Doubleday.

Marks, Linda. Learning Math with Bible Heroes. (Illus.). (J). 1997. pap. text 2.29 (*0-7647-0092-8*) Schaffer Pubns.

— Living with Vision: Reclaiming the Power of the Heart. (Orig.). 1991. pap. 15.95 (*0-904575-53-5*) Sigo Pr.

Marks, Linda, jt. auth. see Feiden, Karyn L.

Marks, Lindy L., et al. Chinoperl Papers,1983, No. 12. Shadick, Harold et al, eds. (Chinoperl Papers). 171p. (Orig.). 1984. pap. 10.00 (*0-318-23301-0*) Chinoperl.

Marks, Londa. Londa Tarot. 1993. pap. 15.00 (*0-88079-664-2*, LD78) US Games Syst.

Marks, Lynn S. Messages from God: 365 Simple Truths for Success. (Illus.). 231p. 1999. 14.95 (*1-888783-31-1*) Golden Halo Prodns.

Marks, Lynne. Revivals & Roller Rinks: Religion, Leisure & Identity in Late-Nineteenth-Century Small-Town Ontario. (Studies in Gender & History). (Illus.). 376p. 1996. text 55.00 (*0-8020-0751-1*); pap. text 19.95 (*0-8020-7800-1*) U of Toronto Pr.

Marks, M. I. Pediatric Infectious Diseases for the Practitioner. (Comprehensive Manuals in Pediatrics Ser.: Vol. 3). (Illus.). 890p. 1984. 185.00 (*0-387-96010-4*) Spr-Verlag.

Marks, M. I., et al, eds. Cystic Fibrosis Pulmonary Infections: Lessons from Around the World. (Respiratory Pharmacology & Pharmacotherapy Ser.). 333p. 1996. 190.00 (*3-7643-5027-X*) Birkhauser.

Marks, M. L. Jews among the Indians: Tales of Adventure & Conflict in the Old West. LC 92-81618. 200p. 1992. 21.95 (*0-9632965-0-7*) Benison Bks.

— Jews among the Indians: Tales of Adventure & Conflict in the Old West. LC 92-81618. 190p. 1995. pap. 14.95 (*0-9632965-1-5*) Benison Bks.

Marks, Malcolm W. & Marks, Charles. Fundamentals of Plastic Surgery. McGrew, Larry, ed. LC 96-8868. 400p. 1997. text 78.00 (*0-7216-6449-0*, W B Saunders Co) Harcrt Hlth Sci Grp.

Marks, Manuel H. & Corn, Herman, eds. Atlas of Adult Orthodontics: Functional & Esthetic Enhancement. LC 86-21469. (Illus.). 645p. 1988. text 149.50 (*0-8121-1023-4*) Lppncott W & W.

An Asterisk (*) at the beginning of an entry indicates that the title is appearing for the first time.

Marks-Maran, Diane. Reconstructing Nursing: Beyond. 1996. pap. text 28.00 (*0-7020-2000-1*, W B Saunders Co) Harcrt Hlth Sci Grp.

Marks, Margaret G. Broadribb's Introductory Pediatric Nursing. 5th ed. LC 97-24540. 544p. 1998. pap. text 29.95 (*0-397-55450-8*) Lppncott W & W.

Marks, Marilyn. Exploring Habitats Resource Guide Vol. 3096: Look Once, Look Again! Baron, Julie A., ed. (Illus.). 80p. (J). (gr. 1-3). 1998. pap. 8.98 (*1-57471-367-1*) Creat Teach Pr.

***Marks, Marilyn.** Life Cycles Resource Guide, Vol. 3086. Kupperstein, Joel, ed. (Illus.). 80p. 1999. pap. text 8.98 (*1-57471-633-6*, 3086) Creat Teach Pr.

***Marks, Mark.** Left on Center. rev. ed. LC 99-93229. 56p. 1999. 15.00 (*1-57579-158-7*) Pine Hill Pr.

Marks, Marlene A. A Woman's Voice: Reflections on Love, Death, Faith, Food & Family Life. LC 98-92267. 240p. 1998. pap. 12.95 (*0-9666432-0-8*) On the Way.

Marks, Marlene A., ed. Nice Jewish Girls: Growing up in America. 352p. 1996. pap. 12.95 (*0-452-27397-8*, Plume) Dutton Plume.

Marks, Martha A. & Blake, Robert. Al Corriente: Curso Intermedio de Espanol. 2nd ed. (SPA.). 1993. pap. text 37.50 (*0-07-040467-4*) McGraw.

— Al Corriente: Curso Intermedio de Espanol. 2nd ed. (SPA.). 1993. pap. text, student ed. 23.50 (*0-07-040469-0*); 31.25 (*0-07-040472-0*) McGraw.

Marks, Martin M. Music & the Silent Film: Contexts & Case Studies, 1895-1924. (Illus.). 320p. 1997. text 45.00 (*0-19-506891-2*) OUP.

Marks, Martin Miller, jt. auth. see Simmon, Scott.

Marks, Mary E. Cooking with Southern Accents: A Collection of Old & New Recipes. (Illus.). (Orig.). 1988. pap. 10.00 (*0-9621561-0-8*) M E Marks.

Marks, Matthew, jt. ed. see Fraenkel, Jeffrey.

Marks, Mel. Yesterday's Warriors. (Illus.). 192p. 1998. 23.00 (*0-9632965-2-3*) Benison Bks.

Marks, Mel, jt. auth. see Maidens, Marion.

***Marks, Michael.** New Testament & the Law: A New Testament Study on the Validity of Jewish Law. 128p. 1999. pap. 10.00 (*0-939513-36-6*) Joy Pub SJC.

Marks, Michael P. The Formation of European Policy in Post-Franco Spain: The Role of Ideas, Interests & Knowledge. 224p. 1997. text 64.95 (*1-85972-377-2*, Pub. by Avebry) Ashgate Pub Co.

Marks, Mitchell L. From Turmoil to Triumph: New Life After Mergers, Acquisitions, & Downsizing. LC 94-4758. 340p. 1994. 24.95 (*0-02-920055-5*) Jossey-Bass.

Marks, Mitchell L. & Mirvis, Philip H. Joining Forces: Making One Plus One Equal Three in Mergers, Alliances & Acquisitions. LC 97-33872. 288p. 1997. per. 26.00 (*0-7879-0350-7*, Scribners Ref) Mac Lib Ref.

Marks, Morton. Haiti on the Hudson: The Formation of the Haitian Communities of Rockland County. St. Fort, Hugues, tr.Tr. of Ki Jan Kominote Ayisyen Yo Te Fome Lan Rockland. (CRP & ENG., Illus.). 32p. 1993. pap. 5.00 (*0-911183-40-X*) Rockland County Hist.

Marks, Nancy. The Winner's Way: Revised Owners & Trainers Manual. Currier, Donald, ed. (Illus.). 112p. 1997. 24.95 (*1-890030-06-6*) Las Vegas Insider.

Marks, Neville & Rodnight, Richard, eds. Research Methods In Neurochemistry, Vol. 5. LC 72-222263. 334p. 1981. 79.50 (*0-306-40583-0*, Plenum Trade) Perseus Pubng.

— Research Methods in Neurochemistry, Vol. 6. 392p. 1985. 95.00 (*0-306-41751-0*, Plenum Trade) Perseus Pubng.

Marks, Norton E., jt. ed. see Durlabhji, Subhash.

Marks, P. L., et al. Late Eighteenth Century Vegetation of Central & Western New York State on the Basis of Original Land Surveys. (New York State Museum Bulletin Ser.: No. 484). (Illus.). 55p. (Orig.). 1992. pap. 7.50 (*1-55557-225-1*) NYS Museum.

Marks, Patricia. Bicycles, Bangs & Boomers: The New Woman in the Popular Press. LC 89-25110. (Illus.). 232p. 1990. text 27.50 (*0-8131-1704-6*) U Pr of Ky.

Marks, Patricia, jt. auth. see Savory, Jerold J.

Marks, Patricia H., ed. Luminaries: Princeton Faculty Remembered. (Illus.). 250p. 1996. text 39.95 (*0-691-01167-2*, Pub. by Princeton U Pr) Cal Prin Full Svc.

Marks, Patricia H., jt. ed. see Logan, John L.

Marks, Patrick. Someone's Making a Monkey Out of You! Florea, Jesse, ed. 104p. (YA). (gr. 6 up). 1995. pap. 6.95 (*0-89051-210-8*, SOMAMO) Master Bks.

Marks, Paul V. & Lavy, Christopher B., eds. A Practical Guide to Head Injury Management. (Illus.). 168p. 1992. text 30.00 (*0-7020-1615-2*, Pub. by W B Saunders) Saunders.

Marks, Paula M. And Die in the West: The Story of the O. K. Corral Gunfight. LC 96-18367. (Illus.). 480p. 1996. pap. 17.95 (*0-8061-2888-7*) U of Okla Pr.

— Hands to the Spindle: Texas Women & Home Textile Production 1822-1880. LC 95-46409. (Clayton Wheat Williams Texas Life Ser.: Vol. 5). (Illus.). 160p. (C). 1996. 19.95 (*0-89096-699-0*) Tex A&M Univ Pr.

***Marks, Paula M.** In a Barren Land: American Indian Dispossession & Survival. LC 97-28377. (Illus.). 451p. 1998. 27.50 (*0-688-14143-9*, Wm Morrow) Morrow Avon.

Marks, Paula M. Precious Dust: The Saga of the Western Gold Rushes. LC 97-50203. (Illus.). 448p. 1998. pap. 17.95 (*0-8032-8247-8*, Bison Books) U of Nebr Pr.

— Turn Your Eyes Toward Texas: Pioneers Sam & Mary Maverick. LC 88-27573. (Centennial Series of the Association of Former Students: No. 30). (Illus.). 344p. 1989. 32.95 (*0-89096-380-0*) Tex A&M Univ Pr.

Marks, Paula M., ed. see Henry, Maridell.

Marks, Paula Mitchell. In a Barren Land: American Indian Dispossession & Survival. 480p. 1999. pap. 16.00 (*0-688-16633-4*, Quil) HarperTrade.

Marks, Percy. The Plastic Age: A Novel. LC 80-17959. (Lost American Fiction Ser.). 352p. 1980. reprint ed. 16.95 (*0-8093-0984-X*) S Ill U Pr.

Marks, Peter, jt. auth. see Luckhurst, Roger.

Marks, Peter, jt. auth. see Marks, Walter.

Marks, Philippa. The British Library Guide to Bookbinding: History & Techniques. LC 98-198940. (British Library Guides Ser.). (Illus.). 96p. 1998. pap. 19.95 (*0-8020-8176-2*) U of Toronto Pr.

Marks, R. & Robinson, A. T. Principles of Weaving. 249p. (C). 1976. pap. text 27.00 (*0-900739-79-7*, Pub. by Textile Inst) St Mut.

Marks, R., jt. ed. see Dyall-Smith, D.

Marks, R. J. & Brodie, B. B. Potato Cyst Nematodes: Biology, Distribution & Control. LC 98-14968. (CAB International Publication). (Illus.). 432p. 1998. text 120.00 (*0-85199-274-9*) OUP.

Marks, R. L. Studying Electrochemical Cells & Reduction Potentials. Neidig, H. Anthony, ed. (Modular Laboratory Program in Chemistry Ser.). 12p. (C). 1992. pap. text 1.50 (*0-87540-418-9*, ELEC 418-9) Chem Educ Res.

Marks, R. M. Roxburgh's Common Skin Diseases. 16th ed. (Illus.). 344p. (gr. 13). 1993. pap. text 35.00 (*0-412-41130-X*, Pub. by E A) OUP.

Marks, R. M., ed. Topics in Topicals. 1985. text 124.50 (*0-85200-891-0*) Kluwer Academic.

Marks, R. M., et al, eds. The Physical Nature of the Skin. (C). 1988. text 144.00 (*0-85200-977-1*) Kluwer Academic.

Marks, R. M. & Payne, P. A. Bioengineering & the Skin. (Illus.). 320p. 1982. text 166.50 (*0-85200-314-5*) Kluwer Academic.

Marks, R. M. & Plewig, Gerd, eds. Stratum Corneum. (Illus.). 300p. 1983. 68.95 (*0-387-11704-0*) Spr-Verlag.

Marks, R. M., et al. Atlas of Skin Pathology. (Current Histopathology Ser.). 1986. text 268.50 (*0-85200-324-2*) Kluwer Academic.

***Marks, Randy.** Outlet Bound: Guide to the Nations Best Outlets. 10th rev. ed. (Illus.). 200p. 1999. pap. 9.95 (*0-9631319-9-0*) Outlet Mktg.

Marks, Raymond F., et al. Lawyer, the Public & Professional Responsibility. LC 70-187314. (American Bar Foundation Publication Ser.). vi, 305p. 1996. pap. 25.00 (*1-57588-321-X*, 304880) W S Hein.

— Shreveport Plan: An Experiment in the Delivery of Legal Services. LC 74-77636. xi, 95p. 1986. pap. 15.00 (*0-910058-61-X*, 305020) W S Hein.

Marks, Richard. Remembering Things of the Good Old Days. LC 93-73607. 48p. 1993. pap. text 8.00 (*1-885935-01-3*) Appalchn Log.

— Stained Glass in England During the Middle Ages. (Illus.). 376p. 1993. text 85.00 (*0-8020-0592-6*) U of Toronto Pr.

Marks, Richard & Morgan, Nigel. The Golden Age of English Manuscript Painting, 1200-1500. LC 80-12985. (Illus.). 120p. 1981. pap. 20.95 (*0-8076-0972-2*, Pub. by Braziller) Norton.

Marks, Richard G. The Image of Bar Kokhba in Traditional Jewish Literature: False Messiah & National Hero. LC 92-34744. (Hermeneutics,Studies in the History of Religions). 224p. 1993. 40.00 (*0-271-00939-X*); pap. 18.95 (*0-271-00940-3*) Pa St U Pr.

Marks, Richard L. Three Men of the Beagle. 272p. 1992. pap. 11.00 (*0-380-71838-3*, Avon Bks) Morrow Avon.

Marks, Rick. America under Attack. LC 95-225351. 1995. mass mkt. 4.99 (*0-503-50400-9*) Carlyle Communications Ltd.

***Marks, Rita.** The Valley of New Beginnings. large type ed. 83p. 1999. pap. 19.95 (*0-9678265-0-0*) Pleasure Wear by Rita.

Marks, Robert. Hamlet: Another Interpretation. LC 80-50694. 1980. 16.00 (*0-9605486-0-2*) Leda Pr.

— Rural Revolution in South China: Peasants & the Making of History in Haifeng County, 1570-1930. LC 83-16980. (Illus.). 367p. reprint ed. pap. 113.80 (*0-608-07005-X*, 206721300009) Bks Demand.

Marks, Robert & Fox, Janet. High Point: Corporate Profiles. LC 96-44897. 1996. 19.95 (*1-885352-41-7*) Community Comm.

— High Point: Reflections of the Past. LC 96-44897. 1996. 28.00 (*1-885352-40-9*) Community Comm.

Marks, Robert, jt. ed. see Dilley, James W.

Marks, Robert B. Tigers, Rice, Silk, & Silt: Environment & Economy in Late Imperial South China. (Studies in Environment & History). (Illus.). 400p. (C). 1998. text 64.95 (*0-521-59177-5*) Cambridge U Pr.

Marks, Robert J., II. Fuzzy Logic Technology & Applications I. LC 94-14291. (IEEE Technology Update Ser.). 470p. 1994. write for info. (*0-7803-1383-6*) Inst Electrical.

Marks, Robert J., II, et al, eds. Computational Intelligence: Imitating Life. LC 94-19065. 448p. 1994. 69.95 (*0-7803-1104-3*, PC4580) Inst Electrical.

Marks, Robert J., II & Thomas, J. B., eds. Advanced Topics in Shannon Sampling & Interpolation Theory. LC 92-25590. (Texts in Electrical Engineering Ser.). (Illus.). 376p. 1992. 87.95 (*0-387-97906-9*) Spr-Verlag.

Marks, Robert J., II, jt. auth. see Reed, Russell D.

Marks, Ron. Personal Selling: A Relationship Approach. 6th ed. LC 96-29159. 585p. (C). 1996. 92.00 (*0-13-242884-9*) P-H.

Marks, Ronald. Practical Problems in Dermatology. 264p. 1996. pap. write for info. (*1-85317-050-X*) Martin Dunitz.

— Sun-Damaged Skin. 1992. 19.95 (*0-614-07393-6*, M Dunitz) Scovill Paterson.

Marks, Ronald, ed. Eczema. 1992. 95.00 (*0-614-06223-3*); 95.00 (*0-614-07391-X*, M Dunitz) Scovill Paterson.

— The Environmental Threat to the Skin. 1992. 115.00 (*0-614-07392-8*, M Dunitz) Scovill Paterson.

— The Environmental Threat to the Skin, Vol. 5. 1992. 115.00 (*0-614-06224-1*) Scovill Paterson.

Marks, Ronald & Cunliffe, W. J., eds. Skin Therapy. 1994. 29.95 (*1-85317-137-9*, M Dunitz) Scovill Paterson.

Marks, Ronald, et al. Clinical Signs & Procedures in Dermatology. 1994. 65.00 (*0-948269-44-8*, M Dunitz) Scovill Paterson.

Marks, Ronald, jt. auth. see Lowe, Nicholas.

Marks, Ronald, jt. auth. see Lowe, Nicholas J.

Marks, Ronald, jt. auth. see Ortonne, Jean-Paul.

Marks, Ross, jt. auth. see Medoff, Mark.

Marks, Ruth A. Through It All. LC 87-73017. 1990. 11.95 (*0-8158-0448-2*) Chris Mass.

Marks, S. J. Something Grazes Our Hair. 80p. (Orig.). 1991. 10.95 (*0-252-06181-0*) U of Ill Pr.

— Something Grazes Our Hair: Poems. fac. rev. ed. LC 90-44637. 84p. 1991. pap. 30.00 (*0-7837-8078-8*, 204783100008) Bks Demand.

Marks, S. N., ed. see Meares, L. G. & Hymowitz, C. E.

Marks, Sally. Innocent Abroad: Belgium at the Paris Peace Conference of 1919. LC 80-13698. 461p. reprint ed. pap. 143.00 (*0-7837-2458-6*, 204261100005) Bks Demand.

Marks, Sandy & Bell, Richard. The Best of the Sports Fan: Sports Trivia Games & More for All Sports Fans. 40p. write for info. (*0-9633505-0-1*) Strike Two Pr.

Marks, Scott, et al. Y2K: Complete Preparedness Guide. LC 98-83022. 369p. 1999. pap. 19.95 (*0-9669039-1-9*, Pub. by Mercury Pubns) ACCESS Pubs Network.

***Marks, Shawnette.** Applehats, Sneakers, & Spraypaint. 44p. 1999. pap. 10.00 (*1-58730-000-1*) S Marks.

Marks, Sheldon. Cancer de la Prostata. LC 97-9313. (SPA.). 332p. 1997. pap. 14.95 (*1-55561-136-2*) Fisher Bks.

— Prostate & Cancer: A Family Guide to Diagnosis, Treatment & Survival. LC 95-17803. (Illus.). 352p. 1995. pap. 14.95 (*1-55561-078-1*) Fisher Bks.

Marks, Sheldon. Prostate & Cancer: A Family Guide to Diagnosis, Treatment & Survival. rev. ed. LC 99-37432. (Illus.). 360p. 1999. pap. 14.95 (*1-55561-206-7*) Fisher Bks.

***Marks, Sheldon.** Prostate & Cancer: A Family Guide to Diagnosis, Treatment & Survival. rev. ed. (Illus.). 352p. 2000. pap. 17.95 (*1-55561-262-8*) Fisher Bks.

Marks, Shelly, jt. auth. see Allen, Marie.

Marks, Shirley F. Please Don't Call My Dog a Dog. LC 92-73384. (Illus.). 96p. 1993. pap. 9.95 (*0-942963-29-6*) Distinctive Pub.

Marks, Shula. The Ambiguities of Dependence in South Africa: Class, Nationalism, & the State in Twentieth-Century Natal. LC 85-7609. (Johns Hopkins Studies in Atlantic History & Culture Ser.). (Illus.). 188p. reprint ed. pap. 58.30 (*0-7837-6189-9*, 204591100009) Bks Demand.

— Class, Race & Gender in South Africa: The Nursing Profession & The Making of Apartheid. LC 93-29470. 1994. text 75.00 (*0-312-10643-2*) St Martin.

Marks, Shula, ed. Not Either an Experimental Doll: The Separate World of Three South African Women. LC 88-12867. (Illus.). 234p. (Orig.). 1988. 31.95 (*0-253-34843-9*); pap. 12.95 (*0-253-28640-9*) Ind U Pr.

— Not Either an Experimental Doll: The Separate Worlds of Three South African Women. (Killie Campbell Africana Library Publication: No. 2). (Illus.). 236p. 1987. pap. write for info. (*0-86980-542-8*, Pub. by Univ Natal Pr) Intl Spec Bk.

Marks, Shula & Trapido, Stanley. POLTCS RACE CLASS NATL20. LC 86-27554. (Illus.). (C). 1987. pap. text 33.50 (*0-582-64490-9*, 74623) Longman.

Marks, Shula, ed. see MacMillan, Hugh.

Marks, Siegfried, ed. Political Constraints on Brazil's Economic Development: (North-South Center, University of Miami, in Cooperation with the Getulio Vargas Foundation & University of Sao Paulo) LC 92-43075. 202p. (C). 1993. pap. 18.95 (*1-56000-683-8*, Pub. by U Miami N-S Ctr) L Rienner.

Marks, Stanley J. If This Be Treason...!, Vol. 1. 135p. (Orig.). 1996. pap. 15.95 (*0-938780-34-4*) Bur Intl Aff.

— If This Be Treason...!, Vol. 1. unabridged ed. 135p. (Orig.). 1996. 22.00 (*0-938780-33-6*) Bur Intl Aff.

— If This Be Treason...! The Reagan-Casey-Bush Conspiracy That Defeated President Jimmy Carter in the 1980 Presidential Election. 160p. (Orig.). 1995. pap. 15.95 (*0-938780-29-8*) Bur Intl Aff.

— If This Be Treason...! The Reagan-Casey-Bush Conspiracy That Defeated President Jimmy Carter in the 1980 Presidential Election. 160p. (Orig.). 1996. write for info. (*0-938780-30-1*) Bur Intl Aff.

— A Year in the Lives of the Damned! Reagan-Reaganism 1986. 1988. pap. 14.95 (*0-685-17796-3*) Bur Intl Aff.

— A Year in the Lives of the Damned! Reagan-Reaganism, 1986. 292p. (Orig.). 1988. pap. 14.95 (*0-938780-18-2*) Bur Intl Aff.

Marks, Stanley J. & Marks, Ethel M. Jews, Judaism & the United States: The Impact of Judaism upon the American People. LC 90-80500. 210p. (Orig.). 1991. 21.95 (*0-938780-20-4*); pap. 19.95 (*0-938780-21-2*) Bur Intl Aff.

— Judaism Looks at Christianity: 7 BC-1985 C. E. 295p. 1986. pap. 13.95 (*0-938780-10-7*) Bur Intl Aff.

— Yes, Americans, a Conspiracy Murdered JFK! LC 92-71289. (Illus.). 220p. (Orig.). 1992. pap. 14.50 (*0-685-59495-5*); pap. 16.95 (*0-938780-25-5*) Bur Intl Aff.

Marks, Stephanie & Assadi, John, eds. Maximizing the Odds: An Attorney's Guide to the Diversity Visa Lottery. 74p. (Orig.). 1995. pap. text 25.00 (*0-934143-77-3*) Lawyers Comm Human.

Marks, Stephanie, ed. see Lewis, Ann E.

Marks, Stephen, ed. Concerning Buildings: Studies in Honour of Sir Bernard Feilden. LC 97-107468. 352p. 1996. text 85.95 (*0-7506-2350-0*) Buttrwrth-Heinemann.

Marks, Stephen, jt. auth. see Samuelson, William F.

Marks, Stephen G., jt. auth. see Samuelson, William F.

Marks, Stephen P., jt. auth. see Weston, Burns H.

Marks, Stephen V. & Maskus, Keith E., eds. The Economics & Politics of World Sugar Policies. LC 92-42179. (Studies In International Trade Policy). 192p. (C). 1993. text 54.50 (*0-472-10428-4*, 10428) U of Mich Pr.

Marks, Steve. Working on Cruise Ships: How to Have the Time of Your Life Working Around the World. (Jobs & Careers Ser.). 119p. 1996. pap. 19.95 (*1-85703-335-3*, Pub. by How To Bks) Trans-Atl Phila.

Marks, Steve & Marks, Cathy. Today's Swingers: The Complete Guide to Successful Swinging. LC 95-78394. 160p. (Orig.). 1995. pap. 16.95 (*0-9640903-1-7*) M S W Pubng.

Marks, Steve, jt. auth. see Marks, Cathy.

Marks, Steven. EDI Purchasing: The Electronic Gateway to the Future. LC 96-8608. 100p. (Orig.). 1997. pap. text 14.95 (*0-945456-27-1*) PT Pubns.

— Gallows Lane. LC 89-51875. (Illus.). 80p. (Orig.). (C). 1989. pap. 8.95 (*0-9624685-0-9*) Tyger Pr.

— Gallows Lane: Playscript. LC 89-51875. 59p. (Orig.). 1993. pap. 6.00 (*0-88734-250-7*) Players Pr.

Marks, Steven, ed. see Grieco, Peter L., Jr.

Marks, Steven C. Nasal & Sinus Surgery. (Illus.). 635p. Date not set. text. write for info. (*0-7216-7804-1*, W B Saunders Co) Harcrt Hlth Sci Grp.

Marks, Steven G. Road to Power: The Trans-Siberian Railroad & the Colonization of Asian Russia, 1850-1917. LC 90-55734. (Illus.). 272p. 1991. text 37.50 (*0-8014-2533-6*) Cornell U Pr.

Marks, Stuart A. Southern Hunting in Black & White: Nature, History & Ritual in a Carolina Community. (Illus.). 345p. 1991. text 49.50 (*0-691-09452-7*, Pub. by Princeton U Pr) Cal Prin Full Svc.

***Marks, Susan.** The Riddle of All Constitutions: International Law, Democracy, & a Critique of Ideology. 200p. 2000. text 74.00 (*0-19-826798-3*) OUP.

Marks, Susan & Black, Bruce. Seven Blessings: Our Jewish Wedding Book. (Illus.). 64p. 1997. 20.00 (*0-8074-0640-6*, 510062) UAHC.

***Marks, Susan Collin.** Watching the Wind: Conflict Resolution During South Africa's Transition to Democracy. 212p. 2000. pap. 14.95 (*1-878379-99-2*) US Inst Peace.

Marks, Susan Moss & Hopkins, William A., Jr. Pharmacy Technician Certification Quick-Study Guide. 2nd ed. 125p. 1999. pap. text 25.00 (*1-58212-000-5*) Am Pharm Assn.

Marks, Sylvia K. Sir Charles Grandison: The Compleat Conduct Book. LC 85-47800. 176p. 1986. 36.50 (*0-8387-5090-7*) Bucknell U Pr.

Marks, T. & Robinson, L. Principles of Weaving. 256p. 1976. 90.00 (*0-7855-7223-6*) St Mut.

Marks, T., jt. auth. see Robinson, S.

Marks-Tarlow, Terry. Creativity Inside Out: Learning Through Multiple Intelligences. Apple, Mali, ed. 400p. (Orig.). 1996. pap. text, teacher ed. 24.95 (*0-201-49044-7*) Supplementary Div.

Marks, Ted, jt. auth. see Mryglot, Gerard.

Marks, Thomas A. Counterrevolution in China: Wang Sheng & the Kuomintang. LC 96-13891. 368p. (Orig.). 1998. 59.50 (*0-7146-4700-4*, Pub. by F Cass Pubs); pap. 24.50 (*0-7146-4238-X*, Pub. by F Cass Pubs) Intl Spec Bk.

— Maoist Insurgency since Vietnam. LC 95-5364. 320p. (C). 1996. pap. 26.50 (*0-7146-4123-5*, Pub. by F Cass Pubs); text 57.50 (*0-7146-4606-7*, Pub. by F Cass Pubs) Intl Spec Bk.

Marks, Thomas C., Jr. & Cooper, John F. State Constitutional Law in a Nutshell. (Nutshell Ser.). 329p. (C). 1988. pap. 22.95 (*0-314-41748-6*) West Pub.

Marks, Thomas C., Jr., jt. auth. see Cooper, John F.

Marks, Tobin J., ed. Bonding Energetics in Organometallic Compounds. LC 90-36268. (ACS Symposium Ser.: No. 428). (Illus.). 292p. 1990. text 72.00 (*0-8412-1791-2*, Pub. by Am Chemical) OUP.

Marks, Tobin J. & Fischer, Dieter, eds. Organometallics of the F-Elements. (NATO Advanced Study Institutes Ser.: C-44). 1979. lib. bdg. 146.00 (*90-277-0990-4*) Kluwer Academic.

Marks, Tobin J. & Fragala, Ignzio L., eds. Fundamental & Technological Aspects of Organo-f-Element Chemistry. 1985. text 195.50 (*90-277-2053-3*) Kluwer Academic.

Marks, Tracy. The Art of Chart Interpretation: A Step-by-Step Method of Analyzing, Synthesizing & Understanding the Birth Chart. LC 86-9683. 176p. (Orig.). 1986. pap. 9.95 (*0-916360-29-6*) CRCS Pubns CA.

— The Art of Chart Synthesis. LC 78-68664. 1979. pap. 7.00 (*0-933620-03-9*) Sag Rising.

— The Astrology of Self-Discovery: An In-Depth Exploration of the Potentials Revealed in the Birth Chart. LC 85-7844. 286p. (Orig.). 1986. pap. 13.95 (*0-916360-20-2*) CRCS Pubns CA.

— Planetary Aspects: From Conflict to Cooperation. rev. ed. LC 86-26445. 225p. (Orig.). 1987. pap. 13.95 (*0-916360-32-6*) CRCS Pubns CA.

— Your Secret Self: Illuminating the Mysteries of the Twelfth House. 264p. (Orig.). 1989. pap. 15.95 (*0-916360-43-1*) CRCS Pubns CA.

Marks, V., jt. ed. see Hubbard, R.

Marks, Vernon J., et al. The Effects of Crushed Particles in Asphalt Mixtures. (Illus.). 48p. (Orig.). (C). 1992. pap. text 25.00 (*1-56806-093-9*) DIANE Pub.

Marks, Vic, jt. ed. see Holmes, Bob.

Marks, Vincent, jt. ed. see Williams, David L.

Marks, Walter & Marks, Peter. The Butler Did It. 1981. pap. 5.25 (*0-8222-0167-4*) Dramatists Play.

Marks, Will. Multi-Level Marketing: The Definitive Guide to America's Top MLM Companies. 2nd rev. ed. LC 96-51294. 211p. 1997. pap. 24.99 (*1-56530-215-X*, Pub. by Summit TX) BookWorld.

M

Marks, William C. No More Mac & Cheese: A Bachelor's Guide to Cooking with Ease. (Illus.). 56p. 1990. ring bd. write for info. (0-9628453-0-2) Marks Pub CA.

Marks, Winifred. How to Give a Speech. 136p. (C). 1980. 40.00 (0-85292-255-8, Pub. by IPM Hse) St Mut.

— Politics & Personnel Management: An Outline History, 1960-1976. 240p. (C). 1978. 50.00 (0-85292-189-6) St Mut.

Marks, Wizard. Letters from Palenque. (U. S. A. Poetry Chapbook Ser.: No. 5). (Illus.). 16p. (Orig.). 1985. pap. 3.00 (0-937724-06-8) Shadow Pr.

Marksbury, Richard A., ed. The Business of Marriage: Transformations in Oceanic Matrimony. LC 93-1008. (Association for Social Anthropology in Oceania Monographs: No. 14). 280p. (C). 1994. pap. 19.95 (0-8229-5511-3); text 49.95 (0-8229-3762-X) U of Pittsburgh Pr.

Marksbury, Tina. Nighty-Night, Teddy Beddy Bear. (Cuddle Cloth Bks.). 12p. (J). (ps). 1986. 4.99 (0-394-88244-X, Pub. by Random Bks Yng Read) Random.

Marksbury, Tom, ed. see McClanahan, Ed.

***Markschies, Christoph.** Between the Worlds. 1998. pap. 26.00 (0-334-02750-0) TPI PA.

Markschies, Christoph, jt. auth. see Boehlig, Alexander.

Markself, Ted. The Seed of Calamity. 240p. mass mkt. 4.99 (1-896329-52-7) Picasso Publ.

Markson, David. The Ballad of Dingus Magee. 200p. 1997. 17.95 (1-889936-07-3) Skyline Pubs Inc.

— The Ballad of Dingus Magee. Gee, Charles G., ed. 250p. 1996. 17.95 (0-9645786-4-6) VYTIS Pub.

— Collected Poems. LC 92-18999. 96p. (Orig.). 1993. pap. 9.95 (1-56478-033-3) Dalkey Arch.

— Reader's Block. LC 96-2323. 194p. (Orig.). 1996. pap. 12.95 (1-56478-132-1) Dalkey Arch.

— Springer's Progress. LC 90-2731. 240p. 1999. reprint ed. pap. 12.95 (1-56478-218-2) Dalkey Arch.

— Wittgenstein's Mistress. 256p. 1999. reprint ed. pap. 12.95 (1-56478-211-5) Dalkey Arch.

Markson, Elizabeth W. & Hollis-Sawyer, Lisa A. Intersections of Aging: Readings in Social Gerontology. LC 98-17848. (C). 2000. pap. text. write for info. (1-891487-06-X) Roxbury Pub Co.

Markson, Elizabeth W., jt. ed. see Hess, Beth B.

Markson, Leona E. & Nash, David B. Accountability & Quality in Health Care: The New Responsibility. (Illus.). 284p. 1995. pap. 65.00 (0-86688-431-9, JC-900) Joint Comm Hlthcare.

Markstein. Developing Reading Skills: Advanced. 3rd ed. (College ESL Ser.). 224p. (C). 1998. pap. 27.95 (0-8384-5276-0) Heinle & Heinle.

Markstein, Linda r. Answer Key-Develop Reading Skills: Beginning. 2nd ed. (College ESL Ser.). (J). 1994. text 7.95 (0-8384-4988-3) Heinle & Heinle.

Markstein, Linda R. Developing Reading Skills. 2nd ed. (College ESL Ser.). (J). 1994. text, suppl. ed. 7.95 (0-8384-5775-4) Heinle & Heinle.

— Developing Reading Skills: Advanced. 2nd ed. 1982. pap. text 13.50 (0-88377-270-1, Newbury) Heinle & Heinle.

— Developing Reading Skills: Beginning. 2nd ed. LC 93-45815. 160p. (J). 1994. mass mkt. 21.95 (0-8384-4987-5) Heinle & Heinle.

— Expanding Reading Skills. 2nd ed. (College ESL Ser.). (J). 1994. mass mkt. 9.95 (0-8384-4208-0) Heinle & Heinle.

Markstein, Linda R. & Grunbaum, Dorien. LEVEL 4 WHATS STORY, 4 bks., Bk. 4, Advanced. (English As a Second Language Bk.). 1981. pap. text 12.40 (0-582-79786-1, 75041) Longman.

— What's the Story? Photographs for Language Practice, 4 bks. (English As a Second Language Bk.). 1981. pap. text 9.50 (0-685-73375-0, 75037); teacher ed. 10.95 (0-582-79787-X, 75042); 95.00 (0-582-79788-8) Longman.

— What's the Story? Photographs for Language Practice, 4 bks., Bk. 3, High-Intermediate. (English As a Second Language Bk.). 1981. pap. text 12.40 (0-582-79785-3, 75040) Longman.

Markstein, Linda R. & Hirasawa, Louise. Developing Reading Skills: Intermediate. 2nd ed. LC 93-46179. 224p. (J). 1994. mass mkt. 21.95 (0-8384-5774-6) Heinle & Heinle.

— Expanding Reading Skills: Advanced. 2nd ed. 222p. (J). 1992. mass mkt. 19.00 (0-8384-3098-8, Newbury) Heinle & Heinle.

— Expanding Reading Skills: Intermediate. 200p. (J). 1982. mass mkt. 16.50 (0-8384-2956-4, Newbury) Heinle & Heinle.

— Expanding Reading Skills: Intermediate 2. 2nd rev. ed. LC 92-27000. 222p. (J). 1992. mass mkt. 21.95 (0-8384-2644-1) Heinle & Heinle.

***Markstein, Peter.** IA-64 & Elementary Functions: Speed & Precision. 298p. 2000. 60.00 (0-13-018348-2) P-H.

Marktanner, T., jt. auth. see Hofmann, H.

***Markulis, Peter M., et al.** Strategic Management for Small & Growing Firms. LC 98-19206. 202p. (C). 1999. pap. text 24.95 (1-55571-465-X, Oasis Pr) PSI Resch.

Markuly, Mark S. & Oslance, Michael. Win the Prize: Game Plan for Life. 1997. 5.25 (0-570-09888-2, 22-2492) Concordia.

Markum, J. A. & Silva, M. P. Beginning Electronic Fabrication. 2nd ed. (Illus.). 160p. 1986. pap. text 8.50 (0-911908-07-2) Tech Ed Pr.

Markum, J. A. & Silva, P. Intermediate Electronic Fabrication. 2nd ed. 192p. 1984. pap. text 8.50 (0-911908-09-9) Tech Ed Pr.

Markun, Leo. Mrs. Grundy: A History of Four Centuries of Morals Intended to Illuminate Present Problems in Great Britain & the United States. 1930. 69.00 (0-403-00130-7) Scholarly.

***Markun, Patricia M.** It's Panama's Canal! LC 99-37092. 1999. lib. bdg. 22.50 (0-208-02499-9) Shoe String.

Markun, Patricia M. The Little Painter of Sabana Grande. LC 91-35230. (Illus.). 32p. (J). (ps-2). 1993. text 14.95 (0-02-762205-3, Bradbury S&S) S&S Childrens.

Markun, Rachael, et al. Attorney's Guide to Pension & Profit-Sharing Plans: September 1994 Update. 3rd ed. Pickus, Bob, ed. LC 80-70006. 764p. 1994. 105.00 (0-88124-791-X, TX-30734) Cont Ed Bar-CA.

Markus. From Augustine to Gregory the Great. 1983. 106.95 (0-86078-117-8) Ashgate Pub Co.

Markus & Jordan, eds. A Midsummer Night's Dream. 1993. text. write for info. (0-582-24590-7, Pub. by Addison-Wesley) Longman.

Markus, jt. auth. see Luck.

Markus, A. F., et al, eds. Information Modelling & Knowledge Bases, Vol. V: Results of the 3rd European-Japanese Seminar, Held in Budapest, Hungary, May 31-June 3, 1993. LC 93-61135. 437p. (YA). (gr. 12). 1994. 124.00 (90-5199-143-6, Pub. by IOS Pr) IOS Press.

Markus, A. F., et al. Psychological Problems in General Practice. (Oxford General Practice Ser.: No. 15). (Illus.). 424p. 1989. pap. 37.50 (0-19-261529-7) OUP.

Markus, Andrew. Australian Race Relations. 266p. 1995. pap. 19.95 (1-86373-554-2, Pub. by Allen & Unwin Pty) Paul & Co Pubs.

Markus, Andrew, jt. ed. see Parkes, Colin M.

Markus, Andrew L. The Willow in Autumn: Ryutei Tanehiko, 1783-1842. (Harvard-Yenching Institute Monographs: No. 35). 300p. (C). 1993. 28.00 (0-674-95351-7) HUP.

Markus, David F. Die Assoziationstheorien Im XVIII, Jahrhundert. (Abhandlungen Zur Philosophie und Ihrer Geschichte Ser.: Bd. 15). (GER.). ix, 72p. 1985. reprint ed. write for info. (3-487-07608-X) G Olms Pubs.

***Markus, Dirk.** Strategische Kooperationen in der Multimediaindustrie: Entstehung, Evolution und Management. (Europaische Hochschulschriften Ser.: Bd. 2535). 359p. 1999. 52.95 (3-631-35615-3) P Lang Pubng.

Markus, Georg. Crime at Mayerling: The Life & Death of Mary Vetsera. De Bussy, Carvel. tr. LC 94-6491. 150p. 1995. pap. 14.95 (0-929497-94-5) Ariadne CA.

Markus, Gilbert. Bartolome de las Casas: The Gospel of Liberation. 1989. pap. 22.00 (1-85390-082-6, Pub. by Veritas Pubns) St Mut.

Markus, Gilbert, jt. auth. see Clancy, Thomas O.

Markus, Gregory B. Analyzing Panel Data. LC 79-91899. (Quantitative Applications in the Social Sciences Ser.: Vol. 18). (Illus.). 72p. 1979. pap. 10.95 (0-8039-1372-9) Sage.

Markus, Gyorgy. Language & Production: A Critique of the Paradigms. 208p. 1986. text 137.50 (90-277-2169-6) Kluwer Academic.

Markus, Hazel R. & Kitayama, Shinobu, eds. Emotion & Culture: Empirical Studies of Mutual Influence. 385p. 1994. 34.95 (1-55798-224-4) Am Psychol.

Markus, Hugh B. The History of the German Public Accounting Profession. rev. ed. Brief, Richard P., ed. LC 97-25944. (New Works in Accounting History). 388p. 1997. text 60.00 (0-8153-3010-3) Garland.

Markus, John. Diccionario de Electronica y Tecnica Nuclear. (SPA.). 1052p. 125.00 (84-267-0003-9, S-14264) Fr & Eur.

— Enciclopedia de Circuitos Electronicos. (SPA.). 888p. 1977. 125.00 (0-8288-5403-3, S14349) Fr & Eur.

— English & Spanish Dictionary of Electronics & Nuclear Technology. (ENG & SPA.). 1052p. 1985. 195.00 (0-8288-0705-1, S14264) Fr & Eur.

— Guidebook of Electronic Circuits. (Illus.). 992p. 1974. text 90.00 (0-07-040445-3) McGraw.

— Introduction to the Spectral Theory of Polynomial Operator Pencils. LC 88-23499. (Translations of Mathematical Monographs: No. 71). 250p. 1988. text 110.00 (0-8218-4523-3, MMONO/71) Am Math.

— Manual de Circuitos Electronicos. 984p. 1974. 125.00 (0-7859-0873-0, S-30723) Fr & Eur.

— Modern Electronic Circuits Reference Manual. (Illus.). 1000p. 1980. 97.00 (0-07-040446-1) McGraw.

— Vocabulario Ingles-Espanol de Electronica y Tecnica Nuclear. 2nd ed. (ENG & SPA.). 196p. pap. 39.95 (84-267-0247-3, S-30684) Fr & Eur.

Markus, John & Sclater, Neil J. McGraw-Hill Dictionary of Electronics. 6th ed. LC 97-16168. (Illus.). 544p. 1997. 55.00 (0-07-057837-0) McGraw.

***Markus, Julia.** Across an Untried Sea: Discovering Lives Hidden in the Shadow of Convention & Time. 2000. 27.95 (0-679-44599-4) Knopf.

Markus, Julia. Angel at My Back. 1999. write for info. (0-679-41031-7) Knopf.

— Dared & Done: The Marriage of Elizabeth Barrett & Robert Browning. LC 94-11573. 1995. 32.50 (0-679-41602-1) Knopf.

— Dared & Done: The Marriage of Elizabeth Barrett Browning & Robert Browning. LC 98-21560. (Illus.). 370p. 1998. reprint ed. pap. 15.95 (0-8214-1246-9) Ohio U Pr.

Markus, Julia, ed. see Browning, Elizabeth Barrett.

Markus, Kurt. Boxers. 112p. 1998. 50.00 (0-944092-36-5) Twin Palms Pub.

— Boxers. limited ed. 112p. 1997. 150.00 (0-944092-37-3) Twin Palms Pub.

Markus, L., jt. auth. see Auslander, Louis.

Markus, Lawrence. Lectures in Differentiable Dynamics. rev. ed. LC 80-16847. (CBMS Regional Conference Series in Mathematics: No. 3). 77p. 1971. pap. 16.00 (0-8218-1695-0, CBMS/3) Am Math.

Markus, Lawrence & Meyer, K. R. Generic Hamiltonian Dynamical Systems Are Neither Integrable Nor Ergodic. LC 74-8095. (Memoirs Ser.: No. 1/144). 52p. 1974. pap. 17.00 (0-8218-1844-9, MEMO/1/144) Am Math.

Markus, Lawrence, jt. auth. see Auslander, Louis.

Markus, Lawrence, jt. auth. see Everitt, W. Norrie.

Markus, M. Lynne. Systems in Organizations: Bugs & Features. LC 83-22121. 256p. 1986. text 29.95 (0-88730-202-5, HarpBusn) HarpInfo.

Markus, Peter. Still Lives with Whiskey Bottle. Bixby, Robert, ed. 41p. 1996. pap. 6.00 (1-882983-31-9) March Street Pr.

Markus, R. A. The End of Ancient Christianity. 276p. (C). 1991. text 54.95 (0-521-32716-4) Cambridge U Pr.

— The End of Ancient Christianity. (Canto Book Ser.). 276p. (C). 1998. pap. 12.95 (0-521-62510-6) Cambridge U Pr.

— Gregory the Great & His World. LC 97-11308. 264p. 1997. text 59.95 (0-521-58430-2); pap. text 22.95 (0-521-58608-9) Cambridge U Pr.

— The Limits of Ancient Christianity: Essays on Late Antique Thought & Culture in Honor of R. A. Markus. Klingshim, William E. & Vessey, Mark, eds. LC 98-51221. (Recentiores Ser.). 376p. 1999. text 54.50 (0-472-10997-9, 10997) U of Mich Pr.

— Sacred & Secular: Studies on Augustine & Latin Christianity. (Collected Studies: CS 465). 350p. 1994. 109.95 (0-86078-450-9, Pub. by Variorum) Ashgate Pub Co.

Markus, Richard M. & Palmer, George H. Trial Handbook for Ohio Lawyers. 3rd ed. LC 90-64031. 354p. 125.00 (0-317-00553-7) West Group.

— Trial Handbook for Ohio Lawyers. 3rd ed. LC 72-97628. 354p. 1993. suppl. ed. 52.50 (0-317-05566-6) West Group.

Markus, Robert A. Saeculum: History & Society in the Theology of St. Augustine. LC 71-87136. 264p. reprint ed. pap. 75.30 (0-608-15750-3, 2031687) Bks Demand.

Markus, T. Domestic Energy & Affordable Warmth. (Illus.). 160p. (C). 1994. pap. 80.00 (0-419-20090-8, E & FN Spon) Routledge.

Markus, Thomas A. Buildings & Power: Freedom & Control in the Origin of Modern Building Types. LC 92-33282. (Illus.). 368p. (C). (gr. 13). 1993. 130.00 (0-415-07664-1, B2360); pap. 40.00 (0-415-07665-X, B2364) Routledge.

Markus, Tom. Actor Behaves: From Audition to Performance. 237p. (Orig.). 1992. pap. 14.95 (0-573-69901-1) S French Trade.

— How to Read a Play. 656p. (C). 1996. pap. text, per. 59.95 (0-7872-1890-1) Kendall-Hunt.

Markus, Tom, jt. auth. see Sarver, Linda.

***Markus, Ustina.** Brassey's Eurasian & East European Security Yearbook, 2000. 2000. 45.00 (1-57488-248-1) Brasseys.

***Markus, Ustina & Nelson, Daniel N.** Brassey's Eurasian & East European Security Yearbook, 2000. 2000. pap. 30.00 (1-57488-249-X) Brasseys.

Markus, Vasyl. Religion & Nationalism in Soviet Ukraine after 1945. 46p. 1994. write for info. (0-9609822-6-4) Ukrainian Studies Fund.

Markusen, Ann R. The Politics of Regions: The Economics & Politics of Territory. LC 87-4359. 320p. (C). 1987. 60.50 (0-8476-7394-4, R7394) Rowman.

— Profit Cycles, Oligopoly & Regional Development. 336p. 1985. 44.00 (0-262-13201-X) MIT Pr.

***Markusen, Ann R., et al, eds.** Second Tier Cities: Rapid Growth Beyond the Metropolis. LC 99-21024. (Globalization & Community Ser.: Vol. 3). 336p. 1999. lib. bdg. 62.95 (0-8166-3373-8, Pub. by U of Minn Pr) Chicago Distribution Ctr.

***Markusen, Ann R. & Costigan, Sean S., eds.** Arming the Future: A Defense Industry for the 21st Century. 442p. 1999. pap. 22.50 (0-87609-246-6) Coun Foreign.

Markusen, Ann R., et al. High Tech America: The What, How, Where & Why of the Sunrise Industries. 256p. 1986. text 39.95 (0-04-338139-1) Routledge.

— The Rise of the Gunbelt: The Military Remapping of Industrial America. (Illus.). 360p. 1991. text 60.00 (0-19-506648-0) OUP.

— Second Tier Cities: Rapid Growth Beyond the Metropolis. LC 99-21024. (Globalization & Community Ser.: Vol. 3). 336p. 1999. pap. 24.95 (0-8166-3374-6, Pub. by U of Minn Pr) Chicago Distribution Ctr.

Markusen, Ann R., jt. auth. see Hall, Peter.

Markusen, Bruce. Baseball's Last Dynasty: The Oakland A's. LC 98-11585. (Illus.). 320p. 1998. pap. 17.95 (1-57028-188-2, 81882H, Mstrs Pr) NTC Contemp Pub Co.

— Roberto Clemente: The Great One. (Illus.). 354p. 1998. 22.95 (1-57167-244-3) Sports Pub.

Markusen, Eric & Kopf, David S. The Holocaust & Strategic Bombing: Genocide & Total War in the Twentieth Century. 230p. 1995. pap. 75.00 (0-8133-7532-0, Pub. by Westview) HarpC.

Markusen, Eric, jt. ed. see Summers, Craig.

Markusen, James R. International Trade: Theory & Evidence. LC 94-24782. 448p. (C). 1994. 65.00 (0-07-040447-X) McGraw.

Markusen, James R., jt. auth. see Scheffman, David T.

Markushevich, A. I. Introduction to the Classical Theory of Abelian Functions. LC 91-36838. (Translations of Mathematical Monographs: Vol. 96). 175p. 1992. text 123.00 (0-8218-4542-X, MMONO/96) Am Math.

— Theory of Functions of a Complex Variable, 3 vols. in 1. 2nd ed. Silverman, Richard A., tr. from RUS. LC 77-8515. 1977. text 48.00 (0-8284-0296-5) Chelsea Pub.

Markuson, Barbara E. & Woods, Elaine W., eds. Networks for Networkers II: Critical Issues for Libraries in the National Network Environment. 250p. 1993. 49.95 (1-55570-128-0) Neal-Schuman.

Markuson, Carolyn, jt. auth. see Tobias, Joyce.

Markuson, Gloria C., jt. auth. see Warren, Oscar L.

Markusse, Jan, jt. auth. see Knippenberg, Hans.

Markussen, Birgitte & Henrik, Hans, eds. Advocacy & Indigenous Film-Making Number One of Intervention: Nordic Papers in Critical Anthropology. 74p. 1995. pap. 15.00 (87-89825-09-8) Smyrna.

Markussen, Birgitte, jt. ed. see Reenberg, Annette.

Markussen, J. Human Insulin by Tryptic Transpeptidations of Porcine Insulin & Biosynthetic Precursors. 1987. text 144.00 (0-7462-0058-7) Kluwer Academic.

Markuszewski, Richard, et al, eds. Gas, Oil & Environmental Biotechnology IV. viii, 540p. 1993. 75.00 (0-910091-85-4) Inst Gas Tech.

Markuszewski, Richard & Blaustein, Bernard D., eds. Fossil Fuels Utilization: Environmental Concerns. LC 86-20673. (ACS Symposium Ser.: No. 319). (Illus.). ix, 385p. 1986. 82.95 (0-8412-0990-1) Am Chemical.

— Fossil Fuels Utilization: Environmental Concerns. LC 86-20673. (ACS Symposium Ser.: Vol. 319). 392p. 1986. reprint ed. pap. 121.60 (0-608-03523-8, 206424200008) Bks Demand.

Markvart, Thomas. Solar Electricity. 2nd ed. pap. text 69.95 (0-471-98853-7) Wiley.

— Solar Electricity 2nd ed. text 125.00 (0-471-98852-9) Wiley.

Markvart, Thomas, ed. Solar Electricity. 248p. 1994. pap. 69.95 (0-471-94161-1) Wiley.

Markwald, R. R., jt. auth. see De la Cruz, M. V.

Markwald, Roger R., jt. auth. see De la Cruz, Maria Victoria.

Markwald, Rudolf K. A Mystic's Passion: The Spirituality of Johannes von Staupitz in His 1520 Lenten Sermons. LC 89-2259. (Renaissance & Baroque Studies & Texts: Vol. 3). XIV, 210p. 1990. text 47.95 (0-8204-0950-2) P Lang Pubng.

Markward, Anne. Monument Valley: Navajo Tribal Park. (Illus.). 64p. 1992. 24.95 (0-944197-22-1); pap. 14.95 (0-944197-20-5) Companion CA.

Markward, Martha, jt. ed. see Pardeck, John.

Markwardt, Bruno. Geschichte der Deutschen Poetik. Incl. Vol. 1. Barock und Fruehaufklaerung. 3rd enl. ed. xii, 512p. 1977. 107.00 (3-11-004020-4); Vol. 2. Aufklaerung, Rokoko, Sturm und Drang. 2nd ed. (GER.). viii, 692p. 1970. 137.00 (3-11-002679-1); Vol. 3. Klassik und Romantik. 2nd ed. viii, 730p. 1971. 148.00 (3-11-003584-7); Vol. 4. Neunzehnte Jahrhundert. viii, 750p. 1959. 112.00 (3-11-005329-2); Vol. 5. Zwanzigste Jahrhundert. viii, 1032p. 1967. 152.00 (3-11-000169-1); (Grundriss der Germanischen Philologie Ser.: Vol. 13, Nos. 1-5). (GER.). (C). write for info. (0-318-51617-9) De Gruyter.

Markway, Barbara G. & Markway, Gregory P. Illuminating the Heart: Steps Toward a More Spiritual Marriage. LC 96-67941. 256p. (Orig.). 1996. pap. 13.95 (1-57224-053-9) New Harbinger.

Markway, Barbara G., et al. Dying of Embarrassment: Help for Social Anxiety & Social Phobia. LC 92-61814. 204p. 1992. pap. 13.95 (1-879237-23-7) New Harbinger.

Markway, Gregory P., jt. auth. see Markway, Barbara G.

Markwell, F. C., jt. auth. see Saul, Pauline.

Markwick, Margaret. Trollope & Women. LC 96-29451. 1997. 40.00 (1-85285-152-X) Hambledon Press.

Markwick, Roger D., jt. auth. see Gill, Graeme J.

Markwiese, James T. & Dahm, Clifford N. Assessment of Biological Treatments to Remediate Cyanide Heap-Leached Ore. (Illus.). 52p. (Orig.). (C). 1996. pap. text 30.00 (0-7881-2338-6) DIANE Pub.

Markwood, Chris. Oklahoma Goverment & Politics: An Introduction. 2nd ed. 262p. (C). per. write for info. (0-7872-6724-4) Kendall-Hunt.

Markwood, Chris. Oklahoma Government & Politics. LC 98-134673. 272p. (C). 1998. per. 40.95 (0-7872-4397-3, 41439701) Kendall-Hunt.

Markytan, M., et al, eds. Multiparticle Dynamics, 1986: Proceedings of the 17th International Symposium on Multiparticle Dynamics Seewinke Austria 16-20 June 1986. 904p. 1987. text 164.00 (9971-5-0177-5) World Scientific Pub.

Marlais, Michael. Conservative Echoes in Fin-de-Siecle Parisian Art Criticism. (Illus.). 272p. 1992. text 45.00 (0-271-00773-7) Pa St U Pr.

Marlan, Stanton, ed. Fire in the Stone: The Alchemy of Soul-Making. LC 97-31742. 206p. 1997. pap. text 19.95 (1-888602-05-8) Chiron Pubns.

— Fire in the Stone: The Alchemy of Soul-Making. LC 97-31742. 206p. 1997. 28.95 (1-888602-06-6) Chiron Pubns.

Marlan, Stanton, ed. & intro. see Jones, Ernest, et al.

Marland. Discovering Poetry. 1987. pap. text. write for info. (0-582-21899-3, Pub. by Addison-Wesley) Longman.

— A Sillitoe Selection. Date not set. pap. text. write for info. (0-582-23373-9, Pub. by Addison-Wesley) Longman.

Marland, Folly, ed. see French Ramblers Association Staff.

Marland, H. & Pelling, M., eds. The Task of Healing: Medicine, Religion & Gender in England & the Netherlands 1450-1800. 352p. 1996. pap. 43.00 (90-5235-096-5, Pub. by Erasmus Pub) Balogh.

Marland, Hilary, ed. Art of Midwifery. (Wellcome Institute Series in the History of Medicine). (Illus.). 256p. (C). 1994. pap. 27.99 (0-415-11675-9) Routledge.

Marland, Hilary & Rafferty, Anne M., eds. Midwives, Society & Childbirth: Debates & Controversies in the Modern Period. LC 96-41125. (Studies in the Social History of Medicine Ser.). 292p. (C). 1997. 74.95 (0-415-13328-9) Routledge.

Marland, Hilary, jt. ed. see Gijswit-Hofstra, Marijke.

Marland, Michael & Rogers, Richard. The Art of the Tutor: Developing Your Role in the Secondary School. LC 97-198779. 192p. 1997. pap. 24.95 (1-85346-479-1, Pub. by David Fulton) Taylor & Francis.

An Asterisk (*) at the beginning of an entry indicates that the title is appearing for the first time.

Marlane, Judith. Women in Television News Revisited. LC 98-48678. 288p. 1999. 40.00 (*0-292-75227-X*); pap. 19.95 (*0-292-75228-8*) U of Tex Pr.

Marlatt, Andrew. Leadership Higher Power 2e. 2nd ed. 1998. 20.50 (*0-07-228208-8*) McGraw.

— Multifacety Ethics 3 Mille. 1997. pap. text 25.50 (*0-07-303668-4*) McGraw.

Marlatt, Daphne. Ana Historic. 160p. 1997. pap. 13.95 (*0-88784-590-8*, Pub. by Hse of Anansi Pr) Genl Dist Srvs.

— Salvage. (Writing West Series). 120p. 1992. pap. 8.95 (*0-88995-074-1*, Pub. by Red Deer) Genl Dist Srvs.

— Selected Writing: Net Work. LC 81-91048. 144p. 1980. pap. 12.95 (*0-88922-175-8*, Pub. by Talonbks) Genl Dist Srvs.

Marlatt, Daphne & Warland, Betsy. Two Women in a Birth. 170p. 1994. pap. 13.00 (*1-55071-003-6*) Guernica Editions.

Marlatt, G. Alan, ed. Harm Reduction: Pragmatic Strategies for Managing High-Risk Behaviors. LC 98-37938. 390p. 1998. lib. bdg. 42.00 (*1-57230-397-2*) Guilford Pubns.

Marlatt, G. Alan & Gordon, Judith R., eds. Relapse Prevention: Maintenance Strategies in the Treatment of Addiction. LC 84-19319. (Clinical Psychology & Psychotherapy Ser.). 558p. 1985. lib. bdg. 57.00 (*0-89862-009-0*) Guilford Pubns.

Marlatt, G. Alan & Nathan, P. E., eds. Behavioral Approaches to Alcoholism. LC 77-620035. (NIAAA-RUCAS Alcoholism Treatment Ser.: No. 2). 1978. pap. 6.00 (*0-911290-48-6*) Rutgers Ctr Alcohol.

Marlatt, G. Alan & VandenBos, Gary R., eds. Addictive Behaviors: Readings on Etiology, Prevention, & Treatment. LC 97-37315. 930p. 1997. pap. 39.95 (*1-55798-468-9*) Am Psychol.

Marlatt, G. Alan, jt. ed. see Donovan, Dennis M.

***Marlatt, Orlo.** Mystic Magic Words. LC 99-93676. 1999. pap. 8.95 (*0-533-13114-6*) Vantage.

Marlatt, Orlo. Mystic Magic Words. 1997. pap. 56.95 (*1-57553-631-5*) Watermrk Pr.

— A Set Order of Words in Poetry & Songs, in Story Form. 1997. pap. write for info. (*1-57553-529-7*) Watermrk Pr.

— A Set Order of Words, in Poetry & Songs, in Story Form. LC 97-91037. 1998. pap. 8.95 (*0-533-12538-3*) Vantage.

Marlatt, William P., ed. see Conejo Valley Genealogical Society, Inc. Staff.

Marlay, Ross & Neher, Clark D. Patriots & Tyrants: Ten Asian Leaders. LC 98-52020. 368p. 1999. pap. 21.95 (*0-8476-8442-3*) Rowman.

Marlay, Ross, et al. Patriots & Tyrants: Ten Asian Leaders. LC 98-52020. 368p. 1999. text 69.00 (*0-8476-8441-5*) Rowman.

Marlay, Ross, jt. auth. see Neher, Clark D.

Marlborough. Churchill, Vol. 1. 1969. lib. bdg. 75.00 (*0-8371-0561-7*, Greenwood Pr) Greenwood.

Marlborough, John C. Letters & Dispatches of John Churchill, First Duke of Marlborough from 1702-1712, 5 vols., Set. Murray, George, ed. LC 68-54801. 1969. reprint ed. lib. bdg. 295.00 (*0-8371-2663-0*, MUJC) Greenwood.

— Letters & Dispatches of John Churchill, First Duke of Marlborough from 1702-1712, 5 vols., Vol. 2. Murray, George, ed. LC 68-54801. 1969. reprint ed. lib. bdg. 75.00 (*0-8371-0829-2*, MUJE) Greenwood.

— Letters & Dispatches of John Churchill, First Duke of Marlborough from 1702-1712, 5 vols., Vol. 3. Murray, George, ed. LC 68-54801. 1969. reprint ed. lib. bdg. 75.00 (*0-8371-0830-6*, MUJF) Greenwood.

— Letters & Dispatches of John Churchill, First Duke of Marlborough from 1702-1712, 5 vols., Vol. 4. Murray, George, ed. LC 68-54801. 1969. reprint ed. lib. bdg. 75.00 (*0-8371-0831-4*, MUJG) Greenwood.

— Letters & Dispatches of John Churchill, First Duke of Marlborough from 1702-1712, 5 vols., Vol. 5. Murray, George, ed. LC 68 54801. 1969. reprint ed. lib. bdg. 75.00 (*0-8371-0832-2*, MUJH) Greenwood.

Marlborough, Sarah J. Letters of Sarah, Duchess of Marlborough. LC 77-37708. reprint ed. 29.50 (*0-404-56766-5*) AMS Pr.

Marle, Charles M. Multiphase Flow in Porous Media. (Illus.). 272p. (C). 1981. 465.00 (*2-7108-0404-2*, Pub. by Edits Technip) Enfield Pubs NH.

Marle, Inc. Staff, ed. see Albert-Robatto, Matilde.

Marle, Jaap Van, see Booij, Geert & Van Marle, Jaap, eds.

Marle, Jaap Van, see Van Marle, Jaap, ed.

Marle, Jaap Van, see Booij, Geert & Van Marle, Jaap, eds.

Marle, Jaap Van, see Booy, Geert & Van Marle, Jaap, eds.

Marle, Jaap Van, see Booij, Geert & Van Marle, Jaap, eds.

Marler, Charles, ed. see Stevens, John C.

Marler, Don C. Historic Hineston. 192p. (Orig.). 1991. pap. 12.95 (*0-9646846-7-5*) Dogwood TX.

— The Neutral Zone: Backdoor to the United States. 238p. (Orig.). 1995. pap. 15.00 (*1-887745-01-7*) Dogwood TX.

Marler, Don C. & McManus, Jane P. The Cherry Winche Country: History of the Redbones. 70p. (Orig.). 1993. pap. 6.00 (*0-9646846-6-7*) Dogwood TX.

Marler, E. E., compiled by. Pharmacological & Chemical Synonyms. 9th ed. 500p. 1990. reprint ed. 275.50 (*0-444-90487-5*) Elsevier.

Marler, E. E., ed. Pharmacological & Chemical Synonyms: A Collection of Names of Drugs, Pesticides & Other Compounds Drawn from the Medical Literature of the World. 10th ed. 602p. 1994. 292.00 (*0-444-82081-7*) Elsevier.

Marler, Jack C., jt. ed. see Kennedy, Leonard A.

Marler, Joan, ed. From the Realm of the Ancestors: Anthology in Honor of Marija Gimbutas. LC 96-49459. (Illus.). 655p. (Orig.). 1997. pap. 45.95 (*1-879198-25-8*) Knwldg Ideas & Trnds.

Marler, John & Wermuth, Andrew. Youth of the Apocalypse: And the Last True Rebellion. (Illus.). 198p. (Orig.). (YA). 1995. pap. 7.00 (*0-938635-89-1*) St Herman Pr.

Marler, Linda M., et al. Color Atlas & Identification Manual of Gram Stain Images. 320p. spiral bd. 45.00 (*0-7817-2663-8*) Lppncott W & W.

Marler, Malcolm. Ideas for Homebound Ministries. Nelson, Becky, ed. (Illus.). 41p. (Orig.). 1993. pap. text 4.95 (*1-56309-072-4*, N934110, New Hope) Womans Mission Union.

Marler, Patti, jt. auth. see Mattia, Jan B.

Marler, Patty & Mattia, Jan B. Getting a Raise Made Easy. (Made Easy Ser.). 96p. (Orig.). 1996. pap. 6.95 (*0-8442-4345-0*, 43450, VGM Career) NTC Contemp Pub Co.

— Hiring Made Easy. LC 98-33527. 96p. 1998. pap. 6.95 (*0-8442-6050-9*, 60509, VGM Career) NTC Contemp Pub Co.

— Networking Made Easy. LC 97-15798. 96p. 1997. pap. 6.95 (*0-8442-4342-6*, 43426) NTC Contemp Pub Co.

— Time Management Made Easy. LC 97-47712. (Illus.). 96p. 1998. pap. 6.95 (*0-8442-4324-8*, 43248, VGM Career) NTC Contemp Pub Co.

Marler, Patty, jt. auth. see Mattia, Jan B.

Marler, Regina. Bloomsbury Pie. 224p. 1997. write for info. (*1-86049-289-4*, Pub. by Virago) Little.

Marler, Regina, ed. Selected Letters of Vanessa Bell. LC 98-2755. (Illus.). 592p. 1998. pap. 14.95 (*1-55921-261-6*) Moyer Bell.

Marler, Tim. Introduction to Oil & Gas Enviornmental Project Management. LC 94-23716. 1994. 79.95 (*0-87814-430-7*) PennWell Bks.

Marles, Fay. The Politics of Nursing in Victorian, 1987. (C). 1989. pap. 65.00 (*0-7300-0691-3*, NPR803, Pub. by Deakin Univ) St Mut.

Marles, J., jt. auth. see Bowen, T.

***Marles, Robin J.** Aboriginal Plant Use in Canada's Northwest Boreal Forest. (Illus.). 256p. 2000. pap. 24.95 (*0-7748-0738-5*) UBC Pr.

Marletta, M., jt. auth. see Light, W. A.

***Marlette, Caroline D.** Denver. LC 99-93682. 2000. pap. 7.95 (*0-533-13121-9*) Vantage.

Marlette, Doug. I Feel Your Pain. (Illus.). 192p. (Orig.). 1996. pap. 9.95 (*0-9654505-0-3*) Loblolly Bks.

Marlette, Jerry. Interstate: A History of Interstate Public Service Rail Operations. Riehle, Ginger, ed. LC 87-35740. (Illus.). 272p. 1991. text 48.00 (*0-933449-07-0*) Transport Trails.

Marlewski-Probert, Bonnie. The Animal Lover's Guide to the Internet: More Than 500 of the Most Educational, Fun Web Sites for Animal Lovers. Stafford, Susan, ed. (Illus.). 135p. (Orig.). 1996. spiral bd. 19.95 (*0-9646181-2-5*) K&B Products.

— Debugging Your Horse: A Simple, Safe Approach to Problem Solving with Your Horse. Stafford, Susan, ed. (Illus.). 325p. (Orig.). 1996. pap. 23.95 (*0-9646181-1-7*, DYH) K&B Products.

— A Parent's Guide to Buying That First Horse: How-to Find the Ideal Horse for Your Family & Avoid Buying a Lemon! Haertel, Kandee, ed. (Illus.). 164p. (Orig.). 1995. pap. 16.95 (*0-9646181-0-9*) K&B Products.

Marley. Accounting for Business. 1994. pap. text. write for info. (*0-582-80076-5*, Pub. by Addison-Wesley) Longman.

— Accounting for Business: Solutions. 1994. pap. text, student ed. write for info. (*0-582-80188-5*, Pub. by Addison-Wesley) Longman.

Marley, jt. auth. see Fernandez.

Marley, A. A., ed. Choice, Decision, & Measurement: Essays in Honor of R. Duncan Luce. LC 96 41621. 400p. 1996. 80.00 (*0-8058-2234-8*) L Erlbaum Assocs.

Marley, Bob. Bob Marley. LC 99-21582. (Illus.). 48p. (gr. 4-7). 1999. 16.95 (*0-7910-5228-1*) Chelsea Hse.

***Marley, Bob.** Bob Marley: Island Prophet. 80p. 1999. 4.95 (*0-7407-0056-1*) Andrews & McMeel.

Marley, C. F. Battleships, Flagships & High-Seas Action. 94p. 1991. pap. 9.90 (*0-9631610-0-8*) Audubon Hills.

Marley, Claire, jt. auth. see Julian, Desmond.

Marley, Daniel T., ed. see Heiserman, Russell L. & Barber, Preston.

Marley, Dave. Employee Incentive Contests: For Improved Marketing, Customer Service, & Morale. (Illus.). 224p. 1995. pap. 19.95 (*0-945442-18-1*) Silverpoint Pr.

***Marley, David F.** Historic Cities of the Americas: An Illustrated Encyclopedia. 2001. lib. bdg. 99.00 (*1-57607-027-1*) ABC-CLIO.

Marley, David F. Pirates: Adventurers of the High Seas. (Illus.). 160p. 1996. 29.95 (*1-85409-215-4*, Pub. by Arms & Armour) Sterling.

— Pirates & Privateers of the Americas: An Illustrated Encyclopedia. LC 94-31348. 458p. 1994. lib. bdg. 75.00 (*0-87436-751-4*) ABC-CLIO.

— Trafalgar, 1805. 1995. pap. 14.95 (*1-85532-479-2*, Pub. by Ospry) Stackpole.

— Wars of the Americas: A Chronology of Armed Conflict in the New World, 1492 to the Present. LC 98-21209. (Illus.). 722p. 1998. lib. bdg. 99.00 (*0-87436-837-5*) ABC-CLIO.

Marley, John. Handwriting Analysis Made Easy. 1978. pap. 10.00 (*0-87980-045-3*) Wilshire.

Marley, Judy. Behold the Man: Seven Meditations on the Passion, Death & Resurrection of Jesus. (Illus.). 48p. (Orig.). 1990. pap. 4.50 (*0-9623410-2-9*, Resurrection Pr) Catholic Bk Pub.

***Marley, Louise.** Glass Harmonica. 2000. pap. 13.95 (*0-441-00729-5*) Ace Bks.

Marley, Louise. Receive the Gift. 304p. 1997. mass mkt. 5.99 (*0-441-00486-5*) Ace Bks.

— Sing the Light. 304p. (Orig.). 1995. mass mkt. 5.50 (*0-441-00272-2*) Ace Bks.

— Sing the Warmth. 1996. mass mkt. 5.99 (*0-441-00386-9*) Ace Bks.

— Small in the Saddle. 50p. (Orig.). 1996. mass mkt. 2.99 (*0-9654318-1-9*) Atomic Wstrn.

— The Terrorists of Irustan. 323p. 1999. pap. 13.00 (*0-441-00619-1*) Ace Bks.

***Marley, Louise.** Terrorists of Irustan. 2000. mass mkt. 5.99 (*0-441-00743-0*) Ace Bks.

Marley, Marie, ed. see Sammartini, Giovanna B.

Marley, Mary L. Organic Brain Pathology. 264p. 1989. 86.00 (*0-205-10142-9*) P-H.

— Organic Brain Pathology & the Bender-Gestalt Test: A Differential Diagnostic. 264p. 1983. text 38.00 (*0-8089-1425-1*, 792683, Grune & Strat) Harcrt Hlth Sci Grp.

Marley, Patty, jt. auth. see Mattia, Jan B.

Marley, Stephen. Dread Dominion. (Judge Dredd Ser.). 1995. mass mkt. 5.95 (*0-352-32929-7*, Pub. by Virgin Bks) London Brdge.

Marliave, Olivier De, see De Marliave, Olivier.

Marlin, A. E. Process Control. 1995. text, wbk. ed. 35.00 (*0-07-040493-3*) McGraw.

Marlin, A. E., ed. Concepts in Pediatric Neurosurgery. (Concepts in Pediatric Neurosurgery Ser.: Vol. 9). (Illus.). viii, 236p. 1989. 184.50 (*3-8055-4835-4*) S Karger.

— Concepts in Pediatric Neurosurgery, Vol. 7. (Illus.). viii, 240p. 1987. 182.75 (*3-8055-4396-4*) S Karger.

— Concepts in Pediatric Neurosurgery, Vol. 8. (Illus.). viii, 224p. 1988. 161.75 (*3-8055-4622-X*) S Karger.

— Concepts in Pediatric Neurosurgery, Vol. 11. (Illus.). viii, 164p. 1991. 187.00 (*3-8055-5328-5*) S Karger.

— Concepts in Pediatric Neurosurgery Series, Vol. 10. (Illus.). 262p. 1990. 220.00 (*3-8055-5022-7*) S Karger.

— Selected Proceedings of the Annual Meeting of the American Society of Pediatric Neurosurgeons, San Juan, Puerto Rico, January 1991. (Journal of Pediatric Neurosurgery: Vol. 18, Nos. 5-6, 1992). (Illus.). iv, 108p. 1992. pap. 96.75 (*3-8055-5711-6*) S Karger.

Marlin, A. Tepper & Council on Economic Priorities. Star Wars: The Economic Fallout. LC 87-22462. 264p. 1987. 24.95 (*0-88730-162-2*, HarpBusn) HarpInfo.

Marlin, Alice T., ed. see Council on Economic Priorities Staff, et al.

Marlin, Arthur E., jt. auth. see Gaskill, Sarah J.

Marlin-Bennett, Renee. Food Fights: International Regimes & the Politics of Agricultural Trade Disputes. LC 93-18535. 276p. 1993. text 44.00 (*2-88124-588-9*) Gordon & Breach.

Marlin, C. D. Coroutines. (Lecture Notes in Computer Science Ser.: Vol. 95). (Illus.). 246p. 1980. 28.00 (*0-387-10256-6*) Spr-Verlag.

Marlin, Debra. Yellowdog. LC 96-45670. 96p. (gr. 8). 1997. 29.95 (*0-8212-2343-7*) Little.

— Yellowpup. LC 99-18351. (Illus.). 80p. 1999. 26.50 (*0-8212-2564-2*, Pub. by Bulfinch Pr) Little.

Marlin, E. Thomas. Process Control: Designing Processes & Control Systems for Dynamic Performance. 1994. pap. text, teacher ed. write for info. (*0-07-040492-5*) McGraw.

Marlin, Emily. Genograms. 160p. (Orig.). 1989. pap. 16.95 (*0-8092-4494-2*, 449420, Contemporary Bks) NTC Contemp Pub Co.

— Relationships in Recovery: Healing Strategies for Couples & Families. LC 89-45687. 288p. 1990. pap. 8.95 (*0-00-001645-4*, Perennial) HarperTrade.

Marlin, George, ed. see Chesterton, G. K.

Marlin, George, ed. see Knox, Ronald.

Marlin, George J. The Politician's Guide to Assisted Suicide, Cloning & Other Current Controversies. 1998. pap. 12.95 (*0-9660597-1-9*) Morley Bks.

Marlin, John. Heavens to Betsy. 224p. 1986. pap. 12.00 (*0-06-272011-2*) HarpC.

Marlin, John T. The Livable Cities Almanac: How over 100 Metropolitan Areas Compare in Economic Health, Air Quality, Water Quality, Crime Rate, Life Expectancy, Health Services, Recreational Opportunities, & More. 384p. 1992. pap. 14.00 (*0-685-52542-2*, Harper Ref) HarpC.

***Marlin, Julie.** Living Room: A Visitor's Guide to Hell & Heaven. (Illus.). 208p. 2000. pap. 14.95 (*0-9700813-7-5*) Wild Grace.

Marlin, Kathryn R. Pencil Puzzle Fun. 96p. teacher ed. 11.99 (*0-86653-747-3*, GA1462) Good Apple.

***Marlin, Matthew.** The Study of Economics: Principles, Concepts & Applications. 6th ed. 480p. (C). 1999. 48.13 (*0-07-366242-9*) McGrw-H Hghr Educ.

Marlin, Michael. The Contemplative Navel Pt. I: The Silliest Prophesies, 3 pts., Set. (Illus.). (Orig.). 1995. pap. write for info. (*0-9649024-0-0*) Imag Nations.

— The Contemplative Navel Pt. 2: Out on a Whim. (Illus.). 124p. (Orig.). 1997. pap. 9.95 (*0-9649024-2-7*) Imag Nations.

Marlin, Robert W. My Sixteen: A Self-Help Guide to Finding Your Sixteen Great-Great Grandparents. LC 96-232653. (Illus.). 229p. (Orig.). 1996. pap. 14.95 (*0-9650513-0-7*) Land Yacht Pr.

Marlin, Thomas E. Process Control: Designing Processes & Control Systems for Dynamic Performance. LC 94-45967. (Chemical Engineering Ser.). 640p. (C). 1995. 93.75 (*0-07-040491-7*) McGraw.

***Marlin, Thomas E.** Process Control: Designing Processes & Control Systems for Dynamic Performance. 2nd ed. LC 99-26739. 1056p. 2000. 93.75 (*0-07-039362-1*) McGraw.

Marling, Arthur E., jt. ed. see Checck, William R.

Marling, Clare F., jt. auth. see Marling, William E.

Marling, Karal A. As Seen on TV: The Visual Culture of Everyday Life in the 1950s. LC 94-2814. (Illus.). 352p. 1994. 24.95 (*0-674-04882-2*, MARSEE) HUP.

— As Seen on TV: The Visual Culture of Everyday Life in the 1950s. (Illus.). 336p. 1996. pap. 17.95 (*0-674-04883-0*) HUP.

— Blue Ribbon: A Social & Pictorial History of the Minnesota State Fair. LC 90-5738. (Illus.). ix, 328p. 1990. 39.95 (*0-87351-251-0*); pap. 24.95 (*0-87351-252-9*) Minn Hist.

— George Washington Slept Here: Colonial Revivals & American Culture, 1876-1896. LC 87-33026. (Illus.). 496p. 1988. text 53.00 (*0-674-34951-2*) HUP.

— Graceland: Going Home with Elvis. LC 96-17477. (Illus.). 288p. 1996. 24.95 (*0-674-35889-9*) HUP.

— Graceland: Going Home with Elvis. (Illus.). 272p. 1996. reprint ed. pap. 14.95 (*0-674-35890-2*) HUP.

— In Search of the Corn Queen: Pictures from the Heartland. (American Scene Ser.). (Illus.). 96p. (C). 1994. pap. 27.50 (*1-881616-18-5*) Dist Art Pubs.

Marling, Karal A., text. Designing Disney's Theme Parks: The Architecture of Reassurance. LC 97-19033. (Illus.). 224p. 1998. 50.00 (*2-08-013639-9*, Pub. by Flammarion) Abbeville Pr.

Marling, Karal A. & Wetenhall, John. Iwo Jima: Monuments, Memories & the American Hero. (Illus.). 312p. (C). 1991. text 24.95 (*0-674-46980-1*) HUP.

Marling, Karal A., jt. ed. see Foy, Jessica H.

***Marling, Karal Ann.** Colossus of Roads: Myth & Symbol along the American Highway. (Illus.). 2000. pap. 16.95 (*0-8166-3672-9*) U of Minn Pr.

— Merry Christmas! Celebrating America's Greatest Holiday. LC 00-31935. (Illus.). 432p. 2000. 27.00 (*0-674-00318-7*) HUP.

— Wall-to-Wall America: Post Office Murals in the Great Depression. (Illus.). 2000. pap. 18.95 (*0-8166-3673-7*) U of Minn Pr.

Marling, Karal Ann & Murphy, Franklin D. Civil Rights in Oz'Images of Kansas in American Popular Art. 1992. 18.00 (*0-913689-44-0*) Spencer Muse Art.

Marling, Karal Ann, et al. Illusions of Eden: Visions of the American Heartland. Stearns, Robert, ed. write for info. (*0-918881-40-4*) Columbus Mus Art.

Marling, William. The American Roman Noir: Hammett, Cain & Chandler. LC 94-25550. 256p. 1995. 35.00 (*0-8203-1658-X*) U of Ga Pr.

— The American Roman Noir: Hammett, Cain & Chandler. 256p. 1998. pap. 18.00 (*0-8203-2081-1*) U of Ga Pr.

Marling, William E. & Marling, Clare F. The Marling Menu-Master for France. 112p. (Orig.). 1971. pap. 8.95 (*0-912818-03-4*) Altarinda Bks.

— The Marling Menu-Master for Germany. 88p. (Orig.). 1970. pap. 8.95 (*0-912818-01-8*) Altarinda Bks.

— The Marling Menu-Master for Italy. 108p. (Orig.). 1971. pap. 8.95 (*0-912818-02-6*) Altarinda Bks.

— The Marling Menu-Master for Spain. 112p. (Orig.). 1973. pap. 8.95 (*0-912818-04-2*) Altarinda Bks.

***Marlis, Stefanie.** Fine. 71p. 2000. pap. 12.95 (*0-9669937-4-8*) Apogee.

— Fine. LC 99-98077. 72p. 2000. pap. 12.95 (*0-9669937-3-X*, Pub. by Apogee) SPD-Small Pr Dist.

Marlis, Stefanie. Rife: Poems. LC 97-10568. 96p. 1998. 20.95 (*1-889330-11-6*); pap. 12.95 (*1-889330-12-4*) Sarabande Bks.

— Sheet of Glass. 40p. (Orig.). 1994. pap. 8.00 (*0-912449-47-0*) Floating Island.

— Slow Joy. LC 89-40260. (Brittingham Prize in Poetry Ser.). 90p. 1989. pap. 11.95 (*0-299-12304-9*) U of Wis Pr.

Marlis, Stefanie, jt. auth. see Arnold, Wally.

Marliss, Garry, jt. auth. see Ben-Menachem, Mordechai.

Marlitt, Richard. Matters of Proportion: The Portland Residential Architecture of Whidden & Lewis. (Illus.). 96p. (Orig.). 1989. pap. 12.95 (*0-87595-177-5*) Oregon Hist.

— Nineteenth Street. rev. ed. LC 78-73291. (Illus.). 218p. 1978. 19.95 (*0-87595-000-0*); pap. 12.95 (*0-87595-138-4*) Oregon Hist.

***Marlo, Shelby.** Shelby Marlo's New Art of Dog Training. LC 98-35005. (Illus.). 256p. 2000. pap. 14.95 (*0-8092-2376-7*, 237670, Contemporary Bks) NTC Contemp Pub Co.

Marlo, Shelby & Mizrahi, Taura S. Shelby Marlo's New Art of Dog Training: Balancing Love & Discipline. LC 98-35005. (Illus.). 256p. 1999. 22.95 (*0-8092-3170-0*) NTC Contemp Pub Co.

Marlock, Dennis & Dowling, John. License to Steal: Traveling Con Artists: Their Games, Their Rules - Your Money. 304p. 1993. text 34.95 (*0-87364-751-3*) Paladin Pr.

Marlor. An Introduction to WordPerfect. (C). 1995. pap. text 10.25 (*0-8053-6361-0*) Benjamin-Cummings.

Marlor, Clark S. Salons of America, 1922-1936. (Illus.). 242p. 1991. 49.00 (*0-932087-15-9*) Sound View Pr.

— The Society of Independent Artists: The Exhibition Record, 1917-1944. LC 84-14867. (Illus.). 600p. 1984. 64.00 (*0-8155-5063-4*) Sound View Pr.

Marlor, Elizabeth A., jt. auth. see Six, Joseph E.

Marlor Press Staff. Boat Log & Record. (Illus.). 128p. 1996. spiral bd. 17.95 (*0-943400-71-6*) Marlor Pr.

— Complete Trip Diary: Write Down, Record, Explore -- & Remember! rev. ed. (Illus.). 96p. 1994. pap. 8.95 (*0-943400-78-3*) Marlor Pr.

— Garden Manager: Plan, Organize & Keep Track of Everything in Your Garden. (Illus.). 128p. 1998. otabind 15.95 (*0-943400-96-1*) Marlor Pr.

— My Camp Book: Campers! Write up Your Own Adventures & Experiences! (Illus.). 96p. (J). 1994. pap. 8.95 (*0-943400-77-5*) Marlor Pr.

M

An Asterisk (*) at the beginning of an entry indicates that the title is appearing for the first time.

— Tale of a Cat: A Journal about the Life & Good Times of Your Feline Friend. (Illus.). 96p. 1996. pap. 8.95 (*0-943400-82-1*) Marlor Pr.

Marlow. Introduction to Electronic Business Communication. (SWC-Business Communication Ser.). 1999. pap. 34.50 (*0-324-01412-0*) Sth-Wstrn College.

***Marlow.** VCR Fault Finding Guide. 2000. pap. write for info. (*0-7506-4634-9*) Buttrwrth-Heinemann.

***Marlow, Alice.** Mermaid's Ground. large type ed. 480p. 1999. 31.99 (*0-7089-4076-5*) Ulverscroft.

Marlow, Christine. Research Methods for Generalist Social Work. 2nd ed. LC 97-9557. 353p. 1997. pap. 59.95 (*0-534-34953-6*) Brooks-Cole.

— Research Methods for Generalist Social Work. 3rd ed. 2000. pap. text 42.75 (*0-534-52571-7*) Thomson Learn.

Marlow, Clare. Beginning to Teach: Primary Teaching Explained. LC 94-163546. 144p. 1994. pap. 23.00 (*1-85346-259-4*) Taylor & Francis.

Marlow, Clayton C. Matt W. Ransom, Confederate General from North Carolina. LC 96-26521. (Illus.). 198p. 1996. lib. bdg. 28.50 (*0-7864-0273-3*) McFarland & Co.

Marlow, Elisabeth. Public Finance. (C). 1994. pap. text, teacher ed. 49.75 (*0-03-007856-3*) Harcourt Coll Pubs.

Marlow, Eugene. Click Here! Internet Advertising: How the Pros Attract, Design, Price, Place & Measure Ads Online. (Business Technology Ser.). 250p. (Orig.). 1997. pap. 29.95 (*0-442-02550-5*, VNR) Wiley.

— Corporate Television Programming. 160p. 1992. 44.95 (*0-86729-312-8*, Focal) Buttrwrth-Heinemann.

— Managing Corporate Media. 2nd ed. (Illus.). 208p. (C). 1989. 47.95 (*0-86729-265-2*, Focal) Buttrwrth-Heinemann.

Marlow, Eugene. Web Visions: An Inside Look at Successful Business Strategies on the Net. 273p. 1996. pap. 30.95 (*0-471-28819-5*, VNR) Wiley.

Marlow, Eugene & Secunda, Eugene. Shifting Time & Space: The Story of Videotape. LC 90-7808. 192p. 1991. 52.95 (*0-275-93408-X*, C3408, Praeger Pubs) Greenwood.

Marlow, Eugene & Sileo, Janice. Electronic Public Relations. 288p. (C). 1995. 24.95 (*0-534-26244-9*) Wadsworth Pub.

— Winners! Producing Effective Electronic Media. LC 94-30435. 158p. 1994. pap. 44.95 (*0-534-24090-9*) Wadsworth Pub.

Marlow, Eugene & Wilson, Patricia O. The Breakdown of Hierarchy: Communicating in the Evolving Workplace. LC 96-39241. 184p. 1997. pap. text 17.95 (*0-7506-9746-6*) Buttrwrth-Heinemann.

Marlow, H. Leroy. Woodcrafting Heritage Toys: A Treasury of Classic Projects. (Illus.). 192p. 1987. 24.95 (*0-8306-7863-8*, 2863) McGraw-Hill Prof.

***Marlow, Herb.** Bruno to the Rescue. (Illus.). 32p. (J). (gr. k-8). 2000. lib. bdg., lab manual ed. 7.95 (*0-9666858-6-5*, BR-1) Four Seasons Bks.

Marlow, Herb. Cougar! large type ed. (Illus.). 40p. (J). (gr. k-8). 1998. lib. bdg. 12.95 (*0-9666858-7-3*, C-2) Four Seasons Bks.

— Dillon's Revenge. LC 96-32099. (Illus.). (J). 1997. write for info. (*1-56763-275-0*); pap. write for info. (*1-56763-276-9*) Ozark Pub.

— Ghost Horse. large type ed. (Illus.). 32p. (J). (gr. k-5). 1995. lib. bdg. 7.95 (*0-9666858-2-2*, GH-1) Four Seasons Bks.

— Max the School House Mouse. large type ed. (Illus.). 32p. (J). (gr. k-5). 1998. lib. bdg. 7.95 (*0-9666858-5-7*, MAX-1) Four Seasons Bks.

— Publish Now! large type ed. (Illus.). 233p. 1999. spiral bd. 24.95 (*0-9666858-3-0*, PN-1) Four Seasons Bks.

— Time Out for Teachers. large type ed. 60p. 1997. spiral bd. 7.95 (*0-9666858-1-4*, TT-1) Four Seasons Bks.

— Twisters, Bronc Riders & Cherry Pie. LC 96-32100. (Illus.). (J). 1997. write for info. (*1-56763-273-4*); pap. write for info. (*1-56763-274-2*) Ozark Pub.

***Marlow, Herb & Marlowe, Lynn.** Max the Rodeo Mouse. large type ed. (Max Ser.). (Illus.). 32p. (J). (gr. k-5). 2000. lib. bdg. 7.95 (*1-893595-07-2*, MAX-2) Four Seasons Bks.

Marlow, Hugh. Managing Change: A Strategy for Our Time. 174p. (C). 1975. 70.00 (*0-85292-122-5*) St Mut.

— Managing Change: A Strategy for Our Time - Key Questions. 68p. (C). 1975. 70.00 (*0-85292-123-3*) St Mut.

— Success: Individual, Corporate & National. 416p. (C). 1984. 125.00 (*0-85292-336-8*) St Mut.

Marlow, James D. Questioning the Postwar Consensus Thesis: Towards an Alternative Account. 192p. 1996. text 77.95 (*1-85521-826-7*, Pub. by Dartmth Pub) Ashgate Pub Co.

Marlow, James E. Charles Dickens: The Uses of Time. LC 92-50683. 1994. 42.50 (*0-945636-48-2*) Susquehanna U Pr.

Marlow, Jean. Classical Audition Speeches for Men. 160p. 1996. pap. 10.95 (*0-435-07026-6*, 07026) Heinemann.

— Classical Audition Speeches for Women. 1996. pap. 10.95 (*0-435-07025-8*, 07025) Heinemann.

Marlow, Jean, ed. Actors' Audition Speeches: For All Ages & Accents. 128p. 1995. pap. 10.95 (*0-435-08664-2*, 08664); pap. 10.95 (*0-435-08663-4*, 08663) Heinemann.

Marlow, Jean, et al. Focus on Microcomputers in the Middle School. Romano, Louis G., ed. 30p. (Orig.). 1986. pap. 3.00 (*0-918449-06-5*) MI Middle Educ.

Marlow, Joyce. Anne. large type ed. 1990. 27.99 (*0-7089-2240-6*) Ulverscroft.

— Country Ways: Secrets for Finding & Keeping a Country Man. LC 98-7596. 192p. 1999. 15.00 (*0-446-52401-8*, Pub. by Warner Bks) Little.

***Marlow, Joyce.** Country Ways: Secrets for Finding & Keeping a Country Man. 224p. 2000. mass mkt. 4.99 (*0-446-60892-0*, Pub. by Warner Bks) Little.

Marlow, Joyce. Perfect Partners. LC 96-95472. 192p. 1997. 18.95 (*0-8034-9198-0*, Avalon Bks) Bouregy.

— Sarah. large type ed. 576p. 1989. 17.95 (*0-7089-2029-2*) Ulverscroft.

— Where the River Rises. large type ed. 520p. 1995. 11.50 (*0-7505-0803-5*, Pub. by Mgna Lrg Print) Ulverscroft.

Marlow, L. & Sauber, S. R. The Handbook of Divorce Mediation. LC 88-18791. (Illus.). 528p. (C). 1990. 85.00 (*0-306-43286-2*, Plenum Trade) Perseus Pubng.

Marlow, Lenard. Divorce & the Myth of Lawyers. 160p. 1992. 19.95 (*0-9632741-0-4*); pap. 10.95 (*0-9632741-1-2*) Harlan Pr.

Marlow, Louis. Seven Friends. LC 76-58445. (English Biography Ser.: No. 31). 1977. lib. bdg. 75.00 (*0-8383-2132-1*) M S G Haskell Hse.

— Seven Friends. (Illus.). 176p. 1992. text 45.00 (*1-872736-07-6*, Pub. by Mandrake Pr) Holmes Pub.

— Welsh Ambassadors: Powys Lives & Letters. LC 73-157126. 273p. 1971. text 29.95 (*0-912568-04-6*) Colgate U Pr.

Marlow, Louise. Hierarchy & Egalitarianism in Islamic Thought. (Cambridge Studies in Islamic Civilization). 214p. (C). 1997. text 54.95 (*0-521-56430-1*) Cambridge U Pr.

Marlow, Mandy, ed. The Oasis Papers: Proceedings from the First International Symposium of the Dakhleh Oasis Project. (Oxbow Monographs: Vol. 97 & 6). (Illus.). 300p. 1999. 81.00 (*1-900188-54-6*, Pub. by Oxbow Bks) David Brown.

Marlow, Mandy & Louth, Charlie. Holderlin & the Dynamics of Translation. (Legenda Studies in Comparative Literature: 2). 280p. (Orig.). 1998. pap. 49.50 (*1-900755-11-4*, Pub. by E H R C) David Brown.

Marlow, Marcia J. The Open Door. 1998. pap. write for info. (*1-58235-016-7*) Watermrk Pr.

Marlow, Mary E. Handbook for the Emerging Woman: Awakening the Unlimited Power of the Feminine Spirit. rev. ed. 216p. 1993. reprint ed. pap. 10.95 (*1-878901-78-8*) Hampton Roads Pub Co.

Marlow, Mary Elizabeth. Jumping Mouse: A Story about Inner Trust. 192p. 1999. pap. text 12.95 (*1-57174-147-X*) Hampton Roads Pub Co.

Marlow, Max. The Burning Rocks. 320p. 1995. 24.00 (*0-7278-4852-6*) Severn Hse.

— The Burning Rocks. large type ed. (Magna Large Print Ser.). 480p. 1996. 27.99 (*0-7505-1048-X*, Pub. by Mgna Lrg Print) Ulverscroft.

— Dry. 320p. 1998. 25.00 (*0-7278-5272-8*) Severn Hse.

— Hell's Children. 320p. 1996. 24.00 (*0-7278-4963-8*) Severn Hse.

— Meltdown. 320p. 1992. 24.95 (*0-450-53785-4*, Pub. by Hodder & Stought Ltd) Trafalgar.

— Shadow at Evening. 1994. lib. bdg. 20.00 (*0-7278-4699-X*) Severn Hse.

— The Trench. 288p. 1999. 26.00 (*0-7278-2237-3*, Pub. by Severn Hse) Chivers N Amer.

— Where the River Rises. 1994. 22.00 (*0-7278-4583-7*) Severn Hse.

Marlow, Michael. Public Finance. 272p. (C). 1995. pap. text, student ed. 34.00 (*0-03-007861-X*) Harcourt Coll Pubs.

Marlow, Tim. Schiele. (Illus.). 112p. 1999. pap. 19.95 (*1-57715-096-1*) Knckerbocker.

Marlow-Trump, Nancy. Ruby Keeler: A Photographic Biography. LC 98-12992. (Illus.). 180p. 1998. boxed set 28.95 (*0-7864-0524-4*) McFarland & Co.

Marlow, W. H. Mathematics for Operations Research. LC 93-24974. (Illus.). 483p. 1993. reprint ed. pap. 12.95 (*0-486-67723-0*) Dover.

***Marlowe.** Mothers, Daughters & Traditions. 2001. write for info. (*0-684-87264-1*, Fireside) S&S Trade Pap.

Marlowe. Stop Time. Date not set. pap. write for info. (*0-465-03151-X*) Basic.

Marlowe, Al. Fly Fishing the Colorado River: An Angler's Guide. LC 97-9294. (Illus.). 164p. 1997. pap. 15.95 (*0-87108-885-1*) Pruett.

— A Hiking & Camping Guide to the Flat Tops Wilderness Area. (Illus.). 215p. 1996. pap. 15.95 (*0-9623868-8-X*) F Pruett.

Marlowe, Ann. How to Stop Time: Heroin from A to Z. LC 99-40908. 304p. 1999. 24.00 (*0-465-03150-1*, Pub. by Basic) HarpC.

***Marlowe, Ann.** How to Stop Time: Heroin from A To Z. LC 00-38980. 304p. 2000. 13.00 (*0-385-72016-5*, Anchor NY) Doubleday.

Marlowe, Bruce A. & Page, Marilyn L. Creating & Sustaining the Constructivist Classroom. LC 97-33745. (Illus.). 200p. 1997. 55.95 (*0-8039-6587-7*); pap. 24.95 (*0-8039-6588-5*) Corwin Pr.

Marlowe, Christopher. The Complete Plays. (Orig.). 1999. pap. 9.95 (*0-460-87968-5*) Tuttle Pubng.

— The Complete Plays. Steanie, J. B., ed. Incl. Dido Queen of Carthage. 1969. Edward II. 1969. Massacre at Paris. 1969. Pts. 1 & 2. Tamburlaine. 1969. (English Library). 608p. (Orig.). 1969. Set pap. 14.95 (*0-14-043037-7*, Penguin Classics) Viking Penguin.

Marlowe, Christopher. The Complete Works of Christopher Marlowe: Translations - All Ovids Elegies, Lucans First Booke, Dido Queene of Carthage & Hero & Leander, Vol. I. Gill, Roma, ed. (Oxford English Texts Ser.). (Illus.). 330p. 1987. text 98.00 (*0-19-811878-3*) OUP.

Marlowe, Christopher. A Concordance to the Plays, Poems & Translations of Christopher Marlowe. Fehrenbach, Robert J. et al, eds. LC 81-67175. (Cornell Concordances Ser.). 1710p. 1982. text 110.00 (*0-8014-1420-2*) Cornell U Pr.

— Doctor Faustus. 208p. 1976. 21.95 (*0-8488-0765-0*) Amereon Ltd.

— Doctor Faustus. (Study Texts Ser.). 1984. pap. text 4.29 (*0-582-35390-4*, 72213) Longman.

— Doctor Faustus. 1969. mass mkt. 4.95 (*0-451-52477-2*, Sig Classics) NAL.

— Doctor Faustus. Jump, John D., ed. (Methuen English Classics Ser.). 176p. (C). 1985. pap. 14.99 (*0-415-03960-6*, NO.2311) Routledge.

— Doctor Faustus. 1969. 10.05 (*0-606-01550-7*, Pub. by Turtleback) Demco.

— Doctor Faustus. Steanie, J. B., ed. (English Library). 1969. write for info. (*0-318-55026-1*) Viking Penguin.

— Doctor Faustus. LC 73-133704. (Tudor Facsimile Texts. Old English Plays Ser.: No. 102). reprint ed. 59.50 (*0-404-53402-3*) AMS Pr.

— Doctor Faustus. unabridged ed. LC 94-7856. (Thrift Editions Ser.). 64p. 1994. pap. text 1.00 (*0-486-28208-2*) Dover.

— Doctor Faustus. 2nd ed. Keefer, Michael, ed. (Literary Texts Ser.). 304p. 2000. pap. 12.95 (*1-55111-210-8*) Broadview Pr.

— Doctor Faustus. 2nd ed. Gill, Roma, ed. (New Mermaids Ser.). (C). 1990. pap. text 11.25 (*0-393-90059-2*) Norton.

— Doctor Faustus, Vol. II. Gill, Roma, ed. (Oxford English Texts Ser.). (Illus.). 184p. 1990. text 80.00 (*0-19-812769-3*) OUP.

— Doctor Faustus: A 1604-Version Edition. Keefer, Michael, ed. 250p. 1991. 29.95 (*0-921149-56-5*); pap. 12.95 (*0-921149-59-X*) Broadview Pr.

***Marlowe, Christopher.** Doctor Faustus: Critical Studies. (Penguin Critical Studies). 106p. 2000. pap. 9.95 (*0-14-077186-7*, Pub. by Pnguin Bks Ltd) Trafalgar.

Marlowe, Christopher. Doctor Faustus: The A-Text. Ormerod, David A. & Wortham, Christopher, eds. 159p. (C). 1993. pap. 14.95 (*0-85564-232-7*, Pub. by Univ of West Aust Pr) Intl Spec Bk.

— Doctor Faustus & Other Plays. Bevington, David & Rasmussen, Eric, eds. (Oxford World's Classics Ser.). 538p. 1998. pap. 10.95 (*0-19-283445-2*) OUP.

— Doctor Faustus & Other Plays: Tamburlaine, Parts I & II; Doctor Faustus, A&B Texts. Bevington, David & Rasmussen, Eric, eds. LC 94-44595. (Oxford World's Classics Ser.). 538p. (C). 1995. text 58.00 (*0-19-812159-8*) OUP.

— Edward II. Forker, Charles, ed. (Revels Plays Ser.). 376p. 1995. text 26.95 (*0-7190-3089-7*, Pub. by Manchester Univ Pr) St Martin.

— Edward II. Landes, William-Alan, ed. LC 96-49197. 71p. 1997. pap. 7.00 (*0-88734-720-7*) Players Pr.

— Edward II. 96p. 1999. pap. 8.95 (*1-85459-410-9*, Pub. by Theatre Comm) Consort Bk Sales.

— Edward II. Charleton, H. B. & Waller, R. D., eds. LC 66-23027. (Works & Life of Christopher Marlowe Ser.: Vol. 6). 226p. 1966. reprint ed. 50.00 (*0-87752-191-3*) Gordian.

— Edward II, Vol. III. Rowland, Richard, ed. LC 94-9290. (English Texts Ser.). (Illus.). 188p. 1995. text 75.00 (*0-19-812278-0*, Clarendon Pr) OUP.

— The Famous Tragedy of the Rich Jew of Malta. LC 70-25427. (English Experience Ser.: No. 334). 76p. 1971. reprint ed. 20.00 (*90-221-0334-X*) Walter J Johnson.

— The Jew of Malta. Bawcutt, N. W., ed. LC 83-80370. (Revels Plays Ser.). 207p. 1988. text 19.95 (*0-7190-1618-5*, Pub. by Manchester Univ Pr) St Martin.

— The Jew of Malta. Landes, William-Alan, ed. & intro. by. LC 96-39956. (Classic Plays Ser.). 1997. pap. 7.00 (*0-88734-717-7*) Players Pr.

— Jew of Malta. 128p. 1997. pap. 6.00 (*1-85459-199-1*) Theatre Comm.

— The Jew of Malta. Bawcutt, N. W., ed. LC 77-17261. (Revels Plays Ser.). 223p. reprint ed. pap. 69.20 (*0-8357-4031-5*, 203672300005) Bks Demand.

— The Jew of Malta. Van Fossen, Richard W., ed. LC 63-14699. (Regents Renaissance Drama Ser.). xxx, 122p. 1991. reprint ed. pap. text 9.95 (*0-8032-5270-6*) U of Nebr Pr.

— The Jew of Malta Vol. IV. Gill, Roma, ed. (Oxford English Texts Ser.). (Illus.). 148p. 1995. text 75.00 (*0-19-812770-7*) OUP.

— The Jew of Malta Vol. IV. Bevington, David, ed. LC 96-38110. 1997. pap., student ed. 9.95 (*0-7190-5180-0*) St Martin.

— Marlowe's Poems. Martin, L. C., ed. LC 66-23027. (Works & Life of Christopher Marlowe Ser.: Vol. 4). 304p. 1966. reprint ed. 50.00 (*0-87752-193-X*) Gordian.

— The Massacre at Paris: With the Death of the Duke of Guise. LC 73-25759. (English Experience Ser.: No. 335). 1971. reprint ed. 15.00 (*90-221-0335-8*) Walter J Johnson.

— New Longman Literature: Doctor Faustus. 1995. pap. text. write for info. (*0-582-25409-4*, Pub. by Addison-Wesley) Longman.

— Tamburlaine the Great. Cunningham, J.S., ed. LC 98-18305. 150p. 1998. pap. 9.95 (*0-7190-5436-2*, Pub. by Manchester Univ Pr) St Martin.

— Tamburlaine the Great. Cunningham, J. S., ed. LC 81-47596. (Revels Plays Ser.). (Illus.). 352p. reprint ed. pap. 109.20 (*0-608-06035-6*, 206636600008) Bks Demand.

— Tamburlaine the Great, 2 pts. Ellis-Fermor, V. M., ed. LC 66-23027. (Works & Life of Christopher Marlowe Ser.: Vol. 2). 321p. 1966. reprint ed. 50.00 (*0-87752-192-1*) Gordian.

— Tamburlaine the Great, Pts. 1 & 2. Jump, John D., ed. LC 67-10666. (Regents Renaissance Drama Ser.). xxvi, 205p. (C). 1967. pap. text 7.95 (*0-8032-5271-4*) U of Nebr Pr.

— Tamburlaine the Great: Christopher Marlowe. (Revels Plays Ser.). 338p. 1999. pap. 19.95 (*0-7190-3096-X*) St Martin.

— Tamburlaine the Great: Parts 1 & 2; The Massacre at Paris, Vol. V. Fuller, David & Esche, Edward J., eds. (Oxford English Texts Ser.). (Illus.). 460p. 1998. text 135.00 (*0-19-818320-8*) OUP.

— The Tragical History of Doctor Faustus. Hope, ed. (Australian National University Press Ser.). 1982. text 35.00 (*0-08-032953-5*, Pergamon Pr) Elsevier.

— The Tragical History of Doctor Faustus. Kocher, Paul H., ed. (Crofts Classics). 96p. 1950. pap. text 4.95 (*0-88295-054-1*) Harlan Davidson.

— The Tragical History of Dr. Faustus. Landes, William-Alan, ed. LC 97-1018. 55p. 1997. pap. 7.00 (*0-88734-721-5*) Players Pr.

— The Tragical History of Doctor Faustus. Boas, Frederick S., ed. (Works & Life of Christopher Marlowe Ser.: Vol. 5). 221p. 1966. reprint ed. 50.00 (*0-87752-190-5*) Gordian.

***Marlowe, Christopher.** The Tragical History of Doctor Faustus. Boas, Frederick S., ed. (Works & Life of Christopher Marlowe Ser.: Vol. 5). 221p. 1999. reprint ed. pap. 12.50 (*0-87752-262-6*) Gordian.

Marlowe, Christopher. Works & Life of Christopher Marlowe, 6 Vols, Set. Case, R. H., ed. 1644p. 1966. reprint ed. 250.00 (*0-87752-067-4*) Gordian.

Marlowe, Christopher & Chapman, George. Hero & Leander. LC 77-172844. (Renaissance Library: No. 1). reprint ed. 27.50 (*0-404-07871-0*) AMS Pr.

Marlowe, Christopher & Nash, Thomas. Dido. LC 70-133703. (Tudor Facsimile Texts. Old English Plays Ser.: No. 72). reprint ed. 59.50 (*0-404-53372-8*) AMS Pr.

Marlowe, Christopher & Rudall, Nicholas. Doctor Faustus. LC 94-17515. (Plays for Performance Ser.). 69p. 1991. pap. 7.95 (*0-929587-56-1*, Pub. by I R Dee); lib. bdg. 15.95 (*0-929587-60-X*, Pub. by I R Dee) Natl Bk Netwk.

Marlowe, Christopher, jt. auth. see Jarman, Derek.

Marlowe, Christopher, jt. auth. see Ule, Louis.

Marlowe, Connie B., photos by. Greatest Mountain: Katahdin's Wilderness. rev. ed. LC 99-14277. (Illus.). 112p. 1999. 35.00 (*0-88448-212-X*) Tilbury Hse.

***Marlowe, David.** Healthcare Marketing Plans That Work. 115p. 1999. pap. 50.00 (*0-9676441-0-0*) Soc Healthcare Strategy.

Marlowe, David, jt. auth. see Crowne, Douglas P.

***Marlowe, David H.** Psychological & Psychosocial Consequences of Combat & Deployment with Special Emphasis on the Gulf War. 2000. pap. 15.00 (*0-8330-2685-2*) Rand Corp.

Marlowe, Derek. Nancy Astor. large type ed. LC 83-26339. 461 P. ;p. 1984. pap. write for info. (*0-89340-773-9*) Chivers N Amer.

— Nancy Astor, the Lady from Virginia: A Novel. LC 84-139731. viii, 246 p. 1982. 6.95 (*0-297-77866-8*) Weidenfeld & Nicolson.

Marlowe, Donald C., et al, eds. Modularity of Orthopedic Implants. LC 97-7308. (STP Ser.: No. 1301). (Illus.). 236p. 1997. text 63.00 (*0-8031-2415-5*, STP1301) ASTM.

Marlowe, Evan. Medico Mnemonica: A Collection of Fun, Fibald, Irreverent & Quite Witty Mnemonics for Medical Students. LC 96-49033. (Illus.). 186p. (Orig.). (C). 1997. pap. text 12.95 (*1-57066-056-5*, ME075) Practice Mgmt Info.

Marlowe, J. Truly Terrible Tales: Explorers. (J). 1997. mass mkt. 7.95 (*0-340-66721-4*, Pub. by Hodder & Stought Ltd) Trafalgar.

— Truly Terrible Tales: Inventors. (J). 1997. mass mkt. 7.95 (*0-340-66722-2*, Pub. by Hodder & Stought Ltd) Trafalgar.

— Truly Terrible Tales: Scientists. (J). 1997. mass mkt. 7.95 (*0-340-66723-0*, Pub. by Hodder & Stought Ltd) Trafalgar.

— Truly Terrible Tales: Writers. (J). 1997. mass mkt. 7.95 (*0-340-66724-9*, Pub. by Hodder & Stought Ltd) Trafalgar.

Marlowe, J. I., jt. auth. see Salomone, L. H.

Marlowe, Joelyn D. & Cummins, Suzanne. Evidence for Paralegals. 2nd ed. LC 98-40613. 1998. pap. text 39.95 (*0-7355-0207-2*) Panel Pubs.

Marlowe, John, jt. auth. see Ross, Victor J.

Marlowe, John, jt. auth. see Skapura, Robert.

Marlowe, Jos, jt. auth. see Stiller, Richard.

Marlowe, Katharine, pseud. Nightfall. 352p. 1994. mass mkt. 4.99 (*0-8125-2415-2*, Pub. by Tor Bks) St Martin.

***Marlowe, Katharine, pseud.** Nightfall. 234p. 1999. reprint ed. pap. 20.00 (*1-892738-28-7*) Isld Nation.

Marlowe, Kenard. Thinking Allowed. LC 94-14750. 1994. pap. 14.95 (*0-9625994-2-5*) Independent.

***Marlowe, Kendall.** The Gift. 51p. 1999. pap. 3.50 (*0-87129-955-0*, G69) Dramatic Pub.

Marlowe, Kevin. MCSD Training Guide: MS Access 97. LC 98-123566. 1997. 59.99 (*1-56205-771-5*) New Riders Pub.

— Using MS Access 97. 290p. 1997. 19.99 (*0-7897-1439-6*) Que.

Marlowe, Lynn, jt. auth. see Marlow, Herb.

Marlowe, Lynn G., et al. California State Capitol Restoration: A Pictorial History. 2nd ed. Worsley, John C. & Dwyer, Dale E., eds. (Orig.). 1988. pap. 5.50 (*0-318-41105-9*) Cal State Leg.

***Marlowe, Pete.** One Arabian Morning. (Illus.). 32p. (J). (gr. k-3). 2000. lib. bdg. 19.95 (*1-55037-659-4*, Pub. by Annick Pr); per. 6.95 (*1-55037-658-6*, Pub. by Annick Pr) Firefly Bks Ltd.

— The Trailer Park Princesses. (Illus.). 32p. (J). (gr. k-2). 2000. lib. bdg. 16.95 (*1-55037-617-9*, Pub. by Annick Pr); per. 6.95 (*1-55037-616-0*, Pub. by Annick Pr) Firefly Bks Ltd.

***Marlowe, Piers.** Hire Me a Hearse. large type ed. 336p. 1999. pap. 18.99 (*0-7089-5507-X*, Linford) Ulverscroft.

***Marlowe, Robert.** The Justice Makers. 334p. 1999. pap. 17.95 (*0-7414-0152-5*) Buy Books.

An Asterisk (*) at the beginning of an entry indicates that the title is appearing for the first time.

Marlowe, Sam. Learning about Dedication from the Life of Frederick Douglass. (Character Building Bk.: Set 2). (Illus.). 24p. (J). (gr. k-4). 1996. lib. bdg. 15.93 (*0-8239-2425-4*, PowerKids) Rosen Group.

Marlowe, Stephen. The Death & Life of Miguel de Cervantes. 512p. 1996. 25.45 (*1-55970-358-X*, Pub. by Arcade Pub Inc) Time Warner.

— The Death & Life of Miguel de Cervantes: A Novel. LC 96-27125. 512p. 1997. pap. 14.45 (*1-55970-403-9*, Pub. by Arcade Pub Inc) Time Warner.

Marlowe, Toby. Beyond a Reasonable Doubt. 352p. 1997. mass mkt. 5.99 (*0-7860-0429-0*, Pinncle Kensgtn) Kensgtn Pub Corp.

Marlowee, Eugene. Webvisions: An Inside Look at Successful Business Strategies on the Net. LC 96-41531. 273p. 1997. text 30.95 (*0-442-02453-3*, VNR) Wiley.

Marlyn, John. Under the Ribs of Death. 264p. 1996. pap. 8.95 (*0-7710-9866-9*) McCland & Stewart.

Marm, Ingvald & Sommerfelt, Alf. Teach Yourself Norwegian. (Teach Yourself Ser.). 1992. 19.95 (*0-8288-8376-9*) Fr & Eur.

— Teach Yourself Norwegian: A Complete Course for Beginners. (NOR.). 304p. 1995. pap. 15.95 (*0-8442-3814-7*, Teach Yrslf) NTC Contemp Pub Co.

Marmain, Jacques, jt. auth. see Belyakov, R. A.

Marmar, Charles R., jt. ed. see Bremner, J. Douglas.

Marmar, Earl S. & Terry, James L., eds. Atomic Processes in Plasma. LC 92-71474. (AIP Conference Proceedings Ser.: No. 257). (Illus.). 200p. (C). 1992. 90.00 (*0-88318-939-9*) Am Inst Physics.

Marmarelis, Vasilis Z., ed. Advanced Methods of Physiological System Modeling, Vol. 2. (Illus.). 310p. (C). 1989. text 85.00 (*0-306-43259-5*, Kluwer Plenum) Kluwer Academic.

— Advanced Methods of Physiological System Modeling, Vol. 3. (Illus.). 284p. (C). 1994. text 95.00 (*0-306-44819-X*, Kluwer Plenum) Kluwer Academic.

Marmarelis, Vasilis Z., intro. Advanced Methods of Physiological System Modeling, Vol. I. (Illus.). 344p. (C). 1987. reprint ed. text 35.00 (*0-941639-01-0*) USC Biomedical.

***Marmaridou, Sophia, ed.** Pragmatic Meaning & Cognition. LC 99-462345. (Pragmatics & Beyond New Ser.: No. 72). xii, 322p. 2000. pap. 24.95 (*1-55619-837-X*) J Benjamins Pubng Co.

***Marmaridou, Sophia S. A., ed.** Pragmatic Meaning & Cognition. LC 99-462345. (Pragmatics & Beyond New Ser.: No. 72). xii, 322p. 2000. 65.00 (*1-55619-919-8*) J Benjamins Pubng Co.

Marmarou, Anthony, et al, eds. Intracranial Pressure & Neuromonitoring in Brain Injury: Proceedings of the Tenth International ICP Symposium, Williamsburg, May 25-29, 1997. LC 98-16255. (Acta Neurochirurgica Supplement Ser.: Vol. 71). (Illus.). 400p. 1998. 199.00 (*3-211-83094-4*) Spr-Verlag.

Marmasse, Claude. Microscopes & Their Uses. xiv, 330p. 1980. text 101.00 (*0-677-05510-2*) Gordon & Breach.

Marmefelt, Thomas. Bank-Industry Networks & Economic Evolution: An Institutional-Evolutionary Approach. LC 98-71397. 154p. 1998. 55.95 (*1-84014-574-9*, Pub. by Ashgate Pub) Ashgate Pub Co.

***Marmel, Elaine.** Microsoft Project 2000 Bible. LC 99-88435. (Bible Ser.). 696p. 2000. pap. 39.99 (*0-7645-3319-3*) IDG Bks.

Marmel, Elaine. Office '97 Visual Learn. LC 97-66154. 432p. 1997. per. 16.99 (*0-7615-1162-8*) Prima Pub.

— 10 Minute Guide to cc: Mail 8. 1997. 14.99 (*0-7897-1311-X*) Que.

Marmel, Elaine, et al. Special Edition Using Ami Pro for Windows 3.11. (Illus.). 1100p. (Orig.). 1995. 34.99 (*0-7897-0363-7*) Que.

Marmel, Elaine, jt. auth. see Koers, Diane.

Marmel, Elaine, jt. auth. see Stevenson, Nancy.

Marmel, Elaine J. Ackerman/Clinicians Guide to Child Custody. 336p. 1994. 85.00 (*0-471-05252-3*) Wiley.

— Building Databases with Approach 3. 336p. 1994. pap. 24.95 (*0-471-05223-X*) Wiley.

— Easy Excel for Windows 95. (Illus.). 250p. (Orig.). 1995. 19.99 (*0-7897-0131-6*) Que.

— Easy Lotus Notes 4.5. 2nd ed. LC 96-70768. 240p. 1997. 24.99 (*0-7897-0946-5*) Que.

***Marmel, Elaine J.** Peachtree for Dummies. (For Dummies Ser.). (Illus.). 384p. 2000. pap. 19.99 (*0-7645-0640-4*) IDG Bks.

Marmel, Elaine J. Sams Teach Yourself Quicken Deluxe 99 in 24 Hours. LC 98-85314. (Teach Yourself Ser.). 1998. pap. 19.99 (*0-672-31358-8*) Sams.

— Windows 98 Fast & Easy. LC 97-69603. (Fast & Easy Ser.). 388p. 2000. pap. 16.99 (*0-7615-1006-0*) Prima Pub.

Marmeladov, Yuri. Dostoevsky's Secret Code: The Allegory of Elijah the Prophet. Macpherson, Jay, tr. from RUS. 125p. (C). 1987. 12.50 (*0-87291-171-3*) Coronado Pr.

Marmelstein, Robert. Programming Games in C. LC 94-22465. 89p. 1994. pap. 34.95 incl. disk (*1-55851-380-9*, M&T Bks) IDG Bks.

Marmini, Paola, jt. auth. see Totaro, Mariella.

Marmion, Daniel M. Handbook of U.S. Colorants: Foods, Drugs, Cosmetics, & Medical Devices. 3rd ed. LC 91-11048. 592p. 1991. 175.00 (*0-471-50074-7*) Wiley.

Marmion, Declan. Spirituality of Everyday Faith. (Louvain Theological & Pastoral Monographs). 1998. pap. text 30.00 (*0-8028-4489-8*) Eerdmans.

Marmion, Shakerley. Dramatic Works of Shakerley Marmion. Maidment, James & Logan, W. H., eds. LC 67-18423. 1972. reprint ed. 24.95 (*0-405-08760-8*, Pub. by Blom Pubns) Ayer.

Marmion, Simon. Book of Hours: Illuminations by Simon Marmion. 48p. 1990. pap. 5.95 (*0-87328-130-6*, 1306) Huntington Lib.

Marmo, Brent. Maestro in the Kitchen Vol. 1: Orchestrating Memorable Occassions. Jack, Bette & Beonar, R. Craig, eds. (Illus.). 240p. 1998. 29.95 (*0-9661034-0-8*) Wamso MN Orch.

Marmo, Costantino, jt. ed. see Eco, Umberto.

Marmo, Giuseppe, et al. Constraint Theory & Quantization Methods- from Relativistic Particles to Field Theory & General Relativity. 460p. 1994. text 99.00 (*981-02-1582-7*) World Scientific Pub.

***Marmol, Jose.** Amalia. Sommer, Dorris, ed. Lane, Helen, tr. (Library of Latin America). 688p. 2000. 35.00 (*0-19-512276-3*); pap. 19.95 (*0-19-512277-1*) OUP.

Marmol, Jose. Amalia. (SPA.). pap. 9.95 (*968-432-461-8*, Pub. by Porrua) Continental Bk.

— Amalia: A Romance of the Argentine. Serrano, Mary J., tr. 1977. lib. bdg. 250.00 (*0-8490-1410-7*) Gordon Pr.

— Antonio Maceo Grajales: El Titan de Bronce. LC 98-87309. (Coleccion Cuba y sus Jueces). (SPA., Illus.). 140p. (Orig.). 1998. pap. 13.00 (*0-89729-880-2*) Ediciones.

Marmolin, Hans, ed. Computer-Supported Cooperative Work: Proceedings of the Fourth European Conference on Computer-Supported Cooperative Work. 353p. (C). 1995. lib. bdg. 144.00 (*0-7923-3697-6*) Kluwer Academic.

Marmolya, Gary A. Gems of the Necklace: Images of the Cleveland Metropolitan Parks. (Illus.). 136p. 1993. 40.00 (*1-883538-00-9*) Photographs Elite.

Marmon, John, et al. Slavery in the Middle East. Marmon, Shaun, ed. LC 97-40143. 172p. (C). 1998. pap. text 16.95 (*1-55876-169-1*) Wiener Pubs Inc.

— Slavery in the Middle East. Marmon, Shaun E., ed. LC 97-40143. 172p. (C). 1998. text 39.95 (*1-55876-168-3*) Wiener Pubs Inc.

Marmon, Shaun. Eunuchs & Sacred Boundaries in Islamic Society. (Studies in Middle Eastern History). (Illus.). 176p. 1995. text 49.95 (*0-19-507101-8*) OUP.

Marmon, Shaun, ed. see Marmon, John, et al.

Marmon, Shaun E., ed. see Marmon, John, et al.

Marmor, Andrei, ed. Law & Interpretation. 474p. 1998. reprint ed. pap. text 39.95 (*0-19-826487-9*) OUP.

Marmor, Judd. Psychiatry in Transition. 2nd ed. 464p. (C). 1994. pap. 29.95 (*1-56000-736-2*) Transaction Pubs.

Marmor, Judd, ed. Modern Psychoanalysis: New Directions & Perspectives. LC 95-16725. 752p. 1995. pap. 44.95 (*1-56000-825-3*) Transaction Pubs.

Marmor, Leonard. Arthritis Surgery. LC 75-45362. 559p. reprint ed. pap. 173.30 (*0-8357-5770-6*, 205601800044) Bks Demand.

Marmor, Leonard, jt. auth. see Houts, Marshall.

Marmor, Michael F. & Ravin, James G. The Eye of the Artist. (Illus.). 256p. (C). (gr. 13). 1996. text 99.95 (*0-8151-7244-3*, 28827) Mosby Inc.

Marmor, Michael F. & Wolfensberger, Thomas J. The Retinal Pigment Epithelium. LC 97-18098. (Illus.). 776p. 1998. text 198.50 (*0-19-510956-2*) OUP.

Marmor, Michael F., jt. ed. see Zinn, Keith M.

Marmor, Theodore R. The Politics of Medicare. 2nd ed. LC 99-52364. (Social Institutions & Social Change Ser.). 228p. 2000. pap. text 16.95 (*0-202-30425-6*); lib. bdg. 35.95 (*0-202-30399-3*) Aldine de Gruyter.

— Social Security: Beyond the Rhetoric of Crisis. Mashaw, Jerry L., ed. LC 88-10238. (Studies from the Project on the Federal Social Role). (Illus.). 265p. reprint ed. pap. 82.20 (*0-608-06489-0*, 206678600009) Bks Demand.

Marmor, Theodore R. Understanding Health Care Reform. LC 94-15886. 288p. 1994. pap. 16.00 (*0-300-05879-9*) Yale U Pr.

Marmor, Theodore R. Understanding Health Care Reform. LC 94-15886. 288p. 1994. 42.50 (*0-300-05878-0*) Yale U Pr.

Marmor, Theodore R., et al, eds. Economic Security & Intergenerational Justice: A Look at North America. LC 94-7382. 376p. 1994. 80.50 (*0-87766-619-9*); pap. 39.00 (*0-87766-620-2*) Urban Inst.

Marmor, Theodore R. & Christianson, Jon B. Health Care Policy: A Political Economy Approach. LC 82-822. 232p. reprint ed. pap. 72.00 (*0-8357-4772-7*, 203770900009) Bks Demand.

Marmor, Theodore R. & De Jong, Philip R., eds. Ageing, Social Security & Affordability. LC 98-71457. (International Studies on Social Security). 394p. 1998. text 76.95 (*1-84014-817-9*, Pub. by Ashgate Pub) Ashgate Pub Co.

Marmor, Theodore R., jt. ed. see De Jong, Peter R.

Marmorstein, Armohom, tr. see Reinman, Jacob J.

Marmorstein, Arthur. Studies in Jewish Theology: The Arthur Marmorstein Memorial. Rabbinowitz, Joseph & Lew, Meyer S., eds. LC 76-39174. (Essay Index Reprint Ser.). 1977. reprint ed. 23.95 (*0-8369-2702-8*) Ayer.

Marmorstein, Gary. Hollywood Rhapsody: Movie, Music & Its Makers, 1900-1975. 2nd ed. LC 97-19891. 400p. 1997. 30.00 (*0-02-864595-2*) Macmillan.

Marmorstein, Jerome & Marmorstein, Nanette. Awakening from Depression: A Mind-Body Approach to Emotional Recovery. LC 91-27523. 160p. (Orig.). 1992. pap. 9.95 (*0-88007-190-7*) Woodbridge Pr.

Marmorstein, Malcolm. Will the Real Jesus Christ Please Stand Up? 1965. pap. 3.25 (*0-8222-1259-5*) Dramatists Play.

Marmorstein, Nanette, jt. auth. see Marmorstein, Jerome.

Marmot. Office Space Planning & Design. (Time-Saver Standards Ser.). 320p. 2000. 44.95 (*0-07-134199-4*) McGraw-Hill Prof.

Marmot, Michael & Wilkinson, Richard, eds. Social Deteremants of Health. LC 99-22942. (Illus.). 306p. 1999. pap. text 35.00 (*0-19-263069-5*) OUP.

Marmouget, C. Rosemary. Scripture Alive: Role-Plays for Youth. 120p. 1997. pap. 19.95 (*0-88489-491-6*) St Marys.

Marmur, Dow. The Star of Return: Judaism after the Holocaust, 29. LC 90-19911. (Contributions to the Study of Religion Ser.: No. 29). 176p. 1991. 55.00 (*0-313-27604-8*, MRJ/, Greenwood Pr) Greenwood.

Marmur, Mildred, tr. see Flaubert, Gustave.

Marmura, Michael. Studies in the Philosophy of Avicenna. 1999. pap. 17.00 (*1-883058-34-1*) Global Pubns.

Marmura, Michael E. Studies in Islamic Philosophy. 1999. pap. 17.00 (*1-883058-33-3*, Nur) Global Pubns.

Marmura, Michael E., ed. Islamic Theology & Philosophy: Studies in Honor of George F. Hourani. 340p. 1996. 64.50 (*0-614-21179-4*, 658); pap. 24.95 (*0-614-21178-6*, 658) Kazi Pubns.

— Islamic Theology & Philosophy: Studies in Honor of George F. Hourani. LC 83-408. 339p. (C). 1984. text 24.50 (*0-87395-746-6*) State U NY Pr.

Marmura, Michael E., tr. The Incoherence of the Philosophers. (Brigham Young University's Islamic Translations Ser.). 580p. 1998. 29.95 (*0-8425-2351-0*, Pub. by Brigham) U Ch Pr.

***Marmura, Michael E., tr.** The Incoherence of the Philosophers. 2nd rev. ed. LC 97-21195. (Islamic Translation Ser.). (ARA & ENG.). 257p. 2000. 29.95 (*0-8425-2466-5*) Brigham.

***Marne, Patricia.** Patricia Marne's Manual of Graphology. (Illus.). 2000. pap. 15.95 (*0-572-02463-0*) W Foulsham.

Marne, Patricia. Reveal the Secrets in Doodles: Learn to Analyse Your Doodles. 214p. 1995. pap. 8.95 (*0-572-01427-9*, Pub. by Foulsham UK) Assoc Pubs Grp.

Marneau. McSd Guide to Analyzing Requirements & Defining Solutions Architecture. (Programming Ser.). (C). 1999. text 43.25 (*0-7600-1178-8*) Course Tech.

Marnef, Guido. Antwerp in the Age of Reformation: Underground Protestantism in a Commercial Metropolis, 1550-1577. (Studies in Historical & Political Science, 112th Series (1994): Vol. 114, Series No. 1). (Illus.). 360p. 1996. text 48.50 (*0-8018-5169-6*) Johns Hopkins.

Marnelius, R., jt. auth. see Brink, L.

Marnelius, R., jt. auth. see Brink, Lars.

Marnell, Tim. Drug Identification Bible. 700p. (Orig.). 1997. pap. 34.95 (*0-9635626-2-2*) Amera-Chem.

— Drug Identification Bible. 2nd ed. LC 94-93967. (Illus.). 458p. (Orig.). 1995. pap. 29.95 (*0-9635626-0-6*) Amera-Chem.

— Drug Identification Bible. 4th rev. ed. (Illus.). 930p. (Orig.). 1999. pap. 34.95 (*0-9635626-3-0*) Amera-Chem.

Marnelli, Shelly, ed. see Hauser, Greg.

Marner, Phyllis. My Little Sticker Album. (Illus.). (J). 1991. pap. text 1.00 (*0-486-26624-9*) Dover.

Marneros, Andreas, et al, eds. Negative vs. Positive Schizophrenia. (Illus.). 464p. 1991. 134.00 (*0-387-54388-0*) Spr-Verlag.

Marneros, Andreas & Tsuang, Ming T., eds. Affective & Schizoaffective Disorders: Similarities & Differences. 304p. 1990. 107.95 (*0-387-52071-6*) Spr-Verlag.

Marnett, Lawrence J. Arachidonic Acid Metabolism & Tumor Initiation. (Prostaglandins, Leukotrienes, & Cancer Ser.). 1985. text 113.50 (*0-89838-729-9*) Kluwer Academic.

Marnett, Lawrence J., ed. Frontiers in Molecular Toxicology. LC 92-10062. (Illus.). 294p. 1992. pap. text 29.95 (*0-8412-2428-5*, Pub. by Am Chemical); student ed. 16.95 (*0-685-59402-5*) Am Chemical.

***Marnett, Lawrence J. & Nigam, S. K.** Eicosanoids & Other Bioactive Lipids in Cancer, Inflammation & Radiation Injury 4. LC 99-40840. (Advances in Experimental Medicine & Biology Ser.). 1999. write for info. (*0-306-46138-2*, Kluwer Plenum) Kluwer Academic.

***Marnette, Sophie.** Narrateur et Points de Vue dans la Litterature Francaise Medievale: Une Approache Linguistique. 262p. 1998. 37.95 (*3-906760-92-8*, Pub. by P Lang) P Lang Pubng.

***Marneweck, Johan, et al.** Basis Administration for SAP. (SAP R/3 Ser.). (Illus.). 579p. 1999. 69.99 (*0-7615-1887-8*, Prima Tech) Prima Pub.

Marney, Carlyle. The Carpenter's Son: But Who Do You Say That I Am? (Sermons) 96p. 1984. reprint ed. pap. 6.95 (*0-913029-02-5*) Stevens Bk Pr.

— The Crucible of Redemption: The Meaning of the Cross-Resurrection Event (Sermons) 64p. 1984. reprint ed. pap. 6.95 (*0-913029-04-1*) Stevens Bk Pr.

— Faith in Conflict. (Abingdon Classics Ser.). (Orig.). 1992. reprint ed. pap. 4.95 (*0-687-12646-0*) Abingdon.

Marney, Dean. The Christmas Tree That Ate My Mother. (J). 1992. 8.60 (*0-606-01795-X*, Pub. by Turtleback) Demco.

— Dirty Socks Don't Win Games. abr. ed. 96p. (J). (gr. 3-7). 1992. pap. 2.95 (*0-590-44880-3*, Apple Paperbacks) Scholastic Inc.

— Jack-O'-Lantern That Ate My Brother. 96p. (J). (gr. 4-7). 1994. pap. 2.95 (*0-590-47731-5*) Scholastic Inc.

Marney, Dean. The Jack-O'-Lantern That Ate My Brother. 1994. 8.05 (*0-606-06502-4*, Pub. by Turtleback) Demco.

Marney, Dean. Just Good Friends. LC 84-40765. (J). 1982. 11.95 (*0-201-15877-9*) HarpC Child Bks.

— Pet-rified! 128p. (J). (gr. 4-9). 1997. pap. 3.99 (*0-590-98830-1*) Scholastic Inc.

— Turkey That Ate My Father. 96p. (J). (gr. 3-7). 1995. pap. 2.99 (*0-590-47730-7*) Scholastic Inc.

Marney, Dean. Turkey That Ate My Father. (J). 1995. 8.09 (*0-606-08323-5*, Pub. by Turtleback) Demco.

Marney, Dean. The Valentine That Ate My Teacher. (J). 1998. pap. text 3.99 (*0-590-93943-2*, Apple Paperbacks) Scholastic Inc.

— The Valentine That Ate My Teacher. (J). 1998. 9.09 (*0-606-13062-4*, Pub. by Turtleback) Demco.

— You, Me, & Gracie Makes Three. (J). (gr. 6-8). 1989. pap. 2.50 (*0-590-41637-5*, Apple Paperbacks) Scholastic Inc.

Marney, John. Chinese by Bygones: Third Semester. (New Program of Chinese Language Study). 184p. Date not set. pap. text 29.95 incl. audio (*0-472-08467-4*, 08467) U of Mich Pr.

Marney, John. Chinese by Bygones: Third Semester. Marney, Steven, ed. (CHI.). 184p. (C). Date not set. audio 16.95 (*0-472-00265-1*, 00265) U of Mich Pr.

Marney, John. Chinese by Bygones: Third Semester. Marney, Steven, ed. (CHI.). 184p. (C). 1997. pap. text 19.95 (*0-472-08434-8*, 08434) U of Mich Pr.

— Chinese by Numbers: First Semester. (New Program of Chinese Language Study). 208p. Date not set. pap. text 29.95 incl. audio (*0-472-08466-6*, 08466) U of Mich Pr.

Marney, John. Chinese by Numbers: First Semester. Marney, Steven, ed. (CHI.). 208p. (C). Date not set. audio 16.95 (*0-472-00266-X*, 00266) U of Mich Pr.

Marney, John. Chinese by Numbers: First Semester. Marney, Steven, ed. (CHI.). 208p. (C). 1997. pap. text 19.95 (*0-472-08404-6*, 08404) U of Mich Pr.

— Chinese by the Book: Second Semester. (New Program of Chinese Language Study). 232p. Date not set. pap. text 29.95 incl. audio (*0-472-08464-X*, 08464) U of Mich Pr.

Marney, John. Chinese by the Book: Second Semester. Marney, Steven, ed. (CHI.). 232p. (C). Date not set. audio 16.95 (*0-472-00264-3*, 00264) U of Mich Pr.

Marney, John. Chinese by the Book: Second Semester. Marney, Steven, ed. LC 97-173148. (CHI.). 232p. (C). 1997. pap. text 19.95 (*0-472-08424-0*, 08424) U of Mich Pr.

Marney, John. Chinese to a T: Fourth Semester. (New Program of Chinese Language Study). 272p. Date not set. pap. text 29.95 incl. audio (*0-472-08468-2*, 08468) U of Mich Pr.

Marney, John. Chinese to a T: Fourth Semester. Marney, Steven, ed. (CHI.). 272p. (C). Date not set. audio 16.95 (*0-472-00268-6*, 00268) U of Mich Pr.

Marney, John. Chinese to a T: Fourth Semester. Marney, Steven, ed. (CHI.). 272p. (C). 1997. pap. text 19.95 (*0-472-08444-5*, 08444) U of Mich Pr.

Marney-Petix, V. C. LANs! LANs! LANs! 3rd expanded rev. ed. LC 98-20998. (Self-Paced Learning Ser.). (Illus.). 325p. (Orig.). 1998. pap. 45.95 (*1-880548-40-2*) Numidia Pr.

Marney-Petix, V. C. & Salins, Andrella. Gigabit Ethernet, ATM & Other High-Speed LANs. (Illus.). 150p. (Orig.). 1997. pap. 45.95 (*1-880548-20-8*) Numidia Pr.

Marney-Petix, Victoria C. Switches, Routers, & Gateways! Self-Paced Learning Series. 2nd rev. ed. LC 98-49881. (Illus.). 210p. 1998. pap. 39.95 (*1-880548-09-7*) Numidia Pr.

Marney, Steven, ed. see Marney, John.

Marnham, Patrick. Dreaming with His Eyes Open: The Life of Diego Rivera. LC 98-6145. (Illus.). 320p. 1998. 35.00 (*0-679-43042-3*) Knopf.

— The Man Who Wasn't Maigret. large type ed. (Illus.). 560p. 1993. 27.99 (*0-7089-8712-5*, Charnwood) Ulverscroft.

— The Man Who Wasn't Maigret: A Portrait of Georges Simenon. LC 92-16351. 1993. 25.00 (*0-374-20171-4*) FS&G.

Marni, Archimede. Allegory in French Heroic Poem of the 17th Century. LC 72-122994. (Studies in French Literature: No. 45). 1970. reprint ed. lib. bdg. 75.00 (*0-8383-1127-X*) M S G Haskell Hse.

Marnie, Eve. LoveStart: Pre-Birth Bonding. (SPA.). 142p. (Orig.). pap. 10.00 (*84-86344-88-3*, 139) Hay House.

Marnik, George F., jt. auth. see Donaldson, Gordon A., Jr.

Marnik, George F., jt. ed. see Donaldson, Gordon A., Jr.

Marnoch, Gordon. Doctors & Management in the National Health Service. LC 96-19931. (Health Services Management). 208p. 1996. 108.00 (*0-335-19345-5*); pap. 30.95 (*0-335-19344-7*) OpUniv Pr.

Marns, Frederick. The Sonnets of William Shakespeare. 168p. 25.00 (*0-85683-013-5*, Pub. by Shepheard-Walwyn Pubs) Paul & Co Pubs.

***Maro, Julia M.** Nursery Rhyme Time. (Eloquence Ser.: Vol. 2). (Illus.). 94p. 1999. pap. 19.95 (*0-9677129-0-4*) AAC Intervent.

Maro, Richard. Prisoner of Fear: My Long Road to Freedom from Anxiety Disease, Panic Attacks & Agoraphobia. 250p. (Orig.). 1990. pap. 12.95 (*0-9628509-0-X*) Hickory Grove Pr.

Marocco, James D. Hawaii's Great Awakening. 52p. (Orig.). 1991. pap. 5.95 (*1-881227-02-2*) Bartimaeus.

— You Can Be a Winner in the Invisible War: The Power of Binding & Loosing. 96p. (Orig.). 1992. pap. 5.95 (*1-881227-00-6*) Bartimaeus.

Marocco, James D. & Yonggi-Cho, Paul. Closing the Forbidden Door: An Expose of the Demonic. 160p. (Orig.). 1992. pap. 9.95 (*1-881227-01-4*) Bartimaeus.

Marochnik, Leonid S. The Milky Way Galaxy. 512p. 1995. text 160.00 (*2-88124-931-0*) Gordon & Breach.

Marochnik, Leonid S., et al. Astrophysics & Space Physics Reviews: The Distribution of Mass & Angular Momentum in the Solar System, Vol. 8. Syunyaev, R. A., ed. (Soviet Scientific Reviews Ser.: Vol. 8, Pt. 3). ii, 62p. 1989. pap. text 64.00 (*3-7186-4986-1*) Gordon & Breach.

Marockie & Henry. West Virginia School Laws: 1997 Edition. 776p. 1997. pap. text 30.00 (*1-55834-684-8*, 36498-12, MICHIE) LEXIS Pub.

Maroda, Karen J. Seduction, Surrender, & Transformation: Emotional Engagement in the Analytic Process. LC 98-50500. (Relational Perspectives Book Ser.: Vol. 13). 216p. 1999. 39.95 (*0-88163-225-2*) Analytic Pr.

Marohn, ed. The "Corrective Emotional Experience" Revisited. (Psychoanalytic Inquiry Ser.: Vol. 10, No. 3). 1994. 20.00 (*0-88163-953-2*) Analytic Pr.

Marohn, Richard C., ed. Adolescent Psychiatry Vol. 20: The Annals of the American Society for Adolescent Psychiatry. 552p. 1995. 49.95 (*0-88163-194-9*) Analytic Pr.

M

Marohn, Richard C., jt. ed. see Feinstein, Sherman C.

Marois, Carmen, jt. auth. see Duchesne, Christiane.

Marois, M., ed. From Theoretical Physics to Biology: Proceedings of the International Conference, 3rd, Versailles, 1971. 1973. 102.75 (*3-8055-1578-2*) S Karger.

Marois, M., ed. see International Conference on Man & Computer Staff.

Marois, Roger. Vocabulaire Francais-Anglais, Anglais-Francais D'archeologie Prehistorique: French - English, English - French Vocabulary of Prehistoric Archaeology. (ENG & FRE.). 116p. 1972. pap. 29.95 (*0-8288-6427-6*, M-6399) Fr & Eur.

Marokvia, Mireille. Immortelles: Memoir of a Will-O'-The-Wisp. LC 96-23011. (Illus.). 197p. 1996. 17.50 (*1-878448-72-2*) MacMurray & Beck.

Marold, Edith. Kenningkunst. viii, 232p. 1983. 100.80 (*3-11-007621-7*) De Gruyter.

Marold, Edith & Zimmermann, Christiane, eds. Nordwestgermanisch. (Ergaenzungsbaende zum Reallexikon der Germanischen Alterrumskunde: Bd. 13). (GER.). x, 299p. (C). 1995. 126.15 (*3-11-014818-8*) De Gruyter.

Marold, Jeffrey. The Complete Guide to Physician Capitation (CWC) Grambo, Michael, ed. 250p. (C). 1996. 399.00 (*1-56329-337-4*) St Anthony Pub.

Marold, Kathryn A., jt. auth. see Larsen.

Marold, Kathryn A., jt. auth. see Larsen, Gwynne.

Marolda, Carmela. Meet the Poet Juan Ramon Jimenez: A Guide for High School Spanish Teachers in the U. S. LC 95-78816. 77p. 1995. pap., teacher ed. 9.95 (*1-882573-07-2*) Serena Bay.

Marolda, Edward J. By Sea, Air, & Land: An Illustrated History of the U. S. Navy & the War in Southeast Asia. LC 91-33197. (Illus.). 410p. (Orig.). 1995. pap. text 43.00 (*0-945274-10-6*) Naval Hist Ctr.

— By Sea, Air, & Land: An Illustrated History of the U. S. Navy & the War in Southeast Asia. (Illus.). 416p. (Orig.). 1996. reprint ed. pap. text 60.00 (*0-7881-3250-4*) DIANE Pub.

Marolda, Edward J. By Sea, Air & Land: Illustrated History of the United States Navy & the War in Southeast Asia. (Illus.). 434p. 1994. per. 58.00 (*0-16-061331-0*) USGPO.

Marolda, Edward J. FDR & the U. S. Navy. LC 98-3749. (Franklin & Eleanor Roosevelt Institute Series on Diplomatic & Economic History). 176p. 1998. text 49.95 (*0-312-21157-0*) St Martin.

***Marolda, Edward J.** Shield & Sword (Cloth Edition) The United States Navy & the Persian Gulf War. LC 98-36937. 1p. 1999. boxed set 59.00 (*0-16-049476-1*) USGPO.

— The Washington Navy Yard: An Illustrated History LC 99-31616. 1999. write for info. (*0-945274-41-6*) Naval Hist Ctr.

— Washington Navy Yard: An Illustrated History. 126p. 1999. per. 17.00 (*0-16-050104-0*, Defense Dept) USGPO.

Marolda, Edward J., ed. Operation End Sweep: A History of Minesweeping Operations in North Vietnam. (Illus.). 129p. (C). 1998. pap. text 30.00 (*0-7881-4802-8*) DIANE Pub.

Marolda, Edward J. & Lesher, James, eds. A Bibliography of the U. S. Navy & the Conflict in Southeast Asia, 1950-1975. 2nd ed. 100p. (Orig.). (C). 1994. pap. text 35.00 (*0-7881-0268-0*) DIANE Pub.

Marolda, Edward J. & Schneller, Robert J. Shield & Sword: The United States Navy & the Persian Gulf War LC 98-36937. 1999. write for info. (*0-16-049878-3*) USGPO.

Marolda, Edward J., ed. see Tensor Industries, Inc. Staff.

Marolda, Maria. Alphabet Book. 1995. pap. 9.50 (*0-201-48007-7*) Addison-Wesley.

— Cuisenaire Alphabet Book. 64p. (J). (gr. k-4). 1980. pap. text 8.95 (*0-914040-78-2*) Cuisenaire.

— Exploring Attributes. 1997. pap. text 13.95 (*0-86651-672-7*) Seymour Pubns.

Marolf, Stacey & Pessano, Laurie. Founding Fathers... & Mothers: A Field Trip to 18th Century America. (Illus.). 128p. (J). (gr. 4-7). 1999. pap. 27.95 incl. audio (*1-892405-12-1*) Good Co Players.

Marolles, Chantal De, see De Marolles, Chantal.

Marolles, Michel De, see De Marolles, Michel.

Marolli, G. Dizionario Tecnico Italiano-Inglese, Inglese-Italiano. (ENG & ITA.). 2048p. 1978. 250.00 (*0-685-42439-1*, M-9197) Fr & Eur.

— Dizionario Tecnico Tedesco-Italiano e Italiano-Tedesco. (ITA.). 2038p. 1991. lib. bdg. 250.00 (*0-685-54279-3*) Fr & Eur.

— English - Italian, Italian - English Technical Dictionary: Dizonarion Tecnico Inglese-Italiano e Italiano-Inglese. 11th ed. (ENG & ITA.). 2216p. 1989. lib. bdg. 275.00 (*0-8288-3367-2*, M9197) Fr & Eur.

— German/Italian/German Technical Dictionary. 7th ed. (GER & ITA.). 2032p. 1994. 295.00 (*0-320-00565-8*) Fr & Eur.

— Italian-English - English-Italian Technical Dictionary. (ENG & ITA.). 1991. 234.00 (*0-7859-8945-5*) Fr & Eur.

— Technical Dictionary Italian-English - English-Italian. 13th ed. Orig. Title: Dizionario Tecnico. (ENG & ITA., Illus.). 1872p. 1996. 205.00 (*88-203-2233-1*, Pub. by Hoepli) IBD Ltd.

— Technical Dictionary, Italian-English/English-Italian. 13th ed. 1872p. 1996. 325.00 (*0-7859-9484-X*) Fr & Eur.

— Technical Dictionary, Italian-English/English-Italian CD-ROM version. 13th ed. 1996. cd-rom 295.00 (*0-7859-9483-1*) Fr & Eur.

Maroln Graphics Staff. Lotus. 1-2-3. Release 4 for Windows. 1994. 6.00 (*1-56884-686-X*) IDG Bks.

Marolt, Bobbi D. Coming Attractions. unabridged ed. LC 96-72553. 256p. (Orig.). 1997. pap. 11.99 (*1-883061-17-2*) Rising AZ.

Marom, E., jt. auth. see NATO Advanced Research Workshop on Unconventional Optical Elements for Information Storage Processing Staff.

***Marom, Emanuel, et al.** Unconventional Optical Elements for Information Storage. 312p. 2000. pap. 64.00 (*0-7923-6191-1*) Kluwer Academic.

Maromonte, Kevin R. Building the Invisible Quality(tm) Corporation: The Executive Guide to Transcending TQM. LC 95-45408. 232p. 1996. 62.95 (*1-56720-008-7*, Quorum Bks) Greenwood.

— Corporate Strategic Business Sourcing. LC 97-30228. 232p. 1998. 59.95 (*1-56720-114-8*, Quorum Bks) Greenwood.

Maron. Numerical Analysis. 3rd ed. (Mathematics Ser.). 1991. teacher ed. 23.25 (*0-534-12373-2*) Brooks-Cole.

Maron, Margaret. Baby Doll Games. 224p. 1995. mass mkt. 5.99 (*0-446-40418-7*, Pub. by Warner Bks) Little.

— Baby Doll Games. large type ed. (Mystery Ser.). 448p. 1992. 27.99 (*0-7089-2775-0*) Ulverscroft.

— Bloody Kin. 224p. 1995. mass mkt. 5.99 (*0-446-40416-0*, Pub. by Warner Bks) Little.

— Bootlegger's Daughter. 272p. 1993. mass mkt. 5.99 (*0-446-40323-7*, Pub. by Warner Bks) Little.

***Maron, Margaret.** Bootlegger's Daughter. large type ed. LC 99-55919. 476p. 2000. pap. 29.95 (*0-7862-2327-8*) Thorndike Pr.

— Bootlegger's Daughter. unabridged ed. 1994. audio 58.00 (*0-7887-0086-3*, 94326) Recorded Bks.

Maron, Margaret. Death in Blue Folders. large type ed. (Mystery Ser.). 400p. 1992. 27.99 (*0-7089-2665-7*) Ulverscroft.

— Death of a Butterfly. large type ed. 1991. 27.99 (*0-7089-2465-4*) Ulverscroft.

— Fugitive Colors. 256p. 1996. mass mkt. 5.99 (*0-446-40393-8*, Pub. by Warner Bks) Little.

— Home Fires. LC 98-6632. Vol. 6. 256p. 1998. 22.00 (*0-89296-655-6*, Pub. by Mysterious Pr) Little.

***Maron, Margaret.** Home Fires. 288p. 2000. mass mkt. 6.50 (*0-446-60810-6*) Warner Bks.

Maron, Margaret. Home Fires. large type ed. LC 98-35938. 354p. 1999. 30.00 (*0-7862-1620-4*, G K Hall Lrg Type) Mac Lib Ref.

— Killer Market. (Deborah Knott Mysteries Ser.). 286p. 1999. mass mkt. 6.50 (*0-446-60619-7*, Pub. by Warner Bks) Little.

— One Coffee With. 192p. 1995. mass mkt. 5.99 (*0-446-40415-2*, Pub. by Warner Bks) Little.

— One Coffee With. large type ed. 1991. 27.99 (*0-7089-2433-6*) Ulverscroft.

— The Right Jack. 224p. 1995. mass mkt. 5.99 (*0-446-40417-9*, Pub. by Warner Bks) Little.

— The Right Jack. large type ed. (Mystery Ser.). 480p. 1992. 27.99 (*0-7089-2730-0*) Ulverscroft.

— Shooting at Loons. 240p. 1994. 18.95 (*0-89296-447-2*) Mysterious Pr.

— Shooting at Loons. 256p. 1995. mass mkt. 5.99 (*0-446-40424-1*, Pub. by Warner Bks) Little.

— Shooting at Loons. large type ed. LC 94-29778. 1994. pap. 19.95 (*1-56895-083-7*) Wheeler Pub.

— Shoveling Smoke: Selected Mystery Stories. LC 97-204862. 248p. 1997. pap. 16.00 (*1-885941-15-3*) Crippen & Landru.

Maron, Margaret. Southern Discomfort. unabridged ed. 1994. audio 49.00 (*0-7887-0032-4*, 94231) Recorded Bks.

Maron, Margaret. Southern Discomfort: A Deborah Knott Mystery. 224p. 1994. mass mkt. 6.50 (*0-446-40080-7*, Pub. by Warner Bks) Little.

***Maron, Margaret.** Southern Discomfort: A Deborah Knott Mystery. large type ed. LC 99-57455. (Mystery Ser.). 358p. 2000. 29.95 (*0-7862-2330-8*) Thorndike Pr.

Maron, Margaret. Southern Discomfort: A Deborah Knott Mystery, Bk. II. 256p. 1993. 17.95 (*0-89296-446-4*) Mysterious Pr.

***Maron, Margaret.** Storm Track. large type ed. LC 00-26167. 352p. 2000. 29.95 (*0-7862-2465-7*) Thorndike Pr.

— Storm Track: A Deborah Knott Mystery. LC 99-51761. 272p. 2000. 22.95 (*0-89296-656-4*, Pub. by Mysterious Pr) Little.

Maron, Margaret. Up Jumps the Devil. 304p. 1997. mass mkt. 5.99 (*0-446-60406-2*, Pub. by Warner Bks) Little.

Maron, Margaret, et al. Margaret Maron Presents: Malice Domestic #8. 256p. 1999. mass mkt. 5.99 (*0-380-79407-1*, Avon Bks) Morrow Avon.

Maron, Margaret, ed. see La Civita, Michael J. L., et al.

Maron, Monika. Animal Triste. Goldstein, Brigitte M., tr. from GER. LC 99-39769. (European Women Writers Ser.). 136p. 2000. text 40.00 (*0-8032-3206-3*) U of Nebr Pr.

***Maron, Monika.** Animal Triste. Goldstein, Brigitte M., tr. from GER. LC 99-39769. (European Women Writers Ser.). 136p. 2000. pap. 15.00 (*0-8032-8255-9*, Bison Books) U of Nebr Pr.

Maron, Monika. The Defector. Marinelli, David N., tr. from GER. 150p. (Orig.). 1988. 16.95 (*0-930523-40-7*); pap. 8.95 (*0-930523-41-5*) Readers Intl.

— Flugasche. Roman. 14th ed. (GER.). 244p. 1996. pap. 15.25 (*3-596-23784-X*, Pub. by Fischer Tasch) Intl Bk Import.

— Silent Close No. 6. Marinelli, David N., tr. from GER. 192p. (C). 1993. 19.95 (*0-930523-93-8*); pap. 11.95 (*0-930523-94-6*) Readers Intl.

— Stille Zeile Sechs, Roman. (GER.). 224p. 1993. pap. 13.50 (*3-596-11804-2*, Pub. by Fischer Tasch) Intl Bk Import.

Marona, Sandra & Shapiro, Mark. ACT TestBuster. 250p. 2000. pap. 17.95 (*0-87891-141-3*) Res & Educ.

Maroncelli, Dorothy. Britain on Your Own: A Guide for Single Mature Travelers. LC 96-90538. (Illus.). 256p. (Orig.). 1997. pap. 12.95 (*0-9653652-5-5*) W Wind Bks.

Maronde, R. F., ed. Topics in Clinical Pharmacology & Therapeutics. (Illus.). 530p. 1986. 138.00 (*0-387-96196-8*) Spr-Verlag.

Marone, Chris J. & Blanpied, M. L., eds. Faulting, Friction & Earthquake Mechanics Pt. II. LC 94-26397. (PAGEOPH Topical Volumes Ser.). 516p. 1994. 42.50 (*0-8176-5099-7*) Birkhauser.

Marone, Gianni, ed. Chemical Mediators & Cellular Interactions in Clinical Immunology. (Journal: International Archives of Allergy & Applied Immunology: Vol. 99 Nos. 2-4). (Illus.). 348p. 1993. 314.00 (*3-8055-5723-X*) S Karger.

— Chemical Mediators & Cellular Interactions in Clinical Immunology. (International Archives of Allergy & Applied Immunology Ser.: Vol. 99, Nos. 2-4, 1992). (Illus.). 346p. 1993. reprint ed. 213.25 (*3-8055-5757-4*) S Karger.

— Human Basophils & Mast Cells, Set. (Chemical Immunology Ser.: Vols. 61 & 62). (Illus.). 470p. 1995. 419.25 (*3-8055-6129-6*) S Karger.

— Human Basophils & Mast Cells: Biological Aspects. (Chemical Immunology Ser.: Vol. 61). (Illus.). xiv, 242p. 1995. 228.00 (*3-8055-6127-X*) S Karger.

— Human Basophils & Mast Cells: Clinical Aspects. (Chemical Immunology Ser.: Vol. 62). (Illus.). x, 240p. 1995. 237.50 (*3-8055-6128-8*) S Karger.

***Marone, Gianni, ed.** Human Eosinophils: Biologic & Clinical Aspects. (Chemical Immunology Ser.: Vol. 76). (Illus.). xiv, 250p. 2000. 207.00 (*3-8055-6974-2*) S Karger.

Marone, Gianni, et al, eds. Asthma & Allergic Diseases: Physiology, Immunopharmacology & Treatment. (Illus.). 439p. 1998. boxed set 95.00 (*0-12-473340-9*) Acad Pr.

Marone, Gianni & Ricci, M., eds. Progress in Clinical Immunology. (Monographs in Allergy: Vol. 18). (Illus.). x, 314p. 1983. 142.75 (*3-8055-3697-6*) S Karger.

***Marone, Gianni, et al.** Mast Cells & Basophils. (Illus.). 450p. 2000. 99.95 (*0-12-473335-2*) Acad Pr.

***Marone, Nicky.** How to Father a Successful Daughter. 1999. pap. 12.95 (*0-449-45914-4*) Fawcett.

Marone, Nicky. How to Father a Successful Daughter. 336p. 1989. reprint ed. mass mkt. 5.99 (*0-449-21687-X*, Crest) Fawcett.

— How to Mother a Successful Daughter: A Practicall Guide to Empowering Girls from Birth to Eighteen. 288p. 1999. pap. 14.00 (*0-609-80276-3*) Harmony Bks.

Marone, Phillip J. Shoulder Injuries in Sports. LC 91-44364. (Illus.). 188p. reprint ed. pap. 58.30 (*0-608-07250-8*, 206747600009) Bks Demand.

Maroney, Tim. Book of Dzyan. 1998. pap. text 13.95 (*1-56882-114-X*) Chaosium.

Maroney, James. Music for Voice & Classical Guitar, 1945-1996: An Annotated Catalog. LC 97-19848. 152p. 1997. lib. bdg. 42.50 (*0-7864-0384-5*) McFarland & Co.

Maroney, John E., jt. auth. see Karnofsky, Brian.

Maroni. Ventilation & Indoor Air Quality in Hospitals: Proceedings of a NATO Advanced Research Workshop, Held in Milano, Italy, on 13-16 September 1995. LC 96-17215. (NATO ASI Series: Partnership Sub-Series 2: Environment). 341p. 1996. text 195.00 (*0-7923-4076-0*) Kluwer Academic.

Maroni, Bradley J., ed. Protein Metabolism in Renal Diseases. (Mineral & Electrolyte Metabolism Ser.: Vol. 24, No. 1, 1998). (Illus.). 102p. 1997. pap. 52.25 (*3-8055-6573-9*) S Karger.

Maroni, Bradley J., jt. auth. see Goodship, Timothy H. J.

Maroni, Gustavo. An Atlas of Drosophila Genes: Sequences & Molecular Features. LC 92-35001. (Illus.). 432p. 1993. text 75.00 (*0-19-507116-6*) OUP.

***Maroni, Gustavo.** Molecular & Genetic Analysis of Human Traits. LC 00-23792. (Illus.). 320p. 2000. pap. 55.95 (*0-632-04369-5*) Blackwell Sci.

***Maroni, Joe.** The Drum Cadence Book for High School Marching Bands. 20p. 1999. pap. 4.95 (*0-7866-3391-3*, 97040) Mel Bay.

Maroni, Joe. Fifty Elementary Duets Snare Dr. 52p. 1992. pap. 5.95 (*1-56222-225-2*, 94628) Mel Bay.

— Fundamental Principles of Drumming. (Building Excellence Ser.). 88p. 1980. spiral bd. 9.95 (*1-56222-057-8*, 94492) Mel Bay.

— Fundamentals of Rhythm for the Drummer. (Building Excellence Ser.). 100p. 1980. spiral bd. 9.95 (*1-56222-058-6*, 94493) Mel Bay.

Maroni, Lisa, tr. see Crocetti, Enzo & Giordano, Mario.

Maroni, Lisa, tr. see Crocetti, Enzo & Giordano, Mario.

Maroni, Marco, et al, eds. Indoor Air Quality: A Comprehensive Reference Book. LC 95-37744. (Air Quality Monographs: Vol. 3). 1100p. 1995. 373.00 (*0-444-81642-9*) Elsevier.

Maroni, Marco, ed. see International Workshop Indoor Air-an Integrated Ap.

Maroni, V. A., et al, eds. Synthesis/Characterization & Novel Applications of Molecular Sieve Materials Vol. 233: Materials Research Society Symposium Proceedings. 303p. 1991. text 30.00 (*1-55899-127-1*) Materials Res.

Maronski, J. & Rupinska, M. Computer Networks Terminology. 73p. 1980. pap. 7.50 (*83-01-01179-3*, M-9061) Fr & Eur.

Maroon, Fred J. Century Ended, Century Begun: The Catholic University of America. LC 90-36773. (Illus.). 144p. 1990. 29.95 (*0-8132-0735-5*) Cath U Pr.

— Jean Louis: Cooking with the Seasons. LC 88-51106. 222p. 1997. 60.00 (*0-934738-49-1*) Lickle Pubng.

— Nixon Years, 1969-1974: White House to Watergate. LC 99-35265. 192p. 1999. 29.95 (*0-7892-0610-2*) Abbeville Pr.

— The United States Capitol. LC 92-35906. (Illus.). 192p. 1993. 45.00 (*1-55670-316-3*); pap. 24.95 (*1-55670-319-8*) Stewart Tabori & Chang.

— White House to Watergate: The Nixon Years, 1970-1974. (Illus.). 192p. 1999. 35.00 (*0-8050-6166-5*, Pub. by H Holt & Co); pap. 22.95 (*0-8050-6165-7*, Pub. by H Holt & Co) VHPS.

Maroon, Fred J., photos by. The Supreme Court of the United States. (Illus.). 176p. 1996. pap. 24.95 (*1-56566-097-8*) Thomasson-Grant.

Maroon, Fred J., photos by. Maroon on Georgetown. 2nd abr. rev. ed. LC 97-17174. (Illus.). 160p. 1997. 50.00 (*1-890674-01-X*) Lickle Pubng.

Maroon, Fred J. & Maroon, Suzy. The Supreme Court of the United States. LC 95-31708. (Illus.). 192p. 1996. 45.00 (*0-9650308-0-6*) Lickle Pubng.

— The Supreme Court of the United States. LC 95-31708. (Illus.). 192p. 1997. pap. 24.95 (*0-9650308-1-4*) Lickle Pubng.

Maroon, Fred J., jt. auth. see Beach, Edward L.

Maroon, Istifan. Becoming a Professional Social Worker. (Hildesheimer Schriftenreihe Zur Sozialpadagogik und Sozialarbeit Ser.: Bd. 10). (GER.). viii, 138p. 1997. write for info. (*3-487-10486-5*) G Olms Pubs.

Maroon, Suzy, jt. auth. see Maroon, Fred J.

Maroone, Al. . . . Just Thought You Auto Know. Winters, Kate, ed. (Illus.). 200p. 1999. write for info. (*1-888069-12-0*) Biography For Everyone.

Marooney, Kimberly. Angel Blessings: Cards of Sacred Guidance & Inspiration. 2nd ed. 147p. Date not set. pap. 4.95 (*0-9615079-8-5*) Merrill-West Pub.

Marosi, E., jt. auth. see Torok, J.

Marosi, Esteban A., jt. auth. see Edwards, Gene.

Maroske, Sara, jt. auth. see Home, R. W.

Marosy, John P. A Manager's Guide to Elder Care & Work. LC 98-6022. 224p. 1998. 55.00 (*1-56720-229-2*, Quorum Bks) Greenwood.

Maroszek, Gina. Buddy Learns about Forgiveness. (Illus.). 24p. (J). (gr. k-3). 1996. pap. 2.95 (*0-9648843-1-3*) GiNancy Pubng.

— Buddy Learns about Teasing. 24p. (J). (gr. k-3). 1995. pap. 2.95 (*0-9648843-0-5*) GiNancy Pubng.

Maroszek, Gina M. Buddy Learns about Fair Play. (Illus.). 24p. (J). (gr. k-3). 1997. pap. 2.95 (*0-9648843-2-1*) GiNancy Pubng.

Marot, Helen. American Labor Unions. LC 70-89754. (American Labor, from Conspiracy to Collective Bargaining Ser., No. 1). 1974. reprint ed. 19.95 (*0-405-02141-0*) Ayer.

— Creative Impulse in Industry: A Proposition for Educators. Stein, Leon, ed. LC 77-70514. 1977. reprint ed. lib. bdg. 19.95 (*0-405-10183-X*) Ayer.

Marot, M., jt. auth. see Rohonyi, K.

Maroti, Peter, et al. Biophysics Problems: A Textbook with Answers. LC 99-176929. 496p. 1998. pap. 75.00 (*963-05-7526-4*) Intl Spec Bk.

Maroto, Angel R., ed. see Ballesteros, Antonio M.

***Maroto, Esteban.** Urania. (Illus.). 64p. 1999. pap. 11.95 (*1-56163-248-1*) NBM.

Marotske, Michelle & Yoakum, Kimberly H. Color Creations Coloring Book: Impressionism, Cubism, Modernism. (Illus.). 60p. (J). (gr. 1-6). 1998. write for info. (*1-893397-00-9*) Painted In.

Marotske, Michelle R. & Yoakum, Kimberly H. Cubism. (Illus.). 20p. (J). (gr. 1-6). 1998. pap. write for info. (*1-893397-02-5*) Painted In.

— Impressionism. (Illus.). 20p. (J). (gr. 1-6). 1998. mass mkt. write for info. (*1-893397-01-7*) Painted In.

— Modernism. (Illus.). 20p. (J). (gr. 1-6). 1998. pap. write for info. (*1-893397-03-3*) Painted In.

Marotta, Kenny. A House in the Piazza. (Prose Ser.: No. 36). 203p. 1995. pap. 18.00 (*1-55071-032-X*) Guernica Editions.

Marotta, P., jt. ed. see Taddei-Ferretti, C.

***Marotta, Priscilla.** Power & Wisdom: The New Path for Women, Millennium Edition. 2nd ed. 256p. 1999. pap. 17.95 (*0-9666339-1-1*, Pub. by Women Wisdom) BookWorld.

Marotta, Robert E., photos by. The Digital Dictionary: A Guide to Digital Equipment Corporation's Technical Terminology. 2nd ed. (Illus.). 659p. 1985. pap. text 39.95 (*0-932376-82-7*, EY-3433E-DP, Digital DEC) Buttrwrth-Heinemann.

Marotta, Sylvia A. & Jennings, Leilani. Gathering Together: A Guidebook for Forming & Developing Associations. 45p. (Orig.). 1996. pap. 9.00 (*1-55833-167-0*) Natl Cath Educ.

Marotta, Terry. I Thought He Was a Speed Bump: And Other Excuses from Life in the Fast Lane. LC 93-35856. 176p. 1994. pap. 9.95 (*0-9638603-0-5*) Ravenscroft.

— The Mountains I Raise: A Garnering in Prose & Verse. LC 96-45289. 115p. 1997. pap. 12.00 (*0-9638603-1-3*) Ravenscroft.

Marotta, Theodore W., jt. auth. see Herubin, Charles A.

***Marotti, Arthur F.** Catholicism & Anti-Catholicism in Early Modern English Texts. LC 98-45552. (Early Modern Literature in History Ser.). 222p. 1999. text 55.00 (*0-312-21871-0*) St Martin.

Marotti, Arthur F. Critical Essays on John Donne. (Critical Essays on British Literature Ser.). 1994. 48.00 (*0-8161-8769-X*, Twyne) Mac Lib Ref.

— Manuscript, Print, & the English Renaissance Lyric. 336p. 1995. text 49.95 (*0-8014-2291-4*); pap. text 21.95 (*0-8014-8238-0*) Cornell U Pr.

Marotti, Arthur F., et al, eds. Reading with a Difference: Gender, Race, & Cultural Identity: A Criticism Book. LC 93-28532. 400p. 1993. pap. 17.95 (*0-8143-2493-2*) Wayne St U Pr.

***Marotti, Arthur F. & Bristol, Michael D., eds.** Print, Manuscript & Performance: The Changing Relations of Media in Early Modern England. LC 99-47596. 320p. (C). 2000. pap. text 24.95 (*0-8142-5049-1*) Ohio St U Pr.

An Asterisk (*) at the beginning of an entry indicates that the title is appearing for the first time.

— Print, Manuscript & Performance: The Changing Relations of the Media in Early Modern England. LC 99-47596. 320p. (C). 2000. text 65.00 (*0-8142-0845-2*) Ohio St U Pr.

Marotti, Arthur F., jt. auth. see Brown, Cedric C.

Marotti, Giorgio. Black Characters in the Brazilian Novel. Marotti, Maria O. & Lawton, Harry, trs. from ITA. (Afro-American Culture & Society Monographs: Vol. 6).Tr. of Il/negro nel romanzo brasiliano. (Illus.). 448p. 1987. 50.95 (*0-934934-24-X*); pap. 19.95 (*0-934934-25-8*) CAAS Pubns.

Marotti, Maria O. The Duplicating Imagination: Twain & the Twain Papers. LC 88-19560. 1990. lib. bdg. 35.00 (*0-271-00650-1*) Pa St U Pr.

Marotti, Maria O., ed. Italian Women Writers from the Renaissance to the Present: Revising the Canon. LC 95-14888. 296p. 1996. 47.50 (*0-271-01505-5*); pap. 19.95 (*0-271-01506-3*) Pa St U Pr.

Marotti, Maria O., tr. see Marotti, Giorgio.

***Marotti, Maria Ornella & Brooke, Gabriella, eds.** Gendering Italian Fiction: Feminist Revisions of Italian History. LC 98-29649. 256p. 1999. 42.50 (*0-8386-3771-X*) Fairleigh Dickinson.

Marotz-Baden, Ramona, et al, eds. Families in Rural America: Stress, Adaptation & Revitalization. 297p. (C). 1988. pap. text 16.00 (*0-916174-21-2*) Natl Coun Family.

Marotz, Lynn R. & Hill, Edna. Health, Safety & Nutrition for the Young Child. 4th ed. LC 96-28773. (Early Childhood Education Ser.). 528p. 1997. pap. 42.95 (*0-8273-7273-6*) Delmar.

Marotz, Lynn R., et al. Health, Safety & Nutrition. 4th ed. LC 96-28773. 608p. (C). 1996. text, mass mkt. 61.95 incl. disk (*0-8273-8353-3*) Delmar.

***Marotz, Lynn R., et al.** Health, Safety & Nutrition for Young Children. 5th ed. (C). 2000. text 47.95 (*0-7668-0946-3*) Delmar.

Marotz, Lynn R., et al. Instructor's Guide for Health, Safety & Nutrition for the Young Child. 3rd ed. 85p. 1993. teacher ed. 14.95 (*0-8273-4933-5*) Delmar.

— Study Guide for Health, Safety & Nutrition for the Young Child. 3rd ed. 169p. 1993. student ed. 14.95 (*0-8273-6060-6*) Delmar.

Marotz, Lynn R., jt. auth. see Allen, K. Eileen.

Marotz, Lynn R., jt. auth. see Cross, Marie Z.

Maroudas, A. & Kuettner, K., eds. Methods in Cartilage Research. 392p. 1990. text 188.00 (*0-12-473280-1*) Acad Pr.

Maroulleti, Lucy. Ar Ri Andhe: Priestess of Cyprogheneia (Aphrodite) (Illus.). 200p. (Orig.). 1996. pap. 13.95 (*1-888447-00-1*) Vsns Two-Thousand.

— Days of Wrath. 2nd ed. (GRE., Illus.). 52p. 1999. reprint ed. pap. 9.95 (*1-888447-08-7*) Vsns Two-Thousand.

— The Diner. (GRE.). 72p. 1999. pap. 11.95 (*1-888447-06-0*) Vsns Two-Thousand.

— Eros Invincible. 2nd rev. ed. (GRE & ENG.). 44p. 1998. pap. 10.00 (*1-888447-03-6*) Vsns Two-Thousand.

— Folk Poetry of Cyprus: 900AD to 1900AD. (Illus.). 300p. 1999. 30.00 (*1-888447-10-9*) Vsns Two-Thousand.

— Of Being Expendable. (Illus.). 120p. 1999. pap. 11.95 (*1-888447-05-2*) Vsns Two-Thousand.

— Paeans & Laments. 2nd ed. (ENG & GRE., Illus.). 48p. (Orig.). 1996. reprint ed. pap. 6.50 (*1-888447-01-X*) Vsns Two-Thousand.

— The Year Being 1990. 3rd ed. (GRE & ENG., Illus.). 76p. 1999. pap. 11.00 (*1-888447-09-5*) Vsns Two-Thousand.

Maroulleti, Lucy, ed. An Anthology of Cypriot Poetry. 150p. 1999. pap. 15.95 (*1-888447-07-9*) Vsns Two-Thousand.

Maroun, F. B. Diastematomyelia. LC 75-17393. (Illus.). 144p. 1976. 12.50 (*0-87527-143-X*) Green.

Maroun, Jack. Decision Making in Business. 3rd rev. ed. LC 90-19566. 176p. (C). 1991. pap. text. write for info. (*0-935732-28-4*) Roxbury Pub Co.

Marousek, Theresa, et al. Laparoscopy & You. (Illus.). 40p. 1994. pap. 3.60 (*0-317-39849-X*) Budlong.

Marousis, Jim, et al. Road School. (Illus.). 256p. 1995. pap. 14.95 (*0-933025-36-X*) Blue Bird Pub.

Marov, Mikhail I. Nonequilibrium Processes in the Planetary & Cometary Atmospheres: Theory & Applications. LC 97-26117. (Astrophysics & Space Science Library). 1997. text 146.00 (*0-7923-4686-6*) Kluwer Academic.

Marov, Mikhail Y. & Grinspoon, David H. The Planet Venus. Owen, Tobias et al, trs. LC 98-10158. (Planetary Exploration Ser.). (Illus.). 464p. 1998. 65.00 (*0-300-04975-7*) Yale U Pr.

Marovic, D. Play the King's Indian Defense. (Chess Ser.). (Illus.). 242p. 1983. 29.95 (*0-08-029727-7*, Pergamon Pr) Elsevier.

— Play the Queen's Gambit. (PECH Pergamon Chess Ser.). 200p. 1991. write for info. (*0-08-029765-X*, 6201, Pub. by CHES); pap. 29.95 (*0-08-029764-1*, 6201, Pub. by CHES) Macmillan.

Marovic, Drazen. An Active Repertoire for Black. 184p. 1995. pap. 16.95 (*0-8050-2320-8*, Pub. by Batsford Chess) H Holt & Co.

***Marovic, Drazen.** Understanding Pawn Play in Chess. 2000. pap. 21.95 (*1-901983-31-5*, Pub. by Gambit) BHB Intl.

Marovitz, Sanford E. Abraham Cahan. LC 96-27133. 1996. 32.00 (*0-8057-3993-9*) Macmillan.

Marovitz, Sanford E., jt. ed. see DeMott, Robert J.

Marovitz, Sanford E., jt. ed. see Gohdes, Clarence.

Marowitz, Charles. Alarums & Excursions: Our Theatres in the '90s. (Applause Critics Circle Ser.). 364p. 1996. pap. 19.95 (*1-55783-261-7*) Applause Theatre Bk Pubs.

— Artaud at Rodez. 1999. pap. 12.95 (*0-7145-3051-4*) M Boyars Pubs.

— Clever Dick. 1989. pap. 5.25 (*0-8222-0216-6*) Dramatists Play.

— Directing the Action: Acting & Directing in Contemporary Theatre. (Acting Ser.). 224p. 1991. pap. 12.95 (*1-55783-072-X*) Applause Theatre Bk Pubs.

— Disciples. 71p. 1987. pap. 5.25 (*0-8222-0313-8*) Dramatists Play.

— The Marowitz Shakespeare: Adaptations & Collages of Hamlet, Macbeth, the Taming of the Shrew, Measure for Measure & The Merchant of Venice. 288p. 1990. pap. 15.00 (*0-7145-2651-7*) M Boyars Pubs.

— Marowitz Shakespeare: Caesar, The Tempest, Timon, Vol. 2. 1999. pap. text 16.95 (*0-7145-3052-2*) M Boyars Pubs.

— The Other Way: An Alternative Approach to Acting & Directing. LC 97-23967. (Illus.). 241p. 1999. 24.95 (*1-55783-303-6*) Applause Theatre Bk Pubs.

— Prospero's Staff: Acting & Directing in the Contemporary Theatre. LC 85-45887. (Indiana Studies in Theatre & Drama). 213p. 1986. pap. 66.10 (*0-608-05032-6*, 205969300004) Bks Demand.

— Recycling Shakespeare. (Illus.). 256p. 1991. pap. 14.95 (*1-55783-094-0*) Applause Theatre Bk Pubs.

— Recycling Shakespeare. (Illus.). 256p. 1991. 32.95 (*1-55783-093-2*) Applause Theatre Bk Pubs.

— Sherlock's Last Case. 1984. pap. 5.25 (*0-8222-1021-5*) Dramatists Play.

— Stage Fright. 1999. pap. 5.25 (*0-8222-1702-3*) Dramatists Play.

— Wilde West. 1988. pap. 5.25 (*0-8222-1256-0*) Dramatists Play.

***Marowitz, Charles, tr.** Boulevard Comedies: Free Adaptions of Becque, Feydeau & Moliere. LC 99-52455. 136p. 1999. pap. 19.95 (*1-57525-210-4*) Smith & Kraus.

Marowitz, Charles, tr. see Ionesco, Eugene.

Marowitz, Charles, tr. see Rostand, Edmond.

***Marowitz, David Z.** Introducing Camus. (Illus.). 176p. 1998. pap. 10.95 (*1-84046-000-8*, Pub. by Totem Bks) Natl Bk Netwk.

Marowski. Classical & Medieval Literature Criticism, Vol. 25. 500p. 1998. 140.00 (*0-7876-2404-7*, GML00198-111928) Visible Ink Pr.

***Marowski.** Poetry for Students, Vol. 4. 350p. 1998. text 60.00 (*0-7876-2725-9*, GML00298-112252) Gale.

Marowski, Daniel G. & Gunton, Sharon R., eds. Contemporary Literary Criticism, Vol. 35. LC 76-38938. 691p. 1985. text 150.00 (*0-8103-4409-2*) Gale.

— Contemporary Literary Criticism, Vol. 36. LC 76-38938. 700p. 1986. text 150.00 (*0-8103-4410-6*) Gale.

— Contemporary Literary Criticism, Vol. 37. LC 76-38938. 600p. 1986. text 150.00 (*0-8103-4411-4*) Gale.

— Contemporary Literary Criticism, Vol. 38. LC 76-38938. 600p. 1986. text 150.00 (*0-8103-4412-2*) Gale.

— Contemporary Literary Criticism, Vol. 39. LC 76-38938. 700p. 1986. text 150.00 (*0-8103-4413-0*) Gale.

— Contemporary Literary Criticism, Vol. 40. LC 76-38938. 600p. 1986. text 150.00 (*0-8103-4414-9*) Gale.

Marowski, Daniel G. & Matuz, Roger. Contemporary Literary Criticism, Vol. 49. 500p. 1988. text 150.00 (*0-8103-4423-8*) Gale.

Marowski, Daniel G. & Matuz, Roger, eds. Contemporary Literary Criticism, Vol. 46. LC 76-38938. 650p. 1987. text 150.00 (*0-8103-4420-3*) Gale.

— Contemporary Literary Criticism, Vol. 41. 500p. 1986. text 150.00 (*0-8103-4415-7*) Gale.

— Contemporary Literary Criticism, Vol. 42. 779p. 1987. text 150.00 (*0-8103-4416-5*) Gale.

— Contemporary Literary Criticism, Vol. 43. 795p. 1987. text 150.00 (*0-8103-4417-3*) Gale.

— Contemporary Literary Criticism, Vol. 44. 626p. 1987. text 150.00 (*0-8103-4418-1*) Gale.

— Contemporary Literary Criticism, Vol. 47. LC 76-38938. 650p. 1988. text 150.00 (*0-8103-4421-1*) Gale.

— Contemporary Literary Criticism, Vol. 50. 600p. 1988. text 150.00 (*0-8103-4424-6*) Gale.

— Contemporary Literary Criticism, Vol. 51. 600p. 1988. text 150.00 (*0-8103-4425-4*) Gale.

— Contemporary Literary Criticism, Vol. 52. 500p. 1989. text 150.00 (*0-8103-5430-6*) Gale.

— Contemporary Literary Criticism, Vol. 53. 500p. 1989. text 150.00 (*0-8103-4427-0*) Gale.

— Contemporary Literary Criticism, Vol. 54. 500p. 1989. text 150.00 (*0-8103-4428-9*) Gale.

— Contemporary Literary Criticism, Vol. 48, Vol. 48. (Contemporary Literary Criticism Ser.). 600p. 1988. text 150.00 (*0-8103-4422-X*) Gale.

Marowski, Daniel G. & Stine, Jean, eds. Contemporary Literary Criticism, Vol. 33. 680p. 1985. text 150.00 (*0-8103-4407-6*) Gale.

Marowski, Daniel G., ed. see Matuz, Roger.

Marowsky, G. & Smirnov, V. V., eds. Coherent Raman Spectroscopy: Recent Advances. (Proceedings in Physics Ser.: Vol. 63). (Illus.). 320p. 1992. 88.95 (*0-387-54993-5*) Spr-Verlag.

Marpet, Mark & Russakoff, Andrew. Visual Basic 5.0 for Windows. LC 97-40519. 1999. write for info. (*0-02-803063-X*); write for info. (*0-02-803064-8*); write for info. (*0-02-803083-4*); write for info. (*0-02-803084-2*) Macmillan.

Marple, Bradley F., jt. auth. see Roland, Peter S.

Marple, Carol, jt. auth. see Marple, Leland.

Marple, Elliot. Man-at-a-Typewriter Journalism: Fifty Years Reporting Pacific Northwest Business. LC 99-93056. (Illus.). 176p. (Orig.). 1999. pap. 12.95 (*0-9670261-0-5*) E Marple.

Marple, Elliot & Olson, Bruce H. National Bank of Commerce of Seattle, 1889-1969: Territorial to Worldwide Banking in Eighty Years, Including the Story of the Marine Bancorporation. LC 72-134228. (Illus.). x, 277p. 1972. 24.95 (*0-87015-189-4*) Pacific Bks.

Marple, Lawrence S., Jr. Digital Special Analysis with Applications in C, FORTRAN & Matlab. (C). 2000. text. write for info. (*0-13-015140-8*) P-H.

Marple, Leland & Marple, Carol. R. S. Prussia: The Art Nouveau Years. 176p. 1998. pap. 29.95 (*0-7643-0508-5*) Schiffer.

— R. S. Prussia: The Early Years. LC 97-184361. (Schiffer Book for Collectors Ser.). (Illus.). 192p. 1997. pap. 29.95 (*0-7643-0268-X*) Schiffer.

Marple, Vivian. I Mention the Garden for Clarity. LC 96-129437. 96p. 1995. pap. 14.95 (*1-55082-142-3*, Pub. by Quarry Pr) LPC InBook.

***Marples, David.** Linin's Revolution Ressia, 1917-1921. 144p. 1999. pap. 11.95 (*0-582-31917-X*) Addison-Wesley.

***Marples, David R.** Belarus: A Denationalized Nation. 130p. 1999. text 33.00 (*90-5702-342-3*, Harwood Acad Pubs); pap. text 19.95 (*90-5702-343-1*, Harwood Acad Pubs) Gordon & Breach.

Marples, David R. Belarus: From Soviet Rule to Nuclear Catastrophe. 208p. 1996. text 49.95 (*0-312-16181-6*) St Martin.

— Necessary Evil: Atomic Energy. (C). 1996. text 49.95 (*0-8133-8858-9*) Westview.

— Stalinism in Ukraine in the 1940s. LC 92-2295. 1992. text 65.00 (*0-312-08401-3*) St Martin.

— Ukraine under Perestroika: Ecology, Economics & the Workers' Revolt. LC 91-8110. 255p. 1991. pap. 16.95 (*0-312-06197-8*) St Martin.

Marples, David R., ed. Nuclear Energy & Security in the Former Soviet Union. LC 97-14352. (C). 1997. pap. 69.00 (*0-8133-9013-3*, Pub. by Westview) HarpC.

Marples, Richard. Aims of Education. 1999. 85.00 (*0-415-15739-0*) Routledge.

Marpurg, Friedrich W. Anfangsgruende der Theoretischen Musik. fac. ed. (Monuments of Music & Music Literature in Facsimile, II Ser.: Vol. 33). (Illus.). 1966. lib. bdg. 40.00 (*0-8450-2233-4*) Broude.

— Anleitung zum Clavierspielen. fac. ed. (Monuments of Music & Music Literature in Facsimile, II Ser.: Vol. 110). (Illus.). 1969. lib. bdg. 40.00 (*0-8450-2310-1*) Broude.

Marquand, C. & Croft, D. Thermofluids: An Integrated Approach to Thermodynamics & Fluid Mechanics Principles. 418p. 1994. pap. 80.00 (*0-471-94184-0*) Wiley.

Marquand, Christina S., jt. auth. see Sedgwick, Sarah C.

Marquand, David. The New Reckoning: Capitalism, States & Citizens. LC 97-39516. 272p. (C). 1998. pap. 26.95 (*0-7456-1745-X*, Pub. by Polity Pr) Blackwell Pubs.

— The New Reckoning: Capitalism, States & Citizens. LC 97-39516. 272p. (C). 1998. 57.95 (*0-7456-1744-1*, Pub. by Polity Pr) Blackwell Pubs.

— The Unprincipled Society: New Demands & Old Politics. LC 88-141389. 292 p. 1988. write for info. (*0-224-01929-5*) Jonathan Cape.

Marquand, David, jt. ed. see Crouch, Colin.

Marquand, Ed. Beyond Soap, Water & a Comb: A Man's Guide to Good Grooming & Fitness. LC 98-12419. (Illus.). 156p. 1999. bds. 14.95 (*0-7892-0445-2*) Abbeville Pr.

— How to Prepare Roughs, Comps & Mockups. LC 84-71518. 96p. 1985. 12.50 (*0-88108-014-4*); pap. 8.95 (*0-88108-019-5*) Art Dir.

— How to Prepare Your Portfolio. rev. ed. Weiler, Marie, ed. LC 81-66881. (Illus.). 128p. 1994. text 14.50 (*0-88108-144-2*); pap. text 10.95 (*0-88108-143-4*) Art Dir.

— How to Prepare Your Portfolio: A Guide for Students & Professionals. (Illus.). 138p. 1981. 12.50 (*0-910158-69-X*); pap. 10.95 (*0-910158-70-3*) Art Dir.

— Smoothies & Juices. LC 97-39200. (Illus.). 84p. 1998. 12.95 (*0-7892-0350-2*) Abbeville Pr.

Marquand, Ed, jt. auth. see Kotz, Susanne.

Marquand, H. A. The Dynamics of Industrial Combination. LC 79-38262. (Evolution of Capitalism Ser.). 218p. 1972. reprint ed. 17.95 (*0-405-04143-8*) Ayer.

Marquand, John P. The Black Cargo. LC 74-26118. (Labor Movement in Fiction & Non-Fiction Ser.). reprint ed. 39.50 (*0-404-58453-5*) AMS Pr.

— H. M. Pulham, Esq. 432p. 1986. reprint ed. pap. 11.00 (*0-89733-231-8*) Academy Chi Pubs.

— Haven's End. LC 77-130064. (Short Story Index Reprint Ser.). 1977. 23.95 (*0-8369-3663-9*) Ayer.

— Last Laugh, Mr. Moto. 192p. Date not set. 20.95 (*0-8488-2363-X*) Amereon Ltd.

— The Late George Aplay. 358p. Date not set. 25.95 (*0-8488-2361-3*) Amereon Ltd.

— The Late George Apley. 1994. lib. bdg. 24.95 (*1-56849-446-7*) Buccaneer Bks.

— The Late George Apley: A Novel in the Form of a Memoir. (YA). (gr. 7 up). 1937. 18.95 (*0-685-03075-X*) Little.

— Mr. Moto Is So Sorry. 1976. 17.95 (*0-89387-016-1*) Amereon Ltd.

— No Hero. reprint ed. lib. bdg. 23.95 (*0-88411-141-5*) Amereon Ltd.

— Point of No Return. 559p. 1985. pap. 12.00 (*0-89733-174-5*) Academy Chi Pubs.

— Right You Are, Mr. Moto. 256p. Date not set. 22.95 (*0-8488-2362-1*) Amereon Ltd.

— Thank You, Mr. Moto. reprint ed. lib. bdg. 23.95 (*0-88411-142-3*) Amereon Ltd.

— Think Fast, Mr. Moto. 150p. 18.95 (*0-8488-2670-1*) Amereon Ltd.

— Wickford Point. 1990. 16.50 (*0-8446-2666-X*) Peter Smith.

— Your Turn, Mr. Moto. 128p. 17.95 (*0-8488-2669-8*) Amereon Ltd.

Marquand, Josephine. Life: Its Nature, Origins & Distribution. (Contemporary Science Library). (Illus.). (C). 1971. reprint ed. pap. 2.00 (*0-393-00589-5*) Norton.

***Marquand, Martine.** Animal Passions. 2000. mass mkt. 6.95 (*0-352-33499-1*) BLA4.

Marquand, Martine. Black Lace: A Feast for the Senses. 1999. mass mkt. 6.95 (*0-352-33310-3*) London Brdge.

— Unhallowed Rites. 1998. mass mkt. 5.95 (*0-352-33222-0*, Pub. by BLA4) London Brdge.

***Marquand, Peter Blondel.** Introduction to Medical Law. 144p. 2000. pap. 40.00 (*0-7506-4239-4*) Buttrwrth-Heinemann.

Marquard, E. A. Luftwaffe Methods in the Selection of Offensive Weapons: Karlsruhe Study, Vol. 2. (USAF Historical Studies: No. 187). 182p. 1955. reprint ed. pap. text 32.95 (*0-89126-150-8*) MA-AH Pub.

Marquard, Jan. Health & Society: A Collection of Articles 131. 1998. text 14.50 (*1-56870-326-0*) RonJon Pub.

— Women & Health 231: A Collection of Articles. 1998. text 16.09 (*1-56870-325-2*) RonJon Pub.

Marquard, Odo. Defense of the Accidental: Philosophical Studies. Wallace, Robert M., tr. 144p. 1991. pap. text 24.95 (*0-19-507252-9*) OUP.

— Farewell to Matters of Principle: Philosophical Studies. Wallace, Robert, tr. (Odeon Ser.). 160p. 1989. text 50.00 (*0-19-505114-9*) OUP.

Marquard, Philip. Called to Build a More Fraternal & Evangelical World: Commentary on the Rule of the Secular Franciscan Order. LC 97-6548. (SFO Resource Library). Date not set. pap. write for info. (*0-8199-0991-2*) Franciscan Pr.

***Marquard, Philip.** Called to Live the Dynamic Power of the Gospel: Commentary on the Rule of the Secular Franciscan Order. (SFO Resource Library: No. III). 103p. 1998. pap. 13.95 (*0-8199-0977-7*) Franciscan Pr.

Marquard, Steven. The Distortion Theory of Macro-Economic Forecasting: A Guide for Economists & Investors. LC 93-42761. 224p. 1994. 67.95 (*0-89930-910-0*, Quorum Bks) Greenwood.

***Marquardt.** Parasitology. 2nd ed. 672p. 1999. 74.95 (*0-12-473275-5*) Acad Pr.

Marquardt, Arthur H. The New Americans. LC 94-71586. 650p. (Orig.). (YA). (gr. 9-12). 1994. pap. 39.95 (*0-940121-19-0*, P212, Cross Roads Bks) Cross Cultural Pubns.

Authored by a Fulbright scholar who studied both Russian & American youth, this book researched the ways young Americans look at current issues like the economy, religious values & racial or ethnic tensions. This work allows high school students from all over the United States to speak for themselves. Clearly written by a long time high school teacher, this is an unusual look into the minds & hearts of our young people. *Publisher Paid Annotation.*

Marquardt, Barbara S. How to Paint from Start to Finish: Tips & Techniques for Practicing Painters. 57p. (Orig.). 1991. student ed. 11.95 (*0-9629638-0-1*) Artmarq.

Marquardt-Cherry, Janet. Objects of Personal Significance. Conrads, David & M. McHenry, Deni, eds. (Illus.). 56p. (Orig.). 1996. pap. 20.00 (*1-882603-03-6*) Mid Am Arts.

Marquardt, Dorothy A. A Guide to the Supreme Court. LC 76-47338. (Illus.). 1977. 7.95 (*0-672-52168-7*, Bobbs) Macmillan.

Marquardt, Dorothy. A., jt. ed. see Ward, Martha E.

Marquardt, Eric P. Designing Omnibus Stock Plans: An Approach to Awarding Incentives. (Building Blocks Ser.: Vol. 36). (Illus.). 24p. 1996. pap. 24.95 (*1-57963-039-1*, A0236) Am Compensation.

Marquardt, Frederic S. Before Bataan & After. LC 73-161770. reprint ed. 41.50 (*0-404-09033-8*) AMS Pr.

***Marquardt, H.** Reflexotherapy of the Feet. (Illus.). 232p. 2000. 49.00 (*0-86577-931-7*) Thieme Med Pubs.

Marquardt, H. Michael. The Joseph Smith Revelations: Text & Commentary. LC 98-46500. (Illus.). 437p. 1999. text 44.95 (*1-56085-126-0*) Signature Bks.

Marquardt, H. Michael & Walters, Wesley P. Inventing Mormonism: Tradition & the Historical Record. LC 93-13603. (Illus.). 286p. 1994. 28.95 (*1-56085-039-6*, Smith Res) Signature Bks.

— Inventing Mormonism: Traditional & the Historical Record. (Illus.). 286p. 1998. pap. 19.95 (*1-56085-108-2*, Smith Res) Signature Bks.

Marquardt, Hanne. Reflex Zone Therapy of the Feet. 160p. (Orig.). 1984. pap. 14.95 (*0-89281-234-6*) Inner Tradit.

***Marquardt, Hans, et al, eds.** Toxicology. LC 98-89314. (Illus.). 1040p. 1999. 159.95 (*0-12-473270-4*) Acad Pr.

Marquardt, James F., Sr., jt. auth. see Gilligan, Lawrence G.

Marquardt, James F., Sr., jt. auth. see Sullivan, James F.

Marquardt, Joachim. Romische Staatsverwaltung, 3 vols. LC 75-7329. (Roman History Ser.). 1975. reprint ed. 121.95 (*0-405-07101-9*) Ayer.

— Romische Staatsverwaltung, 3 vols., Vol. 1. LC 75-7329. (Roman History Ser.). 1972. reprint ed. 32.95 (*0-405-08997-X*) Ayer.

— Romische Staatsverwaltung, 3 vols., Vol. 2. LC 75-7329. (Roman History Ser.). 1975. reprint ed. 40.95 (*0-405-07103-5*) Ayer.

— Romische Staatsverwaltung, 3 vols., Vol. 3. LC 75-7329. (Roman History Ser.). 1975. reprint ed. 40.95 (*0-405-07104-3*) Ayer.

Marquardt, Karl H. Eighteenth-Century Rigs & Rigging. (Illus.). (C). 1992. 56.95 (*1-881093-00-X*) Phoen Pubns.

Marquardt, Karl-Heinz. HMS Beagle, 1820-1870. (Illus.). 1998. 42.95 (*0-85177-703-1*) Brasseys.

Marquardt, Kathleen. Animalscam: The Beastly Abuse of Human Rights. LC 93-24500. 221p. 1993. 24.00 (*0-89526-498-6*) Regnery Pub.

Marquardt, Klaus. Eight Centuries of European Cultlery: An Art Collection. 1997. 95.00 (3-925369-66-X, Pub. by Arnoldsche Art Pubs) Antique Collect.

Marquardt, Linda A., jt. ed. see Heltne, Paul G.

Marquardt, M., jt. auth. see Himmelweit, F.

Marquardt, Manfred. John Wesley's Social Ethics: Praxis & Principles. Gunter, W. Stephen & Steely, John E., trs. 224p. 1992. pap. 19.95 (0-687-20494-1) Abingdon.

Marquardt, Marsha. Colorful Ghost. 16p. (J). (gr. 1). 1989. pap. text 3.00 (1-882225-05-8) Tott Pubns.

— Little Ghost Goes to School. (Illus.). 12p. (Orig.). (J). (gr. 1). 1993. pap. text. write for info. (1-882225-12-0) Tott Pubns.

— Little Ghost's Baby Brother. (Illus.). 12p. (Orig.). (J). (gr. 1). 1994. pap. text. write for info. (1-882225-17-1) Tott Pubns.

— Little Ghost's Vacation. 8p. (J). (gr. 1). 1990. pap. text 2.50 (1-882225-01-5) Tott Pubns.

— Rotten Reggie. 12p. (J). (gr. 1). 1990. pap. text 3.00 (1-882225-00-7) Tott Pubns.

— Tommy Snake. 8p. (J). (gr. 1). 1989. pap. text 3.00 (1-882225-02-3) Tott Pubns.

Marquardt, Max. Wilbur, Orville & the Flying Machine. (Real Readers Ser.: Level Green). (Illus.). 32p. (J). (ps-3). 1989. lib. bdg. 21.40 (0-8172-3530-2) Raintree Steck-V.

— Working Dogs. (Real Reading Ser.). (Illus.). 32p. (J). (ps-3). 1989. pap. 4.95 (0-8114-6711-2) Raintree Steck-V.

Marquardt, Michael. Global Advantage. LC 98-29545. (Improving Human Performance Ser.). 352p. 1999. 39.95 (0-88415-358-4, 5358) Gulf Pub.

***Marquardt, Michael J.** Action Learning in Action: Transforming Problems & People for World-Class Organizational Learning. LC 98-51048. 280p. 1999. 38.95 (0-89106-124-X, 7810, Pub. by Consulting Psychol) Natl Bk Netwk.

Marquardt, Michael J. Building the Learning Organization. (Illus.). 242p. 1995. 27.95 (0-07-040534-4) McGraw.

— Technology-Based Learning: Maximizing Human Performance & Corporate Success. LC 98-23195. 336p. 1998. boxed set 34.95 (1-57444-214-7, SL2147) St Lucie Pr.

***Marquardt, Michael J. & Berger, Nancy O.** Global Leaders for the Twenty-First Century. LC 99-88562. (C). 2000. text 57.50 (0-7914-4661-1) State U NY Pr.

— Global Leaders for the Twenty-First Century. LC 99-88562. 2000. pap. 18.95 (0-7914-4662-X) State U NY Pr.

Marquardt, Michael J. & Engel, Dean W. Global Human Resource Development. LC 92-17719. (Human Resource Development Ser.). 288p. 1992. pap. text 33.00 (0-13-357930-1) P-H.

Marquardt, Michael J., jt. auth. see Schwandt, David R.

Marquardt, Patricia, jt. auth. see Vairavan, Alamelu.

Marquardt, R., jt. ed. see Lemp, M. A.

Marquardt, R. R. & Han, Z. Enzymes in Poultry & Swine Nutrition. 1997. pap. 24.95 (0-88936-821-X, Pub. by IDRC Bks) Stylus Pub VA.

Marquardt, Ronald G., jt. auth. see Karnes, Frances A.

Marquardt, Stacy, ed. see Hart, Anne.

Marquardt, Thomas P., jt. auth. see Peterson, Harold A.

Marquardt, Virginia H., ed. Art & Journals on the Political Front, 1910-1940. LC 97-10342. (Illus.). 336p. 1997. 49.95 (0-8130-1535-9) U Press Fla.

— Survivor from a Dead Age: The Memoirs of Louis Lozowick. (Illus.). 320p. 1997. 36.95 (1-56098-696-4) Smithsonian.

Marquardt, Virginia H., jt. ed. see Roman, Gail H.

Marquardt, William C., jt. ed. see Beaty, Barry J.

***Marquardt, William H., ed.** The Archaeology of Useppa Island. LC 99-41488. (Institute of Archaeology & Paleoenvironmental Studies: No. 3). (Illus.). 265p. 1999. 35.00 (1-881448-07-X); pap. 20.00 (1-881448-08-8) IAPS Bks.

Marquardt, William H., ed. Culture & Environment in the Domain of the Calusa. (Institute of Archaeology & Paleoenvironmental Studies, Monograph: No. 1). 448p. (C). 1992. pap. 25.00 (1-881448-00-2) IAPS Bks.

— Regional Centers in Archaeology: Prospects & Problems. LC 77-82743. (Research Ser.: No. 14). (Illus.). 40p. 1977. pap. 4.00 (0-943414-15-6) MO Arch Soc.

Marquart, Debra. Everything's a Verb. LC 94-67065. (Minnesota Voices Project Ser.: Vol. 70). 80p. 1995. pap. 5.00 (0-89823-162-0) New Rivers Pr.

***Marquart, Debra.** The Hunger Bone: Rock 'n' Roll Stories. (Headwaters Ser.: Vol. 2). 176p. 2000. pap. 14.95 (0-89823-209-0, Pub. by New Rivers Pr) Consort Bk Sales.

***Marquart, James W. & Sorensen, Jonathan R.** Correctional Contexts: Contemporary & Classical Readings. 2nd ed. 500p. 2001. pap. text. write for info. (1-891487-53-1) Roxbury Pub Co.

Marquart, James W. & Sorensen, Jonathan R., eds. Correctional Contexts: Contemporary & Classical Readings. LC 96-19580. 495p. (C). 1997. pap. text. write for info. (0-935732-79-9) Roxbury Pub Co.

Marquart, James W., et al. The Rope, the Chair & the Needle: Capital Punishment in Texas, 1923-1990. (Illus.). 295p. 1998. reprint ed. pap. 12.95 (0-292-75213-X, MARROP) U of Tex Pr.

Marquart, James W., jt. auth. see Crouch, Ben M.

Marquart, Jan. Echoes from the Womb: A Book for Daughters. 190p. 1996. pap. 14.95 (0-9675780-0-0) J Marquart.

Marquart, Josh & Oliveira, Tony. The Sidekick Sourcebook: Advanced & Optional Rules for Blood of Heroes. (Illus.). 184p. 1999. pap. 20.00 (0-9665280-1-8) Pulsar Games.

Marquart, Judith L. Fearless Living. 192p. (Orig.). pap. 9.95 (0-935236-48-1) Genl Med Pub.

Marquart, Kurt E. The Church & Her Fellowship, Ministry, & Governance. Preus, Robert et al, eds. LC 89-84112. (Confessional Lutheran Dogmatics Ser.: Vol. 9). 280p. 1990. 14.50 (0-9622791-9-6) Luther Acad.

Marquart, Kurt E., et al, eds. A Lively Legacy: Essays in Honor of Robert Preus. 224p. (Orig.). 1985. 13.95 (0-9615927-0-2); pap. 11.95 (0-9615927-1-0) Concordia Theo Sem.

Marquerlot, Jean P. & Willems, Michele, eds. Travel & Drama in Shakespeare's Time. 271p. (C). 1996. text 64.95 (0-521-47500-7) Cambridge U Pr.

Marques, A. Scientific Corroborations of Theosophy: H. P. Blavatsky's Secret Doctrine Vindicated (1900) 4th rev. ed. 53p. 1998. reprint ed. pap. 4.00 (0-913510-74-2) Wizards.

Marques, Cavalcante J. English-Portuguese Dictionary of Economic & Commercial Terms: Dicionario Ingles-Portugues de Termos Economicos e Comerciais. (ENG & POR.). 408p. 1982. pap. 49.95 (0-8288-0119-3, M14431) Fr & Eur.

Marques, Eva. 100 Jobs for Kids & Young Adults Vol. 1: A Self-Empowerment Tool. LC 97-90664. (Illus.). 224p. (Orig.). (YA). (gr. 7-12). 1997. pap. 13.95 (0-9658934-0-5, 100-44) WiseChild Pr.

Marques, Lori. Child Safety Mady Easy: Revised ed., 1. 1998. pap. 6.95 (0-9652770-2-X) Screamin Mimi.

***Marques, Lori.** Children's Games Made Easy. (Illus.). (J). 2000. pap. 6.95 (0-9652770-3-8) Screamin Mimi.

Marques, Lori. La Segieridad del Nino Hecha mas Facil. 2nd ed. 1998. pap. text 6.95 (0-9652770-1-1) Screamin Mimi.

Marques, Lori, jt. auth. see Carter, Lisa.

Marques, Luis D. Introduccion a los Estudios Literarios. (SPA.). 300p. (C). 1997. pap. text 15.95 (1-56328-123-6) Edit Plaza Mayor.

Marques, Manual D. Trends in Applications of Mathematics to Mechanics. 1995. lib. bdg. 130.00 (0-582-24874-4, Pub. by Addison-Wesley) Longman.

Marques, Manuel D. Monteiro, see Monteiro Marques, Manuel D.

Marques, Nina M. Diccionari Escolar Catala-Castella, Castella-Catala. 4th ed. (CAT.). 500p. 1991. pap. 27.95 (0-7859-5842-8, 8427304609) Fr & Eur.

Marques, Rene. Mariana O el Alba. (SPA.). 243p. 1968. 7.50 (0-8288-7059-4, S5041) Fr & Eur.

***Marques, Sarah.** La Lengua Que Heredamos: Curso de Espanol para Bilinques. 4th ed. LC 99-33528.Tr. of Spanish for Bilinguals. 464p. 1999. pap. 64.95 (0-471-29746-1) Wiley.

Marques, Villanueva F. Lope de Vega's Vida & Valores. LC 87-25561. 369p. 1988. pap. 20.00 (0-8477-3522-2) U of PR Pr.

Marquess, Harlan E., jt. ed. see Galler, Meyer.

Marquess, Lawrence W. The NLRB & the Appropriate Bargaining Unit. 3rd ed. (Labor Relations & Public Policy Ser.: Vol. 3). 150p. 1998. 35.00 (1-891496-05-0) J M Olin.

Marquess of Anglesey. A History of the British Cavalry Vol. 2: 1851-1871, Vol. 2. (Illus.). 519p. 1989. reprint ed. 75.00 (0-85052-174-2, Pub. by Leo Cooper) Trans-Atl Phila.

— A History of the British Cavalry, 1872-1898, Vol. 3. (Illus.). 478p. 1982. 75.00 (0-436-27327-6, Pub. by Leo Cooper) Trans-Atl Phila.

— A History of the British Cavalry, 1914-1919 Vol. 5: 1914-1919, Egypt, Palestine & Syria. (Illus.). 388p. 1994. 75.00 (0-85052-395-8, Pub. by Leo Cooper) Trans-Atl Phila.

— A History of the British Cavalry, 1816-1919: 1914-1918, Mesopotamia, Vol. 6. (Illus.). 198p. 1995. 75.00 (0-85052-433-4, Pub. by Leo Cooper) Trans-Atl Phila.

Marquess, William H. Lives of the Poet: The First Century of Keats Biography. LC 84-43064. 224p. 1985. 28.50 (0-271-00390-1) Pa St U Pr.

Marquet, Jean F., ed. Surgery & Pathology of the Middle Ear. 1985. text 281.50 (0-89838-707-8) Kluwer Academic.

Marquet, Luis. Diccionari d'Electronica. (CAT.). 208p. 1977. pap. 9.95 (0-8288-5304-5, S50184) Fr & Eur.

Marquet, Luis, jt. auth. see Espunes, I.

***Marquet, Pascal, et al, eds.** Internet-Based Teaching & Learning (IN-TELE) 98: Proceedings of IN-TELE 98. (Internet Communication Ser.: Vol. 2). (Illus.). 570p. 1999. pap. text 74.95 (3-631-35557-2) P Lang Pubng.

Marquette, Catherine M., jt. auth. see Lloyd, Cynthia B.

Marquette County Comm. Educators Staff. Historical Stroll Through Churches of Marquette County. LC 98-91408. 160p. 1998. pap. 9.00 (1-57502-795-X, PO2192) Morris Pubng.

Marquette Electronics Staff. Affinity Reference for Biomedical. 328p. 1995. boxed set 34.95 (0-7872-0065-4) Kendall-Hunt.

Marquette, Jesse, jt. auth. see Malik, Yogendra.

Marquette University College of Engineering Staff. The Education of the Scientist in a Free Society: Papers Delivered at a Conference Commemorating the 50th Anniversary of the Marquette University, College of Engineering, May 20, 21 & 22, 1959. LC 59-15351. 87p. 1959. reprint ed. pap. 30.00 (0-608-04192-0, 206492700011) Bks Demand.

Marquez, Alberto T., ed. War Memories of the Alcala Veterans. (Illus.). 158p. (Orig.). 1992. pap. 13.75 (971-10-0461-5, Pub. by New Day Pub) Cellar.

Marquez, Alex & Marquez, Marta. The New Interpreters Handbook. 116p. (Orig.). (C). 1987. pap. text 20.00 (0-943407-00-1) Iberia Lang.

Marquez, Alfredo. Dalia. (SPA.). pap. 7.99 (968-16-2546-3, Pub. by Fondo) Continental Bk.

***Marquez, Alister Ramirez.** Quien Se Robo Los Colores? (SPA., Illus.). 96p. (YA). (gr. 7-12). 2000. 8.00 (1-877653-72-1) Wayside Pub.

Marquez, Antonio, jt. ed. see Anaya, Rudolfo A.

Marquez, Benjamin. Lulac: The Evolution of a Mexican American Political Organization. LC 92-28983. 159p. 1993. reprint ed. pap. 49.30 (0-608-03571-8, 206439400009) Bks Demand.

Marquez Bessa, Antonio. Diccionario Politico para Occidente. (SPA.). 288p. 1978. pap. 14.95 (0-8288-5149-2, S50003) Fr & Eur.

Marquez, Elizabeth, jt. auth. see Danielson, Charlotte.

Marquez, Enrique. Jose Lezama Lima: Bases y Genesis de un Sistema Poetico. LC 90-41160. (American University Studies: Latin American Literature: Ser. XXII, Vol. 12). IX, 225p. (C). 1991. text 41.95 (0-8204-1377-1) P Lang Pubng.

Marquez, Esther T., jt. auth. see Decker, Robert.

Marquez, Gustavo. El Seguro Social en Venezuela. 56p. 1992. 8.00 (0-940602-54-7) IADB.

Marquez, Gustavo, ed. Reforming the Labor Market in a Liberalized Economy. (Inter-American Development Bank Ser.). 256p. (Orig.). 1996. pap. text 18.50 (0-940602-96-2) IADB.

Marquez, Hector P. La Prefiguracion Como Recurso: Estilistico En Amalia. (SPA.). 14p. (Orig.). 1989. pap. 3.00 (0-89729-552-8) Ediciones.

***Marquez, Herbon.** Latin Sensations. LC 00-8876. 2000. pap. write for info. (0-8225-9695-4) Lerner Pub.

***Marquez, Heron.** Destination San Juan. LC 96-39489. (Port Cities of North America Ser.). 80p. (J). (gr. 3-8). 1998. lib. bdg. 23.93 (0-8225-2792-8, Lerner Publctns) Lerner Pub.

Marquez, Heron. Destination Veracruz. LC 97-16616. (Port Cities of North America Ser.). 72p. (J). (gr. 3-8). 1998. lib. bdg. 23.93 (0-8225-2791-X) Lerner Pub.

Marquez, Hudson. Monkey Island . . . A Fantastic Guide to New Orleans. 1992. pap. 8.95 (0-917905-04-0) Faust Pub Co.

Marquez, Ismael P. La Retorica de la Violencia en Tres Novelas Peruanas. LC 92-27681. (University Texas Studies in Contemporary Spanish-American Fiction: Vol. 7). 130p. (C). 1994. text 35.95 (0-614-00676-7) P Lang Pubng.

Marquez, Jaime, ed. see Klein, Lawrence.

Marquez, Jaime, jt. ed. see Klein, Lawrence Robert.

Marquez, Jay & Alexander, Ted. Building a Data Warehouse with DB2 UDB. 416p. 1999. pap. 44.99 incl. cd-rom (0-471-34405-2) Wiley.

Marquez, Jose, jt. auth. see Taylor, Mark C.

Marquez, Jose A. Ballester y, see Gray, Robin F. & Ballester y Marquez, Jose A.

Marquez, Joseph A., jt. auth. see Simms, Eduard T.

Marquez, Margaret Logan. Hyde Park on the Hudson. LC 96-209982. (Images of America Ser.). 1996. pap. 16.99 (0-7524-0437-7) Arcadia Publng.

Marquez, Maria T., jt. ed. see Rebolledo, Tey D.

Marquez, Marta, jt. auth. see Marquez, Alex.

Marquez, Nancy. Aprendiendo con Movimientos: Metodo TPR Espanol (for Beginners) 2nd ed.Tr. of Learning with Movements. (SPA., Illus.). 50p. 1982. pap. 9.95 (1-56018-471-X, 241) Sky Oaks Prodns.

— L' Enseignement par le Mouvement: Total Physical Response French (for Beginners) 2nd ed. (FRE.). 50p. 1996. pap. 9.95 (1-56018-482-5) Sky Oaks Prodns.

— Learning with Movements: Total Physical Response English (for Beginners) 3rd ed. 50p. 1996. pap. 9.95 (1-56018-483-3) Sky Oaks Prodns.

Marquez, Nancy & Perez, Theresa. Portraits of Mexican Americans. 96p. (J). (gr. 4-8). 1991. 11.99 (0-86653-605-1, GA1324) Good Apple.

***Marquez, Pablo.** Benito's Treasure Hunt. 2000. pap. 7.00 (0-533-13567-2) Vantage.

Marquez, Rene. Las Tortugas Marinas. (Ciencia para Todos Ser.). (SPA.). pap. 6.99 (968-16-4436-0, Pub. by Fondo) Continental Bk.

Marquez, Robert, ed. Latin American Revolutionary Poetry (Poesia Revolucionaria Latinoamericana) A Bilingual Anthology. LC 73-90079. 503p. 1974. reprint ed. pap. 156.00 (0-7837-3907-9, 204375500010) Bks Demand.

Marquez, Robert, ed. & tr. see Guillen, Nicolas.

Marquez-Ruarte, Jorge, jt. auth. see Aghevli, Bijan B.

Marquez, Sandra, jt. auth. see Wagner, Candy.

Marquez-Sterling, Carlos. A la Ingerencia Extrana la Virtud Domestica: Biografia de Manuel Marquez Sterling. LC 86-81071. (Coleccion Cuba y sus Jueces). (SPA., Illus.). 267p. (Orig.). 1986. pap. 12.00 (0-89729-425-4) Ediciones.

Marquez-Sterling, Manuel. Fernan Gonzalez, First Count of Castile: The Man & the Legend. LC 80-15095. (Romance Monographs: No. 40). (Illus.). 160p. 1980. 24.00 (84-499-4056-7) Romance.

***Marquez, Victoria.** Cortejo Calido. (Encanto Ser.). 2000. mass mkt. 3.50 (0-7860-1140-8) Kensgtn Pub Corp.

— In Hot Pursuit. 2000. mass mkt. 5.99 (0-7860-1136-X) Kensgtn Pub Corp.

Marquez-Villanueva, Francisco, ed. Harvard University Conference in Honor of Gabriel Miro (1879-1930) LC 82-83312. (Harvard Studies in Romance Languages: No. 39). (SPA.). (Orig.). 1982. pap. 8.00 (0-940940-39-6) Harvard U Romance Lang & Lit.

Marquie, Jean-Claude, et al, eds. Working with Age. 512p. 1998. text 150.00 (0-7484-0785-5, Pub. by Tay Francis Ltd); pap. text 39.95 (0-7484-0784-7, Pub. by Tay Francis Ltd) Taylor & Francis.

Marquis. Theory & Policy. Date not set. teacher ed. write for info. (0-314-06924-0) West Pub.

Marquis, Annette, jt. auth. see Courter, Gini.

Marquis, Annette, jt. auth. see Marquis Courter, Gini.

Marquis, Arnold. A Guide to America's Indians: Ceremonials, Reservations, & Museums. LC 74-5315. (Illus.). 280p. 1974. pap. 19.95 (0-8061-1148-8) U of Okla Pr.

Marquis, Bernie & Myers, Theresa F., compiled by. How St. Nicholas Became Santa Claus. 38p. (J). (ps). pap. 3.95 (0-8198-3377-0) Pauline Bks.

Marquis, Bessie L. & Huston, Carol J. Leadership Roles & Management Functions in Nursing: Theory & Application. 2nd ed. LC 95-36656. 592p. 1995. pap. text 29.95 (0-397-55236-X) Lppncott W & W.

***Marquis, Bessie L. & Huston, Carol J.** Leadership Roles & Management Functions in Nursing: Theory & Application. 3rd ed. LC 99-14493. 576p. 2000. pap. text 29.95 (0-7817-1923-2) Lppncott W & W.

Marquis, Bessie L. & Huston, Carol J. Management Decision Making for Nurses. 3rd ed. LC 97-24663. 464p. 1997. pap. text 29.95 (0-397-55429-X) Lppncott W & W.

— Management Decision Making for Nurses: 101 Case Studies. (Illus.). 393p. 1987. text 26.95 (0-397-54663-7, Lippncott) Lppncott W & W.

Marquis, Bessie L., jt. auth. see Huston, Carol J.

Marquis Courter, Gini. Mastering Microsoft Outlook 2000. LC 99-60017. (Mastering Ser.). 832p. 1999. 34.99 (0-7821-2472-0) Sybex.

— Microsoft Office 2000 User Specialist Study Guide. 3rd ed. 1008p. 1999. 39.99 (0-7821-2574-3) Sybex.

Marquis Courter, Gini & Marquis, Annette. Excel 2000 Mouse Study Guide. (Illus.). 323p. 1999. pap., student ed. 16.99 (0-7821-2513-1) Sybex.

Marquis Courter, Gini, et al. Word 2000 Mouse Study Guide. 319p. 1999. pap., student ed. 16.99 (0-7821-2515-8) Sybex.

Marquis, Darcy, jt. auth. see Roat, Paul.

Marquis, David M., ed. I Am a Teacher: A Tribute to America's Teachers. (Illus.). 125p. 1999. reprint ed. text 25.00 (0-7881-6177-6) DIANE Pub.

Marquis De Sade, pseud. Aline et Valcourt. (FRE.). 480p. 1986. pap. 45.00 (0-7859-1544-3, 2720201995) Fr & Eur.

— Les Cent Vingt Jours de Sodome. (FRE.). 530p. 1992. pap. 29.95 (0-7859-1555-9, 2867442222) Fr & Eur.

— Les Cent Vingt Jours de Sodome, 2 vols., 1. (FRE.). 320p. 1993. pap. 18.95 (0-7859-3206-2, 2264018798) Fr & Eur.

— Les Cent Vingt Jours de Sodome, 2 vols., 2. (FRE.). 320p. 1993. pap. 18.95 (0-7859-3207-0, 2264018801) Fr & Eur.

— Les Crimes de l'Amour. (FRE.). 1987. pap. 13.95 (0-7859-2914-2) Fr & Eur.

— Les Crimes de l'Amour. (Folio Ser.: No. 1817). (FRE.). 1972. pap. 10.95 (2-07-037817-9) Schoenhof.

— The Crimes of Love. Crosland, Margaret, tr. from FRE. 126p. 1996. 28.95 (0-7206-0957-7, Pub. by P Owen Ltd) Dufour.

— Crimes of Love. 1998. pap. 19.95 (0-7206-0986-0, Pub. by P Owen Ltd) Dufour.

— La Filosofia al Tocador. (SPA.). 208p. 1990. pap. 19.95 (0-7859-5477-5) Fr & Eur.

— Gothic Tales. Crosland, Margaret, tr. from FRE. 183p. 1990. 30.00 (0-7206-0769-8, Pub. by P Owen Ltd) Dufour.

— Histoire de Juliette, Vol. 1. (FRE.). 211p. 1976. pap. 15.95 (0-7859-1474-9, 2264000791) Fr & Eur.

— Histoire de Juliette ou les Prosperites du Vice, 3 vols. (FRE.). 505p. 1976. pap. 14.95 (0-685-73288-6); pap. 14.95 (0-7859-1649-0, 2264000791); pap. 14.95 (0-7859-1651-2, 2264000813) Fr & Eur.

— Idee sur les Romans. (FRE.). 138p. 1970. pap. 14.95 (0-7859-5478-3) Fr & Eur.

— Les Infortunes de la Vertu. (FRE.). 192p. 1969. pap. 11.95 (0-7859-1424-2, 2080702149) Fr & Eur.

— Les Infortunes de la Vertu. Didier, Beatrice, ed. 1977. 16.95 (0-686-55364-0) Fr & Eur.

— Les Infortunes de la Vertu. (Folio Ser.: No. 963). (FRE.). pap. 9.95 (2-07-036963-3) Schoenhof.

— Les Infortunes de la Vertu. unabridged ed. (FRE.). pap. 5.95 (2-87714-161-6, Pub. by Bookking Intl) Distribks Inc.

— Journal Inedit. (FRE.). 192p. 1970. pap. 10.95 (0-7859-1365-3, 2070352218) Fr & Eur.

— Justine ou les Malheurs de la Vertu. (FRE.). 488p. 1981. pap. 11.95 (0-7859-1367-X, 2070354466) Fr & Eur.

— Justine, Philosophy in the Bedroom, & Other Writings. Wainhouse, Austryn & Seaver, Richard, trs. from FRE. LC 90-3153. 784p. 1990. pap. 17.95 (0-8021-3218-9, Grove) Grove-Atltic.

— Letters from Prison. Seaver, Richard, tr. from FRE. & intro. by. LC 97-43150. 7p. 1999. 25.45 (1-55970-411-X, Pub. by Arcade Pub Inc) Time Warner.

— Lusts of the Libertines. Jones, Julian, tr. from FRE. 96p. 1998. reprint ed. pap. 12.95 (1-871592-59-3, Velvet Pub) Creation Books.

— The Mystified Magistrate: Four Stories. Crosland, Margaret, tr. from FRE. Orig. Title: Contes et fabliaux d'un troubadour provencal du XVIII siecle. 158p. 1993. pap. 17.95 (0-7206-0849-X, Pub. by P Owen Ltd) Dufour.

— The Mystified Magistrate: Four Stories. Orig. Title: Contes et fabliaux d'un troubadour provencal du XVIII siecle. 158p. 1996. pap. 18.95 (0-7206-1022-2, Pub. by P Owen Ltd) Dufour.

— The Mystified Magistrate: Four Stories. Crosland, Margaret, tr. from FRE. LC 87-60409. Orig. Title: Contes et fabliaux d'un troubadour provencal du XVIII siecle. 158p. 1986. reprint ed. 27.00 (0-7206-0653-5, Pub. by P Owen Ltd) Dufour.

— La Nouvelle Justine, 2 vols., 1. (FRE.). 448p. 1978. pap. 16.95 (0-686-55369-1) Fr & Eur.

— La Nouvelle Justine, 2 vols., 2. (FRE.). 448p. 1978. pap. 16.95 (0-7859-1479-X, 2264009101) Fr & Eur.

— Oeuvres. (FRE.). 1990. lib. bdg. 125.00 (0-8288-3533-0) Fr & Eur.

— Oeuvres Completes, 30 tomes, Set. 350.00 (0-685-34060-0) Fr & Eur.

— The Passionate Philosopher: A Marquis de Sade Reader. Crosland, Margaret, tr. from FRE. & intro. by. 126p. 1991. 40.00 (0-7206-0826-0, Pub. by P Owen Ltd) Dufour.

— La Philosophie dans le Boudoir. (Folio Ser.: No. 800). (FRE.). pap. 9.95 (2-07-036800-9) Schoenhof.

— La Philosophie dans le Boudoir. unabridged ed. (FRE.). 1997. pap. 6.95 (2-87714-214-0, Pub. by Bookking Intl) Distribks Inc.

— La Philosophie dans le Boudoir: Les Instituteurs Amoureaux. (FRE.). 1976. pap. 10.95 (0-7859-1372-6, 2070368009) Fr & Eur.

— Philosophy in the Boudoir. 3rd ed. (Velvet Ser.: Vol. 1). 160p. 1996. reprint ed. pap. 12.95 (1-871592-09-7) Creation Books.

— The Plays of the Marquis de Sade: Count Oxtiern, The Bedroom, The Madness of Misfortune, The Haunted Tower, The Shyster, Vol. 1. Franceschina, John & Ohmart, Ben, trs. from FRE. LC 92-17131. 250p. (C). 1993. text 35.00 (0-89341-708-4); pap. text 18.50 (0-89341-709-2) Hollowbrook.

— The Plays of the Marquis de Sade: Tancrede, Fanny, The Antique Dealers, Love Makes the Misanthrope, Festival of Friendship, Vol. 3. Franceschina, John & Ohmart, Ben, trs. from FRE. LC 92-17131. 225p. 1995. text 35.00 (0-89341-745-9); pap. text 18.50 (0-89341-746-7) Hollowbrook.

— The Plays of the Marquis de Sade: The Self-Proclaimed Philosopher, Jeanne Laine, The Twins, Truth & Treason, Henriette & St. Clair, Vol. 2. Franceschina, John, tr. from FRE. LC 92-17131. 250p. (C). 1993. text 35.00 (0-89341-710-6); pap. text 18.50 (0-89341-711-4) Hollowbrook.

— The Plays of the Marquis de Sade: The Wedding of the Century, The Marriage of the Arts, The Freak, Prefaces & Theatrical Essays, Vol. 4. Franceschina, John & Ohmart, Ben, trs. from FRE. LC 92-17131. 325p. 1995. text 35.00 (0-89341-747-5); pap. text 18.50 (0-89341-748-3) Hollowbrook.

— Les Prosperites du Vice. (FRE.). 320p. 1969. pap. 16.95 (0-7859-5569-0, 2264008393) Fr & Eur.

— Systeme der Kumulativen Logik. (FRE.). 256p. 1972. pap. 20.95 (0-7859-5479-1) Fr & Eur.

Marquis De Sade, pseud, et al. Oeuvres: Sade, Tome 1. deluxe ed. (Pleiade Ser.). (FRE.). 99.95 (2-07-011190-3) Schoenhof.

Marquis, Derek A. Till Debt Due Us Part: The Step-by-Step Guide to Getting Out of Debt & Managing Your Money. 1993. pap. 16.95 (1-883163-23-4) DC Pubs & Mgmt.

Marquis, Doc. The American Focus on Satanic Crime Vol. 12: The Illuminati's Protocols of the Learned Elders of Zion (Unpublished Edition), 23 vols. Peterson, Alan H., ed. & illus. by. 314p. (C). 1996. 65.00 (1-877858-77-3, AFSC12) Amer Focus Pub.

Marquis, Doc, ed. see Peterson, Alan H.

Marquis, Don. Archyology II (The Final Dig) The Long Lost Tales of Archy & Mehitabel. Adams, Jeff, ed. & pref. by. LC 97-43265. (Illus.). 131p. 1998. 15.95 (0-87451-853-9) U Pr of New Eng.

— Archy & Mehitabel. 1976. 28.95 (0-8488-0831-2) Amereon Ltd.

— Archy & Mehitabel. (Anchor Literary Library). 192p. 1987. pap. 10.95 (0-385-09478-7, Anchor NY) Doubleday.

— Archy & Mehitabel. 207p. 1989. reprint ed. lib. bdg. 21.95 (0-89966-596-9) Buccaneer Bks.

— Archyology: The Long Lost Tales of Archy & Mehitabel. Adams, Jeff, ed. & pref. by. LC 95-39416. (Illus.). 113p. 1996. 15.95 (0-87451-745-1) U Pr of New Eng.

Carter, & Other People. LC 75 142269. (Short Story Index Reprint Ser.). 1977. 20.95 (0-8369-3753-8) Ayer.

— Chapters for the Orthodox. LC 74-130066. (Short Story Index Reprint Ser.). 1977. 21.95 (0-8369-3665-5) Ayer.

— Sun Dial Time. LC 79-132119. (Short Story Index Reprint Ser.). 1977. 20.95 (0-8369-3676-0) Ayer.

— When the Turtles Sing & Other Unusual Tales. LC 70-130065. (Short Story Index Reprint Ser.). 1977. reprint ed. 19.95 (0-8369-3664-7) Ayer.

Marquis, Donald M. In Search of Buddy Bolden: First Man of Jazz. LC 77-10958. (Illus.). xix, 176p. (C). 1993. pap. 14.95 (0-8071-1857-5) La State U Pr.

Marquis, Erna & Silva, Karen. Process for Profit: The How to Approach of TQM. 176p. (C). 1996. pap. text, spiral bd. 32.95 (0-7872-1995-9, 41199501) Kendall-Hunt.

Marquis, F., jt. ed. see Barrera, E. V.

***Marquis, F. D. S., ed.** Powder Materials: Current Research & Industrial Practices. LC 99-75851. 354p. 1999. 116.00 (0-87339-456-9) Minerals Metals.

Marquis, G. & Solin, J., eds. Fatigue Design of Components: A Collection of Papers Presented at Fatigue Design 95, Helsinki, Finland, 5-8 September 1995. LC 97-35379. (ESIS Publication Ser.). 240p. 1997. 136.00 (0-08-043318-9) Elsevier.

Marquis, G., jt. auth. see Socie, Darrell.

Marquis, G., ed. see International Symposium on Fatigue Design Staff.

Marquis, G. Welton. Twentieth-Century Music Idioms. LC 81-4197. 269p. 1981. reprint ed. lib. bdg. 38.50 (0-313-22624-5, MATC, Greenwood Pr) Greenwood.

Marquis, Gary, jt. auth. see Socie, Darrell.

Marquis, Gini. Microsoft Outlook 2000. LC 99-60024. (No Experience Required Ser.). 480p. 1999. pap. 19.99 (0-7821-2483-6) Sybex.

Marquis, Greg. In Armageddon's Shadow: The Civil War & Canada's Maritime Provinces. (Illus.). 384p. 1998. 34.95 (0-7735-1792-8) McG-Queens Univ Pr.

***Marquis, Greg.** In Armageddon's Shadow: The Civil War & Canada's Maritime Provinces. (Illus.). 384p. 2000. pap. 24.95 (0-7735-2079-1, Pub. by McG-Queens Univ Pr) CUP Services.

Marquis, H., jt. auth. see Smith, E.

Marquis, Harold H. The Changing Corporate Image. LC 72-122584. viii, 231p. 1970. write for info. (0-8144-5236-1) AMACOM.

Marquis, John A. Learning to Teach from the Master Teacher (1913) 90p. 1998. reprint ed. pap. 9.95 (0-7661-0509-1) Kessinger Pub.

Marquis, Judith K., ed. Contemporary Issues in Pesticide Toxicology & Pharmacology. (Concepts in Toxicology Ser.: Vol. 2). (Illus.). xii, 108p. 1986. 77.50 (3-8055-4215-1) S Karger.

— A Guide to General Toxicology. 2nd rev. ed. (Continuing Education Ser.: Vol. 5). (Illus.). x, 294p. 1989. 59.25 (3-8055-4924-5) S Karger.

Marquis, June H. Weekends for Two: The Mid-Atlantic Area. 2nd ed. 108p. 1989. pap. 7.95 (0-89709-177-9) Liberty Pub.

Marquis, Kent H. & Ebener, Patricia A. Quality of Prisoner Self-Reports: Arrest & Conviction Response Errors. LC 81-168320. 176p. 1981. pap. 15.00 (0-8330-0300-3, R-2637-DOJ) Rand Corp.

Marquis, M. Ann. Creatures & Critters: Barrier Games for Referential Communication. (Illus.). 63p. 1987. 39.00 (0-7616-7434-9) Commun Skill.

Marquis, M. Ann & Addy-Trout, Elaine. Social Communication: Activities for Improving Peer Interactions & Self-Esteem. LC 92-21826. 1992. pap. 42.00 (0-930599-75-6) Thinking Pubns.

Marquis, Margaret. Lunchtime in Pittsburgh. 40p. (Orig.). 1988. pap. 4.95 (0-9621737-0-3) Pittsburgh Promo.

Marquis, Milton H. Monetary Theory & Policy. 400p. (C). 1996. mass mkt. 95.95 (0-314-06923-2) West Pub.

Marquis of Ruvigny & Raineval. The Blood Royal of Britain: Being a Roll of the Living Descendants of Edward IV & Henry VII, Kings of England & James III, King of Scotland. (Illus.). 632p. 1994. 45.00 (0-8063-1431-1) Genealog Pub.

Marquis of Ruvigny & Raineval. The Blood Royal of Britain & the Plantagenet Roll of the Blood Royal, Set. (Illus.). 3550p. 1994. 175.00 (0-8063-1436-2, 5051) Genealog Pub.

Marquis of Ruvigny & Raineval. The Plantagenet Roll of the Blood Royal: The Anne of Exeter Volume, Containing the Descendants of Anne (Plantagenet), Duchess of Exeter. (Illus.). 842p. 1994. 50.00 (0-8063-1433-8) Genealog Pub.

— The Plantagenet Roll of the Blood Royal: The Clarence Volume, Containing the Descendants of George, Duke of Clarence. (Illus.). 730p. 1994. 50.00 (0-8063-1432-X) Genealog Pub.

— The Plantagenet Roll of the Blood Royal: The Isabel of Essex Volume, Containing the Descendants of Isabel (Plantagenet), Countess of Essex & Eu. (Illus.). 698p. 1994. 45.00 (0-8063-1434-6) Genealog Pub.

— The Plantagenet Roll of the Blood Royal: The Mortimer-Percy Volume, Containing the Descendants of Lady Elizabeth Percy, Nee Mortimer. (Illus.). 650p. 1994. 45.00 (0-8063-1435-4) Genealog Pub.

Marquis, Robert E., jt. ed. see Bennett, Peter B.

Marquis Staff. Who's Who in American Politics 1997-1998, 2 vols., Vol. 1. 16th ed. 1997. write for info. (0-8379-6901-8) Marquis.

— Who's Who in American Politics 1997-1998, 2 vols., Vol. 2. 1997. write for info. (0-8379-6902-6) Marquis.

Marquis Staff, ed. Who Was Who in America, Vol. 12. 1998. 135.00 (0-8379-0231-2) Marquis.

Marquis, Susan L. Unconventional Warfare: Rebuilding U. S. Special Operations Forces. LC 96-53963. 319p. 1997. 49.95 (0-8157-5476-0); pap. 19.95 (0-8157-5475-2) Brookings.

Marquis, Thomas B. The Cheyennes of Montana. Weist, Thomas D., ed. LC 78-59715. 1978. 24.00 (0-917256-04-2) Ref Pubns.

— Keep the Last Bullet for Yourself: The True Story of Custer's Last Stand. Irvine, Keith & Faherty, Robert, eds. LC 75-39093. (Illus.). 192p. 1976. pap. 12.00 (0-917256-14-X) Ref Pubns.

Marquis, Thomas B., tr. Wooden Leg: A Warrior Who Fought Custer. LC 31-10067. (Illus.). xii, 389p. 1962. pap. 14.00 (0-8032-5124-6, Bison Books) U of Nebr Pr.

Marquis, Thomas B., jt. auth. see Leforge, Thomas H.

Marquis, Vincent. A Mortal on the Mend: A Passage to Healing. 107p. 1997. pap. write for info. (1-57502-587-6, PO1680) Morris Pubng.

Marquis Who's Who. Who's Who in the Media & Communications, 1998-1999. 650p. 1997. 259.95 (0-8379-3950-X) Marquis.

Marquis Who's Who Staff. Index to Marquis Who's Who Publications, 1998. 1999. 115.00 (0-8379-1436-1) Marquis.

— Who Was Who in America: Index Volume: 1607-1996, Vol. 1996. 135.00 (0-8379-0227-4) Marquis.

— Who Who's in America, 3 vols., Vol. 1. 51st deluxe ed. 1996. write for info. (0-8379-0180-4) Marquis.

— Who's Who in America, 3 vols. 51st deluxe ed. 1996. write for info. (0-8379-0179-0) Marquis.

— Who's Who in America, 3 vols., Vol. 2. 51st deluxe ed. 1996. write for info. (0-8379-0181-2) Marquis.

— Who's Who in America, 3 vols., Vol. 3. 51st deluxe ed. 1996. write for info. (0-8379-0182-0) Marquis.

— Who's Who in America, 1998, 3 vols. 52nd ed. 1997. 509.95 (0-8379-0183-9) Marquis.

— Who's Who in America, 1998, No. 3. 52nd ed. 1997. 509.95 (0-8379-0184-7) Marquis.

***Marquis Who's Who Staff.** Who's Who in American Art 1999-2000. 23rd ed. 1999. 286.25 (0-8379-6303-6) Marquis.

Marquis Who's Who Staff. Who's Who in American Politics, 1997-1998, 2 vols., Set. 16th ed. 1997. 259.95 (0-8379-6900-X) Marquis.

Marquis Who's Who Staff. Who's Who in Entertainment, 1998-1999. 3rd ed. 833p. 1997. 259.95 (0-8379-1857-X) Marquis.

Marquis Who's Who Staff. Who's Who in Finance & Industry, 1998-1999. 30th ed. 1,025p. 1997. 279.95 (0-8379-0332-7) Marquis.

— Who's Who in Science & Engineering, 1998-1999. 4th ed. 1,672p. 1997. 259.95 (0-8379-5756-7) Marquis.

— Who's Who in the South & Southwest, 1997-1998. 25th ed. 1997. 249.95 (0-8379-0827-2) Marquis.

— Who's Who in the World, 1998. 15th ed. 1998. 369.95 (0-8379-1119-2) Marquis.

— Who's Who West, 1998-1999. 26th ed. 913p. 1997. 272.95 (0-8379-0928-7) Marquis.

Marquis Who's Who Staff, ed. Index to Marquis Who's Who Publications, 1998. 1998. 110.00 (0-8379-1435-3) Marquis.

— The Official ABMS Directory of Board Certified Medical Specialists 2000, Set, 4 vols. 32nd ed. 1999. 510.00 (0-8379-0565-6) Marquis.

***Marquis Who's Who Staff, ed.** The Official ABMS Directory of Board Certified Medical Specialists 2001, Set, 4 vols. 33rd ed. 2000. write for info. (0-8379-0571-0) Marquis.

Marquis Who's Who Staff, ed. Who Was Who, 13 vols., Vol. 11. 1996. 90.00 (0-8379-0225-8) Marquis.

— Who Was Who: Index 1607 - 1996. 1996. 45.00 (0-8379-0226-6) Marquis.

— Who Was Who in America, 14 vols. 12th ed. 1998. 999.95 (0-8379-0228-2) Marquis.

***Marquis Who's Who Staff, ed.** Who Was Who in America. 13th ed. 2000. write for info. (0-8379-0233-9) Marquis.

— Who Was Who in America Index. 13th ed. 2000. write for info. (0-8379-0234-7) Marquis.

Marquis Who's Who Staff, ed. Who's Who in America, 3 vols. 53rd deluxe ed. 1998. 525.00 (0-8379-0191-X) Marquis.

— Who's Who in America 2000, Set, 14 vols. 54th ed. 1999. 549.00 (0-8379-0199-5) Marquis.

***Marquis Who's Who Staff, ed.** Who's Who in America 2001. 55th ed. 2000. write for info. (0-8379-6950-6) Marquis.

Marquis Who's Who Staff, ed. Who's Who in American Art 1999-2000. 23rd ed. 1999. 229.00 (0-8379-6301-X) Marquis.

— Who's Who in American Education, 1996-1997. 5th ed. 1092p. 1995. 159.95 (0-8379-2704-8) Marquis.

— Who's Who in American Law. 9th deluxe ed. 1100p. 1996. 269.95 (0-8379-3512-1) Marquis.

— Who's Who in American Law, 1996-1997. 9th ed. 980p. 1996. 269.95 (0-8379-3511-3) Marquis.

— Who's Who in American Law, 1998-1999. 10th ed. 997p. 1998. 285.00 (0-8379-3513-X) Marquis.

— Who's Who in American Law 2000-2001. 11th ed. 1000p. 1999. 295.00 (0-8379-3516-4) Marquis.

— Who's Who in American Nursing, 1996-1997. 6th ed. 806p. 1995. 149.95 (0-8379-1004-8) Marquis.

— Who's Who in American Politics 1999-2000. 17th ed. 1999. 275.00 (0-8379-6903-4) Marquis.

— Who's Who in Finance & Industry 2000-2001. 31st ed. 1999. 295.00 (0-8379-0334-3) Marquis.

***Marquis Who's Who Staff, ed.** Who's Who in Medical & Healthcare. 3rd ed. 985p. 2000. 249.00 (0-8379-0004-2) Marquis.

Marquis Who's Who Staff, ed. Who's Who in Medicine & Healthcare. 2nd ed. 985p. 1998. 249.95 (0-8379-0002-6) Marquis.

— Who's Who in Medicine & Healthcare, 1997-1998. 1230p. 1996. 249.95 (0-8379-0000-X) Marquis.

— Who's Who in Religion, 1992-1993. 4th ed. 580p. 1992. 129.00 (0-8379-1604-6) Marquis.

— Who's Who in Science & Engineering 2000-2001. 5th ed. 1999. 269.00 (0-8379-5758-3) Marquis.

— Who's Who in the East. 27th ed. 1,213p. 1998. 289.95 (0-8379-0630-X) Marquis.

***Marquis Who's Who Staff, ed.** Who's Who in the East. 28th ed. 2000. write for info. (0-8379-0632-6) Marquis.

Marquis Who's Who Staff, ed. Who's Who in the East, 1997-1998: Classic Edition. 26th ed. 900p. 1996. 279.95 (0-8379-0628-8) Marquis.

— Who's Who in the Midwest. 26th ed. 714p. 1998. 269.95 (0-8379-0728-4) Marquis.

***Marquis Who's Who Staff, ed.** Who's Who in the Midwest. 27th ed. 2000. write for info. (0-8379-0730-6) Marquis.

Marquis Who's Who Staff, ed. Who's Who in the Midwest Deluxe ed. 25th ed. 1996. 259.00 (0-8379-0727-6) Marquis.

— Who's Who in the Midwest, 1996-1997: Classic Edition. 25th ed. 1000p. 1996. 259.95 (0-8379-0726-8) Marquis.

— Who's Who in the South & Southwest. 26th ed. 800p. 1998. 259.95 (0-8379-0829-9) Marquis.

***Marquis Who's Who Staff, ed.** Who's Who in the South & Southwest. 27th ed. 2000. write for info. (0-8379-0831-0) Marquis.

Marquis Who's Who Staff, ed. Who's Who in the West. 27th ed. 1999. 269.00 (0-8379-0930-9) Marquis.

***Marquis Who's Who Staff, ed.** Who's Who in the West. 28th ed. 2000. write for info. (0-8379-0932-5) Marquis.

Marquis Who's Who Staff, ed. Who's Who in the West, 1996-1997. 25th ed. 1055p. 1995. 259.95 (0-8379-0926-0) Marquis.

— Who's Who in the World. 16th ed. 1,620p. 1998. 379.95 (0-8379-1121-4) Marquis.

***Marquis Who's Who Staff, ed.** Who's Who in the World. 18th ed. 2000. write for info. (0-8379-1125-7) Marquis.

Marquis Who's Who Staff, ed. Who's Who in the World, 1995. 12th ed. 1567p. 1995. 329.95 (0-8379-1113-3) Marquis.

— Who's Who in the World, 1996. 13th ed. 1496p. 1995. 339.95 (0-8379-1115-X) Marquis.

— Who's Who in the World, 1997 Classic ed. 14th ed. 1400p. 1996. 359.95 (0-8379-1117-6) Marquis.

— Who's Who in the World 2000. 17th ed. 2000. 389.95 (0-8379-1123-0) Marquis.

— Who's Who of American Women. 21st ed. 1,200p. 1998. 259.00 (0-8379-0424-2) Marquis.

— Who's Who of American Women, 1995-1996. 19th ed. 1150p. 1995. 239.00 (0-8379-0420-X) Marquis.

— Who's Who of American Women, 1997-1998. 20th ed. 1996. 249.00 (0-8379-0422-6) Marquis.

***Marquis Who's Who Staff, ed.** Who's Who of American Women 2000-2001. 22nd ed. 1172p. 2000. 269.00 (0-8379-0426-9) Marquis.

Marquis Who's Who Staff, ed. Who's Who of Emerging Leaders in America, 1993-1994. 4th ed. 758p. 1992. 229.00 (0-8379-7203-5) Marquis.

Marquis Who's Who Staff & American Board of Medical Specialties Staff, eds. The Official ABMS Directory of Board Certified Medical Specialists, 1998, 4 vols. 30th anniversary ed. 1997. 485.00 (0-8379-0551-6) Marquis.

***Marquist, Collen & Frasl, Jack.** Crystalline Communion 2000: Mineral Properties for Healing & Integration. 224p. 1999. pap. 17.95 (0-9620201-3-3) Earthlight WA.

Marquist, Collen & Frasl, Jack. Crystalline Communion, Vol. II: Mineral Properties for Healing & Integration. (Illus.). 48p. (Orig.). 1991. pap. 7.95 (0-9620201-1-7) Earthlight WA.

Marquit, E., tr. see Goldman, I. I. & Krivchenkov, V. D.

Marquit, Erwin. The Socialist Countries: General Features of Political, Economic, & Cultural Life. 2nd ed. LC 83-9329. (Studies in Marxism: Vol. 3). 226p. 1983. 19.95 (0-930656-31-8); pap. 9.95 (0-930656-32-6) MEP Pubns.

Marquit, Erwin, et al, eds. Dialectical Contradictions: Contemporary Marxist Discussions. LC 81-8462. (Studies in Marxism: Vol. 10). 222p. (C). 1982. 19.95 (0-930656-19-9); pap. 9.95 (0-930656-20-2) MEP Pubns.

***Marqusee, Mike.** Redemption Song: Muhammad Ali & the Spirit of the Sixties. LC 99-23701. 310p. 1999. 25.00 (1-85984-717-X, Pub. by Verso) Norton.

— Redemption Song: Muhammad Ali & the Spirit of the Sixties. 320p. 2000. pap. 15.00 (1-85984-293-3, Pub. by Verso) Norton.

Marr, Alexander. Prediction 1. LC 82-71346. 152p. 1981. 14.00 (0-86690-032-2, M2581-014) Am Fed Astrologers.

Marr, C. D. & Stuntz, Daniel E. Ramaria of Western Washington. 1973. 40.00 (3-7682-0902-4) Lubrecht & Cramer.

Marr, Celia, ed. Cardiology of the Horse. (Illus.). 260p. 1997. write for info. (0-7020-2240-3, Pub. by W B Saunders) Saunders.

Marr, David. American Worlds since Emerson. LC 87-5989. 248p. (C). 1988. lib. bdg. 32.50 (0-87023-588-5) U of Mass Pr.

Marr, David & White, Christine, eds. Postwar Vietnam: Dilemmas in Socialist Development. (Southeast Asia Program Ser.: No. 3). (Illus.). x, 254p. (Orig.). (C). 1988. pap. text 12.00 (0-87727-120-8) Cornell SE Asia.

Marr, David, ed. see White, Patrick.

Marr, David G. Vietnam. LC 93-223446. (World Bibliographical Ser.). 472p. 1993. lib. bdg. 110.00 (1-85109-092-4) ABC-CLIO.

— Vietnam, 1945: The Quest for Power. 1997. pap. text 24.95 (0-520-21228-2, Pub. by U CA Pr) Cal Prin Full Svc.

— Vietnamese Tradition on Trial, 1920-1945. (Illus.). 450p. 1981. pap. 19.95 (0-520-05081-9, Pub. by U CA Pr) Cal Prin Full Svc.

Marr, Diane D. Gender Specific Treatment: A Program for Chemically Dependent Women in Recovery. 1994. pap. 21.95 (1-55691-066-5, 665) Learning Pubns.

Marr, Dick. Bicycle Gearing - A Practical Guide: Everything You Will Ever Need to Know to Use & Choose the Best Gearing Strategies for Pleasure & Performance Cycling. LC 89-2986. (Illus.). 136p. (Orig.). 1989. pap. 8.95 (0-89886-184-5) Mountaineers.

Marr, G. V., ed. Handbook on Synchrotron Radiation Vol. 2: Vacuum Ultraviolet & Soft X-Ray Processes. xii, 846p. 1987. 398.25 (0-444-87046-6, North Holland) Elsevier.

Marr, Greg. Short Bike Rides Wisconsin: Rides for the Casual Cyclist. 2nd ed. LC 99-37029. (Short Bike Rides Ser.). (Illus.). 224p. 2000. pap. text 11.95 (0-7627-0406-3) Globe Pequot.

Marr-Hugunin, Lynn. A History of Wrestling at Iowa State University, 1912-1985. (Illus.). 324p. (Orig.). 1987. pap. 24.95 (0-9617912-0-9) Nichols Wrestling.

Marr, J. Joseph & Muller, Miklos, eds. Biochemistry & Molecular Biology of Parasites. (Illus.). 383p. 1995. text 95.00 (0-12-473345-X) Acad Pr.

Marr, Jack J., ed. see Wood, Simeon.

Marr, Jerry, jt. auth. see Bergland, Eric O.

Marr, Jim. Caring for Elderly People. Kershaw, Betty, ed. (Illus.). 304p. (Orig.). 1998. pap. 32.95 (1-56593-764-3, 1486) Singular Publishing.

Marr, John C. Fishery & Resource Management in Southeast Asia. LC 75-36946. (Resources for the Future Ser.). 76p. 1976. pap. 7.50 (0-8018-1826-5) Johns Hopkins.

— Fishery & Resource Management in Southeast Asia. LC 75-36946. (RFF-PISFA Paper Ser.: No. 7). 75p. reprint ed. pap. 30.00 (0-608-18808-5, 203020900067) Bks Demand.

M

Marr, John L., ed. from GRE. Plutarch: Life of Themistocles. (Classical Texts Ser.). 172p. (C). 1998. 59.95 (*0-85668-676-X*, Pub. by Aris & Phillips); pap. 22.00 (*0-85668-677-8*, Pub. by Aris & Phillips) David Brown.

Marr, John N. & Roessler, Richard T. Supervision & Management: A Guide to Modifying Work Behavior. LC 93-36797. (Illus.). 240p. (C). 1994. pap. 20.00 (*1-55728-306-0*) U of Ark Pr.

Marr, John S. A Breath of Air & a Breath of Smoke. LC 70-161362. (Illus.). 48p. (J). (gr. 3 up). 1978. 4.95 (*0-87131-038-4*) M Evans.

***Marr, John S. & Baldwin, James.** The Eleventh Plague: Shea,&John. abr. ed. 1998. audio 18.00 (*0-694-51803-4*, 393107, Pub. by HarperAudio) Lndmrk Audiobks.

Marr, John S. & Baldwin, John. The Eleventh Plague. large type ed. LC 98-29240. 1998. 26.95 (*1-56895-651-7*, Compass) Wheeler Pub.

— The Eleventh Plague: A Novel of Medical Terror. LC PS3563.A7113E44. 528p. 1999. mass mkt. 6.99 (*0-06-109763-2*) HarpC.

Marr, Joseph J., jt. auth. see Boyd, Robert F.

Marr, Katharina. Environmental Impact Assessment in the United Kingdom & Germany: A Comparison of EIA Practice for Wastewater Treatment Plants. LC 97-74455. (Studies in Green Research). (Illus.). 344p. 1997. text 78.95 (*1-84014-147-7*, Pub. by Ashgate Pub) Ashgate Pub Co.

Marr, Lisa. Sexually Transmitted Diseases: A Physician Tells You What You Need to Know. LC 98-25952. (Health Book Ser.). 263p. 1998. 39.95 (*0-8018-6042-3*); pap. 16.95 (*0-8018-6043-1*) Johns Hopkins.

Marr, M. Wayne, ed. Advances in Financial Economics, Vol. 1. 181p. 1995. 73.25 (*1-55938-975-3*) Jai Pr.

Marr, M. Wayne & Hirschey, Mark, eds. Advances in Financial Economics, Vol. 2. 212p. 1996. 78.50 (*0-7623-0123-6*) Jai Pr.

— Advances in Financial Economics, Vol. 3. 212p. 1997. 73.25 (*0-7623-0299-2*) Jai Pr.

Marr, M. Wayne, Jr., et al. Economically Targeted & Social Investment Management & Pension Fund Performance. 28p. (Orig.). 1995. pap. text 20.00 (*0-943205-34-4*) RFICFA.

***Marr, Mary L.** Lighting the Way: A 90-Day Journey in Sharing Your Faith. 152p. 2000. pap. write for info. (*0-8341-1840-8*) Beacon Hill.

Marr, P. The Modern History of Iraq. Date not set. text. write for info. (*0-582-78344-5*, Pub. by Addison-Wesley) Longman.

— Modern History of Iraq. 2nd ed. 2000. pap. 54.95 (*0-8133-8214-9*); pap. 18.95 (*0-8133-8215-7*) Westview.

***Marr, Patt.** Angel in Disguise, Vol. 98. (Love Inspired Ser.). 2000. mass mkt. 4.50 (*0-373-87104-X*, Steeple Hill) Harlequin Bks.

Marr, Phebe. Egypt: Domestic Stability & Regional Role LC 98-54860. 1999. write for info. (*1-57906-022-6*) Natl Defense.

Marr, Rebecca A. The Everytourist Guide to the Springs. (Illus.). 64p. (Orig.). 1992. pap. 4.95 (*0-9631093-0-8*) Marr & Assocs.

Marr, Richard, et al. Insurance Data Quality. 163p. 1995. pap. text 75.00 (*1-877796-13-1*) IDMA.

— Insurance Data Quality Study Guide. 158p. 1995. pap. 25.00 (*1-877796-14-X*) IDMA.

— Systems Development & Project Management Study Guide. 3rd ed. 179p. 1994. pap. text 25.00 (*1-877796-12-3*) IDMA.

Marr, Ron. Christianity That Really Works. 320p. 1993. mass mkt. 5.99 (*0-88368-271-0*) Whitaker Hse.

— Spiritual Dynamite. LC 99-10075. 224p. 1999. pap. 6.99 (*0-88368-576-0*) Whitaker Hse.

Marr, Suzanne, jt. ed. see Wacht, Peter.

Marr, Thomas G., jt. ed. see Bell, George I.

Marr, W. A. & Fairhurst, Charles. Nondestructive & Automated Testing for Soil & Rock Properties. LC 99-23150. 1999. write for info. (*0-8031-2493-7*) ASTM.

***Marr, W. Allen.** Geotechnical Measurements: Lab & Field: Proceedings of Sessions of Geo-Denver 2000: August 5-8, 2000. LC 00-42132. (Geotechnical Special Publications). 2000. write for info. (*0-7844-0518-2*) Am Soc Civil Eng.

Marr, W. Allen, jt. auth. see Durham, Gary N.

Marr, Warren & Ward, Mayhelle. Minorities & the American Dream: A Bicentennial Perspective. 1976. 19.95 (*0-405-09117-6*, 19461) Ayer.

Marr, William. Autumn Window. 2nd rev. ed. 118p. (Orig.). 1996. pap. 10.50 (*0-9637547-9-3*) Arbor Hill Pr.

Marra, Alan A. Technology of Wood Bonding: Principles in Practice. (Structural Engineering Ser.). (Illus.). 608p. (gr. 13). 1992. text 72.95 (*0-442-00797-3*) Chapman & Hall.

Marra, Ben, photos by. Powwow: Images along the Red Road. LC 96-6093. (Illus.). 112p. 1996. pap. 16.95 (*0-8109-2680-6*, Pub. by Abrams) Time Warner.

Marra, Dorothy B., jt. auth. see Medina, Francis X.

Marra, Giulio. Shakespeare & This "Imperfect" World: Dramatic Form & the Nature of Knowing. LC 96-18590. (Studies in Shakespeare: No. 5). 290p. (C). 1997. pap. text 29.95 (*0-8204-3388-8*) P Lang Pubng.

***Marra, James, et al.** Paths to Civilization: Readings in the Intellectual Heritage of the Western World, Vol. 1. 528p. (C). 1999. per. 69.95 (*0-7872-6312-5*) Kendall-Hunt.

— Paths to Civilization: Readings in the Intellectual Heritage of the Western World, Vol. 2. 346p. (C). 1999. per. 55.95 (*0-7872-6313-3*, 41631302) Kendall-Hunt.

— A Student Introduction to Charles Darwin. 170p. (C). 1999. per. 16.95 (*0-7872-6311-7*, 41631102) Kendall-Hunt.

Marra, James C. & Chandler, Gregory T., eds. Environmental Issues & Waste Management Technologies in the Ceramic & Nuclear Industries IV. (Ceramic Transactions Ser.: Vol. 93). 424p. 1999. 95.00 (*1-57498-057-2*, CT093) Am Ceramic.

Marra, James C., jt. ed. see Peeler, David K.

Marra, Julie Mitchell. A Mother's Book of Prayers. 1999. 8.95 (*0-88271-648-4*) Regina Pr.

Marra, Kim, jt. ed. see Schanke, Robert A.

Marra, Michele. The Aesthetics of Discontent: Politics & Reclusion in Medieval Japanese Literature. LC 90-25540. (Illus.). 248p. 1991. text 37.00 (*0-8248-1336-7*); pap. text 16.95 (*0-8248-1364-2*) UH Pr.

— Modern Japanese Aesthetics: A Reader. LC 99-27949. 432p. 1999. 55.00 (*0-8248-2173-4*) UH Pr.

— Representations of Power: The Literary Politics of Medieval Japan. LC 93-10236. (Illus.). 256p. (C). 1993. pap. text 16.95 (*0-8248-1556-4*) UH Pr.

Marra, Reggie. The Quality of Effort: Integrity in Sport & Life for Student-Athletes, Parents, & Coaches. LC 90-84335. 113p. (Orig.). 1991. pap. 11.50 (*0-9627828-0-7*) From Heart Pr.

Marra, William A. Happiness & Christian Hope: Being Joyful in a Fallen World. rev. ed. 202p. 1994. text 13.95 (*0-912141-09-3*) Roman Cath Bks.

Marrable, A. W. The Foal in the Womb. (Illus.). 142p. 1990. pap. 30.00 (*0-85131-345-0*, Pub. by J A Allen) St Mut.

***Marrable, A. W.** Foal in the Womb. 2000. pap. 5.95 (*0-85131-593-3*, Pub. by J A Allen) Trafalgar.

Marraccini, Luigi. You Can Teach Yourself Flamenco Guitar. 96p. 1996. pap. 18.95 incl. audio (*0-7866-1280-0*, 95358P) Mel Bay.

— You Can Teach Yourself Flamenco Guitar. 96p. 1999. pap. 17.95 incl. audio compact disk (*0-7866-4928-3*, 95358BCD) Mel Bay.

Marracini, Luigi. You Can Teach Yourself Flamenco Guitar. (You Can Teach Yourself Ser.). 96p. 1995. pap. 9.95 (*0-7866-0234-1*, MB95358) Mel Bay.

Marrack, Eleanor. Cezanne. 1993. 5.98 (*1-55521-823-7*) Bk Sales Inc.

— Van Gogh. 1992. 5.98 (*1-55521-763-X*) Bk Sales Inc.

Marrack, Philippa, et al. The Harvey Lectures Series, Vol. 89. (Harvey Lectures: No. 89). 191p. 1995. 99.95 (*0-471-11858-3*) Wiley.

***Marraeo, Letisha.** Ricky Martin: Livin' la Vida Loca. 256p. 1999. mass mkt. 5.99 (*0-06-102056-7*, Pub. by Harper SF) HarpC.

Marraffino, Elizabeth. Blue Moon Ruby Tuesday. (Illus.). 60p. (Orig.). 1981. pap. 3.00 (*0-936556-02-1*) Contact Two.

Marrakchi, Abdellatif. Phototonic Switching & Interconnects. (Optical Engineering Ser.: Vol. 40). (Illus.). 464p. 1993. text 199.00 (*0-8247-8931-8*) Dekker.

Marrakchi, Abdellatif, ed. Selected Papers on Photonic Switching, Vol. MS 121. (Milestone Ser.: Vol. 121). 1996. 95.00 (*0-8194-2163-4*) SPIE.

Marran, David. The Cub Fan's Quiz Book. LC 85-12859. 182p. 1985. pap. 7.95 (*0-912083-12-3*) Diamond Communications.

Marranca, Bonnie. Ecologies of Theater. (PAJ Bks.). (Illus.). (C). 1996. pap. text 16.95 (*0-8018-5273-0*) Johns Hopkins.

— Ecologies of Theater: Essays at the Century Turning. (PAJ Bks.). (Illus.). 312p. (C). 1996. text 48.50 (*0-8018-5272-2*) Johns Hopkins.

— The Hudson Valley Reader: Writings from the 17th Century to the Present. (Illus.). 404p. 1995. pap. 15.95 (*0-87951-598-8*, Pub. by Overlook Pr) Penguin Putnam.

— Theatrewritings. 1984. 28.50 (*0-933826-67-2*); pap. 14.95 (*0-933826-68-0*) PAJ Pubns.

Marranca, Bonnie, ed. American Dreams: The Imagination of Sam Shepard. LC 80-85438. 223p. 1981. pap. 15.95 (*0-933826-13-3*) PAJ Pubns.

— The Theatre of Images. LC 95-45775. (PAJ Bks.). (Illus.). 176p. 1996. reprint ed. pap. text 14.95 (*0-8018-5243-9*) Johns Hopkins.

Marranca, Bonnie & Dasgupta, Gautam. Conversations on Art & Performance. LC 98-25840. (PAJ Bks.). 1999. 49.95 (*0-8018-5924-7*); pap. 19.95 (*0-8018-5925-5*) Johns Hopkins.

Marranca, Bonnie & Dasgupta, Gautam, eds. Theatre of the Ridiculous. rev. ed. LC 97-15815. (PAJ Publications). (Illus.). 144p. 1998. text 38.50 (*0-8018-5697-3*); pap. text 14.95 (*0-8018-5698-1*) Johns Hopkins.

Marrance, Bonnie, ed. Plays for the End of the Century. LC 96-21936. (PAJ Bks.). 288p. 1996. text 45.00 (*0-8018-5107-6*); pap. text 16.95 (*0-8018-5108-4*) Johns Hopkins.

Marranda, Bonnie & Dasupta, Gautam, eds. Interculturalism & Performance: Writings from PAJ. 1991. 35.00 (*1-55554-057-0*); pap. 16.95 (*1-55554-058-9*) PAJ Pubns.

Marrano, jt. auth. see DiLouie, Craig.

Marrano, Steven J. & DiLouie, Craig. Electrical System Design & Specification Handbook for Industrial Facilities. LC 98-3948. (Illus.). 1998. 79.00 (*0-88173-194-3*, 0349) Fairmont Pr.

Marrant, John & Aldridge, W. A Narrative of the Lord's Wonderful Dealings with John Marrant, a Black LC 77-27409. (Library of Narratives of North American Indian Captivities). v, 38 p. 1978. write for info. (*0-8240-1641-6*) Garland.

Marrapodi, Betty. Clock That Went Meow: Director's Script. (Illus.). 31p. (J). (gr. k up). 1970. pap. 7.50 (*0-88680-030-7*) I E Clark.

— Clock That Went Meow: In One-Act. (Illus.). 31p. (J). (gr. k up). 1970. pap. 3.25 (*0-88680-029-3*) I E Clark.

— Doctor Hoo: An Environmental Play. (Illus.). 22p. 1973. pap. 3.00 (*0-88680-038-2*) I E Clark.

— Doctor Hoo: Director's Script. (Illus.). 22p. 1973. pap. 7.50 (*0-88680-039-0*) I E Clark.

Marrapodi, Michele. Shakespeare's Italy: Functions of Italian Locations in Renaissance Drama. LC 97-16566. 336p. 1997. pap. 24.95 (*0-7190-5220-3*, Pub. by Manchester Univ Pr) St Martin.

Marrapodi, Michele & Melchiori, Giorgio, eds. Italian Studies is Shakespeare & His Contemporaries. LC 98-36115. 304p. 1999. 45.00 (*0-87413-666-0*) U Delaware Pr.

Marrapodi, Michele, jt. auth. see Klein, Holger.

Marrapodi, Michele, ed. see Hoenselaars, A. J.

Marraro, Howard R. The New Education in Italy. LC 78-63692. (Studies in Fascism: Ideology & Practice). reprint ed. 47.00 (*0-404-16954-6*) AMS Pr.

Marraro, Howard R., ed. Diplomatic Relations Between the United States & the Kingdom of the Two Sicilies, 2 vols., Set. 1951. 45.00 (*0-913298-56-5*) S F Vanni.

Marras, Amerigo, ed. Eco-Tec: Architecture of the In-Between. LC 98-54434. (Storefront Bks.: Vol. 3). (Illus.). 142p. 1999. pap. 15.95 (*1-56898-159-7*) Princeton Arch.

Marras, William S., et al. Dynamic Measures of Low Back Performance. 20p. (C). 1993. pap. 8.00 (*0-932627-52-8*, 174-ER-93) Am Indus Hygiene.

Marras, William S., jt. auth. see Karwowski, Waldemar.

Marrase, Yara. Ingles Facil Para Todos. 153p. 1985. pap. 2.95 (*1-884249-03-5*) Pub Especiales.

— Ingles Para Ciudadania Americana. 48p. 1989. pap. 2.95 (*1-884249-08-6*, TX 2-507-729) Pub Especiales.

— Ingles para Enamorar. 40p. 1995. pap. 3.95 (*1-884249-12-4*, TX 697-375) Pub Especiales.

— Ingles Para la Mujer. 125p. 1988. pap. 2.95 (*1-884249-06-X*, TX 2-278-579) Pub Especiales.

— Ingles Para los Trabajadores. 1993. pap. 2.95 (*1-884249-10-8*, TXU 572-393) Pub Especiales.

— Ingles Primario. 121p. 1981. pap. 2.95 (*1-884249-00-0*, TX 742-377) Pub Especiales.

Marrast, Robert & Marrast, Sylvie. Theatre Espagnol du XVI Siecle. (FRE.). 1983. lib. bdg. 100.00 (*0-7859-3862-1*) Fr & Eur.

Marrast, Sylvie, jt. auth. see Marrast, Robert.

Marrat, Florence. The Dead Man's Message: An Occult Romance. Reginald, R. & Menville, Douglas A., eds. LC 75-46290. (Supernatural & Occult Fiction Ser.). 1976. reprint ed. lib. bdg. 17.95 (*0-405-08150-2*) Ayer.

Marrati-Guenoun, Paola, ed. La Gen Ese et la Trace: Derrida Lecteur de Husserl et Heidegger. LC 97-51250. (Phenomenologica Ser.). 240p. 1998. 100.00 (*0-7923-4969-5*) Kluwer Academic.

Marrazzo, Shirley Virginia. The Adventures of Michael Lee: "Teddy" (Illus.). 40p. (J). (gr. k-4). 1996. pap. 6.99 (*0-9660384-0-1*) S V Marrazzo.

Marre, Louis A. Contemporary Diesel Spotter's Guide. 2nd ed. 352p. 1995. pap. 21.95 (*0-89024-257-7*, 01068) Kalmbach.

— Diesel Locomotives: The First 50 Years. Drury, George H., ed. (Railroad Reference Ser.: No. 10). (Illus.). 480p. 1996. per. 29.95 (*0-89024-258-5*, 01054) Kalmbach.

— Frisco in Color. (Illus.). 1995. 49.95 (*1-878887-50-5*) Morning NJ.

***Marre, Louis A. & Sommers, Gregory J.** Kansas City Southern in the Deramus Era. LC 97-60478. (Illus.). 232p. 1999. 48.00 (*1-881411-14-1*) Withers Pub.

***Marre, Louis A. & Withers, Paul K.** The Contemporary Diesel Spotter's Guide: A Comp[rehensive Reference Manual to Locomotives since 1972. LC 99-69543. 224p. 2000. pap. 24.95 (*1-881411-25-7*) Withers Pub.

Marre, Roland. Die Bedeutung der Unternehmenskultur fur die Personalentwicklung. (Illus.). XIV, 273p. 1997. 54.95 (*3-631-31832-4*) P Lang Pubng.

Marree, Jorgen & Groenewegen, Peter. Back to Bismarck: Eastern European Health Care in Systems Transition. LC 96-79845. 144p. 1997. 59.95 (*1-85972-617-8*, Pub. by Avebry) Ashgate Pub Co.

Marreel-McLellan. Information Management in Health Care. 21st rev. abr. ed. LC 98-51743. 240p. (C). 1999. pap. 53.95 (*0-7668-1255-3*) Delmar.

***Marreel-McLellan.** User's Resource to Accompany Management in Healthcare. 96p. 1999. teacher ed. 17.95 (*0-7668-1256-1*) Delmar.

Marrell, Patrick. Phonics Fun. LC 97-214826. (Illus.). (J). 1997. write for info. (*0-7853-2417-8*) Pubns Intl Ltd.

Marrelli. Geometric Tolerancing: Instructor's Manual. 226p. 1996. teacher ed. 11.33 (*0-02-801889-3*) Glencoe.

— Home Care & Clinical Paths: Effective Care Planning Across the Continuum 97-98. 48p. (C). (gr. 13). 1997. text 19.95 (*0-8151-3419-3*, 31839) Mosby Inc.

Marrelli, Nancy & Dardick, Simon. Cheap Thrills: Great Montreal Meals for under 10 Dollars. 1997. pap. 9.95 (*1-55065-098-X*, Pub. by Vehicule Pr) LPC Group.

***Marrelli, Nancy & Dardick, Simon.** Cheap Thrills: Great Montreal Meals for under $10: The Millennium Edition. (Illus.). 2000. pap. 9.95 (*1-55065-126-9*) Vehicule Pr.

Marrelli, Nancy, jt. auth. see Dardick, Simon.

Marrelli, Richard S. Geometric Tolerancing. LC 82-84363. 1984. pap. text, wbk. ed. 8.00 (*0-02-829810-1*) Macmillan.

Marrelli, Richard S. & McCuistion, Patrick J. Geometric Tolerancing: A Text-Workbook. 2nd ed. LC 95-41232. 1996. text 27.16 (*0-02-801882-6*) Glencoe.

Marrelli, T. M. Home Care & Clinical Paths: Effective Care Planning Across the Continuum. (Illus.). 256p. (C). (gr. 13). 1995. text 62.95 (*0-8151-5853-X*, 26256) Mosby Inc.

Marrelli, T. M., jt. auth. see Ferri, Fred F.

Marrelli, Tina M. Handbook of Home Health Standards & Documentation: Guidelines for Reimbursement, Vol. 3. 3rd ed. (Illus.). 688p. 1997. spiral bd. 29.95 (*0-8151-2399-X*, 31044) Mosby Inc.

— Mosby's Home Care & Hospice Drug Handbook. (Illus.). 816p. (C). (gr. 13). 1999. text 26.95 (*0-8151-1226-2*, 31777) Mosby Inc.

— The Nurse Manager's Survival Guide: Practical Answers to Everyday Problems. 2nd ed. LC 96-37670. (Illus.). 400p. (C). (gr. 13). 1997. pap. text 29.95 (*0-8151-5672-3*, 28206) Mosby Inc.

— The Nurse's Guide to Home Health Care. LC 97-18701. (Illus.). 448p. (C). (gr. 13). 1997. spiral bd. 26.95 (*0-8151-5558-1*, 29633) Mosby Inc.

— Nursing Documentation Handbook. 2nd ed. (Illus.). 384p. (Orig.). (C). (gr. 13). 1995. spiral bd. 28.95 (*0-8151-6405-X*, 26130) Mosby Inc.

Marrelli, Tina M. & Friend, Laura. Home Health Aide - Guidelines for Care: A Resource Guide to Accompany "Home Health Aide: Guidelines for Care" (Illus.). 125p. 1996. teacher ed., ring bd. 89.95 (*0-9647801-1-9*) Marrelli.

Marrelli, Tina M. & Hilliard, Lynda. The Home Health Orientation Manual. LC 99-173195. (Illus.). 304p. (C). (gr. 13). 1997. text 99.95 (*0-8151-4650-7*, 29745) Mosby Inc.

Marrelli, Tina M. & Krulish, Linda H. Home Care Therapy: Quality, Documentation & Reimbursement - A Handbook for Physical Therapists, Speech-Language Pathologists, & Occupational Therapists. 400p. 1999. 34.95 (*0-9647801-2-7*) Marrelli.

Marrelli, Tina M. & Whittier, Sandra M. Home Health Aide - Guidelines for Care: A Handbook for Caregiving at Home. 225p. 1996. spiral bd. 24.95 (*0-9647801-0-0*) Marrelli.

Marren, Joe, jt. auth. see Meyer, Brian.

Marren, Joseph H. Mergers & Acquisitions: A Valuation Handbook. 450p. 1992. text 90.00 (*1-55623-676-X*, Irwn Prfssnl) McGraw-Hill Prof.

Marren, Peter. Britain's Rare Flowers. (Poyser Natural History Ser.). 352p. 1999. 49.95 (*0-85661-114-X*) Poyser.

Marrero, Domingo. El Centauro: Persona y Pensamiento De Ortega y Gasset. (UPREX, Ensayo Ser.: No. 30). 319p. (C). 1974. pap. 1.50 (*0-8477-0030-5*) U of PR Pr.

Marrero, Frank. Lincoln Beachey: The Man Who Owned the Sky. (Illus.). 208p. (Orig.). 1996. pap. 14.95 (*0-942087-12-7*) Scottwall Assocs.

Marrero, Levi. Cuba Economia y Sociedad, 15 vols., Vol. I. (Illus.). 1979. 30.00 (*84-359-0128-9*) Ediciones.

— Cuba Economia y Sociedad, 15 vols., Vol. I. 2nd ed. (Illus.). 1992. 30.00 (*84-399-8831-1*) Ediciones.

— Los Esclavos y la Virgen del Cobre: Dos Siglos de Lucha Por la Libertad en Cuba. LC 79-56290. (Coleccion Cuba y sus Jueces). (SPA., Illus.). 32p. (Orig.). 1982. pap. 3.00 (*0-89729-243-X*) Ediciones.

Marrero, Rafael A., ed. see Ayala, Julio R.

***Marrero, Raul.** Como Escapar del Laberinto Religioso. (SPA.). 1998. 6.99 (*0-8297-1579-7*) Vida Pubs.

Marrero, Robert G. Dracula: The Vampire Legend on Film. (Illus.). 128p. 1992. pap. 12.95 (*0-9634982-0-7*) Fantasma Bks.

— Godzilla-King of the Movie Monsters: An Illustrated Guide to Japanese Monster Movies. Winick, Margot, ed. (Illus.). 144p. (Orig.). 1996. pap. 15.95 (*1-888214-01-5*) Fantasma Bks.

— Vintage Monster Movies. (Illus.). 160p. 1993. pap. 12.95 (*0-9634982-1-5*) Fantasma Bks.

Marrero, Victor D., ed. El Mundo Delicioso de la Papa. deluxe ed. (SPA., Illus.). 112p. 1998. pap. 2.95 (*0-939193-46-9*) Edit Concepts.

Marrese, Michael. Blueprint Soviet Economics. (Illus.). 0.00 (*0-691-04260-8*) Princeton U Pr.

— Blueprint Soviet Economy. (Illus.). pap. 0.00 (*0-691-00379-3*) Princeton U Pr.

Marrese, Michael A., ed. Advances in Electronic Circuit Packaging: Proceedings of the 4th International Electronic Circuit Packaging Symposium, Vol. 4. LC 72-187719. 502p. reprint ed. pap. 155.70 (*0-8357-5159-7*, 202071800018) Bks Demand.

Marrett, Barbara & Neal, John. Mahina Tiare, Pacific Passages. LC 92-91094. (Illus.). 306p. 1993. 27.95 (*0-918074-05-3*) Pacific Intl.

— Mahina Tiare, Pacific Passages. LC 92-91094. (Illus.). 306p. 1994. pap. 19.95 (*0-918074-04-5*) Pacific Intl.

Marretta, Thomas, tr. from SLA. The Great Collection of the Lives of the Saints, Vol. I: September. LC 95-39035. (Illus.). viii, 499p. 1995. 35.00 (*0-9635183-6-4*); pap. 28.00 (*0-9635183-7-2*) Chrysostom Pr.

— The Great Collection of the Lives of the Saints, Vol. II: October. LC 95-39035. (Illus.). x, 460p. 1995. 35.00 (*0-9635183-8-0*); pap. 28.00 (*0-9635183-9-9*) Chrysostom Pr.

— The Great Collection of the Lives of the Saints, Vol. III: November. LC 95-39035. (Illus.). x, 688p. 1997. 35.00 (*1-889814-00-8*); pap. 28.00 (*1-889814-01-6*) Chrysostom Pr.

***Marretta, Thomas, tr. from SLA.** The Great Collection of the Lives of the Saints Vol. IV: December. LC 95-39035. (Illus.). 750p. (YA). (gr. 7-12). 2000. 35.00 (*1-889814-02-4*, L4H, L4S); pap. 28.00 (*1-889814-03-2*, L4H, L4S) Chrysostom Pr.

Marrevee, William. The Popular Guide to the Mass. 174p. (Orig.). 1992. pap. 9.95 (*0-912405-93-7*, Pastoral Press) OR Catholic.

Marrewa, Al. The Feminine Warrior: A Woman's Guide to Verbal, Psychological & Physical Epowerment. LC 97-73756. 288p. 1998. 23.00 (*1-57566-247-7*, Knsington) Kensgtn Pub Corp.

Marrewijk, Charles Van, see Brakman, Steven & Van Marrewijk, Charles.

Marrewijk, Charles Van, see Van Marrewijk, Charles.

An Asterisk (*) at the beginning of an entry indicates that the title is appearing for the first time.

*__Marri, Fabio & Lieber, Maria.__ Die Gluckseligkeit des gemeinen Wesens: Wege der Ideen zwischen Italien und Deutschland im Zeitalter der Aufklarung. 1999. 32.95 (*3-631-35214-X*, Pub. by P Lang) P Lang Pubng.

Marri, Fabio & Lieber, Maria. Lodovico Antonio Muratori und Deutschland: Studien Zur Kultur- und Geistesgeschichte der Fruhaufklarung Unter Mitwirkung Von Christian Weyers. (GER.). 213p. 1997. 32.95 (*3-631-30551-6*) P Lang Pubng.

Marriage & Family Development Committee. A Baha'i Parenting Program. 52p. 1990. pap. 4.95 (*0-909991-37-5*) Bahai.

Marriage & Family of the National Conference of Ca. Tenth Anniversary Edition of "A Family Perspective in Church & Society" 64p. 1998. pap. 7.95 (*1-57455-273-2*) US Catholic.

Marriage, Alwyn. The People of God: A Royal Priesthood. pap. write for info. (*0-232-51989-7*) S Asia.

Marriage, Margaret S., jt. auth. see Mincoff, Elizabeth.

Marrian, Christie, ed. Technology of Proximal Probe Lithography. LC 93-8684. (Institutes for Advanced Optical Technologies Ser.: Vol. IS 10). 1993. pap. 30.00 (*0-8194-1233-3*) SPIE.

— Technology of Proximal Probe Lithography. LC 93-8684. (Institutes for Advanced Optical Technologies Ser.: Vol. IS 10/HC). 1993. 30.00 (*0-8194-1232-5*) SPIE.

Marrian, Christie, jt. ed. see Cerrina, F.

Marric, J. J. Gideon's Month. 1989. mass mkt. 3.95 (*0-8217-2766-4*, Zebra Kensgtn) Kensgtn Pub Corp.

— Gideon's Week. 1989. mass mkt. 3.95 (*0-8217-2722-2*, Zebra Kensgtn) Kensgtn Pub Corp.

*__Marrie, Thomas J.__ Community-Acquired Pneumonia. LC 00-34931. 2000. write for info. (*0-306-46432-2*) Kluwer Academic.

Marrie, Thomas J., ed. Q Fever Vol. 1: The Disease, Vol. 1. LC 96-3686. (Illus.). 545p. 1990. lib. bdg. 179.00 (*0-8493-5984-8*, RC182) CRC Pr.

Marriet, Jane & Topaz, Muriel. Study Guide for Intermediate Labanotation. 2nd rev. ed. (Illus.). 110p. (C). 1970. pap. text 22.95 (*0-932582-58-3*, Pub. by Dance Notation) Princeton Bk Co.

Marriett, Jane, jt. auth. see Miller, Buzz.

Marrin, Albert. Aztecs & Spaniards: Cortes & the Conquest of Mexico. LC 85-28782. (Illus.). 224p. (YA). (gr. 5 up). 1986. text, lib. bdg. 15.95 (*0-689-31176-1*) Atheneum Yung Read.

— Cowboys, Indians, & Gunfighters: The Story of the Cattle Kingdom. LC 92-5727. (Illus.). 208p. (YA). (gr. 5 up). 1993. 22.95 (*0-689-31774-3*) Atheneum Yung Read.

— Empires Lost & Won. LC 96-20851. (Illus.). 224p. (YA). (gr. 5 up). 1997. 19.00 (*0-689-80414-8*) S&S Childrens.

Marrin, Albert. Plains Warrior: Chief Quanah Parker & the Comanches. (Illus.). 208p. (YA). (gr. 5 up). 1996. 18.00 (*0-689-80081-9*) Atheneum Yung Read.

Marrin, Albert. The Sea King: Sir Francis Drake & His Times. (Illus.). 176p. (J). (gr. 5-9). 1995. 20.00 (*0-689-31887-1*) Atheneum Yung Read.

*__Marrin, Albert.__ Sitting Bull & His World. LC 99-42367. (Illus.). 256p. (YA). (gr. 7-12). 2000. 25.99 (*0-525-45944-8*, Dutton Child) Peng Put Young Read.

Marrin, Albert. Stalin: Russia's Man of Steel. 1993. 11.09 (*0-606-06018-9*, Pub. by Turtleback) Demco.

— Struggle for a Continent: The French & Indian Wars, 1690-1760. LC 86-26508. (Illus.). 232p. (YA). (gr. 5 up). 1987. lib. bdg. 15.95 (*0-689-31313-6*) Atheneum Yung Read.

— Terror of the Spanish Main: Sir Henry Morgan & His Buccaneers. LC 98-7819. (Illus.). 256p. (YA). (gr. 6 up). 1999. 19.99 (*0-525-45942-1*, Dutton Child) Peng Put Young Read.

— Unconditional Surrender: U. S. Grant & the Civil War. LC 93-20041. (Illus.). 208p. (YA). (gr. 5 up). 1994. 21.00 (*0-689-31837-5*) Atheneum Yung Read.

— Virginia's General: Robert E. Lee & the Civil War. LC 94-13353. (Illus.). 192p. (J). (gr. 5-9). 1994. 22.00 (*0-689-31838-3*) Atheneum Yung Read.

— The War for Independence: The Story of the American Revolution. LC 87-13711. (Illus.). 288p. (YA). (gr. 5 up). 1988. 19.00 (*0-689-31390-X*) Atheneum Yung Read.

Marrin, Richard B. A Glance Back in Time: Life in Colonial New Jersey (1704-1770) As Depicted in News Accounts of the Day. 359p. (Orig.). 1994. pap. 25.00 (*0-7884-0089-4*) Heritage Bk.

— Passage Point: An Amateur's Dig into New Jersey's Colonial Past. 339p. 1997. pap. 25.50 (*0-7884-0777-5*, MO66) Heritage Bk.

Marriner, Paul. Miramichi River, NB. (River Journal Ser.: Vol. 4, No. 4). (Illus.). 48p. 1997. pap. 15.95 (*1-57188-055-0*) F Amato Pubns.

— Modern Atlantic Salmon Flies. (Illus.). 128p. 1999. pap. 34.95 (*1-57188-152-2*); spiral bd. 44.95 (*1-57188-153-0*) F Amato Pubns.

Marriner, Paul C. Ausable River, NY. (River Journal Ser.: Vol. 1, No. 4). (Illus.). 48p. 1994. pap. 14.95 (*1-878175-43-2*) F Amato Pubns.

Marriner-Tomey, Ann. Guide to Nursing Management & Leadership. 5th ed. (Illus.). 544p. (C). (gr. 13). 1995. pap. text 38.00 (*0-8151-6401-7*, 25500) Mosby Inc.

Marriner-Tomey, Ann. Guide to Nursing Management & Leadership. 5th ed. (Illus.). 544p. 1996. teacher ed. write for info. (*0-8151-6293-6*) Mosby Inc.

*__Marriner-Tomey, Ann, ed.__ Modelos y Teorias de Enfermeri. 4th ed. (C). 1999. text 40.02 (*84-8174-348-8*) Mosby Inc.

Marriner-Tomey, Ann & Alligood, Martha R. Nursing Theorists & Their Work. 4th ed. LC 97-11533. (Illus.). 576p. (C). (gr. 13). 1997. pap. text 38.00 (*0-8151-4421-0*, 30903) Mosby Inc.

Marriner-Tomey, Ann, jt. ed. see Alligood, Martha R.

Marrink, Jan. Amyloidosis. 1986. text 221.50 (*0-89838-844-9*) Kluwer Academic.

Marrion, Alastair R., ed. The Chemistry & Physics of Coatings. 186p. 1994. 42.00 (*0-85186-994-7*, R6994) CRC Pr.

Marrion, Robert & Fosten, Don. The British Army, 1914-18. (Men-at-Arms Ser.: No. 81). (Illus.). 48p. pap. 11.95 (*0-85045-287-2*, 9021, Pub. by Ospry) Stackpole.

— The German Army, 1914-18. (Men-at-Arms Ser.: No. 80). (Illus.). 48p. pap. 11.95 (*0-85045-283-X*, 9020, Pub. by Ospry) Stackpole.

Marriot, F. H. A Dictionary of Statistical Terms. 5th ed. 1996. 76.67 (*0-582-01905-2*, Pub. by Addison-Wesley) Longman.

Marriot, Leo. 80 Years of Civil Aviation. (Illus.). 224p. 1997. 19.98 (*0-7858-0865-5*) Bk Sales Inc.

— Titanic. (Illus.). 160p. 1997. 15.98 (*0-7651-0647-7*) Smithmark.

Marriot, Paul & Argent, Yvonne. The Last Days of T. E. Lawrence: A Leaf in the Wind. LC 97-149225. (Illus.). 208p. 1996. 45.00 (*1-898595-16-X*, Pub. by Alpha Pr Ltd) Intl Spec Bk.

— The Last Days of T. E. Lawrence: A Leaf in the Wind. 208p. 1998. pap. 24.95 (*1-898595-22-4*, Pub. by Alpha Pr Ltd) Intl Spec Bk.

Marriott. Materials Selection in Mechanical Design. 80p. (C). 1994. 48.00 (*0-02-376251-9*, Macmillan Coll) P-H.

Marriott, Alice. Hell on Horses & Women. LC 53-5479. 1993. pap. 15.95 (*0-8061-2482-2*) U of Okla Pr.

— Indians of the Four Corners: The Anasazi & Their Pueblo Descendants. 2nd ed. (Illus.). 182p. (YA). (gr. 6-12). 1996. reprint ed. pap. 12.95 (*0-941270-91-2*) Ancient City Pr.

— Maria: The Potter of San Ildefonso. LC 48-2101. (Civilization of the American Indian Ser.: Vol. 27). (Illus.). 320p. 1987. pap. 16.95 (*0-8061-2048-7*) U of Okla Pr.

— The Ten Grandmothers. LC 45-1584. (Civilization of the American Indian Ser.: Vol. 26). 306p. 1983. pap. 15.95 (*0-8061-1825-3*) U of Okla Pr.

Marriott, Bernadette M., ed. see Institute of Medicine, Committee on Military Nutri.

Marriott, Bernadette M., ed. see Institute of Medicine, Military Nutrition Research.

Marriott, Betty B. Environmental Impact Assessment: A Practical Guide. LC 96-39003. 320p. 1997. 69.95 (*0-07-040410-0*) McGraw.

Marriott, Charles. Modern Movement in Painting. 1977. lib. bdg. 80.00 (*0-8490-2269-X*) Gordon Pr.

*__Marriott, David.__ On Black Men. LC 00-38342. 2000. pap. 16.50 (*0-231-12227-6*); text 49.50 (*0-231-12226-8*) Col U Pr.

Marriott, Donna. Celebrating Father's Day: Father's Day is for Special People, No. 4530. Kupperstein, Joel, ed. (Illus.). 16p. (ps-2). 1999. pap. 2.99 (*1-57471-575-5*) Creat Teach Pr.

— 100 Years Ago, Vol. 4416. Kupperstein, Joel, ed. (Learn to Read Social Studies). (Illus.). 16p. (J). (ps-2). 1998. pap. 2.75 (*1-57471-339-6*, 4416) Creat Teach Pr.

— What Are the Other Kids Doing? . . . While You Teach Small Groups, Vol. 3345. Kupperstein, Joel, ed. LC 98-125034. (Illus.). 160p. (J). (gr. 1-3). 1997. pap. 15.98 (*1-57471-293-4*) Creat Teach Pr.

*__Marriott, Edward.__ The Lost Tribe. 2000. pap. 14.00 (*0-8050-6449-4*) H Holt & Co.

— The Lost Tribe: A Harrowing Passage into New Guinea's Heart of Darkness. 258p. 2000. 23.00 (*0-7881-9341-4*) DIANE Pub.

Marriott, Edward. The Lost Tribe: A Harrowing Passage into New Guinea's Heart of Darkness. LC 97-10420. 1997. 23.00 (*0-8050-5318-2*) H Holt & Co.

— Savage Shore: Life & Death with Nicaragua's Last Shark Hunters. LC 99-43262. 288p. 2000. 24.00 (*0-8050-5555-X*, Metropol Bks) H Holt & Co.

— Savage Shore: Life & Death with Nicaragua's Last Shark Hunters. (Illus.). 320p. 2001. pap. 15.00 (*0-8050-5556-8*, Owl) H Holt & Co.

Marriott, F. H., jt. auth. see Krzanowski, W. J.

Marriott, G. R., tr. see De Laveleye, Emile.

Marriott, Gerard, ed. see Colowick, Sidney P.

Marriott, Henry, et al. Heart Trouble Encyclopedia. LC 99-192855. 368p. (Orig.). 1996. pap. 19.95 (*0-7737-5744-9*) Stoddart Publ.

Marriott, Henry J. Pearls & Pitfalls in Electrocardiography: Pithy Practical Pointers. 2nd ed. LC 97-13639. 1997. write for info. (*0-683-03017-5*) Lppncott W & W.

— Pearls & Pitfalls in Electrocardiography: Pithy Practical Points. LC 90-5594. (Illus.). 157p. 1990. pap. text 29.00 (*0-8121-1334-9*) Lppncott W & W.

— Pearls & Pitfalls in Electrocardiology. 2nd ed. (Illus.). 168p. 1997. pap. 32.00 (*0-683-30170-5*) Lppncott W & W.

— Rhythm Quizlets: Self Assessment. LC 87-2802. (Illus.). 189p. 1987. pap. text 29.00 (*0-8121-1110-9*) Lppncott W & W.

— Rhythm Quizlets: Self Assessment. 2nd ed. LC 87-2802. (Illus.). 288p. 1996. pap. 32.95 (*0-683-05582-8*) Lppncott W & W.

Marriott, Henry J. L. Bedside Cardiac Diagnosis. (Illus.). 315p. 1992. text 54.00 (*0-397-51085-3*) Lppncott W & W.

Marriott, Henry J. L. & Conover, Mary B. Advanced Concepts in Arrhythmias, No. 3. 3rd ed. LC 97-15127. (Illus.). 416p. (C). (gr. 13). 1998. text 42.95 (*0-8151-2090-7*, 28310) Mosby Inc.

Marriott, J. A. English History in Shakespeare. LC 75-174685. (Studies in Shakespeare: No. 24). 1971. reprint ed. lib. bdg. 75.00 (*0-8383-1337-X*) M S G Haskell Hse.

Marriott, J. W., Jr. & Brown, Kathi A. The Spirit to Serve: Marriott's Way. LC 97-22874. (Illus.). 256p. 1997. 25.00 (*0-88730-878-3*, HarpBusn) HarpInfo.

*__Marriott, Jackie.__ How to Have an Obedient Dog. 3rd ed. (Illus.). 128p. 2001. pap. 6.95 (*0-7160-2098-X*, Pub. by Elliot RW Bks) Midpt Trade.

Marriott, James W., ed. Modern Essays & Sketches. LC 68-22928. (Essay Index Reprint Ser.). 1977. 18.95 (*0-8369-0679-9*) Ayer.

Marriott, John. The Culture of Labourism: The East End Between the Wars. 244p. 1994. pap. 28.00 (*0-7486-0285-2*, Pub. by Edinburgh U Pr) Col U Pr.

*__Marriott, John & Matsumura, Masaie.__ The Metropolitan Poor: Semifactual Accounts, 1795-1910, 6 vols. LC 99-52651. 2536p. 1999. 795.00 (*1-85196-524-6*, Pub. by Pickering & Chatto) Ashgate Pub Co.

Marriott, John A. English Political Institutions: An Introductory Study. 4th ed. LC 74-9169. 348p. 1975. reprint ed. lib. bdg. 75.00 (*0-8371-7621-2*, MAEP, Greenwood Pr) Greenwood.

— The Makers of Modern Italy: Napoleon to Mussolini. LC 74-30842. (Illus.). 228p. 1975. reprint ed. lib. bdg. 65.00 (*0-8371-7936-X*, MAMA, Greenwood Pr) Greenwood.

— Second Chambers. LC 78-102250. (Select Bibliographies Reprint Ser.). 1977. 29.95 (*0-8369-5135-2*) Ayer.

— This Realm of England. LC 78-140368. (Select Bibliographies Reprint Ser.). 1977. reprint ed. 23.95 (*0-8369-5611-7*) Ayer.

Marriott, Kim & Meyer, Bernd E., eds. Visual Language Theory. LC 97-38107. (Illus.). 304p. 1998. 49.95 (*0-387-98367-8*) Spr-Verlag.

Marriott, Kim & Stuckey, Peter J. Programming with Constraints: An Introduction. LC 97-40549. (Illus.). 476p. 1998. 49.50 (*0-262-13341-5*) MIT Pr.

Marriott, Leo. ABC British Airways. 2nd ed. 96p. 1998. pap. 12.95 (*1-882663-39-X*) Plymouth VT.

— British Airports Then & Now. (ABC Ser.). (Illus.). 160p. 1994. 19.95 (*0-7110-2076-0*) Spec Mkting Intl.

*__Marriott, Leo.__ Lighthouses. (Illus.). 128p. 1999. 16.98 (*0-7651-1686-3*) Smithmark.

— Portraits of the Civil War: The Men & Women in Blue & Gray. (Illus.). 128p. 1999. 14.98 (*0-7651-1691-X*) Smithmark.

Marriott, Marion. A Tale of Two Seekers. LC 97-91164. 1998. pap. 19.95 (*0-533-12582-0*) Vantage.

Marriott, McKim, ed. India Through Hindu Categories. (Illus.). 228p. (C). 1990. 29.95 (*0-8039-9636-5*) Sage.

— Village India: Studies in the Little Community. LC 55-9326. xx, 270p. 1986. pap. text 15.00 (*0-226-50645-2*) U Ch Pr.

Marriott, Michael. Mountains & Hills of Britain: A Guide to the Uplands of England, Scotland, & Wales. LC 82-194503. 176p. 1982. write for info. (*0-00-218028-6*) Collins.

Marriott, Michelle. Old King Cole & Friends. (Soap Opera Ser.). (Illus.). 8p. (J). (gr. 4 up). 1990. 6.99 (*0-85953-446-4*) Childs Play.

Marriott, Nancy, ed. see Becker, Lyle M.

Marriott, Neil. Small Business Management. (C). 2000. pap. text. write for info. (*0-201-40390-0*) Addison-Wesley.

Marriott, Neil & Chandler, Roy. Management Accounting: A Spreadsheet Approach. LC 92-40486. 1993. 35.90 (*0-13-555152-8*) P-H.

Marriott, Neil, jt. auth. see Olde, Peter.

Marriott, Norman G. Principles of Food Sanitation. 1989. text 59.95 (*0-442-31807-3*) Chapman & Hall.

— Principles of Food Sanitation. 3rd ed. 1993. text 59.95 (*0-442-01201-2*) Chapman & Hall.

— Principles of Food Sanitation. 4th ed. LC 98-43373. 450p. 1999. 63.00 (*0-8342-1232-3*) Aspen Pub.

*__Marriott, Paul & Salmon, Mark, eds.__ Applications of Differential Geometry to Econometrics. LC 99-58375. (Illus.). 344p. 2000. write for info. (*0-521-65116-6*) Cambridge U Pr.

Marriott, Paul D. Saving Historic Roads: Design & Policy Guidelines. LC 97-14443. 256p. 1997. 44.95 (*0-471-19762-9*) Wiley.

*__Marriott, S., et al, eds.__ Floodplains. (Special Publication Ser.: No. 163). 284p. 1999. 108.00 (*1-86239-050-9*, Pub. by Geol Soc Pub Hse) AAPG.

Marriott, Stuart. Extramural Empires: Service & Self-Interest in English University Adult Education 1873-1983. (C). 1984. 70.00 (*0-902031-94-5*, Pub. by Univ Nottingham) St Mut.

— Picture Books in the Primary School Classroom. 160p. 1991. pap. 27.00 (*1-85396-144-2*, Pub. by P Chapman) Taylor & Francis.

Marriott, Stuart, ed. Extra-Mural Empires: Service & Self-Interest in English University Adult Education 1873-1983. 137p. (C). 1984. 60.00 (*0-7855-2392-8*, Pub. by Univ Nottingham) St Mut.

Marriott, Thomas. The Pagan Land. large type ed. 688p. 1983. 27.99 (*0-7089-8124-0*, Charnwood) Ulverscroft.

Marriott, Val & Timblick, Terry, eds. Loneliness: How to Overcome It. (C). 1989. 35.00 (*0-86242-077-6*, Pub. by Age Concern Eng) St Mut.

Marriotte, Jeff, jt. auth. see Golden, Christopher.

Marris. Managerial Capitalism Retrospective. LC 98-16540. 300p. 1998. text 69.95 (*0-312-21578-9*) St Martin.

*__Marris, Paul & Thornham, Sue.__ Media Studies. 2nd ed. LC 99-55968. 2000. pap. text 29.50 (*0-8147-5647-6*) NYU Pr.

Marris, Paul & Thornham, Sue, eds. Media Studies: A Reader. 544p. Date not set. pap. 24.50 (*0-7486-0778-1*, Pub. by Edinburgh U Pr) Col U Pr.

Marris, Peter. The Politics of Uncertainty: Attachment in Private & Public Life. 208p. (C). 1996. 75.00 (*0-415-13171-5*); pap. 24.99 (*0-415-13172-3*) Routledge.

Marris, Peter & Rein, Martin. Dilemmas of Social Reform: Poverty & Community Action in the U. S. 2nd ed. LC 81-16361. 326p. (C). 1996. pap. text 10.00 (*0-226-50657-6*) U Ch Pr.

— Dilemmas of Social Reform: Poverty & Community Action in the United States. 2nd ed. LC 81-16361. 321p. reprint ed. pap. 99.60 (*0-608-09025-5*, 206966000005) Bks Demand.

Marris, Robin. Ending Poverty. LC 98-61513. (Prospects for Tomorrow Ser.). (Illus.). 112p. 1999. pap. 12.95 (*0-500-28114-9*, Pub. by Thames Hudson) Norton.

— Reconstructing Keynesian Economics with Imperfect Competition: A Desk-Top Simulation. 352p. 1991. text 95.00 (*1-85278-541-1*) E Elgar.

Marris, Robin & Wood, Adrian, eds. Corporate Economy: Growth, Competition, & Innovative Potential. (Studies in Technology & Society). 479p. 1971. 52.00 (*0-674-17252-3*) HUP.

Marris, Robin, jt. ed. see Rosenbloom, Richard S.

Marris, Robin L. How to Save the Underclass. LC 96-10521. 200p. 1997. text 45.00 (*0-312-16208-1*) St Martin.

Marris, Stephan. Deficits & the Dollar Summary: The World Economy at Risk. fac. ed. LC 85-17303. (Policy Analyses in International Economics Ser.: Vol. 14). 40p. 1985. reprint ed. pap. 30.00 (*0-7837-7775-2*, 204753000002) Bks Demand.

— Deficits & the Dollar Text: The World Economy at Risk. fac. ed. LC 85-17303. (Policy Analyses in International Economics Ser.: Vol. 14). 384p. 1985. reprint ed. pap. 119.10 (*0-7837-7774-4*, 204753000001) Bks Demand.

Marris, Stephen. Deficits & the Dollar: The World Economy at Risk. LC 87-29887. (Policy Analyses in International Economics Ser.: 14). (Illus.). 416p. 1987. reprint ed. pap. 129.00 (*0-7837-7776-0*, 204753100007) Bks Demand.

— Managing the World Economy: Will We Ever Learn? LC 84-19344. (Essays in International Finance Ser.: No. 155). 30p. 1984. pap. text 10.00 (*0-88165-062-5*) Princeton U Int Finan Econ.

Marris, T. Information Processing with COBOL. (Illus.). 160p. (Orig.). 1989. pap. text 16.95 (*0-7131-3636-7*, Pub. by E A) Routldge.

Marris, Veronica. Lives Worth Living: Women's Experience of Chronic Illness. 256p. 1996. pap. 14.00 (*0-04-440938-9*, Pub. by Rivers Oram) NYU Pr.

Marrison, Andrew. British Business & Protection, 1903-1932. LC 95-37703. (Illus.). 508p. (C). 1996. text 89.00 (*0-19-820298-9*, Clarendon Pr) OUP.

Marrison, Geoffrey, et al. A Catalogue of the South-East Asian History Collections of Dr. D. K. Bassett in the Brynmor Jones Library in the University of Hull LC 98-105724. (Bibliography & Literature Ser.). 86p. 1992. write for info. (*0-85958-590-5*) Univ of Hull Pr.

*__Marrison, Geoffrey E.__ Catalogue of Javanese & Sasak Texts. 235p. 1999. pap. 65.00 (*90-6718-143-9*, Pub. by KITLV Pr) Book Bin.

— Sasak & Javanese Literature of Lombok. (Working Papers: Vol. 14). 223p. 1999. pap. 44.00 (*90-6718-085-8*, Pub. by KITLV Pr) Book Bin.

Marrison, Shelly. Western Americana Catalogue Prices, 1998 Vol. 9: 19,000 Price Entries on Non-Texas Western Americana Offered for Sale in 1995. 242p. (Orig.). 1996. pap. 38.50 (*0-926158-26-0*) W M Morrison.

Marro, Joaquin & Dickman, Ronald. Nonequilibrium Phase Transitions in Lattice Models. LC 98-29461. (Collection Alea - Saclay). (Illus.). 300p. (C). 1998. 100.00 (*0-521-48062-0*) Cambridge U Pr.

Marro, Joaquin & Garrido, P. L. Computational Physics, II: Granada Lectures. 388p. 1993. text 105.00 (*981-02-1163-5*) World Scientific Pub.

Marro, Joaquin, ed. see Thirteenth Sitges Conference Staff.

Marrocco, Mary. The Good News Is Love. 88p. 1998. pap. 9.95 (*0-88489-503-3*) St Marys.

Marrocco, Nancy. Growing in the Dark Vol. 2: Homemade Christians II. (Illus.). 80p. 1998. pap. 9.95 (*0-88489-598-X*) St Marys.

— Homemade Christians. LC 95-900517. (Illus.). 64p. 1995. pap. 7.95 (*0-88489-381-2*) St Marys.

Marrocco, Nancy. Promise in the Storm: Grieving & Dying with Hope. 312p. 1996. teacher ed., spiral bd. 24.95 (*0-88489-367-7*, 1226) St Marys.

Marrocco, Nancy. Promise in the Storm: Grieving & Dying with Hope. LC 97-169638. 208p. 1997. pap. 15.20 (*0-88489-366-9*) St Marys.

Marrocco, W. Thomas. Fourteenth Century Italian Cacce. 2nd rev. ed. LC 60-13484. (Medieval Academy Bks.: No. 39). 1961. 20.00 (*0-910956-16-2*) Medieval Acad.

*__Marrodan, Carlos Losada, ed.__ De Burocratas a Gerentes? Las Ciencias de Gestion Aplicadas a la Administracion del Estado. (SPA.). 464p. 1999. 26.95 (*1-886938-64-4*) IADB.

Marrogi, Aizen J., jt. ed. see Freeman, Scott M.

Marron, jt. auth. see Blancero.

Marron, Aileen. Beach Body Art. (Illus.). 1999. pap. 9.95 (*1-885203-77-2*) Tuttle Pubng.

— Celtic Body Art. (Illus.). 1999. pap. 9.95 (*1-885203-78-0*) Tuttle Pubng.

*__Marron, Aileen & Henna, Halawa.__ The Henna Body Art Kit: Everything You Need to Create Stunning Temporary Tattoos. LC 98-65054. (Illus.). 96p. 1998. pap. 22.95 (*1-885203-64-0*) Jrny Editions.

Marron, Henri, jt. auth. see Leclercq, Dom H.

Marron, J. Function Estimates. LC 86-14203. (Contemporary Mathematics Ser.: Vol. 59). 178p. 1986. pap. 30.00 (*0-8218-5062-8*, CONM/59) Am Math.

Marron, Jamie. Smart Eyes. write for info. (*0-318-59574-5*) Addison-Wesley.

Marron, John, et al, eds. Under the Bridge of Silence: California Poets in the Schools Statewide Anthology 1986. LC 86-71766. 91p. (Orig.). (J). (gr. k-12). 1986. pap. 6.95 (*0-939927-00-4*) Calif Poets Schls.

Marron, Kevin. Fatal Mistakes. 240p. 1993. 27.95 (*0-385-25439-3*) Doubleday.

— Fatal Mistakes. 240p. 1994. mass mkt. 16.95 (*0-385-25482-2*) Doubleday.

— The Slammer. LC 96-163155. 320p. 1997. mass mkt. 19.95 (*0-385-25616-7*) Doubleday.

*__Marron, Maggie.__ The Backstreet Boys. LC 99-47223. (Illus.). 96p. 1999. write for info. (*1-56799-947-6*, Friedman-Fairfax) M Friedman Pub Grp Inc.

— The Backstreet Boys. LC 00-20226. (Illus.). 2000. write for info. (*1-58663-006-7*) M Friedman Pub Grp Inc.

— Britney Spears: Stylin'! 96p. 1999. mass mkt. 9.99 (*0-446-67583-0*, Pub. by Warner Bks) Little.

— Christina Aguilera. (Illus.). 128p. 2000. pap. 12.95 (*0-7893-0479-1*) Universe.

— Ricky Martin. LC 99-37165. 1999. write for info. (*1-56744-916-6*) Kazi Pubns.

— The Ultimate Backstreet Boys Quiz Book. LC 00-30878. (Illus.). 2000. write for info. (*1-58663-037-7*) M Friedman Pub Grp Inc.

— Will Smith: From Rap Star to Mega Star. (Illus.). 96p. 2000. pap. 10.95 (*0-446-67630-6*) Warner Bks.

Marron, Margaret, ed. see Weakland, Steve.

Marrone. Psychology: A Global Perspective. Date not set. write for info. (*1-57259-647-3*) Worth.

*__Marrone, Catherine.__ Professional & Patient Responsibilities in Home Health Care Nursing. LC 99-31118. (Studies in Health & Human Services: Vol. 34). 196p. 1999. text 89.95 (*0-7734-7975-9*) E Mellen.

*__Marrone, Claire.__ Female Journeys: Autobiographical Expressions by French & Italian Women, 180. LC 99-89162. (Contributions in Women's Studies: Vol. 180). 200p. 2000. 59.95 (*0-313-30727-X*, Greenwood Pr) Greenwood.

*__Marrone, Gaetana.__ Cinema Liliana Cavan. LC 99-27242. 2000. 59.50 (*0-691-03193-2*, Pub. by Princeton U Pr) Cal Prin Full Svc.

— The Gaze & the Labyrinth: The Cinema of Liliana Cavani LC 99-27242. 2000. 22.95 (*0-691-00873-6*, Pub. by Princeton U Pr) Cal Prin Full Svc.

Marrone, Mario. Attachment & Interaction. (International Library of Group Analysis). 238p. 1998. pap. 75.00 (*1-85302-587-9*) Taylor & Francis.

Marrone, Robert. Body of Knowledge: An Introduction to Body/Mind Psychology. LC 89-28863. (SUNY Series in Transpersonal & Humanistic Psychology). 160p. (C). 1990. text 54.50 (*0-7914-0387-4*); pap. text 18.95 (*0-7914-0388-2*) State U NY Pr.

Marrone, Robert L. Death, Mourning, & Caring. LC 96-32070. 518p. 1997. mass mkt. 74.95 (*0-314-09979-4*) West Pub.

Marrone, Sandy. St. Louis Blues & Other Song Hits of 1914. 112p. 1990. pap. 9.95 (*0-486-26383-5*) Dover.

Marrone, Steven P. Truth & Scientific Knowledge in the Thought of Henry of Ghent. LC 84-62885. (Speculum Anniversary Monographs: No. 11). 164p. 1985. 20.00 (*0-910956-91-X*); pap. 12.00 (*0-910956-92-8*) Medieval Acad.

— William of Auvergne & Robert Grosseteste: New Ideas of Truth in the Early Thirteenth Century. LC 82-61375. 331p. 1983. reprint ed. pap. 102.70 (*0-7837-9381-2*, 206012500004) Bks Demand.

Marrone, Teresa. The Back-Country Kitchen: Camp Cooking for Canoeists, Hikers, & Anglers. 208p. (Orig.). 1996. pap. 14.95 (*0-9651535-0-9*) Nrthern Trails.

*__Marrone, Teresa.__ The Seasonal Cabin Cookbook. (Illus.). 300p. 2000. 16.95 (*1-885061-79-X*) Adventure Pubns.

Marrone, Teresa, ed. & illus. see Hunt, Dennis.

*__Marrone, Thomas.__ Baby Boomer Thoughts. 56p. 1999. pap. 9.95 (*0-7414-0107-X*) Buy Books.

Marroritis, Basil P. You Make the Credit Call: Interactive Case Studies in Credit Management. Donohue, Teresa G., ed. 314p. (Orig.). 1996. pap. 34.50 (*1-888505-00-1*) NACM.

Marrosu, M. G., et al, eds. Trends in Neuroimmunology. LC 90-6764. (Illus.). 178p. 1990. 55.00 (*0-306-43510-1*, Plenum Trade) Perseus Pubng.

Marrota, Priscila. Power & Wisdom: The New Path for Women. 1. 254p. 1999. pap. text 17.95 (*0-9666339-0-3*) Women Wisdom.

Marrott, Barbara. Getting a Jump on Fitness. LC 96-49159. (Illus.). 192p. 1997. pap. 14.95 (*1-56980-102-9*) Barricade Bks.

Marrou, Henri I. A History of Education in Antiquity. Lamb, George, tr. LC 81-70008. (Wisconsin Studies in Classics). 484p. 1982. reprint ed. pap. 150.10 (*0-7837-9786-9*, 206051500005) Bks Demand.

Marrou, Henri-Irenee, ed. see Moreau, Jacques.

Marrow, Alfred J. The Practical Theorist: The Life & Work of Kurt Lewin. LC 77-1400. 319p. reprint ed. pap. 98.90 (*0-608-13533-X*, 202255100028) Bks Demand.

Marrow, Deborah. The Art Patronage of Maria de'Medici. LC 82-1951. (Studies in Baroque Art History: No. 4). (Illus.). 191p. 1982. reprint ed. pap. 59.30 (*0-8357-1303-2*, 207002600063) Bks Demand.

Marrow, James H. Hans Baldung Grien. 1981. 19.95 (*0-226-94443-3*) U Ch Pr.

— The Hours of Margaret of Cleves. (Illus.). 216p. 1997. pap. 35.00 (*972-8128-04-5*, Pub. by Calouste Gulbenkian) U of Wash Pr.

Marrow, James H. The Hours of Simon de Varie. LC 93-28120. (Illus.). 268p. 1994. 95.00 (*0-89236-284-7*, Pub. by J P Getty Trust) OUP.

Marrow, John, jt. auth. see Ambler, Mark.

Marrow, Linda, ed. see Adams, Faye.

Marrow, Linda, ed. see Andrews, V. C.

Marrow, Linda, ed. see Barnett, Jill.

Marrow, Linda, ed. see Cates, Kimberly.

Marrow, Linda, ed. see Davis, Kathryn L.

Marrow, Linda, ed. see Deveraux, Jude.

Marrow, Linda, ed. see Garwood, Julie.

Marrow, Linda, ed. see Haeger, Diane.

Marrow, Linda, ed. see Hall, Paris.

Marrow, Linda, ed. see Hughes, D. T.

Marrow, Linda, ed. see Jensen, Kathryn.

Marrow, Linda, ed. see Laiman, Leah.

Marrow, Linda, ed. see McNaught, Judith.

Marrow, Linda, ed. see McNaught, Judith, et al.

Marrow, Linda, ed. see Miller, Linda Lael.

Marrow, Linda, ed. see O'Brien, Judith.

Marrow, Linda, ed. see Perry, Michael R.

Marrow, Linda, ed. see Pickard, Nancy.

Marrow, Linda, ed. see Quinn, Elizabeth.

Marrow, Linda, ed. see Schechter, Harold.

Marrow, Linda, ed. see Stewart, Mariah.

Marrow, Linda, ed. see Verge, Lisa A.

Marrow, R. A. Going Around the Bend. 93p. (Orig.). (J). (gr. 5-8). 1998. pap. 9.99 (*0-88092-166-8*, 1668) Royal Fireworks.

Marrow, Raphael W. & Carter, Harriet I. In Pursuit of Crime: The Police of Chicago: Chronicle of a Hundred Years 1833-1933. LC 96-84389. (Illus.). 730p. 1996. lib. bdg. 40.00 (*1-883033-04-7*) Flats Pub.

Marrow, Stanley B. The Gospel of John: A Reading. LC 94-44922. 416p. (Orig.). 1995. pap. 19.95 (*0-8091-3550-7*) Paulist Pr.

— Paul, His Letters & Theology: An Introduction to Paul's Epistles. 288p. (Orig.). 1986. pap. 19.95 (*0-8091-2744-X*) Paulist Pr.

Marrow, Tem. Verses from a Yielded Vessel. 78p. 1998. pap. 10.00 (*1-57502-815-8*, PO2243) Morris Pubng.

Marrs, Carol. The Complete Book of Speech Communication: A Workbook of Ideas & Activities for Students of Speech & Theatre. Zapel, Arthur L., ed. LC 91-47621. (Illus.). 176p. (YA). (gr. 9 up). 1992. pap. 14.95 (*0-916260-87-9*, B142) Meriwether Pub.

Marrs, Christine A. Independent Horsemanship - Beginner Level. iv, 26p. 1997. pap. text, teacher ed. 9.99 (*1-928890-07-5*) I B Hoofinit.

Marrs, Christine A. Independent Horsemanship - Beginner Level: Student Set, 6 vols. (Illus.). 1997. pap. text, student ed. 39.50 (*1-928890-00-8*) I B Hoofinit.

— Independent Horsemanship - Beginner Level Bk. 1: Beginner Basic. iv, 40p. 1997. pap. text 9.99 (*1-928890-01-6*) I B Hoofinit.

— Independent Horsemanship - Beginner Level Bk. 2: The Mechanics of Riding. (Illus.). iv, 32p. 1997. pap. text 5.99 (*1-928890-02-4*) I B Hoofinit.

— Independent Horsemanship - Beginner Level Bk. 3: Objective Riding. (Illus.). iv, 32p. 1997. pap. text 5.99 (*1-928890-03-2*) I B Hoofinit.

— Independent Horsemanship - Beginner Level Bk. 4: ESP Riding. (Illus.). iv, 32p. 1997. pap. text 5.99 (*1-928890-04-0*) I B Hoofinit.

— Independent Horsemanship - Beginner Level Bk. 5: Discipline & Manners. (Illus.). iv, 28p. 1997. pap. text 5.99 (*1-928890-05-9*) I B Hoofinit.

— Independent Horsemanship - Beginner Level Bk. 6: Breed Basics. (Illus.). iv, 28p. 1997. pap. text 5.99 (*1-928890-06-7*) I B Hoofinit.

*__Marrs, David.__ Dinometrics: The Biomechanics of Dinosaurs. 200p. 1999. 40.00 (*0-387-98875-0*) Spr-Verlag.

Marrs, Donald. Executive in Passage: Career in Crisis - The Door to Uncommon Fulfillment. LC 89-6780. 304p. 1990. 19.95 (*0-925887-89-7*) Barring Sky Pub.

Marrs, Edwin W., Jr. A Descriptive Catalogue of the Letters of Charles & Mary Anne Lamb in the W. Hugh Peal Collection, University of Kentucky Libraries. LC 84-50664. (University of Kentucky Libraries Occasional Papers). 48p. 1984. lib. bdg. 15.00 (*0-917519-02-7*) U of KY Libs.

Marrs, Edwin W., Jr., ed. see Carlyle, Thomas.

Marrs, Edwin W., Jr., ed. see Lamb, Charles & Lamb, Mary A.

Marrs, Elijah P. Life & History of the Rev. Elijah P. Marrs. LC 70-89395. (Black Heritage Library Collection). 1977. 16.95 (*0-8369-8625-3*) Ayer.

— Life & History of the Rev. Elijah P. Marrs. (American Biography Ser.). 146p. 1991. reprint ed. lib. bdg. 59.00 (*0-7812-8268-3*) Rprt Serv.

Marrs, Gibson. Broken Rings. Harris, Floyd, ed. LC 95-72491. 360p. 1996. 23.95 (*1-884570-37-2*) Research Triangle.

Marrs, Jim. Alien Agenda. (Illus.). 704p. 1998. mass mkt. 6.99 (*0-06-109686-5*) HarpC.

*__Marrs, Jim.__ Alien Agenda: Investigating the Extraterrestrail Presence Among Us, (Illus.). 480p. 2000. pap. 14.00 (*0-06-095536-8*, Perennial) HarperTrade.

Marrs, Jim. Crossfire: The Plot That Killed Kennedy. 620p. 1990. pap. 13.95 (*0-88184-648-1*) Carroll & Graf.

— Enigma Files. 1995. 24.00 (*0-517-59755-1*) Harmony Bks.

*__Marrs, Jim.__ Rule By Secrecy: The Hidden History that Connects the Trilateral Commision, the Freemasons & the Great Pyramids. LC 99-56174. 480p. 2000. 27.00 (*0-06-019368-9*) HarpC.

Marrs, Jim. The Secret Rule. 2000. pap. 15.00 (*0-06-093184-1*) HarpC.

Marrs, Margie Vathauer, ed. see Turechek, Alma A.

Marrs, Richard, et al. Dr. Richard Marrs' Fertility Book: America's Leading Fertility Expert Tells You Everything You Need to Know about Getting Pregnant. (Illus.). 528p. 1998. pap. 14.95 (*0-440-50803-7*, Delta Trade) Dell.

Marrs, Richard P., ed. Assisted Reproductive Technologies. LC 93-1410. (Illus.). 280p. 1993. 95.00 (*0-86542-203-6*) Blackwell Sci.

Marrs, Ronald W. & Kolm, Kenneth E., eds. Interpretation of Windflow Characteristics from Eolian Landforms. fac. ed. LC 82-15673. (Geological Society of America, Special Paper: No. 192). (Illus.). 114p. 1982. reprint ed. pap. 35.40 (*0-7837-7941-0*, 204769700008) Bks Demand.

Marrs, Samuel. The Angels Laughed: The Promotion of a Dunghill Beggar. Mel, Jeanne, ed. (Illus.). 200p. (Orig.). 1995. pap. 12.95 (*0-9645387-0-9*) Yeshurun Pub.

*__Marrs, Suzanne.__ The Welty Collection: A Guide to the Eudora Welty Manuscripts & Documents at the Mississippi Department of Archives & History. (Illus.). 245p. 1999. reprint ed. text 30.00 (*0-7881-6423-6*) DIANE Pub.

Marrs, Suzanne & Welty, Eudora. The Welty Collection: A Guide to the Eudora Welty Manuscripts & Documents at the Mississippi Department of Archives & History. LC 88-17537. (Illus.). 244p. 1988. text 35.00 (*0-87805-366-2*) U Pr of Miss.

Marrs, Suzanne, jt. ed. see Pollack, Harriet.

*__Marrs, Tex.__ Circle of Intrigue. 2000. pap. 14.95 (*1-930004-05-2*) Rivercrest Pubg.

— Dark Secrets of the New Age: Satan's Plan for a One World Religion. rev. ed. 2000. pap. 12.95 (*0-9667421-4-1*) Rivercrest Pubg.

Marrs, Texe. America Shattered: Unmasking the Plot to Destroy Our Families & Our Country. (Illus.). 160p. (Orig.). 1991. pap. 8.95 (*0-9620086-6-4*) Living Truth Pubs.

— Big Sister Is Watching You: Hillary Clinton & the White House Feminists Who Now Control America - & Tell the President What to Do. 1993. pap. 10.95 (*0-9620086-9-9*) Living Truth Pubs.

— Dark Majesty: The Secret Brotherhood & the Magic of a Thousand Points of Light. (Illus.). 272p. (Orig.). 1992. pap. 12.95 (*0-9620086-7-2*) Living Truth Pubs.

— Days of Hunger, Days of Chaos: The Coming Great Food Shortages in America. LC 98-68372. (Illus.). 238p. 1999. pap. 13.95 (*0-9667421-0-9*) Rivercrest Pubg.

— Mega Forces: Signs & Wonders of the Coming Chaos. 266p. 1989. pap. 8.95 (*0-9620086-0-5*) Living Truth Pubs.

— Millennium: Peace, Promises, & the Day They Take Our Money Away. abr. ed. (Illus.). 272p. (Orig.). 1990. pap. 10.95 (*0-9620086-5-6*) Living Truth Pubs.

— Mystery Mark of the New Age: Satan's Design for World Domination. LC 87-72056. 1988. pap. 11.99 (*0-89107-479-1*) Crossway Bks.

— New Age Cults & Religions. 1990. pap. 13.95 (*0-9620086-8-0*) Living Truth Pubs.

— Project L. U. C. I. D. The Beast 666 Universal Human Control System. (Illus.). 224p. (Orig.). 1996. pap. 12.95 (*1-884302-02-5*) Living Truth Pubs.

— Ravaged by the New Age: Satan's Plan to Destroy Our Kids. LC 88-83897. (Illus.). 272p. (Orig.). 1989. pap. 10.95 (*0-9620086-1-3*) Living Truth Pubs.

Marrs, Texe & Marrs, Wanda. New Age Lies to Women. 256p. 1989. 10.95 (*0-9620086-3-X*) Living Truth Pubs.

Marrs, Texe, et al. Storming Toward Armageddon. James, W. T., ed. LC 92-64450. (Essays in Apocalypse Ser.: Bk. 1). 336p. 1992. pap. 11.95 (*0-89221-228-4*) New Leaf.

Marrs, Texe W. Careers with Robots. LC 87-24550. 221p. reprint ed. pap. 68.60 (*0-8357-3487-0*, 203974600013) Bks Demand.

— Circle of Intrigue: The Hidden Inner Circle of the Illuminati Conspiracy. 1995. pap. 12.95 (*1-884302-00-9*) Living Truth Pubs.

— How to Prepare for the Armed Forces Test (ASVAB) write for info. (*0-318-58787-4*) S&S Trade.

Marrs, Texe W. & Read, Karen. The Woman's Guide to Military Service. 2nd ed. 176p. 1987. pap. 8.95 (*0-89709-152-3*) Liberty Pub.

Marrs, Wanda, jt. auth. see Marrs, Texe.

Marrtay, Captain. Masterman Reader. 390p. Date not set. 27.95 (*0-8488-2364-8*) Amereon Ltd.

Marrus, Michael R. The Holocaust in History. 288p. 1989. pap. 13.95 (*0-452-00953-7*, Mer) NAL.

— Nuremberg War Crimes, 1945-46. LC 96-86777. 276p. 1997. pap. 12.95 (*0-312-13691-9*) St Martin.

— Samuel Bronfman: The Life & Times of Seagram's Mr. Sam. 551p. 1998. text 40.00 (*0-7881-5738-8*) DIANE Pub.

— Samuel Bronfman: The Life & Times of Seagram's Mr. Sam. LC 91-31775. (Illus.). 551p. 1991. 40.00 (*0-87451-571-8*) U Pr of New Eng.

Marrus, Michael R. & Paxton, Robert O. Vichy France & the Jews. 448p. (Orig.). 1995. pap. 17.95 (*0-8047-2499-7*) Stanford U Pr.

Marrus, Stephanie K. Building the Strategic Plan: Find, Analyze, & Present the Right Information. LC 92-47381. 358p. (C). 1994. reprint ed. lib. bdg. 48.50 (*0-89464-835-7*) Krieger.

Marryat, Florence. There Is No Death. 1975. 69.95 (*0-8490-1192-2*) Gordon Pr.

Marryat, Frederick. The Children of the New Forest. (Andre Deutsch Classics). 336p. (J). (gr. 5-8). 1996. 9.95 (*0-233-99077-1*, Pub. by Andre Deutsch) Trafalgar.

Marryat, Frederick. The Children of the New Forest. (Illus.). (J). mass mkt. 8.95 (*0-340-68983-8*, Pub. by Hodder & Stought Ltd) Trafalgar.

Marryat, Frederick. The Children of the New Forest. Butts, Dennis, ed. (World's Classics Ser.). 262p. 1992. pap. 7.95 (*0-19-282725-1*) OUP.

— Frank Mildmay of the Naval Officer. 351p. Date not set. 25.95 (*0-8488-2365-6*) Amereon Ltd.

*__Marryat, Frederick.__ Frank Mildmay: or The Naval Officer. 252p. 2000. pap. 9.95 (*0-594-01531-6*) Eightn Hundrd.

Marryat, Frederick. Frank Mildmay or the Naval Officer. LC 97-3123. (Classics of Nautical Fiction Ser.). 352p. 1997. reprint ed. pap. 14.95 (*0-935526-39-0*) McBooks Pr.

*__Marryat, Frederick.__ Jacob Faithful. 252p. 2000. pap. 9.95 (*0-594-00861-1*) Eightn Hundrd.

— The King's Own. 252p. 2000. pap. 9.95 (*0-594-01750-5*) Eightn Hundrd.

Marryat, Frederick. The King's Own. LC 99-19235. (Classics of Nautical Fiction Ser.). 1999. reprint ed. pap. 15.95 (*0-935526-56-0*) McBooks Pr.

Marryat, Frederick. Mr. Midshipman Easy. Date not set. lib. bdg. 24.95 (*0-8488-1678-1*) Amereon Ltd.

Marryat, Frederick. Mr. Midshipman Easy. LC 98-6699. 368p. 1998. pap. 30.00 (*0-8050-5988-1*) H Holt & Co.

*__Marryat, Frederick.__ Mr. Midshipman Easy. 252p. 2000. pap. 9.95 (*0-594-01690-8*) Eightn Hundrd.

— Mr. Midshipman Easy. LC 97-15354. (Classics of Nautical Fiction Ser.). 352p. 1997. reprint ed. pap. 14.95 (*0-935526-40-4*) McBooks Pr.

Marryat, Frederick. Mr. Midshipman Easy. LC 89-13600. (Classics of Naval Literature Ser.). 448p. 1990. reprint ed. 32.95 (*0-87021-590-6*) Naval Inst Pr.

— Newton Forster or the Merchant Service. LC 98-14726. 1998. pap. 13.95 (*0-935526-44-7*) McBooks Pr.

*__Marryat, Frederick.__ Percival Keene. LC 98-54895. (Heart of Oak Sea Classics Ser.). 416p. 1999. pap. 15.00 (*0-8050-6139-8*, Pub. by H Holt & Co) VHPS.

Marryat, Frederick. Peter Simple. (Heart of Oak Sea Classics Ser.). 512p. 1998. 30.00 (*0-8050-5830-3*, Owl); pap. 15.00 (*0-8050-5565-7*) H Holt & Co.

*__Marryat, Frederick.__ The Phantom Ship. (Classics of Nautical Fiction Ser.). 352p. 2000. pap. 14.95 (*0-935526-85-4*) McBooks Pr.

Marryat, Frederick. The Phantom Ship, 3 vols., 1 bk. LC 79-8168. reprint ed. 44.50 (*0-404-62026-4*) AMS Pr.

*__Marryat, Frederick.__ Snarleyyow: or The Dog Fiend. 252p. 2000. pap. 9.95 (*0-594-01296-1*) Eightn Hundrd.

Marryat, Frederick. Snarleyyow, or the Dog Fiend. (Classics of Nautical Fiction Ser.). 384p. 1999. reprint ed. pap. 16.95 (*0-935526-64-1*, Pub. by McBooks Pr) LPC Group.

Mars. Occupational Crime. 112.95 (*1-85521-382-6*) Ashgate Pub Co.

— Workplace Sabotage. 175.95 (*1-84014-788-1*) Ashgate Pub Co.

*__Mars & Weir.__ Risk Management, Vol. 1+2. 536p. 2000. 165.00 (*1-85521-849-6*) Ashgate Pub Co.

Mars, Brenna. Bobbie's Story: A Feelings Workbook. (Illus.). (J). (gr. k-5). 1999. pap., wbk. ed. 5.95 (*0-87868-735-1*, 7351, CWLA Pr) Child Welfare.

Mars, Brennan. Bobbie's Story: A Guide for Foster Parents. LC 98-24249. vii, 21 p. 1999. pap. 8.95 (*0-87868-701-7*, 7017, CWLA Pr) Child Welfare.

*__Mars, Brigitte.__ Addiction-Free - Naturally: Liberating Yourself from Tobacco, Caffeine, Sugar, Alchol, Prescription Drugs, Cocaine & Narcotics. 160p. 2000. pap. 12.95 (*0-89281-892-1*) Inner Tradit.

Mars, Brigitte. Dandelion Medicine: Remedies & Recipies to Detoxify, Nourish & Stimulate. LC 99-33559. (Storey Medicinal Herb Guide Ser.). (Illus.). 128p. 1999. pap. 12.95 (*1-58017-207-5*) Storey Bks.

— Herbs for Healthy Skin, Hair & Nails. LC 98-23435. (Good Health Guides Ser.). 96p. 1998. pap. 4.95 (*0-87983-838-8*, 38388K, Keats Publng) NTC Contemp Pub Co.

— Natural First Aid. LC 99-32307. 144p. 1999. pap. 12.95 (*1-58017-147-8*) Storey Bks.

Mars, Diana. Matchmaking Mona. (Desire Ser.: No. 1080). 1997. per. 3.50 (*0-373-76080-9*, 1-76080-0) Silhouette.

— Miedo Al Amor (Fear to Love) (Deseo Ser.). (SPA.). 1998. per. 3.50 (*0-373-35226-3*, 1-35226-9) Harlequin Bks.

— Mixed-Up Matrimony. (Desire Ser.). 1995. per. 3.25 (*0-373-05942-6*, 1-05942-7) Silhouette.

— Peril in Paradise. (Desire Ser.). 1995. per. 2.99 (*0-373-05906-X*, 1-05906-2) Silhouette.

Mars, Douglas De, see De Mars, Douglas.

Mars, Florence & Eden, Lynn. Witness in Philadelphia. LC 76-50660. (Illus.). 296p. 1989. pap. 11.95 (*0-8071-1566-5*) La State U Pr.

Mars, Geneva, ed. see Ponthier, Gayle.

Mars, Gerald. Cheats at Work: An Anthology of Workplace Crime. 260p. 1994. 82.95 (*1-85521-379-6*, Pub. by Dartmth Pub); pap. 39.95 (*1-85521-528-4*, Pub. by Dartmth Pub) Ashgate Pub Co.

Mars Hill Productions Staff, jt. auth. see Lifetime Guarantee Ministries Staff.

Mars Hill Productions Staff, jt. contrib. by see National Network of Youth Ministries Staff.

Mars, James. Life of James Mars: A Slave Born & Sold in Connecticut. LC 76-89394. (Black Heritage Library Collection). 1977. 9.00 (*0-8369-8626-1*) Ayer.

Mars, Jenny, jt. auth. see Mars, Ross.

Mars, Jon C. Fitness First Training Diary. rev. ed. (Illus.). 128p. 1995. spiral bd. 14.95 (*0-9626519-2-3*) AOJ Pub Corp.

Mars-Jones, Adam, ed. Mae West Is Dead: Recent Lesbian & Gay Fiction. 2nd ed. 320p. 1987. pap. 11.95 (*0-571-14898-0*) Faber & Faber.

Mars, Julie. Basset Hounds. LC 96-85942. 80p. 1997. 4.95 (*0-8362-2638-0*, Arie Bks) Andrews & McMeel.

*__Mars, Julie.__ The Secret Keepers. LC 99-90345. 288p. 2000. 23.00 (*0-9671851-4-9*, Pub. by GreyCore) Allnce Hse.

Mars, Julie, jt. auth. see Ariel Books Staff.

Mars, Kasey. The Dream. 416p. 1995. mass mkt. 4.99 (*0-7860-0203-4*, Pinncle Kensgtn) Kensgtn Pub Corp.

Mars, Laura, contrib. by. The Complete Mental Health Directory, 2000. 800p. 1999. 190.00 (*0-939300-94-X*); pap. 165.00 (*0-939300-85-0*) Grey Hse Pub.

Mars, Laura, ed. The Complete Directory for People with Chronic Illness, 1999/2000. 4th ed. 1000p. 2000. pap. 165.00 (*1-891482-16-5*) Grey Hse Pub.

— The Complete Directory for People with Chronic Illness, 1999/2000. 4th ed. 1000p. 2000. 190.00 (*1-891482-17-3*) Grey Hse Pub.

An Asterisk (*) at the beginning of an entry indicates that the title is appearing for the first time.

*Mars, Laura, ed. The Complete Directory for People with Disabilities, 1999-2000. 8th rev. ed. 900p. 1999. 190.00 (1-891482-23-8); pap. 165.00 (1-891482-22-X) Grey Hse Pub.
— The Complete Learning Disabilities Directory, 1999-2000. 7th rev. ed. 700p. 1999. 170.00 (1-891482-42-4) Grey Hse Pub.
— The Complete Learning Disabilities Directory, 2000. 7th rev. ed. 702p. 2000. pap. 145.00 (1-891482-41-6) Grey Hse Pub.
Mars, Laura, ed. The Directory of Business Information Resources, 1999. 7th ed. 1622p. 1998. 220.00 (1-891482-15-7); pap. 195.00 (1-891482-14-9) Grey Hse Pub.
***Mars, Laura, ed.** The Directory of Business to Business Catalogs, 1999. 7th rev. ed. 712p. 1999. 190.00 (1-891482-11-4); pap. 165.00 (1-891482-10-6) Grey Hse Pub.
— Educators Resource Directory, 1999-2000. 2nd rev. ed. 591p. 1999. pap. 145.00 (1-891482-75-0) Grey Hse Pub.
— Educators Resource Directory, 1999-00. 2nd rev. ed. 650p. 1999. 145.00 (1-891482-76-9) Grey Hse Pub.
— Food & Beverage Market Place: Suppliers Edition. 800p. 1999. 250.00 (1-891482-71-8) Grey Hse Pub.
— Food & Beverage Market Place: Suppliers Edition. 877p. 1999. pap. 225.00 (1-891482-70-X) Grey Hse Pub.
— Food & Beverage Market Place, 1999-2000. 4th rev. ed. 1700p. 1999. 250.00 (1-891482-21-1); pap. 225.00 (1-891482-20-3) Grey Hse Pub.
— The International Directory of Venture Capital Funds, 2000. 4th rev. ed. 1100p. 1999. pap. 295.00 (1-891482-94-7) Grey Hse Pub.
— The International Directory of Venture Capital Funds, 2000. 4th rev. ed. 1240p. 1999. 295.00 (1-891482-95-5) Grey Hse Pub.
— Older American's Information Directory. 2nd ed. 900p. 2000. 190.00 (1-891482-27-0) Grey Hse Pub.
— Older Americans Information Directory, 1999-2000. 956p. 1998. pap. 165.00 (1-891482-36-X) Grey Hse Pub.
Mars, Laura, ed. Older Americans Information Directory 1999. 956p. 1998. 190.00 (1-891482-37-8) Grey Hse Pub.
***Mars, Laura, ed.** Research Services Directory: A Guide to Independent & Corporate Research Centers. 7th rev. ed. 1100p. 1999. 420.00 (1-891482-31-9) Grey Hse Pub.
— Research Services Directory, 2000: Commercial & Corporate Research Centers. 7th rev. ed. 1089p. 1999. pap. 395.00 (1-891482-30-0) Grey Hse Pub.
Mars, Louis B. Crisis of Possession in Voodoo. Collins, Kathleen, tr. LC 76-51943. 1977. 10.00 (0-918408-07-5); pap. 4.95 (0-918408-00-8) Ishmael Reed.
Mars, Mark. The Dossier: MTVS Aeon Flux. 1995. pap. 18.00 (0-671-54524-8) PB.
Mars, Mick. Polymer Regradeation. 1982. 35.00 (0-02-949640-3) Macmillan.
Mars, N. J. I., ed. Towards Very Large Knowledge Bases. LC 95-75768. (YA). (gr. 12). 1995. 99.00 (90-5199-217-3) IOS Press.
Mars, Perry. Ideology & Change: The Transformation of the Caribbean Left. LC 97-62548. (African American Life Ser.). Date not set. text 34.95 (0-8143-2768-0, Great Lks Bks) Wayne St U Pr.
— Ideology & Change: The Transformation of the Caribbean Left. (African American Life Ser.). 1998. pap. text 17.95 (0-8143-2769-9, Great Lks Bks) Wayne St U Pr.
***Mars, Peter.** A Taste for Money: A Novel Based on the True Story of a Dirty Boston Cop. LC 99-74333. (Illus.). 320p. 1999. pap. 14.95 (0-9664475-1-4, Pub. by Cmmnwlth Publishing) Tabby Hse Bks.
Mars, Peter J. The Tunnel: Drug Dealers Are Missing in Boston - It's Not a Bad Thing but a Good Thing - But What Is Making Them Disappear? LC 98-71888. 312p. 1998. pap. 14.95 (0-9664475-0-6) Cmmnwlth Publishing.
Mars, Phil, et al. Learning Algorithms: Theory & Applications in Signal Processing. LC 96-26721. 240p. 1996. boxed set 84.95 (0-8493-7896-6, 7896) CRC Pr.
***Mars Publishing Staff.** Spec Ops Omega Squad: The Official Strategy Guide from Mars. 80p. 2000. pap. 12.99 (0-9675127-7-8, Pub. by Mars Pubng) IPG Chicago.
Mars, Ross. The Basics of Permaculture Design. (Illus.). 170p. (Orig.). 1996. pap. 24.95 (0-9587626-1-9) RDLE INST Bkstre.
Mars, Ross & Mars, Jenny. Getting Started in Permaculture. (Illus.). 60p. 1994. pap. text 12.50 (0-646-20090-9, Pub. by Candlelight Trust) Rodale Inst.
Marsa, Francisco. Normative Dictionary & Guide to the Spanish Language: Diccionario Normative y Guia de la Lengua Espanol. 2nd ed. (SPA.). 480p. 1990. write for info. (0-7859-4954-2) Fr & Eur.
Marsa, Linda. Prescription for Profits: How the Pharmaceutical Industry Bankrolled the Unholy Marriage between Science & State. LC 96-48440. 1997. 24.50 (0-684-80002-0, Scribners Ref) Mac Lib Ref.
Marsack, Robyn. The Cave of Making: The Poetry of Louis MacNeice. 184p. 1985. pap. text 15.95 (0-19-811732-9) OUP.
— Sylvia Plath. (Open Guides to Literature Ser.). 112p. 1992. pap. 27.95 (0-335-09352-3) OpUniv Pr.
Marsack, Robyn, ed. Thomas Bewick (1753-1828) Selected Work. pap. write for info. (0-85635-780-4, Pub. by Carcanet Pr) Paul & Co Pubs.
Marsack, Robyn, ed. see Blunden, Edmund.
Marsack, Robyn, tr. see Berberova, Nina.
Marsack, Robyn, tr. see Bouvier, Nicolas.
Marsak, L. M., ed. The Nature of Historical Inquiry. LC 74-16092. 220p. 1986. reprint ed. 22.00 (0-88275-221-9) Krieger.
Marsal, D. Logik, Bedeutung und Mathematik: Die Konstruktion Einer Fundamentalsprache der Wissenschaften. viii, 152p. 1987. 29.00 (3-510-65131-6, Pub. by E Schweizerbartsche) Balogh.
— Logik, Dedeutung & Mathematik: Die Konstruktion Einer Fundamentalsprache der Wissenschaften. (GER.). 152p. 1987. pap. 33.60 (0-685-33223-3) Lubrecht & Cramer.
Marsal, K. & Trudinger, B. J., eds. Doppler Ultrasound in Obstetrics. (Progress in Obstetric & Gynecological Sonography Ser.). (Illus.). 150p. 2001. 78.00 (1-85070-644-1) Prthnon Pub.
Marsala, Margaret. The Disappearance of Pegeen. LC 99-64512. 192p. 2000. pap. 11.95 (1-56315-208-8, Pub. by SterlingHse) Natl Bk Netwk.
Marsaldi, Eva, tr. see Obrist, Hans-Ulrich & Altshuler, Bruce.
***Marsalek, J.** Flood Issues in Contemporary Water Management. LC 00-42665. 2000. write for info. (0-7923-6451-1) Kluwer Academic.
Marsalek, J. Head Losses at Selected Sewer Manholes. (Special Reports: No. 52). 87p. (Orig.). 1985. pap. text 35.00 (0-917084-13-6) Am Public Works.
— Hydroinformatics Tools for Planning, Design, Operation, & Rehabilitation of Sewer Systems. LC 98-22933. (NATO Science Ser.). 1998. 244.00 (0-7923-5097-9) Kluwer Academic.
Marsalek, J., et al, eds. Urban Runoff Pollution. LC 86-3930. (NATO ASI Series G: Ecological Sciences: Vol. 10). xi, 893p. 1986. 215.00 (0-387-16090-6) Spr-Verlag.
Marsalek, J. & Torno, Harry C. Urban Storm Drainage, No. WST29/1-2. (Water Science & Technology Ser.: No. 29/1-2). 466p. 1995. pap. 220.00 (0-08-042498-8, Pergamon Pr) Elsevier.
Marsalis, Wynton. Marsalis on Music. Date not set. pap. write for info. (0-393-31530-4) Norton.
— Marsalis on Music. (Illus.). 175p. (YA). (gr. 5 up). 1995. 29.95 (0-393-03881-5) Norton.
— Sweet Swing Blues on the Road. (Illus.). 190p. 1998. pap. text 17.95 (1-56025-155-7, Thunders Mouth) Avalon NY.
Marsalis, Wynton & Stewart, Frank. Sweet Swing Blues on the Road. LC 93-4740. 1994. 29.95 (0-393-03514-X) Norton.
Marsan, C., et al. CD-ROM Atlas of Pathology: Gynecologic Cytopathology: Cervix. (ENG & FRE.). 1998. 149.00 incl. cd-rom (3-540-14655-5) Spr-Verlag.
Marsan, Cosimo A. & Matthies, H., eds. Neuronal Plasticity & Memory Formation. LC 81-21170. (International Brain Research Organization Monograph Ser.: Vol. 9). 681p. 1982. reprint ed. pap. 200.00 (0-608-00321-2, 206103800007) Bks Demand.
Marsan, Cosimo A., jt. ed. see Caputto, R.
Marsan, Jean-Claude. Montreal in Evolution: Historical Analysis of the Development of Montreal's Architecture & Urban Environment. (Illus.). 456p. (C). 1990. reprint ed. pap. text 22.95 (0-7735-0798-1, Pub. by McG-Queens Univ Pr) CUP Services.
Marsan, M. Ajmone, ed. Application & Theory of Petri Nets, 1993: Proceedings of the 14th International Conference, Chicago, Illinois, USA, June 21-25, 1993. (Lecture Notes in Computer Science Ser.: Vol. 691). ix, 591p. 1993. 79.95 (0-387-56863-8) Spr-Verlag.
Marsan, M. Ajmone, et al. Modelling with Generalized Stochastic Petri Nets. (Series in Parallel Computing). 324p. 1995. 120.00 (0-471-93059-8) Wiley.
Marsan, Marc. Who Are You When Noboby's Looking? Discovering the Person You Really Are & Inventing the Life You Really Want. (Illus.). 224p. 1999. pap. 14.95 (1-86204-593-3, Pub. by Element MA) Penguin Putnam.
Marsan, Marco Ajmone, jt. ed. see Obaidat, Mohammad S.
***Marsan, Maricel M.** Un Corazon Dividido (A Split Heart) LC 98-75014. (ENG & SPA.). 64p. 1998. pap. text 8.00 (0-935318-26-7) Edins Hispamerica.
Marsan, Maricel Mayor, see Mayor Marsan, Maricel.
Marsano, Daniel T. In Search of Truth ... An Analytical Approach to the Interview Process. (Illus.). 208p. (C). Date not set. text 40.00 (1-883960-22-3) Henry Quill.
***Marsano, Daniel T.** Sir Day the Knight. rev. ed. (Illus.). 48p. (J). (gr. k-6). 2000. lib. bdg. 15.00 (1-883960-20-7) Henry Quill.
Marsano, Daniel T. Sun Day, the Not-Quite Knight. (Illus.). 48p. (J). (gr. k-6). 1994. lib. bdg. 15.00 (1-883960-13-4) Henry Quill.
Marsch, E. & Schwenn, R., eds. Solar Wind 7: Proceedings of the 3rd COSPAR Colloquium Held in Goslar, Germany, 16-20 September, 1991. LC 92-20040. (COSPAR Colloquia Ser.: Vol. 3). 732p. 1992. 206.25 (0-08-042049-4, Pergamon Pr) Elsevier.
Marsch, E., jt. auth. see Tu, C. Y.
Marschak, Amy. An Angel Cried a Tear Last Night. 36p. (Orig.). 1997. pap. 6.00 (0-9653298-1-X) Human Theatre.
— Poetry for All Those Breathing. 50p. (Orig.). 1996. pap. 10.00 (0-9653298-0-1) Human Theatre.
— Tears from My Heart: A Memorial to Lost Works. (Illus.). 44p. (Orig.). 1997. pap. 8.00 (0-9653298-2-8) Human Theatre.
Marschak, Jacob. Economic Information. 1974. lib. bdg. 158.50 (90-277-0544-5) Kluwer Academic.
— Economic Information, Decision, & Prediction, 3 Vols., Vol. I. (Theory & Decision Library: No. 7). 389p. 1980. pap. text 51.50 (90-277-1195-X) Kluwer Academic.
— Economic Information, Decision, & Prediction, 3 Vols., Vol. III. (Theory & Decision Library: No. 7). 399p. 1981. pap. text 51.50 (90-277-1197-6) Kluwer Academic.
Marschak, Jacob & Radner, Roy. Economic Theory of Teams. LC 78-99832. (Cowles Foundation for Research in Economics at Yale University. Monograph Ser.: No. 22). 357p. reprint ed. pap. 110.70 (0-8357-8107-0, 20338120087) Bks Demand.
Marschak, Thomas, et al. Strategy for R & D: Studies in the Microeconomics of Development. LC 67-28248. (Econometrics & Operations Research Ser.: Vol. 8). (Illus.). 1967. 116.95 (0-387-03945-7) Spr-Verlag.
Marschall, Amy Horning, tr. see Horisch, Jochen.
Marschall, B., tr. see Resch, H. & Beck, E.
Marschall, Ken. Inside The Titanic : Troll Specail: Mini Edition. (J). 1998. 18.95 (0-316-55773-0) Little.
Marschall, Ken. 882 1/2 Amazing Answers to Your Questions about the Titanic. 96p. (gr. 3-7). 1999. pap. 9.99 (0-439-04296-8) Scholastic Inc.
Marschall, Ken, jt. auth. see Tanaka, Shelley.
Marschall, L. A. The Supernova Story. LC 88-17978. (Illus.). 316p. (C). 1988. 22.95 (0-306-42955-1, Plenum Trade) Perseus Pubng.
Marschall, Laurence A. The Supernova Story. LC 93-43454. (Science Library). 344p. (C). 1994. pap. 14.95 (0-691-03633-0, Pub. by Princeton U Pr) Cal Prin Full Svc.
Marschall, R., ed. Aspects of Seismic Reflection Data Processing. (C). 1990. text 195.50 (0-7923-0846-8) Kluwer Academic.
Marschall, Richard. America's Great Comic-Strip Artists. (Illus.). 288p. 1989. 55.00 (0-89659-917-5) Abbeville Pr.
Marschall, Richard, ed. America's Great Comic-Strip Artists. LC 97-4130. (Illus.). 296p. 1997. 45.00 (1-55670-646-4) Stewart Tabori & Chang.
— The Best of Little Nemo. LC 97-11476. (Illus.). 220p. 1997. 45.00 (1-55670-647-2) Stewart Tabori & Chang.
Marschall, Richard, ed. see McCay, Winsor.
Marschall, Richard, ed. see Segar, E. C.
Marschall, Richard A. Numerical Solution of the Helmholtz Equation. 110p. (C). 1993. text 142.00 (0-9636418-0-8) Marschall Acoustics.
Marschall, Rick. Encyclopedia of Country & Western Music. 1988. 14.98 (0-671-07606-X) S&S Trade.
***Marschall, Rick.** The Encyclopedia of Country Music. (Illus.). 208p. 1999. reprint ed. text 25.00 (0-7881-6381-7) DIANE Pub.
Marschall, Susanne. TextTanzTheater: Eine Untersuchung des Dramatischen Motivs und Theatralen Ereignisses Tanz am Beispiel von Frank Wedekinds "Buchse der Pandora" und Hugo von Hofmannsthals "Elektra" Kafitz, Dieter et al, eds. (Studien zur Deutschen und Europaischen Literatur des 19. und 20. Jahrhunderts: Bd. 36). (GER.). 298p. 1996. 57.95 (3-631-30476-5) P Lang Pubng.
Marschall, Veronika. Das Chronogramm: Eine Studie Zu Formen und Funktionen Einer Literarischen Kunstform. Dargestellt Am Beispiel Von Gelegenheitsgedichten des 16 Bis 18. Jahrunderts Aus Den Bestanden der Staatsbibliothek Bamberg. (GER.). 360p. 1997. 63.95 (3-631-31280-6) P Lang Pubng.
Marschall von Bieberstein, F. A. Flora Taurico Caucasicia, Exhibens Stirpes Phaenogamas, in Charsoneso Taurica & Regionibus Caucasicis Sponte Cresentes, 3vols. in 2. 1972. reprint ed. 200.00 (3-7682-0762-5) Lubrecht & Cramer.
Marscharck, Mark, jt. ed. see De Vega, Manuel.
Marschark, Marc. Psychological Development of Deaf Children. (Illus.). 288p. 1997. reprint ed. pap. text 24.95 (0-19-511575-9) OUP.
— Raising & Educating a Deaf Child. (Illus.). 256p. 1998. reprint ed. pap. 13.95 (0-19-512658-0) OUP.
— Relations of Language & Thought: The View from Sign Language & Deaf Children. Everhart, Victoria, ed. LC 96-33363. (Counterpoints Ser.). (Illus.). 208p. 1997. pap. 19.95 (0-19-510058-1) OUP.
Marschark, Marc, et al, eds. Relations of Language & Thought: The View from Sign Language & Deaf Children. LC 96-33363. (Counterpoints Ser.). (Illus.). 208p. 1997. text 45.00 (0-19-510057-3) OUP.
Marschark, Marc & Clark, M. Diane, eds. Psychological Perspectives on Deafness. 400p. 1993. text 79.95 (0-8058-1054-4) L Erlbaum Assocs.
— Psychological Perspectives on Deafness, Vol. II. 300p. 1998. write for info. (0-8058-2709-9); pap. write for info. (0-8058-2710-2) L Erlbaum Assocs.
Marschark, Mark. Raising & Educating a Deaf Child. LC 96-5504. (Illus.). 256p. 1997. 25.00 (0-19-509467-0, RDC-TXT) OUP.
Marschner, Alison, tr. see Destexhe, Alain.
Marschner, Horst. The Mineral Nutrition of Higher Plants. 2nd ed. (Illus.). 912p. 1995. pap. text 62.00 (0-12-473543-6) Acad Pr.
***Marschner, Janice.** California 1850: A Snapshot in Time. LC 99-98054. (Illus.). 225p. 2000. pap. 17.95 (0-9677069-3-9) Coleman Ranch.
Marschner, Walter A. How to Sell Your Home Quickly at the Highest Price. LC 97-76396. 140p. 1998. pap. 18.95 (1-57502-704-6, P01985) Morris Pubng.
Marsden. Basic Complex Analysis. 3rd ed. 1998. teacher ed. 23.90 (0-7167-2772-2); pap. text, student ed. 37.95 (0-7167-3246-7) W H Freeman.
— Basic Complex Analysis. 3rd ed. LC 98-41459. 600p. 1998. pap. text 82.95 (0-7167-2877-X) W H Freeman.
— Bronski House. LC 97-71364. 1998. pap. 11.45 (1-55970-434-9) Arcade Pub Inc.
Marsden. Cold Places. (Oliver & Boyd Georaphy Ser.). (J). 1992. pap. text. write for info. (0-05-005017-6) Addison-Wesley.
Marsden. Equine Behavioural Problems. 2000. text. write for info. (0-7020-1891-0, W B Saunders Co) Harcrt Hlth Sci Grp.
— Marxian & Christian Utopianism: Toward a Socialist Political Theology. 236p. 33.00 (0-85345-831-6, Pub. by Monthly Rev); pap. 19.00 (0-85345-832-4, Pub. by Monthly Rev) NYU Pr.
Marsden. Weather. (Oliver & Boyd Georaphy Ser.). (J). 1992. pap. text. write for info. (0-05-005025-7) Addison-Wesley.
Marsden, tr. see Polo, Marco.
Marsden, A. M., jt. ed. see Coaton, J. R.
Marsden, Alan & Pople, Anthony, eds. Computer Representations & Models in Music. (Illus.). 309p. 1991. text 84.00 (0-12-473545-2) Acad Pr.
Marsden, Andrew K., ed. see International Congress of Emergency Surgery, 5th:.
Marsden, Barry M. The Early Barrow Diggers. (Illus.). 160p. 1999. 32.50 (0-7524-1427-5, Pub. by Tempus Pubng) Arcadia Publng.
Marsden, Bill. Geography 11-16: Rekindling Good Practice. 224p. 1995. pap. text 24.95 (1-85346-296-9, Pub. by David Fulton) Taylor & Francis.
Marsden, Bill & Hughes, Jo, eds. Primary School Geography. LC 94-233197. 176p. 1994. pap. 29.00 (1-85346-281-0, Pub. by David Fulton) Taylor & Francis.
Marsden, C. The Basal Ganglia & New Surgical Treatment for Parkinson's Disease. 376p. 1997. text 126.00 (0-397-51780-7) Lppncott W & W.
Marsden, C. A. & Heal, D. J. Central Serotonin Receptors & Psychotropic Drugs. (Frontiers in Pharmacology & Therapeutics Ser.). (Illus.). 336p. 1992. 145.00 (0-632-02883-1) Blackwell Sci.
Marsden, C. D. Clinical Neurology. 480p. pap. text. write for info. (0-7131-4432-7, Pub. by E A) Routldge.
Marsden, C. David, et al, eds. Madopar HBS. (Journal: European Neurology: Vol. 27, Suppl. 1). (Illus.). vi, 142p. 1987. pap. 45.25 (3-8055-4692-0) S Karger.
Marsden, C. David & Fahn, Stanley, eds. Movement Disorders, No. 3. 3rd ed. (BIMR Ser.: Vol. 12). (Illus.). 529p. 1994. text 105.00 (0-7506-1412-9) Buttrwrth-Heinemann.
Marsden, C. David & Fowler, Timothy J. Clinical Neurology. 2nd ed. LC 97-33688. (An Arnold Publication). (Illus.). 466p. 1998. pap. text 49.95 (0-340-64611-X) OUP.
Marsden, C. David, jt. auth. see Fahn, Stanley.
Marsden, C. R. The Dictionary of Outrageous Quotes. 1999. pap. 11.95 (0-452-27017-0, Plume) Dutton Plume.
Marsden, Carl A., jt. ed. see Andrews, John N.
Marsden, Chantal. Improve Your French. (Improve Your...Ser.). (FRE.). 1995. pap. 79.95 incl. audio (0-8442-1681-X, 1681X, Natl Textbk Co) NTC Contemp Pub Co.
— Practice & Improve Your French. (Practice & Improve Ser.). (FRE.). 1995. pap. 39.95 incl. audio (0-8442-1664-X, 1664X, Natl Textbk Co) NTC Contemp Pub Co.
— Practice & Improve Your French Plus. (Practice & Improve Ser.). (FRE.). 1995. pap. 39.95 incl. audio (0-8442-1678-X, 1678X, Natl Textbk Co) NTC Contemp Pub Co.
***Marsden, Chris & Verhulst, Stefaan, eds.** Convergence in European Digital TV Regulation. LC 99-492085. (Law in Its Social Setting Ser.). 247p. 1999. pap. 40.00 (1-85431-990-6, 18466, Pub. by Blackstone Pr) Gaunt.
Marsden, Christine, jt. auth. see Hadlington, Phillip.
***Marsden, Christopher T.** Regulating the Global Information Society. LC 00-42485. 2000. write for info. (0-415-24218-5) Routledge.
Marsden, David. Original Kawasaki Z1, Z900 & K2900. 128p. 1999. 35.95 (0-7603-0775-X, Pub. by MBI Pubg) Motorbooks Intl.
— A Theory of Employment Systems: Micro-foundations of Diversity. LC 99-21237. (Illus.). 314p. 1999. text 75.00 (0-19-829423-9); pap. text 32.00 (0-19-829422-0) OUP.
Marsden, David, ed. Pay & Employment in the New Europe. 272p. 1992. 95.00 (1-85278-564-0) E Elgar.
Marsden, David, jt. auth. see Kane, Gerard T.
Marsden, David, jt. auth. see Oakley, Peter.
Marsden, David, jt. ed. see Mathur, Hari M.
Marsden, David, jt. ed. see Oakley, Peter.
Marsden, Dennis. Workless: An Exploration of the Social Contract Between Society & the Worker. 2nd enl. rev. ed. (Illus.). 275p. 1982. pap. 14.95 (0-7099-1723-6, Pub. by C Helm) Routldge.
Marsden, Donald & Ames, Kathy. Jonah: The Reluctant Prophet. 1996. 9.95 (1-877871-97-4) Ed Ministries.
Marsden, Eric W. Greek & Roman Artillery: Historical Development. LC 71-440116. 253p. reprint ed. pap. 78.50 (0-608-17746-6, 205224400069) Bks Demand.
— Greek & Roman Artillery: Technical Treatises. LC 74-595763. 312p. reprint ed. pap. 96.80 (0-608-17745-8, 205224300069) Bks Demand.
Marsden, George M. Fundamentalism & American Culture: The Shaping of Twentieth-Century Evangelicalism, 1870-1925. (Illus.). 307p. 1982. pap. text 14.95 (0-19-503083-4) OUP.
— The Outrageous Idea of Christian Scholarship. (Illus.). 152p. 1997. 25.00 (0-19-510565-6) OUP.
— The Outrageous Idea of Christian Scholarship. (Illus.). 160p. 1998. reprint ed. pap. 11.95 (0-19-512290-9) OUP.
— Reforming Fundamentalism: Fuller Seminary & the New Evangelicalism. LC 87-22243. 331p. reprint ed. pap. 102.70 (0-7837-3185-X, 204278900006) Bks Demand.
— Religion & American Culture. 288p. (C). 1990. pap. text 34.00 (0-15-576583-3, Pub. by Harcourt Coll Pubs) Harcourt.
— The Soul of the American University: From Protestant Establishment to Established Nonbelief. (Illus.). 480p. 1996. pap. 18.95 (0-19-510650-4) OUP.
— Understanding Fundamentalism & Evangelicalism. 216p. (Orig.). 1990. pap. 14.00 (0-8028-0539-6) Eerdmans.

An Asterisk (*) at the beginning of an entry indicates that the title is appearing for the first time.

Marsden, Gordon. Victorian Values: Personalities & Perspectives in Nineteenth-Century Society. 2nd ed. LC 98-4601. 304p. (C). 1998. pap. 25.66 (*0-582-29289-1*) Addison-Wesley.

***Marsden, Hilary & MacDonald, Mandy, eds.** Whitaker's Scottish Almanack 2000. (Illus.). 321p. 1999. 28.00 (*0-11-702251-9*, Pub. by Statnry Office) Balogh.

Marsden, Hilda, ed. see Bronte, Anne.

Marsden, J. E., ed. see Bremaud, P.

Marsden, J. E., ed. see Drew, D. A. & Passman, S. L.

Marsden, J. E., ed. see Durran, D. R.

Marsden, J. E., ed. see Feintuch, Avraham.

Marsden, J. E., ed. see Gasquet, C. & Witomski, P.

Marsden, J. E., ed. see Haller, Gyhorgy.

Marsden, J. E., ed. see Ham, Weimin & Reddy, B. D.

Marsden, J. E., ed. see Henningson, Dan S. & Schmid, P.

Marsden, J. E., ed. see Kress, Rainer.

Marsden, J. E., ed. see Kuznetsov, Y. & Kuznetsovi, U. A.

Marsden, J. E., ed. see McCarthy, J. M.

Marsden, J. E., ed. see Mhller, Claus.

Marsden, J. E., ed. see Polderman, J. W. & Willems, J. C.

Marsden, J. E., ed. see Reddy, B. D.

Marsden, J. E., ed. see Sastry, Shankar.

Marsden, J. E., ed. see Sontag, E. D.

Marsden, J. E., ed. see Sulem, C. & Sulem, P. L.

Marsden, J. E., ed. see Tveito, A. & Winther, R.

M

Marsden, Jean I. The Re-Imagined Text: Shakespeare, Adaptation, & Eighteenth-Century Literary Theory. LC 94-3399. 208p. 1995. text 32.00 (*0-8131-1901-4*) U Pr of Ky.

Marsden, Jean I., ed. see Cohen, Derek.

Marsden, Jerrold E. Elementary Classical Analysis. 2nd ed. LC 92-41432. 640p. (C). 1993. pap. text 79.95 (*0-7167-2105-8*) W H Freeman.

— Lectures on Geometric Methods in Mathematical Physics. LC 80-54307. (CBMS-NSF Regional Conference Ser.: No. 37). v, 97p. 1981. pap. text 27.00 (*0-89871-170-3*) Soc Indus-Appl Math.

— Lectures on Mechanics. (London Mathematical Society Lecture Note Ser.: No. 174). (Illus.). 266p. (C). 1992. pap. text 39.95 (*0-521-42844-0*) Cambridge U Pr.

— Multi-Variable Calculus. LC 92-38049. 533p. (C). 1993. pap. text 72.95 (*0-7167-2443-X*) W H Freeman.

— Multivariable Calculus. 1993. pap., student ed. 22.95 (*0-7167-2444-8*) W H Freeman.

— Study Guide Vector Calculus. 3rd ed. 1988. student ed. 16.00 (*0-7167-1980-0*) W H Freeman.

— Vector Calculus. 4th ed. (C). 1996. teacher ed. 16.00 (*0-7167-2445-6*) W H Freeman.

Marsden, Jerrold E., ed. Fluids & Plasmas: Geometry & Dynamics. LC 84-3011. (Contemporary Mathematics Ser.: Vol. 28). 448p. 1984. reprint ed. pap. 49.00 (*0-8218-5028-8*, CONM/28) Am Math.

Marsden, Jerrold E. & Hoffman, Michael. Basic Complex Analysis. 2nd ed. LC 86-18413. (Mathematics Ser.). (Illus.). 620p. (C). 1987. pap. text 77.95 (*0-7167-1814-6*) W H Freeman.

Marsden, Jerrold E. & Hughes, Thomas J. Mathematical Foundations of Elasticity. (Illus.). 576p. 1994. reprint ed. pap. text 14.95 (*0-486-67865-2*) Dover.

Marsden, Jerrold E. & Ratiu, Tudor S. Introduction to Mechanics & Symmetry: A Basic Exposition of Classical Mechanical Systems. LC 94-10793. (Text in Applied Mathematics Ser.: 17). (Illus.). 500p. 1994. 49.95 (*0-387-94347-1*) Spr-Verlag.

— Introduction to Mechanics & Symmetry: A Basic Exposition of Classical Mechanical Systems. LC 94-10793. (Texts in Applied Mathematics Ser.: Vol. 17). (Illus.). 472p. 1994. 70.95 (*0-387-97275-7*) Spr-Verlag.

Marsden, Jerrold E. & Rawtiu, Tudor S. Introduction to Mechanics & Symmetry. 2nd ed. LC 98-44773. (Texts in Applied Mathematics Ser.). 1999. 59.95 (*0-387-98643-X*) Spr-Verlag.

— Introduction to Mechanics & Symmetry: Solutions to Selected Exercises 2nd ed. LC 99-18354. (Texts in Applied Mathematics Ser.). 1999. write for info. (*0-387-98484-4*) Spr-Verlag.

Marsden, Jerrold E. & Sirovich, Lawrence. Chaos, Fractals, & Noise: Stochastic Aspects of Dynamics. 2nd rev. ed. LC 93-10432. (Applied Mathematical Sciences Ser.: Vol. 97). (Illus.). 472p. 1995. 59.95 (*0-387-94049-9*) Spr-Verlag.

Marsden, Jerrold E. & Tromba, Anthony J. Vector Calculus. 3rd ed. LC 87-24595. (Illus.). 704p. (C). 1995. text 42.40 (*0-7167-1856-1*) W H Freeman.

Marsden, Jerrold E. & Weinstein, Alan. Calculus I: Undergraduate Texts in Mathematics. 2nd ed. (Illus.). 300p. 1990. 31.95 (*0-387-90974-5*) Spr-Verlag.

— Calculus II. 2nd ed. (Undergraduate Texts in Mathematics Ser.). (Illus.). 300p. 1996. 31.95 (*0-387-90975-3*) Spr-Verlag.

— Calculus III. 2nd ed. Ewing, J. H. et al, eds. (Undergraduate Texts in Mathematics Ser.). (Illus.). xv, 341p. 1991. reprint ed. 31.95 (*0-387-90985-0*) Spr-Verlag.

Marsden, Jerrold E., et al. Basic Multivariable Calculus. LC 92-38049. 1993. 59.95 (*0-387-97976-X*) Spr-Verlag.

— Basic Multivariable Calculus. xv, 533p. 1993. write for info. (*3-540-97976-X*) Spr-Verlag.

— Dynamics & Control of Multibody Systems. LC 89-15019. (Contemporary Mathematics Ser.: Vol. 97). 468p. 1989. pap. 55.00 (*0-8218-5104-7*, CONM/97) Am Math.

— Integration Algorithms & Classical Mechanics. LC 96-21236. (Fields Institute Communications Ser.: Vol. 10). 244p. 1996. text 79.00 (*0-8218-0259-3*, FIC/10) Am Math.

Marsden, Jerrold E., jt. auth. see Chorin, Alexandre J.

Marsden, Jerrold E., jt. auth. see Tromba, Anthony J.

Marsden, Jerrold E., ed. see Lichtenberg, A. J. & Lieberman, M. A.

***Marsden, John.** Checkers. 128p. (YA). (gr. 7). 2000. mass mkt. 4.99 (*0-440-22860-3*, LLL BDD) BDD Bks Young Read.

Marsden, John. Checkers. LC 97-49405. 128p. (YA). (gr. 7 up). 1998. 15.00 (*0-395-85754-6*) HM.

***Marsden, John.** Darkness, Be My Friend. LC 98-38493. 288p. (J). (gr. 7 up). 1999. 15.00 (*0-395-92274-7*) HM.

Marsden, John. The Dead of Night. 304p. (YA). (gr. 7). 1999. mass mkt. 4.50 (*0-440-22771-2*) BDD Bks Young Read.

— The Dead of Night. LC 96-31656. 288p. (J). (gr. 7). 1997. 16.00 (*0-395-83734-0*) HM.

— The Fury of the Northmen: Saints, Shrines & Sea-Raiders in the Viking Age. (Illus.). 194p. 1997. pap. 19.95 (*1-85626-236-7*, Pub. by Cathie Kyle) Trafalgar.

— A Killing Frost. 320p. (YA). (gr. 8-12). 1999. mass mkt. 4.99 (*0-440-22832-8*) Bantam.

— A Killing Frost. LC 97-2797. 275p. (YA). (gr. 7-12). 1998. 15.00 (*0-395-83735-9*) HM.

— Letters from the Inside. LC 95-174528. 160p. (YA). (gr. 7 up). 1996. mass mkt. 4.99 (*0-440-21951-5*) Dell.

— Letters from the Inside. LC 93-41185. 37p. (J). 1994. 14.95 (*0-395-68985-6*) HM.

— Letters from the Inside. LC 95-174528. 1996. 9.09 (*0-606-09552-7*, Pub. by Turtleback) Demco.

Marsden, John. Letters from the Inside LC 95-174528. 146 p. (J). 1992. write for info. (*0-330-27314-0*, Pub. by Pan) Trafalgar.

Marsden, John. Norton's Hut. 32p. (YA). (gr. 5 up). 1999. 13.95 (*1-887734-64-3*) Star Brght Bks.

— Prayer for the Twenty-First. LC 99-70749. (Illus.). 40p. (YA). (gr. 6-12). 1998. 15.95 (*1-887734-42-2*) Star Brght Bks.

— Sea-Road of the Saints: Celtic Holy Men in the Hebrides. 1996. pap. text 16.95 (*0-86315-210-4*, Pub. by Floris Bks) Gryphon Hse.

— So Much to Tell You. 128p. (YA). (gr. 7 up). 1990. mass mkt. 5.50 (*0-449-70374-6*, Juniper) Fawcett.

— Tomorrow When the War Began. LC 94-29299. 304p. (YA). (gr. 7 up). 1996. mass mkt. 4.99 (*0-440-21985-X*) Dell.

— Tomorrow When the War Began. LC 94-29299. 288p. (J). (gr. 7 up). 1995. 15.00 (*0-395-70673-4*) HM.

— Tomorrow When the War Began. LC 94-29299. 1996. 9.09 (*0-606-10954-4*, Pub. by Turtleback) Demco.

Marsden, Kathryn. Food Combining. (In a Nutshell Ser.). (Illus.). 64p. 1999. 7.95 (*1-86204-479-1*, Pub. by Element MA) Penguin Putnam.

***Marsden, Kathryn.** Food Combining 2-Day Detox: Beat Weight Gain & Protect Your Health. LC 98-70507. 176p. 1998. mass mkt. 8.95 (*1-891696-04-1*) BainBridgeBooks.

Marsden, Kathryn. Super Skin. (Illus.). 1994. reprint ed. pap. 13.00 (*0-7225-2798-5*) Thorsons PA.

Marsden, Keith. African Entrepreneurs: Pioneers of Development. (IFC Discussion Papers: No. 9). 76p. 1990. pap. 22.00 (*0-8213-1693-1*, 11693) World Bank.

***Marsden, Lorna M.** The Singing of New Songs. 1999. pap. 21.00 (*1-85072-169-6*, Pub. by W Sessions) St Mut.

Marsden, Lorna M., ed. The Descent of the God: Continuing Incarnation. 1999. pap. 21.00 (*1-85072-093-2*, Pub. by W Sessions) St Mut.

Marsden, Mary E., jt. auth. see Bray, Robert M.

Marsden, Michael. Practice of Banking 1. 225p. 1985. pap. text 36.00 (*0-86010-563-6*); lib. bdg. 50.00 (*0-86010-580-6*) G & T Inc.

— Practice of Banking 1, Vol. 5. 150p. 1985. pap. text, student ed. 25.00 (*0-86010-588-1*) G & T Inc.

Marsden, Michael T., et al, eds. Eye on the Future: Popular Culture Scholarship into the 21st Century in Honor of Ray B. Browne. LC 94-70244. 294p. (C). 1994. pap. 18.95 (*0-87972-656-3*); text 39.95 (*0-87972-655-5*) Bowling Green Univ Popular Press.

Marsden, Michael T., et al. Movies As Artifacts. LC 82-6300. 288p. (C). 1982. text 36.95 (*0-88229-453-9*) Burnham Inc.

Marsden, Michael T., jt. auth. see Browne, Ray B.

Marsden, Michael T., jt. ed. see Browne, Ray B.

Marsden, Michael T., jt. ed. see Magnaghi, Russell M.

Marsden, P. K. Basic Building Measurement. 158p. pap. 19.95 (*0-86840-133-1*, Pub. by New South Wales Univ Pr) Intl Spec Bk.

Marsden, Pater V. & Lin, Nan, eds. Social Structure & Network Analysis. LC 82-10564. (Sage Focus Editions Ser.: No. 57). 319p. reprint ed. pap. 98.90 (*0-7837-1115-8*, 204164500022) Bks Demand.

Marsden, Paul K. Basic Building Measurement. 180p. 1997. pap. 27.95 (*0-86840-576-0*, Pub. by New South Wales Univ Pr) Intl Spec Bk.

Marsden, Peter. Sociological Methodology. 1993. 74.95 (*1-55786-464-0*) Blackwell Pubs.

— The Taliban: War, Religion & the New Order in Afghanistan. 165p. 1998. text 55.00 (*1-85649-521-3*, Pub. by Zed Books); text 19.95 (*1-85649-522-1*, Pub. by Zed Books) St Martin.

Marsden, Peter, jt. auth. see Serge, Victor.

Marsden, Peter V., ed. Linear Models in Social Research. LC 81-9402. (Illus.). 336p. reprint ed. pap. 104.20 (*0-7837-1114-X*, 204164400022) Bks Demand.

Marsden, Philip. The Bronski House. LC 97-71364. 1997. 23.45 (*1-55970-392-X*, Pub. by Arcade Pub Inc) Time Warner.

Marsden, R. G., ed. Documents Relating to Law & Custom of the Sea, 1915, 2 vols. LC 99-24138. 1999. reprint ed. 175.00 (*1-886363-96-X*) Lawbk Exchange.

— The High Latitude Heliosphere: Proceedings of the 28th ESLAB Symposium, 19-21 April 1994, Friedrichshafen, Germany. LC 94-39754. 498p. 1994. text 166.50 (*0-7923-3229-6*) Kluwer Academic.

— The Sun & the Heliosphere in Three Dimensions. (Astrophysics & Space Science Library). 1986. text 226.50 (*90-277-2198-X*) Kluwer Academic.

Marsden, R. G., jt. auth. see Page, D. E.

Marsden, Ralph W., ed. Politics, Minerals, & Survival: Proceedings of a Symposium. LC 74-27310. 103p. reprint ed. pap. 32.00 (*0-8357-6792-2*, 203546900095) Bks Demand.

Marsden, Rebecca. Tossed Salad from Heaven: Christian Poetry by Rebecca Marsden. 2nd rev. ed. Elliott, Nelson, ed. 96p. 1997. pap. 9.95 (*0-9661177-0-0*) Rebeccas Prod.

Marsden, Richard. The Nature of Capital: Marx after Foucault. LC 99-17994. 288p. 1999. 100.00 (*0-415-19861-5*) Routledge.

— The Text of the Old Testament in Anglo-Saxon England. (Studies in Anglo-Saxon England: No. 15). (Illus.). 534p. (C). 1995. text 89.95 (*0-521-46477-3*) Cambridge U Pr.

Marsden, Simon. Journal of a Ghosthunter: In Search of the Undead from Ireland to Transylvania. LC 94-241997. (Illus.). 128p. 1994. 24.95 (*1-55859-872-3*) Abbeville Pr.

Marsden-Smedley, Philip & Klinke, Jeffery, eds. Views from Abroad 1, 1950-1980: The Spectator Book of Travel Writing. 387p. 1989. 24.95 (*1-85089-330-6*, Pub. by ISIS Lrg Prnt) Transaction Pubs.

Marsden, Terry, et al, eds. Rural Restructuring: Global Processes & Their Responses. (Critical Perspectives on Rural Change Ser.). 208p. 1995. text 110.00 (*0-471-95927-8*, GE11) Wiley.

— Technological Change & the Rural Environment, Vol. 2. (Critical Perspectives on Rural Change Ser.). 224p. (C). 1990. pap. 79.00 (*0-8464-1518-6*) Beekman Pubs.

Marsden, Terry, et al. Constructing the Countryside: An Approach to the Rural Development. (Restructuring Rural Areas Ser.: No. 1). 224p. 1996. pap. 27.95 (*1-85728-040-7*, Pub. by UCL Pr Ltd) Taylor & Francis.

***Marsden, Terry, et al.** Consuming Interests: The Social Provision of Foods. LC 99-27329. (Consumption & Space Ser.). (Illus.). 240p. 1999. 66.00 (*1-85728-899-8*, Pub. by UCL Pr Ltd); pap. 22.95 (*1-85728-900-5*, Pub. by UCL Pr Ltd) Taylor & Francis.

Marsden, Terry, et al. Rural Restructuring: Global Processes & Their Responses. (Critical Perspectives on Rural Change Ser.: Vol. 1). 224p. (C). 1990. text 66.00 (*0-389-20947-3*) B&N Imports.

Marsden, Terry, jt. auth. see Drummond, Ian.

Marsden, Terry, jt. auth. see Murdoch, Jonathan.

Marsden, Victor E. The Protocols of the Learned Elders of Zion. pap. 7.95 (*0-685-17507-3*, Noontide Pr) Legion Survival.

Marsden, Victor E., tr. Protocols of the Learned Elders of Zion. 72p. 1996. pap. 4.00 (*0-944379-42-7*) CPA Bk Pub.

— Protocols of the Learned Elders of Zion. 299p. 1999. pap. 7.00 (*0-944379-41-9*) CPA Bk Pub.

Marsden, Victor E., jt. tr. see Nilus.

Marsden, Vince. Smutter! (Illus.). 24p. (J). (gr. 1-3). 1997. 8.00 (*1-85854-535-8*) Brimax Bks.

Marsden, W. E. An Anglo-Welsh Teaching Dynasty: The Adams Family from the 1840's to the 1930's. 296p. (Orig.). 1997. pap. text 24.50 (*0-7130-4031-9*, Pub. by Woburn Pr) Intl Spec Bk.

Marsden, W. L. The Northern Paiute Language of Oregon. fac. ed. (University of California Publications in American Archaeology & Ethnology: Vol. 20: 11). 19p. (C). 1923. reprint ed. pap. text 2.50 (*1-55567-247-7*) Coyote Press.

Marsden, Walter. Resting Places in East Anglia. 1993. pap. 15.00 (*0-86025-897-1*, Pub. by I Henry Pubns) Empire Pub Srvs.

***Marsden, Walter.** Resting Places in East Anglia: Graves & Memorials in Cambridgeshire, Essex, Norfolk & Suffolk. 2nd unabridged ed. (Illus.). 160p. 1999. pap. 15.00 (*0-86025-479-8*, Pub. by I Henry Pubns) Empire Pub Srvs.

Marsden, William. Malay-English Dictionary. (ENG & MAY.). 1977. reprint ed. 101.95 (*0-518-19003-X*) Ayer.

Marsden, William E. An Anglo-Welsh Teaching Dynasty: The Adams Family from the 1840's to the 1930's. LC 96-52689. (Woburn Education Ser.). (Illus.). 296p. (Orig.). 1997. text 49.50 (*0-7130-0203-4*, Pub. by Woburn Pr) Intl Spec Bk.

— Educating the Respectable: A Study of Fleet Road Board School Hampstead, 1879-1903. 296p. 1991. text 37.50 (*0-7130-0184-4*, Pub. by F Cass Pubs) Intl Spec Bk.

— Unequal Education Provision in England & Wales: The Nineteenth-Century Roots. (Illus.). 269p. 1987. text 30.00 (*0-7130-0178-X*, Pub. by Woburn Pr) Intl Spec Bk.

Marsden, William E., jt. ed. see Goodenow, Ronald K.

Marse, Juan. El Amante Bilingue/The Bilingual Lover, Spanish ed. 1998. pap. text 11.95 (*84-08-02003-X*) Planeta.

— La Muchacha de Las Bragas de Oro. 1999. pap. text 9.95 (*84-08-02372-1*) Planeta Edit.

Marseguerra, Giovanni. Corporate Financial Decisions & Market Value: Studies on Dividend Policy, Price Volatility, & Ownership Structure. LC 97-41523. (Contributions to Management Science Ser.). (Illus.). viii, 181p. 1997. pap. 56.00 (*3-7908-1047-9*) Spr-Verlag.

Marseille, Claudia. Conflict Management: Negotiating Indian Water Rights. LC HD1695.W4M37. (Western Natural Resources Policy Ser.: No. 102). 38p. reprint ed. pap. 30.00 (*0-7837-5766-2*, 204543100006) Bks Demand.

Marsella, Anne. The Lost & Found, & Other Stories. LC 93-46128. 198p. (C). 1994. pap. 13.95 (*0-8147-5503-8*); text 25.00 (*0-8147-5502-X*) NYU Pr.

Marsella, Anthony. Toys from Occupied Japan. LC 95-69835. (Illus.). 144p. (Orig.). 1995. pap. 29.95 (*0-88740-875-3*) Schiffer.

Marsella, Anthony J., et al, eds. Amidst Peril & Pain: The Mental Health & Well-Being of the World's Refugees. LC 93-40308. 1994. pap. text 29.95 (*1-55798-539-1*) Am Psychol.

Marsella, Anthony J., et al, eds. Ethnocultural Aspects of Posttraumatic Stress Disorders: Issues, Research, & Clinical Applications. LC 95-40252. (Illus.). 576p. 1996. 49.95 (*1-55798-319-4*) Am Psychol.

Marsella, Anthony J., et al. Culture & Self: Asian & Western Perspectives. LC 88-18326. 1998. write for info. (*0-415-02926-0*) Routledge.

Marsella, Gail B. Reasoning in Chemistry. LC 95-83552. 100p. (Orig.). (C). 1995. pap. text 10.00 (*0-9646155-9-2*) Branch Text Pr.

— Why an Electron? 100p. (Orig.). (C). 2001. pap. text 10.00 (*0-9646155-8-4*) Branch Text Pr.

Marsella, Joy, jt. auth. see Hilgers, Thomas L.

Marsella, Joy A. The Promise of Destiny: Children & Women in the Stories of Louisa May Alcott, 2. LC 82-15573. (Contributions to the Study of Childhood & Youth Ser.: No. 2). 166p. 1983. 47.95 (*0-313-23603-8*, MLO/, Greenwood Pr) Greenwood.

***Marsella, Richard F.** Welcome to Stress Management. 96p. 1999. pap. 9.95 (*0-9672492-0-1*, Binky Pr) One Hund Health.

Marselli, Mark. Classic Harley-Davidson Big Twins. LC 94-5335. (Enthusiast Color Ser.). (Illus.). 96p. 1994. pap. 13.95 (*0-87938-922-2*) MBI Pubg.

***Marsello, Robert.** A Friend in the Business: Honest Advice for Anyone Trying to Break into Television Writing. LC 99-58604. 257p. 2000. pap. 13.95 (*0-399-52602-1*, Perigee Bks) Berkley Pub.

Marsenich, Bob. Ready, Aim, Change: A Toolbook for Managing Personal Change. 218p. (Orig.). 1989. pap. 11.95 (*0-9622988-3-2*) Seaglass Pubns.

Marsh. Asteroids, Comets, & Meteors. 1996. write for info. (*0-8050-5271-2*) H Holt & Co.

— Australia Can Compete. Date not set. pap. text. write for info. (*0-582-71256-4*, Pub. by Addison-Wesley) Longman.

— Emily Bronte: Wuthering Heights. LC 99-18935. 1999. text 55.00 (*0-312-22376-5*) St Martin.

Marsh. Environmental Geography: In Global Perspective. 243p. 1995. pap. text 28.95 (*0-471-11644-0*) Wiley.

Marsh. Environmental with Environmental Manual. pap. text. write for info. (*0-471-37192-0*) Wiley.

***Marsh.** Grave Mistake. 2000. mass mkt. 5.99 (*0-312-97297-0*) St Martin.

— Great Systmes & Global Enviroment. 2001. pap. text. write for info. (*0-7167-3503-2*) W H Freeman.

Marsh. Jane Austen Novels. LC 97-50415. 288p. 1998. pap. 19.95 (*0-312-21371-9*); text 55.00 (*0-312-21370-0*) St Martin.

— Last Days. Date not set. 24.00 (*0-465-04418-2*, Pub. by Basic) HarpC.

Marsh. Last Days. pap. 14.00 (*0-465-04419-0*, Pub. by Basic) HarpC.

Marsh. Limerick Omnibus. (Reference Library). 464p. 1998. pap. 11.95 (*1-85326-490-3*, 4903WW, Pub. by Wrdsworth Edits) NTC Contemp Pub Co.

— Modern Longman Literature: Autobiographies. 1992. pap. text. write for info. (*0-582-08837-2*, Pub. by Addison-Wesley) Longman.

— New Beginnings V2, 2. 1982. pap. text 15.95 (*0-7710-5457-2*) McCland & Stewart.

— Policy & Politics in American Governments. (C). 1975. pap. text, teacher ed. 16.87 (*0-07-056429-9*) McGraw.

— A Quick & Not Dirty Guide to Business Writing. 170p. (C). 1996. pap. text 14.50 (*0-13-777483-4*) P-H.

— Reason for the Season. 1991. pap. 4.95 (*0-687-35622-9*) Abingdon.

— Shakespeare: The Tragedies. LC 97-48942. 245p. 1998. pap. 19.95 (*0-312-21373-5*); text 55.00 (*0-312-21372-7*) St Martin.

— Virginia Woolf Novels. LC 97-50472. 237p. 1998. pap. 19.95 (*0-312-21375-1*); text 55.00 (*0-312-21374-3*) St Martin.

— Wishful Thinking. Date not set. pap. text. write for info. (*0-582-22453-5*, Pub. by Addison-Wesley) Longman.

Marsh, abr. Emily Bronte: Wuthering Heights. LC 99-18935. 1999. pap. 19.95 (*0-312-22377-3*) St Martin.

Marsh & Willis. Curriculum. 2nd ed. LC 98-19267. 363p. 1998. 69.00 (*0-13-757071-6*) P-H.

Marsh, A., et al. Lone Parents, Work & Benefits. (DSS Research Report Ser.). 1997. write for info. (*0-11-762450-0*, Pub. by Statnry Office) Bernan Associates.

Marsh, A., jt. auth. see Bryson, A.

Marsh, A. H. History of the Court of Chancery & the Rise & Development of the Doctrines of Equity. viii, 140p. 1985. reprint ed. 35.00 (*0-8377-0820-6*, Rothman) W S Hein.

Marsh, A. J. History of the Court of Chancery & of the Rise & Development of the Doctrines of Equity, No. 1. viii, 140p. 1999. reprint ed. 40.00 (*1-56169-458-4*) Gaunt.

Marsh, Alan, jt. auth. see McKay, Stephen.

Marsh, Alec. Money & Modernity: Pound, Williams, & the Spirit of Jefferson. LC 97-45459. 264p. 1998. text 39.95 (*0-8173-0921-7*) U of Ala Pr.

Marsh, Alex & Mullins, David. Housing & Public Policy: Citizenship, Choice, & Control. LC 98-4871. 264p. 1998. 95.00 (*0-335-19926-7*); pap. 29.95 (*0-335-19925-9*) OpUniv Pr.

Marsh, Andrew J. Debates & Proceedings in the Constitutional Convention of the State of Nevada. LC 76-39613. 959p. 1976. reprint ed. lib. bdg. 45.00 (*0-930342-32-1*, 300990) W S Hein.

Marsh, Andy, jt. auth. see Akay, Metin.

An Asterisk (*) at the beginning of an entry indicates that the title is appearing for the first time.

Marsh, Anna, et al, eds. Combining Substance Abuse Treatment with Intermediate Sancations for Adults in the Criminal Justice System. 101p. (C). 1999. pap. text 25.00 (*0-7881-7595-5*) DIANE Pub.

Marsh, Anna & Clunies, Sandra, eds. Intensive Outpatient Treatment for Alcohol & Other Drug Abuse. 104p. (C). 1999. pap. text 25.00 (*0-7881-7596-3*) DIANE Pub.

— Screening & Assessment for Alcohol & Other Drug Abuse among Adults in the Criminal Justice System. (Illus.). 129p. (C). 1999. pap. text 25.00 (*0-7881-7599-8*) DIANE Pub.

Marsh, Anthony. The Groom's Secret Handbook. LC 97-20077. 96p. 1997. per. 9.95 (*0-684-83316-6*) S&S Trade.

Marsh, Anthony S. Fourteen Years in the African Bush: An Account of a Kenyan Game Warden. limited ed. (Illus.). 305p. 1998. 70.00 (*1-57157-079-9*) Safari Pr.

Marsh, Arthur I. & Kaye, Seymour P., eds. International Manual on Collective Bargaining for Public Employees. LC 71-130530. (Special Studies in International Economics & Development). 1973. 52.50 (*0-275-28074-8*) Irvington.

Marsh, Arthur I. & Ryan, Victoria. Historical Directory of Trade Unions: Engineering, Iron & Steel, Coal, Mining, Agriculture, Chemicals, Vol. 2. 379p. 1984. text 86.95 (*0-566-02161-7*, Pub. by Gower) Ashgate Pub Co.

— Historical Directory of Trade Unions: Vol. 1: Non-Manual Unions. 256p. 1980. text 78.95 (*0-566-02160-9*, Pub. by Gower) Ashgate Pub Co.

Marsh, Arthur I., et al. Historical Directory of Trade Unions, Vol. 4: Cotton, Wool & Worsted Linen & Jute & Other Textiles. 574p. 1994. 96.95 (*0-85967-900-4*, Pub. by Scolar Pr) Ashgate Pub Co.

Marsh, B. Ecstasy. 1997. write for info. (*1-86106-094-7*, Pub. by Minerva Pr) Unity Dist.

***Marsh, B.** Eight Bells. 409p. 2000. pap. write for info. (*0-7541-0940-2*, Pub. by Minerva Pr) Unity Dist.

***Marsh, Barbie.** The Pond Story. (Illus.). 26p. (J). (ps-2). 1998. pap. 5.95 (*0-9665222-5-7*) Lve to Read.

Marsh, Benjamin C. An Introduction to City Planning: Democracy's Challenge to the American City. LC 73-11939. (Metropolitan America Ser.). 1977. reprint ed. 13.95 (*0-405-05401-7*) Ayer.

Marsh, Bert. Bert Marsh: Woodturner. (Illus.). 160p. 1996. pap. 26.95 (*0-946819-51-3*, Pub. by Guild Master) Sterling.

Marsh, Betty F. Past & Repast. (Illus.). 88p. (Orig.). 1981. pap. 5.95 (*0-933992-16-5*) Coffee Break.

Marsh, Bill. The Philadelphia Inquirer Map & Guide to Center City Philadelphia & Surrounding Area. Bookman, Ken, ed. (Illus.). 52p. (Orig.). 1993. pap. 7.99 (*0-9634709-2-2*); write for info. (*0-9634709-3-0*) Phila Newspapers.

Marsh, Brian. Baron in Africa: The Adventures of the Remarkable Werner von Alvensleben. (Illus.). 300p. 1997. 35.00 (*1-57157-067-5*) Safari Pr.

— Copying Carol: A Modern Adaptation of Dickens "A Christmas Carol" 22p. (Orig.). 1996. pap. 3.00 (*1-57514-185-X*, 3082) Encore Perform Pub.

— The Last Trophy: Africa Is a Woman. 2nd ed. 304p. 1990. text 16.95 (*0-9624807-1-1*); pap. text 12.95 (*0-9624807-0-3*) PHS Pub Div.

Marsh, Brian, jt. auth. see Holcomb, Tim.

Marsh, Brian T. Overland Models: The First Ten Years. (Illus.). 1987. spiral bd. 39.00 (*0-9617955-1-4*, OMI 2013) Overland Models.

— Overland Models: The First Ten Years. limited ed. (Illus.). 1987. 57.00 (*0-9617955-0-6*, OMI 2014) Overland Models.

Marsh, Carl J. Raleigh & Related Families. LC 88-70909. (Illus.). 1988. 20.00 (*0-9619972-0-6*) C & L Pubns.

Marsh, Carol. Dearest Enemy. large type ed. 268p. 1989. 27.99 (*0-7089-1934-0*) Ulverscroft.

— Enchanted Valley. large type ed. 1990. pap. 16.99 (*0-7089-6911-9*) Ulverscroft.

— For the Love of Lucy. large type ed. 304p. 1989. 27.99 (*0-7089-1996-0*) Ulverscroft.

— Iowa Indian Dictionary for Kids! (Carole Marsh State Bks.). (J). (gr. 2-9). 1996. 29.95 (*0-7933-7689-0*, C Marsh); pap. 19.95 (*0-7933-7690-4*, C Marsh) Gallopade Intl.

— Laird of Imchay. large type ed. (Linford Romance Library). 240p. 1992. pap. 16.99 (*0-7089-7206-3*) Ulverscroft.

— A Match for Melanie. large type ed. 1991. pap. 16.99 (*0-7089-6981-X*) Ulverscroft.

— Nurse under Suspicion. large type ed. 287p. 1989. 27.99 (*0-7089-1962-6*) Ulverscroft.

— A Primrose for Sarah. large type ed. 288p. 1989. 27.99 (*0-7089-2042-X*) Ulverscroft.

— Sex Stuff For Iowa Parents & 1995. 29.95 (*0-7933-2457-2*) Gallopade Intl.

— Sophie in Love. large type ed. 198p. 1995. 27.99 (*0-7505-0791-8*, Pub. by Mgna Lrg Print) Ulverscroft.

— A Young Man's Darling. large type ed. (Lythway Ser.). 160p. 1991. 21.95 (*0-7451-1257-9*, G K Hall Lrg Type) Mac Lib Ref.

Marsh, Carol G., jt. auth. see Harris-Warrick, Rebecca.

Marsh, Carol G., ed. see Cannabich, Christian.

Marsh, Carol G., jt. ed. see Little, Meredith E.

Marsh, Carole. A-Plus Very Good! Secrets of Good Writing for Students. (Quantum Leap Ser.). (Orig.). (J). (gr. 4-12). 1994. 29.95 (*1-55609-272-5*); pap. text 19.95 (*0-935326-63-4*) Gallopade Intl.

— Abstinence Makes the Heart Grow Fonder. (Smart Sex Stuff Ser.). (J). (gr. 2-12). 1994. 29.95 (*1-55609-273-3*); pap. 19.95 (*1-55609-208-3*) Gallopade Intl.

— Ah, So! Japanese for Kids! (Of All the Gall Language Bks.). (J). (gr. 2-9). 1997. 29.95 (*0-7933-7800-1*, C Marsh); pap. 19.95 (*0-7933-7801-X*, C Marsh) Gallopade Intl.

— AIDS-Zits: A "Sextionary" for Kids. (Smart Sex Stuff Ser.). (Orig.). (J). (gr. 2-12). 1994. 29.95 (*1-55609-263-6*); pap. 19.95 (*1-55609-210-5*) Gallopade Intl.

— Alabama & Other State Greats (Biographies) (Carole Marsh Alabama Bks.). (Illus.). (YA). (gr. 3-12). 1994. pap. 19.95 (*1-55609-468-X*); lib. bdg. 29.95 (*1-55609-469-8*) Gallopade Intl.

— Alabama Bandits, Bushwackers, Outlaws, Crooks, Devils, Ghosts, Desperadoes & Other Assorted & Sundry Characters! (Carole Marsh Alabama Bks.). (Illus.). (YA). (gr. 3-12). 1994. pap. 19.95 (*0-7933-0040-1*); lib. bdg. 29.95 (*0-7933-0041-X*) Gallopade Intl.

— Alabama Bingo for Kids! (J). (gr. 2-7). 1997. 24.95 (*0-614-28756-1*); pap. 19.95 (*0-614-28757-X*) Gallopade Intl.

— Alabama "BIO" Bingo! 24 Must Know State People for Kids to Learn about While Having Fun! (Bingo! Ser.). (Illus.). (J). (gr. 2-8). 1998. pap. 14.95 (*0-7933-8525-3*) Gallopade Intl.

— The Alabama Bookstore Book: A Surprising Guide to Our State's Bookstores & Their Specialties for Students, Teachers, Writers & Publishers. (Carole Marsh Alabama Bks.). (Illus.). 1994. pap. 19.95 (*0-7933-2856-X*); lib. bdg. 29.95 (*0-7933-2855-1*) Gallopade Intl.

— Alabama Classic Christmas Trivia: Stories, Recipes, Activities, Legends, Lore & More! (Carole Marsh Alabama Bks.). (Illus.). (YA). (gr. 3-12). 1994. pap. 19.95 (*0-7933-0043-6*); lib. bdg. 29.95 (*0-7933-0044-4*) Gallopade Intl.

— Alabama Coastales! (Carole Marsh Alabama Bks.). (J). 1994. lib. bdg. 29.95 (*0-7933-6938-X*) Gallopade Intl.

— Alabama Coastales! (Carole Marsh Alabama Bks.). (Illus.). (YA). (gr. 3-12). 1994. pap. 19.95 (*1-55609-120-6*); lib. bdg. 29.95 (*1-55609-465-5*) Gallopade Intl.

— Alabama "Crinkum-Crankum" A Funny Word Book about Our State. (Carole Marsh Alabama Bks.). (Illus.). (J). 1994. pap. 19.95 (*0-7933-4811-0*); lib. bdg. 29.95 (*0-7933-4810-2*) Gallopade Intl.

— Alabama Dingbats! Bk. 1: A Fun Book of Games, Stories, Activities & More about Our State That's All in Code! for You to Decipher. (Carole Marsh Alabama Bks.). (Illus.). (J). (gr. 3-12). 1994. pap. 19.95 (*0-7933-3774-7*); lib. bdg. 29.95 (*0-7933-3773-9*) Gallopade Intl.

— Alabama Facts & Factivities. (Carole Marsh State Books Ser.). (J). (gr. 4-7). 1996. write for info. (*0-7933-7847-8*, C Marsh) Gallopade Intl.

— Alabama Festival Fun for Kids! (Carole Marsh Alabama Bks.). (Illus.). (YA). (gr. 3-12). 1994. pap. 19.95 (*0-7933-3927-8*); lib. bdg. 29.95 (*0-7933-3926-X*) Gallopade Intl.

— Alabama "GEO" Bingo! 38 Must Know State Geography Facts for Kids to Learn While Having Fun! (Bingo! Ser.). (Illus.). (J). (gr. 2-8). 1998. pap. 14.95 (*0-7933-8526-1*) Gallopade Intl.

— Alabama Government! The Cornerstone of Everyday Life in Our State! (Carole Marsh Alabama Bks.). (Illus.). (J). (gr. 3-12). 1996. pap. 19.95 (*0-7933-6182-6*); lib. bdg. 29.95 (*0-7933-6181-8*); disk 29.95 (*0-7933-6183-4*) Gallopade Intl.

— Alabama "HISTO" Bingo! 42 Must Know State History Facts for Kids to Learn While Having Fun! (Bingo! Ser.). (Illus.). (J). (gr. 2-8). 1998. pap. 14.95 (*0-7933-8527-X*) Gallopade Intl.

— Alabama History! Surprising Secrets about Our State's Founding Mothers, Fathers & Kids! (Carole Marsh Alabama Bks.). (Illus.). (YA). (gr. 7-12). 1996. pap. 19.95 (*0-7933-6029-3*); lib. bdg. 29.95 (*0-7933-6028-5*); disk 29.95 (*0-7933-6030-7*) Gallopade Intl.

— The Alabama Hot Air Balloon Mystery. (Carole Marsh Alabama Bks.). (Illus.). (J). (gr. 2-9). 1994. 29.95 (*0-7933-2318-5*); pap. 19.95 (*0-7933-2319-3*) Gallopade Intl.

— Alabama Hot Zones! Diseases, Epidemics, Immunization Programs, & Other Germy News from Our State. (J). (gr. 2-7). 1997. 24.95 (*0-614-28754-5*); pap. 19.95 (*0-614-28755-3*) Gallopade Intl.

— Alabama Hot Zones! Viruses, Diseases, & Epidemics in Our State's History. (Hot Zones! Ser.). (Illus.). (J). (gr. 3-12). 1998. pap. 19.95 (*0-7933-8829-5*); lib. bdg. 29.95 (*0-7933-8828-7*) Gallopade Intl.

— Alabama Indian Dictionary for Kids! (Carole Marsh State Bks.). (J). (gr. 2-9). 1996. 29.95 (*0-7933-7644-0*, C Marsh); pap. 19.95 (*0-7933-7645-9*, C Marsh) Gallopade Intl.

— Alabama Jeopardy! Answers & Questions about Our State! (Carole Marsh Alabama Bks.). (Illus.). (J). (gr. 3-12). 1994. pap. 19.95 (*0-7933-4080-2*); lib. bdg. 29.95 (*0-7933-4079-9*) Gallopade Intl.

— Alabama "Jography" A Fun Run Thru Our State! (Carole Marsh Alabama Bks.). (Illus.). (YA). (gr. 3-12). 1994. pap. 19.95 (*1-55609-092-7*); lib. bdg. 29.95 (*1-55609-461-2*) Gallopade Intl.

— Alabama Kid's Cookbook: Recipes, How-to, History, Lore & More! (Carole Marsh Alabama Bks.). (Illus.). (YA). (gr. 3-12). 1994. pap. 19.95 (*0-7933-0081-9*); lib. bdg. 29.95 (*0-7933-0082-7*) Gallopade Intl.

— Alabama Law for Kids! The Cornerstone of Life in Our State. (J). (gr. 2-7). 1997. 24.95 (*0-614-28750-2*); pap. 19.95 (*0-614-28751-0*) Gallopade Intl.

— The Alabama Library Book: A Surprising Guide to the Unusual Special Collections in Libraries Across Our State for Students, Teachers, Writers & Publishers - Includes Reproducible Mailing Labels Plus Activities for Young People! (Carole Marsh Alabama Bks.) (Illus.) 1994. pap. 19.95 (*0-7933-3009-2*); lib. bdg. 29.95 (*0-7933-3008-4*) Gallopade Intl.

— Alabama Math! How It All Adds up in Our State. (Carole Marsh Alabama Bks.). (Illus.). (YA). (gr. 3-12). 1996. pap. 19.95 (*0-7933-6488-4*); lib. bdg. 29.95 (*0-7933-6487-6*) Gallopade Intl.

— The Alabama Media Book: A Surprising Guide to the Amazing Print, Broadcast & Online Media of Our State for Students, Teachers, Writers & Publishers - Includes Reproducible Mailing Labels Plus Activities for Young People! (Carole Marsh Alabama Bks.). (Illus.). 1994. pap. 19.95 (*0-7933-3162-5*); lib. bdg. 29.95 (*0-7933-3161-7*) Gallopade Intl.

— The Alabama Mystery Van Takes Off! Book 1: Handicapped Alabama Kids Sneak Off on a Big Adventure. (Carole Marsh Alabama Bks.). (Illus.). (J). (gr. 3-12). 1994. 29.95 (*0-7933-4964-8*); pap. 19.95 (*0-7933-4965-6*) Gallopade Intl.

— Alabama Quiz Bowl Crash Course! (Carole Marsh Alabama Bks.). (Illus.). (YA). (gr. 3-12). 1994. pap. 19.95 (*1-55609-466-3*); lib. bdg. 29.95 (*1-55609-467-1*) Gallopade Intl.

— Alabama Rollercoasters! (Carole Marsh Alabama Bks.). (Illus.). (YA). (gr. 3-12). 1994. pap. 19.95 (*0-7933-5225-8*); lib. bdg. 29.95 (*0-7933-5224-X*) Gallopade Intl.

— Alabama School Trivia: An Amazing & Fascinating Look at Our State's Teachers, Schools & Students! (Carole Marsh Alabama Bks.). (Illus.). (YA). (gr. 3-12). 1994. pap. 19.95 (*0-7933-0049-5*); lib. bdg. 29.95 (*0-7933-0079-7*) Gallopade Intl.

— Alabama Silly Basketball Sportsmysteries, Vol. I. (Carole Marsh Alabama Bks.). (Illus.). (YA). (gr. 3-12). 1994. pap. 19.95 (*0-7933-0046-0*); lib. bdg. 29.95 (*0-7933-0047-9*) Gallopade Intl.

— Alabama Silly Basketball Sportsmysteries, Vol. II. (Carole Marsh Alabama Bks.). (Illus.). (YA). (gr. 3-12). 1994. pap. 19.95 (*0-7933-1563-8*); lib. bdg. 29.95 (*0-7933-1562-X*); disk 29.95 (*0-7933-1564-6*) Gallopade Intl.

— Alabama Silly Football Sportsmysteries, Vol. I. (Carole Marsh Alabama Bks.). (Illus.). (YA). (gr. 3-12). 1994. pap. 19.95 (*1-55609-463-9*); lib. bdg. 29.95 (*1-55609-464-7*) Gallopade Intl.

— Alabama Silly Football Sportsmysteries, Vol. II. (Carole Marsh Alabama Bks.). (Illus.). (YA). (gr. 3-12). 1994. pap. 19.95 (*0-7933-1340-6*); lib. bdg. 29.95 (*0-7933-1339-2*); disk 29.95 (*0-7933-1341-4*) Gallopade Intl.

— Alabama Silly Trivia! (Carole Marsh Alabama Bks.). (Illus.). (YA). (gr. 3-12). 1994. pap. 19.95 (*1-55609-038-2*); lib. bdg. 29.95 (*1-55609-460-4*) Gallopade Intl.

— Alabama Spelling Bee! Score Big by Correctly Spelling Our State's Unique Names. (Carole Marsh Alabama Bks.). (Illus.). (YA). (gr. 3-12). 1996. pap. 19.95 (*0-7933-6641-0*); lib. bdg. 29.95 (*0-7933-6640-2*) Gallopade Intl.

— Alabama Spelling Bee for Kids! (J). (gr. 2-7). 1997. 24.95 (*0-614-28752-9*); pap. 19.95 (*0-614-28753-7*) Gallopade Intl.

— Alabama Timeline: A Chronology of Alabama History, Mystery, Trivia, Legend, Lore & More. (Carole Marsh Alabama Bks.). (Illus.). (J). (gr. 3-12). 1994. pap. 19.95 (*0-7933-5876-0*); lib. bdg. 29.95 (*0-7933-5875-2*) Gallopade Intl.

— Alabama 2000! Coming Soon to a Calendar Near You - The 21st Century! - Complete Set of AL 2000 Items. (Two Thousand! Ser.). (Illus.). (J). (gr. 3-12). 1998. pap. 75.00 (*0-7933-9309-4*); lib. bdg. 85.00 (*0-7933-9310-8*) Gallopade Intl.

— Alabama 2000! Coming Soon to a Calendar near You--The 21st Century! (Two Thousand! Ser.). (Illus.). (J). (gr. 3-12). 1998. pap. 19.95 (*0-7933-8676-4*); lib. bdg. 29.95 (*0-7933-8675-6*) Gallopade Intl.

— Alabama UFO's & Extraterrestrials! A Look at the Sightings & Science in Our State. (Carole Marsh Alabama Bks.). (Illus.). (J). (gr. 3-12). 1997. pap. 19.95 (*0-7933-6335-7*); lib. bdg. 29.95 (*0-7933-6334-9*) Gallopade Intl.

— Alabama UFOs & Extraterrestrials: The Science Behind the Sightings in Our State. (J). (gr. 2-7). 1997. 24.95 (*0-614-28748-0*); pap. 19.95 (*0-614-28749-9*) Gallopade Intl.

— Alabama's (Most Devastating!) Disasters & (Most Calamitous!) Catastrophies! (Carole Marsh Alabama Bks.). (Illus.). (YA). (gr. 3-12). 1994. pap. 19.95 (*0-7933-0037-1*); lib. bdg. 29.95 (*0-7933-0038-X*) Gallopade Intl.

— Alabama's Unsolved Mysteries (& Their "Solutions") Includes Scientific Information & Other Activities for Students. (Carole Marsh Alabama Bks.). (Illus.). (J). (gr. 3-12). 1994. pap. 19.95 (*0-7933-5723-3*); lib. bdg. 29.95 (*0-7933-5722-5*) Gallopade Intl.

— Alaska & Other State Greats (Biographies) (Carole Marsh Alaska Bks.). (Illus.). (YA). (gr. 3-12). 1994. pap. 19.95 (*1-55609-482-5*); lib. bdg. 29.95 (*1-55609-483-3*) Gallopade Intl.

— Alaska Bandits, Bushwackers, Outlaws, Crooks, Devils, Ghosts, Desperadoes & Other Assorted & Sundry Characters! (Carole Marsh Alaska Bks.). (Illus.). (YA). (gr. 3-12). 1994. pap. 19.95 (*0-7933-0093-2*); lib. bdg. 29.95 (*0-7933-0094-0*) Gallopade Intl.

— Alaska "BIO" Bingo! 24 Must Know State People for Kids to Learn about While Having Fun! (Bingo! Ser.). (Illus.). (J). (gr. 2-8). 1998. pap. 14.95 (*0-7933-8528-8*) Gallopade Intl.

— The Alaska Bookstore Book: A Surprising Guide to Our State's Bookstores & Their Specialties for Students, Teachers, Writers & Publishers. (Carole Marsh Alaska Bks.). (Illus.). 1994. pap. 19.95 (*0-7933-2859-4*); lib. bdg. 29.95 (*0-7933-2858-6*) Gallopade Intl.

— Alaska Classic Christmas Trivia: Stories, Recipes, Activities, Legends, Lore & More! (Carole Marsh Alaska Bks.). (Illus.). (YA). (gr. 3-12). 1994. pap. 19.95 (*0-7933-0096-7*); lib. bdg. 29.95 (*0-7933-0097-5*) Gallopade Intl.

— Alaska Coastales. (Carole Marsh Alaska Bks.). (J). 1994. lib. bdg. 29.95 (*0-7933-7266-6*) Gallopade Intl.

— Alaska Coastales. (Carole Marsh Alaska Bks.). (Illus.). (YA). (gr. 3-12). 1994. pap. 19.95 (*1-55609-478-7*); lib. bdg. 29.95 (*1-55609-479-5*) Gallopade Intl.

— Alaska "Crinkum-Crankum" A Funny Word Book about Our State. (Carole Marsh Alaska Bks.). (Illus.). (J). 1994. pap. 19.95 (*0-7933-4814-5*); lib. bdg. 29.95 (*0-7933-4813-7*) Gallopade Intl.

— Alaska Dingbats! A Fun Book of Games, Stories, Activities & More about Our State That's All in Code! for You to Decipher, Bk. 1. (Carole Marsh Alaska Bks.). (Illus.). (J). (gr. 3-12). 1994. lib. bdg. 29.95 (*0-7933-3776-3*) Gallopade Intl.

— Alaska Dingbats! A Fun Book of Games, Stories, Activities & More about Our State That's All in Code 1 for You to Decipher, Bk. 1. (Carole Marsh Alaska Bks.). (Illus.). (J). (gr. 3-12). 1994. pap. 19.95 (*0-7933-3777-1*) Gallopade Intl.

— Alaska Facts & Factivities. (Carole Marsh State Bks.). (Illus.). (J). (gr. 4-7). 1996. pap., teacher ed. 19.95 (*0-7933-7849-4*, C Marsh) Gallopade Intl.

— Alaska Festival Fun for Kids! (Carole Marsh Alaska Bks.). (Illus.). (YA). (gr. 3-12). 1994. pap. 19.95 (*0-7933-3930-8*); lib. bdg. 29.95 (*0-7933-3929-4*) Gallopade Intl.

— Alaska "GEO" Bingo! 38 Must Know State Geography Facts for Kids to Learn While Having Fun! (Bingo! Ser.). (Illus.). (J). (gr. 2-8). 1998. pap. 14.95 (*0-7933-8529-6*) Gallopade Intl.

— Alaska Government! The Cornerstone of Everyday Life in Our State! (Carole Marsh Alaska Bks.). (Illus.). (J). (gr. 3-12). 1996. pap. 19.95 (*0-7933-6185-0*); lib. bdg. 29.95 (*0-7933-6184-2*); disk 29.95 (*0-7933-6186-9*) Gallopade Intl.

— Alaska "HISTO" Bingo! 42 Must Know State History Facts for Kids to Learn While Having Fun! (Bingo! Ser.). (Illus.). (J). (gr. 2-8). 1998. pap. 14.95 (*0-7933-8530-X*) Gallopade Intl.

— Alaska History! Surprising Secrets about Our State's Founding Mothers, Fathers & Kids! (Carole Marsh Alaska Bks.). (Illus.). (YA). (gr. 7-12). 1996. pap. 19.95 (*0-7933-6032-3*); lib. bdg. 29.95 (*0-7933-6031-5*); disk 29.95 (*0-7933-6033-1*) Gallopade Intl.

— The Alaska Hot Air Balloon Mystery. (Carole Marsh Alaska Bks.). (Illus.). (J). (gr. 2-9). 1994. 29.95 (*0-7933-2327-4*); pap. 19.95 (*0-7933-2328-2*) Gallopade Intl.

— Alaska Hot Zones! Viruses, Diseases, & Epidemics in Our State's History. (Hot Zones! Ser.). (Illus.). (J). (gr. 3-12). 1998. pap. 19.95 (*0-7933-8832-5*); lib. bdg. 29.95 (*0-7933-8831-7*) Gallopade Intl.

— Alaska Indian Dictionary for Kids! (Carole Marsh State Bks.). (J). (gr. 2-9). 1996. 29.95 (*0-7933-7647-5*, C Marsh); pap. 19.95 (*0-7933-7648-3*, C Marsh) Gallopade Intl.

— Alaska Jeopardy! Answers & Questions about Our State! (Carole Marsh Alaska Bks.). (Illus.). (J). (gr. 3-12). 1994. pap. 19.95 (*0-7933-4083-7*); lib. bdg. 29.95 (*0-7933-4082-9*) Gallopade Intl.

— Alaska "Jography" A Fun Run Thru Our State! (Carole Marsh Alaska Bks.). (Illus.). (YA). (gr. 3-12). 1994. pap. 19.95 (*1-55609-472-8*); lib. bdg. 29.95 (*1-55609-473-6*) Gallopade Intl.

— Alaska Kid's Cookbook: Recipes, How-to, History, Lore & More! (Carole Marsh Alaska Bks.). (Illus.). (YA). (gr. 3-12). 1994. pap. 19.95 (*0-7933-0105-X*); lib. bdg. 29.95 (*0-7933-0106-8*) Gallopade Intl.

— The Alaska Library Book: A Surprising Guide to the Unusual Special Collections in Libraries Across Our State for Students, Teachers, Writers & Publishers - Includes Reproducible Mailing Labels Plus Activities for Young People! (Carole Marsh Alaska Bks.). (Illus.). 1994. pap. 19.95 (*0-7933-3012-2*); lib. bdg. 29.95 (*0-7933-3011-4*) Gallopade Intl.

— Alaska Math! How It All Adds up in Our State. (Carole Marsh Alaska Bks.). (Illus.). (YA). (gr. 3-12). 1996. pap. 19.95 (*0-7933-6491-4*); lib. bdg. 29.95 (*0-7933-6490-6*) Gallopade Intl.

— The Alaska Media Book: A Surprising Guide to the Amazing Print, Broadcast & Online Media of Our State for Students, Teachers, Writers & Publishers - Includes Reproducible Mailing Labels Plus Activities for Young People! (Carole Marsh Alaska Bks.). (Illus.). 1994. pap. 19.95 (*0-7933-3165-X*); lib. bdg. 29.95 (*0-7933-3164-1*) Gallopade Intl.

— The Alaska Mystery Van Takes Off! Book 1: Handicapped Alaska Kids Sneak Off on a Big Adventure. (Carole Marsh Alaska Bks.). (Illus.). (J). (gr. 3-12). 1994. 29.95 (*0-7933-4967-2*); pap. 19.95 (*0-7933-4968-0*) Gallopade Intl.

— Alaska Quiz Bowl Crash Course! (Carole Marsh Alaska Bks.). (Illus.). (YA). (gr. 3-12). 1994. pap. 19.95 (*1-55609-480-9*); lib. bdg. 29.95 (*1-55609-481-7*) Gallopade Intl.

— Alaska Rollercoasters! (Carole Marsh Alaska Bks.). (Illus.). (YA). (gr. 3-12). 1994. pap. 19.95 (*0-7933-5228-2*); lib. bdg. 29.95 (*0-7933-5227-4*) Gallopade Intl.

— Alaska School Trivia: An Amazing & Fascinating Look at Our State's Teachers, Schools & Students! (Carole Marsh Alaska Bks.). (Illus.). (YA). (gr. 3-12). 1994. pap. 19.95 (*0-7933-0102-5*); lib. bdg. 29.95 (*0-7933-0103-3*) Gallopade Intl.

— Alaska Silly Basketball Sportsmysteries, Vol. I. (Carole Marsh Alaska Bks.). (Illus.). (YA). (gr. 3-12). 1994. pap. 19.95 (*0-7933-0099-1*); lib. bdg. 29.95 (*0-7933-0100-9*) Gallopade Intl.

M

— Alaska Silly Basketball Sportsmysteries, Vol. II. (Carole Marsh Alaska Bks.). (Illus.). (YA). (gr. 3-12). 1994. pap. 19.95 (*0-7933-1566-2*); lib. bdg. 29.95 (*0-7933-1565-4*); disk 29.95 (*0-7933-1567-0*) Gallopade Intl.

— Alaska Silly Football Sportsmysteries, Vol. I. (Carole Marsh Alaska Bks.). (Illus.). (YA). (gr. 3-12). 1994. pap. 19.95 (*1-55609-476-0*); lib. bdg. 29.95 (*1-55609-477-9*) Gallopade Intl.

— Alaska Silly Football Sportsmysteries, Vol. II. (Carole Marsh Alaska Bks.). (Illus.). (YA). (gr. 3-12). 1994. pap. 19.95 (*0-7933-1347-3*); lib. bdg. 29.95 (*0-7933-1346-5*); disk 29.95 (*0-7933-1348-1*) Gallopade Intl.

— Alaska Silly Trivia! (Carole Marsh Alaska Bks.). (Illus.). (YA). (gr. 3-12). 1994. pap. 19.95 (*1-55609-470-1*); lib. bdg. 29.95 (*1-55609-471-X*) Gallopade Intl.

— Alaska Spelling Bee! Score Big by Correctly Spelling Our State's Unique Names. (Carole Marsh Alaska Bks.). (Illus.). (YA). (gr. 3-12). 1996. pap. 29.95 (*0-7933-6643-7*); pap. 19.95 (*0-7933-6644-5*) Gallopade Intl.

— Alaska Timeline: A Chronology of Alaska History, Mystery, Trivia, Legend, Lore & More. (Carole Marsh Alaska Bks.). (Illus.). (J). (gr. 3-12). 1994. pap. 19.95 (*0-7933-5879-5*); lib. bdg. 29.95 (*0-7933-5878-7*) Gallopade Intl.

— Alaska 2000! Coming Soon to a Calendar Near You - The 21st Century! - Complete Set of AL 2000 Items. (Two Thousand! Ser.). (Illus.). (J). (gr. 3-12). 1998. pap. 75.00 (*0-7933-9311-6*); lib. bdg. 85.00 (*0-7933-9312-4*) Gallopade Intl.

— Alaska 2000! Coming Soon to a Calendar near You--The 21st Century! (Two Thousand! Ser.). (Illus.). (J). (gr. 3-12). 1998. pap. 19.95 (*0-7933-8679-9*); lib. bdg. 29.95 (*0-7933-8678-0*) Gallopade Intl.

— Alaska UFO's & Extraterrestrials! A Look at the Sightings & Science in Our State. (Carole Marsh Alaska Bks.). (Illus.). (J). (gr. 3-12). 1997. pap. 19.95 (*0-7933-6338-1*); lib. bdg. 29.95 (*0-7933-6337-3*) Gallopade Intl.

— Alaska's (Most Devastating!) Disasters & (Most Calamitous!) Catastrophies! (Carole Marsh Alaska Bks.). (Illus.). (YA). (gr. 3-12). 1994. pap. 19.95 (*0-7933-0090-8*); lib. bdg. 29.95 (*0-7933-0091-6*) Gallopade Intl.

— Alaska's Unsolved Mysteries (& Their "Solutions") Includes Scientific Information & Other Activities for Students. (Carole Marsh Alaska Bks.). (Illus.). (J). (gr. 3-12). 1994. pap. 19.95 (*0-7933-5726-8*); lib. bdg. 29.95 (*0-7933-5725-X*) Gallopade Intl.

— Alligators & Crocodiles: The Tooth, the Whole Tooth & Nothing but the Tooth! (Interactive Multimedia Titles Ser.). (J). (gr. 2-9). 1996. 29.95 (*0-7933-7596-7*, C Marsh); pap. 19.95 (*0-7933-7597-5*, C Marsh); pap., teacher ed. 19.95 (*0-7933-7843-5*, C Marsh) Gallopade Intl.

— American Indian Dictionary for Kids! (CD-ROM Titles Ser.). (J). (gr. 2-9). 1997. 29.95 (*0-7933-7601-7*, C Marsh); pap. 19.95 (*0-7933-7600-9*, C Marsh); pap., teacher ed. 19.95 (*0-7933-7829-X*, C Marsh) Gallopade Intl.

— Arizona: A(dama) to Z(oroaster) (Carole Marsh Arizona Bks.). (J). 1994. pap. text 19.95 (*0-7933-7316-6*); lib. bdg. 29.95 (*0-7933-7317-4*) Gallopade Intl.

— Arizona & Other State Greats (Biographies) (Carole Marsh Arizona Bks.). (Illus.). (YA). (gr. 3-12). 1994. pap. 19.95 (*1-55609-506-6*); lib. bdg. 29.95 (*1-55609-507-4*) Gallopade Intl.

— Arizona Bandits, Bushwackers, Outlaws, Crooks, Devils, Ghosts, Desperadoes & Other Assorted & Sundry Characters! (Carole Marsh Arizona Bks.). (Illus.). (YA). (gr. 3-12). 1994. pap. 19.95 (*0-7933-0117-3*); lib. bdg. 29.95 (*0-7933-0118-1*) Gallopade Intl.

— Arizona "BIO" Bingo! 24 Must Know State People for Kids to Learn about While Having Fun! (Bingo! Ser.). (Illus.). 1998. pap. 14.95 (*0-7933-8531-8*) Gallopade Intl.

— The Arizona Bookstore Book: A Surprising Guide to Our State's Bookstores & Their Specialties for Students, Teachers, Writers & Publishers. (Carole Marsh Arizona Bks.). (Illus.). 1994. pap. 19.95 (*0-7933-2862-4*); lib. bdg. 29.95 (*0-7933-2861-6*) Gallopade Intl.

— Arizona Classic Christmas Trivia: Stories, Recipes, Activities, Legends, Lore & More! (Carole Marsh Arizona Bks.). (Illus.). (YA). (gr. 3-12). 1994. pap. 19.95 (*0-7933-0120-3*); lib. bdg. 29.95 (*0-7933-0121-1*) Gallopade Intl.

— Arizona Coastales! (Carole Marsh Arizona Bks.). (J). 1994. lib. bdg. 29.95 (*0-7933-7267-4*) Gallopade Intl.

— Arizona Coastales! (Carole Marsh Arizona Bks.). (Illus.). (YA). (gr. 3-12). 1994. pap. 19.95 (*1-55609-502-3*); lib. bdg. 29.95 (*1-55609-503-1*) Gallopade Intl.

— Arizona "Crinkum-Crankum" A Funny Word Book about Our State. (Carole Marsh Arizona Bks.). (Illus.). (J). 1994. pap. 19.95 (*0-7933-4817-X*); lib. bdg. 29.95 (*0-7933-4816-1*) Gallopade Intl.

— Arizona Dingbats! Bk. 1: A Fun Book of Games, Stories, Activities & More about Our State That's All in Code! for You to Decipher. (Carole Marsh Arizona Bks.). (Illus.). (J). (gr. 3-12). 1994. pap. 19.95 (*0-7933-3780-1*); lib. bdg. 29.95 (*0-7933-3779-8*) Gallopade Intl.

— Arizona Facts & Factivities. (Carole Marsh State Bks.). (Illus.). (J). (gr. 4-7). 1996. pap., teacher ed. 19.95 (*0-7933-7851-6*, C Marsh) Gallopade Intl.

— Arizona Festival Fun for Kids! (Carole Marsh Arizona Bks.). (Illus.). (YA). (gr. 3-12). 1994. pap. 19.95 (*0-7933-3933-2*); lib. bdg. 29.95 (*0-7933-3932-4*) Gallopade Intl.

— Arizona "GEO" Bingo! 38 Must Know State Geography Facts for Kids to Learn While Having Fun! (Bingo! Ser.). (Illus.). (J). (gr. 2-8). 1998. pap. 14.95 (*0-7933-8532-6*) Gallopade Intl.

— Arizona Government! The Cornerstone of Everyday Life in Our State! (Carole Marsh Arizona Bks.). (Illus.). (J). (gr. 3-12). 1996. pap. 19.95 (*0-7933-6188-5*); lib. bdg. 29.95 (*0-7933-6187-7*); disk 29.95 (*0-7933-6189-3*) Gallopade Intl.

— Arizona "HISTO" Bingo! 42 Must Know State History Facts for Kids to Learn While Having Fun! (Bingo! Ser.). (Illus.). (J). (gr. 2-8). 1998. pap. 14.95 (*0-7933-8533-4*) Gallopade Intl.

— Arizona History! Surprising Secrets about Our State's Founding Mothers, Fathers & Kids! (Carole Marsh Arizona Bks.). (Illus.). (J). (gr. 3-12). 1996. pap. 19.95 (*0-7933-6035-8*); lib. bdg. 29.95 (*0-7933-6034-X*); disk 29.95 (*0-7933-6036-6*) Gallopade Intl.

— The Arizona Hot Air Balloon Mystery. (Carole Marsh Arizona Bks.). (Illus.). (J). (gr. 2-9). 1994. 29.95 (*0-7933-2336-3*); pap. 19.95 (*0-7933-2337-1*) Gallopade Intl.

— Arizona Hot Zones! Viruses, Diseases, & Epidemics in Our State's History. (Hot Zones! Ser.). (Illus.). (J). (gr. 3-12). 1998. pap. 19.95 (*0-7933-8835-X*); lib. bdg. 29.95 (*0-7933-8834-1*) Gallopade Intl.

— Arizona Indian Dictionary for Kids! (Carole Marsh State Bks.). (J). (gr. 2-9). 1996. 29.95 (*0-7933-7650-5*, C Marsh); pap. 19.95 (*0-7933-7651-3*, C Marsh) Gallopade Intl.

— Arizona Jeopardy! Answers & Questions about Our State! (Carole Marsh Arizona Bks.). (Illus.). (J). (gr. 3-12). 1994. pap. 19.95 (*0-7933-4086-1*); lib. bdg. 29.95 (*0-7933-4085-3*) Gallopade Intl.

— Arizona "Jography" A Fun Run Thru Our State! (Carole Marsh Arizona Bks.). (Illus.). (YA). (gr. 3-12). 1994. pap. 19.95 (*1-55609-497-3*); lib. bdg. 29.95 (*1-55609-498-1*) Gallopade Intl.

— Arizona Kid's Cookbook: Recipes, How-to, History, Lore & More! (Carole Marsh Arizona Bks.). (Illus.). (YA). (gr. 3-12). 1994. pap. 19.95 (*0-7933-0129-7*); lib. bdg. 29.95 (*0-7933-0130-0*) Gallopade Intl.

— The Arizona Library Book: A Surprising Guide to the Unusual Special Collections in Libraries Across Our State for Students, Teachers, Writers & Publishers - Includes Reproducible Mailing Labels Plus Activities for Young People! (Carole Marsh Arizona Bks.). (Illus.). 1994. pap. 19.95 (*0-7933-3015-7*); lib. bdg. 29.95 (*0-7933-3014-9*) Gallopade Intl.

— Arizona Math! How It All Adds up in Our State. (Carole Marsh Arizona Bks.). (Illus.). (YA). (gr. 3-12). 1996. pap. 19.95 (*0-7933-6494-9*); lib. bdg. 29.95 (*0-7933-6493-0*) Gallopade Intl.

— The Arizona Media Book: A Surprising Guide to the Amazing Print, Broadcast & Online Media of Our State for Students, Teachers, Writers & Publishers - Includes Reproducible Mailing Labels Plus Activities for Young People! (Carole Marsh Arizona Bks.). (Illus.). 1994. pap. 19.95 (*0-7933-3168-4*); lib. bdg. 29.95 (*0-7933-3167-6*) Gallopade Intl.

— The Arizona Mystery Van Takes Off! Book 1: Handicapped Arizona Kids Sneak Off on a Big Adventure. (Carole Marsh Arizona Bks.). (Illus.). (J). (gr. 3-12). 1994. 29.95 (*0-7933-4970-2*); pap. 19.95 (*0-7933-4971-0*) Gallopade Intl.

— Arizona Quiz Bowl Crash Course! (Carole Marsh Arizona Bks.). (Illus.). (YA). (gr. 3-12). 1994. pap. 19.95 (*1-55609-504-X*); lib. bdg. 29.95 (*1-55609-505-8*) Gallopade Intl.

— Arizona Rollercoasters! (Carole Marsh Arizona Bks.). (Illus.). (YA). (gr. 3-12). 1994. pap. 19.95 (*0-7933-5231-2*); lib. bdg. 29.95 (*0-7933-5230-4*) Gallopade Intl.

— Arizona School Trivia: An Amazing & Fascinating Look at Our State's Teachers, Schools & Students! (Carole Marsh Arizona Bks.). (Illus.). (YA). (gr. 3-12). 1994. pap. 19.95 (*0-7933-0126-2*); lib. bdg. 29.95 (*0-7933-0127-0*) Gallopade Intl.

— Arizona Silly Basketball Sportsmysteries, Vol. I. (Carole Marsh Arizona Bks.). (Illus.). (YA). (gr. 3-12). 1994. pap. 19.95 (*0-7933-0123-8*); lib. bdg. 29.95 (*0-7933-0124-6*) Gallopade Intl.

— Arizona Silly Basketball Sportsmysteries, Vol. II. (Carole Marsh Arizona Bks.). (Illus.). (YA). (gr. 3-12). 1994. pap. 19.95 (*0-7933-1569-7*); lib. bdg. 29.95 (*0-7933-1568-9*); disk 29.95 (*0-7933-1570-0*) Gallopade Intl.

— Arizona Silly Football Sportsmysteries, Vol. I. (Carole Marsh Arizona Bks.). (Illus.). (YA). (gr. 3-12). 1994. pap. 19.95 (*1-55609-500-7*); lib. bdg. 29.95 (*1-55609-501-5*) Gallopade Intl.

— Arizona Silly Football Sportsmysteries, Vol. II. (Carole Marsh Arizona Bks.). (Illus.). (YA). (gr. 3-12). 1994. pap. 19.95 (*0-7933-1363-5*); lib. bdg. 29.95 (*0-7933-1362-7*); disk 29.95 (*0-7933-1364-3*) Gallopade Intl.

— Arizona Silly Trivia! (Carole Marsh Arizona Bks.). (Illus.). (YA). (gr. 3-12). 1994. pap. 19.95 (*1-55609-495-7*); lib. bdg. 29.95 (*1-55609-496-5*) Gallopade Intl.

— Arizona Spelling Bee! Score Big by Correctly Spelling Our State's Unique Names. (Carole Marsh Arizona Bks.). (Illus.). (YA). (gr. 3-12). 1996. pap. 19.95 (*0-7933-6647-X*); lib. bdg. 29.95 (*0-7933-6646-1*) Gallopade Intl.

— Arizona Timeline: A Chronology of Arizona History, Mystery, Trivia, Legend, Lore & More. (Carole Marsh Arizona Bks.). (Illus.). (J). (gr. 3-12). 1994. pap. 19.95 (*0-7933-5882-5*); lib. bdg. 29.95 (*0-7933-5881-7*) Gallopade Intl.

— Arizona 2000! Coming Soon to a Calendar near You--The 21st Century! (Two Thousand! Ser.). (Illus.). (J). (gr. 3-12). 1998. pap. 19.95 (*0-7933-8682-9*); lib. bdg. 29.95 (*0-7933-8681-0*) Gallopade Intl.

— Arizona UFO's & Extraterrestrials! A Look at the Sightings & Science in Our State. (Carole Marsh Arizona Bks.). (Illus.). (J). (gr. 3-12). 1997. pap. 19.95 (*0-7933-6341-1*); lib. bdg. 29.95 (*0-7933-6340-3*) Gallopade Intl.

— Arizona's (Most Devastating!) Disasters & (Most Calamitous!) Catastrophies! (Carole Marsh Arizona Bks.). (Illus.). (YA). (gr. 3-12). 1994. pap. 19.95 (*0-7933-0114-9*); lib. bdg. 29.95 (*0-7933-0115-7*) Gallopade Intl.

— Arizona's Unsolved Mysteries (& Their "Solutions") Includes Scientific Information & Other Activities for Students. (Carole Marsh Arizona Bks.). (Illus.). (J). (gr. 3-12). 1994. pap. 19.95 (*0-7933-5729-2*); lib. bdg. 29.95 (*0-7933-5728-4*) Gallopade Intl.

— Arkansas & Other State Greats (Biographies) (Carole Marsh Arkansas Bks.). (Illus.). (YA). (gr. 3-12). 1994. pap. 19.95 (*1-55609-493-0*); lib. bdg. 29.95 (*1-55609-494-9*) Gallopade Intl.

— Arkansas Bandits, Bushwackers, Outlaws, Crooks, Devils, Ghosts, Desperadoes & Other Assorted & Sundry Characters! (Carole Marsh Arkansas Bks.). (Illus.). (YA). (gr. 3-12). 1994. pap. 19.95 (*0-7933-0141-6*); lib. bdg. 29.95 (*0-7933-0142-4*) Gallopade Intl.

— Arkansas "BIO" Bingo! 24 Must Know State People for Kids to Learn about While Having Fun! (Bingo! Ser.). (Illus.). (J). (gr. 2-8). 1998. pap. 14.95 (*0-7933-8534-2*) Gallopade Intl.

— The Arkansas Bookstore Book: A Surprising Guide to Our State's Bookstores & Their Specialties for Students, Teachers, Writers & Publishers. (Carole Marsh Arkansas Bks.). (Illus.). 1994. pap. 19.95 (*0-7933-2865-9*); lib. bdg. 29.95 (*0-7933-2864-0*) Gallopade Intl.

— Arkansas Classic Christmas Trivia: Stories, Recipes, Activities, Legends, Lore & More! (Carole Marsh Arkansas Bks.). (Illus.). (YA). (gr. 3-12). 1994. pap. 19.95 (*0-7933-0144-0*); lib. bdg. 29.95 (*0-7933-0145-9*) Gallopade Intl.

— Arkansas Coastales! (Carole Marsh Arkansas Bks.). (J). 1994. lib. bdg. 29.95 (*0-7933-7268-2*) Gallopade Intl.

— Arkansas Coastales! (Carole Marsh Arkansas Bks.). (Illus.). (YA). (gr. 3-12). 1994. pap. 19.95 (*1-55609-489-2*); lib. bdg. 29.95 (*1-55609-490-6*) Gallopade Intl.

— Arkansas "Crinkum-Crankum" A Funny Word Book about Our State. (Carole Marsh Arkansas Bks.). (Illus.). (J). 1994. pap. 19.95 (*0-7933-4820-X*); lib. bdg. 29.95 (*0-7933-4819-6*) Gallopade Intl.

— Arkansas Dingbats! Bk. 1: A Fun Book of Games, Stories, Activities & More about Our State That's All in Code! for You to Decipher. (Carole Marsh Arkansas Bks.). (Illus.). (J). (gr. 3-12). 1994. pap. 19.95 (*0-7933-3783-6*); lib. bdg. 29.95 (*0-7933-3782-8*) Gallopade Intl.

— Arkansas Facts & Factivities. (Carole Marsh State Bks.). (Illus.). (J). (gr. 4-7). 1996. pap., teacher ed. 19.95 (*0-7933-7853-2*, C Marsh) Gallopade Intl.

— Arkansas Festival for Kids! (Carole Marsh Arkansas Bks.). (Illus.). (YA). (gr. 3-12). 1994. pap. 19.95 (*0-7933-3936-7*); lib. bdg. 29.95 (*0-7933-3935-9*) Gallopade Intl.

— Arkansas "GEO" Bingo! 38 Must Know State Geography Facts for Kids to Learn While Having Fun! (Bingo! Ser.). (Illus.). (J). (gr. 2-8). 1998. pap. 14.95 (*0-7933-8535-0*) Gallopade Intl.

— Arkansas Government! The Cornerstone of Everyday Life in Our State! (Carole Marsh Arkansas Bks.). (Illus.). (J). (gr. 3-12). 1996. pap. 19.95 (*0-7933-6191-5*); lib. bdg. 29.95 (*0-7933-6190-7*); disk 29.95 (*0-7933-6192-3*) Gallopade Intl.

— Arkansas "HISTO" Bingo! 42 Must Know State History Facts for Kids to Learn While Having Fun! (Bingo! Ser.). (Illus.). (J). (gr. 2-8). 1998. pap. 14.95 (*0-7933-8536-9*) Gallopade Intl.

— Arkansas History! Surprising Secrets about Our State's Founding Mothers, Fathers & Kids! (Carole Marsh Arkansas Bks.). (Illus.). (J). (gr. 3-12). 1996. pap. 19.95 (*0-7933-6038-2*); lib. bdg. 29.95 (*0-7933-6037-4*); disk 29.95 (*0-7933-6039-0*) Gallopade Intl.

— The Arkansas Hot Air Balloon Mystery. (Carole Marsh Arkansas Bks.). (Illus.). (J). (gr. 2-9). 1994. 29.95 (*0-7933-2345-2*); pap. 19.95 (*0-7933-2346-0*) Gallopade Intl.

— Arkansas Hot Zones! Viruses, Diseases, & Epidemics in Our State's History. (Hot Zones! Ser.). (Illus.). (J). (gr. 3-12). 1998. pap. 19.95 (*0-7933-8838-4*); lib. bdg. 29.95 (*0-7933-8837-6*) Gallopade Intl.

— Arkansas Indian Dictionary for Kids! (Carole Marsh State Bks.). (J). (gr. 2-9). 1996. 29.95 (*0-7933-7653-X*, C Marsh); pap. 19.95 (*0-7933-7654-8*, C Marsh) Gallopade Intl.

— Arkansas Jeopardy! Answers & Questions about Our State! (Carole Marsh Arkansas Bks.). (Illus.). (J). (gr. 3-12). 1994. pap. 19.95 (*0-7933-4089-6*); lib. bdg. 29.95 (*0-7933-4088-8*) Gallopade Intl.

— Arkansas "Jography" A Fun Run Thru Our State! (Carole Marsh Arkansas Bks.). (Illus.). (YA). (gr. 3-12). 1994. pap. 19.95 (*1-55609-088-9*); lib. bdg. 29.95 (*1-55609-485-X*) Gallopade Intl.

— Arkansas Kid's Cookbook: Recipes, How-to, History, Lore & More! (Carole Marsh Arkansas Bks.). (Illus.). (YA). (gr. 3-12). 1994. pap. 19.95 (*0-7933-0153-X*); lib. bdg. 29.95 (*0-7933-0154-8*) Gallopade Intl.

— The Arkansas Library Book: A Surprising Guide to the Unusual Special Collections in Libraries Across Our State for Students, Teachers, Writers & Publishers - Includes Reproducible Mailing Labels Plus Activities for Young People! (Carole Marsh Arkansas Bks.). (Illus.). 1994. pap. 19.95 (*0-7933-3018-1*); lib. bdg. 29.95 (*0-7933-3017-3*) Gallopade Intl.

— Arkansas Math! How It All Adds up in Our State. (Carole Marsh Arkansas Bks.). (Illus.). (YA). (gr. 3-12). 1996. pap. 19.95 (*0-7933-6497-3*); lib. bdg. 29.95 (*0-7933-6496-5*) Gallopade Intl.

— The Arkansas Media Book: A Surprising Guide to the Amazing Print, Broadcast & Online Media of Our State for Students, Teachers, Writers & Publishers - Includes Reproducible Mailing Labels Plus Activities for Young People! (Carole Marsh Arkansas Bks.). (Illus.). 1994. pap. 19.95 (*0-7933-3171-4*); lib. bdg. 29.95 (*0-7933-3170-6*) Gallopade Intl.

— The Arkansas Mystery Van Takes Off! Book 1: Handicapped Arkansas Kids Sneak Off on a Big Adventure. (Carole Marsh Arkansas Bks.). (Illus.). (J). (gr. 3-12). 1994. 29.95 (*0-7933-4973-7*); pap. 19.95 (*0-7933-4974-5*) Gallopade Intl.

— Arkansas Quiz Bowl Crash Course! (Carole Marsh Arkansas Bks.). (Illus.). (YA). (gr. 3-12). 1994. pap. 19.95 (*1-55609-491-4*); lib. bdg. 29.95 (*1-55609-492-2*) Gallopade Intl.

— Arkansas Rollercoasters! (Carole Marsh Arkansas Bks.). (Illus.). (YA). (gr. 3-12). 1994. pap. 19.95 (*0-7933-5234-7*); lib. bdg. 29.95 (*0-7933-5233-9*) Gallopade Intl.

— Arkansas School Trivia: An Amazing & Fascinating Look at Our State's Teachers, Schools & Students! (Carole Marsh Arkansas Bks.). (Illus.). (YA). (gr. 3-12). 1994. pap. 19.95 (*0-7933-0150-5*); lib. bdg. 29.95 (*0-7933-0151-3*) Gallopade Intl.

— Arkansas Silly Basketball Sportsmysteries, Vol. I. (Carole Marsh Arkansas Bks.). (Illus.). (YA). (gr. 3-12). 1994. pap. 19.95 (*0-7933-0147-5*); lib. bdg. 29.95 (*0-7933-0149-1*) Gallopade Intl.

— Arkansas Silly Basketball Sportsmysteries, Vol. II. (Carole Marsh Arkansas Bks.). (Illus.). (YA). (gr. 3-12). 1994. lib. bdg. 29.95 (*0-7933-1571-9*); disk 29.95 (*0-7933-1573-5*) Gallopade Intl.

— Arkansas Silly Basketball Sportsmysteries, Vol. II. (Carole Marsh Arkansas Bks.). (Illus.). (J). (gr. 3-12). 1997. pap. 19.00 (*0-7933-1572-7*) Gallopade Intl.

— Arkansas Silly Football Sportsmysteries, Vol. I. (Carole Marsh Arkansas Bks.). (Illus.). (YA). (gr. 3-12). 1994. pap. 19.95 (*1-55609-487-6*); lib. bdg. 29.95 (*1-55609-488-4*) Gallopade Intl.

— Arkansas Silly Football Sportsmysteries, Vol. II. (Carole Marsh Arkansas Bks.). (Illus.). (YA). (gr. 3-12). 1994. pap. 19.95 (*0-7933-1379-1*); lib. bdg. 29.95 (*0-7933-1378-3*); disk 29.95 (*0-7933-1380-5*) Gallopade Intl.

— Arkansas Silly Trivia! (Carole Marsh Arkansas Bks.). (Illus.). (YA). (gr. 3-12). 1994. pap. 19.95 (*1-55609-083-8*); lib. bdg. 29.95 (*1-55609-484-1*) Gallopade Intl.

— Arkansas Spelling Bee! Score Big by Correctly Spelling Our State's Unique Names. (Carole Marsh Arkansas Bks.). (Illus.). (YA). (gr. 3-12). 1996. pap. 19.95 (*0-7933-6650-X*); lib. bdg. 29.95 (*0-7933-6649-6*) Gallopade Intl.

— Arkansas Timeline: A Chronology of Arkansas History, Mystery, Trivia, Legend, Lore & More. (Carole Marsh Arkansas Bks.). (Illus.). (J). (gr. 3-12). 1994. pap. 19.95 (*0-7933-5885-X*); lib. bdg. 29.95 (*0-7933-5884-1*) Gallopade Intl.

— Arkansas 2000! Coming Soon to a Calendar Near You - The 21st Century! - Complete Set of AL 2000 Items. (Two Thousand! Ser.). (Illus.). (J). (gr. 3-12). 1998. pap. 75.00 (*0-7933-9313-2*); lib. bdg. 85.00 (*0-7933-9314-0*) Gallopade Intl.

— Arkansas 2000! Coming Soon to a Calendar near You--The 21st Century! (Two Thousand! Ser.). (Illus.). (J). (gr. 3-12). 1998. pap. 19.95 (*0-7933-8685-3*); lib. bdg. 29.95 (*0-7933-8684-5*) Gallopade Intl.

— Arkansas UFO's & Extraterrestrials! A Look at the Sightings & Science in Our State. (Carole Marsh Arkansas Bks.). (Illus.). (J). (gr. 3-12). 1997. pap. 19.95 (*0-7933-6344-6*); lib. bdg. 29.95 (*0-7933-6343-8*) Gallopade Intl.

— Arkansas's (Most Devastating!) Disasters & (Most Calamitous!) Catastrophies! (Carole Marsh Arkansas Bks.). (Illus.). (YA). (gr. 3-12). 1994. pap. 19.95 (*0-7933-0138-6*); lib. bdg. 29.95 (*0-7933-0139-4*) Gallopade Intl.

— Arkansas's Unsolved Mysteries (& Their "Solutions") Includes Scientific Information & Other Activities for Students. (Carole Marsh Arkansas Bks.). (Illus.). (J). (gr. 3-12). 1994. pap. 19.95 (*0-7933-5732-2*); lib. bdg. 29.95 (*0-7933-5731-4*) Gallopade Intl.

— Astronomy for Kids: Milky Way & Mars Bars. (Quantum Leap Ser.). (Illus.). (J). 1994. 29.95 (*0-7933-0012-6*); pap. 19.95 (*0-7933-0013-4*) Gallopade Intl.

— Atlanta! Home of Gone with the Wind, CNN, Coca-Cola & the 1996 Olympic Games. (CD-ROM Titles Ser.). (J). (gr. 2-9). Date not set. pap., teacher ed. 19.95 (*0-7933-7831-1*, C Marsh) Gallopade Intl.

— Autumn: Silly Trivia. (Quantum Leap Ser.). (Orig.). (J). (gr. 2-6). 1994. 29.95 (*1-55609-274-1*) Gallopade Intl.

— Autumn: Silly Trivia. (Quantum Leap Ser.). (Illus.). (Orig.). (J). (gr. 2-6). 1997. pap. 19.95 (*0-685-14606-5*) Gallopade Intl.

— Avast, Ye Slobs! Alabama Pirate Trivia. (Carole Marsh Alabama Bks.). (Illus.). (YA). (gr. 3-12). 1994. pap. 19.95 (*0-7933-0087-8*); lib. bdg. 29.95 (*0-7933-0088-6*) Gallopade Intl.

— Avast, Ye Slobs! Alaska Pirate Trivia. (Carole Marsh Alaska Bks.). (Illus.). (YA). (gr. 3-12). 1994. pap. 19.95 (*0-7933-0111-4*); lib. bdg. 29.95 (*0-7933-0112-2*) Gallopade Intl.

— Avast, Ye Slobs! Arizona Pirate Trivia. (Carole Marsh Arizona Bks.). (Illus.). (YA). (gr. 3-12). 1994. pap. 19.95 (*0-7933-0135-1*); lib. bdg. 29.95 (*0-7933-0136-X*) Gallopade Intl.

M

An Asterisk (*) at the beginning of an entry indicates that the title is appearing for the first time.

— Avast, Ye Slobs! Arkansas Pirate Trivia. (Carole Marsh Arkansas Bks.). (Illus.). (YA). (gr. 3-12). 1994. pap. 19.95 (*0-7933-0159-9*); lib. bdg. 29.95 (*0-7933-0160-2*) Gallopade Intl.

— Avast, Ye Slobs! California Pirate Trivia. (Carole Marsh California Bks.). (Illus.). (YA). (gr. 3-12). 1994. pap. 19.95 (*0-7933-0183-1*); lib. bdg. 29.95 (*0-7933-0184-X*) Gallopade Intl.

— Avast, Ye Slobs! Colorado Pirate Trivia. (Carole Marsh Colorado Bks.). (Illus.). (YA). (gr. 3-12). 1994. pap. 19.95 (*0-7933-0207-2*); lib. bdg. 29.95 (*0-7933-0208-0*) Gallopade Intl.

— Avast, Ye Slobs! Connecticut Pirate Trivia. (Carole Marsh Connecticut Bks.). (Illus.). (YA). (gr. 3-12). 1994. pap. 19.95 (*0-7933-0231-5*); lib. bdg. 29.95 (*0-7933-0232-3*) Gallopade Intl.

— Avast, Ye Slobs! Delaware Pirate Trivia. (Carole Marsh Delaware Bks.). (Illus.). (YA). (gr. 3-12). 1994. pap. 19.95 (*0-7933-0255-2*); lib. bdg. 29.95 (*0-7933-0256-0*) Gallopade Intl.

— Avast, Ye Slobs! Florida Pirate Trivia. (Carole Marsh Florida Bks.). (Illus.). (YA). (gr. 3-12). 1994. pap. 19.95 (*0-7933-0303-6*); lib. bdg. 29.95 (*0-7933-0304-4*) Gallopade Intl.

— Avast, Ye Slobs! Georgia Pirate Trivia. (Carole Marsh Georgia Bks.). (Illus.). (YA). (gr. 3-12). 1994. pap. 19.95 (*0-7933-0327-3*); lib. bdg. 29.95 (*0-7933-0328-1*) Gallopade Intl.

— Avast, Ye Slobs! Hawaii Pirate Trivia. (Carole Marsh Hawaii Bks.). (Illus.). (YA). (gr. 3-12). 1994. pap. 19.95 (*0-7933-0351-6*); lib. bdg. 29.95 (*0-7933-0352-4*) Gallopade Intl.

— Avast, Ye Slobs! Idaho Pirate Trivia. (Carole Marsh Idaho Bks.). (Illus.). (YA). (gr. 3-12). 1994. pap. 19.95 (*0-7933-0375-3*); lib. bdg. 29.95 (*0-7933-0376-1*) Gallopade Intl.

— Avast, Ye Slobs! Illinois Pirate Trivia. (Carole Marsh Illinois Bks.). (Illus.). (YA). (gr. 3-12). 1994. pap. 19.95 (*0-7933-0399-0*); lib. bdg. 29.95 (*0-7933-0400-8*) Gallopade Intl.

— Avast, Ye Slobs! Indiana Pirate Trivia. (Carole Marsh Indiana Bks.). (Illus.). (YA). (gr. 3-12). 1994. pap. 19.95 (*0-7933-0423-7*); lib. bdg. 29.95 (*0-7933-0424-5*) Gallopade Intl.

— Avast, Ye Slobs! Iowa Private Trivia. (Carole Marsh Iowa Bks.). (Illus.). (YA). (gr. 3-12). 1994. pap. 19.95 (*0-7933-0447-4*); lib. bdg. 29.95 (*0-7933-0448-2*) Gallopade Intl.

— Avast, Ye Slobs! Kansas Pirate Trivia. (Carole Marsh Kansas Bks.). (Illus.). (YA). (gr. 3-12). 1994. pap. 19.95 (*0-7933-0471-7*); lib. bdg. 29.95 (*0-7933-0472-5*) Gallopade Intl.

— Avast, Ye Slobs! Kentucky Pirate Trivia. (Carole Marsh Kentucky Bks.). (Illus.). (J). (gr. 3-8). 1994. pap. 19.95 (*0-7933-0495-4*); lib. bdg. 29.95 (*0-7933-0496-2*) Gallopade Intl.

— Avast, Ye Slobs! Louisiana Pirate Trivia. (Carole Marsh Louisiana Bks.). (Illus.). (J). (gr. 3-8). 1994. pap. 19.95 (*0-7933-0519-5*); lib. bdg. 29.95 (*0-7933-0520-9*) Gallopade Intl.

— Avast, Ye Slobs! Maine Pirate Trivia. (Carole Marsh Maine Bks.). (Illus.). (J). (gr. 3-8). 1994. pap. 19.95 (*0-7933-0544-6*); lib. bdg. 29.95 (*0-7933-0545-4*) Gallopade Intl.

— Avast, Ye Slobs! Maryland Pirate Trivia. (Carole Marsh Maryland Bks.). (Illus.). (J). (gr. 3-8). 1994. pap. 19.95 (*0-7933-0568-3*); lib. bdg. 29.95 (*0-7933-0569-1*) Gallopade Intl.

— Avast, Ye Slobs! Massachusetts Pirate Trivia. (Carole Marsh Massachusetts Bks.). (Illus.). (J). (gr. 3-8). 1994. pap. 19.95 (*0-7933-0592-6*); lib. bdg. 29.95 (*0-7933-0593-4*) Gallopade Intl.

— Avast, Ye Slobs! Nevada Pirate Trivia. (Carole Marsh Nevada Bks.). (Illus.). (J). 1994. pap. 19.95 (*0-7933-0762-7*); lib. bdg. 29.95 (*0-7933-0763-5*) Gallopade Intl.

— Avast, Ye Slobs! New Hampshire Pirate Trivia. (Carole Marsh New Hampshire Bks.). (Illus.). (J). 1994. pap. 19.95 (*0-7933-0786-4*); lib. bdg. 29.95 (*0-7933-0787-2*) Gallopade Intl.

— Avast, Ye Slobs! New Jersey Pirate Trivia. (Carole Marsh New Jersey Bks.). (Illus.). (J). 1994. pap. 19.95 (*0-7933-1810-6*); lib. bdg. 29.95 (*0-7933-1809-2*) Gallopade Intl.

— Avast, Ye Slobs! New Mexico Pirate Trivia. (Carole Marsh New Mexico Bks.). (Illus.). (J). 1994. pap. 19.95 (*0-7933-0810-0*); lib. bdg. 29.95 (*0-7933-0811-9*) Gallopade Intl.

— Avast, Ye Slobs! New York Pirate Trivia. (Carole Marsh New York Bks.). (Illus.). (J). 1994. pap. 19.95 (*0-7933-0834-8*); lib. bdg. 29.95 (*0-7933-0835-6*) Gallopade Intl.

— Avast, Ye Slobs! North Carolina Pirate Trivia. (Carole Marsh North Carolina Bks.). (Illus.). (J). 1994. pap. 19.95 (*0-7933-0858-5*); lib. bdg. 29.95 (*0-7933-0859-3*) Gallopade Intl.

— Avast, Ye Slobs! North Dakota Pirate Trivia. (Carole Marsh North Dakota Bks.). (Illus.). (J). 1994. pap. 19.95 (*0-7933-0882-8*); lib. bdg. 29.95 (*0-7933-0883-6*) Gallopade Intl.

— Avast, Ye Slobs! Ohio Pirate Trivia. (Carole Marsh Ohio Bks.). (Illus.). (J). 1994. pap. 19.95 (*0-7933-0907-7*); lib. bdg. 29.95 (*0-7933-0908-5*) Gallopade Intl.

— Avast, Ye Slobs! Oklahoma Pirate Trivia. (Carole Marsh Oklahoma Bks.). (Illus.). (J). 1994. pap. 19.95 (*0-7933-0931-X*); lib. bdg. 29.95 (*0-7933-0932-8*) Gallopade Intl.

— Avast, Ye Slobs! Oregon Pirate Trivia. (Carole Marsh Oregon Bks.). (Illus.). (J). 1994. pap. 19.95 (*0-7933-0955-7*); lib. bdg. 29.95 (*0-7933-0956-5*) Gallopade Intl.

— Avast, Ye Slobs! Pennsylvania Pirate Trivia. (Carole Marsh Pennsylvania Bks.). (Illus.). (J). 1994. pap. 19.95 (*0-7933-0979-4*); lib. bdg. 29.95 (*0-7933-0980-8*) Gallopade Intl.

— Avast, Ye Slobs! Rhode Island Pirate Trivia. (Carole Marsh Rhode Island Bks.). (Illus.). (J). 1994. pap. 19.95 (*0-7933-1003-2*); lib. bdg. 29.95 (*0-7933-1004-0*) Gallopade Intl.

— Avast, Ye Slobs! South Carolina Pirate Trivia. (Carole Marsh South Carolina Bks.). (Illus.). (J). 1994. pap. 19.95 (*0-7933-1027-X*); lib. bdg. 29.95 (*0-7933-1028-8*) Gallopade Intl.

— Avast, Ye Slobs! South Dakota Pirate Trivia. (Carole Marsh South Dakota Bks.). (Illus.). (J). 1994. pap. 19.95 (*0-7933-1051-2*); lib. bdg. 29.95 (*0-7933-1052-0*); disk 29.95 (*0-7933-1053-9*) Gallopade Intl.

— Avast, Ye Slobs! Tennessee Pirate Trivia. (Carole Marsh Tennessee Bks.). (Illus.). (J). 1994. pap. 19.95 (*0-7933-1075-X*); lib. bdg. 29.95 (*0-7933-1076-8*); disk 29.95 (*0-7933-1077-6*) Gallopade Intl.

— Avast, Ye Slobs! Texas Pirate Trivia. (Texas Bks.). (Illus.). (J). 1990. pap. 19.95 (*0-7933-1099-7*); lib. bdg. 29.95 (*0-7933-1100-4*); disk 29.95 (*0-7933-1101-2*) Gallopade Intl.

— Avast, Ye Slobs! The Book of Silly Pirate Trivia. (Triviatime Ser.). (Illus.). (Orig.). (J). (gr. 1-12). 1994. pap. 19.95 (*0-935326-82-0*); lib. bdg. 29.95 (*1-55609-281-4*) Gallopade Intl.

— Avast, Ye Slobs! Utah Pirate Trivia. (Carole Marsh Utah Bks.). (Illus.). (J). 1994. pap. 19.95 (*0-7933-1123-3*); lib. bdg. 29.95 (*0-7933-1124-1*); disk 29.95 (*0-7933-1125-X*) Gallopade Intl.

— Avast, Ye Slobs! Vermont Pirate Trivia. (Carole Marsh Vermont Bks.). (Illus.). (J). 1994. lib. bdg. 29.95 (*0-7933-1148-9*); disk 29.95 (*0-7933-1149-7*) Gallopade Intl.

— Avast, Ye Slobs! Vermont Pirate Trivia. (Carole Marsh Vermont Bks.). (Illus.). (J). 1997. pap. 19.95 (*0-7933-1147-0*) Gallopade Intl.

— Avast, Ye Slobs! Virginia Pirate Trivia. (Carole Marsh Virginia Bks.). (Illus.). (J). 1994. pap. 19.95 (*0-7933-1171-3*); lib. bdg. 29.95 (*0-7933-1172-1*); disk 29.95 (*0-7933-1173-X*) Gallopade Intl.

— Avast, Ye Slobs! Washington, D.C. (Carole Marsh Washington, D.C. Bks.). (Illus.). (YA). (gr. 3-12). 1994. pap. 19.95 (*0-7933-0279-X*); lib. bdg. 29.95 (*0-7933-0280-3*); disk 29.95 (*0-7933-0281-1*) Gallopade Intl.

— Avast, Ye Slobs! Washington Pirate Trivia. (Carole Marsh Washington Bks.). (Illus.). (J). 1994. pap. 19.95 (*0-7933-1195-0*); lib. bdg. 29.95 (*0-7933-1196-9*); disk 29.95 (*0-7933-1197-7*) Gallopade Intl.

— Avast, Ye Slobs! West Virginia Pirate Trivia. (Carole Marsh West Virginia Bks.). (Illus.). (J). 1994. pap. 19.95 (*0-7933-1219-1*); lib. bdg. 29.95 (*0-7933-1220-5*); disk 29.95 (*0-7933-1221-3*) Gallopade Intl.

— Avast, Ye Slobs! Wisconsin Pirate Trivia. (Carole Marsh Wisconsin Bks.). (Illus.). (J). 1994. pap. 19.95 (*0-7933-1243-4*); lib. bdg. 29.95 (*0-7933-1244-2*); disk 29.95 (*0-7933-1245-0*) Gallopade Intl.

— Avast, Ye Slobs! Wyoming Pirate Trivia. (Carole Marsh Wyoming Bks.). (Illus.). (J). 1994. pap. 19.95 (*0-7933-1267-1*); lib. bdg. 29.95 (*0-7933-1268-X*); disk 29.95 (*0-7933-1269-8*) Gallopade Intl.

— Avast, Ye Slobs!: Michigan Pirate Trivia. (Carole Marsh Michigan Bks.). (Illus.). (J). (gr. 3 up). 1994. pap. 19.95 (*0-7933-0616-7*); lib. bdg. 29.95 (*0-7933-0617-5*) Gallopade Intl.

— Avast, Ye Slobs!: Minnesota Pirate Trivia. (Carole Marsh Minnesota Bks.). (Illus.). (J). (gr. 3 up). 1994. pap. 19.95 (*0-7933-0640-X*); lib. bdg. 29.95 (*0-7933-0641-8*) Gallopade Intl.

— Avast, Ye Slobs!: Mississippi Pirate Trivia. (Carole Marsh Mississippi Bks.). (Illus.). (J). (gr. 3 up). 1994. pap. 19.95 (*0-7933-0665-5*); lib. bdg. 29.95 (*0-7933-0666-3*) Gallopade Intl.

— Avast, Ye Slobs!: Missouri Pirate Trivia. (Carole Marsh Missouri Bks.). (Illus.). (J). (gr. 3 up). 1994. pap. 19.95 (*0-7933-0689-2*); lib. bdg. 29.95 (*0-7933-0690-6*) Gallopade Intl.

— Avast, Ye Slobs!: Montana Pirate Trivia. (Carole Marsh Montana Bks.). (Illus.). (J). (gr. 3 up). 1994. pap. 19.95 (*0-7933-0714-7*); lib. bdg. 29.95 (*0-7933-0715-5*) Gallopade Intl.

— Avast, Ye Slobs!: Nebraska Pirate Trivia. (Carole Marsh Nebraska Bks.). (Illus.). (J). (gr. 3 up). 1994. pap. 19.95 (*0-7933-0738-4*); lib. bdg. 29.95 (*0-7933-0739-2*) Gallopade Intl.

— The Backyard Searcher's Extra Terrestrial Log Book. (Quantum Leap Ser.). (Illus.). (J). (gr. 4-9). 1994. pap. 19.95 (*0-935326-27-8*); lib. bdg. 29.95 (*1-55609-282-2*) Gallopade Intl.

— Bat Cave Mystery. (History Mystery Ser.). (Orig.). (J). (gr. 3-8). 1994. pap. 19.95 (*0-935326-72-3*); lib. bdg. 29.95 (*1-55609-154-0*) Gallopade Intl.

— The Battle of Franklin. (Tennessee Bks.). (J). (gr. 2-9). 1997. 29.95 (*0-7933-7824-9*, C Marsh); pap. 19.95 (*0-7933-7825-7*, C Marsh) Gallopade Intl.

— Be a Fourth Grader Forever! How to Live, Love, & Learn with the Open-Minded Optimism, Eagerness & Joy of a Nine Year Old. 1994. 29.95 (*1-55609-900-2*); pap. 19.95 (*1-55609-901-0*) Gallopade Intl.

— Beachy Keen! A Fun & Educational Look at Everything about the Beach for Kids. (CD-ROM Titles Ser.). (J). (gr. 2-9). 1996. pap., teacher ed. 19.95 (*0-7933-7827-3*, C Marsh) Gallopade Intl.

— The Beast & the Kansas Bed & Breakfast. (Carole Marsh Kansas Bks.). (J). (gr. 3-12). 1994. 29.95 (*1-55609-371-3*); pap. 19.95 (*1-55609-372-1*); disk 29.95 (*1-55609-373-X*) Gallopade Intl.

— The Beast of the Alabama Bed & Breakfast. (Carole Marsh Alabama Bks.). (Illus.). (YA). (gr. 3-12). 1994. pap. 19.95 (*0-7933-1331-7*); lib. bdg. 29.95 (*0-7933-1332-5*); disk 29.95 (*0-7933-1330-9*) Gallopade Intl.

— The Beast of the Alaska Bed & Breakfast. (Carole Marsh Alaska Bks.). (Illus.). (J). (gr. 3-12). 1994. pap. 19.95 (*0-7933-1350-3*); lib. bdg. 29.95 (*0-7933-1349-X*) Gallopade Intl.

— The Beast of the Arizona Bed & Breakfast. (Carole Marsh Arizona Bks.). (Illus.). (YA). (gr. 3-12). 1994. pap. 19.95 (*0-7933-1366-X*); lib. bdg. 29.95 (*0-7933-1365-1*); disk 29.95 (*0-7933-1367-8*) Gallopade Intl.

— The Beast of the Arkansas Bed & Breakfast. (Carole Marsh Arkansas Bks.). (Illus.). (YA). (gr. 3-12). 1994. pap. 19.95 (*0-7933-1382-1*); lib. bdg. 29.95 (*0-7933-1381-3*); disk 29.95 (*0-7933-1383-X*) Gallopade Intl.

— The Beast of the California Bed & Breakfast. (Carole Marsh California Bks.). (Illus.). (J). (gr. 3-12). 1994. pap. 19.95 (*0-7933-1398-8*); lib. bdg. 29.95 (*0-7933-1397-X*) Gallopade Intl.

— The Beast of the Colorado Bed & Breakfast. (Carole Marsh Colorado Bks.). (Illus.). (YA). (gr. 3-12). 1994. pap. 19.95 (*0-7933-1414-3*); lib. bdg. 29.95 (*0-7933-1413-5*); disk 29.95 (*0-7933-1415-1*) Gallopade Intl.

— The Beast of the Connecticut Bed & Breakfast. (Carole Marsh Connecticut Bks.). (Illus.). (YA). (gr. 3-12). 1994. pap. 19.95 (*0-7933-1430-5*); lib. bdg. 29.95 (*0-7933-1429-1*); disk 29.95 (*0-7933-1431-3*) Gallopade Intl.

— The Beast of the Delaware Bed & Breakfast. (Carole Marsh Delaware Bks.). (Illus.). (YA). (gr. 3-12). 1994. pap. 19.95 (*0-7933-1448-8*); lib. bdg. 29.95 (*0-7933-1447-X*); disk 29.95 (*0-7933-1449-6*) Gallopade Intl.

— The Beast of the Florida Bed & Breakfast. (Carole Marsh Florida Bks.). (Illus.). (YA). (gr. 3-12). 1994. pap. 19.95 (*0-7933-1494-1*); lib. bdg. 29.95 (*0-7933-1493-3*); disk 29.95 (*0-7933-1495-X*) Gallopade Intl.

— The Beast of the Georgia Bed & Breakfast. (Carole Marsh Georgia Bks.). (Illus.). (YA). (gr. 3-12). 1994. pap. 19.95 (*0-7933-1513-1*); lib. bdg. 29.95 (*0-7933-1512-3*); disk 29.95 (*0-7933-1514-X*) Gallopade Intl.

— The Beast of the Hawaii Bed & Breakfast. (Carole Marsh Hawaii Bks.). (Illus.). (YA). (gr. 3-12). 1919. pap. 19.95 (*0-7933-1532-8*) Gallopade Intl.

— The Beast of the Hawaii Bed & Breakfast. (Carole Marsh Hawaii Bks.). (Illus.). (YA). (gr. 3-12). 1994. lib. bdg. 29.95 (*0-7933-1531-X*); disk 29.95 (*0-7933-1533-6*) Gallopade Intl.

— The Beast of the Idaho Bed & Breakfast. (Carole Marsh Idaho Bks.). (Illus.). (YA). (gr. 3-12). 1994. pap. 19.95 (*0-7933-1551-4*); lib. bdg. 29.95 (*0-7933-1550-6*); disk 29.95 (*0-7933-1552-2*) Gallopade Intl.

— The Beast of the Illinois Bed & Breakfast. (Carole Marsh Illinois Bks.). (Illus.). (YA). (gr. 3-12). 1994. pap. 19.95 (*0-7933-1591-3*); lib. bdg. 29.95 (*0-7933-1590-5*); disk 29.95 (*0-7933-1592-1*) Gallopade Intl.

— The Beast of the Indiana Bed & Breakfast. (Carole Marsh Indiana Bks.). (Illus.). (YA). (gr. 3-12). 1994. pap. 19.95 (*0-7933-1610-3*); lib. bdg. 29.95 (*0-7933-1609-X*); disk 29.95 (*0-7933-1611-1*) Gallopade Intl.

— The Beast of the Iowa Bed & Breakfast. (Carole Marsh Iowa Bks.). (Illus.). (YA). (gr. 3-12). 1994. pap. 19.95 (*0-7933-1629-4*); lib. bdg. 29.95 (*0-7933-1628-6*); disk 29.95 (*0-7933-1630-8*) Gallopade Intl.

— The Beast of the Kentucky Bed & Breakfast. (Carole Marsh Kentucky Bks.). (Illus.). (J). (gr. 3-8). 1994. pap. 19.95 (*0-7933-1651-0*); lib. bdg. 29.95 (*0-7933-1650-2*); disk 29.95 (*0-7933-1652-9*) Gallopade Intl.

— The Beast of the Louisiana Bed & Breakfast. (Carole Marsh Louisiana Bks.). (Illus.). (J). (gr. 3-8). 1994. pap. 19.95 (*0-7933-1670-7*); lib. bdg. 29.95 (*0-7933-1669-3*); disk 29.95 (*0-7933-1671-5*) Gallopade Intl.

— The Beast of the Maine Bed & Breakfast. (Carole Marsh Maine Bks.). (Illus.). (J). (gr. 3-8). 1994. pap. 19.95 (*0-7933-1682-0*); lib. bdg. 29.95 (*0-7933-1681-2*); write for info. (*0-7933-1683-9*) Gallopade Intl.

— The Beast of the Maryland Bed & Breakfast. (Carole Marsh Maryland Bks.). (Illus.). (J). (gr. 3-8). 1994. pap. 19.95 (*0-7933-1691-X*); lib. bdg. 29.95 (*0-7933-1690-1*); disk 29.95 (*0-7933-1692-8*) Gallopade Intl.

— The Beast of the Massachusetts Bed & Breakfast. (Carole Marsh Massachusetts Bks.). (Illus.). (J). (gr. 3-8). 1994. pap. 19.95 (*0-7933-1700-2*); lib. bdg. 29.95 (*0-7933-1699-5*); disk 29.95 (*0-7933-1701-0*) Gallopade Intl.

— The Beast of the Michigan Bed & Breakfast. (Carole Marsh Michigan Bks.). (Illus.). (J). (gr. 3 up). 1994. pap. 19.95 (*0-7933-1709-6*); lib. bdg. 29.95 (*0-7933-1708-8*); disk 29.95 (*0-7933-1710-X*) Gallopade Intl.

— The Beast of the Minnesota Bed & Breakfast. (Minnesota Bks.). (Illus.). (J). (gr. 3 up). 1994. pap. 19.95 (*0-7933-1715-0*); lib. bdg. 29.95 (*0-7933-1714-2*); disk 29.95 (*0-7933-1716-9*) Gallopade Intl.

— The Beast of the Mississippi Bed & Breakfast. (Mississippi Bks.). (Illus.). (J). (gr. 3 up). 1994. pap. 19.95 (*0-7933-1726-6*); lib. bdg. 29.95 (*0-7933-0644-2*); disk 29.95 (*0-7933-1727-4*) Gallopade Intl.

— The Beast of the Missouri Bed & Breakfast. (Missouri Bks.). (Illus.). (J). (gr. 3 up). 1994. pap. 19.95 (*0-7933-1735-5*); lib. bdg. 29.95 (*0-7933-1734-7*) Gallopade Intl.

— The Beast of the Missouri Bed & Breakfast. (Missouri Bks.). (Illus.). (J). (gr. 3 up). 1997. disk 29.95 (*0-7933-1736-3*) Gallopade Intl.

— The Beast of the Montana Bed & Breakfast. (Montana Bks.). (Illus.). (J). (gr. 3 up). 1994. pap. 19.95 (*0-7933-1744-4*); lib. bdg. 29.95 (*0-7933-1743-6*); disk 29.95 (*0-7933-1745-2*) Gallopade Intl.

— The Beast of the Nebraska Bed & Breakfast. (Carole Marsh Nebraska Bks.). (Illus.). (J). (gr. 3 up). 1994. pap. 19.95 (*0-7933-1753-3*); lib. bdg. 29.95 (*0-7933-1752-5*); disk 29.95 (*0-7933-1754-1*) Gallopade Intl.

— The Beast of the Nevada Bed & Breakfast. (Carole Marsh Nevada Bks.). (Illus.). (J). 1994. pap. 19.95 (*0-7933-1762-2*); lib. bdg. 29.95 (*0-7933-1761-4*); disk 29.95 (*0-7933-1763-0*) Gallopade Intl.

— The Beast of the New Hampshire Bed & Breakfast. (Carole Marsh New Hampshire Bks.). (Illus.). (J). 1994. pap. 19.95 (*0-7933-1771-1*); lib. bdg. 29.95 (*0-7933-1770-3*); disk 29.95 (*0-7933-1772-X*) Gallopade Intl.

— The Beast of the New Jersey Bed & Breakfast. (Carole Marsh New Jersey Bks.). (Illus.). (J). 1994. pap. 19.95 (*0-7933-1780-0*); lib. bdg. 29.95 (*0-7933-1779-7*); disk 29.95 (*0-7933-1781-9*) Gallopade Intl.

— The Beast of the New Mexico Bed & Breakfast. (Carole Marsh New Mexico Bks.). (Illus.). (J). 1994. pap. 19.95 (*0-7933-1813-0*); lib. bdg. 29.95 (*0-7933-1812-2*); disk 29.95 (*0-7933-1814-9*) Gallopade Intl.

— The Beast of the New York Bed & Breakfast. (Carole Marsh New York Bks.). (Illus.). (J). 1994. pap. 19.95 (*0-7933-1822-X*); lib. bdg. 29.95 (*0-7933-1821-1*); disk 29.95 (*0-7933-1823-8*) Gallopade Intl.

— The Beast of the North Carolina Bed & Breakfast. (Carole Marsh North Carolina Bks.). (Illus.). (J). 1994. pap. 14.95 (*0-7933-1831-9*); lib. bdg. 29.95 (*0-7933-1830-0*) Gallopade Intl.

— The Beast of the North Dakota Bed & Breakfast. (Carole Marsh North Dakota Bks.). (Illus.). (J). 1994. pap. 19.95 (*0-7933-1840-8*); lib. bdg. 29.95 (*0-7933-1839-4*); disk 29.95 (*0-7933-1841-6*) Gallopade Intl.

— The Beast of the Ohio Bed & Breakfast. (Carole Marsh Ohio Bks.). (Illus.). (J). 1994. pap. 19.95 (*0-7933-1848-3*); lib. bdg. 29.95 (*0-7933-0905-0*); disk 29.95 (*0-7933-1849-1*) Gallopade Intl.

— The Beast of the Oklahoma Bed & Breakfast. (Carole Marsh Oklahoma Bks.). (Illus.). (J). 1994. pap. 19.95 (*0-7933-1870-X*); lib. bdg. 29.95 (*0-7933-1869-6*); disk 29.95 (*0-7933-1871-8*) Gallopade Intl.

— The Beast of the Oregon Bed & Breakfast. (Carole Marsh Oregon Bks.). (Illus.). (J). 1994. pap. 19.95 (*0-7933-1902-1*); lib. bdg. 29.95 (*0-7933-1901-3*); disk 29.95 (*0-7933-1903-X*) Gallopade Intl.

— The Beast of the Pennsylvania Bed & Breakfast. (Carole Marsh Pennsylvania Bks.). (Illus.). (J). 1994. pap. 19.95 (*0-7933-1934-X*); lib. bdg. 29.95 (*0-7933-1933-1*); disk 29.95 (*0-7933-1935-8*) Gallopade Intl.

— The Beast of the Rhode Island Bed & Breakfast. (Carole Marsh Rhode Island Bks.). (Illus.). (J). 1994. pap. 19.95 (*0-7933-1966-8*); lib. bdg. 29.95 (*0-7933-1965-X*); disk 29.95 (*0-7933-1967-6*) Gallopade Intl.

— The Beast of the South Carolina Bed & Breakfast. (Carole Marsh South Carolina Bks.). (Illus.). (J). 1994. pap. 19.95 (*0-7933-1996-X*); lib. bdg. 29.95 (*0-7933-1995-1*); disk 29.95 (*0-7933-1997-8*) Gallopade Intl.

— The Beast of the South Dakota Bed & Breakfast. (Carole Marsh South Dakota Bks.). (Illus.). (J). 1994. pap. 19.95 (*0-7933-2027-5*); lib. bdg. 29.95 (*0-7933-2026-7*); disk 29.95 (*0-7933-2028-3*) Gallopade Intl.

— The Beast of the Tennessee Bed & Breakfast. (Carole Marsh Tennessee Bks.). (Illus.). (J). 1994. pap. 19.95 (*0-7933-2057-7*); lib. bdg. 29.95 (*0-7933-2056-9*); disk 29.95 (*0-7933-2058-5*) Gallopade Intl.

— The Beast of the Texas Bed & Breakfast. (Carole Marsh Texas Bks.). (Illus.). (J). 1994. pap. 19.95 (*0-7933-2087-9*); lib. bdg. 29.95 (*0-7933-2086-0*); disk 29.95 (*0-7933-2088-7*) Gallopade Intl.

— The Beast of the Utah Bed & Breakfast. (Carole Marsh Utah Bks.). (Illus.). (J). 1994. pap. 19.95 (*0-7933-2118-2*); lib. bdg. 29.95 (*0-7933-2117-4*); disk 29.95 (*0-7933-2119-0*) Gallopade Intl.

— The Beast of the Vermont Bed & Breakfast. (Carole Marsh Vermont Bks.). (Illus.). (J). 1994. pap. 19.95 (*0-7933-2150-6*); lib. bdg. 29.95 (*0-7933-2149-2*); disk 29.95 (*0-7933-2151-4*) Gallopade Intl.

— The Beast of the Virginia Bed & Breakfast. (Carole Marsh Virginia Bks.). (Illus.). (J). 1994. pap. 19.95 (*0-7933-2180-8*); lib. bdg. 29.95 (*0-7933-2179-4*); disk 29.95 (*0-7933-2181-6*) Gallopade Intl.

— The Beast of the Washington Bed & Breakfast. (Carole Marsh Washington Bks.). (Illus.). (J). 1994. pap. 19.95 (*0-7933-2213-8*); lib. bdg. 29.95 (*0-7933-2212-X*); disk 29.95 (*0-7933-2214-6*) Gallopade Intl.

— The Beast of the Washington, D.C. Bed & Breakfast. (Carole Marsh Washington, D.C. Bks.). (Illus.). (YA). (gr. 3-12). 1994. pap. 19.95 (*0-7933-1469-0*); lib. bdg. 29.95 (*0-7933-1468-2*); disk 29.95 (*0-7933-1470-4*) Gallopade Intl.

— The Beast of the West Virginia Bed & Breakfast. (Carole Marsh West Virginia Bks.). (Illus.). (J). 1994. pap. 19.95 (*0-7933-2245-6*); lib. bdg. 29.95 (*0-7933-2244-8*); disk 29.95 (*0-7933-2246-4*) Gallopade Intl.

— The Beast of the Wisconsin Bed & Breakfast. (Carole Marsh Wisconsin Bks.). (Illus.). (J). 1994. pap. 19.95 (*0-7933-2277-4*); lib. bdg. 29.95 (*0-7933-2276-6*); disk 29.95 (*0-7933-2278-2*) Gallopade Intl.

— The Beast of the Wyoming Bed & Breakfast. (Carole Marsh Wyoming Bks.). (Illus.). (J). 1994. pap. 19.95 (*0-7933-2301-0*); lib. bdg. 29.95 (*0-7933-2300-2*); disk 29.95 (*0-7933-2302-9*) Gallopade Intl.

— The Best Book of Black Biographies. (Our Black Heritage Ser.). (J). (gr. 3-12). 1994. pap. 19.95 (*1-55609-329-2*); lib. bdg. 29.95 (*1-55609-330-6*); disk 29.95 (*1-55609-331-4*) Gallopade Intl.

***Marsh, Carole.** Big Instruction Book of Small Business. 1999. pap. 29.95 (*0-7933-2478-5*) Gallopade Intl.

Marsh, Carole. The Big Instruction Book of Small Business (Alabama Edition) (Carole Marsh Alabama Bks.). (Illus.). 1994. pap. 29.95 (*0-7933-2779-2*); lib. bdg. 39.95 (*0-7933-2324-X*) Gallopade Intl.

M

— The Big Instruction Book of Small Business: (Alaska Edition) (Carole Marsh Alaska Bks.). (Illus.). 1994. pap. 29.95 (*0-7933-2780-6*); lib. bdg. 39.95 (*0-7933-2325-8*) Gallopade Intl.

— The Big Instruction Book of Small Business: (Arizona Edition) (Carole Marsh Arizona Bks.). (Illus.). 1994. pap. 29.95 (*0-7933-2781-4*); lib. bdg. 39.95 (*0-7933-2342-8*) Gallopade Intl.

— The Big Instruction Book of Small Business: (California Edition) (Carole Marsh California Bks.). (Illus.). 1994. pap. 29.95 (*0-7933-2782-2*); lib. bdg. 39.95 (*0-7933-2360-6*) Gallopade Intl.

— The Big Instruction Book of Small Business: (Colorado Edition) (Carole Marsh Colorado Bks.). (Illus.). 1994. pap. 29.95 (*0-7933-2783-0*); lib. bdg. 39.95 (*0-7933-2369-X*) Gallopade Intl.

— The Big Instruction Book of Small Business: (Connecticut Edition) (Carole Marsh Connecticut Bks.). (Illus.). 1994. pap. 29.95 (*0-7933-2784-9*); lib. bdg. 39.95 (*0-7933-2378-9*) Gallopade Intl.

— The Big Instruction Book of Small Business: (Delaware Edition) (Carole Marsh Delaware Bks.). (Illus.). 1994. pap. 29.95 (*0-7933-2785-7*); lib. bdg. 39.95 (*0-7933-2387-8*) Gallopade Intl.

— The Big Instruction Book of Small Business: (Florida Edition) (Carole Marsh Florida Bks.). (Illus.). 1994. pap. 29.95 (*0-7933-2787-3*); lib. bdg. 39.95 (*0-7933-2405-X*) Gallopade Intl.

— The Big Instruction Book of Small Business: (Georgia Edition) (Carole Marsh Georgia Bks.). (Illus.). 1994. pap. 29.95 (*0-7933-2788-1*); lib. bdg. 39.95 (*0-7933-2414-9*) Gallopade Intl.

— The Big Instruction Book of Small Business: (Hawaii Edition) (Carole Marsh Hawaii Bks.). (Illus.). 1994. pap. 29.95 (*0-7933-2789-X*); lib. bdg. 39.95 (*0-7933-2423-8*) Gallopade Intl.

— The Big Instruction Book of Small Business: (Idaho Edition) (Carole Marsh Idaho Bks.). (Illus.). 1994. pap. 29.95 (*0-7933-2790-3*); lib. bdg. 39.95 (*0-7933-2432-7*) Gallopade Intl.

— The Big Instruction Book of Small Business: (Illinois Edition) (Carole Marsh Illinois Bks.). (Illus.). 1994. pap. 29.95 (*0-7933-2791-1*); lib. bdg. 39.95 (*0-7933-2441-6*) Gallopade Intl.

— The Big Instruction Book of Small Business: (Indiana Edition) (Carole Marsh Indiana Bks.). (Illus.). 1994. pap. 29.95 (*0-7933-2792-X*); lib. bdg. 39.95 (*0-7933-2450-5*) Gallopade Intl.

— The Big Instruction Book of Small Business: (Iowa Edition) (Carole Marsh Iowa Bks.). (Illus.). 1994. pap. 29.95 (*0-7933-2793-8*); lib. bdg. 39.95 (*0-7933-2459-9*) Gallopade Intl.

— The Big Instruction Book of Small Business: (Kansas Edition) (Carole Marsh Kansas Bks.). (Illus.). 1994. pap. 29.95 (*0-7933-2794-6*); lib. bdg. 39.95 (*0-7933-2468-8*) Gallopade Intl.

— The Big Instruction Book of Small Business: (Kentucky Edition) (Carole Marsh Kentucky Bks.). (Illus.). 1994. pap. 29.95 (*0-7933-2795-4*); lib. bdg. 39.95 (*0-7933-2477-7*) Gallopade Intl.

— The Big Instruction Book of Small Business: (Louisiana Edition) (Carole Marsh Louisiana Bks.). (Illus.). 1994. pap. 29.95 (*0-7933-2796-2*) Gallopade Intl.

— The Big Instruction Book of Small Business: (Louisiana Edition) (Carole Marsh Louisiana Bks.). (Illus.). 1997. lib. bdg. 39.95 (*0-7933-2486-6*) Gallopade Intl.

— The Big Instruction Book of Small Business: (Maine Edition) (Carole Marsh Maine Bks.). (Illus.). 1994. pap. 29.95 (*0-7933-2797-0*); lib. bdg. 39.95 (*0-7933-2495-5*) Gallopade Intl.

— The Big Instruction Book of Small Business: (Maryland Edition) (Carole Marsh Maryland Bks.). (Illus.). 1994. pap. 29.95 (*0-7933-2798-9*); lib. bdg. 39.95 (*0-7933-2504-8*) Gallopade Intl.

— The Big Instruction Book of Small Business: (Massachusetts Edition) (Carole Marsh Massachusetts Bks.). (Illus.). 1994. pap. 29.95 (*0-7933-2799-7*); lib. bdg. 39.95 (*0-7933-2513-7*) Gallopade Intl.

— The Big Instruction Book of Small Business: (Michigan Edition) (Carole Marsh Michigan Bks.). (Illus.). 1994. pap. 29.95 (*0-7933-2800-4*); lib. bdg. 39.95 (*0-7933-2522-6*) Gallopade Intl.

— The Big Instruction Book of Small Business: (Minnesota Edition) (Carole Marsh Minnesota Bks.). (Illus.). 1994. pap. 29.95 (*0-7933-2801-2*); lib. bdg. 39.95 (*0-7933-2531-5*) Gallopade Intl.

— The Big Instruction Book of Small Business: (Mississippi Edition) (Carole Marsh Mississippi Bks.). (Illus.). 1994. pap. 29.95 (*0-7933-2802-0*); lib. bdg. 39.95 (*0-7933-2540-4*) Gallopade Intl.

— The Big Instruction Book of Small Business: (Missouri Edition) (Carole Marsh Missouri Bks.). (Illus.). 1994. pap. 29.95 (*0-7933-2803-9*); lib. bdg. 39.95 (*0-7933-2549-8*) Gallopade Intl.

— The Big Instruction Book of Small Business: (Montana Edition) (Carole Marsh Montana Bks.). (Illus.). 1994. pap. 29.95 (*0-7933-2804-7*); lib. bdg. 39.95 (*0-7933-2558-7*) Gallopade Intl.

— The Big Instruction Book of Small Business: (Nebraska Edition) (Carole Marsh Nebraska Bks.). (Illus.). 1994. pap. 29.95 (*0-7933-2805-5*); lib. bdg. 39.95 (*0-7933-2567-6*) Gallopade Intl.

— The Big Instruction Book of Small Business: (Nevada Edition) (Carole Marsh Nevade Bks.). (Illus.). 1994. lib. bdg. 29.95 (*0-7933-2576-5*); ring bd. 29.95 (*0-7933-2806-3*) Gallopade Intl.

— The Big Instruction Book of Small Business: (New Hampshire Edition) (Carole Marsh New Hampshire Bks.). (Illus.). 1994. pap. 29.95 (*0-7933-2807-1*); lib. bdg. 39.95 (*0-7933-2585-4*) Gallopade Intl.

— The Big Instruction Book of Small Business: (New Jersey Edition) (Carole Marsh New Jersey Bks.). (Illus.). 1994. pap. 29.95 (*0-7933-2808-X*); lib. bdg. 39.95 (*0-7933-2594-3*) Gallopade Intl.

— The Big Instruction Book of Small Business: (New Mexico Edition) (Carole Marsh New Mexico Bks.). (Illus.). 1994. pap. 29.95 (*0-7933-2809-8*) Gallopade Intl.

— The Big Instruction Book of Small Business: (New Mexico Edition) (Carole Marsh New Mexico Bks.). (Illus.). 1997. lib. bdg. 39.95 (*0-7933-2603-6*) Gallopade Intl.

— The Big Instruction Book of Small Business: (New York Edition) (Carole Marsh New York Bks.). (Illus.). 1994. pap. 29.95 (*0-7933-2810-1*); lib. bdg. 39.95 (*0-7933-2612-5*) Gallopade Intl.

— The Big Instruction Book of Small Business: (North Carolina Edition) (Carole Marsh North Carolina Bks.). (Illus.). 1994. pap. 29.95 (*0-7933-2811-X*); lib. bdg. 39.95 (*0-7933-2621-4*) Gallopade Intl.

— The Big Instruction Book of Small Business: (North Dakota Edition) (Carole Marsh North Dakota Bks.). (Illus.). 1994. pap. 29.95 (*0-7933-2812-8*); lib. bdg. 39.95 (*0-7933-2630-3*) Gallopade Intl.

— The Big Instruction Book of Small Business: (Ohio Edition) (Carole Marsh Ohio Bks.). (Illus.). 1994. pap. 29.95 (*0-7933-2813-6*); lib. bdg. 39.95 (*0-7933-2639-7*) Gallopade Intl.

— The Big Instruction Book of Small Business: (Oklahoma Edition) (Carole Marsh Oklahoma Bks.). (Illus.). 1994. pap. 29.95 (*0-7933-2814-4*); lib. bdg. 39.95 (*0-7933-2648-6*) Gallopade Intl.

— The Big Instruction Book of Small Business: (Oregon Edition) (Carole Marsh Oregon Bks.). (Illus.). 1994. pap. 29.95 (*0-7933-2815-2*); lib. bdg. 39.95 (*0-7933-2657-5*) Gallopade Intl.

— The Big Instruction Book of Small Business: (Pennsylvania Edition) (Pennsylvania Bks.). (Illus.). 1994. pap. 29.95 (*0-7933-2816-0*); lib. bdg. 39.95 (*0-7933-2666-4*) Gallopade Intl.

— The Big Instruction Book of Small Business: (Rhode Island Edition) (Carole Marsh Rhode Island Bks.). (Illus.). 1994. pap. 29.95 (*0-7933-2817-9*); lib. bdg. 39.95 (*0-7933-2675-3*) Gallopade Intl.

— The Big Instruction Book of Small Business: (South Carolina Edition) (Carole Marsh South Carolina Bks.). (Illus.). 1994. pap. 29.95 (*0-7933-2818-7*); lib. bdg. 39.95 (*0-7933-2684-2*) Gallopade Intl.

— The Big Instruction Book of Small Business: (South Dakota Edition) (Carole Marsh South Dakota Bks.). (Illus.). 1994. pap. 29.95 (*0-7933-2819-5*); lib. bdg. 39.95 (*0-7933-2693-1*) Gallopade Intl.

— The Big Instruction Book of Small Business: (Tennessee Edition) (Carole Marsh Tennessee Bks.). (Illus.). 1994. pap. 29.95 (*0-7933-2820-9*); lib. bdg. 39.95 (*0-7933-2702-4*) Gallopade Intl.

— The Big Instruction Book of Small Business: (Texas Edition) (Carole Marsh Texas Bks.). (Illus.). 1994. pap. 29.95 (*0-7933-2821-7*); lib. bdg. 39.95 (*0-7933-2711-3*) Gallopade Intl.

— The Big Instruction Book of Small Business: (Utah Edition) (Carole Marsh Utah Bks.). (Illus.). 1994. pap. 29.95 (*0-7933-2822-5*); lib. bdg. 39.95 (*0-7933-2720-2*) Gallopade Intl.

— The Big Instruction Book of Small Business: (Vermont Edition) (Carole Marsh Vermont Bks.). (Illus.). 1994. pap. 29.95 (*0-7933-2823-3*); lib. bdg. 39.95 (*0-7933-2729-6*) Gallopade Intl.

— The Big Instruction Book of Small Business: (Virginia Edition) (Carole Marsh Virginia Bks.). (Illus.). 1994. pap. 29.95 (*0-7933-2824-1*); lib. bdg. 39.95 (*0-7933-2738-5*) Gallopade Intl.

— The Big Instruction Book of Small Business: (Washington D. C. Edition) (Washington, D.C. Bks.). (Illus.). 1994. pap. 29.95 (*0-7933-2786-5*); lib. bdg. 39.95 (*0-7933-2396-7*) Gallopade Intl.

— The Big Instruction Book of Small Business: (Washington Edition) (Carole Marsh Washington Bks.). (Illus.). 1994. pap. 29.95 (*0-7933-2825-X*); lib. bdg. 39.95 (*0-7933-2747-4*) Gallopade Intl.

— The Big Instruction Book of Small Business: (West Virginia Edition) (Carole Marsh West Virginia Bks.). (Illus.). 1994. pap. 29.95 (*0-7933-2826-8*); lib. bdg. 39.95 (*0-7933-2756-3*) Gallopade Intl.

— The Big Instruction Book of Small Business: (Wisconsin Edition) (Carole Marsh Wisconsin Bks.). (Illus.). 1994. pap. 29.95 (*0-7933-2827-6*); lib. bdg. 39.95 (*0-7933-2765-2*) Gallopade Intl.

— The Big Instruction Book of Small Business: (Wyoming Edition) (Carole Marsh Wyoming Bks.). (Illus.). 1994. pap. 29.95 (*0-7933-2828-4*); lib. bdg. 39.95 (*0-7933-2774-1*) Gallopade Intl.

— The Big Rio of Ross Perot! (Carole Marsh Biographies Ser.). (J). 1994. pap. text 19.95 (*0-7933-6943-6*); lib. bdg. 29.95 (*0-7933-6942-8*); disk 29.95 (*0-7933-6941-X*) Gallopade Intl.

— Big Trees! (Interactive Multimedia Titles Ser.). (J). (gr. 2-9). 1996. 29.95 (*0-7933-7604-1*, C Marsh); pap. 19.95 (*0-7933-7605-X*, C Marsh); pap., teacher ed. 19.95 (*0-7933-7841-9*, C Marsh) Gallopade Intl.

— Bill S: Shakespeare for Kids. (Quantum Leap Ser.). (Illus.). (J). (gr. 4-12). 1994. pap. 19.95 (*0-935326-10-3*); lib. bdg. 29.95 (*1-55609-156-7*) Gallopade Intl.

— The Biltmore House Classroom Gamebook. (Carole Marsh Bks.). (Illus.). (Orig.). (J). (gr. 1-12). 1994. lib. bdg. 29.95 (*0-935326-83-9*) Gallopade Intl.

— Black Business. (Our Black Heritage Ser.). (J). (gr. 4-12). 1994. pap. 19.95 (*1-55609-326-8*); lib. bdg. 29.95 (*1-55609-327-6*); disk 29.95 (*1-55609-328-4*) Gallopade Intl.

— Black "Jography" The Paths of Our Black Pioneers. (Our Black Heritage Ser.). (J). (gr. 3-12). 1994. pap. 19.95 (*1-55609-320-9*); lib. bdg. 29.95 (*1-55609-321-7*); disk 29.95 (*1-55609-322-5*) Gallopade Intl.

— Black Trivia, A-Z. (Our Black Heritage Ser.). (J). (gr. 3-12). 1994. pap. 19.95 (*1-55609-317-9*); lib. bdg. 29.95 (*1-55609-318-7*); disk 29.95 (*1-55609-319-5*) Gallopade Intl.

— Blackbeard the Pirate's Missing Head Mystery Spook Kit. (S. P. A. R. K. Ser.). (Illus.). (J). (ps-6). 1994. lib. bdg. 29.95 (*0-935326-19-7*) Gallopade Intl.

— The Blood & Guts Dingbats Book. (Carole Marsh Dingbats Bks.). (Illus.). (J). (gr. 3-12). 1994. pap. 19.95 (*0-7933-5399-8*); lib. bdg. 29.95 (*0-7933-5398-X*); disk 29.95 (*0-7933-5400-5*) Gallopade Intl.

— Bone Appetite! Cannabalism for Kids. (Wildly Educational Titles Ser.). (J). (gr. 2-9). 1995. pap. 19.95 (*0-7933-7816-8*, C Marsh) Gallopade Intl.

— Bone Appetite! Cannabalism for Kids. (Wildly Educational Titles Ser.). (J). (gr. 2-9). 1998. 29.95 (*0-7933-7815-X*, C Marsh) Gallopade Intl.

— Bow Wow! Alabama Dogs in History, Mystery, Legend, Lore, Humor & More! (Carole Marsh Alabama Bks.). (Illus.). (J). (gr. 3-12). 1994. pap. 19.95 (*0-7933-3468-3*); lib. bdg. 29.95 (*0-7933-3467-5*); disk 29.95 (*0-7933-3469-1*) Gallopade Intl.

— Bow Wow! Alaska Dogs in History, Mystery, Legend, Lore, Humor & More! (Carole Marsh Alaska Bks.). (Illus.). (J). (gr. 3-12). 1994. pap. 19.95 (*0-7933-3471-3*); lib. bdg. 29.95 (*0-7933-3470-5*); disk 29.95 (*0-7933-3472-1*) Gallopade Intl.

— Bow Wow! Arizona Dogs in History, Mystery, Legend, Lore, Humor & More! (Carole Marsh Arizona Bks.). (Illus.). (J). (gr. 3-12). 1994. pap. 19.95 (*0-7933-3474-8*); lib. bdg. 29.95 (*0-7933-3473-X*); disk 29.95 (*0-7933-3475-6*) Gallopade Intl.

— Bow Wow! Arkansas Dogs in History, Mystery, Legend, Lore, Humor & More! (Carole Marsh Arkansas Bks.). (Illus.). (J). (gr. 3-12). 1994. pap. 19.95 (*0-7933-3477-2*); lib. bdg. 29.95 (*0-7933-3476-4*); disk 29.95 (*0-7933-3478-0*) Gallopade Intl.

— Bow Wow! California Dogs in History, Mystery, Legend, Lore, Humor & More! (Carole Marsh California Bks.). (Illus.). (J). (gr. 3-12). 1994. pap. 19.95 (*0-7933-3480-2*); lib. bdg. 29.95 (*0-7933-3479-9*); disk 29.95 (*0-7933-3481-0*) Gallopade Intl.

— Bow Wow! Colorado Dogs in History, Mystery, Legend, Lore, Humor & More! (Carole Marsh Colorado Bks.). (Illus.). (J). (gr. 3-12). 1994. pap. 19.95 (*0-7933-3483-7*); lib. bdg. 29.95 (*0-7933-3482-9*); disk 29.95 (*0-7933-3484-5*) Gallopade Intl.

— Bow Wow! Connecticut Dogs in History, Mystery, Legend, Lore, Humor & More! (Carole Marsh Connecticut Bks.). (Illus.). (J). (gr. 3-12). 1994. pap. 19.95 (*0-7933-3486-1*); lib. bdg. 29.95 (*0-7933-3485-3*); disk 29.95 (*0-7933-3487-X*) Gallopade Intl.

— Bow Wow! Delaware Dogs in History, Mystery, Legend, Lore, Humor & More! (Carole Marsh Delaware Bks.). (Illus.). (J). (gr. 3-12). 1994. pap. 19.95 (*0-7933-3489-6*); lib. bdg. 29.95 (*0-7933-3488-8*); disk 29.95 (*0-7933-3490-X*) Gallopade Intl.

— Bow Wow! Florida Dogs in History, Mystery, Legend, Lore, Humor & More! (Carole Marsh Florida Bks.). (Illus.). (J). (gr. 3-12). 1994. pap. 19.95 (*0-7933-3495-0*); lib. bdg. 29.95 (*0-7933-3494-2*); disk 29.95 (*0-7933-3496-9*) Gallopade Intl.

— Bow Wow! Georgia Dogs in History, Mystery, Legend, Lore, Humor & More! (Carole Marsh Georgia Bks.). (Illus.). (J). (gr. 3-12). 1994. pap. 19.95 (*0-7933-3498-5*); lib. bdg. 29.95 (*0-7933-3497-7*); disk 29.95 (*0-7933-3499-3*) Gallopade Intl.

— Bow Wow! Hawaii Dogs in History, Mystery, Legend, Lore, Humor & More! (Carole Marsh Hawaii Bks.). (Illus.). (J). (gr. 3-12). 1994. pap. 19.95 (*0-7933-3501-9*); lib. bdg. 29.95 (*0-7933-3500-0*); disk 29.95 (*0-7933-3502-7*) Gallopade Intl.

— Bow Wow! Idaho Dogs in History, Mystery, Legend, Lore, Humor & More! (Carole Marsh Idaho Bks.). (Illus.). (J). (gr. 3-12). 1994. pap. 19.95 (*0-7933-3504-3*); lib. bdg. 29.95 (*0-7933-3503-5*); disk 29.95 (*0-7933-3505-1*) Gallopade Intl.

— Bow Wow! Illinois Dogs in History, Mystery, Legend, Lore, Humor & More! (Carole Marsh Illinois Bks.). (Illus.). (J). (gr. 3-12). 1994. pap. 19.95 (*0-7933-3507-8*); lib. bdg. 29.95 (*0-7933-3506-X*); disk 29.95 (*0-7933-3508-6*) Gallopade Intl.

— Bow Wow! Indiana Dogs in History, Mystery, Legend, Lore, Humor & More! (Carole Marsh Indiana Bks.). (Illus.). (J). (gr. 3-12). 1994. pap. 19.95 (*0-7933-3510-8*); lib. bdg. 29.95 (*0-7933-3509-4*); disk 29.95 (*0-7933-3511-6*) Gallopade Intl.

— Bow Wow! Iowa Dogs in History, Mystery, Legend, Lore, Humor & More! (Carole Marsh Iowa Bks.). (Illus.). (J). (gr. 3-12). 1994. pap. 19.95 (*0-7933-3513-2*); lib. bdg. 29.95 (*0-7933-3512-4*); disk 29.95 (*0-7933-3514-0*) Gallopade Intl.

— Bow Wow! Kansas Dogs in History, Mystery, Legend, Lore, Humor & More! (Carole Marsh Kansas Bks.). (Illus.). (J). (gr. 3-12). 1994. pap. 19.95 (*0-7933-3516-7*); lib. bdg. 29.95 (*0-7933-3515-9*); disk 29.95 (*0-7933-3517-5*) Gallopade Intl.

— Bow Wow! Kentucky Dogs in History, Mystery, Legend, Lore, Humor & More! (Kentucky Bks.). (Illus.). (J). (gr. 3-12). 1994. pap. 19.95 (*0-7933-3519-1*); lib. bdg. 29.95 (*0-7933-3518-3*); disk 29.95 (*0-7933-3520-5*) Gallopade Intl.

— Bow Wow! Louisiana Dogs in History, Mystery, Legend, Lore, Humor & More! (Carole Marsh Louisiana Bks.). (Illus.). (J). (gr. 3-12). 1994. pap. 19.95 (*0-7933-3522-1*); lib. bdg. 29.95 (*0-7933-3521-3*); disk 29.95 (*0-7933-3523-X*) Gallopade Intl.

— Bow Wow! Maine Dogs in History, Mystery, Legend, Lore, Humor & More! (Carole Marsh Maine Bks.). (Illus.). (J). (gr. 3-12). 1994. pap. 19.95 (*0-7933-3525-6*); lib. bdg. 29.95 (*0-7933-3524-8*); disk 29.95 (*0-7933-3526-4*) Gallopade Intl.

— Bow Wow! Maryland Dogs in History, Mystery, Legend, Lore, Humor & More! (Carole Marsh Maryland Bks.). (Illus.). (J). (gr. 3-12). 1994. pap. 19.95 (*0-7933-3528-0*); lib. bdg. 29.95 (*0-7933-3527-2*); disk 29.95 (*0-7933-3529-9*) Gallopade Intl.

— Bow Wow! Massachusetts Dogs in History, Mystery, Legend, Lore, Humor & More! (Massachuseets Bks.). (Illus.). (J). (gr. 3-12). 1994. pap. 19.95 (*0-7933-3531-0*); lib. bdg. 29.95 (*0-7933-3530-2*); disk 29.95 (*0-7933-3532-9*) Gallopade Intl.

— Bow Wow! Michigan Dogs in History, Mystery, Legend, Lore, Humor & More! (Carole Marsh Michigan Bks.). (Illus.). (J). (gr. 3-12). 1994. pap. 19.95 (*0-7933-3534-5*); lib. bdg. 29.95 (*0-7933-3533-7*); disk 29.95 (*0-7933-3535-3*) Gallopade Intl.

— Bow Wow! Minnesota Dogs in History, Mystery, Legend, Lore, Humor & More! (Carole Marsh Minnesota Bks.). (Illus.). (J). (gr. 3-12). 1994. pap. 19.95 (*0-7933-3537-X*); lib. bdg. 29.95 (*0-7933-3536-1*); disk 29.95 (*0-7933-3538-8*) Gallopade Intl.

— Bow Wow! Mississippi Dogs in History, Mystery, Legend, Lore, Humor & More! (Carole Marsh Mississippi Bks.). (Illus.). (J). (gr. 3-12). 1994. pap. 19.95 (*0-7933-3540-X*); lib. bdg. 29.95 (*0-7933-3539-6*); disk 29.95 (*0-7933-3541-8*) Gallopade Intl.

— Bow Wow! Missouri Dogs in History, Mystery, Legend, Lore, Humor & More! (Carole Marsh Missouri Bks.). (Illus.). (J). (gr. 3-12). 1994. pap. 19.95 (*0-7933-3543-4*); lib. bdg. 29.95 (*0-7933-3542-6*); disk 29.95 (*0-7933-3544-2*) Gallopade Intl.

— Bow Wow! Montana Dogs in History, Mystery, Legend, Lore, Humor & More! (Carole Marsh Montana Bks.). (Illus.). (J). (gr. 3-12). 1994. pap. 19.95 (*0-7933-3546-9*); lib. bdg. 29.95 (*0-7933-3545-0*); disk 29.95 (*0-7933-3547-7*) Gallopade Intl.

— Bow Wow! Nebraska Dogs in History, Mystery, Legend, Lore, Humor & More! (Carole Marsh Nebraska Bks.). (Illus.). (J). (gr. 3-12). 1994. pap. 19.95 (*0-7933-3549-3*); lib. bdg. 29.95 (*0-7933-3548-5*); disk 29.95 (*0-7933-3550-7*) Gallopade Intl.

— Bow Wow! Nevada Dogs in History, Mystery, Legend, Lore, Humor & More! (Carole Marsh Nevada Bks.). (Illus.). (J). (gr. 3-12). 1994. pap. 19.95 (*0-7933-3552-3*); lib. bdg. 29.95 (*0-7933-3551-5*); disk 29.95 (*0-7933-3553-1*) Gallopade Intl.

— Bow Wow! New Hampshire Dogs in History, Mystery, Legend, Lore, Humor & More! (Carole Marsh New Hampshire Bks.). (Illus.). (J). (gr. 3-12). 1994. pap. 19.95 (*0-7933-3555-8*); lib. bdg. 29.95 (*0-7933-3554-X*); disk 29.95 (*0-7933-3556-6*) Gallopade Intl.

— Bow Wow! New Jersey Dogs in History, Mystery, Legend, Lore, Humor & More! (Carole Marsh New Jersey Bks.). (Illus.). (J). (gr. 3-12). 1994. pap. 19.95 (*0-7933-3558-2*); lib. bdg. 29.95 (*0-7933-3557-4*); disk 29.95 (*0-7933-3559-0*) Gallopade Intl.

— Bow Wow! New Mexico Dogs in History, Mystery, Legend, Lore, Humor & More! (Carole Marsh New Mexico Bks.). (Illus.). (J). (gr. 3-12). 1994. pap. 19.95 (*0-7933-3561-2*); lib. bdg. 29.95 (*0-7933-3560-4*); disk 29.95 (*0-7933-3562-0*) Gallopade Intl.

— Bow Wow! New York Dogs in History, Mystery, Legend, Lore, Humor & More! (Carole Marsh New York Bks.). (Illus.). (J). (gr. 3-12). 1994. pap. 19.95 (*0-7933-3564-7*); lib. bdg. 29.95 (*0-7933-3563-9*); disk 29.95 (*0-7933-3565-5*) Gallopade Intl.

— Bow Wow! North Carolina Dogs in History, Mystery, Legend, Lore, Humor & More! (Carole Marsh North Carolina Bks.). (Illus.). (J). (gr. 3-12). 1994. pap. 19.95 (*0-7933-3567-1*); lib. bdg. 29.95 (*0-7933-3566-3*); disk 29.95 (*0-7933-3568-X*) Gallopade Intl.

— Bow Wow! North Dakota Dogs in History, Mystery, Legend, Lore, Humor & More! (Carole Marsh North Dakota Bks.). (Illus.). (J). (gr. 3-12). 1994. pap. 19.95 (*0-7933-3570-1*); lib. bdg. 29.95 (*0-7933-3569-8*); disk 29.95 (*0-7933-3571-X*) Gallopade Intl.

— Bow Wow! Ohio Dogs in History, Mystery, Legend, Lore, Humor & More! (Carole Marsh Ohio Bks.). (Illus.). (J). (gr. 3-12). 1994. pap. 19.95 (*0-7933-3573-6*); lib. bdg. 29.95 (*0-7933-3572-8*); disk 29.95 (*0-7933-3574-4*) Gallopade Intl.

— Bow Wow! Oklahoma Dogs in History, Mystery, Legend, Lore, Humor & More! (Carole Marsh Oklahoma Bks.). (Illus.). (J). (gr. 3-12). 1994. pap. 19.95 (*0-7933-3576-0*); lib. bdg. 29.95 (*0-7933-3575-2*); disk 29.95 (*0-7933-3577-9*) Gallopade Intl.

— Bow Wow! Oregon Dogs in History, Mystery, Legend, Lore, Humor & More! (Oregon Bks.). (Illus.). (J). (gr. 3-12). 1994. pap. 19.95 (*0-7933-3579-5*); lib. bdg. 29.95 (*0-7933-3578-7*); disk 29.95 (*0-7933-3580-9*) Gallopade Intl.

— Bow Wow! Pennsylvania Dogs in History, Mystery, Legend, Lore, Humor & More! (Pennsylvania Bks.). (Illus.). (J). (gr. 3-12). 1994. pap. 19.95 (*0-7933-3582-5*); lib. bdg. 29.95 (*0-7933-3581-7*); disk 29.95 (*0-7933-3583-3*) Gallopade Intl.

— Bow Wow! Rhode Island Dogs in History, Mystery, Legend, Lore, Humor & More! (Rhode Island Bks.). (Illus.). (J). (gr. 3-12). 1994. pap. 19.95 (*0-7933-3585-X*); lib. bdg. 29.95 (*0-7933-3584-1*); disk 29.95 (*0-7933-3586-8*) Gallopade Intl.

— Bow Wow! South Carolina Dogs in History, Mystery, Legend, Lore, Humor & More! (South Carolina Bks.). (Illus.). (J). (gr. 3-12). 1994. pap. 19.95 (*0-7933-3588-4*); lib. bdg. 29.95 (*0-7933-3587-6*); disk 29.95 (*0-7933-3589-2*) Gallopade Intl.

— Bow Wow! South Dakota Dogs in History, Mystery, Legend, Lore, Humor & More! (South Dakota Bks.).

M

(Illus.). (J). (gr. 3-12). 1994. pap. 19.95 (*0-7933-3591-4*); lib. bdg. 29.95 (*0-7933-3590-6*); disk 29.95 (*0-7933-3592-2*) Gallopade Intl.

— Bow Wow! Tennessee Dogs in History, Mystery, Legend, Lore, Humor & More! (Tennessee Bks.). (Illus.). (J). (gr. 3-12). 1994. pap. 19.95 (*0-7933-3594-9*); lib. bdg. 29.95 (*0-7933-3593-0*); disk 29.95 (*0-7933-3595-7*) Gallopade Intl.

— Bow Wow! Texas Dogs in History, Mystery, Legend, Lore, Humor & More! (Texas Bks.). (Illus.). (J). (gr. 3-12). 1994. pap. 19.95 (*0-7933-3597-3*); lib. bdg. 29.95 (*0-7933-3596-5*); disk 29.95 (*0-7933-3598-1*) Gallopade Intl.

— Bow Wow! Utah Dogs in History, Mystery, Legend, Lore, Humor & More! (Utah Bks.). (Illus.). (J). (gr. 3-12). 1994. pap. 19.95 (*0-7933-3600-7*); lib. bdg. 29.95 (*0-7933-3599-X*); disk 29.95 (*0-7933-3601-5*) Gallopade Intl.

— Bow Wow! Vermont Dogs in History, Mystery, Legend, Lore, Humor & More! (Vermont Bks.). (Illus.). (J). (gr. 3-12). 1994. pap. 19.95 (*0-7933-3603-1*); lib. bdg. 29.95 (*0-7933-3602-3*); disk 29.95 (*0-7933-3604-X*) Gallopade Intl.

— Bow Wow! Virginia Dogs in History, Mystery, Legend, Lore, Humor & More! (Virginia Bks.). (Illus.). (J). (gr. 3-12). 1994. pap. 19.95 (*0-7933-3606-6*); lib. bdg. 29.95 (*0-7933-3605-8*); disk 29.95 (*0-7933-3607-4*) Gallopade Intl.

— Bow Wow! Washington D. C. Dogs in History, Mystery, Legend, Lore, Humor & More! (Washington, D.C. Bks.). (Illus.). (J). (gr. 3-12). 1994. pap. 19.95 (*0-7933-3492-6*); lib. bdg. 29.95 (*0-7933-3491-8*); disk 29.95 (*0-7933-3493-4*) Gallopade Intl.

— Bow Wow! Washington Dogs in History, Mystery, Legend, Lore, Humor & More! (Washington Bks.). (Illus.). (J). (gr. 3-12). 1994. pap. 19.95 (*0-7933-3609-0*); lib. bdg. 29.95 (*0-7933-3608-2*); disk 29.95 (*0-7933-3610-4*) Gallopade Intl.

— Bow Wow! West Virginia Dogs in History, Mystery, Legend, Lore, Humor & More! (West Virginia Bks.). (Illus.). (J). (gr. 3-12). 1994. pap. 19.95 (*0-7933-3612-0*); lib. bdg. 29.95 (*0-7933-3611-2*); disk 29.95 (*0-7933-3613-9*) Gallopade Intl.

— Bow Wow! Wisconsin Dogs in History, Mystery, Legend, Lore, Humor & More! (Wisconsin Bks.). (Illus.). (J). (gr. 3-12). 1994. pap. 19.95 (*0-7933-3615-5*); lib. bdg. 29.95 (*0-7933-3614-7*); disk 29.95 (*0-7933-3616-3*) Gallopade Intl.

— Bow Wow! Wyoming Dogs in History, Mystery, Legend, Lore, Humor & More! (Wyoming Bks.). (Illus.). (J). (gr. 3-12). 1994. pap. 19.95 (*0-7933-3618-X*); lib. bdg. 29.95 (*0-7933-3617-1*); disk 29.95 (*0-7933-3619-8*) Gallopade Intl.

— The Boy-Is-This-Place-Big Biltmore House Spark Kit. (S. P. A. R. K. Ser.). (Illus.). (Orig.). (J). (gr. 3-12). 1994. lib. bdg. 29.95 (*0-935326-22-7*) Gallopade Intl.

— California & Other State Greats (Biographies) (Carole Marsh California Bks.). (Illus.). (YA). (gr. 3-12). 1994. pap. 19.95 (*1-55609-520-1*); lib. bdg. 29.95 (*1-55609-521-X*); disk 29.95 (*0-7933-1405-4*) Gallopade Intl.

— California Bandits, Bushwackers, Outlaws, Crooks, Devils, Ghosts, Desperadoes & Other Assorted & Sundry Characters! (Carole Marsh California Bks.). (Illus.). (YA). (gr. 3-12). 1994. pap. 19.95 (*0-7933-0165-3*); lib. bdg. 29.95 (*0-7933-0166-1*); disk 29.95 (*0-7933-0167-X*) Gallopade Intl.

— California "BIO" Bingo! 24 Must Know State People for Kids to Learn about While Having Fun! (Bingo! Ser.). (Illus.). (J). (gr. 2-8). 1998. pap. 14.95 (*0-7933-8537-7*) Gallopade Intl.

— The California Bookstore Book: A Surprising Guide to Our State's Bookstores & Their Specialties for Students, Teachers, Writers & Publishers. (Carole Marsh California Bks.). (Illus.). 1994. pap. 19.95 (*0-7933-2868-3*); lib. bdg. 29.95 (*0-7933-2867-5*); disk 29.95 (*0-7933-2869-1*) Gallopade Intl.

— California Classic Christmas Trivia: Stories, Recipes, Activities, Legends, Lore & More! (Carole Marsh California Bks.). (Illus.). (YA). (gr. 3-12). 1994. pap. 19.95 (*0-7933-0168-8*); lib. bdg. 29.95 (*0-7933-0169-6*); disk 29.95 (*0-7933-0170-X*) Gallopade Intl.

— California Coastales! (Carole Marsh California Bks.). (J). 1994. lib. bdg. 29.95 (*0-7933-7269-0*) Gallopade Intl.

— California Coastales! (Carole Marsh California Bks.). (Illus.). (YA). (gr. 3-12). 1994. pap. 19.95 (*1-55609-516-3*); lib. bdg. 29.95 (*1-55609-517-1*); disk 29.95 (*0-7933-1401-1*) Gallopade Intl.

— California "Crinkum-Crankum" A Funny Word Book about Our State. (Carole Marsh California Bks.). (Illus.). (J). 1994. pap. 19.95 (*0-7933-4823-4*); lib. bdg. 29.95 (*0-7933-4822-6*); disk 29.95 (*0-7933-4824-2*) Gallopade Intl.

— California Dingbats! Bk. 1: A Fun Book of Games, Stories, Activities & More about Our State That's All in Code! for You to Decipher. (Carole Marsh California Bks.). (Illus.). (J). (gr. 3-12). 1994. pap. 19.95 (*0-7933-3786-0*); lib. bdg. 29.95 (*0-7933-3785-2*); disk 29.95 (*0-7933-3787-9*) Gallopade Intl.

***Marsh, Carole.** The California Experience Pocket Guide. (California Experience! Ser.). (Illus.). (J). 2000. pap. 6.95 (*0-7933-9447-3*) Gallopade Intl.

Marsh, Carole. California Facts & Factivities. (Carol Marsh State Bks.). (Illus.). (J). (gr. 4-7). 1996. pap., teacher ed. 19.95 (*0-7933-7855-9*) Gallopade Intl.

— California Festival Fun for Kids! (Carole Marsh California Bks.). (Illus.). (YA). (gr. 3-12). 1994. pap. 19.95 (*0-7933-3939-1*); lib. bdg. 29.95 (*0-7933-3938-3*); disk 29.95 (*0-7933-3940-5*) Gallopade Intl.

— California "GEO" Bingo! 38 Must Know State Geography Facts for Kids to Learn While Having Fun! (Bingo! Ser.). (Illus.). (J). (gr. 2-8). 1998. pap. 14.95 (*0-7933-8538-5*) Gallopade Intl.

— California Government! The Cornerstone of Everyday Life in Our State! (Carole Marsh California Bks.). (Illus.). (J). (gr. 3-12). 1996. pap. 19.95 (*0-7933-6194-X*); lib. bdg. 29.95 (*0-7933-6193-1*); disk 29.95 (*0-7933-6195-8*) Gallopade Intl.

— California "HISTO" Bingo! 42 Must Know State History Facts for Kids to Learn While Having Fun! (Bingo! Ser.). (Illus.). (J). (gr. 2-8). 1998. pap. 14.95 (*0-7933-8539-3*) Gallopade Intl.

— California History! Surprising Secrets about Our State's Founding Mothers, Fathers & Kids! (Carole Marsh California Bks.). (Illus.). (J). (gr. 3-12). 1996. pap. 19.95 (*0-7933-6041-2*); lib. bdg. 29.95 (*0-7933-6040-4*); disk 29.95 (*0-7933-6042-0*) Gallopade Intl.

— The California Hot Air Balloon Mystery. (Carole Marsh California Bks.). (Illus.). (J). (gr. 2-9). 1994. 29.95 (*0-7933-2354-1*); pap. 19.95 (*0-7933-2355-X*); disk 29.95 (*0-7933-2356-8*) Gallopade Intl.

— California Hot Zones! Viruses, Diseases, & Epidemics in Our State's History. (Hot Zones! Ser.). (Illus.). (J). (gr. 3-12). 1998. pap. 19.95 (*0-7933-8841-4*); lib. bdg. 29.95 (*0-7933-8840-6*) Gallopade Intl.

— California Indian Dictionary for Kids! (Carole Marsh State Bks.). (J). (gr. 2-9). 1996. 29.95 (*0-7933-7656-4*, C Marsh); pap. 19.95 (*0-7933-7657-2*, C Marsh) Gallopade Intl.

***Marsh, Carole.** California Jeopardy. (California Experience! Ser.). (Illus.). (J). (gr. 2-6). 2000. pap. 7.95 (*0-7933-9504-6*) Gallopade Intl.

Marsh, Carole. California Jeopardy! Answers & Questions about Our State! (Carole Marsh California Bks.). (Illus.). (J). (gr. 3-12). 1994. pap. 19.95 (*0-7933-4092-6*); lib. bdg. 29.95 (*0-7933-4091-8*); disk 29.95 (*0-7933-4093-4*) Gallopade Intl.

***Marsh, Carole.** California Jography. (California Experience! Ser.). (Illus.). (J). (gr. 2-6). 2000. 7.95 (*0-7933-9505-4*) Gallopade Intl.

Marsh, Carole. California "Jography" A Fun Run Thru Our State! (Carole Marsh California Bks.). (Illus.). (YA). (gr. 3-12). 1994. pap. 19.95 (*1-55609-510-4*); lib. bdg. 29.95 (*1-55609-511-2*) Gallopade Intl.

— California "Jography" A Fun Run Thru Our State! (Carole Marsh California Bks.). (Illus.). (J). (gr. 3-12). 1997. disk 29.95 (*0-7933-1391-0*) Gallopade Intl.

— California Kid's Cookbook: Recipes, How-to, History, Lore & More! (Carole Marsh California Bks.). (Illus.). (YA). (gr. 3-12). 1994. pap. 19.95 (*0-7933-0177-7*); lib. bdg. 29.95 (*0-7933-0178-5*); disk 29.95 (*0-7933-0179-3*) Gallopade Intl.

— The California Library Book: A Surprising Guide to the Unusual Special Collections in Libraries Across Our State for Students, Teachers, Writers & Publishers - Includes Reproducible Mailing Labels Plus Activities for Young People! (Carole Marsh California Bks.). (Illus.). 1994. pap. 19.95 (*0-7933-3021-1*); lib. bdg. 29.95 (*0-7933-3020-3*); disk 29.95 (*0-7933-3022-X*) Gallopade Intl.

— California Math! How It All Adds up in Our State. (Carole Marsh California Bks.). (Illus.). (YA). (gr. 3-12). 1996. pap. 19.95 (*0-7933-6500-7*); lib. bdg. 29.95 (*0-7933-6499-X*) Gallopade Intl.

— The California Media Book: A Surprising Guide to the Amazing Print, Broadcast & Online Media of Our State for Students, Teachers, Writers & Publishers - Includes Reproducible Mailing Labels Plus Activities for Young People! (Carole Marsh California Bks.). (Illus.). 1994. pap. 19.95 (*0-7933-3174-9*); lib. bdg. 29.95 (*0-7933-3173-0*); disk 29.95 (*0-7933-3175-7*) Gallopade Intl.

— The California Mystery Van Takes Off! Bk. 1. Handicapped California Kids Sneak Off on a Big Adventure. (Carole Marsh California Bks.). (Illus.). (J). (gr. 3-12). 1994. 29.95 (*0-7933-4976-1*); pap. 19.95 (*0-7933-4977-X*); disk 29.95 (*0-7933-4978-8*) Gallopade Intl.

— California Quiz Bowl Crash Course! (Carole Marsh California Bks.). (Illus.). (YA). (gr. 3-12). 1994. pap. 19.95 (*1-55609-518-X*); lib. bdg. 29.95 (*1-55609-519-8*); disk 29.95 (*0-7933-1400-3*) Gallopade Intl.

— California Rollercoasters! (Carole Marsh California Bks.). (Illus.). (YA). (gr. 3-12). 1994. pap. 19.95 (*0-7933-5237-1*); lib. bdg. 29.95 (*0-7933-5236-3*); disk 29.95 (*0-7933-5238-X*) Gallopade Intl.

— California School Trivia: An Amazing & Fascinating Look at Our State's Teachers, Schools & Students! (Carole Marsh California Bks.). (Illus.). (YA). (gr. 3-12). 1994. pap. 19.95 (*0-7933-0174-2*); lib. bdg. 29.95 (*0-7933-0175-0*); disk 29.95 (*0-7933-0176-9*) Gallopade Intl.

— California Silly Basketball Sportsmysteries, Vol. I. (Carole Marsh California Bks.). (Illus.). (YA). (gr. 3-12). 1994. pap. 19.95 (*0-7933-0171-8*); lib. bdg. 29.95 (*0-7933-0172-6*) Gallopade Intl.

— California Silly Basketball Sportsmysteries, Vol. I. (Carole Marsh California Bks.). (Illus.). (J). (gr. 3-12). 1997. disk 29.95 (*0-7933-0173-4*) Gallopade Intl.

— California Silly Basketball Sportsmysteries, Vol. II. (Carole Marsh California Bks.). (Illus.). (YA). (gr. 3-12). 1994. pap. 19.95 (*0-7933-1575-1*); lib. bdg. 29.95 (*0-7933-1574-3*); disk 29.95 (*0-7933-1576-X*) Gallopade Intl.

— California Silly Football Sportsmysteries, Vol. I. (Carole Marsh California Bks.). (Illus.). (YA). (gr. 3-12). 1994. pap. 19.95 (*1-55609-514-7*); lib. bdg. 29.95 (*1-55609-515-5*); disk 29.95 (*0-7933-1396-1*) Gallopade Intl.

— California Silly Football Sportsmysteries, Vol. II. (Carole Marsh California Bks.). (Illus.). (YA). (gr. 3-12). 1994. pap. 19.95 (*0-7933-1395-3*); lib. bdg. 29.95 (*0-7933-1394-5*) Gallopade Intl.

— California Silly Trivia! (Carole Marsh California Bks.). (Illus.). (YA). (gr. 3-12). 1994. pap. 19.95 (*1-55609-508-2*); lib. bdg. 29.95 (*1-55609-509-0*); disk 29.95 (*0-7933-1390-2*) Gallopade Intl.

— California Spelling Bee! Score Big by Correctly Spelling Our State's Unique Names. (Carole Marsh California Bks.). (Illus.). (YA). (gr. 3-12). 1996. pap. 19.95 (*0-7933-6653-4*); lib. bdg. 29.95 (*0-7933-6652-6*) Gallopade Intl.

— California Timeline: A Chronology of California History, Mystery, Trivia, Legend, Lore & More. (Carole Marsh California Bks.). (Illus.). (J). (gr. 3-12). 1994. pap. 19.95 (*0-7933-5888-4*); lib. bdg. 29.95 (*0-7933-5887-6*); disk 29.95 (*0-7933-5889-2*) Gallopade Intl.

— California 2000! Coming Soon to a Calendar Near You - The 21st Century! - Complete Set of AL 2000 Items. (Two Thousand! Ser.). (Illus.). (J). (gr. 3-12). 1998. pap. 75.00 (*0-7933-9317-5*); lib. bdg. 85.00 (*0-7933-9318-3*) Gallopade Intl.

— California 2000! Coming Soon to a Calendar near You--The 21st Century! (Two Thousand! Ser.). (Illus.). (J). (gr. 3-12). 1998. pap. 19.95 (*0-7933-8688-8*); lib. bdg. 29.95 (*0-7933-8687-X*) Gallopade Intl.

— California UFO's & Extraterrestrials! A Look at the Sightings & Science in Our State. (Carole Marsh California Bks.). (Illus.). (J). (gr. 3-12). 1997. pap. 19.95 (*0-7933-6347-0*); lib. bdg. 29.95 (*0-7933-6346-2*) Gallopade Intl.

***Marsh, Carole.** California's Big Activity Book. (California Experience! Ser.). (Illus.). (J). (gr. k-5). 2000. pap. 9.95 (*0-7933-9457-0*) Gallopade Intl.

Marsh, Carole. California's (Most Devastating!) Disasters & (Most Calamitous!) Catastrophies! (Carole Marsh California Bks.). (Illus.). (YA). (gr. 3-12). 1994. pap. 19.95 (*0-7933-0162-9*); lib. bdg. 29.95 (*0-7933-0163-7*); disk 29.95 (*0-7933-0164-5*) Gallopade Intl.

— California's Unsolved Mysteries (& Their "Solutions") Includes Scientific Information & Other Activities for Students. (Carole Marsh California Bks.). (Illus.). (J). (gr. 3-12). 1994. pap. 19.95 (*0-7933-5735-7*); lib. bdg. 29.95 (*0-7933-5734-9*); disk 29.95 (*0-7933-5736-5*) Gallopade Intl.

***Marsh, Carole.** The Cape Hatteras Lighthouse for Kids! Including the Big Move of 1999. (Hatteras Ser.). (Illus.). (YA). (gr. 3-12). 1999. pap. 19.95 (*0-7933-9436-8*); lib. bdg. 29.95 (*0-7933-9437-6*) Gallopade Intl.

Marsh, Carole. Carole Marsh Alabama Books, 44 bks. (Fullbook State Ser.). (YA). 1994. pap. 587.80 (*0-7933-5122-7*) Gallopade Intl.

— Carole Marsh Alabama Books, 44 bks., Set. (Fullbook State Ser.). (YA). 1994. lib. bdg. 1027.80 (*0-7933-1274-4*) Gallopade Intl.

— Carole Marsh Alaska Books, 44 bks., Set. (Fullbook State Ser.). (YA). 1994. pap. 587.80 (*0-7933-5124-3*); lib. bdg. 1027.80 (*0-7933-1275-2*) Gallopade Intl.

— Carole Marsh Arizona Books, 48 bks., Set. (Fullbook State Ser.). (YA). 1994. pap. 647.60 (*0-7933-5126-X*); lib. bdg. 1127.60 (*0-7933-1276-0*) Gallopade Intl.

— Carole Marsh Arkansas Books, 44 bks., Set. (Fullbook State Ser.). (YA). 1994. pap. 587.80 (*0-7933-5128-6*); lib. bdg. 1027.80 (*0-7933-1277-9*) Gallopade Intl.

— Carole Marsh California Books, 46 bks., Set. (Fullbook State Ser.). (YA). 1994. pap. 617.70 (*0-7933-5130-8*); lib. bdg. 1077.70 (*0-7933-1278-7*) Gallopade Intl.

— Carole Marsh Colorado Books, 44 bks., Set. (Fullbook State Ser.). (YA). 1994. pap. 587.80 (*0-7933-5132-4*); lib. bdg. 1027.80 (*0-7933-1280-9*) Gallopade Intl.

— Carole Marsh Connecticut Books, 44 bks., Set. (Fullbook State Ser.). (YA). 1994. pap. 587.80 (*0-7933-5134-0*); lib. bdg. 1027.80 (*0-7933-1281-7*) Gallopade Intl.

— Carole Marsh Delaware Books, 44 bks., Set. (Fullbook State Ser.). (YA). 1994. pap. 587.80 (*0-7933-5136-7*); lib. bdg. 1027.80 (*0-7933-1282-5*) Gallopade Intl.

— Carole Marsh Florida Books, 46 bks., Set. (Fullbook State Ser.). (YA). 1994. pap. 617.70 (*0-7933-5140-5*); lib. bdg. 1077.70 (*0-7933-1284-1*) Gallopade Intl.

— Carole Marsh Georgia Books, 47 bks., Set. (Fullbook State Ser.). (YA). 1994. pap. 632.65 (*0-7933-5142-1*); lib. bdg. 1102.65 (*0-7933-1285-X*) Gallopade Intl.

— Carole Marsh Hawaii Books, 44 bks., Set. (Fullbook State Ser.). (YA). 1994. pap. 587.80 (*0-7933-5144-8*); lib. bdg. 1027.80 (*0-7933-1286-8*) Gallopade Intl.

— Carole Marsh Idaho Books, 44 bks., Set. (Fullbook State Ser.). (YA). 1994. pap. 587.80 (*0-7933-5146-4*); lib. bdg. 1027.80 (*0-7933-1287-6*) Gallopade Intl.

— Carole Marsh Illinois Books, 44 bks., Set. (Fullbook State Ser.). (YA). 1994. pap. 587.80 (*0-7933-5148-0*); lib. bdg. 1027.80 (*0-7933-1288-4*) Gallopade Intl.

— Carole Marsh Indiana Books, 44 bks. (Fullbook State Ser.). (J). 1994. pap. 587.80 (*0-7933-5150-2*) Gallopade Intl.

— Carole Marsh Indiana Books, 44 bks., Set. (Fullbook State Ser.). (J). 1994. lib. bdg. 1027.80 (*0-7933-1289-2*) Gallopade Intl.

— Carole Marsh Iowa Books, 45 bks., Set. (Fullbook State Ser.). (YA). 1994. pap. 602.75 (*0-7933-5152-9*); lib. bdg. 1052.75 (*0-7933-1290-6*) Gallopade Intl.

— Carole Marsh Kansas Books, 44 bks., Set. (Fullbook State Ser.). (YA). 1994. pap. 587.80 (*0-7933-5154-5*); lib. bdg. 1027.80 (*0-7933-1291-4*) Gallopade Intl.

— Carole Marsh Kentucky Books, 45 bks. (Fullbook State Ser.). (Illus.). (J). (gr. 3-8). 1994. pap. 602.75 (*0-7933-5156-1*) Gallopade Intl.

— Carole Marsh Kentucky Books, 45 bks., Set. (Fullbook State Ser.). (Illus.). (J). (gr. 3-8). 1994. lib. bdg. 1052.75 (*0-7933-1292-2*) Gallopade Intl.

— Carole Marsh Louisiana Books, 44 bks., Set. (Fullbook State Ser.). (Illus.). (J). (gr. 3-8). 1994. pap. 587.80 (*0-7933-5158-8*); lib. bdg. 1027.80 (*0-7933-1293-0*) Gallopade Intl.

— Carole Marsh Maine Books, 44 bks., Set. (Fullbook State Ser.). (Illus.). (J). (gr. 3-8). 1994. pap. 587.80 (*0-7933-5160-X*); lib. bdg. 1027.80 (*0-7933-1294-9*) Gallopade Intl.

— Carole Marsh Massachusetts Books, 44 bks., Set. (Fullbook State Ser.). (Illus.). (J). (gr. 3-8). 1994. pap. 587.80 (*0-7933-5164-2*); lib. bdg. 1027.80 (*0-7933-1296-5*) Gallopade Intl.

— Carole Marsh Michigan Books, 44 bks., Set. (Fullbook State Ser.). (YA). 1997. pap. 587.80 (*0-7933-5166-9*); lib. bdg. 1027.80 (*0-7933-1297-3*) Gallopade Intl.

— Carole Marsh Minnesota Books, 44 bks., Set. (Fullbook State Ser.). (YA). 1994. pap. 587.80 (*0-7933-5168-5*); lib. bdg. 1027.80 (*0-7933-1298-1*) Gallopade Intl.

— Carole Marsh Mississippi Books, 45 bks., Set. (Fullbook State Ser.). (YA). 1994. pap. 602.75 (*0-7933-5170-7*); lib. bdg. 1052.75 (*0-7933-1299-X*) Gallopade Intl.

— Carole Marsh Missouri Books, 44 bks. (Fullbook State Ser.). (YA). 1994. pap. 587.80 (*0-7933-5172-3*) Gallopade Intl.

— Carole Marsh Missouri Books, 44 bks., Set. (Fullbook State Ser.). (YA). 1994. lib. bdg. 1027.80 (*0-7933-1300-7*) Gallopade Intl.

— Carole Marsh Montana Books, 44 bks., Set. (Fullbook State Ser.). (YA). 1994. pap. 587.80 (*0-7933-5174-X*); lib. bdg. 1027.82 (*0-7933-1301-5*) Gallopade Intl.

— Carole Marsh Nebraska Books, 44 bks., Set. (Fullbook State Ser.). (YA). 1994. pap. 587.80 (*0-7933-5176-6*); lib. bdg. 1027.80 (*0-7933-1302-3*) Gallopade Intl.

— Carole Marsh Nevada Books, 44 bks., Set. (Fullbook State Ser.). (YA). 1994. pap. 587.80 (*0-7933-5178-2*); lib. bdg. 1027.80 (*0-7933-1303-1*) Gallopade Intl.

— Carole Marsh New Hampshire Books, 44 bks., Set. (Fullbook State Ser.). (YA). 1994. pap. 587.80 (*0-7933-5180-4*); lib. bdg. 1027.80 (*0-7933-1304-X*) Gallopade Intl.

— Carole Marsh New Jersey Books, 44 bks., Set. (Fullbook State Ser.). (YA). 1994. pap. 587.80 (*0-7933-5182-0*); lib. bdg. 1027.80 (*0-7933-1305-8*) Gallopade Intl.

— Carole Marsh New Mexico Books, 44 bks., Set. (Fullbook State Ser.). (YA). 1994. pap. 587.80 (*0-7933-5184-7*); lib. bdg. 1027.80 (*0-7933-1306-6*) Gallopade Intl.

— Carole Marsh New York Books, 45 bks., Set. (Fullbook State Ser.). (YA). 1994. pap. 602.75 (*0-7933-5186-3*); lib. bdg. 1052.75 (*0-7933-1307-4*) Gallopade Intl.

— Carole Marsh North Carolina Books, 55 bks., Set. (Fullbook State Ser.). (YA). 1994. pap. 767.25 (*0-7933-5188-X*); lib. bdg. 1307.25 (*0-7933-1308-2*) Gallopade Intl.

— Carole Marsh North Dakota Books, 44 bks., Set. (Fullbook State Ser.). (YA). 1994. pap. 587.80 (*0-7933-5190-1*); lib. bdg. 1027.80 (*0-7933-1309-0*) Gallopade Intl.

— Carole Marsh Ohio Books, 44 bks., Set. (Fullbook State Ser.). (YA). 1994. pap. 587.80 (*0-7933-5192-8*); lib. bdg. 1027.80 (*0-7933-1310-4*) Gallopade Intl.

— Carole Marsh Oklahoma Books, 44 bks., Set. (Fullbook State Ser.). (YA). 1994. pap. 587.80 (*0-7933-5194-4*); lib. bdg. 1027.86 (*0-7933-1311-2*) Gallopade Intl.

— Carole Marsh Oregon Books, 44 bks., Set. (Fullbook State Ser.). (YA). 1994. pap. 587.80 (*0-7933-5196-0*); lib. bdg. 1027.80 (*0-7933-1312-0*) Gallopade Intl.

— Carole Marsh Pennsylvania Books, 44 bks., Set. (Fullbook State Ser.). (YA). 1994. pap. 587.80 (*0-7933-5198-7*); lib. bdg. 1027.80 (*0-7933-1313-9*) Gallopade Intl.

— Carole Marsh Rhode Island Books, 44 bks., Set. (Fullbook State Ser.). (YA). 1994. pap. 587.80 (*0-7933-5200-2*); lib. bdg. 1027.80 (*0-7933-1314-7*) Gallopade Intl.

— Carole Marsh South Carolina Books, 45 bks., Set. (Fullbook State Ser.). (YA). 1994. pap. 602.75 (*0-7933-5202-9*); lib. bdg. 1052.75 (*0-7933-1315-5*) Gallopade Intl.

— Carole Marsh South Dakota Books, 44 bks., Set. (Fullbook State Ser.). (YA). 1994. pap. 587.80 (*0-7933-5204-5*); lib. bdg. 1027.80 (*0-7933-1316-3*) Gallopade Intl.

— Carole Marsh Tennessee Books, 44 bks. (Fullbook State Ser.). (YA). 1994. pap. 587.80 (*0-7933-5206-1*) Gallopade Intl.

— Carole Marsh Tennessee Books, 44 bks., Set. (Fullbook State Ser.). (YA). 1994. lib. bdg. 1027.80 (*0-7933-1317-1*) Gallopade Intl.

— Carole Marsh Texas Books, 44 bks., Set. (Fullbook State Ser.). (YA). 1994. pap. 587.80 (*0-7933-5208-8*); lib. bdg. 1027.80 (*0-7933-1318-X*) Gallopade Intl.

— Carole Marsh Utah Books, 44 bks., Set. (Fullbook State Ser.). (YA). 1994. pap. 587.80 (*0-7933-5210-X*); lib. bdg. 1027.80 (*0-7933-1319-8*) Gallopade Intl.

— Carole Marsh Vermont Books, 44 bks., Set. (Fullbook State Ser.). (YA). 1994. pap. 587.80 (*0-7933-5212-6*); lib. bdg. 1027.80 (*0-7933-1320-1*) Gallopade Intl.

— Carole Marsh Virginia Books, 46 bks., Set. (Fullbook State Ser.). (YA). 1994. pap. 617.70 (*0-7933-5214-2*); lib. bdg. 1077.70 (*0-7933-1321-X*) Gallopade Intl.

— Carole Marsh Washington, D. C. Books, 44 bks., Set. (Fullbook State Ser.). (YA). 1994. pap. 587.80 (*0-7933-5138-3*); pap. 587.80 (*0-7933-5216-9*); lib. bdg. 1027.80 (*0-7933-1283-3*); lib. bdg. 1027.80 (*0-7933-1322-8*) Gallopade Intl.

— Carole Marsh West Virginia Books, 44 bks., Set. (Fullbook State Ser.). (YA). 1994. pap. 587.80 (*0-7933-5218-5*); lib. bdg. 1027.80 (*0-7933-1323-6*) Gallopade Intl.

— Carole Marsh Wisconsin Books, 44 bks., Set. (Fullbook State Ser.). (YA). 1994. pap. 587.80 (*0-7933-5220-7*); lib. bdg. 1027.80 (*0-7933-1324-4*) Gallopade Intl.

M

— Carole Marsh Wyoming Books, 44 bks., Set. (Fullbook State Ser.). (YA). 1994. lib. bdg. 1027.80 (*0-7933-1325-2*) Gallopade Intl.
— Castle Hayne. (Carole Marsh Short Story Ser.). (Illus.). 60p. (J). (gr. 4-12). 1994. pap. 19.95 (*1-55609-241-5*); lib. bdg. 29.95 (*1-55609-159-1*) Gallopade Intl.
— The Charming Ghost of Charleston Set. (Carole Marsh Mysteries Ser.). 1994. teacher ed. 125.00 (*0-7933-6958-4*) Gallopade Intl.
— Chill Out: Scary Alabama Tales Based on Frightening Alabama Truths. (Carole Marsh Alabama Bks.). (Illus.). (J). 1994. pap. 19.95 (*0-7933-4658-4*); lib. bdg. 29.95 (*0-7933-4657-6*); disk 29.95 (*0-7933-4659-2*) Gallopade Intl.
— Chill Out: Scary Alaska Tales Based on Frightening Alaska Truths. (Carole Marsh Alaska Bks.). (Illus.). (J). 1994. pap. 19.95 (*0-7933-4661-4*); lib. bdg. 29.95 (*0-7933-4660-6*); disk 29.95 (*0-7933-4662-2*) Gallopade Intl.
— Chill Out: Scary Arizona Tales Based on Frightening Arizona Truths. (Carole Marsh Arizona Bks.). (Illus.). (J). 1994. pap. 19.95 (*0-7933-4664-9*); lib. bdg. 29.95 (*0-7933-4663-0*); disk 29.95 (*0-7933-4665-7*) Gallopade Intl.

M

— Chill Out: Scary Arkansas Tales Based on Frightening Arkansas Truths. (Carole Marsh Arkansas Bks.). (Illus.). (J). 1994. pap. 19.95 (*0-7933-4667-3*); lib. bdg. 29.95 (*0-7933-4666-5*); disk 29.95 (*0-7933-4668-1*) Gallopade Intl.
— Chill Out: Scary California Tales Based on Frightening California Truths. (Carole Marsh California Bks.). (Illus.). (J). 1994. pap. 19.95 (*0-7933-4670-3*); lib. bdg. 29.95 (*0-7933-4669-X*); disk 29.95 (*0-7933-4671-1*) Gallopade Intl.
— Chill Out: Scary Colorado Tales Based on Frightening Colorado Truths. (Carole Marsh Colorado Bks.). (Illus.). (J). 1994. pap. 19.95 (*0-7933-4673-8*); lib. bdg. 29.95 (*0-7933-4672-X*); disk 29.95 (*0-7933-4674-6*) Gallopade Intl.
— Chill Out: Scary Connecticut Tales Based on Frightening Connecticut Truths. (Carole Marsh Connecticut Bks.). (Illus.). (J). 1994. pap. 19.95 (*0-7933-4676-2*); lib. bdg. 29.95 (*0-7933-4675-4*); disk 29.95 (*0-7933-4677-0*) Gallopade Intl.
— Chill Out: Scary Delaware Tales Based on Frightening Delaware Truths. (Carole Marsh Delaware Bks.). (Illus.). (J). 1994. pap. 19.95 (*0-7933-4679-7*); lib. bdg. 29.95 (*0-7933-4678-9*); disk 29.95 (*0-7933-4680-0*) Gallopade Intl.
— Chill Out: Scary Florida Tales Based on Frightening Florida Truths. (Carole Marsh Florida Bks.). (Illus.). (J). 1994. pap. 19.95 (*0-7933-4682-7*); lib. bdg. 29.95 (*0-7933-4681-9*); disk 29.95 (*0-7933-4683-5*) Gallopade Intl.
— Chill Out: Scary Georgia Tales Based on Frightening Georgia Truths. (Carole Marsh Georgia Bks.). (Illus.). (J). 1994. pap. 19.95 (*0-7933-4685-1*); lib. bdg. 29.95 (*0-7933-4684-3*); disk 29.95 (*0-7933-4686-X*) Gallopade Intl.
— Chill Out: Scary Hawaii Tales Based on Frightening Hawaii Truths. (Carole Marsh Hawaii Bks.). (Illus.). (J). 1994. pap. 19.95 (*0-7933-4688-6*); lib. bdg. 29.95 (*0-7933-4687-8*); disk 29.95 (*0-7933-4689-4*) Gallopade Intl.
— Chill Out: Scary Idaho Tales Based on Frightening Idaho Truths. (Carole Marsh Idaho Bks.). (Illus.). (J). 1994. pap. 19.95 (*0-7933-4691-6*); lib. bdg. 29.95 (*0-7933-4690-8*); disk 29.95 (*0-7933-4692-4*) Gallopade Intl.
— Chill Out: Scary Illinois Tales Based on Frightening Illinois Truths. (Carole Marsh Illinois Bks.). (Illus.). (J). 1994. pap. 19.95 (*0-7933-4694-0*); lib. bdg. 29.95 (*0-7933-4693-2*); disk 29.95 (*0-7933-4695-9*) Gallopade Intl.
— Chill Out: Scary Indiana Tales Based on Frightening Indiana Truths. (Carole Marsh Indiana Bks.). (Illus.). (J). 1994. pap. 19.95 (*0-7933-4697-5*); lib. bdg. 29.95 (*0-7933-4696-7*); disk 29.95 (*0-7933-4698-3*) Gallopade Intl.
— Chill Out: Scary Iowa Tales Based on Frightening Iowa Truths. (Carole Marsh Iowa Bks.). (Illus.). (J). 1994. pap. 19.95 (*0-7933-4700-9*); lib. bdg. 29.95 (*0-7933-4699-1*); disk 29.95 (*0-7933-4701-7*) Gallopade Intl.
— Chill Out: Scary Kansas Tales Based on Frightening Kansas Truths. (Carole Marsh Kansas Bks.). (Illus.). (J). 1994. pap. 19.95 (*0-7933-4703-3*); lib. bdg. 29.95 (*0-7933-4702-5*); disk 29.95 (*0-7933-4704-1*) Gallopade Intl.
— Chill Out: Scary Kentucky Tales Based on Frightening Kentucky Truths. (Carole Marsh Kentucky Bks.). (Illus.). (J). 1994. pap. 19.95 (*0-7933-4706-8*); lib. bdg. 29.95 (*0-7933-4705-X*); disk 29.95 (*0-7933-4707-6*) Gallopade Intl.
— Chill Out: Scary Louisiana Tales Based on Frightening Louisiana Truths. (Carole Marsh Louisiana Bks.). (Illus.). (J). 1994. pap. 19.95 (*0-7933-4709-2*); lib. bdg. 29.95 (*0-7933-4708-4*); disk 29.95 (*0-7933-4710-6*) Gallopade Intl.
— Chill Out: Scary Maine Tales Based on Frightening Maine Truths. (Carole Marsh Maine Bks.). (Illus.). (J). 1994. pap. 19.95 (*0-7933-4712-2*); lib. bdg. 29.95 (*0-7933-4711-4*); disk 29.95 (*0-7933-4713-0*) Gallopade Intl.
— Chill Out: Scary Maryland Tales Based on Frightening Maryland Truths. (Carole Marsh Maryland Bks.). (Illus.). (J). 1994. pap. 19.95 (*0-7933-4715-7*); lib. bdg. 29.95 (*0-7933-4714-9*); disk 29.95 (*0-7933-4716-5*) Gallopade Intl.
— Chill Out: Scary Massachusetts Tales Based on Frightening Massachusetts Truths. (Massachuseets Bks.). (Illus.). (J). 1994. pap. 19.95 (*0-7933-4718-1*); lib. bdg. 29.95 (*0-7933-4717-3*); disk 29.95 (*0-7933-4719-X*) Gallopade Intl.
— Chill Out: Scary Michigan Tales Based on Frightening Michigan Truths. (Carole Marsh Michigan Bks.). (Illus.). (J). 1994. pap. 19.95 (*0-7933-4721-1*); lib. bdg. 29.95 (*0-7933-4720-3*); disk 29.95 (*0-7933-4722-X*) Gallopade Intl.
— Chill Out: Scary Minnesota Tales Based on Frightening Minnesota Truths. (Carole Marsh Minnesota Bks.). (Illus.). (J). 1994. pap. 19.95 (*0-7933-4724-6*); lib. bdg. 29.95 (*0-7933-4723-8*); disk 29.95 (*0-7933-4725-4*) Gallopade Intl.
— Chill Out: Scary Mississippi Tales Based on Frightening Mississippi Truths. (Carole Marsh Mississippi Bks.). (Illus.). (J). 1994. pap. 19.95 (*0-7933-4727-0*); lib. bdg. 29.95 (*0-7933-4726-2*); disk 29.95 (*0-7933-4728-9*) Gallopade Intl.
— Chill Out: Scary Missouri Tales Based on Frightening Missouri Truths. (Carole Marsh Missouri Bks.). (Illus.). (J). 1994. pap. 19.95 (*0-7933-4730-0*); lib. bdg. 29.95 (*0-7933-4729-7*); disk 29.95 (*0-7933-4731-9*) Gallopade Intl.
— Chill Out: Scary Montana Tales Based on Frightening Montana Truths. (Carole Marsh Montana Bks.). (Illus.). (J). 1994. pap. 19.95 (*0-7933-4733-5*); lib. bdg. 29.95 (*0-7933-4732-7*); disk 29.95 (*0-7933-4734-3*) Gallopade Intl.
— Chill Out: Scary Nebraska Tales Based on Frightening Nebraska Truths. (Carole Marsh Nebraska Bks.). (Illus.). (J). 1994. pap. 19.95 (*0-7933-4736-X*); lib. bdg. 29.95 (*0-7933-4735-1*); disk 29.95 (*0-7933-4737-8*) Gallopade Intl.
— Chill Out: Scary Nevada Tales Based on Frightening Nevada Truths. (Carole Marsh Nevada Bks.). (Illus.). (J). 1994. pap. 19.95 (*0-7933-4739-4*); lib. bdg. 29.95 (*0-7933-4738-6*); disk 29.95 (*0-7933-4740-8*) Gallopade Intl.
— Chill Out: Scary New Hampshire Tales Based on Frightening New Hampshire Truths. (Carole Marsh New Hampshire Bks.). (Illus.). (J). 1994. pap. 19.95 (*0-7933-4742-4*); lib. bdg. 29.95 (*0-7933-4741-6*); disk 29.95 (*0-7933-4743-2*) Gallopade Intl.
— Chill Out: Scary New Jersey Tales Based on Frightening New Jersey Truths. (Carole Marsh New Jersey Bks.). (Illus.). (J). 1994. pap. 19.95 (*0-7933-4745-9*); lib. bdg. 29.95 (*0-7933-4744-0*); disk 29.95 (*0-7933-4746-7*) Gallopade Intl.
— Chill Out: Scary New Mexico Tales Based on Frightening New Mexico Truths. (Carole Marsh New Mexico Bks.). (Illus.). (J). 1994. pap. 19.95 (*0-7933-4748-3*); lib. bdg. 29.95 (*0-7933-4747-5*); disk 29.95 (*0-7933-4749-1*) Gallopade Intl.
— Chill Out: Scary New York Tales Based on Frightening New York Truths. (Carole Marsh New York Bks.). (Illus.). (J). 1994. pap. 19.95 (*0-7933-4751-3*); lib. bdg. 29.95 (*0-7933-4750-5*); disk 29.95 (*0-7933-4752-1*) Gallopade Intl.
— Chill Out: Scary North Carolina Tales Based on Frightening North Carolina Truths. (Carole Marsh North Carolina Bks.). (Illus.). (J). 1994. pap. 19.95 (*0-7933-4754-8*); lib. bdg. 29.95 (*0-7933-4753-X*); disk 29.95 (*0-7933-4755-6*) Gallopade Intl.
— Chill Out: Scary North Dakota Tales Based on Frightening North Dakota Truths. (Carole Marsh North Dakota Bks.). (Illus.). (J). 1994. pap. 19.95 (*0-7933-4757-2*); lib. bdg. 29.95 (*0-7933-4756-4*); disk 29.95 (*0-7933-4758-0*) Gallopade Intl.
— Chill Out: Scary Ohio Tales Based on Frightening Ohio Truths. (Carole Marsh Ohio Bks.). (Illus.). (J). 1994. pap. 19.95 (*0-7933-4760-2*); lib. bdg. 29.95 (*0-7933-4759-9*); disk 29.95 (*0-7933-4761-0*) Gallopade Intl.
— Chill Out: Scary Oklahoma Tales Based on Frightening Oklahoma Truths. (Oklahoma Bks.). (Illus.). (J). 1994. pap. 19.95 (*0-7933-4763-7*); lib. bdg. 29.95 (*0-7933-4762-9*); disk 29.95 (*0-7933-4764-5*) Gallopade Intl.
— Chill Out: Scary Oregon Tales Based on Frightening Oregon Truths. (Oregon Bks.). (Illus.). (J). 1994. pap. 19.95 (*0-7933-4766-1*); lib. bdg. 29.95 (*0-7933-4765-3*); disk 29.95 (*0-7933-4767-X*) Gallopade Intl.
— Chill Out: Scary Pennsylvania Tales Based on Frightening Pennsylvania Truths. (Pennsylvania Bks.). (Illus.). (J). 1994. pap. 19.95 (*0-7933-4769-6*); lib. bdg. 29.95 (*0-7933-4768-8*); disk 29.95 (*0-7933-4770-X*) Gallopade Intl.
— Chill Out: Scary Rhode Island Tales Based on Frightening Rhode Island Truths. (Rhode Island Bks.). (Illus.). (J). 1994. pap. 19.95 (*0-7933-4772-6*); lib. bdg. 29.95 (*0-7933-4771-8*); disk 29.95 (*0-7933-4773-4*) Gallopade Intl.
— Chill Out: Scary South Carolina Tales Based on Frightening South Carolina Truths. (South Carolina Bks.). (Illus.). (J). 1994. pap. 19.95 (*0-7933-4775-0*); lib. bdg. 29.95 (*0-7933-4774-2*); disk 29.95 (*0-7933-4776-9*) Gallopade Intl.
— Chill Out: Scary South Dakota Tales Based on Frightening South Dakota Truths. (South Dakota Bks.). (Illus.). (J). 1994. pap. 19.95 (*0-7933-4778-5*); lib. bdg. 29.95 (*0-7933-4777-7*); disk 29.95 (*0-7933-4779-3*) Gallopade Intl.
— Chill Out: Scary Tennessee Tales Based on Frightening Tennessee Truths. (Tennessee Bks.). (Illus.). (J). 1994. pap. 19.95 (*0-7933-4781-5*); lib. bdg. 29.95 (*0-7933-4780-7*); disk 29.95 (*0-7933-4782-3*) Gallopade Intl.
— Chill Out: Scary Texas Tales Based on Frightening Texas Truths. (Texas Bks.). (Illus.). (J). 1994. pap. 19.95 (*0-7933-4784-X*); lib. bdg. 29.95 (*0-7933-4783-1*); disk 29.95 (*0-7933-4785-8*) Gallopade Intl.
— Chill Out: Scary Utah Tales Based on Frightening Utah Truths. (Utah Bks.). (Illus.). (J). 1994. pap. 19.95 (*0-7933-4787-4*); lib. bdg. 29.95 (*0-7933-4786-6*); disk 29.95 (*0-7933-4788-2*) Gallopade Intl.
— Chill Out: Scary Vermont Tales Based on Frightening Vermont Truths. (Vermont Bks.). (Illus.). (J). 1994. pap. 19.95 (*0-7933-4790-4*); lib. bdg. 29.95 (*0-7933-4789-0*); disk 29.95 (*0-7933-4791-2*) Gallopade Intl.
— Chill Out: Scary Virginia Tales Based on Frightening Virginia Truths. (Virginia Bks.). (Illus.). (J). 1994. pap. 19.95 (*0-7933-4793-9*); lib. bdg. 29.95 (*0-7933-4792-0*); disk 29.95 (*0-7933-4794-7*) Gallopade Intl.
— Chill Out: Scary Washington D. C. Tales Based on Frightening Washington D. C. Truths. (Washington, D.C. Bks.). (Illus.). (J). 1994. pap. 19.95 (*0-7933-4799-8*); lib. bdg. 29.95 (*0-7933-4798-X*); disk 29.95 (*0-7933-4800-5*) Gallopade Intl.
— Chill Out: Scary Washington Tales Based on Frightening Washington Truths. (Washington Bks.). (Illus.). (J). 1994. pap. 19.95 (*0-7933-4796-3*); lib. bdg. 29.95 (*0-7933-4795-5*); disk 29.95 (*0-7933-4797-1*) Gallopade Intl.
— Chill Out: Scary West Virginia Tales Based on Frightening West Virginia Truths. (West Virginia Bks.). (Illus.). (J). 1994. pap. 19.95 (*0-7933-4802-1*); lib. bdg. 29.95 (*0-7933-4801-3*); disk 29.95 (*0-7933-4803-X*) Gallopade Intl.
— Chill Out: Scary Wisconsin Tales Based on Frightening Wisconsin Truths. (Wisconsin Bks.). (Illus.). (J). 1994. pap. 19.95 (*0-7933-4805-6*); lib. bdg. 29.95 (*0-7933-4804-8*); disk 29.95 (*0-7933-4806-4*) Gallopade Intl.
— Chill Out: Scary Wyoming Tales Based on Frightening Wyoming Truths. (Wyoming Bks.). (Illus.). (J). 1994. pap. 19.95 (*0-7933-4808-0*); lib. bdg. 29.95 (*0-7933-4807-2*); disk 29.95 (*0-7933-4809-9*) Gallopade Intl.
— Choose-Your-Own-Ending Sex Ed Adventures. (Smart Sex Stuff Ser.). 60p. (Orig.). 1994. 29.95 (*1-55609-283-0*); pap. 19.95 (*1-55609-226-1*) Gallopade Intl.
— Christopher Columbus Comes to Alabama! Includes Reproducible Activities for Kids! (Carole Marsh Alabama Bks.). (Illus.). (J). (gr. 3-12). 1994. pap. 19.95 (*0-7933-3621-X*); lib. bdg. 29.95 (*0-7933-3620-1*); disk 29.95 (*0-7933-3622-8*) Gallopade Intl.
— Christopher Columbus Comes to Alaska! Includes Reproducible Activities for Kids! (Carole Marsh Alaska Bks.). (Illus.). (J). (gr. 3-12). 1994. pap. 19.95 (*0-7933-3624-4*); lib. bdg. 29.95 (*0-7933-3623-6*); disk 29.95 (*0-7933-3625-2*) Gallopade Intl.
— Christopher Columbus Comes to Arizona! Includes Reproducible Activities for Kids! (Carole Marsh Arizona Bks.). (Illus.). (J). (gr. 3-12). 1994. pap. 19.95 (*0-7933-3627-9*); lib. bdg. 29.95 (*0-7933-3626-0*); disk 29.95 (*0-7933-3628-7*) Gallopade Intl.
— Christopher Columbus Comes to Arkansas! Includes Reproducible Activities for Kids! (Carole Marsh Arkansas Bks.). (Illus.). (J). (gr. 3-12). 1994. pap. 19.95 (*0-7933-3630-9*); lib. bdg. 29.95 (*0-7933-3629-5*); disk 29.95 (*0-7933-3631-7*) Gallopade Intl.
— Christopher Columbus Comes to California! Includes Reproducible Activities for Kids! (Carole Marsh California Bks.). (Illus.). (J). (gr. 3-12). 1994. pap. 19.95 (*0-7933-3633-3*); lib. bdg. 29.95 (*0-7933-3632-5*); disk 29.95 (*0-7933-3634-1*) Gallopade Intl.
— Christopher Columbus Comes to Colorado! Includes Reproducible Activities for Kids! (Carole Marsh Colorado Bks.). (Illus.). (J). (gr. 3-12). 1994. pap. 19.95 (*0-7933-3636-8*); lib. bdg. 29.95 (*0-7933-3635-X*); disk 29.95 (*0-7933-3637-6*) Gallopade Intl.
— Christopher Columbus Comes to Connecticut! Includes Reproducible Activities for Kids! (Carole Marsh Connecticut Bks.). (Illus.). (J). (gr. 3-12). 1994. pap. 19.95 (*0-7933-3639-2*); lib. bdg. 29.95 (*0-7933-3638-4*); disk 29.95 (*0-7933-3640-6*) Gallopade Intl.
— Christopher Columbus Comes to Delaware! Includes Reproducible Activities for Kids! (Carole Marsh Delaware Bks.). (Illus.). (J). (gr. 3-12). 1994. pap. 19.95 (*0-7933-3642-2*); lib. bdg. 29.95 (*0-7933-3641-4*); disk 29.95 (*0-7933-3643-0*) Gallopade Intl.
— Christopher Columbus Comes to Florida! Includes Reproducible Activities for Kids! (Carole Marsh Florida Bks.). (Illus.). (J). (gr. 3-12). 1994. pap. 19.95 (*0-7933-3648-1*); lib. bdg. 29.95 (*0-7933-3647-3*); disk 29.95 (*0-7933-3649-X*) Gallopade Intl.
— Christopher Columbus Comes to Georgia! Includes Reproducible Activities for Kids! (Carole Marsh Georgia Bks.). (Illus.). (J). (gr. 3-12). 1994. pap. 19.95 (*0-7933-3651-1*); lib. bdg. 29.95 (*0-7933-3650-3*); disk 29.95 (*0-7933-3652-X*) Gallopade Intl.
— Christopher Columbus Comes to Hawaii! Includes Reproducible Activities for Kids! (Carole Marsh Hawaii Bks.). (Illus.). (J). (gr. 3-12). 1994. pap. 19.95 (*0-7933-3654-6*); lib. bdg. 29.95 (*0-7933-3653-8*); disk 29.95 (*0-7933-3655-4*) Gallopade Intl.
— Christopher Columbus Comes to Idaho! Includes Reproducible Activities for Kids! (Carole Marsh Idaho Bks.). (Illus.). (J). (gr. 3-12). 1994. pap. 19.95 (*0-7933-3657-0*); lib. bdg. 29.95 (*0-7933-3656-2*); disk 29.95 (*0-7933-3658-9*) Gallopade Intl.
— Christopher Columbus Comes to Illinois! Includes Reproducible Activities for Kids! (Carole Marsh Illinois Bks.). (Illus.). (J). (gr. 3-12). 1994. pap. 19.95 (*0-7933-3660-0*); lib. bdg. 29.95 (*0-7933-3659-7*); disk 29.95 (*0-7933-3661-9*) Gallopade Intl.
— Christopher Columbus Comes to Indiana! Includes Reproducible Activities for Kids! (Carole Marsh Indiana Bks.). (Illus.). (J). (gr. 3-12). 1994. pap. 19.95 (*0-7933-3663-5*); lib. bdg. 29.95 (*0-7933-3662-7*); disk 29.95 (*0-7933-3664-3*) Gallopade Intl.
— Christopher Columbus Comes to Iowa! Includes Reproducible Activities for Kids! (Carole Marsh Iowa Bks.). (Illus.). (J). (gr. 3-12). 1994. pap. 19.95 (*0-7933-3666-X*); lib. bdg. 29.95 (*0-7933-3665-1*); disk 29.95 (*0-7933-3667-8*) Gallopade Intl.
— Christopher Columbus Comes to Kansas! Includes Reproducible Activities for Kids! (Carole Marsh Kansas Bks.). (Illus.). (J). (gr. 3-12). 1994. pap. 19.95 (*0-7933-3669-4*); lib. bdg. 29.95 (*0-7933-3668-6*); disk 29.95 (*0-7933-3670-8*) Gallopade Intl.
— Christopher Columbus Comes to Kentucky! Includes Reproducible Activities for Kids! (Carole Marsh Kentucky Bks.). (Illus.). (J). (gr. 3-12). 1994. pap. 19.95 (*0-7933-3672-4*); lib. bdg. 29.95 (*0-7933-3671-6*); disk 29.95 (*0-7933-3673-2*) Gallopade Intl.
— Christopher Columbus Comes to Louisiana! Includes Reproducible Activities for Kids! (Carole Marsh Louisiana Bks.). (Illus.). (J). (gr. 3-12). 1994. pap. 19.95 (*0-7933-3675-9*); lib. bdg. 29.95 (*0-7933-3674-0*); disk 29.95 (*0-7933-3676-7*) Gallopade Intl.
— Christopher Columbus Comes to Maine! Includes Reproducible Activities for Kids! (Carole Marsh Maine Bks.). (Illus.). (J). (gr. 3-12). 1994. pap. 19.95 (*0-7933-3678-3*); lib. bdg. 29.95 (*0-7933-3677-5*); disk 29.95 (*0-7933-3679-1*) Gallopade Intl.
— Christopher Columbus Comes to Maryland! Includes Reproducible Activities for Kids! (Carole Marsh Maryland Bks.). (Illus.). (J). (gr. 3-12). 1994. pap. 19.95 (*0-7933-3681-3*); lib. bdg. 29.95 (*0-7933-3680-5*); disk 29.95 (*0-7933-3682-1*) Gallopade Intl.
— Christopher Columbus Comes to Massachusetts! Includes Reproducible Activities for Kids! (Massachuseets Bks.). (Illus.). (J). (gr. 3-12). 1994. pap. 19.95 (*0-7933-3684-8*); lib. bdg. 29.95 (*0-7933-3683-X*); disk 29.95 (*0-7933-3685-6*) Gallopade Intl.
— Christopher Columbus Comes to Michigan! Includes Reproducible Activities for Kids! (Carole Marsh Michigan Bks.). (Illus.). (J). (gr. 3-12). 1994. pap. 19.95 (*0-7933-3687-2*); lib. bdg. 29.95 (*0-7933-3686-4*); disk 29.95 (*0-7933-3688-0*) Gallopade Intl.
— Christopher Columbus Comes to Minnesota! Includes Reproducible Activities for Kids! (Carole Marsh Minnesota Bks.). (Illus.). (J). (gr. 3-12). 1994. pap. 19.95 (*0-7933-3690-2*); lib. bdg. 29.95 (*0-7933-3689-9*); disk 29.95 (*0-7933-3691-0*) Gallopade Intl.
— Christopher Columbus Comes to Mississippi! Includes Reproducible Activities for Kids! (Carole Marsh Mississippi Bks.). (Illus.). (J). (gr. 3-12). 1994. pap. 19.95 (*0-7933-3693-7*); lib. bdg. 29.95 (*0-7933-3692-9*); disk 29.95 (*0-7933-3694-5*) Gallopade Intl.
— Christopher Columbus Comes to Missouri! Includes Reproducible Activities for Kids! (Carole Marsh Missouri Bks.). (Illus.). 36p. (J). (gr. 3-12). 1994. pap. 19.95 (*0-7933-3696-1*); lib. bdg. 24.95 (*0-7933-3695-3*); disk 29.95 (*0-7933-3697-X*) Gallopade Intl.
— Christopher Columbus Comes to Montana! Includes Reproducible Activities for Kids! (Carole Marsh Montana Bks.). (Illus.). (J). (gr. 3-12). 1994. pap. 19.95 (*0-7933-3699-6*); lib. bdg. 29.95 (*0-7933-3698-8*); disk 29.95 (*0-7933-3700-3*) Gallopade Intl.
— Christopher Columbus Comes to Nebraska! Includes Reproducible Activities for Kids! (Carole Marsh Nebraska Bks.). (Illus.). (J). (gr. 3-12). 1994. pap. 19.95 (*0-7933-3702-X*); lib. bdg. 29.95 (*0-7933-3701-1*); disk 29.95 (*0-7933-3703-8*) Gallopade Intl.
— Christopher Columbus Comes to Nevada! Includes Reproducible Activities for Kids! (Carole Marsh Nevada Bks.). (Illus.). (J). (gr. 3-12). 1994. pap. 19.95 (*0-7933-3705-4*); lib. bdg. 29.95 (*0-7933-3704-6*); disk 29.95 (*0-7933-3706-2*) Gallopade Intl.
— Christopher Columbus Comes to New Hampshire! Includes Reproducible Activities for Kids! (Carole Marsh New Hampshire Bks.). (Illus.). (J). (gr. 3-12). 1994. pap. 19.95 (*0-7933-3708-9*); lib. bdg. 29.95 (*0-7933-3707-0*); disk 29.95 (*0-7933-3709-7*) Gallopade Intl.
— Christopher Columbus Comes to New Jersey! Includes Reproducible Activities for Kids! (Carole Marsh New Jersey Bks.). (Illus.). (J). (gr. 3-12). 1994. pap. 19.95 (*0-7933-3711-9*); lib. bdg. 29.95 (*0-7933-3710-0*); disk 29.95 (*0-7933-3712-7*) Gallopade Intl.
— Christopher Columbus Comes to New Mexico! Includes Reproducible Activities for Kids! (Carole Marsh New Mexico Bks.). (Illus.). (J). (gr. 3-12). 1994. pap. 19.95 (*0-7933-3714-3*); lib. bdg. 29.95 (*0-7933-3713-5*); disk 29.95 (*0-7933-3715-1*) Gallopade Intl.
— Christopher Columbus Comes to New York! Includes Reproducible Activities for Kids! (Carole Marsh New York Bks.). (Illus.). (J). (gr. 3-12). 1994. pap. 19.95 (*0-7933-3717-8*); lib. bdg. 29.95 (*0-7933-3716-X*); disk 29.95 (*0-7933-3718-6*) Gallopade Intl.
— Christopher Columbus Comes to North Carolina! Includes Reproducible Activities for Kids! (Carole Marsh North Carolina Bks.). (Illus.). (J). (gr. 3-12). 1994. pap. 19.95 (*0-7933-3720-8*); lib. bdg. 29.95 (*0-7933-3719-4*); disk 29.95 (*0-7933-3721-6*) Gallopade Intl.
— Christopher Columbus Comes to North Dakota! Includes Reproducible Activities for Kids! (Carole Marsh North Dakota Bks.). (Illus.). (J). (gr. 3-12). 1994. pap. 19.95 (*0-7933-3723-2*); lib. bdg. 29.95 (*0-7933-3722-4*); disk 29.95 (*0-7933-3724-0*) Gallopade Intl.
— Christopher Columbus Comes to Ohio! Includes Reproducible Activities for Kids! (Carole Marsh Ohio Bks.). (Illus.). (J). (gr. 3-12). 1994. pap. 19.95 (*0-7933-3726-7*); lib. bdg. 29.95 (*0-7933-3725-9*); disk 29.95 (*0-7933-3727-5*) Gallopade Intl.
— Christopher Columbus Comes to Oklahoma! Includes Reproducible Activities for Kids! (Carole Marsh Oklahoma Bks.). (Illus.). (J). (gr. 3-12). 1994. pap. 19.95 (*0-7933-3729-1*); lib. bdg. 29.95 (*0-7933-3728-3*); disk 29.95 (*0-7933-3730-5*) Gallopade Intl.
— Christopher Columbus Comes to Oregon! Includes

Reproducible Activities for Kids! (Oregon Bks.). (Illus.). (J). (gr. 3-12). 1994. pap. 19.95 (0-7933-3732-1); lib. bdg. 29.95 (0-7933-3731-3); disk 29.95 (0-7933-3733-X) Gallopade Intl.

— Christopher Columbus Comes to Pennsylvania! Includes Reproducible Activities for Kids! (Pennsylvania Bks.). (Illus.). (J). (gr. 3-12). 1994. pap. 19.95 (0-7933-3735-6); lib. bdg. 29.95 (0-7933-3734-8); disk 29.95 (0-7933-3736-4) Gallopade Intl.

— Christopher Columbus Comes to Rhode Island! Includes Reproducible Activities for Kids! (Rhode Island Bks.). (Illus.). (J). (gr. 3-12). 1994. pap. 19.95 (0-7933-3738-0); lib. bdg. 29.95 (0-7933-3737-2); disk 29.95 (0-7933-3739-9) Gallopade Intl.

— Christopher Columbus Comes to South Carolina! Includes Reproducible Activities for Kids! (South Carolina Bks.). (Illus.). (J). (gr. 3-12). 1994. pap. 19.95 (0-7933-3741-0); lib. bdg. 29.95 (0-7933-3740-2); disk 29.95 (0-7933-3742-9) Gallopade Intl.

— Christopher Columbus Comes to South Dakota! Includes Reproducible Activities for Kids! (South Dakota Bks.). (Illus.). (J). (gr. 3-12). 1994. pap. 19.95 (0-7933-3744-5); lib. bdg. 29.95 (0-7933-3743-7); disk 29.95 (0-7933-3745-3) Gallopade Intl.

— Christopher Columbus Comes to Tennessee! Includes Reproducible Activities for Kids! (Tennessee Bks.). (Illus.). (J). (gr. 3-12). 1994. pap. 19.95 (0-7933-3747-X); lib. bdg. 29.95 (0-7933-3746-1); disk 29.95 (0-7933-3748-8) Gallopade Intl.

— Christopher Columbus Comes to Texas! Includes Reproducible Activities for Kids! (Texas Bks.). (Illus.). (J). (gr. 3-12). 1994. pap. 19.95 (0-7933-3750-X); lib. bdg. 29.95 (0-7933-3749-6); disk 29.95 (0-7933-3751-8) Gallopade Intl.

— Christopher Columbus Comes to Utah! Includes Reproducible Activities for Kids! (Utah Bks.). (Illus.). (J). (gr. 3-12). 1994. pap. 19.95 (0-7933-3753-4); lib. bdg. 29.95 (0-7933-3752-6); disk 29.95 (0-7933-3754-2) Gallopade Intl.

— Christopher Columbus Comes to Vermont! Includes Reproducible Activities for Kids! (Vermont Bks.). (Illus.). (J). (gr. 3-12). 1994. pap. 19.95 (0-7933-3756-9); lib. bdg. 29.95 (0-7933-3755-0); disk 29.95 (0-7933-3757-7) Gallopade Intl.

— Christopher Columbus Comes to Virginia! Includes Reproducible Activities for Kids! (Virginia Bks.). (Illus.). (J). (gr. 3-12). 1994. pap. 19.95 (0-7933-3759-3); lib. bdg. 29.95 (0-7933-3758-5); disk 29.95 (0-7933-3760-7) Gallopade Intl.

— Christopher Columbus Comes to Washington! Includes Reproducible Activities for Kids! (Washington Bks.). (Illus.). (J). (gr. 3-12). 1994. pap. 19.95 (0-7933-3762-3); lib. bdg. 29.95 (0-7933-3761-5); disk 29.95 (0-7933-3763-1) Gallopade Intl.

— Christopher Columbus Comes to Washington D. C.! Includes Reproducible Activities for Kids! (Washington, D.C. Bks.). (Illus.). (J). (gr. 3-12). 1994. pap. 19.95 (0-7933-3645-7); lib. bdg. 29.95 (0-7933-3644-9); disk 29.95 (0-7933-3646-5) Gallopade Intl.

— Christopher Columbus Comes to West Virginia! Includes Reproducible Activities for Kids! (West Virginia Bks.). (Illus.). (J). (gr. 3-12). 1994. pap. 19.95 (0-7933-3765-8); lib. bdg. 29.95 (0-7933-3764-X); disk 29.95 (0-7933-3766-6) Gallopade Intl.

— Christopher Columbus Comes to Wisconsin! Includes Reproducible Activities for Kids! (Wisconsin Bks.). (Illus.). (J). (gr. 3-12). 1994. pap. 19.95 (0-7933-3768-2); lib. bdg. 29.95 (0-7933-3767-4); disk 29.95 (0-7933-3769-0) Gallopade Intl.

— Christopher Columbus Comes to Wyoming! Includes Reproducible Activities for Kids! (Wyoming Bks.). (Illus.). (J). (gr. 3-12). 1994. pap. 19.95 (0-7933-3771-2); lib. bdg. 29.95 (0-7933-3770-4); disk 29.95 (0-7933-3772-0) Gallopade Intl.

— Coastales. 1994. 29.95 (1-55609-106-0) Gallopade Intl.

— The Color Purple & All That Jazz. (Our Black Heritage Ser.). (J). (gr. 3-12). 1994. pap. 19.95 (1-55609-314-4); lib. bdg. 29.95 (1-55609-315-2); disk 29.95 (1-55609-316-0) Gallopade Intl.

— Colorado & Other State Greats (Biographies) (Carole Marsh Colorado Bks.). (Illus.). (YA). (gr. 3-12). 1994. pap. 19.95 (1-55609-533-3); lib. bdg. 29.95 (1-55609-534-1); disk 29.95 (0-7933-1421-6) Gallopade Intl.

— Colorado Bandits, Bushwackers, Outlaws, Crooks, Devils, Ghosts, Desperadoes & Other Assorted & Sundry Characters! (Carole Marsh Colorado Bks.). (Illus.). (YA). (gr. 3-12). 1994. pap. 19.95 (0-7933-0189-0); lib. bdg. 29.95 (0-7933-0190-4); disk 29.95 (0-7933-0191-2) Gallopade Intl.

— Colorado "BIO" Bingo! 24 Must Know State People for Kids to Learn about While Having Fun! (Bingo! Ser.). (Illus.). (J). (gr. 2-8). 1998. pap. 14.95 (0-7933-8540-7) Gallopade Intl.

— The Colorado Bookstore Book: A Surprising Guide to Our State's Bookstores & Their Specialties for Students, Teachers, Writers & Publishers. (Carole Marsh Colorado Bks.). (Illus.). 1994. pap. 19.95 (0-7933-2871-3); lib. bdg. 29.95 (0-7933-2870-5); disk 29.95 (0-7933-2872-1) Gallopade Intl.

— Colorado Classic Christmas Trivia: Stories, Recipes, Activities, Legends, Lore & More! (Carole Marsh Colorado Bks.). (Illus.). (YA). (gr. 3-12). 1994. pap. 19.95 (0-7933-0192-0); lib. bdg. 29.95 (0-7933-0193-9); disk 29.95 (0-7933-0194-7) Gallopade Intl.

— Colorado Coastales! (Carole Marsh Colorado Bks.). (J). 1994. lib. bdg. 29.95 (0-7933-7270-4) Gallopade Intl.

— Colorado Coastales! (Carole Marsh Colorado Bks.). (Illus.). (YA). (gr. 3-12). 1994. pap. 19.95 (1-55609-529-5); lib. bdg. 29.95 (1-55609-530-9); disk 29.95 (0-7933-1417-8) Gallopade Intl.

— Colorado "Crinkum-Crankum" A Funny Word Book about Our State. (Carole Marsh Colorado Bks.). (Illus.). (J). 1994. pap. 19.95 (0-7933-4826-9); lib. bdg. 29.95 (0-7933-4825-0); disk 29.95 (0-7933-4827-7) Gallopade Intl.

— Colorado Dingbats! Bk. 1: A Fun Book of Games, Stories, Activities & More about Our State That's All in Code! for You to Decipher. (Carole Marsh Colorado Bks.). (Illus.). (J). (gr. 3-12). 1994. pap. 19.95 (0-7933-3789-5); lib. bdg. 29.95 (0-7933-3788-7); disk 29.95 (0-7933-3790-9) Gallopade Intl.

***Marsh, Carole.** The Colorado Experience Pocket Guide. (Colorado Experience! Ser.). (Illus.). (J). 2000. pap. 6.95 (0-7933-9602-6) Gallopade Intl.

Marsh, Carole. Colorado Facts & Factivities. (Carole Marsh State Bks.). (Illus.). (J). (gr. 4-7). 1996. pap., teacher ed. 19.95 (0-7933-7857-5, C Marsh) Gallopade Intl.

— Colorado Festival Fun for Kids! (Carole Marsh Colorado Bks.). (Illus.). (J). (gr. 3-12). 1994. pap. 19.95 (0-7933-3942-1) Gallopade Intl.

— Colorado Festival Fun for Kids! (Carole Marsh Colorado Bks.). (Illus.). (YA). (gr. 3-12). 1994. lib. bdg. 29.95 (0-7933-3941-3); disk 29.95 (0-7933-3943-X) Gallopade Intl.

— Colorado "GEO" Bingo! 38 Must Know State Geography Facts for Kids to Learn While Having Fun! (Bingo! Ser.). (Illus.). (J). (gr. 2-8). 1998. pap. 14.95 (0-7933-8541-5) Gallopade Intl.

— Colorado Government! The Cornerstone of Everyday Life in Our State! (Carole Marsh Colorado Bks.). (Illus.). (J). (gr. 3-12). 1996. pap. 19.95 (0-7933-6197-4); lib. bdg. 29.95 (0-7933-6196-6); disk 29.95 (0-7933-6198-2) Gallopade Intl.

— Colorado "HISTO" Bingo! 42 Must Know State History Facts for Kids to Learn While Having Fun! (Bingo! Ser.). (Illus.). (J). (gr. 2-8). 1998. pap. 14.95 (0-7933-8542-3) Gallopade Intl.

— Colorado History! Surprising Secrets about Our State's Founding Mothers, Fathers & Kids! (Carole Marsh Colorado Bks.). (Illus.). (J). (gr. 3-12). 1996. pap. 19.95 (0-7933-6044-7); lib. bdg. 29.95 (0-7933-6043-9); disk 29.95 (0-7933-6045-5) Gallopade Intl.

— The Colorado Hot Air Balloon Mystery. (Carole Marsh Colorado Bks.). (Illus.). (J). (gr. 2-9). 1994. 29.95 (0-7933-2363-0); pap. 19.95 (0-7933-2364-9); disk 29.95 (0-7933-2365-7) Gallopade Intl.

— Colorado Hot Zones! Viruses, Diseases, & Epidemics in Our State's History. (Hot Zones! Ser.). (Illus.). (J). (gr. 3-12). 1998. pap. 19.95 (0-7933-8844-9); lib. bdg. 29.95 (0-7933-8843-0) Gallopade Intl.

— Colorado Indian Dictionary for Kids! (Carole Marsh State Bks.). (J). (gr. 2-9). 1996. 29.95 (0-7933-7659-9, C Marsh); pap. 19.95 (0-7933-7660-2, C Marsh) Gallopade Intl.

***Marsh, Carole.** Colorado Jeopardy. (Colorado Experience! Ser.). (Illus.). (J). (gr. 2-6). 2000. pap. 7.95 (0-7933-9604-2) Gallopade Intl.

Marsh, Carole. Colorado Jeopardy! Answers & Questions about Our State! (Carole Marsh Colorado Bks.). (Illus.). (J). (gr. 3-12). 1994. pap. 19.95 (0-7933-4095-0); lib. bdg. 29.95 (0-7933-4094-2); disk 29.95 (0-7933-4096-9) Gallopade Intl.

— Colorado "Jography" A Fun Run Thru Our State! (Carole Marsh Colorado Bks.). (Illus.). (YA). (gr. 3-12). 1994. pap. 19.95 (1-55609-524-4); lib. bdg. 29.95 (1-55609-525-2); disk 29.95 (0-7933-1407-0) Gallopade Intl.

— Colorado Kid's Cookbook: Recipes, How-to, History, Lore & More! (Carole Marsh Colorado Bks.). (Illus.). (YA). (gr. 3-12). 1994. pap. 19.95 (0-7933-0201-3); lib. bdg. 29.95 (0-7933-0202-1); disk 29.95 (0-7933-0203-X) Gallopade Intl.

— The Colorado Library Book: A Surprising Guide to the Unusual Special Collections in Libraries Across Our State for Students, Teachers, Writers & Publishers - Includes Reproducible Mailing Labels Plus Activities for Young People! (Carole Marsh Colorado Bks.). (Illus.). 1994. pap. 19.95 (0-7933-3024-6); lib. bdg. 29.95 (0-7933-3023-8); disk 29.95 (0-7933-3025-4) Gallopade Intl.

— Colorado Math! How It All Adds up in Our State. (Carole Marsh Colorado Bks.). (Illus.). (YA). (gr. 3-12). 1996. pap. 19.95 (0-7933-6503-1); lib. bdg. 29.95 (0-7933-6502-3) Gallopade Intl.

— The Colorado Media Book: A Surprising Guide to the Amazing Print, Broadcast & Online Media of Our State for Students, Teachers, Writers & Publishers - Includes Reproducible Mailing Labels Plus Activities for Young People! (Carole Marsh Colorado Bks.). (Illus.). 1994. pap. 19.95 (0-7933-3177-3); lib. bdg. 29.95 (0-7933-3176-5); disk 29.95 (0-7933-3178-1) Gallopade Intl.

— The Colorado Mystery Van Takes Off! Bk. 1: Handicapped Colorado Kids Sneak Off on a Big Adventure. (Carole Marsh Colorado Bks.). (Illus.). (J). (gr. 3-12). 1994. 29.95 (0-7933-4979-6); pap. 19.95 (0-7933-4980-X); disk 29.95 (0-7933-4981-8) Gallopade Intl.

— Colorado Quiz Bowl Crash Course! (Carole Marsh Colorado Bks.). (Illus.). (YA). (gr. 3-12). 1994. pap. 19.95 (1-55609-531-7); disk 29.95 (0-7933-1416-X) Gallopade Intl.

— Colorado Quiz Bowl Crash Course! (Carole Marsh Colorado Bks.). (Illus.). (J). (gr. 3-12). 1997. lib. bdg. 29.95 (1-55609-532-5) Gallopade Intl.

— Colorado Rollercoasters! (Carole Marsh Colorado Bks.). (Illus.). (YA). (gr. 3-12). 1994. pap. 19.95 (0-7933-5240-1); lib. bdg. 29.95 (0-7933-5239-8); disk 29.95 (0-7933-5241-X) Gallopade Intl.

— Colorado School Trivia: An Amazing & Fascinating Look at Our State's Teachers, Schools & Students! (Carole Marsh Colorado Bks.). (Illus.). (YA). (gr. 3-12). 1994. pap. 19.95 (0-7933-0198-X); lib. bdg. 29.95 (0-7933-0199-8); disk 29.95 (0-7933-0200-5) Gallopade Intl.

— Colorado Silly Basketball Sportsmysteries, Vol. I. (Carole Marsh Colorado Bks.). (Illus.). (YA). (gr. 3-12). 1994. pap. 19.95 (0-7933-0195-5); lib. bdg. 29.95 (0-7933-0196-3); disk 29.95 (0-7933-0197-1) Gallopade Intl.

— Colorado Silly Basketball Sportsmysteries, Vol. II. (Carole Marsh Colorado Bks.). (Illus.). (YA). (gr. 3-12). 1994. pap. 19.95 (0-7933-1578-6); lib. bdg. 29.95 (0-7933-1577-8); disk 29.95 (0-7933-1579-4) Gallopade Intl.

— Colorado Silly Football Sportsmysteries, Vol. I. (Carole Marsh Colorado Bks.). (Illus.). (YA). (gr. 3-12). 1994. pap. 19.95 (1-55609-527-9); lib. bdg. 29.95 (1-55609-528-7); disk 29.95 (0-7933-1409-7) Gallopade Intl.

— Colorado Silly Football Sportsmysteries, Vol. II. (Carole Marsh Colorado Bks.). (Illus.). (YA). (gr. 3-12). 1994. pap. 19.95 (0-7933-1411-9); lib. bdg. 29.95 (0-7933-1410-0); disk 29.95 (0-7933-1412-7) Gallopade Intl.

— Colorado Silly Trivia! (Carole Marsh Colorado Bks.). (Illus.). (YA). (gr. 3-12). 1994. pap. 19.95 (1-55609-522-8); lib. bdg. 29.95 (1-55609-523-6); disk 29.95 (0-7933-1406-2) Gallopade Intl.

— Colorado Spelling Bee! Score Big by Correctly Spelling Our State's Unique Names. (Carole Marsh Colorado Bks.). (Illus.). (YA). (gr. 3-12). 1996. pap. 19.95 (0-7933-6656-9); lib. bdg. 29.95 (0-7933-6655-0) Gallopade Intl.

— Colorado Timeline: A Chronology of Colorado History, Mystery, Trivia, Legend, Lore & More. (Carole Marsh Colorado Bks.). (Illus.). (J). (gr. 3-12). 1994. pap. 19.95 (0-7933-5891-4); lib. bdg. 29.95 (0-7933-5890-6); disk 29.95 (0-7933-5892-2) Gallopade Intl.

— Colorado 2000! Coming Soon to a Calendar Near You - The 21st Century! - Complete Set of AL 2000 Items. (Two Thousand! Ser.). (Illus.). (J). (gr. 3-12). 1998. pap. 75.00 (0-7933-9319-1); lib. bdg. 85.00 (0-7933-9320-5) Gallopade Intl.

— Colorado 2000! Coming Soon to a Calendar near You--The 21st Century! (Two Thousand! Ser.). (Illus.). (J). (gr. 3-12). 1998. pap. 19.95 (0-7933-8691-8); lib. bdg. 29.95 (0-7933-8690-X) Gallopade Intl.

— Colorado UFO's & Extraterrestrials! A Look at the Sightings & Science in Our State. (Carole Marsh Colorado Bks.). (Illus.). (J). (gr. 3-12). 1997. pap. 19.95 (0-7933-6350-0); lib. bdg. 29.95 (0-7933-6349-7) Gallopade Intl.

***Marsh, Carole.** Colorado's Big Activity Book. (Colorado Experience! Ser.). (Illus.). (J). (gr. k-5). 2000. pap. 9.95 (0-7933-9606-9) Gallopade Intl.

Marsh, Carole. Colorado's (Most Devastating!) Disasters & (Most Calamitous!) Catastrophies! (Carole Marsh Colorado Bks.). (Illus.). (YA). (gr. 3-12). 1994. pap. 19.95 (0-7933-0186-6); lib. bdg. 29.95 (0-7933-0187-4); disk 29.95 (0-7933-0188-2) Gallopade Intl.

— Colorado's Unsolved Mysteries (& Their "Solutions") Includes Scientific Information & Other Activities for Students. (Carole Marsh Colorado Bks.). (Illus.). (J). (gr. 3-12). 1994. pap. 19.95 (0-7933-5738-1); lib. bdg. 29.95 (0-7933-5737-3); disk 29.95 (0-7933-5739-X) Gallopade Intl.

— Columbia Lastname: The Schwarzchild Radius, Bk. I. (Columbia Lastname Ser.). (Orig.). (YA). (gr. 4 up). 1994. pap. text 19.95 (0-935326-62-6); lib. bdg. 29.95 (1-55609-284-9) Gallopade Intl.

— Connecticut & Other State Greats (Biographies) (Carole Marsh Connecticut Bks.). (Illus.). (YA). (gr. 3-12). 1994. pap. 19.95 (1-55609-546-5); lib. bdg. 29.95 (1-55609-547-3); disk 29.95 (0-7933-1437-2) Gallopade Intl.

— Connecticut Bandits, Bushwackers, Outlaws, Crooks, Devils, Ghosts, Desperadoes & Other Assorted & Sundry Characters! (Carole Marsh Connecticut Bks.). (Illus.). (YA). (gr. 3-12). 1994. pap. 19.95 (0-7933-0213-7); lib. bdg. 29.95 (0-7933-0214-5); disk 29.95 (0-7933-0215-3) Gallopade Intl.

— Connecticut "BIO" Bingo! 24 Must Know State People for Kids to Learn about While Having Fun! (Bingo! Ser.). (Illus.). (J). (gr. 2-8). 1998. pap. 14.95 (0-7933-8543-1) Gallopade Intl.

— The Connecticut Bookstore Book: A Surprising Guide to Our State's Bookstores & Their Specialties for Students, Teachers, Writers & Publishers. (Carole Marsh Connecticut Bks.). (Illus.). 1994. pap. 19.95 (0-7933-2874-8); lib. bdg. 29.95 (0-7933-2873-X); disk 29.95 (0-7933-2875-6) Gallopade Intl.

— Connecticut Classic Christmas Trivia: Stories, Recipes, Activities, Legends, Lore & More! (Carole Marsh Connecticut Bks.). (Illus.). (YA). (gr. 3-12). 1994. pap. 19.95 (0-7933-0216-1); lib. bdg. 29.95 (0-7933-0217-X); disk 29.95 (0-7933-0218-8) Gallopade Intl.

— Connecticut Coastales. (Carole Marsh Connecticut Bks.). (Illus.). (YA). (gr. 3-12). 1994. pap. 19.95 (1-55609-542-2); lib. bdg. 29.95 (1-55609-543-0); disk 29.95 (0-7933-1433-X) Gallopade Intl.

— Connecticut Coastales! (Carole Marsh Connecticut Bks.). (J). 1994. lib. bdg. 29.95 (0-7933-7271-2) Gallopade Intl.

— Connecticut "Crinkum-Crankum" A Funny Word Book about Our State. (Carole Marsh Connecticut Bks.). (Illus.). (J). 1994. pap. 19.95 (0-7933-4829-3); lib. bdg. 29.95 (0-7933-4828-5); disk 29.95 (0-7933-4830-7) Gallopade Intl.

— Connecticut Dingbats! Bk. 1: A Fun Book of Games, Stories, Activities & More about Our State That's All in Code! for You to Decipher. (Carole Marsh Connecticut Bks.). (Illus.). (J). (gr. 3-12). 1994. pap. 19.95 (0-7933-3792-5); lib. bdg. 29.95 (0-7933-3791-7); disk 29.95 (0-7933-3793-3) Gallopade Intl.

***Marsh, Carole.** The Connecticut Experience Pocket Guide. (Connecticut Experience! Ser.). (Illus.). (J). 2000. pap. 6.95 (0-7933-9578-X) Gallopade Intl.

Marsh, Carole. Connecticut Facts & Factivities. (Carole Marsh State Bks.). (Illus.). (J). (gr. 4-7). 1996. pap., teacher ed. 19.95 (0-7933-7859-1, C Marsh) Gallopade Intl.

— Connecticut Festival Fun for Kids! (Carole Marsh Connecticut Bks.). (Illus.). (YA). (gr. 3-12). 1994. pap. 19.95 (0-7933-3945-6); lib. bdg. 29.95 (0-7933-3944-8); disk 29.95 (0-7933-3946-4) Gallopade Intl.

— Connecticut "GEO" Bingo! 38 Must Know State Geography Facts for Kids to Learn While Having Fun! (Bingo! Ser.). (Illus.). (J). (gr. 2-8). 1998. pap. 14.95 (0-7933-8544-X) Gallopade Intl.

— Connecticut Government! The Cornerstone of Everyday Life in Our State! (Carole Marsh Connecticut Bks.). (Illus.). (J). (gr. 3-12). 1996. pap. 19.95 (0-7933-6200-8); lib. bdg. 29.95 (0-7933-6199-0); disk 29.95 (0-7933-6201-6) Gallopade Intl.

— Connecticut "HISTO" Bingo! 42 Must Know State History Facts for Kids to Learn While Having Fun! (Bingo! Ser.). (Illus.). (J). (gr. 2-8). 1998. pap. 14.95 (0-7933-8545-8) Gallopade Intl.

— Connecticut History! Surprising Secrets about Our State's Founding Mothers, Fathers & Kids! (Carole Marsh Connecticut Bks.). (Illus.). (J). (gr. 3-12). 1996. pap. 19.95 (0-7933-6047-1); lib. bdg. 29.95 (0-7933-6046-3); disk 29.95 (0-7933-6048-X) Gallopade Intl.

— The Connecticut Hot Air Balloon Mystery. (Carole Marsh Connecticut Bks.). (Illus.). (J). (gr. 2-9). 1994. 29.95 (0-7933-2372-X); pap. 19.95 (0-7933-2373-8); disk 29.95 (0-7933-2374-6) Gallopade Intl.

— Connecticut Hot Zones! Viruses, Diseases, & Epidemics in Our State's History. (Hot Zones! Ser.). (Illus.). (J). (gr. 3-12). 1998. pap. 19.95 (0-7933-8847-3); lib. bdg. 29.95 (0-7933-8846-5) Gallopade Intl.

— Connecticut Indian Dictionary for Kids! (Carole Marsh State Bks.). (J). (gr. 2-9). 1996. pap. 19.95 (0-7933-7663-7, C Marsh); disk 29.95 (0-7933-7664-5, C Marsh) Gallopade Intl.

***Marsh, Carole.** Connecticut Jeopardy. (Connecticut Experience! Ser.). (Illus.). (J). (gr. 2-6). 2000. pap. 7.95 (0-7933-9580-1) Gallopade Intl.

Marsh, Carole. Connecticut Jeopardy! Answers & Questions about Our State! (Carole Marsh Connecticut Bks.). (Illus.). (J). (gr. 3-12). 1994. pap. 19.95 (0-7933-4098-5); lib. bdg. 29.95 (0-7933-4097-7); disk 29.95 (0-7933-4099-3) Gallopade Intl.

***Marsh, Carole.** Connecticut Jography. (Connecticut Experience! Ser.). (Illus.). (J). (gr. 2-6). 2000. pap. 7.95 (0-7933-9581-X) Gallopade Intl.

Marsh, Carole. Connecticut "Jography" A Fun Run Thru Our State! (Carole Marsh Connecticut Bks.). (Illus.). (YA). (gr. 3-12). 1994. pap. 19.95 (1-55609-537-6); lib. bdg. 29.95 (1-55609-538-4); disk 29.95 (0-7933-1423-2) Gallopade Intl.

— Connecticut Kid's Cookbook: Recipes, How-to, History, Lore & More! (Carole Marsh Connecticut Bks.). (Illus.). (YA). (gr. 3-12). 1994. pap. 19.95 (0-7933-0225-0); lib. bdg. 29.95 (0-7933-0226-9); disk 29.95 (0-7933-0227-7) Gallopade Intl.

— The Connecticut Library Book: A Surprising Guide to the Unusual Special Collections in Libraries Across Our State for Students, Teachers, Writers & Publishers - Includes Reproducible Mailing Labels Plus Activities for Young People! (Carole Marsh Connecticut Bks.). (Illus.). 1994. pap. 19.95 (0-7933-3159-5); lib. bdg. 29.95 (0-7933-3158-7); disk 29.95 (0-7933-3160-9) Gallopade Intl.

— Connecticut Math! How It All Adds up in Our State. (Carole Marsh Connecticut Bks.). (Illus.). (YA). (gr. 3-12). 1996. pap. 19.95 (0-7933-6506-6); lib. bdg. 29.95 (0-7933-6505-8) Gallopade Intl.

— The Connecticut Media Book: A Surprising Guide to the Amazing Print, Broadcast & Online Media of Our State for Students, Teachers, Writers & Publishers - Includes Reproducible Mailing Labels Plus Activities for Young People! (Carole Marsh Connecticut Bks.). (Illus.). 1994. pap. 19.95 (0-7933-3180-3); lib. bdg. 29.95 (0-7933-3179-X); disk 29.95 (0-7933-3181-1) Gallopade Intl.

— The Connecticut Mystery Van Takes Off! Book 1: Handicapped Connecticut Kids Sneak Off on a Big Adventure. (Carole Marsh Connecticut Bks.). (Illus.). (J). (gr. 3-12). 1994. 29.95 (0-7933-4982-6); pap. 19.95 (0-7933-4983-4); disk 29.95 (0-7933-4984-2) Gallopade Intl.

— Connecticut Quiz Bowl Crash Course! (Carole Marsh Connecticut Bks.). (Illus.). (YA). (gr. 3-12). 1994. pap. 19.95 (1-55609-544-9); lib. bdg. 29.95 (1-55609-545-7); disk 29.95 (0-7933-1432-1) Gallopade Intl.

— Connecticut Rollercoasters! (Carole Marsh Connecticut Bks.). (Illus.). (YA). (gr. 3-12). 1994. pap. 19.95 (0-7933-5243-6); lib. bdg. 29.95 (0-7933-5242-8); disk 29.95 (0-7933-5244-4) Gallopade Intl.

— Connecticut School Trivia: An Amazing & Fascinating Look at Our State's Teachers, Schools & Students! (Carole Marsh Connecticut Bks.). (Illus.). (YA). (gr. 3-12). 1994. pap. 19.95 (0-7933-0222-6); lib. bdg. 29.95 (0-7933-0223-4); disk 29.95 (0-7933-0224-2) Gallopade Intl.

— Connecticut Silly Basketball Sportsmysteries, Vol. I. (Carole Marsh Connecticut Bks.). (Illus.). (YA). (gr. 3-12). 1994. pap. 19.95 (0-7933-0219-6); lib. bdg. 29.95 (0-7933-0220-X); disk 29.95 (0-7933-0221-8) Gallopade Intl.

M

An Asterisk (*) at the beginning of an entry indicates that the title is appearing for the first time.

— Connecticut Silly Basketball Sportsmysteries, Vol. II. (Carole Marsh Connecticut Bks.). (Illus.). (J). (gr. 3-12). 1994. disk 29.95 (*0-7933-1582-4*) Gallopade Intl.

— Connecticut Silly Basketball Sportsmysteries, Vol. II. (Carole Marsh Connecticut Bks.). (Illus.). (YA). (gr. 3-12). 1994. pap. 19.95 (*0-7933-1581-6*); lib. bdg. 29.95 (*0-7933-1580-8*) Gallopade Intl.

— Connecticut Silly Football Sportsmysteries, Vol. I. (Carole Marsh Connecticut Bks.). (Illus.). (YA). (gr. 3-12). 1994. pap. 19.95 (*1-55609-540-6*); lib. bdg. 29.95 (*1-55609-541-4*); disk 29.95 (*0-7933-1425-9*) Gallopade Intl.

— Connecticut Silly Football Sportsmysteries, Vol. II. (Carole Marsh Connecticut Bks.). (Illus.). (YA). (gr. 3-12). 1994. pap. 19.95 (*0-7933-1427-5*); lib. bdg. 29.95 (*0-7933-1426-7*); disk 29.95 (*0-7933-1428-3*) Gallopade Intl.

— Connecticut Silly Trivia! (Carole Marsh Connecticut Bks.). (Illus.). (YA). (gr. 3-12). 1994. pap. 29.95 (*1-55609-535-X*); lib. bdg. 24.95 (*1-55609-536-8*); disk 29.95 (*0-7933-1422-4*) Gallopade Intl.

— Connecticut Spelling Bee! Score Big by Correctly Spelling Our State's Unique Names. (Carole Marsh Connecticut Bks.). (Illus.). (YA). (gr. 3-12). 1996. pap. 19.95 (*0-7933-6659-3*); lib. bdg. 29.95 (*0-7933-6658-5*) Gallopade Intl.

— Connecticut Timeline: A Chronology of Connecticut History, Mystery, Trivia, Legend, Lore & More. (Carole Marsh Connecticut Bks.). (Illus.). (J). (gr. 3-12). 1994. pap. 19.95 (*0-7933-5894-9*); lib. bdg. 29.95 (*0-7933-5893-0*); disk 29.95 (*0-7933-5895-7*) Gallopade Intl.

— Connecticut 2000! Coming Soon to a Calendar Near You - The 21st Century! - Complete Set of AL 2000 Items. (Two Thousand! Ser.). (Illus.). (J). (gr. 3-12). 1998. lib. bdg. 85.00 (*0-7933-9322-1*) Gallopade Intl.

***Marsh, Carole.** Connecticut 2000! Coming Soon to a Calendar Near You - The 21st Century! - Complete Set of AL 2000 Items. (Two Thousand! Ser.). (Illus.). (J). (gr. 3-12). 1998. pap. 75.00 (*0-7933-9321-3*) Gallopade Intl.

Marsh, Carole. Connecticut 2000! Coming Soon to a Calendar near You--The 21st Century! (Two Thousand! Ser.). (Illus.). (J). (gr. 3-12). 1998. pap. 19.95 (*0-7933-8694-2*); lib. bdg. 29.95 (*0-7933-8693-4*) Gallopade Intl.

— Connecticut UFO's & Extraterrestrials! A Look at the Sightings & Science in Our State. (Carole Marsh Connecticut Bks.). (Illus.). (J). (gr. 3-12). 1997. pap. 19.95 (*0-7933-6353-5*); lib. bdg. 29.95 (*0-7933-6352-7*) Gallopade Intl.

***Marsh, Carole.** Connecticut's Big Activity Book. (Connecticut Experience! Ser.). (Illus.). (J). (gr. k-5). 2000. pap. 9.95 (*0-7933-9582-8*) Gallopade Intl.

Marsh, Carole. Connecticut's (Most Devastating!) Disasters & (Most Calamitous!) Catastrophies! (Carole Marsh Connecticut Bks.). (Illus.). (YA). (gr. 3-12). 1994. pap. 19.95 (*0-7933-0210-2*); lib. bdg. 29.95 (*0-7933-0211-0*); disk 29.95 (*0-7933-0212-9*) Gallopade Intl.

— Connecticut's Unsolved Mysteries (& Their "Solutions") Includes Scientific Information & Other Activities for Students. (Carole Marsh Connecticut Bks.). (Illus.). (J). (gr. 3-12). 1994. pap. 19.95 (*0-7933-5741-1*); lib. bdg. 29.95 (*0-7933-5740-3*); disk 29.95 (*0-7933-5742-X*) Gallopade Intl.

***Marsh, Carole.** The Cool California Coloring Book. (California Experience! Ser.). (Illus.). (J). (gr. k-5). 2000. pap. 3.95 (*0-7933-9467-8*) Gallopade Intl.

— The Cool Colorado Coloring Book. (Colorado Experience! Ser.). (Illus.). (J). (gr. k-5). 2000. pap. 3.95 (*0-7933-9607-7*) Gallopade Intl.

— The Cool Connecticut Coloring Book. (Connecticut Experience! Ser.). (Illus.). (J). (gr. k-5). 2000. pap. 3.95 (*0-7933-9583-6*) Gallopade Intl.

Marsh, Carole. Could Your Kid Die "Laughing"? AIDS & Today's Adolescent. (Smart Sex Stuff Ser.). (Orig.). 1994. 29.95 (*1-55609-262-8*); pap. 19.95 (*1-55609-225-3*) Gallopade Intl.

— Crazy Comet Classroom Gamebook. (Carole Marsh Bks.). (Illus.). (Orig.). (J). (gr. 3-12). 1994. pap. 19.95 (*0-935326-87-1*) Gallopade Intl.

— The Crazy Comet Silly Trivia Book. (Gallopade Galaxy Ser.). (Illus.). 60p. (Orig.). (J). (gr. 2-12). 1994. pap. 19.95 (*0-935326-64-2*) Gallopade Intl.

— Cross Staff: A Fictional Journal of Eleanor Dare. (Lost Colony Collection). (Illus.). 200p. (Orig.). 1994. pap. 19.95 (*0-935326-44-8*) Gallopade Intl.

— Crosstaff: Journal Writing Activity Kit. (Carole Marsh Bks.). (Illus.). (Orig.). (J). (gr. 4-12). 1994. pap. 19.95 (*0-935326-23-5*) Gallopade Intl.

— Death Valley! Includes an Original Mystery Story, "The Secret of Scotty's Castle!" (Interactive Multimedia Titles Ser.). (J). (gr. 2-9). 1996. 29.95 (*0-7933-7598-3*, C Marsh); pap. 19.95 (*0-7933-7599-1*, C Marsh); pap., teacher ed. 19.95 (*0-7933-7839-7*, C Marsh) Gallopade Intl.

— Delaware & Other State Greats (Biographies) (Carole Marsh Delaware Bks.). (Illus.). (YA). (gr. 3-12). 1994. pap. 19.95 (*1-55609-557-0*); lib. bdg. 29.95 (*1-55609-558-9*); disk 29.95 (*0-7933-1455-0*) Gallopade Intl.

— Delaware Bandits, Bushwackers, Outlaws, Crooks, Devils, Ghosts, Desperadoes & Other Assorted & Sundry Characters! (Carole Marsh Delaware Bks.). (Illus.). (YA). (gr. 3-12). 1994. pap. 19.95 (*0-7933-0237-4*); lib. bdg. 29.95 (*0-7933-0238-2*); disk 29.95 (*0-7933-0239-0*) Gallopade Intl.

— Delaware "BIO" Bingo! 24 Must Know State People for Kids to Learn about While Having Fun! (Bingo! Ser.). (Illus.). (J). (gr. 2-8). 1998. pap. 14.95 (*0-7933-8546-6*) Gallopade Intl.

— The Delaware Bookstore Book: A Surprising Guide to Our State's Bookstores & Their Specialties for Students, Teachers, Writers & Publishers. (Carole Marsh Delaware Bks.). (Illus.). 1994. pap. 19.95 (*0-7933-2877-2*); lib. bdg. 29.95 (*0-7933-2876-4*); disk 29.95 (*0-7933-2878-0*) Gallopade Intl.

— Delaware Classic Christmas Trivia: Stories, Recipes, Activities, Legends, Lore & More! (Carole Marsh Delaware Bks.). (Illus.). (YA). (gr. 3-12). 1994. pap. 19.95 (*0-7933-0240-4*); lib. bdg. 29.95 (*0-7933-0241-2*); disk 29.95 (*0-7933-0242-0*) Gallopade Intl.

— Delaware Coastales. (Carole Marsh Delaware Bks.). (Illus.). (YA). (gr. 3-12). 1994. pap. 19.95 (*1-55609-553-8*); lib. bdg. 29.95 (*1-55609-554-6*); disk 29.95 (*0-7933-1451-8*) Gallopade Intl.

— Delaware Coastales! (Carole Marsh Delaware Bks.). (J). 1994. lib. bdg. 29.95 (*0-7933-7272-0*) Gallopade Intl.

— Delaware "Crinkum-Crankum" A Funny Word Book about Our State. (Carole Marsh Delaware Bks.). (Illus.). (J). 1994. pap. 19.95 (*0-7933-4832-3*); lib. bdg. 29.95 (*0-7933-4831-5*); disk 29.95 (*0-7933-4833-1*) Gallopade Intl.

— Delaware Dingbats! Bk. 1: A Fun Book of Games, Stories, Activities & More about Our State That's All in Code! for You to Decipher. (Carole Marsh Delaware Bks.). (Illus.). (J). (gr. 3-12). 1994. pap. 19.95 (*0-7933-3795-X*); lib. bdg. 29.95 (*0-7933-3794-1*); disk 29.95 (*0-7933-3796-8*) Gallopade Intl.

— Delaware Facts & Factivities. (Carole Marsh State Bks.). (Illus.). (J). (gr. 4-7). 1996. pap., teacher ed. 19.95 (*0-7933-7861-3*, C Marsh) Gallopade Intl.

— Delaware Festival Fun for Kids! (Carole Marsh Delaware Bks.). (Illus.). (YA). (gr. 3-12). 1994. pap. 19.95 (*0-7933-3948-0*); lib. bdg. 29.95 (*0-7933-3947-2*); disk 29.95 (*0-7933-3949-9*) Gallopade Intl.

— Delaware "GEO" Bingo! 38 Must Know State Geography Facts for Kids to Learn While Having Fun! (Bingo! Ser.). (Illus.). (gr. 2-8). 1998. pap. 14.95 (*0-7933-8547-4*) Gallopade Intl.

— Delaware Government! The Cornerstone of Everyday Life in Our State! (Carole Marsh Delaware Bks.). (Illus.). (J). (gr. 3-12). 1996. pap. 19.95 (*0-7933-6203-2*); lib. bdg. 29.95 (*0-7933-6202-4*); disk 29.95 (*0-7933-6204-0*) Gallopade Intl.

— Delaware "HISTO" Bingo! 42 Must Know State History Facts for Kids to Learn While Having Fun! (Bingo! Ser.). (Illus.). (J). (gr. 2-8). 1998. pap. 14.95 (*0-7933-8548-2*) Gallopade Intl.

— Delaware History! Surprising Secrets about Our State's Founding Mothers, Fathers & Kids! (Carole Marsh Delaware Bks.). (Illus.). (J). (gr. 3-12). 1996. pap. 19.95 (*0-7933-6050-1*); lib. bdg. 29.95 (*0-7933-6049-8*); disk 29.95 (*0-7933-6051-X*) Gallopade Intl.

— The Delaware Hot Air Balloon Mystery. (Carole Marsh Delaware Bks.). (Illus.). (J). (gr. 2-9). 1994. pap. 19.95 (*0-7933-2382-7*); disk 29.95 (*0-7933-2383-5*) Gallopade Intl.

— The Delaware Hot Air Balloon Mystery. (Carole Marsh Delaware Bks.). (Illus.). (J). (gr. 2-9). 1997. 29.95 (*0-7933-2381-9*) Gallopade Intl.

— Delaware Hot Zones! Viruses, Diseases, & Epidemics in Our State's History. (Hot Zones! Ser.). (Illus.). (J). (gr. 3-12). 1998. pap. 19.95 (*0-7933-8850-3*); lib. bdg. 29.95 (*0-7933-8849-X*) Gallopade Intl.

— Delaware Indian Dictionary for Kids! (Carole Marsh State Bks.). (J). (gr. 2-9). 1996. 29.95 (*0-7933-7665-3*, C Marsh); pap. 19.95 (*0-7933-7666-1*, C Marsh) Gallopade Intl.

— Delaware Jeopardy! Answers & Questions about Our State! (Carole Marsh Delaware Bks.). (Illus.). (J). (gr. 3-12). 1994. pap. 19.95 (*0-7933-4101-9*); lib. bdg. 29.95 (*0-7933-4100-0*); disk 29.95 (*0-7933-4102-7*) Gallopade Intl.

— Delaware "Jography" A Fun Run Thru Our State! (Carole Marsh Delaware Bks.). (Illus.). (YA). (gr. 3-12). 1994. pap. 19.95 (*1-55609-550-3*); lib. bdg. 29.95 (*1-55609-551-1*); disk 29.95 (*0-7933-1439-9*) Gallopade Intl.

— Delaware Kid's Cookbook: Recipes, How-to-, History, Lore & More! (Carole Marsh Delaware Bks.). (Illus.). (YA). (gr. 3-12). 1994. pap. 19.95 (*0-7933-0249-8*); lib. bdg. 29.95 (*0-7933-0250-1*); disk 29.95 (*0-7933-0251-X*) Gallopade Intl.

— The Delaware Library Book: A Surprising Guide to the Unusual Special Collections in Libraries Across Our State for Students, Teachers, Writers & Publishers - Includes Reproducible Mailing Labels Plus Activities for Young People! (Carole Marsh Delaware Bks.). (Illus.). 1994. pap. 19.95 (*0-7933-3027-0*); lib. bdg. 29.95 (*0-7933-3026-2*); disk 29.95 (*0-7933-3028-9*) Gallopade Intl.

— Delaware Math! How It All Adds up in Our State. (Carole Marsh Delaware Bks.). (Illus.). (YA). (gr. 3-12). 1996. pap. 19.95 (*0-7933-6509-0*); lib. bdg. 29.95 (*0-7933-6508-2*) Gallopade Intl.

— The Delaware Media Book: A Surprising Guide to the Amazing Print, Broadcast & Online Media of Our State for Students, Teachers, Writers & Publishers - Includes Reproducible Mailing Labels Plus Activities for Young People! (Carole Marsh Delaware Bks.). (Illus.). 1994. pap. 19.95 (*0-7933-3183-8*); lib. bdg. 29.95 (*0-7933-3182-X*); disk 29.95 (*0-7933-3184-6*) Gallopade Intl.

— The Delaware Mystery Van Takes Off! Book 1: Handicapped Delaware Kids Sneak Off on a Big Adventure. (Carole Marsh Delaware Bks.). (Illus.). (J). (gr. 3-12). 1994. 29.95 (*0-7933-4985-0*); pap. 19.95 (*0-7933-4986-9*); disk 29.95 (*0-7933-4987-7*) Gallopade Intl.

— Delaware Quiz Bowl Crash Course! (Carole Marsh Delaware Bks.). (Illus.). (YA). (gr. 3-12). 1994. pap. 19.95 (*1-55609-555-4*); lib. bdg. 29.95 (*1-55609-556-2*); disk 29.95 (*0-7933-1450-X*) Gallopade Intl.

— Delaware Rollercoasters! (Carole Marsh Delaware Bks.). (Illus.). (YA). (gr. 3-12). 1994. pap. 19.95 (*0-7933-5246-0*); lib. bdg. 29.95 (*0-7933-5245-2*); disk 29.95 (*0-7933-5247-9*) Gallopade Intl.

— Delaware School Trivia: An Amazing & Fascinating Look at Our State's Teachers, Schools & Students! (Carole Marsh Delaware Bks.). (Illus.). (YA). (gr. 3-12). 1994. pap. 19.95 (*0-7933-0246-3*); lib. bdg. 29.95 (*0-7933-0247-1*); disk 29.95 (*0-7933-0248-X*) Gallopade Intl.

— Delaware Silly Basketball Sportsmysteries, Vol. I. (Carole Marsh Delaware Bks.). (Illus.). (YA). (gr. 3-12). 1994. pap. 19.95 (*0-7933-0243-9*); lib. bdg. 29.95 (*0-7933-0244-7*); disk 29.95 (*0-7933-0245-5*) Gallopade Intl.

— Delaware Silly Basketball Sportsmysteries, Vol. II. (Carole Marsh Delaware Bks.). (Illus.). (YA). (gr. 3-12). 1994. pap. 19.95 (*0-7933-1457-7*); lib. bdg. 29.95 (*0-7933-1456-9*); disk 29.95 (*0-7933-1458-5*) Gallopade Intl.

— Delaware Silly Football Sportsmysteries, Vol. I. (Carole Marsh Delaware Bks.). (Illus.). (YA). (gr. 3-12). 1994. pap. 19.95 (*0-7933-1442-9*); lib. bdg. 29.95 (*0-7933-1441-0*); disk 29.95 (*0-7933-1443-7*) Gallopade Intl.

— Delaware Silly Football Sportsmysteries, Vol. II. (Carole Marsh Delaware Bks.). (Illus.). (YA). (gr. 3-12). 1994. pap. 19.95 (*0-7933-1445-3*); lib. bdg. 29.95 (*0-7933-1444-5*); disk 29.95 (*0-7933-1446-1*) Gallopade Intl.

— Delaware Silly Trivia! (Carole Marsh Delaware Bks.). (Illus.). (YA). (gr. 3-12). 1994. pap. 19.95 (*1-55609-548-1*); lib. bdg. 29.95 (*1-55609-549-X*); disk 29.95 (*0-7933-1438-0*) Gallopade Intl.

— Delaware Spelling Bee! Score Big by Correctly Spelling Our State's Unique Names. (Carole Marsh Delaware Bks.). (Illus.). (YA). (gr. 3-12). 1996. pap. 19.95 (*0-7933-6662-3*); lib. bdg. 29.95 (*0-7933-6661-5*) Gallopade Intl.

— Delaware Timeline: A Chronology of Delaware History, Mystery, Trivia, Legend, Lore & More. (Carole Marsh Delaware Bks.). (Illus.). (J). (gr. 3-12). 1994. pap. 19.95 (*0-7933-5897-3*); lib. bdg. 29.95 (*0-7933-5896-5*); disk 29.95 (*0-7933-5898-1*) Gallopade Intl.

— Delaware 2000! Coming Soon to a Calendar Near You - The 21st Century! - Complete Set of AL 2000 Items. (Two Thousand! Ser.). (Illus.). (J). (gr. 3-12). 1998. pap. 75.00 (*0-7933-9323-X*); lib. bdg. 85.00 (*0-7933-9324-8*) Gallopade Intl.

— Delaware 2000! Coming Soon to a Calendar Near You-The 21st Century! (Two Thousand! Ser.). (Illus.). (J). (gr. 3-12). 1998. pap. 19.95 (*0-7933-8697-7*); lib. bdg. 29.95 (*0-7933-8696-9*) Gallopade Intl.

— Delaware UFO's & Extraterrestrials! A Look at the Sightings & Science in Our State. (Carole Marsh Delaware Bks.). (Illus.). (J). (gr. 3-12). 1997. pap. 19.95 (*0-7933-6356-X*); lib. bdg. 29.95 (*0-7933-6355-1*) Gallopade Intl.

— Delaware's (Most Devastating!) Disasters & (Most Calamitous!) Catastrophies! (Carole Marsh Delaware Bks.). (Illus.). (YA). (gr. 3-12). 1994. pap. 19.95 (*0-7933-0234-X*); lib. bdg. 29.95 (*0-7933-0235-8*); disk 29.95 (*0-7933-0236-6*) Gallopade Intl.

— Delaware's Unsolved Mysteries (& Their "Solutions") Includes Scientific Information & Other Activities for Students. (Carole Marsh Delaware Bks.). (Illus.). (J). (gr. 3-12). 1994. pap. 19.95 (*0-7933-5744-6*); lib. bdg. 29.95 (*0-7933-5743-8*); disk 29.95 (*0-7933-5745-4*) Gallopade Intl.

— Dinosaur Trivia for Kids: I'm Saury! (Quantum Leap Ser.). (Illus.). (Orig.). (J). (gr. 2 up). 1994. pap. 19.95 (*0-935326-54-5*); lib. bdg. 29.95 (*1-55609-162-1*) Gallopade Intl.

— District of Columbia Government! The Cornerstone of Everyday Life in Our State! (Carole Marsh District of Columbia Bks.). (Illus.). (J). (gr. 3-12). 1996. pap. 19.95 (*0-7933-6206-7*); lib. bdg. 29.95 (*0-7933-6205-9*); disk 29.95 (*0-7933-6207-5*) Gallopade Intl.

— District of Columbia History! Surprising Secrets about Our State's Founding Mothers, Fathers & Kids! (Carole Marsh District of Columbia Bks.). (Illus.). (J). (gr. 3-12). 1996. pap. 19.95 (*0-7933-6053-6*); lib. bdg. 29.95 (*0-7933-6052-8*); disk 29.95 (*0-7933-6054-4*) Gallopade Intl.

— District of Columbia Hot Zones! Viruses, Diseases, & Epidemics in Our State's History. (Hot Zones! Ser.). (Illus.). (J). (gr. 3-12). 1998. pap. 19.95 (*0-7933-8853-8*); lib. bdg. 29.95 (*0-7933-8852-X*) Gallopade Intl.

— District of Columbia Math! How It All Adds up in Our State. (Carole Marsh Washington, D. C. Bks.). (Illus.). (J). (gr. 3-12). 1996. pap. 19.95 (*0-7933-6512-0*); lib. bdg. 29.95 (*0-7933-6511-2*) Gallopade Intl.

— District of Columbia Spelling Bee! Score Big by Correctly Spelling Our State's Unique Names. (Carole Marsh District of Columbia Bks.). (Illus.). (J). (gr. 3-12). 1996. pap. 19.95 (*0-7933-6665-8*); lib. bdg. 29.95 (*0-7933-6664-X*) Gallopade Intl.

— District of Columbia 2000! Coming Soon to a Calendar Near You - The 21st Century! - Complete Set of AL 2000 Items. (Two Thousand! Ser.). (Illus.). (J). (gr. 3-12). 1998. pap. 75.00 (*0-7933-9325-6*); lib. bdg. 85.00 (*0-7933-9326-4*) Gallopade Intl.

— District of Columbia 2000! Coming Soon to a Calendar Near You-The 21st Century! (Two Thousand! Ser.). (Illus.). (J). (gr. 3-12). 1998. pap. 19.95 (*0-7933-8700-0*); lib. bdg. 29.95 (*0-7933-8699-3*) Gallopade Intl.

— The Dragons & Dungeons Dingbats Book. (Carole Marsh Dingbats Bks.). (Illus.). (J). (gr. 3-12). 1994. pap. 19.95 (*0-7933-5396-3*); lib. bdg. 29.95 (*0-7933-5395-5*); disk 29.95 (*0-7933-5397-1*) Gallopade Intl.

— The Drawers of Ocracoke. (Carole Marsh Short Story Ser.). (Illus.). (Orig.). (J). (ps-7). 1994. 29.95 (*1-55609-163-X*); pap. 19.95 (*1-55609-236-9*) Gallopade Intl.

— Evereeady Editorial: How to Write a New Book Every Day! (Lifewrite Ser.). 1994. 29.95 (*1-55609-956-8*); pap. text 19.95 (*1-55609-955-X*); lib. bdg. 29.95 (*1-55609-954-1*); disk 29.95 (*1-55609-957-6*) Gallopade Intl.

***Marsh, Carole.** The Fabulous Florida Coloring Book. (The Florida Experience! Ser.). (Illus.). (J). (gr. k-5). 2000. pap. 3.95 (*0-7933-9468-6*) Gallopade Intl.

Marsh, Carole. First AIDS: Frank Facts for Kids. (Smart Sex Stuff Ser.). (Orig.). 1994. 29.95 (*1-55609-153-2*); pap. 19.95 (*1-55609-205-9*) Gallopade Intl.

***Marsh, Carole.** The First Woman President of the United States of America! When Will We Get One? Who Will It Be?! (First Woman President Ser.). (Illus.). (YA). (gr. 3-12). 1999. pap. 19.95 (*0-7933-9433-3*); lib. bdg. 29.95 (*0-7933-9434-1*) Gallopade Intl.

Marsh, Carole. Florida & Other State Greats (Biographies) Florida Bks. (Illus.). (YA). (gr. 3-12). 1994. pap. 19.95 (*1-55609-425-6*); lib. bdg. 29.95 (*1-55609-426-4*); disk 29.95 (*0-7933-1501-8*) Gallopade Intl.

— Florida Bandits, Bushwackers, Outlaws, Crooks, Devils, Ghosts, Desperadoes & Other Assorted & Sundry Characters! (Carole Marsh Florida Bks.). (Illus.). (YA). (gr. 3-12). 1994. pap. 19.95 (*0-7933-0285-4*); lib. bdg. 29.95 (*0-7933-0286-2*); disk 29.95 (*0-7933-0287-0*) Gallopade Intl.

— Florida "BIO" Bingo! 24 Must Know State People for Kids to Learn about While Having Fun! (Bingo! Ser.). (Illus.). (J). (gr. 2-8). 1998. pap. 14.95 (*0-7933-8549-0*) Gallopade Intl.

— The Florida Bookstore Book: A Surprising Guide to Our State's Bookstores & Their Specialties for Students, Teachers, Writers & Publishers. (Carole Marsh Florida Bks.). (Illus.). 1994. pap. 19.95 (*0-7933-2883-7*); lib. bdg. 29.95 (*0-7933-2882-9*); disk 29.95 (*0-7933-2884-5*) Gallopade Intl.

— Florida Classic Christmas Trivia: Stories, Recipes, Activities, Legends, Lore & More! (Carole Marsh Florida Bks.). (Illus.). (YA). (gr. 3-12). 1994. pap. 19.95 (*0-7933-0288-9*); lib. bdg. 29.95 (*0-7933-0289-7*); disk 29.95 (*0-7933-0290-0*) Gallopade Intl.

— Florida Coastales. (Carole Marsh Florida Bks.). (Illus.). (YA). (gr. 3-12). 1994. pap. 19.95 (*1-55609-118-4*); lib. bdg. 29.95 (*1-55609-422-1*); disk 29.95 (*0-7933-1497-6*) Gallopade Intl.

— Florida Coastales! (Carole Marsh Florida Bks.). (J). 1994. lib. bdg. 29.95 (*0-7933-7274-7*) Gallopade Intl.

— Florida "Crinkum-Crankum" A Funny Word Book about Our State. (Carole Marsh Florida Bks.). (Illus.). (J). 1994. pap. 19.95 (*0-7933-4835-8*); lib. bdg. 29.95 (*0-7933-4834-X*); disk 29.95 (*0-7933-4836-6*) Gallopade Intl.

— Florida Dingbats! Bk. 1: A Fun Book of Games, Stories, Activities & More about Our State That's All in Code! for You to Decipher. (Carole Marsh Florida Bks.). (Illus.). (J). (gr. 3-12). 1994. pap. 19.95 (*0-7933-3801-8*); lib. bdg. 29.95 (*0-7933-3800-X*); disk 29.95 (*0-7933-3802-6*) Gallopade Intl.

***Marsh, Carole.** The Florida Experience Pocket Guide. (Florida Experience! Ser.). (Illus.). (J). 2000. pap. 6.95 (*0-7933-9448-1*) Gallopade Intl.

Marsh, Carole. Florida Facts & Factivities. (Carole Marsh State Bks.). (Illus.). (J). (gr. 4-7). 1996. pap., teacher ed. 19.95 (*0-7933-7865-6*, C Marsh) Gallopade Intl.

— Florida Festival Fun for Kids! (Carole Marsh Florida Bks.). (Illus.). (YA). (gr. 3-12). 1994. pap. 19.95 (*0-7933-3954-5*); lib. bdg. 29.95 (*0-7933-3953-7*); disk 29.95 (*0-7933-3955-3*) Gallopade Intl.

— Florida "GEO" Bingo! 38 Must Know State Geography Facts for Kids to Learn While Having Fun! (Bingo! Ser.). (Illus.). (J). (gr. 2-8). 1998. pap. 14.95 (*0-7933-8550-4*) Gallopade Intl.

— Florida Government! The Cornerstone of Everyday Life in Our State! (Carole Marsh Florida Bks.). (Illus.). (J). (gr. 3-12). 1996. pap. 19.95 (*0-7933-6209-1*); lib. bdg. 29.95 (*0-7933-6208-3*); disk 29.95 (*0-7933-6210-5*) Gallopade Intl.

— Florida "HISTO" Bingo! 42 Must Know State History Facts for Kids to Learn While Having Fun! (Bingo! Ser.). (Illus.). (J). (gr. 2-8). 1998. pap. 14.95 (*0-7933-8551-2*) Gallopade Intl.

— Florida History! Surprising Secrets about Our State's Founding Mothers, Fathers & Kids! (Carole Marsh Florida Bks.). (Illus.). (J). (gr. 3-12). 1996. pap. 19.95 (*0-7933-6056-0*); lib. bdg. 29.95 (*0-7933-6055-2*); disk 29.95 (*0-7933-6057-9*) Gallopade Intl.

— The Florida Hot Air Balloon Mystery. (Carole Marsh Florida Bks.). (Illus.). (J). (gr. 2-9). 1994. 29.95 (*0-7933-2399-1*); pap. 19.95 (*0-7933-2400-9*); disk 29.95 (*0-7933-2401-7*) Gallopade Intl.

— Florida Hot Zones! Viruses, Diseases, & Epidemics in Our State's History. (Hot Zones! Ser.). (Illus.). (J). (gr. 3-12). 1998. pap. 19.95 (*0-7933-8856-2*); lib. bdg. 29.95 (*0-7933-8855-4*) Gallopade Intl.

— Florida Indian Dictionary for Kids! (Carole Marsh State Bks.). (J). (gr. 2-9). 1996. 29.95 (*0-7933-7671-8*, C Marsh); pap. 19.95 (*0-7933-7672-6*, C Marsh) Gallopade Intl.

***Marsh, Carole.** Florida Jeopardy. (Florida Experience! Ser.). (Illus.). (J). (gr. 2-6). 2000. pap. 7.95 (*0-7933-9507-0*) Gallopade Intl.

Marsh, Carole. Florida Jeopardy! Answers & Questions about Our State! (Carole Marsh Florida Bks.). (Illus.). (J). (gr. 3-12). 1994. pap. 19.95 (*0-7933-4107-8*); lib. bdg. 29.95 (*0-7933-4106-X*); disk 29.95 (*0-7933-4108-6*) Gallopade Intl.

An Asterisk (*) at the beginning of an entry indicates that the title is appearing for the first time.

***Marsh, Carole.** Florida Jography. (Florida Experience! Ser.). (Illus.). (J). (gr. 2-6). 2000. pap. 7.95 (*0-7933-9508-9*) Gallopade Intl.

Marsh, Carole. Florida "Jography" A Fun Run Thru Our State! (Carole Marsh Florida Bks.). (Illus.). (YA). (gr. 3-12). 1994. pap. 19.95 (*1-55609-048-X*); lib. bdg. 29.95 (*1-55609-418-3*); disk 29.95 (*0-7933-1487-9*) Gallopade Intl.

— Florida Kid's Cookbook: Recipes, How-To, History, Lore & More! (Carole Marsh Florida Bks.). (Illus.). (YA). (gr. 3-12). 1994. pap. 19.95 (*0-7933-0297-8*); lib. bdg. 29.95 (*0-7933-0298-6*); disk 29.95 (*0-7933-0299-4*) Gallopade Intl.

— The Florida Library Book: A Surprising Guide to the Unusual Special Collections in Libraries Across Our State for Students, Teachers, Writers & Publishers - Includes Reproducible Mailing Labels Plus Activities for Young People! (Carole Marsh Florida Bks.). (Illus.). 1994. pap. 19.95 (*0-7933-3033-5*); lib. bdg. 29.95 (*0-7933-3032-7*); disk 29.95 (*0-7933-3034-3*) Gallopade Intl.

— Florida Math! How It All Adds up in Our State. (Carole Marsh Florida Bks.). (Illus.). (YA). (gr. 3-12). 1996. pap. 19.95 (*0-7933-6515-5*); lib. bdg. 29.95 (*0-7933-6514-7*) Gallopade Intl.

— The Florida Media Book: A Surprising Guide to the Amazing Print, Broadcast & Online Media of Our State for Students, Teachers, Writers & Publishers - Includes Reproducible Mailing Labels Plus Activities for Young People! (Carole Marsh Florida Bks.). (Illus.). 1994. pap. 19.95 (*0-7933-3189-7*); lib. bdg. 29.95 (*0-7933-3188-9*); disk 29.95 (*0-7933-3190-0*) Gallopade Intl.

— The Florida Mystery Van Takes Off! Book 1: Handicapped Florida Kids Sneak Off on a Big Adventure. (Carole Marsh Florida Bks.). (Illus.). (J). (gr. 3-12). 1994. 29.95 (*0-7933-4988-5*); pap. 19.95 (*0-7933-4989-3*); disk 29.95 (*0-7933-4990-7*) Gallopade Intl.

— Florida Quiz Bowl Crash Course! (Carole Marsh Florida Bks.). (Illus.). (YA). (gr. 3-12). 1994. pap. 19.95 (*1-55609-423-X*); lib. bdg. 29.95 (*1-55609-424-8*); disk 29.95 (*0-7933-1496-8*) Gallopade Intl.

— Florida Rollercoasters! (Carole Marsh Florida Bks.). (Illus.). (YA). (gr. 3-12). 1994. pap. 19.95 (*0-7933-5252-5*); lib. bdg. 29.95 (*0-7933-5251-7*); disk 29.95 (*0-7933-5253-3*) Gallopade Intl.

— Florida School Trivia: An Amazing & Fascinating Look at Our State's Teachers, Schools & Students! (Carole Marsh Florida Bks.). (Illus.). (YA). (gr. 3-12). 1994. pap. 19.95 (*0-7933-0294-3*); lib. bdg. 29.95 (*0-7933-0295-1*); disk 29.95 (*0-7933-0296-X*) Gallopade Intl.

— Florida Silly Basketball Sportsmysteries, Vol. I. (Carole Marsh Florida Bks.). (Illus.). (YA). (gr. 3-12). 1994. pap. 19.95 (*0-7933-0291-9*); lib. bdg. 29.95 (*0-7933-0292-7*); disk 29.95 (*0-7933-0293-5*) Gallopade Intl.

— Florida Silly Basketball Sportsmysteries, Vol. II. (Carole Marsh Florida Bks.). (Illus.). (YA). (gr. 3-12). 1994. pap. 19.95 (*0-7933-1503-4*); lib. bdg. 29.95 (*0-7933-1502-6*); disk 29.95 (*0-7933-1504-2*) Gallopade Intl.

— Florida Silly Football Sportsmysteries, Vol. I. (Carole Marsh Florida Bks.). (Illus.). (YA). (gr. 3-12). 1994. pap. 19.95 (*1-55609-420-5*); lib. bdg. 29.95 (*1-55609-421-3*); disk 29.95 (*0-7933-1489-5*) Gallopade Intl.

— Florida Silly Football Sportsmysteries, Vol. II. (Carole Marsh Florida Bks.). (Illus.). (YA). (gr. 3-12). 1994. pap. 19.95 (*0-7933-1491-7*); lib. bdg. 24.95 (*0-7933-1490-9*); disk 29.95 (*0-7933-1492-5*) Gallopade Intl.

— Florida Silly Trivia! (Carole Marsh Florida Bks.). (Illus.). (YA). (gr. 3-12). 1994. pap. 19.95 (*1-55609-037-4*); lib. bdg. 29.95 (*1-55609-417-5*); disk 29.95 (*0-7933-1486-0*) Gallopade Intl.

— Florida Spelling Bee! Score Big by Correctly Spelling Our State's Unique Names. (Carole Marsh Florida Bks.). (Illus.). (YA) (gr. 3-12). 1996. pap. 19.95 (*0-7933-6668-2*); lib. bdg. 29.95 (*0-7933-6667-4*) Gallopade Intl.

— Florida Timeline: A Chronology of Florida History, Mystery, Trivia, Legend, Lore & More. (Carole Marsh Florida Bks.). (Illus.). (J). (gr. 3-12). 1994. pap. 19.95 (*0-7933-5903-1*); lib. bdg. 29.95 (*0-7933-5902-3*); disk 29.95 (*0-7933-5904-X*) Gallopade Intl.

— Florida 2000! Coming Soon to a Calendar Near You - The 21st Century! - Complete Set of AL 2000 Items. (Two Thousand! Ser.). (Illus.). (J). (gr. 3-12). 1998. pap. 75.00 (*0-7933-9327-2*); lib. bdg. 85.00 (*0-7933-9328-0*) Gallopade Intl.

— Florida 2000! Coming Soon to a Calendar Near You-The 21st Century! (Two Thousand! Ser.). (Illus.). (J). (gr. 3-12). 1998. pap. 19.95 (*0-7933-8703-5*); lib. bdg. 29.95 (*0-7933-8702-7*) Gallopade Intl.

— Florida UFO's & Extraterrestrials! A Look at the Sightings & Science in Our State. (Carole Marsh Florida Bks.). (Illus.). (J). (gr. 3-12). 1997. pap. 19.95 (*0-7933-6362-4*); lib. bdg. 29.95 (*0-7933-6361-6*) Gallopade Intl.

***Marsh, Carole.** Florida's Big Activity Book. (Florida Experience! Ser.). (Illus.). (J). (gr. k-5). 2000. pap. 9.95 (*0-7933-9458-9*) Gallopade Intl.

Marsh, Carole. Florida's (Most Devastating!) Disasters & (Most Calamitous!) Catastrophies! (Carole Marsh Florida Bks.). (Illus.). (YA). (gr. 3-12). 1994. pap. 19.95 (*0-7933-0282-X*); lib. bdg. 29.95 (*0-7933-0283-8*); disk 29.95 (*0-7933-0284-6*) Gallopade Intl.

— Florida's Unsolved Mysteries (& Their "Solutions") Includes Scientific Information & Other Activities for Students. (Carole Marsh Florida Bks.). (Illus.). (J). (gr. 3-12). 1994. pap. 19.95 (*0-7933-5750-0*); lib. bdg. 29.95 (*0-7933-5749-7*); disk 29.95 (*0-7933-5751-9*) Gallopade Intl.

— For Your Eyes Only: Silly, Secret & Scary Code & Spy Trivia for Kids. (Carole Marsh Tennessee Bks.). (Illus.). (YA). (gr. 3-12). 1994. pap. 19.95 (*0-7933-5414-5*); lib. bdg. 29.95 (*0-7933-5413-7*); disk 29.95 (*0-7933-5415-3*) Gallopade Intl.

— The Fortune Cookie Christmas. (Illus.). (Orig.). (J). (gr. 3 up). 1994. 29.95 (*1-55609-285-7*); pap. 19.95 (*0-935326-53-7*) Gallopade Intl.

— The Four Hundred Year Old Cookbook. (Naked Gourmet Ser.). (Orig.). 1994. 29.95 (*1-55609-167-2*); pap. 19.95 (*1-55609-000-5*) Gallopade Intl.

***Marsh, Carole.** A Fun Book of Olympic Trivia: A - Z! Special Advance Edition!--2002 Winter Olympics, Salt Lake City, Utah! (Olympic Trivia for Kids! Ser.). (Illus.). (YA). (gr. 3-12). 1999. pap. 19.95 (*0-7933-9439-2*); lib. bdg. 29.95 (*0-7933-9440-6*) Gallopade Intl.

Marsh, Carole. A Fun Book of Olympic Trivia: A-Z! Including the 1998 Winter Olympics, Nagano, Japan! (Olympic Trivia for Kids! Ser.). (Illus.). (J). (gr. 3-12). 1998. pap. 19.95 (*0-7933-8521-0*); lib. bdg. 29.95 (*0-7933-8520-2*) Gallopade Intl.

— A Fun Book of Olympic Trivia: A-Z! Special Advance Edition!--2000 Summer Olympics, Sydney, Australia! (Olympic Trivia for Kids! Ser.). (Illus.). (J). (gr. 3-12). 1998. pap. 19.95 (*0-7933-8982-8*); lib. bdg. 29.95 (*0-7933-8981-X*) Gallopade Intl.

— A Fun Book of Olympic Trivia A-Z: 1886-1996! (J). 1994. pap. text 19.95 (*0-7933-6875-8*); lib. bdg. 29.95 (*0-7933-6876-6*); disk 29.95 (*0-7933-6877-4*) Gallopade Intl.

— Gee! Ology: Trivia for Kids. (Scientifically Speaking Ser.). (Illus.). (J). (gr. 3-12). 1994. pap. 19.95 (*1-55609-306-3*); lib. bdg. 29.95 (*1-55609-305-5*); disk 29.95 (*1-55609-307-1*) Gallopade Intl.

— Georgia & Other State Greats (Biographies) (Carole Marsh Georgia Bks.). (Illus.). (YA). (gr. 3-12). 1994. pap. 19.95 (*1-55609-391-8*); lib. bdg. 29.95 (*1-55609-392-6*); disk 29.95 (*0-7933-1520-4*) Gallopade Intl.

— Georgia Bandits, Bushwackers, Outlaws, Crooks, Devils, Ghosts, Desperadoes & Other Assorted & Sundry Characters! (Carole Marsh Georgia Bks.). (Illus.). (YA). (gr. 3-12). 1994. pap. 19.95 (*0-7933-0309-5*); lib. bdg. 29.95 (*0-7933-0310-9*); disk 29.95 (*0-7933-0311-7*) Gallopade Intl.

— Georgia "BIO" Bingo! 24 Must Know State People for Kids to Learn about While Having Fun! (Bingo! Ser.). (Illus.). (J). (gr. 2-8). 1998. pap. 14.95 (*0-7933-8552-0*) Gallopade Intl.

— The Georgia Bookstore Book: A Surprising Guide to Our State's Bookstores & Their Specialties for Students, Teachers, Writers & Publishers. (Carole Marsh Georgia Bks.). (Illus.). 1994. pap. 19.95 (*0-7933-2886-1*); lib. bdg. 29.95 (*0-7933-2885-3*); disk 29.95 (*0-7933-2887-X*) Gallopade Intl.

— Georgia Classic Christmas Trivia: Stories, Recipes, Activities, Legends, Lore & More! (Carole Marsh Georgia Bks.). (Illus.). (YA). (gr. 3-12). 1994. pap. 19.95 (*0-7933-0312-5*); lib. bdg. 29.95 (*0-7933-0313-3*); disk 29.95 (*0-7933-0314-1*) Gallopade Intl.

— Georgia Coastales. (Carole Marsh Georgia Bks.). (Illus.). (YA). (gr. 3-12). 1994. pap. 19.95 (*1-55609-117-6*); lib. bdg. 29.95 (*1-55609-233-4*); disk 29.95 (*0-7933-1516-6*) Gallopade Intl.

— Georgia Coastales! (Carole Marsh Georgia Bks.). (J). 1994. lib. bdg. 29.95 (*0-7933-7275-5*) Gallopade Intl.

— Georgia "Crinkum-Crankum" A Funny Word Book about Our State. (Carole Marsh Georgia Bks.). (Illus.). (J). 1994. pap. 19.95 (*0-7933-4838-2*); lib. bdg. 29.95 (*0-7933-4837-4*); disk 29.95 (*0-7933-4839-0*) Gallopade Intl.

— Georgia Dingbats! Bk. 1: A Fun Book of Games, Stories, Activities & More about Our State That's All in Code! for You to Decipher. (Carole Marsh Georgia Bks.). (Illus.). (J). (gr. 3-12). 1994. pap. 19.95 (*0-7933-3804-2*); lib. bdg. 29.95 (*0-7933-3803-4*); disk 29.95 (*0-7933-3805-0*) Gallopade Intl.

***Marsh, Carole.** The Georgia Experience Pocket Guide. (Georgia Experience! Ser.). (Illus.). (J). 2000. pap. 6.95 (*0-7933-9449-X*) Gallopade Intl.

Marsh, Carole. Georgia Facts & Factivities. (Carole Marsh State Bks.). (Illus.). (J). (gr. 4-7). 1996. pap., teacher ed. 19.95 (*0-7933-7867-2*) Gallopade Intl.

— Georgia Festival Fun for Kids! (Carole Marsh Georgia Bks.). (Illus.). (YA). (gr. 3-12). 1994. pap. 19.95 (*0-7933-3957-X*); lib. bdg. 29.95 (*0-7933-3956-1*); disk 29.95 (*0-7933-3958-8*) Gallopade Intl.

— Georgia "GEO" Bingo! 38 Must Know State Geography Facts for Kids to Learn While Having Fun! (Bingo! Ser.). (Illus.). (J). (gr. 2-8). 1998. pap. 14.95 (*0-7933-8553-9*) Gallopade Intl.

— Georgia Government! The Cornerstone of Everyday Life in Our State! (Carole Marsh Georgia Bks.). (Illus.). (J). (gr. 3-12). 1996. pap. 19.95 (*0-7933-6212-1*); lib. bdg. 29.95 (*0-7933-6211-3*); disk 29.95 (*0-7933-6213-X*) Gallopade Intl.

— Georgia "HISTO" Bingo! 42 Must Know State History Facts for Kids to Learn While Having Fun! (Bingo! Ser.). (Illus.). (J). (gr. 2-8). 1998. pap. 14.95 (*0-7933-8554-7*) Gallopade Intl.

— Georgia History! Surprising Secrets about Our State's Founding Mothers, Fathers & Kids! (Carole Marsh Georgia Bks.). (Illus.). (J). (gr. 3-12). 1996. pap. 19.95 (*0-7933-6059-5*); lib. bdg. 29.95 (*0-7933-6058-7*); disk 29.95 (*0-7933-6060-9*) Gallopade Intl.

— The Georgia Hot Air Balloon Mystery. (Carole Marsh Georgia Bks.). (Illus.). (J). (gr. 2-9). 1994. 29.95 (*0-7933-2408-4*); pap. 19.95 (*0-7933-2409-2*); disk 29.95 (*0-7933-2410-6*) Gallopade Intl.

— Georgia Hot Zones! Viruses, Diseases, & Epidemics in Our State's History. (Hot Zones! Ser.). (Illus.). (J). (gr. 3-12). 1998. pap. 19.95 (*0-7933-8859-7*); lib. bdg. 29.95 (*0-7933-8858-9*) Gallopade Intl.

— Georgia Indian Dictionary for Kids! (Carole Marsh State Bks.). (J). (gr. 2-9). 1996. 29.95 (*0-7933-7674-2*, C Marsh); pap. 19.95 (*0-7933-7675-0*, C Marsh) Gallopade Intl.

***Marsh, Carole.** Georgia Jeopardy. (Georgia Experience! Ser.). (Illus.). (J). (gr. 2-6). 2000. pap. 7.95 (*0-7933-9510-0*) Gallopade Intl.

Marsh, Carole. Georgia Jeopardy! Answers & Questions about Our State! (Carole Marsh Georgia Bks.). (Illus.). (J). (gr. 3-12). 1994. pap. 19.95 (*0-7933-4110-8*); lib. bdg. 29.95 (*0-7933-4109-4*); disk 29.95 (*0-7933-4111-6*) Gallopade Intl.

***Marsh, Carole.** Georgia Jography. (Georgia Experience! Ser.). (Illus.). (J). (gr. 2-6). 2000. 7.95 (*0-7933-9511-9*) Gallopade Intl.

Marsh, Carole. Georgia Jography: A Fun Run Through the Peach State. abr. ed. (Statemeant Ser.). (Illus.). 50p. (Orig.). (J). (gr. 4-8). 1994. pap. 19.95 (*0-935326-93-6*) Gallopade Intl.

— Georgia Kid's Cookbook: Recipes, How-To, History, Lore & More! (Carole Marsh Georgia Bks.). (Illus.). (YA). (gr. 3-12). 1994. pap. 19.95 (*0-7933-0321-4*); lib. bdg. 29.95 (*0-7933-0322-2*); disk 29.95 (*0-7933-0323-0*) Gallopade Intl.

— The Georgia Library Book: A Surprising Guide to the Unusual Special Collections in Libraries Across Our State for Students, Teachers, Writers & Publishers - Includes Reproducible Mailing Labels Plus Activities for Young People! (Carole Marsh Georgia Bks.). (Illus.). 1994. pap. 19.95 (*0-7933-3036-X*); lib. bdg. 29.95 (*0-7933-3035-1*); disk 29.95 (*0-7933-3037-8*) Gallopade Intl.

— Georgia Math! How It All Adds up in Our State. (Carole Marsh Georgia Bks.). (Illus.). (YA). (gr. 3-12). 1996. pap. 19.95 (*0-7933-6518-X*); lib. bdg. 29.95 (*0-7933-6517-1*) Gallopade Intl.

— The Georgia Media Book: A Surprising Guide to the Amazing Print, Broadcast & Online Media of Our State for Students, Teachers, Writers & Publishers - Includes Reproducible Mailing Labels Plus Activities for Young People! (Carole Marsh Georgia Bks.). (Illus.). 1994. pap. 19.95 (*0-7933-3192-7*); lib. bdg. 29.95 (*0-7933-3191-9*); disk 29.95 (*0-7933-3193-5*) Gallopade Intl.

— The Georgia Mystery Van Takes Off! Book 1: Handicapped Georgia Kids Sneak Off on a Big Adventure. (Carole Marsh Georgia Bks.). (Illus.). (J). (gr. 3-12). 1994. 29.95 (*0-7933-4991-5*); pap. 19.95 (*0-7933-4992-3*); disk 29.95 (*0-7933-4993-1*) Gallopade Intl.

— Georgia Quiz Bowl Crash Course! (Carole Marsh Georgia Bks.). (Illus.). (YA). (gr. 3-12). 1994. pap. 19.95 (*1-55609-383-7*); lib. bdg. 29.95 (*1-55609-384-5*); disk 29.95 (*0-7933-1515-8*) Gallopade Intl.

— Georgia Rollercoasters! (Carole Marsh Georgia Bks.). (Illus.). (YA). (gr. 3-12). 1994. pap. 19.95 (*0-7933-5255-X*); lib. bdg. 29.95 (*0-7933-5254-1*); disk 29.95 (*0-7933-5256-8*) Gallopade Intl.

— Georgia School Trivia: An Amazing & Fascinating Look at Our State's Teachers, Schools & Students! (Carole Marsh Georgia Bks.). (Illus.). (YA). (gr. 3-12). 1994. pap. 19.95 (*0-7933-0318-4*); lib. bdg. 29.95 (*0-7933-0319-2*); disk 29.95 (*0-7933-0320-6*) Gallopade Intl.

— Georgia Silly Basketball Sportsmysteries, Vol. I. (Carole Marsh Georgia Bks.). (Illus.). (YA). (gr. 3-12). 1994. pap. 19.95 (*0-7933-0315-X*); lib. bdg. 29.95 (*0-7933-0316-8*); disk 29.95 (*0-7933-0317-6*) Gallopade Intl.

— Georgia Silly Basketball Sportsmysteries, Vol. II. (Carole Marsh Georgia Bks.). (Illus.). (YA). (gr. 3-12). 1994. pap. 19.95 (*0-7933-1522-0*); lib. bdg. 29.95 (*0-7933-1521-2*); disk 29.95 (*0-7933-1523-9*) Gallopade Intl.

— Georgia Silly Football Sportsmysteries, Vol. I. (Carole Marsh Georgia Bks.). (Illus.). (YA). (gr. 3-12). 1994. pap. 19.95 (*1-55609-393-4*); lib. bdg. 29.95 (*1-55609-394-2*); disk 29.95 (*0-7933-1508-5*) Gallopade Intl.

— Georgia Silly Football Sportsmysteries, Vol. II. (Carole Marsh Georgia Bks.). (Illus.). (YA). (gr. 3-12). 1994. pap. 19.95 (*0-7933-1510-7*); lib. bdg. 29.95 (*0-7933-1509-3*); disk 29.95 (*0-7933-1511-5*) Gallopade Intl.

— Georgia Silly Trivia Book. (Statemeant Ser.). (Illus.). 48p. (Orig.). (J). (gr. 2-12). 1994. pap. 19.95 (*0-935326-61-8*) Gallopade Intl.

— Georgia Spelling Bee! Score Big by Correctly Spelling Our State's Unique Names. (Carole Marsh Georgia Bks.). (Illus.). (YA). (gr. 3-12). 1996. pap. 19.95 (*0-7933-6671-2*); lib. bdg. 29.95 (*0-7933-6670-4*) Gallopade Intl.

— Georgia Timeline: A Chronology of Georgia History, Mystery, Trivia, Legend, Lore & More. (Carole Marsh Georgia Bks.). (Illus.). (J). (gr. 3-12). 1994. pap. 19.95 (*0-7933-5906-6*); lib. bdg. 29.95 (*0-7933-5905-8*); disk 29.95 (*0-7933-5907-4*) Gallopade Intl.

— Georgia 2000! Coming Soon to a Calendar Near You - The 21st Century! - Complete Set of AL 2000 Items. (Two Thousand! Ser.). (Illus.). (J). (gr. 3-12). 1998. pap. 75.00 (*0-7933-9329-9*) Gallopade Intl.

— Georgia 2000! Coming Soon to a Calendar Near You - The 21st Century! - Complete Set of AL 2000 Items. (Two Thousand! Ser.). (Illus.). (YA). (gr. 3-12). 1998. lib. bdg. 85.00 (*0-7933-9330-2*) Gallopade Intl.

— Georgia 2000! Coming Soon to a Calendar Near You-The 21st Century! (Two Thousand! Ser.). (Illus.). (J). (gr. 3-12). 1998. pap. 19.95 (*0-7933-8706-X*); lib. bdg. 29.95 (*0-7933-8705-1*) Gallopade Intl.

— Georgia UFO's & Extraterrestrials! A Look at the Sightings & Science in Our State. (Carole Marsh Georgia Bks.). (J). (gr. 3-12). 1997. pap. 19.95 (*0-7933-6365-9*); lib. bdg. 29.95 (*0-7933-6364-0*) Gallopade Intl.

***Marsh, Carole.** Georgia's Big Activity Book. (Georgia Experience! Ser.). (Illus.). (J). (gr. k-5). 2000. pap. 9.95 (*0-7933-9459-7*) Gallopade Intl.

Marsh, Carole. Georgia's (Most Devastating!) Disasters & (Most Calamitous!) Catastrophies! (Carole Marsh Georgia Bks.). (Illus.). (YA). (gr. 3-12). 1994. pap. 19.95 (*0-7933-0306-0*); lib. bdg. 29.95 (*0-7933-0307-9*); disk 29.95 (*0-7933-0308-7*) Gallopade Intl.

— Georgia's Unsolved Mysteries (& Their "Solutions") Includes Scientific Information & Other Activities for Students. (Carole Marsh Georgia Bks.). (Illus.). (J). (gr. 3-12). 1994. pap. 19.95 (*0-7933-5753-5*); lib. bdg. 29.95 (*0-7933-5752-7*); disk 29.95 (*0-7933-5754-3*) Gallopade Intl.

— The Ghost & Graveyards Dingbats Book. (Carole Marsh Dingbats Bks.). (Illus.). (J). (gr. 3-12). 1994. pap. 19.95 (*0-7933-5387-4*); lib. bdg. 29.95 (*0-7933-5386-6*); disk 29.95 (*0-7933-5388-2*) Gallopade Intl.

— The Ghost of Glencastle Set. (Carole Marsh Mysteries Ser.). 1994. teacher ed. 125.00 (*0-7933-6961-4*) Gallopade Intl.

— Ghost of the Bed & Breakfast. (Ghostest with the Mostest Ser.). (Illus.). 48p. (J). (ps-7). 1994. 29.95 (*1-55609-155-9*); pap. 19.95 (*1-55609-239-3*) Gallopade Intl.

— Gigantic Titanic Trivia for Kids! (Titanic for Kids! Ser.). (Illus.). 1998. pap. 19.95 (*0-7933-8988-7*, C Marsh); pap., teacher ed. 19.95 (*0-7933-8987-9*, C Marsh); pap., teacher ed. 19.95 (*0-7933-8989-5*, C Marsh) Gallopade Intl.

— Gigantic Titanic Trivia for Kids! (Titanic for Kids! Ser.). (Illus.). (J). (gr. 3-6). 1998. pap. 19.95 (*0-7933-8985-2*, C Marsh); lib. bdg. 29.95 (*0-7933-8984-4*, C Marsh) Gallopade Intl.

— Go Queen Go! Chess for Kids. (Quantum Leap Ser.). (Illus.). 48p. (J). (gr. k-12). 1994. 29.95 (*1-55609-160-5*); pap. 19.95 (*0-935326-14-6*) Gallopade Intl.

— Gold Shines Forever! The Discovery & Recovery of the Spanish Treasure Ship Atocha. (Carole Marsh Florida Bks.). (J). 1994. pap. 19.95 (*0-7933-7319-0*); lib. bdg. 29.95 (*0-7933-7586-X*) Gallopade Intl.

— Grand Canyon! A Top to Bottom Look at the Mother of All Holes. (CD-ROM Titles Ser.). (J). (gr. 2-9). 1996. pap. 19.95 (*0-7933-7603-3*, C Marsh); pap., teacher ed. 19.95 (*0-7933-7833-8*, C Marsh) Gallopade Intl.

— Grand Canyon! A Top to Bottom Look at the Mother of All Holes in the Ground. (CD-ROM Titles Ser.). (J). (gr. 2-9). 1996. 29.95 (*0-7933-7602-5*, C Marsh) Gallopade Intl.

— Grits R Us Cookbook. (Naked Gourmet Ser.). (Orig.). 1994. 29.95 (*1-55609-168-0*); pap. 19.95 (*1-55609-003-X*) Gallopade Intl.

***Marsh, Carole.** The Groovy Georgia Coloring Book. (Georgia Experience! Ser.). (Illus.). (J). (gr. k-5). 2000. pap. 3.95 (*0-7933-9469-4*) Gallopade Intl.

Marsh, Carole. The Hairy Horrors Dingbats Book. (Carole Marsh Dingbats Bks.). (Illus.). (J). (gr. 3-12). 1994. pap. 19.95 (*0-7933-5405-6*); lib. bdg. 29.95 (*0-7933-5404-8*); disk 29.95 (*0-7933-5406-4*) Gallopade Intl.

— Halloween: Silly Trivia. (Quantum Leap Ser.). (Illus.). (Orig.). (J). (gr. 2-9). 1994. pap. 19.95 (*1-55609-017-X*); lib. bdg. 29.95 (*1-55609-169-9*) Gallopade Intl.

— The Hard-to-Believe-But-True! Book of Alabama History, Mystery, Trivia, Legend, Lore, Humor & More. (Carole Marsh Alabama Bks.). (Illus.). (YA). (gr. 3-12). 1994. pap. 19.95 (*0-7933-0084-3*); lib. bdg. 29.95 (*0-7933-0085-1*); disk 29.95 (*0-7933-0086-X*) Gallopade Intl.

— The Hard-to-Believe-But-True! Book of Alaska History, Mystery, Trivia, Legend, Lore, Humor & More. (Carole Marsh Alaska Bks.). (Illus.). (YA). (gr. 3-12). 1994. pap. 19.95 (*0-7933-0108-4*); lib. bdg. 29.95 (*0-7933-0109-2*); disk 29.95 (*0-7933-0110-6*) Gallopade Intl.

— The Hard-to-Believe-But-True! Book of Arizona History, Mystery, Trivia, Legend, Lore, Humor & More. (Carole Marsh Arizona Bks.). (Illus.). (YA). (gr. 3-12). 1994. pap. 19.95 (*0-7933-0132-7*); lib. bdg. 29.95 (*0-7933-0133-5*); disk 29.95 (*0-7933-0134-3*) Gallopade Intl.

— The Hard-to-Believe-But-True! Book of Arkansas History, Mystery, Trivia, Legend, Lore, Humor & More. (Carole Marsh Arkansas Bks.). (Illus.). (YA). (gr. 3-12). 1994. pap. 19.95 (*0-7933-0156-4*); lib. bdg. 29.95 (*0-7933-0157-2*); disk 29.95 (*0-7933-0158-0*) Gallopade Intl.

— The Hard-to-Believe-But-True! Book of California History, Mystery, Trivia, Legend, Lore, Humor & More. (Carole Marsh California Bks.). (Illus.). (YA). (gr. 3-12). 1994. pap. 19.95 (*0-7933-0180-7*); lib. bdg. 29.95 (*0-7933-0181-5*); disk 29.95 (*0-7933-0182-3*) Gallopade Intl.

— The Hard-to-Believe-But-True! Book of Colorado History, Mystery, Trivia, Legend, Lore, Humor & More. (Carole Marsh Colorado Bks.). (Illus.). (YA). (gr. 3-12). 1994. pap. 19.95 (*0-7933-0204-8*); lib. bdg. 29.95 (*0-7933-0205-6*); disk 29.95 (*0-7933-0206-4*) Gallopade Intl.

— The Hard-to-Believe-But-True! Book of Connecticut History, Mystery, Trivia, Legend, Lore, Humor & More. (Carole Marsh Connecticut Bks.). (Illus.). (YA). (gr. 3-12). 1994. pap. 19.95 (*0-7933-0228-5*); lib. bdg. 29.95 (*0-7933-0229-3*); disk 29.95 (*0-7933-0230-7*) Gallopade Intl.

— The Hard-to-Believe-But-True! Book of Delaware History, Mystery, Trivia, Legend, Lore, Humor & More. (Carole

M

Marsh Delaware Bks.). (Illus.). (YA). (gr. 3-12). 1994. pap. 19.95 (0-7933-0252-8); lib. bdg. 29.95 (0-7933-0253-6); disk 29.95 (0-7933-0254-4) Gallopade Intl.

— The Hard-to-Believe-But-True! Book of Florida History, Mystery, Trivia, Legend, Lore, Humor & More. (Carole Marsh Florida Bks.). (Illus.). (YA). (gr. 3-12). 1994. pap. 19.95 (0-7933-0300-1); lib. bdg. 29.95 (0-7933-0301-X); disk 29.95 (0-7933-0302-8) Gallopade Intl.

— The Hard-to-Believe-But-True! Book of Georgia History, Mystery, Trivia, Legend, Lore, Humor & More. (Carole Marsh Georgia Bks.). (Illus.). (YA). (gr. 3-12). 1994. pap. 19.95 (0-7933-0324-9); lib. bdg. 29.95 (0-7933-0325-7); disk 29.95 (0-7933-0326-5) Gallopade Intl.

— The Hard-to-Believe-But-True! Book of Hawaii History, Mystery, Trivia, Legend, Lore, Humor & More. (Carole Marsh Hawaii Bks.). (Illus.). (YA). (gr. 3-12). 1994. pap. 19.95 (0-7933-0348-6); lib. bdg. 29.95 (0-7933-0349-4); disk 29.95 (0-7933-0350-8) Gallopade Intl.

— The Hard-to-Believe-But-True! Book of Idaho History, Mystery, Trivia, Legend, Lore, Humor & More. (Carole Marsh Idaho Bks.). (Illus.). (YA). (gr. 3-12). 1994. pap. 19.95 (0-7933-0372-9); lib. bdg. 29.95 (0-7933-0373-7); disk 29.95 (0-7933-0374-5) Gallopade Intl.

— The Hard-to-Believe-But-True! Book of Illinois History, Mystery, Trivia, Legend, Lore, Humor & More. (Carole Marsh Illinois Bks.). (Illus.). (YA). (gr. 3-12). 1994. pap. 19.95 (0-7933-0396-6); lib. bdg. 29.95 (0-7933-0397-4); disk 29.95 (0-7933-0398-2) Gallopade Intl.

— The Hard-to-Believe-But-True! Book of Indiana History, Mystery, Trivia, Legend, Lore, Humor & More. (Carole Marsh Indiana Bks.). (Illus.). (YA). (gr. 3-12). 1994. pap. 19.95 (0-7933-0420-2); lib. bdg. 29.95 (0-7933-0421-0); disk 29.95 (0-7933-0422-9) Gallopade Intl.

— The Hard-to-Believe-But-True! Book of Iowa History, Mystery, Trivia, Legend, Lore, Humor & More. (Carole Marsh Iowa Bks.). (Illus.). (YA). (gr. 3-12). 1994. pap. 19.95 (0-7933-0444-X); lib. bdg. 29.95 (0-7933-0445-8); disk 29.95 (0-7933-0446-6) Gallopade Intl.

— The Hard-to-Believe-But-True! Book of Kansas History, Mystery, Trivia, Legend, Lore, Humor & More. (Carole Marsh Kansas Bks.). (Illus.). (YA). (gr. 3-12). 1994. pap. 19.95 (0-7933-0468-7); lib. bdg. 29.95 (0-7933-0469-5); disk 29.95 (0-7933-0470-9) Gallopade Intl.

— The Hard-to-Believe-But-True! Book of Kentucky History, Mystery, Trivia, Legend, Lore, Humor & More. (Carole Marsh Kentucky Bks.). (Illus.). (J). (gr. 3-8). 1994. pap. 19.95 (0-7933-0492-X); lib. bdg. 29.95 (0-7933-0493-8); disk 29.95 (0-7933-0494-6) Gallopade Intl.

— The Hard-to-Believe-But-True! Book of Louisiana History, Mystery, Trivia, Legend, Lore, Humor & More. (Carole Marsh Louisiana Bks.). (Illus.). (J). (gr. 3-8). 1994. pap. 19.95 (0-7933-0516-0); lib. bdg. 29.95 (0-7933-0517-9); disk 29.95 (0-7933-0518-7) Gallopade Intl.

— The Hard-to-Believe-But-True! Book of Maine History, Mystery, Trivia, Legend, Lore, Humor & More. (Carole Marsh Maine Bks.). (Illus.). (J). (gr. 3-8). 1994. pap. 19.95 (0-7933-0541-1); lib. bdg. 29.95 (0-7933-0542-X); disk 29.95 (0-7933-0543-8) Gallopade Intl.

— The Hard-to-Believe-But-True! Book of Maryland History, Mystery, Trivia, Legend, Lore, Humor & More. (Carole Marsh Maryland Bks.). (Illus.). (J). (gr. 3-8). 1994. pap. 19.95 (0-7933-0565-9); lib. bdg. 29.95 (0-7933-0566-7); disk 29.95 (0-7933-0567-5) Gallopade Intl.

— The Hard-to-Believe-But-True! Book of Massachusetts History, Mystery, Trivia, Legend, Lore, Humor & More. (Carole Marsh Massachusetts Bks.). (Illus.). (J). (gr. 3-8). 1994. pap. 19.95 (0-7933-0589-6); lib. bdg. 29.95 (0-7933-0590-X); disk 29.95 (0-7933-0591-8) Gallopade Intl.

— The Hard-to-Believe-But-True! Book of Michigan History, Mystery, Trivia, Legend, Lore, Humor & More. (Carole Marsh Michigan Bks.). (Illus.). (J). (gr. 3 up). 1994. pap. 19.95 (0-7933-0613-2); lib. bdg. 29.95 (0-7933-0614-0); disk 29.95 (0-7933-0615-9) Gallopade Intl.

— The Hard-to-Believe-But-True! Book of Minnesota History, Mystery, Trivia, Legend, Lore, Humor & More. (Carole Marsh Minnesota Bks.). (Illus.). (J). (gr. 3 up). 1994. pap. 19.95 (0-7933-0637-X); lib. bdg. 29.95 (0-7933-0638-8); disk 29.95 (0-7933-0639-6) Gallopade Intl.

— The Hard-to-Believe-But-True! Book of Mississippi History, Mystery, Trivia, Legend, Lore, Humor & More. (Carole Marsh Mississippi Bks.). (Illus.). (J). (gr. 3 up). 1994. pap. 19.95 (0-7933-0662-0); lib. bdg. 29.95 (0-7933-0663-9); disk 29.95 (0-7933-0664-7) Gallopade Intl.

— The Hard-to-Believe-But-True! Book of Missouri History, Mystery, Trivia, Legend, Lore, Humor & More. (Carole Marsh Missouri Bks.). (Illus.). (J). (gr. 3 up). 1994. pap. 19.95 (0-7933-0686-8); lib. bdg. 29.95 (0-7933-0687-6); disk 29.95 (0-7933-0688-4) Gallopade Intl.

— The Hard-to-Believe-But-True! Book of Montana History, Mystery, Trivia, Legend, Lore, Humor & More. (Carole Marsh Montana Bks.). (Illus.). (J). (gr. 3 up). 1994. pap. 19.95 (0-7933-0711-2); lib. bdg. 29.95 (0-7933-0712-0); disk 29.95 (0-7933-0713-9) Gallopade Intl.

— The Hard-to-Believe-But-True! Book of Nebraska History, Mystery, Trivia, Legend, Lore, Humor & More. (Carole Marsh Nebraska Bks.). (Illus.). (J). (gr. 3 up). 1994. pap. 19.95 (0-7933-0735-X); lib. bdg. 29.95 (0-7933-0736-8); disk 29.95 (0-7933-0737-6) Gallopade Intl.

— The Hard-to-Believe-But-True! Book of Nevada History, Mystery, Trivia, Legend, Lore, Humor & More. (Carole Marsh Nevada Bks.). (Illus.). (J). 1994. pap. 19.95 (0-7933-0759-7); lib. bdg. 29.95 (0-7933-0760-0); disk 29.95 (0-7933-0761-9) Gallopade Intl.

— The Hard-to-Believe-But-True! Book of New Hampshire History, Mystery, Trivia, Legend, Lore, Humor & More. (Carole Marsh New Hampshire Bks.). (Illus.). (J). 1994. pap. 19.95 (0-7933-0783-X); lib. bdg. 29.95 (0-7933-0784-8); disk 29.95 (0-7933-0785-6) Gallopade Intl.

— The Hard-to-Believe-But-True! Book of New Jersey History, Mystery, Trivia, Legend, Lore, Humor & More. (Carole Marsh New Jersey Bks.). (Illus.). (J). 1994. pap. 19.95 (0-7933-1807-6); lib. bdg. 29.95 (0-7933-1806-8); disk 29.95 (0-7933-1808-4) Gallopade Intl.

— The Hard-to-Believe-But-True! Book of New Mexico History, Mystery, Trivia, Legend, Lore, Humor & More. (Carole Marsh New Mexico Bks.). (Illus.). (J). 1994. pap. 19.95 (0-7933-0807-0); lib. bdg. 29.95 (0-7933-0808-9); disk 29.95 (0-7933-0809-7) Gallopade Intl.

— The Hard-to-Believe-But-True! Book of New York History, Mystery, Trivia, Legend, Lore, Humor & More. (Carole Marsh New York Bks.). (Illus.). (J). 1994. pap. 19.95 (0-7933-0831-3); lib. bdg. 29.95 (0-7933-0832-1); disk 29.95 (0-7933-0833-X) Gallopade Intl.

— The Hard-to-Believe-But-True! Book of North Carolina History, Mystery, Trivia, Legend, Lore, Humor & More. (Carole Marsh North Carolina Bks.). (Illus.). (J). 1994. pap. 19.95 (0-7933-0855-0); lib. bdg. 29.95 (0-7933-0856-9); disk 29.95 (0-7933-0857-7) Gallopade Intl.

— The Hard-to-Believe-But-True! Book of North Dakota History, Mystery, Trivia, Legend, Lore, Humor & More. (Carole Marsh North Dakota Bks.). (Illus.). (J). 1994. pap. 19.95 (0-7933-0879-8); lib. bdg. 29.95 (0-7933-0880-1); disk 29.95 (0-7933-0881-X) Gallopade Intl.

— The Hard-to-Believe-But-True! Book of Ohio History, Mystery, Trivia, Legend, Lore, Humor & More. (Carole Marsh Ohio Bks.). (Illus.). (J). 1994. pap. 19.95 (0-7933-0903-4); lib. bdg. 29.95 (0-7933-0904-2); disk 29.95 (0-7933-0906-9) Gallopade Intl.

— The Hard-to-Believe-But-True! Book of Oklahoma History, Mystery, Trivia, Legend, Lore, Humor & More. (Carole Marsh Oklahoma Bks.). (Illus.). (J). 1994. pap. 19.95 (0-7933-0928-X); lib. bdg. 29.95 (0-7933-0929-8); disk 29.95 (0-7933-0930-1) Gallopade Intl.

— The Hard-to-Believe-But-True! Book of Oregon History, Mystery, Trivia, Legend, Lore, Humor & More. (Carole Marsh Oregon Bks.). (Illus.). (J). 1994. pap. 19.95 (0-7933-0952-2); lib. bdg. 29.95 (0-7933-0953-0); disk 29.95 (0-7933-0954-9) Gallopade Intl.

— The Hard-to-Believe-But-True! Book of Pennsylvania History, Mystery, Trivia, Legend, Lore, Humor & More. (Carole Marsh Pennsylvania Bks.). (Illus.). (J). 1994. pap. 19.95 (0-7933-0976-X); lib. bdg. 29.95 (0-7933-0977-8); disk 29.95 (0-7933-0978-6) Gallopade Intl.

— The Hard-to-Believe-But-True! Book of Rhode Island History, Mystery, Trivia, Legend, Lore, Humor & More. (Carole Marsh Rhode Island Bks.). (Illus.). (J). 1994. pap. 19.95 (0-7933-1000-8); lib. bdg. 29.95 (0-7933-1001-6); disk 29.95 (0-7933-1002-4) Gallopade Intl.

— The Hard-to-Believe-But-True! Book of South Carolina History, Mystery, Trivia, Legend, Lore, Humor & More. (Carole Marsh South Carolina Bks.). (Illus.). (J). 1994. pap. 19.95 (0-7933-1024-5); lib. bdg. 29.95 (0-7933-1025-3); disk 29.95 (0-7933-1026-1) Gallopade Intl.

— The Hard-to-Believe-But True! Book of South Dakota History, Mystery, Trivia, Legend, Lore, Humor & More. (Carole Marsh South Dakota Bks.). (Illus.). (J). 1994. pap. 19.95 (0-7933-1048-2); lib. bdg. 29.95 (0-7933-1049-0); disk 29.95 (0-7933-1050-4) Gallopade Intl.

— The Hard-to-Believe-But-True! Book of Tennessee History, Mystery, Trivia, Legend, Lore, Humor & More. (Carole Marsh Tennessee Bks.). (Illus.). (J). 1994. pap. 19.95 (0-7933-1072-5); lib. bdg. 29.95 (0-7933-1073-3); disk 29.95 (0-7933-1074-1) Gallopade Intl.

— The Hard-to-Believe-But-True! Book of Texas History, Mystery, Trivia, Legend, Lore, Humor & More. (Carole Marsh Texas Bks.). (Illus.). (J). 1994. pap. 19.95 (0-7933-1096-2); lib. bdg. 29.95 (0-7933-1097-0); disk 29.95 (0-7933-1098-9) Gallopade Intl.

— The Hard-to-Believe-But-True! Book of Utah History, Mystery, Trivia, Legend, Lore, Humor & More. (Carole Marsh Utah Bks.). (Illus.). (J). 1994. pap. 19.95 (0-7933-1120-9); lib. bdg. 29.95 (0-7933-1121-7); disk 29.95 (0-7933-1122-5) Gallopade Intl.

— The Hard-to-Believe-But-True! Book of Vermont History, Mystery, Trivia, Legend, Lore, Humor & More. (Carole Marsh Vermont Bks.). (Illus.). (J). 1994. write for info. (0-7933-1146-2); pap. 19.95 (0-7933-1144-6); lib. bdg. 29.95 (0-7933-1145-4) Gallopade Intl.

— The Hard-to-Believe-But-True! Book of Virginia History, Mystery, Trivia, Legend, Lore, Humor & More. (Carole Marsh Virginia Bks.). (Illus.). (J). 1994. pap. 19.95 (0-7933-1168-3); lib. bdg. 29.95 (0-7933-1169-1); disk 29.95 (0-7933-1170-5) Gallopade Intl.

— The Hard-to-Believe-But-True! Book of Washington, D.C. History, Mystery, Trivia, Legend, Lore, Humor & More. (Carole Marsh Washington, D.C. Bks.). (Illus.). (J). (gr. 3-12). 1994. lib. bdg. 24.95 (0-7933-0377-X) Gallopade Intl.

— The Hard-to-Believe-But-True! Book of Washington, D.C. History, Mystery, Trivia, Legend, Lore, Humor & More. (Carole Marsh Washington, D.C. Bks.). (Illus.). (YA). (gr. 3-12). 1994. pap. 19.95 (0-7933-0276-5) Gallopade Intl.

— The Hard-to-Believe-But-True! Book of Washington, D.C. History, Mystery, Trivia, Legend, Lore, Humor & More. (Carole Marsh Washington, D.C. Bks.). (Illus.). (J). (gr. 3-12). 1997. disk 29.95 (0-7933-0278-1) Gallopade Intl.

— The Hard-to-Believe-But-True! Book of Washington History, Mystery, Trivia, Legend, Lore, Humor & More. (Carole Marsh Washington Bks.). (Illus.). (J). 1994. pap. 19.95 (0-7933-1192-6); lib. bdg. 29.95 (0-7933-1193-4); disk 29.95 (0-7933-1194-2) Gallopade Intl.

— The Hard-to-Believe-But-True! Book of West Virginia History, Mystery, Trivia, Legend, Lore, Humor & More. (Carole Marsh West Virginia Bks.). (Illus.). (J). 1994. pap. 19.95 (0-7933-1216-7); lib. bdg. 29.95 (0-7933-1217-5); disk 29.95 (0-7933-1218-3) Gallopade Intl.

— The Hard-to-Believe-But-True! Book of Wisconsin History, Mystery, Trivia, Legend, Lore, Humor & More. (Carole Marsh Wisconsin Bks.). (Illus.). (J). 1994. pap. 19.95 (0-7933-1240-X); lib. bdg. 29.95 (0-7933-1241-8); disk 29.95 (0-7933-1242-6) Gallopade Intl.

— The Hard-to-Believe-But-True! Book of Wyoming History, Mystery, Trivia, Legend, Lore, Humor & More. (Carole Marsh Wyoming Bks.). (Illus.). (J). 1994. pap. 19.95 (0-7933-1264-7); lib. bdg. 29.95 (0-7933-1265-5); disk 29.95 (0-7933-1266-3) Gallopade Intl.

— The Haunt of Hope Plantation. (History Mystery Ser.). (Illus.). (Orig.). (J). (gr. 3-9). 1994. 29.95 (1-55609-170-2); pap. 19.95 (0-935326-03-0) Gallopade Intl.

— The Haunt of Hope Plantation S. P. A. R. K. Kit. (S. P. A. R. K. Ser.). (Illus.). (Orig.). (J). (gr. 3-12). 1994. pap. 29.95 (0-935326-21-9) Gallopade Intl.

— The Haunt of Hope Plantation Set. (Carole Marsh Mysteries Ser.). 1994. 125.00 (0-7933-6947-9) Gallopade Intl.

— The Haunted Christmas Tree Mystery. (Carole Marsh Mysteries & Novel Ser.). (Illus.). (J). (gr. 2-9). 1994. 29.95 (1-55609-267-9); pap. 19.95 (1-55609-266-0); disk 29.95 (1-55609-270-9) Gallopade Intl.

— Hawaii: Silly Basketball Sportsmysteries, Vol. I. (Carole Marsh Hawaii Bks.). (Illus.). (YA). (gr. 3-12). 1994. pap. 19.95 (0-7933-0339-7); lib. bdg. 29.95 (0-7933-0340-0); disk 29.95 (0-7933-0341-9) Gallopade Intl.

— Hawaii & Other State Greats (Biographies) (Carole Marsh Hawaii Bks.). (Illus.). (YA). (gr. 3-12). 1994. pap. 19.95 (1-55609-576-7); lib. bdg. 29.95 (1-55609-577-5); disk 29.95 (0-7933-1539-5) Gallopade Intl.

— Hawaii Bandits, Bushwackers, Outlaws, Crooks, Devils, Ghosts, Desperadoes & Other Assorted & Sundry Characters! (Carole Marsh Hawaii Bks.). (Illus.). (YA). (gr. 3-12). 1994. pap. 19.95 (0-7933-0333-8); lib. bdg. 29.95 (0-7933-0334-6); disk 29.95 (0-7933-0335-4) Gallopade Intl.

— Hawaii "Bio" Bingo! 24 Must Know State People for Kids to Learn about While Having Fun! (Bingo! Ser.). (Illus.). (J). (gr. 2-8). 1998. pap. 14.95 (0-7933-8555-5) Gallopade Intl.

— The Hawaii Bookstore Book: A Surprising Guide to Our State's Bookstores & Their Specialties for Students, Teachers, Writers & Publishers. (Carole Marsh Hawaii Bks.). (Illus.). 1994. pap. 19.95 (0-7933-2889-6); lib. bdg. 29.95 (0-7933-2888-8); disk 29.95 (0-7933-2890-X) Gallopade Intl.

— Hawaii Classic Christmas Trivia: Stories, Recipes, Activities, Legends, Lore & More! (Carole Marsh Hawaii Bks.). (Illus.). (YA). (gr. 3-12). 1994. pap. 19.95 (0-7933-0336-2); lib. bdg. 29.95 (0-7933-0337-0); disk 29.95 (0-7933-0338-9) Gallopade Intl.

— Hawaii Coastales. (Carole Marsh Hawaii Bks.). (Illus.). (YA). (gr. 3-12). 1994. pap. 19.95 (1-55609-572-4); lib. bdg. 29.95 (1-55609-573-2); disk 29.95 (0-7933-1535-2) Gallopade Intl.

— Hawaii Coastales! (Hawaii Bks.). (J). 1994. lib. bdg. 29.95 (0-7933-7276-3) Gallopade Intl.

— Hawaii "Crinkum-Crankum" A Funny Word Book about Our State. (Carole Marsh Hawaii Bks.). (Illus.). (J). 1994. pap. 19.95 (0-7933-4841-2); lib. bdg. 29.95 (0-7933-4840-4); disk 29.95 (0-7933-4842-0) Gallopade Intl.

— Hawaii Dingbats! Bk. 1: A Fun Book of Games, Stories, Activities & More about Our State That's All in Code! for You to Decipher. (Carole Marsh Hawaii Bks.). (Illus.). (J). (gr. 3-12). 1994. pap. 19.95 (0-7933-3807-7); lib. bdg. 29.95 (0-7933-3806-9); disk 29.95 (0-7933-3808-5) Gallopade Intl.

— Hawaii Facts & Factivities. (Carole Marsh State Bks.). (Illus.). (J). (gr. 4-7). 1996. pap., teacher ed. 19.95 (0-7933-7869-9) Gallopade Intl.

— Hawaii Festival Fun for Kids! (Carole Marsh Hawaii Bks.). (Illus.). (YA). (gr. 3-12). 1994. pap. 19.95 (0-7933-3960-X); lib. bdg. 29.95 (0-7933-3959-6); disk 29.95 (0-7933-3961-8) Gallopade Intl.

— Hawaii "GEO" Bingo! 38 Must Know State Geography Facts for Kids to Learn While Having Fun! (Bingo! Ser.). (Illus.). (J). (gr. 2-8). 1998. pap. 14.95 (0-7933-8556-3) Gallopade Intl.

— Hawaii Government! The Cornerstone of Everyday Life in Our State! (Carole Marsh Hawaii Bks.). (Illus.). (J). (gr. 3-12). 1996. pap. 19.95 (0-7933-6215-6); lib. bdg. 29.95 (0-7933-6214-8); disk 29.95 (0-7933-6216-4) Gallopade Intl.

— Hawaii "HISTO" Bingo! 42 Must Know State History Facts for Kids to Learn While Having Fun! (Bingo! Ser.). (Illus.). (J). (gr. 2-8). 1998. pap. 14.95 (0-7933-8557-1) Gallopade Intl.

— Hawaii History! Surprising Secrets about Our State's Founding Mothers, Fathers & Kids! (Carole Marsh Hawaii Bks.). (Illus.). (J). (gr. 3-12). 1996. pap. 19.95 (0-7933-6062-5); lib. bdg. 29.95 (0-7933-6061-7); disk 29.95 (0-7933-6063-3) Gallopade Intl.

— The Hawaii Hot Air Balloon Mystery. (Carole Marsh Hawaii Bks.). (Illus.). (J). (gr. 2-9). 1994. 29.95 (0-7933-2417-3); pap. 19.95 (0-7933-2418-1); disk 29.95 (0-7933-2419-X) Gallopade Intl.

— Hawaii Hot Zones! Viruses, Diseases, & Epidemics in Our State's History. (Hot Zones! Ser.). (Illus.). (J). (gr. 3-12). 1998. pap. 19.95 (0-7933-8862-7); lib. bdg. 29.95 (0-7933-8861-9) Gallopade Intl.

— Hawaii Indian Dictionary for Kids! (Carole Marsh State Bks.). (J). (gr. 2-9). 1996. 29.95 (0-7933-7677-7, C Marsh); pap. 19.95 (0-7933-7678-5, C Marsh) Gallopade Intl.

— Hawaii Jeopardy! Answers & Questions about Our State! (Carole Marsh Hawaii Bks.). (Illus.). (J). (gr. 3-12). 1994. pap. 19.95 (0-7933-4113-2); lib. bdg. 29.95 (0-7933-4112-4); disk 29.95 (0-7933-4114-0) Gallopade Intl.

— Hawaii "Jography" A Fun Run Thru Our State! (Carole Marsh Hawaii Bks.). (Illus.). (YA). (gr. 3-12). 1994. pap. 19.95 (1-55609-567-8); lib. bdg. 29.95 (1-55609-568-6); disk 29.95 (0-7933-1525-5) Gallopade Intl.

— Hawaii Kid's Cookbook: Recipes, How-to, History, Lore & More! (Carole Marsh Hawaii Bks.). (Illus.). (YA). (gr. 3-12). 1994. pap. 19.95 (0-7933-0345-1); lib. bdg. 29.95 (0-7933-0346-X); disk 29.95 (0-7933-0347-8) Gallopade Intl.

— The Hawaii Library Book: A Surprising Guide to the Unusual Special Collections in Libraries Across Our State for Students, Teachers, Writers & Publishers - Includes Reproducible Mailing Labels Plus Activities for Young People! (Carole Marsh Hawaii Bks.). (Illus.). 1994. pap. 19.95 (0-7933-3039-4); lib. bdg. 29.95 (0-7933-3038-6); disk 29.95 (0-7933-3040-8) Gallopade Intl.

— Hawaii Math! How It All Adds up in Our State. (Carole Marsh Hawaii Bks.). (Illus.). (YA). (gr. 3-12). 1996. pap. 19.95 (0-7933-6521-X); lib. bdg. 29.95 (0-7933-6520-1) Gallopade Intl.

— The Hawaii Media Book: A Surprising Guide to the Amazing Print, Broadcast & Online Media of Our State for Students, Teachers, Writers & Publishers - Includes Reproducible Mailing Labels Plus Activities for Young People! (Carole Marsh Hawaii Bks.). (Illus.). 1994. pap. 19.95 (0-7933-3195-1); lib. bdg. 29.95 (0-7933-3194-3); disk 29.95 (0-7933-3196-X) Gallopade Intl.

— The Hawaii Mystery Van Takes Off! Book 1: Handicapped Hawaii Kids Sneak Off on a Big Adventure. (Carole Marsh Hawaii Bks.). (Illus.). (J). (gr. 3-12). 1994. 29.95 (0-7933-4994-X); pap. 19.95 (0-7933-4995-8); disk 29.95 (0-7933-4996-6) Gallopade Intl.

— Hawaii Quiz Bowl Crash Course! (Carole Marsh Hawaii Bks.). (Illus.). (YA). (gr. 3-12). 1994. pap. 19.95 (1-55609-574-0); lib. bdg. 29.95 (1-55609-575-9); disk 29.95 (0-7933-1534-4) Gallopade Intl.

— Hawaii Rollercoasters! (Carole Marsh Hawaii Bks.). (Illus.). (YA). (gr. 3-12). 1994. pap. 19.95 (0-7933-5258-4); lib. bdg. 29.95 (0-7933-5257-6); disk 29.95 (0-7933-5259-2) Gallopade Intl.

— Hawaii School Trivia: An Amazing & Fascinating Look at Our State's Teachers, Schools & Students! (Carole Marsh Hawaii Bks.). (Illus.). (YA). (gr. 3-12). 1994. pap. 19.95 (0-7933-0342-7); lib. bdg. 29.95 (0-7933-0343-5); disk 29.95 (0-7933-0344-3) Gallopade Intl.

— Hawaii Silly Basketball Sports Mysteries. (Carole Marsh Hawaii Bks.: Vol. II). (Illus.). (YA). (gr. 3-12). 1994. pap. 19.95 (0-7933-1541-7); lib. bdg. 29.95 (0-7933-1540-9); disk 29.95 (0-7933-1542-5) Gallopade Intl.

— Hawaii Silly Football Sportsmysteries, Vol. I. (Carole Marsh Hawaii Bks.). (Illus.). (YA). (gr. 3-12). 1994. pap. 19.95 (1-55609-570-8); lib. bdg. 29.95 (1-55609-571-6); disk 29.95 (0-7933-1527-1) Gallopade Intl.

— Hawaii Silly Football Sportsmysteries, Vol. II. (Carole Marsh Hawaii Bks.). (Illus.). (YA). (gr. 3-12). 1994. pap. 19.95 (0-7933-1529-8); lib. bdg. 29.95 (0-7933-1528-X); disk 29.95 (0-7933-1530-1) Gallopade Intl.

— Hawaii Silly Trivia! (Carole Marsh Hawaii Bks.). (Illus.). (YA). (gr. 3-12). 1994. pap. 19.95 (1-55609-565-1); lib. bdg. 29.95 (1-55609-566-X); disk 29.95 (0-7933-1524-7) Gallopade Intl.

— Hawaii Spelling Bee! Score Big by Correctly Spelling Our State's Unique Names. (Carole Marsh Hawaii Bks.). (Illus.). (YA). (gr. 3-12). 1996. pap. 19.95 (0-7933-6674-7); lib. bdg. 29.95 (0-7933-6673-9) Gallopade Intl.

— Hawaii Timeline: A Chronology of Hawaii History, Mystery, Trivia, Legend, Lore & More. (Carole Marsh Hawaii Bks.). (Illus.). (J). (gr. 3-12). 1994. pap. 19.95 (0-7933-5909-0); lib. bdg. 29.95 (0-7933-5908-2); disk 29.95 (0-7933-5910-4) Gallopade Intl.

— Hawaii 2000! Coming Soon to a Calendar Near You - The 21st Century! - Complete Set of AL 2000 Items. (Two Thousand! Ser.). (Illus.). (J). (gr. 3-12). 1998. pap. 75.00 (0-7933-9331-0); lib. bdg. 85.00 (0-7933-9332-9) Gallopade Intl.

— Hawaii 2000! Coming Soon to a Calendar Near You-The 21st Century! (Two Thousand! Ser.). (Illus.). (J). (gr. 3-12). 1998. pap. 19.95 (0-7933-8709-4); lib. bdg. 29.95 (0-7933-8708-6) Gallopade Intl.

— Hawaii UFO's & Extraterrestrials! A Look at the Sightings & Science in Our State. (Carole Marsh Hawaii Bks.). (Illus.). (J). (gr. 3-12). 1997. pap. 19.95 (0-7933-6368-3); lib. bdg. 29.95 (0-7933-6367-5) Gallopade Intl.

— Hawaii's (Most Devastating!) Disasters & (Most Calamitous!) Catastrophies! (Carole Marsh Hawaii Bks.). (Illus.). (YA). (gr. 3-12). 1994. pap. 19.95 (0-7933-0330-3); lib. bdg. 29.95 (0-7933-0331-1); disk 29.95 (0-7933-0332-X) Gallopade Intl.

— Hawaii's Unsolved Mysteries (& Their "Solutions") Includes Scientific Information & Other Activities for Students. (Carole Marsh Hawaii Bks.). (Illus.). (J). (gr. 3-12). 1994. pap. 19.95 (0-7933-5756-X); lib. bdg. 29.95 (0-7933-5755-1); disk 29.95 (0-7933-5757-8) Gallopade Intl.

— Hello in There: Poetry to Read to the Unborn Baby. (Unborn Baby Ser.). 1994. 29.95 (1-55609-250-4); pap. 19.95 (1-55609-251-2) Gallopade Intl.

An Asterisk (*) at the beginning of an entry indicates that the title is appearing for the first time.

— Helping Kids Write Better - By Writing on a Computer. (Books for Teachers). (Illus.). 1994. teacher ed. 29.95 (0-7933-0033-9) Gallopade Intl.

— Ho Lee Chow! Chinese for Kids. (Of All the Gaul Ser.). (J). (gr. k-6). 1994. 29.95 (0-7933-7355-7); 19.95 (0-7933-7357-3); pap. 19.95 (0-7933-7356-5); audio 19.95 (0-7933-7360-3); VHS 19.95 (0-7933-7359-X); cd-rom 19.95 (0-7933-7361-1); disk 19.95 (0-7933-7358-1) Gallopade Intl.

— The Hot Air Balloon Mystery. (Carole Marsh Mysteries Ser.). (Illus.). (gr. 2-9). 1994. 29.95 (1-55609-265-2); pap. 19.95 (1-55609-264-4); disk 29.95 (1-55609-268-7) Gallopade Intl.

— Hot Shot: Photography for Kids. (Quantum Leap Ser.). (Illus.). (Orig.). (J). (gr. 3-12). 1994. 29.95 (1-55609-171-0); pap. 19.95 (0-935326-79-0) Gallopade Intl.

— Hot Zones: Disease, Epidemics, Viruses & Bacteria. (Wildly Educational Titles Ser.). (J). (gr. 2-9). Date not set. pap. 19.95 (0-7933-7819-2, C Marsh) Gallopade Intl.

— Hot Zones: Disease, Epidemics, Viruses & Bacteria. (Wildly Educational Titles Ser.). (J). (gr. 2-9). 1998. 29.95 (0-7933-7818-4, C Marsh) Gallopade Intl.

— How to Build a Database. (Budding Genius Titles Ser.). (J). (gr. 2-9). Date not set. 29.95 (0-7933-7806-0, C Marsh); pap. 19.95 (0-7933-7807-9, C Marsh) Gallopade Intl.

— How to Create a Spreadsheet. (Budding Genius Titles Ser.). (J). (gr. 2-9). Date not set. 29.95 (0-7933-7809-5, C Marsh); pap. 19.95 (0-7933-7810-9, C Marsh) Gallopade Intl.

— How to Find an Extra Terrestrial in Your Own Backyard. (Tomorrow's Books for Today's Children). (Illus.). (J). 1994. 29.95 (0-935326-09-X) Gallopade Intl.

— How to Get Your Kid Out of School... Without AIDS, a Disease, or a Baby! (Smart Sex Stuff Ser.). (Orig.). 1994. 29.95 (1-55609-286-5); pap. 19.95 (1-55609-224-5) Gallopade Intl.

— How to Make a Million Writing Books for Kids! (Carole Marsh Life Write Bks.). 1994. 29.95 (0-7933-7371-9); pap. 19.95 (0-7933-7372-7); audio 19.95 (0-7933-7375-1); VHS 19.95 (0-7933-7374-3); disk 19.95 (0-7933-7373-5) Gallopade Intl.

— How to Make a Million Writing for the New Interactive Multimedia & CD-ROM Market. (How to Make a Million! Ser.). (Illus.). (Orig.). 1994. pap. 19.95 (0-7933-7624-6); lib. bdg. 24.95 (0-7933-7623-8) Gallopade Intl.

— How to Raise the Children You Wish Your Parents Had Raised. 1994. 19.95 (1-55609-902-9); pap. 19.95 (1-55609-903-7) Gallopade Intl.

— How to Start a California Library: At Home or School - A Book for All Ages. (Carole Marsh California Bks.). (Illus.). (J). (gr. 3 up). 1994. pap. 19.95 (0-7933-4248-1); lib. bdg. 29.95 (0-7933-4247-3); disk 29.95 (0-7933-4249-X) Gallopade Intl.

— How to Start a Colorado Library: At Home or School - A Book for All Ages. (Carole Marsh Colorado Bks.). (Illus.). (J). (gr. 3 up). 1994. pap. 19.95 (0-7933-4251-1); lib. bdg. 29.95 (0-7933-4250-3); disk 29.95 (0-7933-4252-X) Gallopade Intl.

— How to Start a Connecticut Library: At Home or School - A Book for All Ages. (Carole Marsh Connecticut Bks.). (Illus.). (J). (gr. 3 up). 1994. pap. 19.95 (0-7933-4254-6); lib. bdg. 29.95 (0-7933-4253-8); disk 29.95 (0-7933-4255-4) Gallopade Intl.

— How to Start a Delaware Library: At Home or School - A Book for All Ages. (Carole Marsh Delaware Bks.). (Illus.). (J). (gr. 3 up). 1994. pap. 19.95 (0-7933-4257-0); lib. bdg. 29.95 (0-7933-4256-2); disk 29.95 (0-7933-4258-9) Gallopade Intl.

— How to Start a Florida Library: At Home or School - A Book for All Ages. (Carole Marsh Florida Bks.). (Illus.). (J). (gr. 3 up). 1994. pap. 19.95 (0-7933-4260-0); lib. bdg. 29.95 (0-7933-4259-7); disk 29.95 (0-7933-4261-9) Gallopade Intl.

— How to Start a Georgia Library: At Home or School - A Book for All Ages. (Carole Marsh Georgia Bks.). (Illus.). (J). (gr. 3 up). 1994. pap. 19.95 (0-7933-4263-5); lib. bdg. 29.95 (0-7933-4262-7); disk 29.95 (0-7933-4264-3) Gallopade Intl.

— How to Start a Hawaii Library: At Home or School - A Book for All Ages. (Carole Marsh Hawaii Bks.). (Illus.). (J). (gr. 3 up). 1994. pap. 19.95 (0-7933-4266-X); lib. bdg. 29.95 (0-7933-4265-1); disk 29.95 (0-7933-4267-8) Gallopade Intl.

— How to Start a Kansas Library: At Home or School - A Book for All Ages. (Carole Marsh Kansas Bks.). (Illus.). (J). (gr. 3 up). 1994. pap. 19.95 (0-7933-4281-3); lib. bdg. 29.95 (0-7933-4280-5); disk 29.95 (0-7933-4282-1) Gallopade Intl.

— How to Start a Kentucky Library: At Home or School - A Book for All Ages. (Carole Marsh Kentucky Bks.). (Illus.). (J). (gr. 3 up). 1994. pap. 19.95 (0-7933-4284-8); lib. bdg. 29.95 (0-7933-4283-X); disk 29.95 (0-7933-4285-6) Gallopade Intl.

— How to Start a Louisiana Library: At Home or School - A Book for All Ages. (Carole Marsh Louisiana Bks.). (Illus.). (J). (gr. 3 up). 1994. pap. 19.95 (0-7933-4287-2); lib. bdg. 29.95 (0-7933-4286-4); disk 29.95 (0-7933-4288-0) Gallopade Intl.

— How to Start a Maine Library: At Home or School - A Book for All Ages. (Carole Marsh Maine Bks.). (Illus.). (J). (gr. 3 up). 1994. pap. 19.95 (0-7933-4290-2); lib. bdg. 29.95 (0-7933-4289-9); disk 29.95 (0-7933-4291-0) Gallopade Intl.

— How to Start a Maryland Library: At Home or School - A Book for All Ages. (Carole Marsh Maryland Bks.). (Illus.). (J). (gr. 3 up). 1994. pap. 19.95 (0-7933-4293-7); lib. bdg. 29.95 (0-7933-4292-9); disk 29.95 (0-7933-4294-5) Gallopade Intl.

— How to Start a Massachusetts Library: At Home or School - A Book for All Ages. (Massachuseets Bks.). (Illus.). (J). (gr. 3 up). 1994. pap. 19.95 (0-7933-4296-1); lib. bdg. 29.95 (0-7933-4295-3); disk 29.95 (0-7933-4297-X) Gallopade Intl.

— How to Start a Michigan Library: At Home or School - A Book for All Ages. (Carole Marsh Michigan Bks.). (Illus.). (J). (gr. 3 up). 1994. pap. 19.95 (0-7933-4299-6); lib. bdg. 29.95 (0-7933-4298-8); disk 29.95 (0-7933-4300-3) Gallopade Intl.

— How to Start a Minnesota Library: At Home or School - A Book for All Ages. (Carole Marsh Minnesota Bks.). (Illus.). (J). (gr. 3 up). 1994. pap. 19.95 (0-7933-4302-X); lib. bdg. 29.95 (0-7933-4301-1); disk 29.95 (0-7933-4303-8) Gallopade Intl.

— How to Start a Mississippi Library: At Home or School - A Book for All Ages. (Carole Marsh Mississippi Bks.). (Illus.). (J). (gr. 3 up). 1994. pap. 19.95 (0-7933-4305-4); lib. bdg. 29.95 (0-7933-4304-6); disk 29.95 (0-7933-4306-2) Gallopade Intl.

— How to Start a Missouri Library: At Home or School - A Book for All Ages. (Carole Marsh Missouri Bks.). (Illus.). (J). (gr. 3 up). 1994. pap. 19.95 (0-7933-4308-9); lib. bdg. 29.95 (0-7933-4307-0); disk 29.95 (0-7933-4309-7) Gallopade Intl.

— How to Start a Montana Library: At Home or School - A Book for All Ages. (Carole Marsh Montana Bks.). (Illus.). (J). (gr. 3 up). 1994. pap. 19.95 (0-7933-4311-9); lib. bdg. 29.95 (0-7933-4310-0); disk 29.95 (0-7933-4312-7) Gallopade Intl.

— How to Start a Nebraska Library: At Home or School - A Book for All Ages. (Carole Marsh Nebraska Bks.). (Illus.). (J). (gr. 3 up). 1994. pap. 19.95 (0-7933-4314-3); lib. bdg. 29.95 (0-7933-4313-5); disk 29.95 (0-7933-4315-1) Gallopade Intl.

— How to Start a Nevada Library: At Home or School - A Book for All Ages. (Carole Marsh Nevada Bks.). (Illus.). (J). (gr. 3 up). 1994. pap. 19.95 (0-7933-4317-8); lib. bdg. 29.95 (0-7933-4316-X) Gallopade Intl.

— How to Start a Nevada Library: At Home or School - A Book for All Ages. (Carole Marsh Nevada Bks.). (Illus.). (J). (gr. 3 up). 1997. disk 29.95 (0-7933-4319-4) Gallopade Intl.

— How to Start a New Hampshire Library: At Home or School - A Book for All Ages. (Carole Marsh New Hampshire Bks.). (Illus.). (J). (gr. 3 up). 1994. pap. 19.95 (0-7933-4320-8); lib. bdg. 29.95 (0-685-49562-0) Gallopade Intl.

— How to Start a New Hampshire Library: At Home or School - A Book for All Ages. (Carole Marsh New Hampshire Bks.). (Illus.). (J). (gr. 3 up). 1997. disk 29.95 (0-7933-4321-6) Gallopade Intl.

— How to Start a New Jersey Library: At Home or School - A Book for All Ages. (Carole Marsh New Jersey Bks.). (Illus.). (J). (gr. 3 up). 1994. pap. 19.95 (0-7933-4323-2); lib. bdg. 29.95 (0-7933-4322-4); disk 29.95 (0-7933-4324-0) Gallopade Intl.

— How to Start a New Mexico Library: At Home or School - A Book for All Ages. (Carole Marsh New Mexico Bks.). (Illus.). (J). (gr. 3 up). 1994. pap. 19.95 (0-7933-4326-7); lib. bdg. 29.95 (0-7933-4325-9); disk 29.95 (0-7933-4327-5) Gallopade Intl.

— How to Start a New York Library: At Home or School - A Book for All Ages. (Carole Marsh New York Bks.). (Illus.). (J). (gr. 3 up). 1994. pap. 19.95 (0-7933-4329-1); lib. bdg. 29.95 (0-7933-4328-3); disk 29.95 (0-7933-4330-5) Gallopade Intl.

— How to Start a North Carolina Library: At Home or School - A Book for All Ages. (Carole Marsh North Carolina Bks.). (Illus.). (J). (gr. 3 up). 1994. pap. 19.95 (0-7933-4332-1); lib. bdg. 29.95 (0-7933-4331-3); disk 29.95 (0-7933-4333-X) Gallopade Intl.

— How to Start a North Dakota Library: At Home or School - A Book for All Ages. (Carole Marsh North Dakota Bks.). (Illus.). (J). (gr. 3 up). 1994. pap. 19.95 (0-7933-4335-6); lib. bdg. 29.95 (0-7933-4334-8); disk 29.95 (0-7933-4336-4) Gallopade Intl.

— How to Start a Pennsylvania Library: At Home or School - A Book for All Ages. (Pennsylvania Bks.). (Illus.). (J). (gr. 3 up). 1994. pap. 19.95 (0-7933-4347-X); lib. bdg. 29.95 (0-7933-4346-1); disk 29.95 (0-7933-4348-8) Gallopade Intl.

— How to Start a Rhode Island Library: At Home or School - A Book for All Ages. (Rhode Island Bks.). (Illus.). (J). (gr. 3 up). 1994. pap. 19.95 (0-7933-4350-X); lib. bdg. 29.95 (0-7933-4349-6); disk 29.95 (0-7933-4351-8) Gallopade Intl.

— How to Start a South Carolina Library: At Home or School - A Book for All Ages. (South Carolina Bks.). (Illus.). (J). (gr. 3 up). 1994. pap. 19.95 (0-7933-4353-4); lib. bdg. 29.95 (0-7933-4352-6); disk 29.95 (0-7933-4354-2) Gallopade Intl.

— How to Start a South Dakota Library: At Home or School - A Book for All Ages. (South Dakota Bks.). (Illus.). (J). (gr. 3 up). 1994. pap. 19.95 (0-7933-4356-9); lib. bdg. 29.95 (0-7933-4355-0); disk 29.95 (0-7933-4357-7) Gallopade Intl.

— How to Start a Tennessee Library: At Home or School - A Book for All Ages. (Tennessee Bks.). (Illus.). (J). (gr. 3 up). 1994. pap. 19.95 (0-7933-4359-3); lib. bdg. 29.95 (0-7933-4358-5); disk 29.95 (0-7933-4360-7) Gallopade Intl.

— How to Start a Texas Library: At Home or School - A Book for All Ages. (Texas Bks.). (Illus.). (J). (gr. 3 up). 1994. pap. 19.95 (0-7933-4362-3); lib. bdg. 29.95 (0-7933-4361-5); disk 29.95 (0-7933-4363-1) Gallopade Intl.

— How to Start a Utah Library: At Home or School - A Book for All Ages. (Utah Bks.). (Illus.). (J). (gr. 3 up). 1994. pap. 19.95 (0-7933-4365-8); lib. bdg. 29.95 (0-7933-4364-X); disk 29.95 (0-7933-4366-6) Gallopade Intl.

— How to Start a Vermont Library: At Home or School - A Book for All Ages. (Vermont Bks.). (Illus.). (J). (gr. 3 up). 1994. lib. bdg. 29.95 (0-7933-4367-4); disk 29.95 (0-7933-4369-0) Gallopade Intl.

— How to Start a Vermont Library: At Home or School - A Book for All Ages. (Vermont Bks.). (Illus.). (J). (gr. 3 up). 1997. pap. 19.95 (0-7933-4368-2) Gallopade Intl.

— How to Start a Virginia Library: At Home or School - A Book for All Ages. (Virginia Bks.). (Illus.). (J). (gr. 3 up). 1994. pap. 19.95 (0-7933-4371-2); lib. bdg. 29.95 (0-7933-4370-4); disk 29.95 (0-7933-4372-0) Gallopade Intl.

— How to Start a Washington DC Library: At Home or School - A Book for All Ages. (Washington, D.C. Bks.). (Illus.). (J). (gr. 3 up). 1994. pap. 19.95 (0-7933-4377-1); lib. bdg. 29.95 (0-7933-4376-3); disk 29.95 (0-7933-4378-X) Gallopade Intl.

— How to Start a Washington Library: At Home or School - A Book for All Ages. (Washington Bks.). (Illus.). (J). (gr. 3 up). 1994. pap. 19.95 (0-7933-4374-7); lib. bdg. 29.95 (0-7933-4373-9); disk 29.95 (0-7933-4375-5) Gallopade Intl.

— How to Start a West Virginia Library: At Home or School - A Book for All Ages. (West Virginia Bks.). (Illus.). (J). (gr. 3 up). 1994. pap. 19.95 (0-7933-4380-1); lib. bdg. 29.95 (0-7933-4379-8); disk 29.95 (0-7933-4381-X) Gallopade Intl.

— How to Start a Wisconsin Library: At Home or School - A Book for All Ages. (Wisconsin Bks.). (Illus.). (J). (gr. 3 up). 1994. pap. 19.95 (0-7933-4383-6); lib. bdg. 29.95 (0-7933-4382-8); disk 29.95 (0-7933-4384-4) Gallopade Intl.

— How to Start a Wyoming Library: At Home or School - A Book for All Ages. (Wyoming Bks.). (Illus.). (J). (gr. 3 up). 1994. pap. 19.95 (0-7933-4386-0); lib. bdg. 29.95 (0-7933-4385-2); disk 29.95 (0-7933-4387-9) Gallopade Intl.

— How to Start an Alabama Library: At Home or School - A Book for All Ages. (Carole Marsh Alabama Bks.). (Illus.). (J). (gr. 3 up). 1994. pap. 19.95 (0-7933-4236-8); lib. bdg. 29.95 (0-7933-4235-X); disk 29.95 (0-7933-4237-6) Gallopade Intl.

— How to Start an Alaska Library: At Home or School - A Book for All Ages. (Carole Marsh Alaska Bks.). (Illus.). (J). (gr. 3 up). 1994. pap. 19.95 (0-7933-4239-2); lib. bdg. 29.95 (0-7933-4238-4); disk 29.95 (0-7933-4240-6) Gallopade Intl.

— How to Start an Arizona Library: At Home or School - A Book for All Ages. (Carole Marsh Arizona Bks.). (Illus.). (J). (gr. 3 up). 1994. pap. 19.95 (0-7933-4242-2); lib. bdg. 29.95 (0-7933-4241-4); disk 29.95 (0-7933-4243-0) Gallopade Intl.

— How to Start an Arkansas Library: At Home or School - A Book for All Ages. (Carole Marsh Arkansas Bks.). (Illus.). (J). (gr. 3 up). 1994. pap. 19.95 (0-7933-4245-7); lib. bdg. 29.95 (0-7933-4244-9); disk 29.95 (0-7933-4246-5) Gallopade Intl.

— How to Start an Idaho Library: At Home or School - A Book for All Ages. (Carole Marsh Idaho Bks.). (Illus.). (J). (gr. 3 up). 1994. pap. 19.95 (0-7933-4269-4); lib. bdg. 29.95 (0-7933-4268-6); disk 29.95 (0-7933-4270-8) Gallopade Intl.

— How to Start an Illinois Library: At Home or School - A Book for All Ages. (Carole Marsh Illinois Bks.). (Illus.). (J). (gr. 3 up). 1994. pap. 19.95 (0-7933-4272-4); lib. bdg. 29.95 (0-7933-4271-6); disk 29.95 (0-7933-4273-2) Gallopade Intl.

— How to Start an Indiana Library: At Home or School - A Book for All Ages. (Carole Marsh Indiana Bks.). (Illus.). (J). (gr. 3 up). 1994. pap. 19.95 (0-7933-4275-9); lib. bdg. 29.95 (0-7933-4274-0); disk 29.95 (0-7933-4276-7) Gallopade Intl.

— How to Start an Iowa Library: At Home or School - A Book for All Ages. (Carole Marsh Iowa Bks.). (Illus.). (J). (gr. 3 up). 1994. pap. 19.95 (0-7933-4278-3); lib. bdg. 29.95 (0-7933-4277-5); disk 29.95 (0-7933-4279-1) Gallopade Intl.

— How to Start an Ohio Library: At Home or School - A Book for All Ages. (Carole Marsh Ohio Bks.). (Illus.). (J). (gr. 3 up). 1994. pap. 19.95 (0-7933-4338-0); lib. bdg. 29.95 (0-7933-4337-2); disk 29.95 (0-7933-4339-9) Gallopade Intl.

— How to Start an Oklahoma Library: At Home or School - A Book for All Ages. (Carole Marsh Oklahoma Bks.). (Illus.). (J). (gr. 3 up). 1994. pap. 19.95 (0-7933-4341-0); lib. bdg. 29.95 (0-7933-4340-2); disk 29.95 (0-7933-4342-9) Gallopade Intl.

— How to Start an Oregon Library: At Home or School - A Book for All Ages. (Oregon Bks.). (Illus.). (J). (gr. 3 up). 1994. pap. 19.95 (0-7933-4344-5); lib. bdg. 29.95 (0-7933-4343-7); disk 29.95 (0-7933-4345-3) Gallopade Intl.

— How to Word Process Like a Whiz! (Budding Genius Titles Ser.). (J). (gr. 2-9). Date not set. 29.95 (0-7933-7812-5, C Marsh); pap. 19.95 (0-7933-7813-3, C Marsh) Gallopade Intl.

— How You Know When Your Ass Is Grass. (Of All the Gaul Ser.). (Illus.). 1994. pap. 19.95 (1-55609-203-2) Gallopade Intl.

— How You Know When Your Tush Is Turf. (Of All the Gaul Ser.). (YA). 1994. pap. text 19.95 (0-7933-6923-1); lib. bdg. 29.95 (0-7933-6924-X); disk 29.95 (0-7933-6925-8) Gallopade Intl.

— I Con..If You Con(dom) The Ins & Outs of Contraception for the Sexually Active Girl or Boy. (Smart Sex Stuff Ser.). (Orig.). 1994. pap. 19.95 (1-55609-209-1) Gallopade Intl.

— Idaho & Other State Greats (Biographies) (Carole Marsh Idaho Bks.). (Illus.). (YA). (gr. 3-12). 1994. pap. 19.95 (1-55609-591-0); lib. bdg. 29.95 (1-55609-592-9); disk 29.95 (0-7933-1558-1) Gallopade Intl.

— Idaho Bandits, Bushwackers, Outlaws, Crooks, Devils, Ghosts, Desperadoes & Other Assorted & Sundry Characters! (Carole Marsh Idaho Bks.). (Illus.). (YA). (gr. 3-12). 1994. pap. 19.95 (0-7933-0357-5); lib. bdg. 29.95 (0-7933-0358-3); disk 29.95 (0-7933-0359-1) Gallopade Intl.

— Idaho "BIO" Bingo! 24 Must Know State People for Kids to Learn about While Having Fun! (Bingo! Ser.). (Illus.). (J). (gr. 2-8). 1998. pap. 14.95 (0-7933-8558-X) Gallopade Intl.

— The Idaho Bookstore Book: A Surprising Guide to Our State's Bookstores & Their Specialties for Students, Teachers, Writers & Publishers. (Carole Marsh Idaho Bks.). (Illus.). 1994. pap. 19.95 (0-7933-2892-6); lib. bdg. 29.95 (0-7933-2891-8); disk 29.95 (0-7933-2893-4) Gallopade Intl.

— Idaho Classic Christmas Trivia: Stories, Recipes, Activities, Legends, Lore & More! (Carole Marsh Idaho Bks.). (Illus.). (YA). (gr. 3-12). 1994. pap. 19.95 (0-7933-0360-5); lib. bdg. 29.95 (0-7933-0361-3); disk 29.95 (0-7933-0362-1) Gallopade Intl.

— Idaho Coastales. (Carole Marsh Idaho Bks.). (Illus.). (YA). (gr. 3-12). 1994. pap. 19.95 (1-55609-587-2); lib. bdg. 29.95 (1-55609-588-0); disk 29.95 (0-7933-1554-9) Gallopade Intl.

— Idaho Coastales! (Carole Marsh Idaho Bks.). (J). 1994. lib. bdg. 29.95 (0-7933-7277-1) Gallopade Intl.

— Idaho "Crinkum-Crankum" A Funny Word Book about Our State. (Carole Marsh Idaho Bks.). (Illus.). (J). 1994. pap. 19.95 (0-7933-4844-7); lib. bdg. 29.95 (0-7933-4843-9); disk 29.95 (0-7933-4845-5) Gallopade Intl.

M

— Idaho Dingbats! Bk. 1: A Fun Book of Games, Stories, Activities & More about Our State That's All in Code! for You to Decipher. (Carole Marsh Idaho Bks.). (Illus.). (J). (gr. 3-12). 1994. pap. 19.95 (0-7933-3810-7); lib. bdg. 29.95 (0-7933-3809-3); disk 29.95 (0-7933-3811-5) Gallopade Intl.

— Idaho Facts & Factivities. (Carole Marsh State Bks.). (Illus.). (J). (gr. 4-7). 1996. pap., teacher ed. 19.95 (0-7933-7871-0, C Marsh) Gallopade Intl.

— Idaho Festival Fun for Kids! (Carole Marsh Idaho Bks.). (Illus.). (YA). (gr. 3-12). 1994. pap. 19.95 (0-7933-3963-4); lib. bdg. 29.95 (0-7933-3962-6); disk 29.95 (0-7933-3964-2) Gallopade Intl.

— Idaho "GEO" Bingo! 38 Must Know State Geography Facts for Kids to Learn while Having Fun! (Bingo! Ser.). (Illus.). (J). (gr. 2-8). 1998. pap. 14.95 (0-7933-8559-8) Gallopade Intl.

— Idaho Government! The Cornerstone of Everyday Life in Our State! (Carole Marsh Idaho Bks.). (Illus.). (J). (gr. 3-12). 1996. pap. 19.95 (0-7933-6218-0); lib. bdg. 29.95 (0-7933-6217-2); disk 29.95 (0-7933-6219-9) Gallopade Intl.

— Idaho "HISTO" Bingo! 42 Must Know State History Facts for Kids to Learn While Having Fun! (Bingo! Ser.). (Illus.). (J). (gr. 2-8). 1998. pap. 14.95 (0-7933-8560-1) Gallopade Intl.

— Idaho History! Surprising Secrets about Our State's Founding Mothers, Fathers & Kids! (Carole Marsh Idaho Bks.). (Illus.). (J). (gr. 3-12). 1996. pap. 19.95 (0-7933-6065-X); lib. bdg. 29.95 (0-7933-6064-1); disk 29.95 (0-7933-6066-8) Gallopade Intl.

— The Idaho Hot Air Balloon Mystery. (Idaho Bks.). (Illus.). (J). (gr. 2-9). 1994. 29.95 (0-7933-2426-2); pap. 19.95 (0-7933-2427-0); disk 29.95 (0-7933-2428-9) Gallopade Intl.

— Idaho Hot Zones! Viruses, Diseases, & Epidemics in Our State's History. (Hot Zones! Ser.). (Illus.). (J). (gr. 3-12). 1998. pap. 19.95 (0-7933-8865-1); lib. bdg. 29.95 (0-7933-8864-3) Gallopade Intl.

— Idaho Indian Dictionary for Kids! (Carole Marsh State Bks.). (J). (gr. 2-9). 1996. 29.95 (0-7933-7680-7, C Marsh); pap. 19.95 (0-7933-7681-5, C Marsh) Gallopade Intl.

— Idaho Jeopardy! Answers & Questions about Our State! (Carole Marsh Idaho Bks.). (Illus.). (J). (gr. 3-12). 1994. pap. 19.95 (0-7933-4116-7); lib. bdg. 29.95 (0-7933-4115-9); disk 29.95 (0-7933-4117-5) Gallopade Intl.

— Idaho "Jography" A Fun Run Thru Our State! (Carole Marsh Idaho Bks.). (Illus.). (YA). (gr. 3-12). 1994. pap. 19.95 (1-55609-582-1); lib. bdg. 29.95 (1-55609-583-X); disk 29.95 (0-7933-1544-1) Gallopade Intl.

— Idaho Kid's Cookbook: Recipes, How-to, History, Lore & More! (Carole Marsh Idaho Bks.). (Illus.). (YA). (gr. 3-12). 1994. pap. 19.95 (0-7933-0369-9); lib. bdg. 29.95 (0-7933-0370-2); disk 29.95 (0-7933-0371-0) Gallopade Intl.

— The Idaho Library Book: A Surprising Guide to the Unusual Special Collections in Libraries Across Our State for Students, Teachers, Writers & Publishers - Includes Reproducible Mailing Labels Plus Activities for Young People! (Carole Marsh Idaho Bks.). (Illus.). 1994. pap. 19.95 (0-7933-3042-4); lib. bdg. 29.95 (0-7933-3041-6); disk 29.95 (0-7933-3043-2) Gallopade Intl.

— Idaho Math! How It All Adds up in Our State. (Carole Marsh Idaho Bks.). (Illus.). (YA). (gr. 3-12). 1996. pap. 19.95 (0-7933-6524-4); lib. bdg. 29.95 (0-7933-6523-6) Gallopade Intl.

— The Idaho Media Book: A Surprising Guide to the Amazing Print, Broadcast & Online Media of Our State for Students, Teachers, Writers & Publishers - Includes Reproducible Mailing Labels Plus Activities for Young People! (Carole Marsh Idaho Bks.). (Illus.). 1994. pap. 19.95 (0-7933-3198-6); lib. bdg. 29.95 (0-7933-3197-8); disk 29.95 (0-7933-3199-4) Gallopade Intl.

— The Idaho Mystery Van Takes Off! Book 1: Handicapped Idaho Kids Sneak Off on a Big Adventure. (Carole Marsh Idaho Bks.). (Illus.). (J). (gr. 3-12). 1994. 29.95 (0-7933-4997-4); pap. 19.95 (0-7933-4998-2); disk 29.95 (0-7933-4999-0) Gallopade Intl.

— Idaho Quiz Bowl Crash Course! (Carole Marsh Idaho Bks.). (Illus.). (J). (gr. 3-12). 1994. disk 29.95 (0-7933-1553-0) Gallopade Intl.

— Idaho Quiz Bowl Crash Course! (Carole Marsh Idaho Bks.). (Illus.). (YA). (gr. 3-12). 1994. pap. 19.95 (1-55609-589-9); lib. bdg. 29.95 (1-55609-590-2) Gallopade Intl.

— Idaho Rollercoasters! (Carole Marsh Idaho Bks.). (Illus.). (YA). (gr. 3-12). 1994. pap. 19.95 (0-7933-5261-4); lib. bdg. 29.95 (0-7933-5260-6); disk 29.95 (0-7933-5262-2) Gallopade Intl.

— Idaho School Trivia: An Amazing & Fascinating Look at Our State's Teachers, School & Students! (Carole Marsh Idaho Bks.). (Illus.). (YA). (gr. 3-12). 1994. pap. 19.95 (0-7933-0366-4); lib. bdg. 29.95 (0-7933-0367-2); disk 29.95 (0-7933-0368-0) Gallopade Intl.

— Idaho Silly Basketball Sportsmysteries. (Carole Marsh Idaho Bks.: Vol. II). (Illus.). (YA). (gr. 3-12). 1994. pap. 19.95 (0-7933-1560-3); lib. bdg. 29.95 (0-7933-1559-X); disk 29.95 (0-7933-1561-1) Gallopade Intl.

— Idaho Silly Basketball Sportsmysteries, Vol. I. (Carole Marsh Idaho Bks.). (Illus.). (YA). (gr. 3-12). 1994. pap. 19.95 (0-7933-0363-X); lib. bdg. 29.95 (0-7933-0364-8); disk 29.95 (0-7933-0365-6) Gallopade Intl.

— Idaho Silly Football Sportsmysteries, Vol. I. (Carole Marsh Idaho Bks.). (Illus.). (YA). (gr. 3-12). 1994. pap. 19.95 (1-55609-585-6); lib. bdg. 29.95 (1-55609-586-4); disk 29.95 (0-7933-1546-8) Gallopade Intl.

— Idaho Silly Football Sportsmysteries, Vol. II. (Carole Marsh Idaho Bks.). (Illus.). (YA). (gr. 3-12). 1994. pap. 19.95 (0-7933-1548-4); lib. bdg. 29.95 (0-7933-1547-6); disk 29.95 (0-7933-1549-2) Gallopade Intl.

— Idaho Silly Trivia! (Carole Marsh Idaho Bks.). (Illus.). (YA). (gr. 3-12). 1994. pap. 19.95 (1-55609-580-5); lib. bdg. 29.95 (1-55609-581-3); disk 29.95 (0-7933-1543-3) Gallopade Intl.

— Idaho Spelling Bee! Score Big by Correctly Spelling Our State's Unique Names. (Carole Marsh Idaho Bks.). (Illus.). (YA). (gr. 3-12). 1996. pap. 19.95 (0-7933-6677-1); lib. bdg. 29.95 (0-7933-6676-3) Gallopade Intl.

— Idaho Timeline: A Chronology of Idaho History, Mystery, Trivia, Legend, Lore & More. (Carole Marsh Idaho Bks.). (Illus.). (J). (gr. 3-12). 1994. pap. 19.95 (0-7933-5912-0); lib. bdg. 29.95 (0-7933-5911-2); disk 29.95 (0-7933-5913-9) Gallopade Intl.

— Idaho 2000! Coming Soon to a Calendar Near You - The 21st Century! - Complete Set of AL 2000 Items. (Two Thousand! Ser.). (Illus.). (J). (gr. 3-12). 1998. pap. 75.00 (0-7933-9333-7); lib. bdg. 85.00 (0-7933-9334-5) Gallopade Intl.

— Idaho 2000! Coming Soon to a Calendar Near You-The 21st Century! (Two Thousand! Ser.). (Illus.). (J). (gr. 3-12). 1998. pap. 19.95 (0-7933-8712-4); lib. bdg. 29.95 (0-7933-8711-6) Gallopade Intl.

— Idaho UFO's & Extraterrestrials! A Look at the Sightings & Science in Our State. (Carole Marsh Idaho Bks.). (Illus.). (J). (gr. 3-12). 1997. pap. 19.95 (0-7933-6371-3); lib. bdg. 29.95 (0-7933-6370-5) Gallopade Intl.

— Idaho's (Most Devastating!) Disasters & (Most Calamitous!) Catastrophies! (Carole Marsh Idaho Bks.). (Illus.). (YA). (gr. 3-12). 1994. pap. 19.95 (0-7933-0354-0); lib. bdg. 29.95 (0-7933-0355-9); disk 29.95 (0-7933-0356-7) Gallopade Intl.

— Idaho's Unsolved Mysteries (& Their "Solutions") Includes Scientific Information & Other Activities for Students. (Carole Marsh Idaho Bks.). (Illus.). (J). (gr. 3-12). 1994. pap. 19.95 (0-7933-5759-4); lib. bdg. 29.95 (0-7933-5758-6); disk 29.95 (0-7933-5760-8) Gallopade Intl.

— If My Alabama Mama Ran the World! (Carole Marsh Alabama Bks.). (Illus.). (YA). (gr. 3-12). 1994. pap. 19.95 (0-7933-1336-8); lib. bdg. 29.95 (0-7933-1335-X); disk 29.95 (0-7933-1337-6) Gallopade Intl.

— If My Alaska Mama Ran the World! (Carole Marsh Alaska Bks.). (Illus.). (YA). (gr. 3-12). 1994. pap. 19.95 (0-7933-1356-2); lib. bdg. 29.95 (0-7933-1355-4); disk 29.95 (0-7933-1357-0) Gallopade Intl.

— If My Arizona Mama Ran the World! (Carole Marsh Arizona Bks.). (Illus.). (YA). (gr. 3-12). 1994. pap. 19.95 (0-7933-1371-6); lib. bdg. 29.95 (0-7933-1370-8); disk 29.95 (0-7933-1372-4) Gallopade Intl.

— If My Arkansas Mama Ran the World! (Carole Marsh Arkansas Bks.). (Illus.). (YA). (gr. 3-12). 1994. pap. 19.95 (0-7933-1387-2); lib. bdg. 29.95 (0-7933-1386-4); disk 29.95 (0-7933-1388-0) Gallopade Intl.

— If My California Mama Ran the World! (Carole Marsh California Bks.). (Illus.). (YA). (gr. 3-12). 1994. pap. 19.95 (0-7933-1403-8); lib. bdg. 29.95 (0-7933-1402-X); disk 29.95 (0-7933-1404-6) Gallopade Intl.

— If My Colorado Mama Ran the World! (Carole Marsh Colorado Bks.). (Illus.). (YA). (gr. 3-12). 1994. pap. 19.95 (0-7933-1419-4); lib. bdg. 29.95 (0-7933-1418-6); disk 29.95 (0-7933-1420-8) Gallopade Intl.

— If My Connecticut Mama Ran the World! (Carole Marsh Connecticut Bks.). (Illus.). (YA). (gr. 3-12). 1994. pap. 19.95 (0-7933-1435-6); lib. bdg. 29.95 (0-7933-1434-8); disk 29.95 (0-7933-1436-4) Gallopade Intl.

— If My Delaware Mama Ran the World! (Carole Marsh Delaware Bks.). (Illus.). (YA). (gr. 3-12). 1994. pap. 19.95 (0-7933-1453-4); lib. bdg. 29.95 (0-7933-1452-6); disk 29.95 (0-7933-1454-2) Gallopade Intl.

— If My Florida Mama Ran the World! (Carole Marsh Florida Bks.). (Illus.). (YA). (gr. 3-12). 1994. pap. 19.95 (0-7933-1499-2); lib. bdg. 24.95 (0-7933-1498-4); disk 29.95 (0-7933-1500-X) Gallopade Intl.

— If My Georgia Mama Ran the World! (Carole Marsh Georgia Bks.). (Illus.). (YA). (gr. 3-12). 1994. pap. 19.95 (0-7933-1518-2); lib. bdg. 29.95 (0-7933-1517-4); disk 29.95 (0-7933-1519-0) Gallopade Intl.

— If My Hawaii Mama Ran the World! (Carole Marsh Hawaii Bks.). (Illus.). (YA). (gr. 3-12). 1994. pap. 19.95 (0-7933-1537-9); lib. bdg. 29.95 (0-7933-1536-0); disk 29.95 (0-7933-1538-7) Gallopade Intl.

— If My Idaho Mama Ran the World! (Carole Marsh Idaho Bks.). (Illus.). (YA). (gr. 3-12). 1994. pap. 19.95 (0-7933-1556-5); lib. bdg. 29.95 (0-7933-1555-7); disk 29.95 (0-7933-1557-3) Gallopade Intl.

— If My Illinois Mama Ran the World! (Carole Marsh Illinois Bks.). (Illus.). (YA). (gr. 3-12). 1994. pap. 19.95 (0-7933-1596-4); lib. bdg. 29.95 (0-7933-1595-6); disk 29.95 (0-7933-1597-2) Gallopade Intl.

— If My Indiana Mama Ran the World! (Carole Marsh Indiana Bks.). (Illus.). (YA). (gr. 3-12). 1994. pap. 19.95 (0-7933-1614-6); lib. bdg. 29.95 (0-7933-1613-8); disk 29.95 (0-7933-1615-4) Gallopade Intl.

— If My Iowa Mama Ran the World! (Carole Marsh Iowa Bks.). (Illus.). (YA). (gr. 3-12). 1994. pap. 19.95 (0-7933-1634-0); lib. bdg. 29.95 (0-7933-1633-2); disk 29.95 (0-7933-1635-9) Gallopade Intl.

— If My Kansas Mama Ran the World. (Statemeant Ser.). (J). (gr. 3-12). 1994. 29.95 (1-55609-374-8); pap. 19.95 (1-55609-375-6); disk 29.95 (1-55609-376-4) Gallopade Intl.

— If My Kentucky Mama Ran the World! (Carole Marsh Kentucky Bks.). (Illus.). (J). (gr. 3-8). 1994. pap. 19.95 (0-7933-1656-1); lib. bdg. 29.95 (0-7933-1655-3); disk 29.95 (0-7933-1657-X) Gallopade Intl.

— If My Louisiana Mama Ran the World! (Carole Marsh Louisiana Bks.). (Illus.). (J). (gr. 3-8). 1994. pap. 19.95 (0-7933-1675-8); lib. bdg. 29.95 (0-7933-1674-X); disk 29.95 (0-7933-1676-6) Gallopade Intl.

— If My Maine Mama Ran the World! (Carole Marsh Maine Bks.). (Illus.). (J). (gr. 3-8). 1994. pap. 19.95 (0-7933-1688-X); lib. bdg. 29.95 (0-7933-1687-1); disk 29.95 (0-7933-1689-8) Gallopade Intl.

— If My Mama Ran the World. (J). 1994. 29.95 (1-55609-287-3) Gallopade Intl.

— If My Mama Ran the World. (J). 1997. pap. 14.95 (0-7933-4437-9) Gallopade Intl.

— If My Maryland Mama Ran the World! (Carole Marsh Maryland Bks.). (Illus.). (J). (gr. 3-8). 1994. pap. 19.95 (0-7933-1694-4); lib. bdg. 29.95 (0-7933-1693-6); disk 29.95 (0-7933-1695-2) Gallopade Intl.

— If My Massachusetts Mama Ran the World! (Carole Marsh Massachusetts Bks.). (Illus.). (J). (gr. 3-8). 1994. pap. 19.95 (0-7933-1703-7); lib. bdg. 29.95 (0-7933-1702-9); disk 29.95 (0-7933-1704-5) Gallopade Intl.

— If My Michigan Mama Ran the World! (Carole Marsh Michigan Bks.). (Illus.). (J). (gr. 3 up). 1994. pap. 19.95 (0-7933-1724-X); lib. bdg. 29.95 (0-7933-1723-1); disk 29.95 (0-7933-1725-8) Gallopade Intl.

— If My Minnesota Mama Ran the World! (Carole Marsh Minnesota Bks.). (Illus.). (J). (gr. 3 up). 1994. pap. 19.95 (0-7933-1718-5); lib. bdg. 29.95 (0-7933-1717-7); disk 29.95 (0-7933-1719-3) Gallopade Intl.

— If My Mississippi Mama Ran the World! (Carole Marsh Mississippi Bks.). (Illus.). (J). (gr. 3 up). 1994. pap. 19.95 (0-7933-1729-0); lib. bdg. 29.95 (0-7933-1728-2); disk 29.95 (0-7933-1730-4) Gallopade Intl.

— If My Missouri Mama Ran the World! (Carole Marsh Missouri Bks.). (Illus.). (J). (gr. 3 up). 1994. pap. 19.95 (0-7933-1738-X); lib. bdg. 29.95 (0-7933-1737-1); disk 29.95 (0-7933-1739-8) Gallopade Intl.

— If My Montana Mama Ran the World! (Carole Marsh Montana Bks.). (Illus.). (J). (gr. 3 up). 1994. pap. 19.95 (0-7933-1747-9); lib. bdg. 29.95 (0-7933-1746-0); disk 29.95 (0-7933-1748-7) Gallopade Intl.

— If My Nebraska Mama Ran the World! (Carole Marsh Nebraska Bks.). (Illus.). (J). (gr. 3 up). 1994. pap. 19.95 (0-7933-1756-8); lib. bdg. 29.95 (0-7933-1755-X); disk 29.95 (0-7933-1757-6) Gallopade Intl.

— If My Nevada Mama Ran the World! (Carole Marsh Nevada Bks.). (Illus.). (J). 1994. pap. 19.95 (0-7933-1765-7); lib. bdg. 29.95 (0-7933-1764-9); disk 29.95 (0-7933-1766-5) Gallopade Intl.

— If My New Hampshire Mama Ran the World! (Carole Marsh New Hampshire Bks.). (Illus.). (J). 1994. pap. 19.95 (0-7933-1774-6); lib. bdg. 29.95 (0-7933-1773-8); disk 29.95 (0-7933-1775-4) Gallopade Intl.

— If My New Jersey Mama Ran the World! (Carole Marsh New Jersey Bks.). (Illus.). (J). 1994. pap. 19.95 (0-7933-1783-5); lib. bdg. 29.95 (0-7933-1782-7); disk 29.95 (0-7933-1784-3) Gallopade Intl.

— If My New Mexico Mama Ran The World! (Carole Marsh New Mexico Bks.). (Illus.). (J). 1994. pap. 19.95 (0-7933-1816-5); lib. bdg. 29.95 (0-7933-1815-7); disk 29.95 (0-7933-1817-3) Gallopade Intl.

— If My New York Mama Ran the World! (Carole Marsh New York Bks.). (Illus.). (J). 1994. pap. 19.95 (0-7933-1828-9); lib. bdg. 29.95 (0-7933-1827-0); disk 29.95 (0-7933-1829-7) Gallopade Intl.

— If My North Carolina Mama Ran the World! (Carole Marsh North Carolina Bks.). (Illus.). (J). 1994. pap. 19.95 (0-7933-1834-3); lib. bdg. 29.95 (0-7933-1833-5); disk 29.95 (0-7933-1835-1) Gallopade Intl.

— If My North Dakota Mama Ran the World! (Carole Marsh North Dakota Bks.). (Illus.). (J). 1994. pap. 19.95 (0-7933-1843-2); lib. bdg. 29.95 (0-7933-1842-4); disk 29.95 (0-7933-1844-0) Gallopade Intl.

— If My Ohio Mama Ran the World! (Carole Marsh Ohio Bks.). (Illus.). (J). 1994. pap. 19.95 (0-7933-1851-3); lib. bdg. 29.95 (0-7933-1850-5); disk 29.95 (0-7933-1852-1) Gallopade Intl.

— If My Oklahoma Mama Ran the World! (Carole Marsh Oklahoma Bks.). (Illus.). (J). 1994. pap. 19.95 (0-7933-1876-9); lib. bdg. 29.95 (0-7933-1875-0); disk 29.95 (0-7933-1877-7) Gallopade Intl.

— If My Oregon Mama Ran the World! (Carole Marsh Oregon Bks.). (Illus.). (J). 1994. pap. 19.95 (0-7933-1911-0); lib. bdg. 29.95 (0-7933-1910-2); disk 29.95 (0-7933-1912-9) Gallopade Intl.

— If My Pennsylvania Mama Ran the World! (Carole Marsh Pennsylvania Bks.). (Illus.). (J). 1994. pap. 19.95 (0-7933-1940-4); lib. bdg. 29.95 (0-7933-1939-0); disk 29.95 (0-7933-1941-2) Gallopade Intl.

— If My Rhode Island Mama Ran the World! (Carole Marsh Rhode Island Bks.). (Illus.). (J). 1994. pap. 19.95 (0-7933-1975-7); lib. bdg. 29.95 (0-7933-1974-9); disk 29.95 (0-7933-1976-5) Gallopade Intl.

— If My South Carolina Mama Ran the World! (Carole Marsh South Carolina Bks.). (Illus.). (J). 1994. pap. 19.95 (0-7933-2004-6); lib. bdg. 29.95 (0-7933-2003-8); disk 29.95 (0-7933-2005-4) Gallopade Intl.

— If My South Dakota Mama Ran the World! (Carole Marsh South Dakota Bks.). (Illus.). (J). 1994. pap. 19.95 (0-7933-2036-4); lib. bdg. 29.95 (0-7933-2035-6); disk 29.95 (0-7933-2037-2) Gallopade Intl.

— If My Tennessee Mama Ran the World! (Carole Marsh Tennessee Bks.). (Illus.). (J). 1994. pap. 19.95 (0-7933-2066-6); lib. bdg. 29.95 (0-7933-2065-8); disk 29.95 (0-7933-2067-4) Gallopade Intl.

— If My Texas Mama Ran the World! (Carole Marsh Texas Bks.). (Illus.). (J). 1994. pap. 19.95 (0-7933-2095-X); lib. bdg. 29.95 (0-7933-2094-1); disk 29.95 (0-7933-2096-8) Gallopade Intl.

— If My Utah Mama Ran the World! (Carole Marsh Utah Bks.). (Illus.). (J). 1994. pap. 19.95 (0-7933-2127-1); lib. bdg. 29.95 (0-7933-2126-3); disk 29.95 (0-7933-2128-X) Gallopade Intl.

— If My Vermont Mama Ran the World! (Carole Marsh Vermont Bks.). (Illus.). (J). 1994. pap. 19.95 (0-7933-2159-X); lib. bdg. 29.95 (0-7933-2158-1); disk 29.95 (0-7933-2160-3) Gallopade Intl.

— If My Virginia Mama Ran the World! (Carole Marsh Virginia Bks.). (Illus.). (J). 1994. pap. 19.95 (0-7933-2188-3); lib. bdg. 29.95 (0-7933-2187-5); disk 29.95 (0-7933-2189-1) Gallopade Intl.

— If My Washington, D.C. Mama Ran the World! (Carole Marsh Washington, D.C. Bks.). (Illus.). (YA). (gr. 3-12). 1994. pap. 19.95 (0-7933-1478-X); lib. bdg. 29.95 (0-7933-1477-1); disk 29.95 (0-7933-1479-8) Gallopade Intl.

— If My Washington Mama Ran the World! (Carole Marsh Washington Bks.). (Illus.). (J). 1994. pap. 19.95 (0-7933-2222-7); lib. bdg. 29.95 (0-7933-2221-9); disk 29.95 (0-7933-2223-5) Gallopade Intl.

— If My West Virginia Mama Ran the World! (Carole Marsh West Virginia Bks.). (Illus.). (J). 1994. pap. 19.95 (0-7933-2254-5); lib. bdg. 29.95 (0-7933-2253-7); disk 29.95 (0-7933-2255-3) Gallopade Intl.

— If My Wisconsin Mama Ran the World! (Carole Marsh Wisconsin Bks.). (Illus.). (J). 1994. pap. 19.95 (0-7933-2286-3); lib. bdg. 29.95 (0-7933-2285-5); disk 29.95 (0-7933-2287-1) Gallopade Intl.

— If My Wyoming Mama Ran the World. (Carole Marsh Wyoming Bks.). (Illus.). (J). 1994. pap. 19.95 (0-7933-2310-X); lib. bdg. 29.95 (0-7933-2309-6); disk 29.95 (0-7933-2311-8) Gallopade Intl.

— Illinois & Other State Greats (Biographies) (Carole Marsh Illinois Bks.). (Illus.). (YA). (gr. 3-12). 1994. pap. 19.95 (1-55609-415-9); lib. bdg. 29.95 (1-55609-416-7); disk 29.95 (0-7933-1598-0) Gallopade Intl.

— Illinois Bandits, Bushwackers, Outlaws, Crooks, Devils, Ghosts, Desperadoes & Other Assorted & Sundry Characters! (Carole Marsh Illinois Bks.). (Illus.). (YA). (gr. 3-12). 1994. pap. 19.95 (0-7933-0381-8); lib. bdg. 29.95 (0-7933-0382-6); disk 29.95 (0-7933-0383-4) Gallopade Intl.

— Illinois "BIO" Bingo! 24 Must Know State People for Kids to Learn about While Having Fun! (Bingo! Ser.). (Illus.). (J). (gr. 2-8). 1998. pap. 14.95 (0-7933-8561-X) Gallopade Intl.

— The Illinois Bookstore Book: A Surprising Guide to Our State's Bookstores & Their Specialties for Students, Teachers, Writers & Publishers. (Illinois Bks.). (Illus.). 1994. pap. 19.95 (0-7933-2895-0); lib. bdg. 29.95 (0-7933-2894-2); disk 29.95 (0-7933-2896-9) Gallopade Intl.

— Illinois Classic Christmas Trivia: Stories, Recipes, Activities, Legends, Lore & More! (Carole Marsh Illinois Bks.). (Illus.). (YA). (gr. 3-12). 1994. pap. 19.95 (0-7933-0384-2); lib. bdg. 29.95 (0-7933-0385-0); disk 29.95 (0-7933-0386-9) Gallopade Intl.

— Illinois Coastales. (Carole Marsh Illinois Bks.). (J). 1994. lib. bdg. 29.95 (0-7933-7278-X) Gallopade Intl.

— Illinois Coastales. (Carole Marsh Illinois Bks.). (Illus.). (YA). (gr. 3-12). 1994. pap. 19.95 (1-55609-411-6); lib. bdg. 29.95 (1-55609-412-4); disk 29.95 (0-7933-1594-8) Gallopade Intl.

— Illinois "Crinkum-Crankum" A Funny Word Book about Our State. (Carole Marsh Illinois Bks.). (Illus.). (J). 1994. pap. 19.95 (0-7933-4847-1); lib. bdg. 29.95 (0-7933-4846-3); disk 29.95 (0-7933-4848-X) Gallopade Intl.

— Illinois Dingbats! Bk. 1: A Fun Book of Games, Stories, Activities & More about Our State That's All in Code! for You to Decipher. (Carole Marsh Illinois Bks.). (Illus.). (J). (gr. 3-12). 1994. pap. 19.95 (0-7933-3813-1); lib. bdg. 29.95 (0-7933-3812-3); disk 29.95 (0-7933-3814-X) Gallopade Intl.

***Marsh, Carole.** The Illinois Experience Pocket Guide. (Illinois Experience! Ser.). (Illus.). (J). 2000. pap. 6.95 (0-7933-9450-3) Gallopade Intl.

Marsh, Carole. Illinois Facts & Factivities. (Carole Marsh State Bks.). (Illus.). (J). (gr. 4-7). 1996. pap., teacher ed. 19.95 (0-7933-7873-7, C Marsh) Gallopade Intl.

— Illinois Festival Fun for Kids! (Carole Marsh Illinois Bks.). (Illus.). (YA). (gr. 3-12). 1994. pap. 19.95 (0-7933-3966-9); lib. bdg. 29.95 (0-7933-3965-0); disk 29.95 (0-7933-3967-7) Gallopade Intl.

— Illinois "GEO" Bingo! 38 Must Know State Geography Facts to Learn While Having Fun! (Bingo! Ser.). (Illus.). (J). (gr. 2-8). 1998. pap. 14.95 (0-7933-8562-8) Gallopade Intl.

— Illinois Government! The Cornerstone of Everyday Life in Our State! (Carole Marsh Illinois Bks.). (Illus.). (J). (gr. 3-12). 1996. pap. 19.95 (0-7933-6221-0); lib. bdg. 29.95 (0-7933-6220-2); disk 29.95 (0-7933-6222-9) Gallopade Intl.

— Illinois "HISTO" Bingo! 42 Must Know State History Facts for Kids to Learn While Having Fun! (Bingo! Ser.). (Illus.). (J). (gr. 2-8). 1998. pap. 14.95 (0-7933-8563-6) Gallopade Intl.

— Illinois History! Surprising Secrets about Our State's Founding Mothers, Fathers & Kids! (Carole Marsh Illinois Bks.). (Illus.). (J). (gr. 3-12). 1996. pap. 19.95 (0-7933-6068-4); lib. bdg. 29.95 (0-7933-6067-6); disk 29.95 (0-7933-6069-2) Gallopade Intl.

— The Illinois Hot Air Balloon Mystery. (Carole Marsh Illinois Bks.). (Illus.). (J). (gr. 2-9). 1994. 29.95 (0-7933-2435-1); pap. 19.95 (0-7933-2436-X); disk 29.95 (0-7933-2437-8) Gallopade Intl.

— Illinois Hot Zones! Viruses, Diseases, & Epidemics in Our State's History. (Hot Zones! Ser.). (Illus.). (J). (gr. 3-12). 1998. pap. 19.95 (0-7933-8868-6); lib. bdg. 29.95 (0-7933-8867-8) Gallopade Intl.

— Illinois Indian Dictionary for Kids! (Carole Marsh State Bks.). (J). (gr. 2-9). 1996. 29.95 (0-7933-7683-1, C Marsh); pap. 19.95 (0-7933-7684-X, C Marsh) Gallopade Intl.

***Marsh, Carole.** Illinois Jeopardy. (Illinois Experience! Ser.). (Illus.). (J). (gr. 2-6). 2000. pap. 7.95 (0-7933-9513-5) Gallopade Intl.

Marsh, Carole. Illinois Jeopardy! Answers & Questions about Our State! (Carole Marsh Illinois Bks.). (Illus.). (J). (gr. 3-12). 1994. pap. 19.95 (0-7933-4119-1); lib. bdg. 29.95 (0-7933-4118-3); disk 29.95 (0-7933-4120-5) Gallopade Intl.

***Marsh, Carole.** Illinois Jography. (Illinois Experience! Ser.). (Illus.). (J). (gr. 2-6). 2000. pap. 7.95 (0-7933-9514-3) Gallopade Intl.

Marsh, Carole. Illinois "Jography" A Fun Run Thru Our State! (Carole Marsh Illinois Bks.). (Illus.). (YA). (gr. 3-12). 1994. pap. 19.95 (1-55609-406-X); lib. bdg. 29.95 (1-55609-407-8); disk 29.95 (0-7933-1584-0) Gallopade Intl.

— Illinois Kid's Cookbook: Recipes, How-to, History, Lore & More! (Carole Marsh Illinois Bks.). (Illus.). (YA). (gr. 3-12). 1994. pap. 19.95 (0-7933-0393-1); lib. bdg. 29.95 (0-7933-0394-X); disk 29.95 (0-7933-0395-8) Gallopade Intl.

— The Illinois Library Book: A Surprising Guide to the Unusual Special Collections in Libraries Across Our State for Students, Teachers, Writers & Publishers - Includes Reproducible Mailing Labels Plus Activities for Young People! (Carole Marsh Illinois Bks.). (Illus.). 1994. pap. 19.95 (0-7933-3045-9); lib. bdg. 29.95 (0-7933-3044-0) Gallopade Intl.

— The Illinois Library Book: A Surprising Guide to the Unusual Special Collections in Libraries Across Our State for Students, Teachers, Writers & Publishers - Includes Reproducible Mailing Labels Plus Activities for Young People! (Carole Marsh Illinois Bks.). (Illus.). 1997. disk 29.95 (0-7933-3046-7) Gallopade Intl.

— Illinois Math! How It All Adds up in Our State. (Carole Marsh Illinois Bks.). (Illus.). (YA). (gr. 3-12). 1996. pap. 19.95 (0-7933-6527-9); lib. bdg. 29.95 (0-7933-6526-0) Gallopade Intl.

— The Illinois Media Book: A Surprising Guide to the Amazing Print, Broadcast & Online Media of Our State for Students, Teachers, Writers & Publishers - Includes Reproducible Mailing Labels Plus Activities for Young People! (Carole Marsh Illinois Bks.). (Illus.). 1994. pap. 19.95 (0-7933-3201-X); lib. bdg. 29.95 (0-7933-3200-1); disk 29.95 (0-7933-3202-8) Gallopade Intl.

— The Illinois Mystery Van Takes Off! Book 1: Handicapped Illinois Kids Sneak Off on a Big Adventure. (Carole Marsh Illinois Bks.). (Illus.). (J). (gr. 3-12). 1994. 29.95 (0-7933-5000-X); pap. 19.95 (0-7933-5001-8); disk 29.95 (0-7933-5002-6) Gallopade Intl.

— Illinois Quiz Bowl Crash Course! (Carole Marsh Illinois Bks.). (Illus.). (YA). (gr. 3-12). 1994. pap. 19.95 (1-55609-413-2); lib. bdg. 29.95 (1-55609-414-0); disk 29.95 (0-7933-1593-X) Gallopade Intl.

— Illinois Rollercoasters! (Carole Marsh Illinois Bks.). (Illus.). (YA). (gr. 3-12). 1994. pap. 19.95 (0-7933-5264-9); lib. bdg. 29.95 (0-7933-5263-0); disk 29.95 (0-7933-5265-7) Gallopade Intl.

— Illinois School Trivia: An Amazing & Fascinating Look at Our State's Teachers, Schools & Students! (Carole Marsh Illinois Bks.). (Illus.). (YA). (gr. 3-12). 1994. pap. 19.95 (0-7933-0390-7); lib. bdg. 29.95 (0-7933-0391-5); disk 29.95 (0-7933-0392-3) Gallopade Intl.

— Illinois Silly Basketball Sportsmysteries, Vol. I. (Carole Marsh Illinois Bks.). (Illus.). (YA). (gr. 3-12). 1994. pap. 19.95 (0-7933-0387-7); lib. bdg. 29.95 (0-7933-0388-5); disk 29.95 (0-7933-0389-3) Gallopade Intl.

— Illinois Silly Basketball Sportsmysteries, Vol. II. (Carole Marsh Illinois Bks.). (Illus.). (YA). (gr. 3-12). 1994. pap. 19.95 (0-7933-1600-6); lib. bdg. 29.95 (0-7933-1599-9); disk 29.95 (0-7933-1601-4) Gallopade Intl.

— Illinois Silly Football Sportsmysteries. (Carole Marsh Illinois Bks.: Vol. II). (Illus.). (YA). (gr. 3-12). 1994. pap. 19.95 (0-7933-1588-3); lib. bdg. 29.95 (0-7933-1587-5); disk 29.95 (0-7933-1589-1) Gallopade Intl.

— Illinois Silly Football Sportsmysteries, Vol. I. (Carole Marsh Illinois Bks.). (Illus.). (YA). (gr. 3-12). 1994. pap. 19.95 (1-55609-409-4); lib. bdg. 29.95 (1-55609-410-8); disk 29.95 (0-7933-1586-7) Gallopade Intl.

— Illinois Silly Trivia! (Carole Marsh Illinois Bks.). (Illus.). (YA). (gr. 3-12). 1994. pap. 19.95 (1-55609-113-3); lib. bdg. 29.95 (1-55609-405-1); disk 29.95 (0-7933-1583-2) Gallopade Intl.

— Illinois Spelling Bee! Score Big by Correctly Spelling Our State's Unique Names. (Carole Marsh Illinois Bks.). (Illus.). (YA). (gr. 3-12). 1996. pap. 19.95 (0-7933-6680-1); lib. bdg. 29.95 (0-7933-6679-8) Gallopade Intl.

— Illinois Timeline: A Chronology of Illinois History, Mystery, Trivia, Legend, Lore & More. (Carole Marsh Illinois Bks.). (Illus.). (J). (gr. 3-12). 1994. pap. 19.95 (0-7933-5915-5); lib. bdg. 29.95 (0-7933-5914-7); disk 29.95 (0-7933-5916-3) Gallopade Intl.

— Illinois 2000! Coming Soon to a Calendar Near You - The 21st Century! - Complete Set of AL 2000 Items. (Two Thousand! Ser.). (Illus.). (J). (gr. 3-12). 1998. pap. 75.00 (0-7933-9335-3); lib. bdg. 85.00 (0-7933-9336-1) Gallopade Intl.

— Illinois 2000! Coming Soon to a Calendar Near You-The 21st Century! (Two Thousand! Ser.). (Illus.). (J). (gr. 3-12). 1998. pap. 19.95 (0-7933-8715-9); lib. bdg. 29.95 (0-7933-8714-0) Gallopade Intl.

— Illinois UFO's & Extraterrestrials! A Look at the Sightings & Science in Our State. (Carole Marsh Illinois Bks.). (Illus.). (J). (gr. 3-12). 1997. pap. 19.95 (0-7933-6374-8); lib. bdg. 29.95 (0-7933-6373-X) Gallopade Intl.

***Marsh, Carole.** Illinois's Big Activity Book. (Illinois Experience! Ser.). (Illus.). (J). (gr. k-5). 2000. pap. 9.95 (0-7933-9460-0) Gallopade Intl.

Marsh, Carole. Illinois's (Most Devastating!) Disasters & (Most Calamitous!) Catastrophies! (Carole Marsh Illinois Bks.). (Illus.). (YA). (gr. 3-12). 1994. pap. 19.95 (0-7933-0378-8); lib. bdg. 29.95 (0-7933-0379-6); disk 29.95 (0-7933-0380-X) Gallopade Intl.

— Illinois's Unsolved Mysteries (& Their "Solutions") Includes Scientific Information & Other Activities for Students. (Carole Marsh Illinois Bks.). (Illus.). (J). (gr. 3-12). 1994. pap. 19.95 (0-7933-5762-4); lib. bdg. 29.95 (0-7933-5761-6); disk 29.95 (0-7933-5763-2) Gallopade Intl.

— In Good Taste! Cannibalism - Who Did It, Where, When, How & Why. (Extreme History). 1994. 29.95 (0-7933-7362-X); 19.95 (0-7933-7364-6); pap. 19.95 (0-7933-7363-8); audio 14.95 (0-7933-7367-0); VHS 14.95 (0-7933-7366-2); cd-rom 14.95 (0-7933-7368-9); disk 14.95 (0-7933-7365-4) Gallopade Intl.

***Marsh, Carole.** The Incredible Illinois Coloring Book. (Illinois Experience! Ser.). (Illus.). 2000. pap. 3.95 (0-7933-9470-8) Gallopade Intl.

Marsh, Carole. Indiana & Other State Greats (Biographies) (Carole Marsh Indiana Bks.). (Illus.). (YA). (gr. 3-12). 1994. pap. 19.95 (1-55609-436-1); lib. bdg. 29.95 (1-55609-437-X); disk 29.95 (0-7933-1616-2) Gallopade Intl.

— Indiana Bandits, Bushwackers, Outlaws, Crooks, Devils, Ghosts, Desperadoes & Other Assorted & Sundry Characters! (Carole Marsh Indiana Bks.). (Illus.). (YA). (gr. 3-12). 1994. pap. 19.95 (0-7933-0405-9); lib. bdg. 29.95 (0-7933-0406-7); disk 29.95 (0-7933-0407-5) Gallopade Intl.

— Indiana "BIO" Bingo! 24 Must Know State People for Kids to Learn about While Having Fun! (Bingo! Ser.). (Illus.). (J). (gr. 2-8). 1998. pap. 14.95 (0-7933-8564-4) Gallopade Intl.

— The Indiana Bookstore Book: A Surprising Guide to Our State's Bookstores & Their Specialties for Students, Teachers, Writers & Publishers. (Carole Marsh Indiana Bks.). (Illus.). 1994. pap. 19.95 (0-7933-2898-5); lib. bdg. 29.95 (0-7933-2897-7); disk 29.95 (0-7933-2899-3) Gallopade Intl.

— Indiana Classic Christmas Trivia: Stories, Recipes, Activities, Legends, Lore & More! (Carole Marsh Indiana Bks.). (Illus.). (YA). (gr. 3-12). 1994. pap. 19.95 (0-7933-0408-3); lib. bdg. 29.95 (0-7933-0409-1); disk 29.95 (0-7933-0410-5) Gallopade Intl.

— Indiana Coastales. (Carole Marsh Indiana Bks.). (Illus.). (YA). (gr. 3-12). 1994. pap. 19.95 (1-55609-432-9); lib. bdg. 29.95 (1-55609-433-7); disk 29.95 (0-7933-1617-0) Gallopade Intl.

— Indiana Coastales! (Carole Marsh Indiana Bks.). (J). 1994. lib. bdg. 29.95 (0-7933-7279-8) Gallopade Intl.

— Indiana "Crinkum-Crankum" A Funny Word Book about Our State. (Carole Marsh Indiana Bks.). (Illus.). (J). 1994. pap. 19.95 (0-7933-4851-X); lib. bdg. 29.95 (0-7933-4849-8); disk 29.95 (0-7933-4852-8) Gallopade Intl.

— Indiana Dingbats! Bk. 1: A Fun Book of Games, Stories, Activities & More about Our State That's All in Code! for You to Decipher. (Carole Marsh Indiana Bks.). (Illus.). (J). (gr. 3-12). 1994. pap. 19.95 (0-7933-3816-6); lib. bdg. 29.95 (0-7933-3815-8); disk 29.95 (0-7933-3817-4) Gallopade Intl.

— Indiana Facts & Factivities. (Carole Marsh State Bks.). (Illus.). (J). (gr. 4-7). 1996. pap., teacher ed. 19.95 (0-7933-7875-3, C Marsh) Gallopade Intl.

— Indiana Festival Fun for Kids! (Carole Marsh Indiana Bks.). (Illus.). (YA). (gr. 3-12). 1994. pap. 19.95 (0-7933-3969-3); lib. bdg. 29.95 (0-7933-3968-5); disk 29.95 (0-7933-3970-7) Gallopade Intl.

— Indiana "GEO" Bingo! 38 Must Know State Geography Facts for Kids to Learn While Having Fun! (Bingo! Ser.). (Illus.). (J). (gr. 2-8). 1998. pap. 14.95 (0-7933-8565-2) Gallopade Intl.

— Indiana Government! The Cornerstone of Everyday Life in Our State! (Carole Marsh Indiana Bks.). (Illus.). (J). (gr. 3-12). 1996. pap. 19.95 (0-7933-6224-5); lib. bdg. 29.95 (0-7933-6223-7); disk 29.95 (0-7933-6225-3) Gallopade Intl.

— Indiana "HISTO" Bingo! 42 Must Know State History Facts for Kids to Learn While Having Fun! (Bingo! Ser.). (Illus.). (J). (gr. 2-8). 1998. pap. 14.95 (0-7933-8566-0) Gallopade Intl.

— Indiana History! Surprising Secrets about Our State's Founding Mothers, Fathers & Kids! (Carole Marsh Indiana Bks.). (Illus.). (J). (gr. 3-12). 1996. pap. 19.95 (0-7933-6071-4); lib. bdg. 29.95 (0-7933-6070-6); disk 29.95 (0-7933-6072-2) Gallopade Intl.

— The Indiana Hot Air Balloon Mystery. (Carole Marsh Indiana Bks.). (Illus.). (J). (gr. 2-9). 1994. 29.95 (0-7933-2444-0); pap. 19.95 (0-7933-2445-9); disk 29.95 (0-7933-2446-7) Gallopade Intl.

— Indiana Hot Zones! Viruses, Diseases, & Epidemics in Our State's History. (Hot Zones! Ser.). (Illus.). (J). (gr. 3-12). 1998. pap. 19.95 (0-7933-8871-6); lib. bdg. 29.95 (0-7933-8870-8) Gallopade Intl.

— Indiana Indian Dictionary for Kids! (Carole Marsh State Bks.). (J). (gr. 2-9). 1996. 29.95 (0-7933-7686-6, C Marsh); pap. 19.95 (0-7933-7687-4, C Marsh) Gallopade Intl.

— Indiana Jeopardy! Answers & Questions about Our State! (Carole Marsh Indiana Bks.). (Illus.). (J). (gr. 3-12). 1994. pap. 19.95 (0-7933-4122-1); lib. bdg. 29.95 (0-7933-4121-3); disk 29.95 (0-7933-4123-X) Gallopade Intl.

— Indiana "Jography" A Fun Run Thru Our State! (Carole Marsh Indiana Bks.). (Illus.). (YA). (gr. 3-12). 1994. pap. 19.95 (1-55609-102-8); lib. bdg. 29.95 (1-55609-428-0); disk 29.95 (0-7933-1603-0) Gallopade Intl.

— Indiana Kid's Cookbook: Recipes, How-to, History, Lore & More! (Carole Marsh Indiana Bks.). (Illus.). (YA). (gr. 3-12). 1994. pap. 19.95 (0-7933-0417-2); lib. bdg. 29.95 (0-7933-0418-0); disk 29.95 (0-7933-0419-9) Gallopade Intl.

— The Indiana Library Book: A Surprising Guide to the Unusual Special Collections in Libraries Across Our State for Students, Teachers, Writers & Publishers - Includes Reproducible Mailing Labels Plus Activities for Young People! (Carole Marsh Indiana Bks.). (Illus.). 1994. pap. 19.95 (0-7933-3048-3); lib. bdg. 29.95 (0-7933-3047-5); disk 29.95 (0-7933-3049-1) Gallopade Intl.

— Indiana Math! How It All Adds up in Our State. (Carole Marsh Indiana Bks.). (Illus.). (YA). (gr. 3-12). 1996. pap. 19.95 (0-7933-6530-9); lib. bdg. 29.95 (0-7933-6529-5) Gallopade Intl.

— The Indiana Media Book: A Surprising Guide to the Amazing Print, Broadcast & Online Media of Our State for Students, Teachers, Writers & Publishers - Includes Reproducible Mailing Labels Plus Activities for Young People! (Carole Marsh Indiana Bks.). (Illus.). 1994. pap. 19.95 (0-7933-3204-4); lib. bdg. 29.95 (0-7933-3203-6); disk 29.95 (0-7933-3205-2) Gallopade Intl.

— The Indiana Mystery Van Takes Off! Book 1: Handicapped Indiana Kids Sneak Off on a Big Adventure. (Carole Marsh Indiana Bks.). (Illus.). (J). (gr. 3-12). 1994. 29.95 (0-7933-5003-4); pap. 19.95 (0-7933-5004-2); disk 29.95 (0-7933-5005-0) Gallopade Intl.

— Indiana Quiz Bowl Crash Course! (Carole Marsh Indiana Bks.). (Illus.). (YA). (gr. 3-12). 1994. pap. 19.95 (1-55609-434-5); lib. bdg. 29.95 (1-55609-435-3); disk 29.95 (0-7933-1612-X) Gallopade Intl.

— Indiana Rollercoasters! (Carole Marsh Indiana Bks.). (Illus.). (YA). (gr. 3-12). 1994. pap. 19.95 (0-7933-5267-3); lib. bdg. 29.95 (0-7933-5266-5); disk 29.95 (0-7933-5268-1) Gallopade Intl.

— Indiana School Trivia: An Amazing & Fascinating Look at Our State's Teachers, Schools & Students! (Carole Marsh Indiana Bks.). (Illus.). (YA). (gr. 3-12). 1994. pap. 19.95 (0-7933-0414-8); lib. bdg. 29.95 (0-7933-0415-6); disk 29.95 (0-7933-0416-4) Gallopade Intl.

— Indiana Silly Basketball Sportsmysteries, Vol. I. (Carole Marsh Indiana Bks.). (Illus.). (YA). (gr. 3-12). 1994. pap. 19.95 (0-7933-0411-3); lib. bdg. 29.95 (0-7933-0412-1); disk 29.95 (0-7933-0413-X) Gallopade Intl.

— Indiana Silly Basketball Sportsmysteries, Vol. II. (Carole Marsh Indiana Bks.). (Illus.). (YA). (gr. 3-12). 1994. pap. 19.95 (0-7933-1619-7); lib. bdg. 29.95 (0-7933-1618-9); disk 29.95 (0-7933-1620-0) Gallopade Intl.

— Indiana Silly Football Sportsmysteries, Vol. I. (Carole Marsh Indiana Bks.). (Illus.). (YA). (gr. 3-12). 1994. pap. 19.95 (1-55609-430-2); lib. bdg. 29.95 (1-55609-431-0); disk 29.95 (0-7933-1605-7) Gallopade Intl.

— Indiana Silly Football Sportsmysteries, Vol. II. (Carole Marsh Indiana Bks.). (Illus.). (YA). (gr. 3-12). 1994. pap. 19.95 (0-7933-1607-3); lib. bdg. 29.95 (0-7933-1606-5); disk 29.95 (0-7933-1608-1) Gallopade Intl.

— Indiana Silly Trivia! (Carole Marsh Indiana Bks.). (Illus.). (YA). (gr. 3-12). 1994. pap. 19.95 (1-55609-101-X); lib. bdg. 29.95 (1-55609-427-2); disk 29.95 (0-7933-1602-2) Gallopade Intl.

— Indiana Spelling Bee! Score Big by Correctly Spelling Our State's Unique Names. (Carole Marsh Indiana Bks.). (Illus.). (YA). (gr. 3-12). 1996. pap. 19.95 (0-7933-6683-6); lib. bdg. 29.95 (0-7933-6682-8) Gallopade Intl.

— Indiana Timeline: A Chronology of Indiana History, Mystery, Trivia, Legend, Lore & More. (Carole Marsh Indiana Bks.). (Illus.). (J). (gr. 3-12). 1994. pap. 19.95 (0-7933-5918-X); lib. bdg. 29.95 (0-7933-5917-1); disk 29.95 (0-7933-5919-8) Gallopade Intl.

— Indiana 2000! Coming Soon to a Calendar Near You - The 21st Century! - Complete Set of AL 2000 Items. (Two Thousand! Ser.). (Illus.). (J). (gr. 3-12). 1998. pap. 75.00 (0-7933-9337-X); lib. bdg. 85.00 (0-7933-9338-8) Gallopade Intl.

— Indiana 2000! Coming Soon to a Calendar Near You-The 21st Century! (Two Thousand! Ser.). (Illus.). (J). (gr. 3-12). 1998. pap. 19.95 (0-7933-8718-3); lib. bdg. 29.95 (0-7933-8717-5) Gallopade Intl.

— Indiana UFO's & Extraterrestrials! A Look at the Sightings & Science in Our State. (Carole Marsh Indiana Bks.). (Illus.). (J). (gr. 3-12). 1997. pap. 19.95 (0-7933-6377-2); lib. bdg. 29.95 (0-7933-6376-4) Gallopade Intl.

— Indiana's (Most Devastating!) Disasters & (Most Calamitous!) Catastrophies! (Carole Marsh Indiana Bks.). (Illus.). (YA). (gr. 3-12). 1994. pap. 19.95 (0-7933-0402-4); lib. bdg. 29.95 (0-7933-0403-2); disk 29.95 (0-7933-0404-0) Gallopade Intl.

— Indiana's Unsolved Mysteries (& Their "Solutions") Includes Scientific Information & Other Activities for Students. (Carole Marsh Indiana Bks.). (Illus.). (J). (gr. 3-12). 1994. pap. 19.95 (0-7933-5765-9); lib. bdg. 29.95 (0-7933-5764-0); disk 29.95 (0-7933-5766-7) Gallopade Intl.

— Iowa & Other State Greats (Biographies) (Carole Marsh Iowa Bks.). (Illus.). (YA). (gr. 3-12). 1994. pap. 19.95 (1-55609-458-2); lib. bdg. 29.95 (1-55609-459-0); disk 29.95 (0-7933-1636-7) Gallopade Intl.

— Iowa Bandits, Bushwackers, Outlaws, Crooks, Devils, Ghosts, Desperadoes & Other Assorted & Sundry Characters! (Carole Marsh Iowa Bks.). (Illus.). (YA). (gr. 3-12). 1994. pap. 19.95 (0-7933-0429-6); lib. bdg. 29.95 (0-7933-0430-X); disk 29.95 (0-7933-0431-8) Gallopade Intl.

— Iowa "BIO" Bingo! 24 Must Know State People for Kids to Learn about While Having Fun! (Bingo! Ser.). (Illus.). (J). (gr. 2-8). 1998. pap. 14.95 (0-7933-8567-9) Gallopade Intl.

— The Iowa Bookstore Book: A Surprising Guide to Our State's Bookstores & Their Specialties for Students, Teachers, Writers & Publishers. (Carole Marsh Iowa Bks.). (Illus.). 1994. pap. 19.95 (0-7933-2901-9); lib. bdg. 29.95 (0-7933-2900-0); disk 29.95 (0-7933-2902-7) Gallopade Intl.

— Iowa Classic Christmas Trivia: Stories, Recipes, Activities, Legends, Lore & More! (Carole Marsh Iowa Bks.). (Illus.). (YA). (gr. 3-12). 1994. pap. 19.95 (0-7933-0432-6); lib. bdg. 29.95 (0-7933-0433-4); disk 29.95 (0-7933-0434-2) Gallopade Intl.

— Iowa Coastales. (Carole Marsh Iowa Bks.). (Illus.). (YA). (gr. 3-12). 1994. pap. 19.95 (1-55609-454-X); lib. bdg. 29.95 (1-55609-455-8); disk 29.95 (0-7933-1632-4) Gallopade Intl.

— Iowa Coastales! (Carole Marsh Iowa Bks.). (J). 1994. lib. bdg. 29.95 (0-7933-7280-1) Gallopade Intl.

— Iowa "Crinkum-Crankum" A Funny Word Book about Our State. (Carole Marsh Iowa Bks.). (Illus.). (J). 1994. pap. 19.95 (0-7933-4854-4); lib. bdg. 29.95 (0-7933-4853-6); disk 29.95 (0-7933-4855-2) Gallopade Intl.

— Iowa Dingbats! Bk. 1: A Fun Book of Games, Stories, Activities & More about Our State That's All in Code! for You to Decipher. (Carole Marsh Iowa Bks.). (Illus.). (J). (gr. 3-12). 1994. pap. 19.95 (0-7933-3819-0); lib. bdg. 29.95 (0-7933-3818-2); disk 29.95 (0-7933-3820-4) Gallopade Intl.

— Iowa Festival Fun for Kids! (Carole Marsh Iowa Bks.). (Illus.). (YA). (gr. 3-12). 1994. pap. 19.95 (0-7933-3972-3); lib. bdg. 29.95 (0-7933-3971-5); disk 29.95 (0-7933-3973-1) Gallopade Intl.

— Iowa "GEO" Bingo! 38 Must Know State Geography Facts for Kids to Learn While Having Fun! (Bingo! Ser.). (Illus.). (J). (gr. 2-8). 1998. pap. 14.95 (0-7933-8568-7) Gallopade Intl.

— Iowa Government! The Cornerstone of Everyday Life in Our State! (Carole Marsh Iowa Bks.). (Illus.). (J). (gr. 3-12). 1996. pap. 19.95 (0-7933-6227-X); lib. bdg. 29.95 (0-7933-6226-1); disk 29.95 (0-7933-6228-8) Gallopade Intl.

— Iowa "HISTO" Bingo! 42 Must Know State History Facts for Kids to Learn While Having Fun! (Bingo! Ser.). (Illus.). (J). (gr. 2-8). 1998. pap. 14.95 (0-7933-8569-5) Gallopade Intl.

— Iowa History! Surprising Secrets about Our State's Founding Mothers, Fathers & Kids! (Carole Marsh Iowa Bks.). (Illus.). (J). (gr. 3-12). 1996. pap. 19.95 (0-7933-6074-9); lib. bdg. 29.95 (0-7933-6073-0); disk 29.95 (0-7933-6075-7) Gallopade Intl.

— The Iowa Hot Air Balloon Mystery. (Carole Marsh Iowa Bks.). (Illus.). (J). (gr. 2-9). 1994. 29.95 (0-7933-2453-X); pap. 19.95 (0-7933-2454-8); disk 29.95 (0-7933-2455-6) Gallopade Intl.

— Iowa Hot Zones! Viruses, Diseases, & Epidemics in Our State's History. (Hot Zones! Ser.). (Illus.). (J). (gr. 3-12). 1998. pap. 19.95 (0-7933-8874-0); lib. bdg. 29.95 (0-7933-8873-2) Gallopade Intl.

— Iowa Jeopardy! Answers & Questions about Our State! (Carole Marsh Iowa Bks.). (Illus.). (J). (gr. 3-12). 1994. pap. 19.95 (0-7933-4125-6); lib. bdg. 29.95 (0-7933-4124-8); disk 29.95 (0-7933-4126-4) Gallopade Intl.

— Iowa "Jography" A Fun Run Thru Our State! (Carole Marsh Iowa Bks.). (Illus.). (YA). (gr. 3-12). 1994. pap. 19.95 (1-55609-085-4); lib. bdg. 29.95 (1-55609-450-7); disk 29.95 (0-7933-1622-7) Gallopade Intl.

— Iowa Kid's Cookbook: Recipes, How-To, History, Lore & More! (Carole Marsh Iowa Bks.). (Illus.). (J). (gr. 3-12). 1994. pap. 19.95 (0-7933-0441-5); lib. bdg. 29.95 (0-7933-0442-3); disk 29.95 (0-7933-0443-1) Gallopade Intl.

— The Iowa Library Book: A Surprising Guide to the Unusual Special Collections in Libraries Across Our State for Students, Teachers, Writers & Publishers - Includes Reproducible Mailing Labels Plus Activities for Young People! (Carole Marsh Iowa Bks.). (Illus.). 1994. pap. 19.95 (0-7933-3051-3); lib. bdg. 29.95 (0-7933-3050-5); disk 29.95 (0-7933-3052-1) Gallopade Intl.

— Iowa Math! How It All Adds up in Our State. (Carole Marsh Iowa Bks.). (Illus.). (YA). (gr. 3-12). 1996. pap. 19.95 (0-7933-6533-3); lib. bdg. 29.95 (0-7933-6532-5) Gallopade Intl.

— The Iowa Media Book: A Surprising Guide to the Amazing Print, Broadcast & Online Media of Our State for Students, Teachers, Writers & Publishers - Includes Reproducible Mailing Labels Plus Activities for Young People! (Carole Marsh Iowa Bks.). (Illus.). 1994. pap. 19.95 (0-7933-3207-9); lib. bdg. 29.95 (0-7933-3206-0); disk 29.95 (0-7933-3208-7) Gallopade Intl.

— The Iowa Mystery Van Takes Off! Bk. 1: Handicapped Iowa Kids Sneak off on a Big Adventure. (Carole Marsh Iowa Bks.). (Illus.). (J). (gr. 3-12). 1994. 29.95 (0-7933-5006-9); pap. 19.95 (0-7933-5007-7); disk 29.95 (0-7933-5008-5) Gallopade Intl.

— Iowa Quiz Bowl Crash Course! (Carole Marsh Iowa Bks.). (Illus.). (YA). (gr. 3-12). 1994. pap. 19.95 (1-55609-456-6); lib. bdg. 29.95 (1-55609-457-4); disk 29.95 (0-7933-1631-6) Gallopade Intl.

— Iowa Rollercoasters! (Carole Marsh Iowa Bks.). (Illus.). (YA). (gr. 3-12). 1994. pap. 19.95 (0-7933-5270-3); lib. bdg. 29.95 (0-7933-5269-X); disk 29.95 (0-7933-5271-1) Gallopade Intl.

— Iowa School Trivia: An Amazing & Fascinating Look at Our State's Teachers, Schools & Students! (Carole Marsh Iowa Bks.). (Illus.). (YA). (gr. 3-12). 1994. pap. 19.95 (0-7933-0438-5); lib. bdg. 29.95 (0-7933-0439-3); disk 29.95 (0-7933-0440-7) Gallopade Intl.

— Iowa Silly Basketball Sportsmysteries, Vol. I. (Carole Marsh Iowa Bks.). (Illus.). (YA). (gr. 3-12). 1994. pap. 19.95 (0-7933-0435-0); lib. bdg. 29.95 (0-7933-0436-9); disk 29.95 (0-7933-0437-7) Gallopade Intl.

— Iowa Silly Basketball Sportsmysteries, Vol. II. (Carole Marsh Iowa Bks.). (Illus.). (YA). (gr. 3-12). 1994. pap. 19.95 (0-7933-1638-3); lib. bdg. 29.95 (0-7933-1637-5); disk 29.95 (0-7933-1639-1) Gallopade Intl.

— Iowa Silly Football Sportsmysteries, Vol. I. (Carole Marsh Iowa Bks.). (Illus.). (YA). (gr. 3-12). 1994. pap. 19.95 (1-55609-452-3); lib. bdg. 29.95 (1-55609-453-1); disk 29.95 (0-7933-1624-3) Gallopade Intl.

— Iowa Silly Football Sportsmysteries, Vol. II. (Carole Marsh Iowa Bks.). (Illus.). (YA). (gr. 3-12). 1994. pap. 19.95 (0-7933-1626-X); lib. bdg. 29.95 (0-7933-1625-1); disk 29.95 (0-7933-1627-8) Gallopade Intl.

— Iowa Silly Trivia! (Carole Marsh Iowa Bks.). (Illus.). (YA). (gr. 3-12). 1994. pap. 19.95 (1-55609-084-6); lib. bdg. 29.95 (1-55609-449-3); disk 29.95 (0-7933-1621-9) Gallopade Intl.

— Iowa Spelling Bee! Score Big by Correctly Spelling Our State's Unique Names. (Carole Marsh Iowa Bks.). (Illus.). (YA). (gr. 3-12). 1996. pap. 19.95 (0-7933-6686-0); lib. bdg. 29.95 (0-7933-6685-2) Gallopade Intl.

— Iowa Timeline: A Chronology of Iowa History, Mystery, Trivia, Legend, Lore & More. (Carole Marsh Iowa Bks.). (Illus.). (J). (gr. 3-12). 1994. pap. 19.95 (0-7933-5921-X); lib. bdg. 29.95 (0-7933-5920-1); disk 29.95 (0-7933-5922-8) Gallopade Intl.

— Iowa 2000! Coming Soon to a Calendar Near You - The 21st Century! - Complete Set of AL 2000 Items. (Two Thousand! Ser.). (Illus.). (J). (gr. 3-12). 1998. pap. 75.00 (0-7933-9339-6); lib. bdg. 85.00 (0-7933-9340-X) Gallopade Intl.

— Iowa 2000! Coming Soon to a Calendar Near You-The 21st Century! (Two Thousand! Ser.). (Illus.). (J). (gr. 3-12). 1998. pap. 19.95 (0-7933-8721-3); lib. bdg. 29.95 (0-7933-8720-5) Gallopade Intl.

— Iowa UFO's & Extraterrestrials! A Look at the Sightings & Science in Our State. (Carole Marsh Iowa Bks.). (Illus.). (J). (gr. 3-12). 1997. pap. 19.95 (0-7933-6380-2); lib. bdg. 29.95 (0-7933-6379-9) Gallopade Intl.

— Iowa's (Most Devastating!) Disasters & (Most Calamitous!) Catastrophies! (Carole Marsh Iowa Bks.). (Illus.). (YA). (gr. 3-12). 1994. pap. 19.95 (0-7933-0427-X); lib. bdg. 29.95 (0-7933-0426-1); disk 29.95 (0-7933-0428-8) Gallopade Intl.

— Iowa's Unsolved Mysteries (& Their "Solutions") Includes Scientific Information & Other Activities for Students. (Carole Marsh Iowa Bks.). (Illus.). (J). (gr. 3-12). 1994. pap. 19.95 (0-7933-5768-3); lib. bdg. 29.95 (0-7933-5767-5); disk 29.95 (0-7933-5769-1) Gallopade Intl.

— Is One Enough? Are Two Too Many? (Cloning for Kids! Ser.). (Illus.). 1998. pap., teacher ed. 19.95 (0-7933-8993-3, C Marsh); pap., teacher ed. 19.95 (0-7933-8995-X, C Marsh) Gallopade Intl.

— Is One Enough? Are Two Too Many? (Cloning for Kids! Ser.). (Illus.). (J). (gr. 3-6). 1998. pap. 19.95 (0-7933-8991-7, C Marsh); pap. 19.95 (0-7933-8994-1, C Marsh); lib. bdg. 29.95 (0-7933-8990-9, C Marsh) Gallopade Intl.

— Island of the Calamari. (Carole Marsh Short Story Ser.). (Illus.). (Orig.). (J). (ps-7). 1994. 29.95 (1-55609-172-9) Gallopade Intl.

— Island of the Calamari. (Carole Marsh Short Story Ser.). (Illus.). (Orig.). (J). (ps-7). 1997. pap. 19.95 (1-55609-240-7) Gallopade Intl.

— It Really Is Greek to Me! Greek for Kids. (Of All the Gall Language Bks.). (J). (gr. 2-9). 1997. 29.95 (0-7933-7803-6, C Marsh); pap. 19.95 (0-7933-7804-4, C Marsh) Gallopade Intl.

— Jason Hewitt! German for Kids. (J). 1994. pap. text 19.95 (0-7933-6878-2); lib. bdg. 29.95 (0-7933-6879-0); disk 29.95 (0-7933-6880-4) Gallopade Intl.

— Jungle Gym! A Monkey's Eye View of the World's

M

Jungles Yesterday, Today & Tomorrow? 36p. (J). (gr. 3-5). 1994. pap. 19.95 (0-7933-7347-6); lib. bdg. 29.95 (0-7933-7346-8); disk 29.95 (0-7933-7348-4) Gallopade Intl.

— Jurassic Ark! Alabama Dinosaurs & Other Prehistoric Creatures. (Carole Marsh State Bks.). (J). (gr. k-12). 1994. pap. 19.95 (0-7933-7429-4); lib. bdg. 29.95 (0-7933-7428-6); disk 29.95 (0-7933-7430-8) Gallopade Intl.

— Jurassic Ark! Alaska Dinosaurs & Other Prehistoric Creatures. (Carole Marsh Alaska Bks.). (J). (gr. k-12). 1994. pap. 19.95 (0-7933-7432-4); lib. bdg. 29.95 (0-7933-7431-6); disk 29.95 (0-7933-7433-2) Gallopade Intl.

— Jurassic Ark! Arizona Dinosaurs & Other Prehistoric Creatures. (Carole Marsh State Bks.). (J). (gr. k-12). 1994. pap. 19.95 (0-7933-7435-9); lib. bdg. 29.95 (0-7933-7434-0); disk 29.95 (0-7933-7436-7) Gallopade Intl.

— Jurassic Ark! Arkansas Dinosaurs & Other Prehistoric Creatures. (Carole Marsh State Bks.). (J). (gr. k-12). 1994. pap. 19.95 (0-7933-7438-3); lib. bdg. 29.95 (0-7933-7437-5); disk 29.95 (0-7933-7439-1) Gallopade Intl.

— Jurassic Ark! California Dinosaurs & Other Prehistoric Creatures. (Carole Marsh State Bks.). (J). (gr. k-12). 1994. pap. 19.95 (0-7933-7441-3); lib. bdg. 29.95 (0-7933-7440-5); disk 29.95 (0-7933-7442-1) Gallopade Intl.

— Jurassic Ark! Colorado Dinosaurs & Other Prehistoric Creatures. (Carole Marsh State Bks.). (J). (gr. k-12). 1994. pap. 19.95 (0-7933-7444-8); lib. bdg. 29.95 (0-7933-7443-X); disk 29.95 (0-7933-7445-6) Gallopade Intl.

— Jurassic Ark! Connecticut Dinosaurs & Other Prehistoric Creatures. (Carole Marsh State Bks.). (J). (gr. k-12). 1994. pap. 19.95 (0-7933-7447-2); lib. bdg. 29.95 (0-7933-7446-4); disk 29.95 (0-7933-7448-0) Gallopade Intl.

— Jurassic Ark! Delaware Dinosaurs & Other Prehistoric Creatures. (Carole Marsh State Bks.). (J). (gr. k-12). 1994. pap. 19.95 (0-7933-7450-2); lib. bdg. 29.95 (0-7933-7449-9); disk 29.95 (0-7933-7451-0) Gallopade Intl.

— Jurassic Ark! Florida Dinosaurs & Other Prehistoric Creatures. (Carole Marsh State Bks.). (J). (gr. k-12). 1994. pap. 19.95 (0-7933-7456-1); lib. bdg. 29.95 (0-7933-7455-3); disk 29.95 (0-7933-7457-X) Gallopade Intl.

— Jurassic Ark! Georgia Dinosaurs & Other Prehistoric Creatures. (Carole Marsh State Bks.). (J). (gr. k-12). 1994. pap. 19.95 (0-7933-7459-6); lib. bdg. 29.95 (0-7933-7458-8); disk 29.95 (0-7933-7460-X) Gallopade Intl.

— Jurassic Ark! Hawaii Dinosaurs & Other Prehistoric Creatures. (Carole Marsh State Bks.). (J). (gr. k-12). 1994. pap. 19.95 (0-7933-7462-6); lib. bdg. 29.95 (0-7933-7461-8); disk 29.95 (0-7933-7463-4) Gallopade Intl.

— Jurassic Ark! Idaho Dinosaurs & Other Prehistoric Creatures. (Carole Marsh State Bks.). (J). (gr. k-12). 1994. pap. 19.95 (0-7933-7465-0); lib. bdg. 29.95 (0-7933-7464-2); disk 29.95 (0-7933-7466-9) Gallopade Intl.

— Jurassic Ark! Illinois Dinosaurs & Other Prehistoric Creatures. (Carole Marsh State Bks.). (J). (gr. k-12). 1994. pap. 19.95 (0-7933-7468-5); lib. bdg. 29.95 (0-7933-7467-7); disk 29.95 (0-7933-7469-3) Gallopade Intl.

— Jurassic Ark! Indiana Dinosaurs & Other Prehistoric Creatures. (Carole Marsh State Bks.). (J). (gr. k-12). 1994. pap. 19.95 (0-7933-7471-5); lib. bdg. 29.95 (0-7933-7470-7); disk 29.95 (0-7933-7472-3) Gallopade Intl.

— Jurassic Ark! Iowa Dinosaurs & Other Prehistoric Creatures. (Carole Marsh State Bks.). (J). (gr. k-12). 1994. pap. 19.95 (0-7933-7474-X); lib. bdg. 29.95 (0-7933-7473-1); disk 29.95 (0-7933-7475-8) Gallopade Intl.

— Jurassic Ark! Kansas Dinosaurs & Other Prehistoric Creatures. (Carole Marsh State Bks.). (J). (gr. k-12). 1994. pap. 19.95 (0-7933-7477-4); lib. bdg. 29.95 (0-7933-7476-6); disk 29.95 (0-7933-7478-2) Gallopade Intl.

— Jurassic Ark! Kentucky Dinosaurs & Other Prehistoric Creatures. (Carole Marsh State Bks.). (J). (gr. k-12). 1994. pap. 19.95 (0-7933-7480-4); lib. bdg. 29.95 (0-7933-7479-0); disk 29.95 (0-7933-7481-2) Gallopade Intl.

— Jurassic Ark! Louisiana Dinosaurs & Other Prehistoric Creatures. (Carole Marsh State Bks.). (J). (gr. k-12). 1994. pap. 19.95 (0-7933-7483-9); lib. bdg. 29.95 (0-7933-7482-0); disk 29.95 (0-7933-7484-7) Gallopade Intl.

— Jurassic Ark! Maine Dinosaurs & Other Prehistoric Creatures. (Carole Marsh State Bks.). (J). (gr. k-12). 1994. pap. 19.95 (0-7933-7486-3); lib. bdg. 29.95 (0-7933-7485-5); disk 29.95 (0-7933-7487-1) Gallopade Intl.

— Jurassic Ark! Maryland Dinosaurs & Other Prehistoric Creatures. (Carole Marsh State Bks.). (J). (gr. k-12). 1994. pap. 19.95 (0-7933-7489-8); lib. bdg. 29.95 (0-7933-7488-X); disk 29.95 (0-7933-7490-1) Gallopade Intl.

— Jurassic Ark! Massachusetts Dinosaurs & Other Prehistoric Creatures. (Carole Marsh State Bks.). (J). (gr. k-12). 1994. pap. 19.95 (0-7933-7492-8); lib. bdg. 29.95 (0-7933-7491-X); disk 29.95 (0-7933-7493-6) Gallopade Intl.

— Jurassic Ark! Michigan Dinosaurs & Other Prehistoric Creatures. (Carole Marsh State Bks.). (J). (gr. k-12). 1994. pap. 19.95 (0-7933-7495-2); lib. bdg. 29.95 (0-7933-7494-4); disk 29.95 (0-7933-7496-0) Gallopade Intl.

— Jurassic Ark! Minnesota Dinosaurs & Other Prehistoric Creatures. (Carole Marsh State Bks.). (J). (gr. k-12). 1994. pap. 19.95 (0-7933-7498-7); lib. bdg. 29.95 (0-7933-7497-9); disk 29.95 (0-7933-7499-5) Gallopade Intl.

— Jurassic Ark! Mississippi Dinosaurs & Other Prehistoric Creatures. (Carole Marsh State Bks.). (J). (gr. k-12). 1994. pap. 19.95 (0-7933-7501-0); lib. bdg. 29.95 (0-7933-7500-2); disk 29.95 (0-7933-7502-9) Gallopade Intl.

— Jurassic Ark! Missouri Dinosaurs & Other Prehistoric Creatures. (Carole Marsh State Bks.). (J). (gr. k-12). 1994. pap. 19.95 (0-7933-7504-5); lib. bdg. 29.95 (0-7933-7503-7); disk 29.95 (0-7933-7505-3) Gallopade Intl.

— Jurassic Ark! Montana Dinosaurs & Other Prehistoric Creatures. (Carole Marsh State Bks.). (J). (gr. k-12). 1994. pap. 19.95 (0-7933-7507-X); lib. bdg. 29.95 (0-7933-7506-1); disk 29.95 (0-7933-7508-8) Gallopade Intl.

— Jurassic Ark! Nebraska Dinosaurs & Other Prehistoric Creatures. (Carole Marsh State Bks.). (J). (gr. k-12). 1994. pap. 19.95 (0-7933-7510-X); lib. bdg. 29.95 (0-7933-7509-6); disk 29.95 (0-7933-7511-8) Gallopade Intl.

— Jurassic Ark! Nevada Dinosaurs & Other Prehistoric Creatures. (Carole Marsh State Bks.). (J). (gr. k-12). 1994. pap. 19.95 (0-7933-7513-4); lib. bdg. 29.95 (0-7933-7512-6); disk 29.95 (0-7933-7514-2) Gallopade Intl.

— Jurassic Ark! New Hampshire Dinosaurs & Other Prehistoric Creatures. (Carole Marsh State Bks.). (J). (gr. k-12). 1994. pap. 19.95 (0-7933-7516-9); lib. bdg. 29.95 (0-7933-7515-0); disk 29.95 (0-7933-7517-7) Gallopade Intl.

— Jurassic Ark! New Jersey Dinosaurs & Other Prehistoric Creatures. (Carole Marsh State Bks.). (J). (gr. k-12). 1994. pap. 19.95 (0-7933-7519-3); lib. bdg. 29.95 (0-7933-7518-5); disk 29.95 (0-7933-7520-7) Gallopade Intl.

— Jurassic Ark! New Mexico Dinosaurs & Other Prehistoric Creatures. (Carole Marsh State Bks.). (J). (gr. k-12). 1994. pap. 19.95 (0-7933-7522-3); lib. bdg. 29.95 (0-7933-7521-5); disk 29.95 (0-7933-7523-1) Gallopade Intl.

— Jurassic Ark! New York Dinosaurs & Other Prehistoric Creatures. (Carole Marsh State Bks.). (J). (gr. k-12). 1994. pap. 19.95 (0-7933-7525-8); lib. bdg. 29.95 (0-7933-7524-X); disk 29.95 (0-7933-7526-6) Gallopade Intl.

— Jurassic Ark! North Carolina Dinosaurs & Other Prehistoric Creatures. (Carole Marsh State Bks.). (J). (gr. k-12). 1994. pap. 19.95 (0-7933-7528-2); lib. bdg. 29.95 (0-7933-7527-4); disk 29.95 (0-7933-7529-0) Gallopade Intl.

— Jurassic Ark! North Dakota Dinosaurs & Other Prehistoric Creatures. (Carole Marsh State Bks.). (J). (gr. k-12). 1994. pap. 19.95 (0-7933-7531-2); lib. bdg. 29.95 (0-7933-7530-4); disk 29.95 (0-7933-7532-0) Gallopade Intl.

— Jurassic Ark! Ohio Dinosaurs & Other Prehistoric Creatures. (Carole Marsh State Bks.). (J). (gr. k-12). 1994. pap. 19.95 (0-7933-7534-7); lib. bdg. 29.95 (0-7933-7533-9); disk 29.95 (0-7933-7535-5) Gallopade Intl.

— Jurassic Ark! Oklahoma Dinosaurs & Other Prehistoric Creatures. (Carole Marsh State Bks.). (J). (gr. k-12). 1994. pap. 19.95 (0-7933-7537-1); lib. bdg. 29.95 (0-7933-7536-3); disk 29.95 (0-7933-7538-X) Gallopade Intl.

— Jurassic Ark! Oregon Dinosaurs & Other Prehistoric Creatures. (Carole Marsh State Bks.). (J). (gr. k-12). 1994. pap. 19.95 (0-7933-7540-1); lib. bdg. 29.95 (0-7933-7539-8); disk 29.95 (0-7933-7541-X) Gallopade Intl.

— Jurassic Ark! Pennsylvania Dinosaurs & Other Prehistoric Creatures. (Carole Marsh State Bks.). (J). (gr. k-12). 1994. pap. 19.95 (0-7933-7543-6); lib. bdg. 29.95 (0-7933-7542-8); disk 29.95 (0-7933-7544-4) Gallopade Intl.

— Jurassic Ark! Rhode Island Dinosaurs & Other Prehistoric Creatures. (Carole Marsh State Bks.). (J). (gr. k-12). 1994. pap. 19.95 (0-7933-7546-0); lib. bdg. 29.95 (0-7933-7545-2); disk 29.95 (0-7933-7547-9) Gallopade Intl.

— Jurassic Ark! South Carolina Dinosaurs & Other Prehistoric Creatures. (Carole Marsh State Bks.). (J). (gr. k-12). 1994. pap. 19.95 (0-7933-7549-5); lib. bdg. 29.95 (0-7933-7548-7); disk 29.95 (0-7933-7550-9) Gallopade Intl.

— Jurassic Ark! South Dakota Dinosaurs & Other Prehistoric Creatures. (Carole Marsh State Bks.). (J). (gr. k-12). 1994. pap. 19.95 (0-7933-7552-5); lib. bdg. 29.95 (0-7933-7551-7); disk 29.95 (0-7933-7553-3) Gallopade Intl.

— Jurassic Ark! Tennessee Dinosaurs & Other Prehistoric Creatures. (Carole Marsh State Bks.). (J). (gr. k-12). 1994. pap. 19.95 (0-7933-7555-X); lib. bdg. 29.95 (0-7933-7554-1); disk 29.95 (0-7933-7556-8) Gallopade Intl.

— Jurassic Ark! Texas Dinosaurs & Other Prehistoric Creatures. (Carole Marsh State Bks.). (J). (gr. k-12). 1994. pap. 19.95 (0-7933-7558-4); lib. bdg. 29.95 (0-7933-7557-6); disk 29.95 (0-7933-7559-2) Gallopade Intl.

— Jurassic Ark! Utah Dinosaurs & Other Prehistoric Creatures. (Carole Marsh State Bks.). (J). (gr. k-12). 1994. pap. 19.95 (0-7933-7561-4); lib. bdg. 29.95 (0-7933-7560-6); disk 29.95 (0-7933-7562-2) Gallopade Intl.

— Jurassic Ark! Vermont Dinosaurs & Other Prehistoric Creatures. (Carole Marsh State Bks.). (J). (gr. k-12). 1994. pap. 19.95 (0-7933-7564-9); lib. bdg. 29.95 (0-7933-7563-0); disk 29.95 (0-7933-7565-7) Gallopade Intl.

— Jurassic Ark! Virginia Dinosaurs & Other Prehistoric Creatures. (Carole Marsh State Bks.). (J). (gr. k-12). 1994. pap. 19.95 (0-7933-7567-3); lib. bdg. 29.95 (0-7933-7566-5); disk 29.95 (0-7933-7568-1) Gallopade Intl.

— Jurassic Ark! Washington, D. C. Dinosaurs & Other Prehistoric Creatures. (Carole Marsh State Bks.). (J). (gr. k-12). 1994. pap. 19.95 (0-7933-7453-7); lib. bdg. 29.95 (0-7933-7452-9); disk 29.95 (0-7933-7454-5) Gallopade Intl.

— Jurassic Ark! Washington Dinosaurs & Other Prehistoric Creatures. (Carole Marsh State Bks.). (J). (gr. k-12). 1994. pap. 19.95 (0-7933-7570-3); lib. bdg. 29.95 (0-7933-7569-X); disk 29.95 (0-7933-7571-1) Gallopade Intl.

— Jurassic Ark! West Virginia Dinosaurs & Other Prehistoric Creatures. (Carole Marsh State Bks.). (J). (gr. k-12). 1994. pap. 19.95 (0-7933-7573-8); lib. bdg. 29.95 (0-7933-7572-X); disk 29.95 (0-7933-7574-6) Gallopade Intl.

— Jurassic Ark! Wisconsin Dinosaurs & Other Prehistoric Creatures. (Carole Marsh State Bks.). (J). (gr. k-12). 1994. pap. 19.95 (0-7933-7576-2); lib. bdg. 29.95 (0-7933-7575-4); disk 29.95 (0-7933-7577-0) Gallopade Intl.

— Jurassic Ark! Wyoming Dinosaurs & Other Prehistoric Creatures. (Carole Marsh Wyoming Bks.). (J). (gr. k-12). 1994. pap. 19.95 (0-7933-7579-7); lib. bdg. 29.95 (0-7933-7578-9); disk 29.95 (0-7933-7580-0) Gallopade Intl.

— Just Rushin' Around: Russian for Kids. (Of All the Gall Language Bks.). (J). (gr. 2-9). 1997. 29.95 (0-7933-7797-8, C Marsh); pap. 19.95 (0-7933-7798-6, C Marsh) Gallopade Intl.

— Kansas & Other State Greats (Biographies) (Carole Marsh Kansas Bks.). (J). (gr. 3-12). 1994. 29.95 (1-55609-362-4); pap. 19.95 (1-55609-363-2); disk 29.95 (1-55609-364-0) Gallopade Intl.

— Kansas Bandits, Bushwackers, Outlaws, Crooks, Devils, Ghosts, Desperadoes & Other Assorted & Sundry Characters! (Carole Marsh Kansas Bks.). (Illus.). (YA). (gr. 3-12). 1994. pap. 19.95 (0-7933-0453-9); lib. bdg. 29.95 (0-7933-0454-7); disk 29.95 (0-7933-0455-5) Gallopade Intl.

— Kansas "BIO" Bingo! 24 Must Know State People for Kids to Learn about While Having Fun! (Bingo! Ser.). (Illus.). (J). (gr. 2-8). 1998. pap. 14.95 (0-7933-8570-9) Gallopade Intl.

— The Kansas Bookstore Book: A Surprising Guide to Our State's Bookstores & Their Specialties for Students, Teachers, Writers & Publishers. (Carole Marsh Kansas Bks.). (Illus.). 1994. pap. 19.95 (0-7933-2904-3); lib. bdg. 29.95 (0-7933-2903-5); disk 29.95 (0-7933-2905-1) Gallopade Intl.

— Kansas Classic Christmas Trivia: Stories, Recipes, Activities, Legends, Lore & More! (Carole Marsh Kansas Bks.). (Illus.). (YA). (gr. 3-12). 1994. pap. 19.95 (0-7933-0456-3); lib. bdg. 29.95 (0-7933-0457-1); disk 29.95 (0-7933-0458-X) Gallopade Intl.

— Kansas Coastales. (Statemeant Ser.). (J). 1994. pap. 19.95 (1-55609-366-7); lib. bdg. 29.95 (1-55609-365-9); disk 29.95 (1-55609-367-5) Gallopade Intl.

— Kansas Coastales! (Carole Marsh Kansas Bks.). (J). 1994. lib. bdg. 29.95 (0-7933-7281-X) Gallopade Intl.

— Kansas "Crinkum-Crankum" A Funny Word Book about Our State. (Carole Marsh Kansas Bks.). (Illus.). (J). 1994. pap. 19.95 (0-7933-4857-9); lib. bdg. 29.95 (0-7933-4856-0); disk 29.95 (0-7933-4858-7) Gallopade Intl.

— Kansas Dingbats! Bk. 1: A Fun Book of Games, Stories, Activities & More about Our State That's All in Code! for You to Decipher. (Carole Marsh Kansas Bks.). (Illus.). (J). (gr. 3-12). 1994. pap. 19.95 (0-7933-3822-0); lib. bdg. 29.95 (0-7933-3821-2); disk 29.95 (0-7933-3823-9) Gallopade Intl.

— Kansas Facts & Factivities. (Carole Marsh State Bks.). (Illus.). (J). (gr. 4-7). 1996. pap., teacher ed. 19.95 (0-7933-7879-6, C Marsh) Gallopade Intl.

— Kansas Festival Fun for Kids! (Carole Marsh Kansas Bks.). (Illus.). (YA). (gr. 3-12). 1994. pap. 19.95 (0-7933-3975-8); lib. bdg. 29.95 (0-7933-3974-X); disk 29.95 (0-7933-3976-6) Gallopade Intl.

— Kansas "GEO" Bingo! 38 Must Know State Geography Facts for Kids to Learn While Having Fun! (Bingo! Ser.). (Illus.). (J). (gr. 2-8). 1998. pap. 14.95 (0-7933-8571-7) Gallopade Intl.

— Kansas Government! The Cornerstone of Everyday Life in Our State! (Carole Marsh Kansas Bks.). (Illus.). (J). (gr. 3-12). 1996. pap. 19.95 (0-7933-6230-X); lib. bdg. 29.95 (0-7933-6229-6); disk 29.95 (0-7933-6231-8) Gallopade Intl.

— Kansas "HISTO" Bingo! 42 Must Know State History Facts for Kids to Learn While Having Fun! (Bingo! Ser.). (Illus.). (J). (gr. 2-8). 1998. pap. 14.95 (0-7933-8572-5) Gallopade Intl.

— Kansas History! Surprising Secrets about Our State's Founding Mothers, Fathers & Kids! (Carole Marsh Kansas Bks.). (Illus.). (J). (gr. 3-12). 1996. pap. 19.95 (0-7933-6077-3); lib. bdg. 29.95 (0-7933-6076-5); disk 29.95 (0-7933-6078-1) Gallopade Intl.

— The Kansas Hot Air Balloon Mystery. (Carole Marsh Kansas Bks.). (Illus.). (J). (gr. 2-9). 1994. 29.95 (0-7933-2462-9); pap. 19.95 (0-7933-2463-7); disk 29.95 (0-7933-2464-5) Gallopade Intl.

— Kansas Hot Zones! Viruses, Diseases, & Epidemics in Our State's History. (Hot Zones! Ser.). (Illus.). (J). (gr. 3-12). 1998. pap. 19.95 (0-7933-8877-5); lib. bdg. 29.95 (0-7933-8876-7) Gallopade Intl.

— Kansas Indian Dictionary for Kids! (Carole Marsh State Bks.). (J). (gr. 2-9). 1996. 29.95 (0-7933-7692-0, C Marsh); pap. 19.95 (0-7933-7693-9, C Marsh) Gallopade Intl.

— Kansas Jeopardy! Answers & Questions about Our State! (Carole Marsh Kansas Bks.). (Illus.). (J). (gr. 3-12). 1994. pap. 19.95 (0-7933-4128-0); lib. bdg. 29.95 (0-7933-4127-2); disk 29.95 (0-7933-4129-9) Gallopade Intl.

— Kansas "Jography" A Fun Run Thru Your State. (Statemeant Ser.). (J). (gr. 3-12). 1994. pap. 19.95 (1-55609-354-3); lib. bdg. 29.95 (1-55609-353-5); disk 29.95 (1-55609-355-1) Gallopade Intl.

— Kansas Kid's Cookbook: Recipes, How-To, History, Lore & More! (Carole Marsh Kansas Bks.). (Illus.). (J). (gr. 3-12). 1994. pap. 19.95 (0-7933-0465-2); lib. bdg. 29.95 (0-7933-0466-0); disk 29.95 (0-7933-0467-9) Gallopade Intl.

— The Kansas Library Book: A Surprising Guide to the Unusual Special Collections in Libraries Across Our State for Students, Teachers, Writers & Publishers - Includes Reproducible Mailing Labels Plus Activities for Young People! (Carole Marsh Kansas Bks.). (Illus.). 1994. pap. 19.95 (0-7933-3054-8); lib. bdg. 29.95 (0-7933-3053-X); disk 29.95 (0-7933-3055-6) Gallopade Intl.

— Kansas Math! How It All Adds up in Our State. (Carole Marsh Kansas Bks.). (Illus.). (YA). (gr. 3-12). 1996. pap. 19.95 (0-7933-6536-8); lib. bdg. 29.95 (0-7933-6535-X) Gallopade Intl.

— The Kansas Media Book: A Surprising Guide to the Amazing Print, Broadcast & Online Media of Our State for Students, Teachers, Writers & Publishers - Includes Reproducible Mailing Labels Plus Activities for Young People! (Carole Marsh Kansas Bks.). (Illus.). 1994. pap. 19.95 (0-7933-3210-9); lib. bdg. 29.95 (0-7933-3209-5); disk 29.95 (0-7933-3211-7) Gallopade Intl.

— The Kansas Mystery Van Takes Off! Bk. 1: Handicapped Kansas Kids Sneak off on a Big Adventure. (Carole Marsh Kansas Bks.). (Illus.). (J). (gr. 3-12). 1994. 29.95 (0-7933-5009-3); pap. 19.95 (0-7933-5010-7) Gallopade Intl.

— Kansas Quiz Bowl Crash Course. (Statemeant Ser.). (J). (gr. 3-12). 1994. pap. 19.95 (1-55609-360-8); lib. bdg. 29.95 (1-55609-359-4); disk 29.95 (1-55609-361-6) Gallopade Intl.

— Kansas Rollercoasters! (Carole Marsh Kansas Bks.). (Illus.). (YA). (gr. 3-12). 1994. pap. 19.95 (0-7933-5273-8); lib. bdg. 29.95 (0-7933-5272-X); disk 29.95 (0-7933-5274-6) Gallopade Intl.

— Kansas School Trivia: An Amazing & Fascinating Look at Our State's Teachers, Schools & Students! (Carole Marsh Kansas Bks.). (Illus.). (YA). (gr. 3-12). 1994. pap. 19.95 (0-7933-0462-8); lib. bdg. 29.95 (0-7933-0463-6); disk 29.95 (0-7933-0464-4) Gallopade Intl.

— Kansas Silly Basketball Sportsmysteries, Vol. I. (Carole Marsh Kansas Bks.). (Illus.). (YA). (gr. 3-12). 1994. pap. 19.95 (0-7933-0459-8); lib. bdg. 29.95 (0-7933-0460-1); disk 29.95 (0-7933-0461-X) Gallopade Intl.

— Kansas Silly Basketball Sportsmysteries, Vol. II. (Carole Marsh Kansas Bks.). (Illus.). (YA). (gr. 3-12). 1994. pap. 19.95 (0-7933-1641-3); lib. bdg. 29.95 (0-7933-1640-5); disk 29.95 (0-7933-1642-1) Gallopade Intl.

— Kansas Silly Football Mystery, Vol. I. (Statemeant Ser.). (J). (gr. 3-12). 1994. pap. 19.95 (1-55609-369-1); lib. bdg. 29.95 (1-55609-368-3); disk 29.95 (1-55609-370-5) Gallopade Intl.

— Kansas Silly Football Mystery, Vol. II. (Statemeant Ser.). (J). (gr. 3-12). 1994. lib. bdg. 29.95 (1-55609-377-2); disk 29.95 (1-55609-379-9) Gallopade Intl.

— Kansas Silly Football Mystery, Vol. II. (Statemeant Ser.). (J). (gr. 3-12). 1997. pap. 19.95 (1-55609-378-0) Gallopade Intl.

— Kansas Silly Trivia. (Statemeant Ser.). (J). (gr. 3-12). 1994. pap. 19.95 (1-55609-351-9); disk 29.95 (1-55609-352-7) Gallopade Intl.

— Kansas Silly Trivia. (Statemeant Ser.). (J). (gr. 3-12). 1997. lib. bdg. 29.95 (1-55609-350-0) Gallopade Intl.

— Kansas Spelling Bee! Score Big by Correctly Spelling Our State's Unique Names. (Carole Marsh Kansas Bks.). (Illus.). (YA). (gr. 3-12). 1996. pap. 19.95 (0-7933-6689-5); lib. bdg. 29.95 (0-7933-6688-7) Gallopade Intl.

— Kansas Timeline: A Chronology of Kansas History, Mystery, Trivia, Legend, Lore & More. (Carole Marsh Kansas Bks.). (Illus.). (J). (gr. 3-12). 1994. pap. 19.95 (0-7933-5924-4); lib. bdg. 29.95 (0-7933-5923-6); disk 29.95 (0-7933-5925-2) Gallopade Intl.

— Kansas 2000! Coming Soon to a Calendar Near You - The 21st Century! - Complete Set of AL 2000 Items. (Two Thousand! Ser.). (Illus.). (J). (gr. 3-12). 1998. pap. 75.00 (0-7933-9341-8); lib. bdg. 85.00 (0-7933-9342-6) Gallopade Intl.

— Kansas 2000! Coming Soon to a Calendar Near You-The 21st Century! (Two Thousand! Ser.). (Illus.). (J). (gr. 3-12). 1998. pap. 19.95 (0-7933-8724-8); lib. bdg. 29.95 (0-7933-8723-X) Gallopade Intl.

— Kansas UFO's & Extraterrestrials! A Look at the Sightings & Science in Our State. (Carole Marsh Kansas Bks.). (Illus.). (J). (gr. 2-13). 1997. pap. 19.95 (0-7933-6383-7); lib. bdg. 29.95 (0-7933-6382-9) Gallopade Intl.

— Kansas's (Most Devastating!) Disasters & (Most Calamitous!) Catastrophies! (Carole Marsh Kansas

An Asterisk (*) at the beginning of an entry indicates that the title is appearing for the first time.

Bks.). (Illus.). (YA). (gr. 3-12). 1994. pap. 19.95 (*0-7933-0450-4*); lib. bdg. 29.95 (*0-7933-0451-2*); disk 29.95 (*0-7933-0452-0*) Gallopade Intl.

— Kansas's Unsolved Mysteries (& Their "Solutions") Includes Scientific Information & Other Activities for Students. (Carole Marsh Kansas Bks.). (Illus.). (J). (gr. 3-12). 1994. pap. 19.95 (*0-7933-5771-3*); lib. bdg. 29.95 (*0-7933-5770-5*); disk 29.95 (*0-7933-5772-1*) Gallopade Intl.

— Kentucky & Other State Greats (Biographies) (Carole Marsh Kentucky Bks.). (Illus.). (J). (gr. 3-8). 1994. pap. 19.95 (*1-55609-447-7*); lib. bdg. 29.95 (*1-55609-448-5*); disk 29.95 (*0-7933-1658-8*) Gallopade Intl.

— Kentucky Bandits, Bushwackers, Outlaws, Crooks, Devils, Ghosts, Desperadoes & Other Assorted & Sundry Characters! (Carole Marsh Kentucky Bks.). (Illus.). (J). (gr. 3-8). 1994. pap. 19.95 (*0-7933-0477-6*); lib. bdg. 29.95 (*0-7933-0478-4*); disk 29.95 (*0-7933-0479-2*) Gallopade Intl.

— Kentucky "BIO" Bingo! 24 Must Know State People for Kids to Learn about While Having Fun! (Bingo! Ser.). (Illus.). (J). (gr. 2-8). 1998. pap. 14.95 (*0-7933-8573-3*) Gallopade Intl.

— The Kentucky Bookstore Book: A Surprising Guide to Our State's Bookstores & Their Specialties for Students, Teachers, Writers & Publishers. (Carole Marsh Kentucky Bks.). (Illus.). 1994. pap. 19.95 (*0-7933-2907-8*); lib. bdg. 29.95 (*0-7933-2906-X*); disk 29.95 (*0-7933-2908-6*) Gallopade Intl.

— Kentucky Classic Christmas Trivia: Stories, Recipes, Activities, Legends, Lore & More! (Carole Marsh Kentucky Bks.). (Illus.). (J). (gr. 3-8). 1994. pap. 19.95 (*0-7933-0480-6*); lib. bdg. 29.95 (*0-7933-0481-4*); disk 29.95 (*0-7933-0482-2*) Gallopade Intl.

— Kentucky Coastales. (Carole Marsh Kentucky Bks.). (J). 1994. lib. bdg. 29.95 (*0-7933-7282-8*) Gallopade Intl.

— Kentucky Coastales. (Carole Marsh Kentucky Bks.). (Illus.). (J). (gr. 3-8). 1994. pap. 19.95 (*1-55609-443-4*); lib. bdg. 29.95 (*1-55609-444-2*); disk 29.95 (*0-7933-1654-5*) Gallopade Intl.

***Marsh, Carole.** The Kentucky Coloring Book. (Kentucky Experience! Ser.). (Illus.). (J). (gr. k-5). 2000. pap. 3.95 (*0-7933-9471-6*) Gallopade Intl.

Marsh, Carole. Kentucky "Crinkum-Crankum" A Funny Word Book about Our State. (Carole Marsh Kentucky Bks.). (Illus.). (J). 1994. pap. 19.95 (*0-7933-4860-9*); lib. bdg. 29.95 (*0-7933-4859-5*); disk 29.95 (*0-7933-4861-7*) Gallopade Intl.

— Kentucky Dingbats! A Fun Book of Games, Stories, Activities & More about Our State That's All in Code! for You to Decipher, Bk. 1. (Carole Marsh Kentucky Bks.). (Illus.). (J). (gr. 3-12). 1994. pap. 19.95 (*0-7933-3825-5*); lib. bdg. 29.95 (*0-7933-3824-7*); disk 29.95 (*0-7933-3826-3*) Gallopade Intl.

***Marsh, Carole.** The Kentucky Experience Pocket Guide. (Kentucky Experience! Ser.). (Illus.). (J). 2000. pap. 6.95 (*0-7933-9451-1*) Gallopade Intl.

Marsh, Carole. Kentucky Facts & Factivities. (Carole Marsh State Bks.). (Illus.). 1996. 29.95 (*0-614-11525-6*, C Marsh) Gallopade Intl.

— Kentucky Facts & Factivities. (Carole Marsh State Bks.). (Illus.). (J). (gr. 4-7). 1996. pap., teacher ed. 19.95 (*0-7933-7881-8*, C Marsh) Gallopade Intl.

— Kentucky Festival Fun for Kids! (Carole Marsh Kentucky Bks.). (Illus.). (YA). (gr. 3-12). 1994. pap. 19.95 (*0-7933-3978-2*); lib. bdg. 29.95 (*0-7933-3977-4*); disk 29.95 (*0-7933-3979-0*) Gallopade Intl.

— Kentucky "GEO" Bingo! 38 Must Know State Geography Facts for Kids to Learn While Having Fun! (Bingo! Ser.). (Illus.). (J). (gr. 2-8). 1998. pap. 14.95 (*0-7933-8574-1*) Gallopade Intl.

— Kentucky Government! The Cornerstone of Everyday Life in Our State! (Carole Marsh Kentucky Bks.). (Illus.). (J). (gr. 3-12). 1996. pap. 19.95 (*0-7933-6233-4*); lib. bdg. 29.95 (*0-7933-6232-6*); disk 29.95 (*0-7933-6234-2*) Gallopade Intl.

— Kentucky "HISTO" Bingo! 42 Must Know State History Facts for Kids to Learn While Having Fun! (Bingo! Ser.). (Illus.). (J). (gr. 2-8). 1998. pap. 14.95 (*0-7933-8575-X*) Gallopade Intl.

— Kentucky History! Surprising Secrets about Our State's Founding Mothers, Fathers & Kids! (Carole Marsh Kentucky Bks.). (Illus.). (J). (gr. 3-12). 1996. pap. 19.95 (*0-7933-6080-3*); lib. bdg. 29.95 (*0-7933-6079-X*); disk 29.95 (*0-7933-6081-1*) Gallopade Intl.

— The Kentucky Hot Air Balloon Mystery. (Carole Marsh Kentucky Bks.). (Illus.). (J). (gr. 2-9). 1994. 29.95 (*0-7933-2471-8*); pap. 19.95 (*0-7933-2472-6*); disk 29.95 (*0-7933-2473-4*) Gallopade Intl.

— Kentucky Indian Dictionary for Kids! (Carole Marsh State Bks.). (J). (gr. 2-9). 1996. 29.95 (*0-7933-7695-5*, C Marsh); pap. 19.95 (*0-7933-7696-3*, C Marsh) Gallopade Intl.

***Marsh, Carole.** Kentucky Jeopardy. (Kentucky Experience! Ser.). (Illus.). (J). (gr. 2-6). 2000. pap. 7.95 (*0-7933-9516-X*) Gallopade Intl.

Marsh, Carole. Kentucky Jeopardy! Answers & Questions about Our State! (Carole Marsh Kentucky Bks.). (Illus.). (J). (gr. 3-12). 1994. pap. 19.95 (*0-7933-4131-0*); lib. bdg. 29.95 (*0-7933-4130-2*); disk 29.95 (*0-7933-4132-9*) Gallopade Intl.

***Marsh, Carole.** Kentucky Jography. (Kentucky Experience! Ser.). (Illus.). (J). (gr. 2-6). 2000. pap. 7.95 (*0-7933-9517-8*) Gallopade Intl.

Marsh, Carole. Kentucky "Jography" A Fun Run Thru Our State! (Carole Marsh Kentucky Bks.). (Illus.). (J). (gr. 3-8). 1994. pap. 19.95 (*1-55609-109-5*); lib. bdg. 29.95 (*1-55609-439-6*); disk 29.95 (*0-7933-1644-8*) Gallopade Intl.

— Kentucky Kid's Cookbook: Recipes, How-To, History, Lore & More! (Carole Marsh Kentucky Bks.). (Illus.). (J). (gr. 3-8). 1994. pap. 19.95 (*0-7933-0489-X*); lib. bdg. 29.95 (*0-7933-0490-3*); disk 29.95 (*0-7933-0491-1*) Gallopade Intl.

— The Kentucky Library Book: A Surprising Guide to the Unusual Special Collections in Libraries Across Our State for Students, Teachers, Writers & Publishers - Includes Reproducible Mailing Labels Plus Activities for Young People! (Carole Marsh Kentucky Bks.). (Illus.). 1994. pap. 19.95 (*0-7933-3057-2*); lib. bdg. 29.95 (*0-7933-3056-4*); disk 29.95 (*0-7933-3058-0*) Gallopade Intl.

— Kentucky Math! How It All Adds up in Our State. (Carole Marsh Kentucky Bks.). (Illus.). (YA). (gr. 3-12). 1996. pap. 19.95 (*0-7933-6539-2*); lib. bdg. 29.95 (*0-7933-6538-4*) Gallopade Intl.

— The Kentucky Media Book: A Surprising Guide to the Amazing Print, Broadcast & Online Media of Our State for Students, Teachers, Writers & Publishers - Includes Reproducible Mailing Labels Plus Activities for Young People! (Carole Marsh Kentucky Bks.). (Illus.). 1994. pap. 19.95 (*0-7933-3213-3*); lib. bdg. 29.95 (*0-7933-3212-5*); disk 29.95 (*0-7933-3214-1*) Gallopade Intl.

— The Kentucky Mystery Van Takes Off! Handicapped Kentucky Kids Sneak off on a Big Adventure, Bk. 1. (Carole Marsh Kentucky Bks.). (Illus.). (J). (gr. 3-12). 1994. 29.95 (*0-7933-5012-3*); pap. 19.95 (*0-7933-5013-1*); disk 29.95 (*0-7933-5014-X*) Gallopade Intl.

— Kentucky Quiz Bowl Crash Course! (Carole Marsh Kentucky Bks.). (Illus.). (J). (gr. 3-8). 1994. pap. 19.95 (*1-55609-445-0*); lib. bdg. 29.95 (*1-55609-446-9*); disk 29.95 (*0-7933-1653-7*) Gallopade Intl.

— Kentucky Rollercoasters! (Carole Marsh Kentucky Bks.). (Illus.). (YA). (gr. 3-12). 1994. pap. 19.95 (*0-7933-5276-2*); lib. bdg. 29.95 (*0-7933-5275-4*); disk 29.95 (*0-7933-5277-0*) Gallopade Intl.

— Kentucky School Trivia: An Amazing & Fascinating Look at Our State's Teachers, Schools & Students! (Carole Marsh Kentucky Bks.). (Illus.). (J). (gr. 3-8). 1994. pap. 19.95 (*0-7933-0486-5*); lib. bdg. 29.95 (*0-7933-0487-3*); disk 29.95 (*0-7933-0488-1*) Gallopade Intl.

— Kentucky Silly Basketball Sportsmysteries, Vol. I. (Carole Marsh Kentucky Bks.). (Illus.). (J). (gr. 3-8). 1994. pap. 19.95 (*0-7933-0483-0*); lib. bdg. 29.95 (*0-7933-0484-9*); disk 29.95 (*0-7933-0485-7*) Gallopade Intl.

— Kentucky Silly Basketball Sportsmysteries, Vol. II. (Carole Marsh Kentucky Bks.). (Illus.). (J). (gr. 3-8). 1994. pap. 19.95 (*0-7933-1660-X*); lib. bdg. 29.95 (*0-7933-1659-6*); disk 29.95 (*0-7933-1661-8*) Gallopade Intl.

— Kentucky Silly Football Sportsmysteries, Vol. I. (Carole Marsh Kentucky Bks.). (Illus.). (J). (gr. 3-8). 1994. pap. 19.95 (*1-55609-441-8*); lib. bdg. 29.95 (*1-55609-442-6*); disk 29.95 (*0-7933-1646-4*) Gallopade Intl.

— Kentucky Silly Football Sportsmysteries, Vol. II. (Carole Marsh Kentucky Bks.). (Illus.). (J). (gr. 3-8). 1994. pap. 19.95 (*0-7933-1648-0*); lib. bdg. 29.95 (*0-7933-1647-2*); disk 29.95 (*0-7933-1649-9*) Gallopade Intl.

— Kentucky Silly Trivia! (Carole Marsh Kentucky Bks.). (J). (gr. 3-8). 1994. pap. 19.95 (*1-55609-040-4*); lib. bdg. 29.95 (*1-55609-438-8*); disk 29.95 (*0-7933-1643-X*) Gallopade Intl.

— Kentucky Spelling Bee! Score Big by Correctly Spelling Our State's Unique Names. (Carole Marsh Kentucky Bks.). (Illus.). (YA). (gr. 3-12). 1996. pap. 19.95 (*0-7933-6692-5*); lib. bdg. 29.95 (*0-7933-6691-7*) Gallopade Intl.

— Kentucky Timeline: A Chronology of Kentucky History, Mystery, Trivia, Legend, Lore & More. (Carole Marsh Kentucky Bks.). (Illus.). (J). (gr. 3-12). 1994. pap. 19.95 (*0-7933-5927-9*); lib. bdg. 29.95 (*0-7933-5926-0*); disk 29.95 (*0-7933-5928-7*) Gallopade Intl.

— Kentucky 2000! Coming Soon to a Calendar Near You - The 21st Century! - Complete Set of AL 2000 Items. (Two Thousand! Ser.). (Illus.). (J). (gr. 3-12). 1998. pap. 75.00 (*0-7933-9343-4*); lib. bdg. 85.00 (*0-7933-9344-2*) Gallopade Intl.

— Kentucky 2000! Coming Soon to a Calendar Near You-The 21st Century! (Two Thousand! Ser.). (Illus.). (J). (gr. 3-12). 1998. pap. 19.95 (*0-7933-8727-2*); lib. bdg. 29.95 (*0-7933-8726-4*) Gallopade Intl.

— Kentucky UFO's & Extraterrestrials! A Look at the Sightings & Science in Our State. (Carole Marsh Kentucky Bks.). (Illus.). (J). (gr. 3-12). 1997. pap. 19.95 (*0-7933-6386-1*); lib. bdg. 29.95 (*0-7933-6385-3*) Gallopade Intl.

***Marsh, Carole.** Kentucky's Big Activity Book. (Kentucky Experience! Ser.). (Illus.). (J). (gr. k-5). 2000. pap. 9.95 (*0-7933-9461-9*) Gallopade Intl.

Marsh, Carole. Kentucky's (Most Devastating!) Disasters & (Most Calamitous!) Catastrophies! LC 00-7933. (Carole Marsh Kentucky Bks.). (Illus.). (J). (gr. 3-8). 1970. disk 29.95 (*0-7933-0476-8*) Gallopade Intl.

— Kentucky's (Most Devastating!) Disasters & (Most Calamitous!) Catastrophies! LC 00-7933. (Carole Marsh Kentucky Bks.). (Illus.). (J). (gr. 3-8). 1994. pap. 19.95 (*0-7933-0474-1*); lib. bdg. 29.95 (*0-7933-0475-X*) Gallopade Intl.

— Kentucky's Unsolved Mysteries (And Their "Solutions") Includes Scientific Information & Other Activities for Students. (Carole Marsh Kentucky Bks.). (Illus.). (J). (gr. 3-12). 1994. pap. 19.95 (*0-7933-5774-8*); lib. bdg. 29.95 (*0-7933-5773-X*); disk 29.95 (*0-7933-5775-6*) Gallopade Intl.

— Kids & Space: Look Forward, Plan, Prepare, Go! (Quantum Leap Ser.). (Illus.). (J). (gr. 3-8). 1994. pap. 19.95 (*0-7933-0004-5*); lib. bdg. 29.95 (*0-7933-0003-7*); disk 29.95 (*0-7933-0005-3*) Gallopade Intl.

— A Kid's Book of Smarts: How to Think, Make Decisions, Figure Things Out, Budget Your Time, Money, Plan Your Day, Week, Life & Other Things Adults Wish They'd Learned When They Were Kids! (Quantum Leap Ser.). (Illus.). 68p. (J). (gr. 4-12). 1994. pap. 19.95 (*0-935326-18-9*); lib. bdg. 29.95 (*1-55609-173-7*) Gallopade Intl.

— The Kinky Sex Cookbook. (Naked Gourmet Ser.). (Orig.). 1994. 29.95 (*1-55609-174-5*); pap. 19.95 (*1-55609-005-6*) Gallopade Intl.

— The Kitchen House: How Yesterdays Black Women Created Todays American Foods. (Our Black Heritage Ser.). (J). (gr. 3-12). 1994. pap. 19.95 (*1-55609-308-X*); lib. bdg. 29.95 (*1-55609-309-8*); disk 29.95 (*1-55609-310-1*) Gallopade Intl.

— The Kudzu Cookbook: You Don't Eat It - It Eats You! (Naked Gourmet Ser.). (Orig.). 1994. 29.95 (*1-55609-175-3*); pap. 19.95 (*1-55609-004-8*) Gallopade Intl.

— Latin for Kids: Of All the Gaul. (Of All the Gaul Ser.). (Illus.). (J). (gr. 2-10). 1994. 29.95 (*0-935326-17-0*) Gallopade Intl.

— The Legend of the Devil's Hoofprints. (Carole Marsh Bks.). (Illus.). (Orig.). (J). (gr. 2 up). 1994. pap. 19.95 (*0-935326-57-X*); lib. bdg. 29.95 (*1-55609-177-X*) Gallopade Intl.

— Let's Find Out about Florida! In the Yellow Pages, Dictionary, Encyclopedia, Almanac, Atlas, Who's Who, Bartlett's Quotations & Other Reference Sources! 36p. (J). (gr. 3-5). 1994. pap. 19.95 (*0-7933-7350-6*); lib. bdg. 29.95 (*0-7933-7349-2*); disk 29.95 (*0-7933-7351-4*) Gallopade Intl.

— Let's Quilt Alabama & Stuff It Topographically! (Carole Marsh Alabama Bks.). (Illus.). (YA). (gr. 3-12). 1994. pap. 19.95 (*1-55609-073-0*); lib. bdg. 29.95 (*1-55609-462-0*); disk 29.95 (*0-7933-1328-7*) Gallopade Intl.

— Let's Quilt Alaska & Stuff It Topographically! (Carole Marsh Alaska Bks.). (Illus.). (YA). (gr. 3-12). 1994. pap. 19.95 (*1-55609-094-3*); lib. bdg. 29.95 (*1-55609-475-2*); disk 29.95 (*0-7933-1344-9*) Gallopade Intl.

— Let's Quilt Arizona & Stuff It Topographically! (Carole Marsh Arizona Bks.). (Illus.). (YA). (gr. 3-12). 1994. pap. 19.95 (*1-55609-128-1*); lib. bdg. 29.95 (*1-55609-499-X*); disk 29.95 (*0-7933-1360-0*) Gallopade Intl.

— Let's Quilt Arkansas & Stuff It Topographically! (Carole Marsh Arkansas Bks.). (Illus.). (YA). (gr. 3-12). 1994. pap. 19.95 (*1-55609-078-1*); lib. bdg. 29.95 (*1-55609-486-8*); disk 29.95 (*0-7933-1376-7*) Gallopade Intl.

— Let's Quilt California & Stuff It Topographically! (Carole Marsh California Bks.). (Illus.). (YA). (gr. 3-12). 1994. pap. 19.95 (*1-55609-512-0*); lib. bdg. 29.95 (*1-55609-513-9*); disk 29.95 (*0-7933-1392-9*) Gallopade Intl.

— Let's Quilt Colorado & Stuff It Topographically! (Carole Marsh Colorado Bks.). (Illus.). (YA). (gr. 3-12). 1994. pap. 19.95 (*1-55609-126-5*); lib. bdg. 29.95 (*1-55609-526-0*); disk 29.95 (*0-7933-1408-9*) Gallopade Intl.

— Let's Quilt Connecticut & Stuff It Topographically! (Carole Marsh Connecticut Bks.). (Illus.). (YA). (gr. 3-12). 1994. lib. bdg. 29.95 (*1-55609-539-2*); disk 29.95 (*0-7933-1424-0*) Gallopade Intl.

— Let's Quilt Connecticut & Stuff It Topographically! (Carole Marsh Connecticut Bks.). (Illus.). (J). (gr. 3-12). 1997. pap. 19.95 (*1-55609-061-7*) Gallopade Intl.

— Let's Quilt Delaware & Stuff It Topographically! (Carole Marsh Delaware Bks.). (Illus.). (YA). (gr. 3-12). 1994. pap. 19.95 (*1-55609-063-3*); lib. bdg. 29.95 (*1-55609-552-X*); disk 29.95 (*0-7933-1440-2*) Gallopade Intl.

— Let's Quilt Florida & Stuff It Topographically! (Carole Marsh Florida Bks.). (Illus.). (YA). (gr. 3-12). 1994. pap. 19.95 (*1-55609-055-2*); lib. bdg. 29.95 (*1-55609-419-1*); disk 29.95 (*0-7933-1488-7*) Gallopade Intl.

— Let's Quilt Georgia & Stuff It Topographically! (Carole Marsh Georgia Bks.). (Illus.). (YA). (gr. 3-12). 1994. pap. 19.95 (*1-55609-054-4*); lib. bdg. 29.95 (*1-55609-382-9*); disk 29.95 (*0-7933-1507-7*) Gallopade Intl.

— Let's Quilt Hawaii & Stuff It Topographically! (Carole Marsh Hawaii Bks.). (Illus.). (YA). (gr. 3-12). 1994. pap. 19.95 (*1-55609-093-5*); lib. bdg. 29.95 (*1-55609-569-4*); disk 29.95 (*0-7933-1526-3*) Gallopade Intl.

— Let's Quilt Idaho & Stuff It Topographically! (Carole Marsh Idaho Bks.). (Illus.). (YA). (gr. 3-12). 1994. pap. 19.95 (*1-55609-139-7*); lib. bdg. 29.95 (*1-55609-584-8*); disk 29.95 (*0-7933-1545-X*) Gallopade Intl.

— Let's Quilt Illinois & Stuff It Topographically! (Carole Marsh Illinois Bks.). (Illus.). (YA). (gr. 3-12). 1994. pap. 19.95 (*1-55609-097-8*); lib. bdg. 29.95 (*1-55609-408-6*); disk 29.95 (*0-7933-1585-9*) Gallopade Intl.

— Let's Quilt Indiana & Stuff It Topographically! (Carole Marsh Indiana Bks.). (Illus.). (YA). (gr. 3-12). 1994. pap. 19.95 (*1-55609-096-X*); lib. bdg. 29.95 (*1-55609-429-9*); disk 29.95 (*0-7933-1604-9*) Gallopade Intl.

— Let's Quilt Iowa & Stuff It Topographically! (Carole Marsh Iowa Bks.). (Illus.). (YA). (gr. 3-12). 1994. pap. 19.95 (*1-55609-072-2*); lib. bdg. 29.95 (*1-55609-451-5*); disk 29.95 (*0-7933-1623-5*) Gallopade Intl.

— Let's Quilt Kansas & Stuff It Topographically! (Carol Marsh Kansas Bks.). (J). (gr. 3-12). 1994. pap. 19.95 (*1-55609-357-8*); lib. bdg. 29.95 (*1-55609-356-X*); disk 29.95 (*1-55609-358-6*) Gallopade Intl.

— Let's Quilt Louisiana & Stuff It Topographically! (Carole Marsh Louisiana Bks.). (Illus.). (J). (gr. 3-8). 1994. pap. 19.95 (*1-55609-075-7*); lib. bdg. 29.95 (*1-55609-397-7*); disk 29.95 (*0-7933-1664-2*) Gallopade Intl.

— Let's Quilt Maine & Stuff It Topographically! (Carole Marsh Maine Bks.). (Illus.). (J). (gr. 3-8). 1994. pap. 19.95 (*1-55609-068-4*); lib. bdg. 29.95 (*1-55609-599-6*); disk 29.95 (*1-55609-601-1*) Gallopade Intl.

— Let's Quilt Maryland & Stuff It Topographically! (Carole Marsh Maryland Bks.). (Illus.). (J). (gr. 3-8). 1994. pap. 19.95 (*1-55609-058-7*); lib. bdg. 29.95 (*1-55609-622-4*); disk 29.95 (*1-55609-623-2*) Gallopade Intl.

— Let's Quilt Massachusetts & Stuff It Topographically! (Carole Marsh Massachusetts Bks.). (Illus.). (J). (gr. 3-8). 1994. pap. 19.95 (*1-55609-685-2*); lib. bdg. 29.95 (*1-55609-684-4*); disk 29.95 (*1-55609-686-0*) Gallopade Intl.

— Let's Quilt Michigan & Stuff It Topographically! (Carole Marsh Michigan Bks.). (Illus.). (J). (gr. 3 up). 1994. pap. 19.95 (*1-55609-138-9*); lib. bdg. 29.95 (*1-55609-669-0*); disk 29.95 (*1-55609-670-4*) Gallopade Intl.

— Let's Quilt Minnesota & Stuff It Topographically! (Carole Marsh Minnesota Bks.). (Illus.). (J). (gr. 3 up). 1994. pap. 19.95 (*1-55609-099-4*); lib. bdg. 29.95 (*1-55609-645-3*); disk 29.95 (*1-55609-647-X*) Gallopade Intl.

— Let's Quilt Mississippi & Stuff It Topographically! (Carole Marsh Mississippi Bks.). (Illus.). (J). (gr. 3 up). 1994. pap. 19.95 (*1-55609-074-9*); lib. bdg. 29.95 (*1-55609-710-7*); disk 29.95 (*1-55609-716-6*) Gallopade Intl.

M

— Let's Quilt Missouri & Stuff It Topographically! (Carole Marsh Missouri Bks.). (Illus.). (J). (gr. 3 up). 1994. pap. 19.95 (*1-55609-734-4*); lib. bdg. 29.95 (*1-55609-733-6*); disk 29.95 (*1-55609-735-2*) Gallopade Intl.

— Let's Quilt Montana & Stuff It Topographically! (Carole Marsh Montana Bks.). (Illus.). (J). (gr. 3 up). 1994. pap. 19.95 (*1-55609-131-1*); lib. bdg. 29.95 (*1-55609-757-3*); disk 29.95 (*1-55609-759-X*) Gallopade Intl.

— Let's Quilt Nebraska & Stuff It Topographically! (Carole Marsh Nebraska Bks.). (Illus.). (J). (gr. 3 up). 1994. lib. bdg. 29.95 (*1-55609-781-6*); disk 29.95 (*1-55609-783-2*) Gallopade Intl.

— Let's Quilt Nebraska & Stuff It Topographically! (Carole Marsh Nebraska Bks.). (Illus.). (J). (gr. 3 up). 1997. pap. 19.95 (*1-55609-779-4*) Gallopade Intl.

— Let's Quilt Nevada & Stuff It Topographically! (Carole Marsh Nevada Bks.). (Illus.). (J). 1994. pap. 19.95 (*1-55609-130-3*); lib. bdg. 29.95 (*1-55609-805-7*); disk 29.95 (*1-55609-807-3*) Gallopade Intl.

— Let's Quilt New Hampshire & Stuff It Topographically! (Carole Marsh New Hampshire Bks.). (Illus.). (J). 1994. pap. 19.95 (*1-55609-067-6*); lib. bdg. 29.95 (*1-55609-829-4*); disk 29.95 (*1-55609-831-6*) Gallopade Intl.

— Let's Quilt New Jersey & Stuff It Topographically! (Carole Marsh New Jersey Bks.). (Illus.). (J). 1994. pap. 19.95 (*1-55609-069-2*); lib. bdg. 29.95 (*1-55609-853-7*); disk 29.95 (*1-55609-855-3*) Gallopade Intl.

— Let's Quilt New Mexico & Stuff It Topographically! (Carole Marsh New Mexico Bks.). (Illus.). (J). 1994. pap. 19.95 (*1-55609-127-3*); lib. bdg. 29.95 (*1-55609-877-4*); disk 29.95 (*1-55609-879-0*) Gallopade Intl.

— Let's Quilt New York & Stuff It Topographically! (Carole Marsh New York Bks.). (Illus.). (J). 1994. pap. 19.95 (*1-55609-060-9*); lib. bdg. 29.95 (*1-55609-904-5*); disk 29.95 (*1-55609-905-3*) Gallopade Intl.

— Let's Quilt North Carolina & Stuff It Topographically! (Carole Marsh North Carolina Bks.). (Illus.). (J). 1994. pap. 19.95 (*1-55609-050-1*); lib. bdg. 29.95 (*1-55609-925-8*); disk 29.95 (*1-55609-926-6*) Gallopade Intl.

— Let's Quilt North Dakota & Stuff It Topographically! (Carole Marsh North Dakota Bks.). (Illus.). (J). 1994. pap. 19.95 (*1-55609-135-4*); lib. bdg. 29.95 (*1-55609-946-0*); disk 29.95 (*1-55609-947-9*) Gallopade Intl.

— Let's Quilt Ohio & Stuff It Topographically! (Carole Marsh Ohio Bks.). (Illus.). (J). 1994. pap. 19.95 (*1-55609-095-1*); disk 29.95 (*1-55609-985-1*) Gallopade Intl.

— Let's Quilt Ohio & Stuff It Topographically! (Carole Marsh Ohio Bks.). (Illus.). (J). 1997. lib. bdg. 29.95 (*1-55609-984-3*) Gallopade Intl.

— Let's Quilt Oklahoma & Stuff It Topographically! (Carole Marsh Oklahoma Bks.). (Illus.). (J). 1994. pap. 19.95 (*0-7933-1861-0*); lib. bdg. 29.95 (*0-7933-1860-2*); disk 29.95 (*0-7933-1862-9*) Gallopade Intl.

— Let's Quilt Oregon & Stuff It Topographically! (Carole Marsh Oregon Bks.). (Illus.). (J). 1994. pap. 19.95 (*1-55609-132-X*); lib. bdg. 29.95 (*0-7933-1893-9*); disk 29.95 (*0-7933-1894-7*) Gallopade Intl.

— Let's Quilt Our Alabama County. (Carole Marsh Alabama Bks.). (J). 1994. pap. text 19.95 (*0-7933-6935-5*); lib. bdg. 29.95 (*0-7933-6936-3*); disk 29.95 (*0-7933-6937-1*) Gallopade Intl.

— Let's Quilt Our Alabama Town. (Carole Marsh Alabama Bks.). (J). 1994. pap. text 19.95 (*0-7933-6932-0*); lib. bdg. 29.95 (*0-7933-6933-9*); disk 29.95 (*0-7933-6934-7*) Gallopade Intl.

— Let's Quilt Our Alaska County. (Carole Marsh Alaska Bks.). (J). 1994. pap. text 19.95 (*0-7933-7117-1*); lib. bdg. 29.95 (*0-7933-7116-3*); disk 29.95 (*0-7933-7118-X*) Gallopade Intl.

— Let's Quilt Our Alaska Town. (Carole Marsh Alaska Bks.). (J). 1994. pap. text 19.95 (*0-7933-6967-3*); lib. bdg. 29.95 (*0-685-60854-9*); disk 29.95 (*0-7933-6968-1*) Gallopade Intl.

— Let's Quilt Our Arizona County. (Carole Marsh Arizona Bks.). (J). 1994. pap. text 19.95 (*0-7933-7120-1*); lib. bdg. 29.95 (*0-7933-7119-8*); disk 29.95 (*0-7933-7121-X*) Gallopade Intl.

— Let's Quilt Our Arizona Town. (Carole Marsh Arizona Bks.). (J). 1994. pap. text 19.95 (*0-7933-6970-3*); lib. bdg. 29.95 (*0-7933-6969-X*); disk 29.95 (*0-7933-6971-1*) Gallopade Intl.

— Let's Quilt Our Arkansas County. (Carole Marsh Arkansas Bks.). (J). 1994. pap. text 19.95 (*0-7933-7123-6*); lib. bdg. 29.95 (*0-7933-7122-8*); disk 29.95 (*0-7933-7124-4*) Gallopade Intl.

— Let's Quilt Our Arkansas Town. (Carole Marsh Arkansas Bks.). (J). 1994. pap. text 19.95 (*0-7933-6973-8*); lib. bdg. 29.95 (*0-7933-6972-X*); disk 29.95 (*0-7933-6974-6*) Gallopade Intl.

— Let's Quilt Our Black Heritage. (Our Black Heritage Ser.). 1994. 29.95 (*1-55609-324-1*); pap. 19.95 (*1-55609-323-3*); disk 29.95 (*1-55609-325-X*) Gallopade Intl.

— Let's Quilt Our California County. (Carole Marsh California Bks.). (J). 1994. pap. text 19.95 (*0-7933-7126-0*); lib. bdg. 29.95 (*0-7933-7125-2*); disk 29.95 (*0-7933-7127-9*) Gallopade Intl.

— Let's Quilt Our California Town. (Carole Marsh California Bks.). (J). 1994. pap. text 19.95 (*0-7933-6976-2*); lib. bdg. 29.95 (*0-7933-6975-4*); disk 29.95 (*0-7933-6977-0*) Gallopade Intl.

— Let's Quilt Our Colorado County. (Carole Marsh Colorado Bks.). (J). 1994. pap. text 19.95 (*0-7933-7129-5*); lib. bdg. 29.95 (*0-7933-7128-7*); disk 29.95 (*0-7933-7130-9*) Gallopade Intl.

— Let's Quilt Our Colorado Town. (Carole Marsh Colorado Bks.). (J). 1994. pap. text 19.95 (*0-7933-6979-7*); lib. bdg. 29.95 (*0-7933-6978-9*); disk 29.95 (*0-7933-6980-0*) Gallopade Intl.

— Let's Quilt Our Connecticut County. (Carole Marsh Connecticut Bks.). (J). 1994. pap. text 19.95 (*0-7933-7132-5*); lib. bdg. 29.95 (*0-7933-7131-7*); disk 29.95 (*0-7933-7133-3*) Gallopade Intl.

— Let's Quilt Our Connecticut Town. (Carole Marsh Connecticut Bks.). (J). 1994. pap. text 19.95 (*0-7933-6982-7*); lib. bdg. 29.95 (*0-7933-6981-9*); disk 29.95 (*0-7933-6983-5*) Gallopade Intl.

— Let's Quilt Our Delaware County. (Carole Marsh Delaware Bks.). (J). 1994. pap. text 19.95 (*0-7933-7135-X*); lib. bdg. 29.95 (*0-7933-7134-1*); disk 29.95 (*0-7933-7136-8*) Gallopade Intl.

— Let's Quilt Our Delaware Town. (Carole Marsh Delaware Bks.). (J). 1994. pap. text 19.95 (*0-7933-6985-1*); lib. bdg. 29.95 (*0-7933-6984-3*); disk 29.95 (*0-7933-6986-X*) Gallopade Intl.

— Let's Quilt Our Florida County. (Carole Marsh Florida Bks.). (J). 1994. pap. text 19.95 (*0-7933-7141-4*); lib. bdg. 29.95 (*0-7933-7140-6*); disk 29.95 (*0-7933-7142-2*) Gallopade Intl.

— Let's Quilt Our Florida Town. (Carole Marsh Florida Bks.). (J). 1994. pap. text 19.95 (*0-7933-6991-6*); lib. bdg. 29.95 (*0-7933-6990-8*); disk 29.95 (*0-7933-6992-4*) Gallopade Intl.

— Let's Quilt Our Georgia County. (Carole Marsh Georgia Bks.). (J). 1994. pap. text 19.95 (*0-7933-7144-9*); lib. bdg. 29.95 (*0-7933-7143-0*); disk 29.95 (*0-7933-7145-7*) Gallopade Intl.

— Let's Quilt Our Georgia Town. (Carole Marsh Georgia Bks.). (J). 1994. pap. text 19.95 (*0-7933-6994-0*); lib. bdg. 29.95 (*0-7933-6993-2*); disk 29.95 (*0-7933-6995-9*) Gallopade Intl.

— Let's Quilt Our Hawaii County. (Carole Marsh Hawaii Bks.). (J). 1994. pap. text 19.95 (*0-7933-7147-3*); lib. bdg. 29.95 (*0-7933-7146-5*); disk 29.95 (*0-7933-7148-1*) Gallopade Intl.

— Let's Quilt Our Hawaii Town. (Carole Marsh Hawaii Bks.). (J). 1994. pap. text 19.95 (*0-7933-6997-5*); lib. bdg. 29.95 (*0-7933-6996-7*); disk 29.95 (*0-7933-6998-3*) Gallopade Intl.

— Let's Quilt Our Idaho County. (Carole Marsh Idaho Bks.). (J). 1994. pap. text 19.95 (*0-7933-7150-3*); lib. bdg. 29.95 (*0-7933-7149-X*); disk 29.95 (*0-7933-7151-1*) Gallopade Intl.

— Let's Quilt Our Idaho Town. (Carole Marsh Idaho Bks.). (J). 1994. pap. text 19.95 (*0-7933-7000-0*); lib. bdg. 29.95 (*0-7933-6999-1*); disk 29.95 (*0-7933-7001-9*) Gallopade Intl.

— Let's Quilt Our Illinois County. (Carole Marsh Illinois Bks.). (J). 1994. pap. text 19.95 (*0-7933-7153-8*); lib. bdg. 29.95 (*0-7933-7152-X*); disk 29.95 (*0-7933-7154-6*) Gallopade Intl.

— Let's Quilt Our Illinois Town. (Carole Marsh Illinois Bks.). (J). 1994. pap. text 19.95 (*0-7933-7003-5*); lib. bdg. 29.95 (*0-7933-7002-7*); disk 29.95 (*0-7933-7004-3*) Gallopade Intl.

— Let's Quilt Our Indiana County. (Carole Marsh Indiana Bks.). (J). 1994. pap. text 14.95 (*0-7933-7156-2*); lib. bdg. 29.95 (*0-7933-7155-4*); disk 29.95 (*0-7933-7157-0*) Gallopade Intl.

— Let's Quilt Our Indiana Town. (Carole Marsh Indiana Bks.). (J). 1994. pap. text 19.95 (*0-7933-7006-X*); lib. bdg. 29.95 (*0-7933-7005-1*); disk 29.95 (*0-7933-7007-8*) Gallopade Intl.

— Let's Quilt Our Iowa County. (Carole Marsh Iowa Bks.). (J). 1994. pap. text 19.95 (*0-7933-7159-7*); lib. bdg. 29.95 (*0-7933-7158-9*); disk 29.95 (*0-7933-7160-0*) Gallopade Intl.

— Let's Quilt Our Iowa Town. (Carole Marsh Iowa Bks.). (J). 1994. pap. text 19.95 (*0-7933-7009-4*); lib. bdg. 29.95 (*0-7933-7008-6*); disk 29.95 (*0-7933-7010-8*) Gallopade Intl.

— Let's Quilt Our Kansas County. (Carole Marsh Kansas Bks.). (J). 1994. pap. text 19.95 (*0-7933-7162-7*); lib. bdg. 29.95 (*0-7933-7161-9*); disk 29.95 (*0-7933-7163-5*) Gallopade Intl.

— Let's Quilt Our Kansas Town. (Carole Marsh Kansas Bks.). (J). 1994. pap. text 19.95 (*0-7933-7012-4*); lib. bdg. 29.95 (*0-7933-7011-6*); disk 29.95 (*0-7933-7013-2*) Gallopade Intl.

— Let's Quilt Our Kentucky County. (Carole Marsh Kentucky Bks.). (J). 1994. pap. text 19.95 (*0-7933-7165-1*); lib. bdg. 29.95 (*0-7933-7164-3*); disk 29.95 (*0-7933-7166-X*) Gallopade Intl.

— Let's Quilt Our Kentucky Town. (Carole Marsh Kentucky Bks.). (J). 1994. pap. text 19.95 (*0-7933-7015-9*); lib. bdg. 29.95 (*0-7933-7014-0*); disk 29.95 (*0-7933-7016-7*) Gallopade Intl.

— Let's Quilt Our Louisiana Parish. (Carole Marsh Louisiana Bks.). (J). 1994. pap. text 19.95 (*0-7933-7168-6*); lib. bdg. 29.95 (*0-7933-7167-8*); disk 29.95 (*0-7933-7169-4*) Gallopade Intl.

— Let's Quilt Our Louisiana Town. (Carole Marsh Louisiana Bks.). (J). 1994. pap. text 19.95 (*0-7933-7018-3*); lib. bdg. 29.95 (*0-7933-7017-5*); disk 29.95 (*0-7933-7019-1*) Gallopade Intl.

— Let's Quilt Our Maine County. (Carole Marsh Maine Bks.). (J). 1994. pap. text 19.95 (*0-7933-7171-6*); lib. bdg. 29.95 (*0-7933-7170-8*); disk 29.95 (*0-7933-7172-4*) Gallopade Intl.

— Let's Quilt Our Maine Town. (Carole Marsh Maine Bks.). (J). 1994. pap. text 19.95 (*0-7933-7021-3*); lib. bdg. 29.95 (*0-7933-7020-5*); disk 29.95 (*0-7933-7022-1*) Gallopade Intl.

— Let's Quilt Our Maryland County. (Carole Marsh Maryland Bks.). (J). 1994. pap. text 19.95 (*0-7933-7174-0*); lib. bdg. 29.95 (*0-7933-7173-2*); disk 29.95 (*0-7933-7175-9*) Gallopade Intl.

— Let's Quilt Our Maryland Town. (Carole Marsh Maryland Bks.). (J). 1994. pap. text 19.95 (*0-7933-7024-8*); lib. bdg. 29.95 (*0-7933-7023-X*); disk 29.95 (*0-7933-7025-6*) Gallopade Intl.

— Let's Quilt Our Massachusetts County. (Massachuseets Bks.). (J). 1994. pap. text 19.95 (*0-7933-7177-5*); lib. bdg. 29.95 (*0-7933-7176-7*); disk 29.95 (*0-7933-7178-3*) Gallopade Intl.

— Let's Quilt Our Massachusetts Town. (Massachuseets Bks.). (J). 1994. pap. text 19.95 (*0-7933-7027-2*); lib. bdg. 29.95 (*0-7933-7026-4*); disk 29.95 (*0-7933-7028-0*) Gallopade Intl.

— Let's Quilt Our Michigan County. (Carole Marsh Michigan Bks.). (J). 1994. pap. text 19.95 (*0-7933-7180-5*); lib. bdg. 29.95 (*0-7933-7179-1*); disk 29.95 (*0-7933-7181-3*) Gallopade Intl.

— Let's Quilt Our Michigan Town. (Carole Marsh Michigan Bks.). (J). 1994. pap. text 19.95 (*0-7933-7030-2*); lib. bdg. 29.95 (*0-7933-7029-9*); disk 29.95 (*0-7933-7031-0*) Gallopade Intl.

— Let's Quilt Our Minnesota County. (Carole Marsh Minnesota Bks.). (J). 1994. pap. text 19.95 (*0-7933-7183-X*); lib. bdg. 29.95 (*0-7933-7182-1*); disk 29.95 (*0-7933-7184-8*) Gallopade Intl.

— Let's Quilt Our Minnesota Town. (Carole Marsh Minnesota Bks.). (J). 1994. pap. text 19.95 (*0-7933-7033-7*); lib. bdg. 29.95 (*0-7933-7032-9*); disk 29.95 (*0-7933-7034-5*) Gallopade Intl.

— Let's Quilt Our Mississippi County. (Carole Marsh Mississippi Bks.). (J). 1994. pap. text 19.95 (*0-7933-7186-4*); lib. bdg. 29.95 (*0-7933-7185-6*); disk 29.95 (*0-7933-7187-2*) Gallopade Intl.

— Let's Quilt Our Mississippi Town. (Carole Marsh Mississippi Bks.). (J). 1994. pap. text 19.95 (*0-7933-7036-1*); lib. bdg. 29.95 (*0-7933-7035-3*); disk 29.95 (*0-7933-7037-X*) Gallopade Intl.

— Let's Quilt Our Missouri County. (Carole Marsh Missouri Bks.). (J). 1994. pap. text 19.95 (*0-7933-7189-9*); lib. bdg. 29.95 (*0-7933-7188-0*); disk 29.95 (*0-7933-7190-2*) Gallopade Intl.

— Let's Quilt Our Missouri Town. (Carole Marsh Missouri Bks.). (J). 1994. pap. text 19.95 (*0-7933-7039-6*); lib. bdg. 29.95 (*0-7933-7038-8*); disk 29.95 (*0-7933-7040-X*) Gallopade Intl.

— Let's Quilt Our Montana County. (Carole Marsh Montana Bks.). (J). 1994. pap. text 19.95 (*0-7933-7192-9*); lib. bdg. 29.95 (*0-7933-7191-0*); disk 29.95 (*0-7933-7193-7*) Gallopade Intl.

— Let's Quilt Our Montana Town. (Carole Marsh Montana Bks.). (J). 1994. pap. text 19.95 (*0-7933-7042-6*); lib. bdg. 29.95 (*0-7933-7041-8*); disk 29.95 (*0-7933-7043-4*) Gallopade Intl.

— Let's Quilt Our Nebraska County. (Carole Marsh Nebraska Bks.). (J). 1994. pap. text 19.95 (*0-7933-7195-3*); lib. bdg. 29.95 (*0-7933-7194-5*); disk 29.95 (*0-7933-7196-1*) Gallopade Intl.

— Let's Quilt Our Nebraska Town. (Carole Marsh Nebraska Bks.). (J). 1994. pap. text 19.95 (*0-7933-7045-0*); lib. bdg. 29.95 (*0-7933-7044-2*); disk 29.95 (*0-7933-7046-9*) Gallopade Intl.

— Let's Quilt Our Nevada County. (Carole Marsh Nevada Bks.). (J). 1994. pap. text 19.95 (*0-7933-7198-8*); lib. bdg. 29.95 (*0-7933-7197-X*); disk 29.95 (*0-7933-7199-6*) Gallopade Intl.

— Let's Quilt Our Nevada Town. (Carole Marsh Nevada Bks.). (J). 1994. pap. text 19.95 (*0-7933-7048-5*); lib. bdg. 29.95 (*0-7933-7047-7*); disk 29.95 (*0-7933-7049-3*) Gallopade Intl.

— Let's Quilt Our New Hampshire County. (Carole Marsh New Hampshire Bks.). (J). 1994. pap. text 19.95 (*0-7933-7201-1*); lib. bdg. 29.95 (*0-7933-7200-3*) Gallopade Intl.

— Let's Quilt Our New Hampshire County. (Carole Marsh New Hampshire Bks.). (J). 1997. disk 29.95 (*0-7933-7202-X*) Gallopade Intl.

— Let's Quilt Our New Hampshire Town. (Carole Marsh New Hampshire Bks.). (J). 1994. pap. text 19.95 (*0-7933-7051-5*); lib. bdg. 29.95 (*0-7933-7050-7*); disk 29.95 (*0-7933-7052-3*) Gallopade Intl.

— Let's Quilt Our New Jersey County. (Carole Marsh New Jersey Bks.). (J). 1994. pap. text 19.95 (*0-7933-7204-6*); lib. bdg. 29.95 (*0-7933-7203-8*); disk 29.95 (*0-7933-7205-4*) Gallopade Intl.

— Let's Quilt Our New Jersey Town. (Carole Marsh New Jersey Bks.). (J). 1994. pap. text 19.95 (*0-7933-7054-X*); lib. bdg. 29.95 (*0-7933-7053-1*); disk 29.95 (*0-7933-7055-8*) Gallopade Intl.

— Let's Quilt Our New Mexico County. (Carole Marsh New Mexico Bks.). (J). 1994. pap. text 19.95 (*0-7933-7207-0*); lib. bdg. 29.95 (*0-7933-7206-2*); disk 29.95 (*0-7933-7208-9*) Gallopade Intl.

— Let's Quilt Our New Mexico Town. (Carole Marsh New Mexico Bks.). (J). 1994. pap. text 19.95 (*0-7933-7057-4*); lib. bdg. 29.95 (*0-7933-7056-6*); disk 29.95 (*0-7933-7058-2*) Gallopade Intl.

— Let's Quilt Our New York County. (Carole Marsh New York Bks.). (J). 1994. pap. text 19.95 (*0-7933-7210-0*); lib. bdg. 29.95 (*0-7933-7209-7*); disk 29.95 (*0-7933-7211-9*) Gallopade Intl.

— Let's Quilt Our New York Town. (Carole Marsh New York Bks.). (J). 1994. pap. text 19.95 (*0-7933-7060-4*); lib. bdg. 29.95 (*0-7933-7059-0*); disk 29.95 (*0-7933-7061-2*) Gallopade Intl.

— Let's Quilt Our North Carolina County. (Carole Marsh North Carolina Bks.). (J). 1994. pap. text 19.95 (*0-7933-7213-5*); lib. bdg. 29.95 (*0-7933-7212-7*); disk 29.95 (*0-7933-7214-3*) Gallopade Intl.

— Let's Quilt Our North Carolina Town. (Carole Marsh North Carolina Bks.). (J). 1994. pap. text 19.95 (*0-7933-7063-9*); lib. bdg. 29.95 (*0-7933-7062-0*); disk 29.95 (*0-7933-7064-7*) Gallopade Intl.

— Let's Quilt Our North Dakota County. (Carole Marsh North Dakota Bks.). (J). 1994. pap. text 19.95 (*0-7933-7216-X*); lib. bdg. 29.95 (*0-7933-7215-1*); disk 29.95 (*0-7933-7217-8*) Gallopade Intl.

— Let's Quilt Our North Dakota Town. (Carole Marsh North Dakota Bks.). (J). 1994. pap. text 19.95 (*0-7933-7066-3*); lib. bdg. 29.95 (*0-7933-7065-5*); disk 29.95 (*0-7933-7067-1*) Gallopade Intl.

— Let's Quilt Our Ohio County. (Carole Marsh Ohio Bks.). (J). 1994. pap. text 19.95 (*0-7933-7219-4*); lib. bdg. 29.95 (*0-7933-7218-6*); disk 29.95 (*0-7933-7220-8*) Gallopade Intl.

— Let's Quilt Our Ohio Town. (Carole Marsh Ohio Bks.). (J). 1994. pap. text 19.95 (*0-7933-7069-8*); lib. bdg. 29.95 (*0-7933-7068-X*); disk 29.95 (*0-7933-7070-1*) Gallopade Intl.

— Let's Quilt Our Oklahoma County. (Oklahoma Bks.). (J). 1994. pap. text 19.95 (*0-7933-7222-4*); lib. bdg. 29.95 (*0-7933-7221-6*); disk 29.95 (*0-7933-7223-2*) Gallopade Intl.

— Let's Quilt Our Oklahoma Town. (Carole Marsh Oklahoma Bks.). (J). 1994. pap. text 19.95 (*0-7933-7072-8*); lib. bdg. 29.95 (*0-7933-7071-X*); disk 29.95 (*0-7933-7073-6*) Gallopade Intl.

— Let's Quilt Our Oregon County. (Oregon Bks.). (J). 1994. pap. text 19.95 (*0-7933-7225-9*); lib. bdg. 29.95 (*0-7933-7224-0*); disk 29.95 (*0-7933-7226-7*) Gallopade Intl.

— Let's Quilt Our Oregon Town. (Carole Marsh Oregon Bks.). (J). 1994. pap. text 19.95 (*0-7933-7075-2*); lib. bdg. 29.95 (*0-7933-7074-4*); disk 29.95 (*0-7933-7076-0*) Gallopade Intl.

— Let's Quilt Our Pennsylvania County. (Pennsylvania Bks.). (J). 1994. pap. text 19.95 (*0-7933-7228-3*); lib. bdg. 29.95 (*0-7933-7227-5*); disk 29.95 (*0-7933-7229-1*) Gallopade Intl.

— Let's Quilt Our Pennsylvania Town. (Carole Marsh Pennsylvania Bks.). (J). 1994. pap. text 19.95 (*0-7933-7078-7*); lib. bdg. 29.95 (*0-7933-7077-9*); disk 29.95 (*0-7933-7079-5*) Gallopade Intl.

— Let's Quilt Our Rhode Island County. (Rhode Island Bks.). (J). 1994. pap. text 19.95 (*0-7933-7231-3*); lib. bdg. 29.95 (*0-7933-7230-5*); disk 29.95 (*0-7933-7232-1*) Gallopade Intl.

— Let's Quilt Our Rhode Island Town. (Carole Marsh Rhode Island Bks.). (J). 1994. pap. text 19.95 (*0-7933-7081-7*); lib. bdg. 29.95 (*0-7933-7080-9*); disk 29.95 (*0-7933-7082-5*) Gallopade Intl.

— Let's Quilt Our South Carolina County. (South Carolina Bks.). (J). 1994. pap. text 19.95 (*0-7933-7234-8*); lib. bdg. 29.95 (*0-7933-7233-X*); disk 29.95 (*0-7933-7235-6*) Gallopade Intl.

— Let's Quilt Our South Carolina Town. (Carole Marsh South Carolina Bks.). (J). 1994. pap. text 19.95 (*0-7933-7084-1*); lib. bdg. 29.95 (*0-7933-7083-3*); disk 29.95 (*0-7933-7085-X*) Gallopade Intl.

— Let's Quilt Our South Dakota County. (South Dakota Bks.). (J). 1994. pap. text 19.95 (*0-7933-7237-2*); lib. bdg. 29.95 (*0-7933-7236-4*); disk 29.95 (*0-7933-7238-0*) Gallopade Intl.

— Let's Quilt Our South Dakota Town. (Carole Marsh South Carolina Bks.). (J). 1994. pap. text 19.95 (*0-7933-7087-6*); lib. bdg. 29.95 (*0-7933-7086-8*); disk 29.95 (*0-7933-7088-4*) Gallopade Intl.

— Let's Quilt Our Tennessee County. (Tennessee Bks.). (J). 1994. pap. text 19.95 (*0-7933-7240-2*); lib. bdg. 29.95 (*0-7933-7239-9*); disk 29.95 (*0-7933-7241-0*) Gallopade Intl.

— Let's Quilt Our Tennessee Town. (Carole Marsh Tennessee Bks.). (J). 1994. pap. text 19.95 (*0-7933-7090-6*); lib. bdg. 29.95 (*0-7933-7089-2*); disk 29.95 (*0-7933-7091-4*) Gallopade Intl.

— Let's Quilt Our Texas County. (Texas Bks.). (J). 1994. pap. text 19.95 (*0-7933-7243-7*); lib. bdg. 29.95 (*0-7933-7242-9*); disk 29.95 (*0-7933-7244-5*) Gallopade Intl.

— Let's Quilt Our Texas Town. (Carole Marsh Texas Bks.). (J). 1994. pap. text 19.95 (*0-7933-7093-0*); lib. bdg. 29.95 (*0-7933-7092-2*); disk 29.95 (*0-7933-7094-9*) Gallopade Intl.

— Let's Quilt Our Utah County. (Utah Bks.). (J). 1994. pap. text 19.95 (*0-7933-7246-1*); lib. bdg. 29.95 (*0-7933-7245-3*); disk 29.95 (*0-7933-7247-X*) Gallopade Intl.

— Let's Quilt Our Utah Town. (Carole Marsh Utah Bks.). (J). 1994. pap. text 19.95 (*0-7933-7096-5*); lib. bdg. 29.95 (*0-7933-7095-7*); disk 29.95 (*0-7933-7097-3*) Gallopade Intl.

— Let's Quilt Our Vermont County. (Vermont Bks.). (J). 1994. pap. text 19.95 (*0-7933-7249-6*); lib. bdg. 29.95 (*0-7933-7248-8*); disk 29.95 (*0-7933-7250-X*) Gallopade Intl.

— Let's Quilt Our Vermont Town. (Carole Marsh Vermont Bks.). (J). 1994. pap. text 19.95 (*0-7933-7099-X*); lib. bdg. 29.95 (*0-7933-7098-1*); disk 29.95 (*0-7933-7100-7*) Gallopade Intl.

— Let's Quilt Our Virginia County. (Virginia Bks.). (J). 1992. pap. text 19.95 (*0-7933-7252-6*); lib. bdg. 29.95 (*0-7933-7251-8*); disk 29.95 (*0-7933-7253-4*) Gallopade Intl.

— Let's Quilt Our Virginia Town. (Carole Marsh Virginia Bks.). (J). 1994. pap. text 19.95 (*0-7933-7102-3*); lib. bdg. 29.95 (*0-7933-7101-5*); disk 29.95 (*0-7933-7103-1*) Gallopade Intl.

— Let's Quilt Our Washington County. (Washington Bks.). (J). 1994. pap. text 19.95 (*0-7933-7255-0*); lib. bdg. 29.95 (*0-7933-7254-2*); disk 29.95 (*0-7933-7256-9*) Gallopade Intl.

— Let's Quilt Our Washington Town. (Carol Marsh Washington Bks.). (J). 1994. pap. text 19.95 (*0-7933-7105-8*); lib. bdg. 29.95 (*0-7933-7104-X*); disk 29.95 (*0-7933-7106-6*) Gallopade Intl.

— Let's Quilt Our West Virginia County. (West Virginia Bks.). (J). 1994. pap. text 19.95 (*0-7933-7258-5*); lib. bdg. 29.95 (*0-7933-7257-7*); disk 29.95 (*0-7933-7259-3*) Gallopade Intl.

— Let's Quilt Our West Virginia Town. (Carole Marsh West Virginia Bks.). (J). 1994. pap. text 19.95 (*0-7933-7108-2*); lib. bdg. 29.95 (*0-7933-7107-4*); disk 29.95 (*0-7933-7109-0*) Gallopade Intl.

— Let's Quilt Our Wisconsin County. (Wisconsin Bks.). (J). 1994. pap. text 19.95 (*0-7933-7261-5*); lib. bdg. 29.95 (*0-7933-7260-7*); disk 29.95 (*0-7933-7262-3*) Gallopade Intl.

— Let's Quilt Our Wisconsin Town. (Carole Marsh Wisconsin Bks.). (J). 1994. pap. text 19.95 (*0-7933-7111-2*); lib. bdg. 29.95 (*0-7933-7110-4*); disk 29.95 (*0-7933-7112-0*) Gallopade Intl.

— Let's Quilt Our Wyoming County. (Wyoming Bks.). (J). 1994. pap. text 19.95 (*0-7933-7264-X*); lib. bdg. 29.95 (*0-7933-7263-1*); disk 29.95 (*0-7933-7265-8*) Gallopade Intl.

— Let's Quilt Our Wyoming Town. (Carole Marsh Wyoming Bks.). (J). 1994. pap. text 19.95 (*0-7933-7114-7*); lib. bdg. 29.95 (*0-7933-7113-9*); disk 29.95 (*0-7933-7115-5*) Gallopade Intl.

— Let's Quilt Pennsylvania & Stuff It Topographically! (Carole Marsh Pennsylvania Bks.). (Illus.). (J). 1994. pap. 19.95 (*1-55609-059-5*); lib. bdg. 29.95 (*0-7933-1925-0*); disk 29.95 (*0-7933-1926-9*) Gallopade Intl.

— Let's Quilt Rhode Island & Stuff it Topographically! (Carole Marsh Rhode Island Bks.). (Illus.). (J). 1994. pap. 19.95 (*1-55609-065-X*); lib. bdg. 29.95 (*0-7933-1957-9*); disk 29.95 (*0-7933-1958-7*) Gallopade Intl.

— Let's Quilt South Carolina & Stuff It Topographically! (Carole Marsh South Carolina Bks.). (Illus.). (J). 1994. pap. 19.95 (*1-55609-053-6*); lib. bdg. 29.95 (*0-7933-1987-0*); disk 29.95 (*0-7933-1988-9*) Gallopade Intl.

— Let's Quilt South Dakota & Stuff It Topographically! (Carole Marsh South Dakota Bks.). (Illus.). (J). 1994. pap. 19.95 (*1-55609-136-2*); lib. bdg. 29.95 (*0-7933-2018-6*); disk 29.95 (*0-7933-2019-4*) Gallopade Intl.

— Let's Quilt Tennessee & Stuff It Topographically! (Tennessee Bks.). (Illus.). (J). 1994. pap. 19.95 (*1-55609-079-X*); lib. bdg. 29.95 (*0-7933-2048-8*); disk 29.95 (*0-7933-2049-6*) Gallopade Intl.

— Let's Quilt Texas & Stuff It Topographically! (Carole Marsh Texas Bks.). (Illus.). (J). 1994. pap. 19.95 (*1-55609-077-3*); lib. bdg. 29.95 (*0-7933-2078-X*); disk 29.95 (*0-7933-2079-8*) Gallopade Intl.

— Let's Quilt Utah & Stuff It Topographically! (Carole Marsh Utah Bks.). (Illus.). (J). 1994. pap. 19.95 (*1-55609-129-X*); lib. bdg. 29.95 (*0-7933-2109-3*); disk 29.95 (*0-7933-2110-7*) Gallopade Intl.

— Let's Quilt Vermont & Stuff It Topographically! (Carole Marsh Vermont Bks.). (Illus.). (J). 1994. pap. 19.95 (*1-55609-066-8*); lib. bdg. 29.95 (*0-7933-2141-7*); disk 29.95 (*0-7933-2142-5*) Gallopade Intl.

— Let's Quilt Virginia & Stuff It Topographically! (Carole Marsh Virginia Bks.). (Illus.). (J). 1994. pap. 19.95 (*1-55609-051-X*); lib. bdg. 29.95 (*0-7933-2171-9*); disk 29.95 (*0-7933-2172-7*) Gallopade Intl.

— Let's Quilt Washington & Stuff It Topographically! (Carole Marsh Washington Bks.). (Illus.). (J). 1994. pap. 19.95 (*1-55609-133-8*); lib. bdg. 29.95 (*0-7933-2204-9*); disk 29.95 (*0-7933-2205-7*) Gallopade Intl.

— Let's Quilt Washington, D. C. & Stuff It Topographically! (Carole Marsh Washington, D. C. Bks.). (Illus.). (J). (gr. 3-12). 1994. lib. bdg. 29.95 (*1-55609-564-3*); disk 29.95 (*0-7933-1461-5*) Gallopade Intl.

— Let's Quilt Washington, D. C. & Stuff It Topographically! (Carole Marsh Washington, D. C. Bks.). (Illus.). (J). (gr. 3-12). 1997. pap. 19.95 (*1-55609-563-5*) Gallopade Intl.

— Let's Quilt West Virginia & Stuff It Topographically! (Carole Marsh West Virginia Bks.). (Illus.). (J). 1994. pap. 19.95 (*1-55609-052-8*); lib. bdg. 29.95 (*0-7933-2236-7*); disk 29.95 (*0-7933-2237-5*) Gallopade Intl.

— Let's Quilt Wisconsin & Stuff It Topographically! (Carole Marsh Wisconsin Bks.). (Illus.). (J). 1994. pap. 19.95 (*1-55609-098-6*); lib. bdg. 29.95 (*0-7933-2268-5*); disk 29.95 (*0-7933-2269-3*) Gallopade Intl.

— Let's Quilt Wyoming & Stuff It Topographically! (Carole Marsh Wyoming Bks.). (Illus.). (J). 1994. pap. 19.95 (*1-55609-134-6*); lib. bdg. 29.95 (*1-55609-290-3*); disk 29.95 (*1-55609-291-1*) Gallopade Intl.

An Asterisk (*) at the beginning of an entry indicates that the title is appearing for the first time.

— Life Isn't Fair: Murphy's Laws for Kids. (Quantum Leap Ser.). (Illus.). (J). (gr. 4-12). 1994. 29.95 (*0-935326-08-1*); lib. bdg. 29.95 (*0-7933-6916-9*) Gallopade Intl.

— Life on Mars for Kids! (J). (gr. 2-7). 1997. 24.95 (*0-614-28746-4*); pap. 19.95 (*0-614-28747-2*) Gallopade Intl.

— Like a Virgin: How You Can Convince Your Child to Abstain from Sex. (Smart Sex Stuff Ser.). (Orig.). 1994. pap. 19.95 (*1-55609-223-7*) Gallopade Intl.

— The Little Known, Seldom Told Secrets of Book Distribution for Authors & Small Presses. (Lifewrite Ser.). (Illus.). 1994. 29.95 (*0-7933-2849-7*); pap. text 19.95 (*0-7933-2850-0*); disk 29.95 (*0-7933-2851-9*) Gallopade Intl.

— The Lost Colony Classroom Gamebook. (Carole Marsh Bks.). (Illus.). (Orig.). (J). (gr. 3-12). 1994. pap. 19.95 (*0-935326-86-3*) Gallopade Intl.

— Louisiana! A(lligator) to Z(ydeco) (Carole Marsh Louisiana Bks.). (J). 1994. pap. text 19.95 (*0-7933-7320-4*); lib. bdg. 29.95 (*0-7933-7321-2*); disk 29.95 (*0-7933-7322-0*) Gallopade Intl.

— Louisiana & Other State Greats (Biographies) (Carole Marsh Louisiana Bks.). (Illus.). (J). (gr. 3-8). 1994. pap. 19.95 (*1-55609-403-5*); lib. bdg. 29.95 (*1-55609-404-3*) Gallopade Intl.

— Louisiana & Other State Greats (Biographies) (Carole Marsh Louisiana Bks.). (Illus.). (J). (gr. 3-8). 1997. disk 29.95 (*0-7933-1677-4*) Gallopade Intl.

— Louisiana Bandits, Bushwackers, Outlaws, Crooks, Devils, Ghosts, Desperadoes & Other Assorted & Sundry Characters! (Carole Marsh Louisiana Bks.). (Illus.). (J). (gr. 3-8). 1994. pap. 19.95 (*0-7933-0501-2*); lib. bdg. 29.95 (*0-7933-0502-0*); disk 29.95 (*0-7933-0503-9*) Gallopade Intl.

— Louisiana "BIO" Bingo! 24 Must Know State People for Kids to Learn about While Having Fun! (Bingo! Ser.). (Illus.). (J). (gr. 2-8). 1998. pap. 14.95 (*0-7933-8576-8*) Gallopade Intl.

— The Louisiana Bookstore Book: A Surprising Guide to Our State's Bookstores & Their Specialties for Students, Teachers, Writers & Publishers. (Carole Marsh Louisiana Bks.). (Illus.). 1994. pap. 19.95 (*0-7933-2910-8*); lib. bdg. 29.95 (*0-7933-2909-4*); disk 29.95 (*0-7933-2911-6*) Gallopade Intl.

— Louisiana Classic Christmas Trivia: Stories, Recipes, Activities, Legends, Lore & More! (Carole Marsh Louisiana Bks.). (Illus.). (J). (gr. 3-8). 1994. pap. 19.95 (*0-7933-0504-7*); lib. bdg. 29.95 (*0-7933-0505-5*); disk 29.95 (*0-7933-0506-3*) Gallopade Intl.

— Louisiana Coastales. (Carole Marsh Louisiana Bks.). (J). 1994. lib. bdg. 29.95 (*0-7933-7283-6*) Gallopade Intl.

— Louisiana Coastales. (Carole Marsh Louisiana Bks.). (Illus.). (J). (gr. 3-8). 1994. pap. 19.95 (*1-55609-119-2*); lib. bdg. 29.95 (*1-55609-400-0*); disk 29.95 (*0-7933-1673-1*) Gallopade Intl.

***Marsh, Carole.** The Louisiana Coloring Book. (Louisiana Experience! Ser.). (Illus.). (J). (gr. k-5). 2000. pap. 3.95 (*0-7933-9551-8*) Gallopade Intl.

Marsh, Carole. Louisiana "Crinkum-Crankum" A Funny Word Book about Our State. (Carole Marsh Louisiana Bks.). (Illus.). (J). 1994. pap. 19.95 (*0-7933-4863-3*); lib. bdg. 29.95 (*0-7933-4862-5*); disk 29.95 (*0-7933-4864-1*) Gallopade Intl.

— Louisiana Dingbats! A Fun Book of Games, Stories, Activities & More about Our State That's All in Code! for You to Decipher, Bk. 1. (Carole Marsh Louisiana Bks.). (Illus.). (J). (gr. 3-12). 1994. pap. 19.95 (*0-7933-3828-X*); lib. bdg. 29.95 (*0-7933-3827-1*); disk 29.95 (*0-7933-3829-8*) Gallopade Intl.

***Marsh, Carole.** The Louisiana Experience Pocket Guide. (Louisiana Experience! Ser.). (Illus.). (J). 2000. pap. 6.95 (*0-7933-9546-1*) Gallopade Intl.

Marsh, Carole. Louisiana Facts & Factivities. (Carole Marsh State Bks.). (Illus.). (J). (gr. 4-7). 1996. pap., teacher ed. 19.95 (*0-7933-7883-4*, C Marsh) Gallopade Intl.

— Louisiana Festival Fun for Kids! (Carole Marsh Louisiana Bks.). (Illus.). (YA). (gr. 3-12). 1994. pap. 19.95 (*0-7933-3981-2*); lib. bdg. 29.95 (*0-7933-3980-4*); disk 29.95 (*0-7933-3982-0*) Gallopade Intl.

— Louisiana "GEO" Bingo! 38 Must Know State Geography Facts for Kids to Learn While Having Fun! (Bingo! Ser.). (Illus.). (J). (gr. 2-8). 1998. pap. 14.95 (*0-7933-8577-6*) Gallopade Intl.

— Louisiana Government! The Cornerstone of Everyday Life in Our State! (Carole Marsh Louisiana Bks.). (Illus.). (J). (gr. 3-12). 1996. pap. 19.95 (*0-7933-6236-9*); lib. bdg. 29.95 (*0-7933-6235-0*); disk 29.95 (*0-7933-6237-7*) Gallopade Intl.

— Louisiana "HISTO" Bingo! 42 Must Know State History Facts for Kids to Learn While Having Fun! (Bingo! Ser.). (Illus.). (J). (gr. 2-8). 1998. pap. 14.95 (*0-7933-8578-4*) Gallopade Intl.

— Louisiana History! Surprising Secrets about Our State's Founding Mothers, Fathers & Kids! (Carole Marsh Louisiana Bks.). (Illus.). (J). (gr. 3-12). 1996. pap. 19.95 (*0-7933-6083-8*); lib. bdg. 29.95 (*0-7933-6082-X*); disk 29.95 (*0-7933-6084-6*) Gallopade Intl.

— The Louisiana Hot Air Balloon Mystery. (Carole Marsh Louisiana Bks.). (Illus.). (J). (gr. 2-9). 1994. pap. 19.95 (*0-7933-2481-5*); disk 29.95 (*0-7933-2482-3*) Gallopade Intl.

— The Louisiana Hot Air Balloon Mystery. (Carole Marsh Louisiana Bks.). (Illus.). (J). (gr. 2-9). 1997. 29.95 (*0-7933-2480-7*) Gallopade Intl.

— Louisiana Hot Zones! Viruses, Diseases, & Epidemics in Our State's History. (Hot Zones! Ser.). (Illus.). (J). (gr. 3-12). 1998. pap. 19.95 (*0-7933-8883-X*); lib. bdg. 29.95 (*0-7933-8882-1*) Gallopade Intl.

— Louisiana Indian Dictionary for Kids! (Carole Marsh State Bks.). (J). (gr. 2-9). 1996. 29.95 (*0-7933-7698-X*, C Marsh); pap. 19.95 (*0-7933-7699-8*, C Marsh) Gallopade Intl.

***Marsh, Carole.** Louisiana Jeopardy. (Louisiana Experience! Ser.). (Illus.). (J). (gr. 2-6). 2000. pap. 7.95 (*0-7933-9548-8*) Gallopade Intl.

Marsh, Carole. Louisiana Jeopardy! Answers & Questions about Our State! (Carole Marsh Louisiana Bks.). (Illus.). (J). (gr. 3-12). 1994. pap. 19.95 (*0-7933-4134-5*); lib. bdg. 29.95 (*0-7933-4133-7*); disk 29.95 (*0-7933-4135-3*) Gallopade Intl.

***Marsh, Carole.** Louisiana Jography. (Louisiana Experience! Ser.). (Illus.). (J). (gr. 2-6). 2000. pap. 7.95 (*0-7933-9549-6*) Gallopade Intl.

Marsh, Carole. Louisiana "Jography" A Fun Run Thru Our State! (Carole Marsh Louisiana Bks.). (Illus.). (J). (gr. 3-8). 1994. pap. 19.95 (*1-55609-108-7*); lib. bdg. 29.95 (*1-55609-396-9*); disk 29.95 (*0-7933-1663-4*) Gallopade Intl.

— Louisiana Kid's Cookbook: Recipes, How-To, History, Lore & More! (Carole Marsh Louisiana Bks.). (Illus.). (J). (gr. 3-8). 1994. pap. 19.95 (*0-7933-0513-6*); lib. bdg. 29.95 (*0-7933-0514-4*); disk 29.95 (*0-7933-0515-2*) Gallopade Intl.

— The Louisiana Library Book: A Surprising Guide to the Unusual Special Collections in Libraries Across Our State for Students, Teachers, Writers & Publishers - Includes Reproducible Mailing Labels Plus Activities for Young People! (Carole Marsh Louisiana Bks.). (Illus.). 1994. pap. 19.95 (*0-7933-3060-2*); lib. bdg. 29.95 (*0-7933-3059-9*); disk 29.95 (*0-7933-3061-0*) Gallopade Intl.

— Louisiana Math! How It All Adds up in Our State. (Carole Marsh Louisiana Bks.). (Illus.). (YA). (gr. 3-12). 1996. pap. 19.95 (*0-7933-6542-2*); lib. bdg. 29.95 (*0-7933-6541-4*) Gallopade Intl.

— The Louisiana Media Book: A Surprising Guide to the Amazing Print, Broadcast & Online Media of Our State for Students, Teachers, Writers & Publishers - Includes Reproducible Mailing Labels Plus Activities for Young People! (Carole Marsh Louisiana Bks.). (Illus.). 1994. pap. 19.95 (*0-7933-3216-8*); lib. bdg. 29.95 (*0-7933-3215-X*); disk 29.95 (*0-7933-3217-6*) Gallopade Intl.

— The Louisiana Mystery Van Takes Off! Handicapped Louisiana Kids Sneak off on a Big Adventure, Bk. 1. (Carole Marsh Louisiana Bks.). (Illus.). (J). (gr. 3-12). 1994. 29.95 (*0-7933-5015-8*); pap. 19.95 (*0-7933-5016-6*); disk 29.95 (*0-7933-5017-4*) Gallopade Intl.

— Louisiana Quiz Bowl Crash Course! (Carole Marsh Louisiana Bks.). (Illus.). (YA). 1994. pap. 19.95 (*1-55609-401-9*); lib. bdg. 29.95 (*1-55609-402-7*); disk 29.95 (*0-7933-1672-3*) Gallopade Intl.

— Louisiana Rollercoasters! (Carole Marsh Louisiana Bks.). (Illus.). (YA). (gr. 3-12). 1994. pap. 19.95 (*0-7933-5279-7*); lib. bdg. 29.95 (*0-7933-5278-9*); disk 29.95 (*0-7933-5280-0*) Gallopade Intl.

— Louisiana School Trivia: An Amazing & Fascinating Look at Our State's Teachers, Schools & Students! (Carole Marsh Louisiana Bks.). (Illus.). (J). (gr. 3-8). 1994. pap. 19.95 (*0-7933-0510-1*); lib. bdg. 29.95 (*0-7933-0511-X*); disk 29.95 (*0-7933-0512-8*) Gallopade Intl.

— Louisiana Silly Basketball Sportsmysteries, Vol. I. (Carole Marsh Louisiana Bks.). (Illus.). (J). (gr. 3-8). 1994. pap. 19.95 (*0-7933-0507-1*); lib. bdg. 29.95 (*0-7933-0508-X*); disk 29.95 (*0-7933-0509-8*) Gallopade Intl.

— Louisiana Silly Basketball Sportsmysteries, Vol. II. (Carole Marsh Louisiana Bks.). (Illus.). (J). (gr. 3-8). 1994. pap. 19.95 (*0-7933-1679-0*); lib. bdg. 29.95 (*0-7933-1678-2*); disk 29.95 (*0-7933-1680-4*) Gallopade Intl.

— Louisiana Silly Football Sportsmysteries, Vol. I. (Carole Marsh Louisiana Bks.). (Illus.). (J). (gr. 3-8). 1994. pap. 19.95 (*1-55609-398-5*); lib. bdg. 29.95 (*1-55609-399-3*); disk 29.95 (*0-7933-1665-0*) Gallopade Intl.

— Louisiana Silly Football Sportsmysteries, Vol. II. (Carole Marsh Louisiana Bks.). (Illus.). (J). (gr. 3-8). 1994. pap. 19.95 (*0-7933-1667-7*); lib. bdg. 29.95 (*0-7933-1666-9*); disk 29.95 (*0-7933-1668-5*) Gallopade Intl.

— Louisiana Silly Trivia! (Carole Marsh Louisiana Bks.). (Illus.). (J). (gr. 3-8). 1994. pap. 19.95 (*1-55609-041-2*); lib. bdg. 29.95 (*1-55609-395-0*); disk 29.95 (*0-7933-0522-5*) Gallopade Intl.

— Louisiana Spelling Bee! Score Big by Correctly Spelling Our State's Unique Names. (Carole Marsh Louisiana Bks.). (Illus.). (YA). (gr. 3-12). 1996. pap. 19.95 (*0-7933-6695-X*); lib. bdg. 29.95 (*0-7933-6694-1*) Gallopade Intl.

— Louisiana Timeline: A Chronology of Louisiana History, Mystery, Trivia, Legend, Lore & More. (Carole Marsh Louisiana Bks.). (Illus.). (J). (gr. 3-12). 1994. pap. 19.95 (*0-7933-5930-9*); lib. bdg. 29.95 (*0-7933-5929-5*); disk 29.95 (*0-7933-5931-7*) Gallopade Intl.

— Louisiana 2000! Coming Soon to a Calendar Near You - The 21st Century! - Complete Set of AL 2000 Items. (Two Thousand! Ser.). (Illus.). (J). (gr. 3-12). 1998. pap. 75.00 (*0-7933-9345-0*); lib. bdg. 85.00 (*0-7933-9346-9*) Gallopade Intl.

— Louisiana 2000! Coming Soon to a Calendar Near You-The 21st Century! (Two Thousand! Ser.). (Illus.). (J). (gr. 3-12). 1998. pap. 19.95 (*0-7933-8730-2*); lib. bdg. 29.95 (*0-7933-8729-9*) Gallopade Intl.

— Louisiana UFO's & Extraterrestrials! A Look at the Sightings & Science in Our State. (Carole Marsh Louisiana Bks.). (Illus.). (J). (gr. 3-12). 1997. pap. 19.95 (*0-7933-6389-6*); lib. bdg. 29.95 (*0-7933-6388-8*) Gallopade Intl.

***Marsh, Carole.** Louisiana's BIG Activity Book. (Louisiana Experience! Ser.). (Illus.). (J). (gr. k-5). 2000. pap. 9.95 (*0-7933-9550-X*) Gallopade Intl.

Marsh, Carole. Louisiana's (Most Devastating!) Disasters & (Most Calamitous!) Catastrophies! (Carole Marsh Louisiana Bks.). (Illus.). (J). (gr. 3-8). 1994. pap. 19.95 (*0-7933-0498-9*); lib. bdg. 29.95 (*0-7933-0499-7*) Gallopade Intl.

— Louisiana's (Most Devastating!) Disasters & (Most Calamitous!) Catastrophies! (Carole Marsh Louisiana Bks.). (Illus.). (J). (gr. 3-8). 1997. disk 29.95 (*0-7933-0500-4*) Gallopade Intl.

— Louisiana's Unsolved Mysteries (And Their "Solutions") Includes Scientific Information & Other Activities for Students. (Carole Marsh Louisiana Bks.). (Illus.). (J). (gr. 3-12). 1994. pap. 19.95 (*0-7933-5777-2*); lib. bdg. 29.95 (*0-7933-5776-4*); disk 29.95 (*0-7933-5778-0*) Gallopade Intl.

— The Magic & Sorcery Dingbats Book. (Carole Marsh Dingbats Bks.). (Illus.). (J). (gr. 3-12). 1994. pap. 19.95 (*0-7933-5378-5*); lib. bdg. 29.95 (*0-7933-5377-7*); disk 29.95 (*0-7933-5379-3*) Gallopade Intl.

***Marsh, Carole.** The Magnificent Maryland Coloring Book. (Maryland Experience! Ser.). (Illus.). (J). (gr. k-5). 2000. pap. 3.95 (*0-7933-9615-8*) Gallopade Intl.

— The Magnificent Michigan Coloring Book. (Michigan Experience! Ser.). (Illus.). (J). (gr. k-5). 2000. pap. 3.95 (*0-7933-9567-4*) Gallopade Intl.

— The Magnificent Missouri Coloring Book. (Missouri Experience! Ser.). (Illus.). (J). (gr. k-5). 2000. pap. 3.95 (*0-7933-9575-5*) Gallopade Intl.

— The Magnificent Mississippi Coloring Book. (Mississippi Experience! Ser.). (Illus.). (J). (gr. k-5). 2000. pap. 3.95 (*0-7933-9559-3*) Gallopade Intl.

Marsh, Carole. Maine & Other State Greats (Biographies) (Carole Marsh Maine Bks.). (Illus.). (J). (gr. 3-8). 1994. pap. 19.95 (*1-55609-615-1*); lib. bdg. 29.95 (*1-55609-614-3*); disk 29.95 (*1-55609-616-X*) Gallopade Intl.

— Maine Bandits, Bushwackers, Outlaws, Crooks, Devils, Ghosts, Desperadoes & Other Assorted & Sundry Characters! (Carole Marsh Maine Bks.). (Illus.). (J). (gr. 3-8). 1994. pap. 19.95 (*0-7933-0526-8*); lib. bdg. 29.95 (*0-7933-0527-6*); disk 29.95 (*0-7933-0528-4*) Gallopade Intl.

— Maine "BIO" Bingo! 24 Must Know State People for Kids to Learn about While Having Fun! (Bingo! Ser.). (Illus.). (J). (gr. 2-8). 1998. pap. 14.95 (*0-7933-8579-2*) Gallopade Intl.

— The Maine Bookstore Book: A Surprising Guide to Our State's Bookstores & Their Specialties for Students, Teachers, Writers & Publishers. (Carole Marsh Maine Bks.). (Illus.). 1994. pap. 19.95 (*0-7933-2913-2*); lib. bdg. 29.95 (*0-7933-2912-4*); disk 29.95 (*0-7933-2914-0*) Gallopade Intl.

— Maine Classic Christmas Trivia: Stories, Recipes, Activities, Legends, Lore & More! (Carole Marsh Maine Bks.). (Illus.). (J). (gr. 3-8). 1994. pap. 19.95 (*0-7933-0529-2*); lib. bdg. 29.95 (*0-7933-0530-6*); disk 29.95 (*0-7933-0531-4*) Gallopade Intl.

— Maine Coastales! (Carole Marsh Maine Bks.). (J). 1994. lib. bdg. 29.95 (*0-7933-7284-4*) Gallopade Intl.

— Maine Coastales! (Carole Marsh Maine Bks.). (Illus.). (J). (gr. 3-8). 1994. pap. 19.95 (*1-55609-609-7*); lib. bdg. 29.95 (*1-55609-608-9*); disk 29.95 (*1-55609-610-0*) Gallopade Intl.

— Maine "Crinkum-Crankum" A Funny Word Book about Our State. (Carole Marsh Maine Bks.). (Illus.). (J). 1994. pap. 19.95 (*0-7933-4866-8*); lib. bdg. 29.95 (*0-7933-4865-X*); disk 29.95 (*0-7933-4867-6*) Gallopade Intl.

— Maine Dingbats! Bk. 1: A Fun Book of Games, Stories, Activities & More about Our State That's All in Code! for You to Decipher. (Carole Marsh Maine Bks.). (Illus.). (J). (gr. 3-12). 1994. pap. 19.95 (*0-7933-3831-X*); lib. bdg. 29.95 (*0-7933-3830-1*); disk 29.95 (*0-7933-3832-8*) Gallopade Intl.

— Maine Facts & Factivities. (Carole Marsh State Bks.). (Illus.). (J). (gr. 4-7). 1996. pap., teacher ed. 19.95 (*0-7933-7885-0*, C Marsh) Gallopade Intl.

— Maine Festival Fun for Kids! (Carole Marsh Maine Bks.). (Illus.). (YA). (gr. 3-12). 1994. pap. 19.95 (*0-7933-3984-7*); lib. bdg. 29.95 (*0-7933-3983-9*); disk 29.95 (*0-7933-3985-5*) Gallopade Intl.

— Maine "GEO" Bingo! 38 Must Know State Geography Facts for Kids to Learn While Having Fun! (Bingo! Ser.). (Illus.). (J). (gr. 2-8). 1998. pap. 14.95 (*0-7933-8580-6*) Gallopade Intl.

— Maine Government! The Cornerstone of Everyday Life in Our State! (Carole Marsh Maine Bks.). (Illus.). (J). (gr. 3-12). 1996. pap. 19.95 (*0-7933-6239-3*); pap. 19.95 (*0-7933-6263-6*); lib. bdg. 29.95 (*0-7933-6238-5*); lib. bdg. 29.95 (*0-7933-6262-8*); disk 29.95 (*0-7933-6240-7*); disk 29.95 (*0-7933-6264-4*) Gallopade Intl.

— Maine "HISTO" Bingo! 42 Must Know State History Facts for Kids to Learn While Having Fun! (Bingo! Ser.). (Illus.). (J). (gr. 2-8). 1998. pap. 14.95 (*0-7933-8581-4*) Gallopade Intl.

— Maine History! Surprising Secrets about Our State's Founding Mothers, Fathers & Kids! (Carole Marsh Maine Bks.). (Illus.). (J). (gr. 3-12). 1996. pap. 19.95 (*0-7933-6086-2*); lib. bdg. 29.95 (*0-7933-6085-4*); disk 29.95 (*0-7933-6087-0*) Gallopade Intl.

— The Maine Hot Air Balloon Mystery. (Carole Marsh Maine Bks.). (Illus.). (J). (gr. 2-9). 1994. 29.95 (*0-7933-2489-0*); pap. 19.95 (*0-7933-2490-4*); disk 29.95 (*0-7933-2491-2*) Gallopade Intl.

— Maine Hot Zones! Viruses, Diseases, & Epidemics in Our State's History. (Hot Zones! Ser.). (Illus.). (J). (gr. 3-12). 1998. pap. 19.95 (*0-7933-8886-4*); lib. bdg. 29.95 (*0-7933-8885-6*) Gallopade Intl.

— Maine Indian Dictionary for Kids! (Carole Marsh State Bks.). (J). (gr. 2-9). 1996. 29.95 (*0-7933-7701-3*, C Marsh); pap. 19.95 (*0-7933-7702-1*, C Marsh) Gallopade Intl.

— Maine Jeopardy! Answers & Questions about Our State! (Carole Marsh Maine Bks.). (Illus.). (J). (gr. 3-12). 1994. pap. 19.95 (*0-7933-4137-X*); lib. bdg. 29.95 (*0-7933-4136-1*); disk 29.95 (*0-7933-4138-8*) Gallopade Intl.

— Maine "Jography" A Fun Run Thru Our State! (Carole Marsh Maine Bks.). (Illus.). (J). (gr. 3-8). 1994. pap. 19.95 (*1-55609-597-X*); lib. bdg. 29.95 (*1-55609-596-1*); disk 29.95 (*1-55609-598-8*) Gallopade Intl.

— Maine Kid's Cookbook: Recipes, How-To, History, Lore & More! (Carole Marsh Maine Bks.). (Illus.). (J). (gr. 3-8). 1994. pap. 19.95 (*0-7933-0538-1*); lib. bdg. 29.95 (*0-7933-0539-X*); disk 29.95 (*0-7933-0540-3*) Gallopade Intl.

— The Maine Library Book: A Surprising Guide to the Unusual Special Collections in Libraries Across Our State for Students, Teachers, Writers & Publishers - Includes Reproducible Mailing Labels Plus Activities for Young People! (Carole Marsh Maine Bks.). (Illus.). 1994. pap. 19.95 (*0-7933-3063-7*); lib. bdg. 29.95 (*0-7933-3062-9*); disk 29.95 (*0-7933-3064-5*) Gallopade Intl.

— Maine Math! How It All Adds up in Our State. (Carole Marsh Maine Bks.). (Illus.). (YA). (gr. 3-12). 1996. pap. 19.95 (*0-7933-6545-7*); lib. bdg. 29.95 (*0-7933-6544-9*) Gallopade Intl.

— The Maine Media Book: A Surprising Guide to the Amazing Print, Broadcast & Online Media of Our State for Students, Teachers, Writers & Publishers - Includes Reproducible Mailing Labels Plus Activities for Young People! (Carole Marsh Maine Bks.). (Illus.). 1994. pap. 19.95 (*0-7933-3219-2*); lib. bdg. 29.95 (*0-7933-3218-4*); disk 29.95 (*0-7933-3220-6*) Gallopade Intl.

— The Maine Mystery Van Takes Off! Bk. 1: Handicapped Maine Kids Sneak off on a Big Adventure. (Carole Marsh Maine Bks.). (Illus.). (J). (gr. 3-12). 1994. 29.95 (*0-7933-5018-2*); pap. 19.95 (*0-7933-5019-0*); disk 29.95 (*0-7933-5020-4*) Gallopade Intl.

— Maine Quiz Bowl Crash Course! (Carole Marsh Maine Bks.). (Illus.). (J). (gr. 3-8). 1994. pap. 19.95 (*1-55609-612-7*); lib. bdg. 29.95 (*1-55609-611-9*); disk 29.95 (*1-55609-613-5*) Gallopade Intl.

— Maine Rollercoasters! (Carole Marsh Maine Bks.). (Illus.). (YA). (gr. 3-12). 1994. pap. 19.95 (*0-7933-5282-7*); lib. bdg. 29.95 (*0-7933-5281-9*); disk 29.95 (*0-7933-5283-5*) Gallopade Intl.

— Maine School Trivia: An Amazing & Fascinating Look at Our State's Teachers, Schools & Students! (Carole Marsh Maine Bks.). (Illus.). (J). (gr. 3-8). 1994. pap. 19.95 (*0-7933-0535-7*); lib. bdg. 29.95 (*0-7933-0536-5*); disk 29.95 (*0-7933-0537-3*) Gallopade Intl.

— Maine Silly Basketball Sportsmysteries, Vol. I. (Carole Marsh Maine Bks.). (Illus.). (J). (gr. 3-8). 1994. pap. 19.95 (*0-7933-0532-2*); lib. bdg. 29.95 (*0-7933-0533-0*); disk 29.95 (*0-7933-0534-9*) Gallopade Intl.

— Maine Silly Basketball Sportsmysteries, Vol. II. (Carole Marsh Maine Bks.). (Illus.). (J). (gr. 3-8). 1994. pap. 19.95 (*0-7933-1685-5*); lib. bdg. 29.95 (*0-7933-1684-7*); disk 29.95 (*0-7933-1686-3*) Gallopade Intl.

— Maine Silly Football Sportsmysteries, Vol. I. (Carole Marsh Maine Bks.). (Illus.). (J). (gr. 3-8). 1994. pap. 19.95 (*1-55609-604-6*); lib. bdg. 29.95 (*1-55609-602-X*); disk 29.95 (*1-55609-606-2*) Gallopade Intl.

— Maine Silly Football Sportsmysteries, Vol. II. (Carole Marsh Maine Bks.). (Illus.). (J). (gr. 3-8). 1994. pap. 19.95 (*1-55609-605-4*); lib. bdg. 29.95 (*1-55609-603-8*); disk 29.95 (*1-55609-607-0*) Gallopade Intl.

— Maine Silly Trivia! (Carole Marsh Maine Bks.). (Illus.). (J). (gr. 3-8). 1994. pap. 19.95 (*1-55609-594-5*); lib. bdg. 29.95 (*1-55609-593-7*); disk 29.95 (*1-55609-595-3*) Gallopade Intl.

— Maine Spelling Bee! Score Big by Correctly Spelling Our State's Unique Names. (Carole Marsh Maine Bks.). (Illus.). (YA). (gr. 3-12). 1996. pap. 19.95 (*0-7933-6698-4*); pap. 19.95 (*0-7933-6722-0*); lib. bdg. 29.95 (*0-7933-6697-6*); lib. bdg. 29.95 (*0-7933-6721-2*) Gallopade Intl.

— Maine Timeline: A Chronology of Maine History, Mystery, Trivia, Legend, Lore & More. (Carole Marsh Maine Bks.). (Illus.). (J). (gr. 3-12). 1994. pap. 19.95 (*0-7933-5933-3*); lib. bdg. 29.95 (*0-7933-5932-5*); disk 29.95 (*0-7933-5934-1*) Gallopade Intl.

— Maine 2000! Coming Soon to a Calendar Near You - The 21st Century! - Complete Set of AL 2000 Items. (Two Thousand! Ser.). (Illus.). (J). (gr. 3-12). 1998. pap. 75.00 (*0-7933-9347-7*); lib. bdg. 85.00 (*0-7933-9348-5*) Gallopade Intl.

— Maine 2000! Coming Soon to a Calendar Near You-The 21st Century! (Two Thousand! Ser.). (Illus.). (J). (gr. 3-12). 1998. pap. 19.95 (*0-7933-8733-7*); lib. bdg. 29.95 (*0-7933-8732-9*) Gallopade Intl.

— Maine UFO's & Extraterrestrials! A Look at the Sightings & Science in Our State. (Carole Marsh Maine Bks.). (Illus.). (J). (gr. 3-12). 1997. pap. 19.95 (*0-7933-6392-6*); lib. bdg. 29.95 (*0-7933-6391-8*) Gallopade Intl.

— Maine's (Most Devastating!) Disasters & (Most Calamitous!) Catastrophies! (Carole Marsh Maine Bks.). (Illus.). (J). (gr. 3-8). 1994. pap. 19.95 (*0-7933-0523-3*); lib. bdg. 29.95 (*0-7933-0524-1*, 0-7933-0525-X) Gallopade Intl.

— Maine's (Most Devastating!) Disasters & (Most Calamitous!) Catastrophies! (Carole Marsh Maine Bks.). (Illus.). (J). (gr. 3-8). 1997. disk 29.95 (*0-7933-0525-X*) Gallopade Intl.

— Maine's Unsolved Mysteries (And Their "Solutions") Includes Scientific Information & Other Activities for

M

Students. (Carole Marsh Maine Bks.). (Illus.). (J). (gr. 3-12). 1994. pap. 19.95 (*0-7933-5780-2*); lib. bdg. 29.95 (*0-7933-5779-9*); disk 29.95 (*0-7933-5781-0*) Gallopade Intl.

— Mariner's & More! Virginia People, Places & Things Everyone Should Know. (Carole Marsh Virginia Bks.). (Illus.). (YA). (gr. 9-12). 1994. pap. 19.95 (*0-7933-0001-0*); lib. bdg. 29.95 (*0-7933-0000-2*); disk 29.95 (*0-7933-0002-9*) Gallopade Intl.

— Maryland & Other State Greats (Biographies) (Carole Marsh Maryland Bks.). (Illus.). (J). (gr. 3-8). 1994. pap. 19.95 (*1-55609-637-2*); lib. bdg. 29.95 (*1-55609-636-4*); disk 29.95 (*1-55609-638-0*) Gallopade Intl.

— Maryland Bandits, Bushwackers, Outlaws, Crooks, Devils, Ghosts, Desperadoes & Other Assorted & Sundry Characters! (Carole Marsh Maryland Bks.). (Illus.). (J). (gr. 3-8). 1994. pap. 19.95 (*0-7933-0550-0*); lib. bdg. 29.95 (*0-7933-0551-9*); disk 29.95 (*0-7933-0552-7*) Gallopade Intl.

— Maryland "BIO" Bingo! 24 Must Know State People for Kids to Learn about While Having Fun! (Bingo! Ser.). (Illus.). (J). (gr. 2-8). 1998. pap. 14.95 (*0-7933-8582-2*) Gallopade Intl.

— The Maryland Bookstore Book: A Surprising Guide to Our State's Bookstores & Their Specialties for Students, Teachers, Writers & Publishers. (Carole Marsh Maryland Bks.). (Illus.). 1994. pap. 19.95 (*0-7933-2916-7*); lib. bdg. 29.95 (*0-7933-2915-9*); disk 29.95 (*0-7933-2917-5*) Gallopade Intl.

— Maryland Classic Christmas Trivia: Stories, Recipes, Activities, Legends, Lore & More! (Carole Marsh Maryland Bks.). (Illus.). (J). (gr. 3-8). 1994. pap. 19.95 (*0-7933-0553-5*); lib. bdg. 29.95 (*0-7933-0554-3*); disk 29.95 (*0-7933-0555-1*) Gallopade Intl.

— Maryland Coastales! (Carole Marsh Maryland Bks.). (J). 1994. lib. bdg. 29.95 (*0-7933-7285-2*) Gallopade Intl.

— Maryland Coastales! (Carole Marsh Maryland Bks.). (Illus.). (J). (gr. 3-8). 1994. pap. 19.95 (*1-55609-631-3*); lib. bdg. 29.95 (*1-55609-630-5*); disk 29.95 (*1-55609-632-1*) Gallopade Intl.

— Maryland "Crinkum-Crankum" A Funny Word Book about Our State. (Carole Marsh Maryland Bks.). (Illus.). (J). 1994. pap. 19.95 (*0-7933-4869-2*); lib. bdg. 29.95 (*0-7933-4868-4*); disk 29.95 (*0-7933-4870-6*) Gallopade Intl.

— Maryland Dingbats! Bk. 1: A Fun Book of Games, Stories, Activities & More about Our State That's All in Code! for You to Decipher. (Carole Marsh Maryland Bks.). (Illus.). (J). (gr. 3-12). 1994. pap. 19.95 (*0-7933-3834-4*); lib. bdg. 29.95 (*0-7933-3833-6*); disk 29.95 (*0-7933-3835-2*) Gallopade Intl.

***Marsh, Carole.** The Maryland Experience Pocket Guide. (Maryland Experience! Ser.). (Illus.). (J). 2000. pap. 6.95 (*0-7933-9610-7*) Gallopade Intl.

Marsh, Carole. Maryland Facts & Factivities. (Carole Marsh State Bks.). (Illus.). (J). (gr. 4-7). 1996. pap., teacher ed. 19.95 (*0-7933-7887-7*, C Marsh) Gallopade Intl.

— Maryland Festival Fun for Kids! (Carole Marsh Maryland Bks.). (Illus.). (YA). (gr. 3-12). 1994. pap. 19.95 (*0-7933-3987-1*); lib. bdg. 29.95 (*0-7933-3986-3*); disk 29.95 (*0-7933-3988-X*) Gallopade Intl.

— Maryland "GEO" Bingo! 38 Must Know State Geography Facts for Kids to Learn While Having Fun! (Bingo! Ser.). (Illus.). (J). (gr. 2-8). 1998. pap. 14.95 (*0-7933-8583-0*) Gallopade Intl.

— Maryland Government! The Cornerstone of Everyday Life in Our State! (Carole Marsh Maryland Bks.). (Illus.). (J). (gr. 3-12). 1996. pap. 19.95 (*0-7933-6242-3*); lib. bdg. 29.95 (*0-7933-6241-5*); disk 29.95 (*0-7933-6243-1*) Gallopade Intl.

— Maryland "HISTO" Bingo! 42 Must Know State History Facts for Kids to Learn While Having Fun! (Bingo! Ser.). (Illus.). (J). (gr. 2-8). 1998. pap. 14.95 (*0-7933-8584-9*) Gallopade Intl.

— Maryland History! Surprising Secrets about Our State's Founding Mothers, Fathers & Kids! (Carole Marsh Maryland Bks.). (Illus.). (J). (gr. 3-12). 1996. pap. 19.95 (*0-7933-6089-7*); lib. bdg. 29.95 (*0-7933-6088-9*); disk 29.95 (*0-7933-6090-0*) Gallopade Intl.

— The Maryland Hot Air Balloon Mystery. (Carole Marsh Maryland Bks.). (Illus.). (J). (gr. 2-9). 1994. 29.95 (*0-7933-2498-X*); pap. 19.95 (*0-7933-2499-8*); disk 29.95 (*0-7933-2500-5*) Gallopade Intl.

— Maryland Hot Zones! Viruses, Diseases, & Epidemics in Our State's History. (Hot Zones! Ser.). (Illus.). (J). (gr. 3-12). 1998. pap. 19.95 (*0-7933-8889-9*); lib. bdg. 29.95 (*0-7933-8888-0*) Gallopade Intl.

— Maryland Indian Dictionary for Kids! (Carole Marsh State Bks.). (J). (gr. 2-9). 1996. 29.95 (*0-7933-7704-8*, C Marsh); pap. 19.95 (*0-7933-7705-6*, C Marsh) Gallopade Intl.

***Marsh, Carole.** Maryland Jeopardy. (Maryland Experience! Ser.). (Illus.). (J). (gr. 2-6). 2000. pap. 7.95 (*0-7933-9612-3*) Gallopade Intl.

Marsh, Carole. Maryland Jeopardy! Answers & Questions about Our State! (Carole Marsh Maryland Bks.). (Illus.). (J). (gr. 3-12). 1994. pap. 19.95 (*0-7933-4140-X*); lib. bdg. 29.95 (*0-7933-4139-6*); disk 29.95 (*0-7933-4141-8*) Gallopade Intl.

***Marsh, Carole.** Maryland Jography. (Maryland Experience! Ser.). (Illus.). (J). (gr. 2-6). 2000. 7.95 (*0-7933-9605-0*) Gallopade Intl.

Marsh, Carole. Maryland "Jography" A Fun Run Thru Our State! (Carole Marsh Maryland Bks.). (Illus.). (J). (gr. 3-8). 1994. pap. 19.95 (*1-55609-620-8*); lib. bdg. 29.95 (*1-55609-619-4*); disk 29.95 (*1-55609-621-6*) Gallopade Intl.

— Maryland Kid's Cookbook: Recipes, How-To, History, Lore & More! (Carole Marsh Maryland Bks.). (Illus.). (J). (gr. 3-8). 1994. pap. 19.95 (*0-7933-0562-4*); lib. bdg. 29.95 (*0-7933-0563-2*); disk 29.95 (*0-7933-0564-0*) Gallopade Intl.

— The Maryland Library Book: A Surprising Guide to the Unusual Special Collections in Libraries Across Our State for Students, Teachers, Writers & Publishers - Includes Reproducible Mailing Labels Plus Activities for Young People! (Carole Marsh Maryland Bks.). (Illus.). 1994. pap. 19.95 (*0-7933-3066-1*); lib. bdg. 29.95 (*0-7933-3065-3*); disk 29.95 (*0-7933-3067-X*) Gallopade Intl.

— Maryland Math! How It All Adds up in Our State. (Carole Marsh Maryland Bks.). (Illus.). (YA). (gr. 3-12). 1996. pap. 19.95 (*0-7933-6548-1*); lib. bdg. 29.95 (*0-7933-6547-3*) Gallopade Intl.

— The Maryland Media Book: A Surprising Guide to the Amazing Print, Broadcast & Online Media of Our State for Students, Teachers, Writers & Publishers - Includes Reproducible Mailing Labels Plus Activities for Young People! (Carole Marsh Maryland Bks.). (Illus.). 1994. pap. 19.95 (*0-7933-3222-2*); lib. bdg. 29.95 (*0-7933-3221-4*); disk 29.95 (*0-7933-3223-0*) Gallopade Intl.

— The Maryland Mystery Van Takes Off! Bk. 1: Handicapped Maryland Kids Sneak off on a Big Adventure. (Carole Marsh Maryland Bks.). (Illus.). (J). (gr. 3-12). 1994. 29.95 (*0-7933-5021-2*); pap. 19.95 (*0-7933-5022-0*); disk 29.95 (*0-7933-5023-9*) Gallopade Intl.

— Maryland Quiz Bowl Crash Course! (Carole Marsh Maryland Bks.). (Illus.). (J). (gr. 3-8). 1994. pap. 19.95 (*1-55609-634-8*); lib. bdg. 29.95 (*1-55609-633-X*); disk 29.95 (*1-55609-635-6*) Gallopade Intl.

— Maryland Rollercoasters! (Carole Marsh Maryland Bks.). (Illus.). (YA). (gr. 3-12). 1994. pap. 19.95 (*0-7933-5285-1*); lib. bdg. 29.95 (*0-7933-5284-3*); disk 29.95 (*0-7933-5286-X*) Gallopade Intl.

— Maryland School Trivia: An Amazing & Fascinating Look at Our State's Teachers, Schools & Students! (Carole Marsh Maryland Bks.). (Illus.). (J). (gr. 3-8). 1994. pap. 19.95 (*0-7933-0559-4*); lib. bdg. 29.95 (*0-7933-0560-8*); disk 29.95 (*0-7933-0561-6*) Gallopade Intl.

— Maryland Silly Basketball Sportsmysteries, Vol. I. (Carole Marsh Maryland Bks.). (Illus.). (J). (gr. 3-8). 1994. pap. 19.95 (*0-7933-0556-X*); lib. bdg. 29.95 (*0-7933-0557-8*); disk 29.95 (*0-7933-0558-6*) Gallopade Intl.

— Maryland Silly Basketball Sportsmysteries, Vol. II. (Carole Marsh Maryland Bks.). (Illus.). (J). (gr. 3-8). 1994. pap. 19.95 (*0-7933-1697-9*); lib. bdg. 29.95 (*0-7933-1696-0*); disk 29.95 (*0-7933-1698-7*) Gallopade Intl.

— Maryland Silly Football Sportsmysteries, Vol. I. (Carole Marsh Maryland Bks.). (Illus.). (J). (gr. 3-8). 1994. pap. 19.95 (*1-55609-625-9*); lib. bdg. 29.95 (*1-55609-624-0*); disk 29.95 (*1-55609-626-7*) Gallopade Intl.

— Maryland Silly Football Sportsmysteries, Vol. II. (Carole Marsh Maryland Bks.). (Illus.). (J). (gr. 3-8). 1994. pap. 19.95 (*1-55609-628-3*); lib. bdg. 29.95 (*1-55609-627-5*); disk 29.95 (*1-55609-629-1*) Gallopade Intl.

— Maryland Silly Trivia! (Carole Marsh Maryland Bks.). (Illus.). (J). (gr. 3-8). 1994. pap. 19.95 (*1-55609-042-0*); lib. bdg. 29.95 (*1-55609-617-8*); disk 29.95 (*1-55609-618-6*) Gallopade Intl.

— Maryland Spelling Bee! Score Big by Correctly Spelling Our State's Unique Names. (Carole Marsh Maryland Bks.). (Illus.). (YA). (gr. 3-12). 1996. pap. 19.95 (*0-7933-6701-8*); lib. bdg. 29.95 (*0-7933-6700-X*) Gallopade Intl.

— Maryland Timeline: A Chronology of Maryland History, Mystery, Trivia, Legend, Lore & More. (Carole Marsh Maryland Bks.). (Illus.). (J). (gr. 3-12). 1994. pap. 19.95 (*0-7933-5936-8*); lib. bdg. 29.95 (*0-7933-5935-X*); disk 29.95 (*0-7933-5937-6*) Gallopade Intl.

— Maryland 2000! Coming Soon to a Calendar Near You - The 21st Century! - Complete Set of AL 2000 Items. (Two Thousand! Ser.). (Illus.). (J). (gr. 3-12). 1998. pap. 75.00 (*0-7933-9349-3*); lib. bdg. 85.00 (*0-7933-9350-7*) Gallopade Intl.

— Maryland 2000! Coming Soon to a Calendar Near You-The 21st Century! (Two Thousand! Ser.). (Illus.). (J). (gr. 3-12). 1998. pap. 19.95 (*0-7933-8736-1*); lib. bdg. 29.95 (*0-7933-8735-3*) Gallopade Intl.

— Maryland UFO's & Extraterrestrials! A Look at the Sightings & Science in Our State. (Carole Marsh Maryland Bks.). (Illus.). (J). (gr. 3-12). 1997. pap. 19.95 (*0-7933-6395-0*); lib. bdg. 29.95 (*0-7933-6394-2*) Gallopade Intl.

***Marsh, Carole.** Maryland's Big Activity Book. (Maryland Experience! Ser.). (Illus.). (J). (gr. k-5). 2000. pap. 9.95 (*0-7933-9614-X*) Gallopade Intl.

Marsh, Carole. Maryland's (Most Devastating!) Disasters & (Most Calamitous!) Catastrophies! (Carole Marsh Maryland Bks.). (Illus.). (J). (gr. 3-8). 1994. pap. 19.95 (*0-7933-0547-0*); lib. bdg. 29.95 (*0-7933-0548-9*); disk 29.95 (*0-7933-0549-7*) Gallopade Intl.

— Maryland's Unsolved Mysteries (And Their "Solutions") Includes Scientific Information & Other Activities for Students. (Carole Marsh Maryland Bks.). (Illus.). (J). (gr. 3-12). 1994. pap. 19.95 (*0-7933-5783-7*); lib. bdg. 29.95 (*0-7933-5782-9*); disk 29.95 (*0-7933-5784-5*) Gallopade Intl.

— Massachusetts & Other State Greats (Biographies) (Carole Marsh Massachusetts Bks.). (Illus.). (J). (gr. 3-8). 1994. pap. 19.95 (*1-55609-700-X*); lib. bdg. 29.95 (*1-55609-699-2*); disk 29.95 (*1-55609-701-8*) Gallopade Intl.

— Massachusetts Bandits, Bushwackers, Outlaws, Crooks, Devils, Ghosts, Desperadoes & Other Assorted & Sundry Characters! (Carole Marsh Massachusetts Bks.). (Illus.). (J). (gr. 3-8). 1994. pap. 19.95 (*0-7933-0574-8*); lib. bdg. 29.95 (*0-7933-0575-6*); disk 29.95 (*0-7933-0576-4*) Gallopade Intl.

— Massachusetts "BIO" Bingo! 24 Must Know State People for Kids to Learn about While Having Fun! (Bingo! Ser.). (Illus.). (J). (gr. 2-8). 1998. pap. 14.95 (*0-7933-8585-7*) Gallopade Intl.

— The Massachusetts Bookstore Book: A Surprising Guide to Our State's Bookstores & Their Specialties for Students, Teachers, Writers & Publishers. (Massachuseets Bks.). (Illus.). 1994. pap. 19.95 (*0-7933-2919-1*); lib. bdg. 29.95 (*0-7933-2918-3*); disk 29.95 (*0-7933-2920-5*) Gallopade Intl.

— Massachusetts Classic Christmas Trivia: Stories, Recipes, Activities, Legends, Lore & More! (Carole Marsh Massachusetts Bks.). (Illus.). (J). (gr. 3-8). 1994. pap. 19.95 (*0-7933-0577-2*); lib. bdg. 29.95 (*0-7933-0578-0*); disk 29.95 (*0-7933-0579-9*) Gallopade Intl.

— Massachusetts Coastales. (Massachuseets Bks.). (J). 1994. lib. bdg. 29.95 (*0-7933-7286-0*) Gallopade Intl.

— Massachusetts Coastales. (Carole Marsh Massachusetts Bks.). (Illus.). (J). (gr. 3-8). 1994. pap. 19.95 (*1-55609-694-1*); lib. bdg. 29.95 (*1-55609-693-3*); disk 29.95 (*1-55609-695-X*) Gallopade Intl.

— Massachusetts "Crinkum-Crankum" A Funny Word Book about Our State. (Massachuseets Bks.). (Illus.). (J). 1994. pap. 19.95 (*0-7933-4872-2*); lib. bdg. 29.95 (*0-7933-4871-4*); disk 29.95 (*0-7933-4873-0*) Gallopade Intl.

— Massachusetts Dingbats! A Fun Book of Games, Stories, Activities & More about Our State That's All in Code! for You to Decipher. (Massachuseets Bks.). (Illus.). (J). (gr. 3-12). 1994. pap. 19.95 (*0-7933-3837-9*) Gallopade Intl.

— Massachusetts Dingbats! A Fun Book of Games, Stories, Activities & More about Our State That's All in Code! for You to Decipher, Bk. 1. (Massachuseets Bks.). (Illus.). (J). (gr. 3-12). 1994. lib. bdg. 29.95 (*0-7933-3836-0*); disk 29.95 (*0-7933-3838-7*) Gallopade Intl.

— Massachusetts Facts & Factivities. (Carole Marsh State Bks.). (Illus.). (J). (gr. 4-7). 1996. pap., teacher ed. 19.95 (*0-7933-7889-3*, C Marsh) Gallopade Intl.

— Massachusetts Festival Fun for Kids! (Massachuseets Bks.). (Illus.). (YA). (gr. 3-12). 1994. pap. 19.95 (*0-7933-3990-1*); lib. bdg. 29.95 (*0-7933-3989-8*); disk 29.95 (*0-7933-3991-X*) Gallopade Intl.

— Massachusetts "GEO" Bingo! 38 Must Know State Geography Facts for Kids to Learn While Having Fun! (Bingo! Ser.). (Illus.). (J). (gr. 2-8). 1998. pap. 14.95 (*0-7933-8586-5*) Gallopade Intl.

— Massachusetts Government! The Cornerstone of Everyday Life in Our State! (Carole Marsh Massachusetts Bks.). (Illus.). (J). (gr. 3-12). 1996. pap. 19.95 (*0-7933-6245-8*); lib. bdg. 29.95 (*0-7933-6244-X*); disk 29.95 (*0-7933-6246-6*) Gallopade Intl.

— Massachusetts "HISTO" Bingo! 42 Must Know State History Facts for Kids to Learn While Having Fun! (Bingo! Ser.). (Illus.). (J). (gr. 2-8). 1998. pap. 14.95 (*0-7933-8587-3*) Gallopade Intl.

— Massachusetts History! Surprising Secrets about Our State's Founding Mothers, Fathers & Kids! (Carole Marsh Massachusetts Bks.). (Illus.). (J). (gr. 3-12). 1996. pap. 19.95 (*0-7933-6092-7*); lib. bdg. 29.95 (*0-7933-6091-9*); disk 29.95 (*0-7933-6093-5*) Gallopade Intl.

— The Massachusetts Hot Air Balloon Mystery. (Carole Marsh Massachusetts Bks.). (Illus.). (J). (gr. 2-9). 1994. 29.95 (*0-7933-2507-2*); pap. 19.95 (*0-7933-2508-0*); disk 29.95 (*0-7933-2509-9*) Gallopade Intl.

— Massachusetts Hot Zones! Viruses, Diseases, & Epidemics in Our State's History. (Hot Zones! Ser.). (Illus.). (J). (gr. 3-12). 1998. pap. 19.95 (*0-7933-8892-9*); lib. bdg. 29.95 (*0-7933-8891-0*) Gallopade Intl.

— Massachusetts Indian Dictionary for Kids! (Carole Marsh State Bks.). (J). (gr. 2-9). 1996. 29.95 (*0-7933-7707-2*, C Marsh); pap. 19.95 (*0-7933-7708-0*, C Marsh) Gallopade Intl.

— Massachusetts Jeopardy! Answers & Questions about Our State! (Massachuseets Bks.). (Illus.). (J). (gr. 3-12). 1994. pap. 19.95 (*0-7933-4143-4*); lib. bdg. 29.95 (*0-7933-4142-6*); disk 29.95 (*0-7933-4144-2*) Gallopade Intl.

— Massachusetts "Jography" A Fun Run Thru Our State! (Carole Marsh Massachusetts Bks.). (Illus.). (J). (gr. 3-8). 1994. pap. 19.95 (*1-55609-111-7*); lib. bdg. 29.95 (*1-55609-682-8*); disk 29.95 (*1-55609-683-6*) Gallopade Intl.

— Massachusetts Kid's Cookbook: Recipes, How-To, History, Lore & More! (Carole Marsh Massachusetts Bks.). (Illus.). (J). (gr. 3-8). 1994. pap. 19.95 (*0-7933-0586-1*); lib. bdg. 29.95 (*0-7933-0587-X*); disk 29.95 (*0-7933-0588-8*) Gallopade Intl.

— The Massachusetts Library Book: A Surprising Guide to the Unusual Special Collections in Libraries Across Our State for Students, Teachers, Writers & Publishers - Includes Reproducible Mailing Labels Plus Activities for Young People! (Massachuseets Bks.). (Illus.). 1994. pap. 19.95 (*0-7933-3069-6*); lib. bdg. 29.95 (*0-7933-3068-8*); disk 29.95 (*0-7933-3070-X*) Gallopade Intl.

— Massachusetts Math! How It All Adds up in Our State. (Carole Marsh Massachusetts Bks.). (Illus.). (YA). (gr. 3-12). 1996. pap. 19.95 (*0-7933-6551-1*); lib. bdg. 29.95 (*0-7933-6550-3*) Gallopade Intl.

— The Massachusetts Media Book: A Surprising Guide to the Amazing Print, Broadcast & Online Media of Our State for Students, Teachers, Writers & Publishers - Includes Reproducible Mailing Labels Plus Activities for Young People! (Massachuseets Bks.). (Illus.). 1994. pap. 19.95 (*0-7933-3225-7*); lib. bdg. 29.95 (*0-7933-3224-9*); disk 29.95 (*0-7933-3226-5*) Gallopade Intl.

— Massachusetts' (Most Devastating!) Disasters & (Most Calamitous!) Catastrophies! (Carole Marsh Massachusetts Bks.). (Illus.). (J). (gr. 3-8). 1994. pap. 19.95 (*0-7933-0571-3*); lib. bdg. 29.95 (*0-7933-0572-1*); disk 29.95 (*0-7933-0573-X*) Gallopade Intl.

— The Massachusetts Mystery Van Takes Off! Bk. 1: Handicapped Massachusetts Kids Sneak Off on a Big Adventure. (Massachuseets Bks.). (Illus.). (J). (gr. 3-12). 1994. 29.95 (*0-7933-5024-7*); pap. 19.95 (*0-7933-5025-5*); disk 29.95 (*0-7933-5026-3*) Gallopade Intl.

— Massachusetts Quiz Bowl Crash Course! (Carole Marsh Massachusetts Bks.). (Illus.). (J). (gr. 3-8). 1994. pap. 19.95 (*1-55609-697-6*); lib. bdg. 29.95 (*1-55609-696-8*); disk 29.95 (*1-55609-698-4*) Gallopade Intl.

— Massachusetts Rollercoasters! (Massachuseets Bks.). (Illus.). (YA). (gr. 3-12). 1994. pap. 19.95 (*0-7933-5288-6*); lib. bdg. 29.95 (*0-7933-5287-8*); disk 29.95 (*0-7933-5289-4*) Gallopade Intl.

— Massachusetts School Trivia: An Amazing & Fascinating Look at Our State's Teachers, Schools & Students! (Carole Marsh Massachusetts Bks.). (Illus.). (J). (gr. 3-8). 1994. pap. 19.95 (*0-7933-0583-7*); lib. bdg. 29.95 (*0-7933-0584-5*); disk 29.95 (*0-7933-0585-3*) Gallopade Intl.

— Massachusetts Silly Basketball Sportsmysteries, Vol. I. (Carole Marsh Massachusetts Bks.). (Illus.). (J). (gr. 3-8). 1994. pap. 19.95 (*0-7933-0580-2*); lib. bdg. 29.95 (*0-7933-0581-0*); disk 29.95 (*0-7933-0582-9*) Gallopade Intl.

— Massachusetts Silly Basketball Sportsmysteries, Vol. II. (Carole Marsh Massachusetts Bks.). (Illus.). (J). (gr. 3-8). 1994. pap. 19.95 (*0-7933-1706-1*); lib. bdg. 29.95 (*0-7933-1705-3*); disk 29.95 (*0-7933-1707-X*) Gallopade Intl.

— Massachusetts Silly Football Sportsmysteries, Vol. I. (Carole Marsh Massachusetts Bks.). (Illus.). (J). (gr. 3-8). 1994. pap. 19.95 (*1-55609-688-7*); lib. bdg. 29.95 (*1-55609-687-9*); disk 29.95 (*1-55609-689-5*) Gallopade Intl.

— Massachusetts Silly Football Sportsmysteries, Vol. II. (Carole Marsh Massachusetts Bks.). (Illus.). (J). (gr. 3-8). 1994. pap. 19.95 (*1-55609-691-7*); lib. bdg. 29.95 (*1-55609-690-9*); disk 29.95 (*1-55609-692-5*) Gallopade Intl.

— Massachusetts Silly Trivia! (Carole Marsh Massachusetts Bks.). (Illus.). (J). (gr. 3-8). 1994. pap. 19.95 (*1-55609-110-9*); lib. bdg. 29.95 (*1-55609-680-1*); disk 29.95 (*1-55609-681-X*) Gallopade Intl.

— Massachusetts Spelling Bee! Score Big by Correctly Spelling Our State's Unique Names. (Carole Marsh Massachusetts Bks.). (Illus.). (YA). (gr. 3-12). 1996. pap. 19.95 (*0-7933-6704-2*); lib. bdg. 29.95 (*0-7933-6703-4*) Gallopade Intl.

— Massachusetts Timeline: A Chronology of Massachusetts History, Mystery, Trivia, Legend, Lore & More. (Massachuseets Bks.). (Illus.). (J). (gr. 3-12). 1994. pap. 19.95 (*0-7933-5939-2*); lib. bdg. 29.95 (*0-7933-5938-4*); disk 29.95 (*0-7933-5940-6*) Gallopade Intl.

— Massachusetts 2000! Coming Soon to a Calendar Near You - The 21st Century! - Complete Set of AL 2000 Items. (Two Thousand! Ser.). (Illus.). (J). (gr. 3-12). 1998. pap. 75.00 (*0-7933-9351-5*); lib. bdg. 85.00 (*0-7933-9352-3*) Gallopade Intl.

— Massachusetts 2000! Coming Soon to a Calendar Near You-The 21st Century! (Two Thousand! Ser.). (Illus.). (J). (gr. 3-12). 1998. pap. 19.95 (*0-7933-8739-6*); lib. bdg. 29.95 (*0-7933-8738-8*) Gallopade Intl.

— Massachusetts UFO's & Extraterrestrials! A Look at the Sightings & Science in Our State. (Carole Marsh Massachusetts Bks.). (Illus.). (J). (gr. 3-12). 1997. pap. 19.95 (*0-7933-6398-5*); lib. bdg. 29.95 (*0-7933-6397-7*) Gallopade Intl.

— Massachusetts's Unsolved Mysteries (& Their "Solutions") Includes Scientific Information & Other Activities for Students. (Massachuseets Bks.). (Illus.). (J). (gr. 3-12). 1994. pap. 19.95 (*0-7933-5786-1*); lib. bdg. 29.95 (*0-7933-5785-3*); disk 29.95 (*0-7933-5787-X*) Gallopade Intl.

— Math for Boys: A Book with the Number or Getting Boys to Love & Excel in Math! (Quantum Leap Ser.). (Illus.). (J). (gr. 4-12). 1994. pap. 19.95 (*1-55609-830-8*); lib. bdg. 29.95 (*1-55609-806-5*); disk 29.95 (*1-55609-878-2*) Gallopade Intl.

— Math for Girls: The Book with the Number to Get Girls to Love & Excel in Math! (Quantum Leap Ser.). (Illus.). 60p. (J). (gr. 3-9). 1994. pap. 19.95 (*1-55609-344-6*); lib. bdg. 29.95 (*1-55609-343-8*); disk 29.95 (*1-55609-345-4*) Gallopade Intl.

— Meet in the Middle: The Parents Test - The Kids Test. (Quantum Leap Ser.). (Illus.). (J). (gr. 4 up). 1994. 29.95 (*0-935326-24-3*) Gallopade Intl.

— Meow! Alabama Cats in History, Mystery, Legend, Lore, Humor & More! (Carole Marsh Alabama Bks.). (Illus.). (J). (gr. 3-12). 1994. pap. 19.95 (*0-7933-3315-6*); lib. bdg. 29.95 (*0-7933-3314-8*); disk 29.95 (*0-7933-3316-4*) Gallopade Intl.

— Meow! Alaska Cats in History, Mystery, Legend, Lore, Humor & More! (Carole Marsh Alaska Bks.). (Illus.). (J). (gr. 3-12). 1994. pap. 19.95 (*0-7933-3318-0*); lib. bdg. 29.95 (*0-7933-3317-2*); disk 29.95 (*0-7933-3319-9*) Gallopade Intl.

— Meow! Arizona Cats in History, Mystery, Legend, Lore, Humor & More! (Carole Marsh Arizona Bks.). (Illus.). (J). (gr. 3-12). 1994. pap. 19.95 (*0-7933-3321-0*); lib. bdg. 29.95 (*0-7933-3320-2*); disk 29.95 (*0-7933-3322-9*) Gallopade Intl.

— Meow! Arkansas Cats in History, Mystery, Legend, Lore, Humor & More! (Carole Marsh Arkansas Bks.). (Illus.). (J). (gr. 3-12). 1994. pap. 19.95 (*0-7933-3324-5*); lib. bdg. 29.95 (*0-7933-3323-7*); disk 29.95 (*0-7933-3325-3*) Gallopade Intl.

— Meow! California Cats in History, Mystery, Legend, Lore, Humor & More! (Carole Marsh California Bks.). (Illus.). (J). (gr. 3-12). 1994. pap. 19.95 (*0-7933-3327-X*); lib. bdg. 29.95 (*0-7933-3326-1*); disk 29.95 (*0-7933-3328-8*) Gallopade Intl.

An Asterisk (*) at the beginning of an entry indicates that the title is appearing for the first time.

— Meow! Colorado Cats in History, Mystery, Legend, Lore, Humor & More! (Carole Marsh Colorado Bks.). (Illus.). (J). (gr. 3-12). 1994. pap. 19.95 (*0-7933-3330-X*); lib. bdg. 29.95 (*0-7933-3329-6*); disk 29.95 (*0-7933-3331-8*) Gallopade Intl.

— Meow! Connecticut Cats in History, Mystery, Legend, Lore, Humor & More! (Carole Marsh Connecticut Bks.). (Illus.). (J). (gr. 3-12). 1994. pap. 19.95 (*0-7933-3333-4*); lib. bdg. 29.95 (*0-7933-3332-6*); disk 29.95 (*0-7933-3334-2*) Gallopade Intl.

— Meow! Delaware Cats in History, Mystery, Legend, Lore, Humor & More! (Carole Marsh Delaware Bks.). (Illus.). (J). (gr. 3-12). 1994. pap. 19.95 (*0-7933-3336-9*); lib. bdg. 29.95 (*0-7933-3335-0*); disk 29.95 (*0-7933-3337-7*) Gallopade Intl.

— Meow! Florida Cats in History, Mystery, Legend, Lore, Humor & More! (Carole Marsh Florida Bks.). (Illus.). (J). (gr. 3-12). 1994. pap. 19.95 (*0-7933-3342-3*); lib. bdg. 29.95 (*0-7933-3341-5*); disk 29.95 (*0-7933-3343-1*) Gallopade Intl.

— Meow! Georgia Cats in History, Mystery, Legend, Lore, Humor & More! (Carole Marsh Georgia Bks.). (Illus.). (J). (gr. 3-12). 1994. pap. 19.95 (*0-7933-3345-8*); lib. bdg. 29.95 (*0-7933-3344-X*); disk 29.95 (*0-7933-3346-6*) Gallopade Intl.

— Meow! Hawaii Cats in History, Mystery, Legend, Lore, Humor & More! (Carole Marsh Hawaii Bks.). (Illus.). (J). (gr. 3-12). 1994. pap. 19.95 (*0-7933-3348-2*); lib. bdg. 29.95 (*0-7933-3347-4*); disk 29.95 (*0-7933-3349-0*) Gallopade Intl.

— Meow! Idaho Cats in History, Mystery, Legend, Lore, Humor & More! (Carole Marsh Idaho Bks.). (Illus.). (J). (gr. 3-12). 1994. pap. 19.95 (*0-7933-3351-2*); lib. bdg. 29.95 (*0-7933-3350-4*); disk 29.95 (*0-7933-3352-0*) Gallopade Intl.

— Meow! Illinois Cats in History, Mystery, Legend, Lore, Humor & More! (Carole Marsh Illinois Bks.). (Illus.). (J). (gr. 3-12). 1994. pap. 19.95 (*0-7933-3354-7*); lib. bdg. 29.95 (*0-7933-3353-9*); disk 29.95 (*0-7933-3355-5*) Gallopade Intl.

— Meow! Indiana Cats in History, Mystery, Legend, Lore, Humor & More! (Carole Marsh Indiana Bks.). (Illus.). (J). (gr. 3-12). 1994. pap. 19.95 (*0-7933-3357-1*); lib. bdg. 29.95 (*0-7933-3356-3*); disk 29.95 (*0-7933-3358-X*) Gallopade Intl.

— Meow! Iowa Cats in History, Mystery, Legend, Lore, Humor & More! (Carole Marsh Iowa Bks.). (Illus.). (J). (gr. 3-12). 1994. pap. 19.95 (*0-7933-3360-1*); lib. bdg. 29.95 (*0-7933-3359-8*); disk 29.95 (*0-7933-3361-X*) Gallopade Intl.

— Meow! Kansas Cats in History, Mystery, Legend, Lore, Humor & More! (Carole Marsh Kansas Bks.). (Illus.). (J). (gr. 3-12). 1994. pap. 19.95 (*0-7933-3363-6*); lib. bdg. 29.95 (*0-7933-3362-8*); disk 29.95 (*0-7933-3364-4*) Gallopade Intl.

— Meow! Kentucky Cats in History, Mystery, Legend, Lore, Humor & More! (Carole Marsh Kentucky Bks.). (Illus.). (J). (gr. 3-12). 1994. pap. 19.95 (*0-7933-3366-0*); lib. bdg. 29.95 (*0-7933-3365-2*); disk 29.95 (*0-7933-3367-9*) Gallopade Intl.

— Meow! Louisiana Cats in History, Mystery, Legend, Lore, Humor & More! (Carole Marsh Louisiana Bks.). (Illus.). (J). (gr. 3-12). 1994. pap. 19.95 (*0-7933-3369-5*); lib. bdg. 29.95 (*0-7933-3368-7*); disk 29.95 (*0-7933-3370-9*) Gallopade Intl.

— Meow! Maine Cats in History, Mystery, Legend, Lore, Humor & More! (Carole Marsh Maine Bks.). (Illus.). (J). (gr. 3-12). 1994. pap. 19.95 (*0-7933-3372-5*); lib. bdg. 29.95 (*0-7933-3371-7*); disk 29.95 (*0-7933-3373-3*) Gallopade Intl.

— Meow! Maryland Cats in History, Mystery, Legend, Lore, Humor & More! (Carole Marsh Maryland Bks.). (Illus.). (J). (gr. 3-12). 1994. pap. 19.95 (*0-7933-3375-X*); lib. bdg. 29.95 (*0-7933-3374-1*); disk 29.95 (*0-7933-3376-8*) Gallopade Intl.

— Meow! Massachusetts Cats in History, Mystery, Legend, Lore, Humor & More! (Massachusetts Bks.). (Illus.). (J). (gr. 3-12). 1994. pap. 19.95 (*0-7933-3378-4*); lib. bdg. 29.95 (*0-7933-3377-6*); disk 29.95 (*0-7933-3379-2*) Gallopade Intl.

— Meow! Michigan Cats in History, Mystery, Legend, Lore, Humor & More! (Carole Marsh Michigan Bks.). (Illus.). (J). (gr. 3-12). 1994. pap. 19.95 (*0-7933-3381-4*); lib. bdg. 29.95 (*0-7933-3380-6*); disk 29.95 (*0-7933-3382-2*) Gallopade Intl.

— Meow! Minnesota Cats in History, Mystery, Legend, Lore, Humor & More! (Carole Marsh Minnesota Bks.). (Illus.). (J). (gr. 3-12). 1994. pap. 19.95 (*0-7933-3384-9*); lib. bdg. 29.95 (*0-7933-3383-0*); disk 29.95 (*0-7933-3385-7*) Gallopade Intl.

— Meow! Mississippi Cats in History, Mystery, Legend, Lore, Humor & More! (Carole Marsh Mississippi Bks.). (Illus.). (J). (gr. 3-12). 1994. pap. 19.95 (*0-7933-3387-3*); lib. bdg. 29.95 (*0-7933-3386-5*); disk 29.95 (*0-7933-3388-1*) Gallopade Intl.

— Meow! Missouri Cats in History, Mystery, Legend, Lore, Humor & More! (Carole Marsh Missouri Bks.). (Illus.). (J). (gr. 3-12). 1994. pap. 19.95 (*0-7933-3390-3*); lib. bdg. 29.95 (*0-7933-3389-X*); disk 29.95 (*0-7933-3391-1*) Gallopade Intl.

— Meow! Montana Cats in History, Mystery, Legend, Lore, Humor & More! (Carole Marsh Montana Bks.). (Illus.). (J). (gr. 3-12). 1994. pap. 19.95 (*0-7933-3393-8*); lib. bdg. 29.95 (*0-7933-3392-X*); disk 29.95 (*0-7933-3394-6*) Gallopade Intl.

— Meow! Nebraska Cats in History, Mystery, Legend, Lore, Humor & More! (Carole Marsh Nebraska Bks.). (Illus.). (J). (gr. 3-12). 1994. pap. 19.95 (*0-7933-3396-2*); lib. bdg. 29.95 (*0-7933-3395-4*); disk 29.95 (*0-7933-3397-0*) Gallopade Intl.

— Meow! Nevada Cats in History, Mystery, Legend, Lore, Humor & More! (Carole Marsh Nevada Bks.). (Illus.). (J). (gr. 3-12). 1994. pap. 19.95 (*0-7933-3399-7*); lib. bdg. 29.95 (*0-7933-3398-9*) Gallopade Intl.

— Meow! New Hampshire Cats in History, Mystery, Legend, Lore, Humor & More! (Carole Marsh New Hampshire Bks.). (Illus.). (J). (gr. 3-12). 1994. pap. 19.95 (*0-7933-3401-2*); disk 29.95 (*0-7933-3402-0*) Gallopade Intl.

— Meow! New Hampshire Cats in History, Mystery, Legend, Lore, Humor & More! (Carole Marsh New Hampshire Bks.). (Illus.). (J). (gr. 3-12). 1997. lib. bdg. 29.95 (*0-7933-3400-4*) Gallopade Intl.

— Meow! New Jersey Cats in History, Mystery, Legend, Lore, Humor & More! (Carole Marsh New Jersey Bks.). (Illus.). (J). (gr. 3-12). 1994. lib. bdg. 29.95 (*0-7933-3404-7*); disk 29.95 (*0-7933-3406-3*) Gallopade Intl.

— Meow! New Jersey Cats in History, Mystery, Legend, Lore, Humor & More! (Carole Marsh New Jersey Bks.). (Illus.). (J). (gr. 3-12). 1997. pap. 19.95 (*0-7933-3405-5*) Gallopade Intl.

— Meow! New Mexico Cats in History, Mystery, Legend, Lore, Humor & More! (Carole Marsh New Mexico Bks.). (Illus.). (J). (gr. 3-12). 1994. pap. 19.95 (*0-7933-3408-X*); lib. bdg. 29.95 (*0-7933-3407-1*); disk 29.95 (*0-7933-3409-8*) Gallopade Intl.

— Meow! New York Cats in History, Mystery, Legend, Lore, Humor & More! (Carole Marsh New York Bks.). (Illus.). (J). (gr. 3-12). 1994. pap. 19.95 (*0-7933-3411-X*); lib. bdg. 29.95 (*0-7933-3410-1*); disk 29.95 (*0-7933-3412-8*) Gallopade Intl.

— Meow! North Carolina Cats in History, Mystery, Legend, Lore, Humor & More! (Carole Marsh North Carolina Bks.). (Illus.). (J). (gr. 3-12). 1994. pap. 19.95 (*0-7933-3414-4*); lib. bdg. 29.95 (*0-7933-3413-6*); disk 29.95 (*0-7933-3415-2*) Gallopade Intl.

— Meow! North Dakota Cats in History, Mystery, Legend, Lore, Humor & More! (Carole Marsh North Dakota Bks.). (Illus.). (J). (gr. 3-12). 1994. pap. 19.95 (*0-7933-3417-9*); lib. bdg. 29.95 (*0-7933-3416-0*); disk 29.95 (*0-7933-3418-7*) Gallopade Intl.

— Meow! Ohio Cats in History, Mystery, Legend, Lore, Humor & More! (Carole Marsh Ohio Bks.). (Illus.). (J). (gr. 3-12). 1994. pap. 19.95 (*0-7933-3420-9*); lib. bdg. 29.95 (*0-7933-3419-5*); disk 29.95 (*0-7933-3421-7*) Gallopade Intl.

— Meow! Oklahoma Cats in History, Mystery, Legend, Lore, Humor & More! (Carole Marsh Oklahoma Bks.). (Illus.). (J). (gr. 3-12). 1994. pap. 19.95 (*0-7933-3423-3*); lib. bdg. 29.95 (*0-7933-3422-5*); disk 29.95 (*0-7933-3424-1*) Gallopade Intl.

— Meow! Oregon Cats in History, Mystery, Legend, Lore, Humor & More! (Oregon Bks.). (Illus.). (J). (gr. 3-12). 1994. pap. 19.95 (*0-7933-3426-8*); lib. bdg. 29.95 (*0-7933-3425-X*); disk 29.95 (*0-7933-3427-6*) Gallopade Intl.

— Meow! Pennsylvania Cats in History, Mystery, Legend, Lore, Humor & More! (Pennsylvania Bks.). (Illus.). (J). (gr. 3-12). 1994. pap. 19.95 (*0-7933-3429-2*); lib. bdg. 29.95 (*0-7933-3428-4*); disk 29.95 (*0-7933-3430-6*) Gallopade Intl.

— Meow! Rhode Island Cats in History, Mystery, Legend, Lore, Humor & More! (Rhode Island Bks.). (Illus.). (J). (gr. 3-12). 1994. pap. 19.95 (*0-7933-3432-2*); lib. bdg. 29.95 (*0-7933-3431-4*); disk 29.95 (*0-7933-3433-0*) Gallopade Intl.

— Meow! South Carolina Cats in History, Mystery, Legend, Lore, Humor & More! (South Carolina Bks.). (Illus.). (J). (gr. 3-12). 1994. pap. 19.95 (*0-7933-3435-7*); lib. bdg. 29.95 (*0-7933-3434-9*); disk 29.95 (*0-7933-3436-5*) Gallopade Intl.

— Meow! South Dakota Cats in History, Mystery, Legend, Lore, Humor & More! (South Dakota Bks.). (Illus.). (J). (gr. 3-12). 1994. pap. 19.95 (*0-7933-3438-1*); lib. bdg. 29.95 (*0-7933-3437-3*); disk 29.95 (*0-7933-3439-X*) Gallopade Intl.

— Meow! Tennessee Cats in History, Mystery, Legend, Lore, Humor & More! (Tennessee Bks.). (Illus.). (J). (gr. 3-12). 1994. pap. 19.95 (*0-7933-3441-1*); lib. bdg. 29.95 (*0-7933-3440-3*); disk 29.95 (*0-7933-3442-X*) Gallopade Intl.

— Meow! Texas Cats in History, Mystery, Legend, Lore, Humor & More! (Texas Bks.). (Illus.). (J). (gr. 3-12). 1994. pap. 19.95 (*0-7933-3444-6*); lib. bdg. 29.95 (*0-7933-3443-8*); disk 29.95 (*0-7933-3445-4*) Gallopade Intl.

— Meow! Utah Cats in History, Mystery, Legend, Lore, Humor & More! (Utah Bks.). (Illus.). (J). (gr. 3-12). 1994. pap. 19.95 (*0-7933-3447-0*); lib. bdg. 29.95 (*0-7933-3446-2*); disk 29.95 (*0-7933-3448-9*) Gallopade Intl.

— Meow! Vermont Cats in History, Mystery, Legend, Lore, Humor & More! (Vermont Bks.). (Illus.). (J). (gr. 3-12). 1994. pap. 19.95 (*0-7933-3450-0*); lib. bdg. 29.95 (*0-7933-3449-7*); disk 29.95 (*0-7933-3451-9*) Gallopade Intl.

— Meow! Virginia Cats in History, Mystery, Legend, Lore, Humor & More! (Virginia Bks.). (Illus.). (J). (gr. 3-12). 1994. pap. 19.95 (*0-7933-3453-5*); lib. bdg. 29.95 (*0-7933-3452-7*); disk 29.95 (*0-7933-3454-3*) Gallopade Intl.

— Meow! Washington Cats in History, Mystery, Legend, Lore, Humor & More! (Washington Bks.). (Illus.). (J). (gr. 3-12). 1994. pap. 19.95 (*0-7933-3456-X*); lib. bdg. 29.95 (*0-7933-3455-1*); disk 29.95 (*0-7933-3457-8*) Gallopade Intl.

— Meow! Washington DC Cats in History, Mystery, Legend, Lore, Humor & More! (Washington, D.C. Bks.). (Illus.). (J). (gr. 3-12). 1994. pap. 19.95 (*0-7933-3339-3*); lib. bdg. 29.95 (*0-7933-3338-5*); disk 29.95 (*0-7933-3340-7*) Gallopade Intl.

— Meow! West Virginia Cats in History, Mystery, Legend, Lore, Humor & More! (West Virginia Bks.). (Illus.). (J). (gr. 3-12). 1994. pap. 19.95 (*0-7933-3459-4*); lib. bdg. 29.95 (*0-7933-3458-6*); disk 29.95 (*0-7933-3460-8*) Gallopade Intl.

— Meow! Wisconsin Cats in History, Mystery, Legend, Lore, Humor & More! (Wisconsin Bks.). (Illus.). (J). (gr. 3-12). 1994. pap. 19.95 (*0-7933-3462-4*); lib. bdg. 29.95 (*0-7933-3461-6*); disk 29.95 (*0-7933-3463-2*) Gallopade Intl.

— Meow! Wyoming Cats in History, Mystery, Legend, Lore, Humor & More! (Wyoming Bks.). (Illus.). (J). (gr. 3-12). 1994. pap. 19.95 (*0-7933-3465-9*); lib. bdg. 29.95 (*0-7933-3464-0*); disk 29.95 (*0-7933-3466-7*) Gallopade Intl.

— Michigan & Other State Greats (Biographies) (Carole Marsh Michigan Bks.). (Illus.). (J). (gr. 3 up). 1994. pap. 19.95 (*1-55609-678-X*); lib. bdg. 29.95 (*1-55609-677-1*); disk 29.95 (*1-55609-679-8*) Gallopade Intl.

— Michigan Bandits, Bushwackers, Outlaws, Crooks, Devils, Ghosts, Desperadoes & Other Assorted & Sundry Characters! (Carole Marsh Michigan Bks.). (Illus.). (J). (gr. 3 up). 1994. pap. 19.95 (*0-7933-0598-5*); lib. bdg. 29.95 (*0-7933-0599-3*); disk 29.95 (*0-7933-0600-0*) Gallopade Intl.

— Michigan "BIO" Bingo! 24 Must Know State People for Kids to Learn about While Having Fun! (Bingo! Ser.). (Illus.). (J). (gr. 2-8). 1998. pap. 14.95 (*0-7933-8588-1*) Gallopade Intl.

— The Michigan Bookstore Book: A Surprising Guide to Our State's Bookstores & Their Specialties for Students, Teachers, Writers & Publishers. (Carole Marsh Michigan Bks.). (Illus.). 1994. pap. 19.95 (*0-7933-2922-1*); lib. bdg. 29.95 (*0-7933-2921-3*); disk 29.95 (*0-7933-2923-X*) Gallopade Intl.

— Michigan Classic Christmas Trivia: Stories, Recipes, Activities, Legends, Lore & More! (Carole Marsh Michigan Bks.). (Illus.). (J). (gr. 3 up). 1994. pap. 19.95 (*0-7933-0601-9*); disk 29.95 (*0-7933-0603-5*) Gallopade Intl.

— Michigan Classic Christmas Trivia: Stories, Recipes, Activities, Legends, Lore & More! (Carole Marsh Michigan Bks.). (Illus.). (J). (gr. 3 up). 1997. lib. bdg. 29.95 (*0-7933-0602-7*) Gallopade Intl.

— Michigan Coastales. (Carole Marsh Michigan Bks.). (Illus.). (J). (gr. 3 up). 1994. pap. 19.95 (*1-55609-672-0*); lib. bdg. 29.95 (*1-55609-671-2*); disk 29.95 (*1-55609-673-9*) Gallopade Intl.

— Michigan Coastales! (Carole Marsh Michigan Bks.). (J). 1994. lib. bdg. 29.95 (*0-7933-7287-9*) Gallopade Intl.

— Michigan "Crinkum-Crankum" A Funny Word Book about Our State. (Carole Marsh Michigan Bks.). (Illus.). (J). 1994. pap. 19.95 (*0-7933-4875-7*); lib. bdg. 29.95 (*0-7933-4874-9*); disk 29.95 (*0-7933-4876-5*) Gallopade Intl.

— Michigan Dingbats! Bk. 1: A Fun Book of Games, Stories, Activities & More about Our State That's All in Code! for You to Decipher. (Carole Marsh Michigan Bks.). (Illus.). (J). (gr. 3-12). 1994. pap. 19.95 (*0-7933-3840-9*); lib. bdg. 29.95 (*0-7933-3839-5*); disk 29.95 (*0-7933-3841-7*) Gallopade Intl.

***Marsh, Carole.** The Michigan Experience Pocket Guide. (Michigan Experience! Ser.). (Illus.). (J). 2000. pap. 6.95 (*0-7933-9562-3*) Gallopade Intl.

Marsh, Carole. Michigan Facts & Factivities. (Carole Marsh State Bks.). (Illus.). (J). (gr. 4-7). 1996. pap., teacher ed. 19.95 (*0-7933-7891-5*, C Marsh) Gallopade Intl.

— Michigan Festival Fun for Kids! (Carole Marsh Michigan Bks.). (Illus.). (J). (gr. 3-12). 1994. pap. 19.95 (*0-7933-3993-6*); lib. bdg. 29.95 (*0-7933-3992-8*) Gallopade Intl.

— Michigan Festival Fun for Kids! (Carole Marsh Michigan Bks.). (Illus.). (YA). (gr. 3-12). 1994. disk 29.95 (*0-7933-3994-4*) Gallopade Intl.

— Michigan "GEO" Bingo! 38 Must Know State Geography Facts for Kids to Learn While Having Fun! (Bingo! Ser.). (Illus.). (J). (gr. 2-8). 1998. pap. 14.95 (*0-7933-8589-X*) Gallopade Intl.

— Michigan Government! The Cornerstone of Everyday Life in Our State! (Carole Marsh Michigan Bks.). (Illus.). (J). (gr. 3-12). 1996. pap. 19.95 (*0-7933-6248-2*); lib. bdg. 29.95 (*0-7933-6247-4*); disk 29.95 (*0-7933-6249-0*) Gallopade Intl.

— Michigan "HISTO" Bingo! 42 Must Know State History Facts for Kids to Learn While Having Fun! (Bingo! Ser.). (Illus.). (J). (gr. 2-8). 1998. pap. 14.95 (*0-7933-8590-3*) Gallopade Intl.

— Michigan History! Surprising Secrets about Our State's Founding Mothers, Fathers & Kids! (Carole Marsh Michigan Bks.). (Illus.). (J). (gr. 3-12). 1996. pap. 19.95 (*0-7933-6095-1*); lib. bdg. 29.95 (*0-7933-6094-3*); disk 29.95 (*0-7933-6096-X*) Gallopade Intl.

— The Michigan Hot Air Balloon Mystery. (Carole Marsh Michigan Bks.). (Illus.). (J). (gr. 2-9). 1994. 29.95 (*0-7933-2516-1*); pap. 19.95 (*0-7933-2517-X*); disk 29.95 (*0-7933-2518-8*) Gallopade Intl.

— Michigan Hot Zones! Viruses, Diseases, & Epidemics in Our State's History. (Hot Zones! Ser.). (Illus.). (J). (gr. 3-12). 1998. pap. 19.95 (*0-7933-8895-3*); lib. bdg. 29.95 (*0-7933-8894-5*) Gallopade Intl.

— Michigan Indian Dictionary for Kids! (Carole Marsh State Bks.). (J). (gr. 2-9). 1996. 29.95 (*0-7933-7710-2*, C Marsh); pap. 19.95 (*0-7933-7711-0*, C Marsh) Gallopade Intl.

***Marsh, Carole.** Michigan Jeopardy. (Michigan Experience! Ser.). (Illus.). (J). (gr. 2-6). 2000. pap. 7.95 (*0-7933-9564-X*) Gallopade Intl.

Marsh, Carole. Michigan Jeopardy! Answers & Questions about Our State! (Carole Marsh Michigan Bks.). (Illus.). (J). (gr. 3-12). 1994. pap. 19.95 (*0-7933-4146-9*); lib. bdg. 29.95 (*0-7933-4145-0*); disk 29.95 (*0-7933-4147-7*) Gallopade Intl.

***Marsh, Carole.** Michigan Jography. (Michigan Experience! Ser.). (Illus.). (J). (gr. 2-6). 2000. pap. 7.95 (*0-7933-9565-8*) Gallopade Intl.

Marsh, Carole. Michigan "Jography" A Fun Run Thru Our State. (Carole Marsh Michigan Bks.). (Illus.). (J). (gr. 3 up). 1994. pap. 19.95 (*1-55609-667-4*); lib. bdg. 29.95 (*1-55609-666-6*); disk 29.95 (*1-55609-668-2*) Gallopade Intl.

— Michigan Kid's Cookbook: Recipes, How-To, History, Lore & More! (Carole Marsh Michigan Bks.). (Illus.). (J). (gr. 3 up). 1994. pap. 19.95 (*0-7933-0610-8*); lib. bdg. 29.95 (*0-7933-0611-6*); disk 29.95 (*0-7933-0612-4*) Gallopade Intl.

— The Michigan Library Book: A Surprising Guide to the Unusual Special Collections in Libraries Across Our State for Students, Teachers, Writers & Publishers - Includes Reproducible Mailing Labels Plus Activities for Young People! (Carole Marsh Michigan Bks.). (Illus.). 1994. pap. 19.95 (*0-7933-3072-6*); lib. bdg. 29.95 (*0-7933-3071-8*); disk 29.95 (*0-7933-3073-4*) Gallopade Intl.

— Michigan Math! How It All Adds up in Our State. (Carole Marsh Michigan Bks.). (Illus.). (YA). (gr. 3-12). 1996. pap. 19.95 (*0-7933-6554-6*); lib. bdg. 29.95 (*0-7933-6553-8*) Gallopade Intl.

— The Michigan Media Book: A Surprising Guide to the Amazing Print, Broadcast & Online Media of Our State for Students, Teachers, Writers & Publishers - Includes Reproducible Mailing Labels Plus Activities for Young People! (Carole Marsh Michigan Bks.). (Illus.). 1994. pap. 19.95 (*0-7933-3228-1*); lib. bdg. 29.95 (*0-7933-3227-3*); disk 29.95 (*0-7933-3229-X*) Gallopade Intl.

— The Michigan Mystery Van Takes Off! Book 1: Handicapped Michigan Kids Sneak Off on a Big Adventure. (Carole Marsh Michigan Bks.). (Illus.). (J). (gr. 3-12). 1994. 29.95 (*0-7933-5027-1*); pap. 19.95 (*0-7933-5028-X*); disk 29.95 (*0-7933-5029-8*) Gallopade Intl.

— Michigan Quiz Bowl Crash Course! (Carole Marsh Michigan Bks.). (Illus.). (J). (gr. 3 up). 1994. pap. 19.95 (*1-55609-675-5*); lib. bdg. 29.95 (*1-55609-674-7*); disk 29.95 (*1-55609-676-3*) Gallopade Intl.

— Michigan Rollercoasters! (Carole Marsh Michigan Bks.). (Illus.). (J). (gr. 3-12). 1994. pap. 19.95 (*0-7933-5291-6*); lib. bdg. 29.95 (*0-7933-5290-8*) Gallopade Intl.

— Michigan Rollercoasters! (Carole Marsh Michigan Bks.). (Illus.). (YA). (gr. 3-12). 1994. disk 29.95 (*0-7933-5292-4*) Gallopade Intl.

— Michigan School Trivia: An Amazing & Fascinating Look at Our State's Teachers, Schools & Students! (Carole Marsh Michigan Bks.). (Illus.). (J). (gr. 3 up). 1994. pap. 19.95 (*0-7933-0607-8*); lib. bdg. 29.95 (*0-7933-0608-6*); disk 29.95 (*0-7933-0609-4*) Gallopade Intl.

— Michigan Silly Basketball Sportsmysteries, Vol. I. (Carole Marsh Michigan Bks.). (Illus.). (J). (gr. 3 up). 1994. pap. 19.95 (*0-7933-0604-3*); lib. bdg. 29.95 (*0-7933-0605-1*); disk 29.95 (*0-7933-0606-X*) Gallopade Intl.

— Michigan Silly Basketball Sportsmysteries, Vol. II. (Carole Marsh Michigan Bks.). (Illus.). (J). (gr. 3 up). 1994. pap. 19.95 (*0-7933-1712-6*); lib. bdg. 29.95 (*0-7933-1711-8*); disk 29.95 (*0-7933-1713-4*) Gallopade Intl.

— Michigan Silly Football Sportsmysteries, Vol. I. (Carole Marsh Michigan Bks.). (Illus.). (J). (gr. 3 up). 1994. pap. 19.95 (*1-55609-703-4*); lib. bdg. 29.95 (*1-55609-702-6*); disk 29.95 (*1-55609-704-2*) Gallopade Intl.

— Michigan Silly Football Sportsmysteries, Vol. II. (Carole Marsh Michigan Bks.). (Illus.). (J). (gr. 3 up). 1994. pap. 19.95 (*1-55609-706-9*); lib. bdg. 29.95 (*1-55609-705-0*); disk 29.95 (*1-55609-707-7*) Gallopade Intl.

— Michigan Silly Trivia! (Carole Marsh Michigan Bks.). (Illus.). (J). (gr. 3 up). 1994. pap. 19.95 (*1-55609-664-X*); lib. bdg. 29.95 (*1-55609-663-1*); disk 29.95 (*1-55609-665-8*) Gallopade Intl.

— Michigan Spelling Bee! Score Big by Correctly Spelling Our State's Unique Names. (Carole Marsh Michigan Bks.). (Illus.). (YA). (gr. 3-12). 1996. pap. 19.95 (*0-7933-6707-7*); lib. bdg. 29.95 (*0-7933-6706-9*) Gallopade Intl.

— Michigan Timeline: A Chronology of Michigan History, Mystery, Trivia, Legend, Lore & More. (Carole Marsh Michigan Bks.). (Illus.). (J). (gr. 3-12). 1994. pap. 19.95 (*0-7933-5942-2*); lib. bdg. 29.95 (*0-7933-5941-4*); disk 29.95 (*0-7933-5943-0*) Gallopade Intl.

— Michigan 2000! Coming Soon to a Calendar Near You - The 21st Century! - Complete Set of AL 2000 Items. (Two Thousand! Ser.). (Illus.). (J). (gr. 3-12). 1998. pap. 75.00 (*0-7933-9353-1*); lib. bdg. 85.00 (*0-7933-9354-X*) Gallopade Intl.

— Michigan 2000! Coming Soon to a Calendar near You--The 21st Century! (Two Thousand! Ser.). (Illus.). (J). (gr. 3-12). 1998. pap. 19.95 (*0-7933-8742-6*); lib. bdg. 29.95 (*0-7933-8741-8*) Gallopade Intl.

— Michigan UFO's & Extraterrestrials! A Look at the Sightings & Science in Our State. (Carole Marsh Michigan Bks.). (Illus.). (J). (gr. 3-12). 1997. pap. 19.95 (*0-7933-6401-9*); lib. bdg. 29.95 (*0-7933-6400-0*) Gallopade Intl.

***Marsh, Carole.** Michigan's Big Activity Book. (Michigan Experience! Ser.). (Illus.). (J). (gr. k-5). 2000. pap. 9.95 (*0-7933-9566-6*) Gallopade Intl.

Marsh, Carole. Michigan's (Most Devastating!) Disasters & (Most Calamitous!) Catastrophies! (Carole Marsh Michigan Bks.). (Illus.). (J). (gr. 3 up). 1994. pap. 19.95 (*0-7933-0595-0*); lib. bdg. 29.95 (*0-7933-0596-9*); disk 29.95 (*0-7933-0597-7*) Gallopade Intl.

— Michigan's Unsolved Mysteries (& Their "Solutions") Includes Scientific Information & Other Activities for

Students. (Carole Marsh Michigan Bks.). (Illus.). (J). (gr. 3-12). 1994. pap. 19.95 (0-7933-5789-6); lib. bdg. 29.95 (0-7933-5788-8); disk 29.95 (0-7933-5790-X) Gallopade Intl.

— Minnesota & Other State Greats (Biographies) (Carole Marsh Minnesota Bks.). (Illus.). (J). (gr. 3 up). 1994. pap. 19.95 (1-55609-661-5); lib. bdg. 29.95 (1-55609-660-7); disk 29.95 (1-55609-662-3) Gallopade Intl.

— Minnesota Bandits, Bushwackers, Outlaws, Crooks, Devils, Ghosts, Desperadoes & Other Assorted & Sundry Characters! (Carole Marsh Minnesota Bks.). (Illus.). (J). (gr. 3 up). 1994. pap. 19.95 (0-7933-0622-1); lib. bdg. 29.95 (0-7933-0623-X); disk 29.95 (0-7933-0624-8) Gallopade Intl.

— Minnesota "BIO" Bingo! 24 Must Know State People for Kids to Learn about While Having Fun! (Bingo! Ser.). (Illus.). (J). (gr. 2-8). 1998. pap. 14.95 (0-7933-8591-1) Gallopade Intl.

— The Minnesota Bookstore Book: A Surprising Guide to Our State's Bookstores & Their Specialties for Students, Teachers, Writers & Publishers. (Carole Marsh Minnesota Bks.). (Illus.). 1994. pap. 19.95 (0-7933-2925-6); lib. bdg. 29.95 (0-7933-2924-8); disk 29.95 (0-7933-2926-4) Gallopade Intl.

— Minnesota Classic Christmas Trivia: Stories, Recipes, Activities, Legends, Lore & More! (Carole Marsh Minnesota Bks.). (Illus.). (J). (gr. 3 up). 1994. pap. 19.95 (0-7933-0625-6); lib. bdg. 29.95 (0-7933-0626-4); disk 29.95 (0-7933-0627-2) Gallopade Intl.

— Minnesota Coastales. (Carole Marsh Minnesota Bks.). (Illus.). (J). (gr. 3 up). 1994. pap. 19.95 (1-55609-655-0); lib. bdg. 29.95 (1-55609-654-2); disk 29.95 (1-55609-656-9) Gallopade Intl.

— Minnesota Coastales! (Carole Marsh Minnesota Bks.). (J). 1994. lib. bdg. 29.95 (0-7933-7288-7) Gallopade Intl.

— Minnesota "Crinkum-Crankum" A Funny Word Book about Our State. (Carole Marsh Minnesota Bks.). (Illus.). (J). 1994. pap. 19.95 (0-7933-4878-1); lib. bdg. 29.95 (0-7933-4877-3); disk 29.95 (0-7933-4879-X) Gallopade Intl.

— Minnesota Dingbats! A Fun Book of Games, Stories, Activities & More about Our State That's All in Code! for You to Decipher. Bk. 1. (Carole Marsh Minnesota Bks.). (Illus.). (J). (gr. 3-12). 1994. pap. 19.95 (0-7933-3843-3); lib. bdg. 29.95 (0-7933-3842-5); disk 29.95 (0-7933-3844-1) Gallopade Intl.

— Minnesota Facts & Factivities. (Carole Marsh State Bks.). (Illus.). (J). (gr. 4-7). 1996. pap., teacher ed. 19.95 (0-7933-7893-1, C Marsh) Gallopade Intl.

— Minnesota Festival Fun for Kids! (Carole Marsh Minnesota Bks.). (Illus.). (J). (gr. 3-12). 1994. pap. 19.95 (0-7933-3996-0); lib. bdg. 29.95 (0-7933-3995-2) Gallopade Intl.

— Minnesota Festival Fun for Kids! (Carole Marsh Minnesota Bks.). (Illus.). (YA). (gr. 3-12). 1994. disk 29.95 (0-7933-3997-9) Gallopade Intl.

— Minnesota "GEO" Bingo! 38 Must Know State Geography Facts for Kids to Learn While Having Fun! (Bingo! Ser.). (Illus.). (J). (gr. 2-8). 1998. pap. 14.95 (0-7933-8592-X) Gallopade Intl.

— Minnesota Government! The Cornerstone of Everyday Life in Our State! (Carole Marsh Minnesota Bks.). (Illus.). (J). (gr. 3-12). 1996. pap. 19.95 (0-7933-6251-2); lib. bdg. 29.95 (0-7933-6250-4); disk 29.95 (0-7933-6252-0) Gallopade Intl.

— Minnesota "HISTO" Bingo! 42 Must Know State History Facts for Kids to Learn While Having Fun! (Bingo! Ser.). (Illus.). (J). (gr. 2-8). 1998. pap. 14.95 (0-7933-8593-8) Gallopade Intl.

— Minnesota History! Surprising Secrets about Our State's Founding Mothers, Fathers & Kids! (Carole Marsh Minnesota Bks.). (Illus.). (J). (gr. 3-12). 1996. pap. 19.95 (0-7933-6098-6); lib. bdg. 29.95 (0-7933-6097-8); disk 29.95 (0-7933-6099-4) Gallopade Intl.

— The Minnesota Hot Air Balloon Mystery. (Carole Marsh Minnesota Bks.). (Illus.). (J). (gr. 2-9). 1994. 29.95 (0-7933-2525-0); pap. 19.95 (0-7933-2526-9); disk 29.95 (0-7933-2527-7) Gallopade Intl.

— Minnesota Hot Zones! Viruses, Diseases, & Epidemics in Our State's History. (Hot Zones! Ser.). (Illus.). (J). (gr. 3-12). 1998. pap. 19.95 (0-7933-8898-8); lib. bdg. 29.95 (0-7933-8897-X) Gallopade Intl.

— Minnesota Indian Dictionary for Kids! (Carole Marsh State Bks.). (J). (gr. 2-9). 1996. 29.95 (0-7933-7713-7, C Marsh); pap. 19.95 (0-7933-7714-5, C Marsh) Gallopade Intl.

— Minnesota Jeopardy! Answers & Questions about Our State! (Carole Marsh Minnesota Bks.). (Illus.). (J). (gr. 3-12). 1994. pap. 19.95 (0-7933-4149-3); lib. bdg. 29.95 (0-7933-4148-5); disk 29.95 (0-7933-4150-7) Gallopade Intl.

— Minnesota "Jography" A Fun Run Thru Our State. (Carole Marsh Minnesota Bks.). (Illus.). (J). (gr. 3 up). 1994. pap. 19.95 (1-55609-643-7); lib. bdg. 29.95 (1-55609-642-9); disk 29.95 (1-55609-644-5) Gallopade Intl.

— Minnesota Kid's Cookbook: Recipes, How-To, History, Lore & More. (Carole Marsh Minnesota Bks.). (Illus.). (J). (gr. 3 up). 1994. pap. 19.95 (0-7933-0634-5); lib. bdg. 29.95 (0-7933-0635-3); disk 29.95 (0-7933-0636-1) Gallopade Intl.

— The Minnesota Library Book: A Surprising Guide to the Unusual Special Collections in Libraries Across Our State for Students, Teachers, Writers & Publishers - Includes Reproducible Mailing Labels Plus Activities for Young People! (Carole Marsh Minnesota Bks.). (Illus.). 1994. pap. 19.95 (0-7933-3075-0); lib. bdg. 29.95 (0-7933-3074-2); disk 29.95 (0-7933-3076-9) Gallopade Intl.

— Minnesota Math! How It All Adds up in Our State. (Carole Marsh Minnesota Bks.). (Illus.). (YA). (gr. 3-12). 1996. pap. 19.95 (0-7933-6557-0); lib. bdg. 29.95 (0-7933-6556-2) Gallopade Intl.

— The Minnesota Media Book: A Surprising Guide to the Amazing Print, Broadcast & Online Media of Our State for Students, Teachers, Writers & Publishers - Includes Reproducible Mailing Labels Plus Activities for Young People! (Carole Marsh Minnesota Bks.). (Illus.). 1994. pap. 19.95 (0-7933-3231-1); lib. bdg. 29.95 (0-7933-3230-3); disk 29.95 (0-7933-3232-X) Gallopade Intl.

— The Minnesota Mystery Van Takes Off! Bk. 1: Handicapped Minnesota Kids Sneak off on a Big Adventure. (Carole Marsh Minnesota Bks.). (Illus.). (J). (gr. 3-12). 1994. 29.95 (0-7933-5030-1); pap. 19.95 (0-7933-5031-X); disk 29.95 (0-7933-5032-8) Gallopade Intl.

— Minnesota Quiz Bowl Crash Course! (Carole Marsh Minnesota Bks.). (Illus.). (J). (gr. 3 up). 1994. pap. 19.95 (1-55609-658-5); lib. bdg. 29.95 (1-55609-657-7); disk 29.95 (1-55609-659-3) Gallopade Intl.

— Minnesota Rollercoasters! (Carole Marsh Minnesota Bks.). (Illus.). (J). (gr. 3-12). 1994. pap. 19.95 (0-7933-5294-0); lib. bdg. 29.95 (0-7933-5293-2) Gallopade Intl.

— Minnesota Rollercoasters! (Carole Marsh Minnesota Bks.). (Illus.). (YA). (gr. 3-12). 1994. disk 29.95 (0-7933-5295-9) Gallopade Intl.

— Minnesota School Trivia: An Amazing & Fascinating Look at Our State's Teachers, Schools & Students! (Carole Marsh Minnesota Bks.). (Illus.). (J). (gr. 3 up). 1994. pap. 19.95 (0-7933-0631-0); lib. bdg. 29.95 (0-7933-0632-9); disk 29.95 (0-7933-0633-7) Gallopade Intl.

— Minnesota Silly Basketball Sportsmysteries, Vol. I. (Carole Marsh Minnesota Bks.). (Illus.). (J). (gr. 3 up). 1994. pap. 19.95 (0-7933-0628-0); lib. bdg. 29.95 (0-7933-0629-9); disk 29.95 (0-7933-0630-2) Gallopade Intl.

— Minnesota Silly Basketball Sportsmysteries, Vol. II. (Carole Marsh Minnesota Bks.). (Illus.). (J). (gr. 3 up). 1994. pap. 19.95 (0-7933-1721-5); lib. bdg. 29.95 (0-7933-1720-7); disk 29.95 (0-7933-1722-3) Gallopade Intl.

— Minnesota Silly Football Sportsmysteries, Vol. I. (Carole Marsh Minnesota Bks.). (Illus.). (J). (gr. 3 up). 1994. pap. 19.95 (1-55609-649-6); lib. bdg. 29.95 (1-55609-648-8); disk 29.95 (1-55609-650-X) Gallopade Intl.

— Minnesota Silly Football Sportsmysteries, Vol. II. (Carole Marsh Minnesota Bks.). (Illus.). (J). (gr. 3 up). 1994. pap. 19.95 (1-55609-652-6); lib. bdg. 29.95 (1-55609-651-8); disk 29.95 (1-55609-653-4) Gallopade Intl.

— Minnesota Silly Trivia! (Carole Marsh Minnesota Bks.). (Illus.). (J). (gr. 3 up). 1994. pap. 19.95 (1-55609-640-2); lib. bdg. 29.95 (1-55609-639-9); disk 29.95 (1-55609-641-0) Gallopade Intl.

— Minnesota Spelling Bee! Score Big by Correctly Spelling Our State's Unique Names. (Carole Marsh Minnesota Bks.). (Illus.). (YA). (gr. 3-12). 1996. pap. 19.95 (0-7933-6710-7); lib. bdg. 29.95 (0-7933-6709-3) Gallopade Intl.

— Minnesota Timeline: A Chronology of Minnesota History, Mystery, Trivia, Legend, Lore & More. (Carole Marsh Minnesota Bks.). (Illus.). (J). (gr. 3-12). 1994. pap. 19.95 (0-7933-5945-7); lib. bdg. 29.95 (0-7933-5944-9); disk 29.95 (0-7933-5946-5) Gallopade Intl.

— Minnesota 2000! Coming Soon to a Calendar Near You - The 21st Century! - Complete Set of AL 2000 Items. (Two Thousand! Ser.). (Illus.). (J). (gr. 3-12). 1998. pap. 75.00 (0-7933-9355-8); lib. bdg. 85.00 (0-7933-9356-6) Gallopade Intl.

— Minnesota 2000! Coming Soon to a Calendar near You--The 21st Century! (Two Thousand! Ser.). (Illus.). (J). (gr. 3-12). 1998. pap. 19.95 (0-7933-8745-0); lib. bdg. 29.95 (0-7933-8744-2) Gallopade Intl.

— Minnesota UFO's & Extraterrestrials! A Look at the Sightings & Science in Our State. (Carole Marsh Minnesota Bks.). (Illus.). (J). (gr. 3-12). 1997. pap. 19.95 (0-7933-6404-3); lib. bdg. 29.95 (0-7933-6403-5) Gallopade Intl.

— Minnesota's (Most Devastating!) Disasters & (Most Calamitous!) Catastrophies! (Carole Marsh Minnesota Bks.). (Illus.). (J). (gr. 3 up). 1994. pap. 19.95 (0-7933-0619-1); lib. bdg. 29.95 (0-7933-0620-5); disk 29.95 (0-7933-0621-3) Gallopade Intl.

— Minnesota's Unsolved Mysteries (And Their "Solutions") Includes Scientific Information & Other Activities for Students. (Carole Marsh Minnesota Bks.). (Illus.). (J). (gr. 3-12). 1994. pap. 19.95 (0-7933-5792-6); lib. bdg. 29.95 (0-7933-5791-8); disk 29.95 (0-7933-5793-4) Gallopade Intl.

— The Missing Head Mystery. LC 79-55447. (History Mystery Ser.). (Illus.). (Orig.). (J). (gr. 3-9). 1994. 29.95 (1-55609-179-6); pap. 19.95 (0-935326-01-4) Gallopade Intl.

— The Missing Head Mystery: Classroom Gamebook. (Carole Marsh Bks.). (Illus.). (Orig.). (J). (gr. 3-6). 1994. pap. 19.95 (0-935326-84-7) Gallopade Intl.

— The Missing Head Mystery Set. (Carole Marsh Mysteries Ser.). 1994. teacher ed. 125.00 (0-7933-6944-4) Gallopade Intl.

— Mississippi & Other State Greats (Biographies) (Carole Marsh Mississippi Bks.). (Illus.). (J). (gr. 3 up). 1994. pap. 19.95 (1-55609-726-3); lib. bdg. 29.95 (1-55609-725-5); disk 29.95 (1-55609-727-1) Gallopade Intl.

— Mississippi Bandits, Bushwackers, Outlaws, Crooks, Devils, Ghosts, Desperadoes & Other Assorted & Sundry Characters! (Carole Marsh Mississippi Bks.). (Illus.). (J). (gr. 3 up). 1994. pap. 19.95 (0-7933-0647-7); lib. bdg. 29.95 (0-7933-0648-5); disk 29.95 (0-7933-0649-3) Gallopade Intl.

*Marsh, Carole. Mississippi BIG Activity Book. (Mississippi Experience! Ser.). (Illus.). (J). (gr. k-5). 2000. pap. 9.95 (0-7933-9558-5) Gallopade Intl.

Marsh, Carole. Mississippi "BIO" Bingo! 24 Must Know State People for Kids to Learn about While Having Fun! (Bingo! Ser.). (Illus.). (J). (gr. 2-8). 1998. pap. 14.95 (0-7933-8594-6) Gallopade Intl.

— The Mississippi Bookstore Book: A Surprising Guide to Our State's Bookstores & Their Specialties for Students, Teachers, Writers & Publishers. (Carole Marsh Mississippi Bks.). (Illus.). 1994. pap. 19.95 (0-7933-2928-0); lib. bdg. 29.95 (0-7933-2927-2); disk 29.95 (0-7933-2929-9) Gallopade Intl.

— Mississippi Classic Christmas Trivia: Stories, Recipes, Activities, Legends, Lore & More. (Carole Marsh Mississippi Bks.). (Illus.). (J). (gr. 3 up). 1994. pap. 19.95 (0-7933-0650-7); lib. bdg. 29.95 (0-7933-0651-5); disk 29.95 (0-7933-0652-3) Gallopade Intl.

— Mississippi Coastales. (Carole Marsh Mississippi Bks.). (J). 1994. lib. bdg. 29.95 (0-7933-7289-5) Gallopade Intl.

— Mississippi Coastales. (Carole Marsh Mississippi Bks.). (Illus.). (J). (gr. 3 up). 1994. pap. 19.95 (1-55609-122-2); lib. bdg. 29.95 (1-55609-720-4); disk 29.95 (1-55609-721-2) Gallopade Intl.

— Mississippi "Crinkum-Crankum" A Funny Word Book about Our State. (Carole Marsh Mississippi Bks.). (Illus.). (J). 1994. pap. 19.95 (0-7933-4881-1); lib. bdg. 29.95 (0-7933-4880-3); disk 29.95 (0-7933-4882-X) Gallopade Intl.

— Mississippi Dingbats! Bk. 1: A Fun Book of Games, Stories, Activities & More about Our State That's All in Code! for You to Decipher. (Carole Marsh Mississippi Bks.). (Illus.). (J). (gr. 3-12). 1994. pap. 19.95 (0-7933-3846-8); lib. bdg. 29.95 (0-7933-3845-X); disk 29.95 (0-7933-3847-6) Gallopade Intl.

*Marsh, Carole. The Mississippi Experience Pocket Guide. (Mississippi Experience! Ser.). (Illus.). (J). 2000. pap. 6.95 (0-7933-9554-2) Gallopade Intl.

Marsh, Carole. Mississippi Facts & Factivities. (Carole Marsh State Bks.). (Illus.). (J). (gr. 4-7). 1996. pap., teacher ed. 19.95 (0-7933-7895-8, C Marsh) Gallopade Intl.

— Mississippi Festival Fun for Kids! (Carole Marsh Mississippi Bks.). (Illus.). (J). (gr. 3-12). 1994. pap. 19.95 (0-7933-3999-5); lib. bdg. 29.95 (0-7933-3998-7) Gallopade Intl.

— Mississippi Festival Fun for Kids! (Carole Marsh Mississippi Bks.). (Illus.). (YA). (gr. 3-12). 1994. disk 29.95 (0-7933-4000-4) Gallopade Intl.

— Mississippi "GEO" Bingo! 38 Must Know State Geography Facts for Kids to Learn While Having Fun! (Bingo! Ser.). (Illus.). (J). (gr. 2-8). 1998. pap. 14.95 (0-7933-8595-4) Gallopade Intl.

— Mississippi Government! The Cornerstone of Everyday Life in Our State! (Carole Marsh Mississippi Bks.). (Illus.). (J). (gr. 3-12). 1996. pap. 19.95 (0-7933-6254-7); lib. bdg. 29.95 (0-7933-6253-9); disk 29.95 (0-7933-6255-5) Gallopade Intl.

— Mississippi "HISTO" Bingo! 42 Must Know State History Facts for Kids to Learn While Having Fun! (Bingo! Ser.). (Illus.). (J). (gr. 2-8). 1998. pap. 14.95 (0-7933-8596-2) Gallopade Intl.

— Mississippi History! Surprising Secrets about Our State's Founding Mothers, Fathers & Kids! (Carole Marsh Mississippi Bks.). (Illus.). (J). (gr. 3-12). 1996. pap. 19.95 (0-7933-6101-X); lib. bdg. 29.95 (0-7933-6100-1); disk 29.95 (0-7933-6102-8) Gallopade Intl.

— The Mississippi Hot Air Balloon Mystery. (Carole Marsh Mississippi Bks.). (Illus.). (J). (gr. 2-9). 1994. 29.95 (0-7933-2534-X); pap. 19.95 (0-7933-2535-8); disk 29.95 (0-7933-2536-6) Gallopade Intl.

— Mississippi Hot Zones! Viruses, Diseases, & Epidemics in Our State's History. (Hot Zones! Ser.). (Illus.). (J). (gr. 3-12). 1998. pap. 19.95 (0-7933-8901-1); lib. bdg. 29.95 (0-7933-8900-3) Gallopade Intl.

— Mississippi Indian Dictionary for Kids! (Carole Marsh State Bks.). (J). (gr. 2-9). 1996. 29.95 (0-7933-7716-1, C Marsh); pap. 19.95 (0-7933-7717-X, C Marsh) Gallopade Intl.

*Marsh, Carole. Mississippi Jeopardy. (Mississippi Experience! Ser.). (Illus.). (J). (gr. 2-6). 2000. pap. 7.95 (0-7933-9556-9) Gallopade Intl.

Marsh, Carole. Mississippi Jeopardy! Answers & Questions about Our State! (Carole Marsh Mississippi Bks.). (Illus.). (J). (gr. 3-12). 1994. pap. 19.95 (0-7933-4152-3); lib. bdg. 29.95 (0-7933-4151-5); disk 29.95 (0-7933-4153-1) Gallopade Intl.

*Marsh, Carole. Mississippi Jography. (Mississippi Experience! Ser.). (Illus.). (J). (gr. 2-6). 2000. pap. 7.95 (0-7933-9557-7) Gallopade Intl.

Marsh, Carole. Mississippi "Jography" A Fun Run Thru Our State. (Carole Marsh Mississippi Bks.). (Illus.). (J). (gr. 3 up). 1994. pap. 19.95 (1-55609-091-9); lib. bdg. 29.95 (1-55609-709-3); disk 29.95 (1-55609-715-8) Gallopade Intl.

— Mississippi Kid's Cookbook: Recipes, How-To, History, Lore & More. (Carole Marsh Mississippi Bks.). (Illus.). (J). (gr. 3 up). 1994. pap. 19.95 (0-7933-0659-0); lib. bdg. 29.95 (0-7933-0660-4); disk 29.95 (0-7933-0661-2) Gallopade Intl.

— The Mississippi Library Book: A Surprising Guide to the Unusual Special Collections in Libraries Across Our State for Students, Teachers, Writers & Publishers - Includes Reproducible Mailing Labels Plus Activities for Young People! (Carole Marsh Mississippi Bks.). (Illus.). 1994. pap. 19.95 (0-7933-3078-5); lib. bdg. 29.95 (0-7933-3077-7); disk 29.95 (0-7933-3079-3) Gallopade Intl.

— Mississippi Math! How It All Adds up in Our State. (Carole Marsh Mississippi Bks.). (Illus.). (YA). (gr. 3-12). 1996. pap. 29.95 (0-7933-6559-7); pap. 19.95 (0-7933-6560-0) Gallopade Intl.

— The Mississippi Media Book: A Surprising Guide to the Amazing Print, Broadcast & Online Media of Our State for Students, Teachers, Writers & Publishers - Includes Reproducible Mailing Labels Plus Activities for Young People! (Carole Marsh Mississippi Bks.). (Illus.). 1994. pap. 19.95 (0-7933-3234-6); lib. bdg. 29.95 (0-7933-3233-8); disk 29.95 (0-7933-3235-4) Gallopade Intl.

— The Mississippi Mystery Van Takes Off! Bk. 1: Handicapped Mississippi Kids Sneak Off on a Big Adventure. (Carole Marsh Mississippi Bks.). (Illus.). (J). (gr. 3-12). 1994. 29.95 (0-7933-5033-6); pap. 19.95 (0-7933-5034-4); disk 29.95 (0-7933-5035-2) Gallopade Intl.

— Mississippi Quiz Bowl Crash Course! (Carole Marsh Mississippi Bks.). (Illus.). (J). (gr. 3 up). 1994. pap. 19.95 (1-55609-723-9); lib. bdg. 29.95 (1-55609-722-0); disk 29.95 (1-55609-724-7) Gallopade Intl.

— Mississippi Rollercoasters! (Carole Marsh Mississippi Bks.). (Illus.). (J). (gr. 3-12). 1994. pap. 19.95 (0-7933-5297-5); lib. bdg. 29.95 (0-7933-5296-7) Gallopade Intl.

— Mississippi Rollercoasters! (Carole Marsh Mississippi Bks.). (Illus.). (YA). (gr. 3-12). 1994. disk 29.95 (0-7933-5298-3) Gallopade Intl.

— Mississippi School Trivia: An Amazing & Fascinating Look at Our State's Teachers, Schools & Students! (Carole Marsh Mississippi Bks.). (Illus.). (J). (gr. 3 up). 1994. pap. 19.95 (0-7933-0656-6); lib. bdg. 29.95 (0-7933-0657-4); disk 29.95 (0-7933-0658-2) Gallopade Intl.

— Mississippi Silly Basketball Sportsmysteries, Vol. I. (Carole Marsh Mississippi Bks.). (Illus.). (J). (gr. 3 up). 1994. pap. 19.95 (0-7933-0653-1); lib. bdg. 29.95 (0-7933-0654-X); disk 29.95 (0-7933-0655-8) Gallopade Intl.

— Mississippi Silly Basketball Sportsmysteries, Vol. II. (Carole Marsh Mississippi Bks.). (Illus.). (J). (gr. 3 up). 1994. pap. 19.95 (0-7933-1732-0); lib. bdg. 29.95 (0-7933-1731-2) Gallopade Intl.

— Mississippi Silly Basketball Sportsmysteries, Vol. II. (Carole Marsh Mississippi Bks.). (Illus.). (J). (gr. 3 up). 1997. disk 29.95 (0-7933-1733-9) Gallopade Intl.

— Mississippi Silly Football Sportsmysteries, Vol. I. (Carole Marsh Mississippi Bks.). (Illus.). (J). (gr. 3 up). 1994. pap. 19.95 (1-55609-712-3); lib. bdg. 29.95 (1-55609-711-5); disk 29.95 (1-55609-713-1) Gallopade Intl.

— Mississippi Silly Football Sportsmysteries, Vol. II. (Carole Marsh Mississippi Bks.). (Illus.). (J). (gr. 3 up). 1994. pap. 19.95 (1-55609-718-2); lib. bdg. 29.95 (1-55609-717-4); disk 29.95 (1-55609-719-0) Gallopade Intl.

— Mississippi Silly Trivia! (Carole Marsh Mississippi Bks.). (Illus.). (J). (gr. 3 up). 1994. pap. 19.95 (1-55609-039-0); lib. bdg. 29.95 (1-55609-708-5); disk 29.95 (1-55609-714-X) Gallopade Intl.

— Mississippi Spelling Bee! Score Big by Correctly Spelling Our State's Unique Names. (Carole Marsh Mississippi Bks.). (Illus.). (YA). (gr. 3-12). 1996. pap. 19.95 (0-7933-6713-1); lib. bdg. 29.95 (0-7933-6712-3) Gallopade Intl.

— Mississippi Timeline: A Chronology of Mississippi History, Mystery, Trivia, Legend, Lore & More. (Carole Marsh Mississippi Bks.). (Illus.). (J). (gr. 3-12). 1994. pap. 19.95 (0-7933-5948-1); lib. bdg. 29.95 (0-7933-5947-3); disk 29.95 (0-7933-5949-X) Gallopade Intl.

— Mississippi 2000! Coming Soon to a Calendar Near You - The 21st Century! - Complete Set of AL 2000 Items. (Two Thousand! Ser.). (Illus.). (J). (gr. 3-12). 1998. pap. 75.00 (0-7933-9357-4); lib. bdg. 85.00 (0-7933-9358-2) Gallopade Intl.

— Mississippi 2000! Coming Soon to a Calendar near You--The 21st Century! (Two Thousand! Ser.). (Illus.). (J). (gr. 3-12). 1998. pap. 19.95 (0-7933-8748-5); lib. bdg. 29.95 (0-7933-8747-7) Gallopade Intl.

— Mississippi UFO's & Extraterrestrials! A Look at the Sightings & Science in Our State. (Carole Marsh Mississippi Bks.). (Illus.). (J). (gr. 3-12). 1997. pap. 19.95 (0-7933-6407-8); lib. bdg. 29.95 (0-7933-6406-X) Gallopade Intl.

— Mississippi's (Most Devastating!) Disasters & (Most Calamitous!) Catastrophies! (Carole Marsh Mississippi Bks.). (Illus.). (J). (gr. 3 up). 1994. pap. 19.95 (0-7933-0643-4); lib. bdg. 29.95 (0-7933-0645-0); disk 29.95 (0-7933-0646-9) Gallopade Intl.

— Mississippi's Unsolved Mysteries (& Their "Solutions") Includes Scientific Information & Other Activities for Students. (Carole Marsh Mississippi Bks.). (Illus.). (J). (gr. 3-12). 1994. pap. 19.95 (0-7933-5795-0); lib. bdg. 29.95 (0-7933-5794-2); disk 29.95 (0-7933-5796-9) Gallopade Intl.

— Missouri & Other State Greats (Biographies) (Carole Marsh Missouri Bks.). (Illus.). (J). (gr. 3 up). 1994. pap. 19.95 (1-55609-749-2); lib. bdg. 29.95 (1-55609-748-4); disk 29.95 (1-55609-750-6) Gallopade Intl.

— Missouri Bandits, Bushwackers, Outlaws, Crooks, Devils, Ghosts, Desperadoes & Other Assorted & Sundry Characters! (Carole Marsh Missouri Bks.). (Illus.). (J). (gr. 3 up). 1994. pap. 19.95 (0-7933-0671-X); lib. bdg. 29.95 (0-7933-0672-8); disk 29.95 (0-7933-0673-6) Gallopade Intl.

— Missouri "BIO" Bingo! 24 Must Know State People for Kids to Learn about While Having Fun! (Bingo! Ser.). (Illus.). (J). (gr. 2-8). 1998. pap. 14.95 (0-7933-8597-0) Gallopade Intl.

— The Missouri Bookstore Book: A Surprising Guide to Our

State's Bookstores & Their Specialties for Students, Teachers, Writers & Publishers. (Carole Marsh Missouri Bks.). (Illus.). 1994. pap. 19.95 (*0-7933-2931-0*); lib. bdg. 29.95 (*0-7933-2930-2*); disk 29.95 (*0-7933-2932-9*) Gallopade Intl.

— Missouri Classic Christmas Trivia: Stories, Recipes, Activities, Legends, Lore & More. (Carole Marsh Missouri Bks.). (Illus.). (J). (gr. 3 up). 1994. pap. 19.95 (*0-7933-0674-4*); lib. bdg. 29.95 (*0-7933-0675-2*); disk 29.95 (*0-7933-0676-0*) Gallopade Intl.

— Missouri Coastales. (Carole Marsh Missouri Bks.). (J). 1994. lib. bdg. 29.95 (*0-7933-7290-9*) Gallopade Intl.

— Missouri Coastales. (Carole Marsh Missouri Bks.). (Illus.). (J). (gr. 3 up). 1994. pap. 19.95 (*1-55609-743-3*); lib. bdg. 29.95 (*1-55609-742-5*); disk 29.95 (*1-55609-744-1*) Gallopade Intl.

— Missouri "Crinkum-Crankum" A Funny Word Book about Our State. (Carole Marsh Missouri Bks.). (Illus.). (J). 1994. pap. 19.95 (*0-7933-4884-6*); lib. bdg. 29.95 (*0-7933-4883-8*); disk 29.95 (*0-7933-4885-4*) Gallopade Intl.

— Missouri Dingbats! Bk. 1: A Fun Book of Games, Stories, Activities & More about Our State That's All in Code! for You to Decipher. (Carole Marsh Missouri Bks.). (Illus.). (J). (gr. 3-12). 1994. pap. 19.95 (*0-7933-3849-2*); lib. bdg. 29.95 (*0-7933-3848-4*); disk 29.95 (*0-7933-3850-6*) Gallopade Intl.

***Marsh, Carole.** The Missouri Experience Pocket Guide. (Missouri Experience! Ser.). (Illus.). (J). 2000. pap. 6.95 (*0-7933-9570-4*) Gallopade Intl.

Marsh, Carole. Missouri Facts & Factivities. (Carole Marsh State Bks.). (Illus.). (J). (gr. 4-7). 1996. pap., teacher ed. 19.95 (*0-7933-7897-4*, C Marsh) Gallopade Intl.

— Missouri Festival Fun for Kids! (Carole Marsh Missouri Bks.). (Illus.). (J). (gr. 3-12). 1994. pap. 19.95 (*0-7933-4002-0*); lib. bdg. 29.95 (*0-7933-4001-2*) Gallopade Intl.

— Missouri Festival Fun for Kids! (Carole Marsh Missouri Bks.). (Illus.). (YA). (gr. 3-12). 1994. disk 29.95 (*0-7933-4003-9*) Gallopade Intl.

— Missouri "GEO" Bingo! 38 Must Know State Geography Facts for Kids to Learn While Having Fun! (Bingo! Ser.). (Illus.). (J). (gr. 2-8). 1998. pap. 14.95 (*0-7933-8598-9*) Gallopade Intl.

— Missouri Government! The Cornerstone of Everyday Life in Our State! (Carole Marsh Missouri Bks.). (Illus.). (J). (gr. 3-12). 1996. pap. 19.95 (*0-7933-6257-1*); lib. bdg. 29.95 (*0-7933-6256-3*); disk 29.95 (*0-7933-6258-X*) Gallopade Intl.

— Missouri "HISTO" Bingo! 42 Must Know State History Facts for Kids to Learn While Having Fun! (Bingo! Ser.). (Illus.). (J). (gr. 2-8). 1998. pap. 14.95 (*0-7933-8599-7*) Gallopade Intl.

— Missouri History! Surprising Secrets about Our State's Founding Mothers, Fathers & Kids! (Carole Marsh Missouri Bks.). (Illus.). (J). (gr. 3-12). 1996. pap. 19.95 (*0-7933-6104-4*); lib. bdg. 29.95 (*0-7933-6103-6*); disk 29.95 (*0-7933-6105-2*) Gallopade Intl.

— The Missouri Hot Air Balloon Mystery. (Carole Marsh Missouri Bks.). (Illus.). (J). (gr. 2-9). 1994. 29.95 (*0-7933-2543-9*); pap. 19.95 (*0-7933-2544-7*); disk 29.95 (*0-7933-2545-5*) Gallopade Intl.

— Missouri Hot Zones! Viruses, Diseases, & Epidemics in Our State's History. (Hot Zones! Ser.). (Illus.). (J). (gr. 3-12). 1998. pap. 19.95 (*0-7933-8904-6*); lib. bdg. 29.95 (*0-7933-8903-8*) Gallopade Intl.

— Missouri Indian Dictionary for Kids! (Carole Marsh State Bks.). (J). (gr. 2-9). 1996. 29.95 (*0-7933-7719-6*, C Marsh); pap. 19.95 (*0-7933-7720-X*, C Marsh) Gallopade Intl.

***Marsh, Carole.** Missouri Jeopardy. (Missouri Experience! Ser.). (Illus.). (J). (gr. 2-6). 2000. pap. 7.95 (*0-7933-9572-0*) Gallopade Intl.

Marsh, Carole. Missouri Jeopardy! Answers & Questions about Our State! (Carole Marsh Missouri Bks.). (Illus.). (J). (gr. 3-12). 1994. pap. 19.95 (*0-7933-4155-8*); lib. bdg. 29.95 (*0-7933-4154-X*); disk 29.95 (*0-7933-4156-6*) Gallopade Intl.

***Marsh, Carole.** Missouri Jography. (Missouri Experience! Ser.). (Illus.). (J). (gr. 2-6). 2000. pap. 7.95 (*0-7933-9573-9*) Gallopade Intl.

Marsh, Carole. Missouri "Jography" A Fun Run Thru Our State. (Carole Marsh Missouri Bks.). (Illus.). (J). (gr. 3 up). 1994. pap. 19.95 (*1-55609-731-X*); lib. bdg. 29.95 (*1-55609-730-1*); disk 29.95 (*1-55609-732-8*) Gallopade Intl.

— Missouri Kid's Cookbook: Recipes, How-To, History, Lore & More. (Carole Marsh Missouri Bks.). (Illus.). (J). (gr. 3 up). 1994. pap. 19.95 (*0-7933-0683-3*); lib. bdg. 29.95 (*0-7933-0684-1*); disk 29.95 (*0-7933-0685-X*) Gallopade Intl.

— The Missouri Library Book: A Surprising Guide to the Unusual Special Collections in Libraries Across Our State for Students, Teachers, Writers & Publishers - Includes Reproducible Mailing Labels Plus Activities for Young People! (Carole Marsh Missouri Bks.). (Illus.). 1994. pap. 19.95 (*0-7933-3081-5*); lib. bdg. 29.95 (*0-7933-3080-7*); disk 29.95 (*0-7933-3082-3*) Gallopade Intl.

— Missouri Math! How It All Adds up in Our State. (Carole Marsh Missouri Bks.). (Illus.). (YA). (gr. 3-12). 1996. pap. 19.95 (*0-7933-6563-5*); lib. bdg. 29.95 (*0-7933-6562-7*) Gallopade Intl.

— The Missouri Media Book: A Surprising Guide to the Amazing Print, Broadcast & Online Media of Our State for Students, Teachers, Writers & Publishers - Includes Reproducible Mailing Labels Plus Activities for Young People! (Carole Marsh Missouri Bks.). (Illus.). 1994. pap. 19.95 (*0-7933-3237-0*); lib. bdg. 29.95 (*0-7933-3236-2*); disk 29.95 (*0-7933-3238-9*) Gallopade Intl.

— The Missouri Mystery Van Takes Off! Bk. 1: Handicapped Missouri Kids Sneak off on a Big Adventure. (Carole Marsh Missouri Bks.). (Illus.). (J). (gr. 3-12). 1994. 29.95 (*0-7933-5036-0*); pap. 19.95 (*0-7933-5037-9*); disk 29.95 (*0-7933-5038-7*) Gallopade Intl.

— Missouri Quiz Bowl Crash Course! (Carole Marsh Missouri Bks.). (Illus.). (J). (gr. 3 up). 1994. pap. 19.95 (*1-55609-746-8*); lib. bdg. 29.95 (*1-55609-745-X*); disk 29.95 (*1-55609-747-6*) Gallopade Intl.

— Missouri Rollercoasters! (Carole Marsh Missouri Bks.). (Illus.). (J). (gr. 3-12). 1994. pap. 19.95 (*0-7933-5300-9*); lib. bdg. 29.95 (*0-7933-5299-1*) Gallopade Intl.

— Missouri Rollercoasters! (Carole Marsh Missouri Bks.). (Illus.). (YA). (gr. 3-12). 1994. disk 29.95 (*0-7933-5301-7*) Gallopade Intl.

— Missouri School Trivia: An Amazing & Fascinating Look at Our State's Teachers, Schools & Students! (Carole Marsh Missouri Bks.). (Illus.). (J). (gr. 3 up). 1994. pap. 19.95 (*0-7933-0680-9*); lib. bdg. 29.95 (*0-7933-0681-7*); disk 29.95 (*0-7933-0682-5*) Gallopade Intl.

— Missouri Silly Basketball Sportsmysteries, Vol. I. (Carole Marsh Missouri Bks.). (Illus.). (J). (gr. 3 up). 1994. pap. 19.95 (*0-7933-0677-9*); lib. bdg. 29.95 (*0-7933-0678-7*) Gallopade Intl.

— Missouri Silly Basketball Sportsmysteries, Vol. I. (Carole Marsh Missouri Bks.). (Illus.). (J). (gr. 3 up). 1997. disk 29.95 (*0-7933-0679-5*) Gallopade Intl.

— Missouri Silly Basketball Sportsmysteries, Vol. II. (Carole Marsh Missouri Bks.). (Illus.). (J). (gr. 3 up). 1994. pap. 19.95 (*0-7933-1741-X*); lib. bdg. 29.95 (*0-7933-1740-1*); disk 29.95 (*0-7933-1742-8*) Gallopade Intl.

— Missouri Silly Football Sportsmysteries, Vol. I. (Carole Marsh Missouri Bks.). (Illus.). (J). (gr. 3 up). 1994. pap. 19.95 (*1-55609-737-9*); lib. bdg. 29.95 (*1-55609-736-0*) Gallopade Intl.

— Missouri Silly Football Sportsmysteries, Vol. II. (Carole Marsh Missouri Bks.). (Illus.). (J). (gr. 3 up). 1994. pap. 19.95 (*1-55609-740-9*); lib. bdg. 29.95 (*1-55609-739-5*); disk 29.95 (*1-55609-741-7*) Gallopade Intl.

— Missouri Silly Trivia! (Carole Marsh Missouri Bks.). (Illus.). (J). (gr. 3 up). 1994. pap. 19.95 (*1-55609-100-1*); lib. bdg. 29.95 (*1-55609-728-X*); disk 29.95 (*1-55609-729-8*) Gallopade Intl.

— Missouri Spelling Bee! Score Big by Correctly Spelling Our State's Unique Names. (Carole Marsh Missouri Bks.). (Illus.). (YA). (gr. 3-12). 1996. pap. 19.95 (*0-7933-6716-6*); lib. bdg. 29.95 (*0-7933-6715-8*) Gallopade Intl.

— Missouri Timeline: A Chronology of Missouri History, Mystery, Trivia, Legend, Lore & More. (Carole Marsh Missouri Bks.). (Illus.). (J). (gr. 3-12). 1994. pap. 19.95 (*0-7933-5951-1*); lib. bdg. 29.95 (*0-7933-5950-3*); disk 29.95 (*0-7933-5952-X*) Gallopade Intl.

— Missouri 2000! Coming Soon to a Calendar Near You - The 21st Century! - Complete Set of AL 2000 Items. (Two Thousand! Ser.). (Illus.). (J). (gr. 3-12). 1998. pap. 75.00 (*0-7933-9359-0*); lib. bdg. 85.00 (*0-7933-9360-4*) Gallopade Intl.

— Missouri 2000! Coming Soon to a Calendar near You--The 21st Century! (Two Thousand! Ser.). (Illus.). (J). (gr. 3-12). 1998. pap. 19.95 (*0-7933-8751-5*); lib. bdg. 29.95 (*0-7933-8750-7*) Gallopade Intl.

— Missouri UFO's & Extraterrestrials! A Look at the Sightings & Science in Our State. (Carole Marsh Missouri Bks.). (Illus.). (J). (gr. 3-12). 1997. pap. 19.95 (*0-7933-6410-8*); lib. bdg. 29.95 (*0-7933-6409-4*) Gallopade Intl.

***Marsh, Carole.** Missouri's Big Activity Book. (Missouri Experience! Ser.). (Illus.). (J). (gr. k-5). 2000. pap. 9.95 (*0-7933-9574-7*) Gallopade Intl.

Marsh, Carole. Missouri's (Most Devastating!) Disasters & (Most Calamitous!) Catastrophies! (Carole Marsh Missouri Bks.). (Illus.). (J). (gr. 3 up). 1994. pap. 19.95 (*0-7933-0668-X*); lib. bdg. 29.95 (*0-7933-0669-8*); disk 29.95 (*0-7933-0670-1*) Gallopade Intl.

— Missouri's Unsolved Mysteries (& Their "Solutions") Includes Scientific Information & Other Activities for Students. (Carole Marsh Missouri Bks.). (Illus.). (J). (gr. 3-12). 1994. pap. 19.95 (*0-7933-5798-5*); lib. bdg. 29.95 (*0-7933-5797-7*); disk 29.95 (*0-7933-5799-3*) Gallopade Intl.

— The Monsters, Vampires & Werewolves Dingbats Book. (Carole Marsh Dingbats Bks.). (Illus.). (J). (gr. 3-12). 1994. pap. 19.95 (*0-7933-5393-9*); lib. bdg. 29.95 (*0-7933-5392-0*); disk 29.95 (*0-7933-5394-7*) Gallopade Intl.

— Montana & Other State Greats (Biographies) (Carole Marsh Montana Bks.). (Illus.). (J). (gr. 3 up). 1994. pap. 19.95 (*1-55609-773-5*); lib. bdg. 29.95 (*1-55609-772-7*); disk 29.95 (*1-55609-774-3*) Gallopade Intl.

— Montana Bandits, Bushwackers, Outlaws, Crooks, Devils, Ghosts, Desperadoes & Other Assorted & Sundry Characters! (Carole Marsh Montana Bks.). (Illus.). (J). (gr. 3 up). 1994. pap. 19.95 (*0-7933-0696-5*); lib. bdg. 29.95 (*0-7933-0697-3*); disk 29.95 (*0-7933-0698-1*) Gallopade Intl.

— Montana "BIO" Bingo! 24 Must Know State People for Kids to Learn about While Having Fun! (Bingo! Ser.). (Illus.). (J). (gr. 2-8). 1998. pap. 14.95 (*0-7933-8600-4*) Gallopade Intl.

— The Montana Bookstore Book: A Surprising Guide to Our State's Bookstores & Their Specialties for Students, Teachers, Writers & Publishers. (Carole Marsh Montana Bks.). (Illus.). 1994. pap. 19.95 (*0-7933-2934-5*); lib. bdg. 29.95 (*0-7933-2933-7*); disk 29.95 (*0-7933-2935-3*) Gallopade Intl.

— Montana Classic Christmas Trivia. (Carole Marsh Montana Bks.). (J). (gr. 3 up). 1994. pap. 19.95 (*0-7933-0699-X*); lib. bdg. 29.95 (*0-7933-0700-7*); disk 29.95 (*0-7933-0701-5*) Gallopade Intl.

— Montana Coastales. (Carole Marsh Montana Bks.). (J). 1994. lib. bdg. 29.95 (*0-7933-7291-7*) Gallopade Intl.

— Montana Coastales. (Carole Marsh Montana Bks.). (Illus.). (J). (gr. 3 up). 1994. pap. 19.95 (*1-55609-767-0*); lib. bdg. 29.95 (*1-55609-766-2*); disk 29.95 (*1-55609-768-9*) Gallopade Intl.

— Montana "Crinkum-Crankum" A Funny Word Book about Our State. (Carole Marsh Montana Bks.). (Illus.). (J). 1994. pap. 19.95 (*0-7933-4887-0*); lib. bdg. 29.95 (*0-7933-4886-2*); disk 29.95 (*0-7933-4888-9*) Gallopade Intl.

— Montana Dingbats! Bk. 1: A Fun Book of Games, Stories, Activities & More about Our State That's All in Code! for You to Decipher. (Carole Marsh Montana Bks.). (Illus.). (J). (gr. 3-12). 1994. pap. 19.95 (*0-7933-3852-2*); lib. bdg. 29.95 (*0-7933-3851-4*); disk 29.95 (*0-7933-3853-0*) Gallopade Intl.

— Montana Facts & Factivities. (Carole Marsh State Bks.). (Illus.). (J). (gr. 4-7). 1996. pap., teacher ed. 19.95 (*0-7933-7899-0*, C Marsh) Gallopade Intl.

— Montana Festival Fun for Kids! (Carole Marsh Montana Bks.). (Illus.). (J). (gr. 3-12). 1994. pap. 19.95 (*0-7933-4005-5*); lib. bdg. 29.95 (*0-7933-4004-7*) Gallopade Intl.

— Montana Festival Fun for Kids! (Carole Marsh Montana Bks.). (Illus.). (YA). (gr. 3-12). 1994. disk 29.95 (*0-7933-4006-3*) Gallopade Intl.

— Montana "GEO" Bingo! 38 Must Know State Geography Facts for Kids to Learn While Having Fun! (Bingo! Ser.). (Illus.). (J). (gr. 2-8). 1998. pap. 14.95 (*0-7933-8601-2*) Gallopade Intl.

— Montana Government! The Cornerstone of Everyday Life in Our State! (Carole Marsh Montana Bks.). (Illus.). (J). (gr. 3-12). 1996. pap. 19.95 (*0-7933-6260-1*); lib. bdg. 29.95 (*0-7933-6259-8*); disk 29.95 (*0-7933-6261-X*) Gallopade Intl.

— Montana "HISTO" Bingo! 42 Must Know State History Facts for Kids to Learn While Having Fun! (Bingo! Ser.). (Illus.). (J). (gr. 2-8). 1998. pap. 14.95 (*0-7933-8602-0*) Gallopade Intl.

— Montana History! Surprising Secrets about Our State's Founding Mothers, Fathers & Kids! (Carole Marsh Montana Bks.). (Illus.). (J). (gr. 3-12). 1996. pap. 19.95 (*0-7933-6107-9*); lib. bdg. 29.95 (*0-7933-6106-0*); disk 29.95 (*0-7933-6108-7*) Gallopade Intl.

— The Montana Hot Air Balloon Mystery. (Carole Marsh Montana Bks.). (Illus.). (J). (gr. 2-9). 1994. 29.95 (*0-7933-2552-8*); pap. 19.95 (*0-7933-2553-6*); disk 29.95 (*0-7933-2554-4*) Gallopade Intl.

— Montana Hot Zones! Viruses, Disease, & Epidemics in Our State's History. (Hot Zones! Ser.). (Illus.). (J). (gr. 3-12). 1998. pap. 19.95 (*0-7933-8907-0*); lib. bdg. 29.95 (*0-7933-8906-2*) Gallopade Intl.

— Montana Indian Dictionary for Kids! (Carole Marsh State Bks.). (J). (gr. 2-9). 1996. 29.95 (*0-7933-7722-6*, C Marsh); pap. 19.95 (*0-7933-7723-4*, C Marsh) Gallopade Intl.

— Montana Jeopardy! Answers & Questions about Our State! (Carole Marsh Montana Bks.). (Illus.). (J). (gr. 3-12). 1994. pap. 19.95 (*0-7933-4158-2*); lib. bdg. 29.95 (*0-7933-4157-4*); disk 29.95 (*0-7933-4159-0*) Gallopade Intl.

— Montana "Jography" A Fun Run Thru Our State. (Carole Marsh Montana Bks.). (Illus.). (J). (gr. 3 up). 1994. pap. 19.95 (*1-55609-755-7*); lib. bdg. 29.95 (*1-55609-754-9*); disk 29.95 (*1-55609-756-5*) Gallopade Intl.

— Montana Kid's Cookbook: Recipes, How-To, History, Lore & More. (Carole Marsh Montana Bks.). (Illus.). (J). (gr. 3 up). 1994. pap. 19.95 (*0-7933-0708-2*); lib. bdg. 29.95 (*0-7933-0709-0*); disk 29.95 (*0-7933-0710-4*) Gallopade Intl.

— The Montana Library Book: A Surprising Guide to the Unusual Special Collections in Libraries Across Our State for Students, Teachers, Writers & Publishers - Includes Reproducible Mailing Labels Plus Activities for Young People! (Carole Marsh Montana Bks.). (Illus.). 1994. pap. 19.95 (*0-7933-3084-X*); lib. bdg. 29.95 (*0-7933-3083-1*); disk 29.95 (*0-7933-3085-8*) Gallopade Intl.

— Montana Math! How It All Adds up in Our State. (Carole Marsh Montana Bks.). (Illus.). (YA). (gr. 3-12). 1996. pap. 19.95 (*0-7933-6566-X*); lib. bdg. 29.95 (*0-7933-6565-1*) Gallopade Intl.

— The Montana Media Book: A Surprising Guide to the Amazing Print, Broadcast & Online Media of Our State for Students, Teachers, Writers & Publishers - Includes Reproducible Mailing Labels Plus Activities for Young People! (Carole Marsh Montana Bks.). (Illus.). 1994. pap. 19.95 (*0-7933-3240-0*); lib. bdg. 29.95 (*0-7933-3239-7*); disk 29.95 (*0-7933-3241-9*) Gallopade Intl.

— The Montana Mystery Van Takes Off! Bk. 1: Handicapped Montana Kids Sneak off on a Big Adventure. (Carole Marsh Montana Bks.). (Illus.). (J). (gr. 3-12). 1994. 29.95 (*0-7933-5039-5*); pap. 19.95 (*0-7933-5040-9*); disk 29.95 (*0-7933-5041-7*) Gallopade Intl.

— Montana Quiz Bowl Crash Course! (Carole Marsh Montana Bks.). (Illus.). (J). (gr. 3 up). 1994. pap. 19.95 (*1-55609-770-0*); lib. bdg. 29.95 (*1-55609-769-7*); disk 29.95 (*1-55609-771-9*) Gallopade Intl.

— Montana Rollercoasters! (Carole Marsh Montana Bks.). (Illus.). (J). (gr. 3-12). 1994. pap. 19.95 (*0-7933-5303-3*); lib. bdg. 29.95 (*0-7933-5302-5*) Gallopade Intl.

— Montana Rollercoasters! (Carole Marsh Montana Bks.). (Illus.). (YA). (gr. 3-12). 1994. disk 29.95 (*0-7933-5304-1*) Gallopade Intl.

— Montana School Trivia: An Amazing & Fascinating Look at Our State's Teachers, Schools & Students! (Carole Marsh Montana Bks.). (Illus.). (J). (gr. 3 up). 1994. pap. 19.95 (*0-7933-0705-8*); lib. bdg. 29.95 (*0-7933-0706-6*); disk 29.95 (*0-7933-0707-4*) Gallopade Intl.

— Montana Silly Basketball Sportsmysteries, Vol. I. (Carole Marsh Montana Bks.). (Illus.). (J). (gr. 3 up). 1994. pap. 19.95 (*0-7933-0702-3*); lib. bdg. 29.95 (*0-7933-0703-1*); disk 29.95 (*0-7933-0704-X*) Gallopade Intl.

— Montana Silly Basketball Sportsmysteries, Vol. II. (Carole Marsh Montana Bks.). (Illus.). (J). (gr. 3 up). 1994. pap. 19.95 (*0-7933-1750-9*); lib. bdg. 29.95 (*0-7933-1749-5*); disk 29.95 (*0-7933-1751-7*) Gallopade Intl.

— Montana Silly Football Sportsmysteries, Vol. I. (Carole Marsh Montana Bks.). (Illus.). (J). (gr. 3 up). 1994. pap. 19.95 (*1-55609-761-1*); lib. bdg. 29.95 (*1-55609-760-3*); disk 29.95 (*1-55609-762-X*) Gallopade Intl.

— Montana Silly Football Sportsmysteries, Vol. II. (Carole Marsh Montana Bks.). (Illus.). (J). (gr. 3 up). 1994. pap. 19.95 (*1-55609-764-6*); lib. bdg. 29.95 (*1-55609-763-8*); disk 29.95 (*1-55609-765-4*) Gallopade Intl.

— Montana Silly Trivia! (Carole Marsh Montana Bks.). (Illus.). (J). (gr. 3 up). 1994. pap. 19.95 (*1-55609-752-2*); lib. bdg. 29.95 (*1-55609-751-4*); disk 29.95 (*1-55609-753-0*) Gallopade Intl.

— Montana Spelling Bee! Score Big by Correctly Spelling Our State's Unique Names. (Carole Marsh Montana Bks.). (Illus.). (YA). (gr. 3-12). 1996. pap. 19.95 (*0-7933-6719-0*); lib. bdg. 29.95 (*0-7933-6718-2*) Gallopade Intl.

— Montana Timeline: A Chronology of Montana History, Mystery, Trivia, Legend, Lore & More. (Carole Marsh Montana Bks.). (Illus.). (J). (gr. 3-12). 1994. pap. 19.95 (*0-7933-5954-6*); lib. bdg. 29.95 (*0-7933-5953-8*); disk 29.95 (*0-7933-5955-4*) Gallopade Intl.

— Montana 2000! Coming Soon to a Calendar Near You - The 21st Century! - Complete Set of AL 2000 Items. (Two Thousand! Ser.). (Illus.). (J). (gr. 3-12). 1998. pap. 75.00 (*0-7933-9361-2*); lib. bdg. 85.00 (*0-7933-9362-0*) Gallopade Intl.

— Montana 2000! Coming Soon to a Calendar near You--The 21st Century! (Two Thousand! Ser.). (Illus.). (J). (gr. 3-12). 1998. pap. 19.95 (*0-7933-8754-X*); lib. bdg. 29.95 (*0-7933-8753-1*) Gallopade Intl.

— Montana UFO's & Extraterrestrials! A Look at the Sightings & Science in Our State. (Carole Marsh Montana Bks.). (Illus.). (J). (gr. 3-12). 1997. pap. 19.95 (*0-7933-6413-2*); lib. bdg. 29.95 (*0-7933-6412-4*) Gallopade Intl.

— Montana's (Most Devastating!) Disasters & (Most Calamitous!) Catastrophies! (Carole Marsh Montana Bks.). (Illus.). (J). (gr. 3 up). 1994. pap. 19.95 (*0-7933-0692-2*); lib. bdg. 29.95 (*0-7933-0694-9*); disk 29.95 (*0-7933-0695-7*) Gallopade Intl.

— Montana's Unsolved Mysteries (& Their "Solutions") Includes Scientific Information & Other Activities for Students. (Carole Marsh Montana Bks.). (Illus.). (J). (gr. 3-12). 1994. pap. 19.95 (*0-7933-5801-9*); lib. bdg. 29.95 (*0-7933-5800-0*); disk 29.95 (*0-7933-5802-7*) Gallopade Intl.

— Multipreneur: How a Self-Published Writer Parlayed a Single Children's Mystery into 176 Companies. (MYOB Ser.). (Illus.). 1994. pap. 19.95 (*0-7933-4389-5*); lib. bdg. 29.95 (*0-7933-4388-7*) Gallopade Intl.

— Multipreneur: How a Self-Published Writer Parlayed a Single Children's Mystery into 176 Companies. (MYOB Ser.). (Illus.). 1997. disk 29.95 (*0-7933-4390-9*) Gallopade Intl.

— Mushroom on Mars Hill! The Lowell Observatory & the Discovery of Pluto. (Interactive Multimedia Titles Ser.). (J). (gr. 2-9). 1995. 29.95 (*0-7933-7592-4*, C Marsh); pap. 19.95 (*0-7933-7593-2*, C Marsh) Gallopade Intl.

— Mushroom on Mars Hill! The Lowell Observatory & the Discovery of Pluto. (Interactive Multimedia Titles Ser.). (J). (gr. 2-9). 1996. pap., teacher ed. 19.95 (*0-7933-7837-0*, C Marsh) Gallopade Intl.

— My First Book about Alabama. (Carole Marsh Alabama Bks.). (J). (gr. k-4). 1994. pap. 19.95 (*0-7933-5570-2*); lib. bdg. 29.95 (*0-7933-5569-9*); disk 29.95 (*0-7933-5571-0*) Gallopade Intl.

— My First Book about Alaska. (Carole Marsh Alaska Bks.). (J). (gr. k-4). 1994. pap. 19.95 (*0-7933-5573-7*); lib. bdg. 29.95 (*0-7933-5572-9*); disk 29.95 (*0-7933-5574-5*) Gallopade Intl.

— My First Book about Arizona. (Carole Marsh Arizona Bks.). (J). (gr. k-4). 1994. pap. 19.95 (*0-7933-5576-1*); lib. bdg. 29.95 (*0-7933-5575-3*); disk 29.95 (*0-7933-5577-X*) Gallopade Intl.

— My First Book about Arkansas. (Carole Marsh Arkansas Bks.). (J). (gr. k-4). 1994. pap. 19.95 (*0-7933-5579-6*); lib. bdg. 29.95 (*0-7933-5578-8*); disk 29.95 (*0-7933-5580-X*) Gallopade Intl.

— My First Book about California. (Carole Marsh California Bks.). (J). (gr. k-4). 1994. pap. 19.95 (*0-7933-5582-6*); lib. bdg. 29.95 (*0-7933-5581-8*); disk 29.95 (*0-7933-5583-4*) Gallopade Intl.

***Marsh, Carole.** My First Book about California. (California Experience! Ser.). (Illus.). (J). (gr. 2-6). 2000. pap. 7.95 (*0-7933-9503-8*) Gallopade Intl.

Marsh, Carole. My First Book about Colorado. (Carole Marsh Colorado Bks.). (J). (gr. k-4). 1994. pap. 19.95 (*0-7933-5585-0*); lib. bdg. 29.95 (*0-7933-5584-2*); disk 29.95 (*0-7933-5586-9*) Gallopade Intl.

***Marsh, Carole.** My First Book about Colorado. (Colorado Experience! Ser.). (Illus.). (J). (gr. 2-6). 2000. pap. 7.95 (*0-7933-9603-4*) Gallopade Intl.

Marsh, Carole. My First Book about Connecticut. (Carole Marsh Connecticut Bks.). (J). (gr. k-4). 1994. pap. 19.95 (*0-7933-5588-5*); lib. bdg. 29.95 (*0-7933-5587-7*); disk 29.95 (*0-7933-5589-3*) Gallopade Intl.

***Marsh, Carole.** My First Book about Connecticut. (Connecticut Experience! Ser.). (Illus.). (J). (gr. 2-6). 2000. pap. 7.95 (*0-7933-9579-8*) Gallopade Intl.

Marsh, Carole. My First Book about Delaware. (Carole Marsh Delaware Bks.). (J). (gr. k-4). 1994. pap. 19.95 (*0-7933-5591-5*); lib. bdg. 29.95 (*0-7933-5590-7*); disk 29.95 (*0-7933-5592-3*) Gallopade Intl.

— My First Book about Florida. (Carole Marsh Florida

M

Bks.). (J). (gr. k-4). 1994. pap. 19.95 (*0-7933-5597-4*); lib. bdg. 29.95 (*0-7933-5596-6*); disk 29.95 (*0-7933-5598-2*) Gallopade Intl.

***Marsh, Carole.** My First Book about Florida. (Florida Experience! Ser.). (Illus.). (J). (gr. 2-6). 2000. pap. 7.95 (*0-7933-9506-2*) Gallopade Intl.

Marsh, Carole. My First Book about Georgia. (Carole Marsh Georgia Bks.). (J). (gr. k-4). 1994. pap. 19.95 (*0-7933-5600-8*); lib. bdg. 29.95 (*0-7933-5599-0*); disk 29.95 (*0-7933-5601-6*) Gallopade Intl.

***Marsh, Carole.** My First Book about Georgia. (Georgia Experience! Ser.). (Illus.). (J). (gr. 2-6). 2000. pap. 7.95 (*0-7933-9509-7*) Gallopade Intl.

Marsh, Carole. My First Book about Hawaii. (Carole Marsh Hawaii Bks.). (J). (gr. k-4). 1994. pap. 19.95 (*0-7933-5603-2*); lib. bdg. 29.95 (*0-7933-5602-4*); disk 29.95 (*0-7933-5604-0*) Gallopade Intl.

— My First Book about Idaho. (Carole Marsh Idaho Bks.). (J). (gr. k-4). 1994. pap. 19.95 (*0-7933-5606-7*); lib. bdg. 29.95 (*0-7933-5605-9*); disk 29.95 (*0-7933-5607-5*) Gallopade Intl.

— My First Book about Illinois. (Carole Marsh Illinois Bks.). (J). (gr. k-4). 1994. pap. 19.95 (*0-7933-5609-1*); lib. bdg. 29.95 (*0-7933-5608-3*); disk 29.95 (*0-7933-5610-5*) Gallopade Intl.

M

***Marsh, Carole.** My First Book about Illinois. (Illinois Experience! Ser.). (Illus.). (J). (gr. 2-6). 2000. pap. 7.95 (*0-7933-9512-7*) Gallopade Intl.

Marsh, Carole. My First Book about Indiana. (Carole Marsh Indiana Bks.). (J). (gr. k-4). 1994. pap. 19.95 (*0-7933-5612-1*); lib. bdg. 29.95 (*0-7933-5611-3*); disk 29.95 (*0-7933-5613-X*) Gallopade Intl.

— My First Book about Iowa. (Carole Marsh Iowa Bks.). (J). (gr. k-4). 1994. pap. 19.95 (*0-7933-5615-6*); lib. bdg. 29.95 (*0-7933-5614-8*); disk 29.95 (*0-7933-5616-4*) Gallopade Intl.

— My First Book about Kansas. (Carole Marsh Kansas Bks.). (J). (gr. k-4). 1994. pap. 19.95 (*0-7933-5618-0*); lib. bdg. 29.95 (*0-7933-5617-2*); disk 29.95 (*0-7933-5619-9*) Gallopade Intl.

— My First Book about Kentucky. (Carole Marsh Kentucky Bks.). (J). (gr. k-4). 1994. pap. 19.95 (*0-7933-5621-0*); lib. bdg. 29.95 (*0-7933-5620-2*); disk 29.95 (*0-7933-5622-9*) Gallopade Intl.

***Marsh, Carole.** My First Book about Kentucky. (Kentucky Experience! Ser.). (Illus.). (J). (gr. 2-6). 2000. pap. 7.95 (*0-7933-9515-1*) Gallopade Intl.

Marsh, Carole. My First Book about Louisiana. (Carole Marsh Louisiana Bks.). (J). (gr. k-4). 1994. pap. 19.95 (*0-7933-5624-5*); lib. bdg. 29.95 (*0-7933-5623-7*); disk 29.95 (*0-7933-5625-3*) Gallopade Intl.

***Marsh, Carole.** My First Book about Louisiana. (Louisiana Experience! Ser.). (Illus.). (J). (gr. 2-6). 2000. pap. 7.95 (*0-7933-9547-X*) Gallopade Intl.

Marsh, Carole. My First Book about Maine. (Carole Marsh Maine Bks.). (J). (gr. k-4). 1994. pap. 19.95 (*0-7933-5627-X*); lib. bdg. 29.95 (*0-7933-5626-1*); disk 29.95 (*0-7933-5628-8*) Gallopade Intl.

— My First Book about Maryland. (Carole Marsh Maryland Bks.). (J). (gr. k-4). 1994. pap. 19.95 (*0-7933-5630-X*); lib. bdg. 29.95 (*0-7933-5629-6*); disk 29.95 (*0-7933-5631-8*) Gallopade Intl.

***Marsh, Carole.** My First Book about Maryland. (Maryland Experience! Ser.). (Illus.). (J). (gr. 2-6). 2000. pap. 7.95 (*0-7933-9611-5*) Gallopade Intl.

Marsh, Carole. My First Book about Massachusetts. (Massachuseets Bks.). (J). (gr. k-4). 1994. pap. 19.95 (*0-7933-5633-4*); lib. bdg. 29.95 (*0-7933-5632-6*); disk 29.95 (*0-7933-5634-2*) Gallopade Intl.

— My First Book about Michigan. (Carole Marsh Michigan Bks.). (J). (gr. k-4). 1994. pap. 19.95 (*0-7933-5636-9*); lib. bdg. 29.95 (*0-7933-5635-0*); disk 29.95 (*0-7933-5637-7*) Gallopade Intl.

***Marsh, Carole.** My First Book about Michigan. (Michigan Experience! Ser.). (Illus.). (J). (gr. 2-6). 2000. pap. 7.95 (*0-7933-9563-1*) Gallopade Intl.

Marsh, Carole. My First Book about Minnesota. (Carole Marsh Minnesota Bks.). (J). (gr. k-4). 1994. pap. 19.95 (*0-7933-5639-3*); lib. bdg. 29.95 (*0-7933-5638-5*); disk 29.95 (*0-7933-5640-7*) Gallopade Intl.

— My First Book about Mississippi. (Carole Marsh Mississippi Bks.). (J). (gr. k-4). 1994. pap. 19.95 (*0-7933-5642-3*); lib. bdg. 29.95 (*0-7933-5641-5*); disk 29.95 (*0-7933-5643-1*) Gallopade Intl.

***Marsh, Carole.** My First Book about Mississippi. (Mississippi Experience! Ser.). (Illus.). (J). (gr. 2-6). 2000. pap. 7.95 (*0-7933-9555-0*) Gallopade Intl.

Marsh, Carole. My First Book about Missouri. (Carole Marsh Missouri Bks.). (J). (gr. k-4). 1994. pap. 19.95 (*0-7933-5645-8*); lib. bdg. 29.95 (*0-7933-5644-X*); disk 29.95 (*0-7933-5646-6*) Gallopade Intl.

***Marsh, Carole.** My First Book about Missouri. (Missouri Experience! Ser.). (Illus.). (J). (gr. 2-6). 2000. pap. 7.95 (*0-7933-9571-2*) Gallopade Intl.

Marsh, Carole. My First Book about Montana. (Carole Marsh Montana Ser.). (J). (gr. k-4). 1994. pap. 19.95 (*0-7933-5648-2*); lib. bdg. 29.95 (*0-7933-5647-4*); disk 29.95 (*0-7933-5649-0*) Gallopade Intl.

— My First Book about Nebraska. (Carole Marsh Nebraska Bks.). (J). (gr. k-4). 1994. pap. 19.95 (*0-7933-5651-2*); lib. bdg. 29.95 (*0-7933-5650-4*); disk 29.95 (*0-7933-5652-0*) Gallopade Intl.

— My First Book about Nevada. (Carole Marsh Nevada Bks.). (J). (gr. k-4). 1994. pap. 19.95 (*0-7933-5654-7*); lib. bdg. 29.95 (*0-7933-5653-9*); disk 29.95 (*0-7933-5655-5*) Gallopade Intl.

— My First Book about New Hampshire. (Carole Marsh New Hampshire Bks.). (J). (gr. k-4). 1994. pap. 19.95 (*0-7933-5657-1*); lib. bdg. 24.95 (*0-7933-5656-3*); disk 29.95 (*0-7933-5658-X*) Gallopade Intl.

— My First Book about New Jersey. (Carole Marsh New Jersey Bks.). (J). (gr. k-4). 1994. pap. 19.95 (*0-7933-5660-1*); lib. bdg. 29.95 (*0-7933-5659-8*); disk 29.95 (*0-7933-5661-X*) Gallopade Intl.

***Marsh, Carole.** My First Book about New Jersey. (New Jersey Experience! Ser.). (Illus.). (J). (gr. 2-6). 2000. pap. 7.95 (*0-7933-9521-6*) Gallopade Intl.

Marsh, Carole. My First Book about New Mexico. (Carole Marsh New Mexico Bks.). (J). (gr. k-4). 1994. pap. 19.95 (*0-7933-5663-6*); lib. bdg. 29.95 (*0-7933-5662-8*); disk 29.95 (*0-7933-5664-4*) Gallopade Intl.

— My First Book about New York. (Carole Marsh New York Bks.). (J). (gr. k-4). 1994. pap. 19.95 (*0-7933-5666-0*); lib. bdg. 29.95 (*0-7933-5665-2*); disk 29.95 (*0-7933-5667-9*) Gallopade Intl.

— My First Book about North Carolina. (Carole Marsh North Carolina Bks.). (J). (gr. k-4). 1994. pap. 19.95 (*0-7933-5669-5*); lib. bdg. 29.95 (*0-7933-5668-7*); disk 29.95 (*0-7933-5670-9*) Gallopade Intl.

***Marsh, Carole.** My First Book about North Carolina. (North Carolina Experience! Ser.). (J). (gr. 2-6). 2000. pap. 7.95 (*0-7933-9518-6*) Gallopade Intl.

Marsh, Carole. My First Book about North Dakota. (Carole Marsh North Dakota Bks.). (J). (gr. k-4). 1994. pap. 19.95 (*0-7933-5672-5*); lib. bdg. 29.95 (*0-7933-5671-7*); disk 29.95 (*0-7933-5673-3*) Gallopade Intl.

— My First Book about Ohio. (Carole Marsh Ohio Bks.). (J). (gr. k-4). 1994. pap. 19.95 (*0-7933-5675-X*); lib. bdg. 29.95 (*0-7933-5674-1*); disk 29.95 (*0-7933-5676-8*) Gallopade Intl.

***Marsh, Carole.** My First Book about Ohio. (Ohio Experience! Ser.). (Illus.). (J). (gr. 2-6). 2000. pap. 7.95 (*0-7933-9524-0*) Gallopade Intl.

Marsh, Carole. My First Book about Oklahoma. (Oklahoma Bks.). (J). (gr. k-4). 1994. pap. 19.95 (*0-7933-5678-4*); lib. bdg. 24.95 (*0-7933-5677-6*); disk 29.95 (*0-7933-5679-2*) Gallopade Intl.

***Marsh, Carole.** My First Book about Oklahoma. (Oklahoma Experience! Ser.). (Illus.). (J). (gr. 2-6). 2000. pap. 7.95 (*0-7933-9595-X*) Gallopade Intl.

Marsh, Carole. My First Book about Oregon. (Oregon Bks.). (J). (gr. k-4). 1994. pap. 19.95 (*0-7933-5681-4*); lib. bdg. 29.95 (*0-7933-5680-6*); disk 29.95 (*0-7933-5682-2*) Gallopade Intl.

— My First Book about Pennsylvania. (Pennsylvania Bks.). (J). (gr. k-4). 1994. pap. 19.95 (*0-7933-5684-9*); lib. bdg. 29.95 (*0-7933-5683-0*); disk 29.95 (*0-7933-5685-7*) Gallopade Intl.

***Marsh, Carole.** My First Book about Pennsylvania. (Pennsylvania Experience! Ser.). (Illus.). (J). (gr. 2-6). 2000. pap. 7.95 (*0-7933-9587-9*) Gallopade Intl.

Marsh, Carole. My First Book about Rhode Island. (Rhode Island Bks.). (J). (gr. k-4). 1994. pap. 19.95 (*0-7933-5687-3*); lib. bdg. 29.95 (*0-7933-5686-5*); disk 29.95 (*0-7933-5688-1*) Gallopade Intl.

— My First Book about South Carolina. (South Carolina Bks.). (J). (gr. k-4). 1994. pap. 19.95 (*0-7933-5690-3*); lib. bdg. 29.95 (*0-7933-5689-X*); disk 29.95 (*0-7933-5691-1*) Gallopade Intl.

— My First Book about South Dakota. (South Dakota Bks.). (J). (gr. k-4). 1994. pap. 19.95 (*0-7933-5693-8*); lib. bdg. 29.95 (*0-7933-5692-X*); disk 29.95 (*0-7933-5694-6*) Gallopade Intl.

— My First Book about Tennessee. (Tennessee Bks.). (J). (gr. k-4). 1994. pap. 19.95 (*0-7933-5696-2*); lib. bdg. 29.95 (*0-7933-5695-4*); disk 29.95 (*0-7933-5697-0*) Gallopade Intl.

— My First Book about Texas. (Texas Bks.). (J). (gr. k-4). 1994. pap. 19.95 (*0-7933-5699-7*); lib. bdg. 29.95 (*0-7933-5698-9*); disk 29.95 (*0-7933-5700-4*) Gallopade Intl.

***Marsh, Carole.** My First Book about Texas. (Texas Experience! Ser.). (Illus.). (J). (gr. 2-6). 2000. pap. 7.95 (*0-7933-9527-5*) Gallopade Intl.

Marsh, Carole. My First Book about Utah. (Utah Bks.). (J). (gr. k-4). 1994. pap. 19.95 (*0-7933-5702-0*); lib. bdg. 29.95 (*0-7933-5701-2*); disk 29.95 (*0-7933-5703-9*) Gallopade Intl.

— My First Book about Vermont. (Vermont Bks.). (J). (gr. k-4). 1994. pap. 19.95 (*0-7933-5705-5*); lib. bdg. 29.95 (*0-7933-5704-7*); disk 29.95 (*0-7933-5706-3*) Gallopade Intl.

— My First Book about Virginia. (Virginia Bks.). (J). (gr. k-4). 1994. pap. 19.95 (*0-7933-5708-X*); lib. bdg. 29.95 (*0-7933-5707-1*); disk 29.95 (*0-7933-5709-8*) Gallopade Intl.

***Marsh, Carole.** My First Book about Virginia. (Virginia Experience! Ser.). (Illus.). (J). (gr. 2-6). 2000. pap. 7.95 (*0-7933-9500-3*) Gallopade Intl.

Marsh, Carole. My First Book about Washington D. C. (Washington Bks.). (J). (gr. k-4). 1994. pap. 19.95 (*0-7933-5711-X*); lib. bdg. 29.95 (*0-7933-5710-1*); disk 29.95 (*0-7933-5712-8*) Gallopade Intl.

— My First Book about Washington DC. (Washington, D.C. Bks.). (J). (gr. k-4). 1994. pap. 19.95 (*0-7933-5594-X*); lib. bdg. 29.95 (*0-7933-5593-1*); disk 29.95 (*0-7933-5595-8*) Gallopade Intl.

— My First Book about West Virginia. (West Virginia Bks.). (J). (gr. k-4). 1994. pap. 19.95 (*0-7933-5714-4*); lib. bdg. 29.95 (*0-7933-5713-6*); disk 29.95 (*0-7933-5715-2*) Gallopade Intl.

— My First Book about Wisconsin. (Wisconsin Bks.). (J). (gr. k-4). 1994. pap. 19.95 (*0-7933-5717-9*); lib. bdg. 29.95 (*0-7933-5716-0*); disk 29.95 (*0-7933-5718-7*) Gallopade Intl.

***Marsh, Carole.** My First Book about Wisconsin. (Wisconsin Experience! Ser.). (Illus.). (J). (gr. 2-6). 2000. pap. 7.95 (*0-7933-9539-9*) Gallopade Intl.

Marsh, Carole. My First Book about Wyoming. (Wyoming Bks.). (J). (gr. k-4). 1994. pap. 19.95 (*0-7933-5720-9*); lib. bdg. 29.95 (*0-7933-5719-5*); disk 29.95 (*0-7933-5721-7*) Gallopade Intl.

— My Lifetime of Sex & How to Handle It. (Smart Sex Stuff Ser.). (Orig.). (J). (ps-12). 1994. pap. 19.95 (*1-55609-211-3*) Gallopade Intl.

— The Mystery of Bat Cave Set. (Carole Marsh Mysteries Ser.). 1994. teacher ed. 125.00 (*0-7933-6956-8*) Gallopade Intl.

— Mystery of Old Salem Activity Book. (History Mystery Ser.). 12p. (Orig.). (J). (gr. 4-8). 1994. pap. 19.95 (*0-935326-67-7*) Gallopade Intl.

— Mystery of Old Salem Gamebook. (History Mystery Ser.). (Orig.). (J). (gr. 4-8). 1994. pap. 19.95 (*0-935326-66-9*) Gallopade Intl.

— Mystery of Old Salem S. P. A. R. K. Kit. (History Mystery Ser.). (Illus.). (Orig.). (J). (gr. 3-9). 1994. pap. 19.95 (*0-935326-74-X*) Gallopade Intl.

— The Mystery of Old Salem Set. (Carole Marsh Mysteries Ser.). 1994. teacher ed. 125.00 (*0-7933-6952-5*) Gallopade Intl.

— Mystery of Stone Mountain. (Real People-Real Places Ser.). (Orig.). (J). (gr. 3-7). 1994. pap. 19.95 (*0-935326-25-1*); lib. bdg. 29.95 (*1-55609-180-X*) Gallopade Intl.

— The Mystery of the Biltmore House Set. (Carole Marsh Mysteries Ser.). 1994. teacher ed. 125.00 (*0-7933-6948-7*) Gallopade Intl.

— The Mystery of the Biltmore House Set. (History Mystery Ser.). (Illus.). (J). (gr. 3-9). 1994. 29.95 (*0-935326-07-3*) Gallopade Intl.

— Mystery of the Lost Colony. (History Mystery Ser.). (Illus.). (J). (gr. 4-9). 1994. pap. 19.95 (*0-935326-05-7*); lib. bdg. 29.95 (*1-55609-182-6*) Gallopade Intl.

— The Mystery of the Lost Colony Set. (Carole Marsh Mysteries Ser.). 1994. teacher ed. 125.00 (*0-7933-6949-5*) Gallopade Intl.

— Mystery of the World's Fair. (Real People-Real Places Ser.). (Illus.). (Orig.). (J). (gr. 3-9). 1994. pap. 19.95 (*0-935326-04-9*) Gallopade Intl.

— Mystery of Tryon Palace Activity Book. (History Mystery Ser.). (Orig.). (J). (gr. 3-6). 1994. pap. 19.95 (*0-935326-69-3*) Gallopade Intl.

— Mystery of Tryon Palace Gamebook. (History Mystery Ser.). (Orig.). (J). (gr. 2-6). 1994. pap. 19.95 (*0-935326-70-7*) Gallopade Intl.

— The Mystery of Tryon Palace Set. (Carole Marsh Mysteries Ser.). 1994. teacher ed. 125.00 (*0-7933-6950-9*) Gallopade Intl.

— The Naked Gourmet. (Naked Gourmet Ser.). (Orig.). 1997. 29.95 (*1-55609-001-3*) Gallopade Intl.

— Natchez River Rogues! Pirates, Playboys & the Rest of the Cock-O'-the-Walk Crowd under-the-Hill & along the Natchez Trace. (Carole Marsh Mississippi Bks.). 1994. 29.95 (*0-7933-7369-7*); pap. 19.95 (*0-7933-7370-0*) Gallopade Intl.

— Nebraska & Other State Greats (Biographies) (Carole Marsh Nebraska Bks.). (Illus.). (J). (gr. 3 up). 1994. pap. 19.95 (*1-55609-797-2*); lib. bdg. 29.95 (*1-55609-796-4*); disk 29.95 (*1-55609-798-0*) Gallopade Intl.

— Nebraska Bandits, Bushwackers, Outlaws, Crooks, Devils, Ghosts, Desperadoes & Other Assorted & Sundry Characters! (Carole Marsh Nebraska Bks.). (Illus.). (J). (gr. 3 up). 1994. pap. 19.95 (*0-7933-0720-1*); lib. bdg. 29.95 (*0-7933-0721-X*); disk 29.95 (*0-7933-0722-8*) Gallopade Intl.

— Nebraska Bandits, Bushwackers, Outlaws, Crooks, Devils, Ghosts, Desperadoes & Other Assorted & Sundry Characters. (Carole Marsh Nebraska Bks.). (YA). 1994. student ed. 29.95 (*0-7933-6811-1*) Gallopade Intl.

— Nebraska "BIO" Bingo! 24 Must Know State People for Kids to Learn about While Having Fun! (Bingo! Ser.). (Illus.). (J). (gr. 2-8). 1998. pap. 14.95 (*0-7933-8603-9*) Gallopade Intl.

— The Nebraska Bookstore Book: A Surprising Guide to Our State's Bookstores & Their Specialties for Students, Teachers, Writers & Publishers. (Carole Marsh Nebraska Bks.). (Illus.). 1994. pap. 19.95 (*0-7933-2937-X*); lib. bdg. 29.95 (*0-7933-2936-1*); disk 29.95 (*0-7933-2938-8*) Gallopade Intl.

— Nebraska Classic Christmas Trivia: Stories, Recipes, Activities, Legends, Lore & More! (Carole Marsh Nebraska Bks.). (Illus.). (J). (gr. 3 up). 1994. pap. 19.95 (*0-7933-0723-6*); lib. bdg. 29.95 (*0-7933-0724-4*); disk 29.95 (*0-7933-0725-2*) Gallopade Intl.

— Nebraska Coastales. (Carole Marsh Nebraska Bks.). (J). 1994. lib. bdg. 29.95 (*0-7933-7292-5*) Gallopade Intl.

— Nebraska Coastales. (Carole Marsh Nebraska Bks.). (Illus.). (J). (gr. 3 up). 1994. pap. 19.95 (*1-55609-791-3*); lib. bdg. 29.95 (*1-55609-790-5*); disk 29.95 (*1-55609-792-1*) Gallopade Intl.

— Nebraska "Crinkum-Crankum" A Funny Word Book about Our State. (Carole Marsh Nebraska Bks.). (Illus.). (J). 1994. pap. 19.95 (*0-7933-4890-0*); lib. bdg. 29.95 (*0-7933-4889-7*); disk 29.95 (*0-7933-4891-9*) Gallopade Intl.

— Nebraska Dingbats! Bk. 1: A Fun Book of Games, Stories, Activities & More about Our State That's All in Code! for You to Decipher. (Carole Marsh Nebraska Bks.). (Illus.). (J). (gr. 3-12). 1994. pap. 19.95 (*0-7933-3855-7*); lib. bdg. 29.95 (*0-7933-3854-9*); disk 29.95 (*0-7933-3856-5*) Gallopade Intl.

— Nebraska Facts & Factivities. (Carole Marsh State Bks.). (Illus.). (J). (gr. 4-7). 1996. pap., teacher ed. 19.95 (*0-7933-7901-6*, C Marsh) Gallopade Intl.

— Nebraska Festival Fun for Kids! (Carole Marsh Nebraska Bks.). (Illus.). (J). (gr. 3-12). 1994. pap. 19.95 (*0-7933-4008-X*); lib. bdg. 29.95 (*0-7933-4007-1*) Gallopade Intl.

— Nebraska Festival Fun for Kids! (Carole Marsh Nebraska Bks.). (Illus.). (YA). (gr. 3-12). 1994. disk 29.95 (*0-7933-4009-8*) Gallopade Intl.

— Nebraska "GEO" Bingo! 38 Must Know State Geography Facts for Kids to Learn While Having Fun. (Bingo! Ser.). (Illus.). 1998. pap. 14.95 (*0-7933-8604-7*) Gallopade Intl.

— Nebraska "HISTO" Bingo! 42 Must Know State History Facts for Kids to Learn While Having Fun! (Bingo! Ser.). (Illus.). (J). (gr. 2-8). 1998. pap. 14.95 (*0-7933-8605-5*) Gallopade Intl.

— Nebraska History! Surprising Secrets about Our State's Founding Mothers, Fathers & Kids! (Carole Marsh Nebraska Bks.). (Illus.). (J). (gr. 3-12). 1996. pap. 19.95 (*0-7933-6110-9*); lib. bdg. 29.95 (*0-7933-6109-5*); disk 29.95 (*0-7933-6111-7*) Gallopade Intl.

— The Nebraska Hot Air Balloon Mystery. (Carole Marsh Nebraska Bks.). (Illus.). (J). (gr. 2-9). 1994. 29.95 (*0-7933-2561-7*); pap. 19.95 (*0-7933-2562-5*); disk 29.95 (*0-7933-2563-3*) Gallopade Intl.

— Nebraska Hot Zones! Viruses, Diseases, & Epidemics in Our State's History. (Hot Zones! Ser.). (Illus.). (J). (gr. 3-12). 1998. pap. 19.95 (*0-7933-8910-0*); lib. bdg. 29.95 (*0-7933-8909-7*) Gallopade Intl.

— Nebraska Indian Dictionary for Kids! (Carole Marsh State Bks.). (J). (gr. 2-9). 1996. 29.95 (*0-7933-7725-0*, C Marsh); pap. 19.95 (*0-7933-7726-9*, C Marsh) Gallopade Intl.

— Nebraska Jeopardy! Answers & Questions about Our State! (Carole Marsh Nebraska Bks.). (J). 1994. student ed. 29.95 (*0-7933-6810-3*) Gallopade Intl.

— Nebraska Jeopardy! Answers & Questions about Our State! (Carole Marsh Nebraska Bks.). (Illus.). (J). (gr. 3-12). 1994. pap. 19.95 (*0-7933-4161-2*); lib. bdg. 29.95 (*0-7933-4160-4*); disk 29.95 (*0-7933-4162-0*) Gallopade Intl.

— Nebraska "Jography" A Fun Run thru Our State. (Carole Marsh Nebraska Bks.). (Illus.). (J). (gr. 3 up). 1994. lib. bdg. 29.95 (*1-55609-778-6*); disk 29.95 (*1-55609-780-8*) Gallopade Intl.

— Nebraska Kid's Cookbook: Recipes, How-To, History, Lore & More! (Carole Marsh Nebraska Bks.). (Illus.). (J). (gr. 3 up). 1994. pap. 19.95 (*0-7933-0732-5*); lib. bdg. 29.95 (*0-7933-0733-3*); disk 29.95 (*0-7933-0734-1*) Gallopade Intl.

— The Nebraska Library Book: A Surprising Guide to the Unusual Special Collections in Libraries Across Our State for Students, Teachers, Writers & Publishers - Includes Reproducible Mailing Labels Plus Activities for Young People! (Carole Marsh Nebraska Bks.). (Illus.). 1994. pap. 19.95 (*0-7933-3087-4*); lib. bdg. 29.95 (*0-7933-3086-6*); disk 29.95 (*0-7933-3088-2*) Gallopade Intl.

— Nebraska Math! How It All Adds up in Our State. (Carole Marsh Nebraska Bks.). (Illus.). (YA). (gr. 3-12). 1996. pap. 19.95 (*0-7933-6569-4*); lib. bdg. 29.95 (*0-7933-6568-6*) Gallopade Intl.

— The Nebraska Media Book: A Surprising Guide to the Amazing Print, Broadcast & Online Media of Our State for Students, Teachers, Writers & Publishers - Includes Reproducible Mailing Labels Plus Activities for Young People! (Carole Marsh Nebraska Bks.). (Illus.). 1994. pap. 19.95 (*0-7933-3243-5*); lib. bdg. 29.95 (*0-7933-3242-7*); disk 29.95 (*0-7933-3244-3*) Gallopade Intl.

— The Nebraska Mystery Van Takes Off! Bk. 1: Handicapped Nebraska Kids Sneak off on a Big Adventure. (Carole Marsh Nebraska Bks.). (Illus.). (J). (gr. 3-12). 1994. 29.95 (*0-7933-5042-5*); pap. 19.95 (*0-7933-5043-3*); disk 29.95 (*0-7933-5044-1*) Gallopade Intl.

— Nebraska Quiz Bowl Crash Course! (Carole Marsh Nebraska Bks.). (Illus.). (J). (gr. 3 up). 1994. pap. 19.95 (*1-55609-794-8*); lib. bdg. 29.95 (*1-55609-793-X*); disk 29.95 (*1-55609-795-6*) Gallopade Intl.

— Nebraska Rollercoasters! (Carole Marsh Nebraska Bks.). (Illus.). (J). (gr. 3-12). 1994. pap. 19.95 (*0-7933-5306-8*); lib. bdg. 29.95 (*0-7933-5305-X*) Gallopade Intl.

— Nebraska Rollercoasters! (Carole Marsh Nebraska Bks.). (Illus.). (YA). (gr. 3-12). 1994. disk 29.95 (*0-7933-5307-6*) Gallopade Intl.

— Nebraska School Trivia: An Amazing & Fascinating Look at Our State's Teachers, Schools & Students! (Carole Marsh Nebraska Bks.). (Illus.). (J). (gr. 3 up). 1994. pap. 19.95 (*0-7933-0729-5*); lib. bdg. 29.95 (*0-7933-0730-9*); disk 29.95 (*0-7933-0731-7*) Gallopade Intl.

— Nebraska Silly Basketball Sports Mysteries, Vol. I. (Carole Marsh Nebraska Bks.). (Illus.). (J). (gr. 3 up). 1994. pap. 19.95 (*0-7933-0726-0*); lib. bdg. 29.95 (*0-7933-0727-9*); disk 29.95 (*0-7933-0728-7*) Gallopade Intl.

— Nebraska Silly Basketball Sports Mysteries, Vol. II. (Carole Marsh Nebraska Bks.). (Illus.). (J). (gr. 3 up). 1994. pap. 19.95 (*0-7933-1759-2*); lib. bdg. 29.95 (*0-7933-1758-4*); disk 29.95 (*0-7933-1760-6*) Gallopade Intl.

— Nebraska Silly Football Sports Mysteries, Vol. I. (Carole Marsh Nebraska Bks.). (Illus.). (J). (gr. 3 up). 1994. pap. 19.95 (*1-55609-785-9*); lib. bdg. 29.95 (*1-55609-784-0*); disk 29.95 (*1-55609-786-7*) Gallopade Intl.

— Nebraska Silly Football Sports Mysteries, Vol. II. (Carole Marsh Nebraska Bks.). (Illus.). (J). (gr. 3 up). 1994. pap. 19.95 (*1-55609-788-3*); lib. bdg. 29.95 (*1-55609-787-5*); disk 29.95 (*1-55609-789-1*) Gallopade Intl.

— Nebraska Silly Trivia! (Carole Marsh Nebraska Bks.). (YA). 1994. student ed. 29.95 (*0-7933-6809-X*) Gallopade Intl.

— Nebraska Silly Trivia! (Carole Marsh Nebraska Bks.). (Illus.). (J). (gr. 3 up). 1994. pap. 19.95 (*1-55609-776-X*); lib. bdg. 29.95 (*1-55609-775-1*); disk 29.95 (*1-55609-777-8*) Gallopade Intl.

— Nebraska Timeline: A Chronology of Nebraska History, Mystery, Trivia, Legend, Lore & More. (Carole Marsh

An Asterisk (*) at the beginning of an entry indicates that the title is appearing for the first time.

Nebraska Bks.). (Illus.). (J). (gr. 3-12). 1994. pap. 19.95 (*0-7933-5957-0*); lib. bdg. 29.95 (*0-7933-5956-2*); disk 29.95 (*0-7933-5958-9*) Gallopade Intl.

— Nebraska 2000! Coming Soon to a Calendar Near You - The 21st Century! - Complete Set of AL 2000 Items. (Two Thousand! Ser.). (Illus.). (J). (gr. 3-12). 1998. pap. 75.00 (*0-7933-9363-9*); lib. bdg. 85.00 (*0-7933-9364-7*) Gallopade Intl.

— Nebraska 2000! Coming Soon to a Calendar near You--The 21st Century! (Two Thousand! Ser.). (Illus.). (J). (gr. 3-12). 1998. pap. 19.95 (*0-7933-8757-4*); lib. bdg. 29.95 (*0-7933-8756-6*) Gallopade Intl.

— Nebraska UFO's & Extraterrestrials! A Look at the Sightings & Science in Our State. (Carole Marsh Nebraska Bks.). (Illus.). (J). (gr. 3-12). 1997. pap. 19.95 (*0-7933-6416-7*); lib. bdg. 29.95 (*0-7933-6415-9*) Gallopade Intl.

— Nebraska's (Most Devastating!) Disasters & (Most Calamitous!) Castrophies! (Carole Marsh Nebraska Bks.). (Illus.). (J). (gr. 3 up). 1994. write for info. (*0-7933-0719-8*); pap. 19.95 (*0-7933-0717-1*); lib. bdg. 29.95 (*0-7933-0718-X*) Gallopade Intl.

— Nebraska's Unsolved Mysteries (And Their "Solutions") Includes Scientific Information & Other Activities for Students. (Carole Marsh Nebraska Bks.). (Illus.). (J). (gr. 3-12). 1994. pap. 19.95 (*0-7933-5804-3*); lib. bdg. 29.95 (*0-7933-5803-5*); disk 29.95 (*0-7933-5805-1*) Gallopade Intl.

— Nevada & Other State Greats (Biographies) (Carole Marsh Nevada Bks.). (Illus.). (J). 1994. pap. 19.95 (*1-55609-821-9*); lib. bdg. 29.95 (*1-55609-820-0*); disk 29.95 (*1-55609-822-7*) Gallopade Intl.

— Nevada Bandits, Bushwackers, Outlaws, Crooks, Devils, Ghosts, Desperadoes & Other Assorted & Sundry Characters! (Illus.). (J). 1994. pap. 19.95 (*0-7933-0744-9*); lib. bdg. 29.95 (*0-7933-0745-7*); disk 29.95 (*0-7933-0746-5*) Gallopade Intl.

— Nevada "BIO" Bingo! 24 Must Know State People for Kids to Learn about While Having Fun! (Bingo! Ser.). (Illus.). (J). (gr. 2-8). 1998. pap. 14.95 (*0-7933-8606-3*) Gallopade Intl.

— The Nevada Bookstore Book: A Surprising Guide to Our State's Bookstores & Their Specialties for Students, Teachers, Writers & Publishers. (Carole Marsh Nevada Bks.). (Illus.). 1994. pap. 19.95 (*0-7933-2940-X*); lib. bdg. 29.95 (*0-7933-2939-6*); disk 29.95 (*0-7933-2941-8*) Gallopade Intl.

— Nevada Classic Christmas Trivia: Stories, Recipes, Activities, Legends, Lore & More! (Carole Marsh Nevada Bks.). (Illus.). (J). 1994. pap. 19.95 (*0-7933-0747-3*); lib. bdg. 29.95 (*0-7933-0748-1*); disk 29.95 (*0-7933-0749-X*) Gallopade Intl.

— Nevada Coastales. (Carole Marsh Nevada Bks.). (J). 1994. lib. bdg. 29.95 (*0-7933-7293-3*) Gallopade Intl.

— Nevada Coastales. (Carole Marsh Nevada Bks.). (Illus.). (J). 1994. pap. 19.95 (*1-55609-815-4*); lib. bdg. 29.95 (*1-55609-814-6*); disk 29.95 (*1-55609-816-2*) Gallopade Intl.

— Nevada "Crinkum-Crankum" A Funny Word Book about Our State. (Carole Marsh Nevada Bks.). (Illus.). (J). 1994. pap. 19.95 (*0-7933-4893-5*); lib. bdg. 29.95 (*0-7933-4892-7*); disk 29.95 (*0-7933-4894-3*) Gallopade Intl.

— Nevada Dingbats! Bk. 1: A Fun Book of Games, Stories, Activities & More about Our State That's All in Code! for You to Decipher. (Carole Marsh Nevada Bks.). (Illus.). (J). (gr. 3-12). 1994. pap. 19.95 (*0-7933-3858-1*); lib. bdg. 29.95 (*0-7933-3857-3*); disk 29.95 (*0-7933-3859-X*) Gallopade Intl.

— Nevada Facts & Factivities. (Carole Marsh State Bks.). (Illus.). (J). (gr. 4-7). 1996. pap., teacher ed. 19.95 (*0-7933-7903-2*, C Marsh) Gallopade Intl.

— Nevada Festival Fun for Kids! (Carole Marsh Nevada Bks.). (Illus.). (J). (gr. 3-12). 1994. pap. 19.95 (*0-7933-4011-X*); lib. bdg. 29.95 (*0-7933-4010-1*) Gallopade Intl.

— Nevada Festival Fun for Kids! (Carole Marsh Nevada Bks.). (Illus.). (YA). (gr. 3-12). 1994. disk 29.95 (*0-7933-4012-8*) Gallopade Intl.

— Nevada "GEO" Bingo! 38 Must Know State Geography Facts for Kids to Learn While Having Fun! (Bingo! Ser.). (Illus.). (J). (gr. 2-8). 1998. pap. 14.95 (*0-7933-8607-1*) Gallopade Intl.

— Nevada Government! The Cornerstone of Everyday Life in Our State! (Carole Marsh Nevada Bks.). (Illus.). (J). (gr. 3-12). 1996. pap. 19.95 (*0-7933-6266-0*); lib. bdg. 29.95 (*0-7933-6265-2*); disk 29.95 (*0-7933-6267-9*) Gallopade Intl.

— Nevada "HISTO" Bingo! 42 Must Know State History Facts for Kids to Learn While Having Fun! (Bingo! Ser.). (Illus.). (J). (gr. 2-8). 1998. pap. 14.95 (*0-7933-8608-X*) Gallopade Intl.

— Nevada History! Surprising Secrets about Our State's Founding Mothers, Fathers & Kids! (Carole Marsh Nevada Bks.). (Illus.). (J). (gr. 3-12). 1996. pap. 19.95 (*0-7933-6113-3*); lib. bdg. 29.95 (*0-7933-6112-5*); disk 29.95 (*0-7933-6114-1*) Gallopade Intl.

— The Nevada Hot Air Balloon Mystery. (Carole Marsh Nevada Bks.). (Illus.). (J). (gr. 2-9). 1994. 29.95 (*0-7933-2570-6*); pap. 19.95 (*0-7933-2571-4*); disk 29.95 (*0-7933-2572-2*) Gallopade Intl.

— Nevada Hot Zones! Viruses, Diseases, & Epidemics in Our State's History. (Hot Zones! Ser.). (Illus.). (J). (gr. 3-12). 1998. pap. 19.95 (*0-7933-8913-5*); lib. bdg. 29.95 (*0-7933-8912-7*) Gallopade Intl.

— Nevada Indian Dictionary for Kids! (Carole Marsh State Bks.). (J). (gr. 2-9). 1996. 29.95 (*0-7933-7728-5*, C Marsh); pap. 19.95 (*0-7933-7729-3*, C Marsh) Gallopade Intl.

— Nevada Jeopardy! Answers & Questions about Our State! (Carole Marsh Nevada Bks.). (Illus.). (J). (gr. 3-12). 1994. pap. 19.95 (*0-7933-4164-7*); lib. bdg. 29.95 (*0-7933-4163-9*); disk 29.95 (*0-7933-4165-5*) Gallopade Intl.

— Nevada "Jography" A Fun Run Thru Our State! (Carole Marsh Nevada Bks.). (Illus.). (J). 1994. pap. 19.95 (*1-55609-803-0*); lib. bdg. 29.95 (*1-55609-802-2*); disk 29.95 (*1-55609-804-9*) Gallopade Intl.

— Nevada Kid's Cookbook: Recipes, How-To, History, Lore & More! (Carole Marsh Nevada Bks.). (Illus.). (J). 1994. pap. 19.95 (*0-7933-0756-2*); lib. bdg. 29.95 (*0-7933-0757-0*); disk 29.95 (*0-7933-0758-9*) Gallopade Intl.

— The Nevada Library Book: A Surprising Guide to the Unusual Special Collections in Libraries Across Our State for Students, Teachers, Writers & Publishers - Includes Reproducible Mailing Labels Plus Activities for Young People! (Carole Marsh Nevada Bks.). (Illus.). 1994. pap. 19.95 (*0-7933-3090-4*); lib. bdg. 29.95 (*0-7933-3089-0*); disk 29.95 (*0-7933-3091-2*) Gallopade Intl.

— Nevada Math! How It All Adds up in Our State. (Carole Marsh Nevada Bks.). (Illus.). (J). (gr. 3-12). 1996. pap. 19.95 (*0-7933-6572-4*); lib. bdg. 29.95 (*0-7933-6571-6*) Gallopade Intl.

— The Nevada Media Book: A Surprising Guide to the Amazing Print, Broadcast & Online Media of Our State for Students, Teachers, Writers & Publishers - Includes Reproducible Mailing Labels Plus Activities for Young People! (Carole Marsh Nevada Bks.). (Illus.). 1994. pap. 19.95 (*0-7933-3246-X*); lib. bdg. 29.95 (*0-7933-3245-1*); disk 29.95 (*0-7933-3247-8*) Gallopade Intl.

— The Nevada Mystery Van Takes Off! Bk. 1: Handicapped Nevada Kids Sneak Off on a Big Adventure. (Carole Marsh Nevada Bks.). (Illus.). (J). (gr. 3-12). 1994. 29.95 (*0-7933-5045-X*); pap. 19.95 (*0-7933-5046-8*); disk 29.95 (*0-7933-5047-6*) Gallopade Intl.

— Nevada Quiz Bowl Crash Course! (Carole Marsh Nevada Bks.). (Illus.). (J). 1994. pap. 19.95 (*1-55609-818-9*); lib. bdg. 29.95 (*1-55609-817-0*); disk 29.95 (*1-55609-819-7*) Gallopade Intl.

— Nevada Rollercoasters! (Carole Marsh Nevada Bks.). (Illus.). (J). (gr. 3-12). 1994. pap. 19.95 (*0-7933-5309-2*); lib. bdg. 29.95 (*0-7933-5308-4*) Gallopade Intl.

— Nevada Rollercoasters! (Carole Marsh Nevada Bks.). (Illus.). (YA). (gr. 3-12). 1994. disk 29.95 (*0-7933-5310-6*) Gallopade Intl.

— Nevada School Trivia: An Amazing & Fascinating Look at Our State's Teachers, Schools & Students! (Carole Marsh Nevada Bks.). (Illus.). (J). 1994. pap. 19.95 (*0-7933-0753-8*); lib. bdg. 29.95 (*0-7933-0754-6*); disk 29.95 (*0-7933-0755-4*) Gallopade Intl.

— Nevada Silly Basketball Sportsmysteries, Vol. 1. (Carole Marsh Nevada Bks.). (Illus.). (J). 1994. pap. 19.95 (*0-7933-0750-3*); lib. bdg. 29.95 (*0-7933-0751-1*); disk 29.95 (*0-7933-0752-X*) Gallopade Intl.

— Nevada Silly Basketball Sportsmysteries, Vol. 2. (Carole Marsh Nevada Bks.). (Illus.). (J). 1994. pap. 19.95 (*0-7933-1768-1*); lib. bdg. 29.95 (*0-7933-1767-3*); disk 29.95 (*0-7933-1769-X*) Gallopade Intl.

— Nevada Silly Football Sportsmysteries, Vol. 1. (Carole Marsh Nevada Bks.). (Illus.). (J). 1994. pap. 19.95 (*1-55609-809-X*); lib. bdg. 29.95 (*1-55609-808-1*); disk 29.95 (*1-55609-810-3*) Gallopade Intl.

— Nevada Silly Football Sportsmysteries, Vol. 2. (Carole Marsh Nevada Bks.). (Illus.). (J). 1994. pap. 19.95 (*1-55609-812-X*); lib. bdg. 29.95 (*1-55609-811-1*); disk 29.95 (*1-55609-813-8*) Gallopade Intl.

— Nevada Silly Trivia! (Carole Marsh Nevada Bks.). (Illus.). (J). 1994. pap. 19.95 (*1-55609-800-6*); lib. bdg. 29.95 (*1-55609-799-9*); disk 29.95 (*1-55609-801-4*) Gallopade Intl.

— Nevada Spelling Bee! Score Big by Correctly Spelling Our State's Unique Names. (Carole Marsh Nevada Bks.). (Illus.). (J). (gr. 3-12). 1996. pap. 19.95 (*0-7933-6725-5*) Gallopade Intl.

— Nevada Spelling Bee! Score Big by Correctly Spelling Our State's Unique Names. (Carole Marsh Nevada Bks.). (Illus.). (YA). (gr. 3-12). 1996. lib. bdg. 29.95 (*0-7933-6724-7*) Gallopade Intl.

— Nevada Timeline: A Chronology of Nevada History, Mystery, Trivia, Legend, Lore & More. (Carole Marsh Nevada Bks.). (Illus.). (J). (gr. 3-12). 1994. pap. 19.95 (*0-7933-5960-0*); lib. bdg. 29.95 (*0-7933-5959-7*); disk 29.95 (*0-7933-5961-9*) Gallopade Intl.

— Nevada 2000! Coming Soon to a Calendar Near You - The 21st Century! - Complete Set of AL 2000 Items. (Two Thousand! Ser.). (Illus.). (J). (gr. 3-12). 1998. pap. 75.00 (*0-7933-9365-5*); lib. bdg. 85.00 (*0-7933-9366-3*) Gallopade Intl.

— Nevada 2000! Coming Soon to a Calendar near You--The 21st Century! (Two Thousand! Ser.). (Illus.). (J). (gr. 3-12). 1998. pap. 19.95 (*0-7933-8760-4*); lib. bdg. 29.95 (*0-7933-8759-0*) Gallopade Intl.

— Nevada UFO's & Extraterrestrials! A Look at the Sightings & Science in Our State. (Carole Marsh Nevada Bks.). (Illus.). (J). (gr. 3-12). 1997. pap. 19.95 (*0-7933-6419-1*); lib. bdg. 29.95 (*0-7933-6418-3*) Gallopade Intl.

— Nevada's (Most Devastating!) Disasters & (Most Calamitous!) Castrophies! (Carole Marsh Nevada Bks.). (Illus.). (J). 1994. pap. 19.95 (*0-7933-0741-4*); lib. bdg. 29.95 (*0-7933-0742-2*); disk 29.95 (*0-7933-0743-0*) Gallopade Intl.

— Nevada's Unsolved Mysteries (And Their "Solutions") Includes Scientific Information & Other Activities for Students. (Carole Marsh Nevada Bks.). (Illus.). (J). (gr. 3-12). 1994. pap. 19.95 (*0-7933-5807-8*); lib. bdg. 29.95 (*0-7933-5806-X*); disk 29.95 (*0-7933-5808-6*) Gallopade Intl.

— New Hampshire 2000! Coming Soon to a Calendar near You--The 21st Century! (Two Thousand! Ser.). (Illus.). (J). (gr. 3-12). 1998. pap. 19.95 (*0-7933-8763-9*); lib. bdg. 29.95 (*0-7933-8762-0*) Gallopade Intl.

— New Hampshire & Extraterrestrials! A Look at the Sightings & Science in Our State. (Carole Marsh New Hampshire Bks.). (Illus.). (J). (gr. 3-12). 1997. pap. 19.95 (*0-7933-6422-1*); lib. bdg. 29.95 (*0-7933-6421-3*) Gallopade Intl.

— New Hampshire & Other State Greats (Biographies) (Carole Marsh New Hampshire Bks.). (Illus.). (J). 1994. pap. 19.95 (*1-55609-845-6*); disk 29.95 (*1-55609-846-4*) Gallopade Intl.

— New Hampshire & Other State Greats (Biographies) (Carole Marsh New Hampshire Bks.). (Illus.). (J). 1997. lib. bdg. 29.95 (*1-55609-844-8*) Gallopade Intl.

— New Hampshire Bandits, Bushwackers, Outlaws, Crooks, Devils, Ghosts, Desperadoes & Other Assorted & Sundry Characters! (Carole Marsh New Hampshire Bks.). (Illus.). (J). 1994. pap. 19.95 (*0-7933-0768-6*); lib. bdg. 29.95 (*0-7933-0769-4*); disk 29.95 (*0-7933-0770-8*) Gallopade Intl.

— New Hampshire "BIO" Bingo! 24 Must Know State People for Kids to Learn about While Having Fun! (Bingo! Ser.). (Illus.). (J). (gr. 2-8). 1998. pap. 14.95 (*0-7933-8609-8*) Gallopade Intl.

— The New Hampshire Bookstore Book: A Surprising Guide to Our State's Bookstores & Their Specialties for Students, Teachers, Writers & Publishers. (Carole Marsh New Hampshire Bks.). (Illus.). 1994. pap. 19.95 (*0-7933-2943-4*); lib. bdg. 29.95 (*0-7933-2942-6*); disk 29.95 (*0-7933-2944-2*) Gallopade Intl.

— New Hampshire Classic Christmas Trivia: Stories, Recipes, Activities, Legends, Lore & More! (Carole Marsh New Hampshire Bks.). (Illus.). (J). 1994. pap. 19.95 (*0-7933-0771-6*); lib. bdg. 29.95 (*0-7933-0772-4*); disk 29.95 (*0-7933-0773-2*) Gallopade Intl.

— New Hampshire Coastales. (Carole Marsh New Hampshire Bks.). (J). 1994. lib. bdg. 29.95 (*0-7933-7294-1*) Gallopade Intl.

— New Hampshire Coastales. (Carole Marsh New Hampshire Bks.). (Illus.). (J). 1994. pap. 19.95 (*1-55609-839-1*); lib. bdg. 29.95 (*1-55609-838-3*); disk 29.95 (*1-55609-840-5*) Gallopade Intl.

— New Hampshire "Crinkum-Crankum" A Funny Word Book about Our State. (Carole Marsh New Hampshire Bks.). (Illus.). (J). 1994. pap. 19.95 (*0-7933-4896-X*); lib. bdg. 29.95 (*0-7933-4895-1*); disk 29.95 (*0-7933-4897-8*) Gallopade Intl.

— New Hampshire Dingbats! Bk. 1: A Fun Book of Games, Stories, Activities & More about Our State That's All in Code! for You to Decipher. (Carole Marsh New Hampshire Bks.). (Illus.). (J). (gr. 3-12). 1994. pap. 19.95 (*0-7933-3861-1*); lib. bdg. 29.95 (*0-7933-3860-3*) Gallopade Intl.

— New Hampshire Facts & Factivities. (Carole Marsh State Bks.). (Illus.). (J). (gr. 4-7). 1996. pap., teacher ed. 19.95 (*0-7933-7905-9*, C Marsh) Gallopade Intl.

— New Hampshire Festival Fun for Kids! (Carole Marsh New Hampshire Bks.). (Illus.). (J). (gr. 3-12). 1994. pap. 19.95 (*0-7933-4014-4*); lib. bdg. 29.95 (*0-7933-4013-6*) Gallopade Intl.

— New Hampshire Festival Fun for Kids! (Carole Marsh New Hampshire Bks.). (Illus.). (YA). (gr. 3-12). 1994. disk 29.95 (*0-7933-4015-2*) Gallopade Intl.

— New Hampshire "GEO" Bingo! 38 Must Know State Geography Facts for Kids to Learn While Having Fun! (Bingo! Ser.). (Illus.). (J). (gr. 2-8). 1998. pap. 14.95 (*0-7933-8610-1*) Gallopade Intl.

— New Hampshire Government! The Cornerstone of Everyday Life in Our State! (Carole Marsh New Hampshire Bks.). (Illus.). (J). (gr. 3-12). 1996. pap. 19.95 (*0-7933-6269-5*); lib. bdg. 29.95 (*0-7933-6268-7*); disk 29.95 (*0-7933-6270-9*) Gallopade Intl.

— New Hampshire "HISTO" Bingo! 42 Must Know State History Facts for Kids to Learn While Having Fun! (Bingo! Ser.). (Illus.). (J). (gr. 2-8). 1998. pap. 14.95 (*0-7933-8611-X*) Gallopade Intl.

— New Hampshire History! Surprising Secrets about Our State's Founding Mothers, Fathers & Kids! (Carole Marsh New Hampshire Bks.). (Illus.). (J). (gr. 3-12). 1996. pap. 19.95 (*0-7933-6116-8*); lib. bdg. 29.95 (*0-7933-6115-X*); disk 29.95 (*0-7933-6117-6*) Gallopade Intl.

— The New Hampshire Hot Air Balloon Mystery. (Carole Marsh New Hampshire Bks.). (Illus.). (J). (gr. 2-9). 1994. 29.95 (*0-7933-2579-X*); pap. 19.95 (*0-7933-2580-3*); disk 29.95 (*0-7933-2581-1*) Gallopade Intl.

— New Hampshire Hot Zones! Viruses, Diseases, & Epidemics in Our State's History. (Hot Zones! Ser.). (Illus.). (J). (gr. 3-12). 1998. pap. 19.95 (*0-7933-8916-X*); lib. bdg. 29.95 (*0-7933-8915-1*) Gallopade Intl.

— New Hampshire Indian Dictionary for Kids! (Carole Marsh State Bks.). (J). (gr. 2-9). 1996. 29.95 (*0-7933-7731-5*, C Marsh); pap. 19.95 (*0-7933-7732-3*, C Marsh) Gallopade Intl.

— New Hampshire Jeopardy! Answers & Questions about Our State! (Carole Marsh New Hampshire Bks.). (Illus.). (J). (gr. 3-12). 1994. pap. 19.95 (*0-7933-4167-1*); lib. bdg. 29.95 (*0-7933-4166-3*), disk 29.95 (*0-7933-4168-X*) Gallopade Intl.

— New Hampshire "Jography" A Fun Run Thru Our State! (Carole Marsh New Hampshire Bks.). (Illus.). (J). 1994. pap. 19.95 (*1-55609-827-8*); lib. bdg. 29.95 (*1-55609-826-X*); disk 29.95 (*1-55609-828-6*) Gallopade Intl.

— New Hampshire Kid's Cookbook: Recipes, How-To, History, Lore & More! (Carole Marsh New Hampshire Bks.). (Illus.). (J). 1994. pap. 19.95 (*0-7933-0780-5*); lib. bdg. 29.95 (*0-7933-0781-3*); disk 29.95 (*0-7933-0782-1*) Gallopade Intl.

— The New Hampshire Library Book: A Surprising Guide to the Unusual Special Collections in Libraries Across Our State for Students, Teachers, Writers & Publishers - Includes Reproducible Mailing Labels Plus Activities for Young People! (Carole Marsh New Hampshire Bks.). (Illus.). 1994. pap. 19.95 (*0-7933-3093-9*); lib. bdg. 29.95 (*0-7933-3092-0*); disk 29.95 (*0-7933-3094-7*) Gallopade Intl.

— New Hampshire Math! How It All Adds up in Our State. (Carole Marsh New Hampshire Bks.). (Illus.). (YA). (gr. 3-12). 1996. pap. 19.95 (*0-7933-6575-9*); lib. bdg. 29.95 (*0-7933-6574-0*) Gallopade Intl.

— The New Hampshire Media Book: A Surprising Guide to the Amazing Print, Broadcast & Online Media of Our State for Students, Teachers, Writers & Publishers - Includes Reproducible Mailing Labels Plus Activities for Young People! (Carole Marsh New Hampshire Bks.). (Illus.). 1994. pap. 19.95 (*0-7933-3249-4*); lib. bdg. 29.95 (*0-7933-3248-6*); disk 29.95 (*0-7933-3250-8*) Gallopade Intl.

— The New Hampshire Mystery Van Takes Off! Bk. 1: Handicapped New Hampshire Kids Sneak Off on a Big Adventure. (Carole Marsh New Hampshire Bks.). (Illus.). (J). (gr. 3-12). 1994. 29.95 (*0-7933-5048-4*); pap. 19.95 (*0-7933-5049-2*) Gallopade Intl.

— New Hampshire Quiz Bowl Crash Course! (Carole Marsh New Hampshire Bks.). (Illus.). (J). 1994. pap. 19.95 (*1-55609-842-1*); lib. bdg. 29.95 (*1-55609-841-3*); disk 29.95 (*1-55609-843-X*) Gallopade Intl.

— New Hampshire Rollercoasters! (Carole Marsh New Hampshire Bks.). (Illus.). (J). (gr. 3-12). 1994. pap. 19.95 (*0-7933-5312-2*); lib. bdg. 29.95 (*0-7933-5311-4*) Gallopade Intl.

— New Hampshire Rollercoasters! (Carole Marsh New Hampshire Bks.). (Illus.). (YA). (gr. 3-12). 1994. disk 29.95 (*0-7933-5313-0*) Gallopade Intl.

— New Hampshire School Trivia: An Amazing & Fascinating Look at Our State's Teachers, Schools & Students! (Illus.). (J). 1994. pap. 19.95 (*0-7933-0777-5*); lib. bdg. 29.95 (*0-7933-0778-3*); disk 29.95 (*0-7933-0779-1*) Gallopade Intl.

— New Hampshire Silly Basketball Sportsmysteries, Vol. I. (Carole Marsh New Hampshire Bks.). (Illus.). (J). 1994. pap. 19.95 (*0-7933-0774-0*); lib. bdg. 29.95 (*0-7933-0775-9*); disk 29.95 (*0-7933-0776-7*) Gallopade Intl.

— New Hampshire Silly Basketball Sportsmysteries, Vol. II. (Carole Marsh New Hampshire Bks.). (Illus.). (J). 1994. pap. 19.95 (*0-7933-1777-0*); lib. bdg. 29.95 (*0-7933-1776-2*); disk 29.95 (*0-7933-1778-9*) Gallopade Intl.

— New Hampshire Silly Football Sportsmysteries, Vol. 1. (Carole Marsh New Hampshire Bks.). (Illus.). (J). 1994. pap. 19.95 (*1-55609-833-2*); lib. bdg. 29.95 (*1-55609-832-4*); disk 29.95 (*1-55609-834-0*) Gallopade Intl.

— New Hampshire Silly Football Sportsmysteries, Vol. 2. (Carole Marsh New Hampshire Bks.). (Illus.). (J). 1994. pap. 19.95 (*1-55609-836-7*); lib. bdg. 29.95 (*1-55609-835-9*); disk 29.95 (*1-55609-837-5*) Gallopade Intl.

— New Hampshire Silly Trivia! (Carole Marsh New Hampshire Bks.). (Illus.). (J). 1994. pap. 19.95 (*1-55609-824-3*); lib. bdg. 29.95 (*1-55609-823-5*); disk 29.95 (*1-55609-825-1*) Gallopade Intl.

— New Hampshire Spelling Bee! Score Big by Correctly Spelling Our State's Unique Names. (Carole Marsh New Hampshire Bks.). (Illus.). (YA). (gr. 3-12). 1996. pap. 19.95 (*0-7933-6728-X*); lib. bdg. 29.95 (*0-7933-6727-1*) Gallopade Intl.

— New Hampshire Timeline: A Chronology of New Hampshire History, Mystery, Trivia, Legend, Lore & More. (Carole Marsh New Hampshire Bks.). (Illus.). (J). (gr. 3-12). 1994. pap. 19.95 (*0-7933-5963-5*); lib. bdg. 29.95 (*0-7933-5962-7*); disk 29.95 (*0-7933-5964-3*) Gallopade Intl.

— New Hampshire 2000! Coming Soon to a Calendar Near You - The 21st Century! - Complete Set of AL 2000 Items. (Two Thousand! Ser.). (Illus.). (J). (gr. 3-12). 1998. pap. 75.00 (*0-7933-9367-1*); lib. bdg. 85.00 (*0-7933-9368-X*) Gallopade Intl.

— New Hampshire's (Most Devastating!) Disasters & (Most Calamitous!) Catastrophies! (Carole Marsh New Hampshire Bks.). (Illus.). (J). 1994. pap. 19.95 (*0-7933-0765-1*); lib. bdg. 29.95 (*0-7933-0766-X*); disk 29.95 (*0-7933-0767-8*) Gallopade Intl.

— New Hampshire's Unsolved Mysteries (And Their "Solutions") Includes Scientific Information & Other Activities for Students. (Carole Marsh New Hampshire Bks.). (Illus.). (J). (gr. 3-12). 1994. pap. 19.95 (*0-7933-5810-8*); lib. bdg. 29.95 (*0-7933-5809-4*); disk 29.95 (*0-7933-5811-6*) Gallopade Intl.

— New Jersey & Other State Greats (Biographies) (Carole Marsh New Jersey Bks.). (Illus.). (J). 1994. pap. 19.95 (*1-55609-869-3*); lib. bdg. 29.95 (*1-55609-868-5*); disk 29.95 (*1-55609-870-7*) Gallopade Intl.

— New Jersey Bandits, Bushwackers, Outlaws, Crooks, Devils, Ghosts, Desperadoes & Other Assorted & Sundry Characters! (Carole Marsh New Jersey Bks.). (Illus.). (J). 1994. pap. 19.95 (*0-7933-1789-4*); lib. bdg. 29.95 (*0-7933-1788-6*); disk 29.95 (*0-7933-1790-8*) Gallopade Intl.

— New Jersey "BIO" Bingo! 24 Must Know State People for Kids to Learn about While Having Fun! (Bingo! Ser.). (Illus.). (J). (gr. 2-8). 1998. pap. 14.95 (*0-7933-8612-8*) Gallopade Intl.

— The New Jersey Bookstore Book: A Surprising Guide to Our State's Bookstores & Their Specialties for Students, Teachers, Writers & Publishers. (Carole Marsh New Jersey Bks.). (Illus.). 1994. pap. 19.95 (*0-7933-2946-9*); lib. bdg. 29.95 (*0-7933-2945-0*); disk 29.95 (*0-7933-2947-7*) Gallopade Intl.

M

— New Jersey Classic Christmas Trivia: Stories, Recipes, Activities, Legends, Lore & More! (Carole Marsh New Jersey Bks.). (Illus.). (J). 1994. pap. 19.95 (0-7933-1792-4); lib. bdg. 29.95 (0-7933-1791-6); disk 29.95 (0-7933-1793-2) Gallopade Intl.

— New Jersey Coastales. (Carole Marsh New Jersey Bks.). (J). 1994. lib. bdg. 29.95 (0-7933-7295-X) Gallopade Intl.

— New Jersey Coastales. (Carole Marsh New Jersey Bks.). (Illus.). (J). 1994. pap. 19.95 (1-55609-863-4); lib. bdg. 29.95 (1-55609-862-6); disk 29.95 (1-55609-864-2) Gallopade Intl.

— New Jersey "Crinkum-Crankum" A Funny Word Book about Our State. (Carole Marsh New Jersey Bks.). (Illus.). (J). 1994. pap. 19.95 (0-7933-4899-4); lib. bdg. 29.95 (0-7933-4898-6); disk 29.95 (0-7933-4900-1) Gallopade Intl.

— New Jersey Dingbats! Bk. 1: A Fun Book of Games, Stories, Activities & More about Our State That's All in Code! for You to Decipher. (New Jersey Bks.). (Illus.). (J). (gr. 3-12). 1994. pap. 19.95 (0-7933-3864-6); lib. bdg. 29.95 (0-7933-3863-8); disk 29.95 (0-7933-3865-4) Gallopade Intl.

***Marsh, Carole.** The New Jersey Experience Pocket Guide. (New Jersey Experience! Ser.). (Illus.). (J). 2000. pap. 6.95 (0-7933-9453-8) Gallopade Intl.

Marsh, Carole. New Jersey Facts & Factivities. (Carole Marsh State Bks.). (Illus.). (J). (gr. 4-7). 1996. pap., teacher ed. 19.95 (0-7933-7907-5, C Marsh) Gallopade Intl.

— New Jersey Festival Fun for Kids! (Carole Marsh New Jersey Bks.). (Illus.). (J). (gr. 3-12). 1994. pap. 19.95 (0-7933-4017-9); lib. bdg. 29.95 (0-7933-4016-0) Gallopade Intl.

— New Jersey Festival Fun for Kids! (Carole Marsh New Jersey Bks.). (Illus.). (YA). (gr. 3-12). 1994. disk 29.95 (0-7933-4018-7) Gallopade Intl.

— New Jersey "GEO" Bingo! 38 Must Know State Geography Facts for Kids to Learn While Having Fun! (Bingo! Ser.). (Illus.). (J). (gr. 2-8). 1998. pap. 14.95 (0-7933-8613-6) Gallopade Intl.

— New Jersey Government! The Cornerstone of Everyday Life in Our State! (Carole Marsh New Jersey Bks.). (Illus.). (J). (gr. 3-12). 1996. pap. 19.95 (0-7933-6272-5); lib. bdg. 29.95 (0-7933-6271-7); disk 29.95 (0-7933-6273-3) Gallopade Intl.

— New Jersey "HISTO" Bingo! 42 Must Know State History Facts for Kids to Learn While Having Fun! (Bingo! Ser.). (Illus.). (J). (gr. 2-8). 1998. pap. 14.95 (0-7933-8614-4) Gallopade Intl.

— New Jersey History! Surprising Secrets about Our State's Founding Mothers, Fathers & Kids! (Carole Marsh New Jersey Bks.). (Illus.). (J). (gr. 3-12). 1996. pap. 19.95 (0-7933-6119-2); lib. bdg. 29.95 (0-7933-6118-4); disk 29.95 (0-7933-6120-6) Gallopade Intl.

— The New Jersey Hot Air Balloon Mystery. (Carole Marsh New Jersey Bks.). (Illus.). (J). (gr. 2-9). 1994. 29.95 (0-7933-2588-9); pap. 19.95 (0-7933-2589-7); disk 29.95 (0-7933-2590-0) Gallopade Intl.

— New Jersey Hot Zones! Viruses, Diseases, & Epidemics in Our State's History. (Hot Zones! Ser.). (Illus.). (J). (gr. 3-12). 1998. pap. 19.95 (0-7933-8919-4); lib. bdg. 29.95 (0-7933-8918-6) Gallopade Intl.

— New Jersey Indians! A Kid's Look at Our State's Chiefs, Tribes, Reservations, Powwows, Lore & More from the Past & the Present. (Carole Marsh State Bks.). (J). (gr. 2-9). 1996. 29.95 (0-7933-7734-X, C Marsh); pap. 19.95 (0-7933-7735-8, C Marsh); disk 29.95 (0-7933-7736-6, C Marsh) Gallopade Intl.

***Marsh, Carole.** New Jersey Jeopardy. (New Jersey Experience! Ser.). (Illus.). (J). (gr. 2-6). 2000. pap. 7.95 (0-7933-9522-4) Gallopade Intl.

Marsh, Carole. New Jersey Jeopardy! Answers & Questions about Our State! (Carole Marsh New Jersey Bks.). (Illus.). (J). (gr. 3-12). 1994. pap. 19.95 (0-7933-4170-1); lib. bdg. 29.95 (0-7933-4169-8); disk 29.95 (0-7933-4171-X) Gallopade Intl.

***Marsh, Carole.** New Jersey Jography. (New Jersey Experience! Ser.). (Illus.). 2000. pap. 7.95 (0-7933-9523-2) Gallopade Intl.

Marsh, Carole. New Jersey "Jography" A Fun Run Thru Our State! (Carole Marsh New Jersey Bks.). (Illus.). (J). 1994. pap. 19.95 (1-55609-851-0); lib. bdg. 29.95 (1-55609-850-2); disk 29.95 (1-55609-852-9) Gallopade Intl.

— New Jersey Kid's Cookbook: Recipes, How-to, History, Lore & More. (Carole Marsh New Jersey Bks.). (Illus.). (J). 1994. pap. 19.95 (0-7933-1804-1); lib. bdg. 29.95 (0-7933-1803-3); disk 29.95 (0-7933-1805-X) Gallopade Intl.

— The New Jersey Library Book: A Surprising Guide to the Unusual Special Collections in Libraries Across Our State for Students, Teachers, Writers & Publishers - Includes Reproducible Mailing Labels Plus Activities for Young People! (Carole Marsh New Jersey Bks.). (Illus.). 1994. pap. 19.95 (0-7933-3096-3); lib. bdg. 29.95 (0-7933-3095-5); disk 29.95 (0-7933-3097-1) Gallopade Intl.

— New Jersey Math! How It All Adds up in Our State. (Carole Marsh New Jersey Bks.). (Illus.). (YA). (gr. 3-12). 1996. pap. 19.95 (0-7933-6578-3); lib. bdg. 29.95 (0-7933-6577-5) Gallopade Intl.

— The New Jersey Media Book: A Surprising Guide to the Amazing Print, Broadcast & Online Media of Our State for Students, Teachers, Writers & Publishers - Includes Reproducible Mailing Labels Plus Activities for Young People! (Carole Marsh New Jersey Bks.). (Illus.). 1994. pap. 19.95 (0-7933-3252-4); lib. bdg. 29.95 (0-7933-3251-6); disk 29.95 (0-7933-3253-2) Gallopade Intl.

— The New Jersey Mystery Van Takes Off! Book 1: Handicapped New Jersey Kids Sneak off on a Big Adventure, Bk. 1. (Carole Marsh New Jersey Bks.). (Illus.). (J). (gr. 3-12). 1994. 29.95 (0-7933-5051-4); pap. 19.95 (0-7933-5052-2); disk 29.95 (0-7933-5053-0) Gallopade Intl.

— New Jersey Quiz Bowl Crash Course! (Carole Marsh New Jersey Bks.). (Illus.). (J). 1994. pap. 19.95 (1-55609-866-9); lib. bdg. 29.95 (1-55609-865-0); disk 29.95 (1-55609-867-7) Gallopade Intl.

— New Jersey Rollercoasters! (Carole Marsh New Jersey Bks.). (Illus.). (J). (gr. 3-12). 1994. pap. 19.95 (0-7933-5315-7); lib. bdg. 29.95 (0-7933-5314-9) Gallopade Intl.

— New Jersey Rollercoasters! (Carole Marsh New Jersey Bks.). (Illus.). (YA). (gr. 3-12). 1994. disk 29.95 (0-7933-5316-5) Gallopade Intl.

— New Jersey School Trivia: An Amazing & Fascinating Look at Our State's Teachers, Schools & Students! (Carole Marsh New Jersey Bks.). (Illus.). (J). 1994. pap. 19.95 (0-7933-1801-7); lib. bdg. 29.95 (0-7933-1800-9); disk 29.95 (0-7933-1802-5) Gallopade Intl.

— New Jersey Silly Basketball Sportsmysteries, Vol. 1. (Carole Marsh New Jersey Bks.). (Illus.). (J). 1994. pap. 19.95 (0-7933-1795-9); lib. bdg. 29.95 (0-7933-1794-0); disk 29.95 (0-7933-1796-7) Gallopade Intl.

— New Jersey Silly Basketball Sportsmysteries, Vol. 2. (Carole Marsh New Jersey Bks.). (Illus.). (J). 1994. pap. 19.95 (0-7933-1798-3); lib. bdg. 29.95 (0-7933-1797-5); disk 29.95 (0-7933-1799-1) Gallopade Intl.

— New Jersey Silly Football Sportsmysteries, Vol. 1. (Carole Marsh New Jersey Bks.). (Illus.). (J). 1994. pap. 19.95 (1-55609-857-X); lib. bdg. 29.95 (1-55609-856-1); disk 29.95 (1-55609-858-8) Gallopade Intl.

— New Jersey Silly Football Sportsmysteries, Vol. 2. (Carole Marsh New Jersey Bks.). (Illus.). (J). 1994. pap. 19.95 (1-55609-860-X); lib. bdg. 29.95 (1-55609-859-6); disk 29.95 (1-55609-861-8) Gallopade Intl.

— New Jersey Silly Trivia! (Carole Marsh New Jersey Bks.). (Illus.). (J). 1994. pap. 19.95 (1-55609-848-0); lib. bdg. 29.95 (1-55609-847-2); disk 29.95 (1-55609-849-9) Gallopade Intl.

— New Jersey Spelling Bee! Score Big by Correctly Spelling Our State's Unique Names. (Carole Marsh New Jersey Bks.). (Illus.). (YA). (gr. 3-12). 1996. pap. 19.95 (0-7933-6731-X); lib. bdg. 29.95 (0-7933-6730-1) Gallopade Intl.

— New Jersey Timeline: A Chronology of New Jersey History, Mystery, Trivia, Legend, Lore & More. (Carole Marsh New Jersey Bks.). (Illus.). (J). (gr. 3-12). 1994. pap. 19.95 (0-7933-5966-X); lib. bdg. 29.95 (0-7933-5965-1); disk 29.95 (0-7933-5967-8) Gallopade Intl.

— New Jersey 2000! Coming Soon to a Calendar Near You - The 21st Century! - Complete Set of AL 2000 Items. (Two Thousand! Ser.). (Illus.). (J). (gr. 3-12). 1998. pap. 75.00 (0-7933-9369-8); lib. bdg. 85.00 (0-7933-9370-1) Gallopade Intl.

— New Jersey 2000! Coming Soon to a Calendar near You--The 21st Century! (Two Thousand! Ser.). (Illus.). (J). (gr. 3-12). 1998. pap. 19.95 (0-7933-8766-3); lib. bdg. 29.95 (0-7933-8765-5) Gallopade Intl.

— New Jersey UFO's & Extraterrestrials! A Look at the Sightings & Science in Our State. (Carole Marsh New Jersey Bks.). (Illus.). (J). (gr. 3-12). 1997. pap. 19.95 (0-7933-6425-6); lib. bdg. 29.95 (0-7933-6424-8) Gallopade Intl.

***Marsh, Carole.** New Jersey's Big Activity Book. (New Jersey Experience! Ser.). (Illus.). (J). (gr. k-5). 2000. pap. 9.95 (0-7933-9463-5) Gallopade Intl.

Marsh, Carole. New Jersey's (Most Devastating!) Disasters & (Most Calamitous!) Catastrophies! (Carole Marsh New Jersey Bks.). (Illus.). (J). 1994. pap. 19.95 (0-7933-1786-X); disk 29.95 (0-7933-1787-8) Gallopade Intl.

— New Jersey's (Most Devastating!) Disasters & (Most Calamitous!) Catastrophies! (Carole Marsh New Jersey Bks.). (Illus.). (J). 1997. lib. bdg. 29.95 (0-7933-1785-1) Gallopade Intl.

— New Jersey's Unsolved Mysteries (& Their "Solutions") Includes Scientific Information & Other Activities for Students. (Carole Marsh New Jersey Bks.). (Illus.). (J). (gr. 3-12). 1994. pap. 19.95 (0-7933-5813-2); lib. bdg. 29.95 (0-7933-5812-4); disk 29.95 (0-7933-5814-0) Gallopade Intl.

— New Mexico & Other State Greats (Biographies) (Carole Marsh New Mexico Bks.). (Illus.). (J). 1994. pap. 19.95 (1-55609-893-6); lib. bdg. 29.95 (1-55609-892-8); disk 29.95 (1-55609-894-4) Gallopade Intl.

— New Mexico Bandits, Bushwackers, Outlaws, Crooks, Devils, Ghosts, Desperadoes & Other Assorted & Sundry Characters! (Illus.). (J). 1994. pap. 19.95 (0-7933-0792-9); lib. bdg. 29.95 (0-7933-0793-7); disk 29.95 (0-7933-0794-5) Gallopade Intl.

— New Mexico "BIO" Bingo! 24 Must Know State People for Kids to Learn about While Having Fun! (Bingo! Ser.). (Illus.). (J). (gr. 2-8). 1998. pap. 14.95 (0-7933-8615-2) Gallopade Intl.

— The New Mexico Bookstore Book: A Surprising Guide to Our State's Bookstores & Their Specialties for Students, Teachers, Writers & Publishers. (Carole Marsh New Mexico Bks.). (Illus.). 1994. pap. 19.95 (0-7933-2949-3); lib. bdg. 29.95 (0-7933-2948-5); disk 29.95 (0-7933-2950-7) Gallopade Intl.

— New Mexico Classic Christmas Trivia: Stories, Recipes, Activities, Legends, Lore & More! (Carole Marsh New Mexico Bks.). (Illus.). (J). 1994. pap. 19.95 (0-7933-0795-3); lib. bdg. 29.95 (0-7933-0796-1); disk 29.95 (0-7933-0797-X) Gallopade Intl.

— New Mexico Coastales. (Carole Marsh New Mexico Bks.). (J). 1994. lib. bdg. 29.95 (0-7933-7296-8) Gallopade Intl.

— New Mexico Coastales. (Carole Marsh New Mexico Bks.). (Illus.). (J). 1994. pap. 19.95 (1-55609-887-1); lib. bdg. 29.95 (1-55609-886-3); disk 29.95 (1-55609-888-X) Gallopade Intl.

— New Mexico "Crinkum-Crankum" A Funny Word Book about Our State. (Carole Marsh New Mexico Bks.). (Illus.). (J). 1994. pap. 19.95 (0-7933-4902-8); lib. bdg. 29.95 (0-7933-4901-X); disk 29.95 (0-7933-4903-6) Gallopade Intl.

— New Mexico Dingbats! A Fun Book of Games, Stories, Activities & More about Our State That's All in Code! For You to Decipher, Bk. 1. (Carole Marsh New Mexico Bks.). (Illus.). (J). (gr. 3-12). 1994. pap. 19.95 (0-7933-3867-0); lib. bdg. 29.95 (0-7933-3866-2) Gallopade Intl.

— New Mexico Facts & Factivities. (Carole Marsh State Bks.). (Illus.). (J). (gr. 4-7). 1996. pap., teacher ed. 19.95 (0-7933-7909-1, C Marsh) Gallopade Intl.

— New Mexico Festival Fun for Kids! (Carole Marsh New Mexico Bks.). (Illus.). (J). (gr. 3-12). 1994. pap. 19.95 (0-7933-4020-9); lib. bdg. 29.95 (0-7933-4019-5) Gallopade Intl.

— New Mexico Festival Fun for Kids! (Carole Marsh New Mexico Bks.). (Illus.). (YA). (gr. 3-12). 1994. disk 29.95 (0-7933-4021-7) Gallopade Intl.

— New Mexico "GEO" Bingo! 38 Must Know State Geography Facts for Kids to Learn While Having Fun! (Bingo! Ser.). (Illus.). (J). (gr. 2-8). 1998. pap. 14.95 (0-7933-8616-0) Gallopade Intl.

— New Mexico Government! The Cornerstone of Everyday Life in Our State! (Carole Marsh New Mexico Bks.). (Illus.). (J). (gr. 3-12). 1996. pap. 19.95 (0-7933-6275-X); lib. bdg. 29.95 (0-7933-6274-1); disk 29.95 (0-7933-6276-8) Gallopade Intl.

— New Mexico "HISTO" Bingo! 42 Must Know State History Facts for Kids to Learn While Having Fun! (Bingo! Ser.). (Illus.). (J). (gr. 2-8). 1998. pap. 14.95 (0-7933-8617-9) Gallopade Intl.

— New Mexico History! Surprising Secrets about Our State's Founding Mothers, Fathers & Kids! (Carole Marsh New Mexico Bks.). (Illus.). (J). (gr. 3-12). 1996. pap. 19.95 (0-7933-6122-2); lib. bdg. 29.95 (0-7933-6121-4); disk 29.95 (0-7933-6123-0) Gallopade Intl.

— The New Mexico Hot Air Balloon Mystery. (Carole Marsh New Mexico Bks.). (Illus.). (J). (gr. 2-9). 1994. 29.95 (0-7933-2597-8); pap. 19.95 (0-7933-2598-6); disk 29.95 (0-7933-2599-4) Gallopade Intl.

— New Mexico Hot Zones! Viruses, Diseases, & Epidemics in Our State's History. (Hot Zones! Ser.). (Illus.). (J). (gr. 3-12). 1998. pap. 19.95 (0-7933-8922-4); lib. bdg. 29.95 (0-7933-8921-6) Gallopade Intl.

— New Mexico Indian Dictionary for Kids! (Carole Marsh State Bks.). (J). (gr. 2-9). 1996. 29.95 (0-7933-7737-4, C Marsh); pap. 19.95 (0-7933-7738-2, C Marsh) Gallopade Intl.

— New Mexico Jeopardy! Answers & Questions about Our State! (Carole Marsh New Mexico Bks.). (Illus.). (J). (gr. 3-12). 1994. pap. 19.95 (0-7933-4173-6); lib. bdg. 29.95 (0-7933-4172-8); disk 29.95 (0-7933-4174-4) Gallopade Intl.

— New Mexico "Jography" A Fun Run Thru Our State! (Carole Marsh New Mexico Bks.). (Illus.). (J). 1994. pap. 19.95 (1-55609-875-8); lib. bdg. 29.95 (1-55609-874-X); disk 29.95 (1-55609-876-6) Gallopade Intl.

— New Mexico Kid's Cookbook: Recipes, How-to, History, Lore & More! (Carole Marsh New Mexico Bks.). (Illus.). (J). 1994. pap. 19.95 (0-7933-0804-6); lib. bdg. 29.95 (0-7933-0805-4); disk 29.95 (0-7933-0806-2) Gallopade Intl.

— The New Mexico Library Book: A Surprising Guide to the Unusual Special Collections in Libraries Across Our State for Students, Teachers, Writers & Publishers - Includes Reproducible Mailing Labels Plus Activities for Young People! (Carole Marsh New Mexico Bks.). (Illus.). 1994. pap. 19.95 (0-7933-3099-8); lib. bdg. 29.95 (0-7933-3098-X); disk 29.95 (0-7933-3100-5) Gallopade Intl.

— New Mexico Math! How It All Adds up in Our State. (Carole Marsh New Mexico Bks.). (Illus.). (YA). (gr. 3-12). 1996. pap. 19.95 (0-7933-6581-3); lib. bdg. 29.95 (0-7933-6580-5) Gallopade Intl.

— The New Mexico Media Book: A Surprising Guide to the Amazing Print, Broadcast & Online Media of Our State for Students, Teachers, Writers & Publishers - Includes Reproducible Mailing Labels Plus Activities for Young People! (Carole Marsh New Mexico Bks.). (Illus.). 1994. pap. 19.95 (0-7933-3255-9); lib. bdg. 29.95 (0-7933-3254-0); disk 29.95 (0-7933-3256-7) Gallopade Intl.

— The New Mexico Mystery Van Takes Off! Book 1: Handicapped New Mexico Kids Sneak Off on a Big Adventure, Bk. 1. (Carole Marsh New Mexico Bks.). (Illus.). (J). (gr. 3-12). 1994. 29.95 (0-7933-5054-9); pap. 19.95 (0-7933-5055-7); disk 29.95 (0-7933-5056-5) Gallopade Intl.

— New Mexico Quiz Bowl Crash Course! (Carole Marsh New Mexico Bks.). (Illus.). (J). 1994. pap. 19.95 (1-55609-890-1); lib. bdg. 29.95 (1-55609-889-8); disk 29.95 (1-55609-891-X) Gallopade Intl.

— New Mexico Rollercoasters! (Carole Marsh New Mexico Bks.). (Illus.). (J). (gr. 3-12). 1994. pap. 19.95 (0-7933-5318-1); lib. bdg. 29.95 (0-7933-5317-3) Gallopade Intl.

— New Mexico Rollercoasters! (Carole Marsh New Mexico Bks.). (Illus.). (YA). (gr. 3-12). 1994. disk 29.95 (0-7933-5319-X) Gallopade Intl.

— New Mexico School Trivia: An Amazing & Fascinating Look at Our State's Teachers, Schools & Students! (Carole Marsh New Mexico Bks.). (Illus.). (J). 1994. pap. 19.95 (0-7933-0801-1); lib. bdg. 29.95 (0-7933-0802-X); disk 29.95 (0-7933-0803-8) Gallopade Intl.

— New Mexico Silly Basketball Sportsmystereis, Vol. 1. (Carole Marsh New Mexico Bks.). (Illus.). (J). 1994. pap. 19.95 (0-7933-0798-8); lib. bdg. 29.95 (0-7933-0799-6); disk 29.95 (0-7933-0800-3) Gallopade Intl.

— New Mexico Silly Basketball Sportsmysteries, Vol. 2. (Carole Marsh New Mexico Bks.). (Illus.). (J). 1994. pap. 19.95 (0-7933-1819-X); lib. bdg. 29.95 (0-7933-1818-1); disk 29.95 (0-7933-1820-3) Gallopade Intl.

— New Mexico Silly Football Sportsmysteries. (Carole Marsh New Mexico Bks.). (Illus.). (J). 1994. pap. 19.95 (1-55609-881-2); pap. 19.95 (1-55609-884-7); lib. bdg. 29.95 (1-55609-880-4); disk 29.95 (1-55609-882-0); disk 29.95 (1-55609-885-5) Gallopade Intl.

— New Mexico Silly Trivia! (Carole Marsh New Mexico Bks.). (Illus.). (J). 1994. pap. 19.95 (1-55609-872-3); lib. bdg. 29.95 (1-55609-871-5); disk 29.95 (1-55609-873-1) Gallopade Intl.

— New Mexico Spelling Bee! Score Big by Correctly Spelling Our State's Unique Names. (Carole Marsh New Mexico Bks.). (Illus.). (YA). (gr. 3-12). 1996. pap. 19.95 (0-7933-6734-4); lib. bdg. 29.95 (0-7933-6733-6) Gallopade Intl.

— New Mexico Timeline: A Chronology of New Mexico History, Mystery, Trivia, Legend, Lore & More. (Carole Marsh New Mexico Bks.). (Illus.). (J). (gr. 3-12). 1994. pap. 19.95 (0-7933-5969-4); lib. bdg. 29.95 (0-7933-5968-6); disk 29.95 (0-7933-5970-8) Gallopade Intl.

— New Mexico 2000! Coming Soon to a Calendar Near You - The 21st Century! - Complete Set of AL 2000 Items. (Two Thousand! Ser.). (Illus.). (J). (gr. 3-12). 1998. pap. 75.00 (0-7933-9371-X); lib. bdg. 85.00 (0-7933-9372-8) Gallopade Intl.

— New Mexico 2000! Coming Soon to a Calendar near You--The 21st Century! (Two Thousand! Ser.). (Illus.). (J). (gr. 3-12). 1998. pap. 19.95 (0-7933-8769-8); lib. bdg. 29.95 (0-7933-8768-X) Gallopade Intl.

— New Mexico UFO's & Extraterrestrials! A Look at the Sightings & Science in Our State. (Carole Marsh New Mexico Bks.). (Illus.). (J). (gr. 3-12). 1997. pap. 19.95 (0-7933-6428-0); lib. bdg. 29.95 (0-7933-6427-2) Gallopade Intl.

— New Mexico's (Most Devastating!) Disasters & (Most Calamitous!) Catastrophies! (Carole Marsh New Mexico Bks.). (Illus.). (J). 1994. pap. 19.95 (0-7933-0789-9); lib. bdg. 29.95 (0-7933-0790-2); disk 29.95 (0-7933-0791-0) Gallopade Intl.

— New Mexico's Unsolved Mysteries (& Their "Solutions") Includes Scientific Information & Other Activities for Students. (Carole Marsh New Mexico Bks.). (Illus.). (J). (gr. 3-12). 1994. pap. 19.95 (0-7933-5816-7); lib. bdg. 29.95 (0-7933-5815-9); disk 29.95 (0-7933-5817-5) Gallopade Intl.

— New York & Other State Greats (Biographies) (Carole Marsh New York Bks.). (Illus.). (J). 1994. pap. 19.95 (1-55609-919-3); lib. bdg. 29.95 (1-55609-918-5); disk 29.95 (1-55609-920-7) Gallopade Intl.

— New York Bandits, Bushwackers, Outlaws, Crooks, Devils, Ghosts, Desperadoes & Other Assorted & Sundry Characters! (Carole Marsh New York Bks.). (Illus.). (J). 1994. pap. 19.95 (0-7933-0816-X); lib. bdg. 29.95 (0-7933-0817-8); disk 29.95 (0-7933-0818-6) Gallopade Intl.

— New York "BIO" Bingo! 24 Must Know State People for Kids to Learn about While Having Fun! (Bingo! Ser.). (Illus.). (J). (gr. 2-8). 1998. pap. 14.95 (0-7933-8618-7) Gallopade Intl.

— The New York Bookstore Book: A Surprising Guide to Our State's Bookstores & Their Specialties for Students, Teachers, Writers & Publishers. (Carole Marsh New York Bks.). (Illus.). 1994. pap. 19.95 (0-7933-2952-3); lib. bdg. 29.95 (0-7933-2951-5); disk 29.95 (0-7933-2953-1) Gallopade Intl.

— New York Classic Christmas Trivia: Stories, Recipes, Activities, Legends, Lore & More! (Carole Marsh New York Bks.). (Illus.). (J). 1994. lib. bdg. 29.95 (0-7933-0820-8); disk 29.95 (0-7933-0821-6) Gallopade Intl.

— New York Classic Christmas Trivia: Stories, Recipes, Activities, Legends, Lore & More! (Carole Marsh New York Bks.). (Illus.). (J). 1997. pap. 19.95 (0-7933-0819-4) Gallopade Intl.

— New York Coastales. (Carole Marsh New York Bks.). (J). 1994. lib. bdg. 29.95 (0-7933-7297-6) Gallopade Intl.

— New York Coastales. (Carole Marsh New York Bks.). (Illus.). (J). 1994. pap. 19.95 (1-55609-913-4); lib. bdg. 29.95 (1-55609-912-6); disk 29.95 (1-55609-914-2) Gallopade Intl.

— New York "Crinkum-Crankum" A Funny Word Book about Our State. (Carole Marsh New York Bks.). (Illus.). (J). 1994. pap. 19.95 (0-7933-4905-2); lib. bdg. 29.95 (0-7933-4904-4); disk 29.95 (0-7933-4906-0) Gallopade Intl.

— New York Dingbats! A Fun Book of Games, Stories, Activities & More about Our State That's All in Code! for You to Decipher, Bk. 1. (Carole Marsh New York Bks.). (Illus.). (J). (gr. 3-12). 1994. pap. 19.95 (0-7933-3870-0); lib. bdg. 29.95 (0-7933-3869-7); disk 29.95 (0-7933-3871-9) Gallopade Intl.

— New York Facts & Factivities. (Carole Marsh State Bks.). (Illus.). (J). (gr. 4-7). 1996. pap., teacher ed. 19.95 (0-7933-7911-3, C Marsh) Gallopade Intl.

— New York Festival Fun for Kids! (Carole Marsh New York Bks.). (Illus.). (J). (gr. 3-12). 1994. pap. 19.95 (0-7933-4023-3); lib. bdg. 29.95 (0-7933-4022-5) Gallopade Intl.

An Asterisk (*) at the beginning of an entry indicates that the title is appearing for the first time.

— New York Festival Fun for Kids! (Carole Marsh New York Bks.). (Illus.). (YA). (gr. 3-12). 1994. disk 29.95 (0-7933-4024-1) Gallopade Intl.

— New York "GEO" Bingo! 38 Must Know State Geography Facts for Kids to Learn While Having Fun! (Bingo! Ser.). (Illus.). (J). (gr. 2-8). 1998. pap. 14.95 (0-7933-8619-5) Gallopade Intl.

— New York Government! The Cornerstone of Everyday Life in Our State! (Carole Marsh New York Bks.). (Illus.). (J). (gr. 3-12). 1996. pap. 19.95 (0-7933-6278-4); lib. bdg. 29.95 (0-7933-6277-6); disk 29.95 (0-7933-6279-2) Gallopade Intl.

— New York "HISTO" Bingo! 42 Must Know State History Facts for Kids to Learn While Having Fun! (Bingo! Ser.). (Illus.). (J). (gr. 2-8). 1998. pap. 14.95 (0-7933-8620-9) Gallopade Intl.

— New York History! Surprising Secrets about Our State's Founding Mothers, Fathers & Kids! (Carole Marsh New York Bks.). (Illus.). (J). (gr. 3-12). 1996. pap. 19.95 (0-7933-6125-7); lib. bdg. 29.95 (0-7933-6124-9); disk 29.95 (0-7933-6126-5) Gallopade Intl.

— The New York Hot Air Balloon Mystery. (Carole Marsh New York Bks.). (Illus.). (J). (gr. 2-9). 1994. 29.95 (0-7933-2606-0); pap. 19.95 (0-7933-2607-9); disk 29.95 (0-7933-2608-7) Gallopade Intl.

— New York Hot Zones! Viruses, Diseases, & Epidemics in Our State's History. (Hot Zones! Ser.). (Illus.). (J). (gr. 3-12). 1998. pap. 19.95 (0-7933-8925-9); lib. bdg. 29.95 (0-7933-8924-0) Gallopade Intl.

— New York Indian Dictionary for Kids! (Carole Marsh State Bks.). (J). (gr. 2-9). 1996. 29.95 (0-7933-7740-4, C Marsh); pap. 19.95 (0-7933-7741-2, C Marsh) Gallopade Intl.

— New York Jeopardy! Answers & Questions about Our State! (Carole Marsh New York Bks.). (Illus.). (J). (gr. 3-12). 1994. pap. 19.95 (0-7933-4176-0); lib. bdg. 29.95 (0-7933-4175-2); disk 29.95 (0-7933-4177-9) Gallopade Intl.

— New York "Jography" A Fun Run Thru Our State! (Carole Marsh New York Bks.). (Illus.). (J). 1994. pap. 19.95 (1-55609-898-7); lib. bdg. 29.95 (1-55609-897-9); disk 29.95 (1-55609-899-5) Gallopade Intl.

— New York Kid's Cookbook: Recipes, How-To, History, Lore & More! (Carole Marsh New York Bks.). (Illus.). (J). 1994. pap. 19.95 (0-7933-0828-3); lib. bdg. 29.95 (0-7933-0829-1); disk 29.95 (0-7933-0830-5) Gallopade Intl.

— The New York Library Book: A Surprising Guide to the Unusual Special Collections in Libraries Across Our State for Students, Teachers, Writers & Publishers - Includes Reproducible Mailing Labels Plus Activities for Young People! (Carole Marsh New York Bks.). (Illus.). 1994. pap. 19.95 (0-7933-3102-1); lib. bdg. 29.95 (0-7933-3101-3); disk 29.95 (0-7933-3103-X) Gallopade Intl.

— New York Math! How It All Adds up in Our State. (Carole Marsh New York Bks.). (Illus.). (YA). (gr. 3-12). 1996. pap. 19.95 (0-7933-6584-8); lib. bdg. 29.95 (0-7933-6583-X) Gallopade Intl.

— The New York Media Book: A Surprising Guide to the Amazing Print, Broadcast & Online Media of Our State for Students, Teachers, Writers & Publishers - Includes Reproducible Mailing Labels Plus Activities for Young People! (Carole Marsh New York Bks.). (Illus.). 1994. pap. 19.95 (0-7933-3258-3); lib. bdg. 29.95 (0-7933-3257-5); disk 29.95 (0-7933-3259-1) Gallopade Intl.

— The New York Mystery Van Takes Off! Handicapped New York Kids Sneak Off on a Big Adventure. (Carole Marsh New York Bks.). (Illus.). (J). (gr. 3-12). 1994. pap. 19.95 (0-7933-5058-1); disk 29.95 (0-7933-5059-X) Gallopade Intl.

— The New York Mystery Van Takes Off! Handicapped New York Kids Sneak Off on a Big Adventure, Bk. 1. (Carole Marsh New York Bks.). (Illus.). (J). (gr. 3-12). 1994. 29.95 (0-7933-5057-3) Gallopade Intl.

— New York Quiz Bowl Crash Course! (Carole Marsh New York Bks.). (Illus.). (J). 1994. pap. 19.95 (1-55609-916-9); lib. bdg. 29.95 (1-55609-915-0); disk 29.95 (1-55609-917-7) Gallopade Intl.

— New York Rollercoasters! (Carole Marsh New York Bks.). (Illus.). (J). (gr. 3-12). 1994. pap. 19.95 (0-7933-5321-1); lib. bdg. 29.95 (0-7933-5320-3) Gallopade Intl.

— New York Rollercoasters! (Carole Marsh New York Bks.). (Illus.). (YA). (gr. 3-12). 1994. disk 29.95 (0-7933-5322-X) Gallopade Intl.

— New York School Trivia: An Amazing & Fascinating Look at Our State's Teachers, Schools & Students! (Carole Marsh New York Bks.). (Illus.). (J). 1994. pap. 19.95 (0-7933-0825-9); lib. bdg. 29.95 (0-7933-0826-7); disk 29.95 (0-7933-0827-5) Gallopade Intl.

— New York Silly Basketball Sportsmysteries, Vol. 1. (Carole Marsh New York Bks.). (Illus.). (J). 1994. pap. 19.95 (0-7933-0822-4); lib. bdg. 29.95 (0-7933-0823-2); disk 29.95 (0-7933-0824-0) Gallopade Intl.

— New York Silly Basketball Sportsmysteries, Vol. 2. (Carole Marsh New York Bks.). (Illus.). (J). 1970. lib. bdg. 29.95 (0-7933-1824-6) Gallopade Intl.

— New York Silly Basketball Sportsmysteries, Vol. 2. (Carole Marsh New York Bks.). (Illus.). (J). 1994. pap. 19.95 (0-7933-1825-4); disk 29.95 (0-7933-1826-2) Gallopade Intl.

— New York Silly Football Sportsmysteries, Vol. 1. (Carole Marsh New York Bks.). (Illus.). (J). 1994. pap. 19.95 (1-55609-907-X); lib. bdg. 29.95 (1-55609-906-1); disk 29.95 (1-55609-908-8) Gallopade Intl.

— New York Silly Football Sportsmysteries, Vol. 2. (Carole Marsh New York Bks.). (Illus.). (J). 1994. pap. 19.95 (1-55609-910-X); lib. bdg. 29.95 (1-55609-909-6); disk 29.95 (1-55609-911-8) Gallopade Intl.

— New York Silly Trivia! (Carole Marsh New York Bks.). (Illus.). (J). 1994. pap. 19.95 (1-55609-103-6); lib. bdg. 29.95 (1-55609-895-2); disk 29.95 (1-55609-896-0) Gallopade Intl.

— New York Spelling Bee! Score Big by Correctly Spelling Our State's Unique Names. (Carole Marsh New York Bks.). (Illus.). (YA). (gr. 3-12). 1996. pap. 19.95 (0-7933-6737-9); lib. bdg. 29.95 (0-7933-6736-0) Gallopade Intl.

— New York Timeline: A Chronology of New York History, Mystery, Trivia, Legend, Lore & More. (Carole Marsh New York Bks.). (Illus.). (J). (gr. 3-12). 1994. pap. 19.95 (0-7933-5972-4); lib. bdg. 29.95 (0-7933-5971-6); disk 29.95 (0-7933-5973-2) Gallopade Intl.

— New York 2000! Coming Soon to a Calendar Near You - The 21st Century! - Complete Set of AL 2000 Items. (Two Thousand! Ser.). (Illus.). (J). (gr. 3-12). 1998. pap. 75.00 (0-7933-9373-6); lib. bdg. 85.00 (0-7933-9374-4) Gallopade Intl.

— New York 2000! Coming Soon to a Calendar near You-The 21st Century! (Two Thousand! Ser.). (Illus.). (J). (gr. 3-12). 1998. pap. 19.95 (0-7933-8772-8); lib. bdg. 29.95 (0-7933-8771-X) Gallopade Intl.

— New York UFO's & Extraterrestrials! A Look at the Sightings & Science in Our State. (Carole Marsh New York Bks.). (Illus.). (J). (gr. 3-12). 1997. pap. 19.95 (0-7933-6431-0); lib. bdg. 29.95 (0-7933-6430-2) Gallopade Intl.

— New York's (Most Devastating!) Disasters & (Most Calamitous!) Catastrophies! (Carole Marsh New York Bks.). (Illus.). (J). 1994. pap. 19.95 (0-7933-0813-5); lib. bdg. 29.95 (0-7933-0814-3); disk 29.95 (0-7933-0815-1) Gallopade Intl.

— New York's Unsolved Mysteries (& Their "Solutions") Includes Scientific Information & Other Activities for Students. (Carole Marsh New York Bks.). (Illus.). (J). (gr. 3-12). 1994. pap. 19.95 (0-7933-5819-1); lib. bdg. 29.95 (0-7933-5818-3); disk 29.95 (0-7933-5820-5) Gallopade Intl.

***Marsh, Carole.** The Nifty New Jersey Coloring Book. (New Jersey Experience! Ser.). (Illus.). (J). (gr. k-5). 2000. pap. 3.95 (0-7933-9473-2) Gallopade Intl.

— The Nifty North Carolina Coloring Book. (North Carolina Experience! Ser.). (Illus.). (J). (gr. k-5). 2000. pap. 3.95 (0-7933-9472-4) Gallopade Intl.

Marsh, Carole. North Carolina & Other State Greats (Biographies) (Carole Marsh North Carolina Bks.). (Illus.). (J). 1994. pap. 19.95 (1-55609-938-X); lib. bdg. 29.95 (1-55609-937-1); disk 29.95 (1-55609-939-8) Gallopade Intl.

— North Carolina Bandits, Bushwackers, Outlaws, Crooks, Devils, Ghosts, Desperadoes & Other Assorted & Sundry Characters! (Carole Marsh North Carolina Bks.). (Illus.). (J). 1994. pap. 19.95 (0-7933-0840-2); lib. bdg. 29.95 (0-7933-0841-0); disk 29.95 (0-7933-0842-9) Gallopade Intl.

— North Carolina "BIO" Bingo! 24 Must Know State People for Kids to Learn about While Having Fun! (Bingo! Ser.). (Illus.). (J). (gr. 2-8). 1998. pap. 14.95 (0-7933-8621-7) Gallopade Intl.

— The North Carolina Bookstore Book: A Surprising Guide to Our State's Bookstores & Their Specialties for Students, Teachers, Writers & Publishers. (Carole Marsh North Carolina Bks.). (Illus.). 1994. pap. 19.95 (0-7933-2955-8); lib. bdg. 29.95 (0-7933-2954-X); disk 29.95 (0-7933-2956-6) Gallopade Intl.

— North Carolina Classic Christmas Trivia: Stories, Recipes, Activities, Legends, Lore & More. (Carole Marsh North Carolina Bks.). (Illus.). (J). 1994. pap. 19.95 (0-7933-0843-7); lib. bdg. 29.95 (0-7933-0844-5); disk 29.95 (0-7933-0845-3) Gallopade Intl.

— North Carolina Coastales! (Carole Marsh North Carolina Bks.). (J). 1994. lib. bdg. 29.95 (0-7933-7298-4) Gallopade Intl.

— North Carolina "Crinkum-Crankum" A Funny Word Book about Our State. (Carole Marsh North Carolina Bks.). (Illus.). (J). (gr. 3-12). 1994. 29.95 (0-7933-4907-9); pap. 19.95 (0-7933-4908-7); disk 29.95 (0-7933-4909-5) Gallopade Intl.

— North Carolina Dingbats! Bk. 1: A Fun Book of Games, Stories, Activities & More about Our State That's All in Code! for You to Decipher. (Carole Marsh North Carolina Bks.). (Illus.). (J). (gr. 3-12). 1994. pap. 19.95 (0-7933-3873-5); lib. bdg. 29.95 (0-7933-3872-7); disk 29.95 (0-7933-3874-3) Gallopade Intl.

***Marsh, Carole.** The North Carolina Experience Pocket Guide. (North Carolina Experience! Ser.). (Illus.). (J). 2000. pap. 6.95 (0-7933-9452-X) Gallopade Intl.

Marsh, Carole. North Carolina Facts & Factivities. (Carole Marsh State Bks.). (Illus.). (J). (gr. 4-7). 1996. pap., teacher ed. 19.95 (0-7933-7913-X, C Marsh) Gallopade Intl.

— North Carolina Festival Fun for Kids! (Carole Marsh North Carolina Bks.). (Illus.). (J). (gr. 3-12). 1994. pap. 19.95 (0-7933-4026-8); lib. bdg. 29.95 (0-7933-4025-X) Gallopade Intl.

— North Carolina Festival Fun for Kids! (Carole Marsh North Carolina Bks.). (Illus.). (YA). (gr. 3-12). 1994. disk 29.95 (0-7933-4027-6) Gallopade Intl.

— North Carolina "GEO" Bingo! 38 Must Know State Geography Facts for Kids to Learn While Having Fun! (Bingo! Ser.). (Illus.). (J). (gr. 2-8). 1998. pap. 14.95 (0-7933-8622-5) Gallopade Intl.

— North Carolina Government! The Cornerstone of Everyday Life in Our State! (Carole Marsh North Carolina Bks.). (Illus.). (J). (gr. 3-12). 1996. pap. 19.95 (0-7933-6281-4); lib. bdg. 29.95 (0-7933-6280-6); disk 29.95 (0-7933-6282-2) Gallopade Intl.

— North Carolina "HISTO" Bingo! 42 Must Know State History Facts for Kids to Learn While Having Fun! (Bingo! Ser.). (Illus.). (J). (gr. 2-8). 1998. pap. 14.95 (0-7933-8623-3) Gallopade Intl.

— North Carolina History! Surprising Secrets about Our State's Founding Mothers, Fathers & Kids! (Carole Marsh North Carolina Bks.). (Illus.). (J). (gr. 3-12). 1996. pap. 19.95 (0-7933-6128-1); lib. bdg. 29.95 (0-7933-6127-3); disk 29.95 (0-7933-6129-X) Gallopade Intl.

— The North Carolina Hot Air Balloon Mystery. (Carole Marsh North Carolina Bks.). (Illus.). (J). (gr. 2-9). 1994. 29.95 (0-7933-2615-X); pap. 19.95 (0-7933-2616-8); disk 29.95 (0-7933-2617-6) Gallopade Intl.

— North Carolina Hot Zones! Viruses, Diseases, & Epidemics in Our State's History. (Hot Zones! Ser.). (Illus.). (J). (gr. 3-12). 1998. pap. 19.95 (0-7933-8928-3); lib. bdg. 29.95 (0-7933-8927-5) Gallopade Intl.

— North Carolina Indian Dictionary for Kids! (Carole Marsh State Bks.). (J). (gr. 2-9). 1995. 29.95 (0-7933-7743-9, C Marsh) Gallopade Intl.

— North Carolina Indian Dictionary for Kids! (Carole Marsh State Bks.). (J). (gr. 2-9). 1996. pap. 19.95 (0-7933-7744-7, C Marsh); disk 29.95 (0-7933-7745-5, C Marsh) Gallopade Intl.

***Marsh, Carole.** North Carolina Jeopardy. (North Carolina Experience! Ser.). (Illus.). (J). (gr. 2-6). 2000. pap. 7.95 (0-7933-9519-4) Gallopade Intl.

Marsh, Carole. North Carolina Jeopardy! Answers & Questions about Our State! (Carole Marsh North Carolina Bks.). (Illus.). (J). (gr. 3-12). 1994. pap. 19.95 (0-7933-4179-5); lib. bdg. 29.95 (0-7933-4178-7); disk 29.95 (0-7933-4180-9) Gallopade Intl.

***Marsh, Carole.** North Carolina Jography. (North Carolina Experience! Ser.). (Illus.). (J). (gr. 2-6). 2000. 7.95 (0-7933-9520-8) Gallopade Intl.

Marsh, Carole. North Carolina Jography: A Fun Run Through the Tarheel State. (Statemeant Ser.). (Illus.). 50p. (Orig.). (J). (gr. 4-8). 1994. pap. 19.95 (0-935326-81-2) Gallopade Intl.

— North Carolina Kid's Cookbook: Recipes, How-to, History, Lore & More. (Carole Marsh North Carolina Bks.). (Illus.). (J). 1994. pap. 19.95 (0-7933-0852-6); lib. bdg. 29.95 (0-7933-0853-4); disk 29.95 (0-7933-0854-2) Gallopade Intl.

— The North Carolina Library Book: A Surprising Guide to the Unusual Special Collections in Libraries Across Our State for Students, Teachers, Writers & Publishers - Includes Reproducible Mailing Labels Plus Activities for Young People! (Carole Marsh North Carolina Bks.). (Illus.). 1994. pap. 19.95 (0-7933-3105-6); lib. bdg. 29.95 (0-7933-3104-8); disk 29.95 (0-7933-3106-4) Gallopade Intl.

— North Carolina Math! How It All Adds up in Our State. (Carole Marsh North Carolina Bks.). (Illus.). (YA). (gr. 3-12). 1996. pap. 19.95 (0-7933-6587-2); lib. bdg. 29.95 (0-7933-6586-4) Gallopade Intl.

— The North Carolina Media Book: A Surprising Guide to the Amazing Print, Broadcast & Online Media of Our State for Students, Teachers, Writers & Publishers - Includes Reproducible Mailing Labels Plus Activities for Young People! (Carole Marsh North Carolina Bks.). (Illus.). 1994. pap. 19.95 (0-7933-3261-3); lib. bdg. 29.95 (0-7933-3260-5); disk 29.95 (0-7933-3262-1) Gallopade Intl.

— The North Carolina Mystery Van Takes Off! Book 1: Handicapped North Carolina Kids Sneak Off on a Big Adventure. (Carole Marsh North Carolina Bks.). (Illus.). (J). (gr. 3-12). 1994. 29.95 (0-7933-5060-3); pap. 19.95 (0-7933-5061-1); disk 29.95 (0-7933-5062-X) Gallopade Intl.

— North Carolina Quiz Bowl Crash Course! (Carole Marsh North Carolina Bks.). (Illus.). (J). 1994. pap. 19.95 (1-55609-935-5); lib. bdg. 29.95 (1-55609-934-7); disk 29.95 (1-55609-936-3) Gallopade Intl.

— North Carolina Rollercoasters! (Carole Marsh North Carolina Bks.). (Illus.). (J). (gr. 3-12). 1994. pap. 19.95 (0-7933-5324-6); lib. bdg. 29.95 (0-7933-5323-8) Gallopade Intl.

— North Carolina Rollercoasters! (Carole Marsh North Carolina Bks.). (Illus.). (YA). (gr. 3-12). 1994. disk 29.95 (0-7933-5325-4) Gallopade Intl.

— North Carolina School Trivia: An Amazing & Fascinating Look at Our State's Teachers, Schools & Students! (Carole Marsh North Carolina Bks.). (Illus.). (J). 1994. pap. 19.95 (0-7933-0849-6); lib. bdg. 29.95 (0-7933-0850-X); disk 29.95 (0-7933-0851-8) Gallopade Intl.

— North Carolina Silly Basketball Sportsmysteries, Vol. 1. (Carole Marsh North Carolina Bks.). (Illus.). (J). 1994. pap. 19.95 (0-7933-0846-1); lib. bdg. 29.95 (0-7933-0847-X); disk 29.95 (0-7933-0848-8) Gallopade Intl.

— North Carolina Silly Basketball Sportsmysteries, Vol. 2. (Carole Marsh North Carolina Bks.). (Illus.). (J). 1994. pap. 19.95 (0-7933-1837-8); lib. bdg. 29.95 (0-7933-1836-X); disk 29.95 (0-7933-1838-6) Gallopade Intl.

— North Carolina Silly Football Sportmysteries, Vol. 2. (Carole Marsh North Carolina Bks.). (Illus.). (J). 1994. pap. 19.95 (1-55609-931-2); lib. bdg. 29.95 (1-55609-930-4); disk 29.95 (1-55609-932-0) Gallopade Intl.

— North Carolina Silly Football Sportsmysteries, Vol. 1. (Carole Marsh North Carolina Bks.). (Illus.). (J). 1994. pap. 19.95 (1-55609-928-2); lib. bdg. 29.95 (1-55609-927-4); disk 29.95 (1-55609-929-0) Gallopade Intl.

— North Carolina Silly Trivia! (Carole Marsh North Carolina Bks.). (Illus.). (J). 1994. lib. bdg. 29.95 (1-55609-921-5); disk 29.95 (1-55609-922-3) Gallopade Intl.

— North Carolina Spelling Bee! Score Big by Correctly Spelling Our State's Unique Names. (Carole Marsh North Carolina Bks.). (Illus.). (YA). (gr. 3-12). 1996. pap. 19.95 (0-7933-6740-9); lib. bdg. 29.95 (0-7933-6739-5) Gallopade Intl.

— North Carolina Timeline: A Chronology of North Carolina History, Mystery, Trivia, Legend, Lore & More. (Carole Marsh North Carolina Bks.). (Illus.). (J). (gr. 3-12). 1994. pap. 19.95 (0-7933-5975-9); lib. bdg. 29.95 (0-7933-5974-0); disk 29.95 (0-7933-5976-7) Gallopade Intl.

— North Carolina 2000! Coming Soon to a Calendar Near You - The 21st Century! - Complete Set of AL 2000 Items. (Two Thousand! Ser.). (Illus.). (J). (gr. 3-12). 1998. pap. 75.00 (0-7933-9375-2) Gallopade Intl.

— North Carolina 2000! Coming Soon to a Calendar Near You - The 21st Century! - Complete Set of All 2000 Items. (Two Thousand! Ser.). (Illus.). (J). (gr. 3-12). 1998. lib. bdg. 85.00 (0-7933-9376-0) Gallopade Intl.

— North Carolina 2000! Coming Soon to a Calendar near You--The 21st Century! (Two Thousand! Ser.). (Illus.). (J). (gr. 3-12). 1998. pap. 19.95 (0-7933-8775-2); lib. bdg. 29.95 (0-7933-8774-4) Gallopade Intl.

— North Carolina UFO's & Extraterrestrials! A Look at the Sightings & Science in Our State. (Carole Marsh North Carolina Bks.). (Illus.). (J). (gr. 3-12). 1997. pap. 19.95 (0-7933-6434-5); lib. bdg. 29.95 (0-7933-6433-7) Gallopade Intl.

***Marsh, Carole.** North Carolina's Big Activity Book. (North Carolina Experience! Ser.). (Illus.). (J). (gr. k-5). 2000. pap. 9.95 (0-7933-9462-7) Gallopade Intl.

Marsh, Carole. North Carolina's (Most Devastating!) Disasters & (Most Calamitous!) Catastrophies! (Carole Marsh North Carolina Bks.). (Illus.). (J). 1994. pap. 19.95 (0-7933-0837-2); lib. bdg. 29.95 (0-7933-0838-0); disk 29.95 (0-7933-0839-9) Gallopade Intl.

— North Carolina's Scariest Swamp: The Great Dismal. (North Carolina Bks.). (Illus.). (J). (gr. 3 up). 1994. pap. 19.95 (0-7933-1271-X); lib. bdg. 29.95 (0-7933-1270-1); disk 29.95 (0-7933-1272-8) Gallopade Intl.

— North Carolina's Unsolved Mysteries (& Their "Solutions") Includes Scientific Information & Other Activities for Students. (Carole Marsh North Carolina Bks.). (Illus.). (J). (gr. 3-12). 1994. pap. 19.95 (0-7933-5822-1); lib. bdg. 29.95 (0-7933-5821-3); disk 29.95 (0-7933-5823-X) Gallopade Intl.

— The North Dakota Air Balloon Mystery. (Carole Marsh North Dakota Bks.). (Illus.). (J). (gr. 2-9). 1994. 29.95 (0-7933-2624-9); pap. 19.95 (0-7933-2625-7); disk 29.95 (0-7933-2626-5) Gallopade Intl.

— North Dakota & Other State Greats (Biographies) (Carole Marsh North Dakota Bks.). (Illus.). (J). 1994. pap. 19.95 (1-55609-977-0); lib. bdg. 29.95 (1-55609-976-2) Gallopade Intl.

— North Dakota & Other State Greats (Biographies) (Carole Marsh North Dakota Bks.). (Illus.). (J). 1997. disk 29.95 (1-55609-978-9) Gallopade Intl.

— North Dakota Bandits, Bushwackers, Outlaws, Crooks, Devils, Ghosts, Desperadoes & Other Assorted & Sundry Characters! (Carole Marsh North Dakota Bks.). (Illus.). (J). 1994. pap. 19.95 (0-7933-0864-X); lib. bdg. 29.95 (0-7933-0865-8); disk 29.95 (0-7933-0866-6) Gallopade Intl.

— North Dakota "BIO" Bingo! 24 Must Know State People for Kids to Learn about While Having Fun! (Bingo! Ser.). (Illus.). (J). (gr. 2-8). 1998. pap. 14.95 (0-7933-8624-1) Gallopade Intl.

— The North Dakota Bookstore Book: A Surprising Guide to Our State's Bookstores & Their Specialties for Students, Teachers, Writers & Publishers. (Carole Marsh North Carolina Bks.). (Illus.). 1994. pap. 19.95 (0-7933-2958-2); lib. bdg. 29.95 (0-7933-2957-4); disk 29.95 (0-7933-2959-0) Gallopade Intl.

— North Dakota Classic Christmas Trivia: Stories, Recipes, Activities, Legends, Lore & More! (Carole Marsh North Dakota Bks.). (Illus.). (J). 1994. pap. 19.95 (0-7933-0867-4); lib. bdg. 29.95 (0-7933-0868-2); disk 29.95 (0-7933-0869-0) Gallopade Intl.

— North Dakota Coastales. (Carole Marsh North Dakota Bks.). (Illus.). (J). 1994. pap. 19.95 (1-55609-971-1); disk 29.95 (1-55609-972-X) Gallopade Intl.

— North Dakota Coastales. (Carole Marsh North Dakota Bks.). (Illus.). (J). 1997. lib. bdg. 29.95 (1-55609-970-3) Gallopade Intl.

— North Dakota Coastales! (Carole Marsh North Dakota Bks.). (J). 1994. lib. bdg. 29.95 (0-7933-7299-2) Gallopade Intl.

— North Dakota "Crinkum-Crankum" A Funny Word Book about Our State. (Carole Marsh North Dakota Bks.). (Illus.). (J). (gr. 3-12). 1994. 29.95 (0-7933-4910-9); pap. 19.95 (0-7933-4911-7); disk 29.95 (0-7933-4912-5) Gallopade Intl.

— North Dakota Dingbats! Bk. 1: A Fun Book of Games, Stories, Activities & More about Our State That's All in Code! for You to Decipher. (Carole Marsh North Dakota Bks.). (Illus.). (J). (gr. 3-12). 1994. pap. 19.95 (0-7933-3876-X); lib. bdg. 29.95 (0-7933-3875-1); disk 29.95 (0-7933-3877-8) Gallopade Intl.

— North Dakota Facts & Factivities. (Carole Marsh State Bks.). (Illus.). (J). (gr. 4-7). 1996. pap., teacher ed. 19.95 (0-7933-7915-6, C Marsh) Gallopade Intl.

— North Dakota Festival Fun for Kids! (Carole Marsh North Dakota Bks.). (Illus.). (J). (gr. 3-12). 1994. pap. 19.95 (0-7933-4029-2); lib. bdg. 29.95 (0-7933-4028-4) Gallopade Intl.

— North Dakota Festival Fun for Kids! (Carole Marsh North Dakota Bks.). (Illus.). (YA). (gr. 3-12). 1994. disk 29.95 (0-7933-4030-6) Gallopade Intl.

— North Dakota "GEO" Bingo! 38 Must Know State Geography Facts for Kids to Learn While Having Fun! (Bingo! Ser.). (Illus.). (J). (gr. 2-8). 1998. pap. 14.95 (0-7933-8625-X) Gallopade Intl.

— North Dakota Government! The Cornerstone of Everyday Life in Our State! (Carole Marsh North Dakota Bks.).

M

M

(Illus.). (J). (gr. 3-12). 1996. pap. 19.95 (*0-7933-6284-9*); lib. bdg. 29.95 (*0-7933-6283-0*); disk 29.95 (*0-7933-6285-7*) Gallopade Intl.

— North Dakota "HISTO" Bingo! 42 Must Know State History Facts for Kids to Learn While Having Fun! (Bingo! Ser.). (Illus.). (J). (gr. 2-8). 1998. pap. 14.95 (*0-7933-8626-8*) Gallopade Intl.

— North Dakota History! Surprising Secrets about Our State's Founding Mothers, Fathers & Kids! (Carole Marsh North Dakota Bks.). (Illus.). (J). (gr. 3-12). 1996. pap. 19.95 (*0-7933-6131-1*); lib. bdg. 29.95 (*0-7933-6130-3*); disk 29.95 (*0-7933-6132-X*) Gallopade Intl.

— North Dakota Hot Zones! Viruses, Diseases, & Epidemics in Our State's History. (Hot Zones! Ser.). (Illus.). (J). (gr. 3-12). 1998. pap. 19.95 (*0-7933-8931-3*); lib. bdg. 29.95 (*0-7933-8930-5*) Gallopade Intl.

— North Dakota Indian Dictionary for Kids! (Carole Marsh State Bks.). (J). (gr. 2-9). 1996. 29.95 (*0-7933-7746-3*, C Marsh); pap. 19.95 (*0-7933-7747-1*, C Marsh) Gallopade Intl.

— North Dakota Jeopardy! Answers & Questions about Our State! (Carole Marsh North Dakota Bks.). (Illus.). (J). (gr. 3-12). 1994. pap. 19.95 (*0-7933-4182-5*); lib. bdg. 29.95 (*0-7933-4181-7*); disk 29.95 (*0-7933-4183-3*) Gallopade Intl.

— North Dakota "Jography" A Fun Run Thru Our State! (Carole Marsh North Dakota Bks.). (Illus.). (J). 1994. pap. 19.95 (*1-55609-944-4*); lib. bdg. 29.95 (*1-55609-943-6*); disk 29.95 (*1-55609-945-2*) Gallopade Intl.

— North Dakota Kid's Cookbook: Recipes, How-to, History, Lore & More! (Carole Marsh North Dakota Bks.). (Illus.). (J). 1994. pap. 19.95 (*0-7933-0876-3*); lib. bdg. 29.95 (*0-7933-0877-1*); disk 29.95 (*0-7933-0878-X*) Gallopade Intl.

— The North Dakota Library Book: A Surprising Guide to the Unusual Special Collections in Libraries Across Our State for Students, Teachers, Writers & Publishers - Includes Reproducible Mailing Labels Plus Activities for Young People! (Carole Marsh North Dakota Bks.). (Illus.). 1994. pap. 19.95 (*0-7933-3108-0*); lib. bdg. 29.95 (*0-7933-3107-2*); disk 29.95 (*0-7933-3109-9*) Gallopade Intl.

— North Dakota Math! How It All Adds up in Our State. (Carole Marsh North Dakota Bks.). (Illus.). (J). (gr. 3-12). 1996. pap. 19.95 (*0-7933-6590-2*); lib. bdg. 29.95 (*0-7933-6589-9*) Gallopade Intl.

— The North Dakota Media Book: A Surprising Guide to the Amazing Print, Broadcast & Online Media of Our State for Students, Teachers, Writers & Publishers - Includes Reproducible Mailing Labels Plus Activities for Young People! (Carole Marsh North Dakota Bks.). (Illus.). 1994. pap. 19.95 (*0-7933-3264-8*); lib. bdg. 29.95 (*0-7933-3263-X*); disk 29.95 (*0-7933-3265-6*) Gallopade Intl.

— The North Dakota Mystery Van Takes Off! Book 1: Handicapped North Dakota Kids Sneak Off on a Big Adventure. (Carole Marsh North Dakota Bks.). (Illus.). (J). (gr. 3-12). 1994. 29.95 (*0-7933-5063-8*); pap. 19.95 (*0-7933-5064-6*); disk 29.95 (*0-7933-5065-4*) Gallopade Intl.

— North Dakota Quiz Bowl Crash Course! (Carole Marsh North Dakota Bks.). (Illus.). (J). 1994. pap. 19.95 (*1-55609-974-6*); lib. bdg. 29.95 (*1-55609-973-8*); disk 29.95 (*1-55609-975-4*) Gallopade Intl.

— North Dakota Rollercoasters! (Carole Marsh North Dakota Bks.). (Illus.). (J). (gr. 3-12). 1994. pap. 19.95 (*0-7933-5327-0*); lib. bdg. 29.95 (*0-7933-5326-2*) Gallopade Intl.

— North Dakota Rollercoasters! (Carole Marsh North Dakota Bks.). (Illus.). (YA). (gr. 3-12). 1994. disk 29.95 (*0-7933-5328-9*) Gallopade Intl.

— North Dakota School Trivia: An Amazing & Fascinating Look at Our State's Teachers, Schools & Students! (Carole Marsh North Dakota Bks.). (Illus.). (J). 1994. pap. 19.95 (*0-7933-0873-9*); lib. bdg. 29.95 (*0-7933-0874-7*); disk 29.95 (*0-7933-0875-5*) Gallopade Intl.

— North Dakota Silly Basketball Sportsmysteries, Vol. 1. (Carole Marsh North Dakota Bks.). (Illus.). (J). 1994. pap. 19.95 (*0-7933-0870-4*); lib. bdg. 29.95 (*0-7933-0871-2*) Gallopade Intl.

— North Dakota Silly Basketball Sportsmysteries, Vol. 1. (Carole Marsh North Dakota Bks.). (Illus.). (J). 1997. disk 29.95 (*0-7933-0872-0*) Gallopade Intl.

— North Dakota Silly Basketball Sportsmysteries, Vol. 2. (Carole Marsh North Dakota Bks.). (Illus.). (J). 1994. pap. 19.95 (*0-7933-1846-7*); disk 29.95 (*0-7933-1847-5*) Gallopade Intl.

— North Dakota Silly Basketball Sportsmysteries, Vol. 2. (Carole Marsh North Dakota Bks.). (Illus.). (J). 1997. lib. bdg. 29.95 (*0-7933-1845-9*) Gallopade Intl.

— North Dakota Silly Football Sportsmysteries, Vol. 1. (Carole Marsh North Dakota Bks.). (Illus.). (J). 1994. pap. 19.95 (*1-55609-949-5*); lib. bdg. 29.95 (*1-55609-948-7*) Gallopade Intl.

— North Dakota Silly Football Sportsmysteries, Vol. 2. (Carole Marsh North Dakota Bks.). (Illus.). (J). 1994. pap. 19.95 (*1-55609-968-1*); lib. bdg. 29.95 (*1-55609-967-3*); disk 29.95 (*1-55609-969-X*) Gallopade Intl.

— North Dakota Silly Trivia! (Carole Marsh North Dakota Bks.). (Illus.). (J). 1994. pap. 19.95 (*1-55609-941-X*); lib. bdg. 29.95 (*1-55609-940-1*); disk 29.95 (*1-55609-942-8*) Gallopade Intl.

— North Dakota Spelling Bee! Score Big by Correctly Spelling Our State's Unique Names. (Carole Marsh North Dakota Bks.). (Illus.). (YA). (gr. 3-12). 1996. pap. 19.95 (*0-7933-6743-3*); lib. bdg. 29.95 (*0-7933-6742-5*) Gallopade Intl.

— North Dakota Timeline: A Chronology of North Dakota History, Mystery, Trivia, Legend, Lore & More. (Carole Marsh North Dakota Bks.). (Illus.). (J). (gr. 3-12). 1994. pap. 19.95 (*0-7933-5978-3*); lib. bdg. 29.95 (*0-7933-5977-5*); disk 29.95 (*0-7933-5979-1*) Gallopade Intl.

— North Dakota 2000! Coming Soon to a Calendar Near You - The 21st Century! - Complete Set of AL 2000 Items. (Two Thousand! Ser.). (Illus.). (J). (gr. 3-12). 1998. pap. 75.00 (*0-7933-9377-9*) Gallopade Intl.

— North Dakota 2000! Coming Soon to a Calendar Near You - The 21st Century! - Complete Set of All 2000 Items. (Two Thousand! Ser.). (Illus.). (J). (gr. 3-12). 1998. lib. bdg. 85.00 (*0-7933-9378-7*) Gallopade Intl.

— North Dakota 2000! Coming Soon to a Calendar near You--The 21st Century! (Two Thousand! Ser.). (Illus.). (J). (gr. 3-12). 1998. pap. 19.95 (*0-7933-8778-7*); lib. bdg. 29.95 (*0-7933-8777-9*) Gallopade Intl.

— North Dakota UFO's & Extraterrestrials! A Look at the Sightings & Science in Our State. (Carole Marsh North Dakota Bks.). (Illus.). (J). (gr. 3-12). 1997. pap. 19.95 (*0-7933-6437-X*); lib. bdg. 29.95 (*0-7933-6436-1*) Gallopade Intl.

— North Dakota's (Most Devastating!) Disasters & (Most Calamitous!) Catastrophies! (Carole Marsh North Dakota Bks.). (Illus.). (J). 1994. pap. 19.95 (*0-7933-0861-5*); lib. bdg. 29.95 (*0-7933-0862-3*); disk 29.95 (*0-7933-0863-1*) Gallopade Intl.

— North Dakota's Unsolved Mysteries (& Their "Solutions") Includes Scientific Information & Other Activities for Students. (Carole Marsh North Dakota Bks.). (Illus.). (J). (gr. 3-12). 1994. pap. 19.95 (*0-7933-5825-6*); lib. bdg. 29.95 (*0-7933-5824-8*); disk 29.95 (*0-7933-5826-4*) Gallopade Intl.

— Ohio & Other State Greats (Biographies) (Carole Marsh Ohio Bks.). (Illus.). (J). 1994. pap. 19.95 (*1-55609-999-1*); lib. bdg. 29.95 (*1-55609-998-3*); disk 29.95 (*1-55609-854-5*) Gallopade Intl.

— Ohio Bandits, Bushwackers, Outlaws, Crooks, Devils, Ghosts, Desperadoes & Other Assorted & Sundry Characters! (Illus.). (J). 1994. pap. 19.95 (*0-7933-0888-7*); lib. bdg. 29.95 (*0-7933-0889-5*); disk 29.95 (*0-7933-0890-9*) Gallopade Intl.

— Ohio "BIO" Bingo! 24 Must Know State People for Kids to Learn about While Having Fun! (Bingo! Ser.). (Illus.). (J). (gr. 2-8). 1998. pap. 14.95 (*0-7933-8627-6*) Gallopade Intl.

— The Ohio Bookstore Book: A Surprising Guide to Our State's Bookstores & Their Specialties for Students, Teachers, Writers & Publishers. (Carole Marsh Ohio Bks.). (Illus.). 1994. pap. 19.95 (*0-7933-2961-2*); lib. bdg. 29.95 (*0-7933-2960-4*); disk 29.95 (*0-7933-2962-0*) Gallopade Intl.

— Ohio Classic Christmas Trivia: Stories, Recipes, Activities, Legends, Lore & More! (Carole Marsh Ohio Bks.). (Illus.). (J). 1994. pap. 19.95 (*0-7933-0891-7*); lib. bdg. 29.95 (*0-7933-0892-5*); disk 29.95 (*0-7933-0893-3*) Gallopade Intl.

— Ohio Coastales. (Carole Marsh Ohio Bks.). (Illus.). (J). 1994. pap. 19.95 (*1-55609-993-2*); lib. bdg. 29.95 (*1-55609-992-4*); disk 29.95 (*1-55609-994-0*) Gallopade Intl.

— Ohio Coastales! (Carole Marsh Ohio Bks.). (J). 1994. lib. bdg. 29.95 (*0-7933-7300-X*) Gallopade Intl.

— Ohio "Crinkum-Crankum" A Funny Word Book about Our State. (Carole Marsh Ohio Bks.). (Illus.). (J). (gr. 3-12). 1994. 29.95 (*0-7933-4913-3*); pap. 19.95 (*0-7933-4914-1*); disk 29.95 (*0-7933-4915-X*) Gallopade Intl.

— Ohio Dingbats! Bk. 1: A Fun Book of Games, Stories, Activities & More about Our State That's All in Code! for You to Decipher. (Carole Marsh Ohio Bks.). (Illus.). (J). (gr. 3-12). 1994. pap. 19.95 (*0-7933-3879-4*); lib. bdg. 29.95 (*0-7933-3878-6*); disk 29.95 (*0-7933-3880-8*) Gallopade Intl.

***Marsh, Carole.** The Ohio Experience Pocket Guide. (Ohio Experience! Ser.). (Illus.). (J). 2000. pap. 6.95 (*0-7933-9454-6*) Gallopade Intl.

Marsh, Carole. Ohio Facts & Factivities. (Carole Marsh State Bks.). (Illus.). (J). (gr. 4-7). 1996. pap., teacher ed. 19.95 (*0-7933-7917-2*, C Marsh) Gallopade Intl.

— Ohio Festival Fun for Kids! (Carole Marsh Ohio Bks.). (Illus.). (J). (gr. 3-12). 1994. pap. 19.95 (*0-7933-4032-2*); lib. bdg. 29.95 (*0-7933-4031-4*) Gallopade Intl.

— Ohio Festival Fun for Kids! (Carole Marsh Ohio Bks.). (Illus.). (YA). (gr. 3-12). 1994. disk 29.95 (*0-7933-4033-0*) Gallopade Intl.

— Ohio "GEO" Bingo! 38 Must Know State Geography Facts for Kids to Learn While Having Fun! (Bingo! Ser.). (Illus.). (J). (gr. 2-8). 1998. pap. 14.95 (*0-7933-8628-4*) Gallopade Intl.

— Ohio Government! The Cornerstone of Everyday Life in Our State! (Carole Marsh Ohio Bks.). (Illus.). (J). (gr. 3-12). 1996. pap. 19.95 (*0-7933-6287-3*); lib. bdg. 29.95 (*0-7933-6286-5*); disk 29.95 (*0-7933-6288-1*) Gallopade Intl.

— Ohio "HISTO" Bingo! 42 Must Know State History Facts for Kids to Learn While Having Fun! (Bingo! Ser.). (Illus.). (J). (gr. 2-8). 1998. pap. 14.95 (*0-7933-8629-2*) Gallopade Intl.

— Ohio History! Surprising Secrets about Our State's Founding Mothers, Fathers & Kids! (Carole Marsh Ohio Bks.). (Illus.). (J). (gr. 3-12). 1996. pap. 19.95 (*0-7933-6134-6*); lib. bdg. 29.95 (*0-7933-6133-8*); disk 29.95 (*0-7933-6135-4*) Gallopade Intl.

— The Ohio Hot Air Balloon Mystery. (Carole Marsh Ohio Bks.). (Illus.). (J). (gr. 2-9). 1994. 29.95 (*0-7933-2633-8*); pap. 19.95 (*0-7933-2634-6*); disk 29.95 (*0-7933-2635-4*) Gallopade Intl.

— Ohio Hot Zones! Viruses, Diseases, & Epidemics in Our State's History. (Hot Zones! Ser.). (Illus.). (J). (gr. 3-12). 1998. pap. 19.95 (*0-7933-8934-8*); lib. bdg. 29.95 (*0-7933-8933-X*) Gallopade Intl.

— Ohio Indian Dictionary for Kids! (Carole Marsh State Bks.). (J). (gr. 2-9). 1996. 29.95 (*0-7933-7749-8*, C Marsh); pap. 19.95 (*0-7933-7750-1*, C Marsh) Gallopade Intl.

***Marsh, Carole.** Ohio Jeopardy. (Ohio Experience! Ser.). (J). (gr. 2-6). 2000. pap. 7.95 (*0-7933-9525-9*) Gallopade Intl.

Marsh, Carole. Ohio Jeopardy! Answers & Questions about Our State! (Carole Marsh Ohio Bks.). (Illus.). (J). (gr. 3-12). 1994. pap. 19.95 (*0-7933-4185-X*); lib. bdg. 29.95 (*0-7933-4184-1*); disk 29.95 (*0-7933-4186-8*) Gallopade Intl.

***Marsh, Carole.** Ohio Jography. (Ohio Experience! Ser.). (Illus.). (J). (gr. 2-6). 2000. pap. 7.95 (*0-7933-9526-7*) Gallopade Intl.

Marsh, Carole. Ohio "Jography" A Fun Run Thru Our State! (Carole Marsh Ohio Bks.). (Illus.). (J). 1994. pap. 19.95 (*1-55609-982-7*); lib. bdg. 29.95 (*1-55609-981-9*); disk 29.95 (*1-55609-983-5*) Gallopade Intl.

— Ohio Kid's Cookbook: Recipes, How-To, History, Lore & More! (Carole Marsh Ohio Bks.). (Illus.). (J). 1994. pap. 19.95 (*0-7933-0900-X*); lib. bdg. 29.95 (*0-7933-0901-8*); disk 29.95 (*0-7933-0902-6*) Gallopade Intl.

— The Ohio Library Book: A Surprising Guide to the Unusual Special Collections in Libraries Across Our State for Students, Teachers, Writers & Publishers - Includes Reproducible Mailing Labels Plus Activities for Young People! (Carole Marsh Ohio Bks.). (Illus.). 1994. pap. 19.95 (*0-7933-3111-0*); lib. bdg. 29.95 (*0-7933-3110-2*); disk 29.95 (*0-7933-3112-9*) Gallopade Intl.

— Ohio Math! How It All Adds up in Our State. (Carole Marsh Ohio Bks.). (Illus.). (YA). (gr. 3-12). 1996. pap. 19.95 (*0-7933-6593-7*); lib. bdg. 29.95 (*0-7933-6592-9*) Gallopade Intl.

— The Ohio Media Book: A Surprising Guide to the Amazing Print, Broadcast & Online Media of Our State for Students, Teachers, Writers & Publishers - Includes Reproducible Mailing Labels Plus Activities for Young People! (Carole Marsh Ohio Bks.). (Illus.). 1994. pap. 19.95 (*0-7933-3267-2*); lib. bdg. 29.95 (*0-7933-3266-4*); disk 29.95 (*0-7933-3268-0*) Gallopade Intl.

— The Ohio Mystery Van Takes Off! Handicapped Ohio Kids Sneak off on a Big Adventure, Bk. 1. (Carole Marsh Ohio Bks.). (Illus.). (J). (gr. 3-12). 1994. 29.95 (*0-7933-5066-2*); pap. 19.95 (*0-7933-5067-0*); disk 29.95 (*0-7933-5068-9*) Gallopade Intl.

— Ohio Quiz Crash Course! (Carole Marsh Ohio Bks.). (Illus.). (J). 1994. pap. 19.95 (*1-55609-996-7*); lib. bdg. 29.95 (*1-55609-995-9*); disk 29.95 (*1-55609-997-5*) Gallopade Intl.

— Ohio Rollercoasters! (Carole Marsh Ohio Bks.). (Illus.). (J). (gr. 3-12). 1994. pap. 19.95 (*0-7933-5330-0*); lib. bdg. 29.95 (*0-7933-5329-7*) Gallopade Intl.

— Ohio Rollercoasters! (Carole Marsh Ohio Bks.). (Illus.). (YA). (gr. 3-12). 1994. disk 29.95 (*0-7933-5331-9*) Gallopade Intl.

— Ohio School Trivia: An Amazing & Fascinating Look at Our State's Teachers, Schools & Students! (Carole Marsh Ohio Bks.). (Illus.). (J). 1994. pap. 19.95 (*0-7933-0897-6*); lib. bdg. 29.95 (*0-7933-0898-4*); disk 29.95 (*0-7933-0899-2*) Gallopade Intl.

— Ohio Silly Basketball Sportsmysteries, Vol. 1. (Carole Marsh Ohio Bks.). (Illus.). (J). 1994. pap. 19.95 (*0-7933-0894-1*); lib. bdg. 29.95 (*0-7933-0895-X*); disk 29.95 (*0-7933-0896-8*) Gallopade Intl.

— Ohio Silly Basketball Sportsmysteries, Vol. 2. (Carole Marsh Ohio Bks.). (Illus.). (J). 1994. pap. 19.95 (*0-7933-1854-8*); disk 29.95 (*0-7933-1855-6*) Gallopade Intl.

— Ohio Silly Basketball Sportsmysteries, Vol. 2. (Carole Marsh Ohio Bks.). (Illus.). (J). 1997. lib. bdg. 29.95 (*0-7933-1853-X*) Gallopade Intl.

— Ohio Silly Football Sportsmysteries, Vol. 1. (Carole Marsh Ohio Bks.). (Illus.). (J). 1994. pap. 19.95 (*1-55609-987-8*); lib. bdg. 29.95 (*1-55609-986-X*); disk 29.95 (*1-55609-988-6*) Gallopade Intl.

— Ohio Silly Football Sportsmysteries, Vol. 2. (Carole Marsh Ohio Bks.). (Illus.). (J). 1994. pap. 19.95 (*1-55609-990-8*); lib. bdg. 29.95 (*1-55609-989-4*); disk 29.95 (*1-55609-991-6*) Gallopade Intl.

— Ohio Silly Trivia!. (Carole Marsh Ohio Bks.). (Illus.). (J). 1994. pap. 19.95 (*1-55609-112-5*); lib. bdg. 29.95 (*1-55609-979-7*); disk 29.95 (*1-55609-980-0*) Gallopade Intl.

— Ohio Spelling Bee! Score Big by Correctly Spelling Our State's Unique Names. (Carole Marsh Ohio Bks.). (Illus.). (YA). (gr. 3-12). 1996. pap. 19.95 (*0-7933-6746-8*); lib. bdg. 29.95 (*0-7933-6745-X*) Gallopade Intl.

— Ohio Timeline: A Chronology of Ohio History, Mystery, Trivia, Legend, Lore & More. (Carole Marsh Ohio Bks.). (Illus.). (J). (gr. 3-12). 1994. pap. 19.95 (*0-7933-5981-3*); lib. bdg. 29.95 (*0-7933-5980-5*); disk 29.95 (*0-7933-5982-1*) Gallopade Intl.

— Ohio 2000! Coming Soon to a Calendar Near You - The 21st Century! - Complete Set of AL 2000 Items. (Two Thousand! Ser.). (Illus.). (J). (gr. 3-12). 1998. pap. 75.00 (*0-7933-9379-5*); lib. bdg. 85.00 (*0-7933-9380-9*) Gallopade Intl.

— Ohio 2000! Coming Soon to a Calendar near You-The 21st Century! (Two Thousand! Ser.). (Illus.). (J). (gr. 3-12). 1998. pap. 19.95 (*0-7933-8781-7*); lib. bdg. 29.95 (*0-7933-8780-9*) Gallopade Intl.

— Ohio UFO's & Extraterrestrials! A Look at the Sightings & Science in Our State. (Carole Marsh Ohio Bks.). (Illus.). (J). (gr. 3-12). 1997. pap. 19.95 (*0-7933-6440-X*); lib. bdg. 29.95 (*0-7933-6439-6*) Gallopade Intl.

***Marsh, Carole.** Ohio's Big Activity Book. (Ohio Experience! Ser.). (Illus.). (J). (gr. k-5). 2000. pap. 9.95 (*0-7933-9464-3*) Gallopade Intl.

Marsh, Carole. Ohio's (Most Devastating!) Disasters & (Most Calamitous!) Catastrophies! (Carole Marsh Ohio Bks.). (Illus.). (J). 1994. pap. 19.95 (*0-7933-0885-2*); lib. bdg. 29.95 (*0-7933-0886-0*); disk 29.95 (*0-7933-0887-9*) Gallopade Intl.

— Ohio's Unsolved Mysteries (And Their "Solutions") Includes Scientific Information & Other Activities for Students. (Carole Marsh Ohio Bks.). (Illus.). (J). (gr. 3-12). 1994. pap. 19.95 (*0-7933-5828-0*); lib. bdg. 29.95 (*0-7933-5827-2*); disk 29.95 (*0-7933-5829-9*) Gallopade Intl.

— Oklahoma & Other State Greats (Biographies) (Carole Marsh Oklahoma Bks.). (Illus.). (J). 1994. pap. 19.95 (*0-7933-1879-3*); lib. bdg. 29.95 (*0-7933-1878-5*); disk 29.95 (*0-7933-1880-7*) Gallopade Intl.

— Oklahoma Bandits, Bushwackers, Outlaws, Crooks, Devils, Ghosts, Desperadoes & Other Assorted & Sundry Characters! (Carole Marsh Oklahoma Bks.). (Illus.). (J). 1994. pap. 19.95 (*0-7933-0913-1*); lib. bdg. 29.95 (*0-7933-0914-X*); disk 29.95 (*0-7933-0915-8*) Gallopade Intl.

— Oklahoma "BIO" Bingo! 24 Must Know State People for Kids to Learn about While Having Fun! (Bingo! Ser.). (Illus.). (J). (gr. 2-8). 1998. pap. 14.95 (*0-7933-8630-6*) Gallopade Intl.

— The Oklahoma Bookstore Book: A Surprising Guide to Our State's Bookstores & Their Specialties for Students, Teachers, Writers & Publishers. (Carole Marsh Oklahoma Bks.). (Illus.). 1994. pap. 19.95 (*0-7933-2964-7*); lib. bdg. 29.95 (*0-7933-2963-9*); disk 29.95 (*0-7933-2965-5*) Gallopade Intl.

— Oklahoma Classic Christmas Trivia: Stories, Recipes, Activities, Legends, Lore & More! (Carole Marsh Oklahoma Bks.). (Illus.). (J). 1994. pap. 19.95 (*0-7933-0916-6*); lib. bdg. 29.95 (*0-7933-0917-4*); disk 29.95 (*0-7933-0918-2*) Gallopade Intl.

— Oklahoma Coastales. (Oklahoma Bks.). (J). 1994. lib. bdg. 29.95 (*0-7933-7301-8*) Gallopade Intl.

— Oklahoma Coastales. (Carole Marsh Oklahoma Bks.). (Illus.). (J). 1994. pap. 19.95 (*0-7933-1873-4*); lib. bdg. 29.95 (*0-7933-1872-6*); disk 29.95 (*0-7933-1874-2*) Gallopade Intl.

— Oklahoma "Crinkum-Crankum" A Funny Word Book about Our State. (Oklahoma Bks.). (Illus.). (J). (gr. 3-12). 1994. 29.95 (*0-7933-4916-8*); pap. 19.95 (*0-7933-4917-6*); disk 29.95 (*0-7933-4918-4*) Gallopade Intl.

— Oklahoma Dingbats! Bk. 1: A Fun Book of Games, Stories, Activities & More about Our State That's All in Code! for You to Decipher. (Carole Marsh Oklahoma Bks.). (Illus.). (J). (gr. 3-12). 1994. pap. 19.95 (*0-7933-3882-4*); lib. bdg. 29.95 (*0-7933-3881-6*); disk 29.95 (*0-7933-3883-2*) Gallopade Intl.

***Marsh, Carole.** The Oklahoma Experience Pocket Guide. (Oklahoma Experience! Ser.). (Illus.). (J). 2000. pap. 6.95 (*0-7933-9594-1*) Gallopade Intl.

Marsh, Carole. Oklahoma Facts & Factivities. (Carole Marsh State Bks.). (Illus.). (J). (gr. 4-7). 1996. pap., teacher ed. 19.95 (*0-7933-7919-9*, C Marsh) Gallopade Intl.

— Oklahoma Festival Fun for Kids! (Carole Marsh Oklahoma Bks.). (Illus.). (J). (gr. 3-12). 1994. pap. 19.95 (*0-7933-4035-7*); lib. bdg. 29.95 (*0-7933-4034-9*) Gallopade Intl.

— Oklahoma Festival Fun for Kids! (Carole Marsh Oklahoma Bks.). (Illus.). (YA). (gr. 3-12). 1994. disk 29.95 (*0-7933-4036-5*) Gallopade Intl.

— Oklahoma "GEO" Bingo! 38 Must Know State Geography Facts for Kids to Learn While Having Fun! (Bingo! Ser.). (Illus.). (J). (gr. 2-8). 1998. pap. 14.95 (*0-7933-8631-4*) Gallopade Intl.

— Oklahoma Government! The Cornerstone of Everyday Life in Our State! (Carole Marsh Oklahoma Bks.). (Illus.). (J). (gr. 3-12). 1996. pap. 19.95 (*0-7933-6290-3*); lib. bdg. 29.95 (*0-7933-6289-X*); disk 29.95 (*0-7933-6291-1*) Gallopade Intl.

— Oklahoma "HISTO" Bingo! 42 Must Know State History Facts for Kids to Learn While Having Fun! (Bingo! Ser.). (Illus.). (J). (gr. 2-8). 1998. pap. 14.95 (*0-7933-8632-2*) Gallopade Intl.

— Oklahoma History! Surprising Secrets about Our State's Founding Mothers, Fathers & Kids! (Carole Marsh Oklahoma Bks.). (Illus.). (J). (gr. 3-12). 1996. pap. 19.95 (*0-7933-6137-0*); lib. bdg. 29.95 (*0-7933-6136-2*); disk 29.95 (*0-7933-6138-9*) Gallopade Intl.

— The Oklahoma Hot Air Balloon Mystery. (Carole Marsh Oklahoma Bks.). (Illus.). (J). (gr. 2-9). 1994. 29.95 (*0-7933-2642-7*); pap. 19.95 (*0-7933-2643-5*); disk 29.95 (*0-7933-2644-3*) Gallopade Intl.

— Oklahoma Hot Zones! Viruses, Diseases, & Epidemics in Our State's History. (Hot Zones! Ser.). (Illus.). (J). (gr. 3-12). 1998. pap. 19.95 (*0-7933-8937-2*); lib. bdg. 29.95 (*0-7933-8936-4*) Gallopade Intl.

— Oklahoma Indian Dictionary for Kids! (Carole Marsh State Bks.). (J). (gr. 2-9). 1996. 29.95 (*0-7933-7752-8*, C Marsh); pap. 19.95 (*0-7933-7753-6*, C Marsh) Gallopade Intl.

***Marsh, Carole.** Oklahoma Jeopardy. (Oklahoma Experience! Ser.). (Illus.). (J). (gr. 2-6). 2000. pap. 7.95 (*0-7933-9596-8*) Gallopade Intl.

Marsh, Carole. Oklahoma Jeopardy! Answers & Questions about Our State! (Carole Marsh Oklahoma Bks.). (Illus.). (J). (gr. 3-12). 1994. pap. 19.95 (*0-7933-4188-4*); lib. bdg. 29.95 (*0-7933-4187-6*); disk 29.95 (*0-7933-4189-2*) Gallopade Intl.

***Marsh, Carole.** Oklahoma Jography. (Oklahoma Experience! Ser.). (Illus.). (J). (gr. 2-6). 2000. pap. 7.95 (*0-7933-9597-6*) Gallopade Intl.

An Asterisk (*) at the beginning of an entry indicates that the title is appearing for the first time.

Marsh, Carole. Oklahoma "Jography" A Fun Run Thru Our State! (Carole Marsh Oklahoma Bks.). (Illus.). (J). 1994. pap. 19.95 (*1-55609-086-2*); lib. bdg. 29.95 (*0-7933-1858-0*); disk 29.95 (*0-7933-1859-9*) Gallopade Intl.

— Oklahoma Kid's Cookbook: Recipes, How-To, History, Lore & More! (Carole Marsh Oklahoma Bks.). (Illus.). (J). 1994. pap. 19.95 (*0-7933-0925-5*); lib. bdg. 29.95 (*0-7933-0926-3*); disk 29.95 (*0-7933-0927-1*) Gallopade Intl.

— The Oklahoma Library Book: A Surprising Guide to the Unusual Special Collections in Libraries Across Our State for Students, Teachers, Writers & Publishers - Includes Reproducible Mailing Labels Plus Activities for Young People! (Carole Marsh Oklahoma Bks.). (Illus.). 1994. pap. 19.95 (*0-7933-3114-5*); lib. bdg. 29.95 (*0-7933-3113-7*); disk 29.95 (*0-7933-3115-3*) Gallopade Intl.

— Oklahoma Math! How It All Adds up in Our State. (Carole Marsh Oklahoma Bks.). (Illus.). (YA). (gr. 3-12). 1996. pap. 19.95 (*0-7933-6596-1*); lib. bdg. 29.95 (*0-7933-6595-3*) Gallopade Intl.

— The Oklahoma Media Book: A Surprising Guide to the Amazing Print, Broadcast & Online Media of Our State for Students, Teachers, Writers & Publishers - Includes Reproducible Mailing Labels Plus Activities for Young People! (Carole Marsh Oklahoma Bks.). (Illus.). 1994. pap. 19.95 (*0-7933-3270-2*); lib. bdg. 29.95 (*0-7933-3269-9*); disk 29.95 (*0-7933-3271-0*) Gallopade Intl.

— The Oklahoma Mystery Van Takes Off! Bk. 1: Handicapped Oklahoma Kids Sneak off on a Big Adventure. (Oklahoma Bks.). (Illus.). (J). (gr. 3-12). 1994. 29.95 (*0-7933-5069-7*); pap. 19.95 (*0-7933-5070-0*); disk 29.95 (*0-7933-5071-9*) Gallopade Intl.

— Oklahoma Quiz Bowl Crash Course! (Carole Marsh Oklahoma Bks.). (Illus.). (J). 1994. pap. 19.95 (*0-7933-1882-3*); lib. bdg. 29.95 (*0-7933-1881-5*); disk 29.95 (*0-7933-1883-1*) Gallopade Intl.

— Oklahoma Rollercoasters! (Oklahoma Bks.). (Illus.). (YA). (gr. 3-12). 1994. pap. 19.95 (*0-7933-5333-5*); lib. bdg. 29.95 (*0-7933-5332-7*); disk 29.95 (*0-7933-5334-3*) Gallopade Intl.

— Oklahoma School Trivia: An Amazing & Fascinating Look at Our State's Teachers, Schools & Students! (Carole Marsh Oklahoma Bks.). (Illus.). (J). 1994. pap. 19.95 (*0-7933-0922-0*); lib. bdg. 29.95 (*0-7933-0923-9*); disk 29.95 (*0-7933-0924-7*) Gallopade Intl.

— Oklahoma Silly Basketball Sportsmysteries, Vol. 1. (Carole Marsh Oklahoma Bks.). (Illus.). (J). 1994. pap. 19.95 (*0-7933-0919-0*); lib. bdg. 29.95 (*0-7933-0920-4*); disk 29.95 (*0-7933-0921-2*) Gallopade Intl.

— Oklahoma Silly Basketball Sportsmysteries, Vol. 2. (Carole Marsh Oklahoma Bks.). (Illus.). (J). 1994. pap. 19.95 (*0-7933-1885-8*); lib. bdg. 29.95 (*0-7933-1884-X*); disk 29.95 (*0-7933-1886-6*) Gallopade Intl.

— Oklahoma Silly Football Sportsmysteries, Vol. 1. (Carole Marsh Oklahoma Bks.). (Illus.). (J). 1994. pap. 19.95 (*0-7933-1864-5*); lib. bdg. 29.95 (*0-7933-1863-7*); disk 29.95 (*0-7933-1865-3*) Gallopade Intl.

— Oklahoma Silly Football Sportsmysteries, Vol. 2. (Carole Marsh Oklahoma Bks.). (Illus.). (J). 1994. pap. 19.95 (*0-7933-1867-X*); lib. bdg. 29.95 (*0-7933-1866-1*); disk 29.95 (*0-7933-1868-8*) Gallopade Intl.

— Oklahoma Silly Trivia! (Carole Marsh Oklahoma Bks.). (Illus.). (J). 1994. pap. 19.95 (*1-55609-082-X*); disk 29.95 (*0-7933-1857-2*) Gallopade Intl.

— Oklahoma Silly Trivia! (Carole Marsh Oklahoma Bks.). (Illus.). (J). 1997. lib. bdg. 29.95 (*0-7933-1856-4*) Gallopade Intl.

— Oklahoma Spelling Bee! Score Big by Correctly Spelling Our State's Unique Names. (Carole Marsh Oklahoma Bks.). (Illus.). (YA). (gr. 3-12). 1996. pap. 19.95 (*0-7933-6749-2*); lib. bdg. 29.95 (*0-7933-6748-4*) Gallopade Intl.

— Oklahoma Timeline: A Chronology of Oklahoma History, Mystery, Trivia, Legend, Lore & More. (Oklahoma Bks.). (Illus.). (J). (gr. 3-12). 1994. pap. 19.95 (*0-7933-5984-8*); lib. bdg. 29.95 (*0-7933-5983-X*); disk 29.95 (*0-7933-5985-6*) Gallopade Intl.

— Oklahoma 2000! Coming Soon to a Calendar Near You - The 21st Century! - Complete Set of AL 2000 Items. (Two Thousand! Ser.). (Illus.). (J). (gr. 3-12). 1998. pap. 75.00 (*0-7933-9381-7*); lib. bdg. 85.00 (*0-7933-9382-5*) Gallopade Intl.

— Oklahoma 2000! Coming Soon to a Calendar near You-The 21st Century! (Two Thousand! Ser.). (Illus.). (J). (gr. 3-12). 1998. pap. 19.95 (*0-7933-8784-1*); lib. bdg. 29.95 (*0-7933-8783-3*) Gallopade Intl.

— Oklahoma UFO's & Extraterrestrials! A Look at the Sightings & Science in Our State. (Carole Marsh Oklahoma Bks.). (Illus.). (J). (gr. 3-12). 1997. pap. 19.95 (*0-7933-6443-4*); lib. bdg. 29.95 (*0-7933-6442-6*) Gallopade Intl.

***Marsh, Carole.** Oklahoma's Big Activity Book. (Oklahoma Experience! Ser.). (Illus.). (J). (gr. k-5). 2000. pap. 9.95 (*0-7933-9598-4*) Gallopade Intl.

Marsh, Carole. Oklahoma's (Most Devastating!) Disasters & (Most Calamitous!) Catastrophies! (Oklahoma Bks.). (Illus.). (J). 1994. pap. 19.95 (*0-7933-0910-7*); lib. bdg. 29.95 (*0-7933-0911-5*); disk 29.95 (*0-7933-0912-3*) Gallopade Intl.

— Oklahoma's Unsolved Mysteries (And Their "Solutions") Includes Scientific Information & Other Activities for Students. (Oklahoma Bks.). (Illus.). (J). (gr. 3-12). 1994. pap. 19.95 (*0-7933-5831-0*); lib. bdg. 29.95 (*0-7933-5830-2*); disk 29.95 (*0-7933-5832-9*) Gallopade Intl.

— Old Salem Mystery. (History Mystery Ser.). (Orig.). (J). (gr. 3-12). 1994. 29.95 (*1-55609-184-2*); pap. 19.95 (*0-935326-59-6*) Gallopade Intl.

— Oregon & Other State Greats (Biographies) (Carole Marsh Oregon Bks.). (Illus.). (J). 1994. pap. 19.95 (*0-7933-1914-5*); lib. bdg. 29.95 (*0-7933-1913-7*); disk 29.95 (*0-7933-1915-3*) Gallopade Intl.

— Oregon Bandits, Bushwackers, Outlaws, Crooks, Devils, Ghosts, Desperadoes & Other Assorted & Sundry Characters! (Carole Marsh Oregon Bks.). (Illus.). (J). 1994. pap. 19.95 (*0-7933-0937-9*); lib. bdg. 29.95 (*0-7933-0938-7*); disk 29.95 (*0-7933-0939-5*) Gallopade Intl.

— Oregon "BIO" Bingo! 24 Must Know State People for Kids to Learn about While Having Fun! (Bingo! Ser.). (Illus.). (J). (gr. 2-8). 1998. pap. 14.95 (*0-7933-8633-0*) Gallopade Intl.

— The Oregon Bookstore Book: A Surprising Guide to Our State's Bookstores & Their Specialties for Students, Teachers, Writers & Publishers. (Oregon Bks.). (Illus.). 1994. pap. 19.95 (*0-7933-2967-1*); lib. bdg. 29.95 (*0-7933-2966-3*); disk 29.95 (*0-7933-2968-X*) Gallopade Intl.

— Oregon Classic Christmas Trivia: Stories, Recipes, Activities, Legends, Lore & More! (Carole Marsh Oregon Bks.). (Illus.). (J). 1994. pap. 19.95 (*0-7933-0940-9*); lib. bdg. 29.95 (*0-7933-0941-7*); disk 29.95 (*0-7933-0942-5*) Gallopade Intl.

— Oregon Coastales. (Carole Marsh Oregon Bks.). (Illus.). (J). 1994. lib. bdg. 29.95 (*0-7933-1907-2*) Gallopade Intl.

— Oregon Coastales. (Carole Marsh Oregon Bks.). (Illus.). (J). 1997. pap. 19.95 (*0-7933-1908-0*) Gallopade Intl.

— Oregon Coastales! (Oregon Bks.). (J). 1994. lib. bdg. 29.95 (*0-7933-7302-6*) Gallopade Intl.

— Oregon "Crinkum-Crankum" A Funny Word Book about Our State. (Oregon Bks.). (Illus.). (J). (gr. 3-12). 1994. 29.95 (*0-7933-4919-2*); pap. 19.95 (*0-7933-4920-6*); disk 29.95 (*0-7933-4921-4*) Gallopade Intl.

— Oregon Dingbats! Bk. 1: A Fun Book of Games, Stories, Activities & More about Our State That's All in Code! for You to Decipher. (Oregon Bks.). (Illus.). (J). (gr. 3-12). 1994. pap. 19.95 (*0-7933-3885-9*); lib. bdg. 29.95 (*0-7933-3884-0*); disk 29.95 (*0-7933-3886-7*) Gallopade Intl.

— Oregon Facts & Factivities. (Carole Marsh State Bks.). (Illus.). (J). (gr. 4-7). 1996. pap., teacher ed. 19.95 (*0-7933-7921-0*, C Marsh) Gallopade Intl.

— Oregon Festival Fun for Kids! (Oregon Bks.). (Illus.). (YA). (gr. 3-12). 1994. pap. 19.95 (*0-7933-4038-1*); lib. bdg. 29.95 (*0-7933-4037-3*); disk 29.95 (*0-7933-4039-X*) Gallopade Intl.

— Oregon "GEO" Bingo! 38 Must Know State Geography Facts for Kids to Learn While Having Fun! (Bingo! Ser.). (Illus.). (J). (gr. 2-8). 1998. pap. 14.95 (*0-7933-8634-9*) Gallopade Intl.

— Oregon Government! The Cornerstone of Everyday Life in Our State! (Carole Marsh Oregon Bks.). (Illus.). (J). (gr. 3-12). 1996. pap. 19.95 (*0-7933-6293-8*); lib. bdg. 29.95 (*0-7933-6292-X*); disk 29.95 (*0-7933-6294-6*) Gallopade Intl.

— Oregon "HISTO" Bingo! 42 Must Know State History Facts for Kids to Learn While Having Fun! (Bingo! Ser.). (Illus.). (J). (gr. 2-8). 1998. pap. 14.95 (*0-7933-8635-7*) Gallopade Intl.

— Oregon History! Surprising Secrets about Our State's Founding Mothers, Fathers & Kids! (Carole Marsh Oregon Bks.). (Illus.). (J). (gr. 3-12). 1996. pap. 19.95 (*0-7933-6140-0*); lib. bdg. 29.95 (*0-7933-6139-7*); disk 29.95 (*0-7933-6141-9*) Gallopade Intl.

— The Oregon Hot Air Balloon Mystery. (Carole Marsh Oregon Bks.). (Illus.). (J). (gr. 2-9). 1994. 29.95 (*0-7933-2651-6*); pap. 19.95 (*0-7933-2652-4*); disk 29.95 (*0-7933-2653-2*) Gallopade Intl.

— Oregon Hot Zones! Viruses, Diseases, & Epidemics in Our State's History. (Hot Zones! Ser.). (Illus.). (J). (gr. 3-12). 1998. pap. 19.95 (*0-7933-8940-2*); lib. bdg. 29.95 (*0-7933-8939-9*) Gallopade Intl.

— Oregon Indian Dictionary for Kids! (Carole Marsh State Bks.). (J). (gr. 2-9). 1996. 29.95 (*0-7933-7755-2*, C Marsh); pap. 19.95 (*0-7933-7756-0*, C Marsh) Gallopade Intl.

— Oregon Jeopardy! Answers & Questions about Our State! (Oregon Bks.). (Illus.). (J). (gr. 3-12). 1994. pap. 19.95 (*0-7933-4191-4*); lib. bdg. 29.95 (*0-7933-4190-6*); disk 29.95 (*0-7933-4192-2*) Gallopade Intl.

— Oregon "Jography" A Fun Run Thru Our State. (Carole Marsh Oregon Bks.). (Illus.). (J). 1994. pap. 19.95 (*0-7933-1891-2*); lib. bdg. 29.95 (*0-7933-1890-4*); disk 29.95 (*0-7933-1892-0*) Gallopade Intl.

— Oregon Kid's Cookbook: Recipes, How-to, History, Lore & More! (Carole Marsh Oregon Bks.). (Illus.). (J). 1994. pap. 19.95 (*0-7933-0949-2*); lib. bdg. 29.95 (*0-7933-0950-6*); disk 29.95 (*0-7933-0951-4*) Gallopade Intl.

— The Oregon Library Book: A Surprising Guide to the Unusual Special Collections in Libraries Across Our State for Students, Teachers, Writers & Publishers - Includes Reproducible Mailing Labels Plus Activities for Young People! (Oregon Bks.). (Illus.). 1994. pap. 19.95 (*0-7933-3117-X*); lib. bdg. 29.95 (*0-7933-3116-1*); disk 29.95 (*0-7933-3118-8*) Gallopade Intl.

— Oregon Math! How It All Adds up in Our State. (Carole Marsh Oregon Bks.). (Illus.). (YA). (gr. 3-12). 1996. pap. 19.95 (*0-7933-6599-6*); lib. bdg. 29.95 (*0-7933-6598-8*) Gallopade Intl.

— The Oregon Media Book: A Surprising Guide to the Amazing Print, Broadcast & Online Media of Our State for Students, Teachers, Writers & Publishers - Includes Reproducible Mailing Labels Plus Activities for Young People! (Oregon Bks.). (Illus.). 1994. pap. 19.95 (*0-7933-3273-7*); lib. bdg. 29.95 (*0-7933-3272-9*); disk 29.95 (*0-7933-3274-5*) Gallopade Intl.

— The Oregon Mystery Van Takes Off! Bk. 1: Handicapped Oregon Kids Sneak Off on a Big Adventure. (Oregon Bks.). (Illus.). (J). (gr. 3-12). 1994. 29.95 (*0-7933-5072-7*); pap. 19.95 (*0-7933-5073-5*); disk 29.95 (*0-7933-5074-3*) Gallopade Intl.

— Oregon Quiz Bowl Crash Course! (Carole Marsh Oregon Bks.). (Illus.). (J). 1994. pap. 19.95 (*0-7933-1905-6*); lib. bdg. 29.95 (*0-7933-1904-8*); disk 29.95 (*0-7933-1906-4*) Gallopade Intl.

— Oregon Rollercoasters! (Oregon Bks.). (Illus.). (YA). (gr. 3-12). 1994. pap. 19.95 (*0-7933-5336-X*); lib. bdg. 29.95 (*0-7933-5335-1*); disk 29.95 (*0-7933-5337-8*) Gallopade Intl.

— Oregon School Trivia: An Amazing & Fascinating Look at Our State's Teachers, Schools & Students. (Carole Marsh Oregon Bks.). (Illus.). (J). 1994. pap. 19.95 (*0-7933-0946-8*); lib. bdg. 29.95 (*0-7933-0947-6*); disk 29.95 (*0-7933-0948-4*) Gallopade Intl.

— Oregon Silly Basketball Sportsmysteries, Vol. 1. (Carole Marsh Oregon Bks.). (Illus.). (J). 1994. pap. 19.95 (*0-7933-0943-3*); lib. bdg. 29.95 (*0-7933-0944-1*); disk 29.95 (*0-7933-0945-X*) Gallopade Intl.

— Oregon Silly Basketball Sportsmysteries, Vol. 2. (Carole Marsh Oregon Bks.). (Illus.). (J). 1994. pap. 19.95 (*0-7933-1917-X*); lib. bdg. 29.95 (*0-7933-1916-1*); disk 29.95 (*0-7933-1918-8*) Gallopade Intl.

— Oregon Silly Football Sportsmysteries, Vol. 1. (Carole Marsh Oregon Bks.). (Illus.). (J). 1994. pap. 19.95 (*0-7933-1896-3*); lib. bdg. 29.95 (*0-7933-1895-5*); disk 29.95 (*0-7933-1897-1*) Gallopade Intl.

— Oregon Silly Football Sportsmysteries, Vol. 2. (Carole Marsh Oregon Bks.). (Illus.). (J). 1994. pap. 19.95 (*0-7933-1899-8*); lib. bdg. 29.95 (*0-7933-1898-X*); disk 29.95 (*0-7933-1900-5*) Gallopade Intl.

— Oregon Silly Trivia! (Carole Marsh Oregon Bks.). (Illus.). (J). 1994. pap. 19.95 (*0-7933-1888-2*); lib. bdg. 29.95 (*0-7933-1887-4*); disk 29.95 (*0-7933-1889-0*) Gallopade Intl.

— Oregon Spelling Bee! Score Big by Correctly Spelling Our State's Unique Names. (Carole Marsh Oregon Bks.). (Illus.). (YA). (gr. 3-12). 1996. pap. 19.95 (*0-7933-6752-2*); lib. bdg. 29.95 (*0-7933-6751-4*) Gallopade Intl.

— Oregon Timeline: A Chronology of Oregon History, Mystery, Trivia, Legend, Lore & More. (Oregon Bks.). (Illus.). (J). (gr. 3-12). 1994. pap. 19.95 (*0-7933-5987-2*); lib. bdg. 29.95 (*0-7933-5986-4*); disk 29.95 (*0-7933-5988-0*) Gallopade Intl.

— Oregon 2000! Coming Soon to a Calendar Near You - The 21st Century! - Complete Set of AL 2000 Items. (Two Thousand! Ser.). (Illus.). (J). (gr. 3-12). 1998. pap. 75.00 (*0-7933-9383-3*); lib. bdg. 85.00 (*0-7933-9384-1*) Gallopade Intl.

— Oregon 2000! Coming Soon to a Calendar near You-The 21st Century! (Two Thousand! Ser.). (Illus.). (J). (gr. 3-12). 1998. pap. 19.95 (*0-7933-8787-6*); lib. bdg. 29.95 (*0-7933-8786-8*) Gallopade Intl.

— Oregon UFO's & Extraterrestrials! A Look at the Sightings & Science in Our State. (Carole Marsh Oregon Bks.). (Illus.). (J). (gr. 3-12). 1997. pap. 19.95 (*0-7933-6446-9*); lib. bdg. 29.95 (*0-7933-6445-0*) Gallopade Intl.

— Oregon's (Most Devastating!) Disasters & (Most Calamitous!) Catastrophies! (Carole Marsh Oregon Bks.). (Illus.). (J). 1994. pap. 19.95 (*0-7933-0934-4*); lib. bdg. 29.95 (*0-7933-0935-2*); disk 29.95 (*0-7933-0936-0*) Gallopade Intl.

— Oregon's Unsolved Mysteries (And Their "Solutions") Includes Scientific Information & Other Activities for Students. (Oregon Bks.). (Illus.). (J). (gr. 3-12). 1994. pap. 19.95 (*0-7933-5834-5*); lib. bdg. 29.95 (*0-7933-5833-7*); disk 29.95 (*0-7933-5835-3*) Gallopade Intl.

— Out of the Mouths of Slaves. (Our Black Heritage Ser.). (J). (gr. 3-12). 1994. pap. 19.95 (*1-55609-311-X*); lib. bdg. 29.95 (*1-55609-312-8*); disk 29.95 (*1-55609-313-6*) Gallopade Intl.

***Marsh, Carole.** The Out of This World Ohio Coloring Book. (Ohio Experience! Ser.). (Illus.). (J). (gr. k-5). 2000. pap. 3.95 (*0-7933-9474-0*) Gallopade Intl.

— The Out of This World Oklahoma Coloring Book. (Oklahoma Experience! Ser.). (Illus.). (J). (gr. k-5). 2000. pap. 3.95 (*0-7933-9599-2*) Gallopade Intl.

Marsh, Carole. Palm Fever. (Carole Marsh Short Story Ser.). (Illus.). (J). (gr. 4-12). 1994. 29.95 (*1-55609-185-0*); pap. 19.95 (*1-55609-237-7*) Gallopade Intl.

— Patch, the Pirate Dog: A California Pet Story. (Carole Marsh California Bks.). (J). (ps-4). 1994. pap. 19.95 (*0-7933-5429-3*); lib. bdg. 29.95 (*0-7933-5428-5*); disk 29.95 (*0-7933-5430-7*) Gallopade Intl.

— Patch, the Pirate Dog: A Colorado Pet Story. (Carole Marsh Colorado Bks.). (J). (ps-4). 1994. pap. 19.95 (*0-7933-5432-3*); lib. bdg. 29.95 (*0-7933-5431-5*); disk 29.95 (*0-7933-5433-1*) Gallopade Intl.

— Patch, the Pirate Dog: A Connecticut Pet Story. (Carole Marsh Connecticut Bks.). (J). (ps-4). 1994. pap. 19.95 (*0-7933-5435-8*); lib. bdg. 29.95 (*0-7933-5434-X*); disk 29.95 (*0-7933-5436-6*) Gallopade Intl.

— Patch, the Pirate Dog: A Delaware Pet Story. (Carole Marsh Delaware Bks.). (J). (ps-4). 1994. pap. 19.95 (*0-7933-5438-2*); lib. bdg. 29.95 (*0-7933-5437-4*); disk 29.95 (*0-7933-5439-0*) Gallopade Intl.

— Patch, the Pirate Dog: A Florida Pet Story. (Carole Marsh Florida Bks.). (J). (ps-4). 1994. pap. 19.95 (*0-7933-5444-7*); lib. bdg. 29.95 (*0-7933-5443-9*); disk 29.95 (*0-7933-5445-5*) Gallopade Intl.

— Patch, the Pirate Dog: A Georgia Pet Story. (Carole Marsh Georgia Bks.). (J). (ps-4). 1994. pap. 19.95 (*0-7933-5447-1*); lib. bdg. 29.95 (*0-7933-5446-3*); disk 29.95 (*0-7933-5448-X*) Gallopade Intl.

— Patch, the Pirate Dog: A Hawaii Pet Story. (Carole Marsh Hawaii Bks.). (J). (ps-4). 1994. pap. 19.95 (*0-7933-5450-1*); lib. bdg. 29.95 (*0-7933-5449-8*); disk 29.95 (*0-7933-5451-X*) Gallopade Intl.

— Patch, the Pirate Dog: A Kansas Pet Story. (Carole Marsh Kansas Bks.). (J). (ps-4). 1994. pap. 19.95 (*0-7933-5465-X*); lib. bdg. 29.95 (*0-7933-5464-1*); disk 29.95 (*0-7933-5466-8*) Gallopade Intl.

— Patch, the Pirate Dog: A Kentucky Pet Story. (Carole Marsh Kentucky Bks.). (J). (ps-4). 1994. pap. 19.95 (*0-7933-5468-4*); lib. bdg. 29.95 (*0-7933-5467-6*); disk 29.95 (*0-7933-5469-2*) Gallopade Intl.

— Patch, the Pirate Dog: A Louisiana Pet Story. (Carole Marsh Louisiana Bks.). (J). (ps-4). 1994. pap. 19.95 (*0-7933-5471-4*); lib. bdg. 29.95 (*0-7933-5470-6*); disk 29.95 (*0-7933-5472-2*) Gallopade Intl.

— Patch, the Pirate Dog: A Maine Pet Story. (Carole Marsh Maine Bks.). (J). (ps-4). 1994. pap. 19.95 (*0-7933-5474-9*); lib. bdg. 29.95 (*0-7933-5473-0*); disk 29.95 (*0-7933-5475-7*) Gallopade Intl.

— Patch, the Pirate Dog: A Maryland Pet Story. (Carole Marsh Maryland Bks.). (J). (ps-4). 1994. pap. 19.95 (*0-7933-5477-3*); lib. bdg. 29.95 (*0-7933-5476-5*); disk 29.95 (*0-7933-5478-1*) Gallopade Intl.

— Patch, the Pirate Dog: A Massachusetts Pet Story. (Massachuseets Bks.). (J). (ps-4). 1994. pap. 19.95 (*0-7933-5480-3*); lib. bdg. 29.95 (*0-7933-5479-X*); disk 29.95 (*0-7933-5481-1*) Gallopade Intl.

— Patch, the Pirate Dog: A Michigan Pet Story. (Carole Marsh Michigan Bks.). (J). (ps-4). 1994. pap. 19.95 (*0-7933-5483-8*); lib. bdg. 29.95 (*0-7933-5482-X*); disk 29.95 (*0-7933-5484-6*) Gallopade Intl.

— Patch, the Pirate Dog: A Minnesota Pet Story. (Carole Marsh Minnesota Bks.). (J). (ps-4). 1994. pap. 19.95 (*0-7933-5486-2*); lib. bdg. 29.95 (*0-7933-5485-4*); disk 29.95 (*0-7933-5487-0*) Gallopade Intl.

— Patch, the Pirate Dog: A Mississippi Pet Story. (Carole Marsh Mississippi Bks.). (J). (ps-4). 1994. pap. 19.95 (*0-7933-5489-7*); lib. bdg. 29.95 (*0-7933-5488-9*); disk 29.95 (*0-7933-5490-0*) Gallopade Intl.

— Patch, the Pirate Dog: A Missouri Pet Story. (Carole Marsh Missouri Bks.). (J). (ps-4). 1994. pap. 19.95 (*0-7933-5492-7*); lib. bdg. 29.95 (*0-7933-5491-9*); disk 29.95 (*0-7933-5493-5*) Gallopade Intl.

— Patch, the Pirate Dog: A Montana Pet Story. (Carole Marsh Montana Bks.). (J). (ps-4). 1994. pap. 19.95 (*0-7933-5495-1*); lib. bdg. 29.95 (*0-7933-5494-3*); disk 29.95 (*0-7933-5496-X*) Gallopade Intl.

— Patch, the Pirate Dog: A Nebraska Pet Story. (Carole Marsh Nebraska Bks.). (J). (ps-4). 1994. pap. 19.95 (*0-7933-5498-6*); lib. bdg. 29.95 (*0-7933-5497-8*); disk 29.95 (*0-7933-5499-4*) Gallopade Intl.

— Patch, the Pirate Dog: A Nevada Pet Story. (Carole Marsh Nevada Bks.). (J). (ps-4). 1994. pap. 19.95 (*0-7933-5501-X*); lib. bdg. 29.95 (*0-7933-5500-1*); disk 29.95 (*0-7933-5502-8*) Gallopade Intl.

— Patch, the Pirate Dog: A New Hampshire Pet Story. (Carole Marsh New Hampshire Bks.). (J). (ps-4). 1994. pap. 19.95 (*0-7933-5504-4*); lib. bdg. 29.95 (*0-7933-5503-6*); disk 29.95 (*0-7933-5505-2*) Gallopade Intl.

— Patch, the Pirate Dog: A New Jersey Pet Story. (Carole Marsh New Jersey Bks.). (J). (ps-4). 1994. pap. 19.95 (*0-7933-5507-9*); lib. bdg. 29.95 (*0-7933-5506-0*); disk 29.95 (*0-7933-5508-7*) Gallopade Intl.

— Patch, the Pirate Dog: A New Mexico Pet Story. (Carole Marsh New Mexico Bks.). (J). (ps-4). 1994. pap. 19.95 (*0-7933-5510-9*); lib. bdg. 29.95 (*0-7933-5509-5*); disk 29.95 (*0-7933-5511-7*) Gallopade Intl.

— Patch, the Pirate Dog: A New York Pet Story. (Carole Marsh New York Bks.). (J). (ps-4). 1994. pap. 19.95 (*0-7933-5513-3*); lib. bdg. 29.95 (*0-7933-5512-5*); disk 29.95 (*0-7933-5514-1*) Gallopade Intl.

— Patch, the Pirate Dog: A North Carolina Pet Story. (Carole Marsh North Carolina Bks.). (J). (ps-4). 1994. pap. 19.95 (*0-7933-5516-8*); lib. bdg. 29.95 (*0-7933-5515-X*); disk 29.95 (*0-7933-5517-6*) Gallopade Intl.

— Patch, the Pirate Dog: A North Dakota Pet Story. (Carole Marsh North Dakota Bks.). (J). (ps-4). 1994. pap. 19.95 (*0-7933-5519-2*); lib. bdg. 29.95 (*0-7933-5518-4*); disk 29.95 (*0-7933-5520-6*) Gallopade Intl.

— Patch, the Pirate Dog: A Ohio Pet Story. (Carole Marsh Ohio Bks.). (J). (ps-4). 1994. pap. 19.95 (*0-7933-5522-2*); lib. bdg. 29.95 (*0-7933-5521-4*); disk 29.95 (*0-7933-5523-0*) Gallopade Intl.

— Patch, the Pirate Dog: A Oklahoma Pet Story. (Oklahoma Bks.). (J). (ps-4). 1994. pap. 19.95 (*0-7933-5525-7*); lib. bdg. 29.95 (*0-7933-5524-9*); disk 29.95 (*0-7933-5526-5*) Gallopade Intl.

— Patch, the Pirate Dog: A Oregon Pet Story. (Oregon Bks.). (J). (ps-4). 1994. pap. 19.95 (*0-7933-5528-1*); lib. bdg. 29.95 (*0-7933-5527-3*); disk 29.95 (*0-7933-5529-X*) Gallopade Intl.

— Patch, the Pirate Dog: A Pennsylvania Pet Story. (Pennsylvania Bks.). (J). (ps-4). 1994. pap. 19.95 (*0-7933-5531-1*); lib. bdg. 29.95 (*0-7933-5530-3*); disk 29.95 (*0-7933-5532-X*) Gallopade Intl.

— Patch, the Pirate Dog: A Rhode Island Pet Story. (Rhode Island Bks.). (J). (ps-4). 1994. pap. 19.95 (*0-7933-5534-6*); lib. bdg. 29.95 (*0-7933-5533-8*); disk 29.95 (*0-7933-5535-4*) Gallopade Intl.

— Patch, the Pirate Dog: A South Carolina Pet Story. (South Carolina Bks.). (J). (ps-4). 1994. pap. 19.95 (*0-7933-5537-0*); lib. bdg. 29.95 (*0-7933-5536-2*); disk 29.95 (*0-7933-5538-9*) Gallopade Intl.

— Patch, the Pirate Dog: A South Dakota Pet Story. (South Dakota Bks.). (J). (ps-4). 1994. pap. 19.95 (*0-7933-5540-0*); lib. bdg. 29.95 (*0-7933-5539-7*); disk 29.95 (*0-7933-5541-9*) Gallopade Intl.

— Patch, the Pirate Dog: A Tennessee Pet Story. (Tennessee Bks.). (J). (ps-4). 1994. pap. 19.95 (*0-7933-5543-5*); lib. bdg. 29.95 (*0-7933-5542-7*); disk 29.95 (*0-7933-5544-3*) Gallopade Intl.

M

— Patch, the Pirate Dog: A Texas Pet Story. (Texas Bks.). (J). (ps-4). 1994. pap. 19.95 (*0-7933-5546-X*); lib. bdg. 29.95 (*0-7933-5545-1*); disk 29.95 (*0-7933-5547-8*) Gallopade Intl.

— Patch, the Pirate Dog: A Utah Pet Story. (Utah Bks.). (J). (ps-4). 1994. pap. 19.95 (*0-7933-5549-4*); lib. bdg. 29.95 (*0-7933-5548-6*); disk 29.95 (*0-7933-5550-8*) Gallopade Intl.

— Patch, the Pirate Dog: A Vermont Pet Story. (Vermont Bks.). (J). (ps-4). 1994. pap. 19.95 (*0-7933-5552-4*); lib. bdg. 29.95 (*0-7933-5551-6*); disk 29.95 (*0-7933-5553-2*) Gallopade Intl.

— Patch, the Pirate Dog: A Virginia Pet Story. (Virginia Bks.). (J). (ps-4). 1994. pap. 19.95 (*0-7933-5555-9*); lib. bdg. 29.95 (*0-7933-5554-0*); disk 29.95 (*0-7933-5556-7*) Gallopade Intl.

— Patch, the Pirate Dog: A Washington DC Pet Story. (Washington, D.C. Bks.). (J). (ps-4). 1994. pap. 19.95 (*0-7933-5441-2*); lib. bdg. 29.95 (*0-7933-5440-4*); disk 29.95 (*0-7933-5442-0*) Gallopade Intl.

— Patch, the Pirate Dog: A Washington Pet Story. (Washington Bks.). (J). (ps-4). 1994. pap. 19.95 (*0-7933-5558-3*); lib. bdg. 29.95 (*0-7933-5557-5*); disk 29.95 (*0-7933-5559-1*) Gallopade Intl.

— Patch, the Pirate Dog: A West Virginia Pet Story. (West Virginia Bks.). (J). (ps-4). 1994. pap. 19.95 (*0-7933-5561-3*); lib. bdg. 29.95 (*0-7933-5560-5*); disk 29.95 (*0-7933-5562-1*) Gallopade Intl.

— Patch, the Pirate Dog: A Wisconsin Pet Story. (Wisconsin Bks.). (J). (ps-4). 1994. pap. 19.95 (*0-7933-5564-8*); lib. bdg. 29.95 (*0-7933-5563-X*); disk 29.95 (*0-7933-5565-6*) Gallopade Intl.

— Patch, the Pirate Dog: A Wyoming Pet Story. (Wyoming Bks.). (J). (ps-4). 1994. pap. 19.95 (*0-7933-5567-2*); lib. bdg. 29.95 (*0-7933-5566-4*); disk 29.95 (*0-7933-5568-0*) Gallopade Intl.

— Patch, the Pirate Dog: An Alabama Pet Story. (Carole Marsh Alabama Bks.). (J). (ps-4). 1994. pap. 19.95 (*0-7933-5417-X*); lib. bdg. 29.95 (*0-7933-5416-1*); disk 29.95 (*0-7933-5418-8*) Gallopade Intl.

— Patch, the Pirate Dog: An Alaska Pet Story. (Carole Marsh Alaska Bks.). (J). (ps-4). 1994. pap. 19.95 (*0-7933-5420-X*); lib. bdg. 29.95 (*0-7933-5419-6*); disk 29.95 (*0-7933-5421-8*) Gallopade Intl.

— Patch, the Pirate Dog: An Arizona Pet Story. (Carole Marsh Arizona Bks.). (J). (ps-4). 1994. pap. 19.95 (*0-7933-5423-4*); lib. bdg. 29.95 (*0-7933-5422-6*); disk 29.95 (*0-7933-5424-2*) Gallopade Intl.

— Patch, the Pirate Dog: An Arkansas Pet Story. (Carole Marsh Arkansas Bks.). (J). (ps-4). 1994. pap. 19.95 (*0-7933-5426-9*); lib. bdg. 29.95 (*0-7933-5425-0*); disk 29.95 (*0-7933-5427-7*) Gallopade Intl.

— Patch, the Pirate Dog: An Idaho Pet Story. (Carole Marsh Idaho Bks.). (J). (ps-4). 1994. pap. 19.95 (*0-7933-5453-6*); lib. bdg. 29.95 (*0-7933-5452-8*); disk 29.95 (*0-7933-5454-4*) Gallopade Intl.

— Patch, the Pirate Dog: An Illinois Pet Story. (Carole Marsh Illinois Bks.). (J). (ps-4). 1994. pap. 19.95 (*0-7933-5456-0*); lib. bdg. 29.95 (*0-7933-5455-2*); disk 29.95 (*0-7933-5457-9*) Gallopade Intl.

— Patch, the Pirate Dog: An Indiana Pet Story. (Carole Marsh Indiana Bks.). (J). (ps-4). 1994. pap. 19.95 (*0-7933-5459-5*); lib. bdg. 29.95 (*0-7933-5458-7*); disk 29.95 (*0-7933-5460-9*) Gallopade Intl.

— Patch, the Pirate Dog: An Iowa Pet Story. (Carole Marsh Iowa Bks.). (J). (ps-4). 1994. pap. 19.95 (*0-7933-5462-5*); lib. bdg. 29.95 (*0-7933-5461-7*); disk 29.95 (*0-7933-5463-3*) Gallopade Intl.

— Pennsylvania & Other State Greats (Biographies) (Carole Marsh Pennsylvania Bks.). (Illus.). (J). 1994. pap. 19.95 (*0-7933-1943-9*); lib. bdg. 29.95 (*0-7933-1942-0*); disk 29.95 (*0-7933-1944-7*) Gallopade Intl.

— Pennsylvania Bandits, Bushwackers, Outlaws, Crooks, Devils, Ghosts, Desperadoes & Other Assorted & Sundry Characters! (Carole Marsh Pennsylvania Bks.). (Illus.). (J). 1994. pap. 19.95 (*0-7933-0961-1*); lib. bdg. 29.95 (*0-7933-0962-X*); disk 29.95 (*0-7933-0963-8*) Gallopade Intl.

— Pennsylvania "BIO" Bingo! 24 Must Know State People for Kids to Learn about While Having Fun! (Bingo! Ser.). (Illus.). (J). (gr. 2-8). 1998. pap. 14.95 (*0-7933-8636-5*) Gallopade Intl.

— The Pennsylvania Bookstore Book: A Surprising Guide to Our State's Bookstores & Their Specialties for Students, Teachers, Writers & Publishers. (Pennsylvania Bks.). (Illus.). 1991. pap. 19.95 (*0-7933-2970-1*) Gallopade Intl.

— The Pennsylvania Bookstore Book: A Surprising Guide to Our State's Bookstores & Their Specialties for Students, Teachers, Writers & Publishers. (Pennsylvania Bks.). (Illus.). 1994. lib. bdg. 29.95 (*0-7933-2969-8*); disk 29.95 (*0-7933-2971-X*) Gallopade Intl.

— Pennsylvania Classic Christmas Trivia: Stories, Recipes, Activities, Legends, Lore & More! (Carole Marsh Pennsylvania Bks.). (Illus.). (J). 1994. pap. 19.95 (*0-7933-0964-6*); lib. bdg. 29.95 (*0-7933-0965-4*); disk 29.95 (*0-7933-0966-2*) Gallopade Intl.

— Pennsylvania Coastales. (Pennsylvania Bks.). (J). 1994. lib. bdg. 29.95 (*0-7933-7303-4*) Gallopade Intl.

— Pennsylvania Coastales. (Carole Marsh Pennsylvania Bks.). (Illus.). (J). 1994. pap. 19.95 (*0-7933-1937-4*); lib. bdg. 29.95 (*0-7933-1936-6*); disk 29.95 (*0-7933-1938-2*) Gallopade Intl.

— Pennsylvania "Crinkum-Crankum" A Funny Word Book about Our State. (Pennsylvania Bks.). (Illus.). (J). (gr. 3-12). 1994. 29.95 (*0-7933-4922-2*); pap. 19.95 (*0-7933-4923-0*); disk 29.95 (*0-7933-4924-9*) Gallopade Intl.

— Pennsylvania Dingbats! Bk. 1: A Fun Book of Games, Stories, Activities & More about Our State That's All in Code! for You to Decipher, Bk. 1. (Pennsylvania Bks.). (Illus.). (J). (gr. 3-12). 1994. pap. 19.95 (*0-7933-3888-3*); lib. bdg. 29.95 (*0-7933-3887-5*); disk 29.95 (*0-7933-3889-1*) Gallopade Intl.

***Marsh, Carole.** The Pennsylvania Experience Pocket Guide. (Pennsylvania Experience! Ser.). (Illus.). (J). 2000. pap. 6.95 (*0-7933-9586-0*) Gallopade Intl.

Marsh, Carole. Pennsylvania Facts & Factivities. (Carole Marsh State Bks.). (Illus.). (J). (gr. 4-7). 1996. pap., teacher ed. 19.95 (*0-7933-7923-7*, C Marsh) Gallopade Intl.

— Pennsylvania Festival Fun for Kids! (Pennsylvania Bks.). (Illus.). (YA). (gr. 3-12). 1994. pap. 19.95 (*0-7933-4041-1*); lib. bdg. 29.95 (*0-7933-4040-3*); disk 29.95 (*0-7933-4042-X*) Gallopade Intl.

— Pennsylvania "GEO" Bingo! 38 Must Know State Geography Facts for Kids to Learn While Having Fun! (Bingo! Ser.). (Illus.). (J). (gr. 2-8). 1998. pap. 14.95 (*0-7933-8637-3*) Gallopade Intl.

— Pennsylvania Government! The Cornerstone of Everyday Life in Our State! (Carole Marsh Pennsylvania Bks.). (Illus.). (J). (gr. 3-12). 1996. pap. 19.95 (*0-7933-6296-2*); lib. bdg. 29.95 (*0-7933-6295-4*); disk 29.95 (*0-7933-6297-0*) Gallopade Intl.

— Pennsylvania "HISTO" Bingo! 42 Must Know State History Facts for Kids to Learn While Having Fun! (Bingo! Ser.). (Illus.). (J). (gr. 2-8). 1998. pap. 14.95 (*0-7933-8638-1*) Gallopade Intl.

— Pennsylvania History! Surprising Secrets about Our State's Founding Mothers, Fathers & Kids! (Carole Marsh Pennsylvania Bks.). (Illus.). (J). (gr. 3-12). 1996. pap. 19.95 (*0-7933-6143-5*); lib. bdg. 29.95 (*0-7933-6142-7*); disk 29.95 (*0-7933-6144-3*) Gallopade Intl.

— The Pennsylvania Hot Air Balloon Mystery. (Carole Marsh Pennsylvania Bks.). (Illus.). (J). (gr. 2-9). 1994. 29.95 (*0-7933-2660-5*); pap. 19.95 (*0-7933-2661-3*); disk 29.95 (*0-7933-2662-1*) Gallopade Intl.

— Pennsylvania Hot Zones! Viruses, Diseases, & Epidemics in Our State's History. (Hot Zones! Ser.). (Illus.). (J). (gr. 3-12). 1998. pap. 19.95 (*0-7933-8943-7*); lib. bdg. 29.95 (*0-7933-8942-9*) Gallopade Intl.

— Pennsylvania Indian Dictionary for Kids! (Carole Marsh State Bks.). (J). (gr. 2-9). 1996. 29.95 (*0-7933-7758-7*, C Marsh); pap. 19.95 (*0-7933-7759-5*, C Marsh) Gallopade Intl.

***Marsh, Carole.** Pennsylvania Jeopardy. (Pennsylvania Experience! Ser.). (Illus.). (J). (gr. 2-6). 2000. pap. 7.95 (*0-7933-9588-7*) Gallopade Intl.

Marsh, Carole. Pennsylvania Jeopardy! Answers & Questions about Our State! (Pennsylvania Bks.). (Illus.). (J). (gr. 3-12). 1994. pap. 19.95 (*0-7933-4194-9*); lib. bdg. 29.95 (*0-7933-4193-0*); disk 29.95 (*0-7933-4195-7*) Gallopade Intl.

***Marsh, Carole.** Pennsylvania Jography. (Pennsylvania Experience! Ser.). (Illus.). (J). (gr. 2-6). 2000. pap. 7.95 (*0-7933-9589-5*) Gallopade Intl.

Marsh, Carole. Pennsylvania "Jography" A Fun Run Thru Our State! (Carole Marsh Pennsylvania Bks.). (Illus.). (J). 1994. pap. 19.95 (*0-7933-1923-4*); lib. bdg. 29.95 (*0-7933-1922-6*); disk 29.95 (*0-7933-1924-2*) Gallopade Intl.

— Pennsylvania Kid's Cookbook: Recipes, How-to, History, Lore & More! (Carole Marsh Pennsylvania Bks.). (Illus.). (J). 1994. pap. 19.95 (*0-7933-0973-5*); lib. bdg. 29.95 (*0-7933-0974-3*); disk 29.95 (*0-7933-0975-1*) Gallopade Intl.

— The Pennsylvania Library Book: A Surprising Guide to the Unusual Special Collections in Libraries Across Our State for Students, Teachers, Writers & Publishers - Includes Reproducible Mailing Labels Plus Activities for Young People! (Pennsylvania Bks.). (Illus.). 1994. pap. 19.95 (*0-7933-3120-X*); lib. bdg. 29.95 (*0-7933-3119-6*); disk 29.95 (*0-7933-3121-8*) Gallopade Intl.

— Pennsylvania Math! How It All Adds up in Our State. (Carole Marsh Pennsylvania Bks.). (Illus.). (YA). (gr. 3-12). 1996. pap. 19.95 (*0-7933-6602-X*); lib. bdg. 29.95 (*0-7933-6601-1*) Gallopade Intl.

— The Pennsylvania Media Book: A Surprising Guide to the Amazing Print, Broadcast & Online Media of Our State for Students, Teachers, Writers & Publishers - Includes Reproducible Mailing Labels Plus Activities for Young People! (Pennsylvania Bks.). (Illus.). 1994. pap. 19.95 (*0-7933-3276-1*); lib. bdg. 29.95 (*0-7933-3275-3*); disk 29.95 (*0-7933-3277-X*) Gallopade Intl.

— The Pennsylvania Mystery Van Takes Off! Book 1: Handicapped Pennsylvania Kids Sneak Off on a Big Adventure, Bk. 1. (Pennsylvania Bks.). (Illus.). (J). (gr. 3-12). 1994. 29.95 (*0-7933-5075-1*); pap. 19.95 (*0-7933-5076-X*); disk 29.95 (*0-7933-5077-8*) Gallopade Intl.

— Pennsylvania Quiz Bowl Crash Course! (Carole Marsh Pennsylvania Bks.). (Illus.). (J). 1994. pap. 19.95 (*0-7933-1946-3*); lib. bdg. 29.95 (*0-7933-1945-5*); disk 29.95 (*0-7933-1947-1*) Gallopade Intl.

— Pennsylvania Rollercoasters! (Pennsylvania Bks.). (Illus.). (YA). (gr. 3-12). 1994. pap. 19.95 (*0-7933-5339-4*); lib. bdg. 29.95 (*0-7933-5338-6*); disk 29.95 (*0-7933-5340-8*) Gallopade Intl.

— Pennsylvania School Trivia: An Amazing & Fascinating Look at Ou State's Teachers, Schools & Students! (Carole Marsh Pennsylvania Bks.). (Illus.). (J). 1994. pap. 19.95 (*0-7933-0970-0*); lib. bdg. 29.95 (*0-7933-0971-9*); disk 29.95 (*0-7933-0972-7*) Gallopade Intl.

— Pennsylvania Silly Basketball Sportsmysteries, Vol. 1. (Carole Marsh Pennsylvania Bks.). (Illus.). (J). 1994. pap. 19.95 (*0-7933-0967-0*); lib. bdg. 29.95 (*0-7933-0968-9*); disk 29.95 (*0-7933-0969-7*) Gallopade Intl.

— Pennsylvania Silly Basketball Sportsmysteries, Vol. 2. (Carole Marsh Pennsylvania Bks.). (Illus.). (J). 1994. pap. 19.95 (*0-7933-1949-8*); lib. bdg. 29.95 (*0-7933-1948-X*); disk 29.95 (*0-7933-1950-1*) Gallopade Intl.

— Pennsylvania Silly Football Sportsmysteries, Vol. 1. (Carole Marsh Pennsylvania Bks.). (Illus.). (J). 1994. pap. 19.95 (*0-7933-1928-5*); lib. bdg. 29.95 (*0-7933-1927-7*); disk 29.95 (*0-7933-1929-3*) Gallopade Intl.

— Pennsylvania Silly Football Sportsmysteries, Vol. 2. (Carole Marsh Pennsylvania Bks.). (Illus.). (J). 1994. pap. 19.95 (*0-7933-1931-5*); lib. bdg. 29.95 (*0-7933-1930-7*); disk 29.95 (*0-7933-1932-3*) Gallopade Intl.

— Pennsylvania Silly Trivia! (Carole Marsh Pennsylvania Bks.). (Illus.). (J). 1994. pap. 19.95 (*0-7933-1920-X*); lib. bdg. 29.95 (*0-7933-1919-6*); disk 29.95 (*0-7933-1921-8*) Gallopade Intl.

— Pennsylvania Spelling Bee! Score Big by Correctly Spelling Our State's Unique Names. (Carole Marsh Pennsylvania Bks.). (Illus.). (YA). (gr. 3-12). 1996. pap. 19.95 (*0-7933-6755-7*); lib. bdg. 29.95 (*0-7933-6754-9*) Gallopade Intl.

— Pennsylvania Timeline: A Chronology of Pennsylvania History, Mystery, Trivia, Legend, Lore & More. (Pennsylvania Bks.). (Illus.). (J). (gr. 3-12). 1994. pap. 19.95 (*0-7933-5990-2*); lib. bdg. 29.95 (*0-7933-5989-9*); disk 29.95 (*0-7933-5991-0*) Gallopade Intl.

— Pennsylvania 2000! Coming Soon to a Calendar Near You - The 21st Century! - Complete Set of AL 2000 Items. (Two Thousand! Ser.). (Illus.). (J). (gr. 3-12). 1998. pap. 75.00 (*0-7933-9385-X*); lib. bdg. 85.00 (*0-7933-9386-8*) Gallopade Intl.

— Pennsylvania 2000! Coming Soon to a Calendar near You--The 21st Century! (Two Thousand! Ser.). (Illus.). (J). (gr. 3-12). 1998. pap. 19.95 (*0-7933-8790-6*) Gallopade Intl.

— Pennsylvania 2000! Coming Soon to a Calendar near You-The 21st Century! (Two Thousand! Ser.). (Illus.). (J). (gr. 3-12). 1998. lib. bdg. 29.95 (*0-7933-8789-2*) Gallopade Intl.

— Pennsylvania UFO's & Extraterrestrials! A Look at the Sightings & Science in Our State. (Carole Marsh Pennsylvania Bks.). (Illus.). (J). (gr. 3-12). 1997. pap. 19.95 (*0-7933-6449-3*); lib. bdg. 29.95 (*0-7933-6448-5*) Gallopade Intl.

***Marsh, Carole.** Pennsylvania's Big Activity Book. (Pennsylvania Experience! Ser.). (Illus.). 2000. pap. 9.95 (*0-7933-9590-9*) Gallopade Intl.

Marsh, Carole. Pennsylvania's (Most Devastating!) Disasters & (Most Calamitous!) Catastrophies! (Carole Marsh Pennsylvania Bks.). (Illus.). (J). 1994. pap. 19.95 (*0-7933-0958-1*); lib. bdg. 29.95 (*0-7933-0959-X*); disk 29.95 (*0-7933-0960-3*) Gallopade Intl.

— Pennsylvania's Unsolved Mysteries (& Their "Solutions") Includes Scientific Information & Other Activities for Students. (Pennsylvania Bks.). (Illus.). (J). (gr. 3-12). 1994. pap. 19.95 (*0-7933-5837-X*); lib. bdg. 29.95 (*0-7933-5836-1*); disk 29.95 (*0-7933-5838-8*) Gallopade Intl.

— PG: He's Having Her Baby. 1998. 19.95 (*1-877755-01-X*) Six Hse.

— The Phantastic Painted Desert & the Phenomenal Petrified Forest. (Interactive Multimedia Titles Ser.). (J). (gr. 2-9). 1996. 29.95 (*0-7933-7608-4*, C Marsh); pap. 19.95 (*0-7933-7609-2*, C Marsh); pap., teacher ed. 19.95 (*0-7933-7845-1*, C Marsh) Gallopade Intl.

— Phyzzics for Kids. (Quantum Leap Ser.). (J). (gr. 4-9). 1994. 29.95 (*1-55609-258-X*); pap. 19.95 (*1-55609-245-8*); disk 29.95 (*1-55609-340-3*) Gallopade Intl.

— The Pirate & Treasure Dingbats Book. (Carole Marsh Dingbats Bks.). (Illus.). (J). (gr. 3-12). 1994. pap. 19.95 (*0-7933-5408-0*); lib. bdg. 29.95 (*0-7933-5407-2*); disk 29.95 (*0-7933-5409-9*) Gallopade Intl.

— Pirate's Cookbook. (Naked Gourmet Ser.). (Orig.). 1997. 29.95 (*1-55609-002-1*) Gallopade Intl.

— The Pool Cookbook: Cool Recipes for Lazy Summer Days - Whether You Have a Pool or Not. (Carole Marsh Cookbooks Ser.). (Illus.). 1998. pap. 19.95 (*0-7933-8997-6*, C Marsh); lib. bdg. 29.95 (*0-7933-8996-8*, C Marsh) Gallopade Intl.

***Marsh, Carole.** The Proud Pennsylvania Coloring Book. (Pennsylvania Experience! Ser.). (Illus.). (J). (gr. k-5). 2000. pap. 3.95 (*0-7933-9591-7*) Gallopade Intl.

Marsh, Carole. Publishing on Command: How to Publish & Print 1-1,000 Books at a Time! (ProPub Ser.). 1994. 29.95 (*1-55609-960-6*); pap. 19.95 (*1-55609-959-2*); lib. bdg. 29.95 (*1-55609-958-4*); disk 29.95 (*1-55609-961-4*) Gallopade Intl.

— Quiz Bowl Crash Course. (J). (gr. 5 up). 1994. 29.95 (*1-55609-288-1*); pap. 19.95 (*1-55609-195-8*); disk 29.95 (*1-55609-289-X*) Gallopade Intl.

— Rameses Treasure Tomb: Find of the Century! (Wildly Educational Titles Ser.). (J). (gr. 2-9). 1995. 29.95 (*0-7933-7821-4*, C Marsh); pap. 19.95 (*0-7933-7822-2*, C Marsh) Gallopade Intl.

— Rhode Island "GEO" Bingo! 38 Must Know State Geography Facts for Kids to Learn While Having Fun! (Bingo! Ser.). (Illus.). (J). (gr. 2-8). 1998. pap. 14.95 (*0-7933-8640-3*) Gallopade Intl.

— Rhode Island & Other State Greats (Biographies) (Carole Marsh Rhode Island Bks.). (Illus.). (J). 1994. pap. 19.95 (*0-7933-1978-1*); lib. bdg. 29.95 (*0-7933-1977-3*); disk 29.95 (*0-7933-1979-X*) Gallopade Intl.

— Rhode Island Bandits, Bushwackers, Outlaws, Crooks, Devils, Ghosts, Desperadoes & Other Assorted & Sundry Characters! (Carole Marsh Rhode Island Bks.). (Illus.). (J). 1994. pap. 19.95 (*0-7933-0985-9*); lib. bdg. 29.95 (*0-7933-0986-7*); disk 29.95 (*0-7933-0987-5*) Gallopade Intl.

— Rhode Island "BIO" Bingo! 24 Must Know State People for Kids to Learn about While Having Fun! (Bingo! Ser.). (Illus.). (J). (gr. 2-8). 1998. pap. 14.95 (*0-7933-8639-X*) Gallopade Intl.

— The Rhode Island Bookstore Book: A Surprising Guide to Our State's Bookstores & Their Specialties for Students, Teachers, Writers & Publishers. (Rhode Island Bks.). (Illus.). 1994. pap. 19.95 (*0-7933-2973-6*); lib. bdg. 29.95 (*0-7933-2972-8*); disk 29.95 (*0-7933-2974-4*) Gallopade Intl.

— Rhode Island Classic Christmas Trivia: Stories, Recipes, Activities, Legends, Lore & More! (Carole Marsh Rhode Island Bks.). (Illus.). (J). 1994. pap. 19.95 (*0-7933-0988-3*); lib. bdg. 29.95 (*0-7933-0989-1*); disk 29.95 (*0-7933-0990-5*) Gallopade Intl.

— Rhode Island Coastales! (Rhode Island Bks.). (J). 1994. lib. bdg. 29.95 (*0-7933-7304-2*) Gallopade Intl.

— Rhode Island Coastales! (Carole Marsh Rhode Island Bks.). (Illus.). (J). 1994. pap. 19.95 (*0-7933-1972-2*); lib. bdg. 29.95 (*0-7933-1971-4*); disk 29.95 (*0-7933-1973-0*) Gallopade Intl.

— Rhode Island "Crinkum-Crankum" A Funny Word Book about Our State. (Rhode Island Bks.). (Illus.). (J). (gr. 3-12). 1994. 29.95 (*0-7933-4925-7*); pap. 19.95 (*0-7933-4926-5*); disk 29.95 (*0-7933-4927-3*) Gallopade Intl.

— Rhode Island Dingbats! Bk. 1: A Fun Book of Games, Stories, Activities & More about Our State That's All in Code! for You to Decipher. (Rhode Island Bks.). (Illus.). (J). (gr. 3-12). 1994. pap. 19.95 (*0-7933-3891-3*); lib. bdg. 29.95 (*0-7933-3890-5*); disk 29.95 (*0-7933-3892-1*) Gallopade Intl.

— Rhode Island Facts & Factivities. (Carole Marsh State Bks.). (Illus.). (J). (gr. 4-7). 1996. pap., teacher ed. 19.95 (*0-7933-7925-3*, C Marsh) Gallopade Intl.

— Rhode Island Festival Fun for Kids! (Rhode Island Bks.). (Illus.). (YA). (gr. 3-12). 1994. pap. 19.95 (*0-7933-4044-6*); lib. bdg. 29.95 (*0-7933-4043-8*); disk 29.95 (*0-7933-4045-4*) Gallopade Intl.

— Rhode Island Government! The Cornerstone of Everyday Life in Our State! (Carole Marsh Rhode Island Bks.). (Illus.). (J). (gr. 3-12). 1996. pap. 19.95 (*0-7933-6299-7*); lib. bdg. 29.95 (*0-7933-6298-9*); disk 29.95 (*0-7933-6300-4*) Gallopade Intl.

— Rhode Island "HISTO" Bingo! 42 Must Know State History Facts for Kids to Learn While Having Fun! (Bingo! Ser.). (Illus.). (J). (gr. 2-8). 1998. pap. 14.95 (*0-7933-8641-1*) Gallopade Intl.

— Rhode Island History! Surprising Secrets about Our State's Founding Mothers, Fathers & Kids! (Carole Marsh Rhode Island Bks.). (Illus.). (J). (gr. 3-12). 1996. pap. 19.95 (*0-7933-6146-X*); lib. bdg. 29.95 (*0-7933-6145-1*); disk 29.95 (*0-7933-6147-8*) Gallopade Intl.

— The Rhode Island Hot Air Balloon Mystery. (Carole Marsh Rhode Island Bks.). (Illus.). (J). (gr. 2-9). 1994. 29.95 (*0-7933-2669-9*); pap. 19.95 (*0-7933-2670-2*); disk 29.95 (*0-7933-2671-0*) Gallopade Intl.

— Rhode Island Hot Zones! Viruses, Diseases, & Epidemics in Our State's History. (Hot Zones! Ser.). (Illus.). (J). (gr. 3-12). 1998. pap. 19.95 (*0-7933-8946-1*); lib. bdg. 29.95 (*0-7933-8945-3*) Gallopade Intl.

— Rhode Island Indian Dictionary for Kids! (Carole Marsh State Bks.). (J). (gr. 2-9). 1996. 29.95 (*0-7933-7761-7*, C Marsh); pap. 19.95 (*0-7933-7762-5*, C Marsh) Gallopade Intl.

— Rhode Island Jeopardy! Answers & Questions about Our State! (Rhode Island Bks.). (Illus.). (J). (gr. 3-12). 1994. pap. 19.95 (*0-7933-4197-3*); lib. bdg. 29.95 (*0-7933-4196-5*); disk 29.95 (*0-7933-4198-1*) Gallopade Intl.

— Rhode Island "Jography" A Fun Run Thru Our State! (Carole Marsh Rhode Island Bks.). (Illus.). (J). 1994. pap. 19.95 (*0-7933-1955-2*); lib. bdg. 29.95 (*0-7933-1954-4*); disk 29.95 (*0-7933-1956-0*) Gallopade Intl.

— Rhode Island Kid's Cookbook: Recipes, How-To, History Lore & More! (Carole Marsh Rhode Island Bks.). (Illus.). (J). 1994. pap. 19.95 (*0-7933-0997-2*); lib. bdg. 29.95 (*0-7933-0998-0*); disk 29.95 (*0-7933-0999-9*) Gallopade Intl.

— The Rhode Island Library Book: A Surprising Guide to the Unusual Special Collections in Libraries Across Our State for Students, Teachers, Writers & Publishers - Includes Reproducible Mailing Labels Plus Activities for Young People! (Rhode Island Bks.). (Illus.). 1994. pap. 19.95 (*0-7933-3123-4*); lib. bdg. 29.95 (*0-7933-3122-6*); disk 29.95 (*0-7933-3124-2*) Gallopade Intl.

— Rhode Island Math! How It All Adds up in Our State. (Carole Marsh Rhode Island Bks.). (Illus.). (YA). (gr. 3-12). 1996. pap. 19.95 (*0-7933-6605-4*); lib. bdg. 29.95 (*0-7933-6604-6*) Gallopade Intl.

— The Rhode Island Media Book: A Surprising Guide to the Amazing Print, Broadcast & Online Media of Our State for Students, Teachers, Writers & Publishers - Includes Reproducible Mailing Labels Plus Activities for Young People! (Rhode Island Bks.). (Illus.). 1994. pap. 19.95 (*0-7933-3279-6*); lib. bdg. 29.95 (*0-7933-3278-8*); disk 29.95 (*0-7933-3280-X*) Gallopade Intl.

— The Rhode Island Mystery Van Takes Off! Bk. 1: Handicapped Rhode Island Kids Sneak Off on a Big Adventure. (Rhode Island Bks.). (Illus.). (J). (gr. 3-12). 1994. 29.95 (*0-7933-5078-6*); pap. 19.95 (*0-7933-5079-4*); disk 29.95 (*0-7933-5080-8*) Gallopade Intl.

— Rhode Island Quiz Bowl Crash Course! (Carole Marsh Rhode Island Bks.). (Illus.). (J). 1994. pap. 19.95 (*0-7933-1969-2*); lib. bdg. 29.95 (*0-7933-1968-4*); disk 29.95 (*0-7933-1970-6*) Gallopade Intl.

— Rhode Island Rollercoasters! (Rhode Island Bks.). (Illus.). (YA). (gr. 3-12). 1994. pap. 19.95 (*0-7933-5342-4*); lib. bdg. 29.95 (*0-7933-5341-6*); disk 29.95 (*0-7933-5343-2*) Gallopade Intl.

— Rhode Island School Trivia: An Amazing & Fascinating Look at Our State's Teachers, Schools & Students! (Carole Marsh Rhode Island Bks.). (Illus.). (J). 1994. pap. 19.95 (*0-7933-0994-8*); lib. bdg. 29.95 (*0-7933-0995-6*); disk 29.95 (*0-7933-0996-4*) Gallopade Intl.

— Rhode Island Silly Basketball Sportsmysteries, Vol. 1. (Carole Marsh Rhode Island Bks.). (Illus.). (J). 1994. pap. 19.95 (*0-7933-0991-3*); lib. bdg. 29.95 (*0-7933-0992-1*); disk 29.95 (*0-7933-0993-X*) Gallopade Intl.

— Rhode Island Silly Basketball Sportsmysteries, Vol. 2. (Carole Marsh Rhode Island Bks.). (Illus.). (J). 1994. pap. 19.95 (*0-7933-1981-1*); lib. bdg. 29.95 (*0-7933-1980-3*); disk 29.95 (*0-7933-1982-X*) Gallopade Intl.

— Rhode Island Silly Football Sportsmysteries, Vol. 1. (Carole Marsh Rhode Island Bks.). (Illus.). (J). 1994. pap. 19.95 (*0-7933-1960-9*); lib. bdg. 29.95 (*0-7933-1959-5*); disk 29.95 (*0-7933-1961-7*) Gallopade Intl.

— Rhode Island Silly Football Sportsmysteries, Vol. 2. (Carole Marsh Rhode Island Bks.). (Illus.). (J). 1994. pap. 19.95 (*0-7933-1963-3*); lib. bdg. 29.95 (*0-7933-1962-5*); disk 29.95 (*0-7933-1964-1*) Gallopade Intl.

— Rhode Island Silly Trivia! (Carole Marsh Rhode Island Bks.). (Illus.). (J). 1994. pap. 19.95 (*0-7933-1952-8*); lib. bdg. 29.95 (*0-7933-1951-X*); disk 29.95 (*0-7933-1953-6*) Gallopade Intl.

— Rhode Island Spelling Bee! Score Big by Correctly Spelling Our State's Unique Names. (Carole Marsh Rhode Island Bks.). (Illus.). (YA). (gr. 3-12). 1996. pap. 19.95 (*0-7933-6758-1*); lib. bdg. 29.95 (*0-7933-6757-3*) Gallopade Intl.

— Rhode Island Timeline: A Chronology of Rhode Island History, Mystery, Trivia, Legend, Lore & More. (Rhode Island Bks.). (Illus.). (J). (gr. 3-12). 1994. pap. 19.95 (*0-7933-5993-7*); lib. bdg. 29.95 (*0-7933-5992-9*); disk 29.95 (*0-7933-5994-5*) Gallopade Intl.

— Rhode Island 2000! Coming Soon to a Calendar Near You - The 21st Century! - Complete Set of AL 2000 Items. (Two Thousand! Ser.). (Illus.). (J). (gr. 3-12). 1998. pap. 75.00 (*0-7933-9387-6*); lib. bdg. 85.00 (*0-7933-9388-4*) Gallopade Intl.

— Rhode Island 2000! Coming Soon to a Calendar near You-The 21st Century! (Two Thousand! Ser.). (Illus.). (J). (gr. 3-12). 1998. pap. 19.95 (*0-7933-8793-0*); lib. bdg. 29.95 (*0-7933-8792-2*) Gallopade Intl.

— Rhode Island UFO's & Extraterrestrials! A Look at the Sightings & Science in Our State. (Carole Marsh Rhode Island Bks.). (Illus.). (J). (gr. 3-12). 1997. pap. 19.95 (*0-7933-6452-3*); lib. bdg. 29.95 (*0-7933-6451-5*) Gallopade Intl.

— Rhode Island's (Most Devastating!) Disasters & (Most Calamitous!) Catastrophies! (Carole Marsh Rhode Island Bks.). (Illus.). (J). 1994. pap. 19.95 (*0-7933-0982-4*); lib. bdg. 29.95 (*0-7933-0983-2*) Gallopade Intl.

— Rhode Island's (Most Devastating!) Disasters & (Most Calamitous!) Catastrophies! (Carole Marsh Rhode Island Bks.). (Illus.). (J). 1997. disk 29.95 (*0-7933-0984-0*) Gallopade Intl.

— Rhode Island's Unsolved Mysteries (And Their "Solutions") Includes Scientific Information & Other Activities for Students. (Rhode Island Bks.). (Illus.). (J). (gr. 3-12). 1994. pap. 19.95 (*0-7933-5840-X*); lib. bdg. 29.95 (*0-7933-5839-6*); disk 29.95 (*0-7933-5841-8*) Gallopade Intl.

— River Rogues! Natchez Pirates, Playboys, & the Rest of the Cock-o-the-Walk Crowd under-the-Hill & along the Trace. (Carole Marsh Mississippi Bks.). (J). 1994. pap. 19.95 (*0-7933-7323-9*); lib. bdg. 29.95 (*0-7933-7584-3*) Gallopade Intl.

— Saturnalia. (Carole Marsh Short Story Ser.). (Illus.). (Orig.). (J). (gr. 4-12). 1994. 29.95 (*1-55609-187-7*); pap. 19.95 (*1-55609-238-5*) Gallopade Intl.

— School Trivia: Funny (& Not So Funny) Stuff about Schools, Teachers & Students. (Quantum Leap Ser.). (Illus.). 1994. 29.95 (*0-7933-0007-X*); pap. 19.95 (*0-7933-0008-8*) Gallopade Intl.

— The Secret Mysteries Dingbats Book. (Carole Marsh Dingbats Bks.). (Illus.). (J). (gr. 3-12). 1994. pap. 19.95 (*0-7933-5384-X*); lib. bdg. 29.95 (*0-7933-5383-1*); disk 29.95 (*0-7933-5385-8*) Gallopade Intl.

— The Secret of Scotty's Castle Set. (Carole Marsh Mysteries Ser.). 1994. 125.00 (*0-7933-6964-9*) Gallopade Intl.

— The Secret of Somerset Place. (History Mystery Ser.). (Illus.). (Orig.). (gr. 3-9). 1994. pap. 19.95 (*0-935326-02-2*) Gallopade Intl.

— The Secret of Somerset Place S. P. A. R. K. Kit. (S. P. A. R. K. Ser.). (Illus.). (Orig.). (J). (gr. 3-9). 1994. pap. 19.95 (*0-935326-20-0*) Gallopade Intl.

— The Secret of Somerset Place Set. (Carole Marsh Mysteries Ser.). 1994. teacher ed. 125.00 (*0-7933-6946-0*) Gallopade Intl.

— Self Publishing by the Seat of Your Pants! (ProPub Ser.). 1994. pap. text 19.95 (*1-55609-963-0*); lib. bdg. 29.95 (*1-55609-962-2*); ring bd. 29.95 (*1-55609-964-9*); disk 29.95 (*1-55609-965-7*) Gallopade Intl.

— Sex Stuff for Boys: Sperm, Squirm & Other Squiggly Stuff. (Smart Sex Stuff Ser.). 1994. 29.95 (*1-55609-189-3*); pap. 19.95 (*1-55609-207-5*) Gallopade Intl.

— Sex Stuff for Girls: A Period Is More Than a Punctuation Mark. (Smart Sex Stuff Ser.). (Orig.). 1994. 29.95 (*1-55609-190-7*); pap. 19.95 (*1-55609-206-7*) Gallopade Intl.

— Sex Stuff for Kids 7-17: A Book of Practical Information & Ideas for Kids & Their Teachers & Parents, Contains Chapter on 'AIDS' (J). (gr. 2-12). 1994. 29.95 (*1-55609-200-8*); teacher ed. 29.95 (*1-55609-204-0*); pap. 19.95 (*1-55609-201-6*) Gallopade Intl.

— Sex Stuff for Parents: The Painless, Foolproof, "Really Works!" Way to Teach 7-17-Year-Olds about Sex So They Won't Get AIDS, a Disease or a Baby (& You Won't Get Embarrassed!): For Alabama Parents. (Carole Marsh Montana Bks.). (Illus.). 1994. lib. bdg. 39.95 (*0-7933-2555-2*); lib. bdg. 39.95 (*0-7933-2330-4*); lib. bdg. 39.95 (*0-7933-2339-8*); lib. bdg. 39.95 (*0-7933-2357-6*); lib. bdg. 39.95 (*0-7933-2366-5*); lib. bdg. 39.95 (*0-7933-2375-4*); lib. bdg. 29.95 (*0-685-37842-X*); lib. bdg. 39.95 (*0-7933-2393-2*); lib. bdg. 39.95 (*0-7933-2402-5*); lib. bdg. 39.95 (*0-7933-2411-4*); lib. bdg. 39.95 (*0-7933-2420-3*); lib. bdg. 39.95 (*0-7933-2429-7*); lib. bdg. 39.95 (*0-7933-2438-6*); lib. bdg. 39.95 (*0-7933-2447-5*); lib. bdg. 39.95 (*0-7933-2456-4*); lib. bdg. 39.95 (*0-7933-2465-3*); lib. bdg. 39.95 (*0-7933-2474-2*); lib. bdg. 39.95 (*0-7933-2483-1*); lib. bdg. 39.95 (*0-7933-2492-0*); lib. bdg. 39.95 (*0-7933-2501-3*); lib. bdg. 39.95 (*0-7933-2510-2*); lib. bdg. 39.95 (*0-7933-2519-6*); lib. bdg. 39.95 (*0-7933-2528-5*); lib. bdg. 39.95 (*0-7933-2537-4*); lib. bdg. 39.95 (*0-7933-2546-3*); lib. bdg. 39.95 (*0-7933-2564-1*); lib. bdg. 39.95 (*0-7933-2672-9*); lib. bdg. 39.95 (*0-7933-2573-0*); lib. bdg. 39.95 (*0-7933-2582-X*); lib. bdg. 39.95 (*0-7933-2591-9*); lib. bdg. 39.95 (*0-7933-2600-1*); lib. bdg. 39.95 (*0-7933-2609-5*); lib. bdg. 39.95 (*0-7933-2618-4*); lib. bdg. 39.95 (*0-7933-2627-3*); lib. bdg. 39.95 (*0-7933-2636-2*); lib. bdg. 39.95 (*0-7933-2645-1*); lib. bdg. 39.95 (*0-7933-2654-0*); lib. bdg. 39.95 (*0-7933-2663-X*); lib. bdg. 39.95 (*0-7933-2681-8*); lib. bdg. 39.95 (*0-7933-2690-7*); lib. bdg. 39.95 (*0-7933-2699-0*); lib. bdg. 39.95 (*0-7933-2708-3*); lib. bdg. 39.95 (*0-7933-2717-2*); lib. bdg. 39.95 (*0-7933-2726-1*); lib. bdg. 39.95 (*0-7933-2735-0*); lib. bdg. 39.95 (*0-7933-2744-X*); lib. bdg. 39.95 (*0-7933-2753-9*); lib. bdg. 39.95 (*0-7933-2762-8*); lib. bdg. 39.95 (*0-7933-2771-7*) Gallopade Intl.

— Sex Stuff for Parents: The Painless, Foolproof, "Really Works!" Way to Teach 7-17-Year-Olds about Sex So They Won't Get AIDS, a Disease or a Baby (& You Won't Get Embarrassed!): For Alabama Parents. (Carole Marsh Alabama Bks.). (Illus.). 1997. lib. bdg. 39.95 (*0-7933-2321-5*) Gallopade Intl.

— Sign on the Dotted Line: Two Hundred Years of U. S. Constitution Silly Trivia. (Quantum Leap Ser.). (Illus.). (Orig.). (gr. 3-9). 1994. 29.95 (*1-55609-191-5*); pap. 19.95 (*0-935326-76-6*) Gallopade Intl.

— The Sinister Spies Dingbats Book. (Carole Marsh Dingbats Bks.). (Illus.). (J). (gr. 3-12). 1994. pap. 19.95 (*0-7933-5390-4*); lib. bdg. 29.95 (*0-7933-5389-0*); disk 29.95 (*0-7933-5391-2*) Gallopade Intl.

— Six Puppy Feet: Bridge for Kids. (Quantum Leap Ser.). (Illus.). (J). (gr. k-12). 1994. 29.95 (*1-55609-157-5*); pap. 19.95 (*0-935326-13-8*) Gallopade Intl.

— Snowshoe & Earmuff Go North. (Serendipity Travel Series for Young People). (Illus.). (J). (ps-4). 1994. 29.95 (*1-55609-646-1*); pap. 19.95 (*1-55609-758-1*) Gallopade Intl.

— Snowshoe & Earmuff Go West. (Serendipity Travel Series for Young People). (Illus.). (J). (ps-3). 1994. 29.95 (*1-55609-304-7*); pap. 19.95 (*1-55609-303-9*) Gallopade Intl.

— Sorta Silly, Smart-Aleck Study Tips Even Teens Will Like. (Quantum Leap Ser.). (YA). (gr. 7-12). 1994. pap. 19.95 (*0-7933-7353-0*); lib. bdg. 29.95 (*0-7933-7352-2*); disk 29.95 (*0-7933-7354-9*) Gallopade Intl.

— South Carolina & Other State Greats (Biographies) (Carole Marsh South Carolina Bks.). (Illus.). (J). 1994. pap. 19.95 (*0-7933-2007-0*); lib. bdg. 29.95 (*0-7933-2006-2*); disk 29.95 (*0-7933-2008-9*) Gallopade Intl.

— South Carolina Bandits, Bushwackers, Outlaws, Crooks, Devils, Ghosts, Desperadoes & Other Assorted & Sundry Characters! (Carole Marsh South Carolina Bks.). (Illus.). (J). 1994. pap. 19.95 (*0-7933-1009-1*); lib. bdg. 29.95 (*0-7933-1010-5*); disk 29.95 (*0-7933-1011-3*) Gallopade Intl.

— South Carolina "BIO" Bingo! 24 Must Know State People for Kids to Learn about While Having Fun! (Bingo! Ser.). (Illus.). (J). (gr. 2-8). 1998. pap. 14.95 (*0-7933-8642-X*) Gallopade Intl.

— The South Carolina Bookstore Book: A Surprising Guide to Our State's Bookstores & Their Specialties for Students, Teachers, Writers & Publishers. (South Carolina Bks.). (Illus.). 1994. pap. 19.95 (*0-7933-2976-0*); lib. bdg. 29.95 (*0-7933-2975-2*); disk 29.95 (*0-7933-2977-9*) Gallopade Intl.

— South Carolina Classic Christmas Trivia: Stories, Recipes, Activities, Legends, Lore & More! (Carole Marsh South Carolina Bks.). (Illus.). (J). 1994. pap. 19.95 (*0-7933-1012-1*); lib. bdg. 29.95 (*0-7933-1013-X*); disk 29.95 (*0-7933-1014-8*) Gallopade Intl.

— South Carolina Coastales. (South Carolina Bks.). (J). 1994. lib. bdg. 29.95 (*0-7933-7305-0*) Gallopade Intl.

— South Carolina Coastales. (Carole Marsh South Carolina Bks.). (Illus.). (J). 1994. pap. 19.95 (*1-55609-115-X*); lib. bdg. 29.95 (*0-7933-2001-1*); disk 29.95 (*0-7933-2002-X*) Gallopade Intl.

— South Carolina "Crinkum-Crankum" A Funny Word Book about Our State. (South Carolina Bks.). (Illus.). (J). (gr. 3-12). 1994. 29.95 (*0-7933-4928-1*); pap. 19.95 (*0-7933-4929-X*); disk 29.95 (*0-7933-4930-3*) Gallopade Intl.

— South Carolina Dingbats! Bk. 1: A Fun Book of Games, Stories, Activities & More about Our State That's All in Code! for You to Decipher. (South Carolina Bks.). (Illus.). (J). (gr. 3-12). 1994. pap. 19.95 (*0-7933-3894-8*); lib. bdg. 29.95 (*0-7933-3893-X*); disk 29.95 (*0-7933-3895-6*) Gallopade Intl.

— South Carolina Facts & Factivities. (Carole Marsh State Bks.). (Illus.). (J). (gr. 4-7). 1996. pap., teacher ed. 19.95 (*0-7933-7927-X*, C Marsh) Gallopade Intl.

— South Carolina Festival Fun for Kids! (South Carolina Bks.). (Illus.). (YA). (gr. 3-12). 1994. pap. 19.95 (*0-7933-4047-0*); lib. bdg. 29.95 (*0-7933-4046-2*); disk 29.95 (*0-7933-4048-9*) Gallopade Intl.

— South Carolina "GEO" Bingo! 38 Must Know State Geography Facts for Kids to Learn While Having Fun! (Bingo! Ser.). (Illus.). (J). (gr. 2-8). 1998. pap. 14.95 (*0-7933-8643-8*) Gallopade Intl.

— South Carolina Government! The Cornerstone of Everyday Life in Our State! (Carole Marsh South Carolina Bks.). (Illus.). (J). (gr. 3-12). 1996. pap. 19.95 (*0-7933-6302-0*); lib. bdg. 29.95 (*0-7933-6301-2*); disk 29.95 (*0-7933-6303-9*) Gallopade Intl.

— South Carolina "HISTO" Bingo! 42 Must Know State History Facst for Kids to Learn While Having Fun! (Bingo! Ser.). (Illus.). (J). (gr. 2-8). 1998. pap. 14.95 (*0-7933-8644-6*) Gallopade Intl.

— South Carolina History! Surprising Secrets about Our State's Founding Mothers, Fathers & Kids! (Carole Marsh South Carolina Bks.). (Illus.). (J). (gr. 3-12). 1996. pap. 19.95 (*0-7933-6149-4*); lib. bdg. 29.95 (*0-7933-6148-6*); disk 29.95 (*0-7933-6150-8*) Gallopade Intl.

— The South Carolina Hot Air Balloon Mystery. (Carole Marsh South Carolina Bks.). (Illus.). (J). (gr. 2-9). 1994. 29.95 (*0-7933-2678-8*); pap. 19.95 (*0-7933-2679-6*); disk 29.95 (*0-7933-2680-X*) Gallopade Intl.

— South Carolina Hot Zone! Viruses, Diseases, & Epidemics in Our State's History. (Hot Zones! Ser.). (Illus.). (J). (gr. 3-12). 1998. pap. 19.95 (*0-7933-8949-6*); lib. bdg. 29.95 (*0-7933-8948-8*) Gallopade Intl.

— South Carolina Indian Dictionary for Kids! (Carole Marsh State Bks.). (J). (gr. 2-9). 1996. 29.95 (*0-7933-7764-1*, C Marsh); pap. 19.95 (*0-7933-7765-X*, C Marsh) Gallopade Intl.

— South Carolina Jeopardy! Answers & Questions about Our State! (South Carolina Bks.). (Illus.). (J). (gr. 3-12). 1994. pap. 19.95 (*0-7933-4200-7*); lib. bdg. 29.95 (*0-7933-4199-X*); disk 29.95 (*0-7933-4201-5*) Gallopade Intl.

— South Carolina Jography: A Fun Run Through the Palmetto State. (Statemeant Ser.). (Illus.). 50p. (Orig.). (J). (gr. 3-9). 1994. pap. 19.95 (*0-935326-90-0*) Gallopade Intl.

— South Carolina "Jography" A Fun Run Thru Our State! (Carole Marsh South Carolina Bks.). (Illus.). (J). 1994. pap. 19.95 (*1-55609-049-8*); lib. bdg. 29.95 (*0-7933-1985-4*); disk 29.95 (*0-7933-1986-2*) Gallopade Intl.

— South Carolina Kid's Cookbook: Recipes, How-to, History, Lore & More! (Carole Marsh South Carolina Bks.). (Illus.). (J). 1994. pap. 19.95 (*0-7933-1021-0*); lib. bdg. 29.95 (*0-7933-1022-9*); disk 29.95 (*0-7933-1023-7*) Gallopade Intl.

— The South Carolina Library Book: A Surprising Guide to the Unusual Special Collections in Libraries Across Our State for Students, Teachers, Writers & Publishers - Includes Reproducible Mailing Labels Plus Activities for Young People! (South Carolina Bks.). (Illus.). 1994. pap. 19.95 (*0-7933-3126-9*); lib. bdg. 29.95 (*0-7933-3125-0*); disk 29.95 (*0-7933-3127-7*) Gallopade Intl.

— South Carolina Math! How It All Adds up in Our State. (Carole Marsh South Carolina Bks.). (Illus.). (YA). (gr. 3-12). 1996. pap. 19.95 (*0-7933-6608-9*); lib. bdg. 29.95 (*0-7933-6607-0*) Gallopade Intl.

— The South Carolina Media Book: A Surprising Guide to the Amazing Print, Broadcast & Online Media of Our State for Students, Teachers, Writers & Publishers - Includes Reproducible Mailing Labels Plus Activities for Young People! (South Carolina Bks.). (Illus.). 1994. pap. 19.95 (*0-7933-3282-6*); lib. bdg. 29.95 (*0-7933-3281-8*); disk 29.95 (*0-7933-3283-4*) Gallopade Intl.

— The South Carolina Mystery Van Takes Off! Bk. 1: Handicapped South Carolina Kids Sneak Off on a Big Adventure. (South Carolina Bks.). (Illus.). (J). (gr. 3-12). 1994. 29.95 (*0-7933-5081-6*); pap. 19.95 (*0-7933-5082-4*); disk 29.95 (*0-7933-5083-2*) Gallopade Intl.

— South Carolina Quiz Bowl Crash Course! (Carole Marsh South Carolina Bks.). (Illus.). (J). 1994. pap. 19.95 (*0-7933-1999-4*); lib. bdg. 29.95 (*0-7933-1998-6*); disk 29.95 (*0-7933-2000-3*) Gallopade Intl.

— South Carolina Rollercoasters! (South Carolina Bks.). (Illus.). (YA). (gr. 3-12). 1994. pap. 19.95 (*0-7933-5345-9*); lib. bdg. 29.95 (*0-7933-5344-0*); disk 29.95 (*0-7933-5346-7*) Gallopade Intl.

— South Carolina School Trivia: An Amazing & Fascinating Look at Our State's Teachers, Schools & Students! (Carole Marsh South Carolina Bks.). (Illus.). (J). 1994. pap. 19.95 (*0-7933-1018-0*); lib. bdg. 29.95 (*0-7933-1019-9*); disk 29.95 (*0-7933-1020-2*) Gallopade Intl.

— South Carolina Silly Basketball Sportsmysteries, Vol. 1. (Carole Marsh South Carolina Bks.). (Illus.). (J). 1994. pap. 19.95 (*0-7933-1015-6*); lib. bdg. 29.95 (*0-7933-1016-4*); disk 29.95 (*0-7933-1017-2*) Gallopade Intl.

— South Carolina Silly Basketball Sportsmysteries, Vol. 2. (Carole Marsh South Carolina Bks.). (Illus.). (J). 1994. pap. 19.95 (*0-7933-2010-0*); lib. bdg. 29.95 (*0-7933-2009-7*); disk 29.95 (*0-7933-2011-9*) Gallopade Intl.

— South Carolina Silly Football Sportsmysteries, Vol. 1. (Carole Marsh South Carolina Bks.). (Illus.). (J). 1994. pap. 19.95 (*0-7933-1990-0*); lib. bdg. 29.95 (*0-7933-1989-7*); disk 29.95 (*0-7933-1991-9*) Gallopade Intl.

— South Carolina Silly Football Sportsmysteries, Vol. 2. (Carole Marsh South Carolina Bks.). (Illus.). (J). 1994. pap. 19.95 (*0-7933-1993-5*); lib. bdg. 29.95 (*0-7933-1992-7*); disk 29.95 (*0-7933-1994-3*) Gallopade Intl.

— South Carolina Silly Trivia! (Carole Marsh South Carolina Bks.). (Illus.). (Orig.). (J). 1994. lib. bdg. 29.95 (*0-7933-1983-8*); disk 29.95 (*0-7933-1984-6*) Gallopade Intl.

— South Carolina Spelling Bee! Score Big by Correctly Spelling Our State's Unique Names. (Carole Marsh South Carolina Bks.). (Illus.). (YA). (gr. 3-12). 1996. pap. 19.95 (*0-7933-6761-1*); lib. bdg. 29.95 (*0-7933-6760-3*) Gallopade Intl.

— South Carolina Timeline: A Chronology of South Carolina History, Mystery, Trivia, Legend, Lore & More. (South Carolina Bks.). (Illus.). (J). (gr. 3-12). 1994. pap. 19.95 (*0-7933-5996-1*); lib. bdg. 29.95 (*0-7933-5995-3*); disk 29.95 (*0-7933-5997-X*) Gallopade Intl.

— South Carolina 2000! Coming Soon to a Calendar Near You - The 21st Century! - Complete Set of AL 2000 Items. (Two Thousand! Ser.). (Illus.). (J). (gr. 3-12). 1998. pap. 75.00 (*0-7933-9389-2*); lib. bdg. 85.00 (*0-7933-9390-6*) Gallopade Intl.

— South Carolina 2000! Coming Soon to a Calendar near You--The 21st Century! (Two Thousand! Ser.). (Illus.). (J). (gr. 3-12). 1998. pap. 19.95 (*0-7933-8796-5*); lib. bdg. 29.95 (*0-7933-8795-7*) Gallopade Intl.

— South Carolina UFO's & Extraterrestrials! A Look at the Sightings & Science in Our State. (Carole Marsh South Carolina Bks.). (Illus.). (J). (gr. 3-12). 1997. pap. 19.95 (*0-7933-6455-8*); lib. bdg. 29.95 (*0-7933-6454-X*) Gallopade Intl.

— South Carolina's (Most Devastating!) Disasters & (Most Calamitous!) Catastrophies! (Carole Marsh South Carolina Bks.). (Illus.). (J). 1994. pap. 19.95 (*0-7933-1006-7*); lib. bdg. 29.95 (*0-7933-1007-5*); disk 29.95 (*0-7933-1008-3*) Gallopade Intl.

— South Carolina's Unsolved Mysteries (& Their "Solutions") Includes Scientific Information & Other Activities for Students. (South Carolina Bks.). (Illus.). (J). (gr. 3-12). 1994. pap. 19.95 (*0-7933-5843-4*); lib. bdg. 29.95 (*0-7933-5842-6*); disk 29.95 (*0-7933-5844-2*) Gallopade Intl.

— South Dakota History! Surprising Secrets about Our State's Founding Mothers, Fathers & Kids! (Carole Marsh South Dakota Bks.). (Illus.). (J). (gr. 3-12). 1996. pap. 19.95 (*0-7933-6152-4*); lib. bdg. 29.95 (*0-7933-6151-6*); disk 29.95 (*0-7933-6153-2*) Gallopade Intl.

— South Dakota & Other State Greats (Biographies) (Carole Marsh South Dakota Bks.). (Illus.). (J). 1994. pap. 19.95 (*0-7933-2039-9*); lib. bdg. 29.95 (*0-7933-2038-0*); disk 29.95 (*0-7933-2040-2*) Gallopade Intl.

— South Dakota Bandits, Bushwackers, Outlaws, Crooks, Devils, Ghosts, Desperadoes & Other Assorted & Sundry Characters! (Carole Marsh South Dakota Bks.). (Illus.). (J). 1994. pap. 19.95 (*0-7933-1033-4*); lib. bdg. 29.95 (*0-7933-1034-2*); disk 29.95 (*0-7933-1035-0*) Gallopade Intl.

— South Dakota "BIO" Bingo! 24 Must Know State People for Kids to Learn about While Having Fun! (Bingo! Ser.). (Illus.). (J). (gr. 2-8). 1998. pap. 14.95 (*0-7933-8645-4*) Gallopade Intl.

— The South Dakota Bookstore Book: A Surprising Guide to Our State's Bookstores & Their Specialties for Students, Teachers, Writers & Publishers. (South Dakota Bks.). (Illus.). 1994. pap. 19.95 (*0-7933-2979-5*); lib. bdg. 29.95 (*0-7933-2978-7*); disk 29.95 (*0-7933-2980-9*) Gallopade Intl.

— South Dakota Classic Christmas Trivia: Stories, Recipes, Activities, Legends, Lore & More! (Carole Marsh South Dakota Bks.). (Illus.). (J). 1994. pap. 19.95 (*0-7933-1036-9*); lib. bdg. 29.95 (*0-7933-1037-7*); disk 29.95 (*0-7933-1038-5*) Gallopade Intl.

— South Dakota Coastales. (South Dakota Bks.). (J). 1994. lib. bdg. 29.95 (*0-7933-7306-9*) Gallopade Intl.

— South Dakota Coastales. (Carole Marsh South Dakota Bks.). (Illus.). (J). 1994. pap. 19.95 (*0-7933-2033-X*); lib. bdg. 29.95 (*0-7933-2032-1*); disk 29.95 (*0-7933-2034-8*) Gallopade Intl.

— South Dakota "Crinkum-Crankum" A Funny Word Book about Our State. (South Dakota Bks.). (Illus.). (J). (gr. 3-12). 1994. 29.95 (*0-7933-4931-1*); pap. 19.95 (*0-7933-4932-X*); disk 29.95 (*0-7933-4933-8*) Gallopade Intl.

— South Dakota Dingbats! Bk. 1: A Fun Book of Games, Stories, Activities & More about Our State That's All in Code! for You to Decipher. (South Dakota Bks.). (Illus.). (J). (gr. 3-12). 1994. pap. 19.95 (*0-7933-3897-2*); lib. bdg. 29.95 (*0-7933-3896-4*); disk 29.95 (*0-7933-3898-0*) Gallopade Intl.

— South Dakota Facts & Factivities. (Carole Marsh State Bks.). (Illus.). (J). (gr. 4-7). 1996. pap., teacher ed. 19.95 (*0-7933-7929-6*, C Marsh) Gallopade Intl.

— South Dakota Festival Fun for Kids! (South Dakota Bks.). (Illus.). (YA). (gr. 3-12). 1994. pap. 19.95 (*0-7933-4050-0*); lib. bdg. 29.95 (*0-7933-4049-7*); disk 29.95 (*0-7933-4051-9*) Gallopade Intl.

— South Dakota "GEO" Bingo! 38 Must Know State Geography Facts for Kids to Learn While Having Fun! (Bingo! Ser.). (Illus.). (J). (gr. 2-8). 1998. pap. 14.95 (*0-7933-8646-2*) Gallopade Intl.

— South Dakota Government! The Cornerstone of Everyday Life in Our State! (Carole Marsh South Dakota Bks.). (Illus.). (J). (gr. 3-12). 1996. pap. 19.95 (*0-7933-6305-5*); lib. bdg. 29.95 (*0-7933-6304-7*); disk 29.95 (*0-7933-6306-3*) Gallopade Intl.

— South Dakota "HISTO" Bingo! 42 Must Know State History Facts for Kids to Learn While Having Fun! (Bingo! Ser.). (Illus.). (J). (gr. 2-8). 1998. pap. 14.95 (*0-7933-8647-0*) Gallopade Intl.

— The South Dakota Hot Air Balloon Mystery. (Carole

M

Marsh South Dakota Bks.). (Illus.). (J). (gr. 2-9). 1994. 29.95 (*0-7933-2687-7*); pap. 19.95 (*0-7933-2688-5*); disk 29.95 (*0-7933-2689-3*) Gallopade Intl.

— South Dakota Hot Zones! Viruses, Diseases, & Epidemics in Our State's History. (Hot Zones! Ser.). (Illus.). (J). (gr. 3-12). 1998. pap. 19.95 (*0-7933-8952-6*); lib. bdg. 29.95 (*0-7933-8951-8*) Gallopade Intl.

— South Dakota Indian Dictionary for Kids! (Carole Marsh State Bks.). (J). (gr. 2-9). 1996. 29.95 (*0-7933-7767-6*, C Marsh); pap. 19.95 (*0-7933-7768-4*, C Marsh) Gallopade Intl.

— South Dakota Jeopardy! Answers & Questions about Our State! (South Dakota Bks.). (Illus.). (J). (gr. 3-12). 1994. pap. 19.95 (*0-7933-4203-1*); lib. bdg. 29.95 (*0-7933-4202-3*); disk 29.95 (*0-7933-4204-X*) Gallopade Intl.

— South Dakota "Jography" A Fun Run Thru Our State! (Carole Marsh South Dakota Bks.). (Illus.). (J). 1994. pap. 19.95 (*0-7933-2016-X*); lib. bdg. 29.95 (*0-7933-2015-1*); disk 29.95 (*0-7933-2017-8*) Gallopade Intl.

— South Dakota Kid's Cookbook: Recipes, How-to, History, Lore & More! (Carole Marsh South Dakota Bks.). (Illus.). (J). 1994. pap. 19.95 (*0-7933-1045-8*); lib. bdg. 29.95 (*0-7933-1046-6*); disk 29.95 (*0-7933-1047-4*) Gallopade Intl.

— The South Dakota Library Book: A Surprising Guide to the Unusual Special Collections in Libraries Across Our State for Students, Teachers, Writers & Publishers - Includes Reproducible Mailing Labels Plus Activities for Young People! (South Dakota Bks.). (Illus.). 1994. pap. 19.95 (*0-7933-3129-3*); lib. bdg. 29.95 (*0-7933-3128-5*); disk 29.95 (*0-7933-3130-7*) Gallopade Intl.

— South Dakota Math! How It All Adds up in Our State. (Carole Marsh South Dakota Bks.). (Illus.). (YA). (gr. 3-12). 1996. pap. 19.95 (*0-7933-6611-9*); lib. bdg. 29.95 (*0-7933-6610-0*) Gallopade Intl.

— The South Dakota Media Book: A Surprising Guide to the Amazing Print, Broadcast & Online Media of Our State for Students, Teachers, Writers & Publishers - Includes Reproducible Mailing Labels Plus Activities for Young People! (South Dakota Bks.). (Illus.). 1994. pap. 19.95 (*0-7933-3285-0*); lib. bdg. 29.95 (*0-7933-3284-2*); disk 29.95 (*0-7933-3286-9*) Gallopade Intl.

— The South Dakota Mystery Van Takes Off! Handicapped South Dakota Kids Sneak Off on a Big Adventure, Bk. 1. (South Dakota Bks.). (Illus.). (J). (gr. 3-12). 1994. 29.95 (*0-7933-5084-0*); pap. 19.95 (*0-7933-5085-9*); disk 29.95 (*0-7933-5086-7*) Gallopade Intl.

— South Dakota Quiz Bowl Crash Course! (Carole Marsh South Dakota Bks.). (Illus.). (J). 1994. pap. 19.95 (*0-7933-2030-5*); lib. bdg. 29.95 (*0-7933-2029-1*); disk 29.95 (*0-7933-2031-3*) Gallopade Intl.

— South Dakota Rollercoasters! (South Dakota Bks.). (Illus.). (YA). (gr. 3-12). 1994. pap. 19.95 (*0-7933-5348-3*); lib. bdg. 29.95 (*0-7933-5347-5*); disk 29.95 (*0-7933-5349-1*) Gallopade Intl.

— South Dakota School Trivia: An Amazing & Fascinating Look at Our State's Teachers, Schools & Students! (Carole Marsh South Dakota Bks.). (Illus.). (J). 1994. pap. 19.95 (*0-7933-1042-3*); lib. bdg. 29.95 (*0-7933-1043-1*); disk 29.95 (*0-7933-1044-X*) Gallopade Intl.

— South Dakota Silly Basketball Sportsmysteries, Vol. 1. (Carole Marsh South Dakota Bks.). (Illus.). (J). 1994. pap. 19.95 (*0-7933-1039-3*); lib. bdg. 29.95 (*0-7933-1040-7*); disk 29.95 (*0-7933-1041-5*) Gallopade Intl.

— South Dakota Silly Basketball Sportsmysteries, Vol. 2. (Carole Marsh South Dakota Bks.). (Illus.). (J). 1994. lib. bdg. 29.95 (*0-7933-2041-0*); disk 29.95 (*0-7933-2043-7*) Gallopade Intl.

— South Dakota Silly Basketball Sportsmysteries, Vol. 2. (Carole Marsh South Dakota Bks.). (Illus.). (J). 1997. pap. 19.95 (*0-7933-2042-9*) Gallopade Intl.

— South Dakota Silly Football Sportsmysteries, Vol. 1. (Carole Marsh South Dakota Bks.). (Illus.). (J). 1994. pap. 19.95 (*0-7933-2021-6*); lib. bdg. 29.95 (*0-7933-2020-8*); disk 29.95 (*0-7933-2022-4*) Gallopade Intl.

— South Dakota Silly Football Sportsmysteries, Vol. 2. (Carole Marsh South Dakota Bks.). (Illus.). (J). 1994. lib. bdg. 29.95 (*0-7933-2023-2*); disk 29.95 (*0-7933-2025-9*) Gallopade Intl.

— South Dakota Silly Trvia! (Carole Marsh South Dakota Bks.). (Illus.). (J). 1994. pap. 19.95 (*0-7933-2013-5*); lib. bdg. 29.95 (*0-7933-2012-7*); disk 29.95 (*0-7933-2014-3*) Gallopade Intl.

— South Dakota Spelling Bee! Score Big by Correctly Spelling Our State's Unique Names. (Carole Marsh South Dakota Bks.). (Illus.). (YA). (gr. 3-12). 1996. pap. 19.95 (*0-7933-6764-6*); lib. bdg. 29.95 (*0-7933-6763-8*) Gallopade Intl.

— South Dakota Timeline: A Chronology of South Dakota History, Mystery, Trivia, Legend, Lore & More. (South Dakota Bks.). (Illus.) (J). (gr. 3-12). 1994. pap. 19.95 (*0-7933-5999-6*); lib. bdg. 29.95 (*0-7933-5998-8*); disk 29.95 (*0-7933-6000-5*) Gallopade Intl.

— South Dakota 2000! Coming Soon to a Calendar Near You - The 21st Century! - Complete Set of AL 2000 Items. (Two Thousand! Ser.). (Illus.). (J). (gr. 3-12). 1998. pap. 75.00 (*0-7933-9391-4*); lib. bdg. 85.00 (*0-7933-9392-2*) Gallopade Intl.

— South Dakota 2000! Coming Soon to a Calendar near You--The 21st Century! (Two Thousand! Ser.). (Illus.). (J). (gr. 3-12). 1998. pap. 19.95 (*0-7933-8799-X*); lib. bdg. 29.95 (*0-7933-8798-1*) Gallopade Intl.

— South Dakota UFO's & Extraterrestrials! A Look at the Sightings & Science in Our State. (Carole Marsh South Dakota Bks.). (Illus.). (J). (gr. 3-12). 1997. pap. 19.95 (*0-7933-6458-2*); lib. bdg. 29.95 (*0-7933-6457-4*) Gallopade Intl.

— South Dakota's (Most Devastating!) Disasters & (Most Calamitous!) Catastrophies! (Carole Marsh South Dakota Bks.). (Illus.). (J). 1994. pap. 19.95 (*0-7933-1030-X*); lib. bdg. 29.95 (*0-7933-1031-8*); disk 29.95 (*0-7933-1032-6*) Gallopade Intl.

— South Dakota's Unsolved Mysteries (& Their "Solutions") Includes Scientific Information & Other Activities for Students. (South Dakota Bks.). (Illus.). (J). (gr. 3-12). 1994. pap. 19.95 (*0-7933-5846-9*); lib. bdg. 29.95 (*0-7933-5845-0*); disk 29.95 (*0-7933-5847-7*) Gallopade Intl.

— Stone Mountain Mystery Gamebook. (Carole Marsh Bks.). (Illus.). (Orig.). (J). (gr. 3-9). 1994. pap. 19.95 (*0-935326-80-4*) Gallopade Intl.

— The Stone Mountain Mystery Set. (Carole Marsh Mysteries Ser.). 1994. 125.00 (*0-7933-6957-6*) Gallopade Intl.

— The Super Silly Riddles Dingbats Book. (Carole Marsh Dingbats Bks.). (Illus.). (J). (gr. 3-12). 1994. pap. 19.95 (*0-7933-5411-0*); lib. bdg. 29.95 (*0-7933-5410-2*); disk 29.95 (*0-7933-5412-9*) Gallopade Intl.

— The Super Silly Sports Trivia Dingbats Book. (Carole Marsh Dingbats Bks.). (Illus.). (J). (gr. 3-12). 1994. pap. 19.95 (*0-7933-5381-5*); lib. bdg. 29.95 (*0-7933-5380-7*); disk 29.95 (*0-7933-5382-3*) Gallopade Intl.

— Teachers Guide to Silly Trivia Books. (Books for Teachers). (Illus.). (Orig.). 1994. pap., teacher ed. 19.95 (*0-935326-91-X*) Gallopade Intl.

— The Teddy Bear Company: Economics for Kids. (Quantum Leap Ser.). (Illus.). (J). (gr. 4-8). 1994. 29.95 (*0-935326-16-2*) Gallopade Intl.

— Teddy Bear's Annual Report. (Quantum Leap Ser.). (Illus.). (J). (gr. 4-8). 1994. 29.95 (*0-935326-26-X*) Gallopade Intl.

— Tennessee & Other State Greats (Biographies) (Carole Marsh Tennessee Bks.). (Illus.). (J). 1994. pap. 19.95 (*0-7933-1054-7*); lib. bdg. 29.95 (*0-7933-1055-5*); disk 29.95 (*0-7933-1056-3*) Gallopade Intl.

— Tennessee Bandits, Bushwackers, Outlaws, Crooks, Devils, Ghosts, Desperadoes & Other Assorted & Sundry Characters! (Carole Marsh Tennessee Bks.). (Illus.). (J). 1994. pap. 19.95 (*0-7933-1057-1*); lib. bdg. 29.95 (*0-7933-1058-X*); disk 29.95 (*0-7933-1059-8*) Gallopade Intl.

— Tennessee "BIO" Bingo! 24 Must Know State People for Kids to Learn about While Having Fun! (Bingo! Ser.). (Illus.). (J). (gr. 2-8). 1998. pap. 14.95 (*0-7933-8648-9*) Gallopade Intl.

— The Tennessee Bookstore Book: A Surprising Guide to Our State's Bookstores & Their Specialties for Students, Teachers, Writers & Publishers. (Tennessee Bks.). (Illus.). 1994. pap. 19.95 (*0-7933-2982-5*); lib. bdg. 29.95 (*0-7933-2981-7*); disk 29.95 (*0-7933-2983-3*) Gallopade Intl.

— Tennessee Classic Christmas Trivia: Stories, Recipes, Activities, Legends, Lore & More! (Carole Marsh Tennessee Bks.). (Illus.). (J). 1994. pap. 19.95 (*0-7933-1060-1*); lib. bdg. 29.95 (*0-7933-1061-X*); disk 29.95 (*0-7933-1062-8*) Gallopade Intl.

— Tennessee Coastales. (Carole Marsh Tennessee Bks.). (Illus.). (J). 1994. pap. 19.95 (*0-7933-2063-1*); lib. bdg. 29.95 (*0-7933-2062-3*); disk 29.95 (*0-7933-2064-X*) Gallopade Intl.

— Tennessee Coastales! (Tennessee Bks.). (J). 1994. lib. bdg. 29.95 (*0-7933-7307-7*) Gallopade Intl.

— Tennessee "Crinkum-Crankum" A Funny Word Book about Our State. (Tennessee Bks.). (Illus.). (J). (gr. 3-12). 1994. 29.95 (*0-7933-4934-6*); pap. 19.95 (*0-7933-4935-4*); disk 29.95 (*0-7933-4936-2*) Gallopade Intl.

— Tennessee Dingbats! A Fun Book of Games, Stories, Activities & More about Our State That's All in Code! for You to Decipher, Bk. 1. (Tennessee Bks.). (Illus.). (J). (gr. 3-12). 1994. pap. 19.95 (*0-7933-3900-6*); lib. bdg. 29.95 (*0-7933-3899-9*); disk 29.95 (*0-7933-3901-4*) Gallopade Intl.

— Tennessee Facts & Factivities. (Carole Marsh State Bks.). (Illus.). (J). (gr. 4-7). 1996. pap., teacher ed. 19.95 (*0-7933-7931-8*, C Marsh) Gallopade Intl.

— Tennessee Festival Fun for Kids! (Tennessee Bks.). (Illus.). (YA). (gr. 3-12). 1994. pap. 19.95 (*0-7933-4053-5*); lib. bdg. 29.95 (*0-7933-4052-7*); disk 29.95 (*0-7933-4054-3*) Gallopade Intl.

— Tennessee "GEO" Bingo! 38 Must Know State Geography Facts for Kid to Learn While Having Fun! (Bingo! Ser.). (Illus.). (J). (gr. 2-8). 1998. pap. 14.95 (*0-7933-8649-7*) Gallopade Intl.

— Tennessee Government! The Cornerstone of Everyday Life in Our State! (Carole Marsh Tennessee Bks.). (Illus.). (J). (gr. 3-12). 1996. pap. 19.95 (*0-7933-6308-X*); lib. bdg. 29.95 (*0-7933-6307-1*); disk 29.95 (*0-7933-6309-8*) Gallopade Intl.

— Tennessee "HISTO" Bingo! 42 Must Know State History Facts for Kids to Learn While Having Fun! (Bingo! Ser.). (Illus.). (J). (gr. 2-8). 1998. pap. 14.95 (*0-7933-8650-0*) Gallopade Intl.

— Tennessee History! Surprising Secrets about Our State's Founding Mothers, Fathers & Kids! (Carole Marsh Tennessee Bks.). (J). (gr. 3-12). 1996. pap. 19.95 (*0-7933-6155-9*); lib. bdg. 29.95 (*0-7933-6154-0*); disk 29.95 (*0-7933-6156-7*) Gallopade Intl.

— The Tennessee Hot Air Balloon Mystery. (Carole Marsh Tennessee Bks.). (Illus.). (J). (gr. 2-9). 1994. 29.95 (*0-7933-2696-6*); pap. 19.95 (*0-7933-2697-4*); disk 29.95 (*0-7933-2698-2*) Gallopade Intl.

— Tennessee Hot Zones! Viruses, Diseases, & Epidemics in Our State's History. (Hot Zones! Ser.). (Illus.). (J). (gr. 3-12). 1998. pap. 19.95 (*0-7933-8955-0*); lib. bdg. 29.95 (*0-7933-8954-2*) Gallopade Intl.

— Tennessee Indian Dictionary for Kids! (Carole Marsh State Bks.). (J). (gr. 2-9). 1996. 29.95 (*0-7933-7770-6*, C Marsh); pap. 19.95 (*0-7933-7771-4*, C Marsh) Gallopade Intl.

— Tennessee Jeopardy! Answers & Questions about Our State! (Tennessee Bks.). (Illus.). (J). (gr. 3-12). 1994. pap. 19.95 (*0-7933-4206-6*); lib. bdg. 29.95 (*0-7933-4205-8*); disk 29.95 (*0-7933-4207-4*) Gallopade Intl.

— Tennessee "Jography" A Fun Run Thru Our State! (Carole Marsh Tennessee Bks.). (Illus.). (J). 1994. pap. 19.95 (*1-55609-089-7*); lib. bdg. 29.95 (*0-7933-2046-1*); disk 29.95 (*0-7933-2047-X*) Gallopade Intl.

— Tennessee Kid's Cookbook: Recipes, How-to, History, Lore & More! (Carole Marsh Tennessee Bks.). (Illus.). (J). 1994. pap. 19.95 (*0-7933-1069-5*); lib. bdg. 29.95 (*0-7933-1070-9*); disk 29.95 (*0-7933-1071-7*) Gallopade Intl.

— The Tennessee Library Book: A Surprising Guide to the Unusual Special Collections in Libraries Across Our State for Students, Teachers, Writers & Publishers - Includes Reproducible Mailing Labels Plus Activities for Young People! (Tennessee Bks.). (Illus.). 1994. pap. 19.95 (*0-7933-3132-3*); lib. bdg. 29.95 (*0-7933-3131-5*); disk 29.95 (*0-7933-3133-1*) Gallopade Intl.

— Tennessee Math! How It All Adds up in Our State. (Carole Marsh Tennessee Bks.). (Illus.). (YA). (gr. 3-12). 1996. pap. 19.95 (*0-7933-6614-3*); lib. bdg. 29.95 (*0-7933-6613-5*) Gallopade Intl.

— The Tennessee Media Book: A Surprising Guide to the Amazing Print, Broadcast & Online Media of Our State for Students, Teachers, Writers & Publishers - Includes Reproducible Mailing Labels Plus Activities for Young People! (Tennessee Bks.). (Illus.). 1994. pap. 19.95 (*0-7933-3288-5*); lib. bdg. 29.95 (*0-7933-3287-7*); disk 29.95 (*0-7933-3289-3*) Gallopade Intl.

— The Tennessee Mystery Van Takes Off! Bk. 1: Handicapped Tennessee Kids Sneak Off on a Big Adventure. (Tennessee Bks.). (Illus.). (J). (gr. 3-12). 1994. 29.95 (*0-7933-5087-5*); pap. 19.95 (*0-7933-5088-3*); disk 29.95 (*0-7933-5089-1*) Gallopade Intl.

— Tennessee Quiz Bowl Crash Course! (Carole Marsh Tennessee Bks.). (Illus.). (J). 1994. pap. 19.95 (*0-7933-2060-7*); lib. bdg. 29.95 (*0-7933-2059-3*); disk 29.95 (*0-7933-2061-5*) Gallopade Intl.

— Tennessee Rollercoasters! (Tennessee Bks.). (Illus.). (YA). (gr. 3-12). 1994. pap. 19.95 (*0-7933-5351-3*); lib. bdg. 29.95 (*0-7933-5350-5*); disk 29.95 (*0-7933-5352-1*) Gallopade Intl.

— Tennessee School Trivia: An Amazing & Fascinating Look at Our State's Teachers, Schools & Students! (Carole Marsh Tennessee Bks.). (Illus.). (J). 1994. pap. 19.95 (*0-7933-1066-0*); lib. bdg. 29.95 (*0-7933-1067-9*); disk 29.95 (*0-7933-1068-7*) Gallopade Intl.

— Tennessee Silly Basketball Sportsmysteries, Vol. 1. (Carole Marsh Tennessee Bks.). (Illus.). (J). 1994. pap. 19.95 (*0-7933-1063-6*); lib. bdg. 29.95 (*0-7933-1064-4*); disk 29.95 (*0-7933-1065-2*) Gallopade Intl.

— Tennessee Silly Basketball Sportsmysteries, Vol. 2. (Carole Marsh Tennessee Bks.). (Illus.). (J). 1994. pap. 19.95 (*0-7933-2072-0*); lib. bdg. 29.95 (*0-7933-2071-2*); disk 29.95 (*0-7933-2073-9*) Gallopade Intl.

— Tennessee Silly Football Sportsmysteries, Vol. 1. (Carole Marsh Tennessee Bks.). (Illus.). (J). 1994. pap. 19.95 (*0-7933-2051-8*); lib. bdg. 29.95 (*0-7933-2050-X*); disk 29.95 (*0-7933-2052-6*) Gallopade Intl.

— Tennessee Silly Football Sportsmysteries, Vol. 2. (Carole Marsh Tennessee Bks.). (Illus.). (J). 1994. pap. 19.95 (*0-7933-2054-2*); lib. bdg. 29.95 (*0-7933-2053-4*); disk 29.95 (*0-7933-2055-0*) Gallopade Intl.

— Tennessee Silly Trivia! (Carole Marsh Tennessee Bks.). (Illus.). (J). 1994. pap. 19.95 (*1-55609-036-6*); lib. bdg. 29.95 (*0-7933-2044-5*); disk 29.95 (*0-7933-2045-3*) Gallopade Intl.

— Tennessee Spelling Bee! Score Big by Correctly Spelling Our State's Unique Names. (Carole Marsh Tennessee Bks.). (Illus.). (YA). (gr. 3-12). 1996. pap. 19.95 (*0-7933-6767-0*); lib. bdg. 29.95 (*0-7933-6766-2*) Gallopade Intl.

— Tennessee Timeline: A Chronology of Tennessee History, Mystery, Trivia, Legend, Lore & More. (Tennessee Bks.). (Illus.). (J). (gr. 3-12). 1994. pap. 19.95 (*0-7933-6002-1*); lib. bdg. 29.95 (*0-7933-6001-3*); disk 29.95 (*0-7933-6003-X*) Gallopade Intl.

— Tennessee 2000! Coming Soon to a Calendar Near You - The 21st Century! - Complete Set of AL 2000 Items. (Two Thousand! Ser.). (Illus.). (J). (gr. 3-12). 1998. pap. 75.00 (*0-7933-9393-0*); lib. bdg. 85.00 (*0-7933-9394-9*) Gallopade Intl.

— Tennessee 2000! Coming Soon to a Calendar near You-The 21st Century! (Two Thousand! Ser.). (Illus.). (J). (gr. 3-12). 1998. pap. 19.95 (*0-7933-8802-3*); lib. bdg. 29.95 (*0-7933-8801-5*) Gallopade Intl.

— Tennessee UFO's & Extraterrestrials! A Look at the Sightings & Science in Our State. (Carole Marsh Tennessee Bks.). (Illus.). (J). (gr. 3-12). 1997. pap. 19.95 (*0-7933-6461-2*); lib. bdg. 29.95 (*0-7933-6460-4*) Gallopade Intl.

— Tennessee's (Most Devastating!) Disasters & (Most Calamitous!) Catastrophies! (Carole Marsh Tennessee Bks.). (Illus.). (J). 1994. pap. 19.95 (*0-7933-2069-0*); lib. bdg. 29.95 (*0-7933-2068-2*); disk 29.95 (*0-7933-2070-4*) Gallopade Intl.

— Tennessee's Unsolved Mysteries (& Their "Solutions") Includes Scientific Information & Other Activities for Students. (Tennessee Bks.). (Illus.). (J). (gr. 3-12). 1994. pap. 19.95 (*0-7933-5849-3*); lib. bdg. 29.95 (*0-7933-5848-5*); disk 29.95 (*0-7933-5850-7*) Gallopade Intl.

— The Terror & Tombstones Dingbats Book. (Carole Marsh Dingbats Bks.). (Illus.). (J). (gr. 3-12). 1994. pap. 19.95 (*0-7933-5402-1*); lib. bdg. 29.95 (*0-7933-5401-3*); disk 29.95 (*0-7933-5403-X*) Gallopade Intl.

— Texas & Other State Greats (Biographies) (Carole Marsh Texas Bks.). (Illus.). (J). 1994. pap. 19.95 (*0-7933-2098-4*); lib. bdg. 29.95 (*0-7933-2097-6*); disk 29.95 (*0-7933-2099-2*) Gallopade Intl.

— Texas Bandits, Bushwackers, Outlaws, Crooks, Devils, Ghosts, Desperadoes & Other Assorted & Sundry Characters! (Carole Marsh Texas Bks.). (Illus.). (J). 1994. pap. 19.95 (*0-7933-1081-4*); lib. bdg. 29.95 (*0-7933-1082-2*); disk 29.95 (*0-7933-1083-0*) Gallopade Intl.

— Texas "BIO" Bingo! 24 Must Know State People for Kids to Learn about While Having Fun! (Bingo! Ser.). (Illus.). (J). (gr. 2-8). 1998. pap. 14.95 (*0-7933-8651-9*) Gallopade Intl.

— The Texas Bookstore Book: A Surprising Guide to Our State's Bookstores & Their Specialties for Students, Teachers, Writers & Publishers. (Texas Bks.). (Illus.). 1994. pap. 19.95 (*0-7933-2985-X*); lib. bdg. 29.95 (*0-7933-2984-1*); disk 29.95 (*0-7933-2986-8*) Gallopade Intl.

— Texas Classic Christmas Trivia: Stories, Recipes, Activities, Legends, Lore & More! (Carole Marsh Texas Bks.). (Illus.). (J). 1994. pap. 19.95 (*0-7933-1084-9*); lib. bdg. 29.95 (*0-7933-1085-7*); disk 29.95 (*0-7933-1086-5*) Gallopade Intl.

— Texas Coastales. (Carole Marsh Texas Bks.). (Illus.). (J). 1994. pap. 19.95 (*1-55609-121-4*); lib. bdg. 29.95 (*0-7933-2092-5*); disk 29.95 (*0-7933-2093-3*) Gallopade Intl.

— Texas Coastales! (Texas Bks.). (J). 1994. lib. bdg. 29.95 (*0-7933-7308-5*) Gallopade Intl.

— Texas "Crinkum-Crankum" A Funny Word Book about Our State. (Texas Bks.). (Illus.). (J). (gr. 3-12). 1994. 29.95 (*0-7933-4937-0*); pap. 19.95 (*0-7933-4938-9*); disk 29.95 (*0-7933-4939-7*) Gallopade Intl.

— Texas Dingbats! Bk. 1: A Fun Book of Games, Stories, Activities & More about Our State That's All in Code! for You to Decipher. (Texas Bks.). (Illus.). (J). (gr. 3-12). 1994. pap. 19.95 (*0-7933-3903-0*); lib. bdg. 29.95 (*0-7933-3902-2*); disk 29.95 (*0-7933-3904-9*) Gallopade Intl.

***Marsh, Carole.** The Texas Experience Pocket Guide. (Texas Experience! Ser.). (Illus.). (J). 2000. pap. 6.95 (*0-7933-9455-4*) Gallopade Intl.

Marsh, Carole. Texas Facts & Factivities. (Carole Marsh State Bks.). (Illus.). (J). (gr. 4-7). 1996. pap., teacher ed. 19.95 (*0-7933-7933-4*, C Marsh) Gallopade Intl.

— Texas Festival Fun for Kids! (Texas Bks.). (Illus.). (YA). (gr. 3-12). 1994. pap. 19.95 (*0-7933-4056-X*); lib. bdg. 29.95 (*0-7933-4055-1*); disk 29.95 (*0-7933-4057-8*) Gallopade Intl.

— Texas "GEO" Bingo! 38 Must Know State Geography Facts for Kids to Learn While Having Fun! (Bingo! Ser.). (Illus.). (J). (gr. 2-8). 1998. pap. 14.95 (*0-7933-8652-7*) Gallopade Intl.

— Texas Government! The Cornerstone of Everyday Life in Our State! (Carole Marsh Texas Bks.). (Illus.). (J). (gr. 3-12). 1996. pap. 19.95 (*0-7933-6311-X*); lib. bdg. 29.95 (*0-7933-6310-1*); disk 29.95 (*0-7933-6312-8*) Gallopade Intl.

— Texas "HISTO" Bingo! 42 Must Know State History Facts for Kids to Learn While Having Fun! (Bingo! Ser.). (Illus.). (J). (gr. 2-8). 1998. pap. 14.95 (*0-7933-8653-5*) Gallopade Intl.

— Texas History! Surprising Secrets about Our State's Founding Mothers, Fathers & Kids! (Carole Marsh Texas Bks.). (Illus.). (J). (gr. 3-12). 1996. pap. 19.95 (*0-7933-6158-3*); lib. bdg. 29.95 (*0-7933-6157-5*); disk 29.95 (*0-7933-6159-1*) Gallopade Intl.

— The Texas Hot Air Balloon Mystery. (Carole Marsh Texas Bks.). (Illus.). (J). (gr. 2-9). 1994. 29.95 (*0-7933-2705-9*); pap. 19.95 (*0-7933-2706-7*); disk 29.95 (*0-7933-2707-5*) Gallopade Intl.

— Texas Hot Zones! Viruses, Diseases, & Epidemics in Our State's History. (Hot Zones! Ser.). (Illus.). (J). (gr. 3-12). 1998. pap. 19.95 (*0-7933-8958-5*); lib. bdg. 29.95 (*0-7933-8957-7*) Gallopade Intl.

— Texas Indian Dictionary for Kids! (Carole Marsh State Bks.). (J). (gr. 2-9). 1996. 29.95 (*0-7933-7773-0*, C Marsh); pap. 19.95 (*0-7933-7774-9*, C Marsh) Gallopade Intl.

***Marsh, Carole.** Texas Jeopardy. (Texas Experience! Ser.). (Illus.). (J). (gr. 2-6). 2000. pap. 7.95 (*0-7933-9528-3*); pap. 7.95 (*0-7933-9529-1*) Gallopade Intl.

Marsh, Carole. Texas Jeopardy! Answers & Questions about Our State! (Texas Bks.). (Illus.). (J). (gr. 3-12). 1994. pap. 19.95 (*0-7933-4209-0*); lib. bdg. 29.95 (*0-7933-4208-2*); disk 29.95 (*0-7933-4210-4*) Gallopade Intl.

— Texas "Jography" A Fun Run Thru Our State! (Carole Marsh Texas Bks.). (Illus.). (J). 1994. pap. 19.95 (*1-55609-087-0*); lib. bdg. 29.95 (*0-7933-2076-3*); disk 29.95 (*0-7933-2077-1*) Gallopade Intl.

— Texas Kid's Cookbook: Recipes, How-To, History, Lore & More! (Carole Marsh Texas Bks.). (Illus.). (J). 1994. pap. 19.95 (*0-7933-1093-8*); lib. bdg. 29.95 (*0-7933-1094-6*); disk 29.95 (*0-7933-1095-4*) Gallopade Intl.

— The Texas Library Book: A Surprising Guide to the Unusual Special Collections in Libraries Across Our State for Students, Teachers, Writers & Publishers - Includes Reproducible Mailing Labels Plus Activities for Young People! (Texas Bks.). (Illus.). 1994. pap. 19.95 (*0-7933-3135-8*); lib. bdg. 29.95 (*0-7933-3134-X*); disk 29.95 (*0-7933-3136-6*) Gallopade Intl.

— Texas Math! How It All Adds up in Our State. (Carole Marsh Texas Bks.). (Illus.). (YA). (gr. 3-12). 1996. pap. 19.95 (*0-7933-6617-8*); lib. bdg. 29.95 (*0-7933-6616-X*) Gallopade Intl.

An Asterisk (*) at the beginning of an entry indicates that the title is appearing for the first time.

— The Texas Media Book: A Surprising Guide to the Amazing Print, Broadcast & Online Media of Our State for Students, Teachers, Writers & Publishers - Includes Reproducible Mailing Labels Plus Activities for Young People! (Texas Bks.). (Illus.). 1994. pap. 19.95 (0-7933-3291-5); lib. bdg. 29.95 (0-7933-3290-7); disk 29.95 (0-7933-3292-3) Gallopade Intl.

— The Texas Mystery Van Takes Off! Bk. 1: Handicapped Texas Kids Sneak Off on a Big Adventure. (Texas Bks.). (Illus.). (J). (gr. 3-12). 1994. 29.95 (0-7933-5090-5); pap. 19.95 (0-7933-5091-3); disk 29.95 (0-7933-5092-1) Gallopade Intl.

— Texas Quiz Bowl Crash Course! (Carole Marsh Texas Bks.). (Illus.). (J). 1994. pap. 19.95 (0-7933-2090-9); lib. bdg. 29.95 (0-7933-2089-5); disk 29.95 (0-7933-2091-7) Gallopade Intl.

— Texas Rollercoasters! (Texas Bks.). (Illus.). (YA). (gr. 3-12). 1994. pap. 19.95 (0-7933-5354-8); lib. bdg. 29.95 (0-7933-5353-X); disk 29.95 (0-7933-5355-6) Gallopade Intl.

— Texas School Trivia: An Amazing & Fascinating Look at Our State's Teachers, Schools & Students! (Carole Marsh Texas Bks.). (Illus.). (J). 1994. pap. 19.95 (0-7933-1090-3); lib. bdg. 29.95 (0-7933-1091-1); disk 29.95 (0-7933-1092-X) Gallopade Intl.

— Texas Silly Basketball Sportsmysteries, Vol. 1. (Carole Marsh Texas Bks.). (Illus.). (J). 1994. pap. 19.95 (0-7933-1087-3); lib. bdg. 29.95 (0-7933-1088-1); disk 29.95 (0-7933-1089-X) Gallopade Intl.

— Texas Silly Basketball Sportsmysteries, Vol. 2. (Carole Marsh Texas Bks.). (Illus.). (J). 1994. pap. 19.95 (0-7933-2101-8); lib. bdg. 29.95 (0-7933-2100-X); disk 29.95 (0-7933-2102-6) Gallopade Intl.

— Texas Silly Football Sportsmysteries, Vol. 1. (Carole Marsh Texas Bks.). (Illus.). (J). 1994. pap. 19.95 (0-7933-2081-X); lib. bdg. 29.95 (0-7933-2080-1); disk 29.95 (0-7933-2082-8) Gallopade Intl.

— Texas Silly Football Sportsmysteries, Vol. 2. (Carole Marsh Texas Bks.). (Illus.). (J). 1994. pap. 19.95 (0-7933-2084-4); lib. bdg. 29.95 (0-7933-2083-6); disk 29.95 (0-7933-2085-2) Gallopade Intl.

— Texas Silly Trivia! (Carole Marsh Texas Bks.). (Illus.). (J). 1994. pap. 19.95 (1-55609-081-1); lib. bdg. 29.95 (0-7933-2074-7); disk 29.95 (0-7933-2075-5) Gallopade Intl.

— Texas Spelling Bee! Score Big by Correctly Spelling Our State's Unique Names. (Carole Marsh Texas Bks.). (Illus.). (YA). (gr. 3-12). 1996. pap. 19.95 (0-7933-6770-0); lib. bdg. 29.95 (0-7933-6769-7) Gallopade Intl.

— Texas Timeline: A Chronology of Texas History, Mystery, Trivia, Legend, Lore & More. (Texas Bks.). (Illus.). (J). (gr. 3-12). 1994. pap. 19.95 (0-7933-6005-6); lib. bdg. 29.95 (0-7933-6004-8); disk 29.95 (0-7933-6006-4) Gallopade Intl.

— Texas 2000! Coming Soon to a Calendar Near You - The 21st Century! - Complete Set of AL 2000 Items. (Two Thousand! Ser.). (Illus.). (J). (gr. 3-12). 1998. pap. 75.00 (0-7933-9395-7); lib. bdg. 85.00 (0-7933-9396-5) Gallopade Intl.

— Texas 2000! Coming Soon to a Calendar near You--The 21st Century! (Two Thousand! Ser.). (Illus.). (J). (gr. 3-12). 1998. pap. 19.95 (0-7933-8805-8); lib. bdg. 29.95 (0-7933-8804-X) Gallopade Intl.

— Texas UFO's & Extraterrestrials! A Look at the Sightings & Science in Our State. (Carole Marsh Texas Bks.). (Illus.). (J). (gr. 3-12). 1997. pap. 19.95 (0-7933-6464-7); lib. bdg. 29.95 (0-7933-6463-9) Gallopade Intl.

***Marsh, Carole.** Texas's Big Activity Book. (Texas Experience! Ser.). (Illus.). (J). (gr. k-5). 2000. pap. 9.95 (0-7933-9465-1) Gallopade Intl.

Marsh, Carole. Texas's (Most Devastating!) Disasters & (Most Calamitous!) Catastrophies! (Carole Marsh Texas Bks.). (Illus.). (J). 1994. pap. 19.95 (0-7933-1078-4); lib. bdg. 29.95 (0-7933-1079-2); disk 29.95 (0-7933-1080-6) Gallopade Intl.

— Texas's Unsolved Mysteries (& Their "Solutions") Includes Scientific Information & Other Activities for Students. (Texas Bks.). (Illus.). (J). (gr. 3-12). 1994. pap. 19.95 (0-7933-5852-3); lib. bdg. 29.95 (0-7933-5851-5); disk 29.95 (0-7933-5853-1) Gallopade Intl.

— Thirty Days Has September: Calendar Trivia & Activities for Kids. (Quantum Leap Ser.). (J). (gr. 3-9). 1994. 29.95 (0-7933-0015-0); pap. 19.95 (0-7933-0016-9); disk 29.95 (0-7933-0017-7) Gallopade Intl.

— Thistle Worth: Poetry to Read Aloud. (Illus.). (Orig.). (gr. 2-12). 1994. pap. 19.95 (0-935326-60-X) Gallopade Intl.

— Those Whose Names Were Terrible. (Lost Colony Collection). (Illus.). (Orig.). (J). (gr. 4-8). 1994. pap. 19.95 (0-935326-48-0) Gallopade Intl.

***Marsh, Carole.** The Totally Texas Coloring Book. (Texas Experience! Ser.). (Illus.). (J). (gr. k-5). 2000. pap. 3.95 (0-7933-9475-9) Gallopade Intl.

Marsh, Carole. "Tough Stuff!" How to Talk to Middle-Schoolers about Disturbing Issues, Including the Holocaust, Terrorism, Sex & Politics, Torture & Persecution, War, Drugs, Suicide, Youth Violence, & Much More! -- A Guide for Parents & Teachers. (Tough Stuff! Ser.). (Illus.). 1998. pap. 19.95 (0-7933-8999-2, C Marsh); pap., teacher ed. 19.95 (0-7933-8998-4, C Marsh) Gallopade Intl.

— "Tough Stuff!" How to Talk to Middle-Schoolers about Disturbing Issues, Including the Holocaust, Terrorism, Sex & Politics, War, Drugs, Suicide, Youth Violence, & Much More! -- A Guide for Parents & Teachers. (Tough Stuff! Ser.). (Illus.). 1998. pap., teacher ed. 19.95 (0-7933-9000-1, C Marsh) Gallopade Intl.

— "Tough Stuff!" How to Talk to Middle-Schoolers about Disturbing Issues, Including the Holocaust, Terrorism, Sex & Politics, Torture & Prosecution, War, Drugs, Suicide, Youth Violence, & Much More!--A Guide for Parents & Teachers. (Tough Stuff! Ser.). (Illus.). 1998. pap. 19.95 (0-7933-8524-5); lib. bdg. 29.95 (1-55609-212-1) Gallopade Intl.

— The Truth & Consequences of Sexually Transmitted Diseases. (Smart Sex Stuff Ser.). (Orig.). 1994. pap. 19.95 (1-55609-212-1) Gallopade Intl.

— Tryon Palace Mystery. (History Mystery Ser.). (Orig.). (J). (gr. 3-12). 1994. pap. 19.95 (0-935326-58-8) Gallopade Intl.

— Tryon Palace Mystery. (History Mystery Ser.). (Orig.). (J). (gr. 3-12). 1997. 29.95 (1-55609-193-1) Gallopade Intl.

— 'Twas the Night Before MacChristmas: A Christmas Tale for Macintosh Users. (Lifewrite Ser.). (Illus.). 1994. pap. 19.95 (0-7933-0006-1) Gallopade Intl.

***Marsh, Carole.** 20 Ways to Teach the SOL with Pizzazz! (Virginia Experience! Ser.). (Illus.). 2000. pap. 5.95 (0-7933-9499-6) Gallopade Intl.

Marsh, Carole. Typing in Ten Minutes: On Any Keyboard - At Any Age. (Quantum Leap Ser.). (Illus.). (J). (gr. k-12). 1994. 29.95 (1-55609-194-X); pap. 19.95 (0-935326-12-X) Gallopade Intl.

— Tyrannosaurus & Other Wrecks: Fossil Trivia for Kids. (Quantum Leap Ser.). (Illus.). (Orig.). (J). (gr. 2 up). 1994. 29.95 (1-55609-166-4); pap. 19.95 (0-935326-56-1) Gallopade Intl.

— U. S. A. Jography: A Fun Run Thru the United States, Vol. II. (Jography Ser.). (Illus.). 60p. (J). (gr. k-12). 1994. pap. 19.95 (1-55609-300-4); lib. bdg. 29.95 (1-55609-301-2); disk 29.95 (1-55609-302-0) Gallopade Intl.

— Uncle Rebus: Alabama Picture Stories for Computer Kids. (Carole Marsh Alabama Bks.). (Illus.). (J). (gr. k-3). 1994. pap. 19.95 (0-7933-4505-7); lib. bdg. 29.95 (0-7933-4504-9); disk 29.95 (0-7933-4506-5) Gallopade Intl.

— Uncle Rebus: Alaska Picture Stories for Computer Kids. (Carole Marsh Alaska Bks.). (Illus.). (J). (gr. k-3). 1994. pap. 19.95 (0-7933-4508-1); lib. bdg. 29.95 (0-7933-4507-3); disk 29.95 (0-7933-4509-X) Gallopade Intl.

— Uncle Rebus: Arizona Picture Stories for Computer Kids. (Carole Marsh Arizona Bks.). (Illus.). (J). (gr. k-3). 1994. pap. 19.95 (0-7933-4511-1); lib. bdg. 29.95 (0-7933-4510-3); disk 29.95 (0-7933-4512-X) Gallopade Intl.

— Uncle Rebus: Arkansas Picture Stories for Computer Kids. (Carole Marsh Arkansas Bks.). (Illus.). (J). (gr. k-3). 1994. pap. 19.95 (0-7933-4514-6); lib. bdg. 29.95 (0-7933-4513-8); disk 29.95 (0-7933-4515-4) Gallopade Intl.

— Uncle Rebus: California Picture Stories for Computer Kids. (Carole Marsh California Bks.). (Illus.). (J). (gr. k-3). 1994. pap. 19.95 (0-7933-4517-0); lib. bdg. 29.95 (0-7933-4516-2); disk 29.95 (0-7933-4518-9) Gallopade Intl.

— Uncle Rebus: Colorado Picture Stories for Computer Kids. (Carole Marsh Colorado Bks.). (Illus.). (J). (gr. k-3). 1994. pap. 19.95 (0-7933-4520-0); lib. bdg. 29.95 (0-7933-4519-7); disk 29.95 (0-7933-4521-9) Gallopade Intl.

— Uncle Rebus: Connecticut Picture Stories for Computer Kids. (Carole Marsh Connecticut Bks.). (Illus.). (J). (gr. k-3). 1994. pap. 19.95 (0-7933-4523-5); lib. bdg. 29.95 (0-7933-4522-7); disk 29.95 (0-7933-4524-3) Gallopade Intl.

— Uncle Rebus: Delaware Picture Stories for Computer Kids. (Carole Marsh Delaware Bks.). (Illus.). (J). (gr. k-3). 1994. pap. 19.95 (0-7933-4526-X); lib. bdg. 29.95 (0-7933-4525-1); disk 29.95 (0-7933-4527-8) Gallopade Intl.

— Uncle Rebus: Florida Picture Stories for Computer Kids. (Carole Marsh Florida Bks.). (Illus.). (J). (gr. k-3). 1994. pap. 19.95 (0-7933-4529-4); lib. bdg. 29.95 (0-7933-4528-6); disk 29.95 (0-7933-4530-8) Gallopade Intl.

— Uncle Rebus: Georgia Picture Stories for Computer Kids. (Carole Marsh Georgia Bks.). (Illus.). (J). (gr. k-3). 1994. pap. 19.95 (0-7933-4532-4); lib. bdg. 29.95 (0-7933-4531-6); disk 29.95 (0-7933-4533-2) Gallopade Intl.

— Uncle Rebus: Hawaii Picture Stories for Computer Kids. (Carole Marsh Hawaii Bks.). (Illus.). (J). (gr. k-3). 1994. pap. 19.95 (0-7933-4535-9); lib. bdg. 29.95 (0-7933-4534-0); disk 29.95 (0-7933-4536-7) Gallopade Intl.

— Uncle Rebus: Idaho Picture Stories for Computer Kids. (Carole Marsh Idaho Bks.). (Illus.). (J). (gr. k-3). 1994. pap. 19.95 (0-7933-4538-3); lib. bdg. 29.95 (0-7933-4537-5); disk 29.95 (0-7933-4539-1) Gallopade Intl.

— Uncle Rebus: Illinois Picture Stories for Computer Kids. (Carole Marsh Illinois Bks.). (Illus.). (J). (gr. k-3). 1994. pap. 19.95 (0-7933-4541-3); lib. bdg. 29.95 (0-7933-4540-5); disk 29.95 (0-7933-4542-1) Gallopade Intl.

— Uncle Rebus: Indiana Picture Stories for Computer Kids. (Carole Marsh Indiana Bks.). (Illus.). (J). (gr. k-3). 1994. pap. 19.95 (0-7933-4544-8); lib. bdg. 29.95 (0-7933-4543-X); disk 29.95 (0-7933-4545-6) Gallopade Intl.

— Uncle Rebus: Iowa Picture Stories for Computer Kids. (Carole Marsh Iowa Bks.). (Illus.). (J). (gr. k-3). 1994. pap. 19.95 (0-7933-4547-2); lib. bdg. 29.95 (0-7933-4546-4); disk 29.95 (0-7933-4548-0) Gallopade Intl.

— Uncle Rebus: Kansas Picture Stories for Computer Kids. (Carole Marsh Kansas Bks.). (Illus.). (J). (gr. k-3). 1994. pap. 19.95 (0-7933-4550-2); lib. bdg. 29.95 (0-7933-4549-9); disk 29.95 (0-7933-4551-0) Gallopade Intl.

— Uncle Rebus: Kentucky Picture Stories for Computer Kids. (Carole Marsh Kentucky Bks.). (Illus.). (J). (gr. k-3). 1994. pap. 19.95 (0-7933-4553-7); lib. bdg. 29.95 (0-7933-4552-9); disk 29.95 (0-7933-4554-5) Gallopade Intl.

— Uncle Rebus: Louisiana Picture Stories for Computer Kids. (Carole Marsh Louisiana Bks.). (Illus.). (J). (gr. k-3). 1994. pap. 19.95 (0-7933-4556-1); lib. bdg. 29.95 (0-7933-4555-3); disk 29.95 (0-7933-4557-X) Gallopade Intl.

— Uncle Rebus: Maine Picture Stories for Computer Kids. (Carole Marsh Maine Bks.). (Illus.). (J). (gr. k-3). 1994. pap. 19.95 (0-7933-4559-6); lib. bdg. 29.95 (0-7933-4558-8); disk 29.95 (0-7933-4560-X) Gallopade Intl.

— Uncle Rebus: Maryland Picture Stories for Computer Kids. (Carole Marsh Maryland Bks.). (Illus.). (J). (gr. k-3). 1994. pap. 19.95 (0-7933-4562-6); lib. bdg. 29.95 (0-7933-4561-8); disk 29.95 (0-7933-4563-4) Gallopade Intl.

— Uncle Rebus: Massachusetts Picture Stories for Computer Kids. (Massachuseets Bks.). (Illus.). (J). (gr. k-3). 1994. pap. 19.95 (0-7933-4565-0); lib. bdg. 29.95 (0-7933-4564-2); disk 29.95 (0-7933-4566-9) Gallopade Intl.

— Uncle Rebus: Michigan Picture Stories for Computer Kids. (Carole Marsh Michigan Bks.). (Illus.). (J). (gr. k-3). 1994. pap. 19.95 (0-7933-4568-5); lib. bdg. 29.95 (0-7933-4567-7); disk 29.95 (0-7933-4569-3) Gallopade Intl.

— Uncle Rebus: Minnesota Picture Stories for Computer Kids. (Carole Marsh Minnesota Bks.). (Illus.). (J). (gr. k-3). 1994. pap. 19.95 (0-7933-4571-5); lib. bdg. 29.95 (0-7933-4570-7); disk 29.95 (0-7933-4572-3) Gallopade Intl.

— Uncle Rebus: Mississippi Picture Stories for Computer Kids. (Carole Marsh Mississippi Bks.). (Illus.). (J). (gr. k-3). 1994. pap. 19.95 (0-7933-4574-X); lib. bdg. 29.95 (0-7933-4573-1); disk 29.95 (0-7933-4575-8) Gallopade Intl.

— Uncle Rebus: Missouri Picture Stories for Computer Kids. (Carole Marsh Missouri Bks.). (Illus.). (J). (gr. k-3). 1994. pap. 19.95 (0-7933-4577-4); lib. bdg. 29.95 (0-7933-4576-6); disk 29.95 (0-7933-4578-2) Gallopade Intl.

— Uncle Rebus: Montana Picture Stories for Computer Kids. (Carole Marsh Montana Bks.). (Illus.). (J). (gr. k-3). 1994. pap. 19.95 (0-7933-4580-4); lib. bdg. 29.95 (0-7933-4579-0); disk 29.95 (0-7933-4581-2) Gallopade Intl.

— Uncle Rebus: Nebraska Picture Stories for Computer Kids. (Carole Marsh Nebraska Bks.). (Illus.). (J). (gr. k-3). 1994. pap. 19.95 (0-7933-4583-9); lib. bdg. 29.95 (0-7933-4582-0); disk 29.95 (0-7933-4584-7) Gallopade Intl.

— Uncle Rebus: Nevada Picture Stories for Computer Kids. (Carole Marsh Nevada Bks.). (Illus.). (J). (gr. k-3). 1994. pap. 19.95 (0-7933-4586-3); lib. bdg. 29.95 (0-7933-4585-5); disk 29.95 (0-7933-4587-1) Gallopade Intl.

— Uncle Rebus: New Hampshire Picture Stories for Computer Kids. (Carole Marsh New Hampshire Bks.). (Illus.). (J). (gr. k-3). 1994. pap. 19.95 (0-7933-4589-8); lib. bdg. 29.95 (0-7933-4588-X); disk 29.95 (0-7933-4590-1) Gallopade Intl.

— Uncle Rebus: New Jersey Picture Stories for Computer Kids. (Carole Marsh New Jersey Bks.). (Illus.). (J). (gr. k-3). 1994. pap. 19.95 (0-7933-4592-8); lib. bdg. 29.95 (0-7933-4591-X); disk 29.95 (0-7933-4593-6) Gallopade Intl.

— Uncle Rebus: New Mexico Picture Stories for Computer Kids. (Carole Marsh New Mexico Bks.). (Illus.). (J). (gr. k-3). 1994. pap. 19.95 (0-7933-4595-2); lib. bdg. 29.95 (0-7933-4594-4); disk 29.95 (0-7933-4596-0) Gallopade Intl.

— Uncle Rebus: New York Picture Stories for Computer Kids. (Carole Marsh New York Bks.). (Illus.). (J). (gr. k-3). 1994. pap. 19.95 (0-7933-4598-7); lib. bdg. 29.95 (0-7933-4597-9); disk 29.95 (0-7933-4599-5) Gallopade Intl.

— Uncle Rebus: North Carolina Picture Stories for Computer Kids. (Carole Marsh North Carolina Bks.). (Illus.). (J). (gr. k-3). 1994. pap. 19.95 (0-7933-4601-0); lib. bdg. 29.95 (0-7933-4600-2); disk 29.95 (0-7933-4602-9) Gallopade Intl.

— Uncle Rebus: North Dakota Picture Stories for Computer Kids. (Carole Marsh North Dakota Bks.). (Illus.). (J). (gr. k-3). 1994. pap. 19.95 (0-7933-4604-5); lib. bdg. 29.95 (0-7933-4603-7); disk 29.95 (0-7933-4605-3) Gallopade Intl.

— Uncle Rebus: Ohio Picture Stories for Computer Kids. (Carole Marsh Ohio Bks.). (Illus.). (J). (gr. k-3). 1994. pap. 19.95 (0-7933-4607-X); lib. bdg. 29.95 (0-7933-4606-1); disk 29.95 (0-7933-4608-8) Gallopade Intl.

— Uncle Rebus: Oklahoma Picture Stories for Computer Kids. (Oklahoma Bks.). (Illus.). (J). (gr. k-3). 1994. pap. 19.95 (0-7933-4610-X); lib. bdg. 29.95 (0-7933-4609-6); disk 29.95 (0-7933-4611-8) Gallopade Intl.

— Uncle Rebus: Oregon Picture Stories for Computer Kids. (Oregon Bks.). (Illus.). (J). (gr. k-3). 1994. pap. 19.95 (0-7933-4613-4); lib. bdg. 29.95 (0-7933-4612-6); disk 29.95 (0-7933-4614-2) Gallopade Intl.

— Uncle Rebus: Pennsylvania Picture Stories for Computer Kids. (Pennsylvania Bks.). (Illus.). (J). (gr. k-3). 1994. pap. 19.95 (0-7933-4616-9); lib. bdg. 29.95 (0-7933-4615-0); disk 29.95 (0-7933-4617-7) Gallopade Intl.

— Uncle Rebus: Rhode Island Picture Stories for Computer Kids. (Rhode Island Bks.). (Illus.). (J). (gr. k-3). 1994. pap. 19.95 (0-7933-4619-3); lib. bdg. 29.95 (0-7933-4618-5); disk 29.95 (0-7933-4620-7) Gallopade Intl.

— Uncle Rebus: South Carolina Picture Stories for Computer Kids. (South Carolina Bks.). (Illus.). (J). (gr. k-3). 1994. pap. 19.95 (0-7933-4622-3); lib. bdg. 29.95 (0-7933-4621-5); disk 29.95 (0-7933-4623-1) Gallopade Intl.

— Uncle Rebus: South Dakota Picture Stories for Computer Kids. (South Dakota Bks.). (Illus.). (J). (gr. k-3). 1994. pap. 19.95 (0-7933-4625-8); lib. bdg. 29.95 (0-7933-4624-X); disk 29.95 (0-7933-4626-6) Gallopade Intl.

— Uncle Rebus: Tennessee Picture Stories for Computer Kids. (Tennessee Bks.). (Illus.). (J). (gr. k-3). 1994. pap. 19.95 (0-7933-4628-2); lib. bdg. 29.95 (0-7933-4627-4); disk 29.95 (0-7933-4629-0) Gallopade Intl.

— Uncle Rebus: Texas Picture Stories for Computer Kids. (Texas Bks.). (Illus.). (J). (gr. k-3). 1994. pap. 19.95 (0-7933-4631-2); lib. bdg. 29.95 (0-7933-4630-4); disk 29.95 (0-7933-4632-0) Gallopade Intl.

— Uncle Rebus: Utah Picture Stories for Computer Kids. (Utah Bks.). (Illus.). (J). (gr. k-3). 1994. pap. 19.95 (0-7933-4634-7); lib. bdg. 29.95 (0-7933-4633-9); disk 29.95 (0-7933-4635-5) Gallopade Intl.

— Uncle Rebus: Vermont Picture Stories for Computer Kids. (Vermont Bks.). (Illus.). (J). (gr. k-3). 1994. pap. 19.95 (0-7933-4637-1); lib. bdg. 29.95 (0-7933-4636-3); disk 29.95 (0-7933-4638-X) Gallopade Intl.

— Uncle Rebus: Virginia Picture Stories for Computer Kids. (Virginia Bks.). (Illus.). (J). (gr. k-3). 1994. pap. 19.95 (0-7933-4640-1); lib. bdg. 29.95 (0-7933-4639-8); disk 29.95 (0-7933-4641-X) Gallopade Intl.

— Uncle Rebus: Washington, DC Picture Stories for Computer Kids. (Washington, D.C. Bks.). (Illus.). (J). (gr. k-3). 1994. pap. 19.95 (0-7933-4646-0); lib. bdg. 29.95 (0-7933-4645-2); disk 29.95 (0-7933-4647-9) Gallopade Intl.

— Uncle Rebus: Washington Picture Stories for Computer Kids. (Washington Bks.). (Illus.). (J). (gr. k-3). 1994. pap. 19.95 (0-7933-4643-6); lib. bdg. 29.95 (0-7933-4642-8); disk 29.95 (0-7933-4644-4) Gallopade Intl.

— Uncle Rebus: West Virginia Picture Stories for Computer Kids. (West Virginia Bks.). (Illus.). (J). (gr. k-3). 1994. pap. 19.95 (0-7933-4649-5); lib. bdg. 29.95 (0-7933-4648-7); disk 29.95 (0-7933-4650-9) Gallopade Intl.

— Uncle Rebus: Wisconsin Picture Stories for Computer Kids. (Wisconsin Bks.). (Illus.). (J). (gr. k-3). 1994. pap. 19.95 (0-7933-4652-5); lib. bdg. 29.95 (0-7933-4651-7); disk 29.95 (0-7933-4653-3) Gallopade Intl.

— Uncle Rebus: Wyoming Picture Stories for Computer Kids. (Wyoming Bks.). (Illus.). (J). (gr. k-3). 1994. pap. 19.95 (0-7933-4655-X); lib. bdg. 29.95 (0-7933-4654-1); disk 29.95 (0-7933-4656-8) Gallopade Intl.

— Utah & Other State Greats (Biographies) (Carole Marsh Utah Bks.). (Illus.). (J). 1994. pap. 19.95 (0-7933-2130-1); lib. bdg. 29.95 (0-7933-2129-8); disk 29.95 (0-7933-2131-X) Gallopade Intl.

— Utah Bandits, Bushwackers, Outlaws, Crooks, Devils, Ghosts, Desperadoes & Other Assorted & Sundry Characters! (Carole Marsh Utah Bks.). (Illus.). (J). 1994. lib. bdg. 29.95 (0-7933-1106-3); disk 29.95 (0-7933-1107-1) Gallopade Intl.

— Utah Bandits, Bushwackers, Outlaws, Crooks, Devils, Ghosts, Desperadoes & Other Assorted & Sundry Characters! (Carole Marsh Utah Bks.). (Illus.). (J). 1997. pap. 19.95 (0-7933-1105-5) Gallopade Intl.

— Utah "BIO" Bingo! 24 Must Know State People for Kids to Learn about While Having Fun! (Bingo! Ser.). (Illus.). (J). (gr. 2-8). 1998. pap. 14.95 (0-7933-8654-3) Gallopade Intl.

— The Utah Bookstore Book: A Surprising Guide to Our State's Bookstores & Their Specialties for Students, Teachers, Writers & Publishers. (Utah Bks.). (Illus.). 1994. pap. 19.95 (0-7933-2988-4); lib. bdg. 29.95 (0-7933-2987-6); disk 29.95 (0-7933-2989-2) Gallopade Intl.

— Utah Classic Christmas Trivia: Stories, Recipes, Activities, Legends, Lore & More! (Carole Marsh Utah Bks.). (Illus.). (J). 1994. pap. 19.95 (0-7933-1108-X); lib. bdg. 29.95 (0-7933-1109-8); disk 29.95 (0-7933-1110-1) Gallopade Intl.

— Utah Coastales. (Utah Bks.). (J). 1994. lib. bdg. 29.95 (0-7933-7309-3) Gallopade Intl.

— Utah Coastales. (Carole Marsh Utah Bks.). (Illus.). (J). 1994. pap. 19.95 (0-7933-2124-7); lib. bdg. 29.95 (0-7933-2123-9) Gallopade Intl.

— Utah Coastales. (Carole Marsh Utah Bks.). (Illus.). (J). 1997. disk 29.95 (0-7933-2125-5) Gallopade Intl.

— Utah "Crinkum-Crankum" A Funny Word Book about Our State. (Utah Bks.). (Illus.). (J). (gr. 3-12). 1994. 29.95 (0-7933-4940-0); pap. 19.95 (0-7933-4941-9); disk 29.95 (0-7933-4942-7) Gallopade Intl.

— Utah Dingbats! Bk. 1: A Fun Book of Games, Stories, Activities & More about Our State That's All in Code! for You to Decipher. (Utah Bks.). (Illus.). (J). (gr. 3-12). 1994. pap. 19.95 (0-7933-3906-5); lib. bdg. 29.95 (0-7933-3905-7); disk 29.95 (0-7933-3907-3) Gallopade Intl.

— Utah Facts & Factivities. (Carole Marsh State Bks.). (Illus.). (J). (gr. 4-7). 1996. pap., teacher ed. 19.95 (0-7933-7935-0, C Marsh) Gallopade Intl.

— Utah Festival Fun for Kids! (Utah Bks.). (Illus.). (YA). (gr. 3-12). 1994. pap. 19.95 (0-7933-4059-4); lib. bdg. 29.95 (0-7933-4058-6); disk 29.95 (0-7933-4060-8) Gallopade Intl.

— Utah "GEO" Bingo! 38 Must Know State Geography Facts for Kids to Learn While Having Fun! (Bingo! Ser.). (Illus.). (J). (gr. 2-8). 1998. pap. 14.95 (0-7933-8655-1) Gallopade Intl.

— Utah Government! The Cornerstone of Everyday Life in

M

Our State! (Carole Marsh Utah Bks.). (Illus.). (J). (gr. 3-12). 1996. pap. 19.95 (*0-7933-6314-4*); lib. bdg. 29.95 (*0-7933-6313-6*); disk 29.95 (*0-7933-6315-2*) Gallopade Intl.

— Utah "HISTO" Bingo! 42 Must Know State History Facts for Kids to Learn While Having Fun! (Bingo! Ser.). (Illus.). (J). (gr. 2-8). 1998. pap. 14.95 (*0-7933-8656-X*) Gallopade Intl.

— Utah History! Surprising Secrets about Our State's Founding Mothers, Fathers & Kids! (Carole Marsh Utah Bks.). (Illus.). (J). (gr. 3-12). 1996. pap. 19.95 (*0-7933-6161-3*); lib. bdg. 29.95 (*0-7933-6160-5*); disk 29.95 (*0-7933-6162-1*) Gallopade Intl.

— The Utah Hot Air Balloon Mystery. (Carole Marsh Utah Bks.). (Illus.). (J). (gr. 2-9). 1994. 29.95 (*0-7933-2714-8*); pap. 19.95 (*0-7933-2715-6*); disk 29.95 (*0-7933-2716-4*) Gallopade Intl.

— Utah Hot Zones! Viruses, Diseases, & Epidemics in Our State's History. (Hot Zones! Ser.). (Illus.). (J). (gr. 3-12). 1998. pap. 19.95 (*0-7933-8961-5*); lib. bdg. 29.95 (*0-7933-8960-7*) Gallopade Intl.

— Utah Indian Dictionary for Kids! (Carole Marsh State Bks.). (J). (gr. 2-9). 1996. 29.95 (*0-7933-7776-5*, C Marsh); pap. 19.95 (*0-7933-7777-3*, C Marsh) Gallopade Intl.

— Utah Jeopardy! Answers & Questions about Our State! (Utah Bks.). (Illus.). (J). (gr. 3-12). 1994. pap. 19.95 (*0-7933-4212-0*); lib. bdg. 29.95 (*0-7933-4211-2*); disk 29.95 (*0-7933-4213-9*) Gallopade Intl.

— Utah "Jography" A Fun Run Thru Our State! (Carole Marsh Utah Bks.). (Illus.). (J). 1994. pap. 19.95 (*0-7933-2107-7*); lib. bdg. 29.95 (*0-7933-2106-9*); disk 29.95 (*0-7933-2108-5*) Gallopade Intl.

— Utah Kid's Cookbook: Recipes, How-to, History, Lore & More! (Carole Marsh Utah Bks.). (Illus.). (J). 1994. pap. 19.95 (*0-7933-1117-9*); lib. bdg. 29.95 (*0-7933-1118-7*); disk 29.95 (*0-7933-1119-5*) Gallopade Intl.

— The Utah Library Book: A Surprising Guide to the Unusual Special Collections in Libraries Across Our State for Students, Teachers, Writers & Publishers - Includes Reproducible Mailing Labels Plus Activities for Young People! (Utah Bks.). (Illus.). 1994. pap. 19.95 (*0-7933-3138-2*); lib. bdg. 29.95 (*0-7933-3137-4*); disk 29.95 (*0-7933-3139-0*) Gallopade Intl.

— Utah Math! How It All Adds up in Our State. (Carole Marsh Utah Bks.). (Illus.). (YA). (gr. 3-12). 1996. pap. 19.95 (*0-7933-6620-8*); lib. bdg. 29.95 (*0-7933-6619-4*) Gallopade Intl.

— The Utah Media Book: A Surprising Guide to the Amazing Print, Broadcast & Online Media of Our State for Students, Teachers, Writers & Publishers - Includes Reproducible Mailing Labels Plus Activities for Young People! (Utah Bks.). (Illus.). 1994. pap. 19.95 (*0-7933-3294-X*); lib. bdg. 29.95 (*0-7933-3293-1*); disk 29.95 (*0-7933-3295-8*) Gallopade Intl.

— The Utah Mystery Van Takes Off! Bk. 1: Handicapped Utah Kids Sneak Off on a Big Adventure. (Utah Bks.). (Illus.). (J). (gr. 3-12). 1994. 29.95 (*0-7933-5093-X*); pap. 19.95 (*0-7933-5094-8*); disk 29.95 (*0-7933-5095-6*) Gallopade Intl.

— Utah Quiz Bowl Crash Course! (Carole Marsh Utah Bks.). (Illus.). (J). 1994. pap. 19.95 (*0-7933-2121-2*); lib. bdg. 29.95 (*0-7933-2120-4*); disk 29.95 (*0-7933-2122-0*) Gallopade Intl.

— Utah Rollercoasters! (Utah Bks.). (Illus.). (YA). (gr. 3-12). 1994. pap. 19.95 (*0-7933-5357-2*); lib. bdg. 29.95 (*0-7933-5356-4*); disk 29.95 (*0-7933-5358-0*) Gallopade Intl.

— Utah School Trivia: An Amazing & Fascinating Look at Our State's Teachers, Schools & Students! (Carole Marsh Utah Bks.). (Illus.). (J). 1994. pap. 19.95 (*0-7933-1114-4*); lib. bdg. 29.95 (*0-7933-1115-2*); disk 29.95 (*0-7933-1116-0*) Gallopade Intl.

— Utah Silly Basketball Sportsmysteries, Vol. 1. (Carole Marsh Utah Bks.). (Illus.). (J). 1994. pap. 19.95 (*0-7933-1111-X*); lib. bdg. 29.95 (*0-7933-1112-8*); disk 29.95 (*0-7933-1113-6*) Gallopade Intl.

— Utah Silly Basketball Sportsmysteries, Vol. 2. (Carole Marsh Utah Bks.). (Illus.). (J). 1994. pap. 19.95 (*0-7933-2133-6*); lib. bdg. 29.95 (*0-7933-2132-8*); disk 29.95 (*0-7933-2134-4*) Gallopade Intl.

— Utah Silly Football Sportsmysteries, Vol. 1. (Carole Marsh Utah Bks.). (Illus.). (J). 1994. pap. 19.95 (*0-7933-2112-3*); lib. bdg. 29.95 (*0-7933-2111-5*); disk 29.95 (*0-7933-2113-1*) Gallopade Intl.

— Utah Silly Football Sportsmysteries, Vol. 2. (Carole Marsh Utah Bks.). (Illus.). (J). 1994. pap. 19.95 (*0-7933-2115-8*); lib. bdg. 29.95 (*0-7933-2114-X*); disk 29.95 (*0-7933-2116-6*) Gallopade Intl.

— Utah Silly Trivia! (Carole Marsh Utah Bks.). (Illus.). (J). 1994. pap. 19.95 (*0-7933-2104-2*); lib. bdg. 29.95 (*0-7933-2103-4*); disk 29.95 (*0-7933-2105-0*) Gallopade Intl.

— Utah Spelling Bee! Score Big by Correctly Spelling Our State's Unique Names. (Carole Marsh Utah Bks.). (Illus.). (YA). (gr. 3-12). 1996. pap. 19.95 (*0-7933-6773-5*); lib. bdg. 29.95 (*0-7933-6772-7*) Gallopade Intl.

— Utah Timeline: A Chronology of Utah History, Mystery, Trivia, Legend, Lore & More. (Utah Bks.). (Illus.). (J). (gr. 3-12). 1994. pap. 19.95 (*0-7933-6008-0*); lib. bdg. 29.95 (*0-7933-6007-2*); disk 29.95 (*0-7933-6009-9*) Gallopade Intl.

— Utah 2000! Coming Soon to a Calendar Near You - The 21st Century! - Complete Set of AL 2000 Items. (Two Thousand! Ser.). (Illus.). (J). (gr. 3-12). 1998. pap. 75.00 (*0-7933-9397-3*); lib. bdg. 85.00 (*0-7933-9398-1*) Gallopade Intl.

— Utah 2000! Coming Soon to a Calendar near You--The 21st Century! (Two Thousand! Ser.). (Illus.). (J). (gr. 3-12). 1998. pap. 19.95 (*0-7933-8808-2*); lib. bdg. 29.95 (*0-7933-8807-4*) Gallopade Intl.

— Utah UFO's & Extraterrestrials! A Look at the Sightings & Science in Our State. (Carole Marsh Utah Bks.). (Illus.). (J). (gr. 3-12). 1997. pap. 19.95 (*0-7933-6467-1*); lib. bdg. 29.95 (*0-7933-6466-3*) Gallopade Intl.

— Utah's (Most Devastating!) Disasters & (Most Calamitous!) Catastrophies! (Carole Marsh Utah Bks.). (Illus.). (J). 1994. pap. 19.95 (*0-7933-1102-0*); lib. bdg. 29.95 (*0-7933-1103-9*); write for info. (*0-7933-1104-7*) Gallopade Intl.

— Utah's Unsolved Mysteries (& Their "Solutions") Includes Scientific Information & Other Activities for Students. (Utah Bks.). (Illus.). (J). (gr. 3-12). 1994. pap. 19.95 (*0-7933-5855-8*); lib. bdg. 29.95 (*0-7933-5854-X*); disk 29.95 (*0-7933-5856-6*) Gallopade Intl.

— Vermont & Other State Greats (Biographies) (Carole Marsh Vermont Bks.). (Illus.). (J). 1994. pap. 19.95 (*0-7933-2162-X*); lib. bdg. 29.95 (*0-7933-2161-1*); disk 29.95 (*0-7933-2163-8*) Gallopade Intl.

— Vermont Bandits, Bushwackers, Outlaws, Crooks, Devils, Ghosts, Desperadoes & Other Assorted & Sundry Characters! (Carole Marsh Vermont Bks.). (Illus.). (J). 1994. pap. 19.95 (*0-7933-1129-2*); lib. bdg. 29.95 (*0-7933-1130-6*); write for info. (*0-7933-1131-4*) Gallopade Intl.

— Vermont "BIO" Bingo! 24 Must Know State People for Kids to Learn about While Having Fun! (Bingo! Ser.). (Illus.). (J). (gr. 2-8). 1998. pap. 14.95 (*0-7933-8657-8*) Gallopade Intl.

— The Vermont Bookstore Book: A Surprising Guide to Our State's Bookstores & Their Specialties for Students, Teachers, Writers & Publishers. (Vermont Bks.). (Illus.). 1994. pap. 19.95 (*0-7933-2991-4*); lib. bdg. 29.95 (*0-7933-2990-6*); disk 29.95 (*0-7933-2992-2*) Gallopade Intl.

— Vermont Classic Christmas Trivia: Stories, Recipes, Activities, Legends, Lore & More! (Carole Marsh Vermont Bks.). (Illus.). (J). 1994. pap. 19.95 (*0-7933-1132-2*); lib. bdg. 29.95 (*0-7933-1133-0*); disk 29.95 (*0-7933-1134-9*) Gallopade Intl.

— Vermont Coastales. (Vermont Bks.). (J). 1994. lib. bdg. 29.95 (*0-7933-7310-7*) Gallopade Intl.

— Vermont Coastales. (Carole Marsh Vermont Bks.). (Illus.). (J). 1994. pap. 19.95 (*0-7933-2156-5*); lib. bdg. 29.95 (*0-7933-2155-7*); disk 29.95 (*0-7933-2157-3*) Gallopade Intl.

— Vermont "Crinkum-Crankum" A Funny Word Book about Our State. (Vermont Bks.). (Illus.). (J). (gr. 3-12). 1994. 29.95 (*0-7933-4943-5*); pap. 19.95 (*0-7933-4944-3*); disk 29.95 (*0-7933-4945-1*) Gallopade Intl.

— Vermont Dingbats! Bk. 1: A Fun Book of Games, Stories, Activities & More about Our State That's All in Code! for You to Decipher. (Vermont Bks.). (Illus.). (J). (gr. 3-12). 1994. pap. 19.95 (*0-7933-3909-X*); lib. bdg. 29.95 (*0-7933-3908-1*); disk 29.95 (*0-7933-3910-3*) Gallopade Intl.

— Vermont Facts & Factivities. (Carole Marsh State Bks.). (Illus.). (J). (gr. 4-7). 1996. pap., teacher ed. 19.95 (*0-7933-7937-7*, C Marsh) Gallopade Intl.

— Vermont Festival Fun for Kids! (Vermont Bks.). (Illus.). (YA). (gr. 3-12). 1994. pap. 19.95 (*0-7933-4062-4*); lib. bdg. 29.95 (*0-7933-4061-6*); disk 29.95 (*0-7933-4063-2*) Gallopade Intl.

— Vermont "GEO" Bingo! 38 Must Know State Geography Facts for Kids to Learn While Having Fun! (Bingo! Ser.). (Illus.). (J). (gr. 2-8). 1998. pap. 14.95 (*0-7933-8658-6*) Gallopade Intl.

— Vermont Government! The Cornerstone of Everyday Life in Our State! (Carole Marsh Vermont Bks.). (Illus.). (J). (gr. 3-12). 1996. pap. 19.95 (*0-7933-6317-9*); lib. bdg. 29.95 (*0-7933-6316-0*); disk 29.95 (*0-7933-6318-7*) Gallopade Intl.

— Vermont "HISTO" Bingo! 42 Must Know State History Facts for Kids to Learn While Having Fun! (Bingo! Ser.). (Illus.). (J). (gr. 2-8). 1998. pap. 14.95 (*0-7933-8659-4*) Gallopade Intl.

— Vermont History! Surprising Secrets about Our State's Founding Mothers, Fathers & Kids! (Carole Marsh Vermont Bks.). (Illus.). (J). (gr. 3-12). 1996. pap. 19.95 (*0-7933-6164-8*); lib. bdg. 29.95 (*0-7933-6163-X*); disk 29.95 (*0-7933-6165-6*) Gallopade Intl.

— The Vermont Hot Air Balloon Mystery. (Carole Marsh Vermont Bks.). (Illus.). (J). (gr. 2-9). 1994. 29.95 (*0-7933-2723-7*); pap. 19.95 (*0-7933-2724-5*); disk 29.95 (*0-7933-2725-3*) Gallopade Intl.

— Vermont Hot Zones! Viruses, Disease, & Epidemics in Our State's History. (Hot Zones! Ser.). (Illus.). (J). (gr. 3-12). 1998. pap. 19.95 (*0-7933-8964-X*); lib. bdg. 29.95 (*0-7933-8963-1*) Gallopade Intl.

— Vermont Indian Dictionary for Kids! (Carole Marsh State Bks.). (J). (gr. 2-9). 1996. 29.95 (*0-7933-7779-X*, C Marsh); pap. 19.95 (*0-7933-7780-3*, C Marsh) Gallopade Intl.

— Vermont Jeopardy! Answers & Questions about Our State! (Vermont Bks.). (Illus.). (J). (gr. 3-12). 1994. pap. 19.95 (*0-7933-4215-5*); lib. bdg. 29.95 (*0-7933-4214-7*); disk 29.95 (*0-7933-4216-3*) Gallopade Intl.

— Vermont "Jography" A Fun Run Thru Our State! (Carole Marsh Vermont Bks.). (Illus.). (J). 1994. pap. 19.95 (*0-7933-2139-5*); lib. bdg. 29.95 (*0-7933-2138-7*); disk 29.95 (*0-7933-2140-9*) Gallopade Intl.

— Vermont Kids' Cookbook: Recipes, How-to, History, Lore & More! (Carole Marsh Vermont Bks.). (Illus.). (J). 1994. lib. bdg. 29.95 (*0-7933-1142-X*); disk 29.95 (*0-7933-1143-8*) Gallopade Intl.

— Vermont Kids' Cookbook: Recipes, How-to, History, Lore & More! (Carole Marsh Vermont Bks.). (Illus.). (J). 1997. pap. 19.95 (*0-7933-1141-1*) Gallopade Intl.

— The Vermont Library Book: A Surprising Guide to the Unusual Special Collections in Libraries Across Our State for Students, Teachers, Writers & Publishers - Includes Reproducible Mailing Labels Plus Activities for Young People! (Vermont Bks.). (Illus.). 1994. pap. 19.95 (*0-7933-3141-2*); lib. bdg. 29.95 (*0-7933-3140-4*); disk 29.95 (*0-7933-3142-0*) Gallopade Intl.

— Vermont Math! How It All Adds up in Our State. (Carole Marsh Vermont Bks.). (Illus.). (YA). (gr. 3-12). 1996. pap. 19.95 (*0-7933-6623-2*); lib. bdg. 29.95 (*0-7933-6622-4*) Gallopade Intl.

— The Vermont Media Book: A Surprising Guide to the Amazing Print, Broadcast & Online Media of Our State for Students, Teachers, Writers & Publishers - Includes Reproducible Mailing Labels Plus Activities for Young People! (Vermont Bks.). (Illus.). 1994. pap. 19.95 (*0-7933-3297-4*); lib. bdg. 29.95 (*0-7933-3296-6*); disk 29.95 (*0-7933-3298-2*) Gallopade Intl.

— The Vermont Mystery Van Takes Off! Bk. 1: Handicapped Vermont Kids Sneak Off on a Big Adventure. (Vermont Bks.). (Illus.). (J). (gr. 3-12). 1994. 29.95 (*0-7933-5096-4*); pap. 19.95 (*0-7933-5097-2*); disk 29.95 (*0-7933-5098-0*) Gallopade Intl.

— Vermont Quiz Bowl Crash Course! (Carole Marsh Vermont Bks.). (Illus.). (J). 1994. pap. 19.95 (*0-7933-2153-0*); lib. bdg. 29.95 (*0-7933-2152-2*); disk 29.95 (*0-7933-2154-9*) Gallopade Intl.

— Vermont Rollercoasters! (Vermont Bks.). (Illus.). (YA). (gr. 3-12). 1994. pap. 19.95 (*0-7933-5360-2*); lib. bdg. 29.95 (*0-7933-5359-9*); disk 29.95 (*0-7933-5361-0*) Gallopade Intl.

— Vermont School Trivia: An Amazing & Fascinating Look at Our State's Teachers, Schools & Students! (Carole Marsh Vermont Bks.). (Illus.). (J). 1994. pap. 19.95 (*0-7933-1138-1*); lib. bdg. 29.95 (*0-7933-1139-X*); disk 29.95 (*0-7933-1140-3*) Gallopade Intl.

— Vermont Silly Basketball Sportsmysteries, Vol. 1. (Carole Marsh Vermont Bks.). (Illus.). (J). 1994. pap. 19.95 (*0-7933-1135-7*); lib. bdg. 29.95 (*0-7933-1136-5*); disk 29.95 (*0-7933-1137-3*) Gallopade Intl.

— Vermont Silly Basketball Sportsmysteries, Vol. 2. (Carole Marsh Vermont Bks.). (Illus.). (J). 1994. pap. 19.95 (*0-7933-2165-4*); lib. bdg. 29.95 (*0-7933-2164-6*); 29.95 (*0-7933-2166-2*) Gallopade Intl.

— Vermont Silly Football Sportsmysteries, Vol. 1. (Carole Marsh Vermont Bks.). (Illus.). (J). 1994. pap. 19.95 (*0-7933-2144-1*); lib. bdg. 29.95 (*0-7933-2143-3*); disk 29.95 (*0-7933-2145-X*) Gallopade Intl.

— Vermont Silly Football Sportsmysteries, Vol. 2. (Carole Marsh Vermont Bks.). (Illus.). (J). 1994. pap. 19.95 (*0-7933-2147-6*); lib. bdg. 29.95 (*0-7933-2146-8*); disk 29.95 (*0-7933-2148-4*) Gallopade Intl.

— Vermont Silly Trivia! (Carole Marsh Vermont Bks.). (Illus.). (J). 1994. pap. 19.95 (*0-7933-2136-0*); lib. bdg. 29.95 (*0-7933-2135-2*); disk 29.95 (*0-7933-2137-9*) Gallopade Intl.

— Vermont Spelling Bee! Score Big by Correctly Spelling Our State's Unique Names. (Carole Marsh Vermont Bks.). (Illus.). (YA). (gr. 3-12). 1996. pap. 19.95 (*0-7933-6776-X*); lib. bdg. 29.95 (*0-7933-6775-1*) Gallopade Intl.

— Vermont Timeline: A Chronology of Vermont History, Mystery, Trivia, Legend, Lore & More. (Vermont Bks.). (Illus.). (J). (gr. 3-12). 1994. pap. 19.95 (*0-7933-6011-0*); lib. bdg. 29.95 (*0-7933-6010-2*); disk 29.95 (*0-7933-6012-9*) Gallopade Intl.

— Vermont 2000! Coming Soon to a Calendar Near You - The 21st Century! - Complete Set of AL 2000 Items. (Two Thousand! Ser.). (Illus.). (J). (gr. 3-12). 1998. pap. 75.00 (*0-7933-9399-X*); lib. bdg. 85.00 (*0-7933-9400-7*) Gallopade Intl.

— Vermont 2000! Coming Soon to a Calendar near You--The 21st Century! (Two Thousand! Ser.). (Illus.). (J). (gr. 3-12). 1998. pap. 19.95 (*0-7933-8811-2*); lib. bdg. 29.95 (*0-7933-8810-4*) Gallopade Intl.

— Vermont UFO's & Extraterrestrials! A Look at the Sightings & Science in Our State. (Carole Marsh Vermont Bks.). (Illus.). (J). (gr. 3-12). 1997. pap. 19.95 (*0-7933-6470-1*); lib. bdg. 29.95 (*0-7933-6469-8*) Gallopade Intl.

— Vermont's (Most Devastating!) Disasters & (Most Calamitous!) Catastrophies! (Carole Marsh Vermont Bks.). (Illus.). (J). 1994. pap. 19.95 (*0-7933-1126-8*); lib. bdg. 29.95 (*0-7933-1127-6*); disk 29.95 (*0-7933-1128-4*) Gallopade Intl.

— Vermont's Unsolved Mysteries (& Their "Solutions") Includes Scientific Information & Other Activities for Students. (Vermont Bks.). (Illus.). (J). (gr. 3-12). 1994. pap. 19.95 (*0-7933-5858-2*); lib. bdg. 29.95 (*0-7933-5857-4*); disk 29.95 (*0-7933-5859-0*) Gallopade Intl.

***Marsh, Carole.** The Very Virginia Coloring Book. (Virginia Experience! Ser.). (Illus.). (J). (gr. k-5). 2000. pap. 3.95 (*0-7933-9476-7*) Gallopade Intl.

— The Virginai Experience SOL Virginia Civics for Teachers! (Virginia Experience! Ser.). (Illus.). 2000. pap. 9.95 (*0-7933-9497-X*) Gallopade Intl.

Marsh, Carole. Virginia & Other State Greats (Biographies) (Carole Marsh Virginia Bks.). (Illus.). (J). 1994. pap. 19.95 (*0-7933-2191-3*); lib. bdg. 29.95 (*0-7933-2190-5*); disk 29.95 (*0-7933-2192-1*) Gallopade Intl.

— Virginia Bandits, Bushwackers, Outlaws, Crooks, Devils, Ghosts, Desperadoes & Other Assorted & Sundry Characters! (Carole Marsh Virginia Bks.). (Illus.). (J). 1994. pap. 19.95 (*0-7933-1153-5*); lib. bdg. 29.95 (*0-7933-1154-3*); disk 29.95 (*0-7933-1155-1*) Gallopade Intl.

— Virginia "BIO" Bingo! 24 Must Know State People for Kids to Learn about While Having Fun! (Bingo! Ser.). (Illus.). (J). (gr. 2-8). 1998. pap. 14.95 (*0-7933-8660-8*) Gallopade Intl.

— The Virginia Bookstore Book: A Surprising Guide to Our State's Bookstores & Their Specialties for Students, Teachers, Writers & Publishers. (Virginia Bks.). (Illus.). 1994. pap. 19.95 (*0-7933-2994-9*); lib. bdg. 29.95 (*0-7933-2993-0*); disk 29.95 (*0-7933-2995-7*) Gallopade Intl.

— Virginia Classic Christmas Trivia: Stories, Recipes, Activities, Legends, Lore & More. (Carole Marsh Virginia Bks.). (Illus.). (J). 1994. pap. 19.95 (*0-7933-1156-X*); lib. bdg. 29.95 (*0-7933-1157-8*); disk 29.95 (*0-7933-1158-6*) Gallopade Intl.

— Virginia Coastales. (Virginia Bks.). (J). 1994. lib. bdg. 29.95 (*0-7933-7311-5*) Gallopade Intl.

— Virginia Coastales. (Carole Marsh Virginia Bks.). (Illus.). (J). 1994. pap. 19.95 (*1-55609-116-8*); disk 29.95 (*0-7933-2186-7*) Gallopade Intl.

— Virginia "Crinkum-Crankum" A Funny Word Book about Our State. (Virginia Bks.). (Illus.). (J). (gr. 3-12). 1994. 29.95 (*0-7933-4946-X*); pap. 19.95 (*0-7933-4947-8*); disk 29.95 (*0-7933-4948-6*) Gallopade Intl.

— Virginia Dingbats! Bk. 1: A Fun Book of Games, Stories, Activities & More about Our State That's All in Code! for You to Decipher, Bk. 1. (Virginia Bks.). (Illus.). (J). (gr. 3-12). 1994. pap. 19.95 (*0-7933-3912-X*); lib. bdg. 29.95 (*0-7933-3911-1*); disk 29.95 (*0-7933-3913-8*) Gallopade Intl.

***Marsh, Carole.** The Virginia Experience! (Illus.). 1999. pap. 14.95 (*0-7933-9413-9*); lib. bdg. 24.95 (*0-7933-9414-7*) Gallopade Intl.

— The Virginia Experience! A Virginia Mystery Musical! (Virginia Experience! Ser.). (Illus.). 2000. pap. 20.00 (*0-7933-9496-1*) Gallopade Intl.

— The Virginia Experience! for Eleventh Graders Student Workbook. (Virginia Experience! Ser.). (Illus.). (YA). (gr. 11). 1999. pap., wbk. ed. 6.95 (*0-7933-9421-X*) Gallopade Intl.

— The Virginia Experience! for Eleventh Graders Teacher Resource Book. (Virginia Experience! Ser.). (Illus.). 1999. pap., teacher ed. 9.95 (*0-7933-9430-9*) Gallopade Intl.

— The Virginia Experience! for First Graders Student Workbook. (Virginia Experience! Ser.). (Illus.). (J). (gr. 1). 1999. pap., wbk. ed. 5.95 (*0-7933-9416-3*) Gallopade Intl.

— The Virginia Experience! for First Graders Teacher Resource Book. (Virginia Experience! Ser.). (Illus.). 1999. pap., teacher ed. 9.95 (*0-7933-9425-2*) Gallopade Intl.

— The Virginia Experience! for Fourth Graders Student Workbook. (Virginia Experience! Ser.). (Illus.). (J). (gr. 4). 1999. pap., wbk. ed. 10.95 (*0-7933-9419-8*) Gallopade Intl.

— The Virginia Experience! for Fourth Graders Teacher Resource Book. (Virginia Experience! Ser.). (Illus.). 1999. pap., teacher ed. 9.95 (*0-7933-9428-7*) Gallopade Intl.

— The Virginia Experience! for Kindergarteners: Point-by-Point Guide for Teachers! (Virginia Experience! Ser.). (Illus.). 2000. pap. 5.95 (*0-7933-9530-5*) Gallopade Intl.

— The Virginia Experience! for Kindergarteners Student Workbook. (Virginia Experience! Ser.). (Illus.). (J). (gr. k). 1999. pap., wbk. ed. 5.95 (*0-7933-9415-5*) Gallopade Intl.

— The Virginia Experience! for Kindergarteners Student Workbook. (Virginia Experience! Ser.). (Illus.). (J). 2000. pap. 5.95 (*0-7933-9445-7*) Gallopade Intl.

— The Virginia Experience! for Kindergarteners Teacher Resource Book. (Virginia Experience! Ser.). (Illus.). 1999. pap., teacher ed. 9.95 (*0-7933-9432-5*) Gallopade Intl.

— The Virginia Experience! for Second Graders Student Workbook. (Virginia Experience! Ser.). (Illus.). (J). (gr. 2). 1999. pap., wbk. ed. 5.95 (*0-7933-9417-1*) Gallopade Intl.

— The Virginia Experience! for Second Graders Teacher Resource Book. (Virginia Experience! Ser.). (Illus.). 1999. pap., teacher ed. 9.95 (*0-7933-9426-0*) Gallopade Intl.

— The Virginia Experience! for Seventh Graders Student Workbook. (Virginia Experience! Ser.). (Illus.). (YA). (gr. 7). 1999. pap., wbk. ed. 6.95 (*0-7933-9420-1*) Gallopade Intl.

— The Virginia Experience! for Seventh Graders Teacher Resource Book. (Virginia Experience! Ser.). (Illus.). 1999. pap., teacher ed. 9.95 (*0-7933-9429-5*) Gallopade Intl.

— The Virginia Experience! for Third Graders Student Workbook. (Virginia Experience! Ser.). (Illus.). (J). (gr. 3). 1999. pap., wbk. ed. 5.95 (*0-7933-9418-X*) Gallopade Intl.

— The Virginia Experience! for Third Graders Teacher Resource Book. (Virginia Experience! Ser.). (Illus.). 1999. pap., teacher ed. 9.95 (*0-7933-9427-9*) Gallopade Intl.

— The Virginia Experience! for Twelfth Graders Student Workbook. (Virginia Experience! Ser.). (Illus.). (YA). (gr. 12). 1999. pap., wbk. ed. 6.95 (*0-7933-9422-8*) Gallopade Intl.

— The Virginia Experience Pocket Guide. (Virginia Experience! Ser.). (Illus.). (J). 2000. pap. 6.95 (*0-7933-9456-2*) Gallopade Intl.

— The Virginia Experience SOL Virginia Economics for Teachers! (Virginia Experience! Ser.). (Illus.). 2000. pap. 9.95 (*0-7933-9498-8*) Gallopade Intl.

Marsh, Carole. Virginia Facts & Factivities. (Carole Marsh State Bks.). (Illus.). (J). (gr. 4-7). 1996. pap., teacher ed. 19.95 (*0-7933-7939-3*, C Marsh) Gallopade Intl.

— Virginia Festival Fun for Kids! (Virginia Bks.). (Illus.). (YA). (gr. 3-12). 1994. pap. 19.95 (*0-7933-4065-9*); lib. bdg. 29.95 (*0-7933-4064-0*) Gallopade Intl.

— Virginia Festival Fun for Kids! (Virginia Bks.). (Illus.). (J). (gr. 3-12). 1997. disk 29.95 (*0-7933-4066-7*) Gallopade Intl.

An Asterisk (*) at the beginning of an entry indicates that the title is appearing for the first time.

— Virginia "GEO" Bingo! 38 Must Know State Geography Facts for Kids to Learn While Having Fun! (Bingo! Ser.). (Illus.). (J). (gr. 2-8). 1998. pap. 14.95 (*0-7933-8661-6*) Gallopade Intl.

— Virginia Government! The Cornerstone of Everyday Life in Our State! (Carole Marsh Virginia Bks.). (Illus.). (J). (gr. 3-12). 1996. pap. 19.95 (*0-7933-6320-9*); lib. bdg. 29.95 (*0-7933-6319-5*); disk 29.95 (*0-7933-6321-7*) Gallopade Intl.

— Virginia "HISTO" Bingo! 42 Must Know State History Facts for Kids to Learn While Having Fun! (Bingo! Ser.). (Illus.). (J). (gr. 2-8). 1998. pap. 14.95 (*0-7933-8662-4*) Gallopade Intl.

— Virginia History! Surprising Secrets about Our State's Founding Mothers, Fathers & Kids! (Carole Marsh Virginia Bks.). (Illus.). (J). (gr. 3-12). 1996. pap. 19.95 (*0-7933-6167-2*); lib. bdg. 29.95 (*0-7933-6166-4*); disk 29.95 (*0-7933-6168-0*) Gallopade Intl.

— The Virginia Hot Air Balloon Mystery. (Carole Marsh Virginia Bks.). (Illus.). (J). (gr. 2-9). 1994. 29.95 (*0-7933-2732-6*); pap. 19.95 (*0-7933-2733-4*); disk 29.95 (*0-7933-2734-2*) Gallopade Intl.

— Virginia Hot Zones! Viruses, Diseases, & Epidemics in Our State's History. (Hot Zones! Ser.). (Illus.). (J). (gr. 3-12). 1998. pap. 19.95 (*0-7933-8967-4*); lib. bdg. 29.95 (*0-7933-8966-6*) Gallopade Intl.

— Virginia Indian Dictionary for Kids! (Carole Marsh State Bks.). (J). (gr. 2-9). 1996. 29.95 (*0-7933-7782-X*, C Marsh); pap. 19.95 (*0-7933-7783-8*, C Marsh) Gallopade Intl.

***Marsh, Carole.** Virginia Jeopardy. (Virginia Experience! Ser.). (Illus.). (J). (gr. 2-6). 2000. pap. 7.95 (*0-7933-9501-1*) Gallopade Intl.

Marsh, Carole. Virginia Jeopardy! Answers & Questions about Our State! (Virginia Bks.). (Illus.). (J). (gr. 3-12). 1994. pap. 19.95 (*0-7933-4218-X*); lib. bdg. 29.95 (*0-7933-4217-1*); disk 29.95 (*0-7933-4219-8*) Gallopade Intl.

***Marsh, Carole.** Virginia Jography. (Virginia Experience! Ser.). (Illus.). (J). (gr. 2-6). 2000. pap. 7.95 (*0-7933-9502-X*) Gallopade Intl.

Marsh, Carole. Virginia Jography: A Fun Run Through the Old Dominion State. (Statemeant Ser.). (Illus.). 50p. (Orig.). (J). (gr. 3-12). 1994. pap. 29.95 (*0-935326-99-5*) Gallopade Intl.

— Virginia "Jography" A Fun Run Thru Our State. (Carole Marsh Virginia Bks.). (Illus.). (J). 1994. pap. 19.95 (*1-55609-057-9*); disk 29.95 (*0-7933-2170-0*) Gallopade Intl.

— Virginia "Jography" A Fun Run Thru Our State. (Carole Marsh Virginia Bks.). (Illus.). (J). 1997. lib. bdg. 29.95 (*0-7933-2169-7*) Gallopade Intl.

— Virginia Kid's Cookbook: Recipes, How-to, History, Lore & More! (Carole Marsh Virginia Bks.). (Illus.). (J). 1994. pap. 19.95 (*0-7933-1165-9*); lib. bdg. 29.95 (*0-7933-1166-7*); disk 29.95 (*0-7933-1167-5*) Gallopade Intl.

— The Virginia Library Book: A Surprising Guide to the Unusual Special Collections in Libraries Across Our State for Students, Teachers, Writers & Publishers - Includes Reproducible Mailing Labels Plus Activities for Young People! (Virginia Bks.). (Illus.). 1994. pap. 19.95 (*0-7933-3144-7*); lib. bdg. 29.95 (*0-7933-3143-9*); disk 29.95 (*0-7933-3145-5*) Gallopade Intl.

— Virginia Math! How It All Adds up in Our State. (Carole Marsh Virginia Bks.). (Illus.). (YA). (gr. 3-12). 1996. pap. 19.95 (*0-7933-6626-7*); lib. bdg. 29.95 (*0-7933-6625-9*) Gallopade Intl.

— The Virginia Media Book: A Surprising Guide to the Amazing Print, Broadcast & Online Media of Our State for Students, Teachers, Writers & Publishers - Includes Reproducible Mailing Labels Plus Activities for Young People! (Virginia Bks.). (Illus.). 1994. pap. 19.95 (*0-7933-3300-8*); lib. bdg. 29.95 (*0-7933-3299-0*); disk 29.95 (*0-7933-3301-6*) Gallopade Intl.

— The Virginia Mystery Van Takes Off! Bk. 1: Handicapped Virginia Kids Sneak Off on a Big Adventure. (Virginia Bks.). (Illus.). (J). (gr. 3-12). 1994. 29.95 (*0-7933-5099-9*); pap. 19.95 (*0-7933-5100-6*); disk 29.95 (*0-7933-5101-4*) Gallopade Intl.

— Virginia Quiz Bowl Crash Course! (Carole Marsh Virginia Bks.). (Illus.). (J). 1994. pap. 19.95 (*0-7933-2183-2*); lib. bdg. 29.95 (*0-7933-2182-4*); disk 29.95 (*0-7933-2184-0*) Gallopade Intl.

— Virginia Rollercoasters! (Virginia Bks.). (Illus.). (YA). (gr. 3-12). 1994. pap. 19.95 (*0-7933-5363-7*); lib. bdg. 29.95 (*0-7933-5362-9*); disk 29.95 (*0-7933-5364-5*) Gallopade Intl.

— Virginia School Trivia: An Amazing & Fascinating Look at Our State's Teachers, Schools & Students! (Carole Marsh Virginia Bks.). (Illus.). (J). 1994. pap. 19.95 (*0-7933-1162-4*); lib. bdg. 29.95 (*0-7933-1163-2*); disk 29.95 (*0-7933-1164-0*) Gallopade Intl.

— Virginia Silly Basketball Sportsmysteries, Vol. 1. (Carole Marsh Virginia Bks.). (Illus.). (J). 1994. pap. 19.95 (*0-7933-1159-4*); lib. bdg. 29.95 (*0-7933-1160-8*) Gallopade Intl.

— Virginia Silly Basketball Sportsmysteries, Vol. 1. (Carole Marsh Virginia Bks.). (Illus.). (J). 1997. disk 29.95 (*0-7933-1161-6*) Gallopade Intl.

— Virginia Silly Basketball Sportsmysteries, Vol. 2. (Carole Marsh Virginia Bks.). (Illus.). (J). 1994. pap. 19.95 (*0-7933-2196-4*); lib. bdg. 29.95 (*0-7933-2195-6*); disk 29.95 (*0-7933-2197-2*) Gallopade Intl.

— Virginia Silly Football Sportsmysteries, Vol. 1. (Carole Marsh Virginia Bks.). (Illus.). (J). 1994. pap. 19.95 (*0-7933-2174-3*); disk 29.95 (*0-7933-2175-1*) Gallopade Intl.

— Virginia Silly Football Sportsmysteries, Vol. 2. (Carole Marsh Virginia Bks.). (Illus.). (J). 1994. pap. 19.95 (*0-7933-2177-8*); lib. bdg. 29.95 (*0-7933-2176-X*); disk 29.95 (*0-7933-2178-6*) Gallopade Intl.

— Virginia Silly Trivia! (Carole Marsh Virginia Bks.). (Illus.). 60p. (Orig.). (J). (gr. 3-12). 1994. pap. 19.95 (*0-935326-94-4*); lib. bdg. 29.95 (*0-7933-2167-0*); disk 29.95 (*0-7933-2168-9*) Gallopade Intl.

— Virginia Spelling Bee! Score Big by Correctly Spelling Our State's Unique Names. (Carole Marsh Virginia Bks.). (Illus.). (YA). (gr. 3-12). 1996. pap. 29.95 (*0-7933-6778-6*); pap. 19.95 (*0-7933-6779-4*) Gallopade Intl.

— Virginia Timeline: A Chronology of Virginia History, Mystery, Trivia, Legend, Lore & More. (Virginia Bks.). (Illus.). (J). (gr. 3-12). 1994. pap. 19.95 (*0-7933-6014-5*); lib. bdg. 29.95 (*0-7933-6013-7*); disk 29.95 (*0-7933-6015-3*) Gallopade Intl.

— Virginia 2000! Coming Soon to a Calendar Near You - The 21st Century! - Complete Set of AL 2000 Items. (Two Thousand! Ser.). (Illus.). (J). (gr. 3-12). 1998. pap. 75.00 (*0-7933-9401-5*); lib. bdg. 85.00 (*0-7933-9402-3*) Gallopade Intl.

— Virginia 2000! Coming Soon to a Calendar near You--The 21st Century! (Two Thousand! Ser.). (Illus.). (J). (gr. 3-12). 1998. pap. 19.95 (*0-7933-8814-7*); lib. bdg. 29.95 (*0-7933-8813-9*) Gallopade Intl.

— Virginia UFO's & Extraterrestrials! A Look at the Sightings & Science in Our State. (Carole Marsh Virginia Bks.). (Illus.). (J). (gr. 3-12). 1997. pap. 19.95 (*0-7933-6473-6*); lib. bdg. 29.95 (*0-7933-6472-8*) Gallopade Intl.

***Marsh, Carole.** Virginia's Big Activity Book. (Virginia Experience! Ser.). (Illus.). (J). (gr. k-5). 2000. pap. 9.95 (*0-7933-9466-X*) Gallopade Intl.

Marsh, Carole. Virginia's (Most Devastating!) Disasters & (Most Calamitous!) Catastrophies! (Carole Marsh Virginia Bks.). (Illus.). (J). 1994. pap. 19.95 (*0-7933-1150-0*); lib. bdg. 29.95 (*0-7933-2193-X*); disk 29.95 (*0-7933-2194-8*) Gallopade Intl.

— Virginia's Unsolved Mysteries (& Their "Solutions") Includes Scientific Information & Other Activities for Students. (Virginia Bks.). (Illus.). (J). (gr. 3-12). 1994. pap. 19.95 (*0-7933-5861-2*); lib. bdg. 29.95 (*0-7933-5860-4*); disk 29.95 (*0-7933-5862-0*) Gallopade Intl.

— Volcanoes! Mountains with a Tummyache!! (Interactive Multimedia Titles Ser.). (J). (gr. 2-9). 1996. 29.95 (*0-7933-7607-6*, C Marsh); pap. 19.95 (*0-7933-7606-8*, C Marsh); pap., teacher ed. 19.95 (*0-7933-7835-4*, C Marsh) Gallopade Intl.

— Washington & Other State Greats (Biographies!) (Carole Marsh Washington Bks.). (Illus.). (J). 1994. pap. 19.95 (*0-7933-2225-1*); lib. bdg. 29.95 (*0-7933-2224-3*); disk 29.95 (*0-7933-2226-X*) Gallopade Intl.

— Washington Bandits, Bushwackers, Outlaws, Crooks, Devils, Ghosts, Desperadoes & Other Assorted & Sundry Characters! (Carole Marsh Washington Bks.). (Illus.). (J). 1994. pap. 19.95 (*0-7933-1177-2*); lib. bdg. 29.95 (*0-7933-1178-0*); disk 29.95 (*0-7933-1179-9*) Gallopade Intl.

— Washington "BIO" Bingo! 24 Must Know State People for Kids to Learn about While Having Fun! (Bingo! Ser.). (Illus.). (J). (gr. 2-8). 1998. pap. 14.95 (*0-7933-8663-2*) Gallopade Intl.

— The Washington Bookstore Book: A Surprising Guide to Our State's Bookstores & Their Specialties for Students, Teachers, Writers & Publishers. (Washington Bks.). (Illus.). 1994. pap. 19.95 (*0-7933-2997-3*); lib. bdg. 29.95 (*0-7933-2996-5*); disk 29.95 (*0-7933-2998-1*) Gallopade Intl.

— Washington Classic Christmas Trivia: Stories, Recipes, Activities, Legends, Lore & More! (Washington Bks.). (Illus.). (J). 1994. pap. 19.95 (*0-7933-1180-2*); lib. bdg. 29.95 (*0-7933-1181-0*); disk 29.95 (*0-7933-1182-9*) Gallopade Intl.

— Washington Coastales. (Carole Marsh Washington Bks.). (Illus.). (J). 1994. pap. 19.95 (*0-7933-2219-7*); lib. bdg. 29.95 (*0-7933-2218-9*); disk 29.95 (*0-7933-2220-0*) Gallopade Intl.

— Washington Coastales! (Washington Bks.). (J). 1994. lib. bdg. 29.95 (*0-7933-7312-3*) Gallopade Intl.

— Washington "Crinkum-Crankum" A Funny Word Book about Our State. (Washington Bks.). (Illus.). (J). (gr. 3-12). 1994. 29.95 (*0-7933-4949-4*); pap. 19.95 (*0-7933-4950-8*); disk 29.95 (*0-7933-4951-6*) Gallopade Intl.

— Washington, D. C. & Other State Greats (Biographies) (Washington, D.C. Bks.). (Illus.). (YA). (gr. 3-12). 1994. pap. 19.95 (*0-7933-1481-X*); lib. bdg. 29.95 (*0-7933-1480-1*); disk 29.95 (*0-7933-1482-8*) Gallopade Intl.

— Washington, D. C. Bandits, Bushwackers, Outlaws, Crooks, Devils, Ghosts, Desperadoes & Other Assorted & Sundry Characters! (Carole Marsh Washington, D.C. Bks.). (Illus.). (YA). (gr. 3-12). 1994. pap. 19.95 (*0-7933-0261-7*); lib. bdg. 29.95 (*0-7933-0262-5*); disk 29.95 (*0-7933-0263-3*) Gallopade Intl.

— The Washington, D. C. Bookstore Book: A Surprising Guide to Our State's Bookstores & Their Specialties for Students, Teachers, Writers & Publishers. (Washington, D.C. Bks.). (Illus.). 1994. pap. 19.95 (*0-7933-2880-2*); lib. bdg. 29.95 (*0-7933-2879-9*); disk 29.95 (*0-7933-2881-0*) Gallopade Intl.

— Washington, D. C. Classic Christmas Trivia: Stories, Recipes, Activities, Legends, Lore & More! (Carole Marsh Washington, D.C. Bks.). (Illus.). (YA). (gr. 3-12). 1994. pap. 19.95 (*0-7933-0264-1*); lib. bdg. 29.95 (*0-7933-0265-X*); disk 29.95 (*0-7933-0266-8*) Gallopade Intl.

— Washington, D. C. Coastales. (Carole Marsh Washington, D.C. Bks.). (Illus.). (YA). (gr. 3-12). 1994. pap. 19.95 (*0-7933-1475-5*); lib. bdg. 29.95 (*0-7933-1474-7*); disk 29.95 (*0-7933-1476-3*) Gallopade Intl.

— Washington, D. C. Coastales! (Washington, D.C. Bks.). (J). 1994. lib. bdg. 29.95 (*0-7933-7273-9*) Gallopade Intl.

— Washington D. C. "Crinkum-Crankum" A Funny Word Book about Our State. (Washington, D.C. Bks.). (Illus.). (J). (gr. 3-12). 1994. 29.95 (*0-7933-4952-4*); pap. 19.95 (*0-7933-4953-2*); disk 29.95 (*0-7933-4954-0*) Gallopade Intl.

— Washington, D. C. Dingbats! Bk. 1: A Fun Book of Games, Stories, Activities & More about Our State That's All in Code! for You to Decipher. (Washington, D.C. Bks.). (Illus.). (J). (gr. 3-12). 1994. pap. 29.95 (*0-7933-3798-4*); lib. bdg. 29.95 (*0-7933-3797-6*); disk 29.95 (*0-7933-3799-2*) Gallopade Intl.

— Washington, D. C. Festival Fun for Kids! Includes Reproducible Activities for Kids! (Washington, D.C. Bks.). (Illus.). (J). (gr. 3-12). 1994. pap. 19.95 (*0-7933-3951-0*); lib. bdg. 29.95 (*0-7933-3950-2*); disk 29.95 (*0-7933-3952-9*) Gallopade Intl.

— The Washington D. C. Hot Air Balloon Mystery. (Washington, D.C. Bks.). (Illus.). (J). (gr. 2-9). 1994. 29.95 (*0-7933-2390-8*); pap. 19.95 (*0-7933-2391-6*); disk 29.95 (*0-7933-2392-4*) Gallopade Intl.

— Washington, D. C. Jeopardy! Answers & Questions about Our State! (Washington, D.C. Bks.). (Illus.). (J). (gr. 3-12). 1994. pap. 19.95 (*0-7933-4104-3*); lib. bdg. 29.95 (*0-7933-4103-5*); disk 29.95 (*0-7933-4105-1*) Gallopade Intl.

— Washington, D. C. "Jography" A Fun Run Thru Our State! (Washington, D.C. Bks.). (Illus.). (YA). (gr. 3-12). 1994. pap. 19.95 (*1-55609-561-9*); lib. bdg. 29.95 (*1-55609-562-7*); disk 29.95 (*0-7933-1460-7*) Gallopade Intl.

— Washington, D. C. Kid's Cookbook: Recipes, How-to, History, Lore & More! (Carole Marsh Washington, D.C. Bks.). (Illus.). (YA). (gr. 3-12). 1994. pap. 19.95 (*0-7933-0273-0*); lib. bdg. 29.95 (*0-7933-0274-9*); disk 29.95 (*0-7933-0275-7*) Gallopade Intl.

— The Washington, D. C. Library Book: A Surprising Guide to the Unusual Special Collections in Libraries Across Our State for Students, Teachers, Writers & Publishers. (Washington, D.C. Bks.). (Illus.). 1994. pap. 19.95 (*0-7933-3030-0*); lib. bdg. 29.95 (*0-7933-3029-7*); disk 29.95 (*0-7933-3031-9*) Gallopade Intl.

— The Washington, D. C. Media Book: A Surprising Guide to the Amazing Print, Broadcast & Online Media of Our State for Students, Teachers, Writers & Publishers - Includes Reproducible Mailing Labels Plus Activities for Young People! (Washington, D.C. Bks.). (Illus.). 1994. pap. 19.95 (*0-7933-3186-2*); lib. bdg. 29.95 (*0-7933-3185-4*); disk 29.95 (*0-7933-3187-0*) Gallopade Intl.

— The Washington D. C. Mystery Van Takes Off! Bk. 1: Handicapped Washington D. C. Kids Sneak Off on a Big Adventure. (Washington, D.C. Bks.). (Illus.). (J). (gr. 3-12). 1994. 29.95 (*0-7933-5105-7*); pap. 19.95 (*0-7933-5106-5*); disk 29.95 (*0-7933-5107-3*) Gallopade Intl.

— Washington, D. C. Quiz Bowl Crash Course! (Carole Marsh Washington, D.C. Bks.). (Illus.). (YA). (gr. 3-12). 1994. pap. 19.95 (*0-7933-1472-0*); lib. bdg. 29.95 (*0-7933-1471-2*); disk 29.95 (*0-7933-1473-9*) Gallopade Intl.

— Washington, D. C. Rollercoasters! (Washington, D.C. Bks.). (Illus.). (YA). (gr. 3-12). 1994. pap. 19.95 (*0-7933-5249-5*); lib. bdg. 29.95 (*0-7933-5248-7*); disk 29.95 (*0-7933-5250-9*) Gallopade Intl.

— Washington, D. C. School Trivia: An Amazing & Fascinating Look at Our State's Teachers, Schools & Students! (Washington, D.C. Bks.). (Illus.). (YA). (gr. 3-12). 1994. pap. 19.95 (*0-7933-0270-6*); lib. bdg. 29.95 (*0-7933-0271-4*); disk 29.95 (*0-7933-0272-2*) Gallopade Intl.

— Washington, D. C. Silly Basketball Sportsmysteries, Vol. 1. (Washington, D.C. Bks.). (Illus.). (YA). (gr. 3-12). 1994. pap. 19.95 (*0-7933-0267-6*); lib. bdg. 29.95 (*0-7933-0268-4*); disk 29.95 (*0-7933-0269-2*) Gallopade Intl.

— Washington, D. C. Silly Basketball Sportsmysteries, Vol. 2. (Washington, D.C. Bks.). (Illus.). (YA). (gr. 3-12). 1994. pap. 19.95 (*0-7933-1484-4*); lib. bdg. 29.95 (*0-7933-1483-6*); disk 29.95 (*0-7933-1485-2*) Gallopade Intl.

— Washington, D. C. Silly Football Sportsmysteries, Vol. 1. (Washington, D.C. Bks.). (Illus.). (YA). (gr. 3-12). 1994. pap. 19.95 (*0-7933-1463-1*); lib. bdg. 29.95 (*0-7933-1462-3*); disk 29.95 (*0-7933-1464-X*) Gallopade Intl.

— Washington, D. C. Silly Trivia! (Washington, D.C. Bks.). (Illus.). (YA). (gr. 3-12). 1994. pap. 19.95 (*1-55609-559-7*); lib. bdg. 29.95 (*1-55609-560-0*); disk 29.95 (*0-7933-1459-3*) Gallopade Intl.

— Washington D. C. Timeline: A Chronology of Washington D. C. History, Mystery, Trivia, Legend, Lore & More. (Washington, D.C. Bks.). (Illus.). (J). (gr. 3-12). 1994. pap. 19.95 (*0-7933-5900-7*); lib. bdg. 29.95 (*0-7933-5899-X*); disk 29.95 (*0-7933-5901-5*) Gallopade Intl.

— Washington, D. C. UFO's & Extraterrestrials! A Look at the Sightings & Science in Our State. (Carole Marsh Washington, D.C. Bks.). (Illus.). (J). (gr. 3-12). 1997. pap. 19.95 (*0-7933-6359-4*); lib. bdg. 29.95 (*0-7933-6358-6*) Gallopade Intl.

— Washington, D. C.'s (Most Devastating!) Disasters & (Most Calamitous!) Catastrophies! (Washington, D.C. Bks.). (Illus.). (YA). (gr. 3-12). 1994. pap. 19.95 (*0-7933-0258-7*); lib. bdg. 29.95 (*0-7933-0259-5*); disk 29.95 (*0-7933-0260-9*) Gallopade Intl.

— Washington D. C.'s Unsolved Mysteries (& Their "Solutions") Includes Scientific Information & Other Activities for Students. (Washington, D.C. Bks.). (Illus.). (J). (gr. 3-12). 1994. pap. 19.95 (*0-7933-5747-0*); lib. bdg. 29.95 (*0-7933-5746-2*); disk 29.95 (*0-7933-5748-9*) Gallopade Intl.

— Washington D.C. Facts & Factivities. (Carole Marsh State Bks.). (Illus.). (J). (gr. 4-7). 1996. pap., teacher ed. 19.95 (*0-7933-7863-X*) Gallopade Intl.

— Washington, D.C. Indian Dictionary for Kids! (Carole Marsh State Bks.). (J). (gr. 2-9). 1996. 29.95 (*0-7933-7668-8*, C Marsh); pap. 19.95 (*0-7933-7669-6*, C Marsh) Gallopade Intl.

— Washington, D.C. Silly Football Sportsmysteries, Vol. 2. (Carole Marsh Washington, D.C. Bks.). (Illus.). (YA). (gr. 3-12). 1994. pap. 19.95 (*0-7933-1466-6*); lib. bdg. 29.95 (*0-7933-1465-8*); disk 29.95 (*0-7933-1467-4*) Gallopade Intl.

— Washington Dingbats! Bk. 1: A Fun Book of Games, Stories, Activities & More about Our State That's All in Code! for You to Decipher. (Washington Bks.). (Illus.). (J). (gr. 3-12). 1994. pap. 19.95 (*0-7933-3915-4*); lib. bdg. 29.95 (*0-7933-3914-6*); disk 29.95 (*0-7933-3916-2*) Gallopade Intl.

— Washington Facts & Factivities. (Carole Marsh State Bks.). (Illus.). (J). (gr. 4-7). 1996. pap., teacher ed. 19.95 (*0-7933-7941-5*, C Marsh) Gallopade Intl.

— Washington Festival Fun for Kids! Includes Reproducible Activities for Kids! (Washington Bks.). (Illus.). (J). (gr. 3-12). 1994. pap. 19.95 (*0-7933-4068-3*); lib. bdg. 29.95 (*0-7933-4067-5*); disk 29.95 (*0-7933-4069-1*) Gallopade Intl.

M

— Washington "GEO" Bingo! 38 Must Know State Geography Facts for Kids to Learn While Having Fun! (Bingo! Ser.). (Illus.). (J). (gr. 2-8). 1998. pap. 14.95 (*0-7933-8664-0*) Gallopade Intl.

— Washington Government! The Cornerstone of Everday Life in Our State! (Carole Marsh Washington Bks.). (Illus.). (J). (gr. 3-12). 1996. pap. 19.95 (*0-7933-6323-3*); lib. bdg. 29.95 (*0-7933-6322-5*); disk 29.95 (*0-7933-6324-1*) Gallopade Intl.

— Washington "HISTO" Bingo! 42 Must Know State History Facts for Kids to Learn While Having Fun! (Bingo! Ser.). (Illus.). (J). (gr. 2-8). 1998. pap. 14.95 (*0-7933-8665-9*) Gallopade Intl.

— Washington History! Surprising Secrets about Our State's Founding Mothers, Fathers & Kids! (Carole Marsh Washington Bks.). (Illus.). (J). (gr. 3-12). 1996. pap. 19.95 (*0-7933-6170-2*); lib. bdg. 29.95 (*0-7933-6169-9*); disk 29.95 (*0-7933-6171-0*) Gallopade Intl.

— The Washington Hot Air Balloon Mystery. (Carole Marsh Washington Bks.). (Illus.). (J). (gr. 2-9). 1994. 29.95 (*0-7933-2741-5*); pap. 19.95 (*0-7933-2742-3*); disk 29.95 (*0-7933-2743-1*) Gallopade Intl.

— Washington Hot Zones! Viruses, Diseases, & Epidemics in Our State's History. (Hot Zones! Ser.). (Illus.). (J). (gr. 3-12). 1998. pap. 19.95 (*0-7933-8970-4*); lib. bdg. 29.95 (*0-7933-8969-0*) Gallopade Intl.

— Washington Indian Dictionary for Kids! (Carole Marsh State Bks.). (J). (gr. 2-9). 1996. 29.95 (*0-7933-7785-4*, C Marsh); pap. 19.95 (*0-7933-7786-2*, C Marsh) Gallopade Intl.

— Washington Jeopardy! Answers & Questions about Our State! (Washington Bks.). (Illus.). (J). (gr. 3-12). 1994. pap. 19.95 (*0-7933-4221-X*); lib. bdg. 29.95 (*0-7933-4220-1*); disk 29.95 (*0-7933-4222-8*) Gallopade Intl.

— Washington "Jography" A Fun Run Thru Our State! (Carole Marsh Washington Bks.). (Illus.). (J). 1994. pap. 19.95 (*0-7933-2202-2*); lib. bdg. 29.95 (*0-7933-2201-4*); disk 29.95 (*0-7933-2203-0*) Gallopade Intl.

— Washington Kid's Cookbook: Recipes, How-to, History, Lore & More! (Carole Marsh Washington Bks.). (Illus.). (J). 1994. pap. 19.95 (*0-7933-1189-6*); lib. bdg. 29.95 (*0-7933-1190-X*); disk 29.95 (*0-7933-1191-8*) Gallopade Intl.

— The Washington Library Book: A Surprising Guide to the Unusual Special Collections in Libraries Across Our State for Students, Teachers, Writers & Publishers - Includes Reproducible Mailing Labels Plus Activities for Young People! (Washington Bks.). (Illus.). 1994. pap. 19.95 (*0-7933-3147-1*); lib. bdg. 29.95 (*0-7933-3146-3*); disk 29.95 (*0-7933-3148-X*) Gallopade Intl.

— Washington Math! How It All Adds up in Our State. (Carole Marsh Washington Bks.). (Illus.). (YA). (gr. 3-12). 1996. pap. 19.95 (*0-7933-6629-1*); lib. bdg. 29.95 (*0-7933-6628-3*) Gallopade Intl.

— The Washington Media Book: A Surprising Guide to the Amazing Print, Broadcast & Online Media of Our State for Students, Teachers, Writers & Publishers - Includes Reproducible Mailing Labels Plus Activities for Young People! (Washington Bks.). (Illus.). 1994. pap. 19.95 (*0-7933-3303-2*); lib. bdg. 29.95 (*0-7933-3302-4*); disk 29.95 (*0-7933-3304-0*) Gallopade Intl.

— The Washington Mystery Van Takes Off! Bk. 1: Handicapped Washington Kids Sneak Off on a Big Adventure. (Washington Bks.). (Illus.). (J). (gr. 3-12). 1994. 29.95 (*0-7933-5102-2*); pap. 19.95 (*0-7933-5103-0*); disk 29.95 (*0-7933-5104-9*) Gallopade Intl.

— Washington Quiz Bowl Crash Course! (Carole Marsh Washington Bks.). (Illus.). (J). 1994. pap. 19.95 (*0-7933-2216-2*); lib. bdg. 29.95 (*0-7933-2215-4*); disk 29.95 (*0-7933-2217-0*) Gallopade Intl.

— Washington Rollercoasters! (Washington Bks.). (Illus.). (YA). (gr. 3-12). 1994. pap. 19.95 (*0-7933-5366-1*); lib. bdg. 29.95 (*0-7933-5365-3*); disk 29.95 (*0-7933-5367-X*) Gallopade Intl.

— Washington School Trivia: An Amazing & Fascinating Look at Our State's Teachers, Schools & Students! (Carole Marsh Washington Bks.). (Illus.). (J). 1994. pap. 19.95 (*0-7933-1186-1*); disk 29.95 (*0-7933-1188-8*) Gallopade Intl.

— Washington School Trivia: An Amazing & Fascinating

Look at Our State's Teachers, Schools & Students! (Carole Marsh Washington Bks.). (Illus.). (J). 1997. lib. bdg. 29.95 (*0-7933-1187-X*) Gallopade Intl.

— Washington Silly Basketball Sportsmysteries, Vol. 1. (Carole Marsh Washington Bks.). (Illus.). (J). 1994. pap. 19.95 (*0-7933-1183-7*); lib. bdg. 29.95 (*0-7933-1184-5*); disk 29.95 (*0-7933-1185-3*) Gallopade Intl.

— Washington Silly Basketball Sportsmysteries, Vol. 2. (Carole Marsh Washington Bks.). (Illus.). (J). 1994. pap. 19.95 (*0-7933-2228-6*); lib. bdg. 29.95 (*0-7933-2227-8*); disk 29.95 (*0-7933-2229-4*) Gallopade Intl.

— Washington Silly Football Sportsmysteries, Vol. 1. (Carole Marsh Washington Bks.). (Illus.). (J). 1994. pap. 19.95 (*0-7933-2207-3*); lib. bdg. 29.95 (*0-7933-2206-5*); disk 29.95 (*0-7933-2208-1*) Gallopade Intl.

— Washington Silly Football Sportsmysteries, Vol. 2. (Carole Marsh Washington Bks.). (Illus.). (J). 1994. pap. 19.95 (*0-7933-2210-3*); disk 29.95 (*0-7933-2211-1*) Gallopade Intl.

— Washington Silly Trivia! (Carole Marsh Washington Bks.). (Illus.). (J). 1994. pap. 19.95 (*0-7933-2199-9*); lib. bdg. 29.95 (*0-7933-2198-0*); disk 29.95 (*0-7933-2200-6*) Gallopade Intl.

— Washington Spelling Bee! Score Big by Correctly Spelling Our State's Unique Names. (Carole Marsh Washington Bks.). (Illus.). (YA). (gr. 3-12). 1996. pap. 19.95 (*0-7933-6782-4*); lib. bdg. 29.95 (*0-7933-6781-6*) Gallopade Intl.

— Washington Timeline: A Chronology of Washington History, Mystery, Trivia, Legend, Lore & More. (Washington Bks.). (Illus.). (J). (gr. 3-12). 1994. pap. 19.95 (*0-7933-6017-X*); lib. bdg. 29.95 (*0-7933-6016-1*); disk 29.95 (*0-7933-6018-8*) Gallopade Intl.

— Washington 2000! Coming Soon to a Calendar Near You - The 21st Century! - Complete Set of AL 2000 Items. (Two Thousand! Ser.). (Illus.). (J). (gr. 3-12). 1998. pap. 75.00 (*0-7933-9403-1*); lib. bdg. 85.00 (*0-7933-9404-X*) Gallopade Intl.

— Washington 2000! Coming Soon to a Calendar near You--The 21st Century! (Two Thousand! Ser.). (Illus.). (J). (gr. 3-12). 1998. pap. 19.95 (*0-7933-8817-1*); lib. bdg. 29.95 (*0-7933-8816-3*) Gallopade Intl.

— Washington UFO's & Extraterrestrials! A Look at the Sightings & Science in Our State. (Carole Marsh Washington Bks.). (Illus.). (J). (gr. 3-12). 1997. pap. 19.95 (*0-7933-6476-0*); lib. bdg. 29.95 (*0-7933-6475-2*) Gallopade Intl.

— Washington's (Most Devastating!) Disasters & (Most Calamitous!) Catastrophies! (Carole Marsh Washington Bks.). (Illus.). (J). 1994. pap. 19.95 (*0-7933-1174-8*); lib. bdg. 29.95 (*0-7933-1175-6*); disk 29.95 (*0-7933-1176-4*) Gallopade Intl.

— Washington's Unsolved Mysteries (& Their "Solutions") Includes Scientific Information & Other Activities for Students. (Washington Bks.). (Illus.). (J). (gr. 3-12). 1994. pap. 19.95 (*0-7933-5864-7*); lib. bdg. 29.95 (*0-7933-5863-9*); disk 29.95 (*0-7933-5865-5*) Gallopade Intl.

— West Virginia & Other State Greats (Biographies) (Carole Marsh West Virginia Bks.). (Illus.). (J). 1994. pap. 19.95 (*0-7933-2257-X*); lib. bdg. 29.95 (*0-7933-2256-1*); disk 29.95 (*0-7933-2258-8*) Gallopade Intl.

— West Virginia Bandits, Bushwackers, Outlaws, Crooks, Devils, Ghosts, Desperadoes & Other Assorted & Sundry Characters! (Carole Marsh West Virginia Bks.). (Illus.). (J). 1994. pap. 19.95 (*0-7933-1201-9*); lib. bdg. 29.95 (*0-7933-1202-7*); disk 29.95 (*0-7933-1203-5*) Gallopade Intl.

— West Virginia "BIO" Bingo! 24 Must Know State People for Kids to Learn about While Having Fun! (Bingo! Ser.). (Illus.). (J). (gr. 2-8). 1998. pap. 14.95 (*0-7933-8666-7*) Gallopade Intl.

— The West Virginia Bookstore Book: A Surprising Guide to Our State's Bookstores & Their Specialties for Students, Teachers, Writers & Publishers. (West Virginia Bks.). (Illus.). 1994. pap. 19.95 (*0-7933-3000-9*); lib. bdg. 29.95 (*0-7933-2999-X*); disk 29.95 (*0-7933-3001-7*) Gallopade Intl.

— West Virginia Classic Christmas Trivia: Stories, Recipies, Activities, Legends, Lore & More! (Carole Marsh West Virginia Bks.). (Illus.). (J). 1994. pap. 19.95 (*0-7933-1204-3*); lib. bdg. 29.95 (*0-7933-1205-1*); disk 29.95 (*0-7933-1206-X*) Gallopade Intl.

— West Virginia Coastales. (Carole Marsh West Virginia Bks.). (Illus.). (J). 1994. pap. 19.95 (*0-7933-2251-0*); disk 29.95 (*0-7933-2252-9*) Gallopade Intl.

— West Virginia Coastales. (Carole Marsh West Virginia Bks.). (Illus.). (J). 1997. lib. bdg. 29.95 (*0-7933-2250-2*) Gallopade Intl.

— West Virginia Coastales! (West Virginia Bks.). (J). 1994. lib. bdg. 29.95 (*0-7933-7313-1*) Gallopade Intl.

— West Virginia "Crinkum-Crankum" A Funny Word Book about Our State. (West Virginia Bks.). (Illus.). (J). (gr. 3-12). 1994. 29.95 (*0-7933-4955-9*); pap. 19.95 (*0-7933-4956-7*); disk 29.95 (*0-7933-4957-5*) Gallopade Intl.

— West Virginia Dingbats! Bk. 1: A Fun Book of Games, Stories, Activities & More about Our State That's All in Code! for You to Decipher. (West Virginia Bks.). (Illus.). (J). (gr. 3-12). 1994. pap. 19.95 (*0-7933-3918-9*); lib. bdg. 29.95 (*0-7933-3917-0*); disk 29.95 (*0-7933-3919-7*) Gallopade Intl.

— West Virginia Facts & Factivities. (Carole Marsh State Bks.). (Illus.). (J). (gr. 4-7). 1996. pap., teacher ed. 19.95 (*0-7933-7943-1*, C Marsh) Gallopade Intl.

— West Virginia Festival Fun for Kids! Includes Reproducible Activities for Kids! (West Virginia Bks.). (Illus.). (J). (gr. 3-12). 1994. pap. 19.95 (*0-7933-4071-3*); lib. bdg. 29.95 (*0-7933-4070-5*); disk 29.95 (*0-7933-4072-1*) Gallopade Intl.

— West Virginia "GEO" Bingo! 38 Must Know State Geography Facts for Kids to Learn While Having Fun! (Bingo! Ser.). (Illus.). (J). (gr. 2-8). 1998. pap. 14.95 (*0-7933-8667-5*) Gallopade Intl.

— West Virginia Government! The Cornerstone of Everyday Life in Our State! (Carole Marsh West Virginia Bks.). (Illus.). (J). (gr. 3-12). 1996. pap. 19.95 (*0-7933-6326-8*); lib. bdg. 29.95 (*0-7933-6325-X*); disk 29.95 (*0-7933-6327-6*) Gallopade Intl.

— West Virginia "HISTO" Bingo! 42 Must Know State History Facts for Kids to Learn While Having Fun! (Bingo! Ser.). (Illus.). (J). (gr. 2-8). 1998. pap. 14.95 (*0-7933-8668-3*) Gallopade Intl.

— West Virginia History! Surprising Secrets about Our State's Founding Mothers, Fathers & Kids! (Carole Marsh West Virginia Bks.). (Illus.). (J). (gr. 3-12). 1996. pap. 19.95 (*0-7933-6173-7*); lib. bdg. 29.95 (*0-7933-6172-9*); disk 29.95 (*0-7933-6174-5*) Gallopade Intl.

— The West Virginia Hot Air Balloon Mystery. (Carole Marsh West Virginia Bks.). (Illus.). (J). (gr. 2-9). 1994. 29.95 (*0-7933-2750-4*); pap. 19.95 (*0-7933-2751-2*); disk 29.95 (*0-7933-2752-0*) Gallopade Intl.

— West Virginia Hot Zones! Viruses, Diseases, & Epidemics in Our State's History. (Hot Zones! Ser.). (Illus.). (J). (gr. 3-12). 1998. pap. 19.95 (*0-7933-8973-9*); lib. bdg. 29.95 (*0-7933-8972-0*) Gallopade Intl.

— West Virginia Indian Dictionary for Kids! (Carole Marsh State Bks.). (J). (gr. 2-9). 1996. 29.95 (*0-7933-7788-9*, C Marsh); pap. 19.95 (*0-7933-7789-7*, C Marsh) Gallopade Intl.

— West Virginia Jeopardy! Answers & Questions about Our State! (West Virginia Bks.). (Illus.). (J). (gr. 3-12). 1994. pap. 19.95 (*0-7933-4224-4*); lib. bdg. 29.95 (*0-7933-4223-6*); disk 29.95 (*0-7933-4225-2*) Gallopade Intl.

— West Virginia "Jography" A Fun Run Thru Our State! (Carole Marsh West Virginia Bks.). (Illus.). (J). 1994. pap. 19.95 (*0-7933-2234-0*); lib. bdg. 29.95 (*0-7933-2233-2*); disk 29.95 (*0-7933-2235-9*) Gallopade Intl.

— West Virginia Kid's Cookbook: Recipes, How-to, History, Lore & More! (Carole Marsh West Virginia Bks.). (Illus.). (J). 1994. pap. 19.95 (*0-7933-1213-2*); lib. bdg. 29.95 (*0-7933-1214-0*); disk 29.95 (*0-7933-1215-9*) Gallopade Intl.

— The West Virginia Library Book: A Surprising Guide to the Unusual Special Collections in Libraries Across Our State for Students, Teachers, Writers & Publishers. (West Virginia Bks.). (Illus.). 1994. pap. 19.95 (*0-7933-3150-1*); lib. bdg. 29.95 (*0-7933-3149-8*); disk 29.95 (*0-7933-3151-X*) Gallopade Intl.

— West Virginia Math! How It All Adds up in Our State. (Carole Marsh West Virginia Bks.). (Illus.). (YA). (gr. 3-12). 1996. pap. 19.95 (*0-7933-6632-1*); lib. bdg. 29.95 (*0-7933-6631-3*) Gallopade Intl.

— The West Virginia Media Book: A Surprising Guide to the Amazing Print, Broadcast & Online Media of Our State for Students, Teachers, Writers & Publishers - Includes Reproducible Mailing Labels Plus Activities for Young People! (West Virginia Bks.). (Illus.). 1994. pap. 19.95 (*0-7933-3306-7*); lib. bdg. 29.95 (*0-7933-3305-9*); disk 29.95 (*0-7933-3307-5*) Gallopade Intl.

— The West Virginia Mystery Van Takes Off! Bk. 1: Handicapped West Virginia Kids Sneak Off on a Big Adventure. (West Virginia Bks.). (Illus.). (J). (gr. 3-12). 1994. 29.95 (*0-7933-5108-1*); pap. 19.95 (*0-7933-5109-X*); disk 29.95 (*0-7933-5110-3*) Gallopade Intl.

— West Virginia Quiz Bowl Crash Course! (Carole Marsh West Virginia Bks.). (Illus.). (J). 1994. pap. 19.95 (*0-7933-2248-0*); lib. bdg. 29.95 (*0-7933-2247-2*); disk 29.95 (*0-7933-2249-9*) Gallopade Intl.

— West Virginia Rollercoasters! (West Virginia Bks.). (Illus.). (YA). (gr. 3-12). 1994. pap. 19.95 (*0-7933-5369-6*); lib. bdg. 29.95 (*0-7933-5368-8*); disk 29.95 (*0-7933-5370-X*) Gallopade Intl.

— West Virginia School Trivia: An Amazing & Fascinating Look at Our State's Teachers, Schools & Students! (Carole Marsh West Virginia Bks.). (Illus.). (J). 1994. pap. 19.95 (*0-7933-1210-8*); lib. bdg. 29.95 (*0-7933-1211-6*); disk 29.95 (*0-7933-1212-4*) Gallopade Intl.

— West Virginia Silly Basketball Sportsmysteries, Vol. 1. (Carole Marsh West Virginia Bks.). (Illus.). (J). 1994. pap. 19.95 (*0-7933-1207-8*); lib. bdg. 29.95 (*0-7933-1208-6*); disk 29.95 (*0-7933-1209-4*) Gallopade Intl.

— West Virginia Silly Basketball Sportsmysteries, Vol. 2. (Carole Marsh West Virginia Bks.). (Illus.). (J). 1994. pap. 19.95 (*0-7933-2260-X*); lib. bdg. 29.95 (*0-7933-2259-6*); disk 29.95 (*0-7933-2261-8*) Gallopade Intl.

— West Virginia Silly Football Sportsmysteries, Vol. 1. (Carole Marsh West Virginia Bks.). (Illus.). (J). 1994. pap. 19.95 (*0-7933-2239-1*); lib. bdg. 29.95 (*0-7933-2238-3*); disk 29.95 (*0-7933-2240-5*) Gallopade Intl.

— West Virginia Silly Football Sportsmysteries, Vol. 2. (Carole Marsh West Virginia Bks.). (Illus.). (J). 1994. pap. 19.95 (*0-7933-2242-1*); lib. bdg. 29.95 (*0-7933-2241-3*) Gallopade Intl.

— West Virginia Silly Trivia! (Carole Marsh West Virginia Bks.). (Illus.). (J). 1994. pap. 19.95 (*0-7933-2231-6*); lib. bdg. 29.95 (*0-7933-2230-8*); disk 29.95 (*0-7933-2232-4*) Gallopade Intl.

— West Virginia Spelling Bee! Score Big by Correctly Spelling Our State's Unique Names. (Carole Marsh West Virginia Bks.). (Illus.). (YA). (gr. 3-12). 1996. pap. 19.95 (*0-7933-6785-9*); lib. bdg. 29.95 (*0-7933-6784-0*) Gallopade Intl.

— West Virginia Timeline: A Chronology of West Virginia History, Mystery, Trivia, Legend, Lore & More. (West Virginia Bks.). (Illus.). (J). (gr. 3-12). 1994. pap. 19.95 (*0-7933-6020-X*); lib. bdg. 29.95 (*0-7933-6019-6*); disk 29.95 (*0-7933-6021-8*) Gallopade Intl.

— West Virginia 2000! Coming Soon to a Calendar Near You - The 21st Century! - Complete Set of AL 2000 Items. (Two Thousand! Ser.). (Illus.). (J). (gr. 3-12). 1998. pap. 75.00 (*0-7933-9405-8*); lib. bdg. 85.00 (*0-7933-9406-6*) Gallopade Intl.

— West Virginia 2000! Coming Soon to a Calendar near You--The 21st Century! (Two Thousand! Ser.). (Illus.). (J). (gr. 3-12). 1998. pap. 19.95 (*0-7933-8820-1*); lib. bdg. 29.95 (*0-7933-8819-8*) Gallopade Intl.

— West Virginia UFO's & Extraterrestrials! A Look at the Sightings & Science in Our State. (Carole Marsh West Virginia Bks.). (Illus.). (J). (gr. 3-12). 1997. pap. 19.95 (*0-7933-6479-5*); lib. bdg. 29.95 (*0-7933-6478-7*) Gallopade Intl.

— West Virginia's (Most Devastating!) Disasters & (Most Calamitous!) Catastrophies! (Carole Marsh West Virginia Bks.). (Illus.). (J). 1994. pap. 19.95 (*0-7933-1198-5*); lib. bdg. 29.95 (*0-7933-1199-3*); disk 29.95 (*0-7933-1200-0*) Gallopade Intl.

— West Virginia's Unsolved Mysteries (& Their "Solutions") Includes Scientific Information & Other Activities for Students. (West Virginia Bks.). (Illus.). (J). (gr. 3-12). 1994. pap. 19.95 (*0-7933-5867-1*); lib. bdg. 29.95 (*0-7933-5866-3*); disk 29.95 (*0-7933-5868-X*) Gallopade Intl.

— What the Heck Are Ethics? (Quantum Leap Ser.). (J). (gr. 4-9). 1994. 29.95 (*1-55609-342-X*) Gallopade Intl.

— What the Heck Are Ethics? (Quantum Leap Ser.). (J). (gr. 4-9). 1997. pap. 19.95 (*1-55609-244-X*) Gallopade Intl.

— Will Somebody Hold This Thing a Minute? Statue of Liberty Silly Trivia Book. (Quantum Leap Ser.). (Illus.). 60p. (Orig.). (J). (gr. 3-12). 1994. 29.95 (*1-55609-192-3*); pap. 19.95 (*0-935326-75-8*) Gallopade Intl.

— Wisconsin & Other State Greats (Biographies) (Carole Marsh Wisconsin Bks.). (Illus.). (J). 1994. pap. 19.95 (*0-7933-2289-8*); lib. bdg. 29.95 (*0-7933-2288-X*); disk 29.95 (*0-7933-2290-1*) Gallopade Intl.

— Wisconsin Bandits, Bushwackers, Outlaws, Crooks, Devils, Ghosts, Desperadoes & Other Assorted & Sundry Characters! (Carole Marsh Wisconsin Bks.). (Illus.). (J). 1994. pap. 19.95 (*0-7933-1225-6*); lib. bdg. 29.95 (*0-7933-1226-4*); disk 29.95 (*0-7933-1227-2*) Gallopade Intl.

— Wisconsin "BIO" Bingo! 24 Must Know State People for Kids to Learn about While Having Fun! (Bingo! Ser.). (Illus.). (J). (gr. 2-8). 1998. pap. 14.95 (*0-7933-8669-1*) Gallopade Intl.

— The Wisconsin Bookstore Book: A Surprising Guide to Our State's Bookstores & Their Specialties for Students, Teachers, Writers & Publishers. (Wisconsin Bks.). (Illus.). 1994. pap. 19.95 (*0-7933-3003-3*); lib. bdg. 29.95 (*0-7933-3002-5*); disk 29.95 (*0-7933-3004-1*) Gallopade Intl.

— Wisconsin Classic Christmas Trivia: Stories, Recipes, Activities, Legends, Lore & More. (Carole Marsh Wisconsin Bks.). (Illus.). (J). 1994. pap. 19.95 (*0-7933-1228-0*); lib. bdg. 29.95 (*0-7933-1229-9*); disk 29.95 (*0-7933-1230-2*) Gallopade Intl.

— Wisconsin Coastales. (Carole Marsh Wisconsin Bks.). (Illus.). (J). 1994. 29.95 (*0-7933-2282-0*); pap. 19.95 (*0-7933-2283-9*); disk 29.95 (*0-7933-2284-7*) Gallopade Intl.

— Wisconsin Coastales! (Wisconsin Bks.). (J). 1994. lib. bdg. 29.95 (*0-7933-7314-X*) Gallopade Intl.

— Wisconsin "Crinkum-Crankum" A Funny Word Book about Our State. (Wisconsin Bks.). (Illus.). (J). (gr. 3-12). 1994. 29.95 (*0-7933-4958-3*); pap. 19.95 (*0-7933-4959-1*); disk 29.95 (*0-7933-4960-5*) Gallopade Intl.

— Wisconsin Dingbats! Bk. 1: A Fun Book of Games, Stories, Activities & More about Our State That's All in Code! for You to Decipher. (Wisconsin Bks.). (Illus.). (J). (gr. 3-12). 1994. pap. 19.95 (*0-7933-3921-9*); lib. bdg. 29.95 (*0-7933-3920-0*); disk 29.95 (*0-7933-3922-7*) Gallopade Intl.

***Marsh, Carole.** The Wisconsin Experience Pocket Guide. (Wisconsin Experience! Ser.). (Illus.). (J). 2000. pap. 6.95 (*0-7933-9538-0*) Gallopade Intl.

Marsh, Carole. Wisconsin Facts & Factivities. (Carole Marsh State Bks.). (Illus.). (J). (gr. 4-7). 1996. pap., teacher ed. 19.95 (*0-7933-7945-8*, C Marsh) Gallopade Intl.

— Wisconsin Festival Fun for Kids! Includes Reproducible Activities for Kids! (Wisconsin Bks.). (Illus.). (J). (gr. 3-12). 1994. pap. 19.95 (*0-7933-4074-8*); lib. bdg. 29.95 (*0-7933-4073-X*); disk 29.95 (*0-7933-4075-6*) Gallopade Intl.

— Wisconsin "GEO" Bingo! 38 Must Know State Geography Facts for Kids to Learn While Having Fun! (Bingo! Ser.). (Illus.). (J). (gr. 2-8). 1998. pap. 14.95 (*0-7933-8670-5*) Gallopade Intl.

— Wisconsin Government! The Cornerstone of Everyday Life in Our State! (Carole Marsh Wisconsin Bks.). (Illus.). (J). (gr. 3-12). 1996. pap. 19.95 (*0-7933-6329-2*); lib. bdg. 19.95 (*0-7933-6328-4*); disk 29.95 (*0-7933-6330-6*) Gallopade Intl.

— Wisconsin "HISTO" Bingo! 42 Must Know State History Facts for Kids to Learn While Having Fun! (Bingo! Ser.). (Illus.). (J). (gr. 2-8). 1998. pap. 14.95 (*0-7933-8671-3*) Gallopade Intl.

— Wisconsin History! Surprising Secrets about Our State's Founding Mothers, Fathers & Kids! (Carole Marsh Wisconsin Bks.). (Illus.). (J). (gr. 3-12). 1996. pap. 19.95 (*0-7933-6176-1*); lib. bdg. 29.95 (*0-7933-6175-3*); disk 29.95 (*0-7933-6177-X*) Gallopade Intl.

— The Wisconsin Hot Air Balloon Mystery. (Carole Marsh Wisconsin Bks.). (Illus.). (J). (gr. 2-9). 1994. 29.95 (*0-7933-2759-8*); pap. 19.95 (*0-7933-2760-1*); disk 29.95 (*0-7933-2761-X*) Gallopade Intl.

— Wisconsin Hot Zones! Viruses, Diseases, & Epidemics in Our State's History. (Hot Zones! Ser.). (Illus.). (J). (gr. 3-12). 1998. pap. 19.95 (*0-7933-8976-3*); lib. bdg. 29.95 (*0-7933-8975-5*) Gallopade Intl.

— Wisconsin Indian Dictionary for Kids! (Carole Marsh State Bks.). (J). (gr. 2-9). 1996. 29.95 (*0-7933-7791-9*, C Marsh); pap. 19.95 (*0-7933-7792-7*, C Marsh) Gallopade Intl.

***Marsh, Carole.** Wisconsin Jeopardy. (Wisconsin Experience! Ser.). (Illus.). (J). (gr. 2-6). 2000. pap. 7.95 (*0-7933-9540-2*) Gallopade Intl.

Marsh, Carole. Wisconsin Jeopardy! Answers & Questions about Our State! (Wisconsin Bks.). (Illus.). (J). (gr. 3-12). 1994. pap. 19.95 (*0-7933-4227-9*); lib. bdg. 29.95 (*0-7933-4226-0*); disk 29.95 (*0-7933-4228-7*) Gallopade Intl.

***Marsh, Carole.** Wisconsin Jography. (Wisconsin Experience! Ser.). (Illus.). (J). (gr. 2-6). 2000. pap. 7.95 (*0-7933-9541-0*) Gallopade Intl.

Marsh, Carole. Wisconsin "Jography" A Fun Run Thru Our State! (Carole Marsh Wisconsin Bks.). (Illus.). (J). 1994. pap. 19.95 (*0-7933-2266-9*); lib. bdg. 29.95 (*0-7933-2265-0*); disk 29.95 (*0-7933-2267-7*) Gallopade Intl.

— Wisconsin Kid's Cookbook: Recipes, How-To, History, Lore & More! (Carole Marsh Wisconsin Bks.). (Illus.). (J). 1994. pap. 19.95 (*0-7933-1237-X*); lib. bdg. 29.95 (*0-7933-1238-8*); disk 29.95 (*0-7933-1239-6*) Gallopade Intl.

— The Wisconsin Library Book: A Surprising Guide to the Unusual Special Collections in Libraries Across Our State for Students, Teachers, Writers & Publishers. (Wisconsin Bks.). (Illus.). 1994. pap. 19.95 (*0-7933-3153-6*); lib. bdg. 29.95 (*0-7933-3152-8*); disk 29.95 (*0-7933-3154-4*) Gallopade Intl.

— Wisconsin Math! How It All Adds up in Our State. (Carole Marsh Wisconsin Bks.). (Illus.). (YA). (gr. 3-12). 1996. pap. 19.95 (*0-7933-6635-6*); lib. bdg. 29.95 (*0-7933-6634-8*) Gallopade Intl.

— The Wisconsin Media Book: A Surprising Guide to the Amazing Print, Broadcast & Online Media of Our State for Students, Teachers, Writers & Publishers - Includes Reproducible Mailing Labels Plus Activities for Young People! (Wisconsin Bks.). (Illus.). 1994. pap. 19.95 (*0-7933-3309-1*); lib. bdg. 29.95 (*0-7933-3308-3*); disk 29.95 (*0-7933-3310-5*) Gallopade Intl.

— The Wisconsin Mystery Van Takes Off! Bk. 1: Handicapped Wisconsin Kids Sneak Off on a Big Adventure. (Wisconsin Bks.). (Illus.). (J). (gr. 3-12). 1994. 29.95 (*0-7933-5111-1*); pap. 19.95 (*0-7933-5112-X*); disk 29.95 (*0-7933-5113-8*) Gallopade Intl.

— Wisconsin Quiz Bowl Crash Course! (Carole Marsh Wisconsin Bks.). (Illus.). (J). 1994. pap. 19.95 (*0-7933-2280-4*); lib. bdg. 29.95 (*0-7933-2279-0*); disk 29.95 (*0-7933-2281-2*) Gallopade Intl.

— Wisconsin Rollercoasters! (Wisconsin Bks.). (Illus.). (YA). (gr. 3-12). 1994. pap. 19.95 (*0-7933-5372-6*); lib. bdg. 29.95 (*0-7933-5371-8*); disk 29.95 (*0-7933-5373-4*) Gallopade Intl.

— Wisconsin School Trivia: An Amazing & Fascinating Look at Our State's Teachers, Schools & Students! (Carole Marsh Wisconsin Bks.). (Illus.). (J). 1994. pap. 19.95 (*0-7933-1234-5*); lib. bdg. 29.95 (*0-7933-1235-3*); disk 29.95 (*0-7933-1236-1*) Gallopade Intl.

— Wisconsin Silly Basketball Sportsmysteries, Vol. 1. (Carole Marsh Wisconsin Bks.). (Illus.). (J). 1994. pap. 19.95 (*0-7933-1231-0*); lib. bdg. 29.95 (*0-7933-1232-9*); disk 29.95 (*0-7933-1233-7*) Gallopade Intl.

— Wisconsin Silly Basketball Sportsmysteries, Vol. 2. (Carole Marsh Wisconsin Bks.). (Illus.). (J). 1994. pap. 19.95 (*0-7933-2292-8*); lib. bdg. 29.95 (*0-7933-2291-X*); disk 29.95 (*0-7933-2293-6*) Gallopade Intl.

— Wisconsin Silly Football Sportsmysteries, Vol. 1. (Carole Marsh Wisconsin Bks.). (Illus.). (J). 1994. pap. 19.95 (*0-7933-2271-5*); lib. bdg. 29.95 (*0-7933-2270-7*); disk 29.95 (*0-7933-2272-3*) Gallopade Intl.

— Wisconsin Silly Football Sportsmysteries, Vol. 2. (Carole Marsh Wisconsin Bks.). (Illus.). (J). 1994. pap. 19.95 (*0-7933-2274-X*); lib. bdg. 29.95 (*0-7933-2273-1*); disk 29.95 (*0-7933-2275-8*) Gallopade Intl.

— Wisconsin Silly Trivia! (Carole Marsh Wisconsin Bks.). (Illus.). (J). 1994. pap. 19.95 (*0-7933-2263-4*); lib. bdg. 29.95 (*0-7933-2262-6*); disk 29.95 (*0-7933-2264-2*) Gallopade Intl.

— Wisconsin Spelling Bee! Score Big by Correctly Spelling Our State's Unique Names. (Carole Marsh Wisconsin Bks.). (Illus.). (YA). (gr. 3-12). 1996. pap. 19.95 (*0-7933-6788-3*); lib. bdg. 29.95 (*0-7933-6787-5*) Gallopade Intl.

— Wisconsin Timeline: A Chronology of Wisconsin History, Mystery, Trivia, Legend, Lore & More. (Wisconsin Bks.). (Illus.). (J). (gr. 3-12). 1994. pap. 19.95 (*0-7933-6023-4*); lib. bdg. 29.95 (*0-7933-6022-6*); disk 29.95 (*0-7933-6024-2*) Gallopade Intl.

— Wisconsin 2000! Coming Soon to a Calendar Near You - The 21st Century! - Complete Set of AL 2000 Items. (Two Thousand! Ser.). (Illus.). (J). (gr. 3-12). 1998. pap. 75.00 (*0-7933-9407-4*); lib. bdg. 85.00 (*0-7933-9408-2*) Gallopade Intl.

— Wisconsin 2000! Coming Soon to a Calendar near You--The 21st Century! (Two Thousand! Ser.). (Illus.). (J). (gr. 3-12). 1998. pap. 19.95 (*0-7933-8823-6*); lib. bdg. 29.95 (*0-7933-8822-8*) Gallopade Intl.

— Wisconsin UFO's & Extraterrestrials! A Look at the Sightings & Science in Our State. (Carole Marsh Wisconsin Bks.). (Illus.). (J). (gr. 3-12). 1997. pap. 19.95 (*0-7933-6482-5*); lib. bdg. 29.95 (*0-7933-6481-7*) Gallopade Intl.

M

An Asterisk (*) at the beginning of an entry indicates that the title is appearing for the first time.

***Marsh, Carole.** Wisconsin's BIG Activity Book. (Wisconsin Experience! Ser.). (Illus.). (J). (gr. k-5). 2000. pap. 9.95 (0-7933-9542-9) Gallopade Intl.

Marsh, Carole. Wisconsin's (Most Devastating!) Disasters & (Most Calamitous!) Catastrophies! (Carole Marsh Wisconsin Bks.). (Illus.). (J). 1994. pap. 19.95 (0-7933-1222-1); lib. bdg. 29.95 (0-7933-1223-X); disk 29.95 (0-7933-1224-8) Gallopade Intl.

— Wisconsin's Unsolved Mysteries (& Their "Solutions") Includes Scientific Information & Other Activities for Students. (Wisconsin Bks.). (Illus.). (J). (gr. 3-12). 1994. pap. 19.95 (0-7933-5870-1); lib. bdg. 29.95 (0-7933-5869-8); disk 29.95 (0-7933-5871-X) Gallopade Intl.

***Marsh, Carole.** The Wonderful Wisconsin Coloring Book. (Wisconsin Experience! Ser.). (Illus.). (J). (gr. k-5). 2000. pap. 3.95 (0-7933-9543-7) Gallopade Intl.

Marsh, Carole. World's Fair Fun Trivia Book. (Quantum Leap Ser.). (Illus.). (Orig.). (J). (gr. 4 up). 1994. pap. 19.95 (0-935326-06-5) Gallopade Intl.

— Worlds Fair Kit S. P. A. R. K. (S. P. A. R. K. Ser.). (Illus.). (Orig.). (J). (gr. 3-12). 1994. pap. 19.95 (0-935326-85-5) Gallopade Intl.

— Write Your Own Sports Mystery. (Carole Marsh Bks.). (Illus.). (Orig.). (J). (gr. 3-12). 1994. pap. 19.95 (0-935326-11-1) Gallopade Intl.

— The Writer's Plan: Reproducible Forms to Organize Your Writing for Pleasure & Profit. (Lifewrite Ser.). (Orig.). 1994. pap. 19.95 (1-55609-951-7); lib. bdg. 24.95 (1-55609-950-9); ring bd. 39.95 (1-55609-952-5); Apple II 29.95 (1-55609-953-3) Gallopade Intl.

— Wyoming & Other State Greats (Biographies) (Carole Marsh Wyoming Bks.). (Illus.). (J). 1994. pap. 19.95 (0-7933-2313-4); lib. bdg. 29.95 (0-7933-2312-6); disk 29.95 (0-7933-2314-2) Gallopade Intl.

— Wyoming Bandits, Bushwackers, Outlaws, Crooks, Devils, Ghosts, Desperadoes & Other Assorted & Sundry Characters! (Carole Marsh Wyoming Bks.). (Illus.). (J). 1994. pap. 19.95 (0-7933-1249-3); lib. bdg. 29.95 (0-7933-1250-7); disk 29.95 (0-7933-1251-5) Gallopade Intl.

— Wyoming "BIO" Bingo! 24 Must Know State People for Kid to Learn about While Having Fun! (Bingo! Ser.). (Illus.). (J). (gr. 2-8). 1998. pap. 14.95 (0-7933-8672-1) Gallopade Intl.

— The Wyoming Bookstore Book: A Surprising Guide to Our State's Bookstores & Their Specialties for Students, Teachers, Writers & Publishers. (Wyoming Bks.). (Illus.). 1994. pap. 19.95 (0-7933-3006-8); lib. bdg. 29.95 (0-7933-3005-X); disk 29.95 (0-7933-3007-6) Gallopade Intl.

— Wyoming Classic Christmas Trivia: Stories, Recipes, Activities, Legends, Lore & More! (Carole Marsh Wyoming Bks.). (Illus.). (J). 1994. pap. 19.95 (0-7933-1252-3); lib. bdg. 29.95 (0-7933-1253-1); disk 29.95 (0-7933-1254-X) Gallopade Intl.

— Wyoming Coastales. (Wyoming Bks.). (J). 1994. lib. bdg. 29.95 (0-7933-7315-8) Gallopade Intl.

— Wyoming Coastales. (Carole Marsh Wyoming Bks.). (Illus.). (J). 1994. pap. 19.95 (0-7933-2307-X); lib. bdg. 29.95 (0-7933-2306-1); disk 29.95 (0-7933-2308-8) Gallopade Intl.

— Wyoming "Crinkum-Crankum" A Funny Word Book about Our State. (Wyoming Bks.). (Illus.). (J). (gr. 3-12). 1994. 29.95 (0-7933-4961-3); pap. 19.95 (0-7933-4962-1); disk 29.95 (0-7933-4963-X) Gallopade Intl.

— Wyoming Dingbats! Bk. 1: A Fun Book of Games, Stories, Activities & More about Our State That's All in Code! for You to Decipher, Bk. 1. (Wyoming Bks.). (Illus.). (J). (gr. 3-12). 1994. pap. 19.95 (0-7933-3924-3); lib. bdg. 29.95 (0-7933-3923-5); disk 29.95 (0-7933-3925-1) Gallopade Intl.

— Wyoming Facts & Factivities. (Carole Marsh State Bks.). (Illus.). (J). (gr. 4-7). 1996. pap., teacher ed. 19.95 (0-7933-7947-4, C Marsh) Gallopade Intl.

— Wyoming Festival Fun for Kids! Includes Reproducible Activities for Kids! (Wyoming Bks.). (Illus.). (J). (gr. 3-12). 1994. pap. 19.95 (0-7933-4077-2); lib. bdg. 29.95 (0-7933-4076-4); disk 29.95 (0-7933-4078-0) Gallopade Intl.

— Wyoming "GEO" Bingo! 38 Must Know State Geography Facts for Kids to Learn While Having Fun! (Bingo! Ser.). (Illus.). (J). (gr. 2-8). 1998. pap. 14.95 (0-7933-8673-X) Gallopade Intl.

— Wyoming Government! The Cornerstone of Everyday Life in Our State! (Carole Marsh Wyoming Bks.). (Illus.). (J). (gr. 3-12). 1996. pap. 19.95 (0-7933-6332-2); lib. bdg. 29.95 (0-7933-6331-4); disk 29.95 (0-7933-6333-0) Gallopade Intl.

— Wyoming "HISTO" Bingo! 42 Must Know State History Facts for Kids to Learn While Having Fun! (Bingo! Ser.). (Illus.). (J). (gr. 2-8). 1998. pap. 14.95 (0-7933-8674-8) Gallopade Intl.

— Wyoming History! Surprising Secrets about Our State's Founding Mothers, Fathers & Kids! (Carole Marsh Wyoming Bks.). (Illus.). (J). (gr. 3-12). 1996. pap. 19.95 (0-7933-6179-6); lib. bdg. 29.95 (0-7933-6178-8); disk 29.95 (0-7933-6180-X) Gallopade Intl.

— The Wyoming Hot Air Balloon Mystery. (Carole Marsh Wyoming Bks.). (Illus.). (J). (gr. 2-9). 1994. 29.95 (0-7933-2768-7); pap. 19.95 (0-7933-2769-5); disk 29.95 (0-7933-2770-9) Gallopade Intl.

— Wyoming Hot Zones! Viruses, Diseases, & Epidemics in Our State's History. (Hot Zones! Ser.). (Illus.). (J). (gr. 3-12). 1998. pap. 19.95 (0-7933-8979-8); lib. bdg. 29.95 (0-7933-8978-X) Gallopade Intl.

— Wyoming Indian Dictionary for Kids! (Carole Marsh State Bks.). (J). (gr. 2-9). 1996. 29.95 (0-7933-7794-3, C Marsh); pap. 19.95 (0-7933-7795-1, C Marsh) Gallopade Intl.

— Wyoming Jeopardy! Answers & Questions about Our State! (Wyoming Bks.). (Illus.). (J). (gr. 3-12). 1994. pap. 19.95 (0-7933-4230-9); lib. bdg. 29.95 (0-7933-4229-5); disk 29.95 (0-7933-4231-7) Gallopade Intl.

— Wyoming "Jography" A Fun Run Thru Our State! (Carole Marsh Wyoming Bks.). (Illus.). (J). (gr. 3-12). 1994. pap. 19.95 (1-55609-296-2); lib. bdg. 29.95 (1-55609-295-4); disk 29.95 (1-55609-297-0) Gallopade Intl.

— Wyoming Kid's Cookbook: Recipes, How-To, History, Lore & More. (Carole Marsh Wyoming Bks.). (Illus.). (J). 1994. pap. 19.95 (0-7933-1261-2); lib. bdg. 29.95 (0-7933-1262-0); 29.95 (0-7933-1263-9) Gallopade Intl.

— The Wyoming Library Book: A Surprising Guide to the Unusual Special Collections in Libraries Across Our State for Students, Teachers, Writers & Publishers. (Wyoming Bks.). (Illus.). 1994. pap. 19.95 (0-7933-3156-0); lib. bdg. 29.95 (0-7933-3155-2); disk 29.95 (0-7933-3157-9) Gallopade Intl.

— Wyoming Math! How It All Adds up in Our State. (Carole Marsh Wyoming Bks.). (Illus.). (YA). (gr. 3-12). 1996. pap. 19.95 (0-7933-6638-0); lib. bdg. 29.95 (0-7933-6637-2) Gallopade Intl.

— The Wyoming Media Book: A Surprising Guide to the Amazing Print, Broadcast & Online Media of Our State for Students, Teachers, Writers & Publishers - Includes Reproducible Mailing Labels Plus Activities for Young People! (Wyoming Bks.). (Illus.). 1994. pap. 19.95 (0-7933-3312-1); lib. bdg. 29.95 (0-7933-3311-3); disk 29.95 (0-7933-3313-X) Gallopade Intl.

— The Wyoming Mystery Van Takes Off! Bk. 1: Handicapped Wyoming Kids Sneak Off on a Big Adventure. (Wyoming Bks.). (Illus.). (J). (gr. 3-12). 1994. 29.95 (0-7933-5114-6) Gallopade Intl.

— The Wyoming Mystery Van Takes Off! Bk. 1: Handicapped Wyoming Kids Sneak Off on a Big Adventure, Bk. 1. (Wyoming Bks.). (Illus.). (J). (gr. 3-12). 1994. pap. 19.95 (0-7933-5115-4); disk 29.95 (0-7933-5116-2) Gallopade Intl.

— Wyoming Quiz Bowl Crash Course! (Carole Marsh Wyoming Bks.). (Illus.). (J). 1994. pap. 19.95 (0-7933-2304-5); lib. bdg. 29.95 (0-7933-2303-7); disk 29.95 (0-7933-2305-3) Gallopade Intl.

— Wyoming Rollercoasters! (Wyoming Bks.). (Illus.). (YA). (gr. 3-12). 1994. pap. 19.95 (0-7933-5375-0); lib. bdg. 29.95 (0-7933-5374-2); disk 29.95 (0-7933-5376-9) Gallopade Intl.

— Wyoming School Trivia: An Amazing & Fascinating Look at Our State's Teachers, Schools & Students! (Carole Marsh Wyoming Bks.). (Illus.). (J). 1994. pap. 19.95 (0-7933-1258-2); lib. bdg. 29.95 (0-7933-1259-0); disk 29.95 (0-7933-1260-4) Gallopade Intl.

— Wyoming Silly Basketball Sportsmysteries, Vol. 1. (Carole Marsh Wyoming Bks.). (Illus.). (J). 1994. pap. 19.95 (0-7933-1255-8); lib. bdg. 29.95 (0-7933-1256-6); disk 29.95 (0-7933-1257-4) Gallopade Intl.

— Wyoming Silly Basketball Sportsmysteries, Vol. 2. (Carole Marsh Wyoming Bks.). (Illus.). (J). 1994. pap. 19.95 (0-7933-2316-9); lib. bdg. 29.95 (0-7933-2315-0); disk 29.95 (0-7933-2317-7) Gallopade Intl.

— Wyoming Silly Football Sportsmysteries, Vol. 1. (Carole Marsh Wyoming Bks.). (Illus.). (J). 1994. pap. 19.95 (0-7933-2295-2); lib. bdg. 29.95 (0-7933-2294-4); disk 29.95 (0-7933-2296-0) Gallopade Intl.

— Wyoming Silly Football Sportsmysteries, Vol. 2. (Carole Marsh Wyoming Bks.). (Illus.). (J). 1994. pap. 19.95 (0-7933-2298-7); lib. bdg. 29.95 (0-7933-2297-9); disk 29.95 (0-7933-2299-5) Gallopade Intl.

— Wyoming Silly Trivia. (Carole Marsh Wyoming Bks.). (Illus.). (J). (gr. 3-12). 1994. pap. 19.95 (1-55609-293-8); lib. bdg. 29.95 (1-55609-292-X); disk 29.95 (1-55609-294-6) Gallopade Intl.

— Wyoming Spelling Bee! Score Big by Correctly Spelling Our State's Unique Names. (Carole Marsh Wyoming Bks.). (Illus.). (YA). (gr. 3-12). 1996. pap. 19.95 (0-7933-6791-3); lib. bdg. 29.95 (0-7933-6790-5) Gallopade Intl.

— Wyoming Timeline: A Chronology of Wyoming History, Mystery, Trivia, Legend, Lore & More. (Carole Marsh Wyoming Bks.). (Illus.). (J). (gr. 3-12). 1996. pap. 19.95 (0-7933-6026-9); lib. bdg. 29.95 (0-7933-6025-0); disk 29.95 (0-7933-6027-7) Gallopade Intl.

— Wyoming 2000! Coming Soon to a Calendar near You - The 21st Century! (Two Thousand! Ser.). (Illus.). (J). (gr. 3-12). 1998. pap. 19.95 (0-7933-8826-0); lib. bdg. 29.95 (0-7933-8825-2) Gallopade Intl.

— Wyoming 2000! Coming Soon to a Calendar near You - The 21st Century! - Complete Set of AL 2000 Items. (Two Thousand! Ser.). (Illus.). (J). (gr. 3-12). 1998. pap. 75.00 (0-7933-9409-0); lib. bdg. 85.00 (0-7933-9410-4) Gallopade Intl.

— Wyoming UFO's & Extraterrestrials! A Look at the Sightings & Science in Our State. (Carole Marsh Wyoming Bks.). (Illus.). (J). (gr. 3-12). 1997. pap. 19.95 (0-7933-6485-X); lib. bdg. 29.95 (0-7933-6484-1) Gallopade Intl.

— Wyoming's (Most Devastating!) Disasters & (Most Calamitous!) Catastrophies! (Carole Marsh Wyoming Bks.). (Illus.). (J). 1994. pap. 19.95 (0-7933-1246-9); lib. bdg. 29.95 (0-7933-1247-7); disk 29.95 (0-7933-1248-5) Gallopade Intl.

— Wyoming's Unsolved Mysteries (& Their "Solutions") Includes Scientific Information & Other Activities for Students. (Wyoming Bks.). (Illus.). (J). (gr. 3-12). 1994. pap. 19.95 (0-7933-5873-6); lib. bdg. 29.95 (0-7933-5872-8); disk 29.95 (0-7933-5874-4) Gallopade Intl.

— Yes, You Have to Wipe Your Feet! White House Trivia. (Quantum Leap Ser.). (J). 1994. pap. text 19.95 (0-7933-6872-3); lib. bdg. 29.95 (0-7933-6873-1); disk 29.95 (0-7933-6874-X) Gallopade Intl.

— You'd Betters: The Rule Writers Break That Keep Them from Getting Published - (And How to Stop!) (Lifewrite Ser.). 1994. 29.95 (1-55609-346-2); pap. 19.95 (1-55609-347-0); disk 29.95 (1-55609-600-3) Gallopade Intl.

— You'd Betters: The Rules Writers Break That Keep Them from Getting Published - (And How to Stop!) (Lifewrite Ser.). 1997. ring bd. 39.95 (1-55609-348-9) Gallopade Intl.

Marsh, Catherine. Exploring Data: An Introduction to Data Analysis for Social Scientists. (Illus.). 300p. 1989. pap. 43.95 (0-7456-0172-3) Blackwell Pubs.

— The Survey Method: The Contribution of Surveys to Sociological Explanation. (Contemporary Social Research Ser.: No. 6). 272p. (C). 1982. pap. text 19.95 (0-04-310015-5) Routledge.

Marsh, Charles. God's Long Summer: Stories of Faith & Civil Rights. LC 97-10668. x, 276 p. 1997. 24.95 (0-691-02134-1, Pub. by Princeton U Pr) Cal Prin Full Svc.

***Marsh, Charles.** God's Long Summer: Stories of Faith & Civil Rights. 1999. pap. 15.95 (0-691-02940-7, Pub. by Princeton U Pr) Cal Prin Full Svc.

Marsh, Charles. Reclaiming Dietrich Bonhoeffer: The Promise of His Theology. 216p. 1996. reprint ed. pap. 17.95 (0-19-511144-3) OUP.

Marsh, Charles, jt. auth. see Guth, David W.

Marsh, Charles, jt. ed. see Floyd, Wayne W.

Marsh, Charles S. People of the Shining Mountains: The Utes of Colorado. LC 81-21032. (Illus.). 190p. 1982. pap. 12.95 (0-87108-613-1) Pruett.

Marsh, Christina. Angels in Cross Stitch. (Illus.). 1999. pap. 6.95 (1-85391-716-8) Tuttle Pubng.

***Marsh, Christina.** Country Cross Stitch. 1999. write for info. (1-85391-555-6) J B Fairfax Pr.

Marsh, Christina. Cross Stitch Flower Gardens: From 2 Hours to 2 Weeks. LC 98-228266. 128p. 1998. 24.95 (0-7153-0611-1, Pub. by D & C Pub) Sterling.

Marsh, Christine, jt. auth. see Duncan, Mary.

***Marsh, Christopher.** Making Russian Democracy Work: Social Capital, Economic Development & Democratization. LC 00-29227. (Studies in Russian History: Vol. 4). 202p. 2000. lib. bdg. 89.95 (0-7734-7803-5) E Mellen.

Marsh, Christopher. Popular Religion in Sixteenth-Century England: Holding Their Peace. LC 97-30787. (Social History in Perspective Ser.). 288p. 1998. pap. 19.95 (0-312-21094-9); text. write for info. (0-312-21093-0) St Martin.

Marsh, Christopher C. The Theory & Practice of Bank Book-Keeping & Joint Stock Accounts: Exemplified & Elucidated in a Complete Set of Bank Account Books. Brief, Richard P., ed. LC 77-87278. (Development of Contemporary Accounting Thought Ser.). 1978. reprint ed. lib. bdg. 30.95 (0-405-10906-7) Ayer.

Marsh, Clay B. & Mazzaferri, Ernest L. Internal Medicine Pearls. Sahn, Steven A. & Heffner, John E., eds. (Illus.). 276p. (Orig.). 1992. pap. text 49.95 (1-56053-024-3) Hanley & Belfus.

Marsh, Clifton E. Harford County, Maryland Homeless & Shelter Survey: Housing & Shelter in a Community in Transition. LC 95-41224. 250p. (C). 1995. lib. bdg. 39.50 (0-7618-0123-5) U Pr of Amer.

***Marsh, Clifton E.** The Lost-Found Nation of Islam in America. 240p. 2000. pap. 17.95 (1-57886-008-3) Scarecrow Trade.

Marsh, Clifton E. The Lost-Found Nation of Islam in America. 2nd ed. 240p. 2000. 37.50 (0-8108-3089-2) Scarecrow.

Marsh, Clinton M. Evangelism Is... LC 97-25542. 152p. 1998. pap. 15.95 (0-664-50013-7) Geneva Press.

Marsh, Clive. Albrecht Ritschl & the Problem of the Historical Jesus. LC 92-3639. 248p. 1992. lib. bdg. 89.95 (0-7734-9822-2) E Mellen.

Marsh, Clive & Moyise, Steve. Jesus & The Gospels. 128p. (Orig.). 1999. pap. 15.95 (0-304-70487-3) Continuum.

Marsh, Clive & Ortiz, Gaye, eds. Explorations in Theology & Film: Movies & Meaning. LC 97-10393. (Illus.). 300p. 1997. text 66.95 (0-631-20355-9); pap. text 28.95 (0-631-20356-7) Blackwell Pubs.

Marsh, Colin. Producing a National Curriculum: Plans & Paranoia. LC 95-106398. 160p. 1994. pap. 24.95 (1-86373-741-3, Pub. by Allen & Unwin Pty) Paul & Co Pubs.

Marsh, Colin J. Key Concepts for Understanding Curriculum. (Falmer Press Teachers' Library: No. 5). 236p. 1991. pap. 34.95 (0-7507-0009-2, Falmer Pr) Taylor & Francis.

— Key Concepts for Understanding Curriculum. (Falmer Press Teachers' Library: No. 5). 284p. 1991. 71.00 (0-685-50667-3, Falmer Pr); pap. 27.00 (0-685-50668-1, Falmer Pr) Taylor & Francis.

— Key Concepts for Understanding Curriculum. 2nd ed. LC 97-162456. (Falmer Press Teacher's Library). 272p. 1996. pap. 29.95 (0-7507-0587-6, Falmer Pr) Taylor & Francis.

— Management, Planning & Ideology Vol. 2: Key Concepts for Understanding Curriculum. LC 97-162456. 344p. 1997. pap. 34.95 (0-7507-0663-5, Falmer Pr) Taylor & Francis.

Marsh, Colin J. & Goodson, Ivor. Studying School Subjects: A Guide. LC 97-118307. 176p. 1996. 79.95 (0-7507-0588-4, Falmer Pr); pap. 27.95 (0-7507-0589-2, Falmer Pr) Taylor & Francis.

Marsh, Colin J. & Morris, Paul, eds. Curriculum Development in East Asia. 250p. 1991. 75.00 (1-85000-685-7, Falmer Pr); pap. 34.95 (1-85000-686-5, Falmer Pr) Taylor & Francis.

Marsh, Cynthia. File on Gorky. 96p. 1993. pap. 14.95 (0-413-65060-X, A0686, Methuen Drama) Methn.

Marsh, D. Americas' 25 Favorite Praises. 1995. pap. 6.95 (0-7601-0039-X) Brentwood Music.

— Applied Geometry for Computer Graphics & CAD. LC 99-29057. xii, 304p. 1999. pap. text 39.95 (1-85233-080-5, Pub. by Spr-Verlag) Spr-Verlag.

— Called to Go. 1994. pap. 7.00 (1-55897-809-7) Brentwood Music.

— It Took a Miracle. 1996. pap. 6.95 (0-7601-0567-7) Brentwood Music.

— Let Us Worship. 1993. pap. 6.95 (1-55897-498-9) Brentwood Music.

— Mass Choir Praise. 1994. pap. 6.95 (1-55897-768-6) Brentwood Music.

— Mission Possible. 1997. pap. 7.00 (0-7601-1523-0) Brentwood Music.

Marsh, D. W. Marsh Genealogy, Giving Several Thousand Descendants of John Marsh of Hartford, Connecticut, 1636-1895. (Illus.). 585p. 1989. reprint ed. pap. 87.60 (0-8328-0853-9); reprint ed. lib. bdg. 95.60 (0-8328-0852-0) Higginson Bk Co.

Marsh, D. W., ed. see Hitchcock, E., Sr.

Marsh, Dale. A Liberating Life from Silence. LC 97-61157. 224p. 1997. pap. 13.25 (1-57921-041-4) WinePress Pub.

— The Way of the Painter. 64p. (C). 1990. 100.00 (0-86439-071-8, Pub. by Boolarong Pubns) St Mut.

Marsh, Dale M. The Facilitator. LC 97-60420. (Illus.). 192p. (Orig.). 1997. pap. 12.25 (1-57921-010-4) WinePress Pub.

— A Matter of Convenience. LC 97-60421. 192p. (Orig.). 1997. pap. 12.25 (1-57921-011-2) WinePress Pub.

Marsh, Dave. Before I Get Old: The Story of the Who. (Illus.). 592p. 1983. pap. 10.95 (0-312-07155-8) St Martin.

— Elvis. (Illus.). 256p. 1983. mass mkt. 14.95 (0-446-37219-6, Pub. by Warner Bks) Little.

— Elvis. 2nd ed. LC 98-195112. (Illus.). 248p. 1997. reprint ed. pap. 18.95 (1-56025-118-2, Thunders Mouth) Avalon NY.

— Glory Days. 3rd ed. LC 98-172488. (Illus.). 478p. 1996. pap. 14.95 (1-56025-101-8, Thunders Mouth) Avalon NY.

— The Heart of Rock & Soul: The 1001 Greatest Singles Ever Made. LC 98-49456. 754p. 1999. reprint ed. mass mkt. 19.95 (0-306-80901-X, Pub. by Da Capo) HarpC.

— Louie, Louie: The History & Myth. (Illus.). 256p. (J). 1993. 19.45 (1-56282-865-7, Pub. by Hyperion) Time Warner.

— Louie, Louie: The History & Myth. (Illus.). 256p. (J). 1994. pap. 12.45 (0-7868-8028-7, Pub. by Hyperion) Time Warner.

— Sam & Dave: An Oral History. LC 97-94614. (For the Record Ser.). 128p. 1998. pap. 11.00 (0-380-79375-X, Avon Bks) Morrow Avon.

***Marsh, Dave, ed.** For the Record: George Clinton & P-Funk, Bk. 5. LC 98-158471. (For the Record Ser.: No. 5). 128p. 1998. pap. 12.00 (0-380-79378-4, Avon Bks) Morrow Avon.

— For the Record: Sly & the Family Stone, Bk. 4. LC 98-158552. (For the Record Ser.: No. 4). 128p. 1998. pap. 12.00 (0-380-79377-6, Avon Bks) Morrow Avon.

— For the Record: Women of Motown, Bk. 6. LC 98-158560. (For the Record Ser.: No. 6). 208p. 1998. pap. 12.00 (0-380-79379-2, Avon Bks) Morrow Avon.

Marsh, Dave & Bernard, James. New Book of Rock Lists: From the Beatles, James Brown & Brand Nubian to Elvis Presley, Prince, Pearl Jam & Public Enemy, All You'd Ever Want to Know about the Music, the People, the Hits & the Misses. 624p. 1994. pap. 15.00 (0-671-78700-4, Fireside) S&S Trade Pap.

Marsh, Dave & Floyd, John. For the Records: Sun Records, an Oral History. LC 97-94612. 208p. 1998. pap. 13.00 (0-380-79373-3, Avon Bks) Morrow Avon.

Marsh, Dave & Goldmark, Kathi K. Great Rock & Roll Joke Book. LC 97-19540. 112p. 1997. pap. 7.95 (0-312-16859-4) St Martin.

Marsh, Dave, jt. ed. see Henley, Don.

Marsh, Dave, ed. see Werner, Craig.

Marsh, David. The Germans: A People at the Crossroads. 364p. 1990. 22.95 (0-685-31269-0) St Martin.

— Leon Battista Alberti, Dinner Pieces: A Translation of the "Intercenales" (Medieval & Renaissance Texts & Studies: Vol. 45).Tr. of Intercenales. (Illus.). 288p. 1987. 25.00 (0-86698-028-8, MR45) MRTS.

— Lights! Camera! Celebrate! Hollywood Birthdays, Bashes & Blowouts. LC 95-32223. (Illus.). 64p. 1995. 16.95 (1-883318-26-2) Angel City Pr.

— Lucian & the Latins: Humor & Humanism in the Early Renaissance. LC 98-25390. (Recentiores Ser.). 248p. 1998. text 49.50 (0-472-10846-8, 10846) U of Mich Pr.

— The New Politics of British Trade Unionism: Union Power & the Thatcher Legacy. (Cornell International Industrial & Labor Relations Reports: No. 20). 288p. (Orig.). 1992. 45.00 (0-87546-704-0, ILR Press); pap. 17.95 (0-87546-705-9, ILR Press) Cornell U Pr.

Marsh, David, ed. Capital & Politics in Western Europe. (Illus.). 200p. 1983. 35.00 (0-7146-3225-2, Pub. by F Cass Pubs) Intl Spec Bk.

— Comparing Policy Networks. LC 97-43964. (Public Policy & Management Ser.). (Illus.). 226p. 1998. 110.00 (0-335-19647-0); pap. 36.95 (0-335-19646-2) OpUniv Pr.

Marsh, David & Rhodes, R. A., eds. Policy Networks in British Government. (Illus.). 320p. 1992. 75.00 (0-19-827852-7) OUP.

Marsh, David, et al. Postwar British Politics in Perspective. LC 98-47771. 300p. 1999. 59.95 (0-7456-2029-9); pap. 29.95 (0-7456-2030-2) Blackwell Pubs.

Marsh, David, jt. auth. see Hay, Colin.

Marsh, David, ed. see Gamble, Andrew.

Marsh, David, tr. see Vico, Giambattista.

M

Marsh, David C. The Welfare State: Concept & Development. 2nd ed. LC 79-41439. (Aspects of Modern Sociology: the Social Structure of Modern Britain Ser.). 120p. reprint ed. pap. 37.20 (*0-608-17291-X*, 203032900068) Bks Demand.

Marsh, David D., ed. Preparing Your Schools for the 21st Century: ASCD 1999 Yearbook. 228p. (Orig.). 1999. pap. 20.95 (*0-87120-335-9*, 199000) ASCD.

Marsh, David D., et al. The New American High School. LC 98-9079. (One-Off Ser.). 240p. 1998. pap. 24.95 (*0-8039-6226-6*); lib. bdg. 55.95 (*0-8039-6225-8*, 2795) Corwin Pr.

***Marsh, David E.** PRINCE Companion: Project & Team Manager. 212p. 1998. 70.00 (*0-11-702296-9*, Pub. by Statnry Office) Balogh.

— PRINCE Companion: Project Assurance Function. 200p. 1998. 70.00 (*0-11-702297-7*, Pub. by Statnry Office) Balogh.

— PRINCE Companion: Project Board Member. 203p. 1998. 70.00 (*0-11-702295-0*, Pub. by Statnry Office) Balogh.

Marsh, Derek, ed. Handbook of Lipid Bilayers. 400p. 1990. lib. bdg. 180.95 (*0-8493-3255-9*, QP751) CRC Pr.

Marsh, Diane T. Families & Mental Illness: New Directions in Professional Practice. LC 91-33605. 288p. 1992. 55.00 (*0-275-94018-7*, C4018, Praeger Pubs) Greenwood.

— Families & Mental Retardation: New Directions in Professional Practice. LC 91-38306. 272p. 1992. 59.95 (*0-275-94014-4*, C4014, Praeger Pubs) Greenwood.

— Serious Mental Illness & the Family: The Practitioner's Guide. LC 98-9521. (Couples & Family Dynamics & Treatment Ser.). 374p. 1998. 55.00 (*0-471-18180-3*) Wiley.

Marsh, Diane T., ed. New Directions in the Psychological Treatment of Serious Mental Illness. LC 93-23930. 224p. 1993. 67.95 (*0-275-94428-X*, C4428, Praeger Pubs) Greenwood.

Marsh, Diane T. & Dickens, Rex M. How to Cope with Mental Illness in Your Family: A Guide for Siblings & Offspring. LC 98-12327. 240p. 1998. reprint ed. pap. 13.95 (*0-87477-923-5*, Tarcher Putnam) Putnam Pub Group.

Marsh, Diane T. & Magee, Richard D., eds. Ethical & Legal Issues in Professional Practice with Families. LC 96-46318. 322p. 1997. 69.50 (*0-471-13458-9*) Wiley.

Marsh, Diann. Corona: The Circle City. Parks, Lori, ed. LC 97-78263. (Illus.). 250p. 1998. 39.95 (*1-886483-15-9*) Heritge Media.

— Huntington Beach: The Gem of the South Coast. Parks, Lori M., ed. LC 97-78260. (Illus.). 1999. 39.95 (*1-886483-20-5*) Heritge Media.

— Santa Ana: An Illustrated History, 125th Anniversary Edition. 125th anniversary ed. Parks, Lori, ed. LC 94-79341. (Illus.). 250p. 1994. pap. 19.95 (*1-886483-02-7*) Heritge Media.

Marsh, Diann, jt. auth. see Orton, Charles W.

Marsh, Don. Calligraphy. (First Steps Ser.). (Illus.). 128p. 1996. pap. 18.99 (*0-89134-666-X*, North Lght Bks) F & W Pubns Inc.

— 101 Things You Can Teach Your Kids about Baseball: Actually There's at Least 367 of Them. (Illus.). 120p. (Orig.). 1995. pap. text 9.95 (*0-9647420-9-8*) Campbell Marsh Commun.

— 101 Things You Can Teach Your Kids about Baseball: Actually There's at Least 427 of Them. 2nd ed. (Illus.). 136p. (Orig.). (J). (gr. 1-12). 1998. pap. 9.95 (*0-9647420-4-7*, Pub. by Campbell Marsh Commun) IPG Chicago.

Marsh, Donald F., contrib. by. The Gospel Pianist: 25 Hymn Embellishments for Worship. 64p. 1999. pap. 12.95 (*0-687-07344-8*) Abingdon.

Marsh, Donald J. Renal Physiology. LC 83-11117. (Illus.). 163p. 1983. reprint ed. pap. 50.60 (*0-7837-7516-4*, 204698900005) Bks Demand.

Marsh-Dorward, Doreen. Morel Mushrooms of the Wood River Valley. (Illus.). 8p. (Orig.). 1996. pap. 4.75 (*0-9615729-3-0*) Dorward Photo.

Marsh, Dottie, jt. auth. see Hanft, Barbara.

Marsh, E., jt. auth. see Brooks, T.

Marsh, E. G. The Old Man. 1990. reprint ed. pap. 4.99 (*0-88019-265-8*) Schmul Pub Co.

Marsh, E. L. History of the County of Grey. (Illus.). 487p. 1999. reprint ed. lib. bdg. 52.00 (*0-8328-9816-3*) Higginson Bk Co.

Marsh, Edward, tr. see Fromentin, Eugene.

Marsh, Elias J. Sands of Yesteryear: Arabia Petraea. (Transactions of the Connecticut Academy of Arts & Sciences Ser.: Vol. 52, Pt. 1). 104p. 1994. pap. 16.00 (*1-878508-08-3*) CT Acad Arts & Sciences.

Marsh, Ellen T. Bed & Breakfast. (Special Edition Ser.). 1995. per. 3.75 (*0-373-09978-9*, 1-09978-7) Silhouette.

— A Doctor in the House. (Special Edition Ser.: No. 1110). 1997. per. 3.99 (*0-373-24110-0*, 1-24110-8) Silhouette.

— If This Be Magic. 1990. mass mkt. 4.95 (*0-446-35405-8*, Pub. by Warner Bks) Little.

— Promise Me Paradise. 400p. 1998. mass mkt. 5.99 (*0-8439-4426-9*, Leisure Bks) Dorchester Pub Co.

— Silk & Splendor. 432p. 1986. pap. 3.95 (*0-380-89677-X*, Avon Bks) Morrow Avon.

— Tame the Wild Heart. 448p. 1988. mass mkt. 3.95 (*0-380-75219-0*, Avon Bks) Morrow Avon.

***Marsh, Ellen Tanner.** The Enchanted Prince. 448p. 2000. pap. 5.99 (*0-505-52390-6*, Love Spell) Dorchester Pub Co.

Marsh, F. E. 1000 Bible Study Outlines. LC 75-125115. 496p. 1970. pap. 17.99 (*0-8254-3247-2*) Kregel.

— Why Did Christ Die? LC 85-18093. Orig. Title: The Greatest Theme in the World. 208p. 1985. reprint ed. pap. 10.99 (*0-8254-3249-9*) Kregel.

Marsh, Frank H. & Yarborough, Mark. Medicine & Money: A Study of the Role of Beneficence in Health Care Cost Containment, 30. LC 90-2718. (Contributions in Medical Studies: No. 30). 184p. 1990. 52.95 (*0-313-26357-4*, MMM/, Greenwood Pr) Greenwood.

Marsh, Frank H., jt. auth. see Abel, Charles F.

Marsh, G. Alex & Bane, Leni L. Life along the Mangrove Shore: A Guide to Common Estuarine Plants & Animals of Southern Florida. (Orig.). 1995. pap. 9.95 (*0-912451-31-9*) Florida Classics.

Marsh, G. Barrie. Employer & Employee. (C). 1981. 210.00 (*0-7219-0741-5*, Pub. by Scientific) St Mut.

Marsh, G. E., ed. The Local Plan Inquiry: The Role in Local Plan Preparation, Vol. 19/2. (Illus.). 80p. 1983. pap. 22.00 (*0-08-030442-7*, Pergamon Pr) Elsevier.

Marsh, G. N. Efficient Care in General Practice: How to Look after Even More Patients. (Oxford General Practice Ser.: No. 21). (Illus.). 176p. 1991. 32.50 (*0-19-261953-5*) OUP.

Marsh, G. N., ed. Modern Obstetrics in General Practice. (Oxford General Practice Ser.: No. 9). (Illus.). 1986. pap. 29.95 (*0-19-261419-3*) OUP.

Marsh, G. P. The Origin & History of the English Language. 1972. 59.95 (*0-8490-0774-7*) Gordon Pr.

Marsh, Geoffrey & Renfrew, Mary, eds. Community-Based Maternity Care. LC 98-21742. (Oxford General Practice Ser.). (Illus.). 512p. 1998. pap. text 68.50 (*0-19-262768-6*) OUP.

Marsh, Geoffrey, jt. ed. see Keithley, Jane.

***Marsh, George.** Britten Norman. (Illus.). 128p. 2000. pap. 18.99 (*0-7524-1729-0*, Pub. by Tempus Pubng) Arcadia Publng.

Marsh, George E., II. Computers: Literacy & Learning: A Primer for Administrators. Herman, Jerry J. & Herman, Janice L., eds. (Road Maps to Success Ser.). 72p. 1993. pap. 14.95 (*0-8039-6073-5*) Corwin Pr.

Marsh, George P. The Earth As Modified by Human Action. (American Environmental Studies). 1976. reprint ed. 36.95 (*0-405-02677-3*) Ayer.

— Earth As Modified by Human Action. LC 74-106906. 1970. reprint ed. 32.00 (*0-403-00198-6*) Scholarly.

— Man & Nature. Lowenthal, David, ed. LC 65-11591. (John Harvard Library). 496p. 1965. pap. 19.50 (*0-674-54452-8*) HUP.

Marsh, Graham. Blue Note 2: The Album Cover Art. LC 97-227946. 111p. 1997. pap. text 24.95 (*0-8118-1853-5*) Chronicle Bks.

Marsh, Graham, ed. Blue Note: The Album Cover Art. (Illus.). 112p. (Orig.). 1991. pap. 24.95 (*0-8118-0036-9*) Chronicle Bks.

Marsh, Graham & Callingham, Glyn. California Cool. (GER., Illus.). 128p. 1995. 40.00 incl. 3.5 hd (*3-283-00259-2*) G Olms Pubs.

Marsh, Graham & Callingham, Glyn, eds. California Cool: West Coast Jazz of the 50s & 60s, the Album Cover Art. LC 92-14118. (Illus.). 112p. 1992. pap. 24.95 (*0-8118-0275-2*) Chronicle Bks.

Marsh, Graham & Lewis, Barrie, eds. The Blues: Album Cover Art. 112p. 1996. pap. 24.95 (*0-8118-1168-9*) Chronicle Bks.

Marsh, Graham, jt. ed. see Nourmand, Tony.

Marsh, Harold, Jr. Marsh's California Corporation Law, 3 vols. 2nd ed. 1981. write for info. (*0-318-65477-6*, H39921) P-H.

Marsh, Harold, Jr. & Finkle, R. Roy. Marsh's California Corporation Law, 4 vols. 3rd ed. 4166p. ring bd. 457.00 (*0-13-559014-0*, 55901) Aspen Law.

— Marsh's California Corporation Law, 4 vols., Set. 3rd ed. 3730p. 1990. ring bd. 435.00 (*0-13-564626-X*) Aspen Law.

Marsh, Harold W. & Volk, Robert H. Practice under the California Corporate Securities Laws, 3 vols. 1972. 580.00 (*0-8205-1552-3*) Bender.

Marsh, Harry M., jt. auth. see Marsh, Matthew E.

***Marsh, Helen & Marsh, Tim.** The Burned Deed Index, 1852-1861. 438p. 1999. 42.50 (*0-89308-526-X*) Southern Hist Pr.

Marsh, Helen C. & Marsh, Timothy R. Cemetery Records of Bedford County, Tennessee. rev. ed. (Illus.). 352p. 1986. pap. 25.00 (*0-89308-569-3*, TN 91) Southern Hist Pr.

— Davidson County, Tennessee, Wills & Inventories, 1784-1817, Vol. 1. 272p. 1990. 37.50 (*0-89308-644-4*, TN 117) Southern Hist Pr.

— Davidson County, Tennessee, Wills & Inventories, 1817-1830, Vol. 2. 272p. 1989. 37.50 (*0-89308-665-7*, TN 118) Southern Hist Pr.

— Earliest County Court Records of Bedford County, Tennessee. 184p. 1986. pap. 22.50 (*0-89308-568-5*, TN 90) Southern Hist Pr.

— Land Deed Genealogy of Bedford County, Tennessee. (Illus.). 484p. 1987. 40.00 (*0-89308-610-X*, TN 105) Southern Hist Pr.

— Tennesseans in Texas: As Found in the 1850 Census of Texas. 416p. 1986. 37.50 (*0-89308-561-8*, TN 94) Southern Hist Pr.

Marsh, Helen Crawford & Marsh, Timothy Richard. Land Deed Genealogy of Hancock County, Georgia. LC 97-167563. 1997. write for info. (*0-89308-662-2*) Southern Hist Pr.

Marsh, Henry. Breakthrough Factor. LC 97-12478. 272p. 1997. 22.50 (*0-684-81425-0*) S&S Trade.

— The Breakthrough Factor: Creating Success & Happiness Through a Life of Value. 272p. 1998. pap. 13.00 (*0-684-84798-1*, Fireside) S&S Trade Pap.

Marsh, Henry F., jt. auth. see Cadbury, Warder H.

Marsh, Hugh L., jt. auth. see Swanson, G. A.

Marsh, Hugo. Miller's Antiques Checklist: Toys & Games. (Illus.). 192p. 1995. 14.95 (*1-85732-273-8*, Pub. by Millers Pubns) Antique Collect.

Marsh, Ian. Beyond the Two Party System: Political Representation, Economic Competitiveness & Australian Politics. (Reshaping Australian Institutions Ser.: Vol. 1). (Illus.). 423p. (C). 1995. text 69.95 (*0-521-46223-1*) Cambridge U Pr.

***Marsh, Ian.** Democracy, Governance & Economic Performance: East & Southeast Asia. LC 99-50732. 1999. pap. 24.95 (*92-808-1039-1*) UN Univ Pr.

Marsh, Ian, et al. Classic & Contemporary Readings in Sociology. LC 98-13328. 400p. (C). 1998. pap. 33.53 (*0-582-32023-2*) Addison-Wesley.

— Making Sense Society. 640p. (C). 1996. pap. text 32.75 (*0-582-22895-6*, Pub. by Addison-Wesley) Longman.

Marsh, Ian, jt. auth. see MacDonald, Ronald.

Marsh, Ian A. Policy Making in a Three-Party System Committees, Coalitions & Parliament. 256p. 1986. text 57.50 (*0-416-92090-X*, 1021) Routledge.

Marsh, Irving T. Best Sports Stories, 34 vols. 989.00 (*0-405-12042-7*) Ayer.

— Best Sports Stories. 1980. 25.95 (*0-405-12027-3*) Ayer.

— Best Sports Stories, 1944. 1980. 25.95 (*0-405-12039-7*) Ayer.

— Best Sports Stories, 1945. 1980. 25.95 (*0-405-12038-9*) Ayer.

— Best Sports Stories, 1947. 1980. 25.95 (*0-405-12037-0*) Ayer.

— Best Sports Stories, 1948. 1980. 25.95 (*0-405-12036-2*) Ayer.

— Best Sports Stories, 1949. 1980. 25.95 (*0-405-12035-4*) Ayer.

— Best Sports Stories, 1950. 1980. 25.95 (*0-405-12034-6*) Ayer.

— Best Sports Stories, 1951. 1980. 25.95 (*0-405-12033-8*) Ayer.

— Best Sports Stories, 1952. 1980. 25.95 (*0-405-12032-X*) Ayer.

— Best Sports Stories, 1953. 1980. 25.95 (*0-405-12031-1*) Ayer.

— Best Sports Stories, 1954. 1980. 25.95 (*0-405-12030-3*) Ayer.

— Best Sports Stories, 1955. 1980. 25.95 (*0-405-12029-X*) Ayer.

— Best Sports Stories, 1956. 1980. 25.95 (*0-405-12028-1*) Ayer.

— Best Sports Stories, 1958. 1980. 25.95 (*0-405-12026-5*) Ayer.

— Best Sports Stories, 1959. 1980. 25.95 (*0-405-12025-7*) Ayer.

— Best Sports Stories, 1960. 1980. 25.95 (*0-405-12074-5*) Ayer.

— Best Sports Stories, 1961. 1980. 25.95 (*0-405-12073-7*) Ayer.

— Best Sports Stories, 1962. 1980. 25.95 (*0-405-12072-9*) Ayer.

— Best Sports Stories, 1963. 1980. 25.95 (*0-405-12071-0*) Ayer.

— Best Sports Stories, 1964. 1980. 25.95 (*0-405-12070-2*) Ayer.

— Best Sports Stories, 1965. 1980. 25.95 (*0-405-12069-9*) Ayer.

— Best Sports Stories, 1966. 1980. 25.95 (*0-405-12068-0*) Ayer.

— Best Sports Stories, 1967. 1980. 25.95 (*0-405-12067-2*) Ayer.

— Best Sports Stories, 1968. 1980. 25.95 (*0-405-12066-4*) Ayer.

— Best Sports Stories, 1969. 1980. 25.95 (*0-405-12065-6*) Ayer.

— Best Sports Stories, 1970. 1980. 25.95 (*0-405-12064-8*) Ayer.

— Best Sports Stories, 1973. 1980. 25.95 (*0-405-12061-3*) Ayer.

— Best Sports Stories, 1974. 1980. 25.95 (*0-405-12060-5*) Ayer.

— Best Sports Stories, 1975. 1980. 25.95 (*0-405-12059-1*) Ayer.

— Best Sports Stories, 1976. 1980. 25.95 (*0-405-12058-3*) Ayer.

— Best Sports Stories, 1978. 1980. 25.95 (*0-405-12872-X*) Ayer.

Marsh, Irving T. & Ehre, Edward. Best Sports Stories, 1977. 1980. 25.95 (*0-405-12871-1*) Ayer.

Marsh, J. B. Story of the Jubilee Singers with Their Songs. rev. ed. LC 72-165509. (Illus.). reprint ed. 31.50 (*0-404-04189-2*) AMS Pr.

Marsh, James. The Remains of the Rev. James Marsh, D.D., Late President, & Professor of Moral & Intellectual Philosophy, in the University of Vermont: With a Memoir of His Life. (American Biography Ser.). 642p. 1991. reprint ed. lib. bdg. 109.00 (*0-7812-8269-1*) Rprt Serv.

Marsh, James, et al, eds. Modernity & Its Discontents. LC 91-46765. xiv, 219p. 1992. 32.50 (*0-8232-1344-7*); pap. 19.95 (*0-8232-1345-5*) Fordham.

Marsh, James, intro. Selected Works of James Marsh, 3 vols. LC 76-42199. 2400p. 1976. lib. bdg. 200.00 (*0-8201-1275-5*) Schol Facsimiles.

Marsh, James, tr. see Herder, Johann G.

Marsh, James A. & Kendall, Marion D., eds. The Physiology of Immunity. 464p. 1996. boxed set 139.95 (*0-8493-8033-2*) CRC Pr.

Marsh, James B. Four Years in the Rockies: or The Adventures of Isaac P. Rose. LC 72-9459. (Far Western Frontier Ser.). 266p. 1973. reprint ed. 23.95 (*0-405-04987-0*) Ayer.

Marsh, James B., ed. Resources & Environment in Asia's Marine Sector. 504p. 1992. 150.00 (*0-8448-1708-2*) Taylor & Francis.

Marsh, James G. & Olsen, Johan P. Rediscovering Institutions: The Organizational Basis of Politics. 1989. 32.95 (*0-02-920115-2*) Free Pr.

***Marsh, James H.** The Canadian Encyclopedia: Complete, Unabridged, Expanded, Updated Year 2000 Edition. (Illus.). 2640p. 2000. 64.95 (*0-7710-2099-6*) McCland & Stewart.

Marsh, James L. Critique, Action, & Liberation. LC 93-48999. (SUNY Series in the Philosophy of the Social Sciences). 431p. (C). 1994. text 74.50 (*0-7914-2169-4*); pap. text 24.95 (*0-7914-2170-8*) State U NY Pr.

— Post-Cartesian Meditations: An Essay in Dialectical Phenomenology. LC 88-82135. xiii, 279p. 1988. pap. 17.00 (*0-8232-1217-3*) Fordham.

— Process, Praxis, & Transcendence. LC 98-16746. (SUNY Series in the Philosophy of the Social Sciences). 384p. (C). 1999. text 73.50 (*0-7914-4073-7*); pap. text 24.95 (*0-7914-4074-5*) State U NY Pr.

— Radical Fragments. LC 91-27578. (New Studies in Aesthetics: Vol. 9). 313p. (C). 1992. text 55.95 (*0-8204-1589-8*) P Lang Pubng.

***Marsh, Jan.** Bloomsbury Women. 1999. pap. 17.95 (*1-85793-956-5*, Pub. by Pavilion Bks Ltd) Trafalgar.

Marsh, Jan. Bloomsbury Women: Distinct Figures in Life & Art. LC 95-79117. (Illus.). 88p. 1995. 29.95 (*0-8050-4550-3*) H Holt & Co.

***Marsh, Jan.** Bloomsbury Women: Distinct Figures in Life & Art. (Illus.). 160p. 2000. reprint ed. pap. 17.95 (*1-86205-450-9*, Pub. by Pavilion Bks Ltd) Trafalgar.

Marsh, Jan. Christina Rossetti. 1999. pap. 9.95 (*0-14-013993-1*, Viking) Viking Penguin.

— The Pre-Raphaelite Sisterhood. (Illus.). 416p. 1995. pap. 19.95 (*0-7043-0169-5*, Pub. by Quartet) Interlink Pub.

— The Pre-Raphaelites: Their Lives in Letters & Diaries. LC 96-220485. (Illus.). 160p. 1997. 24.95 (*1-85585-246-2*, Pub. by Collins & Br) Trafalgar.

Marsh, Jan & Nun, Pamela Gerrish. Pre-Raphaelite Women Artists. LC 98-61449. (Illus.). 157p. 1999. pap. 24.95 (*0-500-28104-1*, Pub. by Thames Hudson) Norton.

Marsh, Jan, ed. see Rossetti, Christina Georgina.

Marsh, Jan, ed. see Rossetti, Dante Gabriel.

Marsh, Jayne D., jt. ed. see Boggis, Carol.

Marsh, Jean. The Family at Castle Trevissa. large type ed. (Dales Large Print Ser.). 281p. 1998. pap. 19.99 (*1-85389-800-7*, Dales) Ulverscroft.

***Marsh, Jean.** Iris. 352p. 2000. 24.95 (*0-312-26182-9*) St Martin.

Marsh, Jean. Love in Hazard. large type ed. (Linford Romance Library). 272p. 1993. pap. 16.99 (*0-7089-7325-6*, Linford) Ulverscroft.

— Mission to Argana. large type ed. (Lythway Ser.). 200p. 1990. 19.95 (*0-7451-1127-0*, G K Hall Lrg Type) Mac Lib Ref.

— Shades of Aphrodite. large type ed. (Linford Romance Library). 272p. 1994. pap. 16.99 (*0-7089-7515-1*, Linford) Ulverscroft.

— The Wayward Heart. large type ed. (Lythway Ser.). 208p. 1991. 21.95 (*0-7451-1275-7*, G K Hall Lrg Type) Mac Lib Ref.

Marsh, Jeanne C., et al. Rape & the Limits of Law Reform. LC 81-20621. 170p. 1982. 45.00 (*0-86569-083-9*, Auburn Hse) Greenwood.

Marsh, Jeffery L., jt. auth. see Childs, Marti.

***Marsh, Jeffrey L.** Critical Decisions in Craniofacial Anomalies. 400p. 2000. boxed set 129.00 incl. cd-rom (*1-55009-072-0*) DEKR.

Marsh, Jennifer, jt. auth. see Pfister, Fred.

Marsh, Jerry, ed. see Breakstone, Steve.

Marsh, Joan. The Truth about Janice Henderson. large type ed. (Linford Romance Library). 240p. 1993. pap. 16.99 (*0-7089-7458-9*) Ulverscroft.

Marsh, Joan & Goode, Jamie, eds. Germline Development: Symposium on Germline Development Held at the Ciba Foundation, London, July 1993. LC 93-50785. (CIBA Foundation Symposium Ser.: Vol. 182). 332p. 1994. 128.00 (*0-471-94264-2*) Wiley.

— The GTPase Superfamily - Symposium No. 176. LC 93-10294. (CIBA Foundation Symposium Ser.: Vol. 176). 304p. 1993. 128.00 (*0-471-93914-5*) Wiley.

Marsh, Joan, jt. ed. see Chadwick, Derek J.

Marsh, John. Cumbrian Railways. 1999. pap. text 19.95 (*0-7509-2043-2*) Sutton Pub Ltd.

— House of Echoes. large type ed. (Dales Large Print Ser.). 341p. 1997. pap. 18.99 (*1-85389-740-X*) Ulverscroft.

***Marsh, John.** John Marsh Journals The Life & Times of a Gentleman Composer, 1752-1828. LC 98-44404. 1998. 76.00 (*0-945193-94-7*) Pendragon NY.

Marsh, John. Marketing, Services & Sales. 89p. 1990. pap. 125.00 (*0-85297-371-3*, Pub. by Chartered Bank) St Mut.

— Monk's Hollow. large type ed. (Dales Large Print Ser.). 293p. 1997. pap. 18.99 (*1-85389-782-5*, Dales) Ulverscroft.

— Sketching Landscapes. 1999. pap. 9.95 (*0-304-35118-0*, Pub. by Cassell) Sterling.

— Sketching Street Scenes. LC 99-494980. (Illus.). 48p. 1999. pap. 9.95 (*0-304-35164-4*, Pub. by Cassell) Sterling.

— A Stake in Tomorrow: World Class Lessons in Business Partnerships. LC 99-216984. 1998. 48.00 (*0-7134-8366-0*, Pub. by B T B) Branford.

Marsh, John H. & De La Rue, Richard M., eds. Waveguide Optoelectronics. LC 92-33757. (NATO Advanced Study Institutes Series E, Applied Sciences: Vol. 226). 1992. text 247.50 (*0-7923-2033-6*) Kluwer Academic.

Marsh, Jon, ed. Christina Rossetti. (Everyman's Poetry Ser.). 116p. 1997. pap. 1.95 (*0-460-87820-4*, Everyman's Classic Lib) Tuttle Pubng.

M

An Asterisk (*) at the beginning of an entry indicates that the title is appearing for the first time.

Marsh, Jonathon P., et al. Humane Interfaces: Questions of Method & Practice in Cognitive Technology. LC 99-19385. (Human Factors in Information Technology Ser.). 406p. 1999. 125.00 (*0-444-82874-5*, North Holland) Elsevier.

Marsh, Jordan. Jordan Marsh Illustrated Catalog of 1891: An Unabridged Reprint. (Illus.). 128p. 1991. pap. 9.95 (*0-486-26738-5*) Dover.

Marsh, Joss. Word Crimes. LC 97-49344. 400p. 1998. pap. text 22.50 (*0-226-50691-6*) U Ch Pr.

***Marsh, Joss.** Word Crimes. LC 97-49344. 400p. 1998. lib. bdg. 55.00 (*0-226-50690-8*) U Ch Pr.

Marsh, Julia A. & Vanston, Lawrence K. Interactive Multimedia & Telecommunications: Forecasts of Markets & Technologies. 143p. 1992. pap. 45.00 (*0-614-18108-9*) Tech Futures.

Marsh, K. J., ed. Full-Scale Fatigue Testing: Components & Structures. (Illus.). 331p. 1988. text 79.95 (*0-408-02244-2*) Buttrwrth-Heinemann.

Marsh, K. N., ed. Recommended Reference Materials for Realization of Physicochemical Properties. 1991. 99.00 (*0-632-01718-X*) CRC Pr.

Marsh, K. N., et al, eds. Transport Properties & Related Thermodynamic Data of Binary Mixtures. (DIPPR Ser.: Vol. 5). (Illus.). 110p. 1998. 75.00 (*0-8169-0735-8*, X-129) Am Inst Chem Eng.

Marsh, K. N. & O'Hare, P. A. Solution Calorimetry Experimental Thermodynamics, Pt. IV. (Illus.). 352p. 1994. 105.00 (*0-86542-852-2*) Blackwell Sci.

Marsh, K. N., jt. auth. see Hall, K. R.

Marsh, K. N., jt. ed. see Hall, K. R.

Marsh, K. N., jt. ed. see Martienssen, W.

Marsh, Kathryn, jt. auth. see Collins, Bonnie J.

***Marsh, Ken.** Breakfast at Trout's Place: The Seasons of an Alaska Flyfisher. LC 99-34213. 192p. 1999. pap. 16.00 (*1-55566-247-1*) Johnson Bks.

Marsh, Ken, ed. Battery Book One: Lead Acid Traction Batteries. LC 81-65733. (Illus.). 72p. (Orig.). 1981. pap. 7.95 (*0-939488-00-0*) Curtis Instruments.

Marsh, Kenneth S., jt. ed. see Brody, Aaron L.

Marsh, L. R., ed. see Stewart, Alvan.

Marsh, Laura. Read Me Like a Book: A Special Book about Me. Adams, Deborah B., ed. (Illus.). 88p. 1997. 29.95 (*0-9652420-9-9*, Perspect Publ) Write Perspect.

Marsh, Lee & Western Historical Society Staff. Weston. (Images of America Ser.). (Illus.). 128p. 1998. pap. 16.99 (*0-7524-0947-6*) Arcadia Publng.

Marsh, Leslie, ed. see Riepe, Jack.

Marsh, Linda. Limericks for All Occasions. 429p. 1999. 24.95 (*1-56649-028-6*); pap. 12.95 (*1-56649-027-8*) Welcome Rain.

Marsh, Lindell L., jt. ed. see Porter, Douglas R.

Marsh-Lockett, Carol P. New Critical Essays on Caribbean Literature: Caliban's Turn. 224p. 1998. 37.00 (*0-8153-3081-2*, H2082) Garland.

Marsh-Lockett, Carol P., ed. Black Women Playwrights: Visions on the American Stage. LC 98-42553. (Studies in Modern Drama: Vol. 11). 240p. 1998. 47.00 (*0-8153-2746-3*, H2051) Garland.

Marsh, Lucius B. & Parker, Harriet F. Bronsdon & Box Families. (Illus.). 332p. 1989. reprint ed. pap. 53.00 (*0-8328-0331-6*); reprint ed. lib. bdg. 63.00 (*0-8328-0330-8*) Higginson Bk Co.

Marsh, Lucy A. Real Property Cases. 440p. 1992. pap. text 26.95 (*0-316-54716-6*, Aspen Law & Bus) Aspen Pub.

— Wills, Trusts & Estates: Practical Applications of the Law. LC 98-173206. 352p. 1998. pap. text 26.95 (*1-56706-769-7*) Panel Pubs.

Marsh, M. N. Coeliac Disease. (Illus.). 384p. 1992. 175.00 (*0-632-03097-6*) Blackwell Sci.

Marsh, M. S., jt. auth. see Stevenson, J. C.

***Marsh, Madaleine, ed.** Miller's Collectable Price Guide 1999-2000. (Illus.). 496p. 1999. 29.95 (*1-84000-128-3*) Millers Pubns.

Marsh, Madeleine. Miller's Collecting the 1930s. (Illus.). 144p. 1997. 26.95 (*1-85732-605-9*, Pub. by Mitchell Beazley) Antique Collect.

***Marsh, Madeleine.** Miller's Collecting the 1960s. 1999. 26.95 (*1-84000-258-1*) Millers Pubns.

Marsh, Madeleine. Miller's Collecting the 1960s. (Illus.). 144p. 1999. 26.95 (*1-84000-081-3*, Pub. by Millers Pubns) Antique Collect.

— Perfume Bottles: A Collector's Guide. (Miller's Collector's Guide Ser.). (Illus.). 64p. 1999. 11.95 (*1-84000-162-3*) Antique Collect.

Marsh, Madeleine, ed. Miller's Collectables Price Guide, 1997-1998. (Antique Collectors' Club Ser.). (Illus.). 496p. 1997. 29.95 (*1-85732-860-4*, Pub. by Mitchell Beazley) Antique Collect.

Marsh, Madeleine, jt. auth. see Miller's Publication Staff.

Marsh, Madeleine, ed. see Harris, Carol.

Marsh, Malcolm, et al, eds. Butterworths Road Traffic Service. ring bd. write for info. (*0-406-99654-7*, BRTSASET, MICHIE) LEXIS Pub.

***Marsh, Margaret.** The Empty Cradle: Infertility in America from Colonial Times to the Present. (Henry E. Sigerist Series in the History of Medicine). 1999. pap. text 17.95 (*0-8018-6176-4*) Johns Hopkins.

Marsh, Margaret. Suburban Lives. LC 89-36060. (Illus.). 230p. (Orig.). (C). 1990. text 35.00 (*0-8135-1483-5*); pap. text 16.00 (*0-8135-1484-3*) Rutgers U Pr.

Marsh, Margaret & Ronner, Wanda. The Empty Cradle: Infertility in America from Colonial Times to the Present. (Henry E. Sigerist Series in the History of Medicine). (Illus.). 344p. (C). 1996. 29.95 (*0-8018-5228-5*) Johns Hopkins.

Marsh, Margaret C. Bankers in Bolivia: A Study in American Foreign Investment. LC 76-99250. reprint ed. 27.50 (*0-404-04190-6*) AMS Pr.

Marsh, Mary T. For Any Young Mother Who Lives in a Shoe. 110p. 1991. pap. 12.00 (*0-8170-1170-6*) Judson.

***Marsh, Matthew.** Linux Networking Unleashed. (Illus.). 1100p. 2000. 49.99 (*0-672-31765-6*) Sams.

***Marsh, Matthew E. & Marsh, Harry M.** California Mechanics' Lien Law, Issue 3. 6th ed. 100p. 1999. ring bd. write for info. (*0-327-01571-3*, 8024314) LEXIS Pub.

Marsh, Matthew E. & Marsh, Harry M. California Mechanics' Lien Law & Construction Industry Practice, 2 vols. 5th ed. 810p. 1995. spiral bd. 185.00 (*1-55943-160-1*, MICHIE) LEXIS Pub.

— California Mechanics' Lien Law & Construction Industry Practice, No. 1. 5th ed. 1991. suppl. ed. 30.50 (*0-685-66102-4*, MICHIE) LEXIS Pub.

— California Mechanics' Lien Law & Construction Industry Practice, No. 2. 5th ed. 1992. suppl. ed. 32.00 (*0-685-66103-2*, MICHIE) LEXIS Pub.

— California Mechanics' Lien Law & Construction Industry Practice, No. 3. 5th ed. 1993. suppl. ed. 36.00 (*0-685-74428-0*, MICHIE) LEXIS Pub.

— California Mechanics' Lien Law Handbook. 4th ed. 290p. 1993. pap. 48.00 (*0-250-47227-9*, MICHIE) LEXIS Pub.

Marsh, Michael. Philosophy of the Inner Light. LC 76-50674, (Orig.). 1976. pap. 4.00 (*0-87574-209-2*) Pendle Hill.

— Reaching Toward God. LC 81-81683. 27p. 1981. pap. 4.00 (*0-87574-237-8*) Pendle Hill.

— The Rudelstein Affair. LC 80-29323. 205p. 1981. 9.95 (*0-918056-02-0*) Ariadne Pr.

Marsh, Michael & Mitchell, Paul, eds. How Ireland Voted, 1997. 336p. 1999. pap. text 65.00 (*0-8133-3217-6*); pap. text 25.00 (*0-8133-3218-4*, Pub. by Westview) HarpC.

Marsh, Michael, jt. ed. see Gallagher, Michael.

***Marsh, Michael N., ed.** Celiac Disease: Methods & Protocols. (Methods in Molecular Medicine Ser.: Vol. 41). 304p. 2000. 99.50 (*0-89603-650-2*) Humana.

Marsh, Michael N., ed. Immunopathology of the Small Intestine. LC 86-5620. (Wiley-Medical Publication). 479p. reprint ed. pap. 148.50 (*0-8357-3471-4*, 203973300013) Bks Demand.

Marsh, Michael S. Carolina Hunting Adventures Quest for the Limit. (Illus.). 262p. (Orig.). 1995. pap. 12.95 (*0-937866-50-4*) Atlantic Pub Co.

Marsh, N. H., et al. Structure & Bonding: Atoms & Molecules in Intense Fields, Vol. 86. (Illus.). 256p. 1996. 149.50 (*3-540-61015-4*) Spr-Verlag.

Marsh, Neville. Fibrinolysis. LC 80-42309. (Wiley-Medical Publication). (Illus.). 270p. reprint ed. pap. 83.70 (*0-8357-6305-6*, 203557800096) Bks Demand.

Marsh, Ngaio. Artists in Crime. (Dead Letter Mysteries Ser.). 1997. mass mkt. 5.50 (*0-312-96359-9*) St Martin.

— Artists in Crime. 1976. reprint ed. lib. bdg. 24.95 (*0-88411-471-6*) Amereon Ltd.

— Black As He's Painted. 256p. 1999. mass mkt. 5.99 (*0-312-97279-2*) St Martin.

— Black As He's Painted. 1976. reprint ed. lib. bdg. 23.95 (*0-88411-472-4*) Amereon Ltd.

— Black As He's Painted. 1994. reprint ed. lib. bdg. 27.95 (*1-56849-307-X*) Buccaneer Bks.

— Clutch of Constables. 1999. mass mkt. 5.99 (*0-312-97084-6*) St Martin.

— Clutch of Constables. 1976. reprint ed. lib. bdg. 22.95 (*0-88411-473-2*) Amereon Ltd.

— Clutch of Constables. 1994. reprint ed. lib. bdg. 27.95 (*1-56849-308-8*) Buccaneer Bks.

— Colour Scheme. 1998. mass mkt. 5.99 (*0-312-96603-2*, Pub. by Tor Bks) St Martin.

— Colour Scheme. 1976. reprint ed. lib. bdg. 24.95 (*0-88411-474-0*) Amereon Ltd.

***Marsh, Ngaio.** Dead Water. 1999. mass mkt. 5.99 (*0-312-96990-2*, Thomas Dunne) St Martin.

Marsh, Ngaio. Dead Water. large type ed. LC 99-33137. 1999. 25.95 (*0-7862-2050-3*) Mac Lib Ref.

***Marsh, Ngaio.** Dead Water. large type ed. 368p. 2000. write for info. (*0-7089-4197-4*) Ulverscroft.

Marsh, Ngaio. Dead Water. 1976. reprint ed. lib. bdg. 23.95 (*0-88411-475-9*) Amereon Ltd.

— Death & the Dancing Footman. (Dead Letter Mysteries Ser.). 1998. mass mkt. 5.99 (*0-312-96428-5*) St Martin.

— Death & the Dancing Footman. 1976. reprint ed. lib. bdg. 27.95 (*0-88411-477-5*) Amereon Ltd.

— Death at the Bar. (Dead Letter Mysteries Ser.). 1998. mass mkt. 5.99 (*0-312-96426-9*) St Martin.

— Death at the Bar. 1976. reprint ed. lib. bdg. 25.95 (*0-88411-476-7*) Amereon Ltd.

— Death in a White Tie. 1997. mass mkt. 5.50 (*0-312-96361-0*) St Martin.

— Death in a White Tie. 1976. reprint ed. lib. bdg. 24.95 (*0-88411-479-1*) Amereon Ltd.

— Death in Ecstasy. (Dead Letter Mysteries Ser.). 1997. mass mkt. 5.50 (*0-312-96360-2*) St Martin.

— Death in Ecstasy. 1976. reprint ed. lib. bdg. 24.95 (*0-88411-478-3*) Amereon Ltd.

— Death of a Fool. 1999. mass mkt. 5.99 (*0-312-96832-9*) St Martin.

— Death of a Fool. 1976. reprint ed. lib. bdg. 23.95 (*0-88411-480-5*) Amereon Ltd.

— Death of a Peer. (Dead Letter Mysteries Ser.). 1998. mass mkt. 5.99 (*0-312-96427-7*) St Martin.

— Death of a Peer. 1976. reprint ed. lib. bdg. 26.95 (*0-88411-481-3*) Amereon Ltd.

— Died in the Wool. 256p. 1994. pap. 5.99 (*0-425-14469-0*, Prime Crime) Berkley Pub.

— Died in the Wool. LC 98-51096. 1999. 26.95 (*0-7862-1772-3*) Thorndike Pr.

— Died in the Wool. 1998. 5.99 (*0-312-96604-0*, Pub. by Tor Bks) St Martin.

— Died in the Wool. 1976. reprint ed. lib. bdg. 22.95 (*0-88411-482-1*) Amereon Ltd.

— Enter a Murderer. 1998. 5.99 (*0-312-96670-9*, Pub. by Tor Bks) St Martin.

— Enter a Murderer. 1976. reprint ed. lib. bdg. 22.95 (*0-88411-483-X*) Amereon Ltd.

— False Scent. 1999. mass mkt. 5.99 (*0-312-96898-1*) St Martin.

— False Scent. 1976. reprint ed. lib. bdg. 23.95 (*0-88411-484-8*) Amereon Ltd.

— Final Curtain. 1998. 5.99 (*0-312-96605-9*, Pub. by Tor Bks) St Martin.

— Final Curtain. 1976. reprint ed. lib. bdg. 26.95 (*0-88411-485-6*) Amereon Ltd.

— Grave Mistake. 1976. 22.95 (*0-8488-0577-1*) Amereon Ltd.

— Hand in Glove. 240p. 1983. pap. 3.99 (*0-515-07502-7*, Jove) Berkley Pub.

— Hand in Glove. 1999. mass mkt. 5.99 (*0-312-96908-2*) St Martin.

— Hand in Glove. 1976. reprint ed. lib. bdg. 22.95 (*0-88411-486-4*) Amereon Ltd.

— Killer Dolphin. 1999. mass mkt. 5.99 (*0-312-97010-2*, St Martins Paperbacks) St Martin.

— Killer Dolphin. 1976. reprint ed. lib. bdg. 25.95 (*0-88411-487-2*) Amereon Ltd.

— Last Ditch. 1976. 23.95 (*0-8488-0578-X*) Amereon Ltd.

***Marsh, Ngaio.** Last Ditch. 288p. 2000. mass mkt. 5.99 (*0-312-97286-5*, St Martins Paperbacks) St Martin.

Marsh, Ngaio. Light Thickens. 1976. 21.95 (*0-8488-0579-8*) Amereon Ltd.

***Marsh, Ngaio.** Light Thickens. 5.99p. 2000. mass mkt. 5.99 (*0-312-97314-4*, Minotaur) St Martin.

Marsh, Ngaio. A Man Lay Dead. lib. bdg. 20.95 (*0-8488-2104-1*) Amereon Ltd.

— A Man Lay Dead. (Dead Letter Mysteries Ser.). 192p. 1997. mass mkt. 5.50 (*0-312-96358-0*) St Martin.

— A Man Lay Dead. 1976. reprint ed. lib. bdg. 21.95 (*0-88411-488-0*) Amereon Ltd.

— New Zealand. 1976. reprint ed. lib. bdg. 24.95 (*0-88411-489-9*) Amereon Ltd.

— Night at the Vulcan. 1998. mass mkt. 5.99 (*0-312-96668-7*) St Martin.

— Night at the Vulcan. 1976. reprint ed. lib. bdg. 24.95 (*0-88411-490-2*) Amereon Ltd.

— The Nursing Home Murder. 240p. 1994. mass mkt. 4.50 (*0-425-14242-6*, Prime Crime) Berkley Pub.

— The Nursing Home Murder. 1999. mass mkt. 5.99 (*0-312-96999-6*) St Martin.

— The Nursing Home Murder. 1976. reprint ed. lib. bdg. 22.95 (*0-88411-491-0*) Amereon Ltd.

— Overture to Death. (Dead Letter Mysteries Ser.). 1998. mass mkt. 5.99 (*0-312-96425-0*) St Martin.

— Overture to Death. 1976. reprint ed. lib. bdg. 24.95 (*0-88411-492-9*) Amereon Ltd.

— Photo Finish. 1976. 21.95 (*0-8488-0580-1*) Amereon Ltd.

***Marsh, Ngaio.** Photo Finish. 224p. 2000. mass mkt. 5.99 (*0-312-97301-2*, St Martins Paperbacks) St Martin.

Marsh, Ngaio. Scales of Justice. 1999. mass mkt. 5.99 (*0-312-96671-7*, Pub. by Tor Bks) St Martin.

— Scales of Justice. 1976. reprint ed. lib. bdg. 24.95 (*0-88411-493-7*) Amereon Ltd.

— Singing in the Shrouds. 1976. reprint ed. lib. bdg. 23.95 (*0-88411-494-5*) Amereon Ltd.

— Singing in the Shrounds. 1999. mass mkt. 5.99 (*0-312-96888-4*) St Martin.

— Spinsters in Jeopardy. 1998. mass mkt. 5.99 (*0-312-96669-5*) St Martin.

— Spinsters in Jeopardy. 1976. reprint ed. lib. bdg. 23.95 (*0-88411-495-3*) Amereon Ltd.

— Surfeit of Lampreys. large type ed. 1983. 15.95 (*0-7089-0990-6*) Ulverscroft.

— Tied up in Tinsel. 1976. reprint ed. lib. bdg. 23.95 (*0-88411-496-1*) Amereon Ltd.

— Vintage Murder. 256p. 1999. mass mkt. 5.99 (*0-312-97179-6*, St Martins Paperbacks) St Martin.

— Vintage Murder. 1976. reprint ed. lib. bdg. 22.95 (*0-88411-497-X*) Amereon Ltd.

— When in Rome. 1976. lib. bdg. 23.95 (*0-88411-498-8*) Amereon Ltd.

— When in Rome. 1999. mass mkt. 5.99 (*0-312-97097-8*, St Martins Paperbacks) St Martin.

— Wreath for Rivera. 1998. mass mkt. 5.99 (*0-312-96606-7*, Pub. by Tor Bks) St Martin.

— A Wreath for Rivera. 1976. reprint ed. lib. bdg. 25.95 (*0-88411-499-6*) Amereon Ltd.

***Marsh, Nicholas.** D. H. Lawrence: The Novels. LC 99-59195. (Analysing Texts Ser.). 2000. pap. 19.95 (*0-312-23286-1*) St Martin.

— D.H. Lawrence: The Novels. LC 99-59195. 2000. text 59.95 (*0-312-23284-5*) St Martin.

Marsh, Nim, ed. see SaintLaurent, Robert D.

Marsh, Norma. The Chocolate Touch: A Study Guide. (Novel-Ties Ser.). (J). (gr. 2-4). 1989. pap. text, teacher ed., student ed. 15.95 (*0-88122-043-4*) Lrn Links.

— Follow My Leader: A Study Guide. Friedland, Joyce & Kessler, Rikki, eds. (Novel-Ties Ser.). 18p. (J). (gr. 5-7). 1990. pap. text 15.95 (*0-88122-403-0*) Lrn Links.

— A Gift for Mama: A Study Guide. (Novel-Ties Ser.). (J). (gr. 2-4). 1989. pap. text, teacher ed., student ed. 15.95 (*0-88122-045-0*) Lrn Links.

— Park's Quest: A Study Guide. Friedland, Joyce & Kessler, Rikki, eds. (Novel-Ties Ser.). (J). (gr. 5-7). 1991. pap. text 15.95 (*0-88122-581-9*) Lrn Links.

— The Pushcart War: A Study Guide. (Novel-Ties Ser.). (J). (gr. 5-7). 1988. pap. text, teacher ed., student ed. 15.95 (*0-88122-095-7*) Lrn Links.

— Sarah, Plain & Tall: A Study Guide. (Novel-Ties Ser.). (J). (gr. 3-5). 1988. pap. text, student ed. 15.95 (*0-88122-063-9*) Lrn Links.

— The Secret Garden: A Study Guide. (Novel-Ties Ser.). (J). (gr. 5-7). 1989. pap. text, teacher ed., student ed. 15.95 (*0-88122-057-4*) Lrn Links.

Marsh, Nory. Start to Finish: Developmentally Sequenced Fine Motor Activities for Preschool Children. Anderson, Kirsteen, ed. LC 98-193659. (Illus.). 213p. 1998. spiral bd. 42.50 (*1-883315-29-8*, 8512) Imaginart Intl.

Marsh, P. D. The Art of Tendering. 160p. 1987. text 61.95 (*0-291-39736-0*, Pub. by Gower) Ashgate Pub Co.

— Contract Negotiation Handbook. 412p. (C). 1984. 475.00 (*0-7855-5747-4*, Pub. by Inst Pur & Supply) St Mut.

— Contract Negotiations Handbook. 412p. (C). 1988. 245.00 (*0-7855-3766-X*, Pub. by Inst Pur & Supply) St Mut.

— Contract Negotiations Handbook. 412p. (C). 1989. 525.00 (*0-7855-4639-1*, Pub. by Inst Pur & Supply) St Mut.

— Contracting for Engineering & Construction Projects. 315p. (C). 1988. 156.00 (*0-7855-3773-2*, Pub. by Inst Pur & Supply); 395.00 (*0-7855-5745-8*, Pub. by Inst Pur & Supply) St Mut.

— Contracting for Engineering & Construction Projects. 315p. (C). 1989. 375.00 (*0-7855-4636-7*, Pub. by Inst Pur & Supply) St Mut.

— Successful Bidding & Tendering. (Gower Business Enterprise Ser.). 179p. 1989. text 33.95 (*0-7045-0619-X*, Pub. by Gower) Ashgate Pub Co.

***Marsh, P. D. V.** Contract Negotiation Handbook. 3rd ed. LC 00-39386. 2000. pap. write for info. (*0-566-08021-4*) Ashgate Pub Co.

Marsh, Patrick O. Messages That Work: A Guide to Communication Design. LC 83-1573. 460p. 1983. 49.95 (*0-87778-184-2*) Educ Tech Pubns.

***Marsh, Peter.** Contracting for Engineering & Construction Projects. 5th ed. 272p. 2000. 104.95 (*0-566-08282-9*, Pub. by Ashgate Pub) Ashgate Pub Co.

— Leaving Care in Partnership: Family Involvement with Care Leavers LC 99-201657. (Studies in Evaluating the Children Act 1989). xi, 124p. 1999. write for info. (*0-11-322250-5*, Pub. by Statnry Office) Gale.

Marsh, Peter, ed. Contesting the Boundaries of Liberal & Professional Education: The Syracuse Experiment. (Illus.). 280p. (C). 1988. text 39.95 (*0-8156-2428-X*) Syracuse U Pr.

Marsh, Peter & Crow, Gill. Family Group Conferences in Child Welfare. LC 97-26471. (Working Together for Children, Young People, & Their Families Ser.). 1997. pap. 29.95 (*0-632-04922-7*) Blackwell Sci.

Marsh, Peter & Triseliotis, John. Ready to Practice? Social Workers & Probation Officers: Their Training in the First Year of Work. 250p. 1996. text 58.95 (*1-85972-478-7*, Pub. by Avebry) Ashgate Pub Co.

Marsh, Peter, jt. auth. see Doel, Mark.

Marsh, Peter D. Contracting for Engineering & Construction Projects. 4th ed. 454p. 1995. 96.95 (*0-566-07628-4*, Pub. by Gower) Ashgate Pub Co.

Marsh, Peter D. V. Contract Negotiation Handbook. 3rd ed. 320p. Date not set. text 114.95 (*0-566-02403-9*, Pub. by Ashgate Pub) Ashgate Pub Co.

***Marsh, Peter T.** Bargaining on Europe: Britain & the First Common Market, 1860-1892. LC 99-33406. 256p. 1999. 30.00 (*0-300-08103-0*) Yale U Pr.

Marsh, Peter T. The Discipline of Popular Government: Lord Salisbury's Domestic Statecraft, 1881-1902. (Modern Revivals in History Ser.). 384p. 1993. text 65.95 (*0-7512-0230-4*, Pub. by Gregg Revivals) Ashgate Pub Co.

— Joseph Chamberlain: Entrepreneur in Politics. LC 93-47209. 720p. 1994. 55.00 (*0-300-05801-2*) Yale U Pr.

***Marsh, Philip D. & Martin, Michael.** Oral Microbiology. 4th ed. LC 99-38298. 192p. 2000. pap. text 50.00 (*0-7236-1051-7*) Buttrwrth-Heinemann.

Marsh, Philip D., jt. auth. see Martin, Michael.

Marsh, Philip D., jt. ed. see Hill, Michael J.

Marsh, R., jt. ed. see Surampudi, S.

Marsh, R. E., jt. ed. see Jackson, W. B.

Marsh, R. W., jt. auth. see Olivo, C. Thomas.

Marsh, Rae A. It Could Be Worse: A Jewish Folktale. LC 98-8765. (Illus.). (J). (gr. 1 3). 1998. pap. 16.00 (*1-889397-40-7*, 040) Curiosity Canyon.

Marsh, Ralph, ed. see Emery, J. Gladston.

***Marsh, Rand.** Scorpio Men on Prozac. 2000. pap. 18.00 (*0-7388-2210-8*) Xlibris Corp.

Marsh, Rebecca. Summer in Vermont. large type ed. LC 93-27184. 1994. lib. bdg. 13.95 (*0-7862-0048-0*) Thorndike Pr.

— The Way of the Heart. large type ed. (Linford Romance Library). 256p. 1997. pap. 16.99 (*0-7089-5039-6*) Ulverscroft.

Marsh, Reginald. Anatomy for Artists. LC 75-129078. (Illus.). 209p. 1970. reprint ed. pap. 9.95 (*0-486-22613-1*) Dover.

Marsh, Richard. The Beetle. 1976. 28.95 (*0-405-08151-0*, 18479) Ayer.

Marsh, Richard S. Reading & Understanding Technical Information. (Illus.). (J). (gr. 5). 1986. student ed. 5.25 (*0-89525-758-0*) Ed Activities.

Marsh, Robert. Four Dialectical Theories of Poetry. LC 65-24432. 1995. lib. bdg. 23.00 (*0-226-50689-4*) U Ch Pr.

Marsh, Robert, ed. see Farber, David A.

Marsh, Robert C. Dialogues & Discoveries: The Legendary James Levine Shares Memories of His Life, His Music & His Career. LC 97-44503. (Illus.). 336p. 1998. 27.50 (*0 684 83159 7*, Scribners Ref) Mac Lib Ref.

Marsh, Robert C., ed. see Russell, Bertrand.

Marsh, Robert C., jt. ed. see Russell, Bertrand.

Marsh, Robert M. The Great Transformation: Social Change in Taipei, Taiwan since the 1960s. LC 96-6317. (Taiwan in the Modern World Ser.). 418p. (C). (gr. 13-13). 1996. text 74.95 (*1-56324-787-9*, East Gate Bk) M E Sharpe.

— The Great Transformation: Social Change in Taipei, Taiwan since the 1960s. LC 96-6317. (Taiwan in the Modern World Ser.). (Illus.). 418p. (C). 1996. pap. text 34.95 (*1-56324-788-7*, East Gate Bk) M E Sharpe.

— The Mandarins: The Circulation of Elites in China, 1600

M

to 1900. Zuckerman, Harriet & Merton, Robert K., eds. LC 79-9013. (Dissertations on Sociology Ser.). 1980. lib. bdg. 31.95 (*0-405-12981-5*) Ayer.

Marsh, Robert M. & Manari, Hiroshi. Organizational Change in Japanese Factories. LC 88-19810. (Monographs in Organizational Behavior & Industrial Relations: Vol. 9). 313p. 1989. 78.50 (*0-89232-777-4*) Jai Pr.

Marsh, Robin R. Development Strategies in Rural Colombia: The Case of Caqueta. LC 82-620032. (Latin American Studies: Vol. 55). 1983. text 22.95 (*0-87903-055-0*) UCLA Lat Am Ctr.

Marsh, Rosalind, ed. Women in Russian Culture: Projections & Self-Perceptions. LC 98-16216. (Studies in Slavic Literature, Culture, & Society). 288p. 1998. 49.95 (*1-57181-913-4*) Berghahn Bks.

Marsh, Rosalind J. History & Literature in Contemporary Russia. 240p. (C). 1995. text 42.50 (*0-8147-5527-5*) NYU Pr.

— Images of Dictatorship: Stalin in Literature. 304p. 1989. 45.00 (*0-415-03796-4*, A3493) Routledge.

— Soviet Fiction since Stalin: Science, Politics & Literature. LC 85-30610. 352p. 1986. 56.00 (*0-389-20609-1*, N8172) B&N Imports.

Marsh, Rosalind J., ed. Gender & Russian Literature: New Perspectives. (Studies in Russian Literature). 372p. (C). 1996. text 69.95 (*0-521-55258-3*) Cambridge U Pr.

— Women in Russia & Ukraine. (Illus.). 368p. (C). 1996. text 69.95 (*0-521-49522-9*); pap. text 27.95 (*0-521-49872-4*) Cambridge U Pr.

Marsh, S. Ostwald Ripening. 1999. write for info. (*0-08-042141-5*, Pergamon Pr) Elsevier.

Marsh, S. B. & Soulsby, J. Business Law. 7th ed. 376p. 1999. pap. 48.00 (*0-7487-3415-5*, Pub. by S Thornes Pubs) Trans-Atl Phila.

— Outlines of English Law. 304p. 1982. write for info. (*0-07-084655-3*) McGraw.

***Marsh, S. P., et al, eds.** Solidification, 1999: Proceedings of Symposia Sponsored by the Solidification Committee of the Materials Processing & Manufacturing Division of TMS, Held at the TMS Fall Meeting in Rosemont, Illinois, October 11-15, 1998 & at the TMS Annual Meeting in San Diego, California, February 28-March 4, 1999 LC 98-68636. (Illus.). 19p. 1999. 90.00 (*0-87339-429-1*, 4291) Minerals Metals.

Marsh, Sarah & Moe, Atle. Stars Register of Yachts, Clubs & Flags. (Illus.). 1000p. 1997. 89.50 (*0-9651781-1-0*) Three Stars Co.

Marsh, Stephen, jt. auth. see Andoh, Benjamin.

Marsh, Steve, jt. auth. see Dobson, Alan P.

Marsh, Steven P., et al, eds. Solidification, 1998: Proceedings, Symposium on Solidification, San Antonio, Texas, 1998. LC 97-75876. (Illus.). 542p. 1998. 132.00 (*0-87339-396-1*, TA174) Minerals Metals.

Marsh, Sue, jt. ed. see Baker Library Staff.

Marsh, Susan H., jt. ed. see Kau, Michael Ying-Mao.

Marsh, Susan H., jt. ed. see Kau, Michael Y.

Marsh, T. The Amazing Ark: A Tale about God's Promises. LC 98-33863. (Tale Tellers Ser.). 1999. 7.99 (*0-7814-3085-2*) Chariot Victor.

— The Glory Garden: A Tale about Obedience. LC 98-33862. (Tale Tellers Ser.). 1999. 3.99 (*0-7814-3084-4*) Chariot Victor.

***Marsh, T. F.** The Fantastic Fish: A Tale about Compassion. LC 99-41571. (The Tale Tellers Ser.). (Illus.). (J). 2000. 3.99 (*0-7814-3284-7*) Cook.

— The Grouchy Giant: A Tale about Trusting God. LC 99-41572. (Tale Tellers Ser.). (Illus.). (J). 2000. 3.99 (*0-7814-3283-9*) Chariot Victor.

Marsh, T. F., et al. Tom Kitten. (Classic Tales Ser.). 24p. (J). (gr. 2-4). 1992. lib. bdg. 11.95 (*1-56674-010-X*, HTS Bks) Forest Hse.

— Two Bad Mice. (Classic Tales Ser.). 24p. (J). (gr. 2-4). 1992. lib. bdg. 11.95 (*1-56674-011-8*, HTS Bks) Forest Hse.

Marsh, T. J. & Ward, Jennifer. Way Out in the Desert. LC 97-47220. 32p. (J). (ps-2). 1998. 15.95 (*0-87358-687-5*, Rising Moon Bks) Northland AZ.

***Marsh, Terry.** Essential England. (AAA Essential Guides Ser.). (Illus.). 128p. 2000. pap. 8.95 (*0-658-00374-7*, 003747, Passprt Bks) NTC Contemp Pub Co.

Marsh, Terry. 100 Walks in the French Alps. (Illus.). 221p. 1995. pap. text 34.95 (*0-340-57478-X*, Pub. by Hodder & Stought Ltd) Trafalgar.

Marsh, Theron L., jt. ed. see Sweeney, Mary S.

Marsh, Thomas E. The Official Guide to Collecting Applied Color Label Soda Bottles. (Illus.). 104p. (Orig.). 1992. write for info. (*0-9633682-0-6*) T E Marsh.

— The Official Guide to Collecting Applied Color Soda Bottles, Vol. II. 105p. (J). (ps up). pap., per. write for info. (*0-9633682-1-4*) T E Marsh.

Marsh, Thomas O. Roots of Crime: A Bio-Physical Approach to Crime Prevention & Rehabilitation. 208p. 1984. reprint ed. pap. text 17.95 (*0-8290-1570-1*) Irvington.

Marsh, Tim, jt. auth. see Marsh, Helen.

Marsh, Timothy R., jt. auth. see Marsh, Helen C.

Marsh, Timothy Richard, jt. auth. see Marsh, Helen Crawford.

Marsh, Tracy. Creative Stamping. 1997. pap. 16.95 (*0-85532-827-4*, Pub. by Srch Pr) A Schwartz & Co.

Marsh, Tracy, ed. Victorian Crafts: Over Forty Charming Projects to Make from the Victorian Era. (Illus.). 168p. 1993. 29.95 (*0-943955-75-0*, Trafalgar Sq Pub) Trafalgar.

Marsh, V. & Musat, V. Romania: Investment & Growth. (Illus.). 1995. 170.00 (*1-85564-438-X*, Pub. by Euromoney) Am Educ Systs.

Marsh, Valerie. Beyond Words: Great Stories for Hand & Voice. (Illus.). 80p. 1995. pap., student ed. 14.95 (*0-917846-49-4*, 33902, Alleyside) Highsmith Pr.

— Mystery Fold: Stories to Tell, Draw & Fold. (Illus.). 80p. (J). (ps-5). 1993. pap. 14.95 (*0-913853-31-3*, 32540, Alleyside) Highsmith Pr.

— Paper Cutting Stories for Holidays & Special Events. LC 94-26174. (Illus.). (J). 1994. pap. text 14.95 (*0-917846-42-7*, Alleyside) Highsmith Pr.

— Paper Cutting Stories from A to Z. (Illus.). 80p. 1992. pap. 14.95 (*0-913853-24-0*, 32535, Alleyside) Highsmith Pr.

— Puppet Tales. LC 97-35074. (Alleyside Press Storytelling Ser.). (Illus.). 80p. (J). 1998. pap. 14.95 (*0-917846-92-3*, Alleyside) Highsmith Pr.

— Storyteller's Sampler. (Illus.). 80p. (J). 1996. pap., teacher ed. 14.95 (*0-917846-58-3*, 34006, Alleyside) Highsmith Pr.

— Storytelling with Shapes & Numbers. LC 99-14237. (Illus.). 84p. (J). (gr. k-1). 1999. pap. 15.95 (*1-57950-024-2*, Alleyside) Highsmith Pr.

— Terrific Tales to Tell: From the Storyknifing Tradition. LC 96-43080. 80p. (YA). 1997. pap. 14.95 (*0-917846-60-5*, Alleyside) Highsmith Pr.

— A Treasury of Trickster Tales. LC 97-5208. 80p. 1997. pap. 14.95 (*0-917846-91-5*, Alleyside) Highsmith Pr.

Marsh, Valerie & Luzadder, Patrick K. Story Puzzles: Tales in the Tangram Tradition. LC 96-26676. (Illus.). 80p. (YA). 1996. pap. 14.95 (*0-917846-59-1*, Alleyside) Highsmith Pr.

— True Tales of Heroes & Heroines. LC 98-48774. (Illus.). 95p. (J). (gr. 3-7). 2000. pap. 15.95 (*0-917846-93-1*) Highsmith Pr.

***Marsh, W. Jeffrey.** His Final Hours. LC 00-20908. 2000. write for info. (*1-57345-645-4*) Deseret Bk.

— The Light Within. LC 00-40442. 2000. write for info. (*1-57345-807-4*) Deseret Bk.

Marsh, W. Jeffrey. Unto Us a Child Is Born. 1994. 10.95 (*0-88494-937-0*) Bookcraft Inc.

Marsh, W. Jeffrey & Munns, Ron R. The New Testament for Today: Bible Stories with Modern Parallels. 1995. 10.95 (*0-88494-965-6*) Bookcraft Inc.

***Marsh, Willa.** The Quick & the Dead. large type ed. LC 99-14884. 294p. 1999. 22.95 (*0-7862-1981-5*) Mac Lib Ref.

Marsh, William. Making Flutes. 40p. 1998. 7.00 (*0-937013-85-4*, Pub. by Potes Poets) SPD-Small Pr Dist.

Marsh, William, tr. see Sakaiya, Taichi.

Marsh, William H. Basic Financial Management. LC 94-2856. 640p. 1994. 53.95 (*0-538-84170-2*) S-W Pub.

Marsh, William M. Earthscape a Physical Geography. LC 86-28209. 608p. (C). 1987. text 62.95 (*0-471-85055-1*) Wiley.

— Earthscape a Physical Geography. LC 86-28209. 500p. (C). 1987. 145.00 (*0-471-63018-7*) Wiley.

— Landscape Planning. LC 82-13889. (Earth Science Ser.). (Illus.). 225p. 1981. pap. text 16.00 (*0-201-04102-2*) Addison-Wesley.

— Landscape Planning: Environmental Applications. 3rd ed. LC 97-44579. 448p. 1997. pap. 58.95 (*0-471-24207-1*) Wiley.

Marsh, William M. & Grossa, John. Environmental Geography: Science, Land Use, Earth Systems. LC 95-42701. 448p. 1995. text 77.95 (*0-471-50396-7*) Wiley.

Marsh, William M., et al. Environmental Geography: Science, Land Use & Earth Systems & Rosenthal's Environmental Case Studies. 511p. 1996. 87.90 (*0-471-16988-9*) Wiley.

Marsh, William P., jt. ed. see Bamford, Christopher.

Marsha, M. & Soulsby, S. Business Law. 292p. (C). 1989. 115.00 (*0-7855-5683-4*, Pub. by Inst Pur & Supply) St Mut.

Marshaalek, Kathy. Exploring International Trade Options. 88p. 1995. pap. text 34.50 (*1-883006-13-9*) Intl Busn Pubns.

Marshad, David S. & Lazaro, Judith. Patricia Seybold Group's 1997 User Survey of Electronic Commerce Initiatives. 89p. 1997. pap. 295.00 (*1-892815-25-7*) Patricia Seybold.

***Marshae, Kristina.** Monsters & Wildflowers. 1999. pap. 6.95 (*0-9673675-0-6*) In Flight.

Marshak, Daniel, et al. Strategies for Protein Purification & Characterization: A Laboratory Course Manual. (Illus.). 304p. (C). 1996. pap. 85.00 (*0-87969-385-1*) Cold Spring Harbor.

Marshak, Daniel, ed. see Tobin, Catherine.

Marshak, Daniel R., ed. Techniques in Protein Chemistry, Vol. 7. (Illus.). 533p. 1996. 55.00 (*0-12-473556-8*); text 110.00 (*0-12-473555-X*) Acad Pr.

— Techniques in Protein Chemistry, Vol. 8. (Illus.). 872p. 1997. text 130.00 (*0-12-473557-6*) Morgan Kaufmann.

— Techniques in Protein Chemistry VIII, Vol. 8. (Illus.). 872p. 1997. pap. 75.00 (*0-12-473558-4*) Morgan Kaufmann.

Marshak, Daniel R. & Liu, Darrell T., eds. Therapeutic Peptides & Proteins: Assessing the New Technologies. (Banbury Reports: No. 29). (Illus.). 288p. 1988. text 77.00 (*0-87969-229-4*) Cold Spring Harbor.

— Therapeutic Peptides & Proteins: Formulation, Delivery & Targeting. (Current Communications in Molecular Biology Ser.). (Illus.). (Orig.). 1989. pap. text 24.00 (*0-87969-328-2*) Cold Spring Harbor.

Marshak, David. Action Research on Block Scheduling. LC 97-10138. 250p. 1997. 39.95 (*1-883001-40-4*) Eye On Educ.

— The Common Vision: Parenting & Educating for Wholeness. LC 96-41248. (Counterpoints Studies in the Postmodern Theory of Education Ser.: Vol. 48). (Illus.). 246p. (C). 1997. pap. text 29.95 (*0-8204-3702-6*) P Lang Pubng.

— Encouraging Student Engagement in the Block Period. LC 98-45146. 200p. 1999. pap. 29.95 (*1-883001-65-X*) Eye On Educ.

— HM Study Skills Program: Student Text Level II. rev. ed. Phipps, Paula et al, eds. 104p. 1986. teacher ed. 5.95 (*0-88210-100-5*); pap. text 5.95 (*0-88210-099-8*) Natl Assn Principals.

Marshak, David, jt. auth. see Burkle, Candace R.

Marshak, David, ed. see Andrews, Barry & Hoertdoerfer, Patricia.

Marshak, David, ed. see Branch, Robert C., et al.

Marshak, David, ed. see Burkle, Frank.

Marshak, David, ed. see Fitzpatrick, Elaine M.

Marshak, David, ed. see Goldenberg, Samuel, et al.

Marshak, David, ed. see Keroack, Elizabeth C., et al.

Marshak, David, ed. see Tobin, Catherine D.

Marshak, David, ed. see Wilson, Carol & Krasnow, Gary.

***Marshak, David S.** Bacardi Limited Levages Groupware into Electronic Commerce Providing a View into the Supple/Distribution Chain. (Illus.). 14p. 1998. pap. write for info. (*1-892815-08-7*) Patricia Seybold.

Marshak, David S. Domino Applications. (Illus.). 45p. 1997. pap. 95.00 (*1-892815-21-4*) Patricia Seybold.

Marshak, David S., jt. auth. see Hurwicz, Michael.

Marshak, David S., jt. auth. see Marshak, Ronni T.

***Marshak, Kathy.** Entrepreneurial Couples: Making It Work at Work & at Home. LC 97-49921. xxiii, 272p. 1998. 26.95 (*0-89106-115-0*, 7784, Davies-Black Pub) Consulting Psychol.

Marshak, Laura E. Disability & the Family Life Cycle. 240p. 2000. 42.00 (*0-465-01632-4*, Pub. by Basic) HarpC.

Marshak, Laura E. & Seligman, Milton. Counseling Persons with Physical Disabilities: Theoretical & Clinical Perspectives. LC 92-35809. 234p. (Orig.). (C). 1993. pap. text 29.00 (*0-89079-580-0*, 6594) PRO-ED.

Marshak, Laura E., jt. ed. see Nowell, Richard C.

Marshak, M. L., ed. High Energy Physics with Polarized Beams & Targets (Argonne, 1976) Proceedings. LC 76-50181. (AIP Conference Proceedings Ser., Subseries: Particle & Fields: No. 35, 12). 543p. 1977. 21.50 (*0-88318-134-7*) Am Inst Physics.

Marshak, R. E. Conceptual Foundations of Modern Particle Physics. 704p. 1993. text 99.00 (*981-02-1098-1*); pap. text 53.00 (*981-02-1106-6*) World Scientific Pub.

Marshak, R. R., et al, eds. Advances in Veterinary Science & Comparative Medicine Vol. 38, Pt. B: Comparative Vertebrate Exercise Physiology: Phyletic Adaptations. (Illus.). 236p. 1994. text 104.00 (*0-12-039239-9*) Acad Pr.

— Advances in Veterinary Science & Comparative Medicine Vol. 38A: Comparative Vertebrate Exercise Physiology: Unifying Physiological Principles. (Illus.). 291p. 1994. text 104.00 (*0-12-039238-0*) Acad Pr.

Marshak, R. T., jt. auth. see Seybold, Patricia B.

Marshak, Richard H., et al. Radiology of the Stomach. (Illus.). 656p. 1983. text 180.00 (*0-7216-6124-6*, W B Saunders Co) Harcrt Hlth Sci Grp.

Marshak, Robert E. A Gift of Prophecy: Essays in Celebration of the Life of Robert Eugene Marshak. Sudarshan, E. C., ed. & compiled by by. 584p. 1995. text 109.00 (*981-02-2075-8*) World Scientific Pub.

Marshak, Ronni, et al. Roadmap Set. (Illus.). 230p. 1997. write for info. (*1-892815-10-9*) Patricia Seybold.

Marshak, Ronni T. Document Management Systems Report. (Illus.). 133p. 1997. pap. 295.00 (*1-892815-20-6*) Patricia Seybold.

— Selecting & Implementing Workflow. (Illus.). 46p. 1996. pap. write for info. (*1-892815-13-3*) Patricia Seybold.

Marshak, Ronni T. & Marshak, David S. Selecting & Implementing Groupware. (Illus.). 24p. 1996. pap. write for info. (*1-892815-11-7*) Patricia Seybold.

Marshak, S., tr. see Milne, A. A., pseud.

Marshak, Samuel. The Absent Minded Fellow. Pevear, Richard, tr. from RUS. LC 98-22890. (Illus.). 32p. (YA). (ps-3). 1999. pap. text 16.00 (*0-374-30013-5*) FS&G.

— Hail to Mail. large type ed. Pevear, Richard, tr. from RUS. (Illus.). 1993. 9.50 (*0-614-09826-2*, L-34087-00) Am Printing Hse.

Marshak, Samuel. The Month-Brothers. Whitney, Thomas P., tr. from RUS. LC 82-7927. (Illus.). 32p. (J). (gr. k up). 1983. 15.93 (*0-688-01510-7*, Wm Morrow) Morrow Avon.

Marshak, Samuel. The Pup Grew Up! Pevear, Richard, tr. from RUS. LC 88-28428. (Illus.). 32p. (J). (ps-2). 1995. 13.95 (*0-8050-0952-3*, Bks Young Read) H Holt & Co.

Marshak, Sondra. Prometheus Design, No. 5. 1990. pap. 5.50 (*0-671-72366-9*) S&S Trade.

— Triangle. (Orig.). 1986. per. 3.50 (*0-671-62748-1*) PB.

— Triangle. (Star Trek Ser.: No. 9). (Orig.). 1991. mass mkt. 5.50 (*0-671-74351-1*) PB.

Marshak, Sondra & Culbreath, Myrna. Star Trek, the New Voyages 2. 288p. (Orig.). (J). 1983. mass mkt. 5.50 (*0-553-27933-5*, Spectra) Bantam.

Marshak, Stephen. Structural Geology of Silurian & Devonian Strata in the Mid-Hudson Valley, New York: Fold-Thrust Belt Tectonics in Miniature. (New York State Museum Map & Chart Ser.: No. 41). (Illus.). 66p. (Orig.). 1990. pap. 15.00 (*1-55557-200-6*) NYS Museum.

Marshak, Stephen & Mitra, Gautam. Basic Methods of Structural Geology. 446p. (C). 1988. pap. text 46.67 (*0-13-065178-8*) P-H.

Marshak, Stephen, jt. auth. see Van Der Pluijm, Ben A.

Marshakov, Andrei. Seiberg-Witten Theory & the Integrable Systems. 200p. 1998. 48.00 (*981-02-3636-0*); pap. 24.00 (*981-02-3637-9*) World Scientific Pub.

Marshal, David. Jobs for Everyone. 112p. 1997. pap. 9.95 (*0-8059-4287-4*) Dorrance.

Marshal, Nell. An Investment in Time: What Happens To Your Money When An Investmant Company Folds. LC 98-208008. 243p. 1998. 27.95 (*0-7880-0973-7*) CSS OH.

***Marshal, Rich.** God at Work. 176p. 2000. pap. 11.99 (*0-7684-2101-2*) Destiny Image.

Marshal, Walter G. Through America: or Nine Months in the United States. LC 73-13143. (Foreign Travelers in America, 1810-1935 Ser.). (Illus.). 490p. 1974. reprint ed. 35.95 (*0-405-05466-1*) Ayer.

Marshal, William. O Come Emmanuel: Scripture Verses for Advent Worship. LC 94-12745. 100p. 1994. pap. 7.95 (*0-8192-1629-1*) Morehouse Pub.

Marshalek, Kathy. Exploring International Trade Options. rev. ed. 85p. 1996. pap. text 34.50 (*1-883006-39-2*) Intl Busn Pubns.

— Export Marketing & Sales. 154p. 1992. pap. 67.50 (*1-883006-03-1*) Intl Busn Pubns.

— Export Marketing & Sales. rev. ed. 130p. 1996. pap. text 67.50 (*1-883006-37-6*) Intl Busn Pubns.

— Export Sales Agents & Distributors. rev. ed. 60p. 1996. pap. text 44.50 (*1-883006-45-7*) Intl Busn Pubns.

— International Reference Glossary. 575p. 1997. ring bd. 129.50 (*1-883006-49-X*) Intl Busn Pubns.

Marshalek, Kathy, jt. auth. see Ewert, D. E.

Marshalek, Kathy, jt. auth. see Ewert, Donald E.

Marshall. Accounting. 4th ed. 432p. 1998. pap. 29.38 (*0-256-26854-1*) McGraw.

— Accounting. 4th ed. LC 98-23854. 1998. text 68.00 (*0-256-26843-6*, Irwn McGrw-H) McGrw-H Hghr Educ.

***Marshall.** American Heritage 100 Notebook. 154p. (C). 1998. pap. text 11.04 (*0-536-01323-3*) Pearson Custom.

Marshall. Citizenship & Social Class. 101p. (C). 44.95 (*0-7453-0477-X*, Pub. by Pluto GBR); pap. 14.95 (*0-7453-0476-1*, Pub. by Pluto GBR) Stylus Pub VA.

— Clinical Biochemistry. 3rd ed. 1995. 31.00 (*0-7234-2190-0*) Mosby Inc.

— Cognitive Behavior Therapy. 1997. pap. text 25.95 (*0-7020-1967-4*) Bailliere Tindall.

— Discovering the Arts. 2nd ed. 1996. 19.25 (*0-07-041081-X*) McGraw.

— Diversity in Today's School. (C). 1997. pap. text, teacher ed. 66.00 (*0-15-503215-1*) Harcourt Coll Pubs.

— Diversity in Today's Schools. (C). 2001. pap. text 49.00 (*0-15-503214-3*) Harcourt Coll Pubs.

— Dodge Repair & Remodel '99. 1998. 69.96 (*0-07-134242-7*) McGraw.

— The EKG Technician. LC 89-70794. 272p. 1990. pap. 52.00 (*0-89303-702-8*) P-H.

— Explorations in Biology. 3rd ed. (C). 1994. pap. text, write for info. (*0-07-040819-X*) McGraw.

— Guide to Learning Independently. 2nd ed. 1994. pap. text. write for info. (*0-582-87107-7*, Pub. by Addison-Wesley) Longman.

***Marshall.** A Guide to Learning Independently. 3rd ed. 293p. (C). 1998. pap. text 13.95 (*0-582-81170-8*) Longman.

Marshall. Health Careers Today, Resource Kit. 192p. 1991. 55.00 (*0-8016-3282-X*) Mosby Inc.

— Hygini. (LAT.). 1993. 62.50 (*3-8154-1449-0*, T1449, Pub. by B G Teubner) U of Mich Pr.

— I Hate to Read! (J). 1995. pap. 9.95 (*0-15-200931-0*) Harcourt.

— Instructor's Resource Kit for Nurse Assistant in Long-Term Care: A Rehab Approach. 352p. 1992. pap. text 32.00 (*0-8016-6298-2*) Mosby Inc.

— Libraries & Literature. (C). 1977. text 20.00 (*0-233-96604-8*) Westview.

— Libraries & the Handicapped. (C). 1981. text 27.50 (*0-86531-056-4*) Westview.

— Life Insurance Company Mergers & Consolidations. (C). 1972. 12.95 (*0-256-00653-9*, Irwn McGrw-H) McGrw-H Hghr Educ.

— Mammals from Pouches & Eggs. Graves, Jennifer A. et al, eds. (C). 1990. 60.00 (*0-643-05020-5*, Pub. by CSIRO) Accents Pubns.

— Marketing Management. 2001. write for info. (*0-538-89036-3*) S-W Pub.

***Marshall.** Mental Attitude to Dressage. 2000. pap. 12.95 (*0-85131-739-1*, Pub. by J A Allen) Trafalgar.

Marshall. The 1999 Family Practice Sourcebook: Current Literature & Medical Evidence in Patient Care. LC 98-15925. (Illus.). 405p. (C). (gr. 13). 1998. pap. text 49.95 (*0-8151-2785-5*, 31801) Mosby Inc.

— On Call: Neurology. (C). 1998. text. write for info. (*0-8089-2099-5*, Grune & Strat) Harcrt Hlth Sci Grp.

***Marshall.** Operational Risks. 350p. 2000. 89.95 (*0-471-84595-7*) Wiley.

Marshall. Probability Models for Lifetime Data. 300p. (C). 1998. text. write for info. (*0-12-473940-7*) Acad Pr.

— Professional C++ Programmer. (ITCP-UK Computer Science Ser.). 1997. pap. 42.99 (*1-85032-296-1*) ITCP.

— Recent & Emerging Theoretical Frameworks for Research on Classroom Learning: Contributions & Limitations. (Educational Psychology Ser.: Vol. 31, No. 3-4). 1997. pap. 40.00 (*0-8058-9882-4*) L Erlbaum Assocs.

— Survey Account Text Rn. Odd. Sol. 3rd ed. 1996. 70.25 (*0-256-21667-3*) McGraw.

— The Swaps Market. 2nd ed. 1992. teacher ed. write for info. (*1-55786-753-4*) Blackwell Pubs.

— Telecommunications in the 1990s. 1995. 39.95 (*0-8161-1974-0*, G K Hall & Co) Mac Lib Ref.

— Turning Points: A Contemporary American Memoir. LC 99-36573. 292p. (C). 1999. pap. text 29.00 (*0-02-376451-1*, Macmillan Coll) P-H.

Marshall, ed. The Four-Part Motets of Thomas Crecquillon, Pt. 1. (Wissenschaftliche Abhandlungen-Musicological Studies: Vol. 21). 1981. lib. bdg. 35.00 (*0-912024-91-7*) Inst Mediaeval Mus.

— The Four-Part Motets of Thomas Crecquillon, Pt. 2. (Wissenschaftliche Abhandlungen-Musicological Studies: Vol. 21). 1981. lib. bdg. 42.00 (*0-912024-92-5*) Inst Mediaeval Mus.

An Asterisk (*) at the beginning of an entry indicates that the title is appearing for the first time.

— The Four-Part Motets of Thomas Crecquillon, Pt. 3. (Wissenschaftliche Abhandlungen-Musicological Studies: Vol. 21). 1981. lib. bdg. 42.00 (*0-912024-93-3*) Inst Mediaeval Mus.
— The Four-Part Motets of Thomas Crecquillon, Pt. 4. (Wissenschaftliche Abhandlungen-Musicological Studies: Vol. 21). 1981. lib. bdg. 42.00 (*0-912024-94-1*) Inst Mediaeval Mus.
— Lupi, Servati. (LAT.). 1984. 39.50 (*3-322-00191-1*, T1370, Pub. by B G Teubner) U of Mich Pr.
— Nepotis, Cornelii. (LAT.). 1991. 22.95 (*3-8154-1959-X*, T1959, Pub. by B G Teubner) U of Mich Pr.
Marshall & Briggs, Vernon M. Labor Economics. 6th ed. 656p. (C). 1988. text 48.95 (*0-256-07090-3*, Irwn McGrw-H) McGrw-H Hghr Educ.
Marshall & Flanagan. Project Evaluation in Building Economics. (Foundations of Building Economics Ser.). (Illus.). 256p. 1999. pap. 65.00 (*0-419-19240-9*) Thomson Learn.
Marshall & Misiwicz. Programmed Guide to Tax Research. 4th ed. (SWC-Taxation). (C). 1992. pap. 43.25 (*0-538-82383-6*) Thomson Learn.
Marshall & Morrison. Political History of Jackson County, Missouri. (Illus.). 276p. 1997. reprint ed. pap. 22.00 (*0-7884-0709-0*, M069) Heritage Bk.
Marshall & Swift. Dodge Repair & Remodel Cost Book 1997. 400p. 1997. pap. 59.95 (*0-07-913275-8*) McGraw.
— Dodge Unit Cost Book 1997. 604p. 1996. pap. 59.95 (*0-07-912936-6*) McGraw.
— Home Repair & Remodel Cost Guide 1997. 1996. pap. text 29.95 (*0-07-040858-0*) McGraw.
Marshall, et al. Neuroscience Critical Care: Pathophysiology & Patient Management. (Illus.). 464p. 1990. text 89.00 (*0-7216-2790-0*, W B Saunders Co) Harcrt Hlth Sci Grp.
Marshall, jt. auth. see Archer.
Marshall, jt. auth. see Cournoyer.
Marshall, ed. see Boyle, Marie & Zyla, Gail.
Marshall, ed. see Cataldo, Corinne B., et al.
Marshall, ed. see Cohen, David C.
Marshall, ed. see DeBruyne, Linda K., et al.
Marshall, ed. see Devore, Jay & Peck, Roxy L.
Marshall, ed. see Dintiman, George B., et al.
Marshall, ed. see Fadyn, Joseph N.
Marshall, ed. see Ferraro, Gary.
Marshall, ed. see Graham, Neill.
Marshall, ed. see Hamilton, Eva M., et al.
Marshall, ed. see Hunt, Sara M. & Groff, James L.
Marshall, ed. see Jewell, Linda N. & Siegall, Marc.
Marshall, ed. see Kaplan, Paul S.
Marshall, ed. see Knox, David & Schacht, Caroline.
Marshall, ed. see Napoli, Vincent, et al.
Marshall, ed. see Rolfes, Sharon R., et al.
Marshall, ed. see Shiflet, Angela B.
Marshall, ed. see Sizer, Frances S. & Whitney, Eleanor N.
Marshall, ed. see Territo, Leonard, et al.
Marshall, ed. see Turner, Lori, et al.
Marshall, ed. see Whitney, Eleanor N. & Rolfes, Sharon R.
Marshall, ed. see Whitney, Eleanor N., et al.
Marshall & Swift Staff. Dodge Repair & Remodel Cost Book, 1998. 484p. 1997. pap. 59.95 incl. disk (*0-07-912935-8*) McGraw-Hill Prof.
— Dodge Unit Cost Book 1998. 604p. 1997. pap. 59.95 incl. disk (*0-07-912937-4*) McGraw-Hill Prof.
***Marshall & Swift Staff.** Electrical Cost Book 2000. 296p. 1999. pap. 79.95 (*0-07-135648-7*) McGraw.
Marshall & Swift Staff. Exceptional Homes: A Cost Guide for High-Value & Unique Homes. 400p. 1998. pap. 49.95 (*1-56842-065-X*) Marshall & Swift.
***Marshall & Swift Staff.** Exceptional Homes: A Cost Guide for High-Value & Unique Residences. 2000. pap. 59.95 (*1-56842-078-1*) Marshall & Swift.
Marshall & Swift Staff. Home Repair & Remodel Cost Guide. 1999. 29.95 (*1-56842-071-4*) Marshall & Swift.
***Marshall & Swift Staff.** Home Repair & Remodel Cost Guide. 2000. 39.95 (*1-56842-077-3*) Marshall & Swift.
Marshall & Swift Staff. Illustrated Guide to Houses: Terms, Definitions & Drawings. Cap, Cydney, ed. (Illus.). 132p. (Orig.). 1995. pap. 14.95 (*1-56842-031-5*) Marshall & Swift.
— Log Home Appraisal Training Guide. 1998. pap. 10.00 (*1-56842-070-6*) Marshall & Swift.
— Marshall Valuation Service. 1998. ring bd. 229.95 (*1-56842-067-6*) Marshall & Swift.
— Marshall Valuation Service. 1999. ring bd. 246.95 (*1-56842-073-0*) Marshall & Swift.
***Marshall & Swift Staff.** Marshall Valuation Service. 2000. ring bd. 349.95 incl. cd-rom (*1-56842-079-X*) Marshall & Swift.
— Repair & Remodel Cost Book 2000. 638p. 1999. pap. 79.95 (*0-07-135645-2*) McGraw.
Marshall & Swift Staff. Residential Cost Handbook. Harducy, Richard, ed. 1998. ring bd. 115.95 (*1-56842-066-8*) Marshall & Swift.
— Residential Cost Handbook. 1999. ring bd. 123.95 (*1-56842-072-2*) Marshall & Swift.
***Marshall & Swift Staff.** Residential Cost Handbook. 2000. ring bd. 249.95 incl. cd-rom (*1-56842-081-1*) Marshall & Swift.
— Unit Cost Book 2000. 638p. 1999. pap. 79.95 (*0-07-135642-8*) McGraw.
Marshall & Swift Staff. Valuation Quarterly. 1999. ring bd. 131.95 (*1-56842-074-9*) Marshall & Swift.
***Marshall & Swift Staff.** Valuation Quarterly. 2000. ring bd. 140.95 (*1-56842-082-X*) Marshall & Swift.
Marshall & Swift Staff. Valuation Quaterly. 1998. ring bd. 122.95 (*1-56842-068-4*) Marshall & Swift.
Marshall, A. Games Black Women Play. 112p. 1998. pap. 12.00 (*0-9658299-3-6*) AOP Bks.
— Louis Farrakhan: Made in America. 300p. (Orig.). 1996. pap. 22.95 (*0-9655729-0-0*) BSB Pub.
— Marine Concrete. (gr. 13). 1990. text 155.95 (*0-442-30297-5*) Chapman & Hall.
— Principes d'Economique Politique, 2 vols., Vol. 2. 2nd ed. 1156p. 1971. pap. text 123.00 (*0-677-50535-3*) Gordon & Breach.
Marshall, A. C. Composites Basics. 5th ed. 200p. 1998. 45.00 (*0-938648-35-7*) T-C Pr CA.
Marshall, A. D. & Martin, R. R. Computer Vision, Models & Inspection. (Series in Robotics & Automated Systems: Vol. 4). 456p. (C). 1993. text 53.00 (*981-02-0772-7*) World Scientific Pub.
Marshall, A. G. The Ecology of Ectoparasitic Insects. LC 81-67916. 1982. text 209.00 (*0-12-474080-4*) Acad Pr.
Marshall, A. G. & Verdun, F. R. Fourier Transforms in NMR, Optical & Spectrometry: A User's Handbook. 440p. 1990. 178.50 (*0-444-87360-0*); pap. 77.25 (*0-444-87412-7*) Elsevier.
Marshall, A. Robert. Precalculus Functions & Graphs. (C). 1991. text 53.75 (*0-201-19095-8*) Addison-Wesley.
Marshall, Adre. The Turn of the Mind: Constituting Consciousness in Henry James. LC 97-18972. 280p. 1998. 43.50 (*0-8386-3695-0*) Fairleigh Dickinson.
***Marshall, Alan.** Age of Faction: Court Politics 1660-1702. 1999. pap. 27.95 (*0-7190-4975-X*, Pub. by Manchester Univ Pr); text 79.95 (*0-7190-4974-1*, Pub. by Manchester Univ Pr) St Martin.
Marshall, Alan. America's Best College Towns: What Your Guidance Counselor May Not Tell You. (Illus.). 256p. (Orig.). 1997. pap. 15.95 (*0-9658299-1-X*) AOP Bks.
— The Generation X Relocation Guide. (Illus.). 256p. (Orig.). 1997. pap. 15.95 (*0-9658299-0-1*) AOP Bks.
Marshall, Alan. Lancewood. 233p. pap. 18.95 (*0-9585805-1-0*) Intl Spec Bk.
Marshall, Alan. The Ruffian's Wage: Intelligence & Espionage in the Reign of Charles the Second, 1660-1685. LC 93-44477. (Cambridge Studies in Early Modern British History). (Illus.). 353p. (C). 1994. text 59.95 (*0-521-43180-8*) Cambridge U Pr.
***Marshall, Alan.** Strange Death of Edmund Godfrey: Plots & Politics in Restoration London. 2000. 34.95 (*0-7509-2100-5*) Sutton Pub Ltd.
Marshall, Alan G., ed. Fourier, Hadamard, & Hilbert Transforms in Chemistry. LC 81-20984. 574p. (C). 1982. 125.00 (*0-306-40904-6*, Plenum Trade) Perseus Pubng.
Marshall, Alan J. The Black Musketeers. LC 75-35140. 344p. reprint ed. 49.50 (*0-404-14156-0*) AMS Pr.
— The Men & Birds of Paradise: Journeys Through Equatorial New Guinea. LC 75-35141. reprint ed. 37.50 (*0-404-14157-9*) AMS Pr.
Marshall, Albert & Olkin, Ingram. Inequalities: Theory of Majorization & Its Applications. LC 79-50218. (Mathematics in Science & Engineering Ser.). 1979. text 116.00 (*0-12-473750-1*) Acad Pr.
Marshall, Albert P. The Legendary Four Horsemen of the A. M. E. Church. 24p. (Orig.). 1995. pap. text 5.00 (*1-885066-10-4*) Four-G Pubs.
Marshall, Albert P., ed. Helen Walker McAndrew: Ypsilanti's First Woman Physician. (Illus.). 25p. (Orig.). 1996. pap. 5.00 (*1-882792-36-X*) Proctor Pubns.
Marshall, Alejandro & Bennett, Gordon H. La Salvacion y las Dudas de Algunas Personas. 2nd ed. Bautista, Sara, tr. from SPA. (Serie Diamante).Tr. of God's Way of Salvation. (ENG., Illus.). 36p. 1982. pap. 0.85 (*0-942504-01-1*) Overcomer Pr.
***Marshall, Alex.** How Cities Work: Suburbs, Sprawl & the Roads Not Taken. LC 00-26691. (Illus.). 288p. 2001. 50.00 (*0-292-75239-3*); pap. 24.95 (*0-292-75240-7*) U of Tex Pr.
Marshall, Alex, ed. see Bernstein, Stan.
Marshall, Alexander. Let's Travel Pathways Through Missouri. (Let's Travel Pathways Through America Ser.). (Illus.). 600p. (Orig.). 1998. pap. 16.95 (*0-9626647-4-X*) Clark & Miles.
Marshall, Alexander, ed. Let's Travel Pathways Through Iowa: A Compilation of the Best in Iowa Travel. (Let's Travel Pathways Through America Ser.). (Illus.). 450p. (Orig.). 1995. reprint ed. pap. 16.95 (*0-9626647-3-1*) Clark & Miles.
— Let's Travel Pathways Through Wisconsin: A Compilation of the Best in Wisconsin Travel. (Let's Travel Pathways Through America Ser.). (Illus.). 640p. (Orig.). 1995. reprint ed. pap. 16.95 (*0-9626647-2-3*) Clark & Miles.
Marshall, Alexandra. Gus in Bronze. 256p. 1999. pap. 12.00 (*0-395-92490-1*) HM.
— Something Borrowed. LC 96-29516. 224p. 1997. 22.00 (*0-395-81665-3*) HM.
— Something Borrowed. 240p. 1999. pap. 12.00 (*0-395-92489-8*) HM.
Marshall, Alfred. The Correspondence of Alfred Marshall, Economist, 3 vols., Set, Vols. 1-3. Whitaker, John K., ed. (C). 1996. text 206.00 (*0-521-55889-1*) Cambridge U Pr.
— The Correspondence of Alfred Marshall, Economist Vol. 1: Climbing, 1868-1890, 3 vols. Whitaker, John K., ed. 427p. (C). 1996. text 74.95 (*0-521-55888-3*) Cambridge U Pr.
The Interlinear Greek-English New Testament. 1036p. (C). 1984. 34.95 (*0-310-45240-6*, 12394) Zondervan.
— Memorials of Alfred Marshall. Pigou, A. C., ed. LC 66-24415. (Reprints of Economic Classics Ser.). ix, 518p. 1966. 49.50 (*0-678-00197-9*) Kelley.
— Money, Credit & Commerce. LC 90-43794. (Reprints of Economic Classics Ser.). xvi, 369p. 1991. reprint ed. lib. bdg. 45.00 (*0-678-01463-9*) Kelley.
— New Testament Greek Primer. 176p. (C). 1986. 46.95 (*0-310-20540-9*, 6246) Zondervan.
— Principles of Economics. LC 97-3368. 343p. 1997. pap. 11.95 (*1-57392-140-8*) Prometheus Bks.
— Principles of Economics. 8th ed. (Illus.). xxxii, 731p. 1982. reprint ed. pap. 28.95 (*0-87991-051-8*) Porcupine Pr.
— The Pure Theory of Foreign Trade & the Pure Theory of Domestic Values. LC 73-22013. (Reprints of Economic Classics Ser.). (Illus.). 65p. 1975. reprint ed. lib. bdg. 17.50 (*0-678-01194-X*) Kelley.
Marshall, Alfred & Marshall, Mary P. Economics of Industry: 1879 Edition. 18th ed. (Key Texts Ser.). 248p. 1996. reprint ed. pap. 27.95 (*1-85506-320-4*) Bks Intl VA.
Marshall, Alice K. Pen Names of Women Writers. x, 181p. 1986. pap. 9.95 (*0-9616387-0-2*) A Marshall Collection.
Marshall, An. Aging in Action: A Dynamic Approach to Exercise. (Illus.). (Orig.). 1989. pap. write for info. (*0-318-66585-9*) Marshall Dynamics.
Marshall, And Swift. Electrical Cost Guide. 1998. pap. 69.95 (*0-07-134238-9*) McGraw.
— Unit Cost Guide. 1998. pap. 79.95 (*0-07-134235-4*) McGraw.
Marshall, Andrew W., jt. auth. see Goldhamer, Herbert.
Marshall, Angie. A Woman's Guide to Blackjack: Turning the Tables When the Cards Are Stacked Against You. LC 98-48110. (Illus.). 144p. 1999. pap. 12.00 (*0-8184-0606-2*) Carol Pub Group.
***Marshall, Ann.** Rain: Native Expressions from the American Southwest. 2000. pap. 32.50 (*0-89013-344-1*) Museum NM Pr.
Marshall, Ann, ed. Rain: Native Expressions from the American Southwest. 160p. 1999. pap. 24.95 (*1-57098-291-0*, Pub. by Roberts Rinehart) Publishers Group.
— Rain: Native Expressions from the American Southwest. (Illus.). 160p. 1999. 40.00 (*1-57098-290-2*, Pub. by Roberts Rinehart) Publishers Group.
Marshall, Ann E. Woven with Love. (Illus.). 36p. (Orig.). (J). (gr. 2-5). 1988. pap. 4.50 (*0-934351-02-3*) Heard Mus.
Marshall, Ann E. & Brennan, Mary H. The Heard Museum: History & Collections. rev. ed. 48p. (Orig.). 1995. pap. 9.95 (*0-934351-50-3*) Heard Mus.
Marshall, Anna, jt. auth. see Greenwood, Brian.
Marshall, Anne. The Complete Vegetarian Cookbook. (Illus.). 304p. 1993. 34.95 (*0-8048-1974-2*) Tuttle Pubng.
— Fighting for Survival. (Into the Wild Places Ser.: Vol. 1). (Illus.). 160p. 1999. pap. 14.95 (*1-58382-025-6*) Sagamore Pub.
Marshall, Anne & Huston, James. Under the Double Cross. 295p. 1984. 10.95 (*0-89697-214-3*) Intl Univ Pr.
Marshall, Archibald. Clinton Twins, & Other Stories. LC 70-130062. (Short Story Index Reprint Ser.). 1977. 19.95 (*0-8369-3661-2*) Ayer.
— Clintons, & Others. LC 73-130063. (Short Story Index Reprint Ser.). 1977. 24.95 (*0-8369-3662-0*) Ayer.
Marshall, Arthur. Dictionary of Explosives. (Explosives Ser.). 1989. lib. bdg. 250.00 (*0-8490-3967-3*) Gordon Pr.
— Explosives: Their History, Manufacture, Properties & Tests, 3 vols. 1980. lib. bdg. 900.00 (*0-8490-3151-6*) Gordon Pr.
Marshall, Arthur K. & Garb, Andrew S. California Probate Procedure, Issue 1. 6th ed. 200p. 1999. ring bd. write for info. (*0-327-01356-7*, 8026221) LEXIS Pub.
— California Probate Procedure, 2 vols., Set. 5th ed. 480p. 1995. spiral bd. 160.00 (*1-55943-089-3*, MICHIE) LEXIS Pub.
— California Probate Procedure, Suppl. 1. 1991. 71.50 (*1-55943-087-7*, MICHIE) LEXIS Pub.
— California Probate Procedure, Suppl. 2. 1993. 55.00 (*1-55943-088-5*, MICHIE) LEXIS Pub.
***Marshall, Arthur K. & Garb, Andrew S.** California Probate Procedure: With Judicial Council Forms. 6th ed. LC 98-202744 (Illus.). 1998. write for info. (*0-911110-71-2*); write for info. (*0-911110-72-0*) Parker Pubns.
Marshall, Atwood, jt. auth. see Lyman, Samuel.
Marshall, Audrey & Gorb, Arthur. California Probate Procedures, 2 vols. 6th rev. ed. 1998. ring bd. 195.00 (*0-327-00125-9*, 80258-11) LEXIS Pub.
***Marshall, Barbara.** Configuring Gender: Explorations in Theory & Politics. 170p. 2000. pap. 16.95 (*1-55111-094-6*) Broadview Pr.
— The New Germany & Migration in Europe. pap. write for info. (*0-7190-4336-0*, Pub. by Manchester Univ Pr) St Martin.
Marshall, Barbara. Willy Brandt: A Political Biography. LC 96-28750. (St. Antony's Ser.). 230p. 1997. text 35.00 (*0-312-16438-6*) St Martin.
Marshall, Barbara, jt. auth. see Hackman, Sue.
Marshall, Barbara K., jt. auth. see Clawson, Sharalee S.
Marshall, Barbara L. Engendering Modernity: Feminism, Social Theory, & Social Change. LC 94-13416. 220p. 1994. text 47.50 (*1-55553-212-8*); pap. text 17.95 (*1-55553-213-6*) NE U Pr.
Marshall, Barbara S. The Shining Place of an Image. LC 88-37853. 168p. (C). 1989. lib. bdg. 36.00 (*0-8191-7300-2*) U Pr of Amer.
Marshall, Barry. Dressage from All Angles. 1996. 54.00 (*0-85131-661-1*, Pub. by J A Allen) Trafalgar.
— The Dressage Rider's Problem-Solver. (Illus.). 160p. 1997. 35.00 (*1-86126-002-4*, Pub. by Cro1wood) Trafalgar.
Marshall, Benjamin T., ed. Modern History of New London County, Connecticut, 3 vols. in 2. (Illus.). 1154p. 1997. reprint ed. lib. bdg. 119.00 (*0-8328-5672-X*) Higginson Bk Co.
***Marshall, Bethan.** English Teachers: The Essential Guide. LC 00-42203. 2000. pap. write for info. (*0-415-24078-6*) Routledge.
Marshall, Bette, jt. auth. see Lombardy, William.
Marshall, Bill. Angels, Bulldogs & Dragons: 355th Fighter Group in World War 2. (Illus.). 180p. 1985. pap. 15.95 (*0-685-10425-7*) Champlin Museum.
— Gideon McGee's Dream. LC 97-90165. (Illus.). 136p. (Orig.). 1998. pap. 10.95 (*0-9657575-0-1*) Zacharaias Pr.
— Guy Hocquenghem: Beyond Gay Identity. LC 96-34201. 128p. 1997. pap. text 12.95 (*0-8223-1923-3*); lib. bdg. 39.95 (*0-8223-1930-6*) Duke.
— Victor Serge: The Uses of Dissent. 240p. 1992. 19.50 (*0-85496-766-4*) Berg Pubs.
***Marshall, Bill & Stilwell, Robynn, eds.** Musicals - Hollywood & Beyond. 192p. 2000. pap. 24.95 (*1-84150-003-8*, Pub. by Intellect) Intl Spec Bk.
Marshall, Blaine, ed. see Lewis, Shari & Aesop.
Marshall, Brenda. Teaching the Postmodern. 213p. (C). 1991. pap. 18.99 (*0-415-90455-2*, A5885) Routledge.
Marshall, Brenda, ed. Hollywood Reporter Studio Blu-Book Directory, 1986. 350p. 1986. 40.00 (*0-941140-06-7*) Hollywood Rep.
***Marshall, Brenda DeVore & Mayhead, Molly A., eds.** Navigating Boundaries: The Rhetoric of Women Governors. LC 99-59513. (Praeger Series in Political Communication). 176p. 2000. 59.95 (*0-275-96778-6*, C6778, Praeger Pubs); pap. 18.95 (*0-275-96779-4*, Praeger Pubs) Greenwood.
Marshall, Brian. Motif Programming: The Essentials . . . & More. (X & MOTIF Programming Ser.). (Illus.). 600p. 1992. pap. 39.95 (*1-55558-089-0*, EY-J816E-DP) DEC.
— The Secret of Getting Straight A's: Learn More in Less Time with Little Effort. LC 92-72740. (Illus.). 169p. (Orig.). (YA). (gr. 6 up). 1993. pap. 12.95 (*0-9633357-9-0*) Hathaway Intl.
— The Teradata Database - Application & Archive/Recovery Utilities. 2nd ed. (Illus.). xviii, 428p. 1987. 149.95 (*0-9665493-1-7*, 2) Educ Parallel.
***Marshall, Brian.** The Teradata Database - Implementation for Performance. LC 98-223219. (Illus.). 9p. 1998. 129.99 (*0-9665493-2-5*) Educ Parallel.
Marshall, Brian. The Teradata Database - Introduction & SQL. (Illus.). xii, 464p. 1987. 149.95 (*0-9665493-0-9*, 1) Educ Parallel.
Marshall, Brian & Ford, Wendy. The Secret of Getting Better Grades: Study Smarter, Not Harder. (Illus.). 168p. (Orig.). 1994. pap. 12.95 (*1-57112-061-0*, PA5027) Park Ave.
Marshall, Brian, jt. auth. see Kelly, Jan.
Marshall, Brian G. Bargains, Deals & Steals: How You Can Save up to 99 Percent on Almost Anything at Hidden Sales & Secret Auctions. Thomas, Bill, ed. 160p. (Orig.). 1991. pap. 14.95 (*1-878969-21-8*) Discovery UT.
Marshall, Bridget. Animal Crackers: A Tender Book about Death & Funerals & Love. LC 97-30150. (Illus.). (J). 1997. 6.95 (*1-56123-101-0*) Centering Corp.
Marshall, Bruce. A Foot in the Grave. large type ed. (Linford Mystery Library). 235p. 1988. pap. 16.99 (*0-7089-6559-8*, Linford) Ulverscroft.
— Uniforms of the Republic of Texas: And the Men That Wore Them,1836-1846. 88p. (Orig.). 1999. pap. 19.95 (*0-7643-0682-0*) Schiffer.
— The White Rabbit. LC 87-8663. 243p. 1987. reprint ed. lib. bdg. 65.00 (*0-313-25322-6*, MRWR, Greenwood Pr) Greenwood.
***Marshall, Bruce & Roberts, J. A.** Leaf Development & Canopy Growth. LC 00-27795. (Sheffield Biological Sciences Ser.). 2000. write for info. (*0-8493-9769-3*) CRC Pr.
***Marshall, Bruce D.** Trinity & Truth. LC 99-21509. (Cambridge Studies in Christian Doctrine: No. 3). 302p. (C). 1999. text 64.95 (*0-521-45352-6*); pap. text 22.95 (*0-521-77491-8*) Cambridge U Pr.
Marshall, Bruce D., ed. Theology & Dialogue: Essays in Conversation with George Lindbeck. LC 90-70847. 288p. (C). 1990. text 34.50 (*0-268-01873-1*) U of Notre Dame Pr.
Marshall, Bruce T. A Holy Curiosity: Stories of a Liberal Religious Faith. 125p. (Orig.). 1990. pap. 7.95 (*0-9626716-0-6*) UUF Huntington.
— Taking Pictures of God: Meditations. LC 96-612. 1996. pap. 7.00 (*1-55896-341-3*, Skinner Hse Bks) Unitarian Univ.
Marshall, Bryce & Williams, Paul. Zero at the Bone. McCarthy, Paul, ed. 328p. (Orig.). 1991. mass mkt. 5.50 (*0-671-68511-2*, Pocket Star Bks) PB.
Marshall, Burns. Chemical Engineering. 180p. 1992. 70.50 (*0-13-131418-1*) P-H.
Marshall, Byron K. Academic Freedom & the Japanese Imperial University, 1868-1939. (Illus.). 247p. (C). 1998. text 25.00 (*0-7881-5433-8*) DIANE Pub.
— Academic Freedom & the Japanese Imperial University, 1868-1939. (C). 1992. 48.00 (*0-520-07821-7*, Pub. by U CA Pr) Cal Prin Full Svc.
— Capitalism & Nationalism in Prewar Japan: The Ideology of the Business Elite, 1868-1941. LC 67-26528. 175p. 1967. reprint ed. pap. 30.00 (*0-608-04222-6*, 20649660011) Bks Demand.
Marshall, Byron K., tr. & intro. see Sakae, Osugi.
Marshall, C. C. I. I. Life Assurance Law & Practice, No. 090. (C). 1984. suppl. ed. 230.00 (*0-7855-4286-8*, Pub. by Witherby & Co) St Mut.
— C. I. I. Life Assurance Law & Taxation, No. 130-071. (C). 1984. suppl. ed. 230.00 (*0-7855-4285-X*, Pub. by Witherby & Co) St Mut.
Marshall, C. & Grace, James B., eds. Fruit & Seed Production: Aspects of Development, Environmental Physiology & Ecology. (Society for Experimental Biology Seminar Ser.: No. 48). (Illus.). 268p. (C). 1992. text 85.00 (*0-521-37350-6*) Cambridge U Pr.

M

Marshall, C. A. American Indian Family Support Systems & Implications for the Rehabilitation Process: The Eastern Band of Cherokee Indians & the Mississippi Band of Choctaw Indians: Cherokee Translation of Summary. 200p. 1995. pap. text. write for info. (*1-888557-26-5*, 100017) No Ariz Univ.

— The Assessment of a Model for Determining Community-Based Needs of American Indians with Disabilities: Follow-Up in Denver, Colorado: Final Report. 81p. 1994. pap. text. write for info. (*1-888557-06-0*, 100011) No Ariz Univ.

Marshall, C. A. & Cerveny, L. K. American Indian Family Support Systems & Implications for the Rehabilitation Process: The Eastern Band of Cherokee Indians & the Mississippi Band of Choctaw Indians: Executive Summary. 16p. 1994. pap. text. write for info. (*1-888557-25-7*, 100043) No Ariz Univ.

— American Indian Family Support Systems & Implications for the Rehabilitation Process: The Eastern Band of Cherokee Indians & the Mississippi Band of Choctaw Indians: Final Report. 8p. 1994. pap. text. write for info. (*1-888557-24-9*, 100078) No Ariz Univ.

Marshall, C. A. & Gotto, G. S., 4th. Developing Rehabilitation Researchers in the American Indian Community: A Technical Report of Consumer-Researcher Training. 1998. pap. 10.00 (*1-888557-76-1*) No Ariz Univ.

Marshall, C. A. & Johnson, M. The Utilization of the Family As a Resource in American Indian Vocational Rehabilitation Projects (Section 130 Projects) Final Report. 95p. 1996. pap. text. write for info. (*1-888557-64-8*) No Ariz Univ.

Marshall, C. A., et al. Assessing the Needs of Indigenous People with Disabilities in Mexico: Vecinos y Rehabilitation. 98p. 1996. pap. text. write for info. (*1-888557-58-3*) No Ariz Univ.

— Assessment of a Model for Determining Community-Based Needs of American Indians with Disabilities through Consumer Involvement in Community Planning & Change: Executive Summary. 11p. 1990. pap. text. write for info. (*1-888557-00-1*, 100082) No Ariz Univ.

— Assessment of a Model for Determining Community-Based Needs of American Indians with Disabilities Through Consumer Involvement in Community Planning & Change: Final Report, Phase I. 154p. 1990. pap. text. write for info. (*1-888557-01-X*, 100079) No Ariz Univ.

— An Examination of the Vocational Rehabilitation Needs of American Indians with Behavioral Health Diagnoses in New York State. 111p. 1997. pap. 11.00 (*1-888557-70-2*) No Ariz Univ.

— A National Survey of Indian Health Service Employees & the Development of a Model Job Training Demonstration Project: Identifying Work Opportunities for American Indians & Alaska Natives with Disabilities. 16p. 1994. pap. text. write for info. (*1-888557-17-6*, 100085) No Ariz Univ.

— The Replication of a Model for Determining Community-Based Needs of American Indians with Disabilities Through Consumer Involvement in Community Planning & Change: Executive Summary. 10p. 1992. pap. text. write for info. (*1-888557-02-8*, 100083) No Ariz Univ.

— The Replication of a Model for Determining Community-Based Needs of American Indians with Disabilities Through Consumer Involvement in Community Planning & Change: Final Report, Phase I. 78p. 1992. pap. text. write for info. (*1-888557-03-6*, 100084) No Ariz Univ.

— Vecinos y Rehabilitation Phase II: Assessing the Needs & Resources of Indigenous People with Disabilities in the Mexteca Region of Oaxaca, Mexico. 151p. 1997. pap. 11.00 (*1-888557-71-0*) No Ariz Univ.

Marshall, C. Edmund. The Physical Chemistry & Mineralogy of Soils Vol. 1: Soil Materials. LC 75-22180. 398p. 1975. reprint ed. pap. 32.50 (*0-88275-351-7*) Krieger.

Marshall, Carl. Holy Sex. Lillard, Reshana & Hooper, Angela, eds. LC 95-206552. 74p. (Orig.). 1995. reprint ed. pap. write for info. (*0-9647434-0-X*) GIFFT Minist.

Marshall, Carl & Marshall, David. The Book of Myself: A Do-It-Yourself Autobiography in 201 Questions. LC 96-36072. 208p. (J). 1997. 14.45 (*0-7868-6250-5*, Pub. by Hyperion) Time Warner.

Marshall, Carol, tr. see Comte, Philippe.

Marshall, Carol F., ed. see Eberhart-Wright, Alice.

Marshall, Catherine. Adventures in Prayer. 1987. mass mkt. 5.99 (*0-345-34755-2*) Ballantine Pub Grp.

— Adventures in Prayer. LC 96-216588. (Catherine Marshall Library). 104p. (gr. 10). 1996. pap. 9.99 (*0-8007-9244-0*) Chosen Bks.

— The Assistant Principal: Leadership Choices & Challenges. LC 91-28501. 144p. 1991. pap. 19.95 (*0-8039-6110-3*, D1478) Corwin Pr.

— The Best of Catherine Marshall. LeSourd, Leonard E., ed. LC 93-1606. 350p. (gr. 10). 1993. 14.99 (*0-8007-9209-2*) Chosen Bks.

— Beyond Our Selves. (Catherine Marshall Library). 268p. (gr. 10). 1994. reprint ed. pap. 9.99 (*0-8007-9089-8*) Chosen Bks.

— Beyond Ourselves. 272p. 1976. mass mkt. 4.99 (*0-380-00246-9*, Avon Bks) Morrow Avon.

— Beyond Ourselves. 272p. 1994. pap. 10.00 (*0-380-72202-X*, Avon Bks) Morrow Avon.

— Catherine Marshall: Inspiration Writings. 528p. 1995. 14.99 (*0-88486-118-X*) Arrowood Pr.

— Catherine Marshall's Story Bible. 200p. (J). (ps-5). 1985. pap. 10.95 (*0-380-69961-3*, Avon Bks) Morrow Avon.

Marshall, Catherine. Christy. 501p. 1976. mass mkt. 6.99 (*0-380-00141-1*, Avon Bks) Morrow Avon.

Marshall, Catherine. Christy. 1968. 11.60 (*0-606-00470-X*, Pub. by Turtleback) Demco.

— Christy. abr. ed. LC 94-43919. (Illus.). 160p. (gr. 7-10). 1995. 10.99 (*0-8007-1708-2*) Revell.

— Christy. 1994. reprint ed. lib. bdg. 35.95 (*1-56849-309-6*) Buccaneer Bks.

— Christy Books. 1995. pap., boxed set 19.99 (*0-8499-3947-X*) Word Pub.

— A Closer Walk. 224p. 1987. mass mkt. 4.99 (*0-380-70390-4*, Avon Bks) Morrow Avon.

— Collected Works of Catherine Marshall: Includes to Live Again & Beyond Our Selves. 528p. 1997. 14.99 (*0-88486-176-7*, Inspirational Pr) Arrowood Pr.

— Come into His Light. (Thumbprint Bks.). 92p. (gr. 10). 1996. 4.99 (*0-8007-7150-8*) Revell.

— Designing Qualitative Research. 3rd ed. LC 98-40148. 1999. pap. 24.95 (*0-7619-1340-8*) Sage.

— Hearing God's Voice. (Thumbprint Bks.). 92p. (gr. 10). 1996. 4.99 (*0-8007-7151-6*) Revell.

— The Helper. 1979. pap. 3.95 (*0-380-45583-8*, Avon Bks) Morrow Avon.

— The Helper. LC 77-15875. (Catherine Marshall Library). 240p. (gr. 11). 1994. reprint ed. pap. 9.99 (*0-8007-9131-2*) Chosen Bks.

— The Helper. rev. ed. 192p. 1994. pap. 10.00 (*0-380-72282-8*, Avon Bks) Morrow Avon.

— Inspirational Writings of Catherine Marshall. 1990. 12.98 (*0-88486-025-6*) Arrowood Pr.

— Inspirational Writings of Catherine Marshall. 1991. 12.98 (*0-88486-048-5*, Inspirational Pr) Arrowood Pr.

— Irish Art Masterpieces. (Illus.). 128p. 1995. 35.00 (*0-88363-295-0*) H L Levin.

— Julie. 448p. 1985. mass mkt. 6.99 (*0-380-69891-9*, Avon Bks) Morrow Avon.

— Light in My Darkest Night. 1990. mass mkt. 4.99 (*0-380-71023-4*, Avon Bks) Morrow Avon.

— A Man Called Peter. 93p. 1955. pap. 5.50 (*0-87129-693-4*, M14) Dramatic Pub.

— A Man Called Peter. 1976. mass mkt. 4.95 (*0-380-00894-7*, Avon Bks) Morrow Avon.

— A Man Called Peter. 352p. 1994. pap. 9.00 (*0-380-72204-6*, Avon Bks) Morrow Avon.

— A Man Called Peter: The Story of Peter Marshall. 2nd anniversary ed. 384p. 1999. 18.99 (*0-8007-9264-5*) Chosen Bks.

— A Man Called Peter & the Prayers of Peter Marshall: A Spiritual Life. 512p. 1996. 14.99 (*0-88486-149-X*, Inspirational Pr) Arrowood Pr.

— Meeting God at Every Turn: A Spiritual Autobiography. (Catherine Marshall Library). (Illus.). 256p. (gr. 10). 1995. pap. 9.99 (*0-8007-9231-9*) Chosen Bks.

— Precious in the Father's Sight. abr. ed. (Pocket Devotion Ser.). (Illus.). 384p. 1997. 9.99 (*0-8007-7158-3*, Day by Day with) Revell.

— Something More. 1976. mass mkt. 4.50 (*0-380-00601-4*, Avon Bks) Morrow Avon.

— Something More: In Search of a Deeper Faith. LC 96-4174. (Catherine Marshall Library). 304p. (gr. 11). 1996. pap. 10.99 (*0-8007-9242-4*) Chosen Bks.

— Something More T. rev. ed. 288p. 1994. pap. 9.00 (*0-380-72203-8*, Avon Bks) Morrow Avon.

— To Live Again. (Orig.). 1976. mass mkt. 4.95 (*0-380-01586-2*, Avon Bks) Morrow Avon.

— To Live Again. 336p. (Orig.). 1994. pap. 8.00 (*0-380-72236-4*, Avon Bks) Morrow Avon.

— To Live Again: The Inspiring Story of Catherine Marshall's Triumph Over Grief. LC 57-13338. (Catherine Marshall Library). 340p. (YA). (gr. 10). 1996. pap. 10.99 (*0-8007-9243-2*) Chosen Bks.

— The Unsung Role of the Career Assistant Principal. 68p. (Orig.). (C). 1993. pap. text 11.00 (*0-88210-272-9*) Natl Assn Principals.

Marshall, Catherine, ed. Mr. Jones, Meet the Master: Sermons & Prayers by Peter Marshall. 192p. (gr. 11). 1987. pap. 8.99 (*0-8007-5095-0*) Revell.

— The New Politics of Race & Gender: The 1992 Yearbook of the Politics of Education Association. (Education Policy Perspectives Ser.). 230p. 1993. 69.95 (*0-7507-0176-5*, Falmer Pr) Taylor & Francis.

Marshall, Catherine, ed. The Prayers of Peter Marshall. LC 54-11762. 252p. (gr. 11). 1988. pap. 11.99 (*0-8007-9141-X*) Chosen Bks.

Marshall, Catherine & Kasten, Katherine L. The Administrative Career: A Casebook on Entry, Equity, & Endurance. LC 94-30530. (Illus.). 152p. 1994. pap. 21.95 (*0-8039-6089-1*) Corwin Pr.

Marshall, Catherine & LeSourd, Leonard. Quiet Times with Catherine Marshall. 2nd ed. LC 97-116484. (Catherine Marshall Library). 256p. (gr. 10). 1996. pap. 11.99 (*0-8007-9248-3*) Chosen Bks.

Marshall, Catherine & Rossman, Gretchen B. Designing Qualitative Research. 172p. (C). 1989. text 39.95 (*0-8039-3157-3*); pap. text 17.95 (*0-8039-3158-1*) Sage.

— Designing Qualitative Research. 2nd ed. 188p. 1994. 44.00 (*0-8039-5248-1*); pap. 19.50 (*0-8039-5249-X*) Sage.

***Marshall, Catherine & Rossman, Gretchen B.** Designing Qualitative Research. 3rd ed. LC 98-40148. 224p. 1999. 65.00 (*0-7619-1339-4*) Sage.

Marshall, Catherine, et al. Footprints in the Snow: More Stories about God's Mysterious Ways. LC 92-7548. 128p. (Orig.). 1992. pap. 8.00 (*0-687-13253-3*) Dimen for Liv.

— Vecinos y Rehabilitation Fase II: Evaluacion de las Necesidades y Recursos de los Indigenas con Discapacidades en la Region Mixteca de Oaxaca, Mexico. (ENG & SPA.). 1997. pap. 11.00 (*1-888557-72-9*) No Ariz Univ.

Marshall, Catherine A. & Gotto, George S. Developing Rehabilitation Researchers in the American Indian Community: The Consumer-Researcher Training Model (Final Report) 1998. pap. 7.50 (*1-888557-81-8*) No Ariz Univ.

Marshall Cavendish BK Staff. Exploring Life Science, 11 vols. LC 98-52925. 880p. (J). (gr. 4-6). 2000. 471.36 (*0-7614-7135-9*) Marshall Cavendish.

***Marshall Cavendish Corporation Staff.** Aquatic Life of the World, Vols. 1-10. LC 99-86128. (Illus.). 2000. write for info. (*0-7614-7181-2*) Marshall Cavendish.

Marshall Cavendish Corporation Staff. Dinosaurs of the World, 11 vols. Marshall, Chris, ed. LC 97-43365. (Illus.). 704p. (YA). 1999. 471.36 (*0-7614-7072-7*) Marshall Cavendish.

***Marshall Cavendish Corporation Staff.** Endangered Wildlife & Plants of the World, 13 vols., Set. LC 99-86194. (Illus.). 1872p. 2001. lib. bdg. 459.95 (*0-7614-7194-4*) Marshall Cavendish.

— Peoples of Africa. LC 99-88550. (Illus.). 700p. 2000. lib. bdg. 329.95 (*0-7614-7158-8*) Marshall Cavendish.

Marshall Cavendish Corporation Staff. Wildlife & Plants of the World, 17 vols. LC 97-32139. 1000p. (J). 1999. 471.36 (*0-7614-7099-9*, Benchmark NY) Marshall Cavendish.

Marshall Cavendish Corporation Staff & Benchmark NY USA Staff. Secrets of the Unexplained. (YA). (gr. 4-7). 1999. lib. bdg. 85.50 (*0-7614-0466-X*) Marshall Cavendish.

Marshall Cavendish Staff. Encyclopedia of Earth & Physical Sciences, 11 vols., Set. LC 96-49660. (Illus.). 1500p. (YA). (gr. 10 up). 1998. lib. bdg. 459.95 (*0-7614-0551-8*) Marshall Cavendish.

Marshall, Celia B. A Guide Through the New Testament. LC 93-45517. 176p. (Orig.). 1994. pap. 19.95 (*0-664-25484-5*) Westminster John Knox.

— A Guide Through the Old Testament. 120p. (Orig.). 1989. pap. 19.95 (*0-8042-0124-2*) Westminster John Knox.

***Marshall, Charles.** Lee's Aide-de-Camp. Maurice, Frederick, ed. 352p. 2000. pap. 14.95 (*0-8032-8262-1*, Bison Books) U of Nebr Pr.

Marshall, Charles B. Crisis over Rhodesia: A Skeptical View. LC 67-22896. (Washington Center of Foreign Policy Research, Studies in International Affairs: Vol. 3). 91p. 1967. reprint ed. pap. 30.00 (*0-608-03724-9*, 206454900009) Bks Demand.

— The Exercise of Sovereignty: Papers on Foreign Policy. LC 65-11665. 296p. reprint ed. pap. 91.80 (*0-608-13770-7*, 202054600018) Bks Demand.

— The Limits of Foreign Policy. enl. ed. LC 88-94. 162p. (Orig.). (C). 1988. reprint ed. pap. text 18.50 (*0-8191-6815-7*) U Pr of Amer.

Marshall, Charles F. Discovering the Rommel Murder: Life & Death of the Desert Fox. (Illus.). 267p. 1994. 18.95 (*0-8117-1480-2*) Stackpole.

Marshall, Charles F. Ramble Through My War: Anzio & Other Joys. LC 98-24711. (Illus.). 248296p. 1998. 29.95 (*0-8071-2282-3*) La State U Pr.

***Marshall, Charles F.** Ramble Through My War: Anzio & Other Joys. (Illus.). 312p. 2000. pap. 18.95 (*0-8071-2636-5*) La State U Pr.

Marshall, Charles R. & Schopf, J. William. Evolution & Molecular Revolution. (Life Science Ser.). 176p. (C). 1996. pap. 40.00 (*0-86720-910-0*) Jones & Bartlett.

Marshall, Charles W. Vitamins & Minerals: Help or Harm. 206p. 1985. text 11.95 (*0-397-53060-9*) Lppncott W & W.

— Vitamins & Minerals: Help or Harm? rev. ed. LC RA0784.M35. (People's Health Library Book Ser.). 270p. 1985. reprint ed. pap. 83.70 (*0-608-05770-3*, 205973500007) Bks Demand.

Marshall, Chestar W. & Thompson, Warrent. Final Assault on the Rising Sun: Combat Diaries of B-29 Air Crews over Japan. LC 99-215196. (Illus.). 225p. 1995. 29.95 (*0-933424-59-0*) Specialty Pr.

Marshall, Chester. Hap's War. 1998. 29.95 (*1-885353-05-7*) Global Press.

— Sky Giants over Japan. (Illus.). 220p. (Orig.). 1994. reprint ed. 15.50 (*1-885353-00-6*) Global Press.

Marshall, Chester W. & Thompson, Warren. B-29 Photo Combat Diary: The Superfortress in WWII & Korea. (Illus.). 192p. (Orig.). 1996. pap. 24.95 (*0-933424-60-4*) Specialty Pr.

Marshall, Chris. April Calls: The Sailing Adventure of a Lifetime. 144p. (Orig.). 1993. pap. 9.95 (*0-9637347-3-3*) C W Pub.

— The Complete Book of Chinese Horoscopes: A Unique Guide to Individual Readings Combined with Western Zodiac Signs. LC 96-68727. (Illus.). 144p. 1996. spiral bd. 22.50 (*1-55670-490-9*) Stewart Tabori & Chang.

***Marshall, Chris.** Exhibit A. (Illus.). 96p. 2001. 20.00 (*0-9637347-8-4*); pap. 10.00 (*0-9637347-9-2*) C W Pub.

Marshall, Chris. I Ching: The Ancient Book of Chinese Wisdom for Divining the Future. LC 94-36523. (Illus.). 160p. 1995. per. 20.00 (*0-684-80180-9*) S&S Trade.

— Life Assurance & Pensions Handbook: Taxbriefs. 4th ed. (C). 1988. 250.00 (*0-7855-6048-3*, Pub. by Witherby & Co) St Mut.

— Software Components for the Enterprise: Building Business Objects with UML, Java & XML. LC 99-45160. (Object Technology Ser.). (Illus.). 288p. (C). 1999. pap. 44.95 (*0-201-43313-3*) Addison-Wesley.

— Warfare in the Medieval World. LC 98-11957. (History of Warfare Ser.). 80p. (YA). (gr. 5-12). 1999. 27.12 (*0-8172-5443-9*) Raintree Steck-V.

Marshall, Chris, ed. see Marshall Cavendish Corporation Staff.

Marshall, Christopher. Physical Basis of Computed Tomography. 171p. 1982. 37.50 (*0-87527-314-9*) Green.

— Warfare in the Latin East, 1192-1291. (Cambridge Studies in Medieval Life & Thought: No. 17). (Illus.). 305p. (C). 1994. pap. text 24.95 (*0-521-47742-5*) Cambridge U Pr.

Marshall, Christopher D. & Duane, William, eds. Extracts from the Diary of Christopher Marshall Kept in Philadelphia & Lancaster, During the American Revolution. LC 77-79944. (Eyewitness Accounts of the American Revolution Ser.). 1969. reprint ed. 20.95 (*0-405-01162-8*) Ayer.

***Marshall, Clare P. & Fairbridge, Rhodes W., eds.** Encyclopedia of Geochemistry. LC 98-34743. (Encyclopedia of Earth Sciences Ser.). 712p. 1999. 350.00 (*0-412-75500-9*) Kluwer Academic.

Marshall, Clifford W. & Solomon, Stephen S. Canadian Mortgage Payments. 2nd ed. 320p. 1993. pap. 6.95 (*0-8120-1617-3*) Barron.

Marshall, Clifford W., et al. Real Estate Loans. 2nd ed. (Financial Tables for Better Money Management Ser.). 352p. 1993. pap. 7.95 (*0-8120-1618-1*) Barron.

Marshall, Connie C. From Here to Maternity. 212p. 1986. pap. 9.95 (*0-9613784-1-7*) Conmar Pub.

Marshall County Backboard Club Staff. Lady Marshalls, 1980-1990: The Decade of Howard Beth. LC 90-71725. 88p. 1990. 24.95 (*1-56311-016-4*) Turner Pub KY.

Marshall, Cynthia. Last Things & Last Plays: Shakespearean Eschatology. LC 90-9883. 176p. (C). 1991. 26.95 (*0-8093-1689-7*) S Ill U Pr.

— Monaca Bridge & Selected Poems. 70p. (Orig.). 1996. pap. 6.95 (*1-57502-348-2*, PO1145) Morris Pubng.

Marshall, Cynthia, ed. Essays on C. S. Lewis & George MacDonald: Truth, Fiction, & the Power of Imagination. LC 90-21371. (Studies in British Literature: Vol. 11). 122p. 1991. lib. bdg. 59.95 (*0-88946-494-4*) E Mellen.

Marshall, D. Bruce. The French Colonial Myth & Constitution-Making in the Fourth Republic. LC 71-99833. 376p. reprint ed. pap. 116.60 (*0-608-14022-8*, 202201900024) Bks Demand.

Marshall, D. J. Cathodo-Luminescence of Geological Materials. (Illus.). 128p. 1987. text 125.00 (*0-04-552026-7*) Routledge.

Marshall, D. V., jt. auth. see Ritchie, R.

Marshall, Dale, ed. see Grayson, Jerry.

Marshall, Dale R., et al. Minority Perspectives: Papers. LC 78-186473. (Governance of Metropolitan Regions Ser.: No. 2). 76p. reprint ed. pap. 30.00 (*0-7837-3042-X*, 202382000034) Bks Demand.

Marshall, Dale R., jt. ed. see Montgomery, Roger.

***Marshall, Daniel.** Still Can't See Nothing Coming. 2000. 22.00 (*0-06-019862-1*); pap. 13.95 (*0-06-095826-X*) HarpC.

Marshall, Daniel, jt. ed. see Gregory, Judith.

Marshall, Dave. Scanner Master Ohio Pocket Guide. 168p. 1995. pap. 13.95 (*0-939430-20-7*) Scanner Master.

Marshall, David. Basketball. (Successful Sports Ser.). (J). 1996. lib. bdg. write for info. (*1-57572-073-6*) Heinemann Lib.

— Brazil. LC 95-25034. (Worldfocus Ser.). (J). 1998. 18.50 (*1-57572-029-9*) Heinemann Lib.

— The Figure of Theater: Shaftesbury, Defoe, Adam Smith, & George Eliot. 288p. 1986. text 57.50 (*0-231-06084-X*) Col U Pr.

— Food. Young, Richard, ed. LC 91-20535. (First Technology Library). (Illus.). 32p. (J). (gr. 3-5). 1991. lib. bdg. 15.93 (*1-56074-011-6*) Garrett Ed Corp.

— Footprints of Paul. 1995. pap. text 13.99 (*1-873796-50-1*) Review & Herald.

— God, Muhammad & the Unbelievers. 288p. 1998. 75.00 (*0-7007-1086-8*, Pub. by Curzon Pr Ltd) Paul & Co Pubs.

***Marshall, David.** Guide to Israel. (World Guides Ser.). (Illus.). 32p. (gr. 2-6). 1999. lib. bdg. 21.27 (*1-884756-47-6*) Davidson Titles.

— Guide to Kenya. rev. ed. (World Guides Ser.). (Illus.). 32p. (gr. 2-6). 1999. lib. bdg. 21.27 (*1-884756-50-6*) Davidson Titles.

Marshall, David. Highlander. 320p. 1998. mass mkt. 5.99 (*0-06-105840-8*) HarpC.

— Joy in Jesus. 1998. pap. 9.99 (*1-873796-74-9*) Review & Herald.

— Kenya. (Worldfocus Ser.). (J). 1998. 18.50 (*1-57572-030-2*) Heinemann Lib.

***Marshall, David.** Learn to Play Brazillian Jazz Guitar. 96p. 1999. pap. 19.95 incl. audio compact disk (*0-7866-4159-2*, 97746BCD) Mel Bay.

Marshall, David. Occult Explosion. 1998. pap. 10.99 (*1-873796-68-4*) Review & Herald.

— Soccer. (Successful Sports Ser.). (J). 1998. 18.50 (*1-57572-069-8*) Heinemann Lib.

— The Surprising Effects of Sympathy: Marivaux, Diderot, Rousseau, & Mary Shelley. (Illus.). x, 296p. 1988. 33.00 (*0-226-50710-6*) U Ch Pr.

***Marshall, David & Marshall, Kate.** The Book of Us: A Journal of Your Love Story in 150 Questions. 160p. (J). 1999. pap. 14.95 (*0-7868-6477-X*, Pub. by Hyperion) Time Warner.

Marshall, David & Richardson, Margot. Canada. (Modern Industrial World Ser.). (Illus.). 48p. (J). (gr. 6-8). 1996. lib. bdg. 24.26 (*1-56847-437-7*) Raintree Steck-V.

Marshall, David & Sayer, Geoff. Kenya. LC 95-25032. (Worldforum Ser.). (J). 1996. 18.50 (*1-57572-027-2*) Heinemann Lib.

Marshall, David, jt. auth. see Marshall, Carl.

Marshall, David, jt. auth. see Walker, Jane.

Marshall, David B. Secularizing the Faith: Canadian Protestant Clergy & the Crisis of Belief, 1850-1940. (Illus.). 288p. 1992. text 55.00 (*0-8020-5938-4*); pap. text 19.95 (*0-8020-6879-0*) U of Toronto Pr.

Marshall, David F., ed. Focus on Language Planning: Essays in Honor of Joshua A. Fishman, Vol. 3. LC 91-698. viii, 347p. 1991. 94.00 (*1-55619-118-9*) J Benjamins Pubng Co.

Marshall, David H. A Survey of Accounting: Selected Chapters. 2nd ed. (C). 1994. text 34.00 (*0-256-18085-7*, Irwn McGrw-H) McGrw-H Hghr Educ.

An Asterisk (*) at the beginning of an entry indicates that the title is appearing for the first time.

— A Survey of Accounting: What the Numbers Mean. 2nd ed. (C). 1995. text 37.50 (0-256-21977-X, Irwn McGrw-H) McGrw-H Hghr Educ.
— Survey of Accounting: What the Numbers Mean. 2nd ed. 320p. (C). 1992. text, student ed. 26.87 (0-256-11328-9, Irwn McGrw-H) McGrw-H Hghr Educ.
Marshall, David H. & McManus, Wayne W. Accounting: Ready Notes & Odd Solutions. 3rd ed. 200p. (C). 1996. text, suppl. ed. 10.00 (0-256-21596-0, Irwn McGrw-H) McGrw-H Hghr Educ.
— Accounting: What the Numbers Mean. 3rd ed. LC 95-32359. (Irwin Series in Undergraduate Accounting). 656p. (C). 1995. text 71.75 (0-256-16686-2, Irwn McGrw-H) McGrw-H Hghr Educ.
— Accounting: Working Papers. 3rd ed. 416p. (C). 1995. text, student ed. 26.87 (0-256-16694-3, Irwn McGrw-H) McGrw-H Hghr Educ.
Marshall, David H., et al. Accounting & Finance for Insurance Professionals. LC 97-73244. 515p. (C). 1997. 78.00 (0-89463-078-4, 802) Am Inst FCPCU.
Marshall, Debra. Still Sweet. (Our Town Ser.). 288p. 1997. mass mkt. 5.99 (0-515-12130-4, Jove) Berkley Pub.
Marshall, Delia, jt. auth. see Finch, Peter.
Marshall, Des. Vercors Caves Vol. 1: Classic French Caving. 100p. 1996. pap. 13.95 (1-871890-71-3) Menasha Ridge.
Marshall, Diane. Walking Places in Florida. 400p. 1999. pap. 17.00 (1-893695-01-8) Out There Pr.
Marshall, Diane, jt. auth. see Stann, Kap.
Marshall, Don. Who Discovered the Straits of Juan de Fuca? 27p. 1991. pap. 6.95 (0-87770-493-7) Ye Galleon.
Marshall, Don B. California Shipwrecks: Footsteps in the Sea. LC 78-13767. (Illus.). 176p. 1978. 19.95 (0-87564-223-3) Binford Mort.
— Oregon Shipwrecks. LC 84-71477. (Illus.). 250p. 1984. 24.95 (0-8323-0430-1) Binford Mort.
***Marshall, Don B. & Marshall, John A.** Eh, What's That You Said? Jargon of the Sea. (Illus.). 32p. 1999. pap. 5.95 (0-8323-0530-8) Binford Mort.
Marshall, Don R. The Four Elements of Successful Management: Select*Direct*Evaluate*Reward. LC 98-29548. xvi, 208p. 1999. 24.95 (0-8144-0424-3) AMACOM.
— Successful Techniques for Solving Employees Compensation Problems. LC 77-17964. (Illus.). 212p. reprint ed. pap. 65.80 (0-608-30681-9, 202018900016) Bks Demand.
Marshall, Donald G. Contemporary Critical Theory: A Selective Bibliography. LC 92-33515. ix, 201p. 1993. pap. 15.50 (0-87352-964-2, T126P); lib. bdg. 32.00 (0-87352-963-4, T126C) Modern Lang.
Marshall, Donald G., ed. see Gadamer, Hans-Georg.
Marshall, Donis. ActiveX - OLE Programming: Building Stable Components with Microsoft Foundation Class. 416p. (Orig.). 1998. pap. 49.95 incl. cd-rom (0-87930-516-9) C M P Books.
Marshall, Dorothy. English People in the Eighteenth Century. LC 80-16871. (Illus.). 288p. 1980. reprint ed. lib. bdg. 38.50 (0-313-21080-2, MAENP, Greenwood Pr) Greenwood.
— The Life & Times of Victoria. Fraser, Antonia, ed. (Kings & Queens of England Ser.). (Illus.). 224p. 1992. 24.95 (1-55859-450-7) Abbeville Pr.
— Victoria. (Illus.). 224p. 1998. pap. 18.95 (1-56649-036-7) Welcome Rain.
Marshall, Dorothy W., ed. History of Branch County Michigan, with Index. (Illus.). 527p. 1999. reprint ed. lib. bdg. 55.00 (0-8328-9763-9) Higginson Bk Co.
Marshall, Duncan L. Dividend Potentials: A Productive Determinant for Investment Decision, 1990 Edition. 2nd ed. (Illus.). 68p. (Orig.). 1990. pap. text 25.00 (0-9626505-1-X) D Marshall Pub.
Marshall, E. A., jt. auth. see Oliver, M. C.
Marshall, E. H., ed. History of Obion County: Towns & Communities, Churches, Schools, Farming, Factories, Social & Political. (Illus.). 272p. 1997. reprint ed. lib. bdg. 34.50 (0-8328-6924-4) Higginson Bk Co.
Marshall, E. L., jt. ed. see Owen, Keith.
Marshall, Ed & Lincoln Beta Club Staff. The Way It Is (un-RUSH-ed) Kyle, Jillian, ed. (Illus.). 120p. (Orig.). 1993. pap. 8.95 (0-938041-15-0) Arc Pr AR.
Marshall Editions Staff. Dream Places: A Grand Tour of the World's Best-Loved Destinations. LC 95-17381. (Illus.). 200p. 1995. 39.95 (0-528-83774-5) Rand McNally.
***Marshall Editions Staff.** Scientific American: How Things Work Today. Wright, Michael & Patel, M. N., eds. (Illus.). 288p. 2000. 29.95 (0-375-41023-6) Crown Pub Group.
Marshall Editions Staff. Vietnam: The Decisive Battles. (Illus.). 200p. 1990. text 39.95 (0-02-580171-6) Macmillan.
Marshall Editions Staff & Westland, Pamela. Gifts from the Kitchen. LC 96-29921. (Made for Giving Ser.). 1997. 18.95 (0-89577-955-2, Pub. by RD Assn) Penguin Putnam.
Marshall Editions Staff, jt. auth. see Mason, Antony.
Marshall, Edmund. Business & Society. LC 92-32042. (Elements of Business Ser.). 208p. 1993. pap. 64.95 (0-415-06849-5) Thomson Learn.
— Business & Society. LC 92-32042. (Elements of Business Ser.). 208p. (C). 1993. pap. 22.95 (0-415-06850-9, B0109) Thomson Learn.
Marshall, Edna M. Evaluation of Types of Student-Teaching. LC 73-177054. (Columbia University. Teachers College. Contributions to Education Ser.: No. 488). reprint ed. 37.50 (0-404-55488-1) AMS Pr.
Marshall, Edward. Four on the Shore. LC 84-15610. (Easy-to-Read Bks.: Level 3, Yellow). (Illus.). (J). (ps-3). 1994. pap. 3.99 (0-14-037006-4, PuffinBks) Peng Put Young Read.
Marshall, Edward. Four on the Shore. (Dial Easy-to-Read Ser.). (J). 1985. 9.19 (0-606-06120-7, Pub. by Turtleback) Demco.
Marshall, Edward. Fox & His Friends. (Easy-to-Read Bks.: Level 3, Yellow). (Illus.). (J). (ps-3). 1994. pap. 3.99 (0-14-037007-2, PuffinBks) Peng Put Young Read.
— Fox on Wheels. LC 93-2722. (Easy-to-Read Bks.: Level 3, Yellow). (Illus.). (J). (ps-3). 1993. pap. 3.99 (0-14-036541-9, PuffinBks) Peng Put Young Read.
— Space Case. LC 80-13369. (Illus.). 32p. (J). (ps-3). 1980. 16.99 (0-8037-8005-2, Dial Yng Read) Peng Put Young Read.
Marshall, Edward. Space Case. unabridged ed. (J). (gr. k-4). 1992. pap. 15.90 incl. audio (0-8045-6597-X, 6597) Spoken Arts.
Marshall, Edward. Three by the Sea. LC 80-26097. (Easy-to-Read Bks.: Level 2, Red). (Illus.). 48p. (J). (gr. k-3). 1994. pap. 3.99 (0-14-037004-8, PuffinBks) Peng Put Young Read.
— Three by the Sea. (Puffin Easy-to-Read Ser.). (J). 1994. 8.70 (0-606-00604-4, Pub. by Turtleback) Demco.
— Zorro en la Escuela. (Libro Puffin Facil-de-Leer Ser.). 1996. 8.70 (0-606-10110-1, Pub. by Turtleback) Demco.
— Zorro y Sus Amigos. (Libro Puffin Facil-de-Leer Ser.).Tr. of Fox & His Friends. 1996. 8.70 (0-606-10538-7, Pub. by Turtleback) Demco.
Marshall, Edward & Marshall, James. Fox & His Friends. (Fox Series). 56p. (J). (gr. k-2). pap. 3.99 (0-8072-1350-0) Listening Lib.
— Fox at School. (Fox Series). 48p. (J). (gr. k-2). pap. 3.99 (0-8072-1349-7) Listening Lib.
— Fox in Love. (Fox Series). 48p. (J). (gr. k-2). pap. 3.99 (0-8072-1352-7) Listening Lib.
— Fox on Wheels. (Fox Series). 48p. (J). (gr. k-2). pap. 3.99 (0-8072-1353-5) Listening Lib.
— Three by the Sea. 48p. (J). (gr. k-3). pap. 3.99 (0-8072-1342-X) Listening Lib.
Marshall, Edward C. Grant. Ancestry of General Grant, & Their Contemporaries. (Illus.). 186p. 1997. reprint ed. pap. 27.00 (0-8328-8821-4); reprint ed. lib. bdg. 37.00 (0-8328-8820-6) Higginson Bk Co.
***Marshall, Edward M.** Building Trust at the Speed of Change: The Power of the Relationship-Based Corporation. LC 99-34449. 240p. 1999. 25.00 (0-8144-0478-2) AMACOM.
Marshall, Eileen & Robinson, Colin. The Economics of Energy Self-Sufficiency: British Institute's Joint Energy Policy Programme; Energy Papers, Vol.14. 149p. 1984. text 77.95 (0-435-84518-7, Pub. by Dartmth Pub) Ashgate Pub Co.
Marshall, Eireann, jt. auth. see Hope, Valerie M.
Marshall, Eldon K., et al, eds. Interpersonal Helping Skills. LC 82-17275. (Jossey-Bass Social & Behavioral Science Ser.). (Illus.). 704p. reprint ed. pap. 200.00 (0-8357-4907-X, 203783700009) Bks Demand.
Marshall, Elisabeth. The Remainder of My Bread. limited ed. 64p. 1995. write for info. (0-9649013-0-7) Listning Post Pr.
Marshall, Elizabeth L. Conquering Infertility: Medical Challenges & Moral Dilemmas. LC 96-39440. (Changing Family Ser.). (YA). (gr. 7-12). 1997. 24.00 (0-531-11344-2) Watts.
— High-Tech Harvest. LC 98-8203. (Impact Book Ser.). 144 p. (J). 1999. 24.00 (0-531-11434-1) Watts.
Marshall, Elizabeth L. Human Genome Project. (Illus.). 1996. pap. 17.95 (0-613-13685-3) Econo-Clad Bks.
Marshall, Elizabeth L. The Human Genome Project: Cracking the Code Within Us. LC 95-45975. 128p. (YA). (gr. 7-12). 1996. lib. bdg. 24.00 (0-531-11299-3) Watts.
— The Human Genome Project: Cracking the Code Within Us. (Impact Bks.). 128p. (YA). (gr. 7 up). 1997. pap. 9.95 (0-531-15833-0) Watts.
— A Student's Guide to the Internet: Exploring the World Wide Web, Gopherspace, Electronic Mail, & More! LC 96-5163. (Illus.). 160p. (YA). (gr. 5 up). 1996. lib. bdg. 23.90 (1-56294-923-3) Millbrook Pr.
Marshall, Elva, ed. see Resla, W. J.
Marshall, Emily. Amber on the Line. (Going for the Gold Ser.). 144p. (Orig.). (J). (gr. 3-7). 1997. pap. 3.95 (0-8167-3977-3) Troll Communs.
Marshall, Eric, jt. auth. see Hample, Stuart E.
***Marshall, Evan.** Hanging Hannah. 320p. 2000. 20.00 (1-57566-550-6, Knsington) Kensgtn Pub Corp.
Marshall, Evan. The Marshall Plan for Novel Writing. LC 98-35710. 240p. 1998. 17.99 (0-89879-848-5, Wrtrs Digest Bks) F & W Pubns Inc.
Marshall, Evan. Missing Marlene. 320p. 1999. text 20.00 (1-57566-420-8) Kensgtn Pub Corp.
***Marshall, Evan.** Missing Marlene. (Jane Stuart & Winky Mystery Ser.). 2000. mass mkt. 5.99 (1-57566-555-7) Kensgtn Pub Corp.
Marshall, Evan P. & Sanow, Edwin J. Handgun Stopping Power: The Definitive Study. (Illus.). 240p. 1992. text 39.95 (0-87364-653-3) Paladin Pr.
— Street Stoppers: The Latest Handgun Stopping Power Street Results. 392p. 1996. pap. 39.95 (0-87364-872-2) Paladin Pr.
***Marshall, F. M.** Common-Cause Failure Database & Analysis System: Data Collection & Event Coding. 71p. 1998. pap. 6.00 (0-16-062933-0) USGPO.
— Common-Cause Failure Database & Analysis System: Event Definition & Classification. 60p. 1998. pap. 5.00 (0-16-062932-2) USGPO.
— Common-Cause Failure Database & Analysis System: Overview. 37p. 1998. pap. 3.50 (0-16-062931-4) USGPO.
— Common-Cause Failure Parameter Estimations. 379p. 1998. per. 30.00 (0-16-062969-1) USGPO.
Marshall, F. Ray. Labor in the South. LC 67-22870. (Wertheim Publications in Industrial Relations). (Illus.). 420p. 1967. 29.95 (0-674-50700-2) HUP.
Marshall, F. Ray & Briggs, Vernon M., Jr. Equal Apprenticeship Opportunities: The Nature of the Issue & the New York Experience. LC 68-66987. (Policy Papers in Human Resources & Industrial Relations Ser.: No. 10). (Orig.). 1968. pap. 5.00 (0-87736-110-X) U of Mich Inst Labor.
— The Negro & Apprenticeship. LC 67-18561. 297p. reprint ed. pap. 92.10 (0-608-14631-5, 202310900032) Bks Demand.
Marshall, F. Ray & Godwin, Lamond. Cooperatives & Rural Poverty in the South. LC 70-135534. (Policy Studies in Employment & Welfare: No. 7). 108p. reprint ed. pap. 33.50 (0-608-11903-2, 202312400032) Bks Demand.
Marshall, Felicia. Willa Mae Johnson & the Fayette County Market. LC 96-3392. (J). 1998. 16.00 (0-689-80855-0) S&S Bks Yung.
***Marshall, Felicity.** Sage's Ark. (Illus.). 32p. (J). 2000. 21.95 (1-86368-290-2, Pub. by Fremantle Arts); pap. 12.95 (1-86368-253-8, Pub. by Fremantle Arts) Intl Spec Bk.
Marshall, Fern, jt. auth. see Bradley, Fern M.
Marshall, Fiona. Epilepsy: Practical & Easy-to-Follow Advice. LC 98-36449. (Your Child Ser.). 128p. 1999. pap. 9.95 (1-86204-315-9, Pub. by Element MA) Penguin Putnam.
— Epilepsy: Your Guide to Complementary Therapies, Alternative Techniques & Conventional Treatments. LC 98-4675. (Natural Way Ser.). 128p. 1998. pap. 5.95 (1-86204-194-6, Pub. by Element MA) Penguin Putnam.
— Losing a Parent. LC 93-36599. 168p. (Orig.). 1993. pap. 12.95 (1-55561-056-0) Fisher Bks.
***Marshall, Fiona.** Losing A Parent: Practical Help for You & Other Family Members. 2nd ed. LC 99-88893. 168p. 2000. pap. 14.00 (1-55561-223-7) Fisher Bks.
— Natural Aphrodisiacs. 2000. pap. 10.95 (1-86204-577-1, Pub. by Element MA) Penguin Putnam.
Marshall, Florence. Life & Letters of Mary Wollstonecraft Shelley, 2 vols., Set. LC 70-115181. (Studies in Shelley: No. 25). 1970. reprint ed. lib. bdg. 150.00 (0-8383-1011-7) M S G Haskell Hse.
Marshall, Francine, jt. ed. see Gifford, Diane P.
Marshall, Francis. The Battle of Gettysburg. 337p. 1987. reprint ed. 30.00 (0-942211-26-X) Olde Soldier Bks.
Marshall, Frank, photos by. Ladies & Gentle Men: Women Sharing with Women about the Art of Relating to Men. (Illus.). 134p. (Orig.). 1992. pap. 14.00 (0-9634341-0-1) Orphan Pr.
Marshall, Frank & Hatcher, Carole. Church Visioning Workbook. Date not set. pap. 11.25 (1-56699-178-1, OD121) Alban Inst.
Marshall-Fratani, Ruth, jt. auth. see Corten, Andre.
Marshall, Fray F. Cryptorchidism & Related Anomalies. Elder, Jack S., ed. LC 82-11302. 118p. 1982. 55.00 (0-275-91374-0, C1374, Praeger Pubs) Greenwood.
— Textbook of Operative Urology. Valkhoff, Sandra et al, eds. LC 95-17717. 992p. 1996. text 195.00 (0-7216-5510-6, W B Saunders Co) Harcrt Hlth Sci Grp.
***Marshall, Fray F. & Issa, Muta.** Contemporary Diagnosis & Management of Diseases of the Prostate. (Illus.). 125p. 2000. pap. 29.95 (1-884065-67-8, Hndbks Hlth Care) Assocs in Med.
Marshall, Frederick, ed. see Maydew, Gary L.
Marshall, G., ed. FLAX - Breeding & Utilisation: Proceedings of the EEC Flax Workshop Held in Brussels, Belgium, 4-5 May, 1988. (Advances in Agricultural Biotechnology Ser.). (C). 1988. text 107.50 (0-7923-0065-3) Kluwer Academic.
Marshall, G. A. Coleoptera - Rhynchophora - Curculionidae. (Fauna of British India Ser.). xvi, 370p. 1977. reprint ed 30.00 (0-88065-154-7) Scholarly Pubns.
Marshall, G. F. Laser Beam Scanning: Opto-Mechanical Devices, Systems & Data Storage Optics. (Optical Engineering Ser.: Vol. 8). (Illus.). 448p. 1985. text 165.00 (0-8247-7418-3) Dekker.
Marshall, G. S. Introductory Mathematics, Applications & Methods. LC 97-40061. (Undergraduate Mathematics Ser.). 225p. (C). 1998. pap. 29.95 (3-540-76179-9) Spr-Verlag.
Marshall, Gail. Actresses on the Victorian Stage: Feminine Performance & the Galatea Myth. LC 97-26258. (Studies in Nineteenth-Century Literature & Culture Ser.: Vol. 16). (Illus.). 249p. (C). 1998. text 54.95 (0-521-62016-3) Cambridge U Pr.
Marshall, Garland R., jt. ed. see Rivier, Jean E.
Marshall, Garry & Marshall, Lori. Wake Me When It's Funny: How to Break into Show Business & Stay There. LC 95-6630. (Illus.). 352p. 1997. reprint ed. pap. 14.95 (1-55704-288-8, Pub. by Newmarket) Norton.
***Marshall, Gene.** The Memoirs of Jean Lafitte: From le Journal de Jean Laffite. LC 99-91770. 2000. 25.00 (0-7388-1252-8); pap. 18.00 (0-7388-1253-6) Xlibris Corp.
Marshall, Gene W. The Birth & Rebirth & Rebirth & Rebirth...of Spirit: Some Reflections upon the Origins & Survival Possibilities of the Last Remaining Upright-Walking Primates. (Illus.). 35p. 1996. pap. 8.00 (0-9611552-7-2) Realistic Living.
***Marshall, Gene W.** Fresh Wineskins for the Christian Breakthrough: Fragments of Visionary Brooding on the Sociological Future of Christianity. (Illus.). 68p. 1999. pap. 8.00 (1-890945-03-X) Realistic Living.
Marshall, Gene W. Good Christian Religion As a Social Project: How to View the Jesus Christ Happening As the Central Illumination of My Life Without Becoming a Bigot. (Illus.). 68p. 1997. pap. 8.00 (0-9611552-9-9) Realistic Living.
— Great Thinks, Great Feels, & Great Resolves: Some Reflections on the Essence of Religious Experience. (Illus.). 35p. 1996. pap. 8.00 (0-9611552-8-0) Realistic Living.
— The Infinite Silence Speaks: Poetic Discourses on the Book of Genesis. (Illus.). 56p. 1997. pap. 8.00 (1-890945-00-5) Realistic Living.
— The Infinite Silence Walks among Us: Some Poetic Discourses on the Gospel of John. (Illus.). 68p. 1998. pap. 8.00 (1-890945-02-1) Realistic Living.
***Marshall, Gene W.** Pets, Children & Spirit Maturity: Reflections on the Inner Journey. 42p. 2000. pap. 8.00 (1-890945-04-8) Realistic Living.
Marshall, Gene W. A Primer on Radical Christianity. LC 85-71566. 231p. 1985. pap. 10.00 (0-9611552-1-3) Realistic Living.
***Marshall, Gene W.** The Reincarnation of Paul: A Fictitious dialogue with the New Testament Letter Writer. 33p. 2000. pap. 8.00 (1-890945-05-6) Realistic Living.
Marshall, Gene W. Speaking Back to the Infinite Silence: Some Poetic Discourses on the Psalms. (Illus.). 59p. 1998. pap. 8.00 (1-890945-01-3) Realistic Living.
— To Be or Not to Be a Christian: Meditations & Essays on Authentic Christian Community. LC 94-65447. (Illus.). 336p. (Orig.). 1994. pap. 15.00 (0-9611552-3-X) Realistic Living.
Marshall, Gene W., jt. auth. see Marshall, Joyce.
Marshall, Genevieve E., jt. auth. see O'Brien, Walter J.
Marshall, Geoffrey. Constitutional Conventions: The Rules & Forms of Political Accountability. LC 97-43396. 262p. 1987. pap. text 21.00 (0-19-876202-X) OUP.
Marshall, Geoffrey, ed. Ministerial Responsibility. (Oxford Readings in Politics & Government Ser.). 186p. 1989. 45.00 (0-19-827580-3); pap. 16.95 (0-19-827579-X) OUP.
Marshall, George. Skinhead Nation. 156p. 1996. pap. 26.95 (1-898927-45-6, Pub. by S T Pubng) AK Pr Dist.
— Spirit of '69: A Skinhead Bible. (Illus.). 168p. (Orig.). 1991. pap. 19.95 (0-9518497-0-0, Pub. by S T Pubng) AK Pr Dist.
— Total Madness. (Illus.). (Orig.). 1993. pap. 19.95 (0-9518497-4-3, Pub. by S T Pubng) AK Pr Dist.
— The Two Tone Story. (Illus.). 128p. (Orig.). 1997. pap. 16.95 (0-9518497-3-5, Pub. by S T Pubng) AK Pr Dist.
Marshall, George & Poling, David. Albert Schweitzer: A Biography. rev. ed. (Illus.). 346p. 1991. pap. text 4.00 (1-881815-26-9) Albert Schweitzer.
Marshall, George, ed. & intro. see Marshall, Robert.
Marshall, George C. Biennial Reports of the Chief of Staff of the United States Army to the Secretary of War, 1 July 1939-30 June 1945. 224p. 1996. boxed set 34.00 (0-16-048657-2) USGPO.
— General Marshall's Victory Report on the Winning of World War II in Europe & the Pacific. (Illus.). 140p. 1989. reprint ed. 15.95 (0-9624874-0-6) A A Meverden.
— Marshall's Mission to China: December 1945 to January 1947, 2 vols., Vol. I: The Report. Van Slyke, Lyman P., ed. LC 76-43634. 465p. 1976. lib. bdg. 65.00 (0-313-26910-6, U6910) Greenwood.
— Marshall's Mission to China: December 1945 to January 1947, 2 vols., Vol. 2. Van Slyke, Lyman P., ed. LC 76-43634. 522p. 1976. lib. bdg. 65.00 (0-313-26911-4, U6911) Greenwood.
— The Papers of George Catlett Marshall Vol. 3: "The Right Man for the Job," December 3, 1941-May 31, 1943. Bland, Larry I. & Stevens, Sharon R., eds. (Illus.). 800p. 1991. text 55.00 (0-8018-2967-4) Johns Hopkins.
— Selected Speeches & Statements of General of the Army George C. Marshall. DeWeerd, H. A., ed. LC 72-10365. (FDR & the Era of the New Deal Ser.). 1973. reprint ed. lib. bdg. 37.50 (0-306-70556-7) Da Capo.
Marshall, George C. & Scholarly Resources Inc., Staff. The Complete Records of the Mission of General George C. Marshall to China, December 1945-January 1947. LC 87-20538. 50p. 1987. 10.00 (0-8420-3048-4) Scholarly Res Inc.
Marshall, George C., et al. The Papers of George C. Marshall: Selected World War II Correspondence. LC 93-28320. (World War II Research Collections). 40 p. 1992. write for info. (1-55655-455-9) U Pubns Amer.
Marshall, George J. Angels: An Indexed & Partially Annotated Bibliography of over 4300 Scholarly Books & Articles since the 7th Century B. C. LC 98-47852. 485p. 1999. lib. bdg. 95.00 (0-7864-0555-4) McFarland & Co.
Marshall, George N. Buddha: His Quest for Serenity: A Biography. rev. ed. LC 90-8495. 264p. 1990. 32.95 (0-87047-048-5); pap. 18.95 (0-87047-049-3) Schenkman Bks Inc.
— Challenge of a Liberal Faith. 3rd ed. 256p. (Orig.). 1993. pap. 14.00 (0-933840-31-4, Skinner Hse Bks) Unitarian Univ.
***Marshall, George N. & Poling, David.** Schweitzer: A Biography. LC 99-44065. (Illus.). 362p. 2000. pap. 18.95 (0-8018-6455-0) Johns Hopkins.
Marshall, George W. The Genealogist's Guide: 4th Edition. 4th ed. LC 66-23581. 880p. 1998. reprint ed. pap. 65.00 (0-8063-0235-6) Clearfield Co.
Marshall, Gilbert. Safety Engineering. LC 94-10722. 1994. 34.50 (0-939874-99-7) ASSE.
***Marshall, Gilbert.** Safety Engineering 3rd ed. LC 99-41058. 1999. write for info. (1-885581-28-9) ASSE.
Marshall, Gloria. Butterfly Mornings & Wildflower Afternoons. LC 98-66957. (Illus.). 144p. 1998. pap. 12.95 (1-888345-12-8) Paper Jam.
Marshall, Gloria P. How to Be a Faerie Grandmother: A New Image for the 21st Century. LC 89-81010. (Illus.). 135p. (Orig.). 1990. pap. text 8.95 (1-878323-00-8) Acronym Bks.
Marshall, Gordian, jt. auth. see Hilton, Michael.
Marshall, Gordian, ed. see Blue, Lionel.

M

Marshall, Gordon. In Search of the Spirit of Capitalism: An Essay on Max Weber's Protestant Ethic Thesis. (Modern Revivals in Sociology Ser.). 236p. 1993. 61.95 (*0-7512-0201-0*, Pub. by Gregg Revivals) Ashgate Pub Co.

— Presbyteries & Profits: Calvinism & the Development of Capitalism in Scotland, 1560 - 1707. 416p. 1992. pap. 28.00 (*0-7486-0333-6*, Pub. by Edinburgh U Pr) Col U Pr.

— Repositioning Class: Social Inequality in Industrial Societies. 304p. 1997. 85.00 (*0-7619-5557-7*); pap. 28.00 (*0-7619-5558-5*) Sage.

Marshall, Gordon, ed. A Dictionary of Sociology. 2nd ed. LC 98-3333. (Oxford Paperback Reference Ser.). (Illus.). 720p. (Orig.). 1998. pap. 16.95 (*0-19-280081-7*) OUP.

Marshall, Gordon, et al. Against the Odds? Social Class & Social Justice in Industrial Societies. LC 96-40028. (Illus.). 280p. 1997. text 75.00 (*0-19-829240-6*); pap. text 32.00 (*0-19-829239-2*) OUP.

— Social Class in Modern Britain. 336p. (C). 1989. pap. text 22.95 (*0-04-445416-3*) Routledge.

— Social Class in Modern Britain. 336p. 1989. 49.95 (*0-09-167940-0*) Routledge.

Marshall, Grace L. & Haggblade, Berle. Keyboarding & Computer Applications. LC 92-35186. (J). 1994. text 32.95 (*0-538-61877-9*) S-W Pub.

***Marshall, Grant N., et al.** A Review of the Scientific Literature As It Pertains to Gulf War Illness Vol. 4: Stress. 142p. (C). 2000. 15.00 (*0-8330-2860-X*) Rand Corp.

Marshall, Grant N., et al. A Review of the Scientific Literature As it Pertains to Gulf War Illnesses: Volume 4: Stress, Vol. 4. 130p. 1999. pap. 15.00 (*0-8330-2679-8*, MR-1018/4-OSD) Rand Corp.

***Marshall, Gregory Hugh.** Cuaderno Suplemental: Supplemental Workbook for Intermediate Spanish. (SPA.). 110p. 1999. wbk. ed. write for info. (*0-9702898-1-2*) Monument Bks Pub.

— Cuaderno Suplemental: Supplemental Workbook for Intermediate Spanish. 2nd ed. (SPA.). 2000. wbk. ed. write for info. (*0-9702898-3-9*) Monument Bks Pub.

— Cuaderno Tercero: Review Workbook for Spanish 3. (SPA.). 110p. 1999. wbk. ed. write for info. (*0-9702898-2-0*) Monument Bks Pub.

— Describing Language: An Introduction to the Study of Language. 2000. write for info. (*0-9702898-4-7*) Monument Bks Pub.

— Effective Writing: Basic Grammar & Diagramming Workbook. 1999. wbk. ed. write for info. (*0-9702898-0-4*) Monument Bks Pub.

Marshall, H. Diseases of Plants. 200p. 1991. 100.00 (*81-7158-246-X*, Pub. by Scientific Pubs) St Mut.

Marshall, H., ed. see Mander, Raymond & Mitchinson, J.

Marshall, H. G. & Sorrells, M. E., eds. Oat Science & Technology. LC 92-19551. (Agronomy Ser.: No. 33). 846p. 1992. 48.00 (*0-89118-110-5*) Am Soc Agron.

Marshall, H. H. Like Father Like Son. 1981. 35.00 (*0-7223-1374-8*, Pub. by A H S Ltd) St Mut.

Marshall, H. Jean. Beautiful Words: Inspiring Poems to Live By. 120p. (Orig.). 1996. pap. 6.95 (*1-57502-125-0*) Morris Pubng.

— Hearts of Love: Poetic Passion. 126p. (Orig.). 1997. pap. 11.99 (*0-9655514-0-7*) Inspiring Word.

***Marshall, Hallie.** Disney's Winnie the Pooh's: Telling Time: Book & Watch Set. 24p. (J). (ps-3). 2000. 9.99 (*0-7364-1028-7*, Pub. by Mouse Works) Time Warner.

Marshall, Harold E., jt. ed. see Chapman, Robert E.

Marshall, Harry I. The Karen People of Burma: A Study in Anthropology & Ethnology. LC 77-87046. reprint ed. 47.50 (*0-404-16843-4*) AMS Pr.

Marshall, Helen E. Mary Adelaide Nutting: Pioneer of Modern Nursing. LC 72-174557. 410p. 1972. reprint ed. pap. 127.10 (*0-608-03668-4*, 206449400009) Bks Demand.

Marshall, Helen L. Bright Laughter-Warm Tears. LC 92-71916. 64p. 1990. reprint ed. pap. 5.00 (*1-881598-01-2*) Marshall Ent.

— A Faith That Smiles. LC 92-71917. Orig. Title: Inspirational Resources for Women's Groups. 64p. 1992. reprint ed. pap. 5.00 (*1-881598-00-4*) Marshall Ent.

— Quiet Power. LC 92-71918. 64p. (Orig.). 1992. reprint ed. pap. 5.00 (*1-881598-02-0*) Marshall Ent.

Marshall, Henry. Mantras: A Musical Path to Peace. LC 98-43115. (Illus.). 144p. 1999. pap. 18.95 incl. audio compact disk (*1-885394-34-9*) Bluestar Communs.

Marshall, Henry R. Pain, Pleasure & Aesthetics. LC 75-3281. reprint ed. 29.50 (*0-404-59269-4*) AMS Pr.

Marshall, Herbert. Masters of Soviet Cinema: Vsevolod Pudovkin, Dziga Vertov, Alexander Kovzhenko, Sergei Mikhailovich Eisenstein. (Illus.). 280p. 1983. 35.00 (*0-7100-9287-3*, Routledge Thoemms) Routledge.

Marshall, Herbert, ed. Hamlet Through the Ages. LC 70-148888. (Select Bibliographies Reprint Ser.). 1977. reprint ed. 30.95 (*0-8369-5677-X*) Ayer.

Marshall, Herbert & Stock, Mildred. Ira Aldridge: Negro Tragedian. LC 93-12937. Orig. Title: Ira Aldridge, the Negro Tragedian. 1993. 24.95 (*0-88258-150-3*) Howard U Pr.

Marshall, Herbert, tr. see Eisenstein, Sergei M.

Marshall, Hermine H., ed. Redefining Student Learning: Roots of Educational Challenge. 336p. (C). 1992. pap. 39.50 (*0-89391-917-9*) Ablx Pub.

— Redefining Student Learning: Roots of Educational Change. 336p. (C). 1992. text 73.25 (*0-89391-854-7*) Ablx Pub.

Marshall, Hillie. Good Dating Guide: The Do's & Don'ts of Dating. 1998. pap. 12.95 (*1-84024-017-2*, Pub. by Summers) Howell Pr VA.

Marshall, Howard. Epistle to the Philippians. (Commentary Ser.). 1997. pap. text 16.00 (*0-7162-0485-1*) Epworth Pr.

Marshall, Howard. I Believe in the Historical Jesus. 253p. 1993. reprint ed. pap. 18.95 (*1-57383-019-4*) Regent College.

Marshall, Howard W. Folk Architecture in Little Dixie: A Regional Culture in Missouri. LC 80-26064. (Illus.). 160p. 1981. text 27.50 (*0-8262-0329-9*) U of Mo Pr.

— Paradise Valley, Nevada: The People & Buildings of an American Place. LC 94-26968. (Illus.). 152p. 1995. 57.00 (*0-8165-1310-4*) U of Ariz Pr.

— Vernacular Architecture in Rural & Small Town Missouri: An Introduction. 64p. 1994. pap. 6.00 (*0-614-28313-2*, MP688) Extension Div.

Marshall, Howard W. & Ahlborn, Richard E. Buckaroos in Paradise: Cowboy Life in Northern Nevada. LC 81-10500. (Illus.). 112p. reprint ed. pap. 34.80 (*0-7837-6186-4*, 204590800009) Bks Demand.

Marshall, Hugh. Art-Directing Photography: Choosing a Photographer - Setting up the Shot - Everything You Need to Get the Right Result. (Illus.). 144p. 1998. reprint ed. text 28.00 (*0-7881-5875-9*) DIANE Pub.

— Orestes Brownson & the American Republic: An Historical Perpective. LC 74-142187. 316p. reprint ed. pap. 98.00 (*0-608-15255-2*, 202949300061) Bks Demand.

Marshall, I. H., jt. ed. see Fridlyander, J. N.

Marshall, I. Haen, jt. ed. see Leuw, Ed.

Marshall, I. Howard. Acts of the Apostles. (Tyndale New Testament Commentaries Ser.). (Orig.). 1980. pap. 15.00 (*0-8028-1423-9*) Eerdmans.

— Biblical Inspiration. (Biblical & Theological Classics Library: Vol. 6). 125p. 1995. reprint ed. pap. 9.99 (*0-85364-709-7*, Pub. by Paternoster Pub) OM Literature.

— The Epistles of John. (New International Commentary on the New Testament Ser.). 291p. 1978. 30.00 (*0-8028-2518-4*) Eerdmans.

Marshall, I. Howard. 1 & 2 Thessalonians. (New Century Bible Ser.). 240p. 1983. pap. 19.95 (*0-551-01006-1*, Pub. by Sheffield Acad) CUP Services.

Marshall, I. Howard. The Gospel of Luke. (New International Greek Testament Commentary Ser.). 1978. 45.00 (*0-8028-3512-0*) Eerdmans.

— Kept by the Power of God: A Study of Perservance & Falling Away. (Biblical & Theological Classics Library: Vol. 7). 302p. 1995. reprint ed. pap. 9.99 (*0-85364-642-2*, Pub. by Paternoster Pub) OM Literature.

***Marshall, I. Howard.** Pastoral Epistles. 928p. 1999. 69.95 (*0-567-08661-5*) T&T Clark Pubs.

Marshall, I. Howard. Witness to the Gospel. LC 98-14685. (Theology Ser.). 1998. pap. 45.00 (*0-8028-4435-9*) Eerdmans.

— The Work of Christ. (Biblical Classics Library: Vol. 7). 128p. 1994. reprint ed. mass mkt. 5.99 (*0-85364-629-5*, Pub. by Paternoster Pub) OM Literature.

Marshall, I. Howard, ed. Last Supper & Lord's Supper. (Biblical & Theological Classics Library: Vol. 17). 191p. 1997. reprint ed. pap. 9.99 (*0-85364-856-5*, Pub. by Paternoster Pub) OM Literature.

— New Testament Interpretation. 5th rev. ed. (Biblical & Theological Classics Library: Vol. 16). 406p. 1997. reprint ed. pap. 9.99 (*0-85364-841-7*, Pub. by Paternoster Pub) OM Literature.

— New Testament Interpretation: Essays on Principles & Methods. fac. ed. LC 77-9619. 406p. 1977. reprint ed. pap. 125.90 (*0-7837-7962-3*, 204771800008) Bks Demand.

Marshall, I. Howard, jt. auth. see Bruce, F. F.

Marshall, I. Howard, jt. auth. see Donfried, Karl P.

Marshall, I. Howard, ed. see O'Brien, Peter T.

Marshall, I. Howard, ed. see Wanamaker, Charles A.

Marshall, Ian. Ironclads & Paddlers. 108p. 1997. 80.00 (*1-86227-008-2*, Pub. by Spellmnt Pubs) St Mut.

Marshall, Ian. Passage East. Maxtone-Graham, John, ed. (Illus.). 160p. 1998. 60.00 (*1-57427-069-9*) Howell Pr VA.

— Story Line: Exploring the Literature of the Appalachian Trail. LC 97-44616. 269p. 1998. pap. 19.95 (*0-8139-1798-0*); text 55.00 (*0-8139-1797-2*) U Pr of Va.

Marshall, Ian. Ironclads & Paddlers. 108p. 1993. 34.95 (*0-943231-62-0*) Howell Pr VA.

Marshall, Ian & Morris, Cecilia. Partnering: Starting Life in Another Relationship. 1998. pap. 14.95 (*1-86448-342-3*, Pub. by Allen & Unwin Pty) IPG Chicago.

***Marshall, Ian & Zohar, Danah.** Who's Afraid of Schrodinger' S Cat: All The New Science Ideas You Need To Keep Up With The New Thinking. (Illus.). 432p. 1998. pap. 14.00 (*0-688-16107-3*, Quil) HarperTrade.

Marshall, Ian, jt. auth. see Poyner, David.

Marshall, Ian, jt. auth. see Zohar, Danah.

Marshall, Ineke H., ed. Minorities, Migrants, & Crime: Diversity & Similarity Across Europe & the United States. LC 97-4758. 280p. 1997. text 49.95 (*0-7619-0334-8*); pap. text 22.95 (*0-7619-0335-6*) Sage.

Marshall, Ingeborg. A History & Ethnography of the Beothuk. LC 97-160431. (Illus.). 664p. 1996. 65.00 (*0-7735-1390-6*, Pub. by McG-Queens Univ Pr) CUP Services.

— A History & Ethnography of the Beothuk. (Illus.). 640p. 1998. pap. 29.95 (*0-7735-1774-X*, Pub. by McG-Queens Univ Pr) CUP Services.

Marshall, J. Love One Another. 1990. pap. 36.00 (*0-7220-5175-1*) St Mut.

***Marshall, J. & Cohen, J.** Immune Response in the Critically Ill. Vincent, J. L., ed. LC 99-40677. (Update in Intensive Care & Emergency Medicine Ser.: Vol. 31). (Illus.). 480p. 1999. 179.00 (*3-540-62583-6*) Spr-Verlag.

Marshall, J. A. Archaeological Guide to Taxila. 1987. reprint ed. 95.00 (*81-85046-15-8*, Pub. by Scientific) St Mut.

Marshall, J. Dan, jt. auth. see Sears, James.

Marshall, J. Dan, jt. ed. see Sears, Jim.

***Marshall, J. G. & Willan, R. C.** Nudibranchs of Heron Island, Great Barrier Reef: A Survey of the Opisthobranchia (Sea Slugs) of Heron & Wistari Reefs. (Illus.). 268p. 1999. 60.00 (*90-5782-033-1*, Pub. by Backhuys Pubs) Balogh.

Marshall, J. Howard, II. Done in Oil: An Autobiography. LC 94-10098. (Illus.). 304p. 1994. 34.95 (*0-89096-533-1*) Tex A&M Univ Pr.

— Luke: Historian & Theologian. 252p. 1997. reprint ed. pap. 12.99 (*0-85364-486-1*, Pub. by Paternoster Pub) OM Literature.

***Marshall, J. L.** Nist Calibration Services Users Guide, 1998. 231p. 1998. per. 19.00 (*0-16-054839-X*) USGPO.

Marshall, J. Lawrence. Lightning Protection. LC 73-4415. (Illus.). 206p. reprint ed. pap. 63.90 (*0-608-11499-5*, 200631100058) Bks Demand.

Marshall, J. M., et al, eds. Thin Film Materials & Devices: Developments in Science & Technology Proceedings of the 10th International School on Condensed Matter Physics Varna, Bulgaria 1 - 4 September 1998. 580p. 1999. 96.00 (*981-02-3904-1*) World Scientific Pub.

Marshall, J. M., jt. ed. see Jordan, D.

Marshall, J. N. Services & Space: Aspects of Urban & Regional Development. 294p. (C). 1996. pap. 59.00 (*0-582-25162-1*) Addison-Wesley.

Marshall, J. N., ed. Services & Uneven Development. (Illus.). 328p. 1988. 75.00 (*0-19-823285-3*) OUP.

Marshall, J. T. Miles Expedition of 1874-1875: An Eyewitness Account of the Red River Ear. White, Lonnie J., ed. (Narratives of the American West Ser.: Vol. 1). (Illus.). 1971. 24.95 (*0-88426-014-3*) Encino Pr.

— Miles Expedition of 1874-1875: An Eyewitness Account of the Red River War. (American Biography Ser.). 74p. 1991. reprint ed. lib. bdg. 59.00 (*0-7812-8270-5*) Rprt Serv.

Marshall, J. W., jt. auth. see Gillies, David.

Marshall, Jack. Arabian Nights. LC 86-19273. 112p. (Orig.). 1986. pap. 8.95 (*0-918273-28-5*) Coffee Hse.

— Chaos Comics. (Green Ser.). 32p. (Orig.). 1994. pap. 6.00 (*0-938631-25-X*) Pennywhistle Pr.

— Millennium Fever. LC 96-2773. 96p. (Orig.). 1996. pap. 11.95 (*1-56689-054-3*) Coffee Hse.

— Sesame. LC 93-26494. 96p. (Orig.). 1993. pap. 11.95 (*1-56689-015-2*) Coffee Hse.

Marshall, Jacqueline C. & Shepard-Moore, Marie. My Theory of Life A to Z. Incl. Straws Blowing in the Air. 1988. 99p. 1988. 8.95 (*0-318-35389-X*) Shepherd-Moore Ed Foun.

Marshall, Jacquelyn. Medical Laboratory Assistant. 224p. 1990. pap. 37.60 (*0-89303-693-5*) P-H.

***Marshall, Jacquelyn R.** The Clinical Laboratory Assistant/Phleboromist: Instructor's Guide. Cox-Stevens, Kay, ed. (Clinical Allied Healthcare Ser.). (Illus.). 448p. 1999. teacher ed., ring bd. 99.95 (*0-89262-442-6*) Career Pub.

— The Clinical Laboratory Assistant/Phlebotomist. Cox-Stevens, Kay, ed. LC 98-70063. (Clinical Allied Healthcare Ser.). (Illus.). 500p. 1999. pap. text 44.95 (*0-89262-434-5*) Career Pub.

Marshall, Jacquelyn R. Fundamental Skills for the Clinical Laboratory Professional. LC 92-49234. 698p. (C). 1993. mass mkt. 50.95 (*0-8273-4823-1*) Delmar.

— Fundamental Skills for the Clinical Laboratory Professional Instructor's Guide. 79p. 1993. pap., teacher ed. 14.00 (*0-8273-4825-8*) Delmar.

— Microbiology. 2nd ed. LC 93-38266. (Clinical Laboratory Manual Ser.). 160p. (C). 1994. mass mkt. 28.95 (*0-8273-5363-4*) Delmar.

Marshall, Jacquelyn R. & Harris, Kathleen S. Being a Medical Clerical Worker: An Introductory Core Text. 2nd ed. LC 97-31482. 288p. 1997. pap. text 44.00 (*0-8359-5147-2*) P-H.

Marshall, James. Cut-Ups. (Picture Puffin Ser.). (Illus.). (J). 1986. 10.19 (*0-606-01322-9*, Pub. by Turtleback) Demco.

— The Cut-Ups Carry On. LC 92-40721. (Picture Puffin Ser.). (Illus.). (J). 1993. 10.19 (*0-606-05220-8*, Pub. by Turtleback) Demco.

— Cut-Ups Crack Up. LC 91-37964. (Picture Puffin Ser.). (J). 1994. 10.19 (*0-606-06302-1*, Pub. by Turtleback) Demco.

Marshall, James. Cut-Ups Cut Loose. (J). 1987. 10.19 (*0-606-04189-3*, Pub. by Turtleback) Demco.

***Marshall, James.** Eugene. (Illus.). (J). 2000. pap. 5.95 (*0-618-07319-1*) HM.

Marshall, James. Fox Be Nimble. (Easy-to-Read Bks.: Level 3, Yellow). (Illus.). (J). (ps-3). 1994. pap. 3.99 (*0-14-036842-6*, PuffinBks) Peng Put Young Read.

— Fox in Love. LC 94-223597. (Easy-to-Read Bks.: Level 3, Yellow). (Illus.). 48p. (J). (ps-3). 1994. pap. 3.99 (*0-14-036843-4*, PuffinBks) Peng Put Young Read.

— Fox on Stage Level 3, Yellow. (Easy-to-Read Bks.). (Illus.). 48p. (J). (gr. 1-4). 1996. pap. 3.99 (*0-14-038032-9*, PuffinBks) Peng Put Young Read.

Marshall, James. Fox on the Job. (Puffin Easy-to-Read Ser.). (J). 1995. 9.19 (*0-606-03295-9*, Pub. by Turtleback) Demco.

Marshall, James. Fox Outfoxed. (Puffin Easy-to-Read Ser.). 1996. 8.70 (*0-606-11348-7*, Pub. by Turtleback) Demco.

— Fox Outfoxed. (Illus.). 48p. (J). (ps-3). 1996. pap. 3.99 (*0-14-038113-9*) Viking Penguin.

— Freedom to Be Free. LC 68-58804. (Essay Index Reprint Ser.). 1977. 20.95 (*0-8369-1043-5*) Ayer.

— George & Martha. (Carry-Along Book & Cassette Favorites Ser.). 1p. (J). (gr. 3 up). pap. 9.95 incl. audio (*0-395-45739-4*, 490945) HM.

— George & Martha, 001. LC 74-184250. (Illus.). 48p. (J). (gr. k-3). 1972. 16.00 (*0-395-16619-5*) HM.

— George & Martha, 001. LC 74-184250. (Illus.). 48p. (J). (gr. k-3). 1974. pap. 6.95 (*0-395-19972-7*) HM.

***Marshall, James.** George & Martha. (Carry-Along Book & Cassette Favorites Ser.). (Illus.). 32p. (J). 2000. pap. 9.95 incl. audio (*0-618-04935-5*) HM.

Marshall, James. George & Martha. (J). 1974. 12.15 (*0-606-03394-7*, Pub. by Turtleback) Demco.

— George & Martha: The Complete Stories of Two Best Friends. LC 96-47572. (Illus.). 352p. (J). 1997. 25.00 (*0-395-85158-0*) HM.

— George & Martha Back in Town, 001. LC 83-22842. (Illus.). 32p. (J). (gr. k-3). 1984. 16.00 (*0-395-35386-6*, 5-90939); pap. 3.95 (*0-685-07886-8*) HM.

— George & Martha Back in Town. 1984. 12.15 (*0-606-02800-5*, Pub. by Turtleback) Demco.

— George & Martha Encore, 001. LC 73-5845. (Illus.). 48p. (J). (gr. k-3). 1973. 16.00 (*0-395-17512-7*) HM.

— George & Martha Encore, 001. LC 73-5845. (Illus.). 48p. (J). (ps-3). 1977. pap. 6.95 (*0-395-25379-9*) HM.

— George & Martha Encore. (J). 1973. 12.15 (*0-606-00865-9*, Pub. by Turtleback) Demco.

— George & Martha One Fine Day, 001. (Illus.). 48p. (J). (gr. k-3). 1978. 16.00 (*0-395-27154-1*) HM.

— George & Martha One Fine Day, 001. LC 78-60494. (Illus.). 48p. (J). (ps-3). 1982. pap. 6.95 (*0-395-32921-3*) HM.

George & Martha One Fine Day. (J). 1978. 12.15 (*0-606-02735-1*, Pub. by Turtleback) Demco.

— George & Martha Rise & Shine, 001. (Illus.). 48p. (J). (gr. k-3). 1976. 16.00 (*0-395-24738-1*) HM.

— George & Martha Rise & Shine, 001. (Illus.). 48p. (J). (gr. k-3). 1979. pap. 6.95 (*0-395-28006-0*) HM.

— George & Martha Rise & Shine. (J). 1976. 12.15 (*0-606-02118-3*, Pub. by Turtleback) Demco.

— George & Martha Round & Round. LC 88-14739. (Illus.). 48p. (J). (gr. k-3). 1988. 13.95 (*0-395-46763-2*) HM.

— George & Martha Round & Round. 48p. (J). (ps-3). 1991. pap. 6.95 (*0-395-58410-8*) HM.

— George & Martha Tons of Fun, 001. (Illus.). 48p. (J). (gr. k-3). 1980. 16.00 (*0-395-29524-6*) HM.

— George & Martha Tons of Fun. LC 80-13592. (Illus.). 48p. (J). (ps-3). 1986. pap. 6.95 (*0-395-42646-4*) HM.

— Goldilocks & the Three Bears. LC 87-32983. (Illus.). 32p. (J). (ps-3). 1988. 15.99 (*0-8037-0542-5*, Dial Yng Read) Peng Put Young Read.

— Goldilocks & the Three Bears. (Illus.). 32p. (J). 1998. pap. 5.99 (*0-14-056366-0*, Viking Child) Peng Put Young Read.

— Goldilocks & the Three Bears. (J). 1998. 11.19 (*0-606-12946-4*, Pub. by Turtleback) Demco.

— Hansel & Gretel. (Illus.). 32p. (J). (ps-3). 1994. pap. 5.99 (*0-14-050836-8*, PuffinBks) Peng Put Young Read.

Marshall, James. Hansel & Gretel. LC 89-26011. (Picture Puffin Ser.). 1990. 11.19 (*0-606-06437-0*, Pub. by Turtleback) Demco.

Marshall, James. James Marshall's Mother Goose. LC 79-2574. (Sunburst Ser.). (Illus.). 40p. (J). (ps-6). 1986. pap. 6.95 (*0-374-43723-8*) FS&G.

— James Marshall's Mother Goose. 1986. 12.15 (*0-606-07730-8*, Pub. by Turtleback) Demco.

***Marshall, James.** Jorge y Marta. (SPA., Illus.). (J). 2000. 12.40 (*0-606-18210-1*) Turtleback.

— Jorge y Marta/George & Martha. (SPA & ENG., Illus.). 32p. (J). 2000. 16.00 (*0-618-05075-2*); pap. 6.95 (*0-618-05076-0*) HM.

Marshall, James. The Life & Times of Leith. 220p. (C). 1996. pap. 26.00 (*0-85976-128-2*, Pub. by J Donald) St Mut.

— The Night Before Christmas. abr. ed. (Illus.). (J). (ps-3). 1992. 4.95 (*0-590-45977-5*, Blue Ribbon Bks) Scholastic Inc.

— Old Mother Hubbard & Her Wonderful Dog. 32p. (J). (ps-3). 1991. 13.95 (*0-374-35621-1*) FS&G.

— Old Mother Hubbard & Her Wonderful Dog. 32p. (J). (ps-3). 1993. pap. 4.95 (*0-374-45611-9*) FS&G.

***Marshall, James.** One Fine Day. (Carry-Along Book & Cassette Favorites Ser.). (Illus.). 32p. (J). 2000. pap. 9.95 incl. audio (*0-618-04936-3*) HM.

— Rats on the Range. (Puffin Chapters Ser.). 1997. 9.19 (*0-606-11781-4*, Pub. by Turtleback) Demco.

Marshall, James. Rats on the Range. (Illus.). 80p. (J). (gr. 2-5). 1997. pap. 3.99 (*0-14-038645-9*) Viking Penguin.

Marshall, James. Rats on the Roof. (Puffin Chapters Ser.). 1997. 9.19 (*0-606-11782-2*, Pub. by Turtleback) Demco.

Marshall, James. Rats on the Roof. (Illus.). 80p. (J). (gr. 2-5). 1997. pap. 3.99 (*0-14-038646-7*) Viking Penguin.

— Red Riding Hood. LC 86-16722. (Illus.). 32p. (J). (ps-3). 1987. 15.99 (*0-8037-0344-9*, Dial Yng Read) Peng Put Young Read.

— Red Riding Hood. (J). 1993. pap. 5.99 (*0-14-054693-6*, PuffinBks) Peng Put Young Read.

— Red Riding Hood. (J). 1987. 10.19 (*0-606-00716-4*, Pub. by Turtleback) Demco.

***Marshall, James.** Sing Out, Irene. (Illus.). (J). 2000. pap. 5.95 (*0-618-07321-3*) HM.

— Snake, His Story. (Illus.). (J). 2000. pap. 5.95 (*0-618-07320-5*) HM.

— Someone Is Talking About Hortense. (Illus.). (J). 2000. pap. 5.95 (*0-618-07318-3*) HM.

Marshall, James. Space Case. (Illus.). (J). 1992. pap. 6.99 (*0-14-054704-5*, PuffinBks) Peng Put Young Read.

— Speedboat. (Illus.). 48p. (J). (gr. 1-3). 1999. pap. 5.95 (*0-395-95755-9*) HM.

— A Summer in the South. LC 77-14018. (Illus.). 112p. (J). (gr. 2-5). 1999. pap. 5.95 (*0-395-91361-6*) HM.

***Marshall, James.** Swine Lake. (Illus.). (J). (ps-3). 1999. 15.95 (*0-06-028430-7*) HarpC Child Bks.

Marshall, James. Swine Lake. LC 98-73253. (Michael di Capua Bks.). (Illus.). 40p. (J). (ps-3). 1999. 15.95 (*0-06-205171-7*) HarpC Child Bks.

An Asterisk (*) at the beginning of an entry indicates that the title is appearing for the first time.

— Swine Lake. LC 98-73253. (Michael di Capua Bks.). (Illus.). 40p. (J). 1999. lib. bdg. 15.89 (*0-06-205172-5*) HarpC Child Bks.

***Marshall, James.** Taking Care of Carruthers. (Illus.). (J). 2000. pap. 5.95 (*0-618-07040-0*) HM.

— Three Little Pigs. (Illus.). 32p. (J). (ps-3). 2000. pap. 3.49 (*0-448-42288-3*, Planet Dexter) Peng Put Young Read.

Marshall, James. Three Little Pigs. 1996. 10.19 (*0-606-09966-2*, Pub. by Turtleback) Demco.

— Three up a Tree. LC 86-2163. (Easy-to-Read Bks.). (Illus.). 48p. (J). (ps-3). 1986. lib. bdg. 9.89 (*0-685-13452-0*, Dial Yng Read) Peng Put Young Read.

— Three up a Tree. (Dial Easy-to-Read Ser.). (J). 1986. 9.19 (*0-606-04347-0*, Pub. by Turtleback) Demco.

— Three up a Tree Level 2, Red. LC 86-2163. (Illus.). (J). (gr. k-3). 1994. pap. 3.99 (*0-14-037003-X*, PuffinBks) Peng Put Young Read.

— Tres en un Arbol (Three up a Tree) Baro, Ana B., tr. (SPA., Illus.). 48p. (J). (gr. 2-4). 1990. pap. 9.95 (*84-204-4637-8*) Santillana.

— Tres en un Arbol (Three up a Tree) 1989. 15.15 (*0-606-10519-0*, Pub. by Turtleback) Demco.

— Troll Country. 1999. pap. 11.99 (*0-8037-1669-9*, Dial Yng Read) Peng Put Young Read.

— What's the Matter with Carruthers?, 001. LC 72-75607. (Illus.). 32p. (J). (gr. k-3). 1972. 18.00 (*0-395-13895-7*) HM.

— Yummers!, 001. LC 72-5400. (Illus.). 32p. (J). (gr. k-3). 1973. 16.00 (*0-395-14757-3*) HM.

— Yummers!, 001. LC 72-5400. (Illus.). 32p. (J). (ps-3). 1986. pap. 5.95 (*0-395-39590-9*, Sandpiper) HM.

— Yummers Too: The Second Course. (J). 1986. 11.15 (*0-606-04595-3*, Pub. by Turtleback) Demco.

— Yummers Too: The 2nd Course. (Illus.). 32p. (J). (gr. k-3). 1990. pap. 6.95 (*0-395-53967-6*) HM.

Marshall, James, ed. The Life & Times of Leith. 220p. (C). 1989. text 45.00 (*0-85976-148-7*, Pub. by J Donald) St Mut.

Marshall, James. The Frog Prince. LC 92-25167. (Hello Reader! Ser.). 40p. (J). (ps-3). 1993. pap. 2.95 (*0-590-46571-6*) Scholastic Inc.

— James Marshall's Mother Goose. LC 79-2574. 40p. (J). (ps-3). 1979. 15.00 (*0-374-33653-9*) FS&G.

Marshall, James. The Three Little Pigs. LC 88-33411. (J). (ps-3). 1989. 15.99 (*0-8037-0591-3*, Dial Yng Read) Peng Put Young Read.

Marshall, James, retold by. The Three Little Pigs. (Illus.). 32p. (J). (ps-3). 1996. pap. 6.99 (*0-14-055742-3*, PuffinBks) Peng Put Young Read.

***Marshall, James & Peters, Michael.** Education Policy. LC 99-39711. (International Library of Comparative Public Policy). 828p. 1999. write for info. (*1-85898-792-X*) E Elgar.

Marshall, James, jt. auth. see Allard, Harry.

Marshall, James, jt. auth. see Marshall, Edward.

Marshall, James, jt. auth. see Peters, Michael A.

Marshall, James, ed. see Smeyers, Paul.

Marshall, James D. Michel Foucault: Personal Autonomy & Education. LC 96-11697. (Philosophy & Education Ser.: Vol. 7). 254p. 1996. text 120.50 (*0-7923-4016-7*) Kluwer Academic.

Marshall, James D., et al. The Language of Interpretation: Patterns of Discourse in Discussions of Literature. (Research Reports: No. 27). 158p. 1994. pap. 19.95 (*0-8141-2709-6*) NCTE.

Marshall, James D., jt. auth. see Beach, Richard W.

Marshall, James D., jt. auth. see Peters, Michael A.

Marshall, James D., jt. ed. see Smeyers, Paul.

Marshall, James M. Land Fever: Dispossession & the Frontier Myth. LC 86-4030. 248p. 1986. 29.95 (*0-8131-1568-X*) U Pr of Ky.

Marshall, James N. William J. Fellner: A Bio-Bibliography, 1. LC 92-15462. (Bio-Bibliographies in Economics Ser.: No. 1). 160p. 1992. lib. bdg. 59.95 (*0-313-25856-2*, MWF, Greenwood Pr) Greenwood.

***Marshall, James R.** Lake Superior Journal: Jim Marshall's Views from the Bridge. Hayden, Paul L. & LeMay, Konnie, eds. LC 99-41485. (Illus.). 192p. 1999. pap. 14.95 (*0-942235-40-1*) LSPC Inc.

Marshall, James R. Shipwrecks of Lake Superior. LC 87-80682. (Illus.). 100p. (Orig.). 1987. pap. 19.95 (*0-942235-00-2*) LSPC Inc.

Marshall, James S. Noeth Leith Parish Church. 160p. 1993. 40.00 (*0-86153-161-2*, Pub. by St Andrew); pap. 30.00 (*0-86153-160-4*, Pub. by St Andrew) St Mut.

Marshall, James V. A River Ran Out of Eden. 124p. (J). 1987. pap. 3.95 (*0-88741-026-X*) Sundance Pub.

— Walkabout. 1992. pap. 5.75 (*0-435-27247-0*) Heinemann.

— Walkabout. 158p. 1984. pap. 3.95 (*0-88741-099-5*) Sundance Pub.

Marshall, James V. Walkabout. 1959. 9.05 (*0-606-02369-0*, Pub. by Turtleback) Demco.

***Marshall, James Vance.** White-Out. 2000. 22.00 (*1-56947-224-6*) Soho Press.

Marshall, James W. Presbyterian Churches in Alabama 1811-1936: Sketches of Churches, Outposts, & Preaching Points in the Synod of Alabama, Pt. I: Abbeville-Butler, & Megargel. Foreman, Kenneth J., Jr., ed. (Illus.). 519p. (Orig.). 1985. 29.95 (*0-935883-01-0*); 69.95 incl. disk (*0-935883-02-9*); pap. 14.95 (*0-935883-00-2*) Cooling Spring.

Marshall, Jan. Still Hanging in There . . . Confessions of a Totaled Woman. (Illus.). 216p. 1996. reprint ed. pap. 20.00 incl. audio (*0-9645519-9-3*) Ult Mind Pub.

Marshall, Jane. Going for the Gold: Hakeem Olajuwon. (Illus.). (Orig.). (J). (gr. 3-7). 1996. pap. 4.50 (*0-380-78677-X*, Avon Bks) Morrow Avon.

— Going for the Gold--Hakeem Olajuwon. 1996. 9.70 (*0-606-09331-1*, Pub. by Turtleback) Demco.

— Grace, Noted. Heffley, Rosemary, ed. LC 92-70255. 168p. 1992. pap. 14.95 (*0-916642-45-3*, 956) Hope Pub.

Marshall, Janet. Banana Moon. LC 97-25432. (Illus.). 32p. (J). (ps-3). 1998. 12.95 (*0-688-15768-8*, Grenwillow Bks) HarpC Child Bks.

— A Honey of a Day. LC 99-23175. (Illus.). 24p. (J). (ps-3). 2000. 15.95 (*0-688-16917-1*, Grenwillow Bks) HarpC Child Bks.

— Look Once, Look Twice. LC 94-27259. (Illus.). 64p. (J). (gr. k-3). 1995. 13.95 (*0-395-71644-6*) Ticknor & Flds Bks Yng Read.

Marshall, Jaquelyn. Medical Laboratory Assistant. 1990. pap., teacher ed. 14.00 (*0-89303-737-0*) P-H.

Marshall, Jay W. The Beatitudes of Christmas. LC 96-34215. 100p. 1996. pap. 10.00 (*0-944350-40-2*) Friends United.

— Family Faults: Healing the Hurts That Threaten the Home. LC 97-94378. 142p. 1998. pap. 11.95 (*0-932970-89-3*, AR-101) Prinit Pr.

— The 10 Commandments & Christian Community. LC 95-24084. 128p. (Orig.). 1996. pap. 8.99 (*0-8361-9027-0*) Herald Pr.

Marshall, Jeanie. Affirmations, A Pathway to Transformation: Empowered Development By the Day, by the Month, By the Year. 400p. (Orig.). 1995. pap. 14.00 (*1-885893-01-9*) Jemel Pubng.

— Energetic Meetings: Enhancing Personal & Group Energy & Handling Difficult Behavior. 134p. (Orig.). 1994. pap. 11.00 (*1-885893-00-0*) Jemel Pubng.

Marshall, Jeffrey D. The Life & Legacy of the Reverend Phinehas Bailey. (Occasional Papers: No. 9). (Illus.). 32p. 1985. pap. text 5.00 (*0-944277-14-4*, M37) U VT Ctr Rsch VT.

Marshall, Jeffrey D., ed. A War of the People: Vermont Civil War Letters. LC 98-53635. (Illus.). 377p. 1999. pap. 25.00 (*0-87451-923-3*); text 50.00 (*0-87451-922-5*) U Pr of New Eng.

Marshall, Jeffrey L. & Davis, Bertha S. Wrightstown Township: A Tricentennial History. (Illus.). 96p. (Orig.). 1992. pap. 11.00 (*0-9624245-1-X*) Wrightstown Twp Hist Comm.

Marshall, Jeremy, jt. ed. see McDonald, Fred.

Marshall, Jerilynn, ed. see Arroyo, Stephen.

***Marshall, Jessie N.** Guide to the Nice Agreement Concerning the International Classification of Goods & Services. LC 99-48615. 260p. 1999. text 85.00 (*0-379-21414-8*, 5468043) Oceana.

Marshall, Jim. Book of Rock & Roll Photographs. 1999. write for info. (*0-316-54882-0*) Little.

***Marshall, Jim.** Not Fade Away: The Rock & Roll Photography of Jim Marshall. (Illus.). 144p. 2000. pap. 29.95 (*0-8212-2656-8*, Pub. by Bulfinch Pr) Little.

Marshall, Jim. Not Fade Away: The Rock & Roll Photography of Jim Marshall. LC 97-11245. (Illus.). 144p. (gr. 8). 1997. 50.00 (*0-8212-2362-3*) Little.

Marshall, Jimmie B. Anyone Can Write - Just Let It Come Out. LC 95-83441. (Illus.). 225p. (Orig.). 1997. pap. 9.95 (*0-9625557-4-6*) Excelsior Cee.

— How to Record Your Family History: An Easy & Informative Guide to Writing down & Preserve for Future Generations. rev. ed. 26p. 1999. pap. 3.00 (*0-9625557-5-4*) Excelsior Cee.

— Make Your Home Beautiful. 1997. 4.95 (*0-9625557-7-0*) Excelsior Cee.

— The Marshall Art of Creative Writing. 1998. write for info. (*0-9625557-3-8*) Excelsior Cee.

— Quilted Love: A Patchwork of Thoughts & Feelings. 50p. (Orig.). 1990. pap. 5.00 (*0-9625557-0-3*) Excelsior Cee.

Marshall, Joan. Life Is Our Choice. (Orig.). 1997. pap. write for info. (*1-57553-455-X*) Watermrk Pr.

— A Solitary Pillar: Montreal's Anglican Church & the Quiet Revolution. (McGill-Queen's Studies in Ethnic History). (Illus.). 240p. 1994. 60.00 (*0-7735-1224-1*, Pub. by McG-Queens Univ Pr) CUP Services.

Marshall, Joan K. On Equal Terms. A Thesaurus for Nonsexist Indexing & Cataloging. LC 77-8987. 152p. 1977. 35.00 (*0-918212-02-2*) Neal-Schuman.

***Marshall, Joe T.** The Gray-Cheeked Thrush. LC 00-31933. 2000. write for info. (*1-877973-40-8*) HUP.

Marshall, Joe T. Systematics of Smaller Asian Night Birds Based on Voice. 58p. 1978. 10.00 (*0-943610-25-7*) Am Ornithologists.

Marshall, John. Action Figures of the 1980s. LC 97-80804. 160p. 1998. pap. 29.95 (*0-7643-0494-1*) Schiffer.

***Marshall, John.** Action Figures of the 1960s. (Illus.). 160p. 1998. pap. 29.95 (*0-7643-0428-3*) Schiffer.

Marshall, John. An Autobiographical Sketch. (History - United States Ser.). 48p. 1993. reprint ed. lib. bdg. 59.00 (*0-7812-4880-9*) Rprt Serv.

— An Autobiographical Sketch by John Marshall. Adams, John S., ed. LC 71-160849. (American Constitutional & Legal History Ser). (Illus.). 74p. 1973. reprint ed. lib. bdg. 19.50 (*0-306-70216-9*) Da Capo.

— An Autobiographical Sketch by John Marshall. (American Biography Ser.). 48p. 1991. reprint ed. lib. bdg. 59.00 (*0-7812-8271-3*) Rprt Serv.

— The Buddhist Art of Gandhara. (Illus.). 1981. reprint ed. text 30.00 (*0-685-43580-6*) Coronet Bks.

— Collecting Monster Toys. (Illus.). 160p. 1999. pap. 29.95 (*0-7643-0923-4*) Schiffer.

***Marshall, John.** The Constitutional Decisions of John Marshall, 1905. fac. ed. LC 99-48862. 2000. write for info. (*1-58477-050-3*) Lawbk Exchange.

Marshall, John. Descartes's Moral Theory. LC 98-28008. 208p. 1999. 35.00 (*0-8014-3567-6*) Cornell U Pr.

***Marshall, John.** Dictionary of Financial Engineering. (Financial Engineering Ser.). 256p. 2000. 59.95 (*0-471-24291-8*) Wiley.

Marshall, John. Energy at Work. LC 95-13499. (Read All about Energy & Action Ser.). 24p. (J). (gr. 1-4). 1995. lib. bdg. 18.60 (*1-55916-153-1*) Rourke Bk Co.

— Energy Sources. LC 95-18946. (Energy & Action Ser.). (J). 1995. lib. bdg. 18.60 (*1-55916-156-6*) Rourke Bk Co.

— GI Joe: And Other Backyard Heroes 1970-1979: An Unauthorized Guide. LC 97-65378. (Schiffer Book for Collectors with Values Ser.). (Illus.). 160p. 1997. pap. 29.95 (*0-7643-0201-9*) Schiffer.

— Go & Stop. LC 95-10536. (Read All about Energy & Action Ser.). 24p. (J). (gr. 1-4). 1995. lib. bdg. 18.60 (*1-55916-152-3*) Rourke Bk Co.

— A Guide to Taxila. 154p. (C). 1990. 50.00 (*81-85453-50-0*, Pub. by Print Hse) St Mut.

— John Locke: Resistance, Religion & Responsibility. LC 93-30796. 1993. 27.95 (*0-521-44280-X*) Cambridge U Pr.

— John Locke: Resistance, Religion & Responsibility. (Cambridge Studies in Early Modern British History). 509p. (C). 1994. pap. text 34.95 (*0-521-46687-3*) Cambridge U Pr.

— Life of George Washington, 5 vols. Washington, B., ed. LC 69-19159. 495.00 (*0-404-04250-3*) AMS Pr.

— The Life of George Washington. (Notable American Authors Ser.). 1999. reprint ed. lib. bdg. 125.00 (*0-7812-3948-6*) Rprt Serv.

***Marshall, John.** The Life of George Washington: Special Edition for Schools. Faulkner, Robert & Carrese, Paul, eds. (Illus.). 2000. 25.00 (*0-86597-276-1*) Liberty Fund.

Marshall, John. Make Your Own Japanese Clothes: Patterns & Ideas for Modern Wear. LC 87-82861. (Illus.). 136p. 1988. pap. 25.00 (*0-87011-865-X*) Kodansha.

— Mathematics for Derivatives: Self-Study Workbook. (D. C. Gardner Self-Study Workbook Ser.). 1998. pap., wbk. ed. 295.00 (*1-85564-642-0*) Am Educ Systs.

— Mining the Hard Rock in the Silverton San Juans: A Sense of Place, a Sense of Time. LC 96-94414. (Illus.). 224p. 1996. 34.95 (*0-9632028-2-0*) Simpler Way.

— Mohenjo-Daro & the Indus Civilization: Being an Official Account of Archaeological Excavations at Mohenjo-Daro Carried Out by the Government of India Between the Years 1922 & 1927, 3 vols., Set. 1996. reprint ed. 210.00 (*81-206-1179-9*, Pub. by Asian Educ Servs) S Asia.

— Motion & Speed. LC 95-17283. (Read All about Energy & Action Ser.). 24p. (J). (gr. 1-4). 1995. lib. bdg. 18.60 (*1-55916-154-X*) Rourke Bk Co.

— The Papers of John Marshall: Correspondence, Papers, & Selected Judicial Opinions, 1807-1813. Hobson, Charles, ed. LC 74-9575. (Institute of Early American History & Culture Ser.: Vol. 7). (Illus.). xxxviii, 446p. (C). 1993. 70.00 (*0-8078-2074-1*) U of NC Pr.

— The Papers of John Marshall Vol. I: Correspondence & Papers, November 10, 1775-June 23, 1788, & Account Book, September 1783-June 1788. Johnson, Herbert A. et al, eds. LC 74-9575. (Institute of Early American History & Culture Ser.). (Illus.). xlvi, 448p. 1974. 70.00 (*0-8078-1233-1*) U of NC Pr.

— The Papers of John Marshall Vol. II: Correspondence & Papers, July 1788-December 1795, & Account Book, July 1788-December 1795. Cullen, Charles T. & Johnson, Herbert A., eds. LC 74-9575. (Institute of Early American History & Culture Ser.). xxxvi, 547p. 1977. 70.00 (*0-8078-1302-8*) U of NC Pr.

— The Papers of John Marshall Vol. III: Correspondence & Papers, January 1796-December 1798. Stinchcombe, William C. & Cullen, Charles T., eds. LC 74-9575. (Institute of Early American History & Culture Ser.). (Illus.). xxix, 553p. 1979. 70.00 (*0-8078-1337-0*) U of NC Pr.

— The Papers of John Marshall Vol. IV: Correspondence & Papers, January 1799-October 1800. Cullen, Charles T. & Tobias, Leslie, eds. LC 74-9575. (Institute of Early American History & Culture Ser.). xxxii, 365p. 1984. 70.00 (*0-8078-1586-1*) U of NC Pr.

The Papers of John Marshall Vol. V: Selected Law Cases, 1784-1800. Hobson, Charles F. et al, eds. LC 74-9575. (Institute of Early American History & Culture Ser.). ixx, 583p. 1987. 70.00 (*0-8078-1746-5*) U of NC Pr.

— Papers of John Marshall Vol. VI: Correspondence, Papers, & Selected Judicial Opinions, November 1800-March 1807. Hobson, Charles F., ed. LC 74-9575. (Institute of Early American History & Culture Ser.). (Illus.). xlvi, 568p. (C). 1990. 70.00 (*0-8078-1903-4*) U of NC Pr.

— The Papers of John Marshall Vol. IX: Correspondence, Papers, & Selected Judicial Opinions, January 1820-December 1823. Hobson, Charles F., ed. (Published for the Omohundro Institute of Early American History & Culture, Williamsburg, Virginia Ser.). (Illus.). 440p. 1998. 70.00 (*0-8078-2404-6*) U of NC Pr.

— Sink or Swim. LC 95-18945. (Energy & Action Ser.). (J). 1995. lib. bdg. 18.60 (*1-55916-157-4*) Rourke Bk Co.

— The Structure of Urban Systems. 394p. 1989. text 50.00 (*0-8020-5756-X*); pap. text 24.95 (*0-8020-6735-2*) U of Toronto Pr.

— Super Hero Toys. (Illus.). 176p. 1999. pap. 29.95 (*0-7643-0922-6*) Schiffer.

— The West Coast Trail Poems. 1978. pap. text 4.95 (*0-88982-007-4*, Pub. by Oolichan Bks) Genl Dist Srvs.

— Working Machines. LC 95-16003. (Read All about Energy & Action Ser.). 24p. (J). (gr. 1-4). 1995. lib. bdg. 18.60 (*1-55916-155-8*) Rourke Bk Co.

— The Writing of John Marshall upon the Federal Constitution. (Notable American Authors Ser.). 1999. reprint ed. lib. bdg. 125.00 (*0-7812-3949-4*) Rprt Serv.

Marshall, John, ed. Citizen Participation in Library Decision-Making: The Toronto Experience. LC 84-10617. (Dalhousie University School of Library Service Ser.: No. 1). 436p. 1984. 42.00 (*0-8108-1709-8*) Scarecrow.

Marshall, John, photos by. Portrait of Washington. (Illus.). 80p. 1993. pap. 12.95 (*1-55868-154-X*) Gr Arts Ctr Pub.

— Washington II. LC 98-54905. (Illus.). 1999. 39.95 (*1-55868-464-6*) Gr Arts Ctr Pub.

Marshall, John & Edwards, Wayne, eds. Palace Corbie Seven: The Piano Player Has No Fingers. 330p. 1996. pap. 12.95 (*1-888283-06-8*) Merrimack Bks.

***Marshall, John & Hobson, Charles F., eds.** The Papers of John Marshall: Correspondence, Papers & Selected Judicial Opinions, January 1824 - April 1827. LC 74-9575. (Published for the Omohundro Institute of Early American History & Culture Ser.). (Illus.). 544p. 2000. 60.00 (*0-8078-2520-4*) U of NC Pr.

Marshall, John & Roberts, Jerry. Living (& Dying) in Avalanche Country. (Illus.). 200p. 1998. reprint ed. 29.95 (*0-9632028-0-4*) Simpler Way.

***Marshall, John, et al.** The Life of George Washington: Special Edition for Schools. LC 99-462077. (Illus.). 2000. pap. 14.00 (*0-86597-277-X*) Liberty Fund.

Marshall, John, tr. see Horace.

***Marshall, John A.** But Who Do You Say I Am? LC 99-69331. 286p. 2000. pap. 12.95 (*0-9646439-0-1*) Ambasdr Bks.

Marshall, John A. Find Your Perfect High Without Mind-Altering Substances: Shift Happens When You Train Your Brain. 3rd rev. ed. Phillips, Gay et al, eds. LC 78-112715. (Illus.). 347p. (Orig.). 1997. pap. 12.95 (*0-933426-00-3*) Right Programs.

Marshall, John A., jt. auth. see Marshall, Don B.

Marshall, John B., et al. The Kaskaskia Manuscripts: St. Louis Mound Group - Prehistoric Mussel Faunas. (Missouri Archaeologist Ser.: Vol. 53). (Illus.). iv, 100p. 1995. pap. 7.00 (*0-943414-80-6*) MO Arch Soc.

Marshall, John B., jt. auth. see Cornelius, Temple H.

Marshall, John C., jt. auth. see Halligan, Peter W.

Marshall, John D. Reconciliation Road: A Family Odyssey of War & Honor. (Illus.). 304p. 1993. 34.95 (*0-8156-0274-X*) Syracuse U Pr.

— The Tyranny of the Discrete: A Discussion of the Problems of Local History in England. LC 96-33160. 164p. 1997. text 83.95 (*1-85928-290-3*, Pub. by Scolar Pr) Ashgate Pub Co.

Marshall, John D., ed. Home Field: Nine Writers at Bat. LC 96-49877. (Illus.). 224p. 1997. 21.95 (*1-57061-096-7*) Sasquatch Bks.

Marshall, John D., ed. see Powell, Lawrence C.

***Marshall, John Douglas.** Reconciliation Road: A Family Odyssey. (Illus.). 306p. 2000. pap. 15.95 (*0-295-97949-6*) U of Wash Pr.

Marshall, John F. By the Light of His Lamp. (Spirit & Life Ser.). viii, 62p. 1967. 2.00 (*1-57659-089-5*) Franciscan Inst.

— Conferences on the Our Father. (Spirit & Life Ser.). vi, 54p. 1967. pap. 2.00 (*1-57659-088-7*) Franciscan Inst.

— In the Shadow of His Cross. (Spirit & Life Ser.). viii, 63p. 1969. 2.00 (*1-57659-091-7*) Franciscan Inst.

— The Long Way Home, the Short Way of Love. (Spirit & Life Ser.). viii, 114p. 1968. pap. 3.50 (*1-57659-090-9*) Franciscan Inst.

Marshall, John F. & Ellis, M. E. Investment Banking & Brokerage. 415p. (C). 1994. pap. text 50.95 (*1-878975-38-2*) Blackwell Pubs.

— Investment Banking & Brokerage: The New Rules of the Game. 325p. 1993. text 65.00 (*1-55738-504-1*, Irwn Prfssnl) McGraw-Hill Prof.

Marshall, John F. & Kapner, Kenneth R. Understanding Swaps. (Finance Editions Ser.). 288p. 1993. 69.95 (*0-471-30827-7*) Wiley.

Marshall, John F., jt. auth. see Kapner, Kenneth R.

Marshall, John F., jt. auth. see Weisz, Paul B.

Marshall, John Law School Library Staff, ed. Howard T. Markey on Intellectual Property: A Compilation of His Writings, Opinions, & Speeches, 2 vols., 2 vols. LC 97-81038. 1998. 250.00 (*1-57588-420-8*, 311450) W S Hein.

Marshall, John R. Green White White. 194p. 1999. pap. 17.95 (*0-7414-0075-8*) Buy Books.

Marshall, John R., jt. auth. see Jefferson, James W.

Marshall, Jonathan. To Have & Have Not: Southeast Asia Raw Materials & the Origins of the Pacific War. LC 94-13367. 1994. 35.00 (*0-520-08823-9*, Pub. by U CA Pr) Cal Prin Full Svc.

Marshall, Jonathan, et al. The Iran-Contra Connection. 350p. write for info. (*0-921689-15-2*); pap. write for info. (*0-921689-14-4*) Black Rose.

Marshall, Jonathan, jt. auth. see Heinecke, William.

Marshall, Jonathan, jt. auth. see Scott, Peter D.

Marshall, Joretta L. Counseling Lesbian Partners. LC 96-44113. (Counseling & Pastoral Theology Ser.). 192p. 1997. pap. 18.00 (*0-664-25532-9*) Westminster John Knox.

Marshall, Joseph. The Dance House: Stories from Rosebud. LC 98-20752. (Literature Ser.). (Illus.). 248p. 1998. pap. 13.95 (*1-878610-66-X*) Red Crane Bks.

Marshall, Joseph, 3rd. On Behalf of the Wolf & the First Peoples. LC 95-41844. (Illus.). 256p. 1995. pap. 13.95 (*1-878610-45-7*) Red Crane Bks.

Marshall, Joseph. Travels Through Germany, Russia & Poland in the Years 1769 & 1770. LC 77-135821. (Eastern Europe Collection). 1971. reprint ed. 19.95 (*0-405-02763-X*) Ayer.

Marshall, Joseph, III. Winter of the Holy Iron. (Literature Ser.). (Illus.). 304p. 1994. 19.95 (*1-878610-44-9*) Red Crane Bks.

Marshall, Joseph, jt. auth. see Hulick, Diana E.

Marshall, Joyce. Any Time at All & Other Stories. 224p. 1996. pap. text 6.95 (*0-7710-9893-6*) McCland & Stewart.

— Blood & Bone: Le Retour D'Hiure. (ENG & FRE.). 160p. (Orig.). 1996. pap. 16.95 (*0-88962-602-2*) Mosaic.

— The Queen's Quest & Other Tales: Stories to Live By. (Illus.). 128p. 1994. pap. 13.50 (*0-9611552-6-4*) Realistic Living.

M

Marshall, Joyce & Marshall, Gene W. The Reign of Reality: A Fresh Start for the Earth. LC 87-90621. (Illus.). 267p. 1987. pap. 10.00 (*0-9611552-2-1*) Realistic Living.
Marshall, Joyce, tr. see Roy, Gabrielle.
Marshall, Judi. Women Managers Moving On: Exploring Career & Life Choices. LC 95-1341. 368p. (C). 1995. mass mkt. 17.99 (*0-415-09739-8*) Chapman & Hall.
— Women Managers Moving On: Exploring Career & Life Choices. LC 95-1341. 368p. (C). (gr. 13). 1995. pap. 74.95 (*0-415-09738-X*) Thomson Learn.
Marshall, Judi & Cooper, Cary L. Executives under Pressure: A Psychological Study. LC 78-72594. (Praeger Special Studies). 160p. 1979. 49.95 (*0-275-90388-5*, C0388, Praeger Pubs) Greenwood.
Marshall, Judi & Cooper, Cary L., eds. Coping with Stress at Work. 236p. 1981. text 69.95 (*0-566-02338-5*, Pub. by Gower) Ashgate Pub Co.
Marshall, Judi, jt. auth. see Cooper, Cary L.
Marshall, Judi, jt. ed. see Cooper, Cary L.
Marshall, Judith G. Medicate Me Again. 132p. 1994. pap. text 10.00 (*0-934385-62-9*) Hlth Prof Inst.
— Shattered Silence. 352p. 1993. mass mkt. 4.50 (*1-55817-704-3*, Pinncle Kensgtn) Kensgtn Pub Corp.
— When the Wind Blows. 1992. mass mkt. 4.50 (*1-55817-613-6*, Pinncle Kensgtn) Kensgtn Pub Corp.
Marshall, Judy. Ride a Hole Through the Wind. 92p. (Orig.). (YA). (gr. 9-12). 1994. pap. 9.99 (*0-88092-147-1*) Royal Fireworks.
Marshall, K. C. Advances in Microbial Ecology, Vol. 10. LC 77-649698. (Illus.). 474p. (C). 1988. text 115.00 (*0-306-42710-9*, Kluwer Plenum) Kluwer Academic.
— Advances in Microbial Ecology, Vol. 11. (Illus.). 536p. (C). 1989. text 115.00 (*0-306-43340-0*, Kluwer Plenum) Kluwer Academic.
— Advances in Microbial Ecology, Vol. 12. (Illus.). 550p. (C). 1992. text 115.00 (*0-306-44266-3*, Kluwer Plenum) Kluwer Academic.
— Interfaces in Microbial Ecology. 131p. 1976. 25.00 (*0-674-45822-2*, MAIF) HUP.
Marshall, Kaplan G., jt. auth. see Kahn.
Marshall, Karen, jt. auth. see Alderman, Tracy.
Marshall, Karen, jt. ed. see Brown, Steven R.
***Marshall, Kate.** Book of My Pet. 128p. 2000. 14.95 (*0-7868-6616-0*, Pub. by Disney Pr) Time Warner.
Marshall, Kate, jt. auth. see Marshall, David.
Marshall, Kathleen. What Do You Mean I'm Laid Off? How to Go from Pink Slip to Paycheck. LC 96-112886. (Illus.). 70p. (Orig.). 1995. pap. 9.95 (*0-9649225-0-9*) Career Solns.
Marshall, Kathleen, jt. auth. see Hunt, Nancy.
Marshall, Kathryn. My Sister Gone. LC 91-58685. 240p. 1992. reprint ed. pap. 9.95 (*0-944439-49-7*) Clark City Pr.
Marshall, Kay. The First Step: Guidelines on Care & Recovery Following Colostomy Surgery. 2nd ed. (Illus.). 1990. pap. text. write for info. (*0-916999-06-8*) HERC Inc.
— Moving Forward: A Book for Ileostomy Patients. (Illus.). 32p. 1990. pap. text 3.95 (*0-916999-07-6*) HERC Inc.
— A New Beginning: A Book for Urostomy Patients. (Illus.). 1988. pap. text. write for info. (*0-916999-05-X*) HERC Inc.
Marshall, Kelly. Phoenix. Tayler, Moi, ed. 448p. (Orig.). 1996. pap. 6.99 (*0-9646250-1-6*) Heathchris Bks.
***Marshall, Ken.** Beyond Traditional Training: Develop Your Skills to Maximize Training Impact. 192p. 2000. pap. 24.95 (*0-7494-3028-1*, Kogan Pg Educ) Stylus Pub VA.
Marshall, Kenneth G. Mosby's Family Practice Sourcebook, 2000. (Illus.). 512p. (C). 1999. text 59.00 (*1-55664-468-X*) Mosby Inc.
Marshall, Kerry. A Boy, a Ball, & a Dream: The Marvin Wood Story. (Illus.). 192p. (Orig.). 1991. 19.95 (*0-9630362-0-3*); pap. 10.45 (*0-9630362-1-1*) Scott IN.
— The Ray Crowe Story: A Legend in High School Basketball. 185p. 1992. 20.00 (*0-9636873-0-1*) Good Morn Pub.
— Two of a Kind: The Dick & Tom Vanarsdale Story. (Illus.). 224p. 1992. 18.95 (*0-9630362-2-X*) Scott IN.
***Marshall, Kerry James.** Kerry James Marshall: Momentos. (Illus.). 60p. 2000. 45.00 (*0-941548-40-6*) Ren Soc U Chi.
Marshall, Kevin, jt. auth. see Celentano, Suzanne C.
Marshall, Kevin C., jt. auth. see Characklis, William G.
Marshall, Kimball. CIS-MIS Business: Information Systems for Marketing. (C). 1995. pap. 24.95 (*0-87709-290-7*) Course Tech.
Marshall, Kimberly, ed. Rediscovering the Muses: Women's Musical Traditions. (Illus.). 352p. 1993. pap. text 18.95 (*1-55553-219-5*) NE U Pr.
— Rediscovering the Muses: Women's Musical Traditions. (Illus.). 352p. 1993. text 50.00 (*1-55553-173-3*) NE U Pr.
Marshall, Kit, jt. auth. see Burz, Helen L.
Marshall, Kneale T. & Oliver, Robert M. Decision Making & Forecasting: With Emphasis on Model Building & Policy Analysis. LC 95-869. 384p. (C). 1995. 86.88 (*0-07-048027-3*) McGraw.
Marshall, Kneale T., jt. auth. see Oliver, Robert M.
Marshall, L. & Rowland, F. A Guide to Learning Independently. 2nd ed. 288p. 1993. pap. 2.00 (*0-335-19171-1*) OpUniv Pr.
Marshall, L. A., jt. auth. see Morgan, D. W.
Marshall, Lane. Landscape Architecture: Guidelines to Professional Practice. 160p. 1981. 28.95 (*0-941236-00-5*, 6005) Am Landscape Arch.
Marshall, Laura H., et al. Choosing Employment Goals: Teacher's Manual. (Choice Maker Self-Determination Curriculum Ser.). 282p. 1997. teacher ed., ring bd. 95.00 incl. VHS (*1-57035-122-8*, 88CEG) Sopris.
***Marshall, Laura Huber, et al, contrib. by.** Choosing Personal Goals. (ChoiceMaker Self-Determination Ser.). 140p. 1999. per. 95.00 incl. VHS (*1-57035-211-9*, 88CGP) Sopris.
***Marshall, Laura Huber, et al.** Take Action: Making Goals Happen. (ChoiceMaker Self-Determination Curriculum Ser.). 222p. 1999. pap. 95.00 incl. VHS (*1-57035-196-1*, 88TAKE) Sopris.
Marshall, Lauren & Key, Edd, contrib. by. Rivercide, P. I. 48p. 1998. pap. 5.00 (*0-87440-063-5*) Bakers Plays.
Marshall, Laury, ed. see Firehock, Karen.
Marshall, Leisa L., jt. auth. see Arnett, Kirk P.
Marshall, Lenore. Latest Will. LC 68-56267. (C). 1969. pap. 2.95 (*0-393-04178-6*) Norton.
Marshall, Leonie. An A-Z of Dressage Terms. 1996. pap. 40.00 (*0-85131-633-6*, Pub. by J A Allen) Trafalgar.
— Choosing a Dressage Horse. 1996. pap. 30.00 (*0-85131-634-4*, Pub. by J A Allen) Trafalgar.
— Dressage Terms. 94p. 1990. pap. 30.00 (*0-85131-317-5*, Pub. by J A Allen) St Mut.
— Equitation for the Everyday Rider. (Illus.). 160p. 1997. 35.00 (*1-85223-988-3*, Pub. by Crolwood) Trafalgar.
— Novice to Advanced Dressage. 1990. pap. 21.00 (*0-85131-373-6*, Pub. by J A Allen) St Mut.
— Novice to Advanced Dressage. 1996. pap. 40.00 (*0-85131-631-X*, Pub. by J A Allen) Trafalgar.
— Questions on Dressage. 1990. pap. 40.00 (*0-85131-474-0*, Pub. by J A Allen) St Mut.
— Questions on Dressage. 1996. pap. 40.00 (*0-85131-632-8*, Pub. by J A Allen) Trafalgar.
— Your Horse's Mind. (Illus.). 160p. 1997. 35.00 (*1-85223-978-6*, Pub. by Crolwood) Trafalgar.
Marshall, Leslie B., ed. Infant Care & Feeding in the South Pacific, Vol. 3. LC 85-12648. (Food & Nutrition in History & Anthropology Ser.). xxii, 356p. 1985. text 160.00 (*2-88124-037-2*) Gordon & Breach.
Marshall, Lincoln H., jt. auth. see Rudd, Denis P.
Marshall, Linda. Befitting a Bride. (Illus.). 28p. (Orig.). 1987. pap. 5.95 (*0-933491-21-2*) Hot off Pr.
Marshall, Linda D. What Is a Step? LC 91-67511. (Illus.). 48p. (Orig.). (J). (ps-5). 1992. pap. 10.00 (*1-879289-00-8*) Native Sun Pubs.
Marshall, Logan. The Sinking of the Titanic. abr. ed. Caplan, Bruce M., ed. LC 96-78295. (Illus.). 222p. 1997. reprint ed. pap. 12.95 (*0-9644610-1-3*) Seattle Miracle.
Marshall, Logan, ed. The Sinking of the Titanic & Great Sea Disasters. (Illus.). 384p. 1998. reprint ed. 24.00 (*0-9665233-0-X*) Vsn Forum.
— The Sinking of the Titanic & Great Sea Disasters: Thrilling Stories of Survivors (With Photographs & Sketches) LC 98-20437. (Illus.). 319p. 1998. reprint ed. pap. 30.00 (*1-889059-14-5*) Regent Pr.
Marshall, Lois, jt. auth. see Biggs, Bud.
Marshall, Loren, jt. auth. see Le Fevers, Stephen.
Marshall, Lori, jt. auth. see Marshall, Garry.
***Marshall, Lorna J.** Nyae Nyae Kung: Beliefs & Rites. LC 99-74169. (Peabody Museum Monographs: Vol. 8). (Illus.). 362p. 2000. pap. 25.00 (*0-87365-908-2*); text 45.00 (*0-87365-909-0*) Peabody Harvard.
Marshall, Louise, jt. auth. see Bibus, Ethel.
Marshall, Louise H. & Magoun, Horace W. Discoveries in the Human Brain: Neuroscience Prehistory, Brain Structure & Function. LC 97-42118. (Illus.). 336p. 1997. 69.50 (*0-89603-435-6*) Humana.
Marshall, Lucie, ed. see Tarbell, Jim.
Marshall, Lydie. A Passion for My Provence: Home Cooking from the South of France. LC 98-49394. 320p. 1999. pap. 15.00 (*0-06-093164-7*) HarpC.
— Passion for Potatoes. LC 91-50516. 272p. 1992. pap. 16.00 (*0-06-096910-5*, Perennial) HarperTrade.
Marshall, Lyn. Yogacise: The "No-Sweat" Exercise Programme for the '90s. (Illus.). 95p. 1995. pap. 9.95 (*0-563-36279-0*, Pub. by BBC) Parkwest Pubns.
Marshall, Lyn, jt. auth. see Gosling, Ted.
Marshall, Lynne, jt. auth. see Kirwan, Anna.
***Marshall, M. & Frank, F.** International Encyclopaedia of Energy, 5 vols. 1998. pap. 1500.00 (*81-7020-222-1*, Pub. by Print Hse) St Mut.
Marshall, M. W., jt. auth. see Ferreira, Hugo G.
Marshall, Mac. Weekend Warriors: Alcohol in a Micronesian Culture. Edgerton, Robert B. & Langness, L. L., eds. LC 78-64597. 170p. (C). 1979. pap. 18.95 (*0-87484-455-X*, 455) Mayfield Pub.
Marshall, Mac, ed. Beliefs, Behaviors, & Alcoholic Beverages: A Cross-Cultural Survey. 504p. 1979. pap. text 29.95 (*0-472-08580-8*, 08580) U of Mich Pr.
— Siblingship in Oceania: Studies in the Meaning of Kin Relations. LC 83-14516. (ASAO Monographs: No. 8). (Illus.). 434p. (C). 1983. reprint ed. pap. text 31.00 (*0-8191-3430-9*) U Pr of Amer.
Marshall, Mac & Nason, James D. Micronesia, 1944-1974: A Bibliography of Anthropological & Related Source Materials. LC 75-28587. (Bibliographies Ser.). 348p. 1975. 10.00 (*0-87536-215-X*) HRAFP.
Marshall, Mac, jt. ed. see Kiste, Robert C.
Marshall, Madeleine F. Common Hymnsense. LC 95-2774. 204p. 1995. 19.95 (*0-941050-69-6*, G-4023) GIA Pubns.
— The Poetry of Elizabeth Singer Rowe (1674-1737) LC 87-24399. (Studies in Women & Religion: Vol. 25). (Illus.). 380p. 1987. lib. bdg. 99.95 (*0-88946-524-X*) E Mellen.
— Singer's Manual of English Diction. 208p. 1953. 15.00 (*0-02-871100-9*, Schirmer Books) Mac Lib Ref.
Marshall, Madeleine F. & Todd, Janet M. English Congregational Hymns in the Eighteenth Century. LC 82-40176. 192p. 1982. 24.95 (*0-8131-1470-5*) U Pr of Ky.
Marshall, Marcia, ed. see Pringle, Laurence.
Marshall, Margaret J. Contesting Cultural Rhetorics: Public Discourse & Education 1890-1900. (Illus.). 272p. 1995. text 44.50 (*0-472-10536-1*, 10536) U of Mich Pr.
Marshall, Margaret M. The Dialect of Notre-Dame-de-Sahilhac: A Natural Generative Phonology. (Stanford French & Italian Studies: Vol. 31). 160p. 1984. pap. 56.50 (*0-915838-06-0*) Anma Libri.
Marshall, Margaret R. An Introduction to the World of Children's Books. 2nd ed. 250p. 1988. text 61.95 (*0-566-05461-2*, Pub. by Gower) Ashgate Pub Co.
Marshall, Marguerite M., et al. An Account of Afro-American in Southeast Kansas, 1884-1984. (Illus.). 106p. 1986. pap. 12.95 (*0-89745-091-4*) Sunflower U Pr.
Marshall, Marilyn, ed. People Chow: Favorite Recipes of the Famous & Almost Famous. (Illus.). 336p. 1985. spiral bd. 12.00 (*0-9616537-1-X*) Hays Humane Soc.
Marshall, Marion. Amber Moment. LC 98-87831. 325p. 1998. 25.00 (*0-7388-0121-6*); pap. 15.00 (*0-7388-0122-4*) Xlibris Corp.
Marshall, Mark, jt. auth. see Leung, Helen.
Marshall, Mark G. & National Tech. Info Service Staff. The Nature of Imagery Analysis & Its Place Beside Intelligence Analysis. (Illus.). 300p. (C). 1998. pap. write for info. (*0-9656195-1-6*) Joint Military.
Marshall, Marlene H. Making Bits & Pieces Mosaics: Creative Projects for Home & Garden. LC 97-31831. 1998. 24.95 (*1-58017-015-3*) Storey Bks.
***Marshall, Marlene Hurley.** Making Bits & Pieces Mosaics: Creative Projects for Home & Garden. (Illus.). 96p. 2000. pap. 16.95 (*1-58017-307-1*, 67307) Storey Bks.
Marshall, Martha L. Pronouncing Dictionary of California Names in English & Spanish. (Shorey Historical Ser.). 41p. 1925. reprint ed. pap. 10.00 (*0-8466-0155-9*, S-155) Shoreys Bkstore.
Marshall, Marvin. Fostering Social Responsibility. LC 98-65076. (Fastback Ser.: No. 428). 41p. 1998. pap. 3.00 (*0-87367-628-9*, FB#428) Phi Delta Kappa.
Marshall, Mary. Angel Fire. LC 96-226334. 1996. pap. text 11.99 (*1-56814-525-X*) CCC of America.
— Portraiture of Shakerism. LC 70-134420. reprint ed. 52.00 (*0-404-08461-3*) AMS Pr.
Marshall, Mary, jt. auth. see Foster, D. Glenn.
Marshall, Mary, jt. ed. see Chapman, Alan.
Marshall, Mary A. Music: Careers in Music. LC 93-14832. (Now Hiring Ser.). (Illus.). 48p. (J). (gr. 5-6). 1994. lib. bdg. 15.95 (*0-89686-793-5*, Crstwood Hse) Silver Burdett Pr.
Marshall, Mary E., ed. see Sroufe, L. Alan, et al.
Marshall, Mary M. Main Street Musings, Vol. 1. (Illus.). v, 70p. (Orig.). 1996. pap. 7.25 (*0-9651379-0-2*) M M Marshall.
Marshall, Mary P., jt. auth. see Marshall, Alfred.
Marshall, Maurice & Archer, Douglas L. Food & Health: Study Guide. 336p. (C). 1996. pap. text, student ed. 37.95 (*0-7872-1749-2*) Kendall-Hunt.
Marshall, Mel. How to Make Your Own Fishing Rods. 1982. pap. 4.50 (*0-943822-12-2*) Times Mir Mag Bk Div.
Marshall, Melinda M. Good Enough Mothers: Changing Expectations for Ourselves. LC 93-5838. 344p. 1993. 18.95 (*1-56079-253-1*) Petersons.
— Good Enough Mothers: Changing Expectations for Ourselves. LC 93-5838. 343p. 1994. pap. 10.95 (*1-56079-433-X*) Petersons.
***Marshall, Melissa Rose & Morgulis, Mikhail.** Russia - Between Sword & Cross: Russia's Remarkable Rebel Emigre. (Illus.). 344p. 1999. pap. 24.00 (*0-9675370-0-2*) Pier Pubng.
Marshall, Michael. Great Expectations? Preparing for Evangelism Through Bible Study. LC 91-6600. 145p. (Orig.). 1991. pap. 8.95 (*1-56101-033-2*) Cowley Pubns.
***Marshall, Michael J. & Hirsch, E. D., Jr., eds.** Realms of Gold: A Core Knowledge Reader, Vol. 1. 271p. (YA). (gr. 6-8). 2000. pap. 19.95 (*1-890517-22-4*) Core Knowledge.
— Realms of Gold: A Core Knowledge Reader, Vol. 2. 328p. (YA). (gr. 6-8). 2000. pap. 19.95 (*1-890517-23-2*) Core Knowledge.
— Realms of Gold: A Core Knowledge Reader, Vol. 3. 440p. (YA). (gr. 6-8). 2000. pap. 19.95 (*1-890517-24-0*) Core Knowledge.
Marshall, Michael J., ed. see De Cervantes Saavedra, Miguel.
Marshall, Michael J., ed. see Defoe, Daniel.
Marshall, Michael J., ed. see Doyle, Arthur Conan.
Marshall, Michael J., ed. see Irving, Washington.
Marshall, Michael J., ed. see McSpadden, J. Walker.
Marshall, Michael J., ed. see Porter, Eleanor.
Marshall, Michael J., ed. see Stevenson, Robert Louis.
Marshall, Michael J., ed. see Swift, Jonathan.
Marshall, Michael P., jt. auth. see Hogan, Patrick.
Marshall, Michael W. Ocean Traders: From the Portuguese Discoveries to the Present Day. fac. ed. LC 89-48361. (Illus.). 192p. 1990. reprint ed. pap. 59.60 (*0-7837-8135-0*, 204794200008) Bks Demand.
Marshall, Mike, jt. ed. see Arestis, Philip.
Marshall, Molly. What It Means to Be Human. LC 94-41124. 160p. 1995. pap. 14.00 (*1-880837-85-4*) Smyth & Helwys.
Marshall, Molly T. No Salvation Outside the Church? A Critical Inquiry. LC 93-10803. 280p. 1993. text 89.95 (*0-7734-2854-2*) E Mellen.
Marshall, Monty G. Third World War: Systems, Process, & Conflict Dynamics. LC 99-19221. 328p. 1999. 69.00 (*0-8476-9347-3*) Rowman.
Marshall, Murdena, jt. auth. see Schmidt, David L.
Marshall, Muriel. The Awesome 'Dobie Badlands. LC 99-64982. (Illus.). 123p. 1999. pap. 14.95 (*1-890437-05-0*) Western Reflections.
— Island in the Sky. LC 99-60158. (Illus.). 277p. 1999. pap. 15.95 (*1-890437-07-7*) Western Reflections.
— Red Hole in Time. LC 87-21715. (Elma Dill Russell Spencer Series in the West & Southwest: No. 9). (Illus.). 312p. 1988. 29.50 (*0-89096-316-9*) Tex A&M Univ Pr.
— Uncompahgre: A Guide to the Uncompahgre Plateau. rev. ed. LC 97-62474. (Illus.). 220p. 1998. pap. 15.95 (*1-890437-06-9*) Western Reflections.
— Where Rivers Meet: Lore From The Colorado Frontier. LC 95-40368. (Elma Dill Russell Spencer Series in the West & Southwest: No. 14). (Illus.). 232p. 1996. 32.95 (*0-89096-686-9*); pap. 16.95 (*0-89096-687-7*) Tex A&M Univ Pr.
Marshall, Murry. Spaces of Orderings & Abstract Real Spectra, Vol. 163. LC 96-35288. (Lecture Notes in Mathematics Ser.). ii, 190p. 1996. pap. 35.00 (*3-540-61729-9*) Spr-Verlag.
Marshall, N., jt. auth. see Brook, C.
Marshall, N., ed. see Dawson, Philip.
Marshall, N. B. Explorations in the Life of Fishes. LC 75-129122. (Books in Biology: No. 7). (Illus.). 216p. 1971. 29.00 (*0-674-27951-4*) HUP.
***Marshall, Nancy.** James Tissot: Victorian Life of Modern Love. (Illus.). 216p. 1999. 45.00 (*0-300-08173-1*) Yale U Pr.
Marshall, Natalia. Shelter Now. 144p. 1999. pap. 25.00 (*0-7893-0364-7*) Universe.
Marshall, Nathaniel. Penitential Discipline of the Primitive Church. LC 74-172846. (Library of Anglo-Catholic Theology: No. 13). reprint ed. 44.00 (*0-404-52105-3*) AMS Pr.
Marshall, Neil, jt. auth. see Dollery, Brain.
***Marshall, Nelson.** In the Wake of a Great Yankee Oceanographer: Recollections from the Years Following the Foundations Laid down by Henry Bryant Bigelow. Day Communications Staff, ed. (Illus.). 172p. 1999. pap. 19.95 (*0-9628730-2-0*) Th Anchorage.
Marshall, Nelson. The Scallop Estuary: The Natural History Features of the Niantic River. (Illus.). 150p. 1994. pap. write for info. (*0-9628730-1-2*) Th Anchorage.
— Understanding the Eastern Caribbean & the Antilles, with Checklists Appended. (Illus.). 252p. (Orig.). 1991. pap. 17.95 (*0-9628730-0-4*) Th Anchorage.
Marshall, Nina T. Gardener's Guide to Plant Conservation. 184p. 1993. 12.95 (*0-942635-18-3*) World Wildlife Fund.
Marshall, Nissim, tr. see Puech, Alain.
Marshall, Nissim, tr. see Raabe, Marie.
Marshall-Noke, Dorothy. Feathers. Weinberger, Jane, ed. LC 88-51278. (Illus.). 64p. (J). (ps-4). 1990. pap. 5.95 (*0-932433-52-9*) Windswept Hse.
Marshall, Norman E. That Man Tate & Other Kindred Spirits: With Stories from the Allagash. LC 93-60020. (Orig.). 1993. pap. 12.95 (*0-9636231-0-9*) TreeTop MA.
Marshall, Norman F. & Ripamonti, Aldo. Leonardo da Vinci. (What Made Them Great Ser.). (Illus.). 104p. (J). (gr. 5-8). 1990. 12.95 (*0-382-09982-6*); pap. 5.95 (*0-382-24007-3*) Silver Burdett Pr.
***Marshall, Oliver.** English-Speaking Communities in Latin America since Independence. LC 00-33342. 2000. pap. write for info. (*0-312-23731-6*) St Martin.
Marshall, Oscar J., jt. auth. see Coddington, Edwin F.
***Marshall, Owen.** Sounds of the Oregon Coast. 1999. pap. write for info. (*1-58235-281-X*) Watermrk Pr.
Marshall, P. Geology of Mangaia. (BMB Ser.: No. 36). 1969. reprint ed. pap. 25.00 (*0-527-02139-3*) Periodicals Srv.
— Geology of Rarotonga & Atiu. (BMB Ser.: No. 72). 1969. reprint ed. 25.00 (*0-527-02178-4*) Periodicals Srv.
Marshall, P., tr. see More, Thomas.
Marshall, P. David. Celebrity & Power: Fame in Contemporary Culture. LC 96-31522. 1997. pap. 19.95 (*0-8166-2725-8*) U of Minn Pr.
Marshall, P. J. Bengal: The British Bridgehead. (New Cambridge History of India Ser.: II: 2). (Illus.). 222p. 1988. text 54.95 (*0-521-25330-6*) Cambridge U Pr.
— Trade & Conquest: Studies on the Rise of British Dominance in India. (Collected Studies: No. CS 409). 320p. 1993. 101.95 (*0-86078-373-1*, Pub. by Variorum) Ashgate Pub Co.
Marshall, P. J., ed. The Cambridge Illustrated History of the British Empire. (Illustrated Histories Ser.). (Illus.). 404p. (C). 1996. 39.95 (*0-521-43211-1*) Cambridge U Pr.
Marshall, P. J. & Low, Alaine, eds. The Oxford History of the British Empire: The Eighteenth Century, Vol. 2. (Illus.). 662p. 1998. 45.00 (*0-19-820563-5*) OUP.
Marshall, P. J. & Williams, Thomas G. The Great Map of Mankind: Perceptions of New Worlds in the Age of Enlightenment. LC 82-80225. 320p. 1982. 37.50 (*0-674-36210-1*) HUP.
Marshall, P. J., ed. see Burke, Edmund.
Marshall, P. K., ed. see Gellius, Aulus.
Marshall, P. W. Design of Welded Tubular Connections: Basis & Use of AWS Code Provisions. (Developments in Civil Engineering Ser.: Vol. 37). 412p. 1991. 195.25 (*0-444-88201-4*) Elsevier.
Marshall, Pam, jt. auth. see Hutchinson, Allan C.
Marshall, Patricia. Math Plans. 432p. (C). 1997. pap. 32.00 (*0-205-16270-3*) Allyn.
Marshall, Patricia A., jt. auth. see Thomasma, David C.
***Marshall, Paul.** Heaven is Not My Home: Living in the Now of God's Creation, 1. LC 98-49520. 260p. 1999. 17.99 (*0-8499-1471-X*) Word Pub.
Marshall, Paul. A Kind of Life Imposed on Man: Vocation & Social Order from Tyndale to Locke. 192p. 1996. text 45.00 (*0-8020-0784-8*) U of Toronto Pr.
— Their Blood Cries Out. LC 96-48119. 304p. 1997. pap. 12.99 (*0-8499-4020-6*) Word Pub.
— Thine Is the Kingdom: A Biblical Perspective on the Nature of Government & Politics Today. 160p. 1993. reprint ed. pap. 16.95 (*1-57383-007-0*) Regent College.
Marshall, Paul, ed. Raparapa. 290p. (C). 1990. 90.00 (*0-7316-3328-8*, Pub. by Pascoe Pub) St Mut.

An Asterisk (*) at the beginning of an entry indicates that the title is appearing for the first time.

*Marshall, Paul, ed. Religious Freedom in the World: A Global Report on Freedom & Persecution. 320p. 2000. pap. 14.99 (0-8054-2368-0) Broadman.

Marshall, Paul & Northrup, Lesley. Leaps & Boundaries: The Prayer Book in the 21st Century. LC 97-27226. 224p. 1997. pap. 16.95 (0-8192-1718-2) Morehouse Pub.

Marshall, Paul & Williamson, Nicola. Los Angeles. (Rough Guide Ser.). (Illus.). 288p. (Orig.). 1998. pap. text 14.95 (1-85828-344-2, Pub. by Rough Guides) Penguin Putnam.

Marshall, Paul A., et al, eds. Stained Glass: Worldviews & Social Science. 188p. (Orig.). (C). 1989. pap. text 19.50 (0-8191-7254-5) U Pr of Amer.

Marshall, Paul A. & VanderVennen, Robert E., eds. Social Science in Christian Perspective. (Christian Studies Today). 357p. (Orig.). (C). 1988. lib. bdg. 55.00 (0-8191-7103-4) U Pr of Amer.

Marshall, Paul A., jt. ed. see Chaplin, Jonathan.

Marshall, Paul V. Prayer Book Parallels: The Public Services of the Church Arranged for Comparative Study, Vol. 1. 701p. 1989. 44.95 (0-89869-181-8) Church Pub Inc.

— Prayer Book Parallels: The Public Services of the Church Arranged for Comparative Study, Vol. 2. 576p. 1990. 39.95 (0-89869-209-1) Church Pub Inc.

— Preaching for the Church Today: The Skills, Prayer, & Art of Sermon Preparation. 224p. 1990. 21.95 (0-89869-187-7) Church Pub Inc.

— The Voice of a Stranger: On the Lay Origin of Anglican Liturgies. 269p. 1993. 25.95 (0-89869-236-9) Church Pub Inc.

Marshall, Paula. An Affair of Honour. large type ed. (Mills & Boon Large Print Ser.). 350p. 1997. 23.99 (0-263-15088-7) Ulverscroft.

— The Astrologer's Daughter. large type ed. 350p. 1995. 23.99 (0-263-14187-X, Pub. by Mills & Boon) Ulverscroft.

— A Beckoning Dream. large type ed. (Mills & Boon Large Print Ser.). 350p. 1998. 24.99 (0-263-15527-7, Pub. by Mills & Boon) Ulverscroft.

— Cousin Harry. large type ed. (Magna Large Print Ser.). 384p. 1998. 29.99 (0-7505-1237-7, Pub. by Mgna Lrg Print) Ulverscroft.

*Marshall, Paula. Dear Lady Disdain. (Readers Choice Ser.). 2000. mass mkt. 4.50 (0-373-51115-9, 1-51115-3, Harlequin) Harlequin Bks.

Marshall, Paula. Dear Lady Disdain. large type ed. 350p. 1995. 23.99 (0-263-14425-9, Pub. by Mills & Boon) Ulverscroft.

*Marshall, Paula. The Devil & Drusilla. large type ed. 320p. 1999. 25.99 (0-263-16036-X, Pub. by Mills & Boon) Ulverscroft.

Marshall, Paula. An Improper Duenna. (Regency Romance Ser.). 1993. per. 2.99 (0-373-31207-5, 1-31207-3) Harlequin Bks.

— An Improper Duenna. 1999. per. 3.75 (0-373-31232-6) Harlequin Bks.

— Lady Clairval's Marriage. large type ed. (Mills & Boon Large Print Ser.). 350p. 1997. 23.99 (0-263-15182-4, Pub. by Mills & Boon) Ulverscroft.

— The Lost Princess. 1999. per. 4.99 (0-373-30337-8) Harlequin Bks.

— The Lost Princess. large type ed. (Mills & Boon Large Print Ser.). 350p. 1996. 23.99 (0-263-14759-2, Pub. by Mills & Boon) Ulverscroft.

*Marshall, Paula. Miss Jesmond's Heir. large type ed. 320p. 1999. 25.99 (0-263-16220-6, Pub. by Mills & Boon) Ulverscroft.

Marshall, Paula. Not Quite a Gentleman. large type ed. 350p. 1996. 23.99 (0-263-14528-X, Pub. by Mills & Boon) Ulverscroft.

*Marshall, Paula. The Quiet Man. 320p. 2000. 26.99 (0-263-16417-9, Pub. by Mills & Boon) Ulverscroft.

Marshall, Paula. Step-by-Step Tiling Projects. LC 98-66256. (Illus.). 112p. 1998. pap. 12.95 (0-696-20818-0, Better Homes) Meredith Bks.

*Marshall, Paula. The Wolfe's Mate. large type ed. 320p. 1999. 25.99 (0-263-16185-4, Pub. by Mills & Boon) Ulverscroft.

Marshall, Paula. The Youngest Miss Ashe. large type ed. (Mills & Boon Large Print Ser.). 350p. 1997. 23.99 (0-263-15339-8, Pub. by Mills & Boon) Ulverscroft.

Marshall, Paula & Andrew, Sylvia. Reluctant Bridegrooms: My Lady Love; Darling Amazon. LC 95-13667. (Promo Ser.). 443p. 1995. per. 4.99 (0-373-31218-0, 1-31218-0) Harlequin Bks.

Marshall, Paula, jt. auth. see Hiatt, Brenda.

Marshall, Paule. Brown Girl, Brownstones. 324p. (C). 1981. reprint ed. pap. 10.95 (1-55861-149-5) Feminist Pr.

— The Chosen Place, the Timeless People. LC 84-40073. (Vintage Contemporaries Ser.). 480p. 1984. pap. 15.00 (0-394-72633-2) Vin Bks.

— The Chosen Place, the Timeless People. LC 84-4007. 1992. pap. 13.00 (0-394-23987-3) Vin Bks.

— Daughters. LC 92-53558. (Contemporary Fiction Ser.). 416p. 1992. pap. 13.95 (0-452-26912-1, Plume) Dutton Plume.

*Marshall, Paule. The Fisher King: A Novel. LC 00-28470. 224p. 2000. 23.00 (0-684-87283-8) Scribner.

Marshall, Paule. Paule Marshall: For a Reading on the Occasion of a Reception in Honor of Her MacArthur Fellowship. (InterAmericas Ser.: No. 2). 16p. 1992. 5.00 (0-9633741-2-5) RI Study of Man.

— Praisesong for the Widow. (Contemporary Fiction Ser.). 256p. 1984. pap. 12.95 (0-452-26711-0, Plume) Dutton Plume.

— Reena & Other Stories. LC 83-16592. 224p. 1983. pap. 11.95 (0-935312-24-2) Feminist Pr.

— Soul Clap Hands & Sing. (Howard University Press Library of Contemporary Literature). 208p. 1988. pap. 12.95 (0-88258-155-4) Howard U Pr.

— Third World War: Systems, Process & Conflict Dynamics. LC 99-19221. 328p. 1999. pap. 26.95 (0-8476-9348-1) Rowman.

Marshall, Penny L., jt. auth. see Green, Carol J.

Marshall, Peter. The Catholic Priesthood & the English Reformation. (Oxford Historical Monographs). 282p. 1994. text 65.00 (0-19-820448-5) OUP.

— Enmity in Corinth: Social Conventions in Paul's Relations with the Corinthians. 460p. 1987. lib. bdg. 87.50 (3-16-145070-1, Pub. by JCB Mohr) Coronet Bks.

— The First Easter. LC 87-30876. (Illus.). 126p. (gr. 11). 1995. 11.99 (0-8007-9120-7) Chosen Bks.

— How to Study & Learn: Your Practical Guide to Effective Study Skills. 2nd ed. (Student Handbks.). 144p. 1997. pap. 19.95 (1-85703-435-X, Pub. by How To Bks) Trans-Atl Phila.

— Let's Keep Christmas. LC 53-10628. (Illus.). 48p. (gr. 10). 1995. reprint ed. 9.99 (0-8007-9134-7) Chosen Bks.

*Marshall, Peter. Mastering Bookkeeping. 4th ed. (Illus.). 192p. (Orig.). 1999. pap. 19.95 (1-85703-495-3, Pub. by How To Bks) Trans-Atl Phila.

Marshall, Peter. Maximising Your Memory: How to Train Yourself to Remember More. 128p. 2000. pap. 14.95 (1-85703-234-9, Pub. by How To Bks) Midpt Trade.

Marshall, Peter. Nature's Web: Rethinking Our Place on Earth. LC 96-10481. 523p. (gr. 13). 1996. pap. 29.95 (1-56324-864-6) M E Sharpe.

Marshall, Peter. Nature's Web: Rethinking Our Place on Earth. LC 93-17233. 528p. 1993. reprint ed. 24.95 (1-55778-652-6) Paragon Hse.

— Now I Know Why Tigers Eat Their Young: How to Survive Your Teenagers - with Wisdom & a Little Humor. LC 93-48110. 136p. 1994. pap. 12.95 (1-55958-499-8) Prima Pub.

— Research Methods: How to Design & Conduct a Successful Project. (Student Handbks.). 119p. 1997. pap. 19.95 (1-85703-410-4, Pub. by How To Bks) Trans-Atl Phila.

— Riding the Wind: A New Philosophy for a New Era. 272p. 1999. 24.95 (0-304-33425-1, Pub. by Cassell) Cassell.

— Riding the Wind: A New Philosophy for a New Era. 256p. 1998. 24.95 (0-304-33426-X) Continuum.

*Marshall, Peter. Riding the Wind: A New Philosophy for a New Era. 2000. pap. text 17.95 (0-8264-4703-1) Continuum.

— The Senate Prayers of Peter Marshall. Ogilvie, Lloyd J., ed. 128p. 1997. 16.95 (0-939218-11-9) Chapman Billies.

Marshall, Peter. Unlocking Your Potential: How to Master Your Mind, Life & Destiny. 144p. 1998. pap. 19.95 (1-85703-252-7, Pub. by How To Bks) Trans-Atl Phila.

Marshall, Peter, ed. The Impact of the English Reformation, 1500-1640. LC 96-37853. (Arnold Readers in History Ser.). 356p. 1997. text 65.00 (0-340-67708-2); pap. text 19.95 (0-340-67709-0) OUP.

Marshall, Peter & Manuel, David. From Sea to Shining Sea. LC 85-20428. 444p. (gr. 11). 1985. 21.99 (0-8007-1451-2) Revell.

— From Sea to Shining Sea. LC 85-20428. 444p. (YA). (gr. 10). 1989. pap. 12.99 (0-8007-5308-9) Revell.

— The Light & the Glory: Did God Have a Plan for America? LC 77-23352. 384p. (YA). (gr. 10). 1986. 21.99 (0-8007-0886-5) Revell.

— The Light & the Glory: Did God Have a Plan for America? LC 77-23352. 384p. (YA). (gr. 10). 1987. pap. 12.99 (0-8007-5054-3) Revell.

— The Light & the Glory Children's Activity Book. 72p. (J). (gr. k-7). 1995. pap. 6.99 (0-8007-5574-X) Revell.

Marshall, Peter & Manuel, David. Sounding Forth the Trumpet. LC 97-48640. 560p. (gr. 11 up). 1998. 21.99 (0-8007-1746-5) Revell.

*Marshall, Peter & Manuel, David. Sounding Forth the Trumpet. LC 97-48640. 560p. 1999. pap. 12.99 (0-8007-5703-3) Revell.

Marshall, Peter & Williams, Glyn, eds. British Atlantic Empire Before the American Revolution. 130p. 1980. 35.00 (0-7146-3158-2, Pub. by F Cass Pubs) Intl Spec Bk.

Marshall, Peter, et al. From Sea to Shining Sea Children's Activity Book. 80p. (J). (gr. k-7). 1996. pap. 6.99 (0-8007-5611-8) Revell.

— From Sea to Shining Sea for Children: Discovering God's Plan for America in Her First Half-Century of Independence, 1787-1837. LC 93-10801. (Illus.). 208p. (J). (gr. 7-10). 1993. pap. 9.99 (0-8007-5484-0) Revell.

— The Light & the Glory for Children: Discovering God's Plan for America from Christopher Columbus to George Washington. LC 92-11727. (Illus.). 174p. (J). (gr. 7-10). 1992. pap. 9.99 (0-8007-5448-4) Revell.

— Sounding Forth the Trumpet for Children. LC 98-43952. (Illus.). 208p. (J). (gr. 4-8). 1999. pap. 9.99 (0-8007-5692-4) Baker Bks.

Marshall, Peter, ed. see Burke, Edmund.

Marshall, Peter, ed. see Godwin, William.

Marshall, Peter, jt. ed. see Gordon, Bruce.

Marshall, Peter H. William Godwin: Philosopher, Novelist, Revolutionary. LC 83-19823. (Illus.). 498p. 1984. 57.50 (0-300-03175-0) Yale U Pr.

Marshall, Peter J., ed. The British Discovery of Hinduism in the 18th Century. LC 73-111132. (European Understanding of India Ser.). 320p. reprint ed. pap. 91.20 (0-8357-7422-8, 2024493) Bks Demand.

Marshall, Peter K. Servius & Commentary on Virgil. LC 97-23566. (Occasional Papers, Center for Medieval & Early Renaissance Studies). 44p. 1997. pap. 7.95 (1-889818-03-8) Pegasus Pr.

Marshall, Philip C., jt. ed. see Kelley, Stephen J.

Marshall, Philip H., jt. ed. see Elias, Jeffrey W.

Marshall, Phillip, jt. auth. see Ellis, Cliff.

Marshall, Phyllis F. Calls of God. 38p. (Orig.). 1996. pap. 4.99 (0-9655361-0-6) Eternal Wrd Pub.

Marshall, R. D. & Tipton, Keith F., eds. Essays in Biochemistry, Vol. 21. (Serial Publication Ser.). 176p. 1986. pap. text 62.00 (0-12-158121-7) Acad Pr.

Marshall, R. D., jt. ed. see Campbell, P. N.

Marshall, R. Jackson. Memories of World War I: North Carolina Doughboys on the Western Front. LC 99-171389. (Illus.). xiii, 208p. 1998. pap. 15.00 (0-86526-282-9) NC Archives.

Marshall, R. K., et al. Dynasty: The Royal House of Stewart. (Illus.). 120p. 1995. pap. 17.95 (0-948636-21-1, 6211, Pub. by Natl Mus Scotland) A Schwartz & Co.

Marshall, R. L. The Historical Criticism of Documents. 1977. lib. bdg. 59.95 (0-8490-1956-7) Gordon Pr.

Marshall, R. M. My Cook Book. 136p. 1985. 49.00 (0-906054-34-6) St Mut.

Marshall, Ralph O., et al. Alcohol & Marijuana Use in Texas. 24p. 1981. 2.00 (0-318-02511-6) S Houston Employ.

Marshall, Randolph S. & Mayer, Stephan A. On Call Neurology: Neurology. Schmitt, William, ed. LC 96-36902. 352p. 1997. pap. text 21.95 (0-7216-6523-3, W B Saunders Co) Harcrt Hlth Sci Grp.

Marshall, Ray. The State of Families 3: Losing Direction: Families, Human Resource Development, & Economic Performance. LC 87-24374. 160p. 1991. pap. 16.95 (0-87304-249-2) Manticore Pubs.

Marshall, Ray & Christian, Virgil L., Jr., eds. Employment of Blacks in the South: A Perspective on the 1960s. LC 78-7331. (Illus.). 261p. reprint ed. pap. 81.00 (0-8357-3615-6, 203610900004) Bks Demand.

Marshall, Ray & Osterman, Paul. Workforce Policies for the 1990s: A New Labor Market Agenda & The Possibilities of Employment Policy. LC 89-80284. 1989. 12.00 (0-944826-05-9) Economic Policy Inst.

Marshall, Ray & Tucker, Marc. Thinking for a Living: Education & the Wealth of Nations. LC 91-58596. 304p. 1993. reprint ed. pap. 15.00 (0-465-08557-1, Pub. by Basic) HarpC.

Marshall, Ray, et al. Education, Technology, & the Texas Economy: Can Technology Help Texas Schools?, 3 vols., Vol. 2. (Policy Research Project Report Ser.: No. 85). 148p. 1988. pap. 7.00 (0-89940-691-2) LBJ Sch Pub Aff.

— Education, Technology, & the Texas Economy: Economics of Education, 3 vols., Vol. 1. (Policy Research Project Report Ser.: No. 85). 130p. 1988. pap. 7.00 (0-89940-690-4) LBJ Sch Pub Aff.

— Education, Technology, & the Texas Economy: Vocational Preparation, 3 vols., Vol. 3. (Policy Research Project Report Ser.: No. 85). 50p. 1988. pap. 7.00 (0-89940-692-0) LBJ Sch Pub Aff.

— Employment Discrimination: The Impact of Legal & Administrative Remedies. LC 78-17333. 153p. 1978. 42.95 (0-275-90306-0, C0306, Praeger Pubs) Greenwood.

Marshall, Ray, jt. auth. see Glover, Robert.

Marshall, Ray C., ed. Back to Shared Prosperity: The Growing Inequality of Wealth & Income in America. LC 99-11649. (Illus.). 437p. (gr. 13). 1999. text 84.95 (0-7656-0424-8) M E Sharpe.

Marshall, Ray F. Back to Shared Prosperity: The Growing Inequality of Wealth & Income in America. LC 99-11649. (Illus.). 437p. 1999. pap. text 29.95 (0-7656-0425-6) M E Sharpe.

Marshall, Renee, tr. see Luetke, Frederick.

Marshall, Richard. Edward Ruscha: Los Angeles Apartments. (Illus.). 64p. 1993. pap. 8.95 (0-8109-6808-8, Pub. by Abrams) Time Warner.

— Jean-Michel Basquiat. (Illus.). 272p. 1992. 65.00 (0-8109-6806-1, Pub. by Abrams) Time Warner.

— Jean-Michel Basquiat. (Illus.). 272p. 1994. 35.00 (0-8109-6814-2, Pub. by Abrams) Time Warner.

— Keith Haring, Jean-Michel Basquiat, Kenny Schare: In Your Face. Malca, Leon A., ed. (Illus.). 80p. 1997. pap. text 20.00 (0-9659010-5-X) Malca Fine Art.

— Witchcraft: The History & Mythology. (Illus.). 160p. 1995. write for info. (1-887354-03-4) Saraband CT.

Marshall, Richard, compiled by. Jean-Michel Basquiat. LC 92-19045. 1992. pap. write for info. (0-87427-081-2) Whitney Mus.

Marshall, Richard & Mapplethorpe, Robert. Robert Mapplethorpe. (Illus.). 1990. pap. 39.95 (0-8212-1786-0) Bulfinch Pr.

Marshall, Richard, jt. auth. see Rosenthal, Mark.

Marshall, Richard, jt. ed. see Merrick, David.

Marshall, Richard, ed. see Segar, E. C.

Marshall, Richard D., jt. auth. see Mehta, Kishor C.

Marshall, Richard H., Jr. & Bird, Thomas E., eds. Hryhorij Savyc Skovoroda: An Anthology of Critical Articles. LC 94-931922. xvi, 319p. 44.95 (1-895571-03-0) Ukrainian Acad.

Marshall, Richard J. Home Teaching with Purpose & Power. LC 90-41525. 158p. (Orig.). 1990. pap. 12.95 (0-87579-371-1) Deseret Bk.

Marshall, Richard K. Local Merchants of Prato: Small Entrepreneurs in the Late Medieval Economy. LC 98-43545. Vol. 117. 191p. 1999. 42.50 (0-8018-6057-1) Johns Hopkins.

Marshall, Rick. The Encyclopedia of Country Music. 208p. 1995. write for info. (1-57215-067-X) World Pubns.

Marshall, Rick S., jt. auth. see Saling, Beverly M.

Marshall, Rita. I Hate to Read. (Illus.). 32p. (J). (gr. 4-7). 1995. 19.95 (1-56846-005-8, Creative Eds) Creative Co.

Marshall, Rob. A Guide to Eclectus Parrots, Their Management Care & Breeding. (Illus.). 78p. (Orig.). 1991. pap. 23.95 (0-9587455-4-4) Avian Pubns.

Marshall, Robert. Alaska Wilderness: Exploring the Central Brooks Range. 2nd ed. Marshall, George, ed. & intro. by. LC 73-116025. (Illus.). 1970. pap. 16.95 (0-520-01711-0, Pub. by U CA Pr) Cal Prin Full Svc.

— Arctic Village: A Nineteen Thirties Portrait of Wiseman, Alaska. LC 90-27265. (Classic Reprint Ser.: No. 2). (Illus.). xxviii, 399p. 1991. 28.00 (0-912006-47-1); pap. 20.00 (0-912006-51-X) U of Alaska Pr.

— The Enchanted Golf Clubs. (Illus.). 160p. 1999. reprint ed. pap. 10.95 (1-891369-09-1, Pub. by Breakaway Bks) Consort Bk Sales.

— The Haunted Major. 1998. pap. 12.95 (0-86241-786-4, Pub. by Canongate Books) Interlink Pub.

*Marshall, Robert. The Haunted Major. LC 98-44504. (Illus.). 208p. 1999. 23.00 (0-88001-669-8) HarpC.

Marshall, Robert C. Collective Decision Making in Rural Japan. LC 84-3159. (Michigan Papers in Japanese Studies: No. 11). xiii, 178p. (Orig.). (C). 1984. pap. text 9.95 (0-939512-17-3) U MI Japan.

— Introduction to Group Treatment for Aphasia: Design & Management. 192p. 1998. pap. text 32.50 (0-7506-7013-4) Buttrwrth-Heinemann.

Marshall, Robert G. Pro-Life Precinct Power: A Workbook. (Illus.). 45p. (Orig.). 1990. pap. 2.00 (1-890712-15-9, LW3) Amer Life League.

Marshall, Robert G. & Donovan, Charles A. Blessed Are the Barren: The Social Policy of Planned Parenthood. LC 90-84812. 381p. (Orig.). 1991. pap. 19.95 (0-89870-353-0) Ignatius Pr.

Marshall, Robert G. & St Aubyn, Frederic, eds. Trois Pieces Surrealistes: Les Maries de la Tour Eiffel; L'Armoire a Glace un Beau Soir; Victor ou les Enfants au Pouvoir. LC 75-89864. (FRE., Illus.). 1969. pap. text 14.95 (0-89197-456-3) Irvington.

Marshall, Robert L. The Compositional Process of J. S. Bach: A Study of the Autograph Scores of the Vocal Works, Vol. 1. LC 76-113005. (Princeton Studies in Music: No. 4). (Illus.). 287p. reprint ed. pap. 89.00 (0-8357-4037-4, 203672900001) Bks Demand.

— The Compositional Process of J. S. Bach: A Study of the Autograph Scores of the Vocal Works, Vol. 2. LC 76-113005. (Princeton Studies in Music: No. 4). (Illus.). 195p. reprint ed. pap. 60.50 (0-8357-4038-2, 203672900002) Bks Demand.

*Marshall, Robert L. Mozart Speaks: Views on Music, Musicians & the World. (Illus.). 446p. 2000. reprint ed. pap. 20.00 (0-7881-9321-X) DIANE Pub.

Marshall, Robert L. The Music of Johann Sebastian Bach: The Sources, the Style, the Significance. 375p. 1989. reprint ed. 36.00 (0-02-871781-3, Schirmer Books) Mac Lib Ref.

Marshall, Robert L., ed. Eighteenth Century Keyboard Music. (Studies in Musical Genres & Repertoires). 384p. 1994. 42.00 (0-02-871355-9, Schirmer Books) Mac Lib Ref.

Marshall, Robert W. Finding Rock Art in the Southwest. (Illus.). 32p. reprint ed. pap. 5.95 (0-9659167-0-7) Canyon Moon.

*Marshall, Roger. All about Powerboats: Understanding Design & Performance. (Illus.). 2000. pap. 17.95 (0-07-136204-5) McGraw.

Marshall, Roger. The Complete Guide to Choosing a Cruising Sailboat. LC 98-52773. (Illus.). 214p. 1999. 24.95 (0-07-041998-1) McGraw.

*Marshall, Roger. Essential Sailing. LC 99-27140. 2000. pap. text 16.95 (1-55821-771-1) Lyons Pr.

Marshall, Roger. Sail Better: 101 Tips & Techniques. 1996. pap. text 14.95 (0-07-041077-1) McGraw.

— Sail Better: 101 Tips & Techniques. LC 95-36249. (Illus.). 208p. 1996. pap. 14.95 (0-312-14133-5) St Martin.

Marshall, Ronald F. Kierkegaard the Judge: Condemning & Correcting Christianity. (Illus.). 265p. 1999. pap. 19.95 (0-9672440-1-3) certus sermo.

Marshall, Rosalind. The Winter Queen: The Life of Elizabeth of Bohemia, 1596-1662. (Illus.). 160p. 1998. pap. 25.00 (0-903598-79-5, Pub. by Natl Galleries) Antique Collect.

Marshall, Rosalind K. Queen of Scots. (Illus.). 208p. 1986. pap. 20.00 (0-11-493122-4, Pub. by Statnry Office) Balogh.

— Virgins & Viragos: A History of Women in Scotland from 1080-1980. (Illus.). 340p. 1983. pap. 10.00 (0-89733-075-7) Academy Chi Pubs.

Marshall, Roy K., jt. auth. see Levitt, I. M.

Marshall, Rupel E. The Wails of Palm Trees. 64p. 1999. pap. write for info. (1-56167-460-5) Am Literary Pr.

Marshall, Rush P. Control of Cedar-Apple Rust on Red Cedar. (CT Academy of Arts & Science Transactions Ser.: Vol. 34). 1941. pap. 39.50 (0-686-51364-9) Elliots Bks.

Marshall, Russell. The 40 Safest American Sports Records: With an Analysis of Why They Are Unbreakable. (Illus.). 128p. (Orig.). 1997. pap. 9.95 (0-9657532-0-4) Marshall.

Marshall, Ruth, jt. auth. see Brackelsberg, Phyllis.

Marshall, S., ed. Everyday Science Enrichment Calendar. (Illus.). 28p. 1994. pap. text 24.95 (0-87355-125-7, PB105X) Natl Sci Tchrs.

Marshall, S., et al, eds. Noblesse Workshop on Non-Linear Model Based Image Analysis: Proceedings of NWBIA, 1-3 July 1998, Glasgow. LC 98-20454. (Illus.). xvi, 346p. 1998. pap. 99.00 (3-540-76258-2) Spr-Verlag.

Marshall, S., ed. see Aldridge, Bill G., et al.

Marshall, S. A., jt. auth. see Skevington, J.

Marshall, S. L. Battle at Best. (Battery Classics Ser.). (Illus.). 257p. 1988. reprint ed. 29.95 (0-89839-115-6) Battery Pr.

— Bird. (Illus.). 224p. 1989. mass mkt. 4.50 (0-446-35314-0, Pub. by Warner Bks) Little.

— Bird: The Christmastide Battle. (Vietnam War Ser.: No. 4). (Illus.). 216p. 1983. reprint ed. 27.95 (0-89839-072-9) Battery Pr.

— Crimsoned Prairie: The Indian Wars. (Quality Paperbacks Ser.). (Illus.). 270p. (C). 1984. reprint ed. pap. 12.95 (*0-306-80226-0*) Da Capo.

— Men Against Fire: The Problem of Battle Command in Future War. 1990. 25.00 (*0-8446-4057-3*) Peter Smith.

— The Soldier's Load. 120p. reprint ed. 2.00 (*0-686-31001-2*) Marine Corps.

Marshall, S. L. & Atwood, Lyman. Island Victory: The Battle for Kwajalein. 1983. reprint ed. 23.95 (*0-89201-101-7*) Zenger Pub.

Marshall, S. L. & Davis, W. J. JFK Plus CIA Equals BOP (Bay of Pigs) The Inside Story of the Bay of Pigs. 172p. 1992. pap. 11.00 (*1-885541-01-5*) Marine Bks.

Marshall, S. L., et al. Bastogne: The Story of the First Eight Days in Which the 101st Airborne Division Was Closed Within the Ring of German Forces. LC 88-600068. (United States Army in Action Series. CMH Pub.: No. 22-2). (Illus.). 273p. 1988. reprint ed. pap. 11.00 (*0-16-001972-9*, S/N 008-029-00170-5) USGPO.

***Marshall, S. L. A.** Men Against Fire: The Problem of Battle Command. LC 00-37397. 224p. 2000. write for info. (*0-8061-3280-9*) U of Okla Pr.

— Pork Chop Hill. 256p. 2000. mass mkt. 6.99 (*0-425-17505-7*) Berkley Pub.

— World War I. (Illus.). 528p. 2001. reprint ed. 15.00 (*0-618-05686-6*, Mariner Bks) HM.

Marshall, S. M., et al, eds. The Diabetes Annual. (Diabetes Annual Ser.: Vol. 11). 268p. 1998. 198.50 (*0-444-82895-8*) Elsevier.

— The Diabetes Annual. 7th ed. 384p. 1993. 221.00 (*0-444-89694-5*) Elsevier.

— The Diabetes Annual, 9. 368p. 1995. 231.50 (*0-444-82055-8*) Elsevier.

***Marshall, S. M., et al, eds.** The Diabetes Annual 12. (Diabetes Annual Ser.). (Illus.). 422p. 1999. 195.50 (*0-444-82896-6*) Elsevier.

Marshall, S. M. & Home, P. H., eds. The Diabetes Annual, Vol. 8. 502p. 1994. text 243.25 (*0-444-81788-3*) Elsevier.

Marshall, S. M. & Rizza, R. A., eds. The Diabetes Annual. (Diabetes Annual Ser.: Vol. 10). 404p. 1996. 237.75 (*0-444-82426-X*) Elsevier.

Marshall, Sally, jt. ed. see Marston, Ginna.

Marshall, Sally M., jt. auth. see Kee, Joyce L.

Marshall, Samuel D. Tarantulas & Other Arachnids. LC 96-11352. (Complete Pet Owner's Manual Ser.). (Illus.). 112p. 1996. pap. 6.95 (*0-8120-9315-1*) Barron.

Marshall, Samuel L. The Fields of Bamboo: Dong Tre, Trung Luong & Hoa Hui, Three Battles Just Beyond the South China Sea. (Vietnam War Ser.: No. 7). (Illus.). 242p. 1984. reprint ed. 29.95 (*0-89839-081-8*) Battery Pr.

— Pork Chop Hill: The American Fighting Man in Action: Korea, Spring 1953. (Combat Arms Ser.). (Illus.). 313p. 1986. reprint ed. 29.95 (*0-89839-090-7*) Battery Pr.

— Sinai Victory: Command Decisions in History's Shortest War, Israel's Hundred Hour Conquest of Egypt East of Suez, Autumn 1956. (Combat Arms Ser.: 11th). (Illus.). 280p. 1958. reprint ed. 29.95 (*0-89839-085-0*) Battery Pr.

— West to Cambodia. (Vietnam War Ser.: No. 6). (Illus.). 253p. 1984. reprint ed. 27.95 (*0-89839-078-8*) Battery Pr.

— World War I. LC 85-3968. (American Heritage Library). (Illus.). 384p. (Orig.). 1985. pap. 16.00 (*0-8281-0434-4*) HM.

Marshall, Sandra P. Schemas in Problem Solving. (Illus.). 438p. (C). 1995. text 49.95 (*0-521-43072-0*) Cambridge U Pr.

Marshall, Scott & Waite, John G. The Mount: Home of Edith Wharton. (Illus.). 256p. 1997. pap. 25.00 (*0-9665004-0-7*) E Wharton.

Marshall, Shane A. & Ruedy, John. On Call Principles & Protocols. 2nd ed. (Illus.). 416p. 1993. pap. text 29.95 (*0-7216-3982-8*, W B Saunders Co) Harcrt Hlth Sci Grp.

— On Call Principles & Protocols. 3rd ed. Kersey, Ray, ed. LC 98-32244. (On Call Ser.). (Illus.). 415p. 1999. pap. text. write for info. (*0-7216-5079-1*, W B Saunders Co) Harcrt Hlth Sci Grp.

Marshall, Sheila, jt. ed. see Marcuccio, Phyllis.

Marshall, Shelly. The Book of Karma. 246p. (Orig.). 1994. pap. 12.99 (*1-880197-99-5*) Gylantic Pub.

— Teenage Addicts Can Recover: Treating the Addict, Not the Age. 176p. 1992. pap. 12.95 (*1-880197-02-2*) Gylantic Pub.

Marshall, Shelly, ed. Young, Sober & Free. 137p. 1978. 10.00 (*0-89486-055-0*, 1116A) Hazelden.

Marshall, Sherrill Gibson & Houseman, Clare A. Communication in Nursing. 2nd ed. 400p. pap. text 24.95 (*0-397-55476-1*) Lppncott W & W.

Marshall, Sherrin D. The Dutch Gentry, Fifteen Hundred to Sixteen-Fifty: Family, Faith, & Fortune. 11. LC 86-7647. (Contributions in Family Studies: No. 11). 252p. 1987. 65.00 (*0-313-25021-9*, WYD/, Greenwood Pr) Greenwood.

Marshall, Sherrin D., ed. Women in Reformation & Counter-Reformation Europe: Private & Public Worlds. LC 88-45758. (Illus.). 224p. 1989. 35.00 (*0-253-33678-3*); pap. 11.95 (*0-253-20527-1*, MB-527) Ind U Pr.

Marshall, Sherrin D., jt. ed. see Bebb, Phillip N.

Marshall, Sherrin D., ed. see Rabb, Theodore K.

Marshall, Sidney J. The King of Kor: Or, She's Promise Kept. Reginald, R. & Melville, Douglas, eds. LC 77-84255. (Lost Race & Adult Fantasy Ser.). (Illus.). 1978. reprint ed. lib. bdg. 24.95 (*0-405-10999-7*) Ayer.

Marshall, Stan, jt. auth. see Glass, Richard D.

Marshall, Stephanie P., jt. pref. see Marzano, Robert J.

Marshall, Stephen E. Randax Education Guide to Colleges Seeking Students, 1990. 19th ed. (Illus.). 128p. (Orig.). 1990. pap. 12.95 (*0-914880-20-9*) Educ Guide.

— Randax Education Guide to Colleges Seeking Students, 1992. 21st ed. (Illus.). 128p. (Orig.). 1992. pap. 14.95 (*0-914880-22-5*) Educ Guide.

— Randax Education Guide to Colleges Seeking Students, 1993. 22nd ed. (Illus.). 128p. 1993. pap. 15.95 (*0-914880-23-3*) Educ Guide.

— Randax Education Guide to Colleges Seeking Students, 1994. 23rd ed. (Illus.). 128p. 1994. pap. 16.95 (*0-914880-24-1*) Educ Guide.

***Marshall, Stephen E.** Randax Education Guide to Colleges Seeking Students, 1999 Edition. 28th ed. (Illus.). 128p. 1999. pap. 20.95 (*0-914880-29-2*) Educ Guide.

— Randax Education Guide to Colleges Seeking Students, 2000 Edition. 29th ed. 128p. 2000. pap. 21.95 (*0-914880-30-6*) Educ Guide.

Marshall, Stephen E. Randox Education Guide to Colleges Seeking Students, 1997 Edition. 26th rev. ed. 128p. (Orig.). 1997. pap. 19.95 (*0-914880-27-6*, 27R) Educ Guide.

Marshall, Stephen E., ed. Randax Education Guide to Colleges Seeking Students, 1998. 27th rev. ed. 128p. (YA). 1998. pap. 19.95 (*0-914880-28-4*, 28R) Educ Guide.

Marshall, Steve. Rituals of Terror. 179p. mass mkt. 4.99 (*1-55197-534-3*) Picasso Publ.

Marshall, Steve & Miller-Marshall, Patty, eds. LOL: The Humor of the Internet. LC 99 90710. vii, 157p. Date not set. pap. 12.95 (*0-9673087-0-4*) S Marshall Prodns.

Marshall, Strome. Manual of Otolaryngology: Diagnosis & Therapy. 212p. 1985. 25.50 (*0-316-81967-0*, Little Brwn Med Div) Lppncott W & W.

Marshall, Susan, ed. The Insider's Guide to Hiring & Keeping the Right People. 2nd ed. 175p. 1998. pap. 95.00 (*1-885002-64-5*) Zweig White.

***Marshall, Susan A.** How to Grow a Backbone: 10 Strategies for Gaining Power & Influence at Work. LC 00-29474. (Illus.). 224p. 2000. pap. 14.95 (*0-8092-2494-1*, Contemporary Bks) NTC Contemp Pub Co.

Marshall, Susan E. Human Resources Nuts & Bolts. 136p. 1998. pap. 39.00 (*1-885002-59-9*) Zweig White.

— Splintered Sisterhood: Gender & Class in the Campaign Against Woman Suffrage. LC 96-43666. (Illus.). 320p. 1997. 55.00 (*0-299-15460-2*); pap. 21.95 (*0-299-15464-5*) U of Wis Pr.

Marshall, Susan E. & Esquire Editors. New Hampshire Law Bulletin. 'p. 60.00 (*0-327-01930-1*) LEXIS Pub.

Marshall, Susan E., ed. see Zweig White & Associates Staff.

Marshall, Suzanne. Take-Away Applique. Kurten, Mary Jo, ed. LC 98-2724. (Illus.). 176p. 1998. pap. 22.95 (*1-57432-706-2*, 5012, Am Quilters Soc) Collector Bks.

— Violence in the Black Patch of Kentucky & Tennessee. (Illus.). 232p. 1994. text 34.95 (*0-8262-0971-8*) U of Mo Pr.

***Marshall, Suzanne Greene.** Individuality in Clothing Selection & Personal Appearance: A Guide for the Consumer. 5th ed. LC 99-10378. (Illus.). 436p. 1999. 66.00 (*0-13-011637-8*) P-H.

Marshall, Swift. Repair & Remodel Cost Guide. 1998. pap. 79.95 (*0-07-134241-9*) McGraw.

***Marshall, Sybil.** Fenland Chronicle. 288p. 1998. pap. 13.95 (*0-14-027534-7*, Pub. by Pnguin Bks Ltd) Trafalgar.

— Late Lark Singing. 512p. 1998. pap. 13.95 (*0-14-025840-X*, Pub. by Pnguin Bks Ltd) Trafalgar.

— Sharp through the Hawthorn. 1995. pap. 14.95 (*0-14-023740-2*, Pub. by Pnguin Bks Ltd) Trafalgar.

— Strip the Willow. 576p. 1997. pap. 13.95 (*0-14-025225-8*, Pub. by Pnguin Bks Ltd) Trafalgar.

Marshall, T. Entendiendo el Liderazgo.Tr. of Understanding Leadership. (SPA.). 100. pap. 9.99 (*1-56063-567-3*, 550119) Editorial Unilit.

Marshall, T. Principados y Potestades.Tr. of Principalities & Powers. (SPA.). 3.50 (*1-56063-430-8*, 550014) Editorial Unilit.

Marshall, T. Relaciones Saludables: Como Crearlas y Como Restaurarlas.Tr. of Right Relationships. (SPA.). 100. 6.99 (*1-56063-566-5*, 550129) Editorial Unilit.

— Sanidad de Adentro Hacia Afuera.Tr. of Healing from the Inside Out. (SPA.). 211p. 7.99 (*1-56063-513-4*, 550105) Editorial Unilit.

Marshall, T. G., et al. MCQS in Paediatrics. LC 98-46987. 410p. 1999. pap. text 25.00 (*0-7020-2249-7*, Pub. by W B Saunders) Saunders.

Marshall, T. H. Class, Citizenship, & Social Development. 2000. pap. text 10.00 (*0-226-50702-5*) U Ch Pr.

— Class, Citizenship & Social Development: A Greenwood Archival Edition. LC 73-2879. 334p. 1973. reprint ed. lib. bdg. 55.00 (*0-8371-6778-7*, MACL, Greenwood Pr) Greenwood.

Marshall, T. J., et al. Soil Physics. 3rd ed. (Illus.). 467p. (C). 1996. pap. text 42.95 (*0-521-45766-1*) Cambridge U Pr.

— Soil Physics. 3rd ed. (Illus.). 467p. (C). 1996. text 100.00 (*0-521-45151-5*) Cambridge U Pr.

Marshall-Taylor, Geoffrey, compiled by. The Complete Come & Praise: Words & Music Edition. 256p. 1990. pap. 21.95 (*0-563-34581-0*, Pub. by BBC) Parkwest Pubns.

Marshall, Terry. My Father's Hands. (Northway Ser.). vi, 193p. 1992. 19.95 (*0-89672-274-0*) Tex Tech Univ Pr.

— The Whole World Guide to Language Learning. LC 88-45727. 176p. 1990. pap. 16.95 (*0-933662-75-0*) Intercult Pr.

Marshall, Terry V. Crater Lake. LC 23-939860. (Illus.). 70p. 1977. 16.95 (*0-939860-02-3*); pap. 6.95 (*0-939860-01-5*) Tremaine Graph & Pub.

Marshall, Thomas F. An Analytical Index to American Literature: Vols. I-XXX, Mar. 1929-Jan. 1959, Vols. 1-30, Mar. 1929-Jan. 1959. LC 30-20216. ix, 253p. 1963. text 38.95 (*0-8223-0114-8*) Duke.

Marshall, Thomas M., ed. The Life & Papers of Frederick Bates, 2 vols. LC 75-109. (Mid-American Frontier Ser.). 1975. reprint ed. 57.95 (*0-405-06876-X*) Ayer.

Marshall, Thomas R. Presidential Nominations in a Reform Age. LC 81-1684. 211p. 1981. 45.00 (*0-275-90677-9*, C0677, Praeger Pubs) Greenwood.

— Public Opinion & the Supreme Court. 256p. 1988. text 39.95 (*0-04-497046-3*); pap. text 14.95 (*0-04-497047-1*) Routledge.

Marshall, Thomas R., jt. auth. see Held, Gilbert.

Marshall, Thurgood. Dream Makers, Dream Breakers: The World of Justice. 496p. 1993. 24.95 (*0-316-75918-X*, Aspen Law & Bus) Aspen Pub.

— Thurgood Marshall. LC 96-40129. (Importance of Ser.). (Illus.). (YA). (gr. 4-12). 1997. lib. bdg. 22.45 (*1-56006-061-1*) Lucent Bks.

Marshall, Tim. Man's Greatest Fear: The Final Phase of Human Evolution. LC 96-104113. (Illus.). 180p. (Orig.). 1995. pap. 11.00 (*0-9645750-0-0*) Athena Bks.

Marshall, Timothy. Murdering to Dissect: Graverobbing, Frankenstein & the Anatomy Literature. LC 95-1715. 256p. 1996. text 27.95 (*0-7190-4543-6*, Pub. by Manchester Univ Pr) St Martin.

Marshall, Tom. The Adventures of John Montgomery. LC 96-105586. (Illus.). 398p. 1997. pap. 12.95 (*1-55082-135-0*, Pub. by Quarry Pr) LPC InBook.

— Goddess Disclosing Monologues for Gaia. 160p. 1993. per. 10.95 (*1-55082-039-7*, Pub. by Quarry Pr) LPC InBook.

— Healing from the Inside Out: Understanding God's Touch for Spirit, Soul & Body. 1992. pap. 7.99 (*0-927545-50-0*) Emerald WA.

— Multiple Exposures, Promised Lands: Essays on Canadian Poetry & Fiction. 240p. 1992. pap. 18.95 (*1-55082-047-8*, Pub. by Quarry Pr) LPC InBook.

— The Price of Exit. 1998. mass mkt. 6.99 (*0-8041-1715-2*) Ivy Books.

— Understanding Leadership: Fresh Perspective on the Essentials of New Testament Leadership. 1992. pap. 8.99 (*0-927545-51-9*) Emerald WA.

Marshall, Tom & Muccio, Tom. Leadership: Effective Spiritual Keys for Today's Leaders, 12 pts. 96p. 1993. audio 40.00 (*0-935779-16-7*); VHS 150.00 (*0-935779-17-5*) Crown Min.

— Leadership: Effective Spiritual Keys for Today's Leaders, 12 pts., Set. 96p. 1993. student ed. 10.00 (*0-935779-15-9*) Crown Min.

Marshall, Tony. Community Disorders & Policing. 300p. 1992. 70.00 (*1-871177-25-1*, Pub. by Whiting & Birch); pap. text 29.95 (*1-871177-26-X*, Pub. by Whiting & Birch) Paul & Co Pubs.

Marshall, Tony F. Alternatives to Criminal Courts: The Potential for Non-Judicial Dispute Settlements. 310p. 1985. 87.95 (*0-566-05002-1*, Pub. by Dartmth Pub) Ashgate Pub Co.

Marshall, Tony F., jt. auth. see Rose, Gordon.

***Marshall, Tristan.** Theatre & Empire: Great Britain on the London Stages under James VI & I. LC 00-20183. (Politics, Culture & Society in Early Modern Britain Ser.). 2000. write for info. (*0-7190-5748-5*, Pub. by Manchester Univ Pr) St Martin.

Marshall, V. C. Consequences of Nuclear & Chemical Disasters. (Chemical Engineering Ser.). 350p. (C). 1995. text 115.95 (*0-13-170770-1*, 520805) P-H.

— Disaster at Flixborough. 1980. write for info. (*0-318-57467-5*, Pergamon Pr) Elsevier.

Marshall, Val & Tester, Bronwyn. And Grandpa Sat on Friday. LC 92-34159. (Voyages Ser.). (Illus.). (J). 1993. 4.25 (*0-383-03610-0*) SRA McGraw.

— The Cat's Whiskers. LC 93-11737. (Voyages Ser.). (Illus.). (J). 1994. 4.25 (*0-685-69328-7*) SRA McGraw.

— The Old Car. LC 92-27264. (Voyages Ser.). (Illus.). (J). 1993. 3.75 (*0-383-03644-5*) SRA McGraw.

Marshall, Vance, jt. auth. see Center for Learning Network Staff.

Marshall, Vernon, jt. auth. see Hunt, Philip C.

Marshall, Victor & McPherson, Barry, eds. Aging: Canadian Perspectives. 240p. 1994. pap. text 19.95 (*1-55111-012-1*) Broadview Pr.

Marshall, Victor C. Major Chemical Hazards. LC 86-27611. (Corrosion & Its Prevention Ser.). 587p. 1987. text 118.00 (*0-470-20813-9*) P-H.

Marshall, Victor W., ed. Later Life: The Social Psychology of Aging. LC 85-19581. (Illus.). 352p. 1986. reprint ed. pap. 109.20 (*0-608-01164-9*, 205946400001) Bks Demand.

Marshall, Victor W., jt. ed. see Ryff, Carol D.

Marshall, W. Headfirst. text. write for info. (*0-8050-8034-1*) St Martin.

Marshall, W. G. Through America: or Nine Months in the United States. LC 72-3388. (Essay Index Reprint Ser.). 1977. reprint ed. 39.95 (*0-8369-2913-6*) Ayer.

Marshall, W. Gerald. A Great Stage of Fools: Theatricality & Madness in the Plays of William Wycherley. LC 91-11028. (Studies in the Seventeenth Century: No. 4). 125p. 1993. 37.50 (*0-404-61724-7*) AMS Pr.

Marshall, W. Gerald, ed. The Restoration Mind. LC 96-41595. (Illus.). 280p. 1997. 44.50 (*0-87413-571-0*) U Delaware Pr.

Marshall, W. L., et al. Sourcebook of Treatment Programs for Sexual Offenders. LC 98-21057. (Applied Clinical Psychology Ser.). (Illus.). 516p. (C). 1998. text 85.00 (*0-306-45730-X*, Kluwer Plenum) Kluwer Academic.

Marshall, W. T., jt. auth. see Bhatt, P.

Marshall, Walter H. I've Met Them All. (Illus.). 186p. 1983. 12.95 (*0-317-00339-9*); pap. 8.95 (*0-317-00340-2*) W H Marshall.

Marshall, Wayne E. & Wadsworth, James I., eds. Rice Science & Technology. (Food Science & Technology Ser.: Vol. 59). (Illus.). 488p. 1993. text 185.00 (*0-8247-8887-7*) Dekker.

Marshall, Will, ed. Building the Bridge: 10 Big Ideas to Transform America. LC 96-51532. 188p. 1997. pap. 14.95 (*0-8476-8455-5*) Rowman.

Marshall, William. Inches. 256p. 1995. mass mkt. 5.99 (*0-446-40455-1*, Pub. by Warner Bks) Little.

— The New York Detective. 288p. 1990. mass mkt. 4.95 (*0-445-40921-5*, Pub. by Warner Bks) Little.

— Out of Nowhere. 1989. mass mkt. 3.95 (*0-445-40842-1*, Mysterious Paperbk) Warner Bks.

— To the End. LC 97-39159. 240p. 1998. 22.50 (*0-89296-575-4*, Pub. by Mysterious Pr) Little.

— War Machine. (Yellowthread Street Mystery Ser.). 1989. mass mkt. 3.95 (*0-445-40595-3*, Pub. by Warner Bks) Little.

Marshall, William, tr. see Constantine I.

Marshall, William E. A Phrenologist Amongst the Todas or the Study of a Primitive Tribe in South India: History, Character, Customs, Religion, Infantcide, Polyandry, Language. (C). 1995. 34.00 (*81-206-0899-2*, Pub. by Asian Educ Servs) S Asia.

Marshall, William J. Baseball's Pivotal Era, 1945-1951. LC 98-36951. (Illus.). 513p. 1999. 32.50 (*0-8131-2041-1*) U Pr of Ky.

Marshall, William J. & Bangert, Stephen K., eds. Clinical Biochemistry: Metabolic & Clinical Aspects. LC 95-11348. 854p. 1995. text 141.00 (*0-443-04341-8*) Church.

Marshall, William L., et al, eds. Handbook of Sexual Assault: Issues, Theories, & Treatment of the Offender. LC 89-23174. (Applied Clinical Psychology Ser.). (Illus.). 424p. (C). 1990. 75.00 (*0-306-43272-2*, Plenum Trade) Perseus Pubng.

Marshall, William L. & Eccles, A. The Treatment of Adult Sexual Offenders. LC 99-40981. 220p. 1999. pap. 42.95 (*0-471-97566-4*) Wiley.

Marshall, William S. The Billy Boys: A Concise History of Orangeism in Scotland. 232p. 1996. pap. 52.00 (*1-873644-52-3*, Pub. by Mercat Pr Bks) St Mut.

Marshall, Wolf. The Beatles Hits: Signature Licks. 96p. 1997. pap. 19.95 incl. audio compact disk (*0-7935-6209-0*) H Leonard.

Marshall, Wolf. Beginning Rock Bass Guitar. (Illus.). 24p. 1990. pap. 15.95 incl. audio (*0-8256-1150-4*, AM67430) Music Sales.

— Beginning Rock Rhythm Guitar. (Illus.). 24p. 1990. pap. 17.95 incl. audio (*0-8256-1151-2*, AM67448) Music Sales.

— Beginning Rock Riffs. (Illus.). 24p. 1990. pap. 17.95 incl. audio (*0-8256-1152-0*, AM67455) Music Sales.

— Classical Riffs for Rock Guitar. (Illus.). 24p. 1990. pap. 17.95 incl. audio (*0-8256-1155-5*, AM67463) Music Sales.

***Marshall, Wolf.** The Guitar Style of Mark Knopfler. 72p. 1999. pap. 19.95 incl. audio compact disk (*0-7935-8129-X*) H Leonard.

Marshall, Wolf. Music That Changed Our Lives: An In-Depth Look. (Guitar Presents Ser.). 1999. pap. 14.95 (*1-57560-222-9*) Cherry Lane.

— Original Randy Rhoads. (Illus.). 48p. 1986. pap. 14.95 (*0-8256-1065-6*, AM63850) Music Sales.

— Wolf Marshall Basic Guitar Method, Bk. 3. 80p. 1993. pap. 7.95 (*0-7935-2096-7*, 00697245) H Leonard.

Marshall, Wolf. Wolf Marshall Basic Guitar Method, Bk. 3. 80p. 1993. pap. 14.95 (*0-7935-2097-5*, 00697246) H Leonard.

— Wolf Marshall Basic Guitar Method, Bk. 3. 80p. 1993. pap. 16.95 (*0-7935-2098-3*, 00697247) H Leonard.

Marshall, Wolf. Wolf Marshall Guitar Method, Bk. 1. 64p. 1993. pap. 5.95 (*0-7935-1605-6*, 00697219) H Leonard.

Marshall, Wolf. Wolf Marshall Guitar Method, Bk. 1. 64p. 1993. pap. 12.95 (*0-7935-1606-4*, 00697220); pap. 14.95 (*0-7935-1607-2*, 00697221) H Leonard.

Marshall, Wolf. Wolf Marshall Guitar Method, Bk. 2. 64p. 1993. pap. 5.95 (*0-7935-1608-0*, 00697222) H Leonard.

Marshall, Wolf. Wolf Marshall Guitar Method, Bk. 2. 64p. 1993. pap. 12.95 (*0-7935-1609-9*, 00697223); pap. 14.95 (*0-7935-1610-2*, 00697224) H Leonard.

Marshall, Wolf. Wolf Marshall Guitar Method: Advanced Concepts & Techniques Book. pap. 14.95 incl. audio (*0-7935-2153-X*, 00697254); pap. 16.95 incl. audio compact disk (*0-7935-2154-8*, 00697255) H Leonard.

— Wolf Marshall Guitar Method: Advanced Concepts & Techniques Book. 88p. 1996. pap. 9.95 (*0-7935-2152-1*, 0069725311) H Leonard.

— Wolf Marshall Guitar Method Bk. 1: Power Studies. 144p. 1994. pap. 12.95 (*0-7935-2674-4*, 00697256); pap. 12.95 (*0-7935-2679-5*, 00697259) H Leonard.

Marshall, Wolf. Wolf Marshall Guitar Method Bk. 1: Power Studies. 88p. 1994. pap. 17.95 (*0-7935-2676-0*, 00697258) H Leonard.

— Wolf Marshall Guitar Method Bk. 2: Power Studies. 88p. 1994. pap. 14.95 (*0-7935-2675-2*, 00697257); pap. 17.95 (*0-7935-2681-7*, 00697261) H Leonard.

Marshall, Wolf. Wolf Marshall Guitar Method Bk. 3: Power Studies. 96p. 1994. pap. 12.95 (*0-7935-3274-4*, 00697262) H Leonard.

Marshall, Wolf. Wolf Marshall Guitar Method Bk. 3: Power Studies. 96p. 1994. pap. 14.95 (*0-7935-3275-2*, 00697263); pap. 17.95 (*0-7935-3276-0*) H Leonard.

— The Wolf Marshall Guitar Method Primer: The First Step for Today's Beginning Guitarist. 32p. 1999. pap. 9.95 incl. audio compact disk (*0-7935-9958-X*) H Leonard.

Marshall, Wolf, ed. Ratt Out of Cellar Grv. Guitar Personality Book. (Fretted Ser.). 120p. (Orig.). 1997. pap. 27.95 (*0-88188-764-1*, 00693911) Wrner Bros.

Marshall, Wolf, tr. Iron Maiden Collection. (Recorded Versions Ser.). 183p. 1987. 19.95 (*0-88188-768-4*, HL00693096) H Leonard.

Marshall, Wolf, jt. ed. see Phillips, Mark.

An Asterisk (*) at the beginning of an entry indicates that the title is appearing for the first time.

Marshall, Yale. Singing Fluent American Vowels. Foreman, Edward V., ed. 1993. pap. 37.50 (1-887117-02-4) Pro musica pr.

Marshall, Yana, ed. see Voices from Undercover Staff.

Marshall, Yvonne, ed. Intimate Relations. (World Archaeology Ser.: Vol. 29, Issue 3). 216p. (C). 1998. pap. 27.99 (0-415-18430-4, D6190) Routledge.

***Marshall, Yvonne, et al.** Sigatoka: Shifting Sands of Fiji Prehistory. (Illus.). 129p. (C). 2000. pap. 35.00 (1-84217-011-2, Pub. by Oxbow Bks) David Brown.

Marshalla, Pamela. Drooling: Guidelines & Activities. Boshart, Char, ed. (Little Books with Great Expectations: Vol. 1). (Illus.). 47p. 1997. pap. 25.00 (0-9666844-0-0) Speech Dyn Inc.

***Marshalla, Pamela.** Imitation. Boshart, Char, ed. (Little Books with Great Expectations: Vol. 3). (Illus.). 87p. 1999. pap. 25.00 (0-9666844-5-1) Speech Dyn Inc.

Marshalla, Pamela. Oral-Motor Techniques in Articulation Therapy. Boshart, Char, ed. (Illus.). 95p. 1992. pap. 39.00 (0-9666844-3-5) Speech Dyn Inc.

— Treatise on the Tongue: Analysis & Treatment of Tongue Abnormalities. Boshart, Char, ed. (Illus.). 135p. 1999. pap. 49.00 (0-9666844-2-7) Speech Dyn Inc.

Marshallsay, Diana, et al, eds. Ford List of British Parliamentary Papers, 1974-1983. 742p. 1989. lib. bdg. write for info. (0-85964-188-0) Chadwyck-Healey.

Marshand, La Mer. Awake Beloved: We've Slept Too Long. LC 91-73744. 312p. (Orig.). 1991. pap. 15.95 (0-9630485-0-3) In Print.

Marshay, Lauren. The World According to God: Selections from the Book of Books. 256p. 1999. 12.99 (1-57748-568-8) Barbour Pub.

Marshbum, Sandra, jt. auth. see RanDelle, B. J.

***Marshburn, Beverly.** The Mental Health Worker: Psychiatric Aide. Cox-Stevens, Kay, ed. LC 97-77991. (Clinical Allied Healthcare Ser.). (Illus.). 540p. 1999. pap. text 44.95 (0-89262-437-X) Career Pub.

— The Mental Health Worker: Psychiatric Aide: Instructor's Guide. Cox-Stevens, Kay, ed. (Clinical Allied Healthcare Ser.). (Illus.). 464p. 1999. teacher ed., ring bd. 99.95 (0-89262-445-0) Career Pub.

Marshburn, Sandra. Undertow. 21p. (Orig.). 1992. pap. 6.00 (0-9624453-9-8) March Street Pr.

Marshburn, Tom. Six-Moon Trail: Canada to Mexico along the Pacific Crest. Leishman, Robert K., ed. LC 85-50297. (Illus.). 224p. 1985. 15.95 (0-9614526-0-9) R Leishman.

Marshek, Kurt M., jt. auth. see Juvinall, Robert C.

Marshel, Judy E. PMS Relief: Natural Approaches to Treating Symptoms. 1998. mass mkt. 5.99 (0-425-16395-4) Berkley Pub.

— Trouble-Free Menopause: Manage Your Symptoms & Your Weight. 352p. 1998. pap. 12.00 (0-380-73170-3, Avon Bks) Morrow Avon.

Marshel, Judy E., jt. auth. see Konner, Linda.

Marshell, Robin D. & Tipton, Keith F., eds. Essay in Biochemistry, Vol. 22. 200p. 1987. pap. text 62.00 (0-12-158122-5) Acad Pr.

Marshfield, Alan. The Elektra Poems. 78p. 1982. pap. 13.95 (0-85646-085-0, Pub. by Anvil Press) Dufour.

— Mistress. Date not set. pap. 7.95 (0-900977-42-6, Pub. by Anvil Press) Dufour.

Marshfield Area Genelogy Group & Marshfield Public Library Staff. Index to Births as Reported in the Marshfield News & Marshfield Times Prior to 1908. LC 98-73050. 69, 46p. 1998. write for info. (0-9657421-4-8) Marshfield Hist.

Marshfield Public Library Staff, jt. auth. see Marshfield Area Genelogy Group.

Marshman, Chris. Guide to the EMC Directive 89-336-EEC. 2nd ed. 256p. 1996. pap. 49.95 (0-7803-1169-8, PP5642) Inst Electrical.

Marshment, Margaret, jt. ed. see Gamman, Lorraine.

Marshner, Connaught, jt. compiled by see Weyrich, Paul.

Marshner, William, jt. see Crosby, John, et al.

Marshood, Nabil. Palestinian Teenage Refugees & Immigrants Speak Out. LC 96-44197. (In Their Own Voices Ser.). (Illus.). 64p. (YA). (gr. 7-12). 1997. lib. bdg. 16.95 (0-8239-2442-4, D2442-4) Rosen Group.

Marshu, Ghrighwar M. Maqaddimat Al-Istitba: Al-Sharq Mawjud Bi-Ghayrih la Bi-Dhatih. LC 96-33950. 1996. write for info. (1-56564-241-4) IIIT VA.

Marsi, Randolph P. The Prairie Traveler: The Classic Handbook for American Pioneers. (Illus.). 240p. 1994. pap. 11.95 (0-399-51865-7, Perigee Bks) Berkley Pub.

Marsicano, Ed. All So Good & Rats in White Sauce, Vol. II. 241p. 1996. pap. 9.95 (0-9631022-2-2, MARS2) Ridgefld Pr.

— No Satisfaction & the Happy Time: Two Novels. Milazzo, Richard & Collins, Patricia, eds. LC 93-85692. 229p. (Orig.). 1994. pap. 8.95 (0-9631022-1-4) Ridgefld Pr.

Marsick, Victoria J., ed. Learning in the Workplace. 288p. 1987. lib. bdg. 30.00 (0-7099-4659-7, Pub. by C Helm) Routldge.

Marsick, Victoria J. & Watkins, Karen E. Facilitating Learning Organizations: Making Learning Count. LC 99-21000. 200p. 1999. 78.95 (0-566-08039-7, Pub. by Ashgate Pub) Ashgate Pub Co.

Marsick, Victoria J., jt. auth. see Watkins, Karen E.

Marsigli, Annalita. The Written Script. LC 97-19718. 315p. 1998. 24.95 (0-87951-820-0, Pub. by Overlook Pr) Penguin Putnam.

Marsiglio of Padua. Defensor Minor & de Translatione Imperli. Nederman, Cary J., ed. LC 92-33311. (Cambridge Texts in the History of Political Thought Ser.). 120p. (C). 1993. text 49.95 (0-521-40277-8) Cambridge U Pr.

Marsiglio, William. Fatherhood: Contemporary Theory, Research & Social Policy. (Research on Men & Masculinities Ser.). 320p. 1995. text 58.00 (0-8039-5782-3); pap. text 26.00 (0-8039-5783-1) Sage.

— Procreative Man. LC 97-21089. 1998. text 55.00 (0-8147-5578-X); pap. text 19.00 (0-8147-5579-8) NYU Pr.

Marsili, Mario. Computer Chemistry. 192p. 1989. lib. bdg. 159.00 (0-8493-4554-5, QD39) CRC Pr.

Marsili, Ray, ed. Techniques for Analyzing Food Aroma. LC 96-36593. (Food Science & Technology Ser.: Vol. 79). (Illus.). 400p. 1996. text 165.00 (0-8247-9788-4) Dekker.

***Marsilio, Maria S.** Farming & Poetry in Hesiod's Works & Days. 136p. 2000. 34.50 (0-7618-1684-4) U Pr of Amer.

Marsilius of Padua. Defensor Pacis. Gewirth, Alan, tr. (Medieval Academy Reprints for Teaching Ser.). 1980. reprint ed. pap. text 15.95 (0-8020-6412-4) U of Toronto Pr.

Marsily, Ghislain De, see De Marsily, Ghislain.

Marske, Charles E., ed. Communities of Fate: Readings in the Social Organization of Risk. 246p. (Orig.). (C). 1991. pap. text 27.50 (0-8191-8311-3); lib. bdg. 52.00 (0-8191-8310-5) U Pr of Amer.

Marsland, Amy L., jt. auth. see Marsland, William D.

***Marsland, Bruce.** Lessons from Nothing: Activities for Language Teaching with Limited Time & Resources. LC 98-24907. 1998. write for info. (0-521-62765-6) Cambridge U Pr.

Marsland, Cora. Interpretive Reading. LC 78-86801. (Granger Index Reprint Ser.). 1977. 20.95 (0-8369-6084-X) Ayer.

Marsland, David. Neglect & Betrayal: War & Violence in Modern Sociology. (C). 1990. 60.00 (0-7855-6611-2, Pub. by Inst Euro Def & Strat) St Mut.

— Neglect & Betrayal: War & Violence in Modern Sociology. (C). 1981. pap. 29.00 (0-907967-65-5) St Mut.

— Welfare or Welfare State? Contradictions & Dilemmas in Social Policy. LC 95-33088. 288p. 1996. pap. 19.95 (0-312-12921-1); text 59.95 (0-312-12920-3) St Martin.

Marsland, David, ed. Self Reliance: Reforming Welfare in Advanced Societies. LC 95-18147. 134p. 1995. 32.95 (1-56000-211-5) Transaction Pubs.

— Work & Employment in Liberal Democratic Societies. LC 93-46969. (Liberal Democratic Societies Ser.). 240p. (C). 1994. 24.95 (0-943852-67-6); pap. text 14.95 (0-943852-68-4) Prof World Peace.

Marsland, Stephen E. The Birth of the Japanese Labor Movement: Takano Fusataro & the Rodo Kumiai Kiseikai. LC 88-21622. 288p. 1989. reprint ed. pap. 89.30 (0-608-04389-3, 206517000001) Bks Demand.

***Marsland, Tim & Chew, Jonathan.** 64-Bit Computing. 2000. pap. 45.00 (0-13-022066-3) P-H.

Marsland, William D. & Marsland, Amy L. Venezuela Through Its History. LC 75-40919. (Illus.). 277p. 1976. reprint ed. lib. bdg. 38.50 (0-8371-8690-0, MAVE, Greenwood Pr) Greenwood.

Marslen-Wilson, William, ed. Lexical Representation & Process. (Illus.). 588p. 1991. reprint ed. pap. text 32.50 (0-262-63142-3) MIT Pr.

Marsmann, H., jt. auth. see Kintzinger, J. P.

Marsnik, Nadine C., jt. auth. see Wolff, Florence I.

Marso, Lori J. (Un)Manly Citizens: Jean-Jacques Rousseau's & Germaine de Stael's Subversive Women. LC 98-36624. xiv, 172p. 1999. write for info. (0-8018-6032-6) Johns Hopkins.

Marso, Steven, et al. Manual of Cardiovascular Medicine. LC 99-42919. 600p. 1999. 34.95 (0-683-30685-5) Lppncott W & W.

Marsocci, Fred. Weasel: A Study Guide. Friedland, J. & Kessler, R., eds. (Novel-Ties Ser.). (J). (gr. 4-6). 1993. pap. text, student ed. 15.95 (0-88122-901-6) Lrn Links.

Marsoli, Lisa A. Hercules. 96p. (J). 1997. 7.98 (1-57082-518-1, Pub. by Mouse Works) Time Warner.

Marsoli, Lisa A. & Strong, Stacie. Bow, Wow, & You on the Farm. (Discovery Flap Bks.). (Illus.). (J). 1996. 7.99 (0-85953-541-X) Childs Play.

Marsoli, Lisa Ann. Leap's Friends A-Z. (Illus.). 24p. (J). (gr. k-2). write for info. (1-58605-008-7) Knowledge Kids.

Marsolini, Maxine. Blended Families. 2000. pap. 12.99 (0-8024-3056-2) Moody.

Marson, Charles M. & Giles, Paul R., eds. Synthesis Using Vilsmeier Reagents. 256p. 1994. boxed set 131.95 (0-8493-7869-9, 7869) CRC Pr.

Marson, Chuck. In Your Own Back Yard: A Guide for Great Plains Gardening. (Illus.). 160p. (Orig.). 1983. pap. 8.95 (0-941974-01-4) Baranski Pub Co.

Marson, Iginio, ed. see International Gravity Commission & International G.

Marson, Peg, jt. auth. see Marson, Ron.

Marson, Ron. Analysis. (Task Cards Ser.: No. 10). (Illus.). 48p. 1991. teacher ed. 8.00 (0-941008-80-0) Tops Learning.

— Balancing. LC 81-90443. (Science with Simple Things Ser.: No. 31). (Illus.). 80p. 1981. teacher ed. 15.00 (0-941008-31-2) Tops Learning.

— Balancing. (Task Cards Ser.: No. 4). (Illus.). 48p. 1993. teacher ed. 8.00 (0-941008-74-6) Tops Learning.

— Cohesion-Adhesion. (Task Cards Ser.: No. 13). (Illus.). 64p. 1995. teacher ed. 11.00 (0-941008-83-5) Tops Learning.

— Corn & Beans: Green Thumbs. (Science with Simple Things Ser.: Vol. 39). (Illus.). 80p. 1997. teacher ed. 15.00 (0-941008-49-5) Tops Learning.

— The Earth Moon & Sun. (Science with Simple Things Ser.: No. 40). (Illus.). 72p. 1993. teacher ed. 15.00 (0-941008-40-1) Tops Learning.

— Electricity. (Task Cards Ser.: No. 19). (Illus.). 88p. 1990. teacher ed. 16.00 (0-941008-89-4) Tops Learning.

***Marson, Ron.** Electricity. (Science with Simple Things Ser.: No. 32). (Illus.). 64p. 2000. teacher ed. 15.00 (0-941008-53-3) Tops Learning.

Marson, Ron. Floating & Sinking. (Task Cards Ser.: No. 9). (Illus.). 64p. 1995. teacher ed. 11.00 (0-941008-79-7) Tops Learning.

— Focus Pocus. (Science with Simple Things Ser.: No. 42). (Illus.). 64p. 1996. teacher ed. 15.00 (0-941008-42-8) Tops Learning.

Marson, Ron. Global TOPS: 100 Science Lessons with 15 Simple Things. (Science with Simple Things Ser.: No. 91). (Illus.). 272p. 1988. teacher ed. 69.00 (0-941008-91-6) Tops Learning.

Marson, Ron. Graphing. (Task Cards Ser.: No. 3). (Illus.). 56p. 1990. teacher ed. 9.50 (0-941008-73-8) Tops Learning.

— Heat. (Task Cards Ser.: No. 15). (Illus.). 56p. 1990. teacher ed. 9.50 (0-941008-85-1) Tops Learning.

— Kinetic Model. (Task Cards Ser.: No. 14). (Illus.). 64p. 1992. teacher ed. 11.00 (0-941008-84-3) Tops Learning.

***Marson, Ron.** Lentil Science: Intermediate. (Science with Simple Things Ser.: No. 72). (Illus.). 136p. 1999. teacher ed. 26.00 (0-941008-52-5) Tops Learning.

— Lentil Science: Primary. (Science with Simple Things Ser.: No. 72). (Illus.). 136p. 1999. teacher ed. 26.00 (0-941008-51-7) Tops Learning.

Marson, Ron. Light. (Task Cards Ser.: No. 17). (Illus.). 88p. 1991. teacher ed. 16.00 (0-941008-87-8) Tops Learning.

— Machines. (Task Cards Ser.: No. 22). (Illus.). 48p. 1989. teacher ed. 8.00 (0-941008-99-1) Tops Learning.

— Magnetism. (Task Cards Ser.: No. 19). (Illus.). 88p. 1991. teacher ed. 16.00 (0-941008-90-8) Tops Learning.

***Marson, Ron.** Magnetism. (Science with Simple Things Ser.: No. 33). (Illus.). 64p. 2000. teacher ed. 15.00 (0-941008-54-1) Tops Learning.

Marson, Ron. Math Lab. (Task Cards Ser.: No. 7). (Illus.). 56p. 1994. teacher ed. 9.50 (0-941008-77-0) Tops Learning.

— Measuring Length. (Task Cards Ser.: No. 2). (Illus.). 48p. 1991. teacher ed. 8.00 (0-941008-72-X) Tops Learning.

— Metric Measure. (Task Cards Ser.: No. 6). (Illus.). 56p. 1992. teacher ed. 9.50 (0-941008-76-2) Tops Learning.

— Metric Measuring. LC 81-90446. (Science with Simple Things Ser.: No. 35). (Illus.). 80p. 1984. teacher ed. 15.00 (0-941008-35-5) Tops Learning.

— More Metrics. LC 81-90448. (Science with Simple Things Ser.: No. 36). (Illus.). 80p. 1985. teacher ed. 15.00 (0-941008-36-3) Tops Learning.

— Motion. (Task Cards Ser.: No. 21). (Illus.). 88p. 1990. teacher ed. 16.00 (0-941008-98-3) Tops Learning.

— Oxidation. (Task Cards Ser.: No. 11). (Illus.). 48p. 1995. teacher ed. 8.00 (0-941008-81-9) Tops Learning.

— Pendulums. (Task Cards Ser.: No. 1). (Illus.). 56p. 1992. teacher ed. 9.50 (0-941008-71-1) Tops Learning.

***Marson, Ron.** Pendulums. (Science with Simple Things Ser.: No. 34). (Illus.). 64p. 2000. teacher ed. 15.00 (0-941008-55-X) Tops Learning.

Marson, Ron. The Planets & Stars. (Science with Simple Things Ser.: No. 41). (Illus.). 80p. 1994. teacher ed. 15.00 (0-941008-41-X) Tops Learning.

— Pressure. (Task Cards Ser.: No. 16). (Illus.). 80p. 1992. teacher ed. 14.50 (0-941008-86-X) Tops Learning.

— Radishes: Green Thumbs. (Science with Simple Things Ser.: No. 38). (Illus.). 56p. 1998. teacher ed. 15.00 (0-941008-70-3) Tops Learning.

— Solutions. (Task Cards Ser.: No. 12). (Illus.). 72p. 1990. teacher ed. 13.00 (0-941008-82-7) Tops Learning.

— Sound. (Task Cards Ser.: No. 18). (Illus.). 56p. 1990. teacher ed. 9.50 (0-941008-88-6) Tops Learning.

— Try This on for Science: A Hatrack of Lessons & Teaching Tools Adapted from 41 Tops Books. (Illus.). 96p. 1998. teacher ed. 10.00 (0-941008-95-9) Tops Learning.

— Weighing. (Task Cards Ser.: No. 5). (Illus.). 56p. 1990. teacher ed. 9.50 (0-941008-75-4) Tops Learning.

Marson, Ron & Marson, Peg. Probability. (Task Cards Ser.: No. 8). (Illus.). 64p. 1995. teacher ed. 13.00 (0-941008-78-9) Tops Learning.

Marson, Ron, jt. auth. see Metcalf, Doris H.

Marson, Ron, ed. see Balick, Don.

Marson, Ron, ed. see Fellers, Pat & Gritzmacher, Kathy.

Marson, Ron, ed. see Gritzmacher, Kathy.

Marson, Stuart. Problem Solving with Maps. 48p. 1992. pap. text 14.95 (0-521-42843-2) Cambridge U Pr.

Marsonet, Michele. The Primacy of Practical Reason: An Essay on Nicholas Resher's Philosophy. 284p. (Orig.). (C). 1995. pap. text 32.50 (0-7618-0120-0); lib. bdg. 58.00 (0-7618-0119-7) U Pr of Amer.

— Science, Reality, & Language. LC 94-22357. (SUNY Series in Philosophy). 170p. (C). 1995. text 44.50 (0-7914-2475-8); pap. text 14.95 (0-7914-2476-6) State U NY Pr.

Marsonette, Wayne. Avoiding Potholes, Speed Bumps, & Long Dusty Roads. (Illus.). xviii, 216p. (Orig.). 1996. pap. 12.95 (0-9654885-0-0) GeminImage.

Marsot, Afaf L. Egypt in the Reign of Mohammad Ali. LC 83-5241. (Cambridge Middle East Library: No. 4). (Illus.). 320p. 1984. pap. text 29.95 (0-521-28968-8) Cambridge U Pr.

— A Short History of Modern Egypt. 164p. 1985. pap. text 18.95 (0-521-27234-3) Cambridge U Pr.

— Women & Men in the Late Eighteenth-Century Egypt. LC 95-17236. (Modern Middle East Ser.). (Illus.). 198p. 1995. 35.00 (0-292-75180-X) U of Tex Pr.

Marsrow, Bernadine R. Sketches in Poetry. 1998. pap. 20.00 (1-57553-891-1) Watermrk Pr.

Marstad, Edna M. Thirst for a Rainbow: A Novel. LC 98-41163. 256p. 1999. pap. 12.95 (1-56474-296-2) Fithian Pr.

Marstall, Bob, jt. auth. see Pringle, Laurence P.

Marstall, Bob, jt. illus. see Heinz, Brian J.

Marstein, Nils, jt. auth. see Larsen, Knut Einar.

Marsters, Bridget, jt. auth. see Marsters, Ted.

Marsters, Kate Ferguson, ed. see Park, Mungo.

Marsters, Ted & Marsters, Bridget. The Big Ideas for Little People Book. (Illus.). (Orig.). 1981. pap. 4.00 (0-939562-00-6) Parker Pr.

Marsterson, William. Information Technology & the Role of the Librarian. (Information Technology Ser.). 208p. 1986. 37.50 (0-7099-4610-4, Pub. by C Helm) Routldge.

Marston. Applied Business Statistics. (C). 1982. pap. write for info. (0-03-910366-8) Harcourt Coll Pubs.

— Malcontent. 2nd ed. (New Mermaids Ser.). (C). 1999. pap. 8.00 (0-393-90089-4) Norton.

Marston, jt. auth. see Skitmore.

Marston, A., jt. auth. see Hostettmann, K.

Marston, A., jt. auth. see Oleszek, W.

Marston, A. T. The Swanscombe Skull. LC 78-72701. reprint ed. 27.50 (0-404-18271-2) AMS Pr.

Marston, Adrian. Hamilton Bailey: A Biography. (Illus.). 168p. 1999. text 67.50 (1-84110-024-2) OUP.

Marston, Ann. Broken Blade. 336p. 1999. mass mkt. 5.99 (0-06-105627-8, HarperPrism) HarpC.

— Cloudbearer's Shadow. Vol. 1. 336p. 1999. mass mkt. 5.99 (0-06-105977-3, HarperPrism) HarpC.

— King of Shadows: Second Book in the Sword in Exile Trilogy. 320p. 1999. mass mkt. 5.99 (0-06-102041-9) HarpC.

— Kingmaker's Sword. LC 97-5017. 336p. 1999. mass mkt. 5.99 (0-06-105629-4, HarperPrism) HarpC.

***Marston, Ann.** Sword & Shadow. 336p. 2000. mass mkt. 6.50 (0-06-102042-7, Avon Bks) Morrow Avon.

Marston, Ann. The Western King. 400p. 1999. mass mkt. 5.99 (0-06-105628-6, HarperPrism) HarpC.

***Marston, Christian.** Coverage Evaluation of the Academic Library Survey. 73p. 1999. pap. 7.00 (0-16-050133-4) USGPO.

Marston, D. L. Law for Professional Engineers. xi, 243p. write for info. (0-07-548073-5) McGraw.

Marston, David A., jt. auth. see Burns, Stephen S.

Marston, David A., jt. ed. see Burns, Stephen S.

Marston, Douglas B., jt. auth. see Tindal.

***Marston, Ed, et al.** Colorado, 1870-2000. LC 99-17277. (Illus.). 224p. 1999. 95.00 (1-56579-347-1) Westcliffe Pubs.

Marston, Ed, ed. see High Country News Staff.

Marston, Edward. The Fair Maid of Bohemia: A Novel. LC 96-53925. 1997. 21.95 (0-312-15606-5) St Martin.

***Marston, Edward.** The Hawks of Delamere. (Domesday Bks.: Vol. 7). 256p. 2000. text 22.95 (0-312-20948-7) St Martin.

Marston, Edward. The Laughing Hangman. LC 96-6990. 320p. 1996. text 21.95 (0-312-14305-2) St Martin.

***Marston, Edward.** The Queen's Head. LC 00-102398. (Missing Mystery Ser.: No. 19). 300p. 2000. pap. 14.95 (1-890208-45-0) Poisoned Pen.

Marston, Edward. The Ravens of Blackwater. 1996. mass mkt. 5.99 (0-449-22410-4) Fawcett.

— The Roaring Boy. large type ed. LC 95-8568. 555p. 1995. 23.95 (0-7838-1491-7) Thorndike Pr.

— The Serpents of Harbledown: A Novel. LC 97-34838. 288p. 1998. text 22.95 (0-312-18021-7) St Martin.

— The Stallions of Woodstock. LC 98-50733. Vol. 6. 288p. 1998. text 22.95 (0-312-20021-8) St Martin.

— The Wanton Angel. 2nd ed. LC 99-22062. 288p. 1999. text 23.95 (0-312-20391-8) St Martin.

Marston, Edwin H. The Dynamic Environment: Water, Transportation, & Energy. LC 74-82346. 432p. reprint ed. pap. 134.00 (0-608-11491-X, 201246100081) Bks Demand.

Marston, Elsa. Free As the Desert Wind. (Illus.). 32p. (Orig.). (J). (gr. 2-6). 1996. pap. 7.50 (977-5325-66-8, Pub. by Hoopoe Bks) AMIDEAST.

— Lebanon: New Light in an Ancient Land. LC 93-5402. (Illus.). 128p. (YA). (gr. 5 up). 1994. lib. bdg. 14.95 (0-87518-584-3, Dillon Silver Burdett) Silver Burdett Pr.

Marston, Elsa & Campbell, Anneke. How to Be a Helper. LC 81-43458. vii, 119p. 1982. 3.50 (0-385-17949-9) Doubleday.

Marston, Elsa, jt. auth. see Harik, Ramsay M.

Marston, Frank S. The Peace Conference of 1919: Organization & Procedure. LC 80-28997. 276p. 1981. reprint ed. lib. bdg. 45.00 (0-313-22910-4, MAPEC, Greenwood Pr) Greenwood.

— The Peace Conference of 1919, Organization & Procedure. LC 76-29412. reprint ed. 32.50 (0-404-15349-6) AMS Pr.

Marston, Ginna & Marshall, Sally, eds. Growing up Drug Free: A Parent's Guide to Prevention. (Illus.). 46p. (C). 1999. pap. text 15.00 (0-7881-7802-4) DIANE Pub.

Marston, Gwen. Liberated Quiltmaking. (Illus.). 192p. (Orig.). 1997. 24.95 (0-89145-878-6, 4751, Am Quilters Soc) Collector Bks.

— Twenty Little Amish Quilts: With Full-Size Templates. LC 93-9357. (Needlework Ser.). (Illus.). 56p. 1993. pap. 4.95 (0-486-27582-5) Dover.

— Twenty Little Four-Patch Quilts: With Full-Size Templates. (Illus.). 56p. (Orig.). 1996. pap. 5.95 (0-486-29184-7) Dover.

— Twenty Little Log Cabin Quilts: With Full-Size Templates. LC 95-17401. (Needlework Ser.). (Illus.). 56p. (Orig.). 1995. pap. text 5.95 (0-486-28809-9) Dover.

— Twenty Little Patchwork Quilts. 56p. 1990. pap. 4.95 (0-486-26131-X) Dover.

— Twenty Little Pinwheel Quilts: With Full-Size Templates. (Illus.). 56p. (Orig.). 1994. pap. text 4.95 (0-486-28216-3) Dover.

— Twenty Little Triangle Quilts: With Full-Size Templates. LC 97-7959. (Illus.). 56p. (Orig.). 1997. pap. text 5.95 (0-486-29700-4) Dover.

Marston, Gwen & Cunningham, Joe. Amish Quilting Patterns: Fifty-Six Full-Size Ready-to-Use Designs & Complete Instructions. (Illus.). 96p. (Orig.). 1987. pap. 5.95 (0-486-25326-0) Dover.

Marston, Gwen & Cunningham, Joe. Mary Schafer & Her Quilts. Fitzgerald, Ruth D. & Caltrider, Sue, eds. (Illus.). 64p. (Orig.). 1990. pap. 19.95 (0-944311-04-0) MSU Museum.

— Quilting with Style: Principles for Great Pattern Design. LC 93-7673. 1993. 24.95 (0-89145-814-X, 3470, Am Quilters Soc) Collector Bks.

— Seventy Classic Quilting Patterns: Ready-to-Use Designs & Instructions. (Illus.). 96p. (Orig.). 1987. pap. 5.95 (0-486-25474-7) Dover.

Marston, Hope. By an Unfamiliar Path: The Story of David & Arlene Peters. (Junior Jaffray Collection: Bk. 13). (Illus.). 32p. (J). (ps-2). 1995. pap. 3.99 (0-87509-581-X) Chr Pubns.

— My Little Book of River Otters. LC 97-5958. (Illus.). 32p. (Orig.). (J). (gr. k-5). 1997. pap. 6.95 (1-55971-639-8, NorthWord Pr) Creat Pub Intl.

— The Promise: Junior Jaffray Edition. (Junior Jaffray Collection: Vol. 10). 30p. (J). (ps-2). 1994. pap. 3.99 (0-87509-548-8) Chr Pubns.

— To Vietnam with Love. (Junior Jaffray Collection: Bk. 12). (Illus.). 32p. (J). (ps-2). 1995. pap. 3.99 (0-87509-583-6) Chr Pubns.

Marston, Hope I. Fire Trucks. (Illus.). 48p. (J). (gr. 2-5). 1996. 15.99 (0-525-65231-0) NAL.

— My Little Book of Burrowing Owls. LC 95-36480. (Illus.). 48p. (Orig.). (J). (gr. k-5). 1996. pap. 6.95 (1-55971-547-2, NorthWord Pr) Creat Pub Intl.

— My Little Book of Painted Turtles. LC 96-11583. (Illus.). 36p. (J). (gr. k-5). 1996. pap. 6.95 (1-55971-569-3, NorthWord Pr) Creat Pub Intl.

— My Little Book of Timber Wolves. LC 96-48183. (Illus.). 36p. (Orig.). (J). (ps-5). 1997. pap. 4.95 (1-55971-582-0, NorthWord Pr) Creat Pub Intl.

— My Little Book of Wood Ducks. LC 94-40917. (Illus.). 32p. (Orig.). (J). (gr. 1-5). 1995. pap. 6.95 (1-55971-467-0, NorthWord Pr) Creat Pub Intl.

— Wings in the Water: The Story of a Manta Ray. LC 98-13740. (Smithsonian Oceanic Collection: Vol. 16). (Illus.). 32p. (J). (ps-2). 1998. 15.95 (1-56899-577-6); 19.95 incl. audio (1-56899-579-2, BC4016) Soundprints.

— Wings in the Water: The Story of a Manta Ray, Incl. toy. (Smithsonian Oceanic Collection: No. 16). (Illus.). 32p. (J). (ps-2). 1998. 29.95 (1-56899-581-4) Soundprints.

— Wings in the Water: The Story of a Manta Ray, Incl. toy. (Smithsonian Oceanic Collection: Vol. 16). (Illus.). 32p. (J). (ps-2). 1998. 34.95 incl. audio (1-56899-583-0) Soundprints.

— Wings in the Water: The Story of a Manta Ray - Micro Book. LC 98-13740. (Smithsonian Oceanic Collection: Vol. 16). (Illus.). 32p. (J). (ps-2). 1998. 4.95 (1-56899-578-4) Soundprints.

— Wings in the Water: The Story of a Manta Ray - Micro Book, Incl. micro toy. (Smithsonian Oceanic Collection: Vol. 16). (Illus.). 32p. (J). (ps-2). 1998. 9.95 (1-56899-582-2); 9.95 incl. audio (1-56899-584-9) Soundprints.

— Wings in the Water: The Story of a Manta Ray - Micro Edition. (Smithsonian Oceanic Collection: Vol. 16). (Illus.). 32p. (J). (ps-2). 1998. write for info. incl. audio (1-56899-580-6) Soundprints.

Marston, J. E., tr. see Gneisenau, Count.

Marston, Jerrilyn G. King & Congress: The Transfer of Political Legitimacy, 1774-1776. LC 87-2439. 477p. 1987. reprint ed. pap. 147.90 (0-7837-9382-0, 206012600004) Bks Demand.

Marston, John. Antonio & Mellida: The First Part. Hunter, G. K., ed. LC 64-17229. (Regents Renaissance Drama Ser.). 110p. 1965. reprint ed. pap. 34.10 (0-7837-8896-7, 204960700001) Bks Demand.

— The Dutch Courtesan. 1998. pap. text. write for info. (0-393-90086-X) Norton.

— The Dutch Courtesan. Wine, M. L., ed. LC 65-11519. (Regents Renaissance Drama Ser.). 156p. reprint ed. pap. 48.40 (0-8357-7933-5, 205700600002) Bks Demand.

— The Fawn. Smith, Gerald A., ed. LC 65-11518. (Regents Renaissance Drama Ser.). 143p. 1965. reprint ed. pap. 44.40 (0-608-01857-0, 206250700003) Bks Demand.

— Histriomastix. LC 70-133706. (Tudor Facsimile Texts. Old English Plays Ser.: No. 128). reprint ed. 59.50 (0-404-53428-7) AMS Pr.

— Jack Drum's Entertainment. LC 74-133707. (Tudor Facsimile Texts. Old English Plays Ser.: No. 93). reprint ed. 59.50 (0-404-53393-0) AMS Pr.

— The Malcontent. 1976. 18.95 (0-89190-098-5) Amereon Ltd.

— The Malcontent. Trussler, Simon, ed. (Student Editions of Minor Jacobean Masterpieces Ser.). 192p. (C). 1988. pap. write for info. (0-413-16290-7, A0167, Methuen Drama) Methn.

— The Malcontent. Hunter, George K., ed. (Revels Plays Ser.). (Illus.). 171p. 1999. pap. 19.95 (0-7190-3094-3) St Martin.

— The Malcontent. Wine, M. L., ed. LC 64-17228. (Regents Renaissance Drama Ser.). 151p. reprint ed. pap. 46.90 (0-608-16436-4, 202671000051) Bks Demand.

— The Malcontent & Other Plays. Sturgess, Keith, ed. & notes by. LC 96-48198. (The World's Classics Ser). 428p. 1997. pap. 12.95 (0-19-282250-0) OUP.

Marston, John. Malcontent & Other Plays. 544p. pap. 15.95 (0-14-043635-9, Pub. by Pnguin Bks Ltd) Trafalgar.

Marston, John. Parasitaster: or The Fawn. Blostein, David A., ed. LC 78-60170. (Revels Plays Ser.). 256p. reprint ed. pap. 79.40 (0-608-06031-3, 206636200008) Bks Demand.

— The Plays of John Marston, 3 vols. 1988. reprint ed. lib. bdg. 290.00 (0-7812-0324-4) Rprt Serv.

— The Plays of John Marston, 3 vols. reprint ed. 225.00 (0-403-04206-2) Somerset Pub.

— Public Order: A Guide to the 1986 Public Order Act. 189p. 1987. 105.00 (1-85190-024-1, Pub. by Fourmat Pub) St Mut.

— The Scourge of Villanie. LC 73-21779. (English Literature Ser.: No. 33). 1974. lib. bdg. 75.00 (0-8383-1828-2) M S G Haskell Hse.

Marston, John & Nottridge, Robin E. Police Powers & Duties: A Practical Guide to the Pace Act, 1984. 168p. (C). 1985. 100.00 (0-906840-82-1, Pub. by Fourmat Pub) St Mut.

Marston, Lloyd. Playground Equipment: Do-It-Yourself, Indestructible, Practically Free. LC 83-25565. (Illus.). 160p. 1984. pap. 29.95 (0-89950-104-4) McFarland & Co.

Marston, N., tr. see Chevrel, J. P., ed.

Marston, N. W. Marston Genealogy, 2 pts. (Illus.). 607p. 1989. reprint ed. pap. 91.00 (0-8328-0857-1); reprint ed. lib. bdg. 99.00 (0-8328-0856-3) Higginson Bk Co.

Marston, Nicholas. Beethoven's Piano Sonata in E, Op. 109. LC 94-10762. (Studies in Musical Genesis & Structure). (Illus.). 286p. 1995. text 75.00 (0-19-315332-7) OUP.

Marston, Nicholas. Schumann: "Fantasie, Op. 17" (Cambridge Music Handbooks Ser.). (Illus.). 131p. (C). 1992. text 39.95 (0-521-39284-5); pap. text 12.95 (0-521-39892-4) Cambridge U Pr.

Marston, Paul, jt. auth. see Forster, Roger.

Marston, Peter. The Book of the Conservatory. 1999. pap. 29.95 (0-7538-0501-4) Phoenix.

— The Book of the Conservatory. (Illus.). 176p. 1995. pap. 19.95 (0-297-83477-0, Pub. by Weidenfeld & Nicolson) Trafalgar.

— Garden Room Style. LC 98-66582. (Illus.). 160p. 1998. 35.00 (0-8478-2153-6, Pub. by Rizzoli Intl) St Martin.

Marston, Philip B. Collected Poems. LC 72-148816. reprint ed. 49.50 (0-404-04192-2) AMS Pr.

Marston, Philip L., ed. Selected Papers on Geometrical Aspects of Scattering. LC 93-34227. (Milestone Ser.: Vol. MS 89/HC). 1993. 55.00 (0-8194-1405-0) SPIE.

— Selected Papers on Geometrical Aspects of Scattering. LC 93-34227. (Milestone Ser.: Vol. MS89). 1993. pap. 45.00 (0-8194-1404-2) SPIE.

Marston, R. M. Audio IC Circuits Manual. 1989. 32.00 (0-434-91210-7, TK) CRC Pr.

— Audio IC User's Handbook. LC 97-214587. (Illus.). 192p. 1997. pap. text 32.95 (0-7506-3006-X) Buttrwrth-Heinemann.

Marston, R. M. Newnes Passive & Discrete Circuits Pocket Book. (Illus.). 400p. Date not set. 29.95 (0-7506-4192-4) Buttrwrth-Heinemann.

Marston, R. M. Op-Amp Circuits Manual. 1989. lab manual ed. 32.00 (0-434-91207-7) CRC Pr.

— Optoelectronics Circuits Manual. LC 97-181139. 190p. 1999. pap. text 32.95 (0-7506-0157-4, Newnes) Buttrwrth-Heinemann.

— Optoelectronics Circuits Manual. 2nd ed. LC 99-20871. 1999. 29.95 (0-7506-4166-5) Buttrwrth-Heinemann.

— Security Electronics Circuits Manual. LC 98-22022. (Illus.). 224p. 1998. pap. text 28.95 (0-7506-3007-8, Newnes) Buttrwrth-Heinemann.

Marston, Ralph S., Jr. The Daily Motivator to Go. 200p. 1997. pap. 11.95 (0-9664634-0-4, DM-03) Image Express Inc.

Marston, Ray M. Electronic Circuits Pocket Book Vol. 2: Passive & Discrete Circuits, Vol. 2. (Illus.). 367p. 1993. text 32.95 (0-7506-0857-9) Buttrwrth-Heinemann.

— Instrumentation & Test-Gear Circuits Manual. (Illus.). 400p. 1993. pap. text 44.95 (0-7506-0758-0) Buttrwrth-Heinemann.

— Modern CMOS Circuits Manual. (Illus.). 192p. 1999. pap. text 36.95 (0-7506-2565-1) Buttrwrth-Heinemann.

— Modern TTL Circuits Manual. (EDN Ser.). (Illus.). 224p. 1994. pap. text 36.95 (0-7506-2092-7) Buttrwrth-Heinemann.

— Newnes Digital IC Pocket Book. (Illus.). 256p. 1999. text 29.95 (0-7506-3018-3) Buttrwrth-Heinemann.

Marston, Raymond Micheal. Optoelectronics Circuits Manual. 1988. 32.00 (0-434-91211-5) CRC Pr.

Marston, Richard A., ed. see American Water Resources Association, Summer Sympo.

Marston, Richard A., jt. ed. see Miller, Maynard M.

Marston, Richard C. International Financial Integration: A Study of Interest Differentials Between the Major Industrial Countries. (Japan-U. S. Center Monographs on International Financial Markets: No. 1). (Illus.). 211p. (C). 1995. text 59.95 (0-521-47100-1) Cambridge U Pr.

— International Financial Integration: A Study of Interest Differentials Between the Major Industrial Countries. (Japan-U. S. Center Sanwa Monographs on International Financial Markets: No. 1). 211p. 1997. pap. text 18.95 (0-521-59937-7) Cambridge U Pr.

— Misalignment of Exchange Rates: Effects on Trade & Industry. (National Bureau of Economic Research Project Report Ser.). (Illus.). x, 328p. 1988. lib. bdg. 48.00 (0-226-50723-8) U Ch Pr.

Marston, Richard C., jt. ed. see Bilson, John F.

Marston, Richard C., jt. ed. see Buiter, Willem H.

Marston, Robert B. War, Famine & Our Food Supply. LC 75-26308. (World Food Supply Ser.). (Illus.). 1976. reprint ed. 23.95 (0-405-07787-4) Ayer.

Marston, Robert Q., ed. see Institute of Medicine Staff.

Marston, Sallie, jt. auth. see Knox, Paul L.

Marston, Sallie A., ed. Terminal Disasters: Computer Applications in Emergency Management. (Program on Environment & Behavior Monograph Ser.: No. 39). 218p. (Orig.). (C). 1986. pap. 20.00 (0-685-28113-2) Natural Hazards.

Marston, Stephanie. The Divorced Parent: Success Strategies for Raising Happy Children after Separation. Rubenstein, Julie, ed. 352p. 1995. pap. 10.00 (0-671-51128-9) PB.

Marston, Thomas E., et al. The Vinland Map & the Tartar Relation. LC 95-21114. 291p. 1996. 47.50 (0-300-06520-5) Yale U Pr.

Marston, Thomas E., jt. auth. see Skelton, Raleigh A.

Marston, V. Paul, jt. auth. see Forster, Roger T.

Marston, Wendy. The Hypochondriac's Handbook. LC 98-17271. (Illus.). 144p. 1998. 10.95 (0-8118-2192-7) Chronicle Bks.

Marston, William. Wonder Woman Archives. Kahan, Bob, ed. (Illus.). 240p. 1998. 49.95 (1-56389-402-5, Pub. by DC Comics) Time Warner.

***Marston, William Moulton.** Wonder Woman Archives. 240p. (J). 2000. 49.95 (1-56389-594-3, Pub. by DC Comics) Time Warner.

Marsullo, F. Victoria Sobre los Espiritus Malignos.Tr. of Victory over Demonic Spirits. (SPA.). pap. 6.99 (958-9354-16-5, 550053) Editorial Unilit.

***Marszalec, Elsbieta A. & Trucco, Emanuele, eds.** Polarization & Color Techniques in Industrial Inspection. 324p. 1999. pap. text 72.00 (0-8194-3312-8) SPIE.

Marszalec, Elsbieta A., jt. auth. see Marszalec, Janusz A.

Marszalec, Janusz A. & Marszalec, Elsbieta A. Integration of Lasers & Fiber Optics into Robotic Systems. 144p. 1994. 20.00 (0-8194-1313-5) SPIE.

Marszalek. The Eaton Affair. 1997. 25.00 (0-02-920136-5) Free Pr.

***Marszalek-Gaucher, Ellen & Coffey, Richard J.** Breakthrough Performance: Accelerating the Transformation of Health Care Organizations. LC 00-20567. 321p. 2000. text 44.95 (0-7879-5231-1) Jossey-Bass.

Marszalek-Gaucher, Ellen & Coffey, Richard J. Transforming Healthcare Organizations: How to Achieve & Sustain Organizational Excellence. LC 90-4777. (Health-Management Ser.). 308p. 1990. text 40.95 (1-55542-250-0) Jossey-Bass.

Marszalek, Janet, ed. It's a Darne' Good Cookbook: From Darnestown, Maryland. LC 92-85354. (Illus.). 371p. 1992. ring bd. write for info. (0-9634198-0-3) Great Darnestwn.

Marszalek, John F. Court-Martial: A Black Man in America. LC 73-38282. 336p. reprint ed. pap. 104.20 (0-608-14342-1, 205195400016) Bks Demand.

— Grover Cleveland: A Bibliography, 22. LC 88-9096. (Bibliographies of the Presidents of the United States Ser.: No. 22). 312p. 1988. lib. bdg. 69.50 (0-313-28180-7, AP22, Greenwood Pr) Greenwood.

***Marszalek, John F.** The Petticoat Affair: Manners, Mutiny & Sex in Andrew Jackson's White House. (Illus.). 312p. 2000. pap. 16.95 (0-8071-2634-9) La State U Pr.

Marszalek, John F. The Petticoat Affair: Manners, Sex, & Mutiny in Andrew Jackson's White House. LC 97-16099. (Illus.). 304p. 1998. 24.50 (0-684-82801-4) Free Pr.

— Sherman: A Soldier's Passion for Order. LC 92-24533. 635p. 1992. 35.00 (0-02-920135-7) Free Pr.

— Sherman: A Soldier's Passion for Order. 1994. pap. 19.00 (0-679-74989-6) Random.

***Marszalek, John F.** Sherman's Other War: The General & the Civil War Press. 2nd rev. ed. LC 98-13764. 256p. 1998. pap. 18.00 (0-87338-619-1) Kent St U Pr.

Marszalek, John F., ed. Diary of Miss Emma Holmes, 1861-1866. (Library of Southern Civilization). (Illus.). 528p. 1994. reprint ed. pap. 17.95 (0-8071-1940-7) La State U Pr.

Marszalek, John F., jt. auth. see Conner, Douglas L.

Marszalek, John F., jt. ed. see Lowery, Charles D.

Marszalek, John F., jt. ed. see Miscamble, Wilson D.

Mart, Maria, ed. see Storti-Storchi, Claudia, et al.

Marta-Dajka, Balazs, jt. auth. see Hronszky, Imre-Feher.

Marta, Karen, ed. see Hickey, Dave.

***Martana.** Texas Men: 100 Big Guns, Rising Stars, & Cowboys. LC 00-23650. (Illus.). 224p. 2000. 49.95 (0-9616868-1-2, Pub. by CF Ranch) Ten Speed Pr.

Martanda, Acharya D., tr. Rigveda, Vol. 3. (ENG, HIN & SAN.). 816p. 1984. 17.00 (0-685-72920-6, Pub. by Sarvadeshik Arya) Nataraj Bks.

— Rigveda Vol. 1: With Maharishi Dayananda Sharaswati's Commentary. lx, 952p. 1974. 17.00 (0-685-72918-4, Pub. by Sarvadeshik Arya) Nataraj Bks.

Martanda, Vidya, tr. see Snatak, Brahma D. & Hindi, Surendra K., eds.

Martasudjita, Emanuel P. Die Gegenwart des Mysteriums Christi: Zum Sakramentenverstandnis Bei Gottlieb Sohngen. (Europaische Hochschulschriften Ser.: Reihe 23, Bd. 566). (GER.). 372p. 1996. 61.95 (3-631-49921-3) P Lang Pubng.

***Martbinez, Esperanza & Herbandez, Georgina.** Highlights of Nitrogen Fixation Research. LC 99-32448. (C). 1999. text. write for info. (0-306-46137-4, Kluwer Plenum) Kluwer Academic.

Martchenko, Michael. Birdfeeder Banquet. (Illus.). 32p. (J). (ps-3). 1990. 15.95 (1-55037-147-9, Pub. by Annick); pap. 4.95 (1-55037-146-0, Pub. by Annick) Firefly Bks Ltd.

— A Table, les Oiseaux! - Bird Feeding Banquet. (Droles D'Histories Ser.). (FRE., Illus.). 24p. (J). (ps up). 1992. pap. 6.95 (2-89021-184-3, Pub. by La Courte Ech) Firefly Bks Ltd.

Martchenko, Michael, jt. auth. see Morgan, Allen.

Martchenko, Michael, jt. auth. see Munsch, Robert.

Martchenko, Michael, jt. auth. see Skrypuch, Marsha.

Martchenko, Michael, jt. auth. see Trottier, Maxine.

Martchenko, Michael, ed. see Munsch, Robert.

Marte, Delores, tr. see Erick, Miriam.

Marte, L. F. Political Cycles in International Relations: The Cold War & Africa. 496p. 1994. 57.00 (90-5383-280-7, Pub. by VU Univ Pr) Paul & Co Pubs.

Marte, Rebecca, jt. auth. see Birch, David.

Marteau, Robert. Salamander: Selected Poems of Robert Marteau. LC 78-70307. (Lockert Library of Poetry in Translation). 127p. reprint ed. pap. 39.40 (0-8357-7013-3, 205228800085) Bks Demand.

Marteau, Theresa & Richards, Martin, eds. The Troubled Helix: Social & Psychological Implications of the New Human Genetics. (Illus.). 377p. (C). 1996. text 69.95 (0-521-46288-6) Cambridge U Pr.

— The Troubled Helix: Social & Psychological Implications of the New Human Genetics. (Illus.). 384p. (C). 1999. pap. text 29.95 (0-521-58612-7) Cambridge U Pr.

Marteau, Theresa, jt. ed. see Johnston, Marie.

***Martegani, Paolo & Montenegro, Riccardo.** Digital Design: New Frontiers for the Objects. (Illus.). 96p. 2000. pap. 12.50 (3-7643-6296-0, Pub. by Birkhauser) Princeton Arch.

Martel, Alan. Footprints. 205p. 1996. pap. 13.00 (1-883721-16-4) Silver Mtn Pr.

***Martel, C.** Vocabulario Du Jeu De Boules Provencal. (FRE.). 1999. 34.95 (0-320-01779-6) Fr & Eur.

Martel, Cruz. Yagua Days. (Illus.). (J). (gr. 3). 1995. 8.60 (0-395-73235-2) HM.

— Yagua Days. large type ed. (Illus.). 62p. (J). (gr. 3). 15.50 (0-614-20630-8, L-38177-00 APHB) Am Printing Hse.

***Martel, Frederic.** The Pink & the Black: Homosexuals in France since 1968. LC 99-49932. 444p. 2000. pap. 19.95 (0-8047-3274-4) Stanford U Pr.

Martel, Gloria. Grow Young by Discovering the Cause of Each Wrinkle, & the Ten Steps to Erase Them . . . Forever! McKeever, Ann & Madry, Bobbi R., eds. LC 98-92508. (Illus.). 1998. 29.95 (0-9661774-2-8) Beauty Tech.

Martel, Gordon. Imperial Diplomacy: Roseberry & the Failure of Foreign Policy. 304p. 1986. 65.00 (0-7735-0442-7, Pub. by McG-Queens Univ Pr) CUP Services.

***Martel, Gordon.** Origins of Second World War Reconsidered: A. J. P. Taylor & Historians. 2nd ed. LC 99-18880. 1999. pap. 25.99 (0-415-16325-0) Routledge.

Martel, Gordon. The Origins of the First World War. 2nd ed. LC 95-4505. (Seminar Studies in History). 152p. (C). 1996. pap. text 14.06 (0-582-28697-2, Pub. by Addison-Wesley) Longman.

Martel, Gordon, ed. American Foreign Relations Reconsidered, 1890-1993. LC 93-36339. 304p. (C). 1994. pap. 25.99 (0-415-10477-7, B3807) Routledge.

— Modern Germany Reconsidered. (Illus.). 304p. (C). 1992. 90.00 (0-415-07811-3); pap. 25.99 (0-415-07812-1) Routledge.

***Martel, Gordon, ed.** Origins of Second World War Reconsidered: A. J. P. Taylor & Historians. 2nd ed. LC 99-18880. 304p. (C). 1999. text. write for info. (0-415-16324-2) Routledge.

Martel, Gordon, ed. The Origins of the Second World War Reconsidered: The A. J. P. Taylor Debate after Twenty-Five Years. 292p. 1986. text 75.00 (0-04-940084-3); pap. text 19.95 (0-04-940085-1) Routledge.

— The Origins of the Second World War Reconsidered: The A. J. P. Taylor Debate after Twenty-Five Years. LC 85-20097. (Illus.). 288p. (C). 1986. pap. 24.99 (0-415-08420-2) Routledge.

Martel, Harry, jt. ed. see Selsam, Howard.

Martel, John. The Alternate. LC 98-52776. 432p. 1999. 24.95 (0-525-94487-7) NAL.

***Martel, John.** The Alternate. 544p. 2000. mass mkt. 6.99 (0-451-19996-0, Sig) NAL.

Martel, John. Conflicts of Interest. LC 94-45781. 448p. 1995. 23.00 (0-671-89094-8) PB.

— Conflicts of Interest. 1996. per. 6.99 (0-671-89095-6) PB.

Martel, Jose & Alpern, Hymen. Diez Comedias del Siglo de Oro. 2nd ed. (SPA., Illus.). 865p. (C). 1985. text 30.95 (0-88133-119-8) Waveland Pr.

Martel, Laurence D., jt. auth. see Kline, Peter.

Martel, Lucie, rev. Loss Prevention Test Kit. 2nd ed. (FRE.). 45.00 (0-614-05206-8, LPTK06882M) ASFE.

Martel, Marcel, jt. ed. see Behiels, Michael D.

Martel, Myles. Fire Away: Fielding Tough Questions with Finesse. LC 93-1265. 240p. 1993. 30.00 (1-55623-976-9, Irwn Prfssnl) McGraw-Hill Prof.

Martel, Pierre, et al. Dictionnaire de Frequence des Mots du Francais Parle au Quebec. LC 91-5120. (American University Studies: Linguistics: Ser. XIII, Vol. 26). (FRE.). LIII, 768p. (Orig.). (C). 1992. pap. text 110.95 (0-8204-1740-8) P Lang Pubng.

Martel, Sarah. Not Just Another Low-Fat Recipe Book: Discovering a New Relationship with Food. Ray, Muriel, ed. (Illus.). 105p. 1995. write for info. (0-614-23145-0) Hlth & Food.

***Martel, Simone.** The Expectant Gardener. LC 99-63266. 200p. 2000. pap. 13.95 (0-88739-281-4) Creat Arts Bk.

Martel, Susan K., jt. auth. see Eheart, Brenda K.

Martel, Suzanne. King's Daughter. 1998. 14.95 (0-88899-323-4) Publishers Group.

— The King's Daughter. rev. ed. 192p. 1998. pap. 5.95 (0-88899-218-1) Publishers Group.

Martel, William C. Nuclear Coexistence: Rethinking United States Policy to Promote Stability in an Era of Proliferation. 192p. 1994. per. 15.00 (0-16-061362-0) USGPO.

— Russia's Democratic Moment? Defining United States Policy to Promote Opportunities in Russia. 343p. 1995. per. 21.00 (0-16-061363-9) USGPO.

Martel, William C. & Hailes, Theodore C. Russia's Democratic Moment? Defining U. S. Policy to Promote Democratic Opportunities in Russia. 319p. (C). 1998. reprint ed. pap. text 40.00 (0-7881-4664-5) DIANE Pub.

Martel, William C. & Pendley, William T. Nuclear Coexistence: Rethinking U. S. Policy to Promote Stability in an Era of Proliferation. 178p. (C). 1998. reprint ed. pap. text 35.00 (0-7881-4663-7) DIANE Pub.

An Asterisk (*) at the beginning of an entry indicates that the title is appearing for the first time.

Martel, William C. & Savage, Paul L. Strategic Nuclear War: What the Superpowers Target & Why, 43. LC 85-9869. (Contributions in Military Studies Ser.: No. 43). (Illus.). 269p. 1986. 55.00 (*0-313-24192-9*, SNU/, Greenwood Pr) Greenwood.

Martell, A. E. & Hancock, R. D. Metal Complexes in Aqueous Solutions. LC 96-11162. (Modern Inorganic Chemistry Ser.). (Illus.). 264p. (C). 1996. text 71.00 (*0-306-45248-0*, Kluwer Plenum) Kluwer Academic.

Martell, A. E. & Motekaitis, Ramumas J. Determination & Use of Stability Constants. 2nd ed. 200p. 1992. 79.95 (*0-471-18817-4*) Wiley.

Martell, A. E. & Smith, R. M. Critical Stability Constants, Vol. 5. LC 74-10610. (Illus.). 622p. (C). 1982. text, suppl. ed. 145.00 (*0-306-41005-2*, Kluwer Plenum) Kluwer Academic.

Martell, A. E., jt. auth. see Sawyer, D. T.

Martell, A. E., jt. auth. see Smith, R. M.

Martell, Angela. Splendour in the Sun. (Rainbow Romances Ser.). 160p. 1993. 14.95 (*0-7090-4895-5*) Parkwest Pubns.

— Splendour in the Sun. large type ed. (Linford Romance Ser.). 272p. 1995. pap. 16.99 (*0-7089-7663-8*, Linford) Ulverscroft.

Martell, Arthur E. Inorganic Chemistry in Biology & Medicine. LC 80-23248. (ACS Symposium Ser.: No. 140). 1980. 49.95 (*0-8412-0588-4*) Am Chemical.

Martell, Arthur E., ed. Coordination Chemistry, Vol. 2. LC 74-151255. (ACS Monograph: No. 168 & 174). 636p. 1978. text 98.00 (*0-8412-0292-3*, Pub. by Am Chemical) OUP.

— Coordination Chemistry, Vols. 1-2. LC 74-151255. (ACS Monograph: No. 168 & 174). 49.95 (*0-8412-0275-3*) Am Chemical.

— Inorganic Chemistry in Biology & Medicine. LC 80-23248. (ACS Symposium Ser.: No. 140). (Illus.). 444p. 1980. reprint ed. pap. 137.70 (*0-608-03228-X*, 206374700007) Bks Demand.

Martell, Arthur E. & Motekaitis, Ramumas J. Determination & Use of Stability Constants. 2nd ed. LC 91-45076. 200p. 1993. 45.00 (*1-56081-516-7*, Wiley-VCH) Wiley.

Martell, Arthur E. & Sawyer, Donald T., eds. Oxygen Complexes & Oxygen Activation by Transition Metals. LC 87-32170. (Illus.). 352p. 1988. 95.00 (*0-306-42789-3*, Plenum Trade) Perseus Pubng.

Martell, Arthur E. & Smith, Robert M. Critical Stability Constants Vol. 1: Amino Acids. LC 74-10610. 485p. reprint ed. pap. 150.40 (*0-608-09364-5*, 205411000001) Bks Demand.

— Critical Stability Constants Vol. 2: Amines. LC 74-10610. 429p. reprint ed. pap. 133.00 (*0-608-08573-1*, 206909600002) Bks Demand.

— Critical Stability Constants Vol. 3: Other Organic Ligands. LC 74-10610. 511p. reprint ed. pap. 158.50 (*0-608-08574-X*, 206909600003) Bks Demand.

— Critical Stability Constants Vol. 4: Inorganic Complexes. LC 74-10610. 270p. reprint ed. pap. 83.70 (*0-608-09365-3*, 205411000004) Bks Demand.

Martell, Bill. An Illustrated Guide to Teaching Kids to Wrestle. LC 81-84787. (Illus.). 160p. 1985. reprint ed. pap. 49.60 (*0-608-07082-3*, 206731100009) Bks Demand.

Martell, Charles & Shek, Kitty W. A Guide to the Oral History Collection of Cambodians in California. 84p. 1992. pap. 25.00 (*0-938847-03-1*) CSU Sacto Lib.

Martell, Charles, jt. auth. see Shek, Kitty W.

Martell, Charles A., Jr. The Client-Centered Academic Library: An Organizational Model, 42. LC 82-9378. (Contributions in Librarianship & Information Science Ser.: No. 42). 136p. 1983. 49.95 (*0-313-23213-X*, MLI/, Greenwood Pr) Greenwood.

Martell, Chris, jt. auth. see Campbell, Genie.

Martell, George. A New Education Politics. (Our Schools/Our Selves Ser.). 310p. pap. 19.95 (*1-55028-488-6*, Pub. by J Lorimer) Formac Dist Ltd.

Martell, Hazel. Civilizations of Peru Before 1535. LC 98-20152. (Looking Back Ser.). (Illus.). 64p. (J). (gr. 6-9). 1999. 25.69 (*0-8172-5428-5*) Raintree Steck-V.

— Imperial China, 221 B. C. to A. D. 1294. LC 97-50621. (Looking Back Ser.). (J). 1999. 25.69 (*0-8172-5425-0*) Raintree Steck-V.

— The Myths & Civilization of the Ancient Greeks. (Myths & Civilization Ser.). (Illus.). 48p. (gr. 3-7). 1999. lib. bdg. 16.95 (*0-87226-283-9*, 62839B, P Bedrick Books) NTC Contemp Pub Co.

— Roman Town. LC 97-7072. (Metropolis). (Illus.). 48p. (J). 1998. 24.00 (*0-531-14467-4*) Watts.

— The World of Islam Before 1700. LC 98-9473. (Looking Back Ser.). (J). 1999. 25.69 (*0-8172-5430-7*) Raintree Steck-V.

Martell, Hazel M. The Age of Discovery, 1500-1650. LC 92-18621. (Illustrated History of the World Ser.). (Illus.). 80p. (J). (gr. 2-6). 1993. 19.95 (*0-8160-2789-7*) Facts on File.

— The Celts. LC 95-61265. (See Through History Ser.). (Illus.). 48p. (J). (gr. 3-7). 1995. 19.99 (*0-670-86558-3*, Viking Child) Peng Put Young Read.

— Exploring Africa. LC 97-15230. (Voyages of Discovery Ser.). (Illus.). 48p. (J). (gr. 4-7). 1997. 18.95 (*0-87226-490-4*, 64904B, P Bedrick Books) NTC Contemp Pub Co.

— The Great Pyramid. LC 96-29680. (Great Buildings Ser.). 48p. (J). 1998. lib. bdg. 25.69 (*0-8172-4918-4*) Raintree Steck-V.

— The Kingfisher Book of the Ancient World: From the Ice Age to the Fall of Rome. (Illus.). 160p. 1997. pap. text 17.95 (*0-7534-5009-7*) LKC.

— The Myths & Civilization of the Vikings. (Myths & Civilization Ser.). (Illus.). 48p. (gr. 3 up). 1999. lib. bdg. 16.95 (*0-87226-285-5*, 62855B, P Bedrick Books) NTC Contemp Pub Co.

— Native Americans & Mesa Verde. LC 92-27758. (Hidden Worlds Ser.). (Illus.). 32p. (YA). (gr. 5 up). 1993. lib. bdg. 13.95 (*0-87518-540-1*, Dillon Silver Burdett) Silver Burdett Pr.

— The Normans. LC 91-40970. (Worlds of the Past Ser.). (Illus.). 64p. (YA). (gr. 6 up). 1992. lib. bdg. 21.00 (*0-02-762428-5*, Mac Bks Young Read) S&S Childrens.

— Over 900 Years Ago: With the Vikings. LC 93-2647. (History Detectives Ser.). (Illus.). 32p. (YA). (gr. 6 up). 1993. lib. bdg. 13.95 (*0-02-726325-8*, New Dscvry Bks) Silver Burdett Pr.

— Over Six Thousand Years Ago: In the Stone Age. LC 91-39458. (History Detectives Ser.). (Illus.). 32p. (YA). (gr. 6 up). 1992. lib. bdg. 20.00 (*0-02-762429-3*, Mac Bks Young Read) S&S Childrens.

— The Vikings & Jorvik. LC 92-25215. (Hidden Worlds Ser.). (Illus.). 32p. (J). (gr. 5 up). 1993. lib. bdg. 13.95 (*0-87518-541-X*, Dillon Silver Burdett) Silver Burdett Pr.

— What Do We Know about the Celts? (What Do We Know about...? Ser.). (Illus.). 40p. (YA). (gr. 3 up). 1993. lib. bdg. 18.95 (*0-87226-363-0*, 63630B, P Bedrick Books) NTC Contemp Pub Co.

Martell, Hazel M. & Bahn, Paul. The Kingfisher Book of the Ancient World: From the Ice Age to the Fall of Rome. LC 94-46005. (Illus.). 160p. (J). (gr. 4-8). 1995. 24.95 (*1-85697-565-7*) LKC.

Martell, Hazel Mary. Myths & Civilization of the Celts. (Myths & Civilization Ser.). 48p. 1999. lib. bdg. 16.95 (*0-87226-591-9*, 65919B, P Bedrick Books) NTC Contemp Pub Co.

— Roman Town. (Metropolis Ser.). (Illus.). (J). (gr. 3-7). 1998. pap. 8.95 (*0-531-15345-2*) Watts.

Martell, Helen M. What Do We Know about the Vikings? LC 92-7893. (What Do We Know about...? Ser.). (Illus.). 40p. (YA). (gr. 4-8). 1992. lib. bdg. 18.95 (*0-87226-355-X*, 6355XB, P Bedrick Books) NTC Contemp Pub Co.

Martell, Helvetia, jt. auth. see Kanellos, Nicolas.

***Martell, Joanne.** Millie-Christine: Fearfully & Wonderfully Made. LC 99-52515. (Illus.). 304p. 2000. 17.95 (*0-89587-194-7*); pap. 12.95 (*0-89587-188-2*) Blair.

Martell, Jocelan. Money Watchers: The Four Week Money Management Makeover. 50p. (Orig.). 1989. pap. write for info. (*0-9623255-0-3*) Empire Pubng CO.

Martell, John P. Brokers in Transportation: A Comprehensive History, Study & Guide on Motor Carrier Brokers of Property in the United States. rev. ed. 198p. 1988. pap. text 29.95 (*0-9621540-0-8*) Transmart.

— Today's Highways: A Comprehensive History, Study & Guide on Motor Carriers of Property in the United States. LC 88-51766. 200p. (Orig.). (C). 1989. pap. text 24.95 (*0-9621540-1-6*) Transmart.

Martell, Luke. Ecology & Society: An Introduction. LC 94-12254. 240p. (C). 1994. 45.00 (*0-87023-945-7*); pap. 17.95 (*0-87023-946-5*) U of Mass Pr.

Martell, Luke, jt. auth. see Driver, Stephen.

Martell, Luke, jt. ed. see Outhwaite, William.

Martell, Mary H. The Ancient Chinese. LC 92-9052. (Worlds of the Past Ser.). (Illus.). 64p. (YA). (gr. 6 up). 1993. lib. bdg. 14.95 (*0-02-730653-4*, Mac Bks Young Read) S&S Childrens.

***Martell, Mike.** Operation Hangman. (SEALs Strategic Warfare Ser.). 384p. 2000. mass mkt. 6.99 (*0-380-80827-7*) Morrow Avon.

— Operation No Man's Land. (SEALs Strategic Warfare Ser.). 400p. 2000. mass mkt. 6.99 (*0-380-80828-5*) Morrow Avon.

— Seals Mission, Bk. 3. Date not set. mass mkt. write for info. (*0-380-80829-3*) Morrow Avon.

Martell, Nevin. The Dave Matthews Band: Music for the People. (Illus.). 224p. 1999. per. 14.00 (*0-671-03544-4*, PB Trade Paper) PB.

Martell-Otero, Loida I., jt. ed. see Rodriguez, Jose D.

Martell, Ralph & Aesop. Aesop's Fables in Song. (Illus.). 21p. (J). (gr. k-5). 1987. 9.95 incl. audio (*0-941977-00-5*, RTB-1) Ralmar Enter.

Martell, Ralph G. Fish Tales & Other Stories to Get Hooked On. 1992. 24.95 (*0-9634828-0-7*) Pan Pr NY.

— Small Potatoes. 194p. 19.95 (*0-9634828-1-5*) Pan Pr NY.

Martell, Scott & Embry, Carmen, eds. Sanibel Captiva Review, Vol. I. (Illus.). 134p. 1997. pap. 9.95 (*0-9672431-0-6*) Sanibel Captiva.

— Sanibel Captiva Review, Vol. II. (Illus.). 132p. 1998. pap. 9.95 (*0-9672431-1-4*) Sanibel Captiva.

— Sanibel Captiva Review, Vol. III. (Illus.). 132p. 1999. pap. 9.95 (*0-9672431-2-2*) Sanibel Captiva.

Martell, William A. Greco-Roman Wrestling. LC 92-28782. (Illus.). 176p. 1993. pap. 21.95 (*0-87322-408-6*, PMAR0408) Human Kinetics.

Martella, Maureen. Just a Temp: Expectations & Experiences of Women Clerical Temporary Workers. (Illus.). 128p. 1997. reprint ed. pap. text 25.00 (*0-7881-4615-7*) DIANE Pub.

Martella, Ronald C., et al. Research Methods: Learning to Become a Critical Research Consumer. LC 98-7617. 586p. 1998. 77.00 (*0-205-27125-1*) Allyn.

Martellaro, James T., jt. auth. see Kuritz, Martin.

Martellaro, Joseph A. Economic Development in Southern Italy, 1950-1960. LC 65-15549. 139p. reprint ed. pap. 43.10 (*0-608-18732-1*, 202951500061) Bks Demand.

Martelli, Judith. Ricardo Walks the River Walk. (Illus.). 32p. Date not set. pap. 9.95 (*1-57168-262-7*, Eakin Pr) Sunbelt Media.

— Ricardo Walks the River Walk: The San Antonio River Walk. LC 98-209255. (Illus.). 32p. 1998. 14.95 (*1-57168-224-4*, Eakin Pr) Sunbelt Media.

Martelli, Len, et al. Going Places. (Our Nation, Our World Ser.). (gr. 2). 1983. text 17.20 (*0-07-039942-5*) McGraw.

Martelli, Leonard J., et al. When Someone You Know Has AIDS: A Practical Guide. 256p. 1987. 15.97 (*0-317-52879-3*, Crown) Crown Pub Group.

***Martelli, Mario.** An Introduction to Discrete Dynamical Systems & Chaos. LC 99-25865. 330p. 1999. 69.95 (*0-471-31975-9*) Wiley.

Martelli, Mario, ed. see Castillo-Chavez, C. & Cooke, K.

Martelli, Maurizio, ed. see Busenberg, Stavros N.

Martelli, Maurizio, ed. see Busenberg, Stavros N., et al.

Martello, Leo L. Reading the Tarot: Understanding the Cards of Destiny. LC 89-494121. (Illus.). 208p. (Orig.). 1990. pap. 8.95 (*0-89529-441-9*, Avery) Penguin Putnam.

Martello, Mary A., jt. auth. see Lesko, Matthew.

Martello, Mary A., ed. see Lesko, Matthew.

Martellotti, E. M. & Ernst, H. Physics of Metal Cutting. (Technical Papers: Vol. P226). (Illus.). 66p. 1942. pap. text 30.00 (*1-55589-214-0*) AGMA.

Martellucci, S., et al, eds. Laser Applications for Mechanical Industry. LC 93-10592. (NATO Advanced Study Institutes Series E, Applied Sciences; Vol. 238). 448p. (C). 1993. text 254.00 (*0-7923-2303-3*) Kluwer Academic.

Martellucci, S. & Chester, A. N. Diffractive Optics & Optical Microsystems: Proceedings of the 20th Course of the International School of Quantum Electronics Held in Erice, Italy, November 14-24, 1996. LC 97-40564. (Illus.). 432p. (C). 1997. 125.00 (*0-306-45770-9*, Plenum Trade) Perseus Pubng.

Martellucci, S. & Chester, A. N. Phase Transitions in Liquid Crystals. (NATO ASI Ser.: Vol. 290). (Illus.). 520p. (C). 1992. text 145.00 (*0-306-44213-2*, Kluwer Plenum) Kluwer Academic.

Martellucci, S. & Chester, Arthur N., eds. Optoelectronics for Environmental Science. LC 90-22278. (Ettore Majorana International Science Series, Life Sciences: Vol. 54). (Illus.). 302p. (C). 1990. 132.00 (*0-306-43806-2*, Plenum Trade) Perseus Pubng.

— Progress in Microemulsions. (Ettore Majorana International Science Series, Life Sciences: Vol. 41). (Illus.). 302p. 1989. 95.00 (*0-306-43212-9*, Plenum Trade) Perseus Pubng.

Martellucci, S., et al. Advances in Integrated Optics. (Illus.). 352p. (C). 1994. 105.00 (*0-306-44833-5*, Plenum Trade) Perseus Pubng.

***Martellucci, S., et al.** Optical Sensors & Microsystems: New Concepts, Materials, Technologies. LC 00-23898. 2000. write for info. (*0-306-46380-6*, Kluwer Plenum) Kluwer Academic.

Martelly, I., jt. auth. see Schmitz, W.

Martels, Zweder R. Von, see Von Martels, Zweder R., ed.

Marten, Cyndie. Math & Graphing Skills. Apple, Daniel K., ed. (Illus.). 89p. (C). 1992. pap. text 20.00 (*1-878437-21-6*) Pac Crest Soft.

Marten, G. C., et al. Persistence of Forage Legumes. 596p. 1989. 19.00 (*0-89118-098-2*) Am Soc Agron.

Marten, H. & Seelinger, D., eds. Physics & Chemistry of Fission. 405p. (C). 1992. text 195.00 (*1-56072-023-9*) Nova Sci Pubs.

Marten, Harry. The Art of Knowing: The Poetry & Prose of Conrad Aiken. LC 87-19840. 208p. 1988. text 27.50 (*0-8262-0654-9*) U of Mo Pr.

Marten, Jacqueline. Dream Walker. 1987. pap. 3.95 (*0-317-56906-6*) PB.

— Glory in the Flower. 432p. 1988. pap. 3.95 (*0-317-67363-7*) PB.

— Just a Kiss Away. 448p. 1995. mass mkt. 4.99 (*0-7860-0166-6*, Pinncle Kensgtn) Kensgtn Pub Corp.

Marten, James. The Children's Civil War. LC 97-43647. (Civil War America Ser.). (Illus.). 380p. 1998. 34.95 (*0-8078-2425-9*) U of NC Pr.

***Marten, James.** The Children's Civil War. LC 97-43647. (Civil War America Ser.). (Illus.). 380p. 2000. reprint ed. pap. 17.95 (*0-8078-4904-9*) U of NC Pr.

Marten, James. Texas. LC 93-215090. (World Bibliographical Ser.). 255p. 1992. lib. bdg. 79.25 (*1-85109-184-X*) ABC-CLIO.

— Texas Divided: Loyalty & Dissent in the Lone Star State, 1856-1874. LC 89-48256. 256p. 1990. 29.95 (*0-8131-1700-3*) U Pr of Ky.

Marten, James, ed. see Gist, Gladys L.

Marten, James A. Lessons of War: The Civil War in Children's Magazines. LC 98-15798. 259p. 1998. 55.00 (*0-8420-2654-1*, SR Bks); pap. 18.95 (*0-8420-2656-8*, SR Bks) Scholarly Res Inc.

Marten, Janet L. & Todman, Allen. Lutheran Church Basement Women. LC 91-67641. 1992. 10.95 (*0-9613437-6-1*) Redbird Prods.

Marten, Kay, jt. auth. see Nunn, Ron.

Marten, Laura. Turbio Descubrimiento. (Bianca Ser.). 1996. per. 3.50 (*0-373-33364-1*, 1-33364-0) Harlequin Bks.

Marten, Marty. Problem-Solving: Preventing & Solving Common Horse Problems. Vorhes, Gary, ed. (Illus.). 247p. 1998. pap. 17.95 (*0-911647-43-0*) Western Horseman.

Marten, Michael, jt. auth. see Henbest, Nigel.

Marten, Neville. Giants of Blues: Learn to Play Blues Guitar Like the All-Time Greats. 1999. pap. 25.95 (*1-86074-211-4*) Sanctuary Pubng.

— Star Guitars: Guitars & Players That Have Helped Shape Modern Music. (Illus.). 106p. (Orig.). (YA). (gr. 9-12). 1994. pap. 24.95 (*0-931759-83-8*, HL00000168) Centerstream Pub.

Marten, Phyllis. Why Papa Went Away & Other Stories. (Junior-Teen Companions Ser.). 112p. (YA). (gr. 8 up). 1988. pap. 4.95 (*0-919797-45-8*) Kindred Prods.

Marten, Rainer. Existieren, Wahrsein, und Verstehen: Untersuchung zur ontologischen Basis sprachlicher Verstaendigung. 376p. (C). 1972. 97.70 (*3-11-003583-9*) De Gruyter.

Marten, Timothy J., jt. auth. see Connell, Bruce F.

Martene, Anne Coulter & Sergel, Christopher. Lost Horizon. 133p. 1942. pap. 5.50 (*0-87129-868-6*, L30) Dramatic Pub.

Martens, Ann. Diplomatic Passport. fac. ed. (Illus.). 364p. 1996. pap. 9.00 (*0-614-18191-7*) Visual Studies.

Martens, Anne. Leftisms. 1994. 15.00 (*0-614-18205-0*) Visual Studies.

Martens, Anne C. Home for Christmas. 59p. 1954. pap. 3.50 (*0-87129-167-3*, H24) Dramatic Pub.

— If Boys Wore the Skirts. 1958. 3.25 (*0-87129-497-4*, I11) Dramatic Pub.

— If Girls Asked Boys for Dates. 1952. 3.50 (*0-87129-394-3*, I12) Dramatic Pub.

— Never Trust a Man. 1935. 3.50 (*0-87129-443-5*, N12) Dramatic Pub.

— Pajama Party. 1983. pap. 3.50 (*0-87129-289-0*, P12) Dramatic Pub.

— The Pied Piper. 83p. (J). (gr. 1 up). 1969. pap. 3.50 (*0-87129-784-1*, P23) Dramatic Pub.

— Whodunit? rev. ed. 1981. pap. 3.50 (*0-87129-328-5*, W25) Dramatic Pub.

— You, the Jury. 1965. pap. 3.50 (*0-87129-249-1*, Y12) Dramatic Pub.

Martens, Anne C., jt. auth. see Twain, Mark, pseud.

Martens, Anne C., ed. see Spence, Hartzell.

Martens, Anne Coulter, see Coulter Martens, Anne.

Martens, Bertin. Economic Development That Lasts: Labour Intensive Irrigation Projects in Nepal & the United Republic of Tanzania. xvii, 192p. 1989. pap. 24.75 (*92-2-106400-X*) Intl Labour Office.

Martens, Brian K., jt. auth. see Erchul, William P.

Martens, Charles R. Emulsion & Water-Soluble Paints & Coatings. LC 64-22873. 168p. 1964. 19.50 (*0-442-15558-1*) Krieger.

Martens, Claire. Clever Cornices, Valances, & Unique Window Treatments. LC 97-12798. (Illus.). 128p. 1997. 27.95 (*0-8069-0359-7*) Sterling.

— Great Window Treatments. (Illus.). 128p. 1998. pap. 14.95 (*0-8069-8647-6*) Sterling.

Martens, Claus-Peter, jt. ed. see Scott, Fiona.

Martens, E. A. God's Design: A Focus on Old Testament Theology. 3rd ed. LC 97-43195. 432p. 1997. pap. 19.95 (*0-941037-51-7*, BIBAL Press) D & F Scott.

Martens, Elmer A. Jeremiah. LC 86-9958. (Believers Church Bible Commentary Ser.). 328p. (Orig.). 1986. pap. 21.99 (*0-8361-3405-2*) Herald Pr.

— Old Testament Theology. LC 97-34326. (IBR Bibliographies Ser.). 144p. (C). 1997. pap. 11.99 (*0-8010-2146-4*) Baker Bks.

Martens, Elmer A., jt. auth. see Redekop, John H.

Martens, Els, jt. ed. see Jaccarini, Victor.

Martens, Frederick H. The Art of the Prima Donna & Concert Singer. Farkas, Andrew, ed. (Opera Biographies Ser.). (Illus.). 1977. reprint ed. lib. bdg. 30.95 (*0-405-09693-3*) Ayer.

— The Book of the Opera & the Ballet & the History of the Opera. LC 80-2289. reprint ed. 37.50 (*0-404-18857-5*) AMS Pr.

— The Chinese Fairy Book. LC 97-42627. (Children's Thrift Classics). (J). 1998. pap. 1.00 (*0-486-40140-5*) Dover.

— Leo Ornstein: The Man, His Ideas, & His Work. LC 74-29505. (Modern Jewish Experience Ser.). (Illus.). 1975. reprint ed. 16.95 (*0-405-06732-1*) Ayer.

— A Thousand & One Nights of Opera. LC 77-25416. (Music Reprint Ser.: 1978). 1978. reprint ed. lib. bdg. 49.50 (*0-306-77565-4*) Da Capo.

Martens, Frederick H., tr. see Bachmann, Alberto.

Martens, Frederick H., tr. see Flesch, Carl.

Martens, Frederick H., tr. see Jeritza, Maria.

***Martens, Gunther.** Ein Text Ohne Ende Fur Den Denkenden: Zum Verhaltnis Von Literatur Und Philosophie In Robert Musils Der Mann Ohne Eigenschaften. 199p. 1999. 37.95 (*3-631-34803-7*) P Lang Pubng.

Martens, Harold & Naes, Tormod. Multivariate Calibration. LC 89-14693. 438p. 1992. pap. 145.00 (*0-471-93047-4*) Wiley.

***Martens, Inger.** Paws for a Minute: People Training for Dog Owners. LC 00-29692. (Illus.). 192p. 2000. pap. 13.00 (*0-380-80478-6*) Morrow Avon.

Martens, Ione. The Savor of the Salt. LC 94-70089. 144p. 1994. pap. 9.95 (*0-9637515-1-4*) Dageforde Pub.

Martens, J., jt. ed. see Barth, E. M.

Martens, J. A., et al, eds. Preparation of Catalysts VI: Scientific Bases for the Preparation of Catalysts. (Studies in Surface Science & Catalysis: Vol. 91). 1204p. 1995. 389.50 (*0-444-82078-7*) Elsevier.

Martens, K., ed. Sex & Parthenogenesis - Evolutionary Ecology of Reproductive: Modes in Non-Marine Ostracods. (Illus.). 356p. 1998. 85.50 (*90-5782-017-X*) Backhuys Pubs.

Martens, K., jt. auth. see Horne, David J.

Martens, Karel, et al, eds. Karel Martens: Printed Matter. (Illus.). 144p. (Orig.). 1997. pap. 29.95 (*0-907259-11-1*) Princeton Arch.

Martens, Koen, et al, eds. Speciation in Ancient Lakes. (Advances in Limnology Ser.: Vol. 44). (GER., Illus.). x, 508p. 1994. pap. 112.00 (*3-510-47045-1*, Pub. by E Schweizerbartsche) Balogh.

***Martens, Lorna.** The Promised Land: Feminist Writing in the German Democratic Republic. (C). 2001. pap. text 19.95 (*0-7914-4860-6*) State U NY Pr.

— The Promised Land: Feminist Writing in the German Democratic Republic. (C). 2001. text 59.50 (*0-7914-4859-2*) State U NY Pr.

Martens, Lorna. Shadow Lines: Austrian Literature from Freud to Kafka. LC 95-39266. (Illus.). xii, 293p. 1996. text 49.50 (*0-8032-3186-5*) U of Nebr Pr.

M

Martens, Luc. High-Frequency Characterization of Electronic Packaging. LC 98-39319. (Electronic Packaging & Interconnects Ser.). 1998. 98.00 (*0-7923-8307-9*) Kluwer Academic.

Martens, Lydia. Exclusion & Inclusion: The Gender Composition of British & Dutch Work Forces. LC 96-79153. 265p. 1997. text 69.95 (*1-85972-458-2*, Pub. by Avebry) Ashgate Pub Co.

Martens, Lydia, jt. auth. see Warde, Alan.

Martens, M., ed. see Weurman Flavour Research Symposium Staff.

Martens, M. Hosmer & Mitter, S., eds. Women in Trade Unions: Organizing the Unorganized. xiv, 205p. 1994. pap. 15.75 (*92-2-108759-X*) Intl Labour Office.

Martens, Marianne, tr. see De Beer, Hans.

Martens, Marianne, tr. see Moers, Herman.

Martens, Marianne, tr. see Pfister, Marcus.

Martens, Marianne, tr. see Scheffler, Ursel.

Martens, Mark G., et al. Infectious Diseases in Women. 1020p. 2000. text. write for info. (*0-7216-7379-1*, W B Saunders Co) Harcrt Hlth Sci Grp.

Martens, Maximiliaan P. J., ed. Bruges & the Renaissance: Memling to Pourbus. LC 99-184213. (Illus.). 320p. 1999. 60.00 (*0-8109-6382-5*, Pub. by Abrams) Time Warner.

***Martens, Mert & Anderson, Marilyn.** Teaching American Diplomacy Using Primary Sources: The Establishment of the State of Israel. Bongiorno, Linda & Volker, Karen, eds. (Illus.). 125p. 1999. pap. 19.95 (*0-943804-03-5*) U of Denver Teach.

Martens, Olaf. Olaf Martens: The Recent Work. LC 97-149268. (Illus.). 176p. 1996. 49.95 (*3-908162-40-8*, Pub. by Edit Stemmle) Dist Art Pubs.

— Olaf Marten's Photographs. (Illus.). 128p. 1994. 45.00 (*3-905514-11-7*, Pub. by Edit Stemmle) Dist Art Pubs.

Martens, Phyllis, ed. see Becker, Nancy, et al.

Martens, Phyllis, jt. ed. see Schertz, Mary H.

Martens, Phyllis J. English 550: Teacher's Book of Game Cards. 268p. (Orig.). 1995. pap. 19.95 (*0-9650554-0-X*) English Five Fifty.

Martens, Pierre. Les Gnetophytes. (Handbuch der Pflanzenanatomie Encyclopedia of Plant Anatomy - Traite d' Anatomie Vegetale Ser.: Band XII, Teil 2). (GER., Illus.). 295p. 1997. 80.00 (*3-443-14005-X*, Pub. by Gebruder Borntraeger) Balogh.

Martens, Prisca. I Already Know How to Read: A Child's View of Literacy. LC 96-9461. 1996. pap. text 18.00 (*0-435-07226-9*) Heinemann.

Martens, Rainer. Coaches Guide to Sport Psychology. LC 87-16814. (Illus.). 208p. 1987. pap. text 24.00 (*0-87322-022-6*, BMAR0022) Human Kinetics.

— Indiana Criminal & Traffic Law Manual, 1994 Edition. 264p. 1994. 25.00 (*0-614-05848-1*, MICHIE) LEXIS Pub.

— Parent Guide to U. S. A. Junior Field Hockey. 52p. 1982. 4.00 (*0-317-01164-2*) US Field Hockey.

— Sport Competition Anxiety Test. LC 77-150176. (Illus.). 159p. reprint ed. pap. 49.30 (*0-608-06453-X*, 206729100009) Bks Demand.

— Successful Coaching. 2nd ed. LC 96-31259. (Illus.). 232p. 1996. pap. 19.95 (*0-88011-666-8*, PMAR0666) Human Kinetics.

— Youth Sport Director Guide. LC 94-28875. 264p. 1994. ring bd. 49.00 (*0-87322-751-4*, ACEP0480) Human Kinetics.

Martens, Rainer, ed. Joy & Sadness in Children's Sports. LC 78-107073. (Illus.). 370p. reprint ed. pap. 114.70 (*0-608-20828-0*, 207192700003) Bks Demand.

Martens, Rainer, et al. Competitive Anxiety in Sport. LC 89-38808. (Illus.). 288p. 1990. pap. text 25.00 (*0-87322-935-5*, BMAR0935) Human Kinetics.

***Martens, Rhonda.** Kepler's Philosophy & the New Astronomy. LC 00-36681. (Illus.). 216p. 2000. 37.50 (*0-691-05069-4*) Princeton U Pr.

Martens, Richard A., jt. auth. see Skinner, Sherlyn.

Martens, Ronny & Trachet, Tim. Making Sense of Astrology. LC 98-3528. (Illus.). 250p. 1998. 23.95 (*1-57392-218-8*) Prometheus Bks.

Martens, Sheri. Adam & Andrea Learn & Grow: Understanding Church Words from a Kid's Viewpoint. (Illus.). 80p. (J). (ps-5). 1989. pap. 7.95 (*0-919797-81-4*) Kindred Prods.

Martens, Tom, jt. auth. see Jeneid, Michael.

***Martens, Willem J. & Rotmans, Jan.** Climate Change: An Integrated Perspective. LC 99-52105. (Advances in Global Change Research Ser.). 414p. 2000. write for info. (*0-7923-5996-8*) Kluwer Academic.

Martensen, Daniel F., ed. Concordat of Agreement: Supporting Essays. LC 94-44791. 240p. 1995. pap. 15.00 (*0-8066-2667-4*, 10-26674, Augsburg) Augsburg Fortress.

— Concordat of Agreement--Supporting Essays. 240p. 1995. pap. 15.00 (*0-88028-161-8*, 1311) Forward Movement.

Martensen, Daniel F., jt. ed. see Griffiss, James E.

Martensen, Erich, ed. see Hao, Dinh Nho.

Martensen, Erich, ed. see Nho Hao, Dinh.

Martensen, Kirk. The Chicago Used Car Seller's Guide, Vol. 1. (Orig.). 1989. pap. 6.95 (*0-685-30130-3*) Green Light Pr.

— Used Car Seller's Guide. 144p. (Orig.). 1990. pap. text 6.95 (*0-9624853-0-6*) Green Light Pr.

Martenson, Dennis R. & Johnson, Walter K. Environmental Engineering. LC 82-72214. 763p. 1982. pap. 9.00 (*0-87262-311-4*) Am Soc Civil Eng.

Martenson, Russel E. Myelin: Biology & Chemistry. 976p. 1992. lib. bdg. 229.00 (*0-8493-8849-X*, QP752) CRC Pr.

Martensson, Alf. The Woodworker's Bible. LC 79-7355. (Illus.). 1979. 15.95 (*0-672-52607-7*, Bobbs) Macmillan.

— The Woodworker's Bible. LC 79-7355. 1982. pap. write for info. (*0-672-52717-0*) Macmillan.

— The Woodworkers Bible. 288p. 1985. pap. text 17.95 (*0-02-011940-2*) Macmillan.

Martensson, Bent, jt. auth. see Hinrichsen, Diederich.

Martensson, Kerstin. Applique the Kwik-Sew Way. (Illus.). 77p. 1988. pap. write for info. (*0-913212-11-3*) Kwik Sew.

— Kwik-Sew's Beautiful Lingerie. (Illus.). 80p. (Orig.). 1990. pap. write for info. (*0-913212-14-8*) Kwik Sew.

— Kwik-Sew's Method for Easy Sewing. (Illus.). 80p. (Orig.). 1991. pap. write for info. (*0-913212-15-6*) Kwik Sew.

— Kwik-Sew's Sewing for Baby. (Illus.). 94p. (Orig.). 1987. pap. write for info. (*0-913212-13-X*) Kwik Sew.

— Kwik-Sew's Sewing for Children. (Illus.). 80p. (Orig.). (J). 1993. pap. write for info. (*0-913212-17-2*) Kwik Sew.

— Kwik-Sew's Sewing for Toddlers. (Illus.). 80p. (Orig.). 1992. pap. write for info. (*0-913212-16-4*) Kwik Sew.

— Kwik-Sew's Sweatshirts Unlimited. (Illus.). 79p. (Orig.). 1989. pap. write for info. (*0-913212-12-1*) Kwik Sew.

— Kwik-Sew's Swim & Action Wear. (Illus.). 80p. 1995. pap. write for info. (*0-913212-18-0*) Kwik Sew.

Martenz, Arden. Conflict Resolution Bingo & Activities: A Program for Grades 5-10. 32p. 1995. 13.95 (*1-884063-72-1*) Mar Co Prods.

— Fears Way Series, Set. LC 93-81086. (J). (gr. 2-5). 1994. 32.95 (*1-884063-20-9*) Mar Co Prods.

— I Want What I Want When I Want It: A Program on Dealing with Anger. LC 94-80246. (Illus.). 48p. (Orig.). (J). (gr. 2-5). 1995. pap. 9.95 (*1-884063-48-9*) Mar Co Prods.

— Me & My Job: A Career Awareness Program for Grades 2-4. rev. ed. LC 96-79716. (Illus.). (Orig.). (J). (gr. 2-4). 1997. pap. 10.95 (*1-57543-017-7*) Mar Co Prods.

— Personalized Parenting Program, Grades K-12. (Orig.). 1995. pap. 450.00 (*1-884063-63-2*) Mar Co Prods.

Martenz, Arden & Miele, Robert. The Hate List: A Program on Anger Control. LC 95-75125. (Illus.). 24p. (Orig.). (J). (gr. 2-8). 1995. pap. 6.95 (*1-884063-47-0*) Mar Co Prods.

Martenz, Arden & Smith, Ken. S. C. P. Bingo: Bingo Game & Activity Book. LC 95-81935. (Illus.). 24p. 1996. 13.95 (*1-57543-001-0*) Mar Co Prods.

Martenz, Arden, jt. auth. see Cooper, JoAnn.

Martenz, Arden, jt. auth. see Smith, Ken.

Marter, A., jt. auth. see Johnson, A.

Marter, G. 100 Years of Development Through Science. 1995. pap. 135.00 (*0-85954-394-3*, Pub. by Nat Res Inst) St Mut.

Marter, Joan. Off Limits: Rutgers University & the Avant-Garde, 1957-1963. LC 98-37637. (Illus.). 256p. (C). 1999. 60.00 (*0-8135-2610-8*); pap. 30.00 (*0-8135-2609-4*) Rutgers U Pr.

Marter, Joan M. Alexander Calder. (Illus.). 318p. 1997. pap. text 24.95 (*0-521-58717-4*) Cambridge U Pr.

— Theodore Roszak: The Drawings. (Illus.). 96p. (Orig.). 1992. pap. 29.95 (*0-9633559-0-2*) Drawing Soc.

Marth & Steele, eds. Applied Dairy Microbiology. LC 97-43493. (Food Science & Technology Ser.). (Illus.). 536p. 1998. text 150.00 (*0-8247-0116-X*) Dekker.

***Marth, Del.** Florida Almanac. (Illus.). 488p. 2000. 23.00 (*1-56554-768-3*) Pelican.

— Florida Almanac, 2000-2001. 12th ed. (Illus.). 488p. 2000. pap. 15.95 (*1-56554-769-1*) Pelican.

Marth, Del & Marth, Martha J. The 1996 Florida Almanac. 12th ed. (Illus.). 520p. 1995. pap. 14.50 (*1-885034-03-2*) Suwannee River.

— St. Petersburg: Once Upon a Time: Memories of Places & People - 1890s to 1990s. (Illus.). 196p. (Orig.). 1996. pap. 19.95 (*1-885034-08-3*) Suwannee River.

Marth, Del & Marth, Marty. Marth's 1998 Florida Guide: State's Premier Media & Source Directory. 8th rev. ed. (Illus.). 200p. 1998. spiral bd. 39.50 (*1-885034-10-5*) Suwannee River.

— Marth's 1997 Florida Guide: State's Premier Media & Sources Directory. 7th rev. ed. 192p. (Orig.). 1997. pap., spiral bd. 39.50 (*1-885034-06-7*) Suwannee River.

— The 1998 Florida Almanac. 14th ed. (Illus.). 536p. (Orig.). 1997. pap. 14.50 (*1-885034-09-1*) Suwannee River.

— The 1999 Florida Almanac. 15th ed. 336p. 1998. pap. 14.50 (*1-885034-11-3*) Suwannee River.

— The 1997 Florida Almanac. 13th ed. (Illus.). 520p. (Orig.). 1996. pap. 14.50 (*1-885034-05-9*) Suwannee River.

Marth, Del & Martin, Martha J. Florida Almanac, 1998-1999. 12th ed. McGovern, Bernie, ed. 472p. 1998. pap. 14.95 (*1-56554-476-5*) Pelican.

Marth, Del, et al. Marth's 1999 Florida Guide: State's Premier Media & Source Directory. 9th rev. ed. (Illus.). 220p. 1999. spiral bd. 39.50 (*1-885034-12-1*) Suwannee River.

Marth, Elmer H. Dairy Foods Safety, 1995-1996: A Compendium of Edited Summaries from the World's Literature LC 98-70243. x, 710 p. 1998. write for info. (*0-917678-44-3*) Food & Nut Pr.

Marth, Elmer H., jt. auth. see Ryser, Elliot T.

Marth, Martha J., jt. auth. see Marth, Del.

Marth, Marty. Florida Cat Owner's Handbook. (Illus.). 128p. 1993. pap. 4.95 (*1-56164-008-5*) Pineapple Pr.

— Florida Dog Owner's Handbook. LC 89-49067. (Illus.). 175p. (Orig.). 1990. pap. 6.95 (*0-910923-72-8*) Pineapple Pr.

— Florida Horse Owner's Field Guide. 2nd ed. LC 98-24069. (Illus.). 208p. 1998. pap. 14.95 (*1-56164-154-5*) Pineapple Pr.

Marth, Marty, et al. Marth's 2000 Florida Guide: State's Premier Media & Source Directory. 10th rev. ed. (Illus.). 200p. 2000. spiral bd. 39.50 (*1-885034-14-8*) Suwannee River.

Marth, Marty, jt. auth. see Marth, Del.

Marth, Michael, et al. Four Valley Poets. LC 90-70715. 136p. (Orig.). 1990. pap. 10.95 (*0-9627031-0-9*) Stone & Scott Pubs.

Marth, Roald. Riches from Real Estate Technology. 240p. 1997. 24.95 (*0-7931-1849-2*, 1907-1801) Dearborn.

Martha, J. The Jurisdiction to Tax in International Law: Theory & Practice of Legislative Fiscal Jurisdiction. (Series on International Taxation). 238p. 1989. 106.00 (*90-6544-416-5*) Kluwer Law Intl.

Martha, Pelaez & Paul, Rothman. A Guide to Recalling & Telling Your Life Story. rev. ed. 270p. 1994. mass mkt. 15.00 (*1-893349-00-4*) Hospice Fndt Amer.

Martha Stewart Living. Desserts. LC 98-41866. (Illus.). 144p. 1998. pap. 20.00 (*0-609-80339-5*) C Potter.

***Martha Stewart Living.** Gardening from Seed: The Keys to Success with Flowers & Vegetables. 1999. pap. text 8.95 (*0-609-80665-3*, Crown) Crown Pub Group.

Martha Stewart Living, ed. Good Things. (J). 1997. pap. 20.00 (*0-614-27392-7*) C Potter.

Martha Stewart Living & Mitchell, Carolyn B. Great American Wreaths. (Best of Martha Stewart Living Ser.). (Illus.). 144p. 1996. pap. 20.00 (*0-517-88776-2*) Crown Pub Group.

— Great Parties: The Best of Martha Stewart Living. LC 97-30271. 144p. 1997. pap. 20.00 (*0-609-80099-X*) C Potter.

***Martha Stewart Living & Stewart, Martha.** Best of Martha Stewart Living Weddings. (Illus.). 256p. 1999. 50.00 (*0-609-60426-0*) C Potter.

Martha Stewart Living & Stewart, Martha. Good Things: A Collection of Inspired Household Ideas & Projects. LC 97-9508. (Best of Martha Stewart Living Ser.). 144p. 1997. pap. 20.00 (*0-517-88690-1*) Crown Pub Group.

Martha Stewart Living, et al. How to Decorate: A Guide to Creating Comfortable, Stylish Living Spaces. (Best of Martha Stewart Living Ser.). 144p. 1996. pap. 20.00 (*0-517-88780-0*) Crown Pub Group.

Martha Stewart Living Editors. Giving for the Holidays Vol. 3: Christmas with Martha Stewart Living. 144p. 1999. pap. 22.00 (*0-609-80440-5*) Crown.

***Martha Stewart Living Editors.** Good Things for Organizing. 2001. pap. 22.00 (*0-609-80594-0*) C Potter.

— The Martha Stewart Living Cookbook. Date not set. write for info. (*0-609-50338-3*) Crown Pub Group.

Martha Stewart Living Editors. What to Have for Dinner. 144p. 1996. 20.00 (*0-517-88681-2*) C Potter.

Martha Stewart Living Editors, ed. Handmade Christmas: The Best of Martha Stewart Living. LC 95-21291. 144p. 1995. pap. 20.00 (*0-517-88476-3*) C Potter.

***Martha Stewart Living Editors, ed.** Parties & Projects for the Holidays. (Illus.). 144p. 2000. pap. 22.00 (*0-609-80593-2*) C Potter.

***Martha Stewart Living Magazine Staff, ed.** Martha Stewart Living Cookbook. (Illus.). 2000. 35.00 (*0-609-60750-2*, Crown) Crown Pub Group.

Martha, Wickham. Superstars of Women's Track & Field. LC 96-32154. (Female Sports Stars Ser.). (Illus.). 64p. (J). (gr. 3 up). 1997. lib. bdg. 15.95 (*0-7910-4394-0*) Chelsea Hse.

Marthaler, Berard, ed. see McCarron, Richard E., et al.

Marthaler, Berard, ed. see Meyer, Charles, et al.

Marthaler, Berard, ed. see O'Donnell, Gabriel, et al.

Marthaler, Berard L. Catechism Yesterday & Today: A Short History. 176p. 1995. 21.95 (*0-8146-2353-0*) Liturgical Pr.

— Catechism Yesterday & Today: A Short History. 176p. 1995. pap. 15.95 (*0-8146-2151-1*) Liturgical Pr.

— The Creed: The Apostolic Faith in Contemporary Theology. rev. ed. LC 92-82595. 456p. (C). 1993. pap. 19.95 (*0-89622-537-2*) Twenty-Third.

Marthaler, Berard L., ed. Introducing the Catechism of the Catholic Church. LC 94-2648. 1994. pap. 11.95 (*0-8091-3495-0*) Paulist Pr.

— The Living Light Vol. 32, No. 4: Return to Virtue. 96p. (C). 1996. pap. 8.95 (*1-55586-071-0*) US Catholic.

— The Living Light 34:3 (Spring 1998) Mission & Missions. 96p. 1998. pap. 8.95 (*1-57455-156-6*) US Catholic.

— New Catholic Encyclopedia, Vol. 19. LC 80-84921. (Illus.). 596p. 1995. text 74.50 (*0-614-10331-2*) J Heraty Assocs.

***Marthaler, Berard L., et al.** The Living Light: Special Report - 1997 International Catechetical Congress. 96p. (C). 1998. pap. 8.95 (*1-57455-155-8*) US Catholic.

Marthaler, Berard L., ed. see Borelli, John, et al.

Marthaler, Berard L., ed. see Montague, George T., et al.

Marthaler, Berard L., ed. see O'Keefe, Mark, et al.

Marthaler, Berard L., ed. see Whalen, Michael D., et al.

Marthaler, Dennis G. Zen & the Art of Kicking Butts: The Ultimate Guide for Quitting Smoking Forever. 56p. (Orig.). 1995. pap. 8.95 (*0-9650994-0-7*) D G Marthaler.

Marthaler, L., jt. ed. see Berard.

Marthaler, Nancy. Promises in Poetry, Vol. 1. abr. ed. (Illus.). 100p. (C). 1989. reprint ed. pap. 8.50 (*0-9624310-9-5*) Words From the Heart Pub.

Martham, Anna. The Dark Drums. large type ed. 304p. pap. 18.99 (*0-7089-5411-1*) Ulverscroft.

Marthens, R. S. Advantages of Single Helical Gears. (Technical Papers: Vol. P3). (Illus.). 13p. 1934. pap. text 30.00 (*1-55589-399-6*) AGMA.

— Advantages of Sykes Herringbone Gears. (Technical Papers: Vol. P3A). (Illus.). 13p. 1934. pap. text 30.00 (*1-55589-396-1*) AGMA.

— The Application of Gearmotors. (Technical Papers: Vol. P184). (Illus.). 18p. 1938. pap. text 30.00 (*1-55589-433-X*) AGMA.

— Gearmotors - The New Combined Motor & Speed Reducer Units. (Technical Papers: Vol. P33). (Illus.). 24p. 1933. pap. text 30.00 (*1-55589-424-0*) AGMA.

Marthinsen, J., jt. auth. see Meier, H.

Marthinuss, George & Perry, Larry L. Bank Audit Manual, 3 vols., Vol. 1. LC HG1707.5. (AICPA Integrated Practice System Ser.). 412p. 1992. reprint ed. pap. 127.80 (*0-7837-4864-7*, 204439700001) Bks Demand.

— Bank Audit Manual, 3 vols., Vol. 2. LC HG1707.5. (AICPA Integrated Practice System Ser.). 414p. 1992. reprint ed. pap. 128.40 (*0-7837-4865-5*, 204439700002) Bks Demand.

— Bank Audit Manual, 3 vols., Vol. 3. LC HG1707.5. (AICPA Integrated Practice System Ser.). 396p. 1992. reprint ed. pap. 122.80 (*0-7837-4866-3*, 204439700003) Bks Demand.

— Bank Audit Manual Vol. 3. fac. ed. LC HG1707.5. (AICPA Integrated Practice System Ser.). 396p. 1992. reprint ed. pap. 122.80 (*0-7837-8254-3*, 204902200003) Bks Demand.

— Bank Audit Manual, 1992 Vol. 1. fac. ed. LC HG1707.5. (AICPA Integrated Practice System Ser.). 448p. 1992. pap. 138.90 (*0-7837-8252-7*, 204902200001) Bks Demand.

— Bank Audit Manual, 1992 Vol. 2. fac. ed. LC HG1707.5. (AICPA Integrated Practice System Ser.). 438p. 1992. reprint ed. pap. 135.80 (*0-7837-8253-5*, 204902200002) Bks Demand.

— Comprehensive Engagement Manual, Vol. 1. LC HF5635.M37. (AICPA Integrated Practice System Ser.). 265p. 1992. reprint ed. pap. 82.20 (*0-7837-4872-8*, 204440000001) Bks Demand.

— Comprehensive Engagement Manual, Vol. 2, Pt. 1. LC HF5635.M37. (AICPA Integrated Practice System Ser.). 318p. 1992. reprint ed. pap. 98.60 (*0-7837-4873-6*, 204440000002) Bks Demand.

— Comprehensive Engagement Manual, Vol. 3. fac. ed. LC HF5635.M37. (AICPA Integrated Practice Systems Ser.). 256p. 1992. pap. 79.40 (*0-7837-8244-6*, 204900900003) Bks Demand.

— Comprehensive Engagement Manual, Vol. 3, Pt. 2. LC HF5635.M37. (AICPA Integrated Practice System Ser.). 358p. 1992. reprint ed. pap. 111.00 (*0-7837-4874-4*, 204440000003) Bks Demand.

— Comprehensive Engagement Manual, Vol. 4. fac. ed. LC HF5635.M37. (AICPA Integrated Practice Systems Ser.). 238p. 1992. pap. 73.80 (*0-7837-8245-4*, 204900900004) Bks Demand.

— Comprehensive Engagement Manual, Vol. 4. LC HF5635.M37. (AICPA Integrated Practice System Ser.). 237p. 1992. reprint ed. pap. 73.50 (*0-7837-4875-2*, 204440000004) Bks Demand.

— Comprehensive Engagement Manual Vol. 1. fac. ed. LC HF5635.M37. (AICPA Integrated Practice Systems Ser.). 241p. 1992. pap. 74.80 (*0-7837-8242-X*, 204900900001) Bks Demand.

— Comprehensive Engagement Manual Vol. 2. fac. ed. LC HF5635.M37. (AICPA Integrated Practice Systems Ser.). 264p. 1992. pap. 81.90 (*0-7837-8243-8*, 204900900002) Bks Demand.

— Small Business Audit Manual, Vol. 1. fac. ed. LC HF5667.M25. (AICPA Integrated Practice System Ser.). 140p. 1992. pap. 43.40 (*0-7837-8240-3*, 204900800001) Bks Demand.

— Small Business Audit Manual, 3 vols., Vol. 1. LC HF5667.. (AICPA Integrated Practice System Ser.). (Illus.). 234p. reprint ed. pap. 72.60 (*0-7837-4869-8*, 204439900001) Bks Demand.

— Small Business Audit Manual, Vol. 2. fac. ed. LC HF5667.M25. (AICPA Integrated Practice System Ser.). 610p. 1992. pap. 189.10 (*0-7837-8241-1*, 204900800002) Bks Demand.

— Small Business Audit Manual, 3 vols., Vol. 2. LC HF5667.. (AICPA Integrated Practice System Ser.). (Illus.). 243p. reprint ed. pap. 75.40 (*0-7837-4870-1*, 204439900002) Bks Demand.

— Small Business Audit Manual, 3 vols., Vol. 3. LC HF5667.. (AICPA Integrated Practice System Ser.). (Illus.). 368p. reprint ed. pap. 114.10 (*0-7837-4871-X*, 204439900003) Bks Demand.

Marthinuss, George, et al. Construction Contractors' Audit Manual, Vol. 1. LC HF5686.. (AICPA Integrated Practice System Ser.). 442p. 1992. reprint ed. pap. 137.10 (*0-7837-4863-9*, 204439600001) Bks Demand.

— Construction Contractors' Audit Manual, Vol. 2. LC HF5686.. 434p. 1992. reprint ed. pap. 134.60 (*0-7837-4862-0*, 204439600002) Bks Demand.

— Construction Contractors' Audit Manual: Nonauthoritative Practice Aids, Vol. 1. LC 91-208700. (Small Firm Library). 441p. reprint ed. pap. 136.80 (*0-7837-2434-9*, 204258300001) Bks Demand.

— Construction Contractors' Audit Manual: Nonauthoritative Practice Aids, Vol. 2. LC 91-208700. (Small Firm Library). 217p. reprint ed. pap. 67.30 (*0-7837-2435-7*, 204258300002) Bks Demand.

— Construction Contractors' Audit Manual Vol. 2, Vol. 1. fac. ed. LC HF5686.. (AICPA Integrated Practice System Ser.). 442p. 1992. pap. 137.10 (*0-7837-8246-2*, 204901000001) Bks Demand.

— Construction Contractors' Audit Manual Vol. 2, Vol. 2. fac. ed. LC HF5686.. (AICPA Integrated Practice System Ser.). 464p. 1992. pap. 143.90 (*0-7837-8247-0*, 204901000002) Bks Demand.

M'Arthur, John, ed. see Macpherson, James.

Marthy, H. J., ed. Experimental Embryology in Aquatic Plants & Animals. LC 90-43958. (NATO ASI Ser.: Vol. 195). (Illus.). 418p. (C). 1990. text 156.00 (*0-306-43678-7*, Kluwer Plenum) Kluwer Academic.

Marti. Spirituality of Compassion: Studies in Luke. LC 96-84192. (Covenant Bible Studies). 1996. pap. 5.95 (*0-87178-004-6*) Brethren.

Marti, A., et al. Pequeno Diccionario Espanol-Polaco, Polaco-Espanol. (POL & SPA.). 707p. 1991. 24.95 (*0-8288-5749-0*, S32367) Fr & Eur.

An Asterisk (*) at the beginning of an entry indicates that the title is appearing for the first time.

Marti, Donald B. Historical Directory of American Agricultural Fairs. LC 85-27145. 309p. 1986. lib. bdg. 65.00 (*0-313-24188-0*, MDA/, Greenwood Pr) Greenwood.
— Women of the Grange: Mutuality & Sisterhood in Rural America, 1866-1920, 124. LC 91-11328. (Contributions in Women's Studies: No. 124). 168p. 1991. 47.95 (*0-313-25723-X*, MSG/, Greenwood Pr) Greenwood.

Marti, Donald B., Jr., jt. auth. see Kouhoupt, Rudy.

Marti, Ed & Spano, Michael F. The Credit Saver: How to Protect Yourself from the Credit Bureaus. 108p. 1993. 69.95 (*1-883685-00-1*) Pincushion Pr.

Marti, Ernst. The Four Ethers. LC 83-20156. 64p. (Orig.). 1984. pap. 7.95 (*0-935690-02-6*) Schaumburg Pubns.

Marti, Fritz. Religion, Reason & Man. LC 74-9353. 127p. 1974. 7.50 (*0-87527-141-3*) Green.
— The Unconditional in Human Knowledge: Four Early Essays (1794-1796) by F. W. J. Schelling. Schelling, Friedrich Wilhelm Joseph, tr. LC 77-74407. 272p. 1980. 37.50 (*0-8387-2020-X*) Bucknell U Pr.

Marti, Gerald E. Determining the Role of Environmental Exposures as Risk Factors for B-cell Lymphoproliferative Disorders. 246p. 1997. per. 14.00 (*0-16-061503-8*) USGPO.

Marti, Heinrich, tr. Rufin von Aquileia, De Ieiunio I, II, Zwei Predigten uber das Fasten nach Basileios von Kaisareia: Zwei Predigten uber das Fasten nach Basileios von Kaisareia. LC 89-35687. (Supplements to Vigiliae Christianae Ser.: Vol. 6). (GER.). xxxiii, 56p. 1989. 36.50 (*90-04-08897-0*) Brill Academic Pubs.

Marti i Pol, Miguel. Vacation Notebook Vol. 15: A Translation of Quadern de Vacances. Manye i Marti, Lourdes, ed. Cox, Wayne, tr. from SPA. (Catalan Studies: Translation & Criticism). XV, 100p. (C). 1995. pap. text 19.95 (*0-8204-2598-2*) P Lang Pubng.

Marti-Ibanez, Felix. To Be a Doctor. LC 68-27688. 1968. 4.95 (*0-910922-18-7*) MD Pubns.

Marti, J. RLISP '88: An Evolutionary Approach to Program Design. (Computer Science Ser.). 250p. 1993. text 61.00 (*981-02-1479-0*) World Scientific Pub.

Marti, J. T. Die Toxizitat von Zink, Schwefel und Stickstoffverbindungen auf Flechten-Symbionten. (Bibliotheca Lichenologica Ser.: No. 21). (Illus.). 130p. 1985. pap. text 30.00 (*3-7682-1426-5*) Lubrecht & Cramer.

Marti, J. T., ed. Introduction to Sobolov Spaces & Finite Element Solution of Elliptic Boundary Problems. Whiteman, John R., tr. 218p. 1987. text 70.00 (*0-12-474510-5*) Acad Pr.

Marti, James. Altenative Health & Medicine Encyclopedia. 2nd ed. LC 97-34696. (Illus.). 480p. 1997. 15.95 (*1-57859-020-5*, 00157234) Visible Ink Pr.
— The Alternative Health & Medicine Encyclopedia. 400p. 1994. 15.95 (*0-8103-8303-9*) Visible Ink Pr.
— Ultimate Consumer's Guide to Diets & Nutrition. LC 96-53266. 480p. 1997. pap. 16.00 (*0-395-72860-6*) HM.

Marti, James & Burton, Heather. Holistic Pregnancy & Childbirth. LC 98-27943. 304p. 1999. pap. 16.95 (*0-471-18509-4*) Wiley.

Marti, James E. The Alternative Health & Medicine Encyclopedia 1: The Authoritative Guide to Holistic & Nontraditional Health Practices. 2nd ed. LC 97-31144. 400p. 1997. 47.00 (*0-7876-0073-3*, 00108725) Gale.

Marti, Jed, et al. Semint: Seamless Model Integration. LC 94-27715. 1994. pap. text 7.50 (*0-8330-1567-2*, MR-403-OSD/A) Rand Corp.

Marti, Jorge L. El Periodismo Literario De Jorge Manach. LC 76-27678. (Coleccion Mente y Palabra). 333p. 1977. 5.00 (*0-8477-0542-0*); pap. 4.00 (*0-8477-0543-9*) U of PR Pr.

Marti, Jose. La Edad de Oro (The Golden Age) 5th ed. (SPA.). 1992. pap. 12.99 (*968-16-3503-5*, Pub. by Fondo) Continental Bk.
— Inside the Monster: Writings on the United States & American Imperialism. Randall, Elinor et al, trs. LC 74-21475. 384p. reprint ed. pap. 119.10 (*0-7837-3905-2*, 204375300010) Bks Demand.
— Jose Marti: Como una Lengua de Lava. De La Puebla, Manuel, ed. & intro. by. (SPA.). 152p. 1996. pap. 9.95 (*1-881708-13-6*) Edcnes Mairena.
— Jose Marti: Major Poems. Foner, Philip S., ed. Randall, Elinor, tr. LC 81-20016. 200p. 1982. 29.50 (*0-8419-0761-7*); pap. 17.00 (*0-8419-0834-6*) Holmes & Meier.
— Jose Marti Reader. LC 98-65908. 300p. 1998. pap. 19.95 (*1-875284-12-5*, 93393) Ocean Pr NJ.
— On Art & Literature: Critical Writings. Foner, Philip S., ed. Randall, Elinor, tr. LC 81-81697. 416p. 1982. 23.00 (*0-85345-589-9*, Pub. by Monthly Rev); pap. 15.00 (*0-85345-590-2*, Pub. by Monthly Rev) NYU Pr.
— On Education: Articles on Educational Theory & Pedagogy, & Writings for Children from the Age of Gold. Foner, Philip, ed. Randall, Elinor, tr. LC 79-2326. 320p. 1979. pap. 12.00 (*0-85345-565-1*, Pub. by Monthly Rev) NYU Pr.
— Political Parties & Elections in the United States. Foner, Philip S., ed. Randall, Elinor, tr. from SPA. 208p. (C). 1989. 27.95 (*0-87722-604-0*) Temple U Pr.

***Marti, Jose.** Versos sencillos: From Yo Soy un Hombre Sincero to La Nina de Guatemala. large type ed. Hofmann, Paul, tr. from SPA. 48p. 2000. pap. 5.00 (*0-9700519-0-5*) Hofmann NY.

Marti, Jose. Versos Sencillos (Simple Verses) Simple Verses. Tellechea, Manuel A., tr. LC 97-22189. (Recovering the U. S. - Hispanic Literary Heritage Ser.). (SPA.). 128p. 1997. pap. 12.95 (*1-55885-204-2*) Arte Publico.
— Los Zapaticos de Rosa (The Pink Shoes) (SPA., Illus.). (J). (ps up). 1997. 11.95 (*1-880507-33-1*) Lectorum Pubns.

Marti, Jose, jt. ed. see Granma.

Marti, Jose L., ed. see Gould, Peter & Stearns, Stephen.

Marti, Jose M. La Edad de Oro. 5th ed. (Coleccion Clasicos Cubanos). (SPA., Illus.). 218p. (Orig.). (J). (gr. 5). 1983. reprint ed. pap. 9.95 (*0-89729-028-3*) Ediciones.
— Mujer de Ayer y Hoy. (SPA., Illus.). 28p. (Orig.). 1988. pap. 3.00 (*0-685-24433-4*) Editorial El Coqui.

Marti, Judith, jt. ed. see Womack, Mari.

Marti, Kevin. Body, Heart, & Text in the "Pearl"-Poet. LC 91-29879. (Studies in Medieval Literature: Vol. 12). 220p. 1991. lib. bdg. 89.95 (*0-7734-9764-1*) E Mellen.

Marti, Kurt. Descent Directions & Efficient Solutions in Discretely Distributed Stochastic Programs. (Lecture Notes in Economics & Mathematical Systems Ser.: Vol. 299). 178p. 1988. 32.00 (*0-387-18778-2*) Spr-Verlag.

Marti, Kurt, ed. Stochastic Optimization: Numerical Methods & Technical Applications. (Lecture Notes in Economics & Mathematical Systems Ser.: Vol. 379). (Illus.). vii, 182p. 1992. 50.95 (*0-387-55225-1*) Spr-Verlag.

Marti, Kurt, ed. see GAMM/IFIP-Workshop on "Stochastic Optimization: Nu.

Marti, M. C. & Givel, J. C., eds. Surgery of Anorectal Diseases: With Pre-& Postoperative Management. 2nd ed. LC 98-37795. (Illus.). 500p. 1998. 220.00 (*3-540-63621-8*) Spr-Verlag.

Marti, Manuel, Jr. No Place to Hide: Crisis & Future of American Habitats, 50. LC 83-22762. (Contributions in Sociology Ser.: No. 50). (Illus.). 245p. 1984. 59.95 (*0-313-24271-2*, MNO/, Greenwood Pr) Greenwood.

Marti-Mestres, Gilberte, jt. auth. see Nielloud, Franpcoise.

Marti-Olivella, Jaume, ed. see Castellet, George C.

Marti, Oscar A. Economic Causes of the Reformation in England. LC 83-45586. reprint ed. 32.50 (*0-404-19904-6*) AMS Pr.

Marti, Othmar & Amrein, Matthias. STM & SFM in Biology. (Illus.). 331p. 1993. text 53.00 (*0-12-474500-8*) Acad Pr.

Marti, Othmar & Moller, Rolf, eds. Photons & Local Probes: Proceedings of the NATO Advanced Research Workshop, Reichenau, Germany, September 11-17, 1994. LC 95-37543. (NATO ASI Ser.: Vol. 300). 372p. (C). 1995. text 191.50 (*0-7923-3709-3*) Kluwer Academic.

Marti, Peter. Plastic Analysis of Reinforced Concrete Shear Walls. (IBA Ser.: No. 87). 19p. 1980. 12.50 (*0-8176-1065-0*) Birkhauser.

Marti, Roland, ed. Sauerwein - Girenas - Surowin. (Veroffentlichungen des Landschaftsverbandes Hildesheim Ser.: Bd. 7). 291p. 1997. 50.00 (*3-487-10299-4*) G Olms Pubs.

Marti, Tula. Un Azul Desesperado. LC 85-82349. (SPA.). 105p. (Orig.). 1985. pap. 7.95 (*0-89729-387-8*) Ediciones.

Marti, Willis F., jt. auth. see Pooch, Udo W.

Martial. Epigrams, 2 vols., 2. (Loeb Classical Library: No. 94-95). text 19.95 (*0-674-99106-0*) HUP.
— Martial Bk. V: The Epigrams. Howell, Peter, ed. & tr. by. from LAT. (Classical Texts Ser.). 176p. 1995. 59.99 (*0-85668-589-5*, Pub. by Aris & Phillips); pap. 22.00 (*0-85668-590-9*, Pub. by Aris & Phillips) David Brown.

Martial & Whigham, Peter. Letter to Juvenal. 120p. 1985. 21.95 (*0-85646-141-5*, Pub. by Anvil Press); pap. 14.95 (*0-85646-092-3*, Pub. by Anvil Press) Dufour.

Martial, F. Von, see Von Martial, F.

Martialis, Marcus Valerius Martialis. Epigrams from Martial. O'Connell, Richard, ed. LC 76-3066. (Translation Ser.: No. 3). 1976. pap. 10.00 (*0-912288-07-8*) Perivale Pr.
— Martialis, M. Valerius: Martial-Konkordanz. Siedschlag, Edgar, ed. (Alpha-Omega, Reihe A Ser.: Bd. XXXVIII). iv, 968p. 1979. write for info. (*3-487-06821-4*) G Olms Pubs.

Marticorena, Clodomiro. Bibliografia Botanica Taxonomica De Chile. (Monographs in Systematic Botany from the Missouri Botanical Garden: No. 41). 587p. 1992. 38.95 (*0-685-70546-3*) Miss Botan.

***Martien, Jerry.** Pieces in Place. 128p. 1999. pap. 10.95 (*0-942396-82-0*, Pub. by Blackberry ME) SPD-Small Pr Dist.

Martien, Jerry. Shell Game: A True Account of Beads & Money in North America. 224p. (Orig.). 1996. pap. 14.95 (*1-56279-080-3*) Mercury Hse Inc.

Martienssen, Anthony K. Queen Katharine Parr. LC 75-329565. x, 249p. 1973. write for info. (*0-436-27328-4*) M Secker & Warburg.
— Queen Katharine Parr. LC 73-14768. x, 249p. 1974. write for info. (*0-07-040610-3*) McGraw.

***Martienssen, W.** Landolt-Bornstein. (Numerical Data & Functional Relationships in Science & Technology Ser.). 465p. 1999. write for info. (*3-540-64734-1*) Spr-Verlag.

Martienssen, W. Landolt-Bornstein Vol. 27: Group III: Condensed Matter, Vol. 27. (Illus.). 308p. 1997. 1393.00 (*3-540-60877-X*) Spr-Verlag.
— Phase Diagrams & Physical Properties of Nonequilibrium Alloys: A Nonequilibrium Phase Diagrams of Ternary Amorphous Alloys, Vol. 37. 295p. 1997. 1372.00 (*3-540-60507-X*) Spr-Verlag.

***Martienssen, W., ed.** Compounds from BeBr<g> to ZrC12<g> (Numerical Data & Functional Relationships in Science & Technology Ser.). lviii, 415p. 1999. 2960.00 (*3-540-65344-9*) Spr-Verlag.
— Compounds with 1 to 7 Carbon Atoms. viii, 485p. 1999. 2984.00 (*3-540-66203-0*) Spr-Verlag.

Martienssen, W., ed. Landolt-Bornstein: Magnetic Properties of Non-Metallic Inorganic Compounds Based on Transition Elements, Vol. 27. (Group III Ser.). 345p. 1996. 1372.00 (*3-540-54627-8*) Spr-Verlag.

***Martienssen, W., ed.** Landolt-Bornstein Vol. 27: Group III: Condensed Matter, Set. viii, 388p. 2000. 2933.00 incl. cd-rom (*3-540-65596-4*) Spr-Verlag.

***Martienssen, W., et al, eds.** Landolt-Bornstein. (Numerical Data & Functional Relationships in Science & Technology Ser.). 373p. 1999. write for info. (*3-540-64735-X*) Spr-Verlag.
— Landolt-Bornstein: Alipathic & Aromatic Hydrocarbons, Steroids, Carbohydrates. (Numerical Data & Functional Relationships in Science & Technology - New Series: 35). viii, 310p. 2000. (*3-540-66780-6*) Spr-Verlag.
— Semiconductors: Supplement to Volume III/17 & III/22 Pt. B: II-VI & I-VII Compounds; Semimagnetic Compounds. (Landolt-Boernstein Numerical Data & Functional Relationships in Science & Technology - New Series: Vol. 41). xxvi, 721p. 1999. 4810.00 (*3-540-64964-6*) Spr-Verlag.

***Martienssen, W. & Beke, D. L., eds.** Diffusion in Semiconductors & Nonmetallic Solids Group 3: Condensed Matter. (Numerical Data & Functional Relationships in Science & Technology Ser.: Vol. 33). xviii, 578p. 1999. 3792.00 incl. cd-rom (*3-540-62391-4*) Spr-Verlag.

Martienssen, W. & Fischer, H., eds. Group II - Molecules & Radicals Vol. 18: Radical Reaction Rates in Liquids - Subvolume E - Biradicals, Radicals in Excited States, Carbenes & Related Species. xiii, 424p. 1998. 2500.00 incl. cd-rom (*3-540-62392-2*) Spr-Verlag.

Martienssen, W. & Marsh, K. N., eds. Landolt-Bornstein Vol. 8: Thermodynamic Properties of Organic Compounds & Their Mixtures. (Illus.). 600p. 1995. 2700.95 (*3-540-58854-X*) Spr-Verlag.
— Thermodynamic Properties of Organic Compounds & Their Mixtures Subvolume B: Densities of Aliphatic Hydrocarbons: Alkanes. (Landolt-Bornstein Numerical Data & Functsonal Relationship in Science & Technology New Series: Vol. 8). (Illus.). x, 410p. 1996. 1682.00 (*3-540-61029-4*) Spr-Verlag.

Martienssen, W. & Nelson, D. F., eds. High Frequency Properties of Dielectric Crystals Vol. A: Piezooptic & Electrooptic Constants. (Landolt-Bornstein - Numerical Data & Functional Relationships in Science & Technology Series, Group III: Vol. 30). xii, 497p. 1996. 2027.00 (*0-387-54412-7*) Spr-Verlag.

Martienssen, W. & Schopper, H., eds. Landolt-Bornstein Vol. 13: Production of Radionuclides at Intermediate Energies. (Illus.). 526p. 1995. 2376.95 (*3-540-59049-8*) Spr-Verlag.

***Martienssen, W. & Wijn, H. P. J., eds.** Magnetic Properties of Metals: Supplement to Volume 19 Pt. B: Alloys & Compounds of d-Elements with Main Group Elements, Pt. 1. (Landolt-Boernstein Numerical Data & Functional Relationships in Science & Technology - New Series: Vol. 32). (Illus.). xiv, 348p. 1999. 2402.00 incl. cd-rom (*3-540-62472-4*) Spr-Verlag.

Martienssen, W., jt. auth. see Madelung, Otfried.

Martienssen, W., ed. see Claridge, R. F. & Dohrmann, J.

Martienssen, W., ed. see Demaison, J., et al.

Martienssen, W., ed. see Goldmann, A., et al.

Martienssen, W., ed. see Guelachvili, G. & Rao, K. N.

Martienssen, W., jt. ed. see Kuchitsu, K.

Martienssen, W., ed. see Landolt-Bornstein.

Martienssen, W., jt. ed. see Madelung, Otfried.

Martienssen, W., ed. see Predel, B.

Martienssen, W., jt. ed. see Schopper, H.

Martienssen, W., jt. ed. see Wijn, H. P.

Martienssen, W., ed. see Wohlfahrt, C. & Wohlfahrt, B.

Martienssen, W., ed. see Wohlfarth, C. & Lechner, M. D.

Martig, Renee. Vanishing Wildlife. (Illus.). (Orig.). 1989. pap. 9.95 (*0-9622625-0-1*) Timberline Colorado.

Martignette, Charles G. Great American Pin-Up. (Jumbo Ser.). 1996. 39.99 (*3-8228-8497-9*) Taschen Amer.

Martignette, Charles G & Meisel, Louis K. Gil Elvgren: American Pin-Ups. (Illus.). 280p. 1999. 39.99 (*3-8228-6611-3*) Taschen Amer.

Martignoni, M. & Schonenberger. Precision Fixed Prosthodontics. Clinical & Laboratory Aspects. Pittwood & Rutter, trs. from ITA.Tr. of Precisione e Contorno nella Ricostruzione Protesica. (Illus.). 579p. 1990. text 188.00 (*0-86715-214-1*) Quint Pub Co.

Martignoni, Mauro E. & Iwai, Paul J. A Catalog of Viral Diseases of Insects, Mites, & Ticks. 60p. 1997. reprint ed. 12.75 (*0-89904-617-7*, Wildlife Resrch Grp); reprint ed. pap. 7.00 (*0-89904-618-5*, Wildlife Resrch Grp) Crumb Elbow Pub.

***Martignoni, Steve & Rota, Luciani.** Extreme Mountain Biking. (Illus.). 128p. 2000. pap. 35.99 (*0-7893-0408-2*) Universe.

Martimort, Aime G. Deaconesses: An Historical Study. Whitehead, Kenneth D., ed. LC 86-81423.Tr. of Les Diaconesses essai Historique. 257p. 1996. reprint ed. pap. 14.95 (*0-89870-114-7*) Ignatius Pr.

Martimort, Aime G., ed. Church at Prayer, 4 vols., Set. 1985. pap. 57.50 (*0-8146-1574-0*) Liturgical Pr.
— The Church at Prayer One Volume Edition: An Introduction to the Liturgy. LC 92-28775. 1252p. 1992. 49.95 (*0-8146-2209-7*) Liturgical Pr.

Martimort, Aime G., et al. The Church at Prayer Vol. I: Principles of the Liturgy. O'Connell, Matthew J., ed. & tr. by. 316p. 1987. pap. 15.95 (*0-8146-1363-2*) Liturgical Pr.
— The Church at Prayer Vol. III: The Sacraments. Sicard, Damien, ed. O'Connell, Matthew, tr. from FRE.Tr. of L'/Eglise en Priere. 337p. 1988. pap. 15.95 (*0-8146-1365-9*) Liturgical Pr.

Martimort, Aime G., ed. see Cabie, Robert, et al.

Martimort, Aime G., ed. see Dalmais, I. H. & Jounel, Pierre.

Martimort, David, ed. Agricultural Markets: Mechanisms, Failures, & Regulations. LC 96-16806. (Contributions to Economic Analysis Ser.: Vol. 234). 496p. 1996. text 115.00 (*0-444-82481-2*, North Holland) Elsevier.

Martin. Adult Development. (C). 2000. text. write for info. (*0-15-506821-0*) Harcourt.
— Almanac of Women & Minorities in World Politics. LC 99-57270. 300p. 2000. 49.00 (*0-8133-6805-7*, Pub. by Westview) HarpC.
— America & Its People: Instructor's Resource Manual. 3rd ed. 18.00 (*0-673-97412-X*) Addson-Wesley Educ.
— America Through the Eyes of Its People. 2nd ed. LC 97-148049. 352p. (C). 1997. pap. text 21.00 (*0-673-97738-2*) Addison-Wesley.
— America Thru Their Eyes. (C). 1997. 46.00 (*0-321-80094-X*) Addison-Wesley.

***Martin.** Anatomy & Physiology. 338p. 1999. pap. text 33.00 (*0-536-02835-4*) Pearson Custom.
— Anatomy & Physiology Fetal Pig Dissect. 512p. 2000. spiral bd., lab manual ed. 60.00 (*0-07-231199-1*) McGraw.

Martin. Basic Concepts in Music. (Music Ser.). 1967. pap. 10.50 (*0-534-00636-1*) Wadsworth Pub.
— A Beasty Story. LC 97-49519. 40p. (J). 1999. 16.00 (*0-15-201683-X*, Harcourt Child Bks) Harcourt.
— The Bells of St. Mary. 1999. pap. 8.95 (*0-312-03292-7*) St Martin.

***Martin.** Bird Yard. 1999. mass mkt. write for info. (*0-312-97138-9*) St Martin.

Martin. British Game Shooting. (Illus.). 172p. 1988. 29.95 (*1-57157-008-X*) Safari Pr.
— The Cobbler. 32p. (J). (ps-2). 1998. write for info. (*0-7459-3815-9*, Chariot Bks) Chariot Victor.
— Colonial American Travel Narratives. (C). 1997. pap. text. write for info. (*0-321-02611-X*) Addson-Wesley Educ.
— Command Performance. 256p. 1994. 29.95 (*0-07-103598-2*) McGraw.
— The Complete Guide to Airbrushing Techniques & Materials. 1992. 14.98 (*0-89009-527-2*) Bk Sales Inc.
— Concise History America & Its People. 1998. text (*0-673-98099-5*) Addison-Wesley.
— Contribution to Paleontology West Ct: In Honor of V. Standish Mallory. LC 97-16477. (Thomas Burke Memorial Washington State Museum Research Report Ser.: No. 6). (Illus.). 312p. 1997. pap. 45.00 (*0-295-97560-1*) U of Wash Pr.
— Course Syllabus for Craig Martin. (Adaptable Courseware-Softside Ser.). Date not set. 1.00 (*0-534-56573-5*) Wadsworth Pub.
— Designing Object Oriented C++ 2001. pap. 52.00 (*0-13-597444-5*) P-H.
— Discovering Microsoft Office. 2nd ed. (C). 1999. pap. text 35.50 (*0-03-025618-6*, Pub. by Harcourt Coll Pubs) Harcourt.
— Discovering Microsoft Office 97. LC 97-68511. (C). 1997. pap. text 32.00 (*0-03-025078-1*) Harcourt Coll Pubs.
— Doing Psychology. 2nd ed. (Psychology Ser.). 1985. text. write for info. (*0-534-03808-5*) Brooks-Cole.
— Elementary Algebra. 1995. teacher ed. 45.31 (*0-07-062599-9*) McGraw.
— Elementary Science Methods: A Constructivist Approach. 96p. 1996. teacher ed. 16.00 (*0-8273-7175-6*) Delmar.
— End of Days. 1950. text 25.00 (*0-8050-3918-X*) St Martin.
— Entre Lineas. 2nd ed. (College Spanish Ser.). (SPA.). (C). 1991. teacher ed. 21.95 (*0-8384-2205-5*) Heinle & Heinle.
— Excel 5.0 Windows SFU. (C). 1997. spiral bd. write for info. (*0-15-505061-3*) Harcourt Coll Pubs.
— Fishing & Whaling. (Illus.). 88p. 1995. pap. 6.95 (*0-948636-67-X*, 667X, Pub. by Natl Mus Scotland) A Schwartz & Co.

Martin. General Theory of Secularization. 368p. 1993. 72.95 (*0-7512-0194-4*) Ashgate Pub Co.

Martin. German Writers of the Great War. 1999. text 59.95 (*0-312-22391-9*) St Martin.
— Handbook of Office Gynecology. 1994. 185.00 (*0-07-105450-2*) McGraw.
— Handbook Pharmacy Health Education. 1991. 66.00 (*0-85369-263-7*, Pub. by Pharmaceutical Pr) Rittenhouse.
— Healing Mind. 384p. 1999. pap. 16.95 (*0-312-24300-6*) St Martin.
— How to Help an Alcoholic. 36p. 1986. pap. 2.95 (*0-914733-05-2*) Desert Min.
— Humanities Through Art & Custom Publishing. 1994. 19.25 (*0-07-049380-4*) McGraw.
— Introduction to Language/Theory Computation. 1991. student ed. 13.43 (*0-07-040772-X*) McGraw.

***Martin.** Kat Martin Promotion. 1998. mass mkt. write for info. (*0-312-96758-6*) St Martin.
— Kein Schnaps fur Tamara: Level B. text 8.95 (*0-88436-282-5*) EMC-Paradigm.

Martin. Learn Think Critically. (C). 1997. pap. text 14.00 (*0-673-55217-9*) Addison-Wesley.
— The Maestro Plays. 101. 13.95 (*0-15-200259-6*) Harcourt.
— Mammalogy. 3rd ed. 352p. 2000. spiral bd. 28.13 (*0-697-00643-3*) McGraw.
— Manual of ERCP. (C). 1998. text 169.00 (*0-443-05117-8*, W B Saunders Co) Harcrt Hlth Sci Grp.
— Maryanne & Camp. 1995. pap. 7.98 (*1-57042-265-6*) Warner Bks.
— MAST Tod Sfwr-Microcomputer CO. 3rd ed. (C). 1996. pap. text 26.50 (*0 03 013914-7*, Pub. by Harcourt Coll Pubs) Harcourt.
— MAST TOD SWR-QUATTRO PRO 4.0 M. 2nd ed. LC 95-100838. (C). 1994. pap. text, lab manual ed. 22.50 (*0-03-098228-6*, Pub. by Harcourt Coll Pubs) Harcourt.
— MASTERING TOD SWR-PARADOX 4.0. 2nd ed. LC 94-236560. (C). 1994. pap. text, lab manual ed. 22.50 (*0-03-097925-0*, Pub. by Harcourt Coll Pubs) Harcourt.
— Mastering Today's Software: Access 2000. LC 99-217112. (C). 1999. pap. text 25.50 (*0-03-025992-4*) Harcourt.
— Mastering Today's Software: Access 7.0 for Windows. LC 96-206076. (C). 1996. lab manual ed. write for info. (*0-03-017334-5*) Harcourt Coll Pubs.

— Mastering Today's Software: Approach 97. (C). 1997. pap. write for info. (*0-03-019697-3*) Harcourt Coll Pubs.
— Mastering Today's Software: Custom (Laurentian University) (C). 1995. lab manual ed. write for info. (*0-15-555582-0*) Harcourt Coll Pubs.
— Mastering Today's Software: DBase IV. 2nd ed. (C). 1994. lab manual ed. write for info. (*0-15-555422-0*) Harcourt Coll Pubs.
— Mastering Today's Software: Excel 2000. LC 99-217097. (C). 1999. pap. text 25.50 (*0-03-025993-2*) Harcourt.
— Mastering Today's Software: Extended Microcomputer Concepts. 3rd ed. LC 97-126904. (C). 1996. pap. text 33.50 (*0-03-014067-6*) Harcourt.
— Mastering Today's Software: Freelance Graphics. (C). 1996. pap. text 20.50 (*0-03-019674-4*) Harcourt Coll Pubs.
— Mastering Today's Software: Internet Explorer. (C). 1998. pap. text 24.00 (*0-03-021307-X*) Harcourt Coll Pubs.
— Mastering Today's Software: Lotus Smart Suite 97. (C). 1997. pap. write for info. (*0-03-019568-3*) Harcourt Coll Pubs.
— Mastering Today's Software: Lotus 1-2-3/Windows. LC 95-135860. (C). 1994. pap. text, lab manual ed. 17.50 (*0-03-011073-4*) Harcourt.
— Mastering Today's Software: Microcomputer Concepts. 2nd ed. (C). 1994. pap. text 22.75 (*0-03-098586-2*) Harcourt Coll Pubs.
— Mastering Today's Software: Microsoft Office Windows 95. (C). 1995. pap. text 59.00 (*0-03-018138-0*) Harcourt Coll Pubs.
— Mastering Today's Software: Outlook 2000. LC 99-229998. (C). 1999. pap. text 25.50 (*0-03-025994-0*) Harcourt.
— Mastering Today's Software: PowerPoint 7.0 Windows 95. LC 96-153471. (C). 1996. lab manual ed. write for info. (*0-03-017339-6*) Harcourt Coll Pubs.
— Mastering Today's Software: Windows NT 4.0. (C). 1998. text 24.00 (*0-03-027304-8*) Harcourt Coll Pubs.
— Mastering Today's Software: Windows 3.1. (C). 1994. pap. text, teacher ed. 66.50 (*0-03-004157-0*) Harcourt.
— Mastering Today's Software: Word 2000. (C). 1999. pap. text 25.50 (*0-03-025991-6*) Harcourt.
— Mastering Today's Software: Work Pro. (C). 1997. pap. write for info. (*0-03-019684-1*) Harcourt Coll Pubs.
— Models in Financial Management. 5th ed. (C). 1991. 16.00 (*0-13-060906-4*, Macmillan Coll) P-H.
Martin. Modern Short Stories. 160p. 1993. pap. text 21.33 (*0-13-481805-9*) P-H.
Martin. MTS Lotus1-2-3 Release 5.0 for Windows. LC 96-104040. (C). 1996. pap. text, lab manual ed. 22.50 (*0-03-016307-2*, Pub. by Harcourt Coll Pubs) Harcourt.
— MTS: Wordperfect 6.0 for Windows. LC 95-215612. (C). 1996. pap. text 22.50 (*0-03-016304-8*, Pub. by Harcourt Coll Pubs) Harcourt.
— Netscape Navigator 3.0. LC 99-162391. (C). 1998. pap. text 25.00 (*0-03-024314-9*) Harcourt Coll Pubs.
***Martin.** On Ayer. 2000. pap. 8.25 (*0-534-58370-9*) Wadsworth Pub.
— Organizational Behaviour. (Illus.). 608p. 1999. mass mkt. 32.95 (*0-412-60960-6*, Chap & Hall NY) Chapman & Hall.
Martin. Paradox 4.0, 1993: Production Software Guide. LC 93-71454. (C). 1993. pap. text 9.75 (*0-03-098358-4*) Harcourt Coll Pubs.
***Martin.** PC Concepts. 2nd ed. (C). 1999. pap. text. write for info. (*0-03-025969-X*) Harcourt Coll Pubs.
— Pediatric Balance Program. (C). 1999. pap. text 45.00 (*0-12-785025-2*) Acad Pr.
Martin. Pediatric Balance Program. 1998. 45.00 (*0-7616-6020-8*) Commun Skill.
***Martin.** Plastic Mater Data Handbook. 2002. pap. 125.00 (*0-07-135921-4*) McGraw.
Martin. The Polynesian Journal of Captain Martin. (Australian National University press Ser.). 1996. write for info. (*0-08-033033-9*, Pergamon Pr) Elsevier.
***Martin.** Portfolio Planner. LC 99-160578. viii, 87p. 1999. pap. text. write for info. (*0-13-081314-1*) S&S Trade.
Martin. Practical Food Inspection. 9th ed. (Illus.). 827p. (C). 1978. text 80.95 (*0-7186-0435-0*) Chapman & Hall.
— Preacher. 1999. write for info. (*0-316-54710-7*) Little.
— Prealgebra. 2nd ed. 1997. pap. text, student ed. 29.33 (*0-13-258229-5*) P-H.
— Q-Basic: A Short Course. (C). 1995. lab manual ed. write for info. (*0-15-555519-7*) Harcourt Coll Pubs.
— Q-Basic: A Short Course. (C). 1995. pap. text 20.50 (*0-15-504304-8*) Harcourt Coll Pubs.
— Quattro Pro 4.O: Production Software Guide, 1993. LC 93-71330. (C). 1993. pap. text 9.75 (*0-03-098359-2*) Harcourt Coll Pubs.
— Reaching Your Goal, 8 bks., Set I, Reading Level 2. (Illus.). 192p. (J). (gr. 1-4). 1987. 87.60 (*0-685-58796-7*) Rourke Corp.
— A Recent Martyr. 1989. 7.95 (*0-07-558689-4*) McGraw.
Martin. Roman Land Transportation. (Illus.). (C). text. write for info. (*0-472-10753-4*) U of Mich Pr.
Martin. Sing a Song of Christmas. 1991. pap. 8.95 (*1-55897-213-7*) Brentwood Music.
— Stacey & Mystery, Vol. 1. 1994. 7.98 (*1-57042-143-9*) Warner Bks.
***Martin.** Steps in the Process. 2001. pap. text 23.00 (*0-07-239333-5*) McGraw.
Martin. Successful Engineer. 1993. teacher ed. 26.25 (*0-07-040790-8*) McGraw.
***Martin.** Summers Will Never be the Sam. 2000. 22.95 (*1-85225-232-4*, Pub. by Transworld Publishers Ltd) Trafalgar.
— Summers Will Never Be the Same. 2000. pap. 12.95 (*0-552-99631-9*, Pub. by Transworld Publishers Ltd) Trafalgar.
Martin. Take Look Observation Portfolio. (C). 1994. pap. text 23.96 (*0-201-58857-9*) Addison-Wesley.
— The Theory of Finance. (C). 1988. pap. text, teacher ed. 36.75 (*0-03-063856-9*) Harcourt Coll Pubs.
— Think It - Say It. 1990. 36.00 (*0-7616-7648-1*) Commun Skill.
— Wicked Promise, Vol. 1. 1998. write for info. (*0-312-96733-0*) Tor Bks.
— Windows NT 4.0 Server: Accelerated MCSE Study Guide. LC 98-37009. 1998. pap. 24.99 (*0-07-067697-6*) McGraw.
— WordPerfect 5.2 for Windows, 1995: Production Software Guide. 4th ed. LC 94-76248. (C). 1994. pap. text 9.75 (*0-03-098231-6*) Harcourt Coll Pubs.
— WordPerfect 6.0 for Windows: Production Software Guide. (C). 1995. pap. text 9.75 (*0-03-010817-9*) Harcourt.
Martin. Worked Examples in Strength of Metals & Alloys. 1983. 15.00 (*0-901462-23-3*) Institute of Management Consultants.
Martin. Writing Wisely & Well. 1993. pap. text, teacher ed. 12.81 (*0-07-023473-6*) McGraw.
Martin, ed. America & Its People, Vol. 1. 3rd ed. (C). 1997. pap. text, student ed. 21.56 (*0-673-98076-6*) Addison-Wesley.
— America & Its People, Vol. 2. 3rd ed. (C). 1997. pap. text, student ed. 25.00 (*0-673-98077-4*) Addison-Wesley.
— Lucreti, T. Cari. 6th ed. (LAT.). 1992. reprint ed. pap. 27.95 (*3-8154-1518-7*, T1518, Pub. by B G Teubner) U of Mich Pr.
— Times That Tried Mens Souls. (C). Date not set. pap. write for info. (*0-06-044211-5*) HarpC.
Martin & Archambault, John. Boom Chicka Rock. (J). 14.00 (*0-671-88689-4*) S&S Bks Yung.
Martin & Borteck. New Jersey Estate Planning, Will Drafting & Estate Administration Issue 9, 2 vols. 150p. 1998. ring bd. write for info. (*0-327-00801-6*, 8210214) LEXIS Pub.
Martin & Clark. Introduction to Audiology: Review Manual. 5th ed. LC 99-462666. 265p. 1999. pap. text 28.00 (*0-205-29537-1*) Allyn.
Martin & Ellis, Albert. Cage & Aviary Birds. 1980. pap. 16.95 (*0-685-43766-3*) Viking Penguin.
Martin & Franklin. Analyzing Multicultural Teaching & Learning Styles. 360p. (C). 1998. per. 66.95 (*0-7872-5384-7*, 41538401) Kendall-Hunt.
Martin & Greene. Intermediate Algebra. 1997. pap. text, student ed. 27.40 (*0-13-850306-0*) P-H.
Martin & Gunter. Communicate & Comphrehend Bk. 3. 1994. pap. text. write for info. (*0-582-80147-8*, Pub. by Addison-Wesley) Longman.
— Communicate & Comphrehend Bk. 4. 1994. pap. text. write for info. (*0-582-80146-X*, Pub. by Addison-Wesley) Longman.
— Communicate & Comprehend Bk. 1. 1994. pap. text. write for info. (*0-582-80149-4*, Pub. by Addison-Wesley) Longman.
— Communicate & Comprehend Bk. 5. 1994. pap. text. write for info. (*0-582-80145-1*, Pub. by Addison-Wesley) Longman.
***Martin & Jackson.** Personnel Practice 1997. 192p. 2000. pap. 44.95 (*0-8464-5130-1*) Beekman Pubs.
— Personnel Practice 2000. 208p. 2000. pap. 44.95 (*0-8464-5181-6*) Beekman Pubs.
***Martin & Kotkin, Martin.** Miami: Tempting Tropical Tastes. 1999. pap. 15.95 (*0-8050-5674-2*) St Martin.
Martin & Kramer, Bruce M. Law of Pooling & Utilization: Voluntary, Compulsory, 4 vols. 1957. ring bd. 500.00 (*0-8205-1455-1*) Bender.
Martin & Lieberth. Computer Competency. (C). 2001. pap. 37.00 (*0-205-19444-3*) Allyn.
***Martin & Lii, Battle.** A Guide to Real Estate Licensing Examinations. (C). 2000. text 55.00 (*0-324-05978-7*) Sth-Wstrn College.
Martin & Oughton. Faber & Kell's Heating & Air Conditioning of Buildings. 8th ed. 704p. 1997. pap. 69.95 (*0-7506-3778-1*) Buttrwrth-Heinemann.
Martin & Oughton. Study Guide of Economics. pap. text. write for info. (*0-393-97585-1*) Norton.
Martin & Sexton. Science for All Children. LC 98-26027. 244p. 1998. pap. text 36.00 (*0-205-29373-5*, Longwood Div) Allyn.
Martin & Tuaillon. Atlas Linguistique et Ethnographique du Jura et des Alpes du Nord, Tome I. (FRE.). 175.00 (*0-8288-9901-0*, F136320) Fr & Eur.
Martin & Water. Introduction to Jazz. 400p. 2000. 45.00 (*0-02-864789-0*) S&S Trade.
Martin & Whattam, Al. The Early Days in Photographs: Logging. 16p. 1976. pap. 3.00 (*0-918146-03-8*) Peninsula WA.
— The Early Days in Photographs: Timber. 16p. 1976. pap. 3.00 (*0-918146-02-X*) Peninsula WA.
Martin, et al. Exploring American English: Writing Skills for Classroom. 288p. (C). 1997. per. 35.95 (*0-7872-4335-3*, 41433501) Kendall-Hunt.
Martin, jt. auth. see Bond.
Martin, jt. auth. see Faber, Gary.
Martin, jt. auth. see Fabes.
Martin, jt. auth. see Kaye.
Martin, jt. auth. see Kramer.
Martin, jt. auth. see Lancaster.
Martin, jt. auth. see Morris.
Martin, jt. auth. see Newman.
Martin, jt. auth. see Peacock.
Martin, jt. auth. see Rumelhart.
Martin, jt. auth. see Saltzburg.
Martin, jt. auth. see Scott.
Martin, jt. auth. see Whattam, Al.
Martin, ed. see Council on Technology Teacher Education Staff.
Martin, ed. see Twain, Mark, pseud.
***Martin, Barbara Y. & Moraitis, Dimitri.** The Kingdom of Light: Transforming Your Life with Spiritual Energy. 280p. 2000. pap. 39.95 (*0-9702118-0-5*) WisdomLight.
***Martin, Patricia Preciado.** Amor Eterno: Eleven Lessons in Love. 121p. 2000. 24.95 (*0-8165-1994-3*, Pub. by U of Ariz) U of Ariz Pr.
— Amor Eterno: Eleven Lessons in Love. LC 99-6918. (Camino Del Sol Ser.). 121p. 2000. pap. 11.95 (*0-8165-1995-1*) U of Ariz Pr.
***Martin, Richard K.** Costume & Character in the Age of Ingres. (Illus.). 96p. 1999. 35.00 (*0-8109-6542-9*) Abrams.
Martin, Richard K. Large Scale Linear & Integer Optimization: A Unified Approach. LC 98-46062. xvii, 740 p. 1999. write for info. (*0-7923-8202-1*) Kluwer Academic.
Martin & Dehayes & Dehayes. Managing Information Technology. 3rd ed. LC 98-21991. 716p. 1998. 90.67 (*0-13-860925-X*) P-H.
Martin & Martin Staff, jt. auth. see Martin, Bill, Jr.
Martin, A. America & Its People: Supershell. 3rd ed. 1997. pap. 21.56 (*0-673-97414-6*) Addison-Wesley.
***Martin, A.** Benko Gambit: Hit Back from Move 3! (Illus.). 144p. 1999. pap. 16.95 (*0-7134-8462-4*) B T B.
Martin, A. Health Aspects of Human Settlements: A Review Base on the Technical Discussions Held During 29th WHA, 1976. (Public Health Papers: No. 66). 57p. 1977. pap. text 8.00 (*92-4-130066-3*, 1110066) World Health.
Martin, A. Night Cooling Control Strategies - Final Report. 1996. pap. 80.00 (*0-86022-437-6*, Pub. by Build Servs Info Assn) St Mut.
Martin, A. Ninas Madres - Madres Adolescentes. (Serie Actualidades - Actualities Ser.).Tr. of Child Mothers - Teen Mothers. (SPA.). 2.29 (*1-56063-660-2*, 496253) Editorial Unilit.
— Prostitucion Infantil. (Serie Actualidades - Actualities Ser.).Tr. of Child Prostitution. (SPA.). 40p. 1995. 2.29 (*1-56063-732-3*, 496254) Editorial Unilit.
— The Ring-Net Fishermen. 280p. 1996. pap. 72.00 (*0-85976-443-5*, Pub. by J Donald) St Mut.
Martin, A., jt. auth. see Kendrick, C.
Martin, A. D. The Religion of Wordsworth. LC 72-8965. (Studies in Wordsworth: No. 29). 1973. reprint ed. lib. bdg. 59.00 (*0-8383-1680-8*) M S G Haskell Hse.
Martin, A. D., jt. auth. see Collins, P. D.
Martin, A. E. Common People: Murder in Sideshow Alley. 1999. pap. text 9.95 (*1-86254-303-8*) Wakefield Pr.
— The Misplaced Corpse. (Crime Classics Ser.). 207p. 1999. pap. 9.95 (*1-86254-281-3*, Pub. by Wakefield Pr) BHB Intl.
Martin, A. J. Sensors, Which Way Now? (C). 1988. 105.00 (*0-86022-211-X*, Pub. by Build Servs Info Assn) St Mut.
***Martin, A. Lynn.** Alcohol Sex & Gender in Traditional Europe. 2000. text 59.95 (*0-312-23414-7*) St Martin.
Martin, A. Lynn. Plague? Jesuit Accounts of Epidemic Disease in the 16th Century: Jesuit Accounts of Epidemic Diseases in the Sixteenth Century. LC 94-21215. (Sixteenth Century Essays & Studies: Vol. 28). 268p. 1996. 40.00 (*0-940474-30-1*, SCJP) Truman St Univ.
Martin, A. N. A Life of Principled Obedience. 22p. 1992. pap. 2.00 (*0-85151-634-3*) Banner of Truth.
— Living the Christian Life. 32p. 1986. pap. 2.00 (*0-85151-493-6*) Banner of Truth.
Martin, A. S. & Grover, F., eds. Managing People. 142p. 1988. 30.00 (*0-7277-1354-X*, Pub. by T Telford) RCH.
Martin, A. S., jt. ed. see Rutter, P. A.
***Martin, A. Tony.** The New "Thin" You: The Simple Safe Secret to Lose Weight Once & Forever Naturally. LC 99-75513. 180p. 1999. reprint ed. pap. 9.95 (*1-884820-56-5*) SAFE GOODS.
— Steps to Fight Chronic Fatigue for the Modern Woman. LC 99-75515. 112p. 1999. reprint ed. pap. 9.95 (*1-884820-55-7*) ATN Grp Pub.
— The Truth about Pycnogenol: The Bark with the Bite! LC 99-75514. reprint ed. pap. 8.95 (*1-884820-57-3*) ATN Grp Pub.
Martin, A. W. Robert Menzies: A Life, Vol. I 1894-1943. 456p. 1993. 39.95 (*0-522-84442-1*, Pub. by Melbourne Univ Pr) Paul & Co Pubs.
— Robert Menzies: A Life, 1894-1943, Vol. 1. LC 96-216170. 456p. 1996. pap. 24.95 (*0-522-84711-0*, Pub. by Melbourne Univ Pr) Paul & Co Pubs.
***Martin, A. W.** Robert Menzies, a Life, 1944-1978, Vol. 2. 450p. 2000. 49.95 (*0-522-84864-8*, Pub. by Melbourne Univ Pr) Paul & Co Pubs.
Martin, Abigail A. Bess Streeter Aldrich. LC 92-52529. (Western Writers Ser.: No. 104). (Illus.). 46p. (Orig.). 1992. pap. 4.95 (*0-88430-103-6*) Boise St U W Writ Ser.
— An Irony of Fate: The Fiction of William March. Burgess, Mary A., ed. LC 93-6559. (Milford Series: Popular Writers of Today: Vol. 53). 136p. 1994. pap. 19.00 (*0-89370-282-X*) Millefleurs.
Martin, Ace. Live the Good Life: World Traveling Harley Man. (Illus.). 257p. (Orig.). 1991. pap. 19.95 (*0-9631337-0-5*) A Martin Rd Ink.
Martin-Acena, Pablo & Simpson, James, eds. The Economic Development of Spain since 1870. LC 95-11860. (Economic Development of Modern Europe since 1870 Ser.: Vol. 6). 584p. 1995. 250.00 (*1-85278-793-7*) E Elgar.
Martin, Adrian. Once upon a Time in America. LC 98-229713. (Modern Classics Ser.). (Illus.). 96p. 1998. pap. 10.95 (*0-85170-544-8*) Ind U Pr.
Martin, Adrian R. Brothers from Bataan: POWs, 1942-1945. (Illus.). 334p. (Orig.). 1992. pap. 21.95 (*0-89745-142-2*) Sunflower U Pr.
Martin, Adrienne L. Cervantes & the Burlesque Sonnet. LC 90-39003. 312p. 1991. 45.00 (*0-520-07045-3*, Pub. by U CA Pr) Cal Prin Full Svc.
Martin, Agnes. Writings. 1998. pap. text 24.95 (*3-89322-326-6*, Pub. by Edition Cantz) Dist Art Pubs.
Martin, Alain & Primavesi, Oliver. L' Empedocle de Strasbourg: (P. Strasb. Gr. Inv., 1665-1666) 208p. 1998. 30.00 (*3-11-015129-4*) De Gruyter.
Martin, Alan. Tank Girl 2. (Illus.). 128p. 1995. pap. 17.95 (*1-56971-107-0*) Dark Horse Comics.
Martin, Alan & Hewlett, Jamie. Tank Girl Collection. (Illus.). 136p. 1993. pap. 17.95 (*1-56971-082-1*) Dark Horse Comics.
Martin, Alan D. & Harbison, Samuel A. An Introduction to Radiation Protection. 256p. 1986. 42.50 (*0-412-27800-6*, 9943) Chapman & Hall.
— An Introduction to Radiation Protection. 240p. 1996. pap. text 27.50 (*0-412-63110-5*, Pub. by E A) OUP.
Martin, Alan D., jt. auth. see Halzen, Francis.
Martin, Alastair B. Guennol Collection, Vol. 3. (Illus.). 240p. 1988. 34.95 (*0-87273-124-3*) Bklyn Mus.
Martin, Albert N. A Bad Record & a Bad Heart. 16p. (Orig.). (C). 1989. pap. 1.25 (*0-9622508-1-3*) Simpson NJ.
— Practical Implications of Calvinism. 1979. pap. 2.00 (*0-85151-296-8*) Banner of Truth.
— What's Wrong with Preaching? 32p. 1992. pap. 2.00 (*0-85151-632-7*) Banner of Truth.
Martin, Albert N., frwd. Intercessory Prayer: A Ministerial Task. 42p. (Orig.). 1991. pap. 5.95 (*0-9622508-6-4*) Simpson NJ.
Martin, Albro. James J. Hill & the Opening of the Northwest. LC 90-26749. (Illus.). xxvi, 676p. 1991. reprint ed. pap. 22.50 (*0-87351-261-8*, Borealis Book) Minn Hist.
— Railroads Triumphant: The Growth, Rejection, & Rebirth of a Vital American Force. (Illus.). 448p. 1992. text 35.00 (*0-19-503853-3*) OUP.
Martin, Alex. The Simple Guide to Etiquette in Greece. pap. write for info. (*1-86034-010-5*, 92989, Pub. by Global Bks) Midpt Trade.
Martin, Alex & Hill, Robert, eds. Introductions to Modern English Literature: Modern Poetry/Modern Short Stories. (Illus.). 160p. 1993. pap. text 20.40 (*0-13-481813-X*) P-H.
Martin, Alex, jt. auth. see Grant, Igor.
Martin, Alex, ed. see Lucan, Medlar.
Martin, Alex, ed. see Lucan, Medlar & Gras, Durian.
Martin, Alex, ed. see Lucan, Medlar & Gray, Durian.
Martin, Alexander. UI Design Book for the Applications Programmer. 316p. 1996. pap. text 75.00 (*0-471-95371-7*) Wiley.
***Martin, Alexander C. & Barkley, William D.** Seed Identification Manual. (Illus.). 221p. 2000. reprint ed. 64.95 (*1-930665-03-2*) Blackburn Pr.
Martin, Alexander C., et al. American Wildlife & Plants: A Guide to Wildlife Food Habits. 1998. pap. 10.95 (*0-486-20793-5*) Dover.
Martin, Alexander H. Introduction to Human Anatomy. (Illus.). 576p. (C). 1984. pap. text 38.00 (*0-86577-087-5*) Thieme Med Pubs.
Martin, Alexander M. Romantics, Reformers, Reactionaries: Russian Conservative Thought & Politics in the Reign of Alexander I. LC 96-53558. 288p. 1997. lib. bdg. 35.00 (*0-87580-226-5*) N Ill U Pr.
Martin, Alfred. Acts. (Survey of the Scriptures Study Guides Ser.). 1995. pap. 8.99 (*1-56570-022-8*) Meridian MI.
— Biblical Stewardship. LC 91-150. 107p. 1992. reprint ed. pap. 7.99 (*0-87213-645-0*) Loizeaux.
— Gospel of John. (Survey of the Scriptures Study Guides Ser.). 1995. pap. 8.99 (*1-56570-004-X*) Meridian MI.
— Isaiah. (Everyman's Bible Commentary Ser.). 1967. pap. 9.99 (*0-8024-2023-0*) Moody.
— Isaias; La Salvacion del Senor (Comentario Biblico Portavoz) Orig. Title: Isaiah: The Salvation of Jehovah (Everyman's Bible Commentary). (SPA.). 112p. 1979. pap. 6.99 (*0-8254-1455-5*, Edit Portavoz) Kregel.
— The New Testament. (Survey of the Scriptures Study Guides Ser.). 1995. pap. 8.99 (*1-56570-000-7*) Meridian MI.
— Physical Pharmacy: Text & Solutions Manual Set. 4th ed. 1993. write for info. (*0-8121-1688-7*) Lppncott W & W.
— Problem Solving, Physical Pharmacy IV. 222p. 1993. text 19.50 (*0-8121-1642-9*) Lppncott W & W.
— The Quest for Security. (Synthesis Ser.). 169p. 1979. pap. 1.00 (*0-8199-0371-X*, Frncscn Herld) Franciscan Pr.
Martin, Alfred, et al. Physical Pharmacy. 4th ed. (Illus.). 622p. 1993. text 59.50 (*0-8121-1438-8*) Lppncott W & W.
Martin, Alfred G. Hand-Taming Wild Birds at the Feeder: A Fascinating & Practical Guide to the World of Wild Birds...& How You Can Enter It. LC 63-13599. (Illus.). 144p. 1991. reprint ed. pap. 14.95 (*0-911469-07-9*) A C Hood.
Martin, Alfred W. Faith in a Future Life (1916) 224p. 1998. reprint ed. pap. 17.95 (*0-7661-0684-5*) Kessinger Pub.
— Psychic Tendencies of Today (1918) 172p. 1998. reprint ed. pap. 17.95 (*0-7661-0558-X*) Kessinger Pub.
Martin, Alfred W. Von, see Von Martin, Alfred W.
Martin, Alice, ed. & illus. see Rest, Hillard C.
Martin, Alison, tr. see Irigaray, Luce.
Martin, Allan, et al, eds. Information Technology in the Teaching of History: International Perspectives. 268p. 1997. text 42.00 (*90-5702-023-8*, ECU48, Harwood Acad Pubs); pap. text 17.00 (*90-5702-024-6*, ECU18, Harwood Acad Pubs) Gordon & Breach.
Martin, Allana. Death of a Healing Woman: A Texana Jones Mystery. (WWL Mystery Ser.). 1998. per. 4.99 (*0-373-26281-7*, 1-26281-5, Wrldwide Lib) Harlequin Bks.
— Death of a Healing Woman: A Texana Jones Mystery. large type ed. LC 96-21237. 224p. 1996. text 20.95 (*0-312-14581-0*) St Martin.

An Asterisk (*) at the beginning of an entry indicates that the title is appearing for the first time.

*Martin, Allana. Death of a Myth maker: A Texana Jones Mystery. LC 99-462043. 240p. 2000. text 22.95 (0-312-25241-2, Minotaur) St Martin.

Martin, Allana. Death of a Saint Maker. 1999. per. 4.99 (0-373-26299-X) Harlequin Bks.

— Death of a Saint Maker: A Texana Jones Mystery. LC 97-35441. 288p. 1997. text 22.95 (0-312-18083-7) St Martin.

*Martin, Allana. Death of an Evangelista. (Mystery Ser.: No. 335). 2000. mass mkt. 4.99 (0-373-26335-X, 1-26335-9, Wrldwide Lib) Harlequin Bks.

Martin, Allana. Death of an Evangelista. LC 98-47012. 272p. 1999. text 22.95 (0-312-19853-1) St Martin.

Martin, Alson R. Limited Liability Company & Partnership Answer Book. 816p. boxed set 118.00 (1-56706-313-6, S288) Panel Pubs.

— Limited Liability Company & Partnership Answer Book. annuals 512p. 1995. boxed set 136.00 (1-56706-177-X) Panel Pubs.

Martin, Alvin, jt. auth. see Lynx, David.

Martin, Alvin C. & Borteck, Robert D. New Jersey Estate Planning, Will Drafting & Estate Administration Forms, 2 vols. 1993. ring bd., suppl. ed. 82.00 (0-685-74628-3, MICHIE) LEXIS Pub.

— New Jersey Estate Planning, Will Drafting & Estate Administration Forms, 2 vols., Set. 1120p. 1988. spiral bd. 250.00 (0-87189-072-0, 82098-10, MICHIE) LEXIS Pub.

— New Jersey Estate Planning, Will Drafting & Estate Administration Forms, Set. 1994. disk 75.00 (0-685-74629-1, MICHIE) LEXIS Pub.

Martin, Amanda. Ancient Egypt. LC 97-3532. (My World Ser.). (Illus.). 32p. (J). (gr. 2-7). 1997. write for info. (0-7166-9414-X) World Bk.

*Martin, Amanda. Ancient Egypt. rev. ed. (My Word Ser.). (Illus.). (J). 2000. 9.95 (1-58728-061-2); pap. 5.95 (1-58728-067-1) Two Can Pub.

Martin, Amy. Sanctuary. 1.00 (0-687-08200-5) Abingdon.

Martin, Andre, jt. auth. see Grosse, Harald.

Martin, Andre J. Distribution Resource Planning: The Gateway to True Quick Response & Continuous Improvement. 2nd rev. ed. LC 90-70333. 280p. 1993. 129.00 (0-939246-17-1) Wiley.

Martin, Andre J. Distribution Resource Planning (DRP) The Gateway to True Quick Response & Continuous Replenishment. rev. ed. 352p. 1995. 49.95 (0-471-13222-5) Wiley.

Martin, Andre J. Infopartnering: The Ultimate Strategy for Achieving Efficient Consumer Response. 240p. 1995. 32.50 (0-471-13195-4) Wiley.

— InfoPartnering: Using Quick Response to Create Ultimate Customer Delight. LC 93-61779. 256p. 1994. 68.00 (0-939246-59-7) Wiley.

Martin, Andrea, jt. auth. see Donnelly, Beth.

*Martin, Andreu. No Pidas Sardinas Fuera De Temporada. 1998. pap. text 11.95 (84-204-4796-X) Santillana.

Martin, Andrew. Distribution Resource Planning. 329p. (C). 1990. 400.00 (0-7855-5724-5, Pub. by Inst Pur & Supply) St Mut.

— The Mask of the Prophet: The Extraordinary Fictions of Jules Verne. (Illus.). 236p. 1990. text 59.00 (0-19-815798-3) OUP.

— The New Samisch. 1997. pap. 19.95 (1-85744-065-X) S&S Trade.

— Receptions of War: Vietnam in American Culture. LC 92-33825. (Project for Discourse & Theory Ser.: Vol. 10). 216p. 1994. pap. 13.95 (0-8061-2540-3) U of Okla Pr.

— Scotland's Weather: An Illustrated Anthology. (Illus.). 112p. (Orig.). 1995. pap. 14.95 (0-948636-71-8, 671-8, Pub. by Natl Mus Scotland) A Schwartz & Co.

*Martin, Andrew. Underwear. 160p. 2000. reprint ed. pap. 5.95 (1-930535-02-3) Star Dists.

Martin, Andrew. Union Brand: Economic Democracy. 6p. 1997. ring bd. write for info. (0-9659705-0-7) A Martin.

Martin, Andrew, ed. Scottish Endings: Writings on Death. (Illus.). 128p. (Orig.). 1996. pap. 15.95 (0-948636-86-6, 6866, Pub. by Natl Mus Scotland) A Schwartz & Co.

Martin, Andrew, jt. auth. see Ross, George.

Martin, Andrew, ed. see Keyes, Frank E., Jr.

Martin, Andrew, jt. ed. see Ross, George.

*Martin, Andy. Advanced Level Mathematics Tutorials: Mechanics CD-Rom: Multi-User Version. (Illus.). 2000. audio compact disk 395.00 (0-7487-5471-7, Pub. by S Thornes Pubs) Trans-Atl Phila.

— Advanced Level Mathematics Tutorials: Mechanics CD-Rom: Single-User Version. (Illus.). (YA). 2000. audio compact disk 150.00 (0-7487-5472-5, Pub. by S Thornes Pubs) Trans-Atl Phila.

— Advanced Level Mathematics Tutorials: Statistics CD-Rom: Multi-User Version. (Illus.). (YA). 2000. audio compact disk 395.00 (0-7487-5473-3, Pub. by S Thornes Pubs) Trans-Atl Phila.

Martin, Andy. Blasting Cap Tin Catalog. LC 91-90085. (Illus.). 94p. (Orig.). 1991. pap. 8.00 (0-9628762-0-8) Old Adit.

— County High Points. LC 95-111745. 92p. (Orig.). 1994. pap. 6.00 (0 9628762-1-6) Old Adit.

*Martin, Andy. Napoleon the Novelist. 2001. 57.95 (0-7456-2535-5, Pub. by Polity Pr); pap. 22.95 (0-7456-2536-3, Pub. by Polity Pr) Blackwell Pubs.

— Walking on Water. pap. 13.95 (0-7493-9914-7, Pub. by Random) Trafalgar.

*Martin, Andy, et al. Advanced Level Mathematics Tutorials: Statistics CD-Rom: Single-User Version. (Illus.). (YA). 2000. audio compact disk 150.00 (0-7487-5474-1, Pub. by S Thornes Pubs) Trans-Atl Phila.

Martin, Andy, et al. Pure Mathematics: Complete Advanced Level Mathematics. (Illus.). 736p. (YA). (gr. 11 up). 1999. pap. 43.50 (0-7487-3558-5, Pub. by S Thornes Pubs) Trans-Atl Phila.

Martin, Angela, jt. auth. see Stewart, William.

Martin, Angeles. Diccionario Portugues-Espanol/Espanol-Portugues. (POR & SPA.). 524p. 1995. 39.95 (0-7859-9787-3) Fr & Eur.

Martin, Angus. Kintyre: The Hidden Past. 3rd ed. 240p. 2000. pap. 19.95 (0-85976-119-3, Pub. by J Donald) Dufour.

— The Larch Plantation. (C). 1989. 39.00 (0-86554-019-5, Pub. by Saltire Soc) St Mut.

— The Larch Plantation. 1993. pap. 21.00 (0-86334-069-5, Pub. by Saltire Soc) St Mut.

— The Larch Plantation. 1995. pap. 39.95 (0-7855-2795-8, Pub. by Saltire Soc) St Mut.

— The Song of the Quern. 64p. 1994. pap. 21.00 (1-898218-92-7) St Mut.

Martin, Ann. Abby & the Best Kid Ever. (Baby-Sitters Club Ser.: No. 116). (J). (gr. 3-7). 1998. pap. text 3.99 (0-590-05994-7) Scholastic Inc.

— Building the New School: A Tonka Storybook. LC 95-188943. (Illus.). 32p. (J). (ps-2). 1998. pap. 2.99 (0-590-20308-8) Scholastic Inc.

— Food Pets Die For: Shocking Facts about Pet Food. LC 97-34729. (Illus.). 148p. 1997. pap. text 12.95 (0-939165-31-7) NewSage Press.

Martin, Ann, ed. see Cornell University, Programs for Employment & Work.

*Martin, Ann M. Abby & the Best Kid Ever. (Baby-Sitters Club Ser.: No. 116). (J). 1998. 9.09 (0-606-13160-4, Pub. by Turtleback) Demco.

Martin, Ann M. Abby & the Mystery Baby. (Baby-Sitters Club Mystery Ser.: No. 28). 137p. (J). (gr. 3-7). 1997. pap. 3.99 (0-590-69176-7) Scholastic Inc.

Martin, Ann M. Abby & the Mystery Baby. (Baby-Sitters Club Super Mystery Ser.: No. 28). (J). 1997. 9.09 (0-606-10746-0, Pub. by Turtleback) Demco.

Martin, Ann M. Abby & the Notorious Neighbor. (Baby-Sitters Club Mystery Ser.: No. 35). (J). 1998. pap. 3.99 (0-590-05975-0, Apple Paperbacks) Scholastic Inc.

— Abby & the Secret Society. LC 00-5339. (Baby-Sitters Club Mystery Ser.: No. 23). (J). (gr. 3-7). 1996. pap. text 3.99 (0-590-22867-6) Scholastic Inc.

— Abby & the Secret Society. (Baby-Sitters Club Super Mystery Ser.: No. 23). (YA). 1996. 9.09 (0-606-09037-1, Pub. by Turtleback) Demco.

— Abby in Wonderland. (Baby-Sitters Club Ser.: No. 121). (J). 1998. pap. 3.99 (0-590-50063-5, Apple Paperbacks) Scholastic Inc.

— Abby in Wonderland. (Baby-Sitters Club Ser.: No. 121). (J). 1998. 9.09 (0-606-13165-5, Pub. by Turtleback) Demco.

— Abby the Bad Sport. (Baby-Sitters Club Ser.: No. 110). (J). 1997. pap. text 3.99 (0-590-05988-2, Apple Paperbacks) Scholastic Inc.

— Abby the Bad Sport. (Baby-Sitters Club Ser.: No. 110). 1997. 9.00 (0-606-11070-4, Pub. by Turtleback) Demco.

— Abby's Book. (Baby-Sitters Club Portrait Collection). 160p. (J). (gr. 3-7). 1997. mass mkt. 3.99 (0-590-69182-1) Scholastic Inc.

— Abby's Book. (Baby-Sitters Club Portrait Collection). 1997. 9.09 (0-606-11077-1, Pub. by Turtleback) Demco.

— Abby's Lucky Thirteen. (Baby-Sitters Club Ser.: No. 96). (J). (gr. 3-7). 1996. pap. 3.99 (0-590-22880-3) Scholastic Inc.

— Abby's Lucky Thirteen. (Baby-Sitters Club Ser.: No. 96). 1996. 9.09 (0-606-09032-0, Pub. by Turtleback) Demco.

— Abby's Twin. LC 00-9437. (Baby-Sitters Club Ser.: No. 104). 127p. (J). (gr. 3-7). 1997. mass mkt. 3.99 (0-590-69210-0) Scholastic Inc.

Martin, Ann M. Abby's Twin. (Baby-Sitters Club Ser.: No. 104). 1997. 9.09 (0-606-10744-4, Pub. by Turtleback) Demco.

Martin, Ann M. Abby's Un-Valentine. (Baby-Sitters Club Ser.: No. 127). 160p. (J). (gr. 3-7). 1999. pap. text 4.50 (0-590-50350-2) Scholastic Inc.

*Martin, Ann M. The All-New Mallory Pike. (Baby-Sitters Club Ser.: No. 126). 1999. pap. text 4.50 (0-590-50349-9) Scholastic Inc.

Martin, Ann M. Aloha, Baby-Sitters! (Baby-Sitters Club Super Special Ser.: No. 13). (J). (gr. 4-7). 1996. pap. 4.50 (0-590-22883-8) Scholastic Inc.

— Amalia. (California Diaries). (J). (gr. 6-8). 1997. pap. 3.99 (0-590-29838-0, Little Apple) Scholastic Inc.

Martin, Ann M. Amalia. (California Diaries). (YA). (gr. 6-8). 1997. 9.34 (0-606-12640-6) Turtleback.

— Amalia: Diary Three. (California Diaries: Vol. 14). (Illus.). 144p. (YA). (gr. 3-7). 2000. mass mkt. 4.99 (0-439-09548-4) Scholastic Inc.

Martin, Ann M. Amalia: Diary Two. (California Diaries: Vol. 9). (J). (gr. 6-8). 1998. pap. 3.99 (0-590-02385-3) Scholastic Inc.

— The Amazing True Story of Leo the Magnificat. LC 95-33640. (Illus.). (J). 1996. write for info. (0-614-08630-2) Scholastic Inc.

*Martin, Ann M. Ann M. Martin Mixed Display. 1999. pap. text 51.96 (0-439-05973-9) Scholastic Inc.

Martin, Ann M. Author Day. (Kids in Ms. Colman's Class Ser.: No. 2). (Illus.). (J). (gr. 1-4). 1996. pap. 2.99 (0-614-15777-3, Little Apple) Scholastic Inc.

— Author Day. (Kids in Ms. Colman's Class Ser.: No. 2). (Illus.). (J). (gr. 1-4). 1996. pap. 2.99 (0-590-26216-5) Scholastic Inc.

— Baby Animal Zoo. (Kids in Ms. Colman's Class Ser.: No. 12). (Illus.). (J). (gr. 1-4). 1998. pap. text 3.50 (0-590-06009-0, Little Apple) Scholastic Inc.

— Baby-Sitters at Shadow Lake. (Baby-Sitters Club Super Special Ser.: No. 8). 256p. (J). (gr. 4-6). 1992. pap. 4.50 (0-590-44962-1) Scholastic Inc.

Martin, Ann M. Baby-Sitters at Shadow Lake. (Baby-Sitters Club Super Special Ser.: No. 8). (J). 1992. 9.05 (0-606-01780-1, Pub. by Turtleback) Demco.

Martin, Ann M. Baby-Sitters Beware. (Baby-Sitters Club Super Mystery Ser.: No. 2). (J). (gr. 3-7). 1995. pap. 3.99 (0-590-22871-4) Scholastic Inc.

— Baby-Sitters Beware. (Baby-Sitters Club Super Mystery Ser.: No. 2). (J). 1995. 9.09 (0-606-08483-5, Pub. by Turtleback) Demco.

— Baby-Sitters' Christmas Chiller. (Baby-Sitters Club Super Mystery Ser.: No. 4). (J). 1997. pap. 4.50 (0-590-05977-7, Little Apple) Scholastic Inc.

— Baby-Sitters' Christmas Chiller. (Baby-Sitters Club Super Mystery Ser.: No. 4). (J). 1997. 9.60 (0-606-12884-0, Pub. by Turtleback) Demco.

— The Baby-Sitters Club, Set., No. 5. (Baby-Sitters Club Ser.). (J). (gr. 4 up). 1989. pap. 11.00 (0-590-63344-9) Scholastic Inc.

— The Baby-Sitters Club Boxed Set No. 1 Bks. 1-4: Kristy's Great Idea; Claudia & the Phantom Phone Calls; The Truth about Stacey; Mary Anne Saves the Day. (Baby-Sitters Club Ser.). 1987. pap., boxed set 10.00 (0-590-63218-3); pap., boxed set 11.00 (0-590-63296-5) Scholastic Inc.

— The Baby-Sitters Club Boxed Set No. 1 Bks. 1-4: Kristy's Great Idea; Claudia & the Phantom Phone Calls; The Truth about Stacey; Mary Anne Saves the Day. (Baby-Sitters Club Ser.). (J). 1990. pap., boxed set 14.95 (0-590-63673-1) Scholastic Inc.

— The Baby-Sitters Club Boxed Set No. 12 Bks. 45-48: Kristy & the Baby Parade; Mary Anne Misses Logan; Mallory on Strike; Jessi's Wish. (Baby-Sitters Club Ser.). (J). (gr. 4-7). 1991. pap., boxed set 13.00 (0-590-63963-3) Scholastic Inc.

— The Baby-Sitters Club Boxed Set No. 13 Bks. 49-52: Claudia & the Genius of Elm Street; Dawn's Big Date; Stacey's Ex-Best Friend; Mary Anne & 2 Many Babies. (Baby-Sitters Club Ser.). (J). 1992. pap., boxed set 13.00 (0-590-66141-8) Scholastic Inc.

— The Baby-Sitters Club Boxed Set No. 14 Bks. 53-56: Kristy for President; Mallory & the Dream Horse; Jessi's Gold Medal; Keep Out, Claudia. (Baby-Sitters Club Ser.). 1992. boxed set 13.00 (0-590-66140-X) Scholastic Inc.

— The Baby-Sitters Club Boxed Set No. 16 Bks. 61-64: Jessi & the Awful Secret; Kristy & the Worst Kid Ever; Claudia's Freind Friend; Dawn's Family Feud. (Baby-Sitters Club Ser.). (J). 1993. pap. text, boxed set 14.00 (0-590-66719-X) Scholastic Inc.

— The Baby-Sitters Club Boxed Set No. 17 Bks. 65-68: Stacey's Big Crush; Maid Mary Anne; Dawn's Big Move; Jessi & the Bad Baby-Sitter. (Baby-Sitters Club Ser.). (J). 1993. pap., boxed set 14.00 (0-590-66718-1) Scholastic Inc.

— The Baby-Sitters Club Boxed Set No. 2 Bks. 5-8: Dawn & the Impossible Three; Kristy's Big Day; Claudia & Mean Janine; Boy-Crazy Stacey. (Baby-Sitters Club Ser.). 1987. pap., boxed set 11.00 (0-590-63351-1) Scholastic Inc.

— The Baby-Sitters Club Boxed Set No. 2 Bks. 5-8: Dawn & the Impossible Three; Kristy's Big Day; Claudia & Mean Janine; Boy-Crazy Stacey. (Baby-Sitters Club Ser.). 1987. pap., boxed set 10.00 (0-590-63248-5) Scholastic Inc.

— The Baby-Sitters Club Boxed Set No. 20 Bks. 77-80: Dawn & Whitney, Friends Forever; Claudia & Crazy Peaches; Mary Anne Breaks the Rules; Mallory Pike #1 Fan. (Baby-Sitters Club Ser.). (YA). 1997. pap., boxed set 14.00 (0-590-66935-4) Scholastic Inc.

— The Baby-Sitters Club Boxed Set No. 3 Bks. 9-12: The Ghost at Dawn's House; Logan Likes Mary Anne!; Kristy & the Snobs; Claudia & the New Girl. (Baby-Sitters Club Ser.). 1988. pap., boxed set 11.00 (0-590-63288-4) Scholastic Inc.

— The Baby-Sitters Club Boxed Set No. 4 Bks. 13-16: Good-Bye Stacey, Good-Bye; Hello, Mallory; Little Miss Stoneybrook & Dawn; Jessi's Secret Language. (Baby-Sitters Club Ser.). 1988. pap., boxed set 11.00 (0-590-63335-X) Scholastic Inc.

— The Baby-Sitters Club Boxed Set No. 4 Bks. 13-16: Good-Bye Stacey, Good-Bye; Hello, Mallory; Little Miss Stoneybrook & Dawn; Jessi's Secret Language. (Baby-Sitters Club Ser.). (J). (gr. 3-7). 1991. pap., boxed set 13.00 (0-590-63705-3) Scholastic Inc.

— The Baby-Sitters Club Boxed Set No. 5 Bks. 17-20: Mary Anne's Bad Luck Mystery; Stacey's Mistake; Claudia & the Bad Joke; Kristy & the Walking Disaster. (Baby-Sitters Club Ser.). (J). (gr. 3-7). 1991. pap., boxed set 13.00 (0-590-63704-5) Scholastic Inc.

— The Baby-Sitters Club Boxed Set No. 8 Bks. 29-32: Mallory & the Mystery Diary; Mary Anne & the Great Romance; Dawn's Wicked Stepsister; Kristy & the Secret of Susan. (Baby-Sitters Club Ser.). (J). (gr. 4-7). 1990. pap., boxed set 13.00 (0-590-63583-2) Scholastic Inc.

— The Baby-Sitters Club Boxed Set No. 8 Bks. 57-60: Dawn Saves the Planet; Stacey's Choice; Mallory Hates Boys; Mary Anne's Makeover. (Baby-Sitters Club Ser.). (J). 1993. pap., boxed set 14.00 (0-590-66720-3) Scholastic Inc.

— The Baby-Sitters Club Boxed Set No. 9 Bks. 33-36: Claudia & the Great Search; Mary Anne & Too Many Boys; Stacey & the Mystery of Stoneybrook; Jessi's Baby-Sitter. (Baby-Sitters Club Ser.). (J). (gr. 4-7). 1990. pap., boxed set 13.00 (0-590-63669-3) Scholastic Inc.

— The Baby-Sitters Club Guide to Baby-Sitting. LC 94-148911. (Baby-Sitters Club Ser.). 128p. (J). (gr. 4-7). 1993. pap. 3.50 (0-590-47686-6) Scholastic Inc.

— BSC in the U. S. A. (Baby-Sitters Club Super Special Ser.: No. 14). 246p. (J). (gr. 3-7). 1997. mass mkt. 4.50 (0-590-69216-X) Scholastic Inc.

Martin, Ann M. The Baby-Sitters Club Mystery Boxed Set No. 1 Bks. 1-4: Stacey & the Missing Ring; Beware, Dawn!; Mallory & the Ghost Cat; Kristy & the Missing Child, (Baby-Sitters Club Mystery Ser.). (J). (gr. 3-7). 1993. pap. text, boxed set 14.00 (0-590-66714-9) Scholastic Inc.

Martin, Ann M. The Baby Sitters Club Mystery Boxed Set No. 2 Bks. 5-8: Mary Anne & the Secret in the Attic; The Mystery at Claudia's House; Dawn & the Disappearing Dogs; Jessi & the Jewel Thieves. (Baby-Sitters Club Mystery Ser.). (gr. 4-7). 1993. boxed set 14.00 (0-590-66713-0) Scholastic Inc.

— The Baby-Sitters Club Mystery Boxed Set No. 4 Bks. 13-16: Mary Anne & the Library Mystery; Stacey & the Mystery at the Mall; Kristy & the Vampires; Claudia & the Clue in the Photograph. (Baby-Sitters Club Mystery Ser.). (J). 1997. pap. text, boxed set 14.00 (0-590-66961-3) Scholastic Inc.

— The Baby-Sitters Club Mystery Boxed Set No. 5 Bks. 17-20: Dawn & the Halloween Mystery; Stacey & the Mystery at the Empty House; Kristy & the Missing Fortune; Mary Anne & the Zoo Mystery. (Baby-Sitters Club Mystery Ser.). (J). 1997. pap., boxed set 14.00 (0-590-66962-1) Scholastic Inc.

— The Baby-Sitters Club Postcard Book. (Baby-Sitters Club Ser.). 64p. (J). (gr. 3-7). 1991. pap. 4.95 (0-590-44783-1) Scholastic Inc.

— Baby-Sitters' European Vacation. (Baby-Sitters Club Super Special Ser.: No. 15). (J). (gr. 3-7). 1998. pap. 4.50 (0-590-06000-7) Scholastic Inc.

— Baby-Sitters' Fright Night. (Baby-Sitters Club Super Mystery Ser.: No. 3). (J). (gr. 3-7). Date not set. pap. 4.50 (0-614-19195-5, Apple Paperbacks) Scholastic Inc.

— Baby-Sitters' Fright Night. LC 49-117830. (Baby-Sitters Club Super Mystery Ser.: No. 3). (J). (gr. 3-7). 1996. pap. text 4.50 (0-590-69180-5) Scholastic Inc.

— Baby-Sitters' Fright Night. (Baby-Sitters Club Super Mystery Ser.: No. 3). 1996. 9.60 (0-606-10135-7, Pub. by Turtleback) Demco.

— Baby-Sitters' Haunted House. (Baby-Sitters Club Super Mystery Ser.: No. 1). 256p. (J). (gr. 4-6). 1995. pap. 3.99 (0-590-48311-0) Scholastic Inc.

— Baby-Sitters' Haunted House. (Baby-Sitters Club Super Mystery Ser.: No. 1). (J). 1995. 9.09 (0-606-07237-3, Pub. by Turtleback) Demco.

— Baby-Sitters' Island Adventure. (Baby-Sitters Club Super Special Ser.: No. 4). 240p. (J). (gr. 4-6). 1990. pap. 4.50 (0-590-42493-9) Scholastic Inc.

— Baby-Sitters' Island Adventure. (Baby-Sitters Club Super Special Ser.: No. 4). (J). 1990. 9.05 (0-606-03040-9, Pub. by Turtleback) Demco.

— The Baby-Sitters Little Sister Boxed Set No. 1 Bks. 1-4: Karen's Witch; Karen's Roller Skates; Karen's Worst Day; Karen's Kittycat Club. (Baby-Sitters Little Sister Ser.). (J). 1993. pap., boxed set 11.80 (0-590-66717-3) Scholastic Inc.

— The Baby-Sitters Little Sister Boxed Set No. 14 Bks. 53-56: Karen's School Bus; Karen's Candy; Karen's Magician; Karen's Ice Skates. (Baby-Sitters Little Sister Ser.). (J). 1997. pap., boxed set 11.80 (0-590-66941-9) Scholastic Inc.

— The Baby-Sitters Little Sister Boxed Set No. 15 Bks. 57-60: Karen's School Mystery; Karen's Ski Trip; Karen's Leprechaun; Karen's Pony. (Baby-Sitters Little Sister Ser.). (J). 1997. pap., boxed set 11.80 (0-590-66958-3) Scholastic Inc.

— The Baby-Sitters Little Sister Boxed Set No. 16 Bks. 61-64: Karen's Tattletale; Karen's New Bike; Karen's Movie; Karen's Lemonade Stand. (Baby-Sitters Little Sister Ser.). (J). 1997. pap., boxed set 11.80 (0-590-66959-1) Scholastic Inc.

— The Baby-Sitters Little Sister Boxed Set No. 3 Bks. 9-12: Karen's Sleepover; Karen's Grandmothers; Karen's Prize; Karen's Ghost. (Baby-Sitters Little Sister Ser.). (J). (gr. 2-4). 1990. pap., boxed set 11.00 (0-590-63668-5) Scholastic Inc.

— The Baby-Sitters Little Sister Boxed Set No. 4 Bks. 13-16: Karen's Surprise; Karen's New Year; Karen's In Love; Karen's Goldfish. (Baby-Sitters Little Sister Ser.). (J). (gr. 2-4). 1991. pap., boxed set 11.00 (0-590-63827-0) Scholastic Inc.

— The Baby-Sitters Little Sister Boxed Set No. 5 Bks. 17-20: Karen's Brothers; Karen's Home Run; Karen's Good-Bye; Karen's Carnival. (Baby-Sitters Little Sister Ser.). (J). 1991. pap., boxed set 11.00 (0-590-63950-1) Scholastic Inc.

— The Baby-Sitters Little Sister Boxed Set No. 6 Bks. 21-24: Karen's New Teacher; Karen's Little Witch; Karen's Doll; Karen's School Trip. (Baby-Sitters Little Sister Ser.). (J). (gr. 2-4). 1992. pap., boxed set 11.00 (0-590-63965-X) Scholastic Inc.

— The Baby-Sitters Little Sister Boxed Set No. 7 Bks. 25-28: Karen's Pen Pal; Karen's Ducklings; Karen's Big Joke; Karen's Tea Party. (Baby-Sitters Little Sister Ser.). (J). 1992. pap., boxed set 11.00 (0-590-66125-6) Scholastic Inc.

— The Baby-Sitters Little Sister Boxed Set No. 8 Bks. 29-32: Karen's Cartwheel; Karen's Kittens; Karen's Bully; Karen's Pumpkin Patch. (Baby-Sitters Little Sister Ser.). (J). 1992. pap. 11.00 (0-590-66210-4, Little Apple) Scholastic Inc.

— Baby-Sitters Little Sister Jump Rope Rhymes Pack. (Baby-Sitters Little Sister Ser.). (J). (gr. 2-4). 1995. pap. 5.99 (0-590-25995-4); pap. 5.99 (0-590-55407-7) Scholastic Inc.

— The Baby-Sitters Little Sister Laugh Pack: Baby-Sitters Little Sister Book of Laughs. (Baby-Sitters Little Sister Ser.). (J). 1997. pap. text 6.99 (0-590-13801-4, Little Apple) Scholastic Inc.

— Baby-Sitters Little Sister Photo Scrapbook: Book & Camera. (Baby-Sitters Little Sister Ser.). (J). (gr. 4-7). 1996. pap. 9.99 (0-590-89735-7) Scholastic Inc.

M

— Baby-Sitters Little Sister Playground Games. (Baby-Sitters Little Sister Ser.). (J). (gr. 2-4). 1996. pap. text 5.99 (*0-590-73914-X*) Scholastic Inc.

— Baby-Sitters Little Sister School Scrapbook. (Baby-Sitters Little Sister Ser.). 80p. (J). (gr. 7-9). 1993. pap. 2.95 (*0-590-47677-7*) Scholastic Inc.

— Baby-Sitters Little Sister Summer Fill-In Book. (Baby-Sitters Little Sister Ser.). 96p. (J). (gr. 2-4). 1995. pap. 2.95 (*0-590-26467-2*) Scholastic Inc.

— Baby-Sitters on Board! 240p. (YA). (gr. 4-6). 1988. pap. 4.50 (*0-590-44240-6*) Scholastic Inc.

Martin, Ann M. Baby-Sitters on Board! (Baby-Sitters Club Super Special Ser.: No. 1). (J). 1988. 9.05 (*0-606-03721-7*, Pub. by Turtleback) Demco.

Martin, Ann M. The Baby-Sitters Remember. (Baby-Sitters Club Super Special Ser.: No. 11). 256p. (J). (gr. 3-7). 1994. pap. 3.95 (*0-590-47015-9*) Scholastic Inc.

Martin, Ann M. The Baby-Sitters Remember. (Baby-Sitters Club Super Special Ser.: No. 11). (J). 1994. 9.05 (*0-606-06211-4*, Pub. by Turtleback) Demco.

Martin, Ann M. The Baby-Sitters Special Edition Readers' Reqest Boxed Set: Logan's Story; Logan Bruno, Boy Baby-Sitter; Shannon's Story. (Baby-Sitters Club Special Edition Ser.). (gr. 3-7). 1992. pap. 10.50 (*0-590-66273-2*) Scholastic Inc.

— Baby-Sitters' Summer Vacation. (Baby-Sitters Club Super Special Ser.: No. 2). 256p. (J). (gr. 3-7). 1989. pap. 3.95 (*0-590-44239-2*) Scholastic Inc.

— Baby-Sitters' Summer Vacation. (Baby-Sitters Club Super Special Ser.: No. 2). (J). 1989. 9.05 (*0-606-04165-6*, Pub. by Turtleback) Demco.

— Baby-Sitters' Winter Vacation. (Baby-Sitters Club Super Special Ser.: No. 3). 240p. (J). (gr. 3-7). 1989. pap. 4.50 (*0-590-43973-1*) Scholastic Inc.

— Baby-Sitters' Winter Vacation. (Baby-Sitters Club Super Special Ser.: No. 3). (J). 1989. 9.05 (*0-606-00391-6*, Pub. by Turtleback) Demco.

— Beware, Dawn! (Baby-Sitters Club Mystery Ser.: No. 2). 176p. (J). (gr. 3-7). 1991. pap. 3.99 (*0-590-44085-3*) Scholastic Inc.

— Beware, Dawn! (Baby-Sitters Club Mystery Ser.: No. 2). (J). 1991. 9.09 (*0-606-00309-6*, Pub. by Turtleback) Demco.

— Boy-Crazy Stacey. (Baby-Sitters Club Ser.: No. 8). 192p. (J). (gr. 4-6). 1987. pap. 3.50 (*0-590-43509-4*) Scholastic Inc.

— Boy-Crazy Stacey. LC 88-21510. (Baby-Sitters Club Ser.: No. 8). (J). (gr. 3-7). 1995. pap. 3.50 (*0-590-25163-5*) Scholastic Inc.

Martin, Ann M. Boy-Crazy Stacey. (Baby-Sitters Club Ser.: No. 8). (J). 1987. 8.60 (*0-606-03548-6*, Pub. by Turtleback) Demco.

— BSC in the USA. (Baby-Sitters Club Super Special Ser.). 1997. 9.60 (*0-606-11078-X*, Pub. by Turtleback) Demco.

Martin, Ann M. California Girls! (Baby-Sitters Club Super Special Ser.: No. 5). 272p. (J). (gr. 4-6). 1990. pap. 3.95 (*0-590-43575-2*) Scholastic Inc.

— California Girls! (Baby-Sitters Club Super Special Ser.: No. 5). (J). 1990. 9.60 (*0-606-04622-4*, Pub. by Turtleback) Demco.

— Chain Letter. LC 92-44587. (Baby-Sitters Club Ser.). 40p. (J). (gr. 3-7). 1993. 14.95 (*0-590-47151-1*) Scholastic Inc.

— Class Play. (Kids in Ms. Colman's Class Ser.: No. 3). (Illus.). (J). (gr. 1-4). 1996. pap. text 2.99 (*0-590-69199-6*) Scholastic Inc.

— Claudia & Crazy Peaches. (Baby-Sitters Club Ser.: No. 78). 192p. (J). (gr. 4-6). 1994. pap. 3.50 (*0-590-48222-X*) Scholastic Inc.

— Claudia & Crazy Peaches. (Baby-Sitters Club Ser.: No. 78). 138p. (gr. 4-7). 1999. pap. 3.99 (*0-590-92610-1*) Scholastic Inc.

— Claudia & Crazy Peaches. (Baby-Sitters Club Ser.: No. 78). (J). 1994. 8.60 (*0-606-06204-1*, Pub. by Turtleback) Demco.

— Claudia & Crazy Peaches. (Baby-Sitters Club Ser.: No. 78). 1995. 7.98 (*1-57042-367-9*) Warner Bks.

— Claudia & Mean Janine. (Baby-Sitters Club Ser.: No. 7). 192p. (J). (gr. 4-6). 1987. pap. 3.50 (*0-590-43719-4*) Scholastic Inc.

— Claudia & Mean Janine. (Baby-Sitters Club Ser.: No. 7). (J). (gr. 3-7). 1995. pap. text 3.50 (*0-590-25162-7*) Scholastic Inc.

— Claudia & Mean Janine. (Baby-Sitters Club Ser.: No. 7). (J). 1987. 8.60 (*0-606-00551-X*, Pub. by Turtleback) Demco.

— Claudia & the Bad Joke. (Baby-Sitters Club Ser.: No. 19). 192p. (J). (gr. 4-6). 1988. pap. 3.50 (*0-590-43510-8*) Scholastic Inc.

— Claudia & the Bad Joke. (Baby-Sitters Club Ser.: No. 19). (J). (gr. 3-7). 1996. pap. 3.99 (*0-590-60671-9*) Scholastic Inc.

— Claudia & the Bad Joke. (Baby-Sitters Club Ser.: No. 19). (J). 1988. 9.09 (*0-606-04084-6*, Pub. by Turtleback) Demco.

— Claudia & the Clue in the Photograph. (Baby-Sitters Club Mystery Ser.: No. 16). 176p. (J). (gr. 3-7). 1994. pap. 3.99 (*0-590-47054-X*) Scholastic Inc.

— Claudia & the Clue in the Photograph. (Baby-Sitters Club Mystery Ser.: No. 16). (J). 1994. 9.09 (*0-606-06208-4*, Pub. by Turtleback) Demco.

— Claudia & the First Thanksgiving. (Baby-Sitters Club Ser.: No. 91). (J). (gr. 3-7). 1995. pap. 3.50 (*0-590-22875-7*) Scholastic Inc.

— Claudia & the First Thanksgiving. (Baby-Sitters Club Ser.: No. 91). (J). 1995. 8.60 (*0-606-08480-0*, Pub. by Turtleback) Demco.

***Martin, Ann M.** Claudia & the Friendship Feud. (Baby-Sitters Club Friends Forever Ser.: No. 4). (J). 1999. mass mkt. 4.50 (*0-590-52331-7*, Apple Classics) Scholastic Inc.

Martin, Ann M. Claudia & the Friendship Feud Floor Display. (Baby-Sitters Club Friends Forever Ser.: No. 4). 1999. pap. text 54.00 (*0-439-13481-1*) Scholastic Inc.

— Claudia & the Genius of Elm Street. LC 96-15708. (Baby-Sitters Club Ser.: No. 49). (J). 1996. lib. bdg. 21.27 (*0-8368-1573-4*) Gareth Stevens Inc.

— Claudia & the Genius of Elm Street. (Baby-Sitters Club Ser.: No. 49). 192p. (YA). (gr. 3-7). 1991. pap. 3.25 (*0-590-44970-2*) Scholastic Inc.

— Claudia & the Genius of Elm Street. (Baby-Sitters Club Ser.: No. 49). (J). 1991. 8.35 (*0-606-00357-6*, Pub. by Turtleback) Demco.

— Claudia & the Great Search. (Baby-Sitters Club Ser.: No. 33). 192p. (J). (gr. 3-7). 1990. pap. 3.99 (*0-590-73190-4*) Scholastic Inc.

— Claudia & the Great Search. (Baby-Sitters Club Ser.: No. 33). 192p. (J). (gr. 4-6). 1990. pap. 3.25 (*0-590-42495-5*) Scholastic Inc.

— Claudia & the Great Search. (Baby-Sitters Club Ser.: No. 33). (J). 1990. 9.09 (*0-606-03158-8*, Pub. by Turtleback) Demco.

— Claudia & the Lighthouse Ghost. LC 00-9059. (Baby-Sitters Club Mystery Ser.: No. 27). 154p. (J). (gr. 3-7). 1996. pap. 3.99 (*0-590-69175-9*) Scholastic Inc.

— Claudia & the Lighthouse Ghost. (Baby-Sitters Club Mystery Ser.: No. 27). 1996. 9.09 (*0-606-10134-9*, Pub. by Turtleback) Demco.

— Claudia & the Little Liar. (Baby-Sitters Club Ser.: No. 128). 1999. pap. 4.50 (*0-590-50351-0*) Scholastic Inc.

— Claudia & the Middle School Mystery. (Baby-Sitters Club Ser.: No. 40). 192p. (J). (gr. 4-6). 1991. pap. 3.25 (*0-590-44082-9*) Scholastic Inc.

— Claudia & the Middle School Mystery. (Baby-Sitters Club Ser.: No. 40). (J). 1991. 8.35 (*0-606-04637-2*, Pub. by Turtleback) Demco.

— Claudia & the Mystery at the Museum. LC 94-146924. (Baby-Sitters Club Mystery Ser.: No. 11). 176p. (J). (gr. 3-7). 1993. pap. 3.50 (*0-590-47049-3*) Scholastic Inc.

— Claudia & the Mystery at the Museum. (Baby-Sitters Club Mystery Ser.: No. 11). (J). 1993. 8.60 (*0-606-05142-2*, Pub. by Turtleback) Demco.

— Claudia & the Mystery in the Painting. (Baby-Sitters Club Mystery Ser.: No. 32). 144p. (J). (gr. 3-7). 1997. pap. text 3.99 (*0-590-05972-6*) Scholastic Inc.

Martin, Ann M. Claudia & the Mystery in the Painting. (Baby-Sitters Club Mystery Ser.: No. 32). (YA). 1997. 9.09 (*0-606-11076-3*, Pub. by Turtleback) Demco.

Martin, Ann M. Claudia & the New Girl. (Baby-Sitters Club Ser.: No. 12). 192p. (J). (gr. 4-6). 1988. pap. 3.50 (*0-590-43721-6*) Scholastic Inc.

— Claudia & the New Girl. (Baby-Sitters Club Ser.: No. 12). (J). 1989. 8.60 (*0-606-03758-6*, Pub. by Turtleback) Demco.

— Claudia & the New Girl. rev. ed. (Baby-Sitters Club Ser.: No. 12). 160p. (J). (gr. 3-7). 1996. pap. 3.99 (*0-590-25167-8*) Scholastic Inc.

— Claudia & the Perfect Boy. LC 94-146928. (Baby-Sitters Club Ser.: No. 71). 192p. (J). (gr. 3-7). 1994. pap. 3.99 (*0-590-47009-4*) Scholastic Inc.

— Claudia & the Perfect Boy. (Baby-Sitters Club Ser.: No. 71). (J). 1994. 9.09 (*0-606-05736-6*, Pub. by Turtleback) Demco.

— Claudia & the Phantom Phone Calls. (Baby-Sitters Club Ser.: No. 2). 160p. (J). (gr. 3-7). 1986. pap. 3.50 (*0-590-43513-2*) Scholastic Inc.

— Claudia & the Phantom Phone Calls. (Baby-Sitters Club Ser.: No. 2). (J). (gr. 3-7). 1986. 9.09 (*0-606-03083-2*, Pub. by Turtleback) Demco.

— Claudia & the Phantom Phone Calls. limited ed. (Baby-Sitters Club Ser.: No. 2). 192p. (J). (gr. 3-7). 1995. pap. 3.99 (*0-590-22763-7*) Scholastic Inc.

— Claudia & the Recipe for Danger. LC 00-3586. (Baby-Sitters Club Mystery Ser.: No. 21). 176p. (J). (gr. 3-7). 1995. pap. 3.50 (*0-590-48310-2*) Scholastic Inc.

— Claudia & the Recipe for Danger. (Baby-Sitters Club Mystery Ser.: No. 21). 1995. 8.60 (*0-606-07235-7*, Pub. by Turtleback) Demco.

— Claudia & the Sad Good-Bye. (Baby-Sitters Club Ser.: No. 26). 192p. (J). (gr. 4-6). 1989. pap. 3.50 (*0-590-42503-X*) Scholastic Inc.

— Claudia & the Sad Good-Bye. (Baby-Sitters Club Ser.: No. 26). (J). (gr. 3-7). 1997. pap. 3.99 (*0-590-67394-7*) Scholastic Inc.

— Claudia & the Sad Good-Bye. (Baby-Sitters Club Ser.: No. 26). (J). 1989. 8.60 (*0-606-04187-7*, Pub. by Turtleback) Demco.

— Claudia & the Terrible Truth. (Baby-Sitters Club Ser.: No. 117). (J). 1998. pap. text 3.50 (*0-590-05995-5*, Apple Paperbacks) Scholastic Inc.

***Martin, Ann M.** Claudia & the Terrible Truth. (Baby-Sitters Club Ser.: No. 117). (J). 1998. 9.09 (*0-606-13161-2*, Pub. by Turtleback) Demco.

Martin, Ann M. Claudia & the World's Cutest Baby. (Baby-Sitters Club Ser.: No. 97). (YA). 1996. pap. text 3.99 (*0-590-22881-1*) Scholastic Inc.

— Claudia & the World's Cutest Baby. (Baby-Sitters Club Ser.: No. 97). (YA). 1996. 9.09 (*0-606-09033-9*, Pub. by Turtleback) Demco.

***Martin, Ann M.** Claudia Gets Her Guy. (Baby-Sitters Club Friends Forever Ser.: No. 7). 144p. (J). (gr. 3-7). 2000. pap. 5.50 (*0-590-52338-4*) Scholastic Inc.

Martin, Ann M. Claudia Kishi, Live from WSTO! (Baby-Sitters Club Ser.: No. 85). 1995. pap. text 3.99 (*0-590-94784-2*) Scholastic Inc.

— Claudia Kishi, Live from WSTO! (Baby-Sitters Club Ser.: No. 85). 192p. (J). (gr. 4-6). 1995. pap. text 3.50 (*0-590-48236-X*) Scholastic Inc.

— Claudia Kishi, Live from WSTO! (Baby-Sitters Club Ser.: No. 85). 1995. 9.09 (*0-606-07227-6*, Pub. by Turtleback) Demco.

Martin, Ann M. Claudia Kishi, Live from WTSO!; Mary Anne & Camp BSC; Stacey & the Bad Girls; Farewell Dawn, Bks. 85-88. (Baby-Sitters Club Ser.: 22). 1997. pap., boxed set 14.00 (*0-590-25155-4*) Scholastic Inc.

Martin, Ann M. Claudia Kishi, Middle School Drop Out. LC 49-117780. (Baby-Sitters Club Ser.: No. 101). (J). (gr. 3-7). 1996. pap. text 3.99 (*0-590-69207-0*) Scholastic Inc.

— Claudia Kishi, Middle School Drop Out. (Baby-Sitters Club Ser.: No. 101). 1996. 9.09 (*0-606-10131-4*, Pub. by Turtleback) Demco.

— Claudia Makes up Her Mind. (Baby-Sitters Club Ser.: No. 113). 1997. pap. text 3.99 (*0-590-05991-2*) Scholastic Inc.

Martin, Ann M. Claudia Makes up Her Mind. (Baby-Sitters Club Ser.: No. 113). (J). 1997. 9.09 (*0-606-12882-4*, Pub. by Turtleback) Demco.

Martin, Ann M. Claudia, Queen of the Seventh Grade. (Baby-Sitters Club Ser.: No. 106). (J). 1997. mass mkt. 3.99 (*0-590-69212-7*) Scholastic Inc.

Martin, Ann M. Claudia, Queen of the Seventh Grade. (Baby-Sitters Club Ser.: No. 106). 1997. 9.09 (*0-606-11066-6*, Pub. by Turtleback) Demco.

Martin, Ann M. Claudia's Big Party. (Baby-Sitters Club Ser.: No. 123). 140p. (J) (gr. 3-7). 1998. pap. 3.99 (*0-590-50174-7*) Scholastic Inc.

— Claudia's Book. (Baby-Sitters Club Portrait Collection). 160p. (J). (gr. 4-6). 1995. pap. 3.50 (*0-590-48400-1*) Scholastic Inc.

— Claudia's Book. (Baby-Sitters Club Portrait Collection). (J). 1995. 8.60 (*0-606-07242-X*, Pub. by Turtleback) Demco.

— Claudia's Freind Friend. (Baby-Sitters Club Ser.: No. 63). 192p. (J). (gr. 3-7). 1993. pap. 3.50 (*0-590-45665-2*) Scholastic Inc.

Martin, Ann M. Claudia's Freind Friend. (Baby-Sitters Club Ser.: No. 63). 1993. 8.60 (*0-606-05135-X*, Pub. by Turtleback) Demco.

Martin, Ann M. The Complete Guide to the Baby-Sitters Club. (Baby-Sitters Club Ser.). 240p. (J). (gr. 4-7). 1996. pap. text 4.95 (*0-590-92713-2*) Scholastic Inc.

Martin, Ann M. The Complete Guide to the Baby-Sitters Club. (Baby-Sitters Club Ser.). 1996. 10.05 (*0-606-09036-3*, Pub. by Turtleback) Demco.

Martin, Ann M. Dawn. (California Diaries: Vol. 1). 176p. (YA). (gr. 4-8). 1997. mass mkt. 3.99 (*0-590-29835-6*) Scholastic Inc.

Martin, Ann M. Dawn. (California Diaries). (YA). (gr. 6-8). 1997. 9.09 (*0-606-11179-4*, Pub. by Turtleback) Demco.

Martin, Ann M. Dawn: Diary Three. (California Diaries: Vol. 11). 144p. (gr. 6-8). 1999. pap. text 3.99 (*0-590-02389-6*) Scholastic Inc.

— Dawn: Diary Two. (California Diaries: Vol. 7). (J). (gr. 6-8). 1998. pap. text 3.99 (*0-590-01846-9*) Scholastic Inc.

***Martin, Ann M.** Dawn: Diary Two. (California Diaries). (YA). (gr. 6-8). 1998. 9.09 (*0-606-13238-4*, Pub. by Turtleback) Demco.

Martin, Ann M. Dawn & the Big Sleepover. LC 96-17009. (Baby-Sitters Club Ser.: No. 44). 176p. (J). 1996. lib. bdg. 21.27 (*0-8368-1568-8*) Gareth Stevens Inc.

— Dawn & the Big Sleepover. (Baby-Sitters Club Ser.: No. 44). (J). (gr. 3-7). 1991. pap. 3.99 (*0-590-74244-2*) Scholastic Inc.

— Dawn & the Big Sleepover. (Baby-Sitters Club Ser.: No. 44). 192p. (J). (gr. 4-6). 1991. pap. 3.50 (*0-590-43573-6*) Scholastic Inc.

Martin, Ann M. Dawn & the Big Sleepover. (Baby-Sitters Club Ser.: No. 44). (J). 1991. 9.09 (*0-606-04902-9*, Pub. by Turtleback) Demco.

Martin, Ann M. Dawn & the Disappearing Dogs. (Baby-Sitters Club Mystery Ser.: No. 7). 176p. (J). (gr. 4-6). 1993. pap. 3.50 (*0-590-44960-5*) Scholastic Inc.

— Dawn & the Disappearing Dogs. (Baby-Sitters Club Mystery Ser.: No. 7). (J). 1993. 8.60 (*0-606-02503-0*, Pub. by Turtleback) Demco.

— Dawn & the Halloween Mystery. (Baby-Sitters Club Mystery Ser.: No. 17). 176p. (J). (gr. 3-7). 1994. pap. 3.50 (*0-590-48232-7*) Scholastic Inc.

— Dawn & the Halloween Mystery. (Baby-Sitters Club Mystery Ser.: No. 17). 1994. 8.60 (*0-606-06209-2*, Pub. by Turtleback) Demco.

— Dawn & the Impossible Three. LC 95-21315. (Baby-Sitters Club Ser.: No. 5). 144p. (J). (gr. 4-6). 1987. pap. 3.50 (*0-590-43720-8*) Scholastic Inc.

— Dawn & the Impossible Three. (Baby-Sitters Club Ser.: No. 5). 192p. (J). (gr. 3-7). 1995. pap. text 3.50 (*0-590-25160-0*) Scholastic Inc.

Martin, Ann M. Dawn & the Impossible Three. (Baby-Sitters Club Ser.: No. 5). (J). 1987. 8.60 (*0-606-00545-5*, Pub. by Turtleback) Demco.

Martin, Ann M. Dawn & the Impossible Three. 2nd ed. (Baby-Sitters Club Ser.: No. 5). (J). (gr. 4-6). 1988. pap. 3.50 (*0-590-42232-4*) Scholastic Inc.

— Dawn & the Older Boy. (Baby-Sitters Club Ser.: No. 37). 192p. (J). (gr. 4-6). 1990. pap. 3.25 (*0-590-43566-3*) Scholastic Inc.

— Dawn & the Older Boy. (Baby-Sitters Club Ser.: No. 37). (J). (gr. 3-7). 1997. pap. text 3.99 (*0-590-73337-0*) Scholastic Inc.

— Dawn & the Older Boy. (Baby-Sitters Club Ser.: No. 37). (J). 1990. 9.09 (*0-606-04650-X*, Pub. by Turtleback) Demco.

— Dawn & the School Spirit War. (Baby-Sitters Club Ser.: No. 84). 192p. (J). (gr. 4-6). 1995. pap. 3.50 (*0-590-48228-9*) Scholastic Inc.

Martin, Ann M. Dawn & the School Spirit War. (Baby-Sitters Club Ser.: No. 84). 1995. 8.60 (*0-606-07226-8*, Pub. by Turtleback) Demco.

Martin, Ann M. Dawn & the Surfer Ghost. (Baby-Sitters Club Mystery Ser.: No. 12). 176p. (J). (gr. 4-6). 1993. pap. 3.50 (*0-590-47050-7*) Scholastic Inc.

Martin, Ann M. Dawn & the Surfer Ghost. (Baby-Sitters Club Mystery Ser.: No. 12). (J). 1993. 8.60 (*0-606-05739-0*, Pub. by Turtleback) Demco.

Martin, Ann M. Dawn & the We Love Kids Club. (Baby-Sitters Club Ser.: No. 72). 192p. (J). (gr. 4-6). 1994. pap. 3.99 (*0-590-47010-8*) Scholastic Inc.

— Dawn & the We Love Kids Club. (Baby-Sitters Club Ser.: No. 72). (J). (gr. 4-7). 1997. pap. text 3.99 (*0-590-92603-9*) Scholastic Inc.

Martin, Ann M. Dawn & the We Love Kids Club. (Baby-Sitters Club Ser.: No. 72). (J). 1994. 8.60 (*0-606-05737-4*, Pub. by Turtleback) Demco.

Martin, Ann M. Dawn & Too Many Sitters. LC 00-5843. (Baby-Sitters Club Ser.: No. 98). (J). (gr. 3-7). 1996. pap. text 3.99 (*0-590-22882-X*) Scholastic Inc.

— Dawn & Too Many Sitters. (Baby-Sitters Club Ser.: No. 98). (YA). 1996. 9.09 (*0-606-09034-7*, Pub. by Turtleback) Demco.

— Dawn & Whitney, Friends Forever. (Baby-Sitters Club Ser.: No. 77). 192p. (J). (gr. 3-7). 1994. pap. 3.99 (*0-590-48221-1*) Scholastic Inc.

Martin, Ann M. Dawn & Whitney, Friends Forever. (Baby-Sitters Club Ser.: No. 77). (J). 1994. 9.09 (*0-606-06203-3*, Pub. by Turtleback) Demco.

Martin, Ann M. Dawn on the Coast. (Baby-Sitters Club Ser.: No. 23). (J). pap. 3.95 (*0-590-42007-0*) Scholastic Inc.

— Dawn on the Coast. (Baby-Sitters Club Ser.: No. 23). 192p. (J). (gr. 4-6). 1989. pap. 3.50 (*0-590-43900-6*) Scholastic Inc.

— Dawn on the Coast. (Baby-Sitters Club Ser.: No. 23). 160p. (J). (gr. 3-7). 1997. pap. text 3.99 (*0-590-67391-2*) Scholastic Inc.

— Dawn on the Coast. (Baby-Sitters Club Ser.: No. 23). (J). 1989. 9.09 (*0-606-04085-4*, Pub. by Turtleback) Demco.

— Dawn Saves the Planet. (Baby-Sitters Club Ser.: No. 57). 192p. (J). (gr. 3-7). 1992. 3.50 (*0-590-45658-X*, 052) Scholastic Inc.

Martin, Ann M. Dawn Saves the Planet. (Baby-Sitters Club Ser.: No. 57). (J). 1992. 8.60 (*0-606-01806-9*, Pub. by Turtleback) Demco.

Martin, Ann M. Dawn Schafer, Undercover Baby-Sitter. (Baby-Sitters Club Mystery Ser.: No. 26). (J). (gr. 3-7). 1996. pap. text 3.99 (*0-590-22870-6*) Scholastic Inc.

— Dawn Schafer, Undercover Baby-Sitter. (Baby-Sitters Club Mystery Ser.: No. 26). (YA). 1996. 9.09 (*0-606-09040-1*, Pub. by Turtleback) Demco.

— Dawn y Los Mensajes Aterradores. (El Club de Las Canguro Ser.). 1995. 15.05 (*0-606-10395-3*, Pub. by Turtleback) Demco.

— Dawn's Big Date. LC 96-12304. (Baby-Sitters Club Ser.: No. 50). 176p. (J). (gr. 4 up). 1996. lib. bdg. 21.27 (*0-8368-1574-2*) Gareth Stevens Inc.

— Dawn's Big Date. (Baby-Sitters Club Ser.: No. 50). 192p. (J). (gr. 4-6). 1992. pap. 3.50 (*0-590-44969-9*) Scholastic Inc.

— Dawn's Big Date. (Baby-Sitters Club Ser.: No. 50). 1997. pap. text 3.50 (*0-590-98496-9*) Scholastic Inc.

— Dawn's Big Date. (Baby-Sitters Club Ser.: No. 50). (J). 1992. 9.09 (*0-606-00382-7*, Pub. by Turtleback) Demco.

— Dawn's Big Move. LC 94-146947. (Baby-Sitters Club Ser.: No. 67). 192p. (J). (gr. 3-7). 1993. pap. 3.50 (*0-590-47005-1*) Scholastic Inc.

Martin, Ann M. Dawn's Big Move. (Baby-Sitters Club Ser.: No. 67). (J). 1993. 8.60 (*0-606-05139-2*, Pub. by Turtleback) Demco.

Martin, Ann M. Dawn's Book. (Baby-Sitters Club Portrait Collection). 160p. (J). (gr. 4-6). 1995. mass mkt. 3.50 (*0-590-22864-1*) Scholastic Inc.

— Dawn's Book. (Baby-Sitters Club Portrait Collection). (J). 1995. 8.60 (*0-606-07243-8*, Pub. by Turtleback) Demco.

— Dawn's Family Feud. LC 94-146954. (Baby-Sitters Club Ser.: No. 64). 192p. (J). (gr. 3-7). 1993. pap. 3.50 (*0-590-45666-0*) Scholastic Inc.

Martin, Ann M. Dawn's Family Feud. (Baby-Sitters Club Ser.: No. 64). 1993. 8.60 (*0-606-05136-8*, Pub. by Turtleback) Demco.

Martin, Ann M. Dawn's Wicked Stepsister. (Baby-Sitters Club Ser.: No. 31). 192p. (J). (gr. 4-6). 1990. pap. 3.50 (*0-590-42497-1*) Scholastic Inc.

— Dawn's Wicked Stepsister. (Baby-Sitters Club Ser.: No. 31). (J). (gr. 3-7). 1997. pap. text 3.99 (*0-590-73186-6*) Scholastic Inc.

— Dawn's Wicked Stepsister. (Baby-Sitters Club Ser.: No. 31). (J). 1990. 9.09 (*0-606-00676-1*, Pub. by Turtleback) Demco.

— Don't Give Up, Mallory. (Baby-Sitters Club Ser.: No. 108). (J). 1997. mass mkt. 3.99 (*0-590-69214-3*, Apple Paperbacks) Scholastic Inc.

Martin, Ann M. Don't Give Up, Mallory. (Baby-Sitters Club Ser.: No. 108). 1997. 9.09 (*0-606-11068-2*, Pub. by Turtleback) Demco.

Martin, Ann M. Ducky. (California Diaries: Vol. 5). (J). (gr. 6-8). 1998. pap. text 3.99 (*0-590-29839-9*) Scholastic Inc.

***Martin, Ann M.** Ducky: Diary Three. (California Diaries: Vol. 15). 144p. (YA). (gr. 4-7). 2000. pap. 4.99 (*0-439-09549-2*, Little Apple) Scholastic Inc.

Martin, Ann M. Ducky: Diary Two. (California Diaries). 144p. (J). (gr. 6-8). 1998. pap. 3.99 (*0-590-02387-X*) Scholastic Inc.

***Martin, Ann M.** Ducky: Diary Two. (California Diaries). (YA). (gr. 6-8). 1998. pap. text 71.82 (*0-590-63083-0*) Scholastic Inc.

Martin, Ann M. Eleven Kids, One Summer. 160p. (J). (gr. 4-7). 1993. pap. 3.50 (*0-590-45917-1*) Scholastic Inc.

Martin, Ann M. Eleven Kids, One Summer. (J). 1991. 8.60 (*0-606-05264-X*, Pub. by Turtleback) Demco.

An Asterisk (*) at the beginning of an entry indicates that the title is appearing for the first time.

Martin, Ann M. Everything Changes. (Baby-Sitters Club Friends Forever Ser.). (J). (gr. 3-7). 1999. pap. 4.50 (0-590-50391-X, Pub. by Scholastic Inc) Penguin Putnam.

*Martin, Ann M. Everything Changes. (Baby-Sitters Club Friends Forever Special Ser.). (YA). (gr. 4-7). 1999. pap. text 5.50 (0-439-08324-9) Scholastic Inc.

Martin, Ann M. Farewell, Dawn. (Baby-Sitters Club Ser.: No. 88). 192p. (J). (gr. 4-6). 1995. pap. 3.50 (0-590-22872-2) Scholastic Inc.

— Farewell, Dawn. (Baby-Sitters Club Ser.: No. 88). (J). 1995. 8.60 (0-606-07230-6, Pub. by Turtleback) Demco.

*Martin, Ann M. The Fire at Mary Anne's House. (Baby-Sitters Club Ser.: No. 131). (Illus.). (J). 1999. pap. 4.50 (0-590-50390-1, Apple Classics) Scholastic Inc.

Martin, Ann M. Fire Truck to the Rescue. LC 95-207863. (Tonka Trucks Storybook Ser.). 32p. (J). (ps-3). 1994. pap. 2.99 (0-590-48854-6) Scholastic Inc.

— Get Well Soon, Mallory. (Baby-Sitters Club Ser.: No. 69). 192p. (J). (gr. 4-6). 1993. pap. 3.50 (0-590-47007-8) Scholastic Inc.

— Get Well Soon, Mallory. (Baby-Sitters Club Ser.: No. 69). (J). 1997. pap. text 3.99 (0-590-92600-4) Scholastic Inc.

Martin, Ann M. Get Well Soon, Mallory. (Baby-Sitters Club Ser.: No. 69). (J). 1993. 8.60 (0-606-05734-X, Pub. by Turtleback) Demco.

Martin, Ann M. The Ghost at Dawn's House. LC 88-21506. (Baby-Sitters Club Ser.: No. 9). (J). (gr. 3-7). 1996. pap. text 3.99 (0-590-25164-3) Scholastic Inc.

Martin, Ann M. The Ghost at Dawn's House. (Baby-Sitters Club Ser.: No. 9). (J). 1988. 8.60 (0-606-03549-4, Pub. by Turtleback) Demco.

Martin, Ann M. The Ghost at Dawn's House, No. 9. (Baby-Sitters Club Ser.: No. 9). 192p. (J). (gr. 4-6). 1988. pap. 3.50 (0-590-43508-6) Scholastic Inc.

— Good-Bye Stacey, Good-Bye. (Baby-Sitters Club Ser.: No. 13). 192p. (J). (gr. 4-6). 1988. pap. 3.50 (0-590-43386-5) Scholastic Inc.

— Good-Bye Stacey, Good-Bye. (Baby-Sitters Club Ser.: No. 13). 176p. (J). (gr. 3-7). 1996. pap. text 3.99 (0-590-25168-6) Scholastic Inc.

Martin, Ann M. Good-Bye Stacey, Good-Bye. (Baby-Sitters Club Ser.: No. 13). (J). 1988. 9.09 (0-606-03794-2, Pub. by Turtleback) Demco.

Martin, Ann M. Halloween Parade. (Kids in Ms. Colman's Class Ser.: No. 9). (Illus.). 96p. (J). (gr. 1-4). 1997. pap. text 3.50 (0-590-06001-5) Scholastic Inc.

— Happy Holidays, Jessi. LC 00-9058. (Baby-Sitters Club Ser.: No. 103). 137p. (J). (gr. 3-7). 1996. pap. 3.99 (0-590-69209-7) Scholastic Inc.

— Happy Holidays, Jessi. (Baby-Sitters Club Ser.: No. 103). 1996. 9.09 (0-606-10133-0, Pub. by Turtleback) Demco.

— Hello, Mallory. (Baby-Sitters Club Ser.: No. 14). 192p. (J). (gr. 4-6). 1988. pap. 3.50 (0-590-43385-7) Scholastic Inc.

— Hello, Mallory. (Baby-Sitters Club Ser.: No. 14). (J). (gr. 3-7). 1996. pap. text 3.99 (0-590-25169-4) Scholastic Inc.

Martin, Ann M. Hello, Mallory. (Baby-Sitters Club Ser.: No. 14). (J). 1988. 9.09 (0-606-03809-4, Pub. by Turtleback) Demco.

Martin, Ann M. Here Come the Bridesmaids! (Baby-Sitters Club Super Special Ser.: No. 12). 256p. (J). (gr. 3-7). 1994. pap. 3.95 (0-590-48308-0) Scholastic Inc.

Martin, Ann M. Here Come the Bridesmaids! (Baby-Sitters Club Super Special Ser.: No. 12). 1994. 9.05 (0-606-06923-2, Pub. by Turtleback) Demco.

Martin, Ann M. Holiday Time. (Kids in Ms. Colman's Class Ser.: No. 10). (J). (gr. 1-4). 1997. pap. text 3.50 (0-590-06003-1) Scholastic Inc.

— Jessi & the Awful Secret. (Baby-Sitters Club Ser.: No. 61). 192p. (J). (gr. 4-6). 1993. pap. 3.50 (0-590-45663-6) Scholastic Inc.

— Jessi & the Awful Secret. (Baby-Sitters Club Ser.: No. 61). (J). (gr. 4-7). 1997. pap. text 3.99 (0-590-92589-X) Scholastic Inc.

Martin, Ann M. Jessi & the Awful Secret. (Baby-Sitters Club Ser.: No. 61). (J). 1993. 9.09 (0-606-02499-9, Pub. by Turtleback) Demco.

Martin, Ann M. Jessi & the Bad Baby-Sitter. LC 94-150106. (Baby-Sitters Club Ser.: No. 68). 192p. (J). (gr. 3-7). 1993. pap. 3.50 (0-590-47006-X) Scholastic Inc.

Martin, Ann M. Jessi & the Bad Baby-Sitter. (Baby-Sitters Club Ser.: No. 68). (J). 1993. 8.60 (0-606-05140-6, Pub. by Turtleback) Demco.

Martin, Ann M. Jessi & the Dance School Phantom. LC 96-17007. (Baby-Sitters Club Ser.: No. 42). 144p. (J). (gr. 4 up). 1996. lib. bdg. 21.27 (0-8368-1566-1) Gareth Stevens Inc.

— Jessi & the Dance School Phantom. (Baby-Sitters Club Ser.: No. 42). (J). (gr. 3-7). 1991. pap. text 3.99 (0-590-74242-6) Scholastic Inc.

— Jessi & the Dance School Phantom. (Baby-Sitters Club Ser.: No. 42). 192p. (J). (gr. 4-6). 1991. pap. 3.50 (0-590-44083-7, Apple Paperbacks) Scholastic Inc.

— Jessi & the Dance School Phantom. (Baby-Sitters Club Ser.: No. 42). (J). 1991. 9.09 (0-606-04950-9, Pub. by Turtleback) Demco.

— Jessi & the Jewel Thieves. (Baby-Sitters Club Mystery Ser.: No. 8). 176p. (J). (gr. 4-6). 1993. pap. 3.50 (0-590-44959-1) Scholastic Inc.

Martin, Ann M. Jessi & the Jewel Thieves. (Baby-Sitters Club Mystery Ser.: No. 8). (J). 1993. 9.09 (0-606-05143-0, Pub. by Turtleback) Demco.

Martin, Ann M. Jessi & the Superbrat. (Baby-Sitters Club Ser.: No. 27). 192p. (YA). (gr. 4-6). 1989. pap. 3.50 (0-590-42502-1, Apple Paperbacks) Scholastic Inc.

— Jessi & the Superbrat. (Baby-Sitters Club Ser.: No. 27). 160p. (J). (gr. 3-7). 1997. pap. text 3.99 (0-590-67395-5) Scholastic Inc.

— Jessi & the Superbrat. (Baby-Sitters Club Ser.: No. 27). (J). 1989. 8.60 (0-606-01558-2, Pub. by Turtleback) Demco.

— Jessi & the Troublemaker. (Baby-Sitters Club Ser.: No. 82). 192p. (J). (gr. 4-6). 1995. pap. 3.99 (0-590-48226-2) Scholastic Inc.

— Jessi & the Troublemaker. (Baby-Sitters Club Ser.: No. 82). (J). (gr. 4-7). 1997. pap. text 3.99 (0-590-94777-X) Scholastic Inc.

Martin, Ann M. Jessi & the Troublemaker. (Baby-Sitters Club Ser.: No. 82). 1995. 9.09 (0-606-07224-1, Pub. by Turtleback) Demco.

Martin, Ann M. Jessi Ramsey, Pet-Sitter. (Baby-Sitters Club Ser.: No. 22). 192p. (J). (gr. 4-6). 1989. pap. text 3.50 (0-590-43658-9) Scholastic Inc.

— Jessi Ramsey, Pet-Sitter. (Baby-Sitters Club Ser.: No. 22). (J). (gr. 3-7). 1997. pap. text 3.99 (0-590-67390-4) Scholastic Inc.

— Jessi Ramsey, Pet-Sitter. (Baby-Sitters Club Ser.: No. 22). (J). 1989. 9.09 (0-606-04086-2, Pub. by Turtleback) Demco.

— Jessi Ramsey, Pet-Sitter. large type ed. LC 94-28695. (Baby-Sitters Club Ser.: No. 22). 144p. (J). (gr. 4 up). 1994. lib. bdg. 21.27 (0-8368-1243-3) Gareth Stevens Inc.

— Jessi's Baby-Sitter. (Baby-Sitters Club Ser.: No. 36). (gr. 3-7). 1990. pap. text 3.99 (0-590-73285-4) Scholastic Inc.

— Jessi's Baby-Sitter. (Baby-Sitters Club Ser.: No. 36). 192p. (J). (gr. 4-6). 1990. pap. 3.50 (0-590-43565-5) Scholastic Inc.

Martin, Ann M. Jessi's Baby-Sitter. (Baby-Sitters Club Ser.: No. 36). (J). 1990. 9.09 (0-606-04444-2, Pub. by Turtleback) Demco.

Martin, Ann M. Jessi's Big Break. (Baby-Sitters Club Ser.: No. 115). (J). 1998. pap. text 3.99 (0-590-05993-9, Apple Paperbacks) Scholastic Inc.

*Martin, Ann M. Jessi's Big Break. (Baby-Sitters Club Ser.: No. 115). (J). 1998. 9.09 (0-606-13159-0, Pub. by Turtleback) Demco.

Martin, Ann M. Jessi's Gold Medal. (Baby-Sitters Club Ser.: No. 55). (J). 1992. mass mkt. 3.99 (0-590-92580-6) Scholastic Inc.

— Jessi's Gold Medal. (Baby-Sitters Club Ser.: No. 55). 192p. (J). (gr. 4-6). 1992. pap. 3.25 (0-590-44964-8, Apple Paperbacks) Scholastic Inc.

— Jessi's Gold Medal. (Baby-Sitters Club Ser.: No. 55). (J). 1992. 9.09 (0-606-01858-1, Pub. by Turtleback) Demco.

— Jessi's Horrible Prank. (Baby-Sitters Club Ser.: No. 75). 192p. (J). (gr. 3-7). 1994. pap. 3.50 (0-590-47013-2) Scholastic Inc.

Martin, Ann M. Jessi's Horrible Prank. (Baby-Sitters Club Ser.: No. 75). 1994. 8.60 (0-606-06201-7, Pub. by Turtleback) Demco.

Martin, Ann M. Jessi's Secret Language. (Baby-Sitters Club Ser.: No. 16). 192p. (J). (gr. 4-6). 1988. pap. 3.50 (0-590-44234-1) Scholastic Inc.

— Jessi's Secret Language. (Baby-Sitters Club Ser.: No. 16). (J). (gr. 3-7). 1996. pap. text 3.99 (0-590-60410-4) Scholastic Inc.

— Jessi's Secret Language. (Baby-Sitters Club Ser.: No. 16). (J). 1988. 8.60 (0-606-04087-0, Pub. by Turtleback) Demco.

— Jessi's Secret Language. large type ed. LC 93-15971. (Baby-Sitters Club Ser.: No. 16). 176p. (J). (gr. 4 up). 1993. lib. bdg. 21.27 (0-8368-1020-1) Gareth Stevens Inc.

— Jessi's Wish. LC 96-15684. (Baby-Sitters Club Ser.: No. 48). 144p. (J). (gr. 4 up). 1996. lib. bdg. 21.27 (0-8368-1572-6) Gareth Stevens Inc.

— Jessi's Wish. (Baby-Sitters Club Ser.: No. 48). 192p. (J). (gr. 4-6). 1991. pap. 3.50 (0-590-43571-X) Scholastic Inc.

— Jessi's Wish. (Baby-Sitters Club Ser.: No. 48). (J). (gr. 4 up). 1993. pap. 3.50 (0-685-66003-6) Scholastic Inc.

— Jessi's Wish. (Baby-Sitters Club Ser.: No. 48). (J). 1991. 8.60 (0-606-00523-4, Pub. by Turtleback) Demco.

— Just a Summer Romance. LC 86-46201. 170p. (YA). (gr. 7 up). 1987. 13.95 (0-8234-0649-0) Holiday.

— Just a Summer Romance. 176p. (YA). (gr. 7-9). 1988. pap. 3.50 (0-590-43999-5) Scholastic Inc.

— Karen, Hannie, & Nancy: The Three Musketeers. (Baby-Sitters Little Sister Super Special Ser.: No. 4). 128p. (J). (gr. 2-4). 1992. pap. 2.95 (0-590-45644-X, Little Apple) Scholastic Inc.

— Karen, Hannie, & Nancy: The Three Musketeers. (Baby-Sitters Little Sister Super Special Ser.: No. 4). (J). 1992. 8.05 (0-606-01859-X, Pub. by Turtleback) Demco.

— Karen's Accident. LC 00-9435. (Baby-Sitters Little Sister Ser.: No. 81). 109p. (J). (gr. 2-4). 1997. mass mkt. 2.99 (0-590-69189-9) Scholastic Inc.

Martin, Ann M. Karen's Accident. (Baby-Sitters Little Sister Ser.: No. 81). (J). 1997. 8.09 (0-606-10747-9, Pub. by Turtleback) Demco.

Martin, Ann M. Karen's Angel. (Baby-Sitters Little Sister Ser.: No. 68). (J). 1995. pap. 2.95 (0-590-26025-1) Scholastic Inc.

— Karen's Angel. (Baby-Sitters Little Sister Ser.: No. 68). (J). 1995. 8.05 (0-606-08485-1, Pub. by Turtleback) Demco.

— Karen's Baby. (Baby-Sitters Little Sister Super Special Ser.: No. 5). 128p. (J). (gr. 4-7). 1992. pap. 3.50 (0-590-45649-0) Scholastic Inc.

— Karen's Baby. (Baby-Sitters Little Sister Super Special Ser.: No. 5). (J). 1992. 8.60 (0-606-02512-X, Pub. by Turtleback) Demco.

— Karen's Baby-Sitter. (Baby-Sitters Little Sister Ser.: No. 46). 112p. (J). (gr. 2-4). 1994. pap. 2.95 (0-590-47045-0) Scholastic Inc.

Martin, Ann M. Karen's Baby-Sitter. (Baby-Sitters Little Sister Ser.: No. 46). (J). 1994. 8.05 (0-606-05744-7, Pub. by Turtleback) Demco.

Martin, Ann M. Karen's Big City Mystery. (Baby-Sitters Little Sister Ser.: No. 99). (J). 1998. pap. text 3.50 (0-590-49760-X, Little Apple) Scholastic Inc.

— Karen's Big City Mystery. (Baby-Sitters Little Sister Ser.: No. 99). (J). 1998. 8.60 (0-606-13175-2, Pub. by Turtleback) Demco.

— Karen's Big Fight. (Baby-Sitters Little Sister Ser.: No. 79). (J). (gr. 2-4). 1996. pap. 2.95 (0-590-69187-2) Scholastic Inc.

— Karen's Big Fight. (Baby-Sitters Little Sister Ser.: No. 79). 1996. 8.05 (0-606-10137-3, Pub. by Turtleback) Demco.

— Karen's Big Job. (Baby-Sitters Little Sister Ser.: No. 84). (J). (gr. 4-7). 1997. pap. 3.50 (0-590-69192-9, 691553) Scholastic Inc.

— Karen's Big Job. (Baby-Sitters Little Sister Ser.: No. 84). (YA). 1997. 8.60 (0-606-11081-X, Pub. by Turtleback) Demco.

— Karen's Big Joke. (Baby-Sitters Little Sister Ser.: No. 27). 112p. (J). (gr. 2-4). 1992. pap. 2.95 (0-590-44829-3) Scholastic Inc.

— Karen's Big Joke. (Baby-Sitters Little Sister Ser.: No. 27). (J). 1992. 8.05 (0-606-01860-3, Pub. by Turtleback) Demco.

— Karen's Big Lie. (Baby-Sitters Little Sister Ser.: No. 38). 112p. (J). (gr. 4-7). 1993. pap. 2.95 (0-590-45655-5) Scholastic Inc.

Martin, Ann M. Karen's Big Lie. (Baby-Sitters Little Sister Ser.: No. 38). (J). 1993. 8.05 (0-606-05149-X, Pub. by Turtleback) Demco.

Martin, Ann M. Karen's Big Move. (Baby-Sitters Little Sister Ser.: No. 96). (J). 1998. pap. 3.50 (0-590-06594-7, Little Apple) Scholastic Inc.

— Karen's Big Move. (Baby-Sitters Little Sister Ser.: No. 96). (J). 1998. 8.60 (0-606-13172-8, Pub. by Turtleback) Demco.

— Karen's Big Sister. LC 00-4440. (Baby-Sitters Little Sister Ser.: No. 69). (J). (gr. 2-4). 1996. pap. text 2.95 (0-590-26193-2) Scholastic Inc.

— Karen's Big Sister. (Baby-Sitters Little Sister Ser.: No. 69). (J). 1996. 8.05 (0-606-08486-X, Pub. by Turtleback) Demco.

— Karen's Big Top. (Baby-Sitters Little Sister Ser.: No. 51). 112p. (J). (gr. 4-7). 1994. pap. 2.95 (0-590-48229-7) Scholastic Inc.

Martin, Ann M. Karen's Big Top. (Baby-Sitters Little Sister Ser.: No. 51). 1994. 8.05 (0-606-06215-7, Pub. by Turtleback) Demco.

Martin, Ann M. Karen's Big Weekend. LC 94-150578. (Baby-Sitters Little Sister Ser.: No. 44). 112p. (J). (gr. 2-4). 1993. pap. 2.95 (0-590-47043-4) Scholastic Inc.

Martin, Ann M. Karen's Big Weekend. (Baby-Sitters Little Sister Ser.: No. 44). (J). 1993. 8.05 (0-606-05742-0, Pub. by Turtleback) Demco.

Martin, Ann M. Karen's Birthday. (Baby-Sitters Little Sister Ser.: No. 7). 112p. (J). (gr. 2-4). 1990. pap. 2.95 (0-590-44257-0) Scholastic Inc.

Martin, Ann M. Karen's Birthday. (Baby-Sitters Little Sister Ser.: No. 7). (J). 1990. 8.05 (0-606-04456-6, Pub. by Turtleback) Demco.

Martin, Ann M. Karen's Black Cat. (Baby-Sitters Little Sister Ser.: No. 102). (J). 1998. pap. 3.50 (0-590-50054-6) Scholastic Inc.

— Karen's Book. (Baby-Sitters Little Sister Ser.: No. 100). (J). 1998. pap. 3.50 (0-590-50051-1, Apple Paperbacks) Scholastic Inc.

— Karen's Book. (Baby-Sitters Little Sister Ser.: No. 100). (J). 1998. 8.60 (0-606-13167-1, Pub. by Turtleback) Demco.

— Karen's Brothers. (Baby-Sitters Little Sister Ser.: No. 17). 112p. (J). (gr. 2-4). 1991. pap. 2.95 (0-590-43643-0) Scholastic Inc.

Martin, Ann M. Karen's Brothers. (Baby-Sitters Little Sister Ser.: No. 17). (J). 1991. 8.60 (0-606-04953-3, Pub. by Turtleback) Demco.

Martin, Ann M. Karen's Bully. (Baby-Sitters Little Sister Ser.: No. 31). 112p. (J). (gr. 2-4). 1992. 2.95 (0-590-45646-6, 053) Scholastic Inc.

— Karen's Bully. (Baby-Sitters Little Sister Ser.: No. 31). (J). 1992. 8.05 (0-606-01862-X, Pub. by Turtleback) Demco.

— Karen's Bunny. (Baby-Sitters Little Sister Ser.: No. 83). 112p. (gr. 2-4). 1997. pap. text 3.50 (0-590-69191-0, Apple Paperbacks) Scholastic Inc.

— Karen's Bunny. (Baby-Sitters Little Sister Ser.: No. 83). (YA). 1997. 8.60 (0-606-11080-1, Pub. by Turtleback) Demco.

— Karen's Campout. (Baby-Sitters Little Sister Super Special Ser.: No. 6). 128p. (J). (gr. 3-7). 1993. pap. 3.99 (0-590-46911-8) Scholastic Inc.

Martin, Ann M. Karen's Campout. (Baby-Sitters Little Sister Super Special Ser.: No. 6). (J). 1993. 9.09 (0-606-05147-3, Pub. by Turtleback) Demco.

Martin, Ann M. Karen's Candy. (Baby-Sitters Little Sister Ser.: No. 54). 112p. (J). (gr. 4-7). 1994. pap. 2.95 (0-590-48301-3) Scholastic Inc.

Martin, Ann M. Karen's Candy. (Baby-Sitters Little Sister Ser.: No. 54). (J). 1994. 8.60 (0-606-06218-1, Pub. by Turtleback) Demco.

Martin, Ann M. Karen's Carnival. (Baby-Sitters Little Sister Ser.: No. 20). 112p. (J). (gr. 2-4). 1991. 2.95 (0-590-44823-4) Scholastic Inc.

Martin, Ann M. Karen's Carnival. (Baby-Sitters Little Sister Ser.: No. 20). (J). 1991. 8.60 (0-606-04954-1, Pub. by Turtleback) Demco.

Martin, Ann M. Karen's Cartwheel. LC 94-152641. (Baby-Sitters Little Sister Ser.: No. 29). 112p. (J). (gr. 2-4). 1992. pap. 2.95 (0-590-44825-0) Scholastic Inc.

— Karen's Cartwheel. (Baby-Sitters Little Sister Ser.: No. 29). (J). 1992. 8.05 (0-606-01863-8, Pub. by Turtleback) Demco.

— Karen's Chain Letter. (Baby-Sitters Little Sister Ser.: No. 101). (J). (gr. 2-4). 1998. pap. 3.50 (0-590-50053-8) Scholastic Inc.

— Karen's Chain Letter. (Baby-Sitters Little Sister Ser.: No. 101). (J). 1998. 8.60 (0-606-13168-X, Pub. by Turtleback) Demco.

*Martin, Ann M. Karen's Chicken Pox. Vol. 114. 112p. (gr. 2-4). 1999. mass mkt. 3.99 (0-590-52382-1) Scholastic Inc.

Martin, Ann M. Karen's Christmas Carol. (Baby-Sitters Little Sister Ser.: No. 104). 1998. pap. text 3.50 (0-590-50056-2) Scholastic Inc.

— Karen's Christmas Tree. (Baby-Sitters Little Sister Ser.: No. 80). (J). (gr. 2-4). 1996. pap. 2.99 (0-590-69188-0) Scholastic Inc.

— Karen's Christmas Tree. (Baby-Sitters Little Sister Ser.: No. 80). 1996. 8.09 (0-606-10138-1, Pub. by Turtleback) Demco.

— Karen's Cooking Contest. (Baby-Sitters Little Sister Ser.: No. 93). (J). 1998. pap. text 3.50 (0-590-06591-2, Little Apple) Scholastic Inc.

— Karen's Cooking Contest. (Baby-Sitters Little Sister Ser.: No. 93). (J). 1998. 8.60 (0-606-13169-8, Pub. by Turtleback) Demco.

— Karen's Copycat. (Baby-Sitters Little Sister Ser.: No. 107). 112p. (gr. 2-4). 1999. pap. 3.99 (0-590-50059-7) Scholastic Inc.

— Karen's County Fair. (Baby-Sitters Little Sister Ser.: No. 75). (J). (gr. 2-4). 1996. pap. text 2.95 (0-590-69183-X) Scholastic Inc.

— Karen's County Fair. (Baby-Sitters Little Sister Ser.: No. 75). (YA). 1996. 8.05 (0-606-09050-9, Pub. by Turtleback) Demco.

— Karen's Dinosaur. (Baby-Sitters Little Sister Ser.: No. 73). (J). (gr. 2-4). 1996. pap. text 2.95 (0-590-26301-3) Scholastic Inc.

— Karen's Dinosaur. (Baby-Sitters Little Sister Ser.: No. 73). (YA). 1996. 8.05 (0-606-09048-7, Pub. by Turtleback) Demco.

— Karen's Doll. LC 94-152649. (Baby-Sitters Little Sister Ser.: No. 23). 112p. (J). (gr. 2-4). 1991. pap. 2.95 (0-590-44832-3) Scholastic Inc.

— Karen's Doll. (Baby-Sitters Little Sister Ser.: No. 23). (J). 1991. 8.05 (0-606-00530-7, Pub. by Turtleback) Demco.

— Karen's Doll Hospital. (Baby-Sitters Little Sister Ser.: No. 35). 112p. (J). (gr. 4-7). 1993. pap. 2.95 (0-590-45652-0) Scholastic Inc.

— Karen's Doll Hospital. (Baby-Sitters Little Sister Ser.: No. 35). (J). 1993. 8.05 (0-606-02510-3, Pub. by Turtleback) Demco.

— Karen's Ducklings. (Baby-Sitters Little Sister Ser.: No. 26). 112p. (J). (gr. 2-4). 1992. pap. 2.95 (0-590-44830-7) Scholastic Inc.

— Karen's Ducklings. (Baby-Sitters Little Sister Ser.: No. 26). (J). 1992. 8.05 (0-606-01864-6, Pub. by Turtleback) Demco.

*Martin, Ann M. Karen's Easter Parade. (Baby-Sitters Little Sister Ser.: No. 120). (Illus.). 112p. 2000. mass mkt. 3.99 (0-590-52521-2) Scholastic Inc.

Martin, Ann M. Karen's Field Day. (Baby-Sitters Little Sister Ser.: No. 108). 1999. pap. text 3.99 (0-590-50060-0) Scholastic Inc.

*Martin, Ann M. Karen's Figure Eight. (Baby-Sitters Little Sister Ser.: No. 118). (Illus.). 112p. (J). (gr. 2-4). 2000. pap. 4.99 (0-590-52498-4) Scholastic Inc.

Martin, Ann M. Karen's Fishing Trip. (Baby-Sitters Little Sister Ser.: No. 98). (J). 1998. pap. 3.50 (0-590-06596-3, Little Apple) Scholastic Inc.

*Martin, Ann M. Karen's Fishing Trip. (Baby-Sitters Little Sister Ser.: No. 98). (J). 1998. 8.60 (0-606-13174-4, Pub. by Turtleback) Demco.

Martin, Ann M. Karen's Ghost. (Baby-Sitters Little Sister Ser.: No. 12). 112p. (J). (gr. 2-4). 1990. pap. 2.95 (0-590-43649-X) Scholastic Inc.

— Karen's Ghost. (Baby-Sitters Little Sister Ser.: No. 12). (J). 1990. 8.05 (0-606-04715-8, Pub. by Turtleback) Demco.

— Karen's Goldfish. (Baby-Sitters Little Sister Ser.: No. 16). 112p. (J). (gr. 2-4). 1991. pap. 2.95 (0-590-43644-9) Scholastic Inc.

Martin, Ann M. Karen's Goldfish. (Baby-Sitters Little Sister Ser.: No. 16). (J). 1991. 8.05 (0-606-04955-X, Pub. by Turtleback) Demco.

Martin, Ann M. Karen's Good-Bye. (Baby-Sitters Little Sister Ser.: No. 19). 112p. (J). (gr. 2-4). 1991. pap. 2.95 (0-590-43641-4) Scholastic Inc.

Martin, Ann M. Karen's Good-Bye. (Baby-Sitters Little Sister Ser.: No. 19). 1991. 8.60 (0-606-04956-8, Pub. by Turtleback) Demco.

Martin, Ann M. Karen's Grandad. LC 00-5338. (Baby-Sitters Little Sister Ser.: No. 70). (J). (gr. 2-4). 1996. pap. text 2.95 (0-590-26280-7) Scholastic Inc.

— Karen's Grandad. (Baby-Sitters Little Sister Ser.: No. 70). (YA). 1996. 8.05 (0-606-09045-2, Pub. by Turtleback) Demco.

— Karen's Grandmothers. (Baby-Sitters Little Sister Ser.: No. 10). 112p. (J). (gr. 2-4). 1990. pap. 2.95 (0-590-43651-1) Scholastic Inc.

Martin, Ann M. Karen's Grandmothers. (Baby-Sitters Little Sister Ser.: No. 10). (J). 1990. 8.05 (0-606-04457-4, Pub. by Turtleback) Demco.

Martin, Ann M. Karen's Haircut. (Baby-Sitters Little Sister Ser.: No. 8). 112p. (J). (gr. 2-4). 1990. pap. 2.95 (0-590-42670-2) Scholastic Inc.

Martin, Ann M. Karen's Haircut. (Baby-Sitters Little Sister Ser.: No. 8). (J). 1990. 8.05 (0-606-04458-2, Pub. by Turtleback) Demco.

M

Martin, Ann M. Karen's Half Birthday. LC 49-117840. (Baby-Sitters Little Sister Ser.: No. 78). (J). (gr. 2-4). 1996. pap. text 2.95 (*0-590-69186-4*) Scholastic Inc.

— Karen's Half Birthday. (Baby-Sitters Little Sister Ser.: No. 78). 1996. 8.05 (*0-606-10136-5*, Pub. by Turtleback) Demco.

— Karen's Haunted House. (Baby-Sitters Little Sister Ser.: No. 90). 112p. (J). (gr. 2-5). 1997. pap. text 3.50 (*0-590-06588-2*) Scholastic Inc.

— Karen's Haunted House. (Baby-Sitters Little Sister Ser.: No. 90). (J). 1997. 8.60 (*0-606-11087-9*, Pub. by Turtleback) Demco.

— Karen's Home Run. LC 94-152774. (Baby-Sitters Little Sister Ser.: No. 18). 112p. (J). (gr. 2-4). 1991. pap. 2.95 (*0-590-43642-2*) Scholastic Inc.

Martin, Ann M. Karen's Home Run. (Baby-Sitters Little Sister Ser.: No. 18). (J). 1991. 8.60 (*0-606-04957-6*, Pub. by Turtleback) Demco.

— Karen's Hurricane. (Baby-Sitters Little Sister Ser.: No. 113). (Illus.). (J). 1999. pap. 3.99 (*0-590-52379-1*) Scholastic Inc.

Martin, Ann M. Karen's Ice Skates. (Baby-Sitters Little Sister Ser.: No. 56). 112p. (J). (gr. 4-7). 1994. pap. 2.95 (*0-590-48302-1*) Scholastic Inc.

Martin, Ann M. Karen's Ice Skates. (Baby-Sitters Little Sister Ser.: No. 56). 1994. 8.05 (*0-606-06925-9*, Pub. by Turtleback) Demco.

Martin, Ann M. Karen's in Love. (Baby-Sitters Little Sister Ser.: No. 15). 112p. (J). (gr. 4-7). 1991. pap. 2.95 (*0-590-43645-7*) Scholastic Inc.

— Karen's in Love. (Baby-Sitters Little Sister Ser.: No. 15). (J). 1991. 8.05 (*0-606-04716-6*, Pub. by Turtleback) Demco.

— Karen's Island Adventure. (Baby-Sitters Little Sister Ser.: No. 71). (J). 1996. pap. 2.95 (*0-590-26194-0*) Scholastic Inc.

— Karen's Island Adventure. (Baby-Sitters Little Sister Ser.: No. 71). (YA). 1996. 8.60 (*0-606-09046-0*, Pub. by Turtleback) Demco.

— Karen's Kite. (Baby-Sitters Little Sister Ser.: No. 47). 112p. (J). (gr. 4-7). 1994. pap. 2.95 (*0-590-46913-4*) Scholastic Inc.

Martin, Ann M. Karen's Kite. (Baby-Sitters Little Sister Ser.: No. 47). (J). 1994. 8.05 (*0-606-05745-5*, Pub. by Turtleback) Demco.

Martin, Ann M. Karen's Kittens. (Baby-Sitters Little Sister Ser.: No. 30). 112p. (J). (gr. 2-4). 1992. pap. 2.95 (*0-590-45645-8*) Scholastic Inc.

— Karen's Kittens. (Baby-Sitters Little Sister Ser.: No. 30). (J). 1992. 8.05 (*0-606-01865-4*, Pub. by Turtleback) Demco.

— Karen's Kittycat Club. (Baby-Sitters Little Sister Ser.: No. 4). 112p. (J). (gr. 2-4). 1989. pap. 2.95 (*0-590-44264-3*) Scholastic Inc.

— Karen's Kittycat Club. (Baby-Sitters Little Sister Ser.: No. 4). (J). 1989. 8.05 (*0-606-04259-8*, Pub. by Turtleback) Demco.

— Karen's Lemonade Stand. (Baby-Sitters Little Sister Ser.: No. 64). 112p. (J). (gr. 2-4). 1995. pap. 2.95 (*0-590-25997-0*) Scholastic Inc.

— Karen's Lemonade Stand. (Baby-Sitters Little Sister Ser.: No. 64). (J). 1995. 8.05 (*0-606-07251-9*, Pub. by Turtleback) Demco.

— Karen's Leprechaun. (Baby-Sitters Little Sister Ser.: No. 59). 112p. (J). (gr. 3-7). 1995. pap. 2.95 (*0-590-48231-9*) Scholastic Inc.

— Karen's Leprechaun. (Baby-Sitters Little Sister Ser.: No. 59). (J). 1995. 8.05 (*0-606-07246-2*, Pub. by Turtleback) Demco.

— Karen's Little Sister. (Baby-Sitters Little Sister Ser.: No. 6). 112p. (J). (gr. 2-4). 1989. pap. 2.95 (*0-590-44298-8*) Scholastic Inc.

— Karen's Little Sister. (Baby-Sitters Little Sister Ser.: No. 6). (J). 1989. 8.05 (*0-606-01608-2*, Pub. by Turtleback) Demco.

— Karen's Little Witch. LC 92-106445. (Baby-Sitters Little Sister Ser.: No. 22). 112p. (J). (gr. 2-4). 1991. pap. 2.95 (*0-590-44833-1*) Scholastic Inc.

— Karen's Little Witch. (Baby-Sitters Little Sister Ser.: No. 22). (J). 1991. 8.60 (*0-606-00531-5*, Pub. by Turtleback) Demco.

— Karen's Lucky Penny. (Baby-Sitters Little Sister Ser.: No. 50). 112p. (J). (gr. 2-4). 1994. pap. 2.95 (*0-590-47048-5*) Scholastic Inc.

Martin, Ann M. Karen's Lucky Penny. (Baby-Sitters Little Sister Ser.: No. 50). (J). 1994. 8.05 (*0-606-06214-9*, Pub. by Turtleback) Demco.

Martin, Ann M. Karen's Magic Garden. (Baby-Sitters Little Sister Ser.: No. 76). (J). (gr. 2-4). 1996. pap. text 2.95 (*0-590-69184-8*) Scholastic Inc.

— Karen's Magic Garden. (Baby-Sitters Little Sister Ser.: No. 76). (YA). 1996. 8.05 (*0-606-09051-7*, Pub. by Turtleback) Demco.

— Karen's Magician. (Baby-Sitters Little Sister Ser.: No. 55). 112p. (J). (gr. 4-7). 1994. pap. 2.95 (*0-590-48230-0*) Scholastic Inc.

Martin, Ann M. Karen's Magician. (Baby-Sitters Little Sister Ser.: No. 54). (J). 1994. 8.05 (*0-606-06924-0*, Pub. by Turtleback) Demco.

Martin, Ann M. Karen's Mermaid. (Baby-Sitters Little Sister Ser.: No. 52). 112p. (J). (gr. 4-7). 1994. pap. 2.95 (*0-590-48299-8*) Scholastic Inc.

Martin, Ann M. Karen's Mermaid. (Baby-Sitters Little Sister Ser.: No. 52). (J). 1994. 8.05 (*0-606-06216-5*, Pub. by Turtleback) Demco.

— Karen's Mistake. (Baby-Sitters Little Sister Ser.: No. 117). (Illus.). 112p. (J). (gr. 2-4). 2000. pap. 4.99 (*0-590-52467-4*) Scholastic Inc.

Martin, Ann M. Karen's Monsters. (Baby-Sitters Little Sister Ser.: No. 66). (J). (gr. 2-4). 1995. pap. text 2.95 (*0-590-26279-3*) Scholastic Inc.

— Karen's Monsters. (Baby-Sitters Little Sister Ser.: No. 66). (J). 1995. 8.05 (*0-606-07253-5*, Pub. by Turtleback) Demco.

— Karen's Movie. (Baby-Sitters Little Sister Ser.: No. 63). 112p. (J). (gr. 2-4). 1995. pap. 2.95 (*0-590-25996-2*) Scholastic Inc.

— Karen's Movie. (Baby-Sitters Little Sister Ser.: No. 63). (J). 1995. 8.05 (*0-606-07250-0*, Pub. by Turtleback) Demco.

— Karen's Movie Star. (Baby-Sitters Little Sister Ser.: No. 103). 1998. pap. text 3.50 (*0-590-50055-4*) Scholastic Inc.

— Karen's Mystery. (Baby-Sitters Little Sister Super Special Ser.: No. 3). 128p. (J). (gr. 2-4). 1991. pap. 3.25 (*0-590-44827-7*) Scholastic Inc.

— Karen's Mystery. (Baby-Sitters Little Sister Super Special Ser.: No. 3). (J). 1991. 8.35 (*0-606-00532-3*, Pub. by Turtleback) Demco.

— Karen's Nanny. (Bab-Sitters Club Little Sister Ser.: No. 105). 112p. (gr. 2-4). 1999. pap. text 3.99 (*0-590-50057-0*) Scholastic Inc.

— Karen's New Bike. (Baby-Sitters Little Sister Ser.: No. 62). 112p. (J). (gr. 2-4). 1995. pap. 2.95 (*0-590-48307-2*) Scholastic Inc.

— Karen's New Bike. (Baby-Sitters Little Sister Ser.: No. 62). (J). 1995. 8.05 (*0-606-07249-7*, Pub. by Turtleback) Demco.

— Karen's New Friend. (Baby-Sitters Little Sister Ser.: No. 36). 112p. (J). (gr. 4-7). 1993. pap. 2.95 (*0-590-45651-2*) Scholastic Inc.

— Karen's New Friend. (Baby-Sitters Little Sister Ser.: No. 36). (J). 1993. 8.05 (*0-606-02511-1*, Pub. by Turtleback) Demco.

***Martin, Ann M.** Karen's New Holiday. (Baby-Sitters Little Sister Ser.: No. 112). 112p. (gr. 2-4). 1999. pap. text 3.99 (*0-590-52376-7*) Scholastic Inc.

Martin, Ann M. Karen's New Puppy. (Baby-Sitters Little Sister Ser.: No. 72). (J). 1996. pap. 3.50 (*0-590-26195-9*) Scholastic Inc.

— Karen's New Teacher. (Baby-Sitters Little Sister Ser.: No. 21). 112p. (J). (gr. 2-4). 1991. pap. 2.95 (*0-590-44824-2*) Scholastic Inc.

Martin, Ann M. Karen's New Teacher. (Baby-Sitters Little Sister Ser.: No. 21). (J). 1991. 8.05 (*0-606-00537-4*, Pub. by Turtleback) Demco.

Martin, Ann M. Karen's New Year. (Baby-Sitters Little Sister Ser.: No. 14). 112p. (J). (gr. 2-4). 1991. pap. 2.95 (*0-590-43646-5*) Scholastic Inc.

— Karen's New Year. (Baby-Sitters Little Sister Ser.: No. 15). (J). 1991. 8.05 (*0-606-04717-4*, Pub. by Turtleback) Demco.

— Karen's Newspaper. LC 94-152829. (Baby-Sitters Little Sister Ser.: No. 40). 112p. (J). (gr. 2-4). 1993. pap. 2.95 (*0-590-47040-X*) Scholastic Inc.

— Karen's Newspaper. (Baby-Sitters Little Sister Ser.: No. 40). (J). 1993. 8.05 (*0-606-05151-1*, Pub. by Turtleback) Demco.

— Karen's Paper Route. (Baby-Sitters Little Sister Ser.: No. 97). (Illus.). (J). (gr. 2-4). 1997. pap. text 3.50 (*0-590-06595-5*) Scholastic Inc.

***Martin, Ann M.** Karen's Paper Route. (Baby-Sitters Little Sister Ser.: No. 97). (J). 1998. 8.60 (*0-606-13173-6*, Pub. by Turtleback) Demco.

Martin, Ann M. Karen's Pen Pal. (Baby-Sitters Little Sister Ser.: No. 25). 112p. (J). (gr. 2-4). 1992. pap. 2.95 (*0-590-44831-5*) Scholastic Inc.

— Karen's Pen Pal. (Baby-Sitters Little Sister Ser.: No. 25). (J). 1992. 8.05 (*0-606-00538-2*, Pub. by Turtleback) Demco.

— Karen's Pilgrim. (Baby-Sitters Little Sister Ser.: No. 91). (J). (gr. 2-5). 1997. pap. text 3.50 (*0-590-06589-0*) Scholastic Inc.

Martin, Ann M. Karen's Pilgrim. (Baby-Sitters Little Sister Ser.: No. 91). (J). 1997. 8.60 (*0-606-12885-9*, Pub. by Turtleback) Demco.

Martin, Ann M. Karen's Pizza Party. LC 94-152849. (Baby-Sitters Little Sister Ser.: No. 42). 112p. (J). (gr. 2-4). 1993. pap. 2.99 (*0-590-47042-6*) Scholastic Inc.

— Karen's Pizza Party. (Baby-Sitters Little Sister Ser.: No. 42). (J). 1993. 8.09 (*0-606-05153-8*, Pub. by Turtleback) Demco.

— Karen's Plane Trip. (Baby-Sitters Little Sister Super Special Ser.: No. 2). 128p. (J). (gr. 2-4). 1991. pap. 3.25 (*0-590-44834-X*) Scholastic Inc.

Martin, Ann M. Karen's Plane Trip. (Baby-Sitters Little Sister Super Special Ser.: No. 2). (J). 1991. 8.35 (*0-606-04958-4*, Pub. by Turtleback) Demco.

Martin, Ann M. Karen's Pony. (Baby-Sitters Little Sister Ser.: No. 60). 112p. (J). (gr. 2-4). 1995. pap. 2.95 (*0-590-48305-6*) Scholastic Inc.

— Karen's Pony. (Baby-Sitters Little Sister Ser.: No. 60). (J). 1995. 8.05 (*0-606-07247-0*, Pub. by Turtleback) Demco.

— Karen's Pony Camp. (Baby-Sitters Little Sister Ser.: No. 87). 112p. (J). (gr. 2-4). 1997. pap. text 3.50 (*0-590-06585-8*) Scholastic Inc.

— Karen's Pony Camp. (Baby-Sitters Little Sister Ser.: No. 87). (J). 1997. 8.60 (*0-606-11084-4*, Pub. by Turtleback) Demco.

— Karen's President. (Baby-Sitters Little Sister Ser.: No. 106). 112p. (gr. 2-4). 1999. pap. text 3.99 (*0-590-50058-9*) Scholastic Inc.

— Karen's Prize. (Baby-Sitters Little Sister Ser.: No. 11). 112p. (J). (gr. 2-4). 1990. pap. 2.95 (*0-590-43650-3*) Scholastic Inc.

— Karen's Prize. (Baby-Sitters Little Sister Ser.: No. 11). (J). 1990. 8.05 (*0-606-04718-2*, Pub. by Turtleback) Demco.

— Karen's Promise. (Baby-Sitters Little Sister Ser.: No. 95). (J). 1998. pap. text 3.50 (*0-590-06593-9*, Little Apple) Scholastic Inc.

— Karen's Promise. (Baby-Sitters Little Sister Ser.: No. 95). (J). 1998. 8.60 (*0-606-13171-X*, Pub. by Turtleback) Demco.

— Karen's Pumpkin Patch. LC 94-134295. (Baby-Sitters Little Sister Ser.: No. 32). 112p. (J). (gr. 2-4). 1992. 2.95 (*0-590-45647-4*) Scholastic Inc.

— Karen's Pumpkin Patch. (Baby-Sitters Little Sister Ser.: No. 32). (J). 1992. 8.05 (*0-606-01866-2*, Pub. by Turtleback) Demco.

— Karen's Puppet Show. (Baby-Sitters Little Sister Ser.: No. 88). (J). (gr. 2-4). 1997. pap. text 3.50 (*0-590-06586-6*) Scholastic Inc.

— Karen's Puppet Show. (Baby-Sitters Little Sister Ser.: No. 88). (YA). 1997. 8.60 (*0-606-11085-2*, Pub. by Turtleback) Demco.

***Martin, Ann M.** Karen's Reindeer. (Baby-Sitters Little Sister Ser.: No. 116). 1999. mass mkt. 3.99 (*0-590-52454-2*) Scholastic Inc.

Martin, Ann M. Karen's Roller Skates. (Baby-Sitters Little Sister Ser.: No. 2). 112p. (J). (gr. 2-4). 1988. pap. 2.95 (*0-590-44259-7*) Scholastic Inc.

Martin, Ann M. Karen's Roller Skates. (Baby-Sitters Little Sister Ser.: No. 2). (J). 1988. 8.05 (*0-606-04061-7*, Pub. by Turtleback) Demco.

— Karen's Runaway Turkey. (Baby-Sitters Little Sister Ser.: No. 115). (J). 1999. mass mkt. 3.99 (*0 590 52392 9*) Scholastic Inc.

Martin, Ann M. Karen's School. (Baby-Sitters Little Sister Ser.: No. 41). 112p. (J). (gr. 4-7). 1993. pap. 2.95 (*0-590-47041-8*) Scholastic Inc.

— Karen's School. (Baby-Sitters Little Sister Ser.: No. 41). 112p. (J). (gr. 4-7). 1994. pap. 2.95 (*0-590-48300-5*) Scholastic Inc.

Martin, Ann M. Karen's School. (Baby-Sitters Little Sister Ser.: No. 41). (J). 1993. 8.09 (*0-606-05152-X*, Pub. by Turtleback) Demco.

— Karen's School Bus. (Baby-Sitters Little Sister Ser.: No. 53). (J). 1994. 8.05 (*0-606-06217-3*, Pub. by Turtleback) Demco.

Martin, Ann M. Karen's School Mystery. (Baby-Sitters Little Sister Ser.: No. 57). 112p. (J). (gr. 2-4). 1995. pap. 2.95 (*0-590-48303-X*) Scholastic Inc.

— Karen's School Mystery. (Baby-Sitters Little Sister Ser.: No. 57). (J). 1995. 8.05 (*0-606-07244-6*, Pub. by Turtleback) Demco.

— Karen's School Picture. LC 94-146783. (Baby-Sitters Little Sister Ser.: No. 5). 112p. (J). (gr. 2-4). 1989. pap. 2.95 (*0-590-44258-9*) Scholastic Inc.

— Karen's School Picture. (Baby-Sitters Little Sister Ser.: No. 5). (J). 1989. 8.05 (*0-606-01609-0*, Pub. by Turtleback) Demco.

— Karen's School Surprise. (Baby-Sitters Little Sister Ser.: No. 77). (J). (gr. 4-7). 1996. pap. text 2.95 (*0-590-69185-6*) Scholastic Inc.

— Karen's School Surprise. (Baby-Sitters Little Sister Ser.: No. 77). (YA). 1996. 8.05 (*0-606-09052-5*, Pub. by Turtleback) Demco.

— Karen's School Trip. (Baby-Sitters Little Sister Ser.: No. 24). (J). (gr. 4-7). 1992. pap. 2.95 (*0-590-44859-5*) Scholastic Inc.

— Karen's School Trip. (Baby-Sitters Little Sister Ser.: No. 24). (J). 1992. 8.05 (*0-606-00539-0*, Pub. by Turtleback) Demco.

— Karen's Secret. (Baby-Sitters Little Sister Ser.: No. 33). 112p. (J). (gr. 2-4). 1992. 2.95 (*0-590-45648-2*) Scholastic Inc.

— Karen's Secret. LC 49-242390. (Baby-Sitters Little Sister Ser.: No. 82). 106p. (J). (gr. 2-4). 1997. mass mkt. 3.50 (*0-590-69190-2*) Scholastic Inc.

— Karen's Secret. (Baby-Sitters Little Sister Ser.: No. 33). (J). 1992. 8.05 (*0-606-02508-1*, Pub. by Turtleback) Demco.

Martin, Ann M. Karen's Secret Valentine. (Baby-Sitters Little Sister Ser.: No. 82). (J). 1997. 8.60 (*0-606-10748-7*, Pub. by Turtleback) Demco.

Martin, Ann M. Karen's Show & Share. (Baby-Sitters Little Sister Ser.: No. 109). 112p. (gr. 2-4). 1999. pap. text 3.99 (*0-590-50061-9*) Scholastic Inc.

— Karen's Ski Trip. (Baby-Sitters Little Sister Ser.: No. 58). 112p. (J). (gr. 4-7). 1995. pap. 2.95 (*0-590-48304-8*) Scholastic Inc.

— Karen's Ski Trip. (Baby-Sitters Little Sister Ser.: No. 58). (J). 1995. 8.05 (*0-606-07245-4*, Pub. by Turtleback) Demco.

— Karen's Sleepover. (Baby-Sitters Little Sister Ser.: No. 9). 112p. (J). (gr. 2-4). 1990. pap. 2.95 (*0-590-43652-X*) Scholastic Inc.

Martin, Ann M. Karen's Sleepover. (Baby-Sitters Little Sister Ser.: No. 9). (J). 1990. 8.05 (*0-606-04459-0*, Pub. by Turtleback) Demco.

Martin, Ann M. Karen's Sleigh Ride. (Baby-Sitters Little Sister Ser.: No. 92). (J). 1997. pap. text 3.50 (*0-590-06590-4*, Little Apple) Scholastic Inc.

— Karen's Sleigh Ride. (Baby-Sitters Little Sister Ser.: No. 92). (J). 1997. 8.60 (*0-606-12886-7*, Pub. by Turtleback) Demco.

— Karen's Snow Day. (Baby-Sitters Little Sister Ser.: No. 34). 112p. (J). (gr. 4-7). 1993. pap. 2.95 (*0-590-45650-4*) Scholastic Inc.

— Karen's Snow Day. (Baby-Sitters Little Sister Ser.: No. 34). (J). 1993. 8.05 (*0-606-02509-X*, Pub. by Turtleback) Demco.

— Karen's Snow Princess. (Baby-Sitters Little Sister Ser.: No. 94). (J). (gr. 2-4). 1998. pap. text 3.50 (*0-590-06592-0*) Scholastic Inc.

— Karen's Snow Princess. (Baby-Sitters Little Sister Ser.: No. 94). (J). 1998. 8.60 (*0-606-13170-1*, Pub. by Turtleback) Demco.

— Karen's Softball Mystery. (Baby-Sitters Little Sister Ser.: No. 74). (J). (gr. 2-4). 1996. pap. text 2.95 (*0-590-26214-9*) Scholastic Inc.

— Karen's Softball Mystery. (Baby-Sitters Little Sister Ser.: No. 74). (YA). 1996. 8.05 (*0-606-09049-5*, Pub. by Turtleback) Demco.

***Martin, Ann M.** Karen's Spy Mystery. (Bab-Sitters Club Little Sister Ser.: No. 111). 1999. pap. text 3.99 (*0-590-52356-2*) Scholastic Inc.

Martin, Ann M. Karen's Stepmother. (Baby-Sitters Little Sister Ser.: No. 49). 112p. (J). (gr. 4-7). 1994. pap. 2.95 (*0-590-47047-7*) Scholastic Inc.

Martin, Ann M. Karen's Stepmother. (Baby-Sitters Little Sister Ser.: No. 49). (J). 1994. 8.05 (*0-606-06213-0*, Pub. by Turtleback) Demco.

Martin, Ann M. Karen's Surprise. (Baby-Sitters Little Sister Ser.: No. 13). 112p. (J). (gr. 2-4). 1990. pap. 2.95 (*0-590-43648-1*) Scholastic Inc.

— Karen's Surprise. (Baby-Sitters Little Sister Ser.: No. 13). (J). 1990. 8.05 (*0-606-04719-0*, Pub. by Turtleback) Demco.

***Martin, Ann M.** Karen's Swim Meet. (Baby-Sitters Little Sister Ser.: No. 110). (J). 1999. pap. 3.99 (*0-590-50062-7*, Little Apple) Scholastic Inc.

Martin, Ann M. Karen's Tattletale. (Baby-Sitters Little Sister Ser.: No. 61). 112p. (J). (gr. 2-4). 1995. pap. text 2.95 (*0-590-48306-4*) Scholastic Inc.

— Karen's Tattletale. (Baby-Sitters Little Sister Ser.: No. 61). (J). 1995. 8.05 (*0-606-07248-9*, Pub. by Turtleback) Demco.

— Karen's Tea Party. LC 94-135606. (Baby-Sitters Little Sister Ser.: No. 28). 112p. (J). (gr. 2-4). 1992. pap. 2.95 (*0-590-44828-5*) Scholastic Inc.

— Karen's Tea Party. (Baby-Sitters Little Sister Ser.: No. 28). (J). 1992. 8.05 (*0-606-01868-9*, Pub. by Turtleback) Demco.

— Karen's Telephone Trouble. (Baby-Sitters Little Sister Ser.: No. 86). (J). 1997. pap. text 3.50 (*0-590-69194-5*, Little Apple) Scholastic Inc.

— Karen's Telephone Trouble. (Baby-Sitters Little Sister Ser.: No. 86). (YA). 1997. 8.60 (*0-606-11083-6*, Pub. by Turtleback) Demco.

— Karen's Toothache. LC 94-152866. (Baby-Sitters Little Sister Ser.: No. 43). 112p. (J). (gr. 2-4). 1993. pap. 2.95 (*0-590-46912-6*) Scholastic Inc.

Martin, Ann M. Karen's Toothache. (Baby-Sitters Little Sister Ser.: No. 43). (J). 1993. 8.09 (*0-606-05741-2*, Pub. by Turtleback) Demco.

Martin, Ann M. Karen's Toys. (Baby-Sitters Little Sister Ser.: No. 65). (J). (gr. 2-4). 1995. pap. text 2.95 (*0-590-25998-9*) Scholastic Inc.

— Karen's Toys. (Baby-Sitters Little Sister Ser.: No. 65). (J). 1995. 8.05 (*0-606-07252-7*, Pub. by Turtleback) Demco.

— Karen's Treasure. (Baby-Sitters Little Sister Ser.: No. 85). (J). 1997. pap. text 3.50 (*0-590-69193-7*, Little Apple) Scholastic Inc.

— Karen's Treasure. (Baby-Sitters Little Sister Ser.: No. 85). (YA). 1997. 8.60 (*0-606-11082-8*, Pub. by Turtleback) Demco.

— Karen's Tuba. (Baby-Sitters Little Sister Ser.: No. 37). 112p. (J). (gr. 4-7). 1993. pap. 2.95 (*0-590-45653-9*) Scholastic Inc.

Martin, Ann M. Karen's Tuba. (Baby-Sitters Little Sister Ser.: No. 37). (J). 1993. 8.05 (*0-606-05148-1*, Pub. by Turtleback) Demco.

Martin, Ann M. Karen's Turkey Day. (Baby-Sitters Little Sister Ser.: No. 67). (J). 1995. pap. 2.95 (*0-590-26024-3*) Scholastic Inc.

— Karen's Turkey Day. (Baby-Sitters Little Sister Ser.: No. 67). (J). 1995. 8.05 (*0-606-08484-3*, Pub. by Turtleback) Demco.

— Karen's Twin. LC 94-152888. (Baby-Sitters Little Sister Ser.: No. 45). 112p. (J). (gr. 2-4). 1994. pap. 2.95 (*0-590-47044-2*) Scholastic Inc.

Martin, Ann M. Karen's Twin. (Baby-Sitters Little Sister Ser.: No. 45). (J). 1994. 8.05 (*0-606-05743-9*, Pub. by Turtleback) Demco.

Martin, Ann M. Karen's Two Families. (Baby-Sitters Little Sister Ser.: No. 48). 112p. (J). (gr. 4-7). 1994. pap. 2.95 (*0-590-47046-9*) Scholastic Inc.

Martin, Ann M. Karen's Two Families. (Baby-Sitters Little Sister Ser.: No. 48). (J). 1994. 8.05 (*0-606-06212-2*, Pub. by Turtleback) Demco.

Martin, Ann M. Karen's Unicorn. (Baby-Sitters Little Sister Ser.: No. 89). (Illus.). 112p. (J). (gr. 2-4). 1997. pap. text 3.50 (*0-590-06587-4*) Scholastic Inc.

— Karen's Unicorn. (Baby-Sitters Little Sister Ser.: No. 89). 1997. 8.60 (*0-606-11086-0*, Pub. by Turtleback) Demco.

— Karen's Wedding. (Baby-Sitters Little Sister Ser.: No. 39). 112p. (J). (gr. 2-4). 1993. pap. 2.99 (*0-590-45654-7*) Scholastic Inc.

— Karen's Wedding. (Baby-Sitters Little Sister Ser.: No. 39). (J). 1993. 8.09 (*0-606-05150-3*, Pub. by Turtleback) Demco.

— Karen's Wish. (Baby-Sitters Little Sister Super Special Ser.: No. 1). (Illus.). 128p. (J). (gr. 2-4). 1990. pap. 3.25 (*0-590-43647-3*) Scholastic Inc.

Martin, Ann M. Karen's Wish. (Baby-Sitters Little Sister Super Special Ser.: No. 1). (J). 1990. 8.35 (*0-606-04720-4*, Pub. by Turtleback) Demco.

Martin, Ann M. Karen's Witch. (Baby-Sitters Little Sister Ser.: No. 1). 112p. (J). (gr. 2-4). 1988. pap. 2.95 (*0-590-44300-3*) Scholastic Inc.

Martin, Ann M. Karen's Witch. (Baby-Sitters Little Sister Ser.: No. 1). (J). 1988. 8.05 (*0-606-03838-8*, Pub. by Turtleback) Demco.

Martin, Ann M. Karen's Worst Day. (Baby-Sitters Little Sister Ser.: No. 3). 112p. (J). (gr. 2-4). 1989. pap. 2.95 (*0-590-44299-6*) Scholastic Inc.

Martin, Ann M. Karen's Worst Day. (Baby-Sitters Little Sister Ser.: No. 3). (J). 1989. 8.05 (*0-606-04062-5*, Pub. by Turtleback) Demco.

An Asterisk (*) at the beginning of an entry indicates that the title is appearing for the first time.

— Karen's Yo-Yo. (Baby-Sitters Little Sister Ser.: No. 119). (Illus.). 144p. (J). (gr. 2-4). 2000. mass mkt. 3.99 (*0-590-52511-5*) Scholastic Inc.

Martin, Ann M. Keep Out, Claudia! (Baby-Sitters Club Ser.: No. 56). 192p. (J). (gr. 4-6). 1992. pap. 3.50 (*0-590-45657-1*, Apple Paperbacks) Scholastic Inc.

— Keep Out, Claudia! (Baby-Sitters Club Ser.: No. 56). (J). 1992. 8.60 (*0-606-01870-0*, Pub. by Turtleback) Demco.

— Kristy + Bart = ? (Baby-Sitters Club Ser.: No. 95). (J). (gr. 3-7). 1996. pap. 3.99 (*0-590-22879-X*) Scholastic Inc.

— Kristy + Bart = ? (Baby-Sitters Club Ser.: No. 95). 1996. 9.09 (*0-606-09031-2*, Pub. by Turtleback) Demco.

— Kristy & Mr. Mom. (Baby-Sitters Club Ser.: No. 81). 192p. (J). (gr. 3-7). 1995. pap. 3.50 (*0-590-48225-4*) Scholastic Inc.

— Kristy & Mr. Mom. (Baby-Sitters Club Ser.: No. 81). 1995. 8.60 (*0-606-07223-3*, Pub. by Turtleback) Demco.

— Kristy & Mr. Mom. (Baby-Sitters Club Ser.: No. 81). 1995. 7.98 (*1-57042-368-7*) Warner Bks.

Martin, Ann M. Kristy & Mr. Mom; Jessi & the Troublemaker; Stacey vs. the BSC; Dawn & the School Spirit War, Bks. 81-84. (Baby-Sitters Club Ser.: 21). (YA). 1997. pap., boxed set 14.00 (*0-590-25154-6*) Scholastic Inc.

Martin, Ann M. Kristy & the Baby Parade. LC 96-15687. (Baby-Sitters Club Ser.: No. 45). 176p. (J). (gr. 4 up). 1996. lib. bdg. 21.27 (*0-8368-1569-6*) Gareth Stevens Inc.

— Kristy & the Baby Parade. (Baby-Sitters Club Ser.: No. 45). 192p. (J). (gr. 3-7). 1991. pap. 3.50 (*0-590-43574-4*) Scholastic Inc.

— Kristy & the Baby Parade. (Baby-Sitters Club Ser.: No. 45). (J). 1991. 8.60 (*0-606-04960-6*, Pub. by Turtleback) Demco.

— Kristy & the Cat Burglar. (Baby-Sitters Club Mystery Ser.: No. 36). (J). (gr. 3-7). 1998. pap. 3.99 (*0-590-05976-9*, Apple Paperbacks) Scholastic Inc.

— Kristy & the Copycat. (Baby-Sitters Club Ser.: No. 74). 192p. (J). (gr. 3-7). 1994. pap. 3.99 (*0-590-47012-4*) Scholastic Inc.

— Kristy & the Copycat. (Baby-Sitters Club Ser.: No. 74). (J). 1994. 9.09 (*0-606-06200-9*, Pub. by Turtleback) Demco.

— Kristy & the Dirty Diapers. (Baby-Sitters Club Ser.: No. 89). 192p. (gr. 3-7). 1995. pap. text 3.50 (*0-590-22873-0*) Scholastic Inc.

— Kristy & the Dirty Diapers. (Baby-Sitters Club Ser.: No. 89). (J). 1995. 8.60 (*0-606-07231-4*, Pub. by Turtleback) Demco.

— Kristy & the Haunted Mansion. (Baby-Sitters Club Mystery Ser.: No. 9). 176p. (J). (gr. 3-7). 1993. pap. 3.50 (*0-590-44958-3*) Scholastic Inc.

— Kristy & the Haunted Mansion. (Baby-Sitters Club Mystery Ser.: No. 9). 1993. 8.60 (*0-606-05144-9*, Pub. by Turtleback) Demco.

***Martin, Ann M.** Kristy & the Kidnapper. (Baby-Sitters Club Friends Forever Ser.: No. 9). (Illus.). 144p. (J). (gr. 3-7). 2000. mass mkt. 4.50 (*0-590-52343-0*) Scholastic Inc.

Martin, Ann M. Kristy & the Middle School Vandal. (Baby-Sitters Club Mystery Ser.: No. 25). (J). (gr. 3-7). 1996. pap. 3.99 (*0-590-22869-2*) Scholastic Inc.

— Kristy & the Middle School Vandal. (Baby-Sitters Club Mystery Ser.: No. 25). (YA). 1996. 9.09 (*0-606-09039-8*, Pub. by Turtleback) Demco.

— Kristy & the Missing Child. (Baby-Sitters Club Mystery Ser.: No. 4). 176p. (J). (gr. 3-7). 1992. pap. 3.50 (*0-590-44800-5*) Scholastic Inc.

— Kristy & the Missing Child. (Baby-Sitters Club Mystery Ser.: No. 4). (J). 1992. 8.60 (*0-606-01879-4*, Pub. by Turtleback) Demco.

— Kristy & the Missing Fortune. (Baby-Sitters Club Mystery Ser.: No. 19). 176p. (J). (gr. 3-7). 1995. pap. 3.50 (*0-590-48234-3*) Scholastic Inc.

— Kristy & the Missing Fortune. (Baby-Sitters Club Mystery Ser.: No. 19). (J). 1995. 8.60 (*0-606-07233-0*, Pub. by Turtleback) Demco.

— Kristy & the Mother's Day Surprise. (Baby-Sitters Club Ser.: No. 24). 192p. (J). (gr. 4-6). 1989. pap. 3.50 (*0-590-43506-X*) Scholastic Inc.

— Kristy & the Mother's Day Surprise. (Baby-Sitters Club Ser.: No. 24). 160p. (J). (gr. 3-7). 1997. pap. text 3.99 (*0-590-67392-0*) Scholastic Inc.

— Kristy & the Mother's Day Surprise. (Baby-Sitters Club Ser.: No. 24). (J). 1989. 8.60 (*0-606-04260-1*, Pub. by Turtleback) Demco.

— Kristy & the Mystery Train. (Baby-Sitters Club Mystery Ser.: No. 30). 160p. (J). (gr. 3-7). 1997. mass mkt. 3.99 (*0-590-69178-3*, Apple Paperbacks) Scholastic Inc.

Martin, Ann M. Kristy & the Mystery Train. (Baby-Sitters Club Mystery Ser.: No. 30). 1997. 9.09 (*0-606-11074-7*, Pub. by Turtleback) Demco.

Martin, Ann M. Kristy & the Secret of Susan. (Baby-Sitters Club Ser.: No. 32). 192p. (J). (gr. 4-6). 1990. pap. 3.50 (*0-590-42496-3*) Scholastic Inc.

— Kristy & the Secret of Susan. (Baby-Sitters Club Ser.: No. 32). (J). 1990. 9.09 (*0-606-04462-0*, Pub. by Turtleback) Demco.

— Kristy & the Sister War. (Baby-Sitters Club Ser.: No. 112). 160p. (J). (gr. 3-7). 1997. pap. text 3.99 (*0-590-05990-4*) Scholastic Inc.

Martin, Ann M. Kristy & the Sister War. (Baby-Sitters Club Ser.: No. 112). 1997. 9.09 (*0-606-11072-0*, Pub. by Turtleback) Demco.

Martin, Ann M. Kristy & the Snobs. (Baby-Sitters Club Ser.: No. 11). 192p. (J). (gr. 4-6). 1988. pap. 3.50 (*0-590-43660-0*) Scholastic Inc.

— Kristy & the Snobs. (Baby-Sitters Club Ser.: No. 11). 176p. (J). (gr. 3-7). 1996. pap. 3.99 (*0-590-25166-X*) Scholastic Inc.

— Kristy & the Snobs. (Baby-Sitters Club Ser.: No. 11). (J). 1988. 9.09 (*0-606-03547-8*, Pub. by Turtleback) Demco.

— Kristy & the Vampires. (Baby-Sitters Club Mystery Ser.: No. 15). 176p. (J). (gr. 3-7). 1994. pap. 3.50 (*0-590-47053-1*) Scholastic Inc.

— Kristy & the Vampires. (Baby-Sitters Club Mystery Ser.: No. 14). (J). 1994. 9.09 (*0-606-06207-6*, Pub. by Turtleback) Demco.

— Kristy & the Walking Disaster. (Baby-Sitters Club Ser.: No. 20). 192p. (J). (gr. 4-6). 1989. pap. 3.50 (*0-590-43722-4*) Scholastic Inc.

— Kristy & the Walking Disaster. (Baby-Sitters Club Ser.: No. 20). (J). 1996. pap. 3.99 (*0-590-60692-1*) Scholastic Inc.

— Kristy & the Walking Disaster. (Baby-Sitters Club Ser.: No. 20). (J). 1989. 9.09 (*0-606-04088-9*, Pub. by Turtleback) Demco.

— Kristy & the Worst Kid Ever. (Baby-Sitters Club Ser.: No. 62). 192p. (J). (gr. 3-7). 1993. pap. 3.50 (*0-590-45664-4*) Scholastic Inc.

— Kristy & the Worst Kid Ever. (Baby-Sitters Club Ser.: No. 62). (J). 1993. 8.60 (*0-606-02500-6*, Pub. by Turtleback) Demco.

— Kristy for President. (Baby-Sitters Club Ser.: No. 53). 192p. (J). (gr. 3-7). 1992. pap. 3.25 (*0-590-44967-2*) Scholastic Inc.

— Kristy for President. (Baby-Sitters Club Ser.: No. 53). (J). 1992. 8.35 (*0-606-01880-8*, Pub. by Turtleback) Demco.

— Kristy in Charge. (Baby-Sitters Club Ser.: No. 122). (J). (gr. 3-7). 1998. pap. 3.99 (*0-590-50064-3*) Scholastic Inc.

***Martin, Ann M.** Kristy in Charge. (Baby-Sitters Club Ser.: No. 122). (J). 1998. 9.09 (*0-606-13166-3*, Pub. by Turtleback) Demco.

— Kristy Power! (Baby-Sitters Club Friends Forever Ser.: No. 5). (Illus.). (J). 1999. pap. 4.50 (*0-590-52332-5*) Scholastic Inc.

Martin, Ann M. Kristy Thomas, Dog Trainer. (Baby-Sitters Club Ser.: No. 118). (J). 1998. pap. text 3.99 (*0-590-05996-3*, Apple Paperbacks) Scholastic Inc.

***Martin, Ann M.** Kristy Thomas, Dog Trainer. (Baby-Sitters Club Ser.: No. 118). (J). 1998. 9.09 (*0-606-13162-0*, Pub. by Turtleback) Demco.

Martin, Ann M. Kristy y El Nino Desaparecido. 1995. 15.05 (*0-606-10397-X*, Pub. by Turtleback) Demco.

— Kristy's Big Day. (Baby-Sitters Club Ser.: No. 6). (J). (gr. 4-7). 1987. pap. 3.50 (*0-590-43899-9*) Scholastic Inc.

— Kristy's Big Day. (Baby-Sitters Club Ser.: No. 6). 192p. (J). (gr. 3-7). 1995. pap. 3.50 (*0-590-25161-9*) Scholastic Inc.

— Kristy's Big Day. (Baby-Sitters Club Ser.: No. 6). (J). 1987. 8.60 (*0-606-00549-8*, Pub. by Turtleback) Demco.

— Kristy's Big News. (Baby-Sitters Club Friends Forever Ser.: No. 1). 1999. pap. text 54.00 (*0-439-09611-1*) Scholastic Inc.

***Martin, Ann M.** Kristy's Big News. (Baby-Sitters Club Friends Forever Ser.: No. 1). 136p. (J). (gr. 3-7). 1999. pap. 4.50 (*0-590-52313-9*, Pub. by Scholastic Inc) Penguin Putnam.

Martin, Ann M. Kristy's Book. (Baby-Sitters Club Portrait Collection). (J). (gr. 3-7). Date not set. pap. 3.99 (*0-614-19196-3*, Apple Paperbacks) Scholastic Inc.

— Kristy's Book. (Baby-Sitters Club Portrait Collection). (J). (gr. 3-7). 1996. pap. text 3.99 (*0-590-69181-3*) Scholastic Inc.

— Kristy's Book. (Baby-Sitters Club Portrait Collection). (YA). 1996. 9.09 (*0-606-09043-6*, Pub. by Turtleback) Demco.

— Kristy's Great Idea. (Baby-Sitters Club Ser.: No. 1). (J). 1986. pap. 3.50 (*0-590-43388-1*) Scholastic Inc.

— Kristy's Great Idea. (Baby-Sitters Club Ser.: No. 1). 192p. (J). (gr. 3-7). 1995. pap. 3.50 (*0-590-22473-5*) Scholastic Inc.

— Kristy's Great Idea. (Baby-Sitters Club Ser.: No. 1). (J). 1986. 8.60 (*0-606-03082-4*, Pub. by Turtleback) Demco.

Martin, Ann M. Kristy's Great Idea; Claudia & the Phantom Phone Call; The Truth about Stacey; Mary Anne Saves the Day, Bks. 1-4. (Baby-Sitters Club Ser.: 1). (J). (gr. 3-7). 1993. pap., boxed set 14.00 (*0-590-59887-2*) Scholastic Inc.

Martin, Ann M. Kristy's Mystery Admirer. (Baby-Sitters Club Ser.: No. 38). 1990. pap. text 3.99 (*0-590-73450-4*) Scholastic Inc.

— Kristy's Mystery Admirer. (Baby-Sitters Club Ser.: No. 38). 192p. (J). (gr. 4-6). 1990. pap. 3.25 (*0-590-43567-1*) Scholastic Inc.

— Kristy's Mystery Admirer. (Baby-Sitters Club Ser.: No. 38). (J). 1990. 9.09 (*0-606-04726-3*, Pub. by Turtleback) Demco.

— Kristy's Worst Idea. (Baby-Sitters Club Ser.: No. 100). (J). (gr. 4-7). 1996. pap. text 3.99 (*0-590-69206-2*) Scholastic Inc.

— Kristy's Worst Idea. (Baby-Sitters Club Ser.: No. 100). 1996. 9.09 (*0-606-09029-0*, Pub. by Turtleback) Demco.

— Leo the Magnificat. (J). 1996. pap. write for info. (*0-590-94219-0*) Scholastic Inc.

— Leo the Magnificat. LC 95-33640. (Illus.). 32p. (J). (gr. k-3). 1996. 15.95 (*0-590-48498-2*) Scholastic Inc.

***Martin, Ann M.** Leo the Magnificat. (Illus.). 32p. (J). (gr. k-3). 2000. mass mkt. 5.99 (*0-439-13647-4*) Scholastic Inc.

Martin, Ann M. Little Miss Stoneybrook & Dawn. (Baby-Sitters Club Ser.: No. 15). 192p. (J). (gr. 4-6). 1988. pap. 3.50 (*0-590-43717-8*) Scholastic Inc.

— Little Miss Stoneybrook & Dawn. (Baby-Sitters Club Ser.: No. 15). 1996. pap. text 3.99 (*0-590-25170-8*) Scholastic Inc.

— Logan Bruno, Boy Baby-Sitter. (Baby-Sitters Club Special Edition Ser.). 160p. (J). (gr. 3-7). 1993. pap. 3.50 (*0-590-47118-X*) Scholastic Inc.

Martin, Ann M. Logan Bruno, Boy Baby-Sitter. (Baby-Sitters Club Special Edition Ser.). (J). 1993. 8.60 (*0-606-05145-7*, Pub. by Turtleback) Demco.

Martin, Ann M. Logan Likes Mary Anne! (Baby-Sitters Club Ser.: No. 10). 160p. (J). (gr. 4-6). 1988. pap. 2.75 (*0-590-41124-1*, Apple Paperbacks); pap. 3.50 (*0-590-43387-3*) Scholastic Inc.

— Logan Likes Mary Anne! (Baby-Sitters Club Ser.: No. 10). (J). (gr. 3-7). 1996. pap. text 3.99 (*0-590-25165-1*) Scholastic Inc.

Martin, Ann M. Logan Likes Mary Anne! (Baby-Sitters Club Ser.: No. 10). (J). 1988. 9.09 (*0-606-03546-X*, Pub. by Turtleback) Demco.

Martin, Ann M. Logan's Story. (Baby-Sitters Club Special Edition Ser.: Vol. 1). 160p. (J). (gr. 3-7). 1992. pap. 3.25 (*0-590-45575-3*, Apple Paperbacks) Scholastic Inc.

— Logan's Story. (Baby-Sitters Club Special Edition Ser.). (J). 1992. 8.35 (*0-606-01894-8*, Pub. by Turtleback) Demco.

— Ma & Pa Dracula. 128p. (J). (gr. 4-6). 1991. pap. 2.95 (*0-590-43828-X*) Scholastic Inc.

— Maggie. (California Diaries: Vol. 3). 160p. (YA). (gr. 4-8). 1997. pap. text 3.99 (*0-590-29837-2*) Scholastic Inc.

Martin, Ann M. Maggie. (California Diaries). (YA). (gr. 6-8). 1997. 9.09 (*0-606-11181-6*, Pub. by Turtleback) Demco.

— Maggie: Diary Three. (California Diaries: Vol. 13). 144p. (gr. 6-8). 1999. mass mkt. 4.99 (*0-439-09547-6*) Scholastic Inc.

Martin, Ann M. Maggie: Diary Two. (California Diaries: Vol. 8). (J). (gr. 6-8). 1998. pap. text 3.99 (*0-590-02383-7*) Scholastic Inc.

***Martin, Ann M.** Maggie: Diary Two. (California Diaries). (YA). (gr. 6-8). 1998. 9.09 (*0-606-13239-2*, Pub. by Turtleback) Demco.

Martin, Ann M. Maid Mary Anne. (Baby-Sitters Club Ser.: No. 66). 192p. (J). (gr. 3-7). 1993. pap. 3.50 (*0-590-47004-3*) Scholastic Inc.

Martin, Ann M. Maid Mary Anne. (Baby-Sitters Club Ser.: No. 66). (J). 1993. 8.60 (*0-606-05138-4*, Pub. by Turtleback) Demco.

Martin, Ann M. Mallory & the Dream Horse. LC 94-135668. (Baby-Sitters Club Ser.: No. 54). 192p. (J). (gr. 3-7). 1992. pap. 3.25 (*0-590-44965-6*) Scholastic Inc.

— Mallory & the Dream Horse. (Baby-Sitters Club Ser.: No. 54). (J). 1992. 8.35 (*0-606-01896-4*, Pub. by Turtleback) Demco.

— Mallory & the Ghost Cat. (Baby-Sitters Club Mystery Ser.: No. 3). 160p. (J). 1992. pap. 3.25 (*0-590-44799-8*) Scholastic Inc.

— Mallory & the Ghost Cat. (Baby-Sitters Club Mystery Ser.: No. 3). (J). 1992. 8.35 (*0-606-02501-4*, Pub. by Turtleback) Demco.

— Mallory & the Mystery Diary. (Baby-Sitters Club Ser.: No. 29). (gr. 3-7). 1989. pap. 3.99 (*0-590-67397-1*) Scholastic Inc.

— Mallory & the Mystery Diary. (Baby-Sitters Club Ser.: No. 29). 192p. (J). (gr. 4-6). 1989. pap. 3.50 (*0-590-42500-5*, Apple Paperbacks) Scholastic Inc.

— Mallory & the Mystery Diary. (Baby-Sitters Club Ser.: No. 29). (J). 1989. 9.09 (*0-606-01845-X*, Pub. by Turtleback) Demco.

— Mallory & the Trouble with Twins. (Baby-Sitters Club Ser.: No. 21). (J). 1989. pap. 3.50 (*0-590-43507-8*) Scholastic Inc.

— Mallory & the Trouble with Twins. (Baby-Sitters Club Ser.: No. 21). (J). (gr. 3-7). 1997. pap. text 3.99 (*0-590-67389-0*) Scholastic Inc.

— Mallory & the Trouble with Twins. (Baby-Sitters Club Ser.: No. 21). (J). 1989. 9.09 (*0-606-04089-7*, Pub. by Turtleback) Demco.

— Mallory Hates Boys (& Gym) (Baby-Sitters Club Ser.: No. 59). 192p. (J). (gr. 4-6). 1992. 3.50 (*0-590-45660-1*) Scholastic Inc.

— Mallory on Strike. LC 96-15686. (Baby-Sitters Club Ser.: No. 47). 144p. (J). (gr. 4 up). 1996. lib. bdg. 21.27 (*0-8368-1571-8*) Gareth Stevens Inc.

— Mallory on Strike. (Baby-Sitters Club Ser.: No. 47). 192p. (J). (gr. 4-6). 1991. pap. 3.25 (*0-590-44971-0*) Scholastic Inc.

— Mallory on Strike. (Baby-Sitters Club Ser.: No. 47). (J). 1991. 8.35 (*0-606-00586-2*, Pub. by Turtleback) Demco.

Martin, Ann M. Mallory Pike, #1 Fan. (Baby-Sitters Club Ser.: No. 80). 192p. (J). (gr. 3-7). 1994. pap. 3.99 (*0-590-48224-6*) Scholastic Inc.

Martin, Ann M. Mallory Pike, #1 Fan. (Baby-Sitters Club Ser.: No. 80). (J). 1994. 9.09 (*0-606-06920-8*, Pub. by Turtleback) Demco.

— Mallory y El Gato Fantasma. 1995. 15.05 (*0-606-10396-1*, Pub. by Turtleback) Demco.

— Mallory's Christmas Wish. (Baby-Sitters Club Ser.: No. 92). (J). 1995. pap. 3.50 (*0-590-22876-5*) Scholastic Inc.

— Mallory's Christmas Wish. (Baby-Sitters Club Ser.: No. 92). (J). 1995. 8.60 (*0-606-08481-9*, Pub. by Turtleback) Demco.

— Mary Anne & Camp BSC. (Baby-Sitters Club Ser.: No. 86). 192p. (gr. 4-6). 1995. pap. 3.50 (*0-590-48227-0*) Scholastic Inc.

— Mary Anne & Camp BSC. (Baby-Sitters Club Ser.: No. 86). 1995. 8.60 (*0-606-07228-4*, Pub. by Turtleback) Demco.

— Mary Anne & Miss Priss. (Baby-Sitters Club Ser.: No. 73). 192p. (J). (gr. 3-7). 1994. pap. 3.99 (*0-590-47011-6*) Scholastic Inc.

— Mary Anne & Miss Priss. (Baby-Sitters Club Ser.: No. 73). (J). 1994. 9.09 (*0-606-05738-2*, Pub. by Turtleback) Demco.

— Mary Anne & the Great Romance. (Baby-Sitters Club Ser.: No. 30). 192p. (J). (gr. 4-6). 1990. pap. 3.50 (*0-590-42498-X*) Scholastic Inc.

— Mary Anne & the Great Romance. (Baby-Sitters Club Ser.: No. 30). (J). 1990. 9.09 (*0-606-01876-X*, Pub. by Turtleback) Demco.

— Mary Anne & the Great Romance, Vol. 30. (Baby-Sitters Club Ser.: No. 30). 160p. (J). (gr. 3-7). 1997. pap. text 3.99 (*0-590-67398-X*) Scholastic Inc.

— Mary Anne & the Haunted Bookstore. (Baby-Sitters Club Mystery Ser.: No. 34). (J). 1998. pap. text 3.99 (*0-590-05974-2*, Apple Paperbacks) Scholastic Inc.

— Mary Anne & the Library Mystery. (Baby-Sitters Club Mystery Ser.: No. 13). 176p. (J). (gr. 3-7). 1994. pap. 3.50 (*0-590-47051-5*) Scholastic Inc.

— Mary Anne & the Library Mystery. (Baby-Sitters Club Mystery Ser.: No. 13). (J). 1994. 8.60 (*0-606-05740-4*, Pub. by Turtleback) Demco.

— Mary Anne & the Little Princess. LC 00-9331. (Baby-Sitters Club Ser.: No. 102). 142p. (J). (gr. 3-7). 1996. pap. 3.99 (*0-590-69208-9*) Scholastic Inc.

— Mary Anne & the Little Princess. (Baby-Sitters Club Ser.: No. 102). 1996. 9.09 (*0-606-10132-2*, Pub. by Turtleback) Demco.

— Mary Anne & the Memory Garden. (Baby-Sitters Club Ser.: No. 93). (J). 1996. pap. text 3.99 (*0-590-22877-3*) Scholastic Inc.

— Mary Anne & the Memory Garden. (Baby-Sitters Club Ser.: No. 93). (J). 1996. 9.09 (*0-606-08482-7*, Pub. by Turtleback) Demco.

— Mary Anne & the Music Box Secret. (Baby-Sitters Club Mystery Ser.: No. 31). (J). (gr. 3-7). 1997. mass mkt. 3.99 (*0-590-69179-1*) Scholastic Inc.

Martin, Ann M. Mary Anne & the Music Box Secret. (Baby-Sitters Club Mystery Ser.: No. 31). 1997. 9.09 (*0-606-11075-5*, Pub. by Turtleback) Demco.

Martin, Ann M. Mary Anne & the Playground Fight. (Baby-Sitters Club Ser.: No. 120). (J). 1998. pap. 3.99 (*0-590-05998-X*, Apple Paperbacks) Scholastic Inc.

***Martin, Ann M.** Mary Anne & the Playground Fight. (Baby-Sitters Club Ser.: No. 120). (J). 1998. 9.09 (*0-606-13164-7*, Pub. by Turtleback) Demco.

Martin, Ann M. Mary Anne & the Search for Tigger. (Baby-Sitters Club Ser.: No. 25). 192p. (J). (gr. 4-6). 1989. pap. 3.50 (*0-590-43347-4*) Scholastic Inc.

— Mary Anne & the Search for Tigger. (Baby-Sitters Club Ser.: No. 25). 160p. (J). (gr. 3-7). 1997. pap. text 3.99 (*0-590-67393-9*, Apple Paperbacks) Scholastic Inc.

— Mary Anne & the Search for Tigger. (Baby-Sitters Club Ser.: No. 25). (J). 1989. 8.60 (*0-606-04272-5*, Pub. by Turtleback) Demco.

— Mary Anne & the Secret in the Attic. (Baby-Sitters Club Mystery Ser.: No. 5). 176p. (J). (gr. 3-7). 1992. pap. 3.25 (*0-590-44801-3*, Apple Paperbacks) Scholastic Inc.

— Mary Anne & the Silent Witness. (Baby-Sitters Club Mystery Ser.: No. 24). (J). (gr. 3-7). 1996. pap. 3.99 (*0-590-22868-4*) Scholastic Inc.

— Mary Anne & the Silent Witness. (Baby-Sitters Club Mystery Ser.: No. 24). (YA). 1996. 9.09 (*0-606-09038-X*, Pub. by Turtleback) Demco.

— Mary Anne & the Zoo Mystery. (Baby-Sitters Club Mystery Ser.: No. 20). 176p. (J). (gr. 3-7). 1995. pap. 3.50 (*0-590-48309-9*) Scholastic Inc.

— Mary Anne & the Zoo Mystery. (Baby-Sitters Club Mystery Ser.: No. 20). (J). 1995. 8.60 (*0-606-07234-9*, Pub. by Turtleback) Demco.

— Mary Anne & Too Many Boys. (Baby-Sitters Club Ser.: No. 34). (J). (gr. 3-7). 1990. pap. text 3.99 (*0-590-73283-8*) Scholastic Inc.

— Mary Anne & Too Many Boys. (Baby-Sitters Club Ser.: No. 34). 192p. (J). (gr. 4-6). 1990. pap. 3.50 (*0-590-42494-7*) Scholastic Inc.

— Mary Anne & Too Many Boys. (Baby-Sitters Club Ser.: No. 34). (J). 1990. 8.60 (*0-606-04475-2*, Pub. by Turtleback) Demco.

— Mary Anne & 2 Many Babies. (Baby-Sitters Club Ser.: No. 52). (gr. 3-7). 1948. mass mkt. 3.99 (*0-590-92577-6*) Scholastic Inc.

— Mary Anne & 2 Many Babies. (Baby-Sitters Club Ser.: No. 52). 192p. (J). (gr. 4-6). 1992. pap. 3.50 (*0-590-44966-4*) Scholastic Inc.

— Mary Anne & 2 Many Babies. (Baby-Sitters Club Ser.: No. 52). (J). 1992. 9.09 (*0-606-01897-2*, Pub. by Turtleback) Demco.

— Mary Anne Breaks the Rules. (Baby-Sitters Club Ser.: No. 79). 192p. (J). (gr. 4-6). 1994. pap. 3.50 (*0-590-48223-8*) Scholastic Inc.

— Mary Anne Breaks the Rules. (Baby-Sitters Club Ser.: No. 79). 1994. 8.60 (*0-606-06205-X*, Pub. by Turtleback) Demco.

— Mary Anne in the Middle. (Baby-Sitters Club Ser.: No. 125). 1998. pap. text 3.99 (*0-590-50179-8*) Scholastic Inc.

— Mary Anne Misses Logan. LC 96-15213. (Baby-Sitters Club Ser.: No. 46). 144p. (J). (gr. 4 up). 1996. lib. bdg. 21.27 (*0-8368-1570-X*) Gareth Stevens Inc.

— Mary Anne Misses Logan. (Baby-Sitters Club Ser.: No. 46). 192p. (J). (gr. 4-6). 1991. pap. 3.50 (*0-590-43569-8*) Scholastic Inc.

— Mary Anne Saves the Day. (Baby-Sitters Club Ser.: No. 4). (J). (gr. 3-7). 1987. pap. 3.50 (*0-590-43512-4*) Scholastic Inc.

— Mary Anne Saves the Day. (Baby-Sitters Club Ser.: No. 4). 192p. (J). (gr. 3-7). 1995. pap. text 3.50 (*0-590-25159-7*) Scholastic Inc.

— Mary Anne Saves the Day. (Baby-Sitters Club Ser.: No. 4). (J). (gr. 3-7). 1987. 8.60 (*0-606-03085-9*, Pub. by Turtleback) Demco.

— Mary Anne to the Rescue. (Baby-Sitters Club Ser.: No. 109). 1997. pap. text 3.99 (*0-590-69215-1*, Apple Paperbacks) Scholastic Inc.

Martin, Ann M. Mary Anne to the Rescue. (Baby-Sitters Club Ser.: No. 109). 1997. 9.09 (*0-606-11069-0*, Pub. by Turtleback) Demco.

An Asterisk (*) at the beginning of an entry indicates that the title is appearing for the first time.

Martin, Ann M. Mary Anne vs. Logan. LC 96-17008. (Baby-Sitters Club Ser.: No. 41). 176p. (J). (gr. 4 up). 1996. lib. bdg. 21.27 (*0-8368-1565-3*) Gareth Stevens Inc.

— Mary Anne vs. Logan. (Baby-Sitters Club Ser.: No. 41). 192p. (J). (gr. 4-6). 1991. pap. 3.50 (*0-590-43570-1*) Scholastic Inc.

— Mary Anne vs. Logan. (Baby-Sitters Club Ser.: No. 41). (J). (gr. 4-7). 1997. pap. 3.99 (*0-590-74241-8*, Scholastic Ref) Scholastic Inc.

— Mary Anne vs. Logan. (Baby-Sitters Club Ser.: No. 41). (J). 1991. 8.60 (*0-606-04743-3*, Pub. by Turtleback) Demco.

— Mary Anne's Bad-Luck Mystery. (Baby-Sitters Club Ser.: No. 17). 192p. (J). (gr. 4-6). 1988. 3.50 (*0-590-43659-7*) Scholastic Inc.

— Mary Anne's Bad-Luck Mystery. (Baby-Sitters Club Ser.: No. 17). (J). (gr. 3-7). 1996. pap. text 3.99 (*0-590-60428-7*) Scholastic Inc.

— Mary Anne's Bad-Luck Mystery. (Baby-Sitters Club Ser.: No. 17). (J). 1988. 9.09 (*0-606-04090-0*, Pub. by Turtleback) Demco.

— Mary Anne's Big Breakup. (Baby-Sitters Club Friends Forever Ser.: No. 3). 1999. pap. text 54.00 (*0-439-11739-9*) Scholastic Inc.

*__Martin, Ann M.__ Mary Anne's Big Breakup. Vol. 3. 144p. (J). (gr. 3-7). 1999. mass mkt. 4.50 (*0-590-52326-0*) Scholastic Inc.

Martin, Ann M. Mary Anne's Book. (Baby-Sitters Club Portrait Collection). (J). (gr. 3-7). 1996. pap. 3.99 (*0-590-22865-X*) Scholastic Inc.

— Mary Anne's Book. (Baby-Sitters Club Portrait Collection). (YA). 1996. 9.09 (*0-606-09041-X*, Pub. by Turtleback) Demco.

— Mary Anne's Makeover. (Baby-Sitters Club Ser.: No. 60). 192p. (J). (gr. 3-7). 1993. pap. 3.99 (*0-590-92586-5*) Scholastic Inc.

— Mary Anne's Makeover. (Baby-Sitters Club Ser.: No. 60). 192p. (J). (gr. 4-6). 1993. pap. 3.50 (*0-590-45662-8*) Scholastic Inc.

Martin, Ann M. Mary Anne's Makeover. (Baby-Sitters Club Ser.: No. 60). (J). 1993. 9.09 (*0-606-02498-0*, Pub. by Turtleback) Demco.

— Mary Anne's Revenge. (Baby-Sitters Club Friends Forever Ser.: No. 8). (Illus.). 144p. (J). (gr. 3-7). 2000. mass mkt. 4.50 (*0-590-52340-6*) Scholastic Inc.

— Mind Your Own Business, Kristy! (Baby-Sitters Club Ser.: No. 107). 1997. 9.09 (*0-606-11067-4*, Pub. by Turtleback) Demco.

Martin, Ann M. Mind Your Own Business, Kristy!, Vol. 107. (Baby-Sitters Club Ser.: No. 107). 1997. pap. text 3.99 (*0-590-69213-5*, Little Apple) Scholastic Inc.

— Missing since Monday. LC 86-45390. 176p. (YA). (gr. 7 up). 1987. pap. 3.99 (*0-590-43136-6*) Scholastic Inc.

Martin, Ann M. Missing since Monday. (J). 1986. 9.09 (*0-606-03617-2*, Pub. by Turtleback) Demco.

Martin, Ann M. The Mystery at Claudia's House. (Baby-Sitters Club Mystery Ser.: No. 6). 176p. (J). (gr. 4-6). 1992. 3.50 (*0-590-44961-3*) Scholastic Inc.

— The Mystery at Claudia's House. (Baby-Sitters Club Mystery Ser.: No. 6). (J). 1992. 8.60 (*0-606-02502-2*, Pub. by Turtleback) Demco.

— New York, New York! (Baby-Sitters Club Super Special Ser.: No. 6). 256p. (J). (gr. 3-7). 1991. pap. 4.50 (*0-590-43576-0*) Scholastic Inc.

— New York, New York! (Baby-Sitters Club Super Special Ser.: No. 6). (J). 1991. 9.60 (*0-606-04991-6*, Pub. by Turtleback) Demco.

— Poor Mallory! (Baby-Sitters Club Ser.: No. 39). 160p. (J). 1990. pap. 3.25 (*0-590-43568-X*); mass mkt. 3.99 (*0-590-73451-2*) Scholastic Inc.

Martin, Ann M. Poor Mallory! (Baby-Sitters Club Ser.: No. 39). 1990. 9.09 (*0-606-04775-1*, Pub. by Turtleback) Demco.

Martin, Ann M. Rachel Parker, Kindergarten Show-Off. LC 91-25793. (Illus.). 40p. (J). (gr. k-3). 1992. pap. 6.95 (*0-8234-1067-6*) Holiday.

— Science Fair. (Kids in Ms. Colman's Class Ser.: No. 7). (J). (gr. 1-4). 1997. mass mkt. 3.50 (*0-590-69203-8*) Scholastic Inc.

— Sea City, Here We Come! (Baby-Sitters Club Super Special Ser.: No. 10). 240p. (J). (gr. 4-6). 1993. pap. 4.50 (*0-590-45674-1*) Scholastic Inc.

Martin, Ann M. Sea City, Here We Come! (Baby-Sitters Club Super Special Ser.: No. 10). (J). 1993. 9.60 (*0-606-05146-5*, Pub. by Turtleback) Demco.

Martin, Ann M. Second Grade Baby. (Kids in Ms. Colman's Class Ser.: No. 4). (J). (gr. 1-4). 1996. pap. 2.99 (*0-590-69200-3*) Scholastic Inc.

— Secret Life of Mary Anne Spier. (Baby-Sitters Club Ser.: No. 114). (J). 1997. pap. text 3.99 (*0-590-05992-0*, Little Apple) Scholastic Inc.

— Secret Life of Mary Anne Spier. (Baby-Sitters Club Ser.: No. 114). (J). 1997. 9.09 (*0-606-12883-2*, Pub. by Turtleback) Demco.

— Secret Santa. LC 93-48981. (Baby-Sitters Club Ser.). 40p. (J). (gr. 3-7). 1994. 14.95 (*0-590-48295-5*) Scholastic Inc.

— Shannon's Story. (Baby-Sitters Club Special Edition Ser.). 160p. (J). (gr. 3-7). 1994. pap. 3.50 (*0-590-47756-0*) Scholastic Inc.

Martin, Ann M. Shannon's Story. (Baby-Sitters Club Special Edition Ser.). (J). 1994. 8.60 (*0-606-06210-6*, Pub. by Turtleback) Demco.

Martin, Ann M. Snow War. (Kids in Ms. Colman's Class Ser.: No. 5). 96p. (J). (gr. 1-4). 1997. mass mkt. 2.99 (*0-590-69201-1*) Scholastic Inc.

— Snowbound. (Baby-Sitters Club Super Special Ser.: No. 7). 256p. (J). (gr. 4-6). 1991. pap. 4.50 (*0-590-44963-X*) Scholastic Inc.

— Spelling Bee. (Kids in Ms. Colman's Class Ser.: No. 11). (J). (gr. 1-4). 1998. pap. text 3.50 (*0-590-06005-8*, Little Apple) Scholastic Inc.

— Stacey & the Bad Girls. (Baby-Sitters Club Ser.: No. 87). 139p. (J). (gr. 4-7). 1995. pap. text 3.99 (*0-590-94786-9*) Scholastic Inc.

— Stacey & the Bad Girls. (Baby-Sitters Club Ser.: No. 87). 192p. (J). (gr. 4-6). 1995. pap. 3.50 (*0-590-48237-8*) Scholastic Inc.

— Stacey & the Bad Girls. (Baby-Sitters Club Ser.: No. 87). (J). 1995. 9.09 (*0-606-07229-2*, Pub. by Turtleback) Demco.

*__Martin, Ann M.__ Stacey & the Boyfriend Trap. (Baby-Sitters Club Friends Forever Ser.: No. 6). 144p. (J). (gr. 3-7). 2000. pap. 5.50 (*0-590-52337-6*, Apple Paperbacks) Scholastic Inc.

Martin, Ann M. Stacey & the Cheerleaders. (Baby-Sitters Club Ser.: No. 70). 192p. (J). (gr. 4-6). 1993. pap. 3.50 (*0-590-47008-6*) Scholastic Inc.

— Stacey & the Cheerleaders. (Baby-Sitters Club Ser.: No. 70). (J). 1997. pap. text 3.99 (*0-590-92601-2*) Scholastic Inc.

Martin, Ann M. Stacey & the Cheerleaders. (Baby-Sitters Club Ser.: No. 70). (J). 1993. 9.09 (*0-606-05735-8*, Pub. by Turtleback) Demco.

Martin, Ann M. Stacey & the Fashion Victim. (Baby-Sitters Club Mystery Ser.: No. 29). 144p. (J). (gr. 3-7). 1997. pap. 3.99 (*0-590-69177-5*, 691540) Scholastic Inc.

Martin, Ann M. Stacey & the Fashion Victim. (Baby-Sitters Club Mystery Ser.: No. 29). 1997. 9.09 (*0-606-11073-9*, Pub. by Turtleback) Demco.

Martin, Ann M. Stacey & the Haunted Masquerade. LC 00-3508. (Baby-Sitters Club Mystery Ser.: No. 22). 176p. (J). (gr. 3-7). 1995. pap. text 3.50 (*0-590-22866-8*) Scholastic Inc.

— Stacey & the Haunted Masquerade. (Baby-Sitters Club Mystery Ser.: No. 22). (J). 1995. 8.60 (*0-606-07236-5*, Pub. by Turtleback) Demco.

— Stacey & the Missing Ring. (Baby-Sitters Club Mystery Ser.: No. 1). 176p. (J). (gr. 3-7). 1991. pap. 3.99 (*0-590-44084-5*) Scholastic Inc.

— Stacey & the Missing Ring. (Baby-Sitters Club Mystery Ser.: No. 1). (J). 1991. 9.09 (*0-606-05020-5*, Pub. by Turtleback) Demco.

— Stacey & the Mystery at the Empty House. (Baby-Sitters Club Mystery Ser.: No. 18). 176p. (J). (gr. 4-6). 1994. pap. 3.50 (*0-590-48233-5*) Scholastic Inc.

Martin, Ann M. Stacey & the Mystery at the Empty House. (Baby-Sitters Club Mystery Ser.: No. 18). 1994. 8.60 (*0-606-06921-6*, Pub. by Turtleback) Demco.

Martin, Ann M. Stacey & the Mystery at the Mall. (Baby-Sitters Club Mystery Ser.: No. 14). 176p. (J). (gr. 4-6). 1994. pap. 3.99 (*0-590-47052-3*) Scholastic Inc.

Martin, Ann M. Stacey & the Mystery at the Mall. (Baby-Sitters Club Mystery Ser.: No. 14). (J). 1994. 9.09 (*0-606-06206-8*, Pub. by Turtleback) Demco.

Martin, Ann M. Stacey & the Mystery Money. (Baby-Sitters Club Mystery Ser.: No. 10). 176p. (J). (gr. 4-6). 1993. pap. 3.50 (*0-590-45696-2*) Scholastic Inc.

Martin, Ann M. Stacey & the Mystery Money. (Baby-Sitters Club Mystery Ser.: No. 10). 1993. 8.60 (*0-606-05141-4*, Pub. by Turtleback) Demco.

Martin, Ann M. Stacey & the Mystery of Stoneybrook. (Baby-Sitters Club Ser.: No. 35). 192p. (J). (gr. 4-6). 1990. pap. 3.50 (*0-590-42508-0*) Scholastic Inc.

— Stacey & The Stolen Hearts. (Baby-Sitters Club Mystery Ser.: No. 33). (J). (gr. 3-7). 1998. pap. text 3.99 (*0-590-05973-4*) Scholastic Inc.

— Stacey McGill, Super Sitter. LC 00-5336. (Baby-Sitters Club Ser.: No. 94). (J). (gr. 3-7). 1996. pap. text 3.99 (*0-590-22878-1*) Scholastic Inc.

— Stacey McGill, Super Sitter. (Baby-Sitters Club Ser.: No. 94). 1996. 9.09 (*0-606-09030-4*, Pub. by Turtleback) Demco.

— Stacey McGill...Matchmaker? (Baby-Sitters Club Ser.: No. 124). 160p. (J). (gr. 3-7). 1998. pap. 3.99 (*0-590-50175-5*) Scholastic Inc.

— Stacey the Math Whiz. (Baby-Sitters Club Ser.: No. 105). (J). 1997. mass mkt. 3.99 (*0-590-69211-9*) Scholastic Inc.

Martin, Ann M. Stacey the Math Whiz. (Baby-Sitters Club Ser.: No. 105). 1997. 9.09 (*0-606-10745-2*, Pub. by Turtleback) Demco.

— Stacey vs. Claudia. (Baby-Sitters Club Friends Forever Ser.: No. 2). 1999. pap. 54.00 (*0-439-10721-0*) Scholastic Inc.

— Stacey vs. Claudia. (Baby-Sitters Club Friends Forever Ser.: No. 2). 121p. (J). (gr. 3-7). 1999. pap. 4.50 (*0-590-52318-X*, Pub. by Scholastic Inc) Penguin Putnam.

Martin, Ann M. Stacey vs. the BSC. (Baby-Sitters Club Ser.: No. 83). 192p. (J). (gr. 4-6). 1995. pap. 3.99 (*0-590-48235-1*) Scholastic Inc.

— Stacey vs. the BSC. (Baby-Sitters Club Ser.: No. 83). 1995. 8.60 (*0-606-07225-X*, Pub. by Turtleback) Demco.

— Stacey y El Anillo Perdido. (El Club de Las Canguro Ser.). 1995. 15.05 (*0-606-10394-5*, Pub. by Turtleback) Demco.

— Stacey's Big Crush. (Baby-Sitters Club Ser.: No. 65). 192p. (J). (gr. 3-7). 1993. pap. 3.50 (*0-590-45667-9*) Scholastic Inc.

Martin, Ann M. Stacey's Big Crush. (Baby-Sitters Club Ser.: No. 65). (J). 1993. 8.60 (*0-606-05137-6*, Pub. by Turtleback) Demco.

Martin, Ann M. Stacey's Book. (Baby-Sitters Club Portrait Collection). 160p. (J). (gr. 4-6). 1994. pap. 3.50 (*0-590-48399-4*) Scholastic Inc.

— Stacey's Broken Heart. (Baby-Sitters Club Ser.: No. 99). (J). (gr. 3-7). 1996. pap. text 3.99 (*0-590-69205-4*) Scholastic Inc.

— Stacey's Broken Heart. (Baby-Sitters Club Ser.: No. 99). 1996. 9.09 (*0-606-09035-5*, Pub. by Turtleback) Demco.

— Stacey's Choice. (Baby-Sitters Club Ser.: No. 58). 192p. (J). (gr. 4-6). 1992. 3.50 (*0-590-45659-8*) Scholastic Inc.

— Stacey's Choice. (Baby-Sitters Club Ser.: No. 58). (gr. 3-7). 1997. pap. text 3.50 (*0-590-92584-9*) Scholastic Inc.

— Stacey's Choice. (Baby-Sitters Club Ser.: No. 58). (J). 1992. 9.09 (*0-606-01948-0*, Pub. by Turtleback) Demco.

— Stacey's Emergency. LC 96-17010. (Baby-Sitters Club Ser.: No. 43). 144p. (J). (gr. 4 up). 1996. lib. bdg. 21.27 (*0-8368-1567-X*) Gareth Stevens Inc.

— Stacey's Emergency. (Baby-Sitters Club Ser.: No. 43). 1991. pap. 3.99 (*0-590-74243-4*) Scholastic Inc.

— Stacey's Emergency. (Baby-Sitters Club Ser.: No. 43). 192p. (J). (gr. 4-6). 1991. pap. 3.50 (*0-590-43572-8*) Scholastic Inc.

— Stacey's Emergency. (Baby-Sitters Club Ser.: No. 43). (J). 1991. 8.60 (*0-606-05021-3*, Pub. by Turtleback) Demco.

— Stacey's Ex-Best Friend. (Baby-Sitters Club Ser.: No. 51). 192p. (J). (gr. 3-7). 1992. pap. 3.50 (*0-590-44968-0*) Scholastic Inc.

— Stacey's Ex-Best Friend. (Baby-Sitters Club Ser.: No. 51). (J). 1992. 8.60 (*0-606-00770-9*, Pub. by Turtleback) Demco.

— Stacey's Ex-Boyfriend. (Baby-Sitters Club Ser.: No. 119). (J). (gr. 3-7). 1998. pap. text 3.99 (*0-590-05997-1*) Scholastic Inc.

*__Martin, Ann M.__ Stacey's Ex-Boyfriend. (Baby-Sitters Club Ser.: No. 119). (J). 1998. 9.09 (*0-606-13163-9*, Pub. by Turtleback) Demco.

Martin, Ann M. Stacey's Lie. (Baby-Sitters Club Ser.: No. 76). 192p. (J). (gr. 4-6). 1994. pap. 3.50 (*0-590-47014-0*) Scholastic Inc.

— Stacey's Lie. (Baby-Sitters Club Ser.: No. 76). (J). (gr. 3-7). 1997. pap. text 3.99 (*0-590-92608-X*) Scholastic Inc.

Martin, Ann M. Stacey's Lie. (Baby-Sitters Club Ser.: No. 76). (J). 1994. 9.09 (*0-606-06202-5*, Pub. by Turtleback) Demco.

Martin, Ann M. Stacey's Mistake. (Baby-Sitters Club Ser.: No. 18). 192p. (J). (gr. 4-6). 1988. pap. 3.99 (*0-590-43718-6*) Scholastic Inc.

— Stacey's Mistake. (Baby-Sitters Club Ser.: No. 18). (J). (gr. 3-7). 1996. pap. text 3.99 (*0-590-60534-8*) Scholastic Inc.

— Stacey's Mistake. (Baby-Sitters Club Ser.: No. 18). (J). 1987. 8.60 (*0-606-04091-9*, Pub. by Turtleback) Demco.

— Stacey's Movie. (Baby-Sitters Club Ser.: No. 130). 1999. pap. 4.50 (*0-590-50389-8*) Scholastic Inc.

*__Martin, Ann M.__ Stacey's Problem. (Baby-Sitters Club Friends Forever Ser.: No. 10). (Illus.). 144p. (J). (gr. 3-7). 2000. pap. 4.50 (*0-590-52345-7*) Scholastic Inc.

Martin, Ann M. Stacey's Secret Friend. (Baby-Sitters Club Ser.: No. 111). (Illus.). 160p. (J). (gr. 3-7). 1997. pap. text 3.99 (*0-590-05989-0*) Scholastic Inc.

Martin, Ann M. Stacey's Secret Friend. (Baby-Sitters Club Ser.: No. 111). 1997. 9.09 (*0-606-11071-2*, Pub. by Turtleback) Demco.

Martin, Ann M. Stage Fright: Its Role in Acting. (J). 1986. pap. text 2.50 (*0-590-33758-0*) Scholastic Inc.

— Starring the Baby-Sitters Club! (Baby-Sitters Club Super Special Ser.: No. 9). 256p. (J). (gr. 4-6). 1992. pap. 3.95 (*0-590-45661-X*) Scholastic Inc.

— Summer School. (Kids in Ms. Colman's Class Ser.: No. 8). (J). (gr. 1-4). 1997. pap. text 3.50 (*0-590-69204-6*) Scholastic Inc.

— Sunny. (California Diaries: Vol. 2). 176p. (YA). (gr. 4-8). 1997. mass mkt. 3.99 (*0-590-29836-4*) Scholastic Inc.

— Sunny. (California Diaries). (YA). (gr. 6-8). 1999. pap. text 54.00 (*0-439-09614-6*) Scholastic Inc.

Martin, Ann M. Sunny. (California Diaries). (YA). (gr. 6-8). 1997. 9.09 (*0-606-11180-8*, Pub. by Turtleback) Demco.

— Sunny: Diary Three, (California Diaries: Vol. 12). 160p. (J). (gr. 6-8). 1999. pap. 4.50 (*0-590-02390-X*) Scholastic Inc.

— Sunny: Diary Two. (California Diaries). (YA). (gr. 6-8). 1998. pap. 71.82 (*0-590-65607-4*) Scholastic Inc.

— Sunny: Diary Two. (California Diaries: Vol. 6). (J). (gr. 6-8). 1998. pap. 3.99 (*0-590-29840-2*) Scholastic Inc.

— Sunny: Diary Two. (California Diaries). (YA). (gr. 6-8). 1998. 9.09 (*0-606-13237-6*, Pub. by Turtleback) Demco.

Martin, Ann M. Teacher's Pet. (Kids in Ms. Colman's Class Ser.: No. 1). 96p. (J). (gr. 1-4). 1995. pap. 2.99 (*0-590-26215-7*) Scholastic Inc.

— Teacher's Pet. (Kids in Ms. Colman's Class Ser.: No. 1). (J). (gr. 1-4). 1995. 8.60 (*0-606-07761-8*, Pub. by Turtleback) Demco.

— Ten Kids, No Pets. 176p. (J). (gr. 4-6). 1990. pap. 3.50 (*0-590-43620-1*) Scholastic Inc.

— The Truth about Stacey. (Baby-Sitters Club Ser.: No. 3). (J). 1986. pap. 3.50 (*0-590-43511-6*) Scholastic Inc.

— The Truth about Stacey. (Baby-Sitters Club Ser.: No. 3). 192p. (J). (gr. 3-7). 1995. pap. text 3.99 (*0-590-25158-9*) Scholastic Inc.

Martin, Ann M. The Truth about Stacey. (Baby-Sitters Club Ser.: No. 3). (J). (gr. 3-7). 1986. 9.09 (*0-606-03084-0*, Pub. by Turtleback) Demco.

Martin, Ann M. Welcome Back, Stacey! (Baby-Sitters Club Ser.: No. 28). 160p. (J). (gr. 3-7). 1949. pap. text 3.99 (*0-590-67396-3*) Scholastic Inc.

— Welcome Back, Stacey! (Baby-Sitters Club Ser.: No. 28). 192p. (J). (gr. 4-6). 1989. pap. 3.50 (*0-590-42501-3*, Apple Paperbacks) Scholastic Inc.

— Welcome Back, Stacey! (Baby-Sitters Club Ser.: No. 28). (J). 1989. 9.09 (*0-606-04419-1*, Pub. by Turtleback) Demco.

*__Martin, Ann M.__ Welcome Home, Mary Anne. (Baby-Sitters Club Friends Forever Ser.: Vol. 11). (Illus.). 144p. (J). (gr. 4-7). 2000. pap. 4.50 (*0-590-52346-5*) Scholastic Inc.

Martin, Ann M. Welcome to the BSC, Abby. (Baby-Sitters Club Ser.: No. 90). 192p. (J). (gr. 3-7). 1995. pap. text 3.99 (*0-590-22874-9*) Scholastic Inc.

— Welcome to the BSC, Abby. (Baby-Sitters Club Ser.: No. 90). 1995. 9.09 (*0-606-07232-2*, Pub. by Turtleback) Demco.

Martin, Ann M. & Godwin, Laura. The Doll People. LC 98-12344. (Illus.). 272p. (J). (gr. 4-7). 2000. 15.99 (*0-7868-0361-4*, Pub. by Disney Pr); lib. bdg. 16.49 (*0-7868-2372-0*, Pub. by Disney Pr) Little.

— The Doll People. 96p. (J). (gr. 1-3). 1998. pap. 4.95 (*0-7868-1240-0*, Pub. by Hyprn Ppbks) Little.

Martin, Ann M. & Singer, A.L. The Baby-Sitters Club: The Movie. 144p. (gr. 4-7). 1995. pap. 3.50 (*0-590-60404-X*) Scholastic Inc.

— The Baby-Sitters Club: The Movie. 32p. (ps-3). 1995. pap. 2.95 (*0-590-60403-1*) Scholastic Inc.

Martin, Ann M., jt. auth. see Carr, Jan.

Martin, Ann M., jt. auth. see Danziger, Paula.

Martin, Ann Marie. Joy in Our Hearts: Ann Marie Martin. 2nd ed. (Bellefleur Ser.: Vol. 1). (Illus.). 130p. 2000. mass mkt. 9.95 (*0-9659388-1-6*) Martin Pub Firm.

Martin, Ann Marie & Libby, Stephen E., Sr. Bright Lights & Dice: Ann Marie Martin & Stephen Earl Libby Sr. (Bellefleur Ser.: Vol. 3). (Illus.). 130p. 1998. pap. 9.95 (*0-9659388-3-2*) Martin Pub Firm.

— Gentle Hands Loving Heart: Ann Marie Martin & Stephen Earl Libby Sr. (Bellefleur Ser.: Vol. 2). (Illus.). 130p. 1998. pap. 9.95 (*0-9659388-2-4*) Martin Pub Firm.

*__Martin, Ann Matthews.__ Amalia: Diary Three. (Illus.). (J). 1999. 10.34 (*0-606-18525-9*) Turtleback.

— Claudia & the Disaster Date. (Baby-Sitters Club Friends Forever Ser.: Vol. 12). (Illus.). (J). 2000. pap. 4.50 (*0-590-52348-1*) Scholastic Inc.

— Claudia & the Middle School Mystery. (Illus.). 135p. (gr. 4-7). 1998. pap. 3.99 (*0-590-73452-0*) Scholastic Inc.

— Ducky: Diary Three. (Illus.). (J). 2000. 10.34 (*0-606-18866-5*) Turtleback.

— Karen's Cowboy. (Baby-Sitters Little Sister Ser.: Vol. 122). (Illus.). (J). 2000. pap. 3.99 (*0-590-52528-X*) Scholastic Inc.

— Karen's Gift. Vol. 121. 80p. (J). (gr. 2-5). 2000. pap. 3.99 (*0-590-52527-1*) Scholastic Inc.

— Leo the Magnificent. (Illus.). (J). 2000. 11.44 (*0-606-18573-9*) Turtleback.

— Maggie: Diary Three. (Illus.). (J). 1999. 9.34 (*0-606-18524-0*) Turtleback.

— Sunny: Diary Three. (Illus.). (J). 1999. 9.85 (*0-606-18523-2*) Turtleback.

*__Martin, Ann S.__ Makers & Users: American Decorative Arts, 1620-1830, from the Chipstone Collection. LC 99-38249. (Illus.). 72p. 1999. pap. 19.95 (*0-932900-46-1*) Elvejhem Mus.

Martin, Ann S., ed. see Winterthur, Henry Francis Du Pont Museum Staff.

Martin, Anna, jt. auth. see Women's Co-operative Guild.

Martin, Annamarie, et al. Dothan-Houston County: A Place of Our Own: The Stories of Dothan-Houston County. LC 98-41225. (Illus.). 136p. 1998. 28.00 (*1-885352-34-4*) Community Comm.

Martin, Anne. Quick & Easy Creative Art Lessons. LC 80-17558. 254p. 1981. 18.95 (*0-13-749663-X*, Parker Publishing Co) P-H.

— Reading Your Students: Their Writing & Their Selves. 64p. 1983. pap. 5.95 (*0-915924-32-3*) Tchrs & Writers Coll.

Martin, Anne M., ed. see Ruff, Ken.

Martin, Annette. Annie Sunshine & the White Owl of the Cedars. (Illus.). 128p. (Orig.). (J). (ps-3). 1995. pap. 2.95 (*1-885764-02-2*); pap. 7.95 incl. audio (*1-885764-03-0*) Artistic Visions.

— Discovering Your Psychic World. (Illus.). 176p. (Orig.). 1994. pap. 19.95 (*1-885764-01-4*) Artistic Visions.

Martin, Anthony. Beluga Whales. LC 96-5922. (WorldLife Library). (Illus.). 72p. (Orig.). 1996. pap. 14.95 (*0-89658-306-6*) Voyageur Pr.

Martin, Anthony & Camm, A. John, eds. Geriatric Cardiology: Principles & Practice. LC 93-40107. 832p. 1994. 355.00 (*0-471-94064-X*) Wiley.

— Heart Disease in the Elderly. LC 83-17058. (Wiley Series on Disease Management in the Elderly: No. 2). 285p. reprint ed. pap. 88.40 (*0-8357-3472-2*, 203973400013) Bks Demand.

Martin, Antoinette D., ed. see Martin, Charles A.

Martin, Antoinette Truglio. Famous Seaweed Soup. 1993. 11.15 (*0-606-08741-9*, Pub. by Turtleback) Demco.

Martin, Anton. Handbuch der Gesammten Photographie. Bunnell, Peter C. & Sobieszek, Robert A., eds. LC 76-23057. (Sources of Modern Photography Ser.). (GER.). 1979. reprint ed. lib. bdg. 27.95 (*0-405-09621-6*) Ayer.

Martin, Antonia F. Mangiare E'Squisito - Food Is Love: Antonia's Italian & American Cuisine. 2nd ed. LC 95-95335. (Illus.). 120p. (Orig.). 1996. reprint ed. spiral bd. 15.00 (*0-9653902-0-9*) Food Is Love.

Martin, April. Lesbian & Gay Parenting Handbook: Creating & Raising Our Families. LC 92-54782. 416p. 1993. pap. 16.00 (*0-06-096929-6*, Perennial) HarperTrade.

Martin, April, ed. see Mora, Eddy G.

Martin, Aquinata. The Catholic Church on the Nebraska Frontier: 1854-1885. LC 73-3580. (Catholic University of America. Studies in Romance Languages & Literatures: No. 26). reprint ed. 39.50 (*0-404-57776-8*) AMS Pr.

Martin, Ariadna Y., tr. see Propp, Vladimir.

Martin, Arlan S. Vivaldi Violin Concertos: A Handbook. LC 76-169698. 278p. 1972. 30.00 (*0-8108-0432-8*) Scarecrow.

Martin, Arlene L. Complete Preschool Program. 143p. 1987. pap. text 19.95 (*1-55691-008-8*, 088) Learning Pubns.

An Asterisk (*) at the beginning of an entry indicates that the title is appearing for the first time.

Martin, Arlene L. Psalm 1 Coloring Book. 28p. (J). (ps-2). 1989. pap. 1.55 (*0-7399-0171-0*, 2929) Rod & Staff.

— Psalm 1 Coloring Book. (SPA.). 28p. (J). 1996. pap. 1.40 (*0-7399-0172-9*, 2929.1) Rod & Staff.

— Rhyme & Color. 64p. (J). (gr. 1-3). 1988. pap. 2.35 (*0-7399-0173-7*, 2939) Rod & Staff.

***Martin, Arlene L. & Ashelman, Polly.** Mentoring in Early Childhood Settings. 152p. (C). 1999. per. 20.95 (*0-7872-6014-2*, 41601401) Kendall-Hunt.

Martin, Arlene L. & Prensky, Janet. Every Woman's Guide to Auto Racing: Understanding & Appreciating the Rules, Language, & Obsession with the Sport. 1999. pap. text 5.95 (*0-89529-991-7*, Avery) Penguin Putnam.

Martin, Arthur. Accessing Your Akashic Records. 2nd rev. ed. (Illus.). 130p. 1998. pap. 19.95 (*1-891962-04-3*) Personal Trans.

— Being a Spiritual Being in a Physical Body. 2nd rev. ed. (Illus.). 200p. 1999. pap. 15.95 (*1-891962-03-5*) Personal Trans.

— Journey into the Light. 2nd rev. ed. 105p. 1999. pap. 9.95 (*1-891962-05-1*) Personal Trans.

— Neurokinesiology. 2nd rev. ed. (Illus.). 115p. 1998. pap. 9.95 (*1-891962-07-8*) Personal Trans.

— Recovering Your Lost Self. unabridged ed. 280p. 1999. pap. 18.95 (*1-891962-06-X*) Personal Trans.

— 2011 the New Millennium Begins. 2nd rev. ed. (Illus.). 250p. 1998. pap. 13.95 (*1-891962-02-7*) Personal Trans.

— Your Body Is Talking Are You Listening. 2nd rev. ed. (Illus.). 190p. 1999. pap. 15.95 (*1-891962-01-9*) Personal Trans.

Martin, Arthur, jt. auth. see Cahier, Charles.

Martin, Arthur E. Life in the Slow Lane. (Illus.). 304p. 1990. 25.00 (*0-914339-30-3*) P E Randall Pub.

***Martin, Arthur H.** Opening Communications with God Source: Accessing Your Akashic Records. Orig. Title: Accessing Your Akashic Record. (Illus.). 220p. 2000. pap. 14.95 (*1-891962-09-4*) Personal Trans.

Martin, Asa E. Pennsylvania History Told by Contemporaries. 1993. reprint ed. lib. bdg. 89.00 (*0-7812-5489-2*) Rprt Serv.

Martin, Augustine. Bearing Witness: Essays on Anglo-Irish Literature. Roche, Anthony, ed. LC 96-230781. 260p. 1997. 49.95 (*1-900621-01-0*); pap. 24.95 (*1-900621-02-9*) Dufour.

— W. B. Yeats. 152p. 1990. pap. 10.95 (*0-86140-325-8*) Dufour.

Martin, Augustine, ed. The Works of James Clarence Mangan: With a Biography & Bibliography, 7 vols., Set. Date not set. write for info. (*0-7165-2556-9*, Pub. by Irish Acad Pr) Intl Spec Bk.

Martin, Augustine, ed. Forgiveness: Ireland's Best Contemporary Short Stories. LC 89-17014. 294p. 1989. 25.95 (*0-941423-32-8*); pap. 12.95 (*0-941423-33-6*) FWEW.

Martin, B. Atlas of Scrotal Ultrasound. 200p. 1993. 180.00 (*0-387-53309-5*) Spr-Verlag.

— Panda Bear, Panda Bear. (J). 1995. 13.95 (*0-8050-1758-5*) H Holt & Co.

— Tissue Culture Techniques: An Introduction. LC 94-6357. (Illus.). xi, 247p. 1997. 45.00 (*0-8176-3643-9*) Birkhauser.

— Yo, Grocer. (J). (gr. 4 up). 1995. 12.95 (*0-8050-0329-0*) H Holt & Co.

Martin, B., jt. auth. see Ziegler, K.

Martin, B. Jay. Conundrum Vol. 1: A Cartoon Collection of Concepts, College, & Confounded Connotations. LC 89-4356. (Illus.). 160p. (Orig.). 1988. pap. 5.95 (*0-922073-00-7*) Thought Wave Pr.

Martin-Bagnaudez, Jacqueline. Petit Dictionnaire de l'Architecture. (FRE.). 139p. 1990. pap. 22.95 (*0-7859-8629-4*, 222003139x) Fr & Eur.

Martin, Barb. The Haunted Pogo Stick. (Illus.). 23p. (J). 1995. text 12.50 (*0-930329-92-9*) Kabel Pubs.

Martin, Barbara. The Busy Teacher's Survival Guide. 1996. pap., wbk. ed. 12.95 (*1-55734-029-3*) Tchr Create Mat.

Martin, Barbara. Carryover Activities for the er Sound: Working with er - ir - or - ur. (Illus.). 191p. 1990. pap. text 36.00 (*0-7616-7670-8*) Commun Skill.

Martin, Barbara & Christie, Folla. Landlord & Tenant Law. 2nd ed. 448p. 1994. pap. 39.95 (*0-632-03469-6*) Blackwell Sci.

Martin, Barbara H. The Little Book of Miracles: Collection of Stories of How Simple Faith Can Change Your Daily Life. (Illus.). 56p. (Orig.). 1996. pap. 9.95 (*1-884707-22-X*) Lifestyles.

Martin, Barbara L. & Briggs, Leslie J. The Affective & Cognitive Domains: Integration for Instruction & Research. LC 85-16143. (Illus.). 500p. 1986. 49.95 (*0-87778-193-1*) Educ Tech Pubns.

Martin-Barbero, Jesus & Schlesinger, Philip. Communication, Culture & Hegemony: From Media to Mediations. (Communication & Human Values Ser.). (Illus.). 288p. (C). 1993. text 65.00 (*0-8039-8488-X*); pap. text 24.95 (*0-8039-8489-8*) Sage.

Martin-Barnes, Adrienne, jt. auth. see Paxson, Diana L.

Martin-Baro, Ignacio. Writings for a Liberation Psychology. Aron, Adrianne & Corne, Shawn, eds. LC 94-20987. (Illus.). 256p. 1994. text 37.95 (*0-674-96246-X*, MARWRI) HUP.

— Writings for a Liberation Psychology. Aron, Adrianne & Corne, Shawn, eds. (Illus.). 256p. 1996. pap. 17.50 (*0-674-96247-8*) HUP.

Martin, Barry. Budgies As a New Pet. (Illus.). 64p. (Orig.). 1990. pap. 6.95 (*0-86622-611-7*, TU-004) TFH Pubns.

— Dancing Still. 1999. pap. 20.95 (*0-525-93952-0*) NAL.

— Rabbits As a New Pet. (Illus.). 64p. (Orig.). 1990. pap. 6.95 (*0-86622-618-4*, TU-010) TFH Pubns.

Martin, Belinda B., intro. Pediatric Hospice Care: What Helps. (Illus.). 400p. (C). 1989. write for info. (*0-9623727-0-6*) Child Hosp LA.

***Martin, Ben.** Hollywood at Your Feet: The Story of the World-Famous Chinese Theatre, Millennium Edition. (Illus.). 376p. 2000. pap. 24.95 (*0-938817-21-3*) Pomegranate Pr.

Martin, Ben & Irvine, John. Research Foresight: Creating the Future. 300p. 1989. text 52.00 (*0-86187-510-9*) St Martin.

***Martin, Ben J.** Caught Stealing: A Love Story with a Baseball Background. LC 98-10506. viii, 326 p. 1998. pap. 7.99 (*0-9661852-3-4*) Adams Pr IL.

Martin, Ben R. & Nightingale, Paul, eds. The Political Economy of Science, Technology & Innovation. LC 99-53193. 736p. 2000. 265.00 (*1-85898-961-2*) E Elgar.

Martin, Bengt. Olaf the Ship's Cat. (Illus.). 32p. (J). (ps-3). 1992. 7.95 (*1-56288-266-X*) Checkerboard.

Martin, Benjamin. The Agony of Modernization: Labor & Industrialization in Spain. LC 89-77909. (Cornell International Industrial & Labor Relations Reports: No. 16). 576p. 1990. text 49.95 (*0-87546-165-4*, ILR Press) Cornell U Pr.

Martin, Benjamin, jt. auth. see Boast, William M.

Martin, Benjamin F. Crime & Criminal Justice under the Third Republic: The Shame of Marianne. LC 89-27334. 392p. 1990. text 55.00 (*0-8071-1572-X*) La State U Pr.

— France & the Apres Guerre, 1918-1924. LC 99-14903. (Illus.). 272p. 1999. text 49.95 (*0-8071-2399-4*); pap. text 22.50 (*0-8071-2509-1*) La State U Pr.

— The Hypocrisy of Justice in the Belle Epoque. LC 83-16263. 267p. 1984. pap. 82.80 (*0-7837-8502-X*, 204931000011) Bks Demand.

Martin, Bernard. The Existentialist Theology of Paul Tillich. 1963. pap. 15.95 (*0-8084-0400-8*) NCUP.

Martin, Bernard, jt. auth. see Martin, Bill, Jr.

Martin, Bernd. Japan & Germany in the Modern World. LC 94-42973. 320p. (C). 1995. 59.95 (*1-57181-858-8*) Berghahn Bks.

Martin, Bernice & Lawrence, John. Frontier Eye Witness: Diary of John Lawrence (1867-1908) 183p. 1990. pap. 10.00 (*0-9651079-0-6*) Saguache Cnty.

Martin, Bernice M. Tissue Culture Techniques: An Introduction. LC 94-6357. xi, 247p. 1994. 93.50 (*0-8176-3718-4*) Birkhauser.

Martin, Berta, tr. see McGrath, Susan.

Martin, Beryl. A Family from Barra. LC 98-205052. 200p. 1997. pap. 27.50 (*1-86940-165-4*, Pub. by Auckland Univ) Paul & Co Pubs.

Martin, Bessie. Desertion of Alabama Troops from the Confederate Army. LC 32-34110. (Columbia University. Studies in the Social Sciences: No. 378). reprint ed. 21.50 (*0-404-51378-6*) AMS Pr.

Martin, Bethany, ed. see Martin, LaJoyce.

Martin, Bettina G., ed. The CLMA Guide to Managing a Clinical Laboratory. LC TX 3 260 067. (Illus.). 95p. (Orig.). 1991. pap. text 35.00 (*0-9625414-1-9*) Clinical Lab Mgmnt Assn.

Martin, Betty. Cluster Maps of 117 Colorado I-25 Golf Courses. (Illus.). 1997. spiral bd. 20.00 (*1-890652-05-9*) Bettys Desktop.

— Colorado I-25 Golf Courses Cluster Maps: 117 Golf Courses. (Illus.). 1997. spiral bd. 45.00 (*1-890652-04-0*) Bettys Desktop.

— Colorado Springs Region & Southern Colorado I-25 Golf Courses Vol. 3: 34 Golf Courses. LC 99-213110. (Illus.). 65p. 1997. spiral bd. write for info. (*1-890652-02-4*) Bettys Desktop.

— Denver Region Colorado I-25 Golf Courses: 65 Golf Courses. (Simplified Graphics Maps Ser.: Vol. 2). (Illus.). 80p. 1997. spiral bd. 34.50 (*1-890652-01-6*) Bettys Desktop.

— Glossary of Colorado I-25 Golf Courses Single Point of Destination Location Instruction: 117 Golf Courses. 68p. 1997. spiral bd. 34.00 (*1-890652-03-2*) Bettys Desktop.

— Northern Colorado I-25 Golf Courses: 29 Golf Courses. (Simplified Graphical Maps Ser.: Vol. 1). (Illus.). 45p. 1997. spiral bd. 21.50 (*1-890652-00-8*) Bettys Desktop.

Martin, Betty, jt. auth. see Martin, Don.

Martin, Betty, jt. auth. see Martin, Glen.

Martin, Betty D. Orwell Remembered Vol. II: The Town of Orwell & America's Wars. 230p. 1993. pap. 12.50 (*1-886303-01-0*) Write to Print.

Martin, Betty W., jt. auth. see Martin, Don W.

Martin, Betty Woo, jt. auth. see Martin, Don W.

Martin, Biddy. Femininity Played Straight: Gender, Sexuality, Subjectivity. LC 96-892. 288p. (C). 1997. 70.00 (*0-415-91680-1*); pap. 18.99 (*0-415-91681-X*) Routledge.

— Women & Modernity: The (Life) Styles of Lou Andreas-Salome. LC 90-55718. (Reading Women Writing Ser.). (Illus.). 264p. 1991. text 42.50 (*0-8014-2591-3*); pap. text 15.95 (*0-8014-9907-0*) Cornell U Pr.

***Martin, Bill, Jr.** Avant Rock: Experimental Music from the Beatles to Bjork. (Illus.). 2000. pap. 19.95 (*0-8126-9420-1*) Open Court.

Martin, Bill, Jr. Barn Dance. (J). 1988. 11.15 (*0-606-03724-1*, Pub. by Turtleback) Demco.

— Bill Martin Junior Biography. (J). 1995. write for info. (*0-8050-4074-9*) St Martin.

— Brown Bear, Brown Bear, What Do You See? LC 83 12779. (Illus.). 32p. (J). (ps-k). 1983. lib. bdg. 15.95 (*0-8050-0201-4*, Bks Young Read) H Holt & Co.

— Brown Bear, Brown Bear, What Do You See? (Illus.). 26p. (J). (ps). 1996. bds. 6.95 (*0-8050-4790-5*, B Martin BYR) H Holt & Co.

— Brown Bear, Brown Bear, What Do You See? (SPA., Illus.). 32p. (J). (ps-1). 1998. 15.95 (*0-8050-5967-9*, Bks Young Read) H Holt & Co.

— Brown Bear, Brown Bear, What Do You See? 25th Anniversary Edition. LC 91-29115. (Illus.). 24p. (J). (ps). 1992. 15.95 (*0-8050-1744-5*, Bks Young Read) H Holt & Co.

— Calendar Lion. (J). 1995. 15.95 (*0-8050-2417-4*) H Holt & Co.

— Chicka Chicka ABC. (Illus.). 14p. (J). (ps-k). 1993. pap. 4.95 (*0-671-87893-X*) Litle Simon.

***Martin, Bill, Jr.** Chicka Chicka Boom Boom. (Illus.). (J). 2000. 12.34 (*0-606-18798-7*) Turtleback.

Martin, Bill, Jr. Fire! Fire! Said Mrs. McGuire. LC 94-11258. (Illus.). 32p. (J). 1996. 15.00 (*0-15-227562-2*) Harcourt.

— "Fire! Fire!" Said Mrs. McGuire. LC 94-11258. (Illus.). 32p. (J). 1999. pap. 6.00 (*0-15-202063-2*) Harcourt.

— The Happy Hippopotami. Johnston, Allyn, ed. LC 90-37921. (Illus.). 32p. (J). (ps-3). 1991. 14.00 (*0-15-233380-0*) Harcourt.

— The Happy Hippopotami. LC 90-37921. (Illus.). 32p. (J). (ps-3). 1992. pap. 6.00 (*0-15-233382-7*) Harcourt.

Martin, Bill, Jr. Happy Hippopotami. 1991. 11.20 (*0-606-01024-6*, Pub. by Turtleback) Demco.

Martin, Bill, Jr. Here Are My Hands. (J). (ps-k). 1989. 11.95 (*0-606-01390-3*, Pub. by Turtleback) Demco.

— Humanism & Its Aftermath: The Shared Fate of Deconstruction & Politics. LC 94-39400. 216p. (C). 1995. pap. 15.00 (*0-391-03894-X*) Humanities.

— Humanism & Its Aftermath: The Shared Fate of Deconstruction & Politics. LC 94-39400. 216p. (C). 1995. text 45.00 (*0-391-03893-1*) Humanities.

— Humanism & its Aftermath: The Shared Fate of Deconstruction & Politics LC 98-52765. 1998. write for info. (*1-57392-599-3*) Prometheus Bks.

— The Joy of Drawing. LC 93-9265. (Illus.). 144p. 1993. pap. 22.50 (*0-8230-2370-2*) Watsn-Guptill.

— Knots on a Counting Rope. (Illus.). 32p. (J). (ps-3). 1995. pap. 19.95 (*0-8050-2955-9*, Bks Young Read) H Holt & Co.

— Knots on a Counting Rope. 1997. 11.15 (*0-606-12386-5*, Pub. by Turtleback) Demco.

— Listening to the Future: The Time of Progressive Rock, 1968-1978. LC 97-36495. (Feedback: Vol. 2). 256p. (Orig.). (C). 1997. pap. 19.95 (*0-8126-9368-X*) Open Court.

— The Maestro Plays. (J). 1995. 15.95 (*0-8050-1746-1*, Bks Young Read) H Holt & Co.

— The Maestro Plays. LC 95-49126. (Illus.). 48p. (J). (ps-3). 1996. reprint ed. pap. 6.00 (*0-15-201217-6*, Voyager Bks) Harcourt.

— The Magic Pumpkin. LC 89-11162. (Illus.). 32p. (J). (ps-2). 1996. pap. 5.95 (*0-8050-4904-5*, B Martin BYR) H Holt & Co.

— Matrix & Line: Derrida & the Possibilities of Postmodern Social Theory. LC 91-20980. (SUNY Series in Radical Social & Political Theory). 255p. (C). 1992. text 59.50 (*0-7914-1049-8*); pap. text 19.95 (*0-7914-1050-1*) State U NY Pr.

— Music of Yes: Structure & Vision in Progressive Rock. 298p. (Orig.). 1996. pap. 19.95 (*0-8126-9333-7*) Open Court.

— My Special Place. 136p. (gr. 4-9). 1980. pap. 8.95 (*0-89114-111-1*) Baptist Pub Hse.

***Martin, Bill, Jr.** New Snow. 28p. 1999. 5.00 (*0-938711-62-8*) Tecolote Pubns.

Martin, Bill, Jr. Old Devil Wind. LC 92-37908. (Illus.). 32p. (J). (ps-3). 1993. 13.95 (*0-15-257768-8*) Harcourt.

— Old Devil Wind. LC 92-37908. (Illus.). 32p. (J). 1996. pap. 5.00 (*0-15-201384-9*) Harcourt.

— Old Devil Wind. LC 92-37908. (J). 1996. 10.20 (*0-606-11698-2*, Pub. by Turtleback) Demco.

***Martin, Bill, Jr.** Oso Polar, Oso Polar, Que Es Ese Ruido? LC 99-40728. (SPA., Illus.). 32p. (ps-k). 2000. text 15.95 (*0-8050-6427-3*) H Holt & Co.

Martin, Bill, Jr. Polar Bear, Polar Bear, What Do You Hear? (Illus.). 32p. (J). (ps). 1995. 15.95 (*0-8050-1759-3*, Bks Young Read) H Holt & Co.

— Polar Bear, Polar Bear, What Do You Hear? (Illus.). 32p. (J). (ps-2). 1995. pap. 16.95 (*0-8050-2815-3*, Bks Young Read) H Holt & Co.

— Polar Bear, Polar Bear, What Do You Hear? (Illus.). (J). 1997. bds. 6.95 (*0-8050-5388-3*) H Holt & Co.

— Polar Bear, Polar Bear, What Do You Hear? Big Book. LC 91-13322. (Illus.). 32p. (J). (ps-2). 1995. pap. 19.95 (*0-8050-2346-1*, Bks Young Read) H Holt & Co.

— Politics in the Impasse: Explorations in Postsecular Social Theory. LC 95-13739. (SUNY Series in Radical, Social & Political Theory). 300p. (C). 1996. text 59.50 (*0-7914-2793-5*); pap. text 19.95 (*0-7914-2794-3*) State U NY Pr.

***Martin, Bill, Jr.** Rocket, Socket, Number, Line. 2001. text 16.95 (*0-8050-6304-8*) H Holt & Co.

— Swish! (Illus.). 32p. (gr. k-3). 2000. pap. 6.95 (*0-8050-6578-4*) H Holt & Co.

Martin, Bill, Jr. The Turning of the Year. LC 96-53078. (Illus.). 28p. (J). (ps-2). 1998. lib. bdg. 15.00 (*0-15-201085-8*) Harcourt.

— The Wizard. LC 93-15521. (Illus.). 32p. (J). (ps-3). 1994. 14.95 (*0-15-298926-9*) Harcourt.

Martin, Bill, Jr. The Wizard. 1997. 11.20 (*0-606-13924-9*, Pub. by Turtleback) Demco.

Martin, Bill, Jr. The Wizard. LC 93-15521. (Illus.). 36p. (J). 1997. reprint ed. pap. 6.00 (*0-15-201568-X*, Harcourt Child Bks) Harcourt.

— Words. LC 95 188258. (Illus.). 14p. (J). (ps up). 1993. 4.95 (*0-671-87174-9*) Litle Simon.

***Martin, Bill, Jr.** Yo Grocer. 2001. text 16.95 (*0-8050-6351-X*) St Martin.

Martin, Bill, Jr. & Archambault, John. Barn Dance! LC 86-14225. (Illus.). 32p. (J). (ps-2). 1995. 14.95 (*0-8050-0089-5*, Bks Young Read) H Holt & Co.

— Barn Dance! LC 86-14225. (Illus.). 32p. (J). (ps-3). 1995. pap. 4.95 (*0-8050-0799-7*, Bks Young Read) H Holt & Co.

— Chicka Chicka ABC. (J). 1998. 4.95 (*0-87628-352-0*) Ctr Appl Res.

— Chicka Chicka Boom Boom. (Illus.). 40p. (J). (ps-1). 1989. 15.00 (*0-671-67949-X*) S&S Bks Yung.

— Chicka Chicka Boom Boom. (Illus.). 40p. (J). (ps-3). 1991. 19.95 incl. audio (*0-671-74894-7*) S&S Bks Yung.

— The Ghost-Eye Tree. LC 85-8422. (Illus.). 32p. (Orig.). (J). (ps-2). 1995. 13.95 (*0-8050-0208-1*, Bks Young Read) H Holt & Co.

— The Ghost-Eye Tree. LC 85-8422. (Illus.). 32p. (Orig.). (J). (ps-3). 1995. pap. 5.95 (*0-8050-0947-7*, Bks Young Read) H Holt & Co.

— Here Are My Hands. LC 86-25842. (Illus.). 32p. (J). (ps-2). 1995. 14.95 (*0-8050-0328-2*, Bks Young Read); pap. 5.95 (*0-8050-1168-4*, Owlet BYR) H Holt & Co.

— Knots on a Counting Rope. LC 87-14832. (Illus.). 32p. (J). (ps-2). 1995. 15.95 (*0-8050-0571-4*, Bks Young Read) H Holt & Co.

— Listen to the Rain. LC 88-6502. (Illus.). 32p. (J). (ps-2). 1995. 15.95 (*0-8050-0682-6*, Bks Young Read) H Holt & Co.

— The Magic Pumpkin. LC 89-11162. (Illus.). 32p. (J). (ps-2). 1995. 14.95 (*0-8050-1134-X*, Bks Young Read) H Holt & Co.

— Up & down on the Merry-Go-Round. LC 87-28836. (Illus.). 89p. (J). (ps-2). 1995. 14.95 (*0-8050-0681-8*, Bks Young Read); pap. 4.95 (*0-8050-1638-4*, Bks Young Read) H Holt & Co.

— White Dynamite & Curly Kidd. LC 85-27214. (Illus.). 89p. (J). (ps-2). 1995. 12.95 (*0-8050-0658-3*, Bks Young Read); pap. 5.95 (*0-8050-1018-1*, Bks Young Read) H Holt & Co.

Martin, Bill, Jr. & Martin & Martin Staff. Chicka Chicka Sticka Sticka: An ABC Sticker Book. LC 95-237856. 12p. 1995. pap. 6.95 (*0-689-80096-7*) Litle Simon.

***Martin, Bill, Jr. & Martin, Bernard.** Chicken Chuck. LC 99-37956. (Illus.). 32p. (J). (ps-3). 2000. 16.95 (*1-890817-31-7*, Pub. by Winslow Pr) Publishers Group.

Martin, Bill, Jr & Sampson, Michael. Swish! LC 96-44216. (Illus.). 32p. (J). (gr. k-5). 1995. 14.95 (*0-8050-4498-1*) H Holt & Co.

***Martin, Bill, Jr & Tracy, Wes.** The Christian's Guide to Financial Freedom: Managing Your Money & Your Life from a Biblical Perspective. 2000. pap., wbk. ed. write for info. (*0-8341-1797-5*) Beacon Hill.

Martin, Bill, Jr., et al. Knots on a Counting Rope. LC 87-14858. (Illus.). 32p. (J). (ps-2). 1997. reprint ed. pap. 5.95 (*0-8050-5479-0*) H Holt & Co.

***Martin, Bill, Jr., et al.** The Little Squeegy Bug. LC 00-32085. (Illus.). 2001. write for info. (*1-890817-90-2*) Winslow Pr.

Martin, Bill, Jr., jt. auth. see Archambault, John.

Martin, Bill, Jr., jt. auth. see Sampson, Michael.

Martin, Bob & Martin, Dotty. Arizona's Mountains: A Hiking Guide to the Grand Canyon State. 2nd ed. LC 87-15518. (Illus.). 208p. (Orig.). 1991. pap. 11.95 (*0-917895-37-1*) Johnson Bks.

Martin, Bob, jt. auth. see Garratt, Mike.

Martin, Bob, jt. auth. see Luchenbach, Dave.

Martin, Bobi. Kidding Around San Francisco: A Fun-Packed, Fact-Filled, Travel & Activity Book. LC 96-2400. (Illus.). 144p. (J). (gr. 4-7). 1996. pap. 7.95 (*1-56261-306-5*) Avalon Travel.

Martin, Bobi, ed. see McGuire, Leslie.

Martin, Bobi, ed. see Rubin, Susan G.

Martin, Bobi, ed. see Sherwood, Jonathan.

Martin, Bobi, ed. see Weil, Jennifer C.

Martin, Bonita L. & Momeier, Greta C. Let's Articulate: Reproducible Drill Sheets for Therapy & Carryover. 410p. 1983. student ed., spiral bd. 39.00 (*0-7616-4646-9*) Commun Skill.

Martin, Bonita L. & Momeir, Greta C. More Let's Articulate. 286p. 1987. 33.50 (*0-7616-7341-5*) Commun Skill.

Martin Bossley, Michele. Breathing Not Required. 84p. (J). (gr. 3-8). 1999. pap. 5.50 (*1-55028-474-6*) Formac Dist Ltd.

— The Winning Edge. 87p. (J). (gr. 3-8). 1999. text 5.50 (*1-55028-636-6*) Formac Dist Ltd.

Martin, Brande N. Help, I'm Home! A Self Help Guide for Study Abroad Returnees. (Illus.). 32p. (C). 1997. 5.00 (*0-9660790-0-0*) Globetalk.

Martin, Brendan. In the Public Interest? Privatization & Public Sector Reform. LC 93-5391. 256p. (C). 1993. pap. 19.95 (*1-85649-216-8*, Pub. by Zed Books); text 49.95 (*1-85649-215-X*, Pub. by Zed Books) St Martin.

— Redesigning Public Services: A Partnership Approach. (C). 1998. pap. 25.00 (*1-85649-502-7*, Pub. by Zed Books) St Martin.

Martin, Brent J. Laboratory Cat. LC 98-198506. (Laboratory Animal Pocket Reference Ser.). 160p. 1997. spiral bd. 44.95 (*0-8493-2567-6*) CRC Pr.

Martin, Bret. Strengthen Your Game: Combine a Healthy Body with the Proper Swing Technique to Lower Your Handi, 1. 1998. pap. write for info. (*0-9646775-0-4*) Fairway Publng.

Martin, Brian. Go-Kart Racing/Chassis Setup. (Illus.). 88p. (Orig.). 1996. pap. 14.95 (*0-9605068-4-5*) Martin Motorsports.

— Never Enough. 1994. 26.95 (*0-7737-2688-8*) Stoddart Publ.

— Scientific Knowledge in Controversy: The Social Dynamics of the Fluoridation Debate. LC 90-34740. (SUNY Series in Science, Technology, & Society). 266p. (C). 1991. text 21.50 (*0-7914-0538-9*); pap. text 21.95 (*0-7914-0539-7*) State U NY Pr.

— Strip the Experts. (Anarchist Discussion Ser.). 69p. 1991. pap. 4.50 (*0-900384-63-8*) Left Bank.

— Tales of the Countrymen. large type ed. (Reminiscence Ser.). 24.95 (*1-85695-067-0*, Pub. by ISIS Lrg Prnt) Transaction Pubs.

— Uprooting War. 298p. (Orig.). 1984. pap. 10.00 (*0-900384-26-3*) Left Bank.

M

An Asterisk (*) at the beginning of an entry indicates that the title is appearing for the first time.

***Martin, Brian.** The Whistleblower's Handbook. 104p. 2000. pap. 19.95 (*1-897766-52-1*, Pub. by Jon Carpenter) Paul & Co Pubs.

Martin, Brian, ed. Confronting the Experts. LC 95-19312. 204p. (C). 1996. text 44.50 (*0-7914-2913-X*); pap. text 14.95 (*0-7914-2914-8*) State U NY Pr.

— The Nineteenth Century, 1798-1900, Vol. 4. LC 89-70174. (St. Martin's Anthologies of English Literature Ser.: Vol. No. 4.). 666p. 1990. text 20.00 (*0-312-04476-3*) St Martin.

Martin, Brian, jt. auth. see Carson, Lyn.

Martin, Brian G. The Shanghai Green Gang: Politics & Organized Crime, 1919-1937. LC 95-5017. 279p. (C). 1996. 45.00 (*0-520-20114-0*, Pub. by U CA Pr) Cal Prin Full Svc.

Martin, Brian P. Tales from the Country Pub. 1999. 27.95 (*0-7153-0541-7*) D & C Pub.

***Martin, Brian P.** Tales of the Old Countrywomen. large type unabridged ed. 1999. 25.95 (*0-7531-5459-5*, 154595, Pub. by ISIS Lrg Prnt) ISIS Pub.

***Martin, Bronwen & Ringham, Felizitas.** Cassell Dictionary of Semiotics LC 99-20285. (Illus.). 192p. 1999. 26.95 (*0-304-70636-1*) Continuum.

Martin-Brown, Joan, jt. ed. see Scrageldin, Ismail.

Martin-Brown, Joan, jt. ed. see Serageldin, Ismail.

Martin, Bruce. Martin's MINI Mysteries. LC 98-72684. 186p. 1998. 19.95 (*0-9622899-5-7*) Creative Consort Inc.

— Stock Car Team Secrets: Top NASCAR Teams Reveal Keys to Success. LC 98-46886. (Illus.). 128p. 1999. pap. 17.95 (*0-7603-0535-8*, 128043AP) MBI Pubg.

***Martin, Bruce K.** David Lodge. LC 99-11814. (Twayne's English Authors Ser.: Vol. 553). 188p. 1999. 32.00 (*0-8057-1671-8*, Twayne) Mac Lib Ref.

Martin, Buddy. Down Where the Old Gators Play Vol. II: Reign of the Swamp Fox. 232p. 1996. pap. text, per. 16.95 (*0-7872-2759-5*) Kendall-Hunt.

Martin, C. Fly Fishing in Northern New Mexico. LC 91-11440. (Coyote Bks.). (Illus.). 250p. 1991. pap. 14.95 (*0-8263-1290-X*) U of NM Pr.

Martin, C. & Dieguez, E. Orientation of Single Crystals by Back Reflection Laue Pattern Simulation. LC 98-54444. 164p. 1998. lib. bdg. 27.00 (*981-02-2871-6*) World Scientific Pub.

Martin, C. Dianne, jt. ed. see Blomeyer, Robert L., Jr.

Martin, C. E., ed. see Institute of World Affairs Staff.

Martin, C. F., et al, eds. Systems & Control in the Twenty-First Century. LC 96-45612. (Progress in Systems & Control Theory Ser.). 434p. 1996. 95.00 (*0-8176-3881-4*) Birkhauser.

Martin, C. F., jt. auth. see Hunt, L. R.

Martin, C. F., tr. see Grosseteste, Robert.

Martin, C. G. Maps & Surveys of Malawi. 280p. (C). 1980. text 162.00 (*90-6191-092-7*, Pub. by A A Balkema) Ashgate Pub Co.

Martin, C. J., et al, eds. The Philosopher's Annual, 1985, Vol. VIII. vi, 176p. 1987. pap. text 10.00 (*0-917930-70-3*); lib. bdg. 32.00 (*0-917930-90-8*) Ridgeview.

Martin, C. L. The Blueberry Train. LC 93-31014. (Illus.). 32p. (J). (gr. k-3). 1995. 15.00 (*0-689-80304-4*) S&S Childrens.

— Down Dairy Farm Road. LC 92-42848. (Illus.). 32p. (J). (gr. k-3). 1994. mass mkt. 14.95 (*0-02-762450-1*, Mac Bks Young Read) S&S Childrens.

— Three Brave Women. LC 89-77770. (Illus.). 32p. (J). (ps-3). 1991. 16.00 (*0-02-762445-5*, Mac Bks Young Read) S&S Childrens.

Martin, C. S., ed. see Applied Mechanics, Bioengineering & Fluids Enginee.

***Martin, C. Sunny.** Who's Who in Black Central Ohio: The New Millennium Edition. (Illus.). 200p. 2000. pap. (*0-9634579-2-6*) Whos Who Pub.

Martin, Cabot. No Fish & Our Lives. 224p. 1992. pap. 6.35 (*1-895387-12-4*) Creative Bk Pub.

Martin, Calvin. Keepers of the Game: Indian-Animal Relationship & the Fur Trade. LC 77-78381. 1978. pap. 17.95 (*0-520-04637-4*, Pub. by U CA Pr) Cal Prin Full Svc.

Martin, Calvin, ed. The American Indian & the Problem of History. 246p. 1987. pap. text 19.95 (*0-19-503856-8*) OUP.

Martin, Calvin Luther. The Way of the Human Being. LC 98-44175. 256p. 1999. 30.00 (*0-300-07468-9*) Yale U Pr.

***Martin, Calvin Luther.** The Way of the Human Being. 256p. 1999. pap. 14.95 (*0-300-08552-4*) Yale U Pr.

***Martin, Camille.** Rogue Embryo. (Illus.). 24p. 1999. pap. 3.00 (*0-9663846-3-6*) Lavender Ink.

Martin, Camille, ed. see Reclus, Elisee.

Martin-Canivell, Joaquin. Spain: Criminal Justice Systems in Europe & North America. 63p. 1998. pap. 15.00 (*951-53-1365-1*) Willow Tree NY.

Martin, Cara. The Holistic Educators. LC 98-146471. 1997. pap. 13.95 (*1-900219-08-5*, Pub. by Educ Heretics) Intl Spec Bk.

Martin, Carl R. Genii over Salzburg. LC 97-51437. 104p. 1998. pap. 10.95 (*1-56478-186-0*) Dalkey Arch.

— Go Your Stations, Girl. 1991. pap. 17.50 (*0-910457-36-0*) Arion Pr.

— Go Your Stations, Girl. limited ed. 1991. 75.00 (*0-910457-22-0*) Arion Pr.

***Martin, Carmela.** The Spanish Economy in the New Europe. LC 99-49727. 2000. text 79.95 (*0-312-23006-0*) St Martin.

Martin, Carol. Arthur Lismer. Fetherling, Douglas, ed. (New Views on Canadian Artists Ser.). (Illus.). 96p. 1996. pap. 18.95 (*1-55082-133-4*, Pub. by Quarry Pr) LPC InBook.

***Martin, Carol.** Bertolt Brecht: Critical Anthology. LC 99-41388. 1999. pap. 24.99 (*0-415-20043-1*) Routledge.

Martin, Carol. Dance Marathons: Performing American Culture in the 1920s & 1930s. LC 94-12157. (Performance Studies). (Illus.). 288p. 1994. text 38.50 (*0-87805-673-4*); pap. text 16.95 (*0-87805-701-3*) U Pr of Miss.

Martin, Carol, ed. Ottawa. LC 97-950011. (Colour Guides Ser.). (Illus.). 200p. 1997. pap. 16.95 (*0-88780-396-2*, Pub. by Formac Publ Co) Seven Hills Bk.

— A Sourcebook on Feminist Theatre & Performance: On & Beyond the Stage. LC 96-17794. (Worlds of Performance Ser.). (Illus.). 336p. (C). 1996. 90.00 (*0-415-10644-3*); pap. 25.99 (*0-415-10645-1*) Routledge.

***Martin, Carol & Bial, Henry.** Bertolt Brecht: Critical Anthology. LC 99-41388. (Worlds of Performance Ser.). 256p. (C). 2000. text. write for info. (*0-415-20042-3*) Routledge.

Martin, Carol & Fabes, Richard. Exploring Child Development: Transactions & Transformations. LC 99-31302. 604p. (C). 1999. 81.00 (*0-205-19366-8*, Macmillan Coll) P-H.

Martin, Carol, et al. Severe Learning Disabilities & Challenging Behaviors. 2nd ed. Emerson, Eric, ed. LC 86-5291. 192p. 1993. pap. 49.95 (*1-56593-130-0*, 0442) Singular Publishing.

Martin, Carol, jt. auth. see Martin, Lance.

Martin, Carol, ed. see Cox, Ralph.

Martin, Carol A. George Eliot's Serial Fiction. LC 93-34631. (Studies in Victorian Life & Literature). xi, 348p. 1994. text 55.00 (*0-8142-0625-5*) Ohio St U Pr.

Martin, Carol L., ed. see Weidlinger, Robert.

Martin, Carol O. Exploring the California Missions. 2nd ed. (Illus.). 115p. (Orig.). 1989. pap. 7.95 (*0-9615635-2-4*) Bay Area CA.

— Exploring the California Missions. 2nd ed. Margolin, Malcolm, ed. (Illus.) 115p. (Orig.). 1989. pap. 7.95 (*0-9615635-0-8*) Bay Area CA.

— Exploring the Southwest: Activity Cards. Margolin, Malcolm, ed. (Explorers Ser.: Vol. 1). (Illus.). 110p. (J). (gr. 4-6). 1998. pap. text 10.00 (*0-9615635-1-6*) Bay Area CA.

***Martin, Carol P.** 25 Spanish Science Mini-Books for Emergent Readers: Build Literacy with Easy & Adorable Reproducible Mini-Books on Favorite Science Topics. (SPA & ENG., Illus.). 64p. Date not set. pap. 10.95 (*0-439-15343-3*) Scholastic Inc.

***Martin, Carole.** Imposture Utopique et Proces Colonial: Denis Veiras - Robert Challe. LC 00-27221. (FRE.). 263p. 2000. 49.95 (*1-886365-14-8*) Rookwood Pr.

Martin, Carole A. & Colbert, Karen K. Parenting: A Life Span Perspective. LC 96-22890. 416p. (C). 1996. pap. 42.81 (*0-07-040768-1*) McGraw.

Martin, Carolyn, ed. Children Act Review: A Scottish Experience. 180p. 1994. pap. 45.00 (*0-11-495244-2*, HM52442, Pub. by Statnry Office) Bernan Associates.

Martin, Carolyn A. & Clements, Rhonda. Games, Contest & Relays of Earlier Times. 3rd ed. (Illus.). 365p. 1998. pap. text 27.95 (*0-89641-311-X*) American Pr.

Martin, Carter J., compiled by. 150 Years of American Art: The Amon Carter Museum Collection. LC 96-83425. (Illus.). 40p. (Orig.). 1996. pap. 8.00 (*0-88360-087-0*) Amon Carter.

Martin, Carter W. The True Country: Themes in the Fiction of Flannery O'Connor. LC 68-29047. ix, 253 p. 1969. write for info. (*0-8265-1132-5*) Vanderbilt U Pr.

— The True Country: Themes in the Fiction of Flannery O'Connor. LC 68-29047. 258p. 1994. reprint ed. pap. 16.95 (*0-8265-1249-6*) Vanderbilt U Pr.

***Martin, Casandra.** Paul: By the Grace of God: Early Life Through Second Missionary Journey. (Women Opening the Word Ser.). 1999. pap. 12.99 (*0-89098-254-6*) Twent Cent Christ.

***Martin, Cash.** Convicted. LC 99-97001. ii, 474p. 2000. pap. 19.95 (*0-9677209-0-7*) American Pubng.

Martin, Catherine. An Australian Girl. (Oxford World's Classics Ser.). 512p. 1999. pap. 14.95 (*0-19-283922-5*) OUP.

— Kumihimo: Japanese Silk Braiding Technique. (Illus.). 96p. 1991. pap. 14.95 (*0-937274-59-3*) Lark Books.

— The Silent Sea. Foxton, Rosemary, ed. 569p. 1996. pap. 34.95 (*0-86840-373-3*, Pub. by New South Wales Univ Pr) Intl Spec Bk.

— Strengthening Family Life. (Impact Ser.). 16p. 1996. pap. text 1.95 (*1-55612-866-5*, LL1866) Sheed & Ward WI.

Martin, Catherine, jt. auth. see Martin, Steven.

Martin, Catherine G. The Ruins of Allegory: Paradise Lost & the Metamorphosis of Epic Convention. LC 97-42591. 1998. 69.95 (*0-8223-1980-2*); pap. 23.95 (*0-8223-1989-6*) Duke.

Martin, Cathie J. Shifting the Burden: The Struggle over Growth & Corporate Taxation. (American Politics & Political Economy Ser.). (Illus.). 260p. 1991. pap. text 19.50 (*0-226-50833-1*) U Ch Pr.

— Shifting the Burden: The Struggle over Growth & Corporate Taxation. (American Politics & Political Economy Ser.). (Illus.). 260p. 1991. lib. bdg. 52.00 (*0-226-50832-3*) U Ch Pr.

***Martin, Cathie Jo.** Stuck in Neutral: Business & Politics in the Human Capital Investment Policy. LC 99-22805. 264p. 1999. 49.50 (*0-691-00960-0*, Pub. by Princeton U Pr) Cal Prin Full Svc.

— Stuck in Neutral: Business & Politics in the Human Capital Investment Policy. LC 99-22805. (Studies in American Politics). 264p. 1999. pap. 19.95 (*0-691-00961-9*, Pub. by Princeton U Pr) Cal Prin Full Svc.

Martin, Celine. My Sister Saint Therese: By Sister Genevieve of the Holy Face. LC 97-60610. Orig. Title: A Memoir of My Sister St. Therese (Counseils et Souvenirs). 249p. 1997. reprint ed. pap. 8.00 (*0-89555-598-0*, 1522) TAN Bks Pubs.

Martin, Charles. Catullus. LC 91-40354. (Hermes Bks.). 192p. (C). 1992. 37.50 (*0-300-05199-9*); pap. 16.00 (*0-300-05200-6*) Yale U Pr.

— Godchildren. 1999. pap. 18.95 (*0-14-011880-2*) Viking Penguin.

— Letters from a Headmaster's Study (1949-1977) enl. rev. ed. Piazza, Louise D., ed. (Illus.). 302p. 1986. reprint ed. pap. text 26.50 (*0-8191-5387-7*) U Pr of Amer.

— Letters from a Headmaster's Study (1949-1977) 2nd enl. rev. ed. Piazza, Louise D., ed. (Illus.). 302p. 1986. reprint ed. lib. bdg. 48.00 (*0-8191-5386-9*) U Pr of Amer.

— Passages from Friday: Poems. 1983. 17.50 (*0-317-40788-0*) Abattoir.

— Steal the Bacon. LC 86-46285. (Johns Hopkins Poetry & Fiction Ser.). 88p. 1987. text 14.95 (*0-8018-3493-7*) Johns Hopkins.

— What the Darkness Proposes: Poems. LC 96-18437. (Johns Hopkins). 80p. 1996. 16.95 (*0-8018-5487-3*) Johns Hopkins.

— Your New Business: A Personal Plan for Success. Gerould, Philip, ed. LC 92-54374. (Small Business & Entrepreneurship Ser.). 234p. (Orig.). 1993. pap. 15.95 (*1-56052-170-8*) Crisp Pubns.

Martin, Charles, ed. Registrum Epistolarum Fratris Johannis Peckham, Archiepiscopi Cantuanriensis, 3 vols. (Rolls Ser.: No. 77). 1974. reprint ed. 210.00 (*0-8115-1147-2*) Periodicals Srv.

Martin, Charles, tr. see Catullus, Gaius Valerius.

Martin, Charles A. The Last Great Ace: The Life of Major Thomas B. McGuire, Jr. Martin, Antoinette D., ed. LC 98-96647. (Illus.). 384p. 1999. pap. 19.95 (*0-9667791-0-X*) Fruit Cove.

Martin, Charles A., ed. History of Cass County, Illinois: With Biographical Sketches (Reprinted Without Historical Encyclopedia of Illinois) (Illus.). 376p. 1997. reprint ed. lib. bdg. 42.50 (*0-8328-5722-X*) Higginson Bk Co.

Martin, Charles E. Hollybush: Folk Building & Social Change in an Appalachian Community. LC 83-10201. (Illus.). 132p. (C). 1984. pap. text 18.00 (*0-87049-816-9*) U of Tenn Pr.

— Policy of the United States As Regards Intervention. LC 21-3655. (Columbia University. Studies in the Social Sciences: No. 211). reprint ed. 21.50 (*0-404-51211-9*) AMS Pr.

— Summer Business. (Trophy Picture Bk.). (Illus.). 32p. (J). (gr. k-3). 1990. reprint ed. pap. 4.95 (*0-06-443231-9*, HarpTrophy) HarpC Child Bks.

Martin, Charles H. The Angelo Herndon Case & Southern Justice. LC 73-91777. 256p. reprint ed. pap. 79.40 (*0-8357-5476-6*, 205165300004) Bks Demand.

— Wallenberg's Diary. 224p. Date not set. mass mkt. 4.99 (*1-896329-15-2*) Picasso Publ.

Martin, Charles L. The Digital Estate: Strategies for Competing, Surviving, & Thriving in an Internetworked World. (Illus.). 235p. 1996. 24.95 (*0-07-041045-3*) McGraw.

— Employee Suggestion Systems: A Fifty-Minute Book. LC 96-85016. 1997. pap. text 10.95 (*1-56052-395-6*) Crisp Pubns.

— Owning & Operating a Service Business. LC 95-74739. (Small Business & Entrepreneurship Ser.). 203p. (Orig.). 1996. pap. 15.95 (*1-56052-362-X*) Crisp Pubns.

— A Sketch of Sam Bass: The Bandit. LC 96-35363. (Western Frontier Library Ser.: Vol. 6). (Illus.). 192p. 1997. pap. 9.95 (*0-8061-2915-8*) U of Okla Pr.

— A Sketch of Sam Bass, the Bandit: A Graphic Narrative of His Various Train Robberies, His Death, & Accounts of the Deaths of His Gang & Their History (with an Introduction by Ramon F. Adams) LC 56-5991. (Western Frontier Library: Vol. 6). 190p. reprint ed. pap. 58.90 (*0-608-15168-8*, 205216600046) Bks Demand.

— Starting Your New Business: A Guide for Entrepreneurs. rev. ed. Crisp, Michael G., ed. LC 91-77079. (Fifty-Minute Ser.). (Illus.). 103p. 1992. pap. 10.95 (*1-56052-144-9*) Crisp Pubns.

Martin, Charles L. & Hackett, Donald. Facilitation Skills for Team Leaders: Leading Organized Teams to Greater Productivity. Machoski, Brenda, ed. LC 92-74207. (Fifty-Minute Ser.). 88p. (Orig.). 1993. pap. 10.95 (*1-56052-199-6*) Crisp Pubns.

Martin, Charles R. Looking at Type: The Fundamentals. 68p. 1997. pap. 7.00 (*0-935652-31-0*) Ctr Applications Psych.

Martin, Charles R., ed. see Jones, Jane H. & Sherman, Ruth G.

Martin, Charles T. The Record Interpreter: A Collection of Abbreviations, Latin Words & Names Used in English Historical Manuscripts & Records. 404p. 1910. reprint ed. lib. bdg. 132.00 (*3-487-02295-8*) G Olms Pubs.

— The Record Interpreter: A Collection of Abbreviations, Latin Words & Names Used in English Historical Manuscripts & Records. xv, 464p. 1969. reprint ed. 76.70 (*0-685-66494-5*, 05102295) G Olms Pubs.

Martin, Charles T. The Record Interpreter: A Collection of Abbreviations, Latin Words & Names Used in English Historical Manuscripts & Records. 2nd ed. 464p. 1997. pap. 35.00 (*0-8063-0236-4*) Clearfield Co.

Martin, Charles T., jt. ed. see Brewer, J. S.

Martin, Charles T., jt. ed. see Hardy, Thomas D.

Martin, Charles V. The Rainbow Snakes in a Dream Come True Vol. 1. unabridged ed. Jensen, Shirley M. & MacKendrick, Mary, eds. LC 97-68217. (Illus.). 128p. (J). (gr. 3-7). 1997. pap. write for info. (*0-9658550-0-7*) Rainbow Snakes.

Martin, Charlie. Common Stocks for Ordinary People. Martin, Marcelle, ed. LC 97-94344. (Illus.). vi, 250p. 1998. 20.00 (*0-9667334-0-1*) Kilmartin Pr.

Martin, Charlotte, jt. auth. see Martin, Rick.

Martin-Chauffier, Robert, ed. see La Rochefoucauld, Francois de.

Martin, Cheryl E. Governance & Society in Colonial Mexico: Chihuahua in the Eighteenth Century. LC 95-16036. 280p. 1996. 39.50 (*0-8047-2547-0*) Stanford U Pr.

Martin, Chester. Empire & Commonwealth. LC 74-9227. 385p. 1975. reprint ed. lib. bdg. 79.50 (*0-8371-7626-3*, MAEC, Greenwood Pr) Greenwood.

Martin, Chester B. Lord Selkirk's Work in Canada. (BCL1 - History - Canada Ser.). 240p. 1991. reprint ed. lib. bdg. 79.00 (*0-7812-6374-3*) Rprt Serv.

Martin, Chester O. & Schmidly, David J. Taxonomic Review of the Pallid Bat: Antrozous Pallidus (Le Conte) (Special Publications: No. 18). (Illus.). 48p. 1982. pap. 7.00 (*0-89672-097-7*) Tex Tech Univ Pr.

Martin, Chia. The Art of Touch: A Massage Manual for Young People. LC 95-77754. (Illus.). 72p. (J). (gr. 4-6). 1995. pap. 15.95 (*0-934252-57-2*, Pub. by Hohm Pr) SCB Distributors.

— Rosie: The Shopping Cart Lady. LC 96-4616. (Illus.). 32p. (J). (gr. k-2). 1996. 15.95 (*0-934252-51-3*, Pub. by Hohm Pr) SCB Distributors.

— We Like to Nurse. LC 94-77052. (Illus.). 32p. (Orig.). (J). 1994. pap. 9.95 (*0-934252-45-9*, Pub. by Hohm Pr) SCB Distributors.

***Martin, Chia.** Writing Your Way Through Cancer. 125p. 2000. pap. 11.95 (*1-890772-00-3*, Pub. by Hohm Pr) SCB Distributors.

Martin, Chris. Top Fuel Handbook: Stories, Stats & Stuff about Drag Racing's Most Powerful Class. 1996. pap. 9.95 (*1-880652-58-7*, Pub. by Wichita Eagle) Booksource.

***Martin, Christine.** Fiddle Music of the Scottish Highlands: Ceol Na Fidhle, Vols. 1-2. 1999. pap. 22.95 (*1-871931-32-0*) Taigh Teud.

— Scottish Ceilidh Collection for Fiddlers, 2, Vols.1& 2. 1999. pap. 18.95 (*1-871931-17-7*) Taigh Teud.

— The Scottish Folk Fiddle: Third Position Book. 24p. 2000. pap. text 12.95 (*1-871931-52-5*, TT10064, Pub. by Taigh Teud) Music Sales.

Martin, Christopher. Brontes, Set I. (Life & Work Ser.). (Illus.). 112p. (YA). (gr. 7 up). 1989. lib. bdg. 25.27 (*0-86592-299-3*) Rourke Enter.

— Dickens. (Life & Works Ser.: Set II). (Illus.). 112p. (YA). (gr. 7 up). 1990. lib. bdg. 18.95 (*0-86593-016-3*); lib. bdg. 14.95 (*0-685-36352-X*) Rourke Corp.

— H. G. Wells, Set I. (Life & Works Ser.). (Illus.). 112p. (YA). (gr. 7 up). 1989. lib. bdg. 25.27 (*0-86592-297-7*) Rourke Enter.

— An Introduction to Medieval Philosophy. 136p. 1996. pap. 25.00 (*0-7486-0790-0*, Pub. by Edinburgh U Pr) Col U Pr.

— Lawyer's Guide to the Texas Insurance Code, Article 21.21. LC 95-44175. Date not set. text 95.00 (*0-250-47249-X*, 64625, MICHIE) LEXIS Pub.

— Logistics & Supply Chain Management: Strategies for Reducing Cost & Improving Service. 2nd ed. (Financial Times Ser.). (Illus.). 294p. 1998. 34.95 (*0-273-63049-0*, Pub. by F T P H) Natl Bk Netwk.

***Martin, Christopher.** Mohandas Gandhi. LC 99-28431. (A & E Biography Ser.). (Illus.). 128p. (YA). (gr. 6-9). 2000. lib. bdg. 25.26 (*0-8225-4984-0*, Lerner Publctns) Lerner Pub.

— Pilgrim's Way. 64p. 2000. pap. 6.50 (*1-85311-251-8*) Canterbury Press Norwich.

— Pilgrim's Way: From Winchester to Canterbury. 2000. pap. text. write for info. (*5-550-02611-2*) Nairi.

Martin, Christopher. Policy in Love: Lyric & Public in Ovid, Petrarch & Shakespeare. LC 94-30961. (Duquesne Studies: Language & Literature Ser.: Vol. 17). 240p. (C). 1995. text 44.95 (*0-8207-0260-9*) Duquesne.

— Prairie Patterns: Folk Arts in North Dakota. (Illus.). 126p. (Orig.). 1989. pap. 18.00 (*0-911205-03-9*) N Dak Coun Arts.

— Ruralists: Art & Design 23. 1992. pap. 26.95 (*0-312-07264-3*) St Martin.

— Schooling in Mexico: Educational Austerity in a Developing Country. 235p. 1994. 66.95 (*1-85628-665-7*, Pub. by Avebry) Ashgate Pub Co.

— Shakespeare. (Life & Works). (Illus.). 112p. (J). (gr. 7 up). 1989. 14.95 (*0-685-58633-2*) Rourke Corp.

— Thomas Aquinas: God & Explanations. 224p. 1998. 60.00 (*0-7486-0901-6*, Pub. by Edinburgh U Pr) Col U Pr.

Martin, Christopher, jt. auth. see Mollanen, Tuula.

Martin, Christopher, ed. see Aquinas, Thomas, Saint.

Martin, Christopher J., jt. auth. see Talley, Nicholas J.

***Martin, Chuck.** Net Future: The 7 Cybertrends That Will Drive Your Business, Create New Wealth, & Define Your Future. 224p. 1998. 24.95 (*0-07-041131-X*) McGraw.

— Net Future: The 7 Cybertrends That Will Drive Your Business, Create New Wealth, & Define Your Future. 1999. pap. write for info. (*0-07-134887-5*) McGraw.

***Martin, Clair G.** 100 Heirloom Roses for the American Garden. LC 99-51652. (Illus.). 288p. 2000. pap. 17.95 (*0-7611-1341-X*) Workman Pub.

Martin, Clair G. Smith & Hawken 100 English Roses for the American Garden. LC 97-71. (Illus.). 256p. 1997. pap. 16.95 (*0-7611-0185-3*, 10185) Workman Pub.

Martin, Claire. English - French Lexicon of Electricity. (ENG & FRE.). 51p. 1987. pap. 29.95 (*0-8288-9412-4*) Fr & Eur.

***Martin, Claire & Krebs, Nancy Funnemark, eds.** The Nursing Mother's Problem Solver. 320p. 2000. pap. 13.00 (*0-684-85784-7*, Fireside) S&S Trade Pap.

Martin, Claire & Martin, Steve. My Best Book: A Year-Long Record of "Personal Bests" (Illus.). 40p. (Orig.). (J). (gr. 3-5). 1988. pap. 7.95 (*0-929545-00-1*) Black Birch Bks.

***Martin, Claire Emilie.** Alejo Carpentier y las Cronicas de Indias. (Puertas 88 Ser.: Vol. 6). (SPA.). (C). 1999. 35.00 (*0-910061-61-0*) Ediciones Norte.

An Asterisk (*) at the beginning of an entry indicates that the title is appearing for the first time.

Martin, Clare. Official NBA Trivia: The Ultimate Team-by-Team Challenge for Hoop Fans. 192p. 1999. pap. 10.95 (*0-06-107360-1*) HarpC.

Martin, Clarece. The Historic Roswell Cookbook. rev. ed. Walsh, Darlene M., ed. & photos by. DeNiro, Elaine, photos by. (Illus.). 234p. 1995. reprint ed. pap. 12.95 (*0-9615854-0-4*) Roswell Hist.

Martin, Clarence L. God Is a Verb: Roots of a Rational Religion. LC 88-63981. 140p. (Orig.). 1989. pap. 8.95 (*0-88100-060-4*) Natl Writ Pr.

Martin-Clarke, Daisy E. Culture in Early Anglo-Saxon England. 1979. 18.95 (*0-405-10615-7*) Ayer.

Martin, Claude. Tropical Rain Forests of West Africa: Their Biology, Utilization, Destruction & Conservation. (Illus.). 235p. 1991. 19.50 (*0-8176-2380-9*) Birkhauser.

Martin, Claudia J. & McQueen, David V., eds. Readings for a New Public Health. 250p. 1988. 68.00 (*0-85224-598-X*, Pub. by Edinburgh U Pr) Col U Pr.

— Readings for a New Public Health. 336p. 1991. pap. text 29.00 (*0-85224-616-1*, Pub. by Edinburgh U Pr) Col U Pr.

Martin, Clement G. Low Blood Sugar. 192p. 1985. per. 5.00 (*0-671-76410-1*, Fireside) S&S Trade Pap.

Martin, Clifford E. Math at Work. 1989. pap. 6.95 (*0-87813-924-9*) Christian Light.

Martin-Clouaire, R., jt. ed. see Udink ten Cate, A. J.

Martin, Clyde F. & Hermann, Robert, eds. Ames Research Center (NASA) Conference on Geometric Control Theory, 1976. (Lie Groups: History, Frontiers & Applications Ser.: Vol. 7). 1977. 60.00 (*0-915692-21-X*) Math Sci Pr.

Martin, Clyde F., jt. auth. see Doolin, Brian F.

Martin, Clyde F., jt. ed. see Byrnes, Christopher I.

Martin, Clyde F., ed. see NATO ASI & AMS Summer Seminar in Applied Mathemati.

Martin, Colin. Scotland's Historic Shipwrecks. LC 00-273000. (Historic Scotland Ser.). (Illus.). 128p. 1998. pap. text 24.95 (*0-7134-8327-X*, Pub. by B T B) Branford.

***Martin, Colin & Parker, Geoffrey.** The Spanish Armada. 2nd rev. ed. LC 99-44272. 1999. write for info. (*1-901341-14-3*, Pub. by Mandolin) St Martin.

Martin, Colin A., intro. Australian Aeronautical Conference, 1993, 2 vols. 5th ed. (National Conference Publication Ser.: No. 93-6). (Illus.). 610p. 1993. pap. text 108.00 (*0-85825-576-6*, Pub. by Inst Engrs Aust-EA Bks) Accents Pubns.

Martin, Colleayan, jt. auth. see Currie, Phillip.

Martin-Comin, J., et al. Radiolabeled Blood Elements: Recent Advances in Techniques & Applications. (NATO ASI Ser.: Vol. 262). (Illus.). 382p. (C). 1994. text 125.00 (*0-306-44700-2*, Kluwer Plenum) Kluwer Academic.

***Martin, Constance & West, Richard.** Distant Shores: The Odyssey of Rockwell Kent. LC 00-26272. (Illus.). 128p. 2000. pap. 24.95 (*0-520-22712-3*) U CA Pr.

***Martin, Constance & West, Richard V.** Distant Shores: The Odyssey of Rockwell Kent. LC 00-26272. (Illus.). 128p. 2000. 45.00 (*0-520-22711-5*) U CA Pr.

Martin, Constance R. Dictionary of Endocrinology & Related Biomedical Sciences. (Illus.). 792p. 1995. text 85.00 (*0-19-506033-4*) OUP.

Martin, Corinne. Earthmagic: Finding & Using Medicinal Herbs. LC 91-6330. 240p. 1991. pap. 15.00 (*0-88150-184-0*, Pub. by Countryman) Norton.

— Earthmagic: Using New England Medicinal Herbs. Francis, Ed & Dovner, Sylvia, eds. (Illus.). 250p. (Orig.). 1990. pap. 12.95 (*0-9623199-1-0*) Dirigo Bks.

***Martin, Corinne.** Herbal Remedies from the Wild: Finding & Using Medicinal Herbs. 2nd ed. Orig. Title: Earthmagic. 2000. reprint ed. pap. 15.00 (*0-88150-485-8*, Pub. by Countryman) Norton.

Martin, Cort. Bolt, No. 1: First Blood. (Orig.). 1981. mass mkt. 2.25 (*0-89083-767-8*, Zebra Kensgtn) Kensgtn Pub Corp.

— Bolt, No. 2: Dead Man's Bounty. 1981. mass mkt. 2.25 (*0-89083-783-X*, Zebra Kensgtn) Kensgtn Pub Corp.

— The Hangtown Harlots. (Bolt Ser.: No. 12). 1983. mass mkt. 2.25 (*0-685-07876-0*, Zebra Kensgtn) Kensgtn Pub Corp.

— Montana Mistress. (Bolt Ser.: No. 13). 1984. mass mkt. 2.25 (*0-8217-1316-7*, Zebra Kensgtn) Kensgtn Pub Corp.

Martin, Courtenay. Seven Cigarette Story. (Illus.). viii, 44p. 1999. pap. 12.00 (*0-930324-42-0*) Wings Pr.

Martin, Craig. Enchanted Waters: A Guide to New Mexico's Hot Springs. LC 98-39449. (Illus.). 150p. 1998. pap. 16.95 (*0-87108-891-6*) Pruett.

— Los Alamos Trails. (Illus.). 144p. 1998. pap. 13.95 (*0-9639040-2-7*) All Seasons.

— Mountain Biking in Northern New Mexico: Historical & Natural History Rides. LC 93-49530. (Coyote Book Ser.). (Illus.). 205p. (Orig.). 1994. reprint ed. pap. 63.60 (*0-608-07277-X*, 206750500009) Bks Demand.

— Mountain Water: The Way of the High Country Angler. LC 99-37861. (Illus.). 174p. 2000. pap. 18.95 (*0-87108-896-7*) Pruett.

***Martin, Craig.** Quads, Shoeboxes & Sunken Living Rooms: A History of Los Alamos Housing. (Los Alamos Story Ser.: Vol. 4). 2000. 10.00 (*0-941232-24-7*) Los Alamos Hist Soc.

Martin, Craig. Rio Grande River, NM-CO. (River Journal Ser.: Vol. 5, No. 1). (Illus.). 1998. pap. text 15.95 (*1-57188-089-5*) F Amato Pubns.

— Santa Fe Area Mountain Bike Trails. rev. ed. 100p. (Orig.). 1999. pap. 12.95 (*0-9639040-3-5*) All Seasons.

— 75 Hikes in New Mexico. (Illus.). 224p. 1995. pap. 12.95 (*0-89886-441-0*) Mountaineers.

Martin, Craig & Lehr, Judy. The START Curriculum: Sharing Today & Responsibility Tomorrow. LC 99-60711. (Illus.). 220p. 1999. spiral bd. 34.95 (*0-932796-95-8*) Ed Media Corp.

Martin, Craig & Los Alamos Historical Society Staff. Los Alamos Place Names. LC 98-35807. (Illus.). 131p. 1998. pap. 10.95 (*0-941232-19-0*) Los Alamos Hist Soc.

Martin, Craig, et al. Fly Fishing Southern Colorado: An Angler's Guide. LC 96-44765. (Illus.). 184p. 1997. pap. 17.95 (*0-87108-872-X*) Pruett.

Martin, Craig, jt. auth. see Lehr, Judy B.

Martin, Curits H. & Stronach, Bruce. Politics East & West: A Comparison of Japanese & British Political Culture. LC 92-26273. 352p. (C). (gr. 13). 1992. pap. text 32.95 (*1-56324-108-0*) M E Sharpe.

Martin, Curtis H. President Clinton's Haiti Dilemma. (Pew Case Studies in International Affairs). 50p. (C). 1997. pap. text 3.50 (*1-56927-375-8*) Geo U Inst Dplmcy.

Martin, Curtis H. & Stronach, Bruce. Politics East & West: A Comparison of Japanese & British Political Culture. LC 92-26273. 352p. (C). (gr. 13). 1992. text 75.95 (*0-87332-895-7*) M E Sharpe.

Martin, Cy. Men of the Twentieth: The Story of the 20th Aero Squadron. 127p. 1974. pap. text 37.95 (*0-89126-006-4*) MA-AH Pub.

Martin, Cyd. A Yellowstone ABC. (Illus.). 20p. (J). (ps-2). 1992. pap. 5.95 (*1-879373-12-2*) Roberts Rinehart.

Martin, Cynthia. Beating the Adoption Odds: Using Your Head & Your Heart. LC 97-41249. 416p. 1998. pap. 16.00 (*0-15-600522-0*, Harvest Bks) Harcourt.

— Lover's Knot Placemats. (Illus.). 24p. 1993. 6.95 (*0-922705-45-3*) Quilt Day.

— Machine Quilting Primer. Burns, Eleanor, ed. (Illus.). 96p. (Orig.). 1996. 24.95 (*0-922705-90-9*) Quilt Day.

Martin, Cynthia, tr. see Kabakov, Ilya.

Martin, Cynthia L., et al. The Russian Desk: A Listening & Conversation Course. x, 136p. (Orig.). (C). 1991. pap. text 12.95 (*0-89357-218-7*) Slavica.

— The Russian Desk: Instructor's Manual. vi, 64p. (Orig.). (C). 1991. pap. text 7.95 (*0-89357-219-5*) Slavica.

Martin, D. Cut & Make Wizard of Oz Masks. 1982. pap. text 6.95 (*0-486-24306-0*) Dover.

Martin, D., ed. see Schrag, Norm.

Martin, D., tr. see Soloukhin, Vladimir.

Martin, D. C., et al. Laparoscopic Appearance of Endometriosis, Vol. I. 2nd ed. Martin, Dan C., ed. LC 90-60383. (Illus.). 57p. 1990. pap. text 14.00 (*0-9616747-3-3*) Resurge Pr.

— Laparoscopic Appearance of Endometriosis: Color Atlas, Vol. III. 2nd ed. Martin, Dan C., ed. LC 90-60393. (Illus.). 69p. 1990. pap. text 38.00 (*0-9616747-6-8*) Resurge Pr.

Martin, D. G. Language, Truth & Poetry. 353p. 1975. pap. 14.50 (*0-85224-268-9*, Pub. by Edinburgh U Pr) Col U Pr.

Martin, D. Michael. I, II Thessalonians. LC 95-23281. (New American Commentary Ser.: Vol. 33). 320p. 1995. 29.99 (*0-8054-0133-4*) Broadman.

Martin, D. Roger. No Dreams for Sale. 1983. pap. 6.00 (*0-938566-15-6*) Adastra Pr.

Martin, D. W., ed. Journal of the Acoustical Society of America: Cumulative Index, Vols. 75-84. 625p. 1989. 80.00 (*0-88318-615-2*) Acoustical Soc Am.

Martin, Dale. Into the Primitive: Advanced Trapping Techniques. (Illus.). 176p. 1989. pap. 18.00 (*0-87364-530-8*) Paladin Pr.

— The Trapper's Bible: Traps, Snares, & Pathguards. (Illus.). 72p. 1987. pap. 14.00 (*0-87364-406-9*) Paladin Pr.

***Martin, Dale B.** The Corinthian Body. LC 94-44947. 352p. 1999. 17.00 (*0-300-08172-3*) Yale U Pr.

Martin, Dale B. Slavery As Salvation: The Metaphor of Slavery in Pauline Christianity. 272p. (C). 1990. 35.00 (*0-300-04735-5*) Yale U Pr.

Martin, Dan, jt. auth. see Ahia, C. Emmanuel.

Martin, Dan C., ed. see Martin, D. C., et al.

Martin, Daniel. Database Design & Implementation. 1981. 54.50 (*0-442-30429-3*) Thomson Learn.

— The Guide to the Foundations of Public Administration. LC 89-11813. (Public Administration & Public Policy Ser.: Vol. 37). 478p. reprint ed. pap. 148.20 (*0-608-08956-7*, 206959100005) Bks Demand.

Martin, Daniel C., jt. ed. see Adamson, G. David.

Martin, Daniel R., pref. The Order of Montaigne's Essays: Selected Papers from the Proceedings of the International Montaigne Colloquium Held at UMass-Amherst in Oct. 1988. 247p. 1989. 16.95 (*1-878417-00-2*) Hestia Pr.

Martin, Daniel R. & Cookerly, J. Richard. A Directory of Credentials in Counseling & Psychotherapy. (Reference Bks.). 270p. 1989. 40.00 (*0-8161-9062-3*, Hall Reference) Macmillan.

Martin, Daniel R., ed. see Moliere.

Martin, Daniel W. Henke's California Law Guide. large type ed. LC 99-171315. 389p. 1998. ring bd. 65.00 (*0-327-00208-5*, 64620-11) LEXIS Pub.

Martin, Daniel W., ed. Henke's California Law Guide. 3rd ed. LC 95-76182. 298p. 1995. pap. 55.00 (*0-250-47245-7*, MICHIE) LEXIS Pub.

Martin, Dannie. In the Hat. LC 97-11962. 320p. 1997. 22.50 (*0-684-83335-2*) S&S Trade.

***Martin, Dannie.** In the Hat. 304p. 2000. reprint ed. per. 6.99 (*0-671-02404-3*, Pocket Books) PB.

***Martin, Dannie M.** The Shooter's Job: A Novel. 272p. 2001. 22.50 (*0-684-83336-0*) Simon & Schuster.

Martin, Dannie M. & Sussman, Peter Y. Committing Journalism: The Prison Writings of Red Hog. 352p. 1995. pap. 14.95 (*0-393-31322-0*, Norton Paperbks) Norton.

Martin, Danny B. Mathematics Success - & Failure among African American Youth: The Roles of Sociohistorical Context, Community Forces, School Influence, & Individual Agency. LC 99-34928. (Studies in Mathematical Thinking & Learning). 202p. 1999. write for info. (*0-8058-3042-1*) L Erlbaum Assocs.

***Martin, Darrel.** Fly Fisher's Illustrated Dictionary. (Illus.). 2000. 29.95 (*1-58574-053-5*) Lyons Pr.

Martin, Darrel. Fly-Tying Methods. (Illus.). 320p. 1987. 35.00 (*0-941130-40-1*) Lyons Pr.

— Micropatterns: Tying & Fishing the Small Fly. 336p. 1999. pap. text 29.95 (*1-55821-894-7*) Lyons Pr.

Martin, Darrell. Micropatterns: Tying & Fishing the Small Fly. LC 94-6300. 352p. 1994. 40.00 (*1-55821-260-4*) Lyons Pr.

Martin, Darvin L. Groffdale Mennonite Church Cemetery. LC 96-71677. 118p. 1997. per. 15.00 (*1-55856-254-0*, 250) Closson Pr.

Martin, Darwin J. Schipperkes, AKC Rank No. 50. (KW Dog Ser.). (Illus.). 1996. pap. 9.95 (*0-7938-2352-8*, KW161S) TFH Pubns.

Martin, David. An Arm & a Leg. pap. 11.95 (*0-7493-1965-8*, Pub. by Random) Trafalgar.

Martin, David. Bring Me Children. Zion, Claire, ed. 352p. 1994. reprint ed. mass mkt. 5.99 (*0-671-88611-8*, Pocket Star Bks) PB.

— Camp Vredenburg in the Civil War. (Illus.). 28p. 1993. pap. text 6.00 (*0-944413-27-7*) Longstreet Hse.

— Changing Face of Calcutta. LC 97-901650. (C). 1997. reprint ed. 38.00 (*81-259-0318-6*, Pub. by Vikas) S Asia.

— The Crying Heart Tattoo: A Novel. LC 93-44391. 320p. 1994. pap. 12.95 (*0-8118-0777-0*) Chronicle Bks.

— Cul-de-Sac. 352p. 1998. mass mkt. 6.99 (*0-312-96730-6*) St Martin.

— Does Christianity Cause War? LC 97-26186. 236p. 1998. text 56.00 (*0-19-829267-8*) OUP.

— Europe: An Ever Closer Union. 101p. 1991. 57.50 (*0-85124-537-4*, Pub. by Spkesman); pap. 26.50 (*0-85124-538-2*, Pub. by Spkesman) Coronet Bks.

— Five Little Piggies. LC 97-14667. (Illus.). 40p. (J). (gr. k-2). 1998. 16.99 (*1-56402-918-2*) Candlewick Pr.

***Martin, David.** Five Little Piggies. (Illus.). 40p. (YA). 2000. pap. 6.99 (*0-7636-1081-X*) Candlewick Pr.

Martin, David. Geographic Information Systems: Socioeconomic Applications. 2nd ed. LC 95-15958. (Illus.). 248p. (C). 1995. pap. 25.99 (*0-415-12572-3*) Routledge.

— Geographic Information Systems: Socioeconomic Applications. 2nd ed. LC 95-15958. (Illus.). 248p. (C). (gr. 13). 1995. 85.00 (*0-415-12571-5*) Routledge.

Martin, David. Handbook for Creative Teaching. (Illus.). 960p. 1986. 21.40 (*0-7399-0230-X*, 2481) Rod & Staff.

Martin, David. Heartbeat: Forever Yours. large type ed. (Magna Large Print Ser.). 327p. 1996. 27.99 (*0-7505-1029-3*, Pub. by Mgna Lrg Print) Ulverscroft.

— Lie to Me. 320p. 1991. reprint ed. per. 6.50 (*0-671-73876-3*, Pocket Star Bks) PB.

— Little Chicken Chicken. LC 96-43694. (Illus.). 32p. (J). (ps up). 1997. pap. 5.99 (*0-7636-0121-7*) Candlewick Pr.

Martin, David. Little Chicken Chicken. LC 95-43694. (J). 1997. 11.19 (*0-606-11568-4*, Pub. by Turtleback) Demco.

Martin, David. Manipulating Meetings: How to Get What You Want, When You Want It. rev. ed. (Institute of Management Foundation Ser.). 186p. (Orig.). 1996. pap. 47.50 (*0-273-62193-9*, Pub. by Pitman Pub) Trans-Atl Phila.

***Martin, David.** Monkey & Mom. (Illus.). 8p. (J). (ps-2). 2000. pap. 4.99 (*0-7636-0771-1*) Candlewick Pr.

— Monkey Business. (Illus.). (J). (ps-2). 2000. pap. 5.99 (*0-7636-0773-8*) Candlewick Pr.

Martin, David. Reflections on Sociology & Theology. LC 96-35167. 268p. 1997. text 60.00 (*0-19-827384-3*) OUP.

— Something Never Your Own. (Amelia Chapbooks Ser.). 90p. (Orig.). 1989. pap. 10.95 (*0-936545-10-0*) Amelia.

— Tap, Tap. 1996. mass mkt. 6.99 (*0-614-20521-2*, St Martins Paperbacks) St Martin.

— Tap Tap. 1996. mass mkt. 6.99 (*0-312-95835-8*, Pub. by Tor Bks) St Martin.

Martin, David. Teaching English. 24p. 1977. pap. 2.15 (*0-7399-0237-7*, 2520) Rod & Staff.

Martin, David. Tough Talking: How to Handle Awkward Situations. (Institute of Management Ser.). 192p. (Orig.). 1993. pap. 42.50 (*0-273-62192-0*) Trans-Atlantic Des.

Martin, David, ed. Clara Barton & Hightstown. (Illus.). 32p. 1994. pap. text 6.00 (*0-944413-30-7*) Longstreet Hse.

Martin, David & Johnson, Phyllis. The Struggle for Zimbabwe. LC 81-84556. 400p. (Orig.). 1982. pap. 10.00 (*0-85345-599-6*, Pub. by Monthly Rev) NYU Pr.

***Martin, David & Martin, Pattie.** Songs We Love. (Illus.). 220p. (J). (gr. k-6). 1999. 8.75 (*0-7399-0323-3*, 2177) Rod & Staff.

***Martin, David & Nash, Scott.** Monkey Business. LC 99-48484. (Illus.). 48p. (J). (ps-2). 2000. 10.99 (*0-7636-1178-6*) Candlewick Pr.

— Monkey Trouble. (Illus.). (J). 2000. pap. 10.99 (*0-7636-1179-4*) Candlewick Pr.

Martin, David, jt. auth. see Atkinson, Peter M.

Martin, David, jt. auth. see Johnson, Phyllis.

Martin, David, jt. auth. see Neilsen, Therese.

Martin, David, jt. auth. see Venables, Tony.

Martin, David, ed. see Heelas, Paul.

Martin, David, jt. ed. see Johnson, Phyllis.

Martin, David, ed. see Kowalis, Jeffrey & Kowalis, Loree.

Martin, David, ed. & frwd. see Lehrer, Milton G.

Martin, David, tr. see Sepehry, Sohrab.

Martin, David A., jt. auth. see Aleinikoff, T. Alexander.

Martin, David B. Fight Back! Take Charge! Protect Your Home & Family from Physical Crime. (Illus.). iii, 100p. 1997. write for info. (*0-9658805-7-5*) Desert Drums.

Martin, David C., jt. auth. see Bartol, Kathryn M.

Martin, David C., tr. see Farrokhzaad, Foroogh.

Martin, David E. & Coe, Peter N. Better Training for Distance Runners. 2nd rev. ed. LC 96-43355. (Illus.). 464p. (Orig.). 1997. pap. 22.95 (*0-88011-530-0*, PMAR0530) Human Kinetics.

***Martin, David E. & Gynn, Roger W. H.** The Olympic Marathon. LC 99-57645. (Illus.). 528p. 2000. pap. 27.95 (*0-88011-969-1*) Human Kinetics.

Martin, David E. & Rubinstein, David. Ideology & the Labour Movement: Essays Presented to John Saville. 276p. 1979. 36.00 (*0-8476-6123-7*) Rowman.

Martin, David G. Confederate Monuments at Gettysburg. 256p. 1995. pap. 14.95 (*0-938289-48-9*, 289489) Combined Pub.

***Martin, David G.** Counseling & Therapy Skills. 2nd ed. 313p. (C). 1999. pap. 21.95 (*1-57766-068-4*) Waveland Pr.

Martin, David G. Fluvanna Artillery. (Virginia Regimental Histories Ser.). (Illus.). 165p. 1992. 19.95 (*1-56190-037-0*) H E Howard.

— General James Longstreet & His New Jersey Relations: A Brief Genealogical History of the Families & Common Ancestry of Jonathan Longstreet of Holmdel, New Jersey & Confederate General James Longstreet. rev. ed. 32p. 2000. pap. 6.50 (*0-944413-53-6*, 140) Longstreet Hse.

— OILSR Exemption Handbook. 200p. 45.00 (*0-318-19278-0*) Land Dev Inst.

— The Second Bull Run Campaign, July-August 1862. LC 96-3426. (Great Campaigns Ser.). 1996. 24.95 (*0-938289-80-2*, 289802) Combined Pub.

— The Shiloh Campaign: March - April, 1862. rev. ed. (Great Campaigns Ser.). (Illus.). 256p. 1995. 24.95 (*0-938289-69-1*, 289691) Combined Pub.

— The Vicksburg Campaign: April 1862-July 1863. rev. ed. (Illus.). 256p. 1994. 22.95 (*0-938289-37-3*, 289373) Combined Pub.

Martin, David G., ed. A Casualty at Gettysburg & Andersonville: Selections from the Civil War Diary of Private Austin A. Carr of the 82nd N. Y. Infantry. 2nd ed. LC 99-462545. (Illus.). 44p. (C). 1998. pap. text 9.00 (*0-944413-51-X*, 139) Longstreet Hse.

— Hexamer's First New Jersey Battery in the Civil War. (Illus.). 36p. (C). 1992. pap. text 6.00 (*0-944413-24-2*) Longstreet Hse.

— State of New Jersey: Final Report of the Gettysburg Battlefield Monument Commission. (Illus.). 165p. 1997. reprint ed. 20.00 (*0-944413-41-2*, 209) Longstreet Hse.

Martin, David G. & Moore, Allan D. Basics of Clinical Practice: A Guidebook for Trainees in the Helping Professions. Orig. Title: First Steps in the Art of Intervention. (Illus.). 497p. (C). 1998. reprint ed. pap. text 32.95 (*1-57766-005-6*) Waveland Pr.

— First Steps in the Art of Intervention: A Guidebook for Trainees in the Helping Professions. LC 94-33769. 500p. 1995. text 60.95 (*0-534-22272-2*) Brooks-Cole.

Martin, David G., jt. auth. see Busey, John W.

Martin, David G., jt. auth. see Nofi, Albert A.

Martin, David G., ed. see Busey, John W.

Martin, David G., ed. see Hayward, John.

Martin, David G., ed. see Marbaker, Thomas D.

Martin, David G., ed. see Orr, John W., Jr.

Martin, David J. Elementary Science Methods: A Constructivist Approach. LC 95-46332. (Teaching Methods Ser.). (Illus.). 528p. (C). 1996. mass mkt. 40.00 (*0-8273-7174-8*) Delmar.

***Martin, David J.** Elementary Science Methods: A Constructivist Approach 2nd ed. LC 99-34792. 1999. 62.95 (*0-534-55630-2*) Wadsworth Pub.

Martin, David K. The Eighteenth Century Zimmerman Family of the Mohawk Valley. LC 93-80532. (Illus.). 1994. write for info. (*0-9639300-1-X*) Mouse Hse Bks.

Martin, David K., ed. The Journal of William Gilliland. (Illus.). 146p. 1997. 24.95 (*1-890402-22-2*) Clinton Cnty Hist.

Martin, David L. Alabama's State & Local Governments. 3rd ed. LC 94-3923. (Illus.). 288p. (C). 1994. pap. text 19.95 (*0-8173-0738-9*) U of Ala Pr.

— Running City Hall: Municipal Administration in America. 2nd ed. LC 89-37627. (Illus.). 224p. 1990. pap. text 19.95 (*0-8173-0465-7*) U of Ala Pr.

Martin, David L. & Olsen, Richard W. Gaba in the Nervous System: 50 Years of Progress. 486p. text 125.00 (*0-7817-2267-5*) Lppncott W & W.

***Martin, David Lozell.** Pelikan. LC 99-36099. 320p. 1999. 22.50 (*0-684-85348-5*) S&S Trade.

Martin, David N. Under a Lemon Moon: A Metaphysical Mystery. 288p. (Orig.). 1995. pap. 14.95 (*0-9646601-7-2*) Oaklea Pr.

Martin, David R., et al, eds. Foreign Assistance: U. S. Had Made Slow Progress in Involving Women in Development. (Illus.). 81p. (C). 1997. reprint ed. pap. text 30.00 (*0-7881-4126-0*) DIANE Pub.

Martin, David S., ed. Advances in Cognition, Education, & Deafness. LC 91-10693. (Illus.). 465p. 1991. text 34.95 (*0-930323-79-3*) Gallaudet Univ Pr.

Martin, David S., ed. Cognition, Education, & Deafness: Directions for Research & Instruction. LC 85-12992. 248p. 1985. text 21.95 (*0-930323-12-2*) Gallaudet Univ Pr.

Martin, David S. & Collins, E. Dale, eds. Manual of Acute Hand Injuries. LC 97-17955. (Illus.). 696p. (C). (gr. 13). 1997. pap. text 49.95 (*0-8151-5861-0*, 25196) Mosby Inc.

Martin, David S., jt. auth. see Gewirtz, Herman.

Martin, David W. Doing Psychology Experiments. 2nd ed. LC 84-14987. 246p. (C). 1984. mass mkt. 19.50 (*0-534-03807-7*) Brooks-Cole.

— Doing Psychology Experiments. 3rd ed. (C). 1991. pap. 24.75 (*0-534-14490-X*) Brooks-Cole.

— Doing Psychology Experiments. 4th ed. LC 94-47424. 304p. 1995. mass mkt. 28.50 (*0-534-33840-2*) Brooks-Cole.

— Doing Psychology Experiments. 5th ed. LC 99-16474. 365p. 1999. pap. text 46.95 (*0-534-24871-3*) Brooks-Cole.

M

— Doing Psychology Experiments: Test Items. 4th ed. 1995. mass mkt. write for info. (0-534-33841-0) Brooks-Cole.

Martin, David W., ed. English Texts: British Period to 1900. (Sources for the History of Cyprus Ser.: Vol. VI). 338p. 1999. pap. 70.00 (0-9651704-6-2) Greece & Cyprus Res.

— English Texts: Frankish & Turkish Periods. (Sources for the History of Cyprus Ser.: Vol. V). 320p. 1998. pap. 60.00 (0-9651704-5-4) Greece & Cyprus Res.

Martin, Dawn. Fast Girls Finish Last. LC 98-93804. (Illus.). 255p. (YA). (gr. 8-12). 1999. pap. 19.95 (0-9668718-0-4) Eos Pubg.

— A New Owner's Guide to West Highland White Terriers: AKC Rank #36. (New Owner's Guide to Ser.). (Illus.). 160p. 1996. 12.95 (0-7938-2765-5, JG-116) TFH Pubns.

Martin, Dean F. Marine Chemistry, Vol. 1. 2nd ed. LC 72-169633. (Illus.). 401p. 1972. reprint ed. pap. 124.40 (0-608-08271-6, 205506900001) Bks Demand.

— Marine Chemistry: Theory & Applications, Vol. 2. LC 68-27532. (Illus.). 463p. 1970. reprint ed. pap. 143.60 (0-608-08270-8, 203301100082) Bks Demand.

Martin, Deanna C. & Arendale, David R. Supplemental Instruction: Improving First-Year Student Success in High-Risk Courses. (Freshman Year Experience Monograph: No. 7). 57p. (Orig.). 1993. pap. 30.00 (1-889271-05-5) Nat Res Ctr.

Martin, Deanna C. & Arendale, David R., eds. Supplemental Instruction: Increasing Achievement & Retention. LC 85-644763. (New Directions for Teaching & Learning Ser.: No. TL 60). 110p. (Orig.). 1994. pap. 22.00 (0-7879-9999-7) Jossey-Bass.

Martin, Debbie. The Complete Weightloss Workbook: A Self-Help Guide to Permanent Weight Loss Including Food Journal, Weightloss Tips, Low Fat Recipes, Food Values. (Illus.). 220p. (Orig.). 1993. pap. 15.95 (0-9635558-0-4) Slender Visions.

Martin, Deborah L. An Annotated Guide to Adoption Research. annot. ed. LC 98-207370. 368p. 1998. pap. text 24.95 (0-87868-708-4, 7084, CWLA Pr) Child Welfare.

Martin, Deborah L., ed. 1001 Ingenious Gardening Ideas: New, Fun & Fabulous That Will Change the Way You Garden - Forever. LC 99-6038. 345p. 1999. text 27.95 (0-87596-809-0) Rodale Pr Inc.

Martin, Deborah L., jt. ed. see Gershuny, Grace.

Martin, Debra Bayles, jt. auth. see Eby, Judy W.

Martin, Debra L., jt. ed. see Frayer, David W.

***Martin, Deirdre.** Teaching Children with Speech & Language Difficulties. 80p. 2000. pap. 17.95 (1-85346-585-2) David Fulton.

— 21st C.i. Invest Retire. LC 98-24545. (The 21st Century Investor Ser.). 240p. 1998. pap. 12.50 (0-380-79063-7, Avon Bks) Morrow Avon.

Martin, Deirdre & Miller, Carol. Speech & Language Difficulties in the Classroom. 160p. 1996. pap. 23.95 (1-85346-302-7, Pub. by David Fulton) Taylor & Francis.

Martin, Del. Battered Wives. 1990. mass mkt. 5.99 (0-671-72761-3) PB.

— Battered Wives. rev. ed. LC 81-12985. 281p. 1981. pap. 12.95 (0-912078-70-7) Volcano Pr.

Martin del Campo, jt. auth. see Bogert.

Martin, Della, jt. auth. see Granor, Tamar E.

***Martin, Delores M.** Handbook of Latin American Studies: Humanities, 56. 960p. 1999. 85.00 (0-292-75231-8) U of Tex Pr.

Martin, Delores M., ed. Handbook of Latin American Studies, Vol. 46: Humanities. (ENG, FRE, GER, RUS & SER.). 768p. 1986. text 65.00 (0-292-73035-7) U of Tex Pr.

Martin, Denis & Guild, Elspeth. Martin & Guild: Free Movement of Persons in the European Union. 1996. write for info. (0-406-06564-0, GMMP, MICHIE) LEXIS Pub.

Martin, Dennis. The Operas & Operatic Style of John Frederick Lampe. LC 85-14496. (Detroit Monographs in Musicology: No. 8). xx, 190p. 1985. 40.00 (0-89990-024-0) Harmonie Park Pr.

Martin, Dennis, jt. auth. see Martin, Kymberly.

Martin, Dennis, jt. ed. see Dyck, Cornelius J.

Martin, Dennis D. Fifteenth-Century Carthusian Reform: The World of Nicholas Kempf. LC 92-20135. (Studies in the History of Christian Thought: Vol. 49). xvi, 416p. 1992. 142.00 (90-04-09636-1) Brill Academic Pubs.

Martin, Dennis D., tr. Carthusian Spirituality: The Writings of Hugh of Balma & Guido de Ponte. (Classics of Western Spirituality Ser.: No. 88). 432p. (Orig.). 1996. 32.00 (0-8091-0480-6); pap. 23.00 (0-8091-3664-3) Paulist Pr.

Martin, Dennis D., tr. see Von Balthasar, Hans U.

Martin, Dennis G. & Coons, Robert D. Media Flight Plan III. 3rd ed. 155p. (C). 1996. pap., student ed. 36.00 incl. 3.5 hd (0-9632515-1-1); pap., student ed. 36.00 incl. mac hd (0-9632515-2-X) Deer Creek UT.

Martin, Dennis R., ed. see Root, George F.

Martin, Derek. SWOT Revenue Law. 278p. (C). 1990. 110.00 (0-906322-91-X, Pub. by Blackstone Pr) St Mut.

Martin, Desmond D. & Shell, Richard L. Management of Professionals: Insights for Maximizing Cooperation. (Illus.). 348p. 1988. text 65.00 (0-8247-7847-2) Dekker.

— What Every Engineer Should Know about Human Resources Management. LC 80-22329. (What Every Engineer Should Know Ser.: Vol. 5). (Illus.). 192p. reprint ed. pap. 59.60 (0-608-08955-9, 206959000005) Bks Demand.

Martin, Diana. Graphic Design: Inspirations & Innovations. (Illus.). 144p. write for info. (1-56496-229-6) Rockport Pubs.

Martin, Diana, ed. Graphic Design: Inspirations & Innovations. (Illus.). 144p. 1998. pap. 24.99 (0-89134-898-0, North Lght Bks) F & W Pubns Inc.

Martin, Diana & Cropper, Mary. Fresh Ideas in Letterhead & Business Card Design. (Fresh Ideas Ser.). (Illus.). 144p. 1993. 29.99 (0-89134-505-1, 30481, North Lght Bks) F & W Pubns Inc.

Martin, Diana & Haller, Lynn. Graphic Design: Inspirations & Innovations 2. 2nd ed. LC 96-6553. (Illus.). 144p. 1997. 29.99 (0-89134-773-9, North Lght Bks) F & W Pubns Inc.

Martin, Diana & Haller, Lynn, eds. Street Smart Design. LC 95-53170. (Illus.). 144p. 1996. 29.99 (0-89134-686-4, North Lght Bks) F & W Pubns Inc.

Martin, Diana & White, Ed. How to Airbrush T-Shirts & Other Clothing. (Illus.). 128p. 1994. pap. 24.99 (0-89134-570-1, North Lght Bks) F & W Pubns Inc.

Martin, Diana, jt. auth. see Miller, David.

Martin, Diane. Kill Bugs Dead: An Indoor Gardener's Guide to Eliminating Insects on Houseplants Without Using Harmful Pesticides. (Illus.). 40p. (Orig.). 1992. pap. 7.95 (0-931485-30-4) Scriptorium Pr.

Martin, Diane, ed. see Elgin, Suzette H.

Martin, Diane C. Amazing Grace - The Story Behind the Gospel Navy. (Illus.). (Orig.). 1999. pap. 14.95 (0-9652205-5-9) H Martin.

— Universal Grammar. 1991. pap. text 51.00 (0-7923-1420-4) Kluwer Academic.

Martin, Dianne L., jt. auth. see Ruby, Clayton C.

Martin, Dick. Cut & Assemble the Emerald City. 81st ed. (J). 1980. pap. 6.95 (0-486-24053-3) Dover.

— Cut & Assemble Wizard of Oz Theatre. (J). 1985. pap. 6.95 (0-486-24799-6) Dover.

Martin, Didier. Il Serait un Fois. (FRE.). 1979. pap. 10.95 (0-7859-4116-9) Fr & Eur.

Martin, Dieter. Das Deutsche Versepos im 18. Jahrhundert: Studien & Kommentierte Gattungsbibliographie. (Quellen und Forschungen zur Sprach und Kulturgeschichte der Germanischen Voelker: Bd 103). (GER.). xi, 450p. (C). 1993. lib. bdg. 161.55 (3-11-013816-6) De Gruyter.

Martin, Dolores M. Handbook of Latin American Studies, Vol. 51: Social Sciences. LC 36-32633. 923p. (C). 1992. text 65.00 (0-292-75149-4) U of Tex Pr.

— Handbook of Latin American Studies, Vol. 52: Humanities. 958p. (C). 1993. lib. bdg. 75.00 (0-292-75156-7) U of Tex Pr.

Martin, Dolores M., compiled by. Handbook of Latin American Studies, Vol. 50: Humanities. annot. ed. (ENG & SPA.). 825p. 1991. text 65.00 (0-292-73058-6) U of Tex Pr.

Martin, Dolores M., ed. Handbook of Latin American Studies Vol. 53: Social Sciences. 960p. 1994. text 75.00 (0-292-75166-4) U of Tex Pr.

— Handbook of Latin American Studies Vol. 54: Humanities. 992p. 1996. text 85.00 (0-292-75190-7) U of Tex Pr.

— Handbook of Latin American Studies, Humanities, Vol. 48. 784p. 1988. 65.00 (0-292-73041-1) U of Tex Pr.

— Handbook of Latin American Studies, Vol. 39: Social Sciences, 1977. LC 36-32633. (Handbook of Latin American Studies Ser.). 1997. 59.95 (0-8130-0600-7) U Press Fla.

— Handbook of Latin American Studies, Vol. 40: Humanities 1978. LC 36-32633. 1978. 59.95 (0-8130-0637-6) U Press Fla.

— Handbook of Latin American Studies, Vol. 41: Social Sciences. 814p. 1980. text 65.00 (0-292-73013-6) U of Tex Pr.

— Handbook of Latin American Studies, Vol. 44: Humanities. 795p. 1984. text 65.00 (0-292-73023-3) U of Tex Pr.

— Handbook of Latin American Studies, Vol. 47: Social Sciences. 832p. 1987. text 65.00 (0-292-73038-1) U of Tex Pr.

— Handbook of Latin American Studies, Vol. 49: Social Sciences. 875p. 1989. text 65.00 (0-292-73046-2) U of Tex Pr.

Martin, Dolores M. & Mundell, P. Sue, eds. Handbook of Latin American Studies Vol. 55: Social Sciences. 976p. 1998. 85.00 (0-292-75211-3) U of Tex Pr.

Martin, Dolores M. & Stewart, Donald E., eds. Handbook of Latin American Studies, Vol. 38: Humanities 1976. LC 36-32633. 1976. 59.95 (0-8130-0568-X) U Press Fla.

Martin, Dom. Auschwitz - Humanity's Fingerprint on Time. 1995. text 15.00 (0-9616078-2-3) Trans Gala Pubns.

— An Autobiography of Thoughts. 150p. (Orig.). 1994. pap. 15.00 (0-9616078-3-1) Trans Gala Pubns.

— The Day Before the Day After. (Illus.). 86p. 1985. pap. text 4.95 (0-9616078-0-7) Trans Gala Pubns.

***Martin, Dom.** Et tu, Saiba! (Illus.). 1999. pap. 14.95 (0-9616078-4-X) Trans Gala Pubns.

— Exodus to Eternity. (Illus.). xii, 110p. 2000. pap. 14.95 (0-9616078-5-8) Trans Gala Pubns.

Martin, Dom. The Principles of Zerometrics, Vol. I. 24p. (Orig.). 1989. pap. text 5.00 (0-685-33290-X) Trans Gala Pubns.

— A Thousand Eyes for an Eye. (Illus.). 125p. (Orig.). 1994. pap. 15.00 (0-9616078-1-5) Trans Gala Pubns.

Martin, Don. Don Martin Comes on Strong. (Illus.). 192p. (Orig.). 1989. mass mkt. 3.50 (0-446-35819-3, Pub. by Warner Bks) Little.

— Don Martin Forges Ahead. 1989. mass mkt. 3.95 (0-446-35823-1, Pub. by Warner Bks) Little.

— Don Martin Sails Ahead. 192p. (Orig.). 1989. pap. 3.50 (0-446-35825-8) Warner Bks.

— Don Martin Steps Further Out. (Illus.). 192p. (Orig.). (J). 1984. mass mkt. 2.25 (0-446-32460-4, Pub. by Warner Bks) Little.

— Don Martin's Droll Book. (Illus.). 128p. (Orig.). 1992. pap. 9.95 (1-878574-37-X) Dark Horse Comics.

— Hiking Marin: 133 Great Hikes in Marin County. 2nd ed. (Orig.). 1999. pap. 18.95 (0-9617044-8-9) Martin Press.

Martin, Don & Martin, Betty. Arizona in Your Future: The Complete Relocation Guide for Job-Seekers, Retirees & Snowbirds. 2nd rev. ed. LC 97-66327. (Illus.). 256p. 1998. pap. 15.95 (0-942053-23-0) Pine Cone Pr NV.

— California-Nevada Roads Less Traveled: A Discovery Guide to Places Less Crowded. LC 98-68454. (Illus.). 336p. 1999. pap. 15.95 (0-942053-28-1) Pine Cone Pr NV.

— San Diego: The Best of Sunshine City: An Impertinent Insider's Guide. LC 98-91238. (Best of...Ser.). (Illus.). 256p. 1999. pap. 14.95 (0-942053-27-3) Pine Cone Pr NV.

***Martin, Don & Martin, Betty.** Washington Discovery Guide: A Remarkably Useful Travel Companion for Motorists, RVers & Other Explorers. 2nd rev. ed. (Discovery Guide Ser.). (Illus.). 416p. 2000. pap. 17.95 (0-942053-31-1) Pine Cone Pr NV.

Martin, Don, Jr. & Martin, Karen, eds. Deployed, Not Disconnected. 128p. 1991. pap. 5.50 (0-913991-01-5) Off Christian Fellowship.

Martin, Don & Martin, Kay. MT Tam: A Hiking, Running & Nature Guide. 2nd ed. (Illus.). 102p. 1994. pap. 9.95 (0-9617044-4-6) Martin Press.

Martin, Don & Martin, Key. Point Reyes National Seashore: A Hiking & Nature Guide. 2nd rev. ed. (Illus.). 136p. 1997. pap. 9.95 (0-9617044-6-2) Martin Press.

Martin, Don & Martin, Maggie. Step by Step: A Guide to Stepfamily Living. LC 92-70822. 186p. (Orig.). 1992. pap. text 9.95 (0-932796-38-9) Ed Media Corp.

Martin, Don, et al. Is Your Family Making You Fat? How Your Family Affects Your Weight & What You Can Do about It. 208p. (Orig.). 1995. pap. 11.99 (0-945819-58-7) Sulzburger & Graham Pub.

Martin, Don L., ed. see Martin, Mildred.

Martin, Don W. & Martin, Betty W. Arizona Discovery Guide: A Remarkably Useful Travel Companion for Motorists, RVers & Other Explorers. 3rd ed. (Illus.). 408p. 1996. pap. 15.95 (0-942053-20-6) Pine Cone Pr NV.

— The Best of San Francisco: A Witty & Somewhat Opinionated Insider's Guide to Everybody's Favorite City. 4th ed. LC 96-44567. 1997. pap. 12.95 (0-8118-1571-4) Chronicle Bks.

— The Best of the Gold Country: A Complete, Witty & Remarkably Useful Guide to California's Sierra Foothills & Historic Sacramento. rev. ed. (Best of...Ser.: No. 2). (Illus.). 240p. 1992. pap. 11.95 (0-942053-11-7) Pine Cone Pr NV.

— The Best of the Wine Country: "A Witty, Opinionated & Remarkably Useful Guide to California's Vinelands" 2nd rev. ed. (Best of...Ser.: No. 4). (Illus.). 320p. (Orig.). 1995. pap. 13.95 (0-942053-17-6) Pine Cone Pr NV.

***Martin, Don W. & Martin, Betty W.** Las Vegas, the Best of Glitter City Vol. 1: An Impertinent Insiders' Guide. 2nd ed. LC 97-67633. (Best of...Ser.). (Illus.). 284p. 2000. pap. 15.95 (0-942053-33-8) Pine Cone Pr NV.

Martin, Don W. & Martin, Betty W. Nevada Discovery Guide: A Remarkably Useful Travel Companion for Motorists, RVers & Other Explorers. 2nd ed. (Discovery Guide Ser.). (Illus.). 416p. 1996. pap. 15.95 (0-942053-21-4) Pine Cone Pr NV.

***Martin, Don W. & Martin, Betty W.** Nevada in Your Future: The Complete Relocation Guide for Job-Seekers, Retirees & Snowbirds. (Illus.). 256p. 2000. pap. 16.95 (0-942053-30-3, Pub. by Pine Cone Pr NV) Publishers Group.

Martin, Don W. & Martin, Betty W. New Mexico Discovery Guide: A Remarkably Useful Travel Companion for Motorists, RVers & Other Explorers. LC 97-76165. (Discovery Guide Ser.). (Illus.). 416p. 1998. pap. 16.95 (0-942053-25-7) Pine Cone Pr NV.

— The Toll-Free Traveler: The Complete (800) & (888) Directory for Pleasure & Business Travel. (Illus.). 160p. 1997. pap. 8.95 (0-942053-22-2) Pine Cone Pr NV.

***Martin, Don W. & Martin, Betty W.** Ultimate Wine Book: Everything You Need to Know about Wine Appreciation, Wine with Food, & the. 2nd ed. (Illus.). 192p. 1999. pap. 10.95 (0-942053-29-X, Pub. by Pine Cone Pr NV) Publishers Group.

***Martin, Don W. & Martin, Betty Woo.** The Best of Denver & the Rockies: An Impertinent Insiders' Guide. ("Best of..." City Guides Ser.: No. 6). (Illus.). 236p. 2001. pap. 15.95 (0-942053-35-4, Pub. by Pine Cone Pr NV) Publishers Group.

— The Best of Phoenix & Tucson: An Impertinent Insider's Guide. ("Best of..." City Guides Ser.: No. 5). (Illus.). 236p. 2001. pap. 15.95 (0-942053-34-6, Pub. by Pine Cone Pr NV) Publishers Group.

— Seattle: The Best of Emerald City: An Impertinent Insiders' Guide. (Best of...Ser.). (Illus.). 256p. 2000. pap. 15.95 (0-942053-32-X, Pub. by Pine Cone Pr NV) Publishers Group.

Martin, Donald. How to Be a Successful Student. 2nd ed. (Illus.). 48p. (Orig.). (J). (gr. 8-12). 1991. pap. 5.95 (0-9617044-2-X) Martin Press.

***Martin, Donald.** Killybegs: Then & Now. LC 98-233750. (Illus.). 168p. 1999. pap. 18.95 (1-901737-06-3, Pub. by Anvil Books Ltd) Dufour.

Martin, Donald, tr. see Calvin, John.

Martin, Donald E., jt. ed. see Hensley, Frederick A., Jr.

Martin, Donald E., tr. see Pierdes, G. Philippou.

Martin, Donald E., tr. see Theotokas, George.

***Martin, Donald H.** Communication Satellites. 4th ed. LC 99-87356. 2000. write for info. (1-884989-09-8) Aerospace CA.

Martin, Donald H. Communication Satellites, 1958-1995. 3rd ed. (Illus.). 483p. 1996. pap. 35.00 (1-884989-02-0) Aerospace CA.

Martin, Donald J. Designer Kitchens: A Who's Who in Kitchen Design. 188p. 1995. 24.95 (1-878667-05-X) H & S Media.

— Designer Kitchens: A Who's Who in Kitchen Design. LC 94-79709. (Illus.). 176p. (C). 1995. pap. 15.00 (1-886378-01-0) Kasmar Pubns.

Martin, Donald J., ed. Designer Kitchens: A Who's Who in Kitchen Design. LC 94-79709. (Illus.). 176p. (C). 1995. 24.95 (1-886378-00-2) Kasmar Pubns.

Martin, Donald L. Tidbits for Young Doctors & Their Patients: Journal of a Country Doctor, Pt. II. 1993. pap. 9.95 (1-55673-528-6, Fairway Pr) CSS OH.

Martin, Donna. Food Fun. 2nd rev. ed. (Love 'n Hug Notes Ser.). (Illus.). 10p. (J). 1993. write for info. (1-879127-46-6) Lighten Up Enter.

— Jokes & Riddles. 2nd rev. ed. (Love 'n Hug Notes Ser.). (Illus.). 10p. (J). 1993. write for info. (1-879127-41-5) Lighten Up Enter.

— Let's Remember. 2nd rev. ed. (Love 'n Hug Notes Ser.). (Illus.). 10p. (J). 1993. write for info. (1-879127-42-3) Lighten Up Enter.

— School Bits. 2nd rev. ed. (Love 'n Hug Notes Ser.). (Illus.). 10p. (J). 1993. write for info. (1-879127-45-8) Lighten Up Enter.

— Sports & Play. 2nd rev. ed. (Love 'n Hug Notes Ser.). (Illus.). 10p. (J). 1993. write for info. (1-879127-44-X) Lighten Up Enter.

— You're the Best. 2nd rev. ed. (Love 'n Hug Notes Ser.). (Illus.). 10p. (J). 1993. write for info. (1-879127-43-1) Lighten Up Enter.

Martin, Donna, jt. auth. see Boone, Don.

Martin, Donna, jt. auth. see Brenner, Paul.

Martin, Donna, jt. auth. see Kansas City Jazz Museum Staff.

Martin, Donna B., jt. auth. see Boone, Don.

Martin, Donna Marie, jt. auth. see Andrews, Sharon Vincz.

Martin, Donna R. Ephesians: Reconciled in Christ. LC 94-11717. (Covenant Bible Study Ser.). 62p. 1994. pap. 5.95 (0-87178-221-9, 8219) Brethren.

***Martin, Donna S.** Sams Teach Yourself GTK+ Programming in 21 Days. (Teach Yourself... in 21 Days Ser.). (Illus.). 700p. 2000. pap. 39.99 (0-672-31829-6) Sams.

Martin, Doris. Management for Competitiveness: Maximize Profits, Productivity & Performance. LC 91-90340. 101p. (Orig.). 1991. pap. 15.95 (0-9615541-8-5) Martin Mgmt.

— Managing in Tough Times: One Hundred One New Directions from Big Business. LC 92-90898. 101p. 1992. pap. 15.95 (1-878500-01-5) Martin Mgmt.

Martin, Dorothea A. The Making of a Sino-Marxist World View: Perceptions & Interpretations of World History in the People's Republic of China. LC 89-49161. (Studies on Contemporary China). 160p. (gr. 13). 1990. text 79.95 (0-87332-656-3, East Gate Bk) M E Sharpe.

Martin, Dorothy, tr. Sextette: Translations from the French Symbolists. LC 80-10539. (Symbolists Ser.). reprint ed. 34.50 (0-404-16331-9) AMS Pr.

Martin, Dorothy R. & Cadwallader, Helen A. Lab Studies in Anatomy & Physiology. (Illus.). 328p. (C). 1998. pap. text, lab manual ed. 32.95 (0-88725-277-X) Hunter Textbks.

Martin, Dorothy W. A Collection of Fiction, Poetry & Articles for the Gentle-Hearted. (Gentle Reader Ser.: No. 1). (Illus.). iii, 67p. 1996. pap. 9.95 (0-9665322-1-X) Jewel Pr FL.

Martin, Dotty, jt. auth. see Martin, Bob.

Martin, Doug, ed. see Cade, Blane.

Martin, Douglas, et al. Critical Thinking Handbook--6th-9th Grades: A Guide for Remodelling Lesson Plans in Language Arts, Social Studies, & Science. LC 88-64125. (Orig.). 1995. pap. text 19.95 (0-944583-02-4) Found Critical Think.

Martin, Douglas, tr. see Kapr, Robert.

Martin, Douglas A. My Gradual Demise & Honeysuckle. 84p. 1995. pap. 7.00 (0-9641196-2-5) Champion Bks.

***Martin, Douglas A.** Outline of My Lover: A Novel. 166p. 2000. pap. 12.00 (1-887128-47-6) Soft Skull Pr.

Martin, Douglas C., jt. auth. see Gibson, Helen.

Martin, Douglas C., jt. auth. see Roth, Richard.

Martin, Douglas C., jt. auth. see White, Paul.

Martin, Douglas C., jt. auth. see Wolfe, Tom James.

Martin, Douglas D. Tombstone's "Epitaph" LC 97-16089. (Illus.). 304p. 1997. pap. 16.95 (0-8061-2982-4) U of Okla Pr.

— Yuma Crossing. fac. ed. LC 54-10446. (Illus.). 260p. 1995. pap. 9.95 (0-9632228-1-3) Yuma Cnty Hist.

Martin, Douglas J., jt. auth. see Hatcher, William S.

Martin du Gard, Roger. Confidence Africaine. (FRE.). 67p. 1991. pap. 19.95 (0-7859-1583-4, 29035344458) Fr & Eur.

— Jean Barois. (FRE.). 1972. pap. 10.95 (0-685-67882-2) Fr & Eur.

— Lieutenant-Colonel de Maumort. Brebion, Luc & Crouse, Timothy, trs. from FRE. LC 98-50912. 848p. 1999. 35.00 (0-679-43397-X) Knopf.

— Maumort. (FRE.). 1983. lib. bdg. 110.00 (0-8288-3555-1, M5107) Fr & Eur.

— Oeuvres Completes, Vol. 1. (FRE.). 1955. lib. bdg. 105.00 (0-8288-3556-X, M5105) Fr & Eur.

— Oeuvres Completes, Vol. 2. (FRE.). 1955. lib. bdg. 95.00 (0-7859-0642-8, M5106) Fr & Eur.

— The Postman. Russell, John, tr. from FRE. LC 74-13052. 156p. 1975. reprint ed. 29.50 (0-86527-333-2) Fertig.

— Un Taciturne. (FRE.). 238p. 1932. pap. 12.95 (0-7859-1285-1, 2070242439) Fr & Eur.

— Thibault, 5 tomes, 1. (Folio Ser.: Nos. 788, 140, 164, 165, & 189). (FRE.). 1959. pap. 12.95 (2-07-036788-6) Schoenhof.

— Thibault, 5 tomes, 2. (Folio Ser.: Nos. 788, 140, 164, 165, & 189). (FRE.). 1959. pap. 10.95 (2-07-036140-3) Schoenhof.

An Asterisk (*) at the beginning of an entry indicates that the title is appearing for the first time.

M

An Asterisk (*) at the beginning of an entry indicates that the title is appearing for the first time.

Martin, F. Raoul, ed. see Labbe, John T. & Replinger, Peter J.

Martin, F. X. & Richmond, J. A., eds. From Augustine to Eriugena: Essays on Neoplatonism & Christianity in Honor of John O'Meara. LC 90-33250. 190p. 1991. text 49.95 (*0-8132-0732-0*) Cath U Pr.

Martin, F. X., jt. ed. see Moody, T. W.

Martin, F. X., ed. see Tierney, Michael.

Martin-Fagg, Roger. Making Sense Of The Economy. 1996. pap. text 12.99 (*1-86152-521-4*) Thomson Learn.

Martin-Fagg, Roger, ed. Making Sense of the Economy. LC 96-38882. (Self-Development for Managers Ser.). 144p. 1996. pap. 17.95 (*0-415-10318-5*, Pub. by ITBP) Thomson Learn.

Martin, Faith. Call Me Blessed: The Emerging Christian Woman. 224p. 1998. pap. 14.00 (*0-9669439-0-2*) SpringValley.

Martin, Fay C. Availing Prayer. 120p. reprint ed. pap. 3.00 (*0-686-29098-4*) Faith Pub Hse.

Martin, Fenton & Goehlert, Robert U. Getting Published in Political Science Journals: A Guide for Authors, Editors & Librarians. 4th ed. Orig. Title: Political Science Journal Information. 112p. 1997. 30.00 (*1-878147-24-2*) Am Political.

Martin, Fenton S. & Boehlert, Robert. How to Research the Supreme Court. LC 91-46903. 140p. (YA). (gr. 11). 1992. text 31.95 (*0-87187-697-3*); pap. text 13.17 (*0-87187-633-7*) Congr Quarterly.

Martin, Fenton S. & Goehlert, Robert. American Government & Politics: A Guide to Books for Teachers, Librarians, & Students. LC 97-2513. 204p. 1997. 17.97 (*1-56802-221-2*) Congr Quarterly.

***Martin, Fenton S. & Goehlert, Robert.** How to Research Elections. LC 00-33667. 2000. pap. write for info. (*1-56802-597-1*) CQ Pr.

Martin, Fenton S. & Goehlert, Robert U. The American Presidency: A Bibliography. LC 87-445. 506p. 1987. 105.00 (*0-87187-415-6*) Congr Quarterly.

— American Presidents: A Bibliography. LC 86-30938. 756p. 1987. 155.00 (*0-87187-416-4*) Congr Quarterly.

***Martin, Fenton S. & Goehlert, Robert U.** CQ's Resource Guide to Modern Elections. LC 99-52009. 550p. 1999. 190.00 (*1-56802-326-X*) CQ Pr.

Martin, Fenton S. & Goehlert, Robert U. How to Research the Presidency. LC 96-7488. 134p. (C). (gr. 11). 1996. text 19.97 (*1-56802-029-5*) Congr Quarterly.

— How to Research the Presidency. LC 96-7488. 134p. (YA). (gr. 11). 1996. pap. text 13.77 (*1-56802-028-7*) Congr Quarterly.

Martin, Fenton S. & Goelert, Robert U. How to Research Congress. LC 96-3867. 107p. (C). (gr. 11). 1996. text 19.97 (*0-87187-870-4*) Congr Quarterly.

— How to Research Congress. LC 96-3867. 107p. (YA). (gr. 11). 1996. pap. text 13.77 (*0-87187-869-0*) Congr Quarterly.

Martin, Fern & Woods, Paula. Lafayette: A Pictorial History. (Indiana Pictorial History Ser.). (Illus.). 1994. reprint ed. write for info. (*0-943963-09-5*) G Bradley.

Martin, Fern, jt. auth. see Woods, Paula.

Martin, Fontaine. A History of the Bouligny Family & Allied Families. LC 89-81492. 366p. 1989. 30.00 (*0-940984-51-2*) Univ LA Lafayette.

Martin, Frances G. Cemeteries of Grenada County, Mississippi & Surrounding Areas. rev. ed. 282p. 1999. pap. 35.00 (*1-885480-32-6*) Pioneer Pubng.

Martin, Frances R. Manual for Nursing Care of Children. 352p. 1993. spiral bd. 31.95 (*0-8403-8616-8*) Kendall-Hunt.

Martin, Francesca. Clever Tortoise. LC 98-14206. (Illus.). 32p. (YA). (gr. k up). 2000. 14.99 (*0-7636-0506-9*, Pub. by Candlewick Pr) Penguin Putnam.

— Honey Hunters: A Traditional African Tale. (J). 1994. 11.19 (*0-606-05877-X*, Pub. by Turtleback) Demco.

Martin, Francesca. The Honey Hunters. LC 91-58736. 32p. (J). (ps up). 1992. 14.95 (*1-56402-086-X*) Candlewick Pr.

Martin, Francis. Baptism in the Holy Spirit: A Scriptural Foundation. 62p. (Orig.). 1986. pap. 3.95 (*0-940535-04-1*, UP105) Franciscan U Pr.

— Baptism in the Holy Spirit: Reflections on a Contemporary Grace in the Light of the Catholic Tradition. LC 98-60878. 53p. 1998. pap. 4.95 (*1-879007-31-2*) St Bedes Pubns.

Martin, Francis. The Feminist Question: Feminist Theology in the Light of Christian Tradition. 496p. 1994. pap. 20.00 (*0-8028-0794-1*) Eerdmans.

Martin, Francis. The Life-Changer: How You Can Experience Freedom Power & Refreshment in the Holy Spirit. 2nd rev. ed. LC 98-20142. 170p. 1998. reprint ed. pap. 14.95 (*1-879007-30-4*) St Bedes Pubns.

Martin, Francis, Jr., intro. Western & Wildlife: Selections from the Samuel B & Marion Lawrence Collection. (Illus.). 45p. (Orig.). 1987. pap. 10.00 (*0-9615828-1-2*) Cornell Fine Arts.

Martin, Francis, tr. see Bavarel, Michel.

Martin, Francis G., jt. auth. see Baker, Justine C.

Martin, Francis P. Hung by the Tongue: What You Say Is What You Get. (Illus.). 96p. (Orig.). 1976. mass mkt. 4.95 (*0-9652433-0-3*); mass mkt. 4.95 (*0-9652433-1-1*) F P M Publns.

Martin, Francis X. Friar, Reformer, & Renaissance Scholar: The Life & Work of Giles of Viterbo, 1469-1532. Rotelle, John E. & O'Malley, John W., eds. LC 92-2863. (Augustinian Ser.: Vol. 18). 424p. 1993. 40.00 (*0-941491-51-X*); pap. 28.00 (*0-941491-50-1*) Augustinian Pr.

Martin, Francisco F. & Rights International Staff. International Human Rights Law & Practice: Cases, Treaties, & Materials. LC 97-32815. 1997. 225.00 (*90-411-0616-2*) Kluwer Law Intl.

Martin, Francisco F., et al. The Rights International Companion to Criminal Law & Procedure: An International Human Rights Law Supplement. LC 99-29527. 1999. write for info. (*90-411-9332-4*) Kluwer Law Intl.

Martin, Francois. Francois Martin: Motets for One & Two Voices with Instruments. Cyr, Mary, ed. (Recent Researches in Music of the Classic Era Ser.: Vol. RRC29). xx, 87p. 1988. pap. 35.00 (*0-89579-229-X*) A-R Eds.

— India in the Seventeenth Century, Vol. 2, Pt. 1. Varadarajan, Lotika, ed. 1985. 32.50 (*0-8364-1423-3*, Pub. by Manohar) S Asia.

— India in the Seventeenth Century, Vol. 2, Pt. 2. Varadarajan, Lotika, ed. 1985. 38.00 (*0-8364-1424-1*, Pub. by Manohar) S Asia.

— India in the Seventeenth Century: Social, Economic & Political Memoirs of Francois Martin, Vol. 1. Varadarajan, Lotika, tr. 1982. 36.00 (*0-8364-0818-7*, Pub. by Manohar) S Asia.

Martin, Francois-Xavier, tr. see Pothier, Robert J.

Martin, Frank. Hollywood Continental. (Academy Editions Ser.). (Illus.). 96p. 1989. 29.95 (*0-312-02712-5*) St Martin.

— Rogues' River: Crime on the River Thames in the Eighteenth Century. (Illus.). 200p. 1991. 15.00 (*0-86025-874-2*, Pub. by I Henry Pubns) Empire Pub Srvs.

Martin, Frank, ed. Frank Martin: A Bio-Bibliography, 26. LC 89-78255. (Bio-Bibliographies in Music Ser.: No. 26). 264p. 1990. lib. bdg. 57.95 (*0-313-25418-4*, KFK/, Greenwood Pr) Greenwood.

Martin, Franklin W., ed. Handbook of Tropical Food Crops. 304p. 1984. lib. bdg. 161.00 (*0-8493-0536-5*, SB176) CRC Pr.

Martin, Franklin W. & Ruberte, Ruth M. Edible Leaves of the Tropics. (Tropical Agriculture Ser.). 1980. lib. bdg. 250.00 (*0-8490-3069-2*) Gordon Pr.

— Patiofarming: A Compendium of Useful Tables. (Studies in Tropical Agriculture). 1980. lib. bdg. 69.95 (*0-8490-3075-7*) Gordon Pr.

— The Round Garden: Plans for a Small Intensive Vegetable Garden for Year Round Production in the Tropics. (Studies in Tropical Agriculture). 1980. lib. bdg. 59.95 (*0-8490-3073-0*) Gordon Pr.

Martin, Franklin W., et al. Cultivation of Neglected Tropical Fruits with Promise. (Studies in Tropical Agriculture). 1980. lib. bdg. 59.95 (*0-8490-3074-9*) Gordon Pr.

— Edible Leaves of the Tropics. (Illus.). 194p. 1998. pap. 14.95 (*0-9653360-1-8*, PB84-112549) ECHO Inc.

— Vegetables for the Hot, Humid Tropics. (Studies in Tropical Agriculture). 1980. lib. bdg. 59.95 (*0-8490-3071-4*) Gordon Pr.

Martin, Fred. The Art of Robotics: An Introduction to Engineering. 320p. (C). 2000. text. write for info. (*0-201-49860-X*) Addison-Wesley.

— Art Robotics. 370p. (C). 2001. 95.00 (*0-8053-4336-9*) Addison-Wesley.

— Earthquake. LC 95-38386. (J). 1998. 19.92 (*1-57572-021-3*) Heinemann Lib.

— Flood. LC 95-38334. (J). 1998. (*1-57572-020-5*) Heinemann Lib.

— Italy. LC 98-52757. (Country Studies Ser.). 64p. 1999. 24.22 (*1-57572-894-X*) Heinemann Lib.

— Volcano. LC 95-38352. (J). 1998. (*1-57572-023-X*) Heinemann Lib.

— Weather. LC 95-38353. (J). 1998. (*1-57572-022-1*) Heinemann Lib.

***Martin, Fred G.** The Art of Robotics. 1999. teacher ed. write for info. (*0-201-30876-2*) Addison-Wesley.

Martin, Frederick. The Life of John Clare. (BCL1-PR English Literature Ser.). 301p. 1992. reprint ed. lib. bdg. 89.99 (*0-7812-7497-4*) Rprt Serv.

— The Life of John Clare. 2nd ed. (Illus.). 319p. 1964. 27.50 (*0-7146-2070-X*, Pub. by F Cass Pubs) Intl Spec Bk.

Martin, Frederick N. Clinical Audiometry & Masking. LC 74-183115. (Studies in Communicative Disorders). (C). 1972. pap. 3.25 (*0-672-61282-8*, Bobbs) Macmillan.

— Exercises in Audiometry. 178p. (C). 1997. spiral bd., lab manual ed. 35.00 (*0-205-26825-0*) Allyn.

Martin, Frederick N. & Clark, John G., eds. Hearing Care for Children. LC 95-36484. 416p. 1995. 72.00 (*0-13-124702-6*) Allyn.

***Martin, Frederick N., et al.** Introduction to Audiology. 7th ed. LC 99-21824. 464p. 1999. pap. text 69.00 (*0-205-29536-3*) Allyn.

Martin, Frederick N., jt. ed. see Clark, John Greer.

Martin, Frederick T. The Passing of the Idle Rich. LC 75-1858. (Leisure Class in America Ser.). 1975. reprint ed. 20.95 (*0-405-06924-3*) Ayer.

— Things I Remember. LC 75-1859. (Leisure Class in America Ser.). (Illus.). 1975. reprint ed. 21.95 (*0-405-06925-1*) Ayer.

— Things I Remember. (American Biography Ser.). 255p. 1991. reprint ed. lib. bdg. 69.00 (*0-7812-8272-1*) Rprt Serv.

Martin, Frederick Thomas. Top Secret Intranet: The Story of Intelink- How U.S. Intelligence Built the World's Largest, Most Secure Network. LC 98-35324. 380p. (C). 1998. pap. text 34.99 (*0-13-080898-9*) P-H.

Martin, G., ed. Geographers Vol. 10: Biobibliographical Studies, Vol. 13. (Illus.). 198p. 1991. 100.00 (*0-7201-2081-0*) Continuum.

— Geographers Vol. 10: Biobibliographical Studies, Vol. 14. (Illus.). 128p. 1992. text 99.50 (*0-7201-2116-7*) Continuum.

Martin, G. & Kubin, L. P., eds. Non-Linear Phenomena in Materials Science. 512p. 1988. text 176.00 (*0-87849-565-7*, Pub. by Trans T Pub) Enfield Pubs NH.

— Non Linear Phenomena in Materials Science II. 520p. 1992. text 183.00 (*0-87849-635-1*, Pub. by Trans T Pub) Enfield Pubs NH.

Martin, G. & Laffort, Paul, eds. Odors & Deodorization in the Environment: English Language Edition. rev. ed. 486p. 1994. 199.00 (*0-471-18595-7*) Wiley.

Martin, G., jt. auth. see Gasarch, W.

Martin, G. C. Martin Family, of Ireland, U. S. & Canada. 144p. 1993. reprint ed. pap. 25.00 (*0-8328-3716-4*); reprint ed. lib. bdg. 35.00 (*0-8328-3715-6*) Higginson Bk Co.

Martin, G. E. Foundations of Geometry & the Non-Euclidean Plane. (Undergraduate Texts in Mathematics Ser.). 509p. 1997. 49.95 (*0-387-90694-0*) Spr-Verlag.

— Transformation Geometry: An Introduction to Symmetry. (Undergraduate Texts in Mathematics Ser.). (Illus.). 240p. 1996. 39.95 (*0-387-90636-3*) Spr-Verlag.

Martin, G. E. & Zektzer, Andrew S. Two-Dimensional NMR Methods for Establishing Molecular Connectivity: A Chemist's Guide to Experiment Selection, Performance & Interpretation, 12. (Methods in Stereochemical Analysis Ser.). 508p. 1988. 145.00 (*0-471-18707-0*) Wiley.

Martin, G. H., ed. The Hustings Rolls of Deeds & Wills, 1252-1485: Guide to the Microfilm Edition. 1989. write for info. (*0-85964-213-5*) Chadwyck-Healey.

Martin, G. H. & Highfield, J. R. A History of Merton College. LC 97-34. (Illus.). 458p. 1998. text 80.00 (*0-19-920183-8*) OUP.

Martin, G. H., ed. & tr. see Knighton, Henry.

Martin, G. M., jt. ed. see Esser, Karl.

Martin, G. Neil. Human Neuropsychology. LC 97-11667. 514p. 1998. pap. text 61.00 (*0-13-802331-X*) P-H.

Martin, G. R., jt. auth. see Craine, J. F.

Martin, G. S., jt. auth. see Heap, N. W.

Martin, Gabe. Ooooh . . . Bit Your Tongue? LC 96-84084. (Borderline Cartoons Ser.: Vol. 1). (Illus.). 144p. (Orig.). 1996. pap. 6.95 (*0-9651930-0-4*) Borderline Pub.

***Martin, Gail.** Through the Eyes of a Child: Six Worship Services & Dialogues for Advent Through Epiphany. LC 99-37637. 82p. 1999. pap. 8.50 (*0-7880-1519-2*) CSS OH.

Martin, Gail G. Come, See the Wonder: Four Complete Christmas Services for Schools & Churches. Fittro, Pat, ed. LC 97-185269. 48p. (Orig.). 1997. pap. 3.99 (*0-7847-0701-4*, 08661) Standard Pub.

— Kneel Before the Babe: Four Christmas Services for Worship Planners. LC 96-10701. 68p. (Orig.). 1996. pap. 7.75 (*0-7880-0838-2*) CSS OH.

— We Give You Thanks: Three Services of Thanksgiving. 50p. 1996. pap. 9.50 (*1-57438-002-8*, 2692) Ed Ministries.

***Martin, Gail Gaymer.** Upon a Midnight Clear. (Love Inspired Ser.: Bk. 117). 2000. mass mkt. 4.50 (*0-373-87123-6*, 1-87123-5, Steeple Hill) Harlequin Bks.

Martin-Gaite, Carmen. From Fiction to Metafiction: Essays in Honor of Carmen Martin-Gaite. Servodidio, Mirella & Welles, Marcia L., eds. LC 82-61181. (Illus.). 223p. reprint ed. pap. 69.20 (*0-608-15536-5*, 202971600064) Bks Demand.

Martin, Gale D. Introductory Physical Geology: Laboratory Handouts, GEO 101L. 72p. 1993. spiral bd. 7.95 (*0-8403-8748-2*) Kendall-Hunt.

Martin, Galen, jt. auth. see Fry, Gerald W.

Martin, Garry. Reflective Expressions. 36p. (Orig.). pap. 4.98 (*0-9639912-1-3*) Southeast Pubns.

Martin, Garry & Pear, Joseph. Behavior Modification: What It Is & How to Do It. 6th ed. LC 97-52698. 444p. (C). 1998. pap. text 66.00 (*0-13-080742-7*) P-H.

Martin, Garry L. & Pear, Joseph. Behavior Modification & What It Is & How to Do It. 3rd ed. (Illus.). 576p. 1988. pap. text 42.33 (*0-13-072315-0*) P-H.

Martin, Gary. Art of Comic-Book Inking. (Illus.). 1997. pap. text 14.95 (*1-56971-258-1*) Dark Horse Comics.

— Competitive Karting. Date not set. pap. text 14.95 (*0-614-29805-9*) Martin Motorsports.

— Competitive Karting. rev. ed. Durning, Nancy & Harris, Margaret, eds. LC 80-83189. (Illus.). 144p. 1997. pap. 14.95 (*0-9605068-0-2*) Martin Motorsports.

— Euchre: How to Play & Win. LC 82-90179. 64p. (Orig.). 1982. pap. 4.95 (*0-9605068-1-0*) Martin Motorsports.

— Four-Cycle Kart Engines. rev. ed. (Illus.). 96p. 1986. pap. 14.95 (*0-9605068-2-9*) Martin Motorsports.

***Martin, Gary.** Go-Kart Racing: Just for Kids. (J). (gr. 1-8). 2000. pap. 14.95 (*0-9605068-5-3*) Martin Motorsports.

Martin, Gary. Karting Tools & Tips. (Illus.). 60p. 1992. pap. text 14.95 (*0-9605068-3-7*) Martin Motorsports.

— Welcome to the Professional World. Reyner, David B. & Massey-Reyner, Carole, eds. LC 96-76112. (Illus.). 100p. (Orig.). 1996. pap. 24.95 (*0-9650514-6-3*) Massey-Reyner.

Martin, Gary A. Lazy Way to Wealth, Power, Happiness & Romantic Love. (Illus.). 84p. (Orig.). 1995. pap. 16.95 (*0-9651523-0-8*) Liberty Pubs.

Martin, Gary E. & Zektzer, Andrew S. Two-Dimensional NMR Methods for Establishing Molecular Connectivity: A Chemist's Guide to Experiment Selection, Performance & Interpretation. LC 88-27705. (Methods in Stereochemical Analysis Ser.). (Illus.). xviii, 508p. 1988. 80.00 (*0-89573-703-5*, Wiley-VCH) Wiley.

Martin, Gary J. & Northwestern University (Evanston Ill.) Staff. The Doctor's Book of Symptoms & Treatments: Your Guide to Aches, Pains & Other Physical Problems : Illnesses, Medical Tests & Surgeries. LC 98-183700. 400 p. 1997. write for info. (*0-7853-2594-8*) Pubns Intl Ltd.

Martin, Gary W. Qbasic: A Short Course in Structured Programming. 195p. (C). 1994. pap. text 15.00 (*0-03-098845-4*) Dryden Pr.

— Theory & Practice of Good Programming: ExaMaster Computerized 5.25 IBM Test Bank for Turbo Pascal. (Illus.). 1995. write for info. (*0-15-592377-3*) OUP.

— Theory & Practice of Good Programming: Turbo Pascal. (Illus.). 416p. (C). 1992. pap. text, teacher ed. write for info. (*0-15-592376-5*) OUP.

— Turbo Pascal: Theory & Practice of Good Programming. (Illus.). 1008p. 1995. pap. text 63.95 (*0-19-510730-6*) OUP.

— Turbo Pascal: Theory & Practice of Good Programming. (Illus.). 1008p. (C). 1995. pap. text 56.95 (*0-15-592375-7*) OUP.

***Martin, Gay.** Basic College Mathematics. (C). 1999. text 75.00 (*0-13-084366-0*) P-H.

Martin-Gay. Beginning Albegra. 2nd ed. 1996. pap. text. write for info. (*0-13-568379-3*) Allyn.

— Beginning Algebra. 2nd ed. 1996. text, teacher ed. write for info. (*0-13-568460-9*) Allyn.

— Beginning & Intermediate Algebra. 1996. pap. text, teacher ed. write for info. (*0-13-381278-2*) Allyn.

Martin-Gay. Intermediate Algebra. LC 98-44925. 952p. 1999. pap. text 78.00 (*0-13-228800-1*) P-H.

— Intermediate Algebra. 2nd ed. 1996. pap. text, teacher ed. write for info. (*0-13-258013-6*) Allyn.

— Intermediate Algebra. 2nd ed. 1996. pap. text, teacher ed. write for info. (*0-13-258047-0*) Allyn.

Martin, Gay. Introductory Algebra. 352p. 1998. pap. text, student ed. 30.80 (*0-13-862525-5*) P-H.

***Martin, Gay.** Louisiana: A Guide to Unique Places. 5th ed. (Off the Beaten Path Ser.). (Illus.). 2000. pap. 12.95 (*0-7627-0805-0*) Globe Pequot.

Martin, Gay. Louisiana: Off the Beaten Path: A Guide to Unique Places. 4th ed. Kolb, Carolyn, ed. LC 98-45558. (Off the Beaten Path Ser.). (Illus.). 256p. 1998. pap. 12.95 (*0-7627-0268-0*) Globe Pequot.

***Martin-Gay.** Prealgebra. 2nd ed. 2000. 71.00 (*0-13-026179-3*) P-H.

***Martin, Gay, ed.** Intermediate Algebra. 256p. 1999. pap. text, student ed. 30.80 (*0-13-012869-4*) P-H.

Martin, Gay, ed. Intermediate Algebra. 3rd ed. 816p. 2000. 79.00 (*0-13-016631-6*) P-H.

Martin-Gay, K. Elayn. Beginning Algebra. 2nd ed. LC 96-22904. 678p. (C). 1996. 83.00 (*0-13-353665-3*) P-H.

— Interactive Math for Introductory Algebra. 1999. cd-rom 145.00 (*0-13-281214-2*) P-H.

— Intermediate Algebra. (C). 1999. text 66.00 (*0-13-013144-X*) P-H.

Martin-Gay, K. Elayn. Intermediate Algebra. 2nd ed. LC 96-35376. 760p. (C). 1996. 83.00 (*0-13-242462-2*) P-H.

— Intermediate Algebra: Review, Reference, & Practice. 784p. (C). 1999. pap. text 78.00 (*0-13-012861-9*) P-H.

Martin-Gay, K. Elayn. Introductory Algebra. LC 98-4121. 818p. 1998. pap. text 78.00 (*0-13-228834-6*) P-H.

— Introductory Algebra. LC 98-4121. 880p. (C). 1998. teacher ed. write for info. (*0-13-862467-4*) P-H.

— Introductory & Intermediate Algebra. LC 95-21970. 768p. 1995. 93.00 (*0-13-341504-X*) P-H.

***Martin-Gay, K. Elayn.** Introductory & Intermediate Algebra. LC 99-26184. 1164p. 1999. pap. text 85.20 (*0-13-085048-9*) S&S Trade.

Martin-Gay, K. Elayn. Prealgebra. 2nd ed. LC 97-3525. 710p. (C). 1997. pap. text 78.00 (*0-13-242470-3*) P-H.

***Martin-Gay, K. Elayn.** Prealgebra. 3rd ed. LC 00-35951. 800p. 2000. pap. 72.00 (*0-13-026037-1*) P-H.

Martin-Gay, K. Elayn, et al. Intermediate Algebra: A Graphing Approach. LC 96-53267. 816p. (C). 1997. 83.00 (*0-13-281495-1*) P-H.

***Martin, Gay N.** Alabama: Off the Beaten Path: A Guide to Unique Places. 4th ed. LC 99-43940. 240p. 2000. pap. 12.95 (*0-7627-0530-2*) Globe Pequot.

Martin, Gay N. Alabama's Historic Restaurants & Their Recipes. LC 98-38055. (Historic Restaurants & Their Recipes Ser.). (Illus.). 1998. 16.95 (*0-89587-220-X*) Blair.

Martin, Gene. Tidewater Bobber Fishing for Chinook Salmon. (Illus.). 32p. 1993. pap. 6.95 (*1-878175-54-8*) F Amato Pubns.

— Trail Dust. (Illus.). 60p. 1988. pap. 3.75 (*0-9606648-0-7*) Martin Assocs.

Martin, Genevieve A. Living Language Complete Course: German. (The Living Language Ser.). (GER.). 1998. 22.50 incl. audio (*0-609-60276-4*, 903596) Crown Pub Group.

— Living Language Complete Course: Italian. (ITA.). 1998. 22.50 incl. audio (*0-609-60271-3*, 903598) Crown Pub Group.

Martin, Geo. C., jt. auth. see Salisbury, John E.

Martin, Geoffrey, jt. ed. see Connolly, Philomena.

Martin, Geoffrey J. Ellsworth Huntington: His Life & Thought. LC 73-5682. (Illus.). xx, 315p. (C). 1973. lib. bdg. 39.50 (*0-208-01347-4*, Archon Bks) Shoe String.

Martin, Geoffrey J., ed. Geographers Vol. 10: Biobibliographical Studies, Vol. 15. (Illus.). 160p. 1994. 100.00 (*0-7201-2161-2*) Continuum.

Martin, Geoffrey J. & Armstrong, Patrick H., eds. Geographers Vol. 10: Biobibliographical Studies, Vol. 17. (Illus.). 128p. 1996. 99.50 (*0-7201-2285-6*) Continuum.

Martin, Geoffrey J. & James, Preston E. All Possible Worlds: A History of Geographical Ideas. 3rd ed. LC 92-43050. 608p. 1993. text 95.95 (*0-471-63414-X*) Wiley.

Martin, Geoffrey J., jt. auth. see James, Preston E.

Martin, Geoffrey J., jt. ed. see Armstrong, Patrick H.

Martin, Geoffrey T. A Bibliography of the Amarna Period: The Reigns of Akhenaten Smenkhkare, Tutankhamun & Ay. (Studies in Egyptology). 120p. (C). 1991. text 55.00 (*0-7103-0413-7*, A5621) Routledge.

— Hidden Tombs of Memphis. 1992. pap. 19.95 (*0-500-27666-8*, Pub. by Thames Hudson) Norton.

An Asterisk (*) at the beginning of an entry indicates that the title is appearing for the first time.

Martin, George. God's Word: Reading the Gospels with George Martin. LC 98-65864. 200p. 1998. pap. 8.95 (*0-87973-954-1*) Our Sunday Visitor.
— Polyominoes: A Guide to Puzzles & Problems in Tiling. (Spectrum Ser.). (Illus.). 172p. 1991. pap. text 14.95 (*0-88385-501-1*, POLY) Math Assn.
***Martin, George.** Praying with Jesus: What the Gospels Tell Us about How to Pray. LC BV229.M28 2000. 127p. 2000. pap. 11.95 (*0-8294-1476-2*) Loyola Pr.
Martin, George. Summer of Love: The Making of Sgt. Pepper. (Illus.). 176p. 1994. pap. 17.95 (*0-330-34210-X*, Pub. by Pan) Trans-Atl Phila.
— Twentieth Century Opera: A Guide. rev. ed. LC 99-27953. Orig. Title: The Companion to 20th Century Opera. 688p. 1998. reprint ed. pap. 25.00 (*0-87910-275-6*) Limelight Edns.
Martin, George, tr. from ITA. Italian Folktales. LC 80-11879. (Helen & Kurt Wolff Bk.). (Illus.). 800p. 1990. reprint ed. 27.95 (*0-15-145770-0*) Harcourt.
Martin, George & Burren, Michael. The Obelisk Conspiracy. 224p. 1976. 7.95 (*0-8065-0513-3*, Citadel Pr) Carol Pub Group.
Martin, George & Hornsby, Jeremy. All You Need Is Ears. (Illus.). 288p. 1994. pap. 14.95 (*0-312-11482-6*) St Martin.
Martin, George, jt. auth. see Freund, Peter.
***Martin, George A.** Farm Appliances: And How to Make Them. rev. ed. LC 99-30437. (Illus.). 208p. 1999. pap. 12.95 (*1-55821-888-2*) Lyons Pr.
Martin, George A. Fences, Gates & Bridges: A Practical Manual. LC 92-18206. (Illus.). 192p. 1992. reprint ed. pap. 12.50 (*0-911469-08-7*) A C Hood.
***Martin, George A.** Fences, Gates & Bridges: And How to Build Them. rev. ed. LC 99-30438. (Illus.). 192p. 1999. pap. 12.95 (*1-55821-889-0*) Lyons Pr.
Martin, George A. True Owners of the Soil. LC 90-80408. (Illus.). 92p. (Orig.). 1990. pap. 11.00 (*1-878515-13-6*) W S Dawson.
— Wausau in 1900. rev. ed. Janke, John & Johnson, Jane J., eds. (Illus.). 140p. 1987. 19.95 (*0-9617780-1-6*) Birch Lake Pr.
Martin, George C. Monmouth County the Sharkriver District, Monmouth County & Genealogies of Chambers, Corlies, Drummond, Morris, Potter, Shafto, Webley & White. (Illus.). 99p. 1997. reprint ed. pap. 16.00 (*0-8328-6058-1*) Higginson Bk Co.
Martin, George C., et al, eds. Olive Production Manual. LC 94-60033. (Illus.). 160p. 1994. pap. 32.00 (*1-879906-15-5*, 3353) ANR Pubns CA.
Martin, George C., et al. Castor Family of Pennsylvania, & the Castor Family of New York. (Illus.). 161p. 1994. reprint ed. pap. 26.00 (*0-8328-4306-7*); reprint ed. lib. bdg. 36.00 (*0-8328-4305-9*) Higginson Bk Co.
Martin, George E. Geometric Constructions. LC 97-22885. (Undergraduate Texts in Mathematics Ser.). (Illus.). 160p. (C). 1997. text 34.95 (*0-387-98276-0*) Spr-Verlag.
Martin, George H. Kinematics & Dynamics of Machines. 2nd ed. (Illus.). 492p. (C). 1982. 103.44 (*0-07-040657-X*) McGraw.
***Martin, George I.** The Golden Boy: A Biography of Jackie Jensen. (Illus.). 224p. 2000. pap. 17.95 (*0-914339-86-9*, Pub. by P E Randall Pub) U Pr of New Eng.
Martin, George R. R. The Armageddon Rag. LC 83-13597. 335p. 1983. 25.00 (*0-89366-150-3*) Ultramarine Pub.
— A Clash of Kings. LC 98-37954. (Song of Ice & Fire Ser.: Bk. 2). 768p. 1999. 25.95 (*0-553-10803-4*, Spectra) Bantam.
***Martin, George R. R.** A Clash of Kings. (Song of Ice & Fire Ser.). 1040p. 2000. mass mkt. 6.99 (*0-553-57990-8*) Bantam.
Martin, George R. R. A Game of Thrones. (Song of Ice & Fire Ser.: No. 1). 864p. 1997. mass mkt. 6.99 (*0-553-57340-3*) Bantam.
— Marked Cards. (Wild Cards Ser.: Vol. 2). 448p. (Orig.). 1994. mass mkt. 5.99 (*0-671-72212-3*) Baen Bks.
— Nightflyers. 304p. 1987. reprint ed. pap. 3.50 (*0-8125-4564-8*, Pub. by Tor Bks) St Martin.
Martin, George R. R., creator. Black Trump: Wild Cards. 1995. per. 5.99 (*0-671-87679-1*) Baen Bks.
Martin, George R. R. & Tuttle, Lisa. Windhaven. 1980. 25.00 (*0-671-25277-1*) Ultramarine Pub.
Martin, George R. R., ed. see Zelazny, Roger, et al.
Martin, George T., Jr. & Zald, Mayer M., eds. Social Welfare in Society. LC 81-3837. 614p. reprint ed. pap. 190.40 (*0-8357-6866-X*, 203556400095) Bks Demand.
Martin, George W. Aspects of Verdi. LC 93-13748. (Illus.). 304p. 1993. reprint ed. pap. 15.95 (*0-87910-172-5*) Limelight Edns.
— Causes & Conflicts: The Centennial History of the Association of the Bar of the City of New York, 1870-1970. 2nd ed. LC 96-53609. xiii, 279p. 1997. 17.00 (*0-8232-1735-3*) Fordham.
— The Lay of Threll: A Fantasy Told in Rhyme. 130p. (Orig.). 1996. pap. write for info. (*1-57502-162-5*, PO761) Morris Pubng.
— Let's Communicate: A Self-Help Program on Writing Letters & Memos. LC 71-109516. (Supervisory Management Ser.). 1970. pap. text. write for info. (*0-201-04500-1*) Addison-Wesley.
— Verdi: His Music, Life & Times. LC 92-23999. (Illus.). 522p. 1992. reprint ed. pap. 22.95 (*0-87910-160-1*) Limelight Edns.
— Verdi at the Golden Gate: Opera & San Francisco in the Gold Rush Years. LC 92-18674. 1993. 45.00 (*0-520-08123-4*, Pub. by U CA Pr) Cal Prin Full Svc.
— Verdi, His Music, Life & Times. LC 78-31783. (Music Reprint Ser.). 1979. reprint ed. 59.50 (*0-306-79549-3*) Da Capo.
Martin, George W., et al, eds. The Genera of the Myxomycetes. LC 83-5092. (Illus.). 198p. (C). 1983. text 42.95 (*0-87745-124-9*) U of Iowa Pr.
Martin, George W., jt. auth. see Morris, Jeffrey B.
Martin, Gerald, tr. see Asturias, Miguel Angel.
Martin, Gerald D. Determining Economic Damages. 1988. ring bd. 99.00 (*0-938065-41-6*) James Pub Santa Ana.
Martin, Gerry, jt. auth. see Brayne, Hugh.
***Martin, Gib.** Romans: God's Word for the Biblically-Inept. Richards, Larry, ed. (God's Word for the Biblically-Inept Ser.). 352p. 2000. pap. 16.95 (*1-892016-27-3*, Pub. by Starburst) Natl Bk Netwk.
Martin, Gib, jt. auth. see Richards, Lawrence O.
Martin, Gilbert. Reflections for Organ. 1997. pap. 9.95 (*0-634-00363-1*) H Leonard.
Martin, Gill. Aromatherapy: An Introductory Guide to Professional & Home Use. 120p. 1997. pap. 13.95 (*0-09-181276-3*) Trafalgar.
Martin, Gina & Tucker, Lois. American Painted Tinware: A Guide to Its Identification. (Illus.). xix, 156p. 1997. 42.50 (*1-928855-01-6*) HSEAD.
***Martin, Glen.** The Issachar Factor: Understanding Trends That Confront Your Church & Designing a Strategy for Success. 1999. pap. text 11.99 (*0-8054-2017-7*) Broadman.
Martin, Glen. Life Changing Messages for Busters. Spear, Cindy G., ed. 9p. 1997. ring bd. 44.95 incl. audio (*1-57052-087-9*) Chrch Grwth VA.
Martin, Glen & Gilbert, Larry. Team Decision-Making Inventory. Spear, Cindy G., ed. 4p. 1997. pap. 2.50 (*1-57052-082-8*) Chrch Grwth VA.
***Martin, Glen & Martin, Betty.** To Alaska on a Tractor: 9500 Miles in 126 Days! (Illus.). 149p. 2000. pap. 10.95 (*0-9677147-0-2*) Jericho Pr OH.
Martin, Glen & McIntosh, Gary L. Creating Community: Deeper Fellowship Through Small Group Ministry. LC 97-15829. 192p. 1997. pap. text 11.99 (*0-8054-6100-0*) Broadman.
— Finding Them, Keeping Them. 128p. (Orig.). 1991. pap. 8.99 (*0-8054-6051-9*, 4260-51) Broadman.
Martin, Glen & National Geographic Society Staff. National Geographic's Guide to Wildlife Watching: 100 of the Best Places in America to See Animals in Their Natural Habitats. LC 97-46750. 1998. 21.95 (*0-7922-7131-9*) Natl Geog.
Martin, Glen K., jt. auth. see Lonsbury-Martin, Brenda L.
Martin, Glen S. The Complete Guide to Starting or Evaluating a Singles Ministry, 3 cass., Set. 172p. 1993. ring bd. 99.95 incl. audio (*0-941005-93-3*) Chrch Grwth VA.
— God's Top Ten List: The Ten Commandments. (Guidelines for Living Ser.). 150p. 1999. pap. 9.99 (*0-8024-3097-X*) Moody.
— Single, but Not Alone. 144p. (Orig.). 1993. pap. 9.95 (*0-941005-94-1*) Chrch Grwth VA.
Martin, Glen S., jt. auth. see Wagner, E. Glenn.
Martin, Glen T. From Nietzsche to Wittgenstein: The Problem of Truth & Nihilism in the Modern World. (Literature & the Sciences of Man Ser.: Vol. 1). 420p. (C). 1989. text 60.00 (*0-8204-0917-0*) P Lang Pubng.
Martin, Gonzalez J. Historia de Escultura. 3rd ed. (SPA., Illus.). 326p. 1993. 100.00 (*84-249-3121-1*) Elliots Bks.
— Historia de la Arquitectura. 3rd ed. (SPA., Illus.). 1993. pap. 100.00 (*84-249-3117-3*) Elliots Bks.
— Historia de la Pintura. 3rd ed. (SPA., Illus.). 408p. 1993. 100.00 (*84-249-3119-X*) Elliots Bks.
— Historia del Arte, 2 vols. 6th ed. (SPA., Illus.). 1410p. 1993. pap. 200.00 (*84-249-1022-2*) Elliots Bks.
Martin, Gordon M. & Opitz, Joachim L., eds. The First 50 Years: The American Board of Physical Medicine & Rehabilitation. LC 97-71225. (Illus.). 75p. 1997. text 100.00 (*0-9657664-0-3*) ABPMR.
***Martin, Gordon U. A.** Encyclopedia of Asian Tennis: Who's Who in Asian Tennis. xx, 872p. 2000. 40.00 (*0-9702070-9-3*) Pan Asia Spt.
Martin, Gottfried. Arithmetic & Combinatorics: Kant & His Contemporaries. Wubnig, Judy, ed. & tr. by. from GER. LC 84-5476. (Philosophical Explorations Ser.). 272p. 1985. text 31.95 (*0-8093-1184-4*) S Ill U Pr.
— Arithmetik und Kombinatorik bei Kant. (GER.). 148p. (C). 1972. 70.00 (*3-11-003593-6*) De Gruyter.
— Kant's Metaphysics & Theory of Science. Lucas, P. G., tr. LC 73-15053. 218p. 1974. reprint ed. lib. bdg. 55.00 (*0-8371-7154-7*, MAKM, Greenwood Pr) Greenwood.
— Platons Ideenlehre. LC 72-81562. (C). 1973. 89.25 (*3-11-004135-9*) De Gruyter.
Martin, Gottfried & Loewisch, Dieter-Juergen, eds. Sachindex zu Kants Kritik der Reinen Vernunft. (C). 1967. 29.25 (*3-11-005179-6*) De Gruyter.
Martin, Grace B. An Oregon Schoolma'am: From Rimrocks to Tidelands. (Illus.). 144p. 1981. pap. 7.95 (*0-934784-25-6*) Calapooia Pubns.
— Oregon Schoolma'am Bk. 2: The Depression Years. (Illus.). 200p. pap. 7.95 (*0-934784-26-4*) Calapooia Pubns.
Martin, Graeme R., et al, eds. Advances in Serotonin Receptor Research: Molecular Biology, Signal Transduction & Therapeutics. LC 98-31188. (Annals of the New York Academy of Sciences Ser.: Vol. 861). 297p. 1998. 140.00 (*1-57331-170-7*); pap. 140.00 (*1-57331-171-5*) NY Acad Sci.
Martin, Graham. Birds by Night. (Illus.). 227p. 1990. text (*0-85661-059-3*, 784659) Poyser.
— Great Expectations. (Open Guides to Literature Ser.). 112p. 1985. 102.50 (*0-335-15089-6*); pap. 27.95 (*0-335-15080-2*) OpUniv Pr.
Martin, Graham, ed. see Hammond, Brean.
Martin, Graham, ed. see Morris, Pam.
Martin, Grant. Help! My Child Isn't Learning. 1995. 17.99 (*1-56179-402-3*) Focus Family.
— The Hyperactive Child. 218p. 1992. pap. 10.99 (*0-89693-068-8*, 6-1068, Victor Bks) Chariot Victor.
— The Hyperactive Child. rev. ed. LC 98-4024. 216p. 1998. 10.99 (*1-56476-720-5*, Victor Bks) Chariot Victor.
— When Good Things Become Addictions. 192p. 1991. pap. 8.99 (*0-89693-933-2*) Chariot Victor.
Martin, Grant L. Counseling for Family Violence & Abuse. (Resources for Christian Counseling Ser.). pap. 10.99 (*0-8499-3610-1*) Word Pub.
— Counseling for Family Violence & Abuse. (Resources for Christian Counseling Ser.: Vol. 6). 281p. 18.99 (*0-8499-0587-7*) Word Pub.
— Critical Problems in Children & Youth. (Contemporary Christian Counseling Ser.: Vol. 5). 18.99 (*0-8499-0886-8*) Word Pub.
Martin, Gregorio C., ed. Selected Proceedings of the Mountain Interstate Foreign Conference, 32nd. 415p. (Orig.). 1984. pap. text. write for info. (*0-918401-00-3*) U Wake Forest.
Martin, Gregory. Flemish School, 1600-1900. (National Gallery Publications). (Illus.). 1991. pap. 25.00 (*0-300-06140-4*) Yale U Pr.
— Mountain City. LC 99-56160. 224p. 2000. 23.00 (*0-86547-594-6*) N Point Pr.
Martin, Gregory, et al. The Love of the Soule. LC 78-320571. (English Recusant Literature, 1558-1640 Ser.). 400p. 1978. write for info. (*0-85967-448-7*) Scolar Pr.
***Martin, Guy.** Africa in World Politics: A Pan-African Perspective. LC 00-30616. 2000. pap. write for info. (*0-86543-858-7*) Africa World.
Martin, Guy & Laffort, Paul, eds. Odors & Deodorization in the Environment. LC 94-5422. 1994. 145.00 (*1-56081-666-X*, Wiley-VCH) Wiley.
Martin, Gyorgy. Hungarian Folk Dances. (Hungarian Folk Art Ser.). 134p. 1989. 24.00 (*963-13-2614-4*, Pub. by Corvina Bks) St Mut.
Martin, H. J. Notices Genealogical & Historical of the Martin Family of New England, Who Settled at Weymouth & Hingham in 1635, with Some Account of Their Descendants. 358p. 1989. reprint ed. pap. 53.50 (*0-8328-0859-8*); reprint ed. lib. bdg. 61.50 (*0-8328-0858-X*) Higginson Bk Co.
***Martin, Hall T.** LabVIEW for Telecom, Semiconductor, Automotive, Sound & Vibration & General Test & Measure. 272p. 2000. pap. 39.00 (*0-13-019963-X*) P-H.
Martin, Hank, ed. see Steele, Alexander.
Martin, Hans C., ed. Acidic Precipitation. 1987. text 622.50 (*1-55608-021-2*) Kluwer Academic.
Martin, Hans J. Zebra Finches. (Pet Care Ser.). 80p. 1985. pap. 6.95 (*0-8120-3497-X*) Barron.
***Martin, Hans J.** Zebra Finches. LC 99-89616. (Complete Pet Owner's Manual Ser.). (Illus.). 104p. 2000. pap. 6.95 (*0-7641-1040-3*) Barron.
Martin, Hans-Peter & Schuman, Harald. The Global Trap: An Attack on Democracy & Prosperity. Camiller, Patrick, tr. from GER. LC 97-28037. 1997. text 62.50 (*1-85649-529-9*, Pub. by Zed Books) St Martin.
***Martin, Hans-Peter, et al.** Everything You Need to Know Before You Call the Doctor: A Sound & Sensible Medical Reference for Men, Women, Children & Seniors. LC 00-22018. (Illus.). 960p. 2000. 29.98 (*1-57912-082-2*) Blck Dog & Leventhal.
Martin, Harold, jt. ed. see O'Brien, Robert.
Martin, Harold H. Atlanta & Environs Vol. 3: A Chronicle of Its People & Events: Years of Change & Challenge, 1940s-1970s. LC 86-16158. (Illus.). 632p. 1987. 54.95 (*0-8203-0913-3*) U of Ga Pr.
Martin, Harold H., jt. ed. see O'Brien, Robert.
Martin, Harry. Farm Exports: What's Happening to Our Foreign Markets. (Illus.). 168p. (Orig.). 1983. pap. 3.95 (*0-9611416-0-3*) RRN Bks.
Martin, Harry, jt. auth. see Modlin, Dan.
***Martin-Hart, Terry.** Avondale Estates, GA. (Images of America Ser.). (Illus.). 128p. 1999. pap. 18.99 (*0-7385-0346-0*) Arcadia Pubing.
Martin, Harvey J., III. The Secret Teachings of the Espiritistas: Unravelling the Enigma of Psychic Surgery. Butler, Kathryn R. & Fisher, Ann K., eds. Sepulveda, Seigfreid, tr. from SPA. LC 97-92715. (Illus.). 285p. 1998. 24.95 (*0-9660843-8-1*) Metamind Ent.
Martin, Hattie B., jt. auth. see Crabtree, Alfred B.
Martin, Heather S., jt. auth. see Warner, Caroline H.
Martin, Helen & Edwards, Sam. New Zealand Film, 1912-1995. (Illus.). 222p. 1998. pap. 29.95 (*0-19-558336-1*) OUP.
Martin, Helen M. Out of the Blue. (Orig.). 1996. pap. write for info. (*1-57553-357-X*) Watermrk Pr.
Martin, Helen R. Barnabetta. 1993. reprint ed. lib. bdg. 89.00 (*0-7812-5490-6*) Rprt Serv.
— Betrothal of Elypholate, & Other Tales of the Pennsylvania Dutch. LC 76-128739. (Short Story Index Reprint Ser.). (Illus.). 1977. 19.95 (*0-8369-3630-2*) Ayer.
— Yoked with a Lamb, & Other Stories. LC 76-152948. (Short Story Index Reprint Ser.). 1977. reprint ed. 21.95 (*0-8369-3807-0*) Ayer.
Martin, Helena F. On Some of Shakespeare's Female Characters. 5th ed. LC 75-111773. reprint ed. 49.50 (*0-404-04194-9*) AMS Pr.
Martin, Helene & Pelletier, Claire. Vocabulary of the Telephone. (ENG & FRE.). 39p. 1984. pap. 14.95 (*0-8288-9402-7*) Fr & Eur.
Martin, Helmut. Cult & Canon: The Origins & Development of State Maoism. LC 82-16811. Orig. Title: China Ohne Maoismus?. (Illus.). 245p. 1982. reprint ed. pap. 76.00 (*0-7837-9953-5*, 206068000006) Bks Demand.
Martin, Helmut & Kinkley, Jeffrey C., eds. Modern Chinese Writers: Self-Portrayals. LC 91-31578. (Studies on Modern China). 424p. (C). (gr. 13). 1992. 81.95 (*0-87332-816-7*, East Gate Bk); pap. 30.95 (*0-87332-817-5*, East Gate Bk) M E Sharpe.
Martin, Henri-Jean. The French Book: Religion, Absolutism, & Readership, 1585-1715. Saenger, Paul & Saenger, Nadine, trs. LC 95-49135. (Symposia in Comparative History Ser.). (Illus.). 136p. (C). 1996. text 35.00 (*0-8018-5179-3*); pap. text 13.95 (*0-8018-5419-9*) Johns Hopkins.
— The History & Power of Writing. (Illus.). xvi, 592p. 1995. pap. text 19.00 (*0-226-50836-6*) U Ch Pr.
— History & Power of Writing. LC 93-26718. 608p. 2000. 39.95 (*0-226-50835-8*) U Ch Pr.
— Print, Power, & People in Seventeenth Century France. Gerard, David, tr. LC 91-39016. (Illus.). 758p. 1993. reprint ed. 90.00 (*0-8108-2477-9*) Scarecrow.
Martin, Henry. Charlie Parker & Thematic Improvisation. LC 95-49636. (Studies in Jazz: No. 24). 176p. 1996. text 28.00 (*0-8108-3121-X*) Scarecrow.
Martin, Henry, et al, eds. Annual Review of Jazz Studies Vol. 8: Special Issue on Jazz Music Theory. 300p. 1997. 39.50 (*0-8108-3199-6*) Scarecrow.
Martin, Henry, jt. auth. see Baruchello, Gianfranco.
Martin, Henry, jt. auth. see Glanvill, John.
Martin, Henry, tr. see Manganelli, Giorgio.
Martin, Henry, tr. see Ortese, Anna M.
Martin, Henry, tr. see Zoja, Eva P.
Martin, Henry, tr. & intro. see Ortese, Anna M.
Martin, Henry B. The Polynesian Journal of Henry Byam Martin. Dodd, Edward, ed. (Illus.). 200p. 1981. 16.95 (*0-87577-060-6*, PEMP149, Peabody Museum) Peabody Essex Mus.
Martin, Herb. Places, Please - Musical. 106p. (gr. 10 up). 1978. pap. 5.95 (*0-87129-855-4*, P04) Dramatic Pub.
Martin, Herb & LearnQuick.com Staff. Networking Essentials: Accelerated MCSE Study Guide. LC 98-36279. (Accelerated MCSE Study Guides Ser.). (Illus.). 320p. 1998. pap. 24.99 (*0-07-067685-2*) McGraw.
— TCP/IP: Accelerated MCSE Study Guide. (Accelerated MCSE Study Guides Ser.). (Illus.). 320p. 1998. pap. 24.99 (*0-07-067686-0*) McGraw.
— Windows NT 4.0 Workstation: Accelerated MCSE Study Guide. LC 98-39246. (Accelerated MCSE Study Guides Ser.). (Illus.). 320p. 1998. pap. 24.99 (*0-07-067683-6*) McGraw.
— Windows NT 4.0/Server in the Enterprise: Accelerated MCSE Study Guide. LC 98-39247. (Accelerated MCSE Study Guides Ser.). (Illus.). 320p. 1998. pap. 24.99 (*0-07-067684-4*) McGraw.
Martin, Herbert W. & Stokes, Deborah E. Dunbar: Suns & Dominions. Shevin, David, ed. 72p. 1999. pap. 9.95 (*0-933087-53-5*) Bottom Dog Pr.
Martin, Holger. Heat Exchangers. rev. ed. 160p. 1992. 57.95 (*1-56032-119-9*) Hemisp Pub.
Martin, Hope. Integrating Mathematics Across the Curriculum. LC 96-76990. (Illus.). 256p. (Orig.). 1996. pap. 32.95 (*1-57517-063-9*, 1442) SkyLght.
— Multiple Intelligences in the Mathematics Classroom. LC 95-81187. (Illus.). 208p. (Orig.). 1996. pap. 25.95 (*1-57517-010-8*, 1421) SkyLght.
— What Year Am I? A Math Warmup a Day. (Illus.). ii, 199p. (J). (gr. 3-6). 1997. pap. text 27.95 (*0-9659993-0-0*) Hopes Bks.
***Martin, Hope & Martin, Jill.** Good Morning Math. (Illus.). 122p. (J). (gr. k-4). 1999. pap. 17.95 (*0-9659993-1-9*) Hopes Bks.
Martin, Horace C., ed. see Weidlinger, Robert.
Martin, Howard, jt. auth. see Childre, Doc Lew.
Martin, Howard, ed. see Childre, Doc Lew & Paddison, Sara.
Martin, Howard N. Myths & Folk-Tales of the Alabama-Coushatta Indians. (Illus.). 1976. 22.50 (*0-88426-052-6*) Encino Pr.
Martin, Hugh. The Abiding Presence. LC 83-11337. 256p. 1984. 4.95 (*0-310-28921-1*, 11331P) Zondervan.
— The Atonement: In Its Relations to the Covenant, the Priesthood, the Intercession of Our Lord. 327p. (C). 1998. reprint ed. pap. 11.95 (*1-884416-25-X*) A Press.
— Christ for Us. 261p. 1998. pap. 7.99 (*0-85151-741-2*) Banner of Truth.
— Great Christian Books. LC 71-142666. (Essay Index Reprint Ser.). 1977. reprint ed. 16.95 (*0-8369-2242-5*) Ayer.
— Jonah. (Geneva Series of Commentaries). 359p. 1995. reprint ed. 19.99 (*0-85151-115-5*) Banner of Truth.
— Shadow of Calvary. 1983. pap. 9.99 (*0-85151-373-5*) Banner of Truth.
Martin, Hugh, ed. Christian Social Reformers of the Nineteenth Century. LC 70-107725. (Essay Index Reprint Ser.). 1977. 20.95 (*0-8369-1526-7*) Ayer.
Martin, Hugh, ed. see Bernard of Clairvaux.
Martin, I., jt. auth. see Eysenck, H. J.
Martin, Ian, jt. auth. see Dummett, Ann.
Martin, Ian, jt. auth. see Grant, Lawrence.
Martin, Ian J. Accounting & Control in the Foreign Exchange Market. 2nd ed. 336p. 1993. boxed set 130.00 (*0-406-01362-4*, UK, MICHIE) LEXIS Pub.
Martin, Ian L., jt. auth. see Doble, Adam.
Martin, Ignacio San, see San Martin, Ignacio, ed.
Martin, Ilse, ed. see Smith, George M.
Martin, Ilse, tr. see Wust, Klaus, ed.
Martin, Ilse, tr. see Wust, Klaus, et al, eds.
Martin, Irene. Beach of Heaven: A History of Wahkiakum County. LC 97-29677. (Illus.). 224p. (Orig.). 1997. pap. 19.95 (*0-87422-156-0*) Wash St U Pr.
— Emerald Thorn. 367p. (Orig.). 1991. pap. 12.50 (*1-879366-20-7*) Hearthstone OK.
— Legacy & Testament: The Story of Columbia River Gillnetters. LC 94-14431. (Illus.). 184p. (Orig.). 1994. pap. 19.95 (*0-87422-109-9*) Wash St U Pr.

M

An Asterisk (*) at the beginning of an entry indicates that the title is appearing for the first time.

— Twentieth-Century Russian & East European Painting: The Thyssen-Bornemisza Collection. (Illus.). 1994. 175.00 (*0-302-00619-2*, Pub. by Zwemmer Bks) Intl Spec Bk.

Martin, Irene & Venables, Peter H., eds. Techniques in Psychophysiology. LC 79-42925. (Illus.). 711p. reprint ed. pap. 200.00 (*0-608-18147-1*, 203283400081) Bks Demand.

Martin, Irene, jt. auth. see Boskovits, Miklos.

Martin, Irene, ed. see Vergo, Peter.

Martin, Iris. From Couch to Corporation: Becoming a Successful Corporate Therapist. LC 96-4890. 224p. 1996. 45.00 (*0-471-11958-X*) Wiley.

***Martin, Isabel.** Reading Peter Reading. 2000. 54.95 (*1-85224-466-6*, Pub. by Bloodaxe Bks); pap. 24.95 (*1-85224-467-4*, Pub. by Bloodaxe Bks) Dufour.

Martin, Isabella, ed. see Chesnut, Mary Boykin Miller.

Martin, J. Benedict Arnold, Rev Hero. pap. 18.95 (*0-8147-5646-8*) NYU Pr.

Martin, J. Relativity & Gravitation in General. 350p. 1999. 99.00 (*981-02-3932-7*) World Scientific Pub.

Martin, J. & Hume-Rothery, W. Precipitation Hardening. LC 67-31505. (Selected Readings in Metallurgy Ser.). 1968. reprint ed. 113.00 (*0-08-203608-X*, Pub. by Pergamon Repr) Franklin.

Martin, J. & Trowbridge, T., eds. Platelet Heterogeneity. (Illus.). 286p. 1990. 182.00 (*0-387-19602-1*) Spr-Verlag.

Martin, J. & Wolfe, A. Frogs. LC 96-29879. (Illus.). 32p. (J). (gr. 2-5). 1997. 17.00 (*0-517-70905-8*, Pub. by Crown Bks Yng Read) Random.

Martin, J. A. Voice, Speech, & Language in the Child: Development & Disorder. (Disorders of Human Communication Ser.: Vol. 4). (Illus.). 230p. 1981. 56.95 (*0-387-81629-1*) Spr-Verlag.

Martin, J. C. & Westmoreland, S. D. Readings in the Social Sicences. 2nd ed. 168p. (C). 1990. text 32.00 (*0-536-57805-2*) Pearson Custom.

Martin, J. C., et al. Texas Forever!! The Paintings. (Illus.). 100p. (YA). (gr. 9 up). 1991. 39.95 (*0-9627589-0-6*) Oak Creek Pr.

Martin, J. Campbell. The Successful Engineer: Personal & Professional Skills - A Sourcebook. LC 92-30123. 200p. (C). 1993. 43.13 (*0-07-040725-8*) McGraw.

Martin, J. Colby, jt. auth. see Lee, Ronald R.

Martin, J. D., jt. ed. see Kasonde, J. M.

Martin, J. G. Sharing Music: An Introductory Guide to Music Education. (Academic Ser.). 260p. (C). 1987. pap. 16.95 (*0-910075-06-9*) Hardin-Simmons.

Martin, J. J. Bayesian Decision Problems & Makrov Chains. LC 74-32489. 216p. 1975. reprint ed. 23.50 (*0-88275-277-4*) Krieger.

Martin, J. L., et al, eds. Ultrafast Phenomena Eight: Proceedings of the Eight International Conference, Antibes Juan-les-Pins, France, June 8-12, 1992. LC 93-12330. (Chemical Physics Ser.: Vol. 55). 1993. 99.00 (*0-387-56475-6*) Spr-Verlag.

Martin, J. M. The Spirit-Filled Woman: 365 Daily Devotions. LC 97-36036. 1997. 14.99 (*0-88419-483-3*) Creation House.

Martin, J. M., jt. ed. see Mantoura, R. F.

Martin, J. Malcolm. Herrenrasse. LC 93-85730. 351p. 1993. 22.50 (*0-945319-01-0*) Spes Deo Pubns.

Martin, J. Michael & Martin, Mary E. The Bill Payer by Homefile: Monthly Bill Organizer. (Financial Advantage Ser.). (Illus.). 96p. (Orig.). 1995. pap. 19.95 (*0-9628718-5-0*) HOMEFILE.

— Financial Planning Organizer by Homefile: A Complete Home Filing System. (Financial Advantage Ser.). (Illus.). 71p. 1995. reprint ed. pap. 19.95 (*0-9628718-4-2*) HOMEFILE.

— Homefile: A Complete Home Filing System. (HOMEFILE Home Management Ser.). (Illus.). 71p. (Orig.). 1990. pap. 29.95 (*0-9628718-1-8*) HOMEFILE.

Martin, J. Michael & Martin, Sean M. Life after CDs: A Practical Guide to Safe Investing. (Financial Advantage Ser.). (Illus.). 308p. 1999. reprint ed. pap. 19.95 (*1-882584-51-1*) HOMEFILE.

Martin, J. Michael, jt. auth. see Martin, Mary E.

Martin, J. P., jt. ed. see Carson, M. L.

Martin, J. P., jt. ed. see Stahnke, T.

Martin, J. Paul. A Handbook on Self-Help: Human Rights Education. 28p. (Orig.). 1996. pap. 3.00 (*1-881482-05-7*) Columbia Ctr Stu Human Rts.

Martin, J. Paul & Rangaswamy, R., eds. Twenty-Five Human Rights Documents. rev. ed. 220p. 1994. pap. 10.00 (*1-881482-01-4*) Columbia Ctr Stu Human Rts.

Martin, J. Peter. Adirondack Golf Courses: Past & Present. (Illus.). 112p. (Orig.). 1987. pap. 14.95 (*0-9618820-0-X*) Adirondack Golf.

Martin, J. R. Factual Writing: Exploring & Challenging Social Reality. 101p. (C). 1995. pap. 34.00 (*0-7300-0345-0*, ECS806, Pub. by Deakin Univ) St Mut.

Martin, J. R. & Veel, Robert. Reading Science: Critical & Functional Perspectives on Discourses of Science. LC 97-21777. (Illus.). 384p. (C). 1998. 90.00 (*0-415-16789-2*); pap. 29.99 (*0-415-16790-6*) Routledge.

Martin, J. R., et al. Working with Functional Grammar. 320p. 1997. pap. text 19.95 (*0-340-65250-0*, Pub. by E A) OUP.

Martin, J. R., jt. auth. see Christie, Frances.

Martin, J. R., jt. auth. see Halliday, M. A.

Martin, J. R., jt. ed. see Smith, M. E.

Martin, J. S. Derivative Maths. 1996. 183.00 (*1-873446-38-1*, Pub. by IFR Pub) Am Educ Systs.

Martin, J. W. Precipitation Hardening. 2nd ed. LC 98-33489. 240p. 2000. text 80.00 (*0-7506-3885-0*) Buttrwrth-Heinemann.

— Religious Radicals in Tudor England. 256p. 1989. 55.00 (*1-85285-006-X*) Hambledon Press.

— Strong Materials. (Wykeham Science Ser.: No. 21). 124p. 1972. pap. 18.00 (*0-85109-260-8*) Taylor & Francis.

Martin, J. W. & Hull, R. A. Elementary Science of Metals. LC 73-75479. (Wykeham Science Ser.: No. 1). 148p. (C). 1974. 18.00 (*0-8448-1103-3*, Crane Russak) Taylor & Francis.

— Strong Materials. LC 72-189452. (Wykeham Science Ser.: No. 21). 124p. (C). 1972. 18.00 (*0-8448-1123-8*, Crane Russak) Taylor & Francis.

Martin, J. W., et al. Stability of Microstructure in Metallic Systems. 2nd ed. (Solid State Science Ser.). (Illus.). 442p. 1997. text 115.00 (*0-521-41160-2*); pap. text 47.95 (*0-521-42316-3*) Cambridge U Pr.

Martin, J. Wallis. A Likeness in Stone. LC 98-10286. 288p. 1998. text 22.95 (*0-312-18626-6*) St Martin.

— A Likeness in Stone. large type ed. LC 98-42813. 1999. 30.00 (*0-7862-1684-0*) Thorndike Pr.

— A Likeness in Stone. large type ed. (Ulverscroft Large Print Ser.). 448p. 1998. 29.99 (*0-7089-3895-7*) Ulverscroft.

Martin, Jack. Border Boss: Captain John R. Hughes, Texas Ranger. limited ed. LC 89-48043. (Illus.). 252p. 1990. reprint ed. 60.00 (*0-938349-51-1*) State House Pr.

— Border Boss: Captain John R. Hughes, Texas Ranger. LC 89-48043. (Illus.). 252p. 1990. reprint ed. pap. 14.95 (*0-938349-50-3*) State House Pr.

— The Construction & Understanding of Psychotherapeutic Change: Conversations, Memories, & Theories. LC 93-44505. (Counseling & Development Ser.). 160p. (C). 1994. pap. 16.95 (*0-8077-3336-9*); text 35.00 (*0-8077-3337-7*) Tchrs Coll.

***Martin, Jack.** Follow the Call. Turrentine, Jan, ed. (Illus.). 204p. 1999. pap. 8.99 (*1-56309-691-9*) Womans Mission Union.

Martin, Jack. Weekend Sentences: When Truth Begins. 22p. 1997. pap. 7.95 (*0-944754-43-0*) Pudding Hse Pubns.

Martin, Jack & Hiebert, Bryan A. Instructional Counseling: A Method for Counselors. LC 84-19647. (Illus.). 232p. (C). 1985. pap. 19.95 (*0-8229-5367-6*) U of Pittsburgh Pr.

Martin, Jack & Serich, Mary. Pre-Apprentice Training: Basic Skills. 2nd ed. (Illus.). 223p. (YA). (gr. 10 up). 1995. reprint ed. pap. text 27.95 (*0-9649530-0-5*) J Martin & Assocs.

Martin, Jack & Sugarman, Jeff. Models of Classroom Management: Principles, Applications, & Critical Perspectives. 2nd ed. 184p. (Orig.). (C). 1993. pap. text 19.95 (*1-55059-063-4*) Temeron Bks.

— The Psychology of Human Possibility & Constraint. LC 98-21999. (SUNY Series, Alternatives in Psychology). 192p. (C). 1999. text 59.50 (*0-7914-4123-7*); pap. text 19.95 (*0-7914-4124-5*) State U NY Pr.

Martin, Jack, jt. auth. see Hoshmand, Lisa.

Martin, Jack, jt. auth. see Hoshmand, Lisa L.

Martin, Jack K., jt. ed. see Tuch, Steven A.

Martin, Jacky, jt. auth. see Harding, Wendy.

Martin, Jacqueline & Sauter, Willmar. Understanding Theatre: Performance Analysis in Theory & Practice. (Stockholm Theatre Studies: No. 3). (Illus.). 271p. 1995. pap. 49.50 (*91-22-01679-1*) Coronet Bks.

Martin, Jacqueline B. Birdwashing Song: The Willow Tree Loon. LC 94-11787. (Illus.). (J). 1995. text. write for info. (*0-02-762442-0*) Macmillan.

— Bizzy Bones & the Lost Quilt. LC 87-13577. (Illus.). (J). (ps-3). 1988. 16.00 (*0-688-07407-3*) Lothrop.

— Button, Bucket, Sky. LC 97-16484. (Illus.). 32p. (J). (gr. k-3). 1998. 14.95 (*1-57505-244-X*, Carolrhoda) Lerner Pub.

— The Finest Horse in Town. LC 90-38596. (Illus.). 32p. (J). (gr. k-5). 1992. 15.00 (*0-06-024151-9*); lib. bdg. 14.89 (*0-06-024152-7*) HarpC Child Bks.

— Good Times on Grandfather Mountain. LC 91-17058. (Illus.). 32p. (J). (ps-1). 1992. 15.95 (*0-531-05977-4*) Orchard Bks Watts.

— Good Times on Grandfather Mountain. LC 91-17058. (Illus.). 32p. (J). (ps-1). 1997. pap. 6.95 (*0-531-07087-5*) Orchard Bks Watts.

— The Green Truck Garden Giveaway: A Neighborhood Story & Almanac. (Illus.). (J). (gr. k-4). 1997. 16.00 (*0-614-29060-0*) S&S Childrens.

— Higgins Bend Song & Dance. LC 95-52728. (Illus.). 32p. 1998. 16.00 (*0-395-67583-9*) HM.

— The Second Street Gardens. LC 94-10869. (Illus.). (J). 1995. text 16.00 (*0-02-762460-9*) S&S Bks Yung.

— Washing the Willow Tree Loon. LC 94-11787. (Illus.). 40p. (J). (ps-4). 1995. 16.00 (*0-689-80415-6*) Atheneum Yung Read.

Martin, Jacqueline Briggs. Grandmother Bryant's Pocket. LC 94-31309. (Illus.). 48p. (J). (ps-3). 1996. 14.95 (*0-395-68984-8*) HM.

***Martin, Jacqueline Briggs.** Grandmother Bryant's Pocket. LC 94-31309. (Illus.). 48p. (J). (gr. k-4). 2000. pap. 5.95 (*0-618-03309-2*) HM.

— Grandmother Bryant's Pocket. (Illus.). (J). 2000. 11.40 (*0-606-18209-8*) Turtleback.

Martin, Jacqueline Briggs. The Green Truck Garden Giveaway: A Neighborhood Story & Almanac. LC 94-10869. (Illus.). 32p. (J). (gr. k-4). 1997. per. 16.00 (*0-689-80498-9*) S&S Childrens.

***Martin, Jacqueline Briggs.** Snowflake Bentley. LC 97-12458. (Illus.). 32p. (J). (ps-3). 1998. 16.00 (*0-395-86162-4*) HM.

Martin, Jaime. Diccionario de Expresiones Malsonantes del Espanol. 2nd ed. (SPA.). 370p. 1974. pap. 17.95 (*0-8288-5978-7*, S31400) Fr & Eur.

***Martin, James.** After the Internet: Alien Intelligence. 2000. 27.95 (*0-89526-280-0*) Regnery Pub.

Martin, James. Boa Constrictors. (Illus.). 48p. (J). (gr. 3-7). 1995. lib. bdg. 19.00 (*0-516-35297-0*) Childrens.

— Bobby. (C). 1990. pap. 35.00 (*0-85305-304-9*, Pub. by Arthur James) St Mut.

***Martin, James.** Calgary: Secrets of the City. 196p. 2000. pap. 12.95 (*1-55152-076-1*) Arsenal Pulp.

Martin, James. Cybercorp: The Successful Corporation of the Future . . . 256p. 1996. 27.95 (*0-8144-0351-4*) AMACOM.

— Database Analysis & Design. 1989. 50.00 (*0-13-199688-6*) P-H.

— Design of Man-Computer Dialogues. (Illus.). 496p. 1973. pap. text 60.00 (*0-13-201251-0*) P-H.

— Frogs. LC 96-29879. (Illus.). 32p. (J). (gr. 2-6). 1997. lib. bdg. 18.99 (*0-517-70906-6*) Crown Pub Group.

***Martin, James.** Future Developments in Telecommunications. 3rd ed. 2001. 51.40 (*0-13-345844-X*, Prentice Hall) P-H.

Martin, James. The Great Transition: Using the Seven Disciplines of Enterprise Engineering to Align People, Technology, & Strategy. LC 95-35180. 432p. 1995. 34.95 (*0-8144-0315-8*) AMACOM.

— How Can I Find God? The Famous & the Not-So-Famous Consider the Quintessential Question. LC 97-7900. 224p. (Orig.). 1997. pap. 13.00 (*0-7648-0090-6*, Liguori Triumph) Liguori Pubns.

***Martin, James.** In Good Company: The Fast Track from the Corporate World to Poverty, Chastity & Obedience. 216p. 2000. pap. 15.95 (*1-58051-081-7*) Sheed & Ward WI.

Martin, James. Information Engineering, Bk. 1. 178p. 1989. 94.00 (*0-13-464462-X*) P-H.

— Information Engineering, Bk. 2. 1989. text 94.00 (*0-13-464885-4*) P-H.

— Information Engineering: Design & Construction, Bk. 3. 625p. 1989. 70.60 (*0-13-465501-X*) P-H.

— It's My Belief. 96p. 1993. pap. 35.00 (*0-7152-0648-6*, Pub. by St Andrew) St Mut.

— A Man's Life. LC 94-27683. 150p. 1995. pap. 5.95 (*0-9642188-9-5*) Four Seasns.

— Masters of Disguise: A Natural History of Chameleons. (Illus.). 192p. 1992. 24.95 (*0-8160-2618-1*) Facts on File.

— Non-Subscription to Texas Workers Comp: Lawyer's Edition. 110.00 (*0-685-52373-X*, B10) Sterling TX.

— Restoration. 148p. (Orig.). 1996. pap. 10.00 (*1-57502-318-0*, P01080) Morris Pubng.

***Martin, James.** Restoration: It's Your Time. 50p. 1999. pap. 6.00 (*0-7392-0337-1*, PO3508) Morris Pubng.

Martin, James. The Road to the Aisle. 1993. pap. 22.00 (*0-7152-0375-4*, Pub. by St Andrew) St Mut.

— The Spitting Cobras of Africa. (Illus.). 48p. (J). (gr. 3-7). 1995. 19.00 (*0-516-35239-3*) Childrens.

— The Telematic Society: A Challenge for Tomorrow. (Illus.). 256p. (C). 1981. 35.95 (*0-13-902460-3*) P-H.

— Teleprocessing Network Organization. 1969. 38.00 (*0-13-902452-2*) P-H.

— This Our Exile: A Spiritual Journey with the Refugees in East Africa. LC 98-43648. (Illus.). 224p. 1999. pap. 16.00 (*1-57075-250-8*) Orbis Bks.

— William Barclay: A Personal Memoir. 1985. pap. 3.75 (*0-7152-0579-X*) Outlook.

Martin, James, ed. It's My Belief. 96p. (C). 1991. pap. text 45.00 (*86-15-30648-6*, Pub. by St Andrew) St Mut.

Martin, James, photos by. North Cascades Crest: Notes & Images from America's Alps. LC 98-41006. (Illus.). 128p. 1999. pap. 19.95 (*1-57061-140-8*) Sasquatch Bks.

Martin, James & Grant, Simon. Telecommunications & the Computer. 3rd ed. 640p. 1990. text 86.00 (*0-13-902644-4*) P-H.

Martin, James & Keaveny, Timothy J. Readings & Cases in Labor Relations & Collective Bargaining. Allen, Robert, ed. LC 84-14484. 512p. 1985. pap. text 22.36 (*0-201-12353-3*) Addison-Wesley.

***Martin, James & Kohler, Paula.** Transition from School to Life: A Complete University Course for Special Educators. 1999. ring bd. 195.00 (*0-86586-344-X*) Coun Exc Child.

Martin, James & Leben, Joe. Client - Server Databases: Enterprise Computing. LC 95-10646. (C). 1995. text 41.20 (*0-13-305160-9*) P-H.

— DECnet Phase V: An OSI Implementation Networking. (Illus.). 572p. 1991. pap. text 62.95 (*1-55558-076-9*, EY-H882E-DP, Digital DEC) Buttrwrth-Heinemann.

Martin, James & Leben, Joe. TCP/IP Networking: Architecture, Administration & Programming. 400p. 1994. 45.80 (*0-13-642232-2*) P-H.

Martin, James & Leben, Joseph. Middleware Architectures for Client/Server Computing. (C). 2001. text 48.00 (*0-13-238551-1*, Prentice Hall) P-H.

Martin, James & Martin, Ramela. Out of Darkness: Ramela's Story. LC 97-71582. (Illus.). 224p. (Orig.). 1997. pap. 16.95 (*1-882897-12-9*) Lost Coast.

Martin, James & McClure, Carma L. Structured Techniques: A Basis for CASE. rev. ed. (Illus.). 816p. (C). 1987. 93.00 (*0-13-854936-2*) P-H.

Martin, James & Norman, Adrian R. Computerized Society. (Automatic Computation Ser.). 1970. pap. text 28.67 (*0-13-165977-4*) P-H.

Martin, James & Odell, James J. Object-Oriented Methods. 2nd ed. LC 97-39040. 432p. (C). 1997. 68.00 (*0-13-905597-5*) P-H.

— Principles of Object-Oriented Analysis & Design. 412p. 1992. 46.60 (*0-13-720871-5*) P-H.

Martin, James, et al. Enterprise Networking: Strategies & Transport Protocols. 544p. (C). 1995. 44.20 (*0-13-305186-2*) P-H.

Martin, James, et al. Local Area Networks: Architectures & Implementations. 2nd ed. LC 93-37562. (Illus.). 586p. 1993. 85.00 (*0-13-533035-1*, Pub. by P-H) S&S Trade.

— Merging Colleges for Mutual Growth: A New Strategy for Academic Managers. LC 93-8380. 296p. (C). 1993. text 38.00 (*0-8018-4666-8*) Johns Hopkins.

— VSAM: Services & Programming Techniques. (Illus.). 432p. (C). 1986. text 59.20 (*0-13-944174-3*) P-H.

Martin, James, jt. auth. see Arden Group Staff.

Martin, James, jt. auth. see Twight, Mark.

Martin, James A., Jr. Beauty & Holiness: The Dialogue Between Aesthetics & Religion. (Illus.). 269p. 1990. text 37.50 (*0-691-07357-0*, Pub. by Princeton U Pr) Cal Prin Full Svc.

Martin, James A. Conflict of Law: Cases & Materials. 2nd ed. LC 83-82692. 720p. (C). 1984. 35.00 (*0-316-54856-1*) Little.

— Empirical Philosophies of Religion. LC 78-111850. (Essay Index Reprint Ser.). 1977. 19.95 (*0-8369-1618-2*) Ayer.

***Martin, James A., et al.** The Military Family: A Practice Guide for Human Service Providers. LC 99-55036. 304p. 2000. 59.95 (*0-275-96540-6*) Greenwood.

Martin, James A. Perspectives on Conflict of Laws: Choice of Law. 1980. 15.00 (*0-316-54853-7*, Aspen Law & Bus) Aspen Pub.

Martin, James A., et al, eds. The Gulf War & Mental Health: A Comprehensive Guide. LC 96-2200. 232p. 1996. 55.00 (*0-275-95631-8*, Praeger Pubs) Greenwood.

Martin, James A., jt. auth. see Landers, Jonathan M.

Martin, James A., Jr., jt. ed. see Wohlgelernter, Maurice.

Martin, James C. & Martin, Robert S. Maps of Texas & the Southwest, 1513-1900. (Illus.). 190p. 1998. 39.95 (*0-87611-169-X*) Tex St Hist Assn.

Martin, James C., jt. auth. see Kennedy, Raoul D.

Martin, James C., jt. auth. see Martin, Robert S.

Martin, James D. Davidson's Introductory Hebrew Grammar. 224p. 1993. text 29.95 (*0-567-09642-4*, Pub. by T & T Clark) Bks Intl VA.

Martin, James D. Proverbs. (Old Testament Guides Ser.: No. 16). 104p. 1995. pap. 12.50 (*1-85075-752-6*, Pub. by Sheffield Acad) CUP Services.

Martin, James E. And Then You Die: A Novel. 224p. 1993. mass mkt. 4.99 (*0-380-71696-8*, Avon Bks) Morrow Avon.

— A Fine & Private Place. 256p. 1995. mass mkt. 4.99 (*0-380-71697-6*, Avon Bks) Morrow Avon.

— The Flip Side of Life. 256p. 1991. mass mkt. 3.99 (*0-380-71407-8*, Avon Bks) Morrow Avon.

— The Mercy Trap. 256p. 1990. pap. 3.95 (*0-380-71041-2*, Avon Bks) Morrow Avon.

— The Physics of Radiation Protection. LC 99-38913. 832p. 2000. text 185.00 (*0-471-35373-6*, Wiley-Interscience) Wiley.

— Towards a Theory of Text for Contrastive Rhetoric: An Introduction to Issues of Text for Students & Practitioners of Contrastive Rhetoric. LC 91-40824. (American University Studies: Linguistics: Ser. XIII, Vol. 19). 221p. (C). 1992. text 38.95 (*0-8204-1855-2*) P Lang Pubng.

— Two-Tier Compensation Structures: Their Impact on Unions, Employers, & Employees. LC 89-48881. 280p. 1990. text 35.00 (*0-88099-087-2*); pap. text 17.00 (*0-88099-088-0*) W E Upjohn.

Martin, James E. & Samels, James E. First among Equals: The Role of the Chief Academic Officer. LC 97-11281. 419p. 1997. text 39.95 (*0-8018-5612-4*) Johns Hopkins.

***Martin, James E., et al.** Choosing Education Goals, Set. (ChoiceMaker Self-Determination Ser.). 156p. 2000. per. 95.00 incl. VHS (*1-57035-263-1*, 88EDU) Sopris.

Martin, James E., et al. Self-Directed IEP: Student Workbook, Consumable Workbook, 25 bks. 2nd ed. (ChoiceMaker Self-Determination Curriculum Ser.). (Illus.). 32p. 1996. pap., student ed., wbk. ed. 45.00 (*1-57035-107-4*, 88STU) Sopris.

— Self-Directed IEP: Teacher's Manual. 2nd ed. (ChoiceMaker Self-Determination Curriculum Ser.). (Illus.). 152p. 1996. pap. text, teacher ed., wbk. ed. 120.00 incl. VHS (*1-57035-105-8*, C88DIR) Sopris.

Martin, James G. Ancient Star. (Orig.). 1990. pap. 4.95 (*0-9627587-0-1*) Martin CA.

— The Tolerant Personality. LC 64-15881. (Wayne State University Studies - Sociology: No. 15). (Illus.). 182p. reprint ed. pap. 56.50 (*0-7837-3599-5*, 204346400009) Bks Demand.

Martin, James J. An American Adventure in Bookburning in the Style of 1918. LC 89-3246. 1988. 8.50 (*0-87926-024-6*) R Myles.

— American Liberalism & World Politics, 1931-1941, 2 vol. set. 1963. 35.00 (*0-8159-5005-5*) Devin.

— Charles A. Beard: A Tribute. 1984. lib. bdg. 250.00 (*0-87700-602-4*) Revisionist Pr.

— The Man Who Invented Genocide: The Public Career & Consequences of Raphael Lemkin. LC 84-6682. 360p. 1984. 13.95 (*0-939484-17-X*, 0954, Inst Hist Rev); pap. 7.98 (*0-939484-14-5*, 0953, Inst Hist Rev) Legion Survival.

— Men Against the State: The Expositors of Individualist Anarchism in America, 1827-1908. (Illus.). 1970. pap. 2.50 (*0-87926-006-8*) R Myles.

— Revisionist Viewpoints: Essays in a Dissident Historical Tradition. LC 75-187779. 1977. pap. 5.95 (*0-87926-008-4*) R Myles.

— The Saga of Hog Island & Other Essays in Inconvenient History. LC 76-62654. 1977. pap. 6.95 (*0-87926-021-1*) R Myles.

Martin, James J., ed. see Eltzbacher, Paul.

Martin, James J., jt. ed. see Liggio, Leonard P.

Martin, James J., ed. see Stirner, Max.

Martin, James K. Benedict Arnold, Revolutionary Hero: An American Warrior Reconsidered. LC 97-4631. (Illus.). 540p. 1997. text 35.00 (*0-8147-5560-7*) NYU Pr.

— Concise History of America & Its People. 2nd ed. (C). 1999. pap. text. write for info. (*0-321-00307-1*) Addson-Wesley Educ.

— Concise History of America & Its People, Vol. 1. 2nd ed. (C). 1999. pap. text. write for info. (*0-321-00309-8*) Addson-Wesley Educ.

— Concise History of America & Its People, Vol. 2. 2nd ed. (C). 1999. pap. text. write for info. (*0-321-00311-X*) Addison-Wesley.

— Men in Rebellion: Higher Governmental Leaders & the

An Asterisk (*) at the beginning of an entry indicates that the title is appearing for the first time.

Coming of the American Revolution. LC 72-14142. 271p. reprint ed. pap. 84.10 (*0-7837-5675-5*, 2059102000005) Bks Demand.

Martin, James K., ed. Human Dimensions of Nation Making: Essays on Colonial & Revolutionary America. LC 75-30821. 378p. 1976. 19.95 (*0-87020-158-1*) State Hist Soc Wis.

***Martin, James K., ed.** Ordinary Courage: The Revolutionary War Adventures of Joseph Plumb Martin. 2nd ed. (Illus.). 192p. (C). 1999. pap. text 16.50 (*1-881089-47-9*) Brandywine Press.

Martin, James K., ed. Ordinary Courage: The Revolutionary War Adventures of Private Joseph Plumb Martin. (Illus.). 192p. (C). 1993. pap. text 16.50 (*1-881089-12-6*) Brandywine Press.

Martin, James K. & Lender, Mark E. A Respectable Army: The Military Origins of the Republic, 1763-1789. Franklin, John H. & Eisenstadt, A. S., eds. LC 81-173990. (American History Ser.). (Illus.). 256p. (C). 1982. pap. text 13.95 (*0-88295-812-7*) Harlan Davidson.

Martin, James K. & Stubaus, Karen R. American Revolution: Whose Revolution? LC 76-18740. (American Problem Studies). 158p. 1977. reprint ed. pap. 11.50 (*0-88275-397-5*) Krieger.

Martin, James K., et al. America & Its Peoples, Vol. 2. 3rd ed. LC 96-14563. Vol. 2. 592p. (C). 1997. pap. 60.00 (*0-673-98075-8*) Addson-Wesley Educ.

— CONCISE HIST AMER ITS V2, 2 vols., Vol. II. 2nd ed. LC 92-28837. (C). 1995. text 29.06 (*0-673-46782-1*) Addson-Wesley Educ.

— Concise History America ITS, 2 vols., Vol. I. 2nd ed. LC 92-28837. (C). 1995. text 29.06 (*0-673-46781-3*) Addson-Wesley Educ.

— A Concise History of America & Its People. LC 94-20138. (C). 1995. text 30.00 (*0-673-46780-5*) HarperTrade.

Martin, James K., jt. auth. see Lender, Mark E.

Martin-James, Kathleen. Building Beavers. LC 99-18068. 32p. (J). (gr. k-2). 1999. 21.27 (*0-8225-3628-5*, Lerner Publctns) Lerner Pub.

— Building Beavers. LC 99-18068. (Pull Ahead Bks.). 32p. (J). (gr. k-2). 1999. pap. 6.95 (*0-8225-3632-3*, Lerner Publctns) Lerner Pub.

— Sturdy Turtles. LC 99-11364. (Pull Ahead Bks). 32p. (J). (gr. k-2). 1999. pap. 6.95 (*0-8225-3631-5*, Lerner Publctns) Lerner Pub.

— Sturdy Turtles. LC 99-11364. (Pull Ahead Ser.). 32p. (J). (gr. k-2). 1999. 21.27 (*0-8225-3627-7*, Lerner Publctns) Lerner Pub.

Martin, James L., et al. Hydrodynamics & Transport for Water Quality Modeling. LC 96-24297. 768p. 1999. 89.95 (*0-87371-612-4*) Lewis Pubs.

***Martin, James M.** Restoration: New Evidences, Israel's Downfall & Consequent Struggling for Renewal Provides Imp. 1999. pap. 10.00 (*0-9676111-0-5*) J M Martin Pubs.

Martin, James N. Systems Engineering Guidebook: A Process for Developing Systems & Products. LC 96-36435. (Systems Engineering Ser.). 304p. 1996. boxed set 74.95 (*0-8493-7837-0*) CRC Pr.

Martin, James R. English Text: System & Structure. LC 92-19652. xiv, 620p. 1992. 133.00 (*1-55619-115-4*); pap. 34.95 (*1-55619-485-4*) J Benjamins Pubng Co.

Martin, James T. Active Mind in Aristotle's Psychology. LC 96-20802. (American University Studies: Series V, Vol. 154). 1997. pap. write for info. (*0-8204-2299-1*) P Lang Pubng.

— Immersed: God's Desire for Our Lives. 242p. 1999. pap. write for info. (*0-7392-0175-1*, PO3136) Morris Pubng.

Martin, James T., ed. Philosophies of Being & Mind: Ancient & Medieval. LC 91-27076. 240p. 1992. 50.00 (*0-88206-076-7*) Caravan Bks.

Martin, James W., et al. Surface Mining Equipment. LC 82-81951. (Illus.). 450p. 1982. 37.95 (*0-9609060-0-2*) Martin Consult.

Martin, Jan. The Dynamics of Personal Energy: Exploring the Unseen Dimensions of Self-Esteem & Communication. 2nd ed. (Illus.). 130p. (Orig.). 1995. write for info. (*0-9647055-0-8*) Energy Centre.

Martin, Jan & Gross, Richard. The Dynamics of Personal Energy. (Illus.). 49p. 1996. pap., wbk. ed. 8.95 (*0-9647055-1-6*) Energy Centre.

Martin, Jan, ed. see Robinson, Jan.

Martin, Jana, jt. auth. see Thibodeau, Michael.

Martin, Jane. Coup/Clucks. 1984. pap. 5.25 (*0-8222-0245-X*) Dramatists Play.

— Jane Martin: Collected Plays, 1980-1995. (Contemporary Playwrights Ser.). 320p. 1995. pap. 19.95 (*1-880399-20-2*) Smith & Kraus.

— Jane Martin, 1980-1995: Collected Plays. LC 95-30492. (Contemporary Playwrights Ser.). 320p. 1995. 35.00 (*1-57525-022-5*) Smith & Kraus.

— Women & the Politics of Schooling in Victorian & Edwardian England. LC 97-45897. (Women, Power, & Politics Ser.). 192p. 1998. 75.00 (*0-7185-0053-9*) Bks Intl VA.

Martin, Jane, ed. Funny Dogs. LC 95-60046. (Illus.). 80p. 1995. reprint ed. 15.95 (*0-941807-12-6*) Welcome Enterprises.

— Milestones in Development: A Cumulative Index to Industrial Development, Site Selection Handbook & Related Publications Covering a Quarter-Century of Professional Contribution. 316p. 1981. 11.95 (*0-910436-16-9*) Conway Data.

Martin, Jane D. & Knoohuizen, Nancy. Marketing Basics for Designers: A Sourcebook of Strategies & Ideas. LC 95-13176. 272p. 1995. 45.00 (*0-471-11871-0*) Wiley.

Martin, Jane D. & Rumsey, Barbara M. Name! That Dog. LC 96-94584. (Illus.). 65p. (Orig.). 1996. pap. write for info. (*0-9652923-0-4*) M Rumsey.

Martin, Jane K. School Based Clinics That Work. (Illus.). 73p. (Orig.). (C). 1995. pap. text 20.00 (*0-7881-1885-4*) DIANE Pub.

Martin, Jane R. Changing the Educational Landscape: Philosophy, Women, & Curriculum. 256p. (C). (gr. 13). 1993. pap. 22.99 (*0-415-90795-0*, B0664) Routledge.

— The Schoolhome: Rethinking Schools for Changing Families. 240p. (C). 1992. text 24.95 (*0-674-79265-3*) HUP.

— The Schoolhome: Rethinking Schools for Changing Families. 248p. (C). 1995. pap. text 16.50 (*0-674-79266-1*) HUP.

Martin, Jane R. & Marx, Patricia. Now Everybody Really Hates Me. LC 92-13075. (Illus.). 32p. (J). (ps-3). 1993. 14.95 (*0-06-021293-4*) HarpC Child Bks.

— Now Everybody Really Hates Me. LC 92-13075. (Trophy Picture Bk.). (Illus.). 32p. (J). (gr. k-3). 1996. pap. 6.95 (*0-06-443440-0*, HarpTrophy) HarpC Child Bks.

— Now I Will Never Leave the Dinner Table. LC 94-3209. (Illus.). 32p. (J). (ps-3). 1996. lib. bdg. 14.89 (*0-06-024795-9*) HarpC Child Bks.

— Now I Will Never Leave the Dinner Table. 80th ed. LC 94-3209. (Illus.). 32p. (J). (ps-3). 1996. 14.95 (*0-06-024794-0*) HarpC Child Bks.

***Martin, Jane Roland.** Coming of Age in Academe: Rekindling Women's Hopes & Reforming Academy. LC 99-20656. 240p. (C). 1999. text. write for info. (*0-415-92487-1*) Routledge.

Martin, Jane Roland. Coming of Age in Academy: Rekindling Women's Hopes & Reforming the Academy. LC 99-20656. 1999. pap. 18.99 (*0-415-92488-X*) Routledge.

Martin, Janet & Backhouse, Jane. Good Looking, Easy Swallowing: Creative Catering for Modified Texture Diets. (Illus.). 389p. 1994. text 45.00 (*1-875412-02-6*) Buttrwrth-Heinemann.

Martin, Janet & Todnem, Allen. Cream & Bread. LC 84-60814. (Illus.). 124p. 1984. pap. 8.95 (*0-9613437-0-2*) Redbird Prods.

Martin, Janet L. Helgg Hanson Hotflash Handbook. Nelson, Suzann, ed. LC 97-94290. (Illus.). 56p. 1997. 4.95 (*1-886627-04-5*) Redbird Prods.

— Medieval Russia, 980-1584. (Medieval Textbooks Ser.). (Illus.). 477p. (C). 1996. text 69.95 (*0-521-36276-8*); pap. text 22.95 (*0-521-36832-4*) Cambridge U Pr.

— Shirley Holmquist & Aunt Wilma, Who Dunit? Pearson, Eunice W., ed. (Illus.). 120p. (Orig.). 1988. pap. 7.95 (*0-9613437-2-9*, Martin Hse Pubns) Redbird Prods.

Martin, Janet L. & Lorenz, Ilene L. Our Beloved Sweden: Food, Flowers, Festivals & Faith. 1996. pap. 17.95 (*1-886627-02-9*, Sentel) Redbird Prods.

Martin, Janet L. & Nelson, Suzann J. Cream Peas on Toast: Comfort Food for Norwegian Lutheran Farm Kids (& Others) (Illus.). 1994. 10.95 (*0-9613437-9-6*, Caragana Pr) Redbird Prods.

— Growing up Lutheran: What Does This Mean? LC 97-69403. (Illus.). 232p. 1997. pap. 12.95 (*1-886627-05-3*) Redbird Prods.

— They Glorified Mary: We Glorified Rice. 170p. 1994. pap. 6.95 (*0-9613437-4-5*, Caragana Pr) Redbird Prods.

— They Had Stores . . . We Had Chores. 274p. 1995. pap. 7.95 (*0-9613437-7-X*) Redbird Prods.

— Uffda, But Those Clip-Ons Hurt Them. LC 96-97040. (Illus.). 96p. 1996. 4.95 (*1-886627-03-7*) Redbird Prods.

Martin, Janet L. & Todnem, Allen. Second Helpings of Cream & Bread. Pearson, Eunice W., ed. (Illus.). (Orig.). 1986. pap. 8.95 (*0-9613437-1-0*) Redbird Prods.

Martin, Janet L., jt. auth. see Nelson, Suzann J.

***Martin, Janet Letnes & Nelson, Suzann Johnson.** Luther's Small Dictionary: From Aal to Zululand: This Is Most Certainly True. 252p. 1999. pap. 9.95 (*1-886627-06-1*, Pub. by Redbird Prods) Bookmen Inc.

Martin, Janet M. Lessons from the Hill: The Legislative Journey of an Education Program. 222p. 1993. text 39.95 (*0-312-10685-8*) St Martin.

Martin, Janet M., jt. auth. see Borrelli, Maryanne.

Martin, Janice. Mostly Microwave. Toney, Kitty, ed. (Illus.). 130p. 1984. spiral bd. 6.50 (*0-9614072-0-4*) Mostly Micro.

Martin, Janice, ed. see Bryan, Betsy M. & Cohen, Judith Love.

Martin, Janice, ed. see Gabriel, Diane L. & Cohen, Judith Love.

Martin, Janice, ed. see Siegel, Margot & Cohen, Judith Love.

***Martin, Janis H.** Skills, Drills & Strategies for Bowling. LC 99-40475. (Teach, Coach, Play Ser.). 176p. 2000. 16.00 (*1-890871-16-8*) Holcomb Hath.

Martin, Jay. Robert Lowell. LC 73-629878. (University of Minnesota Pamphlets on American Writers Ser.: No. 92). 48p. (Orig.). reprint ed. pap. 30.00 (*0-7837-2876-X*, 205757900006) Bks Demand.

Martin, Jay G. & Edgley, Gerald J. Environmental Management Systems: A Guide for Planning, Development & Implementation. LC 98-13949. 267p. 1998. pap. text 69.00 (*0-86587-619-3*, 619) Gov Insts.

***Martin, Jean, ed.** The Heritage of Lee County, Alabama. (Heritage of Alabama Ser.: Vol. 41). 320p. 2001. 50.00 (*1-891647-55-5*) Herit Pub Consult.

Martin, Jean, ed. Intrapartum Management Modules: A Perinatal Education Program (Including Implementation Guidelines) 2nd ed. (Illus.). 720p. 1996. write for info. (*0-683-17195-X*) Lppncott W & W.

Martin, Jean-Baptiste. Dictionnaire du Francais Regional de Pilat. (FRE.). 280p. 1989. 59.95 (*0-8288-9486-8*) Fr & Eur.

Martin, Jean-Francois. Little Red Riding Hood. LC 97-23045. (Little Pebbles Ser.). 32p. (J). (ps-1). 1999. 6.95 (*0-7892-0421-5*, Abbeville Kids) Abbeville Pr.

Martin, Jean-Hubert. Man Ray: Photographs. LC 81-53058. (Illus.). 256p. 1997. reprint ed. pap. 34.95 (*0-500-27473-8*, Pub. by Thames Hudson) Norton.

Martin, Jean-Jack. Tour de France d'Un Chasseur de Champignons. (Livres Gourmands et Beaux Livres Collection). (FRE., Illus.). 160p. 1995. pap. 79.95 (*2-86808-093-6*) Intl Scholars.

Martin, Jean L., et al, eds. The Sheldon Memorial Art Gallery Cookbook. LC 78-10588. (Illus.). 212p. 1978. pap. 13.95 (*0-9602018-1-5*) Nebraska Art.

***Martin, Jean M.** Farmington. (Images of America Ser.). 128p. 1999. pap. 18.99 (*0-7385-0255-3*) Arcadia Publng.

Martin, Jeanette S., jt. auth. see Chaney, Lillian H.

Martin, Jeanne I. The Cinnamon Bear Who Wanted to Sing. (Illus.). 24p. (Orig.). (J). (gr. 1-5). 1986. 4.00 (*0-317-51971-9*) Satori Pr.

Martin, Jeanne M. Complete Candida Yeast Guidebook. LC 96-222. 456p. 1996. pap. 18.95 (*0-7615-0167-3*) Prima Pub.

Martin, Jeanne M., jt. auth. see Rona, Zoltan P.

Martin, Jeannette S., jt. auth. see Chaney, Lillian H.

Martin, Jeff. SX-Key Development System Manual Version 1.0. rev. ed. Gracey, Chip, ed. (Illus.). 164p. (YA). (gr. 11 up). Date not set. pap. 19.00 (*1-928982-01-8*) Parallax Inc.

Martin, Jeffrey B. Ben Hecht: Hollywood Screenwriter. Kirkpatrick, Diane, ed. LC 84-16181. (Studies in Cinema: No. 27). 254p. 1985. reprint ed. pap. 78.80 (*0-8357-1571-X*, 207045900093) Bks Demand.

Martin, Jeffrey L., jt. auth. see Stoops, Erik.

Martin, Jeffrey L., jt. auth. see Stoops, Erik D.

Martin, Jennifer. Open Summer. (Chapbook Series II: No. 4). 24p. 1980. pap. 2.50 (*1-880649-10-1*) Writ Ctr Pr.

Martin, Jennifer E. Piccolo. (Orig.). Date not set. pap. write for info. (*0-9643049-1-0*) Cayuse Press.

Martin, Jenny A., ed. The Next Step Forward: Music Therapy with the Terminally Ill. 95p. 1989. spiral bd. 17.95 (*0-930194-46-2*) Ctr Thanatology.

Martin, Jere. Pennsylvania Almanac. LC 97-24386. 416p. 1997. pap. 19.95 (*0-8117-2880-3*) Stackpole.

Martin, Jerome. Carrot-Parrot. (J). (ps). 1991. pap. 9.95 (*0-671-69555-X*) S&S Bks Yung.

Martin, Jerome L., ed. see Altug, Ziya & Hoffman, Janet L.

Martin, Jerry L. Henry L. Brunk & Brunk's Comedians, Tent Repertoire Empire of the Southwest. LC 83-62703. 1984. 25.95 (*0-87972-268-1*); pap. 11.95 (*0-87972-269-X*) Bowling Green Univ Popular Press.

Martin, Jessica, ed. Izaak Walton: Selected Writings. LC 98-101788. 160p. 1997. pap. 18.95 (*1-85754-307-6*, Pub. by Carcanet Pr) Paul & Co Pubs.

Martin, Jessy. I Never Had It So Good: A Spiritual Journey. Reed, Douglas, ed. 100p. 1998. pap. write for info. (*1-889732-13-3*) Word-For-Word.

Martin, Jill, jt. auth. see Martin, Hope.

Martin, Jim. A Bit of a Blue: The Life & Work of Frances Fuller Victor. LC 91-90607. (Illus.). 320p. (Orig.). 1992. pap. 14.95 (*0-9632066-0-5*) Deep Well Pub.

— Factual Writing: Exploring & Challenging Social Reality. (Language Education Ser.). 116p. 1989. pap. text 12.95 (*0-19-437158-1*) OUP.

— Great White Sharks. (Sharks Ser.). (Illus.). 48p. (J). (gr. 3-7). 1995. 19.00 (*0-516-35241-5*) Childrens.

— 1968 & Other Stories. 60p. 1984. pap. 6.00 (*1-878124-00-5*) Flatland.

***Martin, Jim.** Oh Lord! It's the Millennium. 2000. pap. 15.00 (*0-9663249-1-9*) Mustang Publ.

Martin, Jim. Palm Coast. (Illus.). 96p. (Orig.). 1991. pap. 8.00 (*0-918949-10-6*) Martin Jim.

— Policies of Deceit: In Our Public Schools & Colleges. McGavin, Gregor & Martin, Evelyn, eds. 310p. (Orig.). 1998. pap. 16.00 (*0-9663249-0-0*) Mustang Publ.

— Southwestern Cuisine. (Illus.). 64p. (Orig.). 1993. pap. 7.95 (*0-9624640-3-1*) Crow Canyon Archaeol.

Martin, Jo. Apache Women Warriors. (To Know the Land Ser.). (YA). (gr. 8 up). 2000. write for info. (*0-934272-53-0*); pap. write for info. (*0-934272-52-2*) J G Burke Pub.

— Drugs & the Family. (Encyclopedia of Psychoactive Drugs Ser.: No. 2). (Illus.). 128p. (YA). (gr. 7 up). 1989. pap. 8.95 (*0-7910-0797-9*) Chelsea Hse.

Martin, Joan. Reading Quilts: A Study Guide. Friedland, J. & Kessler, R., eds. (Novel-Ties Ser.). 1992. pap. text, student ed. 20.95 (*0-88122-856-7*) Lrn Links.

— Urban Financial Stress: Why Cities Go Broke. LC 81-20659. 217p. 1982. 55.00 (*0-86569-084-7*, Auburn Hse) Greenwood.

Martin, Joan E. Eating Disorders, Food & Occupational Therapy. 1998. pap. text 36.95 (*1-86156-105-9*) Whurr Pub.

Martin, Joan L. Bowling. 8th ed. LC 97-14665. 128p. 1997. pap. 13.13 (*0-697-34539-4*) McGraw.

Martin, Joan M. More Than Chains & Toil: A Christian Work Ethic of Enslaved Women. LC 99-86475. 220p. 2000. pap. 24.95 (*0-664-25800-X*, Pub. by Westminster John Knox) Presbyterian Pub.

Martin, Joan W. Pine Cones & Magnolia Blossoms. LC 99-72740. (Illus.). 100p. 1999. pap. text 8.95 (*1-58521-005-6*) Bks Black Chldn.

Martin, Joanna, ed. A Governess in the Age of Jane Austen: The Journals & Letters of Agnes Porter. LC 97-44890. 256p. 1998. 45.00 (*1-85285-164-3*) Hambledon Press.

Martin, Joanne. Festive Strings: Cello Ensemble. 24p. 1998. pap. text 6.95 (*0-87487-932-9*) Summy-Birchard.

— Festive Strings: Cello Ensemble. 24p. 1998. pap. text 6.95 (*0-87487-975-2*) Summy-Birchard.

— Festive Strings: Solo Cello. 16p. 1998. pap. text 5.95 (*0-87487-946-9*) Summy-Birchard.

— Festive Strings: Solo Cello. 16p. 1998. pap. text 5.95 (*0-87487-978-7*) Summy-Birchard.

— Festive Strings: Solo Viola. 16p. 1998. pap. text 5.95 (*0-87487-934-5*) Summy-Birchard.

— Festive Strings: Solo Viola. 16p. 1998. pap. text 5.95 (*0-87487-977-9*) Summy-Birchard.

— Festive Strings: Solo Violin. 16p. 1998. pap. text 5.95 (*0-87487-933-7*) Summy-Birchard.

— Festive Strings: Solo Violin. 16p. 1998. pap. text 5.95 (*0-87487-976-0*) Summy-Birchard.

— Festive Strings: Viola Ensemble. 24p. 1998. pap. text 6.95 (*0-87487-931-0*) Summy-Birchard.

— Festive Strings: Viola Ensemble. 24p. 1998. pap. text 6.95 (*0-87487-974-4*) Summy-Birchard.

— Festive Strings: Violin Ensemble. 24p. 1998. pap. text 6.95 (*0-87487-930-2*) Summy-Birchard.

— Festive Strings: Violin Ensemble. 24p. 1998. pap. text 6.95 (*0-87487-973-6*) Summy-Birchard.

— Festive Strings for String Quartet or String Orchestra: Cello. 16p. 1998. pap. text 4.95 (*0-87487-985-X*) Summy-Birchard.

— Festive Strings for String Quartet or String Orchestra: Score. 40p. 1998. pap. text 7.95 (*0-87487-929-9*) Summy-Birchard.

— Festive Strings for String Quartet or String Orchestra: String Bass. 16p. 1998. pap. text 4.95 (*0-87487-986-8*) Summy-Birchard.

— Festive Strings for String Quartet or String Orchestra: Viola. 16p. 1998. pap. text 4.95 (*0-87487-927-2*) Summy-Birchard.

— Festive Strings for String Quartet or String Orchestra: 1st Violin. 16p. 1998. pap. text 4.95 (*0-87487-906-X*) Summy-Birchard.

— Festive Strings for String Quartet or String Orchestra: 2nd Violin. 16p. 1998. pap. text 4.95 (*0-87487-911-6*) Summy-Birchard.

— Festive Strings for String Quartet or String Orchestra: 3rd Violin. 16p. 1998. pap. text 4.95 (*0-87487-912-4*) Summy-Birchard.

— Festive Strings Piano Accompaniments. 24p. 1998. pap. text 5.95 (*0-87487-947-7*) Summy-Birchard.

— Festive Strings Piano Accompaniments. 24p. 1998. pap. text 5.95 (*0-87487-979-5*) Summy-Birchard.

— I Can Read Music Vol. 2: Cello. (Illus.). 106p. (J). (gr. k-3). 1997. pap., spiral bd. 12.95 (*0-87487-429-7*, 0429) Summy-Birchard.

— I Can Read Music Vol. 2: Viola. (Illus.). 106p. (J). (gr. k-3). 1997. pap., spiral bd. 12.95 (*0-87487-428-9*, 0428) Summy-Birchard.

— I Can Read Music Vol. 2: Violin. (Illus.). 106p. (J). (gr. k-3). 1997. spiral bd. 12.95 (*0-87487-427-0*, 0427) Summy-Birchard.

— I Can Read Music (for Cello) 106p. 1991. pap. text 12.95 (*0-87487-441-6*) Summy-Birchard.

— I Can Read Music (for Viola) 106p. 1991. pap. text 12.95 (*0-87487-440-8*) Summy-Birchard.

— I Can Read Music (for Violin) 106p. 1991. pap. text 12.95 (*0-87487-439-4*) Summy-Birchard.

— More Festive Strings for String Quartet or String Orchestra: Cello. 16p. 1998. pap. text 4.95 (*0-87487-997-3*) Summy-Birchard.

— More Festive Strings for String Quartet or String Orchestra: Score. 36p. 1998. pap. text 7.95 (*0-87487-971-X*) Summy-Birchard.

— More Festive Strings for String Quartet or String Orchestra: String Bass. 16p. 1998. pap. text 4.95 (*0-87487-998-1*) Summy-Birchard.

— More Festive Strings for String Quartet or String Orchestra: Viola. 16p. 1998. pap. text 4.95 (*0-87487-995-7*) Summy-Birchard.

— More Festive Strings for String Quartet or String Orchestra: 1st Violin. 16p. 1998. pap. text 4.95 (*0-87487-972-8*) Summy-Birchard.

— More Festive Strings for String Quartet or String Orchestra: 2nd Violin. 16p. 1998. pap. text 4.95 (*0-87487-987-6*) Summy-Birchard.

— More Festive Strings for String Quartet or String Orchestra: 3rd Violin. 16p. 1998. pap. text 4.95 (*0-87487-994-9*) Summy-Birchard.

Martin, Joanne, jt. auth. see Daniels, Stephen.

Martin, Joanne M. Cultures in Organizations: Three Perspectives. (Illus.). 240p. (C). 1992. pap. text 27.95 (*0-19-507164-6*) OUP.

Martin, Joanne M., jt. auth. see Martin, Elmer D.

Martin, Joanne M., jt. auth. see Martin, Elmer P.

Martin, Joanne M., jt. ed. see Nordstrom, Carolyn.

Martin, Jody, jt. auth. see Martin, Ned.

Martin, Joe. Conspiracies: Six Plays by Joe Martin. LC 98-221224. x, 340p. (Orig.). 1997. pap. 14.95 (*0-9656712-0-8*) Press Open.

— Foreigners. LC 97-71244. 176p. 1997. pap. 14.00 (*1-57650-074-8*) Hi Jinx Pr.

— Insomnia Suite. Date not set. 9.00 (*0-9632825-4-9*) Tigermoon Ent.

— Legendlore: Tainted Soul. (Illus.). 112p. 1997. pap. 12.95 (*0-941613-94-1*, Caliber Comics) Stabur Pr.

— Mister Boffo: The First Decade. LC 95-83103. (Illus.). 128p. (Orig.). 1996. pap. 9.95 (*0-8362-1442-0*) Andrews & McMeel.

— Mister Boffo Shrink Wrapped. (Illus.). 208p. 1995. pap. 10.95 (*0-8362-1777-2*) Andrews & McMeel.

***Martin, Joe.** Parabola: Shorter Fictions - Including the Novella "Fata Morgana" 176p. 2000. pap. 13.00 (*1-878580-18-3*) Asylum Arts.

Martin, Joe. Tabletop Machining: A Basic Approach to Making Small Parts on Miniature Machine Tools. (Illus.). iv, 238p. 1998. pap. 40.00 (*0-9665433-0-0*) Sherline Prod.

***Martin, Joe & Wujicik, Erick.** Deluxe RECON. Marciniszyn, Alex et al, eds. (RECON Ser.). (Illus.). 224p. (YA). (gr. 8 up). 1999. pap. 20.95 (*1-57457-023-4*, 600) Palladium Bks.

***Martin, Joe & Yockey, Ross.** On Any Given Day. 160p. 2000. 21.95 (*0-89587-233-1*) Blair.

Martin, Joe, tr. see Strindberg, August.

Martin, Joe, tr. & intro. see Bjorneboe, Jens.

M

M

Martin, Joe E. You Had to Be There. Wardell, John, ed. & illus. by. 64p. pap. 11.95 (*0-9673206-0-7*) You Had To Be There.

Martin, Joel. Our Children Forever. 400p. 1996. reprint ed. mass mkt. 7.50 (*0-425-15343-6*) Berkley Pub.

Martin, Joel & Romanowski, Patricia. Love Beyond Life: The Healing Power of After-Death Communications. 336p. 1998. mass mkt. 5.99 (*0-440-22649-X*) Dell.

— Our Children Forever: George Anderson's Message from Children on the Other Side. 336p. (Orig.). 1994. pap. 12.00 (*0-425-14138-1*) Berkley Pub.

— We Are Not Forgotten. 1992. mass mkt. 6.99 (*0-425-13288-9*) Berkley Pub.

Martin, Joel W. Native Ameican Religon. LC 98-50155. 160p. (YA). 1999. lib. bdg. 22.00 (*0-19-511035-8*) OUP.

— Sacred Revolt: The Muskogees' Struggle for a New World. (Illus.). 224p. 1993. pap. 16.50 (*0-8070-5403-8*) Beacon Pr.

— Screening the Sacred: Myth, Ritual & Religion in Popular American Film. 208p. (C). 1995. pap. 24.00 (*0-8133-8830-9*, Pub. by Westview) HarpC.

Martin, Joel W., jt. auth. see Bauer, Raymond T.

Martin, John. Baroque. LC 76-12059. (Icon Editions Ser.). (Illus.). 288p. 1977. pap. 30.00 (*0-06-430077-3*, IN-77, Icon Edns) HarpC.

Martin, John. College Algebra: Instructor's Solution Manual. 1997. teacher ed. write for info. (*1-57259-248-6*) Worth.

— Cruisin' Series, 17 vols. (J). 1992. lib. bdg. 323.00 (*0-516-95002-9*) Childrens.

— The Dance. LC 79-7776. (Dance Ser.). (Illus.). 1980. reprint ed. lib. bdg. 42.95 (*0-8369-9303-9*) Ayer.

***Martin, John.** The Development of Modern Agriculture: British Farming since 1931. LC 99-46108. 2000. text 69.95 (*0-312-22983-6*) St Martin.

Martin, John. Dictators & Democracies Today. LC 68-16953. (Essay Index Reprint Ser.). 1977. 19.95 (*0-8369-0680-2*) Ayer.

— Doc, My Tiger's Got an Itch. LC 96-77318. (Illus.). 150p. 1996. 22.95 (*1-878208-87-X*) Guild Pr IN.

— Elementary Algebra. (C). 1994. pap. text, student ed. 24.06 (*0-07-062600-6*) McGraw.

— In-Line Skating. (Action Sports Ser.). (Illus.). 48p. (J). (gr. 3-4). 1994. lib. bdg. 19.00 (*0-516-35202-4*) Childrens.

— In-Line Skating. LC 93-40644. (Action Sports Ser.). (Illus.). 48p. (J). (gr. 3-7). 1994. pap. 5.95 (*0-516-40202-1*) Childrens.

— Jet Watercraft. (Cruisin' Ser.). (Illus.). 48p. (J). (gr. 3-6). 1994. 19.00 (*0-516-35201-6*) Childrens.

— Languages & the Theory of Computation. 672p. (C). 1990. text 87.00 (*0-07-040659-6*) McGraw.

— Materials for Engineering. (Illus.). 240p. 1997. pap. 29.00 (*1-86125-012-6*, Pub. by Inst Materials) Ashgate Pub Co.

— Organizational Behavior. 768p. 1998. pap. 24.95 (*1-86152-180-4*) Thomson Learn.

***Martin, John.** Organizational Behavior. 2nd ed. 2000. pap. write for info. (*1-86152-583-4*) Thomson Learn.

Martin, John. Organizational Behavior: Lecturers Resource Manual. (ITBP Textbooks Ser.). 768p. 1998. pap., teacher ed. 19.99 (*1-86152-163-4*) Thomson Learn.

— Roses, Fountains & Gold. LC 97-76858. 1998. pap. 14.95 (*0-89870-680-7*) Ignatius Pr.

— Signposts to Heaven. 1998. pap. 4.99 (*0-340-65666-2*, Pub. by Hodder & Stought Ltd) Trafalgar.

— Venice's Hidden Enemies: Italian Heretics in a Renaissance City. LC 92-19220. (Studies on the History of Society & Culture: Vol. 16). 1993. 50.00 (*0-520-07743-1*, Pub. by U CA Pr) Cal Prin Full Svc.

— The World's Fastest Motorcycles. (Wheels Ser.). (Illus.). 48p. (J). (gr. 3-7). 1994. 19.00 (*0-516-35208-3*) Childrens.

— The World's Most Exotic Cars. (Wheels Ser.). (Illus.). 48p. (J). (gr. 3-7). 1994. 19.00 (*0-516-35209-1*) Childrens.

***Martin, John & Romano, Dennis.** Venice Reconsidered: The History & Civilization of an Italian City-State, 1297-1797. LC 00-21349. 460p. 2000. 45.00 (*0-8018-6312-0*) Johns Hopkins.

Martin, John, ed. see Bukowkski, Charles.

Martin, John, ed. see Bukowski, Charles.

Martin, John B. Call It North Country: The Story of Upper Michigan. LC 86-15922. (Great Lakes Bks.: Vol. 4). 299p. reprint ed. pap. 92.70 (*0-608-10540-6*, 2071660) Bks Demand.

— Call It North Country: The Story of Upper Michigan. LC 85-15923. (Great Lakes Bks.). (Illus.). 300p. 1986. reprint ed. pap. 16.95 (*0-8143-1869-X*) Wayne St U Pr.

— Indiana: An Interpretation. LC 92-15855. 352p. 1992. 32.50 (*0-253-33682-1*); pap. 5.95 (*0-253-20754-1*, MB-754) Ind U Pr.

— Indiana: An Interpretation. LC 72-5516. (Biography Index Reprint Ser.). 1977. reprint ed. 33.95 (*0-8369-8136-7*) Ayer.

— Saved to Serve: The Treasure in Earthen Vessels. Nicholson, J. Boyd, ed. 60p. 1994. 4.95 (*1-882701-09-7*) Uplook Min.

Martin, John C. Duties of Junior & Senior Accountants: Supplement of the CPA Handbook. 204p. 1988. text 15.00 (*0-8240-6144-6*) Garland.

— Introduction to Languages & the Theory of Computation. 2nd ed. LC 96-49659. 450p. (C). 1997. 85.00 (*0-07-040845-9*) McGraw.

— Labor Productivity Control: New Approaches for Industrial Engineers & Managers. LC 90-7449. 320p. 1990. 69.50 (*0-275-93663-5*, C3663, Praeger Pubs) Greenwood.

Martin, John C., ed. Nucleotide Analogues As Antiviral Agents. LC 89-15114. (Symposium Ser.: No. 401). (Illus.). 175p. 1989. text 49.95 (*0-8412-1659-2*, Pub. by Am Chemical) OUP.

Martin, John D. Christopher Dock: Pioneer Schoolmaster on Skippack. 1971. pap. 3.10 (*0-87813-906-0*) Christian Light.

Martin, John D. Living Together on God's Earth. rev. ed. (Christian Day School Ser.). (J). (gr. 3). 1996. 14.95 (*0-87813-928-1*) Christian Light.

Martin, John D. Living Together on God's Earth: Teacher's Guidebook. (Christian Day School Ser.). (J). (gr. 3). 1975. teacher ed. 15.75 (*0-87813-910-9*) Christian Light.

Martin, John D., et al, compiled by. Perspectives of Life in Literature. unabridged ed. LC 97-132833. (Illus.). 611p. (YA). (gr. 9). 1996. text 22.95 (*0-87813-927-3*) Christian Light.

Martin, John D. & Ferris, Frank D. I Can't Stop Crying: It's So Hard When Someone You Love Dies. 96p. 1992. pap. 9.95 (*1-55013-407-8*) Firefly Bks Ltd.

Martin, John D. & Kensinger, John W. Exploring the Controversy over Corporate Restructuring. LC 90-84429. 124p. (Orig.). 1990. pap. 20.00 (*0-910586-80-2*, 087-90) Finan Exec.

— New Realities for Stockholder-Management Relations. LC 94-70909. 70p. (Orig.). 1994. pap. text 25.00 (*0-910586-91-8*, 094-01) Finan Exec.

Martin, John D. & Showalter, Lester E. Perspectives of Truth in Literature. (Christian Day School Ser.). (YA). (gr. 12). 1983. 22.95 (*0-87813-921-4*) Christian Light.

— Perspectives of Truth in Literature: Teacher's Guiebook. (Christian Day School Ser.). (YA). (gr. 12). 1983. teacher ed. 12.00 (*0-87813-922-2*) Christian Light.

Martin, John D., jt. auth. see Kensinger, John W.

Martin, John D., jt. auth. see Sanchack, A. J., Jr.

Martin, John E. Holding the Balance: A History of the Department of Labour, 1891-1995. (Illus.). 480p. 1996. 69.95 (*0-908812-62-0*, Pub. by Canterbury Univ); pap. 49.95 (*0-908812-61-2*, Pub. by Canterbury Univ) Accents Pubns.

Martin, John E., pref. Command Performance: The Art of Delivering Quality Service. LC 94-16423. (Harvard Business Review Book Ser.). 256p. 1994. 27.95 (*0-87584-562-2*) Harvard Busn.

Martin, John E., jt. ed. see Miller, William R.

Martin, John F. Profits in the Wilderness: Entrepreneurship & the Founding of New England Towns in the Seventeenth Century. LC 91-2945. xvi, 363p. (C). 1991. 45.00 (*0-8078-2001-6*); pap. 18.95 (*0-8078-4346-6*) U of NC Pr.

— Reorienting a Nation: Consultants & Australian Public Policy. LC 97-39110. (Illus.). 274p. 1998. text 72.95 (*1-84014-073-9*, Pub. by Ashgate Pub) Ashgate Pub Co.

Martin, John G. It Began at Imphal: The Combat Cargo Story. (Illus.). 112p. 1988. pap. 18.95 (*0-89745-111-2*) Sunflower U Pr.

Martin, John H. A Day in the Life of a Ballet Dancer. (J). 1985. 8.05 (*0-606-12239-7*, Pub. by Turtleback) Demco.

— Historical Sketch of Bethlehem in Pennsylvania. LC 72-134382. reprint ed. 38.00 (*0-404-08479-6*) AMS Pr.

— Neuroanatomy Atlas. 2nd ed. 578p. (C). 1996. pap. text 69.95 (*0-8385-6694-4*, A6694-2, Apple Lange Med) McGraw.

Martin, John H., ed. The Corning Flood: Museum Under Water. LC 77-73627. (Illus.). 72p. 1977. pap. 6.00 (*0-87290-063-0*) Corning.

Martin, John H., et al, eds. Journal of Glass Studies, Vol. 30. LC 59-12390. (Illus.). 190p. 1988. pap. 20.00 (*0-87290-030-4*) Corning.

Martin, John H. & Edwards, Charleen K., eds. Journal of Glass Studies, Vol. 25. LC 59-12390. (Illus.). 334p. 1983. pap. 30.00 (*0-87290-025-8*) Corning.

— Journal of Glass Studies, Vol. 26. LC 59-12390. (Illus.). 225p. 1984. pap. 20.00 (*0-87290-026-6*) Corning.

— Journal of Glass Studies, Vol. 27, 1985. LC 59-12390. (Illus.). 176p. 1985. pap. 20.00 (*0-87290-027-4*) Corning.

Martin, John H. & Friedberg, Ardy. Writing to Read. 224p. 1989. reprint ed. mass mkt. 12.95 (*0-446-39051-8*, Pub. by Warner Bks) Little.

Martin, John H. & Martin, Phyllis G. Kyoto: A Cultural Guide. (Illus.). 280p. (Orig.). 1994. pap. 14.95 (*0-8048-1955-6*) Tuttle Pubng.

— Tokyo: A Cultural Guide to Japan's Capital City. LC 96-60059. (Illus.). 312p. (Orig.). 1996. pap. 14.95 (*0-8048-2057-0*) Tuttle Pubng.

Martin, John H. & Price, Richard W., eds. Journal of Glass Studies, Vol. 28, 1986. LC 59-12390. (Illus.). 189p. 1986. pap. 20.00 (*0-87290-028-2*) Corning.

— Journal of Glass Studies, Vol. 29. LC 59-12390. (Illus.). 203p. 1987. pap. 20.00 (*0-87290-029-0*) Corning.

Martin, John H., jt. auth. see Irish, Michael W.

Martin, John Holmes. Principles of Field Crop Production. 3rd ed. 1030p. (C). 1976. 135.00 (*0-02-376720-0*, Macmillan Coll) P-H.

Martin, John J. Ruth Page: An Intimate Biography. LC 76-18427. (Dance Program Ser.: No. 4). (Illus.). 378p. reprint ed. pap. 117.20 (*0-7837-0981-1*, 204128800019) Bks Demand.

Martin, John L. Angel Food. LC 88-7978. 248p. 1989. 16.95 (*0-89407-092-4*) Strawberry Hill.

— Can We Control the Border? A Look at Recent Efforts in San Diego, El Paso & Nogales. (Illus.). 40p. (Orig.). 1995. pap. 7.00 (*1-881290-17-4*) Ctr Immigrat.

Martin, John L. & Bouvier, Leon F. Shaping Georgia: The Effects of Immigration - 1970-2020. (Illus.). 16p. (Orig.). 1995. pap. 6.00 (*1-881290-16-6*) Ctr Immigrat.

— Shaping Texas: The Effects of Immigration - 1970-2020. (Illus.). 16p. (Orig.). 1995. pap. 6.00 (*1-881290-18-2*) Ctr Immigrat.

Martin, John L., jt. auth. see Bouvier, Leon F.

Martin, John M. A Mathematical Skills Primer. Davies Group Staff, ed. & illus. by. 142p. (C). 1996. pap. 12.25 (*1-888570-06-7*) Davies Grp.

Martin, John M. & Romano, Anne T. Multinational Crime: The Challenge of Terrorism, Espionage, Drug, & Arms Trafficking. (Studies in Crime, Law, & Justice: Vol. 9). (Illus.). 220p. 1992. 52.00 (*0-8039-4597-3*); pap. 21.95 (*0-8039-4598-1*) Sage.

Martin, John P., ed. Violence & the Family. LC 77-21846. 377p. reprint ed. pap. 116.90 (*0-8357-3110-3*, 203936600012) Bks Demand.

Martin, John R. Beginning Algebra, Form A. 3rd ed. (C). 1993. pap. text, student ed. 26.25 (*0-07-063019-4*) McGraw.

— The Portrait of John Milton at Princeton. LC 61-14263. (Illus.). 42p. 1961. 15.00 (*0-87811-006-2*) Princeton Lib.

***Martin, John R.** Ventures in Discipleship. 304p. (Orig.). 1998. pap. 26.00 (*1-57910-167-4*) Wipf & Stock.

Martin, John S., ed. see Hawthorne, Nathaniel.

Martin, John T. & Warner, Mark A. Positioning in Anesthesia & Surgery. 3rd ed. Day, Lesley, ed. 352p. 1996. text 79.00 (*0-7216-6674-4*, W B Saunders Co) Harcrt Hlth Sci Grp.

Martin, John V. Never a Ho-Hum Day: Stories of a Kentucky Hill Country Veterinarian & His Doctorin' LC 97-78018. (Illus.). 210p. 1998. 22.95 (*1-57860-052-9*) Guild Pr IN.

Martin, Jonathan W. Methodologies for Predicting the Service Lives of Coating Systems. (Illus.). 68p. (C). 1998. pap. text 35.00 (*0-7881-7185-2*) DIANE Pub.

Martin, Jonathan W., et al. Methodologies for Predicting the Service Lives of Coating Systems. (Illus.). 34p. 1996. pap. 30.00 (*0-934010-33-1*) Fed Soc Coat Tech.

Martin, Jonathan W., jt. ed. see Bauer, David R.

***Martin-Jones, Marilyn & Jones, Kathryn.** Multilingual Literacies: Reading & Writing Different Worlds. LC 00-40369. (Studies in Written Language & Literacy). 2000. write for info. (*1-55619-748-9*) J Benjamins Pubng Co.

Martin-Jones, Marilyn, jt. ed. see Heller, Monica.

Martin, Jose M. Accounting Dictionary: Diccionario de Contabilidad. 4th ed. (SPA.). 270p. 1982. 29.95 (*0-8288-1289-6*, S50180) Fr & Eur.

— Diccionario de Contabilidad. 4th deluxe ed. (SPA.). 1982. 29.95 (*0-685-57710-4*, S-50180) Fr & Eur.

Martin, Joseph. Chalk Talks on Alcohol. LC 82-47750. 192p. 1989. pap. 13.00 (*0-06-250593-9*, Pub. by Harper SF) HarpC.

— Keeper of the Protocols: The Works of Jens Bjorneboe in the Crosscurrents of Western Literature. LC 95-25087. (AUS Series I: Vol. 108). XII, 188p. (C). 1996. text 40.95 (*0-8204-3037-4*) P Lang Pubng.

Martin, Joseph, tr. see Strindberg, August.

Martin, Joseph B. & Barchas, Jack D., eds. Neuropeptides in Neurologic & Psychiatric Disease. LC 85-31183. (Association for Research in Nervous & Mental Disease Research Publications: No. 64). (Illus.). 382p. 1986. reprint ed. pap. 118.50 (*0-608-00637-8*, 206122500007) Bks Demand.

Martin, Joseph B. & Scientific American, Inc. Staff. Scientific American Molecular Neurology. LC 98-5123. (Introduction to Molecular Medicine Ser.). 1998. 69.00 (*0-89454-030-0*) Scientific Am Inc.

Martin, Joseph B., ed. see Institute of Medicine, Committee on a National Neu.

Martin, Joseph H. & Steinberg, Eve P. Real Estate License Examinations: Salesperson & Broker. 4th ed. LC 93-4597. 256p. 1993. per. 15.95 (*0-671-84835-6*, Arc) IDG Bks.

Martin, Joseph P. Private Yankee Doodle. LC 67-29036. (Eyewitness Accounts of the American Revolution Ser.). 1980. reprint ed. 29.95 (*0-405-01137-7*) Ayer.

— Private Yankee Doodle. Scheer, George F., ed. 305p. 1979. reprint ed. pap. 2.25 (*0-915992-10-8*) Eastern National.

— Yankee Doodle Boy. Scheer, George F., ed. (Illus.). (YA). (gr. 7-12). 1995. pap. 8.95 (*0-8234-1180-X*) Holiday.

— Yankee Doodle Boy: A Young Soldier's Adventures in the American Revolution Told by Himself. (American Biography Ser.). 190p. 1991. reprint ed. lib. bdg. 59.00 (*0-7812-8273-X*) Rprt Serv.

Martin, Josephine M., et al. Managing Child Nutrition Programs: Leadership for Excellence. LC 99-13065. 768p. 1999. boxed set 65.00 (*0-8342-0917-9*, 09179) Aspen Pub.

Martin, Joy R. Making Your Marriage Magnificent. (Joyful Living Ser.). 31p. 1983. pap. 2.50 (*0-912623-01-2*) Joyful Woman.

Martin, Joy R., jt. auth. see Handford, Elizabeth R.

Martin, Joyce. Faith Works. Nelson, Becky, ed. LC 96-208601. 160p. 1996. pap. text 9.95 (*1-56309-173-9*, W964146) Womans Mission Union.

— Fallen Words. 1998. pap. write for info. (*1-58235-012-4*) Watermrk Pr.

***Martin, Joyce.** The Holy Spirit & the Second Millennium Disciples. 1999. pap. 12.50 (*0-7392-0351-7*, PO3534) Morris Pubng.

— Profiting from Multiple Intelligence in the Workplace. LC 00-39393. 232p. 2000. 84.95 (*0-566-08312-4*, Pub. by Ashgate Pub) Ashgate Pub Co.

Martin, Joyce A. Triplet Births, Trends & Outcomes, 1971-1994. 26p. 1997. pap. 4.25 (*0-16-061452-X*) USGPO.

Martin, Joyce A., et al. Triplet Births, Trends & Outcomes, 1971-1994. LC 96-50049. (Vital & Health Statistics Ser.: Series 21, No. 55). 1997. write for info. (*0-8406-0524-2*) Natl Ctr Health Stats.

Martin, Joyce L. Light Bright: A Bright Idea for Bright Minds in the Primary Grades. Mackellar, Thompson, ed. (Illus.). 212p. 1989. teacher ed. 49.95 (*0-9621707-0-4*) Port Side Pub.

Martin, Juan. Hasta Que el Tiempo Estalle (Poesias) LC 86-81311. (Coleccion Espejo de Paciencia). (SPA.). 62p. (Orig.). 1987. pap. 9.00 (*0-89729-406-8*) Ediciones.

Martin, Judith. Dandelion. (Illus.). (Orig.). (J). (gr. 1-5). 1978. pap. 4.50 (*0-9606662-0-6*) Paper Bag.

— Everybody Everybody. (Illus.). 79p. 1987. pap. 4.50 (*0-526-67369-9*) Paper Bag.

— I Won't Take a Bath. (Illus.). (Orig.). 1987. pap. write for info. (*0-318-62981-X*) Paper Bag.

— Miss Manner's Basic Training. 1999. 20.01 (*0-609-60052-4*) Crown Pub Group.

— Miss Manners Basic Training: Eating. 1997. 15.00 (*0-614-28222-5*) Crown Pub Group.

— Miss Manner's Basic Training: The Right Thing to Say. LC 97-28967. 192p. 1998. 17.00 (*0-609-60051-6*) Crown Pub Group.

— Miss Manner's Basics: Eat. LC 97-186937. 1997. 15.00 (*0-517-70186-3*, Crown) Crown Pub Group.

— Miss Manners' Citizens Guide to Civility. LC 99-13072. 1999. pap. 18.00 (*0-609-80158-9*) Three Rivers Pr.

— Miss Manners' Guide to Domestic Tranquillity: The Authoritative Manual for Every Civilized Household, However Harried. LC 99-22824. 448p. 1999. 30.00 (*0-517-70165-0*) Random Hse Value.

***Martin, Judith.** Miss Manners' Guide to Domestic Tranquility: The Authoritative Manual for Every Civilized Household, However Harried. (Illus.). 448p. 2000. reprint ed. pap. 18.00 (*0-609-80539-8*, Three Riv Pr) Crown Pub Group.

Martin, Judith. Miss Manners' Guide to Excruciatingly Correct Behavior. 768p. 1991. 14.99 (*0-88365-781-3*) Galahad Bks.

— Miss Manners' Guide to Raising Perfect Children. 432p. 1993. 10.99 (*0-88365-838-0*) Galahad Bks.

— Miss Manner's Guide to the Turn-of-the-Millenium. 768p. 1990. per. 17.00 (*0-671-72228-X*) S&S Trade.

— Miss Manners on Weddings. LC 98-40684. 224p. 1999. 16.00 (*0-609-60431-7*) Crescent Books.

— Miss Manners Rescues Civilization: From Sexual Harassment, Frivolous Lawsuits, Drive-By Shootings & Other Lapses in Civilization. 1996. 30.00 (*0-614-95749-4*, Crown) Crown Pub Group.

— Miss Manner's Weddings. 1999. 11.20 (*0-517-88608-1*) Random.

— Out of the Bag: The Paper Boy Players Book of Plays. LC 94-46006. (Illus.). 48p. (J). 1997. lib. bdg. 16.89 (*0-7868-2148-5*, Pub. by Hyprn Child) Little.

— Reasons to Be Cheerful. (Illus.). 80p. (J). (ps-4). 1985. pap. 4.50 (*0-9606662-1-4*) Paper Bag.

Martin, Judith & Ashwander, Donald. Christmas All over the Place: Playscript. 22p. (J). (ps-12). 1977. 5.00 (*0-87602-113-5*) Anchorage.

— The Lost & Found Christmas. 14p. (J). (ps up). 1977. 5.00 (*0-87602-152-6*) Anchorage.

— The Runaway Presents: Playscript. 16p. (J). (ps up). 1977. 5.00 (*0-87602-197-6*) Anchorage.

— Wiggle Worm's Surprise (Playscript) 16p. (J). (ps up). 1977. 5.00 (*0-87602-218-2*) Anchorage.

Martin, Judith & Paper Bag Players Staff. Out of the Bag. LC 94-46006. (Illus.). 48p. (J). (gr. 1-5). 1997. pap. 13.45 (*0-7868-1061-0*, Pub. by Hyprn Ppbks) Little.

***Martin, Judith A.** Foster Family Care: Theory & Practice. LC 99-56023. 262p. 2000. pap. 36.00 (*0-205-30491-5*) Allyn.

Martin, Judith A., jt. auth. see Kadushin, Alfred.

Martin, Judith N. & Nakayama, Thomas K. Intercultural Communication in Contexts. 2nd ed. LC 99-13995. xxii, 297p. 1999. pap. text 37.95 (*0-7674-0710-5*) Mayfield Pub.

Martin, Judith N., et al. Readings in Cultural Contexts. LC 97-22675. xxiv, 514p. 1997. pap. text 37.95 (*0-7674-0061-5*) Mayfield Pub.

Martin, Judith N., jt. auth. see Nakayama, Thomas K.

Martin, Judy. Airbrush Library: Rendering Transparency. (Airbrush Artist's Library). (Illus.). 64p. 1989. 12.95 (*0-89134-278-8*, 30124, North Lght Bks) F & W Pubns Inc.

— Arizona Walls. 1998. pap. text 14.95 (*0-929526-76-7*) Double B Pubns.

— The Block Book. (Illus.). 144p. 1998. pap. 21.95 (*0-929589-05-X*) Crosley-Griffith.

— Color: How to See It & How to Use It. 144p. 1994. 19.98 (*0-7858-0053-0*) Bk Sales Inc.

— Colour Mixing. (Learn to Paint Ser.). (Illus.). 1999. pap. 15.95 (*0-00-413338-2*, Pub. by HarpC) Trafalgar.

— The Complete Guide to Airbrushing Techniques & Materials. 1992. 14.98 (*0-685-60285-0*) Bk Sales Inc.

— The Complete Guide to Airbrushing Techniques & Materials. 1992. 14.98 (*1-55521-527-0*) Bk Sales Inc.

— Complete Guide to Calligraphy Techniques & Materials. 1993. 14.98 (*0-89009-675-9*) Bk Sales Inc.

***Martin, Judy.** The Creative Pattern Book: Complete Patterns, Intriguing Ideas & Musings on the Creative Process. (Illus.). 176p. 2000. pap. 27.95 (*0-929589-06-8*) Crosley-Griffith.

Martin, Judy. Encyclopedia of Colored Pencil Techniques. 192p. 1997. pap. text 17.95 (*0-7624-0117-6*) Running Pr.

— The Encyclopedia of Printmaking Techniques. (Encyclopedia of Art Ser.). (Illus.). 160p. 1998. pap. 17.95 (*0-7624-0258-X*) Running Pr.

— Impressionism. LC 94-44415. (Art & Artists Ser.). 64p. (J). (gr. 5-10). 1995. lib. bdg. 24.26 (*1-56847-355-9*) Raintree Steck-V.

— Judy Martin's Ultimate Rotary Cutting Reference. (Illus.). 80p. (Orig.). 1997. pap. 14.95 (*0-929589-04-1*) Crosley-Griffith.

***Martin, Judy.** Learn to Paint Colour Mixing. (Illus.). 1999. pap. text. write for info. (*0-00-413337-4*) HarpC.

Martin, Judy. 100 Keys to Great Acrylic Painting. (One Hundred Keys Ser.). (Illus.). 64p. 1995. 16.99 (*0-89134-694-5*, North Lght Bks) F & W Pubns Inc.

— Painting & Drawing. (First Guide Ser.). (Illus.). 96p. (J). (gr. 3-6). 1993. pap. 9.95 (*1-56294-709-5*); lib. bdg. 23.90 (*1-56294-203-4*) Millbrook Pr.

An Asterisk (*) at the beginning of an entry indicates that the title is appearing for the first time.

— Patchwork Book: Easy Lessons for Creative Quilt Design & Construction. (Illus.). 184p. 1994. reprint ed. pap. text 9.95 (*0-486-27844-1*) Dover.
— The Rainbow Collection: Quilt Patterns for Rainbow Colors. 44p. (Orig.). 1987. pap. 10.95 (*0-9602970-2-2*) Leman Pubns.
Martin, Judy. Scrap Quilts. LC 85-72392. (Illus.). 96p. (Orig.). 1985. pap. 12.95 (*0-9602970-9-X*) Leman Pubns.
Martin, Judy. Secret Garden Notebook: A First Gardening Book. (Illus.). 64p. (J). (gr. 4-7). 1991. 12.95 (*0-87923-890-9*) Godine.
— Shining Star Quilts: Lone Star Variations. 144p. 1987. pap. 19.95 (*0-943721-00-8*) Leman Pubns.
— Watercolour Pencils. (Learn to Paint Ser.). (Illus.). 1999. pap. 15.95 (*0-00-413347-1*, Pub. by HarpC) Trafalgar.
Martin, Judy, jt. auth. see Leman, Bonnie.
Martin, Julia. Faiths & Avatars. 1996. 25.00 (*0-7869-0384-8*, Pub. by TSR Inc) Random.
— Rotten to the Core. (Twenty-Three Hundred AD Ser.). (Illus.). 64p. (Orig.). (YA). 1990. pap. 8.00 (*1-55878-059-9*) Game Designers.
Martin, Julia, ed. Ecological Responsibility: A Dialogue with Buddhism: A Collection of Essays & Talks. LC 97-903164. (C). 1997. 26.00 (*81-7030-529-2*, Pub. by Sri Satguru Pubns) S Asia.
Martin, Julia Wallis. The Bird Yard. LC 99-16428. 288p. 1999. text 23.95 (*0-312-20500-7*, Minotaur) St Martin.
— A Likeness in Stone. 1999. mass mkt. 6.50 (*0-312-97077-3*, Minotaur) St Martin.
Martin, Julie, tr. see Karlen, Barbro.
Martin, Juliet. A Puzzle. LC 93-18051. (Illus.). (J). 1994. write for info. (*0-383-03710-7*) SRA McGraw.
Martin, June H. Love's Fools: Aucassin, Troilus, Calisto & the Parody of the Courtly Lover. (Monografias A Ser.: Vol. XXI). 156p. (Orig.). (C). 1972. pap. 41.00 (*0-900411-33-3*, Pub. by Tamesis Bks Ltd) Boydell & Brewer.
Martin, June V., jt. auth. see Martin, Scott V.
***Martin, Justin.** Greenspan: The Man Behind Money. 2000. 27.50 (*0-7382-0275-4*, Pub. by Perseus Pubng) HarpC.
Martin, Justin. 150 Totally Terrific Writing Prompts: Lively, Fun Prompts to Motivate Every Writer in Your Class. 32p. 1999. pap. text 7.95 (*0-439-04086-8*) Scholastic Inc.
Martin, K. Psychology. 2nd ed. (Illus.). 256p. 1997. pap. text 19.95 (*0-7506-3472-3*) Buttrwrth-Heinemann.
Martin, K. & Bastock, T. W., eds. Waste Minimisation: A Chemist's Approach. 155p. 1994. 79.00 (*0-85186-585-2*, R6585) CRC Pr.
Martin, Kady. Let's Party. Martin, William, ed. (Illus.). 160p. (Orig.). 1986. pap. 8.95 (*0-942752-02-3*) C A M Co.
Martin, Karen. Healing the Forgotten Child: Support & Recovery for the Adult Children of Alcoholics (& Other Children of Dysfunctional Families) 60p. (Orig.). (C). 1989. pap., student ed. 79.95 (*0-9623925-0-2*) Resource Dynamics.
— Home Health Client. LC 97-122274. (Illus.). 480p. (C). (gr. 13). 1996. text 68.00 (*0-8151-8593-6*, 28845) Mosby Inc.
— Home Health Client. (Illus.). 170p. (C). (gr. 13). 1998. text, teacher ed. 26.00 (*0-8151-8592-8*, 28844) Mosby Inc.
— Mosby's Home Health Client. (Illus.). 96p. 2000. text, teacher ed. 24.95 (*0-8151-8589-8*, 28841) Mosby Inc.
— Mosby's Home Health Client Teaching. (Illus.). 416p. (C). (gr. 13). 1997. text 114.00 (*0-8151-2296-9*, 29975) Mosby Inc.
— Singing Cowboy. (Illus.). 224p. 1997. pap. 8.95 (*0-936369-60-4*) Son-Rise Pubns.
Martin, Karen, jt. ed. see Clover, Gloria.
Martin, Karen, jt. ed. see Martin, Don, Jr.
Martin, Karen, jt. ed. see Sumida, Stuart.
Martin, Karen S. & Scheet, Nancy J., eds. The Omaha System: Applications for Community Health Nursing. (Illus.). 423p. 1991. pap. text 81.00 (*0-7216-6126-2*, W B Saunders Co); pap. text 30.50 (*0-7216-6123-8*, W B Saunders Co) Harcrt Hlth Sci Grp.
Martin, Karen S., jt. auth. see Reif, Laura.
Martin, Karin A. Puberty, Sexuality & the Self: Girls & Boys at Adolescence. 176p. (C). 1996. 70.00 (*0-415-91424-8*); pap. 17.99 (*0-415-91425-6*) Routledge.
Martin, Kat. Bold Angel. 1994. mass mkt. 6.50 (*0-312-95303-8*) St Martin.
— Dangerous Passions. 1998. mass mkt. 6.99 (*0-312-96247-9*) St Martin.
— Devil's Prize. 1995. mass mkt. 6.99 (*0-312-95478-6*) St Martin.
***Martin, Kat.** The Dream. 432p. 2000. mass mkt. 6.99 (*0-8217-6568-X*, Zebra Kensgtn) Kensgtn Pub Corp.
Martin, Kat. The Duchess of Carbon County. LC 97-9390. 264p. 1997. lib. bdg. 21.95 (*0-7862-1105-9*) Five Star.
— Innocence Undone. 1997. mass mkt. 6.50 (*0-312-96089-1*) St Martin.
— Midnight Rider. 372p. 1996. mass mkt. 5.99 (*0-312-95774-2*) St Martin.
— Midnight Rider. LC 97-47732. 1998. 24.95 (*0-7862-1380-9*) Thorndike Pr.
***Martin, Kat.** Night Secrets. 368p. 1999. mass mkt. 6.99 (*0-312-97002-1*) St Martin.
Martin, Kat. Nothing but Velvet. 1997. mass mkt. 6.50 (*0-312-96243-6*) St Martin.
***Martin, Kat.** Perfect Sin. 368p. 2000. mass mkt. 6.99 (*0-312-97564-3*) St Martin.
Martin, Kat. The Silent Rose. 507p. 1999. mass mkt. 6.99 (*0-8217-6281-8*) Kensgtn Pub Corp.
— Silk & Steel. 368p. (Orig.). 2000. mass mkt. 6.99 (*0-312-97281-4*, St Martins Paperbacks) St Martin.
— Sweet Vengeance. 1993. mass mkt. 6.50 (*0-312-95095-0*) St Martin.
— Wicked Promise, Vol. 1. 344p. 1998. mass mkt. 6.99 (*0-312-96640-7*, Pub. by Tor Bks) St Martin.
Martin, Kate, jt. ed. see Ra'anan, Uri.
Martin, Kate E., tr. see Zahan, Dominique.
Martin, Katherine, ed. Women of Courage: Inspiring Stories from the Women Who Lived Them. LC 97-14204. (Inspiration/Women's Issues). (Illus.). 384p. 1999. pap. 14.95 (*1-57731-093-4*, Pub. by New Wrld Lib) Publishers Group.
Martin, Katherine I. Does My Child Have a Speech Problem? LC 96-35302. 224p. 1997. pap. 16.95 (*1-55652-315-7*) Chicago Review.
Martin, Katheryn, jt. auth. see Martin, Norman.
***Martin, Kathleen.** Penny Maybe. 160p. 1999. pap. write for info. (*1-896764-21-5*) Sec Story Pr.
Martin, Kathryn A., et al. Music Education as Praxis: Reflecting on Music-Making as Human Action. McCarthy, Marie, ed. LC 99-22115. (State-of-the-Arts Ser.: Vol. 3). 142p. (C). 1992. pap. write for info. (*0-9655233-2-2*) Univ MD Coll Pk.
Martin, Kathryn J. Believe It or Not--Mama Likes the Nursing Home! 136p. (Orig.). 1996. pap. 9.99 (*0-8341-1618-9*) Beacon Hill.
Martin, Kathy. Party Shakers. LC 82-21729. (Illus.). 47p. (J). (gr. k-8). 1982. pap. 3.95 (*0-942752-00-7*) C A M Co.
— Party Shakers. Martin, William, ed. (Illus.). 47p. 1982. pap. 3.95 (*0-942752-03-1*) C A M Co.
Martin, Kay. Strategic Recycling: Necessary Revolutions in Local Government Policy. LC 96-96838. (Illus.). xx, 250p. (Orig.). (C). 1996. pap. text 29.99 (*0-9653545-0-4*) Drkhorse Pr.
***Martin, Kay & Willoughby, Tina.** A-Z: Novel Ideas for Reading Teachers. 80p. 2000. pap., teacher ed. 16.95 (*1-877673-42-0*) Cottonwood Pr.
Martin, Kay, jt. auth. see Martin, Don.
Martin, Keith, tr. see Levesque, Jacques.
***Martin, Kelly.** Parent's Book of Baby Names. 1999. mass mkt. 5.98 (*0-345-43643-1*) Ballantine Pub Grp.
Martin, Ken. Digital Integrated Circuit Design. LC 98-53666. (Oxford Series in Electrical & Computer Engineering). (Illus.). 560p. (C). 1999. text 95.00 (*0-19-512584-3*) OUP.
Martin, Ken, jt. auth. see Schroeder, Will.
Martin, Ken, jt. auth. see Willingham, Scott D.
Martin, Kenneth. Tin Islands. 300p. 1996. pap. text 14.95 (*1-873741-27-8*, Pub. by Millvres Bks) LPC InBook.
Martin, Kenneth, ed. see Sperling, Abraham P.
Martin, Kenneth D. & Martin, Vida E. Gold Mining in Washington State, Yesterday & Today: Pioneer Stories. 130p. 1995. pap. text 17.95 (*0-9643300-0-8*) Golden Treas.
Martin, Kenneth R. Delaware Goes Whaling, 1833-1845. (Illus.). 64p. 1974. pap. 1.95 (*0-914650-06-8*) Hagley Museum.
— Heavy Weather & Hard Luck: Portsmouth Goes Whaling. LC 98-28415. (Portsmouth Marine Society Ser.: No. 24). (Illus.). 224p. 1998. 30.00 (*0-915819-23-6*) Portsmouth Marine Soc.
— Home Port - A History of the Navy Federal Credit Union. (Illus.). 136p. 1983. write for info. (*0-9610378-0-6*) Navy Fed Credit.
— Some Very Handsome Work: Scrimshaw at the Cape Cod National Seashore. (Illus.). 56p. 1991. pap. 4.95 (*0-915992-55-8*) Eastern National.
— Whalemen's Paintings & Drawings: Selections from the Kendall Whaling Museum Collection. LC 81-50343. (Illus.). 172p. 1983. 30.00 (*0-87413-191-X*) Kendall Whaling.
— Whalemen's Paintings & Drawings: Selections from the Kendall Whaling Museum Collection. LC 81-50343. (Illus.). 176p. 1982. 30.00 (*0-685-07611-3*) U Delaware Pr.
Martin, Kenneth R. & Lipfert, Nathan R. Lobstering & the Maine Coast. LC 85-61988. (Illus.). 143p. 1985. pap. 16.50 (*0-937410-04-7*) ME Maritime Mus.
Martin, Kenneth R. & Snow, Ralph L. Maine Odyssey: Good Times & Hard Times, Bath, 1936-1986. LC 88-61039. (Illus.). 320p. 1988. 30.00 (*0-9620401-0-X*) Patten Free Lib.
— The Pattens of Bath: A Seagoing Dynasty. LC 96-19324. 1996. pap. 22.95 (*0-937410-15-2*) ME Maritime Mus.
Martin, Kenneth R., ed. see Barnard, Edward C.
Martin, Kenneth W., jt. auth. see Buckwald, Aaron.
Martin, Kenneth W., jt. auth. see Johns, David.
Martin, Kenya R., et al. Love, Faith, & Hope: A Collection of Inspirational Poems, Short Stories, Essays, & Treasures. 210p. 1998. 15.00 (*0-9664022-0-0*) Martin Triplts.
Martin, Kerry & Wakeman, Diana. Sleeping Beauty. LC 92-53435. (Pop-up Bks.). 12p. (J). (ps-k). 1993. 11.95 (*1-56282-369-8*, Pub. by Disney Pr) Little.
Martin, Kevin. Daniel & the Ivory Princess. LC 94-34556. (Illus.). 80p. (J). 1994. 14.95 (*0-942963-50-4*) Distinctive Pub.
***Martin, Kevin.** In Search of a Silent God. Sledge, Bethany, ed. 126p. 1999. pap. write for info. (*0-7392-0321-5*, PO3359) Morris Pubng.
— Official Autograph Collector Price Guide. 2nd ed. (Illus.). 2000. pap. 24.95 (*0-9669710-3-5*) Odyssey Pubs.
Martin, Kevin. Official Autograph Collector Price Guide, 1999 1999. pap. text 24.95 (*0-9669710-0-0*) Odyssey Pubs.
— Signatures of the Stars: An Insider's Guide to Celebrity Autographs. LC 98-70851. (Illus.). 208p. 1998. pap. 16.95 (*0-930625-93-5*, Antique Trader) Krause Pubns.
Martin, Key, jt. auth. see Martin, Don.
***Martin, Kieran & Bonner.** A Great Place to Raise Kids: Interpretation, Science & the Rural-Urban Debate. LC 97-900263. 258p. 1999. pap. 24.95 (*0-7735-2026-0*) McG-Queens Univ Pr.
***Martin, Kim.** Because You Were Here. (Illus.). 24p. (J). (ps-6). 2000. pap. 5.00 (*0-615-11533-0*) Martin Graph.
Martin, Kim, et al. Prep Pak for FLMI 330. (FLMI Insurance Education Program Ser.). 201p. spiral bd., wbk. ed. 24.00 (*0-939921-92-8*, Pub. by Life Office) PBD Inc.
Martin, Kimberly A., jt. auth. see Bertram, Dora R., Jr.
Martin, Kingsley. The Rise of French Liberal Thought: A Study of Political Ideas from Bayle to Condorcet. 2nd ed. Mayer, J. P., ed. LC 80-11662. 316p. 1980. reprint ed. lib. bdg. 65.00 (*0-313-22368-8*, MARF, Greenwood Pr) Greenwood.
***Martin-Kniep, Giselle O.** Capturing the Wisdom of Practice: Professional Portfolios for Educators. LC 99-6646. 119p. 1999. pap. 20.95 (*0-87120-345-6*) ASCD.
Martin-Kniep, Giselle O., et al. Why Am I Doing This? Purposeful Teaching Through Portfolio Assessment. LC 97-51793. 1998. pap. 19.00 (*0-325-00010-7*, Pub. by Boynton Cook Pubs) Heinemann.
Martin, Knute, jt. auth. see Katz, Alfred H.
Martin, Kristine. Tried & True Art: Successful Projects for the Elementary Grades. LC 89-82079. (Illus.). 52p. 1990. pap. 7.95 (*0-9624597-8-X*) Aberdeen Pr.
Martin, Kristyne, ed. The Coxsackie Garden Cookbook. (Illus.). 84p. 1997. pap. 8.95 (*0-931485-31-2*) Scriptorium Pr.
Martin-Kuri, Karyn. A Message for the Millennium. 320p. 1996. 20.00 (*0-345-39522-0*) Ballantine Pub Grp.
Martin, Kurt. Teaching of Development Economics. Knapp, John, ed. 238p. 1967. 30.00 (*0-7146-1014-3*, Pub. by F Cass Pubs) Intl Spec Bk.
Martin, Kurt & Kall, Peter, eds. Stochastic Programming Methods & Technical Applications: Proceedings of the 3rd Gammifip-Workshop on "Stochastic Optimization: Numerical Methods & Technical Applications", Held at the Federal Armed Forces University Munich, Neubiberg Munchen, Germany, June 17-20, 1996. LC 97-48263. (Lecture Notes in Economics & Mathematical Systems Ser.: Vol. 458). (Illus.). x, 437p. 1998. pap. 85.00 (*3-540-63924-1*) Spr-Verlag.
Martin, Kymberly & Martin, Dennis. Espresso Magic. 56p. 1989. pap. 5.95 (*0-9631850-0-4*) Shady Ln Ent.
Martin, L. The Probing Lance. (Illus.). 64p. 12.95 (*0-317-65041-6*) Pleasure Trove.
Martin, L., jt. auth. see Berg, W.
Martin, L. B., jt. auth. see Kimbel, W. H.
Martin, L. C., ed. see Marlowe, Christopher.
Martin, L. Di, see Di Martin, L.
Martin, L. H., jt. auth. see Holmes, Mike.
***Martin, L. J.** Candor Canyon. 2000. mass mkt. 5.99 (*0-7860-1131-9*, Pinncle Kensgtn) Kensgtn Pub Corp.
Martin, L. John. International Propaganda: Its Legal & Diplomatic Control. 1990. 16.50 (*0-8446-0788-6*) Peter Smith.
Martin, L. Joyce. Light in the Evening Time. LC 95-19684. 224p. 1995. pap. 8.99 (*1-56722-132-7*) Word Aflame.
Martin, L. L. Categorization & Differentiation. (Recent Research in Psychology Ser.). vii, 87p. 1985. 36.95 (*0-387-96150-X*) Spr-Verlag.
Martin, LaJoyce. And They All Lived Happily Ever After: Lessons for Writing Your Book of Life. Sledge, Bethany, ed. 100p. 1999. pap. 9.00 (*0-7392-0137-9*, PO3060) Morris Pubng.
***Martin, LaJoyce.** Another Vow. LC 00-35203. 175p. 2000. pap. 8.99 (*1-56722-247-1*) Word Aflame.
Martin, LaJoyce. The Artist's Quest. LC 96-53624. 192p. (Orig.). 1997. pap. 8.99 (*1-56722-199-8*) Word Aflame.
— The Broken Bow. LC 96-11682. 192p. (Orig.). 1996. pap. 8.99 (*1-56722-139-4*, 1567221394) Word Aflame.
— Brother Harry & the Hobo. LC 98-52729. 160p. 1999. pap. 8.99 (*1-56722-228-5*) Word Aflame.
***Martin, LaJoyce.** Dear Grandma, I Like Cookies That Don't Crumble. Love, Ashton: Character Building Stories for Youth. 140p. (J). 2000. pap. write for info. (*0-7392-0501-3*, PO3945) Morris Pubng.
Martin, LaJoyce. Destiny's Winding Road. LC 97-49671. 206p. 1998. pap. 8.99 (*1-56722-211-0*) Word Aflame.
— The Fiddler's Song. 190p. (Orig.). 1996. pap. write for info. (*1-57502-217-6*, D0870) Morris Pubng.
— I'm Coming Apart Lord! Does That Mean I'm a Disciple. Sledge, Bethany, ed. 140p. 1998. pap. 7.99 (*1-57502-685-6*, PO1933) Morris Pubng.
— Love's Golden Wings. LC 87-17346. (Pioneer Trilogy Ser.). (Illus.). 256p. (Orig.). (YA). (gr. 7 up). 1987. pap. 8.99 (*0-932581-19-6*) Word Aflame.
— Love's Mended Wings. LC 86-33955. (Pioneer Trilogy Ser.: Bk. 2). (Illus.). 272p. (Orig.). 1987. pap. 8.99 (*0-932581-09-9*) Word Aflame.
— Love's Velvet Chains. LC 89-24983. (Illus.). 240p. (Orig.). 1989. pap. 8.99 (*0-932581-56-0*) Word Aflame.
— Mister B's Land. LC 98-34552. 219p. 1998. pap. 8.99 (*1-56722-222-6*) Word Aflame.
— Ordered Steps. LC 96-18966. (Path of Promise Ser.). 208p. (Orig.). 1996. pap. 8.99 (*1-56722-190-4*) Word Aflame.
— The Other Side of Jordan. LC 92-14091. 246p. (Orig.). 1992. pap. 8.99 (*0-932581-98-6*) Word Aflame.
***Martin, LaJoyce.** Postmark. 150p. 2000. pap. 8.99 (*1-56722-420-2*) Word Aflame.
Martin, LaJoyce. So Long the Night. LC 94-48229. 196p. (Orig.). (YA). 1995. pap. 8.99 (*1-56722-032-0*) Word Aflame.
— So Swift the Storm. LC 90-35201. (Illus.). 232p. (Orig.). 1990. pap. 8.99 (*0-932581-66-8*) Word Aflame.
— Thread's End. Martin, Bethany, ed. 180p. (Orig.). 1997. pap. 7.99 (*1-57502-419-5*, PO1289) Morris Pubng.
— To Even the Score. LC 93-44338. 200p. (Orig.). 1994. pap. 8.99 (*1-56722-016-9*) Word Aflame.
— To Love a Bent Winged Angel. LC 86-7820. (Pioneer Trilogy Ser.: Bk. 1). (Illus.). 288p. (Orig.). 1986. pap. 8.99 (*0-912315-99-7*) Word Aflame.
— To Love a Runaway. LC 88-31620. 240p. (Orig.). 1989. pap. 8.99 (*0-932581-42-0*) Word Aflame.
***Martin, LaJoyce.** To Say Goodbye. LC 99-41101. (Harris Family Saga Ser.: Vol. 10). 174p. 1999. pap. 8.99 (*1-56722-237-4*) Word Aflame.
Martin, LaJoyce. To Strike a Match. LC 97-25227. 192p. 1997. pap. 8.99 (*1-56722-206-4*) Word Aflame.
— Two Scars Against One. LC 94-3763. 192p. (Orig.). 1995. pap. 8.99 (*1-56722-025-8*) Word Aflame.
— When Love Filled the Gap. LC 87-37241. 150p. (Orig.). 1988. pap. 8.99 (*0-932581-30-7*) Word Aflame.
— The Wooden Heart. LC 91-11965. 235p. (Orig.). 1991. pap. 8.99 (*0-932581-85-4*) Word Aflame.
Martin, Lance. Mariska. (Illus.). 64p. (Orig.). 1995. pap. 19.95 (*0-930400-13-5*) Pleasure Trove.
Martin, Lance & Aagre, Scott. Calligraphy & Related Ornamentation. (Illus.). 98p. 1982. pap. 5.95 (*0-930400-06-2*); lib. bdg. 12.95 (*0-685-57738-4*) Pleasure Trove.
Martin, Lance & Dicke, Robert, Jr. Calligraphy & Ornamental Lettering. Cooper, E., ed. (Illus.). 1979. 12.95 (*0-8024-9953-8*) Pleasure Trove.
Martin, Lance & Martin, Carol. Prayers Against Depression. 124p. 1996. pap. 8.95 (*0-914733-21-4*) Desert Min.
Martin-Larranaga, Ana. The Big Wide-Mouthed Frog. LC 98-33873. (J). 1999. pap. 3.29 (*0-7636-0808-4*) Candlewick Pr.
Martin, Larry. For Sale: The Soul of a Nation. 128p. 1997. pap. 5.95 (*0-9646289-3-7*) Christian Life Bks.
— In the Beginning: Readings on the Origins of the 20th Century Pentecostal Revival & the Birth of the Pentecostal Church of God. (Illus.). 160p. 1994. pap. 7.99 (*0-9646289-0-2*) Christian Life Bks.
— Proven Profits from Pollution Prevention: Case Studies in Resource Conservation & Waste Reduction, Vol. II. White, Diana, ed. LC 85-82638. 130p. 1989. pap. text 20.00 (*0-917582-40-3*) Inst Local Self Re.
Martin, Larry, ed. Holy Ghost Revival on Azusa Street: The True Believers; Eyewitness Accounts of the Revival That Shook the World. (Complete Azusa Street Library: Ser. 2). (Illus.). 160p. 1998. pap. 7.99 (*0-9646289-5-3*) Christian Life Bks.
Martin, Larry & Harrison, Alan. Study Guide. pap. 14.50 (*0-393-97057-4*); pap. 14.50 (*0-393-97056-6*) Norton.
Martin, Larry, jt. auth. see Rothschild, Bruce M.
***Martin, Larry E.** The Life & Ministry of William J. Seymour & a History of the Azusa Street Revival. LC 99-76361. (Complete Azusa Street Library: Vol. 1). (Illus.). 384p. 1999. pap. 12.99 (*0-9646289-4-5*) Christian Life Bks.
Martin, Larry E. The Topeka Outpouring of 1901: Eyewitness Accounts of the Revival That Birthed the 20th Century Pentecostal/Charismatic Revival. (Illus.). 128p. 1997. pap. 5.95 (*0-9646289-2-9*) Christian Life Bks.
***Martin, Larry E., ed.** Holy Ghost Revival on Azusa Street - The True Believers Pt. II: More Eyewitness Accounts. (Complete Azusa Street Library: Vol. 3). (Illus.). 160p. 1999. pap. 7.99 (*0-9646289-6-1*) Christian Life Bks.
Martin, Larry G. Youthful High School Noncompleters: Enhancing Opportunities for Employment & Education. 59p. 1987. 7.00 (*0-318-23415-7*, IN316) Ctr Educ Trng Employ.
Martin, Larry J. Rush to Destiny. 312p. 1998. reprint ed. lib. bdg. 29.95 (*0-7351-0028-4*) Replica Bks.
— Shadow of the Grizzly. large type ed. LC 93-28535. 304p. 1993. lib. bdg. 18.95 (*0-7862-0063-4*) Thorndike Pr.
— Sounding Drum. 352p. 1999. text 23.00 (*1-57566-368-6*) Kensgtn Pub Corp.
— Write from History: Right from History. 131p. 1994. pap. 12.95 (*1-885339-06-2*) Buttonwillow.
***Martin, Larry Jay.** Last Stand, Vol. 1. 1999. pap. 6.99 (*0-7860-1062-2*, Pinncle Kensgtn) Kensgtn Pub Corp.
Martin, Larry L. On My Terms: Against the Current. 450p. 1999. pap. 12.99 (*1-892732-03-3*) J E Ferguson Publ.
Martin, Larry R., jt. auth. see Lewbel, George S.
Martin, Laura. Falling for the Boss. 1999. mass mkt. 3.50 (*0-373-17436-5*, 1-17436-6) Harlequin Bks.
— Florida Gardeners: Wisdom Shared over the Fence. LC 97-22617. (Illus.). 224p. 1997. 19.95 (*0-87833-954-X*) Taylor Pub.
— Living with the Enemy. 1999. pap. 3.50 (*0-373-17420-9*, 1-17420-0, Harlequin) Harlequin Bks.
***Martin, Laura.** Narrative Feminine Identity & the Appearance of Woman in Some of the Shorter Fiction of Goethe, Kleist, Hawthorne & James. LC 00-20027. (Women's Studies: Vol. 23). 224p. 2000. text 89.95 (*0-7734-7809-4*) E Mellen.
Martin, Laura. Perfect Strangers. (Romance Ser.: Vol. 397). 1998. mass mkt. 3.50 (*0-373-17397-0*, 1-17397-0) Harlequin Bks.
— Perfectos Desconocidos. (SPA.). 1997. per. 3.50 (*0-373-33405-2*, 1-33405-1) Harlequin Bks.
— Textos Qanjobales de Santa Eulalia. (MYN & SPA.). 150p. 2000. pap. 12.95 (*1-886502-24-2*) Yax Te Found.
Martin, Laura A., ed. & photos by see Dever, Sean M.
Martin, Laura C. Folklore of Birds. LC 93-39582. (Folklore Ser.). 240p. 1993. 24.95 (*1-56440-216-9*) Globe Pequot.
— Folklore of Birds. LC 92-39582. (Folklore Ser.). (Illus.). 240p. 1996. pap. 16.95 (*1-56440-872-8*) Globe Pequot.
— Gardens of the Heartland. LC 95-37434. (Illus.). 256p. 1996. 45.00 (*1-55859-781-6*) Abbeville Pr.
***Martin, Laura C.** Gifts from a Southern Garden. LC 99-55703. 2000. 32.95 (*0-87833-223-5*) Taylor Pub.
Martin, Laura C. Handmade Gifts from a Country Garden. (Illus.). 160p. 1997. 19.98 (*0-89660-078-5*, Artabras) Abbeville Pr.

M

— Laura C. Martin's Southern Gardens: A Gracious History & Traveler's Guide. LC 92-27281. (Illus.). 256p. 1993. 19.98 (*1-55859-323-3*, Artabras) Abbeville Pr.
— Precious Moments Last Forever. LC 94-27040. (Illus.). 304p. 1994. 17.98 (*1-55859-859-6*) Abbeville Pr.
— Precious Moments Last Forever. (Illus.). 304p. 1997. 17.98 (*0-89660-083-1*, Artabras) Abbeville Pr.
— Texas Gardeners: Answers from the Experts. LC 98-38039. 1999. 14.95 (*0-87833-201-4*) Taylor Pub.
— Wildlife Folklore. (Folklore Ser.). (Illus.). 256p. 1996. reprint ed. pap. 16.95 (*1-56440-974-0*) Globe Pequot.
Martin, Laura M., ed. Sociocultural Psychology: Theory & Practice of Doing & Knowing. (Learning in Doing: Social, Cognitive & Computational Perspectives Ser.). (Illus.). 424p. (C). 1995. text 59.95 (*0-521-46278-9*) Cambridge U Pr.
Martin, Laurelynn G. Searching for Home. LC 96-21539. 192p. (Orig.). 1996. pap. 11.95 (*0-9620507-5-X*) Cosmic Concepts Pr.
Martin, Laurence, ed. Strategic Thought in the Nuclear Age. 1981. 18.50 (*0-8018-2330-7*) Johns Hopkins.
Martin, Laurence & Garnett, John C. British Foreign Policy. LC 97-10240. (Chatham House Papers). 256p. 1997. 46.00 (*1-85567-468-8*); pap. 15.95 (*1-85567-469-6*) Bks Intl VA.
Martin, Laurie. French Vocabulary. (FRE & ENG.). 256p. 1990. pap. 5.95 (*0-8120-4496-7*) Barron.
Martin, Lawrence. All You Really Need to Know to Interpret Arterial Blood Gases. (Illus.). 224p. 1992. pap. 25.00 (*0-8121-1572-4*) Lppncott W & W.
— All You Really Need to Know to Interpret Arterial Blood Gases. LC 98-48608. 1999. write for info. (*0-683-30604-9*) Lppncott W & W.
— Economics: Study Guide. 2nd ed. (C). 1997. pap. text, student ed. 28.00 (*0-393-96896-0*) Norton.
— Pickwickian & Other Stories of Intensive Care: Medical & Ethical Challenges in the ICU. LC 91-61828. 247p. 1991. pap. 10.95 (*1-879653-04-4*) Lakeside Pr.
— Principles of Microeconomics: Study Guide. 2nd ed. (C). 1997. pap., student ed. write for info. (*0-393-96932-0*) Norton.
— Scuba Diving Explained: Questions & Answers on Physiology & Medical Aspects of Scuba Diving. LC 93-79817. (Illus.). 280p. (Orig.). 1995. pap. 20.00 (*1-879653-12-5*) Lakeside Pr.
— Scuba Diving Explained - Questions & Answers on Physiology & Medical Aspects. LC 93-79817. (Illus.). 310p. 1997. pap. 19.95 (*0-941332-56-X*, D883) Best Pub Co.
Martin, Lawrence, et al. Scanning Microscopy of Vertebrate Mineralized Tissues: A Compilation in Memory of Edward J. Reith. (Illus.). viii, 384p. 1989. pap. text 43.00 (*0-931288-41-X*) Scanning Microscopy.
***Martin, Lawrence L.** Contracting for Service Delivery: Local Government Choices. Moulder, Evelina R., ed. (Illus.). 108p. 1999. pap. 36.00i (*0-87326-168-2*) Intl City-Cnty Mgt.
— Financial Management for Human Service Administrators. 288p. 2000. pap. text 37.33 (*0-321-04949-7*) Addison-Wesley.
Martin, Lawrence L. Total Quality Management in Human Service Organizations. (Human Services Guides Ser.: Vol. 67). (Illus.). 112p. (C). 1993. text 42.00 (*0-8039-4949-9*) Sage.
Martin, Lawrence L. & Kettner, Peter M. Measuring the Performance of Human Service Programs. LC 95-41794. (Human Services Guides Ser.: Vol. 71). 139p. 1996. 42.00 (*0-8039-7134-6*); pap. 18.95 (*0-8039-7135-4*) Sage.
Martin, Lawrence L., jt. auth. see Kettner, Peter M.
Martin, Lawrence L., jt. ed. see Lynch, Thomas D.
Martin, Lawrence M. Nursing Home Decision: Easing the Transition for Everyone. 175p. 1999. pap. 14.95 (*0-471-34804-X*) Wiley.
Martin, Lawrence M., tr. see Zahan, Dominique.
Martin, Lawrence R. & Seldman, Neil. An Environmental Review of Incineration Technologies. LC 86-27377. (Illus.). 119p. 1986. pap. 20.00 (*0-917582-45-4*) Inst Local Self Re.
Martin, Lawrence T. & Hurst, Dom D., trs. Homilies on the Gospels by the Venerable Bede, Set, Vols. I & II. (Cistercian Studies: Nos. CS110 & CS111). 1991. 60.00 (*0-685-49216-8*); pap. 25.00 (*0-685-49217-6*) Cistercian Pubns.
— Homilies on the Gospels by the Venerable Bede, Vol. I. (Cistercian Studies: Nos. CS110 & CS111). 1991. pap. 13.95 (*0-87907-710-7*); boxed set 32.95 (*0-87907-610-0*) Cistercian Pubns.
— Homilies on the Gospels by the Venerable Bede, Vol. II. (Cistercian Studies: Nos. CS110 & CS111). 1991. pap. 13.95 (*0-87907-911-8*); boxed set 32.95 (*0-87907-711-5*) Cistercian Pubns.
Martin, Lawrence T., tr. & intro. see Bede.
Martin, Lee. Bird in a Cage. 1997. per. 4.99 (*0-373-26225-6*, 1-26225-2, Wrldwide Lib) Harlequin Bks.
— Death Warmed Over. 1991. mass mkt. 3.50 (*0-373-26065-2*) Harlequin Bks.
***Martin, Lee.** From Our House: A Memoir. LC 99-49707. 208p. 2000. 22.95 (*0-525-94546-6*, Dutt) Dutton Plume.
Martin, Lee. Genealogy of Murder. (Worldwide Library Mysteries: No. 239). 1997. per. 4.99 (*0-373-26239-6*, 1-26239-3, Wrldwide Lib) Harlequin Bks.
— Hacker. (Worldwide Library Mysteries). 1994. per. 3.99 (*0-373-26135-7*, 1-26135-3) Harlequin Bks.
— Hal's Own Murder Case. 1992. mass mkt. 3.99 (*0-373-26087-3*) Harlequin Bks.
— The Least You Need to Know: Stories. LC 95-35647. 192p. 1996. 21.95 (*0-9641151-2-3*); pap. 13.95 (*0-9641151-3-1*) Sarabande Bks.
— The Thursday Club. LC 97-72090. 1997. 14.95 (*1-57008-315-0*) Bookcraft Inc.
***Martin, Lee.** Trail of the Circle Star. large type ed. 288p. 1998. pap. 18.99 (*0-7089-5426-X*) Ulverscroft.
— Trail of the Fast Gun. large type ed. 272p. 1999. pap. 18.99 (*0-7089-5552-5*, Linford) Ulverscroft.
— Trail of the Long Riders. large type ed. 264p. 1999. pap. 18.99 (*0-7089-5573-8*, Linford) Ulverscroft.
— Trail of the Restless Gun. large type ed. 272p. 2000. pap. 18.99 (*0-7089-5667-X*, Linford) Ulverscroft.
Martin, Lee J., jt. auth. see Kroitor, Harry P.
Martin, Lee R., ed. A Survey of Agricultural Economics Literature, Vol. 4. (Illus.). 1064p. (C). 1991. text 59.95 (*0-8166-1942-5*) U of Minn Pr.
Martin, Leland E., et al. A Hearty Band of Firefighters: The Illustrated History of the Danvers Fire Department. LC 97-29889. (Illus.). 1997. pap. write for info. (*1-57864-011-3*) Donning Co.
Martin, Len. Forbes Field - Build-It-Yourself: With an Introduction & History. (Major League Baseball Parks Ser.: No. 2). (Illus.). 102p. (Orig.). 1995. pap. 19.95 (*0-9642887-0-2*) Pt Four Ltd.
Martin, Len D. The Allied Artists Checklist: The Feature Films & Short Subjects of Allied Artists Pictures Corporation, 1947-1978. LC 92-56665. (Illus.). 232p. 1993. lib. bdg. 45.00 (*0-89950-782-4*) McFarland & Co.
— The Columbia Checklist: The Feature Films, Serials, Cartoons & Short Subjects of Columbia Pictures Corporation, 1922-1988. LC 90-53507. 647p. 1991. lib. bdg. 82.00 (*0-89950-556-2*) McFarland & Co.
— The Republic Pictures Checklist: Features, Serials, Cartoons, Short Subjects, & Training Films of Republic Pictures Corporation, 1935-1959. LC 98-12993. (Illus.). 391p. 1998. lib. bdg. 68.50 (*0-7864-0438-8*) McFarland & Co.
***Martin-LeNell, A. Wayne.** Income Taxes for Priests Only - 1998 Tax Year. 102p. 1999. pap. text 15.00 (*1-893060-00-4*) NFPC.
Martin, Lenore G. New Frontiers in Middle East Security. LC 98-44039. 1998. text 49.95 (*0-312-21414-6*) St Martin.
Martin, Leo. The Plain English Guide to IRA Distributions. 9th rev. ed. LC 97-78367. 175p. 1998. ring bd. 99.00 (*0-9664421-0-5*) IRA Doctor.
— The Plain English Guide to IRA Distributions. 10th rev. ed. LC 99-71542. 175p. 1999. ring bd. 99.00 (*0-9664421-1-3*) IRA Doctor.
Martin, Leonard, ed. Bannerman Catalog 1907: Catalog of Military Goods. (Illus.). 256p. 1996. reprint ed. pap. 22.95 (*0-9619727-3-4*) Mil Naval Bks.
Martin, Leonard G. Build-Your-Own Cathedral of Learning. 44p. (Orig.). 1991. pap. 20.00 (*1-878242-00-8*) Fourth River Pr.
Martin, Leonard L. & Tesser, Abraham, eds. The Construction of Social Judgments. (Publication of the University of Georgia's Institute for Behavior Research Ser.). 368p. 1992. text 79.95 (*0-8058-1149-4*) L Erlbaum Assocs.
— Striving & Feeling: Interactions among Goals, Affect, & Self-Regulation. 424p. 1996. text 79.95 (*0-8058-1629-1*) L Erlbaum Assocs.
Martin, Leonard L., jt. auth. see Clore, Gerald L.
Martin, Les. Darkness Falls. (X-Files Ser.). 1995. 9.60 (*0-606-10089-X*, Pub. by Turtleback) Demco.
— Die, Bug, Die! (X-Files Ser.). 1997. 9.60 (*0-606-10977-3*, Pub. by Turtleback) Demco.
— Fear. (X-Files Ser.). 1996. 9.05 (*0-606-10094-6*, Pub. by Turtleback) Demco.
— Fresh Bones. (X Files Young Adult Ser.: No. 6). (Illus.). 144p. (YA). (gr. 12 up). 1997. pap. 4.50 (*0-06-447180-2*, HarpTrophy) HarpC Child Bks.
— The Host. (X Files Young Adult Ser.: No. 8). (Illus.). 128p. (YA). (gr. 7 up). 1997. pap. 4.50 (*0-06-447181-0*, HarpTrophy) HarpC Child Bks.
— Humbug. LC 49-242030. (X-Files Ser.). 1996. 9.05 (*0-606-10092-X*, Pub. by Turtleback) Demco.
Martin, Les. Oliver Twist. LC 89-24279. (Bullseye Step into Classics Ser.). (J). 1994. 9.09 (*0-606-09705-8*, Pub. by Turtleback) Demco.
Martin, Les. Tiger, Tiger. (X-Files Ser.). 1996. 9.60 (*0-606-10090-3*, Pub. by Turtleback) Demco.
— Time Machine. LC 89-39506. (Bullseye Step into Classics Ser.). 1994. 9.09 (*0-606-09973-5*, Pub. by Turtleback) Demco.
Martin, Les. X Files: Darkness Falls, No. 2. (X-Files Ser.: No. 2). 112p. (J). (gr. 5 up). 1995. pap. 4.50 (*0-06-440614-8*, HarpTrophy) HarpC Child Bks.
Martin, Les. X Files: E.B.E. (X-Files Ser.). (J). 1996. 9.05 (*0-606-10978-1*, Pub. by Turtleback) Demco.
Martin, Les. X Files: E.B.E., No. 9. (X-Files Ser.: No. 9). 112p. (YA). (gr. 5 up). 1996. pap. 4.50 (*0-06-440653-9*, HarpTrophy) HarpC Child Bks.
— X Files: Fear, No. 7. (X-Files Ser.: No. 7). 112p. (J). (gr. 4-7). 1996. pap. 3.95 (*0-06-440642-3*, HarpTrophy) HarpC Child Bks.
— X Files: Ghost in the Machine, No. 11. (X-Files Ser.: Vol. 11). 112p. (YA). (gr. 5 up). 1997. pap. 4.50 (*0-06-440678-4*, HarpTrophy) HarpC Child Bks.
— X Files: Humbug, No. 5. (X-Files Ser.: No. 5). 128p. (J). (gr. 5 up). 1996. pap. 3.95 (*0-06-440627-X*, HarpTrophy) HarpC Child Bks.
— X Files: Quarantine, No. 13. (X-Files Ser.: Vol. 13). 128p. (J). (gr. 7 up). 1999. pap. 4.50 (*0-06-447189-6*) HarpC Child Bks.
— X Files: Tiger, Tiger, No. 3. (X-Files Ser.: Vol. 3). 112p. (YA). (gr. 5 up). 1995. pap. 4.50 (*0-06-440626-1*, HarpTrophy) HarpC Child Bks.
— X Files: X Marks the Spot, No. 1. (X-Files Ser.: No. 1). 128p. (YA). (gr. 5 up). 1995. pap. 4.50 (*0-06-440613-X*, HarpTrophy) HarpC Child Bks.
Martin, Les. X Marks the Spot a Novel. (X-Files Ser.). 1995. 10.05 (*0-606-10088-1*, Pub. by Turtleback) Demco.
— Young Indiana Jones & the Tomb of Terror. LC 89-43389. (Young Indiana Jones Ser.: No. 2). 112p. (J). (gr. 4-6). 1990. pap. 3.99 (*0-679-80581-8*) Random Bks Yng Read.
Martin, Lesley, ed. see Hosoe, Eikoh & Holborn, Mark.
Martin, Lesley, ed. see Morgan, Barbara & Patnaik, Deba P.
Martin, Leslie J., jt. ed. see Jones, Mary M.
Martin, Letty. Straight Stitch Machine Applique: Patterns & Instructions for This Easy Technique. LC 94-38946. (Illus.). 158p. 1995. pap. 16.95 (*0-89145-839-5*, 3903, Am Quilters Soc) Collector Bks.
Martin, Levi E. Eberly: Biographic Memorial of John Eberly & Genealogical Family Register of the Eberly Family. 78p. 1997. reprint ed. pap. 15.50 (*0-8328-8426-X*); reprint ed. lib. bdg. 25.50 (*0-8328-8425-1*) Higginson Bk Co.
***Martin, Lexi & Davis, Jessica.** 'N Sync. LC 00-32923. (Illus.). 96p. 2000. 9.98 (*1-58663-061-X*) M Friedman Pub Grp Inc.
Martin, Liam A. The Dharma of History: A West Indian Buddhism. LC 96-94058. xii, 150p. (Orig.). 1996. pap. 19.95 (*0-9650892-0-7*) Gully Pr.
Martin, Liam C. A Walking Tour of Dublin Churches. 64p. 1989. pap. 22.00 (*1-85390-945-9*, Pub. by Veritas Pubns) St Mut.
Martin, Lillian M. Gleams in the Glooming. Martin, Wilfred B., ed. 88p. 1988. pap. 7.95 (*0-920021-60-3*) Creative Bk Pub.
Martin, Lillien J. & De Grucy, Clare. Sweeping the Cobwebs. Kastenbaum, Robert J., ed. LC 78-22209. (Aging & Old Age Ser.). 1979. reprint ed. lib. bdg. 17.95 (*0-405-11823-6*) Ayer.
Martin, Linda. Laboratory Exercises for Animal Sciences & Industry. rev. ed. 160p. (C). 1995. spiral bd. 25.95 (*0-8403-9248-6*) Kendall-Hunt.
— Mesa Verde: The Story Behind the Scenery. LC 93-77024. (Illus.). 48p. (Orig.). 1993. pap. 7.95 (*0-88714-075-0*) KC Pubns.
— Mesa Verde: The Story Behind the Scenery. Morales, Brigitte, tr. (GER., Illus.). 48p. (Orig.). 1993. pap. 8.95 (*0-88714-735-6*) KC Pubns.
— Mesa Verde: The Story Behind the Scenery. Le Bras, Yvon, tr. (FRE., Illus.). 48p. (Orig.). 1993. pap. 8.95 (*0-88714-736-4*) KC Pubns.
— Watch Them Grow. LC 93-25426. (Illus.). 48p. (J). (ps-1). 1994. 14.95 (*1-56458-458-5*) DK Pub Inc.
— When Dinosaurs Go to School. LC 98-34160. (Illus.). 32p. (J). (gr. k-1). 1999. 13.95 (*0-8118-2089-0*) Chronicle Bks.
— When Dinosaurs Go Visiting. (Illus.). 32p. 1997. pap. 4.95 (*0-8118-1707-5*) Chronicle Bks.
Martin, Linda & Segrave, Kerry. Anti-Rock: The Opposition to Rock 'n' Roll. 382p. 1993. reprint ed. pap. 14.95 (*0-306-80502-2*) Da Capo.
— City Parks of Canada. LC 84-98125. (Illus.). 128p. 1995. pap. 12.95 (*0-88962-229-9*) Mosaic.
— Women in Comedy. (Illus.). 312p. 1986. 19.95 (*0-8065-1000-5*, Citadel Pr) Carol Pub Group.
Martin, Linda B., jt. auth. see Weidman, Bette S.
Martin, Linda G. & Preston, Samuel H., eds. Demography of Aging. LC 94-66697. (Illus.). 423p. 1994. pap. 131.20 (*0-608-04832-1*, 206548900004) Bks Demand.
Martin, Linda G., ed. see National Research Council Staff.
Martin, Linda W., ed. New Essays on "Go down, Moses" (American Novel Ser.). 167p. (C). 1996. text 29.95 (*0-521-45431-X*); pap. text 15.95 (*0-521-45609-6*) Cambridge U Pr.
Martin, Linette. Practical Praying. LC 96-49760. (Illus.). 128p. 1997. pap. 10.00 (*0-8028-4233-X*) Eerdmans.
Martin, Lionel. The Early Fidel. 1978. 8.95 (*0-8184-0254-7*) Carol Pub Group.
Martin, Lisa L. Coercive Cooperation: Explaining Multilateral Economic Sanctions. (Illus.). 324p. 1992. text 55.00 (*0-691-08624-9*, Pub. by Princeton U Pr) Cal Prin Full Svc.
***Martin, Lisa L.** Democratic Commitments: Legislatures & International Cooperation. LC 99-49295. (Illus.). 256p. 2000. text 49.50 (*0-691-00923-6*, Pub. by Princeton U Pr) Cal Prin Full Svc.
Martin-Lof, Anders, ed. Harald Cramer: Selected Works. LC 93-25592. 1994. 111.95 (*0-387-56671-6*) Spr-Verlag.
Martin-Lof, Anders, ed. see Cramer, Harald.
Martin, Loren D. Isaiah: An Ensign to the Nations. LC 81-92840. (Isaiah Ser.: Vol. 1). (Illus.). 180p. 1982. 9.95 (*0-9608244-0-5*) Valiant Pubns.
— Isaiah: An Ensign to the Nations, Set. LC 81-92840. (Isaiah Ser.: Vol. 1). (Illus.). 180p. 1982. write for info. (*0-9608244-2-1*) Valiant Pubns.
— Utah Criminal Code. (Orig.). spiral bd. 12.50 (*0-9608244-3-X*) Valiant Pubns.
Martin, Lorraine, jt. auth. see Martin, Scott D.
Martin, Lothar, jt. auth. see Fishman, Sterling.
Martin, Louise. Alligators. (Reptile Discovery Library). (Illus.). 24p. (J). (gr. k-5). 1989. lib. bdg. 14.60 (*0-86592-579-8*) Rourke Enter.
— Aranas Comedoras de Pajaros. (Aranas Ser.).Tr. of Bird Eating Spiders. (SPA.). 24p. (J). (gr. k-4). 1994. lib. bdg. 10.95 (*0-86593-310-3*) Rourke Corp.
— Aranas de Tapadera. (Aranas Ser.).Tr. of Trapdoor Spiders. (SPA.). 24p. (J). (gr. k-4). 1994. lib. bdg. 10.95 (*0-86593-313-8*) Rourke Corp.
— Aranas Pescadores. (Aranas Ser.).Tr. of Fishing Spiders. (SPA.). 24p. (J). (gr. k-4). 1994. lib. bdg. 10.95 (*0-86593-308-1*) Rourke Corp.
— Aranas Tejedoras de Tunel. (Aranas Ser.).Tr. of Funnel Web Spiders. (SPA.). 24p. (J). (gr. k-4). 1994. lib. bdg. 10.95 (*0-86593-309-X*) Rourke Corp.
— Aranas Viuda Negra. (Aranas Ser.).Tr. of Black Widow Spiders. (SPA.). 24p. (J). (gr. k-4). 1994. lib. bdg. 10.95 (*0-86593-312-X*) Rourke Corp.
— Ballenas. (Fauna Silvestre en Peligro Ser.).Tr. of Whales. 24p. (J). (gr. k-4). 1994. lib. bdg. 10.95 (*0-86593-341-3*) Rourke Corp.
— Bird Eating Spiders. (Spider Discovery Library). (Illus.). 24p. (J). (gr. k-5). 1988. lib. bdg. 14.60 (*0-86592-966-1*) Rourke Enter.
— Black Widow Spiders. (Spider Discovery Library). (Illus.). 24p. (J). (gr. k-5). 1988. lib. bdg. 14.60 (*0-86592-965-3*) Rourke Enter.
— Chameleons. (Reptile Discovery Library). (Illus.). 24p. (J). (gr. k-5). 1989. lib. bdg. 14.60 (*0-86592-576-3*) Rourke Enter.
— Elefantes. (Fauna Silvestre en Peligro Ser.).Tr. of Elephants. (SPA.). 24p. (J). (gr. k-4). 1994. lib. bdg. 10.95 (*0-86593-336-7*) Rourke Corp.
— Fishing Spiders. (Spider Discovery Library). (Illus.). 24p. (J). (gr. k-5). 1988. lib. bdg. 14.60 (*0-86592-964-5*) Rourke Enter.
— Focas. (Fauna Silvestre en Peligro Ser.).Tr. of Seals. 24p. (J). (gr. k-4). 1994. lib. bdg. 10.95 (*0-86593-339-1*) Rourke Corp.
— Funnel Web Spiders. (Spider Discovery Library). (Illus.). 24p. (J). (gr. k-5). 1988. lib. bdg. 10.95 (*0-86592-962-9*) Rourke Enter.
— Iguanas. (Reptile Discovery Library). (Illus.). 24p. (J). (gr. k-5). 1989. lib. bdg. 14.60 (*0-86592-575-5*) Rourke Enter.
— Komodo Dragons. (Reptile Discovery Library). (Illus.). 24p. (J). (gr. k-5). 1989. 8.95 (*0-685-58604-9*) Rourke Corp.
— Komodo Dragons. (Reptile Discovery Library). (Illus.). 24p. (J). (gr. k-5). 1989. lib. bdg. 14.60 (*0-86592-574-7*) Rourke Enter.
— Lizards. (Reptile Discovery Library). (Illus.). 24p. (J). (gr. k-5). 1989. 8.95 (*0-685-58605-7*) Rourke Corp.
— Lizards. (Reptile Discovery Library). (Illus.). 24p. (J). (gr. k-5). 1989. lib. bdg. 14.60 (*0-86592-577-1*) Rourke Enter.
— Reptile Discovery Library, 6 bks., Set, Reading Level 2. (Illus.). 144p. (J). (gr. k-5). 1989. lib. bdg. 87.60 (*0-86592-573-9*) Rourke Enter.
— Tarantulas. (Aranas Ser.). 24p. (J). (gr. k-4). 1994. lib. bdg. 17.97 (*0-86593-311-1*) Rourke Corp.
— Tarantulas. (Spider Discovery Library). (Illus.). 24p. (J). (gr. k-5). 1988. lib. bdg. 14.60 (*0-86592-967-X*) Rourke Enter.
— Tigers. (Wildlife in Danger Ser.). (Illus.). 24p. (J). (gr. k-5). 1988. lib. bdg. 8.95 (*0-685-58307-4*) Rourke Corp.
— Tigres. (Fauna Silvestre en Peligro Ser.).Tr. of Tigers. (Illus.). 24p. (J). (gr. k-4). lib. bdg. 10.95 (*0-86593-340-5*) Rourke Corp.
— Trapdoor Spiders. (Spider Discovery Library). (Illus.). 24p. (J). (gr. k-5). 1988. lib. bdg. 8.95 (*0-685-58303-1*) Rourke Corp.
— Trapdoor Spiders. (Spider Discovery Library). (Illus.). 24p. (J). (gr. k-5). 1988. lib. bdg. 14.60 (*0-86592-963-7*) Rourke Enter.
— Turtles. (Reptile Discovery Library). (Illus.). 24p. (J). (gr. k-5). 1989. lib. bdg. 8.95 (*0-685-58607-3*) Rourke Corp.
— Turtles. (Reptile Discovery Library). (Illus.). 24p. (J). (gr. k-5). 1989. lib. bdg. 14.60 (*0-86592-578-X*) Rourke Enter.
— Whales. (Wildlife in Danger Ser.). (Illus.). 24p. (J). (gr. k-5). 1988. lib. bdg. 8.95 (*0-685-67679-X*) Rourke Corp.
Martin, Louise, compiled by. Guide to the Theodore Saloutos Collection. (Illus.). 61p. 1988. pap. 8.00 (*0-932833-08-X*) Immig His Res.
Martin, Lowell A. Enrichment: A History of the Public Library in the United States in the Twentieth Century. LC 97-43171. 224p. 1998. 35.00 (*0-8108-3403-0*) Scarecrow.
— Library Personnel Administration. LC 94-6569. (Library Administration: No. 11). (Illus.). 214p. 1994. text 31.00 (*0-8108-2839-1*) Scarecrow.
— Organizational Structure of Libraries. (Library Administration: No. 12). 1996. 39.50 (*0-8108-3123-6*) Scarecrow.
Martin, Loy D. Browning's Dramatic Monologues & the Post-Romantic Subject. LC 85-9796. 304p. reprint ed. pap. 94.30 (*0-608-06171-9*, 206650400008) Bks Demand.
Martin, Lucien T. & Martin, Melba B. Remember Us. (Illus.). 298p. 1987. 30.00 (*0-9620005-0-7*) Martin Pubs.
Martin, Lucy P., ed. see McCune, Shirley D., et al.
Martin, Lucy P., ed. see O'Brien, Shirley.
Martin, Luis. Daughters of the Conquistadores: Women of the Viceroyalty of Peru. LC 89-42899. (Illus.). 368p. 1989. reprint ed. pap. text 14.95 (*0-87074-297-3*) SMU Press.
— The Intellectual Conquest of Peru: The Jesuit College of San Pablo, 1568-1767. LC 67-26159. 208p. reprint ed. pap. 64.50 (*0-7837-5612-7*, 204551800005) Bks Demand.
Martin, Luke. Issues Related to Parenting. 75p. 1995. pap. 2.60 (*0-7399-0208-3*, 2600) Rod & Staff.
Martin, Luther H. Hellenistic Religions: An Introduction. (Illus.). 192p. 1987. pap. text 21.95 (*0-19-504391-X*) OUP.
Martin, Luther H., ed. Religious Transformations & Socio-Political Change: Eastern Europe & Latin America. LC 93-4333. (Religion & Society Ser.: No. 33). xiv, 457p. (C). 1993. lib. bdg. 152.35 (*3-11-013734-8*) Mouton.
Martin, Luther H., et al, eds. Technologies of the Self: A Seminar with Michel Foucault. LC 87-10756. 176p. (Orig.). (C). 1988. pap. 15.95 (*0-87023-593-1*) U of Mass Pr.
Martin, Luther H., jt. ed. see Jensen, Jeppe S.

An Asterisk (*) at the beginning of an entry indicates that the title is appearing for the first time.

Martin Luther King, Jr. Papers Project Staff. A Guide to Research on Martin Luther King, Jr., & the Modern Black Freedom Struggle. annot. ed. (Occasional Publications in Bibliography Ser.: No. 1). 185p. (Orig.). 1989. pap. 14.50 (*0-911221-09-3*) Stanford U Libraries.

Martin, Lyn E., ed. The Challenge of Internet Literacy: The Instruction-Web Convergence. LC 97-22247. 254p. 1997. pap. 24.95 (*0-7890-0347-3*) Haworth Pr.

— The Challenge of Internet Literacy: The Instruction-Web Convergence. LC 97-22247. 254p. 1997. 45.00 (*0-7890-0346-5*) Haworth Pr.

Martin, Lynda K., ed. see Smith, Kent J. & Bonesteal, Michael.

***Martin, Lynn.** Blue Bowl. 108p. 2000. pap. 13.00 (*0-911287-42-6*) Blue Begonia.

— Where the Yellow Field Widened. (Illus.). 36p. 1994. 25.00 (*0-918116-85-6*) Brooding Heron Pr.

***Martin, Lynn, ed.** Scans: Blueprint for Action: Building Community Coalitions. 67p. (C). 2000. reprint ed. pap. text 20.00 (*0-7881-8671-X*) DIANE Pub.

Martin, Lynn A. The Jesuit Mind: The Mentality of an Elite in Early Modern France. LC 87-47873. (Illus.). 288p. 1988. text 39.95 (*0-8014-2147-0*) Cornell U Pr.

Martin, Lynn J. Traditions We Share: Celebrating the 1997 Folk Arts Apprenticeship Gathering. LC 97-73809. (Illus.). 88p. 1997. pap. 17.50 (*0-937426-39-3*) Honolu Arts.

Martin, Lynn J., ed. Musics of Hawaii: "It all Comes from the Heart": An Anthology of Musical Traditions in Hawaii (Compact Disc/ Book Package) (Illus.). 152p. 1998. pap. text 95.00 (*0-8248-2139-4*) UH Pr.

— Musics of Hawaii: "Talking Story": A Series of Educational Programs Featuring Interviews with Traditional Musicans in Hawaii (Book/Cassette Package) Clarence Lee Design & Associates Staff, tr. & photos by by. (Illus.). 64p. 1998. pap. text 85.00 incl. audio (*0-8248-2140-8*) UH Pr.

Martin, Lynne M., ed. Library Instruction Revisited: Bibliographic Instruction Comes of Age. LC 95-23248. (Reference Librarian Ser.: Nos. 51 & 52). 480p. 1995. 59.95 (*1-56024-759-2*) Haworth Pr.

Martin, Lys, ed. see Rubin, David S.

Martin, M. Wielki Slownik Techni Rosyjsko - Polski. (POL & RUS.). 1151p. 1980. 95.00 (*0-8288-2142-9*, M14452) Fr & Eur.

Martin, M. & Lockwood, Jill. Partnership Taxation Handbook. 528p. 1989. text 79.95 (*0-13-651407-3*) P-H.

Martin, M. & Putinar, M. Lectures on Hyponormal Operators. (Operator Theory Ser.: No. 39). 304p. 1989. 132.00 (*0-8176-2329-9*) Birkhauser.

Martin, M. & Whittle, W. Core Geography: Leisure. (C). 1982. pap. 50.00 (*0-09-144451-9*, Pub. by S Thornes Pubs) St Mut.

— Core Geography: The Developing World. (C). 1985. pap. 65.00 (*0-09-156621-5*, Pub. by S Thornes Pubs) St Mut.

— Core Geography Cities. (C). 1983. pap. 50.00 (*0-09-147521-X*, Pub. by S Thornes Pubs) St Mut.

— Core Geography Work. (C). 1983. pap. 50.00 (*0-09-144461-6*, Pub. by S Thornes Pubs) St Mut.

Martin, M. A., ed. see Menendez Pidal, Ramon.

Martin, M. Dean & Adams, John. Professional Project Management. 154p. 1957. 28.00 (*0-317-54778-X*) Univ Tech.

Martin, M. H., ed. see Applied Mathematics Symposium Staff.

Martin, M. J. Instructional Videotaping: A Teacher's Guide for Making Instructional Videotapes. 32p. 1992. pap., teacher ed. 5.00 (*0-9632211-0-8*) MTCI.

Martin, M. Kay & Voorhies, Barbara. Female of the Species. LC 74-23965. 432p. 1975. pap. text 27.00 (*0-231-03876-3*) Col U Pr.

Martin, M. M. Inheritance: Lincoln's Public Buildings in the Historic District. (Illus.). 115p. (Orig.). 1988. pap. 15.00 (*0-944856-00-4*) Lincoln Hist Soc.

Martin, M. R. Historical Records Survey No. 2: Check List of Minnesota Imprints, 1849-1865. (Historical Records Survey Monographs). 1969. reprint ed. 25.00 (*0-527-01899-6*) Periodicals Srv.

Martin, Mabel W. Land Beneath the Lake: More Factual Folklore. LC 98-87715. 199 P. ;p. 1998. write for info. (*0-9629142-3-1*) Janze Pubns.

— The Ultimate Irony. LC 97-71101. 233p. (Orig.). 1997. mass mkt. 15.00 (*0-9629142-1-5*) Janze Pubns.

Martin, Maggie, jt. auth. see Martin, Don.

Martin, Malachi. Hostage to the Devil - Reissue: The Possession & Exorcism of Five Contemporary Americans. LC 92-53900. 512p. 1999. pap. 16.00 (*0-06-065337-X*, Pub. by Harper SF) HarpC.

— The Jesuits: The Society of Jesus & the Betrayal of the Roman Catholic Church. 528p. 1988. pap. 13.00 (*0-671-65716-X*, Touchstone) S&S Trade Pap.

— The Keys of This Blood: Pope John Paul II vs. Russia & the West for Control of the New World Order. 736p. 1991. per. 15.00 (*0-671-74723-1*) S&S Trade Pap.

— El Ultimo Papa. 1998. 37.95 (*84-08-02503-1*) Planeta.

— Windswept House: A Vatican Novel. 656p. 1998. pap. 14.95 (*0-385-49231-6*) Doubleday.

Martin, Malcolm & Jackson, Tricia. Personnel Practice. 192p. 1997. pap. 60.00 (*0-85292-678-2*, Pub. by IPM Hse) St Mut.

***Martin, Malia.** The Duke's Return. 352p. 1999. mass mkt. 5.99 (*0-380-79898-0*, Avon Bks) Morrow Avon.

Martin, Malia. Her Norman Conqueror. 384p. 1998. mass mkt. 5.99 (*0-380-79896-4*, Avon Bks) Morrow Avon.

***Martin, Malia.** Much Ado About Love. 384p. 2000. mass mkt. 5.99 (*0-380-81517-6*) Morrow Avon.

Martin, Malissa & Yates, William N., Jr. Therapeutic Medications in Sports Medicine. LC 97-45783. 250p. 1997. spiral bd. 29.95 (*0-683-30223-X*) Lppncott W & W.

Martin, Malissa, et al. Fundamentals of Sports Injury Management Student Workbook. LC 96-46312. 209p. 1997. pap., student ed., wbk. ed. 16.95 (*0-683-30212-4*, 85668) Lppncott W & W.

Martin, Malissa, jt. auth. see Anderson, Marcia K.

Martin Mallins, Judy C., jt. ed. see Martin, Norman R.

Martin Management Books Staff. Great Management Quotes: Executives Talk Competitiveness & Success. LC 94-75250. 128p. 1996. pap. 15.95 (*1-878500-03-1*) Martin Mgmt.

— Productive Meetings: How to Structure & Conduct Committee or Group Meetings. 2nd rev. ed. LC 97-74894. 90p. 1997. pap. 14.95 (*1-878500-08-2*) Martin Mgmt.

***Martin Management Books Staff, ed.** Drives, Getaways & Camping for You & Your Dog, USA. LC 99-76180. 200p. 2000. pap. 19.95 (*1-878500-10-4*, Valley Hse Bks) Martin Mgmt.

Martin Management Books Staff, ed. Great Vacations for You & Your Dog, Abroad. LC 95-81616. 237p. (Orig.). 1996. pap. 19.95 (*1-878500-06-6*, Valley Hse Bks) Martin Mgmt.

***Martin Management Books Staff, ed.** Great Vacations for You & Your Dog, U. S. A., 2001-02. 5th ed. 2001. 19.95 (*1-878500-11-2*) Martin Mgmt.

Martin, Manuel, Jr. Rasputin. 66p. (Orig.). 1997. pap. 4.95 (*1-885901-22-4*) Presbyters Peartree.

Martin, Marcelle, ed. see Martin, Charlie.

Martin, Marcia. Dreamseeker. 1998. mass mkt. 5.99 (*0-451-18054-2*, Sig) NAL.

— Southern Storms. 1992. mass mkt. 4.99 (*0-515-10870-7*, Jove) Berkley Pub.

Martin, Marcia G. Architectural Drafting: Procedures & Processes. (Illus.). 88p. (C). 1997. spiral bd. 9.95 (*0-87563-768-X*) Stipes.

Martin, Marcia O. Christmas Memories, 1. 1998. 10.99 (*1-57866-036-X*) Galahad Bks.

Martin, Margaret. Embarazo y Nacimiento: El Libro Ilustrado. LC 97-9312. (SPA., Illus.). 128p. 1997. pap. 9.95 (*1-55561-135-4*) Fisher Bks.

— Husband in Waiting. (Romance Ser.). 1995. per. 2.99 (*0-373-19083-2*, 1-19083-4) Silhouette.

— The Illustrated Book of Pregnancy & Childbirth. LC 91-9050. 126p. 1991. reprint ed. pap. 39.10 (*0-608-02866-5*, 206393000007) Bks Demand.

— Pregnancy & Childbirth: The Basic Illustrated Guide. LC 96-37277. (Illus.). 128p. (Orig.). 1997. pap. 9.95 (*1-55561-114-1*) Fisher Bks.

Martin, Margaret J. & Weiner, Carolyn. More Frequent Error Pairs. 96p. (Orig.). 1982. pap. text 49.00 (*0-7616-3127-5*) Commun Skill.

Martin, Margaret M. The Chambers-Russell-Codman House in Lincoln, Massachusetts. LC 96-36081. (Illus.). 227p. 1996. 30.00 (*0-944856-09-8*) Lincoln Hist Soc.

— No More Wishy-Washy Watercolor. LC 98-39799. (Illus.). 128p. 1999. 27.99 (*0-89134-876-X*, 31183, North Lght Bks) F & W Pubns Inc.

Martin, Margaret M., jt. auth. see Junior League of Buffalo Staff.

Martin, Margaret M., jt. auth. see MacLean, John C.

Martin, Margaret R. Charleston Ghosts. LC 63-22508. (Illus.). xiv, 116p. 1973. 15.95 (*0-87249-091-2*) U of SC Pr.

Martin, Margaret Reid, ed. see Webster, Alan C. & Perry, Paul E.

Martin, Margareta, tr. see Joenpelto, Eeva.

Martin, Margery, jt. ed. see Paulu, Nancy.

Martin, Margery, ed. see Rich, Dorothy.

Martin, Maria R. Estructuras Imaginarias En la Poesia. 47.50 (*0-685-69527-1*) Scripta.

Martin, Marian. European Waterways: A Manual for First Time Users. (Illus.). 192p. 1997. pap. 26.50 (*0-7136-4356-0*) Sheridan.

— The Ravens of Rockhurst. large type ed. LC 97-31793. 1997. 23.95 (*0-7862-1260-8*) Thorndike Pr.

***Martin, Marian & Martin, Sandra.** SAT Savvy: Last Minute Tips & Strategies. 3rd ed. 88p. 1999. 6.00 (*1-57509-045-7*) Octameron Assocs.

Martin, Mariann. Pain & Praise: The Book of Psalms. (Generation Why: Vol. 2:5). 36p. (YA). (gr. 9-12). 1997. pap. 14.95 (*0-87303-270-5*) Faith & Life.

Martin, Mariann, jt. auth. see Glanzer, Brenda.

Martin, Marianne. Love in the Balance. LC 97-52958. 240p. (Orig.). 1998. pap. 11.95 (*1-56280-199-6*) Naiad Pr.

Martin, Marianne K. Dawn of the Dance. LC 98-44749. 224p. 1999. pap. 11.95 (*1-56280-229-1*) Naiad Pr.

— Legacy of Love. LC 97-10005. 240p. (Orig.). 1997. pap. 11.95 (*1-56280-184-8*) Naiad Pr.

***Martin, Marianne K.** Never Ending. LC 98-48233. 256p. 1999. pap. 11.95 (*1-56280-247-X*) Naiad Pr.

Martin, Marie, jt. ed. see Livingston, Donald W.

Martin, Marie A. Cambodia: A Shattered Society. Mcleod, Mark W., tr. LC 93-31837. 383p. 1994. 45.00 (*0-520-07052-6*, Pub. by U CA Pr) Cal Prin Full Svc.

Martin, Marie-Louise. Kimbangu: An African Prophet & His Church. Moore, D. M., tr. LC 75-45371. 222p. reprint ed. pap. 68.90 (*0-608-30460-3*, 201273500083) Bks Demand.

***Martin, Marilyn.** Friends Forever. (Illus.). (YA). 2000. pap. 12.95 (*1-891929-58-5*) Four Seasons.

Martin, Marilyn, et al. The Journal of Decorative & Propaganda Arts. No. 20/1994. (Illus.). 300p. (Orig.). 1994. pap. 25.00 (*0-9631601-3-3*) Wolfson Fnd D&P Arts.

Martin, Marilyn, ed. see Calvin, Robert M.

Martin, Marilyn M., ed. see Calvin, Robert M.

Martin, Marilyn M., ed. see Professional Truck Driver Institute, Inc. Staff.

Martin, Marilyn M., ed. see Professional Truck Driving Institute, Inc. Staff.

Martin, Marilyn M., ed. see Professional Truck Driving Institute of America (P.

Martin, Marilyn S. Pedro. 152p. (J). (gr. 3-6). 1980. 7.65 (*0-7399-0083-8*, 2340) Rod & Staff.

Martin, Marilyn S., tr. Pedro of Guatemala.Tr. of Pedro de Guatemala. (SPA.). 160p. (J). (gr. 3-6). 1997. pap. 4.15 (*0-7399-0084-6*, 2340.1) Rod & Staff.

Martin, Marjorie G. Breakfast at Peppertrees. 150p. 1996. pap. write for info. (*0-9648860-3-0*) Peprtrees B&B Inn.

Martin, Mark. The Ultimate Gnatrat. (Illus.). 120p. 1990. pap. 11.95 (*1-56097-027-8*) Fantagraph Bks.

—**An Unfulfilled Dream. (Illus.). 192p. 1997. pap. 20.00 (*0-87012-568-0*) McClain.**
"When you can go from coaching special teams to something as special & complex as quarterbacks & help a guy break all the records in the history of the franchise it truly says something about that coach. And that's what he did for me." Former NFL Quaterback Vine Ferragamo *Publisher Paid Annotation.*

***Martin, Mark & Macur, Juliet.** Stock Car Racing for Dummies. (For Dummies Ser.). (Illus.). 344p. 2000. pap. 19.99 (*0-7645-5219-8*) IDG Bks.

Martin, Mark, ed. see McCloud, Scott.

Martin, Mark C. Fishing Hot Spots Rhinelander Area. (North Central Wisconsin Area Ser.). (Illus.). 144p. 1988. pap. 9.95 (*0-939314-20-7*) Fishing Hot.

Martin, Mark C., et al. Fishing Northern Illinois' Top 20 Lakes. (Illus.). 112p. 1989. pap. 9.95 (*0-939314-25-8*) Fishing Hot.

— Fishing the Mississippi Pools 11 & 12. (Mississippi River Ser.). (Illus.). 84p. 1989. pap. 9.95 (*0-939314-23-1*) Fishing Hot.

— Fishing the Mississippi Pools 13 & 14. (Mississippi River Ser.). (Illus.). 84p. 1989. pap. 9.95 (*0-939314-24-X*) Fishing Hot.

Martin, Mark O. & Benford, Gregory. A Darker Geometry: A Man-Kzin Novel. 432p. 1996. per. 5.99 (*0-671-87740-2*) Baen Bks.

Martin, Marla. Birthday Friend. (Jewel Book Ser.: Set 4). (Illus.). 32p. (J). (ps-2). 1993. pap. 2.55 (*0-7399-0042-0*, 2136) Rod & Staff.

— Caterpillar Green. (Illus.). 144p. 1977. 7.10 (*0-7399-0069-2*, 2155) Rod & Staff.

— Kitten in the Well. (Illus.). 244p. (J). (ps-2). 1978. 8.95 (*0-7399-0070-6*, 2300) Rod & Staff.

— Kitten in the Well. Fisher, Lois, tr. (SPA., Illus.). 241p. (J). 1995. 7.30 (*0-7399-0071-4*, 2300.1) Rod & Staff.

Martin, Marla. Little Church House by the River. 1994. 14.95 (*0-87813-552-9*) Christian Light.

— Little Church House Takes a Ride. (Illus.). 104p. (J). (ps-5). 1995. 14.95 (*0-87813-553-7*) Christian Light.

Martin, Marla. A Sweet Singer. (Illus.). 56p. (J). 1976. pap. 3.00 (*0-7399-0067-6*, 2425) Rod & Staff.

Martin, Marla & Martinez, Miriam. Locust Story. 62p. (J). (ps-2). 1977. pap. 3.35 (*0-7399-0068-4*, 2320) Rod & Staff.

Martin, Marlene. Practicing the Process: A Basic Text. (C). 1989. text 30.00 (*0-673-18759-4*) Addson-Wesley Educ.

Martin, Marlene & Girard, Maureen. Writing Wisely & Well. LC 92-37244. 512p. (C). 1993. pap. 41.56 (*0-07-023472-8*) McGraw.

***Martin-Marquez, Susan.** Feminist Discourse & Spanish Cinema. (Oxford Hispanic Studies Ser.). (Illus.). 320p. 2000. text 65.00 (*0-19-815979-X*) OUP.

Martin, Marsha A. Heading Home: Breaking the Cycle of Homelessness among America's Veterans: A Post-Summit Action Report & Resource Directory. (Illus.). 114p. (C). 1999. pap. text 20.00 (*0-7881-7696-X*) DIANE Pub.

Martin, Mart. The Almanac of Women & Minorities in American Politics. LC 98-15202. 336p. 1998. 49.95 (*0-8133-6870-7*, Pub. by Westview) HarpC.

— Did He or Didn't He? The Intimate Sex Lives of 201 Famous Men. LC 97-29955. (Illus.). 240p. 1997. pap. text 14.95 (*0-8065-1915-0*, Citadel Pr) Carol Pub Group.

***Martin, Mart.** Did He or Didn't He? The Intimate Sexlives of 201 Famous Men. 1999. pap. text 14.95 (*0-8065-2130-9*, Citadel Pr) Carol Pub Group.

Martin, Mart. Did She or Didn't She? Behind the Bedroom of Two Hundred & One Famous Women. (Illus.). 224p. 1995. pap. 14.00 (*0-8065-1669-0*, Citadel Pr) Carol Pub Group.

Martin, Marta S., jt. auth. see Bonachea, Ramon L.

Martin, Martha. Home in the Bear's Domain. large type ed. 464p. 1987. 27.99 (*0-7089-1578-7*) Ulverscroft.

— O Rugged Land of Gold. (Illus.). 226p. 1989. pap. 12.95 (*0-940055-00-7*) Vanessapress.

Martin, Martha E. The Friendly Stars. rev. ed. Menzel, Donald H., ed. (Illus.). 147p. 1964. pap. 4.95 (*0-486-21099-5*) Dover.

Martin, Martha J., jt. auth. see Marth, Del.

***Martin, Martin.** Description of the Western Islands of Scotland: A Voyage to St. Kilda. 354p. 2000. pap. 19.95 (*1-84158-020-1*, Pub. by Birlinn Ltd) Dufour.

Martin, Martin. A Description of the Western Isles of Scotland. 440p. (C). 1981. 65.00 (*0-901824-01-1*) Mercat Pr Bks.

— Voyage to St. Kilda, 1697. 63p. (C). 1985. 50.00 (*0-7855-3811-9*, Pub. by Mercat Pr Bks) St Mut.

Martin, Martin & MacLeod, Donald. A Description of the Western Islands of Scotland. 540p. pap. 17.95 (*1-874744-19-X*, Pub. by Birlinn Ltd) Dufour.

Martin Martinez, Juan M., ed. see De Rueda, Lope.

Martin Martinez, Juan M., ed. see Ruiz De Alarcon, Juan.

Martin, Marvin. Arthur Ashe: Of Tennis & the Human Spirit. LC 98-8535. (Impact Biography Ser.). 176p. (J). 1999. 24.00 (*0-531-11432-5*) Watts.

— Arthur Ashe: Of Tennis & the Human Spirit. 1999. pap. text 9.95 (*0-531-15959-0*) Watts.

— The Beatles: Music Was Never the Same. LC 96-13932. (Impact Biographies Ser.). 192p. (YA). (gr. 7-12). 1996. lib. bdg. 24.00 (*0-531-11307-8*) Watts.

— The Beatles: Music Was Never the Same. (Impact Biographies Ser.). 208p. (YA). (gr. 7-12). 1997. pap. 9.95 (*0-531-15820-9*) Watts.

Martin, Marvin D., jt. auth. see Nachtigal, Chester.

Martin, Mary, jt. auth. see Bradley, Susan.

Martin, Mary, ed. see Isherwood, Justin.

***Martin, Mary-Anne, intro.** Diego Rivera: Watercolors & Drawings. (Illus.). 48p. 1999. pap. 20.00 (*1-930191-00-6*) M Martin Fine Art.

Martin, Mary Casey, ed. & photos by see Isherwood, Justin.

***Martin, Mary E.** The Luminous Disarray. LC 98-71748. 1998. write for info. (*0-89002-339-5*) Northwoods Pr.

Martin, Mary E. & Martin, J. Michael. The Archives Organizer by Homefile: Guide to Long Term Storage of Personal Records. (Financial Advantage Ser.). (Illus.). 28p. 1997. pap. 9.95 (*0-9628718-9-3*) HOMEFILE.

— Home Filing Made Easy! Guide to Financial Organization. (Financial Organization Ser.). (Illus.). 186p. 1997. pap. 15.95 (*0-9628718-7-7*) HOMEFILE.

— Safe-Deposit Box & Fireproof Safe Organizer Kit: Guide to Protecting Your Valuable Personal Records. (HOMEFILE Organizer Kits). Orig. Title: Papers You Can't Afford to Lose. (Illus.). 32p. 1999. pap. 14.95 (*0-9628718-8-5*) HOMEFILE.

Martin, Mary E., jt. auth. see Martin, J. Michael.

Martin, Mary J. From Anne to Zach. LC 95-80227. (Illus.). 40p. (J). (ps-1). 1996. 15.95 (*1-56397-573-4*) Boyds Mills Pr.

Martin, Mary L. The Fables of Marie de France: An English Translation. 2nd ed. 259p. 1984. 23.95 (*0-917786-34-3*) Summa Pubns.

Martin, Mary L., jt. auth. see Palmer, Erskine L.

Martin, Mary P. Peace: A Thematic Unit. (Thematic Units Ser.). (Illus.). 80p. (J). (gr. 1-3). 1994. student ed. 9.95 (*1-55734-248-2*) Tchr Create Mat.

Martin, MaryJoy. Suicide Legends, Homicide Rumors: The Griffin Mystery. LC 86-232434. (Illus.). 68p. (Orig.). 1986. pap. write for info. (*0-945319-00-2*) Spes Deo Pubns.

Martin, MaryJoy. Twilight Dwellers: Ghosts, Ghouls & Goblins of Colorado. LC 85-16716. (Illus.). 167p. 1985. pap. 13.95 (*0-87108-686-7*) Pruett.

Martin, Maryvonne L., et al. Practical NMR Spectroscopy. LC QD0096.N8M37. 492p. reprint ed. pap. 152.60 (*0-608-12455-9*, 202520200042) Bks Demand.

Martin, Matthew. The Crumbling Facade of African Debt Negotiations: No Winners. LC 91-4014. (International Political Economy Ser.). 408p. 1992. text 69.95 (*0-312-06734-8*) St Martin.

Martin, Maureen, ed. see Reznik, Semyon.

Martin, Maurice A. Urban Policing in Canada: Anatomy of an Aging Craft. 256p. 1995. 65.00 (*0-7735-1284-5*, Pub. by McG-Queens Univ Pr); pap. 24.95 (*0-7735-1294-2*, Pub. by McG-Queens Univ Pr) CUP Services.

***Martin, Maximilian.** Operation Cooperation: Discourses on Joint Ventures & Development. 240p. 1998. pap. text 24.95 (*3-8258-3239-2*, Pub. by CE24) Transaction Pubs.

Martin-McRae, Bettye. Bronc in the Parlor. Boyd, Carol, ed. (Illus.). 120p. (Orig.). 1992. pap. 9.95 (*1-878162-03-9*) Unicorn Pr USA.

Martin, Mel S. How to Hire an Honest Lawyer...& Other Oxymorons. 182p. 1994. pap. text 9.95 (*0-9642951-0-5*) Witty Bks.

Martin, Melba, ed. see Ruth-Heffelbower, Dwayne.

Martin, Melba B., jt. auth. see Martin, Lucien T.

***Martin, Melissa.** For Better or for Worse: A Blessing or a Curse? Domestic Violence in the Christian Home. 248p. 1999. pap. 15.00 (*1-892525-04-6*) ACW Press.

Martin, Melissa & Smathers, James. Current Regulatory Issues in Medical Physics: Proceedings of an American College of Medical Physics Symposium, April 1992. 458p. 1992. pap. text 29.95 (*0-944838-29-4*) Med Physics Pub.

Martin, Melissa, jt. auth. see Jacobus, Charles J.

Martin Mgt. Books Staff, ed. Great Vacations for You & Your Dog, U. S. A., 1999-2000. 4th rev. ed. LC 98-92156. 250 p. 1999. pap. 19.95 (*1-878500-09-0*) Martin Mgmt.

Martin, Mia. Dog Heralding: The Official Collection of Canine Coat-of-Arms. (Illus.). 160p. 1996. 24.95 (*0-87605-532-3*) Howell Bks.

Martin, Michael. The Big Domino in the Sky: And Other Atheistic Tales. LC 96-34925. 244p. (Orig.). 1996. pap. 16.95 (*1-57392-111-4*) Prometheus Bks.

— The Case Against Christianity. 1991. 54.95 (*0-87722-767-5*) Temple U Pr.

— The Case Against Christianity. 290p. 1993. pap. 22.95 (*1-56639-081-8*) Temple U Pr.

— Concepts of Science Education: A Philosophical Analysis. 184p. 1985. reprint ed. pap. text 19.50 (*0-8191-4479-7*) U Pr of Amer.

***Martin, Michael.** The Deserts of Africa. 2000. 50.00 (*1-58479-028-8*) Stewart Tabori & Chang.

Martin, Michael. Legal Realism: American & Scandinavian. LC 96-30774. (American University Studies V: No. 179). IX, 242p. (C). 1997. text 44.95 (*0-8204-3462-0*) P Lang Pubng.

***Martin, Michael.** Understanding the Network: A Practical Guide to Internetworking. LC 99-63274. 550p. 2000. 74.95 (*0-7357-0977-7*) New Riders Pub.

— Verstehen. LC 99-40104. 296p. 1999. 34.95 (*0-7658-0003-9*) Transaction Pubs.

Martin, Michael, ed. Speech Audiometry. 300p. 1987. 64.50 (*0-85066-641-4*, 0047) Singular Publishing.

M

— Speech Audiometry. 2nd ed. LC 97-8329. (Illus.). 360p. 1997. pap. text 58.95 (*1-56593-516-0*, 1190) Thomson Learn.

— Streptokinase Treatment in Chronic Arterial Occlusions & Stenoses. 208p. 1982. 120.00 (*0-8493-5046-8*, RC694, CRC Reprint) Franklin.

Martin, Michael & Gelber, Leonard. Dictionary of American History. enl. rev. ed. (Quality Paperback Ser.: No. 124). 742p. 1981. reprint ed. pap. 16.95 (*0-8226-0124-9*) Littlefield.

Martin, Michael & Greenwood, Cynthia W. Solve Your Child's School-Related Problems. LC 95-20286. 304p. 1995. pap. 19.00 (*0-06-273366-4*, Harper Ref) HarpC.

Martin, Michael & Marsh, Philip D. Oral Microbiology. 2nd ed. LC QR0047.. (Aspects of Microbiology Ser.: No. 1). 128p. reprint ed. pap. 39.70 (*0-7837-4043-3*, 204387300011) Bks Demand.

Martin, Michael & McIntyre, Lee C., eds. Readings in the Philosophy of Social Science. 813p. 1994. 75.00 (*0-262-13296-6*, Bradford Bks); pap. text 37.50 (*0-262-63151-2*, Bradford Bks) MIT Pr.

Martin, Michael, jt. auth. see Marsh, Philip D.

Martin, Michael, jt. auth. see O'Hanlon, William H.

***Martin, Michael Ann.** Women of Grace: A Bible Study on Holiness for Married Women. LC 00-105077. 152p. 2000. 9.95 (*0-9663223-8-X*) Emmaus Road.

Martin, Michael C. Drawing the Line: Reappraising Drawing Past & Present. LC 96-138528. (Illus.). 108p. pap. 24.95 (*1-85332-133-8*) Dist Art Pubs.

Martin, Michael C., jt. auth. see Mihaly, Laszlo.

Martin, Michael J. How to Outsmart the Sun: The Ultimate Guide to Healthy, Young-Looking Skin. 176p. 1994. pap. 14.95 (*1-883955-00-9*) Penmarin Bks.

— Managing Information & Entrepreneurship in Technology-Based Firms. 416p. 1994. 99.00 (*0-471-57219-5*) Wiley.

Martin, Michael M. Basic Problems of Evidence. 6th ed. 498p. 1988. 42.00 (*0-8318-0525-0*, B525) Am Law Inst.

— Invertebrate-Microbial Interactions: Ingested Fungal Enzymes in Arthropod Biology (A Comstock Book) LC 87-47549. (Explorations in Chemical Ecology Ser.). (Illus.). 176p. (C). 1988. pap. text 17.95 (*0-8014-9459-1*) Cornell U Pr.

Martin, Michael M., jt. auth. see Saltzburg, Stephen A.

Martin, Michael N. Angels in Red Hats: Paratroopers of the Second Indochina War. Strode, William, ed. (Illus.). 168p. 1994. 39.95 (*1-56469-025-3*) Harmony Hse Pub.

Martin, Michael O., ed. Third International Mathematics & Science Study Technical Report. LC 96-86397. 250p. 1997. pap. write for info. (*1-889938-06-8*) Intl Study Ctr.

Martin, Michael O. & Kelly, Dana L., eds. Third International Mathematics & Science Study Technical Report Vol. I: Design & Development. LC 96-86397. (Illus.). 250p. (Orig.). 1996. pap. write for info. (*1-889938-00-9*) Intl Study Ctr.

Martin, Michael O. & Mullis, Ina V. Science Achievement in Missouri & Oregon in an International Context: 1997 TIMSS Benchmarking. LC 98-86203. 200p. 1998. write for info. (*1-889938-09-2*) Intl Study Ctr.

Martin, Michael O. & Mullis, Ina V., eds. Third International Mathematics & Science Study (TIMSS) Quality Assurance in Data Collection. LC 96-71249. (Illus.). 220p. (Orig.). 1996. pap. write for info. (*1-889938-01-7*) Intl Study Ctr.

***Martin, Michael O., et al.** School Contexts for Learning Instructions: Third International Mathematics & Science Study (TIMSS) 100p. 1999. write for info. (*1-889938-11-4*) Intl Study Ctr.

Martin, Michael O., et al. Science Achievement in the Primary School Years: IEA's Third International Mathematics & Science Study. LC 97-67234. 200p. (Orig.). 1997. pap. write for info. (*1-889938-03-3*) Intl Study Ctr.

Martin, Michael O., jt. auth. see Mullis, Ina V.

Martin, Michael R. & Lovett, Gabriel H. Encyclopedia of Latin-American History. rev. ed. Hoffman, Fritz L. & Hughes, Robert L., eds. LC 81-715. 348p. 1981. reprint ed. lib. bdg. 35.00 (*0-313-22881-7*, MAELA, Greenwood Pr) Greenwood.

Martin, Michael Rheta & Gelber, Leonard. Adams Dictionary of American History, 8 vols., Set. rev. ed. LC 76-6735. 1977. 700.00 (*0-684-13856-5*, Scribners Ref) Mac Lib Ref.

Martin, Michael T., ed. Cinemas of the Black Diaspora: Diversity, Dependence, & Oppositionality. LC 95-31383. (Contemporary Film & Television Ser.). 540p. (C). 1996. 49.95 (*0-8143-2587-4*); pap. 19.95 (*0-8143-2588-2*) Wayne St U Pr.

— New Latin American Cinema: Studies of National Cinemas, Vol. 2. LC 96-46741. (Contemporary Film & Television Ser.). 480p. 1997. text 49.95 (*0-8143-2706-0*); pap. text 18.95 (*0-8143-2586-6*) Wayne St U Pr.

— New Latin American Cinema: Theory, Practices, & Transcontinental Articulations. LC 96-46741. (Contemporary Film & Television Ser.). 336p. 1997. pap. text 15.95 (*0-8143-2585-8*) Wayne St U Pr.

— New Latin American Cinema Vol. I: Theory, Practices, & Transcontinental Articulations. LC 96-46741. (Contemporary Film & Television Ser.). 336p. 1997. text 39.95 (*0-8143-2705-2*) Wayne St U Pr.

Martin, Michael T. & Kandal, Terry R., eds. Studies of Development & Change in the Modern World. (Illus.). 480p. (C). 1989. pap. text 29.95 (*0-19-505647-7*) OUP.

Martin, Michael W. & Schinzinger, Roland. Ethics in Engineering. 2nd ed. 364p. (C). 1988. text 39.00 (*0-07-040719-3*) McGraw.

Martin, Michaelann, et al. The Catholic Parent Book of Feasts: Celebrating the Church Year with Your Family. LC 98-68198. (Illus.). 191p. 1999. pap. 12.95 (*0-87973-956-8*) Our Sunday Visitor.

***Martin, Micheal.** Freedom to Choose: The Formation of Irish Political Parties, 1918-1932. 290p. 1999. pap. 22.95 (*1-898256-63-2*, Pub. by Collins Press) Dufour.

Martin, Michel, jt. ed. see Greenfeld, Liah.

Martin, Michel L. Warriors to Managers: The French Military Establishment since 1945. LC 79-28114. 446p. reprint ed. pap. 138.30 (*0-7837-2456-X*, 204260900005) Bks Demand.

Martin, Michele. Communication & Mass Media: Culture, Domination, & Opposition. Oulette, Benoit, tr. LC 96-932518.Tr. of Communication et Medias de Masse. (ENG & FRE.). 300p. 1996. pap. 49.27 (*0-13-376807-4*) Allyn.

Martin, Michele. "Hello, Central?" Gender, Technology & Culture in the Formation of Telephone Systems. 232p. 1991. 55.00 (*0-7735-0830-9*, Pub. by McG-Queens Univ Pr) CUP Services.

Martin, Michelle. The Butler Who Laughed. 1997. mass mkt. 4.50 (*0-449-22528-3*) Fawcett.

— Long Shot. 336p. 1998. mass mkt. 5.50 (*0-553-57650-X*) Bantam.

— The Queen of Hearts. 1994. mass mkt. 3.99 (*0-449-22203-9*) Fawcett.

— Stolen Hearts. 304p. 1997. mass mkt. 5.50 (*0-553-57648-8*, Fanfare) Bantam.

— Stolen Moments. 320p. 1997. mass mkt. 5.50 (*0-553-57649-6*) Bantam.

***Martin, Mick.** Video Movie Guide 2000. (Illus.). 1999. 7.99 (*0-345-43957-0*, Ballantine) Ballantine Pub Grp.

— Video Movie Guide 2000. (Illus.). 1999. pap. 18.95 (*0-345-42094-2*) Ballantine Pub Grp.

— Video Movie Guide 2001. 2000. pap. 19.95 (*0-345-42095-0*); mass mkt. 7.99 (*0-345-42099-3*) Ballantine Pub Grp.

Martin, Mick & Porter. Video Movie Guide 1999. 1998. mass mkt. 7.99 (*0-345-42097-7*) Ballantine Pub Grp.

Martin, Mickey J. Bryant: A Creek Indian Nation Townsite. LC 98-92533. (Illus.). 343p. 1998. 64.00 (*0-9638279-4-4*) Fowble Pr.

— Doing Business on the Oklahoma Land Rush Frontier. LC 95-60134. (Illus.). 220p. 1995. 74.00 (*0-9638279-2-8*) Fowble Pr.

— Legacy of the Great Oklahoma Land Rush: A Photographic History of Hoffman Townsite & School in Okmulgee County. LC 93-72854. 489p. 1993. 88.00 (*0-9638279-0-1*) Fowble Pr.

***Martin, Mike.** Small Animal ECGs: An Introductory Guide for Veterinary Surgeons. LC 99-40470. (Illus.). 128p. 2000. pap. text 34.95 (*0-632-05216-3*, Pub. by Blckwell Science) Iowa St U Pr.

Martin, Mike, ed. Stickball, Streetcars & Saturday Matinees. LC 95-69028. 100p. 1995. 14.95 (*0-89821-151-4*, 20106) Reiman Pubns.

Martin, Mike & Corcoran, Brendan. Cardiorespiratory Diseases of the Dog & Cat. (Library of Veterinary Practice). (Illus.). 416p. (Orig.). (C). 1996. pap. text 59.95 (*0-632-03298-7*, Pub. by Blckwll Scitfc UK) Iowa St U Pr.

***Martin, Mike & Martin, Vivian.** By Faith: The Story of King's Garden. LC 99-69285. 304p. 2000. pap. 10.00 (*1-57921-275-1*) WinePress Pub.

Martin, Mike & Rea, Val. Creating Art, Creating Income: A Women's Textile Workshop in Bangladesh, Set. (Illus.). 1994. 36.50 (*1-85339-213-8*, Pub. by Intermed Tech) Stylus Pub VA.

Martin, Mike & Valentine, Don. The Black Tigers: Elite Vietnamese Rangers & Their American Advisors. Strode, William & Butler, William, eds. (Illus.). 136p. 1993. 34.95 (*1-56469-016-4*) Harmony Hse Pub.

Martin, Mike, jt. auth. see Rea, Val.

Martin, Mike, ed. see Reiman Publications Staff.

Martin, Mike W. Everyday Morality: An Introduction. 3rd ed. (Philosophy Ser.). 2000. pap. 36.50 (*0-534-52034-0*) Wadsworth Pub.

— Everyday Morality: An Introduction to Applied Ethics. 320p. (C). 1988. pap. 22.25 (*0-534-09738-3*) Wadsworth Pub.

— Everyday Morality: An Introduction to Applied Ethics. 2nd ed. 384p. 1994. 50.95 (*0-534-20178-4*) Wadsworth Pub.

— Love's Virtues. 224p. 1996. 35.00 (*0-7006-0766-8*); pap. 14.95 (*0-7006-0767-6*) U Pr of KS.

***Martin, Mike W.** Meaningful Work: Rethinking Professional Ethics. LC 99-27536. (Practical & Professional Ethics Ser.). 272p. 2000. 35.00 (*0-19-513325-0*) OUP.

Martin, Mike W. Self-Deception & Morality. LC 86-5467. x, 182p. 1986. 25.00 (*0-7006-0297-6*); pap. 12.95 (*0-7006-0353-0*) U Pr of KS.

— Virtuous Giving: Philanthropy, Voluntary Service, & Caring. LC 93-8027. (Philanthropic Studies). 244p. (C). 1994. 24.95 (*0-253-33677-5*) Ind U Pr.

Martin, Mike W., ed. Self-Deception & Self-Understanding: New Essays in Philosophy & Psychology. LC 84-27013. x, 310p. 1985. pap. 12.95 (*0-7006-0396-4*) U Pr of KS.

Martin, Mike W. & Schinzinger, Roland. Ethics in Engineering. 3rd ed. LC 95-81713. 416p. (C). 1996. pap. 36.25 (*0-07-040849-1*) McGraw.

Martin, Mike W., jt. auth. see Schinzinger, Roland.

Martin, Mikeal. Wicked Pleasures: Sexibition. LC 99-164077. 219p. 1998. 19.99 (*1-892779-01-3*) Cedar Pubg.

***Martin, Mildred.** Prudence & Your Health: Workbook for Prudence & the Millers. Martin, Don L., ed. (Miller Family Ser.). (Illus.). 84p. (J). (gr. 3-6). 2000. pap., wbk. ed. 4.00 (*1-884377-07-6*) Green Psturs Pr.

Martin, Mildred A. Half-Century of Eliot Criticism: Annotated Bibliography of Books & Articles in English, 1916-1965. LC 79-168814. 361p. 1975. 55.00 (*0-8387-7808-9*) Bucknell U Pr.

— Missionary Stories & the Millers. (Miller Family Ser.). (Illus.). 208p. (J). (gr. 3 up). 1993. 9.50 (*0-9627643-7-X*) Green Psturs Pr.

— Missionary Stories & the Millers. (Miller Family Ser.). (Illus.). 208p. (J). (gr. 3 up). 1993. pap. 6.00 (*0-9627643-4-5*) Green Psturs Pr.

— Prudence & the Millers. (Miller Family Ser.). 190p. (J). (gr. 3-8). 1993. 9.50 (*0-9627643-9-6*) Green Psturs Pr.

— Prudence & the Millers. 2nd rev. ed. (Miller Family Ser.). (Illus.). 192p. (J). (gr. 3-8). 1996. pap. 6.00 (*1-884377-03-3*) Green Psturs Pr.

— School Days with the Millers. (Miller Family Ser.). (J). (gr. 3-8). 1995. pap. text 6.00 (*1-884377-01-7*) Green Psturs Pr.

— Storytime with the Millers. 2nd ed. (Miller Family Ser.). (Illus.). 110p. (Orig.). (J). (ps-3). 1994. pap. 5.00 (*1-884377-00-9*) Green Psturs Pr.

— Wisdom & the Millers: Proverbs for Children. 2nd ed. (Miller Family Ser.). (Illus.). 159p. (J). (gr. 2-8). 1993. 9.50 (*0-685-68129-7*); pap. 6.00 (*0-9627643-5-3*) Green Psturs Pr.

— Working with Wisdom. (Miller Family Ser.). (J). (gr. 3-4). 1996. pap. text 4.00 (*1-884377-02-5*) Green Psturs Pr.

Martin, Mildred C. Chinatown's Angry Angel: The Story of Donaldina Cameron. LC 77-2151. (Illus.). 308p. 1986. pap. 14.95 (*0-87015-252-1*) Pacific Bks.

***Martin, Mindy.** Programming Web Store Applications with Microsoft Exchange Server 2000. 2000. pap. 49.99 (*0-7356-0772-9*) Microsoft.

Martin, Mindy. The Secrets to Tender Pie. 1997. 17.95 (*0-614-27968-2*) Ballantine Pub Grp.

Martin, Mindy, jt. auth. see Chester, Thomas.

Martin, Minnie. Basutoland: Its Legends & Customs. LC 75-88997. 174p. 1969. reprint ed. lib. bdg. 49.50 (*0-8371-1756-9*, MAK&) Greenwood.

Martin, Mircea, tr. see Khatskevich, Victor & Shoiykhet, David.

Martin, Mircea, tr. see Krasnoselskii, Alexander M.

Martin, Molly, ed. Hard-Hatted Women: Life on the Job. LC 88-23850. (Illus.). 272p. (Orig.). 1997. pap. 14.95 (*1-878067-91-5*) Seal Pr WA.

Martin-Moreno, Enrique. XII Prophecies for XXI Century. 1998. pap. 40.00 (*88-7838-032-6*) Rockport Pubs.

Martin, Murray S. Academic Library Budgets. LC 91-30103. (Foundations in Library & Information Science: Vol. 28). 270p. 1993. 78.50 (*1-55938-597-9*) Jai Pr.

— Budgetary Control in Academic Libraries. LC 76-5648. (Foundations in Library & Information Science: Vol. 5). 219p. 1987. 78.50 (*0-89232-010-9*) Jai Pr.

— Collection Development & Finance: A Guide to Strategic Library-Materials Budgeting. Intner, Sheila S., ed. LC 94-49211. (Frontiers of Access Ser.: 2). 126p. (Orig.). 1995. pap. text 30.00 (*0-8389-0648-6*) ALA.

— Issues in Personnel Management. Stueart, Robert D., ed. LC 81-81649. (Foundations in Library & Information Science: Vol. 14). 226p. 1979. 78.50 (*0-89232-136-9*) Jai Pr.

Martin, Murray S., ed. Financial Planning for Libraries. LC 82-23346. (Journal of Library Administration: Vol. 3, Nos. 3-4). 131p. 1983. 39.95 (*0-86656-118-8*) Haworth Pr.

— Issues in Collection Management: Librarians, Booksellers, Publishers. (Foundations in Library & Information Science: Vol. 31). 193p. 1995. 78.50 (*1-55938-608-8*) Jai Pr.

Martin, Murray S. & Park, Betsy. Charging & Collecting Fees & Fines: A Handbook for Libraries. LC 97-43635. 146p. 1998. pap. 49.95 (*1-55570-318-6*) Neal-Schuman.

Martin, Murray S. & Wolf, Milton T. Budgeting for Information Access: Managing the Resource Budget for Absolute Access. LC 98-10964. (Frontiers of Access to Library Materials). 174p. 1998. 35.00 (*0-8389-0691-5*) American Library Association National Library.

Martin, Murray S., jt. auth. see Wolf, Milton T.

***Martin, Nadia J.** Disaster Management in the Church & Synagogue Library, No. 18. 24p. 2000. pap. 8.25 (*0-915324-43-1*) CSLA.

Martin, Nancy. Le Combat de Lorna. (Rouge Passion Ser.). (FRE.). 1994. pap. 3.50 (*0-373-37290-6*, 1-37290-3) Harlequin Bks.

— The Cop & the Chorus Girl: (Opposites Attract) (Desire Ser.). 1995. per. 3.25 (*0-373-05927-2*, 1-05927-8) Silhouette.

— The Cowboy & the Calendar Girl. 1998. per. 3.75 (*0-373-76139-2*, 1-76139-4) Silhouette.

— Un Deseo en las Estrellas - A Wish upon a Star. (SPA.). 1997. per. 3.50 (*0-373-35206-9*, 1-35206-1) Harlequin Bks.

— Fortune's Cookie. (Desire Ser.). 1993. per. 2.99 (*0-373-05826-8*, 5-05826-8) Silhouette.

— The Fubs. (Illus.). 32p. (Orig.). (J). (ps up). 1996. pap. 5.99 (*0-938711-35-0*) Tecolote Pubns.

***Martin, Nancy.** Meaning of Life in the World Religions. 256p. 1999. pap. 23.95 (*1-85168-200-7*) One Wrld.

Martin, Nancy. Monkey Wrench. (Tyler Ser.: No. 4). 1992. per. 3.99 (*0-373-82504-8*, 0-82504-2) Harlequin Bks.

— Mostly about Writing. LC 83-9972. 168p. (Orig.). (C). 1983. pap. text 18.50 (*0-86709-069-3*, 0069, Pub. by Boynton Cook Pubs) Heinemann.

— The Pauper & the Pregnant Princess: (Opposites Attract) (Desire Ser.). 1995. per. 3.25 (*0-373-05916-7*, 1-05916-1) Silhouette.

— Prayers Through the Centuries. (C). 1988. 45.00 (*1-85219-018-3*, Pub. by Bishopsgate Pr Ltd) St Mut.

— La Princesa y el Vagabundo. (Deseo Ser.).Tr. of Princess & the Pauper. (SPA.). 1996. per. 3.50 (*0-373-35167-4*, 1-35167-5) Harlequin Bks.

***Martin, Nancy.** Threads from the '30s. LC 99-89520. (Illus.). 112p. 2000. pap. 24.95 (*1-56477-314-0*, B434, Pub. by Martingale & Co) F & W Pubns Inc.

Martin, Nancy. Vanilla Blood. 320p. 1996. pap. 10.95 (*0-938711-36-9*) Tecolote Pubns.

— Whirlwind. (Tyler Ser.: No. 1). 1999. mass mkt. 3.99 (*0-373-82501-3*, 0-82501-8) Harlequin Bks.

— Wish upon a Starr. 1994. per. 2.99 (*0-373-05858-6*) Silhouette.

Martin, Nancy & McCloskey, Marsha R. Variable Star Quilts & How to Make Them. LC 94-41222. (Illus.). 64p. 1995. pap. text 7.95 (*0-486-28595-2*) Dover.

Martin, Nancy, ed. see Colarusso, Ronald P. & Hammill, Donald D.

Martin, Nancy, ed. see Critchlow, Donald E.

Martin, Nancy, jt. ed. see Lightfoot, Martin.

Martin, Nancy, ed. see Lockhart, William E.

Martin, Nancy, ed. see Markoff, Annabelle M.

Martin, Nancy, ed. see Vitale, Barbara M. & Bullock, Waneta B.

Martin, Nancy, ed. see Webster, Raymond.

Martin, Nancy A. The Versatile Labrador Retriever. Foote, Marianne, ed. LC 94-68115. (Pure Breds Ser.). (Illus.). 320p. 1994. pap. 19.95 (*0-944875-43-2*) Doral Pub.

— The Versatile Labrador Retriever. Luther, Luana & Grossman, Alvin, eds. LC 94-68115. (Pure Breds Ser.). (Illus.). 320p. 1994. 26.95 (*0-944875-31-9*) Doral Pub.

Martin, Nancy J. Decorate with Quilts & Collections. Rose, Sharon, ed. LC 96-22451. (Illus.). 224p. 1996. 34.95 (*1-56477-158-X*, B248) Martingale & Co.

— Houses, Cottages & Cabins Patchwork Quilts: With Full-Size Patterns. Orig. Title: Housing Projects. (Illus.). 80p. 1991. reprint ed. pap. 6.95 (*0-486-26907-8*) Dover.

***Martin, Nancy J.** Kitties to Stitch & Quilt: 15 Redwork Designs. LC 99-58874. (Illus.). 80p. 2000. pap. 19.95 (*1-56477-309-4*, B447, Pub. by Martingale & Co) F & W Pubns Inc.

Martin, Nancy J. Make Room for Quilts: Beautiful Decorating Ideas from Nancy J. Martin. 2nd rev. ed. (Illus.). 216p. 1998. 27.95 (*1-56477-221-7*, B167R, That Patchwrk Pl) Martingale & Co.

— Quilters on the Go. LC 98-24781. (Illus.). 32p. 1998. pap. 12.95 (*1-56477-236-5*, B368, That Patchwrk Pl) Martingale & Co.

— Simply Scrappy Quilts. 1995. pap. 24.95 (*1-56477-127-X*, B245) Martingale & Co.

— Tea Party Time: Romantic Quilts & Tasty Tidbits. (Illus.). 64p. (Orig.). 1996. pap. text 8.95 (*0-486-29472-2*) Dover.

***Martin, Nancy J.** 365 Quilt Blocks a Year: Perpetual Calendar. (Illus.). 200p. 1999. pap. 18.95 (*1-56477-273-X*, CI03) Martingale & Co.

— Time-Crunch Quilts. (Illus.). 128p. 2000. pap. 28.95 (*1-56477-291-8*, B407, Pub. by Martingale & Co) F & W Pubns Inc.

Martin, Nancy J. Two-Color Quilts: Ten Romantic Red Quilts & Ten True-Blue Quilts from Nancy J. Martin. Reikes, Ursula, ed. LC 97-46891. (Illus.). 112p. 1998. pap. 25.95 (*1-56477-217-9*, B334, That Patchwrk Pl) Martingale & Co.

Martin, Nancy J. & Hopkins, Judy. 101 Fabulous Rotary-Cut Quilts. LC 98-28906. (Illus.). 272p. 1998. pap. 29.95 (*1-56477-240-3*, B352, Pub. by Martingale & Co) F & W Pubns Inc.

Martin, Nancy J. & Hopkins, Judy D. Rotary Riot: 40 Fast & Fabulous Quilts. LC 91-26050. (Illus.). 128p. 1992. pap. 21.95 (*0-943574-86-2*, B126) Martingale & Co.

Martin, Nancy L. Tips: To Insure Perfect Spanish. (Illus.). 75p. pap. 19.95 (*0-9643508-0-7*) MCL Pubs.

Martin, Ned & Martin, Jody. Bit & Spur Makers in the Vaquero Tradition: A Historical Perspective. (Illus.). 264p. 1999. pap. 25.00 (*0-9659947-1-6*) Hawk Hill.

Martin, Ned, et al. Bit & Spur Makers in the Vaquero Tradition: A Historical Perspective. LC 97-72959. (Illus.). 336p. 1997. 85.00 (*0-9659947-0-8*) Hawk Hill.

***Martin, Neil B.** California Commercial Law II - 9/98 Update. Briggs, Donald R., ed. LC 65-63004. 242p. 1998. ring bd. 87.00 (*0-7626-0265-1*, BU-30045) Cont Ed Bar-CA.

Martin, Neil B., jt. auth. see Crawford, James E.

Martin, Nicholas. Nietzsche & Schiller: Untimely Aesthetics. (Oxford Modern Languages & Literature Monographs). 230p. (C). 1996. text 57.00 (*0-19-815913-7*) OUP.

— An Operator's Manual for Successful Living. LC 88-70784. (Illus.). 160p. (Orig.). 1988. pap. 12.95 (*0-87516-608-3*) DeVorss.

***Martin, Noah.** Tears in a Bottle: Comfort for Life's Hurts. (Illus.). 213p. 2000. 10.00 (*0-9700373-0-9*) Noahs PA.

Martin, Nora. The Eagle's Shadow. LC 96-29902. 176p. (J). (gr. 5-9). 1997. 15.95 (*0-590-36087-6*) Scholastic Inc.

— The Stone Dancers. LC 94-18505. (Illus.). 32p. (J). (ps-2). 1995. 15.00 (*0-689-80312-5*) S&S Bks Yung.

Martin, Nora B. The Federal Census of 1870 for Alleghany County, Virginia. 145p. pap. 12.95 (*0-935931-42-2*) Iberian Pub.

Martin, Norah, jt. ed. see Ludlow, Peter.

Martin, Norman & Martin, Katheryn. Cooking with Katheryn & Friends. (Illus.). 128p. (Orig.). lib. bdg. 7.95 (*0-9646489-4-6*) Martain Pub.

— A Practical Handbook on Year Around Back Yard Gardening: You Can Be an Expert in Your Own Back Yard. 58p. 1996. spiral bd. 8.95 (*0-9646489-3-8*) Martain Pub.

Martin, Norman M. Systems of Logic. 336p. (C). 1989. pap. text 25.95 (*0-521-36770-0*) Cambridge U Pr.

Martin, Norman M. & Pollard, Stephen. Closure Spaces & Logic. LC 96-18772. (Mathematics & Its Applications Ser.). 230p. (C). 1996. text 140.00 (*0-7923-4110-4*) Kluwer Academic.

An Asterisk (*) at the beginning of an entry indicates that the title is appearing for the first time.

Martin, Norman R. Ole Dewey: A Brown Shephard Dog That Belonged to the Martins & Was Claimed by the Author from 1935 to 1952, That Was Written up by "Ripley Believe It or Not" Twice. Mullins, Judy C., ed. (Illus.). 78p. (YA). 1997. lib. bdg. 8.95 (*0-9646489-6-2*) Martain Pub.
— Orphans on the River: Little Red, White & Mississippi Rivers Were Their Home. Mullins, Judy C., ed. (Illus.). 113p. (YA). 1998. pap. 10.00 (*0-9646489-7-0*) Martain Pub.
— Spiritual Relationships: Relationships of Christians, Preachers, Elders, & Teachers. Roper, David, ed. 50p. (Orig.). (C). 1995. pap. 6.95 (*0-9646489-1-1*) Martain Pub.
— Up on Dog Creek: A Time Remembered Foyil, Oklahoma. Speers, Bonnie, ed. (Illus.). 120p. (Orig.). 1995. pap. 8.95 (*0-9646489-0-3*) Martain Pub.
***Martin, Norman R.** Up on Route 66: A Time Remebered Travelers Along the Way 1928 & Foward. Mulling, Judy C., ed. (Illus.). 130p. 2000. pap. 10.00 (*0-9646489-5-4*) Martain Pub.
Martin, Norman R. Upon the Buffalo: Life in the Big Buffalo Valley 1839-1922. Spears, Bonnie, ed. (Illus.). 117p. 1996. lib. bdg. 8.95 (*0-9646489-2-X*) Martain Pub.
***Martin, Norman R. & Martin Mallins, Judy C., eds.** Love along the Way: A Love Story of a Young Army Soldier & a Cherokee Indian Girl, That Started with the "Trail of Tear" Time 1839-1950. (Illus.). 96p. 1999. lib. bdg. 8.85 (*0-9646489-8-9*) Martain Pub.
Martin, Norris, jt. auth. see Texas State Technical College, EDIT Department Sta.
Martin, Olga J. Hollywood's Movie Commandments, a Handbook for Motion Picture Writers & Reviewers. LC 77-124018. (Literature of Cinema, Ser. 1). 1970. reprint ed. 21.95 (*0-405-01624-7*) Ayer.
Martin, Olive. Dial a Christian Message. Oglethorpe, Jean, ed. (C). 1989. pap. 30.00 (*1-85072-022-3*, Pub. by W Sessions) St Mut.
Martin, Oralisa. Oracle: A Text for African American Youth Ministry. 268p. (Orig.). 1994. pap. text 39.95 (*0-9642067-0-6*) Maranatha Pr.
Martin, Ossie H. Spreading Good Cheer Through Song & Verse. 1997. pap. write for info. (*1-57553-579-3*) Watermrk Pr.
Martin, P. Mexico of the Twentieth Century, 2 vols. 1976. lib. bdg. 200.00 (*0-8490-2249-5*) Gordon Pr.
Martin, P. A., jt. ed. see Wickham, Glynne W.
Martin, P. G. Cosmic Dust. (Oxford Studies in Physics). (Illus.). 1979. 34.50 (*0-19-851458-1*) OUP.
Martin, P. G. & Weatherwax, J. Manuals of Food Quality Control No. 1: The Food Control Laboratory. rev. ed. (Food & Nutrition Papers: No. 14-1). (Illus.). 67p. (Orig.). 1987. pap. text 12.00 (*92-5-102489-8*, F3038, Pub. by FAO) Bernan Associates.
Martin, P. S., ed. see International Association for Quaternary Research.
Martin, Pace, jt. auth. see Debelta, Peter.
Martin, Pamela, ed. Telecommuting: The Ride of the Future. 100p. (Orig.). (C). 1992. pap. text 20.00 (*0-941375-93-5*) DIANE Pub.
Martin, Pat. Cherished Czech Recipes. 160p. 1988. spiral bd. 6.95 (*0-941016-46-3*) Penfield.
— Czech & Slovak Touches - Recipes & Traditions: The Czech Book. rev. expanded ed. Crum, Dorothy, ed. (Illus.). 160p. 1999. pap. 12.95 (*1-57216-029-2*) Penfield.
— Czechoslovak Culture: Recipes, History & Folk Arts. Liffring-Zug, Joan & Zug, John, eds. 176p. 1989. pap. 10.95 (*0-941016-61-7*) Penfield.
— Czechoslovak Wit & Wisdom. (Illus.). 40p. 1984. pap. 7.95 (*0-941016-12-9*) Penfield.
Martin, Pat, et al. Rebuses for Readers. ix, 138p. 1992. pap. text 18.00 (*0-87287-920-8*) Teacher Ideas Pr.
Martin, Pat H., jt. auth. see Martin, Earl.
Martin, Patricia. Ancient Echoes: Native American Words of Wisdom. 64p. 1994. 6.50 (*1-56245-035-2*) Great Quotations.
— Glovebox Cookbook. (Illus.). 128p. (Orig.). 1993. pap. 12.95 (*0-86417-515-9*, Pub. by Kangaroo Pr) Seven Hills Bk.
— Growing up in Toyland: Our All Time Best Loved Toys! Caton, Patrick, ed. 168p. 1996. pap. 5.95 (*1-56245-229-0*) Great Quotations.
***Martin, Patricia.** Memory Jug. 236p. (J). (gr. 4-7). 1998. lib. bdg. 16.49 (*0-7868-2368-2*, Pub. by Disney Pr) Little.
Martin, Patricia. Modern Woman: A Stress Relief Manual Just for Women. 78p. 1995. 7.95 (*1-56245-195-2*) Great Quotations.
***Martin, Patricia.** Thoughts from Great Women. 1999. 7.95 (*1-56245-377-7*) Great Quotations.
Martin, Patricia. Travels with Rainie Marie. LC 96-20005. 192p. (J). (gr. 3-7). 1999. pap. 5.99 (*0-7868-1339-3*, Pub. by Hyprn Child) Time Warner.
Martin, Patricia, ed. The Right Side of Forty: Celebrating Timeless Women. LC 97-24308. (Illus.). 128p. 1997. 24.95 (*1-57324-095-8*) Conari Press.
Martin, Patricia A. Animals That Walk on Water. (First Bks.). 1998. pap. 6.95 (*0-531-15896-9*) Watts.
— Chimpanzees LC 99-17068. (Illus.). 48p. (gr. 3-5). 2000. 21.50 (*0-516-21572-8*) Childrens.
***Martin, Patricia A.** Gorillas LC 99-17067. (Illus.). 48p. (gr. 3-5). 2000. 21.50 (*0-516-21570-1*) Childrens.
Martin, Patricia A. Lemurs, Lorises, & Other Lower Primates. LC 99-17066. (Illus.). 48p. (gr. 3-5). 2000. 21.50 (*0-516-21575-2*) Childrens.
— Monkeys from Asia & Africa. LC 99-17064. (Illus.). 48p. (gr. 3-5). 2000. 21.50 (*0-516-21573-6*) Childrens.
— Monkeys from Central & South America LC 99-17063. (Illus.). 48p. (gr. 3-5). 2000. 21.50 (*0-516-21574-4*) Childrens.
— Orangutans LC 99-17065. (Illus.). 48p. (gr. 3-5). 2000. 21.50 (*0-516-21571-X*) Childrens.
— Rivers & Streams. LC 98-10117. (Exploring Ecosystems Ser.). (J). 1999. 24.00 (*0-531-11523-2*) Watts.
***Martin, Patricia A.** Woods & Forests. (Exploring Ecosystems Ser.). (Illus.). (J). 2000. pap. 6.95 (*0-531-16459-4*) Watts.
***Martin, Patricia A., et al.** Woods & Forests. LC 99-33044. (Exploring Ecosystems Ser.). 2000. 24.00 (*0-531-11697-2*) Watts.
***Martin, Patricia A. Fink.** Chimpanzees. (True Bks.). (Illus.). 48p. (J). (gr. 3-5). 2000. pap. 6.95 (*0-516-27013-3*) Childrens.
— Gorillas. (True Bks.). (Illus.). 48p. (J). (gr. 3-5). 2000. pap. 6.95 (*0-516-27014-1*) Childrens.
— Lemurs, Lorises & Other Lower Primates. (True Bks.). (Illus.). 48p. (J). (gr. 3-5). 2000. pap. 6.95 (*0-516-27015-X*) Childrens.
— Monkeys of Asia & Africa. (True Bks.). (Illus.). 48p. (J). (gr. 3-5). 2000. pap. 6.95 (*0-516-27016-8*) Childrens.
— Monkeys of Central & South America. (True Bks.). (Illus.). 48p. (J). (gr. 3-5). 2000. pap. 6.95 (*0-516-27017-6*) Childrens.
— Orangutans. (True Bks.). (Illus.). 48p. (J). (gr. 3-5). 2000. pap. 6.95 (*0-516-27020-6*) Childrens.
Martin, Patricia M. Travels with Rainie Marie. LC 96-20005. 192p. (J). (gr. 4-8). 1997. 15.95 (*0-7868-0257-X*, Pub. by Hyprn Child); lib. bdg. 15.89 (*0-7868-2212-0*, Pub. by Hyprn Child) Little.
Martin, Patricia P. Days of Plenty, Days of Want. LC 88-71438. x, 76p. 1988. pap. 9.00 (*0-916950-88-3*) Biling Rev-Pr.
— El Milagro & Other Stories. LC 95-32550. (Camino Del Sol Ser.). 92p. 1996. pap. 9.95 (*0-8165-1548-4*) U of Ariz Pr.
— Songs My Mother Sang to Me: An Oral History of Mexican American Women. LC 92-6745. (Illus.). 224p. (Orig.). 1992. pap. 17.95 (*0-8165-1329-5*) U of Ariz Pr.
Martin, Patricia S. Beverly Cleary. (Biografias de Triunfadores Ser.). 24p. (J). (gr. 1-4). Date not set. lib. bdg. 13.95 (*0-86593-187-9*) Rourke Corp.
— Bill Cosby: Superstar, Set I. (Reaching Your Goal Ser.). (Illus.). 24p. (J). (gr. 1-4). 1987. lib. bdg. 18.60 (*0-86592-169-5*) Rourke Enter.
— Christa McAuliffe. (Biografias de Triunfadores Ser.). 24p. (J). (gr. 1-4). Date not set. lib. bdg. 13.95 (*0-86593-189-5*) Rourke Corp.
— El Dr. Seuss. (Biografias de Triunfadores Ser.). 24p. (J). (gr. 1-4). Date not set. lib. bdg. 13.95 (*0-86593-188-7*) Rourke Corp.
— Jesse Jackson: A Black Leader, Set I. (Reaching Your Goal Ser.). (Illus.). 24p. (J). (gr. 1-4). 1987. lib. bdg. 18.60 (*0-86592-170-9*) Rourke Enter.
— Reaching Your Goal, 4 bks. (Illus.). 192p. (J). (gr. 1-4). 1987. lib. bdg. 74.40 (*0-86592-166-0*) Rourke Enter.
— Samantha Smith: Little Ambassador. (Reaching Your Goal Bks.). (Illus.). 24p. (J). (gr. 1-4). 1987. 10.95 (*0-685-58131-4*) Rourke Corp.
— Samantha Smith: Little Ambassador. (Reaching Your Goal Bks.). (Illus.). 24p. (J). (gr. 1-4). 1987. lib. bdg. 18.60 (*0-86592-173-3*) Rourke Enter.
— Ted Kennedy Jr. He Faced His Challenge. (Reaching Your Goal Bks.). (Illus.). 24p. (J). (gr. 1-4). 1987. 10.95 (*0-685-58129-2*) Rourke Corp.
— Ted Kennedy Jr. He Faced His Challenge, Set I. (Reaching Your Goal Ser.). (Illus.). 24p. (J). (gr. 1-4). 1987. lib. bdg. 18.60 (*0-86592-174-1*) Rourke Enter.
Martin, Patricia Y., jt. ed. see Ferree, Myra M.
Martin, Patrick. An Inquiry into the Locations & Characteristics of Jacob Bright's Trading House & William Montgomery's Tavern. (Illus.). 101p. 1978. pap. 4.00 (*1-56349-022-6*, RS11) AR Archaeol.
— Tail Code USAF: The Complete History of USAF Tactical Aircraft Tail Code Markings. LC 93-84496. (Illus.). 176p. 1994. 45.00 (*0-88740-513-4*) Schiffer.
Martin, Patrick E. The Mill Creek Site & Pattern Recognition in Historical Archaeology. (Archaeological Completion Reports: No. 10). (Illus.). 265p. (Orig.). 1985. pap. 16.00 (*0-911872-54-X*) Mackinac St Hist Pks.
Martin, Patrick H., jt. auth. see Christie, George C.
Martin, Pattie, jt. auth. see Martin, David.
Martin, Paul. Dictionnaire de Synonymes pour Mots Croises, Par Nombre de Lettres. (FRE.). 110p. 1986. pap. 12.95 (*0-7859-8081-4*, 2853191737) Fr & Eur.
— The Floating World Cycle Poems. 5.00 (*0-686-15307-3*) Great Raven Pr.
— How to Find a Perfect Partner: The Original, Complete & Simplified Scientific Method for Comparing the Energies of Horoscopes for Compatibility. LC 90-83656. 280p. (Orig.). Date not set. pap. 19.95 (*1-878027-48-4*) Channel Media.
— Popular Collecting & the Everyday Self: The Reinvention of Museums? LC 98-17887. 1998. 85.00 (*0-7185-0170-5*) Bks Intl VA.
— Potts Models & Related Problems in Statistical Mechanics. (Advanced Series in Stat Mechanics: Vol. 5). 360p. 1991. text 36.00 (*981-02-0075-7*) World Scientific Pub.
— Songs Visions Traditions of Northwest Indian Tribes. 5.00 (*0-686-15297-2*) Great Raven Pr.
— Victorian Snapshots. LC 72-9219. (Literature of Photography Ser.). 1978. reprint ed. 13.95 (*0-405-04926-9*) Ayer.
— World Encyclopedia of Cocktails: A Compendium of 2500 Mixed Drinks. (Illus.). 408p. 1998. 29.95 (*0-09-475530-2*, Pub. by Constable & Co) Trafalgar.
Martin, Paul & Bateson, Patrick. Design for a Life: How Behavior Develops. LC 99-86972. 272p. 2000. 25.50 (*0-684-86932-2*) S&S Trade.
— Measuring Behaviour: An Introductory Guide. 2nd ed. (Illus.). 238p. (C). 1993. pap. text 18.95 (*0-521-44614-7*) Cambridge U Pr.
Martin, Paul & Brady, Peggy. Port Angeles-Washington: A History, Vol. I. LC 82-82187. (Illus.). 252p. 1983. pap. 18.95 (*0-918146-23-2*) Peninsula WA.
Martin, Paul, jt. auth. see Forster, Anne.
Martin, Paul, ed. see Mugrditchian, Hovhannes.
Martin, Paul C. Measurements & Correlation Functions. x, 98p. 1968. text 195.00 (*0-677-02440-1*) Gordon & Breach.
Martin, Paul D. Mensajeros al Cerebro. Sanz, Maria T. & Larios S, Maia, trs. (Explora y Aprende Ser.). (SPA., Illus.). 96p. (YA). (gr. 3-8). 1994. 15.00 (*0-915741-54-7*) C D Stampley Ent.
— Messengers to the Brain: Your Fantastic Five Senses. Crump, Donald J., ed. LC 82-45636. (Books for World Explorers Series 5: No. 3). 104p. (J). (gr. 3-8). 1984. 8.95 (*0-87044-499-9*); lib. bdg. 12.50 (*0-87044-504-9*) Natl Geog.
— Science: It's Changing Your World. Crump, Donald J., ed. LC 85-2936. (Books for World Explorers Series 6: No. 3). (Illus.). 104p. (J). (gr. 3-8). 1985. lib. bdg. 12.50 (*0-87044-521-9*) Natl Geog.
Martin, Paul K., ed. Airline Handbook. 7th ed. (Illus.). 476p. (Orig.). 1982. pap. 14.00 (*0-686-32833-7*) AeroTravel Res.
— Airline Handbook. 9th ed. (Illus.). 608p. (Orig.). 1985. pap. 16.00 (*0-914553-85-2*) AeroTravel Res.
— Airline Handbook. 10th ed. (Illus.). 700p. (Orig.). 1987. pap. 17.50 (*0-914553-86-0*) AeroTravel Res.
— Airline Handbook: 8th Annual. (Illus.). 500p. (Orig.). 1983. pap. 15.00 (*0-914553-83-6*) AeroTravel Res.
Martin, Paul R. Cult-Proofing Your Kids. 208p. 1993. pap. 9.99 (*0-310-53761-4*) Zondervan.
— Psychological Management of Chronic Headaches. LC 92-48225. (Treatment Manuals for Practitioners Ser.). 266p. 1993. lib. bdg. 42.00 (*0-89862-211-5*) Guilford Pubns.
— Psychological Management of Chronic Headaches. LC 92-48225. (Treatment Manuals for Practitioners Ser.). 266p. 1996. pap. text 23.00 (*1-57230-122-8*, 0122) Guilford Pubns.
— The Wall Street Journal Stylebook. 3rd ed. LC 92-73699. 200p. 1992. 18.00 (*1-881944-00-X*) Dow Jones & Co.
— The Wall Street Journal Stylebook. 4th ed. 1995. 18.00 (*1-881944-03-4*, Wall St Jrnl) Dow Jones & Co.
— The Writer's Little Instruction Book Vol. 1: 385 Secrets for Writing Well & Getting Published. (Illus.). 168p. (Orig.). 1998. pap. 7.95 (*0-9631441-7-0*) Writers Wrld.
***Martin, Paul S.** Anasazi Painted Pottery in the Field Museum Vol. 5: Field Museum, Anthropology Studies, 1940. limited ed. (Illus.). 284p. 2000. 185.00 (*1-57898-244-8*) Martino Pubng.
Martin, Paul S. Archaeological Work in the Ackmen-Lowry Area, Southwestern Colorado, 1937. LC 39-5397. (Field Museum of Natural History Anthropological Ser.: Vol. 23, No. 2). 166p. reprint ed. pap. 51.50 (*0-608-02713-8*, 206337800004) Bks Demand.
— Lowry Ruin in Southwestern Colorado. (Chicago Field Museum of Natural History Fieldiana Anthropology Ser.: Vol. 23). 1969. reprint ed. 70.00 (*0-527-01883-X*) Periodicals Srv.
— Modified Basket Maker Sites, Ackmen-Lowry Area, Southwestern Colorado, 1938. LC 39-30994. (Field Museum of Natural History Anthropological Ser.: Vol. 23, No. 3, June 27, 1939). (Illus.). 238p. 1939. reprint ed. pap. 73.80 (*0-608-02711-1*, 206337600004) Bks Demand.
— The SU Site Excavations at a Mogollon Village, Western New Mexico, Second Season, 1941. LC 43-6439. (Field Museum of Natural History Anthropological Ser.: Vol. 32, No. 2, February 24, 1943). (Illus.). 197p. 1943. reprint ed. pap. 61.10 (*0-608-02702-2*, 206336700004) Bks Demand.
— The SU Site Excavations at a Mogollon Village, Western New Mexico, 1939, with Reports on Pottery & Artifacts & Appendix on Skeletal Material. LC 41-8504. (Field Museum of Natural History Anthropological Ser.: Vol. 32, No. 1). (Illus.). 122p. 1940. reprint ed. pap. 37.90 (*0-608-02718-9*, 206338300004) Bks Demand.
— SU Site Excavations at a Mongollon Village, Western New Mexico, 1st, 2nd, & 3rd Seasons. (Field Museum of Natural History Ser.). (Illus.). 1974. reprint ed. 40.00 (*0-527-01892-9*) Periodicals Srv.
Martin, Paul S. & Klein, Richard G., eds. Quaternary Extinctions: A Prehistoric Revolution. LC 83-18053. 892p. 1989. reprint ed. pap. text 44.00 (*0-8165-1100-4*) U of Ariz Pr.
Martin, Paul S. & Rinaldo, John B. The SU Site Excavations at a Mogollon Village, Western New Mexico, Third Season, 1946. LC 47-30981. (Field Museum of Natural History Anthropological Ser.: Vol. 32, No. 3). (Illus.). 133p. 1947. reprint ed. pap. 41.30 (*0-608-02719-7*, 206338400004) Bks Demand.
— Turkey Foot Ridge Site: A Mogollon Village, Pine Lawn Valley, Western New Mexico. LC 50-12533. (Chicago Natural History Museum. Fieldiana: Anthropology Ser.: Vol. 38, No. 2). 165p. reprint ed. pap. 51.20 (*0-608-15169-6*, 205606800045) Bks Demand.
Martin, Paul S., ed. see Gentry, Howard S.
Martin, Paula. Spanish Armada Prisoners: The Story of the Nuestra Senors del Rosario & Her Crew & of Other Prisoners. 126p. 1984. text 29.00 (*0-85989-305-7*) Univ Exeter Pr.
Martin, Paula & Carss, Marjorie. Giants. Aragon, Laurie W., ed. (Illus.). 83p. (J). (gr. k-3). 1993. pap. 8.99 (*0-614-05561-X*, 4002) COMAP Inc.
Martin, Paula & Tate, Karen. The Project Management Memory Jogger: A Pocket Guide for Project Teams. Oddo, Francine, ed. (Illus.). 164p. 1997. spiral bd. 7.95 (*1-57681-001-1*, 103SE) GOAL-QPC.
Martin, Paula K. The Buck Stops Here: Accountability & the Empowered Manager. LC 98-136040. (Illus.). 1995. 29.95 (*0-943811-02-3*) Renai Educ Services.
— Discovering the WHAT of Management: The Complete Guide to the Kenning Principles of Management. (Illus.). 204p. 1990. 29.95 (*0-943811-01-5*) Renai Educ Services.
Martin, Peggy. 101 Volleyball Drills. LC 98-87714. (Illus.). 128p. 1998. pap. 16.95 (*1-57167-316-4*) Coaches Choice.
***Martin, Peggy-Lou.** Wishes, Wings, & Other Things: Poems for Anytime. 2000. write for info. (*1-57572-399-9*) Heinemann Lib.
Martin, Percy F. Latin America & World War I. 1976. lib. bdg. 59.95 (*0-8490-2130-8*) Gordon Pr.
— Mexico's Treasure House: Guanajuato. 1977. lib. bdg. 59.95 (*0-8490-2255-X*) Gordon Pr.
Martin, Percy F., ed. see De Oliveira Lima, Manuel.
Martin-Perdue, Nancy J. & Perdue, Charles L., Jr. Talk about Trouble: A New Deal Portrait of Virginians in the Great Depression. LC 95-34700. (Illus.). 516p. (C). 1996. pap. 22.50 (*0-8078-4570-1*) U of NC Pr.
— Talk about Trouble: A New Deal Portrait of Virginians in the Great Depression. LC 95-34700. (Illus.). 516p. (C). (gr. 13). 1996. 55.00 (*0-8078-2269-8*) U of NC Pr.
Martin, Perry L. Electronic Failure Analysis Handbook. (Illus.). 750p. 1999. 99.95 (*0-07-041044-5*) McGraw.
Martin, Pete, jt. auth. see Crosby, Bing.
Martin, Peter. The Chrysanthemum Throne: A History of the Emperors of Japan. LC 97-33210. (Illus.). 208p. 1997. 24.95 (*0-8248-2029-0*, Latitude Twenty) UH Pr.
— Edmond Malone, Shakespearean Scholar: A Literary Biography. (Cambridge Studies in Eighteenth-Century English Literature & Thought: 25). (Illus.). 324p. (C). 1995. text 64.95 (*0-521-46030-1*) Cambridge U Pr.
***Martin, Peter.** Life of James Boswell. 624p. 2000. 35.00 (*0-300-08489-7*) Yale U Pr.
Martin, Peter. Real Estate Bargains! 52p. (Orig.). 1990. pap. 7.95 (*1-882066-01-4*) Peters Pr.
Martin, Peter, ed. City Lights (Five Issues), Set. (Avant-Garde Magazines Ser.). 368p. 1974. reprint ed. 36.95 (*0-405-01758-8*) Ayer.
Martin, Peter, et al, eds. Shawcross & Beaumont: Air Law. 4th ed. 1991. ring bd. write for info. (*0-406-99836-1*, SBALASET, MICHIE) LEXIS Pub.
Martin, Peter & Nicholls, John. Creating a Committed Workforce. 224p. (C). 1987. 70.00 (*0-85292-379-1*) St Mut.
Martin, Peter, jt. auth. see Jeck, Steve.
Martin, Peter, jt. auth. see Ritchie, Sheila.
Martin, Peter J. The VCE Mathematics Experiment: An Evaluation. 1993. pap. 65.00 (*0-7300-0814-2*, Pub. by Deakin Univ) St Mut.
Martin, Peter J. & Pierce, Robyn, eds. Elementary Applied Statistics: An Activity Based Approach. 186p. (C). 1995. pap. 70.00 (*0-7300-1387-1*, Pub. by Deakin Univ) St Mut.
Martin, Peter M. Index of Social Security Act Cases Decided by the United States Court of Appeals for the Fourth Circuit. 39p. 1986. pap. 4.00 (*0-685-23188-7*, 28,947C) NCLS Inc.
Martin, Peter W., et al, eds. Language Use & Language Change in Brunei Darussalam. LC 96-31446. (Monographs in International Studies, Southeast Asia Ser.: Vol. 100). 390p. (Orig.). (C). 1996. pap. text 26.00 (*0-89680-193-4*) Ohio U Pr.
Martin, Philip. Farmhouse Fiddlers: Music & Dance Traditions in the Rural Midwest. LC 94-78042. (Illus.). 128p. (Orig.). 1994. pap. 19.95 (*1-883953-06-5*) Midwest Trad.
— The Shortstop's Son. LC 97-14766. 176p. 1997. 22.00 (*1-55728-483-0*); pap. 14.00 (*1-55728-484-9*) U of Ark Pr.
***Martin, Philip.** The Zen Path Through Depression. LC 98-44251. 160p. 2000. pap. 13.00 (*0-06-065446-3*, Pub. by Harper SF) HarpC.
Martin, Philip. The Zen Path Thru Depression. LC 98-44251. 160p. 1999. 19.00 (*0-06-065445-7*, Pub. by Harper SF) HarpC.
Martin, Philip, ed. Immigration Reform & U. S. Agriculture. 592p. 1995. pap. 40.00 (*1-879906-20-1*, 3358) ANR Pubns CA.
— My Midwest: Rural Writings from the Heartland. LC 99-166309. 160p. 1998. pap. 10.95 (*1-883953-26-X*, Face to Face) Midwest Trad.
Martin, Philip, jt. auth. see Gustafsson, Lars.
Martin, Philip L. Promises to Keep: Collective Bargaining in California Agriculture. LC 96-17688. (Illus.). 352p. 1996. text 54.95 (*0-8138-2988-7*) Iowa St U Pr.
Martin, Philip L., jt. ed. see Papademetriou, Demetrious G.
Martin, Philip L., tr. see Spear, Catherine.
Martin, Philip R. Auto Mechanics for the Complete Dummy. 2nd ed. LC 82-62322. (Illus.). 192p. 1983. pap. 9.95 (*0-930968-02-6*) Beach Cities.
— Pilots Wings of the United States: Civilian & Commercial. Ritums, John & Guido, Dennis, eds. LC 93-90426. (Illus.). 268p. 1982. pap. 2.95 (*0-930968-01-8*) Beach Cities.
Martin, Philip W. & Jarvis, Robin, eds. Reviewing Romanticism. LC 91-24823. 244p. 1992. text 55.00 (*0-312-06801-8*) St Martin.
Martin, Phillip, jt. auth. see Lee, James A.
Martin, Phyllis. All about Lorys & Lorikeets. Mathews-Danzer, Reinaldo, ed. (Illus.). 80p. (Orig.). 1998. pap. 10.50 (*1-888417-86-2*, 417862) Dimefast.
— Job-Hunt Success Kit. rev. ed. (Illus.). 147p. 1981. pap. text 13.50 (*0-685-31062-0*) Ctr Career Dev.
— Job-Hunt Success Plan, Adult Learner Edition. abr. rev. ed. (Illus.). 123p. 1989. pap. text 8.50 (*0-685-31059-0*) Ctr Career Dev.

M

— Job-Hunt Success Plan, High School Edition. abr. rev. ed. (Illus.). 118p. (YA). (gr. 11-12). 1989. pap. text 8.50 (*0-685-31060-4*) Ctr Career Dev.

— Return to Chipping Sodbury. 240p. 1997. 21.95 (*0-9656893-0-1*) Credenda.

Martin, Phyllis, jt. auth. see Birmingham, David.

Martin, Phyllis C., jt. auth. see Vincent, Elizabeth L.

Martin, Phyllis G., jt. auth. see Martin, John H.

Martin, Phyllis M. Lesiure & Society in Colonial Brazzaville. (African Studies: No. 87). (Illus.). 295p. (C). 1996. text 64.95 (*0-521-49551-2*) Cambridge U Pr.

Martin, Phyllis M. & O'Meara, Patrick, eds. Africa. 2nd ed. LC 85-45413. (Illus.). 480p. 1986. pap. 17.95 (*0-253-20392-9*, MB-392) Ind U Pr.

— Africa. 3rd ed. LC 95-5772. 472p. 1995. 39.95 (*0-253-32916-7*); pap. 17.95 (*0-253-20984-6*) Ind U Pr.

Martin, Phyllis M., jt. ed. see Birmingham, David.

Martin, Priscilla, ed. Prayers New & Old. rev. ed. 96p. 1993. pap. 1.50 (*0-88028-140-5*, 375) Forward Movement.

Martin, Purvis, ed. Handbook of Office Gynecology. LC 79-2690. 320p. 1985. pap. 31.95 (*0-685-42868-0*, 792690, Grune & Strat) Harcrt Hlth Sci Grp.

Martin, Purvis L. Ambulatory Gynecologic Surgery. LC 78-55286. (Illus.). 394p. 1979. 50.00 (*0-88416-209-5*) Mosby Inc.

Martin, R. Annals, Bk. IV. Tacitus & Woodman, A. J., eds. (Cambridge Greek & Latin Classics Ser.). (Illus.). 289p. (C). 1990. pap. text 22.95 (*0-521-31543-3*) Cambridge U Pr.

— Gel Electrophoresis: Nucleic Acids. (Introduction to Biotechniques Ser.). 160p. (Orig.). 1996. pap. 37.95 (*1-872748-28-7*, Pub. by Bios Sci) Bks Intl VA.

— Tacitus. (Classical Paperbacks Ser.). 256p. 1994. pap. 29.95 (*1-85399-431-6*, Pub. by Brist Class Pr) Focus Pub-R Pullins.

Martin, R., jt. ed. see Bergbreiter, D. E.

Martin, R. A. A Critical Concordance of the Septuagint of Daniel, Vol. 38. 1992. 89.95 (*0-935106-35-9*) E Mellen.

— Syntactical & Critical Concordance to the Greek Text of Baruch & the Epistle of Jeremiah. (Computer Bible Ser.: Vol. 12). (GRE.). 1977. pap. 49.95 (*0-935106-09-X*) E Mellen.

Martin, R. A. & Scorza, Sylvio. Syntactical Concordance to the Correlated Greek & Hebrew Text of Ruth. (Computer Bible Ser.: Vol. 30-A). 279p. (Orig.). 1988. pap. 89.95 (*0-935106-26-X*) E Mellen.

Martin, R. A., jt. auth. see Elliott, John H.

Martin, R. B., et al. Skeletal Tissue Mechanics. LC 98-2906. (Illus.). 384p. 1998. 64.95 (*0-387-98474-7*) Spr-Verlag.

Martin, R. C. The Cities & the Federal System. LC 77-74949. (American Federalism-the Urban Dimension Ser.). 1978. reprint ed. lib. bdg. 23.95 (*0-405-10495-2*) Ayer.

Martin, R. D. Primate Origins & Evolution: A Phylogenetic Reconstruction. (Illus.). 832p. 1990. text 95.00 (*0-691-08565-X*, Pub. by Princeton U Pr) Cal Prin Full Svc.

Martin, R. D., et al, eds. Paternity in Primates: Tests & Theories: Implications of Human DNA Fingerprint. (Illus.). xii, 288p. 1991. 215.75 (*3-8055-5494-X*) S Karger.

Martin, R. D., et al. Motherhood in Human & Nonhuman Primates: Biological & Social Determinants. (Illus.). x, 176p. 1995. 82.75 (*3-8055-6109-1*) S Karger.

Martin, R. D., tr. see Charles-Dominique, Pierre.

Martin, R. E. & Chapman, B. R., eds. Contributions in Mammalogy in Honor of Robert L. Packard. (Special Publications: No. 22). 234p. 1984. 50.00 (*0-89672-124-8*); pap. 25.00 (*0-89672-123-X*) Tex Tech Univ Pr.

Martin, R. H. Applying Information Science & Consensus-Formation Technology Utilization to Do Zeitgeist-Sector Modeling, Scenario Reality Planning Bibliography, No. 3, Nos. 1172-1173. 1976. 12.50 (*0-686-20416-6*, Sage Prdcls Pr) Sage.

Martin, R. H., jt. auth. see Woodman, A. J.

Martin, R. H., ed. see Tacitus.

Martin, R. H., ed. see Terence.

Martin, R. J. The Deity of Christ. 43p. 1998. pap. 1.00 (*1-883858-59-3*) Witness CA.

***Martin, R. L.** Money & the Space Economy. LC 98-29172. 348p. 1999. 115.00 (*0-471-98346-2*); pap. 36.95 (*0-471-98347-0*) Wiley.

Martin, R. M. Logico-Linguistic Papers. (Publications in Language Sciences). xii, 202p. 1981. 67.70 (*90-70176-39-4*); pap. 50.00 (*90-70176-93-9*) Mouton.

— Peirce's Logic of Relations & Other Studies. 156p. 1980. pap. 34.60 (*90-70176-17-3*) Mouton.

Martin, R. M. & Teo, K. L. Optimal Control of Drug Administration in Cancer Chemotherapy. 204p. 1993. text 61.00 (*981-02-1428-6*) World Scientific Pub.

Martin, R. N. Pierre Duhem. LC 91-26643. 286p. (C). 1991. 44.95 (*0-8126-9159-8*); pap. 21.95 (*0-8126-9160-1*) Open Court.

Martin, R. R., jt. auth. see Marshall, A. D.

Martin, R. S. Inanimae: The Secret Way. (Changeling: The Dreaming Ser.). (Illus.). 1998. pap. 16.00 (*1-56504-721-4*, 7307) White Wolf.

***Martin, R. Scott & Manahan, Stanley E.** Environmental Chemistry. 7th ed. (C). 2000. student ed., ring bd. write for info. (*1-56670-532-0*) CRC Pr.

Martin, Rafe. The Boy Who Lived with Seals. LC 91-46023. (Illus.). 32p. (J). (ps-3). 1993. lib. bdg. 15.95 (*0-399-22413-0*, G P Putnam) Peng Put Young Read.

— The Boy Who Lived with the Seals. LC 91-46023. (Illus.). 32p. (J). (ps-3). 1996. pap. 5.99 (*0-698-11352-7*, PapStar) Peng Put Young Read.

Martin, Rafe. A Boy Who Lived with the Seals. LC 91-46023. 1996. 11.15 (*0-606-09100-9*, Pub. by Turtleback) Demco.

Martin, Rafe. The Boy Who Loved Mammoths. (Storytelling-Folklore Ser.). (Illus.). 56p. (Orig.). 1995. pap. 7.95 (*0-938756-42-7*) Yellow Moon.

— The Brave Little Parrot. LC 95-14194. (Illus.). 32p. (J). 1998. 15.99 (*0-399-22825-X*, G P Putnam) Peng Put Young Read.

— The Eagle's Gift. LC 96-3538. (Illus.). 32p. (J). (gr. 1-6). 1997. 15.95 (*0-399-22923-X*, G P Putnam) Peng Put Young Read.

— The Girl & the Sea. LC 97-9459. (Illus.). (J). 1900. 16.00 (*0-15-201322-9*) Harcourt.

— The Hungry Tigress: Buddhist Myths, Legends & Jataka Tales. 3rd rev. ed. (Illus.). 302p. 1998. pap. 16.95 (*0-938756-52-4*) Yellow Moon.

— The Language of Birds. LC 98-48917. (J). 2000. 15.99 (*0-399-22925-6*, G P Putnam) Peng Put Young Read.

— The Lost Princess. LC 98-4335. (J). 1999. 15.95 (*0-399-22924-8*, G P Putnam) Peng Put Young Read.

— Monkey Bridge. LC 96-27974. (Illus.). (J). (ps-2). 1997. 17.00 (*0-679-88106-9*) Random.

— Mysterious Tales of Japan. LC 94-43464. (Illus.). 80p. (YA). (gr. 3 up). 1996. 18.95 (*0-399-22677-X*, G P Putnam) Peng Put Young Read.

— The Rough-Face Girl. LC 91-2921. (Illus.). 32p. (J). (ps-3). 1992. lib. bdg. 15.95 (*0-399-21859-9*, G P Putnam) Peng Put Young Read.

— The Rough-Face Girl. 1998. 11.19 (*0-606-13751-3*, Pub. by Turtleback) Demco.

— A Storyteller's Story. LC 92-7794. (Meet the Author Ser.). (Illus.). 32p. (J). (gr. 2-5). 1992. 14.95 (*0-913461-03-2*, 703) R Owen Pubs.

— Will's Mammoth. (Illus.). 32p. (J). (ps-3). 1989. 15.95 (*0-399-21627-8*, G P Putnam) Peng Put Young Read.

— Will's Mammoth. 1993. 10.15 (*0-606-06103-7*, Pub. by Turtleback) Demco.

Martin, Rafe & Morimoto, Junko. One Hand Clapping: Zen Stories for All Ages. LC 94-35257. (Illus.). 46p. 1995. 16.95 (*0-8478-1853-5*, Pub. by Rizzoli Intl) St Martin.

***Martin, Ralph.** Called to Holiness. 1999. pap. 10.95 (*0-89870-755-2*) Ignatius Pr.

Martin, Ralph. Catholic Church at the End of an Age: What Is the Spirit Saying? 309p. (Orig.). 1994. pap. 12.95 (*0-89870-524-X*) Ignatius Pr.

— Did I Say That? LC 95-61870. (Illus.). viii, 101p. 1995. pap. 19.00 (*0-87875-473-3*) Whitston Pub.

— Is Jesus Coming Soon? A Catholic Perspective on the Second Coming. LC 97-70804. 1997. pap. text 11.95 (*0-89870-635-1*) Ignatius Pr.

Martin, Ralph, ed. The Mathematics of Surfaces II. (Institute of Mathematics & Its Applications Conference Series, New Ser.: New Series 11). (Illus.). 528p. 1987. text 89.00 (*0-19-853619-4*) OUP.

Martin, Ralph & Williamson, Peter, eds. John Paul II & the New Evangelization. LC 94-79294. 290p. (Orig.). pap. 12.95 (*0-89870-536-3*) Ignatius Pr.

Martin, Ralph, et al. Teaching Science for All Children. 2nd ed. (C). 1996. pap., teacher ed. write for info. (*0-205-19586-5*, H9586-2) Allyn.

Martin, Ralph, jt ed. see Goodman, Tim.

Martin, Ralph E. The Peacock Has Landed. LC 97-60659. (Illus.). 52p. 1997. pap. 5.00 (*1-886467-18-8*) WJM Press.

— Sketches in Time. LC 97-90411. (Illus.). 52p. 1997. pap. 5.00 (*1-886467-19-6*) WJM Press.

Martin, Ralph E. & Sexton, Collen. Teaching Science for All Children. 2nd ed. LC 96-19152. 658p. 1996. 75.00 (*0-205-19585-7*) Allyn.

Martin, Ralph E., et al. Science Method. 448p. (J). 1997. pap. text 38.00 (*0-205-27573-7*) P-H.

***Martin, Ralph E., et al.** Teaching Science for All Children. 3rd ed. LC 00-40595. 2001. write for info. (*0-205-32533-5*) Allyn.

***Martin, Ralph P.** Acts (Bible Study Book) (Theology Ser.). 125p. 2000. pap. 6.95 (*1-885216-29-7*) Evan Formosan.

Martin, Ralph P. Colossians: The Church's Lord & the Christian's Liberty. 192p. 1972. 12.50 (*0-85364-125-0*) Attic Pr.

***Martin, Ralph P.** Colossians: The Church's Lord & the Christian's Liberty. 180p. 2000. pap. 18.00 (*1-57910-322-7*) Wipf & Stock.

Martin, Ralph P. Ephesians, Colossians, & Philemon. (Interpretation: a Bible Commentary for Preaching & Teaching Ser.). 160p. 1992. text 21.00 (*0-8042-3139-7*) Westminster John Knox.

— The Epistle of Paul to the Philippians. rev. ed. (Tyndale Bible Commentaries Ser.). 1988. pap. 12.00 (*0-8028-0310-5*) Eerdmans.

— The Family & the Fellowship: New Testament Images of the Church. 142p. 1997. pap. 14.00 (*1-57910-033-3*) Wipf & Stock.

— A Hymn of Christ: Philippians 2:5-11 in Recent Interpretation & in the Setting of Early Christian Worship. 3rd ed. LC 97-35894. 372p. 1997. pap. 29.99 (*0-8308-1894-4*, 1894) InterVarsity.

— James. (Biblical Commentary Ser.: Vol. 48). 29.99 (*0-8499-0247-9*) Word Pub.

— Mark: Evangelist & Theologian. (Contemporary Evangelical Perspective Ser.). 249p. (C). 1986. pap. 12.95 (*0-310-28801-0*, 18118P) Zondervan.

***Martin, Ralph P.** New Testament Foundations Vol. 1: A Guide for Christian Students. 326p. 1999. pap. 26.00 (*1-57910-310-3*) Wipf & Stock.

— New Testament Foundations Vol. 2: A Guide for Christian Students. 470p. 1999. pap. 36.00 (*1-57910-312-X*) Wipf & Stock.

Martin, Ralph P. Reconciliation. 272p. 1989. pap. 14.95 (*0-310-28811-8*) Zondervan.

— Reconciliation: A Study of Paul's Theology. 285p. 1997. pap. 25.00 (*1-57910-034-1*) Wipf & Stock.

— Second Corinthians. (Biblical Commentary Ser.: Vol. 40). 1985. 29.99 (*0-8499-0239-8*) Word Pub.

— The Spirit & the Congregation: Studies in I Corinthians 12-15. 176p. (Orig.). 1997. pap. 16.00 (*1-57910-092-9*) Wipf & Stock.

— La Teologia de la Adoracion (The Theology of Worship. (SPA., Illus.). 270p. (C). 1999. pap. write for info. (*0-7361-0077-6*) Life Pubs Intl.

***Martin, Ralph P.** Where the Action Is: A Bible Commentary for Laymen on Mark. 160p. 1998. pap. 17.00 (*1-57910-165-8*) Wipf & Stock.

Martin, Ralph P. Where the Action Is: Mark - A Bible Commentary for Laypeople. (Theology Series). 165p. 1998. pap. 7.95 (*1-885216-23-8*) Evan Formosan.

— Worship in the Early Church. rev. ed. 144p. 1975. reprint ed. pap. 12.00 (*0-8028-1613-4*) Eerdmans.

Martin, Ralph P. & Davids, Peter H., eds. Dictionary of the Later New Testament & Its Developments. LC 97-36095. 1319p. 1997. 39.99 (*0-8308-1779-4*, 1779) InterVarsity.

Martin, Ralph P. & Dodd, Brian J., eds. Where Christology Began: Essays on Philippians 2. LC 97-44957. 176p. 1998. pap. 25.00 (*0-664-25619-8*) Westminster John Knox.

Martin, Ralph R., jt. auth. see Nutbourne, Anthony W.

Martin, Ramela. Out of Darkness. 1989. write for info. (*0-916431-28-2*) Zoryan Ins.

Martin, Ramela, jt. auth. see Martin, James.

Martin, Randall. Edmund Ironside & Anthony Brewer's the Love-Sick King. rev. ed. LC 91-26246. (Renaissance Imagination Ser.). 488p. 1991. text 20.00 (*0-8153-0454-4*) Garland.

— Women Writrs Renaiss Eng. LC 96-23866. (C). 1997. text 74.06 (*0-582-09621-9*, Pub. by Addison-Wesley); pap. text 29.06 (*0-582-09620-0*, Pub. by Addison-Wesley) Longman.

Martin, Randy. Chalk Lines: The Politics of Work in the Managed University. LC 98-21278. 328p. 1999. 49.95 (*0-8223-2232-3*); pap. 17.95 (*0-8223-2249-8*) Duke.

— Critical Moves: Dance Studies in Theory & Politics. LC 97-49360. 1998. 49.95 (*0-8223-2203-X*); pap. 17.95 (*0-8223-2219-6*) Duke.

— Performance As Political Act: The Embodied Self. LC 89-33473. (Critical Perspectives in Social Theory Ser.). (Illus.). 223p. 1990. 57.95 (*0-89789-174-0*, H174, Greenwood Pr) Greenwood.

— Socialist Ensembles: Theater & State in Cuba & Nicaragua. 208p. 1994. pap. 19.95 (*0-8166-2482-8*); text 49.95 (*0-8166-2480-1*) U of Minn Pr.

— Sport & Culture. LC 98-45941. (Cultural Politics Ser.). 1999. 49.95 (*0-8166-3183-2*) U of Minn Pr.

***Martin, Randy & Miller, Toby.** Sportcult. LC 98-45941. (Cultural Politics Ser.: Vol. 16). 304p. 1999. 19.95 (*0-8166-3184-0*) U of Minn Pr.

Martin, Randy W. Optimal Health: How to Get It - How to Keep It. Rhodes, Sara B., ed. LC 98-83056. (Illus.). 200p. 1999. pap. 19.95 (*1-891850-16-4*) Med Bear.

***Martin, Raquel.** Cartoon Classics Vol. 9: Donald Duck's First 50 Years. (Illus.). (J). 2000. pap. 13.75 (*5-550-00632-4*) Nairi.

Martin, Raquel. Today's Health Alternative. (Illus.). 456p. (Orig.). (C). 1992. pap. text 16.95 (*0-922356-45-9*) Amer West Pubs.

Martin, Raquel & Gerstung, Judi. La Alternativa Al Estrogeno: Terapia de Hormona Natural con Progesterona Botanico. (SPA.). 224p. 1998. pap. 14.95 (*0-89281-589-2*, Inner Trad Espanol) Inner Tradit.

— The Estrogen Alternative: Natural Hormone Therapy with Botanical Progesterone. rev. expanded ed. LC 97-42690. 224p. 1998. pap. 14.95 (*0-89281-780-1*) Inner Tradit.

***Martin, Raquel & Gerstung, Judi.** New Estrogen Alternative: Natural Hormone Therapy with Botanical Progesterone. 3rd rev. ed. LC 99-89914. 240p. 2000. pap. 14.95 (*0-89281-893-X*, Heal Arts VT) Inner Tradit.

***Martin, Raquel & Romano, Karen J.** Preventing & Reversing Arthritis Naturally: The Untold Story. 208p. 2000. pap. 14.95 (*0-89281-891-3*, Heal Arts VT) Inner Tradit.

Martin, Raquel, et al. The Estrogen Alternative: Natural Hormone Therapy with Botanical Progesterone. LC 97-2640. 160p. 1996. pap. 12.95 (*0-89281-645-7*, Heal Arts VT) Inner Tradit.

Martin, Ray. The Ninety-Nine Critical Shots in Pool: Everything You Need to Know to Learn & Master the Game. LC 75-36260. 240p. 1993. pap. 15.00 (*0-8129-2241-7*, Times Bks) Crown Pub Group.

— Your Financial Guide: Advice for Every Stage of Your Life. 304p. 1996. 18.95 (*0-02-861114-4*) Macmillan.

Martin, Ray & Rankin, Lee. Building Garden Furniture: More Than Thirty Beautiful Outdoor Projects. (Illus.). 160p. 1994. pap. 16.95 (*0-8069-8375-2*) Sterling.

Martin, Ray & Reeves, Rosser. The Ninety-Nine Critical Shots in Pool. LC 75-36260. (Illus.). 256p. 1982. write for info. (*0-8129-0618-7*, Times Bks); pap. 12.00 (*0-8129-6313-X*, Times Bks) Crown Pub Group.

***Martin, Raymond.** The Elusive Messiah: A Philosophical Overview of the Quest for the Historical Jesus. LC 99-17104. 256p. 1999. 25.00 (*0-8133-6705-0*, Pub. by Westview) HarpC.

— Elusive Messiah: A Philosophical Overview of the Quest for the Historical Jesus. 2000. pap. 16.00 (*0-8133-9148-2*) Westview.

Martin, Raymond. The Past Within Us: An Empirical Approach to Philosophy of History. LC 88-32244. 176p. reprint ed. pap. 54.60 (*0-608-20158-8*, 205443900011) Bks Demand.

— Ruth: Computer Generated Tools for the Correlated Greek & Hebrew Texts. (Computer Bible Ser.: Vol. 30-C). 272p. 1995. pap. 89.95 (*0-935106-49-9*) E Mellen.

— Self-Concern: An Experiential Approach to What Matters in Survival. LC 97-22320. (Studies in Philosophy). (Illus.). 192p. (C). 1997. text 54.95 (*0-521-59266-6*) Cambridge U Pr.

Martin, Raymond, ed. Success Stories in the American Electronics Industry. 106p. 1991. 15.00 (*1-55822-033-X*) Am Prod & Inventory.

Martin, Raymond, et al, eds. Computer Generated Tools for the Study of the Correlated Greek & Hebrew Texts of Obadiah. (Computer Bible Ser.: Vol. 37). 200p. 1996. pap. 89.95 (*0-935106-34-0*) E Mellen.

***Martin, Raymond & Barresi, John.** Naturalization of the Soul: Self & Personal Identity in the Birth of Modern Psychology. LC 99-38676. (Studies in 18th Century Philosophy). 216p. 1999. 85.00 (*0-415-21645-1*) Routledge.

Martin, Raymond & Scorza, Sylvio. Syntactical Concordance to the Correlated Greek & Hebrew Text of Ruth: The Septuaqint Series. Baird, J. Arthur & Freedman, David N., eds. (Computer Bible Ser.: Vol. 30-B). 209p. 1990. pap. 89.95 (*0-935106-30-8*) E Mellen.

Martin, Raymond & Weadock, Glenn. Bulletproofing Client - Server Systems. LC 97-4056. (Illus.). 384p. 1997. pap. 34.95 (*0-07-067622-4*) McGraw.

Martin, Raymond, jt. auth. see Kolak, Daniel.

Martin, Raymond, jt. ed. see Kolak, Daniel.

Martin, Raymond, ed. see Krishnamurti, Jiddu.

Martin, Raymond A. Studies in the Life & Ministry of the Early Paul & Related Issues. LC 93-20603. (Biblical Press Ser.: Vol. 11). 264p. 1993. text 89.95 (*0-7734-2368-0*, Mellen Biblical Pr) E Mellen.

— Studies in the Life & Ministry of the Historical Jesus. (Illus.). 172p. (C). 1995. pap. text 23.50 (*0-8191-9773-4*); lib. bdg. 48.00 (*0-8191-9772-6*) U Pr of Amer.

— Syntax Criticism of Johannine Literature, the Catholic Epistles & the Gospel Passion Accounts. LC 89-13567. (Studies in the Bible & Early Christianity: Vol. 18). 200p. 1989. lib. bdg. 89.95 (*0-88946-618-1*) E Mellen.

— Syntax Criticism of the Synoptic Gospels. LC 87-5646. (Studies in Bible & Early Christianity: Vol. 10). 232p. 1987. lib. bdg. 99.95 (*0-88946-610-6*) E Mellen.

Martin, Raymond L., ed. Repetitive Manufacturing Specific Industry Group Annotate Bibliography. 3rd ed. 50p. (Orig.). 1995. pap. 10.00 (*1-55822-157-3*) Am Prod & Inventory.

***Martin, Rebecca.** Horse Called Willing. 165p. 1998. pap. 6.95 (*0-87813-576-6*) Christian Light.

Martin, Rebecca. The House with Two Grandmothers. unabridged ed. 125p. (J). (gr. 4-8). 1997. pap. 5.95 (*0-87813-569-3*) Christian Light.

***Martin, Rebecca J., intro.** Wheat People: Celebrating Kansas Harvest. (Illus.). 50p. 2000. write for info. (*0-87726-053-2*) Kansas St Hist.

Martin, Rebecca R. Libraries & the Changing Face of Academia: Responses to Growing Multicultural Populations. LC 93-42118. 273p. 1993. 32.50 (*0-8108-2824-3*) Scarecrow.

Martin, Reed. What Schools Forget to Tell Parents about Their Rights. 48p. (C). 1997. pap. 19.95 (*1-885477-35-X*) Fut Horizons.

Martin, Regina, ed. see Cooper, F. D.

Martin, Reginald. Black Aesthetic Criticism: An Annotated Bibliography. (Bibliographies of Modern Critics & Critical Schools Ser.: Vol. 16). 250p. text 37.00 (*0-8240-6890-4*, H1290) Garland.

— Dark Eros: Black Erotic Writings. 416p. 1999. pap. 14.95 (*0-312-19850-7*) St Martin.

— Dysfunction Junction: Typeface Bombs & Vidnarratives. (Illus.). 108p. 1996. 21.95 (*0-9624889-6-8*) Seymour-Smith.

— Southern Secrets. (Illus.). 80p. 1996. 18.95 (*0-9624889-5-X*) Seymour-Smith.

Martin, Reginald, ed. Dark Eros: Black Erotic Writings. LC 97-8177. 1997. text 25.95 (*0-312-15508-5*) St Martin.

Martin, Reginald, ed. see Andrews, Malachi & Warnette, Ken.

Martin, Regis. Images of Grace: 33 Christian Poems. 50p. 1994. pap. 4.95 (*0-940535-79-3*, UP179) Franciscan U Pr.

— The Last Thing. LC 97-76855. ii, 167p. 1998. pap. text 12.95 (*0-89870-662-9*) Ignatius Pr.

— The Suffering of Love: Christ's Descent into the Hell of Human Hopelessness. LC 95-21586. 173p. 1995. pap. 19.95 (*1-879007-14-2*) St Bedes Pubns.

Martin, Rene. Dictionnaire Culturel de la Mythologie Greco-Romaine. (FRE.). 1992. write for info. (*0-7859-7721-X*, 2091800740) Fr & Eur.

Martin, Renee C. Forgery Forensics: Handwritten Forensic Document Examination. 1999. 59.95 (*0-8493-8124-X*) CRC Pr.

— Forgery Forensics: Modern Document Examination. LC 99-50186. 1999. 59.95 (*0-8493-8125-8*) CRC Pr.

Martin, Renee J., ed. Practicing What We Teach: Confronting Diversity in Teacher Education. LC 94-32933. (Social Context of Education Ser.). 282p. (C). 1995. pap. text 21.95 (*0-7914-2550-9*) State U NY Pr.

Martin, Rex. A System of Rights. 446p. 1997. reprint ed. pap. text 24.00 (*0-19-829293-7*) OUP.

Martin, Rex, ed. see MacCallum, Gerald C., Jr.

Martin, Rex, ed. & intro. see Collingwood, R. G.

Martin-Reynolds, Joanne & Pogacar, Timothy. A Holistic View of Teaching Languages in Elementary & Middle Schools. 274p. (C). 1994. pap. text 24.00 (*1-57074-147-6*) Greyden Pr.

Martin, Rhona. Goodbye, Sally. large type ed. 640p. 1989. 27.99 (*0-7089-2015-2*) Ulverscroft.

— Mango Walk. large type ed. (Ulverscroft Large Print Ser.). 736p. 1997. 27.99 (*0-7089-3762-4*) Ulverscroft.

— The Unicorn Summer. large type ed. (Ulverscroft Large Print Ser.). 544p. 1997. 27.95 (*0-7089-3724-1*) Ulverscroft.

Martin, Rhonda. Writing Historical Fiction. 2nd ed. pap. write for info. (*0-7136-4068-5*, 93321, Pub. by A & C Blk) Midpt Trade.

Martin, Richard. American Ingenuity: Sportswear, 1930s-1970s. LC 98-14956. 1998. write for info. (*0-87099-863-3*) Metro Mus Art.

— The Ceaseless Century: 300 Years of Eighteenth Century Costume. LC 98-215625. 80p. 1998. 16.95 (*0-87099-884-6*) Metro Mus Art.

— Charles James. 80p. 1999. text 18.95 (*0-7893-0378-7*) Universe.

— Cubism & Fashion. LC 98-44882. (Illus.). 160p. 1999. 45.00 (*0-8109-6532-1*, Pub. by Abrams) Time Warner.

— Cubism & Fashion. LC 98-44882. 160p. 1998. 45.00 (*0-87099-888-9*) Metro Mus Art.

***Martin, Richard.** Cubism & Fashion. LC 98-44882. 1998. pap. write for info. (*0-87099-889-7*) Metro Mus Art.

Martin, Richard. Fashion & Surrealism. LC 87-45490. (Illus.). 240p. 1990. pap. 35.00 (*0-8478-1073-9*, Pub. by Rizzoli Intl) St Martin.

— K'aiiroondak: Behind the Willows. Pfisterer, Bill, ed. (Illus.). 321p. (Orig.). (C). 1993. pap. 19.00 (*1-877962-26-0*) Univ AK Ctr CCS.

— Khaki: Cut from the Original Cloth. (Illus.). 176p. 1999. 50.00 (*1-892041-14-6*, Tondo Bks) Arena Editions.

— Mean Streets & Raging Bulls: The Legacy of Film Noir in Contemporary American Cinema. LC 97-11136. 208p. 1997. 29.50 (*0-8108-3337-9*) Scarecrow.

— Mean Streets & Raging Bulls: The Legacy of Film Noir in Contemporary American Cinema. LC 99-17309. 224p. 1999. reprint ed. pap. 22.50 (*0-8108-3642-4*) Scarecrow.

— Modulations: Poems. 112p. 1998. pap. 12.00 (*1-878580-67-1*) Asylum Arts.

— Portraits. (Illus.). 80p. 2000. 75.00 (*2-84323-152-3*, Pub. by Assouline) Rizzoli Intl.

— The St. James Fashion Encyclopedia: A Survey of Style from 1945 to the Present. LC 96-22878. (Illus.). 438p. 1996. 29.95 (*0-7876-1036-4*) Visible Ink Pr.

— Versace. (Illus.). 80p. 1997. 18.95 (*0-7893-0090-7*, Pub. by Universe) St Martin.

Martin, Richard, ed. Contemporary Fashion. 575p. 1995. 140.00 (*1-55862-173-3*, 200201) St James Pr.

— The New Urban Landscape. LC 89-63218. (Illus.). 132p. 1990. pap. 29.95 (*0-9624916-0-8*) Drenttel Doyle.

Martin, Richard & Koda, Harold. Christian Doir. (Illus.). 192p. 1997. 60.00 (*0-8109-6506-2*, Pub. by Abrams) Time Warner.

— Haute Couture. (Illus.). 128p. 1996. 39.95 (*0-8109-6496-1*, Pub. by Abrams) Time Warner.

— Haute Couture. LC 95-45361. 1995. pap. 25.00 (*0-87099-762-9*) Metro Mus Art.

Martin, Richard & Metropolitan Museum of Art (New York, N. Y.) Staff. Our New Clothes: Acquisitions of the 1990s. LC 99-14145. 80p. 1999. pap. 29.95 (*0-8109-6540-2*, Pub. by Abrams) Time Warner.

Martin, Richard & Versace, Gianni. Gianni Versace. LC 97-32249. 1997. pap. 35.00 (*0-87099-843-9*) Metro Mus Art.

Martin, Richard, et al. Christian Dior. LC 96-45943. 201p. 1996. 50.00 (*0-87099-822-6*); pap. 35.00 (*0-87099-823-4*) Metro Mus Art.

— Dorothy Gillespie. (Illus.). 160p. 1997. 35.95 (*0-9633654-3-6*); pap. 22.95 (*0-9633654-4-4*) Radford U Fnd.

— Gianni Versace. LC 97-32249. (Illus.). 192p. 1998. 60.00 (*0-8109-6521-6*, Pub. by Abrams) Time Warner.

— Gianni Versace. LC 97-32249. 1997. 50.00 (*0-87099-842-0*) Metro Mus Art.

— Panfishing. LC 91-60047. (Complete Angler's Library). 278p. 1991. write for info. (*0-914697-37-4*) N Amer Outdoor Grp.

Martin, Richard, jt. auth. see Fay, Judith.

Martin, Richard, jt. auth. see Friedman, Ellen G.

Martin, Richard, ed. see Adams, Jon-K.

Martin, Richard, ed. see Bosch, Susanna A.

Martin, Richard A. 125 Years of Service: St. Lukes Hospital, 1873-1998. (Illus.). 350p. text 31.95 (*1-889668-16-8*) S & D.

Martin, Richard C. Islamic Studies: A History of Religions Approach. 2nd ed. LC 94-41956. 274p. (C). 1995. pap. text 33.20 (*0-13-205543-0*) P-H.

Martin, Richard C., ed. Approaches to Islam in Regious Studies. LC 85-1099. 243p. 1985. 34.00 (*0-8165-0868-2*) U of Ariz Pr.

Martin, Richard C. & Woodward, Mark R. Defenders of Reason in Islam: Mu'tazilism from Medieval School to Modern Symbol. LC 98-177978. 192p. 1997. pap. 20.95 (*1-85168-147-7*, Pub. by Onewrld Pubns) Penguin Putnam.

Martin, Richard C., jt. ed. see Witte, John, Jr.

***Martin, Richard J. & Schallig, Henk D. F. H., eds.** Veterinary Parasitology: Recent Developments in Immunology, Epidemiology & Control. (Parasitology Ser.: Vol. 120). 144p. (C). 2000. pap. write for info. (*0-521-79438-2*) Cambridge U Pr.

Martin, Richard J., jt. auth. see Fanaroff, Avary A.

Martin, Richard J., jt. ed. see Cosentino, Anthony M.

Martin, Richard M. Events, Reference, & Logical Form. LC 77-24685. 271p. reprint ed. pap. 84.10 (*0-608-15253-6*, 202949200061) Bks Demand.

— Logical Semiotics & Mereology. LC 91-41368. (Foundations of Semiotics Ser.: No. 16). xiii, 282p. 1992. 89.00 (*90-272-3288-1*) J Benjamins Pubng Co.

— Metaphysical Foundations: Mereology & Metalogic. (Analytica Ser.). 387p. 1988. 92.00 (*3-88405-053-2*) Philosophia Pr.

— Pragmatics, Truth, & Language. (Boston Studies in the Philosophy of Science: No. XXXVIII). 325p. 1979. pap. text 62.50 (*90-277-0993-9*, D Reidel); lib. bdg. 104.50 (*90-277-0992-0*, D Reidel) Kluwer Academic.

— Semiotics & Linguistic Structure: A Primer of Philosophic Logic. LC 78-6873. 321p. (C). 1978. text 29.50 (*0-87395-381-9*) State U NY Pr.

Martin, Richard M., jt. ed. see Eisele, Carolyn.

Martin, Richard P. The Language of Heroes: Speech & Performance in the "Iliad" LC 89-42889. (Myth & Poetics Ser.). 288p. 1989. text 42.50 (*0-8014-2353-8*) Cornell U Pr.

— The Language of Heroes: Speech & Performance in the "Iliad" LC 89-42889. (Myth & Poetics Ser.). 288p. 1993. pap. text 16.95 (*0-8014-8070-1*) Cornell U Pr.

Martin, Richard P., ed. Bulfinch's Mythology: The Age of Fable, the Age of Chivalry, Legends of Charlemagne. LC 91-55002. (Illus.). 768p. 1991. 45.00 (*0-06-270025-1*, Harper Ref) HarpC.

Martin, Richard P., tr. see Propp, Vladimir.

Martin, Richard T. Dynamic Door Approaches: Fifty Attention-Grabbing Tracting & Telephone Dialogues for Missionaries. 128p. 1998. pap. 9.98 (*0-88290-619-4*, 1083) Horizon Utah.

Martin, Rick & Martin, Charlotte. Vintage Illustration: Discovering America's Calendar Artists. Goldberg, Michael & Manchur, Gail, eds. LC 96-9529. (Illus.). 208p. 1997. 35.00 (*1-888054-00-X*, 5400X) Collectors Pr.

Martin, Rick, jt. auth. see Carpenter, Elizabeth.

Martin, Rick W., jt. ed. see Rivlin, Michel E.

***Martin, Ricky.** Livin' la Vida Loca & Other Hits Recorded by Ricky Martin. 1998. pap. 14.95 (*0-7692-9074-4*) Wrner Bros.

Martin, Riley L. & Wann, O-Qua T. The Coming of Tan: Past, Present & Future of Humanity, Extraterrestrial Attention, Environmental Catastrophe. Cooperman, Curtis L., ed. (Illus.). 369p. (Orig.). 1995. pap. 24.95 (*0-9645745-0-0*) Historicty Prodn.

Martin, Rita & Lesbia de Varona, Ana R., eds. Eugenio Florit, de lo Eterno lo Mejor. (SPA.). Date not set. pap. write for info. (*0-89729-826-8*) Ediciones.

Martin, Robert. Accuracy of Translation. 89p. 1997. reprint ed. pap. 9.99 (*0-85151-735-8*) Banner of Truth.

— Handbook of Hydroxyacetophenones. 544p. 1997. text 307.50 (*0-7923-4564-9*) Kluwer Academic.

Martin, Robert. Media Law. LC 97-175663. (Essentials of Canadian Law Ser.). xiv, 194p. 1996. pap. 30.95 (*1-55221-004-9*, Pub. by Irwin Law) Gaunt.

— More C++ Gems. (SIGS Reference Library: No. 17). 525p. 2000. pap. 44.95 (*0-521-78618-5*) Cambridge U Pr.

— Speaking Freely: Expression & the Law in the Commonwealth. xiii, 706p. 1999. pap. 51.95 (*1-55221-033-2*, Pub. by Irwin Law) Gaunt.

Martin, Robert. Vengeance Is Mine. 220p. (Orig.). 1997. pap. 8.95 (*1-57502-468-3*, P01399) Morris Pubng.

Martin, Robert, jt. auth. see Nyquist, John R.

Martin, Robert, jt. ed. see Winter, Robert.

Martin, Robert A. Critical Essays on Tennessee Williams. LC 97-21446. (Critical Essays on American Literature Ser.). 350p. 1997. 48.00 (*0-7838-0042-8*, G K Hall & Co) Mac Lib Ref.

Martin, Robert A., ed. The Writer's Craft: Hopwood Lectures, 1965-1981. 296p. 1982. pap. text 15.95 (*0-472-06337-5*, 06337) U of Mich Pr.

Martin, Robert A. & Barnosky, Anthony D., eds. Morphological Change in Quaternary Mammals of North America. (Illus.). 427p. (C). 1993. text 74.95 (*0-521-40450-9*) Cambridge U Pr.

Martin, Robert A., ed. see Miller, Arthur.

Martin, Robert C. Designing C Plus Plus Applications Using the Booch Notation. LC 94-47129. 512p. 1995. 62.00 (*0-13-203837-4*) P-H.

Martin, Robert C., et al. Practical Speech for Modern Business. LC 63-7333. 1963. 32.50 (*0-89197-353-2*) Irvington.

Martin, Robert D. Bankruptcy Forms. 1989. write for info. (*0-318-65474-1*, P05824) P-H.

Martin, Robert D. & Doud, Laurel M. Leslie Lewis Doud: His Family & Ancestors. LC 93-80964. (Illus.). 33p. reprint ed. pap. 30.00 (*0-7837-6970-9*, AU0044800004) Bks Demand.

Martin, Robert D., jt. auth. see Ginsberg, Robert E.

Martin, Robert D., tr. see Lorenz, Konrad.

Martin, Robert E., jt. auth. see DeBlase, Anthony F.

Martin, Robert E., jt. ed. see Weise, David R.

Martin, Robert F. Howard Kester & the Struggle for Social Justice in the South, 1904-77. LC 90-39702. (Minds of the New South Ser.). 216p. reprint ed. pap. 67.00 (*0-608-08548-0*, 206907100002) Bks Demand.

— National Income in the United States, 1799-1938. LC 75-22827. (America in Two Centuries Ser.). 1976. reprint ed. 18.95 (*0-405-07699-1*) Ayer.

Martin, Robert J. Economy & International Relations of Azerbaijan: The International Influence. 60p. 1996. pap. text 12.95 (*1-899658-18-1*, Pub. by Royal Inst Intl Affairs) Brookings.

***Martin, Robert J.** Professional Management of Housekeeping Operations. 3rd ed. LC 97-29029. 528p. 1998. 59.95 (*0-471-19862-5*) Wiley.

Martin, Robert J. A Tall Tale from the Short Grass. (Illus.). 90p. 1999. pap. 11.95 (*0-7392-0190-5*, PO3167) Morris Pubng.

— Wise Words to the Graduate. 24p. (YA). (gr. 9 up). 1978. pap. 2.99 (*0-8010-6043-5*) Baker Bks.

Martin, Robert J. & Jones, Tom. Professional Management of Housekeeping Operations. 2nd ed. LC 91-34407. 480p. 1992. 59.95 (*0-471-54779-4*); pap., teacher ed. write for info. (*0-471-55825-7*) Wiley.

Martin, Robert K. The Homosexual Tradition in American Poetry. expanded ed. LC 98-20571. 280p. 1998. pap. 18.95 (*0-87745-648-8*) U of Iowa Pr.

— The Incarnate Ground of Christian Faith: Toward a Christian Theological Epistemology for the Educational Ministry of the Church. LC 98-38404. 384p. (C). 1998. 49.00 (*0-7618-1255-5*) U Pr of Amer.

Martin, Robert K., ed. The Continuing Presence of Walt Whitman: The Life after the Life. LC 91-44249. (Illus.). 282p. 1992. text 28.95 (*0-87745-366-7*) U of Iowa Pr.

Martin, Robert K. & Piggford, George. Queer Forster. LC 97-9960. (Worlds of Desire Ser.). 288p. 1997. pap. text 16.95 (*0-226-50802-1*); lib. bdg. 49.00 (*0-226-50801-3*) U Ch Pr.

Martin, Robert K. & Savoy, Eric, eds. American Gothic: New Inverventions in a National Narrative. LC 97-32722. (Illus.). 264p. 1998. text 32.95 (*0-87745-622-4*) U of Iowa Pr.

Martin, Robert L. The Best of Nuts & Bolts. 106p. 1995. pap. 21.95 (*0-683-18121-1*) Lppncott W & W.

— The City Moves West: Economic & Industrial Growth in Central West Texas. LC 72-89807. 200p. reprint ed. pap. 62.00 (*0-608-17564-1*, 203054700069) Bks Demand.

— The Complete Cadkey Version 8 for DOS & Windows. 1200p. 1996. pap. 59.95 (*0-8273-7992-7*) Delmar.

Martin, Robert L., ed. The Paradox of the Liar. (C). 1979. reprint ed. pap. text 13.00 (*0-917930-10-X*); reprint ed. lib. bdg. 27.00 (*0-917930-30-4*) Ridgeview.

Martin, Robert L., ed. see Clawson, Jeff J. & Dernocoeur, Kate B.

Martin, Robert M. The Meaning of Language. 239p. 1987. pap. text 16.50 (*0-262-63108-3*, Bradford Bks) MIT Pr.

— The Philosopher's Dictionary. 2nd ed. 253p. 1994. pap. 9.95 (*1-55111-044-X*) Broadview Pr.

— Scientific Thinking. 180p. 1997. pap. 19.95 (*1-55111-130-6*) Broadview Pr.

— There Are Two Errors in the Title of This Book: A Sourcebook of Philosophical Puzzles, Problems & Paradoxes. 226p. 1992. pap. 16.95 (*0-921149-98-0*) Broadview Pr.

Martin, Robert P. The Death Penalty: God's Will or Man's Folly? 87p. (Orig.). (C). 1991. pap. 5.95 (*0-9622508-5-6*) Simpson NJ.

— A Guide to the Puritans. 532p. 1997. pap. 25.99 (*0-85151-713-7*) Banner of Truth.

Martin, Robert S. Carnegie Denied: Communities Rejecting Carnegie Library Construction Grants, 1898-1925. 3. LC 92-25741. (Beta Phi Mu Monograph: No. 3). 200p. 1993. 52.95 (*0-313-28609-4*, MNY, Greenwood Pr) Greenwood.

— Luna Rising: PSI Order: ISRA. (Trinity Ser.). (Illus.). 1998. pap. 17.95 (*1-56504-760-5*, 9002) White Wolf.

Martin, Robert S. & Martin, James C. Contours of Discovery: Printed Maps Delineating the Texas & Southwestern Chapters in the Cartographic History of North America, 1513-1930. LC 82-83547. (Illus.). 1982. 49.95 (*0-87611-058-8*) Tex St Hist Assn.

Martin, Robert S., jt. auth. see Fisher, Jeffery.

Martin, Robert S., jt. auth. see Fisher, Jeffrey D.

Martin, Robert S., jt. auth. see Lovell, Douglas D.

Martin, Robert S., jt. auth. see Martin, James C.

Martin, Robin. Protein Synthesis: Methods & Protocols. LC 98-27411. (Methods in Molecular Biology Ser.: Vol. 77). (Illus.). 456p. 1998. 79.50 (*0-89603-397-X*) Humana.

Martin, Robin B. & Krasnow, Erwin G. Radio Financing: A Guide to Lenders & Investors. 51p. (Orig.). 1990. pap. 40.00 (*0-89324-090-7*) Natl Assn Broadcasters.

Martin, Rod & Perry, C. Michael. Improvisation: A Guide to Unlock Your Acting Power: A Workbook for Teachers. (Theatre Book Ser.). 68p. 1996. pap. text 12.95 (*1-57514-014-4*, 5010) Encore Perform Pub.

— Teaching Theatre Through Poetry & Vice-Versa: An Approach to the Essence of Performing Theatre. (Theatre Book Ser.). 26p. 1993. pap. 5.00 (*1-57514-007-1*, 5013) Encore Perform Pub.

Martin, Roderick. Bargaining Power. LC 92-13855. (Illus.). 210p. 1992. text 55.00 (*0-19-827255-3*) OUP.

— New Technology & Industrial Relations in Fleet Street. 1981. 55.00 (*0-19-827243-X*) OUP.

***Martin, Roderick.** Transforming Management in Central & Eastern Europe. LC 99-36417. 224p. 2000. write for info. (*0-19-877568-7*) OUP.

***Martin, Roderick, ed.** Transforming Management in Central & Eastern Europe. LC 99-36417. 224p. 2000. 65.00 (*0-19-877569-5*) OUP.

Martin, Roderick, et al, eds. Workers, Firms & Union: Industrial Relations in Transition. LC 98-20726. (Arbeit - Technik - Organisation - Soziales Ser.: Vol. 4). (Illus.). 284p. (C). 1998. pap. text 48.95 (*0-8204-3578-3*) P Lang Pubng.

— Workers, Firms & Unions: Industrial Relations in Transition. 284p. 1998. 48.95 (*3-631-33205-X*) P Lang Pubng.

Martin, Roderick & Wallace, Judith. Working Women in Recession. (Illus.). 1985. pap. 18.95 (*0-19-878005-2*) OUP.

Martin, Roderick H., ed. Composite Materials Vol. 5: Fatigue & Fracture. (STP, Special Technical Publication Ser.: No. 1230). (Illus.). 550p. 1995. text 126.00 (*0-8031-2012-5*, STP1230) ASTM.

Martin, Roger. Elbert N. Carvel. LC 97-68733. (Oral History Ser.: No. 1, 1997). (Illus.). 168p. 1997. pap. 5.00 (*0-924117-08-7*) Delaware HP.

— Pigs & Other Animals. LC 79-92628. 300p. (C). 1980. 10.95 (*0-936634-00-6*) Myco Pub Hse.

— A Rockport Album: Photographs of Bygone Days. (Illus.). 108p. 1998. pap. 17.95 (*0-9625660-7-1*) Curious Traveller Pr.

— Sherman W. Tribbitt, Oral History Series, 1998, No. 2. LC 98-73231. (Illus.). 1998. pap. 5.00 (*0-924117-11-7*) Delaware HP.

Martin, Roger, ed. Rockport Remembered: An Oral History. (Illus.). 160p. 1997. pap. 16.95 (*0-9625660-5-5*) Curious Traveller Pr.

***Martin, Roger, et al, eds.** Step by Step: Essays on Minimalist Syntax in Honor of Howard Lasnik. LC 99-54610. (Illus.). 381p. 2000. 42.95 (*0-262-13361-X*) MIT Pr.

***Martin, Roger & Handasyde, Katherine.** The Koala: Natural History, Conservation & Management. 2nd ed. 144p. 1999. pap. 28.50 (*1-57524-136-6*) Krieger.

Martin, Roger, et al. Cows Are Freaky When They Look at You: An Oral History of the Kaw Valley Hemp Pickers. (Illus.). 160p. 1991. pap. 15.00 (*0-922820-13-9*) Watermark Pr.

— Writing in the Design Disciplines. Bridwell-Bowles, Lillian et al, eds. (Monographs: Vol. 3). (Illus.). 108p. (Orig.). 1992. pap. 6.00 (*1-881221-02-4*) U Minn Ctr Interdis.

Martin, Roger, jt. auth. see Lee, Anthony.

Martin, Roger A. John J. Zubly: Colonial Georgia Minister. 1981. 27.95 (*0-405-14095-9*) Ayer.

Martin, Roger H. Evangelicals United: Ecumenical Stirrings in Pre-Victorian Britain, 1795-1830. LC 82-10784. (Studies in Evangelicalism: No. 4). 244p. 1983. 26.50 (*0-8108-1586-9*) Scarecrow.

Martin, Roland. Roland Martin's One Hundred One Bass-Catching Secrets. Tucker, Tim, ed. 1988. 19.95 (*0-8329-0457-0*, Winchester Pr) New Win Pub.

Martin, Roland, jt. auth. see Ginouves, Rene.

Martin, Ron. Here Comes Barbell Brock, No. 1: America's Funniest Strongman. (Illus.). 64p. (Orig.). 1988. pap. 3.00 (*0-9621315-0-4*) Christian H & D Pubs.

— Retail Selling Made Easy. 23.95 (*0-9650527-1-0*) Success Dynamic.

— Sales Management Made Easy. 1997. 23.95 (*0-9650527-2-9*) Success Dynamic.

— Success Made Easy. 23.95 (*0-9650527-0-2*) Success Dynamic.

Martin, Ron, et al. Union Retreat & the Regions: The Shrinking Landscape of Organised Labour. LC 96-185818. (Regional Policy & Development Ser.: No. 8). 144p. 1996. pap. 34.95 (*1-85302-255-1*) Taylor & Francis.

Martin, Ron, jt. auth. see Chambers, Pam.

Martin, Ron, jt. ed. see Townroe, Peter.

Martin, Ron G., jt. ed. see Hawthorne, Pat.

Martin, Ronald. One Long Experiment: Scale & Process in Earth History. LC 97-27821. (Perspectives in Paleobiology & Earth History Ser.). (Illus.). 272p. 1998. 85.00 (*0-231-10904-0*) Col U Pr.

— One Long Experiment: Scale & Process in Earth History. LC 97-27821. (Perspectives in Paleobiology & Earth History Ser.). (Illus.). 272p. 1998. pap. 35.00 (*0-231-10905-9*) Col U Pr.

— Watch Out World . . . Here Comes Barbell Brock Vol. 1: America's Funniest Strongman. (Illus.). 64p. (Orig.). 1988. pap. 3.00 (*0-685-22540-2*) Christian H & D Pubs.

Martin, Ronald E. American Literature & the Destruction of Knowledge: Innovative Writing in the Age of Epistemology. LC 90-21088. 416p. 1991. text 37.95 (*0-8223-1125-9*) Duke.

— American Literature & the Universe of Force. LC 81-7806. xviii, 285p. 1983. pap. text 21.95 (*0-8223-0579-8*) Duke.

***Martin, Ronald E.** Environmental Micropaleontology: The Application of Microfossils to Environmental Geology. LC 00-29630. 2000. write for info. (*0-306-46232-X*, Kluwer Plenum) Kluwer Academic.

Martin, Ronald E. Taphonomy: A Process Approach. LC 98-32341. (Paleobiology Ser.). (Illus.). 440p. 1999. pap. 44.95 (*0-521-59833-8*) Cambridge U Pr.

— Taphonomy: A Process Approach. LC 98-32341. (Paleobiology Ser.: No. 4). (Illus.). 440p. 1999. 100.00 (*0-521-59171-6*) Cambridge U Pr.

Martin, Ronald L. Official Guide to Marvel Cave. 2nd ed. (Illus.). 1987. pap. 3.95 (*0-685-18052-2*) Ozark Mtn Pubs.

Martin, Ronda Jackson. Stock Car Legends: The Laughs, Practical Jokes & Fun Stories from Racing's Greats! rev. ed. 128p. 1999. pap. 6.95 (*1-887654-66-6*) Premium Pr TN.

Martin, Rosa, jt. auth. see Risk, Mary.

Martin, Rosa M. NTC's Spanish Grammar. LC 97-36713. (Grammar Ser.). (ENG & SPA., Illus.). 192p. 1997. pap. 7.95 (*0-8442-7225-6*, 72256) NTC Contemp Pub Co.

Martin, Rosa M. & Ellis, Martyn. Pasos Dos: An Intermediate Course in Spanish. (SPA.). 1995. 29.95 incl. audio (*0-8120-8240-0*) Barron.

Martin, Rosa M. & Ellis, Martyn. Pasos II: An Intermediate Course in Spanish. (SPA.). 256p. (YA). (gr. 11-12). 1997. pap. 16.95 (*0-8120-9100-0*) Barron.

Martin, Rosa M. & Ellis, Martyn. Pasos Uno: A First Course in Spanish. (SPA.). 1995. 29.95 incl. audio (*0-8120-8238-9*) Barron.

Martin, Rosa M. & Ellis, Martyns. Pasos I: A First Course in Spanish. (SPA.). 288p. (YA). (gr. 9-10). 1997. pap. 16.95 (*0-8120-9096-9*) Barron.

***Martin, Rosa Marie, ed.** Take off in Spanish (Latin American) A Complete Language Learning Pack. 256p. 2000. 24.95 incl. audio (*0-19-860302-9*); 32.50 incl. audio compact disk (*0-19-860303-7*) OUP.

Martin, Roscoe. The People's Party in Texas: A Study in Third-Party Politics. (Texas History Paperbacks Ser.: No. 7). 280p. 1970. reprint ed. pap. 7.95 (*0-292-70032-6*) U of Tex Pr.

Martin, Roscoe C. Water for New York: A Study in State Administration of Water Resources. LC 60-9946. 1960. 37.95 (*0-8156-2028-4*) Syracuse U Pr.

Martin, Roscoe C., et al. Decisions in Syracuse. LC 68-9709. 368p. 1968. reprint ed. lib. bdg. 69.50 (*0-8371-0160-3*, MADS, Greenwood Pr) Greenwood.

M

Martin, Rose. The Nanny's Helper: The Ultimate Babysitter's Reference Guide. 75p. 1999. ring bd. 39.99 (*0-9643457-1-4*) Achieve Publns.

Martin, Rosemary, ed. Neuroscience Methods: A Guide for Advanced Students. 272p. 1997. text 34.00 (*90-5702-244-3*, Harwood Acad Pubs); pap. text 15.00 (*90-5702-245-1*, Harwood Acad Pubs) Gordon & Breach.

***Martin, Ross M.** The Lancashire Giant: David Shackleton, Labour Leader & Civil Servant. 320p. 1999. 53.95 (*0-85323-934-7*, Pub. by Liverpool Univ Pr); pap. 24.95 (*0-85323-944-4*, Pub. by Liverpool Univ Pr) Intl Spec Bk.

Martin, Ross M. Trade Unionism: Purposes & Forms. (Illus.). 312p. 1989. 75.00 (*0-19-827710-5*) OUP.

— Tuc: The Growth of a Pressure Group Eighteen Sixty-Eight to Nineteen Seventy-Six. 408p. 1980. text 62.00 (*0-19-822475-3*) OUP.

Martin, Roy. Whisper My Name. LC 97-194510. (Illus.). 289p. 1997. 24.95 (*1-884824-10-2*, Timonier Bks) Tryon Pubng.

— Writing & Defending a Thesis or Dissertation in Psychology & Education. 120p. 1980. pap., spiral bd. 26.95 (*0-398-03947-X*) C C Thomas.

***Martin, Roy A.** Inside Nurnberg: Military Justice for Nazi War Criminals. (Illus.). 160p. 2000. pap. 14.95 (*1-57249-227-9*, WM Books) White Mane Pub.

Martin, Roy C. Astronomy on Trial: A Devastating & Complete Repudiation of the Big Bang Fiasco. LC 99-26508. 264p. 1999. pap. 29.50 (*0-7618-1422-1*) U Pr of Amer.

***Martin, Roy C., et al, eds.** Marine & Freshwater Products Handbook. LC 00-101386. 984p. 2000. text 149.95 (*1-56676-889-6*) Technomic.

Martin, Roy E., et al, eds. Fish Inspection, Quality Control, & HACCP: A Global Focus: Proceedings of the Conference Held May 19-24, 1996, Arlington, VA. LC 97-60270. 802p. 1997. text 219.95 (*1-56676-546-3*) Technomic.

Martin, Roy E., jt. ed. see Flick, George J.

Martin, Roy P. Assessment of Personality & Behavior Problems: Infancy Through Adolescence. LC 88-19030. 399p. 1988. lib. bdg. 47.50 (*0-89862-727-3*) Guilford Pubns.

— Assessment of Personality & Behavior Problems: Infancy Through Adolescence. LC 88-19030. 399p. 1992. reprint ed. pap. text 26.00 (*0-89862-026-0*) Guilford Pubns.

***Martin, Russell.** Beethoven's Hair: How a Lock of Hair Solved the Riddle of a Great Composer's Deafness & Helped Save Lives in Nazi Europe. 256p. 2000. 24.95 (*0-7679-0350-1*) Broadway BDD.

Martin, Russell. Out of Silence: An Autistic Boy's Journey into Language & Communication. LC 93-28434. 1995. 22.50 (*0-8050-1998-7*) H Holt & Co.

— Out of Silence: An Autistic Boy's Journey into Language & Communication. 320p. 1995. pap. 12.95 (*0-14-024701-7*, Penguin Bks) Viking Penguin.

***Martin, Russell.** A Story That Stands Like a Dam. (Illus.). 368p. 1999. pap. 15.95 (*0-87480-597-X*) U of Utah Pr.

Martin, Ruth & Brown, Walter. The Ruth Brown Martin Story: How to Market Yourself & Sell 100 Houses Every Year. LC 94-71237. (Illus.). 160p. (Orig.). 1995. reprint ed. pap. 15.95 (*0-923687-31-9*) Celo Valley Bks.

Martin, Ruth R. Oral History in Social Work: Research, Assessment & Intervention. LC 95-17009. (Human Services Guides Ser.: Vol. 69). 144p. 1995. 42.00 (*0-8039-4382-2*); pap. 18.95 (*0-8039-4383-0*) Sage.

Martin, Ruth S. And They Built a Crooked House: An (Unlucky) Homeowner's Account of One of the Largest Residential Construction Cases Ever Tried in Court. LC 91-90070. (Illus.). 257p. (Orig.). 1991. pap. 12.95 (*1-879653-02-8*) Lakeside Pr.

— Crumbling Dreams: What You Must Know Before Building or Buying a New House (or Condo) LC 92-72164. 172p. 1993. pap. 8.00 (*1-879653-06-0*) Lakeside Pr.

Martin, Rux, et al, eds. Eating Well Cookbook. (Illus.). 256p. pap. 15.95 (*1-884943-03-9*) Eat Well Bks.

— The Eating Well Cookbook: Favorite Recipes for Eating Well, the Magazine of Food & Health. LC 94-10042. (Illus.). 256p. 1994. 24.95 (*1-884943-02-0*) Eat Well Bks.

Martin, Rux, jt. auth. see Lawrence, James M.

Martin, Rux, ed. see Bishop, Jack.

Martin, Rux, jt. ed. see Cats-Baril, JoAnne B.

Martin, Rux, ed. see Davis, Deirdre.

Martin, Rux, ed. see Downard, Georgia C. & Righter, Evie.

Martin, Rux, ed. see Fletcher, Anne.

Martin, Rux, ed. see Foo, Susanna.

Martin, Rux, ed. see Mauer, Don.

Martin, Rux, ed. see Mills, Kevin & Mills, Nancy.

Martin, Rux, ed. see Rosbottom, Betty.

Martin, Rux, ed. see Simmons, Marie.

Martin, S. E. Talk to Me, 3. 80p. (gr. 7-12). 1999. mass mkt. 2.99 (*0-590-69142-2*) Scholastic Inc.

Martin, S. I. Incomparable World. LC 98-19986. 213p. 1998. 22.50 (*0-8076-1436-X*) Braziller.

Martin, S. J., jt. auth. see Cotter, T. G.

Martin, S. R. Buzz. (Insomniacs Ser.: Vol. 5). 1999. pap. 2.99 (*0-439-04425-1*) Scholastic Inc.

***Martin, S. R.** Endsville. 112p. (J). (gr. 7-12). 2000. mass mkt. 4.50 (*0-439-10568-4*) Scholastic Inc.

— Tankworld. 112p. (J). (gr. 7-12). 2000. mass mkt. 4.50 (*0-439-10567-6*) Scholastic Inc.

— Vanish. (Insomniacs Ser.: Vol. 6). 80p. (gr. 6-12). 1999. pap. 2.99 (*0-439-04426-X*) Scholastic Inc.

Martin, S. R. Frozen. (Insomniacs Ser.: Vol. 2). 80p. (gr. 7-12). 1999. mass mkt. 1.99 (*0-590-69141-4*) Scholastic Inc.

— Road Kill. (Insomniacs Ser.: Vol. 1). 80p. (gr. 7-12). 1999. mass mkt. 1.99 (*0-590-69130-9*) Scholastic Inc.

***Martin, S. R.** Swampland. 112p. (J). (gr. 7-12). 2000. mass mkt. 4.50 (*0-439-04393-X*) Scholastic Inc.

Martin, S. R. Tunnel, 4. Vol. 4. 80p. (gr. 7-12). 1999. mass mkt. 2.99 (*0-590-69149-X*) Scholastic Inc.

Martin, S. Wayne, et al. Veterinary Epidemiology: Principles & Methods. LC 87-3169. 356p. 1987. text 49.95 (*0-8138-1856-7*) Iowa St U Pr.

Martin, Sadie E. The Life & Professional Career of Emma Abbott. LC 80-2290. reprint ed. 34.50 (*0-404-18858-3*) AMS Pr.

Martin, Sally. Fair Schemer. 224p. (Orig.). 1993. mass mkt. 3.99 (*0-380-77397-X*, Avon Bks) Morrow Avon.

— Sweet Fancy. 224p. (Orig.). 1994. mass mkt. 3.99 (*0-380-77398-8*, Avon Bks) Morrow Avon.

Martin, Sally & Rozakis, Laurie N. ACT English Workbook: American College Testing Program. 224p. 1993. per. 10.95 (*0-671-84775-9*, Arc) IDG Bks.

Martin, Sam & Schroeder, Roger. Making Toys: Heirloom Cars & Trucks in Wood. (Illus.). 103p. 1997. pap. 17.95 (*1-56523-079-5*) Fox Chapel Pub.

Martin, Samuel E. Basic Japanese Conversation Dictionary: English-Japanese & Japanese-English. LC 57-8797. (ENG & JPN.). 266p. 1957. pap. 6.95 (*0-8048-0057-X*) Tuttle Pubng.

— Consonant Lenition in Korean & the Macro-Altaic Question. LC 95-43379. (Center for Korean Studies Monograph Ser.: No. 19). 144p. (Orig.). 1996. pap. text 20.00 (*0-8248-1809-1*) Ctr Korean Studies.

— Easy Japanese: A Direct Approach to Immediate Conversation. LC 57-6763. (JPN.). 272p. (YA). (gr. 9 up). 1965. pap. 7.95 (*0-8048-0157-6*) Tuttle Pubng.

— Essential Japanese: An Introduction to the Standard Colloquial Language. rev. ed. LC 59-5072. (JPN.). 462p. 1962. pap. 16.95 (*0-8048-1862-2*) Tuttle Pubng.

— The Japanese Language Through Time. LC 87-50521. (Language Ser.). 964p. 1988. 72.50 (*0-300-03729-5*) Yale U Pr.

— Korean in a Hurry: A Quick Approach to Spoken Korean. rev. ed. LC 60-8363. 138p. 1954. pap. 6.95 (*0-8048-0349-8*) Tuttle Pubng.

— Martin's Concise Japanese Dictionary: Fully Romanized with Complete Kanji & Kana. (JPN., Illus.). 768p. 1994. pap. 16.95 (*0-8048-1912-2*) Tuttle Pubng.

— Martins Pocket Dictionary: English-Japanese - Japanese-English. 700p. 1989. pap. 9.95 (*0-8048-1588-7*) Tuttle Pubng.

— Reclaiming a Conversation. LC 85-2372. 221p. 1987. pap. 14.00 (*0-300-03999-9*, Y-684) Yale U Pr.

— Reference Grammar of Japanese. 1198p. 1988. 74.95 (*0-8048-1550-X*) Tuttle Pubng.

— A Reference Grammar of Korean. 1040p. 1993. 74.95 (*0-8048-1887-8*) Tuttle Pubng.

Martin, Samuel E. & Chaplin, Hamako I. Japanese: A Manual of Reading & Writing. LC 86-50703. 700p. 1986. reprint ed. boxed set 24.95 (*0-8048-1508-9*) Tuttle Pubng.

Martin, Samuel E. & Lee, Young-Sook C. Beginning Korean. LC 86-50701. (KOR.). 605p. 1986. reprint ed. pap. 24.95 (*0-8048-1507-0*) Tuttle Pubng.

Martin, Samuel E., jt. auth. see Gardner, Elizabeth F.

***Martin, Samuel J.** Kill-Cavalry: The Life of Union General Hugh Judson Kilpatrick. LC 99-47528. (Illus.). 336p. 2000. 27.95 (*0-8117-0887-X*) Stackpole.

Martin, Samuel J. The Road to Glory: Confederate General Richard S. Ewell. 2nd ed. LC 91-58045. 420p. 1991. 29.95 (*1-878208-07-1*); pap. 24.95 (*1-878208-42-X*) Guild Pr IN.

***Martin, Samuel J.** Southern Hero: Mathew Calbraiyth Butler: Confederate General, Hampton Red Shirt & U. S. Senator. 2001. 29.95 (*0-8117-0899-3*) Stackpole.

Martin, Sandra. Programming for the Whole World: A Guide to Internationalization. 320p. (C). 1994. pap. text 33.00 (*0-13-722190-8*) P-H.

— Second Mrs. Adams. large type ed. (Harlequin Romance Ser.). 1997. 20.95 (*0-263-15045-3*) Mac Lib Ref.

— UniForum Technology Guide: Internationalization Explored. 40p. 1992. pap. text 10.00 (*0-936593-18-0*) UniForum.

Martin, Sandra & Hall, Roger. Rupert Brooke in Canada. 154p. 1978. 14.95 (*0-88778-184-5*) Genl Dist Srvs.

Martin, Sandra, jt. auth. see Martin, Marian.

Martin, Sandy D. Black Baptist & African Missions: The Origins of a Movement, 1880-1915. 256p. 1998. pap. text 19.95 (*0-86554-600-2*, P173) Mercer Univ Pr.

— For God & Race: The Religious & Political Leadership of AMEZ Bishop James Walker Hood. LC 98-25444. (Religious Biography Ser.). (Illus.). xxiv, 248p. 1999. 39.95 (*1-57003-261-0*) U of SC Pr.

***Martin-Santos, Luis.** Tiempo de Silencio. 1999. pap. 12.95 (*84-322-0771-3*) E Seix Barral.

Martin-Santos, Luis. Tiempo de Silencio. (SPA.). 1989. 19.95 (*0-8288-2569-6*) Fr & Eur.

— Time of Silence. Leeson, George, tr. 247p. 1989. text 61.50 (*0-231-06984-7*); pap. text 17.50 (*0-231-06985-5*) Col U Pr.

Martin, Sara H. Meeting Needs Through Support Groups. McClain, Cindy, ed. (Illus.). 96p. (Orig.). 1992. pap. text 7.95 (*1-56309-053-8*, N923112, New Hope) Womans Mission Union.

martin, Sarah, tr. see Daeninckx, Didier.

Martin, Sarah C. Old Mother Hubbard. LC 94-210510. 1994. write for info. (*0-7853-0562-9*) Pubns Intl Ltd.

Martin, Sarah C., jt. auth. see Johnson, David.

Martin, Sarah Catherine. Old Mother Hubbard & Her Wonderful Dog. 1991. 10.15 (*0-606-05958-X*, Pub. by Turtleback) Demco.

Martin, Sarah Catherine, jt. auth. see De Paola, Tomie.

Martin-Sayed, Yousry. Organic Chemistry Laboratory Manual with Waste Management & Molecular Modeling. 2nd ed. 124p. 1994. spiral bd. 16.95 (*0-8403-8727-X*) Kendall-Hunt.

Martin-Schiller, Barbara, jt. auth. see Schiller, Jim.

***Martin, Scott.** Insiders' Guide to Golf in the Carolinas. 4th ed. 424p. 2000. pap. text 19.95 (*1-57380-112-7*) IPBI.

Martin, Scott. The Paramedic Survival Handbook. LC 99-226689. 300p. 1999. per. 35.95 (*1-56930-090-9*) Skidmore Roth Pub.

Martin, Scott & Willard, Mitch. The Insiders' Guide to Golf in the Carolinas. 3rd ed. (Insiders' Guide Travel Ser.). (Illus.). 385p. 1997. pap. 16.95 (*1-57380-044-9*, The Insiders Guide) Falcon Pub Inc.

Martin, Scott C. Killing Time: Leisure & Culture in Southwestern, Pennsylvania, 1800-1850. (Illus.). 280p. (C). 1995. text 29.95 (*0-8229-3916-9*) U of Pittsburgh Pr.

Martin, Scott D. Phillywood, Vol. I, Pt. 3. large type ed. LC 96-96210. (Daylight Ser.: No. 2). (Illus.). 100p. (Orig.). 1996. pap. 7.95 (*0-9632177-2-0*, Daylight Bks) Bronx Orig Bks.

Martin, Scott D. & Martin, Lorraine. A Guide to N. Y. Life with Lorraine: Fountain House Journal & the Black Church. large type ed. 50p. (Orig.). 1995. pap. 2.00 (*0-9632177-1-2*, Daylight Bks) Bronx Orig Bks.

Martin, Scott V. Guide to Evaluating Gold & Silver Objects for Appraisers, Collectors, Dealers. Seeffing, D. Albert, ed. 106p. 1995. pap. 24.95 (*0-9645642-0-3*) SM Pubns.

Martin, Scott V. & Martin, June V. The Book of Silver: Flatware Silver Marks & Patterns, Vol. 1R2.A. (Illus.). 800p. (C). 1996. 150.00 (*0-9645642-1-1*) SM Pubns.

Martin-Scramm, James B. Population Perils & the Churches' Response. LC 98-218173. xxiii, 56 p. 1997. write for info. (*2-8254-1226-0*) COE Pubns.

Martin, Seamus J. Apoptosis & Cancer. (Medical Intelligence Unit Ser.). 250p. 1997. 89.95 (*0-412-13511-6*) Chapman & Hall.

— Apoptosis & Cancer. LC 97-10616. (Medical (Karger/Landes Systems) Ser.). 216p. 1997. 98.00 (*1-57059-452-X*) Landes Bioscience.

— Apoptosis & Cancer. LC 97-10616. (Medical (Karger/Landes Systems) Ser.). (Illus.). 216p. 1997. 98.00 (*3-8055-6579-8*) S Karger.

***Martin, Seamus J.** Duggan's Destiny. LC 98-215015. 252p. 1999. pap. text. write for info. (*1-85371-867-X*, Pub. by Poolbeg Pr) Dufour.

Martin, Sean. Scrapbook. (Orig.). 1994. mass mkt. 4.95 (*1-56333-224-8*, Badboy) Masquerade.

Martin, Sean, tr. see Stangerup, Henrik.

Martin, Sean M., jt. auth. see Martin, J. Michael.

Martin, Shane P. Cultural Diversity in Catholic Schools: Challenges & Opportunities for Catholic Educators. LC 97-205616. 83p. 1996. pap. 14.00 (*1-55833-184-0*) Natl Cath Educ.

Martin, Shannon E. Bits, Bytes & Big Brother: Federal Information Control in the Technological Age. LC 94-32929. (Praeger Series in Political Communication). 184p. 1995. 57.95 (*0-275-94900-1*, Praeger Pubs) Greenwood.

Martin, Shannon E. & Hansen, Kathleen A. Newspapers of Record in a Digital Age: From Hot Type to Hot Link. LC 97-47232. (Praeger Series in Political Communication). 176p. 1998. 55.00 (*0-275-95960-0*, Praeger Pubs) Greenwood.

Martin, Sharline M. A Collection: Keys to Self Transformation. Christensen, Leese, ed. (Illus.). 382p. (Orig.). 1996. pap. 19.95 (*1-885260-07-5*) Gathering Pl.

Martin, Sheila. Saying Goodbye with Love: A Step-by-Step Guide Through the Details of Death. LC 98-45462. (Orig.). 1999. pap. 19.95 (*0-8245-1585-4*) Crossroad NY.

Martin, Shelia A., jt. auth. see Brunnermeier, Smita.

Martin, Shelia A., jt. auth. see Gallahera, Michael P.

Martin, Shelley, jt. auth. see Buettner, Linda.

Martin, Sherrill V., jt. ed. see Keck, George R.

Martin, Sidney W. Florida During the Territorial Days. LC 73-19815. (Perspectives in American History Ser.: No. 15). (Illus.). ix, 308p. 1974. reprint ed. lib. bdg. 39.50 (*0-87991-344-4*) Porcupine Pr.

— Henry Flagler, Visionary of the Gilded Age. Orig. Title: Florida's Flagler. (Illus.). 232p. 1998. pap. 18.95 (*0-9631241-1-0*) Tail Tours.

***Martin, Sigrid B. & DK Publishing Staff.** German in Three months. LC 97-47226. (GER.). 1998. pap. 29.95 incl. audio (*0-7894-3230-7*) DK Pub Inc.

Martin, Sigur. History of Our Local Gov., Etc. 1966. 35.00 (*1-57980-027-0*) Claitors.

Martin, Simon. Candida: Your Guide to Complementary Therapies, Alternative Techniques & Conventional Treatments. LC 98-12757. (Natural Way Ser.). 1998. pap. 5.95 (*1-86204-193-8*, Pub. by Element MA) Penguin Putnam.

***Martin, Simon & Grube, Nikolai.** Chronicle of the Maya Kings & Queens: Deciphering the Dynasties of the Ancient Maya. LC 99-69563. (Illus.). 240p. 2000. 34.95 (*0-500-05103-8*, Pub. by Thames Hudson) Norton.

Martin, Sophia S. Smith: Complete Genealogy of the Descendants of Matthew Smith of East Haddam, Ct., with Mention of His Ancestors, 1637-1890. 269p. 1994. reprint ed. pap. 42.00 (*0-8328-4381-4*); reprint ed. lib. bdg. 52.00 (*0-8328-4380-6*) Higginson Bk Co.

Martin-Sperry, A. D., tr. see Laponce, J. A.

Martin-Sperry, Carol, tr. see Cocteau, Jean.

Martin-Sperry, Tony, tr. see Dube, Philippe.

Martin, Stan. Murder in Jamaica: The Adventures of Christiana & the Dreadlocks Cop, Mystery. 359p. 1997. pap. text 18.00 (*0-9682646-1-1*) CPRE.

Martin, Stephanie & Darnley, Lyn. The Teaching Voice. (Illus.). 174p. (Orig.). 1996. pap. 45.00 (*1-56593-790-2*, 1542) Singular Publishing.

Martin, Stephen. Advanced Industrial Economics. LC 92-25471. 1993. pap. 47.95 (*0-631-17852-X*) Blackwell Pubs.

— The Economics of Offsets: Defence Procurement & Countertrade, Vol. 4. (Studies in Defence Economics). 352p. 1996. text 38.00 (*3-7186-5782-1*, Harwood Acad Pubs) Gordon & Breach.

— Industrial Economics: Economic Analysis & Public Policy. 2nd ed. LC 93-427. (Illus.). 582p. (C). 1993. text 72.00 (*0-02-376786-3*, Macmillan Coll) P-H.

Martin, Stephen, ed. The Construction of Europe: Essays in Honor of Emile Noel. LC 94-21318. (Diverse Ser.). 312p. (C). 1994. lib. bdg. 153.00 (*0-7923-2969-4*) Kluwer Academic.

Martin, Stephen & Centre for Industrial Economics Staff. Competition Policies in Europe, Vol. 239. LC 98-20010. (Contributions to Economic Analysis Ser.). 1998. 114.00 (*0-444-82673-4*) Elsevier.

Martin, Stephen & Parker, David. The Impact of Privatization: Ownership & Corporate Performance in the UK. LC 96-25484. (Industrial Economic Strategies for Europe Ser.). 272p. (C). 1997. 75.00 (*0-415-14233-4*) Routledge.

Martin, Stephen F. Organic Synthesis, Vol. 76. 340p. 1999. 49.95 (*0-471-34886-4*) Wiley.

Martin, Stephen H. Beyond Skepticism: All the Way to Enlightenment. 160p. (Orig.). 1995. pap. 11.95 (*0-9646601-4-8*) Oaklea Pr.

— Death in Advertising: A Whodunit. 256p. 1997. pap. 14.95 (*0-9646601-1-3*) Oaklea Pr.

— The Mt. Pelee Redemption: A Metalphysical Mystery. LC 98-71586. 224p. 1998. pap. 12.95 (*1-57174-116-X*) Hampton Roads Pub Co.

— Out of Body, into Mind: A Novel of Suspense. 252p. (Orig.). 1995. pap. 14.95 (*0-9646601-6-4*) Oaklea Pr.

— The Search for Nina Fletcher: A Metaphysical Adventure. 288p. (Orig.). 1995. pap. 14.95 (*0-9646601-3-X*) Oaklea Pr.

— Soul Survivor: A Metaphysical Suspense Novel. 240p. 1996. 18.95 (*0-9646601-8-0*) Oaklea Pr.

Martin, Stephen H., ed. see Clement, Mary.

Martin, Stephen H., ed. see Henderson, Bruce A. & Larco, Jorge L.

***Martin, Stephen Hawley.** Past Fear & Doubt to Amazing Abundance: Secret Knowledge That Brought Me Self-Actualization. 224p. 2000. pap. 14.95 (*1-892538-24-5*) Oaklea Pr.

Martin, Stephen P. Things. (Illus.). 1991. pap. 4.95 (*0-9623693-3-0*) Heaven Bone Pr.

Martin, Stephen-Paul. Advancing Receding. 44p. (Orig.). 1989. pap. 3.00 (*0-926935-21-6*) Runaway Spoon.

— Fear & Philosophy. 1994. pap. 8.95 (*0-938979-40-X*) EG Bksellers.

— The Flood. rev. ed. 88p. 1992. pap. 7.00 (*0-926935-70-4*) Runaway Spoon.

— The Gothic Twilight. LC 92-70668. 100p. (Orig.). 1992. pap. 8.95 (*1-878580-45-0*) Asylum Arts.

— Invading Reagan. (Chapbook Ser.). (Illus.). 26p. (Orig.). 1990. pap. 5.00 (*0-945112-09-2*) Generator Pr.

— Not Quite Fiction. unabridged ed. LC 97-60474. 100p. (Orig.). 1997. pap. 8.95 (*0-9654877-2-5*) Vatic Hum Pr.

— Open Form & the Feminine Imagination: The Politics of Reading in Twentieth-Century Innovative Writing. LC PS228.P6M37. (Post Modern Positions Ser.: Vol. 2). 225p. (Orig.). 1988. lib. bdg. 22.95 (*0-944624-02-2*) Maisonneuve Pr.

— Tales. 24p. (Orig.). 1989. pap. 4.00 (*0-945926-11-1*) Paradigm RI.

— Until It Changes. 48p. 1988. pap. 3.00 (*0-926935-07-0*) Runaway Spoon.

Martin, Stephen W. Decomposing Modernity: Ernest Becker's Images of Humanity at the End of an Age. LC 96-38529. 114p. 1996. pap. text 22.50 (*0-7618-0537-0*); lib. bdg. 42.50 (*0-7618-0536-2*) U Pr of Amer.

Martin, Steve. The Jerk. 1979. mass mkt. 2.25 (*0-446-92626-4*, Pub. by Warner Bks) Little.

— The Judge. 48p. 1997. pap. 6.99 (*0-515-12215-7*, Jove) Berkley Pub.

— L. A. Story & Roxanne: Screenplays. LC 97-1597. 288p. (Orig.). 1997. pap. 12.00 (*0-8021-3512-9*, Grove) Grove-Atltic.

— Picasso at the Lapin Agile & Other Plays. 160p. 1997. pap. 12.00 (*0-8021-3523-4*, Grove) Grove-Atltic.

— Picasso at the Lapin Agile & Other Plays: Picasso at the Lapin Agile; WASP; The Zig-Zag Woman; Patter for a Floating Lady. LC 96-13222. 160p. 1996. 20.00 (*0-8021-1595-0*, Grove) Grove-Atltic.

***Martin, Steve.** Proof: There Is a God! (Illus.). vi, 136p. 2000. pap. 9.95 (*0-9678383-0-4*) J Trombly.

Martin, Steve. Pure Drivel. LC 98-28739. 128p. 1998. 19.95 (*0-7868-6467-2*, Pub. by Hyperion); 19.95 (*0-7868-7915-7*) Hyperion.

***Martin, Steve.** Pure Drivel. large type ed. LC 98-45064. 206p. 1999. 28.95 (*0-7838-0419-9*, G K Hall & Co) Mac Lib Ref.

— Pure Drivel. LC 98-28739. 128p. 1999. reprint ed. pap. text 9.95 (*0-7868-8505-X*, Pub. by Hyperion) Time Warner.

— Shopgirl. 112p. 2001. pap. 10.95 (*0-7868-8568-8*, Pub. by Disney Pr) Time Warner.

— Shopgirl: A Novella. (Illus.). (J). 2000. 17.95 (*0-7868-6658-6*, Pub. by Hyperion) Time Warner.

Martin, Steve. Wasp: A Play in One Act. (Illus.). 65p. 1996. 65.00 (*0-9657858-0-7*) V Dailey.

Martin, Steve, jt. auth. see Martin, Claire.

Martin, Steven & Martin, Catherine. Talk to Me: How to Create Positive Loving Communication. LC 97-92268. viii, 151p. (Orig.). 1997. pap. 12.95 (*0-9659328-0-X*) Posit Publ.

Martin, Steven, jt. auth. see Cranmer, Jeff.

An Asterisk (*) at the beginning of an entry indicates that the title is appearing for the first time.

Martin, Steven W. Wisconsin Construction Lien Law Handbook. 2nd ed. LC 91-9660. 130p. 1991. ring bd. 55.00 incl. disk (0-945574-46-0) State Bar WI.

Martin, Stuart. Schur Algebras & Representation Theory. (Studies in Advanced Mathematics: No. 40). 248p. (C). 1994. text 49.95 (0-521-41591-8) Cambridge U Pr.

Martin, Susan. The Combiners: Understanding Addition & Multiplication Word Problems. large type ed. (Illus.). 80p. (J). (gr. 3-6). 1999. pap. text 14.95 (0-941530-39-6) Move It Math.

— The Separaters: Understanding Subtraction & Division Word Problems. large type ed. (Illus.). 83p. (J). (gr. 3-6). 1997. pap. text 14.95 (0-941530-41-8) Move It Math.

Martin, Susan & Green, Harriet. Research Workout. (Illus.). 144p. (J). (gr. 4-9). 1984. student ed. 13.99 (0-86653-194-7, GA 551) Good Apple.

Martin, Susan, jt. auth. see Jordan, Barbara.

Martin, Susan, ed. see Brandy, Lois S.

Martin, Susan, ed. see Kalman, Maira.

Martin, Susan, jt. ed. see Kennedy, Marla H.

Martin, Susan, ed. see Wells, Carol.

Martin, Susan B., ed. Notable Corporate Chronologies. Vols. 1-2. 1994. 375.00 (0-8103-9217-8, 007660) Gale.

Martin, Susan E. On the Move: The Status of Women in Policing. LC 90-62667. 197p. (Orig.). 1990. pap. text 20.95 (1-884614-06-X) Police Found.

Martin, Susan E., et al, eds. New Directions in the Rehabilitation of Criminal Offenders. LC 81-11287. 508p. reprint ed. pap. 157.50 (0-8357-3183-9, 203945200012) Bks Demand.

Martin, Susan E. & Jurik, Nancy C. Doing Justice, Doing Gender. LC 95-41817. (Women & the Criminal Justice Occupations Ser.: Vol. 1). 216p. 1996. 46.00 (0-8039-5197-3); pap. 21.95 (0-8039-5198-1) Sage.

Martin, Susan E. & Mail, Patricia, eds. Effects of the Mass Media on the Use & Abuse of Alcohol. (Illus.). 302p. (Orig.). (C). 1995. pap. text 45.00 (0-7881-2570-2) DIANE Pub.

Martin, Susan F., compiled by. Refugee Women. LC 92-5754. 140p. (C). 1995. text 22.50 (1-85649-001-7, Pub. by Zed Books) St Martin.

— Refugee Women. LC 92-5754. 256p. (C). 1995. text 59.95 (1-85649-000-9, Pub. by Zed Books) St Martin.

Martin, Susan F., et al, eds. Growing Conifers: Four-Season Plants. (21st-Century Gardening Ser.). (Illus.). 112p. (Orig.). 1997. pap. 9.95 (1-889538-02-7) Bklyn Botanic.

Martin, Susan K. Library Networks, 1986-1987: Libraries in Partnership. LC 86-7438. (Professional Librarian Ser.). 220p. 1986. 40.00 (0-86729-128-1, Hall Reference); 30.00 (0-86729-127-3, Hall Reference) Macmillan.

Martin, Susan M. Palm Oil & Protest: An Economic History of the Ngwa Region, South-eastern Nigeria, 1800-1980. (African Studies: No. 59). (Illus.). 224p. 1988. text 80.00 (0-521-34376-3) Cambridge U Pr.

Martin, Susan R. Wonderful Power: The Story of Ancient Copper Working in the Lake Superior Basin. LC 98-45330. 1999. 49.95 (0-8143-2806-7, Great Lks Bks) Wayne St U Pr.

— Wonderful Power: The Story of Ancient Copper Working in the Lake Superior Basin. 1999. pap. 24.95 (0-8143-2843-1, Great Lks Bks) Wayne St U Pr.

Martin, Suzanne. The Awesome Almanac: Georgia. LC 95-20633. 1995. 20.10 (0-606-09018-5, Pub. by Turtleback) Demco.

— The Awesome Almanac: Texas. LC 92-74714. 1995. 20.10 (0-606-09025-8, Pub. by Turtleback) Demco.

— Awesome Almanacs - Georgia. LC 96-127630. (J). (gr. 4-12). 1995. pap. 14.95 (1-880190-53-2) B&B Pub.

— Awesome Almanacs - Texas. 208p. (J). (gr. 4-12). 1995. pap. 14.95 (1-880190-22-2) B&B Pub.

Martin, Suzanne T., jt. auth. see Cech, Donna.

Martin, Sydney. 1 & 2 Thessalonians, 1 & 2 Timothy, Titus. Greathouse, William M & Taylor, Willard H., eds. (Bible Exposition Ser.: Vol. 10). 248p. 1977. 14.99 (0-8341-0321-4) Beacon Hill.

Martin, T. A Guide to Neophema & Psephotus Grass Parrots. (Illus.). 80p. 1989. pap. 23.95 (0-9587455-1-X) Avian Pubns.

Martin, T., jt. auth. see Brandt, D.

Martin, T. C. The Inventions, Researches & Writings of Nikola Tesla. (Nikola Tesla Ser.). 1986. lib. bdg. 250.00 (0-8490-3835-9) Gordon Pr.

Martin, T. E. 1, 2, 3 John, Jude, Revelation. Greathouse, M., ed. (Bible Exposition Ser.: Vol. 12). 282p. 1983. 14.99 (0-8341-0809-7) Beacon Hill.

Martin, T. H., et al. J. C. Martin on Pulsed Power. (Advances in Pulsed Power Technology Ser.: Vol. 3). (Illus.). 535p. (C). 1996. 150.00 (0-306-45302-9, Plenum Trade) Perseus Pubng.

Martin, T. John, jt. ed. see Mundy, Gregory R.

Martin, T. P., ed. Large Clusters of Atoms & Molecules: Proceedings of the NATO Advanced Study Institute on Large Clusters of Atoms & Molecules: Erice, Sicily, Italy, June 19-29, 1995. LC 96-192. (NATO ASI Series E: Applied Sciences: Vol. 313). 548p. (C). 1996. text 276.00 (0-7923-3937-1) Kluwer Academic.

Martin, Tamara, jt. auth. see Molvar, Erik.

Martin, Tanya. Rockets to the Rescue. 102p. (J). (gr. 4). 1994. pap. 10.95 (0-8464-4840-8) Beekman Pubs.

Martin, Ted. Psychic & Paranormal Phenomena in the Bible: The True Story. LC 96-95063. 304p. (Orig.). 1998. pap. 22.95 (0-9654413-1-8) psychicspacecom.

Martin, Tera, ed. see Kingston, Maxine H.

Martin, Terence. Nathaniel Hawthorne. rev. ed. (United States Authors Ser.: No. 75). 240p. 1983. 32.00 (0-8057-7384-3, Twyne) Mac Lib Ref.

— Parables of Possibility: The American Need for Beginnings. LC 94-17486. 256p. 1995. 32.50 (0-231-07050-0) Col U Pr.

Martin, Terence & Rodenberg, Howard. Aeromedical Transportation: A Clinical Guide. 288p. 1996. text 79.95 (0-291-39842-1, Pub. by Avebury Technical) Ashgate Pub Co.

Martin, Teresa A. Project Cool Guide to XML for Web Designers. LC 99-18992. (Illus.). 298p. 1999. pap. 34.99 (0-471-34401-X) Wiley.

Martin, Teresa A. & Davis, Glenn. The Project Cool Guide to Enhancing Your Web Site. LC 97-31836. 416p. 1998. pap. 29.99 (0-471-19457-3) Wiley.

— The Project Cool Guide to HTML. LC 96-35308. 272p. 1996. pap. 19.95 (0-471-17371-1) Wiley.

Martin, Teresa Castro, jt. auth. see Delgadeo, Margarita.

***Martin, Terrell L.** The Early Woodland Period in Missouri. (Missouri Archaeologist Ser.: Vol. 58). (Illus.). 106p. 1999. pap. 7.50 (0-943414-87-3, 115800) MO Arch Soc.

Martin, Terrell L. Prehistoric Settlement-Subsistence Relationships in the Fishing River Drainage, Western Missouri. Bray, Robert T., ed. (Missouri Archaeologist Ser.: Vol. 37). (Illus.). 170p. (Orig.). 1976. pap. 6.00 (0-943414-54-7) MO Arch Soc.

Martin, Terrence D. Santa Catalina Island: The Story Behind the Scenery. LC 83-83007. (Illus.). 48p. (Orig.). 1984. pap. 7.95 (0-916122-97-2) KC Pubns.

Martin, Terri & Lockhart, William J. Park Waters in Peril. (Illus.). 126p. (C). 1993. pap. text. write for info. (0-940091-33-X) Natl Parks & Cons.

Martin, Terri L. A Family Trait. LC 99-17867. 192p. (J). 1999. 15.95 (0-8234-1467-1) Holiday.

***Martin, Terry.** Row by Row: 10 Easy Bar Quilts. (Illus.). 80p. 2000. pap. 19.95 (1-56477-305-1) Martingale & Co.

— Wishboats. limited ed. (Working Signs Ser.). (Illus.). 48p. 2000. 15.00 (0-911287-40-X) Blue Begonia.

Martin, Terry. Wood Dreaming: The Spirit of Australia Captured in Woodturning. 1999. 29.95 (0-7322-6584-3) HarpC.

Martin, Terry, jt. auth. see Hole, John W., Jr.

Martin, Terry, jt. auth. see Maynard, Christopher.

Martin, Terry, jt. auth. see Perret, Gene.

Martin, Terry, ed. see Bertch, David P.

Martin, Terry, ed. see Bertch, David P. & Bertch, Barbara A.

Martin, Terry J. Rhetorical Deception in the Short Fiction of Hawthorne, Poe & Melville. LC 98-39987. (Studies in Comparative Literature: Vol. 23). 120p. 1998. text 59.95 (0-7734-8240-7) E Mellen.

Martin, Terry P., jt. auth. see Perret, Gene.

Martin, Thea. Bibliography of Forth References. 3rd rev. ed. 1987. pap. 10.00 (0-914593-07-2) Inst Appl Forth.

Martin, Theodore, tr. & intro. see Dante Alighieri.

Martin, Theresa & Simon, Brian. Mountain Biking Marin: 40 Great Rides in Marin County. 112p. 1998. pap. 10.95 (0-9617044-7-0) Martin Press.

Martin, Thomas. Alessandro Vittoria & the Portrait Bust in Renaissance Venice: Remodelling Antiquity. LC 97-43407. (Clarendon Studies in the History of Art: No. 20). (Illus.). 322p. 1999. text 145.00 (0-19-817417-9) OUP.

— Private High. 25p. (YA). (gr. 7 up). 1987. pap. 6.00 (0-87602-267-0) Anchorage.

Martin, Thomas C. The Inventions, Researches & Writings of Nikola Tesla. 496p. 1997. reprint ed. spiral bd. 28.00 (0-7873-0582-0) Hlth Research.

— The Inventions, Researches & Writings of Nikola Tesla, 1894. 510p. 1996. reprint ed. pap. 27.95 (1-56459-711-3) Kessinger Pub.

Martin, Thomas C., jt. auth. see Lancaster, Kent.

Martin, Thomas Commerford, compiled by. Inventions, Researches & Writings of Nikola Tesla. 496p. 1894. 25.00 (0-945001-65-7) GSG & Assocs.

Martin, Thomas E. Military Aircraft Accidents Around Western Massachusetts. LC 94-96095. 180p. 1995. pap. 18.95 (0-9641015-0-5) T E Martin.

Martin, Thomas E. & Finch, Deborah M. Ecology & Management of Neotropical Migratory Birds: A Synthesis & Review of Critical Issues. (Illus.). 512p. 1995. text 85.00 (0-19-508440-3); pap. text 40.00 (0-19-508452-7) OUP.

Martin, Thomas G. If You Only Knew... An Internationally Known Private Investigator Reveals How You Can Take Control of Your Life. Orig. Title: Women, It's Your Turn. 240p. (Orig.). 1997. pap. 16.95 (1-882180-78-X) Griffin CA.

Martin, Thomas H. Etudes Sur le Timee De Platon, 2 vols., Set. LC 75-13279. (History of Ideas in Ancient Greece Ser.). (FRE.). 1976. reprint ed. 60.95 (0-405-07319-4) Ayer.

— Memoire sur les Hypotheses Astronomiques des Plus Ancciens Philosophes de la Grece. Vlastos, Gregory, ed. (History of Ideas in Ancient Times Ser.). 1976. reprint ed. 39.95 (0-405-07320-8) Ayer.

Martin, Thomas J. Old Money. mass mkt. 5.99 (1-55197-289-1) Picasso Publ.

Martin, Thomas J. Old Money. 546p. 1998. 5.95 (1-893627-01-2) T J Martin.

— Old Money. rev. ed. 546p. 1998. pap. 6.95 (1-893627-00-4) T J Martin.

Martin, Thomas K. A Call to Arms. 240p. (Orig.). 1995. mass mkt. 4.99 (0-441-00242-0) Ace Bks.

— Magelord: House of Balm, Vol. 3. (Magelord Trilogy Ser.). 1999. mass mkt. 5.99 (0-441-00623-X) Ace Bks.

— Magelord: The Awakening. (Magelord Trilogy Ser.). 288p. 1997. mass mkt. 5.99 (0-441-00435-0) Ace Bks.

— Magelord: Time of Madness. (Magelord Trilogy Ser.: Vol. 2). 256p. 1998. mass mkt. 5.99 (0-441-00533-0) Ace Bks.

— A Matter of Honor. 224p. (Orig.). 1994. mass mkt. 4.99 (0-441-00107-6) Ace Bks.

— The Two-Edged Sword. LC 94-147972. 272p. (Orig.). 1994. mass mkt. 4.99 (0-441-83344-6) Ace Bks.

***Martin, Thomas L., ed.** Reading the Classics with C. S. Lewis. 416p. (gr. 13 up). 2000. pap. 24.99 (0-8010-2234-7) Baker Bks.

Martin, Thomas L., Jr. & Latham, Donald C. Strategy for Survival. LC 63-17720. (Illus.). 399p. reprint ed. 123.70 (0-8357-9624-8, 201156400079) Bks Demand.

Martin, Thomas L., jt. auth. see Leonard, William F.

Martin, Thomas M. Country Auctioneer: Anecdotes, Admonitions, & Advice. Moore, Amy G., ed. (Illus.). 96p. (Orig.). 1994. pap. 12.95 (1-883912-00-8) Hamiltons.

— Images & the Imageless: A Study in Religious Consciousness & Film. 2nd ed. LC 90-48202. 208p. 1991. 29.50 (0-8387-5212-8) Bucknell U Pr.

Martin, Thomas M., jt. ed. see Voydanoff, Patricia.

Martin, Thomas R. Ancient Greece: From Prehistoric to Hellenistic Times. LC 95-26690. (Illus.). 288p. 1996. 37.00 (0-300-06767-4); pap. 16.00 (0-300-06956-1) Yale U Pr.

***Martin, Thomas R.** Ancient Greece: From Prehistoric to Hellenistic Times. 288p. 2000. pap. 15.95 (0-300-08493-5) Yale U Pr.

Martin, Thomas R., jt. ed. see Nelson, Steve.

Martin, Thomas S. Greening the Past: Towards a Social-Ecological Analysis of History. LC 97-36000. 344p. 1997. 74.95 (1-57309-196-0); pap. 54.95 (1-57309-195-2) Intl Scholars.

— True Whigs & Honest Tories Vol. 1: The Arc of the Empire. LC 96-46452. 424p. 1997. 69.95 (1-57309-131-6); pap. 49.95 (1-57309-130-8) Intl Scholars.

— True Whigs & Honest Tories Vol. 2: A Green Interpretation of the Coming of the American Revolution. 784p. 1997. pap. 49.95 (1-57309-132-4) Intl Scholars.

— True Whigs & Honest Tories Vol. 2: The Unraveling of Empire. 486p. 1997. 69.95 (1-57309-133-2) Intl Scholars.

Martin, Thomas W. French Military Adventures in Alabama, 1818-1828. 1987. pap. 5.95 (0-317-68076-5) Southern U Pr.

***Martin, Ti Adelaide, et al.** Commander's Kitchen: Take Home the True Taste of New Orleans with 200 Recipes from Commander's Palace Restaurant. LC 00-26876. (Illus.). 320p. 2000. 35.00 (0-7679-0290-4) Broadway BDD.

***Martin, Timothy.** There's Nothing Funny about Running: 70 Wacky Short Stories on Running. 208p. 1999. pap. 14.95 (0-9655187-8-7, Pub. by Marathon Pubs Inc) IPG Chicago.

***Martin, Timothy J. & Corbett, James J.** The Requisites in Ophthalmology: Neuro-Ophthalmology. (Illus.). 300p. (C). 1999. text 89.00 (0-323-00182-3) Mosby Inc.

Martin, Timothy L. Angel on My Shoulder. boxed set 16.95 (1-888683-67-8) Wooster Bk.

Martin, Timothy R. Stability of Natural Slopes in the Coastal Plain. LC 98-38681. 88p. 1998. 25.00 (0-7844-0384-8) Am Soc Civil Eng.

Martin, Tom. Creating Local Recycling Markets. 31p. 1994. 6.00 (0-614-18035-X) Inst Local Self Re.

***Martin, Tom.** Day Hikes from the River: A Guide to 75 Hikes from Camps on the Colorado River in Grand Canyon National Park. (Illus.). 172p. 1999. pap. 16.95 (0-9674595-0-8) Vishnu Temple.

— Green History: The Future of the Past. LC 99-88498. 224p. 2000. 54.00 (0-7618-1609-7); pap. 32.50 (0-7618-1610-0) U Pr of Amer.

Martin, Tom. Kentucky Ice: A Winter Adventure. LC 91-90423. (Illus.). 80p. 1991. 16.95 (0-930871-02-2) Search.

— Observations. (Illus.). 155p. (Orig.). 1998. pap. 6.95 (0-930871-04-9) Search.

— Rappelling. 2nd rev. ed. LC 91-90423. (Illus.). 304p. 1995. 16.95 (0-930871-03-0) Search.

Martin, Tom, jt. auth. see Seldman, Neil.

Martin, Tony. Amy Ashwood Garvey: Pan-Africanist, Feminist, & Wife, No. 1. (New Marcus Garvey Library: No. 4). (Illus.). Date not set. pap. text. write for info. (0-912469-07-2) Majority Pr.

— Insurance Direct Marketing. (C). 1989. 690.00 (0-7855-4138-1, Pub. by Witherby & Co) St Mut.

— The Jewish Onslaught: Despatches from the Wellesley Battlefront. xii, 137p. 1993. pap. text 9.95 (0-912469-30-7) Majority Pr.

— Literary Garveyism: Garvey, Black Arts & the Harlem Renaissance. LC 83-60952. (New Marcus Garvey Library: No. 1). (Illus.). xii, 204p. 1983. pap. text 9.95 (0-912469-01-3) Majority Pr.

— Marcus Garvey, Hero: A First Biography. LC 83-61113. (New Marcus Garvey Library: No. 3). (Illus.). x, 179p. 1983. pap. text 9.95 (0-912469-05-6) Majority Pr.

— The Pan-African Connection: From Slavery to Garvey & Beyond. LC 82-19521. (New Marcus Garvey Library: No. 6). (Illus.). xii, 262p. (C). 1984. reprint ed. pap. text 12.95 (0-912469-11-0) Majority Pr.

— The Progress of the African Race since Emancipation & Prospects for the Future. x, 28p. 1998. pap. text 5.00 (0-912469-35-8) Majority Pr.

— Race First: The Ideological & Organizational Struggles of Marcus Garvey & the Universal Negro Improvement Association. (New Marcus Garvey Library: No. 8). (Illus.). x, 421p. (C). 1986. reprint ed. pap. text 12.95 (0-912469-23-4) Majority Pr.

— The Strugglers: Working with Children Who Fail to Learn to Read. 160p. 1989. pap. 29.95 (0-335-09511-9) OpUniv Pr.

Martin, Tony, ed. In Nobody's Backyard - The Grenada Revolutions in Its Own Words Vol. II: Facing the World. (Illus.). xvi, 201p. 1985. 22.95 (0-912469-16-1) Majority Pr.

— The Poetical Works of Marcus Garvey. LC 83-61114. (New Marcus Garvey Library: No. 2). (Illus.). viii, 123p. (C). 1983. 17.95 (0-912469-02-1); pap. 9.95 (0-912469-03-X) Majority Pr.

Martin, Tony, ed. African Fundamentalism: A Literary & Cultural Anthology of Garvey's Harlem Renaissance. (New Marcus Garvey Library: No. 5). (Illus.). xviii, 363p. (C). 1991. pap. text 14.95 (0-912469-09-9) Majority Pr.

Martin, Tony & Leather, Bob. Readers & Texts in the Primary Years. LC 94-12241. (Rethinking Reading Ser.). 144p. 1994. 103.95 (0-335-19228-9); pap. 31.95 (0-335-19227-0) OpUniv Pr.

Martin, Tony, jt. auth. see Rofail, Ash.

Martin, Tony, ed. see Garvey, Marcus.

Martin, Tonya, ed. see Luttery, Kevin.

Martin, Tonya, ed. see Williams-Platt, Kathryn.

Martin, Torry. Under the Circumstances Ten Sketches about the Christian Life. 1999. pap. text 15.99 (0-8341-9980-7) Lillenas.

Martin, Tovah. Garden Whimsy. LC 99-36387. (Illus.). 160p. 1999. 30.00 (0-395-93731-0) HM.

— Heirloom Flowers: Vintage Flowers for Modern Gardens. LC 99-209891. (Illus.). 192p. 1999. per. 16.00 (0-684-85460-0, Fireside) S&S Trade Pap.

— Indoor Gardens. 1998. 24.75 (0-8446-6952-0) Peter Smith.

***Martin, Tovah.** Old-Fashioned Flowers: Classic Blossoms to Grow in Your Garden. (Illus.). 112p. 2000. pap. text 9.95 (1-889538-15-9) Bklyn Botanic.

Martin, Tovah. Tasha Tudor's Heirloom Crafts. LC 95-18605. (Illus.). 160p. 1995. 35.00 (0-395-73527-0) HM.

— Taylor Weekend Guide to Window Boxes. LC 96-44020. (Illus.). 128p. 1997. pap. 12.95 (0-395-81371-9) HM.

— Taylor's Weekend Gardening Guide to Indoor Gardens: Designing & Planting the Interior Landscape. LC 97-38023. (Illus.). 128p. 1997. pap. 12.95 (0-395-82944-5) HM.

— Well-Clad Windowsills: Houseplants for Four Exposures. LC 93-39565. 1994. 27.50 (0-671-85015-6, Hortcultre Bks) Macmillan Gen Ref.

— Window Boxes. 1996. 24.75 (0-8446-6917-2) Peter Smith.

Martin, Tovah, ed. Greenhouses & Garden Rooms. (Plants & Gardens Ser.). (Illus.). 1989. pap. 7.95 (0-945352-47-6) Bklyn Botanic.

— A New Look at Houseplants. (Illus.). 96p. 1994. pap. 7.95 (0-945352-81-6) Bklyn Botanic.

***Martin, Tovah & Brown, Richard W.** Tasha Tudor's Heirloom Crafts. (Illus.). 160p. 2000. pap. 25.00 (0-618-08351-0) HM.

***Martin, Tracie.** Interests in Abortion: A New Perspective on Foetal Potential & the Abortion Debate. (Avebury Series in Philosophy). 118p. 2000. text 56.95 (0-7546-1146-9, Pub. by Ashgate Pub) Ashgate Pub Co.

***Martin, Trent.** Andy, 3 vols., Vol. 1. 318p. 2000. 24.95 (0-9673506-0-3) T Martin Pubns.

— Andy: Madame Justice, 3 vols., Vol. 2. 332p. 2000. 24.95 (0-9673506-1-1) T Martin Pubns.

— Andy: Madame President, 3 vols. (Andy Ser.: Vol. 1). 424p. 2000. 24.95 (0-9673506-2-X) T Martin Pubns.

Martin, Trevor, jt. auth. see Ralescu, Anca L.

***Martin, Troy.** Dazed & Confused: Surviving Life in the Game. (Illus.). 250p. 2000. pap. write for info. (0-9674370-0-8) Trojan Works.

Martin, Troy W. By Philosophy & Empty Deceit: Colossians As Response to a Cynic Critique. LC 96-128715. (Journal for the Study of the New Testament, Supplement Ser.: No. 118). 223p. 1996. 65.00 (1-85075-559-0, Pub. by Sheffield Acad) CUP Services.

Martin, Trude. Obee & Mungedeech. (Illus.). 112p. (J). (gr. 3-7). 1996. mass mkt. 3.99 (0-689-80725-2) Aladdin.

— Obee & Mungedeech. LC 95-43531. (Illus.). 112p. (J). (gr. 4-8). 1996. 15.00 (0-689-80644-2) Aladdin.

— Obee & Mungedeech. LC 95-43531. (J). 1996. 9.09 (0-606-09702-3, Pub. by Turtleback) Demco.

***Martin, Trude.** Obee & Mungedeech. 107p. (J). (gr. 3-6). 1999. reprint ed. text 15.00 (0-7881-6639-5) DIANE Pub.

Martin, Tyrone G. Creating a Legend. LC 97-165653. (Illus.). 128p. (Orig.). 1997. pap. 18.00 (1-884824-20-X, Timonier Bks) Tryon Pubng.

— A Most Fortunate Ship: A Narrative History of Old Ironsides. rev. ed. LC 96-39863. (Illus.). 440p. 1997. 35.00 (1-55750-588-8) Naval Inst Pr.

— Undefeated: "Old Ironsides" in the War of 1812. LC 96-216313. (Illus.). 72p. (Orig.). 1996. pap. 12.00 (1-884824-19-6, Timonier Bks) Tryon Pubng.

Martin, Una, jt. auth. see O'Mahony, Denis.

Martin, Ursula & Wing, Jeannette M., eds. Proceedings of the First International Workshop on Larch, Dedham, U. S. A. 13-15 July 1992. LC 92-36174. (Workshops in Computing Ser.). 1993. 79.00 (0-387-19804-0) Spr-Verlag.

***Martin, V. Kevin.** Mom, I'm Telling on You. 140p. 1999. pap. 8.99 (0-7392-0455-6, PO3760) Morris Pubng.

Martin, Val, ed. see Burt, Al.

Martin, Val, ed. see Ranson, Robert.

Martin, Valerie. Alexandra. 192p. 1991. reprint ed. pap. 10.00 (0-671-73688-4, WSP) PB.

***Martin, Valerie.** Italian Fever. LC 98-31824. 272p. 1999. 22.00 (0-375-40542-9) Knopf.

— Italian Fever. LC 99-54987. 2000. 29.95 (0-7838-8840-6, G K Hall & Co) Mac Lib Ref.

— Italian Fever. (Contemporaries Ser.). 272p. 2000. pap. text 12.00 (0-375-70522-8) Vin Bks.

Martin, Valerie. Love. (Illus.). 1976. pap. 4.50 (0-89924-004-6) Lynx Hse.

***Martin, Valerie.** Love: Short Stories. LC 99-28391. 79p. 1999. pap. 14.95 (0-9668612-3-X, Pub. by Lost Horse) SPD-Small Pr Dist.

M

Martin, Valerie. Mary Reilly. 1994. pap. 10.00 (*0-671-50702-8*, WSP) PB.

— Mary Reilly. 1996. mass mkt. 5.99 (*0-671-52113-6*) PB.

— Set in Motion. 224p. 1991. reprint ed. pap. 10.00 (*0-671-73687-6*, WSP) PB.

Martin, Van J., jt. auth. see Delehanty, Randolph.

Martin, Vance, ed. For the Conservation of the Earth: Proceedings of the 4th World Wilderness Congress. LC 88-16319. 438p. 1988. pap. 18.95 (*1-55591-026-2*) Fulcrum Pub.

Martin, Vance L., jt. ed. see Creedy, John.

Martin, Vanessa. Islam & Modernism: The Iranian Revolution of 1906. LC 89-5942. 245p. 1989. reprint ed. pap. 76.00 (*0-608-07618-X*, 205993300010) Bks Demand.

Martin, Vaughn D. Automotive & Electrical Systems: Troubleshooting & Repair Basics. LC 98-66672. (Illus.). 243p. 1999. pap. 29.95 (*0-7906-1142-2*) Prompt Publns.

— OptoElectronics. LC 96-72184. (Illus.). 264p. 1997. pap. 34.95 (*0-7906-1091-4*) Prompt Publns.

— Optoelectronics: Intermediate Study, Vol. 2. (Illus.). 258p. 1997. pap. 34.95 (*0-7906-1110-4*) Prompt Publns.

— Optoelectronics Vol. 3: Experimental Study. (Illus.). 435p. 1998. pap. 44.95 (*0-7906-1122-8*) Prompt Publns.

Martin, Verna. Stories for Every Season. (Illus.). 268p. (Orig.). (YA). (gr. 4 up). 1996. pap. 7.95 (*0-87813-564-2*) Christian Light.

Martin, Vickee. The Morning after Mourning. 58p. 1999. write for info. (*0-7541-0825-2*, Pub. by Minerva Pr) Unity Dist.

Martin, Vicky. Obey the Moon. large type ed. 545p. 1989. 27.99 (*0-7089-1963-4*) Ulverscroft.

— Tigers of the Night. large type ed. 592p. 1986. 27.99 (*0-7089-1448-9*) Ulverscroft.

Martin, Victor. La Vie Internationale dans la Grece des Cites. Vlastos, Gregory, ed. LC 78-19368. (Morals & Law in Ancient Greece Ser.). 1979. reprint ed. lib. bdg. 48.95 (*0-405-11559-8*) Ayer.

Martin, Vida E., jt. auth. see Martin, Kenneth D.

Martin-Vide, Carlos, ed. Current Issues in Mathematical Linguistics. LC 94-1198. (North-Holland Linguistic Ser.: Vol. 56). 480p. 1994. 171.75 (*0-444-81693-3*, North Holland) Elsevier.

***Martin-Vide, Carlos, ed.** Issues in Mathematical Linguistics: Workshop on Mathematical Linguistics, State College, PA, April, 1998. LC 99-44213. (Studies in Functional & Structural Linguistics: Vol. 47). xii, 214p. 1999. 75.00 (*1-55619-898-1*) J Benjamins Pubng Co.

— Mathematical & Computational Analysis of Natural Language: Selected Papers from the 2nd International Conference on Mathematical Linguistics, Tarragona, 1996. LC 98-26169. (Studies in Functional & Structural Linguistics: No. 45). xviii, 391p. 1998. 79.00 (*1-55619-896-5*) J Benjamins Pubng Co.

Martin, Vince & Marciniszyn, Alex. Phase World Sourcebook. (Rifts Dimension Bk.: No. 3). (Illus.). 112p. (Orig.). 1995. pap. 12.95 (*0-916211-79-7*) Palladium Bks.

Martin, Vincent. A House Divided: The Parting of the Ways Between Synagogue & Church. LC 95-3020. (Stimulus Bks.). 224p. (Orig.). 1995. pap. 11.95 (*0-8091-3569-8*) Paulist Pr.

Martin, Violet F., jt. auth. see Somerville, Edith A.

Martin, Viv. Out of My Head: An Experience of Neurosurgery. 162p. 1997. pap. 22.50 (*1-85776-179-0*, Pub. by Book Guild Ltd) Trans-Atl Phila.

Martin, Vivian, jt. auth. see Martin, Mike.

Martin, W. Fundamentos Educador Evangelico.Tr. of First Steps for Teachers. 120p. 1988. pap. 5.99 (*0-8297-1409-X*) Vida Pubs.

— Women in the Visual Arts. 135p. 1992. pap. text 13.00 (*2-88124-581-1*) Gordon & Breach.

Martin, W. & Macdonell, A. Canadian Education: A Sociological Analysis. 354p. 1978. pap. 13.33 (*0-13-113092-7*) P-H.

***Martin, W. & Tops, Guy A.** Van Dale Groot Woordenboek Engels-Nederlands 3rd ed. LC 99-179338. (Woordenboeken Voor Hedendaags Taalgebruik Ser.). xxix, 1763 p. 1998. write for info. (*90-6648-143-9*, Pub. by Woordenboeken) IBD Ltd.

Martin, W. Allen, jt. ed. see Ellison, Christopher.

***Martin, W. B. & Aitken, I. D.** Diseases of Sheep. 3rd ed. LC 99-36665. (Illus.). 528p. 2000. text 129.95 (*0-632-05139-6*, Pub. by Blckwell Science) Iowa St U Pr.

Martin, W. C. History of Warren County: From Its Earliest Settlement to 1908, with Biographical Sketches of Some Prominent Citizens of the County. (Illus.). 1000p. 1997. reprint ed. lib. bdg. 99.50 (*0-8328-6708-X*) Higginson Bk Co.

Martin, W. C. & Hutchins, R. Flora of New Mexico, 2 vols., Set. (Illus.). 3000p. 1980. lib. bdg. 600.00 (*3-7682-1263-7*) Lubrecht & Cramer.

Martin, W. Coda. A Matter of Life. 1965. 6.95 (*0-8159-6202-9*) Devin.

Martin, W. E. & O'Connell, J. C. Pueblo Indian Vocational Rehabilitation Services Study: Final Report. 85p. 1986. pap. text. write for info. (*1-888557-11-7*, 100109) No Ariz Univ.

Martin, W. L. Loyalty & Integrity. 1996. pap. text 19.99 (*0-9682646-0-3*) CPRE.

Martin, W. L., jt. auth. see Chatto, James.

Martin, W. R., et al, eds. Tobacco Smoking & Nicotine: A Neurobiological Approach. LC 87-18513. (Advances in Behavioral Biology Ser.: Vol. 31). (Illus.). 534p. 1987. 120.00 (*0-306-42611-0*, Plenum Trade) Perseus Pubng.

***Martin, W. R. & Ober, Warren U.** Trees: A Browser's Anthology. LC 99-172531. 264p. 1999. 19.95 (*0-88835-005-8*) P D Meany.

Martin, W. R., ed. see James, Henry.

Martin, W. W. Manual of Ecclesiastical Architecture. 1977. lib. bdg. 75.00 (*0-8490-2206-1*) Gordon Pr.

Martin, Wade E., ed. Environmental Economics & the Mining Industry. LC 93-32888. (Studies in Risk & Uncertainty). 136p. (C). 1993. lib. bdg. 74.50 (*0-7923-9404-6*) Kluwer Academic.

Martin, Wade E., ed. see McDonald, Lisa A.

Martin, Waldo E., Jr. The Mind of Frederick Douglass. LC 84-5140. (Illus.). xii, 334p. 1986. reprint ed. 49.95 (*0-8078-1616-7*); reprint ed. pap. 18.95 (*0-8078-4148-X*) U of NC Pr.

Martin, Waldo E., Jr., ed. see Bond.

Martin, Wallace. Recent Theories of Narrative. LC 85-22401. 248p. (C). 1986. pap. text 14.95 (*0-8014-9355-2*) Cornell U Pr.

Martin, Wallace, ed. Language, Logic, & Genre: Papers from the Poetics & Literary Theory Section, Modern Language Association. 54p. 1974. 10.00 (*0-8387-1446-3*) Bucknell U Pr.

Martin, Walter. Jehovah's Witnesses. 64p. 1968. pap. 4.99 (*0-87123-270-7*) Bethany Hse.

— Mormonism. 32p. 1968. pap. 3.99 (*0-87123-367-3*) Bethany Hse.

— Mormonismo.Tr. of Mormonism. 112p. 1988. 7.99 (*0-88113-208-X*) Caribe Betania.

— The New Age Cult. LC 89-6889. 144p. (Orig.). 1989. pap. 7.99 (*1-55661-077-7*) Bethany Hse.

— La Nueva Era.Tr. of New Age. (SPA.). 144p. (Orig.). 1991. pap. 8.99 (*0-88113-055-9*) Caribe Betania.

— Los Testigos de Jehova.Tr. of Jehovah's Witness. 144p. 1988. 7.99 (*0-88113-285-3*) Caribe Betania.

Martin, Walter, jt. auth. see Rische, Jill M.

Martin, Walter, tr. see Baudelaire, Charles.

Martin, Walter E. Laboratory Exercises for Atmospheric Interactions. 156p. (C). 1996. spiral bd. 14.95 (*0-8403-8389-4*) Kendall-Hunt.

Martin, Walter R. The Kingdom of the Cults. Hanegraaff, Hank, ed. LC 97-33773. 74p. 1997. text 29.99 (*1-55661-714-3*) Bethany Hse.

Martin, Walter R. & Ober, Warren. Henry James's Apprenticeship: The Tales, 1864-1882. 240p. 1993. text 38.00 (*0-88835-034-1*) P D Meany.

Martin, Warren B. A College of Character. LC 82-48392. (Jossey-Bass Series in Higher Education). 247p. reprint ed. pap. 76.60 (*0-8357-4689-5*, 205234400008) Bks Demand.

— Conformity: Standards & Change in Higher Education. LC 72-92894. (Jossey-Bass Higher Education Ser.). 288p. reprint ed. 89.30 (*0-8357-9310-9*, 201395100087) Bks Demand.

Martin, Wayne F. An Insight to Sports. (Illus.). 183p. (Orig.). 1993. pap. 14.95 (*0-9614895-3-7*) Sports Vision.

Martin, Wayne M. Idealism & Objectivity: Understanding Fichte's Jena Project. LC 97-9355. (Studies in Kant & German Idealism). 200p. 1997. 39.50 (*0-8047-3000-8*) Stanford U Pr.

Martin, Wendy. An American Triptych: Anne Bradstreet, Emily Dickinson, & Adrienne Rich. LC 83-6864. x, 272p. 1983. pap. 16.95 (*0-8078-4112-9*) U of NC Pr.

***Martin, Wendy.** A Whole New Poetry Beginning Here: Adrienne Rich in the Eighties & Nineties. 100p. 1998. pap. text 29.00 (*90-5700-544-1*, Harwood Acad Pubs) Gordon & Breach.

Martin, Wendy, ed. The Beacon Book of Essays by Contemporary American Women. 320p. 1997. pap. 16.00 (*0-8070-6347-9*) Beacon Pr.

— Colonial American Travel Narratives. LC 93-47437. 11.95p. (C). 1998. pap. 13.95 (*0-14-039088-X*) Viking Penguin.

— We Are the Stories We Tell: The Best Short Stories by North American Women Since 1945. 272p. 1990. pap. 16.00 (*0-679-72881-3*) Pantheon.

Martin, Wendy Lee, jt. auth. see Axton, W. F.

Martin, Werner, ed. Verzeichnis der Nobelpreistrager, 1901-1987: Mit Preisbegundungen, Kurzkommentaren, Literarischen, Werkbibliographien und einer Biographie Alfred Nobel. 2nd ed. xi, 382p. 1988. lib. bdg. 60.00 (*3-598-10721-8*) K G Saur Verlag.

Martin, Werner, ed. see Agnon, Shmuel Yoseph.

Martin, Werner, ed. see Heyse, Paul.

Martin, Werner, ed. see Solschenizyn, Alexander.

Martin, Wilfred. Voices from the Classroom. 96p. 1985. pap. 8.50 (*0-920021-21-2*) Creative Bk Pub.

Martin, Wilfred B., ed. see Martin, Lillian M.

Martin, Will & Winters, L. Alan. The Uruguay Round: Widening & Deepening the World Trading System. (Directions in Development Ser.). 40p. 1995. pap. 22.00 (*0-8213-3488-3*, 13488) World Bank.

Martin, Will & Winters, L. Alan, eds. The Uruguay Round & the Developing Countries. 493p. 1997. pap. text 28.95 (*0-521-58601-1*) Cambridge U Pr.

— The Uruguay Round & the Developing Economies. (World Bank Discussion Papers: Vol. 307). 476p. 1995. pap. 26.00 (*0-8213-3469-7*, 13469) World Bank.

Martin, Willard E., Jr. Chaucer Bibliography, 1925-1933. LC 72-1042. reprint ed. 31.50 (*0-404-04195-7*) AMS Pr.

Martin, William, Jr. Annapolis. 800p. 1997. reprint ed. mass mkt. 7.99 (*0-446-60420-8*, Pub. by Warner Bks) Little.

Martin, William. Back Bay. 544p. 1992. reprint ed. mass mkt. 6.99 (*0-446-36316-2*, Pub. by Warner Bks) Little.

— Cape Cod. 736p. 1992. reprint ed. mass mkt. 7.99 (*0-446-36317-0*, Pub. by Warner Bks) Little.

— Citizen Washington. LC PS3563.A7297C57 1999. 583p. 1999. 27.00 (*0-446-52172-8*, Pub. by Warner Bks) Little.

— Citizen Washington. 680p. 2000. mass mkt. 7.99 (*0-446-60785-1*, Pub. by Warner Bks) Little.

— Classroom Management. 216p. (C). 1995. pap. text, spiral bd. 34.95 (*0-7872-1030-7*) Kendall-Hunt.

***Martin, William.** Couple's Tao Te Ching Advice for Modern Lovers: A New Interpretation. LC 99-45386. 288p. 2000. pap. text 13.95 (*1-56924-650-5*) Marlowe & Co.

Martin, William. Lammas Alanna. 1998. pap. 17.95 (*1-85224-369-4*, Pub. by Bloodaxe Bks) Dufour.

— Managing Quality Customer Service: A Practical Guide for Establishing a Service Operation. Fritz, Elaine, ed. LC 88-92732. (Fifty-Minute Ser.). (Illus.). 96p. (Orig.). 1989. pap. 10.95 (*0-931961-83-1*) Crisp Pubns.

— Nerve Endings. 480p. 1996. mass mkt. 6.99 (*0-446-36330-8*, Pub. by Warner Bks) Little.

— A Prophet with Honor: The Billy Graham Story. (Illus.). 760p. 1992. pap. 15.00 (*0-688-11906-9*, Quil) HarperTrade.

— Quality Customer Service: A Positive Guide to Superior Service. 3rd rev. ed. Crisp, Michael, ed. LC 92-82933. (Fifty-Minute Ser.). 89p. (Orig.). 1993. pap. 10.95 (*1-56052-203-8*) Crisp Pubns.

— Restaurant Server's Guide to Quality Service. 1988. 6.95 (*0-685-44003-6*, 110) Am Bartenders.

***Martin, William.** Sage's Tao Te Ching: Ancient Advice for the Second Half of Life. 2000. pap. 13.95 (*1-56924-611-4*) Marlowe & Co.

Martin, William. Statesmen of the War in Retrospect, 1918-1928. LC 75-105029. (Essay Index Reprint Ser.). 1977. 23.95 (*0-8369-1675-1*) Ayer.

— The Way of the Word: Contemplative Reflections on the Gospels. (Illus.). 112p. 1997. pap. 9.95 (*1-885121-21-0*) CTS Press.

Martin, William, et al. Hazardous Waste Handbook for Health & Safety. 2nd ed. 240p. 1992. 49.95 (*0-7506-9235-9*) Buttrwrth-Heinemann.

— Marra Familia. 64p. 1994. pap. 14.95 (*1-85224-221-3*, Pub. by Bloodaxe Bks) Dufour.

Martin, William, ed. see Martin, Kady.

Martin, William, ed. see Martin, Kathy.

Martin, William A. A Martin Genealogy: Tied to the History of Germanna, Virginia. 382p. (Orig.). 1995. pap. text 28.50 (*0-7884-0184-X*) Heritage Bk.

— The Siege in Peking: China Against the World. LC 72-79832. (China Library). 190 p. 1972. reprint ed. lib. bdg. 23.00 (*0-8420-1376-8*) Scholarly Res Inc.

Martin, William B. Managing Quality Customer Service. (Better Management Skills Ser.). 1991. pap. 12.95 (*0-7494-0352-7*) Kogan Page Ltd.

— Quality Service: The Restaurant Manager's Bible. 1986. 9.95 (*0-937056-05-7*, FB5) Cornell U Sch Hotel.

— Restaurant Server's Guide: To Quality Customer Service. rev. ed. LC 85-73177. (Fifty-Minute Ser.). (Illus.). 71p. (Orig.). 1987. pap. 10.95 (*0-931961-08-4*) Crisp Pubns.

— Spheres & Satellites. (Hi Map Ser.: No. 12). (Illus.). 60p. pap. text 11.99 (*0-614-05314-5*, HM 5612) COMAP Inc.

— Superior Service! 1995. pap. 24.95 incl. audio (*1-56052-369-7*) Crisp Pubns.

Martin, William B., ed. Texas Plays. LC 89-42893. (Southwest Life & Letters Ser.). (Illus.). 480p. 1990. pap. 16.95 (*0-87074-301-5*); text 35.00 (*0-87074-300-7*) SMU Press.

Martin, William C. The Art of Pastoring: Contemplative Reflections. 92p. (Orig.). 1994. pap. 7.95 (*1-885121-00-8*) CTS Press.

— Christians in Conflict. LC 72-88018. (Studies in Religion & Society). 106p. 1972. 16.95 (*0-913348-01-5*); pap. 12.95 (*0-913348-10-4*) Ctr Sci Study.

***Martin, William C.** The Parent's Tao Te Ching: Ancient Advice for Modern Parents. LC 98-54591. (Illus.). 128p. 1999. pap. 11.95 (*1-56924-662-9*, Pub. by Marlowe & Co) Publishers Group.

Martin, William E., Jr. & Swartz, Jody L., eds. Person-Environment Psychology: Clinical & Counseling Applications for Adolescents & Adults. LC 99-32763. 300p. 2000. write for info. (*0-8058-2953-9*) L Erlbaum Assocs.

Martin, William E., et al. Saving Water in a Desert City. LC 83-43263. 127p. reprint ed. pap. 39.40 (*0-7837-2180-3*, 204251800004) Bks Demand.

Martin, William E., jt. auth. see Padfield, Harland.

Martin, William E., jt. ed. see Swartz, Jody L.

Martin, William F. The Indissoluble Knot. LC 87-17927. 93p. (Orig.). 1987. lib. bdg. 31.00 (*0-8191-6604-9*) U Pr of Amer.

Martin, William F. & Levine, Steven P., eds. Protecting Personnel at Hazardous Waste Sites. 2nd ed. LC 93-28510. 592p. 1993. 79.95 (*0-7506-9457-2*) Buttrwrth-Heinemann.

Martin, William F., et al. Hazardous Waste Handbook for Health & Safety. 480p. 1987. 32.95 (*0-7506-9189-1*) Buttrwrth-Heinemann.

— Maintaining Energy Security in a Global Context. Heck, Charles B., ed. (Triangle Papers: Vol. 48). 142p. (Orig.). 1996. pap. 12.00 (*0-930503-73-2*) Trilateral Comm.

Martin, William G. Out of One, Many Africas: Reconstructing the Study & Meaning of Africa: Reconstructing the Study & Meaning of Africa. LC 98-58006. 1999. 44.95 (*0-252-02471-0*) U of Ill Pr.

Martin, William G., ed. Semiperipheral States in the World-Economy, 113. LC 90-36779. (Contributions in Economics & Economic History Ser.: No. 113). 248p. 1990. 59.95 (*0-313-27489-4*, MGP, Greenwood Pr) Greenwood.

Martin, William G. & West, Michael O. Out of One, Many Africas: Reconstructing the Study & Meaning of Africa. LC 98-58006. 240p. 1999. pap. 19.95 (*0-252-06780-0*) U of Ill Pr.

Martin, William H., et al, eds. Biodiversity of the Southeastern United States: Lowland Terrestrial Communities, Vol. 2, Vol. 2. LC 92-26503. 528p. 1993. 120.00 (*0-471-62883-2*) Wiley.

Martin, William H., et al, eds. Biodiversity of the Southeastern United States Vol. 3: Upland Terrestrial Communities, Vol. 3. 400p. 1993. 110.00 (*0-471-58594-7*) Wiley.

Martin, William H. & Martin, Wilma D. Captain Murrells Savory Seafood Recipes. (Illus.). 133p. 1990. spiral bd. 13.95 (*0-9630689-0-3*) Rum Gully.

Martin, William J. Alaska Methodist Circuit Preacher. (Illus.). 48p. 1998. pap. 8.00 (*0-8059-4364-1*) Dorrance.

— Community Librarianship: Changing the Face of Public Libraries. LC 89-19477. (Looking Forward in Librarianship Ser.). 205p. Date not set. reprint ed. pap. 63.60 (*0-608-20722-5*, 207182000002) Bks Demand.

— The Global Information Society. 249p. 1996. 69.95 (*0-566-07715-9*, Pub. by Gower) Ashgate Pub Co.

— The Global Information Society. 236p. 1996. pap. 34.95 (*0-566-07812-0*, Pub. by Gower) Ashgate Pub Co.

Martin, William O. Metaphysics & Ideology. LC 59-9870. (Aquinas Lectures). 1959. 15.00 (*0-87462-124-0*) Marquette.

— Order & Integration of Knowledge. LC 68-54425. (Illus.). 355p. 1969. reprint ed. lib. bdg. 69.50 (*0-8371-0161-1*, MAKN, Greenwood Pr) Greenwood.

Martin, William O., ed. Settlement of Shallow Foundations on Cohesionless Soils: Design & Performance. LC 86-70535. (Geotechnical Special Publication: No. 5). (Illus.). 98p. reprint ed. pap. 30.40 (*0-8357-6879-1*, 205688400095) Bks Demand.

Martin, William R., jt. auth. see Duderstadt, James J.

Martin, William T. Franklin County, Ohio, History. 1969. reprint ed. 10.00 (*0-935057-48-X*) OH Genealogical.

— History of Franklin County. 480p. 1993. 25.00 (*0-9636036-0-4*) Bergman Bks.

— History of Franklin County, Ohio. 449p. 1993. reprint ed. lib. bdg. 47.50 (*0-8328-2793-2*) Higginson Bk Co.

— Motivation & Productivity in Public Sector Human Service Organizations. LC 88-3099. 161p. 1988. 55.00 (*0-89930-314-5*, MMV/, Quorum Bks) Greenwood.

— Problem Employees & Their Personalities: A Guide to Behaviors, Dynamics, & Intervention Strategies for Personnel Specialists. LC 89-3858. 198p. 1989. 57.95 (*0-89930-417-6*, MEY, Quorum Bks) Greenwood.

Martin, William T., et al. Elementary Differential Equations. 3rd ed. text. write for info. (*0-8162-5435-4*) Holden-Day.

Martin, William W. I accuse! 350p. (C). 1989. 40.00 (*0-924932-01-5*); 100.00 (*0-924932-00-7*) Freedoms Herald.

Martin, Wilma D., jt. auth. see Martin, William H.

Martin, Wiltrud, jt. ed. see Bozarth, George.

Martin, Worthy N. & Aggarwal, J. K., eds. Motion Understanding: Robot & Human Vision. (C). 1988. text 246.00 (*0-89838-258-0*) Kluwer Academic.

***Martin, Xavier D.** Human Nature & the French Revolution: From the Enlightment to the Napoleonic Code. Corcoran, Patrick, tr. (Polygons: Vol. 3). 2000. 69.95 (*1-57181-709-3*) Berghahn Bks.

Martin, Xavier D., ed. Glaucoma Therapy: Effective Pharmacological Approaches. LC 96-77158. (Illus.). 134p. 1996. text 49.00 (*0-88937-176-8*) Hogrefe & Huber Pubs.

Martin, Xavier Sala I., jt. auth. see Barro, Robert.

Martin, Yves, ed. Selected Papers on Scanning Prove Microscopes: Design & Applications. LC 94-42035. (Milestone Ser.: No. 107). 1995. 50.00 (*0-8194-1804-8*, MS107) SPIE.

Martin, Yvonne C. & Willett, Peter, eds. Designing Bioactive Molecules: Three-Dimensional Techniques & Applications. LC 97-41372. (Computer Applications in Chemistry Collection Ser.). (Illus.). 352p. 1997. text 145.00 (*0-8412-3490-6*, Pub. by Am Chemical) OUP.

Martin, Yvonne Connoly, ed. see Kutter, et al.

Martin, Yvonne M. & Macpherson, R. J., eds. Restructuring Administrative Policy in Public Schooling: Canadian & International Case Studies. 285p. (Orig.). (C). 1993. pap. text 22.95 (*1-55059-054-5*) Temeron Bks.

Martina, Alan. Lectures on the Economic Theory of Taxation: Economic Reform, Socially Optimal Piecemeal Consumption Taxation Structures, & Information. LC 92-15323. (Lecture Notes in Economics & Mathematical Systems Ser.: Vol. 384). xii, 313p. 1992. 79.95 (*0-387-55538-2*) Spr-Verlag.

Martinac, Paula. Home Movies. LC 93-17841. 222p. (Orig.). 1993. pap. 10.95 (*1-878067-32-X*) Seal Pr WA.

— The Lesbian & Gay Book of Love & Marriage: Creating the Stories of Our Lives. LC 97-43996. (Illus.). 304p. 1998. pap. 18.00 (*0-7679-0162-2*) Broadway BDD.

— Out of Time. 2nd ed. LC 90-36973. (Djuna Bks.). 224p. 1999. reprint ed. pap. 12.95 (*1-58005-020-4*) Seal Pr WA.

Martinas, Dumitru. The Origins of the Changos. LC 99-195242. 200p. 1998. 42.00 (*973-98391-4-2*, Pub. by Ctr Romanian Studies) Intl Spec Bk.

Martinas, K., et al. Thermodynamics: History & Philosophy - Facts, Trends & Debates. 544p. 1991. text 147.00 (*981-02-0464-7*) World Scientific Pub.

Martinazzi, Toni. From Pavia to Portland: The Enrico Martinazzi Story, 1845-1892 & His Descendants. LC 93-78014. (Illus.). 482p. 1997. 45.00 (*0-9636823-1-8*) T Martinazzi.

Martincek, G. Dynamics of Pavement Structures. (Illus.). 400p. (C). 1994. 175.00 (*0-419-18100-8*, E & FN Spon) Routledge.

Martindale. Online Drug Information Thesaurus. 2nd ed. 1990. 110.00 (*0-85369-229-7*, Pub. by Pharmaceutical Pr) Rittenhouse.

Martindale, Adeline, jt. auth. see Martindale, Robert R.

Martindale, Andrew. Gothic Art. (World of Art Ser.). (Illus.). 288p. 1985. pap. 14.95 (*0-500-20058-0*, Pub. by Thames Hudson) Norton.

An Asterisk (*) at the beginning of an entry indicates that the title is appearing for the first time.

Martindale, Brian, et al. Supervision & Its Vicissitudes. LC 98-150407. (Illus.). 192p. 1997. pap. 29.00 (*1-85575-161-5*, Pub. by H Karnac Bks Ltd) Other Pr LLC.

Martindale, C. C. The Sacraments. (Compact Study Ser.). 23p. (Orig.). 1993. pap. 1.95 (*0-935952-92-6*) Angelus Pr.

Martindale, Carolyn A. The White Press & Black America, 97. LC 85-27219. (Contributions in Afro-American & African Studies: No. 97). 215p. 1986. 57.95 (*0-313-25103-7*, MWP/, Greenwood Pr) Greenwood.

Martindale, Carolyn A., ed. Pluralizing Journalism Education: A Multicultural Handbook. LC 92-35923. 264p. 1993. lib. bdg. 65.00 (*0-313-28592-6*, MZG/) Greenwood.

Martindale, Charles. John Milton & the Transformation of Ancient Epic. LC 86-3408. 256p. 1986. 53.00 (*0-389-20624-5*, N8182) B&N Imports.

— Redeeming the Text: Latin Poetry & the Hermeneutics of Reception. (Roman Literature & Its Contexts Ser.). (Illus.). 135p. (C). 1993. text 54.95 (*0-521-41717-1*); pap. text 17.95 (*0-521-42719-3*) Cambridge U Pr.

— Shakespeare & the Uses of Antiquity: An Introductory Essay. 240p. (C). 1994. pap. 25.99 (*0-415-10426-2*) Routledge.

Martindale, Charles, ed. The Cambridge Companion to Virgil. LC 96-52447. (Cambridge Companions to Literature Ser.). (Illus.). 388p. (C). 1997. text 59.95 (*0-521-49539-3*); pap. text 19.95 (*0-521-49885-6*) Cambridge U Pr.

Martindale, Charles & Hopkins, David, eds. Horace Made New: Horatian Influences on British Writing from the Renaissance to the Twentieth Century. (Illus.). 348p. (C). 1993. text 69.95 (*0-521-38019-7*) Cambridge U Pr.

Martindale, Cyril C. What Are Saints? Fifteen Chapters in Sanctity. LC 68-16954. (Essay Index Reprint Ser.). 1977. 17.95 (*0-8369-0681-0*) Ayer.

Martindale, Cyril C., tr. see Frisch, Hartvig.

Martindale, David. Pufnstuf & Other Stuff: The Weird & Wonderful World of Sid & Marty Krofft. LC 97-51752. (Illus.). 288p. 1998. pap. 16.95 (*1-58063-007-3*) Renaissance.

— Television Detective Shows of the 1970s: Credits, Storylines & Episode Guides for 109 Series. LC 90-53508. (Illus.). 576p. 1991. lib. bdg. 68.50 (*0-89950-557-0*) McFarland & Co.

Martindale, Don & Hanson, R. Galen. Small Town & the Nation: The Conflict of Local & Translocal Forces, 3. LC 79-90793. (Contributions in Sociology Ser.: No. 3). 211p. 1970. 38.50 (*0-8371-1854-9*, MAT/, Greenwood Pr) Greenwood.

Martindale, Don & Martindale, Edith. Social Dimensions of Mental Illness, Alcoholism, & Drug Dependence, 9. LC 72-133499. 330p. 1971. 65.00 (*0-8371-5175-9*, MAM/, Greenwood Pr) Greenwood.

Martindale, Don, jt. ed. see Mohan, Raj P.

Martindale, Don, ed. see Weber, Max M.

Martindale, Don A. The Nature & Types of Sociological Theory. 2nd ed. (Illus.). 656p. (C). 1988. reprint ed. pap. text 33.95 (*0-88133-353-0*) Waveland Pr.

Martindale, Edith, jt. auth. see Martindale, Don.

Martindale, Hilda. Some Victorian Portraits & Others. LC 76-126324. (Biography Index Reprint Ser.). 1977. reprint ed. 17.95 (*0-8369-8030-1*) Ayer.

Martindale-Hubbell Staff. Martindale-Hubbell Bar Register of Preeminent Lawyers, 1998 In The United States, Canada & Other Countries. 1998. 195.00 (*1-56160-321-X*) Martindale-Hubbell.

— Martindale-Hubbell Bar Register of Preeminent Lawyers, 1998: In The United States, Canada & Other Countries. 1998. 195.00 (*1-56160-320-1*) Martindale-Hubbell.

***Martindale-Hubbell Staff, ed.** Martindale Hubbell Law Directory 2000. 2000. 695.00 (*1-56160-376-7*) Martindale-Hubbell.

Martindale-Hubbell Staff, ed. 1997 Martindale-Hubbell International Arbitration & Dispute Resolution Directory. 1997. 170.00 (*1-85739-104-7*) Martindale-Hubbell.

— 1999 Martindale-Hubbell Law Directory, 127 vols. 128th ed. 1998. 695.00 (*1-56160-324-4*) Martindale-Hubbell.

Martindale, J. R., ed. The Prosopography of the Later Roman Empire, Vol. 2, A.D. 395-527. LC 77-118859. (Illus.). 1355p. 1980. text 285.00 (*0-521-20159-4*) Cambridge U Pr.

— The Prosopography of the Later Roman Empire, A.D. 527-641, Vol. 3. 1626p. (C). 1992. text 375.00 (*0-521-20160-8*) Cambridge U Pr.

Martindale, Jane. Status, Authority & Regional Power: Aquitaine & France, 9th-12th Centuries. LC 95-30953. (Collected Studies: Vol. CS488). 400p. 1997. 109.95 (*0-86078-480-0*, Pub. by Variorum) Ashgate Pub Co.

Martindale, Kathleen. Un Popular Culture: Lesbian Writing after the Sex Wars. LC 96-47153. (SUNY Series, Identities in the Classroom). 224p. (C). 1997. text 59.50 (*0-7914-3289-0*); pap. text 19.95 (*0-7914-3290-4*) State U NY Pr.

— Unpopular Culture: Lesbian Writing after the Sex Wars. 1997. 18.95 (*0-614-22147-1*) St U NY Geneseo.

***Martindale, Lee.** Such a Pretty Face: Tales of Power & Abundance. LC 00-8903. 2000. pap. write for info. (*1-892065-27-4*) Meisha Merlin.

***Martindale, Lee, ed.** Such a Pretty Face. 372p. 2000. pap. 16.00 (*1-892065-28-2*) Meisha Merlin.

Martindale, Marianne, ed. Disciplined Ladies: A Cornucopia of Feminine Discipline. 144p. 1997. 34.95 (*0-9524368-7-6*, Pub. by Wildfire Club) LPC InBook.

Martindale, Meredith & Mathews, Nancy M. Lilla Cabot Perry: An American Impressionist. LC 90-61820. (Illus.). 164p. 1991. pap. text 29.95 (*0-940979-14-4*) Natl Museum Women.

Martindale, Meredith, et al. Lilla Cabot Perry: An American Impressionist. (Illus.). 164p. 1995. pap. 35.00 (*0-7892-0045-7*, Cross Riv Pr) Abbeville Pr.

Martindale, Robert R. The 13th Mission: Guest of the Emperor in the Notorius Omori Prison in Tokyo. LC 98-28263. (Illus.). 280p. 1999. 24.95 (*1-57168-252-X*, Eakin Pr) Sunbelt Media.

***Martindale, Robert R. & Martindale, Adeline.** The Elements of Power. LC 99-91891. 2000. 25.00 (*0-7388-1384-2*); pap. 18.00 (*0-7388-1385-0*) Xlibris Corp.

Martindale, Robert R., jt. auth. see Meier, Gladys H.

***Martindale, Robert W.** Alex. LC 00-190577. 2000. 25.00 (*0-7388-1484-9*); pap. 18.00 (*0-7388-1485-7*) Xlibris Corp.

Martindale, T. Chris. Nightblood. 336p. (Orig.). 1990. mass mkt. 4.95 (*0-446-35530-5*) Warner Bks.

— The Voice in the Basement. Zion, Claire, ed. 288p. (Orig.). 1993. mass mkt. 4.99 (*0-671-76012-2*) PB.

— Where the Chill Waits. 1991. mass mkt. 4.95 (*0-446-35532-1*) Warner Bks.

Martindale, Wayne, ed. see Lewis, C. S.

***Martindale, Wink.** Winking at Life. 2000. 24.95 (*0-9677914-1-3*) Century Hill.

Martindell, E. W. A Bibliography of the Works of Rudyard Kipling. LC 72-3118. (English Literature Ser.: No. 33). 1972. reprint ed. lib. bdg. 75.00 (*0-8383-1514-3*) M S G Haskell Hse.

Martine. Sexual Astrology. 251p. 1979. mass mkt. 6.99 (*0-440-18020-1*) Dell.

Martine, Arthur. Martine's Handbook of Etiquette. LC 95-37797. 176p. 1996. reprint ed. pap. 12.95 (*1-55709-429-2*) Applewood.

Martine-Barnes, Adrienne. The Crystal Sword. 224p. 1988. pap. 3.50 (*0-380-75454-1*, Avon Bks) Morrow Avon.

— The Fire Sword. 384p. (Orig.). 1984. pap. 3.95 (*0-380-87718-X*, Avon Bks) Morrow Avon.

— Rainbow Sword. 224p. 1988. pap. 3.50 (*0-380-75455-X*, Avon Bks) Morrow Avon.

— The Sea Sword. 196p. (Orig.). 1989. pap. 3.50 (*0-380-75456-8*, Avon Bks) Morrow Avon.

Martine-Barnes, Adrienne & Paxson, Diana L. The Shield Between the Worlds. 336p. 1995. mass mkt. 4.99 (*0-380-75802-4*, Avon Bks) Morrow Avon.

Martine-Barnes, Adrienne, jt. auth. see Paxson.

Martine-Barnes, Adrienne, jt. auth. see Paxson, Diana L.

Martine, Barrat. Do or Die. 1999. pap. 25.00 (*0-14-023371-7*, Viking) Viking Penguin.

Martine, Brian J. Indeterminacy & Intelligibility. LC 91-38674. (SUNY Series in Systematic Philosophy). 136p. (C). 1992. pap. text 19.95 (*0-7914-1174-5*) State U NY Pr.

— Individuals & Individuality. LC 83-5094. (SUNY Series in Philosophy). 93p. (C). 1984. pap. text 19.95 (*0-87395-828-4*) State U NY Pr.

Martine, George, et al, eds. Reproductive Change in India & Brazil. LC 99-932099. (Illus.). 432p. 1999. text 23.95 (*0-19-564291-0*) OUP.

Martine, James J. Critical Essays on Arthur Miller. (Critical Essays on American Literature Ser.). 240p. 1979. 49.00 (*0-8161-8258-2*, Hall Reference) Macmillan.

— Critical Essays on Eugene O'Neill. (Critical Essays on American Literature Ser.). 224p. 1984. 48.00 (*0-8161-8683-9*, G K Hall & Co) Mac Lib Ref.

— The Crucible: Politics, Property, & Pretense. LC 93-2843. (Masterwork Studies). 160p. 1993. 25.95 (*0-8057-8096-3*, Twyne) Mac Lib Ref.

Martine, James J., ed. American Novelists, 1910-1945, 3 vols., Set. (Dictionary of Literary Biography Ser.: Vol. 9). (Illus.). 1056p. 1981. text 155.00 (*0-8103-0931-9*) Gale.

Martine, Roberta. Basic Traffic Analysis. LC 93-8268. 634p. (C). 1993. 105.00 (*0-13-335407-5*) P-H.

Martine, Roberta & Mercer, Robert. LAN Basics. 89p. (Orig.). 1992. pap. write for info. (*0-917845-20-X*) Intertec IL.

Martine, Roddy. Scotland: The Land & the Whisky. (Illus.). 224p. 1995. 55.00 (*0-7195-5351-2*, Pub. by John Murray) Trafalgar.

— Scottish Clan & Family Names: Their Arms, Origins & Tartans. (Illus.). 224p. 1993. pap. 22.95 (*1-85158-418-8*, Pub. by Mainstream Pubng) Trafalgar.

Martine, Roddy, jt. auth. see Astaire, Lesley.

Martine, Roderick. Single Malt Scotch. LC 97-7238. (Illus.). 144p. 1997. 30.00 (*1-56799-440-7*, Friedman-Fairfax) M Friedman Pub Grp Inc.

Martine, Yvonne, jt. auth. see Clark, Linda.

Martineau, et al. Canada Labour Relations Board Policies & Procedures. braille ed. 608p. 1986. 125.00 (*0-409-81975-1*, MICHIE) LEXIS Pub.

Martineau, ed. see Stendhal, pseud.

***Martineau, Andrea.** What Can I Tell My Child about God? 32p. 1999. reprint ed. pap. 0.70 (*0-88028-207-X*, 719) Forward Movement.

Martineau, Harriet. Deerbrook: A Novel, 3 vols., 2 bks., Set. LC 79-8170. reprint ed. 84.50 (*0-404-62034-5*) AMS Pr.

— The Hour & the Man, 3 vols. in 1. LC 75-148341. reprint ed. 57.50 (*0-404-08890-2*) AMS Pr.

— How to Observe Morals & Manners. 239p. 1988. pap. 24.95 (*0-88738-751-9*) Transaction Pubs.

— Martyr Age of the United States. LC 73-82206. (Anti-Slavery Crusade in America Ser.). 1978. reprint ed. 18.95 (*0-405-00644-6*) Ayer.

— Miscellanies, 2 vols., Set. LC 79-148342. reprint ed. 71.00 (*0-404-08887-2*) AMS Pr.

— Retrospect of Western Travel, 2 Vols. LC 68-24988. (American History & Americana Ser.: No. 47). 1969. reprint ed. lib. bdg. 150.00 (*0-8383-0165-7*) M S G Haskell Hse.

— Retrospect of Western Travel. rev. expanded ed. (American History Through Literature Ser.). 224p. 2000. text 62.95 (*0-7656-0213-X*); pap. text 21.95 (*0-7656-0214-8*) M E Sharpe.

— Retrospect of Western Travel, 3 vols., Set. LC 68-57623. (Illus.). 1970. reprint ed. lib. bdg. 125.00 (*0-8371-0967-1*, MAWT) Greenwood.

— Retrospect of Western Travel, 3 vols., Set. (BCL1 - U. S. History Ser.). 1991. reprint ed. lib. bdg. 225.00 (*0-7812-6013-2*) Rprt Serv.

— Retrospect of Western Travel, 3 vols., Vol. 1. LC 68-57623. (Illus.). 1970. reprint ed. lib. bdg. 55.00 (*0-8371-1969-3*, MAWU) Greenwood.

— Retrospect of Western Travel, 3 vols., Vol. 2. LC 68-57623. (Illus.). 1969. reprint ed. lib. bdg. 55.00 (*0-8371-0968-X*, MAWV) Greenwood.

— Retrospect of Western Travel, 3 vols., Vol. 3. LC 68-57623. (Illus.). 1970. reprint ed. lib. bdg. 55.00 (*0-8371-0969-8*, MAWX) Greenwood.

— Society in America, 3 vols. LC 01-27890. reprint ed. write for info. (*0-404-04260-0*) AMS Pr.

— Society in America. Lipset, Seymour M., ed. LC 80-27647. (Social Science Classics Ser.). 357p. 1981. reprint ed. pap. 24.95 (*0-87855-853-5*) Transaction Pubs.

Martineau, Harriet, tr. see Comte, Auguste.

Martineau, Henri, ed. see Stendhal, pseud.

Martineau, James. A Study of Spinoza. 3rd ed. LC 78-152994. (Select Bibliographies Reprint Ser.). 1977. reprint ed. 25.95 (*0-8369-5746-6*) Ayer.

Martineau, Jane & Robison, Andrew, eds. The Glory of Venice: Art in the Eighteenth Century. LC 94-61010. (Illus.). 528p. 1997. pap. 35.00 (*0-300-06186-2*) Yale U Pr.

Martineau, Jennifer W., jt. auth. see McCauley, Cynthia D.

Martineau, LaVan. The Rocks Begin to Speak. LC 72-85137. (Illus.). 210p. 1973. 19.50 (*0-916122-30-1*) KC Pubns.

— Southern Paiutes: Legends Lore Language & Lineage. LC 92-74128. (Illus.). 336p. 1992. 24.95 (*0-88714-070-X*) KC Pubns.

Martineau, Louis, ed. see Stendhal, pseud.

***Martineau, Lynne, ed.** Pali Workbook: Pali Vocabulary from the 10-Day Vipassana Courses. (Illus.). 159p. 2000. spiral bd., wbk. ed. 14.00 (*1-928706-04-5*) Vipassana Res Pubns.

***Martineau, Michael James.** Let's Get Rowdy! 300p. 2000. pap. 12.98 (*1-930739-17-6*) Internet Bk CA.

Martineau, Robert J. Appellate Justice in England & the United States: A Comparative Analysis. LC 90-84310. xxii, 344p. 1990. lib. bdg. 60.00 (*0-89941-733-7*, 306710) W S Hein.

— Cases & Materials on Appellate Practice & Procedure. (American Casebook Ser.). 565p. (C). 1986. 48.50 (*0-314-30775-3*) West Pub.

— Drafting Legislation & Rules in Plain English. 155p. (C). 1991. pap. 17.00 (*0-314-89023-8*) West Pub.

— Drafting Legislation & Rules in Plain English, of Drafting Exercises. (American Casebook Ser.). 88p. (C). 1991. pap. text, teacher ed. write for info. (*0-314-90368-2*) West Pub.

— Fundamentals of Modern Appellate Advocacy. LC 85-50347. 231p. 1985. pap. 25.00 (*0-318-11702-9*) West Group.

Martineau, Robert J. & Novello, David. Clean Air Act Handbook. LC 97-24110. 1997. write for info. (*1-57073-503-4*) Amer Bar Assn.

***Martineau, Susan.** Gruesome Grub & Disgusting Dishes: Deliciously Edible Recipes! (Illus.). 32p. (J). (gr. 2-7). 2000. pap. 6.95 (*0-7373-0428-6*, 04286W, Pub. by Lowell Hse Juvenile) NTC Contemp Pub Co.

Martinec, Jaroslav, jt. auth. see Hall, Dorothy.

Martinec, Zden E. Boundary-Value Problems for Gravimetric Determination of a Precise Geoid. LC 98 35553. (Lecture in Earth Sciences Ser.: Vol. 73). (Illus.). xii, 240p. 1998. pap. 99.00 (*3-540-64462-8*) Spr-Verlag.

Martinek & Martinkova, eds. Hassensteinii a Lobkowicz Vol. I: Epistulae de re Publica. (LAT.). 1969. 27.95 (*3-322-00195-4*, T1363, Pub. by B G Teubner) U of Mich Pr.

— Hassensteinii a Lobkowicz Vol. II: Epistulae ad Familiares. (LAT.). 1969. 59.50 (*3-322-00194-6*, T1364, Pub. by B G Teubner) U of Mich Pr.

Martinek, Thomas J., et al. Pygmalion in the Gym: Causes & Effects of Expectations in Teaching & Coaching. LC 81-81634. (Illus.). 160p. 1982. reprint ed. pap. 49.60 (*0-608-07103-X*, 206733000009) Bks Demand.

Martinell, Patricia, et al. Study Guide & Manual for the National Certification Examinations for Nurse Practitioners & Other Primary Health Care Providers. 125p. 1989. pap. text 19.95 (*0-8290-1279-6*) Irvington.

Martinelli, Alberto. International Markets & Global Firms: A Comparative Study of Organized Business in the Chemistry Industry. (Studies in Neo-Corporatism). 288p. 1991. text 60.00 (*0-8039-8436-7*) Sage.

Martinelli, Alberto & Smelser, Neil J. Economy & Society: Overviews in Economic Sociology. (International Sociology Ser.). (Illus.). 304p. 1991. 60.00 (*0-8039-8416-2*); pap. 24.00 (*0-8039-8417-0*) Sage.

Martinelli, Alberto, jt. auth. see Chiesi, Antonio M.

***Martinelli Company Staff.** Techniques in Countersurveillance: The Fine Art of Bug Extermination in the Real World of Intelligence Gathering. 120p. 1999. pap. 18.00 (*1-58160-020-8*) Paladin Pr.

Martinelli, Franco, tr. see Cucchi, Enzo.

Martinelli, G. Standard Model, Hadron Phenomenology & Weak Decays on the Lattice: Dir in HEP, Vol. 8, Vol. 8. 350p. 1997. pap. 61.00 (*981-02-0468-X*); text 130.00 (*981-02-0467-1*) World Scientific Pub.

Martinelli, Gabrieli M., jt. auth. see Goldoni, Carlo.

Martinelli, Jeanne E. Across the Spirituality Pole. 32p. (Orig.). 1989. pap. text 5.00 (*0-685-29005-0*) J E Martinelli.

Martinelli, L. W., jt. auth. see Ladiges, P. Y.

Martinelli, Maria C. Al Dente: All the Secrets of Italy's Genuine Home-Style Cooking. Nopar, Charles, tr. from ITA. (Illus.). 192p. 1997. pap. 19.95 (*88-7301-141-1*, Pub. by Gremese Intl) Natl Bk Netwk.

Martinelli, Maria Chiara. How to Eat Out in Italy. (Illus.). 176p. pap. 6.95 (*88-7301-095-4*, Pub. by Gremese Intl) Natl Bk Netwk.

Martinelli, Phylis C., jt. auth. see Sensi-Isolani, Paola A.

Martinello. Interdisciplinary Inquiry. 2nd ed. LC 99-28065. (Illus.). 214p. 1999. pap. text 25.00 (*0-13-923954-5*) P-H.

Martinello, Marian, et al. Hopes, Prayers & Promises. (Texas Ser.: Vol. 2). (Illus.). 48p. (J). (gr. k-8). 1986. 12.95 (*0-935857-05-2*); pap. write for info. (*0-935857-06-0*) Texart.

Martinello, Marian L. Cedar Fever: Story of a German-Texan Girl During World War I. LC 92-73295. (Multicultural Texas Ser.). (Illus.). 212p. (YA). (gr. 7-9). 1992. pap. 7.95 (*0-931722-95-0*) Corona Pub.

— The Search for Emma's Story: A Model For Humanities Detective Work. LC 86-30005. (Illus.). 224p. (Orig.). 1987. pap. 12.95 (*0-87565-070-8*) Tex Christian.

Martinello, Marian L. & Nesmith, Samuel P. With Domingo Leal in San Antonio, 1734. Institute of Texan Cultures Research Staff, ed. (University of Texas Institute of Texan Culture Young Readers Ser.). (Illus.). 78p. (Orig.). (J). (gr. 5-8). 1980. pap. 3.95 (*0-933164-40-8*) U of Tex Inst Tex Culture.

Martinengo-Cesaresco, Evelyn. Essays in the Study of Folksongs. 1976. lib. bdg. 59.95 (*0-8490-1785-8*) Gordon Pr.

Martiner, William. Visual Basic Programmer's Guide to Web Development. LC 97-20877. 460p. 1997. pap. 34.99 (*0-471-19382-8*) Wiley.

Martiner, William, et al. Building Distributed Applications with ADO. LC 98-51575. (Illus.). 464p. 1999. pap. 39.99 (*0-471-31701-2*) Wiley.

Martinerie, Andree. Les Autres Jours. (FRE.). 1974. pap. 10.95 (*0-7859-4033-2*) Fr & Eur.

Martines, Julia, tr. see Brucker, Gene A., ed.

Martines, Lauro. An Italian Renaissance Sextet: Six Tales in Historical Context. Baca, Murtha, tr. from ITA. 250p. 1994. 28.00 (*1-56886-001-3*) Marsilio Pubs.

— Power & Imagination: City-States in Renaissance Italy. LC 87-29843. (Illus.). 400p. (C). 1988. reprint ed. pap. text 17.95 (*0-8018-3643-3*) Johns Hopkins.

Martinet. Comeons Comebacks & Kissoffs. 1997. pap. 95.60 (*0-312-17122-6*) St Martin.

Martinet, A. V., jt. auth. see Thompson, A. J.

Martinet, Andre. From the Steppes to the Seas: Indo-European & the "Indo-Europeans" Weeks, David, tr. from FRE. (Illus.). 272p. 1989. text 60.00 (*0-89241-459-6*) Caratzas.

— Le Langage. (Methodique Ser.). 1544p. 46.95 (*0-686-56443-X*) Fr & Eur.

— Le Langage. deluxe ed. (FRE.). 1544p. 1968. 135.00 (*0-7859-4624-1*) Fr & Eur.

Martinet, Andre & Walter, Henriette. Dictionnaire de la Prononciation Francaise dans Son Usage Reel: Dictionary of French Pronunciation in Its Real Application. (FRE.). 932p. 1973. 125.00 (*0-7859-0729-7*, M-4739) Fr & Eur.

Martinet, Francoise. Ballet Center Work. Crist, Linda A., ed. (Illus.). 87p. (Orig.). (C). 1988. pap. 12.00 (*0-9620289-0-8*) Crist Pubns.

Martinet, Jeanne. The Art of Mingling: Easy, Proven Techniques for Mastering Any Room. 160p. (Orig.). 1992. pap. 9.95 (*0-312-08316-5*) St Martin.

***Martinet, Jeanne.** Artful Dodging. LC 00-27844. 256p. 2000. pap. 11.95 (*0 312 25460 1*) St Martin.

Martinet, Jeanne. Come-Ons, Comebacks & Kiss-Offs. LC 97-20048. (Illus.). 192p. 1997. pap. 11.95 (*0-312-16809-8*) St Martin.

— Getting Beyond "Hello" How to Meet, Mingle & Turn Casual Acquaintances into Friends & Lovers. LC 95-47093. 208p. 1996. pap. 10.95 (*0-8065-1785-9*, Citadel Pr) Carol Pub Group.

Martinet, Jeanne. The Year You Were Born, 1984. LC 91-34577. (Year You Were Born Ser.). (Illus.). 56p. (J). 1992. mass mkt. 7.95 (*0-688-11079-7*, Wm Morrow) Morrow Avon.

Martinet, Jeanne. The Year You Were Born, 1983. LC 91-31605. (Year You Were Born Ser.). (Illus.). 56p. (J). 1992. pap. 7.95 (*0-688-11077-0*, Wm Morrow) Morrow Avon.

Martinet, Jeanne. The Year You Were Born, 1986. (Illus.). 56p. (J). (gr. 2 up). 1993. mass mkt. 7.95 (*0-688-11968-9*, Wm Morrow) Morrow Avon.

— The Year You Were Born, 1987. (Illus.). 56p. (J). (gr. 2 up). 1993. mass mkt. 7.95 (*0-688-11970-0*, Wm Morrow) Morrow Avon.

— The Year You Were Born, 1982. (Illus.). 56p. (J). (gr. 4-7). 1994. mass mkt. 7.95 (*0-688-12877-7*, Wm Morrow) Morrow Avon.

— The Year You Were Born, 1988. (Illus.). 56p. (J). (gr. 1 up). 1995. 15.93 (*0-688-13861-6*, Wm Morrow); mass mkt. 7.95 (*0-688-13862-4*, Wm Morrow) Morrow Avon.

— The Year You Were Born, 1989. (Illus.). 56p. (J). 1996. mass mkt. 7.95 (*0-688-14386-5*, Wm Morrow) Morrow Avon.

Martinet, Jeanne. Year You Were Born, 1989. (Illus.). 56p. (J). 1996. lib. bdg. 14.93 (*0-688-14385-7*, Wm Morrow) Morrow Avon.

Martinet, Y. Clinical & Biological Basis of Lung Cancer Prevention. LC 97-29086. (Respiratory Pharmacology & Pharmacotherapy Ser.). 1997. write for info. (*0-8176-5778-9*) Birkhauser.

M

An Asterisk (*) at the beginning of an entry indicates that the title is appearing for the first time.

Martinet, Y., et al, eds. Clinical & Biological Basis of Lung Cancer Prevention. (Respiratory Pharmacology & Pharmacotherapy Ser.). (Illus.). 350p. 1997. 135.00 (*3-7643-5778-9*) Spr-Verlag.

Martinette, Charles G. & Meisel, Louis K. Pin-Up Poster Book: The Edward Runci Collection. Bennett, Ann, ed. LC 97-69357. (Edward Runci Collection). (Illus.). 48p. 1999. pap. 17.95 (*1-888054-15-8*, 54158) Collectors Pr.

Martinetti. Deformation of Soils, Vol. 4. 1991. 136.00 (*90-5410-005-2*) Ashgate Pub Co.

Martinetti, John. Reasons to Believe Today. (Studies in Theology: Vol. 11).Tr. of Ragioni Per Credere Oggi. 216p. (Orig.). 1996. pap. 25.00 (*0-87462-635-8*) Marquette.

Martinetti, Ron & Hansen, Vagn. The Ultimate James Dean Scrapbook. Pitts, Marty, ed. (American Legends Scrapbook Ser.). 1997. pap. 12.00 (*0-9658671-7-X*) Am Legends.

Martinetti, Ronald. The James Dean Story: A Myth-Shattering Biography of a Hollywood Legend. (Illus.). 192p. 1996. mass mkt. 5.99 (*0-8065-8004-6*, Citadel Stars) Carol Pub Group.

— The James Dean Story: A Myth-Shattering Biography of an Icon. (Illus.). 256p. 1995. 18.95 (*1-55972-270-3*, Birch Ln Pr) Carol Pub Group.

Martinex. Latino Homicide. 2000. 75.00 (*0-8133-6801-4*) HarpC.

***Martinex, Javier & Robinson, Joseph K.** Teacher Templates for Microsoft Office: Intermediate. (Illus.). 112p. 2000. pap., teacher ed. 18.95 (*1-57690-771-6*, TCM 2771) Tchr Create Mat.

Martinex, T. M., et al. Investigating Density, Miscibility, & Solubility. Stanitski, Conrad L., ed. (Modular Laboratory Program in Chemistry Ser.). 12p. (C). 1995. pap. text 1.50 (*0-87540-474-X*, PROP 474-X) Chem Educ Res.

Martinez. Astrophotography II. (Illus.). 172p. 1987. text 18.95 (*0-943396-13-1*) Willmann-Bell.

— Does Turnout Matter? 2000. 55.00 (*0-8133-6851-0*); pap. 20.00 (*0-8133-6850-2*) Westview.

— Zarela Mexican Table. 2000. 25.00 (*0-06-016837-4*) HarperTrade.

Martinez & Howard-Vital. Entering School Leadership. LC 97-220438. 182p. (C). 1997. per. 33.95 (*0-7872-3689-6*, 41368901) Kendall-Hunt.

Martinez & Temple, Charles. Children's Books in Children's Hands. LC 97-9950. 580p. 1997. 67.67 (*0-205-16995-3*) Allyn.

Martinez, A. & Cuttitta, F., eds. Adrenomedullin. LC 97-75046. 340p. Date not set. 81.00 (*90-5199-360-9*, 360-9) IOS Press.

Martinez-A, C., jt. ed. see Kroemer, G.

Martinez, A. Julio, ed. Free Living Amebas: Natural History, Preventions, Diagnosis, Pathology, & Treatment of Disease. 168p. 1985. 99.00 (*0-8493-6631-3*, QR201, CRC Reprint) Franklin.

Martinez, Abelardo, tr. Fertilidad y Esterilidad en Ganado Lechero.Tr. of Dairy Cattle Fertility & Sterility. (SPA., Illus.). 79p. (Orig.). 1996. pap. text 12.00 (*0-932147-29-1*, Hoards Dairyman) Hoard & Sons Co.

Martinez, Adolfo, et al. Agronomic & Economic Evaluation of Urea Placement & Sulfur-Coated Urea for Irrigated Paddy in Farmers' Fields in Eastern India, P-4. Frederick, Ernest D. & Roth, E. N., eds. LC 83-10874. (Papers). (Illus.). 36p. 1983. pap. text 4.00 (*0-88090-044-X*) Intl Fertilizer.

— Fertilizer Use Statistics in Crop Production. LC 82-15856. (Technical Bulletin Ser.: No. T-24). (Illus.). 42p. (Orig.). 1982. pap. text 4.00 (*0-88090-042-3*) Intl Fertilizer.

Martinez, Adolfo, tr. see Brooks, B. David & Dalby, Rex K.

***Martinez, Agustin, ed.** Multicultural Spanish Dictionary. LC 99-22373. 234p. 1999. pap. 24.95 (*1-887563-45-8*, Pub. by Schreiber Pub) Natl Bk Netwk.

***Martinez, Al.** The Last City Room. LC 00-31738. 272p. 2000. 22.95 (*0-312-20901-0*, Thomas Dunne) St Martin.

Martinez, Alba N., tr. see Mora, Pat.

Martinez, Albert B. Baedeker of the Argentine Republic. 1976. lib. bdg. 59.95 (*0-87968-695-2*) Gordon Pr.

Martinez, Alejandro C., et al. The Woman Who Outshone the Sun (La Mujer Que Brillaba Aun Mas Que el Sol) LC 91-16646. (Illus.). 32p. (YA). (ps-3). 1991. 14.95 (*0-89239-101-4*) Childrens Book Pr.

— The Woman Who Outshone the Sun (La Mujer Que Brillaba Aun Mas Que el Sol) LC 91-16646. (ENG & SPA., Illus.). 30p. (YA). (ps-3). 1994. pap. 7.95 (*0-89239-126-X*) Childrens Book Pr.

Martinez, Alicia. Feeling Fit. LC 90-10864. (Smart Talk Ser.). (Illus.). 128p. (J). (gr. 5-9). 1997. pap. 2.95 (*0-8167-2141-6*) Troll Communs.

Martinez Alier, Juan, jt. see Guha, Ramachandra.

Martinez-Alier, Verena. Marriage, Class & Colour in Nineteenth-Century Cuba. 224p. 1989. pap. text 16.95 (*0-472-06405-3*, 06405) U of Mich Pr.

Martinez, Almoyna J. Dicionario de Espanol Portugues - Spanish - Portuguese Dictionary. (POR & SPA.). 1068p. 1990. 75.00 (*0-8288-8541-9*) Fr & Eur.

— Dicionario de Portugues Espanhol.Tr. of Portuguese - Spanish Dictionary. (POR & SPA.). 1332p. 1990. 75.00 (*0-8288-8540-0*) Fr & Eur.

Martinez, Alvarez A. El Tiempo y Yo: Articulos Ensayos, Cronicas. (UPREX, Ensayo Ser.: No. 5). 317p. (C). 1972. pap. 1.50 (*0-8477-0005-4*) U of PR Pr.

***Martinez, Ana Margarita & Montane, Diana.** Estrecho de Traicion: La Historia de la Fatidica Union Entr Ana Margarita Martinez y Juan Pablo Roque. LC 99-66890. (Coleccion Cuba y sus Jueces). (SPA., Illus.). 149p. 1999. pap. 12.00 (*0-89729-912-4*) Ediciones.

Martinez, Andrea P., ed. Planetary & Proto-Planetary Nebulae: From IRAS to ISO. (C). 1987. text 168.00 (*90-277-2517-9*) Kluwer Academic.

***Martinez, Andres.** Doubling Down: A 24/7 Odyssey Through the New Las Vegas. LC 99-29309. 352p. 1999. 25.00 (*0-375-50181-9*) Villard Books.

— 24/7. 352p. 2000. pap. 13.95 (*0-440-50909-2*) Dell.

Martinez, Andrew J. Marine Life of the North Atlantic: Canada to New England. (Illus.). 265p. (Orig.). pap. 30.00 (*0-9640131-0-X*) Martinez & Katz.

— Marine Life of the North Atlantic: Canada to New England. 2nd ed. LC 98-48695. (Illus.). 272p. (Orig.). 1999. pap. 30.00 (*0-89272-455-2*) Down East.

***Martinez, Anne.** Get Certified & Get Ahead. 3rd ed. 2000. pap. 24.99 (*0-07-212395-8*) Osborne-McGraw.

Martinez, Anne. Get Certified & Get Ahead: Millenium Edition. LC 98-55403. (Illus.). 640p. 1999. pap. 24.99 (*0-07-134781-X*) McGraw.

***Martinez, Anne.** Get Cisco Certified & Get Ahead. LC 99-33028. (Illus.). 397p. 1999. pap. 24.99 (*0-07-135258-9*) McGraw.

— Get Linux Certified & Get Ahead. (Computing Careers Ser.). 416p. 1999. 24.99 (*0-07-212333-8*) McGrw-H Intl.

Martinez, Anne. Getting Ahead by Getting Certified. LC 98-9328. 554p. 1998. pap. 24.95 (*0-07-041127-1*) McGraw.

Martinez, Anthony, jt. auth. see Bross, Arthur.

Martinez, Anthony T. The Book of Emmanuel. Zinicola, Barbara D., ed. (Illus.). 112p. 1996. 10.00 (*0-9653802-0-3*) Reliant Pr.

Martinez, Antonio J. Self-Instructional Modules in English As a Second Language for Spanish-Speaking Students, 2 vols., I. (Orig.). (C). 1989. 8.95 (*0-8477-3323-8*) U of PR Pr.

— Self-Instructional Modules in English As a Second Language for Spanish-Speaking Students, 2 vols., Set. (Orig.). (C). 1989. write for info. (*0-8477-3330-0*) U of PR Pr.

— Self-Instructional Modules in English As a Second Language for Spanish-Speaking Students, 2 vols., Vol. II. 88p. (Orig.). (C). 1989. 5.00 (*0-8477-3329-7*) U of PR Pr.

Martinez, Antonio R. Luis Barragan. LC 96-77648. (Illus.). 252p. 1996. 60.00 (*1-885254-44-X*, Pub. by Monacelli Pr) Penguin Putnam.

Martinez, Aquilina, tr. see Dussel, Enrique D.

Martinez, Arthur C., jt. auth. see Madigan, Charles.

Martinez, Beatriz S., tr. see Hume, Maggie.

Martinez, Benjamin & Block, Jacqueline. Visual Forces: An Introduction to Design. 2nd ed. LC 93-29027. 228p. 1994. pap. text 61.33 (*0-13-948290-3*) P-H.

Martinez, Bernice B. Bass De, see Sims, William E. & Bass De Martinez, Bernice B.

Martinez-Bonati, Felix. Don Quixote & the Poetics of the Novel. Fox, Dian, tr. LC 92-5913. 320p. 1992. text 39.95 (*0-8014-2359-7*) Cornell U Pr.

— Fictive Discourse & the Structures of Literature: A Phenomenological Approach. exp. rev. ed. Silver, Philip W., tr. from SPA. LC 80-23628. 200p. 1981. 37.50 (*0-8014-1308-7*) Cornell U Pr.

Martinez-Brawley, Emilia E. Perspectives on the Small Community: Humanistic Views for Practitioners. LC 90-6439. 261p. 1990. 27.95 (*0-87101-183-2*) Natl Assn Soc Wkrs.

— Rural Social & Community Work in the U. S. & U. K. A Cross-Cultural Perspective. LC 81-23464. 279p. 1982. 55.00 (*0-275-90855-0*, C0855, Praeger Pubs) Greenwood.

— Seven Decades of Rural Social Work: From Country Life Commission to Rural Caucus. LC 80-24185. 275p. 1981. 65.00 (*0-275-90678-7*, C0678, Praeger Pubs) Greenwood.

Martinez-Brawley, Emilia E. & Delevan, Sybil M. Transferring Technology in the Personal Social Services. LC 93-16123. 210p. (C). 1993. 24.95 (*0-87101-226-X*) Natl Assn Soc Wkrs.

***Martinez-Brawley, Emilia E. & Zorita, Paz M. B.** Close to Home: Human Services in the Small Community. LC 99-88670. 1999. write for info. (*0-87101-312-6*, NASW Pr) Natl Assn Soc Wkrs.

Martinez Cachero, Jose M., ed. see Azorin, pseud.

Martinez Calvo, Lorenzo. Diccionario Ruso-Espanol. (RUS & SPA.). 2000p. 75.00 (*0-7859-0884-6*, S-50410) Fr & Eur.

Martinez, Carla, et al. Color Voices Place. 120p. (Orig.). 1997. pap. 12.95 (*0-9638843-9-5*) Mille Grazie.

Martinez, Carla, ed. see Punches, Laurie C.

Martinez, Carlos. Breve Historia de Tabasco (Concise History of Tabasco) (Breves Historias de los Estados de Mexico Ser.). (SPA.). 1996. pap. 13.99 (*968-16-4562-6*, Pub. by Fondo) Continental Bk.

— An Unendurable Love. 44p. 1999. 5.00 (*1-889289-30-2*) Ye Olde Font Shoppe.

Martinez, Carlos G. New Mexico Workers' Compensation Manual, 1996-1997. LC 93-27860. 684p. 1997. ring bd. 99.95 (*1-57292-048-3*); ring bd., suppl. ed. 69.95 (*1-57292-047-5*) Austin & Winfield.

***Martinez, Carlos G.** Turning the World Upside Down: How to Be a Radical Witness for Jesus. LC 99-47235. 2000. pap. 8.99 (*0-8163-1760-7*) Pacific Pr Pub Assn.

Martinez, Carol. Paco y Ana Aprenden A Compartir. (Paco y Ana Aprenden Serie).Tr. of Paco & Ana Learn to Share. (SPA., Illus.). 34p. (J). 1996. pap. text 2.50 (*0-311-38593-1*, Edit Mundo) Casa Bautista.

— Paco y Ana Aprenden A Confiar en Dios. (Paco y Ana Aprenden Serie).Tr. of Paco & Ana Learn to Trust God. (SPA., Illus.). 32p. (J). 1996. pap. text 2.50 (*0-311-38594-X*, Edit Mundo) Casa Bautista.

Martinez, Carol. Paco y Ana Aprenden Acerca de la Amabilidad: Frankie & Ann Learn about Kindness. (Paco y Ana Aprenden Ser.). (SPA., Illus.). 32p. (Orig.). (J). (gr. 2-4). 1988. pap. 2.50 (*0-311-38590-7*, Edit Mundo) Casa Bautista.

— Paco y Ana Aprenden Acerca de la Amistad: Frankie & Ann Learn about Friendship. (Paco y Ana Aprenden Ser.). (SPA., Illus.). (Orig.). (J). (gr. 2-4). 1988. pap. 2.50 (*0-311-38589-3*, Edit Mundo) Casa Bautista.

— Paco y Ana Aprenden Acerca de la Honradez: Frankie & Ann Learn about Honesty. (Paco y Ana Aprenden Ser.). (SPA., Illus.). 32p. (Orig.). (J). (gr. 2-4). 1988. pap. 2.50 (*0-311-38587-7*, Edit Mundo) Casa Bautista.

— Paco y Ana Aprenden Acerca de la Obediencia: Frankie & Ann Learn about Obedience. (Paco y Ana Aprenden Ser.). (SPA., Illus.). 32p. (Orig.). (J). (gr. 2-4). 1988. pap. 2.50 (*0-311-38588-5*, Edit Mundo) Casa Bautista.

Martinez, Carol. Paco Y Ana Aprenen Atener Dominio Propio. (Paco y Ana Aprenden Ser.).Tr. of Frankie & Ann Learn Self Control. (SPA., Illus.). 32p. (J). 1995. pap. 2.50 (*0-311-38591-5*, Edit Mundo) Casa Bautista.

— Paco Yana Aprenden Atener Valor. (Paco y Ana Aprenden Ser.).Tr. of Frankie & ann Learn to Have Courage. (SPA., Illus.). 32p. (J). 1995. 2.50 (*0-311-38592-3*, Edit Mundo) Casa Bautista.

Martinez, Carol, tr. see Cooper, Polly.

Martinez, Cathy L., jt. ed. see Long, Robert F.

Martinez, Cecelia, jt. auth. see Geist, Harold.

Martinez, Concha, et al. Truth in Perspective: Recent Issues in Logic, Representation & Ontology. (Avebury Series in Philosophy). 442p. 1998. text 84.95 (*1-85972-698-4*, Pub. by Ashgate Pub) Ashgate Pub Co.

Martinez, Constantino F. Diccionario de la Mitologia Clasica, Vol. 2, I-Z. 8th ed. (SPA.). 304p. 1991. pap. 14.95 (*0-7859-6447-9*) Fr & Eur.

Martinez Cruz, Abelardo. Lexico de Antropologia. 3rd ed. (SPA.). 184p. 1975. pap. 9.95 (*0-8288-5913-2*, S50038) Fr & Eur.

Martinez Cuitino, Luis, ed. see Garcia Lorca, Federico.

***Martinez, D. M.** Crow Cut Cove. LC 99-72984. 225p. 2000. pap. 10.00 (*0-9672246-0-8*) AllensRusk.

Martinez, D. P., ed. The Worlds of Japanese Popular Culture: Gender, Shifting Boundaries & Global Culture. LC 98-7086. (Contemporary Japanese Society Ser.). (Illus.). 224p. (C). 1998. 64.95 (*0-521-63128-9*); pap. 19.95 (*0-521-63729-5*) Cambridge U Pr.

Martinez, D. P., jt. ed. see Van Bremen, Jan.

Martinez Dalmau, Eduardo. Study on the Synoptic Gospels. 1964. 10.00 (*0-8315-0013-1*) Speller.

Martinez, Daniel. The Non-Lawyer Book to Form a Corporation in Cd. Juarez, Chihuahua. 400p. (Orig.). 1994. pap. 49.99 (*0-9642059-2-0*) Infomex.

— The Non-Lawyer Book to Form a Corporation in Guadalajara, Jalisco. 400p. (Orig.). 1994. pap. 49.99 (*0-9642059-5-5*) Infomex.

— The Non-Lawyer Book to Form a Corporation in Mexico City. 400p. (Orig.). 1994. pap. 49.99 (*0-9642059-0-4*) Infomex.

— The Non-Lawyer Book to Form a Corporation in Monterrey, N. L. 400p. (Orig.). 1994. pap. 49.99 (*0-9642059-4-7*) Infomex.

— The Non-Lawyer Book to Form a Corporation in Nuevo Laredo, Tamaulipas. 400p. (Orig.). 1994. pap. 49.99 (*0-9642059-1-2*) Infomex.

— The Non-Lawyer Book to Form a Corporation in Puebla, Puebla. (Orig.). 1994. pap. 49.99 (*0-9642059-8-X*) Infomex.

— The Non-Lawyer Book to Form a Corporation in Queretaro, Mexico. 400p. (Orig.). 1994. pap. 49.99 (*0-9642059-7-1*) Infomex.

— The Non-Lawyer Book to Form a Corporation in San Luis Potosi. 400p. (Orig.). 1994. pap. 49.99 (*0-9642059-6-3*) Infomex.

— The Non-Lawyer Book to Form a Corporation in Tijuana, B. C. 400p. (Orig.). 1994. pap. 49.99 (*0-9642059-3-9*) Infomex.

— The Non-Lawyer Book to Form a Corporation in Veracruz, Jalapa. 400p. (Orig.). 1994. pap. 49.99 (*0-9642059-9-8*) Infomex.

Martinez, David. A Leather Trisagion from Egypt: (P. Mich 799) (Illus.). 100p. (C). text 25.95 (*3-519-07669-1*) B G Teubner.

Martinez de Espinoza, Juan J. Diccionario Marino Espanol-Ingles, Ingles-Espanol Para Uso. (SPA.). 802p. 1989. 35.00 (*0-7859-6218-2*, 8473410483) Fr & Eur.

Martinez de Sousa, Jose. Diccionario de Tipografia y del Libro. 2nd ed. (SPA.). 1981. 55.95 (*0-7859-3680-7*, 8428311323) Fr & Eur.

Martinez De Souza, Jose. General Dictionary of Journalism: Diccionario General de Periodismo. (SPA.). 594p. 1981. pap. 75.00 (*0-8288-1320-5*, S40507) Fr & Eur.

Martinez de Toledo, Alfonso. Arcipreste de Talavera (Corbacho) Ciceri, Marcella, ed. (Nueva Austral Ser.: Vol. 95). (SPA.). 1991. pap. text 24.95 (*84-239-1895-5*) Elliots Bks.

— Atalaya de las Coronicas. Larkin, James B., ed. (Spanish Ser.: No. 10). (Illus.). xvi, 158p. 1983. 25.00 (*0-942260-29-5*) Hispanic Seminary.

Martinez de Velasco, Luis, ed. see Kant, Immanuel.

Martinez, Debbie. Celebrating Chanukah No. 4532: Eight Nights. Kupperstein, Joel, ed. (Illus.). 16p. (J). (ps-2). 1999. pap. 2.99 (*1-57471-577-1*) Creat Teach Pr.

Martinez, Debby. Kindergarten Homework, No. 3347. Ferraro, Mary P. & Lewis, Sue, eds. (Illus.). 96p. (J). 1998. pap. 9.98 (*1-57471-347-7*) Creat Teach Pr.

Martinez, Deborah F., tr. see Erickson, Tim.

Martinez, Demetria. Breathing Between the Lines: Poems. LC 96-45808. (Camino del Sol Ser.). 80p. 1997. 24.95 (*0-8165-1796-7*); pap. 12.95 (*0-8165-1798-3*) U of Ariz Pr.

— Mother Tongue. 1997. pap. 10.00 (*0-345-41656-2*) Ballantine Pub Grp.

Martinez, Dionisio. Bad Alchemy: Poems. 112p. 1996. pap. 12.00 (*0-393-31531-2*) Norton.

***Martinez, Dionisio.** Climbing Back. 2000. 22.00 (*0-393-05006-8*) Norton.

Martinez Doemer, Patricia. How to Open an Adoption. 110p. 1998. pap. 11.95 (*0-9641035-8-3*) R-Squared Pr.

Martinez Dorner, Patricia. Adopcion: Hablando Con Tu Hijo. Martinez, Joseph L., tr.Tr. of Talking to Your Child about Adoption. (ENG & SPA.). 1991. pap. 5.95 (*0-9664480-1-4*) Schaefer Pub Co.

— Talking to Your Child about Adoption. 6th ed. 1998. reprint ed. pap. 5.95 (*0-9664480-0-6*) Schaefer Pub Co.

***Martinez-Duart, J. M.** Materials & Processes for Submicron Technologies. 1999. 127.00 (*0-08-043617-X*, Pub. by Elsevier) Elsevier.

Martinez-Duart, J.M., et al, eds. Coatings & Surface Modifications for Surface Protection & Tribological Applications. LC 98-217371. 1999. write for info. (*0-444-20517-9*) Elsevier.

Martinez, E. G., jt. auth. see Brumana, Fernando G.

Martinez, Ed. Maria de Sautuola: Los Toros de la Cueva. (Remarkable Children Ser.).Tr. of Bulls in the Cave. (SPA.). (J). (gr. k-5). 1997. pap. 5.95 (*0-614-29055-4*, Silver Pr NJ) Silver Burdett Pr.

— Maria de Sautuola: The Bulls in the Cave. (Remarkable Children Ser.). (J). (gr. k-5). 1997. 15.95 (*0-614-29056-2*, Silver Pr NJ); pap. 6.95 (*0-614-29057-0*, Silver Pr NJ) Silver Burdett Pr.

Martinez, Edgar & Brown, Greg. Edgar Martinez: Patience Pays. (Illus.). 32p. (J). 1992. pap. 3.50 (*0-9634650-0-7*) Pos for Kids.

Martinez, Edie, tr. see Apostles for Triumph Staff.

Martinez, Efrain. Classic Spanish Cooking. 1997. 9.99 (*0-88365-982-4*) Galahad Bks.

— Classic Spanish Cooking with Chef Ef. (Illus.). 288p. 1994. pap. 15.00 (*1-56565-119-7*) Lowell Hse.

Martinez, Elena M. Lesbian Voices from Latin America: Breaking Ground. LC 95-37411. (Latin American Studies: Vol. 7). 248p. 1995. text 50.00 (*0-8153-1349-7*, SS907) Garland.

Martinez, Eliseo R. & Martinez, Irma C. French Readiness Skills, Vol. 1. Mahak, Francine T., tr. (Illus.). 87p. (J). 1987. student ed. 9.50 (*1-878300-02-4*) Childrens Work.

— Spanish Readiness Skills, Vol. 1. (Illus.). 78p. (J). (ps-3). 1986. student ed. 8.75 (*1-878300-01-6*) Childrens Work.

— Supplemental Studies in Math, Vol. 1. (Math Ser.). (Illus.). 73p. (J). (ps-1). 1985. student ed. 8.75 (*1-878300-00-8*) Childrens Work.

Martinez, Eliud. The Art of Mariano Azuela: Modernism in la Malhora, el Desquite, la Luciernaga. Miller, Yvette E., ed. LC 79-29682. (Exploration Ser.). 150p. 1980. pap. 7.95 (*0-935480-02-1*) Lat Am Lit Rev Pr.

— Voice-Haunted Journey. LC 89-81825. 264p. 1990. 27.00 (*0-927534-03-7*); pap. 17.00 (*0-927534-04-5*) Biling Rev-Pr.

Martinez, Elizabeth. Dare to Tell. Baca, Phil, ed. (Illus.). 167p. 1996. 29.95 (*1-880470-41-1*); pap. 14.95 (*1-880470-40-3*) Creative Des.

— De Colores Means All of Us: Latina Views for a Multi-Colored Century. LC 98-6841. 268p. 1998. 40.00 (*0-89608-584-8*); pap. 18.00 (*0-89608-583-X*) South End Pr.

Martinez, Elizabeth, ed. The Art of Rini Templeton: Where There Is Life & Struggle, Bi-Lingual: English & Spanish. LC 88-60425. (Illus.). 284p. (Orig.). 1989. pap. 14.95 (*0-941104-24-9*) Real Comet.

— Five Hundred Years of Chicano History in Pictures: 500 Anos del Pueblo Chicano. rev. ed. (ENG & SPA., Illus.). 238p. 1991. 35.00 (*0-9631123-1-7*); pap. 16.00 (*0-9631123-0-9*) SW Organizing Proj.

Martinez, Elizabeth, ed. & tr. see Lopez y Rivas, Gilberto.

Martinez, Elizabeth A. Morpho-Syntactic Erosion Between Two Generational Groups of Spanish Speakers in the United States. LC 92-14656. (Theoretical Studies in Second Language Acquisition: Vol. 4). XIII, 136p. (C). 1994. text 45.95 (*0-8204-1944-3*) P Lang Pubng.

Martinez, Elizabeth C. Edward James Olmos: Mexican-American Actor. LC 93-37659. (Hispanic Heritage Ser.). 32p. (J). (gr. 2-4). 1994. lib. bdg. 19.90 (*1-56294-410-X*) Millbrook Pr.

— Henry Cisneros: Mexican-American Leader. LC 92-21384. (Hispanic Heritage Ser.). (Illus.). 32p. (J). (gr. 2-4). 1993. pap. 4.95 (*1-56294-810-5*); lib. bdg. 19.90 (*1-56294-368-5*) Millbrook Pr.

— The Mexican-American Experience. (Coming to America Ser.). (Illus.). 64p. (J). (gr. 4-6). 1995. lib. bdg. 22.40 (*1-56294-515-7*) Millbrook Pr.

— Sor Juana: A Trailblazing Thinker. (Hispanic Heritage Ser.). (Illus.). 32p. (J). (gr. 2-4). 1994. lib. bdg. 19.90 (*1-56294-406-1*) Millbrook Pr.

Martinez, Elsie & LeCorgne, Margaret. Uptown/ Downtown: Growing up in New Orleans. rev. ed. (Illus.). 177p. 1996. pap. 10.00 (*1-887366-06-7*) Univ LA Lafayette.

Martinez, Eluid L. & Smith, James C., Jr. What Is a New Mexico Santo? Sculpture in New Mexico. LC 77-78519. (Illus.). 1978. pap. 2.95 (*0-913270-76-8*) Sunstone Pr.

Martinez-Esguerra, Maria. Collector's Guide to 1990s Barbie Dolls: Identification & Values. LC 98-221246. 288p. 1998. pap. 12.95 (*1-57432-068-8*) Collector Bks.

Martinez, F. Garcia, ed. Studies in Deuteronomy: In Honour of C. J. Labuschagne on the Occasion of His 65th Birthday. LC 94-4098. (Supplements to Vetus Testamentum Ser.: Vol. 53). 1994. 113.00 (*90-04-10052-0*) Brill Academic Pubs.

Martinez, F. Garcia & Parry, Donald W. A Bibliography of the Finds in the Desert of Judah, 1970-1995. LC 96-175049. (Studies on the Texts of the Desert of Judah: No. 19). 561p. 1996. 168.50 (*90-04-10588-3*) Brill Academic Pubs.

Martinez, F. Garcia, et al. The Scriptures & the Scrolls: Studies in Honour of A. S. Van Der Woude on the Occasion of His 65th Birthday. LC 92-33127. (Supplements to Vetus Testamentum Ser.: Vol. 49). 1992. 114.50 (*90-04-09746-5*) Brill Academic Pubs.

An Asterisk (*) at the beginning of an entry indicates that the title is appearing for the first time.

Martinez, Felix J. & Rosario, Benjamin. Manual Para Comites de Supervision. Bauza, Carmen M., ed. (Cooperatives Ser.). (SPA.). 84p. (Orig.). 1990. 5.95 (*0-934885-03-6*) Edit Nosotros.

Martinez, Felix J., tr. see Bulger, Anthony & Cherel, Jean L.

Martinez-Fernandez, Luis. Fighting Slavery in the Caribbean: The Life & Times of a British Family in Nineteenth-Century Havana. LC 97-32665. (Latin American Realities Ser.). 216p. (C). (gr. 13). 1998. 68.95 (*0-7656-0247-4*) M E Sharpe.

***Martinez-Fernandez, Luis.** Fighting Slavery in the Caribbean: The Life & Times of a British Family in Nineteenth-Century Havana. LC 97-32665. (Latin American Realities Ser.). (Illus.). 216p. (C). (gr. 13). 1998. pap. 28.95 (*0-7656-0248-2*) M E Sharpe.

Martinez, Fernando V. Glossario Espanol-Arabe-Espanol de Terminos Economicos. (Orig.). (ARA & SPA.). 486p. 1986. pap. 19.95 (*0-7859-4939-9*) Fr & Eur.

Martinez, Florentino G. The Dead Sea Scrolls Translated: The Qumran Texts in English. 2nd ed. Watson, Wilfred G., tr. LC 95-52950. 586p. 1996. pap. text 30.00 (*0-8028-4193-7*) Eerdmans.

— The Dead Sea Scrolls Translated: The Qumran Texts in English. 2nd ed. Watson, W. G., tr. lxvii, 519p. 1996. reprint ed. pap. 37.00 (*90-04-10589-1*) Brill Academic Pubs.

— Qumran & Apocalyptic: Studies on the Aramaic Texts from Qumran. LC 91-46425. (Studies on the Texts of the Desert of Judah: Vol. 9). xvi, 233p. 1994. 94.00 (*90-04-09586-1*) Brill Academic Pubs.

Martinez, Florentino G., ed. Qumran Cave 11: 11Q2-18 & 11Q20-22, Vol. II. (Discoveries in the Judaen Desert Ser.: No. XXIII). (Illus.). 560p. 1998. text 175.00 (*0-19-826959-5*) OUP.

Martinez, Florentino G., ed. The Dead Sea Scrolls Translated: The Qumran Texts in English. LC 94-17429. lxvii, 513p. 1994. 106.00 (*90-04-10088-1*) Brill Academic Pubs.

Martinez, Florentino G. & Barrera, Julio T. The People of the Dead Sea Scrolls: Their Literature, Social Organization & Religious Beliefs. Watson, Wilfred G., tr. LC 95-24822. x, 270p. 1995. pap. 23.50 (*90-04-10085-7*) Brill Academic Pubs.

Martinez, Florentino G. & Luttikhuizen, Gerard, eds. Interpretations of the Flood. LC 98-40735. 1999. 87.50 (*90-04-11253-7*) Brill Academic Pubs.

***Martinez, Florentino G. & Tigchelaar, Eibert.** The Dead Sea Scrolls Study Edition, 2 vols. 1384p. 1999. pap. 90.00 (*90-04-11058-5*) Brill Academic Pubs.

Martinez, Florentino G., jt. ed. see Brooke, George J.

Martinez, Florentino Garcia, see Garcia Martinez, Florentino.

Martinez, Floyd. Spirits of the High Mesa. LC 96-50286. 120p. (YA). 1997. pap. 9.95 (*1-55885-198-4*) Arte Publico.

Martinez, Francesco E. & University of Puerto Rico Staff. Futuro Econbomico de Puerto Rico: Antologbia de Ensayos del Proyecto Sobre el Futuro Econbomico de Puerto Rico. LC 98-51528. 1999. write for info. (*0-8477-0368-1*) U of PR Pr.

Martinez, Francisco J. & San Miguel-Carmona, Soledad. Frances Perfeccionamiento. (Illus.). 1990. 24.95 (*2-7005-0153-5*, Pub. by Assimil) Distribks Inc.

Martinez Fuertes, Edelmira, notes. Antologia Poetica del Renacimiento al Barroco. (Clasicos Esenciales Ser.). (SPA.). (C). 1998. pap. 9.95 (*84-294-4560-9*) Santillana.

Martinez, G., ed. Optical Properties of Semiconductors. 1992. text 208.00 (*0-7923-2058-1*) Kluwer Academic.

Martinez, Gabriel Xavier, tr. see Sacchi, Mario Enrique.

Martinez-Garcia, E., jt. ed. see Dallmeyer, R. D.

***Martinez, Gaspar.** Confronting the Mystery of God: Political, Liberation & Public Theologies. 2000. 34.50 (*0-8264-1239-4*) Continuum.

Martinez, Gaule R. Money & Me: Healing Our Relationship with Money. (Illus.). 178p. 1997. pap. 10.95 (*0-9645194-1-0*) Rose Petal.

Martinez, Gayle, ed. see Harvey, Jack B.

Martinez, Gayle R. Journey into Light: The Story of a Woman's Struggle to Heal, Love, & Forgive. 182p. 1992. pap. 10.95 (*0-87604-292-2*) Rose Petal.

— MMBI Handbook: Money & Me Inventory. viii, 43p. 1997. pap. 6.50 (*1-892351-01-3*) Rose Petal.

— Money & Me Workbook. 2nd rev. ed. Twintrees, Marilyn & Twintrees, Thomas, eds. Dixon, Bonnie, tr. (Illus.). 73p. 1997. pap. 9.98 (*1-892351-00-5*) Rose Petal.

***Martinez, Gayle R.** Money & Me Workbook: Revised Edition. Doyle, Jeannine, ed. 51p. 2000. 14.95 (*1-892351-03-X*) Rose Petal.

Martinez, German. Wedding to Marriage. (Worship Ser.). 177p. 1993. pap. 14.95 (*1-56929-009-1*, Pastoral Press) OR Catholic.

Martinez-Gil, Fernando, et al, eds. Issues in the Phonology & Morphology of the Major Iberian Languages. LC 96-47798. (Georgetown Studies in Romance Linguistics). 720p. 1997. 72.00 (*0-87840-647-6*) Georgetown U Pr.

Martinez-Gil, Fernando, jt. ed. see Campos, Hector.

Martinez-Gil, Fernando, jt. ed. see Gutierrez-Rexach, Javier.

Martinez-Gongora, Mar. Discursos Sobre la Mujer en el Humanismo Renacentista Espanol. LC 98-60155. (SPA.). 300p. 1998. 40.00 (*0-938972-30-8*) Spanish Lit Pubns.

Martinez-Gonzalez, E. & Sanz, J. L. The Universe at High-Z, Large-Scale Structure & the Cosmic Microwave Background: Proceedings of an Advanced Summer School, Held at Laredo, Cantabria, Spain, 4-8 September 1995, Vol. 470. LC 96-20317. (Lecture Notes in Physics Ser.). 254p. 1996. 73.00 (*3-540-61225-4*) Spr-Verlag.

Martinez Guridi, G. Evaluation of Loca with Delayed Loop & Loop with Delayed Loca Accident Scenarios: Technical Findings Related to Gs1-171, "ESF Failure from Loop Subsequent to Loca" 233p. 1997. per. 20.00 (*0-16-054679-6*) USGPO.

Martinez, H. Salvador, see Salvador Martinez, H., ed.

Martinez, H. Salvador, ed. see de Ayala, Pero Lopez.

Martinez Hidalgo Teran, Jose M. Diccionario Nautico. deluxe ed.Tr. of Nautical Dictionary. (ENG, FRE & SPA.). 540p. 1977. 125.00 (*0-8288-5356-8*, S50095) Fr & Eur.

Martinez, Homer T., Jr. The Rosary: A Child's Prayer (Coloring Book) (Illus.). 32p. (Orig.). (J). 1995. pap. 1.95 (*0-8091-6622-4*) Paulist Pr.

Martinez, Humberto. Joey the Pony. (Illus.). 16p. (J). (gr. k-2). 1996. pap. 6.95 (*0-8059-3958-X*) Dorrance.

Martinez, Ines. To Know the Moon. LC 93-84222. 238p. (Orig.). 1993. pap. 14.95 (*0-9636433-0-4*) Sandia Pr.

Martinez, Irma C., jt. auth. see Martinez, Eliseo R.

Martinez, Isaac. Ford Windsor Small-Block Performance: Parts & Modifications for High Performance Street & Racing. LC 99-40648. (Illus.). 201p. 1999. pap. text 17.95 (*1-55788-323-8*, HP Books) Berkley Pub.

Martinez, J. D. Combat Mime: A Non-Violent Approach to Stage Violence. LC 82-3578. (Illus.). 224p. (C). 1982. pap. text 30.95 (*0-88229-809-7*) Burnham Inc.

— The Swords of Shakespeare: An Illustrated Guide to Stage Combat Choreography in the Plays of Shakespeare. LC 95-18168. (Illus.). 286p. 1996. lib. bdg. 48.50 (*0-89950-959-2*) McFarland & Co.

Martinez, J. M., ed. see Menendez Pidal, Ramon.

***Martinez, J. Michael, et al, eds.** Confederate Symbols in the Contemporary South. LC 00-24461. (Illus.). 368p. 2000. write for info. (*0-8130-1758-0*) U Press Fla.

Martinez, J. R. & Barbero, B. J., eds. Animal Models for Cystic Fibrosis: The Reserpine-Treated Rat. (Illus.). 1985. 20.00 (*0-911302-54-9*) San Francisco Pr.

***Martinez, Jacqueline.** Journey West. 1999. pap. 8.95 (*1-55517-426-4*) CFI Dist.

***Martinez, Jacqueline M.** Phenomenology of Chicana Experience: Communication & Transformation in Praxis. LC 00-24819. (New Critical Theory Ser.). 2000. pap. 17.95 (*0-7425-0701-7*) Rowman.

***Martinez, Javier.** Teacher Templates for AppleWorks (ClarisWorks) (Illus.). 2000. pap. 18.95 (*1-57690-772-4*) Tchr Create Mat.

Martinez, Javier & Diaz, Alvaro. Chile: The Great Transformation. 156p. 1996. 34.95 (*0-8157-5478-7*) Brookings.

Martinez, Jean, ed. Peptide Hormones As Prohormones: Processing, Biological Activity, Pharmacology. 1989. text 115.00 (*0-470-21262-4*) P-H.

***Martinez, Joe L., Jr.** Tricks of the Grade. 104p. 1999. pap. 12.95 (*0-7392-0470-X*, P02553B) Morris Pubng.

***Martinez, Joe L., Jr. & Desner, Raymond P., eds.** Neurobiology of Learning & Memory. LC 98-84370. (Illus.). 456p. 1998. boxed set 69.96 (*0-12-475655-7*) Acad Pr.

Martinez, Joe L., Jr. & Kesner, Raymond P., eds. Learning & Memory: A Biological View. 2nd ed. (Illus.). 563p. 1991. text 104.00 (*0-12-474992-5*); pap. text 53.00 (*0-12-474993-3*) Acad Pr.

Martinez, Joe L., Jr. & Mendoza, Richard H., eds. Chicano Psychology. 2nd ed. 1984. text 59.95 (*0-12-475660-3*) Acad Pr.

Martinez, Joey, jt. auth. see Schmidt, Fran.

Martinez, John. Fantastic Opera: The Great Operas Illuminated. LC 97-5080. 64p. 1997. pap. 19.95 (*0-8109-2770-5*, Pub. by Abrams) Time Warner.

***Martinez, John & Libonati, Michael E.** State & Local Government. (C). 2000. pap. write for info. (*1-58360-753-6*) Anderson Pub Co.

Martinez, Jorge, ed. Ordered Algebraic Structures. (C). 1989. text 191.50 (*0-7923-0489-6*) Kluwer Academic.

Martinez, Jorge & Holland, C., eds. Ordered Algebraic Structures: The 1991 Conrad Conference. LC 93-18855. 1993. text 169.50 (*0-7923-2258-4*) Kluwer Academic.

Martinez, Jose. Los Espacios Poeticos de Ruben Dario. (American University Studies: Vol. 25). (SPA.). IX, 214p. (C). 1995. text 42.95 (*0-8204-2508-7*) P Lang Pubng.

Martinez, Jose F. Los Del Camino. Cima Communications Staff, ed. (SPA.). (Orig.). 1991. write for info. (*0-9628846-0-X*) J F Martinez.

Martinez, Jose L. Antes de Dar el Si: Before You Say I Do. (SPA.). 128p. (Orig.). 1990. pap. text 10.99 (*0-311-46118-2*) Casa Bautista.

— Apuntes Pastorales: Filipenses, Colosense, Filemon. (Shepherd's Notes Ser.). (SPA.). 100p. 1998. pap. 5.95 (*0-8054-9322-0*) Broadman.

— Apuntes Pastorales: Galatas. (Shepherd's Notes Ser.). (SPA.). 100p. 1998. pap. 5.95 (*0-8054-9323-9*) Broadman.

— Apuntes Pastorales: Genesis. (Shepherd's Notes Ser.). (SPA.). 100p. 1998. pap. 5.95 (*0-8054-9319-0*) Broadman.

— Apuntes Pastorales: Hecho. (Shepherd's Notes Ser.). (SPA.). 100p. 1998. pap. 5.95 (*0-8054-9321-2*) Broadman.

— Apuntes Pastorales: I y II de Timoteo, Tito. (Shepherd's Notes Ser.). (SPA.). 100p. 1998. pap. 5.95 (*0-8054-9324-7*) Broadman.

— Apuntes Pastorales: Mateo. (Shepherd's Notes Ser.). (SPA.). 100p. 1998. pap. 5.95 (*0-8054-9320-4*) Broadman.

— Documentos Cortesianos (The Cortez Documents), Vol. I. (SPA.). 1990. 15.99 (*968-16-3548-5*, Pub. by Fondo) Continental Bk.

— Documentos Cortesianos (The Cortez Documents), Vol. II. (SPA.). 1990. 15.99 (*968-16-3585-X*, Pub. by Fondo) Continental Bk.

— Documentos Cortesianos (The Cortez Documents), Vol. III. (SPA.). 1990. 15.99 (*968-16-3643-0*, Pub. by Fondo) Continental Bk.

— Documentos Cortesianos (The Cortez Documents), Vol. IV. (SPA.). 1990. 15.99 (*968-16-3893-X*, Pub. by Fondo) Continental Bk.

— Hernan Cortez. (SPA.). 1016p. 1990. 17.99 (*968-16-3796-8*, Pub. by Fondo) Continental Bk.

— Hernan Cortez: (Version Abreviada) (Breviarios Ser.). (SPA.). pap. 11.99 (*968-16-4699-1*, Pub. by Fondo) Continental Bk.

— Mas Objetos Que Ensenan de Dios: More Objects That Teach about God. (SPA.). 96p. (Orig.). 1992. pap. 7.99 (*0-311-44008-8*) Casa Bautista.

— Nezahualcoyotl: Vida y Obra (Life & Work) (SPA.). 335p. 1992. reprint ed. 16.99 (*968-16-0509-8*, Pub. by Fondo) Continental Bk.

— Novios - Conversemos Sobre Cosas Que Apenas Se Hablan: Before You Marry, Things That Make a Difference. (SPA.). 80p. 1984. reprint ed. pap. 6.99 (*0-311-46104-2*) Casa Bautista.

Martinez, Jose L., compiled by. Bosquejos de Sermones para Bodas y Funerales: Sermon Outlines for Weddings & Funerals. (SPA.). 112p. (Orig.). 1990. pap. 6.99 (*0-311-43042-2*) Casa Bautista.

— Bosquejos de Sermones Para Celebracion de Bautismo y Cena del Senor: Sermon Outlines on Baptism & The Lord's Supper. (SPA.). 112p. (Orig.). 1988. pap. 7.50 (*0-311-43040-6*) Casa Bautista.

Martinez, Jose L., ed. El Ensayo Mexicano Moderno (The Contemporary Mexican Essay), Vol. I. (SPA.). 552p. 1968. 17.99 (*968-16-1770-3*, Pub. by Fondo) Continental Bk.

— El Ensayo Mexicano Moderno (The Contemporary Mexican Essay), Vol. II. (SPA.). 660p. 1968. 17.99 (*968-16-1771-1*, Pub. by Fondo) Continental Bk.

Martinez, Jose L. & Trenchard, Ernesto. Escogidos en Cristo.Tr. of Chosen in Christ. (SPA.). 320p. 1987. pap. 9.99 (*0-8254-1737-6*, Edit Portavoz) Kregel.

Martinez, Jose L., tr. see Amos, William E., Jr.

Martinez, Jose L., tr. see Hendricks, William.

Martinez, Jose Luis. 503 Ilustraciones Escogidas.Tr. of 503 Selected Illustrations. (SPA.). 320p. (C). 1997. pap. text 13.50 (*0-311-42095-8*) Casa Bautista.

— Es Biblico Restaurar Al Ministro Que Cae en Pecado Sexual?Tr. of Is it Biblical to Restore the Minister Who Has Fallen into Sexual Immorality?. (SPA.). 128p. 1997. pap. text 8.99 (*0-311-46161-1*, Edit Mundo) Casa Bautista.

Martinez, Jose Luis. 502 Illustraciones Escogidas. (SPA.). 320p. 1994. pap. 13.50 (*0-311-42097-4*) Casa Bautista.

Martinez, Jose M. Serrano & King, Russell. A Human Geography of Spain. 300p. 1998. 65.00 (*1-898723-91-5*, Pub. by Sussex Acad Pr); pap. 29.95 (*1-898723-92-3*, Pub. by Sussex Acad Pr) Intl Spec Bk.

Martinez, Joseph, jt. auth. see Martinez, Nancy.

Martinez, Joseph G. Math Without Fear. 167p. (C). 1996. pap. text 33.00 (*0-205-16021-2*) Allyn.

Martinez, Joseph G., jt. auth. see Martinez, Nancy C.

***Martinez, Joseph G. R. & Martinez, Nancy C.** Reading & Writing to Learn Mathematics: A Guide & a Resource Book. LC 00-44148. 2001. write for info. (*0-205-30284-X*) Allyn.

Martinez, Joseph L., tr. see Martinez Dorner, Patricia.

Martinez, Juan A. Cuban Art & National Identity: The Vanguardia Painters, 1927-1950. LC 94-7649. (Illus.). 216p. 1994. 34.95 (*0-8130-1306-2*) U Press Fla.

Martinez, Juan A., ed. see Libby, Gary R.

Martinez, Judas Riley. Mortal. 25p. 1999. pap. 6.00 (*0-9670994-1-2*) Longleaf Meth Coll.

Martinez, Julio A., compiled by. Chicano Scholars & Writers: A Bio-Bibliographical Directory. LC 78-32076. 589p. 1979. 45.00 (*0-8108-1205-3*) Scarecrow.

Martinez, Julio A., ed. Dictionary of Twentieth-Century Cuban Literature. LC 88-35805. 549p. 1990. lib. bdg. 85.00 (*0-313-25185-1*, MZC/, Greenwood Pr) Greenwood.

Martinez, Julio A. & Lomeli, Francisco A., eds. Chicano Literature: A Reference Guide. LC 83-22583. 492p. 1985. lib. bdg. 85.00 (*0-313-23691-7*, MTL/, Greenwood Pr) Greenwood.

Martinez, K., jt. auth. see Hart, J.

Martinez, Katharine A., ed. American Cornucopia: Treasures of the Winterthur Library. LC 90-4115. (Illus.). 115p. 1990. pap. 12.95 (*0-912724-20-X*) Winterthur.

Martinez, Katharine A. & Ames, Kenneth L., eds. The Material Culture of Gender - The Gender of Material Culture. LC 97-29399. (Illus.). 465p. 1997. 40.00 (*0-912724-40-4*) Winterthur.

***Martinez, Katharine A. & Talbott, Page, eds.** Philadelphia's Cultural Landscape: The Sartain Family Legacy. (Illus.). 240p. 2000. 49.50 (*1-56639-791-X*) Temple U Pr.

Martinez, Kerry A., ed. see Dorobiala, James F.

Martinez, L. J., jt. ed. see Hoffmann, S. L.

Martinez, L. S. & Kato, M. M. Spanish-Japanese Dictionary: Diccionario Espanol-Japones. (JPN & SPA.). 1103p. 1982. 150.00 (*0-8288-1021-4*, S40503) Fr & Eur.

Martinez-Lage, jt. auth. see Gutierrez.

Martinez, Larry, jt. auth. see Caggiano, Rosemary.

Martinez, Larry F. Communication Satellites: Power Politics in Space. LC 85-47746. (Artech House Telecommunications Library). 204p. reprint ed. pap. 63.30 (*0-7837-3017-9*, 204292300006) Bks Demand.

***Martinez, Laura L.** Drama for the Dramatically Challenged: Church Plays Made Easy. LC 00-26741. 112p. 2000. pap. 15.00 incl. audio compact disk (*0-8170-1356-3*) Judson.

Martinez, Leticia. Senoritas de Negro. 1997. pap. text 9.98 (*970-661-009-X*) EDAM.

***Martinez, Limon Enrique F.** Tequila: The Spirit of Mexico. (Illus.). 184p. (J). 2000. 35.00 (*0-7892-0621-8*, Abbeville Kids) Abbeville Pr.

Martinez, Lionel. Gold Rushes of North America. 1990. 15.98 (*1-55521-552-1*) Bk Sales Inc.

— Murders in North America. 1991. 15.98 (*1-55521-703-6*) Bk Sales Inc.

Martinez-Lopez, Benjamin. Eduardo Barrios: Vida y Obra. LC 77-10946. (Coleccion Mente y Palabra). 163p. 1977. 5.00 (*0-8477-0550-1*); pap. 4.00 (*0-8477-0551-X*) U of PR Pr.

Martinez Lopez, Cira & Winter, Marcus. Figurillas y Silbatos de Ceramica de Monte Alban. (SPA., Illus.). 148p. 1994. pap. 15.00 (*1-877812-76-5*, UC007) UPLAAP.

Martinez-Lopez, Enrique, jt. ed. see Belchior, Maria D.

Martinez-Lopez, Jorge I., et al. A Casebook of Electrocardiographic Tracings. LC 81-16115. 167p. reprint ed. pap. 51.80 (*0-8357-7873-8*, 203629000002) Bks Demand.

Martinez, Lorri. Where Eagles Fall. 1983. pap. 2.50 (*0-942396-32-4*) Blackberry ME.

Martinez, Lourdes, tr. see Kipling, Rudyard.

Martinez-Lucio, Miguel, jt. ed. see Kirkpatrick, Ian.

Martinez, Luis M. Mis Cuatro Puntos Cardinales. Sardinas, Sergio A., ed. LC 98-89801. (Coleccion Cuba y Sus Jueces Ser.). (SPA., Illus.). 160p. (Orig.). 1999. pap. 13.00 (*0-89729-891-8*) Ediciones.

— The Sanctifier. 324p. 1981. reprint ed. pap. 14.95 (*0-8198-6804-3*) Pauline Bks.

***Martinez, Luis M.** True Devotion to the Holy Spirit. abr. ed. LC 99-88253. Orig. Title: El Espirtu Santo (The Sanctifier). 288p. 2000. pap. 17.95 (*1-928832-05-9*) Sophia Inst Pr.

— When Jesus Sleeps: Finding Spiritual Peace Amid the Storms of Life. 144p. 2000. pap. 11.95 (*1-928832-06-7*) Sophia Inst Pr.

Martinez, Luis R. Epejismo: Poesia. LC 99-63064. (SPA.). 75p. (C). 1999. pap. 19.99 (*1-893231-07-0*) Poet Born.

Martinez, Luz A., ed. Homenaje a Nuestras Curanderas/Honoring Our Healers. (ENG & SPA., Illus.). 53p. (Orig.). 1996. pap. 15.00 (*0-9654674-0-6*) Latina Pr.

Martinez, M. Quier Yo? Dirigir el Estudio Biblico.Tr. of Who Me? Direct Bible Study. (SPA.). 80p. 1995. pap. 4.99 (*0-8297-1909-1*) Vida Pubs.

Martinez,, M. Lina, jt. auth. see Giron, Francisco J.

Martinez, M. R. & Lev, M. C., eds. Computer Integrated Manufacturing. (PED Ser.: Vol. 8). 148p. 1983. pap. text 30.00 (*0-317-02557-0*, H00288) ASME.

Martinez, Magdalena M. National Sovereignty & International Organizations. LC 96-4898. (Legal Aspects of International Organization Ser.: No. 25). 376p. 1996. 108.50 (*90-411-0200-0*) Kluwer Law Intl.

Martinez-Maldonado, Manuel, ed. Mechanisms of Renal Injury & Repair Vol. 21, No. 4-5: Mineral & Electrolyte Metabolism, 1995. (Journal Ser.: Vol. 21, No. 4-5, 1995). (Illus.). 122p. 1995. pap. 86.25 (*3-8055-6209-8*) S Karger.

Martinez, Manuel L. Crossing. LC 98-35881. 128p. 1998. pap. 11.00 (*0-927534-80-0*) Biling Rev-Pr.

Martinez, Margaret. 101 Great Lowfat Mexican Dishes: Hot, Spicy & Healthful! LC 95-5282. (Illus.). 288p. 1995. pap. 12.95 (*0-7615-0009-X*) Prima Pub.

— 101 Great Lowfat Pasta Dishes: Fresh, Zesty & Healthful! LC 96-221. (Illus.). 240p. 1996. per. 12.95 (*0-7615-0414-1*) Prima Pub.

***Martinez, Maria.** Afro-cuban Coordination for Drumset: The Essential Method & Workbook. 80p. 1999. pap. 14.95 incl. audio compact disk (*0-7935-9749-8*) H Leonard.

Martinez, Maria C. Los Cuentos de Juan Bobo. LC 79-52813.Tr. of Juan Bobo Stories. (SPA., Illus.). 59p. Date not set. reprint ed. pap. 8.95 (*0-9601700-6-5*) Editl Libero.

Martinez, Maria C. De, see De Martinez, Maria C.

Martinez, Maria De Lourdes, see Glasser, Ruth.

***Martinez, Maria L.** Open Door to the Universe: A Life's Journey. 1998. 13.50 (*0-926524-53-4*) Granite WI.

Martinez, Maria L., tr. see Martinez, Santiago.

***Martinez, Maria Loreto.** Neighborhood Context & the Development of African American Children. LC 99-43811. (Children of Poverty Ser.). 1999. write for info. (*0-8153-3538-5*) Garland.

Martinez, Maria Lupita. Open Door to the Universe: Finding the Joy of Spirituality along Life's Path. (Illus.). 172p. 1999. pap. 13.50 (*1-893183-00-9*, 505) Granite Pub.

Martinez, Mario. Lady's Men. large type ed. (Large Print Ser.). (Illus.). 384p. 1996. 27.99 (*0-7089-3555-9*) Ulverscroft.

— Lady's Men: The Story of World War II's Mystery Bomber & Her Crew. (Illus.). 208p. 1995. 29.95 (*1-55750-511-X*) Naval Inst Pr.

— Lady's Men: The Story of World War II's Mystery Bomber & Her Crew. 1999. pap. 15.95 (*1-55750-553-5*) Naval Inst Pr.

Martinez, Mario, tr. see Lea, Thomas D. & Latham, Bill.

Martinez, Mario, tr. see Neighbour, Ralph W., Jr.

Martinez, Mario, tr. see Stacker, Joe R. & Wesley, Forbis.

Martinez, Marissa C., jt. ed. see White, Jocelyn C.

Martinez, Marta V., ed. see Dunbaugh, Edwin L.

Martinez, Martha I., et al. A Year of Progress in School-to-Career System Building: The Benchmark Communities Initiative. LC 96-159994. (Illus.). 70p. (Orig.). 1996. pap. 15.00 (*1-887410-83-X*) Jobs for Future.

***Martinez, Martin & Podrebarac, Francis.** The New Prescription: Marijuana As Medicine. 2nd ed. 142p. 2000. pap. text 14.95 (*0-932551-35-1*) Quick Am Pub.

M

***Martinez, Matt, Jr. & Pate, Steve.** Matt Makes a Run for the Border: Recipes & Tales from a Tex-Mex Chef. (Illus.). 192p. 2000. 29.95 (0-86730-768-4) Lebhar Friedman.

Martinez, Max. Layover. LC 96-39824. 140p. 1997. 22.95 (1-55885-199-2) Arte Publico.

— Schoolland. LC 87-35127. 250p. (Orig.). 1988. pap. 9.50 (0-934770-87-5) Arte Publico.

— White Leg. LC 95-33396. 257p. 1996. 19.95 (1-55885-098-8) Arte Publico.

Martinez-Mekler, G. & Seligman, T. H. Dynamics of Nonlinear & Disordered Systems. (World Scientific Series on Nonlinear Science: Vol. 6). 250p. 1995. text 58.00 (981-02-2280-7) World Scientific Pub.

***Martinez, Michael.** Education as the Cultivation of Intelligence. (A Volume in the Educational Psychology Ser.). 272p. 2000. write for info. (0-8058-3251-3) L Erlbaum Assocs.

Martinez-Miller, Orlando. La Etica Judia y la Celestina Como Alegoria. LC 77-89034. 1978. 15.00 (0-89729-179-4) Ediciones.

Martinez, Milton M. Espacio y Albedrio. LC 91-72886. (SPA.). 137p. 1991. 12.00 (0-89729-612-5) Ediciones.

— Sitio de Mascaras. LC 87-72348. (Coleccion Caniqui). (SPA., Illus.). 208p. (Orig.). 1987. pap. 9.95 (0-89729-460-2) Ediciones.

Martinez, Miriam, jt. ed. see Roser, Nancy L.

Martinez, Miriam, jt. illus. see Martin, Marla.

Martinez Moreno, Carlos. El Infierno. Wright, Ann, tr. from SPA. LC 87-63467. (Readers International Ser.). (Illus.). 270p. (Orig.). 1988. 16.95 (0-930523-47-4); pap. 8.95 (0-930523-48-2) Readers Intl.

Martinez, Nancy & Martinez, Joseph. Holt Workbook. 2nd ed. 416p. (C). 1989. pap. text 25.00 (0-03-029809-1) Harcourt Coll Pubs.

Martinez, Nancy C. Basic College Writing: A Text with Readings. 320p. 1990. pap. text 33.00 (0-13-067646-2) P-H.

— Guide to British Poetry Explication: Restoration Through Romantic Period. (Reference Ser.: Vol. 3). 576p. 1993. 65.00 (0-8161-1997-X, G K Hall & Co) Mac Lib Ref.

Martinez, Nancy C. & Martinez, Joseph G. Basic College Writing: A Text with Readings. 320p. (C). 1990. pap. write for info. (0-318-68285-0) P-H.

— Guide to British Poetry Explication Vol. I: Old English - Medieval. 225p. (C). 1991. 65.00 (0-8161-8921-8, Hall Reference) Macmillan.

Martinez, Nancy C., et al. Guide to British Poetry Explication Vol. 4: Victorian-Contemporary. LC 90-49129. (Reference Publication in Literature Ser.). 720p. 1995. 65.00 (0-8161-8988-9, G K Hall & Co) Mac Lib Ref.

Martinez, Nancy C., jt. auth. see Martinez, Joseph G. R.

Martinez, Norma & Farrell, H. Clyde. Texas Routine Case Manual: Access to Attorneys. 66p. pap. 6.50 (0-685-23157-7, 41,575A) NCLS Inc.

Martinez, Oscar J. Border People: Life & Society in the U. S. - Mexico Borderlands. (Illus.). 352p. (Orig.). 1994. pap. 26.95 (0-8165-1414-3) U of Ariz Pr.

— Troublesome Border. LC 87-34294. (PROFMEX Ser.). 177p. 1989. reprint ed. pap. 13.50 (0-8165-1104-7) U of Ariz Pr.

Martinez, Oscar J., ed. U. S.-Mexico Borderlands: Historical & Contemporary Perspectives, Vol. 11. LC 95-21781. (Jaguar Books on Latin America: No. 11). 264p. 1995. pap. 18.95 (0-8420-2447-6); text 55.00 (0-8420-2446-8) Scholarly Res Inc.

Martinez, P. Sistemas Operatives, Teoria y Practica. (SPA.). 254p. 1997. pap. 25.00 (84-7978-262-5, Pub. by Ediciones Diaz) IBD Ltd.

Martinez-Pacheco, Ramon & Conchiero, Angel. Design & Evaluation of Bioavailability & Bioequivalence Studies. (Drugs & the Pharmaceutical Sciences Ser.). Date not set. write for info. (0-8247-9874-0) Dekker.

Martinez-Palomo, Adolfo. The Biology of Entamoeba Histolytica. LC RC0121.A5M3. (Tropical Medicine Research Studies: No. 2). (Illus.). 173p. reprint ed. pap. 53.70 (0-608-18366-0, 203423000089) Bks Demand.

Martinez, Patricia, ed. see Gentry, Robert.

Martinez, Patricia, ed. see Sullivan, Enoch, et al.

Martinez, Patricia Brandon, jt. auth. see Gentry, Robert R.

Martinez, Patrick, ed. The Observer's Guide to Astronomy, 2 vols. Dunlop, Storm, tr. LC 93-29830. (Practical Astronomy Handbooks Ser.). (Illus.). (C). 1992. write for info. (0-521-38088-X); write for info. (0-521-38075-8) Cambridge U Pr.

— The Observer's Guide to Astronomy, Vol. 1. Dunlop, Storm, tr. (Practical Astronomy Handbooks Ser.: No. 4). (Illus.). 610p. (C). 1994. pap. 37.95 (0-521-37945-8); text 85.00 (0-521-37068-X) Cambridge U Pr.

— The Observer's Guide to Astronomy, 2 vols., Vol. 2. Dunlop, Storm, tr. LC 93-29830. (Practical Astronomy Handbooks Ser.). (Illus.). 569p. (C). 1994. pap. 37.95 (0-521-45898-6); text 85.00 (0-521-45265-1) Cambridge U Pr.

Martinez, Patrick & Klotz, Alain. A Practical Guide to CCD Astronomy. Demers, Andre, tr. LC 96-54304. (Practical Astronomy Handbooks Ser.: Vol. 8). (Illus.). 264p. (C). 1997. pap. 30.95 (0-521-59950-4); text 80.00 (0-521-59063-9) Cambridge U Pr.

Martinez, Paul A. & Harbaugh, John W. Simulating Nearshore Environments. LC 93-29269. (Computer Methods in the Geosciences Ser.: Vol. 12). 280p. 1993. 137.25 (0-08-037937-0, Pergamon Pr) Elsevier.

Martinez-Pons, Manuel. Research in the Social Sciences & Education: Principles & Process. LC 96-41348. 346p. 1996. pap. text 34.50 (0-7618-0526-5) U Pr of Amer.

Martinez-Pons, Manuel. Statistics in Modern Research: Applications in the Social Sciences & Education. LC 98-53446. 232p. (C). 1999. pap. 29.50 (0-7618-1333-0) U Pr of Amer.

***Martinez-Pons, Manuel.** Statistics in Modern Research: Applications in the Social Sciences & Education. LC 98-53446. 232p. (C). 1999. 52.00 (0-7618-1332-2) U Pr of Amer.

Martinez, R. Diccionario Biografico Historico Dominicano. (SPA.). write for info. (0-318-56669-9) Fr & Eur.

Martinez, Rafael B., jt. ed. see Barker, Thomas M.

Martinez, Randolf. A Matter of Survival - Burglary. (Illus.). 109p. 1994. write for info. (0-9644652-0-5) Chico Pub.

Martinez, Randolph. Breaking the Ice. 200p. 1998. text. write for info. (0-9644652-1-3) Chico Pub.

Martinez, Raquel. I Hagase Rico: Como Acumular una Fortuna Personal Usando Principalos Sencillos. (SPA.). 186p. (Orig.). 1997. pap. write for info. (1-57502-450-0, PO1348) Morris Pubng.

Martinez, Raquel M. Venid Cantemos. 1.00 (0-687-06167-9) Abingdon.

Martinez, Ray P. Foreigners by Destiny. 1993. pap. write for info. (0-9636523-0-3) R P Martinez.

Martinez, Raymond J. Marie Laveau: Voodoo Queen & Folk Tales along the Mississippi. 96p. 1983. pap. 7.95 (0-911116-83-4) Pelican.

Martinez, Reynel. Six Silent Men: 101st LRP - Rangers, Bk. 1. LC 96-94868. 1997. mass mkt. 5.99 (0-8041-1566-4) Ivy Books.

Martinez, Ricardo, ed. Partners in Progress: National Impaired Driving Goals & Strategies for 2005. 123p. (Orig.). (C). 1997. reprint ed. pap. text 40.00 (0-7881-4030-2) DIANE Pub.

— Traffic Safety Facts (1996) A Compilation of Motor Vehicle Crash Data from the Fatality Analysis Reporting System & the General Estimates System. (Illus.). 192p. (C). 1998. pap. text 35.00 (0-7881-7506-8) DIANE Pub.

Martinez, Ricardo A. The Healing Ritual. LC 83-51345. 174p. 1983. pap. 4.95 (0-89229-014-5) TQS Pubns.

Martinez, Robert E. Business & Democracy in Spain. LC 92-31845. 344p. 1993. 69.50 (0-275-94391-7, C4391, Praeger Pubs) Greenwood.

Martinez, Robert J., ed. see International SAMPE Technical Conference Staff.

Martinez, Rodolfo V. Florula de las Reservas Biologicas de Iquitos, Peru. Lleras, Agustin R. & Taylor, Charlotte M., eds. 1000p. 1997. 85.00 (0-915279-48-7, MSB-63) Miss Botan.

Martinez, Rodolfo V., jt. auth. see Duke, James A.

Martinez Rodriquez, Maria Del Mar, see Del Mar Martinez Rodriquez, Maria, ed.

Martinez, Ronald L., jt. auth. see Durling, Robert.

Martinez, Ronald L., tr. see Agamben, Giorgio.

Martinez, Roy, ed. The Very Idea of Radical Hermeneutics. LC 96-28342. 256p. (C). 1997. text 55.00 (0-391-04008-1) Humanities.

Martinez, Ruben. Managing Casinos: A Guide for Entrepreneurs, Management Personnel & Aspiring Managers. LC 95-31449. (Illus.). 432p. (Orig.). 1995. 75.00 (1-56980-045-6) Barricade Bks.

— The Other Side: The Fault Lines, Guerrilla Saints & True Heart of Rock 'n' Roll. 192p. 1993. pap. 11.00 (0-679-74591-2) Vin Bks.

Martinez, Ruben Gerard. Border Cafe. 50p. 1992. pap. 7.95 (0-944754-14-7) Pudding Hse Pubns.

Martinez, Ruben O. & Anaya, Rudolfo A. Bless Me, Ultima Notes. (Cliffs Notes Ser.). (Illus.). 72p. (Orig.). 1995. pap. text 4.95 (0-8220-0249-3, Cliff) IDG Bks.

Martinez, Ruben O., jt. auth. see Aguirre, Adalberto, Jr.

Martinez, Samuel. Peripheral Migrants: Haitians & Dominican Republic Sugar Plantations. LC 95-4359. 256p. (C). 1995. text 35.00 (0-87049-901-7) U of Tenn Pr.

Martinez San Martin, Angel, ed. see Trigo, Felipe.

Martinez, Santiago. Diccionario Diplomatico. (SPA.). 252p. 1986. pap. 29.95 (0-7859-6199-2, 8472324095) Fr & Eur.

***Martinez, Santiago.** El Silencio de Dios. 1999. 18.95 (84-08-02233-4) Planeta Edit.

Martinez, Santiago. The Ten Commandments of the Law of God. Martinez, Maria L., tr. from SPA. LC 95-72817. 80p. (Orig.). 1996. pap. text 4.95 (1-882972-63-5, 3481) Queenship Pub.

Martinez-Santiago, Adela, jt. auth. see Muckley, Robert L.

Martinez-Serros, Hugo. The Last Laugh & Other Stories. LC 88-6359. 198p. (Orig.). 1988. pap. 9.50 (0-934770-89-1) Arte Publico.

Martinez, Servet. Dynamics of Complex Interacting Systems. Goles, Eric, ed. LC 96-30324. (Nonlinear Phenomena & Complex Systems Ser.). 186p. (C). 1996. text 107.00 (0-7923-4173-2) Kluwer Academic.

Martinez, Servet, jt. auth. see Golaes, E.

Martinez, Servet, jt. auth. see Goles, Eric.

Martinez, Servet, jt. ed. see Goles, Eric.

Martinez-Sicat, Maria T. Imagining the Nation in Four Philippine Novels. LC 95-947023. 164p. (Orig.). 1995. pap. text 18.00 (971-542-043-5, Pub. by U of Philippines Pr) UH Pr.

Martinez-Solanas, Gerardo E. Gobierno Del Pueblo: Opcion para un Nuevo Siglo. LC 97-80442. (Coleccion Cuba y sus Jueces). (SPA.). 114p. 1997. pap. 9.95 (0-89729-861-6) Ediciones.

***Martinez, Soraida.** Soraida's Verdadism: The Intellectual Voice of a Puerto Rican Woman; Unique Controversial Images & Style. LC 99-68364. (Illus.). 108p. 1999. pap. 59.95 (0-9676719-0-6) Artist.

Martinez, Steve K. Materials Testing & Biocompatibility: Index of New Information & Medical Research Bible. rev. ed. 183p. 1997. 47.50 (0-7883-1564-1); pap. 44.50 (0-7883-1565-X) ABBE Pubs Assn.

Martinez, Susan E. Angels & Dreams. Ilse, Sherokee, ed. (Gifts from the Universe Ser.). 116p. (Orig.). 1995. pap. 7.95 (0-9625379-4-2) Safe & Sound Prodns.

Martinez, Susie, et al. Don't Panic... It's in the Freezer! rev. ed. 1997. pap. 13.95 (0-9675379-1-6) Dont Panic.

Martinez, Thomas E. The Peron Novel. (SPA.). 1997. pap. 14.00 (0-679-78146-3) Vin Bks.

Martinez Tolentino, Jaime. Cuentos Fantasticos. LC 81-10292. (UPREX, Estudios Literarios Ser.: No. 62). 70p. 1983. pap. 2.00 (0-8477-0062-3) U of PR Pr.

Martinez, Tomas. The Human Marketplace: An Examination of Private Employment Agencies. LC 74-20196. 176p. 1975. text 34.95 (0-87855-094-1) Transaction Pubs.

Martinez, Tomas E. The Peron Novel. LC 98-46385. 1998. pap. 14.00 (0-679-76801-7) Random.

— Santa Evita. Lane, Helen, tr. 371p. Date not set. 23.00 (0-614-21930-2) Knopf.

— Santa Evita. 1996. 23.00 (0-679-44704-0) Knopf.

— Santa Evita. Lane, Helen, tr. from SPA. LC 97-6676. 1997. pap. 14.00 (0-679-76814-9) Random.

— Santa Evita. (SPA.). 1996. pap. 14.00 (0-679-77629-X) Vin Bks.

Martinez, Tomas Eloy. La Mano del Amo. 1999. pap. text 18.95 (968-406-753-4) F Planeta.

Martinez Torres, Augusto. Diccionario Nuevos Directores Franceses. (SPA.). 176p. 1976. pap. 9.95 (0-8288-5579-X, S50075) Fr & Eur.

Martinez, V. J., et al, eds. New Insights into the Universe: Proceedings of a Summer School, Held in Valencia, Spain, 23-27 September 1991. LC 92 27336. (Lecture Notes in Physics Ser.: Vol. 408). xi, 298p. 1992. 70.95 (0-387-55842-X); write for info. (3-540-55842-X) Spr-Verlag.

Martinez, Valerie. Absence, Luminescent. LC 98-72338. (Levis Poetry Prize Ser.). 67p. 1999. pap. 12.95 (1-884800-23-8, Pub. by Four Way Bks) SPD-Small Pr Dist.

Martinez-Vergne, Teresita. Capitalism in Colonial Puerto Rico: Central San Vicente in the Late Nineteenth Century. (Illus.). 208p. (C). 1992. 49.95 (0-8130-1110-8) U Press Fla.

Martinez Vergne, Teresita. Shaping the Discourse on Space: Charity & Its Wards in Nineteenth-Century San Juan, Puerto Rico. LC 98-20716. 256p. 1999. 32.50 (0-292-75220-2); pap. 17.95 (0-292-75221-0) U of Tex Pr.

Martinez, Victor. Caring for a House. (Illus.). 65p. 1992. pap. 10.00 (0-9624536-4-1) Chusma Hse.

— Parrot in the Oven: Mi Vida: A Novel. LC 96-2119. (Joanna Cotler Bks.). 224p. (J). (gr. 7 up). 1996. 15.95 (0-06-026704-6) HarpC Child Bks.

— Parrot in the Oven: Mi Vida: A Novel. LC 96-2119. (Joanna Cotler Bks.). 224p. (YA). (gr. 12 up). 1996. lib. bdg. 15.89 (0-06-026706-2) HarpC Child Bks.

— Parrot in the Oven: Mi Vida: A Novel. LC 96-2119. 224p. (YA). (gr. 12 up). 1998. pap. 5.95 (0-06-447186-1) HarpC Child Bks.

***Martinez, Victor.** Parrot in the Oven: Mi Vida: A Novel. 1998. 10.05 (0-606-13695-9, Pub. by Turtleback) Demco.

Martinez, Victoria. The Semiotics of a Bourgeois Society: An Analysis of the Aguafuertes Portenas by Roberto Arlt. LC 97-9900. 210p. 1997. pap. 49.95 (1-57309-232-0) Intl Scholars.

Martinez, Victoria J. & Arlt, Roberto. The Semiotics of a Bourgeois Society: An Analysis of the Aguafuertes Porte Nas by Roberto Arlt, Vol. 132. LC 97-9900. (Humanistica Ser.). 1997. write for info. (1-882528-22-0) Scripta.

Martinez, Violeta, ed. see Cowman, Charles E.

Martinez, Wilfred, jt. auth. see Mock, Gloria.

Martinez, William, Jr., jt. auth. see Battenburg, John.

Martinez, Yasmin, ed. see Dounuts, Kevin.

Martinez, Yvonne. God Comes Cable Ready, Are You Connected? unabridged ed. (Illus.). 53p. 1998. pap. 11.95 (0-9668598-0-4) Yvonnes Connection.

Martinez-Zanca, Minerva. Gentleman in the Cane. Chavez, Gloria, ed. (Illus.). (Orig.). 1997. pap. 14.95 (0-9655516-1-X) Obra Hispana.

— Rice, No Beans. Chavez, Gloria, ed. LC 96-92942. (Illus.). 115p. (Orig.). 1997. pap. text 11.00 (0-9655516-0-1) Obra Hispana.

— Trying on Great-Grandma's Boots. Chavez, Gloria, ed. (Illus.). (Orig.). 1997. pap. 14.95 (0-9655516-2-8) Obra Hispana.

Martinez-Zapater, Jose M. & Salinas, Julio, eds. Arabidopsis Protocols. LC 97-44454. (Methods in Molecular Biology Ser.: Vol. 82). (Illus.). 458p. 1998. 89.50 (0-89603-391-0) Humana.

Martinez, Zarela. The Food & Life of Oaxaca: Traditional Recipes from Mexico's Heart. Mendelson, Anne, ed. LC 97-3202. 342p. 1997. 32.50 (0-02-860350-8) Macmillan.

— Food from My Heart: Cuisines of Mexico Remembered & Reimagined. 352p. 1995. 14.00 (0-02-860361-3) Macmillan.

Marting, Diane E. Clarice Lispector: A Bio-Bibliography, 2. LC 93-28537. (Bio-Bibliographies in World Literature Ser.: Vol. 2). 368p. 1993. lib. bdg. 99.50 (0-313-27803-2, Greenwood Pr) Greenwood.

Marting, Diane E., ed. Spanish American Women Writers: A Bio-Bibliographical Source Book. LC 89-27283. 672p. 1990. lib. bdg. 99.50 (0-313-25194-0, MSA/, Greenwood Pr) Greenwood.

— Women Writers of Spanish America: An Annotated Bio-Bibliographical Guide, 5. LC 86-33552. (Bibliographies & Indexes in Women's Studies: No. 5). 464p. 1987. lib. bdg. 89.50 (0-313-24969-5, MWN/, Greenwood Pr) Greenwood.

Marting, Elizabeth. Invitation to Achievement: Your Career in Management. LC HD0020.M35. 35p. reprint ed. pap. 30.00 (0-608-12152-5, 202390800034) Bks Demand.

Marting, Elizabeth, ed. see American Management Association, Research Developm.

Marting, Janet. Commitment, Voice, & Clarity: An Argument Rhetoric & Reader. 1996. teacher ed. 35.95 (0-8442-5906-3); student ed. 24.95 (0-8442-5905-5) NTC Contemp Pub Co.

— The Family Tree: Classic Essays of Family & Ancestors. (Library of Classic Essays). 1998. pap., teacher ed. 23.99 (0-8442-5304-9) NTC Contemp Pub Co.

— The Family Tree: Classic Essays on Family & Ancestors. LC 97-351. (Library of Classic Essays). 320p. (J). 1997. pap., student ed. write for info. (0-8442-5303-0) NTC Contemp Pub Co.

— From the Cradle to the Grave: Classic Essays on Coming of Age & Aging. LC 97-350. (Library of Classic Essays). 304p. 1997. pap., student ed. write for info. (0-8442-5305-7) NTC Contemp Pub Co.

— From the Cradle to the Grave: Classic Essays on Coming of Age & Aging. (Library of Classic Essays). 1998. pap., teacher ed. 23.99 (0-8442-5306-5) NTC Contemp Pub Co.

Marting, Janet, ed. Voice Reflection. LC 94-1385. (C). 1997. 41.40 (0-673-46934-4) Addson-Wesley Educ.

Martingale & Company Staff. Quiltskills: Workshops from the Quilters' Guild. (Illus.). 96p. 1998. pap. text 24.95 (1-56477-213-6) Martingale & Co.

Martingale, Moira. Cannibal Killers. 1995. mass mkt. 5.50 (0-312-95604-5, Pub. by Tor Bks) St Martin.

***Martingale, Moira.** Cannibal Killers: The History of Impossible Murders. 192p. 2000. pap. 11.95 (0-7867-0703-8) Carroll & Graf.

Martini. Appl Manual Essentials Anatomy. 224p. 1996. pap. text 25.00 (0-13-532755-5, Pub. by P-H) S&S Trade.

— Cultural Construction of Parenting. (C). 2000. pap. text 48.50 (0-15-503954-7) Harcourt Coll Pubs.

***Martini.** Essentials of Anatomy & Physiology. 2nd ed. 1999. write for info. (0-13-018834-4) P-H.

Martini. Human Anatomy. 2nd ed. 1996. pap. text, teacher ed. write for info. (0-13-267709-1) Allyn.

— Human Anatomy. 2nd ed. 1997. pap. text, teacher ed. write for info. (0-13-267717-2) Allyn.

***Martini.** Human Body in Health & Disease. LC 99-58973. 596p. 1999. pap. text 50.67 (0-13-856816-2) P-H.

Martini & Bartholomew. Structure & Function of the Human Body. 406p. 1998. pap. text 50.67 (0-13-625377-6) P-H.

***Martini & Timmons.** Human Anatomy. 3rd ed. 1999. suppl. ed. write for info. (0-13-018810-7) P-H.

Martini, Aemidius & Bassi, Domenicus. Catalogus Codicum Graecorum Bibliothecae Ambrosianae, 2 vols. in 1. li, 1297p. 1978. reprint ed. write for info. incl. 3.5 hd (3-487-06499-5) G Olms Pubs.

Martini, Allessandro, ed. Genetics & Hearing Impairment. (Illus.). 348p. (Orig.). 1996. pap. 59.95 (1-56593-792-9, 1546) Singular Publishing.

Martini, Carlo. Bread of the Word. 1989. 4.25 (0-89942-378-7, 378/04) Catholic Bk Pub.

Martini, Carlo C. After Some Years: Reflection on the Ministry of the Priest. 125p. 1991. pap. 9.95 (1-85390-038-9, Pub. by Veritas Pubns) St Mut.

— Drawn to the Lord: Six Stories of Vocation. Rogers, Patrick, tr. from ITA. 80p. (Orig.). 1987. pap. 6.95 (0-86217-248-9, Pub. by Veritas Pubns) St Mut.

— Women & Reconciliation. Griffin, Luke, tr. from ITA. (Cathedral Ser.: No. 3). 66p. (Orig.). 1987. pap. 7.95 (0-86217-239-X, Pub. by Veritas Pubns) St Mut.

— Women & Reconciliation. 66p. (Orig.). 1989. pap. 30.00 (0-86217-293-4, Pub. by Veritas Pubns) St Mut.

Martini, Carlo M. Communicating Christ to the World. Lucas, Thomas, tr. LC 93-35459. 200p. (Orig.). 1994. pap. 14.95 (1-55612-655-7) Sheed & Ward WI.

— In the Thick of His Ministry. 91p. 1991. pap. 6.95 (0-8146-1995-9) Liturgical Pr.

— In the Thick of His Ministry. 96p. 1992. pap. 40.00 (0-85439-336-6, Pub. by St Paul Pubns) St Mut.

— Jacob's Dream: Setting Out on a Spiritual Journey. Lane, Ronald E., tr. from ITA. 72p. (Orig.). 1992. pap. 4.95 (0-8146-2000-0) Liturgical Pr.

— Journeying with the Lord: Reflections for Everyday. 511p. 1987. pap. 14.95 (0-8189-0508-5) Alba.

— The Joy of the Gospel: Meditations for Young People. McGrath, James, tr. 128p. (Orig.). 1994. pap. 8.95 (0-8146-2126-0) Liturgical Pr.

— Letting God Free Us. 128p. 1993. 26.00 (0-85439-452-4, Pub. by St Paul Pubns) St Mut.

— Letting God Free Us: Meditations on Ignatian Spiritual Exercises. Arnandez, Richard, tr. from ITA. LC 93-15187. 128p. (Orig.). 1993. pap. 9.95 (1-56548-053-8) New City.

— Ministers of the Gospel. 1989. pap. 6.95 (0-8245-0959-5) Crossroad NY.

— The New Wine: Christian Witness of the Family. Berger, Mary J., tr. from ITA. 319p. (Orig.). 1994. pap. 11.95 (0-8198-5131-0) Pauline Bks.

— Once More from Emmaus. O'Connell, Matthew J., tr. 120p. (Orig.). 1995. pap. 8.95 (0-8146-2158-9) Liturgical Pr.

— Perseverance in Trials: Reflections on Job. O'Connell, Matthew J., tr. 144p. (Orig.). 1992. pap. 9.95 (0-8146-2060-4) Liturgical Pr.

— A Prophetic Voice in the City: Meditations on the Prophet Jeremiah. Castelli Theisen, Vera, tr. from ITA. LC 97-14655. 160p. 1997. pap. 11.95 (0-8146-2412-X) Liturgical Pr.

— The Testimony of St. Paul. 104p. (C). 1990. 39.00 (0-85439-221-1, Pub. by St Paul Pubns) St Mut.

— What Am I That You Care for Me? Praying with the Psalms. 138p. (Orig.). (C). 1990. 49.00 (0-85439-347-1, Pub. by St Paul Pubns) St Mut.

Martini, Carlo M., ed. Ministers of the Gospel. (C). 1988. 39.00 (0-85439-220-3, Pub. by St Paul Pubns) St Mut.

— The Testimony of St. Paul. (C). 1989. pap. 6.95 (0-8245-0958-7) Crossroad NY.

An Asterisk (*) at the beginning of an entry indicates that the title is appearing for the first time.

Martini, Carlo M., jt. auth. see Eco, Umberto.

Martini, Carlo-Maria. David: Sinner & Believer. 187p. (C). 1996. pap. 39.95 (*0-85439-322-6*, Pub. by St Paul Pubns) St Mut.

— The Dove at Rest. 128p. 1996. pap. 39.95 (*0-85439-511-3*, Pub. by St Paul Pubns) St Mut.

— Promise Fulfilled. 176p. 1996. pap. 39.95 (*0-85439-481-8*, Pub. by St Paul Pubns) St Mut.

***Martini, Carlo-Maria.** Vivir Con la Biblia. 1999. 24.95 (*84-08-02606-2*) Planeta Edit.

Martini, Carlo-Maria & Board of St. Paul Editorial Staff. The Woman among Her People. 136p. (C). 1996. pap. 39.95 (*0-85439-297-1*, Pub. by St Paul Pubns) St Mut.

Martini, Clem. Illegal Entry. 96p. (Orig.). 1999. pap. 13.95 (*0-88754-569-6*, Pub. by Theatre Comm) Consort Bk Sales.

Martini, Clem & Foreman, Kathleen, eds. Something Like a Drug: An Unauthorized Oral History of Theatresports. LC 95-14873. 1995. pap. 14.95 (*0-88734-918-8*, Pub. by Red Deer) Empire Pub Srvs.

Martini, D. Richard, jt. auth. see Dulcan, Mina K.

Martini, Elizabeth B., et al. Long Term Care: For Activity & Social Service Professionals. 2nd ed. (Illus.). 404p. (C). 1996. pap. text 35.00 (*1-882883-28-4*) Idyll Arbor.

Martini, Eric, jt. ed. see Bene, Marie-Christine.

Martini, Francesco De, see De Martini, Francesco.

***Martini, Franklin D.** Meaning of Dreams. 368p. 2001. 9.99 (*0-517-16250-4*) Crown Pub Group.

Martini, Frederic & Welch, Kathleen. Fundamentals of Anatomy & Physiology. 4th ed. LC 97-15117. 1997. pap. text, teacher ed. 14.00 (*0-13-751868-4*) P-H.

***Martini, Frederic, et al.** Human Anatomy. 3rd ed. LC 99-32477. 866p. (C). 1999. 101.33 (*0-13-010011-0*) P-H.

Martini, Frederic H. Clinical Manual Fundamental Anatomy & Physiology. 2nd ed. 1992. pap. text 22.00 (*0-13-335357-5*) P-H.

— Fundamentals of Anatomy & Physiology. 2nd ed. 1120p. (C). 1992. text 97.00 (*0-13-334590-4*) P-H.

Martini, Frederic H. & Bartholomew, Edwin. Essentials of Anatomy & Physiology. 2nd ed. LC 99-32478. 648p. (C). 1999. 79.67 (*0-13-082192-6*) P-H.

***Martini, Frederic H. & Bartholomew, Edwin.** Human Body in Health & Disease: Study Guide. 2000. pap. 25.00 (*0-13-017266-9*) P-H.

Martini, Frederic H. & Karleskint, George. Foundations of Anatomy & Physiology. LC 98-11747. (Illus.). 494p. (C). 1998. pap. text 42.00 (*0-13-592965-2*, Prentice Hall) P-H.

***Martini, Frederick H.** Fundamentals of Anatomy & Physiology & Applications Manual. 4th ed. 1123p. 1998. pap. text 105.00 (*0-13-096292-9*, Prentice Hall) P-H.

Martini, Galen. The Heart's Slow Race: A Farewell to the Lands. LC 76-24956. (Illus.). 1976. 6.95 (*0-87839-029-4*) North Star.

Martini, Harold J. Athletic Injuries: Guidebook for Medicine & Research. LC 87-47678. 150p. 1987. 39.50 (*0-88164-660-1*); pap. 34.50 (*0-88164-661-X*) ABBE Pubs Assn.

Martini, Horst & Soltan, Petru S. Excursions into Combinatorial Theory. LC 96-26787. (Universitext Ser.). (Illus.). 419p. 1997. 59.95 (*3-540-61341-2*) Spr-Verlag.

Martini, I. P. & Chesworth, W. Weathering, Soils & Paleosols. (Developments in Earth Surface Processes Ser.: Vol. 2). 618p. 1992. 197.75 (*0-444-89198-6*) Elsevier.

Martini, I. Peter, ed. Late Glacial & Postglacial Environmental Changes: Quatrnary, Carboniferous-Permian & Proterozoic. LC 95-51665. (Illus.). 360p. 1997. text 70.00 (*0-19-508541-8*) OUP.

Martini, James C. Basic Canoeing Workbook. (Illus.). 98p. (Orig.). 1992. 3.95 (*1-881644-00-6*) P E R Assocs.

***Martini, Jean Marie.** Incredible Edibles: Recipes from Colorado Hotel Chefs. (Illus.). 264p. 1999. pap. 19.99 (*0-9676400-0-8*) CO Hotel.

Martini, Johannes. Four Chansons. (Renaissance Recorder Ser.: No. 1). 1970. 2.75 (*0-913334-06-5*, CM1005) Consort Music.

— Johannes Martini: Secular Pieces. Evans, Edward G., Jr., ed. (Recent Researches in Music of the Middle Ages & Early Renaissance Ser.: Vol. RRM1). xxvi, 90p. 1975. pap. 40.00 (*0-89579-060-2*) A-R Eds.

***Martini, Johannes.** Johannes Martini - Complete Masses Pt.1: Masses Without Known Polyphonic Models. Steib, Murray & Moohan, Elaine, eds. (Illus.). xxiii, 257p. 1999. pap. 95.00 (*0-89579-433-0*, M34) A-R Eds.

— Johannes Martini - Masses Pt. 2: Masses with Known Polyphonic Models. Steib, Murray & Moohan, Elaine, eds. (Illus.). vi, 305p. 1999. 100.00 (*0-89579-434-9*, M35) A-R Eds.

Martini, John. Fortress Alcatraz - Guardian of the Golden Gate. 1991. pap. 11.95 (*0-9629227-0-6*) Pacific Mono.

Martini, John A. Fort Point: Sentry at the Golden Gate. (Illus.). 48p. (Orig.). 1992. pap. 7.95 (*0-9625206-5-9*) Gldn Gate Natl Parks Assoc.

Martini, Juan. El Fantasma Imperfecto: The Imperfect Ghost. 184p. 1995. pap. 14.95 (*0-679-76097-0*) Villard Books.

Martini, Juan C. La Vida Entera. (SPA.). 284p. 1981. pap. 9.50 (*84 02 07874 5*, 3011) Ediciones Norte.

Martini, Leonard J. Practical Seal Design. (Mechanical Engineering Ser.: Vol. 29). (Illus.). 312p. 1984. text 125.00 (*0-8247-7166-4*) Dekker.

Martini, Luciano & Ganong, William F., eds. Frontiers in Neuroendocrinology, Vol. 4. fac. ed. LC 77-82030. (Illus.). 304p. pap. 94.30 (*0-7837-7146-0*, 204714900004) Bks Demand.

— Frontiers in Neuroendocrinology, Vol. 6. LC 77-82030. 428p. 1980. reprint ed. pap. 132.70 (*0-608-00272-0*, 204714900006) Bks Demand.

— Frontiers in Neuroendocrinology, Vol. 10. LC 77-82030. 357p. 1988. reprint ed. pap. 110.70 (*0-608-00275-5*, 204714900010) Bks Demand.

Martini, Luciano, jt. ed. see Ganong, William F.

Martini, Luciano, ed. see International Symposium on Androgens & Antiandroge.

Martini, Luciano, ed. see Meeting on Animal Models in Human Reproduction Sta.

Martini, M., ed. Tuberculosis of the Bones & Joints. (Illus.). 230p. 1988. 118.00 (*0-387-18166-0*) Spr-Verlag.

Martini, Martha R. Marx Not Madison: The Crisis of American Legal Education. LC 96-3341. 180p. 1996. lib. bdg. 36.50 (*0-7618-0485-4*) U Pr of Amer.

Martini, N. & Schell, Josef S. Plant Oils As Fuels: Present State of Science & Future Developments: Proceedings of the Symposium Held in Potsdam, Germany, February 16-18, 1997. LC 98-27941. 1998. pap. write for info. (*3-540-64754-6*) Spr-Verlag.

Martini, R., ed. Geometric Aspects of the Einstein Equation & Integrable Systems. (Lecture Notes in Physics Ser.: Vol. 239). 344p. 1985. 38.95 (*0-387-16039-6*) Spr-Verlag.

Martini, R., jt. ed. see Bongaarts, P. J.

Martini, Regina. Pens & Pencils. rev. ed. (Illus.). 148p. 1998. pap. 24.95 (*0-7643-0313-9*) Schiffer.

Martini, Steve. The Attorney. LC 99-44260. 429p. 2000. 25.95 (*0-399-14536-2*) Putnam Pub Group.

***Martini, Steve.** The Attorney. large type ed. LC 99-87732. (Thorndike Basic Ser.). 2000. 31.95 (*0-7862-2433-9*) Thorndike Pr.

— The Attorney. large type ed. LC 99-87732. 2000. write for info. (*0-7862-2434-7*) Thorndike Pr.

Martini, Steve. Compelling Evidence. 448p. 1993. mass mkt. 7.50 (*0-515-11039-6*, Jove) Berkley Pub.

— Compelling Evidence. large type ed. LC 92-18331. (General Ser.). 657p. 1993. 18.95 (*0-8161-5549-6*, G K Hall Lrg Type) Mac Lib Ref.

— Critical Mass. LC 98-24327. 448p. (YA). (gr. 12 up). 1998. 24.95 (*0-399-14362-9*) Putnam Pub Group.

— Critical Mass. large type ed. LC 98-39406. 1998. 27.95 (*1-56895-668-1*) Wheeler Pub.

— Critical Mass. 1999. reprint ed. mass mkt. 7.99 (*0-515-12583-0*, Jove) Berkley Pub.

***Martini, Steve.** Critical Mass. 1999. reprint ed. mass mkt. 7.99 (*0-515-12648-9*, Jove) Berkley Pub.

— The Judge. abr. ed. 1996. audio 24.00 (*0-671-53453-X*) S&S Audio.

Martini, Steve. The Judge. large type ed. 650p. 1999. lib. bdg. 26.95 (*0-7838-1610-3*, G K Hall Lrg Type) Mac Lib Ref.

— The Judge. large type ed. 1996. pap. 24.95 (*0-7838-1611-1*); pap. 24.95 (*0-614-26605-X*) Thorndike Pr.

— The Judge. 512p. 1996. reprint ed. mass mkt. 6.99 (*0-515-11964-4*, Jove) Berkley Pub.

— El Juramento. 1998. pap. text 11.95 (*84-08-02188-5*) Planeta Edit.

***Martini, Steve.** The Jury. 448p. 2001. 25.95 (*0-399-14672-5*) Putnam Pub Group.

— The List. abr. ed. 1997. audio 25.00 (*0-671-53454-8*, 692868) S&S Audio.

Martini, Steve. The List. large type ed. 451p. 1997. mass mkt. 7.50 (*0-515-12149-5*, Jove) Berkley Pub.

— The List. large type ed. LC 96-54263. 650p. 1997. 28.95 (*0-7838-8089-8*, G K Hall Lrg Type); pap. 26.95 (*0-7838-8090-1*, G K Hall Lrg Type) Mac Lib Ref.

***Martini, Steve.** La Lista. 1999. 29.95 (*84-08-02992-4*) Planeta.

Martini, Steve. Prime Witness. 416p. 1994. mass mkt. 7.99 (*0-515-11264-X*, Jove) Berkley Pub.

— Prime Witness. large type ed. LC 93-34152. 590p. 1993. 23.95 (*0-8161-5869-X*, G K Hall Lrg Type) Mac Lib Ref.

— The Simeon Chamber. large type ed. LC 98-14663. 1998. 25.95 (*1-56895-538-3*, Wheeler) Wheeler Pub.

— The Simeon Chamber. 320p. 1994. reprint ed. mass mkt. 7.50 (*0-515-11371-9*, Jove) Berkley Pub.

— Undue Influence. 480p. 1995. mass mkt. 6.99 (*0-515-11605-X*, Jove) Berkley Pub.

— Undue Influence. 1994. audio 17.00 (*0-671-89520-6*) S&S Trade.

— Undue Influence: TV Movie Tie-In. 1996. mass mkt. 6.99 (*0-515-12072-3*, Jove) Berkley Pub.

Martini, Teri. Christmas for Andy. LC 91-16362. (J). (gr. 3 up). 1991. pap. 3.95 (*0-8091-6603-8*) Paulist Pr.

— Feliz Navidad, Pablo. (Illus.). (J). (gr. 4 up). 1990. pap. 2.95 (*0-8091-6597-X*) Paulist Pr.

— The Secret Is Out. 144p. (J). (gr. 5). 1992. pap. 2.99 (*0-380-71465-5*, Avon Bks) Morrow Avon.

Martini, Therese. Love's Lost Melody. 448p. 1984. mass mkt. 3.50 (*0-446-32236-9*, Pub. by Warner Bks) Little.

Martiniak. DEP Practice Handbook. 312p. 1995. 70.00 (*0-316-54800-6*, Aspen Law & Bus) Aspen Pub.

Martiniak, L. J. Deposition Practice Handbook: How to Take & Defend Depositions. 2nd ed. LC 99-18114. 1999. pap. text 135.00 (*0-7355-0437-7*) Panel Pubs.

Martiniak, Marita, ed. see Worring, Raymond W., et al.

Martinich. Production Operations Management: An Applied Analytical Approach & Wall Street Journal Interactive Guide. 1008p. 1997. text 71.00 (*0-471-28215-4*) Wiley.

Martinich, A. P. Communication & Reference. LC 84-14283. (Foundations of Communication & Cognition Ser.). xiii, 205p. 1984. lib. bdg. 76.15 (*3-11-010067-3*) De Gruyter.

— Hobbes: A Biography. LC 98-36567. (Illus.). 400p. (C). 1999. 34.95 (*0-521-49583-0*) Cambridge U Pr.

— The Philosophy of Language. 3rd ed. 592p. (C). 1996. text 47.95 (*0-19-509368-2*) OUP.

***Martinich, A. P.** The Philosophy of Language. 4th ed. 624p. (C). 2000. pap. text 42.95 (*0-19-513543-1*) OUP.

Martinich, A. P. & White, Michael James Denham, eds. Certainty & Surface in Epistemology & Philosophical Method: Essays in Honor of Avrum Stroll. LC 91-27368. (Problems in Contemporary Philosophy Ser.: Vol. 32). 228p. 1991. lib. bdg. 89.95 (*0-7734-9711-0*) E Mellen.

Martinich, Aloysius P. A Hobbes Dictionary. (The/Blackwell Philosopher Dictionaries Ser.). 400p. 1995. pap. 28.95 (*0-631-19262-X*) Blackwell Pubs.

— Philosphical Writing: An Introduction. 2nd ed. LC 96-7632. 176p. 1996. pap. 18.95 (*0-631-20281-1*) Blackwell Pubs.

— Thomas Hobbes. LC 96-28495. 160p. 1997. pap. 18.95 (*0-312-16494-7*); text 39.95 (*0-312-16493-9*) St Martin.

Martinich, Aloysius P., tr. see Hobbes, Thomas.

Martinich, Joseph S. Production & Operations Management: An Applied Modern Approach. LC 96-28170. 944p. 1996. text 105.95 (*0-471-54632-1*) Wiley.

Martinie, Henri. Art Deco Ornamental Ironwork. LC 94-47177.Tr. of Ferronerie. (Illus.). 112p. 1998. 9.95 (*0-486-28535-9*) Dover.

Martiniello, Marco, ed. Migration, Citizenship & Ethno-National Identities in the European Union. (Research in Ethnic Relations Ser.). 224p. 1995. 72.95 (*1-85972-002-1*, Pub. by Avebry) Ashgate Pub Co.

***Martiniello, Marco, ed.** Multicultural Policies & the State: A Comparison of Two European Societies. (Research in Migration & Ethnic Relations Ser.). 232p. 1999. pap. 20.95 (*90-75719-07-8*, Pub. by Europ Res Centre) Ashgate Pub Co.

Martiniello, Marco, jt. auth. see Body-Gendrot, Sophie.

Martiniez, Louis. New Orleans Voodoo Tarot-Book with Cards. 1992. pap. text 29.95 (*0-89281-363-6*) Inner Tradit.

Martinique, Edward. Preservation of Chinese Traditional Books in Cultural Institutions in Taiwan. LC 98-26409. (Illus.). 168p. 1998. text. write for info. (*0-7734-8290-3*) E Mellen.

Martinis, M., ed. Superstrings, Anomalies & Unification: Proceedings of the Adriatic Meeting on Particle Physics, 5th, Dubrovnik, Yugoslavia, June 16-28, 1986. 584p. 1987. pap. 47.00 (*9971-5-0233-X*); text 110.00 (*9971-5-0232-1*) World Scientific Pub.

Martinis, M., jt. ed. see Tezak, D.

Martinko, Mark, ed. Attribution Theory: An Organizational Perspective. LC 94-17213. (Illus.). 384p. 1995. boxed set 54.95 (*1-884015-19-0*) St Lucie Pr.

Martinkova, jt. ed. see Martinek.

Martino, Cynthia. Eat Your Way Thin. 80p. 1995. pap. 19.00 (*0-9650358-0-8*) C Martino.

— Eat Your Way Thin. LC 96-37197. (Illus.). 194p. 1996. pap. 9.95 (*0-937552-76-3*) Quail Ridge.

Martino, Dennis. Staying in Touch: The Art of Contact Management: Strategic Organization for the Financial Advisor LC 98-93990. 174 p. 1998. write for info. (*1-889800-19-8*) TNT Media Grp.

***Martino, Emanuele.** Mare. 2000. pap. 29.95 (*88-8158-260-0*) Charta.

***Martino, G. & Adorini, L.** Topics in Neuroscience: From Basic Immunology to Immune-Mediated Demyelination. LC 99-17459. 240p. 1999. 155.00 (*88-470-0054-8*, Pub. by Spr-Verlag) Spr-Verlag.

***Martino, James.** Discovering... Alla Scoperta Della Basilicata: An Historical Collection of Italian Recipes from the Region. Mancuso, Olga et al, trs. LC 97-72346. (Illus.). 120p. 1999. 16.95 (*0-9658032-0-1*) Giacomo.

Martino, Joseph P. Research & Development Project Selection. LC 94-30753. (Engineering Management Ser.). 266p. 1995. 90.00 (*0-471-59537-3*) Wiley.

— Science Funding: Politics & Porkbarrel. 336p. (C). 1992. 44.95 (*1-56000-033-3*) Transaction Pubs.

Martino, Joseph P., ed. An Introduction to Technological Forecasting. (Futurist Library). x, 108p. 1973. text 146.00 (*0-677-15050-4*) Gordon & Breach.

Martino, Lino Di, see Kantor, William M. & Di Martino, Lino, eds.

Martino, Lino Di, see Di Martino, Lino.

Martino, Pierre. Naturalisme Francais, 1870-95. 206p. 1969. 29.95 (*0-8288-7431-X*) Fr & Eur.

— Parnasse et Symbolisme. 191p. 1970. 29.95 (*0-8288-7432-8*) Fr & Eur.

Martino, Teresa. Pizza! (Real Readers Ser.: Level Green). (Illus.). 32p. (J). (ps-3). 1989. lib. bdg. 21.40 (*0-8172-3533-7*) Raintree Steck-V.

Martino, Teresa T. The Wolf, the Woman, the Wilderness: A True Story of Returning Home. LC 96-45468. (Illus.). 156p. 1996. pap. text 14.95 (*0-939165-29-5*) NewSage Press.

***Martino, Teresa Tsimmu.** Dancer on the Grass: True Stories about Horses & People. LC 99-52149. (Illus.). 166p. 1999. pap. 12.95 (*0-939165-32-5*) NewSage Press.

Martino, Terry DeFranco. A Town in a Home. 192p. 1999. pap. 11.95 (*1-56315-192-8*, Pub. by SterlingHse) Natl Bk Netwk.

Martino, Tony. Trademark Dilution. LC 95-43641. 156p. 1996. text 90.00 (*0-19-826071-7*) OUP.

Martino, V. Di, see Di Martino, V., ed.

Martino, Vittorio Di, see Yoxen, Edward & Di Martino, Vittorio, eds.

Martino, Vittorio Di, see Chappell, Duncan & Di Martino, Vittorio.

Martino, Vittorio Di, see Di Martino, Vittorio.

Martino, Wayne. From the Margins: Exploring Ethnicity, Gender & Aboriginality. 120p. 1997. pap. 19.95 (*1-86368-215-5*, Pub. by Fremantle Arts) Intl Spec Bk.

***Martino, Wayne & Cook, Chris, eds.** Gender & Texts: A Professional Development Package for Teaching English. 156p. 1999. pap. text 22.50 (*1-875659-13-7*, 659137, Pub. by Aust Assn Teach) Calendar Islands.

***Martino, Wayne & Mellor, Bronwyn.** Gendered Fictions. 100p. 2000. write for info. (*0-8141-1825-9*, 18259) NCTE.

Martinoli, Silvia. How about Parenting? 80p. 1995. pap. 6.95 (*0-9634014-9-1*) S Martinoli.

— Men . . . Wake Up! 1993. pap. 6.95 (*0-9634014-8-3*) S Martinoli.

— No More Detours. 102p. 1992. pap. 6.95 (*0-9634014-7-5*) S Martinoli.

Martinot, Eric. Investments to Improve the Efficiency of Existing Residential Buildings in Countries of the Former Soviet Union. LC 97-29354. (Studies of Economics in Transformation: No. 24). 164p. 1997. pap. 22.00 (*0-8213-4057-3*, 14057) World Bank.

Martinot, Eric & McDoom, Omar. Promoting Energy Efficiency & Renewable Energy: GEF Climate Change Projects & Impacts. 110p. write for info. (*1-884122-93-0*) Global Environ.

Martinot, Steve, tr. see Memmi, Albert.

Martinovitch, Nicholas N. The Turkish Theatre. LC 68-20241. (Illus.). 125p. 1972. reprint ed. 21.95 (*0-405-08761-6*, Pub. by Blom Pubns) Ayer.

***Martinpat.** Memory Jug. 276p. (J). 1998. 15.95 (*0-7868-0357-6*, Pub. by Hyperion) Time Warner.

Martins, Emilia P., ed. Phylogenies & the Comparative Method in Animal Behavior. (Illus.). 432p. (C). 1996. text 65.00 (*0-19-509210-4*) OUP.

***Martins, Felipe, et al.** Professional Access 2000 Programming. 800p. 2000. pap. 49.99 (*1-86100-408-7*) Wrox Pr Inc.

Martins, Felipe, jt. auth. see Mackenzie, Duncan.

Martins, G. R. Modern Drafting Room Practice. (Technical Papers: Vol. P190). (Illus.). 15p. 1939. pap. text 30.00 (*1-55589-446-1*) AGMA.

Martins, George. Reading Scripture As the Word of God: Practical Approaches & Attitudes. 1998. pap. text 11.99 (*1-56955-061-1*) Servant.

Martins, Helen Elizabeth, jt. see Ross, Sue Imrie.

Martins, Helvecio & Grover, Mark. The Autobiography of Elder Helvecio Martins. LC 94-37044. 131p. 1994. 12.95 (*1-56236-218-6*, Pub. by Aspen Bks) Origin Bk Sales.

Martins, Herminio, ed. Knowledge & Passion: Essays in Sociology & Social Theory in Honour of John Rex. 256p. 1993. text 70.00 (*1-85043-323-2*) St Martin.

Martins, Hermino, jt. ed. see Pickering, William S.

Martins, Isabel P., et al, eds. Acquired Aphasia in Children. 328p. 1991. text 171.00 (*0-7923-1315-1*) Kluwer Academic.

Martins, J. A. Diccionario Tecnico Ingles-Portuguese de Maquinas e Ferramentas. (ENG & POR.). 229p. 1983. 35.00 (*0-7859-7152-1*) Fr & Eur.

Martins, J. B., ed. Numerical Methods in Geomechanics. 1982. text 226.00 (*90-277-1461-4*) Kluwer Academic.

Martins, J. M., jt. ed. see Dunlop, David W.

Martins, J. P. & Morgado, E. M., eds. EPIA '89. (Lecture Notes in Artificial Intelligence Ser.: Vol. 390). xii, 400p. 1989. 47.00 (*0-387-51665-4*) Spr-Verlag.

Martins, Joao P. Introduction to Computer Science Using Pascal. 537p. (C). 1989. pap. 56.95 (*0-534-09402-3*) PWS Pubs.

Martins, Michael & Binette, Dennis A. The Commonwealth of Massachusetts vs. Lizzie A. Borden-The Knowlton Papers-1892-1893: A Collection of Previously Unpublished Letters from the Files of Prosecuting Attorney Hosea Morrill Knowlton. (Illus.). 400p. 1994. 49.95 (*0-9641248-3-1*) Fall River Hist Soc.

Martins-Miller, Susan. Betsy Ross. LC 99-25131. 1999. 16.95 (*0-7910-5360-1*) Chelsea Hse.

— Jim Elliot. (Young Reader's Christian Library). (Illus.). 192p. (J). (gr. 3-7). 1998. pap. 1.39 (*1-57748-228-X*) Barbour Pub.

Martins, Onyenekwe C. Voice of Passion. 1998. pap. write for info. (*1-57553-697-8*) Watermrk Pr.

Martins, Peter. New York City Ballet Workout: Fifty Stretches And Exercises Anyone Can Do For A Strong, Graceful, And SculptedBody. 352p. 1997. pap. 22.00 (*0-688-15202-3*, Wm Morrow) Morrow Avon.

— Stretch & Strengthen: The New York City Ballet Workout. Date not set. 40.00 (*0-614-20666-9*, Wm Morrow) Morrow Avon.

— Tributes: Celebrating Fifty Years of New York City Ballet. 75.00 (*0-688-16746-2*, Wm Morrow) Morrow Avon.

— Tributes: Celebrating 50 Years of New York City Ballet. Ramsey, Christopher, ed. LC 98-13671. (Illus.). 176p. 1998. 50.00 (*0-688-15751-3*, Wm Morrow) Morrow Avon.

Martins, Peter & New York City Ballet. The New York City Ballet Workout: Fifty Stretches & Exercises Anyone Can Do for a Strong, Graceful & Sculpted Body. LC 96-36245. 1997. 40.00 (*0-688-14843-3*, Wm Morrow) Morrow Avon.

Martins, Robyn. Fun Facts about the Bible. 256p. 1996. pap. text 2.49 (*1-55748-897-5*) Barbour Pub.

***Martins, Rudolf.** Heaven's Weed: A Rainbow Journey Through the Mennonite Mexican Marijuana Fields. Warren, Sam, ed. 224p. 2000. pap. write for info. (*0-945949-11-1*) Warren Comns.

Martins, Rui, ed. Recent Advances in Hydraulic Physical Modelling. (C). 1989. text 292.50 (*0-7923-0196-X*) Kluwer Academic.

Martins, Susanna W. A Great Estate at Work: The Holkham Estate & Its Inhabitants in the Nineteenth Century. LC 79-51827. 303p. reprint ed. pap. 86.40 (*0-608-15268-4*, 2029223) Bks Demand.

Martins-Swartz, Rosemarie A. Enter Quietly. 96p. (Orig.). 1993. 15.95 (*0-9636337-0-8*); pap. 9.95 (*0-9636337-1-6*) Intricate Lines.

M

Martins, Wilson. The Modernist Idea: A Critical Survey of Brazilian Writing in the Twentieth Century. Tomlins, Jack E., tr. from POR. LC 78-24232. 345p. 1979. reprint ed. lib. bdg. 38.50 (*0-313-20811-5*, MAID, Greenwood Pr) Greenwood.

Martins, Wilson & Menton, Seymour, eds. Teatro Brasileiro Contemporaneo. rev. ed. LC 77-2753. (gr. 11-12). 1978. reprint ed. pap. text 19.95 (*0-89197-640-X*) Irvington.

Martinsen, Deborah A., ed. Literary Journals in Imperial Russia. LC 97-7613. (Studies in Russian Literature). 283p. (C). 1998. text 64.95 (*0-521-57292-4*) Cambridge U Pr.

Martinsen, Ella L. Trail to North Star Gold: True Story of the Alaska-Klondike Gold Rush. 2nd ed. LC 70-98194. (Illus.). 378p. 1991. reprint ed. pap. 14.95 (*0-8323-0242-2*) Binford Mort.

Martinsen, Emily C. & Bolender, Joyce. The Troublesome Triangle: Sons, Wives & Mothers-in-Law. LC 95-72721. 93p. 1995. 9.95 (*0-9651135-0-7*) E C Martinsen.

Martinsen, Harald, jt. auth. see Von Tetzchner, Stephen.

Martinsen, Orjan, jt. auth. see Grimnes, Sverre.

Martinsen. Home Health Care Nursing. 2nd ed. 2000. pap. text. write for info. (*0-7216-7766-5*, W B Saunders Co) Harcrt Hlth Sci Grp.

— The Top 30 Business Schools. 1994. pap. 18.00 (*0-671-86594-3*) S&S Trade.

Martinson, A. D., jt. auth. see Magden, Ronald E.

Martinson, Arthur D. Wilderness above the Sound: The Story of Mount Rainier National Park. 2nd rev. ed. (Illus.). 96p. 1994. pap. 11.95 (*1-879373-76-9*) Roberts Rinehart.

Martinson, Debra, ed. see Martinson, L. Keith & Range, Fritz.

Martinson, Floyd M. Growing up in Norway, 800-1990. 264p. (C). 1992. 29.95 (*0-8093-1778-8*) S Ill U Pr.

— The Sexual Life of Children. LC 93-37847. 168p. 1994. 49.95 (*0-89789-376-X*, Bergin & Garvey) Greenwood.

Martinson, Harry. Aniara: An Epic Science Fiction Poem. LC 98-7891. 180p. 1999. reprint ed. pap. 14.95 (*1-885266-63-4*, 3, Pub. by Story Line) Consort Bk Sales.

— Wild Bouquet: Nature Poems. Smith, William J. & Sjoberg, Leif, trs. from SWE. LC 84-73437. (International Ser.). (Illus.). 80p. 1985. 10.95 (*0-933532-48-2*) BkMk.

Martinson, Ida, jt. ed. see Fitzpatrick, Joyce J.

Martinson, Ida M., jt. auth. see Moldow, D. Gay.

Martinson, Keith. Simple Law Texas Wills & Trusts Form Book. Orig. Title: Do-It-Yourself Texas Wills & Trusts. 62p. 1998. 29.99 incl. cd-rom (*0-9661181-7-0*) Simple Law.

***Martinson, Keith L.** Simple Law Texas Wills & Trusts. (Illus.). 1999. 24.99 (*1-893983-03-X*) Simple Law.

***Martinson, L. Keith.** Simple Law Texas Divorce. 1999. 24.99 (*1-893983-00-5*) Simple Law.

Martinson, L. Keith. Simple Law Texas General Legal Forms, Vol. I. 62p. 1999. 29.99 incl. cd-rom (*1-893983-08-0*, Pub. by Simple Law) Herveys Bklink.

***Martinson, L. Keith.** Simple Law Texas General Legal Forms, Vol. I. 62p. 1999. 19.95 (*1-893983-06-4*, Pub. by Simple Law) Herveys Bklink.

***Martinson, L Keith.** Simple Law Texas Home Equity Loans. 1999. 29.95 (*0-9661181-9-7*) Simple Law.

Martinson, L. Keith. Simple Law Texas Home Equity Loans with CD-ROM. 42p. 1999. 24.95 (*0-9661181-8-9*, Pub. by Simple Law) Herveys Bklink.

— Simple Law Texas Name Change Form. 60p. 1999. 29.99 incl. cd-rom (*0-9661181-6-2*) Simple Law.

***Martinson, L Keith.** Texas Divorce: Complete All The Paperwork for Your Uncontested Texas Divorce in Minutes! 1999. 24.99 (*1-893983-01-3*) Simple Law.

Martinson, L. Keith & Range, Fritz. Simple Law Texas Divorce CD with Form Book: Do It Yourself Pro Se Simplelaw Legal Documents. Martinson, Debra & Range, Diane, eds. (State Specific Do It Yourself Legal Software & Forms Ser.). Orig. Title: Do-It-Yourself Divorce CD & Forms, Simple Texas. 62p. 1999. 29.99 incl. cd-rom (*0-9661181-4-6*) Simple Law.

— Simple Law Texas Divorce Form Book. Martinson, Debra & Range, Diane, eds. (State Specific Do It Yourself Legal Software & Forms Ser.). Orig. Title: Do-it-Yourself, Simple Texas Divorce. 60p. 1999. ring bd. 19.95 (*0-9661181-0-3*) Simple Law.

***Martinson, L. Keith & Range, Fritz.** Simple Law Texas Name Changes Form Book: Do It Yourself Pro Se Simplelaw Legal Documents. Martinson, Debra & Range, Diane, eds. (State Specific Do It Yourself Legal Software & Forms Ser.). 60p. 1999. 19.95 (*0-9661181-5-4*) Simple Law.

Martinson, L. Keith & Range, Fritz. Simple Law Texas Wills & Trusts Form Book. Martinson, Debra & Range, Diane, eds. (State Specific Do It Yourself Legal Software & Forms Ser.). Orig. Title: Do-It-Yourself Wills & Trusts, Simple Texas. 60p. 1999. ring bd. 19.95 (*0-9661181-2-X*) Simple Law.

Martinson, Linda. The Poetry of Pain: Poems of Truth, Acceptance & Hope for Those Who Suffer Chronic Pain. LC 95-92651. 60p. (Orig.). 1996. pap. 9.95 (*0-9648978-2-2*) Simply Books.

— Simply Shrimp: Fresh, Frozen & Canned. (Illus.). 134p. (Orig.). 1988. pap. 5.95 (*0-934363-04-8*) Simply Books.

Martinson, Linda & O'Leary, Joanne. Don't Cut the Apron Strings: An Early Childhood Resource Featuring Integrated Curriculum & Theme Aprons. (Illus.). 114p. (Orig.). 1993. pap. 10.95 (*0-9637759-0-1*) Apron Strings.

Martinson, Moa. My Mother Gets Married. Lacy, Margaret S., tr. & afterword by by. LC 88-21405. 304p. 1988. 35.00 (*0-935312-99-4*); pap. 9.95 (*0-935312-81-1*) Feminist Pr.

— Women & Appletrees. Lacy, Margaret S., tr. & afterword by by. LC 85-6898. 224p. 1985. pap. 11.95 (*0-935312-38-2*) Feminist Pr.

***Martinson, Neil, et al.** Proof Vol. 1: The Magazine of Virtuous Reality. (Illus.). 68p. 1999. pap. 5.95 (*0-9673621-0-5*) Proof Press.

Martinson, Otto B. Cost Accounting in the Service Industry: A Critical Assessment. Barth, Claire, ed. LC 94-207244. 125p. 1994. pap. 40.00 (*0-86641-228-X*, 94291) Inst Mgmt Account.

***Martinson, Paul V.** Families of Faith: An Introduction to World Religions for Christians. LC 99-25953. 1999. 20.00 (*0-8006-3222-2*, Fortress Pr) Augsburg Fortress.

Martinson, Paul V., ed. Islam: An Introduction for Christians. Cox, Stefanie O., tr. from GER. LC 94-2356.Tr. of Was Jeder Vom Islam Wissen Muss. 1994. pap. 17.99 (*0-8066-2583-X*, 9-2583, Augsburg) Augsburg Fortress.

***Martinson, Paul V., ed.** Mission at the Dawn of the 21st Century: A Vision for the Church. LC 99-33588. 416p. 1999. pap. 15.95 (*1-886513-30-9*) Kirk Hse Pubs.

Martinson, Paul Varo. Families of Faith: An Introduction to World Religions for Christians. LC 99-25953. 160p. 1999. pap. 15.99 (*0-8066-3875-3*, 9-3875, Augsburg) Augsburg Fortress.

Martinson, Robert, et al. Rehabilitation, Recidivism & Research. 96p. 1976. 6.00 (*0-318-15372-6*) Natl Coun Crime.

Martinson, Roland D. Effective Youth Ministry: A Congregational Approach. LC 88-6210. 160p. (Orig.). 1988. pap. 13.99 (*0-8066-2311-X*, 10-2030, Augsburg) Augsburg Fortress.

Martinson, Steven D. Harmonious Tensions: The Writings of Friedrich Schiller. LC 95-47381. (Illus.). 448p. 1996. 55.00 (*0-87413-568-0*) U Delaware Pr.

Martinson, Sue Ann. Changing Woman. 60p. 1985. 8.95 (*0-911051-15-5*) Plain View.

Martinson, T. & Apogee Training Staff. GMAT CAT: 1999 Edition. 560p. 1998. 34.95 incl. disk (*0-02-862495-5*, Pub. by Macmillan) S&S Trade.

Martinson, T. L., ed. see Lee, T., et al.

Martinson, Thomas. ArcoTeach Yourself the GRE in 30 Days with CD. 6th ed. (Illus.). 608p. 1999. pap. 19.95 incl. cd-rom (*0-02-862517-X*) S&S Trade.

Martinson, Thomas E. Getting into Graduate Business School. 2nd ed. LC 97-81010. 160p. 1998. pap. 12.95 (*0-02-862209-X*, Arc) IDG Bks.

Martinson, Thomas H. ACT Supercourse. 4th ed. 752p. 1996. 18.95 (*0-02-861186-1*, Arc) IDG Bks.

— ACT Supercourse. 4th ed. 720p. 1998. pap. text 18.95 (*0-02-862484-X*, Arco) Macmillan Gen Ref.

— Arco GMAT: Graduate Management Admission Test. 8th ed. 568p. 1996. pap. text 29.95 incl. disk (*0-02-861310-4*) Macmillan.

— Arco GMAT CAT. 2000th ed. (Arco GMAT CAT Ser.). (Illus.). 580p. 1999. pap. 16.95 incl. cd-rom (*0-02-863223-0*, Arco) Macmillan Gen Ref.

— Arco GRE (Graduate Record Examination) With Computer-Adaptive Tests on Disk. 7th ed. (Illus.). 712p. 1997. pap. text 29.95 incl. disk (*0-02-861923-4*, Arco) Macmillan Gen Ref.

— Arco LSAT: Law School Admission Test. 7th ed. LC 97-117666. 408p. 1996. 29.95 incl. disk (*0-02-861311-2*) Macmillan.

— Arco SAT Supercourse: With Tests. 3rd ed. 1997. pap. 34.95 (*0-02-861596-4*, Arc) IDG Bks.

— Arco Teach Yourself the SAT in 30 Days. 4th ed. (Arco's Teach Yourself to Beat Ser.). 608p. 1999. pap. 19.95 (*0-02-862519-6*, Arco) Macmillan Gen Ref.

— The Best Law Schools. 2nd ed. 1999. 16.95 (*0-02-861084-9*) Macmillan.

— Getting into Graduate Business School. 1995. pap. 12.00 (*0-671-89924-4*) S&S Trade.

— Getting into Law School Today. 2nd ed. 160p. 1994. 12.00 (*0-671-89033-6*, Arco) Macmillan Gen Ref.

***Martinson, Thomas H.** Getting into Law School Today. 3rd ed. LC 97-81129. 160p. 1998. pap. text 12.95 (*0-02-862498-X*, Arc) IDG Bks.

Martinson, Thomas H. GMAT. 7th ed. 1995. pap. 34.95 incl. disk (*0-671-89973-2*) Macmillan USA.

— GMAT: Graduate Management Admission Test. 8th ed. 560p. 1996. 13.95 (*0-02-861073-3*, Arco) Macmillan Gen Ref.

— GMAT: Graduate Management Admission Test 1999. 560p. 1998. pap. text 13.95 (*0-02-862468-8*, Arco) Macmillan Gen Ref.

***Martinson, Thomas H.** GMAT CAT: Graduate Management Admission Test 2000. (Illus.). 580p. 1999. pap. write for info. (*0-02-863222-2*, Arc) IDG Bks.

Martinson, Thomas H. GMAT CAT Supercourse. 6th ed. (Illus.). 720p. 1997. 21.95 (*0-02-861701-0*, Arc) IDG Bks.

— GMAT CAT Supercourse with Tests on Disk: With Computer-Adaptive Tests on Disk. 6th ed. LC 97-81046. (Illus.). 706p. 1997. pap. 39.95 incl. disk (*0-02-861922-6*, Arc) IDG Bks.

— GMAT SuperCourse. 5th ed. LC 95-3266. 832p. 1995. 15.00 (*0-02-860318-4*) Macmillan.

— GMAT Supercourse. 7th ed. 784p. 1998. pap. text 18.95 (*0-02-862485-8*, Arco) Macmillan Gen Ref.

— Graduate Record Exam With Computer-Adaptive Tests on Disk: 1999 Edition. 712p. 1998. pap. 29.95 incl. cd-rom (*0-02-862477-7*, Arco) Macmillan Gen Ref.

— GRE: Graduate Record Examination. 4th ed. 624p. 1992. pap. 13.00 (*0-13-361775-0*, Arco) Macmillan Gen Ref.

— GRE: Graduate Record Examination. 6th ed. 1995. pap. 29.95 incl. 3.5 hd (*0-671-89967-8*) Macmillan USA.

— GRE: Graduate Record Examination. 7th ed. 624p. 1997. 13.95 (*0-02-861699-5*, Arco) Macmillan Gen Ref.

— GRE: Graduate Record Examination. 2000th ed. (Arco GRE: Graduate Record Examination Ser.). (Illus.). 545p. 1999. pap. 16.95 incl. cd-rom (*0-02-863225-7*, Arco) Macmillan Gen Ref.

— GRE: Graduate Record Examination: General Test. 6th ed. LC 95-793. 1995. pap. 14.00 (*0-671-89965-1*) Macmillan.

— GRE Supercourse. 4th ed. 880p. 1995. 18.95 (*0-02-860341-9*) Macmillan.

— GRE Supercourse. 4th ed. 1995. pap. 19.00 (*0-671-89974-0*, Arco) Macmillan Gen Ref.

— GRE Supercourse. 4th ed. 1995. pap. 34.95 incl. disk (*0-671-89976-7*) Macmillan USA.

— GRE Supercourse. 5th ed. (Illus.). 889p. 1997. 21.95 (*0-02-861700-2*, Arc) IDG Bks.

— GRE Supercourse. 6th ed. 864p. 1998. pap. text 18.95 (*0-02-862496-3*, Arco) Macmillan Gen Ref.

— Law School Admission Test: 1999. LC 97-81124. (Illus.). 448p. 1998. pap. text 16.95 (*0-02-862470-X*, Arco) Macmillan Gen Ref.

— Law School Admissions. rev. ed. (Illus.). 320p. 1998. pap. 20.00 (*0-684-84978-X*) S&S Trade.

— LSAT. 6th ed. 1995. pap. 29.00 incl. disk (*0-671-89970-8*) Macmillan USA.

— LSAT: Law School Admission Test. 7th ed. 400p. 1996. pap. 13.95 (*0-02-861072-5*, Arco) Macmillan Gen Ref.

— LSAT: Law School Admission Test, 2000 Edition. 2000th ed. (Illus.). 480p. 1999. pap. 16.95 (*0-02-863216-8*, Arc) IDG Bks.

— LSAT, Law School Admission Test. 6th ed. LC 95-7730. 384p. 1995. pap. 12.95 (*0-02-860326-5*) Macmillan.

— LSAT Law School Admission Test with Tests on CD - Rom: 1999 Edition. LC 97-81121. 392p. 1998. pap. 29.95 incl. cd-rom (*0-02-862480-7*, Arco) Macmillan Gen Ref.

— LSAT Supercourse. 5th ed. LC 96-232940. 752p. 1996. 19.95 (*0-02-861184-5*, Arc) IDG Bks.

— LSAT Supercourse. 5th ed. 1996. 34.95 incl. disk (*0-02-860613-2*, Arc) IDG Bks.

— LSAT Supercourse. 6th ed. 720p. 1998. pap. text 18.95 (*0-02-862486-6*, Arco) Macmillan Gen Ref.

— SAT Supercourse. 2nd ed. (Illus.). 720p. 1994. pap. 17.00 (*0-671-86402-5*, Arco) Macmillan Gen Ref.

— SAT Supercourse. 3rd ed. 752p. 1996. 18.95 (*0-02-861185-3*, Arc) IDG Bks.

— SAT Supercourse. 4th ed. 720p. 1998. pap. text 18.95 (*0-02-862482-3*, Arco) Macmillan Gen Ref.

Martinson, Thomas H. & Crocetti, Gino. Graduate Record Examination General Test (GRE) 2nd ed. (Academic Test Preparation Ser.). 656p. (C). 1987. student ed. 8.95 (*0-317-58457-X*, Arco) Macmillan Gen Ref.

Martinson, Thomas H. & Fazzone, Juliana. ACT SuperCourse. 3rd ed. Bosworth, Stefan et al, eds. LC 93-22327. (Illus.). 720p. 1993. pap. 17.00 (*0-671-86604-4*, Arco) Macmillan Gen Ref.

Martinson, Thomas H. & Fazzone, Julianna. Everything You Need to Score High on SAT II: Subject Test. 3rd ed. 448p. 1998. pap. text 18.95 (*0-02-862483-1*, Arc) IDG Bks.

***Martinson, Tom.** American Dreamscape: The Pursuit of Happiness in Postwar Suburbia. (Illus.). 288p. 2000. 26.00 (*0-7867-0771-2*, Pub. by Carroll & Graf) Publishers Group.

Martinson, Tom, jt. auth. see Gebhard, David.

Martinson, Yvonne. Eroticism, Ethics & Reading: Angela Carter in Dialogue with Roland Barthes. (Stockholm Studies in English: No. LXXXVI). 140p. (Orig.). 1996. pap. 39.50 (*91-22-01704-6*) Coronet Bks.

Martinsons, Maris G., jt. ed. see Burn, Janice M.

Martinsson, A., ed. The Silurian-Devonian Boundary. (International Union of Geological Sciences, Series A: No. 5). vi, 349p. 1977. 58.00 (*3-510-56003-5*, Pub. by E Schweizerbartsche) Balogh.

***Martinsson, Tobias.** ActivePerl with ASP & ADO. 290p. 2000. pap. 39.99 incl. cd-rom (*0-471-38314-7*) Wiley.

Martinsson-Wallin, Helene & Societas Archaeologica Upsaliensis Staff. Ahu--The Ceremonial Stone Structures of Easter Island: Analyses of Variation & Interpretation of Meanings. LC 95-137981. 188p. 1994. pap. 47.50 (*91-506-1043-0*, Pub. by Uppsala Universitet) Coronet Bks.

Martinu, B. First Sonata: Flute & Piano. 36p. 1986. pap. 17.95 (*0-7935-5401-2*) H Leonard.

— Madrigal Sonata: For Flute-Violin-Piano. 1987. pap. 22.00 (*0-7935-5568-X*) H Leonard.

— Trio for Flute, Cello & Piano. 48p. 1986. pap. 17.95 (*0-7935-5538-8*) H Leonard.

Martinus. Opera Omnia. Barlow, Claude W., ed. LC 50-10338. (American Academy in Rome. Papers & Monographs: Vol. 12). 340p. reprint ed. pap. 105.40 (*0-608-16474-7*, 202672800051) Bks Demand.

Martinus, Eivor, tr. see Jonsson, Reidar.

Martinus, Elivor, tr. see Soderbergh, Bengt.

Martinus, F. F. & Asian Educational Services Staff. A Guide to Buddhist Temples. LC 99-932498. 22p. 1999. write for info. (*81-206-1215-9*, Pub. by Asian Educ Servs) S Asia.

***Martinusen, Cindy McCormick.** Winter Passing. LC 00-36411. 2000. pap. write for info. (*0-8423-1906-9*) Tyndale Hse.

Martinussen, John. Democracy, Competition & Choice: Emerging Local Self-Government in Nepal. LC 94-45236. 188p. (C). 1995. 22.95 (*0-8039-9224-6*) Sage.

— State, Society & Market: A Guide to Competing Theories of Development. LC 96-24005. 400p. 1997. pap. 25.00 (*1-85649-442-X*, Pub. by Zed Books) St Martin.

— Transnational Corporations in a Developing Country: The Indian Experience. 228p. (C). 1988. text 24.00 (*0-8039-9584-9*) Sage.

Martinussen, Willy. The Distant Democracy: Social Inequality, Political Resources & Political Influence in Norway. LC 76-18748. 254p. reprint ed. pap. 78.80 (*0-608-13419-8*, 202428100035) Bks Demand.

Martire, Joseph R. & Levinsohn, Mark E. Imaging of Athletic Injuries: Advanced Techniques. 368p. 1991. text 125.00 (*0-07-040728-2*) McGraw-Hill HPD.

Martirena-Mantel, Ana M., ed. External Debt, Savings, & Growth in Latin America. LC 87-21422. xv, 207p. 1987. pap. 12.00 (*0-939934-95-7*) Intl Monetary.

Martis, Kenneth C. Historical Atlas of Political Parties in the U. S. Congress: 1787-1988. 1988. 160.00 (*0-318-32915-8*, Scribners Ref) Mac Lib Ref.

Martis, Kenneth C. & Elmes, Gregory. The Historical Atlas of State Power in Congress, 1790-1990. 190p. 1993. 89.95 (*0-87187-742-2*) Congr Quarterly.

Martius, Joachim, jt. ed. see Elsner, Peter.

Martius, Katharina Von, see Dahlke, Rudiger & Von Martius, Katharina.

Martius, T. Dictionary of International Trade Fairs, 3 vols., Set. 1267p. 1980. 125.00 (*0-569-05140-1*) St Mut.

Martivo, Kyalo. Herufi Zetu: African Traditional Writing Systems: Traditional Graphic Arts As Writing Systems. large type ed. (Illus.). 100p. (J). (gr. 5-8). 1999. pap. 8.95 (*0-9642831-2-3*) Amenta Bk.

Martizez, Juan A. Computer Analysis of Power Systems Transients. 500p. 1996. pap. text 49.95 (*0-7803-2318-1*, EG105) Inst Electrical.

Martlage, Ken. Heart Music: A Poetic Panorama of Healing Possibilities. LC 95-94774. (Illus.). 74p. (Orig.). 1996. pap. 9.95 (*0-9653086-0-X*) Phoenix Images.

Martland, Arthur. E. M. Forster: Passion & Prose. 228p. 1999. pap. 24.95 (*0-85449-268-2*) LPC InBook.

Martland, Peter. Since Records Began: EMI: the First Hundred Years. LC 97-2709. (Illus.). 359p. 1997. 39.95 (*1-57467-033-6*, Amadeus Pr) Timber.

Martland, Thomas R. Religion As Art: An Interpretation. LC 80-27104. (SUNY Series in Philosophy). 221p. (C). 1981. text 49.50 (*0-87395-520-X*) State U NY Pr.

— Religion As Art: An Interpretation. LC 80-27104. (SUNY Series in Philosophy). 221p. (C). 1982. pap. text 16.95 (*0-87395-521-8*) State U NY Pr.

Martlew, Clive. Local Democracy in Practice: The Role & Working Environment of Councillors in Scotland. 184p. 1988. text 72.95 (*0-566-05508-2*, Pub. by Dartmth Pub) Ashgate Pub Co.

Martlew, Gillian V. Electrolytes - The Spark of Life: The Key to Longevity & Quality of Life. 2nd rev. ed. LC 94-65134. Orig. Title: Electrolytes, Trace Minerals, the Spark of Life. 95p. 1998. pap. 12.95 (*0-9640539-0-X*, 101) Natures Pubng.

Martlew, Holley, jt. ed. see Tzedakis, Yannis.

Martlew, Margaret, ed. The Psychology of Written Language: Developmental & Educational Perspectives. LC 82-21933. (Wiley Series in Developmental Psychology & Its Applications). (Illus.). 442p. reprint ed. pap. 137.10 (*0-8357-7544-5*, 203626600001) Bks Demand.

Martley, Ed, jt. auth. see Hauer, Nancy.

Martling, Jackie. Jackie "The Joke Man" Martling's Disgustingly Dirty Joke Book. LC 97-29288. 1997. 20.00 (*0-684-84677-2*) S&S Trade.

— Jackie "The Joke Man" Martling's Disgustingly Dirty Joke Book. 224p. 1998. per. 9.95 (*0-684-85533-X*) S&S Trade Pap.

— Raunchy Riddles. 1988. pap. 2.95 (*1-55817-072-3*) Kensgtn Pub Corp.

— Raunchy Riddles. 192p. 1993. mass mkt. 3.50 (*1-55817-771-X*, Pinncle Kensgtn) Kensgtn Pub Corp.

Martna, Maret, ed. Arctic Bibliography, 2 vols., Vol. 15. LC 53-61783. 1633p. reprint ed. pap. 200.00 (*0-7837-1172-7*, 204170100015) Bks Demand.

— Arctic Bibliography, 2 vols., Vol. 16. LC 53-61783. 1407p. reprint ed. pap. 200.00 (*0-7837-1173-5*, 204170100016) Bks Demand.

Marto, Paul J., ed. see National Heat Transfer Conference Staff.

***Martocchio, Joseph J.** Strategic Compensation: A Human Resource Management Approach. LC 00-55051. 2000. 0.00 (*0-13-028030-5*) P-H.

Martocchio, Joseph J. Strategic Compensation: Human Resource Management Approach. LC 96-50312. 426p. 1997. 82.00 (*0-13-440983-3*) P-H.

Martof, Bernard S., et al. Amphibians & Reptiles of the Carolinas & Virginia. LC 79-11790. (Illus.). 264p. (C). 1989. reprint ed. pap. 21.95 (*0-8078-4252-4*) U of NC Pr.

Martohardjono, Gita, jt. ed. see Klein, Elaine C.

Martome, Michael. Dark Light. LC 73-88291. (Illus.). (Orig.). 1973. pap. 6.95 (*0-912810-11-4*) Lustrum Pr.

Marton, Andrew. Andrew Marton: Interviewed by Joanne D'Antonio. LC 91-26801. (Directors Guild of American Oral History Ser.: No. 12). (Illus.). 557p. 1991. 60.00 (*0-8108-2472-8*) Scarecrow.

***Marton, Andrew M.** China's Spatial Economic Development: Regional Transformation in the Lower Yanzi Delta. LC 00-30826. 2000. write for info. (*0-415-22779-8*) Routledge.

Marton, Andrew M. Urbanization in China's Lower Yangzi Delta: Transactional Relations & the Repositioning of Locality. (East Asian Institute Occasional Paper Ser.). (Illus.). 60p. 1998. pap. 16.95 (*981-02-3757-X*, Pub. by World Scientific Pub) Coronet Bks.

***Marton, Andrew M., ed.** Hong Kong in China. 140p. 1999. 14.00 (*981-02-4103-8*) World Scientific Pub.

Marton, Beryl. The Great Chicken Cookbook for People with Diabetes. LC 98-54450. 192p. 1999. pap. 16.95 (*1-58040-022-1*, 00221Q, Pub. by Am Diabetes) NTC Contemp Pub Co.

An Asterisk (*) at the beginning of an entry indicates that the title is appearing for the first time.

Marton, Betty. Ruben Blades: Panamanian Lawyer & Entertainer. (Hispanics of Achievement Ser.). (Illus.). 12p. (YA). (gr. 5 up). 1992. lib. bdg. 19.95 (*0-7910-1235-2*) Chelsea Hse.

Marton, Brian & Harper, Elizabeth. An Introduction to the Cape d'Aguilar Marine Reserve, Hong Kong. (Illus.). 100p. (Orig.). (C). 1995. pap. 24.00 (*962-209-388-4*, Pub. by HK Univ Pr) Coronet Bks.

Marton, Claire, jt. ed. see Marton, L. L.

Marton, Ference & Booth, Shirley. Learning & Awareness. LC 96-46002. (Educational Psychology Ser.). 240p. 1997. 49.95 (*0-8058-2454-5*); pap. 24.95 (*0-8058-2455-3*) L Erlbaum Assocs.

Marton, Ference & Bowden, John. The University of Learning: Beyond Quality & Competence in Higher Education. 256p. 1998. 59.95 (*0-7494-2292-0*, Kogan Pg Educ) Stylus Pub VA.

Marton, G. S., jt. auth. see Huber, Mark.

Marton, Jirina. Amelia's Celebration. (Illus.). 24p. (J). (ps-3). 1992. pap. 5.95 (*1-55037-220-3*, Pub. by Annick); text 15.95 (*1-55037-221-1*, Pub. by Annick) Firefly Bks Ltd.

— Flores para Mama.Tr. of Flowers for Mom. (SPA., Illus.). 24p. (J). (ps-2). 1994. pap. 6.95 (*1-55037-970-4*, Pub. by Annick) Firefly Bks Ltd.

— Flowers for Mom. (Illus.). 24p. (J). (ps-3). 1991. pap. 5.95 (*1-55037-158-4*, Pub. by Annick); lib. bdg. 15.95 (*1-55037-155-X*, Pub. by Annick) Firefly Bks Ltd.

— I'll Do It Myself. (Illus.). 24p. (J). (ps). 1990. 14.95 (*1-55037-063-4*, Pub. by Annick) Firefly Bks Ltd.

— I'll Do It Myself. (Illus.). 24p. (J). (ps). 1990. pap. 5.95 (*1-55037-062-6*, Pub. by Annick) Firefly Bks Ltd.

— Midnight Visit at Molly's House. (Illus.). 24p. (J). (ps-8). 1988. pap. 4.95 (*0-920303-98-6*, Pub. by Annick) Firefly Bks Ltd.

— You Can Go Home Again. (Illus.). 32p. (J). (gr. k-2). 1994. pap. 5.95 (*1-55037-990-9*, Pub. by Annick); lib. bdg. 15.95 (*1-55037-991-7*, Pub. by Annick) Firefly Bks Ltd.

Marton, Jirina. Lady Kaguya's Secret: A Japanese Tale. 48p. (YA). (ps up). 1997. 19.95 (*1-55037-441-9*, Pub. by Annick) Firefly Bks Ltd.

Marton, Jirina, jt. auth. see Morgan, Allen.

Marton, Joseph, tr. see Bergman, Gunnar.

Marton, Kati. A Death in Jerusalem: The Assassination by Jewish Extremists of the First Arab/Israeli Peacemaker. 336p. 1996. pap. 13.45 (*1-55970-352-0*, Pub. by Arcade Pub Inc) Time Warner.

— Wallenberg: Missing Hero. (Illus.). 224p. 1995. reprint ed. pap. 11.45 (*1-55970-276-1*, Pub. by Arcade Pub Inc) Time Warner.

Marton, L. L. Advances in Electronics & Electron Physics, Vol. 62. (Serial Publication Ser.). 1984. text 151.00 (*0-12-014662-2*) Acad Pr.

— Early History of the Electron Microscope. (Illus.). 1994. pap. 20.00 (*0-911302-73-5*) San Francisco Pr.

Marton, L. L., ed. Advances in Electronics & Electron Physics, Vol. 41. (Serial Publication Ser.). 1976. text 113.00 (*0-12-014541-3*) Acad Pr.

— Advances in Electronics & Electron Physics, Vol. 43. 1977. 99.50 (*0-12-014643-6*) Acad Pr.

— Advances in Electronics & Electron Physics, Vol. 44. (Serial Publication Ser.). 1978. text 130.00 (*0-12-014644-4*) Acad Pr.

— Advances in Electronics & Electron Physics, Vol. 46. LC 49-7504. (Serial Publication Ser.). 1978. text 121.00 (*0-12-014646-0*) Acad Pr.

— Advances in Electronics & Electron Physics, Vol. 49. (Serial Publication Ser.). 1979. text 121.00 (*0-12-014649-5*) Acad Pr.

— Advances in Electronics & Electron Physics, Vol. 60. (Serial Publication Ser.). 424p. 1983. text 158.00 (*0-12-014660-6*) Acad Pr.

— Advances in Electronics & Electron Physics, Vol. 63. (Serial Publication Ser.). 1985. text 151.00 (*0-12-014663-0*) Acad Pr.

— Advances in Electronics & Electron Physics, Vols. 34, 35. (Serial Publication Ser.). 1974. 96.00 (*0-12-014534-0*); text 158.00 (*0-12-014535-9*) Acad Pr.

— Advances in Electronics & Electron Physics, Vols. 36-40, 42 & 45. (Serial Publication Ser.). write for info. (*0-318-50179-1*) Acad Pr.

Marton, L. L. & Marton, Claire, eds. Advances in Electronics & Electron Physics, Vol. 50. LC 49-7504. (Serial Publication Ser.). 1980. text 158.00 (*0-12-014650-9*) Acad Pr.

— Advances in Electronics & Electron Physics, Vol. 51. LC 49-7504. (Serial Publication Ser.). 1980. text 158.00 (*0-12-014651-7*) Acad Pr.

— Advances in Electronics & Electron Physics, Vol. 52. (Serial Publication Ser.). 1980. text 289.00 (*0-12-014652-5*) Acad Pr.

— Advances in Electronics & Electron Physics, Vol. 53. (Serial Publication Ser.). 1980. text 151.00 (*0-12-014653-3*) Acad Pr.

— Advances in Electronics & Electron Physics, Vol. 54. (Serial Publication Ser.). 1980. text 158.00 (*0-12-014654-1*) Acad Pr.

Marton, Laurence J., jt. ed. see Kabra, Pokar M.

Marton, Laurence J., jt. ed. see Morris, David R.

Marton, Paolo, jt. auth. see Muraro, Michelangelo.

Marton, Robert J. Sustaining Total Quality: Achieving Performance Excellence Using the Baldridge Award Criteria. LC 99-43814. 217p. 1999. text 59.00 (*0-86587-610-X*, 610) Gov Insts.

Marton, Ruchama, jt. ed. see Gordon, Neve.

Marton, Sandra. The Bridal Suite: Do Not Disturb. (Presents Ser.: Vol. 1979). 1998. per. 3.75 (*0-373-11979-8*, 1-11979-1) Harlequin Bks.

Marton, Sandra. The Bridal Suite: Do Not Disturb. large type ed. 1994. 25.99 (*0-263-15933-7*, Pub. by Mills & Boon) Ulverscroft.

Marton, Sandra. A Bride for the Taking. LC 95-13570. (Presents Ser.). 189p. 1995. per. 3.25 (*0-373-11751-5*, 1-11751-4) Harlequin Bks.

— A Bride for the Taking. large type ed. 1993. 19.95 (*0-263-13317-6*) Thorndike Pr.

— The Bride Said Never! (Presents Ser.). 1998. per. 3.75 (*0-373-11955-0*, 1-11955-1) Harlequin Bks.

— By Dreams Betrayed. (Presents Ser.: No. 443). 1992. pap. 2.89 (*0-373-11443-5*, 1-11443-8) Harlequin Bks.

— By Dreams Betrayed. large type ed. 1991. reprint ed. lib. bdg. 18.95 (*0-263-12679-X*) Mac Lib Ref.

***Marton, Sandra.** Calor Sureno: The Groom Said Maybe! (Bianca Ser.: No. 149).Tr. of Southern Heat. (SPA.). 1999. per. 3.50 (*0-373-33499-0*, 1-33499-4) Harlequin Bks.

Marton, Sandra. The Corsican Gambit. (Presents Ser.). 1994. per. 2.99 (*0-373-11637-3*, 1-11637-5) Harlequin Bks.

— The Corsican Gambit. large type ed. 1992. 18.95 (*0-263-13030-4*) Mac Lib Ref.

— Deal with the Devil. large type ed. LC 94-20151. (Nightingale Ser.). 257p. 1995. pap. 16.95 (*0-8161-7454-7*, G K Hall Lrg Type) Mac Lib Ref.

— Divorcee Said Yes! large type ed. 1998. 21.95 (*0-263-15561-7*, G K Hall & Co) Mac Lib Ref.

— The Divorcee Said Yes! The Wedding of the Year. (Presents Ser.). 1998. per. 3.75 (*0-373-11962-3*, 1-11962-7) Harlequin Bks.

***Marton, Sandra.** Emerald Fire. 2000. per. 3.99 (*0-373-12100-8*) Harlequin Bks.

Marton, Sandra. Emerald Fire. large type ed. (Harlequin Romance Ser.). 1996. 19.95 (*0-263-14358-9*) Thorndike Pr.

— Ennemis d'un Jour. (Azur Ser.). 1999. mass mkt. 3.50 (*0-373-34764-2*, 1-34764-0) Harlequin Bks.

— Eye of the Storm. large type ed. (Magna Large Print Ser.). 1994. 27.99 (*0-7505-0742-X*, Pub. by Mgna Lrg Print) Ulverscroft.

— Une Femme en Heritage. (Azur Ser.). (FRE.). 1997. pap. 3.50 (*0-373-34649-2*, 1934649-3) Harlequin Bks.

— Garden of Eden. large type ed. 291p. 1994. 27.99 (*0-7505-0662-8*) Ulverscroft.

— The Groom Said Maybe! The Wedding of the Year. (Presents Ser.: Vol. 1968). 1998. per. 3.75 (*0-373-11968-2*, 1-77968-4) Harlequin Bks.

— Guardian Groom. (Landon's Legacy Ser.). 1996. per. 3.50 (*0-373-11813-9*, 1-11813-2) Harlequin Bks.

— Guardian Groom. large type ed. (Harlequin Romance Ser.). 1996. 20.95 (*0-263-14578-6*) Thorndike Pr.

— Hollywood Wedding. 1996. per. 3.50 (*0-373-11819-8*, 1-11819-9) Harlequin Bks.

— Hollywood Wedding. large type ed. (Harlequin Romance Ser.). 1996. 20.95 (*0-263-14593-X*) Mac Lib Ref.

***Marton, Sandra.** El Hombre Mas Atractivo (The Most Handsome Man) The Sexiest Man Alive. (Bianca Ser.: No. 185). 1999. per. 3.50 (*0-373-33535-0*, 1-33535-5) Harlequin Bks.

Marton, Sandra. Hostage of the Hawk. LC 96-418. 186p. 1995. per. 3.25 (*0-373-11780-9*, 1-11780-3) Harlequin Bks.

— An Indecent Proposal. large type ed. (Harlequin Romance Ser.). 1996. 20.95 (*0-263-14551-4*) Mac Lib Ref.

— An Indecent Proposal (Landon's Legacy) LC 96-2360. 186p. 1996. per. 3.50 (*0-373-11808-2*, 1-11808-2) Harlequin Bks.

— Lost in a Dream. (Presents Ser.: No. 457). 1992. per. 2.89 (*0-373-11457-5*, 1-11457-8) Harlequin Bks.

— Lost in a Dream. large type ed. 1991. reprint ed. lib. bdg. 16.95 (*0-263-12685-4*) Mac Lib Ref.

— Lovescenes. large type ed. 298p. 1993. 27.99 (*0-7505-0439-0*) Ulverscroft.

— Mariage a Hollywood. (Azur Ser.). (FRE.). 1997. pap. 3.50 (*0-373-34655-7*, 1-34655-0) Harlequin Bks.

— Marriage on the Edge: The Barons. (Presents Ser.: No. 2027). 1999. per. 3.75 (*0-373-12027-3*, 1-12027-8) Harlequin Bks.

***Marton, Sandra.** Marriage on the Edge: The Barons. large type ed. 288p. 1999. 25.99 (*0-263-16174-9*, Pub. by Mills & Boon) Ulverscroft.

Marton, Sandra. Master of El Corazon. (Presents Ser.: No. 1928). 1997. per. 3.50 (*0-373-11928-3*, 1-11928-8) Harlequin Bks.

***Marton, Sandra.** Mistress of the Sheikh. (Presents Ser.: Bk. 2136). 2000. mass mkt. 3.99 (*0-373-12136-9*, 1-12136-7) Harlequin Bks.

— More Than a Mistress. large type ed. 288p. 2000. 25.99 (*0-263-16312-1*, Pub. by Mills & Boon) Ulverscroft.

Marton, Sandra. More Than a Mistress: The Barons. 1999. per. 3.75 (*0-373-12045-1*, 1-12045-0) Harlequin Bks.

— No Need for Love. 1997. per. 3.50 (*0-373-11880-5*, 1-11880-1) Harlequin Bks.

— No Need for Love. large type ed. (Harlequin Ser.). 1994. lib. bdg. 19.95 (*0-263-13715-5*) Thorndike Pr.

— A Proper Wife. 1997. per. 3.50 (*0-373-11860-0*, 1-11860-3) Silhouette.

— A Proper Wife. large type ed. (Harlequin Romance Ser.). 283p. 1997. 20.95 (*0-263-14910-2*) Mac Lib Ref.

— Roarke's Kingdom. (Presents Ser.). 1993. per. 2.99 (*0-373-11574-1*, 1-11574-0) Harlequin Bks.

— Roarke's Kingdom. large type ed. (Harlequin Ser.). 1992. reprint ed. 18.95 (*0-263-12983-7*) Mac Lib Ref.

— Roman Spring. 1994. per. 2.99 (*0-373-11660-8*, 1-11660-7) Harlequin Bks.

***Marton, Sandra.** Romano's Revenge. (Harlequin Presents Ser.). 2000. mass mkt. 3.99 (*0-373-12117-2*, 1121177) Harlequin Bks.

Marton, Sandra. The Second Mrs. Adams. 1997. per. 3.50 (*0-373-11899-6*, 1-11899-1) Harlequin Bks.

***Marton, Sandra.** The Sexiest Man Alive. 1999. per. 3.75 (*0-373-12008-7*, Harlequin) Harlequin Bks.

— The Sexiest Man Alive. large type ed. 288p. 1999. 25.99 (*0-263-16082-3*, Pub. by Mills & Boon) Ulverscroft.

— Slade Baron's Bride. (Presents Ser.: No. 2063). 1999. per. 3.75 (*0-373-12063-X*, 1-12063-3) Harlequin Bks.

— Slade Baron's Bride. 288p. 2000. 26.99 (*0-263-16372-5*, Pub. by Mills & Boon) Ulverscroft.

Marton, Sandra. Spring Bride. (Harlequin Presents Ser.: No. 1825). 1996. per. 3.50 (*0-373-11825-2*, 1-11825-6) Harlequin Bks.

— Spring Bride. large type ed. (Harlequin Romance Ser.). 1996. 20.95 (*0-263-14668-5*) Thorndike Pr.

***Marton, Sandra.** The Taming of Tyler Kincaid: (The Barons) (Presents Ser.: No. 2081). 2000. per. 3.99 (*0-373-12081-8*, 1-12081-5, Harlequin) Harlequin Bks.

Marton, Sandra. That Long-Ago Summer. large type ed. 285p. 1991. reprint ed. 18.95 (*0-263-12806-7*) Thorndike Pr.

— 'Til Tomorrow. 384p. 1996. mass mkt. 4.99 (*0-7860-0229-8*, Pinncle Kensgtn) Kensgtn Pub Corp.

— Until You. 416p. 1997. mass mkt. 5.50 (*0-7860-0372-3*, Pinncle Kensgtn) Kensgtn Pub Corp.

— Le Vrai Visage de Joanna Adams. (Azur Ser.: No. 710). (FRE.). 1998. pap. 3.50 (*0-373-34710-3*, 1-34710-3) Harlequin Bks.

— A Woman Accused. LC 95-7123. (Presents Ser.). 188p. 1995. per. 3.25 (*0-373-11736-1*, 1-11736-5) Harlequin Bks.

— Yesterday & Forever. large type ed. 1993. reprint ed. lib. bdg. 19.95 (*0-263-13198-X*) Mac Lib Ref.

Marton-Vas-Zoltan, Peter & Tolnai, Marton. Guide to Research & Scholarship in Hungary, 2 vols., Set. 712p. (C). 1989. 150.00 (*963-05-4901-8*, Pub. by Akade Kiado) St Mut.

Martone, Joel, jt. auth. see Lindenberger, Jan.

Martone, John. Far Human Character. 20p. (Orig.). 1991. pap. 3.00 (*0-926935-56-9*) Runaway Spoon.

— Primer. 56p. (Orig.). 1994. pap. 5.00 (*1-57141-008-2*) Runaway Spoon.

— Trousseau. 40p. (Orig.). 1991. pap. 3.00 (*0-926935-46-1*) Runaway Spoon.

***Martone, Michael.** The Flatness & Other Landscapes. LC 99-16606. 171p. 2000. 24.95 (*0-8203-2160-5*) U of Ga Pr.

Martone, Michael. Fort Wayne Is Seventh on Hitler's List: Indiana Stories. enl. ed. LC 93-8645. 160p. 1993. 24.95 (*0-253-33687-2*); pap. 14.95 (*0-253-20851-3*) Ind U Pr.

— Pensees: The Thoughts of Dan Quayle. 100p. (Orig.). 1994. pap. 8.95 (*0-9639885-0-6*) Broad Ripple.

— Return to Powers. 1985. 4.00 (*0-317-19728-2*) Windless Orchard.

— Safety Patrol: Short Stories. LC 87-26868. (Johns Hopkins Ser.). 144p. reprint ed. pap. 44.70 (*0-608-07405-5*, 206763200009) Bks Demand.

— Seeing Eye: Short Stories. LC 95-22744. 192p. 1995. 20.95 (*0-944072-51-8*) Zoland Bks.

Martone, Michael, ed. A Place of Sense: Essays in Search of the Midwest. LC 88-15058. (Bur Oak Original Ser.). (Illus.). 170p. (Orig.). 1988. pap. 12.95 (*0-87745-217-2*) U of Iowa Pr.

— Townships. LC 91-25925. (Bur Oak Original Ser.). (Illus.). 243p. 1992. 32.95 (*0-87745-354-3*); pap. 14.95 (*0-87745-355-1*) U of Iowa Pr.

Martone, Michael, jt. ed. see Williford, Lex.

Martone, Mike. At a Loss. 1977. 4.00 (*0-685-67942-X*) Windless Orchard.

Martone, Robert L., ed. from ITA. Renaissance Comic Tales of Love, Treachery, & Revenge. Martone, Valerie, tr. from ITA. & intro. by. LC 94-16287. (Illus.). 248p. (Orig.). 1994. pap. 15.00 (*0-934977-31-3*) Italica Pr.

Martone, Valerie, tr. see Manetti, Antonio.

Martone, Valerie, tr. & intro. see Martone, Robert L., ed.

Martonen, T. B., ed. Medical Applications of Computer Modelling Vol. 1: Cardiovascular & Ocular Systems. (Advances in Computational Bioengineering Ser.: Vol. 3). 297p. 2000. 139.00 (*1-85312-613-6*, Pub. by WIT Pr) Computational Mech MA.

***Martonen, T. B., ed.** Medical Applications of Computer Modelling Vol. 2: Respiratory System. (Advances in Computational Bioengineering Ser.). 337p. 2000. 157.00 (*1-85312-808-2*, Pub. by WIT Pr) Computational Mech MA.

Martonen, Ted B. Inhaled Particles Fundamentals & Applications. 1999. 59.95 (*0-87371-744-9*) Lewis Pubs.

Martonosi, Anthony N., ed. Enzymes of Biological Membranes Vol. 1: Membrane Structure & Dynamics. 2nd ed. LC 84-8923. (Illus.). 474p. (C). 1985. text 126.00 (*0-306-41451-1*, Kluwer Plenum) Kluwer Academic.

— Enzymes of Biological Membranes Vol. 2: Biosynthesis & Metabolism. 2nd ed. 472p. 1985. 105.00 (*0-306-41452-X*, Plenum Trade) Perseus Pubng.

— Enzymes of Biological Membranes Vol. 3: Membrane Transport. 2nd ed. 700p. 1985. 140.00 (*0-306-41453-8*, Plenum Trade) Perseus Pubng.

— Enzymes of Biological Membranes Vol. 4: Bioenergetics of Electron & Proton Transport. 2nd ed. LC 84-8423. 608p. 1985. 130.00 (*0-306-41454-6*, Plenum Trade) Perseus Pubng.

— Enzymes of Biological Membranes Vol. 4: Bioenergetics of Electron & Proton Transport, Set, Vols. 1-4. 2nd ed. LC 84-8423. 608p. 1985. 380.00 (*0-685-09681-5*, Plenum Trade) Perseus Pubng.

— Membranes & Transport, Vol. 1. LC 82-3690. 722p. 1982. 110.00 (*0-306-40853-8*, Plenum Trade) Perseus Pubng.

— Membranes & Transport, Vol. 2. LC 82-3690. 712p. 1982. 110.00 (*0-306-40854-6*, Plenum Trade) Perseus Pubng.

Martonyi, Csaba L., et al. Clinical Slit Lamp Biomicroscopy & Photo Slit Lamp Biomicrography. 2nd ed. (Illus.). 80p. (C). 1987. pap. 34.50 (*0-9625512-0-1*) Time One Ink.

Martorana, Barbara, jt. auth. see Kane, Andrea L.

Martorana, R. George. Your Pension & Your Spouse: The Joint & Survivor Dilemma. 4th ed. 24p. 1996. pap. 10.00 (*0-89154-503-4*) Intl Found Employ.

Martorana, S. V. & Kuhns, Eileen. Managing Academic Change: Interactive Forces & Leadership in Higher Education. LC 74-27909. (Jossey-Bass Higher Education Ser.). 236p. reprint ed. pap. 73.20 (*0-608-15163-7*, 205216100045) Bks Demand.

***Martorana, Tont.** Your Home Is Not Broken. 1999. pap. 10.00 (*0-9621185-5-9*) Oasis Hse.

Martorano, J. T. & Kildahl, J. P. Beyond Negative Thinking: Breaking the Cycle of Depressing & Anxious Thoughts. (Illus.). 314p. (C). 1989. 24.50 (*0-306-43196-3*, Plen Insight) Perseus Pubng.

Martorano, Joseph, et al. Unmasking PMS. 1994. pap. 5.99 (*0-425-14515-8*) Berkley Pub.

— Unmasking PMS. LC 93-72. 240p. 1993. 21.95 (*0-87131-692-7*) M Evans.

— Unmasking PMS: The Complete PMS Medical Treatment Plan. 272p. 1994. mass mkt. 5.99 (*0-425-14401-1*) Berkley Pub.

Martorano, Joseph T. Stop Smoking, Stay Skinny. LC 97-94078. 160p. 1998. mass mkt. 5.99 (*0-380-79496-9*, Avon Bks) Morrow Avon.

Martorell, Joanot. Tirant Lo Blanc: The Complete Translation. La Fontaine, Ray, tr. from CAT. LC 93-20108. (Catalan Studies: Vol. 1).Tr. of Tirant lo Blanch. X, 820p. (Orig.). (C). 1994. pap. text 39.95 (*0-8204-1688-6*) P Lang Pubng.

Martorell, Joanot & De Galba, Marti J. Tirant Lo Blanc. Rosenthal, David H., tr. LC 95-53756. 688p. (C). 1996. pap. 19.95 (*0-8018-5421-0*) Johns Hopkins.

Martorell, Luis F., jt. auth. see Liogier, Henri A.

Martorella, Peter H. Elementary Social Studies: Developing Reflective, Competent, & Concerned Citizens. (C). 1985. text 27.95 (*0-316-54870-7*) Little.

— Social Studies for Elementary School Children: Developing Young Citizens. 2nd ed. LC 97-18758. 414p. (C). 1997. 72.00 (*0-13-496506-X*) P-H.

— Teaching Social Studies. 1999. pap. text 48.75 (*0-13-022553-3*) PH Diversified.

— Teaching Social Studies in Middle & Secondary Schools. 2nd ed. 433p. (C). 1995. 87.00 (*0-13-442070-5*) P-H.

***Martorella, Peter H.** Teaching Social Studies in Middle & Secondary Schools. 3rd ed. LC 99-89133. 464p. 2000. 72.00 (*0-13-020360-2*, Merrill Coll) P-H.

Martorella, Peter H., ed. Interactive Technologies & the Social Studies: Emerging Issues & Applications. LC 79-5024. (SUNY Series, Theory, Research, & Practice in Social Education). 134p. (C). 1996. text 39.50 (*0-7914-3139-8*); pap. text 12.95 (*0-7914-3140-1*) State U NY Pr.

Martorella, Rosanne. Corporate Art. LC 89-39325. (Illus.). 240p. 1990. 35.00 (*0-8135-1525-4*) Rutgers U Pr.

Martorella, Rosanne, ed. Art & Business: An International Perspective on Sponsorship. LC 95-40583. 288p. 1996. 59.95 (*0-275-95000-X*, Praeger Pubs) Greenwood.

Martorella, Roseanne. The Sociology of Opera: Organization, Production & Performance. 288p. 1982. 59.95 (*0-275-90857-7*, C0857, Praeger Pubs) Greenwood.

Martori, Joe. Street Fights. Stein, Toby, ed. 1987. 17.95 (*0-915643-24-3*) Santa Barb Pr.

Martory, Pierre. The Landscape Is Behind the Door: Bilingual Edition. Ashbery, John, tr. LC 94-11242. 127p. 1994. pap. 13.95 (*1-878818-30-9*, Pub. by Sheep Meadow) U Pr of New Eng.

Martos, Becky B., ed. Disappearances: A Workbook. 168p. (Orig.). 1981. pap. 4.95 (*0-939994-00-3*) Amnesty Intl USA.

Martos, Joseph. Doors to the Sacred: A Historical Introduction to Sacraments in the Catholic Church. LC 91-12298. 488p. 1991. reprint ed. pap. 15.95 (*0-89243-493-7*, Liguori Triumph) Liguori Pubns.

Martos, Joseph & Hegy, Pierre, eds. Equal at the Creation: Sexism, Society, & Christian Thought. LC 98-224666. 240p. 1998. text 50.00 (*0-8020-0868-2*); pap. text 19.95 (*0-8020-7852-4*) U of Toronto Pr.

Martos, Joseph, jt. auth. see Rohr, Richard.

Martos, Juan J., ed. see Christiphori, Ioannis & Stellae, Calveti.

Martosubroto, P., jt. ed. see Pauly, Daniel.

Martres, Laurent. Au Pays des Canyons. (PhotoTripUSA Ser.). (FRE., Illus.). 136p. 1998. pap. 19.95 (*0-916189-02-3*) Graphie Intl.

— Im Land der Canyons. (PhotoTripUSA Ser.). (GER., Illus.). 136p. 1998. pap. 19.95 (*0-916189-03-1*) Graphie Intl.

— Land of the Canyons. (PhotoTripUSA Ser.). (Illus.). 136p. 1998. pap. 14.95 (*0-916189-04-X*) Graphie Intl.

— Land of the Canyons. 2nd rev. ed. (Phototrip U. S. A. Ser.). (Illus.). Date not set. pap. 14.95 (*0-916189-07-4*, Phototrip USA) Graphie Intl.

Martres, Laurent, tr. see Pellier, P.

Martres, Laurent R. Comment Creer une PME aux U. S. A (FRE., Illus.). 144p. (Orig.). 1984. pap. 9.95 (*0-916189-00-7*) Graphie Intl.

— Sumo: Le Sport et le Sacre. (FRE., Illus.). 144p. 1985. pap. text 12.95 (*0-916189-01-5*) Graphie Intl.

Martry, Wagner. Las Freshman Orientation. 58p. (C). 1998. pap. text 5.50 (*0-536-01176-1*) Pearson Custom.

Marts, Eric, jt. ed. see England-Joseph, Judy A.

***Marts, William D. Imagintelligence: Beyond Emotional Intelligence. 352p. (Orig.). 2000. pap. 19.95 (0-9679157-3-2) Imagntion Inst.**

M

An Asterisk (*) at the beginning of an entry indicates that the title is appearing for the first time.

Imagintelligence (coined from imaginational intelligence) is a guide to understanding the mental & physiological processes of mind/body connection. Based on current research that reveals the image as the substrate of all thought, Imagintelligence takes you on a journey from the image - as it occurs in the brain in response to your thoughts - to the body's chemical processes that influence emotions, moods, states of mind, perspectives & spirituality. The imagination has been regarded by most people as a faculty of fantasy or creativity in the arts. Yet it is much more. By focusing on our imaginings, we can intervene between our stimulus/response reactions & eliminate supportive negative thoughts. When negative imaginings cease, illumination, enlightenment, or total peace may be experienced. Imagination Control Therapy & Imagery Management are new thought processes & aids in eliminating stress, developing imaginational & emotional intelligence, avoiding the fight or flight response, changing your emotional & mental responses & imbedding transformation into your emotional system (re-termed as our organic artificial intelligence program). Applied to a Christian metaphysical format, Imagintelligence is a metamorphosis from old school paradigms to modern 21st Century perspectives. http://www.imagination-institute.com. *Publisher Paid Annotation.*

Martschenko, W. G. Deutsch-Russisches Meteorologisches Worterbuch: German - Russian Meteorological Dictionary. (GER & RUS.). 392p. 1973. 19.95 (*0-8288-6234-6*, M-9092) Fr & Eur.

Martschukat, Jurgen, jt. ed. see Finzsch, Norbert.

Martsinkovsky, A. & Todorov, G., eds. Representation Theory & Algebraic Geometry. (London Mathematical Society Lecture Note Ser.: Vol. 238). 131p. (C). 1997. pap. text 35.95 (*0-521-57789-6*) Cambridge U Pr.

Martsinkyavitshute, Victoria. Lithuanian-English - English-Lithuanian Concise Dictionary. (Concise Dictionaries Ser.). (ENG & LIT.). 382p. (Orig.). 1993. pap. 14.95 (*0-7818-0151-6*) Hippocrene Bks.

Marttenin, Arja. Joy of Golf. (Illus.). 40p. (Orig.). 1997. pap. 5.95 (*1-56167-372-2*) Am Literary Pr.

Marttinen, Arja. Little Book of Useful Poems. LC 96-83414. 64p. 1996. 8.95 (*1-56167-249-1*) Am Literary Pr.

Martucci, C. C. How to Become an Outstanding 21st Century Manager. 258p. (Orig.). 1996. pap. 14.00 (*0-933448-02-3*) Outstanding VA.

Martucci, G., jt. auth. see Marathe, Kishore B.

Martucci, Kathleen, et al. Trade Book Publishing 1999: Analysis by Category. 6th rev. ed. (Illus.). 301p. 1998. 1495.00 (*0-88709-021-4*) Simba Info Inc.

Martucci, Kathleen, ed. see Bechard, Matthew.

Martucci, Roberto & Giovannetti, Bruno. A Guide to the Principal Buildings of Florence: History of Architecture & Urban Forms. (Illus.). 160p. 1996. pap. 17.95 (*88-86502-17-6*, Pub. by Canal & Stamperia) Antique Collect.

Martuscelli, Ezio. Advanced Routes for Polymer Testing: Analytical Applications. 1996. write for info. (*0-614-17907-6*) Elsevier.

Martuscelli, Ezio & Marchetta, Carlo. New Polymeric Materials: Reactive Processes & Physical Properties: Invited Papers Presented at a Symposium, Naples, Italy, June, 1986. 194p. 1987. lib. bdg. 85.00 (*90-6764-091-3*, Pub. by VSP) Coronet Bks.

Martuscelli, Ezio, et al. Advanced Routes for Polymer Toughening. LC 96-34584. (Polymer Science Library: Vol. 10). 620p. 1996. 339.50 (*0-444-81960-6*) Elsevier.

Martusewicz, Rebecca A. & Reynolds, William M. Inside-Out: Contemporary Critical Perspectives in Education. 320p. 1994. pap. text 20.00 (*0-312-08067-0*) St Martin.

— Inside/Out: Contemporary Critical Perspectives in Education. 320p. 1995. pap. 32.50 (*0-8058-8004-6*) L Erlbaum Assocs.

Marty. Histopathology of Infectious Diseases. 1997. 165.00 (*0-397-51309-7*, M2964) Lppncott W & W.

Marty, Anton. Untersuchungen Zur Grundlegung der Allgemeinen Grammatik und Sprachphilosophie. (GER.). xxv, 764p. 1976. reprint ed. write for info. (*3-487-06042-6*) G Olms Pubs.

Marty, David R. The Ear Book: A Parent's Guide to Common Ear Disorders of Children. (Illus.). 132p. 1987. pap. 16.95 (*0-943023-12-2*); lib. bdg. 23.95 (*0-943023-11-4*) Lang E N T Pub.

Marty, G. Dictionnaire des Chansons de la Revolution. (FRE.). 1988. lib. bdg. 89.95 (*0-8288-2590-4*, 2235018009) Fr & Eur.

Marty, Jean-Pierre. The Tempo Indications of Mozart. LC 87-29571. 416p. (C). 1989. 52.50 (*0-300-03852-6*) Yale U Pr.

Marty-Laveaux, Charles J. Lexique de la Langue de Pierre Corneille. (Oeuvres De P. Corneille, Eleven - Les Grands Ecrivains De la France Ser.). xcvi, 1060p. 1971. reprint ed. write for info. (*3-487-04032-8*) G Olms Pubs.

Marty, M. & Pappo, M., eds. Ondansetron & Chemotherapy Induced Emesis: 3rd International Congress on Neo-Adjuvant Chemotherapy. viii, 77p. 1992. 49.95 (*0-387-54599-9*) Spr-Verlag.

Marty, Maria C., ed. Bienvenido a la Gran Familia Christiana. (Fe en Accion Ser.).Tr. of Welcome to the Great Christian Family. (SPA.). 32p. (Orig.). 1996. pap. 1.00 (*0-9656265-0-4*) Lion Judah.

— Ven Espiritu Santo, Ayudame. (Fe en Accion Ser.).Tr. of Come Holy Spirit, Help Me. (SPA.). 100p. (Orig.). 1997. pap. 5.00 (*0-9656265-1-2*) Lion Judah.

Marty, Martin. A Cry of Absence: Reflections for the Winter of the Heart. LC 97-16091. (Illus.). 201p. 1997. pap. 12.00 (*0-8028-4328-X*) Eerdmans.

— When True Simplicity Is Gain'd: Finding Spiritual Clarity in a Complex World. LC 98-18065. (Illus.). 112p. 1998. pap. 16.00 (*0-8028-4237-2*) Eerdmans.

Marty, Martin & Marty, Micah. The Promise of Winter: Quickening the Spirit on Ordinary Days & in Fallow Seasons. (Illus.). 111p. (Orig.). 1997. pap. 16.00 (*0-8028-4436-7*) Eerdmans.

Marty, Martin E. Christianity in the New World: From 1500 to 1800. LC 82-83845. (Illustrated History of the Church Ser.). (Illus.). 127p. 1984. 13.45 (*0-86683-173-8*, 1411) Harper SF.

— Faith: Confidence & Doubt in Daily Life. (Intersections: Small Group Ser.). 1995. pap. text 5.49 (*0-8066-0132-9*, 15-167) Augsburg Fortress.

— Fundamentalism & the State: Remaking Politics, Economies, & Millitance. Appleby, R. Scott, ed. (Illus.). 666p. (C). 1996. reprint ed. pap. text 27.50 (*0-226-50884-6*) U Ch Pr.

— Health Medicine & Faith Traditions: An Inquiry into Religion & Medicine. Vaux, Kenneth L., ed. LC 81-71383. 362p. reprint ed. pap. 112.30 (*0-608-17011-9*, 202697500053) Bks Demand.

— The Lord's Supper. expanded ed. LC 97-2472. 88p. (Orig.). 1997. pap. 7.99 (*0-8066-3339-5*, 9-3339, Augsburg) Augsburg Fortress.

Marty, Martin E. The Lutheran People. 32p. 1989. pap. write for info. (*1-889711-03-9*) Cathedral Direct.

— Lutheranism: A Restaurant in Question & Answer Form. 44p. 1989. pap. write for info. (*1-889711-04-7*) Cathedral Direct.

Marty, Martin E. Modern American Religion Vol. 1: The Irony of It All, 1893-1919. LC 86-16524. (Illus.). 398p. (C). 1986. 29.95 (*0-226-50893-5*) U Ch Pr.

— Modern American Religion Vol. 1: The Irony of It All, 1893-1919, 2 vols. 1997. pap. text 16.95 (*0-226-50894-3*) U Ch Pr.

— Modern American Religion Vol. 2: The Noise of Conflict, 1919-1941, 2 vols. 1997. pap. text 18.95 (*0-226-50897-8*) U Ch Pr.

— Modern American Religion Vol. 2: The Noise of Conflict, 1919-1941. LC 85-16524. (Illus.). 480p. 1997. 29.95 (*0-226-50895-1*) U Ch Pr.

— Modern American Religion Vol. 3: Under God Indivisible, 1941-1960. (Modern American Religion Ser.: Vol. 5). 528p. 1996. 34.95 (*0-226-50898-6*) U Ch Pr.

— A Nation of Behavers. LC 76-7997. xii, 256p. 1980. pap. text 12.95 (*0-226-50892-7*, P890) U Ch Pr.

— The One & the Many: America's Struggle for the Common Good. LC 96-48411. (Joanna Jackson Goldman Memorial Lecture on American Civilization & Government Ser.). 288p. 1997. 24.95 (*0-674-63827-1*) HUP.

— The One & the Many: America's Struggle for the Common Good. 256p. 1998. pap. 15.95 (*0-674-63828-X*) HUP.

— Pilgrims in Their Own Land. 512p. 1985. pap. 15.95 (*0-14-008268-9*, Penguin Bks) Viking Penguin.

— Places along the Way: Meditations on the Journey of Faith. LC 94-29532. (Illus.). 112p. 1994. pap. 15.99 (*0-8066-2746-8*, 9-2746, Augsburg) Augsburg Fortress.

— Religion & Republic: The American Circumstance. LC 86-47755. 391p. 1989. pap. 19.00 (*0-8070-1207-6*) Beacon Pr.

— Religious Crises in Modern America. LC 81-80740. (Charles Edmondson Historical Lectures). 40p. (Orig.). 1981. pap. 5.95 (*0-918954-26-6*) Baylor Univ Pr.

— Short History of Christianity. 2nd rev. ed. LC 80-8042. 336p. (Orig.). 1987. pap. 23.00 (*0-8006-1944-7*, 1-1944) Augsburg Fortress.

***Marty, Martin E.** Under God, Indivisible, 1941-1960, Vol. 3. (Modern American Religion Ser.: Vol. 3). 548p. 2000. pap. text 22.00 (*0-226-50899-4*) U Ch Pr.

Marty, Martin E., ed. Modern American Protestantism & Its World, Set. Incl. Vol. 3. Civil Religion, Church & State. 502p. 1992. lib. bdg. 120.00 (*3-598-41533-8*); Vol. 4. Theological Themes in the American Protestant World. 468p. 1992. lib. bdg. 120.00 (*3-598-41535-4*); Vol. 5. Varieties of Protestantism. 272p. 1992. lib. bdg. 120.00 (*3-598-41536-2*); Vol. 6. Protestantism & Social Christianity. 1993. lib. bdg. 120.00 (*3-598-41537-0*); Vol. 7. Protestantism & Regionalism. 248p. 1992. lib. bdg. 120.00 (*3-598-41538-9*); Vol. 8. Ethnic & Non-Protestant Themes. 311p. 1993. lib. bdg. 120.00 (*3-598-41539-7*); Vol. 9. Native American Religion & Black Protestantism. 344p. 1993. lib. bdg. 120.00 (*3-598-41540-0*); Vol. 10. Fundamentalism & Evangelicalism. 356p. 1993. lib. bdg. 120.00 (*3-598-41541-9*); Vol. 11. New & Intense Movements. 404p. 1993. lib. bdg. 120.00 (*3-598-41542-7*); Vol. 12. Women & Women's Issues. 380p. 1993. lib. bdg. 120.00 (*3-598-41543-5*); Vol. 13. Missions & Ecumenical Expressions. 222p. 1993. lib. bdg. 120.00 (*3-598-41544-3*); Vol. 14. Varieties of Religious Expression. 296p. 1993. lib. bdg. 120.00 (*3-598-41545-1*); 1993. Set lib. bdg. 1525.00 (*3-598-41530-3*) K G Saur Verlag.

— Modern American Religion & the Protestant World, Vol. 2. 294p. 1992. lib. bdg. 120.00 (*3-598-41532-X*) K G Saur Verlag.

— The Place of Bonhoeffer: Problems & Possibilities in His Thought. LC 79-8718. 224p. 1981. reprint ed. lib. bdg. 55.00 (*0-313-20812-3*, MAPL, Greenwood Pr) Greenwood.

Marty, Martin E. & Appleby, R. Scott. The Glory & the Power: The Fundamentalist Challenge to the Modern World. (Illus.). 304p. 1992. pap. 17.50 (*0-8070-1217-3*) Beacon Pr.

Marty, Martin E. & Appleby, R. Scott, eds. Accounting for Fundamentalisms: The Dynamic Character of Movements. LC 93-36621. (Fundamentalism Project Ser.: Vol. 4). 862p. (C). 1994. 47.50 (*0-226-50885-4*) U Ch Pr.

— Fundamentalism Observed. xvi, 888p. (C). 1994. pap. text 35.00 (*0-226-50878-1*) U Ch Pr.

— Fundamentalisms & Society: Reclaiming the Sciences, the Family, & Education. LC 92-10259. (Fundamentalism Project Ser.: Vol. 2). 602p. 1993. 45.00 (*0-226-50880-3*) U Ch Pr.

— Fundamentalisms & Society: Reclaiming the Sciences, the Family, & Education. (Fundamentalism Project Ser.). x, 592p. 1997. pap. text 28.00 (*0-226-50881-1*) U Ch Pr.

— Fundamentalisms & the State: Remaking Politics, Militance, & Economies. LC 92-14582. (Fundamentalism Project Ser.: Vol. 3). 676p. (C). 1993. 49.50 (*0-226-50883-8*) U Ch Pr.

— Fundamentalisms Comprehended. LC 94-45338. (Fundamentalism Project Ser.: Vol. 5). 528p. 1995. 45.00 (*0-226-50887-0*) U Ch Pr.

— Fundamentalisms Observed. LC 90-24894. (Fundamentalism Project Ser.: Vol. 1). 896p. 1998. 40.00 (*0-226-50877-3*) U Ch Pr.

— Religion, Ethnicity, & Self-Identity: Nations in Turmoil. LC 96-37268. 151p. 1997. 25.00 (*0-87451-815-6*) U Pr of New Eng.

***Marty, Martin E. & Moore, Jonathan.** Politics, Religion & the Common Good: Advancing a Distinctly American Conversation about Religion's Role in Our Shared Life. LC 99-50450. 240p. 2000. 22.50 (*0-7879-5031-9*) Jossey-Bass.

— Politics, Religion & the Common Good: Advancing a Distinctly American Conversion about Religion's Role in Our Shared Life. 225p. 2000. 23.00 (*0-7879-5033-5*) Jossey-Bass.

Marty, Martin E. & Piscatori, James P. Islamic Fundamentalisms & the Gulf Crisis: A Fundamentalism Project Report. 267p. (Orig.). (C). 1991. pap. 9.95 (*0-9629608-0-2*, Pub. by Fundmtal Project) U Ch Pr.

Marty, Martin E., et al. The Religious Press in America. LC 72-6844. 184p. 1973. reprint ed. lib. bdg. 55.00 (*0-8371-6500-8*, MARP, Greenwood Pr) Greenwood.

Marty, Martin E., jt. auth. see Marty, Micah.

Marty, Martin E., ed. see Palmer, Martin, et al.

Marty, Martin E., ed. & intro. see James, William.

Marty, Micah & Marty, Martin E. Our Hope for Years to Come: The Search for Spiritual Sanctuary. 112p. 1995. pap. 15.99 (*0-8066-2836-7*, 9-2836) Augsburg Fortress.

Marty, Micah, jt. auth. see Marty, Martin.

Marty, Michael. Growth Factors in Clinical Applications: Manual of GM-CSF. 259p. 1995. pap. 89.95 (*0-86542-818-2*) Blackwell Sci.

Marty, Michel E., ed. New Directions in Anti-Cancer Chemotherapy. (Journal: Oncology: Vol. 51, Suppl. 1, 1994). (Illus.). iv, 40p. 1994. pap. 19.25 (*3-8055-6080-X*) S Karger.

Marty, Myron A. Daily Life in the United States, 1960-1990: Decades of Discord. LC 96-53843. (Greenwood Press "Daily Life Through History" Ser.). 400p. 1997. 45.00 (*0-313-29554-9*, Greenwood Pr) Greenwood.

Marty, Myron A. & Marty, Shirley. Frank Lloyd Wright's Taliesin Fellowship. (Illus.). 332p. 1999. pap. 35.00 (*0-943549-73-6*) Truman St Univ.

***Marty, Myron A. & Marty, Shirley.** Frank Lloyd Wright's Taliesin Fellowship. (Illus.). 332p. 1999. 65.00 (*0-943549-74-4*) Truman St Univ.

Marty, Myron A., jt. auth. see Kyvig, David.

Marty, Myron A., jt. auth. see Kyvig, David E.

Marty, R. PISA Programming System for Interactive Production of Application Software. (Informatik-Fachberichte Ser.). 297p. 1981. 32.00 (*0-387-10825-4*) Spr-Verlag.

Marty, Robert. L' Algebre Des Signes: Essai de Semiotique Scientifiqu d' Apres Charles Sanders Peirce. (Foundations of Semiotics Ser.: No. 24). (FRE.). xviii, 409p. 1990. 133.00 (*90-272-3296-2*) J Benjamins Pubng Co.

Marty, Shirley, jt. auth. see Marty, Myron A.

***Marty, Sid.** Leaning on the Wind: Under the Spell of the Great Chinook. 320p. 2001. reprint ed. pap. 18.95 (*0-7710-5671-0*) McCland & Stewart.

Marty, Sid. Men for the Mountains. 270p. 1996. pap. text 18.99 (*0-7710-5851-9*) McCland & Stewart.

***Marty, Sid.** Men for the Mountains. 272p. 2001. pap. 18.95 (*0-7710-5672-9*) McCland & Stewart.

— Switchbacks: True Stories from the Rocky Mountains. 256p. 2001. 24.95 (*0-7710-5669-9*) McCland & Stewart.

Marty, William H. A Survey of the Old Testament: Student Notes. 228p. (C). 1996. pap. text, spiral bd. 19.95 (*0-8403-7603-0*) Kendall-Hunt.

— Surveying the New Testament. 196p. 1996. spiral bd. 21.25 (*0-8403-7025-3*) Kendall-Hunt.

Martyn, Barrie. Nicolas Medtner: His Life & Music. (Illus.). 288p. 1995. 86.95 (*0-85967-959-4*) Ashgate Pub Co.

— Rachmaninoff: Composer, Pianist, Conductor. (Illus.). 672p. 1990. text 96.95 (*0-85967-809-1*, Pub. by Scolar Pr) Ashgate Pub Co.

Martyn, Barry. New Orleans Jazz: The End of the Beginning. LC 98-75089. (Jazzology Press Book #6 Ser.). 200 p. 1998. write for info. (*0-9638890-5-2*) GHB Jazz Fnd.

Martyn, Barry, ed. see Coller, Derek.

Martyn, C. N. & Hughes, R. A., eds. The Epidemiology of Neurological Disorders. (Illus.). 248p. 1998. 77.00 (*0-7279-1149-X*, Pub. by BMJ Pub) Login Brothers Bk Co.

Martyn, Christopher N. Neurology. (Student Notes Ser.). (Illus.). 296p. 1990. pap. text 19.95 (*0-443-03307-2*) Church.

Martyn, D. Climates of the World. (Developments in Atmospheric Science Ser.: Vol. 18). 436p. 1992. 190.25 (*0-444-98739-8*) Elsevier.

Martyn, D., jt. auth. see Jones, Lloyd.

Martyn, David, tr. see Monbrun, Estelle.

Martyn, Dorothy. The Man in the Yellow Hat: Theology & Psychoanalysis in Child Therapy. (American Academy of Religion Academy Ser.). 197p. (C). 1992. 24.95 (*1-55540-630-0*, 010176); pap. 15.95 (*1-55540-631-9*) OUP.

Martyn, Isolde. The Maiden & the Unicorn. 448p. 1999. reprint ed. mass mkt. 5.99 (*0-553-58168-6*) Bantam.

Martyn, J. Louis. Galatians: A New Translation with Introduction & Commentary. LC 96-37760. (Illus.). 640p. 1997. 42.50 (*0-385-08838-8*, Anchor Bib) Doubleday.

— Theological Issues in the Letters of Paul. LC 97-15082. 568p. 1997. 39.95 (*0-687-05622-5*) Abingdon.

Martyn, J. R., ed. D. Iuni Iuvenalis: Satyrae. (LAT.). xxxii, 179p. 1987. pap. 60.00 (*90-256-0923-6*, Pub. by AM Hakkert) BookLink Distributors.

***Martyn, John.** Henry Martyn (1781-1812), Scholar & Missionary to India & Persia: A Biography. LC 99-17083. (Studies in the History of Missions: Vol. 16). 160p. 1999. text 69.95 (*0-7734-8181-8*) E Mellen.

Martyn, John, et al, eds. Information UK 2000. (British Library Research). 293p. 1991. 50.00 (*0-86291-620-8*) Bowker-Saur.

Martyn, John R. The Siege of Mazagao: A Perilous Moment in the Defence of Christendom Against Islam. LC 93-15019. (American University Studies). 264p. (C). 1994. text 43.95 (*0-8204-2210-X*) P Lang Pubng.

Martyn, John R., ed. Andre de Resende - On Court Life. (Bibliotheca Neolatina Ser.: Vol. 3). (Illus.). 230p. 1990. pap. 79.00 (*3-261-04192-7*) P Lang Pubng.

Martyn, John R., ed. & tr. see Pedro, Nunes.

Martyn, John R., tr. see De Resende, Andre.

***Martyn, John R. C.** Henry Martyn (1781-1812), Scholar & Missionary to India & Persia: A Biography. LC 99-17083. (Illus.). 1999. write for info. (*0-88946-068-X*) E Mellen.

Martyn, John R. C., tr. see de Ferreira, Antonia.

Martyn, Lois J., et al. Optic Fundus Signs of Developmental & Neurological Disorders in Children: A Manual for Clinicians. LC 65-80492. (Clinics in Developmental Medicine Ser.: No. 89). (Illus.). 80p. (C). 1991. text 34.95 (*0-521-41209-9*, Pub. by Mc Keith Pr) Cambridge U Pr.

Martyn, Tim, et al. SQL 400: A Professional Programmer's Guide. 1995. 45.00 (*0-07-040799-1*) McGraw.

Martyna, Bobby, jt. auth. see Elbert, Bruce R.

Martynau, V., ed. Etymological Dictionary of the Belorussian Language, Vol. 5. 320p. (C). 1989. 50.00 (*0-7855-6454-3*, Pub. by Collets) St Mut.

Martynenko, Oleg G., jt. auth. see Zukauskas, A. A.

Martynenko, Oleg G., ed. see Idelchik, I. E.

Martynenko, Z., jt. auth. see Soane, David S.

Martyniuk, Andrew O., tr. see Lobko, Hryhoriy.

Martynov, A. & Brix, V. Practical Aerodynamics. LC 63-10019. (International Series of Monographs in Aeronautics & Astronautics: Vol. 4). 1965. 179.00 (*0-08-010137-2*, Pub. by Pergamon Repr) Franklin.

Martynov, Anatoly I. The Ancient Art of Northern Asia. Shimkin, Demitri B. & Shimkin, Edith M., eds. & trs. by. (Illus.). 320p. 1991. text 39.95 (*0-252-01219-4*) U of Ill Pr.

Martynov, G. A. Fundamental Theory of Liquids: Method of Distribution Functions. (Illus.). 492p. 1992. 168.00 (*0-7503-0069-8*) IOP Pub.

Martynov, G. A. & Salem, R. R. Electrical Double Layer at a Metal-dilute Electrolyte Solution Interface. (Lecture Notes in Chemistry Ser.: Vol. 33). 170p. 1983. 29.95 (*0-387-11995-7*) Spr-Verlag.

Martynov, Georgy A. Classical Statistical Mechanics. LC 97-34489. (Fundamentals Theories of Physics Ser.: No. 89). 341p. 1997. text 214.00 (*0-7923-4774-9*) Kluwer Academic.

Martynov, Ivan I. Dimitri Shostakovich, the Man & His Work: Music Book Index. 197p. 1993. reprint ed. lib. bdg. 69.00 (*0-7812-9620-X*) Rprt Serv.

— Dmitri Shostakovich, the Man & His Work. Guralsky, T., tr. LC 75-88903. 197p. 1969. reprint ed. lib. bdg. 65.00 (*0-8371-2100-0*, MAS, Greenwood Pr) Greenwood.

Martynyuk, A. A. Stability Analysis: Nonlinear Mechanical Equations. (Stability & Control: Theory, Methods Ser.). 336p. 1995. text 132.00 (*2-88449-023-X*) Gordon & Breach.

— Stability by Liapunov's Matrix Function Method with Applications, Vol. 214. LC 98-28045. (Pure & Applied Mathematics Ser.). (Illus.). 296p. 1998. text 150.00 (*0-8247-0191-7*) Dekker.

Martynyuk, A. A., jt. auth. see Kato, J.

Martynyuk, A. A., jt. auth. see Sivasundaram, S.

Martyr, jt. auth. see Plint.

Martyr, Anthony, jt. auth. see Plint, M. A.

Martyr, Anthony J., jt. auth. see Plint, Michael A.

Martyr, Debbie. Globetrotter Travel Guide Indonesia. 2nd ed. (Globetrotter Travel Guides Ser.). 128p. 1998. pap. text 10.95 (*1-85368-889-4*, Pub. by New5 Holland) Globe Pequot.

An Asterisk (*) at the beginning of an entry indicates that the title is appearing for the first time.

Martyr, Justin. Saint Justin Martyr: The First Apology, the Second Apology, Dialogue with Trypho, Exhortation to the Greeks, Discourse to the Greeks, the Monarchy, or the Rule of God. Falls, Thomas B., ed. LC 65-18317. (Fathers of the Church Ser.: Vol. 6). 486p. 1977. reprint ed. pap. 150.70 (*0-7837-9146-1*, 204994600004) Bks Demand.

Martyr, Justin, jt. auth. see Felix, Mark.

***Martyr, Paula.** Dial a Times Table. 2000. 7.99 (*0-7858-1234-2*) Bk Sales Inc.

***Martyr, Paula.** Join the Band. (My First Piano Ser.). (J). (ps-3). 1999. 7.98 (*1-57717-113-6*) Todtri Prods.

— A Musical Day. (My First Piano Ser.). (J). 7.98 (*1-57717-112-8*) Todtri Prods.

Martyr, Peter. New World Chronicles, 2 vols. rev. ed. Incl. Vol. 1. New World Chronicles. rev. ed. McNutt, Francis, tr. from LAT. (Illus.). 1996. (*1-887954-08-2*); Vol. 2. New World Chronicles. rev. ed. McNutt, Francis A., tr. from LAT. (Illus.). 1996. (*1-887954-09-0*); 19.95 (*1-887954-07-4*) Athena FL.

Martyshev, F. G. Pond Fisheries. (Russian Translation Ser.: No. 4). 462p. 1983. 162.00 (*90-6191-410-8*, Pub. by A A Balkema) Ashgate Pub Co.

Martyska, Barbara. From Canyons to Highlands. 16p. 1995. pap. text 4.95 (*0-87487-747-4*) Summy-Birchard.

Martz, Adam. SAT Verbal Workbook. (Princeton Review Ser.). 1995. pap. 16.00 (*0-679-75362-1*) Villard Books.

Martz, Arnaud C. Philanthropy's Role in Civilization: Its Contribution to Human Freedom. 206p. (C). 1991. 39.95 (*0-88738-405-6*) Transaction Pubs.

Martz, C. W., ed. Solar Energy Source Book. 2nd ed. (Illus.). 1977. 30.00 (*0-686-23456-1*); pap. 15.00 (*0-686-23457-X*) United Tel.

Martz, Clyde O. Cases & Materials on the Law of Natural Resources. Bruchey, Stuart, ed. LC 78-53553. (Development of Public Land Law in the U. S. Ser.). 1979. reprint ed. lib. bdg. 81.95 (*0-405-11379-X*) Ayer.

Martz, Edwine M., ed. see Walpole, Horace.

Martz, Geoff. Cracking the GED: 2000 Edition. 1999. pap. 18.00 (*0-375-75402-4*) Random.

— Cracking the GMAT CAT 2000. 1999. pap. 20.00 (*0-375-75405-9*) Random.

Martz, Geoffrey. How to Survive Without Your Parents' Money: Making It from College. rev. ed. LC 97-227378. (Princeton Review Ser.). 1996. pap. 10.00 (*0-679-76984-6*) Villard Books.

Martz, Harry F. & Waller, Ray A. Bayesian Reliability Analysis. LC 89-6172. 768p. (C). 1991. reprint ed. lib. bdg. 76.50 (*0-89464-395-9*) Krieger.

Martz, Jim. Hurricane Warning: University of Miami Football. 1989. 17.95 (*0-87397-315-1*, Strode Pubs) Circle Bk Service.

Martz, John D. Accion Democratica: Evolution of a Modern Political Party in Venezuela. LC 65-17147. 457p. 1966. reprint ed. pap. 141.70 (*0-7837-9383-9*, 206012700004) Bks Demand.

— Colombia. LC 75-15694. (Illus.). 384p. 1975. reprint ed. lib. bdg. 69.50 (*0-8371-8215-8*, MACOL, Greenwood Pr) Greenwood.

— Politics & Petroleum in Ecuador. 345p. 1987. 44.95 (*0-88738-132-4*) Transaction Pubs.

— The Politics of Clientelism: Democracy & the State in Colombia. 370p. 1996. text 44.95 (*1-56000-264-6*) Transaction Pubs.

— Venezuela. 2nd ed. LC 85-28268. 489p. 1985. 69.50 (*0-275-91815-7*, C1815, Praeger Pubs); pap. 21.95 (*0-275-92038-0*, B2038, Praeger Pubs) Greenwood.

Martz, John D., ed. United States Policy in Latin America: A Decade of Crisis & Challenge. LC 94-40410. xvii, 407p. (C). 1995. text 60.00 (*0-8032-3162-8*); pap. text 30.00 (*0-8032-8189-7*, Bison Books) U of Nebr Pr.

Martz, John D. & Myers, David J., eds. Venezuela: The Democratic Experience. LC 77-7509. (Praeger Special Studies). 432p. 1977. pap. 18.95 (*0-275-91471-2*, B1471, Praeger Pubs) Greenwood.

Martz, John D., jt. auth. see Baloyra, Enrique A.

Martz, John D., jt. auth. see Jorrin, Miguel.

***Martz, Laura.** Mechanical Desktop 4.0 Update. 2nd ed. Allen, Richard, ed. (Illus.). 179p. 1999. pap. text, teacher ed. 75.00 incl. cd-rom (*1-891502-66-2*, MDT4099) Tech Learn Co.

— Mechanical Desktop 4.0 Update. 2nd unabridged ed. Allen, Richard, ed. (Illus.). 179p. 1999. pap. text, student ed. 105.00 (*1-891502-65-4*, MDT4099U) Tech Learn Co.

Martz, Laura. Mechanical Desktop 3.0: Part Modeling. 2nd ed. Allen, Richard L., ed. (Illus.). 419p. 1998. teacher ed., spiral bd. 125.00 (*1-891502-37-9*, MDT30PARI) Tech Learn Co.

Martz, Laura & Allen, Richard. Mechanical Desktop 3.0: Assembly Modeling: Instructor Manual. 2nd ed. 1998. pap. text, teacher ed. 105.00 (*1-891502-38-7*, MDT30ASMI) Tech Learn Co.

— Mechanical Desktop 3.0: Surface Modeling: Instructor Manual. 2nd ed. 1998. pap. text, teacher ed. 125.00 (*1-891502-39-5*, MDT30SURI) Tech Learn Co.

— Mechanical Desktop 3.0 Part Modeling: Student Manual. 2nd ed. (Illus.). 300p. 1998. pap. text, student ed. 95.00 (*1-891502-31-X*, MDT30SOLI) Tech Learn Co.

— Mechanical Desktop 3.0 Update: Instructor Manual. 2nd ed. 1998. pap., teacher ed. 105.00 incl. cd-rom (*1-891502-36-0*, MDT30UPDI) Tech Learn Co.

***Martz, Laura, et al.** Mechanical Desktop 4: Surface Modeling. (Illus.). 548p. 2000. pap., student ed. 75.00 (*1-891502-71-9*, MDT4SURFSTUD) Tech Learn Co.

— Mechanical Desktop 4: Surface Modeling. 3rd ed. (Illus.). 253p. 2000. pap., teacher ed. 105.00 (*1-891502-72-7*) Tech Learn Co.

— Mechanical Desktop 4.0 - Advanced. 2nd ed. Allen, Richard, ed. (Illus.). 260p. 1999. pap. text, student ed. 75.00 (*1-891502-69-7*, MDT4099) Tech Learn Co.

— Mechanical Desktop 4.0 - Advanced. 2nd ed. Allen, Richard, ed. (Illus.). 260p. 1999. pap. text, teacher ed. 105.00 incl. cd-rom (*1-891502-70-0*, MDT4099) Tech Learn Co.

— Mechanical Desktop 4.0 Fundamentals. 2nd ed. Allen, Richard, ed. (Illus.). 507p. 1999. pap. text, teacher ed. 125.00 incl. cd-rom (*1-891502-68-9*, MDT4099); pap. text, student ed. 95.00 (*1-891502-67-0*, MDT4099) Tech Learn Co.

Martz, Laura, et al. Mechanical Desktop 2.0: Assembly Modeling - Instructor Manual. 2nd large type unabridged ed. (Illus.). 200p. 1998. pap. text, teacher ed. 75.00 (*1-891502-29-8*, MDJ20ASMI) Tech Learn Co.

— Mechanical Desktop 2.0: Solid Modeling - Student Manual. 2nd unabridged ed. (Illus.). 300p. 1998. pap. text, student ed. 95.00 incl. disk (*1-891502-23-9*, MDT20SOL) Tech Learn Co.

Martz, Laura, jt. auth. see Allen, Richard.

Martz, Laura, jt. auth. see Allen, Richard L.

Martz, Laura, ed. see Farricielli, Susan, et al.

Martz, Laura, ed. see Farricrelli, Susan, et al.

Martz, Laura, ed. see Meyers, Ron & Kane, Bill.

Martz, Linda, ed. see Farricrelli, Susan, et al.

Martz, Louis B., ed. Hero & Leander. (Facsimiles Ser.). 1978. 14.00 (*0-918016-35-5*) Folger Bks.

Martz, Louis L. From Renaissance to Baroque: Essays on Literature & Art. (Illus.). 298p. (C). 1991. text 39.95 (*0-8262-0796-0*) U of Mo Pr.

— John Donne in Meditation: The Anniversaries. LC 70-99172. (English Literature Ser.: No. 33). 1970. reprint ed. lib. bdg. 59.00 (*0-8383-0335-8*) M S G Haskell Hse.

— Many Gods & Many Voices: The Role of the Prophet in English & American Modernism. LC 97-40320. (Illus.). 248p. 1998. 34.95 (*0-8262-1148-8*) U of Mo Pr.

— Milton: Poet of Exile. 2nd ed. LC 86-7772. 356p. 1986. pap. 22.00 (*0-300-03736-8*) Yale U Pr.

— The Poetry of Meditation: A Study in English Religious Literature of the Seventeenth Century. rev. ed. LC 54-9520. 405p. reprint ed. pap. 125.60 (*0-8357-8272-7*, 203381400087) Bks Demand.

— Thomas More: The Search for the Inner Man. (Illus.). 128p. (C). 1992. reprint ed. pap. 11.00 (*0-300-05668-0*) Yale U Pr.

Martz, Louis L. & Williams, Aubrey, eds. The Author in His Work: Essays on a Problem in Criticism. LC 77-16309. 427p. reprint ed. pap. 132.40 (*0-8357-5899-0*, 203213600078) Bks Demand.

Martz, Louis L., ed. see H. D., pseud.

Martz, Louis L., ed. & intro. see Lawrence, D. H.

Martz, Louis L., tr. see More, Thomas.

Martz, Mary J. The Central American Soccer War: Historical Patterns & Internal Dynamics of OAS Settlement Procedures. LC 78-11595. (Papers in International Studies: Latin America Ser.: No. 4). 126p. reprint ed. pap. 39.10 (*0-7837-1328-2*, 204147600021) Bks Demand.

Martz, P., et al. Cultural Ecology of Mugu Lagoon. (Illus.). 217p. (C). 1995. reprint ed. pap. text 23.13 (*1-55567-451-8*) Coyote Press.

Martz, Pat & Seid, Judith A., eds. Kumzits! A Festivity of Instant Jewish Songs. LC 97-73644. 90p. 1997. pap. 17.95 (*0-9623668-2-X*) Kopinvant Secular.

Martz, Ron, jt. auth. see Bailey, Lawrence R.

Martz, Ron, jt. auth. see Malcom, Ben S.

Martz, Sandra, ed. Generation to Generation. LC 98-5395. (Illus.). 192p. 1998. pap. 10.95 (*1-57601-072-4*) Papier-Mache Press.

Martz, Sandra H., ed. At Our Core: Women Writing about Power. LC 97-38219. (Illus.). 216p. (Orig.). 1998. pap. 11.00 (*1-57601-007-4*) Papier-Mache Press.

— The Best Is Yet to Be; (Papier-Petite), 6 vols. (Illus.). 64p. 1998. 41.70 (*1-57601-034-1*) Papier-Mache Press.

— The Best Is Yet to Be: Papier-Petite. (Illus.). 64p. 1998. pap. 6.95 (*1-57601-032-5*) Papier-Mache Press.

— Celebrating Women Gift Collection: At Our Core; If I Had a Hammer; I Am Becoming the Woman I've Wanted, 3 bks. in 1. (Illus.). 1998. pap. 32.00 (*1-57601-029-5*) Papier-Mache Press.

— Grow Old along with Me - The Best Is Yet to Be. LC 95-52135. (Illus.). 216p. (Orig.). 1996. pap. 12.00 (*0-918949-86-6*); pap. 20.00 (*0-918949-87-4*) Papier-Mache Press.

— Grow Old along with Me - The Best Is Yet to Be. large type ed. LC 95-52419. (Illus.). 264p. (Orig.). 1996. pap. 17.00 (*0-918949-96-3*) Papier-Mache Press.

— I Am Becoming the Woman I've Wanted. LC 94-19650. (Illus.). 256p. 1994. 18.00 (*0-918949-50-5*); pap. 10.00 (*0-918949-49-1*) Papier-Mache Press.

— I Shall Wear Purple: Papier-Petite. (Illus.). 64p. 1998. pap. 6.95 (*1-57601-036-8*) Papier-Mache Press.

— If I Had a Hammer: Women's Work in Poetry, Fiction, & Photographs. LC 90-7580. (Illus.). 288p. (Orig.). 1990. pap. 11.00 (*0-918949-09-2*) Papier-Mache Press.

— If I Had My Life to Live over I Would Pick More Daisies. LC 92-34059. (Illus.). 224p. (Orig.). 1993. 18.00 (*0-918949-25-4*); pap. 11.00 (*0-918949-24-6*) Papier-Mache Press.

— If I Had My Life to Live over I Would Pick More Daisies. large type ed. LC 95-44949. 240p. (Orig.). 1996. pap. 17.00 (*0-918949-84-X*) Papier-Mache Press.

— If I Had My Life to Live over I Would Pick More Daisies: Reading Card. (Illus.). 24p. 1995. per. 5.00 (*0-918949-71-8*) Papier-Mache Press.

— If I Had My Life to Live Over (papier-petite), 6 vols. (Illus.). 64p. 1998. 41.70 (*1-57601-033-3*) Papier-Mache Press.

— If I Had My Live to Live Over: Papier-Petite. (Illus.). 64p. 1998. pap. 6.95 (*1-57601-031-7*) Papier-Mache Press.

— More Golden Apples: A Further Celebration of Women & Sport. 64p. (Orig.). 1986. pap. 5.95 (*0-918949-01-7*) Martz.

— Multi Title Old Woman/Daisies/Grow Old (Papier-Petite), 12 vols. (Illus.). 64p. 1998. 83.40 (*1-57601-035-X*) Papier-Mache Press.

— 10th Anniversary Gift Set: When I Am an Old Woman I Shall Wear Purple; Daisies; Grow Old along with Me, 3 bks. in 1. anniversary ed. (Illus.). 1997. 56.00 (*1-57601-064-3*); pap. 34.00 (*1-57601-063-5*) Papier-Mache Press.

— There's No Place Like Home for the Holidays. LC 97-15678. (Illus.). 160p. (Orig.). 1997. pap. 9.95 (*1-57601-053-8*) Papier-Mache Press.

— Threads of Experience. LC 95-51733. (Illus.). 64p. 1996. 19.95 (*0-918949-92-0*) Elder Bks.

— The Tie That Binds: A Collection of Writings about Fathers & Daughters - Mothers & Sons. 2nd ed. (Illus.). 192p. 1992. 18.00 (*0-918949-20-3*); pap. 10.00 (*0-918949-19-X*) Martz.

— When I Am an Old Woman I Shall Wear Purple. large type ed. LC 95-44938. 224p. (Orig.). 1996. pap. 17.00 (*0-918949-83-1*) Papier-Mache Press.

— When I Am an Old Woman I Shall Wear Purple. 2nd ed. LC 91-13828. (Illus.). 208p. (Orig.). 1991. 18.00 (*0-918949-15-7*); pap. 11.00 (*0-918949-16-5*) Papier-Mache Press.

— When I Am an Old Woman I Shall Wear Purple: Mini Edition. (Illus.). 64p. 1997. text 6.95 (*1-57601-052-X*) Papier-Mache Press.

— When I Am an Old Woman I Shall Wear Purple: Mini Edition, 6 vols. (Illus.). 64p. 1998. 41.70 (*1-57601-062-7*) Papier-Mache Press.

— When I Am an Old Woman I Shall Wear Purple: Reading Card. (Illus.). 24p. 1995. per. 5.00 (*0-918949-70-X*) Papier-Mache Press.

Martz, Sheryl. Basic Arrhythmia Analysis. 168p. (C). 1994. pap. text, per. 20.63 (*0-8403-9682-1*) Kendall-Hunt.

Martz, Wendelyn, ed. see Evans, Colleen T.

Martz, William J. John Berryman. LC 70-628288. (University of Minnesota Pamphlets on American Writers Ser.: No. 85). 47p. (Orig.). reprint ed. pap. 30.00 (*0-7837-2875-1*, 205758000006) Bks Demand.

— The Place of "Measure for Measure" in Shakespeare's Universe of Comedy. 150p. 1982. 12.50 (*0-87291-159-4*) Coronado Pr.

— The Place of the Merchant of Venice in Shakespeare's Universe of Comedy. 1976. lib. bdg. 250.00 (*0-87700-233-9*) Revisionist Pr.

— The Place of the Tempest in Shakespeare's Universe of Comedy. 1978. 10.00 (*0-87291-098-9*) Coronado Pr.

— Shakespeare's Universe of Comedy. 1976. lib. bdg. 250.00 (*0-87700-268-1*) Revisionist Pr.

Martzloff, Jean-Claude. A History of Chinese Mathematics. Wilson, Stephen S., tr. LC 95-25671. 1995. 63.95 (*3-540-54749-5*) Spr-Verlag.

— A History of Chinese Mathematics. Wilson, Stephen S., tr. LC 95-25671. 509p. 1996. reprint ed. 59.00 (*0-387-54749-5*) Spr-Verlag.

Martzolff, C. F. Swingle: History of the Swingle Family. (Illus.). 212p. 1995. reprint ed. pap. 33.00 (*0-8328-4846-8*); reprint ed. lib. bdg. 43.00 (*0-8328-4845-X*) Higginson Bk Co.

Martzolff, Clement L. Fifty Stories from Ohio History. 1993. reprint ed. lib. bdg. 89.00 (*0-7812-5387-X*) Rprt Serv.

Maru, Hans C., ed. see Symposium on Electrochemical & Thermal Modeling of.

Maru, Hans C., ed. see Symposium on Porous Electrodes, Theory & Practice.

Maru, Olavi. Digest of Bar Association Ethics Opinions: Digest Plus 1970, 1975, 1980 Supplements, 4 vols., Set. LC 74-127109. 1970. suppl. ed. 130.00 (*1-57588-247-7*, 305260) W S Hein.

— Digest of Bar Association Ethics Opinions: 1970 Supplement. LC 74-127109. ix, 366p. 1972. suppl. ed. 30.00 (*0-910058-54-7*, 304780) W S Hein.

— Digest of Bar Association Ethics Opinions: 1980 Supplement. LC 74-127109. ix, 835p. 1982. suppl. ed. 52.00 (*0-910059-01-2*, 304800) W S Hein.

— Research on the Legal Profession: A Review of Work Done. 2nd ed. LC 86-70978. vii, 106p. 1986. pap. 25.00 (*0-910059-11-X*, 306040) W S Hein.

Maruani, J. Molecules in Physics, Chemistry & Biology, 4 vols., Vol. 1: General Introduction to Molecular Sciences. (C). 1988. lib. bdg. 162.50 (*90-277-2596-9*) Kluwer Academic.

— Molecules in Physics, Chemistry & Biology, 4 vols., Vol. 2: Physical Aspects of Molecular Systems. (C). 1988. lib. bdg. 342.00 (*90-277-2597-7*) Kluwer Academic.

— Molecules in Physics, Chemistry & Biology, 4 vols., Vol. 3: Electronic Structure & Chemical Reactivity. (C). 1988. lib. bdg. 224.50 (*90-277-2598-5*) Kluwer Academic.

— Molecules in Physics, Chemistry & Biology, 4 vols., Vol. 4: Molecular Phenomena in Biological Sciences. (C). 1988. lib. bdg. 197.00 (*90-277-2599-3*) Kluwer Academic.

Marubini, Ettore & Valsecchi, Maria G. Analysing Survival Data from Clinical Trials & Observational Studies. LC 94-30632. (Statistics in Practice Ser.). 430p. 1995. 135.00 (*0-471-93987-0*) Wiley.

Maruca, Mary. Exploring National Parks. (Illus.). 32p. (YA). (gr. 1-6). 1998. pap. 8.95 (*1-877856-91-6*) SW Pks Mnmts.

***Maruca, Mary.** A Kid's Guide to Exploring John Muir. LC 99-58592. (Illus.). 16p. (J). (gr. 3-7). 1999. pap. 3.95 (*1-877856-98-3*, E1003) SW Pks Mnmts.

— A Kid's Guide to Exploring San Antonio Missions. LC 99-52165. 16p. (J). (gr. 3-6). 2000. pap. 3.95 (*1-58369-002-6*, E1018) SW Pks Mnmts.

Maruca, Mary, jt. auth. see Southwest Parks & Monuments Editors.

Marucchi, Orazio. Christian Epigraphy. Willis, J. Armine, tr. LC 74-82057. 472p. 1975. pap. 30.00 (*0-89005-070-8*) Ares.

Marucci, Carl J., ed. The Visit of His Holiness Pope John Paul II to the United Nations. 80p. (Orig.). (C). 1996. pap. text 20.00 (*0-9651613-0-7*) Path to Peace.

Marucci, Carl J., et al. Serving the Human Family: The Holy See at the Major United Nations Conferences. LC 97-40759. 1997. 39.95 (*0-9651613-2-3*) Path to Peace.

Marucci, Ferdinando, jt. auth. see Weisz, Ilona.

Marucci, Franco. The Fine Delight That Fathers Thought: Rhetoric & Medievalism in Gerard Manley Hopkins. LC 93-39010. 281p. (C). 1994. 44.95 (*0-8132-0778-9*) Cath U Pr.

***Marucci, Mat.** 15 Minute Warm-Ups for Drums. 24p. 2000. pap. 5.95 incl. audio compact disk (*0-7866-5320-5*, 98652BCD) Mel Bay.

Maruf, Mohammad. Iqbal's Philosophy of Religion. 3rd ed. 260p. 1989. reprint ed. text 29.00 (*1-56744-027-4*) Kazi Pubns.

Maruggi, Edward. Technical Graphics: Electronics Worktext. 2nd ed. 464p. (C). 1990. pap. text 44.20 (*0-675-21378-9*, Merrill Coll) P-H.

— Technology of Drafting. 1990. pap. text, wbk. ed. 39.20 (*0-675-21234-0*, Merrill Coll) P-H.

Maruggi, Edward A. Current Practices for Interpreting Engineering Drawings. LC 94-24210. 432p. (C). 1995. spiral bd. 40.95 (*0-314-04576-7*) West Pub.

— Mushrooms, Sausage & Wine Vol. 1: Life with an Immigrant Father. (Illus.). 153p. (Orig.). 1997. pap. 9.95 (*0-9658870-0-6*) Winston NY.

Maruhn, J. A., jt. auth. see Greiner, Walter.

Marui, Eiji, jt. ed. see Reich, Michael R.

Maruice, F. D., jt. auth. see Dunstan, G. R.

Maruis, Barbara, intro. Famous People of Hispanic Heritage. (Contemporary American Success Stories Ser.). (Illus.). 960p. (YA). (gr. 4-10). 1998. 219.50 (*1-883845-90-4*) Chelsea Hse.

Maruish, Mark E., ed. Handbook of Psychological Assessment in Primary Care Settings. LC 99-48451. 880p. 1999. 250.00 (*0-8058-2999-7*) L Erlbaum Assocs.

— The Use of Psychological Testing for Treatment Planning & Outcome Assessment. 624p. 1994. text 135.00 (*0-8058-1162-1*) L Erlbaum Assocs.

— The Use of Psychological Testing for Treatment Planning & Outcome Assessment. 2nd ed. LC 98-34838. 1507p. 1999. 250.00 (*0-8058-2761-7*) L Erlbaum Assocs.

Maruish, Mark E. & Moses, James A., eds. Clinical Neuropsychology: Theoretical Foundations for Practitioners. 400p. 1996. 79.95 (*0-8058-1343-8*) L Erlbaum Assocs.

Maruki, Toshi. Hiroshima No Pika. LC 82-15365. (Illus.). 48p. (J). (gr. 7 up). 1982. 16.00 (*0-688-01297-3*) Lothrop.

***Marulanda, Angela.** Creciendo con Nuestros Hijos. 2nd ed. 1999. pap. 17.95 (*958-33-0862-5*) Borrero & Gomez.

Marullo, Michael A. Global Automation Profiles Vol. I: The GAP Report. (Illus.). 50p. (Orig.). 1996. spiral bd. 650.00 (*0-614-15050-7*) cfari pr.

— Supplier Profiles Directory of SCADA Products - Systems - Services: The Sourcebook of Products, Systems, & Services for Supervisory Control & Data Acquisition (SCADA) Professionals, 1988-89. 211p. 1988. pap. 40.00 (*0-9622280-0-1*) cfari pr.

— Supplier Profiles Directory of SCADA Products, Systems & Services: 1990-91 Edition. 259p. (Orig.). 1991. pap. 45.00 (*0-685-48472-6*) cfari pr.

Marullo, Michael A., pref. Supplier Profiles Directory of SCADA Products - Systems - Services, 1992-93. 265p. 1993. pap. 50.00 (*0-9622280-2-8*) cfari pr.

Marullo, Rita, jt. auth. see Mound, Laurence A.

Marullo, Sam. Ending the Cold War at Home: From Militarism to a More Peaceful World Order. LC 93-29852. (Lexington Book Series on Social Issues). 74p. 1994. 30.95 (*0-669-24231-4*) Lxngtn Bks.

Marullo, Sam & Lofland, John, eds. Peace Action in the 1980s: Social Science Perspectives. LC 89-49216. 300p. (C). 1990. text 40.00 (*0-8135-1560-2*); pap. text 16.00 (*0-8135-1561-0*) Rutgers U Pr.

Marullo, Thomas G. If You See the Buddha: Studies in the Fiction of Ivan Bunin. LC 98-40491. (Studies in Russian Literature & Theory). 232p. 1998. text 54.95 (*0-8101-1612-X*) Northwestern U Pr.

Marullo, Thomas G., ed. Ivan Bunin - Russian Requiem, 1885-1920: A Portrait from Letters, Diaries, & Fiction. (Illus.). 397p. 1993. text 30.00 (*1-56663-012-6*) I R Dee.

Marullo, Thomas G., ed. Ivan Bunin - From the Other Shore, 1920-1933: Portrait from Letters, Diaries, & Fiction. LC 94-46953. 340p. 1995. text 35.00 (*1-56663-083-5*) I R Dee.

Marullo, Thomas G., tr. see Bunin, Ivan A.

Marum, Andrew & Parise, Frank. Follies & Foibles: A View of 20th Century Fads. LC 82-2355. (Illus.). 238p. reprint ed. pap. 73.80 (*0-7837-1565-X*, 204185700024) Bks Demand.

Marum, Ed, ed. Children & Books in the Modern World: Contemporary Perspectives on Literacy. LC 96-209128. 240p. 1996. 79.95 (*0-7507-0542-6*, Falmer Pr); pap. 27.95 (*0-7507-0543-4*, Falmer Pr) Taylor & Francis.

— Towards 2000: The Future of Childhood, Literacy, & Schooling. LC 95-7254. 1995. 85.00 (*0-7507-0420-9*, Falmer Pr) Taylor & Francis.

Marumo, F., ed. Dynamic Processes of Material Transport & Transformation in the Earth's Interior. (C). 1991. text 385.50 (*0-7923-1075-6*) Kluwer Academic.

Marumoto, Claire, ed. Guide to Government in Hawaii. 11th ed. 1996. 5.00 (*0-318-50041-8*) HI Legis Ref.

Marun, Gioconda. Origenes del Costumbrismo Etico-Social, Addison y Steele: Antecedentes del Articulo Costumbrista Espanol y Argentino. LC 83-80966. (SPA.). 167p. (Orig.). 1983. pap. 19.95 (*0-89729-278-2*) Ediciones.

Maruo, H., jt. ed. see Horikawa, Kiyoshi.

Maruo, Suehiro. Mr. Arashi's Amazing Freak Show. (Illus.). 160p. 1991. pap. 10.95 (*0-922233-06-3*) Blast Bks.

Marus, Joel R., jt. auth. see Eglin, Joseph J., Jr.

Marus, Sheryl M. Kampus Kwestions: How to Bake a Potato & Other Great Mysteries. (Illus.). (Orig.). (C). 1994. pap. 9.99 (*0-9641714-0-6*) STS Instruct.

Marusak, Kathleen, ed. see Janke, Michael Anthony.

Marusak, Kathleene, ed. see Clarke, Mickey.

Maruschak, Laura, jt. auth. see Beck, Allen.

***Marushiakova, Elena & Popov, Vesselin.** Gypsies in the Ottoman Empire: A Contribution to the History of the Balkans. (Interface Collection: Vol. 22). (Illus.). 100p. 2000. pap. 19.95 (*1-902806-02-6*, Pub. by Univ of Herfordshire) Bold Strummer Ltd.

Marushiakova, Elena & Popov, Vesselin. Gypsies (Roma) in Bulgaria. (Studien zur Tsiganologie und Folkloristik: Bd. 18). (Illus.). 216p. 1997. pap. 42.95 (*3-631-30759-4*) P Lang Pubng.

Maruska, Edward J. Salamanders. (Nature Books Ser.). (Illus.). 32p. (J). (gr. 2-6). 1996. lib. bdg. 22.79 (*1-56766-273-0*) Childs World.

Maruskin, Albert F. OCLC, Its Governance, Function, Financing, & Technology. LC 80-23417. (Books in Library & Information Science: No. 32). 157p. reprint ed. pap. 48.70 (*0-7837-0761-4*, 204107500019) Bks Demand.

Maruskin-Mott, Joan. Breakthroughs in Writing & Language. LC 95-42670. 1996. pap., student ed. 11.33 (*0-8092-3298-7*) NTC Contemp Pub Co.

— Breakthroughs in Writing & Language (Text & Exercise Book) 1998. text, wbk. ed. 17.25 (*0-8092-0792-3*) NTC Contemp Pub Co.

Marussi, A. Intrinsic Geodesy. Reilly, I., tr. from ITA. (Illus.). 240p. 1985. 128.95 (*0-387-15133-8*) Spr-Verlag.

Marusso, Adriana, tr. see Sumar, Sonia.

Marusyk, Raymond G., jt. ed. see Kurstak, Edouard.

***Marusza, Julia.** Canal Town Youth: Community Organization & the Development of Adolescent Identity. LC 00-26527. (C). 2000. pap. text 18.95 (*0-7914-4814-2*) State U NY Pr.

— Canal Town Youth: Community Organization & the Development of Adolescent Identity. LC 00-26527. (C). 2001. text 57.50 (*0-7914-4813-4*) State U NY Pr.

Maruszewski, Bodgan. Proceedings of the International Symposium on Trends in Continuum Physics, Trecop' 98, Pozna N, Poland, 17-20 August 1998. LC 98-53243. 350p. 1999. 98.00 (*981-02-3760-X*) World Scientific Pub.

Maruszewski, Mariusz. Language Communication & the Brain: A Neuropsychological Study. Shugar, Grace W., tr. from POL. (Janua Linguarum, Series Major: No. 80). (Illus.). 217p. 1975. text 57.70 (*90-279-3067-8*) Mouton.

Marut, jt. auth. see Yu.

Maruta, Hiroshi & Burgess, Anthony. Regulation of the RAS Signaling Network. LC 96-35747. (Molecular Biology Intelligence Unit Ser.). 188p. 1996. 99.00 (*1-57059-404-X*) Landes Bioscience.

Maruta, Hiroshi, et al. G Proteins, Cytoskeleton, & Cancer. LC 98-20518. (Molecular Biology Intelligence Unit Ser.). 1998. 99.00 (*1-57059-551-8*) Landes Bioscience.

Marutollo, Frank. Organizational Behavior in the Marine Corps: Three Interpretations. LC 89-70913. 232p. 1990. 59.95 (*0-275-93493-4*, C3493, Greenwood Pr) Greenwood.

***Maruvada, P. Sarma.** Corona Performance of High-Voltage Transmission Lines. LC 00-35281. (High Voltage Power Transmission Ser.). 2000. write for info. (*0-86380-254-0*, Pub. by Research Studies Pr Ltd) Taylor & Francis.

Maruya, Saiichi. A Mature Woman. Keene, Dennis, tr. 328p. 1995. 28.00 (*4-7700-1864-9*) Kodansha.

— A Mature Woman. 1997. pap. text 12.00 (*4-7700-2183-6*, Pub. by Kodansha Intl) Kodansha.

— Rain in the Wind: Four Stories. Keene, Dennis, tr. from JPN. 240p. (YA). 1990. 18.95 (*0-87011-940-0*) Kodansha.

— Rain in the Wind: Four Stories. Keene, Dennis, tr. from JPN. 240p. 1992. pap. 8.00 (*4-7700-1558-5*) Kodansha.

Maruyama, E., et al, eds. Recent Advances in Coronary Circulation. 1994. 199.00 (*0-387-70130-3*) Spr-Verlag.

Maruyama, E. & Watanabe, H., eds. Physics & Industry: Proceedings of Academic Session of the XXI General Assembly of the International Union of Pure & Applied Physics Held at Nara, Japan, 22 & 23 September 1993. LC 94-30559. (Lecture Notes in Physics Ser.: Vol. 435). 1994. 59.95 (*3-540-58376-9*) Spr-Verlag.

— Physics & Industry: Proceedings of Academic Session of the XXI General Assembly of the International Union of Pure & Applied Physics Held at Nara, Japan, 22 & 23 September 1993. 435. LC 94-30559. (Lecture Notes in Physics Ser.). 1994. write for info. (*0-387-58376-9*) Spr-Verlag.

Maruyama, Elizabeth, et al. Occupational Therapy Services for Children & Youth under the Individuals with Disabilities Education Act. LC 97-172030. iv, 240 p. 1997. 50.00 (*1-56900-069-7*) Am Occup Therapy.

Maruyama, Geoffrey & Deno, Stanley. Research in Educational Settings. (Applied Social Research Methods Ser.: Vol. 29). 160p. (C). 1992. text 42.00 (*0-8039-4207-9*); pap. text 18.95 (*0-8039-4208-7*) Sage.

Maruyama, Geoffrey M. Basics of Structural Equation Modeling. LC 97-4839. 320p. 1997. 58.00 (*0-8039-7408-6*); pap. 26.95 (*0-8039-7409-4*) Sage.

Maruyama, Hiroshi. XML & Java: Developing Web Applications. LC 99-18618. 400p. (C). 1999. pap. text 39.95 (*0-201-48543-5*) Addison-Wesley.

***Maruyama, Hiroshi, et al.** Xml & Java: Developing Web Applications. LC 99-18618. ix, 386 p. 1999. write for info. incl. cd-rom (*0-201-61611-4*) Addison-Wesley.

Maruyama, K., jt. ed. see Kirchner, R.

Maruyama Kaoru. That Far-Off Self: The Collected Poetry of Maruyama (Family) Kaoru (Given) 2nd rev. ed. Epp, Robert, tr. from JPN. & intro. by. 360p. (C). 1994. text 35.00 (*1-880276-49-6*) Yakusha.

Maruyama, M. & Reniker, S., eds. Context & Complexity: Cultivating Contextual Understanding. (Illus.). xii, 145p. 1991. 47.95 (*0-387-97542-X*) Spr-Verlag.

Maruyama, Magoroh. Management Reform in Eastern & Central Europe: Use of Pre-Communist Cultures. 192p. 1993. 41.95 (*1-85521-343-5*, Pub. by Dartmth Pub) Ashgate Pub Co.

— Mindscapes in Management: Use of Individual Differences in Multicultural Management. 160p. 1994. 41.95 (*1-85521-367-2*, Pub. by Dartmth Pub) Ashgate Pub Co.

Maruyama, Magoroh & Harkins, Arthur M., eds. Cultures of the Future. (World Anthropology Ser.). xxii, 668p. 1978. 100.00 (*90-279-7979-0*) Mouton.

Maruyama, Masaki, ed. Moduli of Vector Bundles. LC 96-641. (Lecture Notes in Pure & Applied Mathematics Ser.: Vol. 179). (Illus.). 336p. 1996. pap. text 145.00 (*0-8247-9738-8*) Dekker.

Maruyama, Masao. Studies in the Intellectual History of Tokugawa Japan. Hane, Mikiso, tr. 422p. 1994. pap. 34.50 (*0-86008-444-2*) Col U Pr.

— Studies in the Intellectual History of Tokugawa Japan. Hane, Mikiso, tr. 424p. (C). 1989. pap. text 24.50 (*0-691-00832-9*, Pub. by Princeton U Pr) Cal Prin Full Svc.

Maruyama, Meredith E., et al. Japan Health Handbook. 320p. 1995. pap. 20.00 (*4-7700-1838-X*) Kodansha.

Maruyama, T. & Tsubokura, M. Current Investigations of the Microbiology of Yersiniae. Une, T. et al, eds. (Contributions to Microbiology & Immunology Ser.: Vol. 12). (Illus.). x, 316p. 1991. 274.00 (*3-8055-5370-6*) S Karger.

Maruyama, T., jt. ed. see Kusuoka, S.

Maruyama, Teresa C. Hospice Care & Culture: A Comparison of the Hospice Movement in the West & Japan. LC R726.8.M3726 1999. (Avebury Series in Philosophy). 204p. (C). 1999. text 61.95 (*1-84014-866-7*, Pub. by Ashgate Pub) Ashgate Pub Co.

Maruyama, Toru & Takahashi, Wataru, eds. Nonlinear & Convex Analysis in Economic Theory. LC 94-39352. (Lecture Notes in Economics & Mathematical Systems Ser.: Vol. 419). 1995. write for info. (*0-387-58767-5*) Spr-Verlag.

Maruyama, Y., et al. Cardiac-Vascular Remodeling & Functional Interaction, Vol. XII. (Illus.). 416p. 1997. 195.00 (*4-431-70188-5*) Spr-Verlag.

Maruyama, Yosh. CF-252 Neutron Brachytherapy, Vol. 1. (Nuclear Science Applications Ser.: Section B, Vol. 1, No. 8). 72p. 1984. pap. text 63.00 (*3-7186-0208-3*) Gordon & Breach.

— International Neutron Therapy Workshop. (Nuclear Science Applications Ser.: Vol. 2). 280p. 1991. pap. text 501.00 (*3-7186-5124-6*, Harwood Acad Pubs) Gordon & Breach.

— International Neutron Therapy Workshop, Pt. 1. (Nuclear Science Applications Ser.: Vol. 1). xx, 228p. 1991. pap. text 448.00 (*3-7186-5123-8*, Harwood Acad Pubs) Gordon & Breach.

— Notes & Abstracts: International Neutron Therapy Workshop. (Nuclear Science Applications Ser.). 56p. 1991. pap. text 101.00 (*3-7186-5122-X*, Harwood Acad Pubs) Gordon & Breach.

Maruyama, Yosh, et al, eds. Cardiac Adaptation & Failure. LC 94-40505. 1995. 195.00 (*0-387-70133-8*) Spr-Verlag.

— Microwave Fixation of Labile Metabolites: Proceedings of an Official Satellite Symposium of the 8th International Congress of Pharmacology Held in Tokyo, Japan, 25 July 1981. (Advances in the Biosciences Ser.: 45). (Illus.). 191p. 1983. 60.50 (*0-08-029829-X*, Pergamon Pr) Elsevier.

Maruyama, Yosh, et al. CF-252 Neutron Brachytherapy & Fast Neutron Beam Therapy, Vol. 2. xxiv, 636p. 1986. text 468.00 (*3-7186-0324-1*) Gordon & Breach.

Maruzen, Benjamin. Hgs Molecular Structure Models: General Chemistry Set. 1p. (C). 1971. 32.00 (*0-8053-6971-6*) Benjamin-Cummings.

— HGS Molecular Structure Models: Organic Chemistry. 2nd ed. 1p. (C). 1988. pap. 33.00 (*0-8053-0260-3*) Benjamin-Cummings.

Maruzzi, Stefano. The Microsoft Windows 95 Developer's Guide. 1040p. 1996. pap. text 49.99 incl. cd-rom (*1-56276-335-0*, Ziff-Davis Pr) Que.

Marval-McNair, Nora de, ed. Selected Proceedings of the Singularidad y Trascendencia Conference. LC 89-64458. (ENG & SPA.). 250p. 1990. pap. 40.00 (*0-89295-059-5*) Society Sp & Sp-Am.

Marvan, P., ed. see Institute of Botany, Czechoslovak Academy of Scien.

Marvano, jt. auth. see Haldeman, Joe.

Marvano, ed. see Haldeman, Joe.

Marvel. The Brood Saga, Pt. 2. (X-Men Ser.). (YA). (gr. 5 up). 1996. pap. 3.99 (*0-614-15790-0*) Tor Bks.

Marvel, Bill. New York Central Trackside with Eugene Van Dusen. LC 97-72732. (Illus.). 128p. 1997. 49.95 (*1-878887-81-5*) Morning NJ.

— Rock Island in Color, 1965-1980, Vol. 2. (Illus.). 1995. 49.95 (*1-878887-39-4*) Morning NJ.

— Santa Fe All the Way, Vol. 1. LC 98-66807. (Illus.). 128p. 1998. 49.95 (*1-58248-009-5*) Morning NJ.

— Under Milwaukee Wires. (Illus.). 1996. 49.95 (*1-878887-69-6*) Morning NJ.

Marvel, Bill, intro. Papers of the Military Historical Society of Massachusetts, 15 vols., Set. 1990. reprint ed. 500.00 (*0-916107-73-6*) Broadfoot.

Marvel Comics Staff. Daredevil, No. 1. (J). (gr. 5). 1996. mass mkt. 3.99 (*0-8125-4346-7*, Pub. by Tor Bks) St Martin.

— Enter the Phoenix. (X-Men Ser.). (J). (gr. 5 up). 1996. pap. 3.99 (*0-614-15789-7*) Tor Bks.

— The Mark of the Man-Wolf. (Spiderman Ser.: No. 3). 1996. mass mkt. 3.99 (*0-8125-4408-0*, Pub. by Tor Bks) St Martin.

— Where Crawls the Lizard? (Spiderman Ser.: No. 2). (J). (gr. 5). 1996. mass mkt. 3.99 (*0-8125-4345-9*, Pub. by Tor Bks) St Martin.

— X-Men, No. 3. Vol. 1. 1996. mass mkt. 3.99 (*0-8125-4405-6*, Pub. by Tor Bks) St Martin.

— X-Men, No. 4. 1996. mass mkt. 3.99 (*0-8125-5540-6*, Pub. by Tor Bks) St Martin.

***Marvel Comics Staff.** X-Men: Beginnings. (Illus.). (J). 2000. pap. 14.95 (*0-7851-0750-9*) Marvel Entrprs.

— X-Men: The Movie. (Illus.). (J). 2000. pap. 14.95 (*0-7851-0749-5*) Marvel Entrprs.

Marvel Entertainment Staff. The Birth of Spiderman. deluxe limited ed. (Illus.). 1997. 100.00 (*1-55709-335-0*) Applewood.

— The Uncanny X-Men. 128p. 1990. pap. 3.99 (*0-8125-1021-6*, Pub. by Tor Bks) St Martin.

Marvel, Karen, ed. see Sherman, Ed.

***Marvel, Laura.** The Taming of the Shrew. LC 99-59318. (Literary Companion Ser.). 224p. (YA). 2000. 13.96 (*0-7377-0237-0*); pap. 13.96 (*0-7377-0236-2*) Greenhaven.

Marvel, Richard. The New Oz: The Wizard Revisited. Schuck, Marjorie M., ed. 86p. (Orig.). 1992. pap. text 10.00 (*0-934616-45-0*) Valkyrie Pub Hse.

Marvel, Terrence L. Thirties America: Prints from the Milwaukee Art Museum. (Illus.). 30p. (Orig.). 1991. pap. 12.00 (*0-944110-30-4*) Milwauk Art Mus.

Marvel, Terrence L., jt. auth. see Bamberger, Tom.

Marvel, Thomas & Moreno, Maria L. Arquitectura de Templos Parroquiales. 2nd ed.Tr. of Architecture of Parish Churches in Puerto Rico. (ENG & SPA., Illus.). 208p. 1994. 29.95 (*0-8477-2118-3*) U of PR Pr.

Marvel, Thomas S. & Brooks, H. Allen. Antonin Nechodoma, Architect, 1877-1928: The Prairie School in the Caribbean. LC 93-32486. (Illus.). 256p. (C). 1994. 49.95 (*0-8130-1269-4*) U Press Fla.

Marvel, William. The Alabama & the Kearsarge: The Sailor's Civil War. LC 96-11144. (Civil War America Ser.). 368p. (C). (gr. 13). 1996. 39.95 (*0-8078-2294-9*) U of NC Pr.

— Andersonville: The Last Depot. LC 93-40101. (Civil War America Ser.). (Illus.). xii, 338p. 1994. 34.95 (*0-8078-2152-7*) U of NC Pr.

— Burnside. LC 91-8419. (Illus.). xiv, 538p. 1991. 45.00 (*0-8078-1983-2*) U of NC Pr.

— The First New Hampshire Battery, Eighteen Sixty-One to Eighteen Sixty-Five. (Illus.). 97p. (Orig.). 1985. pap. 6.95 (*0-9614826-0-5*) Lost Cemetery Pr.

— Fredericksburg. (Civil War Ser.). (Illus.). 56p. 1995. pap. 4.95 (*0-915992-83-3*) Eastern National.

***Marvel, William.** A Place Called Appomattox. LC 00-25593. (Civil War America Ser.). 416p. 2000. 34.95 (*0-8078-2568-9*) U of NC Pr.

Marvel, William. Race of the Soil: "The Ninth New Hampshire Regiment in the Civil War" (Illus.). 534p. 1988. 35.00 (*0-916107-67-1*) Broadfoot.

Marvel, William, contrib. by. Military Order of the Loyal Legion of the United States, 70 vols. (Illus.). 1996. reprint ed. 2400.00 (*1-56837-001-6*) Broadfoot.

Marvel, William, jt. auth. see Cavanaush, Michael A.

Marvell, Andrew. The Complete Poems & Translations. Donno, Elizabeth S., ed. (Poets Ser.). 320p. 1977. pap. 12.95 (*0-14-042213-7*, Penguin Classics) Viking Penguin.

— The Complete Poems of Andrew Marvell. LC 92-54301. 1993. 0.15 (*0-679-42038-X*) Everymns Lib.

— Complete Works in Verse & Prose of Andrew Marvell, 4 vols., Set. LC 77-181955. (Fuller Worthies' Library). reprint ed. 345.00 (*0-404-04270-8*) AMS Pr.

— The Complete Works in Verse & Prose of Andrew Marvell, 4 vols., Set. (BCL1-PR English Literature Ser.). 1992. reprint ed. lib. bdg. 300.00 (*0-7812-7372-2*) Rprt Serv.

— Selected Poems. Hutchings, Bill, ed. (Orig.). 1979. pap. 7.50 (*0-85635-258-6*, Pub. by Carcanet Pr) Paul & Co Pubs.

— "To His Coy Mistress" & Other Poems. LC 96-45478. (Dover Thrift Editions Ser.). 64p. (Orig.). 1997. pap. text 1.00 (*0-486-29544-3*) Dover.

Marvell-Mell, Linaea. Basic Techniques, Bk. 1. rev. ed. Stephens, Lori, ed. (Skill Builder Ser.). (Illus.). 192p. 1989. pap. text, pap., student ed. 12.95 incl. audio (*1-55552-016-2*) Metamorphous Pr.

Marvell, Thomas B. Appellate Courts & Lawyers: Information Gathering in the Adversary System, 4. LC 77-94743. (Contributions in Legal Studies: No. 4). 391p. 1978. 75.00 (*0-313-20312-1*, MAA/, Greenwood Pr) Greenwood.

Marven, Craig. Simple Approach to Digital Signal Processing. LC 96-2518. 248p. 1996. 54.95 (*0-471-15243-9*) Wiley.

***Marven, Nigel.** Incredible Journeys: Featuring the World's Greatest Animal Travellers. (Illus.). 192p. 2000. reprint ed. 25.00 (*0-7881-9309-0*) DIANE Pub.

Marvez, Alex. Wild Ride! The Illustrated History of the Denver Broncos. (Illus.). 240p. 1998. 36.95 (*0-87833-211-1*) Taylor Pub.

Marvick, Elizabeth W. The Young Richelieu: A Psychoanalytic Approach to Leadership. LC 82-24754. (Orig.). 1983. pap. text 14.00 (*0-226-50905-2*) U Ch Pr.

Marvick, Louis W. Mallarme & the Sublime. LC 85-27750. (SUNY Series, Intersections). 211p. (C). 1986. text 64.50 (*0-88706-278-4*); pap. text 21.95 (*0-88706-279-2*) State U NY Pr.

Marvicsin, Dennis J. Maverick. 320p. 1991. mass mkt. 5.99 (*0-515-10662-3*, Jove) Berkley Pub.

Marville, Charles, photos by. Marville: Paris (FRE., Illus.). 450p. 1998. pap. 55.00 (*2-85025-374-X*) Gingko Press.

Marvillet, C., jt. ed. see Vidil, R.

Marvin, Abijah P. History of the Town of Lancaster, Mass., from the First Settlement to the Present Time, 1643-1879. (Illus.). 798p. 1989. reprint ed. lib. bdg. 79.00 (*0-8328-0833-4*, MA0198) Higginson Bk Co.

— History of the Town of Winchendon, Worcester County, Massachusetts. (Illus.). 528p. 1994. reprint ed. lib. bdg. 55.00 (*0-8328-3960-4*) Higginson Bk Co.

— The Life & Times of Cotton Mather. LC 72-1979. (American Biography Ser.: No. 32). 1972. reprint ed. lib. bdg. 75.00 (*0-8383-1454-6*) M S G Haskell Hse.

Marvin, Andrew T. What Every Parent Should Know about Pinewood Derby Cars & More. Marvin, Ann M., ed. (Illus.). 11p. 1998. pap. 3.00 (*0-9664034-0-1*, 1001) A T Marvin.

Marvin, Ann M., ed. see Marvin, Andrew T.

Marvin, Bill. Cashing in on Complaints: Turning Disappointed Diners into Gold. 156p. (Orig.). 1997. pap. 14.95 (*0-9656262-1-0*, HMS-2) Hospitality Masters.

— From Turnover to Teamwork: How to Build & Retain a Customer Oriented Foodservice Staff. 216p. 1994. 54.95 (*0-471-59077-0*) Wiley.

— Guest-Based Marketing: How to Increase Restaurant Sales Without Breaking Your Budget. LC 96-51707. 240p. 1997. 49.95 (*0-471-15394-X*) Wiley.

— Restaurant Basics: Why Guests Don't Come Back...& What You Can Do about It. LC 91-29481. 240p. 1991. 54.95 (*0-471-55174-0*) Wiley.

— There's Got to Be an Easier Way to Run a Business: How to Have a Successful Company . . . And a Life! 172p. 1999. pap. 14.95 (*0-9656262-6-1*) Hospitality Masters.

Marvin, Carolyn. When Old Technologies Were New. 272p. 1990. reprint ed. pap. text 19.95 (*0-19-506341-4*) OUP.

Marvin, Carolyn & Ingle, David. Blood Sacrifice & the Nation: Totem Rituals & the American Flag. LC 97-25640. (Cambridge Cultural Social Studies). (Illus.). 416p. (C). 1998. text 74.95 (*0-521-62345-6*); pap. text 27.95 (*0-521-62609-9*) Cambridge U Pr.

Marvin, Clara, jt. auth. see Marco, Guy A.

Marvin, Elizabeth W. & Hermann, Richard, eds. Concert Music, Rock, & Jazz since 1945: Essays & Analytical Studies. LC 94-30277. (Eastman Studies in Music: No. 2). 464p. (C). 1996. 110.00 (*1-878822-42-X*) Univ Rochester Pr.

Marvin, Francis M. Shafer - Huston - Huston Family History. (Illus.). 470p. 1994. reprint ed. pap. 47.00 (*0-8328-4236-2*); reprint ed. lib. bdg. 57.00 (*0-8328-4235-4*) Higginson Bk Co.

— Van Horn Family History. (Illus.). 464p. 1992. reprint ed. pap. 67.50 (*0-8328-2465-8*); reprint ed. lib. bdg. 77.50 (*0-8328-2464-X*) Higginson Bk Co.

— Van Horn Family History. 464p. 1997. reprint ed. pap. 69.50 (*0-8328-9535-0*); reprint ed. lib. bdg. 79.50 (*0-8328-9534-2*) Higginson Bk Co.

Marvin, Francis S., ed. Evolution of World-Peace: Essays. Unity Ser. 4. LC 68-20318. (Essay Index Reprint Ser.). 1977. 17.95 (*0-8369-0682-9*) Ayer.

— New World-Order: Essays. LC 67-30221. (Essay Index Reprint Ser.). 1977. 19.95 (*0-8369-0683-7*) Ayer.

— Progress & History: Essays. LC 78-84326. (Essay Index Reprint Ser.). 1977. 20.95 (*0-8369-1096-6*) Ayer.

— Recent Developments in European Thought. LC 71-111851. (Essay Index Reprint Ser.). 1977. 21.95 (*0-8369-1619-0*) Ayer.

— Science & Civilization. LC 70-105030. (Essay Index Reprint Ser.). 1977. 23.95 (*0-8369-1581-X*) Ayer.

— Unity of Western Civilization. LC 77-128277. (Essay Index Reprint Ser.). 1977. 21.95 (*0-8369-1889-4*) Ayer.

— Western Races & the World. LC 68-22929. (Unity Ser.: Vol. 5). 1977. reprint ed. 19.95 (*0-8369-0684-5*) Ayer.

Marvin, Francis S. & Clutton-Brock, Alan F., eds. Art & Civilization: Essays. LC 67-26762. (Essay Index Reprint Ser.). 1977. 20.95 (*0-8369-0685-3*) Ayer.

Marvin, Fred. Ready-to-Use Humorous Attention-Getters. (Clip Art Ser.). (Illus.). 64p. 1990. pap. 5.95 (*0-486-26458-0*) Dover.

— Ready-to-Use Money & Savings Illustrations. (Clip Art Ser.). (Illus.). 64p. 1990. pap. text 5.95 (*0-486-26281-2*) Dover.

— Ready-to-Use Performing Arts Illustrations. (Clip Art Ser.). (Illus.). 64p. 1986. pap. 5.95 (*0-486-25184-5*) Dover.

Marvin, Fred. Pinocchio: Geppetto's Surprise. LC 92-54877. (Tiny Changing Pictures Bk.). 10p. (J). (ps). 1993. 4.95 (*1-56282-397-3*, Pub. by Disney Pr) Little.

— Suppertime: Snow White & the Seven Dwarfs. LC 93-71376. (Tiny Changing Pictures Bk.). 10p. (J). (ps-1). 1994. 4.95 (*1-56282-600-X*, Pub. by Disney Pr) Little.

— Walt Disney's Snow White & the Seven Dwarfs. LC 92-53430. (Illustrated Classics Ser.). 96p. (J). 1993. 14.95 (*1-56282-362-0*, Pub. by Disney Pr) Little.

Marvin, Fred & Guell, Fernando. Walt Disney's Snow White & the Seven Dwarfs. LC 92-53430. (Illustrated Classics Ser.). 96p. (J). 1993. lib. bdg. 14.89 (*1-56282-363-9*, Pub. by Disney Pr) Little.

— Walt Disney's Snow White & the Seven Dwarfs. LC 92-53430. (Illustrated Classics Ser.). 96p. (J). 1994. pap. 5.95 (*0-7868-4020-X*, Pub. by Disney Pr) Little.

Marvin, Fred, jt. illus. see Thompson Brothers Staff.

Marvin, Frederic R. Companionship of Books & Other Papers. LC 75-90662. (Essay Index Reprint Ser.). 1977. 23.95 (*0-8369-1227-6*) Ayer.

An Asterisk (*) at the beginning of an entry indicates that the title is appearing for the first time.

— The Excursions of a Book-Lover, Being Papers on Literary Themes. LC 77-92510. (Essay Index in Reprint Ser.). 1978. reprint ed. 30.00 (*0-8486-3004-1*) Roth Pub Inc.

— Fireside Papers. LC 68-8482. (Essay Index Reprint Ser.). 1977. 22.95 (*0-8369-0686-1*) Ayer.

Marvin, G. R., jt. ed. see Holman, M. L.

Marvin, Garry, jt. auth. see Mullan, Bob.

Marvin, Gary. Bullfight. LC 94-15622. 256p. 1994. 18.95 (*0-252-06437-2*) U of Ill Pr.

Marvin, Isabel. Bridge to Freedom. 1997. pap. text 10.95 (*0-8276-0640-0*) JPS Phila.

Marvin, Isabel R. A Bride for Anna's Papa. LC 93-41175. (Illus.). 140p. (J). (gr. 4-8). 1994. pap. 6.95 (*0-915943-93-X*) Milkweed Ed.

— Green Fire. Whitaker, Kate, ed. LC 93-61531. 72p. (J). (gr. 5-8). 1994. pap. 6.95 (*0-932433-15-4*) Windswept Hse.

— Josefina & the Hanging Tree. LC 91-34501. (Chaparral Bks.). 128p. (YA). (gr. 6-9). 1992. pap. 9.95 (*0-87565-103-8*) Tex Christian.

— Mystery of the Ice Cream House. Whitaker, Kate, ed. LC 93-61532. 64p. (J). (gr. 5-8). 1994. pap. 6.95 (*0-932433-87-1*) Windswept Hse.

— Mystery of the Puerto Rican Penny. Weinberger, Jane, ed. LC 93-61533. (The Marisa Blake Mystery Ser.). 72p. (Orig.). (J). (gr. 5-8). 1995. pap. 6.95 (*1-883650-01-1*) Windswept Hse.

— One of Fannin's Men. LC 97-11719. (Illus.). 104p. (YA). (gr. 4 up). 1997. 15.95 (*1-885777-06-X*); pap. 8.95 (*1-885777-19-1*) Hendrick-Long.

— Shipwrecked on Padre Island. LC 92-43073. (Illus.). 160p. (J). (gr. 4 up). 1993. pap. 9.95 (*1-885777-17-5*) Hendrick-Long.

— The Tenth Rifle & the Jesse James Gang. LC 94-61140. (J). 1994. pap. 5.00 (*0-932433-12-X*) Windswept Hse.

Marvin, Isabelle. The Tenth Rifle. (Illus.). 128p. (Orig.). (J). (gr. 3-8). Date not set. pap. 9.95 (*0-89896-109-2*) Larksdale.

Marvin, J. G. Legal Bibliography: or A Thesaurus of American, English, Irish & Scotch Law Books. (Marvin's Legal Bibliography Ser.). vii, 800p. 1992. reprint ed. lib. bdg. 78.00 (*0-89941-349-8*, 502150) W S Hein.

Marvin, Janice K., ed. see Myers, Gary.

Marvin, John T. The Complete West Highland White Terrier. 4th ed. LC 76-58225. (Complete Breed Bk.). (Illus.). 256p. 1977. 25.95 (*0-87605-355-X*) Howell Bks.

***Marvin, Joseph.** White Southern Warrior. Angeletti, Frank, ed. 2000. pap. 12.00 (*0-9701156-0-1*) World Arts.

Marvin, Kathy. Homework Monsters. (Illus.). 16p. (Orig.). (J). 1983. pap. 4.95 (*0-9649170-0-9*) K Tarvin.

Marvin, Larry A. Tiffany. 1997. pap. 56.95 (*1-57553-580-7*) Watermrk Pr.

Marvin, Mary B., ed. see Parrish-Harra, Carol E.

Marvin, Mary J. Preventing Violence Against Women: Not Just a Women's Issue. O'Neil, Jean, ed. (Special Focus Ser.). 100p. (Orig.). 1995. reprint ed. pap. 16.95 (*0-934513-09-0*, M38) Natl Crime DC.

***Marvin, Mary Jo.** Speaking Out for Youth & Justice. O'Neil, Jean & Kirby, Judy, eds. 1999. pap. write for info. (*0-934513-86-4*) Natl Crime DC.

Marvin, Mary Jo, jt. auth. see Kirby, Judy.

Marvin, Nathaniel. Big Deer. 1987. pap. 4.00 (*0-9622903-5-1*) DCHA.

Marvin, Nigel. Identifying Snakes. 1996. 7.98 (*0-7858-0371-8*) Bk Sales Inc.

Marvin, Pamela. Lee: A Romance. 1997. 27.95 (*0-571-19028-6*) Faber & Faber.

— Lee: A Romance. 512p. 1999. pap. 15.95 (*0-571-19550-4*) Faber & Faber.

Marvin, Patrice, jt. ed. see Vrooman, Nicholas.

Marvin, Simon, jt. auth. see Graham, Stephen.

Marvin, T. A. All I Really Needed to Know I Learned While Still in Diapers. 96p. 1991. mass mkt. 5.95 (*0-380-76432-6*, Avon Bks) Morrow Avon.

Marvin, Ursula B. Field & Laboratory Investigations of Meteorites from Victoria Land, Antarctica. Mason, Brian H., ed. LC 83-20087. (Smithsonian Contributions to the Earth Sciences Ser.: No. 26). 138p. reprint ed. pap. 42.80 (*0-608-11949-0*, 202316300032) Bks Demand.

Marvin, Ursula B. & MacPherson, Glenn J., eds. Field & Laboratory Investigations of Meteorites from Victoria & the Thiel Mountains Region, Antarctica, 1982-1983 & 1983-1984. LC 88-600361. (Smithsonian Contributions to the Earth Sciences Ser.: No. 28). (Illus.). 150p. reprint ed. pap. 46.50 (*0-8357-6111-8*, 203432900089) Bks Demand.

Marvin, Ursula B. & Mason, Brian H., eds. Catalog of Meteorites from Victoria Land, Antarctica, 1978-1980. LC 81-607125. (Smithsonian Contributions to the Earth Sciences Ser.: No. 24). 101p. reprint ed. pap. 31.40 (*0-608-30899-4*, 201782700009) Bks Demand.

Marvin, Will. Revolution or Order? 1996. text 28.50 (*0-86531-364-4*) Westview.

***Marvin, William R.** 59 1/2 Money-Making Marketing Ideas: How to Build Volume Without Losing Your Shirt. 1999. pap. 14.95 (*0-9656262-8-8*) Hospitality Masters.

Marvin, William R. The Foolproof Foodservice Selection System: The Complete Manual for Creating a Quality Staff. LC 92-29649. 352p. 1993. 69.95 (*0-471-57431-7*) Wiley.

***Marvin, William R.** Home Remedies: A House Call from the Restaurant Doctor. 160p. 1999. pap. 14.95 (*0-9656262-7-X*) Hospitality Masters.

Marvin, William R., ed. 50 Proven Ways to Build More Profitable Menus. LC 98-102899. (Hospitality Masters Ser.: Vol. HMS-5). 152p. (Orig.). 1997. pap. 14.95 (*0-9656262-4-5*, HMS-5) Hospitality Masters.

— 50 Proven Ways to Build Restaurant Sales & Profit. (Hospitality Masters Ser.: Vol. HMS-1). 160p. (Orig.). 1997. pap. 14.95 (*0-9656262-0-2*, HMS-1) Hospitality Masters.

— 50 Proven Ways to Enhance Guest Service. LC 98-102869. (Hospitality Masters Ser.: Vol. HMS-4). 152p. (Orig.). 1997. pap. 14.95 (*0-9656262-3-7*, HMS-4) Hospitality Masters.

***Marvine, Dee.** Last Chance. 320p. 1999. mass mkt. 4.99 (*0-8439-4475-7*, Leisure Bks) Dorchester Pub Co.

Marvis, B. & DeAngelis, Gina. Crimes Against Children. Sarat, Austin, ed. LC 99-43549. (YA). (gr. 8 up). 2000. 15.95 (*0-7910-4253-7*) Chelsea Hse.

Marvis, B., jt. auth. see Chelsea House Publishing Staff.

Marvis, B., jt. auth. see De Angelis, Gina.

Marvis, Barbara. Rafael Palmeiro. LC 97-21985. (Real Life Reader Biographies Ser.). (Illus.). 32p. (J). (gr. 3-8). 1997. lib. bdg. 15.95 (*1-883845-49-1*) M Lane Pubs.

— Robert Rodriguez. large type ed. LC 97-20752. (Real Life Reader Biographies Ser.). (Illus.). 32p. (J). (gr. 3-8). 1997. lib. bdg. 15.95 (*1-883845-48-3*) M Lane Pubs.

— Selena. large type ed. LC 97-21960. (Real Life Reader Biographies Ser.). (Illus.). 32p. (J). (gr. 3-8). 1997. lib. bdg. 15.95 (*1-883845-47-5*) M Lane Pubs.

— Tommy Nunez: NBA Referee. LC 95-80603. (Illus.). 80p. (YA). (gr. 5 up). pap. 10.95 (*1-883845-28-9*) M Lane Pubs.

Marvis, Barbara & Boulais, Sue. Tommy Nunez. LC 97-21986. (Real Life Reader Biographies Ser.). (Illus.). 32p. (J). (gr. 3-8). 1997. lib. bdg. 15.95 (*1-883845-52-1*) M Lane Pubs.

Marvis, Barbara J. Contemporary American Success Stories Famous People of Asian Ancestry. (Mitchell Lane Multicultural Biography Ser.). 1995. 14.15 (*0-606-08419-3*, Pub. by Turtleback); 16.15 (*0-606-08420-7*, Pub. by Turtleback); 14.15 (*0-606-08421-5*, Pub. by Turtleback); 16.15 (*0-606-08422-3*, Pub. by Turtleback) Demco.

— Contemporary American Success Stories Famous People of Asian Ancestry. (Mitchell Lane Multicultural Biography Ser.). (J). 1995. 16.15 (*0-606-07497-X*, Pub. by Turtleback) Demco.

— Contemporary American Success Stories Famous People of Asian Ancestry. (Mitchell Lane Multicultural Biography Ser.). 1996. 16.15 (*0-606-08423-1*, Pub. by Turtleback); 16.15 (*0-606-10179-9*, Pub. by Turtleback); 16.15 (*0-606-10180-2*, Pub. by Turtleback); 16.15 (*0-606-10181-0*, Pub. by Turtleback) Demco.

— Contemporary American Success Stories Famous People of Asian Ancestry. (Mitchell Lane Multicultural Biography Ser.). (J). 1996. 16.15 (*0-606-07498-8*, Pub. by Turtleback); 15.15 (*0-606-07499-6*, Pub. by Turtleback) Demco.

— Famous People of Asian Ancestry, 5 vols. Incl. Vol. I. LC 93-78991. 96p. (YA). (gr. 5 up). 1993. pap. 10.95 (*1-883845-06-8*); Vol. II. LC 93-78991. 96p. (YA). (gr. 5 up). 1993. pap. 10.95 (*1-883845-07-6*); Vol. III. LC 93-78991. (Illus.). 96p. (YA). (gr. 5 up). 1993. pap. 10.95 (*1-883845-08-4*); Vol. IV. LC 93-78991. (Illus.). 96p. (YA). (gr. 5 up). 1994. pap. 10.95 (*1-883845-09-2*); Vol. V. LC 93-78991. (Illus.). 96p. (YA). (gr. 5 up). 1994. 19.95 (*1-883845-12-2*); Vol. V. LC 93-78991. (Illus.). 96p. (YA). (gr. 5 up). 1994. pap. 10.95 (*1-883845-11-4*); LC 93-78991. (Contemporary American Success Stories Ser.). 54.75 (*1-883845-13-0*); 99.75 (*1-883845-14-9*) M Lane Pubs.

— Famous People of Asian Ancestry. 2nd ed. LC 93-78991. (Contemporary American Success Stories Ser.: Vol. I). (Illus.). 96p. (YA). (gr. 4-10). 1997. reprint ed. lib. bdg. 19.95 (*1-883845-54-8*) M Lane Pubs.

— Famous People of Asian Ancestry. 2nd ed. LC 93-78991. (Contemporary American Success Stories: Vol. II). (Illus.). 96p. (YA). (gr. 4-10). 1997. reprint ed. lib. bdg. 19.95 (*1-883845-55-6*) M Lane Pubs.

— Famous People of Asian Ancestry. 2nd ed. (Contemporary American Success Stories Ser.: Vol. III). (Illus.). 96p. (YA). (gr. 4-10). 1997. reprint ed. lib. bdg. 19.95 (*1-883845-56-4*) M Lane Pubs.

— Famous People of Asian Ancestry. 2nd ed. (Contemporary American Success Stories Ser.: Vol. IV). (Illus.). 96p. (YA). (gr. 4-10). 1997. reprint ed. lib. bdg. 19.95 (*1-883845-57-2*) M Lane Pubs.

— Teacher's Guide: Famous People of Asian Ancestry. 48p. 1994. pap., teacher ed. 11.95 (*1-883845-15-7*) M Lane Pubs.

— Tommy Nunez - NBA Referee, Taking My Best Shot. LC 95-80603. (Mitchell Lane Multicultural Biography Ser.). 1996. 16.15 (*0-606-10347-3*, Pub. by Turtleback) Demco.

Marvis, Jason M. Medical Reactions, Treatments & Therapy of Patients with 'Overdose' Substances. 150p. 1996. 47.50 (*0-7883-0766-5*); pap. 44.50 (*0-7883-0767-3*) ABBE Pubs Assn.

Marvullo, Joseph. Improving Your Color Photography. (Illus.). 176p. 1984. pap. 8.95 (*0-685-08489-2*) P-H.

Marwah, Joe, ed. Neurobiology of Drug Use. (Monographs in Neural Sciences: Vol. 13). (Illus.). viii, 164p. 1987. 128.00 (*3-8055-4561-4*) S Karger.

Marwah, Joe & Teitelbaum, Herman, eds. Advances in Neurodegenerative Disorders Vol. 1: Parkinson's Disease. LC 98-68496. (Illus.). 400p. (C). 1999. text 60.00 (*0-9668997-0-9*) Prominnt Pr.

— Advances in Neurodegenerative Disorders Vol. 2: Alzheimer's & Aging, Vol. 2. LC 98-68496. (Illus.). 400p. (C). 1999. text 60.00 (*0-9668997-1-7*) Prominnt Pr.

Marwah, Kanta. Selected Papers of Lawrence R. Klein: Theoretical Reflections & Econometric Applications. LC 97-18837. 1997. 86.00 (*981-02-2600-4*) World Scientific Pub.

Marwah, Onkar & Pollack, Jonathan D., eds. Military Power & Policy in Asian States: China, India, Japan. LC 79-16241. (Special Studies in Military Affairs). 1983. text 44.00 (*0-89158-407-2*) Westview.

Marwah, Raj. Buy This Book: Understanding Advertising & Making the Most Out of Your Advertising Dollar. (Illus.). 200p. 1991. reprint ed. pap. 24.95 (*0-87757-215-1*) Am Mktg.

Marwah, Ved. Uncivil Wars Pathology of Terrorism in India. (C). 1995. 34.00 (*81-7223-221-7*, Pub. by Indus Pub) S Asia.

Marwaha, J. & Anderson, W. J., eds. Neuroreceptors in Health & Disease. (Monographs in Neural Sciences: Vol. 10). (Illus.). viii, 256p. 1984. 129.75 (*3-8055-3715-8*) S Karger.

Marwak, Joe. Neural Transplantation, CNS Neuronal Injury & Regeneration. 304p. 1994. boxed set 141.95 (*0-8493-8683-7*, RD124) CRC Pr.

Marwali, M., jt. auth. see Shahidehpour, M.

Marwedel, Peter. Code Generation for Embedded Processors. 340p. (C). 1995. text 118.50 (*0-7923-9577-8*) Kluwer Academic.

Marwell, Gerald & Oliver, Pamela. The Critical Mass in Collective Action: A Micro-Social Theory. LC 92-23162. (Studies in Rationality & Social Change). (Illus.). 220p. 1993. text 64.95 (*0-521-30839-9*) Cambridge U Pr.

Marwick. Value at Risk. 1997. text 55.00 (*0-7863-1254-8*, Irwn Prfssnl) McGraw-Hill Prof.

Marwick, Arthur. British Society Since Nineteen Forty-Five. (Pelican Social History of Britain Ser.). 302p. 1984. 15.95 (*0-317-00889-7*, A Lane) Viking Penguin.

Marwick, Arthur. British Society since 1945. 1996. pap. 17.95 (*0-14-024939-7*, Pub. by Pnguin Bks Ltd) Trafalgar.

— A History of the Modern British Isles, 1914-1999: Circumstances, Events & Outcomes. (History of the Modern British Isles Ser.). (Illus.). 448p. 2000. text 62.95 (*0-631-19521-1*); pap. text 32.95 (*0-631-19522-X*) Blackwell Pubs.

Marwick, Arthur. The Nature of History. 3rd rev. ed. LC 89-2786. 442p. (C). 1989. pap. text 39.95 (*0-925065-00-5*) Lyceum IL.

— The Sixties: Cultural Revolution in Britain, France, Italy, & the United States, 1958-1974. LC 98-22105. (Illus.). 924p. 1998. 39.95 (*0-19-210022-X*) OUP.

— The Sixties: Social & Cultural Transformation in Britain, France, Italy & the United States, 1958-1974. (Illus.). 952p. 2000. pap. 22.50 (*0-19-288100-0*) OUP.

Marwick, Arthur, et al, eds. The Illustrated Dictionary of British History. (Illus.). 320p. 1981. 19.95 (*0-500-25072-3*, Pub. by Thames Hudson) Norton.

Marwick, Arthur & Simpson. Documents, Nineteen Hundred to Nineteen Twenty-Nine. 1990. pap. 34.95 (*0-335-09300-0*) OpUniv Pr.

Marwick, Arthur, et al. Europe on Eve of War, Nineteen Hundred to Nineteen Fourteen. 1990. pap. 34.95 (*0-335-09304-3*) OpUniv Pr.

Marwick, Arthur, jt. ed. see Simpson, W.

Marwick, Christine M. Your Right to Government Information. 2nd rev. ed. (ACLU Ser.). 284p. 1985. pap. 8.95 (*0-8093-9960-1*) S Ill U Pr.

Marwick, Hugh. The Orkney Norn. LC 78-72635. (Celtic Language & Literature Ser.: Goidelic & Brythonic). reprint ed. 27.50 (*0-404-17568-6*) AMS Pr.

Marwick, J. S. & Rich, S. G. A Lecture on the Native in the Larger Towns, 1918 & Notes on Natal, 1917. (Colin Webb Natal & Zululand Ser.: No. 4). 56p. 1993. pap. 24.95 (*0-86980-902-4*, Pub. by Univ Natal Pr) Intl Spec Bk.

Marwick, Lawrence. Biblical & Judaic Acronyms. 49.50 (*0-87068-438-8*) Ktav.

Marwick, Merry M. Food Packaging--Variations, Problems & Research: Index of New Information. 160p. Date not set. 47.50 (*0-7883-1918-3*); pap. 44.50 (*0-7883-1919-1*) ABBE Pubs Assn.

Marwick, Peat, jt. auth. see Russell, C. W.

Marwick, Thomas H. Stress Echocardiography: Its Role in the Diagnosis & Evaluation of Coronary Artery Disease, Vol. 149. LC 93-41121. (Developments in Cardiovascular Medicine Ser.: No. 149). 192p. (C). 1994. text 123.00 (*0-7923-2579-6*) Kluwer Academic.

Marwick, Thomas H., ed. Cardiac Stress Testing & Imaging: A Clinician's Guide. LC 96-24943. 638p. 1996. text 105.00 (*0-443-07652-9*) Church.

Marwick, William H. Economic Developments in Victorian Scotland. LC 77-95621. (Reprints of Economic Classics Ser.). 295p. 1973. reprint ed. lib. bdg. 45.00 (*0-678-00739-X*) Kelley.

— Scotland in Modern Times. (Illus.). 209p. 1964. 35.00 (*0-7146-1342-8*, Pub. by F Cass Pubs) Intl Spec Bk.

Marwil, Jonathan L. Frederic Manning: An Unfinished Life. LC 87-15708. xx, 380p. (C). 1988. text 32.95 (*0-8223-0803-7*) Duke.

— A History of Ann Arbor. LC 87-70981. (Illus.). (Orig.). 1987. pap. 9.95 (*0-9618742-0-1*) Ann Arbor Observer.

Marwil, Jonathon L. A History of Ann Arbor. (Illus.). 208p. (Orig.). (C). 1991. 24.95 (*0-472-09463-7*, 09463); pap. 18.95 (*0-472-06463-0*, 06463) U of Mich Pr.

Marwitt, John P. Median Village & Fremont Culture Regional Variation. (Utah Anthropological Papers: No. 95). reprint ed. 24.00 (*0-404-60695-4*) AMS Pr.

— Median Village & Fremont Culture Regional Variation. LC 73-623166. (University of Utah, Anthropological Papers: No. 95). (Illus.). 207p. reprint ed. pap. 64.20 (*0-8357-6852-X*, 203554800095) Bks Demand.

— Pharo Village. (Utah Anthropological Papers: No. 91). reprint ed. 20.00 (*0-404-60691-1*) AMS Pr.

Marwitz, Darlene. Italy Fever: 14 Ways to Satisfy Your Love Affair with Italy. (Illus.). 256p. 1999. 22.95 (*0-9664998-2-4*) Portico Pr TX.

Marwood, Des, jt. auth. see Caffary, Brian.

Marwood, J. F., jt. ed. see Stokes, G. S.

Marx. Now I Will Never Go to Sleep. (Illus.). (J). 14.95 (*0-06-027483-2*); lib. bdg. 14.89 (*0-06-027482-4*) HarpC.

— On Ireland & the Irish Question. (C). text 19.95 (*0-85315-247-0*, Pub. by Lawrence & Wishart) NYU Pr.

Marx, ed. Ciceronis, M. Tulli Fascicule 1: Rhetorica ad Herennium. (LAT.). 1993. reprint ed. pap. 29.95 (*3-8154-1169-6*, T1169, Pub. by B G Teubner) U of Mich Pr.

Marx, jt. auth. see Larsen.

Marx, A. B. Musical Form in the Age of Beethoven: Selected Writings on Theory & Method. Burnham, Scott, ed. LC 96-49875. (Studies in Music Theory & Analysis: Vol. 12). 214p. (C). 1998. text 64.95 (*0-521-45274-0*) Cambridge U Pr.

Marx, Adolf B. Gluck und die Oper, 2 tle. in 1 bd. (GER.). 934p. 1981. reprint ed. write for info. (*3-487-07035-9*) G Olms Pubs.

— Ludwig Van Beethoven: Leben und Schaffen, 2 vols. in 1. 709p. 1979. reprint ed. write for info. (*3-487-06720-X*) G Olms Pubs.

Marx, Alexander. Essays in Jewish Biography. LC 73-2217. (Jewish People; History, Religion, Literature Ser.). 1973. reprint ed. 28.95 (*0-405-05281-2*) Ayer.

— Essays in Jewish Biography. (Brown Classics in Judaica Ser.). 322p. 1986. reprint ed. pap. text 28.00 (*0-8191-5022-3*) U Pr of Amer.

Marx, Alexander & Muller-Hermelink, Hans K., eds. Epithelial Tumors of the Thymus: Pathology, Biology & Treatment. LC 97-1867. 411p. (C). 1997. text 120.00 (*0-306-45591-9*, Kluwer Plenum) Kluwer Academic.

Marx, Alexander, jt. auth. see Finkelstein, Louis.

Marx, Alexander, ed. see Steinschneider, Moritz.

Marx, Alexandria L. How to Write a Money-Making Marketing Plan: The Road to Money - The Key to Survival for Many. LC 96-94512. (Illus.). 256p. 1997. pap. 29.85 (*0-9652820-1-5*) Mktng Dept.

Marx, Alfred. Les Offrandes Vegetales dans l'Ancien Testament: Du Trigut d'Hommage au Repas Eschatologique. (FRE.). 186p. 1994. text 98.00 (*90-04-10136-5*) Brill Academic Pubs.

Marx, Allison. The Clueless Gourmet. 288p. 1995. pap. 14.95 (*0-8092-3443-2*, 344320, Contemporary Bks) NTC Contemp Pub Co.

— Wok This Way. 1994. pap. 4.99 (*0-425-14261-2*); mass mkt. 4.99 (*0-425-14187-X*) Berkley Pub.

Marx, Andrew E. A Practical Guide on Implementing Suggestion Systems. 118p. (C). 1992. pap. text 22.00 (*0-7021-2794-9*, Pub. by Juta & Co) Intl Spec Bk.

Marx, Anne. A Further Semester: New Poems. 96p. 1985. 12.50 (*0-87233-078-8*) Bauhan.

— Love in Late Season: New Poems. LC 92-38177. 1992. 17.50 (*0-87233-108-3*) Bauhan.

Marx, Anthony W. Lessons of Struggle: South African Internal Opposition, 1960-1990. (Illus.). 384p. (C). 1992. pap. text 23.95 (*0-19-507348-7*) OUP.

— Making Race & Nation: A Comparison of the United States, South Africa & Brazil. LC 97-20437. (Cambridge Studies in Comparative Politics). (Illus.). 408p. (C). 1997. 29.95 (*0-521-58455-8*) Cambridge U Pr.

— Making Race & Nation: A Comparison of the United States, South Africa & Brazil. LC 99-162515. (Cambridge Studies in Comparative Politics). 416p. (C). 1998. pap. 18.95 (*0-521-58590-2*) Cambridge U Pr.

Marx, Arthur. My Life with Groucho. LC 91-41254. (Illus.). 287p. 1992. pap. 12.95 (*0-942637-45-3*) Barricade Bks.

— The Secret Life of Bob Hope. LC 92-35525. (Illus.). 480p. 1993. 21.99 (*0-942637-74-7*) Barricade Bks.

— Set to Kill. LC 92-33271. 1993. 17.95 (*0-942637-80-1*) Barricade Bks.

Marx-Aveline, Eleanor, ed. see Ibsen, Henrik.

Marx, Barry, ed. see Miller, Frank.

Marx, Barry, ed. see Moore, Alan.

Marx, C. E. Dictionary of Aquaculture: In English, French, Spanish, German, Italian & Latin. (ENG, FRE, GER, ITA & LAT.). 464p. 187.25 (*0-444-88663-X*) Elsevier.

— Elsevier's Dictionary of Aquaculture. (ENG, FRE, GER, ITA & LAT.). 454p. 1991. 250.00 (*0-8288-9212-1*) Fr & Eur.

Marx, C. W. The Devil's Rights & the Redemption in the Literature of Medieval England. (Illus.). 196p. 1995. 60.00 (*0-85991-455-0*) Boydell & Brewer.

Marx, Daniel. International Shipping Cartels: A Study of Industrial Self-Regulation by Shipping Conferences. LC 69-13988. 323p. 1969. reprint ed. lib. bdg. 65.00 (*0-8371-1174-9*, MASC, Greenwood Pr) Greenwood.

Marx, Dave, jt. auth. see Watson, Jennifer.

Marx, David & Sneed, James H., eds. Antitrust: Challenge of the Health Care Field - Principles & Their Practical Application. 230p. 1990. 30.00 (*0-918945-08-9*) Am Hlth Lawyers.

***Marx, David F.** Baby in the House. (Rookie Readers Ser.). (Illus.). 32p. (J). (gr. 1-2). 2000. pap. 4.95 (*0-516-27045-1*) Childrens.

— Canada. LC 99-37402. (Rookie Read-About Geography Ser.). (J). 2000. 19.00 (*0-516-21550-7*) Childrens.

— Chanukah. (Rookie Read-About Holidays Ser.). (Illus.). (J). 2000. write for info. (*0-516-22204-X*) Childrens.

— Chanukah. (Rookie Read-About Holidays Ser.). (Illus.). 32p. (J). (gr. 1-2). 2000. pap. 5.95 (*0-516-27152-0*) Childrens.

— Christmas. (Rookie Read-About Holidays Ser.). (Illus.). (J). 2000. write for info. (*0-516-22175-2*) Childrens.

— Christmas. (Rookie Read-About Holidays Ser.). (Illus.). 32p. (J). (gr. 1-2). 2000. pap. 5.95 (*0-516-27153-9*) Childrens.

— Earth Day. LC 00-26999. (Rookie Read-About Holidays Ser.). (Illus.). (J). 2001. write for info. (*0-516-22231-7*) Childrens.

M

— Halloween. (Rookie Read-About Holidays Ser.). (Illus.). (J). 2000. write for info. (0-516-22206-6) Childrens.
— Halloween. (Rookie Read-About Holidays Ser.). (Illus.). 32p. (J). (gr. 1-2). 2000. pap. 5.95 (0-516-27154-7) Childrens.
— Hola, Doctor. (Rookie Espanol Ser.). (SPA., Illus.). (J). 2000. 15.00 (0-516-22274-0) Childrens.
— Independence Day. LC 00-26856. (Rookie Read-About Holidays Ser.). (Illus.). (J). 2001. write for info. (0-516-22232-5) Childrens.
— Japan. (Rookie Read-About Geography Ser.). (J). 2000. pap. text 5.95 (0-516-26793-0) Childrens.
— Kwanzaa. (Rookie Read-About Holidays Ser.). (Illus.). (J). 2000. write for info. (0-516-22207-4) Childrens.
— Kwanzaa. (Rookie Read-About Holidays Ser.). (Illus.). 32p. (J). (gr. 1-2). 2000. pap. 5.95 (0-516-27155-5) Childrens.
— Martin Luther King, Jr. Day. LC 00-22638. (Rookie Read-About Holidays Ser.). (Illus.). 2001. write for info. (0-516-22211-2) Childrens.
— New Year's Day. (Illus.). (J). 2000. write for info. (0-516-22205-8) Childrens.
— New Year's Day. (Rookie Read-About Holidays Ser.). (Illus.). 32p. (J). (gr. 1-2). 2000. pap. 5.95 (0-516-27156-3) Childrens.
Marx, David F. New York City. LC 98-37342. (Rookie Read-About Geography Ser.). (Illus.). 32p. (J). (gr. 1-2). 1999. 19.00 (0-516-21552-3) Childrens.
***Marx, David F.** New York City. (Rookie Read-About Geography Ser.). (J). 2000. pap. text 5.95 (0-516-26558-X) Childrens.
— Passover. LC 00-29543. (Rookie Read-About Holidays Ser.). (Illus.). 2000. write for info. (0-516-22214-7) Childrens.
— Que Esta Arriba Cuando Tu Estas Abajo? (Rookie Espanol Ser.). (SPA., Illus.). (J). 2000. 15.00 (0-516-22022-5) Childrens.
— Thanksgiving. (Rookie Read-About Holidays Ser.). (Illus.). (J). 2000. write for info. (0-516-22208-2) Childrens.
— Thanksgiving. (Rookie Read-About Holidays Ser.). (Illus.). 32p. (J). (gr. 1-2). 2000. pap. 5.95 (0-516-27157-1) Childrens.
— Turn It Off! LC 00-30696. (Rookie Readers Ser.). (Illus.). (J). 2001. write for info. (0-516-22229-5) Childrens.
— Valentine's Day. LC 00-22639. (Rookie Read-About Holidays Ser.). (Illus.). 2001. write for info. (0-516-22212-0) Childrens.
— What Is up When You Are Down? (Rookie Readers Ser.). (Illus.). 24p. (J). (gr. k-1). 2000. pap. 4.95 (0-516-27044-3) Childrens.
Marx, David F. & Cornwell, Linda. Japan. LC 99-10670. (Rookie Read-About Geography Ser.). (Illus.). 32p. (J). (gr. 1-2). 1999. 19.00 (0-516-21551-5) Childrens.
***Marx, David F. & Cornwell, Linda.** Mexico. LC 99-43654. (Rookie Read-About Geography Ser.). (Illus.). (YA). 2000. 19.00 (0-516-22041-1) Childrens.
***Marx, David F. & Fisher, Cynthia.** Baby in the House. LC 99-15866. (Rookie Readers Ser.). 2000. 17.50 (0-516-21688-0) Childrens.
***Marx, David F. & Michalak, Paul.** Our Raspberry Jam. LC 99-88534. (Rookie Readers Ser.). (J). 2000. 18.00 (0-516-22174-4) Childrens.
***Marx, David F. & Miller, Susan.** What is up When You Are Down? LC 99-15864. (Rookie Readers Ser.). (J). 2000. 15.00 (0-516-22007-1) Childrens.
Marx, Doug. Gold Gloves. (Baseball Heroes Ser.). 48p. (J). (gr. 3-8). 1991. lib. bdg. 15.95 (0-86593-130-5) Rourke Corp.
— The Homeless. (Troubled Society Ser.). (Illus.). 64p. (YA). (gr. 7 up). 1990. lib. bdg. 17.95 (0-86593-071-6) Rourke Corp.
— Relief Pitchers. (Baseball Heroes Ser.). (J). 1991. lib. bdg. 16.67 (0-685-66096-6) Rourke Corp.
— Relief Pitchers. (Baseball Heroes Ser.). 48p. (J). (gr. 3-8). 1991. lib. bdg. 15.95 (0-86593-131-3) Rourke Corp.
— Rookies. (Baseball Heroes Ser.). (J). 1991. lib. bdg. 16.67 (0-685-66097-4) Rourke Corp.
— Rookies. (Baseball Heroes Ser.). 48p. (J). (gr. 3-8). 1991. lib. bdg. 15.95 (0-86593-132-1) Rourke Corp.
— Running Backs. LC 92-8764. (Football Heroes Ser.). (J). 1992. lib. bdg. 12.95 (0-685-59321-5) Rourke Corp.
— Running Backs. LC 92-8764. (Football Heroes Ser.). 48p. (J). (gr. 3-8). 1992. lib. bdg. 15.95 (0-86593-151-8) Rourke Corp.
— Track & Field. LC 93-27154. (Pro-Am Sports Ser.). 48p. (J). (gr. 3-8). 1993. lib. bdg. 17.95 (0-86593-345-6) Rourke Corp.
— Wrestling. LC 93-36544. (Pro-Am Sports Ser.). 48p. (J). (gr. 3-8). 1993. lib. bdg. 17.95 (0-86593-347-2) Rourke Corp.
Marx, Eileen. Weaving Faith & Family... When You're Hanging on by a Thread! LC 99-31402. 207p. 1999. pap. 14.95 (0-87793-685-4) Ave Maria.
Marx, Eleanor & Aveling, Edward. The Working-Class Movement in America. Le Blanc, Paul, ed. & intro. by. 168p. 1998. pap. 15.00 (0-391-04072-3) Humanities.
***Marx, Eleanor & Aveling, Edward.** The Working-Class Movement in America. LC 99-89708. 200p. 2000. 54.95 (1-57392-626-4, Humanity Bks) Prometheus Bks.
Marx, Eleanor, ed. see Engels, Friedrich.
Marx, Elisabeth. Breaking Through Culture Shock: What You Need to Succeed in International Business. LC 98-46502. 1999. 25.00 (1-85788-220-2) Nicholas Brealey.
Marx, Eloise. I Made It to Broadway - UMW. (Illus.). 115p. (Orig.). 1996. pap. 14.95 (1-886364-00-1) Rabeth Pub Co.
Marx, Eva, et al, eds. Health Is Academic: A Guide to Coordinated School Health Programs. 345p. (C). 1998. pap. 28.00 (0-88210-324-5) Natl Assn Principals.
Marx, Eva, et al. Health Is Academic: A Guide to Coordinated School Health Programs. LC 97-39385. 368p. 1998. pap. 24.95 (0-8077-3713-5) Tchrs Coll.
— Health Is Academic: A Guide to Coordinated School Health Programs. LC 97-39385. 368p. 1998. 55.00 (0-8077-3714-3) Tchrs Coll.
Marx, Frederic J., et al. Massachusetts Nonprofit Organizations, 1996 Supplement, 2 vols. LC 92-85281. 1414p. 1995. ring bd., suppl. ed. 125.00 (1-57589-008-9, 96-04.11-BK) Mass CLE.
Marx, Frederic J., ed. see Allen, Richard C., et al.
Marx, Friedrich, ed. Incerti Auctoris de Ratione Dicendi Ad C. Herennium Libri IV. vi, 554p. 1966. reprint ed. write for info. (0-318-71153-2) G Olms Pubs.
Marx, Gary & Ordovensky, Pat. Working with the News Media. 32p. 1992. pap. 2.50 (0-87652-192-8) Am Assn Sch Admin.
Marx, Gary T. Civil Disorder & the Agents of Social Control. (Reprint Series in Sociology). (C). 1993. reprint ed. pap. text 2.90 (0-8290-2682-7, S-731) Irvington.
— Protest & Prejudice: A Study of Belief in the Black Community. LC 78-23898. 256p. 1979. reprint ed. lib. bdg. 65.00 (0-313-20827-1, MAPT, Greenwood Pr) Greenwood.
— Undercover: Police Surveillance in America. (Twentieth Century Fund Bk.: No. 1). (Illus.). 280p. 1988. 45.00 (0-520-06286-8, Pub. by U CA Pr); pap. 16.95 (0-520-06969-2, Pub. by U CA Pr) Cal Prin Full Svc.
Marx, Gary T., ed. Muckraking Sociology: Research As Social Criticism. LC 71-186711. 240p. 1972. 32.95 (0-87855-036-4); pap. text 18.95 (0-87855-532-3) Transaction Pubs.
Marx, Gary T. & McAdam, Douglas. Collective Behavior & Social Movements: Process & Structure. LC 92-29657. 160p. (C). 1993. pap. text 26.60 (0-13-142100-X) P-H.
Marx, Gary T., jt. ed. see Fijnaut, Cyrille.
Marx, George. The Voice of the Martians. LC 97-196006. 412p. 1997. pap. 135.00 (963-05-7427-6, Pub. by Akade Kiado) St Mut.
Marx, George, ed. Bioastronomy: The Next Steps. (C). 1988. text 237.50 (90-277-2714-7) Kluwer Academic.
***Marx, Gretchen.** Exploring the Internet with Microsoft Internet Explorer 5.0. 403p. 1999. pap. text 42.67 (0-13-086896-5, Prentice Hall) P-H.
Marx, Gretchen & Grauer, Robert. Essentials of Internet. 2nd ed. LC 97-133571. 175p. 1996. spiral bd. 18.67 (0-13-595778-8) P-H.
Marx, Gretchen, jt. auth. see Grauer, Robert T.
Marx, Gretchen, jt. auth. see Kottas, John F.
Marx, Groucho. Groucho & Me. LC 83-46068. (Classics of Modern American Humor Ser.). reprint ed. 35.00 (0-404-19938-0) AMS Pr.
— Groucho & Me. (Illus.). 390p. 1995. reprint ed. pap. 16.00 (0-306-80666-5) Da Capo.
— The Groucho Letters: Letters from & to Groucho Marx. LC 94-15249. 319p. 1994. reprint ed. pap. 13.95 (0-306-80607-X) Da Capo.
— Groucho Marx & Other Short Stories & Tall Tales: Selected Writings of Groucho Marx. Bader, Robert S., ed. 216p. 1996. reprint ed. pap. 12.95 (0-571-19898-8) Faber & Faber.
— Letters of Groucho Marks. 1976. 24.95 (0-8488-1092-9) Amereon Ltd.
— Memoirs of a Mangy Lover. LC 96-46945. (Illus.). 224p. 1997. reprint ed. pap. 13.95 (0-306-80769-6) Da Capo.
Marx, Hans J., jt. ed. see Buelow, George J.
Marx, Harald & Weber, Gregor J. Dresden in the Ages of Splendor & Enlightenment: Eighteenth-Century Paintings from the Old Masters Picture Gallery. Stockman, Russell, tr. from GER. LC 99-234520. Orig. Title: Obras Maestras del Siglo XVIII en la Galeria de Pinturas de Dresde. (SPA & ENG., Illus.). 328p. 1999. 59.95 (0-918881-37-4) Columbus Mus Art.
Marx, Harpo. Harpo Speaks. 1976. 30.95 (0-8488-0181-4) Amereon Ltd.
Marx, Harpo & Barber, Rowland. Harpo Speaks! LC 84-25038. 482p. 1985. pap. 18.95 (0-87910-036-2) Limelight Edns.
Marx, Helen, tr. see Hirigoyen, Marie-France.
Marx, Herbert, jt. ed. see Cotler, Irwin.
Marx, Hymen & Rabb, George B. Phyletic Analysis of 50 Characters of Advanced Snakes. LC 72-85480. (Field Museum of Natural History, Publication 1153, Zoology Ser.: No. 63). 329p. 1972. reprint ed. pap. 102.00 (0-608-02113-X, 206276200004) Bks Demand.
Marx, Ina. Fitness for the Unfit. (Illus.). 152p. 1991. reprint ed. pap. 9.95 (0-8065-1264-4, Citadel Pr) Carol Pub Group.
— Your Are in Charge: The IM Method Total Fitness for the Fit & Not So Fit. 148p. (Orig.). 1990. pap. text 19.95 (0-9626194-0-X) Esperanza Pubns.
Marx, Ina B., et al. Professional Painted Finishes: A Guide to the Art & Business of Decorative Painting. (Illus.). 240p. 1991. 45.00 (0-8230-4418-1, Whitney Lib) Watsn-Guptill.
Marx, Jean L., ed. A Revolution in Biotechnology. (Illus.). 238p. 1989. text 52.95 (0-521-32749-0) Cambridge U Pr.
Marx, Jean L. & Kolata, Gina Bari. Combating the Number One Killer: The Science Report on Heart Research. LC 78-3626. (AAAS Publication Ser.: No. 78-3). (Illus.). 220p. reprint ed. pap. 68.20 (0-608-17716-4, 203011300067) Bks Demand.
Marx, Jeffrey. How to Win a High School Election: Advice & Ideas Collected from Over 1,000 High School Seniors. 1999. pap. text 12.95 (0-9667824-0-2) J Marx.
Marx, Jeffrey & Gruberger, Risa M. What's Right? What's Wrong? A Guide to Talking about Values for Parents & Kids. LC 98-38630. 144p. 1998. 12.95 (0-7621-0099-0, Pub. by RD Assn) Penguin Putnam.
Marx, Jenifer. Gold of the Americas. Dawson, Hal, ed. LC 96-68435. 158p. (Orig.). 1996. pap. text 12.95 (0-915920-89-1) Ram Pub.
— Pirates & Privateers of the Caribbean. 320p. (C). 1992. 32.50 (0-89464-483-1); pap. 23.50 (0-89464-633-8) Krieger.
***Marx, Jenifer, contrib. by.** Advanced IPA Management: Opportunities under the New Medicare. LC 98-53664. 1998. write for info. (0-07-134321-0) McGraw.
Marx, Jenifer, jt. auth. see Marx, Robert.
Marx, Jenifer, jt. auth. see Marx, Robert F.
Marx, John. Organic Chemistry Lab. 80p. (C). 1995. spiral bd. 19.95 (0-7872-1239-3, 41123901) Kendall-Hunt.
Marx, Joseph. Songs of Joseph Marx: High Voice. 64p. 1993. pap. 18.95 (0-7935-1945-4, 00747027) H Leonard.
— Songs of Joseph Marx: Medium Voice. 64p. 1993. pap. 18.95 (0-7935-1944-6, 00747026) H Leonard.
Marx, Jutta. Bidirektionale Sprache. (Sprache und Computer Ser.: Bd. 17). (GER.). x, 227p. 1996. 45.00 (3-487-10286-2) G Olms Pubs.
Marx, Karl. Capital. 464p. Date not set. 29.95 (0-8488-2366-4) Amereon Ltd.
Marx, Karl. Capital, Vol. 1. unabridged ed. Engels, Friedrich, ed. 870p. 1992. reprint ed. pap. 29.95 (1-57002-071-X) Univ Publng Hse.
Marx, Karl. Capital, Vol. 2. Fernbach, David, tr. LC 82-188249. Vol. 2. 624p. 1993. pap. 14.95 (0-14-044569-2, Penguin Classics) Viking Penguin.
— Capital, Vol. 3. Fernbach, David, tr. 1,088p. 1993. pap. 15.95 (0-14-044570-6, Penguin Classics) Viking Penguin.
— Capital: A Critique of Political Economy, Vol. 1. Fowkes, Ben, tr. 1152p. 1992. pap. 22.99 (0-14-044568-4, Penguin Classics) Viking Penguin.
— Capital: A Critique of Political Economy, Vol. 1. Fowkes, Ben, tr. 1977. pap. 18.95 (0-394-72657-X) Vin Bks.
***Marx, Karl.** Capital: An Abridged Edition. McLellan, David, ed. (Oxford World's Classics Ser.). 544p. 1999. pap. 14.95 (0-19-283872-5) OUP.
Marx, Karl. Civil War in France: And Other Writings on the Paris Commune. (Revolutionary Classics Ser.). 144p. 1998. reprint ed. pap. 12.00 (0-88286-236-7) C H Kerr.
— Class Struggles in France. 2nd ed. 220p. 1967. 3.50 (0-935534-07-5) NY Labor News.
— Class Struggles in France, 1848-1850. LC 64-19792. 158p. 1964. pap. 7.95 (0-7178-0030-X) Intl Pubs Co.
— Collected Works of Karl Marx & Frederick Engels Vol. 32: Concludes Theories of Surplus Value, Notebks. XII-XV. LC 73-84671. 1990. 24.95 (0-7178-0532-8) Intl Pubs Co.
— Collected Works of Karl Marx & Frederick Engels Vol. 33: Continues the Economic Manuscripts of 1861-63. LC 73-84671. 552p. 1992. 24.95 (0-7178-0533-6) Intl Pubs Co.
— Collected Works of Karl Marx & Frederick Engels Vol. 34: Concludes the Economic Manuscripts of 1861-63; Chapter 6 from the Manuscript of Capital, 1863-64. LC 73-84671. 580p. 1993. 24.95 (0-7178-0534-4) Intl Pubs Co.
— Collected Works of Karl Marx & Frederick Engels, 1857-58 Vol. 28: Marx: The Major Part of the Grundrisse. Wangermann, Ernst, tr. from GER. LC 73-84671. (Illus.). 590p. 1987. 24.95 (0-7178-0528-X) Intl Pubs Co.
— Collected Works of Karl Marx & Frederick Engels, 1859-61 Vol. 29: Marx: Balance of the Grundrisse, Vol. 29. Golman, Lev I., ed. Schnittke, Victor & Sdobnikov, Kuri, trs. LC 73-84671. (Illus.). xxiv, 592p. 1988. 24.95 (0-7178-0529-8) Intl Pubs Co.
— Contribution to the Critique of Political Economy. pap. 19.95 (0-8464-0303-X) Beekman Pubs.
— Contribution to the Critique of Political Economy. Dobb, Maurice, ed. LC 69-20357. 264p. 1989. pap. 8.95 (0-7178-0041-5) Intl Pubs Co.
— A Contribution to the Critique of Political Economy. 264p. (C). 1972. text 19.95 (0-8464-1287-X) Beekman Pubs.
— Critique of the Gotha Program. LC 69-20357. 116p. (Orig.). 1987. reprint ed. pap. 3.45 (0-7178-0043-1) Intl Pubs Co.
— Early Writings. Benton, Gregor & Livingstone, Rodney, trs. 464p. 1992. pap. 15.95 (0-14-044574-9, Penguin Classics) Viking Penguin.
— The Eastern Question. LC 92-17166. 1992. 45.00 (0-7146-1500-5, Pub. by F Cass Pubs) Intl Spec Bk.
— Economic & Philosophic Manuscripts of 1844. Struik, Dirk J., ed. Milligan, Martin, tr. LC 64-12877. 256p. (C). 1964. pap. 8.95 (0-7178-0053-9) Intl Pubs Co.
— The Eighteenth Brumaire of Louis Bonaparte. LC 63-23036. 128p. 1963. pap. 5.95 (0-7178-0056-3) Intl Pubs Co.
— The German Ideology: Including Theses on Feuerbach & Introduction to the Critique of Political Economy. (Great Books in Philosophy). 200p. 1998. pap. 10.95 (1-57392-258-7) Prometheus Bks.
— Grundrisse: Foundations of the Critique of Political Economy. Nickolaus, Martin, tr. (ENG & GER.). 912p. 1993. pap. 18.95 (0-14-044575-7, Penguin Classics) Viking Penguin.
— Das Kapital. Engels, Friedrich, ed. 356p. 1996. pap. 14.95 (0-89526-711-X, Gateway Editions) Regnery Pub.
— Karl Marx: A Reader. Elster, Jon, ed. 353p. 1986. pap. text 20.95 (0-521-33832-8) Cambridge U Pr.
***Marx, Karl.** Karl Marx: Selected Writings. 2nd ed. McLellan, David, ed. 630p. (C). 2000. pap. text 27.95 (0-19-878265-9) OUP.
Marx, Karl. Marx: Early Political Writings. O'Malley, Joseph, ed. Davis, Richard A., tr. LC 93-31207. (Cambridge Texts in the History of Political Thought Ser.). 230p. (C). 1994. text 44.95 (0-521-34241-4) Cambridge U Pr.
Marx, Karl. Marx: Early Political Writings. O'Malley, Joseph, ed. Davis, Richard A., tr. LC 93-31207. (Cambridge Texts in the History of Political Thought Ser.). 230p. (C). 1994. pap. text 13.95 (0-521-34994-X) Cambridge U Pr.
Marx, Karl. Marx: Later Political Writing. Carver, Terrell, ed. (Cambridge Texts in the History of Political Thought Ser.). 297p. (C). 1996. text 44.95 (0-521-36504-X); pap. text 14.95 (0-521-36739-5) Cambridge U Pr.
— The Marx-Engels Reader. 2nd ed. McLellan, David P., ed. 788p. (C). 1978. pap. 21.00 (0-393-09040-X) Norton.
— Marx on China. 1973. lib. bdg. 250.00 (0-87968-352-X) Gordon Pr.
— Marx on Suicide. Plaut, Eric A. & Anderson, Kevin, eds. & trs. by. from FRE. LC 99-19436. 152p. 1999. 49.95 (0-8101-1632-4); pap. 14.95 (0-8101-1638-3) Northwestern U Pr.
— Marx's Capital. Arthur, C. J., ed. 416p. (C). 1992. pap., student ed. 27.50 (0-85315-777-4, Pub. by Lawrence & Wishart) NYU Pr.
— Oeuvres, Vol. 1. (FRE.). 1963. lib. bdg. 110.00 (0-8288-3558-6, F16290) Fr & Eur.
— Oeuvres, Vol. 2. (FRE.). 1968. lib. bdg. 110.00 (0-8288-3559-4, F16300) Fr & Eur.
— Oeuvres, Vol. 3. (FRE.). 1982. lib. bdg. 125.00 (0-8288-3560-8, F16380) Fr & Eur.
— Oeuvres: Economie: Economie et Philosophie, Salaire, Principes d'un Critique de l'Economie Politique, Le Capital (Livre deuxieme e Livre Troisieme), Vol. 2. 2112p. 52.50 (0-686-56539-8) Fr & Eur.
— Oeuvres: Economie: Le Capital, Livre Premier (1867), Le Manifeste Communiste, Misere de la Philosophie, etc., Vol. 1. 2000p. 45.00 (0-686-56538-X) Fr & Eur.
— On Colonialism. (C). text 15.00 (0-85315-129-6, Pub. by Lawrence & Wishart) NYU Pr.
— On Society & Social Change. Smelser, Neil J., ed. LC 73-78669. (Heritage of Sociology Ser.). xlii, 248p. 1975. reprint ed. pap. text 18.00 (0-226-50918-4, P567) U Ch Pr.
— The Portable Karl Marx. Kamenka, Eugene, ed. 704p. (C). 1983. pap. 15.95 (0-14-015096-X) Viking Penguin.
— The Poverty of Philosophy. LC 63-10632. 160p. 1992. pap. 6.95 (0-7178-0701-0) Intl Pubs Co.
— The Poverty of Philosophy. Quelch, H., tr. from FRE. LC 95-11391. (Great Books in Philosophy). 227p. 1995. pap. 7.95 (0-87975-977-1) Prometheus Bks.
— Poverty of Philosophy. 205p. 1973. pap. 22.95 (0-8464-1331-0) Beekman Pubs.
— Pre-Capitalist Economic Formations. Cohen, Jack, tr. LC 65-16393. 160p. 1989. pap. 4.95 (0-7178-0165-9) Intl Pubs Co.
— Readings from Karl Marx. Sayer, Derek, ed. 256p. 1989. pap. 7.95 (0-415-01810-2) Routledge.
— Selected Essays. Stenning, H. J., tr. LC 68-16955. (Essay Index Reprint Ser.). 1977. 18.95 (0-8369-0687-X) Ayer.
— Selected Writings. Simon, Lawrence H., ed. LC 94-362. 384p. (C). 1994. lib. bdg. 34.95 (0-87220-219-4) Hackett Pub.
— Selected Writings. McLellan, David, ed. (Illus.). 636p. 1977. pap. text 23.95 (0-19-876038-8) OUP.
— Selected Writings in Sociology & Social Philosophy. 267p. (C). 1964. pap. 6.95 (0-07-040672-3) McGraw.
— Selected Writings (Marx) Simon, Lawrence H., ed. (Classics Ser.). 384p. (C). 1994. pap. text 9.95 (0-87220-218-6) Hackett Pub.
— Theories of Surplus Value, 3 vols. 508p. 1970. 135.00 (0-8464-0920-8) Beekman Pubs.
— Theories of Surplus Value, 3 vols. LC 99-42497. (Great Minds Ser.). 506p. 1999. 17.95 (1-57392-777-5) Prometheus Bks.
— Theories of Surplus Value, Pt. II. LC 99-42497. 661p. 1999. pap. 18.95 (1-57392-778-3, Humanity Bks) Prometheus Bks.
***Marx, Karl.** Theories of Surplus Value, Pt. III. LC 99-42497. 637p. 1999. pap. 17.95 (1-57392-779-1, Humanity Bks) Prometheus Bks.
Marx, Karl. Wage-Labor & Capital & Value, Price & Profit. LC 76-10456. (Illus.). 110p. 1976. pap. 4.95 (0-7178-0470-4) Intl Pubs Co.
Marx, Karl & Engels, Friedrich. Birth of the Communist Manifesto. Struik, Dirk J., ed. LC 77-148513. (Illus.). 224p. 1994. reprint ed. pap. 7.95 (0-7178-0320-1) Intl Pubs Co.
— Collected Works, Vol. 8. 1977. pap. 39.95 (0-8464-4438-0) Beekman Pubs.
— Collected Works, Vol. 9. 1977. pap. 39.95 (0-8464-4439-9) Beekman Pubs.
— Collected Works of Karl Marx & Frederick Engels Vol. 30: A Contribution to the Critique of Political Economy, Notebks. I-VI. LC 73-84671. 538p. 1989. 24.95 (0-7178-0530-1) Intl Pubs Co.
— Collected Works of Karl Marx & Frederick Engels Vol. 37: Capital, Vol. 3. (Illus.). 992p. 1998. 34.95 (0-7178-0537-9) Intl Pubs Co.
— Collected Works of Karl Marx & Frederick Engels, 1838-42 Vol. 2: The Early Writings of Engels, Including Poems & Correspondence. LC 73-84671. (ENG & GER., Illus.). 703p. 1975. 24.95 (0-7178-0413-5) Intl Pubs Co.
— Collected Works of Karl Marx & Frederick Engels, 1844-45 Vol. 4: The Holy Family, The Condition of the Working Class in England, Etc. LC 73-84671. (Illus.). 808p. 1975. 24.95 (0-7178-0455-0) Intl Pubs Co.
— Collected Works of Karl Marx & Frederick Engels, 1844-51 Vol. 38: Marx-Engels Correspondence. LC 73-84671. (Illus.). 735p. 1982. 24.95 (0-7178-0538-7) Intl Pubs Co.
— Collected Works of Karl Marx & Frederick Engels,

An Asterisk (*) at the beginning of an entry indicates that the title is appearing for the first time.

1845-48 Vol. 6: The Poverty of Philosophy, the Communist Manifesto, the Polish Question. LC 73-84671. (Illus.). 805p. 1976. 24.95 (*0-7178-0506-9*) Intl Pubs Co.

— Collected Works of Karl Marx & Frederick Engels, 1848 Vol. 7: Demands of the Communist Party in Germany, Articles, Speeches. LC 73-84671. (Illus.). 750p. 1977. 24.95 (*0-7178-0507-7*) Intl Pubs Co.

— Collected Works of Karl Marx & Frederick Engels, 1848-49 Vol. 8: The Journalism & Speeches of the Revolutionary Years in Germany. LC 73-84671. (Illus.). 688p. 1977. 24.95 (*0-7178-0508-5*) Intl Pubs Co.

— Collected Works of Karl Marx & Frederick Engels, 1849 Vol. 9: The Journalism & Speeches of the Revolutionary Years in Germany. LC 73-84671. (Illus.). 688p. 1978. 24.95 (*0-7178-0509-3*) Intl Pubs Co.

— Collected Works of Karl Marx & Frederick Engels, 1849-51 Vol. 10: The Class Struggles in France, the Peasant War in Germany, Etc. LC 73-84671. (Illus.). 814p. 1978. 24.95 (*0-7178-0510-7*) Intl Pubs Co.

— Collected Works of Karl Marx & Frederick Engels, 1851-53 Vol. 11: Revolution & Counter-Revolution in Germany, the 18th Brumaire, Etc. LC 73-84671. (Illus.). 796p. 1979. 24.95 (*0-7178-0511-5*) Intl Pubs Co.

— Collected Works of Karl Marx & Frederick Engels, 1853-54 Vol. 12: Articles from the New York Daily Tribune & the People's Paper. LC 73-84671. (Illus.). 815p. 1979. 24.95 (*0-7178-0512-3*) Intl Pubs Co.

— Collected Works of Karl Marx & Frederick Engels, 1854-55 Vol. 13: The Eastern Question, Spain, England, etc. in Articles from the New York Daily Tribune & Neue Oder Zeitung. LC 73-84671. (Illus.). 825p. 1980. 24.95 (*0-7178-0513-1*) Intl Pubs Co.

— Collected Works of Karl Marx & Frederick Engels, 1855-56 Vol. 14: The Armies of Europe, Articles from the New York Daily Tribune, Neue Oder Zeitung & Unpublished Preparatory Materials. LC 73-84671. (Illus.). 809p. 1980. 24.95 (*0-7178-0514-X*) Intl Pubs Co.

— Collected Works of Karl Marx & Frederick Engels, 1856-58 Vol. 15: Revelations of the Diplomatic History of the 18th Century; Articles from the NY Daily Tribune; Chronicle of the History of Prussia. LC 73-84671. 808p. 1986. 24.95 (*0-7178-0515-8*) Intl Pubs Co.

— Collected Works of Karl Marx & Frederick Engels, 1857-62 Vol. 18: Articles from the New American Cyclopaedia & the Volunteer Journal: Notes on the Art of War. LC 73-84671. (Illus.). 720p. 1982. 24.95 (*0-7178-0518-2*) Intl Pubs Co.

— Collected Works of Karl Marx & Frederick Engels, 1858-60 Vol. 16: Engels' Po & Rhine, Articles from the New York Daily Tribune & das Volk. LC 73-84671. (Illus.). 800p. 1980. 24.95 (*0-7178-0516-6*) Intl Pubs Co.

— Collected Works of Karl Marx & Frederick Engels, 1859-60 Vol. 17: Herr Vogt, Review of International Relations in Europe, Articles from the New York Daily Tribune. LC 73-84671. (Illus.). 704p. 1981. 24.95 (*0-7178-0517-4*) Intl Pubs Co.

— Collected Works of Karl Marx & Frederick Engels, 1861-1864 Vol. 19: History of the Polish Question: Articles on the U. S. Civil War, Intervention in Mexico, Etc., Many from New York Daily Tribune. LC 73-84671. (Illus.). 484p. 1982. 24.95 (*0-7178-0519-0*) Intl Pubs Co.

— Collected Works of Karl Marx & Frederick Engels, 1864-68 Vol. 20: Inaugural Address, Other Documents for the First International: Articles, Speeches on the Polish & Other Questions. LC 73-84671. (Illus.). 614p. 1986. 24.95 (*0-7178-0520-4*) Intl Pubs Co.

— Collected Works of Karl Marx & Frederick Engels, 1867-1870 Vol. 21: The Fenian Prisoners; History of Ireland, Article, Documents, Etc., of the 1st International. LC 73-84671. 645p. 1986. 24.95 (*0-7178-0521-2*) Intl Pubs Co.

— Collected Works of Karl Marx & Frederick Engels, 1870-1871 Vol. 22: Works Written from July, 1870 Thru October, 1871, Addresses to the General Council, International Working Men's Association: The Franco-Prussian War & the Paris Commune, the Civil War in France, Including Drafts & Notes. Selman, Barry, tr. LC 73-84671. (Illus.). 819p. 1987. 24.95 (*0-7178-0522-0*) Intl Pubs Co.

— Collected Works of Karl Marx & Frederick Engels, 1871-74 Vol. 23: Pamphlets, Articles, Etc., of the 1st International; The Housing Question, by Engels. LC 73-84671. (Illus.). 848p. 1988. 24.95 (*0-7178-0523-9*) Intl Pubs Co.

— Collected Works of Karl Marx & Frederick Engels, 1874-88 Vol. 24: Articles & Notes on Germany, the U. S. A. & Russia, 1874-88; Critique of the Gotha Program, Notes on World History, Etc. LC 73-84671. 1989. 24.95 (*0-7178-0524-7*) Intl Pubs Co.

— Collected Works of Karl Marx & Frederick Engels, 1882-89 Vol. 26: Engels, Includes Origin of the Family, Ludwig Feuerbach & the Unfinished "The Role of Force in History," Many of Engels' Prefaces & Major Articles. LC 73-84671. 1991. 24.95 (*0-7178-0526-3*) Intl Pubs Co.

— Collected Works of Karl Marx & Frederick Engels, 1890-95 Vol. 27: Engels: Tsarist Foreign Policy; British Developments; Can Europe Disarm? History of Primitive Christianity; The Peasant Question, More. Chikileva, Tatiana, ed. Fowkes, Ben & Ryazanskaya, S., trs. (Illus.). 728p. 1992. 24.95 (*0-7178-0527-1*) Intl Pubs Co.

— Collected Works of Karl Marx & Friedrich Engels Vol. 31: Theories of Surplus Value, Notebks. VII-XII. LC 73-84671. 1989. 24.95 (*0-7178-0531-X*) Intl Pubs Co.

— Collected Works of Karl Marx & Friedrich Engels Vol. 35: Capital, Vol. 1. 864p. 1996. 24.95 (*0-7178-0535-2*) Intl Pubs Co.

— Collected Works of Karl Marx & Friedrich Engels Vol. 36: Capital, Vol. 2. 1997. 24.95 (*0-7178-0536-0*) Intl Pubs Co.

— Collected Works of Karl Marx & Friedrich Engels, July, 1870-December, 1873 Vol. 44: Marx-Engels Correspondence. LC 73-84671. (Illus.). 822p. 1990. 24.95 (*0-7178-0544-1*) Intl Pubs Co.

— Collected Works of Karl Marx & Frederick Engels, 1845-47 Vol. 5: Theses on Feuerbach, The German Ideology & Related Manuscripts. LC 73-84671. (Illus.). 687p. 1976. 24.95 (*0-7178-0505-0*) Intl Pubs Co.

— Collected Works of Karl Marx & Friedrich Engels, 1852-55 Vol. 39: Marx-Engels Correspondence. LC 73-84671. (Illus.). 780p. 1983. 24.95 (*0-7178-0539-5*) Intl Pubs Co.

— Collected Works of Karl Marx & Friedrich Engels, 1860-64 Vol. 41: Marx-Engels Correspondence. LC 73-84671. 784p. 1983. 24.95 (*0-7178-0541-7*) Intl Pubs Co.

— Collected Works of Karl Marx & Friedrich Engels, 1864-68 Vol. 42: Marx-Engels Correspondence. Upward, Christopher & Peet, John, trs. LC 73-84671. (Illus.). 808p. 1988. 24.95 (*0-7178-0542-5*) Intl Pubs Co.

— Collected Works of Karl Marx & Friedrich Engels, 1868-70 Vol. 43: Marx-Engels Correspondence. LC 73-84671. 800p. 1988. 24.95 (*0-7178-0543-3*) Intl Pubs Co.

— Collected Works of Karl Marx & Friedrich Engels, 1880-83 Vol. 46: Marx-Engels Correspondence. LC 73-84671. 634p. 1993. 24.95 (*0-7178-0546-8*) Intl Pubs Co.

— The Cologne Communist Trial. Livingstone, Rodney, ed. & tr. by. from GER. LC 75-168986. 298p. 1971. 8.50 (*0-7178-0240-X*) Intl Pubs Co.

— The Communist Manifesto. (C). 1997. pap. text. write for info. (*0-321-02590-3*) Addson-Wesley Educ.

***Marx, Karl & Engels, Friedrich.** The Communist Manifesto. 128p. 1998. pap. 4.00 (*0-14-044478-5*) Addison-Wesley Educ.

— The Communist Manifesto. 1976. 18.95 (*0-89190-549-9*) Amereon Ltd.

Marx, Karl & Engels, Friedrich. The Communist Manifesto. 80p. 1992. mass mkt. 4.95 (*0-553-21406-3*, Bantam Classics) Bantam.

— The Communist Manifesto. Beer, Samuel Hutchison, ed. LC 55-10808. (Crofts Classics). 128p. (C). 1955. pap. text 4.95 (*0-88295-055-X*) Harlan Davidson.

— The Communist Manifesto. 48p. (C). 1948. pap. 2.00 (*0-7178-0241-8*) Intl Pubs Co.

— The Communist Manifesto. Huberman, Leo, ed. LC 64-21175. 1977. pap. 10.00 (*0-85345-062-5*, Pub. by Monthly Rev) NYU Pr.

— The Communist Manifesto. LC 99-172611. 1998. mass mkt. 4.95 (*0-451-52710-0*, Sig Classics) NAL.

— The Communist Manifesto. Bender, Frederic L., ed. (Critical Editions Ser.). (C). 1988. pap. text 9.25 (*0-393-95616-4*) Norton.

— The Communist Manifesto. McLellan, David, ed. & intro. by. (Oxford World's Classics Ser.). 90p. 1998. pap. 5.95 (*0-19-283437-1*) OUP.

— The Communist Manifesto. 143p. 1988. mass mkt. 4.99 (*0-671-67881-7*, WSP) PB.

— The Communist Manifesto. pap. 8.95 (*0-7453-1033-8*, Pub. by Pluto GBR) Stylus Pub VA.

— The Communist Manifesto. LC 96-144421. 1995. 20.00 (*0-7453-1034-6*, Pub. by Pluto GBR) Stylus Pub VA.

— The Communist Manifesto. Moore, Samuel, tr. from GER. 60p. 1978. reprint ed. pap. 5.00 (*0-88286-043-7*) C H Kerr.

— The Communist Manifesto. 59p. 1989. reprint ed. pap. 3.95 (*0-87348-140-2*) Pathfinder NY.

***Marx, Karl & Engels, Friedrich.** The Communist Manifesto. 52p. 1999. reprint ed. 14.85 (*0-9663259-1-5*) Queen Publ.

Marx, Karl & Engels, Friedrich. The Communist Manifesto. 150th anniversary ed. Moore, Samuel, tr. 64p. 1998. reprint ed. pap. 5.00 (*0-88286-235-9*) C H Kerr.

— The Communist Manifesto: A Modern Edition. LC 98-17038. 96p. 1998. pap. 13.00 (*1-85984-898-2*, Pub. by Verso) Norton.

— The Communist Manifesto: New Interpretations. Cowling, Mark, ed. LC 97-39361. 224p. 1998. text 55.00 (*0-8147-1576-1*); pap. text 18.50 (*0-8147-1577-X*) NYU Pr.

***Marx, Karl & Engels, Friedrich.** The Communist Manifesto: With Related Documents. Toews, John E., ed. LC 98-87536. 224p. 1999. text 39.95 (*0-312-21812-5*) St Martin.

Marx, Karl & Engels, Friedrich. The Communist Manifesto: With related Documents. Toews, John E., ed. LC 98-87536. 1999. pap. text 11.95 (*0-312-15711-8*) St Martin.

— The Economic & Philosophic Manuscripts of 1884 Karl Marx & the Communist Manfesto. Milligan, Martin, tr. LC 88-60153. (Great Books in Philosophy). 243p. 1988. pap. 6.95 (*0-87975-446-X*) Prometheus Bks.

— Collected Works of Karl Marx & Friedrich Engels, 1856-60 Vol. 40: Marx-Engels Correspondence. LC 73-84671. (Illus.). 780p. 1983. 24.95 (*0-7178-0540-9*) Intl Pubs Co.

— Collected Works of Karl Marx & Friedrich Engels, 1874-79 Vol. 45: Marx-Engels Correspondence. LC 73-84671. 623p. 1992. 24.95 (*0-7178-0545-X*) Intl Pubs Co.

— Feuerbach: Opposition of the Materialistic & Idealistic Outlooks. 128p. 1970. pap. 12.95 (*0-8464-0409-5*) Beekman Pubs.

— German Ideology, Pt. 1 & Selections From Pts 2 & 3. Arthur, C. J., ed. LC 71-148517. (C). 1970. pap. 6.95 (*0-7178-0302-3*) Intl Pubs Co.

— Karl Marx & Friedrich Engels on Literature & Art: A Selection of Writings. Baxandall, Lee, ed. (Documents on Marxist Aesthetics Ser.: Vol.I). 179p. 1974. 37.50 (*0-88477-000-1*) Intl General.

— Karl Marx & Friedrich Engels on Literature & Art: A Selection of Writings. Baxandall, Lee & Morawski, Stefan, eds. (Documents on Marxist Aesthetics Ser.: Vol.I). 179p. 1974. pap. 13.95 (*0-88477-001-X*) Intl General.

— Manifesto of the Communist Party. (Reprint Series in Social Sciences). (C). 1993. reprint ed. pap. text 3.90 (*0-8290-2655-X*, S-455) Irvington.

— El Manifiesto Comunista. Madrid, Luis, ed. (SPA.). 63p. (Orig.). (C). 1992. pap. 5.00 (*0-87348-751-6*) Pathfinder NY.

— Marx & Engels on Ecology, 8. Parsons, Howard L., ed. LC 77-71866. (Contributions in Philosophy Ser.: No.8). 262p. 1977. 65.00 (*0-8371-9538-1*, PME/, Greenwood Pr) Greenwood.

— Marx & Engels on the Means of Communication: A Selection of Texts. De La Haye, Yves, ed. 173p. (Orig.). 1980. pap. 13.95 (*0-88477-013-3*) Intl General.

— Marx & Engels on the Trade Unions. LC 90-43327. xx, 240p. 1990. reprint ed. pap. 8.95 (*0-7178-0676-6*) Intl Pubs Co.

— Marx & Engels on Trade Unions. Lapides, Kenneth, ed. LC 86-25266. 264p. 1986. 55.00 (*0-275-92373-8*, C2373, Praeger Pubs) Greenwood.

— On Historical Materialism. (C). text 17.50 (*0-85315-270-5*, Pub. by Lawrence & Wishart) NYU Pr.

— On Religion. LC 82-17032. (American Academy of Religion, Classics in Religious Studies). 384p. 1982. reprint ed. 25.95 (*0-89130-599-8*, 01 05 03) OUP.

— Revolution in Spain: A Greenwood Archival Edition. LC 74-27667. 255p. 1975. reprint ed. lib. bdg. 52.50 (*0-8371-7909-2*, MARS, Greenwood Pr) Greenwood.

— Selected Correspondence: Eighteen Forty-Six to Eighteen Ninety-Five. LC 75-25261. 551p. 1975. reprint ed. lib. bdg. 38.50 (*0-8371-8385-5*, MAKMF, Greenwood Pr) Greenwood.

— Werke, Vols. 1-39. write for info. (*3-320-01316-5*) Adlers Foreign Bks.

Marx, Karl, et al. The Civil War in France: The Paris Commune. rev. ed. LC 88-24454. 180p. (C). 1993. reprint ed. pap. 8.95 (*0-7178-0666-9*) Intl Pubs Co.

— The Communist Manifesto. 150th anniversary ed. LC 98-9538. 128p. 1998. pap. 10.00 (*0-85345-936-3*, Pub. by Monthly Rev) NYU Pr.

— German Essays on Socialism in the Nineteenth Century. Stassen, Manfred, ed. LC 70-110074. (German Library: Vol. 41). 320p. 1989. 39.50 (*0-8264-0323-9*); pap. 19.95 (*0-8264-0324-7*) Continuum.

— German Socialist Philosophy. Schirmacher, Wolfgang, ed. LC 82-7981. (The German Library: Vol. 40). 324p. 1996. 39.50 (*0-8264-0748-X*) Continuum.

— Writings of the Young Marx on Philosophy & Society. Easton, Loyd D. & Guddat, Kurt H., eds. & trs. by. LC 97-28412. (Hackett Classics Ser.). 512p. 1997. pap. text 14.95 (*0-87220-368-9*); lib. bdg. 37.95 (*0-87220-369-7*) Hackett Pub.

Marx, Karl, jt. auth. see Engels, Friedrich.

Marx, Karl, jt. auth. see Furet, Francois.

Marx, Karl, jt. auth. see Kainz, Howard P.

Marx, Karl, jt. auth. see Trotsky, Leon.

Marx, Laurie & Haskin, Joy, eds. Nursing Quality Assurance Handbook: Developing - Updating Your Program for the 1990's. LC 90-63404. 251p. 1991. pap. 39.95 (*0-944496-19-9*) Precept Pr.

Marx, Leo. Machine in the Garden: Technology & the Pastoral Ideal in America. (Illus.). 400p. 1967. pap. 14.95 (*0-19-500738-7*) OUP.

Marx, Leo. The Machine in the Garden: Technology & the Pastoral Ideal in America. 2nd ed. LC 99-34697. (Illus.). 430p. 2000. pap. text 16.95 (*0-19-513351-X*) OUP.

***Marx, Leo.** The Machine in the Garden: Technology & the Pastoral Ideal in America. 2nd ed. LC 99-34697. (Illus.). 430p. 2000. text 35.00 (*0-19-513350-1*) OUP.

Marx, Leo & Mazlish, Bruce, eds. Progress: Fact or Illusion? LC 95-50970. 248p. (C). 1996. text 47.50 (*0-472-10676-7*, 10676) U of Mich Pr.

— Progress: Fact or Illusion? 248p. (C). 1998. pap. text 24.95 (*0-472-08509-3*, 08509) U of Mich Pr.

Marx, Leo & Trachtenberg, Alan. Three on Technology: New Photographs by Robert Cumming. LC 88-2678. (Illus.). 72p. 1988. pap. 15.00 (*0-938437-21-6*) MIT List Visual Arts.

Marx, Leo, jt. ed. see Smith, Merritt Roe.

Marx, Leonie. Benny Anderson: A Critical Study, 1. LC 83-12945. (Contributions to the Study of World Literature Ser.: No. 1). 161p. 1983. 45.00 (*0-313-24168-6*, MAN/, Greenwood Pr) Greenwood.

Marx, Lesley. Crystals Out of Chaos: John Hawkes & the Shapes of Apocalypse. LC 96-20819. 248p. 1997. 39.50 (*0-8386-3661-6*) Fairleigh Dickinson.

Marx, Maarten. Multi-Dimensional Modal Logic. LC 96-49525. (Applied Logic Ser.: Vol. 4). 256p. (C). 1996. text 104.00 (*0-7923-4345-X*) Kluwer Academic.

Marx, Maarten, et al, eds. Arrow Logic & Multi-Modal Logic. LC 96-24385. (Studies in Logic, Language & Information). 264p. (C). 1996. 64.95 (*1-57586-025-2*); pap. 22.95 (*1-57586-024-4*) CSLI.

Marx-Macdonald, Sherry, tr. see Goldschmidt, Tijs.

Marx, Melvin H. & Cronan-Hillix, W. A. Systems & Theories in Psychology. 4th ed. (Psychology Ser.). 576p. (C). 1986. text 59.74 (*0-07-040680-4*) McGraw.

— Systems & Theories in Psychology. 4th ed. (Psychology Ser.). 576p. (C). 1987. pap. text, teacher ed. 21.56 (*0-07-040681-2*) McGraw.

Marx Memorial Library Staff. Catalog of the Marx Memorial Library. 1979. 380.00 (*0-8161-1520-6*, G K Hall & Co) Mac Lib Ref.

Marx, Michael. Justus - A Utopia: Formation of a Tax Free Constitutional Democracy. 264p. 1998. 30.00 (*1-893395-02-2*) Marx & Marx.

— A War Ends... 256p. 1977. 30.00 (*1-893395-00-6*) Marx & Marx.

Marx, Milton. The Enjoyment of Drama. 2nd ed. LC 61-15689. 1961. pap. text 9.95 (*0-89197-609-4*) Irvington.

Marx, Miriam. Armor & Ashes. Klein, Elizabeth, ed. (Chapbook Ser.: No. 13). 23p. 1983. pap. 3.00 (*0-932884-12-1*) Red Herring.

Marx, Morris L., jt. auth. see Larsen, Richard J.

Marx, Olga, tr. see George, Stefan.

Marx, P., jt. ed. see Dorndorf, W.

Marx, Pamela. Practical Plays. (Illus.). 128p. (Orig.). (J). (gr. 1-5). 1993. pap. 9.95 (*0-673-36049-0*, GoodYrBooks) Addson-Wesley Educ.

— Quick Writes; More Than 60 Short Writing Activities from the Practical to the Poetic. 1999. pap. text 14.95 (*0-673-58643-X*) Addson-Wesley Educ.

— Take a Quick Bow! 26 Short Plays for Classroom Fun. 192p. (J). (gr. 1-4). 1996. pap. 12.95 (*0-673-36316-3*, GoodYrBooks) Addson-Wesley Educ.

— The Travel-the-World Cookbook: For Kids of All Ages. LC 96-222605. (Illus.). (J). (gr. 3-6). 1996. pap. 12.95 (*0-673-36254-X*, GoodYrBooks) Addson-Wesley Educ.

Marx, Pamela & Olson, Pamela. Exploring Contemporary Themes. (Illus.). 300p. (Orig.). (J). (gr. 4-6). 1994. pap. 18.95 (*0-673-36010-5*, GoodYrBooks) Addson-Wesley Educ.

Marx, Patricia. Joey T. & the Missing Cookie. 16p. (J). (ps-1). 1997. per. 12.95 (*0-689-81416-X*) Litle Simon.

— Meet My Staff. LC 96-37678. (Illus.). 40p. (J). (ps-3). 1998. 14.95 (*0-06-027484-0*) HarpC.

Marx, Patricia & Stuart, Charlotte. How to Regain Your Virginity: And Ninety-Nine Other Recent Discoveries About Sex. LC 83-1341. (Illus.). 128p. 1983. pap. 5.95 (*0-89480-365-4*, 365) Workman Pub.

***Marx, Patricia, et al.** 1,003 Great Things about Friends. LC 99-21530. 1999. pap. 8.95 (*0-7407-0021-9*) Andrews & McMeel.

Marx, Patricia, jt. auth. see Hanson, Jeanne.

Marx, Patricia, jt. auth. see Martin, Jane R.

Marx, Patricia, jt. auth. see Read Martin, Jane.

Marx, Patty, et al. The Skinny: What Every Skinny Woman Knows (& Won't Tell You!) LC 98-54824. 192p. 1999. 9.95 (*0-440-50855-X*, Dell Trade Pbks) Dell.

Marx, Patty, jt. auth. see Hodgman, Ann.

Marx, Paul. The Apostle of Life. (Illus.). 204p. 1991. 5.00 (*1-55922-028-7*); pap. 3.00 (*1-55922-029-5*) Human Life Intl.

— Confessions of a Prolife Missionary. 1988. 5.00 (*1-55922-020-1*); pap. 3.00 (*1-55922-021-X*) Human Life Intl.

— Faithful for Life: Telling It Like It Is or at Least As I Saw It. 400p. (Orig.). 1997. 22.00 (*1-55922-044-9*); pap. 16.00 (*1-55922-045-7*) Human Life Intl.

— Fighting for Life: The Further Journeys of Father Paul Marx. (Illus.). 1989. 5.00 (*1-55922-026-0*) Human Life Intl.

— Fighting for Life: The Further Journeys of Fr. Paul Marx. LC 96-2666. (Illus.). vi, 286p. (Orig.). 1989. pap. 3.00 (*1-55922-027-9*) Human Life Intl.

— The Warehouse Priest. (Illus.). 364p. 1994. 8.00 (*1-55922-031-7*); pap. 5.00 (*1-55922-032-5*) Human Life Intl.

Marx, Paul, ed. Modern & Classical Essayists: Twelve Masters. LC 95-17608. xiii, 366p. 1995. pap. text 33.95 (*1-55934-451-2*, 1451) Mayfield Pub.

Marx, Paul, jt. auth. see Byrne, Gary C.

Marx, Pearson. On the Way to the Venus de Milo. LC 94-25976. 1995. 21.00 (*0-671-88335-6*) S&S Trade.

Marx, Peter, ed. Contracts in the Information Industry. 1988. 94.95 (*0-942774-27-2*) Info Indus.

Marx, Peter W. Heiner Muller: "Bildbeschreibung": Eine Analyse aus dem Blickwindel der Greimas' Schen Semiotik. Kafitz, Dieter et al, eds. (Studien zur Deutschen und Europaischen Literatur des 19. und 20. Jahrhunderts: Band 37). (GER., Illus.). 178p. 1998. pap. 37.95 (*3-631-33275-0*) P Lang Pubng.

Marx, R. J., jt. auth. see Franklin, Joe.

***Marx, Raymond J.** The ASTD Media Selection Tool for Workplace Learning. Hudson-Samuels, Karen, ed. LC 99-72433. 158p. 1999. pap. 49.95 (*1-56286-116-6*) Am Soc Train & Devel.

Marx, Robert. Buried Treasures You Can Find. LC 93-84521. (Illus.). 350p. (Orig.). 1993. pap. 14.95 (*0-915920-82-4*) Ram Pub.

— Sunken Teasure: How to Find It. Dawson, Hal, ed. LC 90-63186. (Illus.). 402p. 1990. pap. 14.95 (*0-915920-74-3*) Ram Pub.

Marx, Robert & Marx, Jenifer. New World Shipwrecks, 1492-1825: A Comprehensive Guide. LC 94-65593. (Illus.). 400p. 1994. 16.95 (*0-915920-84-0*) Ram Pub.

Marx, Robert, et al. Management Live! The Video Workbook. 400p. (C). 1991. pap. text 46.00 (*0-13-946781-5*) P-H

Marx, Robert F. Deep, Deeper, Deepest. LC 98-71198. (Illus.). 252p. 1998. 14.95 (*0-941332-66-7*, D983) Best Pub Co.

— History of Underwater Exploration. (Illus.). 240p. 1990. pap. 7.95 (*0-486-26487-4*) Dover.

— Shipwrecks in the Americas. (Illus.). 544p. 1997. reprint ed. pap. 12.95 (*0-486-25514-X*) Dover.

Marx, Robert F. & Marx, Jenifer. The Search for Sunken Treasure: Exploring the World's Great Shipwrecks. (Illus.). 192p. (Orig.). 1996. pap. 19.95 (*1-55013-788-3*) Firefly Bks Ltd.

M

Marx, Robert W., ed. The Census Bureau's TIGER System. (Cartography & Geographic Information Systems Journal Ser.: Vol. 17, No. 1). 107p. 1990. 20.00 (*0-614-06094-X*, AC171) Am Congrs Survey.

Marx, Russell. It's Not Your Fault. 1999. pap. 5.99 (*0-451-18562-5*, Sig) NAL.

Marx, Samuel. Mayer & Thalberg: The Make-Believe Saints. LC 88-31081. (Illus.). 274p. 1988. pap. 12.95 (*0-573-60695-1*) S French Trade.

Marx-Scouras, Danielle. The Cultural Politics of Tel Quel. (Penn State Studies in Romance Literatures). 1996. 45.00 (*0-271-01574-8*); pap. 19.95 (*0-271-01575-6*) Pa St U Pr.

Marx, Siegfried & Pfau, Werner. Astrophotography with the Schmidt Telescope. Lamble, Phillip, tr. (Illus.). 175p. (C). 1992. text 74.95 (*0-521-39549-6*) Cambridge U Pr.

Marx, Steve & Bouvard, Pierre. Radio Advertising's Missing Ingredient! The Optimum Effective Scheduling System. 2nd ed. 136p. (Orig.). 1993. pap. 60.00 (*0-89324-206-3*) Natl Assn Broadcasters.

***Marx, Steven.** Shakespeare & the Bible. (Oxford Shakespeare Topics). 176p. 2000. pap. 18.95 (*0-19-818439-5*); text 39.95 (*0-19-818440-9*) OUP.

Marx, Tracey. Marveling at God's Mysteries: Creative Faith Experiences for Youth. 82p. 1997. pap. 12.95 (*1-57438-010-9*, 8368) Ed Ministries.

Marx, Trish. Echoes of World War Two. LC 92-47369. 96p. (YA). (gr. 5 up). 1993. lib. bdg. 19.93 (*0-8225-4898-4*, Lerner Publctns) Lerner Pub.

— Hanna's Cold Winter. LC 92-27143. (Illus.). (J). (ps-3). 1993. 19.95 (*0-87614-772-4*, Carolrhoda) Lerner Pub.

***Marx, Trish.** One Boy from Kosovo. LC 99-51793. (Illus.). 32p. (YA). (gr. 2-5). 2000. 15.95 (*0-688-17732-8*, Wm Morrow); lib. bdg. 15.89 (*0-688-17733-6*, Wm Morrow) Morrow Avon.

Marx, Trish & Beh-Eger, Dorita. I Heal: The Children of Chernobyl in Cuba. LC 95-53927. (Illus.). (J). 1996. lib. bdg. 21.27 (*0-8225-4897-6*, Lerner Publctns) Lerner Pub.

Marx, Trish, jt. auth. see Nunez, Sandra.

Marx, Walter H. Claimed by Vesuvius. (Illus.). 164p. (C). 1975. pap. text 8.25 (*0-88334-069-0*) Longman.

Marx, Werner. Hegel's Phenomenology of Spirit: A Commentary Based on the Preface & Introduction. Heath, Peter, tr. xxvi, 136p. 1988. pap. text 12.00 (*0-226-50923-0*) U Ch Pr.

— Heidegger & the Tradition. LC 70-126901. (Studies in Phenomenology & Existential Philosophy). 275p. 1971. pap. 19.95 (*0-8101-0656-6*) Northwestern U Pr.

— Introduction to Aristotle's Theory of Being. Schine, Robert S., tr. 75p. 1977. pap. text 49.50 (*90-247-1941-0*, Pub. by M Nijhoff) Kluwer Academic.

— Is There a Measure on Earth? Foundations for a Non-Metaphysical Ethics. Nenon, Thomas J., Jr. & Lilly, Reginald, trs. 184p. (C). 1987. 27.95 (*0-226-50921-4*) U Ch Pr.

— Towards a Phenomenological Ethics: Ethos & the Life-World. LC 90-36907. (SUNY Series in Contemporary Continental Philosophy). 153p. (C). 1992. text 19.50 (*0-7914-0574-5*) State U NY Pr.

Marx, Werner G. Proof Positive. 1992. pap. 8.95 (*1-55673-462-X*, 7915) CSS OH.

***Marx, Werner G.** Thank You, Dr. Luke. 511p. 1998. pap. write for info. (*0-7541-0318-8*, Pub. by Minerva Pr) Unity Dist.

Marx, Wesley. Reason & World: Between Tradition & Another Beginning. 125p. 1971. pap. text 50.50 (*90-247-5048-2*, Pub. by M Nijhoff) Kluwer Academic.

— Vernunft und Welt. (Phaenomenologica Ser.: No. 36). 123p. 1970. lib. bdg. 66.50 (*90-247-5042-3*, Pub. by M Nijhoff) Kluwer Academic.

— Waste. LC 79-137805. (Man & His Environment Ser.). 189p. reprint ed. pap. 58.60 (*0-608-11745-5*, 201323500084) Bks Demand.

Marx, William. The Index of Middle English Prose: Handlist XIV: The National Library of Wales, Vol. 14. LC 99-24806. (Index of Middle English Prose Ser.: Vol. 0267-2472). 136p. 1999. 60.00 (*0-85991-549-2*) Boydell & Brewer.

Marxen. Kindergarten: Teaching & Learning. (C). 2001. 30.00 (*0-02-376892-4*, Macmillan Coll) P-H.

Marxer, Donna & Steis, Drew. Hot Buttons: Jurors on Jurying. Stevens, Marilyn, ed. (Art Calendar Guide Ser.). 33p. 1999. pap. 9.95 (*0-945388-21-7*) Art Calendar.

Marxer, Donna, jt. auth. see Navaretta, Cynthia.

Marxer, Marcy, jt. auth. see Fink, Cathy.

Marxhausen, Joanne. If I Should Die-If I Should Live. (Illus.). 48p. (J). (ps). 1978. pap. 4.99 (*0-570-07793-1*, 56-1317) Concordia.

— Three in One: A Picture of God. (Illus.). 48p. (J). (gr. k-4). 1978. 4.99 (*0-570-07790-7*, 56-1314) Concordia.

Marxhausen, Kim. It Only Takes a Spark: 40 Active Faith-Building Talks. 64p. (gr. 1-4). 1998. pap. 8.99 (*0-570-05329-3*) Concordia.

Marxsen, Willi. The Beginnings of Christology: Together with the Lord's Supper As a Christological Problem. LC 79-7384. 127p. reprint ed. pap. 39.40 (*0-8357-7101-6*, 202929500060) Bks Demand.

— Jesus & the Church: The Beginnings of Christianity. Devenish, Philip E., tr. & intro. by. LC 92-33155. 224p. 1992. pap. 17.00 (*1-56338-053-6*) TPI PA.

— New Testament Foundations for Christian Ethics. Dean, O. C., tr.Tr. of Christliche und Christliche Ethik im Neuen Testament. 320p. 1998. pap. 29.95 (*0-567-29223-1*, Pub. by T & T Clark) Bks Intl VA.

Marxuach, Carmen I. Evaristo Ribera Chevremont: Voz de Vanguardia. 323p. 1987. pap. 15.00 (*0-8477-3524-9*) U of PR Pr.

Mary. All That You Are. 1959. pap. 9.95 (*0-87516-055-7*) DeVorss.

— How Does Your Garden Grow? 2nd ed. (Illus.). 32p. 1995. pap., per. 12.50 (*0-9649466-0-2*) Mary & Me.

— The Love. 1959. pap. 4.50 (*0-87516-056-5*) DeVorss.

Mary & Leigh Block Museum of Art Staff, jt. auth. see Jacob, Mary Jane.

Mary, Andre. Tristan et Iseut. (FRE.). 1973. pap. 11.95 (*0-7859-4014-6*) Fr & Eur.

Mary, Andre, ed. Tristan et Iseut. (Folio Ser.: No. 452). (FRE.). pap. 9.95 (*2-07-036452-6*) Schoenhof.

Mary, Andre, see Eliot, Elaine, pseud.

Mary, Andre, ed. see Villon, Francois.

***Mary Ann & Carey, Kathleen.** Ghost Chat 2000: Ghost Stories for the New Millennium by Mary Ann, Northern Ohio. (Illus.). 60p. 1999. pap. 9.95 (*0-9675677-1-8*) Maka.

— Mary Ann's Funeral Guide: Stories & Advice from Northeast Ohio's Foremost Paranormal. (Illus.). 40p. 1998. pap. 9.95 (*0-9675677-0-X*) Maka.

Mary, Ann C. Christmas Favorites: The Holiday Handbook, Decorating Entertaining & Recipes. 1996. pap. 6.95 (*0-9613770-1-1*) Wimmer Bks.

Mary Ann Liebert Inc. Staff, jt. auth. see Genetic Engineering News Inc. Staff.

Mary, B., ed. Stepping Stones to Recovery for Women. LC 89-17751. 240p. (Orig.). pap. 6.95 (*0-934125-15-5*) Hazelden.

Mary, Bevis, jt. auth. see Jeneanne, Sicek.

Mary Chloe School Craft Saunders Staff. Peace on the Wing: Life's Unfolding, a Personal Journey Possibilities with MCSS. (Illus.). 1997. spiral bd. 12.95 (*0-9662892-0-X*) Possib MCSS.

Mary da Bergamo, Cajetan. Humility of Heart. Vaughan, Herbert C., tr. 240p. 1993. reprint ed. pap. 8.50 (*0-89555-067-9*) TAN Bks Pubs.

Mary Eleanore. Certitudes. LC 68-16956. (Essay Index Reprint Ser.). 1977. 18.95 (*0-8369-0688-8*) Ayer.

Mary, Floreda, ed. see Madison, Guy M.

***Mary, Francis.** Padre Pio: The Wonder Worker. 1999. pap. 12.95 (*0-89870-770-6*) Ignatius Pr.

Mary Ingraham Bunting Institute of Radcliffe Colle. Collected Visions: Women Artist at the Bunting Institute, 1961-1986. 96p. 1986. pap. 7.95 (*0-9601774-2-6*) Radcliffe Coll.

Mary, Johnson A. Ghost along the Erie. LC 95-4165. 1995. pap. 14.95 (*0-925168-34-3*) North Country.

Mary K. Desler & Associates Staff, jt. auth. see Barr, Margaret J.

Mary Louise, ed. Over the Bent World. LC 73-105031. (Essay Index Reprint Ser.). 1977. 44.95 (*0-8369-1676-X*) Ayer.

Mary, Mae. Howdy Doesn't Do It: Say "Hello" in 365 Languages. 1995. pap. 9.95 (*1-887679-75-8*) Foxglove Found.

— Red-Letter Days: A Journal to Track Life's "Periods" 192p. (Orig.). 1995. pap. 9.95 (*1-887679-11-1*) Foxglove Found.

— Red-Letter Days: A Journal to Track Life's "Periods" (JPN.). 192p. (Orig.). 1996. pap. 14.95 (*1-887679-23-5*) Foxglove Found.

— Singing along with Life: Grace Notes. 108p. 1996. pap. 9.95 (*1-887679-04-9*) Foxglove Found.

— Sports: My Life's Track Record. 1995. pap. 9.95 (*1-887679-52-9*) Foxglove Found.

— "True Due" Lists: Things to Do Before You Die. (Orig.). 1997. mass mkt. 4.95 (*0-614-29779-6*) Foxglove Found.

— When Did We Get That Lawn Mower? Our Home Improvements. 1995. pap. 14.95 (*1-887679-57-X*) Foxglove Found.

Mary Of Agreda. Mystical City of God, 4 vols., 1. 610p. 1996. 12.50 (*0-911988-27-0*) AMI Pr.

— Mystical City of God, 4 vols., 2. 608p. 1996. 12.50 (*0-911988-28-9*) AMI Pr.

— Mystical City of God, 4 vols., 3. 790p. 1996. 12.50 (*0-911988-29-7*) AMI Pr.

— Mystical City of God, 4 vols., 4. 661p. 1996. 12.50 (*0-911988-30-0*) AMI Pr.

— Mystical City of God, 4 vols., Set. 2676p. 1996. 50.00 (*0-911988-26-2*, 38229) AMI Pr.

Mary of Agreda & Mary Of Agreda. Mystical City of God. abr. ed. 794p. 1993. pap. 12.50 (*0-911988-31-9*, 38263) AMI Pr.

Mary Of Agreda, jt. auth. see Mary of Agreda.

Mary, Sylvia. Pauline & Johannine Mysticism. 1964. 49.50 (*0-614-00266-4*) Elliots Bks.

Mary, Vincent. Catholicism in the Second Spanish Republic: Religion & Politics in Salamanca 1930-1936. (Oxford Historical Monographs). (Illus.). 300p. (C). 1996. text 75.00 (*0-19-820613-5*) OUP.

Mary, William. Surveying the New Testament. 2nd ed. 252p. (C). 1998. spiral bd. 25.95 (*0-7872-4840-1*, 41484001) Kendall-Hunt.

Maryanoff, Bruce E. & Maryanoff, Cynthia A., eds. Advances in Medicinal Chemistry, Vol. 1. 274p. 1992. 109.50 (*1-55938-170-1*) Jai Pr.

— Advances in Medicinal Chemistry, Vol. 2. 259p. 1993. 109.50 (*1-55938-581-2*) Jai Pr.

— Advances in Medicinal Chemistry, Vol. 3. 187p. 1995. 109.50 (*1-55938-798-X*) Jai Pr.

Maryanoff, Bruce E. & Reitz, Allen. Advances in Medicinal Chemistry, Vol. 4. 1999. 109.50 (*0-7623-0064-7*) Jai Pr.

Maryanoff, Cynthia A., jt. ed. see Maryanoff, Bruce E.

Maryanov, Gerald S. Decentralization in Indonesia as a Political Problem. LC DS0644.M3. (Cornell University, Modern Indonesia Project, Monograph Ser.). 126p. reprint ed. pap. 39.10 (*0-608-30167-1*, 201063700068) Bks Demand.

Maryanski, Alexandra & Turner, Jonathan H. The Social Cage: Human Nature & the Evolution of Society. LC 92-17311. 323p. (C). 1992. 42.50 (*0-8047-2002-9*); pap. 12.95 (*0-8047-2003-7*) Stanford U Pr.

Maryanski, Alexandra, jt. auth. see Turner, Jonathan H.

Maryansky, Glenn, ed. see Piper, Christina.

Marye, George T. Nearing the End in Imperial Russia. LC 71-115562. (Russia Observed, Series I). 1970. reprint ed. 24.95 (*0-405-03048-7*) Ayer.

Marygrove College, Detroit, Michigan Staff. Into Her Own: The Status of Woman from Ancient Times to the End of the Middle Ages. LC 76-38319. (Biography Index Reprint Ser.). 1977. reprint ed. 23.95 (*0-8369-8123-5*) Ayer.

Maryk, Denis, jt. auth. see Samson, Judith.

Maryknoll Sisters Staff. Catholic Children's Treasure Box, Vols. 1-10. 1996. pap. 35.00 (*0-89555-581-6*) TAN Bks Pubs.

Maryknoll Sisters Staff, et al, eds. Catholic Children's Treasure Box, Bk. 11. 2nd ed. (Illus.). 32p. (J). (ps-3). 1998. pap. 4.50 (*0-89555-561-1*, No. 1351) TAN Bks Pubs.

— Catholic Children's Treasure Box, Bk. 12. 2nd ed. (Illus.). 32p. (J). (ps-3). 1998. pap. 4.50 (*0-89555-562-X*, No. 1352) TAN Bks Pubs.

— Catholic Children's Treasure Box, Bk. 13. 2nd ed. (Illus.). 32p. (J). (ps-3). 1998. pap. 4.50 (*0-89555-563-8*, No. 1353) TAN Bks Pubs.

— Catholic Children's Treasure Box, Bk. 14. 2nd ed. (Illus.). 32p. (J). (ps-3). 1998. pap. 4.50 (*0-89555-564-6*, No. 1354) TAN Bks Pubs.

— Catholic Children's Treasure Box, Bk. 15. 2nd ed. (Illus.). 32p. (J). (ps-3). 1998. pap. 4.50 (*0-89555-565-4*, No. 1355) TAN Bks Pubs.

— Catholic Children's Treasure Box, Bk. 16. 2nd ed. (Illus.). 32p. (J). (ps-3). 1998. pap. 4.50 (*0-89555-566-2*, No. 1356) TAN Bks Pubs.

— Catholic Children's Treasure Box, Bk. 17. 2nd ed. (Illus.). 32p. (J). (ps-3). 1998. pap. 4.50 (*0-89555-567-0*, No. 1357) TAN Bks Pubs.

— Catholic Children's Treasure Box, Bk. 18. 2nd ed. (Illus.). 32p. (J). (ps-3). 1998. pap. 4.50 (*0-89555-568-9*, No. 1358) TAN Bks Pubs.

— Catholic Children's Treasure Box, Bk. 19. 2nd ed. (Illus.). 32p. (J). (ps-3). 1998. pap. 4.50 (*0-89555-569-7*, No. 1359) TAN Bks Pubs.

— Catholic Children's Treasure Box, Bk. 20. 2nd ed. (Illus.). 32p. (J). (ps-3). 1998. pap. 4.50 (*0-89555-570-0*, No. 1360) TAN Bks Pubs.

***Maryknoll World Productions Staff.** Children of the Earth: Maryknoll Coloring & Activity Book. (Illus.). 24p. (J). (gr. 3-6). 1999. 2.00 (*0-941395-10-3*) Maryknoll Wrld Prods.

Maryland Association of History Museums Staff, ed. Maryland's Museums & Preservation Organizations: A Historical & Cultural Directory. (Illus.). 155p. 1999. pap. 5.00 (*1-878399-74-8*) Div Hist Cult Progs.

Maryland Department of Agriculture Staff. Maryland Seafood Cookbook, No. I. (Illus.). 48p. 1995. 6.95 (*1-885457-00-6*) Eastwind MD.

— Maryland Seafood Cookbook, No. II. 72p. 1994. pap. 6.95 (*1-885457-02-2*) Eastwind MD.

— Maryland Seafood Cookbook, No. III. 72p. 1994. pap. 6.95 (*1-885457-03-0*) Eastwind MD.

Maryland Fire & Rescue Institute Staff. Rescue Technician: Operational Readiness for Rescue Providers. (Illus.). 240p. (gr. 13). 1997. pap. text 32.95 (*0-8151-8390-9*, 31690) Mosby Inc.

***Maryland Fire & Rescue Institute Staff.** Rescue Technician: Operational Readiness for Rescue Providers. 1998. teacher ed. write for info. (*0-8151-2137-7*) Mosby Inc.

Maryland Genealogies Staff. Maryland Genealogies: A Consolidation of Articles from the Maryland Historical Magazine, 2 vols. LC 80-80064. 1097p. 1997. reprint ed. 75.00 (*0-8063-0887-7*) Genealog Pub.

Maryland Hall of Records Staff. Calendar of Maryland State Papers No. 1: The Black Books. 297p. 1995. reprint ed. pap. 26.50 (*0-8063-0237-2*, 3740) Clearfield Co.

Maryland Head Injury Foundation Staff. Why Did It Happen on a School Day? My Family's Experience with Brain Injury. (Illus.). 40p. (Orig.). (J). (gr. k-6). 1995. pap. 10.00 (*0-927093-02-2*) Brain Injury Assoc.

Maryland Historical Society Staff. Chesapeake Wildfowl Hunting: Maryland's Finest Decoys. (Illus.). 106p. (Orig.). 1991. pap. 16.95 (*0-938420-50-X*) MD Hist.

Maryland House of Correction Writers' Club Staff. Hear My Cry! (Illus.). 64p. 1991. per. 8.95 (*0-932616-36-4*) Brick Hse Bks.

Maryland-National Capital Park & Planning Commissi. Landmarks of Prince George's County: Architectural Photographs. LC 92-39873. (Illus.). 144p. 1993. 29.95 (*0-8018-4628-5*) Johns Hopkins.

Maryland Original Research Society of Baltimore St. The Maryland Original Research Society of Baltimore, 3 vols. Richardson, Albert Levin, ed. LC 67-28606. 1310p. 1999. reprint ed. 16.50 (*0-8063-0546-0*) Genealog Pub.

Maryland Sea Grant College Staff. The Hazards of Diving in Polluted Waters: Proceedings of an International Symposium. LC 92-622817. 1993. pap. text 12.95 (*0-943676-55-X*) MD Sea Grant Col.

Maryland State Archives Staff, abr. Charter of Maryland. 1990. pap. text 5.00 (*0-942370-27-9*) MD St Archives.

Maryland State Dept. of Education, ed. see Cyzyk, Janet L.

Maryme, J. D. Netware User's Guide 4.1. 1995. pap. 29.95 (*1-55851-283-7*, M&T Bks) IDG Bks.

Marymee, J. D. Novell's Guide to Integrating NetWare 5 & NT. LC 99-31811. 480p. 1999. pap. 44.99 (*0-7645-4580-9*) IDG Bks.

Marymee, J. D. & Stevens, Sandy. Novell's Guide to Bordermanager. LC 97-77817. 400p. 1998. pap. 49.99 (*0-7645-4540-X*) IDG Bks.

Maryniak, Barbara. A Hiking Guide to the National Parks & Historic Sites of Newfoundland. (Illus.). 320p. Date not set. pap. 9.95 (*0-86492-150-0*) Genl Dist Srvs.

Maryon, Herbert. Metalwork & Enamelling. 4th ed. (Illus.). 335p. 1971. pap. 8.95 (*0-486-22702-2*) Dover.

Maryon, Laura. Mittens, Mittens, & More Mittens! LC 98-60944. (Illus.). 32p. (J). (ps-4). 1998. pap. 11.99 (*1-57921-138-0*, Pub. by WinePress Pub) BookWorld.

Mary's "Bright Morning Star" Staff. A Call to Obedience in Modern Times. 68p. 1997. pap. 5.00 (*0-9649001-2-2*) Marys Helpers.

***Marysmith, Joan.** Holy Aspic. 224p. (Orig.). 2000. pap. 10.95 (*0-552-99688-2*, Pub. by Transworld Publishers Ltd) Trafalgar.

— Philosophers House. 2000. pap. 10.95 (*0-552-99812-5*, Pub. by Transworld Publishers Ltd) Trafalgar.

— Waterwings. (Illus.). 272p. 2000. pap. 12.95 (*0-552-99689-0*, Pub. by Transworld Publishers Ltd) Trafalgar.

— Waterwings. large type ed. 320p. 31.99 (*0-7089-4037-4*) Ulverscroft.

Maryua, Saiichi. Singular Rebellion. Keene, Dennis, tr. from JPN. 420p. 1990. pap. 6.95 (*0-87011-989-3*) Kodansha.

Marz, Bernd, ed. see Drewermann, Eugen.

Marz, Eduard. Joseph Schumpeter: Scholar, Teacher & Politician. rev. ed. LC 91-25049. 192p. (C). 1992. 42.00 (*0-300-03876-3*) Yale U Pr.

Marz, R. Franz Marc. (Illus.). (C). 1987. text 90.00 (*0-7855-5832-2*, Pub. by Collets) St Mut.

— Marac, Franz. 72p. (C). 1987. 80.00 (*0-7855-4521-2*, Pub. by Collets) St Mut.

Marz, Ron. Batman: Aliens. (Illus.). 128p. (gr. 9-12). 1998. pap. text 14.95 (*1-56971-305-7*) Dark Horse Comics.

***Marz, Ron.** Claws of the Catwoman. (Illus.). 2000. pap. text 10.95 (*1-56971-466-5*) Dark Horse Comics.

Marz, Ron. Green Lantern: A New Dawn. Kahan, Bob, ed. LC 98-123514. (Illus.). 128p. 1997. pap. 9.95 (*1-56389-222-7*, Pub. by DC Comics) Time Warner.

— Green Lantern: Baptism of Fire. (Illus.). 208p. (YA). 1999. pap. text 12.95 (*1-56389-524-2*, Pub. by DC Comics) Time Warner.

***Marz, Ron.** Green Lantern: Emerald Allies. (Green Lantern Ser.). (Illus.). 208p. (J). 2000. pap. text 14.95 (*1-56389-603-6*, Pub. by DC Comics) Time Warner.

Marz, Ron. Green Lantern: Fear Itself. (Illus.). 80p. (YA). 1999. 24.95 (*1-56389-310-X*, Pub. by DC Comics) Time Warner.

***Marz, Ron.** Green Lantern: Fear Itself. (Green Lantern Ser.). (Illus.). 80p. 1999. mass mkt. 14.95 (*1-56389-311-8*, Pub. by DC Comics) Time Warner.

Marz, Ron. Green Lantern/Silver Surfer. Dooley, K., ed. (Illus.). 48p. 1995. pap. 4.95 (*1-56389-258-8*) DC Comics.

Marz, Ron & David, Peter. DC vs. Marvel. Kahan, Bob, ed. LC 97-157633. (Illus.). 192p. 1996. pap. 12.95 (*1-56389-294-4*, Pub. by DC Comics) Time Warner.

Marz, Ron & Dixon, Chuck. Green Lantern: Emerald Knights. (Illus.). 208p. 1998. pap. text 12.95 (*1-56389-475-0*, Pub. by DC Comics) Time Warner.

Marz, Ron, jt. auth. see Kesel, Karl.

Marz, Roy. The Island-Maker. LC 82-17282. 100p. (Orig.). 1982. pap. 6.00 (*0-87886-120-3*, Greenfld Rev Pr) Greenfld Rev Lit.

Marz, Russell B. Medical Nutrition from Marz. 2nd ed. (Illus.). 587p. 1998. text 69.95 (*1-882550-28-5*, Omni Pr) Quiet Lion Pr.

Marz, U., contrib. by. Natural Food Colors: Emphasizing European Technology & Markets. 130p. 1995. 2750.00 (*1-56965-110-8*, GA-089) BCC.

Marz, Ulrich. Biotechnology Production of Food & Feed Ingredients: A Global View. LC 98-120788. 138p. 1997. 3450.00 (*1-56965-021-7*, B-109) BCC.

— Developments & Changes in the Global Compound Feed Sector & Their Impact on the Feed Ingredient Industry. LC 98-143185. 155p. 1998. 3350.00 (*1-56965-121-3*) BCC.

Marzai, Abdol G. Farda dar Esarat-e Dirouz: The Future Held Captive by the Past. (Bibliotheca Iranica: Vol. 10). (PER.). 544p. 1998. pap. text 15.00 (*1-56859-071-7*) Mazda Pubs.

Marzal, Manuel M., et al. The Indian Face of God in Latin America. LC 96-17766. (Faith & Cultures Ser.). 250p. (Orig.). 1996. pap. 22.00 (*1-57075-054-8*) Orbis Bks.

Marzan, Julio. The Numinous Site: The Poetry of Luis Pales Matos. LC 94-47234. 200p. 1995. 35.00 (*0-8386-3581-4*) Fairleigh Dickinson.

— The Spanish American Roots of William Carlos Williams. LC 93-38636. 280p. (C). 1994. text 30.00 (*0-292-75160-5*) U of Tex Pr.

— Translations Without Originals. 50p. 1986. pap. 3.95 (*0-918408-23-7*) Ishmael Reed.

Marzan, Julio, ed. Inventing a Word: An Anthology of Twentieth-Century Puerto Rican Poetry. LC 79-28472. 1980. text 57.50 (*0-231-05010-0*); pap. text 19.50 (*0-231-05011-9*) Col U Pr.

— Luna, Luna: Creative Writing Ideas from Spanish, Latin American, & Latino Literature. LC 96-44822. 248p. (Orig.). 1997. pap. 15.95 (*0-915924-52-8*) Tchrs & Writers Coll.

Marzano, Ferruccio, jt. auth. see Gandolfo, Giancarlo.

Marzano-Fritz, Francesca, jt. auth. see Rohrig, Carl W.

Marzano, Jana S., jt. auth. see Marzano, Robert J.

Marzano, Kathryn M. & Lyons, Pauline D. The Complete Review of Radiography. LC 86-9117. (Red Bks.). 252p. 1989. pap. text 29.95 (*0-8273-4233-0*) Delmar.

***Marzano, Robert J.** Transforming Classroom Grading. LC 00-9790. 2000. write for info. (*0-87120-383-9*) ASCD.

Marzano, Robert J. & Kendall, John S. A Comprehensive Guide to Designing Standards-Based Districts, Schools, & Classrooms. LC 96-36835. 293p. (Orig.). 1996. pap. 29.95 (*0-87120-277-8*) ASCD.

An Asterisk (*) at the beginning of an entry indicates that the title is appearing for the first time.

— The Fall & Rise of Standards-Based Education. 2nd ed. 24p. 1996. pap. 7.50 (*1-58434-008-8*) NASBE.

Marzano, Robert J. & Marshall, Stephanie P., prefs. A Different Kind of Classroom: Teaching with Dimensions of Learning. LC 92-9069. 191p. (Orig.). 1992. pap. 18.95 (*0-87120-192-5*, 611-92107) ASCD.

Marzano, Robert J. & Marzano, Jana S. A Cluster Approach to Elementary Vocabulary Instruction. LC 88-2923. (Reading Aids Ser.). (Illus.). 270p. reprint ed. pap. 83.70 (*0-7837-4589-3*, 204430800002) Bks Demand.

Marzano, Robert J. & Paynter, Diane E. New Approaches to Literacy: Helping Students Develop Reading & Writing Skills. LC 94-9054. (Psychology in the Classroom Ser.). 143p. (Orig.). 1994. pap. text 17.95 (*1-55798-249-X*) Am Psychol.

Marzano, Robert J. & Pickering, Debra J. Dimensiones del Aprendizaje: Manual del Profesor. (SPA.). 276p. 1996. spiral bd. 25.95 (*0-87120-333-2*) ASCD.

— Dimensions of Learning Teacher's Manual. 2nd ed. (Illus.). 352p. 1997. teacher ed., spiral bd. 29.95 (*0-87120-321-9*) ASCD.

— Dimensions of Learning Teacher's Manual & Trainer's Manual, Set. 2nd ed. (Illus.). 1997. teacher ed., ring bd. 106.00 (*0-87120-323-5*) ASCD.

— Dimensions of Learning Trainer's Manual. 2nd ed. (Illus.). 623p. 1997. ring bd. 94.00 (*0-87120-322-7*) ASCD.

— Implementing Dimensions of Learning. (Illus.). 48p. 1992. pap. 4.95 (*0-87120-334-0*) ASCD.

Marzano, Robert J., et al. Assessing Student Outcomes: Performance Assessment Using the Dimensions of Learning Model. LC 93-41882. 138p. 1993. pap. 16.95 (*0-87120-225-5*, 611-93179) ASCD.

— Assessing Student Outcomes: Performance Assessment Using the Dimensions of Learning Model. LC 93-41882. 1993. write for info. (*0-08-720225-5*, Pergamon Pr) Elsevier.

— Dimensions of Thinking: A Framework for Curriculum & Instruction. LC 87-72733. 162p. (Orig.). (C). 1988. pap. 12.00 (*0-87120-148-8*, 611-87040) ASCD.

— Essential Knowledge: The Debate over What American Students Should Know. unabridged ed. LC 99-18024. 450p. 1999. mass mkt. 39.95 (*1-893476-00-6*) McREL Inst.

— Implementing Standards-Based Education. LC 98-43678. (Student Assessment Ser.). 1998. 9.95 (*0-8106-2072-3*) NEA.

Marzano, Robert J., jt. auth. see Kendall, John S.

Marzano, Stefano. Thoughts & Facts Vols. I & II: Creating Value by Design. LC 99-191913. (Illus.). 312p. 1999. pap., boxed set 100.00 (*0-85331-757-7*, Pub. by Lund Humphries) Antique Collect.

Marzaroli, Oscar. Glasgow's People, 1956-1988. (Illus.). 192p. 1994. 34.95 (*1-85158-592-3*, Pub. by Mainstream Pubng) Trafalgar.

Marzaroli, Oscar & Grassie. Shades of Scotland, 1956-1988. (By Appointment Only Ser.). 224p. 1989. 34.95 (*1-85158-213-4*, Pub. by Mainstream Pubng) Trafalgar.

Marzell. Woerterbuch der Deutschen Pflanzennamen. 59.95 (*0-8288-7889-7*, M7031) Fr & Eur.

— Woerterbuch der Deutschen Pflanzennamen, Nos. 1-22. fac. ed. (GER.). 550.00 (*0-686-56642-4*, M-7031) Fr & Eur.

***Marzell, Paul M.** Real Estate Taxpak USA: Hotel/Motel/Inn/Bed & Breakfast. 4th rev. ed. (Illus.). 111p. 2000. spiral bd. 29.95 (*1-889646-10-5*) Marzell Pub.

— Real Estate Taxpak USA: Industrial Building. 4th rev. ed. (Illus.). 118p. 2000. spiral bd. 29.95 (*1-889646-09-1*) Marzell Pub.

— Real Estate Taxpak USA: Office/Professional Building. 4th rev. ed. (Illus.). 116p. 2000. 29.95 (*1-889646-11-3*) Marzell Pub.

Marzell, Paul M. Real Estate Taxpak USA: Residential, 6 vols. Incl. Hotel/Motel/Inn/Bed & Breakfast. (Illus.). 102p. 1996. spiral bd. 29.95 (*1-889646-02-4*); Industrial Building. (Illus.). 112p. 1996. spiral bd. 29.95 (*1-889646-03-2*); Office/Professional Building. (Illus.). 109p. 1996. spiral bd. 29.95 (*1-889646-04-0*); Residential. (Illus.). 115p. 1996. spiral bd. 19.95 (*1-889646-00-8*); Residential Condominium. (Illus.). 114p. 1996. spiral bd. 19.95 (*1-889646-01-6*); Retail/Commercial Building. (Illus.). 113p. 1996. spiral bd. 29.95 (*1-889646-05-9*); spiral bd. write for info. (*1-889646-06-7*) Marzell Pub.

***Marzell, Paul M.** Real Estate Taxpak USA: Residential. 4th rev. ed. (Illus.). 122p. 2000. spiral bd. 19.95 (*1-889646-07-5*) Marzell Pub.

— Real Estate Taxpak USA: Residential Condominium. 4th rev. ed. (Illus.). 120p. 2000. spiral bd. 19.95 (*1-889646-08-3*) Marzell Pub.

— Real Estate Taxpak USA: Retail/Commercial Building. 4th rev. ed. (Illus.). 116p. 2000. spiral bd. 29.95 (*1-889646-12-1*) Marzell Pub.

Marzelli, Robert. Massachusetts Real Estate, 2 vols. LC 83-82338. (Massachusetts Practice Systems Library). Date not set. ring bd. 240.00 (*0-317-00786-6*, 68860, MICHIE) LEXIS Pub.

— Massachusetts Real Estate: A Practice Systems Library Manual, 2 vols. 1983. ring bd. 240.00 (*0-327-00972-1*, 68860, MICHIE) LEXIS Pub.

***Marzelli, Robert.** Massachusetts Real Estate: 1999 Edition. 1800p. 1999. write for info. (*0-327-04926-X*, 6886011) LEXIS Pub.

Marzelli, Robert L. Massachusetts Real Estate. LC 83-82338. (Massachusetts Practice Systems Library). 1993. suppl. ed. 70.00 (*0-317-03242-9*) West Group.

— Real Estate Taxes & Abatements Handbook. 301p. 1980. 34.00 (*0-318-03671-1*) Lawyers Weekly.

***Marzette-Bolivar, C.** Up on the Down Lowe. LC 99-97579. 2000. 19.95 (*0-533-13435-8*) Vantage.

***Marziali, Elsa & Munroe-Blum, Heather.** Interpersonal Group Psychotherapy for Borderline Personality Disorder. 216p. 1999. reprint ed. text 25.00 (*0-7881-6499-6*) DIANE Pub.

***Marziali, Floriano & Mora, Vincenzo.** Coaching the 4- 4-2. (Illus.). 169p. 1998. pap. 14.95 (*0-9651020-8-4*) Reedswain.

Marzials, Frank, tr. see Beckford, William.

Marzillier, John S. & Hall, John, eds. What Is Clinical Psychology? 2nd ed. (Illus.). 384p. 1992. 69.00 (*0-19-262169-6*); pap. text 35.00 (*0-19-262168-8*) OUP.

— What Is Clinical Psychology? 3rd ed. LC 98-37283. (Illus.). 410p. 1999. text 60.00 (*0-19-262929-8*); pap. text 29.95 (*0-19-262928-X*) OUP.

Marzillier, Leon F. Elementary Statistics. 528p. (C). 1989. text 48.75 (*0-697-05931-6*, WCB McGr Hill) McGrw-H Hghr Educ.

— Elementary Statistics. 528p. (C). 1989. text 20.63 (*0-697-10901-1*, WCB McGr Hill) McGrw-H Hghr Educ.

Marzinotto, Paul J. The Connecticut Summary Process Manual. 259p. 1986. ring bd., suppl. ed. 115.00 (*0-910051-04-6*) CT Law Trib.

— Connecticut Summary Process Manual - Second Supplement. 1991. ring bd. 15.00 (*0-910051-14-3*) CT Law Trib.

Marzio, Peter C. The Art Crusade. LC 75-20404. (Smithsonian Studies in History & Technology: No. 34). (Illus.). 102p. reprint ed. pap. 31.70 (*0-8357-5758-7*, 200469100045) Bks Demand.

Marzio, Peter C., et al. The Museum of Fine Arts, Houston: A Permanent Legacy. LC 89-83701. (Illus.). 352p. 1989. 65.00 (*1-55595-022-1*) Hudson Hills.

Marzishevskaya, K., et al. Diccionario Espanol-Ruso, Ruso-Espanol. 2nd ed. (RUS & SPA.). 512p. 1992. pap. 29.95 (*0-7859-1087-5*, 5200021677) Fr & Eur.

Marzluf, G. A., jt. ed. see Brambl, R.

Marzluf, George A., jt. ed. see Brambl, R.

Marzluff, John M. & Balda, Russell P. The Pinyon Jay: Behavioural Ecology of a Colonial & Cooperative Corvid. (Poyser Popular Bird Bks.). (Illus.). 317p. 1992. text 39.00 (*0-85661-064-X*, 784664) Acad Pr.

Marzluff, John M. & Sallabanks, Rex. Avian Conservation: Research & Management. LC 98-10506. 512p. 1998. text 55.00 (*1-55963-569-X*) Island Pr.

Marzo, Luigi Di, see Di Marzo, Luigi.

Marzo, M. & Puigdefabergas, C., eds. Alluvial Sedimentation. LC 92-36455. (International Association of Sedimentologists Special Publication Ser.: No. 17). 1993. pap. 125.00 (*0-632-03545-5*) Blackwell Sci.

Marzo, Peter C., jt. auth. see Nygren, Edward J.

Marzol, Gonzalo C. Aspectos Del Taller Poetico De Jaime Gil de Biedma. 44.70 (*0-685-69529-8*) Scripta.

Marzola, Alessandra & Silva, Francesco, eds. John Maynard Keynes: Language & Method. (Advances in Economic Methodology Ser.). 256p. 1994. 85.00 (*1-85278-923-9*) E Elgar.

Marzolf, Arnold H. Prairie Poems Revisited. 2nd rev. ed. 201p. 1997. pap. 9.95 (*0-9658463-0-X*) A H Marzolf.

— That's the Way It Once Was.Tr. of So Hen Mers Amohl Kaht. 1995. pap. 10.50 (*0-614-23869-2*) Am Hist Soc Ger.

Marzolf, Marion T. The Danish-Language Press in America: Doctoral Dissertation, the University of Michigan, 1972. Scott, Franklyn D., ed. LC 78-15202. (Scandinavians in America Ser.). (Illus.). 1979. lib. bdg. 25.95 (*0-405-11650-0*) Ayer.

Marzoli, G. P. & Versontini, S. Warren's Operation. (Illus.). 90p. 1981. 69.00 (*0-387-10785-1*) Spr-Verlag.

Marzolla, Jean. Veo Navidad. LC 95-6762. (SPA., Illus.). 40p. (J). (ps-3). 1995. 12.95 (*0-590-50197-6*) Scholastic Inc.

***Marzolla, Jean.** Welcome to the Shanna Show. 24p. (J). 2001. 12.99 (*0-7868-0631-1*, Pub. by Disney Pr) Time Warner.

Marzollo, Angelo, jt. ed. see Lasserre, Pierre.

Marzollo, Claudio. Kenny & the Little Kickers. LC 91-16707. (Illus.). 32p. (J). (ps-3). 1992. pap. 3.50 (*0-590-45417-X*) Scholastic Inc.

— Kenny & the Little Kickers. (Hello, Reader! Ser.). (J). 1992. 8.70 (*0-606-01877-8*, Pub. by Turtleback) Demco.

Marzollo, Dan, jt. auth. see Marzollo, Jean.

Marzollo, Dave, jt. auth. see Marzollo, Jean.

Marzollo, Jean. Baseball Brothers. LC 97-30342. (Hello Reader! Ser.). (Illus.). (J). 1998. 3.50 (*0-590-38398-1*) Scholastic Inc.

— Birthday Parties for Children: How to Give Them, How to Survive Them. 1999. 9.99 (*1-57866-056-4*) Galahad Bks.

— Cannonball Chris. LC 86-31512. (Step into Reading Ser.: A Step 3 Book). (Illus.). 48p. (J). (ps-3). 1987. pap. 3.99 (*0-394-88512-0*, Pub. by Random Bks Yng Read) Random.

Marzollo, Jean. Cannonball Chris. (Step into Reading Ser.: A Step 3 Book). (J). (gr. 2-3). 1987. 9.19 (*0-606-12210-9*, Pub. by Turtleback) Demco.

Marzollo, Jean. Christmas Cats. LC 97-7213. (Illus.). 32p. (J). (ps-3). 1997. 2.99 (*0-590-37212-2*) Scholastic Inc.

***Marzollo, Jean.** Close Your Eyes. (Picture Puffin Ser.). (J). 1998. 11.19 (*0-606-13286-4*, Pub. by Turtleback) Demco.

Marzollo, Jean. Companeros en el Futbol, 1 vol. (SPA., Illus.). 48p. (gr. 2-4). 1999. pap. text 3.99 (*0-439-08056-8*) Scholastic Inc.

— Do You Know New. LC 96-34747. (Illus.). 14p. (J). (ps up). 1998. 5.95 (*0-694-00870-2*) HarpC Child Bks.

— Doll-House Christmas. (J). 1986. pap. text 3.95 (*0-590-33093-4*) Scholastic Inc.

— En 1492. (Mariposa Scholastica en Espanol Ser.). 1993. 9.15 (*0-606-06495-8*, Pub. by Turtleback) Demco.

***Marzollo, Jean.** Extreme Challenger. (I Spy Books Ser.). (Illus.). 40p. (J). 2000. 13.95 (*0-439-19900-X*) Scholastic Inc.

Marzollo, Jean. Fathers & Babies: How Babies Grow & What They Need from You from Birth to 18 Months. LC 92-53386. (Illus.). 240p. 1993. pap. 13.00 (*0-06-096908-3*, Perennial) HarperTrade.

— Feliz Cumpleanos, Martin Luther King. Romo, Alberto, tr. from ENG.Tr. of Happy Birthday, Martin Luther King. (SPA., Illus.). 32p. (J). (ps-2). 1994. pap. 4.95 (*0-590-47507-X*) Scholastic Inc.

— Football Friends. LC 97-9096. (Hello Reader! Ser.). (Illus.). (J). (gr. 1-3). 1997. 3.50 (*0-590-38395-7*) Scholastic Inc.

— Halloween Cats. LC 94-228430. 32p. (J). (ps-3). 1992. pap. 2.99 (*0-590-46026-9*) Scholastic Inc.

— Happy Birthday, Martin Luther King. LC 91-42137. (Illus.). 32p. (J). (ps-3). 1993. 5.99 (*0-590-44065-9*) Scholastic Inc.

— Happy Birthday, Martin Luther King. (Illus.). 32p. (J). (ps-3). 1993. 5.99 (*0-590-72828-8*) Scholastic Inc.

***Marzollo, Jean.** Happy Birthday, Martin Luther King. (Illus.). (J). (ps-3). 2000. reprint ed. pap. 5.99 (*0-439-09942-0*) Scholastic Inc.

— Hockey Hero. (Hello, Reader! Ser.). (Illus.). (J). 1999. 8.95 (*0-606-18560-7*) Turtleback.

Marzollo, Jean. Home Sweet Home. LC 96-35410. (Illus.). 32p. (J). (ps-3). 1997. lib. bdg. 14.89 (*0-06-027353-4*) HarpC.

— Home Sweet Home. LC 96-35410. (Illus.). 32p. (J). (ps-3). 1997. 14.95 (*0-06-027562-6*) HarpC Child Bks.

— Home Sweet Home. LC 96-35410. (Illus.). 32p. (J). (ps-3). 1998. pap. 5.95 (*0-06-443501-6*) HarpC Child Bks.

— Home Sweet Home. 1998. 11.15 (*0-606-13483-2*, Pub. by Turtleback) Demco.

— How Kids Grow. LC 97-39190. (Illus.). 32p. (J). (ps-2). 1998. pap. 2.99 (*0-590-45062-X*, Pub. by Scholastic Inc) Penguin Putnam.

— I Am a Leaf. LC 98-5864. (Hello Readers! Ser.: Level 1). (Illus.). 32p. (J). (ps-1). 1999. pap. 3.50 (*0-590-64120-4*, Pub. by Scholastic Inc) Penguin Putnam.

***Marzollo, Jean.** I Am a Rock. (Hello Science Reader! Ser.). 1998. 9.60 (*0-606-13499-9*, Pub. by Turtleback) Demco.

Marzollo, Jean. I Am a Rock, Level 1. LC 97-16373. (Hello Reader! Ser.). (Illus.). (J). 1998. 3.50 (*0-590-37222-X*) Scholastic Inc.

— I Am an Apple. LC 97-6010. (Hello Reader! Ser.). (Illus.). 32p. (J). (ps-1). 1997. 3.50 (*0-590-37223-8*) Scholastic Inc.

— I Am an Apple. (Hello Science Reader! Ser.). (J). 1997. 8.70 (*0-606-11489-0*, Pub. by Turtleback) Demco.

— I Am Fire. LC 95-25750. (Hello Readers! Ser.: Level 1). (Illus.). 32p. (J). (ps-3). 1996. 3.50 (*0-590-84778-3*, Cartwheel) Scholastic Inc.

— I Am Fire. LC 95-25750. (Hello, Reader! Ser.). 1996. 8.70 (*0-606-11491-2*, Pub. by Turtleback) Demco.

— I Am Snow. LC 98-17757. (Hello Reader! Ser.: Level 1). (Illus.). 32p. (J). (ps-1). 2000. pap. 3.50 (*0-590-64174-3*, Pub. by Scholastic Inc) Penguin Putnam.

— I Am Water. LC 95-10528. (Hello Readers! Ser.: Level 1). (Illus.). 32p. (J). (ps-3). 1996. pap. 3.50 (*0-590-26587-3*, Cartwheel) Scholastic Inc.

— I Am Water. (Hello Reader! Level 1 Ser.). (SPA., Illus.). 30p. (ps-1). 1999. pap. text 3.99 (*0-439-08743-0*) Scholastic Inc.

Marzollo, Jean. I Am Water. (Hello, Reader! Ser.). 1996. 8.70 (*0-606-09447-4*, Pub. by Turtleback) Demco.

— I Love You: A Rebus Poem. LC 98-46700. (Illus.). 40p. (J). (ps-1). 2000. 7.95 (*0-590-37656-X*, Pub. by Scholastic Inc) Penguin Putnam.

Marzollo, Jean. I Spy Christmas. (Illus.). 40p. (J). (ps-5). 1992. 12.95 (*0-590-45846-9*, Cartwheel) Scholastic Inc.

— I Spy Fantasy: A Book of Picture Riddles. LC 93-44814. (Illus.). 40p. (J). (ps-5). 1994. 12.95 (*0-590-46295-4*) Scholastic Inc.

— I Spy Fun House: A Book of Picture Riddles. LC 92-16425. (I Spy Books Ser.).Tr. of C'est Moi l'Espion du Parc d'Attractions. (Illus.). 33p. (J). (ps-3). 1993. 12.95 (*0-590-46293-8*) Scholastic Inc.

— I Spy Gold Challenger! A Book of Picture Riddles. LC 98-13982. (I Spy Books Ser.). (Illus.). 40p. (J). 1998. 12.95 (*0-590-04296-3*, Pub. by Scholastic Inc) Penguin Putnam.

— I Spy Little Animals. (Illus.). 26p. (J). (ps). 1998. 6.99 (*0-590-11711-4*, Cartwheel) Scholastic Inc.

— I Spy Little Book. (Illus.). 26p. (J). (ps). 1997. bds. 6.99 (*0-590-34129-4*, Cartwheel) Scholastic Inc.

— I Spy Little Christmas. LC 99-21423. (I Spy Books Ser.). (Illus.). 26p. (J). (ps). 1999. bds. 6.99 (*0-439-08331-1*, Pub. by Scholastic Inc) Penguin Putnam.

***Marzollo, Jean.** I Spy Little Letters. LC 99-36454. (Illus.). 26p. (J). (ps). 2000. bds. 6.99 (*0-439-11496-9*, Cartwheel) Scholastic Inc.

Marzollo, Jean. I Spy Little Numbers, 1. LC 98-40619. (I Spy Little Bks.). (Illus.). 26p. 1999. 6.99 (*0-590-68714-X*, Cartwheel) Scholastic Inc.

***Marzollo, Jean.** I Spy Little Wheels. LC 99-165893. (I Spy Little Board Bks.: No. 3). (Illus.). 26p. (J). (ps). 1998. bds. 6.99 (*0-590-04706-X*, Pub. by Scholastic Inc) Penguin Putnam.

Marzollo, Jean. I Spy, Mystery: A Book of Picture Riddles. LC 92-40863. (Illus.). 37p. (J). (ps-3). 1993. 12.95 (*0-590-46294-6*) Scholastic Inc.

Marzollo, Jean. I Spy School Days. (Illus.). (J). 1995. pap. text. write for info. (*0-590-67441-2*, Cartwheel) Scholastic Inc.

Marzollo, Jean. I Spy School Days: A Book of Picture Riddles. LC 94-43629. (Illus.). 40p. (J). (ps-3). 1995. 12.95 (*0-590-48135-5*, Cartwheel) Scholastic Inc.

— I Spy Spooky Night: A Book of Picture Riddles. LC 95-50528. (Illus.). 40p. (J). (ps-3). 1996. 12.95 (*0-590-48137-1*, Cartwheel) Scholastic Inc.

— I Spy Super Challenger: A Book of Picture Riddles. (Illus.). (J). 1997. 12.95 (*0-614-29294-8*, Cartwheel) Scholastic Inc.

***Marzollo, Jean.** I Spy Treasure Hunt. (ps-3). 1999. 233.10 (*0-439-11749-6*) Scholastic Inc.

Marzollo, Jean. I Spy Treasure Hunt: A Book of Picture Riddles. LC 99-30581. (I Spy Books Ser.). (Illus.). 36p. (J). (ps-3). 1999. 12.95 (*0-439-04244-5*, Pub. by Scholastic Inc) Penguin Putnam.

— I'm a Caterpillar. LC 96-26744. (Hello Reader! Ser.). (Illus.). (J). 1997. 3.50 (*0-590-84779-1*) Scholastic Inc.

Marzollo, Jean. I'm a Caterpillar. (Hello Science Reader! Ser.). (J). 1997. 8.70 (*0-606-11502-1*, Pub. by Turtleback) Demco.

Marzollo, Jean. I'm a Seed. LC 95-13237. (Hello Readers! Ser.: Level 1). (Illus.). 32p. (J). (ps-1). 1996. pap. 3.50 (*0-590-26586-5*, Cartwheel) Scholastic Inc.

— I'm a Seed. (Hello, Reader! Ser.). 1996. 8.70 (*0-606-09454-7*, Pub. by Turtleback) Demco.

— In Fourteen Ninety-Two. 48p. (J). (ps-3). 1994. pap. 4.95 (*0-590-49442-2*) Scholastic Inc.

***Marzollo, Jean.** Mama, Mama. (Illus.). 16p. (J). (ps-k). 1999. 5.95 (*0-694-01245-9*) HarpC Child Bks.

Marzollo, Jean. My First Book of Biographies. LC 92-27623. (Illus.). 80p. (J). (gr. k-4). 1994. 14.95 (*0-590-45014-X*) Scholastic Inc.

— Once upon a Springtime. LC 96-10586. (Hello Reader! Ser.). (Illus.). (J). 1997. 3.50 (*0-590-46017-X*) Scholastic Inc.

***Marzollo, Jean.** Once upon Springtime. 1998. 9.44 (*0-606-13680-0*) Turtleback.

Marzollo, Jean. Papa Papa. LC 99-69950. (Illus.). 14p. (J). (ps up). 2000. 5.95 (*0-694-01246-7*, HarpFestival) HarpC Child Bks.

— Pizza Pie Slugger. (Stepping Stone Bks.). (J). 1989. 9.19 (*0-606-04300-4*, Pub. by Turtleback) Demco.

Marzollo, Jean. Pretend You're a Cat. (Picture Puffin Ser.). (J). 1997. 10.19 (*0-606-11762-8*, Pub. by Turtleback) Demco.

Marzollo, Jean. Read With Me: Thanksgiving Cats. LC 98-26102. (Read with Me Paperback Ser.). (Illus.). 32p. (J). (ps-3). 1999. pap. 3.25 (*0-590-03714-5*, Pub. by Scholastic Inc) Penguin Putnam.

— The Rebus Treasury. 1986. 6.95 (*0-416-95530-4*) Routledge.

— Slam Dunk Saturday. LC 91-25988. (Stepping Stone Bks). (Illus.). 64p. (J). (ps-3). 1994. pap. 3.99 (*0-679-82366-2*, Pub. by Random Bks Yng Read) Random.

— Slam Dunk Saturday. LC 91-25988. (Stepping Stone Bks). (Illus.). 64p. (J). (ps-3). 1994. lib. bdg. 11.99 (*0-679-92366-7*, Pub. by Random Bks Yng Read) Random.

Marzollo, Jean. Slam Dunk Saturday. (J). 1994. 9.19 (*0-606-06743-4*, Pub. by Turtleback) Demco.

Marzollo, Jean. The Snow Angel. LC 94-31997. (Illus.). 32p. (J). (ps-3). 1995. 14.95 (*0-590-48748-5*, Scholastic Hardcover) Scholastic Inc.

— Soccer Cousins. LC 96-7292. (Hello Reader! Ser.). (Illus.). (J). (gr. 2-4). 1997. 3.99 (*0-590-74254-X*) Scholastic Inc.

— Soccer Cousins. 1997. 9.19 (*0-606-11855-1*) Turtleback.

— Soccer Sam. LC 86-47533. (Step into Reading Ser.: A Step 3 Book). (Illus.). 48p. (J). (ps-3). 1987. pap. 3.99 (*0-394-88406-X*, Pub. by Random Bks Yng Read) Random.

Marzollo, Jean. Soccer Sam. (Step into Reading Ser.: A Step 3 Book). (J). (gr. 2-3). 1987. 9.19 (*0-606-03474-9*, Pub. by Turtleback) Demco.

Marzollo, Jean. Sun Song. LC 91-29316. (Picture Bks.). (Illus.). 32p. (J). (ps-3). 1997. pap. 5.95 (*0-06-443476-1*, HarpTrophy) HarpC Child Bks.

— Sun Song. LC 91-29316. (Illus.). 32p. (J). (ps-3). 1995. 14.95 (*0-06-020787-6*) HarperTrade.

— Sun Song. (Trophy Picture Bks.). (J). 1997. 11.15 (*0-606-11937-X*, Pub. by Turtleback) Demco.

— Ten Cats Have Hats. (Illus.). 24p. (J). (ps). 1994. 6.95 (*0-590-20656-7*) Scholastic Inc.

— Valentine Cats. LC 94-47816. (Read with Me Paperback Ser.). (Illus.). 32p. (J). (ps-2). 1996. pap. 2.99 (*0-590-47596-7*, Cartwheel) Scholastic Inc.

— Valentine Cats. (J). 1996. 7.99 (*0-606-08655-2*) Turtleback.

— Veo: Un Libro de Adivinanzas Ilustradas. (SPA., Illus.). 40p. (J). (ps-3). 1994. 12.95 (*0-590-48635-7*, Cartwheel) Scholastic Inc.

— What's the Matter with Mother Goose? LC 99-26423. (Illus.). 32p. (J). (ps-k). 2000. 14.95 (*0-06-027276-7*) HarpC.

Marzollo, Jean & Bjorkman, Steven. In 1492. 40p. (J). (ps-3). 1992. 19.95 (*0-590-72737-0*) Scholastic Inc.

Marzollo, Jean & Carson, Carol D. I Spy: A Book of Picture Riddles. LC 91-28268. (Illus.). 33p. (J). (ps-3). 1991. 12.95 (*0-590-45087-5*, Cartwheel) Scholastic Inc.

Marzollo, Jean & Marzollo, Dan. Basketball Buddies, Level 3. LC 97-29030. (Hello Reader! Ser.). (Illus.). 32p. (J). (gr. 1-3). 1998. pap. 3.50 (*0-590-38401-5*, Pub. by Scholastic Inc) Penguin Putnam.

Marzollo, Jean & Marzollo, Dave. Hockey Hero. LC 97-19281. (Hello Reader! Ser.: Level 3). (Illus.). 32p. (J). (ps-3). 1999. pap. 3.99 (*0-590-38397-3*, Pub. by Scholastic Inc) Penguin Putnam.

Marzollo, Jean & Savage, Beth. Early Learning Mastery Masters. Incl. Colors & Shapes. pap. 5.95 (*0-8224-4477-1*); Concepts. (J). (ps-2). 1981. pap. 5.95 (*0-8224-4478-X*); Letters & Sounds. (J). (ps-2). 1981. pap. 5.95 (*0-8224-4471-2*); Numbers & Number Values. (J). (ps-2). 1981. pap. 5.95 (*0-8224-4472-0*); Storytelling. (J). (ps-2). 1981. pap. 5.95

M

(0-8224-4473-9); Thinking Skills. (J). (ps-2). 1981. pap. 5.95 (0-8224-4474-7); Time. (J). (ps-2). 1981. pap. 5.95 (0-8224-4479-8); Words. (J). (ps-2). pap. 5.95 (0-8224-4480-1); (Makemaster Bk.). (J). (ps-2). 1981. pap. write for info. (0-318-55296-5) Fearon Teacher Aids.

Marzollo, Jean & Wick, Walter. I Spy Christmas. (I Spy Books Ser.). (FRE., Illus.). (J). 16.99 (0-590-24080-3) Scholastic Inc.

— I Spy Fantasy. (I Spy Books Ser.: Bk. 5).Tr. of C'est Moi l'Espion du Monde de la Fantaisie. (FRE., Illus.). (J). 16.99 (0-590-24340-3) Scholastic Inc.

— I Spy Fun House. (I Spy Books Ser.).Tr. of C'est Moi l'Espion du Parc d'Attractions. (FRE., Illus.). (J). 16.99 (0-590-24081-1) Scholastic Inc.

— I Spy Mystery. (I Spy Books Ser.).Tr. of C'est Moi l'Espion du Monde du Mystere. (FRE., Illus.). (J). 16.99 (0-590-24317-9) Scholastic Inc.

— I Spy Spooky Night. LC 96-931225. (I Spy Books Ser.).Tr. of C'est Moi l'Espion du Monde du Frisson. (FRE., Illus.). (J). 1996. 16.99 (0-590-16053-2) Scholastic Inc.

Marzollo, Jean & Widmer, Karherine M. Think! Draw! Write!, Level 2. 48p. (J). (gr. 4-6). 1982. 6.99 (0-8224-6947-2) Fearon Teacher Aids.

Marzollo, Jean & Widmer, Katherine M. Think! Draw! Write!, Level 1. (J). (gr. 1-3). 1982. pap. 6.99 (0-8224-6946-4) Fearon Teacher Aids.

Marzollo, Jean, et al. What's the Matter with Mother Goose? LC 99-26423. (Illus.). 32p. (J). (ps-k). 2000. lib. bdg. 14.89 (0-06-027277-5) HarpC.

Marzollo, Jean, jt. auth. see Wick, Walter.

Marzorati, Gerald, jt. ed. see Whittemore, Katharine.

***Marzorati, Giancarlo.** City Inventions. 2000. pap. 25.00 (88-7838-063-6) L'Arca IT.

Marzotto, Toni, et al. The Evolution of Public Policy: Cars & the Environment. LC 99-25923. 231p. 1999. lib. bdg. 55.00 (1-55587-858-X) L Rienner.

***Marzotto, Toni, et al.** The Evolution of Public Policy: Cars & the Environment. LC 99-25923. 231p. 1999. pap. 19.95 (1-55587-882-2) L Rienner.

Marzuki, S. & Dilts, Robert. Bintang Anda: A Game Process for Community Development. (Technical Notes Ser.: No. 18). 21p. (Orig.). (C). 1982. pap. 2.00 (0-932288-63-4) Ctr Intl Ed U of MA.

Marzulla, Nancie G. & Marzulla, Roger J. Property Rights: Understanding Government Takings & Environmental Regulation. LC 96-47384. 325p. 1997. text 79.00 (0-86587-554-5) Gov Insts.

Marzulla, Roger J., jt. auth. see Marzulla, Nancie G.

Marzulli, Francis N. & Maibach, Howard I., eds. Dermatotoxicology. 4th ed. 800p. 1991. 136.00 (1-56032-055-9) Hemisp Pub.

— Dermatotoxicology. 5th ed. 864p. 1996. boxed set 149.95 (1-56032-356-6) Hemisp Pub.

— Dermatotoxicology Methods: The Laboratory Worker's Ready Reference. 400p. 1997. pap. 59.95 (1-56032-672-7) Hemisp Pub.

Marzulli Larry. Survey of World Regional Geography. 326p. (C). 1990. 45.00 (0-536-57851-6) Pearson Custom.

Marzullo & Snyder. Manual de Liberacion para Obreros Cristianos.Tr. of Manual for the Deliverance Worker. (SPA.). 90p. 1994. 3.99 (958-95462-0-X, 550061) Editorial Unilit.

Marzullo, Evelyn. He Said, "Follow Me" 54p. 1992. pap. write for info. (1-892363-10-0) Christian Covenant.

Marzullo, Frank. The Battle for Your Mind. 19p. 1985. pap. write for info. (1-892363-00-3) Christian Covenant.

— Breaking Satan's Bondage: What Spirits Motivate You. 20p. 1997. pap. write for info. (1-892363-23-2) Christian Covenant.

— Breaking the Curses of Deuteronomy 27 & 28. 14p. 1995. pap. write for info. (1-892363-18-6) Christian Covenant.

— Can a Demon Have a Christian? 12p. 1991. pap. write for info. (1-892363-08-9) Christian Covenant.

— Deliverance from Spirits Named in the Bible. 28p. 1994. pap. write for info. (1-892363-14-3) Christian Covenant.

— Doing the Works of Jesus: Manifesting the Names of God. 20p. 1997. pap. write for info. (1-892363-21-6) Christian Covenant.

— Dying to Self. 12p. 1985. pap. 2.00 (1-892363-01-1) Christian Covenant.

— Escaping Satan's Prison. 48p. 1993. pap. write for info. (1-892363-13-5) Christian Covenant.

— Fighting & Winning the Spiritual Battle. 83p. 1996. pap. write for info. (1-892363-20-8) Christian Covenant.

— Healing the Broken Heart & the Wounded Spirit. 26p. 1987. pap. write for info. (1-892363-05-4) Christian Covenant.

— The Hidden Sin of Witchcraft & the Spirit of Jezebel. 22p. 1996. pap. write for info. (1-892363-19-4) Christian Covenant.

— How to Pray for Healing. 30p. 1988. pap. write for info. (1-892363-06-2) Christian Covenant.

— Incubus & Succubus. 16p. 1995. pap. write for info. (1-892363-15-1) Christian Covenant.

— Loneliness - The Killer. 32p. 1998. pap. write for info. (1-892363-25-9) Christian Covenant.

— Power in the Blood of Jesus. 16p. 1985. pap. write for info. (1-892363-02-X) Christian Covenant.

— Power in the Spoken Word. 19p. 1985. pap. write for info. (1-892363-03-8) Christian Covenant.

— Questions & Answers on Healing & Deliverance. 22p. 1995. pap. write for info. (1-892363-17-8) Christian Covenant.

— Reaching Your Potential. 84p. 1995. pap. write for info. (1-892363-16-X) Christian Covenant.

— Sound Mind, Not Fear: God's Formula for Positive Living Today. 20p. 1986. pap. write for info. (1-892363-04-6) Christian Covenant.

— The Spirit of the Bride of Satan. 16p. 1997. pap. write for info. (1-892363-22-4) Christian Covenant.

— To Conquer Anger. 22p. 1998. pap. write for info. (1-892363-24-0) Christian Covenant.

— Unforgiveness - An Obstacle to Healing. 22p. 1992. pap. write for info. (1-892363-09-7) Christian Covenant.

— Victory over Demonic Spirits. 28p. 1993. pap. write for info. (1-892363-12-7) Christian Covenant.

Marzullo, Frank & Snyder, Nina. The Baker's Son: From Pastry Chef to Evangelist. 67p. 1993. pap. write for info. (1-892363-11-9) Christian Covenant.

Marzullo, Frank & Snyder, Tom. A Manual for the Deliverance Worker. 112p. 1990. pap. write for info. (1-892363-07-0) Christian Covenant.

Marzullo, Giovanni. Month of Birth, Creativity, & the "Two Classes of Men" Vol. 1: A Prenatal Influence of the Sum's Radiation on the Left-Right "Configuration" of the Brain. LC 96-92663. 304p. 1996. 24.95 (0-9652322-9-8, 223) Per Aspera.

Marzzacco, Charles, jt. auth. see Deckey, George.

Marzzacco, Charles J. Determining the Common Ion Effect on the Solubility of Potassium Hydrogen Tartrate. Stanitski, Conrad L., ed. (Modular Laboratory Program in Chemistry Ser.). 12p. (C). 1996. pap. text 1.50 (0-87540-487-1, EQUL 487-1) Chem Educ Res.

Mas, Barbara Pheiffer. All about Nettles: Frequently Asked Questions. (FAQs All about Health Ser.). 96p. 1999. mass mkt. 2.99 (0-89529-971-2, Avery) Penguin Putnam.

Mas-Colell, Andrea. Microeconomic Theory. 1008p. 1995. pap., teacher ed. 34.00 (0-19-510268-1) OUP.

Mas-Colell, Andreu. The Theory of General Economic Equilibrium. (Econometric Society Monographs). 368p. 1985. text 80.00 (0-521-26514-2) Cambridge U Pr.

— The Theory of General Economic Equilibrium. (Econometric Society Monographs: No. 9). (Illus.). 391p. (C). 1990. pap. text 33.95 (0-521-38870-8) Cambridge U Pr.

Mas-Colell, Andreu & Hart, S., eds. Co-operation: Game Theoretic Approaches. LC 96-27102. (NATO ASI Series F: Computer & Systems Science). 315p. 1996. 94.50 (3-540-61311-0) Spr-Verlag.

Mas-Colell, Andreu, et al. Microeconomic Theory. (Illus.). 1008p. 1995. text 72.95 (0-19-507340-1) OUP.

Mas-Lopez, Edita, tr. The Last Poems of Miguel de Unamuno. LC 73-4295. 121p. 1974. 24.50 (0-8386-1288-1) Fairleigh Dickinson.

Mas, Marina & Rallo, John A. My Son, Yo-Yo: A Biography of the Early Years of Yo-Yo Ma. LC 97-195180. (Illus.). 150p. 1997. pap. text 18.95 (962-201-640-5, Pub. by Chinese Univ) U of Mich Pr.

Mas Masumoto, David. Epitaph for a Peach: Four Seasons on My Family Farm. LC 94-39527. 256p. 1996. pap. 13.00 (0-06-251025-8, Perennial) HarperTrade.

Mas Masumoto, David, see Masumoto, David Mas.

Masa, Xose & Virgos, Enrique M. Analysis & Geometry in Foliated Manifolds. 200p. 1995. text 61.00 (981-02-2159-2) World Scientific Pub.

Masaaki Kitahara. Tinnitus. LC 99-12777. (Illus.). 140p. 1988. 66.00 (0-89640-174-X) Igaku-Shoin.

Masabuchi, M., jt. auth. see Yang Wen-Jei.

Masada, E., jt. ed. see De Carli, A.

Masada, Hiroko, jt. auth. see Suleski, Ronald.

***Masagazi, Moses.** Inspirational Guidance. 28p. 1999. pap. write for info. (0-9674089-0-3) M Masagazi.

Masaharu, Takasaki. Takasaki Masaharu: An Architecture of Cosmology. LC 97-22469. (Illus.). 160p. (Orig.). 1998. pap. 35.00 (1-56898-121-X) Princeton Arch.

Masahiko, Aoki & Dore, Ronald, eds. The Japanese Firm: Sources of Competitive Strength. (Illus.). 424p. 1994. text 69.00 (0-19-828815-8) OUP.

Masahiro, Ota, ed. Correct Models of Parallel Computing. LC 96-79141. (Concurrent Systems Engineering Ser.: Vol. 49). 250p. (YA). (gr. 12). 1996. 98.00 (90-5199-310-2, 310-2) IOS Press.

Masai, Gui, tr. see Guisnel, Jean.

***Masaki, Ichiro.** Handbook of Intelligent Transportation. 700p. 1999. 89.00 (0-12-476640-4) Acad Pr.

Masaki, Tomoh, ed. Endothelium-Derived Factors & Vascular Functions: Proceedings of the Fourth International Symposium on Endothelium-Derived Factors, Tokyo, 7-9 December 1993. LC 94-16819. (International Congress Ser.: No. 1051). 270p. 1994. 191.50 (0-444-81669-0, Excerpta Medica) Elsevier.

***Masalha, Nur.** Imperial Israel & the Palestinians: The Politics of Expansion, 1967-2000. LC 00-27698. 2000. write for info. (0-7453-1620-4, Pub. by Pluto GBR) Stylus Pub VA.

Masalha, Nur-Eldeen. Expulsion of the Palestinians: The Concept of 'Transfer' in Zionist Political Thought, 1882-1948. (C). 1992. pap. 11.95 (0-88728-242-3) Inst Palestine.

Masalski, William J. How to Use the Spreadsheet As a Tool in the Secondary School Mathematics Classroom. 2nd ed. LC 99-19972. (Illus.). 76p. 1999. pap. 22.95 (0-87353-468-9) NCTM.

Masana, G. E. How to Advertise & Sell Your Wedding Photography the Easy Way. 2nd rev. ed. 63p. 1995. pap. 19.50 (0-934420-18-1) Studio Pr NE.

Masani, Pesi R. Norbert Wiener, 1894-1964. (Vita Mathematica Ser.). 402p. 1989. 99.50 (0-8176-2246-2) Birkhauser.

Masani, Pesi R., jt. auth. see Mandrekar, V. R.

Masani, Pesi R., ed. see Wiener, Norbert.

Masani, Zareer. Indian Tales of the Raj. (Illus.). 1988. pap. 16.95 (0-520-07127-1, Pub. by U CA Pr) Cal Prin Full Svc.

Masanobu, Abe, jt. auth. see Shirai, Katushiko.

Masanobu, K. History of Ikebana. 1996. pap. 23.95 (4-07-974558-3) Shufu No.

Masanori Fujita & Michihiko Ike. Wastewater Treatment Using Genetically Engineered Microorganisms. LC 94-60490. 185p. 1994. pap. 74.95 (1-56676-139-5) Technomic.

Masanori, Nakamura. The Japanese Monarchy, 1931-1991: Ambassador Grew & the Making of the "Symbol Emperor System" Bix, Herbert P. et al, trs. from JPN. LC 92-14157. (Japan in the Modern World). (Illus.). 224p. (C). (gr. 13). 1992. text 68.95 (1-56324-102-1, East Gate Bk) M E Sharpe.

— The Japanese Monarchy, 1931-1991: Ambassador Grew & the Making of the "Symbol Emperor System" Bix, Herbert P. et al, trs. from JPN. LC 92-14157. (Japan in the Modern World Ser.). (Illus.). 224p. (C). (gr. 13). 1992. pap. text 12.95 (1-56324-109-9, East Gate Bk) M E Sharpe.

***Masao, Kato.** Chinese Opening. (Intermediate to Advanced go Books Ser.). 1998. pap. text. write for info. (4-906574-33-5) KISEIDO.

Masao Miyoshi. Off Center: Power & Culture Relations Between Japan & the United States. (Convergences Ser.). 289p. (C). 1991. 32.00 (0-674-63175-7) HUP.

Masao, Rence I., jt. ed. see Ito, M.

Masao, Ten-Dan K. Kato's Attack & Kill. 1978. pap. 14.95 (4-87187-027-8, G27) Ishi Pr Intl.

Masaoka, Shiki. Songs from a Bamboo Village: Selected Tanka from Takenosato Uta. Goldstein, Sanford & Shinoda, Seishi, trs. 424p. 1998. pap. 16.95 (0-8048-2085-6) Tuttle Pubng.

Masar, Stephen A., ed. Wisconsin Progressives: The Charles R. Van Hise Papers: Guide to a Microfilm Edition. 70p. 1986. pap. write for info. (0-87020-237-5) Chadwyck-Healey.

Masar, Syed A. Schaum's Electric Power Systems. 224p. (C). 1997. pap. 14.95 (0-07-045917-7) McGraw.

Masarik, Al. Excuses to Be Outside. Robertson, Kirk, ed. (Windriver Ser.). 64p. 1986. pap. 6.00 (0-916918-32-7) Duck Down.

— Excuses to Be Outside. deluxe limited ed. Robertson, Kirk, ed. (Windriver Ser.). 64p. 1986. 25.00 (0-916918-33-5) Duck Down.

— Nonesuch Creek: Selected Poems, 1969 to '79. Robertson, Kirk, ed. LC 80-65779. (Windriver Ser.). 112p. (Orig.). 1980. pap. 4.50 (0-916918-12-2) Duck Down.

Masaru Takeuchi. Modern Spherical Functions. Toshinobu Nagura, tr. from JPN. LC 93-24648. (Translations of Mathematical Monographs: Vol. 135). (ENG.). 265p. 1994. text 130.00 (0-8218-4580-2, MMONO/135) Am Math.

Masaryk, J. H., jt. auth. see Gander, Walter.

Masaryk, Thomas G. Constructive Sociological Theory: The Forgotten Legacy of Thomas G. Masaryk. Imber, Jonathan B., ed. LC 93-45995. 347p. (C). 1994. 54.95 (1-56000-164-X) Transaction Pubs.

— Humanistic Ideals. Warren, W. Preston, tr. LC 79-124100. 132p. 1975. 25.00 (0-8387-7664-7) Bucknell U Pr.

— Ideals of Humanity, & How to Work. LC 79-90663. (Essay Index Reprint Ser.). 1977. 19.95 (0-8369-1306-X) Ayer.

— Ideals of Humanity & How to Work: Lectures Delivered in 1898 at the University of Prague. LC 72-135844. (Eastern Europe Collection). 1971. reprint ed. 16.95 (0-405-02786-9) Ayer.

— Modern Man & Religion. LC 74-107816. (Select Bibliographies Reprint Ser.). 1977. 26.95 (0-8369-5216-2) Ayer.

— On Thought & Life: Conversations with Karel Capek. Weatherall, Miles & Weatherall, R., trs. from CZE. LC 78-156689. (Essay Index Reprint Ser.). 1971. reprint ed. 18.95 (0-405-02782-6) Ayer.

— Der Selbstmord als Sociale Massenerscheinung der Modernen Civilisation. Nyiri, J. C., ed. & intro. by. (Philosophia Resources Library). (GER.). xvi, 245p. 1982. lib. bdg. 66.00 (3-88405-014-1) Philosophia Pr.

— Suicide & the Meaning of Civilization. Weist, William B. & Batson, Robert G., trs. LC 74-10877. (Heritage of Sociology Ser.). 1993. pap. text 2.45 (0-226-50933-8, P369) U Ch Pr.

Masashi & Kamon. Environmental Geotechnics, Vol. 1. 620p. 1996. 97.00 (90-5410-849-5) Ashgate Pub Co.

— Environmental Geotechnics, Vol. 2. 587p. 1996. 97.00 (90-5410-850-9) Ashgate Pub Co.

— Environmental Geotechnics, Vol. 3. 1997. 97.00 (90-5410-851-7) Ashgate Pub Co.

Masataka, Tokuda, jt. ed. see Khan, Akhtar S.

Masatomi, H., jt. ed. see Lewis, J. C.

Masatoshi. The Art of Netsuke Carving. (Illus.). 236p. 1992. reprint ed. 80.00 (0-8348-0265-1) Weatherhill.

Masavisut, Nitaya. S.E.A. Write Anthology of Thai Short Stories & Poems, 1. 132p. 1999. pap. text 12.95 (974-7100-68-1) U of Wash Pr.

Masavisut, Nitaya, et al, eds. Gender & Culture in Literature & Film East & West: Issues of Perception & Interpretation. (Literary Studies: Vol. 9). 320p. 1994. pap. text 20.00 (0-8248-1602-1) Coll Lang Ling & Lit.

Masavisut, Nitaya, et al. S.E.A. Write Anthology of Thai Short Stories & Poems. LC 97-941783. xviii, 149 p. 1996. write for info. (974-7047-75-6) AgBe Pub.

Masaya Shiraishi. Japanese Relations with Vietnam, 1951-1987. (Southeast Asia Program Ser.: No. 5). 174p. (Orig.). (C). 1990. pap. text 12.00 (0-87727-122-4) Cornell SE Asia.

Masayesva, Victor & Younger, Erin. Hopi Photographers, Hopi Images. LC 83-1301. (Illus.). 111p. reprint ed. pap. 34.50 (0-608-20410-2, 207166300002) Bks Demand.

Mascagni, P. Cavalleria Rusticana: Vocal Score. (ENG & ITA.). 152p. 1986. pap. 16.95 (0-7935-5367-9, 50338340) H Leonard.

— Cavalleria Rusticana Libretto. 20p. 1986. pap. 4.95 (0-7935-2617-5, 50340230) H Leonard.

Mascagni, Pietro. Cavalleria Rusticana in Full Score. 192p. pap. 12.95 (0-486-27866-2) Dover.

Mascall, Eric L. Importance of Being Human, No. 11--11. LC 74-12849. 118p. 1974. reprint ed. lib. bdg. 35.00 (0-8371-7761-8, MABH, Greenwood Pr) Greenwood.

— Saraband: The Memoirs of E. L. Mascall. (Illus.). 392p. 1993. 25.00 (0-85244-222-X, 961, Pub. by Gra1cewing) Morehouse Pub.

Mascall, Leonard. A Booke of Fishing with Hooke & Line (Taken from the Treatise of Fishing with an Angle) LC 72-6017. (English Experience Ser.: No. 542). 92p. 1973. reprint ed. 25.00 (90-221-0542-3) Walter J Johnson.

— A Booke of the Arte & Manner How to Plant & Graffe All Sortes of Trees. LC 74-80200. (English Experience Ser.: No. 679). 90p. 1974. reprint ed. 25.00 (90-221-0679-9) Walter J Johnson.

Mascara, Cynthia. Book Block for the Internet Resource Guide. 96p. 1999. pap. text. write for info. (0-8053-8433-2) Addison-Wesley.

— Internet Resource Guide for Nurses Package Nurses Pk 1/e 1999 Natnl Bundle. 96p. 1999. pap. text 16.88 (0-8053-8472-3) Benjamin-Cummings.

***Mascarelli, Gloria & Mascarelli, Robert.** The Prayer Connection: A True Story of Miracles. LC 99-74732. x, 230p. 1999. 21.95 (0-9673376-1-5); pap. 14.95 (0-9673376-0-7) Miracle Bk Pubs.

Mascarelli, Robert, jt. auth. see Mascarelli, Gloria.

Mascarello, Maria & Rodino, Luigi. Partial Differential Equations with Multiple Characteristics. LC 98-100498. (Mathematical Topics Ser.). 352 p. 1997. write for info. (3-05-501764-1) Akademie Verlag.

— Partial Differential Equations with Multiple Characteristics. 352p. 1997. 149.95 (3-527-40115-6) Wiley.

***Mascarenhas, A., et al, eds.** Self-Organized Processes in Semiconductor Alloys Vol. 583: Materials Research Society Symposium Proceedings. 2000. text 93.00 (1-55899-491-2) Materials Res.

Mascarenhas, Amyas. Deloitte & Touche: Accounts & Audit of Pension Schemes. 4th ed. 1997. pap. write for info. (0-406-05198-4, TRAA3, MICHIE) LEXIS Pub.

Mascarenhas, Amyas & Sienkiewics, Teresa. Touche Ross: Accounts & Audit of Pension Schemes. 2nd ed. 1991. pap. 84.00 (0-406-00348-3, U.K., MICHIE) LEXIS Pub.

Mascarenhas, Amyas & Turley, Stuart. Spicer's Practical Auditing. 18th ed. 1990. pap. 34.00 (0-406-12300-4, U.K., MICHIE) LEXIS Pub.

Mascarenhas, Lambert. In the Womb of Saudade: Stories of Goan Life. (C). 1994. 9.00 (81-7167-239-6, Pub. by Rupa) S Asia.

Mascarenhas, Mark. My World Cup. LC 97-71687. 1997. 50.00 (0-944142-34-6) Grantha.

Mascarenhas, Ophelia & Mbilinyi, Marjorie. Women in Tanzania: An Analytical Bibliography. 256p. 1983. 20.95 (91-7106-216-5, Pub. by Nordic Africa) Transaction Pubs.

Mascarenhas, Oswald A. Towards Measuring the Technological Impact of Multinational Corporations in the Less Developed Countries. Bruchey, Stuart, ed. LC 80-583. (Multinational Corporations Ser.). 1980. lib. bdg. 44.95 (0-405-13375-8) Ayer.

Mascarenhas, R. C. Comparative Political Economy of East & South Asia: A Critique of Development Policy & Management. LC 98-38454. (Illus.). 270p. 1999. text 75.00 (0-312-21843-5) St Martin.

— Government & the Economy in Australia & New Zealand: The Politics of Economic Policy Making. 454p. 1996. lib. bdg. 69.95 (1-57292-029-7) Austin & Winfield.

Mascarenhas, R. C. Government & the Economy in Australia & New Zealand: The Politics of Economic Policy Making. 454p. 1996. pap. 49.95 (1-57292-028-9) Austin & Winfield.

Mascarenhas, R. C. A Strategy for Rural Development: Dairy Cooperatives in India. 288p. (C). 1988. text 27.50 (0-8039-9548-2) Sage.

Mascarenhas, S. J., jt. auth. see Oswald, A. J.

Mascari, Claude J., ed. see Reid, Charles F., III.

***Mascari, Johnny.** My Light @ Night. Taff, Rebecca, ed. LC 99-97810. (Illus.). 32p. (J). (ps up). 2000. 15.95 (1-930413-00-9) Mascari & Co.

Mascaro, Angelo, jt. auth. see Kowalewski, Kim J.

Mascaro, Francisco. Rita de Casia - Dios Hablara Esta Noche. (SPA.). 134p. (Orig.). 1991. pap. text 10.00 (0-917049-55-1) Saeta.

Mascaro, Joan & Nespor, Marina, eds. Grammar in Progress: Glow Essays for Henk van Riemsdyk. (Studies in Generative Grammar). 300p. (Orig.). (C). 1990. pap. 123.10 (90-6765-417-5) Mouton.

Mascaro, Juan. Upanishads. (Orig.). 1976. 18.95 (0-8488-0339-6) Amereon Ltd.

Mascaro, Juan, tr. see Wyatt, Thomas.

Mascaro, Juan, tr. & intro. see Wyatt, Thomas.

Mascaro Y Porcar, Jose M., prologue by. Diccionario Medico: De Bosillo. 2nd deluxe ed. (SPA.). 632p. 1974. 39.95 (0-8288-5997-3, S13673) Fr & Eur.

Mascaulay, Colman, ed. Sikkim: Report of a Mission to Sikkim & the Tibetan Frontier, with a Memoir on Our Relation with Tibet. (Illus.). 105p. (C). 1977. reprint ed. 55.00 (0-89771-100-9, Pub. by Ratna Pustak Bhandar) St Mut.

Mascelli, Joseph V. The Five C's of Cinematography: Motion Picture Filming Techniques. LC 98-12705. (Illus.). 252p. 1998. reprint ed. pap. 29.95 (1-879505-41-X) Silman James Pr.

Mascenik, John, ed. Ports '80. LC 80-65719. 848p. 1980. pap. 8.00 (0-87262-108-1) Am Soc Civil Eng.

Mascenik, William, ed. see Benest, Frank.

Masceti, Manuela Dunn, jt. ed. see Lorie, Peter.

Mascetta, Joseph A. Chemistry the Easy Way. 3rd ed. 352p. 1996. pap. 12.95 (0-8120-9138-8) Barron.

An Asterisk (*) at the beginning of an entry indicates that the title is appearing for the first time.

— How to Prepare for the SAT II: Chemistry. 6th rev. ed. LC 98-6584. 330p. 1998. pap. 13.95 (*0-7641-0331-8*) Barron.

Mascetti, Daniela & Triossi, Amanda. Bulgari. (Illus.). 256p. 1996. 75.00 (*0-7892-0202-6*) Abbeville Pr.

— Earrings: From Antiquity to the Present. LC 99-70951. (Illus.). 224p. 1999. pap. 34.95 (*0-500-28161-0*, Pub. by Thames Hudson) Norton.

— The Necklace: From Antiquity to the Present. LC 96-48107. (Illus.). 224p. 1997. 60.00 (*0-8109-3682-8*, Pub. by Abrams) Time Warner.

Mascetti, Daniela, jt. auth. see Bennett, David.

Mascetti, Manuela D. Christian Mysticism. LC 97-41749. (Illus.). 224p. (J). 1998. 24.45 (*0-7868-6330-7*, Pub. by Hyperion) Time Warner.

Mascetti, Manuela D. Judaic Mysticism. LC 97-19305. (Illus.). 224p. (J). 1997. 24.45 (*0-7868-6329-3*, Pub. by Hyperion) Time Warner.

Mascetti, Manuela D. Vampire: The Complete Guide to the World of the Undead. (Illus.). 224p. 1994. pap. 14.95 (*0-14-023801-8*, Viking Studio) Studio Bks.

Mascetti, Manuela D., jt. auth. see Lorie, Peter.

Mascetti, Manuela D., jt. compiled by see Lorie, Peter.

Mascetti, Manuela Dunn. Buddha Box. (Illus.). 96p. 1999. 22.95 (*0-8118-1950-7*) Chronicle Bks.

***Mascetti, Manuela Dunn.** The Kama Sutra Box: The Rules of Love & Erotic Practice. 2000. 24.95 (*0-609-60726-X*) Harmony Bks.

Mascetti, Manuela Dunn, jt. auth. see Lorie, Peter.

Masch, M. Kathleen, jt. auth. see Wells, Carolyn C.

Maschal, Richard. Wet-Wall Tattoos: Ben Long & the Art of Fresco. (Illus.). 212p. 1998. pap. 12.95 (*0-89587-215-3*) Blair.

Maschio, G., et al, eds. Hypertension & Renal Disease. (Contributions to Nephrology Ser.: Vol. 54). (Illus.). viii, 232p. 1987. 29.75 (*3-8055-4372-7*) S Karger.

Maschio, Thomas. To Remember the Faces of the Dead: The Plenitude of Memory in Southwestern New Britain. LC 93-32388. 256p. 1994. 50.00 (*0-299-14090-3*); pap. 23.95 (*0-299-14094-6*) U of Wis Pr.

Maschke, Joachim. Moose Als Bioindikatoren Von Schwermetall-Immissionen. (Bryophytorum Bibliotheca Ser.: No. 22). (GER., Illus.). 492p. 1981. lib. bdg. 120.00 (*3-7682-1320-X*) Lubrecht & Cramer.

Maschke, Karen, ed. Educational Equity. LC 96-51812. (Gender & American Law Ser.: Vol. 4). (Illus.). 336p. 1997. text 72.00 (*0-8153-2518-5*) Garland.

— The Employment Context. LC 96-39889. (Gender & American Law Ser.: Vol. 3). (Illus.). 375p. 1997. text 78.00 (*0-8153-2517-7*) Garland.

— Feminist Legal Theories, Pt. 2. LC 96-51825. (Gender & American Law Ser.: Vol. 7). 328p. 1997. text 72.00 (*0-8153-2521-5*) Garland.

— Gender & American Law: The Impact of the Law on the Lives of Women, 7 vols. (Illus.). 2550p. 1997. 494.00 (*0-8153-2514-2*) Garland.

— The Legal Response to Violence Against Women. LC 96-39890. (Gender & American Law Ser.: Vol. 5). 368p. 1997. text 80.00 (*0-8153-2519-3*) Garland.

— Pornography, Sex Work, & Hate Speech, Pt. 1. LC 96-51517. (Gender & American Law Ser.: Vol. 6). 464p. 1997. text 84.00 (*0-8153-2520-7*) Garland.

— Reproduction, Sexuality, & the Family. LC 96-39903. (Gender & American Law Ser.: Vol. 2). (Illus.). 392p. 1997. text 81.00 (*0-8153-2516-9*) Garland.

— Women & the American Legal Order. LC 96-39902. (Gender & American Law Ser.: Vol. 1). (Illus.). 360p. 1997. text 77.00 (*0-8153-2515-0*) Garland.

Maschke, Karen J. Litigation, Courts, Women Workers. LC 88-36993. 118p. 1989. 45.00 (*0-275-93065-3*, C3065, Praeger Pubs) Greenwood.

Maschke, Kathy L., ed. see Fenton, Julia A. & Carlozzi, Annette M.

Maschke, Ruby A. Bible Puzzles for Children. 64p. (J). (gr. 4-6). 1986. pap. 11.00 (*0-8170-1095-5*) Judson.

— Bible Puzzles for Children, Vol. 2. 64p. (J). 1991. pap. 11.00 (*0-8170-1165-X*) Judson.

— Bible Puzzles for Children Vol. 3: The Words of Jesus. 64p. (J). (gr. 1-8). 1998. pap. 11.00 (*0-8170-1295-8*) Judson.

Maschke, Thomas & Burian, Peter K. Minolta Maxxum 800SI, 400SI & 300SI. (Magic Lantern Guides Ser.). (Illus.). 176p. Date not set. pap. 19.95 (*1-883403-57-X*, Silver Pixel Pr) Saunders Photo.

Maschke, Thomas & Burian, Peter K. Minolta Maxxum 600si. Ohlig, Hayley, tr. from GER. (Magic Lantern Guides Ser.). (Illus.). 176p. (Orig.). (C). 1995. pap. 19.95 (*1-883403-34-0*, H 120, Silver Pixel Pr) Saunders Photo.

Maschke, Thomas, jt. auth. see Burian, Peter K.

Maschko, Richard. Die Villdemslekre Im Griechischen Recht. Vlastos, Gregory, ed. LC 78-19369. (Morals & Law in Ancient Greece Ser.). 1979. reprint ed. lib. bdg. 18.95 (*0-405-11560-1*) Ayer.

Maschler, Chaninah, tr. see Duhem, Pierre.

Maschler, Michael B., jt. auth. see Aumann, Robert J.

***Maschmaun, Melita.** Encountering Bliss. 269p. 1999. 150.00 (*81-208-1541-6*, Pub. by Motilal Bnarsidass); pap. 90.00 (*81-208-1571-8*, Pub. by Motilal Bnarsidass) St Mut.

Maschmeyer, A. H. Increasing the Durability of Fine-Pitch Precision Aluminum Gears. (Technical Papers: Vol. P219.06). (Illus.). 38p. 1956. pap. text 30.00 (*1-55589-252-3*) AGMA.

Maschmeyer, Gloria J. & Wedin, John. Paradise of the North: Alaska's Prince William Sound. (Illus.). 90p. 1995. pap. 19.95 (*0-936425-35-0*) Greatland Graphics.

Maschner, H. D. Darwinian Archaeologies. (Interdisciplinary Contributions to Archaeology Ser.). (Illus.). 282p. (C). 1996. 51.00 (*0-306-45328-2*, Plenum Trade) Perseus Pubng.

Maschner, Herbert D., jt. auth. see Ames, Kenneth.

Maschner, Herbert D., jt. auth. see Ames, Kenneth M.

***Maschwitz, David E. & Cook, Edwin F.** Revision of the Nearctic Species of Polypedilum (Polypedilum) & Polypedilum (Uresipedilum) (Diptera: Chironomidae) LC 98-66937. (Bulletin New Ser.: Vol. 12, No. 3). (Illus.). 150p. 2000. pap. text 25.00 (*0-86727-130-2*) Ohio Bio Survey.

Masci, Joseph R. Outpatient Management of HIV Infection. 2nd rev. ed. (Illus.). 448p. (C). (gr. 13). 1996. spiral bd. 39.95 (*0-8151-6144-1*, 25691) Mosby Inc.

Masci, Paul, jt. auth. see Kendall, Philip.

Mascia, Janet L., jt. auth. see Bixler, David P.

***Mascia-Lees, Frances E. & Black, Nancy Johnson.** Gender & Anthropology. 128p. 1999. pap. 9.95 (*1-57766-066-8*) Waveland Pr.

***Mascia-Lees, Frances E. & Sharpe, Patricia.** Taking a Stand in a Postfeminist World: Toward an Engaged Cultural Criticism. LC 99-59783. (C). 2000. pap. text 19.95 (*0-7914-4716-2*) State U NY Pr.

— Taking a Stand in a Postfeminist World: Toward an Engaged Cultural Criticism. LC 99-59783. (C). 2000. text 59.50 (*0-7914-4715-4*) State U NY Pr.

Mascia-Lees, Frances E. & Sharpe, Patricia, eds. Tattoo, Torture, Mutilation, & Adornment: The Denaturalization of the Body in Culture & Text. LC 91-21296. (SUNY Series, The Body in Culture, History, & Religion). 172p. (C). 1992. pap. text 21.95 (*0-7914-1066-8*) State U NY Pr.

Mascia-Less, Frances E., ed. Human Sexuality in Biocultural Perspective: A Special Issue of the Journal of Medical Anthropology. 103p. 1989. pap. text 36.00 (*2-88124-347-9*) Gordon & Breach.

Masciana, Edmond. Shortcuts on Wine: Everything the Wine Lover Needs to Know. 160p. 1996. pap. 10.95 (*0-88496-404-3*) Capra Pr.

Masciandaro, Franco. Dante As Dramatist: The Myth of the Earthly Paradise & Tragic Vision in the "Divine Comedy" LC 91-2536. 224p. (C). 1991. text 32.50 (*0-8122-3069-8*) U of Pa Pr.

Masciantonio, Rudolph. Build Your English Word Power with Latin Numbers. 1997. pap. text, teacher ed. 10.00 (*0-86516-392-8*); pap. text, student ed. write for info. (*0-86516-354-5*) Bolchazy-Carducci.

***Masciantonio, Rudolph.** The Classical Heritage in America: A Curriculum Resource. (Illus.). 100p. 2000. pap. 33.00 (*0-9662763-4-5*, 1672004) Campanian Soc.

Masciantonio, Rudolph. Greco Roman Sports & Games. 64p. (YA). (gr. 7-12). 1991. spiral bd. 4.50 (*0-939507-28-5*, B 314) Amer Classical.

— Latin, the Language of the Health Sciences. (Illus.). 42p. (J). (gr. 7-12). 1992. spiral bd. 4.05 (*0-939507-43-9*, B313) Amer Classical.

— Legal Latin. (ENG, GRE & LAT.). 82p. 1992. spiral bd. 7.75 (*0-939507-22-6*, B312) Amer Classical.

— Star Trek with Latin. 39p. 1991. spiral bd. 4.25 (*0-939507-27-7*, B 311) Amer Classical.

***Masciarelli, James P.** Powerskills: Building Top-Level Relationships for Bottom-Line Results. LC 99-69863. 336p. 2000. 29.95 (*0-9677111-1-8*) Nimbus Pr MA.

Mascie-Taylor, C. G., ed. Biosocial Aspects of Social Class. (Biosocial Society Ser.: No. 2). (Illus.). 160p. 1990. 55.00 (*0-19-857724-9*) OUP.

Mascie-Taylor, C. G. & Bogin, Barry, eds. Human Variability & Plasticity. (Studies in Biological Anthropology: No. 15). (Illus.). 255p. (C). 1995. text 57.95 (*0-521-45399-2*) Cambridge U Pr.

Mascie-Taylor, C. G. & Lasker, Gabriel W., eds. Applications of Biological Anthropology to Human Affairs. (Cambridge Studies in Biological Anthropology: No. 8). (Illus.). 262p. (C). 1991. text 69.95 (*0-521-38112-6*) Cambridge U Pr.

Mascie-Taylor, C. G. & Ulijaszek, Stanley J., eds. Anthropometry: The Individual & the Population. (Studies in Biological Anthropology: No. 13). (Illus.). 227p. (C). 1994. text 57.95 (*0-521-41798-8*) Cambridge U Pr.

Mascie-Taylor, C. G., jt. ed. see Boyce, A. J.

Mascie-Taylor, C. G., jt. ed. see Lasker, G. W.

Mascie-Taylor, C. G., jt. ed. see Lasker, Gabriel W.

Mascie-Taylor, C. G., jt. ed. see Rosetta, L.

Masciello, A. J. Mattino: An Intermediate Italian Grammar Book. 280p. 1995. pap. 16.95 (*0-88962-323-6*) Mosaic.

Mascio, Barbara & Mascio, Richard. Playing the Hand Life Dealt & Winning the Jackpot! Auto-Immune Illness. LC 96-230357. (Illus.). 100p. (Orig.). 1996. pap. 10.95 (*0-9653612-4-1*, AIBM-1) Harmony Publng.

Mascio, Richard, jt. auth. see Mascio, Barbara.

Masciocchi, C. & Barile, A. Radiological Imaging of Sports Injuries. LC 97-12401. (Medical Radiology Ser.). 280p. 1997. write for info. (*3-540-60870-2*) Spr-Verlag.

Mascioli, George, Sr. Jokes & Quotes for Your Answering Machine. 1991. 8.95 (*0-533-09359-7*) GEM Pub NY.

Mascioli, George E. On the Throne Reading. LC 94-96034. 1994. pap. text 12.95 (*0-9644336-0-5*) GEM Pub NY.

Mascitelli. Diccionario de Terminos Marxistos. (SPA.). 416p. 1979. pap. 19.95 (*0-8288-4766-5*, S50073) Fr & Eur.

Mascitelli, Ronald. The Growth Warriors: Creating Sustainable Global Advantage for America's Technology Industries. LC 98-60147. (Illus.). 450p. 1999. 34.95 (*0-9662697-0-5*) Technol Perspect.

Mascle, A., et al, eds. Cenozoic Foreland Basins of Western Europe. (Geological Society Special Publication Ser.: No. 134). 400p. 1998. 117.00 (*1-86239-015-0*, Pub. by Geol Soc Pub Hse) AAPG.

Mascle, Alain, ed. Hydrocarbon & Petroleum Geology of France. LC 94-6892. (Special Publication of the European Association of Petroleum Geoscientists: Vol. 4). 1994. write for info. (*3-540-57732-7*) Spr-Verlag.

— Hydrocarbon & Petroleum Geology of France. LC 94-6892. (Special Publication of the European Association of Petroleum Geoscientists: Vol. 4). 1994. 270.95 (*0-387-57732-7*) Spr-Verlag.

***Mascle, Deanna.** Kentucky Kisses. 1999. mass mkt. 5.99 (*0-8217-6437-3*) Kensgtn Pub Corp.

— Moon Hunter. (Zebra Splendor Historical Romances Ser.). 288p. 2000. mass mkt. 4.99 (*0-8217-6619-8*, Zebra Kensgtn) Kensgtn Pub Corp.

Mascle, George, jt. auth. see Debelmas, Jacques.

Mascola, Marilyn. Charles Schulz. (Reaching Your Goal Ser.: Set II). (Illus.). 24p. (J). (gr. 1-4). 1989. lib. bdg. 18.60 (*0-86592-429-5*) Rourke Enter.

— Ray Kroc. (Reaching Your Goal Ser.: Set II). (Illus.). 24p. (J). (gr. 1-4). 1989. lib. bdg. 18.60 (*0-86592-433-3*) Rourke Enter.

— Ray Kroc, Reading Level 2. (Reaching Your Goal Bks.: Set II). (Illus.). 24p. (J). (gr. 1-4). 1989. 10.95 (*0-685-58802-5*) Rourke Corp.

Mascola, Marilyn, ed. Reaching Your Goal, 7 bks. (Illus.). 192p. (J). (gr. 1-4). 1989. lib. bdg. 130.20 (*0-86592-425-2*) Rourke Enter.

— Reaching Your Goal, 8 bks., Set II, Reading Level 2. (Illus.). 192p. (J). (gr. 1-4). 1989. 87.60 (*0-685-58797-5*) Rourke Corp.

Mascolini, Marcia, jt. auth. see Allen, Roberta.

Mascolo, M. F. & Griffin, S. What Develops in Emotional Development? Perspectives on Nature, Evolution & Function. LC 98-16309. (Emotions, Personality, & Psychotherapy Ser.). (Illus.). 330p. (C). 1998. text 54.50 (*0-306-45722-9*, Kluwer Plenum) Kluwer Academic.

Mascomm Associates Circle Education Staff, ed. see Donofrio, Phyllis.

Mascorro, J. A., jt. ed. see Barber, V. C.

Mascott, Cynthia. Enchanted Summer: A Romantic Guide to Cape Cod, Nantucket & Martha's Vineyard. 1998. pap. text 13.95 (*1-55650-818-2*) Hunter NJ.

***Mascott, Cynthia.** Maine, New Hampshire, Vermont, Massachusetts, Rhode Island, Connecticut. (Rails-to-Trails Ser.). (Illus.). 256p. 2000. pap. 14.95 (*0-7627-0449-7*) Globe Pequot.

Mascrranahas, M. & Justa, H. R., eds. Value Education in Schools & Other Essays. 150p. 1989. text 15.95 (*81-220-0112-2*, Pub. by Konark Pubs Pvt Ltd) Advent Bks Div.

Masdeu, Joseph, et al, eds. Gait Disturbances in the Elderly. LC 97-4217. (Illus.). 272p. 1997. text 83.00 (*0-316-54915-0*, Little Brwn Med Div) Lppncott W & W.

Mase, G. E. Continuum Mechanics. (Schaum's Outline Ser.). 256p. (C). 1996. pap. 15.95 (*0-07-040663-4*) McGraw.

Mase, G. Thomas, jt. auth. see Mase, George E.

Mase, George E. & Mase, G. Thomas. Continuum Mechanics for Engineers. (Illus.). 176p. 1991. lib. bdg. 79.95 (*0-8493-8830-9*, QA808) CRC Pr.

— Continuum Mechanics for Engineers. 2nd ed. LC 99-14604. 400p. 1999. boxed set 79.95 (*0-8493-1855-6*) CRC Pr.

— Solutions Manual for Continuum Mechanics for Engineers. LC 92-42972. 1992. lib. bdg. write for info. (*0-8493-8862-7*, CRC Reprint) Franklin.

Masear, Victoria R. Primary Care Orthopedics. (Illus.). 336p. 1995. text 60.00 (*0-7216-5436-3*, W B Saunders Co) Harcrt Hlth Sci Grp.

Masefield, Constance, jt. ed. see Masefield, John.

Masefield, Geoffrey B. A Short History of Agriculture in the British Colonies. LC 77-26015. 179p. 1978. reprint ed. lib. bdg. 55.00 (*0-313-20094-7*, MAAG, Greenwood Pr) Greenwood.

Masefield, John. Bird of Dawning or the Fortune of the Sea. lib. bdg. 24.95 (*0-8488-2003-7*) Amereon Ltd.

— Jim Davis. 1976. 22.95 (*0-8488-1093-7*) Amereon Ltd.

— Sea Life in Nelson's Time. LC 75-75513. (Select Bibliographies Reprint Ser.). 1977. 24.95 (*0-8369-5011-9*) Ayer.

— Tarpaulin Muster. LC 73-132120. (Short Story Index Reprint Ser.). 1977. 17.95 (*0-8369-3677-9*) Ayer.

Masefield, John, ed. My Favourite English Poems. LC 75-76947. (Granger Index Reprint Ser.). 1977. 21.95 (*0-8369-6028-9*) Ayer.

— Sailor's Garland. LC 70-80376. (Granger Index Reprint Ser.). 1977. 48.36 (*0-8369-6108-0*) Ayer.

Masefield, John & Masefield, Constance, eds. Essays, Moral & Polite, 1660-1714. LC 78-157966. (Essay Index Reprint Ser.). 1977. reprint ed. 19.95 (*0-8369-2243-3*) Ayer.

Masefield, Muriel A. The Story of Fanny Burney. LC 73-21629. (English Biography Ser.: No. 31). 1974. lib. bdg. 75.00 (*0-8383-1786-3*) M S G Haskell Hse.

— Women Novelists from Fanny Burney to George Eliot. LC 67-23244. (Essay Index Reprint Ser.). 1977. 19.95 (*0-8369-0689-6*) Ayer.

Masefield, P., tr. from PLI. Vimana Stories. (C). 1988. 71.00 (*0-86013-272-2*, Pub. by Pali Text) Elsevier.

Masefield, P., jt. tr. see Kyaw, U Ba.

Masefield, Peter. Divine Revelation in Pali Buddhism. 2nd ed. 187p. 1995. pap. 14.00 (*955-9028-02-2*) Paul & Co Pubs.

Masefield, Peter, tr. from PLI. The Udana. 218p. (C). 1994. 37.00 (*0-86013-311-7*) Wisdom MA.

Masefield, Peter & Wiebe, Donald, eds. Aspects of Religion Vol. 18: Essays in Honour of Ninian Smart. LC 94-15794. (Toronto Studies in Religion: Vol. 18). VII, 417p. (C). 1995. text 59.95 (*0-8204-2237-1*) P Lang Pubng.

Masefield, Peter, tr. see Dhammapala.

Masefield, Richard. Brimstone. large type ed. 544p. 1988. 27.99 (*0-7089-1774-7*) Ulverscroft.

— Chalkhill Blue. large type ed. 576p. 1985. 27.99 (*0-7089-1269-9*) Ulverscroft.

Masek, Carrie S., et al, eds. Proceedings: Papers from the Parasession on Language & Behavior. LC 81-82977. 274p. 1981. pap. 8.00 (*0-914203-16-9*) Chicago Ling.

Masel, Richard I. Priniples of Adsorption & Reaction on Solid Surfaces. LC 95-17776. (Chemical Engineering Ser.). 824p. 1996. 94.95 (*0-471-30392-5*, Wiley-Interscience) Wiley.

Maselli, Christopher P. Escape from Jungle Island. LC 98-12277. (Commander Kellie & the Superkids' Early Adventures Ser.). (J). 1998. pap. write for info. (*1-57562-217-3*) K Copeland Pubns.

— In Pursuit of the Enemy. LC 98-12276. (Commander Kellie & the Superkids' Early Adventures Ser.). (J). 1998. pap. write for info. (*1-57562-218-1*) K Copeland Pubns.

— The Mysterious Presence. LC 97-46152. (Commander Kellie & the Superkids' Early Adventures Ser.). 1998. pap. write for info. (*1-57562-215-7*) K Copeland Pubns.

— The Quest for the Second Half. LC 98-12278. (Commander Kellie & the Superkids' Early Adventures Ser.). (J). 1998. pap. write for info. (*1-57562-216-5*) K Copeland Pubns.

Maselli, Daniel & Scottas, Beat, eds. Research Partnership for Common Concerns. 192p. 1996. pap. text 32.95 (*3-8258-2987-1*) Transaction Pubs.

Maselli, Frank. Seminars - The Emotional Dynamic: Advanced Presentation Techniques for Financial Professionals. 230p. (Orig.). 1997. pap. 24.99 (*1-57502-412-8*, PO1276) Morris Pubng.

Masellis, M., ed. The Management of Mass Burn Casualties & Fire Disasters. 352p. (C). 1993. text 178.50 (*0-7923-8804-6*) Kluwer Academic.

Masello, David. Architecture Without Rules: The Houses of Marcel Breuer & Herbert Beckhard. (Illus.). 176p. 1996. pap. 19.95 (*0-393-31375-1*, Norton Paperbks) Norton.

— New York's 50 Best Art in Public Places. LC 99-35693. (Illus.). 128p. 1999. pap. 12.00 (*1-885492-80-4*) City & Co.

Masello, Robert. Fallen Angels... & Spirits of the Dark: Demons, Fiends, & Spirits of the Dark. LC 94-16797. 240p. (Orig.). 1994. pap. 10.00 (*0-399-51889-4*, Perigee Bks) Berkley Pub.

— Raising Hell: A Concise History of the Black Arts & Those Who Dared Practice Them. LC 96-11323. 288p. 1996. pap. 13.95 (*0-399-52238-7*, Perigee Bks) Berkley Pub.

— The Things Your Father Never Taught You. LC 95-12474. (Illus.). 1995. pap. 120.00 (*0-399-52168-2*, Perigee Bks) Berkley Pub.

— The Things Your Father Never Taught You. LC 95-12474. (Illus.). 240p. 1995. pap. 12.00 (*0-399-52167-4*, Perigee Bks) Berkley Pub.

Masemann, Vandra L. & Welch, Anthony R., eds. Tradition, Modernity & Post-Modernity in Comparative Education. LC 97-51803. 248p. 1998. 37.00 (*0-7923-4959-8*) Kluwer Academic.

Masenthal, Basil. The Skippers Pocketbook. (Illus.). 128p. 1999. pap. (*1-898660-58-1*) Fernhurst Bks.

Maser, Chris. Ecological Diversity in Sustainable Development: The Vital & Forgotten Dimension. LC 99-229014. 432p. 1999. 39.95 (*1-56670-377-8*) Lewis Pubs.

— Forest Primeval: The Natural History of an Ancient Forest. LC 89-31775. 1989. 25.00 (*0-87156-683-4*, Pub. by Sierra) Random.

— Leadership & Shared Vision. LC 98-216818. (Sustainable Community Development Ser.). 272p. 1998. per. 39.95 (*1-57444-188-4*) St Lucie Pr.

— Mammals of the Pacific Northwest: From the Coast to the High Cascades. LC 98-7570. (Illus.). 512p. 1998. pap. 26.95 (*0-87071-438-4*) Oreg St U Pr.

— Resolving Environmental Conflict: Towards Sustainable Community Development. 224p. 1995. per. 44.95 (*1-57444-007-1*) St Lucie Pr.

— Sustainable Community Development: Principles & Concepts. 280p. (Orig.). 1996. per. 44.95 (*1-57444-070-5*) St Lucie Pr.

— Sustainable Forestry: Philosophy, Science & Economics. LC 94-5192. (Illus.). 400p. 1994. per. 41.95 (*1-884015-16-6*) St Lucie Pr.

Maser, Chris & Beaton, Charles R. Setting the Stage for Sustainable Community Development. LC 98-161149. (Sustainable Community Development Ser.). 1998. lib. bdg. 34.95 (*1-57444-187-6*) Lewis Pubs.

Maser, Chris & Sidell, James. From the Forest to the Sea: The Ecology of Wood in Streams, Rivers, Estuaries, & Oceans. LC 94-11654. (Illus.). 216p. 1994. boxed set 31.95 (*1-884015-17-4*) St Lucie Pr.

Maser, Chris & Silberstein, Jane. Sustainable Community Development Planning for Conscious Living. (Sustainable Community Development Ser.). 2000. 39.95 (*1-56670-325-5*) Lewis Pubs.

Maser, Chris, jt. auth. see Beaton, Charles R.

Maser, Chris, jt. auth. see Borchers, Jeffrey G.

Maser, Chris, jt. auth. see Li, C. Y.

Maser, Daniel C., jt. ed. see Hoffmann, John M.

Maser, Edward A. Drawings by Johann Michael Rottmayr. LC 80-53676. (Illus.). 124p. (Orig.). 1980. pap. 10.00 (*0-935573-07-0*) D & A Smart Museum.

Maser, Edward A., frwd. Alumni Who Collect I: Drawings from the Sixteenth Century to the Present, Vol. I. LC 82-70634. (Illus.). 78p. (Orig.). 1982. pap. text 3.00 (*0-935573-09-7*) D & A Smart Museum.

Maser, Edward A., frwd. German & Austrian Painting of the Eighteenth Century. LC 78-55418. (Illus.). 56p. (Orig.). 1978. pap. 3.00 (*0-935573-05-4*) D & A Smart Museum.

Maser, Frederick E. How to Write a Local Church History. 10p. 1990. pap. 2.00 (*1-880927-16-0*) Gen Comm Arch.

— Richard Allen. 33p. 1976. pap. 1.00 (*1-880927-07-1*) Gen Comm Arch.

M

An Asterisk (*) at the beginning of an entry indicates that the title is appearing for the first time.

— The Story of John Wesley's Sisters: or Seven Sisters in Search of Love. LC 88-81533. (Illus.). 128p. (Orig.). 1988. 15.95 (*0-914960-89-X*); pap. 12.95 (*0-914960-68-7*) Academy Bks.

— Susanna Wesley. 4th ed. 31p. 1987. reprint ed. pap. 1.00 (*1-880927-01-2*) Gen Comm Arch.

Maser, Frederick E., jt. auth. see Simpson, Robert D.

Maser, H., tr. see Gauss, Karl.

Maser, Jack D. Depression & Expressive Behavior. 128p. (C). 1987. text 29.95 (*0-89859-999-7*) L Erlbaum Assocs.

Maser, Jack D., et al, eds. Handbook of Antisocial Behavior. LC 96-53445. 600p. 1997. 135.00 (*0-471-12452-4*) Wiley.

Maser, Jack D. & Cloninger, C. Robert, eds. Comorbidity of Mood & Anxiety Disorders. 867p. 1990. text 78.00 (*0-88048-324-5*, 8324) Am Psychiatric.

Maser, Jack D. & Rachman, Stanley J., eds. Panic Psychological Perspectives. 392p. 1988. text 89.95 (*0-8058-0091-3*) L Erlbaum Assocs.

Maser, Jack D., jt. ed. see Tuma, Hussain A.

Maser, Jack D., jt. ed. see Wolfe, Barry E.

Maser, Kenneth R. Ground Penetrating Radar Surveys to Characterize Pavement Layer Thickness Variations at GPR Sites. 50p. (C). 1994. pap. text 10.00 (*0-309-05801-5*, SHRP-P-397) SHRP.

M

Maser, Lou, jt. auth. see Raingruber, Bob.

Maser, Peter. Berathung der Armuth: Das Soziale Wirken des Barons Hans Ernst von Kottwitz Zwischen Aufklarung und Erweckungsbewegung in Berlin und Schlesien. (Forschungen zur Praktischen Theologie Ser.: Bd. 10). (GER.). 239p. 1991. 45.80 (*3-631-43679-3*) P Lang Pubng.

Masera, M. & Rilke, O. Dried Flowers: Stylish Arrangements to Decorate Your Home. (Illus.). 160p. 1996. pap. 19.95 (*0-7063-7461-4*, Pub. by WrLock) Sterling.

Masera, Rainer S. An Increasing Role for the ECU: A Character in Search of a Script. LC 87-3747. (Essays in International Finance Ser.: No. 167). 50p. 1987. pap. text 10.00 (*0-88165-074-9*) Princeton U Int Finan Econ.

***Masereel, Frans.** The Idea & Story Without Words. LC 99-54789. (Illus.). 160p. 2000. 25.00 (*1-57062-585-9*, Pub. by Shambhala Pubns) Random.

Masereel, Frans. Passionate Journey: A Novel in 165 Woodcuts. (Illus.). 160p. 1994. reprint ed. 14.00 (*0-87286-174-0*) City Lights.

***Masereel, Frans.** The Sun: A Novel Told in 63 Woodcuts. LC 99-89835. 2000. 25.00 (*1-57062-718-5*, Pub. by Shambhala Pubns) Random.

Maseri, Attilio. Ischemic Heart Disease. LC 95-17707. 1995. text 126.00 (*0-443-07910-2*) Church.

Maseri, Attilio, ed. Hammersmith Cardiology Workshop Series Vol. 2: 1985. LC 85-24360. (Illus.). 244p. 1985. reprint ed. pap. 75.70 (*0-7837-9247-6*, 204715300002) Bks Demand.

Maseri, Attilio, et al, eds. Hammersmith Cardiology Workshop Series, Vol. 3. fac. ed. LC 85-24360. (Illus.). 315p. pap. 97.70 (*0-7837-7141-X*, 204715300003) Bks Demand.

Maseri, Attilio & Goodwin, John F., eds. Hammersmith Cardiology Workshop Series, Vol. 1. LC 85-24360. 349p. 1984. reprint ed. pap. 108.20 (*0-608-00276-3*, 204715300001) Bks Demand.

Masetto, Antonio Dal, see Dal Masetto, Antonio.

***Mash & Wolfe.** Abnormal Child Psychology. 2nd ed. (C). 2001. text 56.25 (*0-534-55413-X*) Wadsworth Pub.

Mash, Eric J. & Barkley, Russell A., eds. Child Psychopathology. LC 96-4857. 650p. 1996. lib. bdg. 66.00 (*1-57230-065-5*) Guilford Pubns.

— Treatment of Childhood Disorders. 2nd ed. LC 98-24806. 771p. 1998. lib. bdg. 69.95 (*1-57230-276-3*, C0276) Guilford Pubns.

Mash, Eric J. & Terdal, Leif G., eds. Assessment of Childhood Disorders. 3rd ed. LC 97-5159. 800p. 1997. lib. bdg. 75.00 (*1-57230-194-5*) Guilford Pubns.

Masha. Singing Words. LC 79-38605. (Granger Index Reprint Ser.). 1977. reprint ed. 18.95 (*0-8369-6337-7*) Ayer.

Mashaba, T. G. & Brink, H. I., eds. Nursing Education: An International Perspective. 332p. (Orig.). (C). 1994. pap. text 46.15 (*0-7021-2620-9*, Pub. by Juta & Co) Intl Spec Bk.

***Mashar, Abeu, et al.** On Historical Astrology: The Book of Religions & Dynasties (On the Great Conjunctions) LC 99-35114. (Islamic Philosophy, Theology & Science Ser.). 1999. write for info. (*90-04-11074-7*) Brill Academic Pubs.

***Mashar, Abu.** Abu Ma'sar on Historical Astrology: The Book of Religions & Dynasties on the Great Conjunctions. Yamamoto, Keiji & Burnett, Charles, eds. LC 99-35114. (Islamic Philosophy, Theology & Science Texts & Studies Ser.). 1198p. 1999. 362.00 (*90-04-11733-4*) Brill Academic Pubs.

Mashat, Mazal, jt. auth. see Dvir, Azriel.

Mashaw, Bijan. BASIC for IBM-PC Etc. 2nd ed. 420p. (C). 1990. pap. text 29.95 (*0-934433-06-2*) Am Comp Pr.

— Programming Byte by Byte: Structured FORTRAN. 3rd rev. ed. 550p. (C). 1992. pap. text 37.45 (*0-934433-08-9*) Am Comp Pr.

— Programming Byte by Byte: Structured FORTRAN 77. 2nd rev. ed. 540p. (Orig.). (C). 1987. reprint ed. pap. 32.20 (*0-934433-02-X*) Am Comp Pr.

Mashaw, Jerry L. Balancing Security & Opportunity: The Challenge of Disability Income Policy: Summary & Overview. (Illus.). 35p. 1996. pap. text. write for info. (*1-884902-14-6*) Natl Acad.

Mashaw, Jerry L. Bureaucratic Justice. LC 82-17506. 242p. 1983. 50.00 (*0-300-02808-3*) Yale U Pr.

— Bureaucratic Justice: Managing Social Security Disability Claims. LC 82-17506. 242p. 1985. reprint ed. pap. 19.00 (*0-300-03403-2*, Y-526) Yale U Pr.

— Greed, Chaos, & Goverance: Using Public Choice to Improve Public Law. 248p. 1999. pap. text 16.00 (*0-300-07870-6*) Yale U Pr.

— Greed, Chaos & Governance: Using Public Choice to Improve Public Law. LC 96-22827. 231p. 1997. 28.00 (*0-300-06677-5*) Yale U Pr.

Mashaw, Jerry L. & Harfst, David L. The Struggle for Auto Safety. 296p. 1990. 43.00 (*0-674-84530-7*) HUP.

Mashaw, Jerry L. & Reno, Virginia P., eds. Balancing Security & Opportunity: The Challenge of Disability Income Policy. 200p. 1996. pap. text 24.00 (*1-884902-04-9*) Natl Acad.

— The Environment of Disability Income Policy: Programs, People, History & Context. 180p. 1996. pap. text 20.00 (*1-884902-05-7*) Natl Acad.

Mashaw, Jerry L., et al. Administrative Law, the American Public Law System, 1995 Supplement To. 3rd ed. (American Casebook Ser.). 82p. (C). 1995. pap. text, suppl. ed. 8.50 (*0-314-06868-6*) West Pub.

— Cases & Materials on Administrative Law, the American Public Law System. 3rd ed. (American Casebook Ser.). 1187p. (C). 1992. reprint ed. text 50.50 (*0-314-00966-3*) West Pub.

— Disability, Work & Cash Benefits. LC 96-22377. 430p. (C). 1996. text 42.00 (*0-88099-168-2*); pap. text 24.00 (*0-88099-167-4*) W E Upjohn.

— Teacher's Manual to Accompany Administrative Law: The American Public Law System, Cases & Materials. 3rd ed. 271p. 1993. pap. text. write for info. (*0-318-70372-6*) West Pub.

Mashaw, Jerry L., jt. auth. see Graetz, Michael J.

Mashaw, Jerry L., ed. see Marmor, Theodore R.

Mashayekhi, Afsaneh, jt. auth. see Julius, DeAnne.

Mashayekhi, Mehrdad, jt. ed. see Farsoun, Samih K.

***Mashberg, Tom.** Stealing Beauty. 2000. write for info. (*0-688-16529-X*, Wm Morrow) Morrow Avon.

Mashburn. The Heart of Dixieland Combos. 1990. 4.95 (*0-685-32204-1*, B063); 4.95 (*0-685-47132-2*, B064) Hansen Ed Mus.

— How to Play Accordion Today. 1990. 6.95 (*0-685-32200-9*, H651) Hansen Ed Mus.

Mashburn, Emma H., ed. see Mashburn, Joseph L.

Mashburn, J. L. Black Postcard Price Guide. 2nd ed. LC 99-25428. Orig. Title: Black Americana Postcard Price Guide. (Illus.). 416p. 1999. pap. 21.95 (*1-885940-06-8*) Colonial House.

— Sports Postcard Price Guide. LC 98-23911. (Illus.). 462p. 1998. pap. 21.95 (*1-885940-04-1*) Colonial House.

Mashburn, Joseph L. The Artist-Signed Postcard Price Guide. Roberts, Ralph, ed. LC 93-60075. (Illus.). 320p. (Orig.). 1993. 21.95 (*1-56664-035-0*); pap. 16.95 (*1-56664-028-8*) WorldComm.

— Black Americana Postcard Price Guide: A Century of History Preserved on Postcards. LC 95-38149. (Illus.). 351p. (Orig.). 1995. pap. 19.95 (*1-885940-01-7*) Colonial House.

— Fantasy Postcards with Price Guide: A Comprehensive Reference. LC 96-9617. (Illus.). 352p. (Orig.). 1996. pap. 19.95 (*1-885940-02-5*) Colonial House.

— The Postcard Price Guide. 2nd ed. Mashburn, Emma H., ed. (Illus.). 464p. 1994. pap. 16.95 (*1-885940-00-9*) Colonial House.

— The Postcard Price Guide. 3rd ed. LC 96-38126. 1997. pap. 19.95 (*1-885940-03-3*) Colonial House.

— The Super Rare Postcards of Harrison Fisher with Price Guide: Eighty-Two Cards. (Illus.). 72p. (Orig.). 1992. pap. 11.95 (*1-56664-005-9*) WorldComm.

Mashburn, William H. Managing Energy Resources in Times of Dynamic Change. LC 86-46135. 300p. 1988. text 65.00 (*0-88173-035-1*) Fairmont Pr.

— Managing Energy Resources in Times of Dynamic Change. 2nd ed. LC 91-3451. 290p. 1993. 74.00 (*0-88173-136-6*) Fairmont Pr.

— Mountain Summer. LC 88-11782. (Appalachian Connection Ser.). (Illus.). 128p. (Orig.). 1990. reprint ed. pap. 8.95 (*0-936015-14-4*) Pocahontas Pr.

Mashburn, William H., jt. auth. see Fairmont Press Staff.

Mashchaninov, Bracha. Tender Skin: And Other Poems. 70p. 1999. pap. 9.95 (*0-7392-0062-3*, PO2893) Morris Pubng.

Masheck, Joseph. Building-Art: Modern Architecture under Cultural Construction. (Contemporary Artists & Their Critics Ser.). (Illus.). 316p. (C). 1993. text 80.00 (*0-521-44013-0*); pap. text 21.95 (*0-521-44785-2*) Cambridge U Pr.

— Historical Present: Essays of the 1970s. LC 83-24104. (Contemporary American Art Critics Ser.: No. 3). 316p. reprint ed. pap. 98.00 (*0-8357-1535-3*, 207056000001) Bks Demand.

— Modernities: Art-Matters in the Present. (Illus.). 272p. 1992. 38.50 (*0-271-00808-3*) Pa St U Pr.

Masheck, Joseph D., ed. Van Gogh One Hundred, 4. LC 94-29206. (Contributions to the Study of Art & Architecture Ser.: No. 4). 424p. 1996. 79.50 (*0-313-29491-7*, Greenwood Pr) Greenwood.

Mashelkar, R. A., et al, eds. Transport Phenomena in Polymeric Systems. 1989. text 99.95 (*0-470-21444-9*) P-H.

Mashelkar, R. A. & Rao, C. N. Solid State Chemistry. Joshi, S. K., ed. LC 94-34672. (Twentieth Century Chemistry Ser.). 740p. 1995. text 86.00 (*981-02-1808-7*) World Scientific Pub.

Mashelkar, R. A., et al. Transport Phenomena in Polymeric Systems, No. I. (C). 1988. 52.50 (*0-85226-542-5*) S Asia.

Mashelkar, R. A., jt. ed. see Mujumdar, Arun S.

Mashiko, Ellen E. Japan. (World Education Ser.). (Illus.). 176p. 1989. pap. text 25.00 (*0-910054-93-2*) Am Assn Coll Registrars.

— Japan. LC 96-15584. (Pelham Guides Ser.). 1996. 22.00 (*0-929851-78-1*) Am Assn Coll Registrars.

Mashinksky, M. L., tr. see Schachnowitz, Selig.

Mashiro, N. Black Medicine IV: The Equalizers. 96p. 1995. pap. 15.00 (*0-87364-815-3*) Paladin Pr.

— Black Medicine II: Weapons at Hand. (Illus.). 128p. 1979. pap. 16.00 (*0-87364-168-X*) Paladin Pr.

— Black Medicine III: Low Blows. (Illus.). 128p. 1981. pap. 16.00 (*0-87364-214-7*) Paladin Pr.

— Black Medicine I: The Dark Art of Death. LC 78-2210. (Illus.). 96p. 1978. pap. 17.00 (*0-87364-101-9*) Paladin Pr.

Mashiter, Rosa. A Little Book of English Teas. (Illus.). 60p. 1995. 7.95 (*0-8118-1011-9*) Chronicle Bks.

— A Little English Cookbook. (Illus.). 60p. 1989. 7.95 (*0-87701-631-3*) Chronicle Bks.

Mashon, Mike, jt. auth. see Keller, Marisa.

Mashoor, S. M. Muslim Heroes of the Twentieth Century. 112p. (Orig.). 1985. pap. 6.95 (*1-56744-342-7*) Kazi Pubns.

Mashruwala, K. G. & Bhave, Vinoba. Gandhi & Marx. 119p. (Orig.). 1981. pap. 1.75 (*0-934676-30-5*) Greenlf Bks.

Mashuta, Mary. Stripes in Quilts. Kuhn, Barbara K., ed. (Illus.). 96p. (Orig.). 1996. pap. 21.95 (*1-57120-008-8*, 10132) C & T Pub.

Masi, Charlie. How to Set up Your Motorcycle Workshop. LC 97-208948. (Tech Ser.). (Illus.). 160p. 1996. pap. 24.95 (*1-884313-04-3*) Whitehorse NH.

***Masi, D. H.** Mystery Manor. Schuyler, Robert G., ed. 78p. 1999. pap. 8.95 (*1-886623-06-6*) Canal Side Pubs.

Masi, Dale A. AIDS Issues in the Workplace: A Response Model for Human Resource Management. LC 90-8912. 232p. 1990. 59.95 (*0-89930-516-4*, MAQ/, Quorum Bks) Greenwood.

Masi, Dale A. & Kuettel, Robin M. Shrink to Fit: Answers to Your Questions about Therapy. LC 98-38164. 200p. 1998. pap. 10.95 (*1-55874-620-X*) Health Comm.

Masi, Doris H. The Breeze & the Rebel. LC 95-83737. 125p. 1996. per. 12.00 (*1-886623-00-7*) Canal Side Pubs.

— Merrick's View. 179p. 1993. per. 12.00 (*0-9628208-7-3*) Canal Side Pubs.

— Milkweed Charley: The Saltsman's Hotel Caper. 54p. 1997. pap. 8.95 (*1-886623-02-3*) Canal Side Pubs.

— Montgomery Hall. LC 94-69573. 74p. 1994. pap. 8.95 (*0-9628208-9-X*) Canal Side Pubs.

— A Place Called Keesler's Corners. 137p. 1991. per. 12.00 (*0-9628208-1-4*) Canal Side Pubs.

— Pride O' the Hilltop. 140p. (J). 1992. per. 12.00 (*0-9628208-6-5*) Canal Side Pubs.

Masi, Frank R., intro. Radio Control Car How-To's: Hot Tech from the Pros. (Illus.). 136p. 1993. pap. 14.95 (*0-911295-25-9*) Air Age.

Masi, Frank R., ed. see Model Airplane News Staff.

Masi, Joseph F., ed. see Thermophysical Properties Symposium Staff.

Masi, Mary. Culinary Arts Career Starter. LC 98-52533. 229p. 1999. pap. 14.95 (*1-57685-205-9*) LrningExprss.

— Firefighter Career Starter. LC 98-6408. (Career Starters Ser.). 1998. pap. 14.95 (*1-57685-112-5*) LrningExprss.

— Real Estate Career Starter. LC 98-24095. (Career Starters Ser.). 208p. 1998. pap. 14.95 (*1-57685-142-7*) LrningExprss.

Masi, Michael. Boethius & the Liberal Arts: A Collection of Essays. (Utah Studies in Literature & Linguistics: Vol. 18). (Illus.). 220p. 1982. pap. 42.00 (*3-261-04722-4*) P Lang Pubng.

Masi, Oliviero. Incisioni - Etchings. (Illus.). 79p. 1987. pap. 25.00 (*0-936598-01-8*) J Szoke Edns.

Masi, Ralph, et al, eds. Health & Cultures: Exploring the Relationships: Policy, Practices, & Education, Vol. I. 300p. 1995. reprint ed. pap. 21.95 (*0-88962-549-2*) Mosaic.

— Health & Cultures: Exploring the Relationships: Programs, Services & Care, Vol. II. 300p. 1995. reprint ed. pap. 21.95 (*0-88962-550-6*) Mosaic.

Masi, Stefania. Deutsche Modalpartikeln und Ihre Entsprechungen Im Italienischen: Aquivalente Fur Doch, Ja, Denn, Schon und Wohl. (Bonner Romanistische Arbeiten Ser.: Bd. 59). (GER.). 287p. 1996. 54.95 (*3-631-30844-2*) P Lang Pubng.

***Masi, Stefano.** Roberto Benigni. 1999. pap. 12.95 (*88-7301-385-6*) Gremese Intl.

Masi, Wendy, jt. auth. see Segal, Marilyn.

***Masi, Wendy S.** Toddler Play. LC 99-17422. (Gymboree Parent's Guide Ser.). 1999. 19.95 (*1-892374-10-2*) Weldon Owen.

Masia, Seth. Alpine Ski Maintenance & Repair. rev. ed. (Illus.). 160p. 1987. pap. 12.95 (*0-8092-4718-6*, 471860, Contemporary Bks) NTC Contemp Pub Co.

Masica, Colin P. Defining a Linguistic Area: South Asia. LC 74-16677. 256p. 1997. lib. bdg. 23.00 (*0-226-50944-3*) U Ch Pr.

— The Indo-Aryan Languages. (Language Surveys Ser.). (Illus.). 555p. (C). 1991. text 125.00 (*0-521-23420-4*) Cambridge U Pr.

— The Indo-Aryan Languages. (Language Surveys Ser.). (Illus.). 557p. (C). 1993. pap. text 44.95 (*0-521-29944-6*) Cambridge U Pr.

Masie, Elliott. Computer Training Handbook. 2nd ed. 1998. 49.00 (*0-943210-37-2*) Lakewood Pubns.

Masiello, Francine. Between Civilization & Barbarism: Women, Nation, & Literary Culture in Modern Argentina. LC 91-45603. (Engendering Latin America Ser.: Vol. 2). x, 246p. 1992. text 50.00 (*0-8032-3158-X*) U of Nebr Pr.

Masiello, Lea. Write at the Start: A Guide for Using Writing in Freshman Seminars. (Freshman Year Experience Monograph: No. 9). 70p. 1993. pap. 30.00 (*1-889271-07-1*) Nat Res Ctr.

Masiello, Robert J. & Weisman, Glen. The Towery Report on Bergen County, NJ. (Towery Report on New American Communities Ser.). (Illus.). 144p. 1995. pap. 9.50 (*1-881096-20-3*) Towery Pub.

Masiero, A. High Energy Physics & Cosmology: Proceedings of the Summer School Ictp, Trieste, Italy 29 June, Vol.15. LC 99-29818. 1999. 88.00 (*981-02-3834-7*) World Scientific Pub.

Masiero, A., ed. see Gava, E.

Masih, Jeneen, ed. see Lawyers Committee for Human Rights.

Masih, Joseph. Armenia: At the Crossroads. 136p. 1999. text 33.00 (*90-5702-344-X*); pap. text 19.95 (*90-5702-345-8*) Gordon & Breach.

Masih, Joseph R., jt. ed. see Adalian, Rouben P.

Masih, Y. Comparative Study of Religions. (C). 1993. 22.00 (*81-208-0743-X*, Pub. by Motilal Bnarsidass) S Asia.

— A Critical History of Western Phil (Greek, Medieval, & Modern) (C). 1994. reprint ed. 16.00 (*81-208-1241-7*, Pub. by Motilal Bnarsidass) S Asia.

— Introduction to Religious Philosophy. (C). 1995. reprint ed. 19.00 (*81 208-0853-3*, Pub. by Motilal Bnarsidass); reprint ed. pap. 14.00 (*81-208-0854-1*, Pub. by Motilal Bnarsidass) S Asia.

— Shankara's Universal Philosophy of Religion. viii, 163p. 1986. text 24.00 (*81-215-0007-9*) Coronet Bks.

Masihi, Edwin. Trade Union Leadership in India: A Sociological Perspective. 1986. 19.00 (*0-8364-1530-2*, Pub. by Ajanta) S Asia.

Masihi, K. Noel, ed. Immunotherapy of Infections. LC 94-16950. (Infectious Disease & Therapy Ser.: Vol. 15). (Illus.). 528p. 1994. text 199.00 (*0-8247-9209-2*) Dekker.

Masihi, K. Noel, jt. ed. see Lange, W.

Masilela, Ntongela. Black Modernity: 20th-Century Discourses Between the United States & South Africa. 300p. 1998. 89.95 (*0-86543-648-7*) Africa World.

— Black Modernity: 20th-Century Discourses Between the United States & South Africa. 300p. 1999. pap. 24.95 (*0-86543-649-5*) Africa World.

Masin, Anton C. Incunabula Typographica: A Catalog of Fifteenth Century Books Held by the University of Notre Dame. 180p. 1979. 29.00 (*0-268-01144-3*) U of Notre Dame Pr.

Masin, Sergio C., ed. Foundations of Perceptual Theory. LC 93-11012. (Advances in Psychology Ser.: Vol. 99). 434p. 1993. 156.25 (*0-444-89496-9*, North Holland) Elsevier.

Masing-Delic, Irene. Abolishing Death: A Salvation Myth of Russian Twentieth-Century Literature. LC 92-13992. 376p. (C). 1992. 45.00 (*0-8047-1935-7*) Stanford U Pr.

***Masing, Milton.** Dearborn County. (Images of America Ser.). 128p. 1999. pap. 18.99 (*0-7385-0306-1*) Arcadia Publng.

***Masing, Milton & Koenker, Jeffrey.** Muncie. (Images of America Ser.). 1999. pap. 18.99 (*0-7385-0111-5*) Arcadia Publng.

***Masing, Milton A.** Dearborn County Indiana Cemetery Records, Vol. A. 888p. 2000. pap. 49.50 (*0-7884-1465-8*, 1465) Heritage Bk.

— Dearborn County Indiana Cemetery Records, Vol. B. 582p. 2000. pap. 49.50 (*0-7884-1505-0*, 1505) Heritage Bk.

Masingila, Joanna. Mathematics for Elementary Teachers Via Problem Solving, Preliminary ed. 394p. 1997. pap. text 38.20 (*0-13-888488-9*) P-H.

***Masini, Beatrice.** A Brave Little Princess. (Illus.). 40p. (J). (ps-3). 2000. 16.99 (*1-84148-267-6*) Barefoot Bks NY.

Masini, Donna. About Yvonne. 304p. 1998. pap. 12.95 (*0-14-027438-3*) Viking Penguin.

— About Yvonne: A Novel. LC 96-45125. 288p. 1997. 23.00 (*0-393-04091-7*) Norton.

— That Kind of Danger. LC 93-36956. (Barnard New Women Poets Ser.). 128p. 1994. pap. 12.00 (*0-8070-6823-3*) Beacon Pr.

Masini, E., ed. Visions of Desirable Societies. LC 82-18069. (Systems Science & World Order Library, Explorations of World Order Ser.). (Illus.). 260p. 1983. text 130.00 (*0-08-026089-6*, Pub. by Pergamon Repr) Franklin.

Masini, Federico, ed. see Jesuit Historical Institute Inc. Staff, et al.

Masini, Gerald, et al, eds. Object-Oriented Languages. (APIC Ser.: No. 34). (Illus.). 512p. (C). 1991. text 65.00 (*0-12-477390-7*) Acad Pr.

Masini, Giancarlo. Florence Invented America. 1999. pap. 14.95 (*1-56886-060-9*) Marsilio.

Masini, Lara V. Art Nouveau. 1995. 24.98 (*0-7858-0257-6*) Bk Sales Inc.

Masino, Anthony. Catharsis Katharsis No. 2: HIV/AIDS Awareness & Prevention Issue. unabridged ed. (Illus.). 32p. (YA). (gr. 6-12). 1997. pap. text 3.00 (*0-9660688-2-3*) Humanity Inc.

Masino, Marcia. Easy Tarot Guide. (Illus.). 288p. (Orig.). 1984. pap. 19.95 (*0-917086-59-7*) ACS Pubns.

Masino, Peg. The Eternal Optimist Carl S. Lytle, M. D. 143p. 1996. 19.95 (*1-884707-24-6*) Lifestyles.

Masironi, R., ed. Trace Elements in Relation to Cardiovascular Diseases: Status of the Joint WHO-IAEA Research Programme. (Offset Publications: No. 5). 1974. pap. text 7.00 (*92-4-170005-X*, 1120005) World Health.

Masiulewicz, Johnny. Professional Cemetery. LC 97-211041. 80p. 1997. pap. 10.00 (*0-9615879-4-6*) Puddinhead Pr.

***Masiunas, John.** Vegetable Gardening Laboratories. (Illus.). 162p. (C). 2000. spiral bd. 19.80 (*0-87563-936-4*) Stipes.

Masius, Morton, tr. see Planck, Max.

An Asterisk (*) at the beginning of an entry indicates that the title is appearing for the first time.

Masjidjamei, Muhammad. The Revolution Which Islam Created. 64p. (Orig.). 1989. pap. text 4.50 (*1-871031-16-8*) Abjad Bk.

Mask, E. Jeffrey. At Liberty under God: Toward a Baptist Ecclesiology. LC 97-33468. 224p. (C). 1997. 42.00 (*0-7618-0898-1*) U Pr of Amer.

Maskaleris, Thanasis, tr. see Kazantzakis, Nikos.

Maskall, Marty, ed. The Athena Treasury: One Hundred One Inspiring Quotations by Women. LC 93-70371. (Illus.). 128p. (Orig.). 1993. pap. 9.95 (*0-9627670-3-4*) Attitude Works.

— The Attitude Treasury: One Hundred One Inspiring Quotations. LC 90-84617. (Illus.). 128p. 1991. pap. 9.95 (*0-9627670-2-6*) Attitude Works.

Maskannec, Gregory G. Nepalese Shaman Oral Texts. LC 98-52681. 707p. 1998. 90.00 (*0-674-60795-3*) HUP.

Maskarinec, Gregory G. The Rulings of the Night: An Ethnography of Nepalese Shaman Oral Texts. LC 94-23024. (Illus.). 1995. 65.50 (*0-299-14490-9*) U of Wis Pr.

Maskawa, T., jt. ed. see Konuma, M.

Maskell. Gas Sensors. (Sensor Physics & Technology Ser.). (Illus.). 320p. 1997. 55.00 (*0-412-72550-9*, Chap & Hall NY) Chapman & Hall.

Maskell, Brian H. Making the Numbers Count: The Management Accountant As Change Agent on the World Class Team. (Illus.). 150p. 1996. 29.00 (*1-56327-070-6*) Productivity Inc.

— Performance Measurement for World Class Manufacturing: A Model for American Companies. (Illus.). 429p. 1991. 55.00 (*0-915299-99-2*) Productivity Inc.

— Sistemas de Datos de Industrias de Primer Nivel Mundial: Un Modelo Para Empresas Avanzadas. (SPA., Illus.). 407p. (Orig.). 1995. pap. 50.00 (*84-87022-15-4*) Productivity Inc.

— Software & the Agile Manufacturer: Computer Systems & World Class Manufacturing. LC 93-33282. (Illus.). 424p. 1994. 50.00 (*1-56327-046-3*) Productivity Inc.

***Maskell, Charles F.** Among the Stones. unabridged ed. Lowey, Warren, ed. 258p. 1999. pap. 29.95 (*0-9676625-0-8*) C F Maskell.

Maskell, Duke. Coleridge's Prose. (C). 1989. 30.00 (*0-907839-09-6*, Pub. by Brynmill Pr Ltd) St Mut.

Maskell, Peter. Competitiveness, Localised Learning & Regional Development: Specialization & Prosperity in Small Business Economies. LC 97-17426. 272p. (C). 1998. write for info. (*0-415-15428-6*) Routledge.

Maskell, Tom. Minolta Maxxum XTSI HTSI. LC 98-36468. (Magic Lantern Guides Ser.). 160 p. 1999. pap. 19.95 (*1-883403-54-5*, Silver Pixel Pr) Saunders Photo.

Maskell, Valerie. Worlds Apart. 352p. 1998. 24.00 (*0-7278-5317-1*) Severn Hse.

***Maskell, Valerie.** Worlds Apart. large type ed. 368p. 1999. 31.99 (*0-7505-1388-8*, Pub. by Mgna Lrg Print) Ulverscroft.

Maskell, William. The Ancient Liturgy of the Church of England. 1977. lib. bdg. 59.95 (*0-8490-1425-5*) Gordon Pr.

— Ancient Liturgy of the Church of England. 3rd ed. LC 71-172848. reprint ed. 62.50 (*0-404-04196-5*) AMS Pr.

Masker, John S. Small States & Security Regimes: The International Politics of Nuclear Non-Proliferation in Nordic Europe & the South Pacific. LC 94-46781. 172p. (C). 1995. lib. bdg. 32.50 (*0-8191-9846-3*) U Pr of Amer.

***Masket, Samuel & Crandall, Alan S., eds.** Atlas of Cataract Surgery. 322p. 1999. 175.00 (*1-85317-557-9*, Pub. by Martin Dunitz) Mosby Inc.

***Maskew, Trish.** Our Own. 1999. 23.95 (*0-9669701-2-8*) Snowcap.

Maskiell, Michelle. Women Between Cultures: The Lives of Kinnaird College Alumnae in British India. (Foreign & Comparative Studies Program, South Asian Ser.: No. 9). (Illus.). 1984. pap. text 10.00 (*0-915984-86-5*) Syracuse U Foreign Comp.

Maskill, Howard. Mechanisms of Organic Reactions. (Oxford Chemistry Primers Ser.: No. 45). (Illus.). 104p. (C). 1996. pap. text 12.95 (*0-19-855822-8*) OUP.

— The Physical Basis of Organic Chemistry. (Illus.). 504p. (C). 1986. pap. text 44.95 (*0-19-855199-1*) OUP.

***Maskill, Howard.** Structure & Reactivity in Organic Chemistry. LC 99-38970. 104p. 2000. write for info. (*0-19-855820-1*) OUP.

Maskin, Eric S., ed. Recent Developments in Game Theory. LC 99-32858. (International Library of Critical Writings in Economics). 520p. 1999. 180.00 (*1-85898-515-3*) E Elgar.

Maskin, Eric S. & Simonovits, Andras, eds. Planning, Shortage & Transformation: Essays in Honor of Janos Kornai. LC 99-37733. (Illus.). 550p. 2000. 60.00 (*0-262-13357-1*) MIT Pr.

Maskit, B. Kleinian Groups. (Grundlehren der Mathematischen Wissenschaften Ser.: Band 287). (Illus.). 287p. 1987. 114.95 (*0-387-17746-9*) Spr-Verlag.

Maskit, B., jt. ed. see Kra, I.

Maskit, Bernard, ed. see Bers, Lipman.

Maskit, Bernard, ed. see Conference on Riemann Surfaces & Related Topics (4.

Maskowski, Alice, jt. auth. see Hauswald, Carol.

Maskrey. The MRCGP Workbook. LC 94-234055. (C). 1994. pap. text, wbk. ed. 34.00 (*0-443-04985-8*) Harcourt.

Maskrey, Andrew. Disaster Mitigation: A Community-Based Approach. (Illus.). 112p. (C). 1989. 39.95 (*0-85598-122-9*, Pub. by Oxfam Pub); pap. 11.95 (*0-85598-123-7*, Pub. by Oxfam Pub) Stylus Pub VA.

Maskrey, Andrew. El Manejo Popular de los Desastres Naturales. (SPA.). 208p. 1989. pap. 19.00 (*1-85339-368-1*, Pub. by Intermed Tech) Stylus Pub VA.

Maskus, Keith E. The Changing Structure of Comparative Advantage in American Manufacturing. Bateman, Fred, ed. LC 83-9209. (Research in Business Economics & Public Policy Ser.: No. 4). 110p. 1983. reprint ed. pap. 34.10 (*0-8357-1443-8*, 207040500088) Bks Demand.

–Intellectual Property Rights in the Global Economy. 2000. pap. 18.95 (*0-88132-282-2*) Inst Intl Eco. Over the past 15 years, intellectual property rights (IPRs) - patents, copyrights & trademarks - have moved from an arcane area of legal analysis & a policy backwater to the forefront of global economic policymaking. In the 1990s dozens of countries unilaterally strengthened their laws & regulations in this area & many others are poised to do likewise. At the multilateral level, the successful conclusion of the Agreement on Trade-Related Aspects of Intellectual Property Rights (TRIPs) in the World Trade Organization elevates the protection & enforcement of IPRs to the level of solemn international commitment. The new IPR system comes with both benefits & costs. Stronger IPRs protection should increase incentives for innovation & raise returns to international technology transfer. However, it also could raise the costs of acquiring new technology & products, shifting the golbal terms of trade in favor of technology producers & against technology transfer. However, it also could raise the cost of acquiring new technology & products, shifting the global terms of trade in favor of technology producers & against technology consumers. In this context, the new regime raises international economic policy questions that evoke impassioned & exaggerated claims from both advocates & opponents of IPRs, particularly concerning sensitive issues such as patent protection of pharmaceuticals & biotechnological inventions & copyright protection for internet transactions. In the first comprehensive economic assessment of the effects of stronger international IPRs, Keith E. Maskus examines these competing claims through an analysis of the economic effects of extended international protection & partial harmonization of IPRs. He presents findings on the potential effects of stronger global IPRs, including likely impacts on foreign direct investment, technology transfer & pricing under enhances market power. The results bear directly on several important policy questions, including the construction of complementary initiatives on market liberalization & competition rules & Maskus discusses whether priority attention should be devoted to them in the upcoming next round of global trade talks. *Publisher Paid Annotation.*

Maskus, Keith E., et al, eds. Quiet Pioneering: Robert M. Stern & His International Legacy. LC 97-37446. 392p. (C). 1997. text 59.50 (*0-472-10839-5*, 10839) U of Mich Pr.

Maskus, Keith E., jt. ed. see Marks, Stephen V.

Masla, Robert, jt. auth. see Goldman, Matthew.

Maslac, Evelyn. Finding a Job for Daddy. LC 95-36718. (Illus.). 24p. (J). (ps-3). 1996. lib. bdg. 13.95 (*0-8075 2437-9*) A Whitman.

Maslach, Christina & Leiter, Michael P. Truth about Burnout: How Organizations Cause Personal Stress & What to Do about It. LC 97-21671. 256p. 1997. per. 24.50 (*0-7879-0874-6*, Scribners Ref) Mac Lib Ref.

Maslach, Christina, jt. auth. see Pines, Ayala M.

Maslak, Mary A. Gentle Whispers: Meditations for a Journey. LC 96-90914. (Illus.). xiv, 90p. (Orig.). 1996. pap. 12.95 (*0-9655795-0-6*) Termar Pub.

Masland, John W., jt. auth. see Lyons, Gene M.

Masland, R., et al, eds. Neuroplasticity: A New Therapeutic Tool in the CNS Pathology. (FIDIA Research Ser.: Vol. 12). 230p. 1988. 112.00 (*0-387-96620-X*) Spr-Verlag.

Masland, Skip. William Willya & the Birthday Cake. (Misadventures of William Willya Ser.). (Illus.). 44p. (J). (gr. k-5). 1995. 9.95 (*1-883016-04-5*) Moonglow.

— William Willya & the Washing Machine. (Misadventures of William Willya Ser.). (Illus.). 44p. (J). (gr. k-5). 1993. 9.95 (*1-883016-01-0*) Moonglow.

Maslanka, Michael P. Texas Employer's Guide to Employee Policy Handbooks. 390p. 1995. ring bd. 187.00 (*0-925773-22-0*) M Lee Smith.

— Wg&l Human Resources Forms with Commentary. LC 98-196240. 1997. write for info. (*0-7913-2237-8*) Warren Gorham & Lamont.

Maslansky, Carol J. Health & Safety at Hazardous Waste Material Sites. 1997. text 59.95 (*0-442-02431-2*, VNR) Wiley.

Maslansky, Carol J. & Maslansky, Steven P. Air Monitoring Instrumentation: A Manual for Emergency, Investigatory, & Remedial Responders. LC 92-10410. 320p. 1993. pap. 62.95 (*0-442-00973-9*, VNR) Wiley.

Maslansky, Carol J. & Maslansky, Steven P. Air Monitoring Instrumentation: A Manual for Emergency, Investigatory, & Remedial Responders. (Industrial Health & Safety Ser.). 320p. 1993. pap. 99.00 (*0-471-28460-2*, VNR) Wiley.

Maslansky, Carol J., jt. auth. see Maslansky, Steven P.

Maslansky, Steven P. & Maslansky, Carol J. Health & Safety at Hazardous Waste Sites: An Investigator's & Remediator's Guide to Hazwoper. LC 97-5909. (Miscellaneous/Catalogs Ser.). 612p. 1997. text 69.95 (*0-442-02398-7*, VNR) Wiley.

Maslansky, Steven P. & Maslansky, Carol J. Health & Safety at Hazardous Waste Sites: An Investigator's & Remediator's Guide to Hazwoper. 624p. 1997. pap. 79.95 (*0-471-28805-5*, VNR) Wiley.

Maslansky, Steven P., jt. auth. see Maslansky, Carol J.

Maslburg, Christoph Von Der, see Eckmiller, Rolf & Von Der Maslburg, Christoph, eds.

Maslen. World Directory Crystal. 1991. pap. text 25.00 (*0-7923-1023-3*) Kluwer Academic.

***Maslen, Bobby L.** Bob Books First!, 12 bks. (Bob Books: Set 1). (Illus.). 14p. (J). (ps-3). 2000. pap. 16.95 (*0-439-14544-9*) Scholastic Inc.

Maslen, Bobby L. Bob Books for Beginning Readers, 12 bks. (Bob Books Ser.: Set 1). (Illus.). 144p. (J). (ps-3). 1994. pap. 14.95 (*0-590-20373-8*) Scholastic Inc.

***Maslen, Bobby L.** Bob Books Fun!, 12 bks. (Bob Books: Set 2). (Illus.). 14p. (J). (ps-3). 2000. pap. 16.95 (*0-439-14545-7*) Scholastic Inc.

— Bob Books Kids!, 10 bks. (Bob Books: Set 1). (Illus.). 15p. (J). (ps-3). 2000. pap. 16.95 (*0-439-14546-5*) Scholastic Inc.

— Bob Books Pals!, 4 bks. (Bob Books: Set 2). (Illus.). 14p. (J). (ps-3). 2000. pap. 16.95 (*0-439-14547-3*) Scholastic Inc.

— Bob Books Wow!, 8 bks. (Bob Books: Set 1). (Illus.). 14p. (J). (ps-3). 2000. pap. 16.95 (*0-439-12198-1*) Scholastic Inc.

Maslen, Bobby L. Even More Bob Books for Young Readers, 8 bks. (Bob Books Ser.: Set 3). (Illus.). 144p. (J). (ps-3). 1994. boxed set 14.95 (*0-590-20375-4*) Scholastic Inc.

— Mat Mopped the Moon. (Bob Books Activity Bks.: No. 1). 32p. (J). (ps up). 1997. pap. 3.99 (*0-590-92172-X*) Scholastic Inc.

— More Bob Books for Young Readers, 8 bks. (Bob Books Ser.: Set 2). (Illus.). 144p. (J). (ps-3). 1994. pap. 14.95 (*0-590-20374-6*) Scholastic Inc.

Maslen, Keith. An Early London Printing House at Work: Studies in the Bowyer Ledgers. LC 93-7766. 272p. 1993. 50.00 (*0-914930-16-8*, 44033) Oak Knoll.

Maslen, Keith & Lancaster, John, eds. The Bowyer Ledgers: The Printing Accounts of William Bowyer Father & Son with a Checklist of Bowyer Printing 1699-1777, a Commentary, Indexes, & Appendixes. (Illus.). 695p. 1991. 295.00 (*0-914930-13-3*, 44064) OUP.

Maslen, Robert W. Elizabethan Fictions: Espionage, Counter-Espionage & the Duplicity of Fiction in Early Elizabethan Prose Narratives. LC 97-927. (Oxford English Monographs). 336p. 1997. text 85.00 (*0-19-811991-7*) OUP.

Maslen, Stuart, jt. ed. see Maresca, Louis.

Maslen, Ted. Fire By Order. 35.00 (*0-85052-557-8*, Pub. by Leo Cooper) Combined Pub.

Maslenikov, Oleg. Frenzied Poet: Andrey Biely & the Russian Symbolists. LC 68-54992. (Illus.). 234p. 1970. reprint ed. lib. bdg. 65.00 (*0-8371-0163-8*, MAFR, Greenwood Pr) Greenwood.

Maslennikov, K. N. German & Russian Dictionary of the Textile Industry: Textilindustrie. 2nd ed. (GER & RUS.). 1981. 85.00 (*0-8288-2382-0*, M15355) Fr & Eur.

Maslennikov, M. V., ed. The Milne Problem with Anisotropic Scattering: Proceedings. (Proceedings of the Steklov Institute of Mathematics Ser.: No. 97). 161p. 1969. pap. 59.00 (*0-8218-1897-X*, STEKLO/97) Am Math.

Maslennikow & Schatrowa. Textile Dictionary, German to Russian. 3rd ed. (GER & RUS.). 826p. 1996. 125.00 (*0-320-00515-1*) Fr & Eur.

Masler, Edward P., jt. ed. see Borkovec, A. B.

Masley, Steven. The 28-Day Antioxidant Diet Program. Gervs, Claire, ed. (Illus.). xii, 308p. 1997. pap. 13.75 (*0-9659977-6-6*) Vitality Bks.

***Maslin.** Angry Marriage. 288p. 2000. 7.98 (*1-56731-386-8*, MJF Bks) Fine Comms.

Maslin. Bailliere's Study Skills for Nurses. 1997. pap. text 18.95 (*0-7020-1979-8*) Bailliere Tindall.

Maslin, Anna M. & Powles, Trevor J., eds. Breast Cancer: Sharing the Decision. LC 98-48316. (Illus.). 282p. 1999. pap. text 34.50 (*0-19-262967-0*) OUP.

Maslin, B. R. & McDonald, M. W. Key to Useful Australian Acacias for the Seasonally Dry Tropics. (Illus.). 84p. 1996. pap. 34.95 (*0-643-05963-6*, Pub. by CSIRO) Accents Pubns.

***Maslin, B. R., et al.** Edible Wattle Seeds of Southern Australia: A Review of Species for Use in Semi-Arid Regions. (Illus.). 108p. 1998. pap. 39.95 (*0-643-06311-0*, Pub. by CSIRO) Accents Pubns.

Maslin, Bonnie. The Angry Marriage: Overcoming the Rage, Reclaiming the Love. LC 93-19272. 288p. (J). 1994. 19.45 (*1-56282-806-1*, Pub. by Hyperion) Time Warner.

Maslin, Bonnie. The Angry Marriage: Overcoming the Rage, Reclaiming the Love. 288p. (J). 1995. pap. 12.45 (*0-7868-8069-4*, Pub. by Hyperion) Time Warner.

***Maslin, Mark.** Earthquakes. LC 99-38578. (Restless Planet Ser.). (Illus.). (J). 2000. pap. 25.69 (*0-7398-1328-5*) Raintree Steck-V.

— Storms. LC 99-56132. (Restless Planet Ser.). 48p. (J). 2000. lib. bdg. 25.69 (*0-7398-1330-7*) Raintree Steck-V.

Maslin, Michael, jt. auth. see Donnelly, Liza.

Maslin, N. M. HF Communications: A Systems Approach. LC 87-42902. (Illus.). 256p. (C). 1988. 65.00 (*0-306-42757-5*, Plenum Trade) Perseus Pubng.

Maslin, Simeon J. What We Believe... What We Do... A Pocket Guide for Reform Jews. 1993. pap. 1.00 (*0-8074-0531-0*, 164030) UAHC.

Maslin, Simeon J., ed. Gates of Mitzvah: Shaarei Mitzvah: A Guide to the Jewish Life Cycle. LC 78-20790. (Illus.). 166p. 1979. pap. 12.95 (*0-916694-53-4*) Central Conf.

Maslin, Simeon J., et al. One God, Sixteen Houses: An Illustrated Introduction to the Churches & Synagogues of the Old York Road Corridor. (Illus.). 197p. (Orig.). 1990. pap. 25.00 (*0-9627062-0-5*) Cong Ken Israel.

Maslin, Zielfa. Management in Occupational Therapy. 1991. 45.95 (*1-56593-009-6*, 0250) Thomson Learn.

— Management of Occupational Therapy. Campling, Jo, ed. (Therapy in Practice Ser.). 144p. 1990. pap. 23.00 (*0-412-33380-5*, A4414) Chapman & Hall.

Masline, Shelaga. Concise Wine Guide. (J Hook Ser.). 192p. 1993. mass mkt. 5.99 (*0-425-13634-5*) Berkley Pub.

Masline, Shelagh A. If We Knew Then What We Know Now: Planning for People with AIDS. (Papers: No. 15). 32p. 1991. 10.00 (*0-934459-64-9*) United Hosp Fund.

Masline, Shelagh R. The A-Z Guide to Healing Herbal Remedies. 320p. 1995. mass mkt. 5.50 (*0-440-22061-0*) Dell.

— The Concise Wine Guide. 192p. (Orig.). 1993. mass mkt. 5.99 (*0-425-13633-7*) Berkley Pub.

***Masline, Shelagh R.** Drug Abuse & Teens: A Hot Issue. LC 99-41408. (Hot Issues Ser.). (Illus.). 64p. (gr. 6 up). 2000. lib. bdg. 19.95 (*0-7660-1372-3*) Enslow Pubs.

Masline, Shelagh R. & Close, Barbara. Aromatherapy: The A-Z Guide to Healing with Essential Oils. (Essential Healing Arts Ser.). 240p. 1997. mass mkt. 5.99 (*0-440-22256-7*) Dell.

Masline, Shelagh R., jt. auth. see Bergfeld, Wilma F.

***Masline, Shelagh Ryan.** Celebrex: Cox-2 Inhibitors: The Amazing New Pain Fighters. 320p. 1999. mass mkt. 5.99 (*0-380-80897-8*, Avon Bks) Morrow Avon.

Masling, Joseph M., ed. Empirical Studies of Psychoanalytic Theories, 3 vols. Incl. Vol. 1. 320p. (C). 1983. text 34.95 (*0-88163-000-4*); Vol. 2. 240p. 1985. text 34.95 (*0-88163-005-5*); Vol. 3. 256p. 1990. text 34.95 (*0-88163-108-6*); Set text 72.50 (*0-88163-137-X*) Analytic Pr.

Masling, Joseph M. & Bornstein, Robert F., eds. Empirical Perspectives on Object Relations Theory. LC 94-31989. (Empirical Studies of Psychoanalytic Theories Ser.: Vol. 5). 263p. 1994. 29.95 (*1-55798-633-9*) Am Psychol.

Masling, Joseph M. & Bornstein, Robert F., eds. Psychoanalytic Perspectives on Developmental Psychology. LC 96-30399. (Empirical Studies of Psychoanalytic Theories: Vol. 6). 351p. 1996. 49.95 (*1-55798-385-2*, 431-6810) Am Psychol.

— Psychoanalytic Perspectives on Psychopathology. LC 93-26281. (Empirical Studies of Psychoanalytic Theories: Vol. 4). 309p. 1993. text 34.95 (*1-55798-211-2*) Am Psychol.

Masling, Joseph M., jt. auth. see Duberstein, Paul Raphael.

Masling, Joseph M., jt. ed. see Bornstein, Robert F.

Masloff, Jacqueline, jt. auth. see Lee, Kaiman.

Masloff, S. Regulations der Fruchtkoerperbildung Bei Dem Ascomyceten Sordaria Macrospora. (Bibliotheca Mycologica: Vol. 172). (GER., Illus.). xii, 144p. 1998. pap. 53.00 (*3-443-59074-8*, Pub. by Gebruder Borntraeger) Balogh.

Maslog, Crispin C., ed. Philippine Communication: An Introduction. 399p. (Orig.). (C). 1989. pap. 16.50 (*971-11-0061-4*, Pub. by New Day Pub) Cellar.

Maslon, Laurence, ed. The Arena Adventure: The First Forty Years. 108p. 1990. pap. 24.95 (*1-55783-092-4*) Applause Theatre Bk Pubs.

Maslon, Laurence, tr. see Slavkin, Viktor.

Maslov, A. A. Inconstancy of the Eternity: Lao-Zi: Myth, Man & His Book. LC 99-28623. (Russian Studies in the Humanities: Vol. 7). (RUS.). 408p. 1999. text 109.95 (*0-7734-3255-8*) E Mellen.

Maslov, A. V. Blood-Sucking Mosquitoes of the Subtribe Culisetina: (Diptera: Culicidae) in World Fauna. (Illus.). 264p. 1990. 57.00 (*90-73348-06-4*, Pub. by Backhuys Pubs) Balogh.

Maslov, Aleksander A. Fallen Soviet Generals: Soviet General Officers Who Were Killed by Enemy Fire in the War Against Nazi Germany, 1941-1945. Glantz, David M., ed. & tr. by. from RUS. LC 97-39035. (Series on Soviet (Russian) Military Institutions). (Illus.). 286p. (C). 1998. 59.50 (*0-7146-4790-X*, Pub. by F Cass Pubs); pap. 26.50 (*0-7146-4346-7*, Pub. by F Cass Pubs) Intl Spec Bk.

Maslov, N. Basic Engineering Geology & Soil Mechanics. 552p. (C). 1987. 90.00 (*0-7855-6291-5*, Pub. by Collets) St Mut.

Maslov, Norman, jt. auth. see Bacon, David.

Maslov, S. Yu. Theory of Deductive Systems & Its Applications. Gelfond, Michael & Lifschitz, Vladimir, trs. 161p. 1987. 24.00 (*0-262-13223-0*) MIT Pr.

Maslov, V. P. & Fedoriuk, M. V. Semi-Classical Approximation in Quantum Mechanics. Niederle, J. & Tolar, J., trs. ix, 294p. 1981. text 176.50 (*90-277-1219-0*) Kluwer Academic.

***Maslov, V. P. & Mosolov, Peter Petrovich.** Nonlinear Wave Equations Perturbed by the Viscous Term. LC 00-43001. (Expositions in Mathematics Ser.). 2000. write for info. (*3-11-015282-7*) De Gruyter.

Maslov, V. P. & Nazaikinskii, V. E. Asymptotics of Operator & Pseudo-Differential Equations. LC 88-3984. (Monographs in Contemporary Mathematics). (Illus.). 320p. (C). 1988. text 110.00 (*0-306-11014-8*, Kluwer Plenum) Kluwer Academic.

Maslov, V. P. & Samborskii, S. N., eds. Idempotent Analysis. LC 91-640741. (Advances in Soviet Mathematics Ser.: Vol. 13). 210p. 1992. text 108.00 (*0-8218-4114-9*, ADVSOV/13) Am Math.

Maslov, V. P., jt. auth. see Karasev, M. V.

Maslov, Victor P., jt. auth. see Kolokoltsov, Vassili N.

Maslova, N. & Pleshakova, T., eds. The Roots of Russia: Paving the Way. 157p. (C). 1995. lib. bdg. 115.00 (*1-56072-210-X*) Nova Sci Pubs.
— The Russian Experience: Ideas in History. 137p. (C). 1995. lib. bdg. 115.00 (*1-56072-211-8*) Nova Sci Pubs.
Maslova, Nina, jt. auth. see Paul, Hilde.
Maslova, Niva B. Nonlinear Evolution Equations. LC 93-7001. (Series on Advances in Mathematics for Applied Sciences: Vol. 10). 208p. 1993. text 74.00 (*981-02-1162-7*) World Scientific Pub.
Maslove, Allan M. & Winer, Stanley L., eds. Knocking on the Back Door: Canadian Perspectives on the Political Economy of Freer Trade with the United States. 1987. pap. text 20.00 (*0-88645-058-6*, Pub. by Inst Res Pub) Ashgate Pub Co.
Maslovskii, E. K., et al. Russian - English - German - French Dictionary of Computer Science Basic Terms. (ENG, FRE, GER & RUS.). 393p. (Orig.). (C). 1990. pap. 15.95 (*0-8285-5290-8*) Firebird NY.
Maslow. Toward Psychology Being. 3rd ed. (Business Technology Ser.). 1998. pap. 29.95 (*0-442-02694-3*, VNR) Wiley.
Maslow, Abraham H. The Farther Reaches of Human Nature. (C). 1971. 25.25 (*0-8446-6069-8*) Peter Smith.
— The Farther Reaches of Human Nature. 432p. 1993. pap 14.95 (*0-14-019470-3*, Arkana) Viking Penguin.
— Journals of A. H. Maslow, 2 Vols. 1980. text 146.95 (*0-8185-0078-6*) Brooks-Cole.
— The Maslow Business Reader. Stephens, Deborah C., ed. LC 99-55086. 304p. 2000. text 29.95 (*0-471-36008-2*) Wiley.
— Queer Birds. (J). 2001. mass mkt. 12.80 (*0-689-80249-8*) Aladdin.
— Religions, Values & Peak Experiences. 1983. 24.25 (*0-8446-6070-1*) Peter Smith.
— Religions, Values & Peak Experiences. 144p. 1994. pap. 12.95 (*0-14-019487-8*) Viking Penguin.
— Toward a Psychology of Being. 2nd ed. 256p. 1968. pap. 38.95 (*0-442-03805-4*, VNR) Wiley.
— Toward a Psychology of Being. 3rd ed. LC 98-3766. 320p. 1998. 35.00 (*0-471-29309-1*, VNR) Wiley.
Maslow, Abraham H., et al. Maslow on Management. LC 98-21068. 336p. 1998. 27.95 (*0-471-24780-4*) Wiley.
Maslow, Alexander. A Study in Wittgenstein's Tractatus. (Wittgenstein Studies). 184p. 1997. pap. 16.00 (*1-85506-538-X*) Thoemmes Pr.
Maslow, Jonathan Evan. Footsteps in the Jungle: Adventures in the Scientific Exploration of the American Tropics. (Illus.). 320p. 1996. text 27.50 (*1-56663-137-8*, Pub. by I R Dee) Natl Bk Netwk.
Maslow, Katie. Hip Fracture Outcomes in People Age Fifty & Over. (Illus.). 95p. (Orig.). (C). 1994. pap. text 35.00 (*0-7881-1414-X*) DIANE Pub.
Maslowski, Karen. How to Start Making Money with Your Sewing. LC 97-49011. (Illus.). 160p. 1998. pap. 18.99 (*1-55870-474-4*, Betrwy Bks) F & W Pubns Inc.
Maslowski, Karen L. Sew up a Storm: All the Way to the Bank!: How to Succeed in a Sewing-Related Business. LC 95-92592. 213p. (Orig.). 1995. pap. 19.95 (*0-9648729-1-9*) SewStorm.
Maslowski, Peter. Armed with Cameras: The American Military Photographers of World War II. LC 93-7957. 1993. 32.95 (*0-02-920265-5*) Free Pr.
Maslowski, Peter, jt. auth. see Millet, Allan R.
Maslowski, Raymond M. & Morgan, Lewis B. Interpersonal Growth & Self Actualization in Groups. LC 72-13775. (Illus.). (C). 1973. 32.50 (*0-8422-5082-4*) Irvington.
***Maslowski, Stephen.** Birds in Fall. LC 99-46947. (Through the Seasons Ser.: Vol. 3). (Illus.). 24p. (J). (gr. 2-7). 2001. lib. bdg. 21.30 (*1-58340-058-3*) Smart Apple.
— Birds in Spring. LC 99-46949. (Through the Seasons Ser.: Vol. 1). (Illus.). 24p. (J). (gr. 2-7). 2001. lib. bdg. 21.30 (*1-58340-056-7*) Smart Apple.
— Birds in Summer. LC 99-46948. (Through the Seasons Ser.: Vol. 2). (Illus.). 24p. (J). (gr. 2-7). 2001. lib. bdg. 21.30 (*1-58340-057-5*) Smart Apple.
— Birds in Winter. LC 99-46946. (Through the Seasons Ser.: Vol. 4). (Illus.). 24p. (J). (gr. 2-7). 2001. lib. bdg. 21.30 (*1-58340-059-1*) Smart Apple.
***Maslowski, Steve.** Through the Seasons, 4 vols. (Illus.). (J). (gr. 2-7). 2001. lib. bdg. 59.80 (*1-58340-015-X*) Smart Apple.
Maslowski, Tadeusz, ed. Ciceronis, M. Tulli Fascicule 23: In P. Vatinium, Pro M. Caelio. (LAT.). 1995. 57.50 (*3-8154-1195-5*, T1195, Pub. by B G Teubner) U of Mich Pr.
Maslowski, Tadeusz, ed. see Cicero, Marcus Tullius.
Maslowsky, Edward. Vibrational Spectra of Organometallic Compounds. LC 76-18694. (Illus.). 542p. reprint ed. pap. 168.10 (*0-608-10313-6*, 201311700085) Bks Demand.
Maslyn, Stacie. Mad Maddie Maxwell. 2000. 7.99 (*0-310-23207-4*) HarpC.
Masnick, George & Bane, Mary J. The Nation's Families: 1960-1990. LC 80-20531. (Illus.). 181p. (Orig.). (C). 1980. 29.95 (*0-86569-050-2*, Auburn Hse); pap. 21.95 (*0-86569-051-0*, Auburn Hse) Greenwood.
***Maso.** Beauty Is Convulsive. 2000. 25.00 (*1-58243-089-6*, Pub. by Counterpt DC) HarpC.
— Music of the Spheres. 2000. 25.00 (*1-58243-088-8*, Pub. by Counterpt DC) HarpC.
Maso, Brian. Visual InterDev Handbook. LC 97-167760. 1997. pap. 29.99 incl. cd-rom (*0-07-882330-7*) Osborne-McGraw.
— Visual J++ LC 97-117442. 1996. pap. text 29.99 (*0-07-882266-1*) Osborne-McGraw.
— Visual J++ 6 from the Ground Up. LC 98-232701. 608p. 1998. pap. 34.99 (*0-07-882505-9*) Osborne-McGraw.
Maso, Calixto. El Caracter Cubano: Apuntes Para un Ensayo de Psicologia Social. LC 96-84337. (Coleccion Cuba y sus Jueces). (SPA.). 160p. (Orig.). 1996. pap. 16.00 (*0-89729-804-7*) Ediciones.
Maso, Calixto C. Historia de Cuba. rev. ed. De la Cuesta, Leonel A., ed. LC 75-23935. (Coleccion Cuba y sus Jueces). (SPA., Illus.). 800p. (Orig.). 1998. pap. 39.95 (*0-89729-875-6*) Ediciones.
Maso, Carole. The American Woman in the Chinese Hat. LC 93-36137. 200p. 1994. 19.95 (*1-56478-045-7*) Dalkey Arch.
— The American Woman in the Chinese Hat. LC 95-23473. 201p. 1995. pap. 11.95 (*0-452-27507-5*, Plume) Dutton Plume.
— Art Lover. LC 94-43655. 249p. 1995. pap. 13.00 (*0-88001-410-5*) HarpC.
— Aureole. LC 96-20641. 224p. 1996. 22.00 (*0-88001-482-2*) HarpC.
— Aureole: An Erotic Sequence. 224p. 1998. pap. 13.00 (*0-88001-564-0*) HarpC.
— Ava. LC 92-35600. 274p. 1993. 19.95 (*1-56478-029-5*) Dalkey Arch.
— Ava. LC 92-35600. 274p. 1995. pap. 12.95 (*1-56478-074-0*) Dalkey Arch.
***Maso, Carole.** Break Every Rule: Essays on Language, Longing & Moments of Desire. 260p. 2000. text 25.00 (*1-58243-063-2*, Pub. by Counterpt DC) HarpC.
Maso, Carole. Defiance. 272p. 1999. pap. 12.95 (*0-452-27829-5*, Plume) Dutton Plume.
— Ghost Dance. LC 94-43667. 1995. pap. 14.00 (*0-88001-409-1*) HarpC.
Maso, G. Dal & Dell'Antonio, G., eds. Composite Media & Homogenization Theory: Proceedings of the Second Workshop, ICTP 20 September - 1 October 1993. 300p. 1995. text 84.00 (*981-02-2457-5*, MMaE-P2929) World Scientific Pub.
Maso, Gianni Dal, see Dal Maso, Gianni.
Maso, Ilja & Wester, Fred, eds. The Deliberate Dialogue: Qualitative Perspectives on the Interview. 140p. 1996. pap. 16.50 (*90-5487-128-8*, Pub. by VUB Univ Pr) Paul & Co Pubs.
Maso, J. C., ed. Interfacial Transition Zone in Concrete. (Rilem Report Ser.: 11). (Illus.). 200p. (C). 1996. 100.00 (*0-419-20010-X*) Routledge.
***Masoff, Joy.** American Revolution, 1700-1800. LC 99-53695. (Illus.). 48p. (J). (gr. 3-7). 2000. 15.95 (*0-439-05109-6*) Scholastic Inc.
— Colonial Times, 1600-1700. LC 99-56243. (Illus.). 48p. (J). (gr. 3-7). 2000. 15.95 (*0-439-05107-X*) Scholastic Inc.
Masoff, Joy. Emergency! LC 97-26995. (Illus.). 48p. (J). (gr. 3-7). 1998. 16.95 (*0-590-97898-5*) Scholastic Inc.
— Fire! LC 97-10928. (Illus.). (J). 1998. pap. 5.99 (*0-590-97585-4*) Scholastic Inc.
— Fire! LC 97-10928. (Illus.). 48p. (J). (gr. 3-7). 1998. 16.95 (*0-590-97872-1*) Scholastic Inc.
***Masoff, Joy.** Oh, Yuck! The Encyclopedia of Everything Nasty. LC 99-43603. (Illus.). 256p. (J). (gr. 3-7). 1999. pap. 15.95 (*0-7611-0771-1*) Workman Pub.
Masoliver, Juan A. Origins of Desire: Modern Spanish Short Stories. (Modern European Short Stories Ser.). 208p. 1994. pap. 13.99 (*1-85242-187-8*) Serpents Tail.
Masolo, D. A. African Philosophy in Search of Identity. LC 93-15353. (African Systems of Thought Ser.). 304p. 1994. 39.95 (*0-253-30271-4*); pap. 16.95 (*0-253-20775-4*) Ind U Pr.
Masolo, D. A., jt. auth. see Karp, Ivan.
Mason. Almanac of Civil Rights. 1994. 24.95 (*0-671-85001-6*); pap. 16.00 (*0-671-85021-0*) S&S Trade.
— Complete Problem Solving for Eesen. 18th Century. 1995. 19.00 (*0-697-29780-2*) McGraw.
***Mason.** Cyberweb. 2000. 20.00 (*0-380-97248-4*) Morrow Avon.
Mason. Educational Psychology. (C). 1995. pap., teacher ed. write for info. (*0-06-502479-6*) Addson-Wesley Educ.
***Mason.** Environmental Democracy. LC 99-15904. 263p. 1999. text 49.95 (*0-312-22700-0*) St Martin.
— Handbook of Plastic Surgery. 2001. pap. text. write for info. (*0-323-01181-0*) Mosby Inc.
Mason. History of the U.S., vol. 1. 1991. text, teacher ed. 81.68 (*0-395-58196-6*) HM.
— History of the U.S., vol. 1. LC 94-236978. 1994. text, student ed. 68.04 (*0-395-68861-2*) HM.
— History of the U.S., vol. 1. LC 94-236978. 1994. text, teacher ed. 101.84 (*0-395-68862-0*) HM.
— A History of United States Posters. 1991. pap. 91.92 (*0-395-58254-7*) HM.
— Hoffman Devlopmental Psychology Today. 6th ed. 1993. text, teacher ed. 20.93 (*0-07-029340-6*) McGraw.
Mason. Journey. 336p. Date not set. write for info. (*0-684-81524-9*) S&S Trade.
Mason. Old Empires, New Nations. 1994. pap. text. write for info. (*0-582-22666-X*, Pub. by Addison-Wesley) Longman.
— Petrology of the Metamorphic Rocks. 2nd ed. (Illus.). 240p. (C). 1990. text 90.50 (*0-04-552027-5*) Routledge.
— Petrology of the Metamorphic Rocks. 2nd ed. (Illus.). 240p. (C). 1990. pap. text 37.95 (*0-04-552028-3*) Thomson Learn.
— Rhapsody. large type ed. LC 98-3732. 1998. 23.95 (*0-7862-1474-0*) Thorndike Pr.
— The Right to Be a Child. 1998. write for info. (*0-201-14941-9*) Addison-Wesley.
— Song of the Paddle. 2nd ed. 1988. 29.95 (*0-07-040798-3*) McGraw.
— Statistical Design. 2nd ed. text. write for info. (*0-471-37216-1*) Wiley.
— Statistics. 4th ed. (C). 1994. pap. text 8.00 (*0-03-097823-8*) Harcourt Coll Pubs.
— Statistics: An Introduction. 4th ed, student ed. 21.50 (*0-534-51071-X*) Brooks-Cole.
— Statistics Easystat Manual: An Introduction. 4th ed. (Statistics Ser.). 1994. pap. 23.95 (*0-534-51072-8*) Wadsworth Pub.
— Twister Theory III. 1996. pap. write for info. (*0-582-20992-7*, Pub. by Addison-Wesley) Longman.
— Twistor Theory. 1995. pap. 72.95 (*0-582-00465-9*) Longman.
— U. N. & Global Issues. 1994. pap. text. write for info. (*0-582-22668-6*, Pub. by Addison-Wesley) Longman.
— Using Mircosoft Excel 97 in Business. (C). 1998. pap. text. write for info. (*0-03-023341-0*) Harcourt Coll Pubs.
— The Writer's Roles. (C). 1994. pap. text, teacher ed. 33.75 (*0-15-500161-2*) Harcourt Coll Pubs.
Mason, ed. Reading Instructions for Today. 3rd ed. (C). 1999. text. write for info. (*0-673-98510-5*) Addison-Wesley.
Mason & Burns. Retailing. 6th ed. LC 97-67114. 1998. 77.95 (*0-87393-535-7*) Dame Pubns.
Mason & Lind. Statistics: An Introduction. 5th ed. (Statistics Ser.). 1998. pap., student ed. 20.75 (*0-534-35381-9*) PWS Pubs.
Mason, et al. Cooperative Occupational Education & Work Experience in the Curriculum. 5th ed. 734p. 1997. 46.95 (*0-8134-3042-9*) Interstate.
***Mason, et al.** Ready Notes for Stats: An Introduction. 5th ed. 1998. pap. 10.50 (*0-534-35653-2*) Thomson Learn.
Mason, jt. auth. see Conger, Sue.
Mason, jt. auth. see Craven.
Mason, Alane Salierno, tr. see Vittorini, Elio.
***Mason, Joseph.** Let My Heart Attack Save Your Life: A Simple, Sound, Workable Weight Management Plan. 240p. 1998. pap. 14.95 (*0-471-34745-0*) Wiley.
Mason, A., jt. auth. see Beetham, P.
***Mason, A. E.** At the Villa Rose. Set. unabridged ed. (YA). (gr. 8 up). 1998. 35.95 incl. audio (*1-55685-590-7*) Audio Bk Con.
Mason, A. E. The Four Feathers. 1999. pap. 14.95 (*0-89526-263-0*) Regnery Pub.
— The Four Feathers. reprint ed. lib. bdg. 22.95 (*0-88411-176-8*) Amereon Ltd.
— The Four Feathers. 1993. reprint ed. lib. bdg. 18.95 (*1-56849-211-1*) Buccaneer Bks.
— The Three Gentlemen. LC 99-72236. 394p. 1999. write for info. (*1-893766-04-7*) Aeon Pub Co.
***Mason, A. E.** The Winding Stair. Set. unabridged ed. 1998. 35.95 incl. audio (*1-55685-588-5*) Audio Bk Con.
Mason, A. E. W. The Prisoner in the Opal. mass mkt. 3.95 (*0-88184-221-4*) Carroll & Graf.
Mason, Abelle. Ports of Entry: Ethnic Impressions. 139p. (C). 1984. pap. text 15.50 (*0-15-570748-5*) Harcourt Coll Pubs.
***Mason, Adelbert.** Herald Before the Mast: The Life & Works of John W. Mason, 19th Century Shipcarver. (Illus.). 80p. 2000. pap. 10.00 (*1-879418-63-0*) Audenreed Pr.
***Mason, Adrienne.** Living Things. (Starting with Science Ser.). 32p. (J). (gr. k-4). 2000. pap. 6.95 (*1-55074-393-7*, Pub. by Kids Can Pr) Genl Dist Srvs.
Mason, Adrienne. Mealworms: Raise Them, Watch Them, See Them Change. unabridged ed. (Illus.). 24p. (J). (gr. 2-4). 1998. pap. 12.95 (*1-55074-448-8*, Pub. by Kids Can Pr) Genl Dist Srvs.
— Oceans: Looking at Beaches & Coral Reefs, Tides & Currents... unabridged ed. (Illus.). 80p. (J). (gr. 3-7). 1997. pap. 16.95 (*1-55074-147-0*, Pub. by Kids Can Pr) Genl Dist Srvs.
***Mason, Adrienne.** The World of Marine Animals. (Illus.). 64p. (J). (gr. 3-7). 1999. pap. 9.95 (*1-55143-046-0*) Orca Bk Pubs.
— World of the Spider. LC 99-18378. (Illus.). 128p. 1999. 29.95 (*1-57805-044-8*, Pub. by Sierra) Random.
Mason, Adrienne & Hodge, Deborah. Living Things. unabridged ed. LC 96-931707. (Starting with Science Ser.). (Illus.). 32p. (J). (gr. k-4). 1998. 14.95 (*1-55074-343-0*, Pub. by Kids Can Pr) Genl Dist Srvs.
— Plants. (Starting with Science Ser.). (Illus.). 32p. (J). (gr. k-4). 1998. 14.95 (*1-55074-193-4*, Pub. by Kids Can Pr) Genl Dist Srvs.
— Simple Machines. unabridged ed. (Starting with Science Ser.). (Illus.). 32p. (J). (ps-4). 1998. 14.59 (*1-55074-311-2*, Pub. by Kids Can Pr) Genl Dist Srvs.
— Solids, Liquids & Gases. unabridged ed. (Starting with Science Ser.). (Illus.). 32p. (J). (ps-4). 1998. 14.95 (*1-55074-195-0*, Pub. by Kids Can Pr) Genl Dist Srvs.
Mason, Alan, tr. see Basov, N. G., ed.
Mason, Alden, ed. see Dolores, Juan.
Mason, Alfred E. Ensign Knightley & Other Stories. LC 70-103525. (Short Story Index Reprint Ser.). 1977. 21.95 (*0-8369-3267-6*) Ayer.
— Sir George Alexander & the St. James' Theatre. LC 72-84520. (Illus.). 1972. 24.95 (*0-405-08762-4*, Pub. by Blom Pubns) Ayer.
Mason, Alice L. Jolly Old Santa Claus. rev. ed. (Illus.). 24p. (J). (ps-3). 1995. 6.95 (*1-57102-081-0*, Ideals Child); pap. 2.49 (*1-57102-075-6*, Ideals Child) Hambleton-Hill.
Mason, Alistair. History of the Society of the Sacred Mission. 344p. 1994. pap. 21.95 (*1-85311-079-5*, 838, Pub. by Canterbury Press Norwich) Morehouse Pub.
Mason, Alpheus T. Organized Labor & the Law. LC 73-89755. (American Labor, from Conspiracy to Collective Bargaining Ser., No. 1). 265p. 1972. reprint ed. 18.95 (*0-405-02142-9*) Ayer.
— The Supreme Court: Palladium of Freedom. LC 62-18443. 217p. reprint ed. pap. 67.30 (*0-608-13967-X*, 205562900029) Bks Demand.
— William Howard Taft: Chief Justice. LC 83-6461. 354p. (C). 1983. reprint ed. pap. text 34.50 (*0-8191-3091-5*) U Pr of Amer.
Mason, Alpheus T. & Baker, Gordon E. Free Government in the Making: Readings in American Political Thought. 4th ed. 812p. 1985. text 49.95 (*0-19-503524-0*) OUP.
Mason, Alpheus T. & Stephenson, D. Grier, Jr. American Constitutional Development. LC 74-32555. (Goldentree Bibliographies Series in American History). (C). 1977. pap. text 14.95 (*0-88295-545-4*) Harlan Davidson.
Mason, Alpheus T. & Stephenson, D. Grier. American Constitutional Law: Introductory Essays & Selected Cases. 2nd ed. LC 97-51707. 718p. (C). 1998. 64.00 (*0-13-080521-1*) P-H.
Mason, Amelia R. Woman in the Golden Ages. 1977. lib. bdg. 250.00 (*0-8490-2833-7*) Gordon Pr.
***Mason, Andrew.** Community, Solidarity & Belonging: Levels of Community & Their Normative Significance. LC 99-57078. 300p. (C). 2000. write for info. (*0-521-63129-7*); pap. write for info. (*0-521-63728-7*) Cambridge U Pr.
Mason, Andrew. Explaining Political Disagreement. LC 92-39228. 182p. (C). 1993. text 49.95 (*0-521-43322-3*) Cambridge U Pr.
— Homes - A Household Model for Economic & Social Studies: Reference Guide for Household Projections, Version 1.0. LC 87-22288. (Papers of the East-West Population Institute: No. 106). (Illus.). x, 114p. (Orig.). 1987. pap. 3.00 (*0-86638-102-3*) EW Ctr HI.
— Victory from Defeat: Learn How & Why Winners Win from History's Greatest Success Stories. LC 97-62445. 178p. 1998. 19.95 (*1-56315-089-1*) SterlingHse.
Mason, Andrew & Tapinos, Georges, eds. Sharing the Wealth: Demographic Change & Economic Transfers between Generations. (Illus.). 344p. 2000. text 85.00 (*0-19-829620-7*) OUP.
Mason, Anita. Reich Angel. LC 94-31322. 373p. 1995. 24.00 (*1-56947-033-2*) Soho Press.
— Reich Angel. LC 94-31322. (Hera Ser.). 373p. 1997. pap. 13.00 (*1-56947-071-5*) Soho Press.
Mason, Anne. The Dancing Meteorite. LC 83-47705. 224p. (YA). (gr. 6-9). 1984. pap. 7.95 (*0-06-024097-0*) HarpC Child Bks.
***Mason, Anthony.** Bruges. (Illus.). 192p. 1999. pap. text 14.95 (*1-86011-953-0*) Cadgn Bks.
Mason, Antony. Around the World in 80 Pages. (Illus.). 80p. (YA). (gr. 3 up). 1995. lib. bdg. 23.40 (*1-56294-626-9*, Copper Beech Bks) Millbrook Pr.
***Mason, Antony.** The Bluffer's Guide to Men. (Bluffer's Guides Ser.). 64p. 1999. pap. 5.95 (*1-902825-12-8*) Oval Bks.
Mason, Antony. Brussels, Bruges, Ghent & Antwerp. LC 93-47110. (Cadogan Guides Ser.). 1994. 10.99 (*0-947754-55-5*, Pub. by Cadgn Bks) Macmillan.
— Brussels, Bruges, Ghent & Antwerp. 2nd ed. LC 93-47110. (Cadogan City Guides Ser.). (Illus.). 384p. 1998. pap. text 18.95 (*1-86011-029-0*, Pub. by Cadgn Bks) Globe Pequot.
Mason, Antony. Cezanne. LC 94-14126. (Famous Artists Ser.). 1994. 12.15 (*0-606-06954-2*, Pub. by Turtleback) Demco.
Mason, Antony. The Children's Atlas of Civilizations. LC 93-23564. (Children's Atlases Ser.). (Illus.). 96p. (J). (gr. 2-6). 1994. pap. 14.95 (*1-56294-733-8*); lib. bdg. 27.40 (*1-56294-494-0*) Millbrook Pr.
— Funpaxs: U. S. A. (Funpax Ser.). (J). (ps-3). 1999. 4.95 (*0-7894-4317-1*) DK Pub Inc.
— If You Were There in Biblical Times. LC 96-199681. (If You Were There Ser.). (Illus.). 32p. (J). (gr. 3-7). 1996. 16.95 (*0-689-80953-0*) S&S Childrens.
— If You Were There in Medieval Times. LC 96-199644. (If You Were There Ser.). (Illus.). 32p. (J). (gr. 3-7). 1996. 16.95 (*0-689-80952-2*) S&S Childrens.
***Mason, Antony.** The Kingfisher First Picture Atlas. 40p. (J). 1999. pap. 7.95 (*0-7534-5260-X*) LKC.
— Leonardo Da Vinci. (Famous Artists Ser.). 1994. 11.15 (*0-606-07023-0*, Pub. by Turtleback) Demco.
— Matisse. (Famous Artists Ser.). 1995. 12.15 (*0-606-08815-6*, Pub. by Turtleback) Demco.
Mason, Antony. Monet. LC 94-22455. (Famous Artists Ser.). (Illus.). 32p. (YA). (gr. 5 up). 1994. 10.95 (*0-8120-6494-1*) Barron.
— Monet. LC 94-22455. (Famous Artists Ser.). (Illus.). 32p. (YA). (gr. 5 up). 1995. pap. 6.95 (*0-8120-9174-4*) Barron.
Mason, Antony. Monet. (Famous Artists Ser.). 1995. 12.15 (*0-606-08824-5*, Pub. by Turtleback) Demco.
Mason, Antony. Peary & Amundsen: Race to the Poles. LC 94-36722. (Beyond the Horizons Ser.). 48p. (J). 1995. lib. bdg. 24.26 (*0-8114-3977-1*) Raintree Steck-V.
— Picasso. (Famous Artists Ser.). (Illus.). 32p. (YA). (gr. 5 up). 1995. 10.95 (*0-8120-6496-8*); pap. 6.95 (*0-8120-9175-2*) Barron.
Mason, Antony. Picasso. (Famous Artists Ser.). 1994. 12.15 (*0-606-08845-8*, Pub. by Turtleback) Demco.
— Romans. LC 95-13711. (Time Trekkers Visit The--). 1995. 11.15 (*0-606-09977-8*, Pub. by Turtleback) Demco.
Mason, Antony. Soccer. (Butterfly Bks.). (ARA., Illus.). 31p. 11.95 (*0-86685-606-4*, LDL6064, Pub. by Librairie du Liban) Intl Bk Ctr.
***Mason, Antony.** Take the Kids to London. (Illus.). 256p. 1999. pap. text 16.95 (*1-86011-992-1*, Pub. by Cadgn Bks) Globe Pequot.
Mason, Antony. Time Trekkers Visit the Romans. (Time Trekkers Ser.). (Illus.). 32p. (J). (gr. 2-4). 1995. lib. bdg. 20.90 (*1-56294-910-1*, Copper Beech Bks) Millbrook Pr.
— Time Trekkers Visit the Stone Age. (Time Trekkers Ser.). (Illus.). 32p. (J). (gr. 2-4). 1996. pap. 5.95 (*0-7613-0480-0*, Copper Beech Bks); lib. bdg. 20.90 (*0-7613-0479-7*, Copper Beech Bks) Millbrook Pr.
Mason, Antony. Time Trekkers Visit the Stone Age. LC 95-39833. (Time Trekkers Visit The--). 1996. 11.15 (*0-606-09978-6*, Pub. by Turtleback) Demco.

An Asterisk (*) at the beginning of an entry indicates that the title is appearing for the first time.

— The Xenophobe's Guide to the Belgians. (Xenophobe's Guides Ser.). 64p. 1999. pap. 5.95 (*1-902825-19-5*) Oval Bks.

Mason, Antony & Hughes, Andrew S. Cezanne. (Famous Artists Ser.). (Illus.). 32p. (YA). (gr. 5 up). 1994. 10.95 (*0-8120-6459-3*) Barron.

— Leonardo da Vinci. (Famous Artists Ser.). (Illus.). 32p. (YA). (gr. 5 up). 1994. 10.95 (*0-8120-6460-7*) Barron.

— Matisse. (Famous Artists Ser.). (Illus.). 32p. (J). (gr. 5 up). 1995. 11.95 (*0-8120-6534-4*) Barron.

Mason, Antony & Lye, Keith. The Children's Atlas of Exploration. LC 92-28856. (Children's Atlases Ser.). (Illus.). 96p. (J). (gr. 2-6). 1993. pap. 14.95 (*1-56294-711-7*); lib. bdg. 27.40 (*1-56294-256-5*) Millbrook Pr.

Mason, Antony & Marshall Editions Staff. Aztec Times. LC 96-53585. (If You Were There Ser.). (Illus.). 32p. (J). (gr. 4-7). 1997. mass mkt. 16.95 (*0-689-81199-3*) S&S Childrens.

— Viking Times. LC 96-40059. (If You Were There Ser.). (Illus.). 32p. (J). (gr. 4-7). 1997. per. 16.95 (*0-689-81198-5*) S&S Childrens.

Mason, Antony, et al. Cezanne. (Famous Artists Ser.). (Illus.). 32p. (YA). (gr. 5 up). 1994. pap. 6.95 (*0-8120-1293-3*) Barron.

— Leonardo da Vinci. (Famous Artists Ser.). (Illus.). 32p. (YA). (gr. 5 up). 1994. pap. 6.95 (*0-8120-1997-0*) Barron.

— Matisse. (Famous Artists Ser.). (Illus.). 32p. (J). (gr. 5 up). 1995. pap. 6.95 (*0-8120-9426-3*) Barron.

— Michelangelo. (Famous Artists Ser.). (Illus.). 32p. (YA). (gr. 5 up). 1994. pap. 6.95 (*0-8120-1998-9*) Barron.

Mason, Antony, jt. auth. see Gumbel, Andrew.

***Mason, Ardenelle.** My View. 1999. pap. write for info. (*1-58235-087-6*) Watermrk Pr.

Mason, Arthur. Cook & the Captain Bold. LC 70-128740. (Short Story Index Reprint Ser.). 1977. 17.95 (*0-8369-3631-0*) Ayer.

Mason, B. J., Jr. Elliott B. in Birds of a Feather. (Illus.). 66p. (Orig.). (J). (gr. 2-4). 1993. 14.95 incl. audio (*0-9640707-0-7*) Color-Me Storybks.

— Elliott B. in Birds of a Feather Teacher's Guide. (Illus.). 12p. (J). (ps-3). 1995. pap., teacher ed. 4.95 (*0-9640707-1-5*) Color-Me Storybks.

Mason, B. J., ed. The Surface Waters Acidification Programme. 562p. (C). 1991. text 120.00 (*0-521-39533-X*) Cambridge U Pr.

Mason, Babbie. Real Monsters: Rosh - O - Monsters. 64p. (J). (gr. 2-5). 1997. 3.99 (*0-689-81155-1*) S&S Childrens.

— Supplementary Cases in Everyday Law. (LA - Business Law Ser.). 1990. mass mkt., wbk. ed. 17.95 (*0-538-60968-0*) S-W Pub.

***Mason, Babbie.** Treasures of Heaven, Stuff of Earth. 2000. pap. 12.99 (*0-88419-725-5*) Creation House.

Mason, Babbie, ed. see Corwin, Edward S.

Mason, Barry. Handing Over: Developing Consistency Across Shifts in Residential & Health Settings. 96p. 1992. pap. text 22.00 (*1-85575-018-X*, Pub. by H Karnac Bks Ltd) Other Pr LLC.

Mason, Basil J. Clouds, Rain, & Rainmaking. 2nd ed. LC 74-16991. 197p. reprint ed. pap. 56.20 (*0-608-12054-5*, 2024497) Bks Demand.

Mason, Bernard S. The Book of Indian Crafts & Costumes. LC 46-6959. 128p. reprint ed. pap. 39.70 (*0-8357-7341-8*, 205516400008) Bks Demand.

— Boomerangs: How to Make & Throw Them. (Illus.). (YA). (gr. 5 up). 1990. 20.25 (*0-8446-5062-5*) Peter Smith.

— Boomerangs: How to Make & Throw Them. LC 73-94346. (Illus.). 99p. 1974. reprint ed. pap. 3.95 (*0-486-23028-7*) Dover.

— Dances & Stories of the American Indian. LC 44-516. (Illus.). 280p. reprint ed. pap. 86.80 (*0-8357-9871-2*, 201340700086) Bks Demand.

— Drums, Tomtoms & Rattles: Primitive Percussion Instruments for Modern Use. (Illus.). (YA). (gr. 5 up). 1990. 21.75 (*0-8446-5063-3*) Peter Smith.

— How to Make Drums, Tom Toms & Rattles. (Illus.). 208p. 1974. reprint ed. pap. 6.95 (*0-486-21889-9*) Dover.

Mason, Bertha, ed. see Jackson, W. Francis.

Mason, Bessie M. Along the Creek. 72p. 1984. pap. 5.00 (*0-916768-06-6*) Sycamore Pr.

— On the Hill. 42p. 1984. 5.00 (*0-916768-07-4*) Sycamore Pr.

Mason, Bethny H. & Brown, Marsha H. The New Complete Junior Showmanship Handbook: A Complete Book of Instruction on How to Begin, How to Handle & How to Win in Junior Showmanship Classes at Dog Shows. 2nd ed. LC 79-25829. (Illus.). 160p. 1980. pap. 16.00 (*0-87605-655-9*) Howell Bks.

Mason, Bill. Bill Mason's No Nonsense Guide to Fly Fishing in Idaho: Learn about Fly Fishing at Idaho's Finest Rivers, Streams, Lakes & Resevoirs. Banks, David et al, eds. (Illus.). 68p. 1995. reprint ed. pap. 14.95 (*0-9637256-1-0*) D Comm.

— Canoescapes. (Illus.). 160p. 1996. 40.00 (*1-55046-141-9*) Boston Mills.

— Path of the Paddle: An Illustrated Guide to the Art of Canoeing. 2nd rev. ed. (Illus.). 200p. 1999. pap. 19.95 (*1-55209-328-X*) Firefly Bks Ltd.

— Song of the Paddle: An Illustrated Guide to Wilderness Camping. (Illus.). 208p. 1997. pap. 19.95 (*1-55209-089-2*) Firefly Bks Ltd.

— Sports Illustrated Fly Fishing: Learn from a Master. (Orig.). 1994. pap. 11.95 (*1-56800-033-2*, Pub. by Sports Illus Bks) Natl Bk Netwk.

***Mason, Bill & Maisner, Larry.** The Rules of Soccer: Simplified. (Illus.). 23p. 1999. pap. 2.50 (*1-889424-01-3*) Yth Sports.

***Mason, Billy.** Askit. rev. ed. 10p. 2000. pap. text 10.00 (*0-942140-12-5*) Kelso.

Mason, Billy. Directory of Recyclable Wastes. (Illus.). 1976. pap. text 11.95 (*0-942140-01-X*) Kelso.

***Mason, Billy.** E. T. C. Echo Tape Casting. rev. ed. 6p. 2000. pap. 10.00 (*0-942140-08-7*) Kelso.

Mason, Billy. A Furniture Stripping Business for the Small Man. 1975. pap. text 7.00 (*0-942140-03-6*) Kelso.

— Grandmaw Old Fashion Soap Making. 1978. 7.00 (*0-942140-04-4*) Kelso.

***Mason, Billy.** How to Win Puzzles 'n Contests. rev. ed. 24p. 2000. pap. text 15.00 (*0-942140-10-9*) Kelso.

— Idea Income. 10p. 2000. pap. text 20.00 (*0-942140-09-5*) Kelso.

Mason, Billy. Making Money with Vending Machine. 1995. pap. 7.00 (*0-942140-06-0*) Kelso.

— Outdoor Advertising. 1976. pap. 5.00 (*0-942140-07-9*) Kelso.

***Mason, Billy.** Your Sur-Name. rev. ed. 6p. 2000. pap. 7.00 (*0-942140-11-7*) Kelso.

Mason, Billy, ed. Directory of Recycable Wastes, Bk. 2. (Orig.). (C). 1981. pap. 11.95 (*0-942140-00-1*) Kelso.

Mason, Bim. Street Theatre & Other Outdoor Performance. LC 91-43615. (Illus.). 240p. (C). (gr. 13). 1992. pap. 25.99 (*0-415-07050-3*, A7103) Routledge.

Mason, Bob. Gamblers, Grifters & Good Ol' Boys. 1986. pap. 7.95 (*0-89746-056-1*) Gambling Times.

Mason, Bob, jt. auth. see Cox, Terry.

Mason, Bob, jt. auth. see Hyman, Jeff.

***Mason, Bobbie A., intro.** Midnight Magic: Selected Stories of Bobbie Ann Mason. LC 97-36369. 301p. 1999. pap. 16.00 (*0-88001-657-4*) HarpC.

***Mason, Bobbie Ann.** Clear Springs: A Family Story. 320p. 2000. pap. 14.00 (*0-06-095629-1*, Perennial) HarperTrade.

Mason, Bobbie Ann. Clear Springs: A Memoir. LC 98-37173. 298p. 1999. 25.00 (*0-679-44925-6*) Random.

— Feather Crowns. LC 92-56227. 464p. 1994. pap. 14.00 (*0-06-092549-3*) HarpC.

— The Girl Sleuth. LC 94-47086. (Illus.). 160p. 1995. pap. 11.95 (*0-8203-1739-X*) U of Ga Pr.

— In Country RI. LC 85-42579. 256p. 1993. reprint ed. pap. 13.00 (*0-06-091530-9*, Perennial) HarperTrade.

— Midnight Magic: Selected Short Stories of Bobbie Ann Mason. LC 97-36369. 320p. 1999. 25.00 (*0-88001-595-0*) HarpC.

— Shiloh & Other Stories. LC 95-16581. 264p. 1995. 18.00 (*0-8131-1948-0*) U Pr of Ky.

— Spence And Lila. LC 97-23997. (Illus.). 176p. 1998. pap. 13.00 (*0-88001-594-2*) HarpC.

Mason, Bonnie N., jt. auth. see Southard, Edna C.

Mason-Bramble. Research in Education & Behavior. 1996. 8.75 (*0-697-20557-6*, WCB McGr Hill) McGrw-H Hghr Educ.

Mason, Brian. Victor Moritz Goldschmidt: Father of Modern Geochemistry. LC 91-78244. (Special Publication: No. 4). (Illus.). xii, 184p. 1992. 40.00 (*0-941809-03-X*) Geochemical Soc.

Mason, Brian H. & Melson, William G. The Lunar Rocks. LC 73-129659. 185p. reprint ed. pap. 57.40 (*0-608-30347-X*, 205512800008) Bks Demand.

Mason, Brian H. & Taylor, S. R. Inclusions in the Allende Meteorite. LC 82-600091. (Smithsonian Contributions to the Earth Sciences Ser.: No. 25). 34p. reprint ed. pap. 30.00 (*0-608-30892-7*, 201930500011) Bks Demand.

Mason, Brian H., ed. see Marvin, Ursula B.

Mason, Brian H., jt. ed. see Marvin, Ursula B.

Mason, Brian K., jt. auth. see Josephson, Barbara S.

Mason, C. A., ed. International Symposium on Teleoperation & Control. (Illus.). 400p. 1988. 174.95 (*0-387-50054-5*) Spr-Verlag.

Mason, C. F. Biology of Freshwater Pollution. 3rd ed. LC 96-166128. (C). 1996. pap. text 45.00 (*0-582-24732-2*) Addison-Wesley.

Mason, C. Russell. The Art & Science of Protective Relaying. LC 56-8964. (General Electric Series for the Advancement of Engineering Practice). 424p. reprint ed. pap. 131.50 (*0-7837-2813-1*, 205765900006) Bks Demand.

Mason, Carleton D. Guns Along the Rio. large type ed. (Dales Large Print Ser.). 1995. pap. 18.99 (*1-85389-548-2*, Dales) Ulverscroft.

Mason, Carol I. Introduction to Wisconsin Indians: Prehistory to Statehood. (Illus.). 327p. 1988. pap. text 18.50 (*0-88133-308-5*) Sheffield WI.

Mason, Caroline. The Simple Guide to Customs & Etiquette in China. 2nd ed. pap. 8.95 (*1-86034-030-X*, 93395) MAGI1 UK.

Mason, Caroline & Murray, Geoffrey. Simple Guide to China: Customs & Etiquette. 3rd rev. ed. (Simple Guides Ser.: Series 1). (Illus.). 80p. 1999. pap. 8.95 (*1-86034-056-3*, Pub. by Global Bks) Midpt Trade.

Mason, Catherine. Making an Herb Garden: Beautiful Designs, Plantings & Ornamentation. LC 97-60005. (Illus.). 96p. 1997. 24.95 (*1-57076-089-6*, Trafalgar Sq Pub) Trafalgar.

Mason, Charles. The Journal of Charles Mason & Jeremiah Dixon. LC 69-17273. (American Philosophical Society, Memoirs Ser.: Vol. 76). 243p. reprint ed. pap. 75.40 (*0-608-14257-3*, 201971000014) Bks Demand.

Mason, Charles. Meaning by All Means: A Vocabulary Text & Workbook for Students of ESL. 144p. (C). 1986. pap. text 19.20 (*0-13-567058-6*) P-H.

Mason, Charles, ed. The Best of Sail Trim. (Illus.). 228p. 1975. 25.00 (*1-57409-119-0*) Sheridan.

Mason, Charles, jt. auth. see Melges, Buddy.

Mason, Charles Q., jt. auth. see Wieseman, Marjorie E.

Mason, Charles W. The Value-Philosophy of Alfred Edward Taylor: A Study in Theistic Implication. LC 79-52512. 1979. pap. text 29.00 (*0-8191-0772-7*) U Pr of Amer.

Mason, Charlotte. Charlotte Mason's Original Homeschooling Series, 6 vols. 1993. boxed set 58.95 (*1-889209-00-7*) C Mason Res.

Mason, Cherie. Everybody's Somebody's Lunch. LC 98-38915. (Illus.). 40p. (J). (gr. 3-6). 1998. 16.95 (*0-88448-198-0*) Tilbury Hse.

— Wild Fox: A True Story. LC 92-74622. (Illus.). 32p. (J). (gr. 2-5). 1993. 15.95 (*0-89272-319-X*) Down East.

Mason, Cherie & Kellogg Markowsky, Judy. Everybody's Somebody's Lunch Teacher's Guide: The Role of Predator & Prey in Nature. (Illus.). 80p. 1998. pap., teacher ed. 9.95 (*0-88448-199-9*) Tilbury Hse.

Mason, Cheryl. Preparing & Directing a Teacher Institute. 32p. 1993. pap. text 6.50 (*0-87355-116-8*) Natl Sci Tchrs.

Mason, Chris, jt. auth. see Macdonald, Sheila.

Mason, Clifford. African-American Bookshelf 100 Must Reads from Before the Civil War through Today. 288p. 2000. 24.95 (*1-55972-539-7*) Carol Pub Group.

***Mason, Colin.** A Short History of Asia: Stone Age to 2000 AD. LC 99-56873. 2000. write for info. (*0-312-23059-1*); pap. 18.95 (*0-312-23060-5*) St Martin.

Mason, Connie. Beyond the Horizon. 448p. (Orig.). 1999. mass mkt. 5.50 (*0-505-52306-X*) Dorchester Pub Co.

***Mason, Connie.** The Black Knight. 400p. 1999. mass mkt. 5.99 (*0-8439-4622-9*, Leisure Bks) Dorchester Pub Co.

Mason, Connie. Bold Land, Bold Love. 384p. 1998. mass mkt. 5.99 (*0-505-52274-8*, Love Spell) Dorchester Pub Co.

— Brave Land, Brave Love. 448p. (Orig.). 1998. mass mkt. 5.50 (*0-505-52282-9*, Love Spell) Dorchester Pub Co.

***Mason, Connie.** Caress & Conquer. 480p. 1999. mass mkt. 5.99 (*0-505-52343-4*, Love Spell) Dorchester Pub Co.

Mason, Connie. Desert Ecstasy. 448p. 1996. pap. text, mass mkt. 5.99 (*0-8439-4195-2*) Dorchester Pub Co.

— For Honor's Sake. 400p. 1998. mass mkt. 5.50 (*0-505-52262-4*, Love Spell) Dorchester Pub Co.

— Gunslinger, 1. (Love Spell Ser.). 400p. 1999. mass mkt. 5.99 (*0-8439-4532-X*) Dorchester Pub Co.

***Mason, Connie.** Ice & Rapture. 448p. 1999. mass mkt. 5.99 (*0-8439-4570-2*, Pub. by Dorchester Pub Co) CMG.

Mason, Connie. The Lion's Bride. 448p. (Orig.). 1995. pap. text, mass mkt. 5.99 (*0-8439-3884-6*) Dorchester Pub Co.

***Mason, Connie.** Lord of the Night. 384p. 1998. reprint ed. mass mkt. 5.50 (*0-505-52254-3*, Love Spell) Dorchester Pub Co.

Mason, Connie. Love Me with Fury. 384p. 1997. mass mkt. 5.50 (*0-505-52215-2*, Love Spell) Dorchester Pub Co.

— Love to Cherish. 1997. mass mkt. 5.99 (*0-380-77999-4*, Avon Bks) Morrow Avon.

***Mason, Connie.** My Lady Vixen. 448p. (Orig.). 1999. pap. 5.99 (*0-8439-4607-5*, Leisure Bks) Dorchester Pub Co.

— The Outlaws: Rafe. (Outlaws Ser.). 400p. 2000. mass mkt. 5.99 (*0-8439-4702-0*, Leisure Bks) Dorchester Pub Co.

Mason, Connie. Pirate. 400p. 1998. mass mkt. 5.99 (*0-8439-4456-0*, Leisure Bks) Dorchester Pub Co.

— Promise Me Forever. 384p. 1998. reprint ed. mass mkt. 5.50 (*0-505-52246-2*, Love Spell) Dorchester Pub Co.

— A Promise of Thunder. 448p. (Orig.). 1996. mass mkt. 5.99 (*0-8439-4194-4*) Dorchester Pub Co.

***Mason, Connie.** Promised Splendor. 448p. (Orig.). 1999. pap. 5.99 (*0-8439-4608-3*, Leisure Bks) Dorchester Pub Co.

Mason, Connie. Pure Temptation. 400p. 2000. mass mkt. 5.99 (*0-8439-4041-7*, Leisure Bks) Dorchester Pub Co.

— Shadow Walker. 400p. (Orig.). 1997. mass mkt. 5.99 (*0-8439-4260-6*, Leisure Bks) Dorchester Pub Co.

***Mason, Connie.** Shadow Walker. 400p. (Orig.). 1999. pap. 5.99 (*0-8439-4606-7*, Leisure Bks) Dorchester Pub Co.

Mason, Connie. Sheik. 400p. (Orig.). 1997. mass mkt. 5.99 (*0-8439-4328-9*, Leisure Bks) Dorchester Pub Co.

— Sierra. 448p. (Orig.). 1995. pap. text, mass mkt. 5.99 (*0-8439-3815-3*) Dorchester Pub Co.

— Surrender to the Fury. 384p. 1998. reprint ed. mass mkt. 5.50 (*0-505-52266-7*, Love Spell) Dorchester Pub Co.

— Taken by You. 1996. mass mkt. 5.50 (*0-380-77998-6*, Avon Bks) Morrow Avon.

***Mason, Connie.** A Taste of Sin. LC 99-96450. 384p. 2000. mass mkt. 5.99 (*0-380-80801-3*, Avon Bks) Morrow Avon.

Mason, Connie. Tears Like Rain. 448p. (Orig.). 1995. mass mkt. 5.99 (*0-8439-4039-5*, Leisure Bks) Dorchester Pub Co.

— Tempt the Devil. 448p. 1998. mass mkt. 5.99 (*0-8439-4366-1*, Leisure Bks) Dorchester Pub Co.

— Tender Fury. 400p. 1996. mass mkt. 5.99 (*0-8439-4196-0*) Dorchester Pub Co.

— To Love a Stranger. 384p. 1997. mass mkt. 5.99 (*0-380-79340-7*, Avon Bks) Morrow Avon.

— To Tame a Renegade. 1998. mass mkt. 5.99 (*0-380-79341-5*, Avon Bks) Morrow Avon.

— To Tempt a Rogue. LC 98-94822. 384p. 1999. mass mkt. 5.99 (*0-380-79342-3*, Avon Bks) Morrow Avon.

— Treasures of the Heart. 448p. (Orig.). 1993. pap. text, mass mkt. 5.99 (*0-8439-3539-1*, Leisure Bks) Dorchester Pub Co.

— Treasures of the Heart. 448p. (Orig.). 1995. mass mkt. 5.99 (*0-8439-4038-7*, Leisure Bks) Dorchester Pub Co.

— Viking! 400p. 1998. mass mkt. 5.99 (*0-8439-4402-1*, Leisure Bks) Dorchester Pub Co.

***Mason, Connie.** Wild Is My Heart. 448p. (Orig.). 1999. pap. 5.99 (*0-8439-4605-9*, Leisure Bks) Dorchester Pub Co.

Mason, Connie. Wild Land, Wild Love. 384p. (Orig.). 1998. mass mkt. 5.50 (*0-505-52278-0*, Love Spell) Dorchester Pub Co.

— Wind Rider. 448p. 1995. mass mkt. 5.99 (*0-8439-4040-9*, Leisure Bks) Dorchester Pub Co.

Mason, D. Investors in People: A Guide to Achieving the Standard. 1996. pap. 129.00 (*1-85953-085-0*, Pub. by Tech Comm) St Mut.

***Mason, D.** Pocket Guide to Lymphoma Classification. (Illus.). 1998. pap. 26.95 (*0-632-05096-9*) Blackwell Sci.

Mason, D. G., ed. see Moody, William Vaughn.

Mason, D. M. Development of Gaslight Emitters with Improved Durability. (Technical Report Ser.: No. 9). vi, 19p. 1964. pap. 25.00 (*1-58222-017-4*) Inst Gas Tech.

Mason, D. M., jt. auth. see Janssen, A. J.

Mason, D. McA., et al. Identification & Determination of Organic Sulfur in Utility Gases. (Research Bulletin Ser.: No. 6). iv, 51p. 1959. pap. 25.00 (*1-58222-025-5*) Inst Gas Tech.

Mason, D. Y. & Harris, Nancy L. Human Lymphoma: Clinical Implications of the Real Classification. LC 98-49714. xiv, 336p. 1999. 275.00 (*1-85233-129-1*) Spr-Verlag.

Mason, Dale J., jt. auth. see Vervoort, Gerardus.

Mason, Dale T., ed. see Van Bebber, Mark & Taylor, Paul S.

Mason, Daniel G. Beethoven & His Forerunners. LC 70-119653. reprint ed. 37.50 (*0-404-04197-3*) AMS Pr.

— Beethoven & His Forerunners. 352p. 1990. reprint ed. lib. bdg. 79.00 (*0-7812-9038-4*) Rprt Serv.

— Chamber Music of Brahms. LC 78-107817. (Select Bibliographies Reprint Ser.). 1977. 26.95 (*0-8369-5209-X*) Ayer.

— Chamber Music of Brahms. LC 70-119653. reprint ed. 27.50 (*0-404-04198-1*) AMS Pr.

— Contemporary Composers. LC 72-1726. reprint ed. 29.50 (*0-404-08327-7*) AMS Pr.

— The Dilemma of American Music & other Essays. 306p. 1990. reprint ed. lib. bdg. 79.00 (*0-7812-9015-5*) Rprt Serv.

— From Grieg to Brahms. enl. ed. LC 79-149689. reprint ed. 27.50 (*0-404-04199-X*) AMS Pr.

— From Grieg to Brahms: Studies of Some Modern Composers & Their Art. 259p. 1990. reprint ed. lib. bdg. 69.00 (*0-7812-9039-2*) Rprt Serv.

— Great Modern Composers: Biographical Sections by M. L. Mason, Appreciation of Music Vol. 2. LC 68-20319. (Essay Index Reprint Ser.). 1977. 19.95 (*0-8369-0690-X*) Ayer.

— Music in My Time: And Other Reminiscences. (American Biography Ser.). 409p. 1991. reprint ed. lib. bdg. 89.00 (*0-7812-8274-8*) Rprt Serv.

— Music in My Time & Other Reminiscences. LC 71-107818. (Select Bibliographies Reprint Ser.). 1977. 36.95 (*0-8369-5189-1*) Ayer.

— Music in My Time & Other Reminiscences. LC 71-109784. 409p. 1970. reprint ed. lib. bdg. 49.50 (*0-8371-4274-1*, MAMT, Greenwood Pr) Greenwood.

— The Orchestral Instruments & What They Do: A Primer for Concert-Goers. 104p. 1990. reprint ed. lib. bdg. 59.00 (*0-7812-9155-0*) Rprt Serv.

— Romantic Composers. LC 73-119654. reprint ed. 29.50 (*0-404-04223-6*) AMS Pr.

— Romantic Composers. LC 69-13990. 353p. 1970. reprint ed. lib. bdg. 69.50 (*0-8371-4096-X*, MARC, Greenwood Pr) Greenwood.

— The Romantic Composers. 353p. 1990. reprint ed. lib. bdg. 79.00 (*0-7812-9040-6*) Rprt Serv.

— Tune in, America. LC 72-90664. (Essay Index Reprint Ser.). 1977. 19.95 (*0-8369-1228-4*) Ayer.

— Tune in America! A Study of Our Coming Musical Independence. LC 72-1720. reprint ed. 31.50 (*0-404-08328-5*) AMS Pr.

Mason, Daniel G., ed. The Art of Music, 14 vols., Set. LC 74-26067. reprint ed. 525.00 (*0-404-13020-8*) AMS Pr.

Mason, Darielle, jt. ed. see Desai, Vishakha N.

Mason, David. The Buried Houses. (Roerich Poetry Prize Winner Ser.). 80p. 1991. pap. 10.95 (*0-934257-84-1*) Story Line.

— The Country I Remember: Poems. 86p. (Orig.). 1996. 21.00 (*1-885266-20-0*); pap. 12.00 (*1-885266-23-5*) Story Line.

***Mason, David.** Improving Articulation Between the Elementary & Junior High Educational Units: In Prince George's County Schools. 32p. 2000. pap. 7.95 (*1-56167-574-1*) Am Literary Pr.

Mason, David. The Poetry of Life: And the Life of Poetry. LC 99-14959. 248p. 2000. pap. 15.95 (*1-885266-80-4*, Pub. by Story Line) Consort Bk Sales.

Mason, David. Race & Ethnicity in Modern Britain. (Illus.). 164p. 1995. pap. text 20.00 (*0-19-878099-0*) OUP.

Mason, David. Small Elegies. 1990. 2.50 (*0-941127-09-5*) Dacotah Terr Pr.

***Mason, David.** Verdun. 2000. reprint ed. pap. 24.95 (*1-900624-41-9*, Pub. by Windrush Pr) Combined Pub.

Mason, David, jt. auth. see Swindells, Philip.

Mason, David, jt. ed. see Jarman, Mark.

Mason, David, jt. ed. see Millard, H. Dean.

***Mason, David A.** Spirit of the Mountains: Korea's SAN-SHIN & Traditions of Mountain-Worship. LC 99-65244. (Illus.). 224p. 1999. 49.95 (*1-56591-107-5*) Hollym Intl.

Mason, David E. Voluntary Nonprofit Enterprise Management. (Nonprofit Management & Finance Ser.). 206p. 1985. 52.50 (*0-306-41582-8*, Plenum Trade) Perseus Pubng.

Mason, David J., jt. auth. see Jurek, Zbigniew J.

Mason, David P. Massacre at Fort Mims. 196p. 1989. pap. 14.95 (*0-926291-02-5*) Greenberry Pub.

Mason, David S. Revolution & Transition in East-Central Europe. 2nd ed. (Dilemmas in World Politics Ser.). 256p. (C). 1996. pap. text 20.00 (*0-8133-2835-7*, Pub. by Westview) HarpC.

***Mason, David S. & Kluegel, James R.** Marketing Democracy: Changing Opinion about Inequality & Politics in East Central Europe. LC 00-37284. 2000. write for info. (*0-7425-0153-1*) Rowman.

Mason, David V. Get a Clue Hell High. LC 98-170290. (Orig.). (YA). (gr. 9 up). 1996. pap. 9.99 (*0-88092-401-2*, 4012) Royal Fireworks.

— School's Out Hell High. LC 97-216295. 108p. (YA). (gr. 9-12). 1996. pap. 9.99 (*0-88092-400-4*) Royal Fireworks.

Mason, Debra, jt. ed. see Buddenbaum, Judith M.

Mason, Diana J. & Leavitt, Judith K. Policy & Politics in Nursing & Health Care. 3rd ed. LC 98-21520. (Illus.). 784p. (C). 1998. pap. text 42.00 (*0-7216-7038-5*, W B Saunders Co) Harcrt Hlth Sci Grp.

Mason, Diana J. & Talbott, Susan W. The Political Action Handbook for Nurses. 640p. (C). 1985. pap. text 29.75 (*0-201-16368-3*, Health Sci) Addison-Wesley.

Mason, Diane. Breastfeeding & the Working Mother. rev. ed. LC 97-2329. 1997. pap. 11.95 (*0-312-15486-0*, St Martin Griffin) St Martin.

Mason, Diane, et al. No More Tantrums. LC 96-34768. 176p. 1997. pap. 12.95 (*0-8092-3070-4*, 307040, Contemporary Bks) NTC Contemp Pub Co.

***Mason, Don.** Transforming Supervision in Health Care. 160p. 1999. pap. 19.95 (*0-304-70463-6*) Continuum.

Mason, Donald B. The Dolphin's Dream - Healing Tales & Stories for Young People. Chapman, Sandy C., ed. (Illus.). xiv, 106p. 1997. pap. 14.00 (*0-9662102-0-4*) Prairie Schooner.

Mason-Dorman, Cheryl & Kenya, Ahmad. Images of the Motherland Teacher Outline of Video Segments: Children of Africa, Dogon of Mali, African Arts & Crafts. (Video & Photo Essay from the Camera of Ahmad Kenya Ser.). (Illus.). 24p. (J). (gr. k-12). 1996. teacher ed. 10.00 (*0-910689-01-6*) Universal Charities Services.

Mason, Dorothy E. Music in Elizabethan England. LC 59-1448. (Folger Guides to the Age of Shakespeare Ser.). 1958. pap. 4.95 (*0-918016-21-5*) Folger Bks.

Mason, Edna W. Isbell. Descendants of Robert Isbell in America. (Illus.). 296p. 1997. reprint ed. pap. 45.00 (*0-8328-9321-8*); reprint ed. lib. bdg. 55.00 (*0-8328-9320-X*) Higginson Bk Co.

Mason, Edward E. Fluid, Electrolyte & Nutrient Therapy in Surgery. LC 73-8805. (Illus.). 360p. reprint ed. 111.60 (*0-8357-9403-2*, 201456100094) Bks Demand.

Mason, Edward S. Controlling World Trade: Cartels & Commodity Agreements. LC 72-4281. (World Affairs Ser.: National & International Viewpoints). 308p. 1972. reprint ed. 23.95 (*0-405-04574-3*) Ayer.

— The Economic & Social Modernization of the Republic of Korea. (East Asian Monographs: No. 92). (Illus.). 584p. 1981. 30.00 (*0-674-23175-9*) HUP.

— Economic Concentration & the Monopoly Problem. LC 57-6351. (Economic Studies: No. 100). (Illus.). 427p. 1957. 25.00 (*0-674-22651-8*) HUP.

— Economic Development in India & Pakistan. LC 77-38764. (Harvard University. Center for International Affairs. Occasional Papers in International Affairs: No. 13). reprint ed. 24.50 (*0-404-54613-7*) AMS Pr.

— Economic Planning in Underdeveloped Areas: Government & Business. LC 58-59763. (Moorhouse I.X. Millar Lecture Ser.: No. 2). 100p. reprint ed. pap. 31.00 (*0-7837-0456-9*, 204077900018) Bks Demand.

— The Harvard Institute for International Development & Its Antecedents. 108p. (Orig.). (C). 1986. pap. text 14.00 (*0-8191-5553-5*); lib. bdg. 33.00 (*0-8191-5552-7*) U Pr of Amer.

— On the Appropriate Size of a Development Program. LC 76-25007. (Harvard University. Center for International Affairs. Occasional Papers in International Affairs: No. 8). reprint ed. 24.50 (*0-404-54608-0*) AMS Pr.

Mason, Edward S. & Asher, Robert E. The World Bank since Bretton Woods. LC 73-1089. 915p. 1973. 44.95 (*0-8157-5492-2*) Brookings.

Mason, Edward T. Samuel Johnson: His Words & His Ways. LC 72-2104. (Studies in Samuel Johnson: No. 97). 1972. reprint ed. lib. bdg. 75.00 (*0-8383-1491-0*) M S G Haskell Hse.

Mason, Elisabeth & Eber, Eric. Investing Tips Grampa Taught Us: A Guide to Financing College Costs. LC 94-37809. (Illus.). 162p. 1994. pap. 13.95 (*0-9643153-0-0*) Finan Pr FL.

Mason, Elizabeth. Cooking Lowfat, Southern & Fabulous. Date not set. pap. text 19.95 (*1-887269-38-X*) J Culler & Sons.

— Cooking Southern Lowfat & Fabulous. 1999. pap. text 19.99 (*1-889893-33-1*) Emerald House Group Inc.

— The Rag Street Journal: The Ultimate Guide to Shopping Thrift & Consignment Stores Throughout the U. S. & Canada. 88p. (Orig.). 1995. pap. 14.95 (*0-8050-3728-4*, Owl) H Holt & Co.

Mason, Elizabeth B. & Starr, Louis M. The Oral History Collection of Columbia University. 4th ed. LC 79-11527. (Illus.). xxx, 306p. 1979. text 22.50 (*0-9602492-0-6*) Columbia U Oral Hist Res.

Mason, Elizabeth J. How to Write Meaningful Nursing Standards. LC 84-13005. 261p. (C). 1989. pap. text 39.95 (*0-8273-4300-0*) Delmar.

Mason, Elliott B. Human Physiology. 575p. 1983. text 52.75 (*0-8053-6885-X*) Benjamin-Cummings.

Mason, Ellsworth. The University of Colorado Library & Its Makers, 1876-1972. LC 93-33714. (Illus.). 401p. 1994. 47.50 (*0-8108-2685-2*) Scarecrow.

Mason, Ellsworth, ed. see Joyce, James.

Mason, Emanuel J. & Bramble, William J. Research in Education & the Behavioral Sciences. LC 95-83257. 512p. (C). 1996. text. write for info. (*0-697-17105-1*) Brown & Benchmark.

Mason, Emilee D. The Unknown Hero. (J). (gr. 3-5). 1996. 6.95 (*1-886706-19-0*) Hickory Hse.

Mason, Emma. Westminster Abbey & Its People c. 1050-c. 1216. (Studies in the History of Medieval Religion: No. 9). (Illus.). 387p. 1996. 110.00 (*0-85115-396-8*) Boydell & Brewer.

***Mason, Et Al.** Island Magic. 320p. 2000. reprint ed. mass mkt. 5.99 (*0-312-97300-4*) St Martin.

Mason, Eudo C. Goethe's Faust: Its Genesis & Purport. LC 67-14969. 435p. reprint ed. pap. 134.90 (*0-608-17963-9*, 202905200058) Bks Demand.

— Rilke, Europe, & the English-speaking World. LC 61-16153. 277p. reprint ed. pap. 79.00 (*0-608-12058-8*, 2024492) Bks Demand.

Mason, Eugene. Aucassin & Nicolette with Other Romances. LC 70-172850. (Illus.). reprint ed. 37.50 (*0-404-07774-9*) AMS Pr.

Mason, Eugene, tr. Arthurian Chronicles: Wace & Layamon. (Medieval Academy Reprints for Teaching Ser.: No. 35). 282p. 1996. reprint ed. pap. text 16.95 (*0-8020-7176-7*) U of Toronto Pr.

Mason, Eugene, tr. see Marie De France.

Mason, F. Van Wyck. At the Villa Rose. 1976. 24.95 (*0-8488-0832-0*) Amereon Ltd.

— Guns for Rebellion. 27.95 (*0-89190-099-3*) Amereon Ltd.

— The Rio Casino Intrigue. reprint ed. lib. bdg. 20.95 (*0-89190-356-9*, Rivercity Pr) Amereon Ltd.

Mason, Felicia. Body & Soul. 288p. 1995. mass mkt. 4.99 (*0-8217-0160-6*, Zebra Kensgtn); mass mkt. 4.99 (*0-7860-0160-7*, Pinncle Kensgtn) Kensgtn Pub Corp.

— Foolish Heart. 240p. 1998. mass mkt. 4.99 (*0-7860-0593-9*, Pinncle Kensgtn) Kensgtn Pub Corp.

***Mason, Felicia.** For the Love of You. (Arabesque Ser.). 284p. 1999. mass mkt. 5.99 (*1-58314-088-3*) BET Bks.

Mason, Felicia. For the Love of You. 288p. 1994. mass mkt. 4.99 (*0-7860-0071-6*, Pinncle Kensgtn) Kensgtn Pub Corp.

***Mason, Felicia.** Forbidden Heart. 1999. mass mkt. 4.99 (*1-58314-050-6*, Arabesq) BET Bks.

— Rhapsody. (Arabesque Ser.). 2000. mass mkt. 5.99 (*1-58314-063-8*) BET Bks.

Mason, Felicia. Rhapsody. 320p. 1997. mass mkt. 4.99 (*0-7860-0404-5*, Pinncle Kensgtn) Kensgtn Pub Corp.

— Seduction. 320p. 1996. mass mkt. 4.99 (*0-7860-0297-2*, Pinncle Kensgtn) Kensgtn Pub Corp.

***Mason, Felicia.** Something to Celebrate. 320p. 1999. 22.00 (*1-58314-045-X*, Arabesq) BET Bks.

— Something to Celebrate. (Arabesque Ser.). 2000. mass mkt. 5.99 (*1-58314-172-3*) BET Bks.

Mason, Florence M. & Dobson, Chris. Information Brokering-How to Make Money Selling Information Services: A How-To-Do-It Manual. LC 98-12371. (How-to-Do-It Manual Ser.). 144p. 1998. pap. 45.00 (*1-55570-342-9*) Neal-Schuman.

Mason, Florence M., jt. auth. see Bierman, Kenneth J.

Mason, Floyd R. John Mason & Mary Ann Miller. 1999. pap. 55.00 (*0-8328-9836-8*) Higginson Bk Co.

— John Mason & Mary Ann Miller of Virginia. 367p. 1999. 65.00 (*0-8328-9835-X*) Higginson Bk Co.

Mason, Floyd R. & Mason, Kathryn G. Garber - Miller. The John H. Garber & Barbara Miller of Pennsylvania, Marland & Va. (Illus.). 1530p. 1998. pap. 155.50 (*0-8328-9657-8*); lib. bdg. 165.50 (*0-8328-9656-X*) Higginson Bk Co.

— Klein. George Klein, Sr., Family Record. (Illus.). 143p. 1997. reprint ed. pap. 21.50 (*0-8328-9443-5*); reprint ed. lib. bdg. 31.50 (*0-8328-9442-7*) Higginson Bk Co.

— Michael Miller & Susanna Bechtol Family Record. 1007p. 1999. 139.00 (*0-8328-9832-5*) Higginson Bk Co.

— Wampler Family Record: John Wampler & Magdalena Garber of Maryland & Virginia. (Illus.). 384p. 1997. pap. 54.00 (*0-8328-9539-3*); lib. bdg. 64.00 (*0-8328-9538-5*) Higginson Bk Co.

— Ziegler Family Record: Ziegler, Zeigler & Zigler. 672p. 1999. 104.50 (*0-8328-9833-3*); pap. 94.50 (*0-8328-9834-1*) Higginson Bk Co.

Mason, Frances B. Great Design: Order & Progress in Nature. LC 72-156690. (Essay Index Reprint Ser.). 1977. reprint ed. 23.95 (*0-8369-2562-9*) Ayer.

Mason, Frances N., ed. John Norton & Sons, Merchants of London & Virginia: Being Papers from Their Counting House for the Years 1750-1795. LC 68-23839. (Illus.). xi, 573p. 1968. reprint ed. 49.50 (*0-678-05614-5*) Kelley.

Mason, Francis, ed. I Remember Balanchine: Recollections of the Ballet Master by Those Who Knew Him. 597p. 1998. text 25.00 (*0-7881-5946-1*) DIANE Pub.

Mason, Francis, jt. auth. see Balanchine, George.

Mason, Francis K. The British Bomber since 1914. (Illus.). 416p. 1994. 49.95 (*1-55750-085-1*) Naval Inst Pr.

— The British Fighter since 1912. (Putnam Aviation Ser.). (Illus.). 448p. 1993. 49.95 (*1-55750-082-7*) Naval Inst Pr.

— Hawker Aircraft since 1920. rev. ed. (Putnam Aviation Ser.). (Illus.). 512p. 1991. 49.95 (*1-55750-351-6*) Naval Inst Pr.

Mason, Francis K., jt. auth. see Windrow, Martin.

Mason, Francis Van Wyck. Saigon Singer. 1976. 24.95 (*0-89190-352-6*) Amereon Ltd.

— Two Tickets for Tangier. 1976. 23.95 (*0-89190-354-2*) Amereon Ltd.

Mason, Franklin. Four Roses in Three Acts. LC 80-68007. 1981. 10.95 (*0-914590-64-2*); pap. 5.95 (*0-914590-65-0*) Fiction Coll.

Mason, G. W. Mason: Ancestors & Descendants of Elisha Mason, Litchfield, Conn., 1759-1858, & His Wife Lucretia Webster, 1766-1853. 120p. 1992. reprint ed. pap. 23.00 (*0-8328-2685-5*); reprint ed. lib. bdg. 33.00 (*0-8328-2684-7*) Higginson Bk Co.

Mason, Gabriel R., ed. Great American Liberals. LC 76-156691. (Essay Index Reprint Ser.). 1977. reprint ed. 18.95 (*0-8369-2413-4*) Ayer.

Mason, Gail & Thomsen, Stephen, eds. Homophobic Violence. LC 97-158830. 160p. 1997. pap. 29.00 (*1-876067-04-7*, Pub. by Federation Pr) Gaunt.

***Mason, Gary.** Coolest Guys: Featuring the Top 35 of the Coolest Guys. 2nd ed. (Illus.). 160p. 2000. pap. 19.95 (*0-7407-1170-9*) Andrews & McMeel.

Mason, Gary, text. The Coolest Guys: Featuring the Top 35 Players from the Coolest Game on Earth. (Lionheart Book Ser.). (Illus.). 160p. 1998. pap. 19.95 (*0-8362-7116-5*) Andrews & McMeel.

Mason, Gene. Save Your License: A Driver's Survival Guide. LC 78-2218. (Illus.). 150p. 1978. text 14.95 (*0-87364-103-5*) Paladin Pr.

Mason, Geoffrey, jt. ed. see Cooperstein, Bruce.

Mason, Geoffrey, jt. ed. see Dong, Chongying.

Mason, George. The Papers of George Mason, 1725-1792, 3 vols., Vol. 1. Rutland, Robert A., ed. LC 70-97016. 613p. reprint ed. pap. 190.10 (*0-7837-0318-X*, 204064000001) Bks Demand.

— The Papers of George Mason, 1725-1792, 3 vols., Vol. 2. Rutland, Robert A., ed. LC 70-97016. 403p. reprint ed. pap. 125.00 (*0-7837-0319-8*, 204064000002) Bks Demand.

— The Papers of George Mason, 1725-1792, 3 vols., Vol. 3. Rutland, Robert A., ed. LC 70-97016. 477p. reprint ed. pap. 147.90 (*0-7837-0320-1*, 204064000003) Bks Demand.

Mason, George H. Life with the Zulus of Natal, South Africa. 232p. 1968. 45.00 (*0-7146-1835-7*, Pub. by F Cass Pubs) Intl Spec Bk.

***Mason, Gilbert R. & Smith, James Patterson.** Beaches, Blood & Ballots: A Black Doctor's Civil Rights Struggle. (Margaret Walker Alexander Series in African American Studies). (Illus.). 256p. 2000. 27.00 (*1-57806-278-0*) U Pr of Miss.

Mason, Grace S. Women Are Queer. LC 77-37278. (Short Story Index Reprint Ser.). 1977. reprint ed. 23.95 (*0-8369-4089-X*) Ayer.

Mason, Gregory, jt. auth. see Mason, Ruth.

Mason, Gregory H., ed. see Nin, Anais & Pollak, Felix.

Mason, Griselda F. Sleigh Ride to Russia: The Quaker Mission to Russia to Try to Avert the Crimean War. (C). 1988. 60.00 (*0-900657-99-5*, Pub. by W Sessions) St Mut.

Mason, H., ed. Voltaire: Candide. (French Texts Ser.). (FRE.). 138p. 1995. pap. 18.95 (*1-85399-369-7*, Pub. by Brist Class Pr) Focus Pub-R Pullins.

Mason, H. A. The Tragic Plane. 200p. 1985. 55.00 (*0-19-812843-6*) OUP.

Mason, H. A., ed. Sir Thomas Wyatt: A Literary Portrait. 344p. 1987. 37.50 (*0-8453-4512-5*) Assoc Univ Prs.

Mason, H. E., ed. Moral Dilemmas & Moral Theory. 256p. 1996. text 52.00 (*0-19-509681-9*) OUP.

Mason, H. L. Toynbee's Approach to World Politics, Vol. 5. LC 60-202. 1958. 11.00 (*0-930598-04-0*) Tulane Stud Pol.

Mason, H. L., ed. see Oldenbourg, Rudolf C. & Sartorius, Hans.

Mason, H. Lee. Before the Horse: Indian Myths & Legends. LC 99-72064. (Illus.). 72p. 1999. 37.50 (*0-938041-42-8*) Arc Pr AR.

— Sermon Outlines for Evangelism. (Sermon Outline Ser.). 48p. 1981. pap. 4.99 (*0-8010-6120-2*) Baker Bks.

Mason, H. Lowell. Hymn-Tunes of Lowell Mason. LC 74-24144. reprint ed. 29.50 (*0-404-13035-6*) AMS Pr.

Mason, Hamilton. French Theatre in New York: 1899-1939. LC 40-14965. reprint ed. 27.50 (*0-404-04224-4*) AMS Pr.

Mason, Harold A. & Wyatt, Thomas. Editing Wyatt: An Examination of Collected Poems of Sir Thomas Wyatt. LC 74-168906. ix, 209p. 1972. write for info. (*0-904274-00-4*) Cambridge Quartely.

Mason, Harriet. The Power of Storytelling: A Step-by-Step Guide to Dramatic Learning in K-12. LC 95-50176. (Illus.). 128p. 1996. pap. 19.95 (*0-8039-6414-5*) Corwin Pr.

— The Power of Storytelling: A Step-by-Step Guide to Dramatic Learning in K-12. LC 95-50176. (Illus.). 128p. 1996. 45.95 (*0-8039-6413-7*) Corwin Pr.

Mason, Harry M. Life on the Dry Line: Working the Land, 1902-1944. LC 92-53038. 224p. 1992. 19.95 (*1-55591-122-6*) Fulcrum Pub.

Mason, Haydn. Candide: Optimism Demolished. (MWS Ser.). 170p. 1992. 23.95 (*0-8057-8085-8*, Twyne); pap. 18.00 (*0-8057-8559-0*, Twyne) Mac Lib Ref.

Mason, Heather, ed. see Arter, Christine, et al.

Mason, Heather L., jt. ed. see Etheridge, David T.

Mason, Helen. Great Careers for People Interested in Food, Vol. 3. 3rd ed. LC 95-62263. (Career Connections Ser.: Series 3). 48p. 1995. text 23.00 (*0-7876-0860-2*, UXL) Gale.

— Great Careers for People Who Like Being Outdoors, Vol. 6. LC 93-78075. (Career Connections Ser.: Series 1). (Illus.). 48p. (J). (gr. 6-9). 1993. text 23.00 (*0-8103-9390-5*, 102108, UXL) Gale.

***Mason, Henry Joseph.** Essay on the Antiquity & Constitution of Parliaments in Ireland. ix,126,xxvip. 1999. reprint ed. 95.00 (*1-56169-554-8*) Gaunt.

Mason, Henry L. College & University Government: A Handbook of Principle & Practice. LC 75-321378. (Tulane Studies in Political Science: No. 14). 249p. Date not set. reprint ed. pap. 77.20 (*0-608-20653-9*, 207209000003) Bks Demand.

— Mass Demonstrations Against Foreign Regimes, Vol. 10. LC 66-8068. 1966. 11.00 (*0-930598-09-1*) Tulane Stud Pol.

— Mass Demonstrations Against Foreign Regimes: A Study of Five Crises. LC 66-8608. (Tulane Studies in Political Science: No. 10). 104p. Date not set. reprint ed. pap. 32.30 (*0-608-20656-3*, 207209300003) Bks Demand.

— Toynbee's Approach to World Politics. LC 60-202. (Tulane Studies in Political Science: No. 5). 163p. Date not set. reprint ed. pap. 50.60 (*0-608-20659-8*, 207209600003) Bks Demand.

Mason, Henry M., tr. see Anjou, Lars A.

***Mason, Herbert.** Disappearances: Poems. LC 99-35310. 1999. 9.95 (*0-933546-72-6*) KNP.

Mason, Herbert. Memoir of a Friend: Louis Massignon. LC 87-40349. 160p. 1988. text 22.00 (*0-268-01365-9*) U of Notre Dame Pr.

— Testimonies & Reflections: Essays of Louis Massignon. 182p. 1996. 24.95 (*0-614-21244-8*, 1225) Kazi Pubns.

— Two Statesmen of Mediaeval Islam: Vizir Ibn Hubayra (499-560 A. H., 1105-1165 A. D.) & Califh an-Nasir Li Din Allah (553-622 A. H., 1158-1225 A. D.) 146p. 1972. text 44.65 (*90-279-6979-5*) Mouton.

Mason, Herbert, ed. from FRE. Testimonies & Reflections: Essays of Louis Massignon. LC 88-40327. (C). 1989. text 29.00 (*0-268-01733-6*) U of Notre Dame Pr.

Mason, Herbert, tr. Gilgamesh: A Verse Narrative. 126p. 1972. mass mkt. 6.99 (*0-451-62718-0*, Ment) NAL.

Mason, Herbert Molloy, Jr. VFW: Our First Century. LC 99-24943. (Illus.). 240p. 1999. 24.95 (*1-886110-72-7*, Pub. by Addax Pubng) Midpt Trade.

Mason, Herbert W. Al-Hallaj. (Curzon Sufi Ser.: No. 2). 128p. (C). 1995. pap. 20.00 (*0-7007-0311-X*) Paul & Co Pubs.

— The Death of Al-Hallaj: A Dramatic Narrative. LC 79-4403. (Illus.). 1991. pap. text 8.00 (*0-268-00843-4*) U of Notre Dame Pr.

Mason, Herbert W., tr. see Massignon, Louis.

Mason, Herman S., Jr. African-American Entertainment in Atlanta. LC 98-85875. (Images of America Ser.). (Illus.). 128p. 1998. pap. 16.99 (*0-7524-0986-7*) Arcadia Publng.

— African-American Life in DeKalb County. LC 98-88063. (Images of America Ser.). (Illus.). 128p. 1998. pap. 18.99 (*0-7385-0034-8*) Arcadia Publng.

Mason, Herman S. African-American Life in Jacksonville. (Images of America Ser.). (Illus.). 128p. (Orig.). 1997. pap. 16.99 (*0-7524-0883-6*) Arcadia Publng.

Mason, Herman S., Jr. Black Atlanta in the Roaring Twenties. (Images of America Ser.). (Illus.). 128p. 1997. pap. 16.99 (*0-7524-0887-9*) Arcadia Publng.

— Politics, Civil Rights & Law in Black Atlanta. (Black America Ser.). (Illus.). 128p. 2000. pap. 18.99 (*0-7524-0985-9*) Arcadia Publng.

***Mason, Herman S.** Washington, GA. (Images of America Ser.). (Illus.). 128p. 1999. pap. 18.99 (*0-7385-0228-6*) Arcadia Publng.

Mason, Hilary, jt. auth. see Mudd, Stephanie.

***Mason, Hillary.** Collections. (Illus.). 2000. pap. 15.95 (*0-947882-31-6*) Belair Pubns Ltd.

Mason Hogue, Marjorie. Amazing Annuals: More Than 300 Container & Garden Plants for Summer-Long Color. (Illus.). 160p. 1998. pap. 24.95 (*1-55209-307-7*) Firefly Bks Ltd.

Mason, I., ed. see International Congress of Animal Production Staff.

Mason, I. J., jt. auth. see Schodde, R.

Mason, I. L. A World Dictionary of Livestock Breeds, Types & Varieties. 4th ed. LC 97-103288. 296p. 1996. text 80.00 (*0-85199-102-5*) OUP.

Mason, I. L., jt. ed. see Hoffmann, B.

Mason, I. S., jt. auth. see Moriello, K. A.

Mason, Ian, jt. auth. see Hatim, Basil.

Mason, Ian A. The Semantics of Destructive Lisp. LC 86-72170. (Center for the Study of Language & Information-Lecture Notes Ser.: No. 5). 290p. 1987. 59.95 (*0-937073-05-9*); pap. 19.95 (*0-937073-06-7*) CSLI.

Mason, Isaac. Life of Isaac Mason As a Slave. LC 72-89393. (Black Heritage Library Collection). 1977. 11.95 (*0-8369-8627-X*) Ayer.

Mason, Ivor, jt. auth. see Sharpe, Paul T.

Mason, J. Evolution Made Plain. 1992. lib. bdg. 250.95 (*0-8490-5567-9*) Gordon Pr.

— Multinuclear NMR. LC 87-12284. (Illus.). 660p. 1987. 155.00 (*0-306-42153-4*, Kluwer Plenum) Kluwer Academic.

Mason, J., ed. Design for Manufacturability, 1994. LC 93-70158. (DE Ser.: Vol. 67). 132p. 1994. 32.50 (*0-7918-1269-3*, H00901) ASME.

Mason, J. & Davis, J. Fostering & Sustaining Mathematics Thinking Through Problem Solving: Thinking Through Problem Solving. 106p. (C). 1995. pap. 50.00 (*0-7300-1264-6*, ECT405, Pub. by Deakin Univ) St Mut.

— Modelling with Mathematics in Primary & Secondary Schools: Modelling with Mathematics in Primary & Secondary Schools. 78p. (C). 1995. pap. 40.00 (*0-7300-1265-4*, ECT404, Pub. by Deakin Univ) St Mut.

***Mason, J. & Nitenberg, G.** Cancer & Nutrition: Prevention & Treatment. (Nestle Nutrition Workshop Series : Clinical & Performance Programme: 4). (Illus.). 316p. 2000. 226.25 (*3-8055-7081-3*) S Karger.

Mason, J., jt. ed. see Shephard.

Mason, J., jt. ed. see Sutherland, R. J.

Mason, J. Alden. The Ethnology of the Salinan Indians. fac. ed. (University of California Publications in American Archaeology & Ethnology: Vol. 10: 4). 143p. (C). 1912. reprint ed. pap. text 15.63 (*1-55567-190-X*) Coyote Press.

— The Language of the Salinan Indians. fac. ed. (University of California Publications in American Archaeology & Ethnology: Vol. 14: 1). 154p. (C). 1918. reprint ed. pap. text 16.88 (*1-55567-217-5*) Coyote Press.

— The Mutsun Dialect of Costanoan Based on the Vocabulary of de la Cuesta. fac. ed. (University of California Publications in American Archaeology & Ethnology: Vol. 11: 7). 73p. (C). 1916. reprint ed. pap. text 8.44 (*1-55567-199-3*) Coyote Press.

— A Preliminary Sketch of the Yaqui Language. fac. ed.

M

An Asterisk (*) at the beginning of an entry indicates that the title is appearing for the first time.

(University of California Publications in American Archaeology & Ethnology: Vol. 20: 12). 20p. (C). 1923. reprint ed. pap. text 2.50 (*1-55567-248-5*) Coyote Press.
— Puerto Rican Folklore. Espinosa, Aurelio M., ed. (Puerto Rico Ser.). 1979. lib. bdg. 59.95 (*0-8490-2989-9*) Gordon Pr.
Mason, J. Barry, et al. Cases & Problems in Contemporary Retailing. 3rd ed. LC 91-73501. 459p. 1992. pap. 31.95 (*0-87393-139-4*) Dame Pubns.
— Retailing. 5th ed. LC 93-21286. (Series in Marketing). 704p. (C). 1993. text 69.95 (*0-256-12002-1*, Irwn Prfssnl) McGraw-Hill Prof.
— Retailing: Canadian Version. 448p. (C). 1990. text 54.95 (*0-256-07865-3*, Irwn McGrw-H) McGrw-H Hghr Educ.
— Retailing, International. 4th ed. (C). 1992. text, student ed. 29.95 (*0-256-11410-2*, Irwn McGrw-H) McGrw-H Hghr Educ.
Mason, J. C. Chebyshev Polynomials. 2000. lib. bdg. 59.95 (*0-8493-0355-9*, Chap & Hall CRC) CRC Pr.
Mason, J. C., ed. Scientific Software Systems. 200p. (gr. 13). 1990. text 74.95 (*0-412-34570-6*, 836) Chapman & Hall.
Mason, J. C. & Cox, M. G. Algorithms for Approximation. 2nd ed. 532p. (gr. 13). 1990. ring bd. 94.95 (*0-412-34580-3*, A3805, Chap & Hall CRC) CRC Pr.
Mason, J. C. & Cox, M. G., eds. Algorithms for Approximation. (Institute of Mathematics & Its Applications Conference Series, New Ser.: New Series 10). (Illus.). 710p. 1987. 125.00 (*0-19-853612-7*) OUP.
***Mason, J. D.** And on the 8th Day She Rested. 244p. 2000. pap. 18.00 (*0-7388-2076-8*) Xlibris Corp.
Mason, J. Day. Speaking to Strangers. (Illus.). 105p. 1987. 40.00 (*0-933858-22-1*) Kennebec River.
Mason, J. J. Coatings for Energy Efficiency & Solar Applications. (C). 1984. 100.00 (*0-7855-4197-7*, Pub. by Interntl Solar Energy Soc) St Mut.
— Coatings for Energy Efficiency & Solar Applications (C38) 89p. (C). 1984. 95.00 (*0-7855-3801-1*, Pub. by Interntl Solar Energy Soc) St Mut.
Mason, J. K. Forensic Medicine for Lawyers. 3rd ed. 490p. 1995. pap. write for info. (*0-406-04999-8*, MFML3, MICHIE) LEXIS Pub.
— Human Life & Medical Practice. 1990. pap. text 25.00 (*0-85224-584-X*, Pub. by Edinburgh U Pr) Col U Pr.
— Medico-Legal Aspects of Reproduction & Parenthood. 2nd ed. LC 97-38226. (Medico-Legal Ser.). 300p. 1998. pap. 48.95 (*1-85521-816-X*, Pub. by Ashgate Pub); text 115.95 (*1-84014-065-8*, Pub. by Ashgate Pub) Ashgate Pub Co.
— The Pathology & Trauma. 2nd ed. 384p. 1993. text 165.00 (*0-340-54820-7*, Pub. by E A) OUP.
Mason, J. M. Comments on the Last Edition of Shakespeare's Plays. LC 73-172851. reprint ed. 52.50 (*0-404-04225-2*) AMS Pr.
— Comments on the Several Editions of Shakespeare's Plays, Extended to Those of Malone & Steevens. LC 77-172852. xv, 608 p. 1973. reprint ed. 76.50 (*0-404-04226-0*) AMS Pr.
Mason, J. P., jt. ed. see Croall, I. F.
Mason, J. S. & Goldberg, A. S. Bulk Solids Handling: An Introduction to the Practice & Technology. 384p. 1986. text 110.00 (*0-412-01251-0*, 9889, Chap & Hall NY) Chapman & Hall.
Mason, J. W. Shinto, 2 vols. 1973. 500.00 (*0-8490-1050-0*) Gordon Pr.
Mason, J. W., & Co. Staff. Furniture Trade Catalog: Illustrated Catalog of Chairs & Furniture by Joel W. Mason. 116p. 1983. reprint ed. pap. 25.00 (*0-87556-653-7*) Saifer.
Mason, Jackie & Berkow, Ira. How to Talk Jewish. 160p. 1991. pap. 9.95 (*0-312-07236-8*) St Martin.
Mason, Jackie & Felder, Raoul. Jackie Mason & Raoul Felder's Survival Guide to New York City. LC 97-22333. (Illus.). 176p. 1997. mass mkt. 16.00 (*0-380-97483-5*, Avon Bks) Morrow Avon.
Mason, Jackie & Gross, Ken. Jackie, Oy! The Birth & Rebirth of Jackie Mason. (Illus.). 224p. 1988. 16.95 (*0-316-54933-9*) Little.
Mason, James. Ancient Greece Resource Book. (Sense of History Ser.). 1991. pap. text 13.32 (*0-582-06819-3*) Longman.
— Art of Chess. 3rd ed. Reinfeld, Fred & Bernstein, Sidney, eds. 378p. 1958. pap. 9.95 (*0-486-20463-4*) Dover.
— Medieval Realms. 1991. pap. text 13.32 (*0-582-20735-5*) Longman.
— Roman Empire. 1991. pap. text 13.32 (*0-582-20736-3*) Longman.
Mason, James D. Combat Handgun Shooting. (Illus.). 286p. 1979. 52.95 (*0-398-03461-3*) C C Thomas.
Mason, James E. The Transformation of Commercial Banking in the United States, 1956-1991. rev. ed. LC 97-40579. (Financial Sector of the American Economy Ser.). (Illus.). 190p. 1997. text 51.00 (*0-8153-2987-3*) Garland.
Mason, James H. The Dudley Genealogies. LC 82-62705. 216p. 1987. 35.00 (*0-9609032-1-6*) J H Mason.
Mason, James H. & Mason, Mary S. Our Dudley Heritage. LC 82-60822. 96p. 1982. 16.50 (*0-9609032-0-8*) J H Mason.
Mason, James J., ed. AIREA Financial Tables. 473p. 1981. 27.50 (*0-911780-54-8*) Appraisal Inst.
***Mason, James P. R.** Messages from Beyond: Spirit-Side Communications after the Passing of the Author's Wife. Vol. 2. 534p. (Orig.). 1999. pap. 19.95 (*0-9699882-1-4*) Alma Bks.
Mason, James P. R. Messages from Beyond: Spirit-Side Communications after the Passing of the Author's Wife. unabridged ed. 479p. (Orig.). 1995. pap. 19.95 (*0-9699882-0-6*, Pub. by Alma Bks) Koen Bk Distributors.
Mason, Jana M., jt. auth. see McCormick, Christine E.
Mason, Jana M., jt. ed. see Allen, JoBeth.
***Mason, Jane.** Flintstones in Viva Rock Vegas: Flintstones Movie Storybook. (Illus.). 32p. (J). (ps-3). 2000. pap. 5.99 (*0-439-17304-3*) Scholastic Inc.
Mason, Jane. Flying Horse: The Story of Pegasus, 1 vol. LC 98-53367. (All Aboard Reading Ser.). (Illus.). 32p. (ps-1). 1999. pap. text 3.99 (*0-448-41980-7*) Putnam Pub Group.
— Hello, Two-Wheeler! LC 94-28633. (All Aboard Reading Ser.: Level 2). (Illus.). 48p. (J). (gr. 1-3). 1995. pap. 3.95 (*0-448-40853-8*, G & D) Peng Put Young Read.
— Jack Frost Movie Storybook. (Illus.). 48p. (gr. 1-5). 1998. pap. text 5.99 (*0-590-66070-5*) Scholastic Inc.
— The Lost World: Jurassic Park: The Movie Storybook. LC 96-80479. (Illus.). 32p. (Orig.). (J). 1997. pap. 8.95 (*0-448-41573-9*, G & D) Peng Put Young Read.
— The Mount People. (C). 1989. 70.00 (*1-85022-057-3*, Pub. by Dyllansow Truran) St Mut.
— Theater. LC 93-5744. (Now Hiring Ser.). (J). 1994. pap. 5.95 (*0-382-24750-7*, Crstwood Hse) Silver Burdett Pr.
Mason, Jane & Gilmour, H. B. Real Monsters: Spontaneously Combustible. (Illus.). 64p. (J). (gr. 2-5). 1997. 3.99 (*0-689-81154-3*) S&S Childrens.
Mason, Jane B. Animaniacs Adventures: Two Wacky Tales in One Cool Book. 48p. (J). (gr. k-2). 1995. pap. 3.95 (*0-590-53528-5*) Scholastic Inc.
— El Autobus Magico Sube Y Baja: Un Libro Sobre Como Flotar Y Hundirse. 1997. 8.19 (*0-606-10797-5*, Pub. by Turtleback) Demco.
— Flik to the Rescue. LC PZ7.M4116Fl 1998. (Disney Chapters Ser.). (Illus.). 43p. (J). (gr. 2-4). 1998. pap. 3.95 (*0-7868-4251-2*, Pub. by Disney Pr) Time Warner.
— Flying Horse: The Story of Pegasus. LC 98-53367. (All Aboard Reading Ser.). 1999. 13.89 (*0-448-42051-1*) Putnam Pub Group.
— The Magic School Bus Ups & Downs: A Book about Floating & Sinking. LC 49-243580. (Magic School Bus Ser.). (Illus.). 32p. (J). (gr. k-2). 1997. pap. 2.99 (*0-590-92158-4*) Scholastic Inc.
— The Magic School Bus Ups & Downs: A Book about Floating & Sinking. (Magic School Bus Ser.). (J). (gr. k-2). 1997. 8.19 (*0-606-10867-X*, Pub. by Turtleback) Demco.
***Mason, Jane B.** The Magic School Bus Ups & Downs: A Book about Sinking & Floating. (Magic School Bus Ser.). (Illus.). (J). (ps-3). 1999. pap. 10.65 (*0-613-00533-3*) Econo-Clad Bks.
Mason, Jane B. The Magic School Bus Ups & Downs: A Book about Sinking & Floating. (Magic School Bus Ser.). (J). (gr. k-2). 1997. pap. 2.99 (*0-614-29014-7*) Scholastic Inc.
— Shadow Stealers. LC 97-195134. (J). (gr. k-2). 1996. pap. text 2.99 (*0-590-50205-0*) Scholastic Inc.
— Tales from Crypt, 2. 48p. (J). (gr. 1-4). 1995. pap. 3.50 (*0-590-25084-1*) Scholastic Inc.
— Tales from the Cryptkeeper. (Tales from the Cryptkeeper Ser.). 1995. 8.70 (*0-606-08264-6*, Pub. by Turtleback) Demco.
— Tales from the Cryptkeeper. (Tales from the Cryptkeeper Ser.). (J). 1995. 8.70 (*0-606-08263-8*, Pub. by Turtleback) Demco.
— Theodore Rex. LC 96-142143. 32p. (J). (ps-3). 1996. pap. 2.99 (*0-590-67784-5*) Scholastic Inc.
Mason, Janet. A Fucking Brief History of Fucking. 26p. 1993. pap. 5.00 (*1-882827-00-7*) Insight to Riot.
— North Carolina Marriage Laws & Procedures. 3rd ed. 31p. (C). 1994. pap. text 2.50 (*1-56011-235-2*, 94.23) Institute Government.
— Reporting Child Abuse & Neglect in North Carolina. LC 96-622240. 115p. 1996. pap. text 8.00 (*1-56011-296-4*, 96.17) Institute Government.
— When I Was Straight. 35p. (Orig.). 1995. pap. 7.00 (*1-882827-06-6*) Insight to Riot.
Mason, Janet, pref. North Carolina Juvenile Code & Related Statutes. annot. ed. 1999. 40.00 (*1-56011-352-9*) Institute Government.
Mason, Janet, jt. auth. see Thomas, Mason P., Jr.
Mason, Janice, ed. see Brewer, Anne.
Mason, Jason B. Star Trek Movie Story Book. 32p. (J). (gr. k-3). 1996. 9.99 (*0-689-80899-2*) S&S Bks Yung.
Mason, Jay W., ed. ECG-SAP I: Electrocardiography Self-Assessment Program. LC 95-75848. (Illus.). 102p. 1995. pap. 95.00 (*1-882764-12-9*, ECGPR) Am Coll Cardiology.
— ECG-SAP II: Electrocardiography Self-Assessment Program II. LC 97-94681. (Illus.). 97p. 1997. pap. 120.00 (*1-882764-19-6*) Am Coll Cardiology.
Mason, Jeff. Philosophical Rhetoric: The Function of Indirection in Philosophical Writings. 192p. 1989. 45.00 (*0-415-03043-9*); pap. 13.95 (*0-415-03044-7*) Routledge.
Mason, Jeff & Washington, Peter. The Future of Thinking: Rhetoric & Liberal Arts Teaching. LC 92-7668. 160p. (C). 1992. pap. 22.99 (*0-415-07319-7*, A7873) Routledge.
Mason, Jeffrey. Wisecracks: The Farces of George S. Kaufman. Brockett, Oscar G., ed. LC 88-11076. (Theater & Dramatic Studies: No. 53). 146p. reprint ed. 45.30 (*0 8357 1887-5*, 207074000004) Bks Demand.
Mason, Jeffrey A. The Philosopher's Address: Writing & the Perception of Philosophy. LC 99-16347. 224p. 1999. 60.00 (*0-7391-0071-8*) Lxngtn Bks.
Mason, Jeffrey D. Melodrama & the Myth of America. LC 92-46375. (Drama & Performance Studies). 268p. 1993. 31.95 (*0-253-33686-4*) Ind U Pr.
Mason, Jeffrey D. & Gainor, J. Ellen, eds. Performing America: Cultural Nationalism in American Theater. LC 99-6219. (Theater: Theory - Text - Performance Ser.). (Illus.). 256p. 1999. text 44.50 (*0-472-10985-5*, 10985) U of Mich Pr.
Mason, Jeffrey M. & McCarthy, Susan. When Elephants Weep: The Emotional Lives of Animals. large type ed. (Large Print Bks.). 1995. 25.95 (*1-56895-267-8*) Wheeler Pub.
Mason, Jennie. Introduction to Word Processing. LC 78-17143. 1979. pap. write for info. (*0-672-97134-8*) Macmillan.
— Word Processing Skills & Simulations. LC 78-15761. 1979. teacher ed. write for info. (*0-672-97135-6*); pap. write for info. (*0-672-97197-6*) Macmillan.
Mason, Jennifer. Qualitative Researching. 208p. 1996. 69.95 (*0-8039-8985-7*); pap. 21.95 (*0-8039-8986-5*) Sage.
Mason, Jennifer, jt. auth. see Finch, Janet.
***Mason, Jerry.** Financial Fitness for Life: Advice from America's Top Financial Planning Program. LC 99-32271. 336p. 1999. pap. 17.95 (*0-7931-3361-0*) Dearborn.
Mason, Jerry, intro. Financial Counseling. 450p. (C). pap. text 30.00 (*0-9639684-0-8*) Accred Finan.
Mason, Jesse D., ed. History of Amador County (CA) (Illus.). 400p. 1994. reprint ed. 47.95 (*0-938121-07-3*); reprint ed. pap. 27.95 (*0-938121-06-5*) Cenotto Pubns.
Mason, Jill, ed. see Chioffi, Nancy & Mead, Gretchen.
Mason, Jill, ed. see Mahnken, Jan.
Mason, Jill, ed. see Pitzer, Sara.
Mason, Jill, ed. see Vargas, Pattie & Gulling, Rich.
Mason, Jill, ed. see Whitehead, Jeffrey.
Mason, Jill, ed. see Woodier, Olwen.
Mason, Jim. An Unnatural Order: Uncovering the Roots of Our Domination of Nature & Each Other. LC 98-10273. 352p. 1997. pap. 17.95 (*0-8264-1028-6*) Continuum.
Mason, Joan. The Flat-Coated Retriever Today. (Illus.). 160p. 1996. 25.95 (*0-87605-124-7*) Macmillan.
Mason, John. Comet Halley Investigations, Results, Interpretations, 2 vols., Vol. 2. (Ellis Horwood Library of Space Science). 1990. text 195.00 (*0-470-21520-8*) P-H.
— Commercial Hydroponics. (Illus.). 172p. reprint ed. 24.95 (*0-86417-300-8*, Pub. by Kangaroo Pr) Seven Hills Bk.
***Mason, John.** Commercial Hydroponics: How to Grow 86 Different Plants in Hydroponics. 172p. 2000. per. 15.00 (*0-684-87202-1*) S&S Trade.
Mason, John. Don't Wait for Your Ship to Come In: Swim Out to Get It! (Portable Book Gift Ser.). 160p. 1996. pap. 5.99 (*1-56292-058-8*, HB-058) Honor Bks OK.
— Farm Management. (Illus.). 160p. 1997. 24.95 (*0-86417-820-4*, Pub. by Kangaroo Pr) Seven Hills Bk.
— Four New World Yoruba Rituals. 3rd rev. ed. LC 93-60567. (Illus.). 174p. (C). 1993. pap. 20.00 (*1-881244-03-2*) Yoruba Theol Arch.
— Growing Australian Natives. (Illus.). 96p. 1997. pap. 14.95 (*0-86417-819-0*, Pub. by Kangaroo Pr) Seven Hills Bk.
— Growing Herbs. LC 93-42021. (Illus.). 116p. (Orig.). 1994. pap. 15.95 (*0-916638-50-2*) Meyerbooks.
***Mason, John.** Haunted Heritage. (Illus.). 160p. 1999. pap. 17.95 (*1-85585-693-X*, Pub. by Collins & Br) Trafalgar.
Mason, John. Highlights in Environmental Research: Professional Inaugural Lectures at Imperial College. 1998. pap. 22.00 (*1-86094-103-6*) World Scientific Pub.
— Idana Fun Orisa: Cooking for Selected Heads. (Illus.). 150p. 1998. pap. 20.00 (*1-881244-07-5*) Yoruba Theol Arch.
***Mason, John.** Know Your Limits - Then Ignore Them. LC 99-73388. 216p. 2000. pap. 11.99 (*1-890900-12-5*, 921-028, Pub. by Insight Intl) BookWorld.
Mason, John. Olookun: Owner of Rivers & Seas. LC 96-60309. (Illus.). 180p. (Orig.). (C). 1996. pap. 20.00 (*1-881244-05-9*) Yoruba Theol Arch.
— Orin Orisa: Songs for Selected Heads. 2nd rev. ed. LC 97-61174. (Illus.). 496p. (Orig.). 1997. pap. text 25.00 (*1-881244-06-7*) Yoruba Theol Arch.
— Proverbs Prayers: Praying the Wisdom of Proverbs into Your Life Every Day. LC 99-73387. 144p. 1999. 12.99 (*1-890900-11-7*) Insight Intl.
— Starting a Nursery or Herb Farm. (Illus.). 180p. 1998. pap. 10.95 (*0-86417-843-3*, Pub. by Kangaroo Pr) Seven Hills Bk.
— Stress Passages: Surviving Life's Transitions Gracefully. LC 86-26904. (Illus.). 269p. (Orig.). 1988. pap. 11.95 (*0-89087-489-1*) Celestial Arts.
Mason, John. Sueltese de Lo Que le Detiene.Tr. of Let Go of Whatever Makes You Stop. (SPA.). 1997. pap. text 7.99 (*0-88113-489-9*) Caribe Betania.
Mason, John. Sustainable Agriculture. 1998. 19.95 (*0-86417-865-4*, Pub. by Kangaroo Pr) Seven Hills Bk.
— Weather & Climate. (Our World Ser.). (Illus.). 48p. (J). (gr. 5-8). 1991. lib. bdg. 12.95 (*0-382-24225-4*) Silver Burdett Pr.
Mason, John, ed. Tigrinya Grammar. LC 95-26821. (ENG & TIR.). 1996. 35.00 (*0-932415-20-2*); pap. 12.95 (*0-932415-21-0*) Red Sea Pr.
Mason, John & Hurtgen, John. Reading the New Testament: Exercises for Beginning Readers of the Greek New Testament. write for info. (*0-88946-791-9*) E Mellen.
— Reading the New Testament: Exercises for Beginning Readers of the Greek New Testament. 171p. 1988. pap. write for info. (*0-7734-9792-7*) E Mellen.
Mason, John & Lawrence, Rosemary. Growing Vegetables. (Growing Ser.). (Illus.). 110p. (Orig.). 1993. pap. 11.95 (*0-86417-377-6*, Pub. by Kangaroo Pr) Seven Hills Bk.
Mason, John, jt. auth. see Edwards, Gary.
Mason, John, jt. auth. see Redmond, Tim.
Mason, John A. Archaeology of Santa Marta, Colombia Pt. 1: The Tairona Culture. Marshall Field Archaeological Expedition to Colombia, 1922-23 - Report on Field Work. LC 32-2747. (Field Museum of Natural History Anthropological Ser.: Vol. 20, No. 1). (Illus.). 265p. reprint ed. pap. 82.20 (*0-608-02720-0*, 206338500001) Bks Demand.
— The Language of the Papago of Arizona. LC 52-81. (University of Pennsylvania, Museum Monographs). 88p. reprint ed. pap. 30.00 (*0-608-13538-0*, 20223820026) Bks Demand.
Mason, John F. & Dickey, Parke A., eds. Oil Field Development Techniques: Proceedings of the Daqing International Meeting, 1982. LC 88-35723. (AAPG Studies in Geology: No. 28). (Illus.). 255p. reprint ed. pap. 79.10 (*0-8357-3071-9*, 203932800012) Bks Demand.
Mason, John H., ed. see Diderot, Denis.
Mason, John L. Ask... Life's Most Important Answers Are Found in Asking the Right Questions. 1996. pap. text 5.99 (*1-888103-07-8*) Trophy Pubng.
— A Brief of the Pequot War. LC 71-152995. (Select Bibliographies Reprint Ser.). 1977. reprint ed. 11.95 (*0-8369-5747-4*) Ayer.
— Conquering an Enemy Called Average: 52 "Nuggets of Truth" That Will Put Mediocrity & Unfulfilled Dreams Where They Belong--Out of Your Life. 128p. 1996. pap. 7.99 (*1-888103-08-6*) Trophy Pubng.
— Un Enemigo Llamado Promedio.Tr. of An Enemy Called Average. (SPA.). 144p. 1996. 7.99 (*0-88113-326-4*, B007-3264) Caribe Betania.
— An Enemy Called Average: Don't Settle for an Average Life, God Wants to Launch You Past the Middle to the Top. 126p. 1990. pap. 7.99 (*0-89274-765-X*, HH-765) Harrison Hse.
— The Identity Crisis Theme in American Feature Films, 1960-1969. 1977. 27.95 (*0-405-09896-0*, 11488) Ayer.
— Usted Nacio Original, No Muera Como una Copia!Tr. of You're Born an Original, Don't Die a Copy!. (SPA.). 128p. 1995. 7.99 (*0-88113-149-0*, B007-1490) Caribe Betania.
Mason, John M. The Human Family & the Creator--God. LC 98-90976. 2000. pap. 13.95 (*0-533-13003-4*) Vantage.
Mason, John M., Jr., jt. ed. see Smith, Bob L.
Mason, John P. The Resurrection According to Paul. LC 92-47029. 168p. 1993. text 79.95 (*0-7734-2358-3*) E Mellen.
Mason, John R. Reading & Responding to Mircea Eliade's History of Religious Ideas. LC 93-15344. 136p. 1993. text 69.95 (*0-7734-9283-6*) E Mellen.
— Switch Engineering Handbook. 482p. 1993. 64.50 (*0-07-040769-X*) McGraw.
Mason, John T., Jr. The Atlantic War Remembered: An Oral History Collection. LC 90-43436. (Illus.). 380p. 1990. text 45.00 (*0-87021-523-X*) Naval Inst Pr.
— The Pacific War Remembered: An Oral History Collection. LC 86-5438. (Illus.). 373p. 1986. text 45.00 (*0-87021-522-1*) Naval Inst Pr.
Mason-John, Vakerie. Talking Black: African, Caribbean, & Asian Lesbians Speak Out. LC 96-176799. (Women on Women Ser.). 256p. 1994. pap. 21.95 (*0-304-32965-7*, Pub. by Cassell) LPC InBook.
Mason-John, Valerie & Khambatta, Ann. Lesbians Talk Making Black Waves. 64p. 1994. pap. 8.50 (*1-85727-007-X*, Pub. by Scarlet Pr) LPC InBook.
Mason, John W. The Cold War, 1945-1991. (Lancaster Pamphlets Ser.). 104p. (C). 1996. pap. 11.99 (*0-415-14278-4*) Routledge.
— The Dissolution of the Austro-Hungarian Empire, 1867-1918. 2nd ed. LC 96-32785. (Seminar Studies in History). 144p. (C). 1997. pap. 15.93 (*0-582-29466-5*) Longman.
Mason, Joseph B., et al. Modern Retailing: Theory & Practice. 6th ed. LC 92-12011. 816p. (C). 1992. text 69.95 (*0-256-10257-0*, Irwn McGrw-H) McGrw-H Hghr Educ.
Mason, Joseph R., jt. auth. see Calomiris, Charles W.
***Mason, Joseph W.** Let My Heart Attack Save Your Life: A Simple, Sound, Workable Weight Management Plan. LC 98-230249. 240p. 1998. pap. 14.95 (*1-56561-134-9*) Wiley.
Mason, Judy S. Mr. Farmer & His Animals. Scoggan, Nita, ed. (Illus.). 52p. (Orig.). (J). (gr. 3 up). 1987. pap. 3.95 (*0-910487-11-1*) Royalty Pub.
Mason, Julian D., Jr., ed. see Wheatley, Phillis.
Mason, Jutta, tr. see Poerksen, Uwe.
Mason, K. & Carter, J. Restitution Law in Australia. LC 96-147121. (Butterworths Australia Ser.). 1088p. 1995. write for info. (*0-409-30135-3*, MICHIE) LEXIS Pub.
Mason, K. L. Advanced Spanish Course. 1967. 11.40 (*0-08-012272-8*, Pergamon Pr); pap. text 9.80 (*0-08-012271-X*, Pergamon Pr) Elsevier.
Mason, K. L. & Sager, J. C. Spanish Oral Drill Book. 1969. pap. text 7.80 (*0-08-013362-2*, Pergamon Pr) Elsevier.
Mason, K. O., et al, eds. The Physics of Accretion onto Compact Objects. (Lecture Notes in Physics Ser.: Vol. 266). viii, 421p. 1986. 59.95 (*0-387-17195-9*) Spr-Verlag.
Mason, Karen Oppenheim. Changing Family in Comparative Perspective: Asia & the United States. xix, 258p. 1999. 40.00 (*0-86638-187-2*) EW Ctr HI.
Mason, Karen Oppenheim & Jensen, An-Magritt, eds. Gender & Family Change in Industrialized Countries. (International Studies in Demography). (Illus.). 338p. 1995. text 75.00 (*0-19-828970-7*) OUP.
Mason, Kate. Cat's Cradle Fun. (Illus.). 24p. (Orig.). (J). (gr. 2-6). 1997. pap. 5.95 (*0-8167-2634-5*, Watermill Pr) Troll Communs.
— The Clock Book: Learn to Tell Time. (Illus.). 16p. (Orig.). (J). (ps-2). 1996. pap. 6.95 (*0-8167-4031-3*) Troll Communs.
— I Can Juggle. (Illus.). 16p. (Orig.). (J). (gr. 3-7). 1997. pap. 6.95 (*0-8167-3968-4*) Troll Communs.
— Make Your Own Cool Crafts. (J). (gr. 4-7). 1994. pap. 5.95 (*0-8167-3226-4*) Troll Communs.

M

An Asterisk (*) at the beginning of an entry indicates that the title is appearing for the first time.

— The Shoe Book: Learn to Tie Your Shoes! (Illus.). 16p. (Orig.). (J). (ps-2). 1996. pap. 6.95 (0-8167-3871-8, Watermill Pr) Troll Communs.

Mason, Kathryn G., jt. auth. see Mason, Floyd R.

Mason, Katrina R. Children of Los Alamos: An Oral History of the Town Where the Atomic Age Began. LC 95-13825. (Twayne's Oral History Ser.). 1995. 29.95 (0-8057-9138-8, Twyne); per. 15.95 (0-8057-9139-6, Twyne) Mac Lib Ref.

Mason, Keith. Medicine for the Twenty-First Century. 1993. pap. 14.95 (1-85230-329-8, Pub. by Element MA) Penguin Putnam.

***Mason, Ken.** Pathology of Trauma. 3rd ed. Purdue, Basil, ed. LC 99-16933. (Illus.). 576p. 2000. text 225.00 (0-340-69189-1, Pub. by E A) OUP.

Mason, Kenneth. African Americans & Race Relations in San Antonio, Texas, 1867-1937. LC 98-42830. (Studies in African American History & Culture). 352p. 1998. 70.00 (0-8153-3076-6) Garland.

Mason, Kermit R. The Roads Taken: A Country Lawyer Looks Back. Taylor, Carl B., ed. & intro. by. 152p. 1986. 12.95 (0-9605948-2-5) C B Taylor.

***Mason, Kevin.** Architect's Business Problem Solver. (Time-Saver Standards Ser.). 400p. 2000. 59.95 (0-07-041106-9) McGraw-Hill Prof.

Mason, Kris, jt. auth. see Lees, Laura.

Mason, Kristin D., jt. auth. see Sandin, Karl J.

Mason, L. & Woodhouse, N. M. Integrability, Self-Duality & Twistor Theory. LC 96-4082. (London Mathematical Society Monographs: Vol. 15). (Illus.). 374p. (C). 1997. text 85.00 (0-19-853498-1, Clarendon Pr) OUP.

***Mason, L. J.** Further Advances in Twistor Theory , Vol. 3. (Research Notes in Mathematics Ser.). 1999. pap. text 69.95 (1-58488-047-3, Chap & Hall CRC) CRC Pr.

Mason, L. John. Guide to Stress Reduction. rev. ed. LC 79-2577. (Illus.). 192p. (Orig.). 1995. pap. 12.95 (0-89087-452-2) Celestial Arts.

Mason, Laura. Singing the French Revolution: Popular Culture & Politics, 1787-1799. LC 96-17694. 280p. 1996. text 39.95 (0-8014-3233-2) Cornell U Pr.

— Sugar-Plums & Sherbet. (Illus.). 250p. 1998. 36.00 (0-907325-83-1) Food Words.

***Mason, Laura.** Sweets & Sweet Shops. 1999. pap. 25.00 (0-7478-0424-9, Pub. by Shire Pubns) St Mut.

***Mason, Laura & Rizzo, Tracey.** The French Revolution. LC 98-72059. xxiii, 357p. 1999. write for info. (0-669-41780-7) HM Trade Div.

Mason, Lauris & Ludman, Joan. George Bellows: The Lithographs. rev. ed. (Illus.). 300p. 1992. 150.00 (1-55660-141-7) A Wofsy Fine Arts.

Mason, Leah. Making Connections: Adult Day Health Care for People with AIDS. LC 92-44741. (Practical Guide Ser.). 1993. 10.00 (1-881277-14-3) United Hosp Fund.

Mason, Leslie C., ed. see Levine, Leslie B.

Mason, Linda. Against All Odds. 133p. 1995. pap. 7.99 (1-882449-26-6, 460013) Messenger Pub.

Mason, Linda & Brown, Roger. Rice, Rivalry & Politics: Managing Cambodian Relief. LC 82-40380. (Illus.). 240p. 1983. pap. 74.40 (0-608-00882-6, 206167600010) Bks Demand.

Mason, Lionel J. & Hughston, L. P., eds. Further Advances in Twistor Theory Vol. 1: Penrose Transform & Its Applications. LC 89-13983. (Pitman Research Notes in Mathematics Ser.: Vol. 231). 399p. 1990. reprint ed. pap. 123.70 (0-608-03599-8, 206442200001) Bks Demand.

Mason, Lisa. Arachne. 272p. 1992. mass mkt. 4.50 (0-380-70911-2, Avon Bks) Morrow Avon.

— Arachne. 272p. 1997. pap. 12.00 (0-380-72971-7, Avon Bks) Morrow Avon.

— Cyberweb. LC 94-32026. 256p. 1995. 20.00 (0-688-13987-6, Avon Bks) Morrow Avon.

— Cyberweb. 272p. 1996. mass mkt. 4.99 (0-380-77486-0, Avon Bks) Morrow Avon.

— Cyberweb. 272p. 1998. pap. 12.00 (0-380-79917-0, Eos) Morrow Avon.

— Pangaea: Bk Ii Imperium Afire. 400p. 2000. mass mkt. 6.50 (0-553-58166-X) Bantam.

— Pangaea Book I Bk. 1: Imperium Without End. 400p. 1999. mass mkt. 6.50 (0-553-57571-6) Bantam.

Mason, Lorna C. America's Past & Promise LC 98-215470. 1998. write for info. (0-395-86708-8) HM.

Mason, Lorna C., ed. see Means, Florence G.

Mason, Lowell. The Pestalozzian Music Teacher. 1977. lib. bdg. 59.95 (0-8490-2425-0) Gordon Pr.

Mason, Lowell & Webb, George J. The Boston Glee Book. LC 76-52481. (Music Reprint Ser.: 1977). 1977. reprint ed. lib. bdg. 35.00 (0-306-70860-4) Da Capo.

***Mason-Lucon, Mirella.** Rainbow. 2000. pap. write for info. (1-58235-419-7) Watermrk Pr.

Mason, Lynn. All That. (Love Stories Super Edition Ser.: No. 10). 224p. (YA). 1999. mass mkt. 4.50 (0-553-49290-X) Bantam.

— As I Am. (Love Stories Ser.). 92p. (YA). (gr. 7-12). 1999. mass mkt. 3.99 (0-553-49274-8) BDD Bks Young Read.

— The "L" Word. (Love Stories Super Edition Ser.: No. 8). (YA). 1998. mass mkt. 4.50 (0-553-49249-7) BDD Bks Young Read.

***Mason, Lynn.** Three Princes. (Love Stories Super Edition Ser.). (YA). (gr. 7-12). 2000. mass mkt. 4.99 (0-553-49329-9) Bantam.

Mason, Lynn, jt. auth. see Mason, Tim.

Mason, M. E., Jr., jt. auth. see McKee, W. Reid.

Mason, Malcolm S., jt. auth. see Dembling, Paul G.

Mason, Marco. Point, Click & Learn Visual Basic 4. 528p. 1996. pap. 34.99 (1-56884-317-8) IDG Bks.

Mason, Marcy, jt. auth. see Rubin, Bonnie M.

Mason, Marcy, jt. auth. see Rubin, Bonnie Miller.

Mason, Marguerite B. 1880 Federal Census Phelps County Missouri. 182p. 1992. pap. 44.00 (1-893474-03-8) Phelps Cnty Gene.

— 1860 Federal Census Dent County Missouri. 85p. 1997. pap. 30.00 (1-893474-17-8) Phelps Cnty Gene.

Mason, Marian. Twin-Souls: Forever in Love. Boggs, Marian, ed. 130p. 1999. pap. 8.95 (0-7392-0077-1) Morris Pubng.

Mason, Marilyn. Intimacy. 24p. (Orig.). 1986. pap. 2.00 (0-89486-365-7, 5309B) Hazelden.

— Seven Mountains: The Inner Climb to Committment & Caring. 240p. 1998. pap. 11.95 (0-452-27417-6) NAL.

Mason, Marilyn Gell. Strategic Management for Today's Libraries. LC 99-17515. 146p. 1999. pap. 35.00 (0-8389-0757-1) ALA.

Mason, Marilyn J., jt. auth. see Fossum, Merle A.

Mason, Marion, et al. The Dynamics of Clinical Dietetics. LC 81-16160. 354p. 1989. text 32.95 (0-8273-4298-5) Delmar.

— Nutrition & the Cell: The Inside Story. LC 72-95734. (Illus.). 92p. reprint ed. 30.00 (0-8357-9636-1, 201310400085) Bks Demand.

Mason, Mark. American Multinationals & Japan: The Political Economy of Japanese Capital Controls, 1899-1980. LC 92-9934. 390p. 1992. text 35.00 (0-674-02630-6) HUP.

— Europe & the Japanese Challenge. LC HG5422.M368 1997. (Illus.). 176p. 1998. text 58.00 (0-19-829264-3) OUP.

— In Search of the Loving God: Resolving the Past Traumas of Christianity, & Bringing to Light Its Healing Spirit. LC 97-68386. 382p. (Orig.). 1997. pap. 16.95 (0-9658477-4-8, 1004) Dwapara Pr.

Mason, Mark & Encarnation, Dennis, eds. Does Ownership Matter? Japanese Multinationals in Europe. (Illus.). 482p. 1995. pap. text 26.00 (0-19-829026-8) OUP.

***Mason, Mary.** Childhood Days at Swarthmoor Hall. 1999. pap. 21.00 (1-85072-210-2, Pub. by W Sessions) St Mut.

Mason, Mary A. From Father's Property to Children's Rights: The History of Child Custody in the United States. LC 93-34524. 256p. 1994. 46,50 (0-231-08046-8) Col U Pr.

— From Father's Property to Children's Rights: The History of Child Custody in the United States. 256p. 1996. pap. 20.50 (0-231-08047-6) Col U Pr.

Mason, Mary A. & Gambrill, Eileen, eds. Debating Children's Lives: Current Controversies. (C). 1993. text 58.00 (0-8039-5458-1); pap. text 26.50 (0-8039-5459-X) Sage.

Mason, Mary A. & Harris, Robert. Using Computers in the Law: Law Office Without Walls. 3rd ed. LC 93-41189. 284p. (C). 1993. pap. 27.50 (0-314-02396-8) West Pub.

Mason, Mary A., jt. ed. see Fass, Paula S.

Mason, Mary Ann. The Custody Wars: Why Children Are Losing the Legal Battle - And What We Can Do about It. LC 98-47890. 240p. 1999. 23.00 (0-465-01532-8, Pub. by Basic) HarpC.

***Mason, Mary Ann.** The Equality Trap. 265p. 2000. pap. 21.95 (0-7658-0740-8) Transaction Pubs.

Mason, Mary Ann, et al, eds. All Our Families: New Policies for a New Century. LC 97-7810. 272p. (C). 1998. pap. 21.95 (0-19-510832-9); text 50.00 (0-19-510831-0) OUP.

Mason, Mary Ann, jt. ed. see Fass, Paula S.

Mason, Mary-Claire. Male Infertility: Men Talking. LC 93-11986. 224p. (C). 1993. text 69.95 (0-415-07289-1, B2423) Routledge.

Mason, Mary E. Active Life & Contemplative Life: A Study of the Concepts from Plato to the Present. Ganss, George E., ed. & frwd. by. LC 60-16598. 151p. 1961. reprint ed. pap. 46.90 (0-608-04188-2, 206492300011) Bks Demand.

Mason, Mary F. Speech Pathology for Tracheostomized & Ventilator Dependent Patients. LC 93-94984. xlii, 598 p. 1993. write for info. (0-9633596-0-6) Voicing.

***Mason, Mary Grimley.** Life Prints: A Memoir of Healing & Discovery. unabridged ed. LC 99-56912. (Cross-Cultural Memoir Ser.). (Illus.). 224p. 2000. 19.95 (1-55861-237-8, Pub. by Feminist Pr) Consort Bk Sales.

Mason, Mary J. The Boy Who Changed. Johnson, Cynthia, ed. (Illus.). 31p. (J). (ps-6). 1996. pap. 12.00 (1-890864-04-8) Breath of Life.

— Church of God in Christ Study Guide. Johnson, Cynthia, ed. (Illus.). 120p. 1997. pap. 29.99 (1-890864-05-6) Breath of Life.

— Jamie Learns a Lesson. Johnson, Cynthia, ed. (Illus.). 25p. (J). (ps-6). 1996. pap. 12.00 (1-890864-00-5) Breath of Life.

— Jaypee Stands Alone. 2nd rev. ed. (Illus.). 13p. (J). (ps-6). 1996. reprint ed. pap. 12.00 (1-890864-06-4) Breath of Life.

— Melvin's Adventure. (Illus.). 16p. (J). (ps-6). 1997. pap. 12.00 (1-890864-01-3) Breath of Life.

Mason, Mary J., ed. see Alston, Regina.

Mason, Mary J., ed. & photos by see Crook, Lydia.

Mason, Mary M. Out of the Shadows: Birthfathers' Stories. (Illus.). 270p. (Orig.). 1995. pap. 14.95 (0-9646259-1-1) O J Howard Pub.

Mason, Mary S., jt. auth. see Mason, James H.

Mason, Matthew T. & Salisbury, J. Kenneth. Robot Hands & the Mechanics of Manipulation. (Artificial Intelligence Ser.). (Illus.). 275p. 1985. 45.00 (0-262-13205-2) MIT Pr.

***Mason, Melvin Rosser.** Martha Mitchell of Possum Walk Road: Texas Quiltmaker. LC 99-39376. (Illus.). 80p. 1999. pap. 19.95 (1-881515-22-2) TX Review Pr.

Mason, Mervyn L. Human Sexuality: A Bibliography & Critical Evaluation of Recent Texts. LC 83-12688. 207p. 1983. lib. bdg. 49.95 (0-313-23932-0, MHU/, Greenwood Pr) Greenwood.

Mason, Michael. Lyrical Ballads. (Annotated Texts Ser.). 336p. (C). 1992. text 58.50 (0-582-03302-0) Longman.

— The Making of Victorian Sexuality. (Illus.). 348p. 1995. pap. 15.95 (0-19-285312-0) OUP.

— The Making of Victorian Sexuality: Sexual Behaviour & Its Understanding. LC 93-28824. (Illus.). 348p. 1994. 30.00 (0-19-812247-0, Clarendon Pr) OUP.

***Mason, Michael.** Park Avenue Chorus Boy. 272p. 2000. 29.95 (1-58374-007-4) Chicago Spectrum.

Mason, Michael. Wonderboys. 170p. 1998. pap. 10.00 (0-7392-0043-7, PO2812) Morris Pubng.

Mason, Michael, ed. see Blake, William.

Mason, Michael, ed. see Wordsworth, William.

Mason, Michael, ed. & intro. see Bronte, Charlotte.

***Mason, Michael A.** The Dream & the Awakening: A True Story That Exposes the Soul Mate Myth. LC 99-91563. vii, 344p. 2000. 23.95 (0-9675724-7-9) Mobius Pubg.

Mason, Michael J. How to Write a Winning College Application Essay. 208p. (YA). (gr. 10 up). 1991. pap. 8.95 (1-55958-083-6) Prima Pub.

— How to Write a Winning College Application Essay. 2nd rev. ed. LC 93-1741. 240p. 1993. pap. 11.95 (1-55958-345-2) Prima Pub.

— How to Write a Winning College Application Essay. 3rd rev. ed. LC 97-13799. 240p. 1997. per. 14.00 (0-7615-1016-8) Prima Pub.

***Mason, Michael James.** How to Write a Winning College Application Essay. 4th rev. ed. LC 00-37361. 256p. 2000. pap. 14.95 (0-7615-2426-6) Prima Pub.

Mason, Micheline. Creating Your Own Work. 108p. 1980. 35.00 (0-905418-80-8, Pub. by Gresham Bks) St Mut.

Mason, Mike. Development & Disorder: A History of the Third World since 1945. LC 97-10706. (Illus.). 526p. 1997. pap. text 30.00 (0-87451-829-6) U Pr of New Eng.

— The Furniture of Heaven: 2 Other Parables for Pilgrims. 260p. 1998. reprint ed. pap. 26.95 (1-57383-102-6, Regent Coll Pub) Regent College.

— The Gospel According to Job: An Honest Look at Pain & Doubt From the Life of One Who Lost Everything. LC 93-42371. 448p. 1994. 19.99 (0-89107-786-3) Crossway Bks.

— The Mystery of Marriage. LC 96-177234. 185p. 1996. 16.99 (0-88070-895-6, Multnomah Bks) Multnomah Pubs.

***Mason, Mike.** Practicing the Presence of People: How We Learn to Love. LC 99-33834. 288p. 1999. pap. 11.95 (1-57856-265-1) Waterbrook Pr.

Mason, Mike & Bruner, Brodie. Pathways to Profits. 100p. (C). 1995. pap. 24.95 (0-9635096-2-4) Telsco Indust.

Mason, Mildred A. & Bates, Grace F. Basic Medical-Surgical Nursing. 3rd ed. 915p. 1991. text, student ed., wbk. ed. 15.95 (0-07-105296-8) McGraw-Hill HPD.

— Basic Medical-Surgical Nursing. 5th ed. 915p. 1991. text 36.95 (0-07-105295-X) McGraw-Hill HPD.

Mason, Miriam E. Mark Twain: Young Writer. LC 90-23768. (Childhood of Famous Americans Ser.). (Illus.). 192p. (J). (gr. 3-7). 1991. reprint ed. mass mkt. 4.95 (0-689-71480-7) Aladdin.

— Smiling Hill Farm. (Illus.). (J). 1995. reprint ed. lib. bdg. 24.95 (1-56849-616-8) Buccaneer Bks.

Mason, Miriam Evangeline. Mark Twain, Boy of Old Missouri. (Childhood of Famous Americans Ser.). (J). 1991. 10.34 (0-606-07843-6) Turtleback.

Mason, Molly, jt. auth. see Ungar, Jay.

Mason, Molly, jt. auth. see Unger, Jay.

Mason, Nancy. Oral History of West Southern Pines, North Carolina. 192p. (Orig.). 1987. 23.45 (0-9617019-0-0); pap. 14.95 (0-9617019-1-9) Southern Pines.

Mason, Nancy A. & Shimp, Leslie A. Building a Pharmacist's Patient Data Base. (Clinical Skills Program, Advancing Pharmaceutical Care Ser.). 96p. 1993. ring bd. 50.00 (1-879907-32-1) Am Soc Hlth-Syst.

Mason, Nancy A., jt. auth. see Shimp, Leslie A.

Mason, Neale B. Leading the Guidebook Astray. 79p. pap. write for info. (3-7052-0437-8, Pub. by Poetry Salzburg) Intl Spec Bk.

Mason, Nick. At the Limit: 21 Classic Race Cars That Shaped a Century of Motorsport. 176p. 1998. 39.95 (0-7603-0570-6) MBI Pubg.

— Pink Floyd. 1995. 40.00 (0-684-81600-8) Simon & Schuster.

— Pink Floyd: The Official History. 1996. 40.00 (0-684-82238-5) S&S Trade.

Mason, Nondita & Otte, George. Writers' Roles: Enactments of the Process. LC 93-77914. (Illus.). 768p. (Orig.). (C). 1993. pap. text 41.50 (0-15-500160-4, Pub. by Harcourt Coll Pubs) Harcourt.

***Mason, Otis T.** Aboriginal American Basketry: Studies in a Textile Art Without Machinery. (LC History-America-E). 548p. 1999. reprint ed. lib. bdg. 129.00 (0-7812-4283-5) Rprt Serv.

Mason, Otis T. Aboriginal American Harpoons. (Shorey Indian Ser.). (Illus.). 154p. reprint ed. pap. 10.00 (0-8466-4058-9, 158) Shoreys Bkstore.

— Aboriginal American Indian Basketry: Studies in Textile Art Without Machinery. LC 71-112623. (Beautiful Rio Grande Classics Ser.). (Illus.). 688p. 1984. reprint ed. lib. bdg. 40.00 (0-87380-012-5) Popular E Commerce.

— The Man's Knife among the Eskimo: A Study in the Collections of the U. S. National Museum. fac. ed. (Shorey Indian Ser.). (Illus.). 20p. 1999. reprint ed. pap. 10.00 (0-8466-4051-1, I-51) Shoreys Bkstore.

— The Man's Knife among the North American Indians: A Study in the Collections of the U. S. National Museum, 1897. 16.95 (0-8488-0035-4, J M C & Co) Amereon Ltd.

— North American Bows, Arrows & Quivers. (Illus.). 216p. 31.95 (0-8488-0037-0, J M C & Co) Amereon Ltd.

— The Origins of Invention: A Study of Industry among Primitive Peoples. LC 77-38362. (Select Bibliographies Reprint Ser.). 1977. reprint ed. 29.95 (0-8369-6779-8) Ayer.

— Traps of the American Indians: A Study in Psychology & Invention. (Illus.). 15p. 1986. reprint ed. pap. 10.00 (0-8466-4007-4, S-7, Shorey Pubns) Shoreys Bkstore.

— Woman's Share in Primitive Culture. 1972. 250.00 (0-87968-460-7) Gordon Pr.

Mason, Owen, et al. Living with the Coast of Alaska. LC 97-15156. (Living with the Shore Ser.). 368p. 1998. lib. bdg. 54.95 (0-8223-2009-6) Duke.

— Living with the Coast of Alaska. LC 97-15156. (Living with the Shore Ser.). xix, 348p. 1998. pap. 19.95 (0-8223-2019-3) Duke.

Mason, P. Maharishi: The Biography of the Man Who Gave Transcendental Meditation to the West. 1994. pap. 24.95 (1-85230-571-1, Pub. by Element MA) Penguin Putnam.

Mason, P. Voyeur. mass mkt. 11.95 (0-340-69501-3, Pub. by Hodder & Stought Ltd) Trafalgar.

Mason, Pamela, jt. ed. see Acutt, Melinda.

Mason, Pamela M. Handbook of Dietary Supplements, Vitamins, & Other Health Supplements. 240p. 1995. pap. text 36.95 (0-632-03923-X) Blackwell Sci.

Mason, Patience. After the War: For the Wives of All Veterans. 12p. 1993. 1.00 (1-892220-02-4) Patience Pr.

— An Explanation of PTSD for 12 Steppers: When I Get Sober, I Feel Crazy. 8p. 1993. 1.00 (1-892220-03-2) Patience Pr.

— Suggested Format for a Twelve Step Group for Trauma Survivors, Families & Friends. 30p. 1997. ring bd. 5.00 (1-892220-06-7) Patience Pr.

— Suggested Format For a Twelve Step Group for Veterans, Families & Friends. 26p. 1995. 5.00 (1-892220-04-0) Patience Pr.

— Why Is Mommy Like She Is? A Book for Children of Women with PTSD. 16p. (J). 1997. spiral bd. 5.00 (1-892220-05-9) Patience Pr.

Mason, Patience & Parker, Sally. Why Is Daddy Like He Is? A Book for Kids about PTSD. 16p. (J). 1992. spiral bd. 5.00 (1-892220-01-6) Patience Pr.

Mason, Patience H. Recovering from the War: A Guide for All Veterans, Family Members, Friends & Therapists. LC 98-192633. 464p. 1998. reprint ed. pap. 12.95 (1-892220-07-5) Patience Pr.

Mason, Patrice G., jt. auth. see Rosenberg, Amye.

***Mason, Patricia.** Return of the Osprey. (Illus.). 32p. (J). (gr. 1-3). 1999. pap. 9.95 (1-55017-203-4) Harbour Pub Co.

Mason, Patricia. Who Cares about Pigs Anyway? 2000. write for info. (0-688-16192-8, Wm Morrow) Morrow Avon.

***Mason, Patrick L., ed.** African Americans, Labor & Society: Organizing for a New Agenda. 280p. 2000. 29.95 (0-8143-2689-7) Wayne St U Pr.

Mason, Patrick L. & Williams, Rhonda M., eds. Race, Markets, & Social Outcomes. LC 97-7145. (Recent Economic Thought Ser.). 1997. lib. bdg. 104.50 (0-7923-9893-9) Kluwer Academic.

***Mason, Paul & Gold, Don.** Producing for Hollywood: A Guide for the Independent Producer. 256p. 2000. pap. 19.95 (1-58115-065-2, Pub. by Allworth Pr) Watsn-Guptill.

***Mason, Paul & Scriver, Mark.** Thrill of the Paddle: The Art of Whitewater Canoeing. (Illus.). 192p. 1999. pap. 22.95 (1-55209-451-0) Firefly Bks Ltd.

Mason, Paul N. Circles of Grace. 1995. 5.50 (0-87129-563-6, C91) Dramatic Pub.

Mason, Paul N. The Discipline Committee. 1995. pap. 5.50 (0-87129-564-4, D63) Dramatic Pub.

Mason, Paul T. & Kreger, Randi. Stop Walking on Eggshells: Taking Your Life Back When Someone You Care about Has Borderline Personality Disorder. LC 97-75479. 240p. 1998. pap. 14.95 (1-57224-108-X) New Harbinger.

Mason, Paul T., jt. ed. see Hunter, Jean E.

Mason, Penelope. History of Japanese Art. LC 92-28698. (Illus.). 432p. 1993. 65.00 (0-8109-1085-3, Pub. by Abrams) Time Warner.

— History of Japanese Art. LC 92-34428. 1993. text 68.67 (0-13-016395-3) Prntice Hall Bks.

Mason, Peter. Bacchanal! The Carnival Culture of Trinidad. LC 98-25019. (Illus.). 192p. 1998. text 49.95 (1-56639-662-X) Temple U Pr.

— Bacchanal! The Carnival Culture of Trinidad. LC 98-25019. (Illus.). 192p. 1999. pap. text 19.95 (1-56639-663-8) Temple U Pr.

— Infelicities: Representations of the Exotic. LC 98-3490. 288p. 1998. 39.95 (0-8018-5880-1) Johns Hopkins.

— Official Assassin: Winston Churchill's SAS Hit Team. Brunner, John & Phillips, Jim, eds. (Illus.). 425p. 1998. 29.95 (0-932572-31-6) Phillips Pubns.

Mason, Peter & Smith, Derrick. Magazine Law: Practical Guide. LC 97-42921. (Blueprint Ser.). 216p. (C). 1998. 85.00 (0-415-15141-4); pap. 27.99 (0-415-15142-2) Routledge.

Mason, Peter, jt. auth. see Egmond, Florike.

Mason, Phil, jt. auth. see Parris, Matthew.

Mason, Philip. The Hammered Dulcimer's Companion. 84p. 1985. spiral bd. 10.95 (0-87166-680-4, 94019) Mel Bay.

Mason, Philip P. The Ambassador Bridge: A Monument to Progress. LC 87-18983. (Great Lakes Bks.). (Illus.). 252p. 1987. pap. 24.95 (0-8143-1840-1) Wayne St U Pr.

— The Birth of a Dilemma: The Conquest & Settlement of Rhodesia. LC 82-9162. (Illus.). 388p. 1982. reprint ed. lib. bdg. 69.50 (0-313-23547-3, MABI, Greenwood Pr) Greenwood.

— Call the Next Witness. LC 86-7122. 218p. 1986. pap. 7.50 (0-226-50955-9) U Ch Pr.

— Detroit, Fort Lernoult, & the American Revolution. LC 64-18967. 34p. reprint ed. pap. 30.00 (0-7837-3634-7, 204350100009) Bks Demand.

An Asterisk (*) at the beginning of an entry indicates that the title is appearing for the first time.

— Directory of Jewish Archival Institutions. LC 75-15504. 77p. reprint ed. pap. 30.00 (*0-7837-3652-5*, 204352300009) Bks Demand.

— Rumrunning & the Roaring Twenties: Prohibition on the Michigan-Ontario Waterway. LC 95-4610. (Illus.). 186p. 1995. 29.95 (*0-8143-2584-X*, Great Lks Bks); 34.95 (*0-8143-2583-1*, Great Lks Bks) Wayne St U Pr.

Mason, Philip P., ed. After Tippecanoe. LC 73-7076. (Illus.). 106p. 1973. reprint ed. lib. bdg. 38.50 (*0-8371-6903-8*, MAAT, Greenwood Pr) Greenwood.

Mason, Philip P., jt. auth. see Woodford, Frank B.

Mason, Philip P., ed. see Hobart, Henry.

Mason, Philip P., jt. ed. see Leab, Daniel J.

Mason, Philip P., ed. see Schoolcraft, Henry R.

Mason, Polly C. Records of Colonial Goucester County, Virginia: A Collection of Abstracts from Original Documents Concerning the Lands & People of Colonial Gloucester County, 2 vols. in 1. (Illus.). 296p. 1997. reprint ed. pap. 45.00 (*0-8063-4720-1*, 9225) Clearfield Co.

Mason, R. Micah, Nahum & Obadiah. (Old Testament Guides Ser.: No. 28). 116p. 1991. pap. 12.50 (*1-85075-702-X*, Pub. by Sheffield Acad) CUP Services.

Mason, R. Petrology of the Metamorphic Rocks. (Textbook of Petrology Ser.). (Illus.). 1978. pap. text 24.95 (*0-04-552014-3*) Routledge.

Mason, R. & Bacsich, P. D., eds. ISDN Applications in Education & Training. 256p. 1993. boxed set 59.00 (*0-85296-860-4*, TE905) INSPEC Inc.

Mason, R., jt. auth. see Hoppe, W.

Mason, R. A., ed. War in the Third Dimension: Essays in Contemporary Air Power. 228p. 1986. 23.00 (*0-08-031188-1*, Pub. by Brasseys) Brasseys.

Mason, R. A., jt. auth. see Armitage, M. J.

Mason, R. A., ed. see Armitage, Michael.

Mason, R. A., ed. see Knight, Michael.

Mason, R. A., ed. see Walker, J. R.

Mason, R. D. Euro-American Pioneer Settlement Systems in the Central Salt River Valley of Northeast Missouri. (Illus.). xi, 99p. 1984. 10.00 (*0-917111-01-X*) Mus Anthro MO.

Mason, R. E. Aerospace Power: Revised Roles & Technology. 152p. 1997. 34.95 (*1-85753-204-X*, Pub. by Brasseys) Brasseys.

Mason, R. H. & Caiger, J. G. A History of Japan. 2nd rev. ed. LC 96-60930. (Illus.). 400p. 1997. pap. 16.95 (*0-8048-2097-X*) Tuttle Pubng.

Mason, R. Hal & Spich, Robert. Management: An International Perspective. 256p. (C). 1987. pap. text 15.95 (*0-256-05631-5*, Irwn McGrw-H) McGrw-H Hghr Educ.

Mason, R. Hunter, jt. auth. see Biernat, Len.

Mason, R. L., jt. auth. see Gunst, R. F.

***Mason-Raley, Dorothy.** Praying Effectively. 221p. 1999. spiral bd. 12.00 (*1-930479-01-8*) C R Pubs.

Mason-Raley, Dorothy, ed. see Raley, Charles W.

Mason, Ralph, et al. Marketing: Practices & Principles. 5th ed. Lynch, Richard, ed. 1995. text 38.25 (*0-02-635601-5*) Glencoe.

Mason, Ralph E., et al. Marketing Practices & Principles. 3rd ed. (Illus.). 1980. text 24.88 (*0-07-040693-6*) McGraw.

— Marketing Practices & Principles. 4th ed. 448p. 1985. text 21.24 (*0-07-040705-3*) McGraw.

Mason, Ranier M. Jean Fautrier's Prints. (FRE., Illus.). 200p. 1986. pap. 75.00 (*1-55660-073-9*) A Wofsy Fine Arts.

— Kurt Seligmann's Graphic Work. (Illus.). 136p. 1982. pap. 150.00 (*1-55660-074-7*) A Wofsy Fine Arts.

Mason, Renee. Homeschooling All the Way Through High School. LC 99-32337. 129p. 1999. pap. 9.99 (*0-8423-3449-1*) Tyndale Hse.

Mason, Rex. Old Testament Pictures of God. LC 93-28067. 216p. 1993. pap. 16.00 (*1-880837-33-1*) Smyth & Helwys.

— Preaching the Tradition: Homily & Hermeneutics after the Exile. 334p. (C). 1990. text 75.00 (*0-521-38304-8*) Cambridge U Pr.

Mason, Rex. Zephaniah, Habakkuk, Joel. (Old Testament Guides Ser.: No. 27). 132p. 1994. pap. 12.50 (*1-85075-718-6*, Pub. by Sheffield Acad) CUP Services.

Mason, Richard. Before Logic. LC 99-59365. (C). 2000. text 49.50 (*0-7914-4531-3*); pap. text 16.95 (*0-7914-4532-1*) State U NY Pr.

— Cambridge Minds. 253p. (C). 1994. pap. text 19.95 (*0-521-45625-8*) Cambridge U Pr.

— The Drowning People. LC 98-50916. 288p. 1999. 24.00 (*0-446-52524-3*, Pub. by Warner Bks) Little.

***Mason, Richard.** The Drowning People. 400p. 2000. mass mkt. 7.50 (*0-446-60800-9*, Pub. by Warner Bks) Little.

Mason, Richard. The God of Spinoza: A Philosophical Study. 286p. (C). 1997. text 59.95 (*0-521-58162-1*) Cambridge U Pr.

— The God of Spinoza: A Philosophical Study. 286p. (C). 1999. pap. 21.95 (*0-521-66585-X*) Cambridge U Pr.

— The Wind Cannot Read. large type ed. 1976. 27.99 (*0-85456-435-7*) Ulverscroft.

— The World of Suzie Wong. 25.95 (*0-8488-0052-4*) Amereon Ltd.

— The World of Suzie Wong. 1993. reprint ed. lib. bdg. 27.95 (*1-56849-097-6*) Buccaneer Bks.

Mason, Richard O., et al. Information & Responsibility: The Ethical Challenge. (Series in Business Ethics: Vol. 2). 320p. (C). 1995. 48.00 (*0-8039-5755-6*); pap. 22.95 (*0-8039-5756-4*) Sage.

Mason, Richard O., jt. auth. see Elam, Joyce J.

Mason, Richard O., jt. auth. see Rowe, Alan J.

Mason, Rita A. A Guide to Dental Radiography. 4th ed. (Illus.). 272p. 1998. text (*0-19-262672-8*) OUP.

***Mason, Rita A. & Bourne, Sarah.** A Guide to Dental Radiography. 4th ed. LC 97-28365. (Illus.). 1998. write for info. (*0-01-926272-8*); pap. write for info. (*0-01-926271-X*) OUP.

Mason, Rita A. & Bourne, Sarah. A Guide to Dental Radiography. 4th ed. (Illus.). 272p. 1998. pap. text 69.50 (*0-19-262671-X*) OUP.

Mason, Robert, IV. S. T. O. R. E. S. Structured Teaching of Research & Experimentation Skills (Middle School) 1991. pap. 15.00 (*0-89824-504-4*) Trillium Pr.

***Mason, Robert, et al.** Statistical Techniques in Business & Economics. 408p. (C). 1998. pap., student ed. 28.13 (*0-07-303928-4*) McGrw-H Hghr Educ.

Mason, Robert C. Chickenhawk. (Illus.). 328p. 1984. pap. 13.95 (*0-14-007218-7*, Penguin Bks) Viking Penguin.

Mason, Robert C., ed. Basement Tectonics, No. 7. (C). 1992. lib. bdg. 251.00 (*0-7923-1582-0*) Kluwer Academic.

Mason, Robert D. Business & Economic Statistics. 1970. text 4.50 (*0-256-01268-7*, Irwn Prfssnl) McGraw-Hill Prof.

— Business & Economic Statistics. 4th ed. (Plaid Ser.). 166p. 1983. text 11.95 (*0-87094-334-0*, Irwn Prfssnl) McGraw-Hill Prof.

Mason, Robert D. & Lind. Statistics: An Introduction. 5th ed. LC 97-34710. 1997. pap. 93.95 (*0-534-35379-7*) Brooks-Cole.

Mason, Robert D. & Lind, Douglas A. Basic Statistics for Business & Economics. 2nd ed. 560p. (C). 1996. text 62.75 (*0-256-19408-4*, Irwn McGrw-H) McGrw-H Hghr Educ.

— Basic Statistics for Business & Economics: Study Guide. 2nd ed. 320p. (C). 1996. text 21.87 (*0-256-21498-0*, Irwn McGrw-H) McGrw-H Hghr Educ.

— Statistical Techniques in Business & Economics. 7th ed. (C). 1989. student ed. 18.95 (*0-256-08054-2*, Irwn McGrw-H) McGrw-H Hghr Educ.

— Statistical Techniques in Business & Economics. 8th ed. LC 92-9933. 896p. (C). 1992. text 71.25 (*0-256-10338-0*, Irwn McGrw-H) McGrw-H Hghr Educ.

— Statistical Techniques in Business & Economics. 9th ed. LC 95-16497. 912p. (C). 1995. text 71.25 (*0-256-13901-6*, Irwn Prfssnl) McGraw-Hill Prof.

— Statistical Techniques in Business & Economics. 9th ed. 352p. (C). 1995. text, student ed. 25.00 (*0-256-17371-0*, Irwn McGrw-H) McGrw-H Hghr Educ.

— Statistical Techniques in Business & Economics. 10th ed. LC 98-26640. 1998. write for info. (*0-07-303935-7*) McGraw.

— Statistical Techniques in Business & Economics. 10th ed. LC 98-26640. xx, 791 p. 1999. write for info. (*0-07-303936-5*) McGraw.

Mason, Robert D., et al. Statistical Techniques in Business & Economics: Business Statistics Software. 9th ed. (C). 1996. pap., text 77.50 incl. disk (*0-256-21184-1*, Irwn McGrw-H) McGrw-H Hghr Educ.

***Mason, Robert D., et al.** Statistics: Introduction. 5th ed. 1998. pap., student ed. 14.00 (*0-534-35655-9*) Thomson Learn.

Mason, Robert D., et al. Statistics: An Intro. 4th ed. (Statistics). 660p. (C). 1995. pap. 60.00 (*0-534-51070-1*) Wadsworth Pub.

Mason, Robert D., jt. auth. see Lind, Douglas A.

Mason, Robert E. A Better School: Who Says So? (Occasional Papers: No. 9). 1976. pap. 10.00 (*0-933669-12-7*) Soc Profs Ed.

— Community of the Young. (Occasional Papers: No. 8). 1975. pap. 10.00 (*0-933669-11-9*) Soc Profs Ed.

Mason, Robert E., III. The Euclid Project: A Computer-Based Geometry Program. (Orig.). (J). (gr. 7-8). 1996. pap. 15.00 (*0-89824-547-8*); pap., teacher ed. 10.00 (*0-89824-548-6*) Royal Fireworks.

***Mason, Robert E.** An Introduction to Geometer's Sketchpad. (Illus.). 1998. pap. 9.99 (*0-89824-545-1*, 5451) Trillium Pr.

Mason, Robert J. Contested Lands: Conflict & Compromise in New Jersey's Pine Barrens. (Conflicts in Urban & Regional Development Ser.). 256p. (C). 1992. 59.95 (*0-87722-925-2*) Temple U Pr.

Mason, Robert J. & Mattson, Mark T. Atlas of United States Environmental Issues. (Illus.). 192p. 1990. 80.00 (*0-685-38861-1*) Macmillan.

Mason, Robert L. The Ultimate Beagle: The Natural Born Rabbit Dog. LC 97-28353. (Illus.). 176p. 1997. 24.95 (*0-940269-14-7*) OTR Pubns.

Mason, Robert L., et al. Statistical Design Analysis of Experiments with Applications to Engineering & Science. LC 88-20893. (Probability & Mathematical Statistics Ser.). 720p. 1989. 115.00 (*0-471-85364-X*) Wiley.

Mason, Robert L., jt. auth. see Gunst, Richard F.

Mason, Robert M. Modern Methods of Music Analysis Using Computers. LC 85-26142. (Illus.). viii, 299p. 1985. lib. bdg. 45.50 (*0-9615669-0-6*) Schoolhouse Pr.

Mason, Robert M., et al. Orofacial Myology: Beyond Tongue Thrust. 63p. 1994. pap. text 40.00 (*0-910329-81-8*, 0111904) Am Speech Lang Hearing.

Mason, Robin. Global Education: Trends & Applications. LC 98-14125. (Studies in Distance Education). 184p. (C). 1998. 75.00 (*0-415-18687-0*); pap. 24.99 (*0-415-18688-9*) Routledge.

Mason, Robin, ed. Shotcrete for Underground Support, Vol. III. 346p. (Orig.). 1980. pap. 30.00 (*0-939204-04-5*, 78-14) Eng Found.

Mason-Robinson, Sally. Developing & Managing Video Collections in Libraries: A How-to-Do-It Manual. LC 96-3058. (How-to-Do-It Manuals Ser.). 130p. 1996. pap. 45.00 (*1-55570-230-9*) Neal-Schuman.

Mason, Roder A. John Knox & the British Reformations. LC 98-35720. (St. Andrews Studies in Reformation History). (Illus.). 288p. (C). 1999. text 86.95 (*1-84014-600-1*, BX9223.J893, Pub. by Ashgate Pub) Ashgate Pub Co.

Mason, Roger. The Economics of Conspicuous Consumption: Theory & Thought since 1700. LC 97-52042. 192p. 1998. 75.00 (*1-85898-833-0*) E Elgar.

***Mason, Roger.** Granny's Village: Memories of the Yorkshire Dales in the 1800's. large type unabridged ed. 2000. 25.95 (*0-7531-5720-9*, 157209, Pub. by ISIS Lrg Prnt) ISIS Pub.

Mason, Roger A., ed. Scots & Britons: Scottish Political Thought & the Union of 1603. LC 93-32399. 337p. (C). 1994. text 64.95 (*0-521-42034-2*) Cambridge U Pr.

Mason, Roger A., ed. see Knox, John.

Mason, Roger B. Franz Johnston. Date not set. 19.95 (*1-55082-179-2*, Pub. by Quarry Pr) LPC InBook.

— Print & Be Damaged: or How I Put My Back Out Saving Letterpress for My Grandchildren's Children. 24p. 1994. pap. 20.00 (*0-930126-46-7*) Typographeum.

— Travels in the Shining Island. LC 96-931561. (Illus.). 96p. pap. 13.95 (*1-896219-16-0*, Pub. by Natural Herit Natural Hist) Birch Brook Pr.

Mason, Ronald J. Rock Island: Historical Indian Archaeology in the Northern Lake Michigan Basin. LC 85-12661. (MCJA Special Paper: No. 6). 228p. reprint ed. pap. 70.70 (*0-7837-1341-X*, 204148900020) Bks Demand.

Mason, Ronald M. Participatory & Workplace Democracy: A Theoretical Development in Critique of Liberalism. LC 81-16687. 268p. 1982. 31.95 (*0-8093-0992-0*) S Ill U Pr.

Mason, Rosalie. Beginners' Guide to Family Preparedness: Food Storage, Back to Basics & Survival Facts. LC 77-79750. (Illus.). 160p. 1977. pap. 11.98 (*0-88290-082-X*) Horizon Utah.

Mason, Russell E. Anxiety Resolution, Relaxation, & Systematic & Flexible Hierarchy Guides, Set-AH. (Train-Ascendance Ser.). 1975. pap. 45.00 incl. audio (*0-89533-009-1*, 58.GT-AR) F I Comm.

— Basic, Advanced Systematic Substitution Training, Set-AS. 1975. pap. 35.00 incl. audio (*0-89533-017-2*) F I Comm.

— Basic, Elementary Systematic Substitution Training, Set-ES. 1973. pap. 35.00 incl. audio (*0-89533-015-6*) F I Comm.

— Basic, Intermediate Systematic Substitution Training, Set-IS. 1973. pap. 35.00 incl. audio (*0-89533-016-4*) F I Comm.

— Brief Outlines for Relaxation Training (& Meditative Relaxation) (Brief Outlines Ser.: No. 1). 1973. pap. 15.00 (*0-89533-022-9*) F I Comm.

— Brief Outlines for Substitution Training & Positive Goal Achievement. (Brief Outlines Ser.: No. 3). 1973. pap. 15.00 (*0-89533-024-5*) F I Comm.

— Continued Feeling Study for Negative Subtypes: Struggle (Anger, Determination, & Others), Set-HS. 1973. audio 9.00 (*0-89533-043-1*) F I Comm.

— Daily Growth for Broader Experiences or Awareness, Achievements, Purposeful Relaxation & Comfort, Set-DG. rev. ed. 1975. pap. 60.00 incl. audio (*0-89533-011-3*) F I Comm.

— De-Sensitization by Systematic Steps with Relaxation, Set-D. 1975. pap. 35.00 incl. audio (*0-89533-005-9*) F I Comm.

— Eighteen Tapes for Comprehensive Training: Relaxation, Feeling & Value Solutions, Set A. pap. 145.00 incl. audio (*0-89533-021-0*, 69.ST-CT) F I Comm.

Mason, Russell E. Extended (Experiential) Awareness, Purposeful Relaxation, Differential (Multiple) Bodily Feeling States & Communication, Set-EA. (Train-Ascendance Ser.). 1975. pap. 55.00 incl. audio (*0-89533-013-X*, GT-LE) F I Comm.

Mason, Russell E. Individual Uses of Positive Substitution & Problem Solutions, Set-IP. 1975. pap. 35.00 incl. audio (*0-89533-007-5*) F I Comm.

— Informational Guides for Groups, Communication, Living & Change: Guides for Groups & Personal Change, Set-GL. 1975. pap. 35.00 incl. audio (*0-89533-019-9*) F I Comm.

— Life-Extension, Purposeful Relaxation, Differential (Multiple) "Feeling" (Psychophysiological) Awareness & Communication, Set. 1975. 70.00 incl. audio (*0-89533-018-0*) F I Comm.

— Multiple Uses: Positive Substitution, Problem Solutions, Relaxation, & Goal Achievements, Set-MS. 1975. pap. 60.00 incl. audio (*0-89533-008-3*) F I Comm.

— Notes: For Applications of Relaxed Training & Feeling Training, Set-AS. 1975. pap. 10.00 (*0-89533-025-3*) F I Comm.

— Positive Experiential Awareness, Purposeful Relaxation, & Differentiated Bodily Feeling States, Set-PA. (Train-Ascendance Cassettes Ser.). 1975. pap. 23.00 incl. audio (*0-89533-012-1*, GT-PA) F I Comm.

— Positive Personalities: Joy, Significance, & Sexual Feelings & Values. LC 70-167784. 1971. 16.00 (*0-89533-000-8*) F I Comm.

Mason, Russell E. Positive Personality Fulfillment, Set-PPF. (Train-Ascendance Cassettes Ser.). 1975. 16.00 incl. audio (*0-89533-048-2*, 71 GT-PF) F I Comm.

Mason, Russell E. Positive Substitution, Purposeful Relaxation, & Goal Achievement Training: A Systematic Positive Beginning, Set-PS. 1975. pap. 60.00 incl. audio (*0-89533-014-8*) F I Comm.

— Relaxation & De-Sensitization Training, Set-RD. (Train-Ascendance Cassettes Ser.). 1975. pap. 45.00 incl. audio (*0-89533-006-7*, 55.GT-RD) F I Comm.

— SET, H. E. S. T. - A Humanistic Endeavor & Surgent Train-Ascendance. 1975. pap. 10.00 (*0-89533-028-8*) F I Comm.

— Simple Guides for Daily Growth, Problem Solving & Purposeful Relaxation, Set. 1975. pap. 23.00 incl. audio (*0-89533-001-6*, 50.GT-GP) F I Comm.

— Simplified Behavior & Feeling State Change & Goal Accomplishments, Set (Train-Ascendance Ser.). 1975. pap. 45.00 incl. audio (*0-89533-002-4*, 51.GT-BF) F I Comm.

— Simplified Extended, Deep, & - or Meditative Relaxation, Set-R. (Train-Ascendance Ser.). 1975. pap. 23.00 incl. audio (*0-89533-004-0*, 53.GT-RM) F I Comm.

— Simplified Purposeful Relaxation for Comfort or Effectiveness, Set-PR. (Train-Ascendance Cassettes Ser.). 1975. pap. 23.00 incl. audio (*0-89533-003-2*, 52.GT-RP) F I Comm.

— Simplified Relaxation, Problem Solutions & Substitutions & Value Considerations, Set-S. (Train-Ascendance Ser.). 1975. pap. 65.00 incl. audio (*0-89533-020-2*, 65.GT-SV) F I Comm.

— Solutions, Relaxation or Understanding of Tense, Anxious, Depressive, Hostile (Irritable) & Disgust States & Problems, Set. 1976. pap. 45.00 incl. audio (*0-89533-010-5*, 59.GT-DH) F I Comm.

Mason, Ruth & Mason, Gregory. Danbury Curve. 15.95 (*0-8084-0370-2*) NCUP.

Mason, Sally & Scholtz, James C. Video for Libraries: Special Interest Video for Small & Medium-Sized Public Libraries. LC 88-22235. 187p. reprint ed. pap. 58.00 (*0-7837-5921-5*, 204572000007) Bks Demand.

Mason, Sammy. Stalls, Spins & Safety. (Illus.). 25.95 (*0-614-13214-2*, 31-13160) EAA Aviation.

Mason, Sandra. Dulcie's Wish. (Illus.). 12p. (J). (gr. 1-4). 1997. pap. 9.95 (*1-890939-02-1*) Century Creations.

***Mason, Sarah J.** Corpse in the Case. large type ed. 392p. 1999. pap. 18.99 (*0-7089-5590-8*, Linford) Ulverscroft.

— Deep-Frozen Death. large type ed. 472p. 1999. pap. 18.99 (*0-7089-5596-7*, Linford) Ulverscroft.

Mason, Sarah J. Dying Breath. 240p. (Orig.). 1994. mass mkt. 5.99 (*0-425-14245-0*, Prime Crime) Berkley Pub.

— Let's Talk of Wills. large type ed. (Linford Mystery Large Print Ser.). 416p. 1995. pap. 16.99 (*0-7089-7731-6*, Linford) Ulverscroft.

***Mason, Sarah J.** Murder from Memory. large type ed. 424p. 1999. pap. 18.99 (*0-7089-5607-6*, Linford) Ulverscroft.

— Murder in the Maze. large type ed. 448p. 1999. pap. 18.99 (*0-7089-5561-4*, Linford) Ulverscroft.

Mason, Sarah J. Seeing Is Deceiving. 208p. 1997. mass mkt. 5.99 (*0-425-15901-9*, Prime Crime) Berkley Pub.

***Mason, Sarah J.** Seeing Is Deceiving. large type ed. 384p. 2000. pap. 18.99 (*0-7089-5673-4*, Linford) Ulverscroft.

— Sew Easy to Kill. large type ed. 392p. 2000. pap. 18.99 (*0-7089-5656-4*, Linford) Ulverscroft.

Mason, Scott. No Dogs in Heaven. (Cleveland Poets Ser.: No. 24). 28p. 1980. pap. 2.50 (*0-914946-21-8*) Cleveland St Univ Poetry Ctr.

Mason, Scott, et al. Cases in Financial Engineering: Applied Studies of Financial Innovation. LC 94-22273. 704p. (C). 1994. 95.00 (*0-13-079419-8*) P-H.

— Diversification & Conversion Strategies for Rural Hospitals. 52p. (Orig.). 1989. pap. 35.00 (*0-87258-524-7*, 184207) Am Hospital.

Mason, Sharon & Dragun, James. Natural Chemicals in Sediments. 204p. (Orig.). (C). 1996. pap. 39.95 (*1-884940-04-8*) Amherst Sci Pubs.

Mason, Sharon, ed. see Davis, Rolanda J.

Mason, Sharon R., ed. see Heyman, Barbara G.

Mason, Shirley L., jt. auth. see Mather, Kirtley F.

Mason, Sophia. Art of Forecasting. 60p. 1977. 12.95 (*0-86690-330-5*, M1322-034) Am Fed Astrologers.

— Card Reading for Astrologers. 2nd unabridged ed. (Illus.). 54p. 1994. spiral bd. 12.00 (*1-889805-20-3*) A-C Tapes.

— Delineation of Progressions. 310p. 1985. 19.95 (*0-86690-280-5*, M2462-014) Am Fed Astrologers.

— Forecasting with New, Full & Quarter Moons. rev. ed. 126p. 1994. pap. 13.00 (*0-86690-362-3*, AFA) Am Fed Astrologers.

— From One House to Another. rev. ed. 64p. 1993. 11.00 (*0-86690-363-1*) Am Fed Astrologers.

— Lunations & Predictions. rev. ed. 66p. 1993. 12.00 (*0-86690-364-X*) Am Fed Astrologers.

— Lunations & Transits - Step-by-Step: New Moon Through Signs & Houses. 2nd unabridged ed. (Illus.). 80p. 1996. spiral bd. 13.00 (*1-889805-06-8*) A-C Tapes.

— Transits from Beginning to End. 2nd rev. ed. (Illus.). 72p. 1996. spiral bd. 16.00 (*1-889805-02-5*) A-C Tapes.

— Understanding Planetary Placements. rev. ed. 86p. 1993. pap. 12.00 (*0-86690-365-8*) Am Fed Astrologers.

Mason, Sophia & Ploscik, Vince. Fatal Accidents (Astrological) 2nd unabridged ed. (Illus.). 202p. (Orig.). 1993. spiral bd. 24.00 (*1-889805-04-1*) A-C Tapes.

— Fatal Accidents with Solar Returns. 2nd unabridged ed. (Illus.). 103p. 1994. spiral bd. 21.00 (*1-889805-03-3*) A-C Tapes.

— Sexuality. 2nd unabridged ed. (Illus.). 158p. (Orig.). 1994. pap., spiral bd. 21.00 (*1-889805-01-7*) A-C Tapes.

Mason, Stanley. Collected Poems. 159p. pap. write for info. (*3-7052-0629-X*, Pub. by Poetry Salzburg) Intl Spec Bk.

Mason, Stanley. Send Out the Dove. limited ed. (New Poetic Drama Ser.). 1986. pap. 5.00 (*0-934218-37-4*) Dragons Teeth.

Mason, Stanley, tr. A German Treasury Pt. 1: German Poetry from 1100 to Rilke. 138p. pap. write for info. (*3-7052-0630-3*, Pub. by Poetry Salzburg) Intl Spec Bk.

— A German Treasury Pt. 2: German Poetry from 1100 to Rilke. 149p. pap. write for info. (*3-7052-0638-9*, Pub. by Poetry Salzburg) Intl Spec Bk.

Mason, Stanley, ed. see Resource Pathway's Editors.

Mason, Stanley I., Jr. Inventing Small Products: For Big Profits Quickly. Christopher, Bill, ed. LC 97-65792. (Management Library). (Illus.). 90p. (Orig.). 1997. pap. 12.95 (*1-56052-436-7*) Crisp Pubns.

M

An Asterisk (*) at the beginning of an entry indicates that the title is appearing for the first time.

M

***Mason, Stephen.** Study Guides for Resource-Efficient Crop Management. 292p. (C). 1999. per. 42.95 (*0-7872-6481-4*, 41648101) Kendall-Hunt.

Mason, Stephen F. History of the Sciences. Orig. Title: Main Currents of Scientific Thought. 640p. 1962. pap. 10.95 (*0-02-093400-9*) Macmillan.

Mason, Stephen F., ed. Optical Activity & Chiral Discrimination. (NATO Advanced Study Institutes Series C, Mathematical & Physical Sciences: No. 48). 1979. text 135.00 (*90-277-0982-3*) Kluwer Academic.

Mason, Stephen T. Catecholamines & Behaviour. LC 83-7722. 480p. 1984. text 85.00 (*0-521-24930-9*); pap. text 39.95 (*0-521-27082-0*) Cambridge U Pr.

Mason, Steve. Flavius Josephus on the Pharisees. LC 90-19845. (Studia Post-Biblica Ser.: Vol. 39). xvi, 424p. 1990. 157.50 (*90-04-09181-5*) Brill Academic Pubs.

— Josephus & the New Testament. LC 92-33067. (Illus.). 248p. (Orig.). 1992. pap. 9.95 (*0-943575-99-0*) Hendrickson MA.

Mason, Steve, ed. Understanding Josephus: Seven Perspectives. (Journal for the Study of the Pseudepigrapha Supplement Ser.: Vol. 32). 260p. 1998. 75.00 (*1-85075-876-6*, Pub. by Sheffield Acad) CUP Services.

Mason, Steve, et al, trs. Flavius Josephus. 300p. 1999. 88.50 (*90 04 10679-0*) Brill Academic Pubs.

***Mason, Steve & Robinson, Thomas.** An Early Christian Reader. 2000. 34.95 (*1-56563-043-2*) Hendrickson MA.

Mason, Steve S., jt. auth. see Goldstein, Niles E.

Mason, Stuart. Bibliography of Oscar Wilde, 2 vols. LC 75-184647. (Reference Ser.: No. 44). 607p. 1972. reprint ed. lib. bdg. 150.00 (*0-8383-1378-7*) M S G Haskell Hse.

***Mason, Stuart.** Bibliography of Oscar Wilde. 605p. 1998. reprint ed. 70.00 (*1-57898-104-2*) Martino Pubng.

Mason, Stuart. Oscar Wilde: Art & Morality. LC 79-174694. (English Literature Ser.: No. 33). 1971. reprint ed. lib. bdg. 75.00 (*0-8383-1334-5*) M S G Haskell Hse.

— Oscar Wilde & the Aesthetic Movement. LC 75-119081. (English Literature Ser.: No. 33). 1970. reprint ed. lib. bdg. 75.00 (*0-8383-1077-X*) M S G Haskell Hse.

***Mason, Stuart & Millard, C. S.** Bibliography of the Poems of Oscar Wilde. fac. ed. (Illus.). 148p. 2000. 45.00 (*1-57898-228-6*) Martino Pubng.

Mason, Susan Garrett, see Garrett Mason, Susan.

Mason, T., jt. auth. see Alty, A.

Mason, T. David, jt. auth. see Holland, Kenneth.

Mason, T. J., ed. Sonochemistry: The Uses of Ultrasound in Chemistry. 1990. 109.00 (*0-85186-293-4*) CRC Pr.

Mason, T. R., ed. Pedro Calderon de la Barca: La Desdicha de la Voz. (SPA.). 288p. 1998. 45.95 (*0-85323-823-5*, Pub. by Liverpool Univ Pr); pap. 23.95 (*0-85323-833-2*, Pub. by Liverpool Univ Pr) Intl Spec Bk.

***Mason, Ted.** Hostage of Fortune. 266p. 1999. pap. 12.95 (*0-910155-38-0*) Bartleby Pr.

Mason, Theodore C. Battleship Sailor, 8 vols. LC 81-85440. (Bluejacket Paperback Ser.). (Illus.). 271p. 1994. pap. 16.95 (*1-55750-579-9*) Naval Inst Pr.

— Rendezvous with Destiny: A Sailor's War. LC 96-44138. (Illus.). 296p. 1997. 29.95 (*1-55750-580-2*) Naval Inst Pr.

— We Will Stand by You: Serving in the Pawnee, 1942-1945. LC 95-24848. (Bluejacket Bks.). (Illus.). 284p. 1996. pap. 15.95 (*1-55750-581-0*) Naval Inst Pr.

Mason, Thomas. Governing Oregon. 272p. (C). 1994. pap. text, per. 39.95 (*0-7872-0005-0*, 41000501) Kendall-Hunt.

— Serving God & Mammon: William Juxon, 1582-1663. LC 83-40507. (Illus.). 208p. 1985. 35.00 (*0-87413-251-7*) U Delaware Pr.

Mason, Thomas A., ed. see Madison, James.

Mason, Thomas D. Art of Hearing Aural Skills for Improvisors. 144p. 1997. otabind 29.95 (*0-7935-7940-6*) H Leonard.

Mason, Tim. Nazism, Fascism & the Working Class. Caplan, Jane, ed. 371p. (C). 1995. text 59.95 (*0-521-43212-X*); pap. text 19.95 (*0-521-43787-3*) Cambridge U Pr.

— The Secret Years: Flight Testing at Boscombe Down, 1939-1945. (Illus.). 320p. 1999. 49.95 (*0-9519899-9-5*, Pub. by Hikoki Pubns) Howell Pr VA.

— Social Policy in the Third Reich: The Working Class & the "National Community", 1918-1939. Kaplan, Jane, ed. Bradwin, John A., tr. 434p. 1993. 60.00 (*0-85496-621-8*, Pub. by Berg Pubs); pap. 22.50 (*0-85496-410-X*, Pub. by Berg Pubs) NYU Pr.

Mason, Tim & Mason, Lynn. Helen Hyde. (American Printmakers Ser.). 112p. 1991. pap. 24.95 (*1-56098-009-5*) Smithsonian.

Mason, Timothy. Ascension Day. 1991. pap. 5.25 (*0-8222-0068-6*) Dramatists Play.

— Babylon Gardens. 1993. pap. 5.25 (*0-8222-1369-9*) Dramatists Play.

— The Fiery Furnace. LC 94-221959. 1994. pap. 5.25 (*0-8222-1355-9*) Dramatists Play.

— In a Northern Landscape. 1985. pap. 5.25 (*0-8222-0558-0*) Dramatists Play.

— Levitation. 1984. pap. 5.25 (*0-8222-0654-4*) Dramatists Play.

— Only You. rev. ed. LC 97-208540. 1995. pap. 5.25 (*0-8222-1488-1*) Dramatists Play.

Mason, Timothy & Children's Theatre Company (Minneapolis, Minn.) St. Timothy Mason: Ten Plays for Children from the Repertory of the Children's Theatre Company of Minneapolis. LC 97-17898. (Young Actors Ser.). 368p. (YA). (gr. 6 up). 1997. pap. 19.95 (*1-57525-120-5*) Smith & Kraus.

Mason, Timothy J. Advances in Sonochemistry, Vol. 2. 322p. 1991. 109.50 (*1-55938-267-8*) Jai Pr.

***Mason, Timothy J.** Sonochemistry. LC 99-15703. (Oxford Chemistry Primers Ser.: No. 70). (Illus.). 96p. 2000. pap. text 12.95 (*0-19-850371-7*) OUP.

Mason, Timothy J., ed. Advances in Sonochemistry, Vol. 1. 275p. 1990. 109.50 (*1-55938-178-7*) Jai Pr.

— Advances in Sonochemistry, Vol. 3. 292p. 1993. 109.50 (*1-55938-476-X*) Jai Pr.

— Advances in Sonochemistry, Vol. 4. 1996. 109.50 (*1-55938-793-9*) Jai Pr.

— Advances in Sonochemistry, Vol. 5. Date not set. 109.50 (*0-7623-0331-X*) Jai Pr.

Mason, Timothy J. & Lorimer, Phillip J. Sonochemistry: Theory, Applications & Uses of Ultrasound in Chemistry. 1989. text 87.95 (*0-470-21373-6*) P-H.

Mason, Todd. Perot: An Unauthorized Biography. 300p. 1990. text 22.95 (*1-55623-236-5*, Irwn Prfssnl) McGraw-Hill Prof.

***Mason, Tom & Mercer, David.** A Sociology of the Mentally Disordered Offender. LC 98-51542. 1999. pap. text. write for info. (*0-582-31741-X*) Longman.

Mason, Tom, jt. ed. see Hopkins, David.

Mason, Tom, ed. see Rybak, Deborah C. & Phelps, David.

Mason, Tony. Only a Game? Sport in the Modern World. (Modern World Issues Ser.). (Illus.). 80p. (C). 1993. pap. text 15.95 (*0-521-39992-0*) Cambridge U Pr.

— Passion of the People: Football in Latin Ameica. (Critical Studies in Latin American Culture). 224p. (C). 1995. 60.00 (*0-86091-403-8*, B3629, Pub. by Verso) Norton.

— Passion of the People: Football in Latin America. (Critical Studies in Latin American Culture). 224p. (C). 1995. pap. 18.00 (*0-86091-667-7*, B3629, Pub. by Verso) Norton.

Mason, Tony, jt. auth. see Holt, Richard.

Mason, Tufton O. American Indian Basketry. (Illus.). 800p. 1988. pap. 17.95 (*0-486-25777-0*) Dover.

***Mason, Tyra & Chekwas, Sam.** Baby Names: Real Names with Real Meanings for African American Children. 2nd rev. large type ed. Taylor, Maxwell, ed. LC 99-47594. (Illus.). 192p. 2000. reprint ed. pap. 11.95 (*1-886433-13-5*) A&B Bks.

Mason, Tyra & Chekwas, Sam. Baby Names: Real Names with Real Meanings for African Children. 192p. 1998. pap. 11.95 (*1-885778-35-X*) Seaburn.

Mason, Val, ed. see Rainford, Laura, et al.

Mason, Valmari M., jt. auth. see Benson-Von der Ohe, Elizabeth E.

Mason, Vicki. Marketing the Continuum of Care: Hospital Marketing Strategies for Developing Community Service. LC 97-25979. 1997. 45.00 (*0-7863-1154-1*, Irwn Prfssnl) McGraw-Hill Prof.

Mason, Victor. The Butterflies of Bali. 256p. 1992. pap. text 19.95 (*0-945971-61-3*) Periplus.

Mason, Virginia, ed. see Mannering, Dennis E.

Mason, Virginia, ed. see Mannering, Dennis E. & Wilde, Kevin.

Mason, W. & Richter, L. Reporting by Key Informants on Labour Markets: An Operational Manual. xi, 41p. (Orig.). 1985. pap. 11.25 (*92-2-105109-9*) Intl Labour Office.

***Mason, W. Dale.** Indian Gaming: Tribal Sovereignty & American Politics. LC 99-54880. 320p. 2000. 29.95 (*0-8061-3213-2*) U of Okla Pr.

— Indian Gaming: Tribal Sovereignty & American Politics. 320p. 2000. pap. text 19.95 (*0-8061-3260-4*) U of Okla Pr.

Mason, W. Everett. Graham-Lewis Family: From Townsend to Holden, Massachusetts & Beyond. LC 97-69707. (Illus.). write for info. (*0-89725-317-5*, Penobscot Pr) Picton Pr.

Mason, W. H., et al. Laboratory Manual in Animal Biology. (Illus.). 156p. (Orig.). (C). 1986. pap. 9.95 (*0-89892-067-1*) Contemp Pub Co of Raleigh.

Mason, W. L., jt. ed. see Aldhous, J. R.

Mason, W. M. & Fienberg, Stephen E., eds. Cohort Analysis in Social Research: Beyond the Identification Problem. (Illus.). 250p. 1985. 102.95 (*0-387-96053-8*) Spr-Verlag.

Mason, W. T. Fluorescent & Luminescent Probes for Biological Activity: A Practical Guide to Technology for Quantitative Analysis. (Biological Techniques Ser.). (Illus.). 433p. 1993. text 104.00 (*0-12-477829-1*) Acad Pr.

Mason, Wendy H. Cyberhound's Guide to Companies on the Internet. 1996. 79.00 (*0-7876-1023-2*) Gale.

Mason, Will E. Classical Versus Neoclassical Monetary Theories: The Roots, Ruts & Resilience of Monetarism & Keynesianism. LC 96-35180. (Recent Economic Thought Ser.). 240p. (C). 1996. lib. bdg. 121.00 (*0-7923-9817-3*) Kluwer Academic.

Mason, William. Dagger. 352p. 1984. mass mkt. 3.50 (*0-8217-1399-X*, Zebra Kensgtn) Kensgtn Pub Corp.

— Memories of a Musical Life. LC 70-133825. 1970. reprint ed. 21.45 (*0-404-07216-X*) AMS Pr.

— Memories of a Musical Life. (American Biography Ser.). 306p. 1991. reprint ed. lib. bdg. 79.00 (*0-7812-8275-6*) Rprt Serv.

Mason, William A. & Mendoza, Sally P., eds. Primate Social Conflict. LC 91-39372. 419p. (C). 1993. pap. text 21.95 (*0-7914-1242-3*) State U NY Pr.

— Primate Social Conflict. LC 91-39372. 419p. (C). 1993. text 64.50 (*0-7914-1241-5*) State U NY Pr.

Mason, William M. The Census of 1790: The Demographic History of Colonial California. Vane, Sylvia B., ed. LC 98-23927. (Anthropological Papers: Vol. 45). (Illus.). 128p. 1998. text 29.95 (*0-87919-137-6*) Ballena Pr.

Mason, William M. & Vane, Sylvia B. The Census of 1790: The Demographic History of Colonial California. LC 98-23927. (Anthropological Papers: Vol. 45). (Illus.). 143p. 1998. pap. 19.95 (*0-87919-138-4*) Ballena Pr.

Mason, William T. Fluorescent & Luminescent Probes 2nd Edition: A Practical Guide to Technology for Quantitative Real-Time Analysis. 2nd ed. LC 99-60998. (Illus.). 630p. 1999. 79.95 (*0-12-447836-0*) Acad Pr.

Mason, Wyatt A., tr. see Michon, Pierre.

Mason, Yvona K., ed. see Kendall, Willmore.

Masoner, Michael. An Audit of the Case Study Method. LC 87-29293. 250p. 1988. 59.95 (*0-275-92761-X*, C2761, Praeger Pubs) Greenwood.

Masonic Service Association of the U. S. Staff. Masonic Poems. 91p. 1992. reprint ed. pap. 12.95 (*1-56459-039-9*) Kessinger Pub.

— Masonry & Americanism. 145p. 1992. reprint ed. pap. 12.95 (*1-56459-038-0*) Kessinger Pub.

Masonic Service Association Staff. Anderson's Constitutions of 1723. 128p. 1997. reprint ed. pap. 17.00 (*0-7661-0073-1*) Kessinger Pub.

Masonry Institute of America Staff. Reinforced Masonry Engineering Handbook. 496p. 1998. boxed set 94.95 (*0-8493-7551-7*) CRC Pr.

Masonry Society Codes & Standards Committee Staff. Commentary to Chapter Twenty-One, Masonry, of the Uniform Building Code: 1994 Edition. (Illus.). 152p. (Orig.). 1995. pap. text 39.00 (*0-9626074-1-X*) Masonry Soc.

***Masonry Society Staff, et al.** Masonry Designers' Guide. 2nd ed. (Illus.). 553p. 1999. write for info. (*0-87031-000-3*) ACI.

Masonry Standards Joint Committee. Building Code Requirements for Masonry Structures, ACI 530 95/ASCE 5-95/TMS 402-95. rev. ed. LC 96-210763. (Illus.). 120p. 1996. pap. 78.00 (*0-7844-0115-2*, TMS-0402-95) Am Soc Civil Eng.

Masonson, Leslie N. Cash, Cash, Cash. 1990. 27.50 (*0-88730-410-9*, HarpBusn) HarpInfo.

***Masonson, Leslie N.** Day Trading on the Edge: A Look-Before-You-Leap Guide to Extreme Investing. 2000. 29.95 (*0-8144-0573-8*) AMACOM.

Masood, Mukhtar. Eyewitnesses of History. 1981. 22.50 (*1-56744-001-0*) Kazi Pubns.

Masood, Rashid. Economic Diversification & Development in Saudi Arabia. (C). 1989. 24.00 (*0-86132-231-2*, Pub. by Popular Prakashan) S Asia.

Masood, Shahla. Cytopathology of the Breast. LC 95-39759. (Illus.). 1995. 116.00 (*0-89189-380-6*) Am Soc Clinical.

Masood, Steven. Into the Light: A Young Muslim's Search for Truth. 157p. 1997. reprint ed. mass mkt. 7.99 (*1-85078-098-6*, Pub. by O M Pubng) OM Literature.

Masopust, Katie P. Fractured Landscape Quilts. Jonsson, Lee, ed. LC 96-5563. (Illus.). 96p. (Orig.). 1996. pap. 21.95 (*1-57120-016-9*) C & T Pub.

Masoro, Edward J. Challenges of Biological Aging. LC 99-25949. (Illus.). 224p. 1999. text 35.95 (*0-8261-1277-3*) Springer Pub.

— Handbook of Physiology Sect. 11: Aging. (Handbook of Physiology). (Illus.). 696p. 1995. text 195.00 (*0-19-507722-9*) OUP.

Masoro, Edward J., ed. Handbook of Physiology in Aging. LC 80-19983. (Series in Clinical Laboratory Science). 520p. 1981. 282.00 (*0-8493-3143-9*, QP86, CRC Reprint) Franklin.

Masotti, Leonardo, jt. ed. see Tortoli, Piero.

Masotti, Louis H., jt. auth. see Lineberry, Robert L.

Masotti, Louis H., jt. auth. see Lineberry, Robert L.

Masotty, Susan, tr. see Durlacher, Gerhard.

Masounave, J. & Hamel, F. G., eds. Fabrication of Particulate Reinforced Metal Composites: Proceedings of an International Conference Held September 17-29, 1990 in Montreal, Quebec, Canada. LC 90-83189. (Conference Proceedings Ser.). (Illus.). 286p. 1990. reprint ed. pap. 88.70 (*0-608-02623-9*, 206328100004) Bks Demand.

Masover, Hal. Invest Like the Pros: Value Investing in Commodity Futures. 2nd rev. ed. (Illus.). 110p. 1997. pap. 24.95 (*0-9664883-0-X*) Crown Futures.

***Masover, Hal.** Value Investing in Commodity Futures: How to Profit with Scale Trading. (Trading Advantage Ser.). 224p. 2000. 69.95 (*0-471-34881-3*) Wiley.

MASP Consulting Staff, jt. auth. see Kuong, J. F.

MASP Consulting Staff, jt. auth. see Kuong, Javier F.

MASP Professional Consulting Staff. Computer Viruses: Realities, Myths & Safeguards. (Illus.). 200p. 1990. 60.00 (*0-940706-24-5*) Management Advisory Pubns.

— Data Communication Networks Audit AP-03. (Audit Plan Ser.). 200p. 1995. student ed., ring bd. 495.00 (*0-940706-26-1*) Management Advisory Pubns.

— Local Area Network Security, Auditing & Controls (MAP-30) (Security, Audit & Control Ser.). (Illus.). 200p. 1996. student ed., ring bd. 250.00 (*0-940706-51-2*) Management Advisory Pubns.

MASP Professional Consulting Staff, ed. see Winters, C. M.

MASP Staff. Year 2000 Testing - Action Plan & Guidelines. Kuong, J. F., ed. (Information Technologies Security, Control, Audit & Contingency Planning Ser.: Vol. 8). (Illus.). 150p. 1998. ring bd. 260.00 (*0-940706-41-5*, MAP-40) Management Advisory Pubns.

Maspero, Emilio. Los Trabajadores Frente a la Crisis. (Coleccion CLAT Ser.). (SPA.). 124p. (Orig.). 1986. pap. 6.00 (*0-917049-04-7*) Saeta.

Maspero, Francois. Cat's Grin. LC 88-34566. 295p. (C). 1989. reprint ed. pap. 9.95 (*0-941533-33-6*, NAB) I R Dee.

— Roissy Express: A Journey Through the Paris Suburbs. Jones, Paul & Bellos, David, trs. LC 93-42235. (Illus.). 330p. (C). (gr. 13). 1994. 65.00 (*0-86091-373-2*, B2577, Pub. by Verso) Norton.

Maspero, Gaston C. The Dawn of Civilization - Map & over Four Hundred Seventy Illustrations & Places. (African Studies). reprint ed. 75.00 (*0-938818-76-7*) ECA Assoc.

— Popular Stories of Ancient Egypt. (African Studies). reprint ed. 40.00 (*0-938818-66-X*) ECA Assoc.

Maspero, Gaston C. & Brugsch, Emile. The Royal Mummies of Deir el-Bahri. Reeves, Nicholas, ed. Raggett, G., tr. (Illus.). 162p. 1993. 49.95 (*0-7103-0392-0*, A5045) Routledge.

Maspero, Jean. L' Organisation Militaire de l'Egypt Byzantine. (Bibliotheque Des Hautes Etudes Ser.: No. 201). 157p. 1974. reprint ed. write for info. (*3-487-05282-2*) G Olms Pubs.

Masquelet, Alain C. & Gilbert, Alain. Flaps in Limb Reconstruction. (Illus.). 256p. 1995. text 152.00 (*0-397-51420-4*) Lppncott W & W.

Masquelet, Alain C., et al. Atlas of Surgical Exposures of the Lower Extremities. 424p. 1993. text 263.00 (*0-397-58325-7*) Lppncott W & W.

***Masquerade Masters Staff.** The New Year's Resolutions Diet, Exercise, & Weight Loss Log Book: A Useful One-Year Self-Help Record to Accomplish Your Health & Fitness Goals. (Illus.). 190p. 1998. vinyl bd. 12.00 (*1-886197-29-6*) Joy Books.

Masquerade Staff. Bondage. 1999. pap. text 10.95 (*1-58419-005-1*) Masq Bks.

— Even Our Fantasies. 1999. pap. text 10.95 (*1-58419-014-0*) Masq Bks.

— Joyful Desires, 1. 1999. pap. text 10.95 (*1-58419-011-6*) Masq Bks.

Masquerier, Lewis. Sociology; Or, the Reconstruction of Society, Government, & Property. LC 76-88504. (Illus.). 213p. 1971. reprint ed. lib. bdg. 59.50 (*0-8371-4967-3*, MASO) Greenwood.

— Sociology: or The Reconstruction of Society, Government & Property. 1973. 59.95 (*0-8490-1073-X*) Gordon Pr.

Masquerotique Studios Staff. Beta Sexus. pap. 13.95 (*1-56097-230-0*, Pub. by Fantagraph Bks) Seven Hills Bk.

Masquet, Georges. Dictionnaire des Grands Evenements de l'Histoire.Tr. of Dictionary of the Great Events of History. (FRE.). 315p. 1973. pap. 15.95 (*0-8288-6260-5*, M-174) Fr & Eur.

Masri, Allan. The Golden Hills of California, Vol. 2. LC 78-65266. (Illus.). 131p. 1983. pap. 7.95 (*0-934136-21-1*) Good Life.

Masri, Sami F., ed. Proceedings of the U. S. National Workshop on Structural Control Research. LC 91-2839. 300p. 1991. 25.00 (*0-9628908-0-4*) USC Schl EDCE.

Masroor, Mehr N. Shadows of Time. (C). 1988. 31.00 (*81-7001-030-6*, Pub. by Chanakya) S Asia.

Masry, Abdullah H. Prehistory in Northeastern Arabia: The Problem of Interregional Interaction. LC 95-35863. (Illus.). 280p. (C). 1996. 212.50 (*0-7103-0536-2*, Pub. by Kegan Paul Intl) Col U Pr.

Mass, jt. auth. see Gorman.

Mass, Arthur. And the Desert Shall Rejoice. (WV Encore Edition Ser.). (C). 1996. pap. text 40.00 (*0-8133-0102-5*) Westview.

Mass, Arthur A. Congress & Water Resources. (Reprint Series in Social Sciences). (C). 1993. reprint ed. pap. text 5.00 (*0-8290-2735-1*, PS-176) Irvington.

Mass Communication Review Yearbook Staff. Mass Communication Review Yearbook, Vol. 4. LC 81-643154. (Illus.). 719p. 1984. reprint ed. pap. 200.00 (*0-608-01171-1*, 205947100004) Bks Demand.

— Mass Communication Review Yearbook, Vol. 5, 1985. LC 81-643154. (Illus.). 658p. 1985. reprint ed. pap. 200.00 (*0-608-01172-X*, 205947100005) Bks Demand.

— Mass Communication Review Yearbook, Vol. 6, 1987. LC 81-643154. (Illus.). 642p. 1987. reprint ed. pap. 199.10 (*0-608-01173-8*, 205947100006) Bks Demand.

Mass, Jeffrey P. Antiquity & Anachronism in Japanese History. 232p. 1995. pap. 14.95 (*0-8047-2592-6*) Stanford U Pr.

— Antiquity & Anachronism in Japanese History. 232p. (C). 1995. 37.50 (*0-8047-1974-8*) Stanford U Pr.

— The Development of Kamakura Rule, 1180-1250: A History with Documents. LC 78-62271. xvi, 312p. 1979. 45.00 (*0-8047-1003-1*) Stanford U Pr.

— The Kamakura Bakufu: A Study in Documents. LC 75-39335. (Illus.). 376p. 1976. 49.50 (*0-8047-0907-6*) Stanford U Pr.

— Lordship & Inheritance in Early Medieval Japan: A Study of the Kamakura Soryo System. 352p. 1989. 45.00 (*0-8047-1540-8*) Stanford U Pr.

— The Origins of Japan's Medieval World: Courtiers, Clerics, Warriors, & Peasants in the Fourteenth Century. LC 97-2475. 544p. 1997. 65.00 (*0-8047-2894-1*) Stanford U Pr.

— Warrior Government in Early Medieval Japan: A Study of the Kamakura Bakufu, Shugo & Jiteo. LC 74-75875. (Yale Historical Publications: Miscellany: No. 103). 269p. reprint ed. pap. 83.40 (*0-8357-8369-3*, 203381500087) Bks Demand.

***Mass, Jeffrey P.** Yoritomo & The Founding of The First Bakufu: The Origins of Dual Government in Japan. LC 99-37920. 1999. 49.50 (*0-8047-3591-3*) Stanford U Pr.

Mass, Jeffrey P., ed. Court & Bakufu in Japan: Essays in Kamakura History. 342p. (C). 1995. 52.50 (*0-8047-2532-2*); pap. 16.95 (*0-8047-2473-3*) Stanford U Pr.

Mass, Jeffrey P. & Hauser, William B., eds. The Bakufu in Japanese History. LC 84-51768. 288p. 1985. 47.50 (*0-8047-1278-6*) Stanford U Pr.

Mass, Jeffrey P., jt. ed. see Hall, John W.

Mass, Larry. We Must Love One Another or Die: Larry Kramer - His Life & Legacy. LC 97-152171. (Sexual Politics Ser.). (Illus.). 320p. 1996. 29.95 (*0-304-33545-2*) Continuum.

Mass, Lawrence. Homosexuality & Sexuality: Dialogues of the Sexual Revolution. LC 90-4985. (Gay & Lesbian Studies: Vol. 1). 184p. 1990. text 49.95 (*1-56024-045-8*) Haworth Pr.

An Asterisk (*) at the beginning of an entry indicates that the title is appearing for the first time.

M

Massaro, Toni M. Constitutional Literacy: A Core Curriculum for a Multicultural Nation. LC 93-10861. (Constitutional Conflicts Ser.). 208p. 1993. text 24.95 (0-8223-1364-2) Duke.

Massaro, Toni M., jt. auth. see Babcock, Barbara Allen.

Massarsky, Cynthia W., jt. auth. see Renz, Loren.

Massart, C., tr. see Zarzycki, J.

Massart, D. L., et al, eds. Chemometrics Tutorials Vols. 1-5: Collected from Chemometrics & Intelligent Laboratory Systems - an International Journal. 428p. 1990. pap. 106.25 (0-444-88837-3) Elsevier.

Massart, D. L. & Lewi, P. J. Principal Components: Manual. 1994. write for info. (0-444-81653-4) Elsevier.

Massart, D. L., et al. Chemometrics: A Textbook. 488p. 1988. 162.50 (0-444-42660-4) Elsevier.

— Handbook of Chemometrics & Qualimetrics. 884p. 1997. 273.00 (0-444-89724-0) Elsevier.

— Handbook of Chemometrics & Qualimetrics Pt. B. LC 98-42544. (Data Handling in Science & Technology Ser.: Vol. 20). 1998. 201.00 (0-444-82853-2) Elsevier.

— Handbook of Chemometrics & Qualimetrics Pts. A & B, 2 vols. (Data Handling in Science & Technology Ser.: Vol. 20). 1998. 307.50 (0-444-82854-0) Elsevier.

Massart, D. Luc & Kaufman, Leonard. The Interpretation of Analytical Chemical Data by the Use of Cluster Analysis. LC 88-32691. 250p. (C). 1989. reprint ed. lib. bdg. 62.50 (0-89464-358-4) Krieger.

Massasati, Ahmad. Islamic Calligraphy Coloring Book. (Illus.). 57p. (Orig.). (J). (gr. 3-6). 1991. pap. 4.95 (0-89259-120-X) Am Trust Pubns.

Massasoit Community College Staff. Laboratory Exercises for Biology of Organisms. 204p. (C). 1994. spiral bd. 23.95 (0-8403-7336-8) Kendall-Hunt.

Massat, Sherry Shepard. Waiting to Be Invited. 40p. 1997. pap. 10.00 (0-929741-55-2) Playsmith.

Massaux, Edouard. The Influence of the Gospel of Saint Matthew on Christian Literature Before Saint Irenaeus: Later Christian Writings. Bellinzoni, Arthur J., ed. Belval, Norman J. & Hecht, Suzanne, trs. (New Gospel Studies: No. 5/2). 1992. text 25.00 (0-86554-382-8, H311) Mercer Univ Pr.

— The Influence of the Gospel of Saint Matthew on Christian Literature Before Saint Irenaeus: The First Ecclesiastical Writers. Bellinzoni, Arthur J., ed. Belval, Norman J. & Hecht, Suzanne, trs. from FRE. LC 90-38747. xxvi, 172p. (C). 1991. text 25.00 (0-86554-381-X, MUP/H309) Mercer Univ Pr.

— Influence of the Gospel of St. Matthew on Christian Literature Before St. Irenaeus Bk. I: The First Ecclesiastical Writers. Bellinzoni, Arthur J., ed. Belval, Norman J. & Hecht, Suzanne, trs. (New Gospel Studies: No. 5/3). 285p. 1993. text 25.00 (0-86554-383-6, MUP/H312) Mercer Univ Pr.

Masschaele, James. Peasants, Merchants, & Markets: Inland Trade in Medieval England, 1150-1350. LC 96-52279. 250p. 1997. text 45.00 (0-312-16035-6) St Martin.

Masschelein, Willy J. Unit Processes in Drinking Water Treatment. LC 92-20757. (Environmental Science & Pollution Ser.: Vol. 3). (Illus.). 656p. 1992. text 230.00 (0-8247-8678-5) Dekker.

Masschelein, Willy J., ed. Ozonization Manual for Water & Wastewater Treatment. LC 81-21986. (Illus.). 346p. reprint ed. pap. 107.30 (0-8357-6650-0, 203531900094) Bks Demand.

Masse, Anthony M. The Decline & Fall of the United States. 275p. 1985. pap. 8.95 (0-9608294-0-7) Bataan Bk Pubs.

***Masse, Gertrude C. E.** A Bibliography of First Editions of the Books Illustrated by Walter Crane. 60p. 1999. reprint ed. 45.00 (1-57898-158-1) Martino Pubng.

Masse, Louis, ed. see Leaverton, Paul E.

Masse, Louis, jt. ed. see Leaverton, Paul E.

Masse, Michelle A. In the Name of Love: Women, Masochism, & the Gothic. LC 91-55552. (Reading Women Writing Ser.). 320p. 1992. text 47.50 (0-8014-2616-2); pap. text 17.95 (0-8014-9918-6) Cornell U Pr.

Masse, N. P., ed. see International Children's Center Conference Staff.

Masse-Raimbault, Anne-Marie, et al, eds. L' Alimentation des Femmes: Etape essentielle au Development de l'Enfant. (FRE.). 152p. (Orig.). 1994. pap. text. write for info. (0-89492-107-X) Acad Educ Dev.

Masse, Sydna & Phillips, Joan. Her Choice to Heal: Finding Spiritual & Emotional Peace after Abortion. LC 98-27035. 144p. 1998. pap. 9.99 (1-56476-734-5) SP Pubns.

Masseau, jt. auth. see Goulemot.

Massee, Robin, tr. see Evans, David & Hoxeng, James, eds.

***Massel, S. R.** Fluid Mechanics for Marine Ecologists. LC 99-34010. (Illus.). xviii, 584p. 1999. 95.00 incl. cd-rom (3-540-65999-4) Spr-Verlag.

Massel, Stanislaw R. Hydrodynamics of Coastal Zones. (Oceanography Ser.: No. 48). 336p. 1989. 168.75 (0-444-87375-9) Elsevier.

— Ocean Waves: Their Physics & Prediction. (Advanced Series in Ocean Engineering). 350p. 1996. pap. text 36.00 (981-02-2109-6) World Scientific Pub.

Masselin, Roselyne. Cuisine Imaginaire: Delicious Menus for Vegetarian Entertaining. (Illus.). 224p. 1994. 27.95 (0-563-36413-0, BBC-Parkwest) Parkwest Pubns.

Massell, Benedict F. Rheumatic Fever & Streptococcal Infection: Unraveling the Mysteries of a Dread Disease. LC 97-205903. (Francis Countway Library of Medicine). 400p. 1997. 25.00 (0-674-76877-9) HUP.

***Massell, David Perera & Forest History Society Staff.** Amassing Power: J. B. Duke & the Saguenay River, 1897-1927. (Studies on the History of Quebec/Etudes d'Histoire du Quebec). (Illus.). 312p. 2000. 39.95 (0-7735-2033-3, Pub. by McG-Queens Univ Pr) CUP Services.

Massell, Gregory J. The Surrogate Proletariat: Moslem Women & Revolutionary Strategies in Soviet Central Asia, 1919-1929. LC 73-16047. 491p. 1974. reprint ed. pap. 152.30 (0-7837-9384-7, 206012800004) Bks Demand.

Masselos, Jim. Indian Nationalism: An History. (C). 1991. reprint ed. write for info. (0-932377-09-2) Sterling Pubs.

***Massen, Ben.** Pathologies of Speech & Language. 1999. pap. text 82.50 (1-86156-122-9) Whurr Pub.

Massena, Robert A. Le, see Le Massena, Robert A.

Massena, Sharon & Smith, Bryan. Pygmy Hedgehogs - The Perfect Pet. LC 97-164947. (Illus.). 80p. (Orig.). (J). 1996. pap. 19.50 (0-9655629-1-3) Bear Tree.

Massenet, Jules. Manon. John, Nicholas, ed. Edmund, Tracey, tr. from FRE. LC 84-755667. (English National Opera Guide Series: Bilingual Libretto, Articles: No. 25). (Illus.). 112p. 1984. pap. 9.95 (0-7145-4041-2) Riverrun NY.

— Manon: Vocal Score: Five Acts. (ENG & FRE.). 396p. 1986. pap. 35.00 (0-7935-2547-0, 50338380) H Leonard.

— Manon in Full Score. 1997. 21.95 (0-486-29871-X, 741688Q) Dover.

Massenet, Jules E. My Recollections. Barnett, H. Villiers, tr. LC 75-107819. (Select Bibliographies Reprint Ser.). 1977. 26.95 (0-8369-5190-5) Ayer.

— My Recollections (1848-1912) 304p. 1990. reprint ed. lib. bdg. 79.00 (0-7812-9073-2) Rprt Serv.

Massengale, Dee. The Guide to a Better Back. Mueller, Phyllis, ed. LC 87-31104. (Illus.). 104p. (Orig.). 1988. pap. 13.95 (0-932419-12-7) Cherokee.

Massengale, Eugene W. Fundamentals of Federal Contract Law. LC 90-40700. 264p. 1990. 65.00 (0-89930-604-7, MFK, Quorum Bks) Greenwood.

Massengale, Jean Montague, text. Fragonard. LC 92-21996. (Masters of Art Ser.). (Illus.). 1993. 24.95 (0-8109-3313-6, Pub. by Abrams) Time Warner.

Massengale, Jeff. My Collective Mind. 1997. pap. 56.95 (1-57553-679-X) Watermrk Pr.

Massengale, John & Swanson, Richard A., eds. The History of Exercise & Sport Science. LC 96-10555. (Illus.). 488p. 1996. text 49.00 (0-87322-524-4, BMAS0524) Human Kinetics.

Massengale, John D. Trends Toward the Future in Physical Education. LC 86-34282. (Illus.). 200p. 1987. reprint ed. pap. 62.00 (0-608-06457-2, 206729500009) Bks Demand.

Massengale, Tim. Let My People Grow! LC 88-31269. (Illus.). 304p. (Orig.). 1989. pap. 8.99 (0-932581-41-2) Word Aflame.

Massengill, Joyce M. From the Hand of God: Words to Enlighten & Encourage. 130p. (Orig.). 1997. pap. 6.95 (1-57502-441-1, PO1334) Morris Pubng.

Massengill, Paul K., ed. see Porter, Patrick K.

Massengill, R. Massengill. LC 96-6072. (Illus.). 64p. 1996. text 13.00 (0-312-14367-2) St Martin.

Massengill, Reed. Portrait of a Racist. 1997. pap. 14.95 (0-312-16725-3) St Martin.

Massengill, Stephen E. Around Southern Pines, North Carolina: A Sandhills Album. (Images of America Ser.). (Illus.). 128p. 1998. pap. 18.99 (0-7524-0951-4) Arcadia Publng.

— Durham, North Carolina: A Postcard History. LC 97-205633. (Images of America Ser.). (Illus.). 128p. 1996. pap. 16.99 (0-7524-0554-3) Arcadia Publng.

***Massengill, Stephen E.** Western North Carolina: A Visual Journey Through Stereo Views & Photographs. (Images of America Ser.). (Illus.). 128p. 1999. pap. 16.99 (0-7385-0104-2) Arcadia Publng.

Massengill, Stephen E., ed. North Carolina Votes on the Constitution: A Roster of Delegates to the State Ratification Conventions of 1788 & 1789. (North Carolina & the Constitution Ser.). (Illus.). xii, 86p. (Orig.). 1988. pap. 6.00 (0-86526-237-3) NC Archives.

Massengill, Stephen E. & Topkins, Robert M. A North Carolina Postcard Album, 1905-1925. (Illus.). xii, 172p. 1988. 55.00 (0-86526-236-5) NC Archives.

Masser & Williams, eds. Learning from Other Countries: The Cross-National Dimension in Urban Policy Making. (Illus.). 220p. (C). 1986. 80.00 (0-86094-210-4) Chapman & Hall.

Masser, Barry Z. How to Make One Hundred Thousand Dollars a Year in Home Mail Order Business. (C). 1992. pap. text 14.95 (0-13-397456-1, Busn) P-H.

Masser, Barry Z. & Leeds, William M. Power Selling by Telephone. 240p. 1982. 19.95 (0-13-686998-X, Parker Publishing Co) P-H.

Masser, I. Handling Geographical Information: Methodology & Potential. 1991. 116.25 (0-582-06730-8, Pub. by Addison-Wesley) Longman.

Masser, Ian. Governments & Geographic Information. LC 98-179222. 160p. 1998. 69.95 (0-7484-0789-8, Pub. by Tay Francis Ltd); pap. 29.95 (0-7484-0706-5, Pub. by Tay Francis Ltd) Taylor & Francis.

Masser, Ian, et al, eds. GIS Diffusion. LC 96-147907. (GISDATA Ser.). 224p. 1996. 89.95 (0-7484-0494-5); pap. 44.95 (0-7484-0495-3) Taylor & Francis.

Masser, Ian & Brown, P. J. Spatial Representation & Spatial Interaction. (Studies in Applied Regional Science: Vol. 10). 1978. pap. text 72.50 (90-207-0717-5) Kluwer Academic.

Masser, Ian & Onsrud, Harlan J., eds. Diffusion & Use of Geographic Information Technologies: Proceedings of the NATO Advanced Research Workshop on Modeling the Diffusion & Use of Geographic Information Technologies, Sounion, Greece, April 8-11, 1992. LC 93-9597. (NATO Advanced Study Institutes Series D, Behavioural & Social Sciences: No. 70). 364p. (C). 1993. lib. bdg. 205.50 (0-7923-2190-1) Kluwer Academic.

Masser, Ian, et al. The Geography of Europe's Future. 224p. 1992. pap. 54.95 (0-471-94714-8) Wiley.

Masser, Ian, jt. auth. see Campbell, Heather.

Masser, Ian, jt. ed. see Friedrich, Peter.

Masserly, John G. Piaget's Conception of Evolution: Beyond Darwin & Lamarck. 184p. 1996. pap. text 23.95 (0-8476-8243-9) Rowman.

— Piaget's Conception of Evolution: Beyond Darwin & Lamarck. 184p. 1996. lib. bdg. 55.50 (0-8476-8242-0) Rowman.

Masserman, Chris, jt. auth. see Masserman, Jules H.

Masserman, Christine M., jt. auth. see Masserman, Jules H.

Masserman, Christine M., jt. ed. see Masserman, Jules H.

Masserman, Jules H. Psychiatry & Health: A Comprehensive Integration. 253p. 1986. 35.95 (0-89885-256-0, Kluwer Acad Hman Sci) Kluwer Academic.

— Theory & Therapy in Dynamic Psychiatry. LC 72-96926. 240p. 1995. pap. 50.00 (1-56821-511-8) Aronson.

— Writing & Editing. 122p. 1996. 14.95 (0-916147-64-9); pap. 9.95 (0-916147-65-7) Regent Pr.

Masserman, Jules H., ed. Current Psychiatric Therapies, Vol. 22. 1984. 53.00 (0-8089-1628-9, 792722, Grune & Strat) Harcrt Hlth Sci Grp.

— Current Psychiatric Therapies, Vols. I & II-XII. Incl. Vol. I. LC 61-9411. (Illus.). 256p. 1961. 47.00 (0-8089-0280-6, W B Saunders Co); Vol V. LC 61-9411. 320p. 1965. text 76.00 (0-8089-0284-9, 792705, W B Saunders Co); Vol VI. LC 61-9411. 400p. 1966. text 81.00 (0-8089-0285-7, 792706, W B Saunders Co); Vol VII. LC 61-9411. (Illus.). 266p. 1967. text 87.00 (0-8089-0286-5, 792707, W B Saunders Co); Vol. VIII. LC 61-9411. 272p. 1968. text 87.00 (0-8089-0287-3, 792708, W B Saunders Co); Vol IX. LC 61-9411. (Illus.). 320p. 1969. text 91.00 (0-8089-0288-1, 792709, W B Saunders Co); LC 61-9411. write for info. (0-318-52856-8, Grune & Strat) Harcrt Hlth Sci Grp.

— Science & Psychoanalysis. Incl. Vol III. Psychoanalysis & Human Values. LC 58-8009. 396p. 1963. text 81.00 (0-8089-0290-3, 792743, W B Saunders Co); Vol XI. Ego. LC 58-8009. 230p. 1967. text 72.00 (0-8089-0298-9, 792751, W B Saunders Co); Vol XVI. Dynamics of Work & Marriage. LC 58-8009. 152p. 1970. 45.50 (0-8089-0303-9, 792756, W B Saunders Co); Vol XX. Dynamics of Power. LC 58-8009. 240p. 1972. 70.50 (0-8089-0737-9, 792760, W B Saunders Co); LC 58-8009. write for info. (0-318-52866-5, Grune & Strat) Harcrt Hlth Sci Grp.

Masserman, Jules H. & Masserman, Chris. Sexual Accusations & Social Turmoil. 160p. 1994. pap. 9.95 (0-916147-42-8, Pub. by Regent Pr) ACCESS Pubs Network.

Masserman, Jules H. & Masserman, Christine M. Sexual Accusations & Social Turmoil. 160p. 1994. 14.95 (0-916147-43-6) Regent Pr.

Masserman, Jules H. & Masserman, Christine M., eds. Social Psychiatry & World Accords. 244p. 1995. 14.95 (0-916147-63-0) Regent Pr.

Masserman, Jules H. & Uribe, Victor M. Adolescent Sexuality. 118p. 1989. pap. 21.95 (0-398-06270-6) C C Thomas.

— Adolescent Sexuality. 118p. (C). 1989. text 33.95 (0-398-05629-3) C C Thomas.

Masseron, Alexandre. Dante Alighieri: The Poet Who Loved St. Francis So Much. Aranadez, Richard, tr. from FRE. (Tau Ser.). 96p. 1979. 2.95 (0-8199-0757-X, Frncscn Herld) Franciscan Pr.

Masseron, Jean. Petroleum Economics. 4th ed. 536p. 1990. 370.00 (2-7108-0597-9, Pub. by Edits Technip) Enfield Pubs NH.

Masset, Evelyn. To Live Each Day Is to Meditate. (Illus.). 42p. 1982. pap. 5.00 (0-318-57339-3) Coleman Pub.

***Massey.** Main Group Chemistry. 2nd ed. LC 99-56863. 2000. text. write for info. (0-471-49037-7) Wiley.

— Main Group Chemistry 2nd ed. LC 99-56863. 2000. pap. text. write for info. (0-471-49039-3) Wiley.

Massey & Taylor. Aluminum in Food & the Environment, No. 73. 1989. 77.00 (0-85186-846-0) CRC Pr.

Massey, Kimbery B., jt. auth. see Baran, Stanley J.

Massey, Adrianne, jt. auth. see Kreuzer, Helen.

Massey, Andrew. Managing the Public Sector: A Comparative Analysis of the United Kingdom & the United States. 240p. 1993. 90.00 (1-85278-333-8) E Elgar.

— Technocrats & Nuclear Politics: The Influence of Professional Experts in Policy-Making. 200p. 1988. text 77.95 (0-566-05644-5, Pub. by Dartmth Pub) Ashgate Pub Co.

Massey, Andrew, jt. auth. see Carr, Fergus.

Massey, Anne. Blue Guide: Berlin & Eastern Germany. 1994. pap. 20.95 (0-393-31197-X, Norton Paperbks) Norton.

***Massey, Anne.** Hollywood Beyond the Screen: Design & Material Culture. (Materializing Culture Ser.). (Illus.). 224p. 2000. 65.00 (1-85973-316-6, Pub. by Berg Pubs); pap. 19.50 (1-85973-321-2, Pub. by Berg Pubs) NYU Pr.

Massey, Anne. The Independent Group: Modernism & Mass Culture in Britain, 1945-1959. LC 95-3509. 1995. text 69.95 (0-7190-4244-5, Pub. by Manchester Univ Pr) St Martin.

— The Independent Group: Modernism & Mass Culture in Britain, 1945-1959. (Illus.). 208p. 1996. text 29.95 (0-7190-4245-3, Pub. by Manchester Univ Pr) St Martin.

— Interior Design of the Twentieth Century. LC 89-52099. (World of Art Ser.). (Illus.). 216p. 1990. pap. 14.95 (0-500-20247-8, Pub. by Thames Hudson) Norton.

Massey, B. Mechanics of Fluids. 6th ed. 704p. 1989. 39.95 (0-278-00047-9) Chapman & Hall.

Massey, B. S. Measures in Science & Engineering: Their Expression, Relation & Interpretation. (Mathematics & Its Applications Ser.). 1986. text 48.95 (0-470-20331-5) P-H.

***Massey, Barbara.** Darby down Under. (Child Like Me Ser.: Vol. 4). (Illus.). (J). 2000. 6.99 (1-56309-766-4, New Hope) Womans Mission Union.

Massey, Barbara & DeLoach, Sylvia. I Can Help Others. (Missions & Me Ser.). 16p. (J). (ps-k). 1998. pap. text 7.95 (1-56309-255-7, W988105) Womans Mission Union.

— Tell Me about God. (Missions & Me Ser.). (Illus.). 16p. (J). (ps-k). 1998. pap. text 7.99 (1-56309-256-5, W988104) Womans Mission Union.

Massey, Barbara & Woodson, Jack. Virginia Wingo: Teacher & Friend. (Meet the Missionary Ser.). 32p. (J). (gr. k-3). 1996. pap. text 5.99 (1-56309-157-7, W947130) Womans Mission Union.

Massey, Barbara, jt. auth. see DeLoach, Sylvia.

Massey, Barbara W., et al. Guide to Birds of the Anza-Borrego Desert. LC 97-39986. (Illus.). 305p. (Orig.). 1998. pap. 23.95 (0-910805-08-3) Anza-Borrego.

Massey, Bernard. Mechanics of Fluids. 7th rev. ed. (Illus.). 734p. (C). 1998. pap. text 42.50 (0-7487-4043-0) St Mut.

***Massey, Bill, et al, eds.** Corporation & Partnership Tax Return Guide, 1999. rev. ed. 144p. 2000. pap. 16.50 (0-7811-0242-1) Res Inst Am.

Massey, Burrows, tr. see Casteret, Norbert.

Massey, C., et al. The Influence of Lubrication on the Onset of Surface Pitting in Machinable Hardness Gear Teeth. (Nineteen Ninety-One Fall Technical Meeting Ser.: Vol. 91FTM17). (Illus.). 21p. 1991. pap. text 30.00 (1-55589-605-7) AGMA.

Massey, Calvin. Property. (Professor Ser.). 410p. 1998. pap. text 17.95 (1-56542-130-2) E Pub Corp.

Massey, Calvin R. Constitutional Law. LC 97-20796. (Aspen Roadmap Ser.). 1997. pap. text 24.95 (1-56706-535-X) Aspen Law.

— Silent Rights: The Ninth Amendments & the Constitution's Unenumerated Rights. 280p. (C). 1995. 69.95 (1-56639-311-6) Temple U Pr.

— Silent Rights: The Ninth Amendments & the Constitution's Unenumerated Rights. (C). 1995. pap. text 24.95 (1-56639-312-4) Temple U Pr.

Massey, Charles, jt. auth. see Kauffman, Nancy.

Massey, Charles C. Thoughts of a Modern Mystic. 1972. 59.95 (0-8490-1209-0) Gordon Pr.

Massey, Charles C., tr. see Du Prel, Carl.

Massey, Charles C., tr. see Zollner, Johann C.

Massey, Craig. Ajustarse o Autodestruirse. Orig. Title: Adjust or Self-Destruct. (SPA.). 144p. 1981. mass mkt. 4.99 (0-8254-1470-9, Edit Portavoz) Kregel.

— Brown Shadow. rev. ed. Moore, Tracy, ed. & illus. by. 136p. (J). (gr. 5-9). 1996. reprint ed. mass mkt. 6.99 (1-891635-02-6) Moore Bks.

— Indian Drums & Broken Arrows. rev. ed. (Illus.). 136p. (J). (gr. 5-9). 1996. reprint ed. mass mkt. 6.99 (1-891635-01-8) Moore Bks.

— Twig the Collie. rev. ed. (Illus.). 106p. (J). (gr. 3-7). 1995. reprint ed. mass mkt. 6.50 (1-891635-00-X) Moore Bks.

Massey, Craig & Massey, Louise. Captain Daley's Crew & the Jungle Ship. rev. ed. (Adventures of Captain Daley's Crew Ser.: Vol. 6). (Illus.). 64p. (J). (gr. 3-7). 1997. reprint ed. mass mkt. 3.50 (1-891635-08-5) Moore Bks.

— Captain Daley's Crew & the Long-Eared Taxicab. rev. ed. (Illus.). 56p. (J). (gr. 3-7). 1997. reprint ed. mass mkt. 3.50 (1-891635-07-7) Moore Bks.

— Captain Daley's Crew & the Missing Houseboat. rev. ed. Moore, Tracy, ed. & illus. by. (Adventures of Captain Daley's Crew Ser.: Vol. 1). 64p. (J). (gr. 3-7). 1997. reprint ed. mass mkt. 3.50 (1-891635-03-4) Moore Bks.

— Captain Daley's Crew at Thunderhead Lake. rev. ed. (Adventures of Captain Daley's Crew Ser.: Vol. 3). (Illus.). 76p. (J). (gr. 3-7). 1997. reprint ed. mass mkt. 3.50 (1-891635-05-0) Moore Bks.

— Captain Daley's Crew in Danger. rev. ed. (Adventures of Captain Daley's Crew Ser.: Vol. 2). (Illus.). 62p. (J). (gr. 3-7). 1997. reprint ed. mass mkt. 3.50 (1-891635-04-2) Moore Bks.

— Captains Daley's Crew the Peg-Legged Tramp. rev. ed. (Adventures of Captain Daley's Crew Ser.: Vol. 4). (Illus.). 80p. (J). (gr. 3-7). 1997. reprint ed. mass mkt. 3.50 (1-891635-06-9) Moore Bks.

Massey, David. The Investor's Guide to New Issues: Profit from Flotations & Initial Public Offerings. 240p. 1995. 45.00 (0-273-61117-8) F T P-H.

Massey, David & Yousefzadeh, Behzad S. The Banking System: Abstract Dimensions for the Next Few Centuries. 64p. (Orig.). 1993. pap. 9.95 (0-9640970-0-1) Hillside Pub GA.

Massey, David B. Le Cycles & Hypersurface Singularities. LC 95-39592. (Lecture Notes in Mathematics Ser.: No. 1615). 131p. 1995. 29.95 (3-540-60395-6) Spr-Verlag.

***Massey-Davis, Lynn.** This Is for You, Mum! (Whispers Ser.). (Illus.). 72p. 2000. 6.99 (1-903222-22-2, Pub. by Wimbledon Publishing Co) Anthem.

Massey, Dennis. Doing Time in American Prisons: A Study of Modern Novels, 24. LC 89-7512. (Contributions in Criminology & Penology Ser.: No. 24). 255p. 1989. 65.00 (0-313-26635-2, MDP/, Greenwood Pr) Greenwood.

***Massey, Don & Davey, Rick.** A Matter of Degree: The Hartford Circus Fire & the Mystery of Little Miss 1565. (Illus.). 320p. 2000. 26.95 (1-930601-24-7); pap. 19.95 (1-930601-23-9) Willow Brook.

Massey, Doreen. Space, Place, & Gender. LC 94-10955. 290p. 1994. pap. 19.95 (0-8166-2617-0); text 44.95 (0-8166-2616-2) U of Minn Pr.

— Spatial Divisions of Labour: Social Structures & the Geography of Production. 2nd ed. LC 94-44809. 410p. (Orig.). (C). 1995. pap. 23.99 (0-415-91296-2, B7279) Routledge.

An Asterisk (*) at the beginning of an entry indicates that the title is appearing for the first time.

Massey, Doreen, ed. Lovers' Guide Encyclopedia: The Definitive Guide to Sex & You. LC 96-61220. (Illus.). 248p. 1997. pap. 24.95 (*1-56025-111-5*, Thunders Mouth) Avalon NY.

Massey, Doreen, et al, eds. Human Geography Today. LC 99-24534. 320p. 1999. 62.95 (*0-7456-2188-0*); pap. 29.95 (*0-7456-2189-9*) Blackwell Pubs.

Massey, Doreen & Allen, John, eds. Geographical Worlds. (Shape of the World Ser.: Vol. 1). (Illus.). 160p. (C). 1996. text 42.95 (*0-19-874184-7*); pap. text 19.95 (*0-19-874185-5*) OUP.

Massey, Doreen & Jess, Pat, eds. A Place in the World: Places, Cultures & Globalization. (Shape of the World Ser.: Bk. 4). (Illus.). 256p. (C). 1996. text 56.95 (*0-19-874190-1*); pap. text 24.95 (*0-19-874191-X*) OUP.

Massey, Doreen & Meegan, Richard, eds. Politics & Method: Contrasting Studies in Industrial Geography. 200p. pap. 14.95 (*0-317-19448-8*, 9123) Routledge.

Massey, Doreen, et al. High-Tech Fantasies: Science Parks in Society, Science & Space. 288p. (C). 1991. pap. 27.99 (*0-415-01339-9*, A6542) Routledge.

Massey, Doreen, ed. see Allen, John, et al.

Massey, Doreen, jt. ed. see Hall, Stuart.

Massey, Doreen B. City Worlds. LC 98-44122. 1998. write for info. (*0-415-20069-5*); pap. write for info. (*0-415-20070-9*) Routledge.

— Global Restructuring, Local Responses LC 88-71668. (Wallace W. Atwood Lecture Ser.). 12 p. 1988. write for info. (*0-914206-30-3*) Clark U Pr.

Massey, Doreen B., jt. auth. see Allen, John.

Massey, Douglas S. & Denton, Nancy A. American Apartheid: Segregation & the Making of the Underclass. (Illus.). 304p. (C). 1993. 43.50 (*0-674-01820-6*) HUP.

— American Apartheid: Segregation & the Making of the Underclass. 304p. 1994. pap. text 16.95 (*0-674-01821-4*, MASAMX) HUP.

Massey, Douglas S., et al. Return to Aztlan: The Social Process of International Migration from Western Mexico. LC 87-5913. (Studies in Demography: Vol. 1). 354p. 1987. pap. 17.95 (*0-520-06970-6*, Pub. by U CA Pr) Cal Prin Full Svc.

— Worlds in Motion: Understanding International Migration at the End of the Millennium. (International Studies in Demography). (Illus.). 376p. 1999. text 85.00 (*0-19-829442-5*) OUP.

Massey, Douglas S., jt. auth. see Durand, Jorge.

Massey, Edwin, Jr. Fifty Cantos from the Land of Nod. (Mucho Somos Ser.: No. 15). 80p. (Orig.). (C). 1993. pap. 5.95 (*0-914370-61-8*) Mothers Hen.

***Massey, Ellen Carpenter, tr.** The Powhatan Cemetery Internment & Lot Records of Powhatan Point, Ohio. LC 99-61483. 344p. 1999. pap. 19.95 (*0-89725-370-1*) Picton Pr.

Massey, Ellen G. And Tyler, Too? LC 98-96069. 192p. 1998. 18.95 (*0-8034-9295-2*) Bouregy.

— Bittersweet Earth. LC 84-20991. (Illus.). 422p. 1985. 29.95 (*0-8061-1927-6*) U of Okla Pr.

— Bittersweet Earth. LC 84-20991. 1993. pap. 15.95 (*0-8061-2528-4*) U of Okla Pr.

— A Candle Within Her Soul: Mary Elizabeth Mahnkey & Her Ozarks, 1877-1948. LC 96-78751. (Illus.). 133p. (Orig.). 1996. pap. 14.95 (*0-934426-71-6*) NAPSAC Reprods.

***Massey, Ellen G.** Home Is the Heart. LC 98-96845. 192p. 1999. lib. bdg. 18.95 (*0-8034-9334-7*, Avalon Bks) Bouregy.

— Merryman's Crossing. LC 99-90717. 192p. 1999. 18.95 (*0-8034-9374-6*, Avalon Bks) Bouregy.

Massey, Ellen G. Music of My Soul. LC 97-97116. 192p. 1998. 18.95 (*0-8034-9277-4*, Avalon Bks) Bouregy.

Massey, Ellen G., ed. Bittersweet Country. LC 86-40091. (Illus.). 464p. (Orig.). 1986. reprint ed. pap. 15.95 (*0-8061-2018-5*) U of Okla Pr.

Massey, Ellen Gray, ed. see Thornton, Carolyn Gray.

Massey, Floyd, Jr. & McKinney, Samuel B. Church Administration in the Black Perspective. LC 76-9804. 176p. 1976. pap. 14.00 (*0-8170-0710-5*) Judson.

Massey, Frank J., Jr., jt. auth. see Dixon, Wilfred J.

Massey, Fred I., tr. & intro. see Najjar, Abdallah M.

Massey, Frederick A. Salvation: Safety, Health, & Deliverance. 40p. 1998. pap. 8.00 (*0-8059-4256-4*) Dorrance.

Massey, Frederick R. Inside the Janitorial Business: How to Start from Scratch & Succeed in Professional Cleaning. 2nd ed. LC 89-2555. (Illus.). 220p. (Orig.). 1989. pap. 39.95 (*0-942144-02-3*) MBM Bks.

Massey, Gale. Grief: Reminders for Healing. (Illus.). 24p. (Orig.). 1994. 1.95 (*0-9640883-0-4*, TX 3 390 733) Massey Pubng.

— Grief...Nuturing the Process. (Illus.). 24p. 1994. 1.95 (*0-9640883-1-2*) Massey Pubng.

— Grief...Reminders for Healing. rev. ed. 19p. 1995. 8.95 (*0-9640883-2-0*) Massey Pubng.

Massey, George M. GI ("Guvmint" Issue) The U. S. Army As Seen by GOBS (Good Ol' Boy Soldier) J. Lamar. (Illus.). 96p. (Orig.). 1997. pap. 11.95 (*1-57736-043-5*, Hillsboro Pr) Providence Hse.

Massey, George V., II. Pennock: The Pennocks of Primitive Hall. (Illus.). 139p. 1991. reprint ed. pap. 22.50 (*0-8328-2228-0*); reprint ed. lib. bdg. 32.50 (*0-8328-2227-2*) Higginson Bk Co.

Massey, Gerald. Ancient Egypt. (African Heritage Classical Research Studies). 944p. reprint ed. 75.00 (*0-938818-57-0*) ECA Assoc.

— Ancient Egypt: The Light of the World, 2 vols. (Illus.). 960p. (Orig.). 1999. reprint ed. spiral bd. 70.00 (*1-885395-85-X*) Book Tree.

— Ancient Egypt: The Light of the World, 2 vols. 944p. (Orig.). 1993. reprint ed. 103.00 (*0-7873-0586-3*) Hlth Research.

— Ancient Egypt: The Light of the World - A Work of Reclamation & Restitution, 2 vols., Set. 1992. lib. bdg. 555.95 (*0-8490-8829-1*) Gordon Pr.

— Ancient Egypt the Light of the World, Set. (Occultism (1897) Ser.: Vols. 1[00ad]2. 944p. 1992. reprint ed. pap. 60.00 (*1-56459-150-6*) Kessinger Pub.

— Ancient Egypt the Light of the World, Vol. 1. Obaba, Al I., ed. (Illus.). 220p. 1990. pap. text 20.00 (*0-916157-53-9*) African Islam Miss Pubns.

— Ancient Egypt the Light of the World, Vol. 2. Obaba, Al I., ed. (Illus.). 236p. 1990. pap. text 20.00 (*0-916157-54-7*) African Islam Miss Pubns.

— Ancient Egypt the Light of the World, Vol. 3. Obaba, Al I., ed. (Illus.). 236p. 1990. pap. text 20.00 (*0-916157-55-5*) African Islam Miss Pubns.

— Ancient Egypt the Light of the World, Vol. 4. Obaba, Al I., ed. (Illus.). 248p. 1990. pap. text 20.00 (*0-916157-56-3*) African Islam Miss Pubns.

— Ancient Egypt the Light of the World, Vol. 5. Obaba, Al I., ed. (Illus.). 190p. 1990. pap. text 20.00 (*0-916157-57-1*) African Islam Miss Pubns.

— Ancient Egypt the Light of the World: A Work of Reclamation & Restitution, Vols. 1 & 2. LC 91-74130. 962p. 1992. reprint ed. pap. 49.95 (*0-933121-31-8*); reprint ed. text 84.95 (*0-933121-33-4*) Black Classic.

— The Book of Beginnings, Pt. 2: Natural Genesis, 2 vols. 535p. 1989. reprint ed. 103.00 (*0-7873-1242-8*) Hlth Research.

— A Book of the Beginnings, 2 vols. LC 95-75937. 1200p. 1995. reprint ed. pap. 49.95 (*0-933121-94-6*) Black Classic.

— Book of the Beginnings. (African Heritage Classical Research Studies). 654p. reprint ed. 75.00 (*0-938818-58-9*) ECA Assoc.

— A Book of the Beginnings, 2 vols., Set. 1286p. 1993. pap. 40.00 (*1-881316-83-1*) A&B Bks.

— A Book of the Beginnings, 2 vols., Set. 1991. lib. bdg. 119.95 (*0-8490-4294-1*) Gordon Pr.

— Book of the Beginnings, 2 vols., Set. 1187p. 1987. 103.00 (*0-7873-0585-5*) Hlth Research.

— Book of the Beginnings, 2 vols., Set. 1995. reprint ed. 84.95 (*0-933121-93-8*) Black Classic.

— A Book of the Beginnings, Vol. I. LC 99-40765. 504p. 1999. pap. 20.00 (*1-881316-80-7*) A&B Bks.

— A Book of the Beginnings, Vol. II. 1996. pap. 25.00 (*1-881316-81-5*) A&B Bks.

***Massey, Gerald.** Book of the Beginnings, Vols. I & II. 1198p. 1999. reprint ed. pap. 70.00 (*0-7661-0837-6*) Kessinger Pub.

Massey, Gerald. A Book of the Beginnings: Egypt, Africa & the Cultural & Historic Heritage of the Black Race, African Origins of Mankind, 2 vols. 1991. lib. bdg. 199.75 (*0-8490-5040-5*) Gordon Pr.

— A Book of the Beginnings, Vols. 1-2: Containing an Attempt to Recover & Reconstitute the Lost Origins of the Myths & Mysteries, Types & Symbols, Religion & Language, with Egypt for the Mouthpiece & Africa as the Birthplace, Set. 1187p. 1992. reprint ed. pap. 57.00 (*1-56459-149-2*) Kessinger Pub.

— Egyptian Book of the Dead & the Ancient Mysteries of Amenta. LC 98-15596. 126p. 1994. pap. 9.95 (*1-881316-75-0*) A&B Bks.

— The Egyptian Book of the Dead & the Mysteries of Amenta. 126p. 1993. reprint ed. spiral bd. 12.50 (*0-7873-0583-9*) Hlth Research.

— Egyptian Book of the Dead & the Mysteries of Amenta (1907) 130p. 1996. reprint ed. pap. 11.95 (*1-56459-891-8*) Kessinger Pub.

— Gerald Massey's Lectures. LC 98-42617. 1998. 24.95 (*1-881316-59-9*) A&B Bks.

— Gerald Massey's Lectures. LC 98-42617. 292p. 1992. reprint ed. pap. text 9.95 (*1-881316-20-3*) A&B Bks.

— Gerald Massey's Lectures. (African Studies). reprint ed. 40.00 (*0-938818-46-5*) ECA Assoc.

— Gerald Massey's Lectures. 287p. 1992. reprint ed. pap. 24.95 (*1-56459-174-3*) Kessinger Pub.

— Gnostic & Historic Christianity. 1985. reprint ed. pap. 6.95 (*0-916411-51-6*, Sure Fire) Holmes Pub.

— The Hebrew & Other Creations. 1987. pap. 6.95 (*0-916411-64-8*, Sure Fire) Holmes Pub.

— The Historic Jesus & the Mythical Christ. 1991. pap. 6.95 (*1-55818-137-7*, Sure Fire) Holmes Pub.

— The Historical Jesus & the Mythical Christ. 248p. 1992. pap. text 9.95 (*1-881316-04-1*) A&B Bks.

— The Historical Jesus & the Mythical Christ. 224p. 1993. reprint ed. spiral bd. 16.50 (*0-7873-0584-7*) Hlth Research.

— The Historical Jesus & the Mythical Christ. 241p. 1996. reprint ed. pap. 9.00 (*1-56459-800-4*) Kessinger Pub.

— Moon Worship: Ancient & Modern. 1990. pap. 6.95 (*1-55818-136-9*) Holmes Pub.

— The Natural Genesis, 2 vols. (Illus.). 1087p. 1998. reprint ed. 84.95 (*1-57478-010-7*); reprint ed. pap. 49.95 (*1-57478-009-3*) Black Classic.

— The Natural Genesis. (African Studies). reprint ed. 75.00 (*0-938818-80-5*) ECA Assoc.

— The Natural Genesis: The Lost Origins of Myths & Mysteries, Types & Symbols, Religion & Language, with Egypt As the Mouthpiece & Africa As the Birthplace, 2 vols., Set. 1991. lib. bdg. 119.95 (*0-8490-4297-6*) Gordon Pr.

— The Natural Genesis: or, The Second Part of a Book of the Beginnings, Set, Vols. 1[00ad]2. 1087p. 1992. reprint ed. pap. 70.00 (*1-56459-151-4*) Kessinger Pub.

***Massey, Gerald.** Poems (1860) 456p. 1999. reprint ed. pap. 29.95 (*0-7661-0743-4*) Kessinger Pub.

Massey, Gerald. Secret Drama of Shakspeare's Sonnets Unfolded. 2nd enl. ed. LC 74-172854. reprint ed. 55.00 (*0-404-04237-6*) AMS Pr.

— Shakespeare's Sonnets Never Before Interpreted. LC 78-172855. reprint ed. 74.50 (*0-404-04238-4*) AMS Pr.

— A Tale of Eternity & Other Poems. 476p. 1995. reprint ed. pap. 33.00 (*1-56459-505-6*) Kessinger Pub.

— World's Great Year: The Esoteric Time Cycle. 1988. reprint ed. pap. 7.95 (*1-55818-116-4*, Sure Fire) Holmes Pub.

Massey, Gerald J., jt. ed. see Horowitz, Tamara.

Massey, Gerard. Concerning Spiritualism. 130p. 1993. reprint ed. pap. 14.95 (*1-56459-395-9*) Kessinger Pub.

Massey, Grace C. Black Science: Old West, Transportation, Safety, Working Easier, Food, Communication, Black Women. Ethridge, Diedria & Davis, Deborah, eds. 56p. 1993. teacher ed. 2.00 (*1-877804-07-X*) Chandler White.

— Black Science Activity Books Teacher's Guide. Ivery, Evelyn L., ed. (Illus.). (Orig.). (J). (gr. 1-6). 1988. pap. text, teacher ed. 2.95 (*0-685-26064-X*) Chandler White.

Massey, Grace C., jt. auth. see Howell, Ann C.

Massey, Harrie S. New Age in Physics. 2nd ed. (Illus.). 1966. 29.95 (*0-8464-0670-5*) Beekman Pubs.

Massey, Harrie S., et al. Electronic & Ionic Impact Phenomena, Vol. 5: Slow Position & Muon Collisions & Notes on Recent Advances. 2nd ed. (International Series of Monographs on Physics). (Illus.). 1975. 115.00 (*0-19-851283-X*) OUP.

Massey, Harrie S., jt. auth. see Haug, A.

Massey, Hart. The Leaky Iron Boat: Nursing an Old Barge Through Holland, Belgium, & France. LC 97-165065. (Illus.). 224p. 1997. pap. 18.95 (*0-7737-5870-4*) Stoddart Publ.

Massey, Howard C. Basic Plumbing with Illustrations. rev. ed. (Illus.). 384p. 1994. pap. 33.00 (*0-934041-99-7*) Craftsman.

***Massey, Howard C.** Behind the Glass: Top Record Producers Tell How They Craft the Hits. (Illus.). 224p. 2000. pap. 22.95 (*0-87930-614-9*, M Freeman Bks) Miller Freeman.

Massey, Howard C. The Complete Sound Blaster. (Illus.). 73p. pap. 14.95 (*0-8256-1351-5*, AM91050) Omnibus NY.

— The MIDI Home Studio. (Illus.). 96p. 1988. pap. 17.95 (*0-8256-1127-X*, AM67182) Music Sales.

— Planning Drain, Waste & Vent Systems. 192p. (Orig.). 1990. pap. 19.25 (*0-934041-51-2*) Craftsman.

— Plumber's Exam Preparation Guide. LC 85-19050. 320p. (Orig.). 1985. pap. 29.00 (*0-934041-04-0*) Craftsman.

— Plumber's Handbook. 3rd rev. ed. LC 98-18088. (Illus.). 352p. 1998. pap. 32.00 (*1-57218-056-0*) Craftsman.

Massey, I. P. Administrative Law. 1995. pap. 30.00 (*81-7012-559-6*, Pub. by Eastern Book) St Mut.

— Administrative Law. 540p. 1985. 180.00 (*0-7855-1292-6*) St Mut.

— Administrative Law. 3rd ed. (C). 1990. text 80.00 (*0-89771-497-0*) St Mut.

Massey, Irving. Find You the Virtue: Ethics, Image & Desire in Literature. (Illus.). 288p. (Orig.). 1987. text 59.00 (*0-8026-0008-5*) Univ Pub Assocs.

— Identity & Community: Reflections on English, Yiddish & French Literature in Canada. LC 94-20233. (Illus.). 206p. 1994. text 29.95 (*0-8143-2518-1*) Wayne St U Pr.

Massey, Irving, contrib. by. Bodleian Manuscript Shelley Adds, No. d.7: Mary Shelley's Copybook of Shelley's Poems. LC 87-21140. (Bodleian Shelley Manuscripts Ser.: Vol. II). 288p. 1987. text 45.00 (*0-8240-6262-0*) Garland.

Massey, Irving, tr. see De Vigny, Alfred.

Massey, Irving J. Uncreating Word: Romanticism & the Object. LC 77-126213. 144p. reprint ed. 44.70 (*0-8357-9250-1*, 201302000083) Bks Demand.

Massey, Isabel A. Interpreting the Sermon on the Mount in the Light of Jewish Tradition As Evidenced in the Palestinian Targums of the Pentateuch: Selected Themes. LC 90-21427. (Studies in the Bible & Early Christianity: Vol. 25). 232p. 1991. lib. bdg. 89.95 (*0-88946-784-6*) E Mellen.

Massey, J. Troy, ed. see Maddox, George T. & Norton, Richard L.

Massey, James. Arts & Crafts Design in America: A State-by-State Guide. 272p. 1998. pap. 22.95 (*0-8118-1886-1*) Chronicle Bks.

— Dalits in India: Religion as a Source of Bondage or Liberation with Special Reference to Christians. (C). 1995. 26.00 (*81-7304-128-8*, Pub. by Manohar) S Asia.

Massey, James. Dalits in India: Religion as a Source of Bondage or Liberation with Special Reference to Christians LC 95-910366. 206p. 1995. write for info. (*81-7304-135-0*, Pub. by Manohar) S Asia.

Massey, James. Doctrine of Ultimate Reality in Sikh Religion. (C). 1991. 15.00 (*81-85425-38-8*, Pub. by Manohar) S Asia.

— Minorities in a Democracy: The Indian Experience LC 99-932118. 224 p. 1999. write for info. (*81-7304-282-9*) S Asia.

— 101 Hot Sex Tips. 160p. (Orig.). 1997. pap. 9.95 (*0-9650574-0-2*) Tristan Pr.

Massey, James & Hayes, Lynne. Coleman vs. Block. 94p. 1986. pap. 5.00 (*0-685-23186-0*, 40,781) NCLS Inc.

Massey, James A., tr. see Feuerbach, Ludwig.

Massey, James C. House Styles in America. 272p. 1999. pap. 27.95 (*0-14-028112-6*) Viking Penguin.

Massey, James E. The Burdensome Joy of Preaching. LC 98-18599. 104p. (Orig.). 1997. pap. 14.95 (*0-687-05069-3*) Abingdon.

Massey, James E. Designing the Sermon: Order & Movement in Preaching. LC 80-17920. (Abingdon Preacher's Library). 128p. (Orig.). 1980. pap. 12.95 (*0-687-10490-4*) Abingdon.

— Preaching from Hebrews. 288p. 1988. pap. 12.95 (*0-310-37181-3*, 12408P) Zondervan.

— Spiritual Disciplines: Growth Through the Practice of Prayer, Fasting, Dialogue, & Worship. rev. ed. Allison, Joseph D., ed. 112p. 1985. pap. 6.95 (*0-310-37151-1*, 12410P) Zondervan.

Massey, James G. & Powell, Arthur J. Windows & Images: Introduction to Humanities. 218p. (C). 1995. text 47.00 (*0-536-59007-9*) Pearson Custom.

Massey, James G., et al. Butterflies & All That Jazz. 206p. (C). 1992. pap. text 51.00 (*0-536-58255-6*) Pearson Custom.

Massey, James P. The Coming Events. LC 96-75144. (Collective Works of James P. Massey Ser.). 116p. (Orig.). 1996. pap. 19.95 (*0-9650514-0-4*) Massey-Reyner.

— The Coming Events. Massey-Reyner, Carole J. et al, eds. (Collective Works of James P. Massey Ser.). 100p. (Orig.). 1996. pap. 9.95 (*0-9650514-4-7*) Massey-Reyner.

— Letters to the Editor. Massey-Reyner, Carole J. & Reyner, David B., eds. LC 96-94329. (Collective Works of James P. Massey Ser.: Vol. II). 125p. (Orig.). 1996. pap. 14.95 (*0-9650514-1-2*) Massey-Reyner.

— Poems from Life. Reyner, David B. & Massey-Reyner, Carole J., eds. LC 96-94327. (Collective Works of James P. Massey Ser.: Vol. III). 80p. (Orig.). 1996. pap. 14.95 (*0-9650514-2-0*) Massey-Reyner.

— Precious Memories. Reyner, David B. & Massey-Reyner, Carole J., eds. LC 96-94328. (Collective Works of James P. Massey Ser.: Vol. IV). 105p. (Orig.). 1996. pap. 14.95 (*0-9650514-3-9*) Massey-Reyner.

Massey, Jamila & Massey, Reginald. Music of India. (C). 1993. 22.00 (*81-7017-332-9*, Pub. by Abhinav) S Asia.

Massey, Jamila, jt. auth. see Massey, Reginald.

Massey, John B. Manual of Dosimetry in Radiotherapy. (Technical Reports: No. 110). (Illus.). (Orig.). 1970. pap. 25.00 (*92-0-115370-8*, IDC110, Pub. by IAEA) Bernan Associates.

Massey, Joseph G. MS-DOS, Lotus 1-2-3, & DBASE. 158p. (Orig.). 1987. pap. text 26.00 (*0-685-21222-X*) Forest Res Syst.

Massey, Julie. Mission Quest: Quest for Courage. (MissionsQuest Ser.). 24p. (J). (gr. 8). 1998. pap. text 3.95 (*1-56309-240-9*, W986112) Womans Mission Union.

— MissionQuest: Quest for Confidence. (MissionsQuest Ser.). (Illus.). 24p. (YA). (gr. 7 up). 1998. pap. text 3.95 (*1-56309-239-5*, W986111) Womans Mission Union.

Massey, Kay P., ed. see Colorado Dietetic Association, Staff.

Massey, Kay P., ed. see Colorado Dietetic Association Staff.

Massey, Kimberley B. & Baran, Stanley J. Television Criticism: Reading, Writing & Analysis. 424p. (C). 1994. pap. text, per. 35.96 (*0-8403-9809-3*) Kendall-Hunt.

Massey, Kimberley K., jt. auth. see Adams, Michael H.

***Massey, Kimberly K.** Readings in Mass Communication: Media Literacy & Culture. LC 98-36731. 1998. pap. text 28.95 (*1-55934-961-1*) Mayfield Pub.

Massey, Lesly F. God & the Working Man. 160p. (Orig.). 1989. pap. 3.50 (*0-933672-80-2*, C-2069) Star Bible.

Massey, Lester G., ed. Coal Gasification: A Symposium Sponsored by the Division of Fuel Chemistry at the 165th Meeting of the American Chemical Society, Dallas, TX, April 9-10, 1973. LC 74-78009. (Advances in Chemistry Ser.: No. 131). (Illus.). 278p. 1974. reprint ed. pap. 86.20 (*0-608-06772-5*, 206696900009) Bks Demand.

Massey, Linton R., jt. auth. see University of Virginia Library Staff.

***Massey, Lorraine.** Yesteryear: America's Twentieth Century. limited ed. LC 99-68586. (Illus.). 256p. 1999. pap. 32.95 (*1-57736-168-7*) Providence Hse.

Massey, Louise, jt. auth. see Massey, Craig.

Massey, M. Slavery in Ancient Rome. (Inside the Ancient World Ser.). 1996. pap. 16.95 (*0-17-439745-3*) Focus Pub-R Pullins.

***Massey, Malcom.** Holiday in Havana. 212p. 2000. pap. 12.95 (*0-595-09466-X*, Writers Club Pr) iUniversecom.

Massey, Margot G. Spring into Winter. (Illus.). (Orig.). 1994. pap. 12.95 (*0-925917-01-X*) Wyman Hse Pubns.

Massey, Marilyn C. Christ Unmasked: The Meaning of the Life of Jesus in German Politics. LC 82-8547. (Studies in Religion). 192p. reprint ed. pap. 59.60 (*0-7837-2463-2*, 204261600005) Bks Demand.

Massey, Marilyn C., ed. In Defense of My Life of Jesus Against the Hegelians. xxxix, 72p. 1983. 59.50 (*0-208-02017-9*) Elliots Bks.

Massey, Mary A., jt. auth. see Heilmann, Ronald W.

Massey, Mary E. Ersatz in the Confederacy: Shortages & Substitutes on the Southern Homefront. LC 92-23314. (Classics in Southern History Ser.). (Illus.). 185p. (C). 1993. reprint ed. pap. 14.95 (*0-87249-877-8*) U of SC Pr.

— Women in the Civil War. LC 93-45580. (Illus.). xxx, 401p. 1994. pap. 17.95 (*0-8032-8213-3*, Bison Books) U of Nebr Pr.

Massey, Michael. Roman Religion. Hodge, Peter, ed. (Aspects of Roman Life Ser.). 48p. (Orig.). (gr. 7-12). 1979. pap. text 9.00 (*0-582-21573-0*, 70846) Longman.

— Women in Ancient Greece & Rome. (Illus.). 40p. (C). 1988. pap. text 10.95 (*0-521-31807-6*) Cambridge U Pr.

Massey, Oliver T. Evaluating Human Resource Development Programs: A Practical Guide to Public Agencies. 304p. (C). 1995. 67.00 (*0-205-15713-0*) Allyn.

***Massey, Peter & Slater, Alison.** Beginner's Guide to Mosaic. (Illus.). 48p. 2000. pap. 11.95 (*0-85532-889-4*, Pub. by Srch Pr) A Schwartz & Co.

***Massey, Peter & Wilson, Jeanne.** 4WD Trails: Central Utah. (Illus.). 148p. 2000. pap. 14.95 (*0-9665675-9-5*, Pub. by Swagman Pubng) Books West CO.

— 4WD Trails: Northern Utah. (Illus.). 148p. 2000. pap. 14.95 (*0-9665675-7-9*, Pub. by Swagman Pubng) Books West CO.

M

An Asterisk (*) at the beginning of an entry indicates that the title is appearing for the first time.

— 4WD Trails: Southeast Utah. (Illus.). 208p. 2000. pap. 14.95 (*0-9665675-6-0*, Pub. by Swagman Pubng) Books West CO.
— 4WD Trails: Southwest Utah. LC QBI99-752. (Illus.). 176p. 2000. pap. 14.95 (*0-9665675-4-4*, Pub. by Swagman Pubng) Books West CO.
— 4WD Adventures in Colorado: How to Explore the Remote Grandeur of Colorado Without Getting Lost. LC QBI98-876. (Illus.). 232p. 1999. pap. 28.95 (*0-9665675-5-2*) Swagman Pubng.
— 4WD Trails: North-Central Colorado. LC QBI99-751. (Illus.). 114p. 1999. pap. 14.95 (*0-9665675-3-6*) Swagman Pubng.
— 4WD Trails: South-Central Colorado. LC QB199-749. (Illus.). 114p. 1999. pap. 14.95 (*0-9665675-2-8*) Swagman Pubng.
***Massey, Peter & Wilson, Joanne.** 4WD Adventures: Utah: The Ultimate Guide to the Utah Backcountry for Anyone with an SUV. (Illus.). 432p. 2000. pap. 32.95 (*0-9665675-1-X*, Pub. by Swagman Pubng) Books West CO.
Massey, Raymond. When I Was Young. (Illus.). 269p. 1976. mass mkt. 5.95 (*0-88780-112-9*, Pub. by Formac Publ Co) Formac Dist Ltd.
Massey, Reginald & Massey, Jamila. The Dances of India: A General Guide & a Users' Handbook. (Illus.). xix, 164p. 1992. 20.00 (*0-317-05152-0*); pap. 13.00 (*0-948725-05-2*) Asia Pub Hse.
Massey, Reginald, jt. auth. see Massey, Jamila.
Massey-Reyner, Carole, ed. see Martin, Gary.
Massey-Reyner, Carole J., ed. see Massey, James P.
Massey, Robert. Formulas for Painters. 224p. 1967. reprint ed. pap. 14.95 (*0-8230-1877-6*) Watsn-Guptill.
Massey, S. Jane, jt. ed. see Tyer, Charlie B.
Massey, Sara. The Pocket Patch, Vol. 4. (Illus.). 72p. (C). 1998. pap. 10.50 (*1-56770-446-8*) S Scheewe Pubns.
***Massey, Sara.** Pocket Patch, Vol. 5. (Illus.). 72p. 2000. pap. 10.50 (*1-56770-486-7*) S Scheewe Pubns.
***Massey, Sara R.** Black Cowboys of Texas. LC 99-55339. 384p. 2000. 29.95 (*0-89096-934-5*) Tex A&M Univ Pr.
Massey, Sheilana. Peace Has No Space for Memories, Vol. 1. Gabel, Barbara, ed. LC 96-92569. 144p. 1996. pap. 11.95 (*0-9651004-1-3*) Spiral Pubs.
***Massey, Sujata.** The Floating Girl. LC 99-88426. 304p. 2000. 24.00 (*0-06-019229-1*) HarpC.
Massey, Sujata. The Flower Master. LC 98-39075. 304p. 1999. 24.00 (*0-06-019228-3*) HarpC.
— The Flower Master. 400p. 2000. mass mkt. 6.99 (*0-06-109734-9*) HarpC.
— The Salaryman's Wife. 432p. 2000. mass mkt. 5.99 (*0-06-104443-1*, Harp PBks) HarpC.
***Massey, Sujata.** Salarymans Wife Arc. 2000. mass mkt. 5.99 (*0-06-104384-2*) HarpC.
Massey, Sujata. Zen Attitude. 320p. 2000. mass mkt. 5.99 (*0-06-104444-X*, HarpTorch) Morrow Avon.
Massey, Thomas A. Healing the Wounds That Divide Us: The Seven Mysteries of Ethical Decision. 1995. pap. text 12.95 (*1-887607-01-3*) Goldn State Pub.
***Massey, Tom.** Gotta Minute? Pratical Tips for Abundant Living: The ABC's of Total Health. 96p. 2000. pap. 9.95 (*1-885003-65-X*, Pub. by R D Reed Pubs) Midpt Trade.
Massey, Truman. Christian Record Book: The Acivator's Calendar. rev. ed. 246p. 1992. student ed. 15.99 (*1-882844-01-7*) TRU Pubns.
Massey, Vera. The Clouded Quaker Star: James Nayler. LC 99-42797. (Illus.). 145p. 1999. pap. 21.50 (*0-944350-46-1*) Friends United.
***Massey, Vera.** James Nayler (1616-1660) 1999. pap. 36.00 (*1-85072-224-2*, Pub. by W Sessions) St Mut.
Massey, Veta H., jt. auth. see Grant, Ann B.
***Massey, Victoria.** The First Lady Diana: Lady Diana Spencer, 1710-1735. 256p. 2000. 29.95 (*1-902809-01-7*, Pub. by Allison & Busby) Intl Pubs Mktg.
Massey, Vincent. Good Neighbourhood & Other Addresses in the United States. LC 69-17584. (Essay Index Reprint Ser.). 1977. 18.95 (*0-8369-0087-1*) Ayer.
Massey, W. C. & Osborne, C. M. A Burial Cave in Baja California: The Palmer Collection, 1887. fac. ed. Rowe, J. H. et al, eds. (University of California Publications: No. 16:8). (Illus.). 31p. (C). 1961. reprint ed. pap. 3.44 (*1-55567-149-7*) Coyote Press.
Massey, W. S. Algebraic Topology: An Introduction. LC 77-22206. (Graduate Texts in Mathematics Ser.: Vol. 56). (Illus.). xxi, 261p. 1996. 49.95 (*0-387-90271-6*) Spr-Verlag.
— A Basic Course in Algebraic Topology. Ewing, J. H. et al, eds. (Graduate Texts in Mathematics Ser.: Vol. 127). (Illus.). 480p. 1997. 49.95 (*0-387-97430-X*) Spr-Verlag.
— Singular Homology Theory. LC 79-23309. (Graduate Texts in Mathematics Ser.: Vol. 70). (Illus.). 280p. 1980. 40.00 (*3-540-90456-5*) Spr-Verlag.
Massey, William & Zemsky, Robert. The Dynamics of Academic Productivity. 1990. 6.00 (*0-614-13569-9*) SHEEO.
Massey, William, ed. see Brown, Kay.
Massey, William S. A Basic Course in Algebraic Topology. 3rd ed. LC 97-198564. (Graduate Texts in Mathematics Ser.). xvi, 428 p. 1997. write for info. (*3-540-97430-X*) Spr-Verlag.
Massey, William S. & Peterson, F. P. The Mod Two Cohomology Structure of Certain Fibre Spaces. LC 52-42839. (Memoirs Ser.: No. 1/74). 97p. 1967. pap. 16.00 (*0-8218-1274-2*, MEMO/1/74) Am Math.
Massi, Jeri. Abandoned. 136p. (J). (gr. 4-6). 1989. pap. 6.49 (*0-89084-467-4*, 044164) Bob Jones Univ.
— The Bridge. (Illus.). 116p. (J). (gr. 4-6). 1986. pap. 6.49 (*0-89084-348-1*, 030148) Bob Jones Univ.
— Crown & Jewel. (Illus.). 154p. (J). (gr. 4-6). 1987. pap. 6.49 (*0-89084-390-2*, 032300) Bob Jones Univ.
— A Dangerous Game. 122p. (J). (gr. 4-6). 1986. pap. 6.49 (*0-89084-347-3*, 030155) Bob Jones Univ.
— Derwood, Inc. 272p. (J). (gr. 4-7). 1986. pap. 6.49 (*0-89084-323-6*, 027458) Bob Jones Univ.
— A Ghost at Horse Creek. 105p. (Orig.). 1989. pap. 5.95 (*1-877778-01-X*) Llama Bks.
— The Lesser Brother. 124p. (Orig.). (YA). (gr. 11). 1989. pap. 5.95 (*1-877778-02-8*) Llama Bks.
— Llamas on the Loose. 140p. (J). 1988. pap. 6.49 (*0-89084-452-6*, 034629) Bob Jones Univ.
— The Myth of the Llama. (Illus.). 118p. (Orig.). (J). (gr. 6). 1989. pap. 5.95 (*1-877778-00-1*) Llama Bks.
— Treasure in the Yukon. (Illus.). 128p. (J). (gr. 4-6). 1986. pap. 6.49 (*0-89084-365-1*, 031070) Bob Jones Univ.
— Two Collars. (Illus.). 164p. (J). 1988. pap. 6.49 (*0-89084-441-0*, 033175) Bob Jones Univ.
Massiah, L., et al, eds. Women in Developing Economies: Making Visible the Invisible. 320p. 1993. 46.50 (*0-85496-345-6*); pap. 19.50 (*0-85496-346-4*) Berg Pubs.
Massialas, Byron G. & Allen, Rodney F. Crucial Issues in Teaching Social Studies, K-12. (C). 1995. pap. 56.95 (*0-534-19752-3*) Wadsworth Pub.
Massialas, Byron G. & Zevin, Jack. Teaching Creatively: Learning Through Discovery. LC 81-19375. 270p. 1983. pap. 19.50 (*0-89874-437-7*) Krieger.
Massicotte, Edouard Z. & Roy, Regis. Armorial du Canada Francais, 2 vols. in 1. LC 74-113783.Tr. of Armorial of French Canada. (Illus.). 332p. 1994. reprint ed. pap. 28.50 (*0-8063-0402-2*) Clearfield Co.
***Massie & Rainey.** Dark Shadows: Dreams of the Dark, Vol. 2. 400p. 1999. mass mkt. 6.99 (*0-06-105752-5*) HarpC.
Massie, Allan. Augustus. 384p. 1995. pap. 13.95 (*0-7867-0267-2*) Carroll & Graf.
— How Should Health Services Be Financed? A Patient's View. (David Hume Papers). 58p. 1988. pap. text 14.00 (*0-08-036585-X*, Pub. by Aberdeen U Pr) Macmillan.
Massie, Annetta, jt. auth. see DeSalvo, Donna.
Massie, Barbara. Craft Malls: Do a Craft Show Everyday! 35p. 1993. pap. text 6.95 (*1-884053-03-3*) Magnolia AR.
— Creating a Small Business: Doing It a Woman's Way. (Illus.). 325p. 1999. pap. 16.95 (*1-884053-09-2*) Magnolia AR.
— Pricing: Hints on How-to-Do-It! 72p. 1995. lib. bdg. 9.95 (*1-884053-07-6*) Magnolia AR.
— So You Want to Be in Business! 80p. 1998. pap. text 9.95 (*1-884053-08-4*) Magnolia AR.
— Survival Guide for Crafters: Dreams Don't Just Happen. 47p. 1994. pap. text 6.95 (*1-884053-06-8*) Magnolia AR.
— Yes, Craft Shows Can Make You Money. 36p. 1992. pap. text 6.50 (*1-884053-00-9*) Magnolia AR.
Massie, Brigid. Selling for People Who Hate to Sell: Successful Selling Skills for the Rest of Us. 208p. 1996. pap., per. 12.00 (*0-7615-0665-9*) Prima Pub.
Massie, Brigid M. & Waters, John. What Do They Say When You Leave the Room? How to Increase Your Personal Effectiveness for Success at Work, at Home & in Your Life. Lee, Paula M., ed. LC 91-22182. 215p. (Orig.). (C). 1991. pap. 10.95 (*0-9629850-0-7*) Eudemonia Pubns.
Massie, Diane R. Chameleon the Spy & the Case of the Vanishing Jewels. LC 83-45050. (Illus.). 48p. (J). (gr. 2-6). 1984. 10.95 (*0-690-04368-6*); lib. bdg. 11.89 (*0-690-04369-4*) HarpC Child Bks.
— Chameleon the Spy & the Terrible Toaster Trap. LC 81-43877. (Illus.). 40p. (J). (gr. 2-6). 1982. 11.95 (*0-690-04223-X*); lib. bdg. 11.89 (*0-690-04224-8*) HarpC Child Bks.
— Chameleon Was a Spy. LC 78-19510. (Illus.). (J). (gr. 2-6). 1979. 11.95 (*0-690-03909-3*); lib. bdg. 11.89 (*0-690-03910-7*) HarpC Child Bks.
***Massie, Diane Redfield.** The Baby Beebee Bird. LC 99-33421. (Illus.). 32p. (J). (ps-1). 2000. 15.95 (*0-06-028083-2*); lib. bdg. 15.89 (*0-06-028084-0*) HarpC Child Bks.
Massie, Elizabeth. Barbara's Escape. (J). 1997. per. 3.99 (*0-671-00134-5*, Minstrel Bks) PB.
— Barbara's Escape. (Daughters of Liberty Ser.). 1997. 9.09 (*0-606-12672-4*, Pub. by Turtleback) Demco.
— California. 144p. 1996. pap. 3.50 (*0-8217-5203-0*) NAL.
***Massie, Elizabeth.** 1870: Not With Our Blood. 192p. 2000. mass mkt. 4.99 (*0-8125-9092-9*) Tor Bks.
— 1863: A House Divided. 4th ed. (Young Founders Ser.: No. 4). 2000. mass mkt. 4.99 (*0-8125-9095-3*) Tor Bks.
Massie, Elizabeth. A Forest Community. 32p. (J). (gr. 2-4). 1999. pap. 5.95 (*0-7398-1480-X*) Raintree Steck-V.
***Massie, Elizabeth.** The Great Chicago Fire, 1871. (YA). 1999. mass mkt. 4.99 (*0-671-03603-3*, Archway) PB.
— Great Chicago Fire, 1871. (Illus.). (J). 1999. 10.34 (*0-606-18370-1*) Turtleback.
Massie, Elizabeth. Maryland: The Night the Harbor Lights Went Out. (American Chills Ser.: No. 1). 144p. 1995. pap. 3.50 (*0-8217-5059-3*, Zebra Kensgtn) Kensgtn Pub Corp.
— Not with Our Blood, 1870. (Young Founders Ser.). 1997. 10.09 (*0-606-13936-2*, Pub. by Turtleback) Demco.
— Patsy & the Declaration. (Daughters of Liberty Ser.: No. 2). (J). (gr. 3-6). 1997. per. 3.99 (*0-671-00133-7*, Minstrel Bks) PB.
— Patsy & the Declaration. (Daughters of Liberty Ser.). 1997. 9.09 (*0-606-12671-6*, Pub. by Turtleback) Demco.
— Patsy's Discovery. (Daughters of Liberty Ser.: No. 1). (J). 1997. per. 3.99 (*0-671-00132-9*) PB.
— Patsy's Discovery. (Daughters of Liberty Ser.). 1997. 9.09 (*0-606-11239-1*, Pub. by Turtleback) Demco.
— Power of Persuasion. (Buffy the Vampire Slayer Ser.: No. 7). 196p. (YA). (gr. 7 up). 1999. per. 4.99 (*0-671-02632-1*) PB.
***Massie, Elizabeth.** 1775: Sons of Liberty. 3rd ed. (Young Founders Ser.: No. 3). 2000. mass mkt. 4.99 (*0-8125-9094-5*) Tor Bks.
Massie, Elizabeth. Sineater. 400p. 1998. reprint ed. mass mkt. 5.99 (*0-8439-4407-2*, Leisure Bks) Dorchester Pub Co.
***Massie, Elizabeth.** 1609: Winter of the Dead. 2nd ed. 192p. (YA). 1998. mass mkt. 4.99 (*0-8125-9093-7*) Tor Bks.
— Welcome Back to the Night. 400p. 1999. mass mkt. 5.99 (*0-8439-4626-1*, Leisure Bks) Dorchester Pub Co.
Massie-Ferch, Kathleen M. & Greenberg, Martin H., eds. Warrior Enchantresses. 352p. 1996. mass mkt. 5.50 (*0-88677-690-2*, Pub. by DAW Bks) Penguin Putnam.
***Massie, Frederick D., ed.** The Uncommon Guide to Common Life of Narragansett Bay. (Illus.). 254p. 1998. pap. 15.00 (*0-9678977-0-X*) Save The Bay.
Massie, Gabriele. Employ Your PC Vol. 1: Businesses That Can Be Run from Home/Put Your Computer to Work for You. Ott, Darlene & Hanf, Linda, eds. LC 96-92069. (Illus.). 320p. (Orig.). 1996. pap. 24.95 (*0-9651225-1-4*) Red Tail.
Massie, Georgia M. Fresh Ideas for Vegetable Cooking. 1985. pap. 19.95 (*0-9614617-0-5*) Fresh Ideas Inc.
Massie, James W. America: The Origin of Her Present Conflict, Her Prospect for the Slave & Her Claim for Anti-Slavery Sympathy. LC 75-83887. (Black Heritage Library Collection). 1977. 21.95 (*0-8369-8628-8*) Ayer.
Massie, Joseph L. Blazer & Ashland Oil: A Study in Management. LC 60-8519. 271p. reprint ed. pap. 84.10 (*0-7837-5794-8*, 204546000006) Bks Demand.
— Essentials of Management. 4th ed. 1986. pap. text 41.00 (*0-13-286337-5*) P-H.
Massie, Larry B. Copper Trails & Iron Rail. 5th rev. ed. (Illus.). 288p. 1998. pap. 12.50 (*1-886167-13-3*) Priscilla Pr.
— Haven, Harbor & Heritage: The Holland, Michigan Story. (Illus.). 200p. 1996. 29.95 (*1-886167-05-2*) Priscilla Pr.
— Michigan Memories: True Stories from Two Peninsulas' Past. LC 95-128553. (Illus.). 288p. 1994. pap. 12.50 (*1-886167-00-1*) Priscilla Pr.
— On the Road to Michigan's Past. (Illus.). 288p. 1995. 18.95 (*1-886167-04-4*); pap. 12.50 (*1-886167-03-6*) Priscilla Pr.
— Pig Boats & River Hogs: Further Voyages into Michigan's Past. 2nd ed. (Illus.). 296p. 1990. pap. 12.50 (*0-9626408-0-8*) Priscilla Pr.
— Potawatomi Tears & Petticoat Pioneers: More of the Romance of Michigan's Past. 2nd ed. (Illus.). 296p. 1992. pap. 12.50 (*0-9626408-3-2*) Priscilla Pr.
— The Romance of Michigan's Past. 2nd ed. (Illus.). 272p. 1991. pap. 12.50 (*0-9626408-1-6*) Priscilla Pr.
— Voyages into Michigan's Past. 8th rev. ed. (Illus.). 288p. 1999. pap. 12.50 (*1-886167-12-5*) Priscilla Pr.
— White Pine Whispers. (Illus.). 288p. 1998. 18.95 (*1-886167-11-7*); pap. 12.50 (*1-886167-10-9*) Priscilla Pr.
Massie, Larry B., ed. Birchbark Belles: Women on the Michigan Frontier. (Illus.). 310p. 1993. pap. 12.50 (*0-9626408-7-5*) Priscilla Pr.
Massie, Larry B. & Schmitt, Peter J. Kalamazoo: The Place Behind the Products. LC 98-73541. (Illus.). 296p. 1998. 32.95 (*0-9654754-8-4*) Am Historical Pr.
Massie, Larry B., jt. auth. see Schmitt, Peter J.
Massie, Lynne. The Buttercup Has My Smile: An Inspiring Journey Through Cancer. Horner, Carolyn, ed. 176p. 1999. per. 17.95 (*0-9669075-0-7*) Cymitar Inc.
Massie, Marian. Soul Never Sleeps: Advanced Perceptions to a More Loving, Purposeful & Joyous Life. 2nd ed. Mueller, Phyllis, ed. 244p. (Orig.). 1992. pap. 11.95 (*0-9633140-2-5*) Advanced Percept.
***Massie, Mary Jane, ed.** Pain: What Psychiatrists Need to Know. (Review of Psychiatry Ser.: Vol. 19, No. 2). 224p. 2000. pap. 28.50 (*0-88048-173-0*) Am Psychiatric.
Massie, Meg. Iran: Key Regional Peacebroker in The Gulf Crisis, August 1990-February 1991. LC 92-156845. 41p. 1991. write for info. (*1-871415-26-8*) Gulf Ctr.
Massie, Paul. Programming IBM Assembly Language. (Illus.). 500p. 1985. pap. text. write for info. (*0-8087-6405-5*) Macmillan.
Massie, Paula. Soccer Mom: A Survival Guide, 1. LC 99-181893. 160p. 1998. pap. 12.95 (*0-9665388-0-3*) Sideline Soccer.
Massie, Randall. When Godly Robes Unravel. 164p. (Orig.). 1990. pap. 5.99 (*0-89900-386-9*) College Pr Pub.
Massie, Rebecca. The Sydney & Frances Lewis Contemporary Art Fund Collection. LC 80-14914. (Illus.). 112p. 1980. pap. 9.95 (*0-917046-09-9*) Va Mus Arts.
Massie, Robert K. Dreadnought: Britain, Germany & the Coming of the Great War. (Illus.). 1040p. 1992. pap. 17.50 (*0-345-37556-4*) Ballantine Pub Grp.
— Nicholas & Alexandra. 624p. 1985. mass mkt. 7.99 (*0-440-36358-6*, LE) Dell.
***Massie, Robert K.** Nicholas & Alexandra: The Story of the Love That Ended an Empire. (Illus.). 624p. 2000. pap. 18.00 (*0-345-43831-0*) Ballantine Pub Grp.
Massie, Robert K. Peter the Great. 928p. 1981. pap. 14.00 (*0-345-29806-3*) Ballantine Pub Grp.
— Peter the Great. 960p. 1986. mass mkt. 7.99 (*0-345-33619-4*) Ballantine Pub Grp.
Massie, Shirley & Lay, Eldonna. Freshet Finds a Way: A Trip Through the Hydrologic Cycle. (Illus.). 16p. (Orig.). (J). (gr. k-4). 1996. pap. 6.95 (*0-9649250-0-1*) Helix Water.
Massie, Somja. Irish Pride: 101 Reasons to Be Proud You're Irish. 224p. 1998. 15.95 (*1-55972-488-9*, Birch Ln Pr); 95.70 (*1-55972-943-0*, Birch Ln Pr) Carol Pub Group.
Massie, Sonja. Betrayal. 384p. 1996. mass mkt. 4.99 (*0-8217-5458-0*, Zebra Kensgtn) Kensgtn Pub Corp.
— The Complete Guide to Irish History & Culture. LC 98-87600. (Complete Idiot's Guides (Lifestyle) Ser.). (Illus.). 268p. 1999. pap. 16.95 (*0-02-862710-5*, Alpha Ref) Macmillan Gen Ref.
— The Dark Mirror. 384p. 1999. mass mkt. 4.99 (*0-8217-5135-2*, Zebra Kensgtn) Kensgtn Pub Corp.
***Massie, Sonja.** Daughter of Ireland. (Irish Eyes Ser.). 304p. 2000. mass mkt. 5.99 (*0-515-12835-X*, Jove) Berkley Pub.
Massie, Sonja. A Friend in Need. LC 96-36729. (Janet Dailey's Love Scenes Ser.). 1997. pap. 3.50 (*1-56853-028-5*, Signal Hill) New Readers.
Massie, Suzanne. Land of the Firebird: The Beauty of Old Russia. 13th ed. LC 80-12860. (Illus.). 493p. (C). 1980. reprint ed. pap. text 30.00 (*0-9644184-1-X*) HeartTree Pr.
— Pavlovsk: The Life of a Russian Palace. (Illus.). 394p. (C). 1990. pap. text 28.00 (*0-9644184-0-1*) HeartTree Pr.
Massie, Winfield. Jungle Tales: Adventures in Meat Inspection. (Illus.). 250p. (Orig.). (C). 1995. pap. 12.95 (*0-9638718-0-3*) Brockton Pubng.
Massieu, Jose F. Ruiz, see Ruiz Massieu, Jose F.
Massieu, Mario R. El Marco Juridico Para el Combate Al Narcotrafico. (SPA.). pap. 5.99 (*968-16-4340-2*, Pub. by Fondo) Continental Bk.
Massignani, Alessandro, jt. auth. see Greene, Jack.
Massignon, Genevieve. Folktales of France. Hyland, Jacqueline, tr. LC 68-14008. (Folktales of the World Ser.). 363p. reprint ed. pap. 112.60 (*0-608-18238-9*, 205665200078) Bks Demand.
Massignon, Louis. Essay on the Origins of the Technical Language of Islamic Mysticism. Clark, Benjamin, tr. from FRE. LC 93-40284. (C). 1996. text 45.00 (*0-268-00928-7*) U of Notre Dame Pr.
— Hallaj: Mystic & Martyr. 300p. 1996. pap. 19.95 (*0-614-21283-9*, 373) Kazi Pubns.
— Hallaj: Mystic & Martyr, 4 vols. Mason, Herbert W., tr. from FRE. LC 80-11085. (Bollingen Ser.: No. XCVIII). 2010p. 1981. text 350.00 (*0-691-09910-3*, Pub. by Princeton U Pr) Cal Prin Full Svc.
Massih & Tabri. Dictionary of Grammar Terminology: Al-Khalil. (ARA.). 525p. 1990. 35.00 (*0-86685-464-9*, LDL4649, Pub. by Librairie du Liban) Intl Bk Ctr.
Massik, Peter, et al, eds. San Francisco Good Life Cookbook: Recipes from the City's Best Restaurants. (Illus.). 288p. 1999. pap. 16.95 (*1-886776-15-6*) Good Life.
Massik, Peter & Chipman, Jeremy. Good Life Bay Area Restaurant Guide: A Comprehensive Guide to Restaurants in San Francisco Wine Country, Silicon Valley, & the East Bay. (Good Life Guides Ser.). (Illus.). 288p. Date not set. pap. 12.95 (*1-886776-13-X*) Good Life.
— Good Life San Francisco Restaurant Guide. 3rd ed. (Good Life Guides Ser.). (Illus.). 288p. 1998. pap. 11.95 (*1-886776-14-8*) Good Life.
Massik, Peter & Good Life Publications Staff, eds. Good Life Peninsula & Silicon Valley Restaurant Guide: The Complete Guide to Dining from San Jose to San Francisco. 2nd ed. (Good Life Guides Ser.). (Illus.). 224p. (Orig.). 1998. pap. 11.95 (*1-886776-10-5*) Good Life.
— Good Life San Francisco Budget Gourmet. (Illus.). 224p. (Orig.). 1997. pap. 9.95 (*1-886776-07-5*) Good Life.
— Good Life San Francisco Restaurant Map. (Good Life Guides Ser.). (Illus.). 32p. (Orig.). 1997. pap. 5.95 (*1-886776-09-1*) Good Life.
Massik, Peter & Good Life Staff. Good Life Peninsula & Silicon Valley Guide: An Insider's Reference for Newcomers, Visitors, & Residents. 3rd ed. (Good Life Guides Ser.). Orig. Title: Good Life Peninsula & San Jose Insider's Guide. (Illus.). 320p. 1998. pap. 14.95 (*1-886776-12-1*) Good Life.
Massil, Stephen, ed. The Jewish Year Book, 1998. 365p. 1998. 32.50 (*0-85303-339-0*, Pub. by M Vallentine & Co) Intl Spec Bk.
— The Jewish Year Book, 1997. 448p. 1997. 32.50 (*0-85303-326-9*, Pub. by M Vallentine & Co) Intl Spec Bk.
Massil, Stephen W. The Jewish Year Book 1995. 1995. 13.50 (*0-85303-269-6*, Pub. by M Vallentine & Co) Intl Spec Bk.
Massil, Stephen W., ed. The Centenary Edition of the Jewish Year Book 1996. 448p. 1996. 30.00 (*0-85303-317-X*, Pub. by M Vallentine & Co) Intl Spec Bk.
— The Jewish Travel Guide, 1997. 400p. (Orig.). 1997. pap. 14.95 (*0-85303-327-7*, Pub. by M Vallentine & Co) Intl Spec Bk.
***Massil, Stephen W., ed.** The Jewish Year Book, 2000. 448p. 2000. 37.50 (*0-85303-381-1*, Pub. by M Vallentine & Co) Intl Spec Bk.
Massil, Stephen W., ed. The Jewish Year Book, 1995. 351p. 1995. 35.00 (*0-85303-296-3*, Pub. by M Vallentine & Co) Intl Spec Bk.
— The Jewish Yearbook, 1999. 400p. 1999. 37.50 (*0-85303-358-7*) Intl Spec Bk.
Massil, Stephen W., pref. The Jewish Year Book, 1896. fac. limited ed. (Illus.). 352p. (YA). 1996. boxed set 25.00 (*0-85303-321-8*, Pub. by M Vallentine & Co) Intl Spec Bk.
Massimello, Giovanni, jt. auth. see Apostolo, Giorgio.
***Massimini, Kathy, ed.** Genetic Disorders Sourcebook: Basic Consumer Health Information about Hereditary Diseases & Disorders. 2nd ed. (Health Reference Ser.). 650p. 2000. lib. bdg. 78.00 (*0-7808-0241-1*) Omnigraphics Inc.
Massimini, Kathy, jt. auth. see Trozzi, Maria.
Massimino, Ferdy, jt. ed. see Sallis, Robert E.
Massimo, L., et al, eds. Oncogenes in Pediatric Tumors. (Ettore Majorana International Life Sciences Ser.). xvii, 269p. 1988. text 195.00 (*3-7186-0469-8*) Gordon & Breach.
— The Role of Pharmacology in Pediatric Oncology. (Developments in Oncology Ser.). 1987. lib. bdg. 197.00 (*0-89838-795-7*) Kluwer Academic.
Massin. Fun with Numbers. Volk, Carol, tr. LC 94-6668. (FRE., Illus.). 40p. (J). (gr. 2-7). 1995. 22.65 (*0-15-200962-0*, Creat Educ) Creative Co.

An Asterisk (*) at the beginning of an entry indicates that the title is appearing for the first time.

Massinelli, Anna Maria. Hardstones. (Gilbert Collection). 288p. 1999. 90.00 (*0-85667-510-5*, Pub. by P Wilson) Antique Collect.

Massing. Art Guys, Think Twice. 1995. pap. 19.95 (*0-936080-36-1*) Cont Arts Museum.

***Massing, Conni L.** The Aberhart Summer. (Illus.). 112p. 1999. pap. 13.95 (*1-896300-40-5*) NeWest Pubs.

***Massing, Michael.** The Fix. LC 99-45376. 335p. 2000. 14.95 (*0-520-22335-7*, Pub. by U CA Pr) Cal Prin Full Svc.

Massing, Michael. The Fix: Under the Nixon Administration, America Had an Effective Drug Policy. We Should Restore It. (Nixon Was Right) LC 98-8618. 336p. 1998. 25.00 (*0-684-80960-5*) Simon & Schuster.

***Massingberd, Hugh M.** Great Houses of England & Wales. LC 00-24925. (Illus.). 240p. 2000. pap. 25.00 (*0-7893-0475-9*) Universe.

Massinger, Philip. Believe As You List. LC 78-133708. (Folio - Tudor Facsimile Texts. Old English Plays Ser.: No. 139). reprint ed. 59.50 (*0-404-53439-2*) AMS Pr.

— The City Madam. fac. ed. Hoy, Cyrus, ed. LC 64-11357. (Regents Renaissance Drama Ser.). 127p. pap. 39.40 (*0-7837-7338-2*, 204729100007) Bks Demand.

— New Way to Pay Old Debt, a Comedie. LC 76-25773. (English Experience Ser.: No. 262). 92p. 1970. reprint ed. 20.00 (*90-221-0262-9*) Walter J Johnson.

— A New Way to Pay Old Debts. (New Mermaids Ser.). (C). 1984. pap. text 9.75 (*0-393-90009-6*) Norton.

— Philip Massinger, 2 vols. (BCL1-PR English Literature Ser.). 1992. reprint ed. lib. bdg. 150.00 (*0-7812-7251-3*) Rprt Serv.

— Philip Massinger, 2 vols., Vols. 1 - 2. Symons, Arthur, ed. (BCL1-PR English Literature Ser.). 1992. reprint ed. lib. bdg. 150.00 (*0-7812-7262-9*) Rprt Serv.

— Philip Massinger: Roman Actor, Maid of Honour, New Way to Pay Old Debts, Believe As You List. (BCL1-PR English Literature Ser.). 416p. 1992. reprint ed. lib. bdg. 99.00 (*0-7812-7263-7*) Rprt Serv.

— Philip Massinger: The Roman Actor, the Maid of Honor, a New Way to Pay Old Debts, Believe As You List. (BCL1-PR English Literature Ser.). 416p. 1992. reprint ed. lib. bdg. 99.00 (*0-7812-7252-1*) Rprt Serv.

— Philip Massinger, 1887-1889. LC 72-108511. 59.00 (*0-403-03683-6*) Scholarly.

— Plays of Philip Massinger, 4 vols., Set. 2nd ed. Gifford, William, ed. LC 12-36722. reprint ed. write for info. (*0-404-04280-5*) AMS Pr.

Massingham & Lancaster. Marketing Case Studies: How to Tackle Them, How To. 214p. 1965. pap. 34.95 (*0-7506-2011-0*) Buttrwrth-Heinemann.

Massingham, Betty. Gertrude Jekyll. (Lifelines Ser.: No. 37). (Illus.). 48p. 1989. pap. 7.50 (*0-85263-304-1*, Pub. by Shire Pubns) Parkwest Pubns.

Massingham, Gordon, ed. see Richmond, Lee.

Massingham, Gordon, ed. see Ronan, John & Ayers, Shirley.

Massingham, Harold J. The Friend of Shelley: A Memoir of Edward John Trelawny. (BCL1-PR English Literature Ser.). 367p. 1992. reprint ed. lib. bdg. 89.00 (*0-7812-7528-8*) Rprt Serv.

— Letters to X. LC 67-26763. (Essay Index Reprint Ser.). 1977. 19.95 (*0-8369-0691-8*) Ayer.

Massingham, Harold J. & Massingham, Hugh, eds. Great Victorians. LC 70-156692. (Essay Index Reprint Ser.). 1977. reprint ed. 20.95 (*0-8369-2284-0*) Ayer.

Massingham, Hugh, jt. ed. see Massingham, Harold J.

Massingham, Lester, jt. auth. see Lancaster, Geoffrey.

Massingill, Randi L. Total Control: The Michael Nesmith Story. (Illus.). 326p. 1997. pap. 18.95 (*0-9658218-3-8*) Flexquarters.

Massini, Mario. Lectio Divina: An Ancient Prayer That Is Ever New. Lane, Edmund C., tr. from ITA. Orig. Title: Lectio Divina: Preghiera Antica e Nuova. 104p. 1998. mass mkt. 5.95 (*0-8189-0813-0*) Alba.

Massion, Francois. Dictionnaire des Belgicismes, 2 vols., Set. (FRE.). 946p. 1987. 295.00 (*0-8288-9464-7*) Fr & Eur.

Massip, Josep M. Diccionari Catala de Falses Etimologies. (CAT.). 224p. 1984. pap. 19.95 (*0-7859-5879-7*, 8429722114) Fr & Eur.

Massip, Renee. La Bete Quaternaire. (FRE.). 1981. pap. 11.95 (*0-7859-4145-2*) Fr & Eur.

— Les Deesses. (FRE.). 1978. pap. 10.95 (*0-7859-4072-3*) Fr & Eur.

— La Regente. (FRE.). 1972. pap. 8.95 (*0-7859-3998-9*) Fr & Eur.

— Le Rire de Sara. (FRE.). 1975. pap. 10.95 (*0-7859-4044-8*) Fr & Eur.

Massis, Bruce E., ed. Serving Print Disabled Library Patrons: A Textbook for Facilitators of Library Service to People with Visual or Physical Impairments. LC 96-12720. 190p. 1996. lib. bdg. 42.50 (*0-7864-0209-1*) McFarland & Co.

Massis, Bruce E. & Vitzansky, Winnie, eds. Interlibrary Loan of Alternative Format Materials: A Balanced Sourcebook. LC 92-40945. (Journal of Interlibrary Loan & Information Supply: Vol. 3, Nos. 1-2). 196p. 1993. lib. bdg. 39.95 (*1-56024-394-5*) Haworth Pr.

Massler, Ina. Hanukkah Activities. (Holiday Activities Ser.). 1994. 2.95 (*1-55734-783-2*) Tchr Create Mat.

Massler, Maury & Schour, Isaac. Atlas of the Mouth. 2nd ed. (Illus.). (C). 22.40 (*0-685-05572-8*) Am Dental.

Massman, Emory A. Hospital Ships of World War II: An Illustrated Reference to 39 United States Military Vessels. LC 99-10813. (Illus.). 509p. 1999. lib. bdg. 75.00 (*0-7864-0556-2*) McFarland & Co.

***Massman, Gordon.** The Numbers. Baratier, David, ed. 88p. 2000. pap. 12.00 (*1-886350-88-4*, Pub. by Pavement Saw); lib. bdg. 75.00 (*1-886350-89-2*, Pavemnt Saw) Pavement Saw.

Massman, Marjorie, ed. see Massman-Wardzala, Joan.

Massman, Virgil F., jt. ed. see Kathman, Michael D.

Massman-Wardzala, Joan. The Story of LittleMouse: LittleMouse Finds Tools for the Adventure of Life. large type ed. Massman, Marjorie, ed. (Illus.). (J). (gr. k-4). 1999. pap. 6.95 (*0-9669902-0-X*) MassAward Pub.

Massmann, H. F. Literatur der Totentanze. 162p. 1963. reprint ed. write for info. (*0-318-71844-8*) G Olms Pubs.

Massmann, John C., ed. see Jaakkola, Terry & Frericks, Julia L.

Massmann, Joseph. Nervousness, Temperament & the Soul. 171p. 1999. reprint ed. 18.95 (*0-912141-75-1*) Roman Cath Bks.

Masso, Jose L. Buenos Dias. (SPA.). 1971. pap. 3.00 (*0-89729-124-7*) Ediciones.

Masso, Phyllis H. Never the Same Again . . . A Young Woman's Story of Life in the Blackstone Valley in the 1820s. LC 98-71875. 150p. (YA). (gr. 5-12). 1998. pap. 14.95 (*1-57960-046-8*) Disc Enter Ltd.

Massof, Robert W. & Lidoff, Lorraine, eds. Issues in Low Vision Rehabilitation: Service Delivery, Policy, & Funding. 272p. 1999. pap. 32.95 (*0-89128-309-9*) Am Foun Blind.

Massoglia, Charlie. Database DDS: A Complete Guide to Creating & Maintaining Physical & Logical File DDS. (Illus.). 312p. (Orig.). 1994. pap. 99.00 (*1-883884-17-9*, 516) Midrange Comput.

Massoglia, Martin. Battalion Attention. LC 95-72492. 198p. (Orig.). 1996. pap. 12.95 (*1-884570-43-7*) Research Triangle.

Massom, Robert. Satellite Remote Sensing of Polar Regions. 1991. 83.00 (*0-87371-607-8*) CRC Pr.

Masson, ed. The Love Poems. (Poetry Library). 240p. 1998. pap. 7.95 (*1-85326-445-8*, 4458WW, Pub. by Wrdsworth Edits) NTC Contemp Pub Co.

Masson, ed. see McDonnel & Kissel.

Masson, Andre. Andre Masson: Paintings 1960-1961 - with an Original Lithograph. (FRE., Illus.). 48p. 1962. pap. 40.00 (*1-55660-269-3*) A Wofsy Fine Arts.

— Andre Masson: Paintings 1962-1968 - with an Original Lithograph. (FRE., Illus.). 62p. 1968. pap. 40.00 (*1-55660-270-7*) A Wofsy Fine Arts.

Masson, Andre, jt. auth. see Sartre, Jean-Paul.

Masson, Andre, ed. see Flaubert, Gustave.

Masson, Andre, jt. ed. see Kessler, Denis.

Masson, Ann M. & Schmalz, Lydia H. Cast Iron & the Crescent City. LC 95-80470. 53p. 1995. pap. 5.00 (*1-879714-07-8*) SW PF LA Land.

Masson, C. R. Metallurgical Slags, Pt. 2. 1982. pap. 67.00 (*0-08-028684-4*, Pergamon Pr) Elsevier.

Masson, Charles. Narrative of Various Journeys in Balochistan, Afghanistan & the Panjab, 1826-1838, 3 vols. (C). 1997. 125.00 (*81-215-0783-9*, Pub. by M Manoharial) Coronet Bks.

Masson, Charles F. Secret Memoirs of the Court of Petersburg: Particularly Towards the End of the Reign of Catherine II & the Commencement of That of Paul I. LC 75-115563. (Russia Observed, Series I). 1970. reprint ed. 20.95 (*0-405-03049-5*) Ayer.

Masson, Christine. Around the World Germany. LC 96-53080. (Around the World Ser.). (Illus.). 112p. 1996. 6.99 (*1-57145-083-1*, Thunder Bay) Advantage Pubs.

— Around the World Spain. Burrett, Tony & Van Splunteren, Carla, trs. from FRE. LC 96-53083. (Around the World Ser.). (Illus.). 112p. 1996. 6.99 (*1-57145-081-5*, Thunder Bay) Advantage Pubs.

Masson, D. Drummond of Hawthornden: The Story of His Life & Writings. LC 68-24912. (English Biography Ser.: No. 31). 1969. reprint ed. lib. bdg. 75.00 (*0-8383-0282-3*) M S G Haskell Hse.

Masson, D. J. & Bochnovic, David A. Treasury Manager's Bookmarks & Favorite Places. (Illus.). i, 98p. 1999. 24.95 (*0-9654739-1-0*) Phoenix-Hecht.

Masson, David. British Novelists & Their Styles. LC 72-10853. (Essay Index Reprint Ser.). 1977. reprint ed. 23.95 (*0-8369-7230-9*) Ayer.

— DeQuincey. Morley, John, ed. LC 68-58385. (English Men of Letters Ser.). reprint ed. lib. bdg. 27.50 (*0-404-51717-X*) AMS Pr.

— Drummond of Hawthornden: The Story of His Life & Writings. (BCL1-PR English Literature Ser.). 490p. 1992. reprint ed. lib. bdg. 99.00 (*0-7812-7207-6*) Rprt Serv.

— Three Devils: Luther's, Milton's & Goethe's. LC 78-128340. reprint ed. 36.00 (*0-404-04247-3*) AMS Pr.

— Wordsworth, Shelley, Keats, & Other Essays. LC 72-13205. (Essay Index Reprint Ser.). 1977. reprint ed. 21.95 (*0-8369-8168-5*) Ayer.

Masson, David, ed. see De Quincey, Thomas.

Masson, Dubos J. The Treasurer's Handbook of Financial Management: Applying the Theories, Concepts & Quantitative Methods of Corporate Finance. Oros, John G. et al, eds. (Illus.). 447p. 1995. 69.95 (*1-55738-884-9*) Treasry Mgmt.

Masson, Dubos J. & Wikoff, David A., eds. Essentials of Cash Management. 5th rev. ed. 350p. (Orig.). (C). 1995. pap. 77.50 (*0-614-09898-X*) Treasry Mgmt.

Masson, Georgina. The Companion Guide to Rome. 5th rev. ed. LC 98 141464. (Illus.). 544p. 1998. pap. 29.95 (*1-900639-21-1*, Pub. by Companion Guide) Boydell & Brewer.

Masson, Helen C., jt. auth. see Erooga, Marcus.

Masson, Helen C., jt. ed. see Erooga, Marcus.

Masson, Herre. Dictionnaire Initiatique. rev. ed. (FRE.). 430p. 1984. 55.00 (*0-7859-4833-3*) Fr & Eur.

Masson, J. M. & Winn-Oakley, Maureen. Out of Hearing: Representing Children in Court. LC 98-35141. (Series in Child Protection & Policy). 190p. 1999. pap. 67.50 (*0-471-98642-9*) Wiley.

***Masson, J. Moussaieff.** Dogs Have the Strangest Friends: Other True Stories of Animal Feelings. LC 99-38945. (Illus.). 128p. (J). (gr. 3-7). 2000. 19.99 (*0-525-45745-3*, Dutton Child) Peng Put Young Read.

Masson, J. Moussaieff. The Oceanic Feeling: The Origins of Religious Sentiment in Ancient India. (Studies of Classical India: No. 3). 228p. 1980. text 140.50 (*90-277-1050-3*, D Reidel) Kluwer Academic.

Masson, James C., ed. Acrylic Fiber Technology & Applications. (Illus.). 408p. 1995. text 199.00 (*0-8247-8977-6*) Dekker.

Masson, Jeffrey M. Against Therapy. LC 93-26695. 1993. reprint ed. pap. 15.95 (*1-56751-022-1*) Common Courage.

— Against Therapy. LC 93-26695. 1994. reprint ed. lib. bdg. 29.95 (*1-56751-023-X*) Common Courage.

— Dogs Never Lie about Love. (Illus.). 1998. pap. 14.00 (*0-609-80201-1*, Crown) Crown Pub Group.

— Dogs Never Lie about Love: Reflections on the Emotional World of Dogs. LC 97-884. 1997. 24.00 (*0-609-60057-5*) Random Hse Value.

— Final Analysis: The Making & Unmaking of a Psychoanalyst. 1990. 18.22 (*0-201-52368-X*) Addison-Wesley.

— Final Analysis: The Making & Unmaking of a Psychoanalyst. 224p. 1998. pap. 14.00 (*0-671-02572-4*, PB Trade Paper) PB.

Masson, Jeffrey M. & McCarthy, Susan. When Elephants Weep: The Emotional Lives of Animals. (Illus.). 320p. 1996. pap. 13.95 (*0-385-31428-0*, Delta Trade) Dell.

Masson, Jeffrey M., ed. & tr. see Freud, Sigmund.

Masson, Jeffrey M., tr. see Freud, Sigmund.

***Masson, Jeffrey Moussaieff.** The Assault on Truth: Freud's Suppression of the Seduction Theory. 320p. 1998. pap. 14.00 (*0-671-02571-6*) PB.

Masson, Jeffrey Moussaieff. The Emperor's Embrace: Reflections on Animal Families & Fatherhood. LC 99-46970. 304p. 1999. 24.00 (*0-671-02083-8*, PB Hardcover) PB.

***Masson, Jeffrey Moussaieff.** My Father's Guru: A Journey Through Spirituality & Disillusion. 192p. 1998. pap. 14.00 (*0-671-02573-2*) PB.

Masson, Joan, et al, eds. Warwick Valley Cooking. (Illus.). 160p. 1989. 7.50 (*0-9623003-0-6*) Friends A Wisner.

Masson, L. R., ed. Bourgeois de la Compagnie du Nord-Ouest, Recits de Voyages, Lettres et Rapports Inedits Relatifs au Nord-Ouest Canadien Avec une Esquisse Historique et des Annotations Vol. 2: McDonald, John-Autobiographical Notes; Keith, George-Letters to Mr. Roderic McKenzie 1807-1817, Johnston, John-an Account of Lake Superior 1792-1807, Wilcooke, Samuel H.-Death of Mr. Benjamin Frobisher 1819, Duncan, Cameron-Nipigon Country 1804, Peter, Grant-Sauteaux Indians, 1804, McKenzie, James-Extracts from His Journal 1799-1800, Athabasca District, McKenzie, James-King's Posts & Journal of a. 499p. 1960. 100.00 (*0-614-01804-8*) Elliots Bks.

Masson, Louis J. Reflections: Essays on Place & Family. LC 95-45267. 128p. (C). 1996. 25.00 (*0-87422-130-7*); pap. 12.95 (*0-87422-131-5*) Wash St U Pr.

Masson, Manju, jt. auth. see Kuenzel, Wayne J.

Masson, Marcelle. A Bag of Bones: Legends of the Wintu Indians of Northern California. LC 66-23398. (Illus.). 130p. 1967. pap. 8.95 (*0-911010-26-2*) Naturegraph.

Masson, Margaret, jt. auth. see George, Ivy.

***Masson, Marilyn A.** In the Realm of Nachan Kan: Postclassic Maya Archaeology at Laguan de On, Belize. (Illus.). 280p. 2000. 65.00 (*0-87081-567-9*) U of Okla Pr.

Masson, Marilyn A., jt. ed. see Smith, Michael E.

Masson, Michael E., jt. ed. see Graf, Peter.

Masson, Mick. Surviving the Dole Years: The 1930s - A Personal Story. 200p. 1994. pap. 27.95 (*0-86840-285-0*, Pub. by New South Wales Univ Pr) Intl Spec Bk.

Masson, Paul M. Berlioz. LC 74-24145. reprint ed. 29.50 (*0-404-13037-2*) AMS Pr.

— L' Opera de Rameau. LC 70-168675. (Music Ser.). (Illus.). 596p. 1972. reprint ed. lib. bdg. 75.00 (*0-306-70262-2*) Da Capo.

Masson, Paul R., ed. France, Financial & Real Sector Issues. LC 95-40587. 1995. 24.00 (*1-55775-491-8*) Intl Monetary.

Masson, Paul R. & Mussa, Michael. The Role of the Fund-Financing & Its Interactions with Adjustments & Surveillance. LC 96-151520. (Pamphlet Ser.: No. 50). 1996. pap. write for info. (*1-55775-551-5*) Intl Monetary.

Masson, Paul R. & Mussa, Michael L. Confronting Budget Deficits. (Economic Issues Ser.: No. 3). 18p. 1996. write for info. (*1-55775-615-5*) Intl Monetary.

Masson, Paul R. & Taylor, Mark P., eds. Policy Issues in the Operation of Currency Unions. LC 92-20210. (Illus.). 324p. (C). 1993. text 59.95 (*0-521-43455-6*) Cambridge U Pr.

Masson, Paul R., et al. EMU & the International Monetary System: Proceedings of a Conference Held in Washington, DC on March 17-18, 1997, Co-Sponsored by the Foundation Camille Gutt & the IMF. LC 97-25671. 1997. write for info. (*1-55775-664-3*) Intl Monetary.

— MULTIMOD Mark II: Revised & Extended Model. LC 90-37502. (Occasional Papers: No. 71). v, 50p. 1990. pap. 10.00 (*1-55775-141-2*) Intl Monetary.

Masson, Paul R., jt. auth. see Ghosh, A. R.

Masson, Pierre. Human Tumors: Histology, Diagnosis, & Techniques. 2nd rev. ed. LC 70-83489. (Illus.). 1360p. reprint ed. pap. 200.00 (*0-608-16049-0*, 203317900084) Bks Demand.

Masson, Robert L., ed. see Jacobs, Edward E., et al.

***Masson, Sophie.** Clementine. LC 00-8912. (Illus.). (J). 2000. pap. write for info. (*0-88489-670-6*) St Marys.

— The First Day. LC 99-50725. (Starmaker Books Ser.). 156p. (J). (gr. 6-9). 2000. pap. 5.50 (*0-88489-490-8*) St Marys.

Masson, Sophie. The House in the Rainforest. 1990. pap. 14.95 (*0-7022-2261-5*, Pub. by Univ Queensland Pr) Intl Spec Bk.

Masson, Sophie. Malkin. LC 00-8079. (J). pap. write for info. (*0-88489-669-2*) St Marys.

— Serafin. (Starmaker Books Ser.). 144p. (YA). (gr. 6-9). 2000. pap. 5.50 (*0-88489-567-X*) St Marys.

Masson, Sophie. The Sun Is Rising. (YA). 1996. pap. 12.95 (*0-7022-2789-7*, Pub. by Univ Queensland Pr) Intl Spec Bk.

Masson Staff. Dictionnaire de Cardiologie. (FRE.). 352p. 1986. 135.00 (*0-7859-7827-5*, 2225802521) Fr & Eur.

— Small Medical Lexicon: French/English/French. 4th ed. (ENG & FRE.). 192p. 1998. 29.95 (*0-320-00160-1*) Fr & Eur.

Masson, Terrence. CG101: A Computer Graphics Industry Reference. (Illus.). 500p. 1999. pap. 39.99 (*0-7357-0046-X*) New Riders Pub.

Masson, Thomas L. Our American Humorists. LC 67-23245. (Essay Index Reprint Ser.). 1977. 26.95 (*0-8369-0692-6*) Ayer.

Masson, V. M. Altyn-Depe. Michael, Henry N., tr. from RUS. (University Museum Monographs: No. 55). (Illus.). xx, 150p. 1988. text 55.00 (*0-934718-54-7*) U Museum Pubns.

Masson, V. M., ed. see Dani, A. H.

Masson, V. M., jt. ed. see Dani, A. H.

Masson-Zwaan, Tanja L. & Mendes de Leon, Pablo M., eds. Air & Space Law - De Lege Ferenda: Essays in Honour of Henri A. Wassenbergh. LC 92-18235. 344p. (C). 1992. lib. bdg. 132.50 (*0-7923-1626-6*) Kluwer Academic.

Massonnet, C. C., et al. Plasticity in Structural Engineering, Fundamentals & Applications. (CISM International Centre for Mechanical Sciences Ser.: Vol. 241). (Illus.). 302p. 1980. 46.95 (*0-387-81350-0*) Spr-Verlag.

***Massonnet, Philippe.** The New China: Money, Sex, & Power. Taiebr, Hannah, tr. from FRE. LC 99-41591. (Illus.). 240p. 1999. 18.95 (*0-8048-2116-X*) Tuttle Pubng.

***Massonxxx, Veneta.** Rehab at the Florida Avenue Grill. LC 99-90707. 102p. 1999. pap. 13.00 (*0-9673688-0-4*) Sage Femme Pr.

Massopust, Peter R. Fractal Functions, Fractal Surfaces, & Wavelets. LC 94-26551. (Illus.). 383p. 1995. text 53.00 (*0-12-478840-8*) Acad Pr.

Massot, R., jt. auth. see Cornu, Aymbe.

Massotty, Susan, tr. from DUT. From Berlin. (Topographics Ser.). 144p. 1997. pap. 18.95 (*0-948462-87-6*, Pub. by Reaktion Bks) Consort Bk Sales.

Massotty, Susan, tr. see Benali, Abdelkader.

Massotty, Susan, tr. see Durlacher, Gerhard.

Massotty, Susan, tr. see Frank, Anne.

Massotty, Susan, tr. see Koppeschaar, Carl.

Massoud, H., jt. auth. see Middlesworth, E. M.

Massoud, H. Z., et al, eds. Physics & Chemistry of SiO2 & the Si-SiO2 Interface: 3rd International Symposium. (Proceedings Ser.: Vol. 96-1). (Illus.). 780p. 1996. 98.00 (*1-56677-151-X*) Electrochem Soc.

— Ultra Large Scale Integration Science & Technology: 6th International Symposium. LC 97-190671. (Proceedings Ser.: Vol. 97-3). (Illus.). 678p. 1997. 72.00 (*1-56677-130-7*) Electrochem Soc.

Massoud, Kathleen. Forever in My Heart. 4p. Date not set. pap. 2.50 (*0-7390-0724-6*, 19706) Alfred Pub.

— The Holly & the Ivy. (Alfred Signature Ser.). 4p. 1995. pap. 1.95 (*0-7390-0769-6*, 14226) Alfred Pub.

— The Ocean Deep: For the Right Hand or Left Hand Alone. 1999. pap. 2.50 (*0-7390-0314-3*, 18991) Alfred Pub.

— What Child Is This? Piano Duet. 8p. 1999. pap. 2.95 (*0-7390-0370-4*, 18975) Alfred Pub.

Massoud, LindaLee. Communicating Beyond the Words: Student Workbook. 55p. 1993. spiral bd., wbk. ed. 21.00 (*1-878819-26-7*) SignQuest Pubs.

— Communicating Beyond the Words: Using Non-Verbal & Non-Manual Clues in English & American Sign Language. 65p. 1991. 22.00 (*1-878819-04-6*) SignQuest Pubs.

— Ehlers-Danlos Syndrome: Medical & Practical Information. 72p. 1997. spiral bd. 5.50 (*1-878819-52-6*) SignQuest Pubs.

***Massoud, LindaLee.** Hard Copy Help Desk: The Computer "How-To" Book. 60p. 1999. pap. 15.95 (*1-878819-63-1*) SignQuest Pubs.

Massoud, LindaLee. Practical Demonstrations: Interpreting vs. Transliterating, 5 cass.; set. 299p. 1996. spiral bd. 130.00 incl. VHS (*1-878819-51-8*) SignQuest Pubs.

— Pre-Interpreting Survey: Introduction to Interpreting. 25p. 1993. 34.00 incl. VHS (*1-878819-23-2*) SignQuest Pubs.

— Pre-Interpreting Survey: Peer Evaluation. 13p. 1993. 28.00 incl. VHS (*1-878819-24-0*) SignQuest Pubs.

— Sign Language Crash Course I. 105p. 1998. spiral bd. 29.95 incl. VHS (*1-878819-42-9*) SignQuest Pubs.

— Sign Language Crash Course II. 125p. 1994. spiral bd. 32.00 incl. VHS (*1-878819-46-1*) SignQuest Pubs.

— SignGlyphics: How to Sketch Sign Pictures. (Illus.). 16p. 1993. 21.60 incl. VHS (*1-878819-32-1*) SignQuest Pubs.

***Massoud, LindaLee.** So You Want to Be a Distance Learning Instructor. 80p. 1998. pap. 24.95 (*1-878819-62-3*) SignQuest Pubs.

Massoud, Mary, ed. Literary Inter-Relations: Ireland, Egypt, & the Far East. (Irish Literary Studies: No. 47). 458p. 1996. text 70.00 (*0-86140-377-0*) OUP.

Massoud, Renee, jt. auth. see Mount, Ellis.

Massoud, Tarik F., jt. auth. see Hademenos, George J.

M

Massoudi, M. & Rajagopal, K. R., eds. Recent Advances in Mechanics of Structured Continua, 1993. LC 93-71574. (AMD Series, Vol. 160; MD: Vol. 41). 159p. 1993. pap. 45.00 (*0-7918-1139-5*, G00783) ASME.

Massoulie, Francois. Middle East Conflicts. LC 98-20065. (Illustrated Histories Ser.). (Illus.). 160p. 1999. pap. 15.00 (*1-56656-237-6*, Interlink Bks) Interlink Pub.

Massoulie, Jean, et al, eds. Cholinesterases: Structure, Function, Mechanism, Genetics, & Cell Biology. LC 91-12371. 414p. 1991. text 98.00 (*0-8412-2008-5*, Pub. by Am Chemical) OUP.

Massoum, Ahmed A., jt. ed. see Lieth, Helmut.

Massry, S. G., jt. auth. see Klahr, S.

Massry, Shaul G., ed. The Charles R. Kleeman Festschrift. (Journal: Mineral & Electrolyte Metabolism Ser.: Vol. 12, Nos. 5-6, 1986). (Illus.). lv, 124p. 1987. pap. 61.00 (*3-8055-4454-5*) S Karger.

— Kidney in Systemic Diseases. (Contributions to Nephrology Ser.: Vol. 7). (Illus.). 1977. 29.75 (*3-8055-2445-5*) S Karger.

Massry, Shaul G., et al, eds. Metabolic & Endocrine Disturbances in Renal Diseases. (Contributions to Nephrology Ser.: Vol. 49). (Illus.). viii, 224p. 1986. 29.75 (*3-8055-4143-0*) S Karger.

— Nutrition & Metabolism in Renal Disease. (Journal: Mineral & Electrolyte Metabolism Ser.: Vol. 18, Nos. 2-5, 1992). (Illus.). 268p. 1992. pap. 250.50 (*3-8055-5691-8*) S Karger.

— Nutrition & Metabolism in Renal Disease Vol. 22, No. 1-3: International Society of Renal Nutrition & Metabolism. (Journal: Mineral & Electrolyte Metabolism Ser.: Vol. 22, No. 1-3, 1996). (Illus.). 202p. 1995. pap. 129.75 (*3-8055-6249-7*) S Karger.

— Phosphate & Mineral Homeostasis. LC 86-30431. (Advances in Experimental Medicine & Biology Ser.: Vol. 208). 568p. 1986. 110.00 (*0-306-42398-7*, Plenum Trade) Perseus Pubng.

— Phosphate & Mineral Metabolism. LC 83-13450. 500p. 1984. 95.00 (*0-306-41731-6*, Plenum Trade) Perseus Pubng.

— Proteinuria: American Journal of Nephrology, Vol. 10, Suppl. 1. (Illus.). iv, 166p. 1990. pap. 35.00 (*3-8055-5245-9*) S Karger.

— Recent Advances in Beta Blockade, 1986. (Journal: American Journal of Nephrology Ser.: Vol. 6, Suppl. 2). (Illus.). iv, 116p. 1986. pap. 36.75 (*3-8055-4442-1*) S Karger.

Massry, Shaul G. & Cinotti, G. A., eds. Pathogenesis, Complications & Treatment of Glomerulonephritis. (Journal: American Journal of Nephrology Ser.: Vol. 9, Suppl. 1, 1989). (Illus.). iv, 84p. 1989. pap. 26.25 (*3-8055-4908-3*) S Karger.

Massry, Shaul G. & Coburn, J. W., eds. Uses & Actions of 1,25 Dihyroxyvitamin D3 in Uremia. (Contributions to Nephrology Ser.: Vol. 18). (Illus.). x, 218p. 1980. 29.75 (*3-8055-3064-1*) S Karger.

Massry, Shaul G. & Fleisch, Herbert, eds. Renal Handling of Phosphate. LC 79-18651. (Illus.). 397p. 1980. reprint ed. pap. 123.10 (*0-608-05428-3*, 206589700006) Bks Demand.

Massry, Shaul G. & Fujita, T., eds. New Actions of Parathyroid Hormone. (Illus.). 494p. 1989. 110.00 (*0-306-43418-0*, Plenum Trade) Perseus Pubng.

Massry, Shaul G. & Glassock, Richard J. Massry & Glassock's Textbook of Nephrology. 4th ed. 2,048p. text 299.00 (*0-683-30488-7*) Lppncott W & W.

Massry, Shaul G. & Glassock, Richard J., eds. Textbook of Nephrology, 2 vols., Set. 3rd ed. LC 94-904. (Illus.). 2144p. 1994. 295.00 (*0-683-05621-2*) Lppncott W & W.

Massry, Shaul G. & Ritz, Eberhard. Cardiocirculatory Function in Renal Disease. (Contributions to Nephrology Ser.: Vol. 41). (Illus.). xii, 460p. 1985. 29.75 (*3-8055-3914-2*) S Karger.

— Pathophysiology of Renal Disease. (Contributions to Nephrology Ser.: Vol. 33). (Illus.). viii, 276p. 1982. pap. 29.75 (*3-8055-3534-1*) S Karger.

Massry, Shaul G., jt. auth. see Suki, Wadi N.

Massry, Shaul G., jt. ed. see Gennari, Carlo.

Massry, Shaul G., jt. ed. see Klahr, Saulo.

Massry, Shaul G., jt. ed. see Kopple, Joel D.

Massry, Shaul G., jt. ed. see Suki, Wadi N.

Massucci, Joseph. Code Alpha. 400p. (Orig.). 1997. mass mkt. 5.99 (*0-8439-4192-8*) Dorchester Pub Co.

***Massucci, Joseph.** Is There a Cricket in the House? Wise, Noreen, ed. (Book-a-Day Collection). 32p. 2000. pap. 5.95 (*1-58584-358-X*) Huckleberry CT.

Massucci, Joseph. The Millennium Project. 368p. 2000. mass mkt. 5.99 (*0-8439-4460-9*, Leisure Bks) Dorchester Pub Co.

Massumi, Brian. A User's Guide to Deleuze & Guattari's Capitalism & Schizophrenia. 236p. 1992. 26.95 (*0-262-13282-6*); pap. text 13.95 (*0-262-63143-1*) MIT Pr.

Massumi, Brian, ed. The Politics of Everyday Fear. (Illus.). 341p. (C). 1993. pap. 19.95 (*0-8166-2163-2*); text 49.95 (*0-8166-2162-4*) U of Minn Pr.

Massumi, Brian, jt. auth. see Dean, Kenneth.

Massumi, Brian, tr. see Attali, Jacques.

Massumi, Brian, tr. see De Certeau, Michel.

Massumi, Brian, tr. see Felman, Shoshana.

Massumi, Brian, tr. see Foucault, Michel & Blanchot, Maurice.

Massumi, Brian, tr. see Lyotard, Jean-Francois.

Massumi, Brian, tr. see Lyotard, Jean-Francois & Thebaud, Jean-Loup.

Massy, P. Essentials of Ikebana. 1996. 31.95 (*4-07-974647-4*) Shufu No.

Massy, William F. Resource Allocation in Higher Education. LC 95-48854. (Economics of Education Ser.). 344p. (C). 1996. text 57.50 (*0-472-10686-4*, 10686) U of Mich Pr.

Massy, William F. & Meyerson, Joel W., eds. Revitalizing Higher Education. 120p. (Orig.). (C). 1995. 34.95 (*1-56079-642-1*) Petersons.

— Strategy & Finance in Higher Education. LC 92-12863. 109p. 1992. 29.95 (*1-56079-178-0*) Petersons.

Massy, William F., jt. auth. see Hopkins, David S.

Mast, Abe. Charm Countryview Favorites: Famous Recipes from the Inn. (Illus.). 160p. 14.95 (*0-9637560-0-1*) Charm Cntryview Inn.

Mast, Anne B., jt. auth. see Mast, Robert H.

***Mast, Brian, ed.** How to Manage One Million Dollars or Less. (Illus.). 2000. pap. 14.99 (*0-88270-796-5*) Bridge-Logos.

Mast, Brian, jt. ed. see Belanger, Ronnie.

Mast, Coleen K. Love & Life: A Christian Sexual Morality Guide for Teens. (Illus.). 155p. 1986. pap., teacher ed. 11.95 (*0-89870-108-2*) Ignatius Pr.

— Sex Respect: The Option of True Sexual Freedom. rev. ed. Forestal, Juliene & Norman, Bill, eds. (Illus.). 182p. (J). (gr. 7-9). 1997. pap., teacher ed. 14.00 (*0-945745-06-0*) Respect Inc.

Mast, Coleen K. Sex Respect: The Option of True Sexual Freedom. rev. ed. Forrestal, Juliene, ed. (Illus.). 180p. (J). (gr. 7-9). 1997. pap., teacher ed., wbk. ed. 10.00i (*0-945745-07-9*) Respect Inc.

Mast, Coleen K. Sex Respect: The Option of True Sexual Freedom. rev. ed. Forrestal, Juliene & Norman, Bill, eds. (Illus.). 118p. (YA). (gr. 7-9). 1997. pap. text, student ed. 10.00 (*0-945745-08-7*) Respect Inc.

— Sex Respect: The Option of True Sexual Freedom: A Public Health Guide for Parents. (Illus.). 61p. (Orig.). (J). (gr. 7-9). 1986. pap. text 8.95 (*0-945745-01-X*) Respect Inc.

— Sex Respect: The Option of True Sexual Freedom: A Public Health Guide for Parents. rev. ed. Forrestal, Julienne, ed. (Illus.). 180p. (Orig.). 1990. pap. text 8.95 (*0-945745-04-4*) Respect Inc.

— Sex Respect: The Option of True Sexual Freedom: A Public Health Manual for Teachers. (Illus.). 61p. (Orig.). (J). (gr. 7-9). 1986. pap. 12.95 (*0-945745-00-1*) Respect Inc.

— Sex Respect: The Option of True Sexual Freedom: A Public Health Manual for Teachers. rev. ed. Forrestal, Julienne, ed. (Illus.). 182p. (Orig.). 1990. pap. text 12.95 (*0-945745-03-6*) Respect Inc.

— Sex Respect: The Option of True Sexual Freedom: A Public Health Workbook for Students. (Illus.). 61p. (Orig.). (J). (gr. 7-9). 1986. pap. text 7.95 (*0-945745-02-8*) Respect Inc.

— Sex Respect: The Option of True Sexual Freedom: A Public Health Workbook for Students. rev. ed. Forrestal, Julienne, ed. (Illus.). 118p. (Orig.). (J). (gr. 7-9). 1990. pap. text 8.95 (*0-945745-05-2*) Respect Inc.

***Mast, Coleen K.** The Sex Respect Video Series Workbook: Freedom Through Abstinence. (Illus.). 154p. (YA). (gr. 7-12). 1998. spiral bd., wbk. ed. 10.95i (*0-945745-09-5*, 430) Respect Inc.

Mast, Coleen K., et al. Love & Life: A Christian Sexual Morality Guide for Teens. LC 86-80693. (Illus.). 119p. 1986. pap. 8.95 (*0-89870-106-6*); pap., teacher ed. 6.95 (*0-89870-107-4*) Ignatius Pr.

Mast, Edward. Wolf Child: The Correction of Joseph. 54p. (J). 1999. pap. 7.00 (*0-87602-368-5*) Anchorage.

Mast, Edward, adapted by. Jungalbook. 60p. (J). 1991. pap. 6.00 (*0-87602-291-3*) Anchorage.

Mast, Edward & Bensinger, Lenore. Dinosaurus: Playscript. (J). 1995. 6.00 (*0-87602-327-8*) Anchorage.

Mast, Gerald. Can't Help Singin' The American Musical on Stage & Screen. LC 87-7986. (Illus.). 388p. 1987. 24.95 (*0-87951-283-0*, Pub. by Overlook Pr) Penguin Putnam.

— The Comic Mind: Comedy & the Movies. LC 78-68546. (Illus.). 382p. 1979. pap. text 19.95 (*0-226-50978-8*, P827) U Ch Pr.

— Film, Cinema, Movie: A Theory of Experience. LC 83-4819. (Illus.). xviii, 304p. 1992. pap. 13.95 (*0-226-50974-5*) U Ch Pr.

— Movies: A Short History. 688p. 1996. pap. text 28.00 (*0-205-19670-5*) P-H.

— A Short History of the Movies. 5th ed. 562p. 1992. 35.00 (*0-02-580510-X*) Macmillan.

Mast, Gerald, ed. Bringing up Baby. (Films in Print Ser.). (Illus.). 233p. (Orig.). (C). 1988. text 35.00 (*0-8135-1340-5*) Rutgers U Pr.

— The Movies in Our Midst: Documents in the Cultural History of Films in America. LC 81-16223. (Illus.). (C). 1983. pap. text 17.95 (*0-226-50981-8*) U Ch Pr.

Mast, Gerald & Kawin, Bruce F. A Short History of the Movies. 7th ed. LC 99-11919. 702p. (C). 1999. pap. text 57.00 (*0-205-29685-8*, Longwood Div) Allyn.

Mast, Greg. State Troops & Volunteers: A Photographic Record of North Carolina's Civil War Soldiers. (Illus.). 381p. 1995. reprint ed. 60.00 (*0-86526-264-0*) NC Archives.

Mast, Gregg. The Eucharistic Service of the Catholic Apostolic Church & Its Influence on Reformed Liturgical Renewals of the Nineteenth Century. LC 98-20703. (Drew Studies in Liturgy). 1998. 52.00 (*0-8108-3553-3*) Scarecrow.

— In Remembrance & Hope: The Ministry & Vision of Howard G. Hageman. LC 98-24503. (Historical Series of the Reformed Church in America). 1998. pap. 18.00 (*0-8028-4613-0*) Eerdmans.

Mast, Gregg, et al. And Grace Shines Through: A Journey of Faith Through the Ordinary Stories of Our Lives. LC 97-6409. 1997. pap. write for info. (*0-916466-05-1*) Reformed Church.

Mast, J. W., et al. Planning & Reduction Technique in Fracture Surgery. (Illus.). 270p. 1995. 265.00 (*0-387-16283-6*) Spr-Verlag.

Mast, Jan, jt. auth. see Gingrich, Ruth A.

Mast, Jan, jt. auth. see Stoltzfus, Louise.

***Mast, Jan S.** Amish Doll Patterns: An Amish Family & Friends. LC 99-51553. (Illus.). 128p. 1999. pap. 16.95 (*1-56148-294-3*) Good Bks PA.

Mast, Jeffrey W., et al. Planning & Reduction Technique in Fracture Surgery. 254p. 1995. 265.00 (*3-540-16283-6*) Spr-Verlag.

Mast, Jennie, jt. auth. see Leonhard, Gwen.

Mast, Jennifer A., ed. Small Business Profiles Vol. 2: A Guide to Today's Top Opportunities for Entrepreneurs. 2nd ed. 361p. 1995. 105.00 (*0-8103-9325-5*, 102052) Gale.

— Ward's Private Company Profiles. 750p. 1993. 139.00 (*0-8103-9140-6*, 101789) Gale.

— Ward's Private Company Profiles, Vol. 2. 2nd ed. 699p. 1994. 139.00 (*0-8103-9311-5*) Gale.

Mast, Jim, jt. auth. see Powell, Nancy.

Mast, Joseph A. The Emerging Self: A Celtic Journey. LC 90-42538. (Illus.). 304p. (Orig.). 1991. 22.95 (*0-931832-77-2*) Fithian Pr.

Mast, Lois A. Mennonite Family History Ten-Year Index, 1982-1991. 1992. pap. 23.00 (*1-883294-05-3*) Masthof Pr.

— The Peter Leibundgutt Journal. 118p. 1991. pap. 9.00 (*1-883294-10-X*) Masthof Pr.

Mast, Lois A., jt. auth. see Lemar, J.

Mast, M. J., ed. County Agents Directory. 62nd ed. 1977. 6.50 (*0-686-20517-0*) C L Mast.

Mast, Richard F., ed. see Spencer, Charles W.

Mast, Robert H., compiled by. Detroit Lives. LC 93-51007. (Conflicts in Urban & Regional Development Ser.). 288p. 1994. 69.95 (*1-56639-225-X*); pap. 22.95 (*1-56639-226-8*) Temple U Pr.

Mast, Robert H. & Mast, Anne B. Autobiography of Protest in Hawai'i. (Illus.). 456p. 1997. pap. 19.95 (*0-8248-1784-2*) UH Pr.

Mast, Roderic B., et al. Lemurs of Madagascar. LC 94-72352. (Illus.). 360p. 1995. pap. 25.00 (*1-881173-08-9*, Pub. by Conser Intl) U Ch Pr.

Mast, William. Faith & Medicine. 78p. (Orig.). 1995. pap. text. write for info. (*0-9648937-0-3*) W Mast.

Mastache, Alba G., et al, eds. Arqueologia Mesoamericana Vol. II: Homenaje a William T. Sanders, II. (ENG & SPA., Illus.). 400p. 1996. pap. 15.00 (*968-29-5193-3*, IN79, Pub. by Dir Gen Pubicaiones) UPLAAP.

Mastache, Alba G., et al. Las Industrias Liticas Coyotlatelco en el Area de Tula. 297p. 1990. pap. 14.00 (*968-6487-12-3*, IN041) UPLAAP.

Mastaglia, Frank L., jt. ed. see Kakulas, Byron A.

Mastaglia, Frank L., jt. ed. see Walton, John.

Mastai, Boleslaw. The Stripes & Stars: The Evolution of the American Flag. (Illus.). 63p. 1999. reprint ed. pap. text 17.00 (*0-7881-6089-3*) DIANE Pub.

Mastalerz, Maria, et al. Coalbed Methane: Scientific, Environmental & Economic Evaluation. LC 99-20461. 1999. write for info. (*0-7923-5698-5*) Kluwer Academic.

Mastalerz, Maria, jt. auth. see Glirkson, Miryam.

Mastalia, Francesco & Pagano, Alfonse. Dreads. LC 99-32436. (Illus.). 144p. 1999. 35.00 (*1-57965-134-8*, 85134) Artisan.

***Mastalia, Francesco & Pagano, Alfonse.** Dreads. LC 99-32436. (Illus.). 144p. 1999. pap. 19.95 (*1-57965-150-X*, 85150) Artisan.

Mastandrea, Paolo. De Fine Versus: Repertorio Di Clausole Riccorenti Nella Poesia Dattilica Latina Dalle Origini a Sidonio Apollinare, 2 vols. (Alpha-Omega, Reihe A Ser.: Bd. CXXXII). (GER.). xxiv, 1172p. 1993. write for info. incl. 3.5 hd (*3-487-09693-5*) G Olms Pubs.

Mastandrea, Paolo, et al. Maximianus: Concordantiae in Maximianum. (GER., Illus.). vi, 196p. 1995. write for info. (*3-487-10019-3*) G Olms Pubs.

Mastanduno, Michael. Economic Containment: CoCom & the Politics of East-West Trade. LC 92-52766. (Cornell Studies in Political Economy). 376p. 1992. 49.95 (*0-8014-2709-6*); pap. text 22.50 (*0-8014-9996-8*) Cornell U Pr.

Mastanduno, Michael, jt. auth. see Kapstein, Ethan B.

Mastanduno, Michael, jt. ed. see Lyons, Gene M.

Mastascusa, E. J. Computer-Assisted Network & System Analysis. LC 87-29831. 318p. reprint ed. pap. 98.60 (*0-7837-2812-3*, 205766000006) Bks Demand.

Mastein, Christof H. Von, see Von Mastein, Christof H.

Mastel, Greg. American Trade Laws after the Uruguay Round. LC 96-11403. 220p. (C). (gr. 13). 1996. text 69.95 (*1-56324-895-6*) M E Sharpe.

Mastel, Greg. American Trade Laws after the Uruguay Round. LC 96-11403. 220p. (C). (gr. 13). 1996. pap. text 32.95 (*1-56324-896-4*) M E Sharpe.

— Antidumping Laws & the U. S. Economy. LC 97-51248. (Illus.). 232p. (C). (gr. 13). 1998. pap. text 30.95 (*0-7656-0326-8*) M E Sharpe.

Mastel, Greg. Antidumping Laws & the U.S. Economy. LC 97-51248. (Illus.). 232p. (C). (gr. 13). 1998. text 72.95 (*0-7656-0325-X*) M E Sharpe.

— The Rise of the Chinese Economy: The Middle Kingdom Emerges. LC 96-53292. 232p. (C). (gr. 13). 1997. text 74.95 (*0-7656-0017-X*); pap. text 34.95 (*0-7656-0018-8*) M E Sharpe.

Masteler, R. A., tr. see Zharkov, V. N.

Mastella, G. & Quinton, P. M., eds. Cellular & Molecular Basis of Cystic Fibrosis. (Illus.). 1988. 20.00 (*0-911302-63-8*) San Francisco Pr.

Masteller, James, jt. auth. see Stoop, David.

Masteller, Richard N. Auto as Icon. (Illus.). (Orig.). (C). 1979. pap. 8.00 (*1-880269-02-3*) D H Sheehan.

— We, the People? Satiric Prints of the 1930s. LC 89-50444. (Illus.). 75p. (Orig.). (C). 1989. pap. 5.00 (*1-880269-05-8*) D H Sheehan.

Mastelli, Rick, ed. see Cooke, Ned & Dunnigan, John.

Mastellone, L. Legal & Commercial Dictionary. (ENG & ITA.). 173p. 1980. write for info. (*0-8288-0397-8*, F 22010) Fr & Eur.

Mastellone, Salvo, jt. auth. see Di Scala, Spencer M.

Masten, Ann, ed. see Pick, A. D.

Masten, Arthur H. History of Cohoes, N.Y. (Illus.). 327p. 1993. reprint ed. lib. bdg. 39.50 (*0-8328-2877-7*) Higginson Bk Co.

Masten, David, jt. auth. see Bierman, Todd.

Masten, Jeffrey & Stallybrass, Peter. Language Machines: Technologies of Literary & Cultural Production. LC 97-7321. (English Institute Ser.). (Illus.). 288p. (C). 1997. pap. 19.99 (*0-415-91864-2*) Routledge.

Masten, Jeffrey & Stallybrass, Peter, eds. Language Machines: Technologies of Literary & Cultural Production. LC 97-7321. (English Institute Ser.). (Illus.). 288p. (C). 1997. 75.00 (*0-415-91863-4*) Routledge.

Masten, Marilyn. Waters of Creation. LC 98-85955. 325p. 1998. 25.00 (*0-7388-0000-7*); pap. 15.00 (*0-7388-0032-5*) Xlibris Corp.

Masten, Michael, et al, eds. Modern Control Systems. 500p. 1996. student ed., wbk. ed. 329.00 (*0-7803-2302-5*, HL5714) Inst Electrical.

***Masten, Michael K. & Stockum, Larry A., eds.** Acquisition, Tracking & Pointing XIII. 430p. 1999. pap. text 92.00 (*0-8194-3166-4*) SPIE.

Masten, Michael K. & Stockum, Larry A., eds. Acquisition, Tracking & Pointing XII. (Proceedings of SPIE Ser.: Vol. 3365). 350p. 1998. 89.00 (*0-8194-2814-0*) SPIE.

— Acquisition, Tracking, & Pointing XI. 46p. 1997. pap. 89.00 (*0-8194-2501-X*) SPIE.

— Selected Papers on Precision Stabilization & Tracking Systems for Acquisition, Pointing, & Control Applications. LC 96-844. (Milestone Ser.: Vol. MS 123). 1996. 118.00 (*0-8194-2259-2*) SPIE.

Masten, Ric. I Know It Isn't Funny but I Love to Make You Laugh: Including the Walt Whitman Extention. 2nd rev. ed. LC 95-92722. (Illus.). 208p. 1996. pap. 12.00 (*0-931104-41-6*) SunInk Pubn.

— Let It Be a Dance. 176p. 1997. pap. 12.95 (*0-931104-45-9*) SunInk Pubn.

— Notice Me! LC 85-82615. 100p. 1986. pap. 6.00 (*0-931104-17-3*) SunInk Pubn.

— Ric Masten Speaking. LC 90-33891. (Illus.). 160p. (Orig.). 1990. pap. 8.00 (*0-918949-11-4*) Masten.

— Stark Naked. LC 80-51980. 1980. 10.00 (*0-931104-04-1*); pap. 6.00 (*0-931104-40-8*) SunInk Pubn.

— Voice of the Hive. rev. ed. LC 78-59786. (Orig.). 1978. pap. 6.00 (*0-931104-02-5*) SunInk Pubn.

Masten, Scott E., ed. Case Studies in Contracting & Organization. (Illus.). 360p. 1996. text 59.95 (*0-19-509251-1*) OUP.

— Case Studies in Contracting & Organization. (Illus.). 360p. (C). 1996. pap. text 34.95 (*0-19-509252-X*) OUP.

Masten, Scott E., jt. ed. see Williamson, Oliver E.

Masten, Yondel. Obstetric Survival Handbook. LC 98-229378. (Illus.). 300p. 1998. per. 39.95 (*1-56930-083-6*) Skidmore Roth Pub.

Mastenbroek, Willem F. Conflict Management & Organization Development. fac. ed. LC 87-10463. 176p. 1987. reprint ed. pap. 54.60 (*0-7837-8285-3*, 204906700009) Bks Demand.

Master, Arthur M., et al. The Electrocardiogram & Chest X-Ray in Diseases of the Heart. LC 63-16703. (Illus.). 565p. reprint ed. 175.20 (*0-608-16113-6*, 201456300096) Bks Demand.

Master Hsuan Hua, Venerable. The Shurangama Sutra Vol. 8: The Fifty Skandha-Demon States, No.8. Buddhist Text Translation Society Staff, tr. LC 77-88845. (Illus.). 402p. 1997. 20.00 (*0-88139-401-7*) Buddhist Text.

— The Wonderful Dharma Lotus Flower Sutra Vol. 11, Chapter 14: Happily Dwelling Conduct, No.11. Buddhist Text Translation Society Staff, tr. LC 77-87782. (Illus.). 210p. 1998. 10.00 (*0-88139-443-2*) Buddhist Text.

— The Wonderful Dharma Lotus Flower Sutra Vol. 12: Chapter 15 Welling Forth from the Earth & Chapter 16 & the Thus Come One's Life Span. Buddhist Text Translation Society Staff, tr. LC 77-87782. (Illus.). 233p. 1998. 10.00 (*0-88139-444-0*) Buddhist Text.

— The Wonderful Dharma Lotus Flower Sutra Vol. 16, Chapters 26-28: Chapter 26 Dharani Chapter 27 The Past Deeds of King Wonderful Adornment Chapter 28 The Encouragement of Universal Worthy Bodhisattva. Buddhist Text Translation Society Staff, tr. LC 77-87782. (Illus.). 121p. 1999. 10.00 (*0-88139-448-3*) Buddhist Text.

Master Hsuan Hua, Venerable & Buddhist Text Translation Society Staff, trs. The Wonderful Dharma Lotus Flower Sutra Vol. 15, Chapter 25: Chapter 25 The Universal Door of Guanshiyin Bodhisattva, No.15. LC 77-87782. (Illus.). 193p. 1999. 10.00 (*0-88139-447-5*) Buddhist Text.

Master Hua, Tripitaka. Herein Lies the Treasure-Trove, Vol. 1. Buddhist Text Translation Society Staff, tr. from CHI. (Illus.). 153p. (Orig.). 1983. pap. 6.50 (*0-88139-001-1*) Buddhist Text.

— Listen to Yourself; Think Everything Over, Vol. II. Buddhist Text Translation Society Staff, tr. from CHI. 172p. 1983. pap. 7.00 (*0-88139-010-0*) Buddhist Text.

— Records of High Sanghans, Vol. I. Buddhist Text Translation Society Staff, tr. from CHI. 146p. (Orig.). 1983. pap. 7.00 (*0-88139-012-7*) Buddhist Text.

— Water Mirror Reflecting Heaven. Buddhist Text Translation Society Staff, tr. from CHI. (Illus.). 77p. (Orig.). 1982. pap. 4.00 (*0-88139-501-3*) Buddhist Text.

Master, John R. Un Estudio del Tabernaculo. Meyer, Richard, ed. (Adult Sunday School Ser.). (SPA.). 102p. 1993. 4.40 (*1-879892-37-5*) Editorial Bautista.

Master Mind Editorial Staff. 2000 Mastermind Goal Achievers Journal. 220p. 1999. 26.95 (*0-88152-160-4*) Master Mind.

Master, Myo-Bong. Gateway to Son (Ch'an) Hye-Am Choi, ed. LC 86-50750. (CHI & KOR.). 359p. (Orig.). 1986. 21.95 (*0-938647-00-8*) Western Son Acad.

Master Ni, Hua-Ching. The Footsteps of the Mystical Child. LC 86-60062. 180p. (C). 1986. pap. text 9.50 (*0-937064-11-4*) SevenStar Comm.

Master, Peter, jt. ed. see Brinton, Donna M.

Master, Peter A. Science, Medicine & Technology: English Grammar & Technical Writing. (Illus.). 320p. (C). 1986. pap. text 16.00 (*0-13-795469-7*) P-H.

— Systems in English Grammar: An Introduction for Language Teachers. LC 95-15946. 480p. (C). 1995. pap. 36.67 (*0-13-156837-X*) P-H.

***Master, Peter A. & Brinton, Donna.** New Ways in English for Specific Purposes. LC 98-60381. (New Ways in Tesol Ser.: 2). 337 p. 1998. 29.95 (*0-939791-49-8*) Tchrs Eng Spkrs.

Master Publishing, Inc. Staff. Installing Your Own Telephones. 2nd ed. (Illus.). 176p. (C). 1986. pap. text 1.80 (*0-8359-3291-5*) P-H.

— Installing Your Own Telephones. 2nd ed. (Illus.). 172p. 1986. 15.50 (*0-8359-3292-3*) P-H.

Master Publishing Staff. Basic Home Theater. (Illus.). 216p. 1998. pap. 24.95 (*0-7906-1154-6*) Prompt Publns.

— The Right Antenna. 2nd ed. (Illus.). 136p. 1998. pap. 24.95 (*0-7906-1152-X*) Prompt Publns.

Master, Roy. How to Survive Your Parents. LC 82-71162. 190p. 1982. pap. 15.95 (*0-933900-10-4*) Foun Human Under.

Master, T. W. Hairdressing in Theory & Practice. LC 84-23946. 280p. 1984. pap. 16.95 (*0-291-39627-5*, Pub. by Gower) Ashgate Pub Co.

Master Teacher Staff. Lesson Plans & Modifications for Inclusion & Collaborative Classrooms. LC 95-79721. 203p. 1995. ring bd. 59.95 (*0-914607-37-5*) Master Tchr.

***Master Teachers Staff & Darlen-De.** The Year of Change. Domzalski, John & Kaplan, Steven, eds. 2000. 11.00 (*0-9672894-1-6*) Twin Angel.

— The Year of Truth. Domzalski, John & Kaplan, Steven, eds. 109p. 1999. pap. 11.00 (*0-9672894-0-8*) Twin Angel.

Master, Wakefield. The Complete Plays of the Wakefield Master. Brown, John R., ed. 1983. pap. 10.95 (*0-87830-584-X*, Thtre Arts Bks) Routledge.

Masteralexis, Lisa P., et al. Principles & Practice of Sport Management. LC 98-12301. 522p. 1998. 49.00 (*0-8342-1021-5*, 10215) Aspen Pub.

MasterCard International Staff & College Student Editors. Mastering (& Succeeding with) the Job Hunt. 149p. (C). 1994. write for info. (*0-9642751-0-4*) Mstercard Intl.

Masterdy, E., ed. One Hundred Alive & Stay Alive! Double Your Life Expectancy. 162p. 1984. 12.95 (*0-8159-6415-3*) Devin.

***Masterfano, Michele.** Managing Transition & Change. 124p. 2000. write for info. (*1-58692-033-2*) Copyright Mgmt.

Masterfield, Maxine. Painting the Spirit of Nature. (Illus.). 144p. 1996. pap. text 24.95 (*0-8230-3867-X*) Watsn-Guptill.

Masterjohn, Ralph J., ed. see Sylligardakis, Titus M.

Masterjohn, Raphael, ed. see Owcharuk, Volodymyr.

Masterman, A. H. & Boyce, R. M. Plumbing & Mechanical Services, Pt. 1. (Illus.). 246p. (C). 1984. pap. 40.00 (*0-7487-0368-3*, Pub. by S Thornes Pubs) Trans-Atl Phila.

— Plumbing & Mechanical Services, Pt. 2. 2nd ed. (Illus.). 224p. (C). 1990. pap. 36.50 (*0-7487-0232-6*, Pub. by S Thornes Pubs) Trans-Atl Phila.

— Plumbing & Mechanical Services, Pt. 3. 3rd ed. 232p. (C). 1990. pap. 36.50 (*0-7487-0233-4*, Pub. by S Thornes Pubs) Trans-Atl Phila.

***Masterman, J. C.** Double-Cross System: The Incredible True Story of How Nazi Spies Were Turned into Double Agents. 2000. pap. 14.95 (*1-58574-130-2*) Lyon Press.

Masterman, J. C. An Oxford Tragedy. (Black Dagger Crime Ser.). 192p. 1997. 19.50 (*0-7451-8707-2*, Black Dagger) Chivers N Amer.

Masterman, L. C. F. G. Masterman. (Illus.). 400p. 1968. 25.00 (*0-7146-1565-X*, Pub. by F Cass Pubs) Intl Spec Bk.

Masterman, Len. Teaching the Media. 2nd ed. (Comedia Bk.). 220p. (C). 1988. pap. 18.99 (*0-415-03974-6*, A4918) Routledge.

Masterman, Lucy B. C. F. G. Masterman: A Biography. LC 68-88329. (Illus.). 400p. 1968. reprint ed. 49.50 (*0-678-05187-9*) Kelley.

***Masterman-Smith, Virginia.** First Mate Tate. LC 00-35867. (Illus.). (J). 2000. write for info. (*0-7614-5075-0*) Marshall Cavendish.

Masterman, Sylvia. The Origins of International Rivalry in Samoa, 1845-1884. LC 75-35205. reprint ed. 32.50 (*0-404-14228-1*) AMS Pr.

Masterman, W. E. An Introduction to Building Procurement Systems. (Illus.). 192p. (C). 1992. 75.00 (*0-419-17720-5*, E & FN Spon) Routledge.

— An Introduction to Building Procurement Systems. LC 92-17960. 1992. write for info. (*0-442-31586-4*, E & FN Spon) Routledge.

Mastern, Jeffrey. Textual Intercourse: Collaboration, Authorship, & Sexualities in Renaissance Drama. LC 96-2949. (Cambridge Studies in Renaissance Literature & Culture: No. 14). (Illus.). 236p. (C). 1997. text 59.95 (*0-521-57260-6*); pap. text 19.95 (*0-521-58920-7*) Cambridge U Pr.

Masteroff, Joe, et al. Cabaret: The Illustrated Book & Lyrics. Sunshine, Linda, ed. LC 99-22945. (Illus.). 128p. 1999. 29.95 (*1-55704-383-3*) Newmarket.

Masterpasqua, Frank & Perna, Phyllis A., eds. The Psychological Meaning of Chaos: Translating Theory into Practice. LC 97-12954. 323p. 1997. text 39.95 (*1-55798-429-8*, 431-7910) Am Psychol.

Masters. Apply & Interview for a Job. (YA - Adult Education Ser.). 1993. pap. 5.95 (*0-538-70844-1*) S-W Pub.

— Career Planning & Development. (YA - Adult Education Ser.). 1992. pap. 9.95 (*0-538-70566-3*) S-W Pub.

— Finding & Holding a Job. (YA - Adult Education Ser.). 1992. pap. 9.95 (*0-538-70570-1*) S-W Pub.

— Listening & Speaking for Job & Personal Use. (YA - Adult Education Ser.). 1992. pap. 9.95 (*0-538-70568-X*) S-W Pub.

— Listening Skills. (YA - Adult Education Ser.). 1993. pap. 5.95 (*0-538-70777-1*) S-W Pub.

Masters. Sangamon. text. write for info. (*0-8052-9620-4*) H Holt & Co.

— She Must Have Known. 2000. pap. 12.95 (*0-552-54536-8*, Pub. by Transworld Publishers Ltd) Trafalgar.

Masters. Speaking Skills. (YA - Adult Education Ser.). 1993. pap. 5.95 (*0-538-70778-X*) S-W Pub.

Masters & Johnson. Heterosexuality. LC 97-49906. 608p. 1998. 11.99 (*0-517-18938-0*) Random Hse Value.

Masters, June, jt. auth. see Brown, Maureen.

***Masters, Aaron.** Queen of Aces. 300p. 2000. pap. 14.95 (*1-929976-02-X*, Pub. by Top Pubns) Herveys Bklink.

***Masters, Alexis.** The Giuliana Legacy: A Novel. 500p. 2000. pap. 14.95 (*1-55874-785-0*) Health Comm.

Masters, Anthony. The Best of the First Ten Years of the Samoyed Quarterly. deluxe ed. (Illus.). 480p. 1995. 75.00 (*0-614-04547-9*) Donald R Hoflin.

***Masters, Anthony.** The Good & the Faithful Servant. large type ed. 320p. 2000. 20.99 (*1-84137-048-7*, Pub. by Mgna Lrg Print) Ulverscroft.

— Greek Myths & Legends. LC 99-27849. 2000. 18.95 (*0-87226-609-5*, 66095B, P Bedrick Books) NTC Contemp Pub Co.

— I Want Him Dead. large type unabridged ed. 1999. 25.95 (*0-7531-5562-1*, 155621, Pub. by ISIS Lrg Prnt) ISIS Pub.

— Possessed. 144p. 1999. pap. (*1-86039-816-2*, Pub. by Orchard Bks) Raincoast Bk.

— Roman Myths. 64p. 2000. write for info. (*0-87226-607-9*, 66079B, P Bedrick Books) NTC Contemp Pub Co.

Masters, Anthony. Roman Myths & Legends. LC 99-25761. (Illus.). 2000. 18.95 (*0-87226-608-7*, 66087B, P Bedrick Books) NTC Contemp Pub Co.

— Serpent Mound. (J). 14.00 (*0-671-79976-2*) S&S Bks Yung.

— Survival. LC 97-24773. (True Stories Ser.). 352p. (YA). (gr. 7 up). 1997. pap. text 7.95 (*0-8069-9657-9*) Sterling.

Masters, Anthony, jt. auth. see James, David.

Masters, Anthony, jt. auth. see Masters, Roger D.

Masters, Ariel, jt. auth. see Lord, Hunter.

Masters, Barry R. Selected Papers on Confocal Microscopy. LC 96-41849. (SPIE Milestone Ser.). 1996. write for info. (*0-8194-2372-6*) SPIE.

Masters, Barry R., ed. Noninvasive Diagnostic Techniques in Ophthalmology. (Illus.). 632p. 1990. 199.00 (*0-387-96992-6*) Spr-Verlag.

Masters, Brian. Killing for Company: The Story of a Man Addicted to Murder. 400p. 1994. mass mkt. 5.99 (*0-440-22043-2*) Dell.

— Moliere Student's Guide to European Literature. (C). 1995. pap. text 7.50 (*0-435-37570-9*, 37570) Heinemann.

Masters, Brien. Patter-Paws the Fox: And Other Stories. (Illus.). 64p. (J). 1992. 10.95 (*0-904693-35-X*, Pub. by Temple Lodge) Anthroposophic.

— A Round of Rounds for the 52 Weeks of the Year: Wir Singen Durch die Jahresrunde, Kanons fur die 52 Wochen. Meuss, Anna R. & Vohringer, Dietgard, trs. 96p. (J). 1990. pap. 15.95 (*0-904693-26-0*, Pub. by Temple Lodge) Anthroposophic.

— Second Waldorf Song Book. pap. 11.95 (*0-86315-135-3*, 1736, Pub. by Floris Bks) Anthroposophic.

***Masters, Brien.** Trumpets of Happiness: And Other Stories. (Illus.). 80p. 1998. pap. 14.95 (*0-904693-96-1*, Pub. by Temple Lodge) Anthroposophic.

Masters, Brien, ed. The Waldorf Song Book. (J). 1988. pap. 8.50 (*0-86315-059-4*, 20243, Pub. by Floris Bks) Gryphon Hse.

Masters, C. L. Amyloid Protein Precursor in Development, Aging, & Alzheimer's Disease. LC 94-4461. (Research & Perspectives in Alzheimer's Disease Ser.). 1994. 132.00 (*0-387-57788-2*) Spr-Verlag.

Masters, Carol. The Peace Terrorist: And Other Stories. LC 93-83979. (Minnesota Voices Project Ser.). 106p. (Orig.). 1994. pap. 9.95 (*0-89823-156-6*) New Rivers Pr.

Masters, Carol, ed. see Goldin, Phyllis R. & Brown, Wanta L.

Masters, Charles J. Glidermen of Neptune: The American D-Day Glider Attack. LC 95-11452. (Illus.). 128p. (C). 1995. 41.95 (*0-8093-2007-X*); pap. 21.95 (*0-8093-2008-8*) S Ill U Pr.

Masters, Christopher. Dali. (Color Library). (Illus.). 128p. (C). 1995. pap. 14.95 (*0-7148-3338-X*, Pub. by Phaidon Press) Phaidon Pr.

Masters, Colin. Sniper. text 22.95 (*0-312-26098-9*) St Martin.

Masters, Colin & Crane, Denis. The Peroxisome: A Vital Organelle. (Illus.). 304p. (C). 1995. text 74.95 (*0-521-48212-7*) Cambridge U Pr.

Masters, Colin & Stroud, Alan. Transfer Pricing. 151p. 1991. boxed set 170.00 (*0-406-00112-X*, U.K., MICHIE) LEXIS Pub.

Masters-Cullen, Roberta, jt. ed. see Gottesman, Roberta.

Masters, Debra & Masters, Will. Business by Design: A Principle Based Business Community. 44p. (Orig.). (C). 1997. pap. text. write for info. (*1-886112-06-1*) Antares.

Masters, Dexter & Way, Katherine, eds. One World or None. LC 71-37858. (Essay Index Reprint Ser.). 1977. reprint ed. 25.95 (*0-8369-2610-2*) Ayer.

Masters, Donald C. A Short History of Canada. LC 80-12913. (Anvil Ser.). 192p. 1980. reprint ed. pap. text 11.50 (*0-89874-201-3*) Krieger.

— The Winnipeg General Strike. LC 51-5058. (Canadian University Paperbooks Ser.: No. 136). (Illus.). 179p. reprint ed. pap. 55.50 (*0-8357-4160-5*, 203693400007) Bks Demand.

Masters, Edgar Lee. Across Spoon River. (Prairie State Bks.). 456p. 14.95 (*0-252-06051-2*) U of Ill Pr.

— Across Spoon River: An Autobiography. (American Biography Ser.). 426p. 1991. reprint ed. lib. bdg. 89.00 (*0-7812-8276-4*) Rprt Serv.

— Along the Illinois. 86p. reprint ed. pap. text 4.95 (*1-877869-20-1*) Mason Cnty Hist Proj.

— Althea: A Play in Four Acts. (Collected Works of Edgar Lee Masters). 120p. 1999. reprint ed. lib. bdg. 88.00 (*1-58201-763-8*, c0763) Classic Bks.

— The Blood of the Prophets. (Collected Works of Edgar Lee Masters). 112p. 1999. reprint ed. lib. bdg. 88.00 (*1-58201-764-6*, c0764) Classic Bks.

— A Book of Verses. (Collected Works of Edgar Lee Masters). 207p. 1999. reprint ed. lib. bdg. 98.00 (*1-58201-765-4*, c0765) Classic Bks.

— The Bread of Idleness: A Play in Four Acts. (Collected Works of Edgar Lee Masters). 173p. 1999. reprint ed. lib. bdg. 88.00 (*1-58201-766-2*, c0766) Classic Bks.

— Children in the Market Place. (Collected Works of Edgar Lee Masters). 468p. 1999. reprint ed. lib. bdg. 118.00 (*1-58201-767-0*, c0767) Classic Bks.

— Domesday Book. (Collected Works of Edgar Lee Masters). 369p. 1999. reprint ed. lib. bdg. 108.00 (*1-58201-768-9*, c0768) Classic Bks.

— Eileen: A Play in Three Acts. (Collected Works of Edgar Lee Masters). 88p. 1999. reprint ed. lib. bdg. 88.00 (*1-58201-769-7*, c0769) Classic Bks.

— The Enduring River: Edgar Lee Masters' Uncollected Spoon River Poems. 104p. (C). 1991. 21.95 (*0-8093-1685-4*) S Ill U Pr.

— The Golden Fleece of California: An Epic Gold Rush Saga. (Illus.). 80p. 1998. pap. 13.95 (*1-885983-28-X*) Turtle Point Pr.

— The Great Valley. (Collected Works of Edgar Lee Masters). 280p. 1999. reprint ed. lib. bdg. 98.00 (*1-58201-770-0*, c0770) Classic Bks.

— Lincoln the Man. 2nd rev. ed. LC 97-40670. (Illus.). 536p. 1997. 29.95 (*0-9623842-6-7*) Fndtn Amer Ed.

— Mark Twain: A Portrait. LC 66-15216. 1938. 30.00 (*0-8196-0171-3*) Biblo.

— Mitch Miller. (Collected Works of Edgar Lee Masters). 269p. 1999. reprint ed. lib. bdg. 98.00 (*1-58201-771-9*, c0771) Classic Bks.

— The New Spoon Rivers. (Collected Works of Edgar Lee Masters). 324p. 1999. reprint ed. lib. bdg. 98.00 (*1-58201-772-7*, c0772) Classic Bks.

— The New Star Chamber & Other Essays. (Collected Works of Edgar Lee Masters). 213p. 1999. reprint ed. lib. bdg. 88.00 (*1-58201-779-4*, c0779) Classic Bks.

— The Open Sea. (Collected Works of Edgar Lee Masters). 302p. 1999. reprint ed. lib. bdg. 88.00 (*1-58201-773-5*, c0773) Classic Bks.

— The Sangamon. LC 88-17510. (Prairie State Bks.). (Illus.). 296p. 1988. 13.95 (*0-252-06038-5*) U of Ill Pr.

— Skeeters Kirby. (Collected Works of Edgar Lee Masters). 394p. 1999. reprint ed. lib. bdg. 108.00 (*1-58201-774-3*, c0774) Classic Bks.

— Songs & Satires. (Collected Works of Edgar Lee Masters). 172p. 1999. reprint ed. lib. bdg. 88.00 (*1-58201-775-1*, c0775) Classic Bks.

Masters, Edgar Lee. Sponn River Antholgy. 1997. mass mkt. 4.99 (*0-8125-3904-4*) Tor Bks.

Masters, Edgar Lee. Spoon River Anthology. 1976. 20.95 (*0-8488-1430-4*) Amereon Ltd.

— Spoon River Anthology. 320p. 1992. mass mkt. 4.95 (*0-451-52530-2*, Sig Classics) NAL.

— Spoon River Anthology. 328p. 1987. 35.00 (*0-02-581780-9*) S&S Trade.

— Spoon River Anthology. 1997. per. 9.00 (*0-684-83825-7*) S&S Trade Pap.

— Spoon River Anthology. 1962. 14.10 (*0-606-01396-2*, Pub. by Turtleback) Demco.

— Spoon River Anthology. 22.95 (*1-56723-075-X*) Yestermorrow.

— Spoon River Anthology. 345p. 1983. reprint ed. lib. bdg. 27.95 (*0-89966-456-3*) Buccaneer Bks.

— Spoon River Anthology. (Collected Works of Edgar Lee Masters). 248p. 1999. reprint ed. lib. bdg. 88.00 (*1-58201-776-X*, c0776) Classic Bks.

— Spoon River Anthology. unabridged ed. 144p. 1992. reprint ed. pap. text 1.50 (*0-486-27275-3*) Dover.

— Spoon River Anthology: An Annotated Edition. Hallwas, John E., ed. (Prairie State Bks.). (Illus.). 464p. 1992. 29.95 (*0-252-01561-4*) U of Ill Pr.

— Spoon River Anthology: An Annotated Edition. Hallwas, John E., ed. (Prairie State Bks.). (Illus.). 464p. 1993. pap. text 15.95 (*0-252-06363-5*) U of Ill Pr.

— Starved Rock. (Collected Works of Edgar Lee Masters). 187p. 1999. reprint ed. lib. bdg. 88.00 (*1-58201-777-8*, c0777) Classic Bks.

— Toward the Gulf. (Collected Works of Edgar Lee Masters). 192p. 1999. reprint ed. lib. bdg. 98.00 (*1-58201-778-6*, c0778) Classic Bks.

— Vachel Lindsay: A Poet in America. LC 68-56452. (Illus.). 1969. reprint ed. pap. 25.00 (*0-8196-0239-6*) Biblo.

— Whitman. LC 68-22695. 1968. reprint ed. 30.00 (*0-8196-0210-8*) Biblo.

Masters, Elaine A. Those Women in White. (Illus.). 386p. 1989. 40.00 (*0-685-26798-9*) E A Masters.

Masters, G. N., jt. auth. see Keeves, J. P.

Masters, Geoff, jt. auth. see Forster, Margaret.

Masters, Geofferey. Profiles of Learning. (C). 1990. pap. 55.00 (*0-86431-067-6*, Pub. by Aust Council Educ Res) St Mut.

Masters, Geofferey N., jt. auth. see Wright, Benjamin D.

Masters, George M., ed. Medieval & Renaissance Studies: Proceedings of the Southeastern Institute of Medieval & Renaissance Studies, Summer 1979. LC 68-54949. (Medieval & Renaissance Monograph: No. 10). (Illus.). 132p. reprint ed. pap. 41.00 (*0-7837-2467-5*, 204262000005) Bks Demand.

Masters, George R., jt. auth. see Allan, Francis C.

Masters, Gilbert M. Introduction to Environmental Engineering & Science. 2nd ed. LC 97-27372. 651p. (C). 1997. 100.00 (*0-13-155384-4*) P-H.

Masters, Helen. The Little Green Tree. (Illus.). 24p. (J). (gr. k-6). 1999. pap. 7.00 (*0-8059-4636-5*) Dorrance.

Masters, Hilary. An American Marriage. LC 81-69038. 1982. reprint ed. 11.00 (*0-941038-00-9*) Coyne & Chenoweth.

— Clemmons. 1991. 10.00 (*0-941038-05-X*) Coyne & Chenoweth.

— Cooper. 1993. reprint ed. pap. text 11.00 (*0-941038-08-4*) Coyne & Chenoweth.

— Hammertown Tales. LC 85-51667. 150p. 1986. 15.00 (*0-913773-18-2*) S Wright.

— Hammertown Tales. LC 85-51667. 128p. 1991. reprint ed. 15.00 (*0-941038-02-5*) Coyne & Chenoweth.

— Home Is the Exile. LC 95-16898. 256p. 1996. 24.00 (*1-877946-73-7*) Permanent Pr.

— In Montaigne's Tower: Essays. LC 99-47635. 192p. 2000. pap. 19.95 (*0-8262-1266-2*) U of Mo Pr.

— Last Stands: Notes from Memory. 1991. 15.00 (*0-941038-04-1*) Coyne & Chenoweth.

— Strickland. 1991. reprint ed. 10.00 (*0-941038-03-3*) Coyne & Chenoweth.

M

Masters, Hilary, contrib. by. In Montaigne's Tower: Essays. 192p. 2000. 34.95 (*0-8262-1262-X*) U of Mo Pr.

Masters, J. G. Sarah Elizabeth: A Tale of Old Colorado. 208p. 1985. 13.95 (*0-940672-29-4*) Shearer Pub.

Masters, Jack. Masters Family History, 1691 to 1989. (Illus.). 576p. 1989. 37.50 (*0-9622761-0-3*) J Masters.

— The Original Basement Waterproofing Handbook. (Illus.). 120p. 1996. pap. 31.95 (*0-9664036-0-6*) Mstr Jack Pubs.

— Smith & Allied Families History: Beaty - Bowers - Hull. (Illus.). 250p. 1991. 35.00 (*0-9622761-1-1*) J Masters.

Masters, James. The Slave Trade. 256p. 1998. mass mkt. 9.95 (*0-352-33228-X*, Pub. by BLA4) London Brdge.

— Working in Sport: How to Use Your Sport to Gain Employment in the UK or Abroad. (Jobs & Careers Ser.). (Illus.). 144p. 1999. pap. 19.95 (*1-85703-427-9*, Pub. by How To Bks) Trans-Atl Phila.

Masters, James I., ed. The Hamptons Guidebook. LC 80-50137. (Illus.). 398p. (Orig.). 1980. 6.95 (*0-89808-002-9*) Masters Pubns.

— North Fork & Shelter Island Guidebook. 3rd ed. LC 81-67384. (Illus.). 320p. (YA). (gr. 9-12). 1981. pap. 4.95 (*0-89808-007-X*) Masters Pubns.

Masters, Jamie. Poetry & Civil War in Lucan's "Bellum Civile" (Cambridge Classical Studies). (Illus.). 285p. (C). 1992. text 59.95 (*0-521-41460-1*) Cambridge U Pr.

Masters, Jamie, jt. ed. see Elsner, Jas.

Masters, Jarvis J. Finding Freedom: Writings from Death Row. LC 97-22092. xxi, 179p. 1997. pap. write for info. (*1-881847-08-X*, Pub. by Padma Pub CA) Bookpeople.

Masters, Jesse & Johnston, Don. Sassy Sayin's & Mountain Badmouth. (Illus.). 80p. (Orig.). 1985. pap. 3.95 (*0-9615347-0-2*) Sassy Sayings.

Masters, John. Bhowani Junction. large type ed. 576p. 1983. 27.99 (*0-7089-1056-4*) Ulverscroft.

— The Himalayan Concerto. large type ed. 475p. 1982. 27.99 (*0-7089-0839-X*) Ulverscroft.

***Masters, John, ed.** Animal Cell Culture: A Practical Approach. (The Practical Approach Ser.: Vol. 232). (Illus.). 320p. 2000. pap. text 55.00 (*0-19-963796-2*) OUP.

— Animal Cell Culture: A Practical Approach. (The Practical Approach Ser.: Vol. 232). (Illus.). 336p. 2000. text 110.00 (*0-19-963797-0*) OUP.

Masters, John A., ed. Elmworth, Case Study of a Deep Basin Gas Field. LC 84-45745. (American Association of Petroleum Geologists. Memoir Ser.: No. 38). 326p. 1984. pap. 101.10 (*0-608-05612-X*, 206607000006) Bks Demand.

Masters, John C. & Smith, William P., eds. Social Comparison, Social Justice, & Relative Deprivation: Theoretical, Empirical, & Policy Perspectives. (Greenwald & Krauss Ser.). 320p. 1987. text 59.95 (*0-89859-632-7*) L Erlbaum Assocs.

Masters, John C., et al. Behavior Therapy: Techniques & Empirical Findings. 3rd ed. 693p. (C). 1987. text 74.00 (*0-15-505376-0*, RIMM 3, Pub. by Harcourt Coll Pubs) Harcourt.

Masters, John E., ed. Damage Detection in Composite Materials. LC 92-24755. (Special Technical Publication Ser.: No. 1128). (Illus.). 290p. 1992. text 83.00 (*0-8031-1474-5*, STP1128) ASTM.

Masters, John E. & Au, Joseph J., eds. Fractography of Modern Engineering Materials: Composites & Metals. LC 87-14970. (Special Technical Publication Ser.: No. 948). (Illus.). 459p. 1987. 59.00 (*0-8031-0950-4*, STP948) ASTM.

Masters, John E. & Gilbertson, Leslie N., eds. Fractography of Modern Engineering Materials Vol. 2: Composites & Metals. (Special Technical Publication Ser.: No. STP 1203). (Illus.). 220p. 1993. text 65.00 (*0-8031-1866-X*, STP1203) ASTM.

Masters, John R. Cancer Cell Lines. LC 99-164711. (Human Cell Culture Ser.). 292 p. 1999. write for info. (*0-7923-5143-6*) Kluwer Academic.

Masters, John R., ed. Human Cancer in Primary Culture. (C). 1991. text 181.00 (*0-7923-1088-8*) Kluwer Academic.

***Masters, John R. W. & Palsson, Bernhard.** Human Cell Culture: Cancer Cell Lines Part 2, Vol. Ii. 400p. 1999. 215.00 (*0-7923-5878-3*) Kluwer Academic.

An Asterisk (*) at the beginning of an entry indicates that the title is appearing for the first time.

Masters, Judith R., tr. see Rousseau, Jean-Jacques.

Masters, Kevin S., et al. Assessing Outcome in Clinical Practice. LC 95-38901. 208p. (C). 1996. 49.00 (*0-205-19353-6*) Allyn.

***Masters, Kim.** The Keys to the Kingdom: How Michael Eisner Lost His Grip. LC 00-26510. (Illus.). 480p. 2000. 27.50 (*0-688-17449-3*, Wm Morrow) Morrow Avon.

Masters, Kim, jt. auth. see Griffin, Nancy.

Masters, L. Ann & Wallace, Harold R. Personality Development for Work. 7th ed. LC 95-16940. 1995. mass mkt. 28.95 (*0-538-63665-3*) S-W Pub.

Masters, Lance A., jt. ed. see Iyer, Gopalkrishnan R.

Masters, Larry W., ed. Problems in Service Life Prediction of Building & Construction Materials. 1985. text 184.00 (*90-247-3181-X*) Kluwer Academic.

Masters, Laurie, ed. see Aldana, Jacquelyn.

Masters, Lowell F. & Richardson, Howard D. Supervision for Successful Team Leadership: Your Personal Analysis with the Quesitons & Answers You Need to Know. Fish, S. A., ed. LC 91-38315. (Illus.). 128p. (Orig.). 1992. pap. 16.95 (*0-9630748-0-6*) Achieve Pr.

Masters, Lowell F., et al. Teaching Secondary Students with Mild Learning & Behavior Problems: Methods, Materials, Strategies. 2nd ed. LC 92-30450. (Illus.). 388p. (C). 1993. text 39.00 (*0-89079-570-3*, 2073) PRO-ED.

— Teaching Secondary Students with Mild Learning & Behavior Problems: Methods, Materials, Strategies. 3rd ed. LC 98-33631. 1999. 42.00 (*0-89079-788-9*) PRO-ED.

Masters, M. The Case of the Chocolate Snatcher. (Can You Solve the Mystery? Ser.). 96p. (J). (gr. 3-8). 1992. 15.98 (*1-56239-173-9*) ABDO Pub Co.

— Case of the Clever Computer Crooks. (Can You Solve the Mystery? Ser.). 96p. (J). (gr. 3-8). 1992. 21.37 (*1-56239-176-3*) ABDO Pub Co.

— The Case of the Famous Chocolate Chip Cookies. (Can You Solve the Mystery? Ser.). 96p. (J). (gr. 3-8). 1992. 21.37 (*1-56239-177-1*) ABDO Pub Co.

— The Case of the Mysterious Dognapper. (Can You Solve the Mystery? Ser.). 96p. (J). (gr. 3-8). 1992. 21.37 (*1-56239-175-5*) ABDO Pub Co.

— Case of the Toilet Paper Decorator. (Can You Solve the Mystery? Ser.). 96p. (J). (gr. 3-8). 1992. 21.37 (*1-56239-180-1*) ABDO Pub Co.

— Case of the Video Game Smuggler. (Can You Solve the Mystery? Ser.). 96p. (J). (gr. 3-8). 1992. 21.37 (*1-56239-174-7*) ABDO Pub Co.

— The Mystery of the Haunted House. (Can You Solve the Mystery? Ser.). 96p. (J). (gr. 3-8). 1992. 21.37 (*1-56239-182-8*) ABDO Pub Co.

— Mystery of the "Star Ship" Movie. (Can You Solve the Mystery? Ser.). 96p. (J). (gr. 3-8). 1992. 21.37 (*1-56239-178-X*) ABDO Pub Co.

— The Secret of the Long Lost Cousin. (Can You Solve the Mystery? Ser.). (YA). (gr. 3-8). 1992. 21.37 (*1-56239-172-0*) ABDO Pub Co.

— The Secret of the Loon Lake Monster. (Can You Solve the Mystery? Ser.). 96p. (J). (gr. 3-8). 1992. 21.37 (*1-56239-181-X*) ABDO Pub Co.

— The Secret of the Software Spy. (Can You Solve the Mystery? Ser.). 96p. (J). (gr. 4-5). 1994. 15.98 (*1-56239-179-8*) ABDO Pub Co.

— Secret of the Video Game Scores. (Can You Solve the Mystery? Ser.). 96p. (J). (gr. 3-8). 1992. 21.37 (*1-56239-183-6*) ABDO Pub Co.

Masters, M. Gay, et al. Central Auditory Processing Disorders: Mostly Management. LC 98-11753. 288p. (C). 1998. 50.00 (*0-205-27361-0*) Allyn.

Masters, Marcia L. Looking Across. 90p. (Orig.). 1990. pap. 7.95 (*0-939395-12-6*) Thorntree Pr.

Masters, Margaret D. Hartley Burr Alexander: Writer-in-Stone. (Illus.). 150p. (Orig.). 1992. 20.00 (*0-9633322-0-1*); pap. 10.00 (*0-9633322-1-X*) M D Masters.

Masters, Marick F. Unions at the Crossroads: Strategic Membership, Financial & Political Perspectives. LC 96-40912. 248p. 1997. 65.00 (*1-56720-129-6*, Quorum Bks) Greenwood.

Masters, Marie, jt. ed. see Olejnik, Renee M.

Masters, Masquerade. The New Year's Resolutions Diet, Exercise & Weight Loss Log Book: A Useful One-Year Self-Help Record to Accomplish Your Health & Fitness Goals. deluxe ed. (Illus.). 190p. 1997. vinyl bd. 24.50 (*1-886197-11-3*) Joy Books.

Masters, Nancy E. Safety for the Forensic Identification Specialist. LC 95-75630. (Illus.). 258p. (C). 1995. pap. 39.95 (*0-9622305-1-0*) Lightning Powder.

Masters, Nancy R. Airplanes of World War II. LC 97-5996. (Wings Ser.). (Illus.). 48p. (J). (gr. 4-7). 1998. 19.00 (*1-56065-531-3*) Capstone Pr.

— Airplanes of World War II. (Wings of War Ser.). (J). 1998. 19.00 (*0-516-21314-8*) Childrens.

— All My Downs Have Been Ups. (Illus.). 190p. 1992. 18.95 (*0-9623563-2-8*) MasAir Pubns.

— Bombers of World War II. LC 97-5998. (Wings Ser.). (Illus.). 48p. (J). (gr. 4-7). 1997. 19.00 (*1-56065-532-1*) Capstone Pr.

— Bombers of World War II. (Wings of War Ser.). (J). 1998. 19.00 (*0-516-21315-6*) Childrens.

— The Fabulous Flying Flag Farm. (Illus.). 32p. (J). (ps-4). 1996. 13.95 (*0-9623563-5-2*) MasAir Pubns.

— Fighter Planes of World War II. LC 97-5999. (Wings Ser.). (Illus.). 48p. (J). (gr. 4-7). 1998. 19.00 (*1-56065-533-X*) Capstone Pr.

— Fighter Planes of World War II. (Wings of War Ser.). (J). 1998. 19.00 (*0-516-21316-4*) Childrens.

— Georgia. LC 98-14036. (America the Beautiful Ser.). 144p. (J). (gr. 5-8). 1999. 32.00 (*0-516-20685-0*) Childrens.

— Guidelines for Freelancers. 2nd rev. ed. 112p. (Orig.). 1996. pap. 13.95 (*0-9623563-7-9*) MasAir Pubns.

— The Horrible, Homemade Halloween Costume. (Ups & Downs Book Ser.). (Illus.). 32p. (J). (gr. 2-4). 1993. 14.95 (*0-9623563-3-6*) MasAir Pubns.

— Training Planes of World War II. LC 97-6000. (Wings Ser.). (J). 1998. 19.00 (*1-56065-534-8*) Capstone Pr.

— Training Planes of World War II. (Wings of War Ser.). (J). 1998. 19.00 (*0-516-21317-2*) Childrens.

— Wing of War. 1999. 76.00 (*0-516-29737-6*) Childrens.

***Masters, Nicholas.** How to Make Money in Commercial Real Estate: For the Small Investor. LC 99-86787. 288p. 2000. text 34.95 (*0-471-35543-7*) Wiley.

Masters, Olga. Collected Stories. (Short Stories from Australia Ser.). 1996. pap. 16.95 (*0-7022-2883-4*, Pub. by Univ Queensland Pr) Intl Spec Bk.

— The Home Girls. LC 82-2709. 194p. 1983. pap. 14.95 (*0-7022-1821-9*, Pub. by Univ Queensland Pr) Intl Spec Bk.

— Loving Daughters. large type ed. LC 93-11696. (General Ser.). 458p. 1993. lib. bdg. 18.95 (*0-7862-0032-4*) Thorndike Pr.

Masters, P. M. Quarternary Coastlines & Marine Archaeology: Towards the Prehistory of Land Bridges & Continental Shelves. Fleming, N. C., ed. LC 82-45021. 1983. text 139.95 (*0-12-479250-2*) Acad Pr.

Masters, Pamela. The Mushroom Years: A Story of Survival. LC 94-93017. (Illus.). xii, 311p. 1998. pap. 19.95 (*0-9664489-2-8*) Hndrson Hse Pubng.

***Masters, Paul.** Meca & the Black Oracle. LC 98-90911. 1999. pap. 15.95 (*0-533-12983-4*) Vantage.

Masters, Peter. Striking Back: A Jewish Commando's War Against the Nazis. LC 97-24416. (Illus.). 320p. 1997. 24.95 (*0-89141-629-3*) Presidio Pr.

Masters, Phil. Artisans Handbook. 1999. pap. text 14.95 (*1-56504-493-2*) White Wolf.

— Gurps Arabian Nights: Magic & Mystery in the Land of the Djinn. Jackson, Steve & Pinsonneault, Susan, eds. (Illus.). 128p. 1998. pap. 19.95 (*1-55634-266-7*, 6062, Pub. by S Jackson Games) BookWorld.

***Masters, Phil.** Swashbucklers Handbook. 2000. pap. text 18.00 (*1-56504-470-3*) White Wolf.

***Masters, Phil, ed.** GURPS Who's Who 1: 52 of History's Most Interesting Characters. 128p. 1999. pap. 19.95 (*1-55634-367-1*, Pub. by S Jackson Games) BookWorld.

— GURPS Who's Who 2. 128p. 1999. pap. 19.95 (*1-55634-407-4*, Pub. by S Jackson Games) BookWorld.

Masters, Phil & Brooks, Alison. Gurp's Places of Mystery. Dupuis, Ann, ed. (Illus.). 1996. pap., suppl. ed. 19.95 (*1-55634-139-3*, 6520) S Jackson Games.

Masters, Phil & Pratchett, Terry. Gurps Discworld. Jackson, Steve, ed. (Illus.). 240p. 1998. pap. 26.95 (*1-55634-261-6*, 6084, Pub. by S Jackson Games) BookWorld.

Masters, Phil, ed. see Desborough, James & Mortimer, Steve.

***Masters, Priscilla.** And None Shall Sleep. large type ed. 336p. 1999. 31.99 (*0-7089-3955-4*) Ulverscroft.

Masters, Priscilla. Catch the Fallen Sparrow. large type ed. (Ulverscroft Large Print Ser.). 400p. 1997. 27.99 (*0-7089-3763-2*) Ulverscroft.

***Masters, Priscilla.** Night Visit. large type ed. LC 99-22225. 1999. pap. 19.95 (*0-7838-8653-5*, G K Hall & Co) Mac Lib Ref.

— Scaring Crows. large type ed. 400p. 1999. 31.99 (*0-7089-4161-3*) Ulverscroft.

Masters, R. E. Eros & Evil: The Sexual Psychopathology of Witchcraft. LC 79-8114. reprint ed. 36.50 (*0-404-18427-8*) AMS Pr.

Masters, Raymond. Social History of the Huntington Wildlife Forest: Which Includes Rich Lake & the Pendleton Settlement. LC 93-12342. 96p. 1993. pap. 9.95 (*0-925168-13-0*) North Country.

Masters, Regina M., jt. auth. see Gylys, Barbara A.

Masters, Robert. Neurospeak: Transforms Your Body While You Read. 124p. 1994. pap. 14.00 (*0-8356-0707-0*, Quest) Theos Pub Hse.

— The Way to Awaken: Exercises to Enliven Body, Self & Soul. LC 96-54724. (Illus.). 288p. 1997. pap. 12.95 (*0-8356-0754-2*, Quest) Theos Pub Hse.

Masters, Robert & Houston, Jean. Mind Games: The Guide to Inner Space. rev. ed. LC 98-20231. (Illus.). 208p. 1998. pap. 14.00 (*0-8356-0753-4*, Pub. by Theos Pub Hse) Natl Bk Netwk.

***Masters, Robert & Houston, Jean.** The Varieties of Psychedelic Experience: The Classic Guide to the Effects of LSD on the Human Psyche. LC 00-26625. 352p. 2000. pap. 16.95 (*0-89281-897-2*) Inner Tradit.

Masters, Robert B. Vu-Calc & Vu-File (The Organizer) LC 83-22489. 176p. 1984. pap. 19.95 (*0-89303-941-1*) P-H.

Masters, Robert J. The Crayon Box. (Coloring Bks.). 64p. (J). 1998. pap. 1.99 (*0-679-89170-6*, Pub. by Random Bks Yng Read) Random.

— Cut up Sisters Color & Snip. (Coloring Book Plus). 24p. (J). 1998. pap. 1.99 (*0-679-89169-2*, Pub. by Random Bks Yng Read) Random.

— Dottie's Dot-to-Dot. 64p. (J). 1998. pap. 1.99 (*0-679-89167-6*, Pub. by Random Bks Yng Read) Random.

— Official Book to Color. 32p. (J). 1998. pap. 1.99 (*0-679-89168-4*, Pub. by Random Bks Yng Read) Random.

— Random House Webster's Concise Dictionary. 1997. 11.95 (*0-679-45855-7*) Random Ref & Info.

Masters, Roger D. Beyond Relativism: Science & Human Values. LC 93-16925. (Illus.). 262p. 1993. 35.00 (*0-87451-634-X*) U Pr of New Eng.

— Fortune Is a River: Leonardo da Vinci & Niccolo Machiavelli's Magnificent Dream to Change the Course of Florentine History. (Illus.). 288p. 1999. pap. 12.95 (*0-452-28090-7*, Plume) Dutton Plume.

— Fortune Is a River: Leonardo da Vinci & Niccolo Machiavelli's Magnificent Dream to Change the Course of Florentine History. LC 97-48447. 288p. 1998. 23.50 (*0-684-84452-4*) Free Pr.

— Machiavelli, Leonardo & the Science of Power. LC 94-40484. (Frank M. Covey, Jr., Loyola Lectures in Political Analysis). (C). 1996. text 32.95 (*0-268-01416-7*) U of Notre Dame Pr.

— Machiavelli, Leonardo, & the Science of Power. LC 94-40484. (Frank M. Covey, Jr., Loyola Lectures in Political Analysis). 384p. (C). 1998. reprint ed. pap. text 24.95 (*0-268-01433-7*) U of Notre Dame Pr.

— The Nature of Politics. LC 88-7652. 320p. (C). 1989. 42.50 (*0-300-04169-1*) Yale U Pr.

— Nature of Politics. 315p. 1991. pap. 19.00 (*0-300-04981-1*) Yale U Pr.

— The Political Philosophy of Rousseau. LC 67-12348. 488p. reprint ed. pap. 151.30 (*0-608-18440-3*, 203263800080) Bks Demand.

Masters, Roger D. & Gruter, Margaret, eds. The Sense of Justice: Biological Foundations of Law. (Focus Editions Ser.: Vol. 136). 288p. (C). 1992. text 59.95 (*0-8039-4397-0*); pap. text 26.00 (*0-8039-4398-9*) Sage.

Masters, Roger D. & Masters, Anthony. Rousseau's First & Second Discourses. 1969. write for info. (*0-318-63175-X*) St Martin.

Masters, Roger D. & Schubert, Glendon A., eds. Primate Politics. LC 93-45842. 1994. pap. 32.00 (*0-8191-9386-0*) U Pr of Amer.

Masters, Roger D., jt. ed. see Gruter, Margaret.

Masters, Roger D., ed. see McGuire, Michael T.

Masters, Roger D., ed. see Rousseau, Jean-Jacques.

Masters, Roger D., ed. & tr. see Rousseau, Jean-Jacques.

Masters, Roy. The Adam & Eve Sindrome. LC 85-80750. 266p. 1985. pap. text 15.95 (*0-933900-11-2*) Foun Human Under.

— Beyond the Known. rev. ed. Baker, Dorothy, ed. LC 88-83553. 255p. (Orig.). 1989. reprint ed. pap. text 15.95 (*0-933900-03-1*) Foun Human Under.

— Eat No Evil. LC 87-80407. 127p. (Orig.). 1987. pap. text 15.95 (*0-933900-12-0*) Foun Human Under.

— Finding God in Physics: Einstein's Missing Relative. Just, Bob & Baker, Dorothy, eds. LC 97-77602. 160p. 1997. pap. write for info. (*0-933900-19-8*) Foun Human Under.

— How to Conquer Negative Emotions. Tappan, Melrose H., ed. & pref. by. LC 88-80163. 325p. 1988. pap. 15.95 (*0-933900-01-5*) Foun Human Under.

— How to Conquer Suffering Without Doctors. LC 76-489. 222p. 1976. pap. 15.95 (*0-933900-04-X*) Foun Human Under.

— How Your Mind Can Keep You Well. 15th ed. Baker, Dorothy, ed. 201p. 1978. pap. 15.95 (*0-933900-09-0*) Foun Human Under.

— The Hypnosis of Life. rev. ed. LC 88-80924. 259p. (Orig.). 1988. pap. 15.95 (*0-933900-05-8*) Foun Human Under.

— Secret Power of Words. Baker, Dorothy, ed. LC 88-81474. 213p. (Orig.). 1988. pap. text 15.95 (*0-933900-14-7*) Foun Human Under.

— Secrets of a Parallel Universe: Why Our Deepest Problems Hold the Key to Ultimate Personal Success & Happiness. Baker, Dorothy, ed. LC 92-81343. 156p. (Orig.). 1992. pap. text 15.95 (*0-933900-17-1*) Foun Human Under.

— Surviving the Comfort Zone. Baker, Dorothy, ed. LC 91-73149. 193p. (Orig.). 1991. pap. text 15.95 (*0-933900-15-5*) Foun Human Under.

— Understanding Sexuality: The Mystery of Our Lost Identities. rev. ed. LC 87-83552. 361p. 1988. reprint ed. pap. 15.95 (*0-933900-13-9*) Foun Human Under.

***Masters, Roy G.** Surgical Options for the Treatment of Heart Failure. 208p. 1999. 96.00 (*0-7923-6130-X*) Kluwer Academic.

Masters, Ruth D. International Law in National Courts. LC 71-76631. (Columbia University. Studies in the Social Sciences: No. 370). reprint ed. 27.50 (*0-404-51370-0*) AMS Pr.

Masters, Ruth E. Counseling Criminal Justice Offenders. 264p. (C). 1994. text 49.95 (*0-8039-5532-4*); pap. text 21.00 (*0-8039-5533-2*) Sage.

Masters, Scott. Bankruptcy . . . You're Not Alone! Famous Members of "the 7-11 Club" LC 94-61342. 350p. 1998. pap. 16.95 (*0-9659487-0-6*) Winston-Fox.

Master's Seminary Faculty Staff & MacArthur, John F., Jr. Rediscovering Expository Preaching. Mayhue, Richard L. & Thomas, Robert L., eds. LC 92-10804. (MacArthur Resource Library). 400p. 1992. 24.99 (*0-8499-0908-2*) Word Pub.

Masters Staff. The Rainbow Masters. (Phoenix Journals). 224p. 1993. pap. 6.00 (*1-56935-017-5*) Phoenix Source.

Masters, Susan Rowan. Libby Bloom. LC 94-43898. (Redfeather Bks.). (Illus.). (J). (gr. 2-4). 1995. 14.95 (*0-8050-3374-2*) H Holt & Co.

— The Secret Life of Hubie Hartzel. LC 89-36402. (Illus.). 144p. (J). (gr. 3-7). 1990. 11.95 (*0-397-32399-9*); lib. bdg. 11.89 (*0-397-32400-6*) HarpC Child Bks.

— Summer Song. LC 94-43684. 137p. (J). (gr. 5-7). 1995. 14.95 (*0-395-71127-4*, Clarion Bks) HM.

Masters, T. W. Salon Management: For Hairdressers & Beauty Therapists. 250p. 1987. text 59.95 (*0-291-39709-3*, Pub. by Gower) Ashgate Pub Co.

Masters, Thomas. How to Buy a House with No or Poor Credit. LC 95-39203. 208p. 1996. pap. 14.95 (*0-471-11996-2*) Wiley.

Masters, Timothy. Advanced Algorithms for Neural Networks: A C++ Sourcebook. LC 94-43390. 448p. 1995. pap. 44.95 incl. disk (*0-471-10588-0*) Wiley.

— Neural, Novel & Hybrid Algorithms for Time Series Prediction. LC 95-31203. 544p. 1995. pap. text 59.99 incl. cd-rom, disk (*0-471-13041-9*) Wiley.

— Practical Neural Network Recipes in C++ (Illus.). 493p. 1993. pap. text 59.00 (*0-12-479040-2*) Acad Pr.

— Signal & Image Processing with Neural Networks: C Sourcebook. 417p. 1994. pap. write for info. incl. disk (*0-471-04963-8*) Wiley.

Masters, Tory Baker & Braddock, Kathy Mayer. How to Live the Good Life in New York. rev. ed. Orig. Title: Intrepid New Yorkers. 336p. 2000. pap. 20.00 (*0-9653080-0-6*, Pub. by Intrepid New Yrker) City & Co.

Masters, W. Stuart, jt. auth. see Shackell, Dora.

***Masters, Wallace.** Personal Development for Life & Work. 8th ed. 2000. pap. 38.95 (*0-538-69795-4*) Sth-Wstrn College.

Masters-Wicks, Karen. Victor Hugo's Les Miserables & the Novels of the Groteque, Vol. 1. LC 92-25009. (Currents in Comparative Romance Languages & Literatures Ser.: Vol. 12). X, 248p. (C). 1994. text 45.95 (*0-8204-2000-X*) P Lang Pubng.

Masters, Will. Heart Spirit: Transforming Work Stress. 25p. (Orig.). (C). 1997. pap. text. write for info. (*1-886112-08-8*) Antares.

Masters, Will, jt. auth. see Masters, Debra.

Masters, William A. Government & Agriculture in Zimbabwe. LC 93-38884. 256p. 1994. 65.00 (*0-275-94755-6*, Praeger Pubs) Greenwood.

Masters, William H. & Johnson, Virginia E. Human Sexual Response. 366p. 1966. text 48.95 (*0-316-54987-8*, Little Brwn Med Div) Lppncott W & W.

Masters, William H., et al. Human Sexuality. 5th ed. LC 94-36210. 769p. (C). 1997. 89.00 (*0-673-46785-6*) Addson-Wesley Educ.

— Masters & Johnson on Sex & Human Loving. 621p. 1988. pap. 21.95 (*0-316-50160-3*, Back Bay) Little.

Masters, Zeke. Ace in the Hole. (Faro Blake Ser.: No. 8). 176p. 1983. pap. 2.25 (*0-671-46485-X*) PB.

Masters, Zominique. Soul of the Heavens. Gray, Etha, ed. 194p. (Orig.). 1991. pap. 12.95 (*1-879940-00-0*) Concepts N Pub.

***Masterson, Abigail.** Nursing & Politics Power Thru Practice. LC 98-31647. 1999. write for info. (*0-443-05991-8*) Church.

Masterson, Aisla. In a Nutshell: Alexander Technique. LC 98-3514. (In a Nutshell Ser.). 1998. 7.95 (*1-86204-195-4*, Pub. by Element MA) Penguin Putnam.

Masterson, B. J. Manual of Gynecologic Surgery. 2nd ed. (Comprehensive Manuals of Surgical Specialties Ser.). (Illus.). 379p. 1986. 290.00 (*0-387-96193-3*) Spr-Verlag.

Masterson, Bat, jt. auth. see Earp, Wyatt.

Masterson, Dan. All Things, Seen & Unseen: Poems New & Selected, 1947-1997. LC 97-34457. 104p. 1997. pap. 14.00 (*1-55728-486-5*) U of Ark Pr.

— All Things, Seen & Unseen: Poems New & Selected, 1947-1997. LC 97-34457. 123p. 1998. 22.00 (*1-55728-485-7*) U of Ark Pr.

— World Without End. LC 90-10890. 84p. 1990. pap. 12.00 (*1-55728-178-5*) U of Ark Pr.

Masterson, Daniel & Dunnigan, James. Way of the Warrior. 224p. 1998. pap. 12.95 (*0-312-19535-4*) St Martin.

Masterson, Daniel, jt. auth. see Dunnigan, James.

Masterson, Daniel M. Japanese in Latin America, 1880 to the Present. 272p. 2000. text 65.00 (*0-8133-2326-6*) Westview.

— Militarism & Politics in Latin America: Peru from Sanchez Cerro to Sendero Luminoso, 111. LC 90-23010. (Contributions in Military Studies Ser.: No. 111). 360p. 1991. 69.50 (*0-313-27213-1*, MLM, Greenwood Pr) Greenwood.

Masterson, Daniel M., ed. Naval History: The 6th Symposium of the U. S. Naval Academy. LC 86-29858. (Illus.). 376p. 1987. 65.00 (*0-8420-2278-3*) Scholarly Res Inc.

Masterson, Dorothy, jt. auth. see Nash, Helen.

Masterson, Elizabeth R. Love Lettes to Elizabeth. v, 114p. 1999. 10.00 (*0-9670541-0-9*) E D Rupp.

Masterson, Eugene. The Word on the Streets: The Unsanctioned Story of Oasis. (Illus.). 96p. 1997. pap. 17.95 (*1-85158-890-6*, Pub. by Mainstream Pubng) Trafalgar.

Masterson, Eugene & Whelan, Ken. Bertie Ahern. LC 98-233928. (Illus.). 224p. 1999. 35.00 (*1-84018-135-4*, Pub. by Mainstream Pubng) Trafalgar.

Masterson-Glen, Josie, jt. ed. see Bliss, Steven.

Masterson-Glen, Josie, ed. see JLC Staff.

Masterson-Glen, Josie, ed. see Randall, Robert.

Masterson-Glen, Josie, ed. see Ransone, Gary.

***Masterson, Graham.** The Chosen Child. 2000. text 23.95 (*0-312-87382-4*) St Martin.

Masterson, Graham. Secrets of the Sexually Irresistible Woman. 272p. 1998. mass mkt. 6.99 (*0-451-19267-2*, Sig) NAL.

Masterson, Helen. Jefferson County: A Contemporary Portrait. (Illus.). 160p. 1999. 49.95 (*1-893619-00-1*, Lammert Pubns) Hist Pub Network.

Masterson, James F. Countertransference & Psychotherapeutic Technique: Teaching Seminars on Psychotherapy of the Borderline Adult. LC 83-3865. 320p. 1983. text 38.95 (*0-87630-334-3*) Brunner-Mazel.

— The Emerging Self: A Developmental, Self, & Object Relations Approach to the Treatment of the Closet Narcissistic Disorder of the Self. LC 93-1604. 340p. 1993. text 39.95 (*0-87630-721-7*) Brunner-Mazel.

— The Narcissistic & Borderline Disorders: An Integrated Developmental Approach. 18th ed. LC 81-38540. 260p. 1989. text 38.95 (*0-87630-292-4*) Brunner-Mazel.

— The Personality Disorders: New Look at the Developmental Self & Object Relations Approach: Theory, Diagnosis & Treatment. LC 99-32777. 2000. 35.95 (*1-891944-33-9*) Zeig Tucker.

An Asterisk (*) at the beginning of an entry indicates that the title is appearing for the first time.

— The Psychiatric Dilemma of Adolescence. 2nd ed. LC 83-24039. 232p. 1986. reprint ed. text 38.95 (*0-87630-356-4*) Brunner-Mazel.
— Psychotherapy of the Borderline Adult: A Developmental Approach. LC 76-16564. 377p. 1988. text 38.95 (*0-87630-127-8*) Brunner-Mazel.
— The Real Self: A Developmental, Self, & Object Relations Approach. LC 85-12824. 192p. 1985. text 34.95 (*0-87630-400-5*) Brunner-Mazel.
— The Search for the Real Self: Unmasking the Personality Disorders of Our Age. 1990. per. 13.95 (*0-02-920292-2*) Free Pr.
— Treatment of the Borderline Adolescent: A Developmental Approach. 5th ed. LC 85-4236. 305p. 1985. reprint ed. text 38.95 (*0-87630-394-7*) Brunner-Mazel.
Masterson, James F. & Costello, Jacinta L. From Borderline Adolescent to Functioning Adult: The Test of Time. 3rd ed. LC 80-14270. 320p. 1986. text 38.95 (*0-87630-234-7*) Brunner-Mazel.
Masterson, James F. & Klein, Ralph, eds. Disorders of the Self: New Therapeutic Horizons - The Masterson Approach. 448p. 1995. 51.95 (*0-87630-786-1*) Brunner-Mazel.
— Psychotherapy of the Disorders of the Self: The Masterson Approach. LC 88-19341. 480p. 1988. text 45.95 (*0-87630-533-8*) Brunner-Mazel.
Masterson, James F., et al. Comparing Psychoanalytic Psychotherapies: Developmental, Self, & Object Relations; Self Psychology; Short-Term Dynamic. LC 91-8288. 312p. 1991. text 39.95 (*0-87630-640-7*) Brunner-Mazel.
Masterson, James J., jt. auth. see Gaetano, Ronald J.
Masterson, James W., et al. Robotics Technology. (Illus.). 320p. (C). 1996. pap. text 37.28 (*1-56637-046-9*) Goodheart.
***Masterson, Jim.** Tribute: The First Collection. 1998. 14.95 (*0-9671281-0-2*) P T Masterson.
Masterson, John T., et al. Invitation to Effective Speech Communication. (C). 1997. 56.00 (*0-673-18565-6*) Addson-Wesley Educ.
Masterson, John T., jt. auth. see Beebe, Steven A.
***Masterson, Josephine.** County Cork, Ireland: A Collection of 1851 Census Records. 117p. 1999. 17.50 (*0-8063-4610-8*) Clearfield Co.
Masterson, Josephine. Ireland: 1841/1851 Census Abstracts: (Northern Ireland) 538p. 1999. 50.00 (*0-8063-1587-3*) Genealog Pub.
***Masterson, Josephine.** Ireland: 1841/1851 Census Abstracts: (Republic of Ireland) 148p. 1999. 25.00 (*0-8063-1586-5*) Genealog Pub.
Masterson, Linda. Summerhaven. (Illus.). 1979. mass mkt. 1.95 (*0-89083-471-7*, Zebra Kensgtn) Kensgtn Pub Corp.
Masterson, Martha G. One Woman's West: Recollections of the Oregon Trail & Settling the Northwest Country. 2nd expanded ed. Barton, Lois, ed. LC 86-15570. (Illus.). 222p. (Orig.). 1986. pap. 9.95 (*0-9609420-2-5*) S Butte Pr.
Masterson, Michael P. Windows NT DNS. 1998. pap. text 32.00 (*1-57870-042-6*) Macmillan Tech.
— Windows NT DNS. LC 98-86490. 1998. pap. 29.99 (*1-56205-943-2*) New Riders Pub.
Masterson, Patrick. Port Orford: A History. LC 94-70323. (Illus.). 380p. 1994. 29.95 (*1-885221-08-8*) BookPartners.
***Masterson, Steve.** Return to Father: A Call for Men to Repent. (Contemporary Christian Living Ser.). 27p. 1999. pap. 1.59 (*0-87509-846-0*) Chr Pubns.
Masterson, Steve & McPeek, George. Out of the Locker Room of the Male Soul: Men Seeking the Heart of God. LC 97-191580. 386p. 1997. pap. 12.99 (*0-88965-136-1*, Pub. by Horizon Books) Chr Pubns.
Masterson, Susie. The Official Hiking Guide Book to Grand County. (Illus.). 44p. 1998. pap. 9.95 (*0-9665375-0-5*) GuestGuide.
Masterson, Thomas. Day-by-Day Colitis 2000 Calendar. (Day-by-Day Year 2000 Calendars Ser.). 120p. 1999. pap. 12.95 (*1-883205-60-3*) Intl Med Pub.
— Day-by-Day HIV 2000 Calendar. (Day-by-Day Year 2000 Calendars Ser.). 120p. 1999. pap. 12.95 (*1-883205-73-5*) Intl Med Pub.
Masterson, Thomas, ed. Pocketful of Prevention: Preventive Care Guidelines. 40p. (C). 1998. pap. 7.50 (*1-883205-44-1*) Intl Med Pub.
Masterson, Thomas, et al. Day-by-Day Dialysis, 1999 Calendar. (Day-by-Day Calendars Ser.). 110p. 1999. pap. 12.95 (*1-883205-48-4*) Intl Med Pub.
Masterson, Thomas M. The Housestaff Book of Forms. 50p. (Orig.). (C). 1993. pap. text 7.50 (*0-9634063-7-X*) Intl Med Pub.
— The Intern Pocket Admission Book. 78p. 1993. pap. text 4.50 (*0-9634063-4-5*) Intl Med Pub.
— The Intern Pocket Survival Guide. 78p. (Orig.). (C). 1992. pap. text 7.50 (*0-9634063-0-2*) Intl Med Pub.
Masterson, Thomas M. & Rothenhaus, Todd C. The CCU Intern Pocket Survival Guide. 2nd ed. 78p. 1992. pap. text 7.50 (*0-9634063-1-0*) Intl Med Pub.
Masterson, Thomas M., et al. The EKG Pocket Survival Guide. (Illus.). 54p. (Orig.). (C). 1993. pap. text 7.50 (*0-9634063-8-8*) Intl Med Pub.
— The ICU Intern Pocket Survival Guide. 78p. (Orig.). (C). 1992. pap. text 7.50 (*0-9634063-3-7*) Intl Med Pub.
— The Wound Management Pocket Survival Guide. (Pocket Survival Guides Ser.). 72p. 1996. pap. 7.50 (*1-883205-30-1*) Intl Med Pub.
Masterson, Thomas M., jt. auth. see Rothenhaus, Todd C.
Masterson, Thomas M., jt. auth. see Tenner, Scott M.
Masterson, Thomas R. & Nunan, J. Carlton. Ethics in Business. 240p. 1969. text 21.50 (*0-8290-0288-X*) Irvington.
Masterson, V. V. The Katy Railroad & the Last Frontier. LC 87-19146. (Illus.). 354p. (C). 1988. reprint ed. pap. 19.95 (*0-8262-0668-9*) U of Mo Pr.
Masterson, Whit. Touch of Evil. (Mystery Scene Bk.). 176p. 1992. mass mkt. 3.95 (*0-88184-886-7*) Carroll & Graf.
Masterson, William B. Famous Gunfighters of the Western Frontier. rev. ed. Jones, William R., ed. & intro. by. (Illus.). 96p. 1995. reprint ed. pap. 6.95 (*0-89646-087-8*) Vistabooks.
Masterson, William H. William Blount. LC 79-88904. 378p. 1970. reprint ed. lib. bdg. 65.00 (*0-8371-2308-9*, MABL, Greenwood Pr) Greenwood.
Masterton. Chemistry Principles & Reactions. 3rd ed. (C). 1996. pap. text, student ed. 22.00 (*0-03-018984-5*, Pub. by Harcourt Coll Pubs) Harcourt.
— Coop Learning T/A Chem: PR. 3rd ed. (C). 1996. wbk. ed. 27.00 (*0-03-019618-3*) Harcourt Coll Pubs.
— Prey. 2000. text 23.95 (*0-312-85103-0*) St Martin.
— Workbook for Chemistry: Principles & Reactions. 3rd ed. (C). 1996. pap. text, student ed. 24.00 (*0-03-018987-X*) Harcourt Coll Pubs.
Masterton, Barbara. Island of Glass. large type ed. 448p. 1987. 27.99 (*0-7089-1644-9*) Ulverscroft.
— Late Harvest. large type ed. 384p. 1989. 27.99 (*0-7089-2043-8*) Ulverscroft.
— Orbs of Jade. large type ed. 1991. 27.99 (*0-7089-2372-0*) Ulverscroft.
Masterton, Graham. Burial. 1996. mass mkt. 4.99 (*0-614-05520-2*); mass mkt. 5.99 (*0-8125-3629-0*, Pub. by Tor Bks) St Martin.
— Drive Him Wild: The Ultimate Guide to Pleasing Your Man in Bed. 224p. (Orig.). 1993. mass mkt. 6.99 (*0-451-17591-3*, Sig) NAL.
— The House That Jack Built. LC 96-32520. 384p. 1996. 24.00 (*0-7867-0353-9*) Carroll & Graf.
***Masterton, Graham.** The House That Jack Built. 400p. 2000. mass mkt. 5.50 (*0-8439-4746-2*, Leisure Bks) Dorchester Pub Co.
Masterton, Graham. How to Drive Your Man Even Wilder in Bed. 224p. (Orig.). 1995. mass mkt. 6.99 (*0-451-18151-4*, Sig) NAL.
— How to Drive Your Man Wild in Bed. 224p. 1976. mass mkt. 6.99 (*0-451-15277-8*, Sig) NAL.
— How to Drive Your Woman Wild in Bed. 1987. mass mkt. 6.99 (*0-451-15657-9*) NAL.
— How to Make His Wildest Dreams Come True. 272p. 1996. mass mkt. 6.99 (*0-451-18753-9*, Sig) NAL.
— How to Make Love Six Nights a Week. 224p. (Orig.). 1991. mass mkt. 6.99 (*0-451-16941-7*, Sig) NAL.
***Masterton, Graham.** Manitou Man. 237p. 1998. pap. 18.95 (*0-9524153-4-8*, Pub. by BFS) Firebird Dist.
Masterton, Graham. Master of Lies. 336p. 1995. 4.99 (*0-8125-1166-2*, Pub. by Tor Bks) St Martin.
— More Ways to Drive Your Man Wild in Bed. 1985. mass mkt. 6.99 (*0-451-16174-2*, Sig) NAL.
— Night Plague. 1991. mass mkt. 4.50 (*0-8125-2204-4*) Tor Bks.
***Masterton, Graham.** Prey. 352p. 1999. mass mkt. 4.99 (*0-8439-4633-4*, Leisure Bks) Dorchester Pub Co.
— Secrets of Sexual Play. 304p. 1999. mass mkt. 7.50 (*0-451-40903-5*, Onyx) NAL.
Masterton, Graham. Seven Secrets of Really Great Sex. LC 99-199882. 288p. 1999. mass mkt. 6.99 (*0-451-19521-3*, Sig) NAL.
***Masterton, Graham.** Snowman. 218p. 2000. 26.00 (*0-7278-5427-5*, Pub. by Severn Hse) Chivers N Amer.
Masterton, Graham. The Terror. 224p. 1998. 24.00 (*0-7278-5300-7*) Severn Hse.
— Wells of Hell. 320p. 1990. pap. 3.95 (*0-8125-2211-7*, Pub. by Tor Bks) St Martin.
— Wild in Bed Together. 256p. (Orig.). 1992. mass mkt. 6.99 (*0-451-17212-4*, Sig) NAL.
Masterton, Jack. Prayers for Use in Church. 152p. 1993. pap. 24.00 (*0-7152-0680-X*, Pub. by St Andrew) St Mut.
Masterton, Murray & Patching, Roger. Now the News in Detail: A Guide to Broadcast Journalism in Australia. 3rd ed. 293p. (C). 1995. pap. 56.00 (*0-7300-1441-X*, Pub. by Deakin Univ) St Mut.
Masterton, Murry & Patching, Roger, eds. How the News in Detail. 1996. pap. 70.00 (*0-949823-68-6*, Pub. by Deakin Univ) St Mut.
Masterton, R. Bruce, jt. ed. see Syka, J.
Masterton, T. H., ed. Worldscapes. 2nd ed. 1987. pap. text 13.05 (*0-05-004028-6*, 70094) Longman.
Masterton, William L. Chemical Principles. 2nd alternate ed. (C). 1983. pap. text, student ed. 27.00 (*0-03-062648-X*) Harcourt Coll Pubs.
— Chemistry. 2nd ed. (C). 1993. pap. text, student ed., wbk. ed. 26.50 (*0-03-028998-X*) Harcourt Coll Pubs.
— Chemistry: Principles & Reactions. (C). 1989. pap. text, teacher ed. 34.00 (*0-03-013642-3*); pap. text, student ed. 28.00 (*0-03-013644-X*, Pub. by Harcourt Coll Pubs) Harcourt.
— Chemistry: Principles & Reactions. 2nd ed. (C). 1993. pap. text, teacher ed. 33.75 (*0-03-028997-1*) Harcourt Coll Pubs.
— Chemistry: Principles & Reactions. 3rd ed. LC 95-72523. (C). 1996. text 73.00 (*0-03-005889-9*, Pub. by Harcourt Coll Pubs) Harcourt.
— Chemistry: Principles & Reactions. 3rd ed. (C). 1996. pap. text, teacher ed. 33.50 (*0-03-018989-6*, Pub. by Harcourt Coll Pubs) Harcourt.
— Chemistry: Principles & Reactions: Lecture Outline. 3rd ed. (C). 1996. teacher ed. 23.50 (*0-03-019048-7*, Pub. by Harcourt Coll Pubs) Harcourt.
— Chemistry: Principles & Reations. 1997. 99.50 (*0-03-053028-8*) Harcourt Coll Pubs.
— Introduction to Chemistry. (C). 1983. pap. text, teacher ed. 17.00 (*0-03-059677-7*) Harcourt Coll Pubs.
— Introduction to Chemistry. (C). 1984. pap. text, teacher ed. 14.75 (*0-03-069572-4*) Harcourt Coll Pubs.
— LEC OUTLN CHEM: PRINC/REAC 1E. (C). 1989. pap. text, teacher ed., suppl. ed. 26.00 (*0-03-013649-0*) Harcourt Coll Pubs.
***Masterton, William L.** Lizzie Didn't Do It. Caso, Adolph, ed. LC 99-88574. 242p. 2000. pap. 19.95 (*0-8283-2052-7*) Branden Bks.
Masterton, William L. & Cherim, Stanley M. Introduction to Chemistry. LC 83-17244. 480p. (C). 1984. text 68.50 (*0-03-059676-9*) SCP.
Masterton, William L. & Slowinski, Emil J. MATH PREPARTN GENER CHEM PB 2E. 2nd ed. 260p. (C). 1982. pap. text 32.00 (*0-03-060119-3*) SCP.
Masterton, William L., et al. Chemical Principles in the Laboratory. 5th ed. 357p. (C). 1989. pap. text, student ed. 58.50 (*0-03-026234-8*) SCP.
— Chemical Principles, with Qualitative Analysis. 6th ed. 1168p. (C). 1986. pap. text, teacher ed. 17.00 (*0-03-008589-6*) SCP.
Masterton, William L., jt. auth. see Slowinski, Emil J.
Masthay, Carl. Schmick's Mahican Dictionary. LC 86-90530. (Memoirs Ser.: Vol. 197). 188p. (C). 1992. 30.00 (*0-87169-197-3*, M197-MAC) Am Philos.
Mastidoro, Maria R. Concordanza Dei Carmina Latina Epigraphica: Compresi Nella Silloge Di J. W. Zarker. (Classical & Byzantine Monographs: No. xxi). (ITA.). xxxi, 259p. 1991. pap. 64.00 (*90-256-1007-2*, Pub. by AM Hakkert) BookLink Distributors.
Mastim, jt. auth. see Dobos.
Mastin, Bettye L. Lexington, 1779. LC 79-90522. 137p. 1979. 12.50 (*0-912839-00-7*) Lexington-Fayette.
Mastin, Catharine. Franklin Carmichael. Fetherling, Douglas, ed. (New Views on Canadian Artists Ser.). (Illus.). 96p. 1996. pap. 18.95 (*1-55082-134-2*, Pub. by Quarry Pr) LPC InBook.
Mastin, Colleayn. The Magic of Mythical Creatures. LC 96-910711. (Illus.). 32p. (J). (gr. 1 up). 1997. 17.95 (*1-895910-45-5*) Grasshopper Bks.
Mastin, Colleayn O. Magic of Mythical Creatures. (Illus.). 32p. (J). (gr. 1). 1999. pap. 9.95 (*1-895910-43-9*, Pub. by Grasshopr Bks) Orca Bk Pubs.
Mastin, Colleyan. North America Arctic Animals. (North American Nature Ser.). (Illus.). 32p. (J). (gr. 1 up). 1997. pap. 9.95 (*1-895910-23-4*) Grasshopper Bks.
— North America Wild Animals, 4 vols. (North American Nature Ser.). (Illus.). 32p. (J). (gr. 1 up). 1997. pap. 9.95 (*1-895910-21-8*) Grasshopper Bks.
— North American Endangered Species, 4 vols. (North American Nature Ser.). (Illus.). 32p. (J). (gr. 1 up). 1997. pap. 9.95 (*1-895910-27-7*) Grasshopper Bks.
— North American Ocean Creatures, 4 vols. (North American Nature Ser.). (Illus.). 32p. (J). (gr. 1 up). 1997. pap. 9.95 (*1-895910-25-0*) Grasshopper Bks.
Mastin, Deborah B. & Hushion, Timothy. The Nuts & Bolts of Copyright. Stevens, Marilyn, ed. (Art Calendar Guide Ser.). 43p. 1999. pap. 9.95 (*0-945388-07-1*) Art Calendar.
Mastin, Deborah B., jt. auth. see Nikkal, Nancy E.
Mastin, Florence R. Across Time's Fence. 1978. pap. 2.00 (*0-911183-07-8*) Rockland County Hist.
Mastin, Ralf. The Ones Who Got Away. 121p. 1998. pap. write for info. (*0-7541-0028-6*, Pub. by Minerva Pr) Unity Dist.
Mastin, Robert. 900 Know-How: How to Succeed with Your Own 900-Number Business. 3rd ed. LC 95-83157. 350p. 1996. pap. 19.95 (*0-9632790-3-3*) Aegis Pub Grp.
Mastin, Robert, ed. Telecom & Networking Glossary: Understanding Communications Technology. LC 98-45440. (Illus.). 144p. 1998. pap. 9.95 (*1-890154-09-1*, TC8) Aegis Pub Grp.
Mastin, Robert, jt. auth. see Ginsburg, Carol M.
Mastin, Tim, ed. see Guay-Woodford, Lisa M. & Chapman, Arlene B.
Mastini, Frank. Ship Modeling Simplified: Tips & Techniques for Model Construction from Kits. 1990. pap. text 18.95 (*0-87742-272-9*) Intl Marine.
— Ship Modeling Simplified: Tips & Techniques for Model Construction from Kits. 224p. 1990. pap. 18.95 (*0-07-155867-5*) McGraw.
Mastny, Vojtech. The Cold War & Soviet Insecurity: The Stalin Years. 304p. 1998. pap. 19.95 (*0-19-512659-9*) OUP.
— Czechoslovakia: Crisis in World Communism. LC 70-166437. (Interim History Ser.). 400p. reprint ed. pap. 124.00 (*0-608-12004-9*, 202291500031) Bks Demand.
— The Helsinki Process & the Reintegration of Europe: Analysis & Documentation, 1986-1990. 380p. (C). 1992. pap. text 25.00 (*0-8147-5477-5*) NYU Pr.
Mastny, Vojtech, ed. Disarmament & Nuclear Tests, 1964-1969. LC 72-122210. (Interim History Ser.). 264p. reprint ed. pap. 81.90 (*0-608-12002-2*, 202291700031) Bks Demand.
— Power & Policy in Transition: Essays Presented on the Tenth Anniversary of the National Committee on American Foreign Policy in Honor of Its Founder, Hans J. Morgenthau. 126. LC 84-15778. (Contributions in Political Science Ser.: No. 126). (Illus.). 271p. 1985. 59.95 (*0-313-24498-7*, MAY/) Greenwood.
Mastny, Vojtech, ed. see Nation, Craig.
Maston, Ann S., ed. Cultural Processes in Child Development. LC 98-47096. (Minnesota Symposia on Child Psychology Ser.: Vol. 29). 168p. 1998. 39.95 (*0-8058-2167-8*) L Erlbaum Assocs.
Maston, T. B. Biblical Ethics--A Survey: A Guide to the Ethical Message of the Scriptures from Genesis Through Revelation. LC 82-6470. 320p. 1982. pap. text 14.95 (*0-86554-312-7*, MUP\P056) Mercer Univ Pr.
— The Ethic of the Christian Life. Hogg, Gayle, ed. (Religious Education Ser.). 152p. (C). 1982. kivar 10.50 (*0-311-72605-4*) Casa Bautista.
— Why Live the Christian Life? LC 96-23690. 200p. 1996. reprint ed. pap. 16.00 (*0-914520-36-9*) Insight Pr.
Mastoon, Adam. The Shared Heart: Portraits & Stories Celebrating Lesbian, Gay, & Bisexual Young People. LC 97-3276. (Illus.). 87p. (YA). (gr. 7 up). 1997. 24.50 (*0-688-14931-6*, Wm Morrow) Morrow Avon.
Mastorakis, Nikos E. Recent Advances in Circuits & Systems. 400p. 84.00 (*981-02-3644-1*) World Scientific Pub.
— Recent Advances in Information Science & Technology. 400p. 82.00 (*981-02-3657-3*) World Scientific Pub.
Mastoris, Stephanos, jt. auth. see Malcolmson, Robert W.
Mastowski, ed. Ciceronis, M. Tulli Fascicule 21: Cum Senatui Gratias Egit. (LAT.). 1981. 29.95 (*3-322-00842-8*, T1192, Pub. by B G Teubner) U of Mich Pr.
Mastracchio, Nicholas J., Jr. Mergers & Acquisitions of CPA Firms: A Guide to Practice Valuation. LC 98-7430. (Illus.). 156p. 1998. pap. 49.00 (*0-87051-205-6*, 090411) Am Inst CPA.
Mastracci, Mark. San Francisco Bay Area School Ratings. LC 97-94473. (Illus.). 224p. 1997. pap. 19.95 (*0-9660448-1-9*) Apollo Sch.
Mastrangelo, Judy. What Do Bunnies Do All Day? (Illus.). 32p. (J). (ps-1). 1991. pap., per. 4.95 (*0-8249-8509-5*, Ideals Child) Hambleton-Hill.
Mastrangelo, R., ed. Central Nervous System Leukemia Prevention & Treatment. (Developments in Oncology Ser.). 1983. text 126.50 (*0-89838-570-9*) Kluwer Academic.
Mastretta, Angeles. Arrancame la Vida. 1998. pap. 14.00 (*0-375-70199-0*) Vin Bks.
— Lovesick. large type ed. Sayers Peden, Margaret, tr. from SPA. LC 97-5817. 538p. 1997. 24.95 (*0-7862-1083-4*) Thorndike Pr.
— Lovesick: A Novel. Peden, Margaret Sayers, tr. 400p. 1998. pap. 13.00 (*1-57322-655-6*, Riverhd Trade) Berkley Pub.
— Mal de Amores. 1998. pap. 15.00 (*0-375-70200-8*) Vin Bks.
— Mujeres de Ojos Grandes.Tr. of Women with Big Eyes. (SPA.). 1997. pap. 12.95 (*84-322-4660-3*, Pub. by E Seix Barral) Continental Bk.
— Tear This Heart Out. 1997. pap. 12.00 (*0-614-27266-1*, Riverhd Trade) Berkley Pub.
— Tear This Heart Out. Peden, Margaret, tr. from SPA. LC 96-39816. 304p. 1997. pap. 12.00 (*1-57322-602-5*, Riverhd Trade) Berkley Pub.
Mastri, Augustus A., jt. auth. see Hatzantonis, Emmanuel.
Mastrianna, Frank B., jt. auth. see Hailstones, Thomas J.
Mastrianna, Frank V. Basic Economics. 10th ed. (SWC-Economics). (C). 1994. mass mkt., student ed. 23.95 (*0-538-84205-9*) S-W Pub.
— Basic Economics. 11th ed. LC 97-7499. (Miscellaneous/Catalogs Ser.). (C). 1997. mass mkt. 63.95 (*0-538-86876-7*); mass mkt., student ed. 22.00 (*0-538-86877-5*) S-W Pub.
***Mastrianna, Frank V.** Basic Economics. 12th ed. 2000. pap. 20.75 (*0-324-02037-6*) Sth-Wstrn College.
— Basic Economics. 12th ed. 2000. pap. 45.00 (*0-324-02036-8*) Thomson Learn.
— Basic Economics. 12th ed. 2000. pap. 19.00 (*0-324-02038-4*) Thomson Learn.
Mastrianna, Frank V. & Hailstones, Thomas J. Basic Economics. 10th ed. LC 94-13025. (C). 1994. pap. 53.95 (*0-538-84204-0*) S-W Pub.
Mastrianna, Frank V., jt. auth. see Hailstones, Thomas J.
Mastrianni, Steven J. Writing OS - 2 2.1 Device Drivers in C. 2nd ed. 416p. 1995. pap. text 39.95 incl. disk (*0-471-13152-0*) Wiley.
Mastrich, James L. & Birnes, William J. Strong Enough for Two. 256p. 1991. pap. 9.95 (*0-02-034520-8*) Macmillan.
Mastrigt, Hans Van, see Uildriks, Niels & Van Mastrigt, Hans.
Mastrini, John & Crosby, Alan. Frommer's Prague & the Best of the Czech Republic. 2nd ed. (Frommer's Travel Guides Ser.). 288p. 1998. pap. 14.95 (*0-02-862092-5*, Frommer) Macmillan Gen Ref.
Mastro, Jim, jt. auth. see Westheimer, Patricia H.
Mastro, Joseph P. U. S. S. R. Calendar of Events Annual, 1987-1991. 97.00 (*0-685-27034-3*) Academic Intl.
— U. S. S. R. Calendar of Events Annual, 1987-1991, 5 vols., Set. 375.00 (*0-87569-113-7*) Academic Intl.
Mastro, M. L. del, see Meisel, Anthony C. & Del Mastro, M. L., trs.
Mastro, M. L. del, see Del Mastro, M. L., tr.
Mastrobuono, Antonio C. Dante's Journey of Sanctification. LC 90-35108. 260p. 1990. pap. 14.95 (*0-89526-741-1*) Regnery Pub.
***Mastroeni, Anthony J., ed.** Is a Culture of Life Still Possible in the U. S.? 185p. 2000. pap. 16.00 (*1-890318-27-2*, Pub. by St Augustines Pr) Chicago Distribution Ctr.
Mastrofski, Stephen D., jt. auth. see Klockars, Carl B.
Mastrofski, Stephen D., jt. ed. see Greene, Jack R.
Mastrogiannopoulos, Elias. The Byzantine Churches of Greece & Cyprus. 136p. 1984. 9.95 (*0-917651-06-5*, Pub. by Holy Cross Orthodox); pap. 5.95 (*0-917651-07-3*, Pub. by Holy Cross Orthodox) BookWorld.
Mastrogiovanni, John L. Beyond Revival Living in the Spirit of Revolution. 102p. 1999. pap. 7.00 (*0-7392-0191-3*, PO3168) Morris Pubng.
Mastrogregori, Massimo, ed. see Glennison, Jean.
Mastroiann, Luigi. Infertility: A Guide for Patients. (Urology & Gyn Ser.). 32p. 1997. pap. text 2.95 (*1-885274-61-0*) Health InfoNet Inc.
Mastroianni, Anna C., ed. see Committee on the Ethical & Legal Issues Relating t.
Mastroianni, Anne C., ed. see Institute of Medicine Staff.

M

Mastroianni, Luigi, Jr., et al, eds. Fertilization & Embryonic Development In Vitro. LC 81-13829. 382p. 1981. 85.00 (0-306-40783-3, Plenum Trade) Perseus Pubng.

— Gamete & Embryo Quality: The Proceedings of the Fourth Organon Round Table Conference, Thessaloniki, Greece, 24-25 June 1993. LC 93-40905. 248p. 1994. 98.00 (1-85070-543-7) Prthnon Pub.

Mastroianni, Luigi, jt. auth. see Coutifaris, Cristos.

Mastroianni, M. J., jt. auth. see Allied Chemical Corporation Staff.

Mastroianni, Michael D. & Dasenbrook, Norman C. Harnessing the Power of Conflict: Optimum Group Performance Through the Self Mediation Method. 170p. (Orig.). 1994. pap. text 9.95 (0-9643949-0-1) Crysand Pr.

Mastroianni, Michael D., jt. auth. see Dasenbrook, Norman C.

Mastrolorenzo, G., jt. auth. see Dvorak, J. J.

Mastromarco, Giuseppe. The Public of Herondas. (London Studies of Classical Philology: Vol. 11). 136p. 1984. text 40.00 (90-70265-94-X, Pub. by Gieben) J Benjamins Pubng Co.

Mastromarino, Anthony J., ed. Biology & Treatment of Colorectal Cancer Metastasis. (Developments in Oncology Ser.). 1986. text 120.50 (0-89838-786-8) Kluwer Academic.

Mastromarino, Anthony J. & Brattain, Michael G., eds. Large Bowel Cancer: Clinical & Basic Science Research, 3. LC 85-515. (Cancer Research Monographs: Vol. 3). 204p. 1985. 55.00 (0-275-91319-8, C1319, Praeger Pubs) Greenwood.

Mastromarino, Anthony J., jt. ed. see Wolman, Sandra R.

Mastromarino, Mark A., ed. The Papers of George Washington Presidential Series Vol. 6: July-November 1790. (Papers of George Washington). 800p. (C). 1996. text 57.50 (0-8139-1637-2) U Pr of Va.

***Mastromattei, Romano & Rigopoulos, Antonio, eds.** Shamanic Cosmos: From India to the North Pole Star. x, 252p. 1999. 27.50 (81-246-0106-2, Pub. by D K Printwrld) Nataraj Bks.

Mastronarde, Donald J. Contact & Discontinuity: Some Conventions of Speech & Action on the Greek Tragic Stage. LC 78-62877. (University of California Publications: No. 21). 153p. pap. 47.50 (0-7837-7491-5, 204921300010) Bks Demand.

— Introduction to Attic Greek. LC 92-21731. (C). 1993. 50.00 (0-520-07843-8, Pub. by U CA Pr); pap. 22.50 (0-520-07844-6, Pub. by U CA Pr) Cal Prin Full Svc.

Mastronarde, Donald J. Introduction to Attic Greek: Answer Key. 1995. pap. 14.95 (0-520-20177-9) U CA Pr.

Mastronarde, Donald J. & Bremer, Jan M. The Textural Tradition of Euripides' "Phoinissai" LC 82-13492. (UC Publications in Classical Studies: Vol. 27). 464p. (C). 1983. pap. 45.00 (0-520-09664-9, Pub. by U CA Pr) Cal Prin Full Svc.

Mastronarde, Donald J., ed. see Euripides.

Mastronardi, G., ed. Mini & Microcomputers & Their Applications - Mimi, 1984: Proceedings, ISMM Symposium, Bari, Italy, June 5-8, 1984. 289p. 1984. 85.00 (0-88986-058-0, 065) Acta Pr.

Mastroni, Nick. The Insider's Guide to Golf Equipment: The Fully Illustrated, Comprehensive Directory of Brand Name Clubs & Accessories. LC 96-30132. (Illus.). 384p. 1997. pap. 13.95 (0-399-52277-8, Perigee Bks) Berkley Pub.

Mastroni, Nick, jt. auth. see Pelz, Dave.

Mastronikola, Katerina. Yield Curves for Gilt-Edged Stocks: A New Model. LC HG4136.. (Bank of England. Discussion Papers. Technical Ser.: No. 49). 40p. reprint ed. pap. 30.00 (0-7837-3208-2, 204320400007) Bks Demand.

Mastropaolo, Joseph. For King & Glory: Knights of the Kingdom of France During the Sixteenth Century. limited ed. LC 98-60289. (Illus.). x, 310p. 1998. 24.95 (0-9640201-1-4) Trisphere Pubs.

Mastropasqua, Corrado. Ibrido: Poesie, 1949-1986. (Essential Poets Ser.: No. 31). (ITA.). 96p. 1988. pap. 8.00 (0-919349-87-0) Guernica Editions.

Mastropasqua, S. The Banking System in the Countries of the EEC: Institutional & Structural Aspects. 170p. 1978. lib. bdg. 52.00 (90-286-0518-5) Kluwer Academic.

Mastropasqua, V. Dizionario Tecnico Nautico: Italiano-Inglese, Inglese-Italiano. (ENG & ITA.). 879p. 1967. pap. 75.00 (0-8288-6683-X, M-9297) Fr & Eur.

Mastropieri. Strats. Effective Mainstream. LC 99-18771. 638p. 1999. pap. text 55.00 (0-13-496472-1) P-H.

Mastropieri, M., jt. auth. see Scruggs, Thomas.

Mastropieri, Margo & Scruggs, Thomas E. Teaching Test Taking Skills: Helping Students Show What They Know. Pressley, Michael, ed. (Cognitive Strategy Training Ser.). 139p. 1992. pap. text 21.95 (0-914797-76-X) Brookline Bks.

Mastropieri, Margo A. & Scruggs, Thomas E. Effective Instruction for Special Education. 2nd ed. LC 93-41947. (Illus.). 419p. (Orig.). (C). 1994. pap. text 37.00 (0-89079-572-X, 6694) PRO-ED.

— A Practical Guide for Teaching Science to Students with Special Needs in Inclusive Settings. (Illus.). 371p. (C). 1993. spiral bd. 34.00 (0-89079-611-4, 6817) PRO-ED.

— Teaching Students Ways to Remember: Strategies for Learning Mnemonically. (Cognitive Strategy Training Ser.). 11p. 1990. pap. text 21.95 (0-914797-67-0) Brookline Bks.

Mastropieri, Margo A., et al. Effective Instruction for Special Education. 2nd ed. (Orig.). 1994. pap., teacher ed. write for info. (0-89079-573-8, 6767) PRO-ED.

Mastropieri, Margo A., jt. ed. see Scruggs, Thomas E.

Mastrorio, Lorraine. Living by the Spirit. 96p. 1998. pap. 9.95 (0-88243-223-0) Gospel Pub.

— Living by the Spirit: Study Guide. 93p. 1997. pap., student ed. 4.95 (0-88243-123-4) Gospel Pub.

Mastrosimone, William. William Mastrosimone: Collected Plays. (Contemporary Playwrights Ser.). 360p. 1993. pap. 19.95 (1-880399-32-6) Smith & Kraus.

Mastry, Cherisse, ed. see Capriola, Arlene & Swensen, Rigmor.

Mastry, Cherisse, ed. see Capriola, Arlene & Swenson, Rigmor.

Mastry, Cherisse, ed. see Watson, Pat & Watson, Janet.

Mastur, Khadija. Cool, Sweet Water: Selected Stories. Memon, Muhammad Umar, ed. Naqvi, Tahira, tr. LC 99-921829. (Pakistan Writers Ser.). 228p. 1999. pap. text 9.95 (0-19-579053-7) OUP.

Masty, Jerome & Hamilton, William P. Atlas of Equine Anatomy: A Fundamental & Applied Approach. 380p. pap. text. write for info. (0-683-30018-0) Lppncott W & W.

Mastyugina, Tatiana & Perepelkin, Lev, eds. An Ethnic History of Russia: Pre-Revolutionary Times to the Present, 35. LC 96-7141. (Contributions in Ethnic Studies: Vol. 35). 264p. 1996. 65.00 (0-313-29315-5, Greenwood Pr) Greenwood.

Masuch, Michael, ed. Organization, Management, & Expert Systems: Models of Automated Reasoning. (Studies in Organization: No. 23). x, 249p. (C). 1990. lib. bdg. 54.95 (3-11-011942-0) De Gruyter.

Masuch, Michael & Polos, Laszlo, eds. Knowledge Representation & Reasoning under Uncertainty: Logic at Work. LC 94-20068. 1994. 39.95 (0-387-58095-6) Spr-Verlag.

Masuch, Michael & Warglien, Massimo. Artificial Intelligence in Organization & Management Theory. 346p. 1992. 154.50 (0-444-89042-4, North Holland) Elsevier.

Masuch, Michael, jt. ed. see Polos, Laszlo.

Masuch, Michael, jt. ed. see Warglien, Massimo.

Mas'Ud Ibn Umar Al-Taftazani. A Commentary on the Creed of Islam. LC 79-52565. (Islam Ser.). 1980. reprint ed. lib. bdg. 23.95 (0-8369-9268-7) Ayer.

Masud, Iqbal. Dream Merchants, Politicians & Partition: Memoirs of an Indian Muslim. LC 98-900025. xviii, 152 p. 1997. write for info. (81-7223-262-4) CE25.

Masud, M., jt. auth. see Khan, R.

Masud, M. Khalid. Islamic Legal Interpretation: Muftis & Their Fatwas. (Illus.). 416p. 1996. 45.00 (0-674-46870-8) HUP.

Masud, Muhammad K. Islamic Legal Philosophy. 1990. pap. 25.50 (1-56744-100-9) Kazi Pubns.

— Shatibi's Philosophy of Islamic Law. 306p. 1997. pap. 29.95 (1-56744-533-0) Kazi Pubns.

***Masud, Muhammad Khalid, ed.** Travellers in Faith: Studies of the Tablighi Fama at as a Transnational Islamic Movement for Faith Renewal. 352p. 2000. 103.00 (90-04-11622-2) Brill Academic Pubs.

***Masud, Naiyer.** Essence of Camphor. 192p. 2000. 21.00 (1-56584-583-8, Pub. by New Press NY) Norton.

Masud-Piloto, Felix. From Welcomed Exiles to Illegal Immigrants: Cuban Migration to the U. S., 1959-1995. 194p. (C). 1995. pap. text 22.95 (0-8476-8149-1); lib. bdg. 53.50 (0-8476-8148-3) Rowman.

— With Open Arms: Cuban Migration to the United States. LC 87-12809. 168p. 1988. 49.50 (0-8476-7566-1, R7566) Rowman.

— With Open Arms? The Evolution of Cuban Migration to the U. S., 1959-1995. rev. ed. 200p. (C). 1995. pap. text 19.95 (0-8476-8038-X); lib. bdg. 49.50 (0-8476-8037-1) Rowman.

Masuda. Words That Wound: Critical Race Theory, Assaultive Speech, & the First Amendment. 2nd ed. 2000. 22.95 (0-8133-6856-1) HarpC.

Masuda, Akiko. The Adventures of Kalakoa: A Hawaiian Rainbow Fantasy. (Illus.). 32p. (J). (gr. k-7). 1991. 7.95 (0-9629842-1-3) Stew & Rice.

— Neil Tofu Luvs Tee-dah Tuna. (Illus.). 32p. (J). (gr. k-8). 1995. pap. write for info. (0-9629842-2-1) Stew & Rice.

Masuda, I. High-Performance BiCMOS Technology & Its Applications to VLSIs, Vol. 3. (Japanese Technology Reviews Ser.: Sec. A). xiv, 86p. 1990. text 107.00 (2-88124-456-4) Gordon & Breach.

Masuda, Jiryo, tr. see Vasu-Mitra.

Masuda, Kohzoh, ed. see United States-Japan Seminar on Energy & Charge Tra.

Masuda, M. Dictionary of Marine Engineering Terms. (ENG & JPN.). 318p. 1980. 125.00 (0-8288-0420-6, M9339) Fr & Eur.

— Kenkyusha's New Pocket Japanese-English Dictionary. 65.00 (0-7859-7130-0, F100790) Fr & Eur.

Masuda, Mutsumi, tr. see Asamiya, Kia.

Masuda, Mutsumi, tr. see Taniguchi, Tomoko.

Masuda, S. & Takahashi, Koichiro, eds. Aerosols: Science, Industry, Health & Environment: Proceedings of the Third International Aerosol Conference, Kyoto, Japan, 24-27 September 1990, 2 vols., Set. (Illus.). 1388p. 1990. pap. 55.25 (0-08-037525-1, Pergamon Pr) Elsevier.

Masuda, Takashi, et al, eds. Worldwide Computing & its Applications: International Conference, WWCA '97, Tsukuba, Japan, March 10-11, 1997. LC 97-27812. (Lecture Notes in Computer Science Ser.: Vol. 1274). xvi, 443p. pap. write for info. (3-540-63343-X) Spr-Verlag.

Masuda, Wataru. Japan & China: Mutual Representations in the Modern Era. Fogel, Joshua, tr. 350p. (C). 1999. text 55.00 (0-7007-1120-1, Pub. by Curzon Pr Ltd) UH Pr.

Masuda, Yoneji. The Information Society As Post-Industrial Society. 178p. (C). 1980. pap. 16.95 (0-930242-15-7) World Future.

Masuda, Yoshio, et al. Analytical Studies on Growing Plant Cell Walls. 50p. 1983. 5.00 (1-55528-084-6, Pub. by Today Tomorrow) Scholarly Pubns.

Masuda, Yuji & Gill, K. S., eds. Human Centred Systems in the Global Economy: Proceedings from the International Workshop on Industrial Cultures & Human Centred Systems, Held by Tokyo Keizai University in Tokyo, May 1990. LC 92-10114. (Artificial Intelligence & Society Ser.). (Illus.). 272p. 1992. 69.00 (3-540-19745-1) Spr-Verlag.

Masuda, Yuji & Gill, Karamjit S., eds. Human Centred Systems in the Global Economy: Proceedings from the International Workshop on Industrial Cultures & Human Centred Systems, Held by Tokyo Keizai University in Tokyo, May 1990. LC 92-10114. (Artificial Intelligence & Society Ser.). (Illus.). 272p. 1992. 69.00 (0-387-19745-1) Spr-Verlag.

Masudi. The Meadows of Gold. Lunde, Paul & Stone, Catherine, trs. 320p. 1987. 65.00 (0-7103-0246-0, A0086) Routledge.

Masudi, H., ed. Tribology Symposium, 1995: Proceedings: The Energy & Environmental EXPO '95 - the Energy-Sources Technology Conference & Exhibition (1995: Houston, TX) LC 93-74682. (PD Ser.: Vol. 72). 177p. 1995. pap. 86.00 (0-7918-1297-9, H00929) ASME.

— Tribology Symposium, 1994, Vol. 61. LC 93-74682. 140p. 1994. pap. 37.50 (0-7918-1189-1) ASME.

Masugi, Ken & Hiraoka, Leona. Japanese-American Internment. The Bill of Rights in Crisis. 1993. student ed. 39.00 (1-56696-004-5) Jackdaw.

Masugi, Ken, jt. ed. see Rusher, William A.

Masugi, Ken, jt. ed. see Wilson, Bradford P.

Masuhara, Hiroshi, ed. see JRDC-KUL Joint International Symposium on "Spectro, et al.

Masui, Kazuko & Yamada, Tomoko. French Cheeses. (Eyewitness Handbooks Ser.). (Illus.). 240p. 1996. pap. 17.95 (0-7894-1070-2) DK Pub Inc.

Masui, Mitsuko. Pandas of the World. Ooka, Diane T., tr. (Illus.). 32p. (J). (gr. k-2). 1989. 12.95 (0-89346-314-0) Heian Intl.

***Masujima, Michio.** Path Integral Quantization & Stochastic Quantization. LC 00-29726. 2000. write for info. (3-540-66542-0) Spr-Verlag.

Masulis, Ronald W. The Debt-Equity Choice. (Financial Management Association Survey & Synthesis Series, the International Investor Series in Finance). 144p. 1988. text 39.95 (0-88730-360-9, HarpBusn); pap. text 18.95 (0-88730-368-4, HarpBusn) HarpInfo.

Masulli, F. & Morasso, P. G. Neural Networks in Biomedicine: Proceedings of the Course. 300p. 1994. text 91.00 (981-02-1744-7) World Scientific Pub.

Masulli, Ignazio. Nature & History: The Evolutionary Approach for Social Scientists, Vol. 1. (World Futures General Evolution Studies). 184p. 1990. text 84.00 (2-88124-376-2) Gordon & Breach.

Masumaga, Reiho, tr. from JPN. A Primer of Soto Zen: A Translation of Dogen's Shobogenzo Zuimonki. LC 76-126044. 128p. (C). 1975. pap. text 8.00 (0-8248-0357-4) EW Ctr HI.

Masumi, Junnosuke. Contemporary Politics in Japan. Carlile, Lonny E., tr. from JPN. LC 94-23660.Tr. of Gendai Seiji. 1995. pap. 30.00 (0-520-05854-2, Pub. by U CA Pr) Cal Prin Full Svc.

Masumi, Junnosuke, jt. auth. see Scalapino, Robert A.

Ma'sumi, M. H. Imam Razi's Ilm-al-Ikhlaq. 1987. 18.50 (1-56744-054-1) Kazi Pubns.

Masumian, Farnaz. Life after Death: A Study of the Afterlife in World Religions. 200p. 1995. pap. 14.95 (1-85168-074-8, Pub. by Onewrld Pubns) Penguin Putnam.

Masumoto, David Mas. Country Voices, the Oral History of a Japanese American Family Farm Community. LC 87-3126. (Illus.). 256p. (Orig.). 1987. pap. 14.95 (0-9614541-0-5) Inaka-Countryside Pubns.

— Harvest Son: Planting Roots in American Soil. LC 98-15702. 256p. 1998. 22.95 (0-393-04673-7) Norton.

— Harvest Son: Planting Roots in American Soil. 304p. 1999. pap. 13.00 (0-393-31974-1, Norton Paperbks) Norton.

Masunaga, Shizuto. Meridian Exercises: The Oriental Way to Health & Vitality. Brown, Stephen, tr. from JPN. Orig. Title: Zen Imagery Exercises. (Illus.). 238p. (Orig.). 1996. pap. 22.00 (0-87040-897-6) Japan Pubns USA.

Masunaga, Shizuto & Ohashi, Wataru. Zen Shiatsu: How to Harmonize Yin & Yang for Better Health. (Illus.). 176p. 1977. pap. 19.95 (0-87040-394-X) Japan Pubns USA.

Masunaga, Y., et al, eds. Worldwide Computing & Its Applications - WWCA '98, Vol. 136. LC 98-14455. (Lecure Notes in Computer Science Ser.: Vol. 1368). xiv, 473p. 1998. pap. 69.00 (3-540-64216-1) Spr-Verlag.

Masunaga, Yoshifumi, ed. see International Conference on Database Systems for A.

Masundire, H. M., ed. see Botswana Wetlands Coordinating Committee., et al.

Masuoka, Jitsuichi & Valien, P., eds. Race Relations. (New Reprints in Essay & General Literature Index Ser.). 1977. reprint ed. 26.95 (0-518-10205-X, 10205) Ayer.

Masuoka, Susan N. En Calavera: The Papier-Mache Art of the Linares Family. LC 94-36635. 1994. 45.00 (0-930741-40-4); pap. 27.00 (0-930741-41-2) UCLA Fowler Mus.

Masur. Viewing America, Vol. 1. Date not set. pap. text. write for info. (0-312-11693-4) St Martin.

Masur, Harold Q. Auto Ben Frank with Fred Doug. 2000. pap. text 13.50 (0-312-14850-X) St Martin.

***Masur, Henry.** Respiratory Infections in Patients with HIV. LC 99-13106. 1999. write for info. (0-7817-2026-5) Lppncott W & W.

Masur, Louis P. The Challenge of American History. LC 98-55163. 330p. 1999. 16.95 (0-8018-6222-1) Johns Hopkins.

***Masur, Louis P.** 1831: Year of Eclipse. (Illus.). 224p. 2001. 25.00 (0-8090-4118-9) Hill & Wang.

Masure, Bruno. Dictionnaire Analphabetique. (FRE.). 202p. 1990. pap. 29.95 (0-7859-8102-0, 2855655986) Fr & Eur.

Masure, Myrle T. The Eight Commandments: A Code of Ethics for Elected Officials. Bonneville, Douglas, ed. & illus. by. 68p. (Orig.). (C). 1996. pap. 12.95 (1-880836-12-2) Pine Isl Pr.

— Eight Commandments for Political Reform: Power in the Elective Process. Goldstein, Wallace L., ed. (Illus.). 80p. (Orig.). 1993. pap. text 10.00 (1-880836-02-5) Pine Isl Pr.

— Eight Commandments for Political Reform: Power in the Elective Process. 2nd ed. Goldstein, Wallace L. & Alward, Edgar C., eds. (Illus.). 80p. (Orig.). (YA). 1994. text 11.00 (1-880836-05-X) Pine Isl Pr.

Masurel, Claire. Christmas Is Coming! LC 98-11951. (Illus.). (J). (ps-1). 1998. 14.95 (0-8118-2106-4) Chronicle Bks.

***Masurel, Claire.** Diez Perros en la Tienda. Moro, Elena, tr.Tr. of Ten Dogs in the Window. (SPA., Illus.). 32p. (J). (ps-1). 2000. 15.95 (0-7358-1302-7, Pub. by North-South Bks NYC); pap. 6.95 (0-7358-1303-5, Pub. by North-South Bks NYC) Chronicle Bks.

— Diez Perros en la Tienda: Un Libro Para Contar. (SPA., Illus.). (J). 2000. 12.40 (0-606-18318-3) Turtleback.

— Dix Chiens dans la Vitrine.Tr. of Ten Dogs in the Window. (FRE., Illus.). (J). (ps-1). pap. 15.95 (3-314-21077-9, Pub. by North-South Bks NYC) Chronicle Bks.

— Emily's First Day of School. (Illus.). 16p. (J). (ps-3). 2000. pap. 6.99 (0-14-056716-X, PuffinBks) Peng Put Young Read.

Masurel, Claire. Good Night! (Illus.). 32p. (J). (ps). 1999. bds. 6.95 (0-8118-2461-6) Chronicle Bks.

— Good Night! (Illus.). 32p. (J). (ps-1). 1999. pap. 5.95 (0-8118-1169-7) Chronicle Bks.

— Good Night! LC 93-30198. 1994. 11.15 (0-606-08921-7, Pub. by Turtleback) Demco.

— No, No, Titus! LC 96-44501. (Illus.). 32p. (J). (ps-1). 1997. lib. bdg. 15.88 (1-55858-726-8, Pub. by North-South Bks NYC) Chronicle Bks.

***Masurel, Claire.** No, No, Titus! LC 96-44501. (Illus.). 32p. (J). (ps-1). 1999. pap. 6.95 (0-7358-1201-2, Pub. by North-South Bks NYC) Chronicle Bks.

— No, Tito, No! Lasconi, Diego, tr. LC 99-20064.Tr. of No, No, Titus!. (SPA., Illus.). 32p. (J). (ps-1). 1999. 15.95 (0-7358-1208-X, Pub. by North-South Bks NYC); pap. 6.95 (0-7358-1209-8, Pub. by North-South Bks NYC) Chronicle Bks.

— Non, Titus, Non!Tr. of No, No, Titus!. (FRE., Illus.). (J). (ps-1). pap. 15.95 (3-314-21050-7, Pub. by North-South Bks NYC) Chronicle Bks.

— Ten Dogs in the Window. LC 97-20945. (Illus.). 32p. (J). (ps-1). 2000. pap. 6.95 (0-7358-1301-9, Pub. by North-South Bks NYC) Chronicle Bks.

Masurel, Claire. Ten Dogs in the Window: A Countdown Book. LC 97-20945. (Illus.). 32p. (J). (ps-1). 1997. 15.95 (1-55858-754-3, Pub. by North-South Bks NYC) Chronicle Bks.

Masurel, Claire. Ten Dogs in the Window: A Countdown Book. LC 97-20945. (Illus.). 32p. (J). (ps-1). 1997. lib. bdg. 15.88 (1-55858-755-1, Pub. by North-South Bks NYC) Chronicle Bks.

Masurel, Claire. Too Big! LC 98-36194. (Illus.). 36p. (J). 1999. 13.95 (0-8118-2090-4) Chronicle Bks.

— Where's Santa? LC 99-190531. 32p. (J). (ps-1). 1998. pap. 6.99 (0-14-056322-9, PuffinBks) Peng Put Young Read.

Masurel, Edouard. L' Annee dans le Monde, 1990. (FRE.). 1991. pap. 11.95 (0-7859-3974-1) Fr & Eur.

Masuren-Matthies. Kunst Lerische Photographie. Sobieszek, Robert A. & Bunnell, Peter C., eds. LC 76-24675. (Sources of Modern Photography Ser.). (GER., Illus.). 1979. reprint ed. lib. bdg. 12.95 (0-405-09651-8) Ayer.

Masuzawa, Tomoko. In Search of Dreamtime: The Quest for the Origin of Religion. LC 93-518. (Religion & Postmodernism Ser.). 232p. 1993. pap. text 15.95 (0-226-50985-0); lib. bdg. 45.00 (0-226-50984-2) U Ch Pr.

***Masuzumi, Alfred.** Caribou Hide: Two Stories of Life on the Land. (Illus.). (J). (gr. 4-7). 1999. pap. 7.95 (1-894303-20-2) RRP.

Maswood, S. Javed. International Political Economy & Globalization. LC 99-40240. 1999. 58.00 (981-02-3854-1) World Scientific Pub.

— International Political Economy & Globalization. LC 99-40240. 300p. 1999. pap. 28.00 (981-02-3855-X) World Scientific Pub.

Masyr, Caryl & Freifeld, Roberta. Space Planning in the Special Library. 1991. 23.00 (0-87111-356-2) SLA.

Maszynska, Maria, ed. see Szmielev, Wanda.

Mata, Angelica, tr. see Mutz, Martha.

Mata, Angelica, tr. see Mutz, Martha, et al.

Mata, Daya. Finding the Joy Within You: Personal Counsel for God-Centered Living. LC 90-63632. (Illus.). 336p. 1990. 14.00 (0-87612-288-8) Self Realization.

— Finding the Joy Within You: Personal Counsel for God-Centered Living. LC 90-63632. (Illus.). 352p. 1998. reprint ed. pap. 11.00 (0-87612-289-6) Self Realization.

— Only Love: Living the Spiritual Life in a Changing World. LC 75-44633. (Illus.). 295p. 1976. 14.00 (0-87612-215-2) Self Realization.

— Only Love: Living the Spiritual Life in a Changing World. LC 75-44633. (Illus.). 295p. 1995. pap. 10.50 (0-87612-216-0) Self Realization.

Mata, Maria E., jt. ed. see Pereira, Pedro T.

***Mata, Marta.** Goldilocks & the Three Bears (Ricitos de Oro y los Tres Sos) Alejandro, Alis, tr. (SPA & ENG., Illus.). 32p. (J). (ps-2). 1998. 12.95 (0-8118-2075-0) Chronicle Bks.

An Asterisk (*) at the beginning of an entry indicates that the title is appearing for the first time.

Mata, Sri D. Enter the Quiet Heart: Creating a Loving Relationship with God. LC 97-62188. 116p. 1998. 10.00 (*0-87612-175-X*) Self Realization.

***Mata-Toledo, Ramon.** Schaum's Outline of Fundamentals of SQL Programming. (Schaum's Outlines Ser.). (Illus.). 352p. 2000. pap. text 16.95 (*0-07-135953-2*, Schaums Outlne) McGraw-Hill Prof.

— Schaum's Outline of Introduction to Computer Science. 240p. 1999. pap. 15.95 (*0-07-134554-X*) McGraw.

***Mata-Toledo, Ramon A.** Schaum's Outline of Fundamentals of Relational Databases. (Schaum's Outlines Ser.). 2000. pap. 16.95 (*0-07-136188-X*) McGraw.

Matacia, Louis J. Finding Treasure: Combining Science & Parapsychology. unabridged ed. LC 99-167473. (Illus.). 112p. (Orig.). 1997. pap. 23.00 (*1-889420-00-X*) Matacia.

Matacia, Louis J. & Cecil. A Canoeing Log of the Shenandoah River. LC 74-17234. (Blue Ridge Voyages Ser.: Vol. 4). (Illus.). (Orig.). 1974. pap. 6.95 (*0-686-08920-0*) Matacia.

Matacia, Louis J. & Corbett, Roger. An Illustrated Guide to Ten White Water Canoe Trips. (Blue Ridge Voyages Ser.: Vol. 3). (Illus.). (Orig.). 1972. pap. 3.50 (*0-686-08919-7*) Matacia.

Matacia, Louis J., jt. auth. see Corbett, Roger.

Matacotta, F. C. & Ottaviani, G., eds. Science & Technology of Thin Films. LC 95-24958. 300p. 1995. text 86.00 (*981-02-2193-2*) World Scientific Pub.

Mataga, Noboru & Kubota, Tanekazu. Molecular Interactions & Electronic Spectra. LC 71-107755. 520p. reprint ed. pap. 161.20 (*0-608-16725-8*, 202782100054) Bks Demand.

Mataga, Theresa A. & Smith, John L. Moving to Las Vegas-1999 Update. 130p. pap. 12.00 (*1-56980-152-5*) Barricade Bks.

Mataga, Thersa & Smith, John L. Moving to Las Vegas. LC 96-47868. 1997. pap. 12.00 (*1-56980-104-5*) Barricade Bks.

***Matai, D. K.** E Risk Management. 384p. 2000. pap. 74.95 (*0-7506-4820-1*) Buttrwrth-Heinemann.

Mataix Lord, Mariano. Diccionario de Electronica, Informatica y Centrales Nucleares. (SPA.). 660p. 1978. 175.00 (*0-8288-4883-1*, S30687) Fr & Eur.

Mataka, Laini. Bein a Strong Black Woman Can Get U Killed. 112p. 2000. pap. 10.95 (*1-57478-002-6*, Du Forcelf) Black Classic.

— Never As Strangers. LC 88-82280. 60p. (Orig.). 1988. pap. 7.95 (*0-933121-75-X*) Black Classic.

— Restoring the Queen. LC 91-74131. 65p. (Orig.). 1991. pap. 8.95 (*0-933121-80-6*) Black Classic.

Mataka, S., et al. Sulphur Nitrides in Organic Chemistry, Vol. 4. 32p. 1984. pap. text 41.00 (*3-7186-0263-6*) Gordon & Breach.

Matalene, Carolyn, jt. auth. see Klement, Alice.

Matalene, Carolyn B., ed. Worlds of Writing. 288p. (C). 1989. pap. 53.44 (*0-07-557260-5*) McGraw.

Matalin, Mary, et al. All's Fair: Love, War, & Running for President. LC 95-234647. (Illus.). 509p. 1995. pap. 13.00 (*0-684-80133-7*, Touchstone) S&S Trade Pap.

Matalon, Ronit. The One Facing Us. Weinstein, Marsha, tr. LC 97-32303. 296p. 1998. 25.00 (*0-8050-4880-4*) H Holt & Co.

— The One Facing Us: A Novel. Weinstein, Marsha, tr. (Illus.). 304p. 1999. pap. 14.00 (*0-8050-6185-1*, Pub. by H Holt & Co) VHPS.

Matalon, Sadis & Sznajder, Jacob I., eds. Acute Respiratory Distress Syndrome: Cellular & Molecular Mechanisms & Clinical Management. LC 98-17227. (NATO ASI Ser.: No. 297). (Illus.). 448p. (C). 1998. text 129.50 (*0-306-45830-6*, Kluwer Plenum) Kluwer Academic.

Matambalya, Francis. The Merits & Demerits of the EU Policies Towards Associated Developing Countries: An Empirical Analysis of EU-SADC Trade & Overall Economic Relations within the Framework of the Lome Countries. 2nd rev. ed. LC 99-32389. (European University Studies, Series 5: Vol. 2211). (Illus.). 288p. 1999. pap. text 48.95 (*0-8204-4333-6*) P Lang Pubng.

Matamoros, Mario P. Conversando con un Martir Cubano: Carlos Gonzalez Vidal. (SPA.). 1997. pap. 9.95 (*0-89729-831-4*) Ediciones.

Matanda, Gcotyelwa, jt. auth. see Matanda, Vuyo.

Matanda, Vuyo & Matanda, Gcotyelwa. Naming Your Child Prophetically: A Dictionary of South African Names. (Illus.). 128p. 1998. mass mkt. 15.95 (*0-9664988-0-1*) Herald Commn.

Matane, Paulias. Trekking Through the New Worlds. 1995. pap. 12.00 (*81-7476-044-X*, Pub. by UBS Pubs) S Asia.

Matane, Paulias. Voyage to Antarctics. (C). 1997. 16.00 (*81-7476-160-8*, Pub. by UBS Pubs Dist) S Asia.

Matanle, Ivor. Collecting & Using Classic Cameras. LC 91-75054. (Illus.). 224p. 1992. pap. 24.95 (*0-500-27656-0*, Pub. by Thames Hudson) Norton.

— Collecting & Using Classic SLRs. LC 96-60139. (Illus.). 264p. 1996. 50.00 (*0-500-01726-3*, Pub. by Thames Hudson) Norton.

— Collecting & Using Classic SLRs. LC 96-60139. (Illus.). 264p. 1997. pap. 27.50 (*0-500-27901-2*, Pub. by Thames Hudson) Norton.

Matano, Robert A. & Doumas, Diana M. Structured Outpatient Approaches to Alcohol & Drug Treatment. (C). 2002. pap. 39.95 (*0-205-27587-7*, Macmillan Coll) P-H.

Matar, jt. auth. see Biletzki, Anat.

Matar, Anat. From Dummett's Philosophical Perspective. LC 97-28723. (Perspectives in Analytical Philosophy Ser.). 260p. (C). 1997. lib. bdg. 125.95 (*3-11-014986-9*) De Gruyter.

Matar, Joseph E., jt. auth. see Lochner, Robert H.

Matar, Muhammad A. Quartet of Joy. Ghazoul, Ferial J. & Verlenden, John, trs. from ARA. LC 97-26841. 1998. pap. 10.00 (*1-55728-488-1*) U of Ark Pr.

Matar, Muhammad A., et al. Quartet of Joy. Ghazoul, Ferial J. & Verlenden, John, trs. from ARA. LC 97-26841. 1998. 16.00 (*1-55728-487-3*) U of Ark Pr.

Matar, N. I., ed. Peter Sterry Vol. 60: Select Writings. LC 92-16212. (University of Kansas Humanistic Studies: Vol. 60). XVI, 225p. (C). 1995. text 45.95 (*0-8204-1953-2*) P Lang Pubng.

Matar, Nabil. Islam in Britain, 1558-1685. LC 97-41874. 262p. (C). 1998. 59.95 (*0-521-62233-6*) Cambridge U Pr.

— Turks, Moors, & Englishman in the Age of Discovery. LC 98-44812. 1999. 32.50 (*0-231-11014-6*) Col U Pr.

***Matar, Nabil.** Turks, Moors, & Englishmen in the Age of Discovery. 2000. reprint ed. pap. 14.50 (*0-231-11015-4*) Col U Pr.

Matar, Nabil I. Islam for Beginners. (Illus.). 160p. 1992. 19.95 (*0-86316-156-1*); pap. 9.00 (*0-86316-155-3*) Writers & Readers.

Matar, Sami, et al, eds. Catalysis in Petrochemical Processes. (C). 1988. text 173.50 (*90-277-2721-X*) Kluwer Academic.

Matar, Sami & Hatch, Lewis F. Chemistry of Petrochemical Processes. LC 93-43441. 850p. 1994. 85.00 (*0-88415-198-0*, 5198) Gulf Pub.

Matar, Sami, jt. auth. see Hatch, Lewis F.

Mataragnon, Rita H., jt. ed. see Ferre, Frederick P.

Matarasso, P. M., tr. The Quest of the Holy Grail. LC 72-12898. (Classics Ser.). 304p. 1969. pap. 12.95 (*0-14-044220-0*, Penguin Classics) Viking Penguin.

Matarasso, Pauline, tr. & intro. see Wyatt, Thomas.

Matarazzo, James. Knowledge & Special Libraries. 265p. 1998. pap. 19.95 (*0-7506-7084-3*) Buttrwrth-Heinemann.

Matarazzo, James M. Closing the Corporate Library: Case Studies on the Decision Making Process. LC 81-14452. 160p. reprint ed. pap. 49.60 (*0-608-12446-X*, 202520700042) Bks Demand.

— Corporate Library Excellence. 137p. 1990. 28.00 (*0-87111-367-8*) SLA.

— Library Problems in Science & Technology. LC 70-164033. (Problem-Centered Approaches to Librarianship Ser.). 191p. reprint ed. 59.30 (*0-8357-9043-6*, 201758900007) Bks Demand.

Matarazzo, James M. & Prusak, Laurence. The Value of Corporate Libraries: Findings from a 1995 Survey of Senior Management. (Illus.). 21p. (Orig.). 1995. pap. 14.50 (*0-87111-449-6*) SLA.

Matarazzo, Jim, jt. auth. see Prusak, Larry.

Matarazzo, Joseph D. & Wechsler, David. Wechsler's Measurement & Appraisal of Adult Intelligence. 5th ed. (Illus.). 572p. 1972. text 49.95 (*0-19-502296-3*) OUP.

Matarazzo, Robert J. Marketing for Success: Creative Marketing Tools for the Agriculture Industry. (Illus.). (Orig.). 1996. pap. 16.95 (*0-9653385-0-9*) Doe Hollow.

Matare, Herbert F. Bioethics: The Ethics of Evolution & Genetic Interference. LC 96-20185. 160p. 1999. 59.95 (*0-89789-461-8*, H461, Bergin & Garvey) Greenwood.

— Energy Facts & Future. LC 88-3999. 208p. 1989. 138.00 (*0-8493-4616-9*, TJ163, CRC Reprint) Franklin.

Matarese, Laura E. & Gottschlich, Michele M. Contemporary Nutrition Support Practice: A Clinical Guide. Connor, Maura, ed. LC 97-1437. (Illus.). 720p. (C). 1998. text 99.00 (*0-7216-5999-3*, W B Saunders Co) Harcrt Hlth Sci Grp.

Matarese, Laura E., et al. Nutrition Support Handbook. (Illus.). 111p. (Orig.). 1997. 20.00 (*0-9615424-5-4*) Cleveland Clinic.

Mataric, Maja, ed. Embodied Cognition & Action: Papers from the 1996 Fall Symosium. (Technical Reports). (Illus.). 155p. 1996. spiral bd. 25.00 (*1-57735-016-2*) AAAI Pr.

Mataric, Mira. Love Affair with Life. LC 98-85388. 325p. 1998. 25.00 (*0-9663501-9-7*); pap. 15.00 (*0-7388-0025-2*) Xlibris Corp.

Matas, Carol. After the War: The Story Behind Exodus. LC 97-13456. 128p. (J). (gr. 7 up). 1996. lib. bdg. 16.00 (*0-689-80350-8*) S&S Bks Yung.

— After the War: The Story Behind Exodus. 128p. (J). (gr. 7-11). 1997. per. 4.50 (*0-689-80722-8*) S&S Childrens.

— After the War: The Story Behind Exodus. (J). 1997. 9.60 (*0-606-13077-2*, Pub. by Turtleback) Demco.

— The Birth of Israel. LC 96-41405. 144p. (J). (gr. 7 up). 1997. per. 15.00 (*0-689-80349-4*) S&S Bks Yung.

— Code Name Kris. LC 90-32656. 160p. (YA). (gr. 7 up). 1990. lib. bdg. 13.95 (*0-684-19208-X*) Scribner.

— Daniel's Story. 144p. (J). (gr. 4-7). 1993. pap. 3.99 (*0-590-46588-0*) Scholastic Inc.

— Daniel's Story. 1993. 9.09 (*0-606-07412-0*, Pub. by Turtleback) Demco.

— The Garden. (YA). (gr. 7 up). 1997. 16.00 (*0-614-29067-8*) S&S Childrens.

— The Garden. LC 96-41405. 144p. (gr. 7-12). 1998. per. 4.99 (*0-689-80723-6*) S&S Childrens.

— Greater Than the Angels. LC 97-27565. 160p. (J). (gr. 6-8). 1998. per. 16.00 (*0-689-81353-8*) S&S Childrens.

— In My Enemy's House. LC 98-16330. 176p. (YA). (gr. 7-10). 1999. per. 16.00 (*0-689-81354-6*) S&S Childrens.

— In My Enemy's House. (YA). (gr. 7-10). 2000. per. 4.50 (*0-689-82400-9*) S&S Childrens.

— More Minds. (J). 1998. pap. text 4.50 (*0-590-39469-X*) Scholastic Inc.

***Matas, Carol.** More Minds. 1998. 9.60 (*0-606-13622-3*, Pub. by Turtleback) Demco.

Matas, Carol. Of Two Minds. 160p. (J). 1997. pap. text 7.95 (*0-921368-44-5*, Pub. by Bain & Cox) Genl Dist Srvs.

— Of Two Minds. 208p. (J). 1998. pap. text 4.50 (*0-590-39468-1*) Scholastic Inc.

— Of Two Minds. 1998. 9.60 (*0-606-13672-X*, Pub. by Turtleback) Demco.

— The Primrose Path. LC 95-225985. 152p. (J). (gr. 7-12). 1997. pap. 7.95 (*0-921368-55-0*) Genl Dist Srvs.

— Safari Adventure in Legoland. 96p. (J). (gr. 4-7). 1993. pap. 2.75 (*0-590-45876-0*) Scholastic Inc.

— Sworn Enemies. 144p. (YA). 1994. mass mkt. 3.99 (*0-440-21900-0*) Dell.

— Sworn Enemies. 1993. 9.09 (*0-606-06043-X*, Pub. by Turtleback) Demco.

Matas, Carol & Nodelman, Perry. More Minds. 192p. (J). (gr. 5-9). 1996. per. 16.00 (*0-689-80388-5*) S&S Bks Yung.

— Out of Their Minds. LC 97-41277. (Illus.). 192p. (J). (gr. 5-9). 1998. 16.00 (*0-689-81946-3*) S&S Bks Yung.

Matas, Carol & Suh, John. Greater Than Angels. Orig. Title: Contagion of Good. 176p. (J). (gr. 4-7). 1999. reprint ed. per. 4.99 (*0-689-83084-X*) Aladdin.

Matas, Carol, jt. auth. see Nodelman, Perry.

Matas, Julio. Erinia. (SPA.). 1971. pap. 9.95 (*0-89729-001-1*) Ediciones.

— El Extravio - La Cronica y el Sucesoaqui Cruza el Cirvo. LC 90-80368. (Coleccion Teatro). (SPA.). 205p. (Orig.). 1990. pap. 12.00 (*0-89729-563-3*) Ediciones.

— Juegos y Rejuegos. LC 91-76709. (Coleccion Teatro). (SPA.). 96p. 1992. pap. 12.00 (*0-89729-628-1*) Ediciones.

— Transiciones, Migraciones. LC 93-72085. (Coleccion Caniqui). (SPA.). 149p. (Orig.). 1993. pap. 16.00 (*0-89729-693-1*) Ediciones.

Matas, Julio, jt. tr. see Colecchia, Francesca.

***Matas, Nodelman, et al.** A Meeting of Minds. LC 99-12239. 199p. (YA). (gr. 5-8). 1999. per. 17.00 (*0-689-81947-1*) S&S Bks Yung.

Matas, V. R. & Krahn, D. Astronomy & Astrophysics Abstracts Vol. 61: Literature 1994, Pt. 1. 1760p. 1995. 374.95 (*3-540-59089-7*) Spr-Verlag.

Matasakis, Aphrodite. I Can't Get over It: A Handbook for Trauma Survivors. 2nd rev. ed. LC 96-67946. 395p. 1996. pap. 16.95 (*1-57224-058-X*) New Harbinger.

— Managing Client Anger: What to Do When a Client Is Angry with You. LC 98-66703. 224p. 1998. 49.95 (*1-57224-123-3*) New Harbinger.

— Post-Traumatic Stress Disorder: A Complete Treatment Guide. LC 93-87082. 384p. 1994. 49.95 (*1-879237-68-7*) New Harbinger.

— Survivor Guilt: A Self-Help Guide. LC 98-68755. 264p. 1999. pap. 14.95 (*1-57224-140-3*) New Harbinger.

— Trust after Trauma: A Guide to Relationships for Survivors & Those Who Love Them. LC 97-75470. 288p. 1998. pap. 15.95 (*1-57224-101-2*) New Harbinger.

— Vietnam Wives: Facing the Challenges of Life with Veterans Suffering Post-Traumatic Stress. 2nd rev. ed. LC 96-67798. viii, 440p. (Orig.). 1996. pap. 19.95 (*1-886968-00-4*, MAVW) Sidran Pr.

— When the Bough Breaks: A Helping Guide for Parents of Sexually Abused Children. LC 90-63758. 272p. (Orig.). 1990. pap. 14.95 (*1-879237-00-8*) New Harbinger.

Matasar, Ann B. Corporate PACs & Federal Campaign Financing Laws: Use or Abuse of Power? LC 85-12280. (Illus.). 171p. 1986. 55.00 (*0-89930-086-3*, MTP/, Quorum Bks) Greenwood.

Matasov, A. I. Estimators for Uncertain Dynamic Systems. LC 98-36911. (Mathematics & Its Applications Ser.). 1998. 186.00 (*0-7923-5278-5*) Kluwer Academic.

Matasovic, Ranko. A Theory of Textual Reconstruction in Indo-European Linguistics. (Schriften uber Sprachen und Texte Ser.: Bd. 2). 195p. 1996. pap. 42.95 (*0-8204-2975-9*) P Lang Pubng.

— A Theory of Textual Reconstruction in Indo-European Linguistics. Holzer, Georg, ed. LC 96-44072. (Schriften uber Sprachen und Texte Ser.: Vol. 2). (GER.). 195p. 1996. pap. 42.95 (*3-631-49751-2*) P Lang Pubng.

Matassarin-Jacobs, Esther. Saunders Review for NCLEX-RN. 2nd ed. LC 93-22879. (Illus.). 800p. 1994. pap. text 32.00 (*0-7216-4993-9*, W B Saunders Co) Harcrt Hlth Sci Grp.

— Saunders Review for NCLEX-RN. 2nd rev. ed. 1995. pap. text 33.00 (*0-7216-6323-0*, W B Saunders Co) Harcrt Hlth Sci Grp.

— Saunder's Review of Practical Nursing for NCLEX-PN. 3rd rev. ed. Connor, Maura, ed. (Illus.). 480p. 1996. pap. text 28.95 (*0-7216-5872-5*, W B Saunders Co) Harcrt Hlth Sci Grp.

Matassarin-Jacobs, Esther, jt. auth. see Black, Joyce M.

Matassarin-Jacobs, Esther, jt. ed. see Black, Joyce M.

Matateyou, Emmanuel. An Anthology of Myths, Legends & Folktales from Cameroon: Storytelling in Africa. LC 97-26520. (Studies in African Literature: Vol. 4). 272p. 1997. text 89.95 (*0-7734-8514-7*) E Mellen.

Matathia, Ira, jt. auth. see Salzman, Marian.

***Matava, Stephen P.** Legacy of the Priest. LC 00-190300. 396p. 2000. 25.00 (*0-7388-1721-X*); pap. 18.00 (*0-7388-1722-8*) Xlibris Corp.

Mataya, Ewa. The Ewa Mataya Pool Guide: Hints, Tips & Championship Strategies from the Two-Time Women's Professional Billboard Association's Player of the Year. LC 94-23367. 128p. (Orig.). 1995. pap. 11.00 (*0-380-77645-6*, Avon Bks) Morrow Avon.

Mataya, Geri. The Salon Biz: Tips for Success. LC 92-9492. (SalonOvations Ser.). 136p. 1992. pap. 20.95 (*1-56253-048-8*) Milady Pub.

Mataya, James M. Policy Statement Manual. 135p. (Orig.). 1994. pap. 95.00 (*1-882097-51-3*) Amers Comm Bank.

— Truth in Savings: Compliance Manual. 250p. (Orig.). 1993. pap. 69.95 (*1-882097-45-9*) Amers Comm Bank.

***Matbias, Pili B.** Just Listen 'n Learn Business Spanish. LC 99-86851. (SPA & ENG., Illus.). 2000. write for info. incl. audio (*0-8442-4618-2*, Passprt Bks) NTC Contemp Pub Co.

Matcha, Duane A. Medical Sociology: A Comparative Perspective. LC 99-13142. 420p. (C). 1999. 57.00 (*0-205-26309-7*) Allyn.

***Matcha, Duane A.** Readings in Medical Sociology. LC 00-38103. 496p. 2000. pap. text 40.00 (*0-205-30861-9*) Allyn.

— The Sociology of Aging. LC 96-13107. 278p. 1996. pap. text 57.00 (*0-205-16468-4*) Allyn.

Matcha, Jack, ed. see Dargan, James F.

Matchan, Don C., jt. auth. see Kaye, Anna.

***Matchar, David B. & Samsa, Gregory P.** Secondary & Teritiary Prevention of Stroke: Patient Outcomes Research Team (PORT) Final Report - Phase 1. 2000. pap. write for info. (*1-58763-009-5*) Agency Healthcare.

Matcheck, Diane. The Sacrifice. LC 97-36408. 208p. (J). (gr. 7-12). 1998. 16.00 (*0-374-36378-1*) FS&G.

— Sacrifice. LC 99-21457. (YA). 1999. pap. 4.99 (*0-14-130640-8*, PuffinBks) Peng Put Young Read.

Matchett, Alastair. Introduction to Accounting for Finance Bankers. Adkins, Kathleen, ed. (Illus.). 200p. 1997. pap. 49.95 (*1-891112-54-6*) Adkins & Match.

Matchett, Alastair, ed. see Adkins, Kathleen.

Matchett, Alastair, ed. see Adkins, Kathleen, et al.

Matchett, Alastair, ed. see Toy, Norman E.

Matchett, D., jt. ed. see Kilpatrick, F.

Matchett, Steve. A Mechanic's Tale: Life in the Pit Lanes of Formula One. LC 99-28946. (Illus.). 208p. 1999. 24.95 (*0-7603-0754-7*, Pub. by MBI Pubg) Motorbooks Intl.

Matchette, Katharine E. Libby's Choice. LC 94-69605. 157p. (YA). (gr. 6-12). 1995. pap. 8.75 (*0-9645045-0-2*) Deka Pr.

— Oh, Suzannah. LC 97-94863. 158p. (YA). (gr. 6 up). 1998. pap. 8.75 (*0-9645045-2-9*) Deka Pr.

— Walk Safe Through the Jungle. LC 74-2085. (Illus.). 140p. (J). (gr. 4-9). 1996. pap. 8.75 (*0-9645045-1-0*) Deka Pr.

Matchette, Robert B., et al, compiled by. Guide to Federal Records in the National Archives of the United States, 3 vols., Set. rev. ed. LC 96-1113. 2428p. 1996. 95.00 (*0-16-048312-3*) National Archives & Recs.

Matchette, Vilma, jt. auth. see Hedrick, Susan.

***Matchinske, Megan.** Writing, Gender & State in Early Modern England: Identity Formation & the Female Subject. LC 97-27259. (Cambridge Studies in Renaissance Literature & Culture: No. 26). 262p. (C). 1998. text 59.95 (*0-521-62254-9*) Cambridge U Pr.

Matcho, Jon. Using Delphi-Special Edition. 1995. 29.99 (*1-56529-823-3*) Que.

Matczak, Sebastian A. Karl Barth on God: Our Knowledge of the Divine Existence. LC 62-15994. 358p. 1962. 25.25 (*0-912116-06-4*) Learned Pubns.

— Philosophy: A Select, Classified Bibliography of Ethics, Economics, Law, Politics, Sociology. LC 72-80678. (Philosophical Questions Ser.: No. 3). 1970. 75.00 (*0-912116-02-1*) Learned Pubns.

— Philosophy: Its Nature, Methods & Basic Sources. LC 70-183043. (Philosophical Questions Ser.: No. 4). 300p. 1976. 50.00 (*0-912116-09-9*) Learned Pubns.

— Le Probleme de Dieu dans la Pensee de Karl Barth. (Philosophical Questions Ser.: No. 1). 1968. pap. 30.00 (*0-912116-00-5*) Learned Pubns.

— Research & Composition in Philosophy. 2nd ed. (Philosophical Questions Ser.: No. 2). (C). 1971. pap. text 55.00 (*0-912116-05-6*) Learned Pubns.

— Unificationism: A New Philosophy & Worldview. LC 81-86036. (Philosophical Questions Ser.: No. 11). 500p. 1982. 55.00 (*0-912116-14-5*) Learned Pubns.

Matczak, Sebastian A., ed. God in Contemporary Thought: A Philosophical Perspective. LC 75-31391. (Philosophical Questions Ser.: No. 10). 1977. 95.00 (*0-912116-12-9*) Learned Pubns.

Matczak, Sebastian A., ed. see Barral, R. M.

Matczak, Sebastian A., ed. see Van Treese, Glenn J.

Matczak, Sebastian A., ed. & intro. see Smith, William A.

Matczuk, Suzanne. Cocktail-O-Matic: The Little Black Book of Cocktails. 128p. 1999. pap. 12.95 (*0-921368-76-3*, Pub. by Bain & Cox) Genl Dist Srvs.

Matczynski, Thomas J., jt. auth. see Lasley.

Matczynski, Thomas J., jt. auth. see Lasley, Thomas J.

Mate, Candace, jt. auth. see Mate, Ferenc.

Mate, Ferenc. Best Boats to Build or Buy. (Illus.). 1992. pap. 29.95 (*0-920256-24-4*) Norton.

— Finely Fitted Yacht. 1994. pap. 25.00 (*0-920256-28-7*) Norton.

— From a Bare Hull: How to Build a Sailboat. 2nd ed. (Illus.). 443p. 1995. pap. 27.50 (*0-920256-31-7*, Norton Paperbks) Norton.

***Mate, Ferenc.** The Hills of Tuscany: A New Life in an Old Land. 256p. 1999. pap. 12.95 (*0-385-33441-9*) Dell.

Mate, Ferenc. The Hills of Tuscany: A New Life in an Old Land. 240p. 1998. text 23.95 (*0-920256-38-4*) Norton.

***Mate, Ferenc.** Hills of Tuscany: A New Life in an Old Land, Vol. 1. large type ed. LC 99-37436. 1999. 26.95 (*0-7838-8742-6*) Macmillan Gen Ref.

Mate, Ferenc. Shipshape: Art of Sailboat Maintenance. 1996. pap. 29.95 (*0-920256-33-3*) Norton.

— The World's Best Sailboats. 1986. 55.00 (*0-920256-11-2*) Norton.

Mate, Ferenc & Mate, Candace. Autumn: A New England Journey. 160p. 1997. pap. 29.95 (*0-920256-27-9*) Norton.

Mate, Gabor. Scattered: How A. D. D. Originates & What You Can Do about It. LC 99-12999. 368p. 1999. 24.95 (*0-525-94412-5*) NAL.

***Mate, Gabor.** Scattered: How Attention Deficit Disorder Originates & What You Can Do about It. 2000. pap. 14.95 (*0-452-27963-1*, Plume) Dutton Plume.

Mate, L. Hilbert Space Methods in Science & Engineering. (Illus.). 200p. 1990. 92.00 (*0-85274-293-2*) IOP Pub.

Mate, Mavis E. Daughters, Wives & Widows after the Black Death: Women in Sussex, 1350-1535. LC 97-42308. 240p. 1998. 75.00 (*0-85115-534-0*, Boydell Pr) Boydell & Brewer.

— Women in Medieval English Society. LC 98-43628. (New

M

Studies in Economic & Social History: No. 39). 110p. 1999. write for info. (*0-521-58322-5*); pap. 10.95 (*0-521-58733-6*) Cambridge U Pr.

***Mateas, Michael & Senger, Phoebe, eds.** Narrative Intelligence: Papers from the AAAI Fall Symposium. (Illus.). 177p. 1999. spiral bd. 25.00 (*1-57735-103-7*) AAAI Pr.

Mateene, Kahombo C., jt. ed. see Biebuyck, Daniel P.

Mateer, Catherine, jt. auth. see Raskin, Sarah.

Mateer, Catherine A., jt. auth. see Sohlberg, McKay M.

Mateer, Charlotte F. & Craft, Louise. Let's Go to the Arctic: A Story & Activities Book about Arctic People & Animals. (Illus.). 60p. (J). (gr. 4-6). 1993. pap. text 7.95 (*1-879373-24-6*) Roberts Rinehart.

Mateer, Constance L. Early Deaths & Marriages in Armstrong County, Pennsylvania. LC 97-65407. 120p. 1997. per. 14.95 (*1-55856-256-7*, 255) Closson Pr.

***Mateer, David, ed.** Courts, Patrons & Poets. (Illus.). 432p. 2000. 45.00 (*0-300-08219-3*); pap. 20.00 (*0-300-08225-8*) Yale U Pr.

Mateer, John. Anachronism. 1997. pap. 14.95 (*1-86368-162-0*, Pub. by Fremantle Arts) Intl Spec Bk.

***Mateer, John.** Barefoot Speech. 2000. pap. 16.95 (*1-86368-266-X*, Pub. by Fremantle Arts) Intl Spec Bk.

Mateer, Niall J., jt. auth. see Okada, H. Richard.

Mateer, Samuel. The Land of Charity: A Descriptive Account of Travancore & Its People. (C). 1991. reprint ed. 29.00 (*81-206-0319-2*, Pub. by Asian Educ Servs) S Asia.

— Native Life in Travancore. 1991. reprint ed. text 34.00 (*81-206-0514-4*, Pub. by Asian Educ Servs) S Asia.

Mateja, Jim. Best Buys in Used Cars. 3rd rev. ed. 232p. 1995. pap. 11.95 (*1-56625-049-8*) Bonus Books.

Mateja, Wendy. Alana & the Dolphins. Orig. Title: Alana, Lady of Light. (Illus.). 16p. (Orig.). 1978. pap. text 4.95 (*0-9601836-0-4*) Magic Unicorn Pubns.

Matejic, Mateja & Milivojevic, Dragan D. An Anthology of Medieval Serbian Literature in English. (Illus.). 205p. 1978. pap. 18.95 (*0-89357-055-9*) Slavica.

Matejic, Mateja, jt. auth. see Mihailovich, Vasa D.

Matejic, Predrag & Thomas, Hannah. Manuscripts on Microform of the Hilandar Research Library (The Ohio State University) Resources in Medieval Slavic Studies, 2 vols., Set. xxix, 1196p. 1992. 79.95 (*0-89357-225-X*) Slavica.

Matejka, D. & Benko, B. Plasma Spraying of Metallic & Ceramic Materials. LC 89-16459. 280p. 1990. 650.00 (*0-471-91876-8*) Wiley.

Matejka, Ken. Why This Horse Won't Drink: How to Win - & Keep - Employee Commitment. LC 90-53215. 256p. 1990. 22.95 (*0-8144-5005-9*) AMACOM.

Matejka, Ken & Ramos, Diane P. Hook'Em: Speaking & Writing to Catch & Keep a Business Audience. 208p. 1996. pap. 17.95 (*0-8144-7901-4*) AMACOM.

Matejka, Ladislav, ed. Cross Currents, 12. (Slavic Studies - Literature). (Illus.). 240p. (C). 1993. pap. 25.00 (*0-300-05838-1*) Yale U Pr.

— Cross Currents, No. 6. (Materials Ser.: No. 28). 1987. 10.00 (*0-930042-65-4*) Mich Slavic Pubns.

— Cross Currents, No. 7. (Michigan Slavic Materials Ser.: No. 29). 1988. pap. 10.00 (*0-930042-66-2*) Mich Slavic Pubns.

— Cross Currents, No. 8. (Michigan Slavic Materials Ser.: No. 30). 1989. pap. 10.00 (*0-930042-67-0*) Mich Slavic Pubns.

— Cross Currents, No. 11. (Illus.). 296p. (C). 1992. pap. 25.00 (*0-300-05242-1*) Yale U Pr.

— Cross Currents: A Yearbook of Central European Culture, No. 10. (Cross Current Yearbooks of Central European Culture Ser.). 272p. (Orig.). 1991. pap. 25.00 (*0-300-04326-0*) Yale U Pr.

— Sound, Sign & Meaning: Quinquagenary of the Prague Linguistic Circle. (Michigan Slavic Contributions Ser.: No. 6). 1978. 25.00 (*0-930042-26-3*) Mich Slavic Pubns.

Matejka, Ladislav, et al, eds. Readings in Soviet Semiotics: Russian Texts. (Michigan Slavic Materials Ser.: No. 15). 1977. pap. 10.00 (*0-930042-08-5*) Mich Slavic Pubns.

Matejka, Ladislav & Stolz, B. A., eds. Cross Currents, No. 3. (Michigan Slavic Materials Ser.: No. 24). 1984. pap. 10.00 (*0-930042-60-3*) Mich Slavic Pubns.

Matejka, Ladislav & Stolz, Benjamin A., eds. Cross Currents, No. 1. (Materials Ser.: No. 20). 1982. pap. 10.00 (*0-930042-43-3*) Mich Slavic Pubns.

Matejka, Ladislav, jt. ed. see Bailey.

Matejka, Ladislav, jt. ed. see Birnbaum, M. D.

Matejka, Ladislav, ed. see Jakobson, Roman.

Matejka, Ladislav, jt. ed. see Konigsberg, Ira.

Matejka, Ladislav, ed. see Reiner, Erica.

Matejka, Ladislav, ed. see Steiner, Wendy, et al.

Matejka, Ladislav, ed. see Veltrusky, Jarmila F.

Matejka, Ladislav, tr. see Volosinov, V. N.

Matejka, Michael G. & Koos, Greg, eds. Bloomington's C & A R. R. Shops: Our Lives Remembered. (Transactions of the Mclean County Historical Society Ser.). (Illus.). 161p. (Orig.). 1987. pap. 11.95 (*0-943788-04-8*) McLean County.

Matejko, Alexander J. A Christian Approach to Work & Industry. LC 88-13824. (Mellen Studies in Business: Vol. 4). 439p. 1989. lib. bdg. 109.95 (*0-88946-156-2*) E Mellen.

— Comparative Work Systems: Ideologies & Reality in Eastern Europe. LC 85-6354. 258p. 1985. 59.95 (*0-275-90216-1*, C0216, Praeger Pubs) Greenwood.

— In Search of New Organizational Paradigms. LC 86-9317. (Illus.). 366p. 1986. 65.00 (*0-275-92099-2*, C2099, Praeger Pubs) Greenwood.

— The Self Defeating Organization. LC 85-9524. 425p. 1986. 65.00 (*0-275-90026-6*, C0026, Praeger Pubs) Greenwood.

Matejko, Alexander J., jt. ed. see Jain, Ajit.

Matejski, Myrtle P., jt. auth. see Swonger, Alvin K.

Matejtschuk, Paul, ed. Affinity Separations: A Practical Approach. LC 96-51855. (The Practical Approach Ser.: No. 179). (Illus.). 272p. 1997. text 105.00 (*0-19-963551-X*); pap. text 55.00 (*0-19-963550-1*) OUP.

Matela, Ray, jt. auth. see Ransom, Robert J.

Mateles, R. I. Directory of Toll Fermentation & Cell Culture Facilities. 3rd ed. LC 97-75083. 200p. 1997. 205.00 (*1-891545-00-0*) Candida.

Mateljan, George. Baking Without Fat. Burns, Jim, ed. LC 93-77482. (Illus.). 175p. (Orig.). 1993. pap. 9.95 (*0-9633608-1-7*) Hlth Valley Foods.

— Cooking Without Fat. 416p. 1992. pap. 14.95 (*0-9633608-0-9*) Hlth Valley Foods.

— Cooking without Fat. Date not set. pap. 17.00 (*0-9633608-2-5*) Hlth Valley Foods.

— Healthy Meals in Minutes. Burns, Jim, ed. (Illus.). 128p. 1995. pap. 5.95 (*0-9633608-3-3*) Hlth Valley Foods.

Matelski, Marilyn J. Soap Operas Worldwide: Cultural & Serial Realities. LC 98-37978. 231p. 1998. lib. bdg. 34.50 (*0-7864-0557-0*) McFarland & Co.

— TV News Ethics. (Electronic Media Guide Ser.). (Illus.). 96p. 1991. pap. text 26.95 (*0-240-80089-3*) Buttrwrth-Heinemann.

— Vatican Radio: Propagation by the Airwaves. LC 94-22656. (Media & Society Ser.). 224p. 1995. 59.95 (*0-275-94760-2*, Praeger Pubs) Greenwood.

Matelski, Marilyn J., jt. auth. see Street, Nancy L.

***Matena, Vlada & Hapner, Mark.** Applying the Enterprise JavaBeans Architecture: Programmer's Guide & Specification. 2000. pap. 39.95 (*0-201-70267-3*) Pearson Custom.

Matenko, Percy. Ludwig Tieck & America. LC 54-62860. (North Carolina. University. Studies in the Germanic Languages & Literatures: No. 12). reprint ed. 27.00 (*0-404-50912-6*) AMS Pr.

Matens, Margaret H. Mandy & the Kookalocka. LC 93-77130. (Illus.). 32p. (J). (gr. k-5). 1993. 14.95 (*1-882959-53-1*) Foxglove TN.

— Wuzzy the Witch. LC 93-77128. (Illus.). 42p. (J). (gr. k-5). 1993. 14.95 (*1-882959-54-X*) Foxglove TN.

Mateo. Refuting the Attack on Mary: A Defense of Marian Doctrines. 2nd ed. 101p. 1999. reprint ed. pap. 6.95 (*1-888992-08-5*) Catholic Answers.

Mateo Diez, Luis. Relato de Babia. (Nueva Austral Ser.: Vol. 213). (SPA.). 1991. pap. text 24.95 (*84-239-7213-5*) Elliots Bks.

Mateo, Franc, jt. illus. see Mateu, Franc.

Mateo, Josep L. Ideas & Buildings, 1992-1995. LC 95-233950. 1996. 58.00 (*3-7643-5595-6*) Birkhauser.

Mateo, Josep Lluis. Mateo Atlas. 1998. pap. text 25.00 (*84-88258-25-9*) Colegio Arquit.

Mateo, Joseph, et al. Berlin. (Illus.). 124p. 1998. 35.00 (*84-604-8113-1*, 810702, Pub. by Actar) Dist Art Pubs.

Mateo, Magdalena A. & Kirchhoff, Karin T. Using & Conducting Nursing Research in the Clinical Settings. 2nd ed. Eoyang, Thomas, ed. LC 98-4260. (Illus.). 380p. (C). 1999. text. write for info. (*0-7216-7165-9*, W B Saunders Co) Harcrt Hlth Sci Grp.

Mateo, Mary A. Portraits of Native American Indians. (Illus.). 96p. (J). (gr. 4-7). 1992. 11.99 (*0-86653-669-8*, GA1322) Good Apple.

Mateo, N. Mountain Agriculture & Crop Genetics Resources. (C). 1989. 44.00 (*81-204-0472-6*) S Asia.

Mateos, Alvarez J. Vocabulario Teologico del Evangelio de San Juan. (SPA.). 310p. 1980. pap. 29.95 (*0-8288-2318-9*, S33107) Fr & Eur.

Mateos, Fernando. Diccionario Chino de la Lengua Espanola. (CHI & SPA.). 1200p. 1987. pap. 75.00 (*0-7859-3350-6*, 8429307621) Fr & Eur.

Mateos, Fernando, et al. Diccionario Espanol de la Lengua China. (SPA.). 1381p. 1990. 339.50 (*84-239-4771-8*) Elliots Bks.

Mateos, Pilar. La Casa Imaginaria (The Imaginary House) (SPA., Illus.). (YA). 1994. pap. 5.99 (*968-16-4038-1*, Pub. by Fondo) Continental Bk.

Mater, Jean. Reinventing the Forest Industry. LC 96-78528. 280p. 1997. pap. 16.95 (*1-885221-58-4*) BookPartners.

Mater, Jean, et al. Marketing Forest Products: Gaining the Competitive Edge. (Illus.). 300p. 1992. 49.00 (*0-87930-193-7*, 412) Miller Freeman.

Mater, John P. Van, see Blavatsky, Helena P. & Van Mater, John P.

Mater, Rick & Wing, Kathy. Date to Win: How to Have More Dates, Find That Lasting Relationship, or Meet Your Ideal Marriage Partner. LC 94-96386. 256p. (Orig.). 1997. pap. 15.95 (*0-9643444-0-8*) Laurel Canyon.

Matera, Dary, jt. auth. see George, Edward.

Matera, Dary, jt. auth. see Theisen, Donna.

Matera, Frances R. & Artigue, Ray J. Public Relations Campaigns. LC 99-48412. 280p. (C). 1999. pap. text 49.00 (*0-205-15815-3*, Macmillan Coll) P-H.

Matera, Frank J. Galatians. (Sacra Pagina Ser.: No. 9). 272p. 29.95 (*0-8146-5811-3*, M Glazier) Liturgical Pr.

— New Testament Christology: The Christology in the Story. LC 98-42257. 304p. 1999. pap. 26.00 (*0-664-25694-5*) Westminster John Knox.

— New Testament Ethics: The Legacies of Jesus & Paul. LC 96-16563. 352p. 1996. 34.95 (*0-664-22069-X*) Westminster John Knox.

***Matera, Frank J.** Strategies for Preaching Paul. LC 00-42840. 2001. write for info. (*0-8146-1966-5*) Liturgical Pr.

***Matera, Joe, ed.** Nelson's Directory of Investment Managers, 1999, 3 vols. 6000p. 1999. pap. 545.00 (*1-891851-05-5*) Nelson Info.

***Matera, Lia.** Counsel for the Defense & Other Stories. LC 00-24237. 173p. 2000. 20.95 (*0-7862-2537-8*) Five Star.

Matera, Lia. Designer Crimes: A Laura Di Palma Mystery. 1996. mass mkt. 5.99 (*0-671-00196-5*) PB.

— Face Value: A Laura Di Palma Mystery. (Illus.). 1995. mass mkt. 5.99 (*0-671-88840-4*) PB.

— Face Value: A Laura Di Palma Mystery. LC 93-27194. 1994. 20.00 (*0-671-74197-7*) S&S Trade.

— Havana Twist: A Willa Jansson Mystery. LC 97-47249. 256p. 1998. 22.00 (*0-684-83470-7*) S&S Trade.

— Havana Twist: A Willa Jansson Mystery. 1999. per. 6.99 (*0-671-00421-2*) S&S Trade.

— Last Chants. (A Willa Jansson Mystery Ser.). 1997. per. 5.99 (*0-671-88096-9*, Pocket Books) PB.

— Last Chants. (Willa Jansson Mystery Ser.). 240p. 1996. 21.00 (*0-684-81085-9*) Simon & Schuster.

— Radical Departure. (Laura Di Palma Ser.). 224p. (Orig.). 1991. mass mkt. 5.99 (*0-345-37126-7*) Ballantine Pub Grp.

— The Smart Money. 192p. (Orig.). 1991. mass mkt. 5.99 (*0-345-37127-5*) Ballantine Pub Grp.

— Star Witness. 1998. per. 6.50 (*0-671-00420-4*, Pocket Books) PB.

— Star Witness. LC 97-1196. 240p. 1997. 21.50 (*0-684-83469-3*) S&S Trade.

— Where Lawyers Fear to Tread. (Willa Jansson Ser.). 1991. mass mkt. 5.99 (*0-345-37125-9*) Ballantine Pub Grp.

***Matera, Lia.** Where Lawyers Fear to Tread. LC 98-55779. 1999. 19.95 (*0-7862-1814-2*) Thorndike Pr.

***Matera, Lia, ed.** Irreconcilable Differences. LC 99-10691. 368p. 1999. 24.00 (*0-06 019225 9*) HarpC

Materassi, Mario & Ramalho de Sousa Santos, Maria I., eds. The American Columbiad: "Discovering" America, Inventing the United States. LC 97-103436. (European Contributions to American Studies: No. 34). 426p. 1997. text 59.50 (*90-5383-423-0*, Pub. by VU Univ Pr) Paul & Co Pubs.

***Materer, Timothy.** James Merrill's Apocalypse. 208p. 2000. 29.95 (*0-8014-3760-1*) Cornell U Pr.

Materer, Timothy. Modernist Alchemy: Poetry & the Occult. (Illus.). 240p. 1996. text 29.95 (*0-8014-3146-8*) Cornell U Pr.

— Wyndham Lewis: The Novelist. LC 75-29310. 189p. reprint ed. pap. 58.60 (*0-7837-3666-5*, 204353900009) Bks Demand.

Materer, Timothy, ed. The Selected Letters of Ezra Pound to John Quinn, 1915-1924. LC 90-23613. 252p. 1991. text 42.95 (*0-8223-1132-1*) Duke.

Materer, Timothy, ed. see Pound, Ezra & Lewis, Wyndham.

Materials & Processes Congress. Process Modeling Tools: Proceedings of American Society for Metals Process Modeling Sessions Processes Congress 1980. LC 81-52303. (Materials-Metalworking Technology Ser.). 224p. reprint ed. pap. 69.50 (*0-608-16435-6*, 202703500053) Bks Demand.

Materials Handling Conference Staff. Unit & Bulk Materials Handling: Presented at the Materials Handling Conference, ASME Century 2 - Emerging Technology Conferences, San Francisco, CA, August 19-21, 1980. Loeffler, F. J. & Proctor, C. R., eds. LC 80-66042. 297p. reprint ed. pap. 92.10 (*0-8357-8772-9*, 203364200087) Bks Demand.

Materials, Metals & Materials Society Staff. Process Control & Automation in Extractive Metallurgy: Proceedings of an International Symposium. fac. ed. Partelpoeg, E. H. & Himmesoete, D. C., eds. LC 88-63685. (Illus.). 233p. reprint ed. pap. 72.30 (*0-7837-6968-7*, 205252500003) Bks Demand.

Materials Research Society Staff. Biomedical Materials & Devices: Symposium Held November 30-December 4, 1987, Boston, MA. Hanker, Jacob S. & Giammara, Beverly L., eds. LC 88-27355. (Material Research Society Symposium Proceedings Ser.: No. 110). (Illus.). 824p. reprint ed. pap. 200.00 (*0-7837-6760-9*, 205915900011) Bks Demand.

— Comparison of Thin Film Transistor & SOI Technologies: Symposium Held February 1984 in Albuquerque, New Mexico, U. S. A. LC 84-24713. (Materials Research Society Symposia Proceedings Ser.: No. 33). (Illus.). 337p. reprint ed. pap. 104.50 (*0-7837-1925-6*, 204214000001) Bks Demand.

— Optical Fiber Materials & Properties: Symposium Held December 3-5, 1986, Boston, Massachusetts, U. S. A. Nagel, Suzanne R., ed. LC 87-7852. (Materials Research Society Symposia Proceedings Ser.: No. 88). (Illus.). 261p. reprint ed. pap. 81.00 (*0-7837-1929-9*, 204214400001) Bks Demand.

— Thin Films: The Relationship of Structure to Properties: Symposium Held April 15-17, 1985, San Francisco, California, U. S. A. Aita, Carolyn & SreeHarsha, K. S., eds. LC 85-21485. (Materials Research Society Symposia Proceedings Ser.: No. 47). (Illus.). 306p. reprint ed. pap. 94.90 (*0-7837-1927-2*, 204214200001) Bks Demand.

Materials Research Society Staff, et al. Biomedical Materials: Symposium Held December 3-6, 1985, Boston, Massachusetts, U. S. A. Williams, J. M., ed. LC 86-23540. (Materials Research Society Symposia Proceedings Ser.: No. 55). (Illus.). 435p. reprint ed. pap. 134.90 (*0-7837-1928-0*, 204214300001) Bks Demand.

— Fly Ash & Coal Conversion By-Products: Characterization, Utilization & Disposal IV: Symposium Held December 1-3, 1987, Boston, Massachusetts, U. S. A. McCarthy, Gregory J., ed. LC 88-9394. (Materials Research Society Symposium Proceedings Ser.: No. 113). 365p. reprint ed. pap. 113.20 (*0-7837-6803-6*, 204663500003) Bks Demand.

— High-Temperature Ordered Intermetallic Alloys: Symposium Held November 26-28, 1984, Boston, Massachusetts, U. S. A. Koch, C. C. et al, eds. LC 85-11488. (Materials Research Society Symposia Proceedings Ser.: No. 39). (Illus.). 572p. reprint ed. pap. 177.40 (*0-7837-1926-4*, 204214100001) Bks Demand.

— High-Temperature Superconductors: Symposium Held November 30-December 4, 1987, Boston, Massachusetts, U. S. A. Brodsky, Merwyn B., ed. LC 88-5130. (Materials Research Society Symposium Proceedings Ser.: No. 99). (Illus.). 1038p. reprint ed. pap. 200.00 (*0-7837-6802-8*, 204663400003) Bks Demand.

— Specialty Cements with Advanced Properties: Symposium Held November 27-29, 1989, Boston, Massachusetts, U. S. A. Scheetz, Barry E., ed. LC 90-41629. (Materials Research Society Symposium Proceedings Ser.: No. 179). (Illus.). 317p. reprint ed. pap. 98.30 (*0-7837-6804-4*, 204663600003) Bks Demand.

Materials Science Seminar Staff. Fatigue & Microstructure: Papers Presented at the 1978 ASM. LC 79-4296. 543p. reprint ed. pap. 168.40 (*0-608-17184-0*, 202699400053) Bks Demand.

Materials Science Seminar, 1976, Metals Park, OH S. Metallic Glasses: Papers Presented at a Seminar of the Materials Science Division of the ASM, September 18 & 19, 1976. LC 77-24014. 360p. reprint ed. pap. 111.60 (*0-608-16822-X*, 202703700053) Bks Demand.

Materials Strategy Commission. Materials Technology Foresight for the U. K. Power Generation Industry. 78p. 1995. pap. 40.00 (*0-901716-86-3*, Pub. by Inst Materials) Ashgate Pub Co.

Materials Technology Institute Staff. Corrosion under Heat-Transfer Conditions: Review of Test Procedures & Some Recent Experimental Work. LC TA0418.74.C6. (MTI Publication Ser.: No. 17) 122p. 1985. reprint ed. pap. 37.90 (*0-608-06689-3*, 206688600009) Bks Demand.

— Furan Reinforced Thermoset Plastics for Chemical Process Equipment. LC TA0455.P55F8. (MTI Publication Ser.: No. 21). 36p. 1986. reprint ed. pap. 30.00 (*0-608-06728-8*, 206692500009) Bks Demand.

Materka, Pat R. Time in, Time Out, Time Enough: A Time Management Guide for Women. 2nd ed. (Illus.). 222p. 1993. pap. 11.95 (*0-9635113-0-0*) Leap Frog.

— Workshops & Seminars: Planning, Promoting, Producing, Profiting. 224p. 1986. 15.95 (*0-13-967795-X*) P-H.

Materlik, G., et al, eds. Resonant Anomalous X-Ray Scattering: Theory & Applications. LC 94-20905. 688p. 1994. 227.25 (*0-444-82025-6*, North Holland) Elsevier.

Matern, B. Spatial Variation. 2nd ed. (Lecture Notes in Statistics Ser.: Vol. 36). (Illus.). 155p. 1986. 47.95 (*0-387-96365-0*) Spr-Verlag.

Matern, S., ed. Clinical Research in Gastroenterology, Vol. I. (C). 1987. text 119.00 (*0-85200-696-9*) Kluwer Academic.

— Clinical Research in Gastroenterology 2. (C). 1989. text 90.50 (*0-7923-8906-9*) Kluwer Academic.

Materna, Gayle, jt. auth. see Astaritta, Tarasa M.

Materne, Yves, ed. The Indian Awakening in Latin America. fac. ed. LC 80-11464. 128p. 1994. pap. 39.70 (*0-7837-7712-4*, 204747300007) Bks Demand.

Maternity Center Association Staff. Birth Atlas. 6th rev. ed. (Illus.). 19p. 1993. reprint ed. 55.00 (*0-912758-00-7*) Maternity Ctr.

***Matero, Robert.** Animals Asleep. LC 00-20884. (Illus.). 2000. lib. bdg. write for info. (*0-7613-1652-3*) Millbrook Pr.

Matero, Robert. The Birth of Humpback Whale. LC 94-10681. (Illus.). 64p. (J). (gr. 3-7). 1996. 16.00 (*0-689-31931-2*) Atheneum Yung Read.

— Eyes on Nature: Reptiles. (Illus.). 32p. (J). 1992. pap. 4.95 (*1-56156-151-7*) Kidsbks.

Materon, L. A., jt. auth. see Beck, D.

Materson. Sins & Needles. 1996. 15.00 (*0-15-200786-5*) Harcourt.

Materson, Richard S., jt. ed. see Gonzalez, Erwin G.

Mates, Barbara T. Adaptive Technology for the Internet: Making Electronic Resources Accessible to All. LC 98-31936. 224p. 1999. pap. 36.00 (*0-8389-0752-0*) ALA.

Mates, Benson. Elementary Logic. 2nd ed. 250p. (C). 1972. text 33.95 (*0-19-501491-X*) OUP.

— The Philosophy of Leibniz: Metaphysics & Language. 256p. 1989. reprint ed. pap. text 19.95 (*0-19-505946-8*) OUP.

— The Skeptic Way: Sextus Empiricus's Outlines of Pyrrhonism. 352p. (C). 1996. text 67.00 (*0-19-509212-0*); pap. text 30.95 (*0-19-509213-9*) OUP.

— Skeptical Essays. LC 80-19553. xii, 188p. (C). 1981. 20.50 (*0-226-50986-9*) U Ch Pr.

— Stoic Logic. LC 53-9918. (California University Publications in Philosophy: Vol. 26). 156p. reprint ed. pap. 48.40 (*0-608-11119-8*, 202117400022) Bks Demand.

Mates, Julian. The American Musical Stage Before Eighteen Hundred. LC 85-30497. 343p. 1986. reprint ed. lib. bdg. 75.00 (*0-313-25324-2*, MAMUS, Greenwood Pr) Greenwood.

— America's Musical Stage: Two Hundred Years of Musical Theatre. (Illus.). 264p. 1987. pap. 19.95 (*0-275-92714-8*, B2714, Praeger Pubs) Greenwood.

— America's Musical Stage: Two Hundred Years of Musical Theatre, 18. LC 85-935. (Contributions in Drama & Theatre Studies: No. 18). (Illus.). 252p. 1985. 57.95 (*0-313-23948-7*, MLY/, Greenwood Pr) Greenwood.

Mates, Julian, intro. More Plays of William Dunlap. LC 95-38126. 336p. 1995. 50.00 (*0-8201-1495-2*) Schol Facsimiles.

Mates, Michael, ed. The Secret Services: Is There a Case for Greater Openness? (C). 1990. 50.00 (*0-907967-07-8*, Pub. by Inst Euro Def & Strat) St Mut.

Mates, R. E., et al, eds. Mechanics of the Coronary Circulation. 94p. 1983. pap. text 24.00 (*0-317-02632-1*, G00221) ASME.

Mates, R. E., jt. ed. see Wod, S.

Mates, Susan O. The Good Doctor. LC 94-18980. (John Simmons Short Fiction Award Ser.). 138p. 1994. 11.50 (*0-87745-467-1*) U of Iowa Pr.

An Asterisk (*) at the beginning of an entry indicates that the title is appearing for the first time.

— The Good Doctor. LC 94-18980. (John Simmons Short Fiction Award Ser.). 138p. 1997. reprint ed. pap. 10.95 (*0-87745-612-7*) U of Iowa Pr.

Matesic, Josep. German - Serbocroatian Phraseological Dictionary: Hrvatsko-Njemacki I Frazeoloski Rjecnik. (GER & SER.). 1987. write for info. (*0-8288-1637-9*, F114950) Fr & Eur.

Matesky, Betty & Womack, Ardelle. Learn to Play Strings/Violin, Bk. 2. (Learn to Play Strings Ser.). 32p. 1971. pap. 5.95 (*0-7390-0311-9*, 761) Alfred Pub.

Matesky, Ralph. Learn to Play in the Orchestra, Cello, Bk. 2. 24p. 1973. pap. 6.95 (*0-7390-0730-0*, 856) Alfred Pub.

— Learn to Play in the Orchestra, Violin II, Bk. 2. 24p. 1973. pap. 6.95 (*0-7390-0560-X*, 854) Alfred Pub.

Matesz, Clara, jt. auth. see Szekely, George.

Matesz, Don & Albert-Matesz, Rachel. The Nourishment for Life Cookbook. Williams, Danielle, ed. LC 94-66937. (Illus.). 500p. (Orig.). 1994. pap. 20.00 (*0-9641267-0-2*) Nourish For Life.

Mateu, Franc. Cinderella: Pop-Up Book. LC 94-71482. 12p. (J). (ps-3). 1995. 12.95 (*0-7868-3025-5*, Pub. by Disney Pr) Little.

— The Jungle Book: Mowgli's Journey. LC 92-53438. (Surprise Lift-the-Flap Bk.). 18p. (J). (ps-1). 1993. 9.95 (*1-56282-374-4*, Pub. by Disney Pr) Time Warner.

Mateu, Franc, et al. The Little Mermaid: Walt Disney Pictures Presents. LC 98-134669. (Golden Super Shape Bks.). Orig. Title: Lille havfrue. 24p. (J). (ps). 1991. pap. 3.29 (*0-307-10027-8*, 10027) Gldn Bks Pub Co.

Mateu, Franc. Snow White & the Seven Dwarfs Whistle While You Work: A Musical Pop-Up Book. LC 92-53432. 10p. (J). (ps-1). 1994. 11.95 (*1-56282-514-3*, Pub. by Disney Pr) Little.

Mateu, Franc & Mateo, Franc. Snow White & the Seven Dwarfs. LC 92-53432. (Pop-up Bks.). 12p. (J). (ps-k). 1993. 11.95 (*1-56282-365-5*, Pub. by Disney Pr) Little.

Mateu, J. M. & Montes, F., eds. Spatial Statistics. (Advances in Ecological Sciences Ser.). 300p. 2000. 157.00 (*1-85312-649-7*, 6497, Pub. by WIT Pr) Computational Mech MA.

Mateu Sancho, Pedro. Diccionario de la Astronomica y Astronautica. (SPA.). 350p. 1962. 49.95 (*0-8288-6806-9*, S-12334) Fr & Eur.

***Mateus, Maria Helena & D'Andrade, Ernesto.** The Phonology of Portuguese. (The Phonology of the World's Languages Ser.). (Illus.). 256p. 2000. text 74.00 (*0-19-823581-X*) OUP.

Matey, Maria. Labor Law & Industrial Relations in Poland. 178p. 1989. lib. bdg. 52.50 (*90-6544-401-7*) Kluwer Academic.

***Mateya, Mark A.** Achiving Academic Excellence: How to Study. unabridged ed. (Illus.). xv, 125p. 2000. pap. 10.95 (*0-9700784-0-4*) Pamaram.

Matfield, Ron. Quality Assurance in Nuclear Power Plants, Vol. 6. (Ispra Courses on Nuclear Engineering & Technology Ser.). xiv, 306p. 1984. text 184.00 (*3-7186-0151-6*) Gordon & Breach.

Math Association of America Staff, ed. Twenty Careers In Math. (Math). 1998. pap. 2.00 (*0-534-36380-6*) Brooks-Cole.

Mathabane, Mark. Kaffir Boy: The True Story of a Black Youth's Coming of Age in Apartheid South Africa. LC 98-25240. 368p. 1998. per. 13.00 (*0-684-84828-7*, Touchstone) S&S Trade Pap.

— Kaffir Boy: The True Story of a Black Youth's Coming of Age in Apartheid South Africa. (J). 1987. 18.05 (*0-606-03837-X*, Pub. by Turtleback) Demco.

— Selected from Kaffir Boy. abr. ed. (Writers' Voices Ser.). 64p. (Orig.). 1991. pap. text 3.95 (*0-929631-28-5*, Signal Hill) New Readers.

***Mathabane, Miriam.** Miriam's Song: A Memoir. LC 00-26552. 320p. 2000. 24.50 (*0-684-83303-4*) Simon & Schuster.

Mathad, G. S., et al, eds. Plasma Processing XII. (Proceedings Ser.: Vol. 98-4). (Illus.). 292p. 1998. 58.00 (*1-56677-198-6*) Electrochem Soc.

— Proceedings of the International Symposium on Plasma Processing, 10th. LC 94-70852. (Processing Ser.: Vol. 94-20). 620p. 1994. 64.00 (*1-56677-077-7*) Electrochem Soc.

— Thin Film Materials, Processes, Reliability & Applications: Thin Film Processes. LC 98-158683. (Proceedings Ser.: Vol. 97-30). 370p. 1997. 66.00 (*1-56677-183-8*) Electrochem Soc.

Mathad, G. S. & Hess, D. W., eds. Proceedings of the International Symposium on Plasma Processing, 9th. LC 92-82777. (Proceedings Ser.: Vol. 92-18). 670p. 1992. 60.00 (*1-56677-020-3*) Electrochem Soc.

Mathad, G. S. & Horiike, Yasuhiro, eds. Proceedings of the Symposium on Highly Selective Dry Etching & Damage Control. LC 93-70068. (Proceedings Ser.: Vol. 93-21). 440p. 1993. 60.00 (*1-56677-066-1*) Electrochem Soc.

Mathad, G. S. & Meyyappan, M., eds. Plasma Processing: 11th International Symposium. (Proceedings Ser.: Vol. 96-12). (Illus.). 720p. 1996. 92.00 (*1-56677-164-1*) Electrochem Soc.

Mathad, G. S., ed. see Symposium on Plasma Processing Staff.

Mathai, A. M. A Handbook of Generalized Special Functions for Statistical & Physical Sciences. (Illus.). 256p. 1993. text 65.00 (*0-19-853595-3*) OUP.

***Mathai, A. M.** An Introduction to Geometrical Probability: Distributional Aspects with Applications. 576p. 2000. text 120.00 (*90-5699-681-9*, G & B Science) Gordon & Breach.

Mathai, A. M. Jacobians of Matrix Transformations & Functions of Matrix Argument. LC 97-3779. 1997. write for info. (*981-02-3095-8*) World Scientific Pub.

Mathai, A. M., ed. Distributions of Test Statistics: Exact & Asymptotic, Null & Non-Null, Methods-Comparisons-Research Frontiers. LC 89-82198. (American Sciences Press Series in Mathematical & Management Sciences: Vol. 18). 1990. 195.00 (*0-935950-20-6*) Am Sciences Pr.

Mathai, A. M. & Provost, S. B. Quadratic Forms in Random Variables: Theory & Applications. (Statistics Ser.: Vol. 126). (Illus.). 424p. 1992. text 175.00 (*0-8247-8691-2*) Dekker.

Mathai, Aleyamma, jt. auth. see Penland, Patrick R.

Mathai, M. O. My Days with Nehru. 270p. 1979. 14.95 (*0-7069-0823-6*) Asia Bk Corp.

Mathamatical Association Staff. Math Talk. 66p. (C). (gr. k). 1990. pap. text 16.50 (*0-435-08307-4*, 08307) Heinemann.

Mathan, Don C., jt. auth. see Kaye, Anna.

Mathangwane, Joyce T. Ikalanga Phonetics & Phonology: A Synchronic & Diachronic Study. LC 98-50448. (Stanford Monographs in African Languages: No. 3). (AFR & ENG.). 160p. (C). 1999. text 34.95 (*1-57586-163-1*) CSLI.

Mathas, Alexander. Der Kalte Kreig in der Deutschen Literaturkritik: Martin Walsers Narrative Prosa in der BRD und DDR. LC 91-48192. (German Life & Civilization Ser.: Vol. 12). (GER.). 243p. (C). 1992. text 46.95 (*0-8204-1824-2*) P Lang Pubng.

Mathas, Andrew. Iwahori-Hecke Algebras & Schur Algebras of the Symmetric Group. LC 99-29310. (University Lecture Ser.). 1999. write for info. (*0-8218-1926-7*) Am Math.

Mathe, G., et al, eds. Lymphocytes, Macrophages, & Cancer. LC 76-26538. (Recent Results in Cancer Research Ser.: Vol. 56). 1976. 35.00 (*3-540-07902-5*) Spr-Verlag.

Mathe, G. & Muggia, Franco M., eds. Cancer Chemo-& Immunopharmacology Part 1: Chemopharmacology. (Recent Results in Cancer Research Ser.: Vol. 74). (Illus.). 315p. 1980. 86.00 (*0-387-10162-4*) Spr-Verlag.

Mathe, G. & Reizenstein, P., eds. Pathophysiological Aspects of Cancer Epidemiology. (Advances in the Biosciences Ser.: No. 50). (Illus.). 276p. 1985. 99.00 (*0-08-030780-9*, Pergamon Pr) Elsevier.

Mathe, Herve & Shapiro, Roy D. Integrating Service Strategy in the Manufacturing Company. LC 92-42178. (Illus.). 336p. 1993. mass mkt. 89.95 (*0-412-46780-1*, A9464) Chapman & Hall.

Mathea-Foertsch, M., ed. see Andreade, B., et al.

Matheeussen, ed. Vivis, Ioannis Lodovici. (LAT.). 1984. 21.95 (*3-322-00196-2*, T1936, Pub. by B G Teubner) U of Mich Pr.

***Matheeussen, C.** J.l. Vives: De Institutione Feminae Christianae, Liber Secundus & Liber Tertius: Introduction, Critical Edition, Translation & Notes. Fantaz, C., tr. (Selected Works of Juan Luis Vives Ser.: Vol. 7). (FRE, ENG & LAT., Illus.). Xii, 256p. 1998. text 91.25 (*90-04-11090-9*) Brill Academic Pubs.

Matheis, G. & Schandelmeier, Heinz, eds. Current Research in African Earth Sciences: Extended Abstracts of the 14th Colloquium on African Geology, Berlin, 18-22 August 1987. 504p. (C). 1987. text 136.00 (*90-6191-709-3*, Pub. by A A Balkema); pap. text 78.00 (*90-6191-710-7*, Pub. by A A Balkema) Ashgate Pub Co.

Matheis, W., jt. auth. see Erb, Bruno.

Mathelin, Catherine. The Broken Piano: Lacanian Psychoanalysis with Children. 1997. pap. text 22.00 (*0-7657-0104-9*) Aronson.

— Lacanian Psychotherapy with Children: The Broken Piano. LC 98-36956. (Lacanian Clinical Field Ser.). (Illus.). 200p. 1998. pap. 17.95 (*1-892746-01-8*, 46018) Other Pr LLC.

Mathelitsch, L. & Plessas, W., eds. Broken Symmetries: Proceedings of the 37th Internationale Universitatswochen fur Kern- Und Teilchenphysik, Schladming, Austria, February 28-March 7, 1998. LC 99-18459. (Lecture Notes in Physics Ser.: Vol. 521). vii, 299p. 1999. 69.95 (*3-540-65667-7*) Spr-Verlag.

— Substructures of Matter As Revealed with Electroweak Probes: Proceedings of the Thirty-Second Internationale Universit Atswochen fur Kern & Teilchenphysik, Schladming, Austria, 24 February-5 March 1993. LC 93-44976. (Lecture Notes in Physics Ser.: Vol. 426). 1994. 104.95 (*0-387-57575-8*) Spr-Verlag.

***Mathema, B. B.** Nepal Struggling for Democracy Big Four the Martyrs Their Revolutionary Stand 1940. 1998. pap. 50.00 (*0-7855-7612-6*) St Mut.

Mathematical Institute of the Polish Academy of Sc & Institute of Mathematics of the Adam Mickiewicz Un. Approximation Theory: Proceedings of the Institute of Mathematics, Poznan, August 22-26, 1972. Ciesielski, Z. & Musielak, J., eds. LC 74-80524. 289p. 1975. text 189.50 (*90-277-0483-X*) Kluwer Academic.

Mathematical Sciences Education Board Staff & National Research Council Staff. Measuring Up: Prototypes for Mathematics Assessment. LC 92-62904. (Illus.). 176p. (Orig.). 1993. pap. text 10.95 (*0-309-04845-1*) Natl Acad Pr.

Mathematical Sciences Education Board Staff, et al. High School Mathematics at Work: Essays & Examples for the Education of All Students. LC 98-19669. 192p. 1998. pap. 27.95 (*0-309-06353-1*) Natl Acad Pr.

Mathematical Social Science Board Conference on th. Essays on a Mature Economy: Britain after 1840. McCloskey, Donald N., ed. LC 73-170254. 455p. 1971. reprint ed. pap. 141.10 (*0-7837-9500-9*, 206024700004) Bks Demand.

Mathematical Society of Japan Staff & Ito, Kiyoshi, eds. Encyclopedic Dictionary of Mathematics, 2 vols. 2nd ed. LC 86-21092. (Illus.). 2168p. (C). 1993. reprint ed. pap. text 90.00 (*0-262-59020-4*) MIT Pr.

Mathematical Society of Japan Staff & Kiyosi Ito, eds. Encyclopedic Dictionary of Mathematics, 4 vols., Set. 2nd ed. (Illus.). 2113p. 1987. 425.00 (*0-262-09026-0*) MIT Pr.

Mathena, Michael. Bonnie Bluebird's Voyages. LC 96-77301. (Illus.). 32p. (Orig.). (J). (gr. 3-5). 1997. pap. 7.95 (*1-884242-89-8*) Multicult Pubns.

Mathenge, Judy Wanijiku. Mcheshi Goes to School: Mcheshi Aenda Shuleni. 1995. 13.15 (*0-606-08817-2*, Pub. by Turtleback) Demco.

Mathenge, Judy Wanjiku. Mcheshi Goes on a Journey: Mcheshi Aenda Safari. 1993. 13.15 (*0-606-08816-4*, Pub. by Turtleback) Demco.

Matheny, Albert R., jt. auth. see Williams, Bruce A.

Matheny, Bradley L., jt. auth. see Wagner, Gary S.

Matheny, Constance O., ed. see Shirkey, Robert J.

Matheny, Edward T., Jr. The Presence of Care: The History of St. Luke's Hospital. Hron, Frederic J., ed. (Illus.). 456p. 1997. 24.95 (*0-9657425-0-4*) St Lukes Hosp.

***Matheny, Edward T., Jr.** The Rise & Fall of Excellence: The Story of Southwest Hight School - RIP. LC 00-90066. 168p. 2000. pap. 15.95 (*1-58597-022-0*) Leathers Pub.

Matheny, Emma R. & Yates, Helen K. Kingston Parish Register: Gloucester & Mathews Counties, Virginia, 1749-1827. 167p. 1996. reprint ed. pap. 18.00 (*0-8063-0832-X*, 3800) Clearfield Co.

— Marriages of Lunenburg County, Virginia, 1746-1853. (Illus.). 177p. 1997. reprint ed. pap. 18.00 (*0-8063-0833-8*, 3805) Clearfield Co.

Matheny, H. E. Major General Thomas Maley Harris. 296p. 1963. reprint ed. pap. 14.95 (*0-87012-003-4*) McClain.

MAJOR GENERAL THOMAS MALEY HARRIS...a member of the Military Commission that tried the President Abraham Lincoln assassination conspirators...& Roster of the 10th West Virginia Volunteer Infantry Regiment, 1861-1865. Reprinted, 1996. *Publisher Paid Annotation.*

Matheny, James F. & Matheny, Marjorie B. Collision Course: The Ram & the Goat of Daniel 8. Esolen, Debra, ed. (Illus.). 185p. (Orig.). 1993. pap. 10.95 (*0-939422-05-0*) Jay & Assocs.

— Come Thou Reign Over Us. 167p. (Orig.). (C). 1981. pap. 7.95 (*0-939422-00-X*) Jay & Assocs.

— The Four Beasts of Daniel Seven: Prophecy for the End Time. Esolen, Debra, ed. (Illus.). 190p. (Orig.). (C). 1992. pap. text 10.95 (*0-939422-04-2*) Jay & Assocs.

— Gold, Silver, Brass, Iron: Rethinking the Kingdoms of Daniel 2. 175p. (Orig.). (C). 1988. pap. 7.95 (*0-939422-02-6*) Jay & Assocs.

— Is There a Russian Connection? An Exposition of Ezekiel 37 & 39. 76p. (Orig.). (J). 1987. pap. 3.95 (*0-939422-01-8*) Jay & Assocs.

Matheny, James F., jt. auth. see Matheny, Marjorie B.

***Matheny, Joseph.** The Incunabula Papers: Ong's Hat & Other Gateways to New Dimensions. (Illus.). 150p. 1999. pap. 14.95 incl. cd-rom, disk (*0-9674890-1-6*) Imedea.

***Matheny, Kenneth B. & McCarthy, Christopher J.** Write Your Own Prescription for Stress. 200p. 2000. pap. 13.95 (*1-57224-215-9*, Pub. by New Harbinger) Publishers Group.

Matheny, Marjorie B. & Matheny, James F. A Kingdom Divided: An Exposition of Daniel 10-12. 195p. 1994. pap. text 10.95 (*0-939422-06-9*) Jay & Assocs.

— The Mark of Blasphemy: An Exposition of Revelation 13:16-18. 108p. 1995. pap. text 6.95 (*0-939422-08-5*) Jay & Assocs.

— The Seventy Weeks of Daniel: An Exposition of Daniel 9: 24-27. 133p. (Orig.). 1990. pap. 9.95 (*0-939422-03-4*) Jay & Assocs.

Matheny, Marjorie B., jt. auth. see Matheny, James F.

Matheny, Meg, ed. Healthcare Leaders Guide to Integrated Delivery Systems. 423p. 1996. ring bd. 195.00 (*1-56925-061-8*, HIDS) Capitol Publns.

Matheny, Nelda & Clark, James. A Photographic Guide to the Evaluation of Hazard Trees in Urban Areas. 2nd ed. 85p. 1993. pap. text 45.00 (*1-881956-04-0*) Int Soc Arboricult.

Matheny, Nelda & Clark, James R. Trees & Development: A Technical Guide to Preservation of Trees During Land Construction. (Illus.). 179p. 1998. pap. text 45.00 (*1-881956-20-2*) Int Soc Arboricult.

Matheny, Nelda, jt. auth. see Clark, James.

Matheny, Richard E. Major Gifts: Solicitation Strategies. LC 95-119607. 167p. 1994. per. 41.50 (*0-89964-309-4*, 25302) Coun Adv & Supp Ed.

Matheny, William G., jt. auth. see Odenwald, Sylvia B.

Matheopoulos, Helena. Diva: Great Sopranos & Mezzos Discuss Their Art. 352p. 1992. text 29.95 (*1-55553-132-6*) NE U Pr.

— Diva: The New Generation: The Sopranos & Mezzos of the Decade Discuss Their Roles. (Illus.). 336p. 1998. 29.95 (*1-55553-358-2*) NE U Pr.

***Matheopoulos, Helena.** The Great Tenors: From Caruso to Pavarotti. LC 99-27958. (Illus.). 128p. 1999. 40.00 (*0-86565-203-1*) Vendome.

***Matheos, Chris.** Bass-Warm-Ups. 32p. 2000. pap. 5.95 incl. audio compact disk (*0-7866-4987-9*, 98433BCD) Mel Bay.

— Building Amazing Bass Technique. 32p. 2000. pap. 5.95 incl. audio compact disk (*0-7866-4988-7*, 98434BCD) Mel Bay.

— Famous Jazz Bass Chord Progressions. 32p. 2000. pap. 5.95 (*0-7866-5076-1*, 98582BCD) Mel Bay.

— Percussive Slap Bass. 72p. 1996. pap. 17.95 (*0-7866-1673-3*, 95703BCP) Mel Bay.

— Reggae Grooves for Electric Bass. 24p. 1998. pap. 9.95 incl. audio compact disk (*0-7866-2940-1*, 96722BCD) Mel Bay.

Mather. Absolutely Typical Too. 1997. 16.95 (*0-413-71790-9*) Methn.

Mather. Afforestation: Policies, Planning & Progress. 224p. 1993. 69.95 (*1-85293-202-3*, Belhaven) Halsted Pr.

— Competitive Manufacturing. 1998. ring bd. 49.95 (*0-8493-0564-0*) CRC Pr.

Mather. Forest Transition. 65.95 (*1-84014-832-2*) Ashgate Pub Co.

Mather, Alexander S. Global Forest Resources. 351p. (C). 1991. text 350.00 (*81-7089-137-X*, Pub. by Intl Bk Distr) St Mut.

Mather, Alexander S., ed. Afforestation: Policies, Planning & Progress. 224p. 1994. text 230.00 (*0-471-94716-4*) Wiley.

Mather, Angus. Offshore Engineering: An Introduction. (Illus.). 290p. 1995. 135.00 (*1-85609-078-7*, Pub. by Witherby & Co) St Mut.

Mather, Anne. Apollo's Seed. large type ed. 278p. (Orig.). 1992. 11.50 (*0-7505-0385-8*, Pub. by Mgna Lrg Print) Ulverscroft.

— Art of Rughooking. LC 98-28321. (Illus.). 128p. 1999. 24.95 (*0-8069-1763-6*) Sterling.

— The Baby Gambit. (Presents Ser.: No. 2055). 1999. per. 3.75 (*0-373-12055-9*, 1-12055-9) Harlequin Bks.

***Mather, Anne.** Baby Gambit. large type ed. (Thorndike Harlequin Romance Ser.). 2000. 22.95 (*0-263-16285-0*) Mills & Boon.

Mather, Anne. Betrayed. (Presents Ser.). 1992. per. 2.89 (*0-373-11492-3*, 1-11492-5) Harlequin Bks.

— Betrayed. large type ed. 1992. reprint ed. 18.95 (*0-263-12892-X*) Mac Lib Ref.

— Blind Passion. (Presents Ser.: No. 444). 1992. pap. 2.89 (*0-373-11444-3*, 1-11444-6) Harlequin Bks.

— Blind Passion. large type ed. 282p. 1991. reprint ed. lib. bdg. 18.95 (*0-263-12694-3*) Mac Lib Ref.

— Brittle Bondage. LC 95-4577. (Presents Ser.). 186p. 1995. per. 3.25 (*0-373-11722-1*, 1-11722-5) Harlequin Bks.

***Mather, Anne.** Une Dangereuse Rivale. 1999. mass mkt. 3.99 (*0-373-34802-9*) Silhouette.

Mather, Anne. Dangerous Sanctuary. (Presents Ser.). 1993. per. 2.89 (*0-373-11553-9*, 1-11553-4) Harlequin Bks.

— Dangerous Sanctuary. large type ed. 1993. reprint ed. 18.95 (*0-263-13183-1*) Mac Lib Ref.

— Dangerous Temptation. (Mira Bks.). 384p. 1997. per. 5.99 (*1-55166-269-8*, 1-66269-1, Mira Bks) Harlequin Bks.

— Dishonourable Intent. (Presents Ser.). 1998. per. 3.75 (*0-373-11947-X*, 1-11947-8) Harlequin Bks.

— Dishonourable Intent. large type ed. 1998. 21.95 (*0-263-15562-5*, G K Hall & Co) Mac Lib Ref.

— En Depit du Soupcon. (Azur Ser.: Bk. 733). 1999. mass mkt. 3.50 (*0-373-34733-2*, 1-34733-5) Harlequin Bks.

— Encadenada a Ti. Orig. Title: Brittle Bondage. (SPA.). 1996. per. 3.50 (*0-373-33354-4*) Harlequin Bks.

— Fever in the Blood. (Presents Ser.: No. 1251). 1990. per. 2.50 (*0-373-11251-3*) Harlequin Bks.

— Guilty. (Presents Ser.). 1993. per. 2.89 (*0-373-11542-3*, 1-11542-7) Harlequin Bks.

— Guilty. large type ed. 1992. reprint ed. lib. bdg. 18.95 (*0-263-13098-3*) Mac Lib Ref.

— Her Guilty Secret. (Presents Ser.: No. 2032). 1999. per. 3.75 (*0-373-12032-X*, 1-12032-8, Harlequin) Harlequin Bks.

***Mather, Anne.** Her Guilty Secret. large type ed. 1999. write for info. (*0-263-16175-7*, Pub. by Mills & Boon) Ulverscroft.

Mather, Anne. Ilusiones Rotas. (Bianca Ser.: Vol. 124).Tr. of Shattered Illusions. 1998. per. 3.50 (*0-373-33474-5*, 1-33474-7) Harlequin Bks.

— Indiscretion. (Presents Ser.: No. 1354). 1991. per. 2.75 (*0-373-11354-4*) Harlequin Bks.

***Mather, Anne.** Innocent Sins. (Presents Ser.: Bk. 2133). 2000. mass mkt. 3.99 (*0-373-12133-4*, 1-12133-4) Harlequin Bks.

Mather, Anne. Inolvidable Pasion: Dishonourable Intent. (Bianca Ser.: No. 137).Tr. of Unforgettable Passion. 1999. mass mkt. 3.50 (*0-373-33487-7*, 1-33487-9) Harlequin Bks.

— Legacy of the Past. large type ed. 316p. 1993. 27.99 (*0-7505-0551-6*, Pub. by Mgna Lrg Print) Ulverscroft.

— Long Night's Loving. (Presents Ser.: No. 1887). 1997. per. 3.50 (*0-373-11887-2*, 1-11887-6) Harlequin Bks.

— Long Night's Loving. large type ed. (Harlequin Ser.). 1997. 20.95 (*0-263-15294-4*) Thorndike Pr.

— The Longest Pleasure. 384p. 1987. mass mkt. 3.50 (*0-373-97030-7*) Harlequin Bks.

***Mather, Anne.** The Millionaire's Virgin: The Greek Tycoons. (Presents Ser.: Bk. 2109). 2000. per. 3.99 (*0-373-12109-1*, 1-12109-4) Harlequin Bks.

Mather, Anne. Monkshood. large type ed. 283p. 1994. 27.99 (*0-7505-0602-4*, Pub. by Mgna Lrg Print) Ulverscroft.

***Mather, Anne.** Morgan's Child. large type ed. (Harlequin Romance Ser.). 2000. 22.95 (*0-263-16409-8*) Mills & Boon.

Mather, Anne. Morgan's Child: (Millenium Celebration) (Presents Ser.: No. 2000). 1998. per. 3.75 (*0-373-12000-1*, 1-12000-5) Harlequin Bks.

***Mather, Anne.** Pacific Heat. 1999. per. 3.75 (*0-373-12019-2*, 1-12019-5, Harlequin) Harlequin Bks.

Mather, Anne. Pacific Heat. 1999. 21.95 (*0-263-15986-8*, G K Hall & Co) Mac Lib Ref.

— Pale Orchid. large type ed. (Magna Romance Ser.). 1992. 11.95 (*0-7505-0226-6*, Pub. by Mgna Lrg Print) Ulverscroft.

— Pecados de Familia. (SPA.). 1997. per. 3.50 (*0-373-33404-4*, 1-33404-4) Harlequin Bks.

— Raw Silk. large type ed. (Harlequin Romance Ser.). 1995. 19.95 (*0-263-14214-0*) Thorndike Pr.

M

— Raw Silk: (Too Hot to Handle) LC 95-7122. (Presents Ser.). 189p. 1995. per. 3.25 (*0-373-11731-0*, 1-11731-6) Harlequin Bks.
— A Relative Betrayal. 1990. per. 2.50 (*0-373-11315-3*) Harlequin Bks.
— Relative Sins. 1996. per. 3.50 (*0-373-11845-7*, 1-11845-4) Harlequin Bks.
— Rich As Sin. (Presents Ser.). 1993. per. 2.99 (*0-373-11567-9*, 1-11567-4) Harlequin Bks.
— A Secret Rebellion. (Presents Ser.). 1994. per. 2.99 (*0-373-11663-2*, 1-11663-1) Harlequin Bks.
— A Secret Rebellion. large type ed. (Harlequin Romance Ser.). 1994. lib. bdg. 19.95 (*0-263-13822-4*) Thorndike Pr.
— Shattered Illusions. 1997. per. 3.50 (*0-373-11911-9*, 1-11911-4) Harlequin Bks.
— Sinful Pleasures. (Presents Ser.). 1998. per. 3.75 (*0-373-11959-3*, 1-11959-3) Harlequin Bks.
— Sinful Pleasures, Vol. 195. 1998. 21.95 (*0-263-15653-2*, Harlequin) Harlequin Bks.
— Les Soupcons d'un Seducteur. (Azur Ser.). (FRE.). 1997. pap. 3.50 (*0-373-34653-0*, 1-34653-5) Harlequin Bks.
— Strange Intimacy. 1994. per. 2.99 (*0-373-11697-7*, 1-11697-9) Harlequin Bks.
— Such Sweet Poison. (Presents Ser.: No. 458). 1992. per. 2.89 (*0-373-11458-3*, 1-11458-6) Harlequin Bks.
— Such Sweet Poison. large type ed. 285p. 1991. reprint ed. 18.95 (*0-263-12807-5*) Thorndike Pr.
— Tender Assault. 1994. per. 2.99 (*0-373-11649-7*) Harlequin Bks.
— Tender Assault. large type ed. (Harlequin Ser.). 1994. lib. bdg. 18.95 (*0-263-13716-3*) Thorndike Pr.
— Tidewater Seduction. (Presents Plus Ser.). 1993. per. 2.99 (*0-373-11591-1*, 1-11591-4) Harlequin Bks.
— Tidewater Seduction. large type ed. (Harlequin Ser.). 1993. 19.95 (*0-263-13356-7*) Mac Lib Ref.
— Treacherous Longings. LC 95-13703. (Presents Ser.). 188p. 1995. per. 3.25 (*0-373-11759-0*, 1-11759-7) Harlequin Bks.
— Treacherous Longings. large type ed. (Harlequin Romance Ser.). 1995. 19.95 (*0-263-14321-X*) Mac Lib Ref.
— Volver a Amarte: Long Night's Loving. (Bianca Ser.: Vol. 458).Tr. of To Love You Again. (SPA.). 1998. per. 3.50 (*0-373-33458-3*, 1-33458-0) Harlequin Bks.
— Wicked Caprice. (Presents Ser.). 1997. per. 3.50 (*0-373-11869-4*, 1-11869-4) Harlequin Bks.
— Wicked Caprice. large type ed. (Harlequin Romance Ser.). 1997. 20.95 (*0-263-15068-2*) Thorndike Pr.
— Wild Concerto. (Bestsellers Ser.). 384p. 1983. mass mkt. 4.95 (*0-373-97006-4*) Harlequin Bks.
— A Woman of Passion. LC 96-702. 188p. 1996. per. 3.50 (*0-373-11797-3*, 1-11797-1) Harlequin Bks.
— A Woman of Passion. large type ed. (Harlequin Romance Ser.). 1996. 19.95 (*0-263-14481-X*) Mac Lib Ref.
Mather, Anne, et al. A Match for Mom: Guilty, a Man for Mom, the Fix-It Man. 1997. per. 5.99 (*0-373-20135-4*, 1-20135-9) Harlequin Bks.
***Mather, Anne D.** The Art of Rug Hooking. 128p. 1999. pap. text 14.95 (*0-8069-1801-2*) Sterling.
— Creative Rug Hooking. LC 00-30132. (Illus.). 2000. pap. write for info. (*0-8069-7146-0*) Sterling.
Mather, Anne D. & Weldon, Louise B. The Cat at the Door & Other Stories to Live By: Affirmations for Children. (Illus.). 200p. (J). (ps-4). pap. 12.00 (*0-89486-758-X*, 5131A) Hazelden.
— Cats in the Classroom: The Sequel to The Cat at the Door & Other Stories to Live By. LC 95-20369. (Illus.). 127p. (J). pap. 11.95 (*1-56838-086-0*) Hazelden.
Mather, Anne D., jt. auth. see Weldon, Louise B.
Mather, Becky R. Creating a Local Area Network in the School Library Media Center. LC 96-50290. (Greenwood Professional Guides in School Librarianship). 160p. 1997. 39.95 (*0-313-30094-1*, Greenwood Pr) Greenwood.
Mather, Berkely. The Pagoda Tree. large type ed. 576p. 1982. 27.99 (*0-7089-0892-6*) Ulverscroft.
Mather, Betty B. Interpretation of French Music from 1675-1775 for Woodwind & Other Performers. LC 74-168244. 1973. 20.00 (*0-941084-03-5*) McGinnis & Marx.
Mather, Betty B. & Gavin, Gail. The French Noel: With an Anthology of 1725 Arranged for Flute Duet. LC 95-10193. 120p. (C). 1996. 20.00 (*0-253-21025-9*) Ind U Pr.
Mather, Betty B. & Lasocki, David. The Art of Preluding, 1700-1830. LC 84-758576. 1983. 12.00 (*0-941084-08-6*) McGinnis & Marx.
— Free Ornamentation in Woodwind Music. LC 87-753698. 1976. 22.00 (*0-941084-05-1*) McGinnis & Marx.
Mather, Betty B., jt. auth. see Lasocki, David.
Mather, Charlotte. Kissed by an Angel. 57p. 15.00 (*0-934172-12-9*) WIM Pubns.
Mather, Christine. Native America: Arts, Traditions, & Celebrations. (Illus.). 1990. 40.00 (*0-517-57436-5*) C Potter.
Mather, Christine & Woods, Sharon. Santa Fe Style. LC 86-42715. (Illus.). 256p. 1993. 42.50 (*0-8478-0734-7*, Pub. by Rizzoli Intl) St Martin.
Mather, Cotton. The Angel of Bethesda. Jones, Gordon W., ed. LC 72-185323. 384p. 1972. 30.00 (*0-8271-7220-6*) Oak Knoll.
— The Angel of Bethsada. (Notable American Authors Ser.). 1999. reprint ed. lib. bdg. 125.00 (*0-7812-3968-0*) Rprt Serv.
— Bonifacius: An Essay upon the Good. Levin, David, ed. LC 66-14448. 215p. reprint ed. pap. 66.70 (*0-8357-7340-X*, 201465400093) Bks Demand.
— Bonifacius: An Essay...to Do Good. LC 67-18712. 218p. 1967. reprint ed. 50.00 (*0-8201-1032-9*) Schol Facsimiles.
— Bonnifacius (Essays to Do Good) (Notable American Authors Ser.). 1999. reprint ed. lib. bdg. 125.00 (*0-7812-3964-8*) Rprt Serv.
— Brethren Dwelling Together in Unity. (Notable American Authors Ser.). 1999. reprint ed. lib. bdg. 125.00 (*0-7812-3965-6*) Rprt Serv.
***Mather, Cotton.** The Christian Philosopher. Solberg, Winton U., ed. 2000. 29.95 (*0-252-06893-9*) U of Ill Pr.
Mather, Cotton. The Christian Philosopher. (Notable American Authors Ser.). 1999. reprint ed. lib. bdg. 125.00 (*0-7812-3967-2*) Rprt Serv.
— Christian Philosopher: A Collection of the Best Discoveries in Nature, with Religious Improvements. LC 68-29082. 328p. 1968. reprint ed. 50.00 (*0-8201-1033-7*) Schol Facsimiles.
— Corderius Americanus or: The Good Education of Children. (Notable American Authors Ser.). 1999. reprint ed. lib. bdg. 125.00 (*0-7812-3963-X*) Rprt Serv.
— Day of Humiliation: Times of Affliction & Disaster. LC 68-24211. 406p. 1970. 60.00 (*0-8201-1067-1*) Schol Facsimiles.
— Declaration of the Gentlemen, Merchants & Inhabitants of Boston. (Notable American Authors Ser.). 1999. reprint ed. lib. bdg. 125.00 (*0-7812-3951-6*) Rprt Serv.
— Diary. (Notable American Authors Ser.). 1999. reprint ed. lib. bdg. 125.00 (*0-7812-3972-9*) Rprt Serv.
— Eleutheria or an Idea of the Reformation in England. (Notable American Authors Ser.). 1999. reprint ed. lib. bdg. 125.00 (*0-7812-3956-7*) Rprt Serv.
— A Faithful Man: Michael Wiglesworth. (Notable American Authors Ser.). 1999. reprint ed. lib. bdg. 125.00 (*0-7812-3961-3*) Rprt Serv.
— Family Well Ordered. (Notable American Authors Ser.). 1999. reprint ed. lib. bdg. 125.00 (*0-7812-3958-3*) Rprt Serv.
— The Life of Sir William Phips. LC 75-137260. reprint ed. 31.50 (*0-404-04249-X*) AMS Pr.
— The Life of Sir William Phips. (BCL1 - United States Local History Ser.). 208p. 1991. reprint ed. lib. bdg. 79.00 (*0-7812-6266-6*) Rprt Serv.
— Magnalia Christi Americana, Bks. I & II. Murdock, Kenneth B. & Miller, Elizabeth W., eds. LC 73-76383. (John Harvard Library). (Illus.). 512p. reprint ed. pap. 158.80 (*0-7837-2496-9*, 205745900005) Bks Demand.
— Magnalia Christi Americana or: The Ecclesiastical History of New England from Its First Planting. (Notable American Authors Ser.). 1999. reprint ed. lib. bdg. 125.00 (*0-7812-3960-5*) Rprt Serv.
— Magnalia Christi Americana, or the Ecclesiastical History of New-England from the Year 1620, Unto the Year 1698, 7 bks., Set. LC 74-141092. (Research Library of Colonial Americana). (Illus.). 1972. reprint ed. 63.95 (*0-405-03297-8*) Ayer.
— Manductio ad Ministerium. (Notable American Authors Ser.). 1999. reprint ed. lib. bdg. 125.00 (*0-7812-3971-0*) Rprt Serv.
— Manuductio Administerium, Directions for a Candidate of the Ministry. LC 75-41190. reprint ed. 36.50 (*0-404-14685-6*) AMS Pr.
— Memorable Providences: Relating to Witchcrafts & Possessions. (Notable American Authors Ser.). 1999. reprint ed. lib. bdg. 125.00 (*0-7812-3952-4*) Rprt Serv.
— The Negro Christianized. (Notable American Authors Ser.). 1999. reprint ed. lib. bdg. 125.00 (*0-7812-3962-1*) Rprt Serv.
— Ornaments for the Daughters of Zion. LC 78-8588. 128p. 1978. 50.00 (*0-8201-1311-5*) Schol Facsimiles.
— Parentator (Life of Increase Mather) (Notable American Authors Ser.). 1999. reprint ed. lib. bdg. 125.00 (*0-7812-3969-9*) Rprt Serv.
— Pastoral Letter to the English Captives in Africa. (Notable American Authors Ser.). 1999. reprint ed. lib. bdg. 125.00 (*0-7812-3957-5*) Rprt Serv.
— Paterna: The Autobiography of Cotton Mather. Bosco, Ronald A., ed. LC 76-10595. (Center for Editions of American Authors). 504p. 1976. lib. bdg. 75.00 (*0-8201-1273-9*) Schol Facsimiles.
— Pietas in Patrian (Life of Sir William Phips) (Notable American Authors Ser.). 1999. reprint ed. lib. bdg. 125.00 (*0-7812-3955-9*) Rprt Serv.
— A Poem to the Memory of Mr. Urian Oakes. (Notable American Authors Ser.). 1999. reprint ed. lib. bdg. 125.00 (*0-7812-3950-8*) Rprt Serv.
— The Present State of New England. LC 68-24989. (American History & Americana Ser.: No. 47). 1969. reprint ed. lib. bdg. 75.00 (*0-8383-0214-9*) M S G Haskell Hse.
— The Present State of New England. (BCL1 - U. S. History Ser.). 52p. 1991. reprint ed. lib. bdg. 59.00 (*0-7812-6099-X*) Rprt Serv.
— The Present State of New England. (Notable American Authors Ser.). 1999. reprint ed. lib. bdg. 125.00 (*0-7812-3953-2*) Rprt Serv.
— Ratio Disciplinae Fratrum Novanglorum: A Faithful Account of the Discipline Professed & Practised, in the Churches of New-England. LC 71-141114. (Research Library of Colonial Americana). 1972. reprint ed. 25.95 (*0-405-03327-3*) Ayer.
— Ration Disciplinae. (Notable American Authors Ser.). 1999. reprint ed. lib. bdg. 125.00 (*0-7812-3970-2*) Rprt Serv.
— Reasonable Religion. (Notable American Authors Ser.). 1999. reprint ed. lib. bdg. 125.00 (*0-7812-3959-1*) Rprt Serv.
— Selected Letters of Cotton Mather. Silverman, Kenneth, ed. LC 78-142338. 472p. reprint ed. pap. 146.40 (*0-608-14363-4*, 201956500013) Bks Demand.
— Sentiments of the Small Pox Inoculated. (Notable American Authors Ser.). 1999. reprint ed. lib. bdg. 125.00 (*0-7812-3966-4*) Rprt Serv.
— The Threefold Paradise of Cotton Mather: An Edition of Triparadisus. Smolinski, Reiner, ed. LC 92-29850. 520p. 1995. 75.00 (*0-8203-1519-2*) U of Ga Pr.
— The Wonders of the Invisible World. (Notable American Authors Ser.). 1999. reprint ed. lib. bdg. 125.00 (*0-7812-3954-0*) Rprt Serv.
Mather, Cotton & Karan, P. P. Beyond the Great Divide: Denver to the Grand Canyon. LC 92-10534. (Touring North America Ser.). (Illus.). 194p. 1992. 25.00 (*0-8135-1882-2*); pap. 9.95 (*0-8135-1883-0*) Rutgers U Pr.
Mather, Cotton & Thompson, George F. Registered Places of New Mexico: The Land of Enchantment. 1995. 19.95 (*0-9643841-0-8*) NMex Geograp.
Mather, Cotton, et al. Japanese Landscapes: Where Land & Culture Merge: A Concise Visual Guide. LC 98-16082. 1998. 24.95 (*0-8131-2090-X*) U Pr of Ky.
Mather, Cotton, jt. auth. see Janeway, James.
Mather, Cotton, jt. auth. see Karan, P. P.
Mather, Cotton, jt. ed. see De Souza, Anthony R.
Mather, Cotton, jt. ed. see Karan, P. P.
Mather, Cynthia L. & Debye, Kristina E. How Long Does It Hurt? A Guide to Recovering from Incest for Teenagers, Their Friends, & Their Families. LC 94-12536. (Social & Behavioral Sciences Ser.). 283p. 1994. mass mkt. 16.50 (*1-55542-674-3*) Jossey-Bass.
Mather, Eleanore P. Anna Brinton: A Study in Quaker Character. LC 74-152086. (Illus.). (Orig.). 1971. pap. 4.00 (*0-87574-176-2*) Pendle Hill.
Mather, Eleanore P. Barclay in Brief. (C). 1944. pap. 1.00 (*0-87574-028-6*) Pendle Hill.
Mather, Eleanore P. Edward Hicks: Primitive Quaker. LC 75-110287. (Illus.). (Orig.). 1970. pap. 4.00 (*0-87574-170-3*) Pendle Hill.
Mather, Eleanore P. & Miller, Dorothy C. Edward Hicks: His Peaceable Kingdoms & Other Paintings. LC 81-71405. (Illus.). 224p. 1983. 40.00 (*0-8453-4760-8*, Cornwall Bks) Assoc Univ Prs.
Mather, Eleanore P. & Price, Charles. A Quaker Experiement in Education & Community. LC 79-93378. 128p. 1993. 7.00 (*0-87574-954-2*, 1064) Pendle Hill.
Mather, Eleanore P., ed. see Fogelklou-Norlind, Emilia.
Mather, Eleanore P., ed. see Murphy, Carol R.
Mather, Eleanore P., ed. see Robinson, Jo A.
Mather, Elsie, tr. see Greenglass, Esther R.
Mather, F. C. High Church Prophet: Bishop Samuel Horsley (1733-1806) & the Caroline Tradition in the Later Georgian Church. (Illus.). 344p. 1992. text 85.00 (*0-19-820227-X*) OUP.
Mather, F. C., ed. Chartism & Society. LC 80-15587. 488p. 1980. 54.50 (*0-8419-0625-4*) Holmes & Meier.
Mather, Frank J. Estimates in Art. LC 79-137261. (Illus.). reprint ed. 39.50 (*0-404-04256-2*) AMS Pr.
— Estimates in Art, Ser. 2. LC 70-93356. (Essay Index Reprint Ser.). 1977. 23.95 (*0-8369-1527-5*) Ayer.
Mather, Frank J., Jr. Mahonri M. Young. (Illus.). 59p. (Orig.). 1940. pap. write for info. (*1-879886-05-7*) Addison Gallery.
Mather, Frank J. Western European Painting of the Renaissance. LC 65-28209. (Illus.). reprint ed. lib. bdg. 72.00 (*0-8154-0148-5*) Cooper Sq.
Mather, Frederick G., jt. auth. see Roberts, James A.
Mather, George & Nichols, Larry. Discovering the Plain Truth: How the Worldwide Church of God Embraced the Gospel of Grace. LC 97-43047. 140p. 1997. pap. 9.99 (*0-8308-1969-X*, 1969) InterVarsity.
Mather, George, et al. The Motion Aftereffect: A Modern Perspective. LC 97-52191. (Illus.). 232p. 1998. 27.50 (*0-262-13343-1*, Bradford Bks) MIT Pr.
Mather, George A. & Nichols, Larry A. Dictionary of Cults, Sects, Religions & the Occult. (Illus.). 376p. 1993. 29.99 (*0-310-53100-4*) Zondervan.
Mather, H. E. Mather: Lineage of Rev. Richard Mather. (Illus.). 540p. 1990. reprint ed. pap. 81.00 (*0-8328-1613-2*); reprint ed. lib. bdg. 89.00 (*0-8328-1612-4*) Higginson Bk Co.
Mather, Hal. Bills of Materials. 200p. 1986. text 45.00 (*0-87094-947-0*, Irwn Prfssnl) McGraw-Hill Prof.
— Competitive Manufacturing. 241p. (C). 1988. 310.00 (*0-7855-5730-X*, Pub. by Inst Pur & Supply) St Mut.
— Competitive Manufacturing. 241p. (C). 1989. 280.00 (*0-7855-6112-9*, Pub. by Inst Pur & Supply) St Mut.
— Competitive Manufacturing. 2nd ed. 288p. 1998. text 69.95 (*1-85573-380-3*) Buttrwrth-Heinemann.
— How to Profitably Delight Your Customers. 192p. 69.95 (*1-85573-381-1*) Buttrwrth-Heinemann.
Mather, Henry. Contract Law & Morality, 90. LC 98-41418. (Contributions in Legal Studies: Vol. 90). 200p. 1999. 57.95 (*0-313-30868-3*, Greenwood Pr) Greenwood.
Mather, Herb. Lay Speakers Lead in Stewardship: Advanced Course. 16p. 1997. pap. 5.95 (*0-88177-197-X*, DR197) Discipleship Res.
Mather, Herb, jt. auth. see Christopher, J. Clif.
Mather, Herbert. Don't Shoot the Horse ('Til You Know How to Drive the Tractor) Moving from Annual Fund Raising to a Life of Giving. LC 94-72156. 104p. 1994. pap. 11.95 (*0-88177-136-8*, DR136) Discipleship Res.
— Letters for All Seasons: A Year of Letters Designed to Increase Giving in Your Church. LC 93-12892. 80p. (Orig.). 1993. pap. 6.95 (*0-687-39343-4*) Abingdon.
Mather, Increase. A Brief History of the War with the indians. (Notable American Authors Ser.). 1999. reprint ed. lib. bdg. 125.00 (*0-7812-3976-1*) Rprt Serv.
— Cases of Conscience Concerning Evil Spirits. (Notable American Authors Ser.). 1999. reprint ed. lib. bdg. 125.00 (*0-7812-3981-8*) Rprt Serv.
— Cometographia: or A Discourse Concerning Comets. (Notable American Authors Ser.). 1999. reprint ed. lib. bdg. 125.00 (*0-7812-3978-8*) Rprt Serv.
— Departing Glory: Eight Jeremiads of Increase Mather. LC 86-31349. 328p. 1987. 50.00 (*0-8201-1415-4*) Schol Facsimiles.
— A Discourse Concerning Baptism & the Consecration of Churches. (Notable American Authors Ser.). 1999. reprint ed. lib. bdg. 125.00 (*0-7812-3975-3*) Rprt Serv.
— The Dying Pastor's Legacy. (Notable American Authors Ser.). 1999. reprint ed. lib. bdg. 125.00 (*0-7812-3984-2*) Rprt Serv.
— An Essay for the Recording of Illustrious Providences. LC 77-17526. 424p. 1977. reprint ed. lib. bdg. 60.00 (*0-8201-1299-2*) Schol Facsimiles.
— Essay for the Recording of Illustrius Providences. (Notable American Authors Ser.). 1999. reprint ed. lib. bdg. 125.00 (*0-7812-3979-6*) Rprt Serv.
— The Great Blessings of the Primitive Counsellours. (Notable American Authors Ser.). 1999. reprint ed. lib. bdg. 125.00 (*0-7812-3982-6*) Rprt Serv.
— Important Truths about Conversion. (Notable American Authors Ser.). 1999. reprint ed. lib. bdg. 125.00 (*0-7812-3974-5*) Rprt Serv.
— Life & Death of That Reverend Man of God, Mr. Richard Mather. (Notable American Authors Ser.). 1999. reprint ed. lib. bdg. 125.00 (*0-7812-3973-7*) Rprt Serv.
— Relation of the Troubles Which Have Happened in New-England, by Reason of the Indians There from the Year 1614 to the Year 1675. LC 78-141093. (Research Library of Colonial Americana). 1972. reprint ed. 16.95 (*0-405-03298-6*) Ayer.
— Remarkable Providences. LC 97-72584. 262p. (YA). 1997. reprint ed. 24.95 (*1-880045-18-4*) Back Home Indust.
— Remarkable Providences Illustrative of the Earlier Days of American Colonisation. Dorsen, Richard M., ed. LC 77-70610. (International Folklore Ser.). 1977. reprint ed. lib. bdg. 26.95 (*0-405-10107-4*) Ayer.
— Several Papers Relating to the State of New England. (Notable American Authors Ser.). 1999. reprint ed. lib. bdg. 125.00 (*0-7812-3980-X*) Rprt Serv.
— The Surest Way to the Greatest Honour. (Notable American Authors Ser.). 1999. reprint ed. lib. bdg. 125.00 (*0-7812-3983-4*) Rprt Serv.
Mather, Increase & Stoddard, Solomon. Increase Mather Vs. Solomon Stoddard: Two Puritan Tracts. LC 72-141117. (Research Library of Colonial Americana). 1972. reprint ed. 25.95 (*0-405-03328-1*) Ayer.
Mather, J., et al, eds. Groundwater Contaminants & Their Migrations. LC 99-207718. (Geological Society Special Publication Ser.: No. 128). (Illus.). 320p. 1997. 115.00 (*1-897799-95-0*, Pub. by Geol Soc Pub Hse) AAPG.
Mather, J. & Roberts, P. Introduction to Cell & Tissue Culture: Theory & Techniques. LC 98-27597. (Introductory Cell & Molecular Biology Techniques Ser.: Vol. 1). (Illus.). 230p. (C). 1998. text 29.50 (*0-306-45859-4*, Kluwer Plenum) Kluwer Academic.
Mather, J. E. & Boswell, F. E. Gold Camp Desperadoes: A Study of Violence, Crime, & Punishment on the Mining Frontier. LC 92-50724. 1993. reprint ed. 13.95 (*0-8061-2521-7*) U of Okla Pr.
Mather Jackson, Edward A. Nathaniel Hawthorne, A Modest Man. LC 77-110834. 356p. 1971. reprint ed. lib. bdg. 35.00 (*0-8371-2594-4*, MANH, Greenwood Pr) Greenwood.
Mather, Jan. Designing Alberta Gardens: The Complete Guide to Beautiful Gardens. (Prairie Garden Bks.). (Illus.). 176p. 1994. pap. 24.95 (*0-88995-111-X*, Pub. by Red Deer) Genl Dist Srvs.
— The Prairie Garden Planner: A Personal Journal. (Prairie Garden Bks.). (Illus.). 256p. 1996. pap. 22.95 (*0-88995-144-6*, Pub. by Red Deer) Genl Dist Srvs.
— The Prairie Rose Garden. LC 96-910777. (Prairie Garden Bks.). (Illus.). 80p. 1997. pap. 10.95 (*0-88995-163-2*, Pub. by Red Deer) Genl Dist Srvs.
***Mather, Janet.** The European Union & British Democracy: Towards Convergence. LC 00-33347. 2000. write for info. (*0-312-23577-1*) St Martin.
Mather, Jay & Maharidge, Dale. Yosemite - A Landscape of Life. Hennessy, Terry, ed. LC 90-41607. (Illus.). 120p. (Orig.). 1990. pap. 14.95 (*0-939666-56-1*) Yosemite Assn.
Mather, Jean & Alden, Richard. Fundamentals of Grammar & Writing: English 301. 178p. (C). 1992. pap. text 24.18 (*1-56226-130-4*) CAT Pub.
Mather, Jennie P., ed. Mammalian Cell Culture: The Use of Serum-Free Hormone-Supplemented Media. LC 84-1985. 312p. 1984. 79.50 (*0-306-41584-4*, Plenum Trade) Perseus Pubng.
Mather, Jennie P., jt. ed. see Barnes, David.
Mather, Jim, ed. see Green, Madge.
Mather, John. Very First Light: The True Inside Story of the Scientific Journey Back to the Dawn of the Universe. 352p. 2000. pap. 16.00 (*0-465-01576-X*, Pub. by Basic) HarpC.
Mather, John & Boslough, John. The Very First Light. 320p. 1996. 27.50 (*0-465-01575-1*, Pub. by Basic) HarpC.
Mather, John R. Water Resources: Distribution, Use & Management. (Environmental Science & Technology Ser.: No. 1-121). 439p. 1983. 150.00 (*0-471-89401-X*) Wiley.
Mather, John R. & Sanderson, Marie. The Genius of C. Warren Thornthwaite, Climatologist-Geographer. LC 95-14239. 226p. 1996. 29.95 (*0-8061-2787-2*) U of Okla Pr.
Mather, John R. & Sdasyuk, Galina V., eds. Global Change: Geographical Approaches. LC 91-14025. (Geographical Dialogue: Soviet & American Views Ser.). (Illus.). 293p. 1991. 53.00 (*0-8165-1272-8*) U of Ariz Pr.
Mather, Karen T. Silas, the Bookstore Cat. LC 94-72357. (Illus.). 32p. (J). (gr. 1-3). 1994. 14.95 (*0-89272-352-1*) Down East.

An Asterisk (*) at the beginning of an entry indicates that the title is appearing for the first time.

Mather, Kelli & Ellington, Linda. School-Based Student Support Groups No. 3: A Step-by-Step Curriculum Guide for Facilitators. 244p. 1998. pap. 29.95 (*0-8309-0784-X*) Herald Pub Hse.

Mather, Kelli E. & Ellington, Linda K. School-Based Student Support Groups: A Step-by-Step Curriculum Guide for Facilitators. LC 94-168073. 1994. write for info. (*0-8309-0687-8*) Herald Pub Hse.

Mather, Kirtley F. & Mason, Shirley L. A Source Book in Geology, 1400-1900. LC 67-12100. (Source Books in the History of the Sciences). (Illus.). 726p. reprint ed. pap. 200.00 (*0-7837-3850-1*, 204367200010) Bks Demand.

Mather, Marshall. John Ruskin. LC 72-881. (English Biography Ser.: No. 31). 1972. reprint ed. lib. bdg. 75.00 (*0-8383-1425-2*) M S G Haskell Hse.

Mather, Mary. Pocket Guide to Outdoor Photography. (Illus.). 28p. 1993. spiral bd. 12.95 (*0-9633024-5-0*) Greycliff Pub.

Mather, Maurice W. & Hewitt, Joseph W. Xenophon's Anabasis, Bks. 1-4. LC 62-18051. (Illus.). 522p. 1976. pap. 24.95 (*0-8061-1347-2*) U of Okla Pr.

Mather, McGregor. Grimoire of Armadel. 1994. 22.95 (*0-87728-712-0*) Weiser.

Mather, Mike. Tomorrow's Headlines. 1999. pap. 16.95 (*0-7414-0043-X*) Buy Books.

Mather, Mort. Gardening for Independence. 1977. pap. 3.95 (*0-911764-19-4*) M Mather.

Mather, Nancy. An Instructional Guide to the Woodcock-Johnson Psycho-Educational Battery. rev. ed. LC 90-82412. (Illus.). 305p. (C). 1990. pap. text 42.50 (*0-88422-108-3*) Clinical Psych.

— An Instructional Guide to the Woodcock-Johnson Psycho-Educational Battery. rev. ed. LC 96-21576. 336p. 1996. pap. 49.95 (*0-471-16189-6*) Wiley.

Mather, Nancy & Jaffe, Lynne. The Woodcock-Johnson Psycho-Educational Battery: Recommendations & Reports. rev. ed. LC 96-20245. 400p. 1996. pap. 49.95 (*0-471-16210-8*) Wiley.

Mather, Nancy & Jaffe, Lynne E. The Woodcock-Johnson Psycho-Educational Battery: Recommendations & Reports. rev. ed. LC 91-75518. 396p. 1992. pap. text 39.50 (*0-88422-115-6*) Clinical Psych.

Mather, Nancy & Roberts, Rhia. Informal Assessment & Instruction in Written Language: A Practitioner's Guide for Students with Learning Disabilities. LC 96-24701. 400p. 1996. pap. 49.95 (*0-471-16208-6*) Wiley.

— Informal Assessment & Remediation of Written Language: A Practitioner's Guide for Students with Learning Disabilities. LC 94-29759. 460p. 1995. 44.95 (*0-88422-153-9*) Clinical Psych.

Mather, Nancy, jt. auth. see Goldstein, Sam.

Mather, Otis M. Mather Papers: History of Larue County, Kentucky. 57p. 1995. pap. 7.00 (*1-889221-26-0*) Ancestral Trails.

Mather, Paul D. M. I. A. Accounting for the Missing in Southeast Asia. (Illus.). 207p. (Orig.). (C). 1995. pap. text 40.00 (*0-7881-2533-8*) DIANE Pub.

— M. I. A. Accounting for the Missing in Southeast Asia. 231p. (Orig.). 1995. per. 10.00 (*0-16-036391-8*) USGPO.

Mather, Paul M. Computer Applications in Geography. LC 90-43734. 270p. 1991. pap. 80.00 (*0-471-92615-9*) Wiley.

***Mather, Paul M.** Computer Processing of Remotely Sensed Images: An Introduction. 2nd ed. LC 98-37544. 306p. 1999. pap. 59.95 (*0-471-98550-3*) Wiley.

Mather, Paul M., ed. Geographical Information Handling-Research & Applications. LC 93-8835. 356p. 1994. 125.00 (*0-471-94060-7*) Wiley.

— TERRA-1: Understanding the Terrestrial Environment - The Role of Earth Observations from Space. LC 92-18705. 1992. 99.00 (*0-7484-0044-3*, Pub. by Tay Francis Ltd) Taylor & Francis.

Terra 2: Understanding the Terrestrial Environment: Remote Sensing Data Systems & Networks. LC 94-23083. 254p. 1995. 180.00 (*0-471-95405-5*) Wiley.

Mather, Peter & McCarthy, Rita. Reading & All That Jazz: Tuning-Up Your Reading, Thinking, & Study Skills. LC 98-18568. 448p. 1999. pap. 36.56 (*0-07-041099-2*) McGraw.

Mather, R. E. The Cottonwood Murders--Unsolved. LC 98-50075. 1999. 15.95 (*0-9625069-4-X*) Hist West Pub.

— Scandal of the West: Domestic Violence on the Frontier. unabridged ed. LC 98-4063. (Illus.). vi, 213p. 1998. pap. 15.95 (*0-9625069-2-3*) Hist West Pub.

Mather, R. E. & Boswell, F. E. Hanging the Sheriff: A Biography of Henry Plummer. LC 98-42521. 1998. pap. write for info. (*0-9663355-0-3*) Hist Montana.

Mather, Rachel R. The Heirs of Jane Austen: Twentieth-Century Writers of the Comedy of Manners. (American University Studies IV: Vol. 180). XII, 142p. (C). 1997. text 34.95 (*0-8204-2624-5*) P Lang Pubng.

Mather, Richard. Church Covenant: Two Tracts. LC 75-141115. (Research Library of Colonial Americana). 1972. reprint ed. 25.95 (*0-405-03329-X*) Ayer.

Mather, Richard B. The Poet Shen Yueh, (441-513) The Reticent Marquis. LC 88-1138. 272p. 1988. reprint ed. pap. 84.40 (*0-608-06469-6*, 206670200009) Bks Demand.

Mather, Richard B., tr. & intro. see Liu, I-ching.

Mather, Ruth E. & Boswell, F. E. Hanging the Sheriff: A Biography of Henry Plummer. LC 87-2125. (University of Utah Publications in the American West: No. 21). 236p. reprint ed. pap. 73.20 (*0-8357-3271-1*, 203949200013) Bks Demand.

— John David Borthwick: Artist of the Goldrush. LC 88-20671. (University of Utah Publications in the American West: No. 23). 230p. 1989. pap. 71.30 (*0-7837-8566-6*, 204938200011) Bks Demand.

Mather, Ruth E. & Boswell, Fred E. The Bannack Gallows. LC 98-24666. viii, 207p. 1998. pap. 15.95 (*0-9625069-3-1*) Hist West Pub.

— Gold Camp Desperadoes: A Study of Violence, Crime & Punishment on the Mining Frontier. LC 89-77024. (Illus.). 224p. 1990. 24.95 (*0-9625069-0-7*) Hist West Pub.

— Vigilante Victims: Montana's 1864 Hanging. LC 90-41114. (Illus.). 208p. 1991. 24.95 (*0-9625069-1-5*) Hist West Pub.

Mather, S. B., jt. ed. see Kahn, Robert P.

Mather, Sheila. Leaving Food Behind: An Inspiring Personal Story of Recovery from Bulimia, Starving, Overeating. 144p. 1999. pap. 12.95 (*0-9681812-0-1*) ACCESS Pubs Network.

Mather, Stephen J., ed. Current Directions in Radiopharmaceutical Research & Development. LC 96-38428. (Developments in Nuclear Medicine Ser.: Vol. 30). 1996. lib. bdg. 136.00 (*0-7923-4254-2*) Kluwer Academic.

Mather, Stephen J. & Hughes, David G., eds. A Handbook of Paediatric Anaesthesia. (Illus.). 320p. 1991. pap. 35.00 (*0-19-263011-3*) OUP.

Mather, Stephen J., jt. auth. see Peutrell, Jane M.

Mather, Susan M., jt. auth. see Carroll, Cathryn.

Mather, Thomas M., jt. auth. see Sonenshine, Daniel E.

***Mather, Timothy C.** Prophetic Deliverence. 128p. 2000. pap. 7.99 (*1-930027-01-X*) Insight Intl.

Mather, Tom. The Cheeseburger. 96p. (Orig.). 1997. pap. 12.00 (*1-57502-552-3*, P01611) Morris Pubng.

— Voyages in the Toilet Dimension. 90p. 1999. pap. 5.99 (*0-9671155-0-7*) Cheeseburger Pubg.

***Mather, Victoria.** Absolutely Typical Too. 2000. pap. 9.95 (*0-413-72100-0*) Methn.

Matherly. Access 2: Essentials for Windows. LC 94-69262. 181p. 1995. 22.99 (*0-7897-0110-3*) Que.

Matherly. Works 4 for Windows 95 Essentials. 2nd ed. LC 97-66318. 497p. 1997. 49.99 (*1-57576-831-3*) Sams.

Matherly, Cheryl, jt. auth. see Sanborn, Robert.

Matherly, Donna. Excel 97 Smartstart. 1997. teacher ed. 39.99 (*1-57576-817-8*) Que Educ & Trng.

Matherly, Donna. Excel 97 Smartstart. LC 97-65620. (Illus.). 384p. 1997. 29.99 (*1-57576-816-X*) Sams.

Matherly, Donna. Microsoft Office 97 Professional Essentials AIE. 1997. 39.99 (*1-57576-788-0*) Que Educ & Trng.

Matherly, Donna M. Access 2 for Windows Essentials. 1995. 39.99 (*0-7897-0116-2*) Macmillan USA.

Matherly, Donna M. dBASE 5.0 for Windows Smartstart. 272p. 1995. pap. text 22.67 (*0-7897-0439-0*) Macmillan USA.

Matherly, Donna M. dBASE 5.0 Smartstart. 1995. teacher ed. 39.99 incl. disk (*0-7897-0443-9*) Macmillan USA.

Matherly, Donna M. & O'Hara. Paradox 5 for Windows Essentials. 1995. teacher ed. 39.99 (*0-7897-0120-0*) Que.

Matherly, Donna M., jt. auth. see Goforth, Laura J.

Matherly, Sandra & Hodges, Shannon. Telephone Nursing: The Process. Pramik, Janice, ed. 132p. (Orig.). (C). 1990. pap. text 44.00 (*0-933948-23-9*, 2550) Ctr Res Ambulatory.

***Mathern, G. W., ed.** Pediatric Epilepsy & Epilepsy Surgery. (Developmental Neuroscience Ser.: Vol. 21, No. 3-5). (Illus.). 250p. 1999. pap. 48.75 (*3-8055-6925-4*) S Karger.

Matherne, Beverly. Je Me Souviens de la Louisiane. Bixby, Robert, ed. 31p. 1993. pap. 6.00 (*1-882983-06-8*) March Street Pr.

Matheron, G. Estimating & Choosing. (Illus.). 170p. 1989. 76.95 (*0-387-50087-1*) Spr-Verlag.

Matheron, G. & Armstrong, M., eds. Geostatistical Case Studies. 1987. text 154.00 (*1-55608-019-0*) Kluwer Academic.

Mathers, Debra. Suffering from Guilt. (Master's Touch Bible Study Ser.). 1994. pap. 4.50 (*0-570-09437-2*, 20-2458) Concordia.

Mathers, Douglas. Brain. LC 90-42883. (Illus.). 32p. (J). (gr. 4-6). 1992. lib. bdg. 18.60 (*0-8167-2090-8*) Troll Communs.

— Ears. LC 90-42176. (Illus.). 32p. (J). (gr. 4-6). 1992. lib. bdg. 18.60 (*0-8167-2092-4*) Troll Communs.

— Ears. LC 90-42176. (Illus.). 32p. (J). (gr. 4-6). 1997. pap. 4.95 (*0-8167-2093-2*) Troll Communs.

Mathers, E. P. Sung to Sharyar. 128p. 1987. 70.00 (*1-85077-146-4*, Pub. by Darf Pubs Ltd) St Mut.

Mathers, E. P. & Mardrus, J. C., eds. Book of the Thousand Nights & One Night, 4 vols., Set. 1200p. (C). (gr. 13). 1987. pap. 65.00 (*0-415-04543-6*) Routledge.

Mathers, E. Powys. The Book of the Thousand Nights & One Night, 4 vols. 1986. 12.95 (*0-685-73835-3*, A5329, Routledge Thoemms); 12.95 (*0-318-61561-4*, Routledge Thoemms); 12.95 (*0-318-61562-2*, Routledge Thoemms) Routledge.

— The Book of the Thousand Nights & One Night, 4 vols., Set. 1986. 37.50 (*0-7102-0869-3*, A5329, Routledge Thoemms) Routledge.

Mathers, E. Powys, tr. see Suikaku, Ilara.

Mathers, Edward P., ed. Coloured Stars: Oriental Love Poetry. pap. 5.95 (*0-8283 1432-2*, 11) Branden Bks.

Mathers, James. The Motorist's Guide to the Law. 90p. 1986. 100.00 (*0-906840-95-3*, Pub. by Fourmat Pub) St Mut.

Mathers, James M. The Constitutional Common-Law Trust. 182p. 1996. 29.95 (*0-9628640-2-1*) Helion Pub.

— The Recovery Handbook. LC 90-86083. (Orig.). 1992. pap. 15.95 (*0-9628640-0-5*) Helion Pub.

***Mathers, Jennifer G.** The Russian Nuclear Shield from Stalin to Yeltsin. LC 00-31128. (Illus.). 2000. write for info. (*0-312-23578-X*) St Martin.

Mathers, Jerry. . . . And Jerry Mathers as "The Beaver" 272p. 1998. pap. text 14.00 (*0-425-16370-9*) Berkley Pub.

Mathers, John C., jt. ed. see Widdowson, Elsie M.

Mathers, John G., jt. auth. see Daniels, William R.

Mathers, Lawrence H., Jr. Clinical Anatomy Principles. LC 95-10657. 1995. write for info. (*0-614-07820-2*) Mosby Inc.

Mathers, Lawrence H., Jr., et al. Principles of Clinical Anatomy. (Illus.). 816p. (C). (gr. 13). 1995. text 57.00 (*0-8016-6356-3*, 06356) Mosby Inc.

Mathers, Lawrence J., Jr. The Peripheral Nervous System: Structure, Function, & Clinical Correlations. (Illus.). 227p. (C). 1984. reprint ed. 37.50 (*0-409-90074-5*) Buttrwrth-Heinemann.

Mathers-MacGregor, S. L. Book of the Sacred Magic of Abra-Melin. 318p. 1998. reprint ed. pap. 24.95 (*0-7661-0425-7*) Kessinger Pub.

Mathers, Mayo, jt. auth. see Zeiler, Jean Lovelace.

Mathers, Norman W. Beyond Desert Storm: Hope for Days Ahead. (Illus.). 96p. 1993. pap. 12.95 (*0-9634654-0-6*) ATS Pubns.

***Mathers, Norman W.** Beyond Our Time: What the Bible Says about America in Prophecy. LC 98-93747. 120p. 1999. pap. 17.95 (*0-9634654-2-2*) ATS Pubns.

— Explaining Violence: What the Bible Says about Violent Times. LC 99-95517. 120p. 2000. pap. 17.95 (*0-9634654-4-9*) ATS Pubns.

Mathers, Norman W. The New Beyond: Psychics - A Global Issue. 116p. Date not set. pap. 16.95 (*0-9634654-1-4*) ATS Pubns.

***Mathers, Petra.** A Cake for Herbie. LC 99-24881. Orig. Title: A Poem for Lottie. 32p. (J). 2000. pap. 15.00 (*0-689-83017-3*) Atheneum Yung Read.

— A Cake for Herbie. Orig. Title: A Poem for Lottie. (J). 2000. 15.00 (*0-689-01506-2*) Atheneum Yung Read.

— Dodo Gets Married. LC 99-86369. (J). 2001. write for info. (*0-689-83018-1*) Atheneum Yung Read.

Mathers, Petra. Lottie's New Beach Towel. LC 97-6689. 32p. (J). (ps-k). 1998. 15.00 (*0-689-81606-5*) Atheneum Yung Read.

— Lottie's New Friend. LC 98-21625. 32p. (J). (ps-3). 1999. 15.00 (*0-689-82014-3*) S&S Childrens.

— Maria Theresa. LC 84-48346. (Illus.). 32p. (J). (ps-3). 1985. 13.95 (*0-06-024109-8*) HarpC Child Bks.

— Maria Theresa. LC 84-48346. (Trophy Picture Bk.). (Illus.). 32p. (J). (gr. k-3). 1992. pap. 4.95 (*0-06-443282-3*, HarpTrophy) HarpC Child Bks.

Mathers, Petra, jt. illus. see Jonell, Lynne.

Mathers, S. L. The Book of the Sacred Magic of Abramelin the Mage. LC 75-12248. 268p. 1975. reprint ed. pap. 8.95 (*0-486-23211-5*) Dover.

— The Greater Key of Solomon (1914) 145p. 1996. reprint ed. pap. 16.95 (*1-56459-843-8*) Kessinger Pub.

— The Kabbalah Unveiled. 359p. (Orig.). 1996. reprint ed. spiral bd. 22.00 (*0-7873-1270-3*) Hlth Research.

— The Kabbalah Unveiled, 1887. 365p. 1996. reprint ed. pap. 19.95 (*1-56459-814-4*) Kessinger Pub.

— The Tarot. 1973. 59.95 (*0-8490-1177-9*) Gordon Pr.

— The Tarot: A Short Treatise on Reading Cards. 1997. pap. text 5.95 (*0-88079-723-1*, BK137) US Games Syst.

Mathers, S. L., tr. The Kabbala Unveiled: Books of the Zohar. 1973. lib. bdg. 250.00 (*0-87968-124-1*) Krishna Pr.

***Mathers, S. L., et al.** Golden Dawn Legacy of MacGregor Mathers. (Golden Dawn Studies Ser.: Vol. 23). 1998. pap. 8.95 (*1-55818-410-4*) Holmes Pub.

Mathers, S. L., et al. The Secret Knowledge of the Neophyte. Kuntz, Darcy, ed. (Golden Dawn Studies Ser.: Vol. 18). 1997. pap. 8.95 (*1-55818-394-9*) Holmes Pub.

Mathers, S. L. MacGregor. The Kabbalah Unveiled. 374p. (Orig.). 1983. reprint ed. pap. 14.95 (*0-87728-557-8*) Weiser.

— The Tarot: A Short Treatise on Reading Cards. rev. ed. LC 71-17150. (Illus.). 96p. 1969. pap. 5.95 (*0-87728-754-6*) Weiser.

Mathers, S. L. MacGregor, tr. The Grimoire of Armadel. rev. ed. LC 95-16140. (FRE.). 88p. 1979. 22.95 (*0-87728-839-9*) Weiser.

Mathers, S. L. MacGregor, tr. see Crowley, Aleister, ed.

***Mathers, S. Liddell MacGregor.** The Key of Solomon the King: Clavicula Salomonis. (Illus.). 144p. 2000. 35.00 (*0-87728-945-X*) Weiser.

— The Key of Solomon the King: Clavicula Salomonis. rev. ed. LC 99-48471. (Illus.). 144p. 2000. pap. 14.95 (*0-87728-931-X*) Weiser.

Mathers, Todd W. Windows NT Thin Client Solutions. LC 98-84224. 550p. 1998. pap. 35.00 (*1-57870-065-5*) Macmillan Tech.

Mathers, William M. Treasure of the Concepcion. (Illus.). 164p. (C). 1994. 24.50 (*0-931234-56-5*, D666) Best Pub Co.

Matherson, Charles & Byrum, C. Stephen. A War Still Raging. (Illus.). 376p. 1991. 19.95 (*1-879908-01-8*) Milton Pub.

Matherson, Francois, ed. see Althusser, Louis.

Matherson, Robert. Scandal at the Oak Beach Inn. 1998. 22.00 (*1-56980-133-9*) Barricade Bks.

Mathes, C. Hodge. In the Shadow of Old Smoky: Stories of the Mountains & Their People. Maynard, Charles W., ed. (Illus.). 142p. 1994. pap. text 8.95 (*0-9630682-5-3*) Panther TN.

Mathes, C. Hodge. In the Shadow of Old Smoky: Stories of the Mountains & Their People. Maynard, Charles W., ed. (Illus.). 142p. 1994. text 12.00 (*0-9630682-6-1*) Panther TN.

Mathes, C. Hodge. Tall Tales from Old Smoky. 252p. 1991. reprint ed. 14.95 (*0-932807-59-3*) Overmountain Pr.

***Mathes, Charles.** The Girl at the End of the Line. 2000. per. 4.99 (*0-373-26341-4*) Harlequin Bks.

Mathes, Charles. The Girl at the End of the Line. LC 98-46784. 288p. 1999. text 22.95 (*0-312-19887-6*) St Martin.

— The Girl Who Remembered Snow. 1997. per. 4.99 (*0-373-26257-4*, 1-26257-5, Wrldwide Lib) Harlequin Bks.

— The Girl with the Phony Name. 48p. 1997. per. 4.99 (*0-373-26246-9*, 1-26246-8, Wrldwide Lib) Harlequin Bks.

Mathes, Eugene W. Jealousy: The Psychological Data. 218p. (C). 1992. lib. bdg. 42.50 (*0-8191-8521-3*) U Pr of Amer.

Mathes, Jerry D., II. Power Focus: Reconstruction of Self Through Mental Imagery. LC 94-24971. 1994. 16.95 (*1-885018-04-5*); pap. 9.95 (*1-885018-05-3*) Logo Press.

Mathes, John, jt. auth. see Brunner, Ingrid.

Mathes, P., ed. Secondary Prevention in Coronary Artery Disease & Myocardial Infarction. (Developments in Cardiovascular Medicine Ser.). 1985. lib. bdg. 223.50 (*0-89838-736-1*) Kluwer Academic.

Mathes, P. & Halhuber, M. J., eds. Controversies in Cardiac Rehabilitation. (Illus.). 240p. 1982. 39.95 (*0-387-11234-0*) Spr-Verlag.

Mathes, Patricia G. & Irby, Beverly J. Teen Pregnancy & Parenting Handbook. LC 92-85264. (Illus.). 440p. (Orig.). 1993. pap. text 19.95 (*0-87822-333-9*, 4660) Res Press.

Mathes, Patricia G. & Irby, Beverly J. Teen Pregnancy & Parenting Handbook: Discussion Guide. LC 92-85263. (Illus.). 64p. 1993. student ed., spiral bd. 6.95 (*0-87822-334-7*, 4661) Res Press.

Mathes, Patricia G., jt. auth. see Torgesen, Joseph K.

Mathes, Stephen J. & Nahai, Foad. Clinical Atlas of Muscle & Musculocutaneous Flaps. LC 79-10739. (Illus.). 520p. (C). (gr. 13). 1979. text 90.95 (*0-8016-3141-6*, 03141) Mosby Inc.

— Reconstructive Surgery: Principles, Anatomy & Technique, 2 vols. LC 96-29462. 1997. text 499.00 (*0-443-07981-1*) Church.

— Reconstructive Surgery: Principles, Anatomy & Technique, 2 vols., Set. LC 96-29462. (Illus.). 1625p. 1996. 499.00 (*0-942219-02-3*) Quality Med Pub.

Mathes, Valerie S. Helen Hunt Jackson & Her Indian Reform Legacy. LC 97-10883. (Illus.). 256p. 1997. pap. 13.95 (*0-8061-2963-8*) U of Okla Pr.

Mathes, Valerie S., ed. see Jackson, Helen H.

Mathes, W. Michael. The America's First Academic Library: Santa Cruz de Tlatelolco. 101p. 1985. 8.95 (*0-929722-05-1*) CA State Library Fndtn.

Mathes, W. Michael, intro. Ethnology of the Baja California Indians. LC 92-4023. 544p. 1992. text 30.00 (*0-8240-0793-X*) Garland.

***Mathesius, Peter.** Daily Exercise Log. 2nd ed. 134p. (C). 1998. spiral bd. 16.95 (*0-7872-4343-4*) Kendall-Hunt.

Mathesius, Vilem. A Functional Analysis of Present Day English on a General Linguistic Basis. Vachek, Josef, ed. Duskova, Libuse, tr. from CZE. (Janua Linguarum, Series Practica: No. 208). 228p. 1975. pap. text 50.00 (*90-279-3077-5*) Mouton.

Matheson, A. C., jt. auth. see Williams, E. R.

Matheson, Andrew, et al, eds. The Conservation of Bees. (Syposia of the Linnean Society of London Ser.: No. 18). (Illus.). 272p. 1996. text 79.95 (*0-12-479740-7*) Acad Pr.

Matheson, Andrew J. Molecular Acoustics. LC 73-147401. (Illus.). 308p. reprint ed. pap. 95.50 (*0-608-17551-X*, 203053100069) Bks Demand.

Matheson, Ann. Theories of Rhetoric in the 18th-Century Scottish Sermon. LC 93-42728. 308p. 1994. text 99.95 (*0-7734-9413-8*) E Mellen.

Matheson, B. S. Invented Personages in Shakespeare's Plays. LC 71-144656. reprint ed. 27.50 (*0-404-04258-9*) AMS Pr.

Matheson, Boyd C. A Champion Lives Within. text 16.95 (*1-882441-24-9*); pap. text 10.95 (*1-882441-25-7*) InANutshell Bks.

— Elephants Don't Bite but Fleas Do. 200p. text 19.95 (*1-882441-75-3*); pap. text 12.95 (*1-882441-76-1*) InANutshell Bks.

Matheson, Boyd C., jt. auth. see Packer, Barry.

Matheson, Carl, jt. ed. see Davies, David.

***Matheson, David.** An Introduction to the Study of Education: An Outline for the Intending Student. 1999. 29.95 (*1-85346-612-3*) David Fulton.

Matheson, David & Matheson, Jim. The Smart Organization: Creating Value Through Strategic R&D. 320p. 1997. 29.95 (*0-87584-765-X*, HBS Pr) Harvard Busn.

Matheson, Don. Stray Cat. 1988. pap. 3.50 (*0-671-66508-1*) PB.

Matheson, Douglas W. Experimental Psychology: Research, Design & Analysis. 3rd ed. LC 77-25185. 390p. (C). 1978. text 43.25 (*0-03-089891-9*) Harcourt Coll Pubs.

Matheson, Duncan. Legal Aid - the New Framework. 180p. 1988. pap. 34.00 (*0-406-50295-1*, UK, MICHIE) LEXIS Pub.

Matheson, Duncan, ed. see Ough, R. & McClelland, Alan M.

Matheson, Elizabeth. Blithe Air: Photographs from England, Wales, & Ireland. (Illus.). 84p. 1995. 40.00 (*0-912330-76-7*) Jargon Soc.

— Blithe Air: Photographs from England, Wales, & Ireland. deluxe ed. (Illus.). 84p. 1995. 150.00 (*0-912330-77-5*) Jargon Soc.

Matheson, Elizabeth & McFee, Michael. To See. LC 91-62756. 80p. 1991. 24.95 (*0-933598-34-3*) NC Wesleyan Pr.

— To See. limited ed. LC 91-62756. 80p. 1991. 150.00 (*0-933598-35-1*) NC Wesleyan Pr.

Matheson, Elizabeth M., ed. see Hart, Robert.

M

Matheson, Eve. The Modeling Handbook: The Complete Guide to Breaking into Local, Regional & International Modeling. 3rd ed. 240p. 1995. pap. 12.00 (0-8050-3830-2, Owl) H Holt & Co.

— The Modeling Handbook: The Complete Guide to Breaking into Local, Regional & International Modeling. 4th ed. 192p. 2000. pap. 15.95 (0-87314-300-0, Pub. by Peter Glenn) SCB Distributors.

Matheson, Ewing. The Depreciation of Factories, Mines & Industrial Undertakings & Their Valuation. 2nd ed. LC 75-18476. (History of Accounting Ser.). (Illus.). 1979. reprint ed. 18.95 (0-405-07558-8) Ayer.

Matheson-Ferrey, Juanita. One Hundred One Inexpensive Ways to Entertain Children. LC 88-72476. 125p. (Orig.). 1987. pap. write for info. (0-317-59719-1, 662-4685) AFCOM Pub.

Matheson, George. Portraits of Bible Men. LC 96-16868. (Bible Portrait Ser.: Vol. 1). 144p. 1996. pap. 9.99 (0-8254-3292-8) Kregel.

— Portraits of Bible Men. LC 96-16868. (Bible Portrait Ser.: Vol. 2). 144p. 1996. pap. 9.99 (0-8254-3293-6) Kregel.

— Portraits of Bible Men. LC 96-16868. (Bible Portrait Ser.: Vol. 3). 144p. 1996. pap. 9.99 (0-8254-3294-4) Kregel.

— Portraits of Bible Men. LC 96-16868. (Bible Portrait Ser.: Vol. 4). 144p. 1996. pap. 9.99 (0-8254-3295-2) Kregel.

— Portraits of Bible Women. LC 86-7429. 144p. 1993. reprint ed. pap. 9.99 (0-8254-3250-2) Kregel.

Matheson, Gordon & American Society of Civil Engineers Staff. Design with Residual Materials: Proceedings of Sessions Sponsored by the ASCE Geotechnical Engineering Division in Conjunction with the ASCE National Convention, November 10-14, 1996. LC 96-36649. (Geotechnical Special Publications). 88p. 1996. 20.00 (0-7844-0207-8) Am Soc Civil Eng.

Matheson, James. Smart Organization: Creating Value Through Strategic R & D. 1997. 29.95 (0-07-105054-X) McGraw.

***Matheson, Jil & Holding, Alison.** Focus on London 99. 205p. 1999. pap. 90.00 incl. cd-rom (0-11-621159-8, Pub. by Statnry Office) Balogh.

Matheson, Jim, jt. auth. see Matheson, David.

Matheson, John, jt. auth. see Kelsey, Hugh.

Matheson, John H. Publicly Traded Corporation Governance, Operation & Regulation, 1 vol. (Corporate Law Ser.). 1993. 110.00 (0-685-68838-0) West Group.

— Publicly Traded Corporations: Governance, Operation & Regulation. 1993. 130.00 (0-318-72145-7) West Group.

Matheson, John H. & Garon, Philip S. Minnesota Corporation Law & Practice. LC 92-32448. (National Corporation Law Ser.). 1992. 110.00 (0-13-145996-1) Aspen Law.

Matheson, John H., jt. auth. see Adams, Edward S.

Matheson, Katy & Duclow, Geraldine. Performing Arts Resources Vol. 21: Pleasure Gardens. Vallillo, Stephen M. & Chach, Maryann, eds. LC 75-646287. Date not set. 30.00 (0-932610-18-8) Theatre Lib.

Matheson, Lance A. Statistical Quality Control in High Reliability Systems. LC 93-34976. (Studies on Industrial Productivity). 120p. 1993. text 44.00 (0-8153-1628-3) Garland.

Matheson, Lister M. The Prose Brut: The Development of a Middle English Chronicle. LC 98-11574. (Medieval & Renaissance Texts & Studies: Vol. 180). 424p. 1998. 30.00 (0-86698-222-1, MR180) MRTS.

Matheson, Lister M., ed. Death & Dissent Vol. 2: Two Fifteenth-Century Chronicles: The Dethe of the Kynge of Scotis; Warkworth's Chronicles. LC 98-52326. (Medieval Chronicles Ser.). 168p. 1999. 75.00 (0-85115-725-4, Boydell Pr) Boydell & Brewer.

— Popular & Practical Science of Medieval England. LC 93-72666. (Medieval Texts & Studies: No. 11). (Illus.). 425p. 1994. 68.00 (0-937191-30-2) Mich St U Pr.

Matheson, M., tr. see Schuon, Frithjof.

Matheson, Nancey, et al. Education Indicators: An International Perspective. (Illus.). 312p. (Orig.). 1997. pap. text 50.00 (0-7881-4267-4) DIANE Pub.

Matheson, Nancy. Education Indicators: An International Perspective. 330p. 1996. pap. 23.00 (0-16-063587-X) USGPO.

Matheson, Peter. The Collected Works of Thomas Muntzer. 504p. pap. 45.95 (0-567-29252-5, Pub. by T & T Clark) Bks Intl VA.

— A Just Peace: A Theological Exploration. LC BT0736.4.M37. 156p. 1981. reprint ed. pap. 48.40 (0-608-00247-X, 206074900006) Bks Demand.

— The Rhetoric of the Reformation. 288p. 1998. 47.95 (0-567-08593-7, Pub. by T & T Clark) Bks Intl VA.

— The Third Reich & the Christian Churches. 128p. pap. 19.95 (0-567-29105-7, Pub. by T & T Clark) Bks Intl VA.

Matheson, Peter, ed. from GER. Argula von Grumbach: A Woman's Voice in the Reformation. 224p. 44.95 (0-567-09707-2, Pub. by T & T Clark) Bks Intl VA.

— The Collected Works of Thomas Muntzer. 544p. 1988. 59.95 (0-567-09495-2, Pub. by T & T Clark) Bks Intl VA.

Matheson, Richard. The Beardless Warriors. 1994. lib. bdg. 24.95 (1-56849-431-9) Buccaneer Bks.

— Bid Time Return. 280p. 1986. reprint ed. lib. bdg. 38.95 (0-89966-514-4) Buccaneer Bks.

— By the Gun. 1994. 18.95 (0-87131-747-8) M Evans.

— Collected Stories. 920p. 1989. lib. bdg. 39.95 (0-910489-10-6) Scream Pr.

— Darker: Three Novels of Suspense. 1989. lib. bdg. 30.00 (0-910489-05-X) Scream Pr.

— Earthbound. 224p. 1995. 4.99 (0-8125-4810-8, Pub. by Tor Bks) St Martin.

— Ghost Trilogy. 1988. lib. bdg. 30.00 (0-910489-16-5) Scream Pr.

— The Gunfight. large type ed. LC 93-37092. 326p. 1993. lib. bdg. 18.95 (0-7862-0002-2) Thorndike Pr.

— Hell House. 1994. lib. bdg. 27.95 (1-56849-435-1) Buccaneer Bks.

— Hell House. LC 99-38407. 301p. 1999. pap. 13.95 (0-312-86885-5, Pub. by Tor Bks) St Martin.

— Hell House. limited ed. (Classics Revisited Ser.). 1996. boxed set 65.00 (1-887368-07-8) Gauntlet.

— I Am Legend. 1976. 29.95 (0-8488-1432-0) Amereon Ltd.

— I Am Legend. 400p. 1991. reprint ed. lib. bdg. 27.95 (0-89966-838-0) Buccaneer Bks.

— I Am Legend. 320p. 1995. reprint ed. 4.99 (0-8125-2300-8, Pub. by Tor Bks) St Martin.

— The Incredible Shrinking Man. 320p. 1995. reprint ed. 4.99 (0-8125-2299-0, Pub. by Tor Bks) St Martin.

— Now You See It. 1996. mass mkt. write for info. (0-614-05531-8); mass mkt. 6.99 (0-8125-4811-6, Pub. by Tor Bks) St Martin.

— The Path: A New Look at Reality. LC 99-12398. 1999. 13.95 (0-312-87057-4, Pub. by Tor Bks) St Martin.

— The Path: Metaphysics for the 90's. 2nd ed. 152p. (Orig.). 1998. reprint ed. pap. 10.95 (0-911650-13-X) Word Foun.

— Robert Bloch: Appreciations of the Master: A Collection of Tributes to & Fiction by Robert Bloch. Mainhardt, Ricia, ed. 320p. 1995. 24.95 (0-312-85976-7) Tor Bks.

— 7 Steps to Midnight. 320p. 1995. pap. 5.99 (0-8125-5057-9, Pub. by Tor Bks) St Martin.

— The Shrinking Man. 1993. reprint ed. lib. bdg. 27.95 (0-89968-352-5, Lghtyr Pr) Buccaneer Bks.

— Somewhere in Time. 288p. 1976. 28.95 (0-8488-1094-5) Amereon Ltd.

— Somewhere in Time. 304p. 2000. 13.95 (0-312-86886-3, Pub. by Tor Bks) St Martin.

— Somewhere in Time. aut. limited ed. 323p. 1999. 50.00 (1-887368-21-3) Gauntlet.

— Somewhere in Time & What Dreams May Come. rev. ed. 512p. 1991. reprint ed. 25.00 (0-910489-06-8) Scream Pr.

Matheson, Richard, ed. Robert Bloch: Appreciations of. 1995. 24.95 (0-614-08649-3) Tor Bks.

— Robert Bloch Tribute Anthology. 1995. 24.95 (0-614-03859-6) Tor Bks.

Matheson, Richard, et al, eds. The Twilight Zone: The Original Stories. 576p. 1985. pap. 8.95 (0-380-89601-X, Avon Bks) Morrow Avon.

***Matheson, Richard C.** Dystopia: Collected Stories. 402p. 2000. 50.00 (1-887368-24-8) Gauntlet.

Matheson, Richard C. I Am Legend. 5th ed. LC 97-13698. 1997. pap. 12.95 (0-312-86504-X) St Martin.

— What Dreams May Come. 1998. mass mkt. 6.99 (0-8125-7094-4, Pub. by Tor Bks) St Martin.

— What Dreams May Come. aut. limited annot. ed. 320p. 1998. 50.00 (1-887368-17-5) Gauntlet.

***Matheson, Richard Christian.** A Stir of Echoes, Vol. 1. 1999. mass mkt. 5.99 (0-8125-7212-2, Pub. by Forge NYC) St Martin.

Matheson, Robert E. Official Varieties & Synonyms of Surnames & Christian Names in Ireland for the Guidance of Registration Officers & the Public in Searching the Indexes of Births, Deaths, & Marriages. 94p. 1995. reprint ed. pap. 11.00 (0-7884-0301-X) Heritage Bk.

— Special Report on Surnames in Ireland: Together with Varieties & Synonymes of Surnames & Christian Names in Ireland, 2 vols. in 1. LC 68-54684. 172p. 1994. reprint ed. 18.50 (0-8063-0187-2, 3830) Genealog Pub.

Matheson, Shirlee S. City Pictures. 160p. (J). (gr. 4-7). pap. 9.99 (0-7710-5860-8) McCland & Stewart.

— Flying the Frontiers Vol. 2: More Hours of Aviation Adventure! (Illus.). 320p. 1996. write for info. (1-55059-131-2) Detselig Ents.

— Prairie Pictures. 128p. (J). (gr. 4-7). pap. 9.99 (0-7710-5857-8) McCland & Stewart.

— Youngblood of the Peace. (Illus.). 235p. (Orig.). 1991. pap. 14.95 (1-55059-033-2) Temeron Bks.

Matheson, Shirley S., jt. auth. see Pollon, Earl K.

Matheson, Shirley Smith, see Smith Matheson, Shirley.

Matheson, Susan B. Ancient Glass in the Yale University Art Gallery. 1980. pap. 13.00 (0-89467-010-7) Yale Art Gallery.

— Dura-Europos: The Ancient City & the Yale Collection. (Illus.). 48p. (Orig.). 1982. pap. 4.95 (0-89467-022-0) Yale Art Gallery.

— Greek Vases: A Guide to the Yale Collection. LC 88-50027. (Illus.). 43p. (Orig.). 1988. pap. 6.00 (0-89467-048-4) Yale Art Gallery.

— Polygnotos & Vase Painting in Classical Athens. LC 95-9683. (Studies in Classics). 558p. 1995. 60.00 (0-299-13870-4) U of Wis Pr.

Matheson, Susan B., jt. auth. see Kleiner, Diana E.

Matheson, Susan B., ed. see Kleiner, Diana E. E.

Matheson, Sylvia A. The Tigers of Baluchistan. 2nd ed. LC 97-930622. (Illus.). 242p. 1999. text 24.95 (0-19-577763-8) OUP.

Matheson, Terry. Alien Abductions: Creating a Modern Phenomenon. LC 98-30816. (Illus.). 398p. 1998. 26.95 (1-57392-244-7) Prometheus Bks.

Matheson, Tim. Traffic Tickets, Fines & Other Annoying Things. 72p. 1984. pap. 4.95 (0-8065-0883-3, Citadel Pr) Carol Pub Group.

Matheson, Wayne, et al. Performance Evaluation in the Human Services. LC 93-23223. (Illus.). 145p. 1995. lib. bdg. 39.95 (1-56024-379-1) Haworth Pr.

Matheson, William H. The Sufferings of Light: Selected Poems of William H. Matheson. LC 96-69808. 122p. (Orig.). 1996. pap. 25.00 (1-889087-01-7) P S A Pr.

Matheus, James & Scherger, Joseph E., eds. Patient Care Emergency Handbook. 650p. (C). 1991. text 60.00 (1-878487-30-2, 5421M) Practice Mgmt Info.

Mathew. Socratic Physics: Mechanics. (Physics Ser.). 1998. pap. 25.95 (0-534-36581-7) Brooks-Cole.

Mathew, Arnold H., tr. Old Catholic Missal & Ritual. LC 73-84708. reprint ed. 37.50 (0-404-01949-8) AMS Pr.

***Mathew, Arnold Harris.** Old Catholic Missal & Ritual. Elijah, ed. LC 73-84708. 652p. 2000. reprint ed. 34.95 (1-883938-65-1) Dry Bones Pr.

Mathew, Asha. Fair Sex in Unfair Society: Women & Crime. (Illus.). viii, 202p. 1992. 22.95 (1-881338-31-2) Nataraj Bks.

— Fair Sex in Unfair Society (Women & Crime) (C). 1992. 24.00 (81-7024-491-9, Pub. by Ashish Pub Hse) S Asia.

***Mathew, Biju.** Taxi! Behind the Wheel of New York's Cabs. 1999. 25.00 (1-85984-748-X, Pub. by Verso) Norton.

Mathew, Brian. Bulbs: The Four Seasons. (Illus.). 144p. 1998. 24.95 (1-85793-504-7, Pub. by Pavilion Bks Ltd) Trafalgar.

Mathew, Brian. Bulbs: The Four Seasons: A Guide to Selecting & Growing Bulbs All Year Round. (Illus.). 144p. reprint ed. pap. 19.95 (1-86205-200-X, Pub. by Pavilion Bks Ltd) Trafalgar.

Mathew, Brian. A Review of Allium Section. (Illus.). 1996. pap. 42.00 (0-947643-93-1, Pub. by Royal Botnic Grdns) Balogh.

Mathew, Christopher G., ed. Protocols in Human Molecular Genetics. LC 91-25466. (Methods in Molecular Biology Ser.: Vol. 9). (Illus.). 472p. 1991. 89.50 (0-89603-205-1) Humana.

Mathew, David. Catholicism in England, 1535-1935. 1977. lib. bdg. 59.95 (0-8490-1587-1) Gordon Pr.

— Celtic Peoples & Renaissance Europe: A Study of the Celtic & Spanish Influences on Elizabethan History (1933) (Illus.). 540p. 1975. reprint ed. 20.00 (0-911858-27-X) Appel.

Mathew, Elangikal T. Employment & Unemployment in Kerala: Some Negelected Aspects. LC 97-27341. 1997. 32.00 (0-7619-9205-7) Sage.

Mathew, Frank. An Image of Shakespeare. LC 72-3654. (Studies in Shakespeare: No. 24). 1972. reprint ed. lib. bdg. 75.00 (0-8383-1550-X) M S G Haskell Hse.

Mathew, George. Communal Road to a Secular Kerala. 1989. 28.50 (81-7022-282-6, Pub. by Concept) S Asia.

— Electricity & Magnetism: Quick & Short Conceptionally Guided Questions. (Illus.). 278p. (Orig.). (C). 1995. pap. text 23.95 (0-9647223-2-1) Ross Pub OH.

Mathew, George, ed. Dignity for All: Essays in Socialism & Democracy. (C). 1991. 25.00 (81-202-0318-6, Pub. by Ajanta) S Asia.

— Panchayati Raj in Jammu & Kashmir. (C). 1990. text 23.00 (81-7022-315-6, Pub. by Concept) S Asia.

Mathew, Jan, ed. see Junior League of Sarasota FL, Inc. Staff.

***Mathew, Joseph C.** Ethnic Conflict in Bhutan. LC 99-934067. (Illus.). 1999. 29.50 (81-85693-68-4, Pub. by Nirala Pubns) S Asia.

Mathew, K., jt. auth. see Ho, G.

Mathew, K. K. Democracy, Quality & Freedom. 468p. 1978. 235.00 (0-7855-1291-8) St Mut.

— Three Lectures. 75p. 1983. 105.00 (0-7855-1290-X) St Mut.

Mathew, K. M. History of the Portuguese Navigation in India. 352p. (C). 1987. 37.00 (81-7099-046-7, Pub. by Mittal Pubs Dist) S Asia.

***Mathew, K. S.** French in India & Indian Nationalism (1700 A. D. - 1963 A. D.) 1999. 110.00 (81-7646-053-2, Pub. by BR Pub) S Asia.

Mathew, K. S. Indo-Portuguese Trade & the Fuggers of Germany: Sixteenth Century. LC 98-905185. (C). 1997. 44.00 (81-7304-137-7, Pub. by Manohar) S Asia.

— Mariners, Merchants & Oceans: Studies Maritime History. LC 95-905821. (C). 1995. 38.00 (81-7304-075-3, Pub. by Manohar) S Asia.

— Portuguese Trade with India in the 16th Century. 1983. 24.00 (0-8364-0996-5, Pub. by Manohar) S Asia.

— Ship-Building & Navigation in the Indian Ocean Region, A. D. 1400-1800. LC 97-904132. (C). 1997. 32.00 (81-215-0739-1, Pub. by M Manoharial) Coronet Bks.

Mathew, K. S., jt. auth. see Behiels, Michael D.

Mathew, L. P. & Karikari, S. K. Horticulture: Principals & Practices. 202p. 1990. 13.95 (0-333-45306-9) Macmillan.

Mathew, Laura J., jt. ed. see Sloane, Philip D.

Mathew, M. P., jt. auth. see Naidu, Prabhakar S.

Mathew, Mary T. Female Development in the Novels of Rabindranath Tagore: A Cross-Cultural Analysis of Gender & Literature in British India. LC 95-33502. 242p. (C). 1996. text 89.95 (0-7734-4236-7) E Mellen.

Mathew, Mohan. Dimensions of Dialogue. LC 84-17009. 145p. 1984. pap. 6.70 (0-918833-00-0) Comm Wholistic Growth.

Mathew, N. M., jt. ed. see Sethuraj, M. R.

Mathew, Ninan T., jt. auth. see Evans, Randolph W.

Mathew, P. M. Women's Organizations & Women's Interests. 177p. 1986. 25.00 (81-7024-036-0, Pub. by Ashish Pub Hse) S Asia.

Mathew, P. M. & Philip, Omana. Studies in the Pollen Morphology of South Indian Rubiaceae. (Advances in Pollen Spore Research Ser.: Vol. 10). viii, 80p. 1983. 20.00 (1-55528-056-0, Pub. by Today Tomorrow) Scholarly Pubns.

Mathew, Paul & Ludwig, Barbara. Clinical Application of Blood Gases. 5th ed. 128p. 1994. pap. text, wbk. ed. 15.95 (0-8151-7586-8, 23839) Mosby Inc.

Mathew, Roy J., ed. Treatment of Migraine: Pharmacological & Biofeedback Considerations. (Illus.). 170p. 1981. text 27.50 (0-88331-209-3) R B Luce.

Mathew, Sydney, jt. auth. see Stewart, Tom.

Mathew, Vadakeparambil M. The Due Process of Law: 5th & 14th Amendments of the U. S. Constitution. 49p. (Orig.). (C). 1980. pap. text 5.00 (0-9614320-0-4) Mathew.

***Mathewes-Green, Frederica.** At the Corner of East & Now: A Modern Life in Ancient Christian Orthodoxy. LC 99-29731. 256p. 1999. 23.95 (0-87477-987-1, Tarcher Putnam) Putnam Pub Group.

— At the Corner of East & Now: A Modern Life in Ancient Christian Orthodoxy. 288p. 2000. reprint ed. pap. 13.95 (1-58542-044-1, Tarcher Putnam) Putnam Pub Group.

Mathewes-Green, Frederica. Facing East: A Pilgrim's Journey into the Mysteries of Orthodoxy. LC 96-36700. 1997. 12.00 (0-06-065499-6) HarpC.

— Facing East: A Pilgrim's Journey into the Mysteries of Orthodoxy. LC 96-36700. 272p. 1997. 22.00 (0-06-065498-8, Pub. by Harper SF) HarpC.

— Real Choices: Listening to Women, Looking for Alternatives to Abortion. LC 97-24460. 1997. write for info. (1-888212-07-1) Conciliar Pr.

Mathewman, Tony. The History of Trix HO/OO: Model Railways in Britain, 1935-1992. LC 95-949328. (Illus.). 424p. 1995. 75.00 (0-904568-76-8) Pincushion Pr.

Mathews. Adaptive Filters. 2001. text, student ed. write for info. (0-02-377131-3) P-H.

— Art History & Feminism. 1998. 26.95 (0-8057-9779-3, Twyne); per. 14.95 (0-8057-9780-7, Twyne) Mac Lib Ref.

— Atlas of Descriptive Embryology. 5th ed. LC 98-115859. 266p. (C). 1997. pap. text 52.00 (0-13-593740-X, Prentice Hall) P-H.

— Fantasy. LC 97-4356. 1997. 33.00 (0-8057-0958-1, Twyne) Mac Lib Ref.

— Numerical Methods with MATLAB. 3rd ed. 680p. 1998. 89.33 (0-13-270042-5) P-H.

— Passionate Discontent. LC 99-22167. 2000. 35.00 (0-226-51018-2) U Ch Pr.

— Social Work Practice. (C). 2000. 40.00 (0-205-28589-9, Macmillan Coll) P-H.

— Wind Is Blowing Again. 1996. pap. 5.95 (0-7601-0574-X) Brentwood Music.

Mathews & Brotchie. Oulipo Compendium. 320p. 1998. pap. 19.99 (0-947757-96-1, Pub. by Atlas Pr) Serpents Tail.

Mathews, jt. see Johnston.

Mathews, Adrian. The Hat of Victor Noir. 288p. 1997. pap. 12.95 (1-85702-569-5) Trafalgar.

— Vienna Blood. 2000. mass mkt. 6.99 (0-06-109810-8) HarpC.

— Vienna Blood: A Novel. LC 99-12848. 400p. 1999. 24.00 (0-06-019341-7) HarpC.

Mathews, Aidan C. Exit & Entrance. 64p. 1990. pap. 12.95 (1-85235-054-7) Dufour.

— Immediate Man: Cuimhni As Chearbhall o Dalaigh. 80p. 1983. pap. 21.00 (0-85105-416-1, Pub. by Smyth) Dufour.

— Minding Ruth. 68p. 1983. pap. 12.95 (0-904011-40-2) Dufour.

Mathews, Alfred. History of Wayne, Pike & Monroe Counties, PA. (Illus.). 1283p. 1994. reprint ed. lib. bdg. 119.50 (0-8328-3632-X) Higginson Bk Co.

Mathews, Alfred & Hungerford, Austin N. History of the Counties of Lehigh & Carbon, PA. (Illus.). 802p. 1993. reprint ed. lib. bdg. 81.00 (0-8328-2848-3) Higginson Bk Co.

Mathews, Alice. A Woman God Can Use. LC 90-41671. 180p. 1990. pap. 10.99 (0-929239-30-X) Discovery Hse Pubs.

— A Woman Jesus Can Teach. 150p. 1991. pap. 9.99 (0-929239-44-X) Discovery Hse Pubs.

Mathews, Alice P. My Treasured Pleasures: "Down Home Cooking" Central Louisiana Style. large type ed. Mathews, Marita, ed. (Illus.). 416p. 1998. pap. 22.98 (1-887303-20-0) Blu Lantern Pub.

Mathews, Allison & Hardingham, Martin. Medical & Hygiene Textile Production: A Handbook. 56p. (Orig.). 1994. pap. 14.00 (1-85339-211-1, Pub. by Intermed Tech) Stylus Pub VA.

Mathews, Andrew, et al. Platzangst: Ein Uebungsprogramm Fuer Betroffene und Angehoerige. (Unveraenderte Auflage Ser.: Vol. 3, 1997). viii, 132p. 1997. pap. 28.00 (3-8055-6522-4) S Karger.

Mathews, Anne J. Communicate: A Librarian's Guide to Interpersonal Relations. LC 83-2557. 88p. reprint ed. pap. 30.00 (0-7837-5972-X, 204577400007) Bks Demand.

Mathews, Annette L., tr. see Perez, Ramon.

Mathews, Anthony S., tr. see Adam, Jean-Pierre.

Mathews, Arlene, jt. auth. see Cooper, Mimi.

Mathews, Arthur F., jt. auth. see Law & Business Inc. Staff.

Mathews, Basil J., ed. East & West: Conflict or Cooperation. LC 67-26764. (Essay Index Reprint Ser.). 1977. 17.95 (0-8369-0694-2) Ayer.

Mathews, Binny. Recipes: A Notebook for Cooks. 142p. 1988. 14.95 (0-948751-02-9) Interlink Pub.

Mathews, C. K., jt. auth. see Borgstedt, H. U.

Mathews, Caitlin & Pollack, Rachel. Tarot Tales. 1996. mass mkt. 5.99 (0-441-00352-4) Ace Bks.

Mathews, Catharine V. Andrew Ellicott: His Life & Letters. LC 97-1142. (Illus.). 192p. 1997. reprint ed. pap. 14.99 (1-56664-111-X) WorldComm.

Mathews, Chester O. The Grade Placement of Curriculum Materials in the Social Studies. LC 78-177058. (Columbia University. Teachers College. Contributions to Education Ser.: No. 241). reprint ed. 37.50 (0-404-55241-2) AMS Pr.

Mathews, Christopher K. & Van Holde, Kensal E. Biochemistry. Bowen, Diane, ed. 1100p. (C). 1990. trans. 215.25 (0-8053-5016-0) Benjamin-Cummings.

— IBM PC Testing Software. Bowen, Diane, ed. 1100p. (C). 1990. sl. 17.25 (0-8053-5017-9) Benjamin-Cummings.

***Mathews, Christopher K., et al.** Biochemistry. 3rd ed. LC 99-43683. 1200p. (C). 1999. 109.33 (0-8053-3066-6) Benjamin-Cummings.

An Asterisk (*) at the beginning of an entry indicates that the title is appearing for the first time.

Mathews, Claire R. Defending Zion: Edom's Desolation & Jacob's Restoration (Isaiah 34-35) in Context. (Beiheft zur Zeitschrift fuer die Alttestamentliche Wissenschaft Ser.: Vol. 236). vii, 190p. (C). 1995. lib. bdg. 98.50 (*3-11-014665-7*) De Gruyter.

***Mathews, Claire R.** Isaiah 1-39. (Berit Olam (The Everlasting Covenant) Ser.). 2000. 0.00 (*0-8146-5057-0*) Liturgical Pr.

Mathews, Cornelius. Behemoth: A Legend of the Mound-Builders. LC 77-93643. (American Fiction Ser.). xv, vi, 192p. 1970. write for info. (*0-512-00515-X*) Irvington.

— Behemoth: A Legend of the Mound-Builders. 1972. reprint ed. 27.50 (*0-8422-8138-X*) Irvington.

— Behemoth: A Legend of the Mound Builders. (Notable American Authors Ser.). 1999. reprint ed. lib. bdg. 125.00 (*0-7812-3985-0*) Rprt Serv.

— Big Abel & the Little Manhattan. LC 73-93642. (American Fiction Ser.). xv, 93p. 1970. write for info. (*0-512-00514-1*) Irvington.

— Big Abel & the Little Manhattan. 1972. reprint ed. 27.50 (*0-8422-8093-6*) Irvington.

— The Career of Puffer Hopkins. LC 70-93644. (American Fiction Ser.). xv, viii, 319p. 1970. write for info. (*0-512-00516-8*) Irvington.

— The Career of Puffer Hopkins. 1972. reprint ed. 31.00 (*0-8422-8094-4*) Irvington.

— False Pretenses or Both Sides of Good Society. (Notable American Authors Ser.). 1999. reprint ed. lib. bdg. 125.00 (*0-7812-3990-7*) Rprt Serv.

— Jacob Leisler. (Notable American Authors Ser.). 1999. reprint ed. lib. bdg. 125.00 (*0-7812-3989-3*) Rprt Serv.

— Poems on Man in His Various Aspects under the American Republic. (Notable American Authors Ser.). 1999. reprint ed. lib. bdg. 125.00 (*0-7812-3987-7*) Rprt Serv.

— The Politicians. (Notable American Authors Ser.). 1999. reprint ed. lib. bdg. 125.00 (*0-7812-3986-9*) Rprt Serv.

— The Various Writings of Cornelius Mathews. LC 72-144659. 370p. 1972. reprint ed. 47.50 (*0-404-04265-1*) AMS Pr.

— The Various Writings of Cornelius Mathews. (BCL1-PS American Literature Ser.). 370p. 1992. reprint ed. lib. bdg. 89.00 (*0-7812-6791-9*) Rprt Serv.

— Witchcraft. Meserve, Walter J. & Meserve, Mollie A., eds. (When Conscience Trod the Stage Ser.). 1998. pap., spiral bd. 4.95 (*0-937657-40-9*) Feedbk Theabks & Prospero.

— Witchcraft or the Martyrs of Salem. (Notable American Authors Ser.). 1999. reprint ed. lib. bdg. 125.00 (*0-7812-3988-5*) Rprt Serv.

Mathews, Cornelius, ed. Enchanted Moccasins & Other Legends of the American Indians. LC 73-119646. reprint ed. 32.50 (*0-404-04264-3*) AMS Pr.

Mathews, Craig. Fishing Yellowstone Hatches. 104p. 1992. 19.95 (*1-55821-178-0*) Lyons Pr.

— Western Fly-Fishing Strategies. LC 97-23800. (Illus.). 208p. 1998. 29.95 (*1-55821-641-3*) Lyons Pr.

Mathews, Craig & Juracek, John. Fly Patterns of Yellowstone. (Illus.). 88p. 1989. 17.95 (*1-55821-030-X*) Lyons Pr.

Mathews, Craig & Molinero, Clayton. The Yellowstone Fly-Fishing Guide. LC 97-6966. (Illus.). 150p. (Orig.). 1997. pap. 16.95 (*1-55821-545-X*) Lyons Pr.

***Mathews, D. J.** Let's Run Our Schools Together. 101p. 1999. pap. 9.95 (*0-7414-0006-5*) Buy Books.

Mathews, Daniel. Cascade-Olympic Natural History. 2nd rev. ed. LC 99-32445. (Illus.). 640p. 1999. pap. 24.00 (*0-9620782-1-2*) Raven Edit.

Mathews-Danzer, R. All about Australian Birds. (Illus.). 140p. 2000. pap. 14.50 (*1-888417-90-0*) Dimefast.

— All about Cockatoos. (Exotic Bird Ser.). (Illus.). 80p. 1996. pap. 9.00 (*1-888417-80-3*) Dimefast.

— All about Macaws. (Illus.). 80p. 1999. pap. 14.00 (*1-888417-89-7*) Dimefast.

— All about Rosellas. (Illus.). 70p. 1999. pap. 9.50 (*1-888417-87-0*) Dimefast.

— Dead Puppys Can't Play Games. 160p. 1999. pap. 14.95 (*1-888417-40-4*) Dimefast.

— Masters of Fear, Vol. 2. Mathews, Rinaldo, ed. (Wizard, Ghost & Heroes Ser.). (Illus.). 165p. 2000. pap. 18.00 (*1-888417-03-X*) Dimefast.

— Murder at the Mouse Factory. 1999. 14.95 (*1-888417-51-X*) Dimefast.

— The Mystery Writer. 1999. pap. 14.95 (*1-888417-41-2*) Dimefast.

***Mathews-Danzer, R.** Mystery Writers Work Book. (Illus.). 130p. 1999. pap. 14.99 (*1-888417-69-2*) Dimefast.

Mathews-Danzer, R. Origin of Terror, Vol. 1. Mathews, Rinaldo, ed. (Wizard, Ghost & Heroes Ser.). (Illus.). 170p. 2000. pap. 18.00 (*1-888417-02-1*) Dimefast.

— Penguins with Guns. 2000. pap. 14.95 (*1-888417-42-0*) Dimefast.

— Planning an Aviary. (Exotic Bird Ser.). 140p. 1996. pap. 14.00 (*1-888417-81-1*) Dimefast.

— Third Side of the Coin. 780p. 1997. pap. 21.50 (*1-888417-00-5*) Dimefast.

— Wizards, Ghosts & Heroes, Vol. 3. Mathews, Rinaldo, ed. (Illus.). 210p. 2000. pap. 18.00 (*1-888417-04-8*) Dimefast.

Mathews-Danzer, R., ed. All about Amazons. (Exotic Bird Care Ser.). (Illus.). 71p. (Orig.). 1998. pap. 9.00 (*1-888417-83-8*, 417838) Dimefast.

— All about Ferrets: Animal Care Booklet. (Illus.). 1999. pap. 12.95 (*1-888417-70-6*) Dimefast.

Mathews-Danzer, R. & Cestero, Emmett. All about Exotic Birds: With CD-ROM. (Exotic Bird Ser.). (Illus.). 1999. pap. 49.95 incl. cd-rom (*1-888417-94-3*) Dimefast.

— Planning an Aviary: With CD-ROM. (Exotic Bird Ser.). (Illus.). 1999. pap. write for info. incl. cd-rom (*1-888417-93-5*) Dimefast.

Mathews-Danzer, R. & Mathews, Rinaldo. Murder at Fort Christmas. 2000. 14.95 (*1-888417-50-1*) Dimefast.

Mathews-Danzer, R., et al. Exotic Bird Series - Set, 10 vols. (Illus.). 380p. 2000. pap. 90.00 (*1-888417-91-9*) Dimefast.

Mathews-Danzer, R., ed. see Cestero, Emmett.

Mathews-Danzer, Reinaldo. Business of Aviculture. Mathews, Rinaldo, ed. (Exotic Bird Ser.). (Illus.). 150p. (Orig.). 1998. pap. 16.00 (*1-888417-88-9*, 417889) Dimefast.

Mathews-Danzer, Reinaldo, ed. see Martin, Phyllis.

Mathews, David. Politics for People: Finding a Responsible Public Voice. Talhouk, Afif, tr. (ARA.). 235p. 1997. pap. write for info. (*1-886604-05-3*) Lebanese Ctr.

— Politics for People: Finding a Responsible Public Voice. LC 93-5794. 240p. 1994. text 24.95 (*0-252-02088-X*) U of Ill Pr.

Mathews, David, jt. auth. see Frigon, Normand L.

Mathews, David J. Foundations for Violence-Free Living: A Step-by-Step Guide to Facilitating Men's Domestic Abuse Groups. Hyman, Vincent, ed. LC 95-36815. 240p. (Orig.). 1995. pap. text 45.00 (*0-940069-05-9*) A H Wilder.

— On the Level: Foundations for Violence-Free Living Participant's Workbook. Hyman, Vincent, ed. LC 95-36815. 160p. (Orig.). 1995. pap. text, student ed. 15.00 (*0-940069-06-7*) A H Wilder.

Mathews, David M. Precalculus Investigations Using Derive. LC 93-33006. 144p. (C). 1997. 28.00 (*0-673-99097-4*) Addson-Wesley Educ.

— Precalculus Investigations Using Maple V. (C). 1997. 26.73 (*0-673-99410-4*) Addson-Wesley Educ.

Mathews-Deacon, Saundra. Magic Theatre I Children's Musical Revue. (J). 1977. pap. 5.50 (*0-87129-230-0*, M12) Dramatic Pub.

— Magic Theatre II Children's Musical Revue. 1981. 5.50 (*0-87129-396-X*, M45) Dramatic Pub.

Mathews, Donald G. Religion in the Old South. LC 77-587. 294p. 1979. pap. text 16.95 (*0-226-51002-6*, P819) U Ch Pr.

— Slavery & Methodism: A Chapter in American Morality, 1780-1845. LC 78-13249. 329p. 1978. reprint ed. lib. bdg. 35.00 (*0-313-21045-4*, MASAM, Greenwood Pr) Greenwood.

Mathews, Donald G. & De Hart, Jane S. Sex, Gender & the Politics of ERA: A State & the Nation. (Illus.). 304p. 1992. reprint ed. pap. text 21.00 (*0-19-507852-7*) OUP.

Mathews, Dorothy, jt. auth. see Schaffter, Dorothy.

Mathews, Eddie & Buege, Bob. Eddie Mathews & the National Pastime. LC 94-71074. (Illus.). 347p. 1994. 22.95 (*1-882134-41-9*) Douglas Amer Sports Pubns.

Mathews, Edward. Autobiography of Rev. E. Mathews, the Father Dickson of Mrs. Stowe's 'Dred' LC 79-89392. (Black Heritage Library Collection). 1977. 27.95 (*0-8369-8629-6*) Ayer.

Mathews, Edward G., Jr., tr. see St. Ephrem the Syrian.

Mathews, F. Neil. Entomology: Investigative Activities for Could-Be Bug Buffs. Smith, Linda H., ed. (Triad Prototype Ser.). 1978. pap. 5.00 (*0-936386-03-7*) Creative Learning.

Mathews, F. X., ed. & tr. see Secundus, Joannes.

Mathews, Forrest D. Is There a Public for Public Schools? LC 96-76709. 86p. (Orig.). 1996. per. 9.50 (*0-923993-02-9*) Kettering Found.

— Politics for People: Finding a Responsible Public Voice. 2nd ed. LC 98-18786. 1998. write for info. (*0-252-02456-7*) U of Ill Pr.

— Politics For People: Finding a Responsible Public Voice. 2nd ed. LC 98-18786. 1998. pap. 12.95 (*0-252-06763-0*) U of Ill Pr.

***Mathews, Francine.** The Cutout. LC 00-31651. 2001. write for info. (*0 553 10893 X*) Bantam.

Mathews, Francine. Death in a Cold Hard Light. 352p. 1999. reprint ed. mass mkt. 5.99 (*0-553-57625-9*) Bantam.

— Death in a Mood Indigo. 352p. 1998. mass mkt. 5.99 (*0-553-57624-0*) Bantam.

— Death in Rough Water: A Merry Folger Mystery. 288p. 1996. mass mkt. 5.50 (*0-380-72335-2*, Avon Bks) Morrow Avon.

— Death in the Off-Season. 352p. 1995. mass mkt. 4.99 (*0-380-72334-4*, Avon Bks) Morrow Avon.

Mathews, Freya. The Ecological Self. 200p. (C). 1991. text 78.50 (*0-389-20935-X*) Rowman.

Mathews, Freya, ed. Ecology & Democracy. LC 96-14009. 288p. (Orig.). (C). 1996. pap. 24.00 (*0-7146-4252-5*, Pub. by F Cass Pubs) Intl Spec Bk.

Mathews, G. J. Origin & Distribution of the Elements: Proceedings of the Symposium (New Orleans) 780p. (C). 1988. text 138.00 (*9971-5-0455-3*) World Scientific Pub.

Mathews, Garret. Baseball Days: Recollections of America's Favorite Pastime. LC 99-10738. (Illus.). 160p. 2000. pap. 16.95 (*0-8092-2561-1*, 256110, Contemporary Bks) NTC Contemp Pub Co.

Mathews, George B. Theory of Numbers. 2nd ed. LC 61-17958. 18.95 (*0-8284-0156-X*) Chelsea Pub.

***Mathews, Gordon.** Global Culture/Individual Identity: Searching for Home in Cultural Supermarket. LC 99-41333. 232p. 2000. pap. 24.99 (*0-415-20616-2*) Routledge.

— Global Culture/Individual Identity: Searching for Home in Cultural Supermarket. LC 99-41333. 240p. (C). 2000. text 75.00 (*0-415-20615-4*) Routledge.

Mathews, Gordon. What Makes Life Worth Living? How Japanese & Americans Make Sense of Their Worlds. LC 95-22263. (Illus.). 296p. 1996. pap. 17.95 (*0-520-20133-7*, Pub. by U CA Pr) Cal Prin Full Svc.

— What Makes Life Worth Living? How Japanese & Americans Make Sense of Their Worlds. LC 95-22263. (Illus.). 296p. (C). 1996. 48.00 (*0-520-20132-9*, Pub. by U CA Pr) Cal Prin Full Svc.

Mathews, Harry. Armenian Papers: Poems 1954-1984. 120p. 1987. pap. 11.95 (*0-691-01440-X*, Pub. by Princeton U Pr) Cal Prin Full Svc.

— Cigarettes. LC 98-23363. 304p. 1998. reprint ed. pap. 13.50 (*1-56478-203-4*) Dalkey Arch.

— The Conversions. LC 97-23674. 192p. 1997. reprint ed. pap. 11.95 (*1-56478-166-6*) Dalkey Arch.

— The Journalist. 256p. 1994. 21.95 (*1-56792-007-1*) Godine.

— The Journalist. LC 97-23675. 256p. 1997. reprint ed. pap. 12.95 (*1-56478-165-8*) Dalkey Arch.

— The Orchard. 48p. (Orig.). (C). 1988. pap. 7.00 (*0-917453-18-2*) Bamberger.

— Out of Bounds: Poems. (Burning Deck Poetry Chapbooks Ser.). 44p. 1989. pap. 5.00 (*0-930901-61-4*) Burning Deck.

— Selected Declarations of Dependence. (Sun & Moon Classics Ser.: No. 128). (Illus.). 200p. (Orig.). 1995. pap. 10.95 (*1-55713-234-8*) Sun & Moon CA.

***Mathews, Harry.** Singular Pleasures. LC 92-29478. (Illus.). 144p. 1999. pap. 12.95 (*1-56478-233-6*, Pub. by Dalkey Arch) Chicago Distribution Ctr.

— The Sinking of the Odradek Stadium. LC 99-35094. 197p. 1999. reprint ed. pap. 11.95 (*1-56478-207-7*, Pub. by Dalkey Arch) Chicago Distribution Ctr.

Mathews, Harry. Tlooth. LC 98-23364. 192p. 1998. reprint ed. pap. 12.50 (*1-56478-194-1*) Dalkey Arch.

— 20 Lines a Day. LC 87-73070. 136p. 1997. pap. 10.95 (*1-56478-168-2*) Dalkey Arch.

— The Way Home: Collected Longer Prose. 214p. 1999. pap. text 15.99 (*1-900565-05-6*, Pub. by Atlas Pr) SPD-Small Pr Dist.

Mathews, Harry, et al. S. A Novel. LC 97-2553.Tr. of Semaines de Suzuane. 124p. 1997. pap. 15.95 (*1-57129-043-5*, Lumen Eds) Brookline Bks.

— 2000 & What? Short Stories about the Turn of the Millennium. Roeseler, Karl & Gilbert, David, eds. 238p. 1996. pap. 12.00 (*0-9639192-2-9*, Pub. by Trip St Pr) SPD-Small Pr Dist.

Mathews, Harry, ed. see Perec, Georges.

Mathews, Harry, tr. see Perec, Georges & Bober, Robert.

Mathews, Heyward. Oceanography Text Flash Card. 320p. (C). 1995. pap. text, spiral bd. 18.95 (*0-7872-1120-6*) Kendall-Hunt.

Mathews, Ian, jt. auth. see Fox, Russel.

Mathews, J. P. A Command of the Heart. LC 96-95471. 192p. 1997. 18.95 (*0-8034-9197-2*, Avalon Bks) Bouregy.

Mathews, J. W., tr. see Legouis, Emile.

Mathews, Jack. The Battle of Brazil: Terry Gilliam V. Universal Pictures. rev. ed. (Illus.). 272p. 1998. pap. text 19.95 (*1-55783-347-8*) Applause Theatre Bk Pubs.

Mathews, Jackson, ed. see Baudelaire, Charles.

Mathews, Jackson, tr. see Valery, Paul.

Mathews, James, jt. auth. see Judge, Ken.

Mathews, James A. How to Prepare for the Air Traffic Controller Exam. 2nd ed. LC 96-47496. 432p. 1997. pap. 13.95 (*0-8120-9646-0*) Barron.

Mathews, James K. The Matchless Weapon - Satyagraha. 210p. 1994. pap. 15.00 (*0-934676-77-1*) Greenlf Bks.

Mathews, James W., jt. ed. see Dameron, J. Lasley.

Mathews, Jana B., jt. auth. see Rice, Mark P.

Mathews, Jane. Not for Sadie. (Illus.). 48p. (Orig.). (J). (gr. k-3). 1993. pap. 9.95 (*1-880812-05-3*) S Ink WA.

— Sadie Learns a Lesson. (Illus.). 48p. (Orig.). (J). (ps-3). 1989. pap. 9.95 (*1-880812-18-5*) S Ink WA.

Mathews, Jane G. & Mathews, Richard A. The Manor & Cottages: Albemarle Park, Asheville, North Carolina, a Historic Planned Residential Community. (Illus.). 112p. (Orig.). 1991. pap. 19.95 (*0-9630437-0-6*) Albemarle Pk.

Mathews, Jay. Class Struggle: What's Wrong. 1999. pap. 15.00 (*0-8129-3140-8*, Times Bks) Crown Pub Group.

— Escalante: The Best Teacher in America. LC 88-11960. 336p. 1995. pap. 12.95 (*0-8050-1195-1*, Owl) H Holt & Co.

Mathews, Jay, jt. auth. see Goldstein, Steven M.

Mathews, Jerold, jt. auth. see Johnston, Elgin.

Mathews, Jessica T., ed. Preserving the Global Environment: The Challenge of Shared Leadership. 384p. (C). 1990. pap. text 15.50 (*0-393-96093-5*) Norton.

Mathews, John. Complex Variables for Math & Engineering. 2nd ed. 368p. (C). 1988. text 63.75 (*0-697-06764-5*, WCB McGr Hill) McGrw-H Hghr Educ.

— Curriculum Exposed. 144p. (Orig.). 1990. pap. 26.95 (*0-8464-1486-4*) Beekman Pubs.

Mathews, John, jt. auth. see Winter, Dave.

Mathews, John, tr. see Gramsci, Antonio.

Mathews, John A. Catching the Wave: Workplace Reform in Australia. LC 94-25504. (Cornell International Industrial & Labor Relations Reports: No. 26). 359p. 1994. pap. 21.95 (*0-87546-706-7*, ILR Press) Cornell U Pr.

— Catching the Wave: Workplace Reform in Australia. LC 94-25504. (Cornell International Industrial & Labor Relations Reports: No. 36). 376p. 1994. 45.00 (*0-87546-707-5*, ILR Press) Cornell U Pr.

Mathews, John A. & Cho, Dong-Sung. Tiger Technology: The Creation of a Semiconductor Industry in East Asia. LC 99-35365. (Cambridge Asia-Pacific Studies). (Illus.). 304p. 2000. 54.95 (*0-521-66269-9*) Cambridge U Pr.

Mathews, John J. Life & Death of an Oilman: The Career of E. W. Marland. LC 89-70455. 1974. reprint ed. pap. 14.95 (*0-8061-1238-7*) U of Okla Pr.

— Osages: Children of the Middle Waters. LC 61-9006. (Civilization of the American Indian Ser.: No. 60). (Illus.). 848p. 1981. reprint ed. pap. 27.95 (*0-8061-1770-2*) U of Okla Pr.

— Sundown. LC 88-40214. 328p. 1988. pap. 15.95 (*0-8061-2160-2*) U of Okla Pr.

— Talking to the Moon. LC 81-137822. (Illus.). 256p. (Orig.). 1987. pap. 13.95 (*0-8061-2083-5*) U of Okla Pr.

— Wah'Kon-Tah: The Osage & the White Man's Road. (Civilization of the American Indian Ser.: Vol. 3). (Illus.). 359p. 1981. pap. 16.95 (*0-8061-1699-4*) U of Okla Pr.

Mathews, John M. & Hart, James, eds. Essays in Political Science in Honor of Westel Woodbury Willoughby. LC 68-8458. (Essay Index Reprint Ser.). 1977. reprint ed. 21.95 (*0-8369-0428-1*) Ayer.

— Essays in Political Science in Honor of Westel Woodbury Willoughby. LC 68-8458. (Essay Index Reprint Ser.). 374p. 1982. reprint ed. lib. bdg. 21.00 (*0-8290-0831-4*) Irvington.

Mathews, Jon & Walker, Robert L. Mathematical Methods of Physics. 2nd ed. 501p. (C). 1971. pap. text 101.00 (*0-8053-7002-1*) Addison-Wesley.

Mathews, Joseph M. How to Succeed in the Practice of Medicine. LC 74-180582. (Medicine & Society in America Ser.). (Illus.). 244p. 1972. reprint ed. 19.95 (*0-405-03959-X*) Ayer.

Mathews, Judith. There's Nothing to D-o-o-o! LC 97-32540. (Illus.). 32p. (J). 1999. 16.00 (*0-15-201647-3*) Harcourt.

Mathews, Judith, ed. Two of Everything. LC 92-29880. (Illus.). 32p. (J). (gr. k-3). 1993. lib. bdg. 15.95 (*0-8075-8157-7*) A Whitman.

Mathews, Judith & Robinson, Fay. Nathaniel Willy, Scared Silly. (Illus.). 32p. (J). (gr. k-3). 1999. per. 5.99 (*0-689-82955-8*) Aladdin.

Mathews, Judith, ed. see Baden, Robert.

Mathews, Judith, ed. see Berleth, Richard.

Mathews, Judith, ed. see Coleman, Mary A.

Mathews, Judith, ed. see Hamm, Diane J.

Mathews, Judith, ed. see Helfman, Elizabeth.

Mathews, Judith, ed. see Kroll, Virginia L.

Mathews, Judith, ed. see Muldoon, Kathleen M.

Mathews, Judith, ed. see Nerlove, Miriam.

Mathews, Judith, ed. see Nodar, Carmen M.

Mathews, Judith, ed. see Nodar, Carmen S.

Mathews, Judith, ed. see Patneaude, David.

Mathews, Judith, ed. see Schlieper, Anne.

Mathews, Judith, ed. see Seltzer, Meyer.

Mathews, Judith, ed. see Stowe, Cynthia.

Mathews, Judith, ed. see Zimelman, Nathan.

Mathews, Kate. Molas! Patterns, Techniques, & Projects for Colorful Applique. LC 97-31249. (Illus.). 128p. 1998. 24.95 (*1-57990-020-8*, Pub. by Lark Books) Random.

— Quick & Easy Vests & Jackets: Creative Fashions to Sew. LC 98-22045. (Illus.). 128p. 1999. 24.95 (*1-57990-083-6*, Pub. by Lark Books) Random.

— Sewing a Travel Wardrobe: Versatile Clothes & Stylish Accessories for Every Adventure. LC 98-52373. (Illus.). 128p. 1999. 24.95 (*1-57990-125-5*, Pub. by Lark Books) Random.

Mathews, Kate. The Weekend Sewer's Guide to Pants & Skirts: Time-Saving Sewing with a Creative Touch. LC 98-4631. (Weekend Sewer's Guide Ser.). (Illus.). 128p. 1998. 24.95 (*1-57990-056-9*, Pub. by Lark Books) Random.

***Mathews, Kate.** The Weekend Sewer's Guide to Pants & Skirts: Time-Saving Sewing with a Creative Touch. (Illus.). 2000. pap. 14.95 (*1-57990-159-X*) Lark Books.

Mathews, Kay. Hiking Trails of the Sandia & Manzano Mountains. (Illus.). 104p. (Orig.). 1985. pap. 7.50 (*0-910467-02-1*) Heritage Assocs.

Mathews, Kenneth A. Genesis 1-11, Vol. 1A. (New AMERICAN Commentary Ser.: Vol. 1). 528p. 1996. 36.99 (*0-8054-0101-6*) Broadman.

Mathews, Kenneth E., jt. auth. see Stotland, Ezra.

Mathews, Larry. Norman Levine & His Works. 46p. (C). 1989. pap. text 9.95 (*1-55022-034-9*, Pub. by ECW) Genl Dist Srvs.

Mathews, Lou. L. A. Breakdown. 256p. 1999. 24.95 (*0-947993-80-0*, Pub. by Mlvrn Pubg Co) Brit Bk Co Inc.

Mathews, Louise. Bunches & Bunches of Bunnies. (Illus.). 32p. (J). (gr. k-3). 1989. reprint ed. pap. 4.99 (*0-590-44766-1*) Scholastic Inc.

— Gator Pie. (Illus.). 38p. (J). (gr. 1-4). 1995. pap. 4.95 (*0-7608-0005-7*) Sundance Pub.

Mathews, Loulie A. Not Every Sea Hath Pearls. 173p. (Orig.). 1986. pap. 7.95 (*0-87961-165-0*) Naturegraph.

Mathews, M. Cash. Strategic Intervention in Organizations: Resolving Ethical Dilemmas. (Library of Social Research: Vol. 169). 160p. (C). 1988. 59.95 (*0-8039-3303-7*); pap. 26.00 (*0-8039-3304-5*) Sage.

Mathews, M. R. An Introduction to Cost & Management Accounting. 280p. 1981. pap. 36.00 (*0-409-60105-5*, NZ, MICHIE) LEXIS Pub.

— Socially Responsible Accounting. LC 92-38135. 260p. 1993. mass mkt. 34.95 (*0-412-47340-2*) Chapman & Hall.

Mathews, Marcia M. Henry Ossawa Tanner: American Artist. LC 69-10279. (Illus.). 278p. 1995. pap. 12.95 (*0-226-51006-9*) U Ch Pr.

Mathews, Marita, ed. see Mathews, Alice P.

Mathews, Marthiel, ed. see Baudelaire, Charles.

Mathews, Marthiel, tr. see Male, Emile.

Mathews, Marthiel, tr. see Valery, Paul.

Mathews, Martin S. Web Publishing with Microsoft FrontPage. 464p. 1996. pap. text 27.95 (*0-07-882224-6*) Osborne-McGraw.

Mathews, Mary, et al, eds. Policing the Conflict in South Africa. LC 93-7218. 240p. 1993. 49.95 (*0-8130-1224-4*) U Press Fla.

Mathews, Mary, jt. auth. see Gillespie, Patricia.

An Asterisk (*) at the beginning of an entry indicates that the title is appearing for the first time.

Mathews, Mary M. Ten Years in Nevada; or, Life on the Pacific Coast. LC 84-20813. (Illus.). vi, 343p. 1985. reprint ed. pap. 7.50 (*0-8032-8124-2*, Bison Books) U of Nebr Pr.

Mathews, Max V. & Pierce, John R., eds. Current Directions in Computer Music Research. (System Development Foundation, Benchmark Ser.). 440p. 1991. pap. text 25.00 (*0-262-63139-3*) MIT Pr.

Mathews, Michael B., ed. Translational Control. LC 87-132738. (Current Communications in Molecular Biology Ser.). 202p. (Orig.). reprint ed. pap. 62.70 (*0-608-08844-7*, 206948300004) Bks Demand.

Mathews, Michelle, ed. see Baums, Roosevelt.

Mathews, Mitford M., ed. Americanisms: A Dictionary of Selected Americanisms on Historical Principles. LC 69-19279. (Orig.). 1993. pap. text 1.95 (*0-226-51012-3*, P229) U Ch Pr.

Mathews, Nancy J. The Beeper. 2000. pap. 12.00 (*1-888417-25-0*) Dimefast.

Mathews, Nancy M. An American Perspective: Paintings from the Maier Museum of Art, Randolph-Macon Woman's College. LC 85-63217. (Illus.). 24p. (Orig.). 1985. pap. 4.00 (*0-88259-950-X*) NCMA.

— The Art of Charles Prendergast from the Collections of the Williams College Museum of Art & Mrs. Charles Prendergast. LC 93-22826. (Exhibit Catalog Ser.). (Illus.). 120p. (Orig.). 1993. pap. 25.00 (*0-913697-16-8*) Williams Art.

— Mary Cassatt. LC 86-17224. (Illus.). 160p. 1987. 45.00 (*0-8109-0793-3*, Pub. by Abrams) Time Warner.

— Mary Cassatt. LC 92-15548. (Rizzoli Art Ser.). (Illus.). 24p. 1992. pap. 7.95 (*0-8478-1611-7*, Pub. by Rizzoli Intl) St Martin.

— Mary Cassatt: A Life. LC 98-8028. (Illus.). 383p. 1998. pap. 18.00 (*0-300-07754-8*) Yale U Pr.

Mathews, Nancy M., ed. Cassatt: A Retrospective. 376p. 1996. 75.00 (*0-88363-256-X*) H L Levin.

Mathews, Nancy M., et al. Maurice Prendergast. (Illus.). 196p. 1990. 65.00 (*3-7913-0966-8*, Pub. by Prestel) te Neues.

Mathews, Nancy M., jt. auth. see Martindale, Meredith.

Mathews, Nathan. Abstracts of Georgia Land Plat Books A & B. (Illus.). 294p. (C). 1995. text 30.00 (*1-883793-15-7*) Wolfe Pubng.

Mathews, Neal, Jr. The Nashville Numbering System. 64p. 1984. pap. 7.95 (*0-88188-335-2*, HL 00704491) H Leonard.

Mathews, Nieves. Francis Bacon: The Story of a Character Assassination. LC 96-60105. 459p. 1996. 50.00 (*0-300-06441-1*) Yale U Pr.

Mathews, Oliver. The Album of Carte-de-Visite & Cabinet Portrait Photographs 1854-1914. (Illus.). 148p. 1987. 14.95 (*0-85945-002-3*, Pub. by Bishopsgte Pr) Intl Spec Bk.

Mathews, P., jt. auth. see Brickell, G.

Mathews, P. M., et al, eds. Gravitation, Quantum Fields & Superstrings. 480p. (C). 1988. text 108.00 (*9971-5-0582-7*) World Scientific Pub.

Mathews, Patricia. Thursday & the Lady. 408p. 1987. per. 4.50 (*0-373-97047-1*) Harlequin Bks.

Mathews, Patricia, tr. see Miro, Joan.

Mathews, Patricia T. Aurier's Symbolist Art Criticism & Theory. LC 85-20944. (Studies in the Fine Arts: Criticism: No. 18). (Illus.). 230p. reprint ed. pap. 71.30 (*0-8357-1686-4*, 207061000005) Bks Demand.

Mathews, Peggy. Farmer Boy: (Hmong/English Edition) Vang, Va, tr. (MUL., Illus.). 30p. (J). (gr. 1-5). 1994. 15.95 (*1-879600-09-9*) Pac Asia Pr.

— Farmer Boy: (Tr. from Hmong) (Illus.). 30p. (J). (gr. 1-4). 1994. 14.95 (*1-879600-08-0*) Pac Asia Pr.

Mathews, Peter. Corpus of Maya Hieroglyphic Inscriptions: Tonina, Vol. 6, Pt. 1. LC 75-19760. (Illus.). 64p. 1983. pap. 50.00 (*0-87365-804-3*) Peabody Harvard.

— Exporting to the Republic of Ireland. O'Brien, Gerry & Jolly, Adam, eds. (Illus.). 173p. 1999. pap. 25.00 (*0-7494-2750-7*) Nichols Pub.

Mathews, Peter & McKechnie, Ann, eds. Australian Education Directory, 1996. 187p. 1996. pap. 125.00 (*0-7855-2836-9*, Pub. by Aust Council Educ Res) St Mut.

Mathews, Peter, jt. auth. see Graham, Ian.

Mathews, Peter, jt. auth. see Houston, Stephen D.

Mathews, Peter, jt. auth. see Schele, Linda.

Mathews, Peter, jt. auth. see Willey, Gordon R.

***Mathews, Phillip.** Spectacular Australia. (Spectacular Ser.). (Illus.). 132p. 2000. 75.00 (*0-88363-846-0*) H L Levin.

Mathews, R. Belladonna. 2000. pap. 14.00 (*1-888417-05-6*) Dimefast.

Mathews, R. Arthur. Ready for Battle: Thirty-One Studies on Christian Discipline. LC 93-35784. 144p. 1993. pap. 7.99 (*0-87788-727-6*) OMF Bks.

Mathews, R. Mark & Fawcett, Stephen B. Matching Clients & Services: Information & Referral. LC 81-4337. (Sage Human Services Guide Ser.: No. 21). (Illus.). 160p. 1981. reprint ed. pap. 49.60 (*0-608-01174-6*, 205947200001) Bks Demand.

Mathews, Race. Australia's First Fabians: Middle-Class Radicals, Labour Activists, & the Early Labour Movement. LC 92-45211. (Illus.). 288p. (C). 1993. pap. write for info. (*0-521-44678-3*); text 64.95 (*0-521-44133-1*) Cambridge U Pr.

Mathews, Ranjiv, jt. auth. see Gearhart, John P.

Mathews, Reinaldo. And He Created Animals. 450p. (Orig.). 1997. pap. 16.50 (*1-888417-01-3*, 417015) Dimefast.

Mathews, Reinaldo, ed. All about Conures. (Exotic Bird Care Ser.). (Illus.). 70p. (Orig.). 1997. pap. 9.50 (*1-888417-84-6*, 417846) Dimefast.

Mathews, Richard. Aldiss Unbound: The Science Fiction of Brian W. Aldiss. LC 77-24582. (Milford Series: Popular Writers of Today: Vol. 9). 64p. 1977. pap. 13.00 (*0-89370-213-7*) Millefleurs.

— Worlds Beyond the World: The Fantastic Vision of William Morris. LC 78-247. (Milford Series: Popular Writers of Today: Vol. 13). 63p. 1978. pap. 13.00 (*0-89370-218-8*) Millefleurs.

Mathews, Richard & Wilber, Rick, eds. Subtropical Speculations: An Anthology of Florida Science Fiction. LC 90-37793. 304p. 1991. pap. 8.95 (*0-910923-82-5*) Pineapple Pr.

Mathews, Richard, ed. see Brown, Canter.

Mathews, Richard A., jt. auth. see Mathews, Jane G.

Mathews, Rinaldo. Hallow Gods. 200p. 2000. pap. 14.00 (*1-888417-06-4*) Dimefast.

Mathews, Rinaldo, jt. auth. see Mathews-Danzer, R.

Mathews, Rinaldo, ed. see Mathews-Danzer, R.

Mathews, Rinaldo, ed. see Mathews-Danzer, Reinaldo.

Mathews, Robert H. Chinese-English Dictionary: A Chinese-English Dictionary Compiled for the China Inland Mission. rev. ed. (Harvard-Yenching Institute Publications). 1250p. (C). 1943. 39.50 (*0-674-12350-6*) HUP.

Mathews, Ruth, et al. Female Sexual Offenders: An Exploratory Study. Bear, Euan, ed. 112p. (Orig.). 1989. pap. 17.50 (*1-884444-28-8*) Safer Soc.

Mathews, S. Mentoring & Coaching. (Financial Times Management Briefings Ser.). 1997. pap. 94.50 (*0-273-63252-3*, Pub. by F T P-H) Trans-Atl Phila.

Mathews, S. & Knight, A. Managing Stress. A Practical Survival Guide. 1996. pap. 129.00 (*1-85953-081-8*, Pub. by Tech Comm) St Mut.

Mathews, S. & Sutherland, S. Equal Opportunities: A Management Strategy. 1996. pap. 129.00 (*1-85953-055-9*, Pub. by Tech Comm) St Mut.

Mathews, Sally S. The Sad Night: The Story of an Aztec Victory & a Spanish Loss. LC 92-25119. (Illus.). 40p. (J). (gr. 1-4). 1994. 16.95 (*0-395-63035-5*, Clarion Bks) HM.

— Travel & Learn Florida. LC 98-38946. (Illus.). 48p. 1998. pap. 9.00 (*1-883114-10-1*) Waterview Pr.

***Mathews, Sally Schofer.** The Sad Night: The Story of an Aztec Victory & a Spanish Loss. (Illus.). 36p. (J). (gr. 4-6). 1999. text 17.00 (*0-7881-6762-6*) DIANE Pub.

Mathews, Shailer. Faith of Modernism. LC 71-108117. reprint ed. 20.00 (*0-404-04266-X*) AMS Pr.

— Select Medieval Documents & Other Material Illustrative in the History of Church & Empire, 754 A.D.-1254 A.D. LC 70-178566. (LAT.). reprint ed. 34.50 (*0-404-56628-6*) AMS Pr.

— The Spiritual Interpretation of History. 1977. lib. bdg. 250.00 (*0-8490-2661-X*) Gordon Pr.

Mathews, Shailer, et al. Contributions of Science to Religion. LC 79-117822. (Essay Index Reprint Ser.). 1977. 30.95 (*0-8369-1763-4*) Ayer.

Mathews, Sue. Designing & Managing a Training & Development Strategy. (Financial Times Management Briefings Ser.). 1997. pap. 89.50 (*0-273-63199-3*, Pub. by F T P-H) Trans-Atl Phila.

Mathews, Sue & Sutherland, Sybil. Equal Opportunities. (Financial Times Management Briefings Ser.). 1997. pap. 94.50 (*0-273-63177-2*, Pub. by F T P-H) Trans-Atl Phila.

Mathews, T. F. & Wieck, R. S., eds. Treasures in Heaven: Armenian Illuminated Manuscripts. 296p. 1994. text 75.00 (*0-691-03752-3*, Pub. by Princeton U Pr) Cal Prin Full Svc.

Mathews, Thomas. Art & Architecture in Byzantium & Armenia: Liturgical & Exegetical Approaches. (Collected Studies: Vol. CS510). 312p. 1995. 147.95 (*0-86078-537-8*, Pub. by Variorum) Ashgate Pub Co.

— La Politica Puertorriquena y el Nuevo Trato. Colorado, Antonio J., tr. 349p. (C). 1975. 4.00 (*0-8477-0831-4*); pap. 3.00 (*0-8477-0832-2*) U of PR Pr.

Mathews, Thomas F. Byzantium: From Antiquity to the Renaissance. LC 97-42413. (Illus.). 176p. 1998. pap. 18.95 (*0-8109-2700-4*, Pub. by Abrams) Time Warner.

***Mathews, Thomas F.** Clash of Gods: Reinterpretation of Early Christian Art. rev. expanded ed. LC 98-51583. (Princeton Paperbacks Ser.). 1999. pap. text 26.95 (*0-691-00939-2*, Pub. by Princeton U Pr) Cal Prin Full Svc.

Mathews, Thomas F. Clash of the Gods: A Reinterpretation of Early Christian Art. 233p. 1993. pap. text 24.95 (*0-691-00159-6*) Princeton U Pr.

— Treasures in Heaven: Armenian Illuminated Manuscripts. 296p. 1994. pap. text 39.50 (*0-691-03751-5*, Pub. by Princeton U Pr) Cal Prin Full Svc.

Mathews, Thomas F. & Sanjian, Avedis K. Armenian Gospel Iconography: The Tradition of the Glajor Gospel. LC 90-2723. (Dumbarton Oaks Studies: No. 29). (Illus.). 440p. 1991. 50.00 (*0-88402-183-1*, MSAG) Dumbarton Oaks.

Mathews, Thomas F. & Wieck, Roger S., eds. Treasures in Heaven: Armenian Illuminated Manuscripts. LC 93-40269. 1994. write for info. (*0-87598-100-3*) Pierpont Morgan.

Mathews, Thomas F., et al. Treasures in Heaven: Armenian Art, Religion, & Society. LC 97-34874. 192p. 1997. 35.00 (*0-87598-120-8*) Pierpont Morgan.

Mathews, Thomas W. Introduction to Electronics K6640. (C). 2000. pap. text, lab manual ed. write for info. (*0-201-61089-2*) Addison-Wesley.

Mathews, Tom, jt. auth. see Wilkins, Roy.

Mathews, V., ed. see Arnold, Caroline.

Mathews, V., ed. see Liptak, Karen.

Mathews, V., ed. see Nourse, Alan E.

Mathews, Victor, jt. ed. see Coleson, Joseph.

Mathews, Vince, jt. auth. see Prima Publishing Staff.

Mathews, Virginia H., ed. Library Services for Children & Youth: Dollars & Sense. 68p. 1995. pap. 21.95 (*1-55570-176-0*) Neal-Schuman.

Mathews, Walter. Restaurant Newsletters That Pay Off. LC 97-1969. 187p. 1997. 49.95 (*0-471-16912-9*) Wiley.

Mathews Weinbender, Miriam. Water Seed: Poems of the Nestucca River Valley. LC 99-60084. (Illus.). 80p. (Orig.). 1999. pap. 8.50 (*1-892076-07-1*) Dancing Moon.

Mathews, Wendell G., jt. auth. see Brown, Donald R.

Mathews, Wendell G., jt. ed. see Betts, Janice L.

Mathews, William, ed. see Pepys, Samuel.

Mathews, William S. How to Understand Music: A Concise Course in Musical Culture by Object Lessons & Essays, 2 vols. 5th ed. LC 75-144657. reprint ed. 65.00 (*0-404-07213-5*) AMS Pr.

— Masters & Their Music. LC 78-153364. reprint ed. 39.50 (*0-404-07209-7*) AMS Pr.

— Music: Its Ideals & Methods, a Collection of Essays for Young Teachers, Amateurs, & Students. LC 70-173057. reprint ed. 41.00 (*0-404-07211-9*) AMS Pr.

— Popular History of Music from the Earliest Times until the Present. rev. ed. LC 74-173058. reprint ed. 49.50 (*0-404-07212-7*) AMS Pr.

Mathews, William S., ed. Hundred Years of Music in America. LC 73-135725. reprint ed. 52.50 (*0-404-04259-7*) AMS Pr.

Mathews, William S. & Liebling, Emil. Pronouncing & Defining Dictionary of Music. LC 78-173059. reprint ed. 42.00 (*0-404-07210-0*) AMS Pr.

Mathews, Wilma K. Effective Media Relations: A Practical Guide for Communicators. (Strategic Communicator Ser.). 139p. 1998. 185.00 (*1-888015-10-1*) IABC.

Mathews, Winifred. Dauntless Women: Stories of Pioneer Wives. LC 70-126325. (Biography Index Reprint Ser.). (Illus.). 1977. reprint ed. 18.95 (*0-8369-8031-X*) Ayer.

Mathewson. I Corinthians. 1997. pap. 8.99 (*1-56570-078-3*) Meridian.

Mathewson, C. H. Critical Shear Stress & Incongruent Shear in Plastic Deformation. (Connecticut Academy of Arts & Sciences Ser., Trans.: Vol. 38). 1951. pap. 39.50 (*0-685-22898-3*) Elliots Bks.

Mathewson, Champion H. Zinc, the Science & Technology of the Metal, Its Alloys & Compounds. LC 74-105708. 733p. reprint ed. pap. 200.00 (*0-608-11167-8*, 201523800094) Bks Demand.

Mathewson, Christopher. Pitching in a Pinch: or Baseball from the Inside. (American Biography Ser.). 306p. 1991. reprint ed. lib. bdg. 79.00 (*0-7812-8277-2*) Rprt Serv.

Mathewson, Christy. First Base Faulkner. 1976. 30.95 (*0-8488-1547-5*) Amereon Ltd.

— Pitching in a Pinch. 1976. 29.95 (*0-8488-1546-7*) Amereon Ltd.

— Pitching in a Pinch: or Baseball from the Inside. LC 93-42716. (Illus.). xxii, 320p. 1994. pap. 15.00 (*0-8032-8212-5*, Bison Books) U of Nebr Pr.

Mathewson, Dean. How Smart Are You? Test Your Baseball IQ. 64p. pap. 2.95 (*0-9637056-5-2*) Blck Dog & Leventhal.

Mathewson, G. Bradley. Asking for Money: The Entrepreneur's Guide to the Financing Process. 261p. 1989. 24.95 (*0-9623770-0-7*) Fin Systs Assocs.

Mathewson, G. Frank. Fiscal Transfer Pricing in Multinational Corporations. LC 79-314786. (Ontario Economic Council Research Studies: No. 16). 170p. reprint ed. pap. 52.70 (*0-8357-3998-8*, 203669800005) Bks Demand.

— Information, Entry, & Regulation in Markets for Life Insurance. LC 82-190622. (Ontario Economic Council Research Studies: No. 24). (Illus.). 125p. reprint ed. pap. 38.80 (*0-7837-4284-3*, 204397600012) Bks Demand.

Mathewson, G. Frank, jt. ed. see Stiglitz, Joseph E.

Mathewson, Henry S., ed. see Holt, Marian C.

Mathewson, Kent, ed. Culture, Form & Place. LC 93-37168. (Geoscience & Man Ser.: Vol. 32). (Illus.). 384p. (C). 1994. pap. text 24.95 (*0-938909-55-X*) Geosci Pubns LSU.

Mathewson, Kent & Neenan, William B., eds. Financing the Metropolis. LC 80-15718. 480p. 1980. 69.50 (*0-275-90518-7*, C0518, Praeger Pubs) Greenwood.

Mathewson, Paul R. & Finley, John W., eds. Biosensor Design & Application. LC 92-31003. (ACS Symposium Ser.: No. 511). (Illus.). 202p. 1992. text 59.00 (*0-8412-2494-3*, Pub. by Am Chemical) OUP.

Mathewson, R. Duncan, III. Treasure of the Atocha. 2nd ed. (Orig.). 1998. pap. 18.95 (*0-88415-875-6*, 5875, Pisces Books) Lonely Planet.

Mathewson, Richard J. & Primosch, Robert E. Fundamentals of Pediatric Dentistry. 3rd ed. LC 94-43277. (Illus.). 400p. (Orig.). 1995. pap. text 58.00 (*0-86715-262-1*, B2621) Quint Pub Co.

***Mathewson, Rufus W., Jr.** The Positive Hero in Russian Literature. 2nd ed. LC 99-49407. 392p. 1999. pap. 22.95 (*0-8101-1716-9*) Northwestern U Pr.

Mathewson, Rufus W., Jr. The Positive Hero in Russian Literature. 2nd ed. LC 72-97207. xviii, 366p. 1975. pap. 15.95 (*0-8047-0976-9*) Stanford U Pr.

Mathewson, W. Upland Tales. 271p. 1999. 29.95 (*1-57157-152-3*) Safari Pr.

***Mathewson, Worth.** Big December Canvasbacks. LC 99-89449. (Illus.). 176p. 2000. pap. 19.95 (*1-56833-153-3*) Madison Bks UPA.

***Mathewson, Worth, ed.** Western Bird Hunting: Bird-Hunting Tales from the American West. (Illus.). 289p. 2000. 29.95 (*1-57157-209-0*) Safari Pr.

Mathey, Francois. Molecular Chemistry of the Transition Elements: An Introductory Course. LC 95-48041. (Inorganic Chemistry Ser.). 242p. 1996. 135.00 (*0-471-95919-7*) Wiley.

Mathey, Francois & Sevin, Alain. Molecular Chemistry of the Transition Elements: An Introductory Course. LC 95-48041. (Inorganic Chemistry Ser.). 242p. 1996. pap. 59.95 (*0-471-95687-2*) Wiley.

Mathey, Kosta, ed. Housing Policies in the Socialist Third World. 342p. 1990. text 110.00 (*0-7201-2049-7*) Continuum.

Mathez, Edmond A., ed. see Holden, Martin.

Mathhewman, Jim. HR Effectiveness. 176p. 1993. 75.00 (*0-85292-535-2*, Pub. by IPM Hse) St Mut.

Mathia, Myrna E. & Yamine, Lorena S., eds. Nursing Education in the Middle East: Community Health Needs & Curriculum Development. 244p. 1983. text 24.95 (*0-8156-6066-9*, Pub. by Am U Beirut) Syracuse U Pr.

Mathiak, K. Valuations of Skew Fields & Projective Hjelmslev Spaces. (Lecture Notes in Mathematics Ser.). vii, 116p. 1986. 29.95 (*0-387-16099-X*) Spr-Verlag.

Mathiane, Nomavenda. South Africa: Diary of Troubled Times. Finn, James, ed. LC 88-33590. (Focus on Issues Ser.: No. 7). (Illus.). 189p. 1989. 23.95 (*0-932088-38-4*); pap. 12.95 (*0-932088-37-6*) Freedom Hse.

Mathias, Barbara & French, Mary A. 40 Ways to Raise a Nonracist Child. LC 96-7389. 176p. 1996. pap. 11.00 (*0-06-273322-2*) HarpC.

Mathias, Barbara & Mills, Pamela. DOS for WordPerfect Users. LC 93-70781. (Computer Ser.). (Illus.). 116p. 1994. pap. 11.95 (*1-56052-216-X*) Crisp Pubns.

Mathias, Barry. Power in the Dark. (Illus.). 256p. 1997. pap. 11.95 (*1-894012-00-3*, Pub. by SalPress) Firebird Dist.

Mathias, Beverley. A Treasury of Christmas Stories. LC 93-50708. (Illus.). 160p. (J). (ps-4). 1994. pap. 6.95 (*1-85697-985-7*) LKC.

Mathias, C. J. & Bannister, Roger, eds. Autonomic Failure: A Textbook of Clinical Disorders of the Autonomic Nervous System. 4th ed. LC RC407.A95 1999. (Illus.). 592p. 1999. text 250.00 (*0-19-262851-8*) OUP.

Mathias, Christopher, jt. auth. see Turino, Kenneth.

Mathias, Dietmar. Die Geschichtstheologie der Geschichtssummarien in Den Psalmen. (Beitrage zur Erforschung des Alten Testaments & Antiken Judentums Ser.: Bd. 35). (GER., Illus.). 297p. 1993. 44.95 (*3-631-44223-8*) P Lang Pubng.

Mathias, Dietmar, ed. see Wagner, Siegfried.

Mathias, Don. Misuse of Drugs. 251p. 1988. pap. 54.00 (*0-409-78816-3*, NZ, MICHIE) LEXIS Pub.

Mathias, Dot & Floyd, Sally. Speedbuilding for Court Reporting, Vol. 1. Ritter, Beverly L., ed. (Realtime Machine Shorthand Ser.). 252p. (C). 1990. reprint ed. pap. text 40.00 (*0-938643-03-7*) Stenotype Educ.

Mathias, Dot, jt. auth. see Floyd, Sally.

Mathias, Elizabeth & Raspa, Richard. Italian Folktales in America: The Verbal Art of an Immigrant Woman. LC 88-6598. (Illus.). 346p. 1988. pap. 19.95 (*0-8143-2122-4*) Wayne St U Pr.

— Italian Folktales in America: The Verbal Art of an Immigrant Woman. LC 85-10659. (Wayne State University Folklore Archive Study Ser.). 345p. reprint ed. pap. 107.00 (*0-608-10572-4*, 2071192) Bks Demand.

***Mathias, Frank F.** The G. I. Generation: A Memoir. LC 99-89854. (Illus.). 300p. 2000. 25.00 (*0-8131-2157-4*) U Pr of Ky.

Mathias, Frank F. G. I. Jive: An Army Bandsman in World War II. LC 82-4792. (Illus.). 256p. 1982. 26.00 (*0-8131-1462-4*) U Pr of Ky.

Mathias, Gerald B., jt. auth. see Habein, Yaeko S.

Mathias, Idris. The Last of the Mwldan. 1997. pap. 26.95 (*0-8464-4578-6*) Beekman Pubs.

— The Last of the Mwldan. 1997. pap. 40.00 (*1-85902-428-9*, Pub. by Gomer Pr) St Mut.

Mathias, J. & Hixson, Sandra. A Compilation of Chinese Dictionaries. (CHI.). 1975. 11.95 (*0-88710-020-1*) Yale Far Eastern Pubns.

Mathias, Jack, jt. ed. see Li, Sifa.

Mathias, Jack A., et al. Integrated Fish Farming: Proceedings of a Workshop on Integrated Fish Farming Held in Wuxi, Jiangsu Province, People's Republic of China, October 11-15, 1994. Charles, Anthony T., ed. LC 97-27473. 432p. 1997. boxed set 79.95 (*1-56670-260-7*) CRC Pr.

Mathias, Jim, ed. Shanghai Common Expressions. LC 88-51589. 79p. 1989. 39.00 (*0-931745-38-1*) Dunwoody Pr.

Mathias, Jim & Kennedy, Thomas L., eds. Computers, Language Reform & Lexicography in China: A Report by the CETA Delegation. LC 81-112015. 84p. reprint ed. pap. 30.00 (*0-608-18348-2*, 203302900083) Bks Demand.

Mathias, John, jt. auth. see Jones, Jeff.

Mathias, L. J. Solid State NMR of Polymers. (Illus.). 464p. (C). 1991. text 129.50 (*0-306-44015-6*, Kluwer Plenum) Kluwer Academic.

Mathias, M. E. & Constance, L. Flora of Ecuador No. 145: Umbelliferae. (Opera Botanica Series B). 71p. 1976. pap. 20.00 (*91-546-0197-5*, Pub. by Coun Nordic Pubs) Balogh.

***Mathias, Matt.** Generations: A Family Story 1000 B. C. to 2000 A. D. 150p. 2000. 15.00 (*0-9672197-2-8*) CrocusplusDBR.

Mathias, Mildred E., ed. Flowering Plants in the Landscape. LC 81-16310. (Illus.). 215p. 1982. pap. 24.95 (*0-520-05414-8*, Pub. by U CA Pr) Cal Prin Full Svc.

Mathias-Mundy, Evelyn & McCorkle, Constance M. Ethnoveterinary Medicine: An Annotated Bibliography. (Bibliographies in Technology & Social Change Ser.: No. 6). 209p. (C). 1989. pap. 18.00 (*0-945271-16-6*) ISU-CIKARD.

Mathias-Mundy, Evelyn, et al. Indigenous Technical Knowledge of Private Tree Management: A Bibliographic Report. (Bibliographies in Technology & Social Change Ser.: No. 7). 175p. (C). 1992. pap. 18.00 (*0-945271-30-1*) ISU-CIKARD.

Mathias, P. & Pollard, Sidney, eds. The Cambridge Economic History of Europe Vol. 8: The Industrial Economies: The Development of Economic & Social Policies. (Illus.). 1280p. 1989. text 195.00 (*0-521-22504-3*) Cambridge U Pr.

An Asterisk (*) at the beginning of an entry indicates that the title is appearing for the first time.

Mathias, P. & Postan, M. M., eds. The Cambridge Economic History of Europe: The Industrial Economies: Capital, Labour & Enterprise: The United States, Japan & Russia, Vol. 7, Pt 2. 651p. 1982. pap. text 49.95 (*0-521-28801-0*) Cambridge U Pr.

Mathias, Peter. The Brewing Industry in England, 1700-1830. (Modern Revivals in Economic & Social History Ser.). 624p. 1993. 95.95 (*0-7512-0150-2*, Pub. by Gregg Revivals) Ashgate Pub Co.

— First Industrial Nation: Economic History of Britain, 1700-1914. 2nd ed. 512p. (C). 1983. pap. 22.99 (*0-415-02756-X*) Routledge.

Mathias, Peter, ed. Science & Society, 1600-1900. LC 76-172833. 174p. reprint ed. pap. 49.60 (*0-608-15751-1*, 2031688) Bks Demand.

Mathias, Peter & Davis, John A., eds. Agriculture & Industrialization: From the Eighteenth Cenury to the Present Day. (Illus.). 240p. 1996. 50.95 (*0-631-18115-6*) Blackwell Pubs.

— Enterprise & Labour: From the Eighteenth Century to the Present. (Nature of Industrialization Ser.: Vol. 3). 240p. (C). 1996. 52.95 (*0-631-17407-9*) Blackwell Pubs.

— International Trade & British Economic Growth: From the Eighteenth Century to the Present Day. (Nature of Industrialization Ser.). 224p. 1997. 48.95 (*0-631-18116-4*) Blackwell Pubs.

Mathias, Robert & Steelman, Diane. Controlling Prison Populations: An Assessment of Current Mechanisms, 1982. 1982. 1.50 (*0-318-02050-5*) Natl Coun Crime.

Mathias, Roland. Burning Brambles: Selected Poems 1944-1979. 163p. (C). 1983. 30.00 (*0-85088-728-3*, Pub. by Gomer Pr) St Mut.

— A Field at Vallorcines. 63p. 1996. pap. 14.85 (*0-8464-4623-5*) Beekman Pubs.

Mathias, Roland, ed. David Jones. 144p. (C). 1976. pap. 35.00 (*0-85088-372-5*, Pub. by Gomer Pr) St Mut.

Mathias, Roland, jt. auth. see Adams, Sam.

Mathias, Roland, jt. ed. see Adams, Sam.

Mathias, Roland, jt. ed. see Garlick, Raymond.

Mathias, Rowland. A Field at Vallarcines. 63p. 1996. pap. 14.95 (*0-8464-4760-6*) Beekman Pubs.

Mathias, Sara. Electing Justice: A Handbook of Judicial Election Reforms. LC 90-82925. 160p. (Orig.). 1990. pap. 6.00 (*0-938870-45-9*) Am Judicature.

Mathias, Sara, ed. Judicial Discipline & Disability Digest: 1989-1991 Supplement. LC 81-65601. 399p. 1993. 140.00 (*0-938870-61-0*) Am Judicature.

Mathias, Sara, et al, eds. Judicial Discipline & Disability Digest: July 1986-December 1988 Supplement. LC 81-65601. 352p. 1990. 200.00 (*0-938870-48-3*) Am Judicature.

Mathias, Sean. Windows NT Workstation 4 Unleashed: MCSE. 850p. 1997. 59.99 (*0-672-31188-7*) Sams.

Mathias, Sheila F., jt. ed. see Franks, Felix.

Mathias, William F. Dictionary of Sport Fishing, Tropical Eastern Pacific Ocean, English-Spanish. unabridged ed. 54p. 1998. spiral bd. 10.00 (*0-9668682-0-X*) W F Mathias.

Mathiasen, Carolyn. The SEC & Social Policy Shareholder Resolutions in the 1990s. LC 95-125151. 100p. (Orig.). 1994. pap. 25.00 (*1-879775-22-0*) IRRC Inc DC.

Mathiasen, Carolyn, ed. How Institutions Voted on Social Policy Shareholder Resolutions in the Proxy Season, 1991. 144p. 1991. pap. 35.00 (*0-931035-92-9*) IRRC Inc DC.

Mathiasen, Carolyn & Welsh, Heidi, contrib. by. Social Policy Shareholder Resolutions in 1977: Issues, Votes & Views of Institutional Investors. 78p. 1998. pap. 55.00 (*1-879775-54-9*) IRRC Inc DC.

Mathiasen, Carolyn, ed. see Booth, Helen E.

Mathiasen, Carolyn, ed. see Bradley, Adrienne.

Mathiasen, Carolyn, ed. see Ortigoza, Brenda.

Mathiasen, Carolyn, ed. see Shaw, Linda S., et al.

Mathiasen, Carolyn, ed. see Williams, Susan.

Mathiasen, Karl, III. Board Passages: Three Key Stages in a Nonprofit Board's Life Cycle. (Nonprofit Governance Ser.: No. 07). 20p. (Orig.). 1990. pap. text 12.00 (*0-925299-09-X*) Natl Ctr Nonprofit.

— Evolucao Dos Conselhos: Tres Estagios Importantes Na Vida do Conselho Diretor de Uma Organizacao.Tr. of Board Passages. (POR.). 20p. (Orig.). 1996. pap. write for info. (*0-925299-70-7*) Natl Ctr Nonprofit.

Mathiasen, Patrick. An Ocean of Time: Alzheimer's: Tales of Hope & Forgetting. LC 96-29679. 1997. 22.50 (*0-684-82252-0*) S&S Trade.

Mathiassen, Lars, jt. auth. see Dahlbom, Bo.

Mathiassen, Lars, jt. ed. see Kyng, Morten.

Mathiassen, Terje. A Short Grammar of Latvian. LC 97-190866. 236p. 1997. pap. 22.95 (*0-89357-270-5*) Slavica.

— A Short Grammar of Lithuanian. 256p. (Orig.). 1996. pap. 22.95 (*0-89357-267-5*) Slavica.

Mathiassen, Therkel. Archaeological Collections from the Western Eskimos. LC 76-21673. (Thule Expedition, 5th, 1921-1924 Ser.: Vol. 10, No. 1). reprint ed. 37.50 (*0-404-58325-3*) AMS Pr.

— Archaeology of the Central Eskimos, 2 pts. in 1 vol. LC 76-21669. (Thule Expedition, 5th, 1921-1924 Ser.: No. 4). reprint ed. 137.50 (*0-404-58315-6*) AMS Pr.

— Contributions to the Geography of Baffin Land & Melville Peninsula. LC 76-21640. (Thule Expedition, 5th, 1921-1924 Ser.: Vol. 1, No. 3). reprint ed. 39.50 (*0-404-58303-2*) AMS Pr.

— Contributions to the Physiography of Southampton Island. LC 76-21639. (Thule Expedition, 5th, 1921-1924 Ser.: Vol. 1, No. 2). reprint ed. 32.50 (*0-404-58302-4*) AMS Pr.

— Material Culture of the Iglulik Eskimos. LC 76-21671. (Thule Expedition. 5th. 1921-1924 Ser.: Vol. 6, No. 1). reprint ed. 67.50 (*0-404-58317-2*) AMS Pr.

— Report on the Expedition. LC 76-21664. (Thule Expedition, 5th, 1921-1924 Ser.: Vol. 1, No. 1). reprint ed. 39.50 (*0-404-58301-6*) AMS Pr.

Mathie. Chemical Treatment of Cooling Water. 182p. (C). 1998. pap. text 84.00 (*0-13-975186-6*, Pub. by P-H) S&S Trade.

Mathie, Alton J. Chemical Treatment for Cooling Water. LC 98-5957. (Illus.). 168p. 1998. pap. 79.00 (*0-88173-253-2*, 0394) Fairmont Pr.

Mathie, Mellisa. Celebrating Oregon. Bishop, Janice, ed. (Illus.). 40p. 1993. pap. 30.00 (*0-9636258-0-2*) Will Creek W.

Mathie, Robert T. & Griffith, Tudor M., eds. The Haemodynamic Effects of Nitric Oxide. 400p. 1998. 78.00 (*1-86094-081-1*, Pub. by Imperial College) World Scientific Pub.

Mathie, Robert T., jt. auth. see Grace, Pierce A.

Mathie, Vonne, jt. auth. see Brown, Hazel.

Mathiesen, C. F., jt. auth. see Johansen, John.

Mathiesen, Egon. Jungle in the Wheat Field. (Illus.). (J). (gr. k-3). 1960. 9.95 (*0-8392-3014-1*) Astor-Honor.

— Oswald the Monkey. (Illus.). (J). (gr. k-3). 1959. 9.95 (*0-8392-3025-7*) Astor-Honor.

Mathiesen, Hans E. Failka/Ilaros No. 1: The Hellenistic Settlements Danish Archaeological Investigations in Kuwait - The Terracotta Figurines. (Jutland Archaeological Society Publications: No. 16). (Illus.). 94p. (C). 1983. 18.95 (*87-00-53651-2*, Pub. by Aarhus Univ Pr) David Brown.

— Sculpture in the Parthian Empire: A Study in Chronology, 2 vols., Set. (Illus.). 232p. (C). 1993. 51.00 (*87-7288-311-1*, Pub. by Aarhus Univ Pr) David Brown.

Mathiesen, Michael. The New American Bible: Ecology of Mind, Pt. II. G. O. D., ed. (Collaboration Ser.). 500p. pap. 20.00 (*0-939887-87-8*) Millennium Sta Cruz.

Mathiesen, Thomas. Prison on Trial: A Critical Assessment. 192p. (C). 1990. text 45.00 (*0-8039-8224-0*); pap. text 17.95 (*0-8039-8225-9*) Sage.

— Source Readings: Greek Views. rev. ed. LC 98-106574. 7p. (C). 1997. pap. text 15.50 (*0-393-96694-1*) Norton.

Mathiesen, Thomas J. Apollo's Lyre: Greek Music & Music Theory in Antiquity & the Middle Ages. LC 99-35248. (Publications of the Center for the History of Music Theory & Literature). 824p. 2000. text 75.00 (*0-8032-3079-6*, Bison Books) U of Nebr Pr.

Mathiesen, Thomas J., ed. Thesaurus Musicarum Latinarum: Canon of Data Files. LC 99-10606. (Publications of the Center for History of Music Theory & Literature). (Illus.). 324p. 1999. pap. text 45.00 (*0-8032-8233-8*, Bison Books) U of Nebr Pr.

Mathiesen, Thomas J. & Rivera, Benito V., eds. Festa Musicologica: Essays in Honor of George J. Buelow. LC 94-46264. (Festschrift Ser.: No. 14). 1995. 54.00 (*0-945193-70-X*) Pendragon NY.

Mathieson. Tourism. 1999. pap. write for info. (*0-582-49475-3*) Addison-Wesley.

Mathieson, David S., jt. auth. see Jaensch, Dean.

Mathieson, A. C. Morphological Studies of the Marine Brown Alga Taonia Lennebackerae Farlow Ex. J. Agardh L. (Illus.). 1966. pap. 12.00 (*3-7682-0439-1*) Lubrecht & Cramer.

Mathieson, Carol Fisher. Music of Many Cultures. (Illus.). 80p. (J). (gr. 10-13). 1996. pap. text 9.95 (*1-58037-102-7*, Pub. by M Twain Media) Carson-Dellos.

Mathieson, Craig. Hi Fi Days: The Future of Australian Rock. LC 97-106262. (Illus.). 144p. (Orig.). 1997. pap. 12.95 (*1-86448-232-X*, Pub. by Allen & Unwin Pty) IPG Chicago.

Mathieson, D. L. Cross on Evidence. 677p. 1989. pap. 87.00 (*0-409-78883-X*, NZ, MICHIE) LEXIS Pub.

— Cross on Evidence. 4th ed. 677p. 1989. boxed set 108.00 (*0-409-78790-6*, NZ, MICHIE) LEXIS Pub.

Mathieson, Donald J. & Rojas-Suarez, Liliana. Liberalization of the Capital Account: Experiences & Issues. LC 93-16797. (Occasional Paper - International Fund: No. 103). 39p. 1993. 15.00 (*1-55775-280-X*) Intl Monetary.

Mathieson, Donald J., et al. Managing Financial Risks in Indebted Developing Countries. (Occasional Papers: No. 65). 47p. 1989. pap. 10.00 (*1-55775-116-1*) Intl Monetary.

Mathieson, Donald J., jt. auth. see Folkerts-Landau, David.

Mathieson, Jim. What's Your Golf IQ? All You Ever Wanted to Know about Golf (And Probably More) Goskie, Gloria, ed. 245p. 1998. pap. 13.95 (*0-9665939-0-1*) Twin Pr.

Mathieson, John A., jt. auth. see Sewell, John W.

Mathieson, John A., jt. auth. see Yeung, Ophelia M.

Mathieson, Judy. Mariner's Compass Quilts: New Directions. LC 95-18374. (Illus.). 80p. 1995. pap. 21.95 (*0-914881-97-3*, 10119) C & T Pub.

***Mathieson, Kenny.** Celtic Music: Great Musicians, Influential Groups. (Illus.). 2000. pap. 19.95 (*0-87930-623-8*) Miller Freeman.

— Giant Steps: The Story of Bebop. (Illus.). 2000. pap. 16.95 (*0-86241-859-3*, Pub. by Canongate Books) Interlink Pub.

Mathieson, Margaret, jt. auth. see McCulloch, Ros.

Mathieson, Neil, jt. auth. see McIvor, Doug.

Mathieson, Peter. The Complete Pub Trivia Night Book. 176p. 1998. pap. text. write for info. (*0-9698461-7-7*) Master Pt Pr.

Mathieson, Raymond S. Japan's Role in Soviet Economic Growth: Transfer of Technology since 1965. LC 78-19790. 277p. 1979. 65.00 (*0-275-90389-3*, C0389, Praeger Pubs) Greenwood.

Mathieson, Robert, ed. Japan & NAFTA. 128p. (Orig.). 1993. pap. 9.95 (*1-883223-01-6*) Pacific NY.

Mathieson, T. L., jt. ed. see Adams, J. S.

Mathieu, Agnes. The Three Little Pigs: A Fairy Tale by Perrault. LC 97-23044. (Little Pebbles Ser.). 32p. (J). (ps-1). 1999. 6.95 (*0-7892-0423-1*, Abbeville Kids) Abbeville Pr.

Mathieu, Aron. The Book Market: How to Write, Publish & Market Your Book. LC 80-71059. 474p. 1981. 19.95 (*0-939014-00-9*) Andover Pr.

Mathieu, Bertrand. Orpheus in Brooklyn: Orphism, Rimbaud, & Henry Miller LC 77-366292. xii, 230p. 1976. write for info. (*90-279-3036-8*) Mouton.

Mathieu, Bertrand, tr. see Cendrars, Blaise.

Mathieu, Bertrand, tr. see Rimbaud, Arthur.

Mathieu, Clement, jt. auth. see Lozet, J.

Mathieu, Clement, jt. auth. see Lozet, Jean.

Mathieu, Deborah R. Preventing Prenatal Harm: Should the State Intervene? LC 95-36923. (Clinical Medical Ethics Ser.). 208p. 1996. pap. 19.95 (*0-87840-600-X*) Georgetown U Pr.

— Preventing Prenatal Harm: Should the State Intervene? 168p. 1991. lib. bdg. 88.00 (*0-7923-0984-7*, Pub. by Kluwer Academic) Kluwer Academic.

Mathieu, Didier, jt. auth. see Lewis, Gareth.

Mathieu, Gilbert. Vocabulaire de L'Economie. (FRE.). 35.00 (*0-8288-7890-0*, M6401); pap. 35.00 (*0-686-57041-3*, M-6401) Fr & Eur.

Mathieu, Gustave B. Introduction to German Poetry. 176p. 1991. pap. 4.95 (*0-486-26713-X*) Dover.

Mathieu, Gustave B. & Stern, Guy. Say It in German. (Orig.). 1950. pap. 3.50 (*0-486-20804-4*) Dover.

Mathieu, Gustave B., jt. auth. see Haas, Werner.

Mathieu, Gustave B., ed. see Haas, Werner & Merrifield, Doris F.

Mathieu, Gustave B., tr. see Dover Staff.

Mathieu, H. J., et al, eds. Ecasia '95: 6th European Conference on Applications of Surface & Interface Analysis, Congress Centre, Montreux, Switzerland, October 9-13, 1995. 95th ed. LC 96-11157. 1999. text 310.00 (*0-471-95899-9*) Wiley.

Mathieu, J. & Fleury, P. Physics Dictionary: Dictionnaire de Physique. 3rd rev. ed. (FRE.). 567p. 1991. 135.00 (*0-8288-2233-6*, F23760) Fr & Eur.

Mathieu, J., jt. ed. see Comte-Bellot, G.

Mathieu, J. P., ed. Advances in Raman Spectroscopy: Proceedings of the Third International Conference on Raman Spectroscopy: University of Reims, France, September, 1972. LC 73-76120. 655p. reprint ed. pap. 200.00 (*0-8357-5182-1*, 202399600001) Bks Demand.

Mathieu, J. P., jt. auth. see Poulet, H.

***Mathieu, Jean & Scott, Julian.** Turbulent Flows: An Introduction. (Illus.). 464p. (C). 2000. text 100.00 (*0-521-57066-2*); pap. text 44.95 (*0-521-77538-8*) Cambridge U Pr.

Mathieu, Jean, jt. auth. see Chevray, Rene.

Mathieu, Jean P. Optics, 2 pts. Incl. Pt. 1. Electromagnetic Optics. LC 73-10408. 1975. Pt. 2. Quantum Optics. LC 73-10408. 1975. LC 73-10408. 1975. 243.00 (*0-08-017157-5*, Pub. by Pergamon Repr) Franklin.

Mathieu, Jean P. & Desnuelle, P. Selected Constants Optical Rotatory Power: Amino Acids. (Tables of Constants & Numerical Data Ser.: Vol. 10). 1959. 35.00 (*0-08-009202-0*, Pub. by Pergamon Repr) Franklin.

Mathieu, Jean P. & Jacques, J. Selected Constants Optical Rotary Power: IA Steroids. (Tables of Constants & Numerical Data Ser.: Vol. 14). 453.00 (*0-08-010982-9*, Pub. by Pergamon Repr) Franklin.

Mathieu, Jean P. & Janot, M. Selected Constants Optical Rotatory Power: Alkaloids. (Tables of Constants & Numerical Data Ser.). 1959. 104.00 (*0-08-009312-4*, Pub. by Pergamon Repr) Franklin.

Mathieu, Joan. Zulu: An Irish Journey. LC 97-37229. 224p. 1998. 22.00 (*0-374-29957-9*) FS&G.

***Mathieu, Joan.** Zulu: An Irish Journey. LC 99-38925. 212p. 1999. pap. text 17.95 (*0-8156-0613-3*) Syracuse U Pr.

Mathieu, Joe. Big Bird's Big Book. (Illus.). 12p. (J). (ps-1). 1987. 39.95 (*0-394-89128-7*, Pub. by Random Bks Yng Read) Random.

— Elmo Wants a Bath. (Sesame Street Bathtime Bks.). (Illus.). 10p. (J). (ps). 1992. 4.99 (*0-679-83066-9*, Pub. by Random Bks Yng Read) Random.

— Sesame Street Lift-&-Peek Party! LC 99-182530. (Great Big Flap Book Ser.). (Illus.). 12p. (J). (ps). 1998. 11.99 (*0-679-88979-5*) Random.

Mathieu, Joe. Sesame Street Stays up Late: Based on the Television Special by Lou Berger. LC 94-32232. (Picturebacks Ser.). 24p. (J). (ps-3). 1995. pap. 3.25 (*0-679-86743-0*) Random.

Mathieu, Joe & Siede, George. Counting. LC 97-196632. (Illus.). (J). 1997. write for info. (*0-7853-2227-2*) Pubns Intl Ltd.

Mathieu, Joe, et al. Colors. LC 97-198441. (Illus.). (J). 1997. write for info. (*0-7853-2226-4*) Pubns Intl Ltd.

— Sounds. LC 97-196656. (Illus.). (J). 1997. write for info. (*0-7853-2228-0*) Pubns Intl Ltd.

Mathieu, Joe, jt. illus. see Gikow, Louise.

Mathieu, Joseph. Big Joe's Trailer Truck. LC 74-2538. (Pictureback Ser.). (Illus.). 32p. (Orig.). (J). (ps-1). 1974. pap. 3.25 (*0-394-82925-5*, Pub. by Random Bks Yng Read) Random.

— Sesame Street Treasury: ABC & 1,2,3. Random House Staff & Children's TV Workshop Staff, eds. LC 99-165389. 1998. 9.99 (*0-375-80042-5*) Random.

Mathieu, Joseph, jt. auth. see LeSieg, Theo, pseud.

Mathieu, Kristen & LTD Publications International Staff. Counting Songs / LC 98-182040. 1998. write for info. (*0-7853-2673-1*) Pubns Intl Ltd.

Mathieu, M. Elementary Operators & Applications: In Memory of Domingo a Herroro. 300p. 1992. text 86.00 (*981-02-0914-2*) World Scientific Pub.

Mathieu, Mark. New Drug Approval in the United States. (Worldwide Pharmaceutical Regulation Ser.). (Orig.). 1995. pap. 100.00 (*1-882615-13-1*) Parexel Intl.

— New Drug Development: A Regulatory Overview. 3rd ed. 327p. 1994. 125.00 (*1-882615-01-8*) Parexel Intl.

Mathieu, Mark, ed. Biologics Development: A Regulatory Overview. LC 92-62597. 310p. 1993. 135.00 (*1-882615-00-X*) Parexel Intl.

— Handbook of CDER Staffing & Review. 213p. (Orig.). 1996. pap. 125.00 (*1-882615-28-X*) Parexel Intl.

Mathieu, Martin, jt. auth. see Albrecht, Ernst.

Mathieu, Nicolas. Financial Sector Reform: A Review of World Bank Assistance. 104p. 1998. pap. 22.00 (*0-8213-4291-6*, 14291) World Bank.

— Industrial Restructuring: World Bank Experience, Future Challenges. (Operations Evaluation Studies). 144p. 1996. pap. 22.00 (*0-8213-3614-2*, 13614) World Bank.

Mathieu, Nicole, jt. ed. see Audouze, Jean.

Mathieu, Paul. The Druid's Lodge Confederacy. 224p. 1990. 60.00 (*0-85131-525-9*, Pub. by J A Allen) St Mut.

Mathieu, Philippe. Teach Yourself Word 3.0. 189p. 1989. ring bd. 79.95 incl. disk (*0-929533-10-0*) Tutorland.

Mathieu, Pierre, jt. auth. see Di Francesco, Philippe.

Mathieu, Pierre L. The Symbolist Generation. LC 89-43610. (Illus.). 250p. 1991. 50.00 (*0-8478-1218-9*, Pub. by Rizzoli Intl) St Martin.

Mathieu, Pierre-Louis. Gustave Moreau. (Illus.). 320p. 1996. 125.00 (*2-08-013574-0*, Pub. by Flammarion) Abbeville Pr.

Mathieu, Renee. Diccionari Catala-Frances i Frances-Catala. (CAT & FRE.). 288p. 1990. pap. 11.95 (*0-7859-6037-6*, 8440461984) Fr & Eur.

— Diccionari Escolar Catala-Frances i Frances-Catala. (FRE.). 208p. 1988. pap. 19.95 (*0-7859-6197-6*, 8472111598) Fr & Eur.

Mathieu, Richard, jt. auth. see Letheren, Carole A.

Mathieu, Richard G. Manufacturing & the Internet: An Information Guide for Professionals in Manufacturing... LC 96-17830. 480p. 1996. pap. text 34.95 (*0-89806-164-4*, MFGNET) Eng Mgmt Pr.

Mathieu-Rosay, Jean. Dictionnaire du Christianisme. (FRE.). 316p. 1990. pap. 17.95 (*0-7859-7888-7*, 2501012887) Fr & Eur.

— Dictionnaire Etymologique Marabout. (FRE.). 544p. 1985. pap. 17.95 (*0-7859-8641-3*, 250100664x) Fr & Eur.

Mathieu, W. A. The Listening Book: Discovering Your Own Music. LC 90-53384. 144p. (Orig.). 1991. pap. 14.00 (*0-87773-610-3*, Pub. by Shambhala Pubns) Random.

— The Musical Life: Reflections on What It Is & How to Live It. LC 93-39776. 1994. pap. 17.00 (*0-87773-670-7*, Pub. by Shambhala Pubns) Random.

Mathiew, Mark, ed. Parexel's Pharmaceutical R&D Statistical Sourcebook, 1996. 180p. 1996. 195.00 (*1-882615-26-3*) Parexel Intl.

Mathiew, W. A. Harmonic Experience: Tonal Harmony from Its Natural Origins to Its Modern Expression. LC 96-40069. (Illus.). 512p. 1997. 39.95 (*0-89281-560-4*, Inner Trad) Inner Tradit.

Mathiews, David. Politics for People. Talhouk, Afif, tr. 1997. text 9.00 (*1-886604-06-1*) Lebanese Ctr.

Mathiopoulos, Margarita. History & Progress: In Search of European & American Identity. LC 89-8841. 459p. 1989. 75.00 (*0-275-92792-X*, C2792, Praeger Pubs) Greenwood.

Mathios, Alan D., jt. auth. see Knoppers, Bartha M.

Mathiot, Elizabeth M. NGOs & Grassroots in Development Work in South India: Elizabeth Moen Mathiot. Charlton, Sue M. & Everett, Jana, eds. LC 97-37089. 152p. (C). 1997. text 36.00 (*0-7618-0931-7*) U Pr of Amer.

Mathiot, Madeleine. A Dictionary of Papago Usage, Vol. 1, B-K. (Language Science Ser.: No. 8-1). 504p. 1974. pap. text 82.35 (*90-279-2677-8*) Mouton.

***Mathiowetz, Nancy A. & Wunderlich, Gooloo S.** Survey Measurement of Work Disability: Summary of a Workshop. 110p. 2000. pap. 26.25 (*0-309-06899-1*) Natl Acad Pr.

Mathiowitz, Edith. Encyclopedia of Controlled Drug Delivery, 2 vols. LC 99-24907. 1088p. 1999. 595.00 (*0-471-14828-8*) Wiley.

***Mathiowitz, Edith.** Encyclopedia of Controlled Drug Delivery, Vol. 1. LC 99-24907. 1999. text 495.00 (*0-471-16662-6*) Wiley.

— Encyclopedia of Controlled Drug Delivery, Vol. 2. LC 99-24907. 1999. text 55.01 (*0-471-16663-4*) Wiley.

***Mathiowitz, Edith, et al.** Bioadhesive Drug Delivery Systems: Fundamentals, Novel Approaches & Development. LC 99-32806. (Drugs & the Pharmaceutical Sciences Ser.). (Illus.). 696p. 1999. text 195.00 (*0-8247-1995-6*) Dekker.

Mathiprakasam, B. & Heenan, Patrick, eds. Thirteenth International Conference on Thermoelectrics. (AIP Conference Proceedings Ser.: No. 316). (Illus.). 359p. 1995. text 140.00 (*1-56396-444-9*, AIP Pr) Spr-Verlag.

Mathis. Human Resource Management. 7th ed. Date not set. pap. text, teacher ed. write for info. (*0-314-03589-3*) West Pub.

— Photosynthesis, Vol. 1. 1995. lib. bdg. write for info. (*0-7923-3857-X*) Kluwer Academic.

— Resource Gde Hum Res Mgt 7e. 7th ed. (SWC-Management). 1993. mass mkt., suppl. ed. 17.50 (*0-314-03590-7*) West Pub.

— Wooden Biscuit: A Kwanzaa Tale. 1996. pap. 3.95 (*0-15-200097-6*) Harcourt.

— Wooden Biscuit: A Kwanzaa Tale. 2001. 10.95 (*0-15-200095-X*) Harcourt.

***Mathis & Jackson.** Human Resource Management. 10th ed. 2001. pap., student ed. 25.00 (*0-324-07156-6*) Sth-Wstrn College.

Mathis & Jackson. Human Resources Management: Eessential Perspectives. LC 98-21500. (SWC-Management Ser.). 1998. pap. 47.95 (*0-324-00207-6*) Thomson Learn.

Mathis, Andrew G., jt. auth. see Lillibridge, E. Michael.

An Asterisk (*) at the beginning of an entry indicates that the title is appearing for the first time.

M

Mathis, Averil. Antiques & Collectible Thimbles & Accessories. (Illus.). 184p. 1995. 19.95 (*0-89145-322-9*, 1712) Collector Bks.

Mathis, Carla M. & Connor, Helen V. The Triumph of Individual Style: A Guide to Dressing Your Body, Your Beauty, Your Self. (Illus.). 192p. 1993. pap. 28.95 (*0-9632223-0-9*) Timeless Edits.

Mathis, Carmen, ed. see Jones, B. Keith.

Mathis, Cleopatra. Aerial View of Louisiana. LC 79-90841. 85p. 1979. 12.95 (*0-935296-00-X*, Pub. by Sheep Meadow) U Pr of New Eng.

— The Bottom Land. LC 83-60967. 64p. 1983. 13.95 (*0-935296-40-9*, Pub. by Sheep Meadow) U Pr of New Eng.

— The Center for Cold Weather. LC 89-10838. 89p. 1990. pap. 12.95 (*0-935296-85-9*, Pub. by Sheep Meadow); text 25.00 (*0-935296-84-0*, Pub. by Sheep Meadow) U Pr of New Eng.

— Guardian: Poems. LC 95-39158. 115p. 1995. 25.00 (*1-878818-49-X*, Pub. by Sheep Meadow) U Pr of New Eng.

— Guardian: Poems. LC 95-39158. 115p. 1996. pap. 13.95 (*1-878818-58-9*, Pub. by Sheep Meadow) U Pr of New Eng.

Mathis, D. K., jt. auth. see Gardiner, Gareth S.

Mathis, Darlene. Latino Women of Color. Date not set. mass mkt. write for info. (*0-345-40692-3*) Ballantine Pub Grp.

— Women of Color: The Multinational Fashion Guide to Fashion & Beauty. 1999. pap. text 15.95 (*1-892123-05-3*) Capital VA.

Mathis-Eddy, Darlene. Leaf Threads, Wind Rhymes. LC 84-71936. 64p. (Orig.). 1985. pap. 6.95 (*0-935306-31-5*) Barnwood Pr.

Mathis, Edward G. The Fifth Level: A Dan Roman Mystery. 256p. 1992. text 20.00 (*0-684-19386-8*, Scribners Ref) Mac Lib Ref.

Mathis, Emily D. & Doody, John E. Grant Proposals: A Primer for Writers. LC 94-188383. (Development Fastbacks Ser.). (Illus.). 56p. 1994. pap. 8.00 (*1-55833-129-8*) Natl Cath Educ.

Mathis, Erma H. The Mission Arlington Story: Tillie's Vision. 80p. (Orig.). 1996. pap. 11.95 (*1-889730-02-5*, SPI0038) Scripta Pubng.

Mathis, F. John, jt. auth. see Taylor, Jon G.

Mathis, J. J. A Review of Russellism, Et Cetera, Et Cetera. 66p. 1988. reprint ed. pap. 2.95 (*1-883858-41-0*) Witness CA.

Mathis, Jackson. Human Resource Management. 9th ed. LC 99-15314. (SWC-Management Ser.). 1999. pap. 91.95 (*0-538-89004-5*) S-W Pub.

***Mathis, Jackson.** Human Resource Management Professional Review Web Tutor-Online. 9th ed. 1999. pap. text 33.00 (*0-534-76812-1*) Thomson Learn.

Mathis, James L. Psychiatric Medicine: A Handbook. Gardner, James F., ed. (Allied Health Professions Monograph). 212p. (C). 1984. 22.50 (*0-87527-320-3*) Green.

Mathis, Johnny, jt. auth. see Mancini, Henry.

Mathis, Jon & Shomon, Mary J. Scratching the Net: Web Sites for Cats. LC 98-25110. (Illus.). 96p. 1998. pap. 9.95 (*0-8362-6818-0*) Andrews & McMeel.

Mathis, Mark A., ed. see Phelps, David S., et al.

Mathis, Mary, jt. auth. see Mathis, Ray.

Mathis, Melissa B. Animal House. LC 98-36597. (Illus.). 32p. (J). 1999. 15.95 (*0-689-81594-8*) S&S Bks Yung.

Mathis, Michael. Marple & Newtown Townships. LC 98-87697. (Images of America Ser.). (Illus.). 128p. 1998. pap. 16.99 (*0-7524-1246-9*) Arcadia Publng.

Mathis, Michael J., jt. ed. see Dinchak, William G.

***Mathis, Mike.** Cherry Hill. (Images of America Ser.). 128p. 1999. pap. 18.99 (*0-7385-0193-X*) Arcadia Publng.

Mathis, Paul, ed. Photosynthesis - From Light to Biosphere: Proceedings of the 10th International Congress, Montpellier, France, 20-25 August 1995, Set. 5168p. (C). 1996. text 1618.00 (*0-7923-3862-6*) Kluwer Academic.

Mathis, Ray & Mathis, Mary. Introduction & Index to the John Horry Dent Farm Journals & Account Books, 1840-1892. 206p. 1977. 11.00 (*0-8173-5251-1*) Hist Chattahoochee.

Mathis, Richard, jt. auth. see Coronado, Karen.

Mathis, Rick. The Christ-Centered Heart: Peaceful Living in Difficult Times. LC 98-47860. 160p. 1999. pap. 14.95 (*0-7648-0387-5*, Liguori Triumph) Liguori Pubns.

***Mathis, Rick.** Prayer-Centered Healing: Finding the God Who Heals. LC 00-29603. 2000. pap. 14.95 (*0-7648-0660-2*) Liguori Pubns.

Mathis, Robert L. Human Resource Manual. 8th ed. LC 96-26109. 650p. 1996. pap. 84.95 (*0-314-06246-7*) West Pub.

Mathis, Robert L. & Jackson, John H. Human Resource Management. 7th ed. Perlee, Simon, ed. LC 93-4430. (SWC-Management). 650p. (C). 1993. text 67.50 (*0-314-02529-4*) West Pub.

Mathis, Sharon B. The Hundred Penny Box. (Illus.). (J). (gr. 5). 1995. 9.32 (*0-395-73254-9*) HM.

— The Hundred Penny Box. (Newbery Library). (Illus.). 48p. (J). (gr. 1-4). 1986. pap. 5.99 (*0-14-032169-1*, PuffinBks) Peng Put Young Read.

— The Hundred Penny Box. (J). 1986. 10.19 (*0-606-01280-X*, Pub. by Turtleback) Demco.

— The Hundred Penny Box. large type ed. (Illus.). 62p. (J). (gr. 5). 15.50 (*0-614-20595-6*, L-38191-00 APHB) Am Printing Hse.

— Teacup Full of Roses. (Novels Ser.). (J). (gr. 7). 1987. pap. 4.99 (*0-14-032328-7*, PuffinBks) Peng Put Young Read.

Mathis, Sharon Bell. Running Girl: The Diary of Ebonee Rose. LC 96-29066. (Illus.). 64p. (J). (gr. 3). 1997. 17.00 (*0-15-200674-5*) Harcourt.

Mathis, Sharon Bell. Sidewalk Story. 1986. 9.19 (*0-606-12514-0*, Pub. by Turtleback) Demco.

Mathis, Sharon Bell. Teacup Full of Roses. LC 74-162675. 1987. 10.09 (*0-606-03482-X*, Pub. by Turtleback) Demco.

Mathis, Shawn D., ed. Man of God: Essays on the Life & Work of the Preacher. 256p. 1996. pap. 12.99 (*0-89225-459-9*, G54599) Gospel Advocate.

***Mathis, Stephen.** United in Christ: A Study in Philippians. LC 00-100638. (Streams of Mercy Study Ser.: Vol. 11). 45p. 2000. pap. 5.95 (*0-89112-245-1*) Abilene Christ U.

Mathis, Wayne N. Studies of Gymnomyzinae: Diptera: Ephydridae: A Revision of the Genus Glenanthe Haliday from the New World, Pt. 6. LC 94-28014. (Smithsonian Contributions to Zoology Ser.: Vol. 567). 30p. 1994. reprint ed. pap. 30.00 (*0-7837-8868-1*, 204957900001) Bks Demand.

— Studies of Gymnomyzinae: Diptera: Ephydridae, IV: A Revision of the Shore-Fly Genus Hecamede Haliday, Pt. 5. LC 91-14038. (Smithsonian Contributions to Zoology Ser.: No. 541). (Illus.). 50p. reprint ed. pap. 30.00 (*0-7837-5896-0*, 204568700007) Bks Demand.

— Studies of Parydrinae: Diptera: Ephydridae: Revision of the Shore Fly Genus Pelinoides Cresson, Pt. 2. LC 84-600299. (Smithsonian Contributions to Zoology Ser.: No. 410). 51p. reprint ed. pap. 30.00 (*0-608-14522-X*, 202535600043) Bks Demand.

Mathis, Wayne N. & Ghorpade, Kumar D. Studies of Parydrinae: Diptera: Ephydridae: A Review of the Genus Brachydeutere Loew from the Oriental, Australian & Oceanian Regions, Pt. 1. LC 84-600345. (Smithsonian Contributions to Zoology Ser.: No. 406). 29p. reprint ed. pap. 30.00 (*0-608-14455-X*, 202504300041) Bks Demand.

Mathis, Wayne N. & Munari, Lorenzo. A World Catalog of the Family Tethinidae: Diptera. LC 96-32911. (Smithsonian Contributions to Zoology Ser.: No. 584). (Illus.). 33p. 1996. reprint ed. pap. 30.00 (*0-608-04255-2*, 206501000012) Bks Demand.

Mathis, Wayne N. & Zatwarnicki, Tadeusz. A World Catalog of Shore Files (Diptera - Ephydridae) Gupta, Virendra K., ed. LC 95-79418. (Memoirs on Entomology, International Ser.: Vol. 4). 430p. 1995. 60.00 (*1-56665-059-3*) Assoc Pubs FL.

Mathis, Wayne N., et al. Studies of Gymnomyzinae: A Revision of the Shore-Fly Genus Mosillus Latreille, Pt. 5. LC 93-24454. (Smithsonian Contributions to Zoology Ser.: No. 548). 42p. reprint ed. pap. 30.00 (*0-7837-6416-2*, 204639600012) Bks Demand.

Mathis, Wayne N., jt. auth. see Baptista, Alessandra R.

Mathis, Wayne N., jt. auth. see Freidberg, Amnon.

Mathis, William J., ed. Field Guide to Educational Renewal. (Illus.). 348p. (Orig.). (C). 1994. pap. text 15.00 (*0-9627232-5-8*) Psychology Pr.

Mathis, William R. Mustang Performance Handbook. LC 94-18029. 224p. (Orig.). 1994. pap. 17.95 (*1-55788-193-6*, HP Books) Berkley Pub.

— Mustang Performance Handbook 2: Chassis & Suspension Modifications for Street, Strip, & Road Racing Use for All Models of the Ford Mustand, 1979 to Present, No. 2. LC 94-24719. (Illus.). 188p. (Orig.). 1995. pap. 17.95 (*1-55788-202-9*, HP Books) Berkley Pub.

Mathisen. People, Personal Expression & Social Relations in Late Antiquity: Text from Gaul & Western Europe, Vol. 1. (Illus.). (C). text. write for info. (*0-472-10771-2*) U of Mich Pr.

— People, Personal Expression & Social Relations in Late Antiquity: Texts from Gaul & Western Europe, Vol. 2. (Illus.). (C). text. write for info. (*0-472-10772-0*) U of Mich Pr.

Mathisen, Carl W. My Trusty Indian Guide: And Other Alaskan Tales. 256p. (Orig.). 1992. pap. 12.95 (*1-882756-00-2*) Alaska Eagle.

Mathisen, Carolyn. U. S. Social Policy Shareholder Resolutions: Including Voting Practices of Institutional Investors. 71p. (Orig.). 1996. pap. 50.00 (*1-879775-37-9*) IRRC Inc DC.

Mathisen, James A., jt. auth. see Ladd, Tony.

Mathisen, James I. CareerMAX! Career Planning Workbook. (Illus.). 228p. 1998. wbk. ed. 69.95 (*0-9668338-2-1*) CareerMax.

— CareerMAX! Your Guide to Total Career Development. (Illus.). 149p. 1998. wbk. ed. 69.95 (*0-9668338-1-3*) CareerMax.

Mathisen, Marilyn. Apparel & Accessories. Lynch, Richard L., ed. (Career Competencies in Marketing Ser.). (Illus.). 1979. text 12.04 (*0-07-040905-6*) McGraw.

Mathisen, Ralph. Ruricius of Limoges & Friends: A Collection of Letters from Visigoth Gaul. (Translated Text for Historians Ser.). (Illus.). 272p. 1998. pap. 19.95 (*0-85323-703-4*, Pub. by Liverpool Univ Pr) U of Pa Pr.

Mathisen, Ralph W. Ecclesiastical Factionalism & Religious Controversy in Fifth-Century Gaul. LC 88-18922. 367p. 1989. reprint ed. pap. 113.80 (*0-7837-9194-1*, 204989500004) Bks Demand.

— Roman Aristocrats in Barbarian Gaul: Strategies for Survival in an Age of Transition. LC 92-22725. (Illus.). 293p. 1993. text 35.00 (*0-292-77051-0*) U of Tex Pr.

Mathisen, Ralph W. & Sivan, Hagith, eds. Shifting Frontiers in Late Antiquity. 400p. 1996. 95.95 (*0-86078-588-2*, Pub. by Variorum) Ashgate Pub Co.

Mathisen, Robert R. The Role of Religion in American Life: An Interpretive Historical Anthology. 2nd ed. 368p. (Orig.). (C). 1996. per. 41.95 (*0-8403-9367-9*) Kendall-Hunt.

Mathisen, Robert R. The Role of Religion in American Life: An Interpretive Historical Anthology. 3rd ed. 418p. (Orig.). (C). per. 48.95 (*0-7872-6618-3*) Kendall-Hunt.

Mathison, Dirk. The Book of Good Habits: Simple & Creative Ways to Enrich Your Life. LC 97-18710. 224p. (Orig.). 1997. pap. 9.95 (*0-9639946-6-2*, 46-6-2) Snta Monica.

Mathison, George. Winning Thoughts: For Any Season . . . of Life. (Illus.). 192p. 1997. pap. 12.95 (*0-9649877-1-6*) Auburn Netwrk.

Mathison, Keith A. Dispensationalism: Rightly Dividing the People of God? 176p. (Orig.). 1995. pap. 9.99 (*0-87552-359-5*) P & R Pubng.

— Postmillennialism: An Eschatology of Hope; An Eschatology of Hope. LC 98-55539. 1999. pap. 14.99 (*0-87552-389-7*) P & R Pubng.

Mathison, Ruby L. Synthetic Fuels Research: A Bibliography. 4th ed. 218p. 1980. pap. 15.00 (*0-318-12717-2*, H01980) Am Gas Assn.

Mathison, Sheila R., ed. see Whippel, Frank W.

***Mathison, Vicki.** Dog Works: The Meaning & Magic of Canine Constructions. (Illus.). 96p. 2000. pap. 16.95 (*1-58008-244-0*) Ten Speed Pr.

Mathiu, Joe & Siede, George. On the Go. LC 97-196617. (Illus.). 1997. write for info. (*0-7853-2225-6*) Pubns Intl Ltd.

*** Mathlouthi, M.** Food Packaging & Preservation. 292p. 1998. 159.00 (*0-8342-1349-4*) Aspen Pub.

Mathmann, Jakob M., jt. auth. see Kobel, Fritz X.

Mathmann, Jakob M., jt. auth. see Zobel, Fritz X.

Mathog, Robert H. Atlas of Cranifacial Trauma. 1991. text 147.00 (*0-7216-3204-1*, W B Saunders Co) Harcrt Hlth Sci Grp.

Mathog, Robert H., et al. Trauma of the Nose & Paranasal Sinuses. Levine, Howard, ed. LC 94-26571. (Rhinology & Sinusology Ser.). (Illus.). 184p. 1994. 75.00 (*0-86577-526-5*) Thieme Med Pubs.

Mathosian, Mark. First Byte: Taking the Mystery Out of Buying a Personal Computer. (Illus.). 16p. pap. 2.95 (*0-9631924-2-6*) Inkwell Pubs.

— Prime Time Computing: A Seniors Guide to Home Computing. (Illus.). 164p. 1993. lib. bdg. 14.95 (*0-9631924-1-8*) Inkwell Pubs.

— Up & Running with Your Personal Computer: A Beginner's Guide to Buying, Using & Enjoying an IBM or Compatible Personal Computer. (Illus.). 168p. 1992. pap. 16.95 (*0-9631924-0-X*) Inkwell Pubs.

Mathot, Vincent B., ed. Calorimetry & Thermal Analysis of Polymers. LC 93-48558. 369p. 1994. 99.50 (*1-56990-126-0*) Hanser-Gardner.

Mathpal, Yashodhar. Rock Art in Kumaon Himalaya. LC 96-901530. (Illus.). xxii, 92p. (C). 1995. 68.00 (*81-7305-057-0*, Pub. by Aryan Bks Intl) Nataraj Bks.

Mathre, D. E., ed. Compendium of Barley Diseases. 2nd rev. ed. LC 97-75001. 120p. 1997. pap. 42.00 (*0-89054-180-9*) Am Phytopathol Soc.

Mathre, Mary L., ed. Cannabis in Medical Practice: A Legal, Historical & Pharmacological Overview of the Therapeutic Use of Marijuana. LC 97-10944. 247p. 1997. pap. 29.95 (*0-7864-0361-6*) McFarland & Co.

Mathsoft, Incorporated Staff. The Essential Roark's. 1996. pap. text 59.95 (*0-942075-61-7*) McGraw.

Mathson, Patricia. Give Thanks & Praise: Children's Liturgies & Celebrations for Sundays, Weekdays & Saints Days. LC 97-154974. (Illus.). 208p. (J). 1997. pap. 12.95 (*0-87793-605-6*) Ave Maria.

— Seasons of Celebrations: Prayers, Plays & Projects for the Church Year. LC 95-77475. (Illus.). 168p. (J). (ps-10). 1995. pap., teacher ed. 9.95 (*0-87793-566-1*) Ave Maria.

***Mathson, Patricia L.** Bundles of Faith & Tons of Fun: Easy Activities, Prayers & Projects for Children. LC 00-8521. (Illus.). 112p. 2000. pap., teacher ed. 12.95 (*0-87793-942-X*) Ave Maria.

Mathuna, Seamus M. & Corrain, Ailbhe O., eds. Miscellanea Celtica in Memoriam Henrich Wagner. LC 98-116831. (Acta Universitatis Upsaliensis Studia Celtica Upsaliensia: No. 2). (Illus.). 366p. 1997. 67.50 (*91-554-3951-9*, Pub. by Almqvist Wiksell) Coronet Bks.

***Mathur.** Marvels of Kishangarh Paintings: From the Collection of the National Museum, New Delhi. 2000. 140.00 (*81-86050-43-4*, Pub. by Bharat Vidya) S Asia.

Mathur, A. P. Commentaries on Gambling Acts in India. 513p. 1973. 110.00 (*0-7855-1374-4*) St Mut.

— Commentaries on Motor Vehicles Act. 9th ed. (C). 1990. 400.00 (*0-7855-5107-7*) St Mut.

— Commentaries on Motor Vehicles Act, 2 vols., Set. 2000p. 1982. 720.00 (*0-7855-1373-6*) St Mut.

— Commentaries on Prevention of Corruption Act, 1947. 699p. 1981. 240.00 (*0-7855-1372-8*) St Mut.

— Commentaries on Prevention of Corruption Act, 1947: With Supplement of New Act. 3rd rev. ed. (C). 1990. 80.00 (*0-7855-5608-7*) St Mut.

— Law Relating to Motor Vehicles. (C). 1990. text 400.00 (*0-89771-498-9*) St Mut.

— Law Relating to Motor Vehicles. 9th ed. (C). 1993. 225.00 (*81-7012-416-6*, Pub. by Eastern Book) St Mut.

— Prevention of Food Adulteration Act. 838p. 1983. 320.00 (*0-7855-1289-6*) St Mut.

— Prevention of Food Adulteration Act, 1954. (C). 1990. 125.00 (*0-7855-5338-X*) St Mut.

— Prevention of Food Adulteration Act, 1989, with Supplement. 9th ed. (C). 1990. text 225.00 (*0-7855-6596-5*) St Mut.

Mathur, A. P., ed. Commentaries on Gambling Acts in India, 1973: With Supplement. 2nd rev. ed. (C). 1990. 65.00 (*0-7855-5551-X*) St Mut.

— Commentaries on Prevention of Corruption Act, 1947. 3rd ed. (C). 1981. 130.00 (*0-7855-4701-0*) St Mut.

Mathur, A. P., rev. Prevention of Food Adulteration Act, 1989, with Supplement. 9th rev. ed. (C). 1990. 225.00 (*0-7855-5557-9*) St Mut.

Mathur, Ajeet N. Labour Institutions & Economic Development: A Study of Nepal. 1997. pap. 25.00 (*0-7855-7429-8*, Pub. by Ratna Pustak Bhandar) St Mut.

***Mathur, Ambika.** Miss Panda in Great Britain. (Miss Panda Ser.). (Illus.). 40p. (J). (ps-5). 2000. pap. 10.00 (*1-883573-01-7*, Little Blue) Pride & Imprints.

Mathur, Anurag, jt. ed. see Suraiya, Jug.

Mathur, Ashok. Once upon an Elephant. LC 99-166689. 1999. pap. 13.95 (*1-55152-058-3*) Arsenal Pulp.

Mathur, B. B. Women & Depressed Caste Population in India. (C). 1994. text 32.00 (*81-85613-79-6*, Pub. by Chugh Pubns) S Asia.

***Mathur, Brij M., ed.** Public Health Policy & Administration. 1998. 38.00 (*81-7169-510-8*, Pub. by Commonwealth) S Asia.

Mathur, D., ed. Physics of Ion Impact Phenomena. (Chemical Physics Ser.: Vol. 54). (Illus.). 304p. 1991. 79.95 (*0-387-53429-6*) Spr-Verlag.

Mathur, D. C. Contract Labour in India. (C). 1989. 105.00 (*0-7855-4769-X*) St Mut.

— Naturalistic Philosophies of Experience: Studies in James, Dewey & Farber Against the Background of Husserl's Phenomenology. LC 79-117613. 192p. 1971. 12.00 (*0-87527-052-2*) Green.

Mathur, Deepa. Women, Family & Work. (C). 1992. 18.00 (*81-7033-147-1*, Pub. by Rawat Pubns) S Asia.

***Mathur, Dinesh S.** Predictive Astrology: An Insight. LC 99-932617. 435p. 1999. pap. 100.00 (*81-208-1627-7*, Pub. by Motilal Banarsidass) St Mut.

Mathur, G. Economic Justice in a Free Society. 1994. write for info. (*81-224-0604-1*, Pub. by Wiley Estrn) Franklin.

Mathur, G. C. Commentaries on Prevention of Food Adulteration Act, 1954. 1995. 95.00 (*0-7855-2844-X*, Pub. by Eastern Book) St Mut.

— Conveyancing, Precedents & Forms. 1995. pap. 35.00 (*81-7012-189-2*, Pub. by Eastern Book) St Mut.

— Government Servants: Appointment, Promotion & Disciplinary Actions. 1995. 125.00 (*81-7012-420-4*, Pub. by Eastern Book) St Mut.

— Law of Land Acquisition & Compensation. 1995. 195.00 (*81-7012-571-5*, Pub. by Eastern Book) St Mut.

— Low-Cost Housing in Developing Countries. (C). 1993. 24.00 (*81-204-0774-1*, Pub. by Oxford IBH) S Asia.

Mathur, G. C., ed. Government Servants: Appointment, Promotion & Disciplinary Actions. (C). 1990. 205.00 (*0-7855-6695-3*); 205.00 (*0-7855-5426-2*) St Mut.

Mathur, G. C., rev. Prevention of Food Adulteration Act. 9th rev. ed. (C). 1989. 225.00 (*0-7855-5108-5*) St Mut.

Mathur, G. C., ed. see Singh, S. D.

Mathur, H. C. Patanjali's Model of Human Mind. 345p. 1987. 59.95 (*81-7071-065-0*) Asia Bk Corp.

Mathur, Hari M. Anthropology & Development in Traditional Societies. (C). 1995. 28.00 (*0-7069-8857-4*, Pub. by Vikas) S Asia.

— Improving Agricultural Administration. (C). 1989. 14.00 (*81-204-0392-4*, Pub. by Oxford IBH) S Asia.

Mathur, Hari M., ed. Development, Displacement & Resettlement: Focus on Asian Experiences. LC 94-907543. (C). 1995. 29.00 (*0-7069-8858-2*, Pub. by Vikas) S Asia.

Mathur, Hari M., ed. Family Welfare Programme in India. 1995. 29.50 (*0-7069-9854-5*, Pub. by Vikas) S Asia.

Mathur, Hari M. & Marsden, David, eds. Development Projects & Impoverishment Risks: Resettling Project-Affected People in India. LC 98-907626. 312p. 1998. text 27.00 (*0-19-564469-7*) OUP.

Mathur, Ike. Personal Finance. (Thomson Executive Press). (C). 1983. pap. 40.00 (*0-538-06010-7*, F01) S-W Pub.

Mathur, Ike, ed. Financial Management in Post-1992 Europe. LC 93-3802. (Journal of Multinational Financial Management: Vol. 2, Nos. 3-4). (Illus.). 219p. 1993. lib. bdg. 6.95 (*1-56024-439-9*) Haworth Pr.

Mathur, Ike & Jai-Sheng, Chen. Strategies for Joint Ventures in the People's Republic of China. LC 87-7033. 204p. 1987. 57.95 (*0-275-92354-1*, C2354, Praeger Pubs) Greenwood.

Mathur, Ike, jt. ed. see Doukas, John.

Mathur, Indu & Sharma, Sanjay, eds. Health Hazards, Gender, & Society. (C). 1995. 22.50 (*81-7033-239-7*, Pub. by Rawat Pubns) S Asia.

Mathur, Justice G. Amin & Sastri's Law of Easements. rev. ed. 839p. 1984. 360.00 (*0-7855-1420-1*) St Mut.

— Government Servants: Appointment, Promotion & Disciplinary Actions. (C). 1990. text 200.00 (*0-89771-500-4*) St Mut.

Mathur, K. M. Administration of Police Training in India. (C). 1987. 58.50 (*81-212-0100-4*, Pub. by Gian Publng Hse) S Asia.

Mathur-Kamat, Ambika. Miss Panda in Australia. (Illus.). 16p. (J). (gr. k-2). 1998. pap. 8.00 (*0-8059-4316-1*) Dorrance.

— Miss Panda in China. (Miss Panda Ser.). (Illus.). 40p. (J). (ps-5). 2000. pap. 10.00 (*1-886383-98-7*, Little Blue) Pride & Imprints.

— Miss Panda in Egypt. (Miss Panda Ser.). (Illus.). 40p. (J). (ps-5). 2000. pap. 10.00 (*1-886383-99-5*, Little Blue) Pride & Imprints.

Mathur, Kamlesh, jt. auth. see Salkin, Harvey.

Mathur, Krishna M. Crime, Human Rights & National Security. LC 96-905171. 399p. 1996. 46.00 (*81-212-0516-6*, Pub. by Gyan Publishing Hse) Nataraj Bks.

— Indian Police: Role & Challenges. 1994. 32.00 (*81-212-0460-7*, Pub. by Gian Publng Hse) S Asia.

— Police, Law & Internal Security. (C). 1994. 32.00 (*81-212-0455-0*, Pub. by Gian Publng Hse) S Asia.

Mathur, Kuldeep, ed. Development Policy & Administration. LC 96-28725. (Readings in Indian Government & Politics: Vol. 1). 276p. 1996. 38.00 (*0-8039-9340-4*) Sage.

Mathur, Kuldeep & Jayal, Niraja G. Drought, Policy & Politics in India: The Need for a Long-Term Perspective. (Illus.). 140p. (C). 1993. text 26.00 (*0-8039-9122-3*) Sage.

Mathur, L. P. Indian Revolutionary Movement in the U. S. A. 1970. text 20.00 (*0-685-14077-6*) Coronet Bks.

An Asterisk (*) at the beginning of an entry indicates that the title is appearing for the first time.

Mathur, Lalit M. Tree Plantation & Environment Awareness. (Illus.). xvi, 443p. 1993. 59.00 (81-7024-489-7, Pub. by Ashish Pub Hse) Nataraj Bks.
Mathur, M. V. & Arora, R. K. Indian University System: Revitalization & Reform. (C). 1994. 34.00 (81-224-0602-5, Pub. by Wiley Estrn) Franklin.
Mathur, P. C. Government & Politics in South Asia, 22 vols., Set. (C). 1985. 390.00 (0-7855-4748-7) St Mut.
— Water & Land Management in Arid Ecology: Policy & Socio-Scientific Perspectives on Soil-Crop-Water Synergy. 1991. 34.00 (81-7033-126-9, Pub. by Rawat Pubns) S Asia.
Mathur, P. C., jt. auth. see Jha, Shree N.
Mathur, P. C., jt. auth. see Narain, Iqbal.
Mathur, P. C., jt. ed. see Mehra, R. M.
Mathur, P. L. Role of Governor in Non-Congress States. (C). 1988. 32.00 (81-7033-050-5, Pub. by Rawat Pubns) S Asia.
Mathur, P. N., jt. ed. see Bolliger, C. T.
Mathur, Paul. Take Me There: Oasis, the Story. LC 97-30593. 1997. pap. 17.95 (0-87951-853-7, Pub. by Overlook Pr) Penguin Putnam.
Mathur, Praveen N., jt. auth. see Colt, Henri.
Mathur, Praveen N., jt. ed. see Beamis, John F., Jr.
Mathur, Pushpa R. Costumes of the Rulers of Mewar: With Patterns & Construction Techniques. (C). 1994. text 82.00 (81-7017-293-4, Pub. by Abhinav) S Asia.
Mathur, R., ed. Latest Advances in Environmental Conservation - A Publication of Forum for Environmental Protection. 1998. pap. 150.00 (81-7233-175-4, Pub. by Scientifc Pubs) St Mut.
Mathur, R. Mohan & Varma, Rajiv K. Static Controllers for Electrical Transmission Systems. 500p. 2001. 69.95 (0-7803-3412-4, PC5683-QOE) Inst Electrical.
Mathur, R. N. Quality of Working Life of Women Construction Workers. 1989. 26.50 (81-7169-000-9, Pub. by Commonwealth) S Asia.
Mathur, S. B. American Fiction: The Technique of Point of View. (Orig.). 1979. pap. 3.95 (0-89684-087-5, Pub. by Arnold-Heinemann Pubs) Humanities.
Mathur, Sharad C., jt. auth. see Henry, John H.
Mathur, Shiv S. Creating Value: Shaping Tommorrow's Business. 468p. 1998. pap. text 38.95 (0-7506-3954-7) Buttrwrth-Heinemann.
— Creating Value: Shaping Tomorrow's Business. LC 97-158690. 432p. 1997. text 59.95 (0-7506-3339-5) Buttrwrth-Heinemann.
Mathur, Suman. Art & Culture under the Kusanas. LC 98-900600. 1998. 68.00 (81-86050-09-4, Pub. by B K Prakashan) S Asia.
Mathur, Y. B. The Growth Muslim Politics in India. 296p. 1979. 25.95 (0-318-36575-8) Asia Bk Corp.
Mathureshwar das. Devotion at Home. 32p. (Orig.). 1988. pap. 2.00 (0-931889-08-1) Epistemology Pubs.
***Mathurin, D. Emerson.** Soccer Linesmanship: An Instructional Manual for the Assistant Refree. (Illus.). 92p. 1999. pap. 12.95 (1-890946-13-3) Reedswain.
Mathurin, Owen C. Henry Sylvester Williams & the Origins of the Pan-African Movement, 1869-1911, 21. LC 75-35348. (Contributions in Afro-American & African Studies: No. 21). 183p. 1976. 29.95 (0-8371-8594-7, MHW/, Greenwood Pr) Greenwood.
Mathus, S. Liddel, ed. The Greater Key of Solomon: Including a Clear & Precise Explanation of King Solomon's Secret. (Illus.). 148p. 1998. reprint ed. pap. 9.95 (1-881316-67-X) A&B Bks.
Mathus-Vliegen, Lisabeth M. The Role of Laser in Gastroenterology: Analysis of Eight Years' Experience. (Developments in Gastroenterology Ser.). (C). 1989. text 191.50 (0-7923-0425-X) Kluwer Academic.
Mathy, Francis, tr. see Endo, Shusaku.
Mathy, Jean-Philippe. Extreme-Occident: French Intellectuals & America. LC 93-16456. 324p. (C). 1993. lib. bdg. 54.00 (0-226-51063-8) U Ch Pr.
— Extreme-Occident: French Intellectuals & America. LC 93-16456. 324p. (C). 2000. pap. 16.95 (0-226-51064-6) U Ch Pr.
***Mathy, Jean-Philippe.** French Resistance: The French-American Culture Wars. LC 99-57336. (Illus.). 2000. pap. write for info. (0-8166-3443-2) U of Minn Pr.
Mathy, P., ed. Air Pollution & Ecosystems. (C). 1987. text 405.50 (90-277-2611-6) Kluwer Academic.
Mathy, Robin M., jt. auth. see Whitman, Frederick L.
Mathys, H. P. Liebe Deinen Nachsten Wie Dich Selbst: Untersuchungen zum Alttestamentlichen Gebot der Nachstenliebe (Lev 19, 18) 2nd ed. (Orbis Biblicus et Orientalis Ser.). (GER.). 1990. text 45.00 (3-7278-0357-6, Pub. by Presses Univ Fribourg) Eisenbrauns.
Mathys, Hans-Peter. Dichter und Beter: Theologen Aus Spataltestamentlicher Zeit. (Orbis Biblicus et Orientalis Ser.: Vol. 132). (GER.). 374p. 1994. text 77.00 (3-7278-0931-0, Pub. by Presses Univ Fribourg) Eisenbrauns.
Mathys, Nicholas J., jt. auth. see Burack, Elmer H.
Mathys, Robert, Sr., ed. Isoelastic Hip Prosthesis: Manual of Surgical & Operative Techniques. LC 92-1481. (Illus.). 110p. 1992. pap. text 56.00 (0-88937-094-X) Hogrefe & Huber Pubs.
Mati, J. K. Contemporary Issues in Maternal Health Care in Africa. 118p. 1995. pap. text 27.00 (3 7186 5561-6) Gordon & Breach.
Mati, J. K., et al. Contemporary Issues in Maternal Health Care in Africa. 448p. 1995. text 132.00 (3-7186-5560-8, Harwood Acad Pubs) Gordon & Breach.
Matias, David. Fifth Season. LC 99-199895. 135p. 1998. 35.00 (0-944854-38-9); pap. 10.00 (0-944854-37-0) Provincetown Arts.
Matias, Manuel. Las Chilenas. LC 91-73140. 128p. 1991. 13.00 (0-89729-611-7) Ediciones.
Matias, Manuel, tr. see Triester, Kenneth.
Matiasz, George A. End Time: Notes on the Apocalypse. (Illus.). 320p. 1996. pap. 10.00 (1-873176-24-4, AK Pr San Fran) AK Pr Dist.
Matiasz, George Z. How to Survive on per Diem. 1974. pap. 1.00 (0-686-11777-8) Matiasz.
Matibag, Eugenio. Afro-Cuban Religious Experience: Cultural Reflections in Narrative. LC 95-46559. (Illus.). 352p. (C). 1996. 49.95 (0-8130-1431-X) U Press Fla.
Matich, Olga. Paradox in the Religious Poetry of Zinaida Gippius. bds. 40.00 (3-7705-0653-7) Adlers Foreign Bks.
Matick, Richard E. Transmission Lines for Digital & Communications Networks: An Introduction to Transmission Lines, High-Frequency, & High-Speed Pulse Characteristics & Applications. LC 94-32639. 392p. 1994. 69.95 (0-7803-1121-3, PC4853) Inst Electrical.
— Transmission Lines for Digital & Communications Networks: An Introduction to Transmission Lines, High-Frequency & High-Speed Pulse Characteristics & Applications. LC 68-30561. 382p. reprint ed. pap. 108.90 (0-608-18559-0, 2052038) Bks Demand.
Matiella, Ana C. Cultural Pride Curriculum Unit. (Latino Family Life Education Curriculum Ser.). 182p. (Orig.). 1988. pap., teacher ed. 29.95 (0-941816-67-2) ETR Assocs.
— Cultural Pride Student Workbook. (Latino Family Life Education Curriculum Ser.). (Illus.). 96p. (Orig.). (J). (gr. 5-8). 1988. pap. 7.95 (0-941816-68-0) ETR Assocs.
— La Familia Curriculum Unit. (Latino Family Life Education Curriculum Ser.). 188p. (Orig.). 1988. pap., teacher ed. 29.95 (0-941816-69-9) ETR Assocs.
— La Familia Student Workbook. (Latino Family Life Education Curriculum Ser.). (Illus.). 96p. (Orig.). (J). (gr. 5-8). 1988. pap., wbk. ed. 7.95 (0-941816-70-2) ETR Assocs.
— The Multicultural Challenge in Health Education. LC 93-44540. 1994. 34.95 (1-56071-355-0) ETR Assocs.
Matiella, Ana C., tr. see Stewart, Deborah D.
Matieu, Kristen & Publications International, Ltd. Editorial Staff. Lullabies, 1 Vol. LC 98-193914. (Baby Looney Tunes Song Bks.). (Illus.). (J). 1998. write for info. (0-7853-2672-3) Pubns Intl Ltd.
Matignon, Jeanne, jt. auth. see Montreynaud, Florence.
Matijasevich, Yuri. Hilbert's Tenth Problem. (Foundations of Computing Ser.). (Illus.). 288p. 1993. 45.00 (0-262-13295-8) MIT Pr.
Matijevic, Egon, ed. Surface & Colloid Science, Vol. 12. LC 67-29459. 484p. 1982. 115.00 (0-306-40616-0, Plenum Trade) Perseus Pubng.
— Surface & Colloid Science, Vol. 14. LC 67-29459. (Illus.). 404p. (C). 1987. text 138.00 (0-306-42421-5, Kluwer Plenum) Kluwer Academic.
Matijevic, Egon & Good, Robert J., eds. Surface & Colloid Science, Vol. 13. 288p. 1984. 95.00 (0-306-41322-1, Plenum Trade) Perseus Pubng.
Matijevich, Elke. The Zeitroman of the Late Weimar Republic, Vol. 77. (Studies in Modern German Literature). VIII, 198p. (C). 1995. text 45.95 (0-8204-2751-9) P Lang Pubng.
Matik, Wendy-o. Love Like Rage. 64p. (Orig.). 1994. pap. 7.00 (0-916397-31-9) Manic D Pr.
Matilal, Bimal K. Language & Reality: An Introduction to Indian Philosophical Studies. 450p. 1986. 31.00 (0-317-53529-3, Pub. by Motilal Bnarsidass) S Asia.
— Logic, Language & Reality: An Introduction to Indian Philosophical Studies. 447p. 1985. 29.50 (81-208-0008-7, Pub. by Motilal Bnarsidass) S Asia.
— Navya-Nyaya Doctrine of Negation: The Semantics & Ontology of Negative Statements in Navya-Navya Pgilosophy. LC 67-27088. (Oriental Ser.: No. 46). (Illus.). 219p. 1968. 15.00 (0-674-60650-7) HUP.
Matilal, Bimal K. Perception: An Essay on Classical Indian Theories of Knowledge. 454p. 1992. reprint ed. pap. text 39.95 (0-19-823976-9) OUP.
Matilal, Bimal K. Philosophy of Indian Languages: India's Contribution to the Study of Language. 198p. 1991. text 24.95 (0-19-562515-3) OUP.
Matilal, Bimal K., ed. Knowing from Words: Western & Indian Philosophical Analysis of Understanding & Testimony. LC 93-1731. (Synthese Library). 396p. (C). 1994. lib. bdg. 236.00 (0-7923-2345-9, Pub. by Kluwer Academic) Kluwer Academic.
— Moral Dilemmas in the Mahabharata. (C). 1989. 18.00 (81-208-0603-4, Pub. by Motilal Bnarsidass) S Asia.
Matilal, Bimal K. & Shaw, Jaysankar L., eds. Analytical Philosophy in Comparative Perspective. (Synthese Library: No. 178). 415p. 1984. text 179.50 (90-277-1870-9, D Reidel) Kluwer Academic.
Matilal, Bimal K., et al. The Character of Logic in India. Ganeri, Jonardon & Tiwari, Heeraman, eds. LC 97-19873. (SUNY Series in Indian Thought). 180p. (C). 1998. text 59.50 (0-7914-3739-6); pap. text 19.95 (0-7914-3740-X) State U NY Pr.
***Matilal, Bimal Krishna.** The Character of Logic in India. Ganeri, Jonardon & Tiwari, Heeraman, eds. (Illus.). 192p. 2000. text 12.95 (0-19-564896-X) OUP.
Matilal, Bimal Krishna, jt. ed. see Evans.
Matilda, Martin, ed. see Jacobson, Paul.
Matile, P. The Lytic Compartment of Plant Cells. LC 75-5931. (Cell Biology Monographs: Vol. 1). (Illus.). xiii, 183p. 1975. 87.95 (0-387-81296-2) Spr-Verlag.
Matilla Rivas, Alfredo, ed. see Pietri, Pedro.
Matilla Rivas, Alfredo, tr. & prologue by see Pietri, Pedro.
Matilsky, Barbara. The Spirit of Place: Art, Environment, Community. LC 98-73647. (Illus.). 20p. 1998. pap. 8.00 (0-9653805-1-3) Ackland Art Mus.
Matilsky, Barbara C. The Expressionist Surface: Contemporary Art in Plaster. (Illus.). 48p. 1990. pap. text 9.25 (0-9604514-2-0) Queens Mus.
Matimore, P. Henry. Heroes of God's Church. (Illus.). 286p. (YA). (gr. 5-8). Date not set. reprint ed. text 19.00 (0-911845-44-5) Neumann Pr.
Matin, Abdul. Muslims in India & Abroad: Caste & Ethnicity. (C). 1996. 26.00 (81-7024-755-1, Pub. by Ashish Pub Hse) S Asia.
Matin, Abdul, jt. ed. see Mohammad, Noor.
Matin-asgari, Afshin. Iranian Student Opposition to the Shah Mohammad Reza Pahlavi. LC 99-35107. (Illus.). 314p. 1999. 35.00 (1-56859-079-2) Mazda Pubs.
Matinko-Wald, Ruth A., ed. Three Decades of Exploration: Homage to Leo Castelli. LC 87-62753. 16p. (Orig.). 1987. pap. write for info. (0-942461-02-9) Mus Art Fl.
Matinko-Wald, Ruth A., ed. see Jones, Arthur F.
Matinko-Wald, Ruth A., ed. see Larsen, Susan C.
Matinko-Wald, Ruth A., ed. see Van der Marck, Jan.
***Matinuddin, Kamal.** Taliban Phenomenon: Afghanistan (1994-1997) LC 99-203425. (Illus.). 306p. 1999. text 28.00 (0-19-577903-7) OUP.
— The Taliban Phenomenon: Afghanistan 1994-1997. (Illus.). 315p. 2000. pap. 16.95 (0-19-579274-2) OUP.
Matinuddin, Kamal, jt. ed. see Rose, Leo E.
Matis, Catherine S. & Fleming, Mary K. Breakfast in Bed: Health-Smart Recipes for Muffins, Cakes, & Breads. LC 96-216393. (Illus.). 128p. 1996. pap. 12.95 (1-57427-055-9) Howell Pr VA.
Matis, Dave & Toole, Jobe H. Paint Contractor's Manual. LC 84-29315. (Illus.). 224p. 1985. pap. 26.00 (0-910460-46-9) Craftsman.
Matis, Gretchen, ed. see Hilliard, Cheryl.
Matis, Herbert, ed. The Economic Development of Austria since 1870. (Economic Development of Modern Europe since 1870 Ser.: Vol. 4). (Illus.). 624p. 1994. 265.00 (1-85278-719-8) E Elgar.
Matis, J. H., et al, eds. Compartmental Analysis of Ecosystem Models. (Statistical Ecology Ser.: Vol. 10). 1979. 45.00 (0-89974-007-3) Intl Co-Op.
***Matis, J. H. & Kiffe, T. R.** Stochastic Population Models: A Compartmental Perspective. (Lecture Notes in Statistics Ser.: Vol. 145). (Illus.). 216p. (C). 2000. pap. text 49.95 (0-387-98657-X) Spr-Verlag.
Matis, K. A. Flotation Science & Engineering. (Illus.). 584p. 1994. text 210.00 (0-8247-9264-5) Dekker.
Matis, K. A., jt. auth. see Gallios, G. P.
Matis, K. A., jt. ed. see Mavros, P.
Matisoff, Barnard S. The Handbook of Electronic Manufacturing. 3rd ed. (Electrical Engineering Ser.). 1992. write for info. (0-442-01334-5, VNR) Wiley.
Matisoff, Bernard S., et al. Surface Mount Technology: The Handbook of Materials & Methods. (Illus.). 448p. 1989. 48.50 (0-8306-3130-5, 3130) McGraw-Hill Prof.
Matisoff, James A. The Dictionary of Lahu. (Publications in Linguistics: Vol. III). 1989. 125.00 (0-520-09711-4, Pub. by U CA Pr) Cal Prin Full Svc.
Matisoff, James A., ed. Languages & Dialects of Tibeto-Burman. (STEDT Monograph Ser.: Vol. 2). 180p. 1996. pap. text 20.00 (0-944613-26-8) UC Berkeley Ctrs SE Asia.
Matisoff, James A., ed. see LaPolla, Randy J. & Lowe, John B.
Matison, Jim & Hess, Karen. Cashing in on Consulting for Private Security Professionals. 160p. 1997. 19.95 (1-889373-03-6, PTR10) Prof Trning.
Matison, Sumner, jt. ed. see Wiedeman, George H.
Matisse, Henri. Drawings: Themes & Variations. LC 94-40925.Tr. of Dessins, Themes et Variations. (Illus.). 168p. 1995. pap. text 12.95 (0-486-28520-0) Dover.
***Matisse, Henri.** Henri Matisse: Femmes et fleurs. (Illus.). 192p. 2000. 60.00 (3-87909-566-3, Pub. by Wienand) Nazraeli Press.
Matisse, Henri. Jazz. Hawkes, Sophie, tr. from FRE. LC 83-11934. (Illus.). 176p. 1983. pap. 29.50 (0-8076-1131-X) Braziller.
— Matisse. 1998. 1.00 (0-486-40394-7) Dover.
***Matisse, Henri.** Matisse: Jazz. (Pegasus Library). (Illus.). 136p. 2000. 25.00 (3-7913-2392-X) Prestel Pub NY.
— Matisse Cut-Outs Postcard Book. (Illus.). 1995. pap. 5.99 (3-8228-9443-5) Benedikt Taschen.
Matisse, Henri. Matisse Line Drawings & Prints. (Fine Art Ser.). (Illus.). 48p. 1980. pap. 3.95 (0-486-23877-6) Dover.
— Matisse on Art. Flam, Jack D., ed. & intro. by. (Documents of Twentieth-Century Art Ser.). (Illus.). 300p. 1995. pap. 18.95 (0-520-20032-2, Pub. by U CA Pr) Cal Prin Full Svc.
— Matisse on Art. rev. ed. Flam, Jack D., ed. & intro. by. (Documents of Twentieth-Century Art Ser.). (Illus.). 300p. 1995. 35.00 (0-520-20037-3, Pub. by U CA Pr) Cal Prin Full Svc.
— Portrait Drawings: Forty-Five Plates. (Illus.). 48p. 1990. pap. 4.95 (0-486-26438-6) Dover.
Matisse, Henri & Castleman, Riva. Jazz. Hawkes, Sophie, tr. (Illus.). 96p. 1992. 14.95 (0-8076-1291-X) Braziller.
Matisse, Paul, ed. & tr. see Duchamp, Marcel.
Matissek, R., jt. ed. see Wittkowski, R.
Mativo, Kyalo. Amenta. LC 95-115241. 1994. pap. 14.00 (0-9642831-1-5) Amenta Bk.
— Kiongozi: A Teacher's Guide to Africa: Basic Information about Africa for Elementary Schools. (Kiongozi: Introducing a Continent Ser.: Vol. 1). (Illus.). 120p. (Orig.). (J). (gr. 4-12). 1997. pap. 7.95 (0-9642831-0-7) Amenta Bk.
Matiyasevich, Y. V., jt. ed. see Nerode, Anil.
Matje, Martin. Celeste: A Day in the Park. LC 98-21628. (Illus.). 40p. (J). (ps-2). 1999. 12.00 (0-689-82100-X) S&S Childrens.
Matjevic, E. Surface & Colloid Science, Vol. 15. (Illus.). 288p. (C). 1992. text 105.00 (0-306-44150-0, Kluwer Plenum) Kluwer Academic.
Matkin, Craig. An Observer's Guide to the Whales of Prince William Sound. (Illus.). 112p. (Orig.). 1994. pap. 12.95 (1-877900-03-6) Prince W Sound.
Matkin, Craig, et al. Killer Whales of Southern Alaska. (Illus.). 96p. 1999. pap. 14.95 (0-9633467-9-2) N Gulf Oceanic.
***Matkin, Gary W.** Technology Transfer 7 the University. LC 00-44177. (American Council on Education). 2000. write for info. (1-57356-471-0) Oryx Pr.
Matkin, Gary W. Using Financial Information in Continuing Education: Accepted Methods & New Approaches. LC 96-36577. 334p. 1997. boxed set 39.95 (0-89774-941-3) Oryx Pr.
Matkin, James G. Principled Bargaining. LC 86-156970. 11 p. 1986. write for info. (0-88886-128-1) Que8ens U Indus Relat.
Matkin, Noel, jt. ed. see Roush, Jackson.
Matkin, R. E., jt. auth. see Riggar, T. F.
Matkin, Ralph E. Insurance Rehabilitation: Service Applications in Disability Compensation Systems. LC 85-593. 360p. 1985. pap. text 34.00 (0-936104-55-4, 1279) PRO-ED.
Matkin, Ralph E. & Riggar, T. F. Persist & Publish: Helpful Hints for Academic Writing & Publishing. (Illus.). 176p. (Orig.). 1991. pap. text 17.50 (0-87081-227-0) Univ Pr Colo.
Matkov, Rebecca R., jt. auth. see O'Brien, Dawn.
Matkovic, V., jt. auth. see Sch Onau, Eckhardshop.
Matkovics, B., et al. Radicals, Ions & Tissue Damage. (Illus.). 323p. (C). 1990. 39.00 (963-05-5879-3, Pub. by Akade Kiado) Intl Spec Bk.
Matla, Ihor, jt. auth. see Bisset, William P.
Matlack, Lucius C. History of American Slavery & Methodism from 1780 to 1849. LC 77-138342. (Black Heritage Library Collection). 1977. 31.95 (0-8369-8734-9) Ayer.
— Life of Rev. Orange Scott. LC 70-138343. (Black Heritage Library Collection). 1977. 30.95 (0-8369-8735-7) Ayer.
Matlak, Raymond E. Samuel Taylor Coleridge Revisited. 1996. 23.95 (0-8057-7064-X, Twyne) Mac Lib Ref.
Matlak, Richard. The Poetry of Relationship: The Wordsworths & Coleridge, 1797-1800. LC 96-48921. 244p. 1997. text 39.95 (0-312-10166-X) St Martin.
Matlak, Richard E., ed. Approaches to Teaching Coleridge's Poetry & Prose. LC 91-21906. (Approaches to Teaching World Literature Ser.: No. 38). x, 185p. 1991. pap. 18.00 (0-87352-700-3, AP38P); lib. bdg. 37.50 (0-87352-549-3, AP38C) Modern Lang.
Matlak, Richard E., jt. auth. see Mellor, Anne K.
Matlary. Energy Policy in the European Union. LC 96-47729. 208p. 1997. text 55.00 (0-312-17295-8) St Martin.
Matlaw, Myron. American Popular Entertainment: Paper & Proceedings of the Conference on the History of American Popular Entertainment, 1. LC 78-74655. (Contributions in Drama & Theatre Studies: No. 1). (Illus.). 338p. 1979. 35.00 (0-313-21072-1, MEN/) Greenwood.
— Nineteenth Century American Plays. 272p. Date not set. 22.95 (0-8488-2367-2) Amereon Ltd.
Matlaw, Myron, ed. Nineteenth-Century American Plays. rev. ed. Orig. Title: Black Crook & Other 19th Century American Plays. 262p. 1988. reprint ed. 24.95 (1-55783-017-7); reprint ed. pap. 14.95 (1-55783-018-5) Applause Theatre Bk Pubs.
Matlaw, Ralph E., ed. see Chekhov, Anton.
Matlaw, Ralph E., ed. see Dostoyevsky, Fyodor.
Matlaw, Ralph E., tr. see Odoevski, I. V.
Matlay, J., jt. auth. see Sharp & Matlay Staff.
Matless, David. Landscape & Englishness. (Picturing History Ser.). (Illus.). 304p. 1998. 45.00 (1-86189-022-2, Pub. by Reaktion Bks) Consort Bk Sales.
Matley, Ian M. The Geography of International Tourism. (C). 1987. text 30.00 (81-85046-56-5, Pub. by Scientific Pubs) St Mut.
Matley, John F., jt. auth. see Fowler, Don D.
Matlick, Len. B.S.Ing: The Secrets of Success in the Business World. 120p. 1987. pap. 14.00 (0-87364-428-X) Paladin Pr.
Matlick, Richard. Metaphoresis: Do We Know What We Are Talking About? 224p. 1999. pap. 11.95 (1-893162-01-X) Erica Hse.
Matlin. Introduction to Psychology. 2nd ed. (C). 1994. student ed. 100.00 (0-15-503095-7) Harcourt.
— Psychology. 2nd ed. (C). 1994. pap. text, teacher ed. 35.00 incl. VHS (0-15-502107-9) Harcourt Coll Pubs.
— Psychology. 3rd ed. (C). 1998. pap. text, teacher ed. 26.75 (0-15-508401-1) Harcourt Coll Pubs.
— The Psychology of Women. 3rd ed. (C). 1996. pap. text, teacher ed. 42.00 (0-15-503301-8) Harcourt Coll Pubs.
— The Psychology of Women. 4th ed. (C). Date not set. pap. write for info. (0-15-507896-8) Harcourt Coll Pubs.
— Psycology. 3rd ed. (C). 1998. pap. text, student ed. 25.00 (0-15-508400-3, Pub. by Harcourt Coll Pubs) Harcourt.
Matlin, David. China Beach. (Orig.). 1998. pap. 10.95 (1-886449-76-7, P9767, Pub. by Barrytown Ltd) Consort Bk Sales.
— Dressed in Protective Fashion. (Illus.). 96p. (Orig.). 1990. pap. 8.00 (0-9626046-0-7) OtherWind Pr.
***Matlin, David.** A Halfman Dreamer. (Poetry New York Pamphlet Ser.: No. 16). 16p. 1999. pap. 5.00 (0-923389-27-X) Meet Eyes Bind.
Matlin, David. How the Night Is Divided: A Novel. LC 93-12587. 201p. 1993. 20.00 (0-929701-33-X) McPherson & Co.
***Matlin, David.** Vernooykill Creek: The Crisis of Prisons in America. (Illus.). 115p. 1998. pap. 15.00 (1-879691-47-7) SDSU Press.
***Matlin, Eric.** The Procrastinator's Guide to Wills & Estates. 2001. pap. 12.95 (1-57071-617-X) Sourcebks.

M

Matlin, Margaret W. Cognition. 4th ed. LC 96-79969. 594p. (C). 1997. text 74.00 (0-15-504081-2, Pub. by Harcourt Coll Pubs) Harcourt.
— Psychology. 2nd ed. (C). 1994. pap. text, student ed. 25.00 (0-15-502108-7) Harcourt Coll Pubs.
— Psychology. 3rd ed. LC 98-71493. (C). 1998. text 77.50 (0-15-505495-3, Pub. by Harcourt Coll Pubs) Harcourt.
— Psychology: Test Bank. 2nd ed. (C). 1994. pap. text 41.50 (0-15-502109-5, Pub. by Harcourt Coll Pubs) Harcourt.
— The Psychology of Women. 3rd ed. LC 95-79405. (C). 1996. text 46.00 (0-15-503008-6, Pub. by Harcourt Coll Pubs) Harcourt.
— Sensation & Perception. 2nd ed. 550p. (C). 1988. pap. text 49.33 (0-205-11125-4, H11257) Allyn.
— Sensation & Perception. 3rd ed. LC 91-26132. 533p. 1992. 55.00 (0-205-13519-6) Allyn.
— Sensation & Perception. 4th ed. LC 96-38560. 554p. 1996. 88.00 (0-205-26382-8) Allyn.

Matlin, Myna L., jt. auth. see Wortman, Bob.

Matlin, Myna L., jt. ed. see Su Pinnell, Gay.

Matlin, Samuel, jt. auth. see Neimark, Paul.

***Matlins, Antoinette L.** Gems & Jewelry at Auction: The Definitive Buying & Selling Guide at the Auction House or on the Internet. 200p. 2000. pap. 19.95 (0-943763-29-0) GemStone Pr.
— Pearl Book: The Definite Buying Guide: How to Select, Buy, Care for & Enjoy Pearls. 2nd ed. LC 99-55463. 2000. pap. text 19.95 (0-943763-28-2) GemStone Pr.

Matlins, Antoinette L. & Bonanno, Antonio C. Gem Identification Made Easy: A Hands-on Guide to More Confident Buying & Selling. LC 89-1611. (Illus.). 296p. 1989. 29.95 (0-943763-03-7) GemStone Pr.
— Gem Identification Made Easy: A Hands-on Guide to More Confident Buying & Selling. 2nd rev. ed. LC 97-25444. 344p. 1997. 34.95 (0-943763-16-9) GemStone Pr.
— Jewelry & Gems, the Buying Guide: How to Buy Diamonds, Pearls, Colored Gemstones, Gold & Jewelry with Confidence & Knowledge. 4th rev. ed. LC 98-34996. (Illus.). 304p. 1998. 24.95 (0-943763-19-3) GemStone Pr.

Matlins, Antoinette L., et al. Engagement & Wedding Rings: The Definitive Buying Guide for People in Love. LC 89-77334. (Illus.). 304p. 1990. pap. 14.95 (0-943763-05-3) GemStone Pr.
— Engagement & Wedding Rings: The Definitive Buying Guide for People in Love. 2nd rev. ed. LC 98-47788. (Illus.). 304p. 1999. pap. 16.95 (0-943763-20-7) GemStone Pr.

Matlins, Antoinette Leonard & Bonanno, Antonio C. Jewelry & Gems, the Buying Guide: How to Buy Diamonds, Pearls, Colored Gemstones, Gold & Jewelry with Confidence & Knowledge. 4th rev. ed. LC 98-34996. (Illus.). 261p. 1998. pap. 17.95 (0-943763-22-3) GemStone Pr.

***Matlins, Stuart M.** The Jewish Lights Spirituality Handbook: A Guide to Understanding, Exploring & Living a Spiritual Life. 2000. 24.95 (1-58023-100-4) Jewish Lights.

***Matlins, Stuart M., ed.** The Jewish Lights Spirituality Handbook: A Guide to Understanding, Exploring & Living a Spiritual Life. 2000. pap. 16.95 (1-58023-093-8) Jewish Lights.
— The Perfect STranger's Guide to Funerals & Grieving Practices: A Guide to Etiquette in Other People's Religious Ceremonies. 2000. pap. 16.95 (1-893361-20-9) SkyLight Paths.
— The Perfect Stranger's Guide to Wedding Ceremonies: A Guide to Etiquette in Other People's Religious Ceremonies. 2000. pap. 16.95 (1-893361-19-5) SkyLight Paths.

Matlins, Stuart M. & Magida, Arthur J., eds. How to Be a Perfect Stranger Vol. 2: A Guide to Etiquette in Other People's Religious Ceremonies. LC 95-37474. 416p. 1996. 24.95 (1-879045-63-X) Jewish Lights.

Matlins, Stuart M., jt. ed. see Magida, Arthur J.

Matlis, Eben. Cotorsion Modules. LC QA0003.A57. (Memoirs of the American Mathematical Society Ser.: No. 49). 74p. reprint ed. pap. 30.00 (0-7837-1633-8, 204192600024) Bks Demand.
— Torsion-Free Modules. (Chicago Lectures in Mathematics). 174p. (C). 1973. pap. text 15.00 (0-226-51074-3) U Ch Pr.

Matlock-Abdullah, Arriama, ed. see Olusegun, Ayobumi.

Matlock, Bill J., jt. auth. see Schell, Frank R.

***Matlock, C. Marshall.** 21st Edition: The Best of Newspaper Design. (SPA & ENG., Illus.). 256p. 2000. text 35.00 (1-878107-12-7) Soc News Design.

Matlock, C. Marshall, ed. The Best of Newspaper Design. 14th ed. (ENG & SPA., Illus.). 256p. (Orig.). 1992. pap. 35.00 (1-878107-03-8) Soc News Design.
— The Best of Newspaper Design. 17th ed. (Illus.). 256p. (Orig.). 1996. pap. 45.00 (1-878107-06-2) Soc News Design.
— The Best of Newspaper Design. 19th ed. (ENG & SPA., Illus.). 272p. (Orig.). 1998. pap. 45.00 (1-878107-09-7) Soc News Design.
— The Best of Newspaper Design, 18. 18th ed. (ENG & SPA., Illus.). 256p. (Orig.). 1997. 45.00 (1-878107-07-0) Soc News Design.

Matlock, Curtiss Ann. Annie in the Morning. (Here Come the Grooms Ser.: No. 31). 1996. per. 3.99 (0-373-30131-6, 1-30131-6) Harlequin Bks.
— The Forever Rose. (Men at Work Ser.: Vol. 20). 1998. mass mkt. 4.50 (0-373-81032-6, 1-81032-4) Harlequin Bks.
— Heaven in Texas. (Winner's Circle Ser.). 1996. per. 3.99 (0-373-60075-5, 1-60075-8) Harlequin Bks.
— If Wishes Were Horses. 384p. 1998. mass mkt. 5.99 (0-380-79344-X, Avon Bks) Morrow Avon.
— Last Chance Cafe, Bk. 36. (Born in the U. S. A. Ser.). 1997. per. 4.50 (0-373-47186-6, 1-47186-1) Harlequin Bks.
— Lost Highways. 1999. mass mkt. 5.99 (1-55166-499-2, 1-66499-4, Mira Bks) Harlequin Bks.
— Love in a Small Town. 1997. mass mkt. 5.99 (0-380-78107-7, Avon Bks) Morrow Avon.
— Loves of Ruby Dee. 1996. mass mkt. 5.99 (0-380-78106-9, Avon Bks) Morrow Avon.
— Miracle on I-40. rev. ed. (Illus.). 126p. 1999. pap. 11.95 (0-9654499-2-0, Madeira Bks) Windows on Hist.
— More Than a Mother. 1992. per. 4.99 (0-373-48239-6, 5-48239-3) Harlequin Bks.
— A Time & a Season. (Men Made in America Ser.). 1995. per. 3.99 (0-373-45186-5, 1-45186-3) Harlequin Bks.
— A Time to Keep. 1994. per. 3.59 (0-373-45166-0) Harlequin Bks.
— True Blue Hearts. 1993. per. 3.39 (0-373-09805-7, 5-09805-8) Silhouette.
— White Gold. LC 95-7110. (Historical Ser.). 354p. 1995. per. 3.99 (0-373-28851-4, 1-28851-3) Harlequin Bks.

***Matlock, Curtiss Ann.** Driving Lessons. 448p. 2000. mass mkt. 5.99 (1-55166-599-9, 1-66599-1, Mira Bks) Harlequin Bks.

Matlock, David. Russiawalks. 286p. 1995. pap. 12.95 (0-8050-1204-4, Owl) H Holt & Co.

Matlock, David K., ed. see Minerals, Metals & Materials Society Staff.

Matlock, Gary, jt. auth. see Duke, Philip.

Matlock, Gary, jt. ed. see Duke, Philip.

Matlock, Gene D. Jesus & Moses Are Buried in India. (Illus.). 100p. (Orig.). 1991. pap. 8.00 (0-9627739-0-5) Geo-Mind Pubns.

Matlock, Jann. Scenes of Seduction: Prostitution, Hysteria, & Reading Difference in Nineteenth-Century France. LC 93-13966. 422p. 1994. 69.50 (0-231-07206-6); pap. 22.00 (0-231-07207-4) Col U Pr.

Matlock, Mark. Avoiding Stupidity: The Art & Science of Decision-Making. (Wise Guides Ser.). 48p. (YA). 1998. pap. 5.95 (1-888237-20-1) Baxter Pr.
— Have a Friend - Be a Friend: Wisdom on Friendship. (Wise Guides Ser.). 48p. (YA). 1998. pap. 5.95 (1-888237-21-X) Baxter Pr.
— Truth Puzzlers. (Wise Guides Ser.). 48p. (YA). 1998. pap. 5.95 (1-888237-22-8) Baxter Pr.

Matlock, Matthew. Inside New York, 1999: The Ultimate Guidebook. (Illus.). 368p. 1998. pap. 16.95 (1-892768-00-3) Inside NY.

Matlock, R. Barry. Unveiling the Apocalyptic Paul: Paul's Interpreters & the Rhetoric of Criticism. LC 96-131834. (Journal for the Study of the New Testament, Supplement Ser.: No. 127). 361p. 1996. 85.00 (1-85075-590-6, Pub. by Sheffield Acad) CUP Services.

Matlock, W. G. Realistic Planning for Arid Lands: Natural Resource Limitations to Agricultural Development, Vol. 2. (Advances in Desert & Arid Land Technology & Development Ser.). iv, 262p. 1981. text 235.00 (3-7186-0051-X) Gordon & Breach.

Matloff, Gregory L. Telescope Power: Fantastic Activities & Easy Projects for Young Astronomers. LC 92-39602. 128p. (Orig.). 1993. pap. 12.95 (0-471-58039-2) Wiley.
— The Urban Astronomer: A Practical Guide to Celestial Objects for Observers in Cities & Suburbs. LC 91-9316. (Science Editions Ser.: No. 1800). 224p. 1991. 39.95 (0-471-53142-1); pap. 16.95 (0-471-53143-X) Wiley.

Matloff, Gregory L., jt. auth. see Mallove, Eugene F.

Matloff, Jack, jt. auth. see Denton, Timothy.

Matloff, Jack M., ed. Cardiac Valve Replacement: Current Status. 1985. text 160.50 (0-89838-722-1) Kluwer Academic.

Matloff, Maurice. United States Army in World War 2, War Department, Strategic Planning for Coalition Warfare, 1943- 1944. 660p. 1959. boxed set 23.00 (0-16-061290-X) USGPO.

Matloff, Maurice, ed. American Military History Vol. 1: 1775-1902. (Illus.). 752p. 1996. 29.95 (0-938289-72-1) Combined Pub.
— American Military History Vol. 1: 1775-1902, 1, 1. (Illus.). 752p. 1996. pap. 17.95 (0-938289-70-5, 289705) Combined Pub.
— American Military History Vol. 2: 1902-1985, 2, 2. (Illus.). 384p. 1996. 29.95 (0-938289-73-X, 28973X); pap. 17.95 (0-938289-71-3, 289713) Combined Pub.
— World War I: Concise Military Histories of America's Major Wars. (Illus.). 1979. 7.95 (0-679-51450-3) McKay.

Matloff, Norman S. IBM Microcomputer Architecture & Assembly: A Look Under the Hood. 416p. 1991. 47.20 (0-13-451998-1) P-H.

Matlon, Ronald J. Opening Statements & Closing Arguments. LC 92-34211. (Trial Consultant Handbook Ser.: Vol. 1). 1992. 25.00 (0-9624181-2-9) Stuart Allen.

Matlon, Ronald J. & Ortiz, Sylvia P., eds. Index to Journals in Communication Studies Through 1995. 692p. (C). 1997. pap. text 80.00 (0-944811-21-3, 111) Natl Comm Assn.

Matluck, C. Marshall. The Best of Newspaper Design. 20th ed. (ENG & SPA., Illus.). 272p. 1999. pap. 45.00 (1-878107-10-0) Soc News Design.

Matney, Roy M., II & Roth, C. H., Jr. Parallel Computing Structures & Algorithms for Logic Design Problems. LC 72-133318. 124p. 1969. 19.00 (0-403-04518-5) Scholarly.

Mato, Jose M. Phospholipid Metabolism in Cellular Signaling. 160p. 1990. lib. bdg. 142.00 (0-8493-5978-3, QP752) CRC Pr.

Mato, Tataya. The Black Madonna Within: Drawings, Dreams, Reflections. LC 94-5690. (Dreamcatchers Ser.: Vol. 1). 216p. 1994. 44.95 (0-8126-9248-9); pap. 18.95 (0-8126-9249-7) Open Court.

Matocha, Linda & Sussman, Marvin B., eds. Publishing in Journals on the Family: Essays on Publishing. LC 93-9424. (Marriage & Family Review Ser.: Vol. 18, Nos. 1-2). (Illus.). 272p. 1993. lib. bdg. 49.95 (1-56024-341-4) Haworth Pr.

Matochik, Michael J., ed. The Civil War, 1861-1865, Pt. 1. (Bibliographic Guide to the Microfiche Collection Ser.). ix, 144p. reprint ed. 40.00 (0-8357-0719-9) Univ Microfilms.

***Matocq, Lisa M., ed.** Truth & Consequences of the Genetic Revolution: Human Genetic Research, April 8, 1966 Informational Hearing, California Select committee on Genetics & Public Policy. 103p. (C). 2000. reprint ed. pap. text 25.00 (0-7881-8879-8) DIANE Pub.

***Matocq, Lisa M. & Gibson, Rachel, eds.** Truth & Consequences of the Genetic Revolution: Animal Pharm : Old MacDonald Had a Lab. 131p. 2000. pap. text 25.00 (0-7881-8877-1) DIANE Pub.
— Truth & Consequences of the Genetic Revolution: DNA on Trial. 91p. 2000. pap. text 20.00 (0-7881-8878-X) DIANE Pub.

Matoesian, Gregory M. Reproducing Rape: Domination Through Talk in the Courtroom. LC 92-40155. (Language & Legal Discourse Ser.). viii, 264p. 1993. pap. text 15.95 (0-226-51080-8); lib. bdg. 40.00 (0-226-51079-4) U Ch Pr.

Matolcsi, Tamas. Concept of Mathematical Physics: Models in Mechanics. 336p. (C). 1986. 250.00 (0-569-09012-1, Pub. by Collets) St Mut.
— A Concept of Mathematical Physics Models for Space-Time. 236p. (C). 1984. 95.00 (963-05-3245-X, Pub. by Akade Kiado) St Mut.
— A Concept of Mathematical Physics: Models for Space-Time. 236p. 1984. 210.00 (0-569-08814-3, Pub. by Collets) St Mut.
— A Concept of Mathematical Physics Models in Mechanics: Models in Mechanics. 335p. (C). 1986. 130.00 (963-05-3627-7, Pub. by Akade Kiado) St Mut.
— Spacetime Without Reference Frames. (Illus.). 411p. (C). 1993. pap. 129.00 (963-05-6433-5, Pub. by Akade Kiado) St Mut.

Matolcsy, G., et al, eds. Pesticide Chemistry. (Studies in Environmental Science: No. 32). 800p. 1989. 401.25 (0-444-98903-X) Elsevier.

Matomors, Clemencia, jt. auth. see Horemis, George.

Maton, A., et al. Housing of Animals: Construction & Equipment of Animal Houses. (Developments in Agricultural Engineering Ser.: No. 8). 458p. 1985. 211.25 (0-444-42528-4) Elsevier.

Maton, Michael. National Honours & Awards of Australia. (Illus.). 136p. 1995. 42.50 (0-86417-679-1, Pub. by Kangaroo Pr) Seven Hills Bk.

Maton, Paul N., jt. auth. see Decker, John L.

Matoni, Charles J. I Call You Friend: Dialogues with Jesus. 143p. (Orig.). 1995. pap. 9.95 (1-883520-08-8) Jeremiah Pr.

Matoni, Charles J. & Matos, Paul C. California Decedent Estate Practice: May 1994 Update, Vol. 3. Tom, Janette, ed. LC 86-70193. 582p. 1994. 42.00 (0-88124-751-0, ES-30866) Cont Ed Bar-CA.

Matonis, A. T. & Melia, Daniel F., eds. Celtic Language - Celtic Culture: A Festschrift for Eric P. Hamp. xix, 415p. 1990. 45.00 (0-926689-01-0) Ford & Bailie Pubs.

Mator, Carlos A. El Narrador Picaro: Guzman de Alfarache. vi, 132p. 1985. 12.50 (0-942260-51-1) Hispanic Seminary.

Matore, Georges. Dictionnaire du Vocabulaire Essentiel. 6th ed.Tr. of Dictionary of Essential Vocabulary. (FRE.). 360p. 1980. pap. 23.95 (0-8288-1945-9, M6652) Fr & Eur.

Matore, Georges, ed. see Gautier, Theophile.

Matoren, Gary M. The Clinical Research Process in the Pharmaceutical Industry. (Drugs & the Pharmaceutical Sciences Ser.: Vol. 19). (Illus.). 576p. 1983. text 165.00 (0-8247-1914-X) Dekker.

Matory, W. Earle, ed. Ethnic Considerations in Facial Aesthetic Surgery. LC 97-22014. (Illus.). 400p. 1997. text 194.00 (0-7817-0292-5) Lppncott W & W.

***Matos, Candi & Matos, Chris.** Pants with Pockets: And Other Tips on Managing an ADD/ADHD Child. 2nd ed. Crews, Ethel Maxam & Richter, Patricia, eds. (SPA.). 138p. 1999. pap. 13.95 (1-891990-02-0) Herbal Way.

Matos, Candi & Matos, Chris. Pants with Pockets & Other Tips on Managing an ADD/ADHD Child. 2nd rev. ed. Crews, Ethel Maxam, ed. (Illus.). x, 200p. 1998. reprint ed. pap. 13.95 (1-891990-00-4, 18891990004) Herbal Way.

Matos, Carlos A. Rodriguez, see Villanueva-Collado, Alfredo & Rodriguez Matos, Carlos A.

Matos, Chris, jt. auth. see Matos, Candi.

Matos, Eduardo, ed. Trabajos Arqueologicos en el Centro de la Ciudad de Mexico. 2nd ed. (SPA.). 584p. 1990. pap. 14.00 (968-6487-42-5, IN021) UPLAAP.

Matos, Gustavo P. Gustavo Pales Matos: Obras. LC 86-7094. 512p. 1986. 15.00 (0-8477-3235-5, 19865) U of PR Pr.

Matos, Libio & Abreu, Ivan. El ABC Del Credito y La Inversion. (SPA.). 480p. 1999. lib. bdg., mass mkt. 19.95 (0-9670951-0-7, Eagle Lithographers) ABC Pubg.

Matos, Maria A. Pinto de, see Pinto de Matos, Maria A.

Matos Paoli, Francisco. El Cerco de Dios. (SPA., Illus.). 157p. 1995. pap. 9.95 (1-881708-09-8) Edcnes Mairena.

Matos-Paoli, Francisco. Hacia el Hondo Vuelo. LC 80-26395. (UPREX, Poesia Ser.: No. 61). (SPA.). 200p. (Orig.). 1983. pap. 3.00 (0-8477-0061-5) U of PR Pr.
— Testigo de la Esperanza. (UPREX, Poesia Ser.: No. 29). 132p. (C). 1975. pap. 1.50 (0-8477-0029-1) U of PR Pr.

Matos, Paul C. California Decedent Estate Practice: 6/96 Update. 3rd ed. Tom, Janette, ed. LC 86-70193. 452p. 1996. ring bd. 51.00 (0-7626-0001-2, ES-30868) Cont Ed Bar-CA.

Matos, Paul C., jt. auth. see Matoni, Charles J.

Matos, Paula C. California Decedent Estate Practice No. 3: June 1995 Update. Tom, Jannette, ed. LC 86-70193. 434p. 1995. ring bd. 46.00 (0-88124-881-9, ES-30867) Cont Ed Bar-CA.
— California Decedent Estate Practice No. 3: March 1992 Update. Dworin, Christopher D., ed. LC 86-70193. 480p. 1992. ring bd. 40.00 (0-88124-469-4, ES-30864) Cont Ed Bar-CA.
— California Decedent Estate Practice Vol. 3: 1987. Dworin, Christopher D., ed. LC 86-70193. 850p. 1987. ring bd. 95.00 (0-88124-157-1, ES-30860) Cont Ed Bar-CA.

***Matos, Paula C.** California Decedent Estate Practice - 5-99 Update, Vol. 3. Tom, Janette, ed. LC 86-70193. 542p. 1999. ring bd. 59.00 (0-7626-0326-7, ES-30862) Cont Ed Bar-CA.
— California Decedent Estate Practice, 5/98 Update, Vol. 3. Tom, Janette, ed. LC 86-70193. 575p. 1998. ring bd. 56.00 (0-7626-0225-2, ES-30861) Cont Ed Bar-CA.
— California Decendent Estate Practice 3. Tom, Janette, ed. LC 86-70193. 414p. 1997. ring bd. 51.00 (0-7626-0109-4, ES-30869) Cont Ed Bar-CA.

Matos, Paula C., jt. auth. see Lee, Richard D.

Matos-Rodriguez, Felix V. & Delgado, Linda C., eds. Puerto Rican Women's History: New Perspectives. LC 98-10750. (Perspectives on Latin America & the Caribbean Ser.). 272p. (C). (gr. 13). 1998. pap. text 27.95 (0-7656-0246-6) M E Sharpe.

Matos-Rodriguez, Felix V. & Delgado, Linda C., eds. Puerto Rican Women's History: New Perspectives. LC 98-10750. (Perspectives on Latin America & the Caribbean Ser.). 272p. (C). (gr. 13). 1998. text 66.95 (0-7656-0245-8) M E Sharpe.

Matossian, Mary K. Food, Weather & History. (Essays in World History Ser.). (C). 1996. text 30.00 (0-8133-1571-9); pap. text 10.95 (0-8133-1572-7) Westview.
— Poisons of the Past: Molds, Epidemics, & History. (Illus.). 208p. (C). 1991. reprint ed. pap. 14.00 (0-300-05121-2) Yale U Pr.
— Shaping World History: Breakthroughs in Ecology, Technology, Science, & Politics. LC 96-29807. (Sources & Studies in World History). 264p. (C). (gr. 13). 1997. 74.95 (0-7656-0061-7) M E Sharpe.

Matossian, Mary K. Shaping World History: Breakthroughs in Ecology, Technology, Science, & Politics. LC 96-29807. (Sources & Studies in World History). 264p. (C). (gr. 13). 1997. pap. 30.95 (0-7656-0062-5) M E Sharpe.

Matossian, Mary K., jt. auth. see Villa, Susie H.

Matossian, Michele. Sams Teach Yourself 3D Studio MAX 2 in 14 Days. LC 98-84317. (Teach Yourself Ser.). 480p. 1998. pap. text 39.99 (0-672-31268-9) Sams.
— 3D Studio MAX Three: Visual QuickStart Guide. (Illus.). 360p. (C). 1999. pap. text 19.95 (0-201-35350-4) Peachpit Pr.

***Matossian, Nouritza.** Black Angel: The Life of Arshile Gorky. (Illus.). 576p. 2000. 40.00 (1-58567-006-5, Pub. by Overlook Pr) Penguin Putnam.

Matossian, Nouritza. Xenakis. 1991. pap. 19.95 (0-912483-35-0) Pro-Am Music.

***Matott, Justin.** Drinking Fountain Joe. (Illus.). 32p. 2000. 16.95 (1-889191-12-4) Clove Publns.
— Independence Days: Still Just Boys & Other Stories. 2000. pap. 18.00 (0-937381-75-6) Brewers Pubns.

Matott, Justin. Lesson's from the Garden - Harvest of Reflections. LC 97-46879. 1998. 19.95 (0-345-42091-8) Ballantine Pub Grp.
— My Garden Visits. LC 96-46792. 1997. 18.00 (0-345-41251-6) Ballantine Pub Grp.
— Ol' Lady Grizelda. LC 99-159840. (Illus.). 36p. (J). (gr. 2-6). 1998. 16.95 (1-889191-09-4) Clove Publns.

***Matott, Justin.** When Did I Meet You Grandma. (Illus.). 32p. 2000. 16.95 (1-889191-11-6) Gulf Pub.

Matousek, Clifford H., jt. auth. see Gray, Al.

Matousek, Jiri. Geometric Discrepancy: An Illustrated Guide. LC 99-15547. (Algorithms & Combinatorics Ser.: Vol. 18). xi, 221p. 1999. 94.00 (3-540-65528-X) Spr-Verlag.

Matousek, Jiri & Nesetril, Jaroslav. Invitation to Discrete Mathematics. LC 98-14008. (Illus.). 432p. 1998. text 79.00 (0-19-850208-7); pap. text 35.00 (0-19-850207-9) OUP.

***Matousek, Mark.** The Boy He Left Behind: A Man's Search for His Lost Father. LC 99-54721. 220p. 2000. 23.95 (1-57322-154-6, Riverhead Books) Putnam Pub Group.

Matousek, Mark. Sex Death Enlightenment: A True Story. 365p. 1997. reprint ed. pap. 12.00 (1-57322-581-9, Riverhd Trade) Berkley Pub.

Matousek, Mark & Harvey, Andrew. Dialogues with a Modern Mystic. (Illus.). 276p. 1994. pap. 12.00 (0-8356-0704-6, Quest) Theos Pub Hse.

Matousek, Vaclav. Flow Mechanism of Sand-Water Mixtures in Pipelines. (Illus.). 254p. 1997. pap. 57.50 (90-407-1602-1, Pub. by Delft U Pr) Coronet Bks.

***Matousek, Vaclav, et al, eds.** Text, Speech & Dialogue: Proceedings of the 2nd International Workshop, TSD'99, Plzen, Czech Republic, September 13-17, 1999. LC 99-47531. (Lecture Notes in Artificial Intelligence Ser.: Vol. 1692). xi, 396p. 1999. pap. 69.00 (3-540-66494-7) Spr-Verlag.

Matov, G. Tales of Tzaddikim: Bereishis. Weinbach, Shaindel, tr. from HEB. (ArtScroll Youth Ser.). (Illus.). 320p. (YA). (gr. 7-12). 1987. 15.99 (0-89906-825-1); pap. 11.99 (0-89906-826-X) Mesorah Pubns.
— Tales of Tzaddikim: Devarim. Weinbach, Shaindel, tr. (ArtScroll Youth Ser.). (Illus.). 320p. (YA). (gr. 7-12). 1988. 15.99 (0-89906-833-2); pap. 11.99 (0-89906-834-0) Mesorah Pubns.
— Tales of Tzaddikim: Sh'emos. Weinbach, Shaindel, tr.

M

An Asterisk (*) at the beginning of an entry indicates that the title is appearing for the first time.

from HEB. (ArtScroll Youth Ser.). (Illus.). 320p. (YA). (gr. 7-12). 1988. 15.99 (*0-89906-827-8*); pap. 11.99 (*0-89906-828-6*) Mesorah Pubns.

— Tales of Tzaddikim. Weinbach, Shaindel, tr. (Illus.). (J). boxed set 84.99 (*0-89906-841-3*, TA6H); pap., boxed set 56.99 (*0-89906-842-1*) Mesorah Pubns.

Matovcik, Gerard. Academic Sportfolio: Excuse Notes Are No Excuse. Pranzo, Donard, ed. (Sports Singles Ser.). (Illus.). (YA). (gr. 9-12). 1989. 50.00 (*0-924086-11-4*) Acad Sportfolio.

Matovich, Richard M. A Concordance to the Collected Poems of Sylvia Plath. LC 85-45126. 623p. 1986. text 20.00 (*0-8240-8664-3*, H618) Garland.

Matovina, Dan. Without You: The Tragic Story of Badfinger. LC 97-75125. (Illus.). 456p. 1997. pap. 19.95 (*0-9657122-1-4*) F Glover Bks.

***Matovina, Dan.** Without You: The Tragic Story of Badfinger. (Illus.). 2000. pap. 29.95 (*0-9657122-2-2*) F Glover Bks.

Matovina, Timothy M. The Alamo Remembered: Tejano Accounts. LC 95-10131. (Illus.). 144p. 1995. pap. 11.95 (*0-292-75186-9*); text 25.00 (*0-292-75185-0*) U of Tex Pr.

— Perspectivas: Hispanic Ministry. Tarango, Yolanda et al, eds. LC 95-8617. 152p. (Orig.). 1995. pap. 12.95 (*1-55612-770-7*) Sheed & Ward WI.

— Tejano Religion & Ethnicity: San Antonio, 1821-1860. 176p. 1995. 24.95 (*0-292-75170-2*) U of Tex Pr.

***Matovina, Timothy M., et al, eds.** Presente! U. S. Latino Catholics from Colonial Origins to the Present. (American Catholic Identities Ser.). 288p. 2000. 50.00 (*1-57075-347-4*) Orbis Bks.

— Presente! U. S. Latino Catholics from Colonial Origins to the Present. (American Catholic Identities Ser.). (Illus.). 288p. 2000. pap. 30.00 (*1-57075-328-8*) Orbis Bks.

Matovina, Timothy M. & Navarro, Jose A. Defending Mexican Valor in Texas: Jose Antonio Navarro's Historical Writings, 1853-1857. McDonald, David R., ed. LC 95-38156. (Illus.). 128p. 1995. pap. 14.95 (*1-880510-32-4*) State House Pr.

Matovina, Timothy M., jt. auth. see Elizondo, Virgilio P.

Matovina, Timothy M., ed. see Elizondo, Virgilio, et al.

Matovina, Timothy M., ed. see Navarro, Jose A.

Matoy, Ray R. Thunderbird Tracks: Early History of the Will Rogers Council Boy Scouts of America. LC 89-63385. (Illus.). 235p. 1991. 14.95 (*0-9615098-5-6*) Prairie Imp.

Matranga, Frances C. I'm Glad I'm Me! Beegle, Shirley, ed. (Happy Day Bks.). (Illus.). 24p. (J). (ps). 1994. reprint ed. pap. 1.99 (*0-7847-0259-4*, 04209) Standard Pub.

Matranga, Petrus, ed. Anecdota Graeca. 799p. 1971. reprint ed. write for info. (*3-487-04163-4*) G Olms Pubs.

Matranga, Victoria K. America at Home: A Celebration of Twentieth-Century Housewares. (Illus.). 208p. 1996. 44.95 (*0-9655487-0-8*) Natl Housewares Mnfctrs.

Matrangelo, Stella, tr. see Coelho, Raquel.

Matras, Christian. Seeing & Remembering. Johnston, George, tr. 48p. 1988. 7.95 (*0-921254-09-1*, Pub. by Penumbra Pr) U of Toronto Pr.

Matras, John L. Mazda RX-7. (Sports Car Color History Ser.). (Illus.). 128p. 1994. pap. 21.95 (*0-87938-938-9*) MBI Pubg.

Matras, Yaron, et al, eds. The Typology & Dialectology of Romani. LC 97-42187. (Current Issues in Linguistic Theory Ser.: Vol. 156). xxxii, 223p. 1997. lib. bdg. 65.00 (*1-55619-872-8*) J Benjamins Pubng Co.

Matras, Yaron & International Conference on Romani Linguistics Sta, eds. Romani in Contact: The History, Structure & Sociology of a Language. LC 95-15437. (Current Issues in Linguistic Theory Ser.: No. 126). xvii, 208p. 1995. lib. bdg. 55.00 (*1-55619-580-X*) J Benjamins Pubng Co.

Matrau, Henry. Letters Home: Henry Matrau of the Iron Brigade. Reid-Green, Marcia M., ed. LC 92-26862. (Illus.). xix, 170p. 1993. text 30.00 (*0-8032-3151-2*) U of Nebr Pr.

— Letters Home: Henry Matrau of the Iron Brigade. Reid-Green, Marcia, ed. LC 92-26862. (Illus.). xix, 170p. 1998. pap. 11.00 (*0-8032-8242-7*, Bison Books) U of Nebr Pr.

Matravers, Derek. Art & Emotion. LC 98-197730. 246p. (C). 1998. text 65.00 (*0-19-823638-7*) OUP.

***Matravers, Matt.** Justice & Punishment: The Rationale of Coercion. 280p. 2000. text 60.00 (*0-19-829573-1*) OUP.

Matravers, Matt, ed. Punishment & Political Theory. 224p. 1998. 50.00 (*1-901362-88-4*, Pub. by Hart Pub) Intl Spec Bk.

***Matray, James.** Japan's Emergence as a Global Power. LC 00-39356. 224p. 2000. 40.00 (*0-313-29972-2*, GR9972, Greenwood Pr) Greenwood.

Matray, James I., ed. Historical Dictionary of the Korean War. LC 90-22833. 662p. 1991. lib. bdg. 89.50 (*0-313-25924-0*, MYK, Greenwood Pr) Greenwood.

Matrazzo, Donna. Corporate Scriptwriting Book. 2nd ed. LC 80-81823. (Illus.). 210p. 1985. reprint ed. pap. 16.95 (*0-932617-07-7*) Communicom.

Matrceta, et al. Invitation to Enlightenment: Letter to the Great King Kani Ska. LC 98-14406. (Tibetan Translation Ser.). 1998. write for info. (*0-89800-299-0*); pap. 25.00 (*0-89800-298-2*) Dharma Pub.

Matre, Nancy A. Van, see Poppe, Carol A. & Van Matre, Nancy A.

Matricardi, Connie. Preschool Puppet Plays. (Illus.). 36p. (Orig.). (J). (gr. k). 1993. pap. 9.95 (*1-884555-00-4*) P Depke Bks.

Matrinelli, Maria C. Al Dente: All the Secrets of Italy's Genuine Home-Style Cooking. 1996. 29.95 (*88-7301-069-5*, Pub. by Gremese Intl) Natl Bk Netwk.

Matrisciana, Patrick. The Clinton Chronicles Book. 320p. 1994. pap. 12.95 (*1-878993-63-1*) Jeremiah Films.

Matriscrana, Patrick & Miller, Dorothy. Dual Citizenship. 76p. (Orig.). 1995. pap. 4.95 (*1-878993-66-6*) Jeremiah Films.

Matrix, Cherie & Feminists Against Censorship Staff, eds. Tales from the Clitoris: A Female Experience of Pornography. 128p. 1996. pap. 10.95 (*1-873176-09-0*, AK Pr San Fran) AK Pr Dist.

Matrone, Gennard, jt. auth. see Beeson, Kenneth C.

Matros, Yu S. Unsteady State Processes in Catalysis. (Illus.). 724p. 1990. 225.00 (*90-6764-127-8*, Pub. by VSP) Coronet Bks.

Matrosov, V. M. Methods of Nonlinear Dynamical Analysis: Lecture Notes. (Soviet & East European Mathematics Ser.). 1993. text 68.00 (*981-02-1112-0*) World Scientific Pub.

Matrullo, Fondano. Exotic Baking: A Culinary Extravaganza. Lafortezza, Angela & Antonio, Fausto, eds. LC 95-83589. (Orig.). 1995. spiral bd. 9.99 (*0-9650334-0-6*) Dirusso Internat.

Matsagouras, George, ed. The American Church & the Ecumenical Patriarch: Governance, Diaspore, Role of Women. 1998. pap. 5.95 (*1-880971-36-4*) Light&Life Pub Co MN.

***Matsakis, Aphrodite.** Emotional Claustrophobia: Getting over Your Fear of Being Engulfed by People/Situation. 140p. 2000. pap. 12.95 (*1-57224-211-6*, Pub. by New Harbinger) Publishers Group.

Matsas, Michael. The Illusion of Safety: The Story of the Greek Jews During the Second World War. LC 98-144547. (Illus.). 448p. 1997. pap. text 25.00 (*0-918618-66-5*) Pella Pub.

***Matsas, Rebecca & Tsacopoulos, Marco.** The Functional Roles of Glial Cells in Health & Disease: Dialogue Between Glia & Neurons. LC 99-42891. (Advances in Experimental Medicine & Biology Ser.). 389p. 1999. pap. write for info. (*0-306-46205-2*, Kluwer Plenum) Kluwer Academic.

Matsch, Charles L., jt. ed. see Goldthwait, R. P.

Matsch, Leander W. & Morgan, J. Derald. Electromagnetic & Electromechanical Machines. 3rd ed. 592p. 1986. text 103.95 (*0-471-60364-3*); pap. text, teacher ed. 10.00 (*0-471-60421-6*) Wiley.

Matschat, Cecile H. Suwannee River: Strange Green Land. lib. bdg. 23.95 (*0-8488-2004-5*) Amereon Ltd.

Matschek, Cheryl A. The Principled Practice: A Comprehensive Guide to the Non-Clinical Aspects of Dentistry. LC 94-47411. 1995. write for info. (*0-943367-05-0*) Princess Pub.

Matscher, Cheryl A. Cooking for Health: Without Meat, Dairy or Refined Sugar. LC 98-31928. 154p. 1998. 19.95 (*0-943367-06-9*) Princess Pub.

***Matscher, Cheryl A.** For the Love of Princess: Surviving the Loss of Your Pet. 2nd rev. ed. 150p. 1999. pap. 14.95 (*0-943367-07-7*) Princess Pub.

***Matschinsky, F. M. & Magnuson, M. A., eds.** Molecular Pathogenesis of MODYs. (Frontiers in Diabetes Ser.: Vol. 15). (Illus.). x, 272p. 2000. 168.00 (*3-8055-6950-5*) S Karger.

***Matschinsky, Wolfgang.** Road Vehicle Suspensions. Baker, Alan, tr. 359p. 2000. 169.00 (*1-86058-202-8*) Prof Eng Pubng.

Matschoss, Conrad. Great Engineers. Hatfield, H. Stafford, tr. LC 70-128278. (Essay Index Reprint Ser.). 1977. 30.95 (*0-8369-1837-1*) Ayer.

Matsdorf, Gary, jt. auth. see Hilderbrand, K. Micheal.

Matseiko, Youri & Miller, Steven E., eds. Safeguarding Ukraine's Security: Dilemmas & Options. (CSIA Studies in International Security: No. 9). (Illus.). 350p. Date not set. 39.95 (*0-262-13310-5*) MIT Pr.

— Safeguarding Ukraine's Security: Dilemmas & Options. (CSIA Studies in International Security: Vol. No. 9). (Illus.). 350p. Date not set. pap. text 17.95 (*0-262-63164-4*) MIT Pr.

Matsell, George W. The Secret Language of Crime. LC 97 60112. 212p. 1997. pap. 12.95 (*0-87243-228-9*) Templegate.

Matsen, Bradford. Faces of Fishing: People, Food & the Sea at the Beginning of the Twenty-First Century. LC 97-36387. (Illus.). 120p. 1998. pap. 19.95 (*1-878244-20-5*, 97509) Monterey Bay Aquarium.

— Fishing up North: Stories of Luck & Loss in Alaskan Seas. LC 97-44588. 224p. 1998. 14.95 (*0-88240-502-0*, Alaska NW Bks) Gr Arts Ctr Pub.

Matsen, Bradford, jt. auth. see Troll, Ray.

Matsen, Bradford, ed. see Caldwell, Francis E.

Matsen, Frederick A., III, et al, eds. The Shoulder: A Balance of Mobility & Stability. LC 93-30015. 653p. 1993. 105.00 (*0-89203-091-7*) Amer Acad Ortho Surg.

Matsen, Fredrick A., III, et al. Practical Evaluation & Management of the Shoulder. LC 93-41664. 1994. text 85.00 (*0-7216-4819-3*, W B Saunders Co) Harcrt Hlth Sci Grp.

Matsen, Herbert S., ed. Alessandro Achillini & His Doctrine of Universals & Transcendentals: A Study in Renaissance Ockhamism. 1975. 45.00 (*0-8387-1221-5*) Fairleigh Dickinson.

Matsen, III, Frederick A., 3rd, jt. auth. see Rockwood, Charles A., Jr.

Matsen, Jonn. Eating Alive: Prevention Thru Good Digestion. (Illus.). 300p. (Orig.). 1991. pap. 19.95 (*0-9693586-0-1*) Gordon Soules Bk.

***Matsen, Jonn, et al.** The Secrets to Great Health: From Your Nine Liver Dwarves. 1999. pap. text 24.95 (*0-9682853-0-9*) Goodwin Bks.

Matsen, Kenneth, jt. auth. see Slocum, Robert.

Matsen, Patricia P., et al, eds. Readings from Classical Rhetoric. LC 89-36897. 400p. (C). 1990. pap. 19.95 (*0-8093-1593-9*) S Ill U Pr.

— Readings from Classical Rhetoric. LC 89-36897. 400p. (C). 1990. 36.95 (*0-8093-1592-0*) S Ill U Pr.

Matsen, Wallace C. Old Is Not A Dirty Word: Aging Observed...aging Experienced, 1. 1998. pap. text 12.50 (*1-881907-27-9*) Two Bytes Pub.

Matsen, William E. The Great War & the American Novel: Versions of Reality & the Writer's Craft in Selected Fiction of the First World War. LC 92-40772. (American University Studies: American Literature: Ser. XXIV, Vol. 48). VIII, 226p. (C). 1993. text 39.95 (*0-8204-2093-X*) P Lang Pubng.

Matshazi, Meshack J. & Tillfors, Christina. A Survey of Workers' Education Activities in Zimbabwe, 1980-1981. (Research Report Ser.: No. 69). 85p. 1983. write for info. (*91-7106-217-3*, Pub. by Nordic Africa) Transaction Pubs.

Matsheru, M. Income Tax Made Simple. 165p. 1991. pap. 20.00 (*0-409-10495-7*, SA, MICHIE) LEXIS Pub.

Matshoba, Mtutuzeli. Call Me Not a Man. (African Classics Ser.). (C). 1995. pap. text 15.73 (*0-582-00242-7*, 76386) Longman.

***Matsik, Brian.** Professional E-Commerce Site Security. 500p. 2000. pap. 59.99 (*1-86100-339-0*) Wrox Pr Inc.

Matske. Government in America. 2nd abr. ed. (C). 1997. text, student ed. 23.33 (*0-673-99659-X*) Addson-Wesley Educ.

***Matsko Hood, Karen Jean.** Icelandic Horse Activity & Coloring Book: Educational Activity & Coloring Book Series. (Icelandic Horse Activity & Coloring Book: 1). 160p. (J). (gr. k-1). 2000. pap. 9.95 (*0-9679368-0-2*) Whsprng Pine.

Matsler, Franklin G. & Hines, Edward R. State Policy Formation in Illinois Higher Education. (Orig.). (C). 1987. pap. text 7.50 (*0-944498-00-0*) ISU Ctr High Educ.

Matsmura, John, et al. Rapid Force Projection Technologies: Assessing the Performance of Advanced Ground Acoustic Sensors. (Illus.). xiv, 68p. 1999. pap. 30.00 (*0-8330-2724-7*, DB-262-A/OSD) Rand Corp.

Matsner Gruenberg, Sidonie. Los Hijos: Enciclopedia Grafica Para Su Crianza y Educacion. 35.00 (*0-8288-7891-9*, S13986) Fr & Eur.

Matson. A New History of Philosophy, Vol. 1. 2nd ed. (C). 1999. text 44.50 (*0-15-507848-8*, Pub. by Harcourt Coll Pubs) Harcourt.

— Social Skills. (Applied Research in Mental Retardation). 1984. pap. 18.25 (*0-08-030959-3*, Pergamon Pr) Elsevier.

Matson, Alex, tr. see Kallas, Aino J.

Matson, Arthur J., ed. see Samp, Ardyce H.

***Matson, Bruce H.** Hermitage Country Club: A History of Its First 100 Years, 1900-2000. LC 99-56161. (Illus.). 2000. write for info. (*1-57864-095-4*) Donning Co.

Matson, Cathy D. Merchants & Empire: Trading in Colonial New York. LC 97-2768. (Early America). (Illus.). 480p. 1997. text 45.00 (*0-8018-5602-7*) Johns Hopkins.

Matson, Cathy D. & Onuf, Peter S. A Union of Interests: Political & Economic Thought in Revolutionary America. LC 89-16749. (American Political Thought Ser.). x, 238p. 1990. 25.00 (*0-7006-0417-0*) U Pr of KS.

Matson, Christopher, jt. auth. see Batchelor, Peter F.

Matson, Clive. Equal in Desire. 1989. pap. 4.50 (*0-914433-43-1*) Man-Root.

— Let the Crazy Child Write! Finding Your Creative Writing Voice. LC 98-21570. 256p. 1998. pap. 14.00 (*1-880032-35-X*) New Wrld Lib.

— On the Inside. LC 82-14621. (Illus.). 70p. (Orig.). 1982. pap. 4.00 (*0-916156-65-6*) Cherry Valley.

Matson, D. L., et al, eds. Spacecraft Exploration of the Outer Solar System. 162p. 1998. pap. 123.50 (*0-08-043463-0*, Pergamon Pr) Elsevier.

Matson, Daniel S. & Fontana, Bernard L., eds. Friar Bringas Reports to the King: Methods of Indoctrination on the Frontier of New Spain, 1796-97. LC 76-11987. 177p. 1977. pap. 11.95 (*0-8165-0524-1*) U of Ariz Pr.

Matson, Daniel S., tr. see Fontana, Bernard L., ed.

Matson, David L. Household Conversion Narratives in Acts: Pattern & Interpretation. LC 96-133148. (JSNT Supplement Ser.: No. 123). 224p. 1996. 65.00 (*1-85075-586-8*, Pub. by Sheffield Acad) CUP Services.

Matson, Donald D., jt. auth. see Shillito, John, Jr.

Matson, Elizabeth & Stotts, Stuart. The Bookcase Ghost: A Storyteller's Collection of Wisconsin Ghost Stories. LC 96-28978. 112p. (Orig.). 1996. pap. 12.95 (*1-883953-16-2*) Midwest Trad.

Matson, Emerson N. Legends of the Great Chiefs. (Illus.). 144p. (YA). (gr. 8-12). 1984. reprint ed. pap. 6.95 (*0-9609940-0-9*) Storypole.

Matson, Emerson N. Storypole Legends: Legends of the Indians of Puget Sound. 2nd ed. Orig. Title: Longhouse Legends. (Illus.). 108p. (YA). (gr. 4-9). 1996. reprint ed. pap. 8.95 (*0-89992-141-8*) Coun India Ed.

Matson, Eva J., ed. see Griffin, Marcus.

Matson, Floyd. Walking Alone & Marching Together: A History of the Organized Blind Movement in the United States, 1940-1990. (Illus.). 1117p. 1990. text 30.00 (*0-9624122-1-X*) Natl Fed Blind.

Matson, Ghastgifvar E. The Middle East in Pictures, 4 Vols. 1980. 192.95 (*0-405-12212-8*, 19456) Ayer.

— The Middle East in Pictures, Vol. 4. 1980. 49.95 (*0-405-18868-4*) Ayer.

Matson, Henrietta. The Mississippi Schoolmaster. LC 72-1511. (Black Heritage Library Collection). 1977. reprint ed. 25.95 (*0-8369-9035-8*) Ayer.

***Matson, Hugo W.** Deep Game. LC 99-64392. 1999. 25.00 (*0-7388-0496-7*); pap. 18.00 (*0-7388-0497-5*) Xlibris Corp.

— Killer's Gift. LC 00-190482. 2000. 25.00 (*0-7388-1758-9*); pap. 18.00 (*0-7388-1759-7*) Xlibris Corp.

Matson, J. L. Handbook of Behavior Modification with the Mentally Retarded. 2nd ed. LC 89-23235. (Applied Clinical Psychology Ser.). (Illus.). 544p. (C). 1990. 100.00 (*0-306-43309-5*, Plenum Trade) Perseus Pubng.

Matson, J. L. Handbook of Treatment Approaches in Childhood Psychopathology. LC 88-19648. (Applied Clinical Psychology Ser.). (Illus.). 612p. (C). 1988. 110.00 (*0-306-42844-X*, Plenum Trade) Perseus Pubng.

Matson, J. L., jt. auth. see Frame, C. L.

Matson, J. V. How to Fail Successfully: A Bold Approach to Meeting Your Goals Through Intelligent Fast Failure. 130p. 1991. pap. text 15.00 (*0-9629789-0-6*) Dynamo Pub.

Matson, Jack V. Effective Expert Witnessing. 2nd ed. LC 94-15811. 224p. 1994. boxed set 75.00 (*1-56670-002-7*) CRC Pr.

— Effective Expert Witnessing. 3rd ed. LC 98-45935. 225p. 1999. 69.95 (*1-56670-340-9*) Lewis Pubs.

— Effective Expert Witnessing: A Handbook for Technical Professionals. (Illus.). 160p. 1990. 61.95 (*0-87371-297-8*, L297) Lewis Pubs.

— Innovate or Die: A Personal Perspective on the Art Innovation. LC 96-70197. (Illus.). 192p. 1996. pap. 16.99 (*0-9654449-0-2*) Paradigm Pr MI.

Matson, Johnny L. Behavior Therapy for Dev. & Physically Disabled. Hersen, Michel & Hasselt, Vincent B., eds. 49.00 (*0-12-343050-X*) Acad Pr.

— Handbook of Hyperactivity in Children. LC 91-2459. 416p. (C). 1993. 85.00 (*0-205-14591-4*, H45917, Longwood Div) Allyn.

— Philosophy & Care of the Mentally Retarded: A Worldwide Status Report. 120p. 1983. pap. 15.25 (*0-08-028093-5*, Pergamon Pr) Elsevier.

Matson, Johnny L., ed. Autism in Children & Adults: Etiology, Assessment & Intervention. 275p. (C). 1994. 46.50 (*0-534-23826-2*) Thomson Learn.

— Psychopathology in the Mentally Retarded. 312p. (C). 1991. write for info. (*0-205-13463-7*) Allyn.

Matson, Johnny L. & Andrasik, Frank, eds. Treatment Issues & Innovations in Mental Retardation. (Applied Clinical Psychology Ser.). 666p. 1983. 95.00 (*0-306-40935-6*, Plenum Trade) Perseus Pubng.

Matson, Johnny L. & Frame, Cynthia L. Psychopathology among Mentally Retarded Children & Adolescents. LC 85-14388. (Developmental Clinical Psychology & Psychiatry Ser.: No. 6). 119p. (Orig.). 1986. reprint ed. pap. 36.90 (*0-608-01463-X*, 205950700001) Bks Demand.

Matson, Johnny L. & Mulick, James A., eds. Handbook of Mental Retardation. (General Psychology Ser.: No. 121). (Illus.). 650p. 1983. 100.00 (*0-08-028060-9*, Pergamon Pr) Elsevier.

Matson, Johnny L., jt. ed. see Barrett, Rowland P.

Matson, Leslie. Meini, The Blasket Nurse: The Blasket Nurse. LC 96-133756. 176p. 1997. pap. 12.95 (*1-85635-133-5*, Pub. by Mercier Pr) Irish Amer Bk.

Matson, Madeline. Food in Missouri: A Cultural Stew. LC 93-50819. (Missouri Heritage Readers Ser.). (Illus.). 168p. (C). 1994. pap. 8.95 (*0-8262-0960-2*) U of Mo Pr.

Matson, Mary K., ed. see Bane, William F.

Matson, Molly, ed. see Guerrier, Edith.

***Matson, N.** The French & Indians of the Illinois River. LC 00-30812. (Shawnee Classics). (Illus.). 2000. write for info. (*0-8093-2364-8*) S Ill U Pr.

Matson, N. Reminiscences of Bureau County, Illinois. (Illus.). 406p. 1993. lib. bdg. 42.00 (*0-8328-3527-7*) Higginson Bk Co.

Matson, Nancy. The Boy Trap. LC 99-16089. (Illus.). 112p. (J). (gr. 3-6). 1999. 14.95 (*0-8126-2663-X*, Pub. by Front St-Cricket Bks) Publishers Group.

Matson, P., ed. Biogenic Trace Gas Emissions. (Methods in Ecology Ser.). (Illus.). 384p. 1995. pap. 55.00 (*0-632-03641-9*) Blackwell Sci.

Matson, R. G. The Origins of Southwestern Agriculture. LC 91-14054. (Illus.). 356p. 1991. 66.00 (*0-8165-1196-9*) U of Ariz Pr.

Matson, R. G. & Coupland, Gary. The Prehistory of the Northwest Coast. (Illus.). 364p. 1994. text 75.00 (*0-12-480260-5*) Acad Pr.

Matson, Robert W. Neutrality & Navicerts: Britain, the United States, & Economic Warfare, 1939-1940. LC 93-43702. (Modern American History Ser.). 216p. 1994. text 65.00 (*0-8153-1651-8*) Garland.

Matson, Robert W., ed. see Paulaharju, Samuli.

Matson, Suzanne. Durable Goods. LC 93-14958. 72p. (Orig.). 1993. pap. 9.95 (*1-882295-00-5*) Alice James Bks.

— The Hunger Moon: A Novel. LC 98-96707. 256p. 1999. pap. 12.00 (*0-345-42553-7*) Ballantine Pub Grp.

— The Hunger Moon: A Novel. LC 96-45286. 252p. 1997. 23.00 (*0-393-04099-2*) Norton.

— Sea Level. LC 90-4952. 72p. (Orig.). 1990. pap. 9.95 (*0-914086-84-7*) Alice James Bks.

***Matson, Suzanne.** A Trick of Nature: A Novel. LC 99-51815. 256p. 2000. 23.95 (*0-393-04854-3*) Norton.

Matson, Theodore A., jt. ed. see Donovan, Michelle R.

Matson, Tim. Earth Ponds: The Country Pond Maker's Guide to Building, Maintenance & Restoration. 2nd rev. ed. LC 90-26957. (Illus.). 160p. 1982. pap. 18.00 (*0-88150-155-7*, Pub. by Countryman) Norton.

— Earth Ponds Sourcebook: The Pond Owner's Manual & Resource Guide. LC 97-10388. (Illus.). 208p. (Orig.). 1997. pap. 18.95 (*0-88150-358-4*, Pub. by Countryman) Norton.

***Matson, Tim.** Round Trip to Deadsville: A Year in the Funeral Underground. 220p. 2000. 22.95 (*1-890132-17-9*) Chelsea Green Pub.

Matson, Wallace I. A New History of Philosophy, Vol. 1. (C). 1997. pap. text 32.50 (*0-15-517661-7*) Harcourt.

— A New History of Philosophy, Vol. 1: Ancient & Medieval. (Illus.). 249p. (C). 1987. pap. text 30.25 (*0-15-565728-3*) Harcourt Coll Pubs.

— A New History of Philosophy, Vol. 2: Modern. (Illus.). 236p. (C). 1987. pap. text 38.50 (*0-15-565729-1*, Pub. by Harcourt Coll Pubs) Harcourt.

M

Matson, Wallace I., jt. auth. see Warren, Thomas B.

Matson, Wayne R., ed. Cosmonautics: A Colorful History: History of Soviet-Russian Space Programs. 212p. 1994. 49.95 (*1-885609-01-9*) Cosmos Books.

Matsoukas, G., jt. auth. see Sfekas, S.

Matsov, Akhmat G. Chechen Grammar. O'Sullivan, Patrick, ed. LC 95-68410. 74p. 1995. 39.00 (*1-881265-23-4*) Dunwoody Pr.

Matsson, L., ed. Nonlinear Cooperative Phenomena in Biological Systems: Proceedings of the Adriatico Research Conference ICTP, Trieste, Italy 19-22 August 1997. LC 98-34936. 350p. 1998. 74.00 (*981-02-3454-6*) World Scientific Pub.

Matsson, Per, et al, eds. Clinical Impact of the Monitoring of Allergic Inflammation. (Illus.). 272p. 1991. text 83.00 (*0-12-480265-6*) Acad Pr.

Matsuba, Kazukiyo. Ando, Architect. 1998. 35.00 (*4-7700-2171-2*, Pub. by Kodansha Intl) Kodansha.

Matsuba, Shoichi, jt. auth. see Tymieniecka, Anna-Teresa.

Matsubara, Tatsuo. Introduction to Water Color Painting, Set. (Easy Start Guide Ser.). (Illus.). 1991. 37.95 (*4-7661-0622-9*, Pub. by Graphic-Sha) Bks Nippan.

Matsubara, Hiroaki. Mastering New Architectural Techniques. (Illus.). 160p. (Orig.). 1996. pap. 49.95 (*4-7661-0820-5*, Pub. by Graphic-Sha) Bks Nippan.

Matsubara, Mitsunori. Pancaratra Samhitas & Early Vaisnava Theology. (C). 1995. 22.50 (*81-208-1221-2*, Pub. by Motilal Bnarsidass) S Asia.

Matsubara, Naoko. In Praise of Trees. (Illus.). 96p. 1994. pap. 14.95 (*0-88962-178-0*) Mosaic.

Matsubara, T., ed. The Structure & Properties of Matter. (Solid-State Sciences Ser.: Vol. 28). (Illus.). 450p. 1982. 89.95 (*0-387-11098-4*) Spr-Verlag.

Matsubara, T. & Kotani, A., eds. Superconductiving in Magnetic & Exotic Materials: Proceedings of the Sixth Taniguchi International Symposium, Kashikojima, Japan, Nov. 14-18, 1983. (Solid-State Sciences Ser.: Vol. 52). (Illus.). 225p. 1984. 59.95 (*0-387-13324-0*) Spr-Verlag.

Matsuda, Fukumatsu, tr. see Tsuda, Sokichi.

***Matsuda, H., ed.** Rotary Blood Pumps: New Developments & Current Applications. (Illus.). 150p. 2000. 64.00 (*4-431-70280-6*) Spr-Verlag.

Matsuda, Kazuo, jt. ed. see Sandford, Paul A.

Matsuda, Mari J. Where Is Your Body? And Other Essays on Race, Gender, & the Law. LC 96-25498. 224p. 1997. pap. 12.50 (*0-8070-6781-4*) Beacon Pr.

Matsuda, Mari J., ed. Called from Within: Early Women Lawyers of Hawai'i. LC 92-11002. (Biography Monograph Ser.). 400p. 1992. pap. 24.95 (*0-8248-1448-7*); text 45.00 (*0-8248-1430-4*) UH Pr.

Matsuda, Mari J., et al. Words That Wound: Critical Race Theory, Assaultive Speech & the First Amendment. (New Perspectives on Law, Culture, & Society Ser.). 168p. (C). 1993. pap. 25.00 (*0-8133-8428-1*, Pub. by Westview) HarpC.

Matsuda, Mari J., jt. auth. see Lawrence, Charles R., III.

Matsuda, Matt K. The Memory of the Modern. LC 95-30287. (Illus.). 264p. (C). 1996. pap. 21.00 (*0-19-509365-8*); text 65.00 (*0-19-509364-X*) OUP.

Matsuda, Naonori. Process Architecture No. 133: Cityscape of Hong Kong. (Illus.). 144p. 1997. pap. 37.95 (*4-89331-133-6*, Pub. by Process Archit) Bks Nippan.

Matsuda, Paul, jt. ed. see Silva, Tony.

Matsuda, S., et al, eds. Perspectives on Particle Physics: Festschrift in Honor of Prof. H. Miyazawa. 424p. (C). 1989. text 99.00 (*9971-5-0589-4*) World Scientific Pub.

Matsuda, T. & Niitsuma, N. Collision Tectonics in the South Fossa Magna, Central Japan: A Special Issue of the Journal Modern Geoleogy. 152p. 1989. pap. text 283.00 (*0-677-25920-4*) Gordon & Breach.

Matsuda, Tadayoshi, ed. Cancer Treatment by Hyperthermia, Radiation & Drugs. 380p. 1993. 160.00 (*0-85066-837-9*, Pub. by Tay Francis Ltd) Taylor & Francis.

Matsuda, Takami. Death & Purgatory in Middle English Didactic Poetry. LC 97-18534. 288p. 1997. 60.00 (*0-85991-507-7*) Boydell & Brewer.

Matsuda, Yoshiro, jt. auth. see Kurabayashi, Koshimasa.

***Matsudaira, Lori.** Year Round Crafts & Activities for Children. (Illus.). 175p. (J). (ps-8). 1998. 14.95 (*1-887188-04-5*) Silesia Cos.

Matsudaira, Paul, jt. ed. see Silva, Tony.

Matsudaira, Paul, jt. ed. see Wilson, Leslie.

Matsudaira, Paul T., ed. A Practical Guide to Protein & Peptide Purification for Microsequencing. 2nd ed. (Illus.). 188p. 1993. 42.00 (*0-12-480282-6*) Acad Pr.

Matsudaira, Paul T., et al, eds. Methods in Cell Biology: Cell Biological Applications of Confocal Microscopy, Vol. 38. (Illus.). 380p. 1993. text 104.00 (*0-12-564138-9*) Acad Pr.

Matsudaira, Paul T. & Osborne, Barbara A. Methods in Cell Biology Vol. 46: Cell Death, Vol. 46. (Illus.). 459p. 1995. text 100.00 (*0-12-564147-8*) Acad Pr.

Matsudaira, Paul T. & Robinson, J. Paul. Methods in Cell Biology Vol. 42: Flow Cytometry, Pt. B. 2nd ed. (Illus.). 697p. 1994. text 125.00 (*0-12-564143-5*) Acad Pr.

Matsueda, Pat. The Fish Catcher. 1985. pap. 3.50 (*0-932136-08-7*) Petronium HI.

Matsueda, Pat. Theoretical Traditions. 148.95 (*1-85521-804-6*) Ashgate Pub Co.

Matsuhashi, Ann. Writing in Real Time: Modeling Production Processes. Farr, Marcia, ed. LC 86-22214. (Writing Research Ser.: Vol. 16). 320p. (C). 1987. pap. 39.50 (*0-89391-417-7*); text 73.25 (*0-89391-400-2*) Ablx Pub.

Matsui. Women in the New Asia. 2000. text 55.00 (*1-85649-625-2*); pap. text 19.95 (*1-85649-626-0*, Pub. by Zed Books) St Martin.

Matsui-Haag, Kazue, tr. see Collinwood, Dean W., et al.

Matsui, Hideji, ed. see International Congress of Biomechanics (8th, 1981, Nagoya, Japan) Staff.

Matsui, Hideji, ed. see International Congress of Biomechanics Staff.

Matsui, Isao. Theory & Practice of Eel Culture. Gopal, Alamelu, tr. from JPN. 141p. 1983. text 78.00 (*90-6191-036-6*, Pub. by A A Balkema) Ashgate Pub Co.

Matsui, Nobuo. Practice of Shrimp Culture. rev. ed. (Illus.). 166p. (C). 1997. text 104.00 (*90-5410-277-2*, Pub. by A A Balkema) Ashgate Pub Co.

Matsui, S. Hazard Assessment & Control of Environmental Contaminants in Water. (Water Science & Technology Ser.: Vol. 25). 494p. 1993. 231.00 (*0-08-042190-3*, Pergamon Pr) Elsevier.

Matsui, Susan, tr. see Akio, Terumasa.

Matsui, Susan, tr. see Nakawatari, Harutaka.

Matsui, Susan, tr. see Tejima, Keizaburo.

Matsui, Tetsuo & Rosenblatt, Richard H. Review of the Deep-Sea Fish Family Platytroctidae: Pisces: Salmoniformes. LC 86-25088. (Bulletin of the Scripps Institution of Oceanography, University of California, San Diego Ser.: No. 26). 169p. 1987. pap. 52.40 (*0-7837-7492-3*, 204921400010) Bks Demand.

***Matsui, Tomoko.** Bridging & Relevance. LC 00-22619. (Pragmatics & Beyond New Ser.: Vol. 76). xii, 248p. 2000. 75.00 (*1-55619-924-4*) J Benjamins Pubng Co.

Matsui, Y., jt. auth. see Narlal, K.

Matsui, Yoshiichi. Goldfish Guide. 3rd ed. (Illus.). 325p. 1991. 23.95 (*0-86622-605-2*, PL2011) TFH Pubns.

***Matsuka, Mitsuo, et al, eds.** Asian Bees & Beekeeping: Progress of Research & Development. (Illus.). 264p. 1999. text 47.50 (*1-57808-084-3*) Science Pubs.

Matsukas, Aristarhos. Greek: A Complete Course for Beginners. (ENG & GRE.). 320p. 1998. pap. 19.95 incl. audio (*0-8442-3785-X*, Teach Yrslf) NTC Contemp Pub Co.

Matsukata, Masayoshi. Report on the Adoption of the Gold Standard in Japan. Wilkins, Mira, ed. LC 78-3937. (International Finance Ser.). (Illus.). 1979. reprint ed. lib. bdg. 40.95 (*0-405-11238-6*) Ayer.

Matsukawa, Michiya. The Japanese Trade Surplus & Capital Outflow. (Occasional Paper Ser.: No. 22). 30p. 1987. pap. 10.00 (*1-56708-021-9*) Grp of Thirty.

Matsuki, Akitomo, jt. auth. see McIntyre, John W.

Matsuki, Kenji. Introduction to Mori's Program. 1999. pap. text 49.95 (*0-387-98465-8*) Spr-Verlag.

— Weyl Groups & Birational Transformations among Minimal Models. LC 95-15922. (Memoirs Ser.: No. 557). 133p. 1995. pap. 36.00 (*0-8218-0341-7*, MEMO/116/557) Am Math.

Matsukus, Aristarhos. Teach Yourself Greek Complete Course. 2nd ed. (GRE., Illus.). 320p. 1996. pap. 14.95 (*0-8442-3705-1*) NTC Contemp Pub Co.

Matsumakia, Marc M. Opacite Referentielle et Quantification: Une Introduction a la Semantique Intensionnelle. (Publications Universitaires Europeennes, Serie 28: Vol. 517). (FRE.). 272p. 1997. 40.95 (*3-906754-74-X*, Pub. by P Lang) P Lang Pubng.

Matsumoto. Culture & Psychology. 2nd ed. LC 99-51518. (Psychology Ser.). 570p. (C). 1999. mass mkt. 35.95 (*0-534-35436-X*) Brooks-Cole.

Matsumoto. Developing Your Diversity. (Psychology Ser.). (YA). 1996. 49.95 incl. VHS (*0-534-23230-2*) Brooks-Cole.

***Matsumoto, Akira.** Sexual Differentiation of the Brain. LC 99-37571. 323p. 1999. boxed set 89.95 (*0-8493-1165-9*) CRC Pr.

Matsumoto, Akira & Ishii, Susumu, eds. Atlas of Endocrine Organs: Vertebrates & Invertebrates. Urano, A., tr. from JPN. LC 92-28888. (Illus.). 320p. 1992. 272.95 (*0-387-53158-0*) Spr-Verlag.

Matsumoto, Alan. Non-Cardiac Thoracic Interventions. LC 96-52547. (Radiologic Interventions Ser.). (Illus.). 384p. 1997. write for info. (*0-89640-288-6*) Igaku-Shoin.

Matsumoto, Alan H. Radiologic Interventions: Noncardiac Thoracic Interventions. LC 96-52547. (Radiologic Interventions Ser.). 440p. 1997. 79.00 (*0-683-30338-4*) Lppncott W & W.

Matsumoto, David. Cultural Influences on Research Methods & Statistics. LC 93-41938. 60p. 1994. mass mkt. 6.25 (*0-534-23766-5*) Brooks-Cole.

***Matsumoto, David.** Cultural Influences on Research Methods & Statistics. 65p. (C). 2000. pap. 8.95 (*1-57766-112-5*) Waveland Pr.

Matsumoto, David. Culture & Modern Life. LC 96-30685. (Psychology Ser.). 132p. 1996. mass mkt. 16.95 (*0-534-49688-1*) Brooks-Cole.

***Matsumoto, David.** People: Psychology from a Cultural Perspective. 184p. (C). 2000. pap. 14.95 (*1-57766-113-3*) Waveland Pr.

Matsumoto, David R. Unmasking Japan: Myths & Realities about the Emotions of the Japanese. 1996. 29.50 (*0-8047-2719-8*); pap. write for info. (*0-8047-2755-4*) Stanford U Pr.

Matsumoto, G., jt. auth. see Kaminuma, T.

Matsumoto, Gen & Kontani, Masao, eds. Nerve Membrane: Biochemistry & Function of Channel Proteins. LC QP0552.M44N4. 258p. 1981. reprint ed. pap. 80.00 (*0-608-01243-2*, 206193100001) Bks Demand.

Matsumoto, Gen, jt. ed. see Yamakawa, Takeshi.

Matsumoto, H., ed. Modern Radio Science, 1993. LC 93-22988. (Illus.). 264p. 1993. text 39.95 (*0-19-856379-5*) OUP.

Matsumoto, H. & Sato, T. Computer Simulation of Space Plasmas. 1985. text 233.50 (*90-277-1952-7*) Kluwer Academic.

Matsumoto, Hiroshi. The Relationship Between Various Types of Teachers' Language & Comprehension in the Acquisition of Intermediate Japanese. 240p. (C). 1998. 52.00 (*0-7618-0936-8*); pap. 32.50 (*0-7618-0937-6*) U Pr of Amer.

Matsumoto, Isamu, ed. Advances in Chemical Diagnosis & Treatment of Metabolic Disorders. LC 93-173045. (Illus.). 183p. 1992. reprint ed. pap. 56.80 (*0-608-06836-5*, 206703300001) Bks Demand.

Matsumoto, Kazuko, jt. ed. see Stiefel, Edward I.

Matsumoto, Kiiko & Birch, Stephen. Extraordinary Vessels. 294p. (Orig.). 1986. pap. 20.00 (*0-912111-14-3*) Paradigm Publns.

— Extraordinary Vessels. Felt, Robert L., ed. 220p. (Orig.). 1993. pap. text 22.00 (*0-912111-35-6*) Paradigm Publns.

— Five Elements & Ten Stems: Nan-Ching Theory, Diagnosis, & Practice. Felt, Robert L., ed. (Illus.). 236p. 1993. reprint ed. pap. text 18.95 (*0-912111-25-9*) Paradigm Publns.

— Hara Diagnosis: Reflections on the Sea. (Illus.). 496p. 1993. text 68.95 (*0-912111-13-5*) Paradigm Publns.

Matsumoto, Kiyoshi & Acheson, Roy M. Organic Synthesis at High Pressures. LC 90-31171. 456p. 1991. 175.00 (*0-471-62761-5*) Wiley.

Matsumoto, Koji. Organizing for Higher Productivity: An Analysis of Japanese Systems & Practices. 2nd ed. (Illus.). 75p. 1986. reprint ed. text 18.00 (*92-833-1065-9*, 310659); reprint ed. pap. text 13.75 (*92-833-1066-7*, 310667) Productivity Inc.

— The Rise of the Japanese Corporate System: The Inside View of a MITI Official. (Japanese Studies). 220p. (C). 1991. text 89.95 (*0-7103-0407-2*, A5593) Routledge.

— The Rise of the Japanese Corporate System: The Inside View of a MITI Official. (Japanese Studies). 280p. 1994. pap. 25.50 (*0-7103-0488-9*) Routledge.

Matsumoto, Kunio, jt. ed. see Nakamura, Toshikazu.

Matsumoto, Leiji. Galaxy Express 999. (Illus.). 232p. 1999. pap. text 16.95 (*1-56931-324-5*, Viz Comics) Viz Commns Inc.

***Matsumoto, Leiji.** Galaxy Express, 1999, Vol. 2. 1999. pap. 16.95 (*1-56931-380-6*) Viz Commns Inc.

Matsumoto, Lisa. Beyond 'Ohi'a Valley: Adventures in a Hawaiian Rainforest. (Illus.). 36p. (J). (gr. 3-6). 1996. 16.95 (*0-9647491-2-2*) Lehua.

— How the B-52 Cockroach Learned to Fly. (Illus.). 32p. (J). (gr. 2-5). 1995. 16.95 (*0-9647491-0-6*) Lehua.

***Matsumoto, Pat.** Cows on Parade: Charity Cattle Auction. (Illus.). 32p. 1999. pap. 10.00 (*0-938903-28-4*) Cty of Chicago.

Matsumoto, Pat, ed. Chicago Designs: Fashion, Photography, Architecture. (Illus.). 16p. (Orig.). 1990. pap. 10.00 (*0-938903-11-X*) Cty of Chicago.

Matsumoto, Pat, jt. auth. see Terry, Cliff.

Matsumoto, Pat, ed. see Bonesteel, Michael.

***Matsumoto, S. & Sato, H., eds.** Spina Bifida. (Illus.). xvi, 556p. 2000. pap. 179.00 (*4-431-70260-1*) Spr-Verlag.

Matsumoto, Seicho. Inspector Imanishi Investigates. LC 89-34038. (Soho Crime Ser.). 310p. 1994. pap. 12.00 (*1-56947-019-7*) Soho Press.

— Points & Lines. Yamamoto, Makiko & Blum, Paul C., trs. 160p. pap. 9.00 (*4-7700-0937-2*) FS&G.

— Points & Lines. Shaw, ed. Tamamoto, Makiko & Blum, Paul C., trs. from JPN. LC 72-117385. 160p. 1986. pap. 11.95 (*0-87011-456-5*) Kodansha.

— The Voice & Other Stories. Kabat, Adam, tr. 180p. 1995. pap. 9.00 (*4-7700-1949-1*) Kodansha.

Matsumoto, Seiichi, ed. Sexuality & Human Bonding: Proceedings of the XII World Congress of Sexology, Yokohama, Japan, 12-16 August, 1995. LC 96-533. (International Congress Ser.: Vol. 1095). 536p. 1996. 222.25 (*0-444-82195-3*) Elsevier.

Matsumoto, Shigeru. Motoori Norinaga, 1730-1801. LC 77-95928. (Harvard East Asian Ser.: No. 44). 275p. reprint ed. pap. 85.30 (*0-608-10090-0*, 200549700054) Bks Demand.

Matsumoto, Shoichi, ed. Electronic Display Devices. LC 89-27756. 396p. 1990. 335.00 (*0-471-92218-8*) Wiley.

— Recent Advances in Fertility Control: Proceedings of the 2nd International Symposium on Recent Advances in Fertility Control, Tokyo, Japan, Oct. 24, 1987, Vol. 2. (Current Clinical Practice Ser.: No. 50). 40p. 1989. 25.75 (*90-219-1676-2*, Excerpta Medica) Elsevier.

Matsumoto, Shoichi, et al, eds. Annual Review of Hydrocephalus, 1988, Vol. 6. (Illus.). xvi, 171p. 1990. 128.00 (*0-387-52204-2*) Spr-Verlag.

— Annual Review of Hydrocephalus, 1989, Vol. 7. 176p. 1990. 128.00 (*0-387-52937-3*) Spr-Verlag.

— Annual Review of Hydrocephalus, 1990, Vol. 8. 192p. 1992. 137.00 (*0-387-54846-7*) Spr-Verlag.

Matsumoto, Shoichi & Tamaki, N., eds. Hydrocephalus: Pathogenesis & Treatment. (Illus.). 720p. 1992. 292.00 (*0-387-70080-3*) Spr-Verlag.

Matsumoto, Shoichi, tr. see Sone, T.

Matsumoto, Shoji & Tabrah, Ruth. The Natural Way of Shin Buddhism. LC 93-43084. 176p. (Orig.). (C). 1993. pap. 9.95 (*0-938474-14-6*) Buddhist Study.

Matsumoto, Shoji & Tabrah, Ruth M. Ajatasatru: The Story of Who We Are. LC 88-16813. 84p. (Orig.). 1988. pap. 9.95 (*0-938474-08-1*) Buddhist Study.

Matsumoto, Shoji, tr. see Tabrah, Ruth M., ed.

***Matsumoto, Sumiko.** Japanese Healthy, High-Style Cooking: Step-by-Step Winning Recipes As Used in Lake Forest, IL LaJolla & Palm Springs, CA & Boca Raton, FL. Donahue, Alice K., ed. LC 98-61067. (Illus.). 194p. 1999. lib. bdg. 16.95 (*0-9666131-0-4*, 1) Triangle Pk.

Matsumoto, T. Age & Nature of the Circum-Pacific Orogenesis. 1967. 42.50 (*0-686-43415-3*) Elsevier.

Matsumoto, T., et al, eds. Computations, Glassy Materials, Microgravity & Non-Destructive Testing: Proceedings of a Symposia of the Third International Conference on Advanced Materials, Sunshine City, Ikebukuro, Tokyo, Japan, August 31-September 4, 1993. LC 95-3190. 1660p. 1994. 645.25 (*0-444-81993-2*) Elsevier.

Matsumoto, Taiyo. Black & White. (Illus.). 216p. 1999. pap. text 15.95 (*1-56931-322-9*, Viz Comics) Viz Commns Inc.

***Matsumoto, Taiyo.** Black & White, Vol. 2. (Illus.). 205p. 1999. pap. text 15.95 (*1-56931-432-2*, Pub. by Viz Commns Inc) Publishers Group.

— Black & White, Vol. 3. 2000. pap. 15.95 (*1-56931-490-X*) Viz Commns Inc.

Matsumoto, Teruo. Laser Disobstruction & Laser-Assisted Balloon Angioplasty: A Color Atlas. Hacke, Gregory, ed. (Illus.). 97p. 1991. 75.00 (*0-912791-66-7*, Ishiyaku EuroAmerica) Med Dent Media.

Matsumoto, Tomone, ed. see Gessel, Van C.

Matsumoto, Tomone, tr. see Mukoda, Kuniko.

Matsumoto, Toru. Beyond Prejudice. Daniels, Roger, ed. LC 78-54826. (Asian Experience in North America Ser.). 1979. reprint ed. lib. bdg. 15.95 (*0-405-11283-1*) Ayer.

Matsumoto, Valerie J. Farming the Home Place: A Japanese American Community in California, 1919-1982. LC 92-56774. (Illus.). 280p. 1993. pap. text 16.95 (*0-8014-8115-5*) Cornell U Pr.

Matsumoto, Valerie J. & Allmendinger, Blake. Over the Edge: Remapping Western Experience. LC 97-39311. 1998. 48.00 (*0-520-21148-0*, Pub. by U CA Pr); pap. 19.95 (*0-520-21149-9*, Pub. by U CA Pr) Cal Prin Full Svc.

Matsumoto, Y. & Morita, S., eds. Aspects of Low Dimensional Manifolds. (Advanced Studies in Pure Mathematics: Vol. 20). 376p. 1993. 70.00 (*4-314-10077-X*, ASPM/20C, Pub. by Kinokuniya) Am Math.

Matsumoto, Y., jt. ed. see Ichimura, S.

Matsumoto, Yo. Complex Predicates in Japanese: A Syntactic & Semantic Study of the Notion "Word" LC 96-32128. (Studies in Japanese Linguistics). 352p. 1997. pap. 25.95 (*1-57586-060-0*) Cambridge U Pr.

— Complex Predicates in Japanese: A Syntactic & Semantic Study of the Notion 'Word' (Studies in Japanese Linguistics). 352p. 1996. text 70.00 (*1-57586-065-1*) CSLI.

— Complex Predicates in Japanese: A Syntactic & Semantic Study of the Notion Word. (Studies in Japanese Linguistics). 352p. (C). 1996. pap. text 24.95 (*1-57586-064-3*) CSLI.

— Complex Predicates in Japanese: A Syntactic & Semantic Study of the Notion Word. LC 96-32128. (Studies in Japanese Linguistics). 359p. 1997. 69.95 (*1-57586-061-9*) Cambridge U Pr.

Matsumoto, Yoshihio & Ohno, Yutaka. Japanese Perspectives in Software Engineering. (Illus.). 320p. (C). 1989. pap. text 40.33 (*0-201-41629-8*) Addison-Wesley.

Matsumoto, Yoshiko. Noun-Modifying Constructions in Japanese: A Frame-Semantic Approach. LC 97-5309. (Studies in Language Companion Ser.: Vol. 35). 300p. 1997. lib. bdg. 74.00 (*1-55619-846-9*) J Benjamins Pubng Co.

Matsumura, Akihiro. Tokyo Portraits: An Enigmatic View of the City. (Illus.). 144p. 1997. write for info. (*4-07-976534-7*, Pub. by Shufunotomo) Weatherhill.

***Matsumura, Ella Mae, et al.** Member Segmentation & Profitability: Current Practice & Future Possibilities. 58p. 1999. pap. 100.00 (*1-880572-38-9*, 1752-45) Filene Res.

Matsumura, Fumio, et al, eds. Biodegradation of Pesticides. LC 82-7570. 326p. 1982. 59.50 (*0-306-40857-0*, Plenum Trade) Perseus Pubng.

Matsumura, Fumio, jt. ed. see Clark, J. Marshall.

Matsumura, Hideyuki. Commutative Ring Theory. (Cambridge Studies in Advanced Mathematics: No. 8). 336p. 1989. pap. text 39.95 (*0-521-36764-6*) Cambridge U Pr.

Matsumura, Janice. More Than a Momentary Nightmare: The Yokohama Incident & Wartime Japan. LC 99-179200. (Cornell East Asia Ser.: Vol. 92). 172p. (C). 1998. 18.70 (*1-885445-52-0*); pap. 11.90 (*1-885445-92-X*) Cornell East Asia Pgm.

***Matsumura, John.** Lightning over Water: Sharpening America's Light Forces for Rapid-Reaction Missions. LC 00-36920. 2000. write for info. (*0-8330-2845-6*) Rand Corp.

Matsumura, John, et al. Analytical Support to the Defense Science Board: Tactics & Technology for 21st Century Military Superiority. LC 97-179486. 68p. 1997. pap. 6.00 (*0-8330-2482-5*, DB-198-A) Rand Corp.

***Matsumura, John, et al.** The Army after Next: Exploring New Concepts & Technologies for the Light Battle. (Illus.). xvi, 40p. (C). 1999. pap. 15.00 (*0-8330-2782-4*, DB258-A) Rand Corp.

Matsumura, John, et al. Joint Operations Superiority in the 21st Century. (Illus.). xxi, 50p. 1999. pap. 30.00 (*0-8330-2714-X*, DB-260-A/OSD) Rand Corp.

Matsumura, John M., et al. Assessment of Crusader: The Army's Next Self-Propelled Howitzer & Resupply Vehicle. LC 98-14849. (Illus.). 44p. 1998. pap. 10.00 (*0-8330-2596-1*, MR-930-A) Rand Corp.

Matsumura, K. N. & Hamilton, William L. After Fifteen Years: Artificial Liver & Artificial Pancreas. 2nd ed. LC 78-56092. (Illus.). 1978. 19.95 (*0-9606924-0-1*) Alin Found Pr.

Matsumura, Kenneth. Heterosexual AIDS: Myth or Fact? LC 88-70310. 1988. pap. 9.95 (*0-9606924-3-6*) Alin Found Pr.

Matsumura, Masaie, jt. auth. see Marriott, John.

Matsumura, Molleen, ed. Voices for Evolution. LC 95-70815. 176p. 1995. pap. 10.00 (*0-939873-53-2*) Natl Ctr Sci Educ.

Matsumura, Molleen, jt. auth. see Rogers, Judith.

Matsumura, Molleen, ed. see Komuta, Kensaburo.

Matsunaga, Akira. Chitosan: The Ultimate Health Builder. LC 97-91350. 1998. pap. 14.95 (*0-533-12629-0*) Vantage.

An Asterisk (*) at the beginning of an entry indicates that the title is appearing for the first time.

Matsunaga, Alicia & Matsunaga, Daigan. Foundation of Japanese Buddhism: The Mass Movement, Vol. 2. LC 74-83654. 1976. pap. 14.50 (*0-914910-28-0*) Buddhist Bks.

Matsunaga, Alicia, jt. auth. see Matsunaga, Daigan.

Matsunaga, Daigan & Matsunaga, Alicia. Foundation of Japanese Buddhism: The Aristocratic Age, Vol. I. 5th rev. ed. LC 74-83654. 1996. pap. 12.50 (*0-914910-26-4*) Buddhist Bks.

Matsunaga, Daigan, jt. auth. see Matsunaga, Alicia.

Matsunaga, Ichiro, et al. Encounter at Sea: And a Heroic Lifeboat Journey. LC 94-5792. (Illus.). 232p. 1994. pap. 15.95 (*1-879094-27-4*, Sabre Pr) Momentum Bks.

Matsunaga, Karen K. Japanese Country Quilting: Sashiko Patterns & Projects for the Beginner. (Illus.). 96p. (Orig.). 1990. pap. 22.00 (*0-87011-936-2*) Kodansha.

***Matsunaga, Louella.** The Changing Face of Japanese Retail: Working in a Chain Store. LC 00-42482. 2000. write for info. (*0-415-22975-8*) Routledge.

Matsunaga, Louella, tr. see Kobayashi, Shigenori.

Matsunaga, Sachiko. The Role of Phonological Coding in Reading Kanji: A Research Report & Some Pedagogical Implications. (Technical Reports: No. 6). 64p. (Orig.). (C). 1995. pap. text 10.00 (*0-8248-1734-6*) Sec Lang Tching.

Matsunaka, Ryoji, jt. ed. see Nakagawa, Dai.

Matsunami, H. Silicon Carbide & Related Materials 1995: Proceedings of the Sixth International Conference, Kyoto, Japan, 18-21 September 1995. Nakashima, S. et al, eds. LC 96-11373. (Institute of Physics Conference Ser.: Vol. 142). (Illus.). 1200p. 1996. 497.00 (*0-7503-0335-2*) IOP Pub.

Matsunami, Kodo. International Handbook of Funeral Customs. LC 97-43929. 232p. 1998. lib. bdg. 75.00 (*0-313-30443-2*, Greenwood Pr) Greenwood.

Matsunami, Niichiro. Japanese Constitution & Politics. LC 78-78356. (Studies in Japanese Law & Government). 577p. 1979. lib. bdg. 95.00 (*0-313-27028-7*, U7028, Greenwood Pr) Greenwood.

Matsuno, Koichiro. Protobiology: Physical Basis of Biology. 272p. 1989. 136.00 (*0-8493-6403-5*, QH505, CRC Reprint) Franklin.

Matsuno, Koichiro, et al, eds. Molecular Evolution & Protobiology. LC 83-24465. 480p. 1984. 110.00 (*0-306-41509-7*, Plenum Trade) Perseus Pubng.

Matsuno, Koichiro & Hartman, H. Origin & Evolution of Prokaryotic & Eukaryotic Cells. 442p. 1993. text 106.00 (*981-02-1262-3*) World Scientific Pub.

Matsuno, T. Dynamics of the Middle Atmosphere. Holton, James S., ed. LC 84-8291. 550p. 1984. text 274.00 (*90-277-1758-3*) Kluwer Academic.

***Matsuo, Basheo & Hamill, Sam.** Narrow Road to the Interior: And Other Writings. LC 00-38786. 2000. pap. 14.95 (*1-57062-716-9*, Pub. by Shambhala Pubns) Random.

Matsuo, Dorothy. Boyhood to War: History & Anecdotes of the 442nd Regimental Combat Team. (Illus.). 240p. 1992. boxed set 35.00 (*1-56647-019-6*) Mutual Pub HI.

Matsuo, Hiro, ed. The Japan Business Study Program: Trade, Foreign Investment, & Competition. (Illus.). 100p. (Orig.). 1990. pap. 15.00 (*0-87755-321-1*) Bureau Busn TX.

Matsuo, Hirofumi. Understanding Japanese Business. (Illus.). 74p. (Orig.). (C). 1995. pap. text 25.00 (*0-7881-2332-7*) DIANE Pub.

Matsuo, Hosaku. The Logic of Unity: The Discovery of Zero & Emptiness in Prajnaparamita Thought. Inada, Kenneth K., tr. LC 86-5916. (SUNY Series in Buddhist Studies). 148p. (C). 1987. text 21.50 (*0-88706-391-8*) State U NY Pr.

Matsuo, Nobutake, ed. Growth Hormones: Research & Therapy: Asian Pacific Symposium, Kobe, September 1996. (Hormone Research Ser.: Vol. 49, Suppl. 1, 1998). (Illus.). iv, 58p. 1998. pap. 27.00 (*3-8055-6600-X*) S Karger.

Matsuo, T., ed. Water Quality & Pollution Control in Asia: Selected Proceedings of Asian Waterqual '95, the 5th IAWQ Asian Regional Conference on Water Quality & Pollution Control, Held in Manila, the Philippines, 7-9 February 1995. 296p. 1997. pap. write for info. (*0-08-043289-1*) Elsevier.

Matsuo, T., et al. Biological Mass Spectrometry: Present & Future. LC 93-33841. 688p. 1994. 550.00 (*0-471-93896-3*) Wiley.

Matsuo, Takane, ed. Adaptability in Plants: With Special References to Crop Yield. LC 80-472254. (JIBP Synthesis Ser.: No. 6). 227p. 1975. reprint ed. pap. 70.40 (*0-608-01586-5*, 206200600001) Bks Demand.

— Gene Conservation: Exploration, Collection, Preservation, & Utilization of Genetic Resources. LC 78-304419. (JIBP Synthesis Ser.: No. 5). 245p. 1975. reprint ed. pap. 76.00 (*0-608-01585-7*, 206200500001) Bks Demand.

Matsuo, Yukio. Ice Sculpture: Secrets of a Japanese Master. LC 91-26696. 200p. 1992. 89.95 (*0-471-55409-X*) Wiley.

Matsuoka, Fumitaka. The Color of Faith: Building Community in a Multiracial Society. LC 98-26845. 144p. 1998. pap. 15.95 (*0 8298-1281-4*) Pilgrim OH.

— Out of Silence: Emerging Themes in Asian American Churches. LC 94-33659. 152p. (Orig.). 1995. pap. 11.95 (*0-8298-1025-0*) Pilgrim OH.

Matsuoka, Kazuko, tr. see Seibu Museum of Art Staff.

Matsuoka, M. Infrared Absorbing Dyes. LC 90-40052. (Topics in Applied Chemistry Ser.). (Illus.). 234p. (C). 1990. text 79.50 (*0-306-43478-4*, Kluwer Plenum) Kluwer Academic.

Matsuoka, Mikihiro & Rose, Brian. The DIR Guide to Japanese Economic Statistics. (Illus.). 304p. 1994. text 49.95 (*0-19-828861-1*) OUP.

***Matsuoka, Satoshi & Oldehoeft, Rodney R., eds.** Computing in Object-Oriented Parallel Environments: Third International Symposium, ISCOPE 99, San Francisco, CA, USA, December 1999, Proceedings. LC 99-58793. viii, 205p. 1999. pap. 45.00 (*3-540-66818-7*) Spr-Verlag.

Matsuoka, Satoshi, jt. ed. see Futatsugi, Kokichi.

Matsuoka, Shiro. Relaxation Phenomena in Polymers. 322p. 1992. 67.50 (*1-56990-060-4*) Hanser-Gardner.

Matsurra, Takeshi. Synthetic Membranes & Membrane Separation Processes. 480p. 1993. boxed set 147.95 (*0-8493-4202-3*) CRC Pr.

***Matsusaka, Yoshihisa Tak.** Making of Japanese Manchuria, 1904-1932. (Illus.). 475p. 2000. 49.50 (*0-674-00369-1*) HUP.

Matsushima, E., jt. ed. see Kojima, T.

Matsushima, Yozo. Differentiable Manifolds. Kobayashi, E. T., tr. LC 71-182215. (Pure & Applied Mathematics Ser.: No. 9). 315p. reprint ed. pap. 97.70 (*0-8357-6094-4*, 203454700090) Bks Demand.

— Holomorphic Vector Fields on Compact Kahler Manifolds. LC 77-145641. (CBMS Regional Conference Series in Mathematics: No. 7). 38p. 1971. pap. 16.00 (*0-8218-1656-X*, CBMS/7) Am Math.

Matsushita, Fumiko. Design & Construction Practice in Japan: A Practical Guide. (ENG & JPN., Illus.). 380p. 1997. pap. 69.95 (*4-87571-857-8*, Pub. by Hokuseido Pr) Book East.

Matsushita, Konosuke. Not for Bread Alone. 176p. (Orig.). 1994. pap. 12.00 (*0-425-14133-0*) Berkley Pub.

Matsushita, Masatoshi. Japan in the League of Nations. LC 68-58606. (Columbia University. Studies in the Social Sciences: No. 314). reprint ed. 20.00 (*0-404-51314-X*) AMS Pr.

Matsushita, Mitsuo. International Trade & Competition Law in Japan. (Modern Japanese Law: No. 1). 364p. 1993. text 48.00 (*0-19-825440-7*) OUP.

Matsushita, Mitsuo & Schoenbaum, Thomas J. Japanese International Trade & Investment Law. 240p. 1989. 54.50 (*0-86008-449-3*, Pub. by U of Tokyo) Col U Pr.

Matsushita, Shutaro. Economic Effects of Public Debts. LC 73-78012. (Columbia University. Studies in the Social Sciences: No. 309). reprint ed. 20.00 (*0-404-51309-3*) AMS Pr.

Matsushita, Tomonori, ed. A Glossarial Concordance to William Langland's The Vision of Pier's Plowman: B-Text, 3 vols. (Alpha-Omega Series C. English Authors). 1650p. Date not set. write for info. (*3-487-10373-7*) G Olms Pubs.

***Matsushita, Yutaka, ed.** Designing Communication & Collaboration Support Systems. (Advanced Information Processing Technology Ser.). 216p. 1999. text 95.00 (*90-5699-116-7*) Gordon & Breach.

***Matsuura, Jeffrey H.** A Manager's Guide to the Law & Economics of Data Networks. LC 99-89514. (Intellectual Property & Communications Law Library). 2000. 83.00 (*1-58053-020-6*) Artech Hse.

Matsuura, Jeffrey H., jt. auth. see Delta, George B.

Matsuura, Kumiko, et al. Annual Review of United Nations Affairs: Covering Years from 1961 Thru 1998, 56 vols. annuals LC 50-548. 1962. lib. bdg. 2892.50 (*0-379-12300-2*) Oceana.

Matsuura, Richard & Matsuura, Ruth. Ali'i Kai. (Illus.). (J). 7.95 (*1-887916-05-9*) Orch Isle Pub.

— Angels Masquerading on Earth. (Illus.). (J). 7.95 (*1-887916-07-5*) Orch Isle Pub.

— Birthday Wish. (Illus.). (J). 8.95 (*1-887916-04-0*) Orch Isle Pub.

— Fruit, the Tree & the Flower. (J). 8.95 (*1-887916-02-4*) Orch Isle Pub.

— Gift from Santa. (Illus.). (J). 7.95 (*1-887916-06-7*) Orch Isle Pub.

— Hawaiian Christmas Story. (Illus.). (J). 8.95 (*1 887916 01 6*) Orch Isle Pub.

— Kalani & Primo. (Illus.). (J). 8.95 (*1-887916-03-2*) Orch Isle Pub.

— King Who Wanted to See God. (Illus.). (J). 8.95 (*1-887916-00-8*) Orch Isle Pub.

Matsuura, Ruth, jt. auth. see Matsuura, Richard.

Matsuura, Takeshi, jt. ed. see Sourirajann, S.

Matsuya Piece-Goods Store Staff, ed. Japanese Design Motifs: 4260 Illustrations of Heraldic Crests. Adachi, Fumie, tr. from JPN. & intro. by. (Pictorial Archive Ser.). (Illus.). 213p. 1972. reprint ed. pap. 11.95 (*0-486-22874-6*) Dover.

Matsuyama, Keisuke, jt. ed. see Matthews, Ron.

Matsuyama, T. & Hwang, V. S. Sigma: A Knowledge-Based Aerial Image Understanding System. LC 89-29221. (Advances in Computer Vision & Machine Intelligence Ser.). (Illus.). 296p. (C). 1990. 85.00 (*0-306-43301-X*, Plenum Trade) Perseus Pubng.

Matsuyama, Takashi, jt. ed. see Nagao, Makoto.

Matsuzaki, K., et al. NMR Spectroscopy & Stereoregularity of Polymers. (Illus.). xviii, 278p. 1996. 287.00 (*3-8055-6298-5*) S Karger.

Matsuzaki, Katsuhiko & Taniguchi, Masahiko. Hyperbolic Manifolds. (Oxford Mathematical Monographs). (Illus.). 264p. 1998. text 115.00 (*0-19-850062-9*) OUP.

Matsuzaki, Yuji & Wada, Ben K., eds. Proceedings of the Second International Conference on Adaptive Structures. LC 92-54123. 890p. 1992. text 39.95 (*0-87762-932-3*) Technomic.

Matsuzawa, T. Clinical Pet on Oncology: Proceedings of the Second International Symposium. 452p. 1994. text 109.00 (*981-02-1825-7*) World Scientific Pub.

Matsuzawa, Toshiaki. An Introduction to Contract Safety Laboratories of the World. (Illus.). 246p. 1996. 67.50 (*1-56386-042-2*, Ishiyaku EuroAmerica) Med Dent Media.

Matt, Colleen, ed. see Quinlan, Susan C.

Matt, Daniel C. The Essential Kabbalah. 221p. 1997. 7.98 (*0-7858-0870-1*) Bk Sales Inc.

Matt, Daniel C. God & the Big Bang: Discovering Harmony Between Science & Spirituality. LC 96-6100. 216p. 1996. 21.95 (*1-879045-48-6*) Jewish Lights.

— God & the Big Bang: Discovering Harmony Between Science & Spirituality. LC 96-6106. 216p. 1998. pap. 16.95 (*1-879045-89-3*) Jewish Lights.

— God & the Big Bang: Discovering Harmony Between Science & Spirituality, Set. abr. ed. text 17.95 incl. audio (*1-57453-150-6*) Audio Lit.

— Zohar, The Book of Enlightment. (Classics of Western Spirituality Ser.). 320p. 1982. pap. 19.95 (*0-8091-2387-8*) Paulist Pr.

Matt, Daniel C., tr. The Essential Kabbalah: The Heart of Jewish Mysticism. LC 94-40147. 240p. 1996. pap. 13.00 (*0-06-251163-7*, Pub. by Harper SF) HarpC.

Matt, Dick, et al. The EAA Air Adventure Museum: EAA Museum Guide Book. 48p. (Orig.). 1991. pap. 9.95 (*0-940000-42-3*) EAA Aviation.

Matt, Gerald. Photography in Japan: Desire & Void. (Illus.). 176p. 1997. 49.95 (*3-908162-70-X*) Dist Art Pubs.

Matt, Gerald, ed. see Miller, Arthur, et al.

***Matt, Joe.** Peepshow: A Cartoon Diary. (Illus.). 104p. 1999. pap. 14.95 (*1-896597-27-0*, Pub. by Drawn & Quarterly) LPC InBook.

Matt, Joe. The Poor Bastard. 172p. 1997. pap. 12.95 (*1-896597-04-1*, Pub. by Drawn & Quarterly) LPC InBook.

Matt, John. Crewdog: A Saga of a Young American. 512p. 1992. 24.95 (*1-881429-00-8*) Waterford Bks.

Matt, Margaret, et al. Human Anatomy Coloring Book. (Illus.). 48p. (Orig.). (J). (gr. 5 up). 1982. pap. 2.95 (*0-486-24138-6*) Dover.

Matt, Michael, ed. see Davies, Michael, et al.

Matt, Pamela. A Kinesthetic Legacy: The Life & Works of Barbara Clark. (Illus.). 340p. (C). 1993. pap. 29.50 (*1-881914-25-9*) C Manuals Trust.

Matt, Paul. Aeronca, Best of Paul Matt. (Illus.). 96p. 1993. pap. text 19.95 (*0-943691-02-8*) Aviation Heritage.

— Paul Matt Scale Airplane Drawings, Vol. 1. (Illus.). 160p. 1993. pap. text 24.95 (*0-943691-04-4*) Aviation Heritage.

— Paul Matt Scale Airplane Drawings, Vol. 2. (Illus.). 158p. 1993. pap. text 24.95 (*0-943691-05-2*) Aviation Heritage.

Matt, Paul, jt. ed. see Rust, Kenn C.

Matt, Stephen R. Electricity & Basic Electronics. LC 97-11853. (Illus.). 364p. 1997. 38.64 (*1-56637-406-5*) Goodheart.

Matt Stoddard, Sonia von, see Von Matt Stoddard, Sonia.

Matta-Clark, Gordon, jt. auth. see Lee, Pamela M.

Matta, George J., Jr. A POW Diary - My Father's Struggle. (Illus.). 252p. (Orig.). 1997. pap. 12.00 (*0-9658080-0-9*) DarRyan Pr.

Matta, Michael S. & Wilbraham, Antony C. Biochemistry. 2nd ed. LC 85-15765. (Illus.). 800p. (C). 1986. pap. text, teacher ed. 20.50 (*0-8053-9633-0*) Benjamin-Cummings.

— Chemistry: Intro General Organic Biolg Chem. 2nd ed. LC 85-15765. (Illus.). 800p. (C). 1986. pap. text, student ed. 17.25 (*0-8053-9632-2*) Benjamin-Cummings.

— General, Organic & Biological Chemistry. 2nd ed. LC 85-15765. (Illus.). 800p. (C). 1986. text 47.50 (*0-8053-9630-6*) Benjamin-Cummings.

Matta, Michael S., et al. Introduction to Chemistry: Instructor Supplements. (C). 1996. text, teacher ed. 2.66 (*0-669-33310-7*); text, teacher ed. 28.36 (*0-669-39923-X*) HM Trade Div.

— Introduction to General, Organic, & Biological Chemistry. 10th ed. 883p. (C). 1996. text 74.76 (*0-669-33309-3*); pap. text, student ed. 27.96 (*0-669-33311-5*); pap. text, student ed. 19.96 (*0-669-33312-3*) HM Trade Div.

— Introduction to Organic & Biological Chemistry. 572p. (C). 1996. text 67.96 (*0-669-39922-1*); pap. text, student ed. 25.96 (*0-669-41707-6*); pap. text, student ed. 19.96 (*0-669-41708-4*) HM Trade Div.

Matta, Paula, ed. Children's Books by Small Presses: An Exhibition, May 15-June 23, 1989, at the Small Press Center. 100p. (Orig.). 1989. pap. 5.00 (*0-9622769-1-X*) Small Pr Ctr.

— The Environment: Books by Small Presses: An Exhibition, April 22-May 31, 1990, at the Small Press Center. 64p. (Orig.). 1990. pap. 5.00 (*0-9622769-2-8*) Small Pr Ctr.

— Roots in Print: A Multicultural Exhibit of Small Press Books on Ethnic History, Culture, Customs & Neighborhoods: An Exhibition, May 15-June 25, 1992, at the Small Press Center. annot. ed. 208p. (Orig.). 1992. pap. 6.00 (*0-9622769-3-6*) Small Pr Ctr.

Mattachine Society Staff. The Mattachine Review, 5 vols., Set. LC 75-12336. (Homosexuality Ser.). 1975. reprint ed. 242.95 (*0-405-07373-9*) Ayer.

Mattaei, Julia A., jt. auth. see Amott, Teresa.

Mattaei, Julie A., jt. auth. see Amott, Teresa.

Mattai, Ravi J. The Rural University: The Jawaja Experiment in Educational Innovation. 1985. 27.50 (*0-8364-1406-3*, Pub. by Popular Prakashan) S Asia.

Mattaini, Mark A. Clinical Practice with Individuals. LC 96-42938. (Illus.). 195p. (Orig.). (C). 1996. pap. text 28.95 (*0-87101-270-7*) Natl Assn Soc Wkrs.

— More Than a Thousand Words: Graphics for Clinical Practice. LC 93-6591. (Illus.). 297p. (C). 1993. 28.95 (*0-87101-224-3*); disk 60.95 (*0-87101-227-8*); disk 60.95 (*0-87101-229-4*) Natl Assn Soc Wkrs.

Mattaini, Mark A. & NASW Press Staff. Clinical Intervention with Families. LC 99-20801. 1999. 32.95 (*0-87101-308-8*, NASW Pr) Natl Assn Soc Wkrs.

Mattaini, Mark A. & Thyer, Bruce A., eds. Finding Solutions to Social Problems: Behavioral Strategies for Changes. LC 96-9216. (Illus.). 427p. 1996. text 39.95 (*1-55798-367-4*); pap. text 19.95 (*1-55798-390-9*) Am Psychol.

Mattaini, Mark A., et al. The Foundations of Social Work Practice: A Graduate Text. 2nd ed. LC 98-28663. 384p. 1998. pap. 34.95 (*0-87101-297-9*) Natl Assn Soc Wkrs.

Mattaini, Mark A., jt. ed. see Meyer, Carol H.

Mattaj, I., jt. ed. see Nagai, K.

Mattalia, Sonia. La Figura En El Tapiz: Teoria y Practica Narrativa En Juan Carlos Onetti. (Monagrafias A Ser.: Vol. CXXXVII). 240p. (Orig.). (C). 1990. pap. 45.00 (*0-7293-0295-4*, Pub. by Tamesis Bks Ltd) Boydell & Brewer.

Mattaliano, Jane & Omonde, Lois G. Milestones: A Pictorial History of Philippi, West Virginia 1844-1994. LC 94-17015. 1994. write for info. (*0-89865-902-7*) Donning Co.

Mattalino, Angelo, jt. auth. see Ellenbecker, Todd S.

***Mattani.** Dance, Drama & Theatre in Thailand: The Process of Development & Modernization. LC 97-947850. (Illus.). 300p. 1998. pap. 24.95 (*974-390-006-3*) Suriwong Bk Ctr.

Mattapash, Shmuel. Reshimos Maamorei Dach. 128p. 1981. reprint ed. 10.00 (*0-8266-5443-6*) Kehot Pubn Soc.

Mattar, Farid. Columns of Stars. LC 95-94760. (Orig.). 1996. pap. 12.95 (*0-533-11629-5*) Vantage.

Mattar, Marriam. At Home in the Fourth Dimension. 208p. 1994. 95.00 (*1-898162-90-5*, Pub. by IMMEL Pubng) St Mut.

Mattar, Nabil. A Study in Bohairic Coptic: A Bohairic Grammar with Arabic & English Translations. LC 90-33325. (ARA, COP & ENG., Illus.). 641p. (C). 1990. pap. text 34.95 (*0-932727-41-7*); lib. bdg. 44.95 (*0-932727-42-5*) Hope Pub Hse.

— A Study of Bohairic Coptic. (ARA & ENG., Illus.). 725p. (Orig.). (C). 1989. pap. write for info. (*0-318-65809-7*) Holy Virgin Mary.

Mattar, Philip. The Mufti of Jerusalem. rev. ed. 176p. 1991. pap. text 18.50 (*0-231-06463-2*) Col U Pr.

— The Mufti of Jerusalem: Al-Hajj Amin Al-Husayni & the Palestinian National Movement. rev. ed. (Illus.). 191p. (C). 1998. pap. text 20.00 (*0-7881-5502-4*) DIANE Pub.

Mattar, Philip, ed. Encyclopedia of the Palestinians. LC 99-23510. 304p. 2000. 75.00 (*0-8160-3043-X*) Facts on File.

Mattauer, Maurice. Berge und Gebirge: Werden und Vergehen Geologischer Grossstrukturen. (GER., Illus.). viii, 191p. 1998. 37.00 (*3-510-65184-7*, Pub. by E Schweizerbartsche) Balogh.

Mattausch, Jutta. Tibetan Power Yoga: The Essence of All Yogas - A Tibetaan Exercise for Physical Vitality & Mental Power. LC 97-71447. (Illus.). 112p. (Orig.). 1997. pap. 9.95 (*0-914955-30-6*) Lotus Pr.

Mattavelli, L. & Novelli, L., eds. Advances in Organic Geochemistry, 1987: Organic Geochemistry in Petroleum Exploration & Analytical Geochemistry: Proceedings of the 13th International Meeting on Organic Geochemistry, Venice, September 21-25, 1987, Pts. 1 & 2. (Organic Geochemistry Ser.). (Illus.). 1199p. 1989. 280.25 (*0-08-037236-8*, Pergamon Pr) Elsevier.

Mattavi, James N., ed. see Symposium on Combustion Modeling in Reciprocating.

Mattawa, Khaled. Ismailia Eclipse: Poems. LC 95-39156. 93p. 1995. pap. 12.95 (*1-878818-44-9*, Pub. by Sheep Meadow) U Pr of New Eng.

Mattawa, Khaled, jt. ed. see Akash, Munir.

Mattawa, Khaled, tr. see Janabi, Hatif.

Mattax, Charlotte. Accompaniment on Theorbo & Harpsichord: Denis Delair's Treatise of 1690. LC 90-49917. (Publications of the Early Music Institute). (Illus.). 176 Pgsp. (Orig.). 1991. pap. 16.95 (*0-253-28592-5*) Ind U Pr.

Mattax, Charlotte, tr. & comment see Delair, Denis.

Mattay, J., ed. Electron Transfer I. (Topics in Current Chemistry Ser.: Vol. 169). (Illus.). 385p. 1994. 219.95 (*0-387-57565-0*) Spr-Verlag.

— Photoinduced Electron Transfer V. (Topics in Current Chemistry Ser.: Vol. 168). (Illus.). 290p. 1993. 189.95 (*0-387-56746-1*) Spr-Verlag.

— Photoinduced Electron Transfer IV. (Topics in Current Chemistry Ser.: Vol. 163). (Illus.). xiii, 250p. 1992. 142.95 (*0-387-55117-4*) Spr-Verlag.

— Photoinduced Electron Transfer I. (Topics in Current Chemistry Ser.: Vol. 156). 256p. 1990. 135.95 (*0-387-52379-0*) Spr-Verlag.

— Photoinduced Electron Transfer III. (Topics in Current Chemistry Ser.: Vol. 159). (Illus.). xii, 259p. 1991. 111.95 (*0-387-53257-9*) Spr-Verlag.

Mattay, J., et al, eds. Topics in Current Chemistry Vol. 177: Electron Transfer II. (Illus.). viii, 268p. 1995. 207.95 (*3-540-60110-4*) Spr-Verlag.

Mattay, J. & Griesbeck, A., eds. Photochemical Key Steps in Organic Synthesis: An Experimental Course Book. LC 95-158496. (Illus.). 350p. 1994. pap. 94.95 (*3-527-29214-4*, Wiley-VCH) Wiley.

***Matte-Blanco, Ignacio.** The Unconscious As Infinite Sets. 504p. 1998. reprint ed. pap. 42.00 (*1-85575-202-6*, Pub. by H Karnac Bks Ltd) Other Pr LLC.

Matte-Blanco, Ignacio. Thinking, Feeling & Being. 300p. 1987. text 37.50 (*0-415-00677-5*) Routledge.

Matte, Edouard J. Structures de la Pensee: Modes - Temps - Aspects - Modes De Proces En Anglais et En Francais. LC 92-15123. (American University Studies: Linguistics: Ser. XIII, Vol. 27). (FRE.). XXXVIII, 420p. 1993. 62.95 (*0-8204-1880-3*) P Lang Pubng.

Matte, Edward. French & English Verbal Systems: A Descriptive & Contrastive Synthesis. (American University Studies: Linguistics: Ser. XIII, Vol. 7). XX, 338p. (C). 1988. text 44.95 (*0-8204-0756-9*) P Lang Pubng.

M

Matte, Gerard & Davis, Jessica M. Readings from the 7th International Conference on Humour. (Illus.). 180p. 1997. pap. 26.95 (*0-86840-440-3*, Pub. by New South Wales Univ Pr) Intl Spec Bk.

Matte, Jacqueline. Austin from Boston. LC 97-60783. 1997. 14.95 (*0-9654721-0-8*) Fat Cat Pub.

Matte, Jacqueline A., jt. auth. see Hamilton, Virginia V.

Matte, James A. The Art & Science of the Polygraph Technique. (Illus.). 296p. 1980. pap. 36.95 (*0-398-06271-4*) C C Thomas.

— The Art & Science of the Polygraph Technique. fac. ed. (Illus.). 296p. 1980. 49.95 (*0-398-04044-3*) C C Thomas.

— Forensic Psychophysiology Using the Polygraph: Scientific Truth Verification - Lie Detection. (Illus.). 800p. (Orig.). (C). 1996. text 89.00 (*0-9655794-0-9*) J A M Pubns.

Matte, Jaqueline A. The History of Washington County: First County in Alabama. LC 82-70721. (Illus.). 486p. 1982. 30.00 (*0-9608434-0-X*); 5.00 (*0-685-05992-8*) WA County Hist.

***Matte, Lisa.** City Smart: Boston. (City Smart Ser.). (Illus.). 272p. 2000. pap. 15.95 (*1-56261-483-5*, City Smart) Avalon Travel.

Matte, Nancy L. & Henderson, Susan H. Success, Your Style! Right & Left Brain Techniques for Learning. LC 94-41287. 219p. 1995. 38.95 (*0-534-24468-8*) Wadsworth Pub.

Matte, Nicolas M. & Jakhu, Ram S. Law of International Telecommunications in Canada. (Law & Economics of International Telecommunications Ser.). 131p. 1987. 45.00 (*3-7890-1309-9*, Pub. by Nomos Verlags) Intl Bk Import.

Matte, Robert, Jr. Asylum Picnic. Robertson, Kirk, ed. LC 77-73205. 1980. pap. 3.00 (*0-916918-07-6*) Duck Down.

— Eating the English Army. 1975. 4.00 (*0-685-67935-7*) Windless Orchard.

Mattei, James F. The "Comp" Rehensive Guide to the Casino Game: How to Vacation Free. 160p. 1999. spiral bd. 14.95 (*0-9669549-2-0*) Bald Terney.

— The "Comp"rehensive Guide to Atlantic City: How to Vacation Free in A. C. 133p. 1998. spiral bd. 14.95 (*0-9669549-0-4*) Bald Terney.

— The "Comp"rehensive Guide to the Gulf Coast: How to Make the Most of the Gulf Coast. 140p. 1999. spiral bd. 14.95 (*0-9669549-1-2*) Bald Terney.

Mattei, Janet A., et al, compiled by. AH Herculis Light Curves, 1963-1995. (AAVSO Monographs: No. 8). (Illus.). 74p. (Orig.). 1996. pap. text 10.00 (*1-878174-19-3*) Am Assn Var Star.

— AM Herculis Light Curves 1977-1995. (AAVSO Monographs: No. 10). (Illus.). 48p. (Orig.). 1997. pap. text 10.00 (*1-878174-21-5*) Am Assn Var Star.

— Maxima & Minima of Long Period Variables, 1949-1975. 128p. 1990. pap. text 15.00 (*1-878174-09-6*) Am Assn Var Star.

— PU Vulpeculae Light Curves, 1979-1995. (AAVSO Monographs: No. 11). (Illus.). 25p. 1997. pap. text 10.00 (*1-878174-22-3*) Am Assn Var Star.

— R Coronae Borealis Light Curves, 1843-1990. (AAVSO Monograph: No. 4). (Illus.). 27p. 1991. pap. text 10.00 (*1-878174-03-7*) Am Assn Var Star.

— R Scuti Light Curves, 1985-1990. (AAVSO Monographs: No. 3, Supplement 1). (Illus.). 16p. 1991. pap. text 10.00 (*1-878174-07-X*) Am Assn Var Star.

— R Scuti Light Curves, 1991-1995: AAVSO Monograph 3, Supplement 2. (AAVSO Monographs: No. 3, Supplement 2). (Illus.). 15p. 1996. pap. text, suppl. ed. 10.00 (*1-878174-16-9*) Am Assn Var Star.

— R Scuti Light Curves, 1963-1985. (AAVSO Monographs: No. 3). (Illus.). 29p. 1988. pap. text 10.00 (*1-878174-08-8*) Am Assn Var Star.

— RS Ophiuchi Light Curves, 1890-1995: AAVSO Monograph 7. (AAVSO Monographs: No. 7). (Illus.). 38p. 1996. pap. text 10.00 (*1-878174-13-4*) Am Assn Var Star.

— RX Andromedae Light Curves, 1963-1995. (AAVSO Monographs: No. 9). (Illus.). 76p. (Orig.). 1996. pap. text 10.00 (*1-878174-20-7*) Am Assn Var Star.

— RY Sagittarii Light Curves, 1892-1990: AAVSO Monograph 5. (AAVSO Monographs: No. 5). (Illus.). 22p. 1994. pap. text 10.00 (*1-878174-04-5*) Am Assn Var Star.

— RY Sagittarii Light Curves, 1991-1995: AAVSO Monograph 5, Supplement 1. (AAVSO Monographs: No. 5, Supplement 1). (Illus.). 12p. 1996. pap. text, suppl. ed. 10.00 (*1-878174-18-5*) Am Assn Var Star.

— SS Cygni Light Curves, 1896-1985. (AAVSO Monographs: No. 1). (Illus.). 53p. 1985. pap. text 10.00 (*1-878174-01-0*) Am Assn Var Star.

— SS Cygni Light Curves, 1985-1990. (AAVSO Monographs: No. 1, Supplement 1). (Illus.). 23p. 1991. pap. text 10.00 (*1-878174-05-3*) Am Assn Var Star.

— SS Cygni Light Curves, 1991-1995. (AAVSO Monographs: No. 1, Supplement 2). (Illus.). 21p. 1996. pap. text, suppl. ed. 10.00 (*1-878174-14-2*) Am Assn Var Star.

— TT Arietis Light Curves, 1974-1995. (Monograph Ser.: No. 12). (Illus.). 50p. 1997. pap. text 10.00 (*1-878174-23-1*) Am Assn Var Star.

— U Geminorum Light Curves, 1855-1985. (Monograph Ser.: No. 2). (Illus.). 53p. 1987. pap. text 10.00 (*1-878174-02-9*) Am Assn Var Star.

— U Geminorum Light Curves, 1985-1990. (AAVSO Monograph: No. 2, Supplement 1). (Illus.). 22p. 1991. pap. text 10.00 (*1-878174-06-1*) Am Assn Var Star.

— U Geminorum Light Curves, 1991-1995: AAVSO Monograph 2, Supplement 2. (AAVSO Monographs: No. 2, Supplement 2). (Illus.). 20p. 1996. pap. text, suppl. ed. 10.00 (*1-878174-15-0*) Am Assn Var Star.

— Z Camelopardalis Light Curves, 1927-1995: AAVSO Monograph 6. (AAVSO Monographs: No. 6). (Illus.). 72p. 1996. pap. text 10.00 (*1-878174-12-6*) Am Assn Var Star.

Mattei, Janet A., et al. R Coronae Borealis Light Curves, 1991-1995: AAVSO Monograph 4, Supplement 1. (AAVSO Monographs: No. 4, Supplement 1). (Illus.). 14p. 1996. pap. text, suppl. ed. 10.00 (*1-878174-17-7*) Am Assn Var Star.

Mattei, Marie D., jt. ed. see Coll, Cynthia G.

***Mattei, Ugo.** Basic Principles of Property Law: A Comparative Legal & Economic Introduction, 93. LC 99-31575. Vol. 93. 232p. 2000. 65.00 (*0-313-31186-2*) Greenwood.

Mattei, Ugo. Comparative Law & Economics. LC 96-45860. 288p. (C). 1997. text 52.50 (*0-472-09649-4*, 09649) U of Mich Pr.

— Comparative Law & Economics. LC 96-45860. 288p. 1998. pap. text 22.95 (*0-472-06649-8*, 06649) U of Mich Pr.

Matteis, Francesco De, see De Matteis, Francesco, ed.

Mattel, Jean-Francois, jt. auth. see Janicaud, Dominique.

Mattelart, Armand. The Invention of Communication. Emanuel, Susan, tr. LC 96-14993. 320p. (C). 1996. pap. 21.95 (*0-8166-2697-9*); text 54.95 (*0-8166-2696-0*) U of Minn Pr.

— Mapping World Communication: War, Progress, Culture. Emanuel, Susan & Cohen, James A., trs. from FRE. LC 93-32250. 1994. pap. 19.95 (*0-8166-2262-0*); text 49.95 (*0-8166-2261-2*) U of Minn Pr.

***Mattelart, Armand.** Networking the World, 1794-2000. (Illus.). 2000. pap. 16.95 (*0-8166-3288-X*) U of Minn Pr.

Mattelart, Armand. Transnationals & the Third World: The Struggle for Culture. (Illus.). 192p. 1985. 34.95 (*0-89789-030-2*, Bergin & Garvey); pap. 14.95 (*0-89789-100-7*, Bergin & Garvey) Greenwood.

Mattelart, Armand, ed. Communicating in Popular Nicaragua. (Illus.). 140p. 1986. pap. 15.95 (*0-88477-024-9*) Intl General.

Mattelart, Armand & Mattelart, Michele. Rethinking Media Theory: Signposts & New Directions. Cohen, James A. & Urquidi, Marina, trs. from FRE. (Media & Society Ser.: Vol. 5). 208p. (C). 1992. pap. 17.95 (*0-8166-1910-7*) U of Minn Pr.

Mattelart, Armand & Schmucler, Hector. Communication & Info Technologies: Freedom of Choice for Latin America. Voigt, Melvin J., ed. Buxton, David, tr. from FRE. (Communication & Information Science Ser.). 192p. 1985. text 73.25 (*0-89391-214-X*) Ablx Pub.

Mattelart, Armand & Siegelaub, Seth, eds. Communication & Class Struggle: Capitalism, Imperialism, Vol. 1. (Illus.). 445p. (Orig.). 1979. pap. 54.95 (*0-88477-011-7*) Intl General.

— Communication & Class Struggle: Liberation, Socialism, Vol. 2. LC 80-110213. (Illus.). 438p. (Orig.). 1983. pap. 54.95 (*0-88477-018-4*) Intl General.

Mattelart, Armand, jt. auth. see Dorfman, Ariel.

Mattelart, Armand, jt. auth. see Mattelart, Michele.

Mattelart, Michele & Mattelart, Armand. The Carnival of Images: Brazilian Television Fiction. LC 90-36026. 192p. 1990. 52.95 (*0-89789-212-7*, H212, Bergin & Garvey) Greenwood.

Mattelart, Michele, jt. auth. see Mattelart, Armand.

Mattelon, Kate S., jt. ed. see Tobias, Michael.

Mattelon, Patrice, jt. auth. see Solisti-Mattelon, Kate.

***Matten.** Managing Bank Capital: Capital Allocation & Performance Measurement. 2nd ed. LC 99-59514. 350p. 2000. text 95.00 (*0-471-85196-5*) Wiley.

Matten, Chris. Managing Bank Capital: Capital Allocation & Performance Measurement. LC 95-53023. 224p. 1996. 155.00 (*0-471-96116-7*) Wiley.

Mattenheimer, A. & Beutter, Manfred H. Cartridges for Breech-Loading Rifles: A Contribution to Firearms Instruction. 1991. 29.95 (*0-939683-05-9*) Armory Pubns.

Mattens, W. C., ed. see Boom, Rob, et al.

Matteo, Anthony M. Quest for the Absolute: The Philosophical Vision of Joseph Marechal. LC 91-26367. 202p. 1992. lib. bdg. 32.00 (*0-87580-165-X*) N Ill U Pr.

Matteo, Henry S. Denationalization vs. "The Right to Have Rights" The Standard of Intent in Citizenship Loss. LC 97-18826. 144p. 1997. 46.50 (*0-7618-0781-0*); pap. 24.50 (*0-7618-0782-9*) U Pr of Amer.

Matteo, Laura, ed. Who's Who among Top Executives. (Illus.). 415p. 1997. 199.00 (*0-9652836-1-5*) Kaleo Publns.

Matteo, M. Di, see Di Matteo, M.

Matteo, Michael A. How To Survive the Public School System: A Guide for Students, Parents & Teachers. LC 91-90383. 100p. (Orig.). 1991. pap. 8.50 (*0-9629771-9-5*) M&P Pub.

Matteo, Sante & Peer, Larry H. The Reasonable Romantic: Essays on Alessandro Manzoni. X, 156p. 1989. text 36.50 (*0-8204-0372-5*) P Lang Pubng.

Matteo, Sherri, ed. American Women in the Nineties: Today's Critical Issues. 288p. 1993. text 47.50 (*1-55553-150-4*); pap. text 18.95 (*1-55553-151-2*) NE U Pr.

Matteo, Stephen. Bob Dylan: The Life & Music of America's Folk-Rock Icon. LC 97-51265. (Illus.). 120p. 1998. 19.98 (*1-56799-634-5*, MetroBooks) M Friedman Pub Grp Inc.

Matteoli, Enrico, jt. ed. see Mansoori, G. Ali.

Matteoni, Norman E. & Veit, Henry. Condemnation Practice in California. 2nd ed. Chapin, John K., ed. LC 95-69144. 444p. 1997. ring bd. 45.00 (*0-7626-0131-0*, RE-32412) Cont Ed Bar-CA.

— Condemnation Practice in California - 6-99 Update, Vols. 1 & 2. Briggs, Donald R., ed. LC 95-69144. 390p. 1999. ring bd. 60.00 (*0-7626-0335-6*, RE-32414) Cont Ed Bar-CA.

— Condemnation Practice in California, 6/98 Update, 2 vols. 2nd ed. Chapin, John K., ed. LC 95-69144. 512p. 1998. ring bd. 54.00 (*0-7626-0238-4*, RE-32413) Cont Ed Bar-CA.

Matter. Material Science. 1996. cd-rom 99.50 (*0-412-80080-2*, Chap & Hall CRC) CRC Pr.

Matter, E. Ann & Coakley, John, eds. Creative Women in Medieval & Early Modern Italy: A Religious & Artistic Renaissance. (Middle Ages Ser.). (Illus.). 376p. (C). 1994. text 38.50 (*0-8122-3236-4*) U of Pa Pr.

Matter, Jacques. Saint-Martin, Vol. VIII. Amadou, Robert, ed. 329p. reprint ed. write for info. (*0-318-71419-1*) G Olms Pubs.

***Matter, Norman L.** An Angel's Story. Taucher, Gina, ed. xi, 305p. 2000. pap. 14.00 (*0-9700005-0-2*) Tourek Bks.

Matter, Robert M. Pre-Seminole Florida: Spanish Soldiers, Friars, & Indian Missions, 1513-1763. LC 90-21600. (Evolution of North American Indians Ser.: Vol. 13). 208p. 1991. reprint ed. text 10.00 (*0-8240-2508-3*) Garland.

Matter, William D. If It Takes All Summer: The Battle of Spotsylvania. LC 87-31950. (Illus.). xvi, 455p. (C). 1988. 37.50 (*0-8078-1781-3*) U of NC Pr.

Mattera, John. Abra Cadaver. 1982. pap. 3.60 (*0-87129-202-5*, A28) Dramatic Pub.

— Restless in Peace. 82p. 1987. pap. 5.00 (*0-87129-000-6*, R49) Dramatic Pub.

— You Don't Have to Die. 71p. 1991. pap. 5.50 (*0-87129-083-9*, Y16) Dramatic Pub.

Mattera, Philip. Inside U.S. Business: A Concise Encyclopedia of Leading Industries. 3rd ed. LC 93-23940. 636p. 1993. text 65.00 (*1-55623-731-6*, Irwn Prfssnl) McGraw-Hill Prof.

— World Class Business: A Guide to the 100 Most Powerful Global Corporations. 784p. 1995. 50.00 (*0-8050-1681-3*) H Holt & Co.

Mattern. The Bighorn Sheep. LC 98-3624. (Wildlife of North America Ser.). (Illus.). 48p. (J). 1998. 19.00 (*0-7368-0028-X*) Capstone Pr.

— The Coyote. LC 98-6342. (Wildlife of North America Ser.). (Illus.). 48p. (J). 1998. 19.00 (*0-7368-0029-8*) Capstone Pr.

Mattern, Carolyn J., ed. The Papers of Nathaniel P. Tallmadge: Guide to a Microfilm Edition. 45p. 1973. pap. write for info. (*0-89887-185-9*) Chadwyck-Healey.

— Papers of the International Workingmen's Association: Guide to a Microfilm Edition. (Guides to Historical Resources Ser.). 132p. 1972. pap. 1.00 (*0-87020-151-4*) State Hist Soc Wis.

— The Papers of the International Workingmen's Association, 1868-1877: Guide to a Microfilm Edition. 15p. 1972. pap. write for info. (*0-89887-181-6*) Chadwyck-Healey.

Mattern, Carolyn J., jt. auth. see Behrnd-Klodt, Menzi L.

Mattern, David B. Benjamin Lincoln & the American Revolution. LC 95-4399. 317p. 1998. pap. 14.95 (*1-57003-260-2*) U of SC Pr.

***Mattern, David B., et al, eds.** The Papers of James Madison, Vol. 5. Vol. 5. 704p. 2000. text 67.50 (*0-8139-1941-X*) U Pr of Va.

Mattern, David B., ed. see Madison, James.

Mattern, Evelyn & Brancato, Helen D. Why Not Become Fire? Encounters with Women Mystics. LC 99-30550. 128p. 1999. pap. 14.95 (*0-87793-690-0*) Ave Maria.

***Mattern, Joanne.** The Abyssinian Cat. LC 00-25667. (Learning about Cats Ser.). (Illus.). 48p. (YA). (gr. 5 up). 2000. lib. bdg. 21.26 (*0-7368-0564-8*, Capstone Bks) Capstone Pr.

Mattern, Joanne. The Adventures of Robin Hood. (Wishbone Classics Ser.). 1996. 9.09 (*0-606-10369-4*, Pub. by Turtleback) Demco.

— Baby Animals. LC 91-40282. (Illus.). 24p. (J). (gr. 4-7). 1993. pap. text 1.95 (*0-8167-2958-1*) Troll Communs.

***Mattern, Joanne.** Balance Beam & Floor Exercises. LC 99-27924. (Compete Like A Champion Gymnastics Ser.). 48p. (J). 1999. lib. bdg. write for info. (*0-86593-567-X*) Rourke Corp.

Mattern, Joanne. Bears. LC 92-20176. (Illus.). 24p. (J). (gr. 4-7). 1992. pap. 1.95 (*0-8167-2952-2*) Troll Communs.

— The Big Horn Sheep. (Wildlife of North America Ser.). (Illus.). (J). 1998. 19.00 (*0-516-21480-2*) Childrens.

— Coyote, Vol. 6. (Wildlife of North America Ser.). (J). 1998. 19.00 (*0-516-21481-0*) Childrens.

***Mattern, Joanne.** Ferdinand Magellan. LC 99-55480. (Explorers & Exploration Ser.). (Illus.). 48p. (YA). 2000. lib. bdg. 22.83 (*0-7398-1484-2*) Raintree Steck-V.

Mattern, Joanne. Good Night, Bear! LC 97-221925. (Illus.). 32p. (J). (gr. k-2). 1998. pap. 2.95 (*0-8167-4517-X*) Troll Communs.

— Ivanhoe. (Wishbone Mysteries Ser.). (J). 1997. 9.09 (*0-606-12105-6*, Pub. by Turtleback) Demco.

— Lions & Tigers. LC 92-19053. (Illus.). 24p. (J). (gr. 4-7). 1992. pap. 1.95 (*0-8167-2956-5*) Troll Communs.

***Mattern, Joanne.** The Maine Coon Cat. (Learning about Cats Ser.). 48p. (YA). (gr. 5 up). 2000. lib. bdg. 21.26 (*0-7368-0565-6*, Capstone Bks) Capstone Pr.

Mattern, Joanne. Monkeys & Apes. LC 92-28080. (Illus.). 24p. (J). (gr. 4-7). 1992. pap. text 1.95 (*0-8167-2962-X*) Troll Communs.

— The Odyssey. (Wishbone Classics Ser.). 1996. 9.09 (*0-606-10365-1*, Pub. by Turtleback) Demco.

— Oliver Twist. (Wishbone Classics Ser.). 1996. 9.09 (*0-606-10368-6*, Pub. by Turtleback) Demco.

***Mattern, Joanne.** Parallel Bars & Horizontal Bars. LC 99-27924. 48p. (J). 1999. lib. bdg. write for info. (*0-86593-570-X*) Rourke Corp.

— The Persian Cat. (Learning about Cats Ser.). 48p. (YA). (gr. 5 up). 2000. lib. bdg. 21.26 (*0-7368-0566-4*, Capstone Bks) Capstone Pr.

Mattern, Joanne. A Picture Book of Butterflies & Moths. LC 92-5225. (Picture Book of...Ser.). (Illus.). 24p. (J). (gr. 1-4). 1992. lib. bdg. 9.95 (*0-8167-2796-1*, BP089) Troll Communs.

— A Picture Book of Butterflies & Moths. LC 92-5225. (Picture Book of...Ser.). (Illus.). 24p. (J). (gr. 1-4). 1996. pap. 2.95 (*0-8167-2797-X*) Troll Communs.

— Picture Book of Cats. LC 90-42548. (Picture Book of...Ser.). (Illus.). 24p. (J). (gr. 1-4). 1991. lib. bdg. 14.50 (*0-8167-2146-7*) Troll Communs.

— Picture Book of Cats. LC 90-42548. (Picture Book of...Ser.). (Illus.). 24p. (J). (gr. 4-7). 1991. pap. 2.95 (*0-8167-2147-5*) Troll Communs.

— A Picture Book of Insects. LC 90-11211. (Picture Book of...Ser.). (Illus.). 24p. (J). (gr. 1-4). 1991. lib. bdg. 14.50 (*0-8167-2154-8*) Troll Communs.

— A Picture Book of Insects. LC 90-11211. (Picture Book of...Ser.). (Illus.). 24p. (J). (gr. 1-4). 1997. pap. 2.95 (*0-8167-2155-6*) Troll Communs.

***Mattern, Joanne.** Pommel Horse & the Rings. LC 99-27924. 48p. (J). 1999. write for info. (*0-86593-568-8*) Rourke Corp.

Mattern, Joanne. Reptiles & Amphibians. LC 92-20189. (Illus.). 24p. (J). (gr. 4-7). 1992. pap. 1.95 (*0-8167-2954-9*) Troll Communs.

— Safety at Home. LC 98-5530. (Safety First Ser.). (Illus.). 24p. (J). 1999. lib. bdg. 18.60 (*1-57765-071-9*, Checkerboard Library) ABDO Pub Co.

— Safety at School. LC 98-5529. (Safety First Ser.). (Illus.). 24p. (J). (gr. k-3). 1999. lib. bdg. 18.60 (*1-57765-070-0*, Checkerboard Library) ABDO Pub Co.

— Safety in Public Places. LC 98-13897. (Safety First Ser.). (Illus.). 24p. (J). (gr. k-3). 1999. lib. bdg. 18.60 (*1-57765-074-3*, Checkerboard Library) ABDO Pub Co.

— Safety in the Water. LC 98-17278. (Safety First Ser.). (Illus.). 24p. (J). (gr. k-3). 1999. lib. bdg. 18.60 (*1-57765-072-7*, Checkerboard Library) ABDO Pub Co.

— Safety on the Go. LC 98-17272. (Safety First Ser.). (Illus.). 24p. (J). (gr. k-3). 1998. lib. bdg. 18.60 (*1-57765-075-1*, Checkerboard Library) ABDO Pub Co.

— Safety on Your Bicycle. LC 98-17277. (Safety First Ser.). (Illus.). 24p. (J). (gr. k-3). 1999. lib. bdg. 18.60 (*1-57765-073-5*, Checkerboard Library) ABDO Pub Co.

***Mattern, Joanne.** The Siamese Cat. (Learning about Cats Ser.). 48p. (YA). (gr. 5 up). 2001. lib. bdg. 21.26 (*0-7368-0567-2*, Capstone Bks) Capstone Pr.

Mattern, Joanne. The Strange Case of Dr. Jekyll & Mr. Hyde. (Wishbone Classics Ser.). 1996. 9.09 (*0-606-10371-6*, Pub. by Turtleback) Demco.

— Tiger Woods. LC 99-169803. (History Makers Ser.). (Illus.). 48p. (J). (gr. 4-6). 1998. pap. 3.95 (*0-8167-4551-X*) Troll Communs.

***Mattern, Joanne.** Training & Fitness. LC 99-27924. 48p. (J). 1999. lib. bdg. write for info. (*0-86593-571-8*) Rourke Corp.

— Uneven Parallel Bars. LC 99-27924. 48p. (J). 1999. lib. bdg. write for info. (*0-86593-569-6*) Rourke Corp.

— The Vault. LC 99-27924. (J). 1999. lib. bdg. write for info. (*0-86593-566-1*) Rourke Corp.

Mattern, Joanne. Young Martin Luther King, Jr. I Have a Dream. LC 91-26478. (Illus.). 32p. (J). (gr. k-2). 1991. pap. 3.50 (*0-8167-2545-4*) Troll Communs.

— Young Martin Luther King, Jr. I Have a Dream. LC 91-26478. (Illus.). 32p. (J). (gr. k-2). 1997. text 17.25 (*0-8167-2544-6*) Troll Communs.

***Mattern, Joanne, contrib. by.** Henry Hudson. LC 99-55476. (Explorers & Exploration Ser.). 48p. (J). 2000. lib. bdg. write for info. (*0-7398-1483-4*) Raintree Steck-V.

Mattern, Joanne, ed. see Payle, Howard.

Mattern, Joanne, ed. see Pyle, Howard.

Mattern, Johannes. Bavaria & the Reich: The Conflict over the Law for the Protection of the Republic. LC 78-64111. (Johns Hopkins University. Studies in the Social Sciences. Thirtieth Ser. 1912: 3). reprint ed. 27.50 (*0-404-61226-1*) AMS Pr.

— Geopolitik Doctrine of Self-Sufficiency & Empire. LC 78-64186. (Johns Hopkins University. Studies in the Social Sciences. Thirtieth Ser. 1912: 2). reprint ed. 29.50 (*0-404-61293-8*) AMS Pr.

Mattern, Mark. Acting in Concert: Music, Community & Political Action. LC 97-21868. 184p. 1998. 50.00 (*0-8135-2483-0*); pap. 20.00 (*0-8135-2484-9*) Rutgers U Pr.

Mattern, Susan P. Wasteland Called Peace: Roman Imperial Strategy, 31 B.C.-A.D. 235: Imperial Strategy in the Principate. LC 98-40630. 260p. 1999. 35.00 (*0-520-21166-9*, Pub. by U CA Pr) Cal Prin Full Svc.

Matters, C. Virginia, ed. Riding & Roping: The Memoirs of J. Will Harris. LC 74-78373. (Illus.). 211p. 1977. 20.00 (*0-913480-23-1*); pap. 6.00 (*0-913480-34-7*) Inter Am U Pr.

Matters, M. Single-Electron & Copper Pair Transport in Circuits of Small Tunnel Junctions. (Illus.). 112p. (Orig.). 1996. pap. 62.50 (*90-407-1315-4*, Pub. by Delft U Pr) Coronet Bks.

Matters, Marion. Introduction to the USMARC Format for Archival & Manuscripts Control. 24p. 1990. pap. 10.00 (*0-614-01638-X*) Soc Am Archivists.

Matters, Marion, compiled by. Oral History Cataloging Manual. LC 95-8672. 112p. 1995. pap. 25.00 (*0-931828-97-X*) Soc Am Archivists.

Matters, Marion, ed. Automated Records & Techniques in Archives: A Resource Directory. 75p. (C). 1990. pap. 16.00 (*0-931828-80-5*) Soc Am Archivists.

Matterson, Elizabeth. Play with a Purpose for under Sevens. pap. 15.95 (*0-14-010493-3*, Pub. by Pnguin Bks Ltd) Trafalgar.

— This Little Puffin. (Illus.). (J). 1991. pap. 12.95 (*0-14-034048-3*, Pub. by Pnguin Bks Ltd) Trafalgar.

An Asterisk (*) at the beginning of an entry indicates that the title is appearing for the first time.

***Matterson, Stephen.** Studying Poetry. 192p. 2000. pap. text 18.95 (*0-340-75942-9*, Pub. by E A) OUP.

***Matterson, Stephen & Jones, Darryl.** Studying Poetry. (An Arnold Publication). 192p. (C). 2000. text 59.95 (*0-340-75941-0*) E A.

Matterson, Stephen, ed. & intro. see Melville, Herman.

Matterson, Steven. Berryman & Lowell: The Art of Losing. LC 87-1824. 144p. 1987. 49.00 (*0-389-20730-6*, N8288) B&N Imports.

Mattes, Aaron L. Active Isolated Stretching. Sommer, Eleanor K., ed. (Illus.). 122p. 1995. pap. 30.00 (*0-9656396-0-6*) A L Mattes.

Mattes, Eleanor B. In Memoriam - The Way of a Soul: A Study of Some Influences That Shaped Tennyson's Poem. 128p. (C). 1990. reprint ed. lib. bdg. 75.00 (*0-8383-0594-6*) M S G Haskell Hse.

— Myth for Moderns: Erwin Ramsdell Goodenough & Religious Studies in America, 1938-1955. LC 97-8875. (ATLA Monograph Ser.: No. 43). 256p. 1997. 42.00 (*0-8108-3339-5*) Scarecrow.

Mattes, Jane. Single Mothers by Choice: A Guidebook for Single Women Who Are Considering or Have Chosen. LC 94-13460. 243p. 1994. pap. 15.00 (*0-8129-2246-8*, Times Bks) Crown Pub Group.

Mattes, Larry J. Bilingual Language, Speech, & Hearing Dictionary. 96p. (Orig.). 1985. pap. text 9.00 (*0-930951-01-8*) Acad Comm.

— Criterion-Referenced Articulation Profile. 1986. pap. text 45.00 (*0-930951-06-9*) Acad Comm.

— Handbook of Consonant Speech Drills. 175p. 1986. pap. text 22.00 (*0-930951-04-2*) Acad Comm.

— Spanish Language Assessment Procedures: A Communication Skills Inventory. (Illus.). 1985. pap. text 38.00 (*0-930951-03-4*) Acad Comm.

Mattes, Larry J. & Eddo, Debe. Adventures in Pragmatic Problem-Solving: Stories & Language Activities for Children. (Illus.). 174p. 1989. pap. text 22.95 (*0-930951-11-5*) Acad Comm.

Mattes, Larry J. & Santiago, George. Teaching Spanish Speech Sounds: Drills for Articulation Therapy. (Illus.). 122p. 1985. pap. text 18.50 (*0-930951-02-6*) Acad Comm.

Mattes, Merrill J. The Great Platte River Road. LC 87-10844. (Illus.). xl, 600p. 1987. reprint ed. pap. 19.95 (*0-8032-8153-6*, Bison Books) U of Nebr Pr.

— Jackson Hole, Crossroads of the Western Fur Trade, 1807-1840. LC 94-37582. (Center Bks.: Vol. 1). 1994. pap. 7.95 (*1-886402-00-0*) Jackson Hole Hist.

— Platte River Road Narratives: A Descriptive Bibliography of Travel over the Great Central Overland Route to Oregon, California, Utah, Colorado, Montana, & Other Western States & Territories, 1812-1866. LC 87-1668. (Illus.). 648p. 1988. text 95.00 (*0-252-01342-5*) U of Ill Pr.

Mattesini, Fabrizio. Financial Markets, Asymmetric Information & Macroeconomic Equilibrium. 200p. 1993. 77.95 (*1-85521-177-7*, Pub. by Dartmth Pub) Ashgate Pub Co.

Matteson. Mat/women Health. 2001. text. write for info. (*0-323-00915-8*) Harcourt.

Matteson, Antonette. The Occult Family Physician & Botanic Guide to Health. 1992. lib. bdg. 89.95 (*0-8490-8744-9*) Gordon Pr.

— The Occult Family Physician & Botanic Guide to Health. 317p. 1996. reprint ed. spiral bd. 22.50 (*0-7873-0587-1*) Hlth Research.

— The Occult Family Physician & Botanic Guide to Health: A Description of American & Foreign Plants & Their Medical Virtues. enl. rev. ed. (Illus.). 327p. 1993. reprint ed. pap. 12.50 (*0-916638-24-3*) Meyerbooks.

— The Occult Family Physician & Botanic Guide to Health, 1894. 324p. 1996. reprint ed. pap. 24.95 (*1-56459-709-1*) Kessinger Pub.

Matteson, Barbara J. Mystic Minerals: Wisdom of the Ancients. rev. ed. LC 86-71607. (Illus.). 64p. 1986. pap. 4.95 (*0-9620524-0-X*) Cosmic Resources.

***Matteson, Calvin.** Civil War Veterans: In & Around Allegany County. Wightman, Christina C., ed. 200p. 1999. pap. write for info. (*1-888911-17-4*) Benson Smythe.

Matteson, D. M. List of Manuscripts Concerning American History Preserved in European Libraries. (Carnegie Institute Ser.: Vol. 10). 1925. 30.00 (*0-527-00690-4*) Periodicals Srv.

Matteson, D. S. Stereodirected Synthesis with Organoboranes. Rees, C. W. et al, eds. (Reactivity & Structure Ser.: Vol. 32). (Illus.). 400p. 1995. 174.95 (*3-540-59182-6*) Spr-Verlag.

Matteson, David M. Organization of the Government under the Constitution. LC 72-118201. (American Constitutional & Legal History Ser). 1970. reprint ed. lib. bdg. 47.50 (*0-306-71935-5*) Da Capo.

Matteson, Edith, tr. see Bergnian, Bo.

Matteson, Edith, tr. see Madsen, Benedicte & Willert, Soren.

Matteson, Edith M., jt. auth. see Matteson, Jean M.

Matteson, Edith M., tr. see Sandberg, Gosta.

Matteson, Esther, et al. Comparative Studies in Amerindian Languages. (Janua Linguarum, Ser. Practica: No. 127). 251p. (Orig.). 1972. pap. text 70.80 (*90-279-2110-5*) Mouton.

Matteson, H. P., ed. see Aydelott, George C.

Matteson, Jean M. & Matteson, Edith M. Blossoms of the Prairie: The History of the Danish Lutheran Churches in Nebraska. 247p. 1988. 30.95 (*0-9620787-0-0*) Blossoms Prairie.

Matteson, Marguerite C., ed. Better Than Strangers, 2 vols. Incl. Vol. 1. (Illus.). xx, 340p. (Orig.). 1996. pap. (*0-9654092-0-1*); Vol. 2. (Illus.). xii, 316p. (Orig.). 1996. pap. (*0-9654092-1-X*); 65.00 (*0-9654092-2-8*) Cynosure Pubng.

Matteson, Marianna M. Manuel Diaz Rodriguez: Evolution & Dynamics of the Stylist, Vol. 107. LC 93-18340. (Scripta Humanistica Ser.). 101 p. 1993. 48.50 (*1-882528-02-6*) Scripta.

Matteson, Mary A., et al. Gerontological Nursing: Concepts & Practice. 2nd ed. Rader, Ilze, ed. (Illus.). 1024p. 1996. text 58.00 (*0-7216-3785-X*, W B Saunders Co) Harcrt Hlth Sci Grp.

— Introductory Nursing Care of Adults. (Illus.). 1216p. 1995. text 49.00 (*0-7216-3319-6*, W B Saunders Co) Harcrt Hlth Sci Grp.

Matteson, Michael J. Filtration: Principles & Practices. 2nd enl. rev. ed. Orr, Clive, ed. (Chemical Industries Ser.: Vol. 27). (Illus.). 760p. 1986. text 250.00 (*0-8247-7582-1*) Dekker.

— Legends of Christmas. large type ed. (Illus.). 144p. (J). (gr. 3-8). 1998. pap. 9.50 (*1-890740-05-5*) Remnant Pr.

Matteson, Michael T. & Ivancevich, John M., eds. Management & Organizational Behavior Classics. 6th ed. LC 94-49391. 480p. (C). 1995. text 37.25 (*0-256-16204-2*, Irwn McGrw-H) McGrw-H Hghr Educ.

Matteson, Michael T. & Joinvancevich, John M. Management & Organizational Behavior Classics. 7th ed. LC 98-23853. 1998. 45.03 (*0-256-26457-0*, Irwn Prfssnl) McGraw-Hill Prof.

Matteson, Michael T., jt. auth. see Invancevich, John M.

Matteson, Michael T., jt. auth. see Ivancevich, John M.

Matteson, Patricia. Resolving the DDT Dilemma: Protecting Biodiversity & Human Health. (Illus.). 52p. (C). 1999. pap. text 20.00 (*0-7881-7793-1*) DIANE Pub.

Matteson, Peggy. Advocating for Self: Women's Decisions Concerning Contraception. LC 95-14297. (Illus.). 146p. (C). 1995. pap. 14.95 (*1-56023-868-2*); lib. bdg. 54.95 (*1-56024-948-X*) Haworth Jrnl Co-Edits.

Matteson, Peggy, ed. Teaching Nursing in the Neighborhoods: The Northeastern University Model. (Teaching of Nursing Ser.). (Illus.). 256p. 1995. 34.95 (*0-8261-9100-2*) Springer Pub.

Matteson, Richard, Sr. Appalachian Folk Songs for Piano & Voice: Beginning-Intermediate Level. 80p. 1996. spiral bd. 10.95 (*0-7866-1798-5*, 95740) Mel Bay.

Matteson, Richard L. An Appalachian Christmas. 80p. 1993. pap. 7.95 (*1-56222-885-4*, 95057) Mel Bay.

***Matteson, Richard L., Jr.** Early Music Favorites for Acoustic Guitar: Intermediate Level. 88p. 1998. pap. 19.95 incl. audio compact disk (*0-7866-2085-4*, 95779BCD) Mel Bay.

Matteson, Richard L., jt. auth. see Harris, Janis L.

Matteson, Ronald G. Introduction to Document Image Processing Techniques. LC 95-15177. 259p. 1995. 37.00 (*0-89006-492-X*) Artech Hse.

Matteson, Rosemary. Nothing Gold Can Stay. Ingham, Donna, ed. LC 98-61620. 260p. 1999. pap. 17.95 (*1-881636-73-9*) Windsor Hse Pub Grp.

Matteson, Stefanie. Murder among the Angels. 256p. 1996. pap. 19.95 (*0-425-15149-2*, Prime Crime) Berkley Pub.

— Murder among the Angels. 256p. 1996. mass mkt. 5.99 (*0-425-15548-X*, Prime Crime) Berkley Pub.

***Matteson, Stefanie.** Murder on High. large type ed. LC 99-59387. (Mystery Ser.). 2000. 24.95 (*1-57490-261-X*, Beeler LP Bks) T T Beeler.

Matteson, Stefanie. Murder on the Silk Road. 1992. mass mkt. 5.50 (*0-425-14820-3*, Prime Crime) Berkley Pub.

— Murder under the Palms. LC 96-31429. Vol. 3. 256p. 1997. pap. 21.95 (*0-425-15628-1*, Prime Crime) Berkley Pub.

— Murder under the Palms. large type ed. LC 98-5876. 1998. 24.95 (*1-57490-137-0*) T T Beeler.

— Murder under the Palms. 256p. 1997. reprint ed. mass mkt. 5.99 (*0-425-16035-1*, Prime Crime) Berkley Pub.

Matteson, Stephen R., et al. Dental Radiology. 4th rev. ed. LC 87-16258. (Dental Assisting Manuals Ser.). (Illus.). viii, 155p. (C). 1988. pap. 27.50 (*0-8078-4205-2*) U of NC Pr.

Matteson, Sumner. Hawks for Kids. LC 94-40922. (Wildlife for Kids Ser.). (Illus.). 48p. (Orig.). (J). (gr. 3-7). 1995. pap. 6.95 (*1-55971-462-X*, NorthWord Pr) Creat Pub Intl.

Mattessich, Paul & Monsey, Barbara. Community Building: What Makes It Work: A Literature Review of Factors Influencing Successful Community Building. Hyman, Vincent, ed. LC 97-12500. (Orig.). 1997. per., wbk. ed. 20.00 (*0-940069-12-1*) A H Wilder.

Mattessich, Paul W. & Monsey, Barbara R. Collaboration: What Makes It Work: A Review of Research Literature on Factors Influencing Successful Collaboration. LC 92-72633. 53p. (Orig.). 1992. pap. 15.00 (*0-940069-02-4*) A H Wilder.

***Mattessich, Richard.** The Beginnings of Accounting Thought: Accounting Practice in the Middle East, 8000 B. C. to 2000 B. C. & Accounting Thought in India, 300 B.C. & the Middle Ages. LC 00-34726. (New Works in Accounting History Ser.). 2000. write for info. (*0-8153-3445-1*) Garland.

Mattessich, Richard V. Critique of Accounting: Examination of the Foundations & Normative Structure of an Applied Discipline. LC 95-3776. 304p. 1995. 69.50 (*0-89930-863-5*, Quorum Bks) Greenwood.

Matteucci, Mario. Dictionnaire Juridique. (FRE & ITA.). 1963. write for info. (*0-7859-4892-9*) Fr & Eur.

Matteucci, N., jt. auth. see Bobbio, Norberto.

Mattews, Caitlin & Matthews, John. Hallowquest. 1998. pap. 21.00 (*0-7225-3448-5*) Genl Dist Srvs.

Mattews, Keith & Friedland, Jay. The Mac ROM Reference: A Programmer's Guide to Manintosh Macros. (Illus.). 650p. 1988. 29.95 (*0-685-18871-X*) P-H.

Mattews, Patricia & Matthews, Clayton. The Sound of Murder. large type ed. LC 94-33231. 360p. 1995. 23.95 (*1-56054-335-3*) Thorndike Pr.

Mattey, Angela M. The Key to Spiritual & Psychic Development - Table Tipping: Guided Meditation & Energy Circle Protection Process for Table Tipping. unabridged ed. LC 92-91268. (Illus.). 359p. 1993. pap. 13.95 incl. audio (*1-882836-00-6*) TAM Ent.

Mattey, Joe P. The Timber Bubble That Burst: Government Policy & the Bailout of 1984. (Illus.). 120p. 1990. text 55.00 (*0-19-506275-2*) OUP.

Mattfeld, Jacquelyn, ed. see M.I.T. Symposium Staff.

Mattfeld, Julius. A Hundred Years of Grand Opera in New York: 1825-1925. reprint ed. 21.50 (*0-404-13038-0*) AMS Pr.

Mattfeld, Victor. Georg Rhaw's Publications for Vespers. (Wissenschaftliche Abhandlungen-Musicological Studies: Vol. 11). 361p. 1967. lib. bdg. 40.00 (*0-912024-81-X*) Inst Mediaeval Mus.

Mattfield, tr. see Banus, Maria.

Mattfield, Julius. The Folk Music of the Western Hemisphere: A List of References in the New York Public Library. Dorson, Richard M., ed. LC 80-796. (Folklore of the World Ser.). 1981. reprint ed. lib. bdg. 17.95 (*0-405-13335-9*) Ayer.

Matthaei, C. F., ed. see Emesenus, Nemesius.

Matthaei, G. L., et al. Microwave Filters, Impedance-Matching Networks, & Coupling Structures. LC 80-68976. (Artech Microwave Library). (Illus.). 1096p. 1980. reprint ed. 99.00 (*0-89006-099-1*) Artech Hse.

Matthaei, Gay & Grutman, Jewel H. The Journal Julia Singing Bear. LC 95-31738. (Illus.). 80p. (J). 1996. 19.95 (*1-56566-095-1*) Lickle Pubng.

Matthaei, Gaye, jt. auth. see Grutman, Jewel.

Matthaei, Sondra H. Faith Matters: Faith Mentoring in the Faith Community. LC 96-8128. 160p. (Orig.). 1996. pap. 15.00 (*1-56338-140-0*) TPI PA.

— The God We Worship. LC 93-8154. (We Believe Ser.). 144p. (Orig.). 1993. pap. 8.95 (*0-687-15203-8*) Abingdon.

***Matthaei, Sondra Higgins.** Making Disciples: Faith Formation in the Wesleyan Tradition. LC 00-38578. 2000. write for info. (*0-687-02475-7*) Abingdon.

Matthaeus, Antonius. De Criminibus on Crimes Vol. 2: A Commentary on Books XLVII & XLVIII of the Digest. Hewett, M. L., ed. & tr. by. Stoop, B. C., ed. 1993. 75.00 (*0-86981-799-X*, Pub. by Juta & Co) Gaunt.

Matthai, William C. Microbiology: A Laboratory Textbook. 3rd ed. 356p. (C). 1997. pap. text 31.95 (*1-890871-27-3*) Holcomb Hath.

Matthaiou, Anna. Aspects de l'Alimentation en Grece sous la Domination Ottomane: Des Reglementations au Discours Normatif. (Studien Zur Geschichte Sudosteuropas Ser.: Bd. 14). (FRE., Illus.). 390p. 1997. 63.95 (*3-631-31033-1*) P Lang Pubng.

Matthas, Ursula. Die Laubwerfenden Eichenwaelder Kretas. (Dissertationes Botanicae Ser.: Band 119). (GER., Illus.). 172p. 1988. pap. 53.00 (*3-443-64031-1*, Pub. by Gebruder Borntraeger) Balogh.

Matthay, Eileen. Counseling for College. 2nd ed. LC 95-15060. 464p. 1995. pap. 32.95 (*1-56079-534-4*) Petersons.

Matthay, Michael A. & Ingbar, David H. Pulmonary Edema. LC 98-3647. (Lung Biology in Health & Disease Ser.). (Illus.). 688p. 1998. text 195.00 (*0-8247-0150-X*) Dekker.

Matthay, Tobias A. Musical Interpretation: Its Laws & Principles, No. 3713. 1913. pap. text 8.95 (*0-686-30014-9*) Boston Music.

— Musical Interpretation, Its Laws & Principles, & Their Application in Teaching & Performing. LC 70-107820. (Select Bibliographies Reprint Ser.). 1977. 17.95 (*0-8369-5191-3*) Ayer.

— Musical Interpretation, Its Laws & Principles, & Their Application in Teaching & Performing. LC 72-109787. 163p. 1970. reprint ed. lib. bdg. 35.00 (*0-8371-4277-6*, MAMU, Greenwood Pr) Greenwood.

— Musical Interpretation, Its Laws & Principles, & Their Application in Teaching & Performing. 163p. 1990. reprint ed. lib. bdg. 59.00 (*0-7812-9152-6*) Rprt Serv.

Matthe, G. Die Beschaffenheit des Grundwassers. (Lehrbuch der Hydrogeologie Ser.). x, 498p. 1994. 82.00 (*3-443-01008-3*, Pub. by Gebruder Borntraeger) Balogh.

Matthe, Georg, ed. see Ubell, K.

Mattheck, C. Design in Nature: Learning from Trees. Linnard, W., tr. from GER. LC 97-34438. (Illus.). 290p. 1998. pap. 44.95 (*3-540-62937-8*) Spr-Verlag.

Mattheck, Claus, et al. The Body Language of Trees: A Handbook for Failure Analysis. Department of the Environment Staff, tr. (Research for Amenity Trees Ser.: No. 4). xx, 240p. 1995. 39.95 (*0-11-753067-0*, Pub. by Statnry Office) Balogh.

Mattheck, G. Claus. Trees: The Mechanical Design. (Illus.). 125p. 1996. 39.00 (*0-387-54276-0*) Spr-Verlag.

Mattheck, G. Claus, jt. auth. see Kubler, Hans.

Matthee, Dalene. Fiela's Child. 1990. pap. text. write for info. (*0-582-05293-9*, Pub. by Addison-Wesley) Longman.

— Fiela's Child. LC 92-12963. (Phoenix Fiction Ser.). (AFR & ENG.). x, 360p. 1992. pap. 13.95 (*0-226-51083-2*) U Ch Pr.

***Matthee, Rudi & Baron, Beth, eds.** Iran & Beyond: Essays in Middle Eastern History in Honor of Nikki R. Keddie. (Illus.). 310p. 2000. text 45.00 (*1-56859-099-7*) Mazda Pubs.

Matthee, Rudolph P. The Politics of Trade in Safavid Iran: Silk for Silver, 1600-1730. LC 99-12830. (Cambridge Studies in Islamic Civilization). (Illus.). 312p. (C). 2000. 64.95 (*0-521-64131-4*) Cambridge U Pr.

Matthei, Wesley G. (Mis)Managing the System: How to Change the System. LC 94-73196. 368p. (Orig.). 1997. pap. 19.95 (*0-9658493-0-9*) Nusystems.

Mattheier, Klaus J., ed. Norm und Variation. (Forum Angewandte Linguistik Ser.: Bd. 32). (Illus.). 201p. 1997. 42.95 (*3-631-32106-6*) P Lang Pubng.

Mattheier, Klaus J. & Radtke, Edgar, eds. Standardisierung und Destandardisierung Europaischer Nationalsprachen. (Variolingua, Nonstandard - Standard - Substandard Ser.: bD. 1). (Illus.). IX, 290p. 1997. 51.95 (*3-631-31663-1*) P Lang Pubng.

Mattheisen, Paul F., et al, eds. The Collected Letters of George Gissing Vol. 1: 1863-1880. LC 89-26577. 399p. (C). 1990. text 70.00 (*0-8214-0955-7*) Ohio U Pr.

— The Collected Letters of George Gissing Vol. 5: 1892-1895. LC 89-26577. 407p. (C). 1994. text 70.00 (*0-8214-1067-9*) Ohio U Pr.

— The Collected Letters of George Gissing, 1881-1885, Vol. 2. (Illus.). 429p. (C). 1991. text 70.00 (*0-8214-0984-0*) Ohio U Pr.

— The Collected Letters of George Gissing, 1895-1897, Vol. 6. LC 89-26577. (Illus.). 390p. 1994. text 70.00 (*0-8214-1098-9*) Ohio U Pr.

— The Collected Letters of George Gissing, 1900-1902, Vol. 8. LC 89-26577. 495p. (C). 1996. text 70.00 (*0-8214-1144-6*) Ohio U Pr.

***Mattheisen, Paul F., et al, eds.** With Gissing in Italy: The Memoirs of Brain Boru Dunne. LC 98-50127. (Illus.). 208p. 1999. 36.95 (*0-8214-1258-2*) Ohio U Pr.

Mattheisen, Paul F., ed. see Gissing, George R.

Mattheisen, Paul F., ed. see Gissing, George R., et al.

Mattheou, Antonia S. Tracing Your Greek Ancestry - Reference to Cyprus, Vol. 1. (Illus.). 54p. (Orig.). 1992. pap. 12.00 (*0-9635648-0-3*) A S Mattheou.

Matthes, ed. Hermagorae Temnitae. (GRE.). 1962. 18.95 (*3-322-00871-1*, T1428, Pub. by B G Teubner) U of Mich Pr.

Matthes, Chip, ed. see Banks, Michael A.

Matthes, Dieter, et al. Suctoria und Urceolariidae (Peritricha) (Protozoenfauna Ser.: Vol. 7-1). (GER., Illus.). 309p. 1988. lib. bdg. 160.00 (*3-437-30497-6*) Lubrecht & Cramer.

Matthes, Francois E. The Incomparable Valley: A Geologic Interpretation of the Yosemite. Fryxell, Fritiof, ed. (Illus.). 1950. pap. 16.95 (*0-520-00827-8*, Pub. by U CA Pr) Cal Prin Full Svc.

Matthes, Gayle B. Discovering the Kingdom of Heaven. 157p. (C). 1988. reprint ed. pap. 5.95 (*0-944386-07-5*) SOM Pub.

Matthes, Georg. Die Beschaffenheit Des Grundwassers. 1990. 2nd ed. (Lehrbuch der Hydrobiologie Ser.: Vol. 2). (GER., Illus.). 498p. 1990. text 97.50 (*3-443-01007-5*, Pub. by Gebruder Borntraeger) Balogh.

Matthes, Gertrud P. A Little German Cookbook. (Illus.). 60p. 1995. 7.95 (*0-8118-1013-5*) Chronicle Bks.

Matthes, Joachim. Lebenswelt und Soziale Probleme. (GER.). 561p. 1982. 49.50 (*3-593-32695-7*) Irvington.

Matthes, William A., jt. ed. see Case, Charles W.

Mattheson, Johann. Das Neu-Eroffnete Orchestre. (GER.). xviii, 349p. 1993. reprint ed. write for info. (*3-487-09612-9*) G Olms Pubs.

Mattheson, Johann. Pieces de Clavecin. fac. ed. (Monuments of Music & Music Literature in Facsimile, I Ser.: Vol. 5). (Illus.). 1965. lib. bdg. 50.00 (*0-8450-2005-6*) Broude.

Matthew. Caring for God's People. 1993. pap. 13.90 (*0-7152-0707-5*) St Mut.

***Matthew, et al.** Jesus Christ's Meteorite Prophecy. LC 99-90649. (Illus.). 128p. 2000. pap. text 19.50 (*0-9672554-0-6*) Alinement Adver.

Matthew, et al. Ligonier, Indiana: Memories of the First One Hundred Fifty Years, 1835-1985. Zimmerman, Ben, ed. 1985. 25.00 (*0-318-18809-0*) Ligonier Comm.

Matthew Bende Staff. Federal Litigation Guide: New York & Connecticut. LC 98-20120. 1998. 530.00 (*0-8205-3925-2*) Bender.

Matthew Bender Publishers Staff, jt. ed. see New York State Staff.

***Matthew Bender Staff, ed.** Civil Practice Annual of New York 2000. annuals 2000. text 110.00 (*0 8205 4192 3*) Bender.

Matthew Bender Tax Staff, ed. see Lassila, Dennis.

Matthew, Brian, jt. auth. see Petersen, Kris.

***Matthew, C.** A Nightingale Sang in Fernhurst Road. 1998. text 29.95 (*0-7195-5899-9*, Pub. by John Murray) Trafalgar.

Matthew Cahill, Advertising Staff, ed. see Springhouse Publishing Company Staff.

Matthew, Carole B. Windows 98 Instant Ref. LC 98-84264. 336p. 1998. 14.99 (*0-7821-2191-8*) Sybex.

***Matthew, Colin.** Nineteenth Century. (Short History of the British Isle Ser.). 280p. 2000. pap. 19.95 (*0-19-873143-4*) OUP.

Matthew, Colin, compiled by. Brief Lives: Twentieth Century Pen Portraits from the Dictionary of National Biography. 620p. 1997. (*0-19-860087-9*) OUP.

Matthew, Colin, ed. Brief Lives: Twentieth Century Pen Portraits from the Dictionary of National Biography. 624p. 2000. pap. 16.95 (*0-19-280089-2*) OUP.

***Matthew, Colin, ed.** The Nineteenth Century: The British Isles, 1815-1901. (Short Oxford History of the British Isles Ser.). (Illus.). 280p. 2000. text 65.00 (*0-19-873144-2*) OUP.

Matthew, Colin, jt. ed. see Garnett, Jane.

***Matthew, Dawn D., ed.** Disabilities Sourcebook. LC 99-56930. (Health Reference Ser.). (Illus.). 600p. 2000. lib. bdg. 78.00 (*0-7808-0389-2*) Omnigraphics Inc.

Matthew, Donald. Atlas of Medieval Europe. (Cultural Atlas Ser.). (Illus.). 240p. 1983. 45.00 (*0-87196-133-4*) Facts on File.

— The Norman Kingdom of Sicily. (Medieval Textbooks Ser.). 434p. (C). 1992. text 80.00 (*0-521-26284-4*); pap. text 26.95 (*0-521-26911-3*) Cambridge U Pr.

***Matthew, Fort & Heathcote, Paul.** Paul Heathcote's Rhubarb & Black Pudding. (Illus.). 252p. 1998. 45.00 (*1-85702-500-8*, Pub. by Fourth Estate) Trafalgar.

Matthew, H. C. Gladstone, 1809-1898. LC 98-107796. (Illus.). 706p. 1997. pap. text 32.00 (*0-19-820696-8*) OUP.

— Gladstone, Eighteen Nine to Eighteen Seventy-Four. (Illus.). 288p. 1989. reprint ed. pap. text 24.00 (*0-19-282122-9*) OUP.

— Gladstone, 1875-1898. LC 97-117492. (Illus.). 458p. 1995. 39.95 (*0-19-820405-1*) OUP.

— The Liberal Imperialists: The Ideas & Politics of a Post-Gladstonian Elite. (Oxford Historical Monographs). 1973. 36.00 (*0-19-821842-7*) OUP.

Matthew, H. C., ed. see Gladstone, William E.

Matthew, James E. Literature of Music. LC 69-12688. (Music Ser.). 1969. reprint ed. lib. bdg. 37.50 (*0-306-71227-X*) Da Capo.

Matthew, James E., tr. see Borren, Charles V.

Matthew, Jean F. Does Anybody Know Where My Son Is Tonight? 103p. (Orig.). 1997. pap. 10.95 (*0-9644574-1-5*) Shoeless Pub.

— We Never Wore Shoes: Growing up on Ft. Myers Beach. (Illus.). 593p. (YA). 1994. 29.95 (*0-9644574-6-6*) Shoeless Pub.

Matthew, Jean R. Testimony: Stories. LC 86-16126. 80p. 1987. pap. 12.95 (*0-8262-0623-9*, 83-36315) U of Mo Pr.

Matthew, John. The Quiet Corner. 96p. (C). 1991. pap. text 50.00 (*86-15-30645-1*, Pub. by St Andrew) St Mut.

Matthew, John, ed. The Quiet Corner. 96p. (C). 1989. pap. 59.00 (*0-7855-6810-7*, Pub. by St Andrew) St Mut.

Matthew, John & Matthew, Stewart. The Quiet Corner. 96p. 1993. pap. 30.00 (*0-7152-0645-1*, Pub. by St Andrew) St Mut.

Matthew, K. M. An Excursion of Tamilnadu, India. (Illus.). 728p. (C). 1995. text 122.00 (*90-5410-286-1*, Pub. by A A Balkema) Ashgate Pub Co.

— Illustration of the Flora of Tamilnadu Carnatic. (C). 1988. text 60.00 (*0-7855-3160-2*, Pub. by Scientific) St Mut.

Matthew, L., ed. Professional Care for the Elderly Mentally Ill. 288p. 1995. pap. 44.75 (*1-56593-327-3*, 0657) Singular Publishing.

Matthew, Margaret, et al. Our Sunday Visitor's Encyclopedia of Saints. LC 97-69277. (Illus.). 800p. 1998. 39.95 (*0-87973-588-0*) Our Sunday Visitor.

*__Matthew, Neil & Stones, Richard.__ Beginning Linux Programming. 2nd ed. 1999. pap. 39.99 (*1-86100-297-1*) Wrox Pr Inc.

Matthew of Westminster. Flowers of History, Especially Such As Relate to the Affairs of Britain, 2 vols. Yonge, C. D., ed. LC 68-57870. (Bohn's Antiquarian Library). reprint ed. 115.00 (*0-404-50030-7*) AMS Pr.

Matthew, Oommen P. & Sant'Ambrogio. Respiratory Function of the Upper Airway. (Lung Biology in Health & Disease Ser.: Vol. 35). (Illus.). 672p. 1988. text 215.00 (*0-8247-7802-2*) Dekker.

Matthew, R. G., jt. auth. see Falconer, R. A.

Matthew, Richard A., jt. ed. see Deudney, Daniel H.

Matthew, Robert H., et al. The Conservation of Georgian Edinburgh: The Proceedings & Outcome of a Conference Organized by the Scottish Civic Trust in Association with the Edinburgh Architectural Association & in Conjunction with the Civic Trust, London. LC 72-77764. xv, 130 p. 1972. write for info. (*0-85224-215-8*, Pub. by Edinburgh U Pr) Col U Pr.

*__Matthew, Sidney L.__ Bobby Jones Golf Tips: Secrets of the Master. LC 99-34608. (Illus.). 144p. 1999. 19.95 (*1-886947-86-4*) Sleepng Bear.

Matthew, Sidney L. History of Bobby Jones Clubs. 300p. 1992. 49.95 (*0-9634887-0-8*) Impreg Quadrilat.

— The Life & Times of Bobby Jones: Portrait of a Gentleman. (Illus.). 454p. 1995. text 25.00 (*0-9634887-1-6*) Impreg Quadrilat.

*__Matthew, Sidney L.__ Wry Stories on the Road Hole. (Illus.). 144p. 2000. 22.00 (*1-58536-017-1*) Sleepng Bear.

Matthew, Sidney L., ed. see Jones, Bobby.

Matthew, Sidney L., ed. see Jones, Robert.

Matthew, Stewart. Session Matters: A Handbook for Elders. 88p. 1993. pap. 30.00 (*0-7152-0644-3*, Pub. by St Andrew) St Mut.

Matthew, Stewart, tr. Session Matters: A Handbook for Elders. 88p. (C). 1989. 35.00 (*0-7855-6808-5*, Pub. by St Andrew) St Mut.

Matthew, Stewart & Lawson, Ken. Caring for God's People: Handbook for Elders & Ministers on Pastoral Care. 128p. (C). 1988. pap. text 60.00 (*0-7152-0634-6*) St Mut.

Matthew, Stewart & Scott, Kenneth. Leading God's People: A Handbook for Elders. 116p. (C). 1989. pap. 35.00 (*0-7855-6818-2*, Pub. by St Andrew) St Mut.

— Leading God's People: A Handbook for Elders. 116p. 1993. pap. 40.00 (*0-7152-0696-6*, Pub. by St Andrew) St Mut.

— Leading God's People: A Handbook for Elders. 116p. (C). 1988. pap. text 35.00 (*0-7152-0591-9*) St Mut.

Matthew, Stewart, jt. auth. see Matthew, John.

Matthew the Poor. Communion of Love. LC 84-10561. 234p. (Orig.). 1984. pap. text 11.95 (*0-88141-036-5*) St Vladimirs.

Matthew, Tobie, jt. auth. see Lessius, Leonardus.

*__Matthew-Walker, Robert.__ Broadway to Hollywood: The Musical & the Cinema. (Illus.). 225p. 2000. reprint ed. pap. text 19.00 (*0-7881-9039-3*) DIANE Pub.

Matthew, William D. Climate & Evolution. LC 73-17830. (Natural Sciences in America Ser.). (Illus.). 150p. 1974. reprint ed. 15.95 (*0-405-05748-2*) Ayer.

— Outline & General Principles of the History of Life: University of California Syllabus Series, Vol. 213. Gould, Stephen Jay, ed. LC 79-8335. (History of Paleontology Ser.). (Illus.). 1980. reprint ed. lib. bdg. 24.95 (*0-405-12719-7*) Ayer.

Matthewman, Jim. HR Effectiveness. 160p. (C). 1993. 50.00 (*0-7855-2659-5*, Pub. by IPM Hse) St Mut.

— HR Effectiveness. 160p. (C). 1994. pap. 34.00 (*0-85292-570-0*, Pub. by IPM Hse) St Mut.

Matthewman, Jim, et al. Tolley's Social Security & State Benefits Handbook, 1995-96. 580p. 1995. pap. 310.00 (*1-86012-072-5*, Pub. by Tolley Pubng) St Mut.

— Tolley's Social Security & State Benefits, 1993-94. 580p. 1993. 120.00 (*0-85459-744-1*, Pub. by Tolley Pubng) St Mut.

*__Matthewman, M. F. G.__ Examination Results: Processing, Analysis & Presentation. LC 00-29112. 2000. write for info. (*0-415-23226-0*) Routledge.

Matthewman, Phyllis. Robert Morrison. unabridged ed. 71p. 1995. reprint ed. pap. 5.99 (*0-88019-343-3*) Schmul Pub Co.

Matthewman, R., jt. auth. see Morton, J.

Matthews. Annotated Guide to IRS Employee Benefit Plan Audits. 275p. Date not set. 125.00 (*1-56706-318-7*) Aspen Pub.

— Byzantium. 176p. (C). 1998. pap. text. write for info. (*0-13-080744-3*) P-H.

— Improve Your Paragraphs. 560p. 1994. pap. 50.94 (*0-07-041062-3*) McGraw.

— Internal Combustion Engines & Automotive Engineering. (C). 1998. text. write for info. (*0-321-01064-7*) Addson-Wesley Educ.

— Legumes: Chemistry, Technology, & Human Nutrition. (Food Science & Technology Ser.: Vol. 32). (Illus.). 408p. 1989. text 155.00 (*0-8247-8042-6*) Dekker.

— Pesticide Application Methods. 2nd ed. 1992. pap. text. write for info. (*0-582-40905-5*) Longman.

*__Matthews.__ Wild Nights. 2000. text. write for info. (*0-86547-560-1*) N Point Pr.

Matthews. World Religions. 3rd ed. (Religion). 1999. mass mkt., student ed. 16.50 (*0-534-56692-8*) Wadsworth Pub.

Matthews, ed. Marx One Hundred Years On. (C). 1983. pap. 19.50 (*0-85315-566-6*, Pub. by Lawrence & Wishart) NYU Pr.

Matthews & Boldman, Craig. Every Excuse in the Book. 288p. 1999. 6.98 (*1-56731-354-X*, MJF Bks) Fine Comms.

Matthews & Marino. Professional Interactions: Oral Communication Skills of Science, Technology & Medicine. 320p. 1990. pap. text 23.80 (*0-13-726084-9*) P-H.

Matthews & Reynold. New Mexico Creditor/Debtor Law, Issue 10. 101p. 1998. ring bd. 120.00 (*0-327-00762-1*, 8213514) LEXIS Pub.

Matthews, jt. auth. see Evans.

Matthews, jt. auth. see Fung.

Matthews, jt. auth. see Johnston.

Matthews, jt. auth. see Read.

*__Matthews, A., et al, eds.__ Metallurgical Coatings & Thin Films 1999. 1520p. 1999. 353.00 (*0-444-50399-4*, North Holland) Elsevier.

Matthews, A. & Rickerby, D. S. Advanced Surface Coatings: A Handbook of Surface Engineering. (Illus.). 384p. (C). 1991. text 173.50 (*0-216-92899-0*, Pub. by B Acad & Prof) Routldge.

Matthews, A. & Truscott, P. Disability, Household Income & Expenditure. (DSS Research Report Ser.). 1990. 14.00 (*0-11-761755-5*, Pub. by Statnry Office) Bernan Associates.

Matthews, A., jt. ed. see Rickerby, D. S.

Matthews, A. G., ed. Walker Revised: Being a Revision of John Walker's Sufferings of the Clergy During the Grand Rebellion, 1642-60. (Illus.). 496p. 1988. 98.00 (*0-19-821264-X*) OUP.

Matthews, A. M. The Seven Keys to Calm. 176p. 1998. pap. 12.00 (*0-671-00027-6*, Pocket Books) PB.

— The Seven Keys to Calm: Essential Steps for Staying Calm under Any Circumstances. LC 98-158138. 176p. 1997. 16.00 (*0-671-00026-8*) PB.

*__Matthews, Alan.__ Farm Incomes - Myths & Realities. 72p. 2000. pap. 8.95 (*1-85918-241-0*, Pub. by Cork Univ) Stylus Pub VA.

*__Matthews, Alex.__ Cat's Claw. LC 99-88369. (Cassidy McCabe Mysteries Ser.: No. 5). 288p. 2000. 22.95 (*1-890768-22-7*) Intrigue Press.

Matthews, Alex. Satan's Silence. Ellison, Lee, ed. LC 96-79331. (Cassidy McCabe Mystery Ser.: No. 2). 304p. 1997. 22.50 (*0-9643161-5-3*) Intrigue Press.

— Satan's Silence. LC 96-79331. (Cassidy McCabe Mystery Ser.: No. 2). 368p. 1998. mass mkt. 5.50 (*1-890768-04-9*) Intrigue Press.

— Secret's Shadow: The First Cassidy McCabe Mystery. LC 95-80820. (Cassidy McCabe Mystery Ser.: Vol. 1). 352p. 1998. mass mkt. 5.50 (*1-890768-03-0*) Intrigue Press.

— Vendetta's Victim: The Third Cassidy McCabe Mystery. LC 98-10176. (Cassidy McCabe Mystery Ser.: No. 3). 222p. 1998. 22.95 (*0-9643161-9-6*) Intrigue Press.

— Vendetta's Victim: The Third Cassidy McCabe Mystery. 256p. 1999. mass mkt. 5.95 (*1-890768-14-6*) Intrigue Press.

*__Matthews, Alex.__ Wanton's Web. LC 98-51072. (Cassidy McCabe Mystery Ser.). 316p. 1999. 22.95 (*1-890768-12-X*) Intrigue Press.

Matthews, Alfred W. World Religions. 2nd ed. LC 94-26811. 528p. (C). 1994. 41.25 (*0-314-04598-8*) West Pub.

— World Religions. 3rd ed. LC 98-16562. 1998. 64.95 (*0-534-56691-X*) Wadsworth Pub.

Matthews, Alison, ed. see Olsen, Margaret.

Matthews, Alison F., jt. auth. see Olsen, Margaret A.

Matthews, Allan. Sovereigns - Peacefully - Take Charge: An Agenda for Liberty & Justice. LC 96-92954. (Illus.). x, 149p. (Orig.). 1997. pap. 8.00 (*0-9655953-0-7*) Sovereign People Press.

Matthews, Allan, jt. auth. see Holmberg, Kenneth.

Matthews, Andrew. Being Happy. (Illus.). 1990. pap. 14.95 (*0-8431-2868-2*, Price Stern) Peng Put Young Read.

Matthews, Andrew. Dixie's Demon. large type ed. (Illus.). (J). 1996. pap. 16.95 (*0-7451-4815-8*, Galaxy Child Lrg Print) Chivers N Amer.

Matthews, Andrew. Follow Your Heart: Finding Purpose in Your Life & Work. LC 98-47058. (Illus.). 144p. 1999. pap. 14.95 (*0-8431-7491-9*, Price Stern) Peng Put Young Read.

Matthews, Andrew. Libro de los Amigos. (SPA.). 1997. pap. text 8.98 (*968-403-604-3*) Selector.

— Making Friends. (Illus.). 144p. 1991. pap. 14.95 (*0-8431-2969-7*, Price Stern) Peng Put Young Read.

Matthews, Andrew. Marduk the Mighty & Other Stories of Creation. LC 96-41710. (Illus.). 96p. (J). (gr. 2 up). 1997. lib. bdg. 22.40 (*0-7613-0204-2*) Millbrook Pr.

— Mouse Flute. (Blue Bananas Ser.). (Illus.). (J). 1997. pap. 4.99 (*0-7497-2634-2*) Dell.

— Por Favor, Sea Feliz. 1997. pap. text 7.98 (*968-403-545-4*) Selector.

Matthews, Andrew & Todd, Justin. The Jar of the Sun. (Illus.). 32p. (J). (gr. k-3). 1992. 16.95 (*0-09-176400-9*, Pub. by Hutchnson) Trafalgar.

*__Matthews, Andrews.__ Revolution & Reaction: European History 1789-1849. (Cambridge Perspectives in History Ser.). 160p. 2000. pap. write for info. (*0-521-56734-3*) Cambridge U Pr.

Matthews, Anis. A Guide for Haj & Umra. 1991. pap. 14.50 (*1-56744-029-0*) Kazi Pubns.

Matthews, Anne. Bright College Years: Inside the American Campus Today. LC 96-50197. 1997. 22.50 (*0-684-81541-9*) S&S Trade.

*__Matthews, Anne.__ Bright College Years: Inside the American Campus Today. LC 98-20987. 1998. pap. 14.00 (*0-226-51092-1*) U Ch Pr.

— Essential Australia. (AAA Essential Guides Ser.). (Illus.). 128p. 2000. pap. 8.95 (*0-658-00377-1*, 003771, Passprt Bks) NTC Contemp Pub Co.

Matthews, Anne. Scenic Australia. (Illus.). 112p. 1998. 24.95 (*1-86436-268-5*, Pub. by New5 Holland) Sterling.

— Sydney & New South Wales. (Illustrated Travel Guides from Thomas Cook Ser.). (Illus.). 192p. 1994. pap. 12.95 (*0-8442-9050-5*, Passprt Bks) NTC Contemp Pub Co.

Matthews, Anne M. The Cave. 320p. 1998. mass mkt. 6.50 (*0-446-60509-3*, Pub. by Warner Bks) Little.

— The Cave. large type ed. LC 97-19946. (Basic Ser.). 403p. 1997. 24.95 (*0-7862-1148-2*) Thorndike Pr.

Matthews, Arlene M. Excited, Exhausted, Expecting: The Emotional Life of Mothers-to-Be. LC 94-27694. 224p. (Orig.). 1995. pap. 10.00 (*0-399-51885-1*, Perigee Bks) Berkley Pub.

Matthews, Arline & Welan, Janet. In Charge of the Ward. 3rd ed. LC 93-25221. 288p. 1993. pap. 26.95 (*0-632-03448-3*) Blackwell Sci.

Matthews, Arthur D. & Emery, Clark M., eds. Studies in Shakespeare. LC 79-144658. reprint ed. 20.00 (*0-404-04267-8*) AMS Pr.

Matthews, Arthur H. Standing up, Standing Together: The Emergence of the National Association of Evangelicals. (Illus.). xiv, 187p. (Orig.). 1992. pap. 8.95 (*1-880844-00-1*) Nat Assn Evan.

— The Wall of Light: Nikola Tesla & the Venusian Space Ship, the X-12. 140p. 1996. reprint ed. spiral bd. 17.00 (*0-7873-0588-X*) Hlth Research.

Matthews, B., jt. auth. see Khan, M. A.

*__Matthews, Bay.__ Rambler's Rest. 2000. mass mkt. 4.50 (*0-373-82216-2*, 1-82216-2) Harlequin Bks.

Matthews, Bay. Worth Waiting For. (Special Edition Ser.). 1993. mass mkt. 3.50 (*0-373-09825-1*, 5-09825-6) Silhouette.

Matthews, Becky, ed. see Snell, Alma Hogan.

Matthews, Ben & Schwope, Charles. Mastering Netrunner. LC 96-39506. 192p. 1996. pap. 9.95 (*1-55622-531-8*) Wordware Pub.

Matthews, Bernard E. An Introduction to Parasitology. (Studies in Biology). (Illus.). 208p. (C). 1998. pap. text 18.95 (*0-521-57691-1*) Cambridge U Pr.

Matthews, Beth, et al. I Only See My Dad on Weekends: Kids Tell Their Stories about Divorce & Blended Families. Norton, LoraBeth, ed. LC 94-4733. (Kids Helping Kids Ser.). 48p. (J). (gr. 3-8). 1994. pap. 4.99 (*0-7814-0110-0*, Chariot Bks) Chariot Victor.

*__Matthews, Bette.__ Cakes. LC 00-21286. (For Your Wedding Ser.). (Illus.). 96p. 2000. write for info. (*1-56799-961-1*, Friedman-Fairfax) M Friedman Pub Grp Inc.

Matthews, Betty. Marx: A Hundred Years On. LC 97-187380. 312 p. 1983. write for info. (*0-85315-565-8*) Lawrence & Wishart.

*__Matthews, Betty, compiled by.__ My Picture Dictionary. (Illus.). (J). (ps-2). 1999. pap. 29.00 (*0-7217-0390-9*, Pub. by Schofield) St Mut.

Matthews, Bill, ed. The English Boxing Champions, 1872-1910: And Record Book. 176p. (C). 1989. pap. 35.00 (*0-7223-2413-8*, Pub. by A H S Ltd) St Mut.

Matthews, Billie L. & Hurlburt, Virginia E. Davy's Dawg. (Illus.). 64p. (J). (gr. 3-8). 1989. pap. 4.95 (*1-885777-02-7*) Hendrick-Long.

Matthews, Billie P. & Chichester, A. Lee. Secret of the Cibolo. Roberts, Melissa, ed. (Illus.). 88p. (J). (gr. 6-7). 1988. 9.95 (*0-89015-638-7*) Sunbelt Media.

Matthews, Birch. Wet Wings & Droptanks: Recollections of American Transcontinental Air Racing 1928-1970. LC 93-84497. (Illus.). 268p. 1993. 45.00 (*0-88740-530-4*) Schiffer.

Matthews, Birch J. Cobra! The Bell Aircraft Corporation 1934-1946. (Illus.). 432p. (C). (gr. 13). 1996. 59.95 (*0-88740-911-3*) Schiffer.

Matthews, Birch J., jt. auth. see Carter, Dustin W.

Matthews, Bonnye L. Chemical Sensitivity: A Guide to Coping with Hypersensitivity Syndrome, Sick Building Syndrome & Other Environmental Illnesses. LC 92-54089. 291p. 1992. lib. bdg. 39.95 (*0-89950-731-X*) McFarland & Co.

Matthews, Bonnye L., ed. Defining Multiple Chemical Sensitivity. LC 98-3762. 212p. 1998. lib. bdg. 39.50 (*0-7864-0413-2*) McFarland & Co.

Matthews, Boris, tr. The Herder Dictionary of Symbols: Symbols from Art, Archaeology, Mythology, Literature, & Religion. LC 93-17017. (Illus.). 228p. 1993. 14.95 (*0-933029-84-5*) Chiron Pubns.

Matthews, Boris, tr. see Barz, Ellynor.

Matthews, Boris, tr. see Dieckmann, Hans.

Matthews, Boris, tr. see Neumann, Erich.

Matthews, Boris, tr. see Schellenbaum, Peter.

Matthews, Boris L., tr. see Abt, Theodor.

Matthews, Brander. American of the Future, & Other Essays. LC 68-57330. (Essay Index Reprint Ser.). 1977. 21.95 (*0-8369-0693-4*) Ayer.

— Bookbinding Old & New, Vol. 12. (History of Bookbinding & Design Ser.). (Illus.). 350p. 1990. text 50.00 (*0-8240-4039-2*) Garland.

— Books & Play-Books: Essays on Literature & the Drama. LC 71-37795. (Essay Index Reprint Ser.). 1977. reprint ed. 19.95 (*0-8369-2612-9*) Ayer.

— Bookshelf of Brander Matthews. LC 79-134610. reprint ed. 31.50 (*0-404-04268-6*) AMS Pr.

— The Development of the Drama. LC 79-39199. (Select Bibliographies Reprint Ser.). 1977. reprint ed. 23.95 (*0-8369-6801-8*) Ayer.

— Essays on English. LC 73-156693. (Essay Index Reprint Ser.). 1977. reprint ed. 21.95 (*0-8369-2285-9*) Ayer.

— French Dramatists of the Nineteenth Century. LC 68-20240. 1972. reprint ed. 24.95 (*0-405-08782-9*, Pub. by Blom Pubns) Ayer.

— Gateways to Literature: And Other Essays. LC 70-142667. (Essay Index Reprint Ser.). 1977. reprint ed. 20.95 (*0-8369-2414-2*) Ayer.

— Historical Novel, & Other Essays. LC 68-20320. (Essay Index Reprint Ser.). 1977. reprint ed. 20.95 (*0-8369-0695-0*) Ayer.

— Inquiries & Opinions. LC 68-22930. (Essay Index Reprint Ser.). 1977. reprint ed. 20.95 (*0-8369-0696-9*) Ayer.

— Outlines in Local Color. LC 76-98584. (Short Story Index Reprint Ser.). 1977. 20.95 (*0-8369-3158-0*) Ayer.

— Parts of Speech. LC 68-54361. (Essay Index Reprint Ser.). 1977. 22.95 (*0-8369-0697-7*) Ayer.

— Pen & Ink. LC 73-37120. (Essay Index Reprint Ser.). 1977. reprint ed. 18.95 (*0-8369-2515-7*) Ayer.

— Playwrights on Playmaking: Other Studies of the Stage. LC 67-26765. (Essay Index Reprint Ser.). 1977. 23.95 (*0-8369-0698-5*) Ayer.

— Principles of Playmaking. LC 79-134113. (Essay Index Reprint Ser.). 1977. 23.95 (*0-8369-1989-0*) Ayer.

— Recreations of an Anthologist. LC 67-26766. (Essay Index Reprint Ser.). 1977. 19.95 (*0-8369-0699-3*) Ayer.

— Secret of the Sea & C. LC 74-160942. (Short Story Index Reprint Ser.). 1977. reprint ed. 19.95 (*0-8369-3921-2*) Ayer.

— Shakespeare As a Playwright. LC 13-21467. reprint ed. 45.00 (*0-404-04269-4*) AMS Pr.

— Story of a Story & Other Stories. LC 70-98585. (Short Story Index Reprint Ser.). 1977. 20.95 (*0-8369-3159-9*) Ayer.

— Studies of the Stage. LC 72-294. (Essay Index Reprint Ser.). 1977. reprint ed. 20.95 (*0-8369-2806-7*) Ayer.

— Tales of Fantasy & Fact. LC 73-98586. (Short Story Index Reprint Ser.). 1977. 19.95 (*0-8369-3160-2*) Ayer.

— Vignettes of Manhattan. LC 70-90587. (Short Story Index Reprint Ser.). 1977. 20.95 (*0-8369-3070-3*) Ayer.

— Vistas of New York. LC 70-37279. (Short Story Index Reprint Ser.). 1977. reprint ed. 20.95 (*0-8369-4090-3*) Ayer.

— With My Friends: Tales Told in Partnership; with an Introductory Essay on the Art & Mystery of Collaboration, Vol. 1. LC 72-3372. (Short Story Index Reprint Ser.). 1977. reprint ed. 23.95 (*0-8369-4155-1*) Ayer.

Matthews, Brander, ed. Ballads of Books. LC 77-94814. (Granger Poetry Library). (Illus.). 1978. reprint ed. 20.00 (*0-89609-089-2*) Roth Pub Inc.

— Papers on Playmaking. LC 75-111852. (Essay Index Reprint Ser.). 1977. 21.95 (*0-8369-1890-8*) Ayer.

— Poems of American Patriotism. LC 70-133072. (Granger Index Reprint Ser.). 1977. 19.95 (*0-8369-6202-8*) Ayer.

Matthews, Brander, et al. Stories of the Army. LC 76-113683. (Short Story Index Reprint Ser.). 1977. reprint ed. 19.95 (*0-8369-3412-1*) Ayer.

Matthews, Brander, ed. see Bernard, John.

Matthews, Brenda. Niagara Flavours Guidebook & Cookbook. (Illus.). 128p. 1999. pap. 16.95 (*1-55028-606-4*, Pub. by J Lorimer) Formac Dist Ltd.

Matthews, Brian. AutoCAD 2000 3D F/X & Design. LC 99-42712. 1999. pap. text 49.99 (*1-57610-406-0*) Coriolis Grp.

— Louisa: 50th Anniversary Edition. LC 99-208738. 1998. reprint ed. pap. 19.95 (*0-7022-3071-5*, Pub. by Univ Queensland Pr) Intl Spec Bk.

Matthews, Byron, ed. Current Municipal Problems: 1974-1990, 15 vols., Set. 160.00 (*0-317-12012-3*) West Group.

Matthews, Byron, jt. auth. see Matthews, Thomas.

*__Matthews, C.__ Celtic Love. LC 99-40709. 1999. pap. 10.01 (*0-06-251610-8*) HarpC.

Matthews, C. Little Book of Celtic Blessings. 48p. 1994. pap. 5.95 (*1-85230-564-9*, Pub. by Element MA) Penguin Putnam.

*__Matthews, C. Robert, et al, eds.__ Advances in Protein Chemistry: Protein Folding Mechanisms. Vol. 53. (Illus.). 345p. 2000. 85.00 (*0-12-034253-7*) Acad Pr.

An Asterisk (*) at the beginning of an entry indicates that the title is appearing for the first time.

Matthews, C. S. & Russell, D. G. Pressure Buildup & Flow Tests in Wells. 163p. 1967. 47.00 (0-89520-200-X, FEMONO001) Soc Petrol Engineers.

Matthews, Caitlin. The Barefoot Book of Princesses. (Illus.). 64p. (J). (gr. k-3). 1998. 17.95 (1-901223-74-4) Barefoot Bks NY.

— The Blessing Seed: A Creation Myth for the New Millennium. (Illus.). 32p. (J). (gr. k-7). 1998. 14.95 (1-901223-28-0) Barefoot Bks NY.

***Matthews, Caitlin.** The Blessing Seed: A Creation Myth for the New Millennium. (Illus.). 32p. (J). (gr. k-7). 2000. pap. 6.99 (1-84148-154-8) Barefoot Bks NY.

Matthews, Caitlin. The Celtic Book of Days: A Guide to Celtic Spirituality & Wisdom. LC 95-11996. (Illus.). 128p. 1996. 24.95 (0-89281-565-5, Destiny Bks) Inner Tradit.

— The Celtic Book of the Dead. 128p. 1992. text 27.95 (0-312-07241-4) St Martin.

— Celtic Devotional. 1996. 14.00 (0-517-70413-7) Random.

— Celtic Love: Ten Enchanted Stories. LC 99-40709. (Illus.). 240p. 2000. 18.00 (0-06-251609-4, Pub. by Harper SF) HarpC.

— The Celtic Spirit: Daily Meditations for the Turning Year. LC 98-27087. 416p. 1999. pap. 14.00 (0-06-251538-1, Pub. by Harper SF) HarpC.

***Matthews, Caitlin.** The Celtic Wisdom Tarot: Book & Deck. LC 98-49370. (Illus.). 128p. 1999. boxed set 35.00 (0-89281-720-8) Inner Tradit.

Matthews, Caitlin. Elements of Celtic Tradition. (Element Library). (Illus.). 96p. 1995. pap. 14.95 (1-85230-709-9, Pub. by Element MA) Penguin Putnam.

— Elements of Celtic Tradition. (Elements of...Ser.). 1997. pap. 9.95 (1-86204-028-1, Pub. by Element MA) Penguin Putnam.

Matthews, Caitlin. Elements of Goddess. 130p. 1993. pap. 9.95 (1-85230-085-X, Pub. by Element MA) Penguin Putnam.

Matthews, Caitlin. Elements of Goddess. (Elements of...Ser.). 144p. 1997. pap. 9.95 (1-86204-147-4, Pub. by Element MA) Penguin Putnam.

— Hallowquest. 1990. 16.00 (0-85030-963-8, Pub. by Aqrn Pr) Harper SF.

— In Search of Women's Passionate Soul: Revealing the Daimon Lover Within. LC 96-40133. 256p. 1997. pap. 16.95 (1-85230-942-3, Pub. by Element MA) Penguin Putnam.

— Singing the Soul Back Home: Shamanism in Daily Life. 268p. 1995. pap. 14.95 (1-85230-616-5, Pub. by Element MA) Penguin Putnam.

***Matthews, Caitlin.** While the Bear Sleeps: Winter Tales & Traditions. (Illus.). 80p. (YA). (gr. 1 up). 1999. 19.95 (1-902283-81-3) Barefoot Bks NY.

***Matthews, Caitlin & Matthews, John.** The Little Book of Celtic Lore. LC 98-22914. (Illus.). 48p. 1998. 5.95 (1-86204-229-2, Pub. by Element MA) Penguin Putnam.

Matthews, Caitlin, jt. auth. see Matthews, John.

Matthews, Candace. Business Interactions. (Illus.). 224p. (C). 1987. pap. text 31.53 (0-13-100876-5) P-H.

Matthews, Candace & Edmondson, Phillip. Speaking Solutions: Interaction, Presentation, Listening, & Pronunciation. LC 93-45923. 240p. (C). 1994. pap. text 32.67 (0-13-701229-2) P-H.

Matthews, Candice Smith. Gregorio Esparza: Alamo Hero. LC 95-36585. (Illus.). 96p. (J). (gr. 5-6). 1996. 12.95 (1-57168-061-6) Sunbelt Media.

Matthews, Cari P. Federal Civil Trialbook. 240p. 1991. ring bd. 70.00 (0-314-00815-2) West Pub.

Matthews, Carol L. Environmental Science Experiments & Activies Teacher Pack: Teacher & Student Manuals Photocopy Rights Edition. enl. rev. ed. Matthews, Douglas L., ed. & illus. by. (Expert Systems for Teachers Ser.). 536p. 1999. pap., student ed. 258.00 (0-9629357-5-1) Water Pr.

— Environmental Science Experiments & Activities: Student Lab Manual. rev. ed. Matthews, Douglas L., ed. & illus. by. (Expert Systems for Teachers Ser.). 208p. 1999. pap. 16.00 (0-9629357-4-3) Water Pr.

— Environmental Science Experiments & Activities: Teacher & Student Manuals. large type rev. ed. Matthews, Douglas L., ed. & illus. by. (Expert Systems for Teachers). 536p. 1999. teacher ed. 238.00 incl. cd-rom (0-9629357-6-X) Water Pr.

— Freshwater Science: Experiments & Activities Student Lab Manual. Matthews, Douglas L., ed. & illus. by. (Expert Systems for Teachers Ser.). 1999. pap., student ed., lab manual ed. 9.00 (0-9629357-7-8) Water Pr.

— Freshwater Science: Experiments & Activities Teacher Pack. rev. ed. Matthews, Douglas L., ed. & illus. by. (Expert Systems for Teachers Ser.). 1999. pap., teacher ed. 163.00 (0-9629357-8-6) Water Pr.

— Freshwater Science: Experiments & Activities Teacher Pack. 3rd large type rev. ed. Matthews, Douglas L., ed. & illus. by. (Expert Systems for Teachers Ser.). 62p. 1999. pap. 143.00 (0-9629357-9-4) Water Pr.

— Marine & Oceanography: Experiments & Activities. 7th enl. rev. ed. Matthews, Douglas L., ed. & illus. by. (Expert Systems for Teachers Ser.). 636p. 1999. teacher ed. 238.00 incl. cd-rom (0-9629357-3-5) Water Pr.

— Marine Biology & Oceanography: Experiments & Activities. 7th ed. Matthews, Douglas L., ed. & illus. by. (Expert Systems for Teachers Ser.). 636p. 1991. pap., teacher ed. 258.00 (0-9629357-2-7); pap., student ed. 16.00 (0-9629357-1-9) Water Pr.

— Marine Biology, Oceanography, Environmental & Freshwater Science Professional Sample Copy: Experiments & Activities. 7th ed. Matthews, Douglas L., ed. & illus. by. (Expert Systems for Teachers Ser.). 302p. 1991. pap., teacher ed. 18.00 (0-9629357-0-0) Water Pr.

Matthews, Carole B., jt. auth. see Matthews, Martin S.

Matthews, Cecily. Captain Orinoco's Onion. LC 93-2802. (Illus.). (J). 1994. write for info. (0-383-03680-1) SRA McGraw.

— Mr. Clutterbus. LC 92-34257. (Voyages Ser.). (Illus.). (J). 1993. 4.25 (0-383-03642-9) SRA McGraw.

— Monster Magic. LC 97-122010. 96p. (J). 1996. pap. 10.95 (0-7022-2796-X, Pub. by Univ Queensland Pr) Intl Spec Bk.

— My Dog Ben. LC 92-31946. (Voyages Ser.). (Illus.). (J). 1993. 3.75 (0-383-03585-6) SRA McGraw.

— Why Not? LC 93-9280. (Voyages Ser.). (Illus.). (J). 1994. write for info. (0-383-03727-1) SRA McGraw.

Matthews, Charles. The Oscar Encyclopedia. LC 94-47288. 1280p. 1995. pap. 24.95 (0-385-47364-8, Main St Bks) Doubleday.

***Matthews, Charles.** Teach Yourself Go. 192p. 1999. pap. 9.95 (0-8442-2677-7, Teach Yrslf) NTC Contemp Pub Co.

Matthews, Charles, ed. see Ibn Al-Firkah & Ibrahim ibn Abd Al-Rahman.

Matthews, Cheryl & Hailey, Karen, eds. Mixed with Love. 250p. (Orig.). 1985. pap. 11.00 (0-685-08482-5) Chattanooga Christ.

Matthews, Chris. Asset Management. (Illus.). 414p. 1995. teacher ed., ring bd. 100.00 (1-928594-36-0); student ed., ring bd. 100.00 (1-928594-35-2) BOMI Inst.

Matthews, Christine. Lethal Ladies II. 1998. mass mkt. 6.99 (0-425-16268-0) Berkley Pub.

Matthews, Christine & Randisi, Robert J. Murder Is the Deal of the Day. 240p. 1998. text 22.95 (0-312-19928-7) St Martin.

***Matthews, Christopher.** Hardball with Chris Matthews: How Politics Is Played - Told by One Who Knows the Game. rev. ed. LC 99-45398. 240p. 1999. 13.00 (0-684-84559-8) S&S Trade.

Matthews, Christopher. Kennedy & Nixon: The Rivalry That Shaped Postwar America. (Illus.). 377p. 1996. 25.00 (0-684-81030-1) S&S Trade.

— Kennedy & Nixon: The Rivalry That Shaped Postwar America. 416p. 1997. per. 14.00 (0-684-83246-1) S&S Trade Pap.

Matthews, Christopher K., ed. see American Society for Microbiology Staff.

Matthews, Clayton, jt. auth. see Mattews, Patricia.

Matthews, Clayton, jt. auth. see Matthews, Patricia.

***Matthews, Clifford N.** Case Studies in Engineering Design. LC 98-214280. (Illus.). 288p. 1998. pap. 49.95 (0-470-32363-9) Halsted Pr.

Matthews, Clifford N. & Cheung, Oswald, eds. Dispersal & Renewal: Hong Kong University During the War Years. (Illus.). 462p. 1998. 42.50 (962-209-472-4, Pub. by HK Univ Pr) Coronet Bks.

***Matthews, Clive.** An Introduction to Natural Language Processing Through Prolog. LC 98-24258. 1998. pap. text 33.52 (0-582-06622-0) Longman.

Matthews, D. E. & Farewell, Vernon T. Using & Understanding Medical Statistics. 3rd rev. ed. (Illus.). xiv, 246p. 1996. pap. 35.00 (3-8055-6276-4) S Karger.

Matthews, D. J. Iqbal: A Selection of the Urdu Verse-Text & Translation. (C). 1993. pap. 38.00 (0-7286-0215-6) S Asia.

Matthews, D. M., jt. auth. see Ford, M. J.

Matthews, Dakin, tr. see Moreto, Augustin.

Matthews, Dale. Triumph of the Cross: Vocal Score (Lent Cantata) 84p. 1986. pap. 9.95 (0-7935-4944-2, 50324260) H Leonard.

Matthews, Dale & Clark, Connie. The Faith Factor: Proof of the Healing Power of Prayer. 320p. 1999. pap. 13.95 (0-14-027575-4) Penguin Putnam.

Matthews, Dan. Force Option. (Slam Ser.). 1993. mass mkt. 3.50 (0-373-63407-2, 1-63407-0) Harlequin Bks.

— Shadow Warriors. (Slam Ser.). 1993. per. 3.50 (0-373-63409-9, 1-63409-6) Harlequin Bks.

— White Powder, Black Death. (Slam Ser.). 1993. mass mkt. 3.50 (0-373-63408-0, 1-63408-8) Harlequin Bks.

Matthews, Daniel N., jt. auth. see Walker, Deward E., Jr.

Matthews, David. A Course in Nepali. 1984. pap. 42.50 (0-8364-1061-0, Pub. by Sch Orient & African Stud) S Asia.

— I Saw the Welsh Revival: An Eyewitness Account of the 1904 Revival in Wales. 144p. 1992. reprint ed. pap. 6.95 (0-9626908-2-1) Pioneer Goshen.

***Matthews, David.** The Invention of Middle English: An Anthology of Primary Sources. LC 00-28411. 2000. pap. write for info. (0-271-02082-2) Pa St U Pr.

Matthews, David. The Making of Middle English, 1765-1910 LC 98-53478. (Medieval Cultures Ser.). 1999. write for info. (0-8166-3186-7) U of Minn Pr.

***Matthews, David.** The Making of Middle English, 1765-1910. LC 98-53478. 1999. 39.95 (0-8166-3185-9) U of Minn Pr.

Matthews, David. Understanding Fundamental Principles of Wisdom, Creation, the Adam Man & Knowledge. 140p. 1999. pap. 8.99 (1-884369-59-6, Serenity Bks) McDougal Pubng.

— Urdu Complete Course. (Teach Yourself Ser.). 320p. 1999. pap. 31.95 (0-8442-3673-X) NTC Contemp Pub Co.

Matthews, David, ed. An Anthology of Urdu Verse in English: With the Original Poems in Devanagari. (ENG & URD.). 148p. 1995. text 17.95 (0-19-563462-4) OUP.

Matthews, David, tr. Battle of Karbala: Marsiya of Anis. (C). 1994. 16.00 (81-7167-213-2, Pub. by Rupa) S Asia.

Matthews, David, tr. An Anthology of Urdu Verse in English: With the Original Poems in Devanagari. (Oxford India Paperbacks Ser.). 146p. 1998. reprint ed. pap. text 8.95 (0-19-563927-8) OUP.

Matthews, David & Bukharaev, Ravil, trs. Historical Anthology of Kazan Tatar Verse. 320p. 1998. 55.00 (0-7007-1077-9, Pub. by Curzon Pr Ltd) Paul & Co Pubs.

Matthews, David, ed. see Mitchell, Donald.

Matthews, David, tr. see Rusva, Mirza M.

Matthews, David A. & Picken, Fiona M. Medical Librarianship. LC 79-40833. (Outlines of Modern Librarianship Ser.: No. 12). 173p. reprint ed. pap. 53.70 (0-7837-5317-9, 204505600005) Bks Demand.

Matthews, David C. Crashing Without Burning: Life after Failure. LC 97-8705. 144p. 1997. 17.00 (1-57312-155-X) Smyth & Helwys.

Matthews, David J., tr. see Siddiqi, Shaukat.

Matthews, David L., 3rd. The Richest Man There Ever Was or Ever Will Be: The Financial Laws of Your Future. Collins, Mike, ed. LC 94-69820. 106p. 1994. pap. 14.95 (0-9644282-0-2) Stick To The Word.

Matthews, David M., jt. auth. see Ford, Michael J.

Matthews, David O. Managing the Intramural-Recreational Sports Program. Zeigler, Earle F., ed. (Monograph Series on Sport & Physical Education Management). 62p. (Orig.). 1984. pap. text 4.00 (0-87563-255-6) Stipes.

Matthews, David O., ed. Managing Collegiate Sport Clubs. LC 86-27633. (Illus.). 255p. 1987. reprint ed. pap. 79.10 (0-608-07093-9, 206732000009) Bks Demand.

Matthews, David R. Controlling Common Property Regulating Canada's East Coast Fishery. LC 93-93870. 277p. 1993. text 55.00 (0-8020-2932-9) U of Toronto Pr.

***Matthews, Dawn.** Food Safety Sourcebook: Basic Consumer Health Information about the Safe Handling of Meat. LC 99-37611. (Health Reference Ser.). 1999. lib. bdg. 48.00 (0-7808-0326-4) Omnigraphics Inc.

***Matthews, Dawn D., ed.** Health Resources Sourcebook: Basic Consumer Health Information about Sources of Medical Assistance. (Health Reference Ser.). 500p. 2000. lib. bdg. 78.00 (0-7808-0328-0) Omnigraphics Inc.

— Healthy Heart Sourcebook for Women. (Health Reference Ser.). (Illus.). 400p. 2000. 48.00 (0-7808-0329-9) Omnigraphics Inc.

— Sexually Transmitted Diseases Sourcebook: Basic Consumer Health Information about Sexually Transmitted Diseases. 2nd ed. (Health Reference Ser.). 600p. 2000. lib. bdg. 78.00 (0-7808-0249-7) Omnigraphics Inc.

Matthews, Denis K. Blame It On Vanity! 1999. write for info. (1-878898-22-1) Christian Pub.

Matthews, Denny, et al. Play-by-Play: 25 Years of Royals on the Radio. LC 99-19435. (Illus.). 240p. 1999. pap. 14.95 (1-886110-78-6, Pub. by Addax Pubng) Midpt Trade.

Matthews, Derek, et al. The Priesthood of Industry: The Rise of the Professional Accountant in British Management. LC 97-33637. (Illus.). 372p. 1998. text 78.00 (0-19-828960-X) OUP.

Matthews, Donald H. Honoring the Ancestors: An African Cultural Interpretation of Black Religion & Literature. (Illus.). 192p. 1998. 24.95 (0-19-509104-3) OUP.

Matthews, Donald M. The Early Glyptic of Tell Brak: Cylinder Seals of Third Millennium Syria. (Orbis Biblicus et Orientalis Ser.: Vol. 15). 311p. 1997. text 84.00 (3-7278-1104-8, Pub. by Presses Univ Fribourg) Eisenbrauns.

— The Kassite Glyptic of Nippur. (Orbis Biblicus et Orientalis Ser.: Vol. 116). 153p. 1992. text 38.00 (3-7278-0807-1, Pub. by Presses Univ Fribourg) Eisenbrauns.

— Principles of Composition in Near Eastern Glyptic of the Later Second Millennium BC. (Orbis Biblicus et Orientalis Ser.: Vol. 8). 176p. 1990. text 58.25 (3-7278-0698-2, Pub. by Presses Univ Fribourg) Eisenbrauns.

Matthews, Donald N., jt. ed. see Gorman, Lyn.

Matthews, Donald R. U. S. Senators & Their World. LC 80-17163. (Illus.). 303p. 1980. reprint ed. lib. bdg. 65.00 (0-313-22664-4, MASE, Greenwood Pr) Greenwood.

Matthews, Donald R., ed. Perspectives on Presidential Selection. LC 73-1078. (Brookings Insitution Studies in Presidential Selection). 258p. reprint ed. pap. 80.00 (0-608-12717-5, 202539000043) Bks Demand.

Matthews, Donald R. & Prothro, James W. Negro Political Participation Study, 1961-1962. 2nd ed. 1975. write for info. (0-89138-112-0) ICPSR.

Matthews, Donald R. & Valen, Henry. Parliamentary Representation: The Case of the Norwegian Storting. LC 98-35317. (Parliaments & Legislatures Ser.). 1999. text 60.00 (0-8142-0798-7); pap. text 23.95 (0-8142-5002-5) Ohio St U Pr.

Matthews, Donald R., jt. auth. see Keech, William R.

Matthews, Donna, jt. auth. see Smith, Barbara Sweetland.

Matthews, Dorothy L. The Crucified Life. Stancil, Mary H., ed. & illus. by. 40p. 1998. pap. 4.95 (1-892212-00-5) Love Pubg Co.

Matthews, Douglas, jt. auth. see Rifkin, Glenn.

Matthews, Douglas L., ed. & illus. see Matthews, Carol L.

Matthews, Downs. Arctic Foxes. LC 94-6012. (Illus.). (YA). (gr. 5 up). 1995. write for info. (0-671-86563-3) S&S Bks Yung.

— Beneath the Canopy: Wildlife of the Latin American Rain Forest. LC 98-43588. (Illus.). 144p. 1999. pap. 24.95 (0-8118-2243-5) Chronicle Bks.

— Harp Seal Pups. LC 95-2314. (Illus.). 40p. (J). (gr. 2-5). 1997. mass mkt. 17.00 (0-689-80014-2) S&S Bks Yung.

Matthews, E., jt. auth. see Fraser, P. M.

Matthews, E. C. How to Paint Signs & Sho' Cards. 3rd ed. (Classic Reprint Ser.). 140p. 1924. reprint ed. pap. 4.95 (0-921335-19-9, Pub. by LVTL) Veritas Tools.

Matthews, E. G. & Kitching, R. L. Insect Ecology. 2nd ed. LC 83-7015. (Australian Ecology Ser.). (Illus.). 212p. 1988. pap. text 24.95 (0-7022-1812-X, Pub. by Univ Queensland Pr) Intl Spec Bk.

Matthews, E. T. George, the Friendly Dragon. Mitchell, Francis, ed. (Illus.). 40p. (Orig.). (J). (ps-6). 1997. pap. 9.95 (1-895814-02-2) NewWorld Pub.

Matthews, Edith V., tr. see Halevy, Ludovic.

Matthews, Edward. St. Stephen's Handbook for Altar Servers. 64p. 1994. pap. 4.95 (0-85244-277-7, 969, Pub. by Gra1cewing) Morehouse Pub.

Matthews, Edward, jt. auth. see Brusselmans, Christiane.

Matthews, Edward M. The Ancient Path. 56p. 1989. reprint ed. pap. 2.50 (0-935461-23-X) St Alban Pr CA.

— Deceptio, Falsum et Dissimulatio: A Critique. 96p. 1984. reprint ed. pap. 7.50 (0-935461-09-4) St Alban Pr CA.

— A Means of Grace. 58p. 1946. pap. 3.00 (0-935461-08-6) St Alban Pr CA.

— Principles or Expediency? 64p. 1989. reprint ed. pap. 3.00 (0-935461-17-5) St Alban Pr CA.

Matthews, Elaine, jt. ed. see Fraser, Peter.

Matthews, Elaine, jt. ed. see Hornblower, Simon.

Matthews, Elizabeth W. Access Points to the Law Library: Card Catalog Interpretation. LC 82-80900. vi, 66p. 1982. lib. bdg. 30.00 (0-89941-156-8, 302290) W S Hein.

— The Law Library Reference Shelf: Annotated Subject Guide. 3rd rev. ed. LC 95-42097. v, 229p. 1996. 47.50 (0-89941-991-7, 305600) W S Hein.

***Matthews, Elizabeth W.** The Law Library Reference Shelf: Annotated Subject Guide. 4th rev. ed. LC 99-21881. vii, 213p. 1999. 48.50 (1-57588-501-8, 323850) W S Hein.

Matthews, Elizabeth W. Lincoln As a Lawyer: An Annotated Bibliography. LC 90-39143. 272p. (C). 1991. 31.95 (0-8093-1644-7) S Ill U Pr.

Matthews, Elmora M. Neighbor & Kin: Life in a Tennessee Ridge Community. LC 66-15287. 216p. reprint ed. pap. 67.00 (0-8357-3259-2, 203948000013) Bks Demand.

***Matthews, Emily & Hammond, Al.** Critical Consumption Trends & Implications: Degrading Earth's Ecosystems. 72p. 1999. pap. 20.00 (1-56973-410-0) World Resources Inst.

Matthews, Eric. Twentieth-Century French Philosophy. 240p. 1996. pap. 16.95 (0-19-289248-7) OUP.

Matthews, Eric, jt. ed. see Dalgarno, Melvin.

Matthews, Eric, tr. see Kant, Immanuel.

Matthews, Eric, tr. see Weber, Max.

***Matthews, F. L.** Composite Materials. 1999. 49.99 (0-8493-0621-3) CRC Pr.

— Finite Element Modeling of Composite Materials & Structures. LC 00-31152. 2001. write for info. (0-8493-0846-1) CRC Pr.

***Matthews, F. L., et al, eds.** Finite Element Modeling of Composite Materials & Structures. 220p. 2000. boxed set 153.00 (1-85573-422-2) Am Educ Systs.

***Matthews, F. L. & Rawlings, R. D.** Composite Materials: Engineering & Science. 480p. 1999. 49.50 (1-85573-473-7, Pub. by Woodhead Pubng) Am Educ Systs.

Matthews, Fred H. The Quest for an American Sociology: Robert E. Park & the Chicago School. LC 77-373940. 288p. reprint ed. pap. 89.30 (0-7837-1029-1, 204134000020) Bks Demand.

Matthews, Frederick. American Merchant Ships Eighteen Fifty to Nineteen Hundred, 2 vols., Vol. I. (Illus.). 960p. 1988. reprint ed. pap. 11.95 (0-486-25538-7) Dover.

— American Merchant Ships Eighteen Fifty to Nineteen Hundred, 2 vols., Vol. II. (Illus.). 960p. 1988. reprint ed. pap. 11.95 (0-486-25539-5) Dover.

Matthews, Frederick C., jt. auth. see Howe, Octavius T.

Matthews, G. The Normative Structure of Black Nationalism. 77p. 1998. pap. text 12.00 (1-56411-171-7) Untd Bros & Sis.

— PVC: Production, Properties & Uses. 512p. 1997. 90.00 (0-901716-59-6, Pub. by Inst Materials) Ashgate Pub Co.

Matthews, G. & Tunstall, Jeremy. Insect Pests of Cotton. LC 93-171734. (Illus.). 592p. 1994. text 170.00 (0-85198-724-9) OUP.

Matthews, G., jt. auth. see Kelly, P.

***Matthews, G. A.** Application of Pesticides to Crops. LC 99-25181. 1999. pap. text 40.00 (1-86094-175-3) Imperial College.

***Matthews, G A.** Application of Pesticides to Crops. LC 99-25181. 300p. 1999. 60.00 (1-86094-168-0, Pub. by Imperial College) World Scientific Pub.

***Matthews, G. A.** Pesticide Application Methods. 3rd ed. LC 00-33746. 2000. write for info. (0-632-05473-5) Blackwell Sci.

Matthews, G. A. & Hislop, E. C., eds. Application Technology for Crop Protection. (Illus.). 368p. 1993. text 130.00 (0-85198-834-2) OUP.

Matthews, G. A. & Thronhill, E. W. Pesticide Application Equipment for Use in Agriculture: Manually Carried. LC 95-214726. (Agricultural Services Bulletin Ser.: No. 112-1). (Illus.). 163p. 1994. pap. 25.00 (92-5-103582-2, F35822, Pub. by FAO) Bernan Associates.

Matthews, G. E. & Williams, R. T., eds. Defects in Insulating Materials: ICDIM 96. (Materials Science Forum Ser.: Vols. 239-241). (Illus.). 812p. (C). 1997. text 280.00 (0-87849-756-0, Pub. by Trans T Pub) Enfield Pubs NH.

Matthews, Gareth B. The Augustinian Tradition. LC 97-35854. (Philosophical Traditions Ser.). 450p. 1998. 55.00 (0-520-20999-0, Pub. by U CA Pr); pap. 24.95 (0-520-21001-8, Pub. by U CA Pr) Cal Prin Full Svc.

— Dialogues with Children. 136p. 1984. 17.95 (0-674-20282-1) HUP.

— Dialogues with Children. 136p. 1992. pap. 13.00 (0-674-20284-8) HUP.

— Philosophy & the Young Child. LC 80-14494. 123p. 1980. 23.95 (0-674-66605-4) HUP.

— Philosophy & the Young Child. 123p. 1982. pap. text 9.50 (0-674-66606-2) HUP.

— The Philosophy of Childhood. LC 94-16178. 144p. 1994. 18.95 (0-674-66480-9, MATPHC) HUP.

— The Philosophy of Childhood. LC 96-215909. 144p. 1996. pap. 12.95 (0-674-66481-7) HUP.

— Socratic Perplexity & the Nature of Philosophy. LC 99-10366. 148p. 1999. text 29.95 (*0-19-823828-2*) OUP.

— Thought's Ego in Augustine & Descartes. LC 92-52767. 240p. (C). 1992. text 32.50 (*0-8014-2775-4*) Cornell U Pr.

Matthews, Gareth B., jt. ed. see Turner, Susan M.

Matthews, Gareth B., tr. see Ammonius.

***Matthews, Gary.** Neurobiology: Molecules, Cells & Systems. 2nd ed. 2000. 75.95 (*0-632-04496-9*) Blackwell Sci.

Matthews, Gary G. Cellular Physiology of Nerve & Muscle. 3rd ed. LC 97-14314. (Illus.). 1997. pap. 41.95 (*0-632-04354-7*) Blackwell Sci.

— Introduction to Neuroscience. LC 99-23051. (11th Hour Ser.). (Illus.). 1999. pap. 18.95 (*0-632-04414-4*) Blackwell Sci.

Matthews, Gary G. Neurobiology: Molecules, Cells & Systems. LC 96-45522. (Illus.). 600p. 1997. pap. 56.95 (*0-86542-404-7*) Blackwell Sci.

Matthews, Gary L. The Challenge of Baha'u'llah. 284p. (Orig.). 1993. pap. 9.95 (*0-85398-360-7*) G Ronald Pub.

Matthews, Geoffery. The Reconquest of Burma, 1943-1945. pap. 3.95 (*0-685-56071-6*) Beachcomber Bks.

Matthews, Geoffrey, jt. auth. see Everest, Kelvin.

Matthews, Geoffrey, ed. see Shelley, Percy Bysshe.

Matthews, Geoffrey V. Bird Navigation. 2nd ed. LC 68-23181. (Cambridge Monographs in Experimental Biology: Vol. 3). 207p. reprint ed. pap. 59.00 (*0-8357-7270-5*, 2027236) Bks Demand.

Matthews, George, jt. ed. see King, Francis.

Matthews, Gerald. Cognitive Science Perspectives on Personality & Emotion, Vol. 124. LC 97-45697. (Advances in Psychology Ser.). 574p. 1997. 149.50 (*0-444-82450-2*) Elsevier.

***Matthews, Gerald.** Human Performance: Cognition, Stress & Individual Differences. LC 99-87641. 2000. pap. write for info. (*0-415-04407-3*) Routledge.

Matthews, Gerald & Deary, Ian J. Personality Traits. LC 97-14349. 320p. (C). 1998. text 59.95 (*0-521-49739-6*); pap. text 19.95 (*0-521-49759-0*) Cambridge U Pr.

Matthews, Gerald, jt. auth. see Wells, Adrian.

Matthews, Gerald E. A Declaration of Independence for Black Americans: An Essay for Change & Growth. 123p. (Orig.). reprint ed. pap. 9.00 (*1-56411-132-6*) Untd Bros & Sis.

Matthews, Gilda. Soul Vibrations: Astrology for African Americans. LC 95-35908. 1996. pap. 10.00 (*0-688-14601-5*, Quil) HarperTrade.

Matthews, Glen P. Water Resources Geography & Law. 1987. reprint ed. 60.00 (*81-85046-45-X*, Pub. by Scientific) St Mut.

Matthews, Glenice L. Enamels, Enameling, Enamelists. LC 83-70776. (Illus.). 192p. 1984. 29.95 (*0-8019-7285-X*) Krause Pubns.

Matthews, Glenna. American Women's History: A Student Companion. (Student Companions to American History Ser.). (Illus.). 368p. (YA). 2000. text 45.00 (*0-19-511317-9*) OUP.

— The Rise of Public Woman: Woman's Power & Woman's Place in the United States, 1630-1970. (Illus.). 320p. 1994. reprint ed. pap. 11.95 (*0-19-509045-4*) OUP.

Matthews, Gordon. Dire Straits. (Orig.). 1987. mass mkt. 2.95 (*0-345-33885-5*) Ballantine Pub Grp.

— Madonna. Arico, Diane, ed. LC 85-10587. (Hot Rock Ser.). (Illus.). 64p. (YA). (gr. 8-12). 1985. pap. 3.50 (*0-685-10385-4*) S&S Trade.

Matthews, Graham. Disaster Management in British Libraries: Project Report with Guidelines for Library Managers. LC 98-155588. (Information Research Reports). x, 176 p. 1996. write for info. (*0-7123-3306-1*) B23tish Library.

Matthews, Graham P., Jr. Children's Bible Stories with Questions. LC 93-19623. (Illus.). (J). (gr. 3 up). 1993. write for info. (*0-910683-18-2*) Townsnd-Pr.

Matthews, Grant J., ed. Strong, Weak, & Electromagnetic Interactions in Nuclei, Atoms, & Astrophysics: A Workshop in Honor of Stewart D. Bloom's Retirement. LC 91-76876. (AIP Conference Proceedings Ser.: No. 242). 248p. 1992. 88.00 (*0-88318-943-7*) Am Inst Physics.

Matthews, Greg. Come to Dust. large type ed. LC 98-12212. (Keith Moody Mystery Ser.). 246p. 1998. 23.95 (*0-8027-3317-4*) Walker & Co.

— Far from Heaven: A Keith Moody Mystery. LC 97-9608. 276p. 1997. 20.95 (*0-8027-3303-4*) Walker & Co.

— Heart of the Country. 704p. 1990. mass mkt. 5.99 (*0-8217-4677-4*, Zebra Kensgtn) Kensgtn Pub Corp.

— Heart of the Country. 704p. 1997. mass mkt. 6.99 (*0-7860-0460-6*, Pinncle Kensgtn) Kensgtn Pub Corp.

— One True Thing. 320p. 1992. reprint ed. mass mkt. 4.99 (*0-8217-3994-8*, Zebra Kensgtn) Kensgtn Pub Corp.

***Matthews, Gregory E.** Payroll Answer Book. LC 99-188134. 1999. write for info. (*1-56706-305-5*) Panel Pubs.

Matthews, Guy, jt. auth. see James, David.

Matthews, Gwenyth F. Voices from the Shadows: Women with Disabilities Speak Out. 200p. pap. 8.95 (*0-88961-080-0*, Pub. by Womens Pr) LPC InBook.

Matthews, Harry, tr. see Bataille, Georges.

Matthews, Harry G. International Tourism: A Political & Social Analysis. LC 77-24764. (Illus.). 100p. 1978. pap. 13.95 (*0-87073-945-X*); text 18.95 (*0-87073-944-1*) Schenkman Bks Inc.

— Multinational Corporations & Black Power. 136p. 1976. text 32.95 (*0-87073-776-7*) Transaction Pubs.

Matthews, Harry R., et al. Biochemistry: A Short Course. LC 96-16469. 505p. 1997. pap. 59.95 (*0-471-02205-5*) Wiley.

Matthews, Heidi & Walser, Eric. On the Road Review. 156p. 1999. 29.95 (*1-889366-10-2*) Cramer Prods.

Matthews, Hellen, ed. A Hairst o' Words: New Writing from the North East of Scotland. (Aberdeen University Press Bks.). (Illus.). 160p. 1991. pap. text 13.90 (*0-08-041198-3*, Pub. by Aberdeen U Pr) Macmillan.

Matthews, Henry. Kirtland Cutter: Architect in the Land of Promise. LC 98-14470. (McLellan Book Ser.). (Illus.). 432p. 1998. 60.00 (*0-295-97609-8*) U of Wash Pr.

Matthews, Herbert, ed. Surface Wave Filters: Design, Construction & Use. LC 77-3913. 535p. reprint ed. pap. 165.90 (*0-608-10272-5*, 201952200012) Bks Demand.

Matthews, Herbert L. The Education of a Correspondent. LC 76-106672. 550p. 1970. reprint ed. lib. bdg. 79.50 (*0-8371-3369-6*, MACO, Greenwood Pr) Greenwood.

— The Fruits of Fascism. LC 78-63694. (Studies in Fascism: Ideology & Practice). 352p. 1983. reprint ed. 34.50 (*0-404-16955-4*) AMS Pr.

Matthews, Herbert L., ed. The United States & Latin America. rev. ed. LC 59-15532. 1963. reprint ed. pap. 1.95 (*0-317-02968-1*, 93840-C) Am Assembly.

Matthews, Hodin, jt. auth. see Brooks, Ashley.

Matthews, Hugoe, jt. auth. see Miller, George, II.

Matthews, Irene, tr. see Campobello, Nellie.

Matthews, Irene, tr. & afterword by see Felinto, Marilene.

Matthews, J. Little Book of Arthurian Wisdom. 48p. 1994. pap. 5.95 (*1-85230-565-7*, Pub. by Element MA) Penguin Putnam.

— The Park. (Longman African Writers Ser.). (C). 1995. pap. text 8.95 (*0-582-26435-9*) Addison-Wesley.

Matthews, J. F. Western Aristocracies & Imperial Court, AD 364-425. 460p. 1990. pap. text 29.95 (*0-19-814499-7*) OUP.

Matthews, J. H. Andre Breton: Sketch for an Early Portrait. LC 86-20741. (Purdue University Monographs in Romance Languages: No. 22). xii, 176p. (Orig.). 1986. pap. 46.00 (*0-915027-71-2*) J Benjamins Pubng Co.

— Benjamin Peret. LC 74-30229. (Twayne's World Authors Ser.). 176p. (C). 1975. lib. bdg. 20.95 (*0-8057-2691-8*) Irvington.

— Eight Painters: The Surrealist Context. (Illus.). 160p. 1983. pap. text 29.95 (*0-8156-2302-X*) Syracuse U Pr.

— Eight Painters: The Surrealist Context. LC 82-10801. (Illus.). 164p. 1982. reprint ed. pap. 50.90 (*0-608-07616-3*, 205993100010) Bks Demand.

— The Imagery of Surrealism. LC 77-7927. (Illus.). 320p. 1977. reprint ed. pap. 99.20 (*0-608-06984-1*, 206719200009) Bks Demand.

— The Inner Dream: Celine As Novelist. 1978. 39.95 (*0-8156-2197-3*) Syracuse U Pr.

— The Inner Dream: Celine As Novelist. LC 78-11324. 246p. 1978. reprint ed. pap. 76.30 (*0-608-07617-1*, 205993200010) Bks Demand.

— Surrealism & Film. LC 75-163624. 226p. reprint ed. pap. 70.10 (*0-608-16941-2*, 205614600050) Bks Demand.

— The Surrealist Mind. LC 88-43398. 240p. 1991. 40.00 (*0-945636-06-7*) Susquehanna U Pr.

— Surrealist Poetry in France. LC 71-96815. 254p. reprint ed. pap. 78.80 (*0-8357-3125-1*, 203938600012) Bks Demand.

— Theatre in Dada & Surrealism. LC 73-16286. 300p. reprint ed. pap. 93.00 (*0-8357-7052-4*, 203344300086) Bks Demand.

— Toward the Poetics of Surrealism. LC 75-43974. 255p. 1976. reprint ed. pap. 79.10 (*0-608-06977-9*, 206718500009) Bks Demand.

***Matthews, J. N. S.** Introduction to Randomised Controlled Clinical Trials. (An Arnold Publication). (Illus.). 208p. 2000. pap. text 34.95 (*0-340-76143-1*, Pub. by E A) OUP.

Matthews, J. Rosser. Quantification & the Quest for Medical Certainty. LC 94-24091. 200p. 1995. text 39.50 (*0-691-03794-9*, Pub. by Princeton U Pr) Cal Prin Full Svc.

Matthews, Jack. An Almanac for Twilight. LC 92-70688. (Classic Contemporaries Ser.). 1992. reprint ed. pap. 12.95 (*0-88748-143-4*) Carnegie-Mellon.

— Booking in the Heartland. LC 86-7150. 176p. reprint ed. pap. 54.60 (*0-608-07401-2*, 206762800009) Bks Demand.

— Booking Pleasures. LC 95-31740. 191p. 1995. 24.95 (*0-8214-1129-2*) Ohio U Pr.

— Crazy Women. LC 84-25112. (Poetry & Fiction Ser.). 176p. 1987. reprint ed. pap. 9.95 (*0-8018-3469-4*) Johns Hopkins.

— Crazy Women: Short Stories. LC 84-25112. (Johns Hopkins Ser.). 170p. reprint ed. pap. 52.70 (*0-608-07403-9*, 206763000009) Bks Demand.

— Dirty Tricks. LC 90-30832. (Poetry & Fiction Ser.). 168p. 1990. pap. 10.95 (*0-8018-4054-6*) Johns Hopkins.

— Dirty Tricks: Short Stories. LC 90-30832. (Johns Hopkins Ser.). 184p. reprint ed. pap. 57.10 (*0-608-07402-0*, 206762900009) Bks Demand.

— Dubious Persuasions: Short Stories. LC 81-47591. (Johns Hopkins Ser.). 168p. reprint ed. pap. 52.10 (*0-608-07404-7*, 206763100009) Bks Demand.

— Ghostly Populations: Short Stories. LC 86-45439. (Johns Hopkins, Poetry & Fiction Ser.). 184p. 1986. reprint ed. pap. 57.10 (*0-608-06713-X*, 206691000009) Bks Demand.

— Memoirs of a Bookman. LC 89-37615. 178p. 1989. 15.95 (*0-8214-0937-9*) Ohio U Pr.

— Memoirs of a Bookman. LC 89-37615. 178p. 1991. pap. 14.95 (*0-8214-0974-3*) Ohio U Pr.

— On the Shore of That Beautiful Shore. 1991. pap. 3.50 (*0-87129-082-0*, O46) Dramatic Pub.

***Matthews, Jack.** Reading Matter: Rhetorical Muses of a Rabid Bibliophile. LC 00-31361. 2000. write for info. (*1-58456-027-4*) Oak Knoll.

Matthews, Jack. Storyhood As We Know It & Other Tales. (Poetry & Fiction Ser.). 208p. 1993. pap. 12.95 (*0-8018-4623-4*) Johns Hopkins.

— Storyhood As We Know It & Other Tales. LC 92-42477. (Johns Hopkins Ser.). 123p. reprint ed. pap. 66.10 (*0-608-07399-7*, 206762600009) Bks Demand.

— Tales of the Ohio Land. (Illus.). 186p. 1978. 11.95 (*0-87758-011-1*) Ohio Hist Soc.

***Matthews, Jack.** Time & Money.com: Create Wealth by Profiting from the Explosive Growth of E-Commerce. 96p. 2000. pap. 9.95 (*0-938716-50-6*, Possible Pr) Markowski Intl.

Matthews, Jack. Toys Go to War: World War II Military Toys, Games, Puzzles & Books. Chenoweth, Candace A., ed. LC 94-73995. (Illus.). 272p. (Orig.). (C). 1995. pap. 29.95 (*0-929521-95-1*) Pictorial Hist.

Matthews, Jack, ed. see Wessen, Ernest J.

Matthews, Jack L. Sales Driven: Turning Your Company into a Marketing Machine. 250p. 1992. text 24.95 (*1-55738-417-7*, Irwn Prfssnl) McGraw-Hill Prof.

Matthews, James. Frank O'Connor. LC 75-125470. (Irish Writers Ser.). 94p. 1975. pap. 1.95 (*0-8387-7609-4*) Bucknell U Pr.

— Statutes at Large of the Provisional Government of the Confederate States of America. LC 87-83739. 922p. 1988. reprint ed. lib. bdg. 95.00 (*0-89941-629-2*, 305500) W S Hein.

Matthews, James, ed. High Energy Gamma-Ray Astronomy. LC 91-70876. (AIP Conference Proceedings Ser.: No. 220). (Illus.). 360p. 1991. 85.00 (*0-88318-812-0*) Am Inst Physics.

***Matthews, James K.** So Many, So Much, So Far, So Fast: United States Transportation Command & Strategic Deployment For Operation Desert Shield/desert Storm (clothbound) 340p. 2000. boxed set 29.00 (*0-16-059187-2*) USGPO.

— So Many, So Much, So Far, So Fast: United States Transportation Command & Strategic Deployment for Operation Desert Shield/desert Storm (paperbound) 340p. 1996. per. 24.00 (*0-16-061113-X*) USGPO.

Matthews, James M. High Energy Astrophysics: Theory & Observations from MeV to TeV. 296p. 1994. text 86.00 (*981-02-1680-7*) World Scientific Pub.

Matthews, James R., ed. Acoustic Emission. LC 82-20928. (Nondestructive Testing Monographs & Tracts: Vol. 2). (Illus.). viii, 167p. 1983. text 171.00 (*0-677-16490-4*) Gordon & Breach.

Matthews, Jan & Eastaway, Nigel. Tolley's Self-Assessment 1998-99 Fifth Edition. 5th ed. 1998. pap. 195.00 (*1-86012-830-0*) Tolley Pubng.

Matthews, Jan, jt. auth. see Eastaway, Nigel A.

Matthews, Janet R. & Walker, C. Eugene, eds. Basic Skills & Professional Issues in Clinical Psychology. LC 96-38506. 366p. (C). 1997. 55.00 (*0-205-16970-8*) Allyn.

Matthews, Janet S. Edge of Wilderness: A Settlement History of Manatee River & Sarasota Bay, 1528-1885. LC 83-72562. (Illus.). 464p. 1994. reprint ed. 21.50 (*0-914381-00-8*) Coastal Pr FL.

— Historic Spanish Point: Cooking Then & Now. Newton, Frances & Gootee, Diane F., eds. (Illus.). 256p. 1993. spiral bd. 13.95 (*0-9660576-1-9*) Gulf Coast Herit.

— Sarasota: Journey to Centennial: A Pictorial & Entertaining Commentary on Growth & Development of Sarasota. rev. ed. LC 97-61782. (Illus.). 242p. 1997. 29.95 (*0-9621986-2-5*) Coastal Pr FL.

— Venice: Journey from Horse & Chaise. LC 89-60490. (Illus.). 394p. 1989. 20.00 (*0-9621986-0-9*) Coastal Pr FL.

Matthews, Janet Wright. Clouds Before the Sun. 320p. 26.00 (*0-7278-5540-9*) Severn Hse.

— A Silver Flood. 464p. 2000. 31.99 (*0-7505-1492-2*) Ulverscroft.

Matthews, Janice R. What's Inside a Mud Dauber's Nest? A Teachers' Guide with Identification Keys. (Illus.). 32p. 1996. pap. 4.95 (*1-888499-07-9*) Riverview GA.

Matthews, Janice R., et al. Successful Scientific Writing: A Step-by-Step Guide for the Biological & Medical Sciences. (Illus.). 195p. (C). 1996. spiral bd. 20.95 (*0-521-55948-0*) Cambridge U Pr.

***Matthews, Janice R., et al.** Successful Scientific Writing: A Step-by-Step Guide for the Biological & Medical Sciences. 2nd ed. (Illus.). 292p. 2000. pap. write for info. (*0-521-78962-1*) Cambridge U Pr.

Matthews, Janice R., ed. see Jackson Scandinavian American Society Staff.

Matthews, Jay, ed. Business Focus: Newspaper Travel & Entertainment Expense Policies & Guidelines. (Illus.). 68p. (Orig.). (C). 1990. pap. 39.95 (*1-877888-12-5*) Intl Newspaper.

Matthews, Jay & Rozak, Chester. Newspaper Financial Management: An Introduction. 72p. (Orig.). 1988. pap. 49.95 (*1-877888-05-2*) Intl Newspaper.

Matthews, Jay, jt. auth. see Pew, David.

Matthews, Jaymie M., jt. ed. see Nemec, James M.

Matthews, Jean, tr. see Rodinson, Maxime.

Matthews, Jean V. Toward a New Society: American Thought & Culture, 1800-1830. (Illus.). 208p. 1990. 33.00 (*0-8057-9052-7*); pap. 20.00 (*0-8057-9057-8*) Macmillan.

— Women's Struggle for Equality: The First Phase, 1828-1876. LC 96-47500. (American Ways Ser.). 224p. 1997. 24.95 (*1-56663-145-9*, Pub. by I R Dee); pap. text 12.95 (*1-56663-146-7*, Pub. by I R Dee) Natl Bk Netwk.

***Matthews, Jeanie.** Colors of His Grace. 120p. 2000. pap. write for info. (*0-9701439-0-7*, PO4517) M K Clark.

Matthews, Jenny, jt. auth. see Brearley, Sue.

Matthews, Jerold & Eidswick, Jack. Hp 48G Calculus Companion Hp Forty Eight G Calculus Companion. (C). 1997. 39.06 (*0-06-500165-6*) Addson-Wesley Educ.

Matthews, Jerry. Motorcycling: A Beginner's Manual. 64p. (C). 1990. text 65.00 (*0-906754-53-4*, Pub. by Fernhurst Bks) St Mut.

***Matthews, Jessica.** Babies on Her Mind. large type ed. 288p. 2000. 25.99 (*0-263-16179-X*, Pub. by Mills & Boon) Ulverscroft.

Matthews, Jessica. Beginning Over. 1999. pap. write for info. (*0-679-77546-3*) Vin Bks.

— Dr. Prescott's Dilemma. (Promo Ser.). 1999. per. 3.75 (*0-373-83380-6*, 1-83380-5) Harlequin Bks.

— For a Child's Sake. large type ed. (Mills & Boon Large Print Ser.). 288p. 1998. 24.99 (*0-263-15411-4*, Pub. by Mills & Boon) Ulverscroft.

— A Heart of Gold. large type ed. (Mills & Boon Large Print Ser.). 288p. 1998. 24.99 (*0-263-15448-3*, Pub. by Mills & Boon) Ulverscroft.

***Matthews, Jessica.** His Made to Order Bride. 288p. 2000. 26.99 (*0-263-16360-1*, Pub. by Mills & Boon) Ulverscroft.

Matthews, Jessica. Too Close for Comfort. large type ed. (Mills & Boon Large Print Ser.). 288p. 1998. 24.99 (*0-263-15454-8*, Pub. by Mills & Boon) Ulverscroft.

Matthews, Jessica T. Beginning Over. 1998. write for info. (*0-679-45129-3*) Knopf.

Matthews, Jill. Cocktails & Cigarettes. Spafford, John M., ed. 98p. (Orig.). 1994. pap. 9.95 (*1-890538-13-2*, Nghtlight Pub) Rhiannon Pubns.

— Hanson. Mummbop to the Top. LC 99-200324. (J). 1997. per. 3.99 (*0-671-01913-9*, Archway) PB.

— The Lives & Loves of New Kids on the Block. 1990. pap. 3.95 (*0-685-33337-X*) PB.

— The Love Touch, Vol. 1. Spafford, John M., ed. (Illus.). 50p. (Orig.). 1996. pap. 3.95 (*1-890538-00-0*, Pulp Friction) Rhiannon Pubns.

— The Love Touch, Vol. 2. Spafford, John M., ed. (Illus.). 50p. (Orig.). 1996. pap. 3.95 (*1-890538-01-9*, Pulp Friction) Rhiannon Pubns.

— The Love Touch, Vol. 3. Spafford, John M., ed. (Illus.). 50p. (Orig.). 1996. pap. 3.95 (*1-890538-02-7*, Pulp Friction) Rhiannon Pubns.

— The Love Touch, Vol. 4. Spafford, John M., ed. (Illus.). 50p. (Orig.). 1996. pap. 3.95 (*1-890538-03-5*, Pulp Friction) Rhiannon Pubns.

— The Love Touch, Vol. 5. Spafford, John M., ed. (Illus.). 50p. (Orig.). 1996. pap. 3.95 (*1-890538-04-3*, Pulp Friction) Rhiannon Pubns.

— The Love Touch, Vol. 6. Spafford, John M., ed. (Illus.). 50p. (Orig.). 1996. pap. 3.95 (*1-890538-05-1*, Pulp Friction) Rhiannon Pubns.

— The Love Touch, Vol. 7. Spafford, John M., ed. (Illus.). 50p. (Orig.). 1996. pap. 3.95 (*1-890538-06-X*, Pulp Friction) Rhiannon Pubns.

— The Love Touch, Vol. 8. Spafford, John M., ed. (Illus.). 50p. (Orig.). 1996. pap. 3.95 (*1-890538-07-8*, Pulp Friction) Rhiannon Pubns.

— The Love Touch, Vol. 9. Spafford, John M., ed. (Illus.). 50p. (Orig.). 1996. pap. 3.95 (*1-890538-08-6*, Pulp Friction) Rhiannon Pubns.

— The Love Touch, Vol. 10. Spafford, John M., ed. (Illus.). 50p. (Orig.). 2000. pap. 3.95 (*1-890538-09-4*, Pulp Friction) Rhiannon Pubns.

— The Love Touch, Vol. 11. Spafford, John M., ed. (Illus.). 50p. (Orig.). 2000. pap. 3.95 (*1-890538-10-8*, Pulp Friction) Rhiannon Pubns.

— The Love Touch, Vol. 12. Spafford, John M., ed. (Illus.). 50p. (Orig.). 2000. pap. 3.95 (*1-890538-11-6*, Pulp Friction) Rhiannon Pubns.

— The Love Touch, Vol. 13. Spafford, John M., ed. (Illus.). 50p. (Orig.). 2000. pap. 3.95 (*1-890538-12-4*, Pulp Friction) Rhiannon Pubns.

Matthews, Jill & Gollihare, Jarrod. Hanson: The Official Book. LC 97-41726. (Illus.). 96p. (J). 1997. pap. text 10.95 (*0-8230-8323-3*) Watsn-Guptill.

Matthews, Jill J., ed. Sex in Public: Austrialian Sexual Cultures. LC 97-217255. (Illus.). 232p. 1997. pap. 24.95 (*1-86448-049-1*) Paul & Co Pubs.

Matthews, Jim, jt. auth. see Eastaway, Nigel A.

Matthews, Jo. I Remember Somalia. LC 94-25547. (Why We Left Ser.). (Illus.). (J). 1994. lib. bdg. 22.83 (*0-8114-5606-4*) Raintree Steck-V.

Matthews, Joan, jt. auth. see Stone, Julie.

Matthews, Joan L. Secrets of the Heart. 352p. 1998. mass mkt. 4.99 (*0-8217-5845-4*, Zebra Kensgtn) Kensgtn Pub Corp.

Matthews, Joan M., et al, eds. From Politics to Policy: A Case Study in Educational Reform. LC 91-8074. 336p. 1991. 59.95 (*0-275-93736-4*, C3736, Praeger Pubs) Greenwood.

Matthews, John. Art of Childhood & Adolescence: The Construction of Meaning. LC 99-168718. 177p. 1998. 85.00 (*0-7507-0766-6*, Falmer Pr); pap. 27.95 (*0-7507-0765-8*, Falmer Pr) Taylor & Francis.

— Arthur & the Mystic Grail. LC 98-106740. (Illus.). 96p. 1997. 12.95 (*0-8069-9604-8*) Sterling.

— Arthurian Tradition. (Element Library). (Illus.). 96p. 1995. pap. 14.95 (*1-85230-713-7*, Pub. by Element MA) Penguin Putnam.

— Bardic Source Book: Inspirational Legacy & Teachings of the Ancient Celts. 1999. pap. text 14.95 (*0-7137-2785-3*) Blandford Pr.

— Bardic Sourcebook. LC 98-139404. (Illus.). 320p. 1998. 24.95 (*0-7137-2664-4*, Pub. by Blandford Pr) Sterling.

— The Barefoot Book of Giants, Ghost & Goblins: Traditional Tales from Around the World. (Illus.). 80p. (J). (gr. 1-5). 1999. 19.95 (*1-902283-27-9*) Barefoot Bks NY.

— The Beginning Entrepreneur. LC 93-1466. (Illus.). 224p. 1995. pap. 13.95 (*0-8442-4141-5*, 41415, VGM Career) NTC Contemp Pub Co.

— A Celtic Reader: Selections from Celtic Legend, Scholarship, & Story. 1991. 26.95 (*0-85030-935-2*, Pub. by Aqrn Pr) Harper SF.

An Asterisk (*) at the beginning of an entry indicates that the title is appearing for the first time.

*Matthews, John. The Celtic Seers' Source Book: Vision & Magic in the Druid Tradition. 288p. 1999. 29.95 (0-7137-2780-2) Strlng Pub CA.

Matthews, John. The Celtic Shaman: A Handbook. (Illus.). 206p. 1993. pap. 14.95 (1-85230-245-3, Pub. by Element MA) Penguin Putnam.

— The Celtic Shaman's Pack: Exploring the Inner Worlds. LC 94-22046. (Illus.). 208p. 1995. pap. 29.95 (1-85230-481-2, Pub. by Element MA) Penguin Putnam.

*Matthews, John. Celtic Totem Animals: The Complete Guide to Discovering Your Natural Shamanic Power. 2000. pap. 25.95 (1-86204-840-1) Element MA.

Matthews, John. Classic Celtic Fairy Tales. LC 98-100835. (Illus.). 192p. (J). (gr. 7). 1997. 24.95 (0-7137-2618-0, Pub. by Blandford Pr) Sterling.

— Classic Celtic Fairy Tales. (Illus.). 208p. (J). (gr. 4-7). 1999. pap. text 14.95 (0-7137-2783-7) Blandford Pr.

— Drinking from the Sacred Well. LC 98-30395. 1998. 12.00 (0-06-251562-4) HarpC.

— Drinking from the Sacred Well: Personal Voyages of Discovery with the Celtic Saints. LC 98-30395. 304p. 1998. 19.00 (0-06-251561-6, Pub. by Harper SF) HarpC.

— Druid Sourcebook. (Illus.). 384p. 1998. 14.95 (0-7137-2710-1, Pub. by Blandford Pr) Sterling.

— Elements of Arthurian Tradition. (Elements of...Ser.). (Illus.). 144p. 1997. pap. 9.95 (1-86204-025-7, Pub. by Element MA) Penguin Putnam.

— Elements of Grail Tradition. LC 98-196618. (Illus.). 144p. 1997. pap. 9.95 (1-86204-033-8, Pub. by Element MA) Penguin Putnam.

— The Eyeball Killer. 320p. 1996. pap. 5.99 (0-7860-0242-5, Pinncle Kensgtn) Kensgtn Pub Corp.

— Fourth: Applications in Engineering & Industry. 1989. text 71.95 (0-470-21442-2) P-H.

— Gawain: Knight of the Goddess - Restoring an Archetype. 1990. 22.95 (0-85030-783-X, Pub. by Aqrn Pr) Harper SF.

— Gawain: Knight of the Goddess: Restoring an Archetype. (Illus.). 1992. reprint ed. pap. 14.00 (1-85538-172-9, Pub. by Aqrn Pr) Harper SF.

— The Grail: Quest for the Eternal. LC 90-71439. (Art & Imagination Ser.). (Illus.). 96p. 1991. pap. 15.95 (0-500-81027-3, Pub. by Thames Hudson) Norton.

— Healing the Wounded King: Soul Work & the Quest for the Grail. LC 96-52056. 192p. 1997. pap. 16.95 (1-85230-955-5, Pub. by Element MA) Penguin Putnam.

— King Arthur & the Grail Quest: Myth & Vision from Celtic Times to the Present. (Illus.). 160p. 1997. pap. 16.95 (0-7137-2587-7, Pub. by Blandford Pr) Sterling.

— Landscapes of Legend. LC 98-117298. (Illus.). 160p. 1998. 29.95 (0-7137-2650-4, Pub. by Blandford Pr) Sterling.

— Secret Camelot. LC 97-172211. (Illus.). 176 p. 1997. 29.95 (0-7137-2646-6, Pub. by Blandford Pr) Sterling.

— The Song of Taliesin: Stories & Poems from the Books of Broceliande. 1992. pap. 15.00 (1-85538-114-1, Pub. by Aqrn Pr) HarpC.

— Tales of the Celtic Otherworld. (Illus.). 176p. 1998. 24.95 (0-7137-2656-3) Sterling.

— Taliesin: Shamanism & the Bardic Mysteries in Britain & Ireland. (Illus.). 368p. 1991. pap. 18.00 (1-85538-109-5, Pub. by Aqrn Pr) HarpC.

— Taliesin: Shamanism & the Bardic Mysteries in Britain & Ireland. (Illus.). 256p. 1990. pap. 13.95 (0-04-440586-3) Routledge.

Matthews, John, ed. An Arthurian Reader: Selections from Arthurian Legend, Scholarship & Story. (Illus.). 432p. 1988. 24.95 (0-85030-778-3, Pub. by Aqrn Pr) Harper SF.

— An Arthurian Reader: Selections from Arthurian Legend, Scholarship, & Story. (Illus.). 352p. 1991. pap. 16.00 (1-85030-909-3, Pub. by Aqrn Pr) Harper SF.

— Choirs of the God: Revisioning Masculinity. 256p. (Orig.). 1991. pap. 14.95 (1-85274-110-4, Pub. by Mandala) IBD Ltd.

*Matthews, John, ed. The Encyclopaedic Dictionary of Environmental Change. (An Arnold Publication). (Illus.). 448p. 2000. text 150.00 (0-340-74109-0, Pub. by E A) OUP.

Matthews, John, ed. From Isles of Dream: Visionary Stories from the Celtic Renaissance. 304p. (Orig.). 1993. pap. 17.95 (0-940262-61-4, Lindisfarne) Anthroposophic.

— A Glastonbury Reader: Selections from the Myths, Legends & Stories of Ancient Avalon. (Illus.). 320p. 1991. 25.95 (0-85030-999-9, Pub. by Aqrn Pr) Harper SF.

— A Glastonbury Reader: Selections from the Myths, Legends & Stories of Ancient Avalon. (Illus.). 320p. 1993. reprint ed. 17.00 (1-85538-276-8, Pub. by Aqrn Pr) Harper SF.

— Progress in Agricultural Physics & Engineering. (Illus.). 352p. 1991. text 130.00 (0-85198-705-2) OUP.

Matthews, John, ed. Sources of the Grail: An Anthology. 576p. 1997. pap. 19.95 (0-940262-87-8, 2026, Lindisfarne) Anthroposophic.

Matthews, John, intro. Within the Hollow Hills: An Anthology of New Celtic Writing. 336p. (Orig.). 1995. pap. 17.95 (0-940262-70-3, Lindisfarne) Anthroposophic.

Matthews, John & Green, Marian. The Grail Seeker's Companion: A Guide to the Grail Quest in the Aquarian Age. (Illus.). 208p. 1986. pap. 12.95 (0-85030-478-4, Pub. by Aqrn Pr) HarpC.

Matthews, John & Havell. Complex Analysis for Mathematics & Engineering. 1996. 66.25 (0-7637-0270-6) Jones & Bartlett.

Matthews, John & Matthews, Caitlin. The Encyclopedia of Celtic Wisdom: A Celtic Shaman's Sourcebook. 456p. 2000. reprint ed. pap. 16.95 (1-85230-786-2, Pub. by Element MA) Penguin Putnam.

— A Fairy Tale Reader: A Collection of Story, Lore & Vision. 1993. 16.00 (1-85538-283-0, Pub. by Aqrn Pr) Harper SF.

— The Winter Solstice: The Sacred Traditions of Christmas. LC 98-11784. 256p. 1998. 29.95 (0-8356-0769-0, Pub. by Theos Pub Hse) Natl Bk Netwk.

— The Wizard King: And Other Spellbinding Tales. (Illus.). 80p. (J). (gr. k-3). 1998. 18.95 (1-901223-84-1) Barefoot Bks NY.

Matthews, John & Stewart, Bob. Celtic Warrior Chiefs. (Illus.). 192p. 1993. pap. 14.95 (1-85314-116-X, Pub. by Frebird Bks) Sterling.

Matthews, John, jt. auth. see Mattews, Caitlin.

Matthews, John, jt. auth. see Matthews, Caitlin.

Matthews, John, ed. see Baring-Gould, Sabine.

Matthews, John, ed. see Burch, Monte.

Matthews, John, jt. ed. see Stewart, R. J.

Matthews, John, jt. tr. see Heather, Peter.

Matthews, John A. The Ecology of Recently-Deglaciated Terrain: A Geoecological Approach to Glacier Forelands Succession. (Studies in Ecology). (Illus.). 406p. (C). 1992. text 120.00 (0-521-36109-5) Cambridge U Pr.

Matthews, John B., et al. Policies & Persons: A Casebook in Ethics. 2nd ed. 512p. (C). 1991. teacher ed. write for info. (0-318-72116-3); text 49.00 (0-07-040999-4) McGraw.

Matthews, John C. Fundamentals of Receptor, Enzyme & Transport Kinetics. 192p. 1993. boxed set 83.95 (0-8493-4426-3, QP517) CRC Pr.

Matthews, John D. Silvicultural Systems. (Illus.). 296p. 1991. reprint ed. pap. text 45.00 (0-19-854670-X) OUP.

Matthews, John E. The Copywriter. large type ed. 180p. 1964. 25.00 (1-887229-08-6) Copy Wrkshp.

*Matthews, John F. Laying down the Law: A Study of the Theodosian Code. LC 00-35198. (Illus.). 320p. 2000. 40.00 (0-300-07900-1) Yale U Pr.

Matthews, John F. The Roman Empire of Ammianus. LC 89-45756. 623p. 1989. reprint ed. pap. 193.20 (0-608-07735-4, 206456000009) Bks Demand.

*Matthews, John G. Diseases of the Goat. 2nd rev. ed. LC 99-34208. (Illus.). 364p. 1999. pap. 51.95 (0-632-05167-1, Pub. by Blckwell Science) Iowa St U Pr.

Matthews, John H. Introduction to the Design & Analysis of Building Electrical Systems. LC 92-26279. 1993. text 59.95 (0-442-00874-0, VNR) Wiley.

Matthews, John M. Legislative & Judicial History of the 15th Amendment. LC 77-129081. (American Constitutional & Legal History Ser). 1971. reprint ed. 22.50 (0-306-70063-8) Da Capo.

Matthews, John O. Struggle & Survival on Wall Street: The Economics of Competition Among Securities Firms. LC 93-98. (Illus.). 288p. 1994. text 49.95 (0-19-505063-0) OUP.

Matthews, John R. Eating Disorders. (Library in a Book). (Illus.). 176p. (YA). (gr. 9-12). 1991. 26.95 (0-8160-1911-8) Facts on File.

*Matthews, John R. The Rise & Fall of the Soviet Union. LC 99-34059. (World History Ser.). (Illus.). 128p. (YA). (gr. 6-9). 2000. lib. bdg. 23.70 (1-56006-567-2) Lucent Bks.

Matthews, John R., jt. auth. see Cornell, Jim.

Matthews, John T. The Sound & the Fury: Faulkner & the Lost Cause. Lecker, Robert, ed. LC 90-43606. (Twayne's Masterworks Ser.). 152p. 1990. 29.00 (0-8057-7965-5, MWS 61) Macmillan.

*Matthews, Joseph L. Beat the Nursing Home Trap: A Consumer's Guide to Choosing & Financing Long-Term Care. 3rd ed. LC 98-51467. 291p. 1999. 21.95 (0-87337-515-7) Nolo com.

Matthews, Joseph L. How to Win Your Personal Injury Claim. 3rd ed. LC 99-24192. 244p. 1999. pap. 29.95 (0-87337-529-7) Nolo com.

— The Lawyer Who Blew up His Desk: And Other Tales of Legal Madness. LC 97-47373. 242p. 1998. pap. 11.95 (0-89815-974-1) Ten Speed Pr.

— Shades of Resistance. 347p. 1996. pap. 15.95 (0-9647760-0-6) Creat Arts-Headlands.

— Social Security, Medicare & Pensions. large type ed. 288p. 1991. lib. bdg. 14.95 (1-56054-989-0) Thorndike Pr.

Matthews, Joseph L. & Berman, Dorothy M. Social Security, Medicare & Pensions. 7th ed. 320p. 1999. pap. 19.95 (0-87337-289-1) Nolo com.

— Social Security, Medicare, & Pensions: Get the Most Out of Your Retirement & Medical Benefits. 7th ed. LC 98-22231. 1999. 21.95 (0-87337-487-8) Nolo com.

Matthews, Joseph L., et al. Social Security, Medicare & Pensions: Get the Most Out of Your Retirement & Medical Benefits. 6th large type ed. LC 96-38562. (Spec-Hall Ser.). 651p. 1996. lib. bdg. 25.95 (0-7838-1983-8, G K Hall Lrg Type) Mac Lib Ref.

— Social Security, Medicare & Pensions: Get the Most Out of Your Retirement & Medical Benefits. 6th large type ed. LC 96-38562. 1997. pap. 20.00 (0-7838-1984-6, G K Hall Lrg Type) Mac Lib Ref.

Matthews, Judith & Robinson, Fay. Nathaniel Willy, Scared Silly. LC 92-4052. (Illus.). 32p. (J). (gr. k-3). 1994. mass mkt. 15.00 (0-02-765285-8, Bradbury S&S) S&S Childrens.

Matthews, Judith & Wood, Jeanne. Talk German. LC 98-33765. (Talk...Language Ser.). (GER.). 128p. 1999. pap. 18.95 incl. audio (0-8442-1735-2, 17352, Passprt Bks) NTC Contemp Pub Co.

Matthews, Judy G., et al. Clipart & Dynamic Designs for Libraries & Media Centers: Books & Basics, Vol. 1. xii, 193p. 1987. pap. text 28.00 (0-87287-636-5) Libs Unl.

Matthews, Julia. Seasonal Activities. Quilliam, Sue & Scholastic, Inc. Staff, eds. 1984. pap. 14.95 (0-590-70831-7, Scholastic Hardcover) Scholastic Inc.

Matthews, Julia, jt. auth. see Daw, Kurt.

Matthews, Julian G., tr. see Legrand, B.

Matthews, K. Great Blueberry Recipes. LC 97-50634. 1998. pap. 2.95 (0-88266-979-6, Storey Pub) Storey Bks.

Matthews, K., jt. ed. see Namazi, N. M.

Matthews, Kate. The Weekend Sewer's Guide to Blouses: Time Saving Sewing with a Creative Touch. LC 97-43021. (Weekend Sewers Guide Ser.). (Illus.). 144p. 1998. 24.95 (1-57990-032-1, Pub. by Lark Books) Random.

— The Weekend Sewer's Guide to Dresses: Time-Saving Sewing with a Creative Touch. LC 97-18402. (Illus.). 144p. 1998. 24.95 (1-57990-015-1, Pub. by Lark Books) Random.

Matthews, Kate, ed. see Morris, Mary & McCann, Sally.

Matthews, Kathy, jt. auth. see Gallin, Pamela.

Matthews, Kathy, jt. auth. see Gallin, Pamela F.

Matthews, Kathy, jt. auth. see Giller, Robert M.

Matthews, Kay. An Anasazi Welcome. LC 92-796. (Illus.). 40p. (J). (gr. 4-7). 1992. pap. 6.95 (1-878610-27-9) Red Crane Bks.

— Cross-Country Skiing in Northern New Mexico: An Introduction & Trail Guide. rev. ed. (Illus.). 166p. 1993. pap. 10.95 (0-940875-00-4) Acequia Madre.

— Day Hikes in the Taos Area. 2nd rev. ed. (Illus.). 106p. 1997. pap. 10.95 (0-940875-07-1) Acequia Madre.

Matthews, Kay. Hiking the Mountain Trails of Santa Fe: A Guide to Trails, People, Places, & Events. 146p. 1995. pap. 10.95 (0-940875-05-5) Acequia Madre.

Matthews, Kay. Hiking the Wilderness: A Backpacking Guide to the Wheeler Peak, Pecos, & San Pedro Parks Wilderness Areas. (Illus.). 140p. (Orig.). 1992. pap. 10.95 (0-940875-02-0) Acequia Madre.

— Hiking the Wilderness: A Backpacking Guide to the Wheeler Peak, Pecos, & San Pedro Parks Wilderness Areas. 2nd rev. ed. (Illus.). 145p. (Orig.). 1999. pap. 12.95 (0-940875-08-X, Pub. by Acequia Madre) Books West CO.

Matthews, Kay. Hiking Trails of the Sandia & Manzano Mountains. 175p. 1995. pap. 12.95 (0-940875-06-3) Acequia Madre.

Matthews, Kay. I'm Glad You Asked. LC 94-70246. (Illus.). 32p. (Orig.). (J). (ps-3). 1994. pap. 7.50 (0-940875-03-9) Acequia Madre.

Matthews, Ken. The Gulf Conflict & International Relations. LC 92-47343. (Illus.). 352p. (C). 1993. pap. 27.99 (0-415-07519-X, A7695) Routledge.

Matthews, Kent, ed. see Walters, A. A.

Matthews, Kermit D. Matthews, Page, Wilson, Dean, Bartlett & Related Families. (Illus.). 290p. 1993. pap. 45.00 (0-8328-3616-8); lib. bdg. 55.00 (0-8328-3615-X) Higginson Bk Co.

Matthews, Kevin M. The Great Buildings Collection: A Designer's Library of Architecture on CD-ROM. (Illus.). 104p. 1994. 149.00 incl. cd-rom (0-9667098-0-2, 83526-81851) Artifice.

*Matthews, Kezi. John Riley's Daughter. LC 99-58255. 160p. (YA). (gr. 7 up). 2000. 15.95 (0-8126-2775-X, Pub. by Front St-Cricket Bks) Publishers Group.

Matthews, Kimberly T. Promise You Won't Tell Nobody. 2nd rev. ed. 130p. 1998. pap. 11.00 (0-9667609-0-5) Kissed Pubns.

Matthews, L. Joseph, jt. auth. see Crow, Gary M.

Matthews, L. R. Cardiopulmonary Anatomy & Physiology. (Illus.). 352p. (C). 1996. pap. text 27.95 (0-397-54954-7, Lippnctt) Lppncott W & W.

Matthews, Larry E. Cumberland Caverns. 316p. 1989. pap. 9.95 (0-9615093-4-1, 07-0003) Natl Speleological.

Matthews, Laura. A Curious Courting. large type ed. LC 93-37450. 353p. 1994. lib. bdg. 19.95 (0-7862-0095-2) Thorndike Pr.

— In My Lady's Chamber. large type ed. LC 93-33460. 334p. (Orig.). 1994. lib. bdg. 19.95 (0-7862-0096-0) Thorndike Pr.

— The Lady Next Door. 1999. pap. 3.99 (0-451-17732-0, Sig) NAL.

— Lord Clayborne's Fancy. 256p. 1989. mass mkt. 3.50 (0-446-35412-0, Pub. by Warner Bks) Little.

*Matthews, Laura. Prudent Match. (Regency Romance Ser.). 2000. mass mkt. 4.99 (0-451-20070-5, Sig) NAL.

Matthews, Laura. The Village Spinster. large type ed. LC 93-1107. 275p. 1993. lib. bdg. 18.95 (1-56054-742-1) Thorndike Pr.

Matthews, Leonard. Gunfighters, Set I. (The Wild West in American History Ser.). 32p. (J). (gr. 3-8). Date not set. lib. bdg. 23.93 (1-57103-361-0) Rourke Pr.

— Indians. (Wild West in American History Ser.: Set I). (Illus.). 32p. (J). (gr. 3-8). 1989. lib. bdg. 23.93 (0-86625-364-5) Rourke Pubns.

— Pioneers. (Wild West in American History Ser.). (Illus.). 32p. (J). (gr. 3-8). 1989. 13.50 (0-685-73975-9) Rourke Corp.

— Pioneers. (Wild West in American History Ser.). (Illus.). 32p. (J). (gr. 3-8). 1989. lib. bdg. 18.00 (0-86625-362-9) Rourke Pubns.

— The Railroaders. (Wild West in American History Ser.: Set I). (Illus.). 32p. (J). (gr. 3-8). 1989. lib. bdg. 23.93 (0-86625-366-1) Rourke Pubns.

— Soldiers. (Wild West in American History Ser.). (Illus.). 32p. (J). (gr. 3-8). 1989. lib. bdg. 23.93 (0-86625-365-3) Rourke Pubns.

*Matthews, Leonard J. Soldiers: The Wild West in American History. 29p. (J). (gr. 4-7). 2000. reprint ed. 20.00 (0-7881-9446-1) DIANE Pub.

Matthews, Lewis. Proteas of the World. (Illus.). 256p. 1993. 45.00 (0-88192-235-8) Timber.

Matthews, Liz. Teeny Witch & Christmas Magic. LC 90-11206. (Teeny Witch Ser.). (Illus.). 48p. (J). (gr. k-1). 1991. pap. 3.95 (0-8167-2271-4) Troll Communs.

— Teeny Witch & the Great Halloween Ride. LC 90-11207. (Teeny Witch Ser.). (Illus.). 48p. (J). (gr. k-1). 1991. pap. 3.95 (0-8167-2275-7) Troll Communs.

— Teeny Witch & the Perfect Valentine. LC 90-11204. (Teeny Witch Ser.). (Illus.). 48p. (J). (gr. k-1). 1996. pap. 3.95 (0-8167-2281-1) Troll Communs.

— Teeny Witch & the Tricky Easter Bunny. LC 90-11205. (Teeny Witch Ser.). (Illus.). 48p. (J). (gr. k-1). 1997. pap. 3.95 (0-8167-2273-0) Troll Communs.

— Teeny Witch Goes on Vacation. LC 90-11141. (Teeny Witch Ser.). (Illus.). 48p. (J). (gr. k-1). 1997. pap. 3.95 (0-8167-2279-X) Troll Communs.

— Teeny Witch Goes to School. LC 90-11208. (Teeny Witch Ser.). (Illus.). 48p. (J). (gr. k-1). 1997. pap. 3.95 (0-8167-2277-3) Troll Communs.

— Teeny Witch Goes to the Library. LC 90-11140. (Illus.). 48p. (J). (gr. k-1). 1997. pap. 3.95 (0-8167-2269-2) Troll Communs.

*Matthews, Lloyd J. & Pavri, Tinaz, eds. Population Diversity & the U. S. Army. 143p. 1999. pap. write for info. (1-58487-002-8) SSI US Army.

Matthews, Lydia. The Voice of Citizenry: Artists & Communities in Collaboration. (Illus.). 36p. (Orig.). 1993. pap. write for info. (0-930495-22-5) San Fran Art Inst.

Matthews, M. Classification of the Heliothinae. 195p. 1991. pap. 75.00 (0-85954-292-0, Pub. by Nat Res Inst) St Mut.

Matthews, M. & Jago, N. D. Millet Pests of the Sahel: An Identification Guide. 80p. 1993. pap. 45.00 (0-85954-331-5, Pub. by Nat Res Inst) St Mut.

Matthews, M. H. Making Sense of Place: Children's Understanding of Large-Scale Environments. (Illus.). 352p. (C). 1992. text 68.00 (0-389-20987-2) B&N Imports.

Matthews, M. H., jt. auth. see Gardiner, V.

Matthews, M. H., jt. ed. see Bondi, L.

Matthews, M. H., jt. ed. see Gardiner, Vince.

*Matthews, M. R. Time for Science Education: How Teaching the History & Philosophy of Pendulum Motion Can Contribute to Science Literacy. (Innovations in Science Education & Technology Ser.). 390p. 1999. pap. write for info. (0-306-45880-2, Kluwer Plenum) Kluwer Academic.

Matthews, Marci M. Every Star a Wish. Date not set. 17.00 (0-9658069-0-1); 27.00 (0-9658069-1-X) off to see.

*Matthews, Marcus C. Heliothine Moths of Australia: A Reference Guide to Pest Bollworms & Related Noctuid Groups. 1999. pap. 90.00 incl. cd-rom (0-643-06305-6, Pub. by CSIRO) Accents Pubns.

Matthews, Margaret, jt. auth. see Lubelska, Diana.

Matthews, Margery I., et al. Churches of Foster: A History of Religious Life in Rural Rhode Island. (Illus.). 169p. (Orig.). 1978. pap. 5.00 (0-917012-20-8) N Foster Baptist.

Matthews, Marian. New Mexico Creditor - Debtor Law, 1989-1992. 300p. 1993. suppl. ed. 53.50 (1-56257-976-2, MICHIE) LEXIS Pub.

Matthews, Mark. The Horseman: Obsessions of a Zoophile. LC 94-38329. 208p. (C). 1994. 27.95 (0-87975-902-X) Prometheus Bks.

Matthews, Marsha, jt. auth. see Kaplan, Jared.

Matthews, Martin. Microsoft Windows 98 Companion. 704p. 29.99 (1-57231-931-3) Microsoft.

Matthews, Martin H., jt. auth. see Beatson, Jack.

Matthews, Martin S. Access from the Ground Up. (Illus.). 368p. (Orig.). 1993. pap. 19.95 (1-55958-303-7) Prima Pub.

— Access from the Ground Up. 2nd ed. LC 93-87187. (Orig.). 1994. pap. 19.95 (1-55958-511-0) Prima Pub.

— Excel for Windows 95 Made Easy: The Basics & Beyond! 2nd rev. ed. (Made Easy Ser.). 560p. 1995. pap. text 24.95 (0-07-882151-7) McGraw.

— Excel for Windows 95 Made Easy: The Basics & Beyond! 5th deluxe ed. Cuthbertson, Joanne, ed. 560p. 1995. 34.95 incl. cd rom (0 07 882162 2) McGraw.

— Office 2000 Answers! 1999. pap. text 24.99 (0-07-211888-1) Osborne-McGraw.

— Outlook 98 Made Easy: The Basics & Beyond. LC 98-216395. (Made Easy Ser.). 608p. 1998. pap. 24.99 (0-07-882525-3) Osborne-McGraw.

— The Power of Windows & DOS Together: Work Faster & Smarter by Combining the Strengths of Both. LC 93-3791. 1993. pap. 24.95 (1-55958-339-8) Prima Pub.

— Web Publishing with FrontPage 97. 2nd ed. LC 97-138996. 1997. pap. text 29.99 (0-07-882312-9) Osborne-McGraw.

— Windows 98 Answers! Certified Tech Support. LC 98-235186. 1998. pap. text 24.99 (0-07-882455-9) Osborne-McGraw.

*Matthews, Martin S. Windows 2000: A Beginner's Guide. (Network Professional's Library). 2000. pap. 39.99 (0-07-212324-9) Osborne-McGraw.

Matthews, Martin S. Your FoxPro for Windows Consultant: From the Ground Up. (Illus.). 560p. (Orig.). 1993. pap. 39.95 (1-55958-305-3) Prima Pub.

Matthews, Martin S. & Matthews, Carole B. Office 97 Answers! Certified Tech Support. LC 97-209564. (Illus.). 448p. (Orig.). 1997. pap. text 24.99 (0-07-882403-6) Osborne-McGraw.

— The Official Guide to CorelDRAW! 6 for Windows 95. (Illus.). 742p. 1995. pap. text 34.95 (0-07-882168-1) McGraw.

— Windows 95 Answers! Certified Tech Support. 2nd ed. LC 97-209702. (Illus.). 448p. 1997. pap. text 24.99 (0-07-882399-4, Oracle Press) Osborne-McGraw.

Matthews, Martin S. & Poulsen, Erik B. FrontPage 98: The Complete Reference. LC 98-126690. (Illus.). 728p. (Orig.). 1998. pap. 39.99 incl. cd-rom (0-07-882394-3, Oracle Press) Osborne-McGraw.

— FrontPage 2000. (Complete Reference Ser.). (Illus.). 953p. 1999. pap. 49.99 incl. cd-rom (0-07-211939-X) Osborne-McGraw.

M

Matthews, Marvin A. Ozark's Seasons of the Heart. LC 99-173716. (Illus.). 288p. 1998. pap. 22.95 (*0-938041-34-7*) Arc Pr AR.

Matthews, Mary. As Close As Possible. 24p. 1996. pap. 7.00 (*1-886226-02-4*) Flume Pr.

Matthews, Mary. Magid Fasts for Ramadan. LC 95-10452. (Illus.). 48p. (J). (ps-3). 1996. 15.95 (*0-395-66589-2*, Clarion Bks) HM.

***Matthews, Mary.** Magid Fasts for Ramadan. (Illus.). 48p. (J). (gr. 1-5). 2000. pap. 6.95 (*0-618-04035-8*, Clarion Bks) HM.

***Matthews, Mason L.** The Horse That Fell Through the Stage: And Other Tales of a Texas Veterinarian. LC 99-47734. (Illus.). 64p. 1999. pap. 9.95 (*1-893271-10-2*) Maverick Publng.

***Matthews, Melanie A., ed.** The Healthcare Industry Market Yearbook. 2nd ed. 715p. 1999. per. 545.50 (*1-882364-29-5*, Amer Busn Pub) Hlth Res Pub.

— The Managed Care Yearbook. 4th ed. 478p. 1998. per. 253.50 (*1-882364-26-0*, Amer Busn Pub) Hlth Res Pub.

Matthews, Melvyn. Rediscovering Holiness: The Search for the Sacred Today. 112p. 1995. pap. 11.95 (*0-687-06639-5*) Abingdon.

Matthews, Merdith M. Mother Wore Combat Boots & Chased Troop Trains: A Young Woman's Adventure Story As an Army Nurse in World War II. unabridged ed. LC 98-93842. (Illus.). xxl, 180p. 1998. pap. 14.95 (*0-9667358-0-3*, 080798) Grapevine OH.

Matthews, Merrill. What Do You Do with an Ousted Liberal?, Vol. 6. LC 95-80936. (Salt Ser.). (Illus.). 48p. 1996. pap. 3.49 (*1-56384-112-6*) Huntington Hse.

Matthews, Merrill, Jr. & Goodman, John C. Myths about Our Health Care System: Lessons for Policy Makers. 18p. 1995. pap. 5.00 (*1-56808-055-7*, BG136) Natl Ctr Pol.

Matthews, Merrill, Jr., jt. auth. see Goodman, John C.

Matthews, Mervyn. Education in the Soviet Union: Policies & Institutions since Stalin. LC 82-6656. 239p. reprint ed. pap. 74.10 (*0-608-11931-8*, 202327400032) Bks Demand.

— Patterns of Deprivation in the Soviet Union under Brezhnev & Gorbachev. (Publication Ser.: No. 383). 158p. (C). 1989. pap. text 18.95 (*0-8179-8832-7*) Hoover Inst Pr.

— Poverty in the Soviet Union. (Illus.). 227p. 1986. text 64.95 (*0-521-32544-7*); pap. text 19.95 (*0-521-31059-8*) Cambridge U Pr.

— Privilege in the Soviet Union. (Illus.). 1978. pap. text 16.95 (*0-04-323021-0*) Routledge.

Matthews, Mervyn, ed. Party, State & Citizen in the Soviet Union: A Collection of Documents. LC 89-34446. 428p. (gr. 13). 1990. text 97.95 (*0-87332-430-7*) M E Sharpe.

Matthews, Michael, jt. ed. see Rounds, Laura.

Matthews, Michael D. Money Clips (Mini) The Little Book of Big Money Ideas. LC 94-15351. 160p. 1994. pap. 5.99 (*0-88070-687-2*, Multnomah Bks) Multnomah Pubs.

Matthews, Michael J. How to Find the Best Quality Child Care. LC 97-61132. x, 308p. 1998. pap. 24.00 (*1-890877-07-7*) Autumn Pub Grp.

Matthews, Michael R. Constructivism in Science Education: A Philosophical Examination. LC 97-47347. 1998. 49.00 (*0-7923-4924-5*) Kluwer Academic.

— History, Philosophy, & Science Teaching. LC 93-32237. (Philosophy of Education Research Library). 256p. (C). 1994. pap. 22.99 (*0-415-90899-X*) Routledge.

— History, Philosophy & Science Teaching: Selected Readings. 240p. (C). 1990. pap. 24.95 (*0-8077-3094-7*) Tchrs Coll.

Matthews, Michael R., ed. Constructivism in Science Education: A Philosophical Examination. 234p. 1998. pap. 98.00 (*0-7923-5033-2*) Kluwer Academic.

— The Scientific Background to Modern Philosophy: Selected Readings. LC 88-32012. 174p. (C). 1989. 24.95 (*0-87220-075-2*); pap. 6.95 (*0-87220-074-4*) Hackett Pub.

Matthews, Mildred S., jt. ed. see Burns, Joseph A.

Matthews, Mildred S., jt. ed. see Gehrels, Tom.

***Matthews, Monte L.** How to Implement Assessment Feedback. LC 99-22811. 370p. 1999. 29.95 (*1-57444-229-5*) St Lucie Pr.

Matthews, N. F. Unification of Electromagnetism, Kinematics & Gravitation. 282p. 1999. lib. bdg. write for info. (*0-9671473-0-1*) NC U Coll Eng.

Matthews, Nancy. Wilderness Preservation. (Earth at Risk Ser.). (Illus.). 128p. (YA). (gr. 5 up). 1991. lib. bdg. 19.95 (*0-7910-1580-7*) Chelsea Hse.

***Matthews, Nancy & Gibson, Eric.** Outward Bound: American Art at the Brink of the Twenty-First Century. LC 99-62969. (Illus.). 100p. 1999. pap. 25.00 (*0-9661013-1-6*) Meridian Int Ctr.

Matthews, Nancy, et al. A Winding River: The Journey of Contemporary Art in Vietnam. LC 97-80482. (Illus.). 100p. 1997. pap. 20.00 (*0-9661013-0-8*) Meridian Int Ctr.

Matthews, Nancy A. Managing Rape: The Feminist Anti-Rape Movement & the State. LC 93-49037. (International Library of Sociology Ser.). 224p. (C). (gr. 13). 1994. 75.00 (*0-415-06491-0*, B3816) Routledge.

Matthews, Nathan. Municipal Charters: A Discussion of the Essentials of a City Charter with Forms or Models for Adoption. 18.95 (*0-405-19037-9*) Ayer.

Matthews, Olen P. Water Resources, Geography & Law. LC 84-70006. 1984. pap. 15.00 (*0-89291-174-3*) Assn Am Geographers.

Matthews, P. & MacLean, R. Working with Children. 116p. (C). 1986. 50.00 (*0-7300-0389-2*, Pub. by Deakin Univ) St Mut.

Matthews, P. C. Vector Calculus. LC 97-41192. (Undergraduate Mathematics Ser.). (Illus.). ix, 182p. 1998. pap. 29.95 (*3-540-76180-2*) Spr-Verlag.

Matthews, P. H. Grammatical Theory in the United States: From Bloomfield to Chomsky. LC 92-41067. (Studies in Linguistics: Vol. 67). 286p. (C). 1993. pap. text 27.95 (*0-521-45847-1*) Cambridge U Pr.

— Morphology. 2nd ed. (Cambridge Textbooks in Linguistics Ser.). 263p. (C). 1991. text 59.95 (*0-521-41043-6*); pap. text 19.95 (*0-521-42256-6*) Cambridge U Pr.

***Matthews, P. J.** New Voices in Irish Criticism. 272p. 2000. pap. 19.95 (*1-85182-545-2*, Pub. by Four Cts Pr) Intl Spec Bk.

***Matthews, P. J., ed.** New Voices in Irish Criticism. 272p. 2000. 35.00 (*1-85182-544-4*, Pub. by Four Cts Pr) Intl Spec Bk.

Matthews, Pamela E. & Chisko, Ann M. Elementary Algebra: An Analytical Approach. LC 85-12204. 366p. 1986. text 40.50 (*0-471-87995-9*) P-H.

Matthews, Pamela R. Ellen Glasgow & a Woman's Traditions. (Feminist Issues Ser.). 288p. (C). 1994. text 32.50 (*0-8139-1539-2*) U Pr of Va.

Matthews, Pamela R., ed. see Glasgow, Ellen.

Matthews, Patricia. Dead Man Riding. LC 99-475998. (Thumbprint Mysteries Ser.). 128p. (J). (gr. 1). 1999. pap. 5.95 (*0-8092-0607-2*, 060720) NTC Contemp Pub Co.

***Matthews, Patricia.** Death in the Desert. (Thumbprint Mysteries Ser.). 128p. 1999. pap. 5.95 (*0-8092-0608-0*, 060800) NTC Contemp Pub Co.

Matthews, Patricia. The Dreaming Tree. 384p. (Orig.). 1989. spiral bd. 4.50 (*0-373-97103-6*) Harlequin Bks.

— Oasis. 352p. (Orig.). 1988. pap. 4.50 (*0-373-97094-3*) Harlequin Bks.

— Oasis. large type ed. LC 88-36823. 503p. (Orig.). 1989. reprint ed. lib. bdg. 7.95 (*0-89621-857-0*) Thorndike Pr.

— The Secret of Secco Canyon. LC 99-189230. (Thumbprint Mysteries Ser.). 128p. 1999. pap. 5.95 (*0-8092-0606-4*, 060640) NTC Contemp Pub Co.

— Taste of Evil. large type ed. LC 93-42206. 1994. lib. bdg. 21.95 (*1-56054-334-5*) Thorndike Pr.

— Touch of Terror. 256p. 1995. 20.00 (*0-7278-4746-5*) Severn Hse.

Matthews, Patricia & Matthews, Clayton. The Scent of Fear. large type ed. LC 92-23099. 351p. 1992. reprint ed. lib. bdg. 19.95 (*1-56054-336-1*) Thorndike Pr.

— Vision of Death. 256p. 1993. lib. bdg. 19.00 (*0-7278-4397-4*) Severn Hse.

Matthews, Patricia M. The Significance of Beauty: Kant on Feeling & the System of the Mind. LC 97-30596. (New Synthese Historical Library). 252p. 1997. lib. bdg. 120.50 (*0-7923-4764-1*) Kluwer Academic.

***Matthews, Patrick.** Real Wine: The Rediscovery of Natural Winemaking. (Illus.). 192p. 2000. 24.95 (*1-84000-257-3*, Pub. by Mitchell Beazley) Antique Collect.

Matthews, Patrick. Wild Bunch: Great Wines from Small Producers. 288p. 1997. pap. 13.95 (*0-571-19043-X*) Faber & Faber.

Matthews, Paul. Forty Years with .45-70. (Illus.). 148p. (Orig.). 1989. pap. 11.50 (*0-935632-84-0*) Wolfe Pub Co.

— Ground That Love Seeks. 1996. pap. 15.95 (*0-947960-09-0*) Five Seas Pr.

— Loading the Black Powder Rifle Cartridge. 1993. 22.50 (*1-879356-20-1*) Wolfe Pub Co.

— The Paper Jacket. 1991. 13.50 (*1-879356-02-3*) Wolfe Pub Co.

— Sing Me the Creation. 226p. 1995. pap. 16.95 (*1-869890-60-4*, Pub. by Hawthorn Press) Anthroposophic.

— Sixty Years of Rifles. 1991. 19.50 (*1-879356-03-1*) Wolfe Pub Co.

***Matthews, Paul.** Trusts & Estate Disputes: Practice & Procedure. 200p. 1999. 79.50 (*1-85811-202-8*, Pub. by CLT Prof) Gaunt.

Matthews, Paul, ed. With My Heart in My Mouth: A Gathering of Poems. 154p. 1994. pap. 21.95 (*1-85584-016-2*, Pub. by R Steiner Pr) Anthroposophic.

Matthews, Paul & Millichap, Denzil. Guide to Leasehold Reform, Housing & Urban Development Act 1993. 400p. 1993. pap. text 48.00 (*0-406-02650-5*, UK, MICHIE) LEXIS Pub.

Matthews, Paul, jt. auth. see Barraclough, Hugh.

Matthews, Paul, jt. ed. see Bradford, Katie.

Matthews, Paul A. Shooting the Black Powder Cartridge Rifle. 129p. 1994. 22.50 (*1-879356-38-4*) Wolfe Pub Co.

Matthews, Paul C. How to Try a Federal Criminal Case, 2 vols. LC 60-8096. lxxii, 1347p. 1960. lib. bdg. 68.00 (*0-89941-601-2*, 500450) W S Hein.

Matthews, Paul H., et al. Athens for All: A Bilingual Guide to Spending an Hour or a Lifetime in Georgia's Classic City. LC 96-208831. (ENG & SPA., Illus.). 208p. (Orig.). 1996. pap. 11.95 (*1-888499-01-X*) Riverview GA.

Matthews, Penny. Hair-Raising: Ten Horror Stories. 152p. (YA). (gr. 7-9). 1995. pap. 3.50 (*0-590-48403-6*) Scholastic Inc.

Matthews, Pete, jt. auth. see Boldman, Craig.

Matthews, Peter, photos by. Bravo! Recipes, Legends, & Lore Celebrating 120 Years of the University Musical Society. (Illus.). 224p. 1999. 29.95 (*0-9670787-0-9*) Univ Music Soc.

Matthews, Peter, et al. A Global Atlas of Wastewater Sludge & Biosolids Use & Disposal. LC 98-196659. ix, 197 p. 1996. write for info. (*1-900222-01-9*) Intl Assn Water.

Matthews, Peter, jt. auth. see Maitland, Sara.

Matthews, Peter H. The Concise Oxford Dictionary of Linguistics. LC 97-12848. (Oxford Paperback Reference Ser.). (Illus.). 422p. 1998. pap. 13.95 (*0-19-280008-6*) OUP.

Matthews, Phoebe. The Boy on the Cover. (YA). (gr. 7 up). 1988. pap. 2.75 (*0-380-75407-X*, Avon Bks) Morrow Avon.

— Switchstance. 176p. (Orig.). (YA). (gr. 7 up). 1989. pap. 2.95 (*0-380-75729-X*, Avon Bks) Morrow Avon.

Matthews, R., jt. auth. see Aizerman, M.

Matthews, R. Arthur. Born for Battle: 31 Studies on Spiritual Warfare. 190p. 1993. pap. 7.99 (*0-87788-090-5*) OMF Bks.

— Nascido para a Batalha. Orig. Title: Born for Battle. (POR.). 192p. 1987. pap. 5.95 (*0-8297-1606-8*) Vida Pubs.

Matthews, R. B., et al, eds. Modelling the Impact of Climate Change on Rice Production in Asia. (Illus.). 304p. 1995. text 105.00 (*0-85198-959-4*) OUP.

Matthews, R. C., et al. British Economic Growth, 1856-1973. LC 80-53222. (Studies of Economic Growth in Industrialized Countries). 736p. 1982. 85.00 (*0-8047-1110-0*) Stanford U Pr.

Matthews, R. E. A Critical Appraisal of Viral Taxonomy. 264p. 1983. 152.00 (*0-8493-5648-2*, QR394, CRC Reprint) Franklin.

— Fundamentals of Plant Virology. (Illus.). 403p. 1992. text 42.00 (*0-12-480558-2*) Acad Pr.

— Plant Virology. 3rd ed. (Illus.). 835p. (C). 1991. text 53.00 (*0-12-480553-1*) Acad Pr.

Matthews, R. E., ed. Classification & Nomenclature of Viruses. (Journal: Intervirology: Vol. 17, No. 1-3, 1982). (Illus.). 200p. 1982. 31.50 (*3-8055-3557-0*) S Karger.

Matthews, R. E. F., ed. Diagnosis of Plant Virus Diseases. 384p. 1993. boxed set 157.95 (*0-8493-4284-8*, SB736) CRC Pr.

Matthews, R. H. Reliability 1991. 864p. 1991. ring bd. 325.95 (*1-85166-643-5*, Chap & Hall CRC) CRC Pr.

Matthews, Ralph. The Creation of Regional Dependency. 336p. 1983. text 40.00 (*0-8020-5617-2*); pap. text 15.95 (*0-8020-6510-4*) U of Toronto Pr.

Matthews, Ray. The Tiltable Book: How to Turn the Tables on Your Railroad. (Illus.). 96p. (Orig.). 1996. pap. 14.95 (*1-884570-48-8*) Research Triangle.

Matthews, Rex, ed. see Copeland, Warren R.

Matthews, Rex, ed. see Culpepper, R. Alan.

Matthews, Rex, ed. see Maddox, Randy L.

Matthews, Rex, ed. see Nelson, Richard D.

Matthews, Rex, ed. see Roels, Shirley J., et al.

Matthews, Rex, jt. ed. see Rowe, Kenneth E.

Matthews, Rex, ed. see Wesley, John & Kurewa, Zwomunondita.

Matthews, Richard. Fordism, Flexibility & Regional Productivity Growth. rev. ed. LC 96-36713. (Studies on Industrial Productivity). (Illus.). 280p. 1996. text 65.00 (*0-8153-2736-6*) Garland.

Matthews, Richard & Hoyle, Mark. Matrimonial & Commercial Injunctions. 130p. 1994. 175.00 (*0-85459-823-5*, Pub. by Tolley Pubng) St Mut.

Matthews, Richard, ed. see Tenhover, Gregory R.

Matthews, Richard E. The 149th Pennsylvania Volunteer Infantry Unit in the Civil War. LC 94-21041. (Illus.). 346p. 1994. lib. bdg. 42.00 (*0-89950-993-2*) McFarland & Co.

Matthews, Richard K. If Men Were Angels: James Madison & the Heartless Empire of Reason. LC 94-36168. (American Political Thought Ser.). 320p. 1996. 25.00 (*0-7006-0643-2*); pap. 14.95 (*0-7006-0807-9*) U Pr of KS.

— Radical Politics of Thomas Jefferson. LC 84-5240. xii, 172p. 1984. reprint ed. pap. 9.95 (*0-7006-0293-3*) U Pr of KS.

Matthews, Richard K., ed. Virtue, Corruption, & Self-Interest: Political Values in the Eighteenth Century. LC 93-55063. 1994. 48.50 (*0-934223-26-2*) Lehigh Univ Pr.

Matthews, Rob. Beyond Two Thousand: A Minimum Model for the Global Future. (Illus.). 230p. (Orig.). (C). 1989. pap. 16.00 (*0-9622962-0-1*) Global Dynamics.

Matthews, Robert. Unravelling the Mind of God. 1995. mass mkt. 6.95 (*0-86369-671-6*, Pub. by Virgin Bks) London Bridge.

Matthews, Robert J. A Plainer Translation: Joseph Smith's Translation of the Bible: A History & Commentary. LC 75-5937. xxvii, 468p. 1975. pap. 11.95 (*0-8425-2237-9*, Friends of the Library) Brigham.

***Matthews, Robert J.** The Selected Writings of Robert J. Matthews. LC 99-41731. (Gospel Scholars Ser.). 1999. write for info. (*1-57345-552-0*) Deseret Bk.

Matthews, Robert J. & Demopoulos, William, eds. Learnability & Linguistic Theory. (C). 1989. lib. bdg. 114.50 (*0-7923-0247-8*) Kluwer Academic.

Matthews, Robert J., jt. ed. see Millet, Robert L.

Matthews, Robert O. & Pratt, Cranford, eds. Human Rights in Canadian Foreign Policy. 400p. (C). 1988. pap. text 24.95 (*0-7735-0683-7*, Pub. by McG-Queens Univ Pr) CUP Services.

Matthews, Robert O. & Rubinof, Arthur G. Internal Conflict & Conflict Management. 2nd ed. 624p. (C). 1989. pap. text 29.00 (*0-13-470832-6*) P-H.

Matthews, Robert O., et al. International Conflict & Conflict Management. 2nd ed. 624p. (C). 1989. pap. text 31.20 (*0-13-471665-5*) P-H.

Matthews, Robert O., jt. ed. see Ali, Taisier M.

Matthews, Robert W., et al. WOWBugs: New Life for Life Science. LC 97-176650. (Illus.). 320p. 1996. pap. 19.95 (*1-888499-06-0*) Riverview GA.

Matthews, Robert W., jt. ed. see Ross, Kenneth G.

Matthews, Rodney. Countdown to Millennium. LC 96-49517. (Illus.). 144p. (Orig.). 1997. pap. 24.95 (*0-87951-780-8*, Pub. by Overlook Pr) Penguin Putnam.

Matthews, Roger. Informal Justice. (Contemporary Criminology Ser.). 224p. (C). 1988. text 69.95 (*0-8039-8148-1*); pap. text 16.95 (*0-8039-8149-X*) Sage.

Matthews, Roger, ed. Imprisonment. LC 99-28907. (International Library of Criminology, Criminal Justice & Penology). 480p. 1999. text 148.95 (*1-85521-827-5*, Pub. by Ashgate Pub) Ashgate Pub Co.

— Privatizing Criminal Justice. (Contemporary Criminology Ser.). 224p. (C). 1989. text 69.95 (*0-8039-8240-2*); pap. text 18.95 (*0-8039-8241-0*) Sage.

Matthews, Roger & Francis, Peter, eds. Prisons 2000: An International Perspective on the Current State & Future of Imprisonment. 288p. 1996. text 69.95 (*0-312-16096-8*) St Martin.

Matthews, Roger & Young, Jock, eds. Confronting Crime. LC 85-62748. 256p. (Orig.). (C). 1986. text 39.95 (*0-8039-9731-0*); pap. text 16.95 (*0-8039-9732-9*) Sage.

— Issues in Realist Criminology: A Reader. (Contemporary Criminology Ser.). (Illus.). 176p. 1992. 49.95 (*0-8039-8624-6*); pap. 19.95 (*0-8039-8625-4*) Sage.

— Rethinking Criminology: The Realist Debate. (Contemporary Criminology Ser.). (Illus.). 176p. 1992. 49.95 (*0-8039-8620-3*); pap. 19.95 (*0-8039-8485-5*) Sage.

Matthews, Ron. European Armaments Collaboration: Policy Problems & Prospects, Vol. 1. LC 92-17039. 198p. 1992. text 48.00 (*3-7186-5244-7*) Gordon & Breach.

— Nandi's Magic Garden. LC 97-11612. (Illus.). (YA). (gr. 3-7). 1997. 16.95 (*1-881316-21-1*); pap. 7.95 (*1-881316-34-3*) A&B Bks.

Matthews, Ron & Matsuyama, Keisuke, eds. Japan's Military Renaissance? LC 92-37814. 264p. 1993. text 65.00 (*0-312-09150-8*) St Martin.

Matthews, Ronald. English Messiahs: Studies of Six English Religious Pretenders, 1656-1927. LC 76-172553. 1972. reprint ed. 15.95 (*0-405-18187-6*, Pub. by Blom Pubns) Ayer.

Matthews, Roy & Holden, John. Archery in Earnest. (Illus.). 112p. 1998. pap. 29.95 (*1-86126-089-X*, Pub. by Crolwood) Trafalgar.

Matthews, Roy A. Canada & the Little Dragons. (Essays in International Economics Ser.). 192p. (Orig.). 1996. pap. 11.95 (*0-920380-87-5*, Pub. by Inst Res Pub) Ashgate Pub Co.

Matthews, Roy T. & Platt, F. Dewitt. The Western Humanities. 3rd ed. LC 96-53229. xxiv, 616p. 1997. pap. text 54.95 (*1-55934-433-4*, 1433) Mayfield Pub.

Matthews, Roy T. & Platt, F. DeWitt. The Western Humanities. 3rd ed. xxiii, 360p. 1997. pap. text 48.95 (*1-55934-944-1*, 1944) Mayfield Pub.

— The Western Humanities: Instructor's Manual. 3rd rev. ed. vii, 407p. 1997. pap. text, teacher ed. write for info. (*1-55934-967-0*) Mayfield Pub.

— The Western Humanities No. 2: Renaissance to the Present. 3rd ed. LC 96-53229. (Illus.). 367p. (C). 1997. pap. text 48.95 (*1-55934-945-X*, 1945) Mayfield Pub.

Matthews, Roy T. & Platt, F. DeWitt, eds. Readings in the Western Humanities Vol. 1: Beginnings Through the Renaissance. 3rd rev. ed. LC 96-52519. xii, 238p. (C). 1997. pap. text 19.95 (*1-55934-577-2*, 1577) Mayfield Pub.

Matthews, Roy T. & Platt, F. Dewitt, eds. Readings in the Western Humanities Vol. 2: The Renaissance to the Present. 3rd rev. ed. LC 96-52519. xi, 323p. (C). 1997. pap. text 19.95 (*1-55934-578-0*, 1578) Mayfield Pub.

Matthews, Rupert. Ancient Egyptians at a Glance. LC 97-40031. (At a Glance Ser.). (Illus.). 32p. (YA). (gr. 3 up). 1997. 14.95 (*0-87226-554-4*, 65544B, P Bedrick Books) NTC Contemp Pub Co.

— Cooking A Meal LC 99-12309. (Everyday History Ser.). 2000. 20.00 (*0-531-14545-X*) Watts.

***Matthews, Rupert.** Cooking a Meal. (Everyday History Ser.). (Illus.). (YA). 2000. pap. 6.95 (*0-531-15399-1*) Watts.

— Explorer. (Eyewitness Books). (J). (gr. 4-7). 2000. 19.99 (*0-7894-6580-9*) DK Pub Inc.

— Explorer. (Eyewitness Books). (J). (gr. 4-7). 2000. 15.95 (*0-7894-5762-8*) DK Pub Inc.

Matthews, Rupert. Frederic Remington. 1999. 14.99 (*0-7628-2432-8*) Alva Pr.

— Frederic Remington. (Illus.). 111p. 1998. text 30.00 (*0-7881-5630-6*) DIANE Pub.

***Matthews, Rupert.** Going to School. LC 99-46770. (Everyday History Ser.). 2000. 20.00 (*0-531-14554-9*) Watts.

— Telling the Time. LC 99-46859. (Everyday History Ser.). 2000. 20.00 (*0-531-14588-3*) Watts.

— Telling the Time. (Everyday History Ser.). (Illus.). (J). 2000. pap. 6.95 (*0-531-15985-X*) Watts.

Matthews, Rupert O. Dictionnaire des Dinosaures. (FRE.). 48p. 1990. 22.95 (*0-7859-7960-3*, 2719215236) Fr & Eur.

— The Power Brokers: Kingmakers & Usurpers Throughout History. LC 89-31332. 336p. 1989. reprint ed. pap. 104.20 (*0-608-02857-6*, 206392100007) Bks Demand.

Matthews, Ruth. Heat Shock Proteins in Fungal Infections. Burnie, James P., ed. LC 95-18862. (Molecular Biology Intelligence Unit Ser.). 170p. 1995. 99.00 (*1-57059-275-6*) Landes Bioscience.

Matthews, Ruth H., jt. auth. see Gebhardt, Susan E.

Matthews, S. Training & Development: Needs, Planning & Implementation. 1996. pap. 145.00 (*1-85953-077-X*, Pub. by Tech Comm) St Mut.

Matthews, S., jt. auth. see Thompson, J.

Matthews, S., jt. ed. see Thompson, J.

Matthews, Sallie R. Interwoven: A Pioneer Chronicle. LC 81-48373. (Illus.). 248p. 1992. reprint ed. 24.95 (*0-89096-123-9*) Tex A&M Univ Pr.

Matthews, Sam. Apostolic Teams: Penetrating the Nations. xiii, 115p. 1999. pap. 10.00 (*0-9669755-0-2*) Matthews Pub Co.

***Matthews, Sandra & Wexler, Laura.** Pregnant Pictures. LC 99-53026. (Illus.). 2000. 35.00 (*0-415-92120-1*) Routledge.

Matthews, Sandra & Wexler, Laura. Pregnant Pictures. LC 99-53026. (Illus.). 288p. (C). (gr. 13). 2000. 85.00 (*0-415-90449-8*) Routledge.

An Asterisk (*) at the beginning of an entry indicates that the title is appearing for the first time.

Matthews, Sarah, ed. Short Stories by Arthur Conan Doyle. (Thornes Classic Short Stories Ser.). (Illus.). 107p. 1996. pap. 10.95 (*0-7487-2483-4*, Pub. by S Thornes Pubs) Trans-Atl Phila.

Matthews, Sarah & Parker, Huw. From Telling to Selling: Language at Work. (Illus.). 224p. (YA). (gr. 9-11). 1998. pap. 22.50 (*0-7487-2979-8*, Pub. by S Thornes Pubs) Trans-Atl Phila.

Matthews, Sarah & Royston, Mike, eds. Short Stories by Hans Christian Andersen. Haugaard, Erik, tr. (Thornes Classic Short Stories Ser.). (Illus.). 100p. 1996. pap. 10.95 (*0-7487-2484-2*, Pub. by S Thornes Pubs) Trans-Atl Phila.

Matthews, Sarah, ed. see Doyle, Arthur Conan.

Matthews, Sarah, ed. see Twain, Mark, pseud.

Matthews, Sarah, tr. see Bombarde, Odile & Moatti, Claude.

Matthews, Sarah, tr. see Braudel, Fernand.

Matthews, Sarah, tr. see Brice, Raphaelle.

Matthews, Sarah, tr. see De Sairigne, Catherine.

Matthews, Sarah, tr. see Farre, Marie.

Matthews, Sarah, tr. see Jobin, Claire.

Matthews, Sarah, tr. see Limousin, Odile.

Matthews, Sarah, tr. see Pfeffer, Pierre.

Matthews, Sarah, tr. see Planche, Bernard.

Matthews, Sarah, tr. see Ruffault, Charlotte.

Matthews, Sarah, tr. see Segalen, Martine.

Matthews, Sarah, tr. see Singh, Anne.

Matthews, Scott. Stuck in the Seventies: One Hundred Thirteen Things That Screwed up the Twentysomething Generation. 2nd ed. (Illus.). 228p. 1995. pap. 12.95 (*1-56625-051-X*) Bonus Books.

Matthews, Scott & Alpert, Barbara. How to Be a Christmas Angel. 96p. 1995. mass mkt. 5.99 (*0-7860-0199-2*, Pinncle Kensgtn) Kensgtn Pub Corp.

— Santa's Little Instruction Book. 1997. pap. 5.99 (*0-7860-0459-2*) Kensgtn Pub Corp.

— Santa's Little Instruction Book: His Checklist to See Who's Been Naughty or Nice. 96p. 1994. 4.99 (*0-7860-0129-1*, Pinncle Kensgtn) Kensgtn Pub Corp.

— You Know You're a Scrooge When . . . 96p. 1996. 5.99 (*0-7860-0323-5*, Pinncle Kensgtn) Kensgtn Pub Corp.

Matthews, Scott & Nikuradse, Tamara. Dear Grandma, Thank You for... 1996. mass mkt. 5.99 (*0-7860-0253-0*, Pinncle Kensgtn) Kensgtn Pub Corp.

— Dear Granpa, Thank You For . . . 96p. 1996. pap. 5.99 (*0-7860-0266-2*, Pinncle Kensgtn) Kensgtn Pub Corp.

— To the Woman I Love, Thank You for Being Mine. 160p. (Orig.). 1994. pap. 5.99 (*0-449-90915-8*, Columbine) Fawcett.

Matthews, Scott, jt. auth. see Nikuradse, Tamara.

Matthews, Stanley L., jt. ed. see Powell, Frank J.

Matthews, Stephanie. Stompin' Hard. 1998. pap. 7.95 (*0-944754-57-0*) Pudding Hse Pubns.

Matthews, Stephanie, et al. Up from the Soles of Our Feet: A Women's Reader. LaGattuta, Margo, ed. (New Voices Ser.: Vol. 10). 220p. (Orig.). 1998. pap. 17.95 (*0-911051-98-8*) Plain View.

Matthews, Stephen & Yip, Virginia. Cantonese: A Comprehensive Grammar. LC 93-36173. 440p. (C). (gr. 13). 1994. pap. 32.99 (*0-415-08945-X*) Routledge.

Matthews, Stephen, jt. auth. see Yip, Virginia.

***Matthews, Steven.** Yeats as Precursor: Readings in Irish, British & American Poetry. LC 99-43510. 2000. text 49.95 (*0-312-22930-5*) St Martin.

Matthews, Stewart & Lawson, Ken. Caring for God's People: A Handbook for Elders & Ministers on Pastoral Care. 128p. (C). 1992. pap. 39.00 (*0-7855-6824-7*, Pub. by St Andrew) St Mut.

***Matthews, Stuart.** Aerodynamics. (How Does It Work? Ser.). (Illus.). 24p. (J). (gr. 2-7). 2001. lib. bdg. 21.30 (*1-58340-065-6*) Smart Apple.

— Electromagnetics. (How Does It Work? Ser.). (Illus.). 24p. (J). (gr. 2-7). 2001. lib. bdg. 21.30 (*1-58340-066-4*) Smart Apple.

— How Does It Work?, 4 vols. (Illus.). (J). (gr. 2-7). 2001. lib. bdg. 85.20 (*1-58340-069-9*) Smart Apple.

— Hydraulics. (How Does It Work? Ser.). (Illus.). 24p. (J). (gr. 2-7). 2001. lib. bdg. 21.30 (*1-58340-067-2*) Smart Apple.

— Levers & Pulleys. (How Does It Work? Ser.). (Illus.). 24p. (J). (gr. 2-7). 2001. lib. bdg. 21.30 (*1-58340-068-0*) Smart Apple.

Matthews, Susan M., jt. ed. see Keith, Samuel J.

***Matthews, Susan R.** Avalanche Soldier. 288p. 1999. mass mkt. 6.50 (*0-380-80315-1*, Avon Bks) Morrow Avon.

— Colony Fleet. 304p. 2000. mass mkt. 6.50 (*0-380-80316-X*) Morrow Avon.

Matthews, Susan R. Exchange of Hostages. 384p. 1997. mass mkt. 5.99 (*0-380-78913-2*, Avon Bks) Morrow Avon.

— Hour of Judgement. 272p. 1999. mass mkt. 5.99 (*0-380-80314-3*, Avon Bks) Morrow Avon.

— Prisoner of Conscience. 320p. 1998. mass mkt. 3.99 (*0-380-78914-0*, Avon Bks) Morrow Avon.

Matthews, T. W., tr. see Legouis, Emile.

Matthews, Tanya S. War in Algeria: Background for Crisis. LC 62-10305. 165p. reprint ed. pap. 51.20 (*0-7837-0457-7*, 204078000018) Bks Demand.

Matthews, Thomas & Matthews, Byron. Matthews Municipal Ordinances, 1963-1992, 7 Vols. LC 72-80615. 700.00 (*0-685-09238-0*) West Group.

Matthews, Timothy. UFO Revelation: The Secret Technology Exposed? 1999. pap. text 12.95 (*0-7137-2733-0*) Blandford Pr.

Matthews, Tom. The African Mural. (Illus.). 168p. (C). 1989. 250.00 (*1-85368-062-1*, Pub. by New5 Holland) St Mut.

***Matthews, Tom L.** Always Inventing: A Photobiography of Alexander Graham Bell. LC 98-27209. (Illus.). 64p. (J). (gr. 4-6). 1999. 16.95 (*0-7922-7391-5*, Pub. by Natl Geog) S&S Trade.

Matthews, Tom L. Light Shining Through the Mist: A Photobiography of Dian Fossey. (Illus.). 64p. (YA). (gr. 5). 1998. per. 17.95 (*0-7922-7300-1*, T07300C, Pub. by Natl Geog) Publishers Group.

***Matthews, Tony.** Paper Trees: Genealogical Clip-Art. LC 98-75467. 100p. 1999. pap. 14.95 (*0-8063-1607-1*) Genealog Pub.

Matthews, Tony. This Dawning Land. 116p. (C). 1990. 45.00 (*0-86439-010-6*, Pub. by Boolarong Pubns) St Mut.

Matthews, Tristan & BradyGAMES Staff. Totally Unauthorized Guide to Killer Instinct. (Illus.). 160p. (Orig.). 1995. 9.99 (*1-56686-320-1*) Brady Pub.

Matthews, V. J. St. Philip Neri. LC 84-50406. 120p. 1984. reprint ed. pap. 5.50 (*0-89555-237-X*) TAN Bks Pubs.

Matthews, Valerie, ed. see Kirk, Douglas.

Matthews, Victor H. Manners & Customs in the Bible. rev. ed. (Illus.). 284p. 1991. 17.95 (*0-943575-77-X*); pap. 9.95 (*0-943575-81-8*) Hendrickson MA.

***Matthews, Victor H.** Old Testament Themes. 2000. pap. 15.99 (*0-8272-2712-4*) Chalice Pr.

***Matthews, Victor H., et al, eds.** Gender & Law in the Hebrew Bible & the Ancient Near East. (JSOT Supplement Ser.: No. 262). 251p. 1998. 75.00 (*1-85075-886-7*, Pub. by Sheffield Acad) CUP Services.

Matthews, Victor H. & Benjamin, Don C. Old Testament Parallels: Laws & Stories from the Ancient Near East. 2nd expanded rev. ed. LC 97-15575. 384p. 1997. pap. 19.95 (*0-8091-3731-3*, 3731-3) Paulist Pr.

— Social World of Ancient Israel: 1250-587 BCE. LC 93-34183. 328p. 1993. 24.95 (*0-913573-89-2*) Hendrickson MA.

Matthews, Victor H. & Moyer, James C. The Old Testament: Text & Context. LC 97-2428. 308p. (C). 1997. 29.95 (*1-56563-168-4*) Hendrickson MA.

Matthews, Victor H., jt. auth. see Walton, John H.

Matthews, Victor J. Antimachus of Colophon: Text & Commentary. (Mnemosyne, Bibliotheca Classica Batava Ser.: Vol. 155). 1995. suppl. ed. 152.50 (*90-04-10468-2*) Brill Academic Pubs.

Matthews, Victoria, jt. auth. see Grey-Wilson, Christopher.

Matthews, Victoria, ed. see White, James, et al.

Matthews, Vince. Playstation: The Unauthorized Edition, Vol. 2. 128p. 1996. pap. text 12.99 (*0-7615-0515-6*) Prima Pub.

— Playstation Game Secrets: The Unauthorized Edition, Vol. 1. 128p. 1996. pap. text 12.99 (*0-7615-0200-9*) Prima Pub.

Matthews, Vince, jt. auth. see Prima Creative Services Staff.

Matthews, Vincent, ed. Laramide Folding Associated with Basement Block Faulting in the Western United States. LC 78-54346. (Geological Society of America, Memoir Ser.: No. 151). 400p. reprint ed. pap. 124.00 (*0-608-13879-7*, 202373100033) Bks Demand.

Matthews, W. B., et al. McAlpine's Multiple Sclerosis. 2nd ed. (Illus.). 401p. 1990. text 131.00 (*0-443-04047-8*) Church.

Matthews, W. H., III. The Geologic Story of Longhorn Cavern. (Guidebook Ser.: GB 4). (Illus.). 50p. 1963. reprint ed. pap. 3.00 (*0-686-29313-4*) Bur Econ Geology.

— The Geologic Story of Palo Duro Canyon. (Guidebook Ser.: GB 8). (Illus.). 51p. 1969. reprint ed. pap. 2.00 (*0-686-29316-9*) Bur Econ Geology.

Matthews, W. H. Mazes & Labyrinths: Their History & Development. (Illus.). 254p. 1970. reprint ed. pap. 8.95 (*0-486-22614-X*) Dover.

Matthews, W. R., ed. Christian Faith: Essays in Explanation & Defence. LC 73-152162. (Essay Index Reprint Ser.). 1977. reprint ed. 23.95 (*0-8369-2348-0*) Ayer.

Matthews, Warren. World Religions. Baxter, ed. 491p. (C). 1991. pap. text 42.50 (*0-314-78261-3*) West Pub.

Matthews, Washington. Grammar & Dictionary of the Language of the Hidatsa. LC 76-44080. (Shea's American Linguistics, Ser. 2: Nos. 1 & 2). reprint ed. 49.50 (*0-404-15787-4*) AMS Pr.

— The Mountain Chant: A Navajo Ceremony. LC 97-25249. 120p. 1997. pap. 14.95 (*0-87480-542-2*) U of Utah Pr.

— Navaho Myths Prayers & Songs with Texts & Translations. fac. ed. Goddard, P. E., ed. (University of California Publications in American Archaeology & Ethnology: Vol. 5: 2). 43p. (C). 1907. reprint ed. pap. text 4.69 (*1-55567-170-5*) Coyote Press.

— Navajo Weavers & Silversmiths. LC 70-97218. (Wild & Woolly West Ser., No. 7). (Illus.). 44p. 1968. pap. 4.00 (*0-910584-07-9*) Filter.

— The Night Chant: A Navaho Ceremony. LC 74-7991. reprint ed. 94.50 (*0-404-11880-1*) AMS Pr.

— The Night Chant: A Navaho Ceremony. (Illus.). 376p. 1995. reprint ed. pap. 19.95 (*0-87480-491-4*); reprint ed. text 45.00 (*0-87480-490-6*) U of Utah Pr.

Matthews, Washington, tr. from NAV. Navaho Legends. (Illus.). 320p. 1993. reprint ed. pap. 19.95 (*0-87480-424-8*) U of Utah Pr.

Matthews, Wendy. The Gift of a Traveler. LC 94-35307. (Illus.). 32p. 1996. pap. 4.95 (*0-8167-3657-X*, Troll Medallion) Troll Communs.

Matthews, Wendy L., jt. auth. see McClay, John B.

Matthews, William. After All: Last Poems. LC 98-22909. 64p. 1998. 20.00 (*0-395-91340-3*) HM.

***Matthews, William.** After All: Last Poems. 72p. 2000. pap. 13.00 (*0-618-05685-8*) HM.

Matthews, William. British Autobiographies: An Annotated Bibliography of British Autobiographies Published or Written Before 1951. LC Z 2027.A9M3. (California Library Reprint Edition). 390p. reprint ed. pap. 120.90 (*0-7837-4836-1*, 204448300003) Bks Demand.

— British Diaries: An Annotated Bibliography of British Diaries Written Between 1442-1942. LC Z 2014.D5M3. (California Library Reprint). 373p. reprint ed. pap. 115.70 (*0-7837-4838-8*, 204448500003) Bks Demand.

— Canadian Diaries & Autobiographies. LC 50-62732. 144p. reprint ed. pap. 44.70 (*0-8357-7994-7*, 205205400031) Bks Demand.

— Cowboys & Images: The Watercolors of William Matthews. West, Thomas, ed. LC 94-1187. (Illus.). 136p. 1994. 40.00 (*0-8118-0768-1*) Chronicle Bks.

— Curiosities. LC 89-5127. 172p. 1989. pap. 13.95 (*0-472-06388-X*, 06388); text 39.50 (*0-472-09388-6*, 09388) U of Mich Pr.

— A Happy Childhood. LC 84-803. 71p. 1984. 12.95 (*0-316-55073-6*) Little.

— The Mortal City One-Hundred Epigrams from Martial. 128p. (Orig.). 1995. pap. 15.00 (*0-942148-17-7*) Ohio Review.

— Night Life. Wheatcroft, John, ed. (Bucknell University Fine Editions, a Series in Contemporary Poetry). (Illus.). 60p. 1997. 150.00 (*0-916375-28-5*) Press Alley.

Matthews, William. Selected Poems & Translations, 1969-1991. 224p. 1993. pap. 15.00 (*0-395-66993-6*) HM.

Matthews, William. Time & Money: New Poems. 76p. 1996. pap. 14.00 (*0-395-82526-1*) HM.

— Words: Their Use & Abuse. LC 70-37792. (Essay Index Reprint Ser.). 1977. reprint ed. 25.95 (*0-8369-2611-0*) Ayer.

Matthews, William, ed. Later Medieval English Prose. LC 63-9439. (Goldentree Books in English Literature). (Orig.). 1963. pap. text 17.95 (*0-89197-270-6*) Irvington.

Matthews, William & Edgette, John H., eds. Current Thinking & Research in Brief Therapy Vol. 2: Solutions, Strategies & Narratives, Vol. 2. 2nd ed. 304p. 1998. 59.95 (*0-87630-867-1*) Brunner-Mazel.

Matthews, William, ed. see Pepys, Samuel.

Matthews, William, jt. ed. see Spisak, James W.

Matthews, William, tr. see Horace.

Matthews, William H., III, ed. Man's Impact on the Global Environment: Assessment & Recommendations for Action. (Study of Critical Environmental Problems Ser.). 1970. pap. text 10.95 (*0-262-69027-6*) MIT Pr.

Matthews, William J. Patterns in Freshwater Fish Ecology. LC 97-21339. 784p. 1998. write for info. (*0-412-02831-X*) Kluwer Academic.

Matthews, William J. & Edgette, John H., eds. Current Thinking & Research in Brief Therapy Vol. 1: Solutions, Strategies, Narratives, Vol. 1. 304p. 1997. 37.95 (*0-87630-819-1*) Brunner-Mazel.

Matthews, William K. Structure & Development of Russian. LC 77-90152. 224p. 1969. reprint ed. lib. bdg. 59.50 (*0-8371-2246-5*, MARU, Greenwood Pr) Greenwood.

Matthews, William R. & Leetch, Robert N. 101 Ways to Power up Your Job Search. 1997. pap. 12.95 (*0-614-20466-6*) McGraw.

***Matthewson, M. John, ed.** Optical Fiber Reliability & Testing. 1999. pap. text 72.00 (*0-8194-3441-8*) SPIE.

Matthewson, P. Treasure of the Atocha: A 16 Year Undersea Adventure. LC 85-30978. (Illus.). 192p. 1987. 19.95 (*0-525-24497-2*, 9EP1, Pisces Books) Lonely Planet.

Matthey, Marinette. Apprentissage d'une Langue et Interaction Verbale: Solicitation, Transmission et Construction de Connaissances Linguistiques en Situation Exolingue. (Exploration Ser.). (FRE.). 225p. 1996. 35.95 (*3-906754-61-8*, Pub. by P Lang) P Lang Pubng.

Matthiae, Paolo, et al, eds. Resurrecting the Past: A Joint Tribute to Adnan Bounni. xxxvi, 407p. 1990. pap. text 105.00 (*90-6258-067-X*, Pub. by Netherlands Inst) Eisenbrauns.

Matthias, Ann, jt. auth. see Green, Andrew.

Matthias, Catherine. I Love Cats. LC 83-7215. (Rookie Readers Ser.). (Illus.). 32p. (J). (gr. k-2). 1983. lib. bdg. 17.00 (*0-516-02041-2*) Childrens.

— I Love Cats. LC 83-7215. (Rookie Readers Ser.). (Illus.). 32p. (J). (ps-3). 1983. pap. 4.95 (*0-516-42041-0*) Childrens.

— Over-Under. LC 83-21005. (Rookie Readers Ser.). (Illus.). 32p. (J). (ps-2). 1984. pap. 4.95 (*0-516-42048-8*) Childrens.

— Too Many Balloons. LC 81-15520. (Rookie Readers Ser.). (Illus.). 32p. (J). (gr. k-2). 1982. lib. bdg. 17.00 (*0-516-03633-5*) Childrens.

— Too Many Balloons. LC 81-15520. (Rookie Readers Ser.). (Illus.). 32p. (J). (ps-2). 1982. pap. 4.95 (*0-516-43633-3*) Childrens.

Matthias, Howard. The Korean War: Reflections of a Young Combat Platoon Leader. (Illus.). 1992. 15.95 (*0-942407-17-2*) Father & Son.

Matthias, John. Beltane at Aphelion: Longer Poems. 203p. 1995. text 32.95 (*0-8040-0983-X*) Swallow.

— Crossing. Date not set. pap. 14.95 (*0-85646-035-4*, Pub. by Anvil Press) Dufour.

— A Gathering of Ways. LC 90-20684. 136p. 1991. 19.95 (*0-8040-0941-4*); pap. 10.95 (*0-8040-0945-7*) Swallow.

— Northern Summer: New & Selected Poems, 1963-1983. LC 83-18199. 224p. 1984. pap. 12.95 (*0-8040-0853-1*); text 24.95 (*0-8040-0852-3*) Swallow.

***Matthias, John.** Pages: New Poems & Cuttings. LC 99-32582. 160p. 2000. 28.95 (*0-8040-1019-6*); pap. 14.95 (*0-8040-1020-X*) Ohio U Pr.

Matthias, John. Reading Old Friends: Essays, Reviews, & Poems on Poetics 1975-1990. LC 90-28980. (SUNY Series, The Margins of Literature). 348p. (C). 1992. pap. text 21.95 (*0-7914-0880-9*) State U NY Pr.

— Swimming at Midnight: Selected Shorter Poems. LC 95-1278. 132p. 1995. text 26.95 (*0-8040-0984-8*); pap. text 12.95 (*0-8040-0985-6*) Swallow.

— Turns. Date not set. pap. 14.95 (*0-85646-023-0*, Pub. by Anvil Press) Dufour.

Matthias, John, ed. David Jones: Man & Poet. (Man & Poet Ser.). 580p. 1989. 55.00 (*0-943373-03-4*); pap. 30.00 (*0-943373-04-2*) Natl Poet Foun.

— Selected Works of David Jones. (Poetry & Literature Ser.). 237p. 1993. pap. 14.95 (*0-943373-19-0*) Natl Poet Foun.

— Selected Works of David Jones. (Poetry & Literature Ser.). 237p. 1993. 25.00 (*0-943373-18-2*) Natl Poet Foun.

Matthias, John, jt. ed. see O'Rourke, William.

Matthias, Kurt E. Citizen "M" Speaks, Vol. 1. LC 82-74183. (Illus.). 125p. 1983. pap. 5.00 (*0-9609110-0-6*) Creative Lit.

Matthias, Lu. Critical Theoretical Inquiry on the Notion of Act (Entelechy) in the Metaphysics of Aristotle & Saint Thomas Aquinas. LC 89-78078. (American University Studies: Ser. V, Vol. 85). (Illus.). 359p. (C). 1992. text 53.00 (*0-8204-1171-X*) P Lang Pubng.

Matthias, Margaret & Gulley, Beverly, eds. Celebrating Family Literacy Through Intergenerational Programming. 1995. 15.00 (*0-87173-135-5*) ACEI.

***Matthias, Rebecca.** You Can Do It: How a Young Mother Started a Business on a Shoestring & Built It into a Multimillion Dollar Company. 272p. 1999. 24.95 (*0-385-49590-0*) Doubleday.

***Matthias, Willard C.** Behind the Scenes: A History of the Use, Misuse & Non-Use of Strategic Intelligence Analysis During the Long War of 1936-1991. LC 00-22029. 2001. write for info. (*0-271-02066-0*) Pa St U Pr.

Matthiasson, John. Living on the Land: Change among the Inuit of Northern Baffin Island. 180p. 1992. pap. text 14.95 (*0-921149-93-X*) Broadview Pr.

Matthie-Jacobs, Linda & Morrish, Sheri. The Fire 'n' Ice Cookbook: Mexican Food with a Bold New Attitude. (Illus.). 141p. 1995. pap. 14.95 (*1-895292-40-9*) BookWorld.

Matthieben, Wilhelm, jt. ed. see Sudhoff, Karl.

Matthies, Anke, ed. School Library - Centre of Communication: Conference Proceedings of the 12th Annual Conference of the IASL. 225p. 1983. pap. 25.00 (*1-890861-02-2*) IASL.

Matthies, Dennis. Precision in Questioning. (Illus.). 430p. (C). 1996. spiral bd. 35.00 (*1-887981-03-9*) Stanford Bookstore.

— Question Driven Writing. 400p. 1996. spiral bd. 35.00 (*1-887981-05-5*) Stanford Bookstore.

— Self Coached Reading. (C). 1996. spiral bd. write for info. (*1-887981-07-1*) Stanford Bookstore.

— Self Teaching: Techniques for Mastering Difficult Abstract Concepts. (Illus.). 250p. (C). 1996. spiral bd. 18.00 (*1-887981-06-3*) Stanford Bookstore.

— Think on Your Feet. (Illus.). 350p. (C). 1996. spiral bd. 35.00 (*1-887981-04-7*) Stanford Bookstore.

Matthies, H., ed. Learning & Memory: Mechanisms of Information Storage in the Nervous System. 427p. 1986. 120.00 (*0-08-034186-1*, H222, H223, Pergamon Pr) Elsevier.

Matthies, H., jt. ed. see Marsan, Cosimo A.

Matthies, Michael, jt. auth. see Trapp, Stefan.

Matthies, S., et al. Standard Distribution in Texture Analysis: Maps for the Case of Cubic - Orthorhombic Symmetry, Vol. 2. 256p. 1988. lib. bdg. 70.00 (*3-05-500248-2*, Pub. by Akademie Verlag) Wiley.

— Standard Distribution in Texture Analysis: Maps for the Case of Cubic - Orthorhombic Symmetry, Vol. 3. 480p. 1990. lib. bdg. 103.00 (*3-05-500249-0*, Pub. by Akademie Verlag) Wiley.

***Matthiesen, Bill, ed.** Argentinean Tangos for Keyboard. 96p. 1999. pap. 17.95 (*0-7866-3534-7*, 97207) Mel Bay.

***Matthiesen, Steven J.** Essential Words for the TOEFL. 2nd rev. ed. LC 98-51852. 294p. 1999. pap. 8.95 (*0-7641-0466-7*) Barron.

Matthiessen, Christian & Strohmeier, K. Peter. Innovation & Urban Population Dynamics: A Multi-Level Process. (Urban Europe Ser.). 320p. 1992. 82.95 (*1-85628-143-4*, Pub. by Avebry) Ashgate Pub Co.

Matthiessen, Christian M. I. M., jt. auth. see Halliday, M. A.

Matthiessen, F. O., ed. see James, Henry.

Matthiessen, Francis O. American Renaissance. (BCL1-PS American Literature Ser.). 678p. 1993. reprint ed. lib. bdg. 149.00 (*0-7812-6577-0*) Rprt Serv.

— American Renaissance: Art & Expression in the Age of Emerson & Whitman. (Illus.). 704p. (C). 1968. reprint ed. pap. text 19.95 (*0-19-500759-X*) OUP.

— Oxford Book of American Verse. 1188p. (YA). (gr. 9 up). 1950. text 49.95 (*0-19-500049-8*) OUP.

— Sarah Orne Jewett. (BCL1-PS American Literature Ser.). 159p. 1992. reprint ed. lib. bdg. 69.00 (*0-7812-6775-7*) Rprt Serv.

— Theodore Dreiser. LC 72-7876. (American Men of Letters Ser.). (Illus.). 267p. 1973. reprint ed. lib. bdg. 35.00 (*0-8371-6550-4*, MATD, Greenwood Pr) Greenwood.

— Translation, an Elizabethan Art. (BCL1-PR English Literature Ser.). 232p. 1992. reprint ed. lib. bdg. 79.00 (*0-7812-7034-0*) Rprt Serv.

Matthiessen, Maria Von, see Von Matthiessen, Maria, photos by.

Matthiessen, Peter. African Silences. 1992. pap. 13.00 (*0-679-73102-4*) Vin Bks.

— At Play in the Fields of the Lord. 1992. 25.00 (*0-8446-6636-X*) Peter Smith.

— At Play in the Fields of the Lord. LC 91-50228. 384p. 1991. pap. 13.00 (*0-679-73741-3*) Vin Bks.

— Blue Meridian: The Search for the Great White Shark. LC 97-178650. 204p. 1997. pap. 12.95 (*0-14-026513-9*) Viking Penguin.

M

— Bone by Bone. LC 98-46180. 410p. 1999. 26.95 (*0-375-50102-9*) Random.
— The Cloud Forest. 1992. 23.75 (*0-8446-6605-X*) Peter Smith.
— The Cloud Forest. (Illus.). 320p. 1987. pap. 13.95 (*0-14-025507-9*) Viking Penguin.
— East of Lo Monthang: In the Land of Mustang. (Illus.). 192p. 1998. pap. 25.00 (*0-7881-5600-4*) DIANE Pub.
— East of Lo Monthang: In the Land of Mustang. (Illus.). 192p. 1996. pap. 25.00 (*1-57062-226-4*, Pub. by Shambhala Pubns) Random.
— East of Lo Monthang: In the Land of Mustang. limited ed. (Illus.). 192p. 1995. 150.00 (*1-57062-159-4*) Shambhala Pubns.
— Far Tortuga. LC 87-40154. 416p. 1988. pap. 14.00 (*0-394-75667-3*) Vin Bks.
— In the Spirit of Crazy Horse. (Illus.). 645p. 1992. pap. 17.95 (*0-14-014456-0*, Penguin Bks) Viking Penguin.
— Indian Country. 352p. 1992. pap. 14.95 (*0-14-013023-3*, Penguin Bks) Viking Penguin.
— Killing Mister Watson. LC 90-50631. 384p. 1991. pap. 14.00 (*0-679-73405-8*) Vin Bks.
— Lost Man's River. LC 97-10124. 1998. pap. 14.00 (*0-679-73564-X*) Random.
— The Man Who Killed Belle Starr. (International Ser.). 432p. 2000. pap. 14.00 (*0-375-70181-8*) Vin Bks.
— Men's Lives: Surfmen & Baymen of the South Fork. LC 87-40095. 352p. 1988. pap. 15.00 (*0-394-75560-X*) Vin Bks.
— Nine-Headed Dragon River: Zen Journals, 1969-1985. 1998. pap. 17.00 (*1-57062-367-8*, Pub. by Shambhala Pubns) Random.
— The Not-So-Wicked Stepmother. (Illus.). (J). 1999. pap. write for info. (*0-14-054080-6*) NAL.
— On the River Styx & Other Stories. LC 89-40508. 224p. 1990. pap. 8.95 (*0-685-29463-3*) Vin Bks.
— On the River Styx & Other Stories. LC 89-40508. 224p. 1991. pap. 12.00 (*0-679-72852-X*) Vin Bks.
— The Peter Matthiessen Reader. Jenkins, McKay, ed. & intro. by. LC 99-35246. 359p. 2000. pap. 14.00 (*0-375-70272-5*) Vin Bks.
***Matthiessen, Peter.** Sal Si Puedes (Escape If You Can) Cesar Chavez & the New American Revolution. 392p. 2000. pap. 17.95 (*0-520-22584-8*) U CA Pr.
Matthiessen, Peter. The Snow Leopard. 1981. mass mkt. 3.95 (*0-553-20651-6*) Bantam.
***Matthiessen, Peter.** The Snow Leopard. 2000. 25.50 (*0-8446-7128-2*) Peter Smith.
— Tigers in the Snow. LC 99-44866. (Illus.). 160p. 2000. 25.00 (*0-86547-576-8*) N Point Pr.
Matthiessen, Peter. The Tree Where Man Was Born. 1996. 25.25 (*0-8446-6892-3*) Peter Smith.
— The Tree Where Man Was Born. (Nature Classics Ser.). 448p. 1995. pap. 14.95 (*0-14-023934-0*, Penguin Bks) Viking Penguin.
— The Tree Where Man Was Born. (Illus.). 248p. 1996. reprint ed. 19.98 (*1-56731-102-4*, MJF Bks) Fine Comms.
— Under the Mountain Wall: A Chronicle of Two Seasons in Stone Age New Guinea. Hoagland, Edward, ed. LC 96-155866. (Illus.). 320p. 1987. pap. 12.95 (*0-14-025270-3*, Penguin Bks) Viking Penguin.
— Wildlife in America. 1996. 23.75 (*0-8446-6893-1*) Peter Smith.
***Matthiessen, Peter.** The Wind Birds: Shorebirds of North America. 1999. 25.00 (*0-8446-7016-2*) Peter Smith.
Matthiessen, Peter. The Wind Birds: Shorebirds of North America. LC 93-48005. (Curious Naturalist Ser.). (Illus.). 168p. 1994. reprint ed. pap. 12.95 (*1-881527-37-9*, Chapters Bks) HM.
Matthiessen, Peter, jt. auth. see Catlin, George.
Matthiessen, Peter, jt. auth. see Pintauro, Joe.
Matthieu. Tablettes de la Vie et la Mort. Smith, ed. (Exeter French Texts Ser.: Vol. 40). (FRE.). 82p. Date not set. pap. text 19.95 (*0-85989-196-8*, Pub. by Univ Exeter Pr) Northwestern U Pr.
Matthieu, Carol Y., ed. see Coleman, Craig S.
Matthieu, Carol Y., jt. ed. see Coleman, Craig S.
***Matthijssen, Luuk.** Interfacing Between Lawyers & Computers: An Architecture for Knowledge-Based Interfaces to Legal Databases. LC 99-21512. (Law & Electronic Commerce Ser.). xii, 268 p. 1999. 99.00 (*90-411-1181-6*) Kluwer Law Intl.
Matthioulus, P. A. Compendium. 921p. (C). 1992. 825.00 (*963-05-0200-3*, Pub. by Akade Kiado) St Mut.
Matthis, Irene & Szecsody, Imre, eds. On Freud's Couch: Seven New Interpretations of Freud's Case Histories. LC 97-29931. (Illus.). 288p. 1998. 50.00 (*0-7657-0115-4*) Aronson.
Matthys, E. F. & Truckner, W. G., eds. Melt-Spinning, Strip Casting, & Slab Casting: A Collection of Papers from the 1996 TMS Annual Meeting & Exhibition in Anaheim, California, February 4-8, 1996. (Illus.). 247p. 1996. 20.00 (*0-87339-314-7*, 3147) Minerals Metals.
Matthys, Eric F. & Kushner, Brian, eds. Advanced Sensing, Modelling & Control of Materials Processing. LC 92-80676. (Illus.). 321p. 1992. pap. 99.60 (*0-608-04982-4*, 206560000004) Bks Demand.
Matthys, H., ed. see International Titisee Conference Staff.
Matthys, John H., ed. Masonry: Components to Assemblages. LC 90-36037. (Special Technical Publication (STP) Ser.: STP 1063). (Illus.). 450p. 1990. text 42.00 (*0-8031-1453-2*, STP1063) ASTM.
Matthys, Robert J. Crystal Oscillator Circuits. rev. ed. 266p. (C). 1992. lib. bdg. 44.50 (*0-89464-552-8*) Krieger.
Matthysee, J. G. & Colbo, M. H. Ixodid Ticks of Uganda. (Illus.). 426p. 1987. pap. 22.50 (*0-938522-31-0*, ESATICKU) Entomol Soc.
Matthysen, Erik. The Nuthatches. (Poyser Bird Bks.). (Illus.). 303p. 1998. text 39.95 (*0-85661-101-8*) Acad Pr.
Matthysse, Steven, et al, eds. Psychopathology: The Evolving Sciences of Mental Disorder. (Illus.). 647p. (C). 1996. text 69.95 (*0-521-44469-1*) Cambridge U Pr.
Matthysse, Steven & Kety, Seymour S. Catecholamines & Their Enzymes in the Neuropathology of Schizophrenia. LC 75-4093. (Illus.). 382p. 1975. 175.00 (*0-08-018242-9*, Pub. by Pergamon Repr) Franklin.
Matti, Jonathan C., et al. Silurian & Lower Devonian Basin & Basin-Slope Limestones, Copenhagen Canyon, Nevada. LC 74-19734. (Geological Society of America, Special Paper: No. 159). 56p. reprint ed. pap. 30.00 (*0-608-13553-4*, 202545800044) Bks Demand.
Matti, Jonathan C., jt. auth. see Murphy, Michael A.
Mattia, Anthony, jt. auth. see Belchen, Richard P.
Mattia, F. Benedetto. Elsevier's Dictionary of Acronyms, Initialisms, Symbols & Abbreviations. LC 96-37915. 662p. 1997. 187.00 (*0-444-82589-4*) Elsevier.
Mattia, Jan B. & Marler, Patti. Resumes Made Easy. Kennedy, Sarah, ed. (Made Easy Ser.). 96p. (Orig.). 1995. pap. 6.95 (*0-8442-4348-5*, 43485, VGM Career) NTC Contemp Pub Co.
Mattia, Jan B. & Marler, Patty. Choosing a Career Made Easy. LC 96-40422. 96p. 1997. pap. 6.95 (*0-8442-4343-4*, 43434) NTC Contemp Pub Co.
— College Applications Made Easy. LC 96-27779. 96p. 1996. pap. 6.95 (*0-8442-4344-2*, 43442, VGM Career) NTC Contemp Pub Co.
— Job Hunting Made Easy. (Made Easy Ser.). 96p. (Orig.). 1995. pap. 6.95 (*0-8442-4347-7*, 43477, VGM Career) NTC Contemp Pub Co.
Mattia, Jan B. & Marley, Patty. Cover Letters Made Easy. LC 95-30110. (Made Easy Ser.). 96p. 1995. pap. 6.95 (*0-8442-4346-9*, 43469, VGM Career) NTC Contemp Pub Co.
Mattia, Jan B. & Morler, Patty. Job Interviews Made Easy. Kennedy, Sarah, ed. LC 95-775. (Made Easy Ser.). 96p. (Orig.). 1995. pap. 6.95 (*0-8442-4349-3*, 43493, VGM Career) NTC Contemp Pub Co.
Mattia, Jan B., jt. auth. see Marler, Patty.
Mattiasson, Bo, ed. Immobilized Cells & Organelles, Vol. I. 152p. 1983. 121.00 (*0-8493-6440-X*, QH585) Franklin.
— Immobilized Cells & Organelles, Vol. II. 168p. 1983. 100.00 (*0-8493-6441-8*, QH585) Franklin.
Mattiasson, Bo. & Holst, Olle, eds. Extractive Bioconversions. (Bioprocess Technology Ser.: Vol. 11). (Illus.). 352p. 1990. text 155.00 (*0-8247-8272-0*) Dekker.
Mattiasson, K., et al, eds. Numiform 86: Proceedings of the International Conference on Numerical Methods in Industrial Forming Processes, Gothenburg, 25-29 August 1986. 404p. (C). 1986. text 220.00 (*90-6191-659-3*, Pub. by A A Balkema) Ashgate Pub Co.
Mattiat, Oskar E., ed. Ultrasonic Transducer Materials. LC 71-131885. 186p. 1971. 69.50 (*0-306-30501-1*, Plenum Trade) Perseus Pubng.
Mattice, Dave, ed. see Black, Robert U.
Mattice, Wayne L. & Suter, Ulrich W. Conformational Theory of Large Molecules: The Rotational Isomeric State Model in Macromolecular Systems. 449p. 1994. 87.95 (*0-471-84338-5*) Wiley.
Mattick, Hans W. A Selected Bibliography on the American Jail with Special Emphasis on Illinois Jails, No. 821. 1975. 8.50 (*0-686-20357-7*, Sage Prdcls Pr) Sage.
Mattick, Leonard R. & Szymanski, Herman A., eds. Lectures on Gas Chromatography, 1966. LC 67-9658. (Illus.). 235p. 1967. reprint ed. pap. 72.90 (*0-608-05760-6*, 205972400007) Bks Demand.
Mattick, Paul. Economic Crisis & Crisis Theory. LC 80-5459. 235p. reprint ed. pap. 72.90 (*0-608-17078-X*, 202762200055) Bks Demand.
— Economics, Politics & the Age of Inflation. LC 78-68044. 151p. reprint ed. pap. 46.90 (*0-608-14912-8*, 202613100048) Bks Demand.
— Marx & Keynes: The Limits of the Mixed Economy. LC 69-15526. (Extending Horizons Ser.). 384p. (C). 1969. 6.95 (*0-87558-045-9*); pap. 3.45 (*0-87558-069-6*) Porter Sargent.
Mattick, Paul, Jr., ed. Marxism: Last Refuge of the Bourgeoisie? LC 83-620. 333p. 1983. reprint ed. pap. 103.30 (*0-7837-9956-X*, 206068300006) Bks Demand.
Mattick, Paul, Jr., ed. Marxism - Last Refuge of the Bourgeoisie? LC 83-620. 336p. (gr. 13). 1983. pap. text 36.95 (*0-87332-261-4*) M E Sharpe.
Mattick, Richard P. & Hall, Wayne. Methadone Maintenance Treatment & Other Opioid Replacement Therapies. Ward, Jeff, ed. LC 99-459989. 480p. 1997. text 34.00 (*90-5702-238-9*, Harwood Acad Pubs); pap. text 15.00 (*90-5702-239-7*, Harwood Acad Pubs) Gordon & Breach.
Mattie, Erik. World's Fairs. LC 98-34047. (Illus.). 256p. 1998. 65.00 (*1-56898-132-5*) Princeton Arch.
Mattie, Joan I. Folk Art in Canada. 1981. pap. 4.50 (*1-890402-03-6*) Clinton Cnty Hist.
Mattielli, Sandra, ed. Virtues in Conflict: Tradition & the Korean Woman Today. 214p. Date not set. pap. 22.00 (*0-614-12688-6*) E Rock Pr.
Mattila, John M., jt. auth. see Thompson, Wilbur R.
Mattila, Markku & Karwowski, Waldemar, eds. Computer Applications in Ergonomics, Occupational Safety, & Health: Proceedings of the International Conference on Computer-Aided Ergonomics & Safety '92: CAES '92, Tampere, Finland, 18-20 May 1992. LC 92-10527. 514p. 1992. 192.00 (*0-444-89605-8*, North Holland) Elsevier.
Mattila, Markku, ed. see Satellite Symposium on Alcohol, Drugs & Driving Staff.
Mattila, Pertti. Geometry of Sets & Measures in Euclidean Spaces: Fractals & Rectifiability. (Studies in Advanced Mathematics: No. 44). 355p. (C). 1999. pap. text 32.95 (*0-521-65595-1*) Cambridge U Pr.
***Mattila, Raiji.** The King's Magnates: A Study of the Highest Officials of the Neo-Assyrian Empire. xvi, 201p. 2000. pap. text 35.00 (*951-45-9042-2*, Pub. by Neo-Assyrian Text) Eisenbrauns.
Mattill, A. J., Jr., jt. auth. see Schweitzer, Albert.
Mattimore, Bryan W. 99 Percent Inspiration: Tips, Tales & Techniques for Liberating Your Business Creativity. LC 93-28469. 176p. 1993. pap. 17.95 (*0-8144-7788-7*) AMACOM.
Mattina, Anthony, ed. The Golden Woman: The Colville Narrative of Peter J. Seymour. DeSautel, Madeline, tr. LC 85-1156. 357p. 1985. 34.95 (*0-8165-0915-8*) U of Ariz Pr.
Mattina, Anthony & Montler, Timothy, eds. American Indian Linguistics & Ethnography in Honor of Laurence C. Thompson. LC 93-61213. (Occasional Papers in Linguistics: No. 10). xi, 497p. 1993. 25.00 (*1-879763-50-8*); pap. 15.00 (*1-879763-10-9*) U MT UMOPL.
Mattingley, Christobel. The Miracle Tree. LC 86-4541. (Illus.). 28p. (J). (gr. 3 up). 1986. 11.95 (*0-15-200530-7*, Gulliver Bks) Harcourt.
Mattingley, Cristobel. The Magic Saddle. LC 95-72230. (Illus.). 40p. (J). (ps-3). 1996. 16.00 (*0-689-80959-X*) S&S Bks Yung.
Mattingley, Jason B., jt. auth. see Bradshaw, John L.
Mattingly, Ben. The Miracle of Aloe Vera: Everything You Should Know about Aloe. LC 97-12785. (Illus.). 192p. Date not set. per. 12.00 (*0-7615-0861-9*) Prima Pub.
Mattingly, Carol. Well-Tempered Women: Nineteenth-Century Temperance Rhetoric. LC 98-16297. (Illus.). 272p. 1999. 34.95 (*0-8093-2209-9*) S Ill U Pr.
Mattingly, Cheryl. Healing Dramas & Clinical Plots: The Narrative Structure of Experience. LC 97-38627. 206p. (C). 1998. text 59.95 (*0-521-63004-5*); pap. text 22.95 (*0-521-63994-8*) Cambridge U Pr.
Mattingly, Cheryl & Fleming, Maureen H. Clinical Reasoning: Forms of Inquiry in Occupational Therapy. (Illus.). 378p. (C). 1993. text 35.95 (*0-8036-5937-7*) Davis Co.
***Mattingly, Cheryl & Garro, Linda C., eds.** Narrative & the Cultural Construction of Illness & Healing. LC 00-31629. 217p. 2000. 45.00 (*0-520-21824-8*); pap. 17.95 (*0-520-21825-6*, Pub. by U CA Pr) Cal Prin Full Svc.
***Mattingly, D. J. & Salmon, John.** Economies Beyond Agriculture in the Classical World. LC 00-26104. (Leicester-Nottingham Studies in Ancient Society). 2000. write for info. (*0-415-21253-7*) Routledge.
Mattingly, D. J., et al. Dialogues in Roman Imperialism: Power, Discourse, & Discrepant Experience in the Roman Empire. LC 97-160791. (JRA Supplementary Ser.: Vol. 23). (Illus.). 200p. (Orig.). 1997. pap. 29.95 (*1-887829-23-7*) Jour Roman Arch.
Mattingly, D. J., jt. auth. see Lazreg, N. Ben.
Mattingly, D. J., jt. ed. see Potter, D. S.
***Mattingly, David.** Book of Changes. Thompson, Robert, ed. (Spectrum Universal Edition Ser.). 44p. 2000. pap. 14.95 (*1-893686-02-7*, Pub. by Univ Ed) Wrner Bros.
Mattingly, David J. Tripolitania. LC 94-46968. 265p. (C). 1995. text 62.00 (*0-472-10658-9*, 10658) U of Mich Pr.
Mattingly, David M. & Seward, Charles. Seward's Bedside Diagnosis. 13th ed. (Illus.). 373p. 1989. pap. text 45.00 (*0-443-04077-X*) Church.
Mattingly, Garrett. The Armada. 001. 464p. 1974. pap. 16.00 (*0-395-08366-4*, 17, SenEd) HM.
— Catherine of Aragon. LC 83-45808. reprint ed. 32.50 (*0-404-20169-5*) AMS Pr.
— The Invincible Armada & Elizabethean England. LC 79-65984. (Folger Guides to the Age of Shakespeare Ser.). 1979. pap. 4.95 (*0-918016-11-8*) Folger Bks.
— Renaissance Diplomacy. 284p. 1988. reprint ed. pap. 8.95 (*0-486-25570-0*) Dover.
Mattingly, George. Breathing Space. LC 75-5515. (Illus.). (Orig.). 1975. pap. 19.95 (*0-912652-11-X*) Blue Wind.
Mattingly, H. Roman Coins. LC 85-71345. (Illus.). 1986. lib. bdg. 35.00 (*0-942666-46-1*) S J Durst.
Mattingly, Harold B. Aes & Pecvnia: Records of Roman Currency Down to 269 B.C. 19p. 1979. pap. 5.00 (*0-916710-51-3*) Obol Intl.
— The Athenian Empire Restored: Epigraphic & Historical Studies. 584p. (C). 1996. text 69.00 (*0-472-10656-2*, 10656) U of Mich Pr.
— The Coinage of the Civil Wars of 68-69 A.D. 1977. 3.75 (*0-915018-21-7*) Attic Bks.
— Fel Temp Reparatio. (Illus.). 1977. 3.75 (*0-915018-22-5*) Attic Bks.
— Man in the Roman Street. 1966. pap. 7.95 (*0-393-00337-X*) Norton.
— The Various Styles of the Roman Republican Coinage. 18p. 1977. 5.00 (*0-916710-31-9*) Obol Intl.
Mattingly, Harold B., jt. auth. see Robinson, E. S.
Mattingly, Harold B., tr. see Alfoldi, Andras.
Mattingly, Harold B., tr. & intro. see Tacitus, Cornelius.
Mattingly, I. G. & Studdert-Kennedy, Michael, eds. Modularity & the Motor Theory of Speech Perception: Proceedings of a Conference to Honor Alvin M. Liberman. 480p. 1990. text 89.95 (*0-8058-0331-9*) L Erlbaum Assocs.
Mattingly, J., et al. Aircraft Engine Design, Set. (Educ Ser.). 582p. 1987. 86.95 (*0-930403-23-1*, 23-1) AIAA.
Mattingly, Jack D. Elements of Gas Turbine Propulsion. 1995. 68.00 (*0-07-041019-4*) McGraw.
— Elements of Gas Turbine Propulsion. LC 95-897. (Mechanical Engineering Series; Aeronautical & Aerospace Engineering Ser.). 960p. 1996. 86.88 (*0-07-912196-9*) McGraw.
Mattingly, James, et al. Connecticut's Saltwater Fishing & Shoreline Recreation Guide. 1992. pap. text 3.95 (*1-881514-02-1*) Red Bk Atlas.
Mattingly, Jim, et al. Connecticut's Bass Fishing: Guides to the Best Bass Lakes & Ponds. 60p. 1992. pap. 3.95 (*1-881514-00-5*) Red Bk Atlas.
— Connecticut's Trout Fishing: Guides to the Best Lakes & Ponds, Rivers & Streams. 64p. 1992. pap. 3.95 (*1-881514-01-3*) Red Bk Atlas.
Mattingly, John. Management of Health Information: Functions & Applications. 64p. (C). 1996. pap. text, teacher ed. 15.95 (*0-8273-7892-0*) Delmar.
Mattingly, John, ed. & intro. see Branfield, Wilfred.
Mattingly, M. R. The Catholic Church on the Kentucky Frontier: 1785-1812. LC 73-3579. (Catholic University of America. Studies in Romance Languages & Literatures: No. 25). reprint ed. 40.00 (*0-404-57775-X*) AMS Pr.
Mattingly, Mary, ed. see Dickhoner, Elaine M.
Mattingly, Matt. The Long Walk Home. (Illus.). 168p. 1998. pap. 12.95 (*1-880710-38-2*) Monterey Pacific.
***Mattingly, Nancy Ann.** Pieces of My Heart. 136p. 1999. 12.95 (*0-9630274-6-8*) J D Huff.
***Mattingly, Phyllis.** No Vaseline on My Teeth: The Memoirs of Phyllis Mattingly. (Illus.). 1998. pap. 14.95 (*0-9669482-0-3*) Style Media.
Mattingly, Rick. Creative Timekeeping for the Contemporary Jazz Drummer. 64p. 1992. pap. 8.95 (*0-7935-1951-9*, 06621764) H Leonard.
***Mattingly, Rick.** The Drummer's Time: Conversations with the Great Drummers of Jazz. 84p. 1998. per. 12.95 (*0-634-00146-9*) H Leonard.
Mattingly, Rick, jt. auth. see Morgenstein, Rod.
Mattingly, Rick, ed. see Pinksterboer, Hugo.
Mattingly, Rick, ed. see Weinberg, Norman.
Mattingly, Rozella. Management of Health Information: Functions & Applications. (Allied Health Ser.). (Illus.). 400p. (C). 1996. mass mkt. 55.95 (*0-8273-6057-6*) Delmar.
Mattingly, Tom. Tennessee Football, the Peyton Manning Years. LC 99-178659. (Illus.). 160p. 1998. 39.95 (*0-943860-13-X*) UMI Pubns.
Mattioli, Leone, jt. ed. see Miller, Herbert C.
Mattioli, Maria, tr. see Swart, Susan.
Mattione, Richard P. OPEC's Investments & the International Financial System. LC 84-23242. 201p. 1985. 34.95 (*0-8157-5510-4*); pap. 14.95 (*0-8157-5509-0*) Brookings.
Mattione, Richard P., jt. auth. see Dale, Richard S.
Mattione, Richard P., jt. auth. see Enders, Thomas O.
Mattioni, Mattioni, & Mattioni, Ltd. Staff. Pennsylvania Environmental Law Handbook. 5th ed. 408p. 1997. pap. text 95.00 (*0-86587-604-5*, 604) Gov Insts.
Mattis, jt. auth. see Gaubatz.
Mattis, Ann, ed. A Society for International Development: Prospectus 1984. LC 83-16550. (Duke Press Policy Studies). xxi, 249p. (C). 1983. text 35.95 (*0-8223-0561-5*); pap. text 19.95 (*0-8223-0562-3*) Duke.
Mattis, D. C. The Many-Body Problem: An Encyclopedia of Exactly Solved Models. 984p. 1994. pap. text 74.00 (*981-02-1476-6*) World Scientific Pub.
— The Theory of Magnetism I. (Solid-State Sciences Ser.: Vol. 17). (Illus.). xv, 300p. 1988. 53.95 (*0-387-18425-2*) Spr-Verlag.
— The Theory of Magnetism II. (Solid-State Sciences Ser.: Vol. 55). (Illus.). 190p. 1985. 69.00 (*0-387-15025-0*) Spr-Verlag.
Mattis, D. C., jt. ed. see Lieb, Elliott H.
Mattis, Mary C., jt. auth. see Burke, Ronald J.
Mattis, Michael & Mottola, Emil, eds. Baryon Number Violation at the SSC? Proceedings of the Santa Fe Workshop, Santa Fe, U. S. A., April 27-30, 1990. 224p. 1990. text 67.00 (*981-02-0364-0*) World Scientific Pub.
***Mattis, Nancy M.** An Inside View into Maine's Nursing Homes. 2000. 24.95 incl. cd-rom (*0-9679320-2-5*) Healthwrite.
— An Inside View into Maine's Nursing Homes. (Illus.). 276p. 2000. pap. 24.95 (*0-9679320-0-9*) Healthwrite.
***Mattisoff, James A.** Blessings, Curses, Hopes & Fears: Psycho-Ostensive Expressions in Yiddish. (Contraversions--Jews & Other Differences Ser.). 2000. pap. text 14.95 (*0-8047-3394-5*) Stanford U Pr.
Mattison. Lizards. (Of the World Ser.). (Illus.). 224p. 1998. pap. 17.95 (*0-7137-2357-2*, Pub. by Blandford Pr) Sterling.
— Warehousing: Strategies, Technologies & Techniques. (Illus.). 512p. 1996. 55.00 (*0-07-041034-8*) McGraw.
Mattison, Alice. Animals. LC 79-54884. 72p. 1979. pap. 3.95 (*0-914086-29-4*) Alice James Bks.
***Mattison, Alice.** The Book Borrower: A Novel. 288p. 2000. pap. 13.00 (*0-688-17786-7*, Quil) HarperTrade.
Mattison, Alice. The Book Borrower: A Novel. LC 99-21961. 288p. 1999. 24.00 (*0-688-16824-8*, Wm Morrow) Morrow Avon.
— Hilda & Pearl. large type ed. LC 95-16375. 426p. 1995. 23.95 (*0-7862-0494-X*) Thorndike Pr.
— Men Giving Money, Women Yelling: Intersecting Stories. LC 96-47658. 244p. 1997. 22.00 (*0-688-15109-4*, Wm Morrow) Morrow Avon.
— Men Giving Money, Women Yelling: Intersecting Stories. 256p. 1998. reprint ed. pap. 13.00 (*0-688-16106-5*, Wm Morrow) Morrow Avon.
Mattison, Andrew M., jt. auth. see McWhirter, David P.
Mattison, Chris. The Care of Reptiles & Amphibians in Captivity. (Illus.). 334p. 1992. pap. 19.95 (*0-7137-2338-6*, Pub. by Blandford Pr) Sterling.
— The Encyclopedia of Snakes. LC 95-2501. (Illus.). 288p. (YA). 1995. 35.00 (*0-8160-3072-3*) Facts on File.
— The Encyclopedia of Snakes. (Illus.). 288p. 1999. pap. 18.95 (*0-8160-3931-3*, Checkmark) Facts on File.
***Mattison, Chris.** Frogs & Toads. LC 98-210630. (Of the World Ser.). (Illus.). 192p. 1998. pap. 17.95 (*0-7137-2355-6*, Pub. by Blandford Pr) Sterling.

An Asterisk (*) at the beginning of an entry indicates that the title is appearing for the first time.

Mattison, Chris. Frogs & Toads of the World. (Illus.). 191p. 1987. 29.95 (*0-8160-1602-X*) Facts on File.
— Keeping & Breeding Lizards. (Illus.). 224p. (Orig.). 1996. pap. 24.95 (*0-7137-2632-6*, Pub. by Blandford Pr) Sterling.
— Keeping & Breeding Snakes. (Illus.). 224p. 1996. pap. 16.95 (*0-7137-2579-6*, Pub. by Blandford Pr) Sterling.
— Keeping & Breeding Snakes. rev. ed. LC 99-182212. (Illus.). 1999. 24.95 (*0-7137-2709-8*, Pub. by Blandford Pr) Sterling.
— Lizards of the World. (Of the World Ser.). (Illus.). 192p. (J). 1989. 29.95 (*0-8160-1900-2*) Facts on File.
— A Practical Guide to Exotic Pets: How to Keep & Enjoy a Wide Range of Unusual Pets. 1999. pap. 9.99 (*1-84100-244-5*) Quadrillion Media.
— Rattler! (Illus.). 144p. 1998. pap. 19.95 (*0-7137-2731-4*, Pub. by Blandford Pr) Sterling.
— Rattler! A Natural History of Rattlesnakes. (Illus.). 144p. 1996. 29.95 (*0-7137-2534-6*, Pub. by Blandford Pr) Sterling.
— Snakes of the World. (Illus.). 192p. 1998. pap. 17.95 (*0-7137-2340-8*, Pub. by Blandford Pr) Sterling.
— Snakes of the World. (Of the World Ser.). (Illus.). 190p. 1986. 29.95 (*0-8160-1082-X*) Facts on File.
— Snakes Photoguide. (Gems Ser.). (GER.). (J). 1995. pap. 8.00 (*0-00-470825-3*) Collins SF.

Mattison, Christopher. Snake. LC 99-19957. 192p. 1999. 29.95 (*0-7894-4660-X*) DK Pub Inc.
— The Snake Book. LC 96-38294. (Illus.). 32p. (J). 1997. 12.95 (*0-7894-1526-7*) DK Pub Inc.

Mattison, D. R. & Olshan, A. F., eds. Male-Mediated Developmental Toxicity. (Reproductive Biology Ser.). (Illus.). 418p. (C). 1994. text 125.00 (*0-306-44815-7*, Kluwer Plenum) Kluwer Academic.

Mattison, H. Impending Crisis of Eighteen Sixty: The Present Connection of the Methodist Episcopal Church with Slavery. LC 75-149870. (Black Heritage Library Collection). 1977. 20.95 (*0-8369-8750-0*) Ayer.

Mattison, Harry, et al, eds. El Salvador. 1983. 29.95 (*0-86316-063-8*); pap. 14.95 (*0-86316-064-6*) Writers & Readers.

Mattison, Judith. The Seven Last Words of Christ: The Message of the Cross for Today. LC 92-19355. 80p. 1992. pap. 8.99 (*0-8066-2628-3*, 9-2628) Augsburg Fortress.

Mattison, Phillip E. Practical Digital Video Programming with Examples in C. LC 94-215942. 522p. 1994. pap. write for info. (*0-471-31015-8*) Wiley.

Mattison, Richard E. & Hynd, George W. Child Psychopathology Developmental Disorders: Diagnostic Criteria & Clinical Assessment, 2 vols., Set. (C). 1991. text 120.00 (*0-8058-0330-0*) L Erlbaum Assocs.
— Child Psychopathology Developmental Disorders: Diagnostic Criteria & Clinical Assessment, Vol. 1: Diagnostic Criteria. 504p. (C). 1991. text 89.95 (*0-8058-0328-9*) L Erlbaum Assocs.
— Child Psychopathology Developmental Disorders: Diagnostic Criteria & Clinical Assessment, Vol. 1, Diagnostic Criteria. 520p. (C). 1993. pap. text 45.00 (*0-8058-1368-3*) L Erlbaum Assocs.
— Child Psychopathology Developmental Disorders: Diagnostic Criteria & Clinical Assessment, Vol. 2: Developmental Disorders. 336p. (C). 1991. pap. 59.95 (*0-8058-0329-7*) L Erlbaum Assocs.

Mattison, Rob. Understanding Database Management Systems Handbook. 2nd ed. LC 97-30319. (Illus.). 666p. 1997. pap. 54.95 (*0-07-049999-3*) McGraw.
— Web Warehousing & Knowledge Management. Kilger-Mattison, Brigitte, ed. & illus. by. LC 99-18755. (McGraw Hill Series on Data Warehousing). 576p. 1999. pap. 49.00 (*0-07-041103-4*) McGraw.

***Mattison, Rob.** Winning Telco Customers Using Marketing Databases. LC 99-36699. 344p. 1999. 69.00 (*1-58053-036-2*) Artech Hse.

Mattison, Robert. Data Warehousing & Data Mining for Telecommunications. LC 97-22863. 250p. 1997. 75.00 (*0-89006-952-2*) Artech Hse.

Mattison, Robert S. Grace Hartigan: A Painter's World. LC 90-80947. (Illus.). 156p. 1990. 50.00 (*1-55595-041-8*) Hudson Hills.
— Robert Motherwell: The Formative Years. Foster, Stephen, ed. LC 87-10742. (Studies in the Fine Arts: The Avant-Garde: No. 56). (Illus.). 256p. 1987. reprint ed. pap. 79.40 (*0-8357-1810-7*, 207074100004) Bks Demand.

Mattison, Robin, et al. New Proclamation: Easter to All Saints. LC 99-210103. (Proclamation: Aids for Interpreting the Church Year, 1999, Series A). 224p. 1998. pap. 24.99 (*0-8006-4240-6*, 1-4240) Augsburg Fortress.

Mattison, Steve. Ceramics, 2 bks. in 1. LC 98-48457. (Two Books in One). (Illus.). 128p. 1998. 24.95 (*0-8069-6323-9*) Sterling.

Mattison, Wendy & Scareth, Thomas, eds. Hmong Lives: From Laos to La Crosse. Lo, Laotou, tr. (Illus.). 232p. (Orig.). 1994. pap. text 12.95 (*0-9647337-0-6*) Pump Hse Regional Ctr.

Mattiuda, Don. Radionic/Homeopathic Manual: Radionic Instruction. unabridged ed. 230p. 1997. ring bd. 95.00 (*1-57179-072-1*) Intern Guild ASRS.

Mattix, Rick, jt. auth. see Helmer, William J.

Mattiza, Dorothy B. One Hundred Texas Wildflowers. Foreman, Ronald J., ed. LC 93-84561. (Illus.). 72p. (Orig.). 1993. pap. 7.95 (*1-877856-35-5*) SW Pks Mnmts.

Mattle, Heinrich, jt. auth. see Mumenthaler, Mark.

Mattler, Leon E. Facial Improvement Therapy. 45p. 1996. reprint ed. spiral bd. 9.00 (*0-7873-1195-2*) Hlth Research.

Mattli, Walter. The Logic of Regional Integration: Europe & Beyond. LC 98-11655. (Illus.). 214p. (C). 1999. text 54.95 (*0-521-63227-7*) Cambridge U Pr.

***Mattli, Walter.** The Logic of Regional Integration: Europe & Beyond. LC 98-11655. (Cambridge Studies in Comparative Politics). (Illus.). 240p. (C). 1999. pap. text 18.95 (*0-521-63536-5*) Cambridge U Pr.

Mattlin, Everett, jt. auth. see Wanger, Ralph.

Mattman, Jurg W. & Kaufer, Steve, eds. The Complete Workplace Violence Prevention Manual. (Illus.). 800p. 1994. student ed. 387.00 (*0-9637790-5-2*) Inter-Act Assocs.

Mattman, Jurg W., jt. auth. see Kaufer, Steven C.

Mattman, Lida H. Cell Wall Deficient Forms Stealth Pathogens. 2nd ed. 432p. 1992. boxed set 57.95 (*0-8493-4405-0*, QR77) CRC Pr.
— Cell Wall Deficient Forms Stealth Pathogens. 3rd ed. Date not set. 99.95 (*0-8493-8767-1*, 8767) CRC Pr.

Matto de Turner, Clorinda. Birds Without a Nest: A Novel. (Texas Pan American Ser.). 208p. 1996. pap. 12.95 (*0-292-75195-8*) U of Tex Pr.
— Birds Without a Nest: A Novel. Hudson, J. G., tr. (Texas Pan American Ser.). 208p. 1996. text 30.00 (*0-292-75194-X*) U of Tex Pr.
— Birds Without a Nest: A Story of Indian Life in Peru. 1977. lib. bdg. 59.95 (*0-8490-1508-1*) Gordon Pr.
— Torn from the Nest. 224p. 1999. pap. 13.95 (*0-19-511006-4*) OUP.

Matto, Edward A. A Manager's Guide to the Antitrust Laws. LC 79-54843. 207p. reprint ed. pap. 64.20 (*0-608-12149-5*, 202390700034) Bks Demand.

Mattock, G., jt. auth. see Eilbeck, W. J.

Mattock, John. Identifying Guide to Roses. 80p. 1994. 6.98 (*0-7858-0052-2*) Bk Sales Inc.
— International Management: A Guide to Cross-Cultural Business. 2nd ed. 1999. 24.95 (*0-7494-2827-9*) Kogan Page Educ.

Mattock, John & Ehrenborg, Jons. How to Be a Better Negotiator. (How to Be a Better...Ser.). 1997. pap. 15.95 (*0-7494-2093-6*) Kogan Page Ltd.

Mattock, John & Newdick, Jane. Step-by-Step Guide to Growing & Displaying Roses. (Illus.). 124p. 1993. pap. 12.95 (*1-55110-076-2*) Whitecap Bks.

Mattock, John, jt. auth. see Guy, Vincent.

Mattock, Michael G., et al. New Capabilities for Strategic Mobility Analysis Using Mathematical Programming. LC 94-42766. (Illus.). 103p. 1995. pap. text 15.00 (*0-8330-1610-5*, MR-296-JS) Rand Corp.

Mattock, N. M. & Abeykoon, P. Innovative Programmes of Medical Education in South-East Asia. (WHO Regional Publications, South-East Asia Ser.: No. 21). viii, 119p. 1993. pap. text 20.00 (*92-9022-163-1*, 1560021) World Health.

Mattogno, Carlo. Auschwitz - The End of a Legend: A Critique of Jean-Claude Pressac. Granata, Russ, tr. (Illus.). xiii, 138p. (Orig.). (C). 1994. pap. 5.95 (*0-939484-50-1*, 0995, Inst Hist Rev) Legion Survival.

Matton, Mary-Ann, ed. Berlin 1986: The Archetype of Shadow in a Split World. LC 97-46830. 456p. 1987. 35.00 (*3-85630-514-9*) Continuum.
— Berlin 1986: The Archetype of Shadow in a Split World. 456p. 1995. pap. 19.95 (*3-85630-506-8*) Continuum.

Mattoni, Rudi. Butterflies of Greater Los Angeles. (Illus.). (Orig.). (C). 1990. pap. text 8.00 (*0-9611464-4-3*) Lepidoptera.

Mattoo, Amitabh, jt. ed. see Cortright, David.

Mattoo, Autar K. & Suttle, Jeffrey C. The Plant Hormone Ethylene. (Illus.). 352p. 1991. boxed set 249.00 (*0-8493-4566-9*, QK898) CRC Pr.

Mattoo, Mehraj. Structured Derivatives: New Tools for Investment Management. 300p. 1996. 75.00 (*0-273-61120-8*) F T P-H.

Mattoo, Neerga. The Stranger Beside Me: Short Stories from Kashmir. (C). pap. 8.50 (*81-86112-14-6*, Pub. by UBS Pubs Dist) S Asia.

Mattoo, Neerja. Best of Kashmiri Cooking. 131p. 1998. pap. 9.95 (*0-7818-0612-7*) Hippocrene Bks.
— Best of Kashmiri Cooking. (C). 1995. pap. 10.00 (*81-85944-50-4*, Pub. by UBS Pubs Dist) S Asia.

Mattoon, Ashley T., jt. auth. see Abramovitz, Janet N.

Mattoon, D. P., jt. auth. see Mattoon, L. G.

Mattoon, John S., jt. auth. see Nyland, Thomas G.

Mattoon, L. G. & Mattoon, D. P. Mattoon: A Genealogy of the Descendants of Philip Mattoon of Deerfield, Mass. (Illus.). 339p. 1995. reprint ed. pap. 52.50 (*0-8328-4800-X*); reprint ed. lib. bdg. 62.50 (*0-8328-4799-2*) Higginson Bk Co.

Mattoon, Mary A. Chicago 1992. 550p. 1995. 35.00 (*3-85630-538-6*); pap. 25.00 (*3-85630-537-8*) Continuum.
— Paris Eighty-Nine: Personal & Archetypal Dynamics in the Analytical Relationship. LC 81-3357. 530p. 1995. 35.00 (*3-85630-529-7*); pap. 25.00 (*3-85630-524-6*) Continuum.
— Understanding Dreams. LC 84-5523. Orig. Title: Applied Dream Analysis: A Jungian Approach. vii, 248p. 1978. pap. 19.00 (*0-88214-326-3*) Spring Pubns.
— Zurich, 1995: Open Questions in Analytical Psychology. 36p. 1996. pap. 29.95 (*3-85630-556-4*) Continuum.

Mattoon, Mary A., ed. Zurich, 1995: Open Questions in Analytical Psychology. 36p. 1996. 39.95 (*3-85630-555-6*) Continuum.

***Mattoon, Mary Ann.** Forence '98: Destruction & Creation: Personal & Cultural Transformations. 2000. 39.80 (*3-85630-584-X*); pap. 29.80 (*3-85630-583-1*) Daimon Pubs.

Mattoon, Mary-Ann. Jungian Psychology after Jung. LC 93-45880. 64p. (Orig.). 1994. pap. 7.95 (*1-882275-03-9*) Rnd Table Pr.
— Jungian Psychology in Perspective. 352p. 1985. pap. 18.95 (*0-02-920650-2*) Free Pr.

Mattoon, Richard W., jt. ed. see Forman, Donald T.

Mattoon, Steven. S. W. A. T. Training & Employment. (Illus.). 152p. 1987. pap. 25.00 (*0-87364-439-5*) Paladin Pr.

Mattos Bicudo, Carlos E. de, see De Mattos Bicudo, Carlos E.

Mattos, N. M. An Approach to Knowledge Base Management. Siekmann, Joerg H., ed. (Lecture Notes in Artificial Intelligence Ser.: Vol. 513). xi, 247p. 1991. pap. 31.00 (*0-387-54268-X*) Spr-Verlag.

Mattoso, Katia M. De Queiros, see De Queiros Mattoso, Katia M.

***Mattox & Moore.** Trauma. 4th ed. LC 99-12957. 1514p. 1999. pap. 185.00 (*0-8385-9012-8*) McGraw.

Mattox, Addie & Tuemmler, Denise. Bringing the Business Case to Management. 48p. 1997. 100.00 (*0-89258-313-4*, D060) Assn Inform & Image Mgmt.

Mattox, Beverly. I Could Not Call Him Father. (Illus.). 176p. 1997. pap. 8.95 (*0-9656737-0-7*) K Mattox Minist.
— I Could Not Call Him Father. LC 97-21548. 175p. 1997. pap. 12.99 (*0-88368-505-1*) Whitaker Hse.

***Mattox, Brenda Sneathen.** Victorian Family Paper Dolls. (Illus.). (J). 1999. pap. 4.95 (*0-486-40811-6*) Dover.

Mattox, Cheryl & Mattox, Cheryl W. Let's Get the Rhythm of the Band. (J). 1997. pap. 19.95 incl. audio (*0-938971-96-4*) JTG Nashville.

Mattox, Cheryl W. Let's Get the Rhythm of the Band. (J). (ps-3). 1993. pap. 8.95 (*0-938971-97-2*) JTG Nashville.
— My Play a Tune Book: Shake It to the One That You Love the Best. (Sing a Song, Play along Series with Electronic Keyboard). (J). 1991. 14.95 (*0-938971-11-5*) JTG Nashville.

Mattox, Cheryl W., ed. Shake It to the One That You Love the Best: Play Songs & Lullabies from Black Musical Traditions. (Illus.). (Orig.). (J). (ps-6). 1990. pap. 7.95 (*0-9623381-0-9*) Warren-Mattox.

Mattox, Cheryl W., jt. auth. see Mattox, Cheryl.

Mattox, D. M., et al, eds. Adhesion in Solids. (Symposium Proceedings Ser.: Vol. 119). 1988. text 17.50 (*0-931837-89-8*) Materials Res.

Mattox, Donald M. Handbook of Physical Vapor Deposition (PVD) Processing: Film Formation, Adhesion, Surface Preparation & Contamination Control. LC 97-44664. (Illus.). 917p. 1998. 195.00 (*0-8155-1422-0*) Noyes.

Mattox, Gale A., et al, eds. Germany in Transition: A Unified Nation's Search for Identity. LC 98-54301. 288p. 1999. 65.00 (*0-8133-9150-4*, Pub. by Westview); pap. write for info. (*0-8133-9151-2*) Westview.

***Mattox, Gale A. & Rachwald, Arthur R., eds.** Enlarging NATO: The National Debates. 300p. 2001. 55.00 (*1-55587-906-4*) L Rienner.

Mattox, Henry E. The Twilight of Amateur Diplomacy: The American Foreign Service & Its Senior Officers in the 1890s. LC 88-29022. (American Diplomatic History Ser.: No. 2). (Illus.). 228p. 1989. 21.00 (*0-87338-375-3*) Kent St U Pr.

Mattox, K. K. Down in the Mouth but on Top of the World. LC 97-40104. (Illus.). 100p. 1997. pap. 12.95 (*1-884363-13-X*) Odenwald Pr.

Mattox, Karl R. & Bold, Harold C. Phycological Studies Vol. 3: The Taxonomy of Certain Ulotrichacean Algae. (University Texas Publication: No. 6222). (Illus.). 66p. 1975. reprint ed. pap. 37.40 (*3-87429-098-0*, 007822, Pub. by Koeltz Sci Bks) Lubrecht & Cramer.

Mattox, Kenneth L. Atlas of Head & Neck Surgery, Vol. 2. 2nd ed. 350p. (C). 1999. text 125.00 (*1-55664-254-7*) Mosby Inc.
— Core Textbook of Obstetrics & Gynecology. LC 96-49800. (Illus.). 624p. (C). (gr. 13). 1997. pap. text 36.95 (*0-8151-6035-6*, 24828) Mosby Inc.

Mattox, Kenneth L., ed. Complications of Trauma. (Illus.). 616p. 1994. text 178.00 (*0-443-08851-9*) Church.
— The History of Surgery in Houston. limited ed. LC 98-28964. (Illus.). 488p. 1998. lthr. 100.00 (*1-57168-258-9*) Sunbelt Media.

***Mattox, Kent.** No High Like the Most High: Divine Direction for Destiny. 176p. 1999. pap. 9.99 (*1-884369-90-1*) McDougal Pubng.

Mattox, Rick E. Minnesota Legal Forms: Criminal Law Forms. 240p. 1993. ring bd., wbk. ed. 69.95 incl. disk (*0-614-05902-X*, MICHIE) LEXIS Pub.
— Minnesota Legal Forms, 1981-1993: Criminal Law Forms. (Minnesota Legal Forms Ser.). 240p. ring bd. 69.95 incl. disk (*0-917126-83-1*, MICHIE) LEXIS Pub.
— Minnesota Legal Forms, 1981-1993: Criminal Law Forms. (Minnesota Legal Forms Ser.). 240p. 1993. suppl. ed. 28.50 (*0-86678-030-0*, MICHIE) LEXIS Pub.

Mattox, Robert. Christian Employee: Revised & Updated. LC 77-20588. 1998. pap. text 10.99 (*0-88270-761-2*) Bridge-Logos.

Mattox, Stephen R. Petrology, Age, Geochemistry & Correlation of the Tertiary Volcanic Rocks of the Awapa Plateau, Garfield, Piute & Wayne Counties, Utah. (Miscellaneous Publication Ser.: Vol. 91-5). (Illus.). 46p. 1991. pap. 6.25 (*1-55791-314-5*, MP-91-5) Utah Geological Survey.

Mattozz. Jeremy Bible Bookworm, 4 Vols., Set. (Jeremy the Bible Bookworm Ser.). (J). 1996. pap. 15.75 (*0-88271-578-X*) Regina Pr.

Mattozzi, Patricia R. Eastertime. (Little Lessons for Little Learners Ser.). (Illus.). (J). 1992. 4.50 (*0-8378-2459-1*) Gibson.
— The Greatest Gift. (Little Lessons for Little Learners Ser.). (J). 1990. 4.50 (*0-8378-1887-7*) Gibson.
— Little Lessons for Little Learners: Birthdays Are Special. 1993. 4.50 (*0-8378-5315-X*) Gibson.
— Little Lessons for Little Lerners: The New Baby. (Illus.). 24p. 1994. 4.50 (*0-8378-7689-3*) Gibson.

Mattozzi, Patricia R. Prayer. (Little Lessons for Little Learners Ser.). (J). 4.95 (*0-614-22068-8*) Regina Pr.

Mattozzi, Patti. Little Lessons for Little Learners: Angels. 32p. (J). (gr. 2 up). 1989. pap. 4.50 (*0-8378-1843-5*) Gibson.
— Little Lessons for Little Learners: Heaven. (J). (gr. 3 up). 1991. 4.50 (*0-8378-1986-5*) Gibson.
— Little Lessons for Little Learners: Prayer. 32p. (J). (gr. 1 up). 1989. 4.50 (*0-8378-1844-3*) Gibson.

Matts, Abraham & Sperling. Reasons for Jewish Customs & Traditions. LC 68-31711. 310p. 1989. pap. 11.95 (*0-8197-0184-X*) Bloch.

Mattson. Statistics: Difficult Concepts Understandable Explanations. LC 80-24947. 1984. 24.00 (*0-86516-056-2*) Bolchazy-Carducci.

Mattson, Andrea L. Roots: Foundation Quarter Horse Bloodlines. (Illus.). 160p. 1992. pap. 16.95 (*1-879984-78-4*) Premier KS.

Mattson, Andrea L., ed. The Stallion Finder, 1995: Premier Publishing Equine. 328p. 1995. pap. 34.95 (*1-879984-50-4*) Premier KS.
— The Stallion Finder, 1996: Premier Publishing Equine. 328p. 1995. pap. 34.95 (*1-879984-51-2*) Premier KS.

Mattson, Catherine & Mattson, Mark T. Contemporary Atlas of the United States. (Illus.). 160p. 1990. 115.00 (*0-02-897281-3*) Macmillan.

Mattson, Donald E., et al. Old Fort Snelling Instruction Book for Fife, with Music of Early America. 2nd ed. LC 74-7298. (Minnesota Historic Sites Pamphlet Ser: No. 11). 112p. 1976. pap. 11.95 (*0-87351-090-9*) Minn Hist.

Mattson, Einar. Basic Corrosion Technology for Scientists & Engineers. 2nd ed. (Illus.). 208p. 1997. 40.00 (*1-86125-011-8*, Pub. by Inst Materials) Ashgate Pub Co.

Mattson, Elmer W. Professionalism: How to Enhance & Enrich Your Profession. LC 82-99894. (Illus.). (Orig.). 1982. pap. 4.95 (*0-9609084-0-4*) Motiv Unltd.

Mattson, Francis O. Edna St. Vincent Millay, 1892-1950. (Illus.). 48p. 1991. pap. 6.00 (*0-87104-429-3*) NY Pub Lib.
— Walt Whitman: In Life or Death Forever. (Illus.). 45p. 1992. pap. 10.00 (*0-87104-431-5*) NY Pub Lib.

Mattson, Francis O., ed. E. E. Cummings at 100. (Illus.). 80p. 1994. pap. 14.95 (*0-87104-436-6*) NY Pub Lib.
— Virginia Woolf & Her Circle: Manuscripts, Books, & Images from the Berg Collection. (Illus.). 72p. 1993. pap. 11.95 (*0-87104-434-X*) NY Pub Lib.

Mattson, George E. Black Belt Test Guide. LC 88-92266. (Illus.). 300p. (Orig.). 1988. pap. 20.00 (*0-930559-01-0*) Peabody Pub.

Mattson, George E. The Black Belt Test Guide: The Complete Uechi-ryu System. (Illus.). 299p. 1988. pap. 20.00 (*0-930559-07-X*) Peabody Pub.

Mattson, George E. Uechiryu Karate Do. LC 75-5978. (Illus.). 492p. (Orig.). 1974. 40.00 (*0-686-10569-9*); pap. 25.00 (*0-685-03984-6*) Peabody Pub.
— The Way of Karate. (Illus.). 200p. 1992. pap. 18.95 (*0-8048-1852-5*) Tuttle Pubng.
— The Way of Karate. 21.95 (*0-685-22157-1*) Wehman.

Mattson, George E., ed. see Rabesa, Arthur.

Mattson, Hans. Reminiscences: Story of an Emigrant. Scott, Franklyn D., ed. LC 78-15201. (Scandinavians in America Ser.). (Illus.). 1979. reprint ed. lib. bdg. 28.95 (*0-405-11651-9*) Ayer.
— Reminiscences: The Story of an Emigrant. (American Biography Ser.). 314p. 1991. reprint ed. lib. bdg. 79.00 (*0-7812-8278-0*) Rprt Serv.

Mattson, Harold F. Discrete Mathematics with Applications to Computer Science. LC 92-33772. 672p. 1993. text 92.95 (*0-471-60672-3*) Wiley.

Mattson, Harold F., et al, eds. Applied Algebra, Algebraic Algorithms & Error-Correcting Codes: 9th International Symposium, AAECC-9 New Orleans, LA, U. S. A., October 7-11, 1991 Proceedings. (Lecture Notes in Computer Science Ser.: Vol. 539). xi, 489p. 1991. 47.95 (*0-387-54522-0*) Spr-Verlag.

Mattson, Heidi. Ivy League Stripper. LC 94-23871. (Illus.). 288p. 1995. 21.45 (*1-55970-290-7*, Pub. by Arcade Pub Inc) Time Warner.
— Ivy League Stripper. 1996. mass mkt. 6.99 (*0-312-95955-9*) St Martin.

Mattson, Ivar T. Simon. King, Ella M., ed. 188p. (Orig.). 1992. pap. 6.99 (*0-9625584-5-1*) Super G Pub Co.

Mattson, James S. Computer-Assisted Instruction in Chemistry Part A: General Approach. LC 73-89669. (Computers in Chemistry & Instrumentation Ser.: No. 4). 287p. 1974. reprint ed. pap. 89.00 (*0-7837-8641-7*, 204100000001) Bks Demand.

Mattson, James S., et al, eds. Computer-Assisted Instruction in Chemistry Pt. B: Applications. LC 73-89669. (Computers in Chemistry & Instrumentation Ser.: No. 4). (Illus.). 278p. 1974. reprint ed. pap. 86.20 (*0-7837-0664-2*, 204100000002) Bks Demand.
— Computer Fundamentals for Chemists. LC 72-91432. (Computers in Chemistry & Instrumentation Ser.: No. 1). (Illus.). 380p. reprint ed. pap. 117.80 (*0-7837-3377-1*, 204333500008) Bks Demand.
— Computers in Polymer Sciences. LC 75-40603. (Computers in Chemistry & Instrumentation Ser.: No. 6). (Illus.). 390p. reprint ed. pap. 120.90 (*0-7837-0732-0*, 204105600019) Bks Demand.
— Infrared, Correlation, & Fourier Transform Spectroscopy. LC 77-9460. (Computers in Chemistry & Instrumentation Ser.: No. 7). (Illus.). 247p. reprint ed. pap. 76.60 (*0-7837-0862-9*, 204117000019) Bks Demand.
— Laboratory Systems & Spectroscopy. LC 75-32388. (Computers in Chemistry & Instrumentation Ser.: No. 5). (Illus.). 300p. reprint ed. pap. 93.00 (*0-7837-0729-0*, 204105300019) Bks Demand.
— Spectroscopy & Kinetics. LC 72-91433. (Computers in Chemistry & Instrumentation Ser.: Vol. 3). 346p. 1973. reprint ed. pap. 107.30 (*0-608-00733-1*, 206150900009) Bks Demand.

M

Mattson, James S. & Mark, Harry B., Jr. Activated Carbon: Surface Chemistry & Adsorption from Solution. LC 74-138502. (Illus.). 247p. reprint ed. pap. 76.60 (*0-8357-6004-9*, 203454800090) Bks Demand.

Mattson, James S. & Simon, Merrill. The Pioneers of NMR & Magnetic Resonance in Medicine: The Story of MRI. (Illus.). 838p. 1996. lib. bdg. 75.00 (*0-9619243-1-4*) Dean Bks.

Mattson, James S., ed. see Mark, Harry B., Jr.

Mattson, Jean M. Playwriting for the Puppet Theatre. LC 97-8165. 235p. 1997. pap. 24.95 (*0-8108-3324-7*) Scarecrow.

Mattson, Jennifer A., tr. see Stavans, Ilan.

Mattson, Jerauld, jt. ed. see Fossum, John A.

Mattson, Jerauld, jt. ed. see Fossum, John.

Mattson, Karen. Relapse Prevention Workbook for Women. 48p. 1992. pap. 5.50 (*1-56246-030-7*, 3227, HazeldenJohnson Inst) Hazelden.

Mattson, Kevin. Creating a Democratic Public: The Struggle for Urban Participatory Democracy During the Progressive Era. LC 96-53211. 1997. 45.00 (*0-271-01722-8*); pap. 16.95 (*0-271-01723-6*) Pa St U Pr.

Mattson, Lloyd. Christian Camping Today: A Complete Handbook for the Short-Term Staff. LC 97-51483. 144p. 1998. pap. text 6.99 (*0-87788-611-3*, H Shaw Pubs) Waterbrook Pr.

Mattson, Margaret E., jt. auth. see Donovan, Dennis M.

Mattson, Mark P., ed. Neuroprotective Signal Transduction. LC 97-37497. (Contemporary Neuroscience Ser.). (Illus.). 360p. 1997. 145.00 (*0-89603-473-9*) Humana.

Mattson, Mark P. & Geddes, James W., eds. Advances in Cell Aging & Gerontology Vol. 2: The Aging Brain. 347p. 1997. 128.50 (*0-7623-0265-8*) Jai Pr.

Mattson, Mark T. Macmillan Family Reference Atlas of the U. S. A. (Illus.). 377p. 1997. 27.95 (*0-02-864889-7*) Mac Lib Ref.

— The Scholastic Environmental Atlas of the United States. LC 92-46757. 80p. (gr. 4-7). 1993. 14.95 (*0-590-49354-X*, Scholastic Ref) Scholastic Inc.

Mattson, Mark T., compiled by. Factbook on Elementary, Middle & Secondary Schools. LC 92-34283. 1995. 39.95 (*0-590-49225-X*, 2846m3985 1993) Scholastic Inc.

Mattson, Mark T. & Asante, Molefi K. The African American Atlas: Black History & Culture: An Illustrated Reference. 2nd ed. LC 98-25556. (Illus.). 251p. 1998. 115.00 (*0-02-864984-2*) Macmillan.

Mattson, Mark T., jt. auth. see Asante, Molefi K.

Mattson, Mark T., jt. auth. see Cuff, David J.

Mattson, Mark T., jt. auth. see Mason, Robert J.

Mattson, Mark T., jt. auth. see Mattson, Catherine.

Mattson, Marlon R., ed. Manual of Psychiatric Quality Assurance: A Report of the APA Committee on Quality Assurance. LC 91-25954. 254p. 1992. pap. text 27.50 (*0-89042-232-X*, 2232) Am Psychiatric.

Mattson, Mart T., jt. auth. see Asante, Molefi K.

Mattson, Martha. Amazons the Forgotten Tribe: Understanding Sexual Orientations. LC 97-73679. (Illus.). 416p. 1998. pap. 16.95 (*0-9658947-4-6*) Amazon Press.

Mattson, Michelle M. Franz Xaver Kroetz: The Construction of a Political Aesthetic. LC 96-25504. 256p. 1996. 49.50 (*1-85973-079-5*) Berg Pubs.

Mattson, Patrick. Air Traffic Control Test Prep: #ASA-ATC. 2nd ed. (Illus.). 216p. 1996. reprint ed. pap. 19.95 (*1-56027-254-6*, ASA-ATC) ASA Inc.

Mattson, Paul R. The Real American Quarter Horse: Versatile Athletes Who Proved Supreme. LC 91-90201. (Illus.). 160p. 1991. pap. 26.00 (*1-879984-77-6*) Premier KS.

*__Mattson, Ralph T.__ Finding a Job You Can Love. 1999. pap. 9.99 (*0-87552-393-5*) P & R Pubng.

Mattson, Robin. Soap Opera Cafe: The Skinny on Food from a Daytime Star. LC 97-15269. (Illus.). 224p. 1997. 20.00 (*0-446-52056-X*, Pub. by Warner Bks) Little.

*__Mattson, Robin.__ Soap Opera Cafe: The Skinny on Food from a Daytime Star. 304p. 1999. mass mkt. 13.99 (*0-446-67489-3*, Pub. by Warner Bks) Little.

Mattson, Sue, ed. see Nelson, Sharlene & Nelson, Ted.

Mattson, Susan, ed. see Organization for Obstetric, Gynecologic & Neonatal.

Mattson, Ted. Adventures of the Iditarod Air Force: True Stories about the Pilots Who Fly for Alaska's Famous Sled Dog Race. LC 96-61936. (Illus.). 160p. (C). 1997. pap. 14.95 (*0-945397-59-3*, Pub. by Epicenter Pr) Gr Arts Ctr Pub.

Mattson, Thomas. Small Town: Reflections on People, History, Religion & Nature in Central New England. (Illus.). 366p. 1992. pap. 12.95 (*0-9633929-0-5*) Northfld Pr.

Mattson, Timothy G., ed. Parallel Computing in Computational Chemistry. LC 95-1232. (ACS Symposium Ser.: No. 592). (Illus.). 232p. 1995. text 78.00 (*0-8412-3166-4*, Pub. by Am Chemical) OUP.

Mattson, W. J., et al, eds. Mechanisms of Woody Plant Defenses Against Insects. (Illus.). 435p. 1987. 141.00 (*0-387-96673-0*) Spr-Verlag.

*__Mattson, William J., et al, eds.__ Dynamics of Forest Herbivory: Quest for Pattern & Principle. (Illus.). 286p. (C). 1999. reprint ed. pap. text 35.00 (*0-7881-8235-8*) DIANE Pub.

Mattsson. Urban Land Property Markets Sweden. 256p. 1995. 75.00 (*1-85728-052-0*, Pub. by UCL Pr Ltd) Taylor & Francis.

*__Mattsson, Jan Eric, et al, eds.__ Swedish Lichenology: Dedicated to Roland Moberg. (Illus.). 210p. 1999. 58.50 (*91-554-4452-0*, Pub. by Uppsala Universitet) Coronet Bks.

Mattsson, Bengt. The Ascia Symbol on Latin Epitaphs. (Studies in Mediterranean Archaeology & Literature: No. 70). 153p. (Orig.). 1990. pap. 53.50 (*91-86098-83-7*, Pub. by P Astroms) Coronet Bks.

Mattsson, Einar. Basic Corrosion Technology Scientists & Engineers. 1989. text 59.95 (*0-470-21464-3*) P-H.

Mattsson, L., jt. auth. see Bennett, J. M.

Mattsson, L. G. & Stymne, B., eds. Corporate & Industry Strategies for Europe: Adaptations to the European Single Market in a Global Industrial Environment. (Advanced Series in Management: Vol. 15). 388p. 1995. 101.25 (*0-444-89182-X*, North Holland) Elsevier.

Mattsson, Lars-Goran, jt. ed. see Johansson, Borge.

Mattuck. First Course in Analysis. LC 98-25850. 460p. 1998. 76.00 (*0-13-081132-7*) P-H.

Mattuck, Richard D. A Guide to Feynman Diagrams in the Many-Body Problem. (Illus.). xv, 429p. 1992. reprint ed. pap. 11.95 (*0-486-67047-3*) Dover.

*__Mattusch, C. C., et al, eds.__ From the Parts to the Whole: ACTA of the 13th International Bronze Congress Held at Cambridge, MA, May 28 - June 1, 1996, Vol. 1. (Journal of Roman Archaeology Supplementary Ser.: Vol. 39). (Illus.). 288p. 2000. 129.00 (*1-887829-39-3*) Jour Roman Arch.

Mattusch, Carol C. Bronzeworkers in the Athenian Agora. (Excavations of the Athenian Agora Picture Bks.: No. 20). (Illus.). 32p. 1982. pap. 3.00 (*0-87661-624-4*) Am Sch Athens.

— Classical Bronzes: The Art & Craft of Greek & Roman Statuary. LC 95-36843. (Illus.). 280p. 1996. text 47.50 (*0-8014-3182-4*) Cornell U Pr.

— Greek Bronze Statuary: From the Beginnings Through the Fifth Century B. C. LC 88-47737. (Illus.). 288p. 1988. text 49.95 (*0-8014-2148-9*) Cornell U Pr.

— The Victorious Youth. LC 97-6758. (Getty Museum Studies on Art). 110p. 1997. pap. 17.50 (*0-89236-470-X*, Pub. by J P Getty Trust) OUP.

Mattusch, Max Hans-Jurgen. Vielsprachigkeit: Fluch Oder Segen fur die Menschheit? Zu Fragen Einer Europaischen und Globalen Fremdsprachenpolitik. (GER., Illus.). 321p. 1998. 51.95 (*3-631-30587-7*) P Lang Pubng.

Mattutat, Heinrich. Harrap's Compact Dictionary: German-French, French-German. rev. ed. (FRE & GER.). 646p. 1992. 49.95 (*0-7859-8591-3*, 055053783X) Fr & Eur.

Mattutat, Heinrich, jt. auth. see Weis, E.

Mattutat, Heinrich, jt. auth. see Weis, Erich.

Matty, Paul. Planning Publications: An Annotated Bibliography & Reference Guide. (CPL Bibliographies Ser.: No. 68). 100p. 1981. 10.00 (*0-86602-068-3*, Sage Prdcls Pr) Sage.

Matual, David. Tolstoy's Translation of the Gospels: A Critical Study. LC 92-6906. 212p. 1992. lib. bdg. 89.95 (*0-7734-9502-9*) E Mellen.

Matula, Arturo. Western Wildflowers. 48p. 1998. pap. 9.95 (*0-929526-83-X*) Green Grows Pr.

Matula, Janice, ed. Reading Across Disciplines. 4th ed. 168p. (C). 1998. pap. text 24.75 (*0-536-01545-7*) Pearson Custom.

Matula, Richard A., ed. see American Society of Mechanical Engineers Staff.

Matula, Susan, ed. see Goldberg, Mark.

Matulay, L. Aristophanes, Five Comedies: The Knights; Lysistrata; The Clouds; The Birds; The Frogs. 20.00 (*0-8196-2863-8*) Biblo.

Matulef, Mark L., et al. National Evaluation of the Supportive Housing Demonstration Program: Final Report. (Illus.). 300p. (Orig.). (C). 1995. pap. text 45.00 (*0-7881-1994-X*) DIANE Pub.

*__Matulic, Rusko.__ Bibliography of Sources on the Region of Former Yugoslavia. LC 98-72877. 450p. 1998. 63.00 (*0-88033-402-9*, 504, Pub. by East Eur Monographs) Col U Pr.

Matulic, Rusko. Bibliography of Sources on Yugoslavia. LC 80-53861. 260p. 1981. pap. 20.00 (*0-918660-13-0*) Ragusan Pr.

Matulich & Lamb, Charles W. Marketing. 3rd ed. (SB - Marketing Education Ser.). 1995. mass mkt., student ed. 22.95 (*0-538-84949-5*) S-W Pub.

Matulich, Loretta K. A Cross-Disciplinary Study of the European Immigrants of 1870 to 1925. Corasco, Francesco, ed. LC 80-878. (American Ethnic Groups Ser.). 1981. lib. bdg. 30.95 (*0-405-13439-8*) Ayer.

Matulich, Serge. Financial Accounting. 2nd ed. LC 94-5626. (Illus.). 876p. (C). 1994. text 60.00 (*1-881934-14-4*) Unicorn Res.

Matulka, Denise I. Picture This: Picture Books for Use with Young Adults a Curriculum-Related Annotated Bibliography. LC 97-2234. 296p. 1997. 39.95 (*0-313-30182-4*, Greenwood Pr) Greenwood.

Matunas, Edward A., jt. auth. see Zwirz, R. W.

Matura, Mustapha. The Coup: A Play of Revolutionary Dreams. (Methuen Modern Plays Ser.). 69p. (Orig.). (C). 1991. pap. write for info. (*0-413-65260-2*, AO563, Methuen Drama) Methn.

— Matura: Six Plays. 374p. (C). 1992. pap. 13.95 (*0-413-66070-2*, A0631, Methuen Drama) Methn.

— Playboy of the West Indies. 1988. pap. 6.95 (*0-88145-060-X*) Broadway Play.

Matura, Thaddee. A Dwelling Place for the Most High: Meditations with Francis of Assisi: or Fifteen Days with Francis of Assisi. Lachance, Paul, tr. from ENG. LC 98-11296. 1999. pap. 11.95 (*0-8199-0985-8*) Franciscan Pr.

— Francis of Assisi: The Message in His Writings. (Franciscan Sources Ser.). 208p. 1997. pap. text 18.00 (*1-57659-127-1*) Franciscan Inst.

— Gospel Radicalism: The Hard Sayings of Jesus. Despot, Maggi & Lachance, Paul, trs. from FRE. LC 83-6249. 208p. reprint ed. pap. 64.50 (*0-8357-2684-3*, 204022000015) Bks Demand.

Matura, Thaddee, jt. auth. see Flood, David.

Maturano, Humberto R. & Varela, Francisco J. The Tree of Knowledge: The Biological Roots of Human Understanding. rev. ed. LC 91-50781. (Illus.). 264p. pap. 29.95 (*0-87773-642-1*, Pub. by Shambhala Pubns) Random.

Maturi, Mary B. & Maturi, Richard J. Cultural Gems: An Eclectic Look at Unique United States Libraries. LC 95-90555. (Illus.). 208p. 1996. 29.95 (*0-9607298-1-X*) Twntyfirst Cent Pubs.

Maturi, Mary B., jt. auth. see Maturi, Richard J.

Maturi, Mary Buckingham, jt. auth. see Maturi, Richard J.

Maturi, Richard J. Divining the Dow: One Hundred of the World's Most Widely Followed Stock Market Prediction Systems. 200p. 1993. text 24.95 (*1-55738-475-4*) Twntyfirst Cent Pubs.

— Investor's Guide to Making MegaBucks on Mergers: How to Profit from Mergers, Acquisitions, Spinoffs, Stock Splits, & Other Corporate Restructurings. LC 96-90004. 224p. 1996. 24.95 (*0-9607298-2-8*) Twntyfirst Cent Pubs.

— Main Street Beats Wall Street: How the Top Investment Clubs Are Outperforming the Investment. 200p. 1994. text 24.95 (*1-55738-804-0*) Twntyfirst Cent Pubs.

— Money Making Investments Your Broker Doesn't Tell You About. LC 94-152197. 200p. 1993. text 24.95 (*1-55738-537-8*) Twntyfirst Cent Pubs.

— Stock Picking: The Eleven Best Tactics for Beating the Market. LC 93-36. 208p. 1993. pap. 14.95 (*0-07-040938-2*) McGraw.

— Wall Street Words: From Annuities to Zero Coupon Bonds, Revised Edition. rev. ed. 150p. 1995. per. 16.95 (*1-55738-865-2*, Irwn Prfssnl) McGraw-Hill Prof.

— Wall Street Words: The Basics & Beyond. (Investor's Quick Reference Ser.). 150p. 1991. per. 14.95 (*1-55738-195-X*, Irwn Prfssnl) McGraw-Hill Prof.

Maturi, Richard J. & Maturi, Mary B. Will Rogers, Performer: An Illustrated Biography with a Filmography. LC 99-14629. (Illus.). 285p. 1999. lib. bdg. 60.00 (*0-7864-0637-2*) McFarland & Co.

*__Maturi, Richard J. & Maturi, Mary Buckingham.__ Beverly Bayne, Queen of the Movies: A Biography with a Filmography & a Listing of Stage, Radio & Television Appearances. (Illus.). 212p. 2000. lib. bdg. 29.95 (*0-7864-0796-4*) McFarland & Co.

Maturi, Richard J. & Maturi, Mary Buckingham. Francis X Bushman: A Biography & Filmography. LC 98-7400. (Illus.). 264p. 1998. lib. bdg. 39.95 (*0-7864-0485-X*) McFarland & Co.

Maturi, Richard J., jt. auth. see Maturi, Mary B.

Maturi, Richard J., jt. auth. see Sosnowy, John K.

Maturin, B. W. Self-Knowledge & Self-Discipline. vi, 276p. 1995. text 18.95 (*0-912141-16-6*) Roman Cath Bks.

Maturin, Charles R. The Albigenses: A Romance, 4 vols., Set. LC 73-22768. (Gothic Novels II Ser.). 1979. reprint ed. 96.95 (*0-405-06017-3*) Ayer.

— Bertram, 1816. LC 92-36902. (Revolution & Romanticism Ser.). 110p. 1992. reprint ed. 48.00 (*1-85477-120-5*) Continuum.

— The Fatal Revenge: The Family of Montorio, 3 vols., Set. LC 73-22767. (Gothic Novels II Ser.). 1979. reprint ed. 94.95 (*0-405-06018-1*) Ayer.

— Melmoth the Wanderer. LC 88-37955. (Oxford World's Classics Ser.). 584p. 1998. pap. 11.95 (*0-19-283592-0*) OUP.

— Melmoth the Wanderer: A Tale. LC 61-5561. 434p. reprint ed. pap. 134.60 (*0-608-16019-9*, 203311400083) Bks Demand.

— The Milesian Chief: A Romance, 4 vols., 2 bks., Set. LC 79-8172. reprint ed. 84.50 (*0-404-62038-8*) AMS Pr.

— The Wild Irish Boy. Varma, Devendra P., ed. LC 77-2043. (Gothic Novels Ser.: No. III). 1977. lib. bdg. 72.95 (*0-405-10141-4*) Ayer.

— Women: or Pour et Contre, 3 vols., 2 bks., Set. LC 79-8173. reprint ed. 84.50 (*0-404-62043-4*) AMS Pr.

Maturo, Cathy, ed. see Maturo, Jeffrey.

Maturo, Jeffrey. The ABCs of Handguns & Shooting. Maturo, Cathy, ed. (Illus.). 41p. 1995. pap. 8.95 (*0-9645196-0-7*) Ambass Prod.

Matus. Toni Morrison: Contemporary Critical Essays. 150p. 1998. pap. 19.95 (*0-7190-4448-0*, Pub. by Manchester Univ Pr); text 59.95 (*0-7190-4447-2*, Pub. by Manchester Univ Pr) St Martin.

Matus, Irvin Leigh. Shakespeare, in Fact. LC 96-23394. 336p. 1997. pap. 22.50 (*0-8264-0928-8*) Continuum.

— Shakespeare, the Living Record. LC 92-128349. xii, 174 p. 1991. write for info. (*0-333-51981-7*) Macmillan.

Matus, Irwin. Wrestling with Parenthood: Contemporary Dilemmas. LC 94-41833. 180p. 1995. pap. 12.95 (*1-880197-12-X*) Gylantic Pub.

Matus, Jean L. Pip of Weeville. LC 88-70820. (Illus.). 16p. (J). (ps-2). 1987. lib. bdg. 11.95 (*0-945938-00-4*) Peartree.

Matus, Thomas. Bede Griffiths: A Universal Monk. (Modern Spiritual Masters Ser.). 128p. 1998. pap. 13.00 (*1-57075-200-1*) Orbis Bks.

— Nazarena an American Anchoress. LC 98-14691. 208p. 1998. pap. 16.95 (*0-8091-3792-5*, 3792-5) Paulist Pr.

Matus, Thomas, et al. Mystery of Master Romuald: History of Camaldolese Benedictines. LC 94-31045. 220p. 1994. pap. 12.95 (*0-940147-33-5*) Source Bks CA.

Matus, Todd. Broken Views: A Document of Eastern Europe. Chapp, Belena S., ed. LC 97-60124. (Illus.). 64p. (Orig.). 1997. pap. 15.00 (*1-887421-02-5*) Univ Gall U of DE.

Matusak, Larraine R. Finding Your Voice: Learning to Lead-- Anywhere You Want to Make a Difference. LC 96-25322. 1996. pap. 17.95 (*0-7879-0305-1*) Jossey-Bass.

Matusak, Larraine R., jt. auth. see Kellerman, Barbara.

Matuschak, George M. Multiple Systems Organ Failure: Hepatic Regulation of Systemic Host Defense. (Illus.). 408p. 1993. text 199.00 (*0-8247-9059-6*) Dekker.

Matuschka, James C. Alter Universe. 178p. mass mkt. 4.99 (*1-55197-322-7*) Picasso Publ.

Matusiak, John. Orthodox Clip Art. (Illus.). 87p. 1987. pap. 17.95 (*1-880971-55-0*) Light&Life Pub Co MN.

Matusita, K., et al, eds. Statistical Sciences & Data Analysis: Proceedings of the Third Pacific Area Statistica Conference. x, 570p. 1993. 245.00 (*90-6764-150-2*) Coronet Bks.

Matusky, Gregory, jt. auth. see Raab, Steven S.

Matusmura, Fumio. Toxicology of Insecticides. 2nd ed. LC 85-12371. 618p. 1985. 75.00 (*0-306-41979-3*, Plenum Trade) Perseus Pubng.

Matusof, Eliyahu, ed. Maamarei Admur Hatzemach Tzedek, 5614-5615. (HEB.). 326p. 1998. 18.00 (*0-8266-6014-2*) Kehot Pubn Soc.

Matusow, Allen J. Farm Policies & Politics in the Truman Years. LC 67-12101. (Historical Studies: No. 80). 279p. 1967. 17.50 (*0-674-29500-5*) HUP.

— Joseph R. McCarthy. vii, 181p. 1970. 8.95 (*0-13-566729-1*, Spectrum IN) Macmillan Gen Ref.

— Nixon's Economy: Booms, Busts, Dollars, & Votes. LC 97-49995. 288p. 1998. 35.00 (*0-7006-0888-5*) U Pr of KS.

Matusow, David G. Sna, Appn, Hpr & Tcp/Ip Integration. (Illus.). 452p. 1996. 55.00 (*0-07-041051-8*) McGraw.

Matussek, N., jt. ed. see Hippius, H.

Matussek, Paul, jt. auth. see Egenter, Richard.

Matustik, Martin J. Specters of Liberation: Great Refusals in the New World Order. LC 97-17277. (SUNY Series in Radical Social & Political Theory). 320p. (C). 1998. pap. text 23.95 (*0-7914-3692-6*) State U NY Pr.

— Specters of Liberation: Great Refusals in the New World Order. LC 97-17277. (SUNY Series in Radical Social & Political Theory). 320p. (C). 1998. text 71.50 (*0-7914-3691-8*) State U NY Pr.

Matustik, Martin J. & Havel, Vaclav. Postnational Identity: Critical Theory & Existential Philosophy in Habermas, Kierkegaard & Havel. LC 92-42692. (Critical Perspectives Ser.). 328p. 1993. pap. text 18.95 (*0-89862-270-0*) Guilford Pubns.

Matustik, Martin J. & Westphal, Merold, eds. Kierkegaard in Post-Modernity. LC 94-46241. (Studies in Continental Thought). 320p. 1995. text 39.95 (*0-253-32888-8*); pap. text 18.95 (*0-253-20967-6*) Ind U Pr.

Matuszak, David F. Nelson Point: Portrait of a Northern Gold Rush Town. large type ed. LC 92-64297. (Illus.). 270p. (Orig.). 1993. pap. 19.95 (*0-9633582-0-0*) Pacific Sunset.

*__Matuszewski, Barbara B.__ 70 Years of Pioneering & Professionalism: A Celebration of Culinary Excellence by the American Culinary Federation. (Illus.). 80p. 1999. 29.95 (*0-9673403-0-6*) Am Culinary Fed.

Matuszewski, Daniel, jt. ed. see Thambipillai, Pushpa.

Matutano, Jose R. Diccionario Terminologico de Quimica. 2nd ed. (ENG, GER & SPA.). 786p. 1982. pap. 105.00 (*0-7859-5095-8*) Fr & Eur.

Matute. Historias de la Artamila Level C. text 8.95 (*0-88436-889-0*) EMC-Paradigm.

Matute, Ana M. Algunos Muchachos. (SPA.). pap. 13.95 (*84-233-1182-1*, Pub. by Destino) Continental Bk.

— El Arrepentido y Otras Narraciones. (SPA.). 1989. 13.50 (*0-8288-2570-X*, S2295) Fr & Eur.

— Celebration in the Northwest. Porter, Phoebe A., tr. from SPA. & intro. by. LC 96-18583. (European Women Writers Ser.). xvii, 86p. 1997. pap. 12.00 (*0-8032-8196-X*); text 35.00 (*0-8032-3180-6*) U of Nebr Pr.

— Celebration in the Northwest. Porter, Phoebe A., tr. & intro. by. LC 96-18583. (European Women Writers Ser.). x, 139p. 1998. pap. 12.00 (*0-8032-8229-X*, Bison Books) U of Nebr Pr.

— Fiesta al Noroeste. (SPA.). pap. 13.95 (*84-233-1072-8*, Pub. by Destino) Continental Bk.

— Fiesta al Noroeste. (SPA.). pap. 14.95 (*84-376-0150-9*, Pub. by Ediciones Catedra) Continental Bk.

— Fireflies. Glafyra, Ennis, tr. LC 98-22630. (Catalan Studies: Vol. 21). 241p. (C). 1998. pap. 39.95 (*0-8204-3015-3*) P Lang Pubng.

— The Heliotrope Wall & Other Stories. Doyle, Michael S., tr. 160p. 1989. text 44.50 (*0-231-06556-6*) Col U Pr.

— Historia de Artamila. (SPA.). pap. 14.50 (*84-233-2323-4*, Pub. by Destino) Continental Bk.

— Los de Abel. (SPA.). pap. 15.50 (*84-233-1108-2*, Pub. by Destino) Continental Bk.

— Los Ninos Tontos. (SPA.). pap. 11.95 (*84-233-0958-4*, Pub. by Destino) Continental Bk.

— Primera Memoria. (SPA.). pap. 17.95 (*84-233-0726-3*, Pub. by Destino) Continental Bk.

— School of the Sun. 256p. 1989. text 61.50 (*0-231-06916-2*); pap. text 18.50 (*0-231-06917-0*) Col U Pr.

— Los Soldados Lloran de Noche. (SPA.). pap. 15.50 (*84-233-0243-1*, Pub. by Destino) Continental Bk.

— Soldiers Cry by Night. Miller, Yvette E., ed. Nugent, Robert & De la Camara, Maria, trs. from SPA. LC 94-25087. (Discoveries Ser.). 160p. 1995. pap. 16.95 (*0-935480-67-6*) Lat Am Lit Rev Pr.

— El Tiempo. (SPA.). pap. 17.95 (*84-233-1157-0*, Pub. by Destino) Continental Bk.

— La Trampa. (SPA.). pap. 15.95 (*84-233-1069-8*, Pub. by Destino) Continental Bk.

— The Trap. Jose De La Camara, Maria & Nugent, Robert, trs. from SPA. LC 96-17096. (Discoveries Ser.).Tr. of La Trampa. 220p. (C). 1996. pap. 15.95 (*0-935480-81-1*) Lat Am Lit Rev Pr.

Matute, Leonel M. Manual de Interpretacion - LSM Dictionary: Mexican Sign Language Dictionary. (ENG & SPA., Illus.). 254p. 1997. pap. 19.95 (*0-915035-70-7*) Dawn Sign.

***Matutes, Estella.** T-Cell Lymphoproliferative Disorders: Classification, Clinical & Laboratory Aspects. 104p. 1998. text 65.00 (*90-5702-352-0*, Harwood Acad Pubs) Gordon & Breach.

Matuz, Roger. Contemporary Literary Criticism, Vol. 45. Marowski, Daniel G., ed. 792p. 1987. text 150.00 (*0-8103-4419-X*) Gale.

— Contemporary Literary Criticism, Vol. 64. 500p. 1991. text 150.00 (*0-8103-4438-6*) Gale.

— Contemporary Literary Criticism, Vol. 65. 500p. 1991. text 150.00 (*0-8103-4439-4*) Gale.

— Contemporary Literary Criticism, Vol. 66. 500p. 1991. text 150.00 (*0-8103-4440-8*) Gale.

— Contemporary Literary Criticism, Vol. 67. 500p. 1991. text 150.00 (*0-8103-4975-2*) Gale.

Matuz, Roger. Contemporary Literary Criticism, Vol. 68. 1992. 150.00 (*0-8103-4442-4*) Gale.

Matuz, Roger. Contemporary Literary Criticism, Vol. 69. 500p. 1992. text 150.00 (*0-8103-4446-7*) Gale.

— Contemporary Literary Criticism, Vol. 70. 500p. 1992. text 150.00 (*0-8103-4447-5*) Gale.

— Contemporary Literary Criticism, Vol. 71. 500p. 1992. text 150.00 (*0-8103-4448-3*) Gale.

— Contemporary Literary Criticism, Vol. 72. 500p. 1992. text 150.00 (*0-8103-4976-0*) Gale.

— Contemporary Literary Criticism, Vol. 72. 500p. 1992. text 140.00 (*0-8103-4977-9*) Gale.

Matuz, Roger. Contemporary Literary Criticism, Vol. 74. 1993. 150.00 (*0-8103-4978-7*) Gale.

Matuz, Roger. Contemporary Literary Criticism, Vol. 74. 500p. 1993. text 150.00 (*0-8103-4980-9*) Gale.

— Contemporary Literary Criticism, Vol. 75. 500p. 1993. text 150.00 (*0-8103-4981-7*) Gale.

— Contemporary Literary Criticism, Vol. 76. 500p. 1993. text 150.00 (*0-8103-4982-5*) Gale.

— Contemporary Literary Criticism, Vol. 77. 500p. 1993. text 150.00 (*0-8103-4983-3*) Gale.

— Contemporary Literary Criticism, Vol. 78. 500p. 1993. text 150.00 (*0-8103-4986-8*) Gale.

— Contemporary Literary Criticism, Vol. 79. 500p. 1994. text 150.00 (*0-8103-4987-6*) Gale.

Matuz, Roger. Contemporary Literary Criticism, Vol. 79. 1994. 140.00 (*0-8103-4984-1*) Gale.

Matuz, Roger. Contemporary Literary Criticism, Vol. 80. 500p. 1994. text 150.00 (*0-8103-4988-4*) Gale.

— Contemporary Literary Criticism, Vol. 82. 500p. 1994. text 150.00 (*0-8103-4990-6*) Gale.

— Contemporary Literary Criticism Vol. 63: In, Vol. 63. 500p. 1991. text 150.00 (*0-8103-4437-8*) Gale.

— Contemporary Literary Criticism Vol. 81: Yb 93, Vol. 81. 8th ed. 500p. 1994. text 150.00 (*0-8103-4989-2*) Gale.

— Contemporary Literary Criticism & Index, Vol. 68. 500p. 1992. text 140.00 (*0-8103-4445-9*) Gale.

Matuz, Roger. Contemporary Southern Writers. LC 98-35875. 442p. 1999. 140.00 (*1-55862-370-1*) St James Pr.

— The Handy Sports Answer Book. LC 98-16994. 1998. write for info. (*1-57859-065-5*) Visible Ink Pr.

— Inside Sports: Golf Encyclopedia. LC 97-12946. (Illus.). 640p. 1997. 19.95 (*1-57859-007-8*, 00156950) Visible Ink Pr.

Matuz, Roger, ed. Contemporary Literary Criticism, Vol. 55. 600p. 1989. text 150.00 (*0-8103-4429-7*) Gale.

— Contemporary Literary Criticism, Vol. 56. 535p. 1989. text 150.00 (*0-8103-4430-0*) Gale.

— Contemporary Literary Criticism, Vol. 58. 435p. 1990. text 150.00 (*0-8103-4432-7*) Gale.

— Contemporary Literary Criticism, Vol. 60. (Illus.). 525p. 1990. text 150.00 (*0-8103-4434-3*) Gale.

— Contemporary Literary Criticism, Vol. 61. (Illus.). 525p. 1990. text 150.00 (*0-8103-4435-1*) Gale.

— Contemporary Literary Criticism & Index, Vol. 57. 500p. 1990. text 140.00 (*0-8103-4449-1*) Gale.

Matuz, Roger, et al. The Handy Sports Answer Book. LC 98-16994. (Illus.). 546p. 1998. pap. 19.95 (*1-57859-075-2*) Visible Ink Pr.

Matuz, Roger, jt. auth. see Marowski, Daniel G.

Matuz, Roger, jt. ed. see Marowski, Daniel G.

***Matveev, A. & Savkin, A.** Qualitative Theory of Hybrid Dynamical Systems. (Control Engineering Ser.). 352p. 2000. 69.95 (*0-8176-4141-6*, Pub. by Birkhauser) Spr-Verlag.

Matveev, L. T. Cloud Dynamics. 1984. text 247.50 (*90-277-1737-0*) Kluwer Academic.

Matveev, S. V., jt. auth. see Fomenko, A. T.

Matveev, V. A., et al. Particles & Cosmology: International School, Bakson Valley, Moscow, 6-12 May 1991. Alexeev, E. N. et al, eds. 400p. 1992. text 109.00 (*981-02-1002-7*) World Scientific Pub.

Matveev, V. B. & Salle, M. A. Darboux Transformations & Solitons. (Nonlinear Dynamics Ser.). (Illus.). 144p. 1991. 98.95 (*0-387-50660-8*) Spr-Verlag.

Matveeva, Anna. The North Caucasus: Russia's Fragile Borderland. (Central Asian & Caucasian Prospects Ser.). 96p. 1998. pap. 12.95 (*1-86203-062-6*, Pub. by Royal Inst Intl Affairs) Brookings.

Matveeva, N., jt. ed. see Makarov, V.

Matveeva, N. M. & Kozlov, E. V. Ordered Phases in Metallic Systems. (Illus.). 237p. (C). 1996. lib. bdg. 135.00 (*1-56072-357-2*) Nova Sci Pubs.

***Matvejevic, Predrag.** Mediterranean: A Cultural Landscape. LC 98-47186. 210p. 1999. 29.95 (*0-520-20738-6*, Pub. by U CA Pr) Cal Prin Full Svc.

Matveyev, Vladimir. The Hermitage: Selected Treasures from One of the World's Great Museums. Booth-Clibbon, Edward, ed. (Illus.). 164p. 1999. reprint ed. text 25.00 (*0-7881-6442-2*) DIANE Pub.

Matwiyoff, Nicholas A. Magnetic Resonance. LC 89-10774. (Illus.). 134p. reprint ed. pap., wbk. ed. 41.60 (*0-608-07189-7*, 206741400009) Bks Demand.

Matyakin, E. G. Oncology Reviews Vol. 4, Pt. 2: Oropharyngeal Region Cancer - Modern Problems of Diagnosis, Treatment & Prognosis - the Oncological Service in the U. S. S. R., Vol. 4. (Soviet Medical Reviews Ser.: Section F). 108p. 1991. pap. text 130.00 (*3-7186-5230-7*, Harwood Acad Pubs) Gordon & Breach.

Matyas, Csaba, jt. auth. see Giertych, Maciej.

Matyas, David E. Legal Issues in Healthcare Fraud & Abuse: Navigating the Uncertainties. 2nd ed. LC 96-70114. (NHLA Focus Ser.). 403p. 1997. 75.00 (*0-918945-19-4*) Am Hlth Lawyers.

Matyas, Laslo, ed. Generalized Method of Moments Estimation. LC 98-51529. (Themes in Modern Econometrics Ser.: Vol. 5). (Illus.). 328p. (C). 1999. 54.95 (*0-521-66013-0*) Cambridge U Pr.

***Matyas, Laslo, ed.** Generalized Method of Moments Estimation. LC 98-51529. (Themes in Modern Econometrics Ser.: Vol. 5). (Illus.). 328p. (C). 1999. pap. 19.95 (*0-521-66967-7*) Cambridge U Pr.

Matyas, Laszlo & Sevestre, Patrick, eds. The Econometrics of Panel Data: A Handbook of the Theory with Applications. 2nd rev. ed. (Advanced Studies in Theoretical & Applied Econometrics: Vol. 33). 948p. (C). 1996. lib. bdg. 150.00 (*0-7923-3787-5*) Kluwer Academic.

— The Econometrics of Panel Data: Handbook of Theory & Applications. LC 92-35605. (Advanced Studies in Theoretical & Applied Econometrics: Vol. 28). 1992. lib. bdg. 194.50 (*0-7923-2043-3*) Kluwer Academic.

Matyas, Marsha L. & Malcom, Shirley M. Investing in Human Potential: Science & Engineering at the Crossroads. 165p. 1991. 9.95 (*0-87168-430-6*, 91-39S) AAAS.

Matyas, Marsha L. & Triana, Estrella, eds. Proyecto Futuro: Science & Mathematics Activities in English & Spanish. (Illus.). 450p. 1992. pap. write for info. (*0-87168-507-8*, 92-38B) AAAS.

Matyas, Marsha L., ed. see National Research Council Staff.

Matyas, Robert M., et al. Construction Dispute Review Board Manual. LC 95-32923. 175p. 1995. 49.95 (*0-07-041060-7*) McGraw.

Matyas, Stephen M., jt. auth. see Meyer, Carl H.

Matyi, Robert. My God - They're Real! LC 78-32013. 1979. 22.95 (*0-87949-150-7*) Ashley Bks.

Matyja, H. & Zielenski, P. G., eds. Amorphous Metals: Proceedings of the Summer School on Amorphous Metals, Wilga, Poland, Sept. 16-21, 1985. 352p. 1987. text 131.00 (*9971-5-0109-0*) World Scientific Pub.

Matyjaszewski, Krzysztof. Cationic Polymerization: Mechanisms, Synthesis & Applications. (Plastics Engineering Ser.: Vol. 35). (Illus.). 784p. 1996. text 225.00 (*0-8247-9463-X*) Dekker.

***Matyjaszewski, K.** Controlled/Living Radical Polymerization: Progress in ATRP, NMP & Raft. LC 00-32254. (Symposium Ser.). 480p. 2000. text. write for info. (*0-8412-3707-7*) Am Chemical.

Matyjaszewski, Krzysztof, ed. Controlled Radical Polymerization, Vol. 685. LC 97-43731. (ACS Symposium Ser.: No. 685). (Illus.). 484p. 1998. text 135.00 (*0-8412-3545-7*, Pub. by Am Chemical) OUP.

Matyssek, H. Handbuch der Notizentechnik fur Dolmetscher, 2 vols. (GER.). 893p. 1989. pap. 70.00 (*3-87276-616-3*, Pub. by Julius Groos) IBD Ltd.

***Matystik, Walter F., et al.** State Environmental Agencies on the Internet. LC 99-53924. 344p. 1999. pap. 59.00 (*0-86587-685-1*, 685) Gov Insts.

Matz, Adolph. Cost Accounting: Planning & Control. 8th ed. (Thomson Executive Press). (C). 1983. pap. 43.00 (*0-538-01870-4*, A87) S-W Pub.

Matz, B. W. The Inns & Taverns of Pickwick. LC 72-6718. (Studies in Dickens: No. 52). (Illus.). 261p. 1972. reprint ed. lib. bdg. 75.00 (*0-8383-1644-1*) M S G Haskell Hse.

***Matz, Benjamin.** The History & Development of the Quartz Watch. (Illus.). 64p. 1999. pap. text 14.95 (*0-9653053-0-9*) Kalbe Pr.

Matz, Carol, ed. see Faber, Nancy & Faber, Randall.

Matz, Dale, jt. auth. see Edgar, Pamela.

Matz, David. An Ancient Rome Chronology, 264-27 B. C. LC 96-46861. 236p. 1997. lib. bdg. 42.50 (*0-7864-0161-3*) McFarland & Co.

— Ancient World Lists & Numbers: Numerical Phrases & Rosters in the Greco-Roman Civilizations. LC 95-3197. 264p. 1995. lib. bdg. 46.50 (*0-7864-0039-0*) McFarland & Co.

***Matz, David.** Famous Firsts in the Ancient Greek & Roman World. LC 99-52497. 160p. 2000. lib. bdg. 35.00 (*0-7864-0599-6*) McFarland & Co.

Matz, David. Greek & Roman Sport: A Dictionary of Athletes & Events from the Eighth Century B.C. to the Third Century A.D. LC 90-53509. 175p. 1991. lib. bdg. 32.50 (*0-89950-558-9*) McFarland & Co.

Matz, David E., jt. auth. see Hoffman, David A.

Matz, Karl A. Themes Across the Curriculum: Ready-to-Use Activities & Projects for the Elementary Classroom. 338p. 1995. pap. text 27.95 (*0-87628-907-3*) Ctr Appl Res.

— Themes & Bulletin Boards Across the Curriculum: Ready-to-Use Activities & Projects for the Elementary Classroom. 338p. 1998. pap. 27.50 (*0-87628-139-0*) Ctr Appl Res.

Matz, Leonard M. Banker's Guide To Investing in Mortgage-Backed Securities LC 94-225375. (Financial Management Ser.). 1994. write for info. (*1-55827-161-9*) Sheshunoff.

— Self-Paced Bank Investment Training LC 99-186331. 1998. write for info. (*1-55827-262-3*) Sheshunoff.

Matz, Leonard M. & Sheshunoff Information Services Staff. Corporate Investment Guide Series. LC 98-177643. 1997. write for info. (*1-55827-196-1*) Sheshunoff.

Matz, Marc. Nocturne for a Dangerous Man. LC 99-22968. 448p. 1999. 25.95 (*0-312-86935-5*, Pub. by Tor Bks) St Martin.

***Matz, Marc.** Nocturne for a Dangerous Man. 2000. mass mkt. 6.99 (*0-8125-7537-7*, Pub. by Tor Bks) St Martin.

Matz, Michael G. Succeding. What It Is. How to Do It: Featuring the Triad Formula for Success. Snodgrass, Kay, ed. 144p. 1998. pap. 17.97 (*0-9667641-3-7*) Pinnacle Rock.

Matz, Nancy J. Two Worlds: Developing Your Psychic Skills. 2nd ed. Douglas, Marion, ed. (Illus.). 134p. 1994. reprint ed. pap. 11.95 (*0-9647802-0-8*) N Matz Coun.

Matz, Onas P. History of the Second Ferrying Group Ferrying Division, Air Transport Command: New Castle Army Air Base, Wilmington, Delaware. LC 92-63231. (Illus.). 419p. 1993. lib. bdg. 49.95 (*0-9635652-0-6*) Modet Ent.

***Matz, Robert.** Defending Literature in Early Modern England: Renaissance Literary Theory in Social Context. (Cambridge Studies in Renaissance Literature & Culture: Vol. 37). 240p. 2000. 59.95 (*0-521-66080-7*) Cambridge U Pr.

Matz, Ruth G., jt. auth. see Botsford, Margot.

Matz, Samuel A. Bakery Technology: Nutrition, Packaging, Product Development, QA. LC 88-33634. (Illus.). 384p. 1989. text 69.00 (*0-942849-03-5*) Pan Tech Intl.

— Bakery Technology & Engineering. 3rd ed. (Illus.). 850p. 1991. text 149.00 (*0-942849-07-8*) Pan Tech Intl.

— The Chemistry & Technology of Cereals As Food & Feed. 2nd ed. (Illus.). 650p. 1991. text 99.00 (*0-942849-06-X*) Pan Tech Intl.

— Cookie & Cracker Technology. 3rd ed. (Illus.). 420p. 1992. 79.00 (*0-942849-09-4*) Pan Tech Intl.

— Equipment for Bakers. LC 88-9747. (Illus.). 494p. (C). 1988. 69.00 (*0-942849-02-7*) Pan Tech Intl.

— Formulas & Processes for Bakers. 2nd ed. (Illus.). 416p. (C). 1997. 79.00 (*0-942849-15-9*) Pan Tech Intl.

— Formulating & Processing Dietetic Foods. unabridged ed. (Illus.). 312p. 1996. text 89.00 (*0-942849-13-2*) Pan Tech Intl.

— Glossary of Cereal Science & Technology. LC 94-48585. 220p. (C). 1995. text 29.00 (*0-942849-14-0*) Pan Tech Intl.

— Glossary of Milling & Baking Terms. 120p. (C). 1993. lib. bdg. 19.00 (*0-942849-10-8*) Pan Tech Intl.

Matz, Samuel A. Ingredients for Bakers. 1996. text 126.00 (*1-85573-414-1*, Pub. by Woodhead Pubng) Am Educ Systs.

Matz, Samuel A. Ingredients for Bakers. 2nd rev. ed. (Illus.). 348p. (C). 1996. text 89.00 (*0-942849-17-5*) Pan Tech Intl.

— Snack Food Technology. 3rd ed. 415p. (gr. 13). 1992. 138.00 (*0-442-30893-0*) Chapman & Hall.

— Snack Food Technology. 3rd rev. ed. LC 92-31152. (Illus.). 450p. (C). 1993. text 79.00 (*0-942849-08-6*) Pan Tech Intl.

— Technology of Food Product Development. 300p. 1993. 79.00 (*0-942849-11-6*) Pan Tech Intl.

Matz, Terry. Lost in God: Rediscovering Modern Prayer Form in Traditional Saints. LC 94-76023. 64p. (Orig.). 1994. pap. 2.95 (*0-89243-674-3*) Liguori Pubns.

Matza, Aleks. The Video Production Organizer: A Guide for Businesses, Schools, Government Agencies & Professional Associations. LC 94-44269. (Illus.). 248p. 1995. pap. 36.95 (*0-240-80229-2*, Focal) Buttrwrth-Heinemann.

Matza, David. Delinquency & Drift. 224p. 1989. pap. 21.95 (*0-88738-804-3*) Transaction Pubs.

Matza, David, jt. auth. see Sykes, Gresham M.

Matza, Diane, ed. Sephardic-American Voices: Two Hundred Years of a Literary Legacy. LC 96-25559. (Brandeis Series in American Jewish History, Culture, & Life). (Illus.). 377p. 1997. pap. 19.95 (*0-87451-890-3*); text 50.00 (*0-87451-786-9*) U Pr of New Eng.

Matzaganian, Edward. Middle Eastern Recipes for Healthy Eating. 104p. 1998. pap. 17.95 (*0-931541-43-3*) Mancorp Pub.

Matzat, B. H., et al, eds. Algorithmic Algebra & Number Theory: Selected Papers of a Conference Held at the University of Heidelberg in October 1997. x, 490p. 1998. pap. 85.00 (*3-540-64670-1*) Spr-Verlag.

Matzat, B. Heinrich, jt. auth. see Malle, Gunter.

Matzat, Don. Christ-Esteem. LC 89-27039. 207p. 1990. pap. 8.99 (*0-89081-784-7*) Harvest Hse.

Matzdorff, Axel C., tr. see Virchow, Rudolf L.

Matze, Claire S. The Stars in My Geddoh's Sky. LC 98-39185. (Illus.). (J). (gr. k-3). 1999. pap. 14.95 (*0-8075-5332-8*) A Whitman.

Matzen, Mary, ed. see Byham, William C. & Pickett, Debra.

Matzen, Richard N. Clinical Preventive Medicine. (Illus.). 1263p. (C). (gr. 13). 1993. text 105.00 (*0-8016-3176-9*, 03176) Mosby Inc.

Matzen, Robert D. Carole Lombard: A Bio-Bibliography, 4. LC 88-15429. (Bio-Bibliographies in the Performing Arts Ser.: No. 4). 181p. 1988. lib. bdg. 52.95 (*0-313-26286-1*, MZL/, Greenwood Pr) Greenwood.

Matzen, Tom. Start & Run a Profitable Coffee Bar. (Business Ser.). 1999. pap. 16.95 (*1-55180-253-8*) Self-Counsel Pr.

Matzer, John, Jr., ed. Advanced Supervisory Practices. LC 92-15124. (Municipal Management Ser.). 196p. 1992. pap. 29.95 (*0-87326-087-2*) Intl City-Cnty Mgt.

Matzer, John, Jr., ed. Capital Financing Strategies for Local Governments. (Practical Management Ser.). (Illus.). 208p. (Orig.). 1983. pap. 23.95 (*0-87326-037-6*) Intl City-Cnty Mgt.

— Capital Projects: New Strategies for Planning, Management, & Finance. LC 89-27321. (Practical Management Ser.). 230p. 1989. pap. 23.95 (*0-87326-059-7*) Intl City-Cnty Mgt.

— Pay & Benefits: New Ideas for Local Government. (Practical Management Ser.). (Orig.). 1988. pap. text 23.95 (*0-87326-056-2*) Intl City-Cnty Mgt.

— Personnel Practices for the Nineties: A Local Government Guide. (Practical Management Ser.). (Orig.). 1988. pap. text 23.95 (*0-87326-055-4*) Intl City-Cnty Mgt.

— Practical Financial Management: New Techniques for Local Governments. (Practical Management Ser.). (Illus.). 207p. 1984. pap. text 23.95 (*0-87326-043-0*) Intl City-Cnty Mgt.

Matzer, Mario & Hafellner, Josef. Eine Revision der Lichenicolen Arten der Sammelgattung Rosellina (Ascomycetes) Wirth, Volkmar et al, eds. (Bibliotheca Lichenologica: Vol. 37). (GER., Illus.). 146p. 1990. 48.00 (*3-443-58016-5*, Pub. by Gebruder Borntraeger) Balogh.

Matzerath, Horst, jt. ed. see Engeli, Christian.

Matzeu, M. & Vignoli, A., eds. Topological Nonlinear Analysis II. LC 97-167225. (Progress in Nonlinear Differential Equations & Their Applications Ser.). 325p. 1997. 120.00 (*0-8176-3886-5*) Birkhauser.

Matzeu, Michele & Vignoli, Alfonso, eds. Topological Nonlinear Analysis: Degree, Singularity, & Variations. LC 94-5251. (Progress in Nonlinear Differential Equations & Their Applications Ser.: Vol. 15). ix, 531p. 1994. 104.50 (*0-8176-3742-7*) Birkhauser.

Matzig, Stefan, tr. see Dockray, Tracy A. & Grimm, Wilhelm K.

Matzinger-Tchakerian, Margit & Odell, John. European Community Enlargement & the United States. (Pew Case Studies in International Affairs). 54p. (C). 1992. pap. text 3.50 (*1-56927-130-5*) Geo U Inst Dplmcy.

***Matzkanin, George A.** World Heritage Wilderness: From the Wrangells to Glacier Bay, Vol. 26, No. 2. Rennick, Penny, ed. LC 72-92087. (Illus.). 100p. 1999. pap. 21.95 (*1-56661-045-1*) Alaska Geog Soc.

***Matzkanin, George A. & Easter, Jacob K.** NDE of Hidden Corrosion. (Illus.). 61p. 1998. pap. 75.00 (*1-890596-05-1*, NTIAC-SR-98-03) TX Res Inst.

Matzkanin, George A. & Hansen, George P. Heat Damage in Graphite Epoxy Composites. (Illus.). 67p. 1998. pap. 75.00 (*1-890596-07-8*, NTIAC-SR-98-02) TX Res Inst.

Matzkanin, George A., jt. auth. see Easter, Jacob K.

Matzkanin, George A., jt. auth. see Rummel, Ward D.

Matzkanin, George A., jt. ed. see Kenny, Paul G.

Matzkanin, George A., jt. ed. see Palmer, Donald D.

Matzke, Bernd. ABAP-4: A Guide to the Language of the R-3 System. Weinland, Audrey, tr. LC 97-180511. 448p. (C). 1997. 45.95 (*0-201-92471-4*) Addison-Wesley.

Matzke, Frederick & Schuetze, Armin W. The Counseling Shepherd. LC 88-61281. 255p. 1988. 21.99 (*0-8100-0295-7*, 15N0463) Northwest Pub.

Matzke, H., ed. Indentation Fracture & Mechanical Properties of Ceramic Fuels & Glasses. (Applied Research Reports). 246p. 1987. pap. text 240.00 (*3-7186-0443-4*) Gordon & Breach.

Matzku, Siegfried & Stahel, Rolf A., eds. Antibodies in Diagnosis & Therapy: Technologies Mechanisms & Clinical Data. (Studies in Medicinal Chemistry Ser.: Vol. 3). 328p. 1999. text 79.00 (*90-5702-310-5*, ECU113, Harwood Acad Pubs) Gordon & Breach.

Matzler, C. Applications of the Interaction of Microwaves with the Natural Snow Cover, Vol.2. Becker, F., ed. (Remote Sensing Reviews Ser.: Vol. 2, No. 2). ii, 132p. 1987. pap. text 182.00 (*3-7186-0416-7*) Gordon & Breach.

Matzner. Muselmann: Holocaust Memoirs. LC 92-47104. 1993. 20.00 (*0-88125-457-6*) Ktav.

Matzner, Egon & Streck, Wolfgang, eds. Beyond Keynesianism: The Socio-Economics of Production & Full Employment. 288p. 1991. pap. 35.00 (*1-85898-072-0*) E Elgar.

***Matzner, Florian.** Wolfgang Winter. 2000. pap. 14.95 (*3-7757-0843-X*) Gerd Hatje.

Matzner, Joseph. She Loves Me, She Loves Me Knot. (Illus.). 32p. (Orig.). 1993. pap. 8.95 (*0-317-05730-8*) J Matzner.

Matzner, William, et al. Miscarriages Can Be Prevented: Hope & Help for Couples Who Thought They Could Never Have a Baby. (Illus.). 110p. 1998. pap. write for info. (*1-57502-778-X*, P02153) Morris Pubng.

Matzo, Marianne, jt. ed. see Fulmer, Terry.

***Matzuk, Martin, et al, eds.** Transgenics in Endocrinology. 350p. 2000. 135.00 (*0-89603-764-9*) Humana.

Matzulewitsch, Leonid. Byzantinische Antike: Studien auf Grund der Silbergefaesse der Ermitage. (Archaologische Mitteilungen aus Russischen Sammlungen Ser.: Vol. 2). (GER., Illus.). xi, 150p. (C). 1974. reprint ed. 542.30 (*3-11-002245-1*) De Gruyter.

Mau, August. Pompeii: Its Life & Art. 2nd ed. Kelsey, Francis W., tr. from GER. (Illus.). xxv, 557p. (C). 1982. reprint ed. lib. bdg. 60.00 (*0-89241-346-8*) Caratzas.

— Pompeii, Its Life & Art. 1982. 64.95 (*0-8434-0138-9*) McGrath NH.

Mau, Bruce, jt. auth. see Koolhaas, Rem.

Mau, Hoanh L. Do, see Do Mau, Hoanh L.

Mau, Jacob, jt. auth. see Kepler, Kay.

Mau, James. Social Change & Images of the Future. 192p. 1968. 18.95 (*0-87073-048-7*) Schenkman Bks Inc.

Mau, James, jt. ed. see Bell, Wendell.

Mau, L. Y., jt. auth. see Liu, F. C.

Mau, Rennie, jt. auth. see Wheeler, Eugene D.

Maubrey, Pierre. L' Expression de la Passion Interieure dans le Style de Bernanos Romancier. LC 70-94195. (Catholic University of America. Studies in Romance Languages & Literatures: No. 59). (FRE.). reprint ed. 37.50 (*0-404-50359-4*) AMS Pr.

M

An Asterisk (*) at the beginning of an entry indicates that the title is appearing for the first time.

M

Mauceri, Joseoh. Therapy or Theology: Religion & Mental Health. (Orig.). 1995. pap. 8.00 (*0-9626257-8-7*) CBCCU Amer.

Mauceri, Joseph. The Great Break: A Short History of the Separation of Medical Science from Religion. 156p. 1987. pap. 9.95 (*0-940170-13-2*) Station Hill Pr.

Mauceri, Philip. State under Siege: Development & Policy Making in Peru. 192p. 1996. pap. text 23.00 (*0-8133-3607-4*, Pub. by Westview) HarpC.

Mauceri, Philip, jt. ed. see Cameron, Maxwell A.

Mauch & Birch. Guide to the Successful Thesis & Dissertation: A Handbook for Students & Faculty. 4th ed. LC 98-6702. (Illus.). 368p. 1998. text 59.75 (*0-8247-0169-0*) Dekker.

Mauch, James E. & Birch, Jack W. Guide to the Successful Thesis & Dissertation: Conception to Publication: A Handbook for Students & Faculty. LC 83-2112. (Books in Library & Information Science: No. 43). (Illus.). 252p. reprint ed. pap. 78.20 (*0-8357-6135-5*, 203454900090) Bks Demand.

Mauch, James E. & Sabloff, Paula L., eds. Reform & Change in Higher Education: International Perspectives. LC 94-31729. (Garland Studies in Higher Education: No. 2). (Illus.). 336p. 1994. text 55.00 (*0-8153-1706-9*, SS961) Garland.

Mauch, James E., et al. The Emeritus Professor: Old Rank - New Meaning. Fife, Jonathan D., ed. LC 90-60888. (ASHE-ERIC Higher Education Reports: No. 90-2). 88p. (Orig.). (C). 1990. pap. 24.00 (*0-9623882-9-7*) GWU Grad Schl E&HD.

Mauch, John, jt. auth. see Ehrenkranz, David.

Mauch, Mercedes. Senecas Frauenbild in den Philosophischen Schriften. (Studien zur Klassischen Philologie: Bd. 106). (GER.). 176p. 1997. 42.95 (*3-631-31267-9*) P Lang Pubng.

Mauch, Peter & Loeffler, Jay, eds. Radiation Oncology: Technology & Biology. LC 93-31650. 1994. text 125.00 (*0-7216-6724-4*, W B Saunders Co) Harcrt Hlth Sci Grp.

Mauch, Peter M. Hodgkin's Disease. LC 98-55677. 1999. write for info. (*0-7817-1502-4*) Lppncott W & W.

Mauch, Robert P., Jr. The Consumer Guide to Over-the-Counter Drugs. LC 97-6639. 160p. (Orig.). 1997. pap. 12.95 (*0-9657918-0-7*) Strategies Growth.

Mauch, Thomas, ed. & tr. see Boccaccio, Giovanni.

Mauch, Werner & Papen, Uta, eds. Making a Difference: Innovations in Adult Education. LC 97-26319. 216p. 1997. 19.95 (*3-631-32038-8*) P Lang Pubng.

Mauche, Christopher W., ed. Accretion-Powered Compact Binaries. (Illus.). 496p. (C). 1990. text 80.00 (*0-521-40212-3*) Cambridge U Pr.

Mauchline, John, ed. see Davidson, A. B.

Mauck, Christine K., et al, eds. Barrier Contraceptives: Current Status & Future Trends. 384p. 1994. 178.50 (*0-471-30440-9*, Wiley-Interscience) Wiley.

Mauck, Dave, ed. see Herrick, Rodney.

Mauck, Diane & Jenkins, Janet. Teaching Primaries. 1983. pap. 5.45 (*0-89137-610-0*); pap., student ed. 4.35 (*0-89137-612-7*) Quality Pubns.

Mauck, Jeffrey. The Education of a Soldier: Ulysses S. Grant in the War with Mexico. (Illus.). 28p. 1996. pap. 9.95 (*0-913415-10-3*) Amer Kestrel.

Mauck, Jeffrey G., jt. auth. see Haecker, Charles M.

Mauck, Marchita. Places for Worship: A Guide to Building & Renovating. LC 94-7252. (American Essays in Liturgy Ser.). 72p. (Orig.). 1995. pap. write for info. (*0-8146-2283-6*) Liturgical Pr.

— Shaping a House for the Church. 105p. (Orig.). 1990. pap. 12.00 (*0-929650-06-9*, HOUSE) Liturgy Tr Pubns.

Mauck, Scott, jt. auth. see Haynes, J. H.

Mauck, Sheila, ed. see Clark, Marge.

Mauck, Sue I., jt. auth. see Clapp, Steve.

Mauck, Sue I., jt. auth. see Schriner, Chris.

Mauck, Sue I., ed. see Herrick, Rodney.

Mauclair, Camille. Turner. Shaw, E. B., tr. (Illus.). 168p. 1939. lib. bdg. 35.00 (*0-8288-3930-1*) Fr & Eur.

***Maucourant, F.** A Pocket Retreat for Catholics: Thirty Simple Steps to Holiness - In Just Ten Minute a Day! Orig. Title: The Life of Union with OUr Divine Lord. 224p. 2000. reprint ed. pap. 10.95 (*1-928832-12-1*) Sophia Inst Pr.

Maud, Aylmer, tr. see Tolstoy, Leo.

Maud, Peter J. & Foster, Carl, eds. Physiological Assessment of Human Fitness. LC 94-40072. (Illus.). 304p. 1995. text 50.00 (*0-87322-776-X*, BMAU0776) Human Kinetics.

Maud, R. R., jt. ed. see Heine, K.

Maud, Ralph. Charles Olson's Reading: A Biography. LC 94-44403. 1995. 44.95 (*0-8093-1995-0*) S Ill U Pr.

— Dylan Thomas in Print: A Bibliographical History. LC 78-101190. 273p. reprint ed. pap. 84.70 (*0-8357-9753-8*, 201779300008) Bks Demand.

— A Guide to B. C. Indian Myth & Legend. LC 83-148600. 224p. 1982. reprint ed. pap. 14.95 (*0-88922-189-8*, Pub. by Talonbks) Genl Dist Srvs.

— Guide to Welsh Wales. 1994. 22.95 (*0-86243-335-5*, Pub. by Y Lolfa) St Mut.

— Guide to Welsh Wales. 1994. 22.95 (*0-86243-332-0*, Pub. by Y Lolfa); pap. 13.95 (*0-86243-310-X*, Pub. by Y Lolfa) Intl Spec Bk.

— What Does Not Change? The Significance of Charles Olson's "The Kingfishers" LC 97-14291. 1997. write for info. (*0-8386-3731-0*) Fairleigh Dickinson.

Maud, Ralph, ed. The Porcupine Hunter & Other Stories: The Original Tshimshian Texts of Henry Tate. 112p. 1994. pap. 13.95 (*0-88922-333-5*, Pub. by Talonbks) Genl Dist Srvs.

— Wales in His Arms: Dylan Thomas's Choice of Welsh Poetry. LC 94-230112. 112p. 1994. pap. write for info. (*0-7083-1248-9*, Pub. by Univ Wales Pr) Paul & Co Pubs.

Maud, Ralph, jt. auth. see Hill-Tout, Charles.

Maud, Ralph, jt. auth. see Olson, Charles.

Maud, Ralph, ed. see Hill-Tout, Charles.

Maud, Ralph, ed. see Olson, Charles & Boldereff, Frances.

Maud, Rodney R., jt. ed. see Partridge, Timothy C.

Maud, Timothy J. The Internet Investor: A Practical & Time-Saving Guide to Financial Information on the Internet. 422p. 1999. pap. 19.95 (*1-57112-101-3*) Park Ave.

Maudadi, A. A. Tafhimul - Quran: Urdu Translation & Commentary, 6 vols., Set. 1993. 150.00 (*0-933511-70-1*) Kazi Pubns.

Maude. The Life of Jenny Lind. Farkas, Andrew & Moran, W. R., eds. LC 76-29953. (Illus.). 222p. 1997. reprint ed. pap. 19.95 (*0-88143-201-6*) Ayer.

Maude, A. D., jt. auth. see Maude, R.

Maude, Alymer, tr. see Tolstoy, Leo.

Maude, Angus. South Asia. LC 66-18564. 1966. 18.95 (*0-8023-1076-1*) Dufour.

Maude, Aylmer. Leo Tolstoy. LC 75-20491. (Studies in Tolstoy: No. 62). 1974. lib. bdg. 75.00 (*0-8383-2001-5*) M S G Haskell Hse.

— Leo Tolstoy & His Works. LC 74-6377. (Studies in Tolstoy: No. 62). 1974. lib. bdg. 75.00 (*0-8383-2009-0*) M S G Haskell Hse.

— Peculiar People, the Dukhobors. LC 72-131033. reprint ed. 32.50 (*0-404-04275-9*) AMS Pr.

— Tolstoy & His Problems. 1973. 250.00 (*0-8490-1220-1*) Gordon Pr.

— Tolstoy & His Problems. LC 74-7137. (Studies in Tolstoy: No. 62). 1974. lib. bdg. 75.00 (*0-8383-1999-8*) M S G Haskell Hse.

— Tolstoy on Art. LC 72-2134. (Studies in European Literature: No. 56). 1972. reprint ed. lib. bdg. 75.00 (*0-8383-1459-7*) M S G Haskell Hse.

Maude, Aylmer, tr. see Tolstoy, Leo.

Maude, D., jt. auth. see Molyneux, P.

Maude, F. N. The Jena Campaign, 1806. LC 97-38292. (Napoleonic Library). 202p. 1998. 40.00 (*1-85367-310-2*, Pub. by Greenhill Bks) Stackpole.

Maude, George. Historical Dictionary of Finland. LC 94-20484. (European Historical Dictionaries Ser.: No. 8). 384p. 1995. 63.00 (*0-8108-2995-9*) Scarecrow.

Maude, H. E. Of Islands & Men: Studies in Pacific History. 1969. 23.50 (*0-19-550177-2*) OUP.

Maude, H. E., ed. see Grimble, Arthur F.

Maude, J. Internet Investor. 1997. pap. 23.00 (*0-00-638556-7*) HarpC.

***Maude, J. Timothy.** The Internet Investor. 430p. 1999. pap. 80.00 (*0-85297-498-1*, Pub. by Chartered Bank) St Mut.

Maude, Jenny M. The Life of Jenny Lind. Farkas, Andrew, ed. LC 76-29953. (Opera Biographies Ser.). (Illus.). 1977. reprint ed. lib. bdg. 21.95 (*0-405-09694-1*) Ayer.

— The Life of Jenny Lind: Briefly Told by Her Daughter. LC 74-24149. (Illus.). reprint ed. 32.50 (*0-404-13041-0*) AMS Pr.

Maude, Louise, tr. see Tolstoy, Leo.

Maude, R. & Maude, A. D. The Servant, the General & Armageddon. LC 98-202033. (Illus.). 110p. 1998. pap. 11.95 (*0-85398-424-7*) G Ronald Pub.

Maude, R. B. Seedborne Diseases & Their Control. LC 96-214887. (A CAB International Publication). 288p. 1996. text 80.00 (*0-85198-922-5*) OUP.

Maude, Zoe. Lists of Clay. 272p. 1998. pap. 16.95 (*1-892745-01-1*) Petals of Life.

Mauderly, Joe L., jt. ed. see McCunney, Robert J.

Maudgal, P. C. & Missotten, L., eds. Herpetic Eye Diseases. (Documenta Ophthalmologica Proceedings Ser.). 1985. text 247.50 (*90-6193-527-X*) Kluwer Academic.

— Superficial Keratitis. 1981. text 141.50 (*90-6193-801-5*) Kluwer Academic.

Maudoodi, Syed A. An Introduction to Understanding the Quaran. Ansari, Zafar I., tr. 48p. 1990. pap. write for info. (*1-882837-21-5*) W A M Y Intl.

Maudslay, A. P. Archaeology: Biologia Centrali-America or, Contibutions to the Knowledge of the Fauna & Flora of Mexico & Central America. Godman, F. Ducane & Salvin, Osbert, eds. LC 74-30688. (Illus.). 907p. 1983. 285.00 (*0-8061-9919-9*) U of Okla Pr.

Maudslay, A. P., tr. see Diaz Del Castillo, Bernal.

Maudslay, Alfred P., jt. auth. see Maudslay, Anne C.

Maudslay, Anne C. & Maudslay, Alfred P. A Glimpse at Guatemala: And Some Notes on the Ancient Monuments of Central America. LC 92-85006. (Illus.). 289p. 1992. reprint ed. 40.00 (*0-9633895-0-5*) F Silver Bks.

Maudslay, Robert. Texas Sheepman. Kupper, Winifred, ed. LC 78-157347. (Select Bibliographies Reprint Ser.). (Illus.). 1977. reprint ed. 20.95 (*0-8369-5808-X*) Ayer.

Maudsley, Henry. Body & Mind. 207p. 55.00 (*1-85506-659-9*) Thoemmes Pr.

Maudsley, Henry. The Physiology & Pathology of Mind, 2 vols. 3rd enl. rev. ed. LC 78-72810. reprint ed. 75.00 (*0-404-60878-7*) AMS Pr.

— Physiology & Pathology of the Mind, 4. LC 77-72191. (Contributions to the History of Psychology Ser.: Pt. C, Vol. IV, Medical Psychology). 442p. 1977. reprint ed. lib. bdg. 79.50 (*0-313-26943-2*, U6943, Greenwood Pr) Greenwood.

— Responsibility in Mental Disease, 3. LC 77-72191. (Contributions to the History of Psychology Ser.: Vol. III, Pt. C, Medical Psychology). 603p. 1977. reprint ed. lib. bdg. 95.00 (*0-313-26942-4*, U6942, Greenwood Pr) Greenwood.

Maududi, Mawlana. Rights of Non Muslims in the Islamic State. 64p. 1996. pap. 3.00 (*0-614-21475-0*, 1607) Kazi Pubns.

Maududi, S. Abul Ala. Economic Problems of Man & Its Islamic Solution. 1989. pap. 3.50 (*0-935782-84-2*) Kazi Pubns.

— Economic System of Islam. 315p. 1993. pap. 12.50 (*1-56744-263-3*) Kazi Pubns.

— Ethical Viewpoint of Islam. 1978. pap. 3.00 (*0-935782-99-0*) Kazi Pubns.

— First Principles of Islamic State. 1992. pap. 3.00 (*1-56744-008-8*) Kazi Pubns.

— Fundamentals of Islam (Khutabat) 1992. pap. 14.50 (*0-935782-09-5*) Kazi Pubns.

— Holy Quran Arabic English Translation & Brief Footnotes. 1983. 29.95 (*1-56744-041-X*) Kazi Pubns.

— Human Rights in Islam. 39p. (Orig.). 1981. pap. 1.95 (*0-9503954-9-8*, Pub. by Islamic Fnd) New Era Publns MI.

— Islam & Ignorance. 42p. (Orig.). 1992. pap. 3.00 (*1-56744-468-7*) Kazi Pubns.

— Islamic Law & Constitution. 1991. 16.95 (*1-56744-099-1*) Kazi Pubns.

— Islamic Sermons (Khutabat) 262p. 1992. pap. 12.50 (*1-56744-312-5*) Kazi Pubns.

— Islamic Way of Life. 80p. 1992. pap. 4.95 (*1-56744-107-6*) Kazi Pubns.

— The Meaning of the Quran, 6 vols., Set. (ARA & ENG.). 1991. 160.00 (*1-56744-134-3*) Kazi Pubns.

— Political Theory of Islam. 1994. pap. 3.00 (*1-56744-189-0*) Kazi Pubns.

— Process of Islamic Revolution. 1990. pap. 3.00 (*1-56744-195-5*) Kazi Pubns.

— Purdah & the Status of Women in Islam. 1991. 12.00 (*0-934905-00-2*, Library of Islam); pap. 7.50 (*1-56744-200-5*) Kazi Pubns.

— The Religion of Truth. 1989. pap. 3.00 (*0-933511-36-1*) Kazi Pubns.

— Rights of Non-Muslims in the Islamic State. 1992. pap. 3.00 (*0-933511-41-8*) Kazi Pubns.

— The Road to Peace & Salvation. 1088p. 1987. pap. 3.00 (*0-933511-42-6*) Kazi Pubns.

— Towards Understanding Islam. 130p. 1992. pap. 7.50 (*0-933511-79-5*) Kazi Pubns.

— Towards Understanding Islam. Ahmad, Khurshid, tr. from URD. 116p. pap. 5.95 (*0-86037-053-4*, Pub. by Islamic Fnd) New Era Publns MI.

— Towards Understanding Islam. Ahmad, Khurshid, tr. from URD.Tr. of Risala-e-Diniyat. 126p. (Orig.). 1977. pap. 4.00 (*0-89259-151-X*) Am Trust Pubns.

— Towards Understanding Islam. Ahmad, Khurshid, tr. from URD.Tr. of Risala-e-Diniyat. 179p. (Orig.). 1980. pap. 5.95 (*0-939830-22-1*, Pub. by IIFSO KW) New Era Publns MI.

Mauduit, Israel. Observations upon the Conduct of Sir William Howe at the White Plains: As Related in the Gazette of December 30, 1776. LC 71-140874. (Eyewitness Accounts of the American Revolution Ser.). 1971. reprint ed. 14.95 (*0-405-01219-5*) Ayer.

Maue-Dickson, Wilma, et al. Computed Tomographic Atlas of the Head & Neck. 453p. 1983. 145.00 (*0-316-55081-7*, Little Brwn Med Div) Lppncott W & W.

Maue-Dickson, Wilma, jt. auth. see Dickson, David.

Mauelshagen, Carl. The Salzburg Lutheran Expulsion & Its Impact. (Illus.). 167p. 1994. pap. text 17.50 (*0-7884-0002-9*) Heritage Bk.

Mauer, Alison K. & Mauer, Edgar F., eds. George Dock, M.D. A Bibliography of His Writings. 2nd ed. (Illus.). 36p. 1991. pap. text 20.00 (*0-9631270-0-4*) Fr Lib LA Cty Med.

Mauer, Alvin M., ed. The Biology of Human Leukemia. LC 89-15499. (Johns Hopkins Series in Contemporary Medicine & Public Health). (Illus.). 251p. reprint ed. pap. 77.90 (*0-608-07400-4*, 206762700009) Bks Demand.

***Mauer, Don.** A Guys Guide to Great Eating: Big-Flavored, Fat-Reduced Recipes for Men Who Love to Eat. LC 99-11028. (Illus.). 350p. 1999. pap. 17.00 (*0-395-91536-8*) HM.

Mauer, Don. Lean & Lovin' It: Exceptionally Delicious Recipes for Low-Fat Living & Permanent Weight Loss. Martin, Rux, ed. (Illus.). 448p. 1996. pap. 16.95 (*1-881527-97-2*, Chapters Bks) HM.

Mauer, Don, jt. auth. see Jacobson, Don.

Mauer, Edgar F., jt. ed. see Mauer, Alison K.

Mauer, Friedrich, ed. see Hartmann Von Aue.

Mauer, G. P. Hobs & the Factors Influencing Their Standardization. (Technical Papers: Vol. P240). (Illus.). 25p. 1943. pap. text 30.00 (*1-55589-169-1*) AGMA.

Mauer, Gerlinde & Magen, Ursula. Ad Bene et Fideliter Seminandum: Festgabe fur Karlheinz Deller zum 21. Februar 1987. (Alter Orient und Altes Testament Ser.: Vol. 220). (GER.). xv, 333p. 1988. text 79.50 (*3-7887-1280-5*) NeukirchenerV.

Mauer, John W. Technology & Culture: A Textbook for Hss 105. 122p. (C). 1998. per. 36.95 (*0-7872-5291-3*, 41529101) Kendall-Hunt.

Mauer, Lowell. Sams Teach Yourself More Visual Basic X in 21 Days. 2nd ed. LC 98-84136. (Teach Yourself Ser.). 1998. pap. 35.00 (*0-672-31307-3*) Sams.

Mauer, Marc. The Race to Incarcerate. LC 98-46750. 224p. 1998. pap. 22.95 (*1-56584-429-7*, Pub. by New Press NY) Norton.

Mauer, Shelley M., jt. auth. see Morford, Ted R.

Mauer, Walt. Amish Portrait. (Illus.). 32p. 1998. pap. 4.00 (*1-890541-36-2*) Americana Souvenirs & Gifts.

— Hex Signs...& Their Meanings. (Illus.). 12p. 1996. pap. 2.50 (*1-890541-33-8*) Americana Souvenirs & Gifts.

Mauermayer, W. Transurethral Surgery. (Illus.). 477p. 1982. 535.00 (*0-387-11869-1*) Spr-Verlag.

Mauermeyer, Carol & Simcoe, Annell L. Keyboarding for the Automated Office Level 1 Working Papers. 2nd ed. 1991. 19.20 (*0-13-513151-0*) P-H.

Mauet, Thomas A. Fundamentals of Trial Techniques: Canadian Edition. 2nd ed. 340p. 1995. pap. text 50.00 (*0-316-55113-9*, Aspen Law & Bus) Aspen Pub.

— Materials in Pretrial Litigation: Problems & Cases. 800p. 1992. teacher ed. write for info. (*0-316-55106-6*, 51066) Aspen Law.

— Materials in Pretrial Litigation: Problems & Cases. 800p. 1992. pap. 31.00 (*0-316-55102-3*, 51023) Aspen Law.

— Materials on Trial Advocacy. 3rd ed. LC 93-80974. 992p. 1994. lib. bdg. 36.00 (*0-316-55110-4*, Aspen Law & Bus) Aspen Pub.

— Mauet's Trial Notebook. pap. 80.00 incl. disk (*0-316-55111-2*, 51090) Aspen Law.

— Mauet's Trial Notebook. 2nd ed. LC 98-9798. 1998. write for info. (*1-56706-942-8*); ring bd. 89.00 (*1-56706-941-X*) Aspen Law.

— Pretrial. 3rd ed. 448p. 1995. 31.00 (*0-316-55108-2*, Aspen Law & Bus) Aspen Pub.

— Pretrial. 4th ed. 1999. pap. text 38.95 (*0-7355-0052-5*) Panel Pubs.

— Trial Evidence: Artistry & Advocacy in the Courtroom. Orig. Title: Trial Evidence: Artistry & Advocacy in the Courtroom. (Illus.). 128p. 1997. pap. 185.00 incl. audio (*0-943380-94-4*) PEG MN.

— Trial Notebook. LC 93-80290. 1994. lib. bdg. 80.00 (*0-316-55109-0*) Little.

— Trial Tech. 4th ed. LC 95-80361. 536p. 1996. 32.95 (*0-316-55061-2*, Aspen Law & Bus) Aspen Pub.

— Trial Techniques. 5th ed. LC 99-34132. 1999. pap. text 42.00 (*0-7355-0635-3*) Panel Pubs.

Mauet, Thomas A. & Gianna, Dominic J. A Day on Trial: Advocacy for the New Milleniem. 172p. 1992. pap. 185.00 incl. audio (*0-943380-93-6*) PEG MN.

Mauet, Thomas A. & Maerowitz, Marlene A. Fundamentals of Litigation for Paralegals. 2nd ed. LC 95-76313. 576p. 1995. 49.95 (*0-316-55114-7*, 551147) Aspen Law.

— Fundamentals of Litigation for Paralegals. 3rd ed. LC 98-42452. 1999. boxed set 65.95 (*0-7355-0275-7*) Panel Pubs.

— Fundamentals of Litigation for Paralegals Including Instructor's Guide. 2nd ed. 308p. 1995. pap., wbk. ed. write for info. (*0-316-54896-0*, 548960) Aspen Law.

Mauet, Thomas A. & Wolfson, Warren D. Materials in Trial Advocacy: Problems & Cases. 992p. 1994. teacher ed. write for info. (*0-316-55069-8*, 50698) Aspen Law.

— Materials in Trial Advocacy: Problems & Cases. 4th ed. LC 97-46974. 1998. pap. text 40.00 (*1-56706-693-3*) Aspen Law.

— Trial Evidence. LC 97-13788. 400p. 1997. pap. text 26.95 (*1-56706-554-6*) Aspen Law.

Maufer, Thomas. Deploying IP Multicast in the Enterprise. LC 97-41591. 304p. (C). 1997. 59.00 (*0-13-897687-2*) P-H.

Maufler, Thomas A. IP Fundamentals: Addressing, Routing, & Troubleshooting. LC 99-21033. 450p. 1999. pap. 49.99 (*0-13-975483-0*) P-H.

Maufort, Marc. Songs of American Experience: The Vision of O'Neill & Melville. LC 90-41225. (American University Studies: American Literature: Ser. XXIV, Vol. 24). (Illus.). XIV, 226p. (C). 1991. text 35.00 (*0-8204-1407-7*) P Lang Pubng.

Maufort, Marc, ed. Staging Difference: Cultural Pluralism in American Theatre & Drama. (American University Studies: Ser. XXVI, Vol. 25). 396p. (C). 1996. text 69.95 (*0-8204-2732-2*) P Lang Pubng.

Maufrrij-Sherower, T. S., ed. see Sherower, Abbott W.

Maugans, Debby. Beyond the Bowl. LC 97-22433. (Illus.). 224p. 1997. pap. 12.95 (*0-8092-3005-4*, 300540, Contemporary Bks) NTC Contemp Pub Co.

Maugans, James D. The Grammatical Lawyer II. LC 79-50329. 321p. 1996. text 37.00 (*0-8318-0753-9*, B753) Am Law Inst.

Maugans, Jayne E. Aging Parents, Ambivalent Baby Boomers: A Critical Approach to Gerontology. LC 93-79472. 192p. (Orig.). 1994. text 35.95 (*0-930390-49-0*); pap. text 18.95 (*0-930390-23-7*) Gen Hall.

Mauge, Conrad E. The Lost Orisha. (Illus.). 224p. (Orig.). 1996. pap. 19.95 (*0-9637516-4-6*) Hse of Providence.

— ODU IFA Bk. 1: Sacred Scriptures of IFA. 48p. 1994. pap. 6.95 (*0-9637516-2-X*) Hse of Providence.

— ODU IFA Bk. 2: Sacred Scriptures of IFA. 48p. 1995. pap. 6.95 (*0-9637516-3-8*) Hse of Providence.

— ODU IFA Bk. 3: Iwori Meji. (ODU IFA Ser.). (YOR.). 54p. 1997. pap. 6.95 (*0-9637516-6-2*) Hse of Providence.

— ODU IFA Bk. 4: Idi Meji. (ODU IFA Ser.). (YOR.). 36p. 1997. pap. text 6.95 (*0-9637516-7-0*) Hse of Providence.

— The Yoruba Religion: Introduction to Its Practice. 112p. (Orig.). 1993. pap. text 12.95 (*0-9637516-0-3*) Hse of Providence.

— Yoruba Self Help Using Adimu, Vol. 1. 128p. 1997. pap. 12.95 (*0-9637516-5-4*) Hse of Providence.

— The Yoruba World of Good & Evil. (Illus.). 180p. (Orig.). 1994. pap. 12.95 (*0-9637516-1-1*) Hse of Providence.

Maugel, T. K., jt. auth. see Pierce, S. K.

Mauger, Being. Songs from the Womb: Healing the Wounded Mother. LC 99-495093. 1999. pap. text 17.95 (*1-898256-54-3*) Collins Press.

***Mauger, Bill.** Profit from Home Using a Computer: How to Turn Your Computer into a Cash Machine. 63p. 1999. pap. 109.00 (*0-9686587-0-9*) IV-DS.

Mauger, Gaston. Cours de Langue et de Civilisation Francaise, 4 Vols, 1. 16.95 (*2-01-008054-8*) Schoenhof.

— Cours de Langue et de Civilisation Francaise, 4 Vols, 2. 15.95 (*2-01-007944-2*) Schoenhof.

— Cours de Langue et de Civilisation Francaise, 4 Vols, 3. 16.95 (*2-01-001554-1*) Schoenhof.

— Cours de Langue et de Civilisation Francaise, 4 Vols, 4. 24.95 (*2-01-007945-0*) Schoenhof.

— Cours de Langue et de Civilisation Francaise a L'usage des Etrangers, 4 tomes. Incl. Tome I. 18.95 (*0-8288-9904-5*, F138130); Tome II. 19.95

An Asterisk (*) at the beginning of an entry indicates that the title is appearing for the first time.

(*0-8288-9905-3*, F138131); Tome III. 24.95 (*0-8288-9906-1*, F138132); Tome IV. 29.95 (*0-8288-9907-X*, F138133); (FRE.). write for info. (*0-318-51975-5*) Fr & Eur.
— Francais Accelere. (FRE.). 186p. 1964. 14.95 (*0-8288-7497-2*) Fr & Eur.
— Grammaire Pratique du Francais d Aujourd Hui, Lanque Parlee, Laugue Ecrite. (Coll. F). 19.95 (*0-685-36653-7*) Fr & Eur.
— Grammaire Pratique du Francais d'Aujourd Hui, Lanque Parlee, Laugue Ecrite. 8th ed. (FRE.). 1978. pap. 25.95 (*0-7859-4728-0*) Fr & Eur.
— Scenes de la Vie Francaise. 6.95 (*0-685-36697-9*) Fr & Eur.
Mauger, Gaston, jt. auth. see Mosby Staff.
Mauger, Thierry. The Ark of the Desert. (Illus.). 160p. 1991. 49.95 (*0-7103-0436-6*, A6715) Routledge.
— The Bedouins of Arabia. (Illus.). 139p. 1990. 45.00 (*0-7103-0366-1*, A4185) Routledge.
— Flowered Men & Green Slopes of Arabia. (Illus.). 189p. 1990. 45.00 (*0-7103-0365-3*, A4188) Routledge.
— Impressions of Arabia: Architecture & Frescoes of the 'Asir Region. (Illus.). 200p. 1996. 55.00 (*2-08-013624-0*, Pub. by Flammarion) Abbeville Pr.
— Undiscovered Asir. (Illus.). 160p. 1990. boxed set 69.95 (*0-905743-70-9*, Pub. by Stacey Intl) Intl Bk Ctr.
Maugeri, A., jt. auth. see Giannessi, F.
Maugeri, Antonio. Elliptic & Parabolic Equations with Discontinuous Coefficients. 250p. 1994. text 125.00 (*3-527-40135-0*) Wiley.
Maugeri, Marilyn, jt. auth. see Maugeri, Rudy.
Maugeri, Rudy & Maugeri, Marilyn. How to Become Fully Alive. 1983. pap. 4.95 (*0-913907-00-6*) Rumar Ent.
***Maugeri, Rudy, et al.** A Ten Step Journey to Becoming Fully Alive: A Spiritual Connection. 79p. 1999. pap. 9.95 (*0-913907-01-4*) Rumar Ent.
***Maugham.** Napoleon's Line Cavalry Recreated in Color Photographs: Europa Militaria #10. 96p. 2000. pap. 23.95 (*1-86126-266-3*, Pub. by Crolwood) Motorbooks Intl.
— Napoleon's Line Infantry Recreated in Color Photographs: Europa Militaria #11. 96p. 2000. pap. 23.95 (*1-86126-267-1*, Pub. by Crolwood) Motorbooks Intl.
Maugham, M., jt. auth. see Peace, P.
Maugham, Robin. Conversations with Willie: Recollections of W. Somerset Maugham. LC 78-316547. 184p. 1978. 5.00 (*0-491-02303-0*) Virgin Bks.
— Enemy! 1994. pap. 12.95 (*1-873741-18-9*, Pub. by Millvres Bks) LPC InBook.
— Escape from the Shadows: An Autobiography. LC 72-7418. (Illus.). xii, 273p. 1973. write for info. (*0-07-040969-2*) McGraw.
— Escape From the Shadows: Robin Maugham, his Autobiography. LC 73-169647. 278p. 1972. write for info. (*0-340-14949-3*) St Martin.
— Search for Nirvana: Korean Monks' Life. LC 76-353663. 236 p. 1975. 4.50 (*0-491-01704-9*) Virgin Bks.
***Maugham, Robin.** The Servant. (Film Ink Ser.). 2000. pap. 12.00 (*1-85375-389-0*, Pub. by Prion) Trafalgar.
Maugham, Robin. Somerset & All the Maughams. LC 75-22759. (Illus.). 270p. 1977. reprint ed. lib. bdg. 65.00 (*0-8371-8236-0*, MASOM, Greenwood Pr) Greenwood.
Maugham, W. Somerset. Ah King. LC 75-26127. (Works of W. Somerset Maugham). 1977. reprint ed. 23.95 (*0-405-07850-1*) Ayer.
— Andalusia: The Land of the Blessed Virgin. LC 75-25381. (Works of W. Somerset Maugham). 1977. reprint ed. 23.95 (*0-405-07833-1*) Ayer.
— Ashenden, or, the British Agent. 24.95 (*0-89190-213-9*) Amereon Ltd.
— Ashenden, or, The British Agent. large type ed. 512p. 1992. 22.95 (*1-85290-034-2*, Pub. by ISIS Lrg Prnt) Transaction Pubs.
— Ashenden, or, The British Agent. LC 76-178451. (Short Story Index Reprint Ser.). reprint ed. 14.50 (*0-8369-4052-0*) Ayer.
— Ashenden, or, The British Agent. LC 75-25348. (Works of W. Somerset Maugham). 1977. reprint ed. 27.95 (*0-405-07805-6*) Ayer.
— Cakes & Ale. 208p. 1993. pap. 12.95 (*0-14-018588-7*, Penguin Classics) Viking Penguin.
— Catalina: A Romance. LC 75-25350. (Works of W. Somerset Maugham). 1977. reprint ed. 23.95 (*0-405-07808-0*) Ayer.
— Christmas Holiday. LC 75-25351. (Works of W. Somerset Maugham). 1977. reprint ed. 23.95 (*0-405-07809-9*) Ayer.
— Collected Short Stories. 448p. 1992. pap. 13.95 (*0-14-018589-5*, Penguin Classics) Viking Penguin.
— Collected Short Stories, Vol. 2. 256p. 1992. pap. 13.95 (*0-14-018590-9*, Penguin Classics) Viking Penguin.
— Collected Short Stories, Vol. 3. 256p. 1993. pap. 13.95 (*0-14-018591-7*) Viking Penguin.
— Collected Short Stories, Vol. 4. 464p. 1993. pap. 14.95 (*0-14-018592-5*, Penguin Classics) Viking Penguin.
***Maugham, W. Somerset.** Creatures of Circumstance. 325p. 2000. text 32.95 (*0-7658-0784-X*) Transaction Pubs.
Maugham, W. Somerset. Creatures of Circumstance. LC 75-26130. (Works of W. Somerset Maugham). 1977. reprint ed. 23.95 (*0-405-07853-6*) Ayer.
— Don Fernando. 269p. 1994. pap. 10.95 (*1-56924-902-4*) Marlowe & Co.
— Don Fernando: Or Variations on Some Spanish Themes. LC 75-25382. (Works of W. Somerset Maugham). 1977. reprint ed. 23.95 (*0-405-07834-X*) Ayer.
— East of Suez: A Play in Seven Scenes. LC 75-25386. (Works of W. Somerset Maugham). 1977. reprint ed. 23.95 (*0-405-07838-2*) Ayer.
— Explorer. Date not set. lib. bdg. 23.95 (*0-8488-1676-5*) Amereon Ltd.
— The Explorer: With Four Illustrations by F. Graham Cootes. LC 75-25353. (Works of W. Somerset Maugham). 1977. reprint ed. 23.95 (*0-405-07810-2*) Ayer.
— For Services Rendered: A Play in Three Acts. LC 75-25388. (Works of W. Somerset Maugham). 1977. reprint ed. 23.95 (*0-405-07839-0*) Ayer.
— France at War. LC 75-25373. (Works of W. Somerset Maugham). 1977. reprint ed. 23.95 (*0-405-07835-8*) Ayer.
— Gentleman in the Parlour. 300p. 1994. pap. 10.95 (*1-56924-903-2*) Marlowe & Co.
***Maugham, W. Somerset.** The Great Exotic Novels & Short Stories of Somerset Maugham. 812p. 2001. reprint ed. pap. 16.95 (*0-7867-0813-1*, Pub. by Carroll & Graf) Publishers Group.
— The Kite. (Short Stories Ser.). 22p. 2000. pap. 3.95 (*1-86092-044-6*, Pub. by Travelman Pub) IPG Chicago.
Maugham, W. Somerset. The Letter: A Play in Three Acts. LC 75-25389. (Works of W. Somerset Maugham). 1977. reprint ed. 23.95 (*0-405-07841-2*) Ayer.
— Liza of Lambeth. 126p. 1992. pap. 10.95 (*0-14-018593-3*, Penguin Classics) Viking Penguin.
***Maugham, W. Somerset.** The Magician. 288p. 1999. 26.95 (*0-7351-0175-2*) Replica Bks.
Maugham, W. Somerset. The Magician. 208p. 1992. pap. 12.95 (*0-14-018595-X*, Viking) Viking Penguin.
— The Magician. 233p. 1974. reprint ed. spiral bd. 11.50 (*0-7873-0589-8*) Hlth Research.
— The Making of a Saint: A Romance of Mediaeval Italy. LC 75-30388. (Works of W. Somerset Maugham). 1977. reprint ed. 26.95 (*0-405-07815-3*) Ayer.
— The Mixture As Before. LC 75-26134. (Works of W. Somerset Maugham). 1977. reprint ed. 23.95 (*0-405-07855-2*) Ayer.
— Moon & Sixpence. 22.95 (*0-8488-2653-1*) Amereon Ltd.
— Moon & Sixpence. 224p. 1993. pap. 9.95 (*0-14-018597-6*) Viking Penguin.
— The Moon & Sixpence. (Ghosts of Fear Street Ser.). (gr. 3-6). 1984. per. 1.50 (*0-671-00851-X*, Minstrel Bks) PB.
***Maugham, W. Somerset.** The Moon & Sixpence. LC 99-57094. (International Ser.). 160p. 2000. pap. 11.00 (*0-375-72456-7*) Vin Bks.
Maugham, W. Somerset. The Moon & Sixpence. large type ed. 384p. 1995. lib. bdg. 24.00 (*0-939495-78-3*) North Bks.
— The Moon & Sixpence. large type ed. LC 98-52327. 327p. 1999. 27.95 (*1-56000-483-5*) Transaction Pubs.
— The Moon & Sixpence. LC 75-25357. (Works of W. Somerset Maugham). 1977. reprint ed. 23.95 (*0-405-07816-1*) Ayer.
— The Moon & Sixpence. 242p. 1998. reprint ed. lib. bdg. 24.00 (*1-58287-050-0*) North Bks.
— Moon & Sixpence. unabridged ed. 156p. 1997. reprint ed. pap. 14.95 (*1-57002-016-7*) Univ Publng Hse.
— The Moon & Sixpence. unabridged ed. LC 95-34752. (Thrift Editions Ser.). 176p. 1995. reprint ed. pap. text 2.00 (*0-486-28731-9*) Dover.
— Mrs. Craddock. 256p. 1992. pap. 11.95 (*0-14-018594-1*, Penguin Classics) Viking Penguin.
— Mrs. Craddock. LC 75-25358. (Works of W. Somerset Maugham). 1977. reprint ed. 26.95 (*0-405-07817-X*) Ayer.
— The Narrow Corner. 224p. 1993. pap. 13.95 (*0-14-018598-4*, Penguin Classics) Viking Penguin.
— The Narrow Corner. LC 75-25359. (Works of W. Somerset Maugham). 1977. reprint ed. 23.95 (*0-405-07818-8*) Ayer.
— Of Human Bondage. 1976. 31.95 (*0-8488-1095-3*) Amereon Ltd.
— Of Human Bondage. 656p. 1991. mass mkt. 5.95 (*0-553-21392-X*, Bantam Classics) Bantam.
— Of Human Bondage. 704p. 1991. mass mkt. 5.95 (*0-451-52556-6*, Sig Classics) NAL.
— Of Human Bondage. 1915. 17.05 (*0-606-01173-0*, Pub. by Turtleback) Demco.
— Of Human Bondage. LC 92-225714. (Twentieth-Century Classics Ser.). 608p. 1992. pap. 11.95 (*0-14-018522-4*, Penguin Classics) Viking Penguin.
***Maugham, W. Somerset.** Of Human Bondage. 2000. pap. 14.00 (*0-375-72466-4*) Vin Bks.
Maugham, W. Somerset. Of Human Bondage. large type ed. LC 98-49474. 375p. 1998. 27.95 (*1-56000-500-9*) Transaction Pubs.
— Of Human Bondage. 1981. reprint ed. lib. bdg. 41.95 (*0-89966-386-9*) Buccaneer Bks.
— Of Human Bondage. 774p. 1999. reprint ed. 39.95 (*0-7351-0121-3*) Replica Bks.
— Of Human Bondage. (Illus.). 684p. 1992. reprint ed. 33.95 (*1-877767-71-9*) Univ Publng Hse.
— Of Human Bondage: One of Modern Library's 100 Best Novels. LC 98-46169. 1999. pap. 11.95 (*0-375-75315-X*) Modern Lib NY.
***Maugham, W. Somerset.** The Painted Veil. 290p. 1999. 27.95 (*0-7351-0173-6*) Replica Bks.
Maugham, W. Somerset. The Painted Veil. 256p. 1992. pap. 12.95 (*0-14-018599-2*, Penguin Classics) Viking Penguin.
The Painted Veil. large type ed. 1974. 27.99 (*0-85456-255-9*) Ulverscroft.
— Points of View: Five Essays. LC 75-25374. (Works of W. Somerset Maugham). 1977. reprint ed. 23.95 (*0-405-07827-7*) Ayer.
— Princess September & the Nightingale. LC 98-9230. (The Iona & Peter Opie Library of Children's Literature). (Illus.). 48p. (YA). (gr. k-6). 1998. 16.95 (*0-19-512480-4*) OUP.
— The Razor's Edge. 1978. 17.05 (*0-606-03057-3*, Pub. by Turtleback) Demco.
— The Razor's Edge. (Penguin Twentieth-Century Classics Ser.). 314p. 1992. pap. 12.95 (*0-14-018523-2*, Penguin Classics) Viking Penguin.
— The Sacred Flame: A Play in Three Acts. LC 75-25390. (Works of W. Somerset Maugham). 1977. reprint ed. 23.95 (*0-405-07847-1*) Ayer.
— Selected Prefaces & Introductions. LC 75-25375. (Works of W. Somerset Maugham). 1977. reprint ed. 23.95 (*0-405-07828-5*) Ayer.
— Sheppey: A Play in Three Acts. LC 75-30396. (Works of W. Somerset Maugham). 1977. reprint ed. 23.95 (*0-405-07848-X*) Ayer.
— Six Comedies. LC 75-25391. (Works of W. Somerset Maugham). 1977. reprint ed. 35.95 (*0-405-07849-8*) Ayer.
— Six Stories Written in the First Person Singular. LC 75-26133. (Works of W. Somerset Maugham). 1977. reprint ed. 23.95 (*0-405-07854-4*) Ayer.
— Strictly Personal. LC 75-25376. (Works of W. Somerset Maugham). 1977. reprint ed. 23.95 (*0-405-07829-3*) Ayer.
— The Summing Up. 208p. 1992. pap. 12.95 (*0-14-018600-X*, Penguin Classics) Viking Penguin.
— The Summing Up. LC 75-25377. (Works of W. Somerset Maugham). 1978. reprint ed. 23.95 (*0-405-07830-7*) Ayer.
— Ten Novels & Their Authors. 301p. 1978. pap. 6.95 (*0-330-25497-9*) Academy Chi Pubs.
— Theatre. LC 75-25365. (Works of W. Somerset Maugham). 1977. reprint ed. 23.95 (*0-405-07823-4*) Ayer.
— Then & Now: A Novel. LC 75-25364. (Works of W. Somerset Maugham). 1977. reprint ed. 25.95 (*0-405-07822-6*) Ayer.
— The Trembling of a Leaf. LC 75-26136. (Works of W. Somerset Maugham). 1977. reprint ed. 23.95 (*0-405-07857-9*) Ayer.
— The Trembling of a Leaf. 302p. 1985. reprint ed. mass mkt. 4.95 (*0-935180-21-4*) Mutual Pub HI.
***Maugham, W. Somerset.** The Trembling of a Leaf: Little Stories of the South Sea Islands. 304p. 1999. write for info. (*0-7351-0189-2*); pap. 19.95 (*0-7351-0193-0*) Replica Bks.
— Up at the Villa. LC 99-56315. (International Ser.). 192p. 2000. pap. 11.00 (*0-375-72462-1*) Vin Bks.
Maugham, W. Somerset. Up at the Villa. LC 75-25366. (Works of W. Somerset Maugham). 1977. reprint ed. 28.95 (*0-405-07824-2*) Ayer.
— The Vagrant Mood: Six Essays. LC 75-25378. (Works of W. Somerset Maugham). 1977. reprint ed. 23.95 (*0-405-07831-5*) Ayer.
Maugham, W. Somerset, jt. auth. see Copper, Basil.
Maugham, W. Somerset, ed. see Kipling, Rudyard.
***Maugham, William S.** Ashenden the British Agent. 2000. 34.95 (*0-7658-0779-3*) Transaction Pubs.
Maughan, Barbara, jt. ed. see Hill, Jonathan.
Maughan, Caroline & Webb, Julian. Maughan & Webb: Lawyering Skills & the Legal Process. 1995. pap. write for info. (*0-406-04466-X*, WMLS, MICHIE) LEXIS Pub.
Maughan, Caroline, jt. auth. see Webb, Julian.
Maughan, Esther, jt. ed. see Clifton, Rita.
Maughan, Jackie J. Hiking Idaho. LC 96-21415. (Illus.). 352p. 1996. pap. 16.95 (*1-56044-469-X*) Falcon Pub Inc.
— Yellowstone on My Mind. (On My Mind Ser.). (Illus.). 120p. 1998. 32.95 (*1-56044-380-4*) Falcon Pub Inc.
Maughan, Jackie J., et al. Go Tell It on the Mountain. 224p. 1996. 22.95 (*0-8117-0738-5*) Stackpole.
Maughan, James T. Ecological Assessment of Hazardous Waste Sites. LC 92-27826. 352p. 1992. text 72.95 (*0-442-01091-5*, VNR) Wiley.
Maughan, James T. Ecological Assessment of Hazardous Waste Sites. (Industrial Health & Safety Ser.). 352p. 1992. 110.00 (*0-471-28476-9*, VNR) Wiley.
Maughan, Ron, et al. Biochemistry of Exercise & Training. LC 97-31837. (Illus.). 256p. 1997. text 95.00 (*0-19-262742-2*); pap. text 52.50 (*0-19-262741-4*) OUP.
***Maughan, Ron J. & Murray, Robert.** Sports Drinks: Basic Science & Practical Aspects. LC 00-34307. (Nutrition in Exercise & Sport Ser.). 2000. write for info. (*0-8493-7008-6*) CRC Pr.
Maughan, Ron J. Basic Sciences for Sports Medicine. LC 99-17155. 368p. 1999. pap. text 45.00 (*0-7506-3466-9*) Buttrwrth-Heinemann.
Maughan, Ron J. & Shirreffs, Susan M., eds. Biochemistry of Exercise IX, Vol. 9. LC 96-10897. (International Series on Sport Sciences). (Illus.). 608p. 1996. text 69.00 (*0-88011-486-X*, BMAU0486) Human Kinetics.
Maughan, Ron J., jt. ed. see Rogozkin, Victor A.
Maughan, Ronald J., et al. Nutrition in Sport. LC 99-12066. (Olympic Encyclopaedia of Sports Medicine Ser.: Vol. VII). (Illus.). 704p. 2000. 125.00 (*0-632-05094-2*) Blackwell Sci.
Maughan, Stephen. Echoes of Glory: The Napoleonic Soldier Recreated in Color Photographs. (Illus.). 1998. 39.95 (*1-85915-004-7*, Pub. by W & G) Motorbooks Intl.
— Napoleon's Imperial Guard. (Illus.). 96p. 1999. pap. 22.95 (*1-86126-290-6*, Pub. by Crolwood) Motorbooks Intl.
— Napoleon's Line Cavalry: Recreated in Color Photographs. (Illus.). 1997. pap. text 19.95 (*1-85915-038-1*, Pub. by W & G) Motorbooks Intl.
— Napoleon's Line Infantry & Artillery: Recreated in Color Photographs. (Illus.). 1997. pap. text 19.95 (*1-85915-053-5*, Pub. by W & G) Motorbooks Intl.
***Maughan, Stephen E.** The Napoleonic Soldier. LC 99-490336. (Illus.). 144p. 2000. 52.95 (*1-86126-281-7*, 129758AE, Pub. by Crolwood) Motorbooks Intl.
Maughon, Donna, ed. see Maughon, Robert M.
Maughon, Martha. Why Am I Crying? 1983. pap. 6.95 (*0-310-37671-8*, 11221P) Zondervan.
— Why Am I Crying? A Helpful & Honest Look at Depression. LC 89-19681. 128p. 1989. pap. 8.99 (*0-929239-17-2*) Discovery Hse Pubs.
Maughon, Robert M. Elvis Is Alive. Maughon, Donna, ed. 1997. 24.95 (*0-9650366-1-8*) Cinnamon Moon.
— Elvis Is Alive. 2nd ed. Maughon, Donna, ed. 254p. 1999. pap. 19.95 (*0-9650366-2-6*) Cinnamon Moon.
— New Orleans E. R. 18th ed. Copple, Curry, ed. 315p. (Orig.). 1999. pap. 14.95 (*0-9650366-0-X*) Cinnamon Moon.
Maugin, Gerard A. Continuum Mechanics of Electromagnetics Solids. (Applied Mathematics & Mechanics Ser.: Vol. 33). 598p. 1988. 299.00 (*0-444-70399-3*, North Holland) Elsevier.
— Material Inhomogeneities in Elasticity. LC 93-6887. 280p. (gr. 13). 1993. ring bd. 78.95 (*0-412-49520-1*, Chap & Hall CRC) CRC Pr.
— Nonlinear Electromechanical Effects & Applications. (Series in Theoretical & Applied Mechanics: Vol. 1). 184p. 1986. text 47.00 (*9971-978-43-1*); pap. text 28.00 (*9971-5-0096-5*) World Scientific Pub.
***Maugin, Gerard A.** Nonlinear Waves in Elastic Crystals. LC 99-44815. (Oxford Mathematical Monographs). (Illus.). 320p. 2000. text 95.00 (*0-19-853484-1*) OUP.
Maugin, Gerard A. Thermomechanics of Nonlinear Irreversible Behaviours: An Introduction. LC 99-45822. (Nonlinear Science Ser.). 350p. 1999. 62.00 (*981-02-3375-2*) World Scientific Pub.
— The Thermomechanics of Plasticity & Fracture. (Cambridge Texts in Applied Mathematics Ser.: No. 7). (Illus.). 370p. (C). 1992. text 115.00 (*0-521-39476-7*); pap. text 42.95 (*0-521-39780-4*) Cambridge U Pr.
Maugin, Gerard A., jt. auth. see Eringen, A. Cemal.
***Maugis, D.** Contact, Adhesion & Rupture of Elastic Solids. LC 99-50194. (Illus.). 465p. 2000. 99.00 (*3-540-66113-1*) Spr-Verlag.
Maugnan, Mark & Wilson, Daniel. Wholistic Taxes: Good Advice You Never Thought You Would Hear from a CPA. LC 96-94805. (Illus.). 240p. (Orig.). 1996. pap. 11.95 (*1-57502-319-9*, P01083) Morris Pubng.
Maugras, M. Dictionnaire Biologie Cellulaire. (FRE.). 174p. 1996. 49.95 (*0-320-00659-X*) Fr & Eur.
Mauguiere, Benedicte N. Traversee des Ideologies et Exploration des Identites dans les Ecritures de Femmes au Quebec (1970-1980) (Francophone Cultures & Literatures Ser.: Vol. 17). (FRE.). 385p. (C). 1997. text 59.95 (*0-8204-3021-8*) P Lang Pubng.
Mauguiere, Benedicte N., ed. Cultural Identities in Canadian Literature (Identites Culturelles dans la Litterature Canadienne) LC 97-10690. VIII, 230p. (C). 1998. pap. text 32.95 (*0-8204-3389-6*) P Lang Pubng.
Mauguiere, Francois, jt. auth. see Rossini, P. M.
Maui Association for Family & Community Education. Best of Our Favorite Recipes. spiral bd. 22.95 (*0-9641882-1-X*) Maui Assn.
Maui Cooks Inc. Staff. Maui Cooks Again. (Illus.). pap. 15.95 (*0-9639120-0-3*) Maui Cooks.
Mauila, A., et al. Dictionnaire Francais de Medicine et de Biologie, Vol. 3. (FRE.). 1200p. 1972. 195.00 (*0-7859-0746-7*, M-6394) Fr & Eur.
Mauiner, Dan, ed. see Podjen, India J.
Mauk, A. Grant, jt. auth. see Scott, Robert A.
Mauk, Barbara R., jt. auth. see Fatooh, Audrey.
Mauk, David & Oakland, John. American Civilization: An Introduction. 2nd ed. LC 97-240. (Illus.). 443p. (C). 1998. pap. 20.99 (*0-415-16523-7*) Routledge.
Mauk, David C. The Colony That Rose from the Sea: Norwegian Maritime Migration & Community in Brooklyn, 1850-1910. Lovboll, Odd S., ed. (Special Publications). (Illus.). 272p. 1997. 44.95 (*0-87732-086-1*) Norwegian-Am Hist Assn.
— Colony that Rose from the Sea: Norwegian Maritime Migration & Community in Brooklyn, 1850-1930. 368p. 1998. text 44.95 (*0-252-02400-1*) U of Ill Pr.
Mauk, Jonathan Van Dorn. The Gallery of Legends Book: An Historical Overview of Racing in the Daytona Beach Florida Area From 1903-1995 covering World Land Speed Records, Stock Car, Sports Car & Motorcycle Racing. (Illus.). 166p. (Orig.). 1995. pap., per. 9.95 (*1-889516-00-7*) Intl Speedway.
Mauk, Laura. Daddy & Me: A Children's Collection of Thoughts. Caton, Patrick, ed. LC 97-71650. 168p. 1997. pap. 5.95 (*1-56245-312-2*) Great Quotations.
— The Essence of Music: An Ensemble of Musical Quotes. 64p. 1995. 6.50 (*1-56245-216-9*) Great Quotations.
— Home Sweet Home. 366p. 1995. pap., spiral bd. 6.50 (*1-56245-175-8*) Great Quotations.
— Mommy & Me: A Children's Collection of Thoughts. Caton, Patrick, ed. LC 97-71651. 168p. 1997. pap. 5.95 (*1-56245-311-4*) Great Quotations.
Mauksch, Mary. Fabulous & Flourless. LC 97-19003. 212p. 1997. 19.95 (*0-02-862002-X*) Macmillan.
***Maul, Bill.** Fuzzy Zoeller: Have You Heard the One About??? LC 99-94948. 208p. 1999. 49.98 (*0-9673241-0-6*) Fashn Fun Cl Inc.
Maul, Dianna, jt. auth. see Barlow, Janelle.
Maul, George A. Introduction to Satellite Oceanography. 1984. text 269.50 (*90-247-3096-1*) Kluwer Academic.
Maul, George A., ed. Climatic Change in the Intra-Americas Sea. LC 93-6852. 1993. write for info. (*0-340-58981-7*, Pub. by E A) Routldge.
Maul, George A. & American Geophysical Union Staff. Small Islands: Marine Science & Sustainable Development. LC 96-29237. (Coastal & Estaurine Studies: Vol. 51). 467p. 1996. 65.00 (*0-87590-265-0*) Am Geophysical.
Maul, George A., ed. see Kumar, M.
Maul, Lyle R. & Mayfield, Dianne C. The Entrepreneur's Road Map to Business Success. rev. ed. LC 92-50275. (Illus.). 350p. 1992. pap. 14.95 (*0-929382-60-9*) Saxtons River Pubns.

M

Maul, Richard W. An Analysis of the Constitutional Provisions Pertaining to Legislative Organization in South Dakota. 1952. 5.00 (*1-55614-019-3*) U of SD Gov Res Bur.

Maul, Susan K. & Adams, Jeanette N. Childhood Cancer: A Nursing Overview. (C). 1987. 62.50 (*0-86720-381-1*) Jones & Bartlett.

Maulana, Abdul M. Khutubat-i-Jumu'ah. 110p. (Orig.). 1985. pap. 7.50 (*1-56744-317-6*) Kazi Pubns.

— Tafsir ul-Quran, 4 vol. set. 2800p. (C). 1985. text 69.00 (*1-56744-216-1*) Kazi Pubns.

Maulana, Jalal al-Din Rumi. Night & Sleep. Barks, Coleman & Bly, Robert, trs. from PER. (Illus.). 48p. (Orig.). 1980. pap. 6.00 (*0-938756-02-8*) Yellow Moon.

Maulana, Muhammad A. The New World Order. 4th ed. 86p. 1989. pap. 4.95 (*0-913321-33-8*) Ahmadiyya Anjuman.

— The Religion of Islam. 617p. 1992. reprint ed. 20.95 (*0-913321-32-X*) Ahmadiyya Anjuman.

— The Religions of Islam. 808p. 1986. 90.00 (*0-7855-1201-2*) St Mut.

Maulana, Muhammad K. Hayatus Sahabah: The Lives of the Sahabah, 2 vol. set. Majiid Ali Khan, tr. 450p. (C). 1991. text 69.00 (*1-56744-287-0*) Kazi Pubns.

Maulana Muhammad Kandhlawi. Hayatus Sahabah: The Lives of the Sahabah, Vol. 1. Mojid Ali Khan, tr. 430p. (C). 1991. text. write for info. (*1-56744-288-9*) Kazi Pubns.

Maulana Muhammed Ali. Holy Qur'an. rev. ed. (ARA & ENG.). vi, 1256p. 1991. reprint ed. 19.95 (*0-913321-01-X*) Ahmadiyya Anjuman.

Maulana S. Tilmiz H. Rizvi. Guide Book of Qur'an. 1990. pap. 3.95 (*0-940368-76-5*, 126) Tahrike Tarsile Quran.

Maulbetsch, J. S., et al. Basic Research in Heat Transfer. 158p. 1977. pap. 7.25 (*0-318-12589-7*, M60177) Am Gas Assn.

Maulde, L. De, see De Maulde, L.

Mauldin. Always Ready to Sing. 1993. pap. 6.95 (*1-55897-584-5*) Brentwood Music.

— Christmas I Love to Tell the Story. 1990. pap. 6.95 (*1-55897-036-3*) Brentwood Music.

— He's Still the Lamb. 1995. pap. 6.95 (*0-7601-0242-2*) Brentwood Music.

— Life Prescription. 128p. 1996. text 24.95 (*0-7872-2456-1*) Kendall-Hunt.

— More Ready to Sing. 1992. pap. 6.95 (*1-55897-395-8*) Brentwood Music.

Mauldin, John. How to Profit from the Y2K Recession. LC 99-17334. 256p. 1999. text 24.95 (*0-312-20706-9*) St Martin.

Mauldin, Barbara. Masks of Mexico. (Illus.). 128p. 1999. pap. 24.95 (*0-89013-325-5*) Museum NM Pr.

***Mauldin, Barbara.** Masks of Mexico. (Illus.). 128p. 1999. 45.00 (*0-89013-329-8*) Museum NM Pr.

Mauldin, Bill. Back Home. 25.95 (*0-89190-856-0*) Amereon Ltd.

— Bill Mauldin's Army: Bill Mauldin's Greatest World War II Cartoons. LC 82-23141. (Illus.). 384p. 1983. reprint ed. pap. 18.95 (*0-89141-159-3*) Presidio Pr.

— Mud & Guts: A Look at the Common Soldier of the American Revolution. (Illus.). 58p. 1996. reprint ed. pap. text 20.00 (*0-7881-3267-9*) DIANE Pub.

Mauldin, Bill. Mud & Guts: The Common Soldier of the American Revolution. 64p. 1995. pap. 8.50 (*0-16-061670-0*) USGPO.

Mauldin, Bill. Up Front. (Illus.). 240p. 21.95 (*0-89190-896-X*) Amereon Ltd.

— Up Front. 1994. lib. bdg. 24.95 (*1-56849-444-0*) Buccaneer Bks.

Mauldin, Bill. Up Front. 24.95 (*0-393-05031-9*) Norton.

Mauldin, Bill. Up Front. 50th fac. ed. 240p. 1995. 23.95 (*0-393-03816-5*) Norton.

Mauldin, Carol. Mrs. Mauldin's Make-Over Magic: A Diet of Choice (The Absolutely Last Diet You'll Ever Need!) 1997. pap. text 19.95 (*0-9661090-0-7*) C Mauldin.

Mauldin, Christopher A. Honor Bound: The Life of Harvey P. Everest. (Oklahoma Commerce & Industry Hall of Honor Ser.). (Illus.). 149p. (Orig.). (C). 1989. text 24.95 (*0-9623357-0-3*); pap. text 12.95 (*0-685-26157-3*) Okla City Univ Pr.

Mauldin, Henry. Mountains & Pioneers of Lake County. 2nd ed. Greenlee, Carolyn W., ed. 56p. 1998. pap. 6.95 (*1-887400-22-2*, EUB-1010) Earthen Vessel Prodns.

Mauldin, Jane E. Glory, Hallelujah! Now Please Pick up Your Socks: Meditations. LC 98-16742. 72p. 1998. pap. 7.00 (*1-55896-365-0*, Skinner Hse Bks) Unitarian Univ.

Mauldin, John H. Light, Lasers & Optics. (Illus.). 240p. 1988. 22.95 (*0-8306-9038-7*, 3038); pap. 16.95 (*0-8306-9338-6*, 3038) McGraw-Hill Prof.

— Particles in Nature: The Chronological Discovery of the New Physics. (Illus.). 288p. 1986. 23.95 (*0-8306-0416-2*, 2616); pap. 16.95 (*0-8306-0516-9*, 2616P) McGraw-Hill Prof.

— Prospects for Interstellar Travel. LC 57-43769. (Science & Technology Ser.: Vol. 80). (Illus.). 390p. 1992. 50.00 (*0-87703-344-7*, Am Astronaut Soc) Univelt Inc.

— Sun Spaces-Home Additions for Year-Round Natural Living. LC 87-21913. (Illus.). 256p. 1987. 21.95 (*0-8306-7816-6*, 2816) McGraw-Hill Prof.

Mauldin, Lynn C. Lea County, New Mexico: A Pictorial History. LC 97-35685. 1997. write for info. (*1-57864-010-5*) Donning Co.

Mauldin, Michael L. Conceptual Information Retrieval: A Case Study in Adaptive Partial Parsing. 240p. (C). 1991. text 102.00 (*0-7923-9214-0*) Kluwer Academic.

Mauldin, R., et al. Measure & Measurable Dynamics. LC 89-14914. (Contemporary Mathematics Ser.: Vol. 94). 326p. 1989. pap. 57.00 (*0-8218-5099-7*, CONM/94) Am Math.

Mauldin, W. Parker, jt. ed. see Ross, J. A.

Maulding, Shoni. Hitched Horsehair: The Complete Guide for Self Learning. LC 97-92318. (Illus.). 186p. 1998. pap. 25.95 (*0-9659624-6-6*) River Publ.

Mauldon. Teaching Gymnastics. 2nd ed. 1989. pap. text. write for info. (*0-582-02950-3*, Pub. by Addison-Wesley) Longman.

Mauldon, Margaret, tr. see Huysmans, Joris-Karl.

Mauldon, Margaret, tr. see Stendhal, pseud.

Mauldon, Margaret, tr. see Zola, Emile.

Maule, A. J., jt. auth. see Svenson, O.

Maule, Christopher, jt. auth. see Acheson, Keith.

Maule, Elizabeth M. Bird's Eye Views of Wisconsin Communities: A Preliminary Checklist. LC 77-24430. 1977. pap. 2.00 (*0-87020-168-9*) State Hist Soc Wis.

Maule, Graham, jt. auth. see Bell, John.

Maule, Graham, jt. auth. see Bell, John L.

Maule, Harry E., ed. Great Tales of the American West. reprint ed. lib. bdg. 27.95 (*0-88411-875-4*) Amereon Ltd.

Maule, James E. Better That 100 Witches Should Live: The 1696 Acquittal of Thomas Maule of Salem, Massachusetts, on Charges of Seditious Libel & Its Impact on the Development of First Amendment Freedoms. LC 95-94567. 684p. 1995. text 60.00 (*0-9647362-2-5*) JEMBk Pub.

This book is both a biography of Thomas Maule of Salem, Massachusetts (1645-1724) & an analysis of the 1696 trial in which he was acquitted of seditious libel charges. Maule, an outspoken Quaker who criticized the Puritans for their religious persecution & intolerance, their attempts to impose their religious views on everyone, & their mismanagement of the witchcraft crisis, persuaded a Puritan jury to disregard the Court's direction to convict, arguing that the court had no right to suppress his expression of religious belief. Maule's triumph over a coercive theocracy influenced the development of the First Amendment & contributed significantly to the establishment of the freedom of religious expression. Contains: Reprints of Thomas Maule's four extant writings, including the offending treatise, its sequel, & the two letters, & Joseph R. Maule's previously unpublished M. A. thesis, BASIS FOR THE MAULE CHARACTERIZATIONS IN THE ROMANCE, HOUSE OF THE SEVEN GABLES. Author: A law professor at Villanova University School of Law, has written two genealogies & numerous tax books, & received a 1993 BNA Tax Management Distinguished Author award. To order: JEMBook Publishing Company, 219 Comrie Drive, Villanova, PA 19085.
Publisher Paid Annotation.

— The History & Genealogy of the Maules. 830p. 1982. 30.00 (*0-9647362-0-9*) JEMBk Pub.

— S Corporations: State Law & Taxation, 2 vols., Set. 1990. 250.00 (*0-685-28165-5*) West Group.

— A Zappone Family History. 153p. 1986. pap. 12.00 (*0-9647362-1-7*) JEMBk Pub.

Maule, James E., jt. auth. see Clay, Alvin A., III.

Maule, Jeremy, jt. ed. see Poole, Adrian.

***Maule, John.** Congregation of the Damned. LC 00-190735. (Illus.). 160p. 2000. pap. write for info. (*1-57579-189-7*) Pine Hill Pr.

Maule, Linda S., jt. auth. see Sheldon, Charles H.

Maule, R. William. Information, Communications & Technology in Organizations: An Introduction to Information Studies & Organizational Informatics. (Illus.). 464p. (C). 1996. pap. text 45.00 (*0-9647905-0-5*) Info Assocs Pr.

— Information Networks & Services: An Overview of Foundations, Standards & Practices for Modern Information Management. (Illus.). 500p. (Orig.). (C). 1998. pap. text 45.00 (*0-9647905-1-3*) Info Assocs Pr.

— Information Theory & Research: An Introduction to the Disciplines & Methodologies of Information Studies & Organizational Informatics. (Illus.). 500p. (Orig.). (C). 1998. pap. text 45.00 (*0-9647905-2-1*) Info Assocs Pr.

— Internet & WWW 1: Internet Foundation Technologies, Services & Practices. (Illus.). 230p. (C). 1999. pap. text 35.00 (*0-9647905-4-8*) Info Assocs Pr.

— Internet & WWW 3: Interent E-Business & E-Commerce. (Illus.). 220p. (C). 2000. pap. text 35.00 (*0-9647905-6-4*) Info Assocs Pr.

— Internet & WWW 2: Internet Network Design, Implementation & Management. (Illus.). 240p. (C). 1999. pap. text 35.00 (*0-9647905-5-6*) Info Assocs Pr.

Mauleon, Rebeca. The Salsa Guidebook for Piano & Ensemble. (Illus.). 259p. (C). 1993. pap. 20.00 (*0-9614701-9-4*) Sher Music.

Mauleon, Rebecca. 101 Montunos. (Illus.). 250p. 1999. text 28.00 (*1-883217-07-5*) Sher Music.

Maulhardt, Jeffrey W. The Day the New York Giants Came to Oxnard: November 11, 1913. (Illus.). 48p. 1997. pap. text 14.95 (*0-9657515-0-3*) J W Maulhardt.

Maulik, Beth. Schoolhouse Magazine: An Educator's Guide to Families on the Move - Minnesota. Gendler, Neal, ed. (Illus.). 88p. 1998. pap. 6.95 (*0-9663804-0-1*) Schoolhse Mag.

***Maulik, Beth.** Schoolhouse Magazine: Regional Guide to Minnesota Schools. Gendler, Neal, ed. (Illus.). 96p. 2000. pap. 6.95 (*0-9663804-3-6*) Schoolhse Mag.

Maulik, Dev. Doppler Ultrasound in Obstetrics & Gynecology. LC 96-11916. 752p. 1996. 159.00 (*0-387-94240-8*) Spr-Verlag.

***Maulik, Dev, ed.** Asphyxia & Fetal Brain Damage. LC 97-52695. 372p. 1998. 119.95 (*0-471-18427-6*, Wiley-Liss) Wiley.

Maulik, S. Coleoptera - Phytophaga - Chrysomelidae: Chrysomelinae & Halticinae. (Fauna of British India Ser.). (Illus.). xiv, 442p. 1977. reprint ed. 30.00 (*0-88065-156-3*) Scholarly Pubns.

— Coleoptera - Phytophaga - Chrysomelidae: Galerucinae. (Fauna of British India Ser.). (Illus.). xiv, 658p. 1979. reprint ed. 30.00 (*0-88065-157-1*) Scholarly Pubns.

— Coleoptera - Phytophaga - Chrysomelidae: Hispinae & Cossidinae. (Fauna of British India Ser.). xii, 442p. 1973. reprint ed. 16.00 (*0-88065-155-5*) Scholarly Pubns.

Maulik, Sunil & Patel, Salil. Molecular Biotechnology: Therapeutic Applications & Strategies. LC 96-2733. 223p. 1996. pap. 59.95 (*0-471-11681-5*, Wiley-Liss) Wiley.

Maulitz, Russell C., ed. Unnatural Causes: The Three Leading Killer Diseases in America. 210p. 1989. text 37.00 (*0-8135-1405-3*); pap. text 18.00 (*0-8135-1406-1*) Rutgers U Pr.

Maull, jt. auth. see Breckler.

Maull, B. Maull Bailey. R. F., ed. 241p. 1991. reprint ed. pap. 43.00 (*0-8328-2054-7*); reprint ed. lib. bdg. 53.00 (*0-8328-2053-9*) Higginson Bk Co.

Maull, Diana, jt. auth. see Carmicheal, David W.

Maull, Hanns, jt. ed. see Segal, Gerald.

Maull, Hanns W. Energy, Minerals, & Western Security. LC 84-15410. 431p. reprint ed. pap. 133.70 (*0-7837-2190-0*, 204252800004) Bks Demand.

— Natural Gas & Economic Security. (Atlantic Papers: No. 43). 60p. (Orig.). 1981. pap. text 10.50 (*0-86598-082-9*) Rowman.

Maull, Kimball I. Advances in Trauma, Vol. 11. 270p. 1996. 69.95 (*0-8151-6203-0*) Mosby Inc.

Maull, Kimball I. & Augenstein, Jeffrey S., eds. Trauma Informatics. LC 97-8491. (Computers in Health Care Ser.). (Illus.). 328p. 1997. 59.00 (*0-387-94359-5*) Spr-Verlag.

Maull, Kimball I., et al. Complications of Trauma & Critical Care. 135th ed. LC 95-15497. (Illus.). 528p. 1996. text 120.00 (*0-7216-4940-8*, W B Saunders Co) Harcrt Hlth Sci Grp.

— Trauma Update for the EMT. 272p. (C). 1992. pap. 24.00 (*0-89303-889-X*, 740503) P-H.

Maull, Kimball I., ed. see Advances in Trauma & Critical Care Staff.

Maulmier, Thierrey. Diccionario Terminologia Politica. (SPA.). 340p. 1977. pap. 19.95 (*0-8288-5366-5*, S50250) Fr & Eur.

Maultsby, Maxie C., Jr. Coping Better . . . Anytime Anywhere: The Handbook of Rational Self-Counseling. (Illus.). 259p. 1998. reprint ed. pap. 14.95 (*0-932838-05-7*) Tangrm Bks.

— Guia Ilustrada del Medico para el Auto-Tratamiento Emocional. Munoz, Gabriela & Maultsby, Rossnilda O., trs. from ENG.Tr. of You & Your Emotions. (ENG & SPA., Illus.). 109p. 1977. reprint ed. pap. 8.95 (*0-932838-06-5*) Tangrm Bks.

— Rational Behavior Therapy. (Illus.). 288p. (C). 1984. pap. 28.95 (*0-13-752907-4*) P-H.

— Rational Behavior Therapy: The Self-Help Psychotherapy. (Illus.). 254p. 1990. reprint ed. pap. 18.95 (*0-932838-08-1*) Tangrm Bks.

— The Rational Behavioral Alcoholic-Relapse Prevention Treatment Method: An Illustrated Guide for the New Self-Help Treatment Techniques for Alcoholics & Other Substance Abusers. Orig. Title: A Million Dollars for Your Hangover. (Illus.). 233p. 1978. pap. 13.95 (*0-932838-00-6*) Tangrm Bks.

— Relapse Prevention Treatment for Alcoholics & Other Addicted People. (Illus.). 233p. 1990. reprint ed. pap. 13.95 (*0-932838-03-0*) Tangrm Bks.

Maultsby, Maxie C., Jr. & Hendricks, Allie. You & Your Emotions. (Illus.). 109p. 1990. reprint ed. pap. 8.95 (*0-932838-01-4*) Tangrm Bks.

Maultsby, Rossnilda O., tr. see Maultsby, Maxie C., Jr.

Maulucci, Anthony. Adriana's Eyes & Other Stories. LC 98-75406. 151p. 1999. pap. 11.95 (*0-9645226-1-6*) Lorenzo Pr.

— The Discovery of Luminous Being. LC 94-96880. 112p. 1995. pap. 8.95 (*0-9645226-0-8*) Lorenzo Pr.

Maum, Ima G., pseud. Beyond Ramen Noodles: How to Feed Yourself When You Don't Have the Time, the Space, or the Equipment, & You Can't Afford to Eat Every Meal Out. (Illus.). 132p. (Orig.). 1993. pap. 6.00 (*1-883770-00-9*, El Moro Pr) El Moro Pub.

Maume, Patrick. The Long Gestation: Irish Nationalist Life, 1891-1918. LC 99-22052. 2000. text 55.00 (*0-312-22549-0*) St Martin.

Maumee Valley Herb Society Staff, et al. There's More to Life Than Parsley. LC 95-171231. (Illus.). 192p. (Orig.). 1994. pap. 12.95 (*0-9644350-0-4*) Maumee Vall Herb Soc.

Maumenee, A. Edward. A. Edward Maumenee, M. D. The Wilmer Ophthalmological Institute at the Johns Hopkins University & the Stanford Medical School. (Ophthalmology Oral History Ser.). (Illus.). xxx, 267p. 1994. pap. 45.00 (*1-56055-068-6*) FAAO.

Maun, Clint & Haacker, Robert. Power Tools for Long-Term Care Marketing. 85p. 1992. 149.00 incl. audio (*0-929442-15-6*, 2221pp) Prof Prnting & Pub.

Maun, Clint & Thorson, James A. Are You Still Working at the Home? A Book for Human Service Professionals. (Long Term Care Ser.). 96p. 1992. pap. 7.95 (*0-9631371-1-5*) James A Thorson.

Maun, Clint, jt. auth. see Haacker, Robert.

***Maun, Ian.** Radical! A Practical Guide to French: Makes French Grammar Easy. LC 99-47308. 256p. 2000. pap. 15.95 (*0-658-00415-8*, 004158) NTC Contemp Pub Co.

Maund, Alfred. The Big Boxcar. LC 98-35208. (Radical Novel Reconsidered Ser.). 1999. pap. 14.95 (*0-252-06754-1*) U of Ill Pr.

Maund, K. L. Handlist of the Acts of Native Welsh Rulers, 1132-1283. Pryce, Huw, ed. 176p. 1996. 50.00 (*0-7083-1333-7*, Pub. by Univ Wales Pr) Paul & Co Pubs.

— Ireland, Wales & England in the Eleventh Century. (Studies in Celtic History: Vol. 12). (Illus.). 247p. (C). 1991. 75.00 (*0-85115-533-2*) Boydell & Brewer.

Maund, K. L., ed. Gruffudd ap Cynan: A Collaborative Biography. LC 96-24757. (Studies in Celtic History: Vol. 16). (Illus.). 232p. 1997. 75.00 (*0-85115-389-5*) Boydell & Brewer.

Maunder, Andrew, ed. see Wood.

Maunder, C. R. Algebraic Topology. unabridged ed. (Illus.). 384p. 1996. reprint ed. pap. text 10.95 (*0-486-69131-4*) Dover.

Maunder, Chris, jt. ed. see Bettenson, Henry.

Maunder, Elwood R. & Davidson, Margaret, eds. First National Colloquium on the History of Forest Products Industry. vii, 221p. 1967. pap. text 16.00 (*0-8223 0266 7*) Duke.

Maunder, Michael & Moore, Patrick. The Sun in Eclipse. LC 97-42031. (Illus.). 260p. 1997. pap. 39.00 (*3-540-76146-2*) Spr-Verlag.

***Maunder, Michael J. de F. & Moore, Patrick.** Transit: When Planets Cross the Sun. LC 99-31314. (Illus.). viii, 164p. 1999. pap. 39.95 (*1-85233-621-8*, Pub. by Spr-Verlag) Spr-Verlag.

Maunder, Richard. Keyboard Instruments in Eighteenth-Century Vienna. (Illus.). 288p. 1998. text 95.00 (*0-19-816637-0*) OUP.

Maunder, Richard, ed. Domenico Corri's a Select Collection of the Most Admired Songs, Duetts, &C., Volume 4, & the Singer's Preceptor, Vols. 1-2. LC 93-8550. (Domenico Corri's Treatises on Singing Ser.: Vol. 3). 328p. 1995. text 40.00 (*0-8153-0681-4*) Garland.

— Domenico Corri's, Vols. 1-3: A Select Collection of the Most Admired Songs, Duetts, & C. LC 93-8550. (Domenico Corri's Treatises on Singing Ser.: No.1). 364p. 1993. text 40.00 (*0-8153-0679-2*) Garland.

— The Musical Sources for Domenico Corri's: A Select Collection of the Most Admired Songs, Duets, & C., 3 Vols., Vols. 1 - 3. LC 93-8550. (Domenico Corri's Treatises on Singing Ser.: No. 2). 608p. 1994. text 40.00 (*0-8153-0680-6*) Garland.

— The Musical Sources for Domenico Corri's: A Select Collection of the Most Admired Songs, Duetts, & C., the Singer's Preceptor. LC 93-8550. (Domenico Corri's Treatises on Singing Ser.: Vol. 4). 272p. 1995. text 40.00 (*0-8153-0845-0*) Garland.

Maunder, W. F. Employment in an Underdeveloped Area, 3--3. LC 73-19566. (Caribbean Ser.). 215p. 1974. reprint ed. lib. bdg. 59.50 (*0-8371-7296-9*, MAUA, Greenwood Pr) Greenwood.

Maunder, W. F., ed. see Baxter, R. E. & Phillips, C.

Maunder, W. F., ed. see Mark, J., et al.

Maunder, W. F., ed. see Moir, C. B. & Dawson, J.

Maunder, W. F., ed. see Wilson, R. A. & Bosworth, D. L.

Maunder, W. John. The Human Impact of Climate Uncertainty: Weather Information, Economic Planning, & Business Management. 240p. 1989. 49.95 (*0-415-04076-0*, A3673); pap. 14.95 (*0-415-04077-9*, A3677) Routledge.

—.The Uncertainty Business. 1987. 55.00 (*0-416-36100-5*) Routledge.

Maunders, Richard, ed. Domenico Corri's: A Select Collection of the Most Admired Songs, Duetts, & C., 4 Vols., Set. LC 93-8550. 1572p. 1995. 499.00 (*0-8153-0678-4*) Garland.

Maundril, Marlene. Mind Massage: 60 Creative Visualizations. 1997. pap. 19.95 (*1-86163-005-0*, Pub. by Capall Bann Pubng) Holmes Pub.

Mauner, George. Three Swiss Painters: Cuno Amiet, Giovanni Giacometti, Augusto Giacometti: Exhibition Catalogue. (Illus.). 166p. 1973. pap. 7.50 (*0-911209-02-6*) Palmer Mus Art.

Mauner, George, et al, eds. Paris: Center of Artistic Enlightenment. (Papers in Art History: Vol. IV). (Illus.). 250p. (Orig.). 1988. pap. 22.00 (*0-915773-03-1*) Penn St Univ Dept Art Hist.

***Mauner, George L., et al.** Manet: The Still-Life Paintings. LC 00-42009. 2000. write for info. (*0-8109-4391-3*) Abrams.

Maung, E. Burmese Buddhist Law. LC 77-87483. reprint ed. 25.00 (*0-404-16812-4*) AMS Pr.

***Maung Maung, U.** The 1988 Uprising in Burma. (Monograph Series, Yale Southeast Asia Studies: Vol. 49). 306p. 1999. pap. 22.00 (*0-938692-72-0*); lib. bdg. 35.00 (*0-938692-71-2*) Yale U SE Asia.

Maung, Mya. The Burma Road to Capitalism: Economic Growth Versus Democracy. LC 97-43959. 320p. 1998. 65.00 (*0-275-96216-4*, Praeger Pubs) Greenwood.

— The Burma Road to Poverty. LC 90-27555. 360p. 1991. 75.00 (*0-275-93613-9*, C3613, Praeger Pubs) Greenwood.

Maung Tin, tr. see Buddhaghosa.

***Maunger, Benig.** Reclaiming the Spirituality of Birth: Healing for Mothers & Babies. 216p. 2000. pap. 14.95 (*0-89281-896-4*) Inner Transform.

Maunsbach, Arvid B. & Afzelius, Bjorn A. Biomedical Electron Microscopy: Illustrated Methods & Interpretations. LC 98-85235. (Illus.). 548p. (C). 1998. text 99.95 (*0-12-480610-4*) Acad Pr.

M

An Asterisk (*) at the beginning of an entry indicates that the title is appearing for the first time.

Maunsell Party, Limited Staff & Asia Pacific Economic Cooperation (Organization) Staff. Congestion Points Study Phase III: Best Practices Manual &Technical Report. LC 98-945507. 1997. write for info. (*981-00-8936-8*, Pub. by AgBe Pub) Balogh.
Maunuhal Singh. Strategy of International Business. 240p. 1986. 19.00 (*81-7003-069-2*, Pub. by S Asia Pubs) S Asia.
Maunupau, Thomas K. Huakai Makaika A Kaupo, Maui: A Visit to Kaupo, Maui: As Published in Kanupepa Kuokoa, June 1, 1922-March 15, 1923. LC 98-44377. 1999. pap. 18.00 (*1-58178-001-X*) Bishop Mus.
— Huakai Makaika a Kaupo, Maui: A Visit to Kaupo, Maui: As Published in Kanupepa Kuokoa, June 1, 1922-March 15, 1923. LC 98-44377. 1999. 30.00 (*1-58178-000-1*) Bishop Mus.
Mauny, M., jt. auth. see Cousineau, G.
Maupas, P., jt. ed. see Melnick, Joseph L.
Maupassant, Guy de. Afloat: A Journal of His Days at Sea. Johnston, Marlo, tr. from FRE. (Illus.). 144p. 1996. 32.00 (*0-7206-0966-6*, Pub. by P Owen Ltd) Dufour.
— L' Ami Maupassant. (FRE.). 1992. pap. 10.95 (*0-7859-3277-1*, 2277220477) Fr & Eur.
— Apparition et Autre Contes d'Angoisse. (FRE.). 1987. pap. 10.95 (*0-7859-2985-1*) Fr & Eur.
— Bel Ami. Deliasement, ed. write for info. (*0-318-63435-X*) Fr & Eur.
— Bel Ami. Delaisement, ed. (Folio Ser.: No. 865). (FRE.). 9.95 (*2-07-036865-3*) Schoenhof.
— Bel Ami. Parmee, Douglas, tr. from FRE. (Classics Ser.). 416p. 1975. pap. 11.95 (*0-14-044315-0*, Penguin Classics) Viking Penguin.
— Bel-Ami. unabridged ed. (FRE.). pap. 7.95 (*2-87714-150-0*, Pub. by Bookking Intl) Distribks Inc.
— Best Ghost Stories. (Classics Library). 1998. pap. 3.95 (*1-85326-189-0*, 1890WW, Pub. by Wrdsworth Edits) NTC Contemp Pub Co.
— Best Short Stories - Les Meilleurs Contes: A Dual-Language Book. Jupiter, Steven, tr. 256p. (Orig.). 1996. pap. text 8.95 (*0-486-28918-4*) Dover.
— Boule de Suif. 1999. pap. 8.95 (*2-266-08297-3*) Midwest European Pubns.
— Boule de Suif. (Folio Ser.: No. 904). (FRE.). 1961. pap. 9.95 (*2-07-036904-8*, 650) Schoenhof.
— Boule de Suif: La Maison Tellier. (FRE.). (C). pap. 11.95 (*0-8442-1823-5*, VF1823-5) NTC Contemp Pub Co.
— Boule de Suif & Other Stories: Collected Novels & Stories, Vol. 1. Boyd, Ernest A., tr. LC 76-157786. (Short Story Index Reprint Ser.). 1977. reprint ed. 18.95 (*0-8369-3898-4*) Ayer.
— Boule de Suif et Autres Contes Normands. Bancquart, Marie-Claire, ed. (Coll. Prestige). 10.95 (*0-8288-9610-0*, M2452) Fr & Eur.
— Boule de Suif, Mademoiselle Fifi. unabridged ed. (FRE.). pap. 5.95 (*2-87714-194-2*, Pub. by Bookking Intl) Distribks Inc.
— The Complete Novels. 13.95 (*0-7867-0823-9*) Carroll & Graf.
— The Complete Novels of Guy de Maupassant. 776p. 1992. pap. 13.95 (*0-88184-823-9*) Carroll & Graf.
— Contes: A Selection. Jotcham, N., ed. 176p. (C). 1984. pap. text 16.95 (*0-521-27135-5*) Cambridge U Pr.
— Contes Choisis. (FRE.). 19.95 (*0-8288-9611-9*, F67610) Fr & Eur.
— Les Contes de la Becasse. (Folio Ser.: No. 1144). (FRE.). 8.95 (*2-07-037144-1*) Schoenhof.
— Contes de la Becasse. write for info. (*0-318-63465-1*) Fr & Eur.
— Les Contes de la Becasse. unabridged ed. (FRE.). pap. 5.95 (*2-87714-230-2*, Pub. by Bookking Intl) Distribks Inc.
— Contes du Jour et de la Nuit. (FRE.). 1984. pap. 12.95 (*0-7859-2906-1*) Fr & Eur.
— Les Contes du Jour et de la Nuit - le Horla. unabridged ed. (FRE.). pap. 7.95 (*2-87714-220-5*, Pub. by Bookking Intl) Distribks Inc.
Maupassant, Guy de. Contes du Jour et la Nuit. text 8.95 (*0-88436-989-7*) EMC-Paradigm.
Maupassant, Guy de. Contes et Nouvelles, Tome 1. deluxe ed. (Pleiade Ser.). (FRE.). 1670p. 1974. pap. 82.95 (*2-07-010805-8*) Schoenhof.
— Contes et Nouvelles, Tome 2. deluxe ed. (Pleiade Ser.). (FRE.). 1766p. 1987. pap. 85.95 (*2-07-010943-7*) Schoenhof.
— Contes et Nouvelles Vol. 1: 1875-1884. (FRE.). 248p. 1988. pap. write for info. (*0-7859-4764-7*) Fr & Eur.
— Contes Fantastiques Complets. (FRE.). 377p. 1977. 10.95 (*0-8288-9614-3*, M2454) Fr & Eur.
— The Dark Side: Tales of Terror & the Supernatural. LC 96-54509. 256p. 1997. pap. 10.95 (*0-7867-0419-5*) Carroll & Graf.
— Day & Night Stories: Collected Novels & Stories, Vol. 9. Boyd, Ernest A., ed. Jameson, Storm, tr. from FRE. LC 70-157787. (Short Story Index Reprint Ser.). 1977. reprint ed. 18.95 (*0-8369-3899-2*) Ayer.
***Maupassant, Guy de.** A Day in the Country & Other Stories. Coward, David, tr. from FRE. LC 99-186616. (Oxford World's Classics Ser.). 336p. 1998. pap. 8.95 (*0-19-283863-6*) OUP.
Maupassant, Guy de. De Tunis a Kairouan. (FRE.). 1993. pap. 24.95 (*0-7859-3326-3*, 2870274785) Fr & Eur.
— Les Dimanches d'un Bourgeois de Paris. (FRE.). 93p. 1988. pap. 19.95 (*0-7859-4763-9*) Fr & Eur.
— En Sicile. (FRE.). 1993. pap. 24.95 (*0-7859-3325-5*, 2870274777) Fr & Eur.
— Fort Comme la Mort. 1963. write for info. (*0-318-63472-4*, 1084) Fr & Eur.
— Fort Comme la Mort. (Folio Ser.: No. 1450). (FRE.). 1963. pap. 12.95 (*2-07-037450-5*) Schoenhof.
— Histoires Fantastiques. (FRE.). 1982. pap. 10.95 (*0-7859-3022-1*) Fr & Eur.
— Le Horla. 1999. pap. 8.95 (*2-266-08298-1*) Midwest European Pubns.
— Le Horla. (Folio Ser.: No. 1711). (FRE.). 1962. pap. 6.95 (*2-07-037711-3*, 840) Schoenhof.
***Maupassant, Guy de.** The Horla. (Classic Frights Ser.). (Illus.). 64p. (J). (gr. 5). 1998. pap. 5.95 (*0-929605-84-5*, Pub. by Books of Wonder) Morrow.
Maupassant, Guy de. Le Horla: Et Autres Contes Cruels et Fantastiques. (FRE.). 693p. 1976. 10.95 (*0-685-57719-8*, F67670) Fr & Eur.
— In the Country. (Short Stories Ser.). (Illus.). 32p. (YA). (gr. 4 up). 1992. lib. bdg. 18.60 (*0-88682-503-2*, Creat Educ) Creative Co.
— A Life: The Humble Truth. Pearson, Roger, tr. from FRE. LC 98-32139. (Oxford World's Classics Ser.). 245p. 1999. pap. 8.95 (*0-19-283298-0*) OUP.
— Little Rogue, & Other Stories Vol. 10: Collected Novels & Stories. Boyd, Ernest A., ed. Jameson, Storm, tr. from FRE. LC 73-157788. (Short Story Index Reprint Ser.). 1977. reprint ed. 18.95 (*0-8369-3900-X*) Ayer.
— Mademoiselle Fifi. (FRE.). 1977. 10.95 (*0-8288-9618-6*, M12713) Fr & Eur.
— Mademoiselle Fifi. (Folio Ser.: No. 945). 1960. pap. 8.95 (*2-07-036945-5*, 583) Schoenhof.
— Mademoiselle Fifi & Other Stories. Coward, David, tr. & intro. by. LC 92-10105. (World's Classics Ser.). 288p. 1993. pap. 8.95 (*0-19-282923-8*) OUP.
***Maupassant, Guy de.** Mademoiselle Fifi & Other Stories. (Oxford World's Classics Ser.). 288p. 1999. pap. 9.95 (*0-19-283752-4*) OUP.
Maupassant, Guy de. Mademoiselle Fifi & Other Stories. 1993. reprint ed. lib. bdg. 22.95 (*1-56849-174-3*) Buccaneer Bks.
— Mademoiselle Fifi & Other Stories Vol. 2: Collected Novels & Stories. Boyd, Ernest A., ed. LC 77-157789. (Short Story Index Reprint Ser.). 1977. reprint ed. 18.95 (*0-8369-3901-8*) Ayer.
— La Main Gauche. 9.95 (*0-686-54795-0*) Fr & Eur.
— La Main Gauche. (FRE.). 1978. pap. 10.95 (*0-7859-2972-X*, 2080703005) Fr & Eur.
— La Maison Tellier. (FRE.). 254p. 1978. pap. 11.95 (*0-7859-4689-6*) Fr & Eur.
— La Maison Tellier: Une Partie de Campagne. (FRE.). 1980. pap. 10.95 (*0-7859-3088-4*) Fr & Eur.
— Miss Harriet. 1978. pap. 10.95 (*0-7859-2892-8*) Fr & Eur.
— Miss Harriet. (Folio Ser.: No. 1036). (FRE.). pap. 8.95 (*2-07-037036-4*) Schoenhof.
— Miss Harriett, & Other Stories Vol. 6: Collected Novels & Stories. Boyd, Ernest A., ed. LC 71-157790. (Short Story Index Reprint Ser.). 1977. reprint ed. 18.95 (*0-8369-3902-6*) Ayer.
— Misti. pap. 9.95 (*0-685-23907-1*, 2156) Fr & Eur.
Maupassant, Guy de. Mon Oncle Jules: Level D. text 8.95 (*0-88436-044-X*) EMC-Paradigm.
Maupassant, Guy de. Monsieur Parent. (Folio Ser.: No. 1913). (FRE.). 248p. 1988. pap. 9.95 (*2-07-037913-2*) Schoenhof.
— Mont-Oriol. (Folio Ser.: No. 811). (FRE.). (Orig.). pap. 9.95 (*2-07-036811-4*) Schoenhof.
— Mont Oriol. (FRE.). 1976. pap. 12.95 (*0-7859-2886-3*) Fr & Eur.
— Mont-Oriol. unabridged ed. (FRE.). (Orig.). 1996. pap. 5.95 (*2-87714-337-6*, Pub. by Bookking Intl) Distribks Inc.
Maupassant, Guy de. The Necklace. (Illus.). (J). (gr. 4 up). 1992. 26.60 (*1-56846-006-6*, Creat Educ) Creative Co.
Maupassant, Guy de. The Necklace. 35p. (YA). (gr. 10 up). 1969. pap. 3.50 (*0-87129-853-8*, N10) Dramatic Pub.
— The Necklace. rev. ed. Weissenhorn, Mathilde, tr. from FRE. (Read-Along Radio Dramas Ser.). (J). (gr. 6-10). 1993. reprint ed. ring bd. 38.00 (*1-878298-16-X*) Balance Pub.
— The Necklace & Other Short Stories. (Thrift Editions Ser.). Orig. Title: The Works of Guy de Maupassant: Short Stories. 128p. 1992. reprint ed. pap. 1.00 (*0-486-27064-5*) Dover.
— Notre Coeur. (FRE.). 1993. pap. 10.95 (*0-7859-3176-7*, 2253062553) Fr & Eur.
— Oeuvres Completes, 16 tomes, Set. Pia, ed. 2450.00 (*0-685-34942-X*) Fr & Eur.
— The Olive Orchard & Other Stories. Boyd, Ernest A., ed. Jameson, Storm, tr. from FRE. LC 75-157791. (Collected Novels & Stories Ser.: Vol. 14). 1977. reprint ed. 18.95 (*0-8369-3903-4*) Ayer.
— A Parisian Bourgeois' Sundays & Other Stories. Johnston, Marlo, tr. from FRE. LC 98-111578. 176p. 1998. 29.95 (*0-7206-1033-8*, Pub. by P Owen Ltd) Dufour.
— La Petite Rogue. 9.95 (*0-686-54792-6*) Fr & Eur.
— La Petite Rogue. (FRE.). 1972. pap. 10.95 (*0-7859-3109-0*) Fr & Eur.
— Pierre & Jean. 1976. 19.95 (*0-8488-0472-4*) Amereon Ltd.
— Pierre & Jean. Tancock, Leonard W., tr. & intro. by. (Classics Ser.). 176p. 1979. pap. 9.95 (*0-14-044358-4*, Penguin Classics) Viking Penguin.
— Pierre et Jean. (FRE.). (C). pap. 11.95 (*0-8442-1813-8*, VF1813-8) NTC Contemp Pub Co.
— Pierre et Jean. (Folio Ser.: No. 1414). (FRE.). 1962. pap. 9.95 (*2-07-037414-9*) Schoenhof.
— Pierre et Jean. unabridged ed. (FRE.). pap. 5.95 (*2-87714-163-2*, Pub. by Bookking Intl) Distribks Inc.
— Pierrot, et Autres Nouvelles. (FRE.). 1991. pap. 16.95 (*0-7859-3162-7*, 2253055816) Fr & Eur.
— Quinze Contes. Green, F. C., ed. 131p. 1943. pap. text 16.95 (*0-521-05693-4*) Cambridge U Pr.
— Romans. deluxe ed. (Pleiade Ser.). (FRE.). 1959. 93.95 (*2-07-011118-0*) Schoenhof.
— Le Rosier de Madame Husson. (Folio Ser.: No. 2153). (FRE.). pap. 8.95 (*2-07-038243-5*) Schoenhof.
— St. Anthony & Other Stories. Hearn, Lafcadio, tr. from FRE. LC 79-150479. (Short Story Index Reprint Ser.). 1977. reprint ed. 18.95 (*0-8369-3820-8*) Ayer.
— Scenes de la Vie Parisienne. (FRE.). 192p. 1985. pap. 10.95 (*0-7859-4690-X*) Fr & Eur.
— Selected Short Stories. Colet, Roger, tr. (Classics Ser.). 368p. 1971. pap. 11.95 (*0-14-044243-X*, Penguin Classics) Viking Penguin.
***Maupassant, Guy de.** A Selection of the Political Journalism: With Introduction & Notes. Ritchie, Adrian C., ed. (Illus.). 179p. 1999. pap. 28.95 (*3-906762-93-9*, Pub. by P Lang) P Lang Pubng.
Maupassant, Guy de. Sisters Rondoli, & Other Stories: Collected Novels & Stories, Vol. 5. Boyd, Ernest A., ed. LC 79-157792. (Short Story Index Reprint Ser.). 1977. reprint ed. 23.95 (*0-8369-3904-2*) Ayer.
— Six Contes de Maupassant. (FRE.). (C). 1994. pap. 6.99 (*0-8442-1019-6*, VF1019-6) NTC Contemp Pub Co.
— Les Soeurs Rondoli. 1992. pap. 10.95 (*0-7859-3171-6*, 2253060097) Fr & Eur.
— Sur L'Eau. (FRE.). 1972. 10.95 (*0-8288-9623-2*, M2458) Fr & Eur.
— Toine. 1991. pap. 12.95 (*0-7859-2926-6*) Fr & Eur.
— Toine. (Folio Ser.: No. 2278). (FRE.). pap. 10.95 (*2-07-038380-6*) Schoenhof.
— Une Vie. 1959. write for info. (*0-318-63613-1*, 478) Fr & Eur.
— Une Vie. (Folio Ser.: No. 544). (FRE.). 1959. pap. 9.95 (*2-07-036544-1*, 478) Schoenhof.
— Une Vie. unabridged ed. (FRE.). pap. 5.95 (*2-87714-134-9*, Pub. by Bookking Intl) Distribks Inc.
— When Chickens Grow Teeth: A Story from the French of Guy de Maupassant. LC 95-53797. (Illus.). 32p. (J). (ps-2). 1996. 15.95 (*0-531-09526-6*); lib. bdg. 16.99 (*0-531-08876-6*) Orchard Bks Watts.
— Who Knows? (Classic Frights Ser.). (Illus.). 64p. (J). (gr. 5-7). 1998. pap. 5.95 (*0-929605-80-2*, Classic Frights) Books of Wonder.
— A Woman's Life. Sloman, H. N., tr. (Classics Ser.). 208p. 1978. pap. 10.95 (*0-14-044161-1*, Penguin Classics) Viking Penguin.
— Yvette - A Novelette, & Ten Other Stories. Galsworthy, John, tr. LC 70-150550. (Short Story Index Reprint Ser.). 1977. reprint ed. 18.95 (*0-8369-3847-X*) Ayer.
Maupassant, Guy de & Bismut, Roger. Contes du Jour et de la Nuit. (Folio Ser.: No. 1558). (FRE.). 251p. 1977. 9.95 (*2-07-037558-7*) Schoenhof.
Maupassant, Guy de & Cogny, Pierre. Le Rosier de Madame Husson. (FRE.). 1976. 10.95 (*0-8288-9625-9*, F67790) Fr & Eur.
Maupassant, Guy de & Kellett, Arnold. The Dark Side of Guy de Maupassant: A Selection & Translation. LC 89-511. 252 p. 1989. write for info. (*0-88184-459-4*) Carroll & Graf.
Maupassant, Guy de, et al. A Trio of Terror & Suspense. abr. ed. Baxter, Beth, ed. 1987. pap. 5.95 incl. audio (*1-882071-11-5*, 013) B&B Audio.
Maupassant, Guy de, jt. auth. see Greimas, Algirdas Julien.
Maupeou, Patrick De, see Giraudy, Daniele & De Maupeou, Patrick.
Maupertius, Pierre L. Oeuvres, 4 vols., Set. liii, 1590p. 1974. reprint ed. write for info. (*3-487-01056-9*) G Olms Pubs.
***Maupin.** Flying Cadets of WWII. LC 99-33029. 324p. 1999. 29.95 (*0-07-134843-3*) McGraw.
Maupin, Armis. Almost Anyone. Date not set. pap. 13.00 (*0-06-093090-X*) HarpC.
Maupin, Armistead. Babycakes. LC 94-133601. Vol. 4. 336p. 1994. pap. 13.00 (*0-06-092483-7*, Perennial) HarperTrade.
— Back to Barbary Lane: The Final Tales of the City Omnibus. LC 90-56366. 720p. 1991. 32.50 (*0-06-016649-5*) HarperTrade.
— Further Tales of the City. 384p. 1991. pap. 13.00 (*0-06-092492-6*, Perennial) HarperTrade.
— Maybe the Moon: A Novel. LC 92-52596. 320p. 1993. reprint ed. pap. 13.00 (*0-06-092434-9*, Perennial) HarperTrade.
— More Tales of the City. LC 92-52596. (Tales of the City Ser.). 320p. 1992. 11.00 (*0-685-60778-X*, Perennial) HarperTrade.
— More Tales of the City TV Tie In. LC 79-1710. Vol. 2. (Illus.). 352p. 1998. pap. 13.00 (*0-06-092938-3*, Perennial) HarperTrade.
— The Night Listener: A Novel. LC 00-38907. 352p. 2000. 26.00 (*0-06-017143-X*, HarpCollins) HarperTrade.
— Significant Others. LC 94-113536. Vol. 5. 336p. 1994. pap. 13.00 (*0-06-092481-0*, Perennial) HarperTrade.
— Sure of You. LC 94-141694. Vol. 6. 272p. 1994. pap. 13.00 (*0-06-092484-5*, Perennial) HarperTrade.
— Tales of the City. annuals LC 77-11781. Vol. 1. 384p. 1993. pap. 13.00 (*0-06-096404-9*) HarpC.
Maupin, Armistead. 28 Barbary Lane: A "Tales of the City" Omnibus. 768p. 1990. 32.50 (*0-06-016466-2*) HarperTrade.
Maupin, Edward W. In Pursuit of the Wild Prostate. (Illus.). 128p. (Orig.). 1996. pap. 12.95 (*0-9654257-0-3*) Dawn Eve Prod.
Maupin, G. W., Jr., et al, eds. Extending the Life of Bridges. LC 90-40769. (Special Technical Publication (STP) Ser.: STP 1100). (Illus.). 140p. 1990. text 35.00 (*0-8031-1402-8*, STP1100) ASTM.
***Maupin, Melissa.** Benjamin Banneker. LC 99-18148. (Journey to Freedom Ser.). (Illus.). 32p. (YA). (gr. 4 up). 1999. lib. bdg. 24.21 (*1-56766-618-3*) Childs World.
— Computer Engineer. (Career Explorations Ser.). 48p. (YA). (gr. 5 up). 2001. lib. bdg. 21.26 (*0-7368-0591-5*, Capstone Bks) Capstone Pr.
— Landscaper. LC 99-53793. (Career Explorations Ser.). 48p. (YA). (gr. 5 up). 2000. lib. bdg. 21.26 (*0-7368-0490-0*, Capstone Bks) Capstone Pr.
Maupin, Melissa. The Story of Coca-Cola. LC 98-31889. (Illus.). 48p. (YA). (gr. 5 up). 1999. lib. bdg. 23.95 (*1-58340-001-X*) Smart Apple.
— Texas Outdoor Adventure Guide for Kids. Zappler, George, ed. (Illus.). 154p. (J). 1998. pap. 14.95 (*1-885696-28-0*, Pub. by TX Prks & Wldlife) U of Tex Pr.
Mauquoy-Hendrickx, Marie. Van Dyck's Prints (L'Iconographie d'Antoine van Dyck), Catalogue Raisonne, 2 vols. 2nd ed. (FRE., Illus.). 450p. 1991. pap. 120.00 (*1-55660-226-X*) A Wofsy Fine Arts.
— Wierix Family Prints (Les Estampes des Wierix), Catalogue Raisonne, 4 vols. (Illus.). 1983. pap. 295.00 (*1-55660-225-1*) A Wofsy Fine Arts.
Maur, Karin Von, see Von Maur, Karin.
Maura, Anne. Heart's Journey: Reclaiming Your Power of Choice. LC 99-90613. xiv, 160p. 1999. pap. 15.95 (*0-9672558-0-5*) Yng Millionrs.
Maura, Juan F. What We Women Know. 3rd ed. (Vagrom Chap Bk.: No. 15). 41p. 1981. 3.95 (*0-935552-05-7*) Sparrow Pr.
— Women in the Conquest of the Americas. Deredita, John F., tr. from SPA. LC 92-26545. XIV, 278p. (C). 1997. pap. text 29.95 (*0-8204-2043-3*) P Lang Pubng.
Maura, P. Roderick. Dr. Morgan's Guide to North American Wild Life: 1992-1993 Edition. 258p. 1992. pap. 16.95 (*0-9630814-7-0*) Dr Morgans.
Maurais, Jacques. Lexicon of Carbonated Beverages: Lexiques des Boissons Gazeuses. (ENG & FRE.). 40p. 1980. pap. 14.95 (*0-8288-4818-1*, M9241) Fr & Eur.
— Lexicon of Food Chemistry: Lexique de la Chimie Alimentaire. 10th ed. (ENG & FRE.). 119p. 1981. pap. 9.95 (*0-8288-0837-6*, M6656) Fr & Eur.
— Lexicon of Spices & Seasonings: Lexique des Epices et Assaisonnements. (ENG & FRE.). 44p. 1980. pap. 14.95 (*0-8288-4817-3*, M9236) Fr & Eur.
— Quebec's Aboriginal Languages: History, Planning & Development, Vol. 107. LC 96-16507. 260p. 1996. 59.00 (*1-85359-361-3*, Pub. by Multilingual Matters) Taylor & Francis.
Maurais, Jacques & Villa, T. Guide de Redaction des Menus Anglais-Francais. 10th ed.Tr. of English-French Menu Translation Guide. (ENG & FRE.). 153p. 1980. pap. 9.95 (*0-8288-0838-4*, M9237) Fr & Eur.
Maurais, Jacques, et al. Lexicon of Pasta, 1982. 3rd ed. (ENG & FRE.). 43p. 1980. pap. 14.95 (*0-8288-0839-2*, M9243) Fr & Eur.
Maurakami, Ryu & McCarthy, Ralph F. 69. 184p. 1993. 20.00 (*4-7700-1736-7*) Kodansha.
Mauran, J. E. & Stockbridge, J. C. Memorials of the Mauran Family. 171p. 1993. reprint ed. pap. 29.50 (*0-8328-3800-4*); reprint ed. lib. bdg. 39.50 (*0-8328-3799-7*) Higginson Bk Co.
Maurande, G., jt. auth. see Pierre, C.
Mauranen, Anna, jt. ed. see Ventola, Eija.
Maureau, Paul M. The Masardis Saga: Nineteenth Century Life in Aroostook County, Maine. LC 83-50686. (Illus.). 160p. (Orig.). 1985. pap. 10.95 (*0-931474-28-0*) TBW Bks.
Maurel, Martine. Malaria: A Layman's Guide. 120p. pap. 12.95 (*1-86812-534-3*) Menasha Ridge.
Maurel, Martine, jt. auth. see Drooker, Penelope B.
Maurel, Sylvie. Jean Rhys. LC 98-21227. 200p. 1999. text 35.00 (*0-312-21687-4*) St Martin.
Maurel, Victor. Dix Ans de Carriere, 1887-1897. Farkas, Andrew, ed. LC 76-29954. (Opera Biographies Ser.).Tr. of Ten Years of My Career, 1887-1897. (FRE., Illus.). 1977. reprint ed. lib. bdg. 35.95 (*0-405-09695-X*) Ayer.
Maurel, W., et al. Biomechanical Models for Soft Tissue Simulation, Vol. 166. LC 97-48783. (ESPRIT Basic Research Ser.). xvi, 173p. 1998. 56.00 (*3-540-63742-7*) Spr-Verlag.
Mauren, Mary L. Creating Communities of Good News: A Handbook for Small-Group Facilitators. LC 92-64035. 84p. (Orig.). 1992. pap. 8.95 (*1-55612-473-2*, LL1473) Sheed & Ward WI.
Maurenbrecher, Berthold. Forschungen Zur Lateinischen Sprachgeschichte und Metrik. (GER.). 269p. 1979. reprint ed. write for info. (*3-487-06049-3*) G Olms Pubs.
Maurenbrecher, Manfred. Subjekt und Koerper, Vol. 698. (European University Studies: German Language & Literature: Ser. 1). (GER.). 599p. 1983. 41.00 (*3-261-03298-7*) P Lang Pubng.
Maurens, Jacques, ed. see Voltaire.
Maurensig, Paolo. Canone Inverso: A Novel. McPhee, Jenny, tr. LC 98-10774. 160p. 1998. 21.00 (*0-8050-5538-X*) H Holt & Co.
— Canone Iverso: A Novel. 208p. 1999. pap. text 12.00 (*0-8050-6302-1*, Owl) H Holt & Co.
***Maurensig, Paolo.** The Luneberg Variation. LC 98-34459. 144p. 1998. pap. 11.00 (*0-8050-6028-6*, Owl) H Holt & Co.
Maurer. Combat Squadrons of the Air Force in World War II: History & Insignia. 1983. reprint ed. 35.00 (*0-89201-097-5*) Zenger Pub.
— Mathematic Elements. 4th ed. 1996. pap. text, student ed. 29.33 (*0-13-259185-5*) P-H.
***Maurer.** True Colors: Level 2. 336p. 1998. pap. text, teacher ed. 22.05 (*0-201-19082-6*) S&S Trade.
— True Colors: Level 1. 1998. wbk. ed. 8.95 (*0-201-60377-2*) Addison-Wesley.
— True Colors: Level 1. 336p. 1998. pap. text 21.00 (*0-201-19081-8*) S&S Trade.
Maurer. Untangling Ecological. LC 98-26199. 1999. lib. bdg. 50.00 (*0-226-51132-4*) U Ch Pr.
***Maurer.** Untangling Ecological. LC 98-26199. 251p. 1999. pap. text 18.00 (*0-226-51133-2*) U Ch Pr.
Maurer & Gilbert, James B., eds. Air Force Combat Units of World War II. LC 79-7285. (Flight: Its First Seventy-Five Years Ser.). 1980. reprint ed. lib. bdg. 44.95 (*0-405-12194-6*) Ayer.

M

An Asterisk (*) at the beginning of an entry indicates that the title is appearing for the first time.

Maurer, jt. auth. see Berger.
Maurer, A. E., ed. The Works of John Dryden Vol. XX: Prose: 1691-1698, De Arte Graphica & Shorter Works, Vol. XX. LC 55-7149. (Illus.). 546p. 1990. 80.00 (*0-520-02133-9*, Pub. by U CA Pr) Cal Prin Full Svc.
Maurer, Adah. Corporal Punishment Handbook. (Illus.). 32p. 1981. 3.50 (*0-932141-01-3*) End Violence.
— Instead of Spanking Vol. 2: 1001 Alternatives. (Illus.). 1986. 6.50 (*0-932141-06-4*) End Violence.
— One-Thousand-One Alternatives to Corporal Punishment, Vol. 1. (Illus.). 58p. 1984. 5.95 (*0-932141-03-X*) End Violence.
Maurer, Adah, jt. auth. see Taylor, Leslie.
Maurer, Alfons V. Homo Agens: Handlungstheoretische Untersuchungen Zum Theologisch-Ethischen Verstandnis des Sittlichen. (Forum Interdisziplinare Ethik Ser.: Bd. 8). (GER., Illus.). 433p. 1994. 59.95 (*3-631-46618-8*) P Lang Pubng.
Maurer-Alvarez, Pansy. Dolores: The Alpine Years. 1996. 20.00 (*1-882413-31-8*); pap. 12.00 (*1-882413-30-X*) Hanging Loose.
***Maurer, Andreas.** What Next for the European Parliament? 2000. pap. 16.00 (*0-901573-90-6*) Fed Trust Ed Res.
Maurer, Armand A. About Beauty: A Thomistic Interpretation. LC 83-70939. 141p. (Orig.). 1983. pap. text 6.95 (*0-9603456-1-1*, 85-00065) U of St Thomas.
— Medieval Philosophy. 2nd ed. xxii, 455p. pap. text 26.29 (*0-88844-704-3*) Brill Academic Pubs.
— St. Thomas & Historicity. LC 79-84278. (Aquinas Lectures). 1979. 15.00 (*0-87462-144-5*) Marquette.
Maurer, Armand A., tr. see Eckhart.
Maurer, B. R&D, Innovation & Industrial Structure: Essays on the Theory of Technological Competition. (Contributions to Economics Ser.). 158p. 1996. 59.00 (*3-7908-0900-4*) Spr-Verlag.

M

Maurer, B. B., ed. Mountain Heritage. (Illus.). 352p. 1975. reprint ed. pap. 14.60 (0-87012-279-7) McClain. The most complete one volume work available on the Appalachian Cultural Heritage of West Virginians. Written by a group of West Virginia's finest scholars. The twelve chapters cover Man & the Appalachian Wilderness, Culture, Arts & Crafts, Language, Folklore & Literature, Family & Home, Music, Religion, Black Culture, The Mountain State, Songs, & Dances. Scholarly yet easily readable, the book is a ready resource for home, school, office & community. Seventh Edition, 1996. ***Publisher Paid Annotation.***

***Maurer, Bill.** Recharting the Caribbean. (Illus.). 320p. (C). 2000. pap. text 22.95 (*0-472-08693-6*, 08693) U of Mich Pr.
Maurer, Bill. Recharting the Caribbean: Land, Law, & Citizenship in the British Virgin Islands. LC 96-51247. 320p. (C). 1997. text 44.50 (*0-472-10811-5*, 10811) U of Mich Pr.
Maurer, Bill, jt. ed. see Collier, Jane.
Maurer, Charles B. Call to Revolution: The Mystical Anarchism of Gustav Landauer. LC 75-148270. 219p. reprint ed. pap. 67.90 (*0-8357-7976-9*, 202765900055) Bks Demand.
Maurer, Christopher. Federico Garcia Lorca, 1898-1936. 1999. 55.00 (*84-8048-267-2*) Vanderbilt U Pr.
Maurer, Christopher, ed. Born to Rule. write for info. (*0-614-16414-1*) Doubleday.
— A Moral Anatomy. 1995. write for info. (*0-614-16413-3*) Doubleday.
Maurer, Christopher, ed. see Garcia Lorca, Federico.
Maurer, Christopher, ed. & intro. see Garcia Lorca, Federico.
Maurer, Christopher, ed. & tr. see Garcia Lorca, Federico.
Maurer, Christopher, tr. see Garcia Lorca, Federico.
Maurer, Christopher, tr. see Gracian, Baltasar.
***Maurer, Crescenia.** Rio + 8: An Assessment of National Councils for Sustainable Development. 12p. 1999. 5.00 (*1-56973-426-7*) World Resources Inst.
Maurer, D. W. The Argot of the Racetrack. (Publications of the American Dialect Society: No. 16). 70p. 1951. pap. text 7.15 (*0-8173-0616-1*) U of Ala Pr.
Maurer, David W. The American Confidence Man. 316p. 1974. 49.95 (*0-398-02974-1*); pap. 33.95 (*0-398-06272-2*) C C Thomas.
— The Big Con: The Story of the Confidence Man. LC 99-25494. 336p. 1999. pap. 12.95 (*0-385-49538-2*) Doubleday.
— Whiz Mob. 1964. pap. 15.95 (*0-8084-0321-4*) NCUP.
Maurer, David W. & Pearl, Quinn. Kentucky Moonshine. LC 74-7880. (Kentucky Bicentennial Bookshelf Ser.). (Illus.). 162p. reprint ed. pap. 50.30 (*0-8357-4295-4*, 203709400007) Bks Demand.
Maurer, David W., jt. auth. see Babcock, C. Merton.
***Maurer, Dennis.** At the Foot of the Cross: Lent & Easter Dramas. 2000. pap. 7.25 (*0-7880-1549-4*) CSS OH.
Maurer, Diane V. Marbling: A Complete Guide to Creating Beautiful Patterned Papers & Fabrics. (Illus.). 120p. 1994. pap. 11.95 (*1-56799-113-0*, Friedman-Fairfax) M Friedman Pub Grp Inc.
Maurer, Donna. Annie, Bea & Chi Chi Dolores. LC 92-25104. (Illus.). 32p. (J). (ps-k). 1998. pap. 6.95 (*0-531-07092-1*) Orchard Bks Watts.
— Annie, Bea & Chi Chi Dolores. (J). 1998. 12.15 (*0-606-13144-2*, Pub. by Turtleback) Demco.
— Annie, Bea & Chi Chi Dolores: A School Day Alphabet. LC 92-25104. (Illus.). 32p. (J). (ps-k). 1993. 15.95 (*0-531-05467-5*); lib. bdg. 16.99 (*0-531-08617-8*) Orchard Bks Watts.
Maurer, Donna & Sobal, Jeffery. Eating Agendas: Food & Nutrition As Social Problems. (Social Problems & Social Issues Ser.). 359p. 1995. pap. text 28.95 (*0-202-30508-2*) Aldine de Gruyter.
Maurer, Donna & Sobal, Jeffery, eds. Eating Agendas: Food & Nutrition As Social Problems. (Social Problems & Social Issues Ser.). 359p. 1995. lib. bdg. 51.95 (*0-202-30507-4*) Aldine de Gruyter.
Maurer, Donna, jt. auth. see Sobal, Jeffery.
Maurer, Eduard & Abel, R. Christopher. The Magic & Music of Perfumes. 1996. reprint ed. pap. 4.95 (*1-55818-351-5*, Sure Fire) Holmes Pub.
Maurer, Edward S. Perfumes & Their Production. LC 59-17885. 328p. reprint ed. pap. 101.70 (*0-608-12620-9*, 202542400043) Bks Demand.
Maurer, Ernest W. The Dream Is Alive: Space Flight & Operations in Earth Orbit. (Illus.). 320p. (Orig.). (C). 1991. pap. text 29.95 (*0-9628591-0-9*) Geosync Pubns.
Maurer, Evan E. Gerome Kamrowski: A Retrospective Exhibition. (Illus.). 120p. 1983. pap. 7.95 (*0-912303-27-1*) Michigan Mus.
Maurer, Evan E., intro. Sculpture of Africa: Selections from a Private Collection. (Illus.). 52p. 1984. 5.00 (*0-912303-41-7*) Michigan Mus.
Maurer, Evan M., pref. Mignonette Yin Cheng. (Illus.). 46p. (Orig.) (C). 1988. pap. 5.00 (*0-912303-40-9*) Michigan Mus.
***Maurer, Evan M. & Batulukisi, Niangi.** Spirits Embodied: Art of the Congo. LC 99-74258. (Illus.). 153p. 2000. pap. 34.95 (*0-8166-3655-9*) U of Minn Pr.
Maurer, Evan M. & Roberts, Allen F. The Rising of a New Moon: A Century of Tabwa Art. (Illus.). 288p. (Orig.). (C). 1986. pap. 39.95 (*0-912303-32-8*) Michigan Mus.
Maurer-Fazio, Margaret, jt. ed. see Cook, Sarah.
Maurer, Frances A., jt. auth. see Smith, Claudia M.
Maurer, Frances A., jt. ed. see Smith, Claudia M.
Maurer, Friedrich & Rupp, Heinz, eds. Deutsche Wortgeschichte, Vol. 1. 3rd ed. LC 73-88302. (Grundriss der Germanischen Philologie Ser.: Vol. 17, Pt. 1). 581p. (C). 1974. 157.70 (*3-11-003627-4*) De Gruyter.
— Deutsche Wortgeschichte, Vol. 2. 3rd rev. ed. (Grundriss der Germanischen Philologie Ser.: Vol. 17, Pt. 2). (GER.), vi, 698p. (C). 1974. 169.25 (*3-11-003619-3*) De Gruyter.
— Deutsche Wortgeschichte, Vol. 3. 3rd ed. (Grundriss der Germanischen Philologie Ser.: Vol. 17, Pt. 3). (C). 1978. 113.10 (*3-11-003620-7*) De Gruyter.
Maurer, Friedrich, ed. see Von Strassburg, Gottfried.
Maurer, G. P. Recent Durability Tests on Helical Gears. (Technical Papers: Vol. P169). (Illus.). 21p. (Orig.). 1938. pap. text 30.00 incl. audio compact disk (*1-55589-390-2*) AGMA.
Maurer, George E. & Elser, Bernard P. Fundamentals of Building a Bamboo Fly-Rod. LC 98-15376. (Illus.). 240p. 1998. 50.00 (*0-88150-416-5*, Pub. by Countryman) Norton.
Maurer, Greg. Mountain Bike Adventures in Southwest British Columbia: 50 Rides. LC 99-6060. (Mountain Bike Adventures Ser.). 224p. 1999. pap. 16.95 (*0-89886-626-8*) Mountaineers.
Maurer, Gretchen. Business of Bridal Beauty. LC 97-38364. (Milady - Cosmetology). 192p. (C). 1998. 31.95 (*1-56253-338-X*) Thomson Learn.
Maurer, H., et al, eds. J. UCS. The Journal of Universal Computer Science: Annual Print & CD-ROM Archive Edition. xxxiv, 860p. 1997. 198.00 incl. cd-rom (*3-540-63210-7*) Spr-Verlag.
— J. UCS, the Journal of Universal Computer Science Vol. XXXIV: Annual Print & CD-ROM Archive Edition, 1995, Vol. 1. 827p. 1997. 225.00 incl. cd-rom (*3-540-62047-8*) Spr-Verlag.
— J.UCS. The Journal of Universal Computer Science: Annual Print & CD-ROM Archive Edition, Vol. 3, 1997. xxvii, 1417p. 1999. 199.00 incl. cd-rom (*3-540-65392-9*) Spr-Verlag.
Maurer, H. A., ed. Automata, Languages & Programming: Sixth Colloquium. (Lecture Notes in Computer Science Ser.: Vol. 71). 1979. 48.00 (*0-387-09510-1*) Spr-Verlag.
— New Results & New Trends in Computer Science: Graz, Austria, June 20-21, 1991 Proceedings. (Lecture Notes in Computer Science Ser.: Vol. 555). viii, 403p. 1991. 48.00 (*0-387-54869-6*) Spr-Verlag.
Maurer, H. W., jt. ed. see Kearney, R. L.
Maurer, Hans W., jt. ed. see Kearney, Robert L.
Maurer, Harold M., ed. Pediatrics. LC 82-9423. 1097p. reprint ed. pap. 200.00 (*0-7837-6247-X*, 204595900010) Bks Demand.
Maurer, Harold M. & Ruymann, Frederick B. Rhabdomyosarcoma & Related Tumors in Children & Adolescents. (Illus.). 504p. 1991. lib. bdg. 189.00 (*0-8493-6902-9*, RC281) CRC Pr.
Maurer, Harry. Sex: Real People Talk about What They Really Do. 560p. 1995. pap. 20.99 (*0-14-017145-2*, Penguin Bks) Viking Penguin.
— Strange Ground: Americans in Vietnam, 1945-1975. 656p. 1990. reprint ed. pap. 12.95 (*0-380-70931-7*, Avon Bks) Morrow Avon.
— Strange Ground: An Oral History of Americans in Vietnam, 1945-1975. LC 97-40136. 656p. 1998. reprint ed. pap. 17.95 (*0-306-80839-0*) Da Capo.
Maurer, Heinz F., jt. auth. see Mange, Maria A.
Maurer, Hermann A., et al. From Databases to Hypermedia: With 26 CAI Lessons. LC 98-36068. xii, 312p. 1998. pap. 44.95 incl. cd-rom (*3-540-63754-0*) Spr-Verlag.
Maurer, Herrymon. The Power of Truth. (C). 1950. pap. 4.00 (*0-87574-053-7*) Pendle Hill.
Maurer, Herrymon, ed. Pendle Hill Reader. LC 74-142668. (Essay Index Reprint Ser.). 1977. reprint ed. 20.95 (*0-8369-2415-0*) Ayer.
***Maurer, Ingo & Andrew, Susan, eds.** International Design Yearbook 15. (Illus.). 240p. (J). 2000. 85.00 (*0-7892-0638-2*, Abbeville Kids) Abbeville Pr.
Maurer, Jack R. Developments in the Power Industry: Heat Exchanger Technologies & Materials Improvements. LC 93-73003. (PWR Ser.: Vol. 23). 124p. 1993. 35.00 (*0-7918-0998-6*, H00830) ASME.
Maurer, Jack R., ed. Heat Exchanger Technology for the Global Environment: International Joint Power Generation Conference, Phoenix, AZ, 1994. 173p. 1994. pap. 40.00 (*0-7918-1381-9*) ASME.
Maurer, Jan, et al. Otoacoustic Emissions. LC 96-50973. (Self-Instructional Ser.). (Illus.). 60p. (Orig.). 1997. pap. text 25.00 (*1-56772-055-2*, 5506305) AAO-HNS.
Maurer, Janet R. Building a New Dream: A Family Guide to Coping with Chronic Illness & Disability. 1990. pap. 9.57 (*0-201-55098-9*) Addison-Wesley.
Maurer, Jay. Focus on Grammar: Advanced Level. 176p. 1995. pap. text, teacher ed. 26.97 (*0-201-65694-9*) Addison-Wesley.
Maurer, Jay. Focus on Grammar: Advanced Level. 1996. 42.56 incl. audio (*0-201-69428-X*) Addison-Wesley.
Maurer, Jay. Focus on Grammar: An Advanced Course for Reference & Grammar. 1995. pap. text, student ed. 24.00 (*0-8013-1423-2*) P-H.
— Focus on Grammar: An Advanced Course for Reference & Practice. LC 94-39043. 384p. 1995. pap. text 27.92 (*0-201-65693-0*) Addison-Wesley.
— Focus on Grammar Vol. A: Advanced Students Book. 224p. (J). 1995. pap. text 13.97 (*0-201-82584-8*) Addison-Wesley.
— Keystone Bk. 2: An EFL Course. LC 97-12071. 160p. 1997. pap. text, student ed. 15.05 (*0-201-69515-4*) Addison-Wesley.
— True Colors: Real Voices, Communication Workbook 2. 64p. 1997. pap. text 8.82 (*0-201-18636-5*) Addison-Wesley.
— True Colors: Real Voices, Real Communication Student Book 3. 160p. 1998. pap. text, student ed. 15.04 (*0-201-18730-2*) Addison-Wesley.
***Maurer, Jay.** True Colors: Real Voices, Real Communication Student Book 3. 160p. 1998. pap. text, student ed. 11.28 (*0-201-18788-4*) Addison-Wesley.
— True Colors: Real Voices, Real Communication Student Book 4. 160p. 1998. pap. text, student ed. 15.04 (*0-201-19052-4*) Addison-Wesley.
Maurer, Jay. True Colors: Real Voices, Real Communication Workbook Basic Level. 64p. 1998. pap. text, wbk. ed. 8.83 (*0-201-18634-9*) Addison-Wesley.
— True Colors: Real Voices, Real Communication Workbook 1. 64p. 1997. pap. text 8.82 (*0-201-18635-7*) Addison-Wesley.
— True Colors: Real Voices, Real Communication Workbook 3. 64p. 1998. pap. text, wbk. ed. 8.83 (*0-201-18637-3*) Addison-Wesley.
— True Colors Bk. 1: Real Voices Real Communication. LC 97-12071. 160p. 1997. pap. text, student ed. 15.05 (*0-201-87808-9*) Addison-Wesley.
— True Colors Video Workbook, Level 1. 64p. 1998. pap. text, wbk. ed. 11.13 (*0-201-35116-1*) Addison-Wesley.
Maurer, Joan H. Curly: An Illustrated Biography of the Superstooge. (Illus.). 256p. 1985. 19.95 (*0-8065-0979-1*, Citadel Pr) Carol Pub Group.
— Curly: An Illustrated Biography of the Superstooge. (Illus.). 224p. 1988. pap. 14.95 (*0-8065-1086-2*, Citadel Pr) Carol Pub Group.
— The Three Stooges Book of Scripts. LC 84-17614. (Illus.). 256p. 1984. 19.95 (*0-8065-0933-3*) Carol Pub Group.
Maurer, Joan H. & Maurer, Norman. The Three Stooges Book of Scripts, Vol. II. (Illus.). 256p. 1987. 19.95 (*0-8065-1018-8*, Citadel Pr) Carol Pub Group.
Maurer, Joan H., et al. The Three Stooges Scrapbook. (Illus.). 256p. 1985. reprint ed. pap. 16.95 (*0-8065-0946-5*, Citadel Pr) Carol Pub Group.
Maurer, John, jt. ed. see Goldstein, Erik.
Maurer, John H. The Outbreak of the First World War: Strategic Planning, Crisis Decision Making, & Deterrence Failure. LC 95-22012. (Studies in Diplomacy & Strategic Thought). 168p. 1995. 55.00 (*0-275-94998-2*, Praeger Pubs) Greenwood.
Maurer, John H. & Porth, Richard H. Military Intervention in the Third World: Threats, Constraints, & Options. LC 84-11685. (Foreign Policy Issues Ser.). 1984. 62.95 (*0-275-91223-X*, C1223, Praeger Pubs) Greenwood.
***Maurer, Jorge.** Get a Lean Body: The #1 Online Interactive Fitness Book. (Jorge Maurer's Online Interactive Fitness Bks.: Vol. 1). (Illus.). 261p. 2000. pap. 49.95 (*1-891542-02-8*) Maurer Power.
Maurer, Karl. Interpolation in Thucydides. LC 95-10386. (Mnemosyne, Bibliotheca Classica Batava: Supplementum Ser.: Vol. 150). 1995. 92.00 (*90-04-10300-7*) Brill Academic Pubs.
Maurer, Katharine. Intellectual Status at Maturity As a Criterion for Selecting Items in Preschool Tests, Vol. 21. LC 46-5115. (Illus.). 166p. 1970. reprint ed. lib. bdg. 45.00 (*0-8371-7895-9*, CWMP, Greenwood Pr) Greenwood.
Maurer, Katharine, jt. auth. see Goodenough, Florence L.
Maurer, Kent L., jt. auth. see Locke, David R.
Maurer, Konrad, ed. Imaging of the Brain in Psychiatry & Related Fields. LC 92-49551. 1993. 159.00 (*0-387-54785-1*) Spr-Verlag.
Maurer, Konrad, et al, eds. Alzheimer's Disease Epidemiology, Neuropathology, Neurochemistry, & Clinics: Proceedings, International Congress on Alzheimer's Disease, Wurzburg, June 1989. (Key Topics in Brain Research Ser.). (Illus.). 600p. 1990. 127.95 (*0-387-82197-X*) Spr-Verlag.
Maurer, Konrad & Dierks, T. Atlas of Brain Mapping: Topographic Mapping of EEG & Evoked Potentials. (Illus.). xi, 103p. 1991. 86.95 (*0-387-53090-8*) Spr-Verlag.
Maurer, Linda K. I Don't Know How to Help Them: A Book for Friends & Families of Bereaved Parents. 2nd rev. ed. LC 96-94092. 64p. 1996. reprint ed. pap. 8.95 (*0-9636977-2-2*) L K Maurer.
— Standing Beside You: A Book for Bereaved Parents. LC 97-93340. 88p. (Orig.). 1996. pap. 9.95 (*0-9636977-1-4*) L K Maurer.
***Maurer, Marc, ed.** Oh, Wow! large type ed. (Kernel Bk.: Vol. 18). (Illus.). 96p. 2000. pap. 3.00 (*1-885218-18-4*) Natl Fed Blind.
— Reflecting the Flame. large type ed. (Kernel Bk.: Vol. 17). (Illus.). 96p. 2000. pap. 3.00 (*1-885218-17-6*) Natl Fed Blind.
***Maurer, Marc, et al.** I Can Feel Blue on Monday. large type ed. (Kernel Book Ser.: Vol. 19). (Illus.). 96p. 2000. pap. 3.00 (*1-885218-21-4*) Natl Fed Blind.
Maurer, Marc, ed. see Jernigan, Kenneth.
***Maurer, Marsha.** In the Garden: A Collection of Prayers for Everyday. 2000. 12.99 (*1-57748-742-7*) Barbour Pub.
Maurer, Martha E. Coalition Command & Control: Key Considerations. 161p. 1994. per. 8.50 (*0-16-045138-8*) USGPO.
***Maurer-Mathison, Diane V.** Art of the Scrapbook: A Guide to Handbinding & Decorating Memory Books, Albums & Art Journals. LC 99-89949. (Illus.). 144p. 2000. pap. 24.95 (*0-8230-1019-8*) Watsn-Guptill.
Maurer-Mathison, Diane V. The Ultimate Marbling Handbook: A Guide to Basic & Advanced Techniques for Marbling Paper & Fabric. LC 98-47000. (Illus.). 144p. 1999. pap. text 24.95 (*0-8230-5575-2*) Watsn-Guptill.
Maurer-Mathison, Diane V. & Philippoff, Jennifer. Paper Art: The Complete Guide to Papercraft Techniques. LC 97-28466. (Crafts Ser.). (Illus.). 144p. 1997. pap. 27.50 (*0-8230-3840-8*) Watsn-Guptill.
— Papercraft: Making & Decorating Paper. LC 94-27976. (Illus.). 120p. 1995. 11.95 (*1-56799-151-3*, Friedman-Fairfax) M Friedman Pub Grp Inc.
Maurer, Matthew M. & Davidson, George. Leadership in Instructional Technology. LC 96-50444. 333p. 1997. pap. text 52.00 (*0-13-239849-4*) P-H.
Maurer, Maurer. Air Force Combat Units of World War II. 1982. reprint ed. 35.00 (*0-89201-092-4*) Zenger Pub.
Maurer, Maurer, ed. Air Force Combat Units of World War II. LC 94-13389. 360p. 1994. 12.98 (*0-7858-0194-4*, Chrtwell) Bk Sales Inc.
***Maurer, Naomi, et al.** The Pursuit of Spiritual Wisdom: The Thought & Art of Vincent Van Gogh & Paul Gauguin. LC 98-16272. (Illus.). 330p. 1998. 65.00 (*0-8386-3749-3*) Fairleigh Dickinson.
Maurer, Norman, jt. auth. see Maurer, Joan H.
***Maurer, Peter.** My Way: The Universe & the Truth. 224p. 2000. pap. write for info. (*1-57733-068-4*) B Dolphin Pub.
Maurer, Pierre, jt. auth. see Milivojevic, Marko.
***Maurer, Rainer H.** Economic Growth & International Trade with Capital Goods: Theories & Empirical Evidence. LC 98-212680. (Illus.). 246p. (C). 1998. text 69.50 (*3-16-146922-4*) JCB Mohr.
Maurer, Richard. Rocket! How a Toy Launched the Space Age. LC 94-19243. 64p. (J). 1995. lib. bdg. 17.99 (*0-517-59629-6*, Pub. by Crown Bks Yng Read) Random.
— Wild Colorado. LC 98-33892. 96p. 1999. 18.00 (*0-517-70945-7*) C Potter.
— The Wild Colorado: The True Adventures of Fred Dellenbaugh, Age 17, on the Second Powell Expedition into the Grand Canyon. LC 98-33892. (Illus.). 120p. (YA). (gr. 5-8). 1999. lib. bdg. 19.99 (*0-517-70946-5*) Crown Pub Group.
Maurer, Richard E. Interdisciplinary Curriculum: Restructuring Secondary Schools. LC 93-723. 304p. 1993. pap. text 38.00 (*0-205-14117-X*) Allyn.
— Special Educator's Discipline Handbook. 232p. 1988. text 29.95 (*0-87628-771-2*) Ctr Appl Res.
Maurer, Rick. Beyond the Wall of Resistance: Unconventional Strategies That Build Support for Change. (Illus.). 208p. 1995. 24.95 (*1-885167-07-5*) Bard Press.
— Caught in the Middle: A Leadership Guide for Partnership in the Workplace. LC 91-23238. 258p. 1992. 30.00 (*1-56327-004-8*) Productivity Inc.
***Maurer, Rick.** The Cycle of Change 5p. 1998. (*0-88886-500-7*) Que8ens U Indus Relat.
Maurer, Rick. The Feedback Toolkit: 16 Tools for Better Communication in the Workplace. LC 94-11842. (Illus.). 50p. (Orig.). 1994. pap. 12.00 (*1-56327-056-0*) Productivity Inc.
Maurer, Robert J. Drug-Free Workplace. 198p. (Orig.). 1989. pap. 85.00 (*0-317-93916-5*); pap. 40.00 (*0-317-93917-3*) ACET NY.
— Drug-Free Workplace Employer's Handbook. 198p. (Orig.). 1989. pap. 85.00 (*0-685-25974-9*) ACET NY.
Maurer, Ruth. An Electronic Companion to Operations Management. Venable, Alan, ed. (Electronic Companion Ser.). (Illus.). 300p. 1997. pap. text, wbk. ed. write for info. (*1-58032-011-2*) Cogito Lrning.
— An Electronic Companion to Operations Management. (Illus.). 300p. 1998. pap., wbk. ed. 29.95 incl. cd-rom (*1-58032-012-0*) Cogito Lrning.
Maurer, Ruth A., jt. auth. see Parker, Joni M.
Maurer, Shawn L. Proposing Men: Dialectics of Gender & Class in the Eighteenth-Century English Periodical. LC 98-16809. 320p. 1998. 49.50 (*0-8047-3353-8*); pap. write for info. (*0-8047-3357-0*) Stanford U Pr.
Maurer, Shawn L., ed. see Inchbald, Elizabeth S.

An Asterisk (*) at the beginning of an entry indicates that the title is appearing for the first time.

Maurice, Thomas. The History of Hindostan: It's Arts, & It's Science, As Connected with the History of the Other Great Empires of Asia, During the Itos & Ancient Periods of the World. LC 78-60888. (Myth & Romanticism Ser.). 1359p. 1984. text 20.00 (*0-8240-3566-6*) Garland.

Maurice-Williams, R. S. Spinal Degenerative Disease. (Illus.). 356p. 1981. 48.00 (*0-685-24837-2*) Mosby Inc.

— Subarachnoid Hemorrhage: Aneurysms & Vascular Malformations of the Central Nervous System. (Illus.). 448p. 1987. 131.50 (*0-685-24836-4*) Mosby Inc.

Maurice, Yvon T., ed. Proceedings of the 8th Quadrennial IAGOD-Symposium Held in Ottawa, Canada, August 12-18, 1990. (International Association on the Genesis of Ore Deposits (IAGOD) Symposia Ser.). (Illus.). xiii, 901p. 1993. lib. bdg. 200.00 (*3-510-65153-7*, Pub. by E Schweizerbartsche) Balogh.

Mauriceau, A. M. The Married Woman's Private Medical Companion. LC 73-20635. (Sex, Marriage & Society Ser.). 256p. 1974. reprint ed. 23.95 (*0-405-05811-X*) Ayer.

Mauricio, Rufino, jt. auth. see Fry, Gerald W.

Mauriel, John J. Strategic Leadership for Schools: Creating & Sustaining Productive Change. LC 89-45592. (Education-Higher Education Ser.). 373p. 1989. text 38.45 (*1-55542-184-9*) Jossey-Bass.

***Mauriello, Barbara.** Making Memory Boxes: Box Projects to Make, Give & Keep. 2000. pap. 22.00 (*1-56496-711-5*) Rockport Pubs.

Mauriello, Joseph. Management of Orbital & Ocular Tumors. 1990. 145.00 (*0-938607-19-7*) Field & Wood Inc Medical.

***Mauriello, Joseph A., Jr.** Unfavorable Results of Eyelid & Lacrimal Surgery Prevention. LC 99-54758. (Illus.). 688p. 2000. 195.00 (*0-7506-7016-9*) Buttrwrth-Heinemann.

Mauriello, Sally M., et al. Radiographic Imaging for the Dental Team. (Illus.). 400p. (C). 1995. text 40.00 (*0-397-55020-0*, Lippnctt) Lppncott W & W.

Mauriello, Thomas, jt. auth. see Ingraham, Barton I.

Maurier, Anina, ed. see Pascal, Alana.

Maurier, Anina, ed. see Pascal, Alana & VanderKar, Lynne.

Maurier, Daphne de, see Center for Learning Network Staff & de Maurier, Daphne.

Maurier, George Du, see Du Maurier, George.

Maurier, George L. Du, see Du Maurier, George L.

Mauries. Sonia Rykiel. 80p. 1998. 18.95 (*0-7893-0204-7*, Pub. by Universe) St Martin.

Mauries, Patrick. Fornasetti: Designer of Dreams. LC 97-62080. (Illus.). 288p. 1998. pap. 34.95 (*0-500-28051-7*, Pub. by Thames Hudson) Norton.

— Jewelry by Chanel. (Illus.). 144p. 2000. pap. 35.00 (*0-8212-2550-2*, Pub. by Bulfinch Pr) Little.

— Your World & Welcome to It: A Rogue's Gallery of Interior Design. Philipps, Christopher, tr. LC 98-6317. (Illus.). 96p. 1998. 24.50 (*0-684-84420-6*) S&S Trade.

Mauries, Patrick, jt. auth. see Pelle, Marie P.

Mauries, Patrick, jt. auth. see Pelle, Marie-Paule.

Mauries, Patrick, ed. see Lacroix, Christian.

Maurik, John van, see Van Maurik, John.

Maurin, Jacques. Virologie Medicale. (Collection Traites). (FRE., Illus.). 930p. 1985. 150.00 (*2-257-10435-8*) S M P F Inc.

Maurin, Krzysztof. Analysis: Integration, Distributions, Holomorphic Functions, Tensor & Harmonic Analysis, Pt. 2. 1980. lib. bdg. 187.00 (*90-277-0865-7*) Kluwer Academic.

— Analysis, Part 1: Elements. Lepa, Eugene, tr. from POL. LC 74-80525. 672p. 1976. lib. bdg. 146.00 (*90-277-0484-8*) Kluwer Academic.

Maurin, Krzysztof & Raczka, R., eds. Mathematical Physics & Physical Mathematics. LC 74-34289. (Mathematical Physics & Applied Mathematics Ser: No. 2). 1976. text 176.50 (*90-277-0537-2*) Kluwer Academic.

Maurin, Mario. Henri de Regnier: Le Labyrinthe et le Double. LC 72-339689. (FRE.). 301p. 1972. reprint ed. pap. 93.40 (*0-7837-6942-3*, 204677100003) Bks Demand.

Maurin, Peter. Easy Essays. pap. 3.95 (*0-89979-015-1*) British Am Bks.

— Easy Essays. 216p. 1977. pap. 6.95 (*0-8199-0681-6*, Frncscn Herld) Franciscan Pr.

Maurin, Vladimir M., tr. see Okladnikov, Aleksei P.

Maurin, Vladimir M., tr. see Oshanin, L. V.

Maurin, Vladimir M., tr. see Tretiakov, P. N. & Mongait, A. L.

Maurine, jt. auth. see Moon, Margaret.

Maurine Brooks, Christopher & Hansen, George P. The Milbourne Christopher Library. LC 93-77302. 1994. write for info. (*0-915181-26-6*) Magic Words.

Maurino, Daniel E. & Reason, James. Beyond Aviation Human Factors. 181p. 1995. 67.95 (*0-291-39822-7*) Ashgate Pub Co.

Maurino, Daniel E., et al. Beyond Aviation Human Factors. 192p. 1998. pap. 33.95 (*1-84014-948-5*) Ashgate Pub Co.

Maurino, Ferdinando D. Salvatore Di Giacomo & Neapolitan Dialectal Literature. 1951. 15.95 (*0-913298-30-1*) S F Vanni.

Maurio, Don J. A Practical Guide to Antibacterial Agents. 40p. (Orig.). Date not set. pap. 15.95 (*0-9657721-1-X*) Grp Tech.

Mauritzson, Jules. Looking West: Three Essays on Swedish American Life. Bergendoff, Conrad, tr. xx, 73p. 1994. pap. 12.00 (*0-910184-42-9*) Augustana.

Maurizi, Vincenzo. History of Seyd Said: Sultan of Muscat; Together with an Account of the Countries & People on the Shores of the Persian Gulf, by Sheik Mansur. (Arabia Past & Present Ser.: Vol. 13). 208p. 1984. 35.00 (*0-906672-33-3*) Oleander Pr.

***Maurizio, Valerio.** Top Rated Bird Hunting. (Illus.). 260p. 2000. pap. 18.95 (*1-58667-004-2*) Derrydale Pr.

— Top Rated Freshwater Fishing. (Illus.). 410p. 2000. pap. 18.95 (*1-58667-002-6*) Derrydale Pr.

— Top Rated Paddling Adventures. (Illus.). 270p. 2000. pap. 18.95 (*1-58667-005-0*) Derrydale Pr.

— Top Rated Saltwater Fishing: Bays, Estuaries, Flats & Offshore in North America. (Illus.). 300p. (Orig.). 2000. pap. 18.95 (*1-58667-001-8*) Derrydale Pr.

***Maurizio, Valerio, ed.** Top Rated Big Game Hunting in North America. (Illus.). 315p. 2000. pap. 18.95 (*1-58667-003-4*) Derrydale Pr.

— Top Rated Fly Fishing: Salt & Freshwaters in North America. (Illus.). 250p. (Orig.). 2000. pap. 18.95 (*1-58667-000-X*) Derrydale Pr.

— Top Rated Western Adventures: Guest Ranches, Pack Trips & Cattle Drives in North America. (Illus.). 240p. (Orig.). 2000. pap. 18.95 (*1-58667-006-9*) Derrydale Pr.

Mauro, Alexander, ed. Muscle Regeneration. fac. ed. LC 77-90593. (Illus.). 576p. pap. 178.60 (*0-7837-7263-7*, 204704200005) Bks Demand.

***Mauro, Anthony.** Illustrated Great Decisions of the Supreme Court. LC 00-29758. (Illus.). 400p. 2000. 59.95 (*1-56802-482-7*) CQ Pr.

Mauro, Buzz, jt. auth. see Gottesman, Deb.

Mauro, Claudia. Reading the River. 38p. 1999. pap. 13.95 (*0-9653800-3-3*, Pub. by Whiteaker Pr) SPD-Small Pr Dist.

— Stealing Fire. 54p. (Orig.). 1997. pap. 12.95 (*0-9653800-0-9*) Whiteaker Pr.

Mauro-Cochrane, Jeanette. Self-Respect & Sexual Assault. LC 92-38938. 1993. pap. 12.60 (*0-8306-4289-7*) McGraw-Hill Prof.

Mauro, Francesco, jt. auth. see Gledhill, Barton.

Mauro, Garry. Beaches Bureaucrats & Big Oil. 1998. pap. 8.95 (*0-9658344-1-7*) Look Away Bks.

Mauro, J. P. Al Franken Is a Bucktoothed Moron--And Other Observations The Right Strikes Back! 1996. 21.95 (*0-9652966-0-1*) Payback Pub.

Mauro, Jim, jt. auth. see McDougall, Richard.

Mauro, John B. Statistical Deception at Work. (Communication Textbook Ser.). 128p. (C). 1992. pap. 17.50 (*0-8058-1232-6*) L Erlbaum Assocs.

Mauro, Joseph V. & Meyrowitz, Michael R. Oral Pathology: Mucous Membrane Lesions. 64p. 1984. 30.00 (*0-318-17795-1*); write for info. (*0-318-17796-X*) Am Dental Hygienists.

Mauro, Judith A., jt. auth. see Delmar Staff.

Mauro, Louis F. Di, see DiMauro, Louis F.

Mauro, Lucia. Careers for Fashion Plates & Other Trendsetters. (Careers for You Ser.). (Illus.). 160p. 1996. 14.95 (*0-8442-4477-5*, 44775, VGM Career); pap. 9.95 (*0-8442-4478-3*, 44783, VGM Career) NTC Contemp Pub Co.

— Careers for the Stagestruck & Other Dramatic Types. LC 97-1935. (Illus.). 144p. 1997. 14.95 (*0-8442-4327-2*, 43272); pap. 9.95 (*0-8442-4328-0*, 43280) NTC Contemp Pub Co.

— Fashion. LC 95-18547. (VGM Career Portraits Ser.). (Illus.). 96p. (J). (gr. 4-6). 1995. 13.95 (*0-8442-4363-9*, 43639, VGM Career) NTC Contemp Pub Co.

Mauro, Paolo, et al. Perspectives on Regional Unemployment in Europe. LC 99-26825. (Occasional Paper Ser.). 1999. write for info. (*1-55775-800-X*) Intl Monetary.

Mauro, Philip. Champion of Kingdom. pap. 2.99 (*0-87377-047-1*) GAM Pubns.

— Chronology of the Bible. 1980. lib. bdg. 49.95 (*0-8490-3140-0*) Gordon Pr.

— Kingdom Heresies of S. D. Gordon. pap. 2.99 (*0-87377-009-9*) GAM Pubns.

— Of the Things Which Must Soon Come to Pass: Commentary on Revelation. 1984. reprint ed. 17.99 (*0-87377-056-0*) GAM Pubns.

— The World & Its God. 95p. 1981. reprint ed. pap. 4.00 (*0-89084-151-9*, 016527) Bob Jones Univ.

Mauro, Raf. Fitting In. LC 96-107437. 64p. (Orig.). (J). (gr. 1-3). 1995. pap. 8.95 (*0-940669-31-5*, D-37) Dramaline Pubns.

— Modern Monologues for Modern Kids. LC 95-167520. 64p. (J). (gr. 1-3). 1994. pap. 8.95 (*0-940669-29-3*, D-33) Dramaline Pubns.

— When Kids Achieve: Positive Monologues for Preteen Boys & Girls. LC 97-18324. 64p. (J). (gr. 4-7). 1997. pap. 8.95 (*0-940669-37-4*, D-43) Dramaline Pubns.

Mauro, Robert. Engineering Electronics: A Practical Approach. 1120p. (C). 1989. text 63.00 (*0-13-278029-1*) P-H.

— Finding Love & Intimacy. Garee, Betty, ed. 200p. 1994. pap. 8.95 (*0-915708-37-X*) Cheever Pub.

— The Landscape of My Disability: Poems by Robert Mauro. 36p. 1997. pap. 6.00 (*1-891420-05-4*) Lemonade Factory.

— On Stage! Short Plays for Acting Students. Zapel, Arthur L., ed. LC 90-52982. 240p. (Orig.). (YA). (gr. 9-12). 1990. pap. text 15.95 (*0-916260-67-4*, B165) Meriwether Pub.

— Two-Character Plays for Student Actors: A Collection of 15 One-Act Plays. Zapel, Arthur L., ed. LC 88-60078. 192p. (Orig.). (YA). (gr. 7-12). 1988. pap. 16.95 (*0-916260-53-4*, B174) Meriwether Pub.

Mauro, Robert, jt. auth. see Becker, Elle.

Mauro, Tullio De, see De Mauro, Tullio, ed.

Maurois, Andre. Adrienne ou la Vie de Madame de La Fayette. (FRE.). 1968. pap. 29.95 (*0-7859-5109-1*) Fr & Eur.

— Ariel ou la Vie de Shelley. (Coll. Diamant). 1970. pap. write for info. (*0-7859-5275-6*) Fr & Eur.

— Un Art de Vivre. (FRE.). 256p. 1973. 6.95 (*0-7859-0110-8*, M3759) Fr & Eur.

— Aspects de la Biographie. 1930. 13.95 (*0-7859-5271-3*) Fr & Eur.

— Aux Innocents les Mains Pleines. (FRE.). pap. 9.95 (*0-7859-5571-2*) Fr & Eur.

— Balzac. (FRE., Illus.). 1976. 49.95 (*0-8288-9740-9*, 2080607464) Fr & Eur.

— Bernard Quesnay. 1963. pap. 17.50 (*0-685-11045-1*) Fr & Eur.

— Bernard Quesnay. (FRE.). 192p. 1973. pap. 10.95 (*0-7859-0109-4*, M3757) Fr & Eur.

— Cercle de Famille. (Coll. Diamant). 1959. 23.25 (*0-685-11071-0*) Fr & Eur.

— Le Cercle de Famille. (FRE.). 437p. 1977. 10.95 (*0-8288-9882-0*, F114050) Fr & Eur.

— Chantiers Americains. (FRE.). pap. 6.95 (*0-8288-9872-3*, F113470) Fr & Eur.

— Choses Nues. (Coll. Soleil). (FRE.). 284p. 1963. pap. 15.95 (*0-7859-1286-X*, 2070243125) Fr & Eur.

— Climates of Love. Levien, Michael, ed. Schiff, Violet & Cook, Esme, trs. from FRE. LC 87-60486. (Modern Romance Classics Ser.). 214p. 1986. reprint ed. 27.00 (*0-7206-0671-3*, Pub. by P Owen Ltd) Dufour.

— Climats. 9.95 (*0-686-55489-2*) Fr & Eur.

— Climats. (Coll. Diamant). (FRE.). 1955. 39.95 (*0-7859-0049-7*, FC1394) Fr & Eur.

— La Conquete de l'Angleterre par les normands. (Coll. Le Memorial des Siecles). (FRE.). 19.95 (*0-8288-9873-1*, F113500) Fr & Eur.

— Le Cote de Chelsea. 144p. 1967. pap. 21.95 (*0-7859-5272-1*) Fr & Eur.

— Cours de Bonheur Conjugal. (FRE.). pap. 10.95 (*0-8288-9875-8*, F113530) Fr & Eur.

— D'Aragon a Montherlant et De Shakespeare a Churchill. (FRE.). 12.95 (*0-8288-9876-6*, F113540) Fr & Eur.

— De Gide a Sartre. (FRE.). 12.95 (*0-8288-9877-4*, F113550) Fr & Eur.

— De la Bruyere a Proust: Lecture Mon Doux Plaisir. (Coll. Les Grands Evenements Litteraires). (FRE.). 11.95 (*0-8288-9878-2*, F113560) Fr & Eur.

— Dialogues sur le Commandement. (FRE.). 1924. pap. 13.95 (*0-7859-5316-7*) Fr & Eur.

— Les Discours du Docteur O'Grady. (FRE.). 1968. pap. 26.95 (*0-7859-5549-6*) Fr & Eur.

— Don Juan ou la Vie de Byron. 1969. pap. write for info. (*0-7859-5274-8*) Fr & Eur.

— France. (Illus.). 37.50 (*0-686-55492-2*) Fr & Eur.

— Histoire d'Angleterre. 26.25 (*0-685-36938-2*) Fr & Eur.

— Histoire de la France. 34.90 (*0-685-36939-0*) Fr & Eur.

— Histoire des Etats-Unis, 2 vols. 48.25 (*0-685-36940-4*) Fr & Eur.

— Les Illusions. (Coll. Les Soirees du Luxembourg). 26.95 (*0-685-36941-2*) Fr & Eur.

— L' Instinct du Bonheur. pap. 8.95 (*0-685-36942-0*) Fr & Eur.

— Lelia ou la Vie de George Sand. 22.95 (*0-685-36943-9*) Fr & Eur.

— Lettre Ouverte a un Jeune Homme sur la Conduite de la Vie. (Coll. Lettre Ouverte). pap. 9.95 (*0-685-36944-7*) Fr & Eur.

— Lyautey. 17.95 (*0-685-36945-5*) Fr & Eur.

— Memoires I: Les Annees d'Apprentissage. 19.95 (*0-685-36946-3*) Fr & Eur.

— Mes Songes Que Voici. pap. 17.50 (*0-685-36948-X*) Fr & Eur.

— Les Mondes Imaginaires. pap. 18.50 (*0-685-36949-8*) Fr & Eur.

— Ni Ange, Ni Bete. (FRE.). 1927. 10.95 (*0-8288-9883-9*, F114080) Fr & Eur.

— Nico le Petit Garcon Change en Chien. 9.95 (*0-686-55495-7*) Fr & Eur.

— Nouveaux Discours du Docteur O'Grady. pap. 9.95 (*0-685-36950-1*) Fr & Eur.

— Olympio Ou la Vie de Victor Hugo. 28.50 (*0-685-36951-X*) Fr & Eur.

— Le Pays des 36000 Volontes. (FRE.). 94p. 1990. pap. 11.95 (*0-7859-4614-4*) Fr & Eur.

— Le Poeme de Versailles. pap. 9.50 (*0-685-36952-8*) Fr & Eur.

— Portrait d'un Ami qui s'appelait Moi. (Coll. Les Auteurs Juges par leurs Oeuvres). pap. 17.50 (*0-685-36953-6*) Fr & Eur.

— Pour Piano Seul. pap. 19.50 (*0-685-36954-4*) Fr & Eur.

— Private Universe. Miles, Hamish, tr. LC 70-177963. (Essay Index Reprint Ser.). 1977. reprint ed. 22.95 (*0-8369-2564-5*) Ayer.

— Promethee: ou La Vie de Balzac. 27.50 (*0-685-36955-2*) Fr & Eur.

— Promethee: ou La Vie de Balzac; Olympio: ou La View de Victor Hugo. (FRE.). 1993. pap. 60.00 (*0-7859-3406-5*) Fr & Eur.

— Prometheus: The Life of Balzac. 573p. 1983. pap. 11.95 (*0-88184-023-8*) Carroll & Graf.

— Proust: Portrait of a Genius. (Illus.). 336p. 1984. pap. 10.95 (*0-88184-104-8*) Carroll & Graf.

— Quatre Etudes Anglaises. pap. 17.95 (*0-685-36956-0*) Fr & Eur.

— Rene Ou la Vie de Chateaubriand. (Coll. Diamant). 25.50 (*0-685-36957-9*) Fr & Eur.

— Rene ou la Vie de Chateaubriand. (FRE.). 315p. 1985. pap. 39.95 (*0-7859-4613-6*) Fr & Eur.

— Ricochets: Miniature Tales of Human Life. Miles, Hamish, tr. from FRE. LC 73-150551. (Short Story Index Reprint Ser.). 1977. reprint ed. 16.95 (*0-8369-3848-8*) Ayer.

— Robert et Elizabeth Browning. pap. 17.50 (*0-685-36958-7*) Fr & Eur.

— Les Roses de Septembre. 123.50 (*0-685-36968-4*) Fr & Eur.

— Sentiments et Coutumes. pap. 17.50 (*0-685-36959-5*) Fr & Eur.

— Seven Faces of Love. 1977. reprint ed. 20.95 (*0-518-10169-X*) Ayer.

— Les Silences de Colonel Bramble. Dicours. Nouveau Discours du Dr. O'Grady. (FRE.). 1992. pap. 12.95 (*0-7859-3085-X*, 2253012769) Fr & Eur.

— Les Silences du Colonel Bramble. pap. 6.50 (*0-685-23886-5*, 90) Fr & Eur.

— Les Silences du Colonel Bramble: Avec: Discours, Nouveaux Discours du Dr. O'Grady. 14.50 (*0-686-55498-1*) Fr & Eur.

— Soixante Ans de Ma Vie Litteraire. Incl. Role de l'Ecrivain dans le Monde d'Aujourd'hui. 9.95 write for info. (*0-318-52265-9*) Fr & Eur.

— Terre Promise. 340p. 9.95 (*0-686-55499-X*); pap. 16.50 (*0-685-36962-5*) Fr & Eur.

— Les Titans Ou les Trois Dumas. pap. 12.50 (*0-685-36963-3*) Fr & Eur.

— Tourgueniev. (Coll. Grandes Figures Litteraires). pap. 16.50 (*0-685-36964-1*) Fr & Eur.

— Les Trois Dumas. 25.95 (*0-685-36969-2*) Fr & Eur.

— Trois Portraits de Femme: La Duchesse de Devonshire, la Comtesse D'Albany, Henriette de France. (Coll. Les Soirees du Luxembourg). 21.50 (*0-685-36965-X*) Fr & Eur.

— La Vie de Disraeli. (Coll. Leurs Figures). pap. 32.50 (*0-685-36967-6*) Fr & Eur.

— La Vie de Disraeli. (FRE.). 1978. pap. 11.95 (*0-7859-4494-X*, 207036884X) Fr & Eur.

Maurois, Andre, tr. see Hopkins, Gerard Manley.

Mauron, Jean, ed. Nutrition Adequacy: Nutrients Available & Needs. (Experientia Supplementa Ser.: Vol. 44). 384p. (C). 1983. text 52.95 (*3-7643-1479-6*) Birkhauser.

***Mauroni, Albert J.** America's Struggle with Chemical-biological Warfare. LC 99-41136. 320p. 2000. 65.00 (*0-275-96756-5*, Praeger Pubs) Greenwood.

Mauroni, Albert J. Chemical-Biological Defense: U. S. Military Policies & Decisions in the Gulf War. LC 97-46531. 280p. 1998. 65.00 (*0-275-96243-1*, B6765, Praeger Pubs) Greenwood.

***Mauroni, Albert J.** Chemical-Biological Defense: U. S. Military Policies & Decisions in the Gulf War. 280p. 1999. pap. 27.95 (*0-275-96765-4*, B6765, Praeger Pubs) Greenwood.

Maurus, Hrabanus. De Institutione Clericorum Libri Tres: Studien und Edition von Detlev Zimpel. (Freiburger Beitraege zur Mittelalterlichen Geschichte, Studien und Texte: Bd. 7). (GER.). XXV, 617p. 1996. 95.95 (*3-631-30736-5*) P Lang Pubng.

***Maurus, Marc.** Used Books. 66p. 1999. pap. 12.95 (*0-9669897-0-8*) Gravity Presses.

Maurus, Rhabanus. The Life of Saint Mary Magdalene & of Her Sister Saint Martha. Mycoff, David, tr. (Cistercian Studies: No. 108). 166p. 1989. 31.95 (*0-87907-608-9*); pap. 15.95 (*0-87907-908-8*) Cistercian Pubns.

Maurus, Terentianus. Concordantia in Terentianum Maurum. Beck, Jan-Wilhelm, ed. (Alpha-Omega, Reihe A Ser.: Bd. CXXXVI). (GER.). 268p. 1993. write for info. (*3-487-09723-0*) G Olms Pubs.

Maurus, Walt. A Complete Introduction to Bettas. (Complete Introduction to...Ser.). (Illus.). 128p. 1987. pap. 8.95 (*0-86622-288-X*, CO005S) TFH Pubns.

Maury, C. J. Recent Mollusks of the Gulf of Mexico & Pleistocene & Pliocene Species from the Gulf States No. 10: Special Publication. 282p. 1971. reprint ed. 9.00 (*0-87710-361-5*) Paleo Res.

Maury, E. A. Drainage in Homeopathy. 105p. 1982. pap. 5.95 (*0-85032-069-0*, Pub. by C W Daniel) Natl Bk Netwk.

— Drainage in Homoeopathy. (C). 1980. pap. 8.95 (*0-8464-1007-9*) Beekman Pubs.

Maury, Emmerick-Armand. Dictionnaire Familial d'Homeopathie. (FRE.). 1982. write for info. (*0-7859-7938-7*, 2-7113-0026-9) Fr & Eur.

— Dictionnaire Familial d'Homeopathie. 1991. write for info. (*0-7859-7896-8*, 2-501-01546-0) Fr & Eur.

Maury, Emmerick-Armand & De Rudder, Chantal. Dictionnaire Familial des Medecines Naturelles. (FRE.). 1982. 105.00 (*0-8288-9523-6*, M6832) Fr & Eur.

Maury, Emmerick-Armand & Rudder, C. Diccionario Familiar de Medicina Natural: Colloquial Dictionary of Natural Medicine. (SPA.). 441p. 1981. 19.95 (*0-8288-1867-3*, S37815) Fr & Eur.

Maury, Inez. My Mother & I Are Growing Strong (Mi Mama y Yo Nos Hacemos Fuertes) Munoz, Anna, tr. (Illus.). 28p. (J). (ps-5). 1979. pap. 5.95 (*1-884244-17-3*) Volcano Pr.

— My Mother the Mail Carrier - Mi Mama la Cartera. Alemany, Norah, tr. LC 76-14275. (ENG & SPA., Illus.). 32p. (J). (ps-4). 1976. pap. 7.95 (*0-935312-23-4*) Feminist Pr.

Maury, Jean-Pierre. Newton: The Father of Modern Astronomy. Paris, I. Mark, tr. (Discoveries Ser.). (Illus.). 144p. 1992. pap. 12.95 (*0-8109-2835-3*, Pub. by Abrams) Time Warner.

— The Turtleons Are Coming. (I Love to Read Collection). (Illus.). 46p. (J). (ps-3). 1992. lib. bdg. 12.79 (*0-89565-810-0*) Childs World.

Maury, Louis F. La Magie Et l'Astrologie Dans l'Antiquite et au Moyen-Age. (Volkskundliche Quellen Ser.: Reihe II). iv, 484p. 1980. reprint ed. write for info. (*3-487-06956-3*) G Olms Pubs.

Maury, Pierre. Two Hundred Examples of Letters: Deux Cents Modeles de Lettres. (FRE.). 285p. 1986. pap. 17.95 (*0-8288-1557-7*, F113580) Fr & Eur.

Maury, R. C., jt. auth. see Juteau, Thierry.

An Asterisk (*) at the beginning of an entry indicates that the title is appearing for the first time.

Maury, Richard. The Saga of Cimba. (Illus.). 1973. 7.25 (*0-8286-0063-5*) J De Graff.

Maury, Vincent & Fourmaintraux, D., eds. Rock at Great Depth: Rock Mechanics & Rock Physics at Great Depth - Proceedings of an International Symposium, Pau, 28 - 31 August 1989, 3 vols. (Illus.). 1620p. (C). 1989. text 324.00 (*90-6191-975-4*, Pub. by A A Balkema) Ashgate Pub Co.

Maurya, S. D. Population & Housing Problems in India, 2 vols., Set. (C). 1989. 76.00 (*81-85076-79-0*, Pub. by Chugh Pubns) S Asia.

— Women in India. (C). 1988. 31.00 (*81-85076-49-9*, Pub. by Chugh Pubns) S Asia.

Maurya, S. D. & Devi, Gayatri. Social Environment of India. (C). 1989. 34.00 (*81-85076-65-0*, Pub. by Chugh Pubns) S Asia.

Maus, Cynthia P. Puerto Rico in Pictures & Poetry. 1976. lib. bdg. 250.00 (*0-8490-1385-2*) Gordon Pr.

***Maus, Derek C.** Readings on "Crime & Punishment" LC 99-55780. (Literary Companion Ser.). 127p. (gr. 9-12). 2000. lib. bdg. 21.96 (*0-7377-0235-4*) Greenhaven.

— Readings on "Crime & Punishment" LC 99-55780. (Literary Companion Ser.). 224p. (YA). (gr. 9-12). 2000. pap. 13.96 (*0-7377-0234-6*) Greenhaven.

Maus, Janet, ed. see Jordan, Joe.

Maus, Katharine E. Ben Jonson & the Roman Frame of Mind. LC 84-17691. 223p. reprint ed. pap. 69.20 (*0-7837-6767-6*, 204659700003) Bks Demand.

— Inwardness & Theater in the English Renaissance. LC 94-43099. 232p. 1995. pap. text 14.95 (*0-226-51124-3*); lib. bdg. 37.50 (*0-226-51123-5*) U Ch Pr.

Maus, Katharine E., ed. Four Revenge Tragedies: The Spanish Tragedy; The Revenger's Tragedy; The Revenge of Bussy D'Ambois; & The Atheist's Tragedy. (Oxford World's Classics Ser.). 464p. 1995. text 59.00 (*0-19-812170-9*) OUP.

— Four Revenge Tragedies: The Spanish Tragedy; The Revenger's Tragedy; The Revenge of Bussy D'Ambois; & The Atheist's Tragedy. (Oxford World's Classics Ser.). 464p. 2000. pap. 10.95 (*0-19-283878-4*) OUP.

Maus, Katharine E., jt. ed. see Harvey, Elizabeth D.

Maus, Rex & Huggard, Susan. The CAP GEMINI Reference to Expert Systems. (CAP GEMINI America Ser.). 256p. 1988. text 24.95 (*0-07-040981-1*) McGraw.

Mausberg, Burkhard & Muldoon, Paul. A Taste of Canada: Comments & Analyses on Toxic Chemicals in Your Meals & Bioengineered Food Made in Canada. (Illus.). 55p. 1998. pap. text 20.00 (*0-7881-4897-4*) DIANE Pub.

Mausberg, Burkhard, et al. The Citizen's Guide to Biotechnology. (Illus.). 73p. 1996. reprint ed. pap. text 25.00 (*0-7881-3772-7*) DIANE Pub.

Mauser. American Business: An Introduction. 6th ed. (C). 1996. pap. write for info. (*0-15-503615-7*) Harcourt Coll Pubs.

— Patti's Pet Gorilla. (J). 1987. pap. 7.00 (*0-385-22416-8*) Doubleday.

Mauser, Ferdinand F. & Schwartz, David J. American Business: An Introduction. 6th ed. 729p. (C). 1986. pap. text 32.00 (*0-15-502315-2*) Dryden Pr.

Mauser, Gary A. Political Marketing: An Approach to Campaign Strategy. Permut, Steven E., ed. LC 82-25973. (Praeger Series in Public & Nonprofit Sector Marketing). 304p. 1983. 57.95 (*0-275-91721-5*, C1721, Praeger Pubs) Greenwood.

— Political Marketing: An Approach to Campaign Strategy. LC 82-25973. 1983. 34.95 (*0-03-052591-8*) Holt R&W.

Mauser, H. & Gauglitz, G. Photokinetics: Theoretical Fundamentals & Applications. LC 98-26516. (Chemical Kinetics Ser.). 556p. 1998. 362.00 (*0-444-82536-3*) Elsevier.

Mauser, Patricia R. Love Is for the Dogs. (J). 1989. pap. 2.50 (*0-380-75723-0*, Avon Bks) Morrow Avon.

— Patti's Pet Gorilla. 64p. (J). 1991. pap. 2.95 (*0-380-71039-0*, Avon Bks) Morrow Avon.

Mausert, Otto. Herbs for Health. (Longevity Ser.). 1991. lib. bdg. 75.00 (*0-8490-4195-3*) Gordon Pr.

— Herbs for Health. 200p. 1996. reprint ed. spiral bd. 19.00 (*0-7873-0590-1*) Hlth Research.

Mauseth. Botany: Introduction to Plant Biology. 3rd ed. 1995. pap. text 87.50 (*0-03-013882-5*, Pub. by Harcourt Coll Pubs) Harcourt.

— Introduction to Plant Biology. 2nd ed. (C). 1995. pap. text 31.00 (*0-03-005893-7*) Harcourt Coll Pubs.

Mauseth, James. Botany: An Introduction to Plant Biology. 2nd ed. LC 94-69539. (Life Science Ser.). (C). 1995. text 72.50 (*0-03-096842-9*) Jones & Bartlett.

— Botany: Introduction to Plant Biology. 2nd ed. (Life Science Ser.). 864p. 1997. 72.50 (*0-7637-0669-8*) Jones & Bartlett.

— Botany: Introduction to Plant Biology, Test Bank. 2nd ed. (Life Science Ser.). (C). 1995. pap., teacher ed. 10.00 (*0-03-005892-9*) Jones & Bartlett.

Mauseth, James D. Botany: An Introduction to Plant Biology. 2nd ed. LC 97-42599. 862p. 1998. 75.00 (*0-7637-0746-5*) Jones & Bartlett.

— Plant Anatomy. 600p. (C). 1988. text 63.95 (*0-8053-4570-1*) Benjamin-Cummings.

Mausfield. Perception Theory. text. write for info. (*0-471-49149-7*) Wiley.

Maushard, Lawrence J. Made in Managua: A Nonfiction Account of One Journalist's Trip Through a Telling Place & Time. (Illus.). 162p. (Orig.). 1990. pap. 5.95 (*0-9626912-0-8*) Quimby Archives.

Maushart, Susan. The Mask of Motherhood: How Becoming a Mother Changes Everything & Why We Pretend It Doesn't. LC 98-27830. 266p. 1999. 24.00 (*1-56584-483-1*, Pub. by New Press NY) Norton.

***Maushart, Susan.** Mask of Motherhood: How Becoming a Mother Changes Our Lives & Why We Never Talk about It. 2000. pap. 12.95 (*0-14-029178-4*) Viking Penguin.

Mauskopf, Norman. A History of Chemistry & the Earth Sciences During the Enlightenment. 1999. 26.95 (*0-8057-9517-0*, Twyne) Mac Lib Ref.

Mauskopf, Norman, photos by. Dark Horses. (Illus.). 112p. 1988. 50.00 (*0-944092-04-7*) Twin Palms Pub.

Mauskopf, Seymour H., ed. Chemical Sciences in the Modern World. (Chemical Sciences in Society Ser.). (Illus.). 448p. (C). 1994. text 45.00 (*0-8122-3156-2*) U of Pa Pr.

Mauskopf, Seymour H. & McVaugh, Michael R. The Elusive Science: Origins of Experimental Psychical Research. LC 80-7991. 392p. 1980. reprint ed. pap. 121.60 (*0-608-03736-2*, 206456100009) Bks Demand.

Mausner, Judith S. & Kramer, Shira. Mausner & Bahn Epidemiology: An Introductory Text. 2nd ed. (Illus.). 361p. 1985. pap. text 40.95 (*0-7216-6181-5*, W B Saunders Co) Harcrt Hlth Sci Grp.

Mauss, Armand L. The Angel & the Beehive: The Mormon Struggle with Assimilation. LC 93-11328. 280p. 1994. text 29.95 (*0-252-02071-5*) U of Ill Pr.

Mauss, Marcel. A General Theory of Magic. Brain, Robert, tr. from FRE. 152p. 1972. 19.95 (*0-7100-7338-0*, Routledge Thoemms) Routledge.

— Gift: The Form & Reason for Exchange in Archaic Societies. 1990. pap. 10.95 (*0-393-30698-4*) Norton.

***Mauss, Marcel.** Gift: The Form & Reason for Exchange in Archaic Societies. 184p. 2000. pap. 12.95 (*0-393-32043-X*) Norton.

Mauss, Marcel, jt. auth. see Durkheim, Emile.

Mauss, Marcel, jt. auth. see Hubert, Henri.

Mausser, Wayne. Black & Blue Rivalry. 1998. 25.00 (*0-939995-20-4*) Angel Pr WI.

— Chicago Cubs Facts & Trivia. (Illus.). 192p. 1996. pap. 12.99 (*0-938313-14-2*) E B Houchin.

Maust, John. Un Canto Nuevo en los Andes. Windle, Jeanette, tr. LC 89-35170.Tr. of New Song in the Andes. (SPA., Illus.). 163p. 1995. pap. 6.00 (*0-9617490-7-5*) Gospel Missionary.

— New Song in the Andes. LC 89-35170. (Illus.). 173p. (Orig.). 1992. pap. 9.95 (*0-87808-219-0*, WCL219-0) William Carey Lib.

Mauterer, Erin Marie. The Three Little Pigs. 2nd ed. (We Both Read Ser.). 48p. (J). (gr. k-1). 1999. pap. 3.99 (*1-891327-09-7*) Treas Bay Inc.

Mauthner, Fritz. Der Atheismus und Seine Geschichte Im Abendlande. (GER.). xxii, 2201p. 1985. reprint ed. text. write for info. (*3-487-00379-1*) G Olms Pubs.

Mautino, Robert A. & Endelman, Gary, eds. Nationality & Citizenship Handbook. 130p. 1996. 49.00 (*1-878677-95-0*, 52.40) Amer Immi Law Assn.

Mautner, Diane. Draw Me a Story. (Illus.). 151p. 1994. pap. 24.95 (*0-9626939-8-7*) Janelle Pubns.

Mautner, Richard, jt. auth. see Bluestone, Morton D.

Mautner, Thomas. Penguin Dictionary of Philosophy. LC 98-155375. 672p. 1998. pap. 15.95 (*0-14-051250-0*) Viking Penguin.

Mautner, Thomas, ed. see Hutcheson, Francis.

Mautor, Claudette, jt. auth. see Pulleyn, Rob.

Mautz, Carl, et al. Biographies of Western Photographers: A Reference Guide to Photographers Working in the 19th Century American West. (Illus.). 600p. 1997. 85.00 (*0-9621940-7-7*) C Mautz Pubng.

Mautz, Robert K. Duties of Junior & Senior Accountants. 344p. 1988. text 15.00 (*0-8240-6143-8*) Garland.

— Financial Reporting for Nonprofit Organizations: A Fresh Look. LC 93-40062. (New Works in Accounting History). 136p. 1994. text 15.00 (*0-8153-1718-2*) Garland.

— Fundamentals of Auditing. 2nd ed. LC 64-20075. 593p. reprint ed. pap. 183.90 (*0-608-10950-9*, 201258700082) Bks Demand.

Mautz, Robert K. & Sharaf, Hussein A. The Philosophy of Auditing. (Monograph No. 6). 248p. 1961. 12.00 (*0-86539-002-9*) Am Accounting.

Mauvais-Jarvis, P. & Lafire, Fernand. Medecine de la Reproduction Tome 1: Gynecologie Endocrinienne. (Illus.). 520p. 1982. 58.00 (*0-318-04526-5*) S M P F Inc.

— Medecine de la Reproduction Tome 2: Medecine de la Reproduction Masculine. (Illus.). 1984. 65.00 (*0-318-04527-3*) S M P F Inc.

Mauw, S. & Veltink, G. J. Algebraic Specification of Communication Protocols. (Tracts in Theoretical Computer Science Ser.: No. 36). 209p. (C). 1993. text 49.95 (*0-521-41883-6*) Cambridge U Pr.

Mauze, Marie. Present Is Past: Some Uses of Tradition in Native Societies. LC 96-51052. 250p. 1997. write for info. (*0-7618-0684-9*); pap. write for info. (*0-7618-0685-7*) U Pr of Amer.

Mauzy, Barbara. Bakelite in the Kitchen. LC 97-80327. (Illus.). 192p. 1998. pap. 29.95 (*0-7643-0455-0*) Schiffer.

***Mauzy, Barbara.** Pyrex, the Unauthorized Collector's Guide. (Illus.). 160p. 2000. pap. 29.95 (*0-7643-1069-0*) Schiffer.

***Mauzy, Barbara & Mauzy, Jim.** Mauzy's Comprehensive Handbook of Depression Glass Prices. 2nd rev. ed. (Illus.). 192p. (Orig.). 2000. pap. 9.95 (*0-7643-0992-7*) Schiffer.

Mauzy, Barbara & Mauzy, Jim. Mauzy's Comprehensive Handbook of Depression Glass Prices. (Illus.). 160p. (Orig.). 1999. pap. 9.95 (*0-7643-0834-3*) Schiffer.

Mauzy, Barbara E. Peanut Butter Glasses. LC 96-35800. 128p. (YA). (gr. 10). 1997. pap. 19.95 (*0-7643-0107-1*) Schiffer.

***Mauzy, Barbara E. & Mauzy, Jim.** Mauzy's Comprehensive Handbook of Depression Glass Prices. LC 98-83095. 192 p. 1999. write for info. (*0-7643-0827-0*) Schiffer.

Mauzy, Charles, jt. ed. see Kirk, Ruth.

Mauzy, Diane K., jt. auth. see Milne, R. S.

Mauzy, Jim, jt. auth. see Mauzy, Barbara.

Mauzy, Jim, jt. auth. see Mauzy, Barbara.

Mauzy, Jim, jt. auth. see Mauzy, Barbara E.

Mavaddat, R. Network Scattering Parameters. (Advanced Series on Circuits & Systems). 350p. 1996. text 68.00 (*981-02-2305-6*) World Scientific Pub.

Maval Medical Education Staff, ed. see Waintrub, Valentin & Luder, Maria.

Mavalankar, Damodar K. The Service of Humanity. (Sangam Texts Ser.). 132p. 1986. pap. 12.75 (*0-88695-025-2*) Concord Grove.

Mavalwala, Jamshed, ed. Dermatoglyphics: An International Bibliography (World Anthropology) xvi, 306p. 1978. text 53.85 (*90-279-7999-5*) Mouton.

— Dermatoglypics: An International Perspective. (World Anthropology Ser.). (Illus.). xxii, 382p. 1978. text 61.55 (*90-279-7580-9*) Mouton.

MaVeciana, Jose, ed. SME's: Internationalization, Networks & Strategy. 736p. 1994. 126.95 (*1-85628-696-7*, Pub. by Avebry) Ashgate Pub Co.

Maveety, Elaine A., jt. ed. see Ward, Jean M.

Maveety, Nancy. Justice Sandra Day O'Connor: Strategist on the Supreme Court. LC 95-52533. (Studies in American Constitutionalism). 160p. 1996. pap. text 23.95 (*0-8476-8195-5*) Rowman.

— Justice Sandra Day O'Connor: Strategist on the Supreme Court. LC 95-52533. (Studies in American Constitutionalism). 160p. 1996. lib. bdg. 55.50 (*0-8476-8194-7*) Rowman.

— Representation Rights & the Burger Years. 272p. (C). 1991. text 49.50 (*0-472-10227-3*, 10227) U of Mich Pr.

Mavel, Alain. Dictionnaire de Gynecologie et D'Obstetrique: Termes Usuels S'Hier et D'Aujourd'Hui. (FRE.). 592p. 1990. pap. write for info. (*0-7859-0499-9*, 2718404957) Fr & Eur.

Maver, Igor. Readings in Contemporary Australian Poetry. Jurgensen, Manfred, ed. (German-Australian Studies: Vol. 12). 150p. 1997. pap. 28.95 (*3-906757-30-7*, Pub. by P Lang) P Lang Pubng.

— Readings in Contemporary Australian Poetry. LC 97-11727. (German-Australian Studies/Deutsch-Australische Studien: Vol. 12). 150p. (C). 1997. pap. text 28.95 (*0-8204-3401-9*, Pub. by P Lang) P Lang Pubng.

Maver, Igor, ed. Ethnic Literature & Culture in the U. S. A., Canada, & Australia. 306p. 1996. 57.95 (*3-631-49747-4*) P Lang Pubng.

Maverick, Augustus. Henry J. Raymond & the New York Press: The Progress of American Journalism from 1840-1870. LC 78-125708. (American Journalists Ser.). 1971. reprint ed. 29.95 (*0-405-01689-1*) Ayer.

Maverick, Mary A. Memoirs. 1993. reprint ed. lib. bdg. 75.00 (*0-7812-5944-4*) Rprt Serv.

— Memoirs of Mary A. Maverick. Green, Rena M., ed. LC 88-31141. (Illus.). 152p. 1989. pap. 47.20 (*0-608-05116-0*, 206567500005) Bks Demand.

Maverick, Maury. Maverick American. 1993. reprint ed. lib. bdg. 75.00 (*0-7812-5969-X*) Rprt Serv.

Maverick, Maury, Jr. Texas Iconoclast: Maury Maverick, Jr. Kownslar, Allan O., ed. LC 96-31443. (Illus.). 300p. (Orig.). 1997. pap. 16.95 (*0-87565-172-0*) Tex Christian.

Maves, Carolyn, jt. auth. see Maves, Paul B.

***Maves, D. Roger.** WinRef 98-95: In-Your-Pocket. LC 99-76892. 576p. 2000. pap. 9.95 (*1-885071-22-1*) Sequoia Pub Inc.

Maves, Paul B. & Maves, Carolyn. Finding Your Way Through the Bible: Revised NRSV Edition. 176p. (Orig.). (J). (gr. 2-5). 1992. pap. 4.95 (*0-687-13046-8*) Abingdon.

Mavi, H. S. Introduction to Agrometeorology. (C). 1986. 14.00 (*81-204-0122-0*, Pub. by Oxford IBH) S Asia.

Mavian, Vahram. Selected Writings of Vahram Mavian, 1926-1983: A Unique Voice in Armenian Diaspora Literature. Hacikyan, Agop J., ed. & tr. by. from ARM. Mamourian, Arsene, tr. from ARM. LC 92-21428. 296p. 1992. text 89.95 (*0-7734-9198-8*) E Mellen.

Maviglia, Joseph. A God Hangs Upside Down. 128p. 1994. pap. 10.00 (*1-55071-014-1*) Guernica Editions.

Mavigliano, George J. & Lawson, Richard A. The Federal Art Project in Illinois, 1939-1943. LC 89-6172. (Illus.). 192p. (C). 1990. 26.95 (*0-8093-1580-7*) S Ill U Pr.

Mavigliano, George J., jt. auth. see Lawson, Richard A.

Maviglio. Catalutic Combusters. 1985. pap. 2.95 (*0-88266-337-2*) Storey Bks.

Mavil, jt. auth. see Doherty.

Mavinkurva. Namasmarana. 1986. pap. 2.50 (*1-57836-090-0*, BW-110) Sathya Sai Bk Ctr.

Mavis, B., jt. auth. see Chelsea House Publishing Staff.

***Mavis, Janice.** Feelings Inside of Me. 24p. 1999. pap. 6.95 (*1-56167-521-0*) Am Literary Pr.

Mavis, Ross & Mavis, Willa. Tide's Table: Maritime Cooking from Inn on the Cove. (Illus.). 284p. 1997. pap. 16.95 (*0-86492-208-6*, Pub. by Goose Ln Edits) Genl Dist Srvs.

Mavis, Willa, jt. auth. see Mavis, Ross.

Mavissaka, Matig & Barlow, David H., eds. Phobia: Psychological & Pharmacological Treatment. LC 80-15306. 256p. 1981. lib. bdg. 35.00 (*0-89862-602-1*) Guilford Pubns.

Mavissakalian, Matig R., jt. ed. see Prien, Robert F.

Mavituna, Ferda, et al, eds. Plant Cell Biotechnology. (NATO ASI Series H: Vol. 18). (Illus.). xx, 500p. 1988. 207.00 (*0-387-18556-9*) Spr-Verlag.

Mavko, Gary, et al. The Rock Physics Handbook: Tools for Seismic Analysis in Porous Media. LC 97-36653. (Illus.). 340p. (C). 1998. text 64.95 (*0-521-62068-6*) Cambridge U Pr.

Mavlin, George J. & Mygak, Joe. The Guidebook to Municipal Bonds: The History, the Industry, the Mechanics. (Illus.). 228p. 1991. 29.95 (*0-9618162-7-9*) Thomson Financial.

Mavor, Anne. Strong Hearts, Inspired Minds: 21 Artists Who Are Mothers Tell Their Stories. LC 96-92485. (Illus.). 256p. (Orig.). 1996. pap. 24.95 (*0-9653724-0-5*) Rowanberry Bks.

Mavor, Anne S., ed. see Commission on Behavioral & Social Sciences & Educa.

Mavor, Anne S., ed. see National Research Council Staff.

***Mavor, Carol.** Becoming: The Photographs of Clementina, Viscountess Hawarden. LC 99-10105. (Illus.). 264p. 1999. 59.95 (*0-8223-2355-9*) Duke.

Mavor, Carol. Pleasures Taken: Performances of Sexuality & Loss in Victorian Photographs. LC 94-41559. (Illus.). 208p. 1995. text 49.95 (*0-8223-1603-X*); pap. text 17.95 (*0-8223-1619-6*) Duke.

Mavor, Carol & Hawarden, Clementina. Becoming: The Photographs of Clementina, Viscountess Hawarden. LC 99-10105. (Illus.). 264p. 1999. pap. 19.95 (*0-8223-2389-3*) Duke.

Mavor, J., ed. M. O. S. T. Integrated Circuit Engineering. LC 73-87027. (Illus.). 172p. reprint ed. pap. 53.40 (*0-608-17790-3*, 203225500079) Bks Demand.

Mavor, James W., Jr. Voyage to Atlantis: The Discovery of a Legendary Land. rev. ed. (Illus.). 320p. 1996. reprint ed. pap. 16.95 (*0-89281-634-1*) Inner Tradit.

Mavor, James W. & Dix, Byron E. Manitou: The Sacred Landscape of New England's Native Civilization. LC 89-17106. (Illus.). 392p. 1992. pap. 18.95 (*0-89281-078-5*) Inner Tradit.

Mavor, Michael B. Joseph Andrews Notes. (Cliffs Notes Ser.). 80p. 1963. pap. 3.75 (*0-8220-0682-0*, Cliff) IDG Bks.

Mavor, Salley. You & Me: Poems of Friendship. LC 97-10062. 32p. (J). (ps-3). 1997. 16.95 (*0-531-30045-5*); lib. bdg. 17.99 (*0-531-33045-1*) Orchard Bks Watts.

Mavor, Sunny, jt. auth. see White, Linda B.

Mavragis, Edward P. Writing: The Essay. 91p. 1991. student ed. 4.95 (*1-56078-025-8*) Comp Pr.

Mavragis, Edward P., jt. auth. see Craz, Albert G.

Mavredakis, John G., jt. auth. see Zukin, James H.

Mavrich, Dorothy L. Rialto Square Theatre. (Illus.). 16p. 1993. 8.00 (*0-9635264-0-5*) D Mavrich.

Mavrides, Marios. Triangular Arbitrage in the Foreign Exchange Market: Inefficiencies, Technology, & Investment Opportunities. LC 91-47075. 200p. 1992. 57.95 (*0-89930-718-3*, Quorum Bks) Greenwood.

Mavrigian, Mike. Performance Wheels & Tires. LC 97-45832. 176p. 1998. pap. 16.95 (*1-55788-286-X*, HP Books) Berkley Pub.

Mavrikis, Anna. The Ice Pick Technique. LC 99-61093. 272p. 2000. pap. 14.95 (*0-88739-258-X*) Creat Arts Bk.

Mavrikis, Peter, ed. see Altman, Linda Jacobs.

Mavrikis, Peter, ed. see Hinds, Kathryn.

Mavrikis, Peter, ed. see Schafer, Susan.

Mavrikis, Peter, ed. see Stefoff, Rebecca.

Mavrocordatos, Nicolas. Les Loisirs de Philothee. LC 90-189048. (FRE & GRE., Illus.). 253p. reprint ed. pap. 78.50 (*0-7837-6949-0*, 204677800003) Bks Demand.

Mavrodiev, Strachimir C. Applied Ecology if the Black Sea. LC 98-34037. 1998. 75.00 (*1-56072-613-X*) Nova Sci Pubs.

Mavrodineanu, Radu. & Boiteux, Henri. Flame Spectroscopy. LC 64-20088. (Wiley Series in Pure & Applied Spectroscopy). 741p. reprint ed. pap. 200.00 (*0-608-09946-5*, 200747600062) Bks Demand.

Mavrogordato, Alice, tr. see Hadamovsky, Eugen.

Mavroidis, Petros & Cottier, Thomas, eds. The World Trade Forum Vol. 1: State Trading in the Twenty-First Century. LC 99-179462. (Illus.). 464p. 1998. text 65.00 (*0-472-10996-0*, 10996) U of Mich Pr.

Mavroidis, Petros C., jt. auth. see Palmeter, N. David.

Mavroidis, Petros C., jt. ed. see Hoekman, Bernard M.

Mavrolas, Pamela & Schechtman, Michael. Coal Mine Subsidence: Proceedings from a Citizens' Conference. 2nd ed. Henderson, Harold, ed. 46p. 1982. reprint ed. 4.00 (*0-943724-01-5*) Illinois South.

Mavrolas, Pamela, ed. see Boulding, Russell.

Mavromatis, Andreas, ed. Hypnogogia: The Unique State of Consciousness Between Wakefullness & Sleep. 353p. 1987. text 70.00 (*0-7102-0282-2*, Routledge Thoemms) Routledge.

Mavromatis, Harry A. Exercises in Quantum Mechanics: A Collection of Illustrative Problems & Their Solutions. 1986. text 122.00 (*90-277-2288-9*) Kluwer Academic.

Mavronicolas, Mario & Tsigas, Philippas. Distributed Algorithms: 11th International Workshop, WDAG '97, Saarbrucken, Germany, September 24-26, 1997: Proceedings, Vol. 132. LC 97-34775. (Lecture Notes in Computer Science Ser.). 1997. write for info. (*3-540-63575-0*) Spr-Verlag.

Mavronicolas, Marios, et al. Networks in Distributed Computing. LC 98-37246. (Dimacs Series in Discrete Mathematics & Theoretical Computer Science). 1998. write for info. (*0-8218-0992-X*) Am Math.

Mavros, P. & Matis, K. A., eds. Innovations in Flotation Technology. (C). 1991. text 264.50 (*0-7923-1560-X*) Kluwer Academic.

Mavrovitis, Basil B., ed. The Treasurer's Handbook of Financial Management. Date not set. write for info. (*0-614-30098-3*) Treasry Mgmt.

Mavrovitis, Basil P. Cashflow, Credit & Collection: Over 100 Proven Techniques for Protecting & Strengthening Your Balance Sheet. 2nd ed. LC 94-150137. 400p. 1993. per. 32.50 (*1-55738-522-X*, Irwn Prfssnl) McGraw-Hill Prof.

Mavterer, Erin M. The Three Little Pigs. (We Both Read Ser.). 48p. (J). (gr. k-1). 1998. 7.99 (*1-891327-05-4*) Treas Bay Inc.

M

An Asterisk (*) at the beginning of an entry indicates that the title is appearing for the first time.

Maw, G. A. Biochemistry of S-Methyl-L-Cysteine & Its Principal Derivatives, Vol. 2. (Sulfur Reports). 38p. (Orig.). 1982. pap. text 106.00 (*3-7186-0112-5*) Gordon & Breach.

Maw, Geoffrey Waring. Pilgrims in Hindu Holy Land. Conacher, Gillian M. & Sykes, Marjorie, eds. 176p. 1999. pap. 23.00 (*1-85072-190-4*, Pub. by W Sessions) St Mut.

Maw, Joan E. Swahili for Starters: A Practical Introductory Course. (School of Oriental & African Studies). (Illus.). 342p. 1999. pap. text 35.00 (*0-19-823783-9*) OUP.

Maw, Nigel G., et al. Maw on Corporate Governance. Alsbury, Alison, ed. LC 93-41372. 208p. (C). 1994. 48.95 (*1-85521-378-8*, Pub. by Dartmth Pub) Ashgate Pub Co.

Maw, Taylor. The Incredible Jelly Bean Day. Thatch, Nancy R., ed. LC 97-18801. (Books for Students by Students). (Illus.). 32p. (J). 1997. lib. bdg. 15.95 (*0-933849-66-4*) Landmark Edns.

***Mawadza, Aquilina.** Shona-English, English-Shona Dictionary & Phrasebook. (ENG & SHO.). 160p. 2000. pap. 11.95 (*0-7818-0813-8*) Hippocrene Bks.

Mawby. Containing Germany: Britain & the Arming of the Federal Republic. LC 98-42166. 256p. 1999. text 65.00 (*0-312-21914-8*) St Martin.

Mawby, Colin. Hymns for Occasions for Manuals. 224p. 1998. pap. 27.95 (*0-7866-3793-5*, 97495) Mel Bay.

Mawby, Janet. Writers & Politics in Modern Scandinavia. LC 78-18931. (Writers & Politics Ser.). 53p. 1978. pap. text 10.50 (*0-8419-0417-0*) Holmes & Meier.

Mawby, Larry, ed. see Sisson, Linda & Sisson, John.

Mawby, R. I. Policing Across the World: Issues for the Twenty-First Century. LC 99-175617. 1999. 72.00 (*1-85728-488-7*); pap. text 23.95 (*1-85728-489-5*) UCL Pr Ltd.

Mawby, R. I. & Gill, M. L. Crime Victims: Needs, Services, & the Voluntary Sector. (Illus.). 272p. (C). 1987. pap. text 25.00 (*0-422-61450-5*, Pub. by Tavistock) Routldge.

Mawby, R. I. & Walklate, Sandra. Critical Victimology: International Perspectives. 240p. (C). 1994. text 65.00 (*0-8039-8511-8*); pap. text 19.95 (*0-8039-8512-6*) Sage.

Mawby, R. I., jt. auth. see Gill, M. L.

Mawcroft, Michael, ed. see L'Abbe-D'Aubignac.

Mawdesley, M. J. Planning & Controlling Construction Projects. LC 97-144702. 432p. (C). 1997. 100.00 (*0-582-23409-3*) Addison-Wesley.

Mawdesley-Thomas, Lionel E., et al. Diseases of Fish. 277p. (C). 1974. text 27.50 (*0-8422-7178-3*) Irvington.

Mawdsley. The Stalin Years. LC 98-222091. 192p. 1998. text 79.95 (*0-7190-4599-1*, Pub. by Manchester Univ Pr) St Martin.

Mawdsley, Andres A., pref. Palau: A Challenge to the Rule of Law in Micronesia: Report of a Mission by William J. Butler, Esq., The Hon. George C. Edwards, The Hon. Michael D. Kirby, C.M.G. 58p. (Orig.). (C). 1988. pap. text 5.00 (*0-916265-04-8*) Am Assn Intl Comm Jurists.

Mawdsley, Dean L. The America of Eric Sloane: A Collector's Bibliography. 1990. 9.95 (*0-918676-24-X*) Conn Hist Com.

— Cruise Books of the United States Navy in World War II: A Bibliography. LC 92-41498. 162p. 1993. 6.00 (*0-945274-13-0*) Naval Hist Ctr.

Mawdsley, Evan. Moscow & Leningrad. 2nd ed. 1991. pap. 22.50 (*0-393-30773-5*) Norton.

— The Russian Civil War. (Illus.). 320p. (C). 1987. text 55.00 (*0-04-947024-8*); pap. text 18.95 (*0-04-947025-6*) Routledge.

— The Stalin Years. LC 98-222091. 192p. 1998. pap. 19.95 (*0-7190-4600-9*, Pub. by Manchester Univ Pr) St Martin.

Mawdsley, Evan & Munck, Thomas. Computing for Historians: An Introductory Guide. (Illus.). 200p. 1993. pap. 19.95 (*0-7190-3454-X*, Pub. by Manchester Univ Pr) St Martin.

***Mawdsley, Evan & White, Stephen.** The Soviet Elite from Lenin to Gorbachev: The Central Committee & Its Members. 352p. 2000. text 39.95 (*0-19-829738-6*) OUP.

***Mawdsley, Ian.** AutoCAD 2000: An Introductory Course. 288p. 2000. pap. 29.95 (*0-7506-4722-1*, Newnes) Buttrwrth-Heinemann.

Mawdsley, Ralph. Academic Misconduct: Cheating & Plagiarism. (Monograph Ser.: No. 51). 121p. 1994. pap. 27.00 (*1-56534-082-5*) Ed Law Assn.

***Mawdsley, Ralph D.** Legal Problems of Religious & Private Schools. 4th ed. 300p. 2000. write for info. (*1-56534-101-5*) Ed Law Assn.

Mawdsley, Ralph D. Pupil Transportation & the Law. 2nd ed. 100p. (C). 1996. text 27.00 (*1-56534-091-4*) Ed Law Assn.

Mawdudi, S. Abul. Human Rights in Islam. 40p. 1996. pap. 4.50 (*0-614-21510-2*, 469) Kazi Pubns.

— Towards Understanding the Quran, Vols. I-IV. Ansari, Zafar I., tr. 380p. 1996. pap. 16.50 (*0-614-21074-7*, 1248) Kazi Pubns.

Mawe, S. M. Grown Men. LC 96-46831. 240p. 1997. mass mkt. 22.00 (*0-380-97432-0*, Avon Bks) Morrow Avon.

— Grown Men: A Novel. 240p. 1998. pap. 12.00 (*0-380-79048-3*, Avon Bks) Morrow Avon.

Mawe, Sheelagh M. Dandelion: The Triumphant Life of a Misfit, a Story for All Ages. 165p. (Orig.). (J). (gr. 4). 1994. pap. 7.95 (*0-9642168-0-9*) Totally Unique.

Mawer, Deborah. Darius Milhaud: Modality & Structure in Music of the 1920s. LC 97-3007. (Illus.). 432p. 1997. text 86.95 (*1-85928-249-0*, Pub. by Ashgate Pub) Ashgate Pub Co.

***Mawer, Deborah, ed.** The Cambridge Companion to Ravel. LC 99-47568. (Cambridge Companions to Music Ser.). (Illus.). 324p. (C). 2000. write for info. (*0-521-64026-1*); pap. write for info. (*0-521-64856-4*) Cambridge U Pr.

Mawer, Giselle & Fletcher, Lee. Language & Literacy in Workplace Education. LC 98-35999. (Language in Social Life Ser.). 1999. write for info. (*0-582-25764-6*) Longman.

Mawer, Giseller. Language & Literacy in Workplace Education. LC 98-35999. 336p. 1999. pap. text 29.68 (*0-582-25765-4*) Addison-Wesley.

***Mawer, Granville A.** Ahab's Trade: The/Saga of South Sea Whaling. LC 99-38992. (Illus.). 393p. 2000. text 29.95 (*0-312-22809-0*) St Martin.

Mawer, Granville A. Most Perfectly Safe: The Convict Shipwreck Disasters of 1833-42. LC 97-147977. (Illus.). 208p. 1997. pap. 24.95 (*1-86448-186-2*, Pub. by Allen & Unwin Pty) Paul & Co Pubs.

Mawer, Mick. The Effective Teaching of Physical Education. LC 94-38241. (Effective Teacher Ser.). 1995. pap. text. write for info. (*0-582-09522-0*, Pub. by Addison-Wesley) Longman.

— Mentoring in Physical Education: Issues & Insights. LC 96-18405. 224p. 1996. 79.95 (*0-7507-0564-7*, Falmer Pr); pap. 27.95 (*0-7507-0565-5*, Falmer Pr) Taylor & Francis.

Mawer, Mick, jt. ed. see Hardy, Colin C.

Mawer, Simon. Mendel's Dwarf. 1999. pap. 12.95 (*0-14-028155-X*) Viking Penguin.

— Mendel's Dwarf. large type ed. LC 98-23615. 1998. 26.95 (*0-7862-1519-4*) Thorndike Pr.

Mawhin, J. L. & Willem, M. Critical Point Theory & Hamiltonian Systems. (Applied Mathematical Sciences Ser.: Vol. 74). (Illus.). xiv, 277p. 1989. 79.95 (*0-387-96908-X*) Spr-Verlag.

Mawhin, Jean. Topological Degree Methods in Non-Linear Boundary Value Problems. LC 78-31906. (CBMS Regional Conference Series in Mathematics: No. 40). 122p. 1979. reprint ed. pap. 18.00 (*0-8218-1690-X*, CBMS/40) Am Math.

Mawhiney, A. R. Good Morning Doctor. 100p. 1971. pap. 5.95 (*0-931764-00-9*) Roberts Pub Co.

Mawhiney, Anne-Marie. Towards Aboriginal Self-Government: Relations Between Status Indian Peoples & the Government of Canada. LC 93-18018. 160p. 1993. text 15.00 (*0-8153-0823-X*, 93-18018) Garland.

Mawhiney, R. B. Clinical Hypnosis in Chiropractic. 88p. 1979. 50.00 (*0-931764-10-6*) Roberts Pub Co.

— History of Chiropractic in Wisconsin, 1950-1990, No. 1. (Illus.). 268p. 1988. 50.00 (*0-931764-05-X*) Roberts Pub Co.

— History of Chiropractic in Wisconsin, 1950-1990, No. 2. (Illus.). 206p. 1993. 50.00 (*0-931764-09-2*) Roberts Pub Co.

— Madame President. 80p. 1984. mass mkt. 7.95 (*0-931764-04-1*) Roberts Pub Co.

— Scoliosis: Collection of Published Articles. (Illus.). 66p. 1989. 45.00 (*0-931764-08-4*) Roberts Pub Co.

— Scoliosis Care. (Illus.). 100p. 1998. pap. 12.95 (*0-931764-01-7*) Roberts Pub Co.

— Scoliosis Manual. (Illus.). 113p. 1995. 45.00 (*0-931764-03-3*) Roberts Pub Co.

— Scoliosis Treatment Manual. (Illus.). 90p. 1989. 50.00 (*0-931764-07-6*) Roberts Pub Co.

Mawhiney, R. W. Holy Criers. 100p. 1998. pap. 7.95 (*0-931764-02-5*) Roberts Pub Co.

Mawhinney, Bruce. Preaching with Freshness: Avoiding Burnout & Renewing Enthusiasm for Biblical Preaching. LC 96-52007. 264p. 1997. pap. 12.99 (*0-8254-3198-0*) Kregel.

Mawhinney, Charles H. A Modular Approach to dBASE IV: IBM Version. 96p. (C). 1992. spiral bd. write for info. (*0-697-13252-8*) Bus & Educ Tech.

Mawhinney, M. H., jt. auth. see Trinks, Willibald.

Mawhinney, Paul C., ed. Music Master: The CD-Five Singles Directory, 1994, Vol. One. 2nd ed. 194p. 1994. reprint ed. pap. 30.00 (*0-910925-07-0*) Record-Rama.

— Music Master: The Forty-Five RPM Christmas Singles Directory, 1994, Vol. One. 2nd ed. 142p. 1994. reprint ed. pap. 30.00 (*0-910925-08-9*) Record-Rama.

— MusicMaster: The 45 RPM Record Directory by Artist (1997 Edition) rev. ed. 1500p. 1997. pap. 100.00 (*0-910925-09-7*) Record-Rama.

— MusicMaster: The 45 RPM Record Directory by Label (1997 Edition) rev. ed. 1500p. 1997. pap. 100.00 (*0-910925-11-9*) Record-Rama.

— MusicMaster: The 45 RPM Record Directory by Title (1997 Edition) rev. ed. 1500p. 1997. pap. 100.00 (*0-910925-10-0*) Record-Rama.

Mawhinney, Thomas C., ed. Organizational Behavior Management & Statistical Process Control: Theory, Technology & Research. LC 87-32520. (Journal of Organizational Behavior Management: Vol. 9, No. 1). (Illus.). 159p. 1988. text 49.95 (*0-86656-751-8*) Haworth Pr.

— Organizational Culture, Rule-Governed Behavior & Organizational Behavior Management: Theoretical Foundations & Implications for Research & Practice. LC 92-30026. (Journal of Organizational Behavior Management: Vol. 12, No. 2). (Illus.). 137p. 1993. 39.95 (*1-56024-359-7*) Haworth Pr.

— Organizational Culture, Rule-Governed Behavior & Organizational Behavior Management: Theoretical Foundations & Implications for Research & Practice. LC 92-30026. (Journal of Organizational Behavior Management: Vol. 12, No. 2). 137p. 1996. pap. 17.95 (*0-7890-0068-7*) Haworth Pr.

— Pay for Performance: History, Controversy, & Evidence. LC 91-41350. (Journal of Organizational Behavior Management: Vol. 12, No. 1). 1992. text 49.95 (*1-56024-254-X*) Haworth Pr.

— Pay for Performance: History, Controversy, & Evidence. LC 91-41350. (Journal of Organizational Behavior Management: Vol. 12, No. 1). 1992. pap. text 19.95 (*1-56024-255-8*) Haworth Pr.

Mawhood, Philip, ed. Local Government in the Third World: The Experience of Tropical Africa. LC 82-11176. (Wiley Series on Public Administration in Developing Countries). (Illus.). 275p. reprint ed. pap. 85.30 (*0-8357-2954-0*, 203921000011) Bks Demand.

Mawley, Edward, jt. auth. see Jekyll, Gertrude.

Mawn, Thomas, jt. auth. see Gottlieb, Bert.

Mawson, Anthony R. Guide to Area Schools & Day Care Centers: New Orleans Region. 168p. (Orig.). 1989. pap. 9.95 (*0-9622274-0-4*) S & DCIS Inc.

— Transient Criminality: A Model of Stress-Induced Crime. LC 87-11741. 345p. 1987. 65.00 (*0-275-92552-8*, C2552, Praeger Pubs) Greenwood.

Mawson, C. O., ed. Roget's Pocket Thesaurus. 1987. pap. 3.95 (*0-317-56742-X*) PB.

Mawson, Dave, et al. Design & Make It! Electronic Products. 144p. 1998. pap. 30.00 (*0-7487-2473-7*) St Mut.

Mawson, Douglas. Home of the Blizzard: A True Story of Antarctic Survival. LC 98-3748. (Illus.). 568p. 1998. text 27.95 (*0-312-21125-2*) St Martin.

***Mawson, Douglas.** Home of the Blizzard: A True Story of Arctic Survival. (Illus.). 2000. pap. 17.95 (*0-312-23072-9*) St Martin.

Mawson, John, jt. ed. see Bradbury, Jonathan.

Mawson, Robert. The Lazarus Child. 400p. 1999. mass mkt. 6.50 (*0-553-58005-1*) Bantam.

— The Lazarus Child. 303p. 1998. 32.95 (*0-385-25741-4*) Dov Press.

— The Lazarus Child. LC 98-49018. (Wheeler Large Print Book Ser.). 450 p. 1998. write for info. (*1-56895-696-7*) Wheeler Pub.

***Mawson, Steve.** The Fundamentals of Hospitality Marketing. 128p. 2000. pap. 16.95 (*0-8264-4832-1*) Continuum.

***Mawson, Stuart.** Arnhem Doctor. 176p. 2000. pap. 19.95 (*1-86227-088-0*, Pub. by Spellmnt Pubs) St Mut.

Mawson, Thomas. The Imperial Obligation: Industrial Villages for the Partialy Disabled Soldiers & Sailors. Phillips, William R. & Rosenberg, Janet, eds. LC 79-6918. (Physically Handicapped in Society Ser.). 1980. reprint ed. lib. bdg. 17.95 (*0-405-13125-9*) Ayer.

Mawson, Timothy. The Garden Room: Bringing Nature Indoors. LC 99-218268. 1999. pap. 24.00 (*0-609-80282-8*) Crown Pub Group.

Mawyer, Martin. Defending the American Family. LC 95-69892. 224p. 1995. pap. 10.95 (*0-89221-296-9*) New Leaf.

— Pathways to Success: 1st Steps for Becoming a Christian in Action. LC 94-67320. 176p. (Orig.). 1994. pap. 9.95 (*0-89221-270-5*) New Leaf.

Max. Book of Be: Rules for Life. 50p. 1997. pap. 35.00 (*0-922070-40-7*) M Tecton Pub.

— Bribery of Congress & State Legislators. (Illus.). 45p. 1997. pap. 35.00 (*0-922070-94-6*) M Tecton Pub.

— Clinton! Liar! Liar! Pants on Fire! (Illus.). 50p. 1997. pap. 32.00 (*0-922070-70-9*) M Tecton Pub.

— Clinton's Pornography & Lies. 50p. 1997. pap. 32.00 (*0-922070-83-0*) M Tecton Pub.

— Conquests of Europe by the Negro Race. 50p. 1997. pap. 40.00 (*0-922070-84-9*) M Tecton Pub.

— Constitutional Secret Teachings. 50p. 1997. pap. 35.00 (*0-922070-86-5*) M Tecton Pub.

— Crazy Congress. (Illus.). 50p. 1997. pap. 32.00 (*0-922070-72-5*) M Tecton Pub.

— Crazy Ross Perot. (Illus.). 50p. 1997. pap. 32.00 (*0-922070-71-7*) M Tecton Pub.

— Cults of the Circumcised: On the Practice of Circumcision. (Illus.). 50p. 1997. pap. 45.00 (*0-922070-33-4*) M Tecton Pub.

— Extended Dream of Mr. D. 1999. pap. text 12.95 (*1-896597-26-2*) LPC InBook.

— Goddamn Yankees. (Illus.). 45p. 1997. pap. 35.00 (*0-922070-95-4*) M Tecton Pub.

— Guns are Legal! 50p. 1997. pap. 32.00 (*0-922070-32-6*) M Tecton Pub.

— How to Cure Toenail Fungus. (Illus.). 50p. 1997. pap. 40.00 (*0-922070-55-5*) M Tecton Pub.

— How to Prevent Arthritis. 50p. 1997. pap. 35.00 (*0-922070-37-7*) M Tecton Pub.

— How to Prevent Headaches. (Illus.). 50p. 1997. pap. 40.00 (*0-922070-90-3*) M Tecton Pub.

— Illegal Affirmative Action. 50p. 1997. pap. 40.00 (*0-922070-77-6*) M Tecton Pub.

— Illegal F. B. I., B. A. T. F., D. E. A., I. R. S. 50p. 1997. pap. 35.00 (*0-922070-39-3*) M Tecton Pub.

— Illegal Property Taxes. 50p. 1997. pap. 32.00 (*0-922070-48-2*) M Tecton Pub.

— Illegal Tobacco Taxes. 50p. 1997. pap. 40.00 (*0-922070-47-4*) M Tecton Pub.

— Illegal U. S. Prisons. (Illus.). 45p. 1997. pap. 75.00 (*0-922070-66-0*) M Tecton Pub.

— Illegality of Corporations, Foundations, Trusts. 50p. 1997. pap. 42.00 (*0-922070-78-4*) M Tecton Pub.

— Illegality of Drug Arrests. (Illus.). 45p. 1997. pap. 45.00 (*0-922070-68-7*) M Tecton Pub.

— Illegality of Federal Reserve. (Illus.). 45p. 1997. pap. 35.00 (*0-922070-96-2*) M Tecton Pub.

— Illegality of Lawyers & Their Monopoly. (Illus.). 45p. 1997. pap. 40.00 (*0-922070-92-X*) M Tecton Pub.

— Illegality of Welfare. 50p. 1997. pap. 32.00 (*0-922070-87-3*) M Tecton Pub.

— Live Better & Longer/Healthy Eating. 50p. 1997. pap. 32.00 (*0-922070-35-0*) M Tecton Pub.

— McVeigh is Innocent. (Illus.). 45p. 1997. pap. 35.00 (*0-922070-93-8*) M Tecton Pub.

— Illegal Withholding Tax. (Illus.). 45p. (Orig.). 1997. pap. 35.00 (*0-922070-30-X*) M Tecton Pub.

— Paula Jones, Hero! (Illus.). 45p. 1997. pap. 35.00 (*0-922070-91-1*) M Tecton Pub.

— Prevent Gas on Stomach. (Illus.). 50p. 1997. pap. 40.00 (*0-922070-89-X*) M Tecton Pub.

— Prevent Hemorrhoids/How To. 50p. 1997. pap. 32.00 (*0-922070-36-9*) M Tecton Pub.

— Prevent the Common Cold: It's Ridiculous to Catch a Cold in This Modern Age. 50p. 1997. pap. 40.00 (*0-922070-34-2*) M Tecton Pub.

— Prevent Tooth Decay. 50p. 1997. pap. 40.00 (*0-922070-42-3*) M Tecton Pub.

— Prophet Stathopulos: Right Living. 50p. 1997. pap. 40.00 (*0-922070-41-5*) M Tecton Pub.

— Religious/Philosophical Dictionary & Phonetic History. 50p. 1997. pap. 50.00 (*0-922070-69-5*) M Tecton Pub.

— Secret History of the Hittites, Philistines, Greeks, Hebrews, Galalians & Nazzarians. 50p. 1997. pap. 45.00 (*0-922070-82-2*) M Tecton Pub.

— Social Security, Medicare, Welfare Are Unconstitutional. 50p. 1997. pap. 40.00 (*0-922070-80-6*) M Tecton Pub.

— Supreme Thoughts to Live By. 50p. 1997. pap. 32.00 (*0-922070-38-5*) M Tecton Pub.

— Tax Protestor's Handbook. 50p. 1997. pap. 35.00 (*0-922070-44-X*) M Tecton Pub.

— Tax Religions, Foundations, Unions, Charities, Etc. 50p. 1997. pap. 40.00 (*0-922070-75-X*) M Tecton Pub.

— U. S. A. Slavery Today. 50p. 1997. pap. 40.00 (*0-922070-76-8*) M Tecton Pub.

— Up the I. R. S. Cartoons. (Illus.). 50p. 1997. pap. 35.00 (*0-922070-43-1*) M Tecton Pub.

— The Waco Texas Massacre. 50p. 1997. pap. 35.00 (*0-922070-79-2*) M Tecton Pub.

***Max Born Symposium Staff.** Theoretical Physics: Fin de Siaecle: Proceedings of the XII Max Born Symposium, Held in Wroclaw, Poland, 23-26 September, 1998. Borowiec, Andrzej et al, eds. LC 99-89490. (Lecture Notes in Physics Ser.: Vol. 539). xx, 319p. 2000. 82.80 (*3-540-66801-2*) Spr-Verlag.

***Max, Charles.** Entwicklung Von Kompetenz - Ein Neues Paradigma fur das Lernen In Schule und Arbeitswelt: Ertrag und Perspektiven der Franzosischsprachigen Kompetenzforschung und Ihre Bedeutung Als Gestaltungsprinzip Von Bildung. (Europaische Hochschulschriften: Reihe 11, Padagogik Ser.). 506p. 1999. 68.95 (*3-631-35378-2*) P Lang Pubng.

Max, Derrick A., jt. auth. see Bradford, David F.

Max, Gerry. Concerto for Ten Broken Fingers. 162p. 1978. pap. 14.95 (*0-686-38100-9*, 101) William of Orange.

— Ixion's Wheel. 118p. 1979. pap. 14.95 (*0-686-38099-1*, 102) William of Orange.

Max, Gertie. The Finalizer. (Illus.). 15p. (YA). (gr. 9-12). 1994. pap. text 8.95 (*1-886695-31-8*) Study System.

— Gertie Max Study Systemizer: Includes the Finalizer. rev. ed. (Illus.). 105p. (J). (gr. 4-12). 1998. 49.95 (*1-886695-21-0*) Study System.

— The Systemizer. (Illus.). 47p. (J). (gr. 4-12). 1995. pap. text 9.95 (*1-886695-15-6*) Study System.

Max, Herbert B. Business Investment & Loan Agreements: Forms & Authorities. 1985. suppl. ed. 75.00 (*0-317-29386-9*, #H43902) Harcourt.

Max, Herbert B., jt. auth. see Brown, J. Robert, Jr.

Max, Herbert B., jt. auth. see Frome, Robert L.

Max, Ingolf & Stelzner, Werner, eds. Logik und Mathematik: Frege-Kolloquium, 1993. (Perspektiven der Analytischen Philosophie - Perspectives in Analytical Philosophy Ser.: Bd. 5). (GER.). xi, 553p. (C). 1995. lib. bdg. 207.70 (*3-11-014545-6*) De Gruyter.

Max, Jill. Spider Spins a Story: 14 Legends from Native America. LC 97-18970. (Illus.). 72p. (J). (gr. 3-7). 1997. 16.95 (*0-87358-611-5*, Rising Moon Bks) Northland AZ.

Max, Jill, ed. see Bohlke, Dorothee.

Max, Jill, ed. see Duncklee, John.

Max, Jill, ed. see Mann, Marek.

Max, Louise Reinoehl. Nine Lives: A Journal for My Cat. 80p. 1999. 12.95 (*0-87905-889-7*) Gibbs Smith Pub.

Max, Lucado. Inspirational Bible: Life Lessons from the Inspired Word of God. 1997. 29.97 (*90-71676-47-1*); 39.97 (*90-71676-48-X*) Word Pub.

— Inspirational Bible, Life's Lessons Fron The Inspired Word Of God, Supersaver Ed., 1. 1997. pap. text 19.97 (*90-71676-46-3*) Word Pub.

Max, M. D., jt. ed. see Fleming, N. C.

Max, Mitchell B., et al. The Design of Analgesic Clinical Trials. (Advances in Pain Research & Therapy Ser.: Vol. 18). 752p. 1991. text 147.00 (*0-88167-736-1*) Lppncott W & W.

Max, Mitchell B., ed. see IASP Refresher Courses on Pain Management Staff & IASP Scientific Program Committee.

Max Mueller, F. Keshub Chunder Sen. rev. ed. Mookerjee, Nanda, ed. 1976. 6.00 (*0-88386-862-8*) S Asia.

Max-Muller, F. & Fleet, J. F. Indian Paleography from about B.C. 350 to about A.D. 1300: With a Life Sketch of Buhler. (Illus.). 140p. 1987. reprint ed. 20.00 (*0-88065-073-7*) Scholarly Pubns.

Max-Neef, Manfred. From the Outside Looking In: Experiences in "Barefoot Economics" (Illus.). 208p. (C). 1992. text 62.50 (*1-85649-187-0*, Pub. by Zed Books); text 22.50 (*1-85649-188-9*, Pub. by Zed Books) St Martin.

Max-Neef, Manfred, jt. ed. see Ekins, Paul.

Max-Neef, Manfred A. Human Scale Development: Conception, Application & Further Reflections. LC 91-12713. (Illus.). 128p. (Orig.). 1991. pap. 12.95 (*0-945257-35-X*) Apex Pr.

Max-Planck-Institut fuer Geschichte Klaus Scholz S, ed. Germania Sacra: Historisch-Statistische Beschreibung der Kirche des Alten Reiches. (GER.). viii, 595p. (C). 1995. lib. bdg. 229.29 (*3-11-014533-2*) De Gruyter.

Max-Planck-Institut fuer Geschichte Staff, ed. Germania Sacra: Historisch-Statistische Beschreibung der Kirche Des Alten Reiches. (GER., Illus.). xvii, 768p. (C). 1991. lib. bdg. 252.35 (*3-11-012927-2*) De Gruyter.

An Asterisk (*) at the beginning of an entry indicates that the title is appearing for the first time.

— Germania Sacra: Historisch-Statistische Beschreibung der Kirche Des Alten Reiches. (GER.). xii, 358p. (C). 1992. lib. bdg. 144.65 (*3-11-013223-0*) De Gruyter.
— Germania Sacra Vol. NF 35.1: Historisch-Statistische Beschreibung der Kirche des Alten Reiches: Die Dioezese. (GER.). xx, 237p. (C). 1996. lib. bdg. 241.50 (*3-11-015193-6*) De Gruyter.
— Germania Sacra Vol. NF 36: Historisch-Statistische Beschreibung der Kirche des Alten Reiches: Die Sifte in Schmalkalden und Roemhild. (GER.). xiii, 262p. (C). 1996. lib. bdg. 200.00 (*3-11-015280-0*) De Gruyter.
— Germania Sacra Neue Folge: Historisch-Statistische Bechreibung der Kirche des Alten Reiches, No. 31. (GER., Illus.). xii, 560p. (C). 1993. lib. bdg. 203.10 (*3-11-013657-0*) De Gruyter.
Max Planck Institute for Comparative Public Law &, ed. World Court Digest, 1991-1995 Vol. 2, Vol. 2. 453p. 1997. 79.95 (*3-540-62083-4*) Spr-Verlag.
Max Planck Institute Staff. Justification & Excuse, Set. 2453p. 1989. write for info. (*0-929179-22-6*) Juris Pubng.
Max-Plank-Institut fuer Geschichte Staff, ed. see Becker, Petrus.
Max Plank Institute for History Staff & Theil, Bernhard, eds. Germania Sacra: Historisch-Statistische Beschreibung der Kirche des Alten Reiches. (GER.). xii, 224p. (C). 1994. lib. bdg. 169.25 (*3-11-014214-7*) De Gruyter.
Max, Robert R. & Cerny, Sarah P. Power Writing. rev. ed. 167p. reprint ed. spiral bd. 120.00 incl. audio, VHS (*1-55678-006-0*, 3000) Learn Inc.
Max, Robert R. & Cerny, Sarah P. Power Writing. rev. ed. 167p. 1988. reprint ed. teacher ed. 75.00 (*1-55678-008-7*) Learn Inc.
Max, Stanley M. The United States Great Britain & the Sovietization of Hungary 1945-1948. 1985. text 55.50 (*0-88033-069-4*, 177, Pub. by East Eur Monographs) Col U Pr.
Max, Timothy A., et al. The Pacific Northwest Region Vegetation & Inventory Monitoring System. (Illus.). 28p. 1997. reprint ed. pap. 4.00 (*0-89904-569-3*, Bear Meadows Resrch Grp) Crumb Elbow Pub.
Max, Tung A. Preserving World's Cities. 2001. 40.00 (*0-517-70148-0*) Random.
Maxa, Kathleen, jt. auth. see Pulitzer, Roxanne.
Maxcy, jt. auth. see Hanson.
Maxcy, David J., jt. auth. see Hanson, Jarice.
Maxcy, Kenneth F., ed. see Frost, Wade H.
Maxcy, Larry. Garden Wisdom: Tips, Lore & Old-Fashioned Good Advice for Creating a Beautiful, Healthy Garden. LC 99-50085. (Illus.). 160p. 2000. text 16.00 (*1-56799-767-8*, Friedman-Fairfax) M Friedman Pub Grp Inc.
Maxcy, Spencer J. Democracy, Chaos, & the New School Order. LC 94-23544. 224p. 1995. 61.95 (*0-8039-6198-7*); pap. 27.95 (*0-8039-6199-5*) Corwin Pr.
— Educational Leadership: A Critical Pragmatic Perspective. LC 91-4637. (Critical Studies in Education & Culture). 240p. 1991. 55.00 (*0-89789-258-5*, H258, Bergin & Garvey); pap. 16.95 (*0-89789-259-3*, G259, Bergin & Garvey) Greenwood.
Maxcy, Spencer J., ed. Postmodern School Leadership: Meeting the Crisis in Educational Administration. LC 93-2868. 200p. 1993. 55.00 (*0-275-94565-0*, C4565, Praeger Pubs) Greenwood.
Maxeiner, James R. Policy & Methods in German & American Antitrust Law: A Comparative Study. LC 86-8108. 188p. 1986. 57.95 (*0-275-92113-1*, C2113, Praeger Pubs) Greenwood.
Maxeiner, James R. & Schotthhofer, Peter W. Advertising Law in Europe & North America. 2nd ed. LC 99-11602. 1999. 165.00 (*90-411-0646-4*) Kluwer Law Intl.
Maxell, Ronald F. Gettysburg: The Screenplay. LC 97-76410. 176p. 1998. pap. 19.95 (*1-891961-00-4*) Prsn to Prsn.
***Maxemilian Productions Staff.** Harp Almanac, 2000: International Resource Guide for All Harps. (Illus.). 1999. pap. 24.98 (*0-9662113-3-2*) Maxemilian Prods.
Maxey, David, jt. auth. see Schulman, Andrew.
Maxey, Gary S. The Latent Power of Mammon. pap. 2.99 (*0-88019-159-7*) Schmul Pub Co.
Maxey, I. Parker. The Cornerstone of Living. 1991. pap. 8.99 (*0-88019-276-3*) Schmul Pub Co.
— Man's Ascent to God. 1993. pap. 12.99 (*0-88019-306-9*) Schmul Pub Co.
— Ministerial Ethics & Etiquette. 1987. pap. 14.99 (*0-88019-222-4*) Schmul Pub Co.
Maxey, James, et al. Hadrosaur Tales: A Review of Literary Science Fiction, Vol. III. Summers, David L., ed. 100p. (Orig.). 1997. pap. 5.95 (*1-885093-10-1*) Hadrosaur Pr.
***Maxey, Lisa & Magnusson, Jim.** Rehabilitation for the Post-Surgical Patient: Procedures & Protocols. (Illus.). 416p. (C). 1999. text. write for info. (*0-323-00166-1*) Mosby Inc.
Maxey, M., jt. auth. see Park, M. E.
Maxey, Margaret N. & Kuhn, Robert L. Regulatory Reform: New Vision or Old Curse. LC 84-26261. 254p. 1985. 40.95 (*0-275-90145-9*, C0145, Praeger Pubs) Greenwood.
Maxey, Randy. Upgrading to AutoCAD 13. (Illus.). 400p. (Orig.). 1995. pap. 30.00 (*1-56205-249-7*) New Riders Pub.
Maxey, Robert T. Alexander Campbell & the Peculiar Institution. 332p. pap. 12.99 (*0-89900-291-9*) College Pr Pub.
Maxey, Russell. Airports of Columbia: A Photographic History. (Illus.). 300p. 1987. 19.50 (*0-317-56064-6*) Palmetto Pub.
— Columbia's Bicentennial Seventeen Eighty-Six to Nineteen Eighty-Six. LC 86-60217. (Illus.). 180p. 1986. pap. 16.00 (*0-317-45809-4*) Palmetto Pub.
Maxey, Susan, jt. auth. see Gordon, Stephen P.
Maxfield, ed. The Saxon Shore. (Illus.). 192p. 1989. pap. text 15.95 (*0-85989-330-8*, Pub. by Univ Exeter Pr) Northwestern U Pr.
Maxfield & Babbie. Research Methods for Criminal Justice & Criminology. 3rd ed. (Criminal Justice Ser.). 2000. pap. text 56.00 (*0-534-51664-5*) Wadsworth Pub.
— Research Methods for Criminal Justice with Infotrac. 2nd ed. (Criminal Justice Ser.). 1997. pap. text 56.00 (*0-534-52170-3*) Wadsworth Pub.
Maxfield, Albert & Brady, Robert. Company D, Eleventh Regiment Maine Infantry Volunteers. 85p. 1995. reprint ed. pap. 9.95 (*0-9642029-5-6*) Union Pubng.
Maxfield, Christa. Sacred Springs. (Orig.). 1998. pap. text 10.95 (*1-57532-072-X*) Press-Tige Pub.
Maxfield, Clive. Bebop to the Boolean Boogie: An Unconventional Guide to Electronics Fundamentals, Components & Processes. LC 94-41062. (Illus.). 504p. 1995. pap. 35.00 (*1-878707-22-1*) LLH Tech Pub.
Maxfield, Clive & Brown, Alvin. Bebop Bytes Back: An Unconventional Guide to Computers. LC 97-65591. (Illus.). 872p. (Orig.). 1997. pap. 49.95 (*0-9651934-0-3*) Doone Publns.
Maxfield, Clive M. Designus Maximus Unleashed! LC 98-154344. 472p. 1998. pap. text 39.95 (*0-7506-9089-5*, Newnes) Buttrwrth-Heinemann.
Maxfield, Doris. Charitable Organizations of the U. S. A Descriptive & Financial Information Guide. 2nd ed. 1991. 150.00 (*0-8103-8081-1*) Gale.
Maxfield, Duncan. My Valentine Counting Book. (Chubby Board Bk.). (Illus.). 8p. (J). (ps). 1999. bds. 2.99 (*0-689-82237-5*) S&S Childrens.
— Things I Love. (Chubby Board Bk.). (Illus.). 8p. (J). (ps). 1999. bds. 2.99 (*0-689-82236-7*) S&S Childrens.
— Where the Sharks Are. (Rugrats Ser.). (Illus.). 24p. (J). (ps-2). 1998. pap. 3.25 (*0-689-81978-1*, Simon Spot) Litle Simon.
Maxfield, Georgie. The Novel Approach to Sexuality & Disability. Toner, Fanny, ed. (Illus.). 195p. (Orig.). 1996. pap. 7.95 (*0-9654069-0-3*) Nrthrn NV Amputee.
Maxfield, James F. The Fatal Woman: Sources of Male Anxiety in American Film Noir, 1941-1991. LC 95-42165. (Illus.). 192p. 1996. 32.50 (*0-8386-3662-4*) Fairleigh Dickinson.
Maxfield, John. Carla & the Wolves. unabridged ed. Landes, William-Alan, ed. LC 97-27818. 55p. (Orig.). 1997. pap. 6.00 (*0-88734-701-0*) Players Pr.
Maxfield, John E. & Maxfield, Margaret W. Abstract Algebra & Solution by Radicals. (Illus.). xi, 209p. 1992. reprint ed. pap. 8.95 (*0-486-67121-6*) Dover.
Maxfield, Kathryn E. & Bucholz, Sandra. A Social Maturity Scale for Blind Preschool Children: A Guide to Its Use. 57p. 1957. pap. 9.95 (*0-89128-059-6*) Am Foun Blind.
Maxfield, Margaret W., jt. auth. see Maxfield, John E.
Maxfield, Michael & Maxfield, Myrica. The Sound of Success: Musical Motivation. 32p. (YA). 1992. 19.95 (*0-9634682-1-9*, 232822) Myrichael Way.
Maxfield, Michael G. Research Methods for Criminal Justice. (Criminal Justice Ser.). 1995. pap., student ed. 18.95 (*0-534-23157-8*) Wadsworth Pub.
— Research Methods for Criminal Justice. 2nd ed. (Criminal Justice Ser.). (C). 1997. 16.00 (*0-534-52165-7*) Wadsworth Pub.
Maxfield, Michael G. & Babbie, Earl. Research Methods for Criminal Justice & Criminology. LC 94-37944. 395p. 1994. mass mkt. 44.00 (*0-534-23154-3*) Wadsworth Pub.
— Research Methods for Criminal Justice & Criminology. 2nd ed. LC 97-28501. (Criminal Justice Ser.). (C). 1997. 49.75 (*0-534-52164-9*) Wadsworth Pub.
Maxfield, Myrica, jt. auth. see Maxfield, Michael.
Maxfield, Peter C. Taxation of Mining Operations. 1981. 215.00 (*0-8205-1418-7*, 418) Bender.
Maxfield, Peter C. & Houghton, James L. Federal Income Taxation of Oil & Gas & Natural Resources Transactions, Cases & Materials on The. Garr, James R., ed. 335p. 1990. pap. text 23.95 (*0-88277-781-5*) Foundation Pr.
Maxfield, Sylvia. Gatekeepers of Growth: The International Political Economy of Central Banking in Developing Countries. 192p. 1997. pap. text 15.95 (*0-691-00243-6*, Pub. by Princeton U Pr) Cal Prin Full Svc.
— Gatekeepers of Growth: The International Political Economy of Central Banking in Developing Countries. LC 96-27217. 192p. 1997. text 35.00 (*0-691-02687-4*, Pub. by Princeton U Pr) Cal Prin Full Svc.
— Governing Capital: International Finance & Mexican Politics. LC 90-55137. 208p. 1990. text 32.50 (*0-8014-2458-5*) Cornell U Pr.
— North American Economic Integration: Monetary & Exchange Rate Aspects. (Pew Case Studies in International Affairs). 50p. (C). 1995. pap. text 3.50 (*1-56927-212-3*, GU Schl Foreign) Geo U Inst Dplmcy.
Maxfield, Sylvia & Anzaldua, Ricardo, eds. Government & Private Sector in Contemporary Mexico. (Monographs: No. 20). 144p. (Orig.). (C). 1987. pap. 12.50 (*0-935391-71-1*, MN-20) UCSD Ctr US-Mex.
Maxfield, Sylvia & Schneider, Ben R., eds. Business & the State in Developing Countries. LC 97-3385. (Cornell Studies in Political Economy). (Illus.). 360p. 1996. text 45.00 (*0-8014-3371-1*); pap. text 17.95 (*0-8014-8406-5*) Cornell U Pr.
Maxford, Howard. The A-Z of Horror Films. LC 96-43726. 1996. 59.95 (*0-253-33253-2*); pap. 29.95 (*0-253-21107-7*) Ind U Pr.
— A-Z of Science Fiction & Fantasy Films. 1998. pap. text 24.95 (*0-7134-8265-6*, Pub. by B T B) Branford.
***Maxford, Howard.** David Lean. 2000. pap. 23.95 (*0-7134-8680-5*, Pub. by B T B) Bks Intl VA.
— George Lucas Companion: The Complete Guide to Hollywood's Most Influential Film-Maker. (Illus.). 178p. 1999. pap. text 19.95 (*0-7134-8425-X*) B T B.
Maxford, Howard. Hammer, House of Horror: Behind the Screams. 1996. 27.95 (*0-87951-652-6*, Pub. by Overlook Pr) Penguin Putnam.
Maxham, Mintcy D., jt. auth. see Houck, Peter W.
Maxham, Robert, tr. see Tarrasch, S.
Maxian, Bruce, ed. ASIS '94: "The Economics of Information" - Proceedings of the 57th Annual Meeting of the American Society for Information Science. 128p. (Orig.). 1994. pap. 29.50 (*0-938734-93-8*) Info Today Inc.
Maxian, M., jt. auth. see Hrdina, L.
Maxim. Social Studies & Elementary School Children. 6th ed. LC 98-22993. 656p. (C). 1998. 72.00 (*0-13-649898-1*) P-H.
Maxim, A. & Coppage. Wulfeck's Virginia Marriages. (Second Ser.). 280p. 1990. 42.50 (*0-317-02847-2*) A M Coppage.
Maxim, Bruce R., jt. auth. see Koffman, Elliot B.
Maxim, Daniel, et al. Covert German Rearmament, 1919-1939: Deception & Misperception. LC 84-11891. 149p. 1984. lib. bdg. 49.50 (*0-313-27012-0*, U7012, Greenwood Pr) Greenwood.
Maxim, George W. The Sourcebook: Activities for Infants & Young Children. 2nd ed. 336p. (C). 1990. pap. text 42.00 (*0-675-21055-0*, Merrill Coll) P-H.
— The Very Young: Guiding Children from Infancy Through the Early Years. 5th ed. LC 96-36068. 556p. 1997. 71.00 (*0-13-490210-6*, Merrill Coll) P-H.
Maxim, Jane & Bryan, Karen. Language & the Elderly: A Clinical Perspective. LC 94-185437. (Illus.). 298p. (Orig.). (C). 1994. pap. text 59.95 (*1-56593-254-4*, 0048) Thomson Learn.
Maxim, Jane, jt. ed. see Bryan, Karen.
***Maxim, John R.** The Bannerman Effect. Hershey, J. H., ed. 400p. 2000. mass mkt. 6.99 (*0-380-73009-X*, Avon Bks) Morrow Avon.
Maxim, John R. The Bannerman Solution. 432p. 1999. mass mkt. 6.99 (*0-380-73008-1*, Avon Bks) Morrow Avon.
***Maxim, John R.** Bannerman's Law. 480p. 2000. mass mkt. 6.99 (*0-380-73010-3*, Avon Bks) Morrow Avon.
Maxim, John R. Haven. LC 96-52147. 384p. 1997. mass mkt. 24.00 (*0-380-97301-4*, Avon Bks) Morrow Avon.
— Haven. LC 96-52147. 405p. 1998. mass mkt. 6.99 (*0-380-78669-9*, Avon Bks) Morrow Avon.
***Maxim, John R.** Mosaic. LC 98-46869. 384p. 1999. 24.00 (*0-380-97544-0*, Avon Bks) Morrow Avon.
— Mosaic. LC 98-46869. 448p. 2000. mass mkt. 6.99 (*0-380-79354-7*, Avon Bks) Morrow Avon.
— Platforms. Date not set. mass mkt. write for info. (*0-380-73005-7*) Morrow Avon.
Maxim, John R. Shadow Box. LC 96-6789. 393p. 1997. mass mkt. 6.99 (*0-380-78668-0*, Avon Bks) Morrow Avon.
***Maxim, John R.** Time Out of Mind. LC 85-21896. 528p. 1999. mass mkt. 6.99 (*0-380-73006-5*, Avon Bks) Morrow Avon.
Maxim, L. Daniel & Cook, Frank X. Financial Risk Analysis. LC 72-182226. (AMA Management Briefing Ser.). (Illus.). 70p. reprint ed. pap. 30.00 (*0-608-10239-3*, 205038600078) Bks Demand.
Maxim, Paul & Whitehead, Paul. Explaining Crime. 4th ed. LC 97-32804. 464p. 1998. 46.95 (*0-7506-9784-9*) Buttrwrth-Heinemann.
Maxim, Paul S. Quantitative Research Methods in the Social Sciences. LC 98-18953. (Illus.). 416p. (C). 1999. text 55.00 (*0-19-511465-5*) OUP.
Maxim, Peter E. The Seattle Psychotherapy Language Analysis Schema. 66p. 1986. pap., ring bd. 24.95 (*0-295-96459-6*) U of Wash Pr.
Maxim, Silas P., jt. auth. see Lapham, William B.
***Maximenko, A.** Rook vs. Minor Pieces. (Illus.). 190p. 1999. pap. 19.95 (*1-879479-81-8*) ICE WA.
Maximilian, C. Encyclopedic Dictionary of Genetics: Dictionar Enciclopedic de Genetica. (RUM.). 1984. write for info. (*0-8288-1445-7*, M15835) Fr & Eur.
Maximin, Anita & Stevic-Rust, Lori. The Stop Smoking Workbook. 192p. 1997. 9.98 (*1-56731-207-1*, MJF Bks) Fine Comms.
— The Stop Smoking Workbook: Your Guide to Healthy Quitting. LC 95-61240. (Illus.). 171p. 1996. pap. 17.95 (*1-57224-037-7*) New Harbinger.
Maximin, Anita, et al. Heart Therapy: Regaining Your Cardiac Health. LC 97-75473. 260p. 1998. pap. 13.95 (*1-57224-104-7*) New Harbinger.
Maximin, Anita, jt. auth. see Stevic-Rust, Lori.
Maximin, Daniel. Lone Sun. LC 89-30992. (CARAF Bks.). 352p. 1989. text 35.00 (*0-8139-1224-5*) U Pr of Va.
Maximoff, Gregory P. The Guillotine at Work. Nowlin, William G., Jr., ed. 1979. pap. 13.00 (*0-932366-06-6*) Black Thorn Bks.
— The Guillotine at Work: Twenty Years of Terror in Soviet Russia, 2 vols., Set. 1973. 600.00 (*0-87700-203-7*) Revisionist Pr.
Maximov, V., compiled by. Uranium Carbides, Nitrides & Silicides. (Bibliographical Ser.: No. 14). 175p. 1964. pap. 17.00 (*92-0-044064-9*, ISP21 14, Pub. by IAEA) Bernan Associates.
— Uranium Carbides, Nitrides & Silicides. (Bibliographical Ser.: No. 33). 110p. 1968. pap. 16.00 (*92-0-044368-0*, ISP21 33, Pub. by IAEA) Bernan Associates.
— Uranium Carbides, Nitrides & Silicides II, 1963-1965. (Bibliographical Ser.: No. 21). 172p. 1966. pap. 17.00 (*92-0-044166-1*, ISP21 21, Pub. by IAEA) Bernan Associates.
Maximov, V. I., ed. Illustrated Concise Dictionary of Russian Scientific & Technical Terms. (RUS.). 800p. 1994. 59.95 (*0-8285-5449-8*) Firebird NY.
Maximov, Vladimir, ed. see Solzhenitsyn, Aleksandr, et al.
Maximova, T. A., tr. see Gogotsi, Yu & Lavrenko, V. A.
***Maximovich, Stanley P.** 101 Ways to Feel & Look Great! A Plastic Surgeon's Guide to Improve Your Life from the Inside Out. LC 99-93136. 280p. 1999. 29.95 (*0-9671054-2-0*) Biddle Hse Pubng.
Maximovitch, John. The Orthodox Veneration of Mary the Birthgiver of God: Orthodox Theological Texts. 4th rev. ed. St. Herman of Alaska Brotherhood Staff, ed. Rose, Seraphim, tr. from RUS. & intro. by. LC 94-66189. (Illus.). 88p. 1994. pap. 7.00 (*0-938635-68-9*) St Herman Pr.
Maximus of Tyre. Maximus of Tyre: The Philosophical Orations. Trapp, M. B., tr. & intro. by. LC 96-21022. 458p. (C). 1997. text 98.00 (*0-19-814989-1*) OUP.
Maximus, Valerius. Factorum et Dictorum Memorabilium Libri IX. Cum Inserti Auctoris Fragmento de Paraenominibus. Recensuit et Emendavit. (LAT.). vi, 792p. 1976. reprint ed. lib. bdg. write for info. (*3-487-06117-1*) Lubrecht & Cramer.
— Valerius Maxiums' Memorable Deeds & Sayings, Bk. 1. Wardle, D., ed. & tr. by. LC 97-44272. 312p. 1998. text 70.00 (*0-19-815016-4*) OUP.
Maxine, Cassin. Turnip's Blood. Maddox, Everette et al, eds. (Illus.). 112p. (Orig.). 1985. pap. 15.00 (*0-9614371-0-3*) Sisters Grim Pr.
Maxine, David, ed. see Baum, L. Frank.
Maxine, David, ed. see Baum, L. Frank & Denslow, W. W.
Maxine, David, ed. see Baum, L. Frank & McGraw, Eloise J.
Maxine, David, ed. see Baum, L. Frank, et al.
Maxine, David, ed. see Snow, Jack.
Maxine, David, ed. & illus. see Baum, L. Frank & Payes, Rachel C.
Maxmanian, Paul E., jt. auth. see Fox, Robert D.
Maxmen. Psychotropic Drugs. 3rd ed. 480p. 1999. 45.00 (*0-393-70301-0*) Norton.
Maxmen, Jerrold S. The Post-Physician Era: Medicine in the Twenty-First Century. LC 93-42557. 256p. reprint ed. pap. 79.40 (*0-608-08653-3*, 206917600003) Bks Demand.
Maxmen, Jerrold S. & Ward, Nicholas G. Essential Psychopathology & Its Treatment. 2nd ed. (Illus.). 539p. (C). 1995. 45.00 (*0-393-70173-5*) Norton.
— Psychotropic Drugs: Fast Facts. 2nd ed. 421p. 1995. pap. 35.00 (*0-393-70181-6*) Norton.
Maxner, Joyce. Nicholas Cricket. LC 88-33076. (Illus.). 32p. (J). (gr. k-3). 1989. 14.00 (*0-06-024216-7*); lib. bdg. 13.89 (*0-06-024222-1*) HarpC Child Bks.
— Nicholas Cricket. LC 88-33076. (Trophy Picture Bk.). (Illus.). 28p. (J). (gr. k-3). 1991. pap. 4.95 (*0-06-443275-0*, HarpTrophy) HarpC Child Bks.
***Maxon, Antonia B.** The Hearing-Impaired Child. 224p. 2001. 45.00 (*0-7506-7094-0*) Buttrwrth-Heinemann.
Maxon, Gayle. Douglas Johnson: Birds of Magic & Other New Paintings. LC 90-60857. (Illus.). 31p. 1990. text 8.00 (*0-935037-31-4*) G Peters Gallery.
— Edward Borein: Artist of the Old West. LC 84-61996. (Illus.). 60p. 1984. pap. 18.00 (*0-935037-02-0*) G Peters Gallery.
— A Selection of Paintings from the Gerald Peters Collection. LC 83-62810. (Illus.). 98p. 1983. pap. 25.00 (*0-935037-05-5*) G Peters Gallery.
— Still Life, 1963-1993. LC 93-85072. (Illus.). 79p. 1993. pap. 18.00 (*0-935037-51-9*) G Peters Gallery.
Maxon, Gayle, ed. Beverly Pepper, Small Scale Sculpture & Drawings. LC 89-83479. (Illus.). 32p. 1989. 8.00 (*0-935037-28-4*) G Peters Gallery.
Maxon, Gayle & Hopkins, Quincie, eds. Carol Mothner: A Room of One's Own. LC 86-60902. (Illus.). 31p. 1986. 15.00 (*0-935037-09-8*) G Peters Gallery.
— Michael Coleman: Wilderness Artist. LC 86-60905. (Illus.). 53p. 1986. pap. 12.00 (*0-935037-11-X*) G Peters Gallery.
Maxon, Gayle, ed. see Campbell, Lawrence.
Maxon, Gayle, ed. see Carlson, George A.
Maxon, Gayle, ed. see Waldrum, Harold J.
Maxon, Gayle, jt. intro. see Peters, Gerald P.
Maxon, H. A. The Younger. 1999. pap. 7.50 (*1-892614-19-7*) Briarwood VA.
Maxon, Helen. D. Howard Hitchcock. 1986. 39.95 (*0-914916-63-7*) Ku Paa.
Maxon, James C. Lake Mead & Hoover Dam: The Story Behind the Scenery. LC 79-87573. (Illus.). 48p. (Orig.). 1980. pap. 7.95 (*0-916122-61-1*) KC Pubns.
— Lake Mead & Hoover Dam: The Story Behind the Scenery. Morales, Brigitte, tr. (GER., Illus.). 48p. (Orig.). 1993. pap. 8.95 (*0-88714-734-8*) KC Pubns.
— Lake Mead & Hoover Dam: The Story Behind the Scenery. Lee, Frances Y., tr. (CHI., Illus.). (Orig.). 1993. pap. 8.95 (*0-88714-780-1*) KC Pubns.
— Lake Mead & Hoover Dam: The Story Behind the Scenery. Petzinger, Saori, tr. (JPN., Illus.). 48p. (Orig.). 1993. pap. 8.95 (*0-88714-781-X*) KC Pubns.
Maxon, Peter. Building a Better Team: A Handbook for Managers & Facilitators. LC 93-20443. 208p. 1993. 69.95 (*0-566-07424-9*, Pub. by Gower) Ashgate Pub Co.
Maxon, Robert M. Conflict & Accommodation in Western Kenya: The Gusii & the British, 1907-1963. LC 88-45734. (Illus.). 216p. 1989. 37.50 (*0-8386-3350-1*) Fairleigh Dickinson.
— East Africa: An Introductory History. 289p. 1986. pap. 18.95 (*0-937058-24-6*) West Va U Pr.
— East Africa: An Introductory History. 2nd rev. ed. LC 94-60994. 300p. 1994. pap. 25.00 (*0-937058-35-1*) West Va U Pr.
— Struggle for Kenya: The Loss & Reassertion of Imperial Initiative, 1912-1923. LC 91-58952. (Illus.). 352p. 1993. 47.50 (*0-8386-3486-9*) Fairleigh Dickinson.
Maxon, Robert M., jt. auth. see Ofcansky, Thomas P.

M

An Asterisk (*) at the beginning of an entry indicates that the title is appearing for the first time.

M

*Maxon, Ronald E., Jr., ed. Rural Utilities Service: Opportunities to Operate Electricity & Telecommunications Loan Programs More Effectively. (Illus.). 48p. (C). 1999. pap. text 20.00 (0-7881-8312-5) DIANE Pub.
Maxon, Yale C. Control of Japanese Foreign Policy, Vol. 5--5. LC 72-12330. 286p. 1973. reprint ed. lib. bdg. 59.75 (0-8371-6728-0, MACJ, Greenwood Pr) Greenwood.
Max's Word Services Staff, ed. see Browning, Beverly A.
Maxsenti, Michael A., compiled by. Ronchetti Design: The Structures, Their Builders & Artisans. LC 97-92757. (Architectural Monograph Ser.). (Illus.). 56p. 1997. 24.00 (0-9660793-0-2) Max Co.
*Maxson, Cheryl L. & Klein, Malcolm W. The Modern Gang Reader. 2nd ed. Miller, Jody A., ed. (Illus.). 335p. (C). 2000. pap. text. write for info. (1-891487-44-2) Roxbury Pub Co.
Maxson, Cheryl L., jt. auth. see Klein, Malcolm W.
Maxson, H. A. On the Sonnets of Robert Frost: A Critical Examination of the 37 Poems. LC 97-34951. 157p. 1997. lib. bdg. 32.50 (0-7864-0389-6) McFarland & Co.
Maxson, Mary L., et al. Arimatsu Shibori: A Japanese Tradition of Indigo Dyeing. (Illus.). 100p. (Orig.). 1995. pap. text 25.00 (0-925895-02-4) Mead Brook Art.
Maxted, jt. auth. see Pigeon.
*Maxted, Anna. Getting over It: An Autobiography. LC 99-462222. 416p. 2000. 24.00 (0-06-039320-3, ReganBks) HarperTrade.
Maxted, I. Canterbury & Whitstable Railway. (C). 1985. 39.00 (0-85361-089-4) St Mut.
Maxted, Nigel, et al, eds. Plant Genetic Conservation: The In Situ Approach. LC 96-86665. 472p. 1997. pap. 54.95 (0-412-63730-8) Kluwer Academic.
— Plant Genetic Conservation: The In Situ Approach. LC 96-86665. (Illus.). 472p. (C). 1997. write for info. (0-412-63400-7) Kluwer Academic.
Maxton, Graeme. Driving over a Cliff? Strategy & Analysis of the World's Car Industry. 263p. (C). 1994. 33.75 (0-201-59392-0) Addison-Wesley.
Maxton, Hugh. At the Protestant Museum. 53p. 1986. pap. 10.95 (0-85105-443-9, Pub. by Smyth) Dufour.
— The Engraved Passion: (New & Selected Poems) 120p. (C). 1991. 24.00 (0-948268-96-4, Pub. by Dedalus); pap. 30.00 (0-948268-95-6, Pub. by Dedalus) St Mut.
— Jubilee for Renegades. 80p. 1982. pap. 10.95 (0-85105-392-0, Pub. by Smyth) Dufour.
Maxton, Hugh, tr. Between: Selected Poems of Agnes Nemes Nagy. (C). 1988. pap. 15.00 (0-948268-39-5, Pub. by Dedalus) St Mut.
Maxton, Hugh, ed. see Clarke, Austin.
*Maxtone-Graham, John. Cruise Savvy: An Invaluable Primer for First-Time Passengers. (Illus.). 192p. 2000. pap. 17.95 (1-57409-071-2) Sheridan.
Maxtone-Graham, John. From Song to Sovereign. (Illus.). 96p. 1987. 15.00 (0-945335-00-8) Intl Voyage.
— From Song to Sovereign. rev. ed. (Illus.). 112p. 1987. 15.00 (0-945335-01-6); pap. 10.95 (0-945335-02-4) Intl Voyage.
*Maxtone-Graham, John. Liners to the Sun. LC 99-89712. (Illus.). 512p. 1999. 35.00 (1-57409-108-5); pap. 19.95 (1-57409-107-7) Sheridan.
— Passage East. 160p. 1997. 160.00 (1-86227-039-2, Pub. by Spellmnt Pubs) St Mut.
*Maxtone-Graham, John, ed. Titanic Survivor: The Memoirs of Violet Jessop Stewardess. large type ed. 408p. 1999. 31.99 (0-7089-9126-2) Ulverscroft.
Maxtone-Graham, John, ed. see Marshall, Ian.
Maxtone-Graham, John, ed. & anno. see Jessop, Violet.
Maxtone-Graham, Katrina. An Adopted Woman. 1982. write for info. (0-318-56975-2) Eleventh Hour.
— An Adopted Woman. LC 87-71563. 365p. 1983. 21.95 (0-943362-00-8) Remi Bks.
— Pregnant by Mistake: The Stories of Seventeen Women. rev. ed. LC 87-28353. 440p. 1990. reprint ed. 21.95 (0-943362-01-6); reprint ed. pap. 12.95 (0-943362-02-4) Remi Bks.
*Maxwell. The Disciple: A Message from Heaven. 256p. 1999. pap. text 12.95 (0-9656406-0-4) Emerald City UT.
Maxwell. Environment of Life. 2nd ed. (Biology Ser.). 1976. 17.75 (0-8221-0167-X) Brooks-Cole.
— Environment of Life. 3rd ed. (Biology Ser.). 1980. mass mkt. 18.50 (0-8185-0355-6) Brooks-Cole.
— Financial Markets. Date not set. pap. text, teacher ed. write for info. (0-314-03392-0) West Pub.
— Plastic Surgery of the Breast. (Illus.). 900p. 1993. text 250.00 (0-8016-5821-7) Mosby Inc.
*Maxwell. Plastics: A Laymans Guide. 160p. 1999. pap. 30.00 (1-86125-085-1) Institute of Management Consultants.
Maxwell. Principles of Economics: Theory & Practice. (Illus.). 704p. 1989. 12.95 (0-8016-2423-1) Mosby Inc.
— Psychotherapy. 2nd ed. 168p. 1991. pap. 43.95 (1-56593-574-8, 0304) Singular Publishing.
— Rational Health Care. 1995. text 92.00 (0-443-05336-7, W B Saunders Co) Harcrt Hlth Sci Grp.
— S.g. Texas Politics Today. 8th ed. (Political Science). (C). 1997. 15.75 (0-534-54062-7) Wadsworth Pub.
*Maxwell. Shadow & Silk. LC 98-44601. 1999. 30.00 (0-7862-1716-2) Thorndike Pr.
Maxwell. Texas Politics. 7th ed. (Political Science Ser.). (C). 1995. pap., student ed. 14.25 (0-314-05992-X) West Pub.
— Texas Politics Today. 9th ed. LC 99-22999. (Political Science Ser.). 1999. 50.95 (0-534-56979-X) Wadsworth Pub.
— Texas Politics Today. 9th ed. (Political Science Ser.). 1999. pap. text, student ed. 18.00 (0-534-56980-3) Wadsworth Pub.
— Writing Our Lives. LC 98-41799. 313p. 1999. pap. text 32.00 (0-205-27380-7) Allyn.
Maxwell & Satake, Eiki. Theory of Probability for Clinical Diagnostic Testing. 123p. (C). 1993. student ed. 17.88 (1-56870-062-8) RonJon Pub.
Maxwell, et al. Oil & Gas: 1996 Case Supplement. 6th ed. 1998. 9.95 (1-56662-413-4) Foundation Pr.
Maxwell, A. E. Just Enough Light to Kill. 336p. 1993. mass mkt. 4.99 (0-06-104111-4, Harp PBks) HarpC.
— The King of Nothing. large type ed. 375p. 1993. reprint ed. lib. bdg. 17.95 (1-56054-594-1) Thorndike Pr.
— Multivariate Analysis in Behavioral Research: For Medical & Social Science Students. 2nd ed. 164p. (gr. 13). 1977. pap. 54.95 (0-412-14300-3, NO. 6193) CRC Pr.
— Redwood Empire. 416p. 1987. mass mkt. 3.95 (0-373-97049-8) Harlequin Bks.
— Redwood Empire. LC 95-13554. (Historical Ser.). 440p. 1995. per. 4.50 (0-373-28867-0, 1-28867-9) Harlequin Bks.
Maxwell, A. Graham. Be Careful Who You Trust! LC 96-41279. (Illus.). 1996. write for info. (1-56652-006-1); pap. write for info. (1-56652-005-3) Pine Knoll Pubns.
Maxwell, Aileen & Maxwell, Thomas. Canyonlands of Utah: A Pictorial of the Needles District. (Illus.). 32p. (Orig.). 1985. pap. 4.95 (0-9614389-0-8) Rigelle Pubns.
Maxwell, Alice. The Gift of Laughter & Nineteen Other Short Stories. 1974. 10.00 (0-685-41736-0) Fountainhead.
Maxwell, Alice S. & Dunlevy, Marion B. Virago! The Story of Anne Newport Royall 1769-1854. LC 84-42731. 1991. pap. 19.98 (0-9629706-0-3) Dunwell Pr.
Maxwell, Allen, jt. ed. see Hudson, Wilson M.
Maxwell, Alma, ed. see Oswald, Diane.
Maxwell, Ann. Change. 1996. mass mkt. 5.99 (0-7860-0294-8, Pinncle Kensgtn) Kensgtn Pub Corp.
— Colonial Photography & Exhibitions: Representations of the 'Native' & the Making of European Identities. LC 98-25112. 1999. 85.00 (0-7185-0169-1) Bks Intl VA.
— Dancer's Illusion. 1996. mass mkt. 5.99 (0-7860-0250-6, Pinncle Kensgtn) Kensgtn Pub Corp.
— Dancer's Luck. 1995. mass mkt. 5.99 (0-7860-0207-7, Pinncle Kensgtn) Kensgtn Pub Corp.
— The Diamond Tiger. 480p. 1992. mass mkt. 4.99 (0-06-104181-5, Harp PBks) HarpC.
— The Diamond Tiger. 472p. 1999. mass mkt. 5.99 (0-06-104079-7, Harp PBks) HarpC.
*Maxwell, Ann. The Diamond Tiger. large type ed. LC 99-46550. (G. K. Hall Core Ser.). 1999. 28.95 (0-7838-8789-2, G K Hall Lrg Type) Mac Lib Ref.
Maxwell, Ann. The Ruby. 384p. 1999. mass mkt. 5.99 (0-06-104269-2, Harp PBks) HarpC.
— The Secret Sisters. 469p. 1999. mass mkt. 5.99 (0-06-104236-6, Harp PBks) HarpC.
— Shadow & Silk. 432p. 1997. mass mkt. 6.50 (0-8217-5547-1, Zebra Kensgtn) Kensgtn Pub Corp.
— Shadow & Silk. large type ed. LC 97-20273. 1997. lib. bdg. 25.95 (1-57490-085-4, Beeler LP Bks) T T Beeler.
— Timeshadow Rider. 320p. 1997. mass mkt. 5.99 (0-7860-0368-5, Pinncle Kensgtn) Kensgtn Pub Corp.
Maxwell, Ann M., jt. auth. see Rattana.
Maxwell, Arthur. Bedtime Stories Classics, 5 vols. 128p. (Orig.). (J). 1986. pap. 24.99 (0-8280-0518-4) Review & Herald.
— Bedtime Story Classics, 5 vols. (J). (gr. k-3). 1998. pap. 24.99 (0-8280-1275-X) Review & Herald.
— Uncle Arthur's Bible Book. 512p. (J). (gr. 1-3). 1968. 29.99 (0-8280-0997-X) Review & Herald.
Maxwell, Arthur S. Jesus Friend of Children. (J). 1988. pap. 5.99 (0-8280-0464-1) Review & Herald.
— Storytime. 128p. (J). 1989. 19.99 (1-877773-00-X) Review & Herald.
Maxwell, Arthur S. & Holloway, Cheryl W. Uncle Arthur's Storytime. (Children's True Adventures Classic Edition Ser.: Vol. 3). (Illus.). 128p. (J). 1989. 29.90 (1-877773-03-4) Fam Media.
— Uncle Arthur's Storytime, Vol. 1. (Children's True Adventures Classic Edition Ser.). (Illus.). 128p. (J). 1989. lib. bdg. 29.90 (1-877773-01-8) Fam Media.
— Uncle Arthur's Storytime, Vol. 2. (Children's True Adventures Classic Edition Ser.). (Illus.). 128p. (YA). 1989. lib. bdg. 29.90 (1-877773-02-6) Fam Media.
Maxwell-Batten, C. Araminta's Message: Reflections of a Fairy. 2nd ed. (Reflections Ser.). (Illus.). xiv, 60p. (Orig.). 1998. pap. 10.00 (0-9672283-0-1) Sita Shiva.
Maxwell, Bernard J., et al. Easter for Fifty Days. LC 88-51302. 96p. (Orig.). 1989. pap. 12.95 (0-89622-367-1) Twenty-Third.
Maxwell, Bob. Beginner's Best Shot at Video Poker, Vol. 1. Maxwell, Sandra K., ed. 96p. (Orig.). 1996. mass mkt. 7.95 (0-9650990-0-8) KayLine Prods.
Maxwell, Bruce. How to Access Federal Government Information on the Internet, 1998: Washington Online. 300p. (YA). (gr. 11). 1997. pap. text 28.95 (1-56802-295-6) Congr Quarterly.
— How to Access the Federal Government on the Internet, 1999: Washington Online. 4th ed. 300p. 1998. pap. 29.95 (1-56802-387-1) Congr Quarterly.
— How to Access the Government's Electronic Bulletin Boards, 1997: Washington Online. 332p. (C). 1997. pap. text 26.95 (1-56802-238-7) Congr Quarterly.
— How to Find Health Information on the Internet. LC 98-20101. 332p. (C). 1998. pap. text 35.95 (1-56802-271-9) Congr Quarterly.
*Maxwell, Bruce. How to Track Politics on the Internet. 200p. 1999. pap. 29.95 (1-56802-472-X) CQ Pr.
Maxwell, Bruce. Insider's Guide to Finding a Job in Washington: Contacts & Strategies to Build Your Career in Public Policy. LC 99-47835. 300p. 1999. pap. 24.95 (1-56802-473-8) Congr Quarterly.
Maxwell, Bruce & Jacobson, Michael F. Marketing Disease to Hispanics. (Illus.). 100p. (Orig.). 1989. pap., per. 6.95 (0-89329-020-3) Ctr Sci Public.
Maxwell, C. The Pergamon Dictionary of Perfect Spelling. 2nd ed. LC 78-40291. 335p. 1978. pap. 11.75 (0-08-022865-8, Pergamon Pr) Elsevier.
Maxwell, C. Bede. The New German Shorthaired Pointer. 3rd ed. LC 74-75758. 12.95 (0-87605-156-5) Howell Bks.
Maxwell, C. J. Minear, Descendants of John Minear (1732-1781) 232p. 1993. reprint ed. pap. 36.50 (0-8328-3244-8); reprint ed. lib. bdg. 46.50 (0-8328-3243-X) Higginson Bk Co.
Maxwell, C. Mervyn. God Cares, Vol. 1. 1981. pap. 13.99 (0-8163-1417-9) Pacific Pr Pub Assn.
— God Cares, Vol. 2. 2nd ed. 1985. pap. 18.99 (0-8163-1418-7) Pacific Pr Pub Assn.
Maxwell, C. Mervyn. Tell It to the World: The Story of Seventh-day Adventists. (Illus.). 287p. 1976. pap. 12.99 (0-8163-1390-3) Pacific Pr Pub Assn.
Maxwell, Carolyn, ed. Haydn: Solo Piano Literature-A Comprehensive Guide Annotated & Evaluated with Thematics. (Maxwell Music Evaluation Bks.). (Illus.). 200p. (Orig.). (C). 1983. pap. 7.95 (0-912531-00-2) Maxwell Mus Eval.
— Mozart - Solo Piano Literature: A Comprehensive Guide: Annotated & Evaluated with Thematics. (Maxwell Music Evaluation Bks.). (Illus.). 347p. (Orig.). 1987. pap. 13.95 (0-912531-04-5) Maxwell Mus Eval.
— Scarlatti: Solo Piano Literature-A Comprehensive Guide Annotated & Evaluated with Thematics. (Maxwell Music Evaluation Bks.). (Illus.). 412p. (Orig.). 1985. pap. 13.95 (0-912531-02-9) Maxwell Mus Eval.
— Schubert - Solo Piano Literature: A Comprehensive Guide: Annotated & Evaluated with Thematics. (Maxwell Music Evaluation Bks.). (Illus.). (Orig.). 1986. pap. 12.95 (0-912531-03-7) Maxwell Mus Eval.
Maxwell, Carolyn & DeVan, William, eds. Schumann - Solo Piano Literature: A Comprehensive Guide: Annotated & Evaluated with Thematics. (Maxwell Music Evaluation Bks.). (Illus.). 339p. (Orig.). 1984. pap. 11.95 (0-912531-01-0) Maxwell Mus Eval.
Maxwell, Carolyn, ed. see Owens, Vivian.
Maxwell, Carolyn, ed. see Owens, Vivian W.
Maxwell, Cassandre. Bright Star, Bright Star, What Do You See? LC 89-82551. (Illus.). 32p. (J). (ps). 1990. pap. 6.99 (0-8066-2462-0, 9-2462) Augsburg Fortress.
— Yosef's Gift of Many Colors: An Easter Story. LC 92-44189. (Illus.). 32p. (J). (ps-3). 1993. 16.99 (0-8066-2627-5, 9-2627) Augsburg Fortress.
Maxwell, Catherine, ed. Swinburne. (Everyman's Poetry Ser.). 128p. 1997. pap. 3.50 (0-460-87871-9, Everyman's Classic Lib) Tuttle Pubng.
Maxwell, Cathy. Because of You. LC 98-93459. (Avon Romantic Treasure Ser.). 384p. 1999. mass mkt. 5.99 (0-380-79710-0, Avon Bks) Morrow Avon.
— Falling in Love Again. LC 96-95485. 384p. (Orig.). 1997. mass mkt. 5.99 (0-380-78718-0, Avon Bks) Morrow Avon.
*Maxwell, Cathy. Married in Haste. LC 99-94774. 372p. 1999. mass mkt. 6.50 (0-380-80831-5, Avon Bks) Morrow Avon.
— A Scandalous Marriage. 384p. 2000. mass mkt. 6.50 (0-380-80832-3, Avon Bks) Morrow Avon.
Maxwell, Cathy. When Dreams Come True. 384p. 1998. mass mkt. 5.99 (0-380-79709-7, Avon Bks) Morrow Avon.
— You & No Other. LC 96-96079. 375p. (Orig.). 1996. mass mkt. 5.99 (0-380-78716-4, Avon Bks) Morrow Avon.
Maxwell, Christine & Gregory, O. B. Spelling Basics. 128p. (C). 1993. pap. text 13.95 (1-56118-091-2) Paradigm MN.
— Spelling Basics. 128p. (C). 1993. pap. text, teacher ed. 8.00 (1-56118-092-0) Paradigm MN.
Maxwell, Christine & Grycz, Czeslaw J. New Riders' Official Internet Yellow Pages. 2nd ed. LC 94-34785. 802p. 1994. pap. 29.99 (1-56205-408-2) New Riders Pub.
Maxwell, Christine, et al. McKinley Official Internet Yellow Pages. 3rd ed. (Illus.). 900p. (Orig.). 1995. pap. 29.99 (1-56205-440-6) New Riders Pub.
Maxwell-Cook, John C. Fundamental Structural Diagrams. (Viewpoint Publication Ser.). (Illus.). 1978. text 45.00 (0-7210-1073-3, Pub. by C & CA) Scholium Intl.
*Maxwell, Corey. The Big Little Lie. (Illus.). 32p. (J). (gr. k-3). 1999. 12.95 (1-890145-04-1, Paw Island Ent) PetCare.
Maxwell, Corey. The Mixed-Up Pup. (Paw Island Presents...Ser.). (Illus.). 16p. (J). (ps-3). 1997. pap. 8.95 (1-890145-01-7) PetCare.
*Maxwell, Corey. The Mixed-Up Pup. (Illus.). 32p. 1999. 12.95 (1-890145-03-3, Paw Island Ent) PetCare.
— A Paw Island Christmas. (Illus.). 16p. (J). (gr. k-3). 1996. pap. 9.95 (1-890145-00-9) PetCare.
*Maxwell, Corey. A Paw Island Christmas. (Illus.). 32p. (J). 1999. 12.95 (1-890145-02-5, Paw Island Ent) PetCare.
Maxwell, Cory H. The Neal A. Maxwell Quote Book. 1997. 19.95 (1-57008-325-8) Bookcraft Inc.
Maxwell, D. & Miller, S. Taurhievel Domain Sourcebook. 1996. 7.95 (0-7869-0398-8, Pub. by TSR Inc) Random.
Maxwell, D. E. Brian Friel. LC 76-125299. (Irish Writers Ser.). 110p. 1975. pap. 1.95 (0-8387-7666-3) Bucknell U Pr.
Maxwell, D. R. EC Study-Lessons Learnt from Emergencies after Accidents in Ireland Involving Dangerous Substances: EUR 15565. 98p. 1994. pap. 25.00 (92-826-7516-5, Pub. by Comm Europ Commun) Bernan Associates.
Maxwell, Dan, et al, eds. New Directions in Machine Language. (Distributed Language Translation Ser.). 259p. (C). 1988. 90.80 (90-6765-377-2); pap. 61.55 (90-6765-378-0) Mouton.
Maxwell, Dan & Schubert, Klaus, eds. Metataxis in Practice: Dependency Syntax for Multilingual Machine Translation. (Distributed Language Translation Ser.). 323p. (Orig.). (C). 1989. 98.60 (90-6765-422-1); pap. 80.00 (90-6765-421-3) Mouton.
Maxwell, Dan, jt. ed. see Schubert, Klaus.
*Maxwell, Daniel. Urban Livelihoods & Food & Nutrition Security in Greater Accra, Ghana. LC 99-87101. (Research Report Ser.). 1999. write for info. (0-89629-115-4) Intl Food Policy.
Maxwell, Daniel & Wiebe, Keith. Land Tenure & Food Security: A Review of Concepts, Evidence, & Methods. (Research Paper Ser.: Vol. 129). (Illus.). iii, 37p. (C). 1998. pap. 4.00 (0-934519-77-3, RP129) U of Wis Land.
Maxwell, David. Private Security Law: Case Studies. 440p. 1992. 59.95 (0-7506-9034-8) Buttrwrth-Heinemann.
Maxwell, David, jt. auth. see Barefoot, J. Kirk.
Maxwell, David L. & Satake, Eiki. Research & Statistical Methods in Communication Disorders. LC 96-29698. (Illus.). 336p. 1997. pap. 35.00 (0-683-05655-7) Lppncott W & W.
Maxwell, Donald. Economics. 3rd ed. 736p. (C). 1993. text, student ed. 22.50 (0-256-11808-6, Irwn McGrw-H) McGrw-H Hghr Educ.
*Maxwell, Donald R. The Abacus & the Rainbow: Bergson, Proust & the Digital-Analogic Opposition. LC 98-46160. (Studies in the Humanities: Vol. 50). xiv, 263p. (C). 1999. text 52.95 (0-8204-4435-9) P Lang Pubng.
Maxwell, Donald W. Literature of the Great Lakes Region: An Annotated Bibliography. LC 91-14663. 502p. 1991. text 20.00 (0-8240-7027-5, H1252) Garland.
Maxwell, Dorothy B. A Florida Guidebook . . . Five Hundred Free or Exceptionally Low-Cost Places to Go & Things to Do in Florida (Nothing over 2.50) 112p. (Orig.). 1988. pap. 6.95 (0-929731-00-X) Ariel Publishing.
Maxwell, Douglas F. Inside Out: Psychological Self-Portraiture. (Illus.). 80p. 1995. pap. 12.00 (1-888332-04-2) Aldrich Mus.
Maxwell, Duane, ed. see Lee, Tony.
Maxwell, E. A Mind of My Own. 23.00 (0-685-69284-1) HarperTrade.
*Maxwell, Earl. Service, Prosperity & Sanity: Positioning the Professional Service Firm for the Future. (Illus.). 228p. 1998. pap. 19.95 (0-9666011-0-6) Maxwell Locke Ritter.
Maxwell, Edith. Just Dial a Number. 1990. pap. 2.99 (0-671-72867-9) PB.
Maxwell, Edwin A. Fallacies in Mathematics. 96p. 1959. text 25.95 (0-521-05700-0) Cambridge U Pr.
Maxwell, Elizabeth. A Flowing Stream: An Informal History of Montreat, NC 1897-1997. LC 97-60336. (Illus.). 192p. (Orig.). 1997. pap. 14.95 (1-56664-116-0) WorldComm.
Maxwell, Emily. An Easter Disguise. 320p. 1994. mass mkt. 3.99 (0-8217-4515-8, Zebra Kensgtn) Kensgtn Pub Corp.
— Queen of Hearts. 1992. mass mkt. 3.50 (0-8217-3639-6, Zebra Kensgtn) Kensgtn Pub Corp.
— Wicked Count. 1990. mass mkt. 2.95 (0-8217-2994-2, Zebra Kensgtn) Kensgtn Pub Corp.
Maxwell, Ernest. Trees of the San Jacinto Mountains. 32p. 1976. pap. 1.75 (0-913612-02-2) Strawberry Valley.
Maxwell, Evan. All the Winters That Have Been. 240p. 1996. mass mkt. 5.50 (0-06-100903-2, Harp PBks) HarpC.
— Season of the Swan. large type ed. LC 97-51358. 1998. 23.95 (1-57490-132-X, Beeler LP Bks) T T Beeler.
Maxwell, Evelyn. At Eden's Gate: Whole Health & Well-Being. LC 97-213864. (Illus.). xii, 254p. (Orig.). 1997. pap., per. 19.00 (0-944996-18-3) Carlsons.
Maxwell, Fay. Carroll & Harrison County, Ohio: Eckley & Perry 1921 Ohio History Index. 24p. 1983. 12.00 (1-885463-01-4) Ohio Genealogy.
— The 1880 Franklin & Pickaway Counties, Ohio: History Illustrations Index. (Illus.). 4p. 1984. 8.00 (1-885463-12-X) Ohio Genealogy.
— Fairfield County, Ohio: Hervey Scott's 1795-1876 History Index & C. M. L. Wiseman History Index Plus Fairfield County 1806 Taxables & Fairfield County, Lancaster 1803-1865 Will Index. 102p. 1971. 20.00 (1-885463-02-2) Ohio Genealogy.
— Franklin County, Ohio: Columbus 1843 City Directory Indexed Including Important Events in Columbus 1797-1843 Plus Franklin County Death Records 1811-1832 from Area Newspapers. 55p. 1977. 15.00 (1-885463-03-0) Ohio Genealogy.
— Franklin County, Ohio: Franklinton Cemetery Records. 14p. 1985. 8.00 (1-885463-10-3) Ohio Genealogy.
— Franklin County, Ohio: German Village & Brewery History Including Index. 57p. 1971. 14.00 (1-885463-07-3) Ohio Genealogy.
— Franklin County, Ohio: Living in a Landmark, a Pictorial of German Village. 54p. 1971. 10.00 (1-885463-08-1) Ohio Genealogy.
— Franklin County, Ohio: Scotch-Irish Accadian Nova Scotia Refugee Tract History Traces Them Back to Scotland, a First. 160p. 1974. 30.00 (1-885463-11-1) Ohio Genealogy.
— Franklin County, Ohio: Taxables of 1806, 1810 & 1814 Plus Franklin County 1803-1865 Will Index. 43p. 1976. 12.00 (1-885463-04-9) Ohio Genealogy.
— Franklin County, Ohio: 1826, 1832 & 1842 Chattels. 120p. 1978. 35.00 (1-885463-05-7) Ohio Genealogy.
— Franklin County, Ohio: 1860 Mortality Schedules, Complete Death Records. 24p. 1977. 8.00 (1-885463-09-X) Ohio Genealogy.
— Franklin County, Ohio: 1864 Civil War Military Roster Index. 98p. 1984. 25.00 (1-885463-06-5) Ohio Genealogy.

An Asterisk (*) at the beginning of an entry indicates that the title is appearing for the first time.

M

Maxwell, John C. The Winning Attitude. 288p. 1996. mass mkt. 5.99 (0-7852-7535-5) Nelson.

Maxwell, John C. Your Bridge to a Better Future. LC 97-6699. 208p. 1997. 12.99 (0-7852-7433-2) Nelson.

*Maxwell, John C. Your Bridge to a Better Future. 2000. 9.97 (0-7852-6831-6) Tommy Nelson.

Maxwell, John C. & Dornan, Jim. Becoming a Person of Influence. LC 97-23001. 224p. 1997. 19.99 (0-7852-7100-7, Oliver-Nelson) Nelson.

*Maxwell, John W., Jr. & VonHagen, Jhurgen. Empirical Studies of Environmental Policies in Europe. LC 00-37085. (Zei Studies in European Economics & Law). (Illus.). 2000. write for info. (0-7923-7752-4, Kluwer Plenum) Kluwer Academic.

*Maxwell, Jonathan. Blitz Theory: How to Win at Blitz Chess. (Illus.). 112p. 1999. pap. 11.95 (0-9677752-0-5) Silent Lyric Prod.

Maxwell, Jonathan, jt. ed. see Geyl, Roland.

Maxwell, Joseph. The Tarot. Powell, Ivor C., tr. from FRE. 224p. (Orig.). pap. 26.95 (0-8464-4297-3) Beekman Pubs.

— The Tarot. 190p. (Orig.). 1988. pap. 17.95 (0-85207-206-6, Pub. by C W Daniel) Natl Bk Netwk.

Maxwell, Joseph A. Qualitative Research Design: An Interactive Approach. LC 95-50209. (Applied Social Research Methods Ser.: Vol. 41). 204p. (C). 1996. 42.00 (0-8039-7328-4); pap. 18.95 (0-8039-7329-2) Sage.

Maxwell, Josie G. Joy Is to Know Him. 180p. (Orig.). 1994. pap. 12.95 (0-9638758-1-7) Brockton Pubng.

Maxwell, Judith. Full Circle: The Phase II Manual: A Support Group Guidebook for Battered Women. Farias, Helen G. & Janezic, Shirley, eds. LC 92-83703. 230p. 1993. reprint ed. pap. text 12.95 (0-9632698-0-1) Veda Vangarde.

— Textos Chujes de San Mateo Ixtatan. (MYN & SPA.). 100p. 2000. pap. 9.95 (1-886502-27-7) Yax Te Found.

Maxwell, Judith & Maxwell, Jessica. The Feminist Revised Mother Goose: A 21st-Century Children's Edition. 2nd ed. (Illus.). (J). (gr. 2-8). 1995. pap. text 7.95 (0-9632698-7-9) Veda Vangarde.

— The Feminist Revised Mother Goose Rhymes: A 21st Century Children's Edition. LC 92-81770. 32p. (J). (gr. 1-9). 1992. pap. 7.95 (0-9632698-1-X) Veda Vangarde.

Maxwell, Judith B., ed. Restructuring the Incentive System. LC 75-308268. (Policy Review & Outlook Ser.: No. 1975). 170p. 1974. reprint ed. pap. 52.70 (0-608-01372-2, 206211500002) Bks Demand.

Maxwell, Judith B. & Beigie, Carl E. The Disappearance of the Status Quo. LC 74-169370. (Policy Review & Outlook Ser.: No. 1974). 110p. 1974. reprint ed. pap. 34.10 (0-608-01373-0, 206211600002) Bks Demand.

Maxwell, Judith B. & Pestieau, Caroline. Economic Realities of Contemporary Confederation. LC 80-494656. (Accent Quebec Ser.). 142p. 1980. reprint ed. pap. 44.10 (0-608-01371-4, 206211100002) Bks Demand.

Maxwell, Kathryn & Maxwell, Shami. International Price Guide of Old & Unusual Playing Cards. (Illus.). 120p. (Orig.). 1988. pap. 14.95 (0-940649-00-4) Parnell Pub.

Maxwell, Kathryn, jt. auth. see Maxwell, Shami.

Maxwell, Kathryn S. Pioneer Cooking. (Illus.). 184p. (Orig.). 1987. pap. 4.95 (0-940649-02-0) Parnell Pub.

Maxwell, Katie. Bedside Manners: A Practical Guide to Visiting the Ill. 112p. (gr. 11). 1990. pap. 8.99 (0-8010-6265-9) Baker Bks.

Maxwell, Kenneth. The Making of Portuguese Democracy. 264p. (C). 1995. text 59.95 (0-521-46077-8) Cambridge U Pr.

— The Making of Portuguese Democracy. 264p. 1997. pap. text 19.95 (0-521-58596-1) Cambridge U Pr.

— Pombal, Paradox of the Enlightenment. (Illus.). 218p. (C). 1995. text 54.95 (0-521-45044-6) Cambridge U Pr.

Maxwell, Kenneth, ed. Portugal in the Nineteen Eighties: Dilemmas of Democratic Consolidation, 138. LC 85-9872. (Contributions in Political Science Ser.: No. 138). (Illus.). 268p. 1986. 65.00 (0-313-24889-3, MPG/, Greenwood Pr) Greenwood.

— The Press & the Rebirth of Iberian Democracy, 99. LC 82-24201. (Contributions in Political Science Ser.: No. 99). (Illus.). 198p. 1983. 57.95 (0-313-23100-1, MPI/, Greenwood Pr) Greenwood.

Maxwell, Kenneth & Haltzel, Michael H., eds. Portugal: Ancient Country, Young Democracy. (Illus.). 136p. (C). 1990. lib. bdg. 22.25 (0-943875-20-X) W Wilson Ctr Pr.

Maxwell, Kenneth R. Conflicts & Conspiracies: Brazil & Portugal, 1750-1808. LC 72-89813. (Cambridge Latin American Studies: No. 16). 301p. reprint ed. pap. 85.80 (0-608-18398-9, 2030608) Bks Demand.

Maxwell, Kim. Residential Broadband: An Insider's Guide to the Battle for the Last Mile. LC 98-29310. 400p. 1998. pap. 39.99 (0-471-25165-8) Wiley.

Maxwell, Kimera K. & Reinsch, Roger W. A Lawyer's Guide to Public Relations: The Art of Promoting Your Practice. LC 89-161995. x, 221 p. 1989. write for info. (0-941161-64-1) PES Inc WI.

Maxwell, L. E. Women in Ministry: An Historical & Biblical Look at the Role of Women in Christian Leadership. 1995. pap. 9.99 (0-87509-587-9) Chr Pubns.

Maxwell, Larry. Becoming a Dynamic Youth Leader: A Guide for Equipping Volunteer Youth Workers. Spear, Cindy G., ed. 208p. (Orig.). 1993. pap. 10.95 (0-941005-88-7) Chrch Grwth VA.

— The Complete Guide to Starting or Evaluating Dynamic Youth Ministry. Johnson, Tamara & Spear, Cindy G., eds. 164p. 1993. 99.95 incl. audio (0-941005-87-9) Chrch Grwth VA.

— Gaining Personal Financial Freedom: Through the Biblical Principles of Finances. Spear, Cindy G. & Johnson, Tamara, eds. 158p. 1992. pap. 9.95 (0-941005-55-0); pap., student ed. 4.35 (0-941005-53-4); pap., wbk. ed. 3.25 (0-941005-54-2) Chrch Grwth VA.

— How to Start a Local Church Bible Institute. 127p. 1994. ring bd., vinyl bd. 99.95 (1-57052-020-8) Chrch Grwth VA.

Maxwell, Larry A. 175 Ways to Fund Your Youth Ministry. Spear, Cindy G., ed. 26p. 1995. ring bd. 54.95 (1-57052-048-8) Chrch Grwth VA.

Maxwell, Lee A. Altar Guild Manual. 1997. pap. 13.99 (0-570-04896-6, 12-3309) Concordia.

Maxwell, Leigh. The Ashanti Ring: Sir Garnet Wolseley's Campaigns, 1870-1882 LC 86-156095. 248p. 1985. write for info. (0-436-27447-7) M Secker & Warburg.

*Maxwell, Lizzie. Little Fish in a Big Pond: A Support Guide for Actors. Dudley, Nan T. et al, eds. 193p. 1999. pap. 14.95 (0-9671273-0-0) DreamLover Pubg.

Maxwell, Lorraine E. Designing Child Care Settings. (Illus.). 110p. 1998. pap. 15.75 (1-57753-232-5, 327DCCS) Corn Coop Ext.

Maxwell, M. H. A Christmas Song of Old Boston: A String of Pearls, 1852 Replica. 31p. 1973. 6.50 (1-881946-04-5) Gauntlet Bks.

Maxwell Maltz Foundation Staff & Sommer, Bobbe. Psycho-Cybernetics 2000. 352p. 1993. 29.95 (0-13-735903-9) P-H.

*Maxwell Maltz Foundation Staff, et al. Psycho-Cybernetics. rev. ed. 384p. 1999. 7.98 (1-56731-306-X, MJF Bks) Fine Comms.

Maxwell, Marcus. Revelation: A Bible Commentary for Every Day. LC 98-2543. (Doubleday Bible Commentaries Ser.). 224p. 1998. pap. 12.95 (0-385-49028-3) Doubleday.

Maxwell, Margaret. African Studies Handbook for Teachers. 3rd ed. 221p. (C). 1983. teacher ed., spiral bd. 6.00 (0-932288-69-3) Ctr Intl Ed U of MA.

— Narodniki Women: Russian Women Who Sacrificed Themselves for the Dream of Freedom. (Athene Ser.). 310p. 1990. text 36.00 (0-08-037462-X, Pergamon Pr); pap. text 14.50 (0-08-037461-1, Pergamon Pr) Elsevier.

— Narodniki Women: Russian Women Who Sacrificed Themselves for the Dream of Freedom. (Athene Ser.). 360p. (C). 1990. text 36.00 (0-8077-6247-4); pap. text 17.95 (0-8077-6246-6) Tchrs Coll.

Maxwell, Margaret F. A Passion for Freedom: The Life of Sharlot Hall. LC 82-4866. (Illus.). 234p. 1995. pap. 18.95 (0-8165-1506-9) U of Ariz Pr.

Maxwell, Margaret F., jt. auth. see Maxwell, Robert L.

Maxwell, Margaret M. Let's Visit Texas Missions. (Illus.). xi, 68 p. (J). (gr. 4-5). 1998. 13.95 (1-57168-197-3) Sunbelt Media.

Maxwell, Margaret M., ed. see Kriplen, Nancy.

Maxwell, Margie, jt. auth. see Maxwell, Jim.

Maxwell, Marilyn C., ed. see Newell, Coke.

Maxwell, Marion. A Little Irish Baking Book. (Little Irish Book Ser.). (Illus.). 60p. 1995. 9.95 (0-86281-534-7, Pub. by Appletree Pr) Irish Bks Media.

Maxwell, Marion & McWilliams, Catherine. A Little Book of Scottish Baking. LC 97-1655. 60p. 1997. 8.95 (1-56554-290-8) Pelican.

Maxwell, Mark. Nixoncarver. LC 97-40068. 192p. 1998. text 19.95 (0-312-18146-9) St Martin.

— NixonCarver: A Novel. 1999. pap. 11.95 (0-312-20664-X, St Martin Griffin) St Martin.

Maxwell, Martha. Improving Student Learning Skills. LC 79-83582. (Jossey-Bass Series in Higher Education). (Illus.). 538p. reprint ed. pap. 166.80 (0-7837-6518-5, 204563000007) Bks Demand.

— Improving Student Learning Skills: A New Edition. LC 96-79453. 428p. (Orig.). 1997. pap. 38.95 (0-943202-61-2) H & H Pub.

Maxwell, Martha, ed. From Access to Success: A Book of Readings on College Developmental Education & Learning Assistance Programs. LC 94-79104. 318p. (Orig.). 1994. pap. 29.95 (0-943202-47-7) H & H Pub.

— When Tutor Meets Student. 2nd ed. 296p. (C). 1994. text 32.50 (0-472-09532-3, 09532); pap. text 17.95 (0-472-06532-7, 06532) U of Mich Pr.

Maxwell, Mary. Human Evolution: A Philosophical Anthropology. 288p. 1984. text 71.50 (0-231-05946-9, King's Crown Paperbacks) Col U Pr.

— Morality among Nations: An Evolutionary View. LC 89-27881. (SUNY Series in Bio-politics). 198p. (C). 1990. pap. text 19.95 (0-7914-0350-5) State U NY Pr.

— Playing with Fire. (Desire Ser.). 1993. per. 2.99 (0-373-05825-X, 5-05825-0) Silhouette.

Maxwell, Mary, ed. The Sociobiological Imagination. LC 90-10336. (SUNY Series in Philosophy & Biology). 376p. (C). 1991. text 59.50 (0-7914-0767-5); pap. text 21.95 (0-7914-0768-3) State U NY Pr.

Maxwell, Mary B. Benson. Genealogy of the Benson, Latimer, Reed, Durham & Associated Families. 57p. 1997. reprint ed. pap. 11.00 (0-8328-7497-3); reprint ed. lib. bdg. 21.00 (0-8328-7496-5) Higginson Bk Co.

*Maxwell, Mary E. Among the Hills of Camillus. (Illus.). 140p. 1999. reprint ed. pap. 18.00 (1-890691-04-6) Pine Grve Pr.

Maxwell, Mary E. The Doctor's Wife, 3 vols., 2 bks., Set. LC 79-8426. reprint ed. 84.50 (0-404-62047-7) AMS Pr.

— To Walk a Country Mile. LC 99-161495. 176p. 1998. pap. text 20.95 (1-896867-03-0) Moulin Publ.

Maxwell, Mary L. & Savage, C. Wade, eds. Science, Mind, & Psychology: Essays in Honor of Grover Maxwell. LC 89-36360. 476p. (Orig.). (C). 1989. lib. bdg. 65.00 (0-8191-7557-9) U Pr of Amer.

*Maxwell, Mary R. Sauce for the Goose. 2000. mass mkt. 6.95 (0-352-33492-4) BLA4.

*Maxwell, Max. Love & Bile: Sayings of a Gadfly. (Illus.). xiv, 142p. 2000. pap. 12.95 (0-9679344-0-0) Gadfly Pr PA.

Maxwell, Michael. Manual of Policy & Procedure for Your Internal Security Force. 1992. pap. 149.50 (0-614-05762-0) Abbott Langer Assocs.

Maxwell, Michael, jt. auth. see Maxwell, Helen.

Maxwell, Michelle, jt. auth. see Cain, Sandra.

Maxwell, Milicent. How to Save on Your Long Distance, Fight Back & Win. LC 98-92328. (Illus.). 28p. pap. 9.99 (1-893839-00-1, Pub. by M & M Pubg) Baker & Taylor.

— In a Black Womans Eyes. 1999. pap. 19.99 (1-893839-01-X, Pub. by M & M Pubg) Baker & Taylor.

— We Didn't Know He Was That Way. 1999. pap. 19.99 (1-893839-02-8, Pub. by M & M Pubg) Baker & Taylor.

Maxwell, Mimi. Monster MASH. 1998. pap. text 6.99 (0-9680678-8-3) Tumbleweed Pr.

Maxwell, Moreau S., ed. Eastern Arctic Prehistory: Paleoeskimo Problems. (Memoir Ser.: No. 31). 176p. 1976. pap. 8.00 (0-932839-01-0) Soc Am Arch.

Maxwell, Nan L. Income Inequality in the United States, 1947-1985, 101. LC 89-11971. (Contributions in Economics & Economic History Ser.: No. 101). 227p. 1989. 59.95 (0-313-26411-2, MIQ/, Greenwood Pr) Greenwood.

*Maxwell, Nan L. & Rubin, Victor. High School Career Academies: A Pathway to Educational Reform in Urban School Districts. (C). 2000. write for info. (0-88099-214-X); pap. write for info. (0-88099-213-1) W E Upjohn.

Maxwell, Nancy. Washington County, Arkansas, Miscellaneous Record Book, 1841-1879. LC 98-116031. vi, 142p. 1997. pap. 24.00 (0-7884-0760-0, M099) Heritage Bk.

— Washington County, Arkansas, Sheriff's Census for 1865. 67p. (Orig.). 1994. pap. text 16.50 (1-55613-885-7) Heritage Bk.

Maxwell, Neal A. The Christmas Scene. 1994. pap. 1.95 (0-88494-962-1) Bookcraft Inc.

— If Thou Endure It Well. 1996. 13.95 (1-57008-233-2) Bookcraft Inc.

— Lord, Increase Our Faith. 1994. 11.95 (0-88494-919-2) Bookcraft Inc.

— Meek & Lowly. LC 86-32784. xii, 127p. 1994. pap. 6.95 (0-87579-945-0) Deseret Bk.

— Men & Women of Christ. 1991. 12.95 (0-88494-785-8) Bookcraft Inc.

— Neal A. Maxwell, Set. 1992. reprint ed. boxed set 24.95 (0-87579-607-9) Deseret Bk.

— Not My Will, but Thine. 1988. 14.95 (0-88494-672-X) Bookcraft Inc.

— "Oh, Divine Redeemer" & "Notwithstanding My Weakness" & a More Determined Discipleship LC 98-72590. (Classic Talk Ser.). 69 p. 1998. write for info. (0-87579-984-1) Deseret Bk.

— That Ye May Believe. 1992. 11.95 (0-88494-843-9) Bookcraft Inc.

Maxwell, Nicholas. The Comprehensibility of the Universe: A New Conception of Science. (Illus.). 332p. 1999. text 60.00 (0-19-823776-6) OUP.

*Maxwell, Nicole. Witch Doctor's Apprentice: Hunting for Medicinal Plants in the Amazon. 400p. 1999. 9.98 (1-56731-303-5, MJF Bks) Fine Comms.

Maxwell, Nilda, jt. auth. see Cooper, Judy.

Maxwell, Patrick, jt. auth. see Diesel, Alleyn.

Maxwell, Peter B. On the Interpretation of Statutes. xxxii, 458p. 1991. reprint ed. 48.50 (0-8377-2440-6, Rothman) W S Hein.

Maxwell-Plath, Susan, jt. auth. see Cornelius, Nelarine.

Maxwell, R. The Northern Wastes (Realm) (Middle-Earth Role Playing Ser.). (Illus.). 192p. 1997. pap. 28.00 (1-55806-296-3, 2025) Iron Crown Ent Inc.

Maxwell, R. A. Mineral Resources of South Texas: Region Served Through the Port of Corpus Christi. (Reports of Investigations: RI 43). (Illus.). 140p. 1962. pap. 3.50 (0-686-29333-9) Bur Econ Geology.

Maxwell, R. M. Jimmie Stewart - Frontiersman. 116p. (C). 1989. text 65.00 (1-872795-53-6, Pub. by Pentland Pr) St Mut.

— Villiers-Stuart Goes to War. 349p. (C). 1989. text 69.00 (0-946270-85-6, Pub. by Pentland Pr) St Mut.

— Villiers-Stuart on the Frontier. 209p. (C). 1989. text 50.00 (0-946270-57-0, Pub. by Pentland Pr) St Mut.

Maxwell, Rachel R., et al. Susan Rothenberg - The Prints: A Catalogue Raisonne. (Illus.). 104p. (Orig.). (C). 1987. pap. 20.00 (0-944751-00-8) Maxwells Busn.

*Maxwell, Randy. Bring Back the Glory: What Happens When God's People Pray for Revival. Thomas, Jerry D., ed. LC 00-23569. 191p. 2000. pap. 12.99 (0-8163-1788-7) Pacific Pr Pub Assn.

Maxwell, Randy. If My People Pray: An Eleventh Hour Call to Prayer & Revival. LC 94-37661. 1995. pap. 10.99 (0-8163-1246-X) Pacific Pr Pub Assn.

— On Eagles' Wings: How to Let Jesus Bear Your Burdens. McFarland, Ken, ed. LC 85-17036. (Illus.). 64p. 1986. pap. 4.99 (0-8163-1345-8) Pacific Pr Pub Assn.

Maxwell, Raymond A. Dress Black: A Collection of Poetry. 80p. (Orig.). 1992. pap. 10.00 (0-9634108-0-6) ASWAD.

Maxwell, Rhoda J. Images of Mothers in Literature for Young Adults. LC 93-9534. (American University Studies, XXIV, American Literature: Vol. 51). 139p. (C). 1994. text 36.95 (0-8204-2175-8) P Lang Pubng.

— Writing Across the Curriculum in Middle & High Schools. LC 95-456. 208p. 1995. pap. text 33.33 (0-205-15325-9) Allyn.

*Maxwell, Rhoda J. & Meiser, Mary. Teaching English in Middle & Secondary Schools. 3rd ed. 480p. 2000. pap. 52.00 (0-13-021362-4) P-H.

Maxwell, Rhoda J. & Meiser, Mary. Teaching English in the Middle & Secondary School. 2nd ed. 480p. (C). 1996. pap. text 60.00 (0-13-461666-9) P-H.

Maxwell, Richard. The Mysteries of Paris & London. (Victorian Literature & Culture Ser.). (Illus.). 416p. 1992. text 39.50 (0-8139-1341-1) U Pr of Va.

— The Spectacle of Democracy: Spanish Television, Nationalism, & Political Transition. LC 94-18784. 256p. 1994. pap. 17.95 (0-8166-2358-9) U of Minn Pr.

Maxwell, Richard & Sharples, Johanna. From Birth to Backing: The Complete Handling of the Young Horse. (Illus.). 160p. 1998. 27.50 (1-57076-120-5, Trafalgar Sq Pub) Trafalgar.

Maxwell, Richard C., et al. California Cases on Security Transactions in Land. 4th ed. (American Casebook Ser.). 778p. (C). 1991. 57.50 (0-314-89955-3) West Pub.

— California Cases on Security Transactions in Land, Teacher's Manual to Accompany. 4th ed. (American Casebook Ser.). 194p. (C). 1992. pap. text. write for info. (0-314-01383-0) West Pub.

— Cases & Materials on the Law of Oil & Gas. 6th ed. LC 92-5650. 1060p. 1992. text 45.95 (0-88277-983-4) Foundation Pr.

— Law of Oil & Gas: Teacher's Manual for Cases & Materials on The. 6th ed. (University Casebook Ser.). 177p. (C). 1992. pap. text. write for info. (1-56662-030-9) Foundation Pr.

Maxwell, Richard E., et al. Ohio School Finance: A Practitioner's Guide. 2nd ed. LC 96-4100. 300p. 1996. pap. 35.00 (0-87084-785-6) Anderson Pub Co.

Maxwell, Richared, jt. auth. see Bayley, Lesley.

Maxwell, Robert. Desperate Encounters: The Fifth Royal Gurkha Rifles (the Punjab Frontier Force) 264p. (C). 1989. text 65.00 (0-946270-35-X, Pub. by Pentland Pr) St Mut.

James Stirling: Writings on Architecture. (Illus.). 288p. 1999. 24.95 (88-8118-323-4, Pub. by Skira IT) Abbeville Pr.

— James Stirling - Michael Wilford. LC 98-38516. (Studio Paperback Ser.). (ENG & GER.). 1998. pap. write for info. (0-8176-5291-4) Birkhauser.

— James Stirling, Michael Wilford. LC 98-38516. 1999. pap. 29.95 (3-7643-5291-4) Birkhauser.

— Sweet Disorder & the Carefully Careless. LC 93-32943. (Princeton Papers on Architecture: No. 2). (Illus.). 336p. (Orig.). 1994. pap. 19.95 (1-56898-005-1) Princeton Arch.

Maxwell, Robert, et al, contrib. by. Contemporary British Architects. (Illus.). 240p. 1994. 65.00 (3-7913-1349-5, Pub. by Prestel) te Neues.

Maxwell, Robert, ed. Reshaping the National Health Service, Vol. II. (Reshaping the Public Sector Ser.). 256p. 1987. 34.95 (0-946967-18-0); pap. 21.95 (0-946967-30-X) Transaction Pubs.

*Maxwell, Robert, photos by. Robert Maxwell: Photographs. (Illus.). 156p. 2000. 60.00 (1-892041-32-4) Arena Editions.

Maxwell, Robert & Muirhead, Thomas. James Stirling & Michael Wilford: Buildings & Projects, 1975-1992. LC 93-60420. (Illus.). 320p. 1994. 80.00 (0-500-34126-5, Pub. by Thames Hudson) Norton.

Maxwell, Robert & Murray, Peter, contrib. by. Contemporary British Architects. (Illus.). 240p. 1997. pap. text 29.95 (3-7913-1825-X, Pub. by Prestel) te Neues.

Maxwell, Robert, ed. see Deans, David & Beaver, Benjamin.

Maxwell, Robert A. & Eckhardt, Shohreh B. Drug Discovery: A Casebook & Analysis. LC 90-4915. 463p. 1990. 109.50 (0-89603-180-2) Humana.

Maxwell, Robert J., jt. auth. see Watkin, David.

Maxwell, Robert L. & Maxwell, Margaret F. Maxwell's Handbook for AACR2R: Explaining & Illustrating the Anglo-American Cataloging Rules & the 1993 Amendments. LC 97-1449. 456p. 1997. 60.00 (0-8389-0704-0) ALA.

Maxwell, Robert S. Texas Economic Growth, 1890 to World War II: From Frontier to Industrial Giant. (Texas History Ser.). (Illus.). 42p. 1982. pap. text 9.95 (0-89641-099-4) American Pr.

— Whistle in the Piney Woods: Paul Bremond & the Houston, East & West Texas Railway. LC 98-33659. 384p. 1999. reprint ed. 24.95 (1-57441-061-X) UNTX Pr.

Maxwell, Robert W. Maxwell Quick Medical Reference. (Illus.). 32p. (Orig.). (C). 1995. pap. text 7.95 (0-9645191-0-0) Mxwll Pub.

— Maxwell Quick Medical Reference. 3rd rev. ed. (Illus.). 32p. (Orig.). (C). 1996. pap. text 7.95 (0-9645191-1-9) Mxwll Pub.

Maxwell, Robin. The Queen's Bastard. LC 98-50502. 448p. 1999. 24.95 (1-55970-475-6, Pub. by Arcade Pub Inc) Time Warner.

*Maxwell, Robin. The Queen's Bastard. LC 00-22781. 448p. 2000. pap. 13.00 (0-684-85760-X, Fireside) S&S Trade Pap.

Maxwell, Robin. The Secret Diary of Anne Boleyn: A Novel. LC 96-49275. 288p. 1997. 23.45 (1-55970-375-X, Pub. by Arcade Pub Inc) Time Warner.

— The Secret Diary of Anne Boleyn: A Novel. LC 97-53056. 288p. 1998. per. 11.00 (0-684-84969-0) S&S Trade Pap.

*Maxwell, Robin. The Secret Diary of Anne Boleyn: A Novel. large type ed. 512p. 2000. write for info. (0-7089-4198-2) Ulverscroft.

Maxwell, Ronald F., jt. auth. see Roda, Bot.

Maxwell, Ross A. The Big Bend Country. Pearson, John R., ed. (Illus.). 88p. 1986. 9.95 (0-912001-13-5); pap. 6.95 (0-912001-12-7) Big Bend.

Maxwell, Ross A., et al. Geology of Big Bend National Park, Brewster County, Texas. LC 68-65757. (University of Texas Publications: No. 6711). 621p. reprint ed. pap. 192.60 (0-7837-3157-4, 204282800006) Bks Demand.

Maxwell, S. Vegetarian Pasta Recipes. 1996. 6.98 (0-7858-0674-1) Bk Sales Inc.

Maxwell, Sandra K., ed. see Maxwell, Bob.

Maxwell, Sarah. Bagels & Lox & Lots More. 96p. 1995. 12.98 (0-7858-0245-2) Bk Sales Inc.

— Greek Meze Cooking. 128p. 1992. 12.98 (1-55521-774-5) Bk Sales Inc.

An Asterisk (*) at the beginning of an entry indicates that the title is appearing for the first time.

***Maxwell, Sarah.** I Can Cook: How-to-Cook Activity Projects for the Very Young. (Show Me How Ser.). (J). 1999. write for info. (*1-84038-282-1*) Hermes Hse.
— I Can Cook: How to Cook Activity Projects for the Very Young. (Show Me How Ser.). (Illus.). 40p. (J). 2000. pap. 7.95 (*0-7548-0096-2*, Lorenz Bks) Anness Pub.
Maxwell, Sarah. Vegetarian Pasta. 128p. 1994. 12.98 (*0-7858-0092-1*) Bk Sales Inc.
***Maxwell, Sarah & Nightingale, Hugh.** I Can Make Magic: How to Make Magic Tricks for Children. (Show Me How Ser.). (Illus.). 40p. (J). 2000. pap. 7.95 (*0-7548-0097-0*, Lorenz Bks) Anness Pub.
***Maxwell, Sarah & Nilsen, Angela.** Irresistable Cakes. 96p. 2000. pap. 12.95 (*0-7548-0313-9*) Anness Pub.
Maxwell, Sarah, jt. auth. see Nilsen, Angela.
Maxwell, Scott E. Linux Core Kernel Commentary. LC 99-45422. 575p. 1999. pap. text 39.99 (*1-57610-469-9*) Coriolis Grp.
Maxwell, Scott E. & Delaney, Harold D. Designing Experiments & Analyzing Data: A Model Comparison Perspective. 1990. mass mkt., teacher ed. write for info. (*0-534-10375-8*) Brooks-Cole.
Maxwell, Scott E., jt. auth. see Bray, James H.
Maxwell, Shami & Maxwell, Kathryn. Playing Card Price Guide. (Illus.). 128p. 1992. lib. bdg. 12.95 (*0-940649-11-X*) Parnell Pub.
— Self Publish to Success: Make Money Publishing. (Illus.). 128p. (Orig.). 1988. pap. 9.95 (*0-940649-03-9*) Parnell Pub.
Maxwell, Shami, jt. auth. see Maxwell, Kathryn.
Maxwell, Sheri. Book of Mark: The Story of Jesus. 160p. 1999. pap. 6.99 (*0-87788-518-4*, H Shaw Pubs) Waterbrook Pr.
Maxwell, Sidney D. The Suburbs of Cincinnati: Sketches, Historical & Descriptive. LC 73-2907. (Metropolitan America Ser.). 190p. 1977. reprint ed. 15.95 (*0-405-05402-5*) Ayer.
Maxwell, Sonia. Scandinavian Cooking. 128p. 1995. 12.98 (*0-7858-0186-3*) Bk Sales Inc.
Maxwell, Stanley M. The Man Who Couldn't be Killed: An Incredible Story of Faith & Courage During China's Cultural Revolution. LC 94-26486. 222p. 1995. pap. 10.99 (*0-8163-1235-4*) Pacific Pr Pub Assn.
Maxwell, Stanley M. The Man Who Lived Twice: A Father Risks All for His Family's Freedom. LC 96-35460. 1997. pap. 10.99 (*0-8163-1372-5*) Pacific Pr Pub Assn.
***Maxwell, Steve.** Linux Network Management Tools. (Illus.). 2000. pap. 49.99 (*0-07-212262-5*) McGrw-H Intl.
Maxwell, Steve. UNIX Network Management Tools. LC 99-17145. 448p. 1999. pap. 39.99 (*0-07-913782-2*) McGraw.
Maxwell, Steve & Hall, Bruce, intros. Conference on Railway Engineering, 1993: Contracting Railways-Safety, Standards & the Surroundings. (National Conference Publication Ser.: No. 93-12). (Illus.). 288p. (Orig.). 1993. pap. text 54.00 (*0-85825-582-0*, Pub. by Inst Engrs Aust-EA Bks) Accents Pubns.
***Maxwell-Stuart, P. G.** Martin Del Rio: Investigation into Magic. 2000. text. write for info. (*0-7190-4976-8*, Pub. by Manchester Univ Pr) St Martin.
Maxwell-Stuart, P. G. The Occult in Early Modern Europe: A Documentary History. LC 98-7748. (Documents in History Ser.). 264p. 1999. pap. 21.95 (*0-312-21753-6*); text 65.00 (*0-312-21752-8*) St Martin.
Maxwell-Stuart, Peter. Chronicle of the Popes: The Reign-by-Reign Record of the Papacy over 2000 Years. LC 97-60230. (Illus.). 240p. 1997. 29.95 (*0-500-01798-0*, Pub. by Thames Hudson) Norton.
Maxwell, T. G., jt. auth. see Bates, David.
Maxwell, T. S. The Gods of Asia: Image, Text & Meaning. (Illus.). 352p. 1999. pap. 16.95 (*0-19-564733-5*) OUP.
— Visvarupa. (Illus.). 320p. 1989. text 29.95 (*0-19-562117-4*) OUP.
Maxwell, Terry B. & Hughes, Joan E. The CompuResource Book: A Collection of Activities to Integrate Curriculum & Computers. (Illus.). 146p. (C). 1994. teacher ed., spiral bd. 21.50 (*1-885401-00-0*) Maxwell Grp.
Maxwell, Terry G. Diversified Mutual Fund Investment Strategies: How to Build a High-Return, Low-Risk Portfolio of Mutual Funds. Stankiewicz, Ilene, ed. LC 91-75315. (Illus.). 165p. 1991. 19.95 (*0-9630625-0-6*) Capital MI.
Maxwell, Thomas. Kiss Me Once. 336p. 1986. 16.45 (*0-89296-163-5*, Pub. by Mysterious Pr) Little.
— Kiss Me Once. 1987. mass mkt. 3.95 (*0-445-40537-6*, Pub. by Warner Bks) Little.
— Kiss Me Once. 1988. mass mkt. 4.95 (*0-445-40750-6*, Pub. by Warner Bks) Little.
— Kiss Me Twice. 304p. 1989. mass mkt. 4.95 (*0-445-40539-2*, Pub. by Warner Bks) Little.
— The Saberdene Variations. LC 87-42700. 320p. 1987. 16.95 (*0-89296-166-X*, Pub. by Mysterious Pr) Little.
— The Saberdene Variations. 1988. mass mkt. 4.95 (*0-445-40743-3*, Pub. by Warner Bks) Little.
— The Suspense Is Killing Me. 272p. 1991. mass mkt. 4.99 (*0-446-40042-4*, Pub. by Warner Bks) Little.
Maxwell, Thomas, jt. auth. see Maxwell, Aileen.
Maxwell, Timothy T. & Jones, Jesse C. Alternative Fuels: Emissions, Economics & Performance. 243p. 1994. 49.00 (*1-56091-523-4*, R-143) Soc Auto Engineers.
Maxwell, Victor. Alive in Me. 1997. pap. 5.99 (*1-898787-11-5*) Emerald House Group Inc.
— Authenic Servant. 1997. pap. text 9.99 (*1-898787-58-1*) Emerald House Group Inc.
***Maxwell, Victor.** Belfast's Halls of Faith & Fame. (Illus.). 1999. pap. 11.99 (*1-84030-051-5*) Ambassador Prodns Ltd.
— Mission to Millions. 183p. 2000. pap. 9.99 (*1-84030-069-8*, Ambassador-Emerald) Emerald House Group Inc.
Maxwell, Victor. Singing We Go: Fifty Years with the Woodvale. 1999. pap. text 8.99 (*1-84030-041-8*) Ambassador Prodns Ltd.
Maxwell, Victor & Woods, Bill. Angel of the Amazon. 213p. 1997. pap. 9.99 (*1-84030-004-3*) Emerald House Group Inc.
Maxwell, W. H., jt. ed. see Beard, Leo R.
Maxwell, W. Harold & Brown, C. R., eds. A Complete List of British & Colonial Law Reports & Legal Periodicals: Arranged in Alphabetical & in Chronological Order with Bibliographical Notes with a Check List of Canadian Statutes, 1937. 3rd ed. viii, 190p. 1995. reprint ed. lib. bdg. 70.00 (*1-886363-11-0*) Lawbk Exchange.
Maxwell, William. All the Days & Nights: The Collected Stories of William Maxwell. 432p. 1995. pap. 13.00 (*0-679-76102-0*) Vin Bks.
— Ancestors: A Family History. LC 94-31109. 1995. pap. 13.00 (*0-679-75929-8*) Vin Bks.
— Billie Dyer & Other Stories. large type ed. LC 92-45885. (General Ser.). 187p. 1993. pap. 17.95 (*0-8161-5572-0*, G K Hall Lrg Type) Mac Lib Ref.
— The Folded Leaf. LC 78-63992. (Gay Experience Ser.). 320p. reprint ed. 45.00 (*0-404-61510-4*) AMS Pr.
— Folded Leaf, Vol. 1. LC 96-5454. 1996. pap. 12.00 (*0-679-77256-1*) AMS Pr.
— Heavenly Tenants. (Illus.). 57p. (J). (gr. 4-7). 1992. reprint ed. 13.95 (*0-930407-25-3*) Parabola Bks.
— The Old Man at the Railroad Crossing: And Other Tales. LC 86-46248. 192p. (Orig.). 1987. pap. 10.95 (*0-87923-676-0*) Godine.
— The Outermost Dream: Literary Sketches. LC 97-70220. (Graywolf Rediscovery Ser.). 240p. 1997. pap. 12.95 (*1-55597-264-0*) Graywolf.
— Over by the River. LC 76-30608. 256p. 1984. pap. 10.95 (*0-87923-561-1*) Godine.
— So Long, See You Tomorrow. 160p. 1996. pap. 10.00 (*0-679-76720-7*) Random.
— They Came Like Swallows. LC 96-46880. 1997. pap. 12.00 (*0-679-77257-X*) McKay.
— Time Will Darken It, Vol. 1. LC 96-25027. 1997. pap. 13.00 (*0-679-77258-8*) McKay.
Maxwell, William, ed. Thinking: The Expanding Frontier. (Problem Solving Ser.). 304p. 1983. text 59.95 (*0-89859-731-5*) L Erlbaum Assocs.
Maxwell, William E. & Crain, Ernest. Texas Politics Today. 6th ed. Simon, ed. 416p. (C). 1992. text 36.50 (*0-314-89956-1*) West Pub.
— Texas Politics Today. 7th ed. LC 94-3694. 396p. (C). 1995. mass mkt. 37.00 (*0-314-04324-1*) West Pub.
Maxwell, William E., et al. Texas Politics Today. 8th ed. LC 97-24349. (Political Science). (C). 1997. 32.50 (*0-314-12781-X*) Wadsworth Pub.
***Maxwell, William J.** New Negro, Old Left: African-American Writing & Cmmunism Between the Wars. LC 98-52487. (Illus.). 10p. 1999. 49.50 (*0-231-11424-9*) Col U Pr.
— New Negro, Old Left: African-American Writing & Communism Between the Wars. LC 98-52487. (Illus.). 272p. 1999. pap. 17.50 (*0-231-11425-7*) Col U Pr.
Maxwell, William W. Finding Yourself: A Spiritual Journey Through a Florida Garden. (Illus.). 48p. pap. 12.95 (*0-9623313-1-7*) Bok Tower.
Maxx. Mac Without Drugs. 1994. 395.00 (*0-316-99689-0*) Little.
Maxx, Elliot. Oregon's Best Jokes. (Illus.). 96p. (Orig.). 1995. pap. 7.95 (*0-935735-03-8*) Fiasco Productions.
— The Seattle Joke Book III. (Illus.). 128p. (Orig.). 1995. pap. 8.95 (*0-935735-06-2*) Fiasco Productions.
***Maxym, Carol & York, Leslie B.** Teens in Turmoil: A Path to Change for Parents, Adolescents & their Families. LC 99-38963. 268p. 2000. 23.95 (*0-670-88754-4*) Viking Penguin.
Maxym, Lucy. The Lucy Maxym Collection of Russian Lacquer. (Illus.). 50p. (Orig.). 1989. 15.00 (*0-940202-10-7*) Crnrs of the Wrld.
— Russian Lacquer, Legends & Fairy Tales. LC 81-51492. (Illus.). 80p. 1981. 39.00 (*0-940202-01-8*) Crnrs of the Wrld.
— Russian Lacquer, Legends & Fairy Tales, Vol. II. (Illus.). 80p. 1986. 39.00 (*0-940202-03-4*) Crnrs of the Wrld.
Maxymuk, John. Using Desktop Publishing to Create Newsletters, Library Guides & Web Pages: A How-to-Do-It Manual for Librarians. LC 97-3980. (How-to-Do-It Manuals Ser.). 200p. 1997. pap. 55.00 (*1-55570-265-1*) Neal-Schuman.
Maxymuk, John, ed. Finding Government Information on the Internet: A How-To-Do-It Manual. LC 95-30716. 175p. (Orig.). 1995. pap. 49.95 (*1-55570-228-7*) Neal-Schuman.
May. Conversations with Conjunctions. 1994. 59.00 (*0-7616-7191-9*) Commun Skill.
— Economic Social History of Britain. 2nd ed. 1996. pap. text. write for info. (*0-582-25721-2*, Pub. by Addison-Wesley) Longman.
— Effective Writing. 5th ed. LC 98-55174. (Illus.). 288p. (C). 1999. pap. text 26.00 (*0-13-011897-4*) P-H.
— Emergency Medicine. 2nd ed. 1992. 87.50 (*0-316-55186-4*, Little Brwn Med Div) Lppncott W & W.
— Emergency Medicine, Vol. 2. 1992. 87.50 (*0-316-55187-2*, Little Brwn Med Div) Lppncott W & W.
***May.** The Facial Nerve. 2nd ed. LC 99-34435. (Illus.). 912p. 1999. 199.00 (*0-86577-821-3*) Thieme Med Pubs.
May. Social Research Issues, Methods: Issues, Methods & Process. 2nd ed. LC 97-20094. 1997. pap. 24.95 (*0-335-20005-2*) OpUniv Pr.
May, ed. Ethics in the Accounting Curriculum: Cases & Readings. 1990. 45.00 (*0-86539-074-6*) Am Accounting.
May & MacDonald. Financial Accounting. (AB - Accounting Principles Ser.). (C). 1994. 77.95 (*0-538-84498-1*) S-W Pub.
May & Mehlmeister. Student Workbook for Comprehensive Maternity Nursing: Nursing Process & the Childbearing Family. 2nd ed. 272p. 1990. text 15.95 (*0-397-54754-4*) Lppncott W & W.
May, et al. Effective Writing: A Handfbook for Finance People. LC 98-36415. 256p. 1998. pap. text 26.60 (*0-13-759408-9*) P-H.
May, jt. auth. see Spiller.
May, Ena. Close Shave with the Devil. LC 99-211575. 1999. pap. text 15.95 (*1-901866-17-3*, Liplop) Goodfellow.
May, T. Knowing the Social World. LC 98-13161. 1998. 85.00 (*0-335-19768-X*) OpUniv Pr.
May, A. J., jt. auth. see Bird, J. O.
May, A. R. Mental Health Services in Europe. (Offset Publications: No. 23). 1976. pap. text 12.00 (*92-4-170023-8*, 1120023) World Health.
May, A. R., et al. Mental Health of Adolescents & Young Persons. Proceedings of the WHO Technical Conference, Stockholm, 1969. (Public Health Papers: No. 41). 72p. 1971. pap. 5.00 (*92-4-130041-8*, 1110041) World Health.
May, Alex. Britain & Europe since 1945. LC 98-28607. (Seminar Studies in History Ser.). 160p. (C). 1998. pap. 15.73 (*0-582-30778-3*) Longman.
***May, Alex.** Multimedia: Digital Photography. LC 99-54350. (Essential Computers Ser.). 72p. 2000. pap. text 6.95 (*0-7894-5531-5*, D K Ink) DK Pub Inc.
May, Alex & May, Nancy. Bed, Breakfast & Bike Mid-Atlantic: A Cycling Guide to Country Inns. LC 92-60539. (Illus.). 276p. (Orig.). 1992. pap. 14.95 (*0-933855-06-0*) Anacus Pr.
— Ride Guide: South Jersey. 2nd rev. ed. LC 97-77818. (Illus.). 128p. (Orig.). 1998. pap. 12.95 (*0-933855-14-1*) Anacus Pr.
May, Alf. Out of Grimsby. 161p. (C). 1989. text 42.00 (*0-902662-86-4*, Pub. by R K Pubns); pap. text 21.00 (*0-902662-87-2*, Pub. by R K Pubns) St Mut.
***May, Alice G.** Surviving Betrayal: Hope & Help for Women Whose Partners Have Been Unfaithful* 365ons. LC 99-37159. 384p. 1999. pap. 14.00 (*0-06-251804-6*) HarpC.
May, Alice G., jt. auth. see May, Angelo M.
***May, Allan.** Longstreet Highroad Guide to the Northwest Coast. LC 00-104186. (Illus.). 352p. 2000. pap. 18.95 (*1-56352-595-X*) Longstreet.
May, Allan. Longstreet Highroad Guide to the Washington Cascades. LC 99-61768. (Illus.). 352p. 1999. pap. 18.95 (*1-56352-536-4*) Arthritis Found.
***May, Allen R.** Mob Stories. 2000. 19.95 (*1-56072-779-9*, Nova Kroshka Bks) Nova Sci Pubs.
May, Andrew P. Amsterdam Scene: Gay Guide. (Illus.). 192p. 1997. pap. 11.95 (*0-85449-264-X*, Pub. by Gay Mens Pr) LPC InBook.
May, Angelo M. & May, Alice G. The Two Lions of Lyons: The Tale of Two Surgeons - Alexis Carrel & Rene Leriche. rev. ed. (Illus.). 319p. (C). 1994. 49.50 (*0-930329-45-7*) Kabel Pubs.
May, Anne. Epidurals for Childbirth. LC 94-8975. (Oxford Medical Publications). (Illus.). 216p. 1994. text 59.95 (*0-19-262439-3*); pap. text 29.50 (*0-19-262438-5*) OUP.
May, Anne C. Manipulatives for Keyboard Capers. 40p. 1993. 37.95 (*1-884098-03-7*); 20.00 (*1-884098-02-9*) Elijah Co.
May, Annelise & National Conference of State Legislatures Staff. Comparison Of Digital Signature Legislation. LC 98-118323. (Information Policy & Technology Ser.). 1997. write for info. (*1-55516-997-X*) Natl Conf State Legis.
May, Annette A., jt. auth. see Knepflar, Kenneth J.
May, Antionette. Free Spirit. Hickman, Irene, ed. 196p. (Orig.). 1985. pap. 5.95 (*0-915689-07-3*) Hickman Systems.
— Psychic Women. 1984. pap. 6.95 (*0-915689-03-0*) Hickman Systems.
May, Antoinette. Haunted Houses of California. 2nd ed. (Illus.). 208p. 1993. pap. 10.95 (*0-933174-91-8*) Wide World-Tetra.
— The Yucatan: A Guide to the Land of Maya Mysteries. 3rd ed. (Illus.). 296p. (Orig.). 1993. pap. text 10.95 (*0-933174-90-X*) Wide World-Tetra.
May, Antoinette, jt. auth. see Browne, Sylvia.
May, Arthur J. Hapsburg Monarchy, 1867-1914. LC 51-7368. 544p. reprint ed. pap. 168.70 (*0-8357-9162-9*, 200378000033) Bks Demand.
May, Beatrice. Sister to Jane. large type ed. (Historical Romance Ser.). 320p. 1992. 27.99 (*0-7089-2696-7*) Ulverscroft.
May, Bella J. Amputations & Prosthetics: A Case Study Approach. LC 96-15601. (Illus.). 246p. (C). 1996. pap. text 34.95 (*0-8036-0043-7*) Davis Co.
— Home Health & Rehabilitation: Concepts of Care. 2nd ed. LC 98-17364. 368p. 1998. 65.00 (*0-8036-0382-7*) Davis Co.
May, Betty M. Best Little Hors d'oeuvres in Kansas. (Illus.). 81p. (Orig.). 1987. pap. 9.95 (*0-9619522-0-2*) B M May.
May, Bill. I'd Like to Be a Cowboy Poet. 98p. (Orig.). 1997. pap. write for info. (*1-57502-391-1*, P01226) Morris Pubng.
***May, Billie.** A Kiss for Wilhelmina. 181p. 1999. pap. 13.95 (*0-7414-0137-1*) Buy Books.
May, Bonnie, ed. Treasury of Classic Spanish Love Short Stories in Spanish & English. LC 97-15375. (ENG & SPA.). 128p. 1997. 11.95 (*0-7818-0512-0*) Hippocrene Bks.
May, Brian. The Modernist As Pragmatist: E. M. Forster & the Fate of Liberalism. 240p. (C). 1996. 37.50 (*0-8262-1096-1*) U of Mo Pr.
May, Brian, jt. auth. see Tomoda, Takako.
May, Caroline, ed. The American Female Poets. reprint ed. 32.50 (*0-8422-8095-2*) Irvington.
May, Cecilia & Russo, Phyllis. The Great Chefs of Naples. (Illus.). 68p. (Orig.). 1996. ring bd. 18.00 (*0-9656613-0-X*) Great Chefs Naples.
May, Charles. The Short Story. (Studies in Genre). 1995. 33.00 (*0-8057-0953-3*, Twyne) Mac Lib Ref.
— The Short Story: The Reality of Artifice. 1995. pap. 14.95 (*0-8057-9238-4*, Hall Reference) Macmillan.
May, Charles E. Edgar Allan Poe: A Study of the Short Fiction. (Twayne's Studies in Short Fiction: No. 28). 192p. 1991. 29.00 (*0-8057-8337-7*) Macmillan.
— Fiction's Many Worlds. 766p. (C). 1993. pap. text 39.56 (*0-669-27762-2*); teacher ed. 2.66 (*0-669-27765-7*) HM Trade Div.
— Interacting with Essays. (C). 1996. text, teacher ed. 31.56 (*0-669-35525-9*); pap. text 30.36 (*0-669-35524-0*) HM Trade Div.
— Twentieth Century European Short Story: An Annotated Bibliography. (Magill Bibliographies Ser.). 178p. 1989. 42.00 (*0-8108-2807-3*) Scarecrow.
May, Charles E., ed. The New Short Story Theories. LC 94-7037. 363p. (Orig.). (C). 1994. pap. text 16.95 (*0-8214-1087-3*) Ohio U Pr.
— Short Story Theories. LC 75-36982. 265p. 1977. pap. text 9.95 (*0-8214-0221-8*) Ohio U Pr.
May, Charles W. Charles E. Duryea - Automobile Maker. 2nd ed. 202p. 1996. reprint ed. pap. 9.95 (*1-889849-02-2*) Riverbeach Pub.
May, Cheryl. Legacy: Engineering at Kansas State University. (Illus.). 105p. (Orig.). 1983. pap. text 5.00 (*0-9609342-0-0*) College Engineering KS.
May, Chris. The Horse Care Manual: How to Keep Your Horse Healthy, Fit & Happy. 160p. 1994. pap. 16.95 (*0-8120-1133-3*) Barron.
May, Christina R. Pioneer Clothing on the Oregon Trail. LC 98-183244. (Illus.). 90p. 1998. pap. 10.95 (*1-57502-690-2*, PO1950) Morris Pubng.
***May, Christopher.** A Global Political Economy of Intellectual Property Rights: The New Enclosures? LC 99-57173. (Ripe Series in Global Political Economy). 2000. write for info. (*0-415-22904-9*) Routledge.
May, Christopher. Nonlinear Pricing: Theory & Applications. LC 98-37590. (Trading Advantage Ser.). 361p. 1999. 69.95 (*0-471-24551-8*) Wiley.
May, Christopher N. In the Name of War: Judicial Review & the War Powers since 1918. LC 88-9444. 370p. 1989. 46.50 (*0-674-44549-X*) HUP.
— Presidential Defiance of 'Unconstitutional' Laws: Reviving the Royal Prerogative, 86. LC 98-11095. (Contributions in Legal Studies: Vol. 86). 232p. 1998. 59.95 (*0-313-30064-X*, GM0064, Greenwood Pr) Greenwood.
May, Christopher N. & Ides, Allan. Constitutional Law--National Power & Federalism: Examples & Explanations. LC 97-43054. (Examples & Explanations Ser.). 376p. 1998. pap. text. write for info. (*1-56706-635-6*) Panel Pubs.
May, Christopher N., jt. auth. see Ides, Allan.
May, Claire A., jt. auth. see Braine, George.
May, Clayton, ed. Epoxy Resins: Chemistry & Technology. 2nd expanded rev. ed. (Illus.). 1288p. 1987. text 299.00 (*0-8247-7690-9*) Dekker.
May, Clayton A., ed. Chemorheology of Thermosetting Polymers. LC 83-12280. (ACS Symposium Ser.: No. 227). 338p. 1983. lib. bdg. 49.95 (*0-8412-0794-1*) Am Chemical.
— Chemorheology of Thermosetting Polymers. LC 83-12280. (ACS Symposium Ser.: Vol. 227). 335p. 1983. reprint ed. pap. 103.90 (*0-608-03076-7*, 206352900007) Bks Demand.
— Resins for Aerospace. LC 80-15342. (ACS Symposium Ser.: No. 132). 1980. 54.95 (*0-8412-0567-1*) Am Chemical.
— Resins for Aerospace. LC 80-15342. (ACS Symposium Ser.: No. 132). (Illus.). 511p. 1980. reprint ed. pap. 158.50 (*0-608-03234-4*, 206375300007) Bks Demand.
May, Cliff & Sunset Magazine & Books Staff. Western Ranch Houses by Cliff May: A Sunset Book. LC 97-72541. (California Architecture & Architects Ser.: No. 10). (Illus.). 176p. 1997. pap. 32.50 (*0-940512-04-1*) Hennessey.
May, Cliff, jt. auth. see Sunset Magazine Editorial Staff.
May, D. Situating Social Theory. LC 96-23676. 208p. 1996. 82.95 (*0-335-19287-4*) OpUniv Pr.
May, D., jt. ed. see Kunii, Toshiyasu L.
May, D. J. Mr. Marble's Moose. (Illus.). 52p. (J). (ps-3). 1993. 9.99 (*0-8499-0969-4*) Tommy Nelson.
May, Dan. There's an Old Southern Saying: The Wit & Wisdom of Dan May. 130p. (Orig.). 1995. pap. 13.95 (*0-9638911-0-3*) Crabby Keys.
May, Daniel L. Legal Periodicals in English, 6 vols., Set. annuals LC 75-42308. 1976. ring bd., suppl. ed. 525.00 (*0-87802-054-3*) Glanville.
May, Danny & Sharpe, Andy. Everything Wine Book. LC 97-18140. (Illus.). 352p. 1997. pap. 12.95 (*1-55850-808-2*) Adams Media.
May, Darcy. Elves & Fairies Stickers. (Illus.). (J). (gr. 4-7). 1993. pap. 1.00 (*0-486-27717-8*) Dover.
— Twelve Days of Christmas. (Illus.). 12p. (J). 1993. 5.00 (*1-55670-336-8*) Stewart Tabori & Chang.
— Victorian Dollhouse Sticker Picture. 1998. 4.50 (*0-486-40375-0*) Dover.
May, Darcy. The Nutcracker Ballet. (Read with Me Paperback Ser.). 32p. (J). (ps-3). 1994. pap. 2.99 (*0-590-48197-5*, Cartwheel) Scholastic Inc.
May, Daryl & Bansemer, Roger. Rachael's Splendifilous Adventure. Little, Carl, ed. LC 91-66032. (Illus.). 40p. (Orig.). (J). (ps-4). 1992. 10.95 (*0-932433-83-9*) Windswept Hse.

M

An Asterisk (*) at the beginning of an entry indicates that the title is appearing for the first time.

M

May, David. Madrugada. (Orig.). 1997. mass mkt. 6.95 (*1-56333-574-3*, Badboy) Masquerade.

May, Dawn. Aboriginal Labour & the Cattle Industry: Queensland from White Settlement to the Present. (Studies in Australian History: No. 13). (Illus.). 254p. (C). 1994. text 64.95 (*0-521-46506-0*) Cambridge U Pr.

May, Dean. Utah: A People's History. LC 87-17898. (Bonneville Bks.). (Illus.). 1987. pap. 15.95 (*0-87480-284-9*) U of Utah Pr.

May, Dean L. Three Frontiers: Family, Land, & Society in the American West, 1850-1900. LC 93-43560. (Interdisciplinary Perspectives on Modern History Ser.). (Illus.). 329p. (C). 1994. text 49.95 (*0-521-43499-8*) Cambridge U Pr.

— Three Frontiers: Family, Land, & Society in the American West, 1850-1900. (Interdisciplinary Perspectives on Modern History Ser.). (Illus.). 329p. 1997. pap. 18.95 (*0-521-58575-9*) Cambridge U Pr.

May, Debra H. Everyday Letters for Busy People: Hundreds of Sample Letters You Can Copy or Adapt on a Minute's Notice. LC 98-19879. 250p. 1998. pap. 15.99 (*1-56414-339-2*) Career Pr Inc.

— Proofreading Plain & Simple. LC 97-8273. (In Plain English Ser.). 192p. (Orig.). 1997. pap. 11.99 (*1-56414-291-4*) Career Pr Inc.

May, Derwent. The New Times Nature Diary. (Illus.). 127p. 1995. 18.95 (*0-86051-850-7*, Robson-Parkwest) Parkwest Pubns.

— The New Times Nature Diary. LC 94-77100. (Illus.). 128p. 1996. pap. 9.95 (*0-86051-946-5*, Robson-Parkwest) Parkwest Pubns.

***May, Dorothy.** Archetypal Reiki: Book & Cards for Spiritual, Emotional & Physical Healing. LC 99-40403. (Illus.). 112p. 2000. pap. 22.95 (*1-885203-90-X*, Pub. by Jrny Editions) Tuttle Pubng.

May, Dorothy. Codependency: PowerLoss, SoulLoss. LC 94-60569. 320p. 1994. pap. 12.95 (*0-8091-3532-9*) Paulist Pr.

— Codependency: PowerLoss SoulLoss. 300p. 1994. pap. 12.95 (*1-882195-02-7*) Whales Tale Pr.

***May, Dorothy.** How Do You Do It? The Key to Satisfying Relationships in Every Area of Life. 80p. 1999. pap. 6.95 (*1-58169-023-1*, Gazelle Pr) Genesis Comm Inc.

May, Dorothy. Windblown: An Unveiling of the Soul. 118p. 1998. pap. 12.50 (*1-892193-00-0*, Patchwrk Pr) Tenacity Pr.

May, Douglas B. Contracting Out Instructional Services: Education's New Frontier. (Issue Papers: No. 18-93). 10p. 1993. pap. write for info. (*1-57655-070-2*) Independ Inst.

— To Improve School Productivity, Bid Out Instructional Services. 10p. 1989. pap. text 8.00 (*1-57655-084-2*) Independ Inst.

May Dugan Center Staff & Horton, Charlene. Raising Money & Having Fun (Sort Of) A "How-to" Book for Small Non-Profit Groups. LC 91-66345. (Illus.). 132p. 1991. pap. text 18.95 (*0-9630760-0-0*) M Dugan Ctr.

May, Ed, ed. Contemporary Authors, Vol. 109. 552p. 1983. text 150.00 (*0-8103-1909-8*) Gale.

May, Edgar. The Wasted Americans: Cost of Our Welfare Dilemma. LC 80-19500. (Illus.). 227p. 1980. reprint ed. lib. bdg. 65.00 (*0-313-22674-1*, MAWAM, Greenwood Pr) Greenwood.

May, Elaine. Adaptation. 1970. pap. 3.25 (*0-8222-0009-0*) Dramatists Play.

— The Birdcage: The Shooting Script. LC 96-28600. 176p. 1997. pap. 14.95 (*1-55704-277-2*, Pub. by Newmarket) Norton.

May, Elaine T. Barren in the Promised Land: Childless Americans & the Pursuit of Happiness. (Illus.). 336p. 1997. 14.95 (*0-674-06182-9*) HUP.

— Great Expectations: Marriage & Divorce in Post-Victorian America. LC 80-10590. (Illus.). 208p. 1983. pap. text 11.95 (*0-226-51170-7*) U Ch Pr.

— Homeward Bound: American Families in the Cold War Era. 304p. 1990. pap. 18.50 (*0-465-03055-6*, Pub. by Basic) HarpC.

— Pushing the Limits: American Women 1940-1961, Vol. 9. (Young Oxford History of Women in the United States Ser.). (Illus.). 144p. (J). 1998. reprint ed. pap. 10.95 (*0-19-512407-3*) OUP.

May, Elaine Tyler, jt. ed. see Wagnleitner, Reinhold.

May, Eleanor R. Unlisted Numbers. 59p. (Orig.). 1995. pap. 10.00 (*1-880994-15-1*) Mt Olive Coll Pr.

May, Elizabeth, ed. Musics of Many Cultures: An Introduction. LC 76-50251. (Illus.). 454p. 1980. pap. 27.50 (*0-520-04778-8*, Pub. by U CA Pr) Cal Prin Full Svc.

May, Ernest, ed. see Godson, Roy S.

May, Ernest, jt. ed. see Stauffer, George B.

May, Ernest, jt. ed. see Stauffer, George.

May, Ernest R. American Imperialism: A Speculative Essay. 1991. 14.95 (*1-879176-03-3*) Imprint Pubns.

— Imperial Democracy: The Emergence of America As a Great Power. 1991. 15.95 (*1-879176-04-1*) Imprint Pubns.

— The Lessons of the Past: The Use & Misuse of History in American Foreign Policy. LC 73-82670. 236p. 1975. reprint ed. pap. text 10.95 (*0-19-501890-7*) OUP.

— The Making of the Monroe Doctrine. (Illus.). 328p. (C). 1992. pap. 14.95 (*0-674-54341-6*) Belknap Pr.

— Strange Victory: Hitler's Conquest of France. LC 99-53619. (Illus.). 384p. 2000. 26.00 (*0-8090-8906-8*) Hill & Wang.

May, Ernest R., ed. Knowing One's Enemies: Intelligence Assessment Before the Two World Wars. LC 84-42573. 577p. reprint ed. pap. 178.90 (*0-7837-0239-6*, 204054700017) Bks Demand.

— NSC Sixty-Eight: Blueprint for American Strategy in the Cold War. 176p. 1993. text 35.00 (*0-312-09445-0*); pap. text 15.95 (*0-312-06637-6*) St Martin.

May, Ernest R. & Fairbank, John K., eds. America's China Trade in Historical Perspective: The Chinese & American Performance. (Studies in American-East Asian Relations: No. 11). 390p. 1986. 27.50 (*0-674-03075-3*) HUP.

May, Ernest R. & Fraser, Janet. Campaign Seventy-Two: The Managers Speak. LC 73-85182. 224p. 1973. 29.00 (*0-674-09141-8*); pap. 15.50 (*0-674-09143-4*) HUP.

May, Ernest R. & Laiou, Angeliki E. The Dumbarton Oaks Conversations & the United Nations, 1944-1994. LC 97-48477. 144p. 1998. 20.00 (*0-88402-255-2*) Dumbarton Oaks.

May, Ernest R. & Thomson, James C., Jr., eds. American-East Asian Relations: A Survey. LC 70-188970. (Harvard Studies in American-East Asian Relations: No. 1). 440p. reprint ed. pap. 136.40 (*0-7837-4141-3*, 205796400011) Bks Demand.

May, Ernest R. & Zelikow, Philip D., eds. The Kennedy Tapes: Inside the White House During the Cuban Missile Crisis. LC 97-14216. (Illus.). 800p. 1997. 35.00 (*0-674-17926-9*) HUP.

— The Kennedy Tapes: Inside the White House During the Cuban Missile Crisis. 468p. 1998. pap. 16.95 (*0-674-17927-7*) HUP.

May, Ernest R., jt. auth. see Neustadt, Richard E.

May, F. Geology of the Invermoriston District: Memoir for 1:50,000 Geological Sheet 73W (Scotland) (Memoirs of the Geo. Survey of Gt. Brit (Scotland) Ser.: No. 81027261). (Illus.). x, 78p. 1998. pap. 70.00 (*0-11-884532-2*, HM45322, Pub. by Statnry Office) Balogh.

— Music Director's Guide to the Drum Set. 32p. 1992. pap. 7.95 (*0-7935-1791-5*, 06621760) H Leonard.

May, F. J. The Book of Acts & Church Growth. 1990. pap. 7.99 (*0-87148-113-8*) Pathway Pr.

May, F. L. Catalogue of Laces & Embroideries in the Collection. (Illus.). 1936. 10.00 (*0-87535-038-0*) Hispanic Soc.

May, Fiona, jt. auth. see Manias, Paul.

May, Florence. The Life of Johannes Brahms, 2 vols., Set. 1976. lib. bdg. 79.00 (*0-403-03630-5*) Scholarly.

— The Life of Johannes Brahms, 2 vols., Set. 1988. reprint ed. lib. bdg. 99.00 (*0-7812-0192-6*) Rprt Serv.

May, Florence L. Hispanic Lace & Lacemaking. 1980. reprint ed. 12.00 (*0-87535-048-8*) Hispanic Soc.

May, Frances. The Poets' Cat. 69p. 1990. pap. 7.00 (*1-878660-09-8*) Fireweed WI.

— Singposts, New & Selected Poems. 124p. 1986. pap. 14.95 (*1-887649-05-0*) Black Hat Pr.

May, Frank. Reading As Communication. 5th ed. LC 97-3811. 557p. 1997. 72.00 (*0-13-494683-9*) P-H.

***May, Frank B.** Unraveling the Seven Myths of Reading &Counteracting Their Effects: Assessment & Intervention Practices Forcounteracting Their Effects. 224p. 2000. pap. text 44.00 (*0-205-30914-3*) Allyn.

May, Frank P., jt. auth. see Tyner, Mack.

May, Gabriele S. Tradition im Umbruch: Zur Sophokles-Rezeption im Deutschen Vormarz. (American University Studies: Germanic Languages & Literature: Ser. I, Vol. 76). 163p. (C). 1989. text 32.95 (*0-8204-1007-1*) P Lang Pubng.

May, Gary. Un-American Activities: The Trials of William Remington. LC 93-25321. (Illus.). 416p. (C). 1994. 30.00 (*0-19-504980-2*) OUP.

May, Gayl L., et al, eds. Space: A Vital Stimulus to Our National Well-Being, 31st Goddard Memorial Symposium, March 9-10, 1983, Arlington, Virginia, & World Space Programs & Fiscal Reality, 30th Goddard Memorial Symposium, April 9-10, 1992, Alexandria, Virginia. LC 95-175703. (Science & Technology Ser.: Vol. 83). (Illus.). 334p. 1994. 70.00 (*0-87703-389-7*, Am Astronaut Soc); pap. 50.00 (*0-87703-390-0*, Am Astronaut Soc) Univelt Inc.

— Space Exploitation & Utilization, First AAS/JRS Symposium, Dec. 15-19, 1985, Honolulu, HI. LC 57-43769. (Advances in the Astronautical Sciences Ser.: Vol. 60). (Illus.). 740p. 1986. 70.00 (*0-87703-254-8*, Am Astronaut Soc); pap. 55.00 (*0-87703-255-6*, Am Astronaut Soc) Univelt Inc.

May, Georg. Das Recht des Gottesdienstes in der Diozese Mainz zur Zeit von Bischhof Joseph Ludwig Colmar (1802-1818), Band 2. (Kanonistische Studien und Texte Ser.: Vol. 37). (GER.). xii, 692p. 1987. 60.00 (*90-6032-290-8*, Pub. by B R Gruner) Humanities.

May, George. Doctor's Secret Journal: A True Account of Violence at Fort Michilimackinac. (Illus.). 47p. 1960. pap. 3.00 (*0-911872-30-2*) Mackinac St Hist Pks.

— Massac Biographies. (Illus.). 209p. 1998. 10.00 (*0-9605566-2-1*, 500) G W May.

— Stewards of the State: The Governors of Michigan. Kirk, Robert, ed. (Illus.). 193p. 1987. 20.95 (*0-9614344-2-2*) Historical Soc MI.

— War 1812. (Illus.). 43p. (Orig.). 1962. pap. 3.00 (*0-911872-28-0*) Mackinac St Hist Pks.

May, George O. Financial Accounting: A Distillation of Experience. 1972. reprint ed. text 30.00 (*0-914348-05-1*) Scholars Bk.

— Twenty-Five Years of Accounting Responsibility, 1911-1936, Vols. I & II. Hunt, Carleton, ed. 1971. reprint ed. text 35.00 (*0-914348-03-5*) Scholars Bk.

May, George S. A Most Unique Machine: The Michigan Origins of the American Automobile Industry. LC 74-19230. (Illus.). 406p. reprint ed. pap. 125.90 (*0-608-10735-2*, 201273600083) Bks Demand.

May, George S., ed. Automobile Industry, 1896-1920. (Encyclopedia of American Business History & Biography Ser.). 1990. 99.00 (*0-8160-2084-1*) Facts on File.

— Automobile Industry, 1920-1980. (Encyclopedia of American Business History & Biography Ser.). (Illus.). 544p. 1989. 99.00 (*0-8160-2083-3*) Facts on File.

— Michigan Civil War History: An Annotated Bibliography. LC 61-14050. 140p. reprint ed. pap. 43.40 (*0-7837-3670-3*, 204354400009) Bks Demand.

May, George S., jt. auth. see Dunbar, Willis F.

May, George W. Down Illinois Rivers. (Illus.). 400p. 1981. 16.00 (*0-9605566-5-6*) G W May.

— History of Massac County, Illinois. (Illus.). 232p. 1983. reprint ed. 6.00 (*0-9605566-4-8*) G W May.

— History Papers on Massac County, Illinois. (Illus.). 200p. 1990. 12.00 (*0-9605566-7-2*) G W May.

— Massac County, 1955 to 1982: Accompanies History of Massac County. 1983. pap. 1.00 (*0-9605566-6-4*) G W May.

— Walter West's Probation: The Birth of Massac County, a Novel of the Regulator-Flathead War. (Illus.). 322p. 1993. 12.00 (*0-9605566-8-0*) G W May.

May, Gerald G. Addiction & Grace: Love & Spirituality in the Healing of Addictions. LC 88-45147. (Illus.). 208p. 1991. reprint ed. pap. 13.00 (*0-06-065537-2*, Pub. by Harper SF) HarpC.

— The Awakened Heart: Living Beyond Addiction. LC 91-55086. 272p. 1993. reprint ed. pap. 15.00 (*0-06-065473-2*, Pub. by Harper SF) HarpC.

— Care of Mind/Care of Spirit: A Psychiatrist Explores Spiritual Direction. LC 91-58190. 256p. 1992. reprint ed. pap. 14.00 (*0-06-065567-4*, Pub. by Harper SF) HarpC.

— Simply Sane: The Spirituality of Mental Health. enl. ed. LC 93-2581. 176p. 1993. pap. 11.95 (*0-8245-1366-5*) Crossroad NY.

— Will & Spirit: A Contemplative Psychology. LC 82-47751. (Illus.). 368p. 1987. pap. 22.00 (*0-06-250582-3*, Pub. by Harper SF) HarpC.

May, Gerald R. & Gardiner, Richard. Clinical Imaging of the Pancreas. LC 86-42592. (Clinical Imaging of the Gastrointestinal Tract Ser.). 192p. 1987. reprint ed. pap. 59.60 (*0-608-00359-X*, 206107600007) Bks Demand.

May, Gerhard. Creatio Ex Nihilo: The Doctrine of 'Creation Out of Nothing' in Early Christian Thought. Worral, A. S., tr. from GER. 216p. 1994. text 44.95 (*0-567-09695-5*, Pub. by T & T Clark) Bks Intl VA.

— Schoepfung aus dem Nichts: Die Entstehung der Lehre von der Creatio Ex Nihilo. (Arbeiten zur Kirchengeschichte Ser.: Vol. 48). (C). 1978. 86.95 (*3-11-007204-1*) De Gruyter.

May, Gerhard, jt. auth. see Wilson, Joanna.

May, Gideon S. The Croft & the Ceilidh. 1980. pap. 30.00 (*0-907526-60-8*, Pub. by Alloway Publ) St Mut.

— Gideon's Way. 1980. pap. 30.00 (*0-907526-61-6*, Pub. by Alloway Publ) St Mut.

— The Kilt for Keeps. 1980. pap. 30.00 (*0-907526-59-4*, Pub. by Alloway Publ) St Mut.

May, Glenn A. Battle for Batangas: A Philippine Province at War. LC 90-45074. (Illus.). 405p. 1991. reprint ed. pap. 125.60 (*0-608-07833-6*, 205400900010) Bks Demand.

— Inventing a Hero: The Posthumour Re-Creation of Andres Bonifacio. LC 96-85119. (Monographs). 200p. (C). 1996. pap. 19.95 (*1-881261-19-0*); lib. bdg. 40.00 (*1-881261-18-2*) U Wisc Ctr SE Asian.

— A Past Recovered. 267p. (Orig.). (C). 1987. pap. 17.50 (*971-10-0260-4*, Pub. by New Day Pub) Cellar.

— Social Engineering in the Philippines: The Aims, Execution & Impact of American Colonial Policy, 1900-1913, 2. LC 79-7467. (Contributions in Comparative Colonial Studies: No. 2). 268p. 1980. 65.00 (*0-313-20978-2*, MAE, Greenwood Pr) Greenwood.

May, Gordon S. The Encyclopedia of Journal Entries. unabridged ed. 758p. 1994. pap. text 80.50 (*1-884826-00-8*) AIPB.

May, Graham H. The Future Is Ours: Foreseeing, Managing & Creating the Future. LC 96-15310. (Studies on the Twenty-First Century). 272p. 1996. 69.50 (*0-275-95678-4*, Praeger Pubs); pap. 22.95 (*0-275-95679-2*, Praeger Pubs) Greenwood.

May, Hal, ed. Contemporary Authors, Vol. 119. 600p. 1986. text 150.00 (*0-8103-1919-5*) Gale.

— Contemporary Authors, Vol. 120. 760p. 1987. text 150.00 (*0-8103-1920-9*) Gale.

— Contemporary Authors, Vol. 121. 475p. 1987. text 150.00 (*0-8103-1921-7*) Gale.

— Contemporary Authors, Vol. 122. 500p. 1987. text 150.00 (*0-8103-1922-5*) Gale.

May, Hal & Evory, Ann, eds. Contemporary Authors, Vol. 107. 600p. 1983. text 150.00 (*0-8103-1907-1*) Gale.

— Contemporary Authors, Vol. 108. 824p. 1983. text 150.00 (*0-8103-1908-X*) Gale.

— Contemporary Authors, Vol. 110. LC 62-52046. 833p. 1984. text 150.00 (*0-8103-1910-1*) Gale.

— Contemporary Authors, Vol. 111. LC 62-52046. 528p. 1984. text 150.00 (*0-8103-1911-X*) Gale.

— Contemporary Authors, Vol. 112. LC 62-52046. 528p. 1984. text 150.00 (*0-8103-1912-8*) Gale.

— Contemporary Authors, Vol. 113. LC 65-52046. 536p. 1985. text 150.00 (*0-8103-1913-6*) Gale.

— Contemporary Authors, Vol. 114. 792p. 1985. text 150.00 (*0-8103-1914-4*) Gale.

— Contemporary Authors, Vol. 115. LC 62-52046. 492p. 1985. text 150.00 (*0-8103-1915-2*) Gale.

— Contemporary Authors, Vol. 116. 600p. 1986. text 150.00 (*0-8103-1916-0*) Gale.

— Contemporary Authors, Vol. 117. 800p. 1986. text 150.00 (*0-8103-1917-9*) Gale.

— Contemporary Authors, Vol. 118. 500p. 1986. text 150.00 (*0-8103-1918-7*) Gale.

May, Hal & Lesniak, James. Contemporary Authors: New Revision Series, Vol. 36. (New Revision Ser.). 500p. 1992. text 150.00 (*0-8103-1990-X*) Gale.

— Contemporary Authors Vol. 35: Index, Vol. 35. rev. ed. 500p. 1991. text 150.00 (*0-8103-1996-9*) Gale.

— Contemporary Authors Vol. 37: Index, Vol. 37. rev. ed. 500p. 1992. text 150.00 (*0-8103-1997-7*) Gale.

May, Hal & Lesniak, James, eds. Contemporary Authors, Vol. 27. (New Revision Ser.). 500p. 1989. text 150.00 (*0-8103-1981-0*) Gale.

— Contemporary Authors, Vol. 28. (New Revision Ser.). 500p. 1989. text 150.00 (*0-8103-1982-9*) Gale.

— Contemporary Authors, Vol. 29. (New Revision Ser.). 500p. 1990. text 150.00 (*0-8103-1983-7*) Gale.

May, Hal & Straub, Deborah A., eds. Contemporary Authors, New Revision Series, Vol. 25. (New Revision Ser.). 500p. 1988. text 150.00 (*0-8103-1979-9*) Gale.

May, Hal & Trosky, Susan M. Contemporary Authors, Vol. 124. 500p. 1988. text 150.00 (*0-8103-1924-1*) Gale.

May, Hal & Trosky, Susan M., eds. Contemporary Authors, Vol. 123. 488p. 1988. text 150.00 (*0-8103-1923-3*) Gale.

— Contemporary Authors, Vol. 125. 500p. 1988. text 150.00 (*0-8103-1950-0*) Gale.

May, Hal, ed. see Gale Research Staff.

May, Harold L., ed. Emergency Medicine, 2 vols. 2nd ed. 2416p. 1992. text 75.00 (*0-316-55185-6*) Lppncott W & W.

May, Harriett J. Enterostomal Therapy. fac. ed. LC 76-19894. (Illus.). 286p. pap. 88.70 (*0-7837-7195-9*, 204710400005) Bks Demand.

May, Harvey. The Beswick Price Guide. 3rd ed. (Illus.). 144p. 1995. pap. 23.95 (*1-870703-11-1*, Pub. by Francis Jos Pubns) Krause Pubns.

May-Hayes, Gila. Effective Defense: The Woman, the Plan, the Gun. (Illus.). 200p. (Orig.). 1994. pap. 13.95 (*1-885036-01-9*) FAS Bks.

May, Helen. The Discovery of Early Childhood. LC 97-161522. 264p. 1997. pap. 29.95 (*1-86940-166-2*, Pub. by Auckland Univ) Paul & Co Pubs.

May, Henry F. The Divided Heart: Essays on Protestantism & the Enlightment in America. 240p. 1991. text 50.00 (*0-19-505899-2*) OUP.

— The End of American Innocence: A Study of the First Years of Our Own Time, 1912-1917. LC 93-33225. 439p. 1994. 57.50 (*0-231-09652-6*); pap. 22.00 (*0-231-09653-4*) Col U Pr.

— The Enlightenment in America. LC 75-32349. 448p. 1978. pap. text 24.95 (*0-19-502367-6*) OUP.

— Three Faces of Berkeley: Competing Ideologies in the Wheeler Era, 1899-1919. Brentano, Carroll & Rothblatt, Sheldon, eds. LC 93-30444. (Chapters in the History of the University of California Ser.: No. 1). 53p. (Orig.). 1994. pap. 10.00 (*0-87772-342-7*) UCB IGS.

May, Henry W. A Treatise of the Statutes of Elizabeth Against Fraudulent Conveyances: The Bills of Sale Registration Acts & the Law of Voluntary Dispositions of Property Independently of Those Statutes with an Appendix Containing the above Acts & the Married Women's Property Act, 1870, Also Some Unpublished Cases (1700-1733) xlviii, 564p. 1998. reprint ed. 185.00 (*1-56169-378-2*) Gaunt.

May, Herbert G., ed. Oxford Bible Atlas. 3rd ed. (Illus.). 144p. 1985. 30.00 (*0-19-143452-3*); pap. 21.95 (*0-19-143451-5*) OUP.

May, Herbert Gordon. Material Remains of Megiddo Cult. 1972. lib. bdg. 5.00 (*0-226-51177-4*) U Ch Pr.

May, Huguette D. & Smith, Anthea. Finding Charm in Charm City: Affectionate Views of Baltimore. LC 98-11466. 192p. 1998. 29.95 (*0-8018-5929-8*) Johns Hopkins.

May, Irvin M., Jr. Marvin Jones: The Public Life of an Agrarian Advocate. LC 79-5282. (Centennial Series of the Association of Former Students: No. 8). (Illus.). 312p. 1980. 29.95 (*0-89096-093-3*) Tex A&M Univ Pr.

May, Irvin M., jt. auth. see Dethloff, Henry C.

May, Isobel. Italian-English - English-Italian Dictionary. (ENG & ITA.). 672p. 1988. 39.50 (*0-87557-045-3*) Saphrograph.

May, J. Divers. (Illus.). (J). 1996. mass mkt. 13.95 (*0-340-64906-2*, Pub. by Hodder & Stought Ltd) Trafalgar.

May, J. C. & Brown, F., eds. Biological Product Freeze-Drying & Formulation. (Developments in Biological Standardization Ser.: Vol. 74). (Illus.). x, 382p. 1992. pap. 61.00 (*3-8055-5466-4*) S Karger.

May, J. J. Danforth Genealogy: Nicholas Danforth of Framingham, England & Cambridge, Mass. (1589-1638) & William of Newbury, Mass. (1640-1771) & Their Descendants. 492p. 1989. reprint ed. pap. 62.00 (*0-8328-0453-3*); reprint ed. lib. bdg. 72.00 (*0-8328-0452-5*) Higginson Bk Co.

May, J. L., ed. see France, Anatole, pseud.

May, J. O., ed. Roofs & Roofing: New Materials, Industrial Applications, Uses & Performance. 440p. 1988. text 101.00 (*0-470-21109-1*) P-H.

May, J. P. E-Zero-Zero Ring Spaces & F-Zero-Zero Ring Spectra. (Lecture Notes in Mathematics Ser.: Vol. 577). 1977. 31.95 (*0-387-08136-4*) Spr-Verlag.

— The Geometry of Iterated Loop Spaces. LC 72-85090. (Lecture Notes in Mathematics Ser.: Vol. 271). ix, 175p. 1972. 34.95 (*0-387-05904-0*) Spr-Verlag.

May, J. P., jt. auth. see Greenlees, J. P.

May, J. Peter. Classifying Spaces & Fibrations. (Memoirs Ser.: No. 1/155). 98p. 1989. reprint ed. pap. 19.00 (*0-8218-1855-4*, MEMO/1/155) Am Math.

***May, J. Peter.** A Concise Course in Algebraic Topology. LC 99-29613. (Lectures in Mathematics). vii, 247p. 1999. pap. text 18.00 (*0-226-51183-9*) U Ch Pr.

May, J. Peter. Concise Course in Algebraic Topology. LC 99-29613. (Chicago Lectures in Mathematics). vii, 247p. 1999. lib. bdg. 40.00 (*0-226-51182-0*) U Ch Pr.

— Simplicial Objects in Algebraic Topology. LC 82-51078. (Chicago Lectures in Mathematics). viii, 170p. (C). 1992. pap. text 26.50 (*0-226-51181-2*) U Ch Pr.

An Asterisk (*) at the beginning of an entry indicates that the title is appearing for the first time.

May, J. Peter & Thomas, Charles B., eds. The Selected Works of J. Frank Adams, Vol. 1. 552p. 1992. text 90.00 (*0-521-41063-0*) Cambridge U Pr.

May, J. Peter, et al. Equivariant Homotopy & Cohomology Theory: Dedicated to the Memory of Robert J. Piacenza. LC 96-28298. (Regional Conference Series in Mathematics: Vol. 91). 366p. 1996. pap. 49.00 (*0-8218-0319-0*, CBMS/91) Am Math.

May, J. Peter, jt. auth. see Gugenheim, V. M.

May, J. Peter, ed. see Adams, J. Frank.

May, J. R. & Shahinpoor, Mo, eds. High Pressure Shock Compression of Solids. LC 92-37371. (High Pressure Shock Compression of Materials Ser.). 464p. 1993. 139.95 (*0-387-97964-6*) Spr-Verlag.

May, Jacob L., jt. ed. see Gorayska, Barbara.

May, James F., ed. The Citizen's Guide to U. S. Supreme Court Opinions, 1996-97 Term. LC 98-11517. 832p. 1998. pap. 79.00 (*1-884925-62-6*) Toucan Valley.

May, James Lewis, ed. see France, Anatole, pseud.

May, James M. Trials of Character: The Eloquence of Ciceronian Ethos. LC 87-13884. viii, 216p. (C). 1988. 45.00 (*0-8078-1759-7*) U of NC Pr.

May, James M., jt. auth. see Groton, Anne H.

May, James V. Mental Diseases: A Public Health Problem. Grob, Gerald N., ed. LC 78-22574. (Historical Issues in Mental Health Ser.). 1980. reprint ed. lib. bdg. 40.95 (*0-405-11927-5*) Ayer.

May, Jan. Equus Caballus-On Horses & Handling. 1995. 59.00 (*0-85131-616-6*, Pub. by J A Allen) St Mut.

May, Janet G. Return to Chewelah: A Story of Innocence & Loss. LC 97-12093. 256p. 1997. pap. 11.95 (*0-9641357-5-2*) Storm Peak.

May, Janice. The Texas State Constitution: A Reference Guide, 26. LC 96-539. (Reference Guides to the State Constitutions of the United States: No. 26). 504p. 1996. lib. bdg. 99.50 (*0-313-26637-9*, Greenwood Pr) Greenwood.

May, Jayne & Murdock, Dick. Love Lines. 4th ed. 130p. 1978. pap. 5.00 (*0-932916-01-5*) May-Murdock.

May, Jeffery. Dragonby: Report on Excavations at an Iron Age & Romano-British Settlement in North Lincolnshire, 2 vols. (Monographs in Archaeology: Vol. 61). (Illus.). 728p. 1996. 120.00 (*1-900188-14-7*, Pub. by Oxbow Bks) David Brown.

May, Jeffrey A., jt. ed. see Abbott, Patrick L.

May, Jeffrey V., jt. auth. see Keel, Brooks A.

May, Jerry, jt. ed. see Muir, Roy.

***May, Jesse.** The Gambler's Guide to the World: The Insider Scoop from a Professional Player on Finding the Action, Beating the Odds & Living It up Around the Globe. LC 00-31188. (Illus.). 400p. 2000. pap. 17.50 (*0-7679-0552-0*) Broadway BDD.

May, Jesse. Shut up & Deal. LC 97-34619. 224p. 1998. pap. 12.95 (*0-385-48940-4*, Anchor NY) Doubleday.

May, Jill P. Children's Literature & Critical Theory: Reading & Writing for Understanding. 264p. (C). 1995. text 41.95 (*0-19-509584-7*); pap. text 25.95 (*0-19-509585-5*) OUP.

— Lloyd Alexander. (Twayne's United States Authors Ser.: No. 576). 200p. 1991. 21.95 (*0-8057-7622-2*, Twyne) Mac Lib Ref.

May, Jill P., jt. ed. see Nodelman, Perry.

May, Jim. The Boo Baby Girl Meets the Ghost of Mable's Gable. LC 92-72702. (Illus.). 32p. (J). (ps-5). 1992. lib. bdg. 14.95 (*1-878925-03-2*) Brotherstone Pubs.

— The Farm on Nippersink Creek. 192p. 1993. 18.95 (*0-87483-339-6*) August Hse.

— Farm on Nippersink Creek. (gr. 6 up). 1996. pap. text 12.95 (*0-87483-446-5*) August Hse.

May, Joan C., jt. auth. see Rey, Louis.

May, Joe, compiled by. The Way We Were: A Pictorial History of Clark County, Arkansas. (Illus.). 134p. 1996. 35.00 (*0 88107-260-5*) Curtis Media.

May, John. Baccarat for the Clueless: A Beginner's Guide to Playing & Winning. LC 98-19278. (Illus.). 1998. pap. 12.00 (*0-8184-0604-6*, L Stuart) Carol Pub Group.

— A Declaration of the Estate of Clothing Now Used Within This Realme of England. LC 71-171775. (English Experience Ser.: No. 400). 60p. 1971. reprint ed. 20.00 (*90-221-0400-1*) Walter J Johnson.

***May, John.** Get the Edge at Blackjack: Revolutionary Advantage Play Methods that Work. 160p. 2000. pap. 13.95 (*1-56625-151-6*) Bonus Books.

May, John. Pluralism & the Religions: The Theological & Political Dimensions. LC 98-187158. 99p. 1998. pap. text 17.95 (*0-304-70259-5*) Continuum.

— Reference Wales. LC 95-137131. 300p. 1994. pap. 19.95 (*0-7083-1234-9*, Pub. by Univ Wales Pr) Paul & Co Pubs.

— The RIF Survival Handbook: How to Manage Your Money if You're Unemployed. LC 82-80357. 132p. (Orig.). 1982. pap. 4.95 (*0-9605750-2-2*) Tilden Pr.

May, John & Whittle, Judy. Symantec C++ for the Macintosh: The Basics. 1995. pap. 34.95 incl. disk (*1-55828-276-9*, MIS Pr) IDG Bks.

— Symantec C++ for Windows: The Basics. LC 94-17483. 1994. pap. 29.95 incl. disk (*1-55828-327-7*, MIS Pr) IDG Bks.

May, John G., compiled by. Historical Studies in the Physical Sciences: A Subject Index to Vols. 1-10, 1969-1979. LC 84-51371. 51p. (Orig.). 1984. pap. 3.00 (*0-918102-11-1*) U Cal Hist Sci Tech.

May, John R. The New Image of Religious Film. LC 97-5897. (Communication, Culture & Theology Ser.). (Illus.). 288p. (Orig.). 1997. pap. 24.95 (*1-55612-761-8*, LL1761) Sheed & Ward WI.

— The Pruning Word: The Parables of Flannery O'Connor. LC 75-19878. 204p. reprint ed. pap. 63.30 (*0-608-14225-5*, 202207500024) Bks Demand.

— Toward a New Earth: Apocalypse in the American Novel. LC 72-3510. 264p. 1972. reprint ed. pap. 81.90 (*0-608-00891-5*, 206168500010) Bks Demand.

May, John R., ed. Image & Likeness: Religious Visions in American Film Classics. 1991. pap. 14.95 (*0-8091-3286-9*) Paulist Pr.

May, John R. & Bird, Michael, eds. Religion in Film. LC 81-23983. (Illus.). 276p. 1982. pap. text 18.00 (*0-87049-368-X*) U of Tenn Pr.

May, John W. Law of Crimes. xxii, 239p. 1985. reprint ed. 35.00 (*0-8377-0823-0*, Rothman) W S Hein.

May, Jon. Divers: From Piper Alpha to the Gulf War, a Deep Sea Story. 178p. 1996. 35.00 (*0-340-63529-0*, Pub. by Hodder & Stought Ltd) Trafalgar.

May, Judith V. & Wildavsky, Aaron B., eds. The Policy Cycle. LC 78-15351. (Sage Yearbooks in Politics & Public Policy Ser.: No. 5). (Illus.). 332p. reprint ed. pap. 103.00 (*0-8357-4775-1*, 203771200009) Bks Demand.

May, Julian. Billie Jean King, Tennis Champion. LC 74-82744. 46 p. 1974. write for info. (*0-913940-09-7*, Crstwood Hse) Silver Burdett Pr.

— Diamond Mask. (Galactic Milieu Ser.: Bk. 2). 448p. 1995. mass mkt. 5.99 (*0-345-36248-9*, Del Rey) Ballantine Pub Grp.

— The Golden Torc. (Saga of Pliocene Exile Ser.: Vol. II). 416p. 1985. mass mkt. 5.99 (*0-345-32419-6*, Del Rey) Ballantine Pub Grp.

— Jack the Bodiless. (Galactic Milieu Trilogy Ser.: Book 1). 480p. 1993. mass mkt. 5.99 (*0-345-36247-0*, Del Rey) Ballantine Pub Grp.

— Magnificat, Vol. 3. 1997. mass mkt. 6.99 (*0-345-36249-7*, Del Rey) Ballantine Pub Grp.

— The Many-Colored Land. 480p. 1985. mass mkt. 5.99 (*0-345-32444-7*, Del Rey) Ballantine Pub Grp.

— Orion Arm Bk. 2: The Rampart Worlds. 2000. mass mkt. 6.99 (*0-345-39519-0*, Del Rey) Ballantine Pub Grp.

— Perseus Spur. 1999. mass mkt. 6.99 (*0-345-39510-7*) Ballantine Pub Grp.

***May, Julian.** Poverty & Inequality in South Africa: Meeting the Challenge. LC 99-54460. 320p. 1999. pap. 29.95 (*1-85649-808-5*) Zed Books.

— Poverty & Inequality South Africa: Meeting the Challenge. LC 99-54460. 320p. 1999. text 69.95 (*1-85649-807-7*) St Martin.

May, Julian. Sky Trillium. 1998. mass mkt. 6.99 (*0-345-38001-0*, Del Rey) Ballantine Pub Grp.

***May, Kara.** Joe Lion's Big Boots. (I Am Reading Ser.). (Illus.). 48p. (YA). 2000. pap. 3.95 (*0-7534-5318-5*, Kingfisher) LKC.

May, Karl. In the Desert. Billerbeck-Gentz, F., tr. from GER. (Illus.). 318p. 1955. pap. 17.50 (*0-945345-74-7*) Lubrecht & Cramer.

— Jubilaeumsbildhand: Sein Leben & Werk in Bildern & Dokumenten. rev. ed. Klussmeier, H. & Plaul, Heiner, eds. (GER., Illus.). 305p. 1992. lib. bdg. 63.50 (*0-614-97981-1*) G Olms Pubs.

— Jubilaums-Bildband. (GER.). 305p. 1992. write for info. (*3-487-08169-5*) G Olms Pubs.

— Mein Leben und Streben. xiii, 570p. 1975. reprint ed. write for info. (*3-487-08084-2*) G Olms Pubs.

— Der Weg zum Gluck Bande 1 & 2, 2 vols. (Quellen zur Trivial-Literatur Ser.). (GER.). 2616p. 1971. reprint ed. write for info. (*3-487-00111-X*) G Olms Pubs.

— Winnetou. LC 98-164851. 762p. 1998. reprint ed. pap. 19.95 (*0-8264-1092-8*) Continuum.

May, Karl F. Winnetou. abr. ed. Koblick, David, tr. from GER. & abr. by. LC 99-18364. 256p. 1999. pap. 16.95 (*0-87422-179-X*) Wash St U Pr.

May, Kathie D. Science. 1992. 6.95 (*1-55708-378-9*, C907) McDonald Pub Co.

***May, Kathleen M.** Feminist Family Therapy. LC 00-35569. 2000. write for info. (*1-55620-207-5*) Am Coun Assn.

May, Kathryn A. & Mahlmeister, Laura R. Maternal & Neonatal Nursing: Family-Centered Care. 3rd ed. (Illus.). 1232p. (C). 1993. text 61.95 (*0-397-54953-9*, Lippnctt) Lppncott W & W.

— Pocket Guide to Maternal & Neonatal Nursing. LC 93-30921. 1993. write for info. (*0-397-55125-8*) Lppncott W & W.

May, Kathryn E., jt. auth. see Messer, Ellen.

***May, Kathy.** Molasses Man. LC 98-21223. (Illus.). 32p. (J). (ps-3). 2000. 16.95 (*0-8234-1438-8*) Holiday.

May, Katja. African Americans & Native Americans in the Cherokee & Creek Nations, 1830s-1920s: Collision & Collusion. rev. ed. LC 95-52635. (Studies in African American History & Culture). 312p. 1996. text 77.00 (*0-8153-2449-9*) Garland.

May, Keith F. A Field Guide to Historic Pendleton. (Illus.). 214p. (Orig.). 1997. pap. 16.95 (*1-57502-427-6*, P01307) Morris Pubng.

— A Field Guide to the Historic Dalles Area. LC 97-93112. (Illus.). 180p. (Orig.). 1997. pap. 15.95 (*1-57502-446-2*, PO1343) Morris Pubng.

— Finding the Trail in Oregon: A Guide to Sites, Museums & Ruts on the Oregon Trail. 220p. (Orig.). 1996. pap. 14.95 (*1-57502-136-6*) Morris Pubng.

— Ghosts of Times Past: A Road Trip of Eastern Oregon Ghost Towns. (Illus.). 96p. (Orig.). 1996. pap. 11.95 (*1-57502-107-2*) Morris Pubng.

— Living on the Dry Side of Oregon: Comments from the Cosmic Cowboy. LC 98-118984. (Illus.). 90p. 1997. pap. 8.95 (*1-57502-648-1*, PO1835) Morris Pubng.

— A Tour of Pendleton's Historic Homes. (Illus.). 72p. (Orig.). 1995. pap. 9.95 (*1-57502-090-4*) Morris Pubng.

May, Kenneth M., ed. Electronic Underwriter: Artificial Intelligence & Insurance. (Illus.). 183p. 1991. pap. 35.00 (*0-614-05733-7*) CPCU Society.

May, Kerry P. Test Flights. 71p. (Orig.). 1995. pap. 8.95 (*0-931122-79-1*) West End.

May, Kyi W., jt. auth. see Guillermo, Artemio R.

May, L., et al, eds. Rotifer Symposium, No. IV. (C). 1987. lib. bdg. 267.00 (*90-6193-645-4*) Kluwer Academic.

May, L. & Gardner, C. M. Gardner History & Genealogy. 407p. 1989. reprint ed. pap. 52.50 (*0-8328-0584-X*); reprint ed. lib. bdg. 62.50 (*0-8328-0583-1*) Higginson Bk Co.

***May, Larry.** The Big Tomorrow: Hollywood & the Politics of the American Way. LC 99-57265. (Illus.). 328p. 2000. 32.50 (*0-226-51162-6*) U Ch Pr.

May, Larry. Masculinity & Morality. LC 97-37785. 240p. 1998. pap. 15.95 (*0-8014-8442-1*); text 39.95 (*0-8014-3418-1*) Cornell U Pr.

— The Morality of Groups: Collective Responsibility, Group-Based Harm & Corporate Rights. LC 87-40350. (Soundings: A Series in Ethics, Economics & Business: Vol. 1). 216p. (C). 1989. pap. text 13.00 (*0-268-01378-0*) U of Notre Dame Pr.

— Screening out the Past: The Birth of Mass Culture & the Motion Picture Industry. LC 83-4927. (Illus.). 320p. (C). 1983. reprint ed. pap. text 15.00 (*0-226-51173-1*) U Ch Pr.

— Sharing Responsibility. LC 92-12658. 216p. 1992. 34.95 (*0-226-51168-5*) U Ch Pr.

— Sharing Responsibility. 204p. 1996. reprint ed. pap. text 15.95 (*0-226-51169-3*) U Ch Pr.

— The Socially Responsive Self: Social Theory & Professional Ethics. 216p. 1996. pap. text 15.95 (*0-226-51172-3*); lib. bdg. 35.00 (*0-226-51171-5*) U Ch Pr.

May, Larry, ed. Recasting America: Culture & Politics in the Age of Cold War. LC 88-21618. (Illus.). 320p. 1988. pap. text 18.00 (*0-226-51176-6*) U Ch Pr.

— Recasting America: Culture & Politics in the Age of Cold War. LC 88-21618. (Illus.). 320p. 1989. lib. bdg. 60.00 (*0-226-51175-8*) U Ch Pr.

May, Larry, et al, eds. Liberty, Equality, & Plurality. LC 97-3124. 312p. 1997. 45.00 (*0-7006-0847-8*) U Pr of KS.

— Mind & Morals: Essays on Ethics & Cognitive Science. (Illus.). 325p. 1996. 42.50 (*0-262-13313-X*, Bradford Bks); pap. text 21.00 (*0-262-63165-2*, Bradford Bks) MIT Pr.

— Rethinking Masculinity: Philosophical Explorations in Light of Feminism. LC 92-22430. (New Feminist Perspectives Ser.). 244p. (C). 1992. 50.00 (*0-8476-7773-7*) Rowman.

— Rethinking Masculinity: Philosophical Explorations in Light of Feminism. 2nd ed. LC 96-21390. 346p. 1996. 66.00 (*0-8476-8256-0*); pap. 16.95 (*0-8476-8257-9*) Rowman.

May, Larry & Collins-Chobanian, Shari. Applied Ethics. 2nd ed. LC 97-29594. 654p. 1997. pap. text 49.00 (*0-13-575291-4*) P-H.

May, Larry & Hoffman, Stacey. Collective Responsibility. 320p. (C). 1991. text 57.50 (*0-8476-7691-9*); pap. text 21.00 (*0-8476-7692-7*) Rowman.

May, Larry & Kohn, Jerome, eds. Hannah Arendt: Twenty Years Later. (Studies in Contemporary German Social Thought). 384p. 1996. 42.00 (*0-262-13319-9*) MIT Pr.

— Hannah Arendt: Twenty Years Later. (Studies in Contemporary German Social Thought). (Illus.). 392p. 1997. reprint ed. pap. text 21.00 (*0-262-63182-2*) MIT Pr.

May, Larry, et al. Globalization & Global Governance: Medical Ethics in Conflict with Religious Freedom. Vayrynen, Raimo V., ed. (Point/Counterpoint Ser.). 288p. 1999. pap. 23.95 (*0-8476-8774-0*) Rowman.

May, Lawrence A. Classic Descriptions of Physical Signs in Medicine. LC 77-10533. 273 p. 1977. write for info. (*0-89561-022-1*) Dabor Sci Pubns.

May, Lee. Gardening Life. LC 98-66364. 240p. 1998. 22.00 (*1-56352-497-X*) Longstreet.

— In My Father's Garden: Estranged for 39 Years, a Father & Son Find Common Ground in the Garden. 208p. 1995. 19.95 (*1 56352 192 X*) Longstreet.

May, Leland C. Parodies of the Gothic Novel. Varma, Devendra P., ed. LC 79-8464. (Gothic Studies & Dissertations). 1980. lib. bdg. 19.95 (*0-405-12654-9*) Ayer.

May, Leondra, jt. auth. see Zaboly, Gary S.

May, Leopold, ed. see Danon, Jacques, et al.

May, Lewis, tr. see De Pourtales, Guy.

May, Lowell A. Camp Concordia: German POWs in the Midwest. (Illus.). 146p. 1996. pap. 20.95 (*0-89745-192-9*) Sunflower U Pr.

May, Lynn E. Church History Committee Handbook. Deweese, Charles W., ed. (Resource Kit for Your Church's History Ser.). 20p. 1984. pap. 2.95 (*0-939804-13-1*) Hist Comm S Baptist.

May, M., jt. auth. see James, D.

May, M. D., et al. Networks, Routers & Transputers. LC 93-77461. (Transputer & Occam Engineering Ser.: Vol. 32). 221p. (gr. 12). 1993. 80.00 (*90-5199-129-0*, Pub. by IOS Pr) IOS Press.

***May, Margaret.** Transforming the Finance Function to Add Company Wide Value. (Management Briefings Ser.). (Illus.). 1999. pap. 137.50 (*0-273-64313-4*, Pub. by F T P-H) Trans-Atl Phila.

May, Marge & Hall, John, eds. Memories of Little Traverse Bay. (Illus.). 112p. (Orig.). 1989. pap. 10.00 (*0-685-26072-0*) Little Traverse.

May, Margie. Inspirational Poetry. 1996. pap. 6.00 (*0-7880-0919-2*, Fairway Pr) CSS OH.

May, Marianne, jt. auth. see Apple, Loyal E.

May, Mark, jt. auth. see Hartshorne, Hugh.

May, Mark, jt. auth. see Levine, Howard L.

May, Mark A. A Social Psychology of War & Peace. 1943. 79.50 (*0-686-51314-2*) Elliots Bks.

May, Martha & Urofsky, Melvin I. The New Christian Right: Political & Social Issues. LC 96-24441. 504p. 1996. text 85.00 (*0-8153-2581-9*) Garland.

May, Matthew. Admissions Guide to Selective Business Schools. 192p. 1993. 29.95 (*0-8442-8550-1*, Passprt Bks) NTC Contemp Pub Co.

— Admissions Guide to Selective Business Schools. 176p. 1994. pap. 16.95 (*0-8442-8556-0*, VGM Career) NTC Contemp Pub Co.

May, Maurice I., et al. Managing Institutional Long-Term Care for the Elderly. 336p. 1991. 79.00 (*0-8342-0275-1*) Aspen Pub.

May, Melanie A. A Body Knows: A Theopoetics of Death & Resurrection. 132p. 1995. 17.95 (*0-8264-0849-4*) Continuum.

May, Melanie A., ed. For All the Saints: The Practice of Ministry in the Faith Community. LC 90-42737. 146p. 1990. reprint ed. pap. 45.30 (*0-608-02165-2*, 206283400004) Bks Demand.

May, Michael. Energy & Security in East Asia. vi, 50p. 1998. pap. 7.50 (*0-9653935-2-6*) Asia-Pacific Res.

— A Start Proposal. (CISA Research Note Ser.: No. 14). 1983. 10.00 (*0-86682-055-8*) Ctr Intl Relations.

May, Michael L., jt. auth. see Westfall, Minter J., Jr.

May, Michael M., et al. Strategic Arms Reductions. 73p. 1988. pap. 8.95 (*0-8157-5525-2*) Brookings.

May, Michael W. Radio Personality Basics. (Illus.). 170p. 1992. pap. text 14.95 (*0-9612074-1-8*) M May Ent.

May, Nancy, jt. auth. see May, Alex.

May, Nola. Classic Earring Designs. LC 94-70725. (Illus.). 96p. (Orig.). 1994. pap. 9.95 (*0-943604-43-5*, BOO/32) Eagles View.

***May, Paul Richard.** The Business of E-Commerce: From Corporate Strategy to Technology. (Breakthroughs in Application Development Ser.: No. 1). 300p. 2000. pap. 34.95 (*0-521-77698-8*) Cambridge U Pr.

May, Peter. Exam Classes. 174p. 1996. pap. text 13.95 (*0-19-437208-1*) OUP.

— The Last Banner. LC 96-35854. 1996. 22.50 (*0-684-80085-3*) S&S Trade.

— The Last Banner: The Story of the 1985-86 Celtics, the NBA's Greatest Team of All Time. LC 97-51731. 304p. 1998. pap. 9.95 (*1-55850-835-X*) Adams Media.

***May, Peter.** Natural Resource Valuation & Policy in Brazil. 352p. 1999. 55.00 (*0-231-10826-5*) Col U Pr.

May, Peter H. Natural Resource Valuation & Policy in Brazil: Methods & Cases. LC 99-25861. (Methods & Cases in Conservation Science Ser.). 352p. 1999. pap. 28.00 (*0-231-10827-3*) Col U Pr.

***May, Peter H.** Pricing the Planet: Economic Analysis for Sustainable Development. 2000. pap. text 20.00 (*0-231-10175-9*) Col U Pr.

May, Peter H. & DaMotta, Ronaldo S. Pricing the Planet: Economic Analysis for Sustainable Development. (Illus.). 220p. 1996. 45.00 (*0-231-10174-0*) Col U Pr.

May, Peter J. Biological Balance. 1999. 17.95 (*1-85279-098-9*) TFH Pubns.

— Physical & Mechanical Problems. 1999. 15.95 (*1-85279-099-7*) TFH Pubns.

— Recovering from Catastrophes: Federal Disaster Relief Policy & Politics, 128. LC 84-19731. (Contributions in Political Science Ser.: No. 128). (Illus.). 186p. 1985. 57.95 (*0-313-24698-X*, MYR/, Greenwood Pr) Greenwood.

May, Peter J. & Williams, Walter. Disaster Policy Implementation: Managing Programs under Shared Governance. LC 86-22653. (Disaster Research in Practice Ser.). (Illus.). 210p. (C). 1986. 65.00 (*0-306-42179-8*, Plenum Trade) Perseus Pubng.

May, Peter J., et al. Environmental Management & Governance: Intergovernmental Approaches to Hazards & Sustainability. (Illus.). 272p. (C). 1996. 85.00 (*0-415-14445-0*); pap. 25.99 (*0-415-14446-9*) Routledge.

May, Peter J., jt. ed. see Leiggi, Patrick.

May, Philip R. Origins of Hydraulic Mining in California. limited ed. (Illus.). 88p. 1970. 6.95 (*0-910740-17-8*) Holmes.

May, R. Rudolph Red Nosed. (Illus.). (J). pap. 14.95 incl. audio compact disk (*1-55709-136-6*) Applewood.

May, R., Jr. The Urbanization Revolution: Planning a New Agenda for Human Settlements. (Urban Innovation Abroad Ser.). (Illus.). 288p. (C). 1989. 85.00 (*0-306-43222-6*, Plenum Trade) Perseus Pubng.

May, R., jt. auth. see Gottlob, R.

May, R. A., ed. see Beit-Arie, Malachi.

May, Rachel. Love in a Chinese Garden. 1997. per. 5.99 (*0-373-83348-2*, 1-83348-2) Harlequin Bks.

— The Translator in the Text: On Reading Russian Literature in English. LC 94-22792. (Studies in Russian Literature & Theory). 209p. 1994. pap. text 15.95 (*0-8101-1158-6*) Northwestern U Pr.

— The Translator in the Text: On Reading Russian Literature in English. LC 94-22792. (Studies in Russian Literature & Theory). 220p. (C). 1994. text 49.95 (*0-8101-1157-8*) Northwestern U Pr.

May, Rachel, tr. see Tertz, Abram, pseud.

May, Raoul M., jt. ed. see Anderson, R. C.

May, Raoul M., tr. see DeFelipe, Javier & Jones, Edward G., eds.

May, Reinhard. Heidegger's Hidden Sources: East-Asian Influences on His Work. Parkes, Graham, ed. & tr. by. LC 96-5493. 144p. (C). 1996. 65.00 (*0-415-14037-4*); pap. 20.99 (*0-415-14038-2*) Routledge.

May, Rex. Gesundheit, Dummy! The Best of Baloo. (Illus.). 92p. 1999. pap. 7.95 (*0-9657929-3-5*) JONA Bks.

May, Richard E., jt. auth. see Wolfe, Susan M.

May, Richard L. Reducing New Home Costs As Much As 30,000 Dollars. rev. ed. LC 90-70961. (Orig.). 1990. 7.95 (*0-9627119-0-X*) J Zachary Pub.

May, Richard M. The Shreek of Wagons. 154p. 1993. 29.95 (*1-883543-00-2*); pap. 19.95 (*1-883543-01-0*) Rigel Pubns.

M

An Asterisk (*) at the beginning of an entry indicates that the title is appearing for the first time.

— A Sketch of a Migrating Family to California in 1848. 66p. 1991. 16.95 (*0-87770-494-5*); pap. 9.95 (*0-87770-499-6*) Ye Galleon.

May, Robert. Logical Form: Its Structure & Derivation. 280p. 1985. pap. text 21.00 (*0-262-63102-4*) MIT Pr.

— Rudolph the Red Nosed Reindeer. LC 91-156221. (Illus.). 32p. (J). (ps-2). 1998. 9.95 (*1-55709-139-0*) Applewood.

May, Robert, ed. Psychoanalytic Psychotherapy in a College Context. LC 87-2836. 214p. 1988. 55.00 (*0-275-92733-4*, C2733, Praeger Pubs) Greenwood.

May, Robert & Koster, Jan, eds. Levels of Syntactic Representation. (Studies in Generative Grammar). 350p. 1981. pap. 69.25 (*90-70176-30-0*) Mouton.

May, Robert, jt. auth. see Fiengo, Robert.

May, Robert, jt. auth. see Huang, C. T.

May, Robert, jt. ed. see Huang, C. T.

May, Robert E. How Billy Joe Bobtail Met Texas Slim. (Bobtail Chronicles Ser.). (Illus.). 32p. (J). (ps-3). 1987. pap. 5.95 (*0-87397-300-3*, Strode Pubs); lib. bdg. 11.89 (*0-87397-303-8*, Strode Pubs) Circle Bk Service.

— John A. Quitman: Old South Crusader. LC 84-10019. (Southern Biography Ser.). (Illus.). 465p. 1995. pap. 19.95 (*0-8071-1207-0*) La State U Pr.

— Poppa & Elizabeth: A Bobtail Romance. (Bobtail Chronicles Ser.). (Illus.). 32p. (Orig.). (J). (ps-3). 1988. pap. 5.95 (*0-87397-313-5*, Strode Pubs); lib. bdg. 11.89 (*0-87397-314-3*, Strode Pubs) Circle Bk Service.

May, Robert E., ed. see McPherson, James M., et al.

May, Robert L. Rudolph the Red-Nosed Reindeer. 32p. (J). 1993. spiral bd. 5.95 incl. audio (*1-55709-137-4*) Applewood.

May, Robert L. Rudolph the Red-Nosed Reindeer. LC 94-20997. (Illus.). 32p. (J). (ps-3). 1994. 9.95 (*1-55709-294-X*) Applewood.

— Rudolph's Second Christmas. LC 92-18416. (Illus.). 32p. (J). (ps-3). 1992. 9.95 (*1-55709-192-7*) Applewood.

May, Robert M. Cosmic Consciousness Revisited: The Modern Origins & Development of Western Spiritual Psychology. rev. ed. 276p. 1993. pap. 19.95 (*1-85230-280-1*, Pub. by Element MA) Penguin Putnam.

May, Robert M., jt. ed. see Lawton, John H.

May, Robert M., jt. ed. see Magurran, Anne E.

May, Robert M., ed. see Tilman, David.

May, Robin. The British Army in North America. (Men-at-Arms Ser.: No. 39). (Illus.). 48p. pap. 11.95 (*0-85045-195-7*, 9161, Pub. by Osprey) Stackpole.

— British Army in North America 1775-1783, Vol. 39. rev. ed. 1998. pap. text 12.95 (*1-85532-735-X*, Osprey Bks) Chapman & Hall.

— Plains Indians of North America. (Original People Ser.). (Illus.). 48p. (J). (gr. 4-8). 1987. lib. bdg. 16.67 (*0-86625-258-4*) Rourke Pubns.

— Wolfe's Army. (Men-at-Arms Ser.: No. 48). (Illus.). 48p. pap. 11.95 (*0-85045-193-0*, 9163, Pub. by Osprey) Stackpole.

May, Robin & Ross, David. Royal Canadian Mounted Police. (Men-at-Arms Ser.: No. 197). (Illus.). 48p. pap. 11.95 (*0-85045-834-X*, 9130, Pub. by Ospry) Stackpole.

May, Robin, jt. auth. see Rosa, Joseph G.

May, Robin, ed. see Alighieri, Dante.

May, Robin, ed. see Thornton, Arlean.

May, Roger J., jt. auth. see Chopra, Sanjiv.

May, Rollo. The Art of Counseling. rev. ed. LC 88-30155. 1990. pap. text 23.95 (*0-89876-156-5*) Gardner Pr.

— The Courage to Create. LC 93-43718. 144p. 1994. pap. 10.95 (*0-393-31106-6*) Norton.

— The Courage to Create. 1995. 24.00 (*0-8446-6854-0*) Peter Smith.

— The Discovery of Being. 1995. 24.00 (*0-8446-6855-9*) Peter Smith.

— Freedom & Destiny. 288p. 1999. pap. 14.00 (*0-393-31842-7*, Norton Paperbks) Norton.

***May, Rollo.** Freedom & Destiny. 1999. 27.50 (*0-8446-7021-9*) Peter Smith.

May, Rollo. The Meaning of Anxiety. 448p. 1996. pap. 15.95 (*0-393-31456-1*, Norton Paperbks) Norton.

— My Quest for Beauty. LC 85-61687. 243p. 1985. 9.95 (*0-933071-01-9*) Saybrook Pub Co.

— My Quest for Beauty. LC 85-61687. (Illus.). 244p. 1987. reprint ed. pap. 9.95 (*0-933071-13-2*) Saybrook Pub Co.

— Power & Innocence: A Search for the Sources of Violence. 288p. 1998. pap. 13.00 (*0-393-31703-X*) Norton.

— Psychology & the Human Dilemma. 336p. 1996. pap. 13.00 (*0-393-31455-3*, Norton Paperbks) Norton.

May, Rollo, ed. Existential Psychology. 2nd ed. 128p. (C). 1969. pap. 18.75 (*0-07-553578-5*) McGraw.

May, Rollo, et al, eds. Existence. LC 94-71311. 456p. 1994. pap. 40.00 (*1-56821-271-2*) Aronson.

May, Rollo, jt. auth. see Schneider, Kirk J.

May, Ronald V. An Archaeological Salvage Report on the Excavation at Kitchen Creek: An Investigation of a Subsidiary Hakataya Resource Camp & Associated Milling Stations. (Illus.). 135p. (C). 1975. reprint ed. pap. text 15.00 (*1-55567-452-6*) Coyote Press.

May, Ronald V. An Evaluation of Mexican Majolica in Alta California. 1980. reprint ed. pap. 4.95 (*0-686-31787-4*) Acoma Bks.

May, Ronald V. Mexican Majolica in Northern New Spain: A Model for Interpreting Ceramic Change. (Illus.). 147p. 1975. pap. text 16.25 (*1-55567-031-8*) Coyote Press.

— The Table Mountain Complex as Derived from a Synthesis of 124 Archaeological Sites Clustered in Stratified Biological, Geographical & Geological Zones. (Illus.). 119p. (C). 1987. reprint ed. pap. text 13.13 (*1-55567-431-3*) Coyote Press.

May, Ronald V., jt. auth. see Barnes, Mark.

May, Roy, jt. ed. see Furley, Oliver.

May, Roy H., Jr. The Poor of the Land: A Christian Case for Land Reform. LC 90-46980. 160p. reprint ed. pap. 49.60 (*0-608-20248-7*, 207150700012) Bks Demand.

May, S. Case Studies in Business. 146p. (C). 1984. 90.00 (*0-7855-5654-0*, Pub. by Inst Pur & Supply) St Mut.

— Costa Rica. 1976. lib. bdg. 59.95 (*0-8490-1677-0*) Gordon Pr.

— The Descendants of Richard Sares (Sears) of Yarmouth, Mass., 1638-1888, with Some Notices of Other Families by the Name of Sears. 676p. 1989. reprint ed. pap. 98.00 (*0-8328-1053-3*); reprint ed. lib. bdg. 108.00 (*0-8328-6555-9*) Higginson Bk Co.

May, S. R. & Dogo, G., eds. Care of the Burn Wound. (Illus.). xiv, 246p. 1985. 191.50 (*3-8055-3991-6*) S Karger.

May, Sally Ruth. Master Paintings in the Art Institute of Chicago. 2nd rev. ed. LC 88-9367. (Illus.). 168p. 1999. 50.00 (*0-86559-175-X*, Pub. by Art Inst Chi) Hudson Hills.

May, Samuel J. Fugitive Slave Law & Its Victims. LC 77-133161. (Black Heritage Library Collection). 1977. 15.95 (*0-8369-8716-0*) Ayer.

— Some Recollections of Our Anti-Slavery Conflict. LC 79-83888. (Black Heritage Library Collection). 1977. 17.95 (*0-8369-8630-X*) Ayer.

— Some Recollections of Our Anti-Slavery Conflict. LC 68-29010. (American Negro: His History & Literature. Series 1). 1968. reprint ed. 17.95 (*0-405-01829-0*) Ayer.

May, Scott. Surfing. LC 93-32164. (Pro-Am Sports Ser.). 48p. (J). (gr. 3-8). 1993. lib. bdg. 17.95 (*0-86593-349-9*) Rourke Corp.

May, Scottie & Kenney, Cindy. Children's Curriculum for Grades 1-6. (Nineteen Ninety-Eight Fifty-Day Spiritual Adventure Ser.). (Illus.). 128p. Date not set. wbk. ed. 25.00 (*1-57849-057-X*) Mainstay Church.

— Children's Curriculum for Grades 1-6. (Nineteen Ninety-Nine 50-Day Spiritual Adventure Ser.). (Illus.). 128p. (J). 1998. pap. 25.00 (*1-57849-123-1*) Mainstay Church.

May, Scottie, et al. Children's Curriculum for Grades 1-6. (Nineteen Ninety-Seven 50-Day Spiritual Adventure Ser.). (Illus.). 128p. Date not set. pap., wbk. ed. 25.00 (*1-57849-016-2*) Chapel of Air.

— 1996 50-Day Spiritual Adventure: Grades 1-6 Leader's Guide. Hiebert, Charlene, ed. (Illus.). 128p. (Orig.). 1995. pap., wbk. ed. 20.00 (*1-879050-76-5*) Chapel of Air.

May, Scottie, jt. auth. see Kenney, Cindy.

May, Sheila. Case Studies in Business. 146p. (C). 1989. 73.00 (*0-7855-4630-8*, Pub. by Inst Pur & Supply) St Mut.

***May, Signora.** Community Development: Extent of Federal Influence on "Urban Sprawl" Is Unclear. 81p. (C). 2000. pap. text 20.00 (*0-7881-8492-X*) DIANE Pub.

May, Simon. Nietzsche's Ethics & His War on 'Morality' LC 99-28678. 232p. 2000. 45.00 (*0-19-823846-0*) OUP.

May, Simon, jt. auth. see Creasey, Pauline.

May, Stacy, jt. auth. see Hamilton, Walton H.

May, Stacy, jt. auth. see Keezer, Dexter M.

May, Stephen. Critical Multiculturalism. LC 99-179371. 1998. 85.00 (*0-7507-0768-2*, Falmer Pr) Taylor & Francis.

— Critical Multiculturalism: Uncommon Voices in a Common Struggle. LC 99-179371. 1998. pap. text 28.95 (*0-7507-0767-4*) Taylor & Francis.

— Footloose on the Santa Fe Trail. (Illus.). 144p. 1993. pap. 14.95 (*0-87081-295-5*) Univ Pr Colo.

***May, Stephen.** Indigenous Community-Based Education. LC 99-23922. 1999. 49.95 (*1-85359-450-4*) Taylor & Francis.

May, Stephen. Making Multicultural Education Work. LC 94-9690. (Language & Education Library: Vol. 7). 1994. 74.95 (*1-85359-237-4*, Pub. by Multilingual Matters) Taylor & Francis.

— Making Multicultural Education Work. LC 94-9690. (Language & Education Library: Vol. 7). 223p. 1994. pap. 29.95 (*1-85359-236-6*) Taylor & Francis.

— Pilgrimage: A Journey Through Colorado's History & Culture. LC 82-76537. (Illus.). 200p. 1986. pap. 8.95 (*0-8040-0883-3*); text 18.95 (*0-8040-0882-5*) Swallow.

May, Stephen C. Self-Assessment Color Review of Equine Orthopedics & Rheumatology. LC 99-169788. (Illus.). 176p. 1998. pap. text 34.95 (*0-8138-2137-1*) Iowa St U Pr.

***May, Stephen J.** Maverick Heart: The Further Adventures of Zane Grey. (Illus.). 272p. 2000. 29.95 (*0-8214-1316-3*, Ohio U Ctr Intl); pap. 16.95 (*0-8214-1317-1*, Ohio U Ctr Intl) Ohio U Pr.

May, Stephen J. Zane Grey: Romancing the West. LC 97-353. (Illus.). 196p. (Orig.). 1997. pap. 14.95 (*0-8214-1182-9*); text 29.95 (*0-8214-1181-0*) Ohio U Pr.

May, Steve. Sermon Illustrator: A Database of Illustrations for Preaching & Teaching, Electronic Ed. 1997. 50.00 (*0-687-06136-9*) Abingdon.

— The Story File: 1,001 Contemporary Illustrations for Speakers, Writers & Preachers with CD Rom. LC 99-59632. (Illus.). 2000. 19.95 (*1-56563-524-8*) Hendrickson MA.

May, Steven W. Elizabethan Courtier Poets: The Poems & Their Contexts. LC 99-24514. 424p. 1998. 19.95 (*1-889818-05-4*) Pegasus Pr.

— Sir Walter Raleigh. (Twayne's English Authors Ser.: No. 469). 400p. 1989. 23.95 (*0-8057-6983-8*) Macmillan.

***May, Susan E.** Twins: The Two of Us. (Illus.). 32p. (J). (ps-k). 1999. pap. 9.95 (*1-891846-13-2*) Busn Word.

May, Suzanne D., jt. auth. see Ashby, Clifford.

May, T. W. & Wood, A. E. Fungi of Australia, Vol. 2A. (Illus.). 1996. pap. 54.95 (*0-643-05930-X*, Pub. by CSIRO) Accents Pubns.

May, Theodore W. & Dana, Richard, eds. Internship Training in Professional Psychology. 527p. 1987. pap. 38.95 (*0-89116-773-0*) Hemisp Pub.

— Internship Training in Professional Psychology. 527p. 1987. 79.95 (*0-89116-580-0*) Hemisp Pub.

May, Theresa, jt. auth. see Fried, Larry K.

May, Thomas. Autonomy, Authority & Moral Responsibility. LC 97-44701. (Law & Philosophy Library: No. 33). 200p. 1997. 117.50 (*0-7923-4851-6*) Kluwer Academic.

***May, Thomas & Schmitz, Gotz.** The Reigne of King Henry the Second, Written in Seauen Books. LC 99-55552. (Renaissance English Text Society Ser.: Vol. 195). 1999. 35.00 (*0-86698-237-X*) MRTS.

May, Thomas & Tudice, Paul, eds. Advance Directives & Surrogate Decision Making in Illinois. 122p. 1999. pap. write for info. (*0-9623335-3-0*) HSP IL.

May, Thomas E. Constitutional History of England since the Accession of George Third, 1760-1860, 2 vols., Set. 1080p. 1986. reprint ed. 85.00 (*0-8377-2429-5*, Rothman) W S Hein.

— Treatise upon the Law, Privileges, Proceedings & Usage of Parliament. (Parliamentary & Congressional Ser.). vi, 40p. 1971. reprint ed. 47.00 (*0-7165-2014-1*) W S Hein.

May, Thomastine Le, see Le May, Thomastine.

May, Tim. Situating Social Theory. LC 96-23676. 208p. 1996. pap. 23.95 (*0-335-19286-6*) OpUniv Pr.

— Social Research: Issues, Methods & Process. 2nd ed. LC 97-20094. 1997. 88.00 (*0-335-20006-0*) OpUniv Pr.

May, Tim & Vass, Antony A. Working with Offenders: Issues, Contexts & Outcomes. (New Directions in Social Work Ser.). 256p. 1996. 75.00 (*0-8039-7621-6*); pap. 24.95 (*0-8039-7622-4*) Sage.

May, Tim & Williams, Malcolm. Knowing the Social World. LC 98-13161. 224p. 1998. pap. 24.95 (*0-335-19767-1*) OpUniv Pr.

May, Timothy. Probation: Politics, Policy & Practice. 176p. 1990. pap. 34.95 (*0-335-09377-9*) OpUniv Pr.

May, Timothy, jt. auth. see Barberis, Peter.

May, Timothy, jt. auth. see Hobbs, Dick.

May, Timothy C. Trade Unions & Pressure Group Politics. 160p. 1975. 17.95 (*0-347-01058-X*, 94631-1) Ashgate Pub Co.

May, Todd. Between Genealogy & Epistemology: Psychology, Politics, & Knowledge in the Thought of Michel Foucault. LC 92-29112. 144p. (C). 1993. 30.00 (*0-271-00905-5*) Pa St U Pr.

— The Moral Theory of Poststructuralism. LC 94-45435. 152p. 1995. 35.00 (*0-271-01468-7*); pap. 16.95 (*0-271-01469-5*) Pa St U Pr.

***May, Todd.** Our Practices, Our Selves or, What It Means to Be Human. LC 00-32367. 2001. write for info. (*0-271-02086-5*) Pa St U Pr.

May, Todd. The Political Philosophy of Poststructuralist Anarchism. LC 93-30551. 1994. 32.50 (*0-271-01045-2*); pap. 15.95 (*0-271-01046-0*) Pa St U Pr.

— Reconsidering Difference: Nancy, Derrida, Levinas, & Deleuze. LC 96-42210. 1997. 60.00 (*0-271-01657-4*); pap. 19.95 (*0-271-01658-2*) Pa St U Pr.

May, Todd, ed. Twentieth Century Continental Philosophy: A Reader. LC 96-6794. 321p. 1996. pap. text 55.00 (*0-13-450826-2*) P-H.

May, Tom, jt. auth. see McAllister, Dawson.

May, Trevor. An Economic & Social History of Britain, 1760-1970. LC 86-143. (Illus.). 360p. (C). 1987. pap. text 14.95 (*0-582-35280-0*) Longman.

***May, Trevor.** Victorian & Edwardian Horse Cabs. 1999. pap. 25.00 (*0-7478-0430-3*, Pub. by Shire Pubns) St Mut.

May, Trevor. The Victorian Domestic Servant. (Album Ser.: No. 338). (Illus.). 32p. 1998. pap. 6.25 (*0-7478-0368-4*, Pub. by Shire Pubns) Parkwest Pubns.

— The Victorian Schoolroom. (Album Ser.: No. 302). (Illus.). 32p. 1998. pap. 6.25 (*0-7478-0243-2*, Pub. by Shire Pubns) Parkwest Pubns.

— The Victorian Undertaker. (Album Ser.: No. 32). 32p. 1996. pap. 4.75 (*0-7478-0331-5*, Pub. by Shire Pubns) Parkwest Pubns.

— The Victorian Workhouse. (Album Ser.: No. 334). (Illus.). 32p. 1997. pap. 6.25 (*0-7478-0355-2*, Pub. by Shire Pubns) Parkwest Pubns.

May, Vicki. Riverbend. 105p. 1984. 4.95 (*0-89697-131-7*) Intl Univ Pr.

May, Vicki & Rodberg, C. V. Medicine Wheel Ceremonies: Ancient Philosophies for Use in Modern Day Life. LC 95-50749. (Illus.). 48p. (Orig.). (C). 1996. pap. 8.95 (*0-87961-242-8*) Naturegraph.

***May, Volkhard, et al.** Charge & Energy Transfer Dynamics in Molecular Systems: A Theoretical Introduction. 416p. 2000. 125.00 (*3-527-29608-5*) Wiley.

***May, W.** Definitions of Terms & Modes Used at NIST for Value Assignment of Reference Materials for Chemical Measurements. 18p. 2000. pap. 2.25 (*0-16-059015-9*) USGPO.

May, W., jt. auth. see Lawler, R.

***May, W. E.** The Boats of Men-of-War. rev. ed. (Illus.). 128p. 2000. 34.95 (*1-55750-190-4*) Naval Inst Pr.

May, William. An Introduction to Moral Theology. rev. ed. LC 90-60638. 288p. (C). 1999. pap. 9.95 (*0-87973-453-1*, 453) Our Sunday Visitor.

***May, William D.** So Much Data So Little Math: How to Predict Data Trends - 5 Easy Profitable Methods. (Illus.). 192p. 2000. pap. 27.50 (*0-7618-1640-2*) U Pr of Amer.

***May, William E.** Catholic Bioethics & the Gift of Human Life. LC 00-130461. 272p. 2000. pap. 17.95 (*0-87973-683-6*) Our Sunday Visitor.

May, William E. The Church's Mission of Evangelization. 1998. pap. text 17.95 (*0-940535-92-0*, UP192) Franciscan U Pr.

— Marriage: The Rock on Which the Family Is Built. LC 94-79300. 143p. (Orig.). 1995. pap. 9.95 (*0-89870-537-1*) Ignatius Pr.

— Moral Absolutes, Catholic Traditions, Current Trends & the Truth. LC 88-44163. (Pere Marquette Lectures). 1989. text 15.00 (*0-87462-544-0*, PM-20) Marquette.

— Sex & the Sanctity of Human Life. 141p. (Orig.). 1984. pap. 6.95 (*0-931888-17-4*) Christendom Pr.

— Sex, Marriage & Chastity: Reflections of a Catholic Layman, Spouse & Parent. 2nd ed. 170p. 1981. reprint ed. pap. 8.95 (*0-8199-0821-5*, 0821-5, Frncscn Herld) Franciscan Pr.

— The Unity of the Moral & Spiritual Life. (Synthesis Ser.). 1978. pap. 1.00 (*0-8199-0745-6*, Frncscn Herld) Franciscan Pr.

***May, William E. & Whitehead, Kenneth D., eds.** The Battle for the Catholic Mind: Catholic Faith & Catholic Intellect in the Work of the Fellowship of Catholic Scholars 1978-95. 480p. 2000. pap. 28.00 (*1-890318-06-X*, Pub. by St Augustines Pr) U Ch Pr.

May, William E., tr. see De Haro, Ramon G.

***May, William F.** Ethics of Giving & Receiving: Am I My Foolish Brother's Keeper? LC 00-26740. 224p. 2000. write for info. (*0-87074-452-6*, Pub. by SMU Press) Tex A&M Univ Pr.

May, William F. The Patient's Ordeal. LC 90-45841. (Medical Ethics Ser.). 240p. 1991. 26.95 (*0-253-33717-8*) Ind U Pr.

— The Patient's Ordeal. LC 90-45841. (Medical Ethics Ser.). 240p. 1994. pap. 11.95 (*0-253-20870-X*) Ind U Pr.

***May, William F.** Physician's Covenant: Images of the Healer in Medical Ethics. 2nd ed. 232p. 2000. pap. 19.95 (*0-664-22274-9*) Westminster John Knox.

May, William V. & Tolin, Craig. Pronunciation Guide for Choral Literature: French, German, Hebrew, Italian, Latin, Spanish. 100p. (Orig.). 1987. pap. 20.00 (*0-940796-47-3*, 1040) MENC.

May, William V., et al. World's Greatest Music Video with Teacher's Guide. 1989. pap., teacher ed. 42.00 incl. VHS (*0-940796-58-9*, 3021) MENC.

May, William W. Business Ethics & the Law: Beyond Compliance. LC 91-23017. (Rockwell Lectures: Vol. 2). 99p. (C). 1992. text 16.95 (*0-8204-1728-9*) P Lang Pubng.

— Ethics & Higher Education. LC 90-31898. (American Council on Education/Macmillan Series on Higher Education). 408p. reprint ed. pap. 126.50 (*0-608-20859-0*, 207195800003) Bks Demand.

— Ethics & Higher Education. LC 98-12123. 408p. 1990. reprint ed. pap. 27.95 (*1-57356-216-5*) Oryx Pr.

May, Willie & Sahadi, Lou. Say Hey: The Autobiography of Willie Mays. 1989. mass mkt. 4.50 (*0-671-67836-1*) PB.

Maya. Mortal Sins. Duncan, Robert E., ed. (Illus.). 175p. 2000. mass mkt. 15.95 (*1-888347-28-7*, Enigma) Donnchad.

Maya, Love P. Off the Village Mat. LC 97-91048. 1998. pap. 12.95 (*0-533-12548-0*) Vantage.

Mayada, Maruja Del Castillo De, see Ackerman, James D. & Del Castillo De Mayada, Maruja.

Mayadas, Azim L. NGCSA: A Retrospective. 14p. 1985. 15.00 (*0-318-21719-8*) NGCSA.

Mayadas, Azim L., jt. auth. see Intermarkon Inc. Staff.

Mayadas, Nazneen S., et al, eds. International Handbook on Social Work Theory & Practice. LC 96-53520. 480p. 1997. lib. bdg. 99.50 (*0-313-27914-4*, Greenwood Pr) Greenwood.

Mayaguez Institute of Tropical Agriculture Staff. The Mayaguez Institute of Tropical Agriculture, Puerto Rico: A Bibliography of Publications. (Studies in Tropical Agriculture). 1980. lib. bdg. 59.95 (*0-8490-3072-2*) Gordon Pr.

Mayakovsky, Stanislaw, pseud & Geary, Rick. Cyberantics. (Illus.). 56p. (Orig.). (J). 1992. 14.95 (*1-878574-29-9*) Dark Horse Comics.

Mayakovsky, Vladimir. The Bedbug & Selected Poetry. Blake, Patricia, ed. Hayward, Max & Reavey, George, trs. LC 75-10805. 320p. 1975. reprint ed. pap. 14.95 (*0-253-20189-6*, MB-189) Ind U Pr.

— Legends! Early Poems. Enzensberger, Maria, tr. from RUS. 64p. (Orig.). 1991. pap. 5.95 (*0-87286-255-0*) City Lights.

— Mayakovsky--Plays. Daniels, Guy, tr. (European Drama Classics Ser.). 276p. 1995. pap. 15.95 (*0-8101-1339-2*) Northwestern U Pr.

***Mayakovsky, Vladimir & Lissitzky, El.** For the Voice, Vols. 1 & 2. (Illus.). 400p. (C). 2000. pap., boxed set 44.95 (*0-262-13377-6*) MIT Pr.

Mayali, Laurent & Tibbetts, Stephanie J., eds. The Two Laws: Studies in Medieval Legal History Dedicated to Stephan Kuttner. LC 90-1686. (Studies in Medieval & Early Modern Canon Law). 248p. 1990. 39.95 (*0-8132-0725-8*) Cath U Pr.

Mayali, Laurent, ed. see Storti-Storchi, Claudia, et al.

Mayall. Music Appreciation. (Music Ser.). 2002. 30.00 (*0-534-54522-X*) Brooks-Cole.

Mayall, Berry, ed. Children's Childhoods: Observed & Experienced. LC 94-36526. 192p. 1994. 85.00 (*0-7507-0369-5*, Falmer Pr); pap. 27.95 (*0-7507-0370-9*, Falmer Pr) Taylor & Francis.

Mayall, Berry, et al. Children's Health in Primary Schools. 240p. 1996. 79.95 (*0-7507-0544-2*, Falmer Pr); pap. 27.95 (*0-7507-0545-0*, Falmer Pr) Taylor & Francis.

***Mayall, Beth.** Get Over It! How to Survive Break-Ups, Backstabbing Friends & Bad Haircuts And... (Illus.). 128p. (J). (gr. 7-12). 2000. mass mkt. 4.99 (*0-439-11465-9*) Scholastic Inc.

— What's Your Guy-Q? 25+ Cool Quizzes to Help Discover the Real You! 128p. (YA). (gr. 7-12). 2000. mass mkt. 4.99 (*0-439-11466-7*) Scholastic Inc.

Mayall, David. English Gypsies & State Policies. (Interface Collection: Vol. 7). (Illus.). 98p. (C). 1995. pap. 17.95 (*0-900458-64-X*, Pub. by Univ of Herfordshire) Bold Strummer Ltd.

An Asterisk (*) at the beginning of an entry indicates that the title is appearing for the first time.

Mayall, David. Gypsy-Travellers in Nineteenth Century Society. (Illus.). 272p. 1988. text 85.00 (*0-521-32397-5*) Cambridge U Pr.

Mayall, David & Cronin, Michael, eds. Sporting Nationalisms: Identity, Ethnicity, Immigration & Assimilation. LC 98-18870. (Sport in the Global Society Ser.: No. 6). 160p. 1998. 52.50 (*0-7146-4896-5*, Pub. by F Cass Pubs); pap. 24.50 (*0-7146-4449-8*, Pub. by F Cass Pubs) Intl Spec Bk.

Mayall, Don, compiled by. The Worker Traits Data Book: Specific Details on the 12,741 Jobs Listed in the Dictionary of Occupational Titles. LC 93-33412. 344p. 1994. pap. 49.95 (*1-56370-110-3*, WTDB) JIST Works.

Mayall, Donald. Careers in Banking & Finance: How to Achieve Your Professional Goal. American Institute of Banking Staff & Lubow, Joseph, eds. LC 85-18691. 143p. (Orig.). 1985. pap. 10.50 (*0-935183-00-0*) Amer Inst Bank.

Mayall, James. Nationalism & International Society. (Cambridge Studies in International Relations: No. 10). 181p. (C). 1990. pap. text 18.95 (*0-521-38961-5*) Cambridge U Pr.

***Mayall, James.** World Politics. 2001. 56.95 (*0-7456-2589-4*, Pub. by Polity Pr); pap. 21.95 (*0-7456-2590-8*, Pub. by Polity Pr) Blackwell Pubs.

Mayall, James, ed. The New Interventionism 1991-1994: United Nations Experience in Cambodia, Former Yugoslavia & Somalia. (London School of Economics Monographs in International Studies). 248p. (C). 1996. text 59.95 (*0-521-55197-8*); pap. text 18.95 (*0-521-55856-5*) Cambridge U Pr.

Mayall, Jan K. & Desharnais, Guylaine. Positioning in a Wheelchair: A Guide for Professional Caregivers of the Disabled Adult. 2nd ed. LC 94-27090. 176p. 1995. pap. 23.00 (*1-55642-251-2*, 42512) SLACK Inc.

Mayall, John. Festival Play: A Comedy. LC 99-166896. 38 p. 1997. write for info. (*0-573-12109-5*) French.

Mayall, M. W., jt. auth. see Mayall, N.

Mayall, Margaret B. Children & Health at Home & School. LC 95-37675. 192p. (C). 1996. 91.95 (*0-335-19283-1*); pap. 31.95 (*0-335-19282-3*) OpUniv Pr.

Mayall, Margaret W., jt. auth. see Mayall, R. Newton.

***Mayall, N. & Mayall, M. W.** Sundials: Their Construction & Use. 2000. pap. 9.95 (*0-486-41146-X*) Dover.

Mayall, R. Newton. Sky Observer's Guide, a Handbook for Amateur Astronomers. (Golden Guide Ser.). 11.05 (*0-606-11848-9*, Pub. by Turtleback) Demco.

Mayall, R. Newton & Mayall, Margaret W. Sundials: Their Construction & Use. 3rd ed. LC 73-76242. 256p. 1994. pap. 16.95 (*0-933346-71-9*) Sky Pub.

Mayall, Simon V. Turkey: Thwarted Ambition. 117p. (C). 1997. pap. text 25.00 (*0-7881-4669-6*) DIANE Pub.

Mayall, Simon V. Turkey: Thwarted Ambition. 121p. 1997. per. 9.00 (*0-16-061196-2*) USGPO.

***Mayama, Shigeki, et al, eds.** Proceedings of the 14th International Diatom Symposium. (Illus.). 638p. 1999. 228.00 (*3-87429-401-3*, Pub. by Koeltz Sci Bks) Lubrecht & Cramer.

Mayan, Wayne W. Is It Possible to Be a Christian & Modern? LC 93-11069. 90p. (Orig.). (C). 1993. pap. text 19.50 (*0-8191-9159-0*); lib. bdg. 37.50 (*0-8191-9158-2*) U Pr of Amer.

Mayanathan, Saha D., jt. auth. see Salleh, Ismail.

Mayants, Lazar. Beyond the Quantum Paradox: Probability Riddles... Quantum Riddles... Other Riddles... LC 94-1214. 102p. 1994. write for info. (*0-7484-0206-3*, Pub. by Tay Francis Ltd); pap. 49.50 (*0-7484-0207-1*, Pub. by Tay Francis Ltd) Taylor & Francis.

— The Enigma of Probability & Physics. 392p. 1984. text 219.50 (*90-277-1674-9*) Kluwer Academic.

Mayar, M. P. Elsevier's Dictionary of Cancer. 500p. 1999. write for info. (*0-444-82950-4*) Elsevier.

Mayaram, Kartikeya, jt. auth. see Pederson, Donald O.

Mayaram, Shail. Resisting Regimes: Myth, Memory & the Shaping of a Muslim Identity. LC 97-900355. (Illus.). 312p. 1997. text 32.00 (*0-19-563955-3*) OUP.

Mayasandra, Venogopal. Chemical Characterization of Liquefaction Products of an Inertinite Enriched Northern Alaska Coal. (MIRL Reports: No. 86). (Illus.). 56p. (Orig.). (C). 1989. pap. 7.00 (*0-911043-10-1*) UAKF Min Ind Res Lab.

Mayaud, P. N. Derivation, Meaning, & Use of Geomagnetic Indices. (Geophysical Monograph Ser.: Vol. 22). 154p. 1980. 26.00 (*0-87590-022-4*, GM2200) Am Geophysical.

Maybank, Burnet R., et al. The Law of Automobile Insurance in South Carolina. LC 97-150000. 1997. pap. write for info. (*0-943856-43-4*, 535) SC Bar CLE.

Maybank, Stephen. Theory of Reconstruction from Image Motion. Huang, T. S. et al, eds. LC 92-17979. (Information Sciences Ser.: Vol. 28). (Illus.). 264p. 1992. 75.95 (*0-387-55537-4*) Spr-Verlag.

***Maybarduk, Linda.** The Dancer Who Flew: A Memoir of Rudolf Nureyev. LC 99-70969. (Illus.). 180p. (YA). (gr. 5 up). 1999. 18.95 (*0-88776-415-0*) Tundra Bks.

Maybaum. Creation & Guilt. 1969. 13.50 (*0-85303-029-4*, Pub. by M Vallentine & Co) Intl Spec Bk.

Maybaum, Klaus. Fachhochschulen in the Federal Republic of Germany: Material Concerning Functions & Organization. 431p. 1989. pap. 41.00 (*3-7890-1790-6*, Pub. by Nomos Verlags) Intl Bk Import.

Maybe, Ellyn. The Cowardice of Amnesia: Poetry. Cervenkova, Exene, ed. LC 98-215536. 140p. 1998. pap. 10.00 (*1-880985-58-6*) Two Thirteen Sixty-one.

— The Ellyn Maybe Coloring Book. (Illus.). 50p. (Orig.). 1997. pap. write for info. (*0-9652048-5-5*) Sacred Beverage.

Maybeck, Jacomena. People & Places: A Memoir. (Illus.). 152p. (Orig.). 1992. pap. 9.95 (*1-879042-01-0*) Stonegarden Pr.

Maybeck, Peter S. Stochastic Models, Estimation & Control, Vol. 3. (Mathematics in Science & Engineering Ser.). 270p. 1982. text 88.00 (*0-12-480703-8*) Acad Pr.

Maybee, Rolland H. Railroad Competition & the Oil Trade, 1855-1873. LC 73-16234. (Perspectives in American History Ser.: No. 16). (Illus.). x, 451p. 1974. reprint ed. lib. bdg. 49.50 (*0-87991-341-X*) Porcupine Pr.

Mayberry. Argument Sake Lester Cit. 2ntl ed. (C). 1996. 32.00 (*0-201-38266-0*) Addison-Wesley.

— For Argument's Sake: A Guide to Writing Effective Arguments. 3rd ed. LC 98-21403. 208p. (C). 1998. pap. text 35.66 (*0-321-01467-7*) Addison-Wesley.

Mayberry, ed. For Argument's Sake with Readings. (C). 1998. text. write for info. (*0-321-01193-7*) Addison-Wesley Educ.

Mayberry, Bob. Theatre of Discord: Dissonance in Beckett, Albee, & Pinter. LC 88-45786. 96p. 1989. 22.50 (*0-8386-3353-6*) Fairleigh Dickinson.

Mayberry, Claude. Discovering Seeds of Change. (YA). 1993. pap., wbk. ed. 4.95 (*0-201-49003-X*) Addison-Wesley.

— Discovering Seeds of Change. (J). (gr. 4-7). 1993. pap., wbk. ed. 4.95 (*0-201-49002-1*) Addison-Wesley.

— Discovering Seeds of Change. (J). (ps-3). 1993. pap., wbk. ed. 4.95 (*0-201-49001-3*) Addison-Wesley.

Mayberry, Edward, jt. auth. see Prince, Thomas.

Mayberry, G., jt. auth. see Houze, H.

Mayberry, James D., jt. auth. see Czaplicki, Jon S.

Mayberry, Jodine. Business Leaders Who Built Financial Empires. (Twenty Events Ser.). (Illus.). 48p. (J). (gr. 5-6). 1994. lib. bdg. 24.26 (*0-8114-4934-3*) Raintree Steck-V.

— Leaders Who Changed the Twentieth Century. LC 93-19032. (Twenty Events Ser.). (Illus.). 48p. (J). (gr. 5-7). 1993. lib. bdg. 24.26 (*0-8114-4926-2*) Raintree Steck-V.

Mayberry, Katherine J. Christina Rossetti & the Poetry of Discovery. LC 89-33163. 160p. 1989. text 27.50 (*0-8071-1529-0*) La State U Pr.

Mayberry, Katherine J., ed. Teaching What You're Not: Identity Politics in Higher Education. (C). 1996. pap. text 20.00 (*0-8147-5547-X*) NYU Pr.

— Teaching What You're Not: Identity Politics in Higher Education. 380p. (C). 1996. text 55.00 (*0-8147-5531-3*) NYU Pr.

Mayberry, Katherine J. & Golden, Robert E. For Argument's Sake: A Guide to Writing Effective Arguments. 2nd ed. LC 95-15722. 224p. (C). 1996. text 29.06 (*0-673-52459-0*) Addison-Wesley Educ.

Mayberry, Maralee. Meeting the Challenge: Innovative Feminist Pedagogies in Action. LC 98-37302. 1999. 80.00 (*0-415-92248-8*) Routledge.

Mayberry, Maralee & Rose, Ellen C. Meeting the Challenge: Innovative Feminist Pedagogies in Action. LC 98-37302. 1999. pap. 22.99 (*0-415-92249-6*) Routledge.

Mayberry, Maralee, et al. Home Schooling: Parents As Educators. LC 94-23543. (Illus.). 144p. 1995. 49.95 (*0-8039-6075-1*); pap. 21.95 (*0-8039-6076-X*) Corwin Pr.

Mayberry, Maralee, jt. auth. see Stockard, Jean.

Mayberry, Mark, jt. auth. see Scriven, John.

Mayberry, Nancy, jt. auth. see Mayberry, Robert.

Mayberry, Nancy, ed. see Fernandez de Mesa, Blas.

Mayberry, Robert & Mayberry, Nancy. Francisco Martinez de la Rosa. (Twayne's World Authors Ser.: No. 618). 176p. (C). 1988. 28.95 (*0-8057-6460-7*, TWAS 618) Macmillan.

Mayberry, Sara O., ed. Healthcare Design. LC 96-12446. (Series in Healthcare & Senior Living Design). 340p. 1996. 80.00 (*0-471-13349-3*) Wiley.

Mayberry, Susanah. My Amiable Uncle: Recollections about Booth Tarkington. LC 82-81021. (Illus.). 160p. 1983. 24.95 (*0-911198-66-0*) Purdue U Pr.

— Of Love & Leland: A World War II Generation Memoir. 110p. 1997. 19.95 (*1-57860-003-0*) Guild Pr IN.

***Mayberry, Tom.** Coleridge & Wordsworth: The Crucible of Friendship. 2000. reprint ed. pap. 16.95 (*0-7509-2507-8*, Pub. by Sutton Publng) Intl Pubs Mktg.

Mayberry, Tom. Coleridge & Wordsworth in the West Country. (Illus.). 224p. 1994. pap. 22.95 (*0-7509-0628-6*, Pub. by Sutton Pub Ltd) Intl Pubs Mktg.

Maybery, Paul, ed. see Line, Lorie.

Maybin, ed. Using English. LC 96-207979. (Illus.). 352p. (C). 1996. 75.00 (*0-415-13119-7*); pap. 24.99 (*0-415-13120-0*) Routledge.

Maybin, Janet, ed. Language & Literacy in Social Practice. LC 93-29932. 264p. 1993. 74.95 (*1-85359-216-1*, Pub. by Multilingual Matters); pap. 29.95 (*1-85359-215-3*, Pub. by Multilingual Matters) Taylor & Francis.

Maybin, Janet, jt. ed. see Stierer, Barry.

Maybon, Charles B. & Fredet, Jean. Histoire de la Concession Francaise de Changhai. LC 78-38077. reprint ed. 82.50 (*0-404-56941-2*) AMS Pr.

Maybury, Anne. I Am Gabriella! large type ed. 1983. 15.95 (*0-7089-0979-5*) Ulverscroft.

— Midnight Dancers. large type ed. LC 91-8483. 498p. 1991. reprint ed. lib. bdg. 20.95 (*1-56054-160-1*) Thorndike Pr.

— The Moonlit Door. large type ed. 448p. 1995. 27.99 (*0-7089-3222-3*) Ulverscroft.

***Maybury, Anne.** Shadow of a Stranger. large type ed. LC 99-56103. 288p. 2000. lib. bdg. 25.95 (*1-58547-019-8*) Ctr Point Pubg.

Maybury, Anne. Walk in the Paradise Garden. large type ed. 1983. 15.95 (*0-7089-1004-1*) Ulverscroft.

Maybury, Jennifer. Take a Number: Poetry in E-Motion. LC 97-65874. (Illus.). 128p. (Orig.). 1997. pap. 10.95 (*1-889120-08-1*) StarsEnd Creations.

Maybury-Lewis, Biorn. The Politics of the Possible: The Brazilian Rural Workers' Trade Union Movement, 1964-1985. LC 93-26985. 320p. 1994. 69.95 (*1-56639-166-0*); pap. 22.95 (*1-56639-167-9*) Temple U Pr.

Maybury-Lewis, David. Indigenous People, Ethnic Groups, & the State. LC 98-122570. 168p. 1996. pap. text 20.00 (*0-205-19816-3*) Allyn.

***Maybury-Lewis, David.** Millennium: Tribal Wisdom & the Modern World. (Illus.). 397p. 1999. reprint ed. text 25.00 (*0-7881-6418-X*) DIANE Pub.

Maybury-Lewis, David, ed. Dialectical Societies: The Ge & Bororo of Central Brazil. LC 79-10689. (Harvard Studies in Cultural Anthropology: No. 1). (Illus.). 354p. 1979. 43.50 (*0-674-20285-6*) HUP.

Maybury-Lewis, David & Almagor, Uri, eds. The Attraction of Opposites: Thought & Society in a Dualistic Mode. 384p. 1989. text 65.00 (*0-472-10094-7*, 10094); pap. text 24.95 (*0-472-08086-5*, 08086) U of Mich Pr.

Maybury, Mark & Wahlster, Wolfgang. Readings in Intelligent User Interfaces. LC 98-16058. 736p. 1998. pap. 59.95 (*1-55860-444-8*) Morgan Kaufmann.

Maybury, Mark T., ed. Intelligent Multimedia Information Retrieval. LC 97-591. (AAAI Press Ser.). (Illus.). 500p. 1997. pap. text 40.00 (*0-262-63179-2*) MIT Pr.

— Intelligent Multimedia Interfaces. (AAAI Press Ser.). (Illus.). 413p. 1993. pap. text 44.00 (*0-262-63150-4*) MIT Pr.

Maybury, Mark T., jt. ed. see Mani, Inderjeet.

Maybury, Richard J. Ancient Rome: How It Affects You Today. Williams, Jane A., ed. LC 95-14032. (Uncle Eric Bk.). (Illus.). 93p. (Orig.). 1995. pap. 8.95 (*0-942617-22-3*) Blstckng Pr.

— Are You Liberal? Conservative? or Confused? Williams, Jane A., ed. LC 95-12484. (Uncle Eric Bk.). (Illus.). 139p. (Orig.). 1995. pap. 9.95 (*0-942617-23-1*) Blstckng Pr.

— The Clipper Ship Strategy: For Success in Your Career, Business & Investments. LC 97-14454. (An "Uncle Eric" Bks.). 265p. (YA). (gr. 9 up). 1997. 15.95 (*0-942617-28-2*) Blstckng Pr.

— Evaluating Books - What Would Thomas Jefferson Think about This? Guidelines for Selecting Books: Consistent with the Principles of America's Founders. 106p. (YA). (gr. 7 up). 1994. 8.95 (*0-942617-14-2*) Blstckng Pr.

***Maybury, Richard J.** The Money Mystery: The Hidden Force Affecting Your Career, Business & Investments. 2nd ed. LC 99-29734. ("Uncle Eric" Book Ser.). 1999. 9.95 (*0-942617-34-7*) Blstckng Pr.

— The Thousand Year War: How It Affects You Today in the Mideast. Williams, Jane A., ed. LC 99-11076. (Uncle Eric Bks.). (YA). (gr. 7 up). 1999. pap. 17.95 (*0-942617-32-0*) Blstckng Pr.

Maybury, Richard J. Uncle Eric Talks about Personal, Career & Financial Security. LC 94-11733. (Uncle Eric Bk.). 45p. (YA). (gr. 7 up). 1994. 7.95 (*0-942617-20-7*) Blstckng Pr.

— Whatever Happened to Justice? Williams, Jane A., ed. (Uncle Eric Bks.). (Illus.). 256p. (Orig.). (J). (gr. 7 up). 1993. pap. 14.95 (*0-942617-10-X*) Blstckng Pr.

***Maybury, Rick.** Whatever Happened to Penny Candy? A Fast, Clear & Fun Explanation of the Economics You Need for Success in Your Career, Business & Investments. 4th rev. ed. Williams, Jane A., ed. LC 00-24350. (Uncle Eric Bks.). (Illus.). 192p. (J). 2000. pap. 12.95 (*0-942617-31-2*) Blstckng Pr.

Maychell, Karen, jt. auth. see Stillman, Andy.

Maychick, Diana. Audrey Hepburn: An Intimate Portrait. (Citadel Stars Ser.). (Illus.). 256p. 1996. mass mkt. 5.99 (*0-8065-8000-3*, Citadel Pr) Carol Pub Group.

Mayck, Arthur & Waddell, Gene. Charleston in Eighteen Eighty-Three. (Illus.). 176p. 1984. reprint ed. pap. 15.00 (*0-89308-428-X*) Southern Hist Pr.

Maycock, A. L. Nicholas Ferrar of Little Gidding. LC 80-16684. 334p. reprint ed. pap. 103.60 (*0-8357-9131-9*, 201934500011) Bks Demand.

Maycock, Stephen. Miller's Rock & Pop Memorabilia. (Illus.). 160p. 1997. 24.95 (*1-85732-270-3*, Pub. by Millers Pubns) Antique Collect.

Maycock, Stephen, jt. auth. see Ould, Alan.

Maycock, Susan E. An Architectural History of Carbondale, Illinois. LC 82-19189. (Illus.). 256p. 1983. pap. 17.95 (*0-8093-1120-8*) S Ill U Pr.

Maycroft, Elizabeth. The Wondrous World of Winter: Photographs from the Heart. (Illus.). 256p. 1998. 60.00 (*1-888122-03-X*) Status Pubs.

Maycunich, Ann, jt. auth. see Gilley, Jerry W.

Mayda, Jaro. Francois Geny & Modern Jurisprudence. fac. ed. LC 78-17864. 288p. 1978. reprint ed. pap. 89.30 (*0-7837-7930-5*, 204768600008) Bks Demand.

***Maydak, Mike.** Endangered Animals. (Wild Stickers Ser.). (Illus.). 2000. pap. 2.50 (*0-941042-28-6*) Dog Eared Pubns.

Mayden, Bronwyn. First Talk: A Teen Pregnancy Prevention Dialogue among Latinos. 1999. pap. 14.95 (*0-87868-761-0*) Child Welfare.

— Sexuality Education for Youths in Care: A State-by-State Survey. 1996. pap. text 6.95 (*0-87868-639-8*) Child Welfare.

Mayden, Bronwyn & Brooks, Thomas R. Welfare Reform & Teen Parents: An Issue Brief. 24p. 1996. pap. 6.95 (*0-87868-657-6*) Child Welfare.

Mayden, Richard L. Phylogenetic Studies of North American Minnows, with Emphasis on the Genus Cyprinella: Teleostei: Cypiniformes. (Miscellaneous Publications: No. 80). (Illus.). 189p. 1989. pap. text 15.00 (*0-89338-029-6*) U KS Nat Hist Mus.

Mayden, Richard L., ed. Systematics, Historical Ecology, & North American Freshwater Fishes. LC 92-19781. xvi, 969p. 1992. 99.50 (*0-8047-2162-9*) Stanford U Pr.

Mayden, Richard L. & Burr, Brooks M. Life History of the Slender Madtom, Noturus Exilis, in Southern Illinois: Pisces: Ictaluridae. (Occasional Papers: No. 93). 64p. 1981. 1.00 (*0-317-04827-9*) U KS Nat Hist Mus.

Mayden, Richard L., jt. auth. see Burr, Brooks M.

Maydew, Gary L. Agribusiness Accounting & Taxation. Tuszynski, Judith & Higgins, Kathleen, eds. 572p. 1997. text 65.00 (*0-8080-0149-3*) CCH INC.

***Maydew, Gary L.** Agribusiness Accounting & Taxation: Cumulative Supplement. 2nd ed. 60p. 1999. pap. text, suppl. ed. 20.00 (*0-8080-0418-2*) CCH INC.

Maydew, Gary L. Small Business Taxation: Planning & Practice. 2nd ed. Marshall, Frederick, ed. LC 98-141970. xiv, 552p. (C). 1997. 74.95 (*0-8080-0199-X*) CCH INC.

Maydew, Randall C. America's Lost H-Bomb! Palomares, Spain, 1966. LC 98-162850. (Illus.). xi, 160p. 1997. pap. 16.95 (*0-89745-214-3*) Sunflower U Pr.

***Maye, Beth.** The Marble. Wise, Noreen, ed. (Lemonade Collection). 96p. (YA). (gr. 4 up). 2000. pap. 6.95 (*1-58584-264-8*) Huckleberry CT.

Maye, Jennifer. The ABC Approach to Financial Aid. Rovenal, Cynthia, ed. LC 96-71661. (Orig.). 1997. pap. 14.95 (*0-9655725-0-1*) Natl Student Finan.

Maye, John. Colorado Corporate Forms, 3 vols. 3rd rev. ed. 1501p. 1998. ring bd. 275.00 (*0-327-00130-5*, 80301-11) LEXIS Pub.

Mayeda, Sengaku & Koller, John M., eds. A Thousand Teachings: The Upadesasahasri of Sankara. LC 91-9641. 265p. (C). 1992. text 20.50 (*0-7914-0943-0*) State U NY Pr.

Mayeell, Mark, jt. auth. see Natural Health Magazine Editors.

Mayekiso, Mzwanele. Township Politics: Civic Struggles for a New South Africa. (Illus.). 288p. (Orig.). (C). 1995. 30.00 (*0-85345-966-5*, Pub. by Monthly Rev); pap. 18.00 (*0-85345-965-7*, Pub. by Monthly Rev) NYU Pr.

Mayell, Mark. Natural Energy: A Consumer's Guide to Legal, Mind-Altering & Mood-Brightening Herbs & Supplements. LC 97-24045. 304p. 1998. pap. 15.00 (*0-517-88812-2*) Harmony Bks.

***Mayell, Mark, ed.** The Natural health First-Aid Guide: The Definitive Handbook of Natural Remedies for Treating Minor Emergencies. 544p. 2000. reprint ed. text 24.00 (*0-7881-6986-6*) DIANE Pub.

Mayell, Mark, jt. auth. see Cousens, Gabriel.

Mayell, Mark, jt. auth. see Natural Health Magazine Editors.

***Mayer.** ACT! X for Windows for Dummies. (For Dummies Ser.). 384p. 1999. pap. 19.99 (*0-7645-0561-0*) IDG Bks.

Mayer. The Alien. LC 93-73762. (Magic Days Ser.). (Illus.). 32p. (J). (ps-3). 1995. pap. text 4.69 (*0-307-16661-9*, 16661, Goldn Books) Gldn Bks Pub Co.

***Mayer.** Articulated Peasant. 2000. 65.00 (*0-8133-3715-1*, Pub. by Westview); pap. 24.00 (*0-8133-3716-X*, Pub. by Westview) HarpC.

Mayer. Embalming: History, Theory & Practice. 3rd ed. 683p. (C). 2000. 75.00 (*0-8385-2187-8*, Apple Lange Med) McGraw.

— Fundamentals of Voice & Articulation. 11th ed. 1995. teacher ed. 11.87 (*0-697-27067-X*, WCB McGr Hill) McGrw-H Hghr Educ.

— Fundamentals of Voice & Articulation. 12th ed. 336p. 1998. pap. 39.69 (*0-697-35508-X*) McGraw.

— International Auction Records, 1993. (Illus.). 2130p. 1993. 179.00 (*1-56466-053-2*) Archer Fields.

***Mayer.** Just a New Neighbor. (Mercer Mayer's Little Critter Ser.). 24p. (J). 2000. pap. text. write for info. (*0-307-13265-X*) Gldn Bks Pub Co.

— Just Me & My Family. (Mercer Mayer's Little Critter Ser.). (Illus.). 160p. (J). 1999. 9.99 (*0-307-34094-5*, Goldn Books) Gldn Bks Pub Co.

Mayer. The Prince. LC 94-77863. (Magic Days Ser.). (Illus.). 32p. (J). (ps-3). 1995. pap. text 4.69 (*0-307-16665-1*, 16665, Goldn Books) Gldn Bks Pub Co.

— Swamp Thing. LC 93-73742. (Magic Days Ser.). (Illus.). 32p. (J). (ps-3). 1995. pap. text 4.69 (*0-307-16660-0*, 16660, Goldn Books) Gldn Bks Pub Co.

— What Can a Man Do? 1993. lib. bdg. 25.00 (*0-226-51348-3*) U Ch Pr.

Mayer & Rimini. Ion Beam Handbook for Material Analysis. 488p. 1977. 125.00 (*0-12-480860-3*) Acad Pr.

Mayer, et al. Old Maryland. (Historical Ser.). (Illus.). 1976. pap. 3.50 (*0-8940-022-7*, SB-022) Sun Pub.

Mayer, A. L., jt. auth. see Deutschen Akademie der Wissenschaften Staff.

Mayer, A. M. & Poljakoff-Mayber, A. The Germination of Seeds. 3rd ed. (Illus.). 212p. 1982. text 51.00 (*0-08-028854-5*, Pergamon Pr); pap. text 35.00 (*0-08-028853-7*, Pergamon Pr) Elsevier.

Mayer, Adele. Repressed Memories of Sexual Abuse. 1995. pap. 11.95 (*1-55691-117-3*, 173) Learning Pubns.

— Sex Offenders: Perspectives & Approaches to Understanding & Management. LC 86-45796. 300p. 1988. pap. 19.95 (*0-918452-95-3*, 953) Learning Pubns.

— Sexual Abuse: Causes, Consequences & Treatment of Incestuous & Pedophilic Acts. LC 84-80657. 176p. 1985. pap. 19.95 (*1-55691-059-2*, 592) Learning Pubns.

— Walking Victims: Understanding & Treating Abused Women Who Repeat the Cycle. LC 97-147699. 134p. 1997. pap. 15.95 (*1-55691-126-2*, 262) Learning Pubns.

— Women Sex Offenders: Treatment & Dynamics. 1991. pap. 16.95 (*1-55691-063-0*, 630) Learning Pubns.

Mayer, Adrian C. Land & Society in Malabar. LC 73-13032. 158p. 1974. reprint ed. lib. bdg. 55.00 (*0-8371-7103-2*, MASM, Greenwood Pr) Greenwood.

Mayer, Albert, et al. Pilot Project, India. LC 72-12332. (Illus.). 367p. 1973. reprint ed. lib. bdg. 75.00 (*0-8371-6729-9*, MAPI, Greenwood Pr) Greenwood.

Mayer, Albert I., Jr. Olympiad. LC 61-12875. (Illus.). (YA). (gr. 7 up). 1938. 22.00 (*0-8196-0115-2*) Biblo.

M

Mayer, Albert J., III. Real Estate Office Management: People, Functions, Systems. 2nd ed. LC 88-31636. (Illus.). 350p. 1988. reprint ed. pap. 23.00 (*0-913652-64-4*, 113) Realtors Natl.

Mayer, Alfred, compiled by. Annals of European Civilization, 1501-1900. LC 83-45811. reprint ed. 42.00 (*0-404-20172-5*) AMS Pr.

Mayer, Alois. Mayer's Best of Vermont: A Pictorial Collection of the Green Mountain State. (Illus.). 80p. (Orig.). 1997. pap. 13.95 (*0-9657583-0-3*, 51395) Mayer Photo-graphics.

Mayer, Andrew, et al, eds. Protect the President: Outrageous Editorials from the Ultra-Right Newspaper Publisher William Loeb. LC 79-87929. (Illus.). 1979. pap. 9.95 (*0-932400-01-9*) Intervale Pub Co.

Mayer, Andy. Good Dog, Millie: A Day in the Life of America's Most Influential Canine. 30p. 1992. 8.95 (*0-02-508201-9*) Macmillan.

Mayer, Andy & Becker, Jim. Fire Trucks. LC 92-61195. (Look & Listen Board Books Ser.). (Illus.). 10p. (J). (ps). 1993. bds. 6.95 (*0-590-46298-9*, Cartwheel) Scholastic Inc.

— The Official Book of Thumb Wrestling. LC 80-51513. (Illus.). 1983. bds. 5.95 (*0-89480-363-8*, 363) Workman Pub.

— Work Trucks. LC 92-61194. (Look & Listen Board Books Ser.). (Illus.). 10p. (J). (ps). 1993. pap. 6.95 (*0-590-46299-7*, Cartwheel) Scholastic Inc.

Mayer, Andy, jt. auth. see Becker, Jim.

Mayer, Anita L. Clothing from the Hands That Weave. LC 84-81051. (Illus.). 168p. 1986. pap., spiral bd. 18.00 (*0-934026-14-9*) Interweave.

— Handwoven Clothing Felted to Wear. LC 87-63347. (Illus.). 100p. 1988. pap. 16.95 (*0-916658-45-7*) Shuttle Craft.

Mayer, Ann E. Artists in Dylan Thomas's Prose Works: Adam Naming & Aesop Fabling. LC 96-149581. 208p. 1996. 55.00 (*0-7735-1306-X*, Pub. by McG-Queens Univ Pr) CUP Services.

— Islam & Human Rights. 250p. 1996. 64.95 (*0-614-21485-8*, 543); pap. 23.95 (*0-614-21484-X*, 543) Kazi Pubns.

— Islam & Human Rights: Tradition & Politics. 3rd ed. LC 98-20762. 280p. 1998. text 69.00 (*0-8133-3564-7*, Pub. by Westview); pap. text 26.00 (*0-8133-3504-3*, Pub. by Westview) HarpC.

***Mayer, Arno J.** The Furies: Violence & Terror in the French & Russian Revolutions. LC 99-59145. 700p. 2000. 35.00 (*0-691-04897-5*, Pub. by Princeton U Pr) Cal Prin Full Svc.

Mayer, Augusto. El Estilo Gotico en Espana. 3rd ed. (SPA., Illus.). 307p. 1960. lib. bdg. 35.00 (*0-8288-3937-9*, S16754) Fr & Eur.

Mayer, B. Mexico: Aztec, Spanish & Republican, 2 vols. 1976. lib. bdg. 250.00 (*0-8490-2246-0*) Gordon Pr.

***Mayer, B., et al, eds.** Nitric Oxide. LC 99-87335. (Handbook of Experimental Pharmacology Ser.: 413). x, 630p. 2000. 399.00 (*3-540-66122-0*) Spr-Verlag.

Mayer, Barbara. The College Survival Guide. (Illus.). 160p. 1992. pap. 6.95 (*0-8442-6674-4*, VGM Career) NTC Contemp Pub Co.

— Complete Book of Home Decorating. 256p. 1994. pap. 19.95 (*1-56799-063-0*, Friedman-Fairfax) M Friedman Pub Grp Inc.

— The High School Survival Guide. (Illus.). 160p. 1994. pap. 6.95 (*0-8442-6670-1*, VGM Career) NTC Contemp Pub Co.

— How to Succeed in High School. (Illus.). 176p. 1995. pap. 8.95 (*0-8442-8121-2*, Natl Textbk Co) NTC Contemp Pub Co.

— How to Succeed in High School. 2nd rev. ed. LC 99-23655. 176p. 1999. pap. 11.95 (*0-8442-2941-5*, VGM Career) NTC Contemp Pub Co.

— In the Arts & Crafts Style. (Illus.). 224p. 1992. 40.00 (*0-8118-0202-7*) Chronicle Bks.

— Succeed in College. LC 98-8249. (Here's How Ser.). 160p. 1998. pap. 12.95 (*0-8442-2489-8*) NTC Contemp Pub Co.

— Succeed in High School. LC 97-30879. (Here's How Ser.). (Illus.). 176p. 1997. pap. 12.95 (*0-8442-2478-2*, 24782, NTC Learningworks) NTC Contemp Pub Co.

Mayer, Becker, ed. The Hungry Traveler Vol. 1: Mexico. LC 96-86643. (Hungry Traveler Ser.). (Illus.). 224p. (Orig.). 1997. pap. 8.95 (*0-8362-2724-7*) Andrews & McMeel.

— The Hungry Traveler Vol. 2: Germany. LC 96-86642. (Hungry Traveler Ser.). (Illus.). 304p. (Orig.). 1997. pap. 8.95 (*0-8362-2725-5*) Andrews & McMeel.

— The Hungry Traveler Vol. 3: Italy. LC 96-86641. (Hungry Traveler Ser.). (Illus.). 256p. (Orig.). 1997. pap. 8.95 (*0-8362-2726-3*) Andrews & McMeel.

— The Hungry Traveler Vol. 4: France. LC 96-86639. (Hungry Traveler Ser.). (Illus.). 208p. (Orig.). 1997. pap. 8.95 (*0-8362-2727-1*) Andrews & McMeel.

Mayer, Becker, jt. auth. see Zullo, Kathryn.

Mayer, Becker J., jt. auth. see Depue, Anne.

Mayer, Becker J., jt. auth. see Garrity, John.

Mayer, Ben S., jt. auth. see Liller, William.

Mayer, Bernadette. Another Smashed Pinecone. 96p. 1998. pap. 10.00 (*0-935992-20-0*) United Art Bks.

— A Bernadette Mayer Reader. LC 91-43995. 144p. (Orig.). 1992. pap. 11.95 (*0-8112-1203-3*, NDP739, Pub. by New Directions) Norton.

— The Desires of Mothers to Please Others in Letters. 346p. 1994. pap. 12.95 (*0-9638433-1-1*) Hard Pr MA.

— The Formal Field of Kissing. 32p. 1990. pap. 6.00 (*0-685-56988-8*) SPD-Small Pr Dist.

— Memory. 150p. 1975. pap. 4.00 (*0-913028-39-8*) North Atlantic.

— Midwinter Day. LC 98-54649. 119p. 1999. reprint ed. pap. 12.95 (*0-8112-1406-0*, NDP876, Pub. by New Directions) SPD-Small Pr Dist.

— Poetry. 1976. 7.00 (*0-686-16289-7*); pap. 3.50 (*0-686-16290-0*) Kulchur Foun.

— Proper Name & Other Stories. 144p. (Orig.). 1996. pap. 13.95 (*0-8112-1325-0*, NDP824, Pub. by New Directions) Norton.

Mayer, Bernadette, jt. auth. see Worsley, Dale.

Mayer, Bernard. Entombed: My True Story: How Forty-Five Jews Lived Underground & Survived the Holocaust. LC 94-71465. (Illus.). 206p. (Orig.). (YA). (gr. 8-12). 1994. pap. 9.95 (*0-9641508-0-8*) Aleric Pr.

***Mayer, Bernard S.** The Dynamics of Conflict Resolution: A Practitioner's Guide. LC 99-50576. 2000. 34.95 (*0-7879-5019-X*) Jossey-Bass.

Mayer, Bill. Longing. 90p. (Orig.). 1993. pap. 9.95 (*0-9636556-0-4*) Pangaea Bks.

Mayer, Bill. Shadow Games: A Book of Hand & Puppet Shadows. 40p. (J). (ps-2). 1995. spiral bd. 10.95 (*1-57054-030-6*) Klutz.

Mayer, Bill, jt. auth. see Harris, Joel Chandler.

Mayer, Brantz, ed. Captain Canot, or Twenty Years of an African Slaver. LC 68-29011. (American Negro: His History & Literature. Series 1). 1969. reprint ed. 32.95 (*0-405-01830-4*) Ayer.

Mayer, Brantz, ed. see Carroll, Charles H.

Mayer, Brown & Platt Staff, ed. see Allison, Courtney D., et al.

Mayer-Browne, Elizabeth. Best of Austrian Cuisine. LC 96-6559. (Cookbook Classics Ser.). 224p. 1997. reprint ed. pap. 11.95 (*0-7818-0526-0*) Hippocrene Bks.

Mayer, C. H. The Continuing Struggle: Autobiography of a Labor Activist. LC 89-62399. 187p. 1989. pap. 11.95 (*0-938875-20-5*) Pittenbruach Pr.

Mayer, C. P., jt. auth. see Davis, E. P.

Mayer, Carl, jt. auth. see Meringer, Rudolf.

Mayer, Charles S., jt. auth. see Adler, Lee.

Mayer, Charles W., jt. ed. see Logsdon, Loren.

Mayer, Christine A., jt. auth. see Cummings, Kevin S.

Mayer, Colin & Vives, Xavier, eds. Capital Markets & Financial Intermediation. (Illus.). 377p. (C). 1995. pap. text 22.95 (*0-521-55853-0*) Cambridge U Pr.

— Financial Intermediation. 377p. (C). 1993. text 59.95 (*0-521-44397-0*) Cambridge U Pr.

Mayer, Colin, jt. auth. see Franks, Julian.

Mayer, Colin, jt. auth. see Jenkinson, Tim.

Mayer, Colin, jt. ed. see Giovannini, Alberto.

Mayer Culpepper, Marilyn & Gianakos, Perry E. Writing for Life: A Writer's Reader. (C). 1988. pap., teacher ed. write for info. (*0-02-341790-0*, U2558-7) Allyn.

Mayer, Cynthia, jt. auth. see Liggett, Twila C.

Mayer, D. P. & Kemper, F. H., eds. Acesulfame-K. (Food Science & Technology Ser.: Vol. 47). (Illus.). 256p. 1991. text 150.00 (*0-8247-8530-4*) Dekker.

Mayer, Dale C. Dining with the Hoover Family: A Collection of Reminiscences & Recipes. (Illus.). 96p. (Orig.). 1991. pap. 5.00 (*0-938469-11-8*) Hoover Lib.

Mayer, Dale C., ed. Lou Henry Hoover: Essays on a Busy Life. LC 93-78297. (Illus.). 160p. 1994. 23.50 (*1-881019-04-7*) High Plns WY.

Mayer, Daniel F., jt. auth. see Johansen, Carl A.

Mayer, David. Harlequin in His Element: The English Pantomine, 1806-1836. LC 79-88809. 420p. 1969. reprint ed. pap. 130.20 (*0-7837-2297-4*, 205738500004) Bks Demand.

— Playing Out the Empire: Ben-Hur & Other Toga Plays & Films, 1883-1908. A Critical Anthology. (Illus.). 336p. (C). 1994. text 65.00 (*0-19-811990-9*) OUP.

— Sergei M. Eisenstein's Potemkin: A Shot-by-Shot Presentation. (Quality Paperbacks Ser.). (Illus.). 256p. 1990. reprint ed. pap. 12.95 (*0-306-80388-7*) Da Capo.

Mayer, David, jt. ed. see Melanson, Richard A.

Mayer, David, ed. & intro. see Wallace, Lew.

Mayer, David C., jt. auth. see Mullins, Charles E.

Mayer, David N. The Constitutional Thought of Thomas Jefferson. LC 93-29649. 416p. (C). 1995. pap. text 19.50 (*0-8139-1485-X*) U Pr of Va.

Mayer, David P., et al. Foot & Ankle: A Sectional Imaging Atlas. LC 93-9264. (Illus.). 228p. 1993. text 120.00 (*0-7216-3199-1*, W B Saunders Co) Harcrt Hlth Sci Grp.

Mayer, Debby. Literary Agents: The Essential Guide for Writers. LC 97-34446. 172p. 1998. pap. 12.95 (*0-14-026873-1*) Viking Penguin.

Mayer, Dorothy M. Angelica Kauffmann, R. A. 1741-1807. 192p. 1972. 50.00 (*0-900675-68-3*, Pub. by Smyth) Dufour.

— The Forgotten Master: The Life & Times of Louis Spohr. LC 80-27659. (Music Reprint Ser.). 208p. 1981. reprint ed. 29.50 (*0-306-76099-1*) Da Capo.

Mayer, Doug. The Slightly Skewed Computer Dictionary. LC 94-19285. 96p. 1994. pap. 8.95 (*1-55958-432-7*) Prima Pub.

Mayer, Douglas F., jt. auth. see Clemens, John K.

***Mayer, E. & Saper, C., eds.** The Biological Basis for Mind Body Interactions. LC 99-59943. (Progress in Brain Research Ser.). 1999. write for info. (*0-444-50049-9*, Excerpta Medica) Elsevier.

Mayer, Edgar. Die Reiseerzahlung des Lukas (Lk 9, 51 - 19, 10) Entscheidung in der Wuste. (Europaische Hochschulschriften Ser.: Reihe 23, Bd. 554). (GER.). 358p. 1996. 61.95 (*3-631-49638-9*) P Lang Pubng.

Mayer, Edgar N. Structure of French: A Programmed Course on the Linguistic Structure of French. (C). 1969. pap. text 9.75 (*0-89197-429-6*) Irvington.

Mayer, Eduard V. Schopenhauers Aesthetik und Ihr Verhaeltnis zu den Aesthetischen Lehren Kants und Schellings. (Abhandlungen Zur Philosophie und Ihrer Geschichte Ser.: Bd. 9). (GER.). vi, 82p. 1980. reprint ed. write for info. (*3-487-06772-2*) G Olms Pubs.

Mayer, Egon. Children of Intermarriage: A Study in Pattern of Identification & Family Life. LC 83-82077. 56p. 1983. pap. 2.50 (*0-87495-055-4*) Am Jewish Comm.

— Love & Tradition: Marriage Between Jews & Christians. LC 85-6588. 311p. reprint ed. pap. 96.50 (*0-608-08571-5*, 206909400002) Bks Demand.

Mayer, Egon & Avgar, Amy. Conversion among the Intermarried: Choosing to Become Jewish. LC 87-70999. 44p. (Orig.). 1987. pap. 5.00 (*0-87495-091-0*) Am Jewish Comm.

Mayer, Egon & Sheingold, Carl. Intermarriage & the Jewish Future. LC 79-63378. 46p. 1980. pap. 2.00 (*0-87495-031-7*) Am Jewish Comm.

Mayer, Elise, ed. see Barley, Chris S.

Mayer, Elizabeth, tr. see Goethe, Johann Wolfgang Von.

Mayer, Elizabeth, tr. see Stifter, Adalbert.

Mayer, Elizabeth L. Basic Learning Skills Bk. II: How Music Can Contribute, Bk. II. (Music Makes a Difference Ser.). 12p. 1994. pap. 1.95 (*1-886380-01-5*) Langstaff Vid.

— Let's Keep Singing! John Langstaff Sings with Children Ages 6-10. (Making Music with John Langstaff Ser.). (J). (gr. 2-5). 1997. pap. 4.95 (*1-886380-23-6*) Langstaff Vid.

— Let's Sing! John Langstaff Sings with Children Ages 3-7. (Making Music with John Langstaff Ser.). (J). (ps-2). 1997. pap. 4.95 (*1-886380-22-8*) Langstaff Vid.

— Let's Sing & Let's Keep Singing! John Langstaff Sings with Children, 2 vols., Set. (Making Music with John Langstaff Ser.). (J). (gr. k-5). 1997. pap. 8.95 (*1-886380-24-4*) Langstaff Vid.

— Making Music in the Classroom: Ages 3 - 7. (Making Music with John Langstaff Ser.). 24p. (J). (ps-2). 1994. pap., per. 4.95 (*1-886380-07-4*) Langstaff Vid.

— Making Music in the Classroom: Ages 7-11. (Making Music with John Langstaff Ser.). 24p. (J). (gr. 2-6). 1994. pap. 4.95 (*1-886380-08-2*) Langstaff Vid.

— Making Music with Children: Ages 3-7. (Making Music with John Langstaff Ser.). 24p. (J). (ps-2). 1994. pap. 4.95 (*1-886380-05-8*) Langstaff Vid.

— Making Music with Children: Ages 7-11. (Making Music with John Langstaff Ser.). 24p. (J). (gr. 2-7). 1994. pap. 4.95 (*1-886380-06-6*) Langstaff Vid.

— Making Music with Children Bk. I: Why It Matters, Bk. I. (Music Makes a Difference Ser.). 12p. 1994. pap. text, per. 1.95 (*1-886380-00-7*) Langstaff Vid.

— Making Music with John Langstaff Series. 96p. (J). (ps). 1994. pap. 10.95 (*1-886380-09-0*) Langstaff Vid.

— The Whole Child Bk. III: How Music Fits In, Bk. III. (Music Makes a Difference Ser.). 12p. 1994. pap. 1.95 (*1-886380-02-3*) Langstaff Vid.

Mayer, Elizabeth L. & Langstaff, John M. Music Makes a Difference Series, Bks. I. 48p. 1994. pap. 5.95 (*1-886380-04-X*) Langstaff Vid.

Mayer, Emeran A. & Raybould, Helen, eds. Basic & Clinical Aspects of Chronic Abdominal Pain. LC 93-11488. (Pain Research & Clinical Management Ser.: Vol. 9). 356p. 1993. 252.00 (*0-444-89437-3*) Elsevier.

Mayer, Enrique. Dictionnaire des Meubles et Objets D'Art: 8,000 Prix En Ventes Publiques. (FRE.). 720p. 1993. 450.00 (*0-7859-7836-4*, 2226059601) Fr & Eur.

Mayer, Eric, jt. auth. see Reed, Mary.

Mayer, Eva M. As Shadows Darken. LC 96-90125. xii, 305p. (Orig.). 1996. pap. 10.99 (*0-9651539-0-8*) Tri-Cross.

Mayer, F. E. & Piepkorn, Arthur C. The Religious Bodies of America. 616p. 1968. 25.00 (*0-570-03294-6*, 15-1714) Concordia.

Mayer, F. L. & Hamelink, J. L., eds. Aquatic Toxicology & Hazard Evaluation: First Conference- STP 634. 315p. 1977. 30.75 (*0-8031-0278-X*, STP634) ASTM.

Mayer, F. Stephan & Sutton, Karen. Personality: An Integrative Approach. LC 95-38601. 652p. 1996. 87.00 (*0-02-378180-7*, Macmillan Coll) P-H.

Mayer, Fanny H. Ancient Tales in Modern Japan: An Anthology of Japanese Folk Tales. LC 84-47746. (Illus.). 382p. reprint ed. pap. 118.50 (*0-8357-3940-6*, 205703500004) Bks Demand.

Mayer, Fanny H., ed. from JPN. The Yanagita Kunio Guide to the Japanese Folk Tale. LC 85-45291. (Illus.). 392p. (C). 1986. 31.50 (*0-253-36812-X*) Ind U Pr.

Mayer, Fanny H., tr. see Yanagita, Kunio.

Mayer, Francis. The 47th Proposition of Euclid. 50p. 1996. reprint ed. pap. 14.95 (*1-56459-987-6*) Kessinger Pub.

Mayer, Frank. Cytology & Morphogenesis of Bacteria. (Handbuch der Pflanzenanatomie Encyclopedia of Plant Anatomy - Traite d' Anatomie Vegetale Ser.: Vol. 6, Pt. 2). (Illus.). x, 290p. 1986. 88.00 (*3-443-14017-3*, Pub. by Gebruder Borntraeger) Balogh.

Mayer, Frank & Norris, John R., eds. Methods in Microbiology Vol. 20: Electron Microscopy in Microbiology. 431p. 1988. text 125.00 (*0-12-521520-7*) Acad Pr.

Mayer, Frank A. Adenauer & Kennedy: A Study in German-American Relations, 1961-1963. LC 95-37633. (Franklin & Eleanor Roosevelt Institute Series on Diplomatic & Economic History). 160p. 1996. text 45.00 (*0-312-12952-1*) St Martin.

— The Opposition Years: Winston Churchill & the Conservative Party, 1945- 1951. LC 91-4348. (American University Studies: History: Ser. IX, Vols. 116). 187p. (C). 1992. text 36.95 (*0-8204-1661-4*) P Lang Pubng.

Mayer, Frank B. With Pen & Pencil on the Frontier in 1851: The Diary & Sketches of Frank Blackwell Mayer. LC 75-103. (Mid-American Frontier Ser.). (Illus.). 1975. reprint ed. 15.95 (*0-405-06871-9*) Ayer.

— With Pen & Pencil on the Frontier in 1851: The Diary & Sketches of Frank Blackwell Mayer. Heilbron, Bertha L., ed. LC 86-717. xvii, 256p. 1986. reprint ed. pap. 9.95 (*0-87351-195-6*, Borealis Book) Minn Hist.

Mayer, Frank H. & Roth, Charles B. The Buffalo Harvest. 1995. reprint ed. pap. 8.50 (*1-877704-19-9*) Pioneer Pr.

Mayer, Fred. Forgotten Peoples of Siberia. 1993. 50.00 (*1-881616-08-8*, Pub. by Scalo Pubs) Dist Art Pubs.

Mayer, Frederick. Creative Universities. 1961. pap. 18.95 (*0-8084-0094-0*) NCUP.

— Interpreting NAFTA: The Nature of Politics & the Art of Political Analysis. LC 98-3019. 368p. 1998. 47.50 (*0-231-10980-6*); pap. 18.50 (*0-231-10981-4*) Col U Pr.

— Man, Morals & Education. 1962. 16.95 (*0-8084-0206-4*) NCUP.

Mayer, G. Roy, jt. auth. see Sulzer-Azaroff, Beth.

Mayer, Garry F., ed. Ecological Stress & the New York Blight: Science & Management. LC 82-71795. (Illus.). x, 717p. (Orig.). (C). 1982. pap. text 10.00 (*0-9608990-0-6*) Estuarine Res.

Mayer, Gebhard. Die D-Mark als Leitwahrung in Europa? Eine Untersuchung uber die Sonderstellungen der Bundesbank und der D-Mark in Europa. (GER.). 284p. 1996. pap. 54.95 (*3-631-49530-7*) P Lang Pubng.

Mayer, Geoff, jt. auth. see McFarlane, Brian.

Mayer, George H. The Political Career of Floyd B. Olson. LC 86-33332. xxii, 329p. 1987. reprint ed. pap. 10.95 (*0-87351-206-5*, Borealis Book) Minn Hist.

Mayer, George L. Famous Old New Orleans Recipes. rev. ed. 96p. Date not set. mass mkt. 11.95 (*0-9665279-0-9*) Progress Market.

Mayer, Gerald S. The Divorced Dad Dilemma. 2nd ed. LC 94-92268. 85p. 1997. reprint ed. pap. 9.95 (*0-9649210-7-3*) Motivo Pubng.

— The Divorced Dad Dilemma: A Father's Guide to Understanding, Grieving, & Growing Beyond the Losses of Divorce & to Developing a Deeper, Ongoing Relationship to His Children. 96p. 1994. pap. 9.95 (*0-9642504-0-3*) Desert City Pr.

— When It Hurts Too Much to Quit: Smoking & Depression. (Quit Smart Smoking Cessation Ser.). 12p. 1997. pap. 2.95 (*0-9642504-1-1*) Desert City Pr.

Mayer, Gertrude T. Women of Letters, 2 vols. LC 73-1197. (Essay Index Reprint Ser.). 1977. reprint ed. 53.95 (*0-518-10059-6*) Ayer.

Mayer, Gina. Just a Bully. (Mercer Mayer's Little Critter Ser.). 24p. 1999. pap. 3.29 (*0-307-13200-5*) Gldn Bks Pub Co.

***Mayer, Gina.** Just a Toy. (Mercer Mayer's Little Critter Ser.). (Illus.). (J). 2000. pap. 3.29 (*0-307-13279-X*, Goldn Books) Gldn Bks Pub Co.

Mayer, Gina. Just Lost! (Look-Look Bks.). (Illus.). 24p. (J). (ps-3). 1994. 3.29 (*0-307-12844-X*, 12844) Gldn Bks Pub Co.

Mayer, Gina. Just Me in the Tub. (Look-Look Bks.). (Illus.). 24p. (J). (ps-3). 1994. pap. 3.29 (*0-307-12816-4*, 12816) Gldn Bks Pub Co.

Mayer, Gina. Just Say Please. (Little Golden Bks.). 24p. (J). 1998. 2.29 (*0-307-96017-X*, 96017, Goldn Books) Gldn Bks Pub Co.

— This Is My Body. (Little Golden Bks.). 24p. (J). 1998. 2.29 (*0-307-96013-7*, 96013, Goldn Books) Gldn Bks Pub Co.

— Trick or Treat, Little Critter. (Look-Look Bks.). (Illus.). 24p. (J). (ps-3). 1993. pap. 3.29 (*0-307-12791-5*, 12791, Goldn Books) Gldn Bks Pub Co.

Mayer, Gina & Mayer, Mercer. Just a Bad Day. (Little Golden Storybks.). (Illus.). 24p. (J). 1998. 3.99 (*0-307-16029-7*, 16029, Goldn Books) Gldn Bks Pub Co.

— Just a Bad Day. (Little Golden Bks.). (Illus.). 24p. (J). (gr. 3-5). 1998. 2.29 (*0-307-98873-2*, 98873, Goldn Books) Gldn Bks Pub Co.

— Just a Little Different. (Little Golden Storybks.). (Illus.). 24p. (J). 1998. 3.99 (*0-307-16009-2*, 16009, Goldn Books) Gldn Bks Pub Co.

— Just a Little Different. (Little Golden Bks.). (Illus.). 24p. (J). (gr. 3-5). 1998. 2.29 (*0-307-98875-9*, 98875, Goldn Books) Gldn Bks Pub Co.

— Just a Thunderstorm. (Little Look-Look Bks.). (Illus.). 24p. (J). (ps). 1993. pap. 1.79 (*0-307-11540-2*, 11540) Gldn Bks Pub Co.

— Just Like Dad. (Little Golden Storybks.). (Illus.). 24p. (J). 1998. 3.99 (*0-307-16057-2*, 16057, Goldn Books) Gldn Bks Pub Co.

— Just Like Dad. (Little Golden Bks.). (Illus.). 24p. (J). (gr. 3-5). 1998. 2.29 (*0-307-98876-7*, 98876, Goldn Books) Gldn Bks Pub Co.

— My Big Sister. (Look-Look Bks.). (Illus.). (J). 1997. pap. text 1.79 (*0-307-11619-0*, 11619, Goldn Books) Gldn Bks Pub Co.

— The New Potty: Gina & Mercer Mayer. (Little Look-Look Bks.). (Illus.). 24p. (J). (ps-3). 1992. 1.79 (*0-307-11523-2*, 11523, Goldn Books) Gldn Bks Pub Co.

***Mayer, Gina & Mayer, Mercer.** The School Play: A Complete Handbook. (Illus.). 24p. (J). 1999. 3.99 (*0-307-16143-9*, Goldn Books) Gldn Bks Pub Co.

Mayer, Gina & Mayer, Mercer. Taking Care of Mom. (Little Golden Bks.). (Illus.). 24p. (J). 1998. 2.29 (*0-307-98880-5*, 98880, Goldn Books) Gldn Bks Pub Co.

— A Very Special Critter. (Look-Look Bks.). (Illus.). 24p. (J). (ps-3). 1993. pap. 3.29 (*0-307-12763-X*, 12763, Goldn Books) Gldn Bks Pub Co.

Mayer, Gladys. Behind the Veils of Death & Sleep. 1973. lib. bdg. 250.00 (*0-87968-541-7*) Krishna Pr.

— Color & Healing. 1973. lib. bdg. 250.00 (*0-87968-309-0*) Krishna Pr.

— Color & the Human Soul. 1973. lib. bdg. 250.00 (*0-87968-542-5*) Krishna Pr.

— Colour & Healing: How Color Affects Us. 29p. 1996. reprint ed. pap. 10.00 (*0-7873-0591-X*) Hlth Research.

Mayer, Gloria G., et al, eds. Making Capitation Work: Clinical Operations in an Integrated Delivery System. Date not set. ring bd. 189.00 (*0-8342-0677-3*, S178) Aspen Pub.

***Mayer, Gloria G. & Kuklierus, Ann.** Que Hacer Cuando Su Nino Se Enferme: Facil de Leer & Facil de Usar. (SPA., Illus.). 181p. 2000. pap. 14.95 (*0-9701245-1-1*) IHA.

— Que Hacer para la Salud de los Adolescentes. (Illus.). 2000. pap. 14.95 (*0-9701245-3-8*) IHA.

— What to Do for Teen Health. (Illus.). 2000. pap. 14.95 (*0-9701245-2-X*) IHA.

— What to Do When Your Child Gets Sick. (Illus.). 181p. 2000. pap. 14.95 (*0-9701245-0-3*) IHA.

***Mayer, Gloria G. & Mayer, Thomas.** Goldilocks on Management: 27 Revisionist Fairy Tales for Serious Managers. LC 99-31250. (Illus.). 224p. 1999. 21.95 (*0-8144-0481-2*) AMACOM.

Mayer, Gloria G., jt. ed. see Barnett, Albert E.

Mayer, Guenter. Index Philoneus. LC 73-81702. 312p. (C). 1974. text 211.55 (*3-11-004536-2*) De Gruyter.

Mayer, Gustav. Erinnerungen. (Bibliothek des Deutschen Judentums Ser.: Abt. 5). (GER.). 380p. 1993. reprint ed. write for info. (*3-487-09688-9*) G Olms Pubs.

***Mayer, H., ed.** Minimally Invasive Spine Surgery: A Surgical Manual. 290p. 2000. (*3-540-65631-6*) Spr-Verlag.

Mayer, H. M. & Brock, M., eds. Percutaneous Lumbar Discectomy. (Illus.). 225p. 1989. 86.95 (*0-387-51032-X*) Spr-Verlag.

Mayer, Hans. Outsiders: A Study in Life & Letters. Sweet, Denis, tr. 422p. 1982. 49.50 (*0-262-13175-7*) MIT Pr.

Mayer, Hans, jt. auth. see Stewart, Bruce W.

Mayer, Hans E. The Crusades. 2nd ed. Gillingham, John, tr. (Illus.). 364p. 1988. pap. text 24.00 (*0-19-873097-7*) OUP.

Mayer, Hans E. Kings & Lords in the Latin Kingdom of Jerusalem. (Collected Studies: No. CS 437). 352p. 1994. 117.95 (*0-86078-416-9*, Pub. by Variorum) Ashgate Pub Co.

— Kreuzzuge und Lateinischer Osten. (Collected Studies: No. CS171). (GER.). (C). 1983. reprint ed. lib. bdg. 124.95 (*0-86078-119-4*, Pub. by Variorum) Ashgate Pub Co.

— Probleme des Lateinischen Konigreichs Jerusalem. (Collected Studies: No. CS178). (GER., Illus.). 356p. (C). 1983. reprint ed. lib. bdg. 124.95 (*0-86078-126-7*, Pub. by Variorum) Ashgate Pub Co.

Mayer, Hans-Georg. German Trucks & Cars in WW II Vol. VI: VW Beetle at War. Force, Edward, tr. from GER. (Illus.). 48p. 1992. pap. 9.95 (*0-88740-400-6*) Schiffer.

Mayer, Harold M. & Hayes, Charles R. Land Uses in American Cities. LC 82-81036. (Illus.). 200p. (Orig.). (C). 1983. pap. text 9.95 (*0-941226-02-6*) Park Pr Co.

Mayer, Harold M. & Kohn, Clyde F., eds. Readings in Urban Geography. LC 59-11973. (Illus.). 633p. reprint ed. pap. 196.30 (*0-8357-7002-8*, 205677600085) Bks Demand.

Mayer, Harold M. & Wade, Richard C. Chicago: Growth of a Metropolis. LC 68-54054. (Illus.). 522p. 1969. 60.00 (*0-226-51273-8*) U Ch Pr.

— Chicago: Growth of a Metropolis. LC 68-54054. (Illus.). 522p. 1973. pap. 30.00 (*0-226-51274-6*, P546) U Ch Pr.

Mayer, Harry, ed. Modern Reader's Book of Psalms. (Black & Gold Library). 1968. 6.95 (*0-87140-879-1*, Pub. by Liveright) Norton.

Mayer, Hartwig. Die Althochdeutsche Griffelglossen der Handschrift Ottob. Lat. 3295 (Biblioteca Vaticana) (Canadian Studies in German Language & Literature: Vol. 27). (GER.). 192p. 1982. 31.00 (*3-261-04965-0*) P Lang Pubng.

Mayer, Henry. All on Fire: William LLoyd Garrison & the Abolition of American Slavery. LC 98-19406. 707p. 1998. 32.50 (*0-312-18740-8*) St Martin.

***Mayer, Henry.** All on Fire: William Lloyd Garrison & the Abolition of Slavery. (Illus.). 704p. 2000. pap. 18.95 (*0-312-25367-2*) St Martin.

Mayer, Henry. Mayer on the Media: Issues & Arguments. Tiffen, Rodney, ed. 208p. 1995. pap. 22.95 (*1-86373-625-5*, Pub. by Allen & Unwin Pty) Paul & Co Pubs.

— A Son of Thunder: Patrick Henry & the American Republic. 544p. 1992. reprint ed. pap. text 20.00 (*0-8139-1376-4*) U Pr of Va.

Mayer, Henry & Kirby, Liz. ARGAP 2, a Second Research Guide to Australian Politics & Cognate Subjects. LC 85-120697. xiii, 254p. 1984. write for info. (*0-582-71495-8*) Longman.

Mayer, Herbert. Advanced C Programming on the IBM PC. (Orig.). 1991. 24.95 (*0-8306-8694-0*); 24.95 (*0-8306-8695-9*) McGraw-Hill Prof.

Mayer, Herbert T. The Care & Feeding of Authentic Christians. 1996. 15.95 (*0-7880-0649-5*, Fairway Pr) CSS OH.

Mayer, Holly A. Belonging to the Army: Camp Followers & Community During the American Revolution. 321p. 1999. pap. 18.95 (*1-57003-339-0*) U of SC Pr.

Mayer, Ira. 21 Forces Shaping the 21st Century Consumer. LC 99-230470. 1999. write for info. (*1-885747-19-5*) EPM Communs.

Mayer, Ira, ed. see Raugust, Karen.

Mayer, Ira, ed. see Rauqust, Karen.

Mayer, J. E. The Herbalist. (Alternative Medicine Ser.). 1992. lib. bdg. 79.99 (*0-8490-5409-5*) Gordon Pr.

Mayer, J. P. Alexis de Tocqueville. LC 78-67399. (European Political Thought Ser.). (GER.). 1980. reprint ed. lib. bdg. 17.95 (*0-405-11716-7*) Ayer.

— British Cinemas & Their Audiences. Jowett, Garth S., ed. LC 77-11387. (Aspects of Film Ser.). (Illus.). 1978. lib. bdg. 20.95 (*0-405-11141-X*) Ayer.

— Max Weber & German Politics. LC 98-26544. (Max Weber Classic Monographs). 1998. write for info. (*0-415-17455-4*) Routledge.

— Max Weber & German Politics. 3rd rev. ed. LC 78-67371. (European Political Thought Ser.). 1979. reprint ed. lib. bdg. 17.95 (*0-405-11717-5*) Ayer.

— Political Thought in France. LC 78-67367. (European Political Thought Ser.). 1980. reprint ed. lib. bdg. 17.95 (*0-405-11718-3*) Ayer.

— Sociology of Film: Studies & Documents. LC 73-169334. (Literature of Cinema, Ser. 2). (Illus.). 398p. 1976. reprint ed. 26.95 (*0-405-03901-8*) Ayer.

Mayer, J. P., ed. Considerations sur les Principaux Evenemens de la Revolution Francoise, Madame la Baronne Stael, 3 vols., Set. LC 78-67391. (European Political Thought Ser.). (FRE.). 1980. reprint ed. lib. bdg. 94.95 (*0-405-11742-6*) Ayer.

— Considerations sur les Principaux Evenemens de la Revolution Francoise, Madame la Baronne Stael, 3 vols., Vol. 1. LC 78-67391. (European Political Thought Ser.). (FRE.). 1980. reprint ed. lib. bdg. 47.95 (*0-405-11743-4*) Ayer.

— Considerations sur les Principaux Evenemens de la Revolution Francoise, Madame la Baronne Stael, 3 vols., Vol. 2. LC 78-67391. (European Political Thought Ser.). (FRE.). 1980. reprint ed. lib. bdg. 47.95 (*0-405-11744-2*) Ayer.

— European Political Thought Series: Traditions & Endurance, 67 bks., Set. (Illus.). 1979. lib. bdg. 2593.00 (*0-405-11670-5*) Ayer.

— European Political Thought Series: Traditions & Endurance, 67 bks., Vol. 21. (Illus.). 1979. lib. bdg. 724.00 (*0-405-18995-8*) Ayer.

— European Political Thought Series: Traditions & Endurance, 67 bks., Vol. 36. (Illus.). 1979. lib. bdg. 858.00 (*0-405-18996-6*) Ayer.

— European Political Thought Series: Traditions & Endurance, 67 bks., Vols. 1[00ad]20. (Illus.). 1979. lib. bdg. 662.00 (*0-685-00508-9*) Ayer.

— Fundamental Studies of Jean Bodin: An Original Anthology. LC 78-67314. (European Political Thought Ser.). (FRE & GER.). 1979. lib. bdg. 50.95 (*0-405-11671-3*) Ayer.

— The Impact of the Eighteenth Brumaire: An Original Anthology. LC 78-67322. (European Political Thought Ser.). (ENG & GER.). 1979. lib. bdg. 40.95 (*0-405-11672-1*) Ayer.

Mayer, J. P., jt. auth. see Pierson.

Mayer, J. P., ed. see Althusius, Johannes.

Mayer, J. P., ed. see Bagge, Dominique.

Mayer, J. P., ed. see Baudrillart, Henri J.

Mayer, J. P., ed. see Bayle, Francis & Rohden, Peter R.

Mayer, J. P., ed. see Beer, Max.

Mayer, J. P., ed. see Bluntschli, Johann C.

Mayer, J. P., ed. see Bodin, Jean.

Mayer, J. P., ed. see Bougle, Celestin C.

Mayer, J. P., ed. see Burchhardt, Jacob, et al.

Mayer, J. P., ed. see Chaix-Ruy, Jules.

Mayer, J. P., ed. see Chalres, Celestin, et al.

Mayer, J. P., ed. see Chinard, Gilbert.

Mayer, J. P., ed. see Constant de Rebecque, Henri B.

Mayer, J. P., ed. see Cortes, Juan D. & Schramm, Edmund.

Mayer, J. P., ed. see Cotta, Sergio.

Mayer, J. P., ed. see Cottu, Charles.

Mayer, J. P., ed. see Cranston, Maurice W.

Mayer, J. P., ed. see De Lolme, J. L. & Machelon, Jean-Pierre.

Mayer, J. P., ed. see De Remusat, Charles F.

Mayer, J. P., ed. see De Tocqueville, Alexis.

Mayer, J. P., ed. see Dempf, Alois.

Mayer, J. P., ed. see Dolleans, Edouard.

Mayer, J. P., ed. see Gadave, Renne.

Mayer, J. P., ed. see Gewirth, Alan.

Mayer, J. P., ed. see Guizot, Francois P.

Mayer, J. P., ed. see Hubert, Rene.

Mayer, J. P., ed. see Huit, Charles.

Mayer, J. P., ed. see Jannet, Claudio.

Mayer, J. P., ed. see Jefferson, Thomas.

Mayer, J. P., ed. see Lanson, Gustave.

Mayer, J. P., ed. see Lehmann, William C.

Mayer, J. P., ed. see Leroy, Andre L.

Mayer, J. P., ed. see Luccioni, Jean.

Mayer, J. P., ed. see MacCunn, John.

Mayer, J. P., ed. see Martin, Kingsley.

Mayer, J. P., ed. see McIlwain, Charles H.

Mayer, J. P., ed. see Mommsen, Theodor.

Mayer, J. P., ed. see Morley, John M.

Mayer, J. P., ed. see Moulinie, Henri.

Mayer, J. P., ed. see Pellissier, Georges.

Mayer, J. P., ed. see Perthes, Clemens T.

Mayer, J. P., ed. see Remond, Gabriel.

Mayer, J. P., ed. see Reybaud, Louis.

Mayer, J. P., ed. see Robin, Leon.

Mayer, J. P., ed. see Rommen, Heinrich A.

Mayer, J. P., ed. see Saresberiensis, Ioannis.

Mayer, J. P., ed. see Schemann, Ludwig.

Mayer, J. P., ed. see See, Henri E.

Mayer, J. P., ed. see Sidney, Algernon.

Mayer, J. P., ed. see Sieyes, Emmanuel & Sainte-Beuve, Charles-Augustin.

Mayer, J. P., ed. see Sorel, Georges.

Mayer, J. P., ed. see Troeltsch, Ernst.

Mayer, J. P., ed. see Vinet, Alexandre R.

Mayer, J. P., ed. see Von Ulrich & Wiliamovitz-Moellendorff, B. Niese.

Mayer, J. P., ed. see Vorlander, Franz.

Mayer, J. P., ed. see Waitz, Georg.

Mayer, J. P., ed. & intro. see De Tocqueville, Alexis.

Mayer, J. P., ed. & intro. see Flint, Robert.

***Mayer, J. Richard.** Connections in Environmental Sciece: A Case Study Approach. 352p. (C). 2000. pap. 49.69 (*0-07-229726-3*) McGrw-H Hghr Educ.

Mayer, J. W., jt. auth. see Taft, W. Stanley.

Mayer, Jack, ed. see Schwartz, Bob & Schwartz, Leah.

Mayer, Jacob, et al. Political Thought. LC 72-134114. (Essay Index Reprint Ser.). 1977. 29.95 (*0-8369-1932-7*) Ayer.

Mayer, James M., jt. auth. see Nugent, William A.

Mayer, Jan. City & Port: The Transformation of Port Cities - London, Barcelona, New York & Rotterdam. LC 99-236082. (Illus.). 432p. 1998. 65.00 (*90-5727-020-X*, Pub. by Intl Bks) Paul & Co Pubs.

Mayer, Jan, tr. see Evans, Joy & Moore, Jo E.

Mayer, Janos. Stochastic Linear Programming Algorithms. (Optimization Theory & Applications Ser.). 163p. 1998. text 31.00 (*90-5699-144-2*) Gordon & Breach.

Mayer, Jean, ed. Bringing Jobs to People: Employment Promotion at Regional & Local Levels. vi, 211p. (Orig.). 1988. 36.00 (*92-2-106326-7*); pap. 22.50 (*92-2-106325-9*) Intl Labour Office.

Mayer, Jeffrey J. ACT! 4 for Windows for Dummies. LC 98-84964. (For Dummies Ser.). 384p. 1998. pap. 19.99 (*0-7645-0282-4*) IDG Bks.

Mayer, Jeffrey J. ACT! 3 for Windows for Dummies. LC 96-77072. (For Dummies Ser.). 380p. 1996. pap. 19.99 (*0-7645-0027-9*) IDG Bks.

Mayer, Jeffrey J. If You Haven't Got the Time to Do It Right, When Will You Find the Time to Do It Over? (Illus.). 160p. 1991. pap. 10.00 (*0-671-73364-8*, Fireside) S&S Trade Pap.

— Success Is a Journey: 7 Steps to Achieving Success in Business & Life. LC 98-42939. 224p. 1999. pap. 17.95 (*0-07-041129-8*) McGraw.

***Mayer, Jeffrey J.** Success Is a Journey: 7 Steps to Achieving Success in Business & Life. 2001. pap. 12.95 (*0-07-136514-1*) McGraw.

Mayer, Jeffrey J. Time Management for Dummies. 2nd ed. LC 99-62837. (For Dummies Ser.). 384p. 1999. pap. 19.99 (*0-7645-5145-0*) IDG Bks.

Mayer, Jeffrey J. Time Management for Dummies: A Reference for the Rest of Us. abr. ed. (For Dummies Ser.). 1996. audio 12.00 (*0-694-51744-5*, CPN 10094) HarperAudio.

Mayer, Jeffrey J. Time Management for Dummies: Briefcase Edition. abr. ed. (For Dummies Ser.). 161p. 1995. pap. 9.99 (*1-56884-973-7*) IDG Bks.

— Time Management Survival Guide for Dummies. 202p. 1995. pap. 12.99 (*1-56884-972-9*) IDG Bks.

— Winning the Fight Between You & Your Desk, Your Office, & Your Computer. LC 93-48256. (Illus.). 160p. 1994. 18.00 (*0-88730-674-8*, HarpBusn) HarpInfo.

Mayer, Jill S., ed. Space - The Next Renaissance: Proceedings of the 7th Annual International Space Development Conference. 518p. 1991. pap. 30.00 (*0-912183-06-3*) Univelt Inc.

Mayer, Jim. Groundwater. McClurg, Sue, ed. (Layperson's Guide Ser.). (Illus.). 20p. 1998. pap. 5.00 (*1-893246-64-7*) Water Educ.

— Water Pollution. McClurg, Sue, ed. (Layperson's Guide Ser.). (Illus.). 20p. 1996. pap. 5.00 (*1-893246-56-6*) Water Educ.

Mayer, John. Mathematics & Choice. 156p. (C). 1996. pap. text, spiral bd. 18.95 (*0-7872-1348-9*) Kendall-Hunt.

— Youth Baseball: Great Practices, Great Games. (Illus.). 192p. 2000. pap. 16.95 (*1-57167-392-X*) Coaches Choice.

***Mayer, John & Pingatore, Gene.** Coaching Youth Basketball: Great Practices, Great Games. (Illus.). 125p. 2000. pap. 12.95 (*1-57167-447-0*) Coaches Choice.

***Mayer, John C.** Runework: A Practical Guide for Beginners. (Illus.). 50p. 2000. pap. 8.00 (*0-9700036-0-9*) Vanaheim Pubng.

Mayer, John D., ed. Strange of Balcaskie: Strangus de Caledonia, Vol. 3. 3rd ed. (Extraneus Ser.: Vol. III, Bk. IX). xxvi, 814p. 1999. 80.00 (*0-9638665-7-5*) Arapacana Pr.

Mayer, John E. Jewish-Gentile Courtships: An Exploratory Study of a Social Process. LC 80-16130. 240p. 1980. reprint ed. lib. bdg. 59.50 (*0-313-22465-X*, MAJG, Greenwood Pr) Greenwood.

Mayer, John E. & Timms, Noel. The Client Speaks: Working Class Impressions of Casework. 193p. 1970. pap. 19.50 (*0-932400-03-5*) Intervale Pub Co.

Mayer, John R. Strange: The Alloway Strange (Family) 2nd ed. (Illus.). 285p. 1995. reprint ed. pap. 42.00 (*0-8328-4736-4*); reprint ed. lib. bdg. 52.00 (*0-8328-4735-6*) Higginson Bk Co.

— Strange. "Extraneus" Strange (Family) of Eastern America. 2nd ed. (Illus.). 398p. 1995. reprint ed. pap. 59.50 (*0-8328-4734-8*); reprint ed. lib. bdg. 69.50 (*0-8328-4733-X*) Higginson Bk Co.

— Strange. Extraneus Bk. IX: Strange of Balcaskie & the Clans Outlandish Strang & Stronge, Strangus de Caledonia et Hibernia et America. 2nd ed. (Illus.). 542p. 1997. reprint ed. pap. 75.00 (*0-8328-9519-9*); reprint ed. lib. bdg. 85.00 (*0-8328-9518-0*) Higginson Bk Co.

— Strange of the Carolinas. 3rd rev. ed. LC 99-68154. (Extraneus Ser.: Vol. XII). (Illus.). xxvi, 666p. 1999. 75.00 (*0-9638665-9-1*) Arapacana Pr.

Mayer, John R., ed. The Alloway Strange: Alva Extraneus de Virginia. 2nd ed. LC 90-148997. (Extraneus Ser.: Vol. III, Bk. X). (Illus.). xxiv, 256p. (C). 1994. pap. 32.00 (*0-9638665-3-2*) Arapacana Pr.

— L' Estrange of Moystown. (Extraneus Ser.: Vol. II, Bk. VIII). 1996. pap. write for info. (*0-9638665-4-0*, B08BA) Arapacana Pr.

— Strange of Blisland: Extraneus De Terra Felicitas. 2nd rev. ed. LC 90-148997. (Extranus Ser.: Vol. IV, Bk. XI). xl, 708p. (C). 1995. pap. 67.00 (*0-9638665-6-7*) Arapacana Pr.

— Strange of Eastern America: Extraneus de America Orientalis. 2nd rev. ed. LC 90-148997. (Extraneus Ser.: Vol. I, Bk. V). (Illus.). xviii, 380p. (Orig.). (C). 1993. pap. 41.00 (*0-9638665-0-8*) Arapacana Pr.

— Strange of the Carolinas: Extraneus de Carolina. 2nd ed. (Extraneus Ser.: Vol. IV, Bk. XII). (Illus.). xxvi, 548p. (C). 1993. pap. 58.00 (*0-9638665-2-4*) Arapacana Pr.

Mayer, Jorg, et al. Development Policies in Natural Resource Economies. LC 98-30463. (In Association with UNCTAD Ser.). 240p. 1999. 80.00 (*1-84064-009-X*) E Elgar.

Mayer, Judith, jt. auth. see Lipschutz, Ronnie D.

Mayer, Karen A. Prima's Official Guide to Crystal Reports 7. LC 98-66121. 456p. 1999. pap. 29.99 (*0-7615-1656-5*) Prima Pub.

Mayer, Karl H. Maya Monuments: Sculptures of Unknown Provenance in Europe. Brizee, Sandra L., tr. from GER. (Illus.). 1978. pap. 20.00 (*0-916552-11-X*) Acoma Bks.

— Maya Monuments: Sculptures of Unknown Provenance in the U. S. (Illus.). 1980. pap. 30.00 (*0-916552-16-0*) Acoma Bks.

— Mushroom Stones of Meso-America. (Illus.). 1977. pap. 7.95 (*0-916552-09-8*) Acoma Bks.

Mayer, Karl U., jt. ed. see Baltes, Paul B.

Mayer, Karl U., ed. see Blossfeld, Hans-Peter & Hamerle, Alfred M.

Mayer, Karl U., jt. ed. see Leschinsky, Achim.

Mayer, Karl Ulrich, jt. ed. see Leschinsky, Achim.

Mayer, Ken. Real Women Don't Diet! 224p. 1995. pap. 4.99 (*0-7860-0247-6*, Pinncle Kensgtn) Kensgtn Pub Corp.

— Real Women Don't Diet! One Man's Praise of Large Women & His Outrage at the Society That Rejects Them. LC 93-36312. (Illus.). 1993. 18.95 (*0-910155-27-5*) Bartleby Pr.

Mayer, Kenneth R. The Politics of Defense Contracting. 240p. 1991. 37.50 (*0-300-04524-7*) Yale U Pr.

Mayer, Kenneth R., jt. auth. see Canon, David T.

Mayer-Kress, G., ed. Dimensions & Entropies in Chaotic Systems. (Synergetics Ser.: Vol. 32). (Illus.). 280p. 1989. 83.00 (*0-387-16254-2*) Spr-Verlag.

Mayer, Kurt B. & Goldstein, Sidney. Migration & Economic Development in Rhode Island. LC 58-10480. 72p. 1958. reprint ed. 30.00 (*0-608-16581-6*, 202751700055) Bks Demand.

Mayer, Lance, et al. The Devotion Family: The Lives & Possessions of Three Generations in Eighteenth-Century Connecticut. (Illus.). 64p. (Orig.). 1991. pap. 14.95 (*1-878541-03-X*) Lyman Allyn.

Mayer, Larry. Montana from the Big Sky. (Illus.). 144p. 1990. 29.95 (*0-9627618-1-8*) Billings Gazette.

Mayer, Larry, ed. Extensional Tectonics of the Southwestern United States: A Perspective on Processes & Kinematics. fac. ed. LC 86-22853. (Geological Society of America, Special Paper: No. 208). (Illus.). 130p. 1986. reprint ed. pap. 40.30 (*0-7837-8039-7*, 204779500008) Bks Demand.

Mayer, Larry, ed. see Lord, Marc, et al.

Mayer, Larry, jt. photos by see Sample, Michael S.

Mayer, Laurence, ed. see Ba, Jean-Claude & Wilson, David E.

Mayer, Laurence P., ed. see Carpenter, Judith A.

Mayer, Laurence P., ed. see Kidane, Amine H.

Mayer, Laurence P., ed. see McCullen, Wendy H.

Mayer, Lawrence C. Redefining Comparative Politics: Promise Versus Performance. (Library of Social Research). 320p. (C). 1989. text 59.95 (*0-8039-3463-7*) Sage.

— Redefining Comparative Politics: Promise Versus Performance, Vol. 173. (Library of Social Research). 320p. (C). 1989. pap. text 26.00 (*0-8039-3464-5*) Sage.

— Redefining Comparative Politics: Promise vs. Performance. LC 89-34765. (Sage Library of Social Research: No. 173). (Illus.). 303p. 1989. reprint ed. pap. 94.00 (*0-608-04318-4*, 206509700012) Bks Demand.

Mayer, Lawrence C. & Burnett, John A. Politics in Industrial Societies: A Comparative Perspective. LC 76-54694. 399p. reprint ed. pap. 123.70 (*0-608-30092-6*, 205549100022) Bks Demand.

Mayer, Lawrence C., et al. Comparative Politics: Nations & Theories in a Changing World. 2nd ed. LC 95-34433. 423p. (C). 1996. 69.00 (*0-13-373325-4*) P-H.

Mayer, Lene, jt. auth. see Gipson, Morrell.

Mayer, Leonard. Design & Planning of Research & Clinical Laboratory Facilities. 536p. 1995. 99.00 (*0-471-30623-1*) Wiley.

Mayer, Levy, ed. see Rorer, David.

Mayer, Lloyd F., jt. ed. see Weiner, Howard L.

Mayer, Lorenzo, jt. auth. see Aldrich, Daniel G., Jr.

Mayer, Lyle V. Fundamentals of Voice & Articulation. (C). 1995. audio. write for info. (*0-697-27068-8*) Brown & Benchmark.

— Fundamentals of Voice & Articulation. 11th ed. 352p. (C). 1995. text. write for info. (*0-697-27066-1*) Brown & Benchmark.

— Fundamentals of Voice & Diction. 10th ed. (C). 1993. audio. write for info. (*0-697-13934-4*) Brown & Benchmark.

Mayer, M., jt. auth. see Bekka, B.

Mayer, Marc, text. Being & Time: The Emergence of Video Projection. LC 95-50260. (Illus.). 98p. (Orig.). 1996. pap. 29.95 (*0-914782-94-0*, 620462) Buffalo Fine-Albrght-Knox.

Mayer, Marc, jt. auth. see Brutvan, Cheryl A.

Mayer, Margaret M. & Castagner, Claude. The American Dream: American Popular Music. rev. ed. (Illus.). 218p. (C). 1994. pap. text. write for info. (*0-9640120-3-0*) Front Desk LLC.

Mayer, Margarita. Breathing & Relaxation: In Theory & Practice. Callender, Vesta & Clark, Winifred, eds. Mayer, Thomas, tr. from GER. (Illus.). 45p. (Orig.). (C). 1988. pap. text. write for info. (*0-318-62904-6*) W Clark.

M

An Asterisk (*) at the beginning of an entry indicates that the title is appearing for the first time.

Mayer, Margery. The Virtual Edge: Embracing Technology for Distributed Project Team Success. LC 98-6265. (Illus.). 104p. 1998. pap. 32.95 (*1-880410-16-8*) Proj Mgmt Inst.

Mayer, Margit & Ely, John. The German Greens: Paradox Between Movement & Party. LC 96-3065. 352p. 1998. 69.95 (*1-56639-515-1*); pap. 24.95 (*1-56639-516-X*) Temple U Pr.

Mayer, Maria. The Rusyns of Hungary: Political & Social Developments, 1860-1910. LC 97-61165. 250p. 1998. 35.00 (*0-88033-387-1*, 490, Pub. by East Eur Monographs) Col U Pr.

Mayer, Marianna. Baba Yaga & Vasilisa the Brave. LC 90-38514. (Illus.). 40p. (J). (ps-3). 1994. 16.95 (*0-688-08500-8*, Wm Morrow); lib. bdg. 15.93 (*0-688-08501-6*, Wm Morrow) Morrow Avon.

***Mayer, Marianna.** Beauty & the Beast. (Illus.). (J). 2000. 15.95 (*1-58717-017-5*) SeaStar.

Mayer, Marianna. Beauty & the Beast. LC 87-1095. (Illus.). 48p. (J). (gr. k up). 1987. reprint ed. mass mkt. 6.95 (*0-689-71151-4*) Aladdin.

— A Boy, a Dog, a Frog & a Friend. 1993. pap. 4.99 (*0-14-054610-3*, PuffinBks) Peng Put Young Read.

— Iduna & the Magic Apples. LC 88-2494. (Illus.). 40p. (J). (gr. k-4). 1988. lib. bdg. 16.95 (*0-02-765120-7*, Mac Bks Young Read) S&S Childrens.

***Mayer, Marianna.** Iron John. LC 97-45664. 40p. (J). 1999. 15.89 (*0-688-11555-1*, Wm Morrow) Morrow Avon.

Mayer, Marianna. Iron John. LC 97-45664. (Illus.). 40p. (J). (gr. k-3). 1999. 16.00 (*0-688-11554-3*, Wm Morrow) Morrow Avon.

***Mayer, Marianna.** Merlin. (J). 1999. 15.99 (*0-8037-2187-0*, Dial Yng Read) Peng Put Young Read.

Mayer, Marianna. The Mother Goose Cookbook: Rhymes & Recipes for the Very Young. LC 97-5942. (Illus.). 37p. (J). (ps-3). 1998. 11.95 (*0-688-15242-2*, Wm Morrow) Morrow Avon.

***Mayer, Marianna.** Parsifal. (J). 2001. 15.99 (*0-8037-2012-2*, Dial Yng Read) Peng Put Young Read.

Mayer, Marianna. Pegasus. LC 96-32442. (Illus.). 40p. (J). (gr. k-3). 1998. 16.00 (*0-688-13382-7*, Wm Morrow) Morrow Avon.

***Mayer, Marianna.** Pegasus. LC 96-32442. (Illus.). 40p. (J). (gr. k-3). 1998. 15.89 (*0-688-13383-5*, Wm Morrow) Morrow Avon.

Mayer, Marianna. The Prince & the Pauper. deluxe ed. Arico, Diane, ed. LC 98-36176. (Illus.). 48p. (J). (gr. 2-4). 1999. 17.99 (*0-8037-2099-8*, Dial Yng Read) Peng Put Young Read.

— Turandot. LC 93-27033. (Illus.). 48p. (J). (ps up). 1995. 16.00 (*0-688-09073-7*, Wm Morrow) Morrow Avon.

***Mayer, Marianna.** Twelve Apostles. (Illus.). 32p. (J). (ps up). 2000. 16.99 (*0-8037-2533-7*, Dial Yng Read) Peng Put Young Read.

Mayer, Marianna. Twelve Dancing Princesses. (J). 1998. mass mkt. 5.95 (*0-688-14392-X*, Wm Morrow) Morrow Avon.

— The Twelve Dancing Princesses. LC 83-1034. (Illus.). 40p. (J). (ps-3). 1989. 17.00 (*0-688-08051-0*, Wm Morrow) Morrow Avon.

— Women Warriors: Myths & Legends of Heroic Women. LC 98-45697. (Illus.). 80p. (J). (gr. 4-7). 1999. 18.00 (*0-688-15522-7*, Wm Morrow) Morrow Avon.

***Mayer, Marianna.** Young Jesus of Nazareth. 32p. (J). 1999. 15.93 (*0-688-16728-4*, Wm Morrow) Morrow Avon.

Mayer, Marianna. Young Jesus of Nazareth. LC 98-47474. (Illus.). 32p. (J). (ps-3). 1999. 16.00 (*0-688-16727-6*, Wm Morrow) Morrow Avon.

— Young Mary of Nazareth. LC 97-38944. (Illus.). 40p. (J). (gr. 4-7). 1998. 16.00 (*0-688-14061-0*, Wm Morrow) Morrow Avon.

***Mayer, Marianna.** Young Mary of Nazareth. LC 97-38944. (Illus.). 40p. (J). (gr. 4-7). 1998. 15.93 (*0-688-14062-9*, Wm Morrow) Morrow Avon.

***Mayer, Marianna & Mayer, Mercer.** Beauty & the Beast. LC 00-26181. (Illus.). (J). 2000. 15.88 (*1-58717-018-3*) SeaStar.

Mayer, Marion. History of a Family Dispersed. (Illus.). 300p. 1995. 35.00 (*0-9644869-0-3*) Mayer Pr.

Mayer, Marion S. Handbook of Insect Pheromones & Sex Attractants. 1096p. 1990. lib. bdg. 355.00 (*0-8493-2934-5*, QD557) CRC Pr.

Mayer, Martin. The Asian Disease: Plausible Diagnoses, Possible Remedies. (Public Policy Brief Highlights Ser.: Vol. 44A). 6p. 1998. pap. write for info. (*0-941276-54-6*) J Levy.

— The Asian Disease: Plausible Diagnoses Possible Remedies: Regulation of Cross-Border Interbank Lending & Derivatives Trade. (Public Policy Brief Ser.: Vol. 44). 40p. 1998. pap. write for info. (*0-941276-53-8*) J Levy.

Mayer, Martin. The Bankers. 1975. mass mkt. 2.25 (*0-345-24750-7*) Ballantine Pub Grp.

— The Bankers. 1977. mass mkt. 2.25 (*0-345-27541-1*) Ballantine Pub Grp.

— The Bankers. 1979. mass mkt. 2.75 (*0-345-28581-6*) Ballantine Pub Grp.

Mayer, Martin. The Bankers. 608p. 1980. mass mkt. 5.99 (*0-345-29569-2*) Ballantine Pub Grp.

— The Bankers: The Next Generation. LC 96-34801. 528p. 1997. 29.95 (*0-525-93865-6*, Truman Talley) St Martin.

— The Bankers: The Next Generation: The New Worlds of Money, Credit, & Banking in an Electronic Age. 528p. 1998. pap. 16.95 (*0-452-27264-5*) NAL.

— The Greatest Ever Bank Robbery: The Collapse of the Savings & Loan Industry. 384p. 1992. reprint ed. pap. 12.95 (*0-02-012620-4*) Macmillan.

— Madison Avenue, U. S. A. (NTC's Business Classics Ser.). (Illus.). 304p. 1994. pap. 11.95 (*0-8442-3247-5*, NTC Business Bks) NTC Contemp Pub Co.

***Mayer, Martin.** Risk Reduction in the New Financial Architecture. (Public Policy Briefs Highlights Ser.: Vol. 56A). 6p. 1999. pap. write for info. (*0-941276-80-5*) J Levy.

— Risk Reduction in the New Financial Architecture: Realities & Fallacies in International Financial Reform. (Public Policy Brief Ser.). 56p. 1999. pap. write for info. (*0-941276-79-1*) J Levy.

Mayer, Martin & Faria, Deborah G. New York: Metropolis of the American Dream. LC 95-38123. (Urban Tapestry Ser.). (Illus.). 384p. 1995. 39.50 (*1-881096-22-X*) Towery Pub.

Mayer, Martin & Finn, David. Children of the World: Learning Together at the United Nations International School. (Illus.). 160p. 1990. 34.95 (*0-8191-7681-8*) Madison Bks UPA.

Mayer, Martin & Young, James W. How to Become an Advertising Man. LC 97-31590. (NTC's Business Classics Ser.). 96p. 1993. pap. 12.95 (*0-8442-3002-2*, NTC Business Bks) NTC Contemp Pub Co.

Mayer, Martin, jt. auth. see Linowitz, Sol M.

Mayer-Martin, Donna. Thematic Catalogue of Troubadour & Trouvere Melody. (Thematic Catalogues Ser.: No. 18). (Illus.). 2000. lib. bdg. 76.00 (*0-918728-82-7*) Pendragon NY.

Mayer, Martin P. Gay, Lesbian, & Heterosexual Teachers: An Investigation of Acceptance of Self, Acceptance of Others, Affectional & Lifestyle Orientation: Their Rightful Place. LC 93-26785. 196p. 1993. text 79.95 (*0-7734-2236-6*) E Mellen.

Mayer, Mary H., tr. see Fitzpatrick, Edward A., ed.

Mayer, Melanie J. Klondike Women: True Tales of the 1897-1898 Gold Rush. LC 89-33517. (Illus.). 280p. 1989. 34.95 (*0-8040-0926-0*); pap. 18.95 (*0-8040-0927-9*) Swallow.

***Mayer, Melanie J. & DeArmond, R. N.** Staking Her Claim: The Life of Belinda Mulrooney, Klondike & Alaska Entrepreneur. LC 99-36187. 390p. 2000. 39.95 (*0-8040-1021-8*) Ohio U Pr.

— Staking Her Claim: The Life of Belinda Mulrooney, Klondike & Alaska Entrepreneur. LC 99-36187. (Illus.). 390p. 2000. pap. 19.95 (*0-8040-1022-6*) Ohio U Pr.

Mayer, Mercer. All by Myself. (J). 1985. 9.15 (*0-606-12162-5*, Pub. by Turtleback) Demco.

— All by Myself. (Look-Look Bks.). (Illus.). 24p. (J). (ps-3). 1985. reprint ed. pap. 3.29 (*0-307-11938-6*, 11938, Goldn Books) Gldn Bks Pub Co.

— Appelard & Liverwurst. LC 89-13803. (Illus.). 40p. (J). (gr. k up). 1990. 13.95 (*0-688-09659-X*, Wm Morrow) Morrow Avon.

— Baby Sister Says No. LC 86-82368. (Look-Look Bks.). (Illus.). 24p. (J). (gr. 4-8). 1987. pap. 3.29 (*0-307-11949-1*, 11949) Gldn Bks Pub Co.

***Mayer, Mercer.** Best Present. (Road to Reading Mile 2 Ser.). (Illus.). (J). 2000. 10.99 (*0-307-46215-3*, Goldn Books) Gldn Bks Pub Co.

Mayer, Mercer. Bubble Bubble. rev. ed. (Illus.). 48p. (J). 1992. reprint ed. pap. 5.95 (*1-879920-03-4*) Rain Bird Prods.

— The Cat's Meow. (Schooltime Tales Ser.). (Illus.). 48p. (J). (ps-3). 1994. 4.69 (*0-307-15984-1*, 15984, Goldn Books) Gldn Bks Pub Co.

— Critters of the Night: Mummy Pancakes. (Tattoo Tales Ser.). (J). (ps-1). 1997. pap. 5.99 (*0-614-28931-9*) Random Bks Yng Read.

— Critters of the Night Glow-in-the-Dark. (J). 1998. 9.99 (*0-679-88707-5*, Pub. by Random Bks Yng Read) Random.

— Dog, & a Frog. (J). (ps-3). 1992. pap. 4.99 (*0-14-054611-1*, Viking Child) Peng Put Young Read.

— The E-Mail Mystery: Mercer Mayer's LC & The Critter Kids. LC 94-73091. (Mini Novels Ser.: Vol. 8). (Illus.). 72p. (J). (ps-3). 1995. per. 4.69 (*0-307-16181-1*, 16181, Goldn Books) Gldn Bks Pub Co.

— East of the Sun & West of the Moon. 1987. 12.19 (*0-606-01468-3*, Pub. by Turtleback) Demco.

— East of the Sun & West of the Moon. LC 86-20578. (Illus.). 48p. (J). (gr. k up). 1987. reprint ed. mass mkt. 6.99 (*0-689-71113-1*) Aladdin.

— Frog Goes to Dinner. (J). (ps). 1992. pap. 4.99 (*0-14-054633-2*, PuffinBks) Peng Put Young Read.

Mayer, Mercer. Frog Goes to Dinner. (J). 1977. 9.19 (*0-606-03303-3*, Pub. by Turtleback) Demco.

Mayer, Mercer. Frog on His Own. 1993. pap. 3.99 (*0-14-054634-0*) NAL.

— Frog on His Own. (J). 1973. 9.19 (*0-606-02116-7*, Pub. by Turtleback) Demco.

— The Ghost of Goose Island: Mercer Mayer's LC & The Critter Kids. (Schooltime Tales Ser.: Vol. 5). (Illus.). 48p. (J). (ps-3). 1995. per. 4.69 (*0-307-16030-0*, 16030, Goldn Books) Gldn Bks Pub Co.

— Great Cat Chase. (Illus.). 32p. (J). (ps-3). 1994. pap. 5.95 (*1-879920-07-7*) Rain Bird Prods.

— Happy Easter, Little Critter. LC 87-81759. (Look-Look Bks.). (Illus.). 24p. (J). (ps-3). 1988. pap. 3.29 (*0-307-11723-5*, 11723, Goldn Books) Gldn Bks Pub Co.

— Hiccup. (J). 1976. 9.19 (*0-606-01721-6*, Pub. by Turtleback) Demco.

— I Am Helping. LC 94-68287. (Illus.). 1995. 4.99 (*0-679-87348-1*) Random.

— I Am Sharing. LC 94-68288. (Illus.). 1995. 4.99 (*0-679-87349-X*) Random.

Mayer, Mercer. I Just Forgot. LC 87-81779. (Look-Look Bks.). (Illus.). 24p. (J). (ps-3). 1988. pap. 3.29 (*0-307-11975-0*, 11975, Goldn Books) Gldn Bks Pub Co.

— I Just Forgot. (Golden Look-Look Bks.). 1988. 8.15 (*0-606-12351-2*, Pub. by Turtleback) Demco.

Mayer, Mercer. If I Had a Gorilla. (Illus.). 32p. (J). (ps-3). 1994. pap. 5.95 (*1-879920-06-9*) Rain Bird Prods.

— Just a Daydream. (Look-Look Bks.). (Illus.). 24p. (J). (ps-3). 1989. pap. 3.29 (*0-307-11973-4*, 11973) Gldn Bks Pub Co.

Mayer, Mercer. Just a Daydream. (Golden Look-Look Bks.). (J). 1989. 7.89 (*0-606-12371-7*, Pub. by Turtleback) Demco.

Mayer, Mercer. Just a Mess. LC 86-82369. (Look-Look Bks.). (Illus.). 24p. (J). (ps-3). 1987. pap. 3.29 (*0-307-11948-3*, 11948) Gldn Bks Pub Co.

Mayer, Mercer. Just A Mess: Look Look Book. (J). 1987. 8.74 (*0-606-12372-5*) Turtleback.

Mayer, Mercer. Just a Nap. (Little Look-Look Bks.). (Illus.). 24p. (J). (ps). 1989. pap. 1.79 (*0-307-11713-8*, 11713) Gldn Bks Pub Co.

Mayer, Mercer. Just a Rainy Day. (Little Look-Look Bks.). (Illus.). 24p. (J). (ps). 1990. pap. 1.79 (*0-307-11682-4*, 11682) Gldn Bks Pub Co.

Mayer, Mercer. Just a Snowy Day. (Golden Touch & Feel Bks.). (Illus.). 24p. (J). (gr. k). 1983. spiral bd. 7.99 (*0-307-12156-9*, 12156) Gldn Bks Pub Co.

— Just Camping Out: Mercer Mayer. (Little Look-Look Bks.). (Illus.). 24p. (J). (ps). 1989. pap. 1.79 (*0-307-11714-6*, 11714) Gldn Bks Pub Co.

— Just for You. (Look-Look Bks.). (Illus.). 24p. (J). (ps-3). 1975. pap. 3.29 (*0-307-11838-X*, 11838) Gldn Bks Pub Co.

— Just for You. (J). 1982. 7.45 (*0-606-12373-3*, Pub. by Turtleback) Demco.

— Just Go to Bed. rev. ed. (Look-Look Bks.). (Illus.). 24p. (J). (ps-3). 1985. reprint ed. pap. 3.29 (*0-307-11940-8*, 11940) Gldn Bks Pub Co.

— Just Going to the Dentist. (Look-Look Bks.). (Illus.). 24p. (J). (ps-3). 1990. pap. 3.29 (*0-307-12583-1*, 12583) Gldn Bks Pub Co.

— Just Going to the Dentist-OS. (J). 1998. 8.20 (*0-606-12374-1*, Pub. by Turtleback) Demco.

— Just Grandma & Me. (Look-Look Bks.). (Illus.). 24p. (J). (ps-3). 1985. reprint ed. pap. 3.29 (*0-307-11893-2*, 11893) Gldn Bks Pub Co.

— Just Grandpa & Me. (Look-Look Bks.). (Illus.). 24p. (J). (ps-3). 1985. pap. 3.29 (*0-307-11936-X*, 11936) Gldn Bks Pub Co.

— Just Grandpa & Me. (Golden Look-Look Bks.). 1985. 8.20 (*0-606-12375-X*, Pub. by Turtleback) Demco.

— Just Me & My Babysitter. (Look-Look Bks.). (Illus.). 24p. (J). (ps-3). 1986. pap. 3.29 (*0-307-11945-9*, 11945) Gldn Bks Pub Co.

— Just Me & My Babysitter, a Look Look Book. (J). 1986. 8.20 (*0-606-12376-8*, Pub. by Turtleback) Demco.

Mayer, Mercer. Just Me & My Cousin. (Look-Look Bks.). (Illus.). 24p. (J). (ps-3). 1992. pap. 3.29 (*0-307-12688-9*, 12688) Gldn Bks Pub Co.

Mayer, Mercer. Just Me & My Dad, 2 vols. (Look-Look Bks.). (Illus.). 24p. (J). (ps-3). 1982. pap. 3.29 (*0-307-11839-8*, 11839) Gldn Bks Pub Co.

— Just Me & My Dad. (J). 1982. 9.15 (*0-606-12377-6*, Pub. by Turtleback) Demco.

Mayer, Mercer. Just Me & My Little Brother. (J). 1991. 9.15 (*0-606-12378-4*, Pub. by Turtleback) Demco.

Mayer, Mercer. Just Me & My Mom. (Look-Look Bks.). (Illus.). 24p. (J). (ps-3). 1990. pap. 3.29 (*0-307-12584-X*, 12584) Gldn Bks Pub Co.

— Just Me & My Puppy. (Look-Look Bks.). (Illus.). 24p. (J). (ps-3). 1985. pap. 3.29 (*0-307-11937-8*, 11937) Gldn Bks Pub Co.

— Just Me & My Puppy, Look Look Book. (J). 1985. 7.70 (*0-606-12380-6*, Pub. by Turtleback) Demco.

— Just My Friend & Me. (Look-Look Bks.). (Illus.). 24p. (J). (ps-3). 1988. 3.29 (*0-307-11947-5*, 11947, Goldn Books) Gldn Bks Pub Co.

Mayer, Mercer. Just My Friend & Me, Look Look Book. (J). 1988. 7.35 (*0-606-12381-4*, Pub. by Turtleback) Demco.

Mayer, Mercer. Just Shopping with Mom. (Look-Look Bks.). (Illus.). 24p. (J). (ps-3). 1989. pap. 3.29 (*0-307-11972-6*, 11972, Goldn Books) Gldn Bks Pub Co.

Mayer, Mercer. Just Shopping with Mom. (J). 1989. 9.15 (*0-606-12382-2*, Pub. by Turtleback) Demco.

Mayer, Mercer. Little Critter Just a Pirate. (Magic Touch Talking Bks.). (Illus.). 22p. (J). (ps-2). 1996. 19.99 (*1-888208-12-0*) Hasbro.

— Little Critter Just Going to the Moon. (Magic Touch Talking Bks.). (Illus.). 22p. (J). (ps-2). 1996. 19.99 (*1-888208-11-2*) Hasbro.

***Mayer, Mercer.** Little Critter Sleeps Over. LC 97-80729. (Road to Reading Ser.). (Illus.). 32p. (J). (gr. 1-2). 1999. 10.99 (*0-307-46203-X*, Goldn Books) Gldn Bks Pub Co.

Mayer, Mercer. Little Critter Sleeps Over. LC 97-80729. (Road to Reading Ser.). (Illus.). 32p. (J). 1999. pap. text 3.99 (*0-307-26203-0*, Goldn Books) Gldn Bks Pub Co.

— Little Critter's Holiday Fun Sticker Book. (Illus.). 16p. (J). (ps-1). 1994. bds. 4.95 (*0-590-48640-3*, Cartwheel) Scholastic Inc.

— Little Critter's Joke Book. (Look-Look Bks.). (Illus.). 24p. (J). (ps-3). 1993. pap. 3.29 (*0-307-12790-7*, 12790) Gldn Bks Pub Co.

— Little Critter's Little Red Riding Hood: Little Critter Chunky Flap Book. LC 94-68286. (Illus.). 1995. 3.99 (*0-679-87346-5*) Random.

— Little Critter's Read-It-Yourself Storybook: Six Funny Easy-to-Read Stories. (Illus.). 196p. (J). (gr. k-2). 1993. 17.95 (*0-307-16840-9*, 16840) Gldn Bks Pub Co.

— Little Critters Search for the Beautiful Princess. (Illus.). 1995. 12.00 (*0-679-87351-1*) McKay.

***Mayer, Mercer.** Little Critter's the Best Present. LC 99-89570. (Road to Reading Ser.). (Illus.). (J). 2000. pap. 3.99 (*0-307-26215-4*) Gldn Bks Pub Co.

Mayer, Mercer. Little Monster's Moving Day. (Little Monster Sticker Bks.). (Illus.). 24p. (J). (ps-1). 1995. bds. 4.95 (*0-590-48643-8*, Cartwheel) Scholastic Inc.

— Little Monster's Sports Fun. (Little Monster Sticker Bks.). (Illus.). 24p. (Orig.). (J). (ps-1). 1995. bds. 4.95 (*0-590-48644-6*, Cartwheel) Scholastic Inc.

— Liverwurst Is Missing. LC 90-5435. (Illus.). 32p. (J). (gr. k up). 1990. 16.00 (*0-688-09657-3*, Wm Morrow) Morrow Avon.

— Liverwurst Is Missing. (J). 1981. 10.95 (*0-590-07793-7*) Scholastic Inc.

— Liza Lou & the Yeller Belly Swamp. LC 80-16605. (Illus.). 48p. (J). (gr. k-3). 1997. per. 5.99 (*0-689-81505-0*) Aladdin.

Mayer, Mercer. Liza Lou & the Yeller Belly Swamp. LC 80-16605. (J). 1997. 11.19 (*0-606-11572-2*, Pub. by Turtleback) Demco.

— Me Too! (J). 1985. 7.45 (*0-606-12422-5*, Pub. by Turtleback) Demco.

— Me Too! (Look-Look Bks.). (Illus.). 24p. (J). (ps-3). 1985. reprint ed. pap. 3.29 (*0-307-11941-6*, 11941) Gldn Bks Pub Co.

Mayer, Mercer. Mercer Mayer's Little Critter's, 2 vols., Set. (Early Childhood First Bks.). (Illus.). 40p. (J). (gr. k-1). 1999. lib. bdg. 27.90 (*1-56674-943-3*) Forest Hse.

— Mercer Mayer's Little Critter's Vol. 1: The Picnic. large type ed. (Early Childhood First Bks.: No. 1). (Illus.). 20p. (J). (gr. k-2). 1999. lib. bdg. 13.95 (*1-56674-219-6*) Forest Hse.

— Mercer Mayer's Little Critter's Vol. 2: The Trip. (Early Childhood First Bks.: No. 2). (Illus.). 20p. (J). (gr. k-2). 1999. lib. bdg. 13.95 (*1-56674-254-4*) Forest Hse.

Mayer, Mercer. Merry Christmas, Mom & Dad. (Look-Look Bks.). (Illus.). 24p. (J). (ps-3). 1982. pap. 3.29 (*0-307-11886-X*, 11886, Goldn Books) Gldn Bks Pub Co.

Mayer, Mercer. Midnight Snack. (Step into Reading Ser.: A Step 1 Book). (J). 1997. lib. bdg. 11.99 (*0-679-98706-1*, Pub. by Random Bks Yng Read) Random.

— My Teacher Is a Vampire. (Schooltime Tales Ser.). (Illus.). 48p. (J). (gr. 1-3). 1994. 4.69 (*0-307-15957-4*, 15957) Gldn Bks Pub Co.

— The New Baby. (Look-Look Bks.). (Illus.). 24p. (J). (ps-3). 1985. reprint ed. pap. 3.29 (*0-307-11942-4*, 11942, Goldn Books) Gldn Bks Pub Co.

— No Dancing in the Bathtub. (Pictureback Ser.). (J). 1998. pap. 3.25 (*0-679-88708-3*, Pub. by Random Bks Yng Read) Random.

— No Flying in the Hall. LC 96-45318. (J). 1997. pap. 3.25 (*0-679-87377-5*, Pub. by Random Bks Yng Read) Random.

— One Frog Too Many. 1992. pap. 4.99 (*0-14-054679-0*) NAL.

— One Frog Too Many. (J). 1977. 9.19 (*0-606-03306-8*, Pub. by Turtleback) Demco.

— One Monster after Another. (Illus.). 48p. (J). (ps-3). 1993. pap. 5.95 (*1-879920-05-0*) Rain Bird Prods.

— Una Pesadilla En Mi Armario. 1996. 12.70 (*0-606-10528-X*, Pub. by Turtleback) Demco.

— The Pizza War: Mercer Mayer's LC & The Critter Kids. LC 94-75364. (Mini Novels Ser.: Vol. 5). (Illus.). 72p. (J). (ps-3). 1995. per. 4.69 (*0-307-15979-5*, 15979, Goldn Books) Gldn Bks Pub Co.

— Professor Wormbog in Search for the Zipperump-a-Zoo. (Illus.). 48p. (J). (ps up). 1992. pap. 5.95 (*1-879920-04-2*) Rain Bird Prods.

— The Purple Kiss. LC 93-80651. (LC & the Critter Kids Mini-Novels Ser.). (Illus.). 72p. (J). (ps-3). 1994. 4.69 (*0-307-15980-9*, 15980, Goldn Books) Gldn Bks Pub Co.

— The Secret Code. (LC & the Critter Kids Mini-Novels Ser.). (Illus.). 72p. (J). (ps-3). 1994. pap. 4.69 (*0-307-15983-3*, 15983, Goldn Books) Gldn Bks Pub Co.

***Mayer, Mercer.** Shibumi & the Kitemaker. LC 98-49700. (Illus.). 48p. (J). (ps-3). 1999. 18.95 (*0-7614-5054-8*, Cav Child Bks) Marshall Cavendish.

Mayer, Mercer. Showdown at the Aracade. LC 93-73740. (Schooltime Tales Ser.). (Illus.). 48p. (J). (ps-3). 1994. 4.69 (*0-307-15958-2*, 15958, Goldn Books) Gldn Bks Pub Co.

— A Silly Story: Nothing Less Nothing More. (Illus.). 48p. (J). 1992. reprint ed. pap. 5.95 (*1-879920-02-6*) Rain Bird Prods.

— Tale of Two Zombies. LC 98-16811. (Pictureback Ser.). 48p. (J). 1998. pap. 3.99 (*0-679-88710-5*, Pub. by Random Bks Yng Read) Random.

— There's a Nightmare in My Closet. 28p. (J). (ps-3). 1992. pap. 5.99 (*0-14-054712-6*, PuffinBks) Peng Put Young Read.

— There's a Nightmare in My Closet. (Pied Piper Bks.). (J). 1968. 11.19 (*0-606-01852-2*, Pub. by Turtleback) Demco.

— There's a Nightmare in My Closet (Una Pesadilla en Mi Armario) (SPA.). (J). 7.50 (*84-372-1754-7*) Santillana.

Mayer, Mercer. There's An Alligator In My School. (J). write for info. (*0-8037-0621-9*, Dial Yng Read); write for info. (*0-8037-0622-7*, Dial Yng Read) Peng Put Young Read.

Mayer, Mercer. There's an Alligator under My Bed. LC 86-19944. (Illus.). 32p. (J). (ps-3). 1987. 15.99 (*0-8037-0374-0*, Dial Yng Read) Peng Put Young Read.

— There's Something in My Attic. (Illus.). 32p. (J). (ps-3). 1992. pap. 5.99 (*0-14-054813-0*, PuffinBks) Peng Put Young Read.

Mayer, Mercer. There's Something in My Attic. (J). 1988. 11.19 (*0-606-01749-6*, Pub. by Turtleback) Demco.

Mayer, Mercer. This Is My Family. (Little Golden Storybks.). (J). 1997. 3.99 (*0-307-16068-8*, 16068, Goldn Books) Gldn Bks Pub Co.

M

An Asterisk (*) at the beginning of an entry indicates that the title is appearing for the first time.

— Top Dog. (LC & the Critter Kids Mini-Novels Ser.). (Illus.). 72p. (J). (gr. 2-5). 1994. 4.69 (*0-307-15981-7*, 15981) Gldn Bks Pub Co.

— What a Bad Dream. (Look-Look Bks.). (Illus.). 24p. (J). (ps-3). 1992. 3.29 (*0-307-12685-4*, 12685, Goldn Books) Gldn Bks Pub Co.

— What Do You Do with a Kangaroo? (J). 1973. 11.19 (*0-606-01210-9*, Pub. by Turtleback) Demco.

— What Do You Do with a Kangaroo. LC 72-87073. 48p. (J). (ps-3). 1987. pap. 5.99 (*0-590-44850-1*) Scholastic Inc.

— When I Get Bigger. (Look-Look Bks.). (Illus.). 24p. (J). (ps-3). 1985. reprint ed. pap. 3.29 (*0-307-11943-2*, 11943) Gldn Bks Pub Co.

— When I Get Bigger, Look-Look Book. (J). 1985. 9.15 (*0-606-12571-X*, Pub. by Turtleback) Demco.

— Whinnie the Lovesick Dragon. LC 85-18886. (Illus.). 32p. (J). (gr. k-3). 1986. lib. bdg. 14.95 (*0-02-765180-0*, Mac Bks Young Read) S&S Childrens.

— The Wizard Comes to Town. (Illus.). 40p. (J). 1991. reprint ed. pap. 5.95 (*1-879920-00-X*) Rain Bird Prods.

— You're the Scaredy-Cat. (Illus.). 40p. (J). 1991. reprint ed. pap. 5.95 (*1-879920-01-8*) Rain Bird Prods.

Mayer, Mercer & Farber, Erica. No Howling in the House. (Step into Reading Ser.: A Step 2 Book). (Illus.). (J). (ps-3). 1996. lib. bdg. 11.99 (*0-679-97365-6*) McKay.

— No Howling in the House. LC 95-13690. (Step into Reading Ser.: A Step 2 Book). 48p. (J). (gr. k-2). 1996. pap. 3.99 (*0-679-87365-1*) Random.

— No Howling in the House. LC 95-13690. (Step into Reading Ser.: A Step 2 Book). (J). (gr. 1-3). 1996. 9.19 (*0-606-09690-6*, Pub. by Turtleback) Demco.

Mayer, Mercer, et al. Midnight Snack. LC 97-67476. (Step into Reading Ser.: A Step 1 Book). (Illus.). (J). (ps-3). 1997. pap. 3.99 (*0-679-88706-7*, Pub. by Random Bks Yng Read) Random.

Mayer, Mercer, jt. auth. see Fitzgerald, John D.

Mayer, Mercer, jt. auth. see Mayer, Gina.

Mayer, Mercer, jt. auth. see Mayer, Marianna.

Mayer, Michael F. Foreign Films on American Screens. LC 82-49212. (Cinema Classics Ser.). 126p. 1985. lib. bdg. 27.00 (*0-8240-5769-4*) Garland.

— The Libel Revolution: A New Look at Defamation & Privacy. 28.75 (*0-317-67926-0*) Law Arts.

— Rights of Privacy. 251p. (C). 1972. text 7.95 (*0-317-67878-7*) Law Arts.

Mayer, Michael J. How to Love, Understand & Cope with Teenagers. LC 78-61586. 1979. 10.95 (*0-87212-123-2*) Libra.

Mayer, Milton. The Nature of the Beast. Gustafson, W. Eric, ed. LC 74-21243. 376p. 1975. 40.00 (*0-87023-176-6*) U of Mass Pr.

— Robert Maynard Hutchins: A Memoir. Hicks, John H., ed. LC 92-16512. 1993. 45.00 (*0-520-07091-7*, Pub. by U CA Pr) Cal Prin Full Svc.

— They Thought They Were Free: The Germans, 1933-45. 2nd ed. LC 55-5137. 368p. 1966. pap. text 16.50 (*0-226-51192-8*, P222) U Ch Pr.

Mayer, Milton, jt. auth. see Boulding, Kenneth E.

Mayer, Milton S. What Can a Man Do? A Selection of His Most Challenging Writings. Gustafson, W. Eric, ed. LC 64-15801. 320p. reprint ed. pap. 99.20 (*0-608-18548-5*, 202011800016) Bks Demand.

Mayer, Mordecai. Israel's Wisdom in Modern Life: Essays & Interpretations of Religious & Cultural Problems Based on the Talmudic & Midrashic Literature. 32.50 (*0-87559-147-7*) Shalom.

Mayer, Morris F. A Guide for Child-Care Workers. LC 58-10171. 184p. 1958. pap. 16.95 (*0-87868-066-7*) Child Welfare.

Mayer, Morris F. & Melancon, Richard. The University of Alabama: College of Commerce & Business Administration. (First 75 Years Ser.). 250p. 1995. 49.95 (*0-9644291-0-1*) U Ala Coll of C & B A.

***Mayer, Musa.** Advanced Breast Cancer: A Guide to Living with Metastatic Disease. 2nd ed. Lamb, Linda, ed. LC 98-38919. (Illus.). 540p. 1998. pap. 24.95 (*1-56592-522-X*) OReilly & Assocs.

Mayer, Musa. Night Studio: A Memoir of Philip Guston. LC 96-43818. (Illus.). 320p. 1997. pap. 17.95 (*0-306-80767-X*) Da Capo.

Mayer, Nancy K. Rainy Day Activities for the Commodore 64. write for info. (*0-318-58231-7*) P-H.

Mayer, Nathan. Beyond a Reasonable Doubt. 1992. pap. 5.60 (*0-87129-166-5*, B71) Dramatic Pub.

Mayer, Nonna, jt. ed. see Boy, Daniel.

Mayer, O. B., et al. The Dutch Fork. Holcomb, Brent, ed. (Illus.). 155p. (C). 1982. 20.00 (*0-9611610-0-0*) Dutch Fork Pr.

Mayer-Oakes, Thomas F., ed. see Kumao, Harada.

***Mayer, Otto G. & Scharrer, Hans-Eckart, eds.** Transatlantic Relations in a Global Economy. LC 99-213686. (Verhoffentlichungen des Hwwa-Institut Fhur Wirtschaftsforschung-Hamburg Ser.). 186p. 1999. write for info. (*3-7890-5935-8*, Pub. by Nomos Verlags) Intl Bk Import.

***Mayer, Pamela S. & Center for Creative Leadership Staff.** The Human Side of Knowledge Management: An Annotated Bibliography. LC 00-27960. 2000. write for info. (*1-882197-56-9*) Ctr Creat Leader.

***Mayer, Paola.** Jena Romanticism & Its Appropriation of Jakob Bhohme: Theosophy, Hagiography, Literature. 1999. 65.00 (*0-7735-1852-5*) McG-Queens Univ Pr.

Mayer, Patricia E., ed. see Holden, William M.

***Mayer, Paul A., ed.** Computer Media & Communication: A Reader. 354p. 2000. pap. text 24.95 (*0-19-874257-6*) OUP.

***Mayer, Peter, et al.** HAPM Workmanship Checklists. LC 99-37102. 352p. 2000. pap. 110.00 (*0-419-24730-0*) Routledge.

Mayer, Peter J. Miwok Balanophagy: Implications for the Cultural Development of Some California Acorn-Eaters. (Archaeological Research Facility, Dept. of Anthropology, Miscellaneous Papers, Berkeley CA). 43p. (C). 1976. pap. 4.38 (*1-55567-648-0*) Coyote Press.

Mayer, Peter P., et al, eds. Quality Care for Elderly People. LC 97-65432. (Illus.). 256p. 1997. text 55.00 (*0-412-61830-3*, Pub. by E A) OUP.

***Mayer, Peter W., et al.** Residential End Uses of Water LC 99-41861. 1999. write for info. (*1-58321-016-4*) Am Water Wks Assn.

Mayer, Philip. The Lineage Principle in Gusii Society. LC 79-320820. (International African Institute Ser.: No. 24). 35p. reprint ed. pap. 30.00 (*0-8357-3020-4*, 205710600010) Bks Demand.

Mayer, Philip, ed. Black Villagers in an Industrial Society: Anthropological Perspectives on Labour Migration in South Africa. (Illus.). 1981. 35.00 (*0-19-570191-7*) OUP.

***Mayer, Philip & Gilliam, Kenneth P.** Multiple Choice Questions: For Macroeconomics. 102p. (C). 1999. spiral bd. 10.00 (*1-929659-01-6*) P Mayer.

— Mutiple Choice Questions: For Microeconomics. 90p. (C). 1999. spiral bd. 10.00 (*1-929659-02-4*) P Mayer.

***Mayer, Philip & Gillian, Kenneth P.** Multiple Choice Questions: For Microeconomics & Macroeconomics. 164p. (C). 1999. spiral bd. 15.00 (*1-929659-00-8*) P Mayer.

Mayer, Philipp M. Freedome in Architecture Design: An Image of Tomorrow. LC 93-87103. 1995. 29.95 (*0-9638694-0-X*) Pegasus Pubng.

Mayer, R. Orientation on Quantitative IR-Thermografy in Wall-Shear Stress Measurements. (Series 01 - Aerodynamics: No. 09). (Illus.). 102p. 1998. pap. 22.50 (*90-407-1572-6*, Pub. by Delft U Pr) Coronet Bks.

Mayer, R. & Thiel, W. Darstellung und Reaktionen Von Thiooxalsauren und Thiooxalsaurederivaten, Vol. 8. Senning, Alexander, ed. (Sulfer Reports: Vol. 8, No. 1). (GER.). 58p. 1988. pap. text 90.00 (*3-7186-4807-5*) Gordon & Breach.

Mayer, R., jt. auth. see Hoepelman, J.

Mayer, R., jt. auth. see Hoepleman, J.

Mayer, R., ed. see Lucan.

Mayer, R. G., jt. ed. see Adams, J. N.

Mayer, R. John & Brown, I. R., eds. Heat Shock Proteins in the Nervous System. (Neuroscience Perspectives Ser.). (Illus.). 297p. 1994. text 83.00 (*0-12-480960-X*) Acad Pr.

Mayer, R. John & Walker, J. H., eds. Immunochemical Methods in Cell & Molecular Biology. (Biological Techniques Ser.). 325p. 1988. text 83.00 (*0-12-480855-7*) Acad Pr.

Mayer, R. John, jt. auth. see Doherty, Fergus J.

Mayer, Ralph. The Artist's Handbook of Materials & Techniques. 5th rev. ed. LC 90-50357. (Illus.). 800p. 1991. 45.00 (*0-670-83701-6*) Viking Penguin.

— HarCol Dict Art Term. 2nd ed. LC 91-55395. (Illus.). 480p. 1992. pap. 18.00 (*0-06-461012-8*, Perennial) HarperTrade.

— Making CAD-CAM Data Transfer Work: IGES & Other Solutions (a Hands-On Guide) Linden, Jonathan, ed. (Illus.). 250p. 1987. 295.00 (*0-932007-13-9*) Mgmt Roundtable.

Mayer, Reinhard. Fremdlinge im Eigenen Haus: Clemens Brentano als Vorbild fur Adrian Leverkuhn und Clemens der Ire in den Romanen Doktor Faustus und Der Erwahlte von Thomas Mann. (Literature & the Sciences of Man Ser.: Vol. 8). 138p. (C). 1996. text 41.95 (*0-8204-2344-0*) P Lang Pubng.

Mayer, Richard E. Environmental Science Case Studies. (C). 1998. pap. text. write for info. (*0-8053-0658-7*) Addison-Wesley.

— The Promise of Cognitive Psychology. (Illus.). 136p. (C). 1990. reprint ed. pap. text 17.50 (*0-8191-7653-2*) U Pr of Amer.

— The Promise of Educational Psychology: Learning in the Content Areas. LC 98-9789. 280p. (C). 1998. pap. text 32.00 (*0-13-913013-6*, Merrill Coll) P-H.

— Thinking, Problem Solving, Cognition. 2nd ed. 560p. (C). 1991. pap. 39.95 (*0-7167-2215-1*) W H Freeman.

Mayer, Richard E., ed. Teaching & Learning Computer Programming: Multiple Research Perspectives. 336p. 1988. 59.95 (*0-8058-0073-5*) L Erlbaum Assocs.

Mayer, Richard J. Conflict Management: The Courage to Confront. 2nd ed. LC 94-30934. 176p. 1997. 49.95 (*0-935470-82-4*) Battelle.

Mayer, Richard T., jt. auth. see Harmon, Michael M.

Mayer, Richard T., jt. auth. see Soufi, Wahib A.

Mayer, Richard T., jt. ed. see Bailey, Mary T.

Mayer, Richard T., jt. ed. see Fisher, Joseph L.

Mayer, Robern N. The Consumer Movement: Guardians of the Marketplace. (Social Movements Past & Present Ser.). 216p. 1989. pap. 15.95 (*0-8057-9719-X*, Twyne) Mac Lib Ref.

— The Consumer Movement: Guardians of the Marketplace. (Social Movements Past & Present Ser.). 216p. 1989. 26.95 (*0-8057-9718-1*, Twyne) Mac Lib Ref.

Mayer, Robert. History & the Early English Novel: Matters of Fact from Bacon to Defoe. LC 96-9608. (Cambridge Studies in Eighteenth-Century English Literature & Thought Ser.: No. 33). (Illus.). 260p. (C). 1997. text 59.95 (*0-521-56377-1*) Cambridge U Pr.

— Sweet Salt, A Novel. 132p. (Orig.). 1984. 15.95 (*0-933553-02-1*); pap. 11.95 (*0-933553-03-X*) Mariposa Print Pub.

— The Vidyadharas of Vajrakumara: A Scripture of the Ancient Tantra Collection. (Critical Studies in Buddhism: Vol. 14). 450p. 1999. text 55.00 (*0-7007-1178-3*, Pub. by Curzon Pr Ltd) UH Pr.

Mayer, Robert A., intro. Blacks in America: A Photographic Record. LC 86-80319. (Illus.). 60p. (Orig.). 1986. pap. 12.50 (*0-935398-12-0*, 030) G Eastman Hse.

Mayer, Robert E. Minolta Classic Cameras. (Magic Lantern Guides). (Illus.). 176p. (Orig.). (C). 1998. pap. 19.95 (*1-883403-17-0*, H 195, Silver Pixel Pr) Saunders Photo.

Mayer, Robert E., et al. Photography Careers. (Opportunities in...Ser.). (Illus.). 160p. 1988. 13.95 (*0-8442-6180-7*, VGM Career) NTC Contemp Pub Co.

Mayer, Robert G. Embalming: History, Theory & Practice. 2nd rev. ed. (C). 1996. pap. text 77.50 (*0-8385-1468-5*, A1468-6, Apple Lange Med) McGraw.

Mayer, Robert J. & Griswold, Millie H., eds. Advent Christian Catechism. 70p. 1987. student ed. 3.00 (*1-881909-02-6*) Advent Christ Gen Conf.

Mayer, Robert N., ed. Enhancing Consumer Choice: Proceedings, Second International Conference on Research in the Consumer Interest. (Orig.). 1991. pap. text 15.00 (*0-945857-01-2*) Am Coun Consumer.

Mayer, Robert R. Social Science & Institutional Change. LC 81-2705. 202p. 1982. text 34.95 (*0-87855-432-7*) Transaction Pubs.

Mayer, Robert S. Satan's Children. 272p. 1992. mass mkt. 4.99 (*0-380-71830-8*, Avon Bks) Morrow Avon.

— Through Divided Minds. 304p. 1992. mass mkt. 4.99 (*0-380-71920-7*, Avon Bks) Morrow Avon.

— Through Divided Minds: Probing the Mysteries of Multiple Personalites - A Doctor's First-Person Story. 304p. 1990. pap. 8.95 (*0-380-70905-8*, Avon Bks) Morrow Avon.

Mayer, Robert T., tr. Bernard of Clairvaux: The Irishman. LC 78-768. (Cistercian Fathers Ser.). 1978. 11.95 (*0-87907-110-9*) Cistercian Pubns.

Mayer, Roland, ed. see Horace.

Mayer, Roland H. & Rudd, Niall. Epistles Two & 'Ars Poetica' (Cambridge Greek & Latin Classics Ser.). 256p. (C). 1990. pap. text 22.95 (*0-521-31292-2*) Cambridge U Pr.

Mayer, Ronald A. 1937 Newark Bears: A Baseball Legend. (Illus.). 300p. (C). 1994. reprint ed. pap. 14.95 (*0-8135-2153-X*) Rutgers U Pr.

Mayer, Ronald A., jt. auth. see Tomlinson, Gerald.

Mayer, Rosemary. Pontormo's Diary. (Illus.). 200p. (C). 1983. 26.95 (*0-915570-17-3*); pap. 16.95 (*0-686-86541-3*) Oolp Pr.

Mayer, S. J. NRC Antitrust Licensing Actions, 1978-1996. 144p. 1997. per. 14.00 (*0-16-062862-8*) USGPO.

***Mayer, Sandro.** Love Letter: The Heartbreaking Tale of the Incredible Bond. 2000. pap. 12.95 (*88-7301-404-6*) Gremese Intl.

Mayer, Sandy, ed. see Knott, Tara D.

Mayer, Shelly. Preparing Dairy Cattle for Show. LC 95-167817. (Illus.). 48p. (C). 1995. pap. text 4.00 (*0-932147-25-9*) Hoard & Sons Co.

Mayer, Sigrid. The Critical Reception of the Short Fiction by Joyce Carol Oates & Gabriele Wohmann. LC 97-42961. (Literary Criticism in Perspective Ser.). 220p. 1998. 55.00 (*1-57113-083-7*) Camden Hse.

Mayer, Sigrid, jt. auth. see Eggers, Walter.

Mayer-Skumanz, Lene. The Tower. (Illus.). (J). (gr. 2-5). 1993. 12.95 (*965-465-000-2*) Pitspopany.

Mayer-Spitzweck, E., jt. auth. see Hussain, Maria.

Mayer-St, Hans-Georg. The Medium PKW of the German Wehrmacht, 1937-1945. LC 98-182541. 48p. 1998. pap. 9.95 (*0-7643-0570-0*) Schiffer.

Mayer, Stefan & Weber, Michael. Bibliographie Zur Linguistischen Gesprachsforschung. (Germanistische Linguistik Ser.). 216p. 1983. write for info. (*3-487-07399-4*) G Olms Pubs.

Mayer, Stephan A., jt. auth. see Marshall, Randolph S.

***Mayer, Stephanie.** First Exposure: The Statchbooks & Photographs of Theodore Robinson. (MAA G Sources).Tr. of Theodore Robinson: Esquisses et photographies. (Illus.). 2000. pap. 13.00 (*0-932171-11-7*, Museed Art) Terra Found Arts.

— Theodore Robinson: Esquisses et photographies. Rose, Francesca, ed. (MAA G Sources).Tr. of First Exposure: The Sketchbooks & Photographs of Theodore Robinson. (FRE., Illus.). 56p. 2000. pap. 13.00 (*0-932171-12-5*, Museed Art) Terra Found Arts.

Mayer, Steve. Bishop vs. Knight. LC 97-71891. (Illus.). 192p. (Orig.). 1997. pap. 22.50 (*1-879479-73-7*) ICE WA.

***Mayer, Steve.** Jaw Dropping Chess: Openings. (Chess Bks.). (Illus.). 1999. pap. text 17.95 (*0-7134-8579-5*) B T B.

Mayer, Steve. The Soltis Variation of the Yugoslav Attack. LC 94-72924. (Studies in Contemporary Opening Theory). 280p. (Orig.). 1994. pap. 22.95 (*1-886040-16-8*) Hypermodern Pr.

Mayer, Steven E. Building Community Capacity: The Potential of Community Foundations. (Illus.). 222p. (Orig.). 1994. pap. 17.50 (*0-9624428-4-4*, 313a1) Rainbow Research.

Mayer, Steven E. & Scheie, David. Supporting Low Income Neighborhood Organizations: A Guide for Community Foundations. Lilya, Mary, ed. (Illus.). 1989. write for info. (*0-9624428-2-8*) Rainbow Research.

Mayer Stinchecum, Amanda, tr. see Yagu, G.

Mayer-Stinehecum, Amanda, tr. see Hidaka, Masako.

Mayer, Susan & Peterson, Paul E., eds. Earning & Learning: How Schools Matter. LC 99-6383. 1999. 42.95 (*0-8157-5528-7*); pap. 18.95 (*0-8157-5529-5*) Brookings.

Mayer, Susan B. & Rogers, Donna C. Kuba: People of Central Africa. (Illus.). 16p. 1978. pap. 4.95 (*0-614-02732-2*) J S Blanton Mus.

Mayer, Susan E. What Money Can't Buy: Family Income & Children's Life Chances. LC 96-34429. (Illus.). 256p. 1997. 37.95 (*0-674-58733-2*) HUP.

Mayer, Susan E. What Money Can't Buy: Family Income & Children's Life Chances. (Illus.). 240p. 1998. pap. 17.95 (*0-674-58734-0*) HUP.

Mayer, Susan M. & Reese, Becky D. American Images: Selections from the James & Mari Michener Collection of 20th Century American Art. 2nd ed. (Illus.). 28p. 1981. pap. 12.95 (*0-935213-06-6*) J S Blanton Mus.

— A Woman's Place. (Illus.). 20p. 1977. pap. 4.95 (*0-935213-05-8*) J S Blanton Mus.

Mayer, T., tr. Al-Ghazi's Letter to a Disciple. 1996. text 32.50 (*0-946621-62-4*, Pub. by Islamic Texts); pap. text 19.95 (*0-946621-63-2*, Pub. by Islamic Texts) Intl Spec Bk.

Mayer, T. F. Thomas Starkey: A Dialogue Between Pole & Lupset. (Camden Fourth Ser.: No. 37). 172p. 27.00 (*0-86193-119-X*) David Brown.

Mayer, T. W. The Caribbean & Its People. (People & Places Ser.). (Illus.). 48p. (J). (gr. 5-8). 1995. lib. bdg. 24.26 (*1-56847-338-9*) Raintree Steck-V.

Mayer, T. Y. The Writing Workshop: Morals of Aesop's Fables. (Writing Workshop, Human Condition Ser.: Vol. 1). 100p. 1996. teacher ed., spiral bd. 40.00 (*1-889008-04-4*) Projects.

Mayer, Tamar. The Gender Ironies of Nationalism: Sexing the Nation. LC 98-52189. 1999. 85.00 (*0-415-16254-8*) Routledge.

— Women & the Israeli Occupation: The Politics of Change. LC 94-3886. (International Studies of Women & Places). (Illus.). 240p. (C). (gr. 13). 1994. 85.00 (*0-415-09545-X*, B0129) Routledge.

Mayer, Tamar, ed. The Gender Ironies of Nationalism: Sexing the Nation. LC 98-52189. 362p. 1999. pap. 29.95 (*0-415-16255-6*) Routledge.

— Women & the Israeli Occupation: The Politics of Change. LC 94-3886. (International Studies of Women & Places). (Illus.). 240p. (C). 1994. pap. 25.99 (*0-415-09546-8*, B0133) Routledge.

Mayer, Thom. Emergency Management of Pediatric Trauma. (Illus.). 531p. 1985. text 135.00 (*0-7216-6189-0*, W B Saunders Co) Harcrt Hlth Sci Grp.

Mayer, Thom, jt. auth. see Edwards, Tanise.

Mayer, Thom, ed. see Cayten, C. Gene, et al.

Mayer, Thom A., ed. see Salluzzo.

Mayer, Thomas. The Changing Past: Egyptian Historiography of the Urabi Revolt, 1882-1983. LC 87-25410. 117p. 1988. pap. 18.95 (*0-8130-0889-1*) U Press Fla.

— Doing Economic Research: Essays on the Applied Methodology of Economics. (Economists of the Twentieth Century Ser.). 192p. 1995. 90.00 (*1-85278-939-5*) E Elgar.

— Monetary Policy & the Great Inflation in the United States: The Federal Reserve & the Failure of Macroeconomic Policy, 1965-79. LC 98-24137. 168p. 1999. 75.00 (*1-85898-953-1*) E Elgar.

— Truth Versus Precision in Economics. (Advances in Economic Methodology Ser.). 208p. 1992. 85.00 (*1-85278-546-2*); pap. 25.00 (*1-85278-552-7*) E Elgar.

Mayer, Thomas, ed. Monetary Theory. (International Library of Critical Writings in Economics: Vol. 7). 384p. 1990. text 210.00 (*1-85278-180-7*) E Elgar.

— The Political Economy of American Monetary Policy. (Illus.). 324p. (C). 1993. pap. text 21.95 (*0-521-44651-1*) Cambridge U Pr.

Mayer, Thomas & Duesenberry, James. Money, Banking, & the Economy: Test Item File. 6th ed. (C). 1996. pap. text, teacher ed., suppl. ed. write for info. (*0-393-96850-2*) Norton.

Mayer, Thomas & Sheffrin, Steven M., eds. Fiscal & Monetary Policy, 2 vols., Set. LC 94-46730. (International Library of Critical Writings in Economics: Vol. 52). 724p. 1995. 305.00 (*1-85898-009-7*) E Elgar.

Mayer, Thomas & Spinelli, Franco. Macroeconomics & Macroeconomic Policy Issues. 271p. 1991. text 82.95 (*1-85628-219-8*, Pub. by Avebry) Ashgate Pub Co.

Mayer, Thomas, et al. Money, Banking, & the Economy. 6th ed. LC 95-13313. (C). 1996. 85.50 (*0-393-96848-0*) Norton.

— Money, Banking, & the Economy: Study Guide. 6th ed. LC 96-215061. (C). 1996. pap., student ed. 16.00 (*0-393-96849-9*) Norton.

Mayer, Thomas, jt. auth. see Mayer, Gloria G.

Mayer, Thomas, tr. see Mayer, Margarita.

Mayer, Thomas A. & Barnett, Albert E. A Guide to Forming Physician Networks. 95p. 1997. pap. 93.00 (*0-929156-30-7*) Atlantic Info Services Inc.

Mayer, Thomas F. Analytical Marxism. LC 94-4601. (Contemporary Social Theory Ser.). 1994. 56.00 (*0-8039-4680-5*); pap. 26.95 (*0-8039-4681-3*) Sage.

— Mathematical Models of Group Structure. LC 74-1031. (Studies in Sociology). (C). 1975. pap. text 3.00 (*0-672-61212-7*, Bobbs) Macmillan.

***Mayer, Thomas F.** Reginald Pole: Prince & Prophet. (Illus.). 450p. 2000. write for info. (*0-521-37188-0*) Cambridge U Pr.

— A Reluctant Author. LC 99-48301. (Transactions Ser.). 115p. 1999. pap. write for info. (*0-87169-894-3*) Am Psychol.

Mayer, Thomas F. & Woolf, D. R., eds. The Rhetorics of Life-Writing in Early Modern Europe: Forms of Biography from Cassandra Fedele to Louis XIV. LC 95-1859. (Studies in Medieval & Early Modern Civilization). 400p. 1995. text 57.50 (*0-472-10591-4*, 10591) U of Mich Pr.

Mayer, Thomas F., jt. ed. see Greenberg, Edward S.

Mayer, Toby G., jt. auth. see Fleming, Richard W.

Mayer, Tom G., et al. Contemporary Conservative Care for Painful Spinal Disorders. LC 91-9298. (Illus.). 588p. 1991. text 99.00 (*0-8121-1344-6*) Lppncott W & W.

Mayer, Tommye K. One-Handed in a Two-Handed World. (Illus.). 229p. 1999. reprint ed. pap. 16.95 (*0-9652805-0-0*) Prince-Gallison.

M

*Mayer, Tommye-Karen. One-Handed in a Two-Handed World. 2nd ed. LC 99-90859. (Illus.). 2000. 20.00 (0-9652805-1-9) Prince-Gallison.

— Teaching Me to Run. Date not set. write for info. (0-9652805-2-7) Prince-Gallison.

Mayer, Virginia. Festival Marketplaces: The Formula for Success. Murphy, Jenny & Kailo, Andrea, eds. 28p. (Orig.). 1986. pap. 17.00 (0-317-04910-0) Natl Coun Econ Dev.

Mayer, Walter. Nuzi-Studien I: Die Archive des Palastes und die Prosopographie der Berufe. (Alter Orient und Altes Testament Ser.: Vol. 205). (GER.). xiii, 221p. 1978. text 17.50 (3-7887-0574-4) NeukirchenerV.

— Politik und Kriegskunst der Assyrer. (Abhandlvorgen zur Literatur Alt-Syrien-Palastinas und Mesopatamieus Ser.: No. 9). xvi, 545p. 1995. text 122.00 (3-927120-26-X, Pub. by UGARIT) Eisenbrauns.

Mayer, Walter G., jt. ed. see Alippi, Adriano.

*Mayer, Wendy & Allen, Pauline. John Chrysostom. LC 99-17709. 256p. (C). 1999. text. write for info. (0-415-18252-2) Routledge.

Mayer, Wendy, et al. John Chrysostom. LC 99-17709. (Early Church Fathers Ser.). 1999. pap. 24.99 (0-415-18253-0) Routledge.

Mayer, Werner R., jt. auth. see Loretz, Oswald.

Mayer, William, et al. Perspectives on the Educational Use of Animals. (Illus.). 77p. 1980. pap. 3.00 (0-913098-38-8) Orion Society.

Mayer, William G. The Changing American Mind: How & Why American Public Opinion Changed Between 1960 & 1988. LC 92-26578. 518p. (C). 1992. text 57.50 (0-472-09498-X, 09498); pap. text 20.95 (0-472-06498-3, 06498) U of Mich Pr.

— The Divided Democrats: Ideological Unity, Party Reform & Presidential Elections. (Transforming American Politics Ser.). 1996. text 75.00 (0-8133-2679-6, Pub. by Westview) HarpC.

*Mayer, William G., ed. In Pursuit of the White House 2000: How We Choose Our Presidential Nominees. LC 99-6575. 384p. (C). 2000. pap. 24.95 (1-889119-17-2, Pub. by Seven Bridges) Stylus Pub VA.

Mayer, William V. & Van Gelder, R. G., eds. Physiological Mammalogy, 2 vols. Incl. Vol. 1. 1964. 63.00 (0-12-481001-2); Vol. 2. 1964. 63.00 (0-12-481002-0); 1964. write for info. (0-318-50336-0) Acad Pr.

Mayer, Wolf. Images in Stone: A Guide to the Building Stones of Parliament House. unabridged ed. LC 95-11121. (Illus.). 48p. (Orig.). 1996. pap. 12.95 (0-644-35725-8, Pub. by AGPS Pr) Intl Spec Bk.

Mayerchak, Patrick M. East Asia & the Western Pacific, 1996. 29th ed. 168p. 1996. pap. 11.50 (0-943448-98-0) Stryker-Post.

— Scholars' Guide to Washington, D. C., for Southeast Asian Studies: Brunei, Burma, Cambodia, Indonesia, Laos, Malaysia, Philippines, Singapore, Thailand, & Vietnam. David, Zdenek V., ed. LC 82-19454. 412p. 1991. 29.95 (0-87474-626-4); pap. text 12.95 (0-87474-625-6) W Wilson Ctr Pr.

Mayerchak, Patrick N., jt. auth. see Indorf, Hans H.

Mayerfeld, Jamie. Suffering & Moral Repsonsibility. LC 98-19813. (Oxford Ethics Ser.). (Illus.). 256p. 1999. text 45.00 (0-19-511599-6) OUP.

Mayergoyz, I. D. & Lawson, W. Basic Electric Circuit Theory: A One-Semester Text. LC 96-18904. (Illus.). 449p. (C). 1996. text 62.00 (0-12-480865-4) Acad Pr.

Mayergoyz, Isaak D. Nonlinear Diffusion of Electromagnetic Fields. LC 98-12650. (Electromagnetism Ser.). (Illus.). 412p. 1998. boxed set 120.00 (0-12-480870-0) Acad Pr.

Mayerhofer, Gottfried, jt. auth. see Lorber, Jakob.

Mayeroff, Jerry M., ed. see Sagarin, James L.

Mayeroff, Milton. On Caring Ri. LC 90-55052. 144p. 1990. reprint ed. pap. 11.00 (0-06-092024-6, Perennial) HarperTrade.

Mayers & Readman. Dynamic Landscape. Date not set. pap. text. write for info. (0-05-003806-0) Addison-Wesley.

Mayers, Bonney, ed. see North, Bill.

Mayers, D. F., jt. auth. see Morton, K. W.

Mayers, David. The Ambassadors & America's Soviet Policy. (Illus.). 368p. 1995. text 55.00 (0-19-506802-5) OUP.

— The Ambassadors & America's Soviet Policy. (Illus.). 368p. 1997. reprint ed. pap. 22.00 (0-19-511576-7) OUP.

*Mayers, David. Wars & Peace: The Future Americans Revisioned, 1861-1991. LC 98-15550. 184p. 1999. pap. 18.95 (0-312-22770-1) St Martin.

Mayers, Florence C. ABC: The Wild West. LC 90-440. (Illus.). 32p. (J). 1990. 7.50 (0-8109-1903-6) Abrams.

— ABC - The Alef-Bet Book: The Israel Museum, Jerusalem. LC 88-27501. (ABC Ser.). (Illus.). 32p. (J). (gr. k up). 1989. 12.95 (0-8109-1885-4, Pub. by Abrams) Time Warner.

— The ABC Museum of Modern Art, New York. (ABC Ser.). (Illus.). 32p. 1986. 12.95 (0-8109-1849-8, Pub. by Abrams) Time Warner.

— Baseball ABC. LC 94-1167. (Illus.). 40p. (J). 1994. 12.95 (0-8109-1938-9, Pub. by Abrams) Time Warner.

— Basketball ABC. LC 95-78670. (Illus.). 40p. 1996. 12.95 (0-8109-3143-5, Pub. by Abrams) Time Warner.

— A Russian ABC: Featuring Masterpieces from the Hermitage, St. Petersburg. (ABC Ser.). (Illus.). 36p. (J). 1992. 12.95 (0-8109-1919-2, Pub. by Abrams) Time Warner.

Mayers, Gregory. Listen to the Desert. 128p. 1997. pap. 35.00 (0-86012-272-7, Pub. by Srch Pr) St Mut.

— Listen to the Desert: Secrets of Spiritual Maturity from the Desert Fathers & Mothers. LC 96-12888. (Illus.). 160p. (Orig.). 1996. pap. 11.00 (0-89243-930-0, Liguori Triumph) Liguori Pubns.

Mayers, Keith. A Dictionary of Locksmithing. 72p. 1980. reprint ed. pap., spiral bd. 12.95 (0-9604860-0-3) Keith Mayers Pub.

— Kyros: Lessons of a Startup. iv, 203p. 1999. pap. 16.95 (0-9604860-3-8) Keith Mayers Pub.

— Step into the Sun. (Orig.). 1999. pap. 14.95 (0-9604860-2-X) Keith Mayers Pub.

Mayers, Keith, jt. auth. see Lonidier, Lynn.

Mayers, Lewis. American Legal System: The Administration of Justice in the United States by Judicial, Administrative, Military & Arbitral Tribunals. rev. ed. xi, 594p. 1981. reprint ed. 52.50 (0-8377-0839-7, Rothman) W S Hein.

— Federal Service: A Study of the System of Personnel Administration of the United States Government. (Brookings Institution Reprint Ser.). reprint ed. lib. bdg. 39.50 (0-697-00165-2) Irvington.

— Shall We Amend the Fifth Amendment? LC 78-6206. 350p. 1978. reprint ed. lib. bdg. 69.50 (0-313-20394-6, MASH, Greenwood Pr) Greenwood.

*Mayers, Lise B. & Rabatin, Diana L. Brief Employee Assistance Homework Planner. (Practice Planners Ser.). (Illus.). 256p. 2000. pap. 49.95 (0-471-38088-1) Wiley.

Mayers, Marlene G. & Jacobson, Annette L., eds. Clinical Care Plans for Pediatric Nursing. 2nd ed. (McGraw-Hill Clinical Care Plans Ser.). 330p. 1994. text 26.00 (0-07-105462-6) McGraw-Hill HPD.

— Clinical Care Plans for Perinatal-Neonatal Nursing. 2nd ed. (McGraw-Hill Clinical Care Plans Ser.). 298p. 1994. text 26.00 (0-07-105463-4) McGraw-Hill HPD.

Mayers, Marlene G. & Pankratz, Carol, eds. Clinical Care Plans for Medical-Surgical Nursing. 2nd ed. (McGraw-Hill Clinical Care Plans Ser.). 362p. 1994. text 26.00 (0-07-105464-2) McGraw-Hill HPD.

Mayers, Marlene G., jt. auth. see Watson, Annita.

Mayers, Marvin K. A Look at Latin American Lifestyles. 2nd ed. (International Museum of Cultures Ser.: No. 2). 138p. 1982. pap. 12.50 (0-88312-170-0) S I L Intl.

Mayers, Marvin K., ed. Languages of Guatemala. (Janua Linguarum, Ser. Practica: No. 23). (Orig.). 1966. pap. text 67.70 (90-279-0642-4) Mouton.

Mayers, Marvin K. & Rath, Daniel D., eds. Nucleation in Papua New Guinea Cultures. LC 88-81188. (International Museum of Cultures Publications: No. 23). 120p. (Orig.). 1988. pap. 22.00 (0-88312-177-8) S I L Intl.

Mayers, Marvin K., jt. auth. see Grunlan, Stephen A.

Mayers, Marvin K., jt. auth. see Lingenfelter, Sherwood G.

*Mayers, Mary. Faces of Deception. LC 99-91172. 1999. 25.00 (0-7388-0654-4); pap. 18.00 (0-7388-0655-2) Xlibris Corp.

— Silent Insanity. LC 99-91173. 1999. 25.00 (0-7388-0656-0); pap. 18.00 (0-7388-0657-9) Xlibris Corp.

Mayers, Phil D. Give Us This Day Our Daily Bread: Spiritual-Simple-Educational, a Step-by-Step Guide to Baking Bread. (Illus.). 32p. 1993. 14.99 (0-9635606-1-1) P D Mayers.

— Hungry Hog. 1995. 14.99 (0-9635606-2-X) P D Mayers.

Mayers, R. Stewart, jt. auth. see Zepeda, Sally J.

Mayers, Raymond S. Financial Management for Nonprofit Human Service Agencies: Text - Cases - Readings. (Illus.). 358p. 1989. pap. 45.95 (0-398-06273-0) C C Thomas.

— Financial Management for Nonprofit Human Service Agencies: Text - Cases - Readings. (Illus.). 358p. (C). 1989. text 71.95 (0-398-05571-8) C C Thomas.

Mayers, Raymond S., et al, eds. Hispanic Substance Abuse. LC 92-43848. (Illus.). 258p. 1993. pap. 37.95 (0-398-06274-9) C C Thomas.

— Hispanic Substance Abuse. LC 92-43848. (Illus.). 258p. (C). 1993. text 54.95 (0-398-05849-0) C C Thomas.

Mayers, Raymond S., et al. Dilemmas in Human Service Management. LC 93-50540. (Social Work Ser.: Vol. 23). 184p. (C). 1994. text 28.95 (0-8261-7740-9) Springer Pub.

Mayers, Ronald B. Balanced Apologetics: Using Evidences & Presuppositions in Defense of the Faith. 252p. 1996. pap. 13.99 (0-8254-3265-0) Kregel.

— Evangelical Perspectives: Toward a Biblical Balance. LC 86-28966. 204p. (Orig.). 1987. lib. bdg. 44.00 (0-8191-6062-8) U Pr of Amer.

Mayers, Susan, jt. ed. see Berry, Nancy.

Mayers, T. K. Understanding Weapons & Arms Control Vol. I(b) A Guide to the Issues. 4th rev. ed. (Illus.). 157p. 1991. 9.95 (0-08-037438-7, 3827M) Brasseys.

Mayersberg, Paul. The Siege. 1999. pap. write for info. (0-670-81367-2) Viking Penguin.

Mayerson, Arlene B. Americans with Disabilities Act Annotated: Legislative History, Regulations & Commentary. 1994. 350.00 (0-318-72575-4) West Group.

Mayerson, C., et al. And We'll Live Happliy Ever After: Three Generations of Women & Their Lives in Marriage. 320p. 1995. write for info. (0-471-31074-3) Wiley.

Mayerson, Chaim, ed. see Waysman, Dvora.

Mayerson, Evelyn W. The Cat Who Escaped from Steerage. LC 90-32890. 64p. (J). (gr. 4-6). 1990. 15.00 (0-684-19209-8) Scribner.

— Miami: A Saga. large type ed. LC 94-17035. 778p. 1994. lib. bdg. 23.95 (0-7862-0267-X) Thorndike Pr.

— Well & Truly. large type ed. LC 90-22548. 622p. 1991. reprint ed. 19.95 (1-56054-084-2) Thorndike Pr.

Mayes. The Behavioral & Social Contexts of HIV Infection Risk in Lesbians & Other Women Who Have Sex with Women: A Special Issue of "Women's Health", Vol. 2, No. 2, 1996. 1996. pap. 20.00 (0-8058-9885-9) L Erlbaum Assocs.

— Financial Analysis with Lotus Window Disk. (C). 1995. student ed. 40.00 (0-03-018064-3) Harcourt.

— Financial Analysis with Microsoft Excel. (C). 1995. student ed. 40.00 incl. disk (0-03-018083-X) Harcourt.

— Financial Analysis with Microsoft Excel. (C). 1995. pap. text, teacher ed. 209.50 (0-03-016012-X) Harcourt.

— Supervision for Midwives. LC 97-144815. 227p. 1997. pap. text 32.50 (1-898507-14-7) Buttrwrth-Heinemann.

Mayes & Lesser. ACT in Algebra: Applications, Concepts & Technology in Learning Algebra. 2nd ed. 2001. pap. text 33.25 (0-07-232575-5) McGraw.

*Mayes, Linda C., et al. The Yale Child Study Center Guide to Understanding Your Child. LC 00-39116. 704p. 2001. pap. 24.95 (0-316-79432-5) Little.

Mayes, A. D. H. Deuteronomy. (New Century Bible Ser.). 416p. 1991. pap. 28.50 (0-551-00895-4, Pub. by Sheffield Acad) CUP Services.

Mayes, A. D. H., ed. see Society for Old Testament Study.

Mayes, Andrew A., ed. see Lindars, Barnabas.

Mayes, Andrew D. Deuteronomy. (New Century Bible Ser.). 352p. 1979. 15.95 (0-551-00804-0) Attic Pr.

— Judges. (Old Testament Guides Ser.: Vol. 8). 98p. 1986. pap. 12.50 (0-905774-58-2, Pub. by Sheffield Acad) CUP Services.

Mayes, Andrew R. Human Organic Memory Disorders. (Problems in the Behavioral Sciences Ser.: No. 7). (Illus.). 312p. 1988. pap. text 31.95 (0-521-34879-X) Cambridge U Pr.

Mayes, Angie. Great American Stock Car Racing Trivia. LC 97-66713. 1997. pap. 6.95 (1-887654-26-7) Premium Pr TN.

*Mayes, Angie. Stock Car Trivia: Fast Facts for Racing Fans! LC 99-70379. 128p. 1999. pap. 6.95 (1-887654-72-0) Premium Pr TN.

Mayes, Anne C. & Mayes, David G. Introductory Economic Statistics. LC 75-15838. 233p. reprint ed. pap. 72.30 (0-608-17344-4, 202980100065) Bks Demand.

Mayes, Brigett G. Soul of a Woman. LC 98-90539. 1999. pap. 8.95 (0-533-12833-1) Vantage.

Mayes, C., tr. see Schlichting, Hermann T. & Gersten, K.

Mayes, Catherine S., contrib. by. Bill Viola: The City of Man. (Illus.). 10p. 1989. 5.00 (0-934358-24-9) Fuller Mus Art.

Mayes, Dave, jt. auth. see Davis, Kathleen.

Mayes, David, et al. Inefficiency in Industry. 250p. (C). 1995. pap. text 32.00 (0-13-342908-3) P-H.

Mayes, David, jt. auth. see Britton, Andrew.

Mayes, David G., ed. The European Challenge: Industry's Response to the 1992 Programme. 456p. (C). 1992. text 68.50 (0-472-10372-5, 10372) U of Mich Pr.

— The Evolution of the Single European Market. LC 97-14362. 296p. 1997. 90.00 (1-85898-649-4) E Elgar.

— The External Implications of European Integration. 224p. 1993. text 79.50 (0-472-10452-7, 10452) U of Mich Pr.

— Sources of Productivity Growth. (National Institute of Economic & Social Research Occasional Papers: No. 49). (Illus.). 407p. (C). 1996. text 64.95 (0-521-55437-3) Cambridge U Pr.

Mayes, David G. & Hart, Peter. The Single Market Programme As Stimulus to Change: Britain & Germany. (National Institute of Economic & Social Research Occasional Papers: No. 47). (Illus.). 264p. (C). 1994. text 59.95 (0-521-47156-7) Cambridge U Pr.

Mayes, David G., jt. auth. see Mayes, Anne C.

Mayes, Desiree. Opera Unveiled. LC 99-19508. 1999. pap. 12.00 (0-942668-53-7) Katydid Bks.

Mayes, Donald S. Managed Dental Care: A Guide to Dental HMOs. Brennan, Mary, ed. LC 93-78068. 248p. (Orig.). 1993. pap. 40.00 (0-89154-464-X) Intl Found Employ.

Mayes, Doris. Oatmeal Sandwiches: A History of the Will T. Austin Family. limited ed. 160p. 1998. pap. write for info. (1-887303-18-9) Blu Lantern Pub.

Mayes, Doug, et al. Charlotte: Nothing Could Be Finer. LC 96-9574. (Urban Tapestry Ser.). (Illus.). 368p. 1996. 44.95 (1-881096-33-5) Towery Pub.

Mayes, Edward. Lucius Q. C. Lamar: His Life, Times & Speeches, 1825-1893. LC 70-173065. reprint ed. 115.00 (0-404-04613-4) AMS Pr.

Mayes, Edward K. Speed of Life. LC 99-72276. 57p. 1999. pap. 12.95 (0-9669937-0-5, 01, Pub. by Apogee) SPD-Small Pr Dist.

— Works & Days. LC 99-6960. (Pitt Poetry Ser.). 80p. 1999. pap. 12.95 (0-8229-5708-6) U of Pittsburgh Pr.

Mayes, Eric A., Jr. Church-Related Position Descriptions for Presidents, Directors, Chairpersons, Coordinators, Etc. 2nd rev. ed. Woodberry, Reginia, ed. vi, 54p. (Orig.). 1993. pap. write for info. (1-890025-00-3) B E A M Oklhma City.

— Deacon Training in the Black Church: A Two-Part Manual: A Self-Study Plan & a Pastor-Directed Plan. rev. ed. Brown, Robert, ed. viii, 133p. 1991. pap. write for info. (1-890025-04-6) B E A M Oklhma City.

— The Preaching Values of a Church Covenant. Brown, Robert, ed. xii, 188p. (Orig.). 1991. pap. write for info. (1-890025-01-1) B E A M Oklhma City.

— The Seven Greatest Signs Ever Performed: A Contemporary Treatment. Brown, Robert, ed. 84p. (Orig.). 1994. pap. write for info. (1-890025-03-8) B E A M Oklhma City.

— Suit up Your Workers for Christian Service. Brown, Robert, ed. viii, 95p. (Orig.). 1992. pap. write for info. (1-890025-02-X) B E A M Oklhma City.

Mayes, Eric A., Jr., ed. & photos by see Roland, Dewitt.

Mayes, Frances. Bella Tuscany: The Sweet Life in Italy. LC 99-24880. (Illus.). 304p. 1999. 25.00 (0-7679-0283-1) Broadway BDD.

*Mayes, Frances. Bella Tuscany: The Sweet Life in Italy. 1999. mass mkt. 7.99 (0-7679-0480-X) Broadway BDD.

— Bella Tuscany: The Sweet Life in Italy. 288p. 2000. pap. 15.00 (0-7679-0284-X) Broadway BDD.

— Bella Tuscany/Under Tuscan Sky, 2 vols. 2000. pap. 30.00 (0-7679-9905-3) Broadway BDD.

Mayes, Frances. The Book of Summer. (Illus.). 61p. 1995. 295.00 (0-940592-27-4) Heyeck Pr.

— The Discovery of Poetry. 2nd ed. LC 92-75794. 600p. (C). 1994. pap. text 41.50 (0-15-500162-0, Pub. by Harcourt Coll Pubs); pap. text, teacher ed. 5.00 (0-15-500163-9) Harcourt Coll Pubs.

— Ex Voto. (Lost Road Poetry Ser.: No. 42). 64p. (Orig.). 1995. pap. 12.00 (0-918786-47-9) Lost Roads.

— Under the Tuscan Sun: At Home in Italy. 352p. 1998. mass mkt. 7.50 (0-7679-0280-7) Bantam.

— Under the Tuscan Sun: At Home in Italy. 280p. 1996. 22.95 (0-8118-0842-4) Chronicle Bks.

— Under the Tuscan Sun: At Home in Italy. large type ed. (Basic Ser.). 1998. lib. bdg. 26.95 (0-7862-1432-5) Thorndike Pr.

Mayes, Frances. Under the Tuscan Sun: At Home in Italy. LC 97-20218. 288p. 1997. reprint ed. pap. 15.00 (0-7679-0038-3) Broadway BDD.

Mayes, Fred & Joyce, Mary. Alternatives to Traditional Transportation Fuels 1994. (Illus.). 73p. (Orig.). (C). 1997. pap. text 25.00 (0-7881-3761-1) DIANE Pub.

Mayes, Gary, jt. auth. see Spader, Dann.

Mayes, Gary R. Now What! Resting in the Lord When Life Doesn't Make Sense. LC 95-14652. 176p. 1995. pap. 9.99 (0-89107-856-8) Crossway Bks.

Mayes, Herb. Smoke No More: A Journey Through Life's Dangerous Health Hazards from Smoking Cigarettes. 137p. (Orig.). 1997. pap. write for info. (1-57502-553-1, P01612) Morris Pubng.

Mayes, Herbert F. True Confessions of My Life. 208p. 1999. pap. write for info. (0-7392-0050-X, PO2719) Morris Pubng.

Mayes, Herbert R. Alger: A Biography Without a Hero. (Illus.). 247p. 1978. reprint ed. 33.00 (0-686-35758-2) G K Westgard.

Mayes, J. T., jt. ed. see Kibby, Michael R.

Mayes, Janis A., jt. ed. see Adams, Anne V.

Mayes, Janis A., ed. see African Literature Association Staff.

Mayes, Janis A., tr. see Dadie, Bernard B.

Mayes, John A. Quantum Velocity of Light: The Unification of Quantum & Classical Physics. LC 83-61674. (C). 1984. text 35.00 (0-9611548-0-2) Quantum Pubns.

Mayes, John B. & Thurston, Rosemary P. Instructor-Student Workbook & Study Guide: For Anatomy & Physiology Text Book. (Illus.). 118p. 1994. 16.50 (0-916973-06-9) Burnell Co.

Mayes, Joseph R., ed. Virginia Lawyer: A Basic Practice Handbook. 1991. suppl. ed. 50.00 (0-87473-907-1, MICHIE) LEXIS Pub.

Mayes, Joseph R., ed. see Virginia Bar Association, Virginia Lawyer Committe.

Mayes, Julian, jt. auth. see Wheeler, Dennis.

Mayes, Kathleen. Muffin Magic . . . And More: Baking Secrets Your Mother Never Told You. LC 93-25105. (Illus.). 208p. (Orig.). 1993. 12.95 (0-88007-201-6) Woodbridge Pr.

Mayes, Kathleen & Gottfried, Sandra. Boutique Bean Pot: Exciting Bean Varieties in Superb New Recipes! LC 92-7572. (Illus.). 208p. (Orig.). 1992. pap. 12.95 (0-88007-196-6) Woodbridge Pr.

— Roots: A Vegetarian Bounty: Delicious Ways with Root Vegetables. LC 94-48213. (Illus.). 208p. (Orig.). 1995. pap. 14.95 (0-88007-206-7) Woodbridge Pr.

Mayes, M. A. & Barrow, M. G., eds. Aquatic Toxicology & Risk Assessment: Fourteenth Volume. (Special Technical Publication Ser.: No. 1124). (Illus.). 385p. 1992. text 89.00 (0-8031-1425-7, STP1124) ASTM.

Mayes, Maureen D. The Scleroderma Book: A Guide for Patients & Families. LC 98-54669. (Illus.). 192p. 1999. 23.00 (0-19-511507-4) OUP.

Mayes, Paul, jt. auth. see Cooke, Ian.

Mayes, Philip E., jt. ed. see Bentz, Valerie M.

Mayes, Robert L. & Lesser, Lawrence M. ACT in Algebra: Applications, Concepts & Technology in Learning Algebra. LC 97-34698. 704p. (C). 1997. pap. 55.31 (0-07-041093-3) McGraw.

Mayes, Robert L., jt. auth. see Gaudry, Marc J.

Mayes, Scott P. Daydreams. 137p. 1996. mass mkt. 4.99 (1-55197-136-4) Picasso Publ.

*Mayes, Sean. Life on Tour with David Bowie: We Can Be Heros. 2000. pap. text 12.95 (1-897783-17-5) Indep Music Pr.

Mayes, Stephen, ed. The Critical Mirror: A History of Postwar Journalism. LC 95-60603. (Illus.). 240p. (Orig.). 1996. pap. 29.95 (0-500-27848-2, Pub. by Thames Hudson) Norton.

Mayes, Stephen & Stein, Lyndall, eds. Positive Lives - Responses to HIV: A Photodocumentary. LC 93-40472. 1993. 60.00 (0-304-32846-4) Continuum.

Mayes, Susan. Baby Animals. (Young Nature Ser.). (Illus.). 32p. (J). (ps-2). 1995. pap. 6.95 (0-7460-1652-2, Usborne); lib. bdg. 14.95 (0-88110-725-5, Usborne) EDC.

Mayes, Susan. Baby Animals Board Book. (Young Nature Ser.). (Illus.). 12p. (J). (ps up). 1995. bds. 4.95 (0-7460-1976-9, Usborne) EDC.

Mayes, Susan. Dinosaurs. (Young Nature Ser.). (Illus.). 32p. (J). (ps-2). 1993. pap. 6.95 (0-7460-1020-6, Usborne) EDC.

Mayes, Susan. Dinosaurs. (Young Nature Ser.). (Illus.). 32p. (J). (ps-3). 1993. lib. bdg. 14.95 (0-88110-641-0, Usborne) EDC.

Mayes, Susan. Earth & Space. (Starting Point Science Ser.). (Illus.). 144p. (J). (gr. 1 up). 1995. 17.95 (0-7460-1971-8, Usborne) EDC.

Mayes, Susan. How Do Animals Talk? (Starting Point Science Ser.). (Illus.). 24p. (J). (gr. 1-4). 1991. pap. 4.95 (0-7460-0600-4, Usborne) EDC.

An Asterisk (*) at the beginning of an entry indicates that the title is appearing for the first time.

Mayes, Susan. How Do Animals Talk? (Starting Point Science Ser.). (Illus.). 24p. (J). (gr. 1 up). 1991. lib. bdg. 12.95 (0-88110-549-X, Usborne) EDC.
— How Does a Bird Fly? (Starting Point Science Ser.). (Illus.). 24p. (J). (gr. 1 up). 1991. pap. 3.95 (0-7460-0694-2, Usborne); lib. bdg. 12.95 (0-88110-546-5, Usborne) EDC.
— Life on Earth. (Starting Point Science Ser.). (Illus.). 144p. (J). (gr. 1 up). 1995. pap. 17.95 (0-7460-1973-4, Usborne) EDC.
***Mayes, Susan.** School Families: A Peer Mentoring Program for Students Entering Middle School or Junior High School. LC 99-60077. (Illus.). 104p. (YA). (gr. 6-8). 1999. pap. text. write for info. (1-57543-071-1) Mar Co Prods.
Mayes, Susan. Starting Painting. (First Skills Ser.). (Illus.). 32p. (J). (gr. k-3). 1996. pap. 4.95 (0-7460-2375-8, Usborne); lib. bdg. 12.95 (0-88110-847-2, Usborne) EDC.
— The Usborne Book of Dinosaurs. (Usborne Kid Kits Ser.). (Illus.). (J). (ps-2). 1999. 13.95 (0-88110-781-6, Usborne) EDC.
— What Makes a Flower Grow? (Starting Point Science Ser.). (Illus.). 24p. (J). (gr. 1 up). 1989. lib. bdg. 12.95 (0-88110-381-0, Usborne) EDC.
— What Makes a Flower Grow? (Starting Point Science Ser.). (Illus.). 24p. (J). (gr. 1-4). 1989. pap. text 3.95 (0-7460-0275-0, Usborne) EDC.
— What Makes It Rain? (Starting Point Science Ser.). (Illus.). 24p. (J). (gr. 1 up). 1989. lib. bdg. 12.95 (0-88110-379-9, Usborne) EDC.
— What Makes It Rain? (Starting Point Science Ser.). (Illus.). 24p. (J). (gr. 1 up). 1989. pap. 3.95 (0-7460-0274-2, Usborne) EDC.
— What's Inside You? (Starting Point Science Ser.). (Illus.). 24p. (J). (gr. 1-4). 1991. pap. 3.95 (0-7460-0602-0, Usborne) EDC.
— What's Inside You? (Starting Point Science Ser.). (Illus.). 24p. (J). (gr. 1 up). 1991. lib. bdg. 12.95 (0-88110-550-3, Usborne) EDC.
— What's Out in Space? (Starting Point Science Ser.). (Illus.). 24p. (J). (gr. 1-4). 1990. lib. bdg. 12.95 (0-88110-443-4, Usborne) EDC.
— What's Out in Space? (Starting Point Science Ser.). (Illus.). 24p. (J). (gr. 1-4). 1991. pap. 3.95 (0-7460-0430-3, Usborne) EDC.
— What's the Earth Made Of? (Starting Point Science Ser.). (Illus.). 24p. (J). (gr. 1-4). 1995. pap. 4.95 (0-7460-1709-X, Usborne) EDC.
Mayes, Susan. What's the Earth Made Of? (Starting Point Science Ser.). (Illus.). 24p. (J). (gr. 4-7). 1995. lib. bdg. 12.95 (0-88110-752-2, Usborne) EDC.
Mayes, Susan. What's under the Ground? (Starting Point Science Ser.). (Illus.). 24p. (J). (gr. 1-4). 1989. pap. 3.95 (0-7460-0357-9, Usborne) EDC.
— Where Do Babies Come From? (Starting Point Science Ser.). (Illus.). 24p. (J). (gr. 1-4). 1992. pap. 3.95 (0-7460-0690-X, Usborne) EDC.
— Where Do Babies Come From? (Starting Point Science Ser.). (Illus.). 24p. (J). (gr. 1 up). 1992. lib. bdg. 12.95 (0-88110-547-3, Usborne) EDC.
— Where Does Electricity Come From? (Starting Point Science Ser.). (Illus.). 24p. (J). (gr. 1 up). 1989. pap. text 3.95 (0-7460-0358-7, Usborne) EDC.
— Where Does Rubbish Go? (Starting Point Science Ser.). (Illus.). 24p. (J). (gr. 1-4). 1992. pap. 3.95 (0-7460-0627-6, Usborne) EDC.
— Where Does Rubbish Go? (Starting Point Science Ser.). (Illus.). 24p. (J). (gr. 1 up). 1992. lib. bdg. 12.95 (0-88110-551-1, Usborne) EDC.
— Why Is Night Dark? (Starting Point Science Ser.). (Illus.). 24p. (J). (gr. 1-4). 1990. lib. bdg. 12.95 (0-88110-442-6, Usborne) EDC.
— Why Is Night Dark? (Starting Point Science Ser.). (Illus.). 24p. (J). (gr. 1 up). 1990. pap. 3.95 (0-7460-0428-1, Usborne) EDC.
Mayes, Susan, jt. auth. see Khanduri, Kamini.
Mayes, Thorn L. Wireless Communication in the United States: The Early Development of American Radio Operating Companies. Goodnow, Arthur C. et al, eds. (Illus.). 248p. 1989. pap. text 29.95 (0-9625170-0-3) NE Wireless & Steam Mus.
Mayes, Timothy R. Advanced Financial Analysis with Microsoft Excel. 1997. pap. 31.00 (0-03-024112-X, Pub. by Harcourt Coll Pubs) Harcourt.
Mayes, Timothy R. & Shank, Todd M. Financial Analysis with Lotus 1-2-3 for Windows. 318p. (C). 1996. text, student ed. 43.50 (0-03-016014-6) Dryden Pr.
Mayes, Timothy R. & Shark, Todd M. Financial Analysis with Microsoft Excel. LC 96-170563. 312p. (C). 1995. text, student ed. 43.50 (0-03-015502-9) Dryden Pr.
***Mayes, Tony & Mortimore, Sara.** Making the Most of HACCP: Learning from Others' Experience. 320p. 2000. text 108.00 (1-85573-504-0, Pub. by Woodhead Pubng) Am Educ Systs.
***Mayes, Tracy.** Days of June: Recollections of a Country Sheriff. LC 99-94212. 60p. 1999. pap. 8.00 (1-889622-67-2) Leathers Pub.
Mayes, Vernon O. Nanise: A Navajo Herbal. 1990. pap. 27.00 (0-912586-62-1) Dine College Pr.
Mayes, Vernon O. & Rominger, James M. Navajoland Plant Catalog. LC 94-67167. viii, 72p. (Orig.). (C). 1994. pap. 7.00 (0-9628075-5-9) Natl Woodlands Pub.
Mayeski, Marie A. Dhuoda: Ninth Century Mother & Theologian. 1995. pap. 25.00 (0-940866-47-1) U Scranton Pr.
— Dhuoda: Ninth Century Mother & Theologian. iix, 168p. (C). 1995. text 25.00 (0-940866-46-3) U Scranton Pr.
— Women: Models of Liberation. LC 87-62399. 256p. (Orig.). (C). 1989. pap. 12.95 (1-55612-086-9) Sheed & Ward WI.
Mayeski, Marie A., ed. A Rocking-Horse Catholic: A Caryll Houselander Reader. LC 90-62084. 224p. (Orig.). (C). 1991. pap. 12.95 (1-55612-401-5) Sheed & Ward WI.
Mayesky, Mary. Creative Activities. 6th ed. LC 97-12925. 576p. (C). 1997. mass mkt. 63.95 (0-8273-8363-0) Delmar.
Mayesky, Mary E. Creative Activities for Children in the Early Primary Grades. 250p. 1986. pap. 21.50 (0-8273-2573-8) Delmar.
— Creative Activities for Young Children. 5th ed. LC 94-21328. 701p. (C). 1994. mass mkt. 57.95 (0-8273-5886-5) Delmar.
— Creative Activities for Young Children. 5th ed. 1995. teacher ed. 14.00 (0-8273-5887-3) Delmar.
Mayesky, Mary E. & Nueman, Donald. Creative Activities for Young Children. 4th ed. Wlodkowski, Raymond J., ed. LC 94-21328. 560p. 1990. pap., teacher ed. 14.00 (0-8273-3959-3) Delmar.
— Creative Activities for Young Children. 4th ed. Wlodkowski, Raymond J., ed. LC 94-21328. 560p. 1990. pap. 32.00 (0-8273-3958-5) Delmar.
Mayeur, Jean-Marie & Hilaire, Yves-Marie. Dictionnaire du Monde Religieux dans la France Contemporaine Vol. 1: Les Jesuites. Duclos, Paul, ed. (FRE.). 272p. 1985. 135.00 (0-8288-9489-2) Fr & Eur.
— Dictionnaire du Monde Religieux dans la France Contemporaine Vol. 3: La Bretagne. Lagree, Michel, ed. (FRE.). 428p. 1985. pap. 135.00 (0-7859-5243-8) Fr & Eur.
— Dictionnaire du Monde Religieux dans la France Contemporaine Vol. 4: Lille-Flandres. Caudron, Andre, ed. (FRE.). 504p. 1990. 125.00 (0-8288-9492-2) Fr & Eur.
— Dictionnaire du Monde Religieux dans la France Contemporaine, Vol. 2: L'Alsace. Vogler, Bernard, ed. (FRE.). 483p. 1987. 125.00 (0-8288-9490-6) Fr & Eur.
Mayeur, Jean-Marie & Reberioux, Madeleine. The Third Republic from Its Origins to the Great War, 1871-1914. (Cambridge History of Modern France Ser.: No. 4). (Illus.). 314p. 1988. pap. text 19.95 (0-521-35857-4) Cambridge U Pr.
Mayeux. Broadcast News: Writing & Reporting. 2nd ed. 1995. teacher ed. 10.62 (0-697-20152-X, WCB McGr Hill) McGrw-H Hghr Educ.
Mayeux, Peter. Broadcast News: Writing & Reporting. 2nd ed. LC 95-77993. 432p. (C). 1995. text 44.00 (0-697-20151-1) Brown & Benchmark.
— Writing for the Electronic Media. 2nd ed. 464p. (C). 1993. text 46.25 (0-697-14399-6) Brown & Benchmark.
***Mayeux, Peter E.** Broadcast News Writing & Reporting. 2nd ed. 432p. (C). 2000. pap. 37.95 (1-57766-146-X) Waveland Pr.
Mayeux, Richard & Christen, Y., eds. Epidemiology of Alzheimer's Disease: From Gene to Prevention. LC 98-54192. (Research & Perspectives in Alzheimer's Disease Ser.). (Illus.). xi, 136p. 1999. 95.00 (3-540-65413-5) Spr-Verlag.
Mayeux, Richard & Rosen, Wilma G., eds. The Dementias. LC 83-4273. (Advances in Neurology Ser.: No. 38). (Illus.). 286p. 1983. reprint ed. pap. 88.70 (0-608-05774-6, 205973900007) Bks Demand.
Mayeux, Terry. Cosmically Incorrect: Using Astrology to Get What You Want from the People in Your Life. 1999. pap. 10.95 (0-8362-7868-2) Andrews & McMeel.
Mayfair. Empire Builder Game. 1988. 30.00 (0-425-11026-5) Berkley Pub.
Mayfair Games Staff. Angry Wizard Game. 1992. pap. 7.00 (0-912771-21-6) Mayfair Games.
— Apocalypse. 1993. 25.00 (0-923763-97-X) Mayfair Games.
— The Beast Within. 1993. 17.00 (0-923763-59-7) Mayfair Games.
— Beneath 2 Suns Game. 1986. pap. 7.00 (0-912771-74-7) Mayfair Games.
— Blood & Steel. 1994. 25.00 (0-923763-98-8) Mayfair Games.
— Bridgette. 1996. 15.00 (1-56905-075-9) Mayfair Games.
— British Rails. 1994. 25.00 (0-923763-70-8) Mayfair Games.
— Chill. 1994. pap. 20.00 (0-923763-85-6) Mayfair Games.
— Chill Companion. 1994. pap. 12.00 (0-923763-86-4) Mayfair Games.
— Crystal Barrier Game. Date not set. pap. 7.00 (0-912771-67-4) Mayfair Games.
— Dark Folk. 1988. pap. 10.00 (0-912771-06-2) Mayfair Games.
— Demons. 1992. 20.00 (0-923763-61-9) Mayfair Games.
— Denizens of Diannor. 1994. 11.00 (1-56905-007-4) Mayfair Games.
— Denizens of Og. 1993. 11.00 (0-923763-95-3) Mayfair Games.
— Denizens of Vecheron. 1993. 11.00 (0-923763-75-9) Mayfair Games.
— Denizens of Verekna. 1993. 14.00 (0-923763-80-5) Mayfair Games.
— Dragons Game. 1986. pap. 10.00 (0-912771-22-4) Mayfair Games.
— Dwarves. 1986. pap. 10.00 (0-912771-03-8) Mayfair Games.
— Elves. 1988. pap. 10.00 (0-912771-10-0) Mayfair Games.
— Family Business. 1989. pap. 12.50 (0-912771-65-8) Mayfair Games.
— Fantastic Treasures. 1988. pap. 10.00 (0-912771-20-8) Mayfair Games.
— Final Challenge Game. 1988. pap. 7.00 (0-912771-23-2) Mayfair Games.
— Giants Game. 1987. pap. 10.00 (0-912771-80-1) Mayfair Games.
— Hell Bent. 1994. 8.95 (1-56905-063-5) Mayfair Games.
— Iron Dragon. 1995. 30.00 (0-923763-90-2) Mayfair Games.
— Lich Lords Game. 1988. pap. 7.00 (0-912771-33-X) Mayfair Games.
— Lizardmen. 1991. 12.00 (0-923763-26-0) Mayfair Games.
— Lycanthropes. 1991. 12.00 (0-923763-30-9) Mayfair Games.
— Modern Art. 1996. 30.00 (1-56905-088-0) Mayfair Games.
— Monsters Myth & Legend 3. 1992. 10.00 (0-923763-56-2) Mayfair Games.
— Monsters Myth Game. Date not set. pap. 10.00 (0-912771-29-1) Mayfair Games.
— More Cosmic Encounters. 1994. 35.00 (0-923763-58-9) Mayfair Games.
— Nippon Rails. 1992. 25.00 (0-923763-68-6) Mayfair Games.
— North American Rails. Date not set. 25.00 (0-923763-69-4) Mayfair Games.
— Pinnacle Game. 1986. pap. 7.00 (0-912771-41-0) Mayfair Games.
— Power Lunch. Date not set. 15.00 (1-56905-055-4) Mayfair Games.
— Psionics. 1991. 12.00 (0-923763-31-7) Mayfair Games.
— Seed of Darkness. 1994. 4.99 (0-923763-78-3) Mayfair Games.
— Sentinels. Date not set. 25.00 (0-923763-79-1) Mayfair Games.
— Simply Cosmic. 1996. 20.00 (1-56905-072-4) Mayfair Games.
— Steel Deep. 1996. 18.00 (1-56905-015-5) Mayfair Games.
— Streets Tell Stories. 1993. 25.00 (0-923763-89-9) Mayfair Games.
— Things. Date not set. 16.00 (0-923763-84-8) Mayfair Games.
— Throne of Evil Game. Date not set. pap. 7.00 (0-912771-24-0) Mayfair Games.
— To Hell & Back Again. 1993. 20.00 (0-923763-62-7) Mayfair Games.
— Undead: Army of Night. Date not set. 25.00 (0-923763-92-9) Mayfair Games.
— Underground Companion. 1994. 18.00 (1-56905-065-1) Mayfair Games.
— Underground Notebook. 1993. 30.00 (0-923763-91-0) Mayfair Games.
— Voodoo. 1992. 12.00 (0-923763-57-0) Mayfair Games.
— War of Darkness Game. 1986. pap. 7.00 (0-912771-66-6) Mayfair Games.
— Ways & Means. 1996. 25.00 (1-56905-021-X) Mayfair Games.
— Wizards. 1986. pap. 10.00 (0-912771-07-0) Mayfair Games.
— Wizards Betrayal Game. Date not set. pap. 7.00 (0-912771-78-X) Mayfair Games.
— Wizard's Dilemma. 1989. pap. 7.00 (0-912771-85-2) Mayfair Games.
— Wizards Revenge Game. 1989. pap. 7.00 (0-912771-32-1) Mayfair Games.
— Wizards Vale Game. 1987. pap. 7.00 (0-912771-02-X) Mayfair Games.
Mayfiel. America's Kids. 1992. pap. 6.95 (1-55897-267-6) Brentwood Music.
***Mayfield.** Early Childhood Education & Care in Canada: Contexts, Dimensions & Issues. 2001. 87.93 (0-13-080039-2) Prntice Hall Bks.
Mayfield. Solomon's Legacy: History of Ancient Israel. 1992. pap. text. write for info. (0-582-87121-2, Pub. by Addison-Wesley) Longman.
— Theory Essentials. (Music Ser.). 2000. 36.00 (0-534-57231-6) Wadsworth Pub.
— Thinking for Yourself. 2nd ed. (Freshman English/Advanced Writing Ser.). 1990. mass mkt., teacher ed. write for info. (0-534-13813-6) Wadsworth Pub.
***Mayfield.** Thinking for Yourself. 5th ed. (Developmental Study/Stdy Skill). 2000. 36.50 (0-534-51861-3) Wadsworth Pub.
Mayfield, Al A. The Word for Children: An Illustrated Beginner's Bible about Jesus Christ, the Son of God. (Illus.). 16p. (J). (gr. k-3). 1998. pap. 7.00 (0-8059-4390-0) Dorrance.
Mayfield, Barbara J. Kid's Club: Nutrition Learning Activities for Young Children. (Illus.). 605p. 1997. teacher ed., ring bd. 299.95 (1-883983-06-1) Noteworthy Creat.
— The Kid's Club Cubs & the Search for the Treasures of the Pyramid. LC 94-68042. (Illus.). 40p. (Orig.). (J). (ps-2). 1994. pap. 24.95 incl. audio (1-883983-15-0) Noteworthy Creat.
— Nutrition Notes: Musical Nutrition Education to Sing & Color. 3rd rev. ed. (Illus.). 88p. (Orig.). (J). (ps-2). 1997. pap. 17.95 incl. audio (1-883983-04-5) Noteworthy Creat.
— Teaching for a Lifetime: Nutrition Education for Young Children. 70p. 1994. 45.95 incl. VHS (1-883983-25-8) Noteworthy Creat.
Mayfield, Carl. Sandia Mountain Sequence. 20p. 1982. pap. 2.00 (0-913719-57-9, High Coo Pr) Brooks Books.
Mayfield, Chris, ed. Growing up Southern. (Southern Exposure Ser.). (Illus.). 128p. (Orig.). (C). 1980. pap. 4.00 (0-943810-73-6) Inst Southern Studies.
Mayfield, Dianne C., jt. auth. see Maul, Lyle R.
***Mayfield, George.** Gold Harvest. 98p. 2000. pap. 14.99 (0-9530460-0-1, Pub. by Green Magic Prodns) SCB Distributors.
Mayfield-Ingram, Karen, jt. auth. see Thompson, Virginia.
Mayfield, James. Discovering Grace. 1994. 8.95 (0-687-60246-7) Abingdon.
— Discovering Grace in Grief. LC 93-61043. 112p. 1994. pap. 10.00 (0-8358-0696-0) Upper Room Bks.
Mayfield, James, jt. ed. see Nicholas, Charles K.
Mayfield, James B. Go to the People: Releasing the Rural Poor Through the People's School System. LC 85-23714. (Library of Management for Development Ser.). 220p. Date not set. reprint ed. pap. 68.20 (0-608-20740-3, 205449900003) Bks Demand.
— Local Government in Egypt. LC 96-960426. 432p. 1996. 49.00 (977-424-373-0, Pub. by Am Univ Cairo Pr) Col U Pr.
— One Can Make a Difference: The Challenges & Opportunities of Dealing with World Poverty - The Role of Rural Development Facilitators (RDFs) in the Process of Rural Development. LC 97-5519. 514p. 1997. 69.50 (0-7618-0714-4); pap. 46.50 (0-7618-0715-2) U Pr of Amer.
Mayfield, Janis B., ed. see Zuber, William P.
Mayfield, Julian. The Hit & the Long Night. (Northeastern Library of Black Literature). 310p. 1989. reprint ed. pap. text 16.95 (1-55553-065-6) NE U Pr.
***Mayfield, Julie.** The Magical First Day. LC 98-35734. (Illus.). (J). 1998. write for info. (1-56763-336-6); pap. write for info. (1-56763-337-4) Ozark Pub.
Mayfield, Karen, et al, eds. Equals Investigations: Scatter Matters: A Middle-School Mathematics Unit Focusing on Scatterplots, Correlation, & Cause & Effect. Coates, Grace & Franco, Jose, trs. (Equals Ser.). (Illus.). 76p. (J). (gr. 6-9). 1996. pap. 21.95 (0-912511-56-7, EQUALS) Lawrence Science.
Mayfield, Karen & Whitlow, Robert, eds. Equals Investigations: Flea-Sized Surgeons: A Middle-School Mathematics Unit Focusing on Surface Area, Volume & Scale. Coates, Grace & Franco, Jose, trs. (Equals Ser.). (Illus.). 140p. (J). (gr. 6-9). 1996. pap. 21.95 (0-912511-25-7, EQUALS) Lawrence Science.
— Equals Investigations: Growth Patterns: A Middle-School Mathematics Unit Focusing on Linear & Exponential Growth Functions. Coates, Grace & Franco, Jose, trs. (Equals Ser.). (Illus.). 154p. (J). (gr. 6-9). 1996. pap. 21.95 (0-912511-57-5, EQUALS) Lawrence Science.
— Equals Investigations: Remote Rulers: A Middle-School Mathematics Unit Focusing on the Relationship Between Algebraic Graphs & Graphs from Real Data Involving Direct & Inverse Variation. Coates, Grace & Franco, Jose, trs. (Equals Ser.). (Illus.). 134p. (J). (gr. 6-9). 1996. pap. 21.95 (0-912511-58-3, EQUALS) Lawrence Science.
— Equals Investigations: Telling Someone Where to Go: A Middle-School Mathematics Unit Focusing on Measurement of Distance & Angle. Coates, Grace & Franco, Jose, trs. (Equals Ser.). (Illus.). 140p. (J). (gr. 6-9). 1996. pap. 21.95 (0-912511-59-1, EQUALS) Lawrence Science.
Mayfield, Katherine. Acting A to Z: The Young Person's Guide to a Stage or Screen Career. LC 98-50540. (Illus.). 144p. 1998. pap. 16.95 (0-8230-8801-4) Watsn-Guptill.
— Smart Actors, Foolish Choices: A Self-Help Guide to Coping with the Emotional Stresses. 176p. 1996. pap. text 16.95 (0-8230-8424-8) Watsn-Guptill.
Mayfield, Larry, jt. auth. see Hawthorne, Grace.
Mayfield, M. J., jt. ed. see Carpenter, C. P., 2nd.
***Mayfield, Marilyn.** A New Owner's Guide to Old English Sheepdogs. 160p. 2000. 12.95 (0-7938-2795-7) TFH Pubns.
***Mayfield, Mark & Southern Style Editorial Staff.** Southern Style. LC 99-11138. (Illus.). 208p. 1999. 45.00 (0-8212-2611-8, Pub. by Bulfinch Pr) Little.
Mayfield, Mark, jt. auth. see Coad, Pete.
Mayfield, Mark, jt. auth. see Coad, Peter.
Mayfield, Marlys. Thinking for Yourself: Developing Critical Thinking Skills Through Reading & Writing. 3rd ed. LC 93-9950. 440p. 1993. mass mkt. 27.25 (0-534-20334-5) Wadsworth Pub.
— Thinking for Yourself: Developing Critical Thinking Skills Through Reading & Writing. 4th ed. LC 96-8677. (Freshman English/Advanced Writing Ser.). (C). 1996. 32.50 (0-534-51858-3) Wadsworth Pub.
— Thinking for Yourself: Developing Critical Thinking Skills Through Writing. 2nd ed. 424p. (C). 1990. pap. 27.95 (0-534-13812-8) Wadsworth Pub.
Mayfield, Marlys, jt. auth. see Bothwell, Dorr.
Mayfield, Martha. Prayer, a Weekly Outline. 122p. 1997. pap. 16.50 (0-9657149-1-8) Stress Pr TX.
Mayfield, Michael W. & Gallo, Rafael E. The Rivers of Costa Rica: A Canoeing, Kayaking, & Rafting Guide. LC 88-22783. (Illus.). 136p. 1988. pap. 10.95 (0-89732-083-2) Menasha Ridge.
Mayfield Publishing Company Staff, jt. auth. see Kolak, Daniel.
Mayfield, Rich & Mann, Bob. Kinabalu Escape: The Soldier's Story. 224p. 1998. pap. 15.95 (0-09-478070-6, Pub. by Constable & Co) Trafalgar.
***Mayfield, Ruth.** You Can Be Somebody, No. 2. 224p. 2000. pap. 11.95 (0-9701193-0-5) R Mayfield.
Mayfield, Sandra. Purpose & Process. 650p. (C). 1994. text 37.20 (0-536-58629-2) Pearson Custom.
Mayfield, Signe. Christopher Brown: Works on Paper. 1995. pap. text 29.95 (0-9636922-3-2) Palo Alto Art.
***Mayfield, Signe.** The Thought of Things: Jewelry by Kiff Slemmons. Craighead, Linda, ed. (Illus.). 24p. 2000. pap. text. write for info. (0-9636922-5-9) Palo Alto Art.
Mayfield, Signe, et al. Christopher Brown: Works on Paper. 1997. pap. text 25.00 (0-9636922-4-0) Palo Alto Art.
Mayfield, Stacey E., ed. see Mayfield, Terry L.
Mayfield, Terry L. 118 Tips for Creating the Perfect Customer. Mayfield, Stacey E., ed. 16p. 1997. 5.00 (1-890805-15-7) Motivat Discov.
Mayfield, Thomas J. Adopted by Indians: A True Story. Margolin, Malcolm, ed. Orig. Title: Indian Summer. (Illus.). 144p. (J). (gr. 4-6). 1997. pap. 10.95 (0-930588-93-2) Heyday Bks.

M

— Indian Summer: Traditional Life among the Choinumne Indians of California's San Joaquin Valley. (Illus.). 144p. (Orig.). 1993. pap. 16.00 (0-930588-64-9) Heyday Bks.

Mayfield, Vincent. Teach Yourself Activex Controls with Visual C++ in 14 Days. 900p. Date not set. pap. text 39.99 incl. cd-rom (1-57521-294-3) Sams.

Mayfield, William D., jt. ed. see Anthony, W. S.

Mayfield, William P., photos by. William Preston Mayfield Photographer: Six Decades of Imagemaking. LC 97-91281. (Illus.). 128p. 1997. 39.95 (0-9661758-1-6); pap. 27.50 (0-9661758-0-8) Viewpt Pubns.

Mayflower Culinary Editors. Bakery Cooking. LC 98-131553. (The Everyday Chef Ser.). 64p. 1997. pap. text 5.99 (1-58029-018-3, Everywhere) Hambleton-Hill.

— Cooking with Kids. LC 98-134056. (The Everyday Chef Ser.). 64p. 1997. pap. text 5.99 (1-58029-013-2, Everywhere) Hambleton-Hill.

— Desserts. LC 98-131555. (The Everyday Chef Ser.). 64p. 1997. pap. text 5.99 (1-58029-017-5, Everywhere) Hambleton-Hill.

— Fast & Delicious. LC 98-134054. (The Everyday Chef Ser.). 64p. 1997. pap. text 5.99 (1-58029-014-0, Everywhere) Hambleton-Hill.

— Holiday Favorites. LC 98-131553. (The Everyday Chef Ser.). 64p. 1997. pap. text 5.99 (1-58029-016-7, Everywhere) Hambleton Hill.

— Light & Easy. LC 98-134045. (The Everyday Chef Ser.). 64p. 1997. pap. text 5.99 (1-58029-010-8, Everywhere) Hambleton-Hill.

— Pasta Favorites. LC 98-134039. (The Everyday Chef Ser.). 64p. 1997. pap. text 5.99 (1-58029-015-9, Everywhere) Hambleton-Hill.

— Taste of the Sea. LC 98-134062. (The Everyday Chef Ser.). 64p. 1997. pap. text 5.99 (1-58029-011-6, Everywhere) Hambleton-Hill.

Maygay, Tomas. Hungarian-English Standard Dictionary. 650p. 1995. pap. 40.00 (0-7818-0390-X) Hippocrene Bks.

Mayglothing, Rosie. Rowing. (Skills of the Game Ser.). (Illus.). 144p. pap. text 19.95 (1-85223-753-8, Pub. by Crolwood) Trafalgar.

Mayhall, C. Glen. Hospital Epidemiology & Infection Control. 2nd ed. LC 99-19467. 1565p. 1999. text 169.00 (0-683-30608-1) Lppncott W & W.

***Mayhall, Carole.** Come Walk with Me: A Practical Guide to Knowing Christ Intimately & Passing It On. LC 97-42277. 224p. 1998. pap. 11.95 (1-57856-005-5) Waterbrook Pr.

Mayhall, Carole. Help Lord, I'm Sinking: Lessons from My Rocking Boat. LC 97-31605. 1998. write for info. (1-57683-075-6) NavPress.

***Mayhall, Carole.** Here I Am Again, Lord: Confessions of a Slow Learner. LC 99-33835. 192p. 2000. pap. 9.95 (1-57856-263-5) Waterbrook Pr.

Mayhall, Carole. Para Que Valga la Pena Escuchard (Your Words Can Make a Difference) (Serie Realidades - Realities Ser.). (SPA.). 75p. 1994. write for info. (1-56063-281-X) Editorial Unilit.

— When God Whispers. 1997. pap. text 8.00 (0-89109-948-4) NavPress.

— Words That Hurt, Words That Heal. LC 86-61136. 108p. 1986. pap. 8.00 (0-89109-179-3) NavPress.

Mayhall, Carole, jt. auth. see Mayhall, Jack.

Mayhall, Jack. Cuando No Estamos de Acuerdo - When You Disagree. (SPA.). 90p. 1995. write for info. (0-7899-0006-8) Editorial Unilit.

Mayhall, Jack & Mayhall, Carole. Marriage Takes More Than Love. (NavClassics Ser.). 1996. pap. 12.00 (0-89109-946-8) NavPress.

Mayhall, Jane. Givers & Takers. 1968. pap. 7.50 (0-87130-013-3) Eakins.

— Givers & Takers 2. LC 68-55445. 78p. 1973. 10.00 (0-87130-032-X); pap. 7.50 (0-87130-033-8) Eakins.

— Ready for the Ha Ha. LC 66-23198. 102p. 1966. 30.00 (0-87130-014-1) Eakins.

Mayhall, Mildred P. The Kiowas. LC 62-16477. (Civilization of the American Indian Ser.: Vol. 63). (Illus.). 384p. 1984. pap. 18.95 (0-8061-0987-4) U of Okla Pr.

***Mayhall, Pamela D.** Police Community Relations & the Administration of Justice. 5th ed. LC 99-36908. (Illus.). 402p. 1999. 78.67 (0-13-020997-X) P-H.

Mayhall, Robin M., intro. Cranking up a Fine War: A Louisiana Soldier from Boot Camp to General's Aide. LC 98-89821. (Illus.). 256p. 1999. 24.95 (1-892958-01-5) ByrenLee Pr.

Mayhall, Yolanda. The Sumi-E Book. (Illus.). 128p. 1989. pap. 16.95 (0-8230-5022-X) Watsn-Guptill.

Mayhan, Benton. Peter & His Friend Jesus. 1999. pap. text 3.95 (0-687-05338-2) Abingdon.

Mayhan, Robert J. Discrete Time & Continuous Time Linear Systems. LC 83-5999. (Electrical Engineering Ser.). (Illus.). 640p. 1984. pap. text, teacher ed. 34.25 (0-201-05597-X) Addison-Wesley.

— Discrete Time & Continuous Time Linear Systems. 2nd ed. (C). 1998. text. write for info. (0-201-50807-9) Addison-Wesley.

Mayhar, Ardath. A Road of Stars: Stories. LC 98-85956. 325p. 1998. 25.00 (0-7388-0001-5); pap. 15.00 (0-7388-0042-2) Xlibris Corp.

— Slewfoot Sally & the Flying Mule: And Other Tales from Cotton County. Richards, J., ed. LC 95-76456. (Illus.). 226p. (Orig.). (YA). (gr. 7-12). 1995. pap. 12.00 (1-887303-00-6) Blu Lantern Pub.

— Through a Stone Wall: A Writer's Handbook & Literary Autobiography. Richards, J., ed. LC 95-76457. 200p. (Orig.). 1995. pap. 9.98 (1-887303-07-3) Blu Lantern Pub.

— The Wall. LC 86-31453. (Illus.). 136p. (Orig.). 1987. pap. 6.95 (0-917053-06-0) Space And.

— The World Ends in Hickory Hollow. 190p. 1998. pap. 12.95 (1-892884-03-8, B1009) Cascade Mntn Pubg.

Mayhar, Ardath & Dunn, Marylois. Timber Pirates. limited ed. Richards, Jerri S., ed. LC 98-225932. (YA). (gr. 6-12). 1998. pap. write for info. (1-887303-19-7) Blu Lantern Pub.

Mayhawk, Robert. Mayhawk's Law. (Illus.). 128p. 1986. write for info. (0-940959-00-3) Murre Co.

Mayhead, Molly A., jt. ed. see Marshall, Brenda DeVore.

Mayhead, Robin. Walter Scott. LC 72-88622. (British Authors-Introductory Critical Studies). 142p. reprint ed. pap. 40.50 (0-608-16460-7, 2026348) Bks Demand.

Mayher, Bill. The College Admissions Mystique. LC 97-14576. 256p. 1998. pap. 13.00 (0-374-52513-7) FS&G.

Mayher, John S. Uncommon Sense: Theoretical Practice in Language Education. LC 89-31482. 302p. (Orig.). (C). 1989. pap. text 25.00 (0-86709-247-5, 0247, Pub. by Boynton Cook Pubs) Heinemann.

Mayher, John S., et al. Learning to Write/Learning to Learn. LC 83-15154. 152p. (Orig.). (C). 1983. pap. text 20.00 (0-86709-073-1, 0073, Pub. by Boynton Cook Pubs) Heinemann.

Mayher, John S., jt. ed. see Brause, Rita S.

***Mayhew.** Crew. 2000. 27.95 (0-385-40937-0, Pub. by Transworld Publishers Ltd); pap. 10.95 (0-552-14492-4, Pub. by Transworld Publishers Ltd) Trafalgar.

Mayhew. A Father's Book of Prayers. 1996. 5.95 (0-88271-495-3) Regina Pr.

— Friendship. 1996. 5.95 (0-88271-499-6) Regina Pr.

— Love & Marriage. 1996. 5.95 (0-88271-498-8) Regina Pr.

— A Mother's Book of Prayers. 1996. 5.95 (0-88271-494-5) Regina Pr.

— Prayers in Time of Sorrow. 1996. 5.95 (0-88271-497-X) Regina Pr.

— Strength for Tomorrow. 1996. 5.95 (0-88271-496-1) Regina Pr.

— A War of Words. 1998. text 35.00 (1-86064-267-5) I B T.

***Mayhew, A.** Education of India: A Study of British Educational Policy in India. 1999. 35.00 (81-7020-708-8, Pub. by Cosmo Pubn) S Asia.

***Mayhew, A. J.** Sensational South Carolina. LC 98-66161. 128p. 1999. pap. 6.95 (1-887654-40-2) Premium Pr TN.

Mayhew, A. L., ed. Promptorium Parvulorum: The First English-Latin Dictionary. (EETS. ES Ser.: No. 102). 1974. reprint ed. 75.00 (0-527-00306-9) Periodicals Srv.

Mayhew, A. L., ed. see Skeat, Walter W.

Mayhew, Alan. Recreating Europe: The European Union's Policy Towards Central & Eastern Europe. LC 97-38835. 432p. (C). 1998. text 59.95 (0-521-63086-X); pap. text 22.95 (0-521-63897-6) Cambridge U Pr.

Mayhew, Anthony L., ed. see Skeat, Walter W.

Mayhew, Arthur B. Christianity in India. (C). 1988. 32.50 (81-212-0143-8, Pub. by Gian Publng Hse) S Asia.

Mayhew, Augustus. Paved with Gold: The Romance & Reality of the London Street. 2nd ed. (Illus.). 408p. 1971. reprint ed. 25.00 (0-7146-1412-2, BHA-01412, Pub. by F Cass Pubs) Intl Spec Bk.

Mayhew, Bob & Birdsall, John. The Art of Western Riding. (Illus.). 160p. 1996. 35.00 (1-85223-181-5, Pub. by Crolwood) Trafalgar.

— The Art of Western Riding. (Illus.). 160p. 1990. 24.00 (0-87605-886-1) Howell Bks.

Mayhew, Bradley. Lonely Planet Tibet. 4th ed. 320p. 1999. pap. 17.95 (0-86442-637-2) Lonely Planet.

***Mayhew, Bradley.** Shanghai. 2001. pap. 15.99 (0-86442-507-4) Lonely Planet.

Mayhew, Bradley & Huhti, Thomas. Lonely Planet South-West China. (Illus.). 600p. 1998. pap. 19.95 (0-86442-596-1) Lonely Planet.

Mayhew, Bradley, jt. auth. see Greenway, Paul.

Mayhew, Bradley, jt. auth. see MacLeod, Calum.

***Mayhew, David R.** America's Congress: Actions in the Public Sphere, James Madison Through Newt Gingrich. LC 99-86055. (Illus.). 288p. 2000. 30.00 (0-300-08049-2) Yale U Pr.

Mayhew, David R. Congress: The Electoral Connection. LC 74-78471. (Studies in Political Science: No. 26). (Illus.). 192p. 1975. pap. 14.00 (0-300-01809-6) Yale U Pr.

— Divided We Govern: Party Control, Lawmaking & Investigations, 1946-1990. LC 91-13216. 192p. (Orig.). 1991. 32.50 (0-300-04835-1) Yale U Pr.

— Divided We Govern: Party Control, Lawmaking & Investigations, 1946-1990. 192p. (Orig.). 1993. pap. 17.00 (0-300-04837-8) Yale U Pr.

— Placing Parties in American Politics: Organization, Electoral Settings, & Government Activity in the Twentieth Century. LC 85-43298. 412p. 1986. reprint ed. pap. 127.80 (0-608-06485-8, 206678200009) Bks Demand.

Mayhew, Deborah J. Principles & Guidelines in Software User Interface Design. 544p. (C). 1991. text 60.80 (0-13-721929-6) P-H.

— The Usability Engineering Lifecycle: A Practitioner's Handbook for User Interface Design. Neilsen, Jakob et al, eds. LC 99-19111. (Interactive Technologies Ser.). 550p. 1999. pap. text 49.95 (1-55860-561-4, Pub. by Morgan Kaufmann) Harcourt.

Mayhew, Deborah J., jt. ed. see Bias, Randolph G.

Mayhew, Diane. Dark Interlude. write for info. (0-7860-0569-6) Kensgtn Pub Corp.

Mayhew, Dianne. Impetuous. 1999. mass mkt. 4.99 (1-58314-043-3) BET Bks.

***Mayhew, Dianne.** Playing with Fire. (Arabesque Ser.). 2000. mass mkt. 5.99 (1-58314-161-8) BET Bks.

Mayhew, Dianne. Playing with Fire. 304p. 1997. mass mkt. 4.99 (0-7860-0457-6, Pinncle Kensgtn) Kensgtn Pub Corp.

***Mayhew, Dianne.** Stolen Moments. 2000. mass mkt. 5.99 (1-58314-119-7) BET Bks.

Mayhew, Dianne V. Dark Interlude. (Arabesque Ser.). 288p. 1998. mass mkt. 4.99 (0-7860-0594-7, Pinncle Kensgtn) Kensgtn Pub Corp.

— Secret Passions. 150p. 1993. mass mkt. 3.79 (0-9634431-0-0) C Y Pub Grp.

Mayhew, Ed & Mayhew, Mary. Educating Your Star Child. Charles, Rodney & Pasco, Elizabeth, eds. LC 96-69528. 250p. (Orig.). 1997. pap. text 16.95 (1-887472-17-7) Sunstar Pubng.

Mayhew, Edgar D. & Colahan. Equine Medicine & Surgery. 5th ed. LC 98-24941. (Illus.). 2076p. (gr. 13). 1998. text 239.00 (0-8151-1743-4, 28580) Mosby Inc.

Mayhew, Elisabeth. The Dark Mountain. large type ed. 352p. 1985. 27.99 (0-7089-1285-0) Ulverscroft.

Mayhew, Eugene J., ed. Shalom: Essays in Honor of Dr. Charles H. Shaw. 231p. 1983. pap. 11.95 (0-912407-01-8) William Tyndale Col Pr.

Mayhew, Henry. London Labour & the London Poor, 4 vols., 2. (Illus.). 1982. pap. 9.95 (0-486-21935-6) Dover.

— London Labour & the London Poor, 4 vols., 3. (Illus.). 1982. pap. 9.95 (0-486-21936-4) Dover.

— Mormons: or Latter Day Saints. LC 71-134398. reprint ed. 45.00 (0-404-08440-0) AMS Pr.

— Voices of the Poor: Selections from the "Morning Chronicle" & "Labour & the Poor", 1849-1950. Humphreys, Anne, ed. (Illus.). 280p. 1971. 37.50 (0-7146-2929-4, Pub. by F Cass Pubs) Intl Spec Bk.

Mayhew, Henry, jt. auth. see Thomas, Donald S.

Mayhew, Ian G. Large Animal Neurology: A Handbook for Veterinary Clinicians. LC 88-34037. (Illus.). 380p. 1989. pap. text 58.00 (0-8121-1183-4) Lppncott W & W.

Mayhew, Isabel, ed. see Smith, Charles W.

Mayhew, J. E. & Newton, Adrian C. The Silviculture of Mahogany: Swietenia Macrophylla. LC 98-34213. 240p. 1998. 45.00 (0-85199-307-9) OUP.

Mayhew, James. Katie & the Mona Lisa. LC 98-41162. (Illus.). 32p. (J). (ps-2). 1999. 15.95 (0-531-30177-X) Orchard Bks Watts.

— Katie Meets the Impressionists. LC 98-34693. (Illus.). 32p. (J). (ps-2). 1999. 15.95 (0-531-30151-6) Orchard Bks Watts.

***Mayhew, James.** The Kingfisher Book of Tales From Russia. (Illus.). 80p. (YA). 2000. pap. 12.95 (0-7534-5293-6, Kingfisher) LKC.

Mayhew, Jayne N. Four Seasons in Cross Stitch. LC 97-191499. (Illus.). 128p. 1997. 24.95 (0-7153-0486-0) Sterling.

Mayhew, Jayne N. & Wheeler, Nicki. Animals in Cross Stitch. (Illus.). 128p. 1995. 24.95 (0-7153-0199-3, Pub. by D & C Pub) Sterling.

Mayhew, Jayne Netley & Wheeler, Nicki. The Water's Edge in Cross Stitch. (Illus.). 128p. 1999. 24.95 (0-7153-0703-7, Pub. by D & C Pub) Sterling.

Mayhew, John, jt. auth. see Ince, William.

Mayhew, Jonathan. Claudio Rodriguez & the Language of Poetic Vision. LC 89-42931. 160p. 1990. 32.50 (0-8387-5174-1) Bucknell U Pr.

— Observations on the Charter & Conduct of the Society for the Propagation of the Gospel in Foreign Parts, Designed to Show Their Non-Conformity to Each Other. LC 72-38456. (Religion in America, Series 2). 180p. 1972. reprint ed. 18.95 (0-405-04077-6) Ayer.

— The Poetics of Self-Consciousness: Twentieth-Century Spanish Poetry. LC 92-56608. 1994. 29.50 (0-8387-5256-X) Bucknell U Pr.

— Sermons. LC 76-83429. (Religion in America, Ser. 1). 1975. reprint ed. 21.95 (0-405-00254-8) Ayer.

Mayhew, Lenore, tr. see Akhmatova, Anna Andreevena.

Mayhew, Lenore, tr. see Basho, Matsu, et al.

Mayhew, Leon H. The New Public: Professional Communication & the Means of Social Influence. LC 96-49355. (Cultural Social Studies). 344p. (C). 1997. text 59.95 (0-521-48146-5) Cambridge U Pr.

— The New Public: Professional Communication & the Means of Social Influence. LC 96-49355. (Cultural Social Studies). 332p. (C). 1997. pap. 22.95 (0-521-48493-6) Cambridge U Pr.

Mayhew, Leon H., ed. see Parsons, Talcott.

Mayhew, Leonard, tr. see Truffaut, Francois.

Mayhew, Leslie. Urban Hospital Location. LC 85-15820. (London Research Series in Geography: No. 4). (Illus.). 176p. 1985. text 60.00 (0-04-362054-X) Routledge.

Mayhew, Lewis B. Colleges Today & Tomorrow. LC 74-75939. (Jossey-Bass Higher Education Ser.). 272p. reprint ed. 84.40 (0-8357-9308-7, 201395200092) Bks Demand.

— The Literature of Higher Education, 1971. LC 74-155167. (Higher Education Ser.). 176p. reprint ed. 54.60 (0-8357-9332-X, 201381800087) Bks Demand.

— The Literature of Higher Education, 1972. LC 74-155167. (Jossey-Bass Higher Education Ser.). 198p. reprint ed. 61.40 (0-8357-9333-8, 201385900088) Bks Demand.

— Surviving the '80s. LC 79-88773. (Jossey-Bass Series in Higher Education). 366p. reprint ed. pap. 113.50 (0-7837-0183-7, 204047900017) Bks Demand.

Mayhew, Lewis B. & Ford, Patrick J. Changing the Curriculum. LC 79-159265. (Jossey-Bass Higher Education Ser.). 206p. reprint ed. pap. 63.90 (0-8357-9302-8, 201723700006) Bks Demand.

— Reform in Graduate & Professional Education. LC 73-20968. (Jossey-Bass Higher Education Ser.). 270p. reprint ed. pap. 83.70 (0-608-16951-X, 202776200056) Bks Demand.

Mayhew, Lewis B., et al. The Quest for Quality: The Challenge for Undergraduate Education in the 1990s. LC 90-34307. (Higher & Adult Education Ser.). 320p. 1990. text 38.45 (1-55542-254-3) Jossey-Bass.

Mayhew, Lewis B., jt. auth. see Dressel, Paul L.

Mayhew, Maren S., jt. ed. see Edmunds, Marilyn W.

***Mayhew, Margaret.** Bluebirds. 2000. pap. 10.95 (0-552-13910-6, Pub. by Transworld Publishers Ltd) Trafalgar.

Mayhew, Margaret. The Flame & the Furnace. large type ed. 432p. 1982. 27.99 (0-7089-0888-8) Ulverscroft.

— The Master of Aysgarth. large type ed. 368p. 1983. 27.99 (0-7089-1058-0) Ulverscroft.

***Mayhew, Margaret.** Old Soldiers Never Die. 224p. 2000. 25.00 (0-7278-5441-0, Pub. by Severn Hse) Chivers N Amer.

— Regency Charade. LC 86-9110. 192p. 1986. 15.95 (0-8027-0912-5) Walker & Co.

Mayhew, Mary. Your Star Child: Birthing an Evolved Soul. Charles, Rodney, ed. LC 95-68465. (Illus.). 400p. (Orig.). 1995. pap. 16.95 (0-9638502-2-9) Sunstar Pubng.

Mayhew, Mary, jt. auth. see Mayhew, Ed.

Mayhew, Michael, ed. Harvest Tales & Midnight Revels: Stories for the Waning of the Year. LC 98-96146. (Illus.). 240p. 1998. 23.95 (0-9661664-2-6); pap. 14.95 (0-9661664-3-4) Bald Mtn Bks.

Mayhew, Miriam, jt. auth. see Carver, John.

***Mayhew, Nicholas.** Sterling: The History of a Currency. LC 99-59989. (Illus.). 304p. 2000. 27.95 (0-471-38535-2) Wiley.

Mayhew, Nicholas, jt. auth. see Gemmill, Elizabeth.

Mayhew, Patrick, ed. One Family's War: Wartime Letters from Many Fronts 1939-1945. (Illus.). 264p. (Orig.). 1997. pap. 15.95 (1-873376-47-2, Pub. by Spellmnt Pubs) St Mut.

Mayhew, Richard L. Divine Healing Today. 1983. pap. 8.99 (0-88469-154-3) BMH Bks.

Mayhew, Robert. Aristotle's Criticism of Plato's "Republic" LC 97-20980. 176p. 1997. 56.00 (0-8476-8654-X); pap. 23.95 (0-8476-8655-8) Rowman.

***Mayhew, Robert, ed.** The Art of Nonfiction: A Guide for Writers & Readers. 2001. pap. 13.00 (0-452-28231-4, Plume) Dutton Plume.

Mayhew, Robert, ed. & intro. see Rand, Ayn.

Mayhew, Robert, tr. & intro. see Aristophanes.

***Mayhew, Robert J.** Enlightenment Geography: The Political Languages of British Geography, 1650-1850. LC 00-27247. (Illus.). 2000. write for info. (0-312-23475-9) St Martin.

***Mayhew-Smith, Peter.** Guardian Career Guide. 2000. pap. 19.95 (1-85702-545-8, Pub. by Fourth Estate) Trafalgar.

Mayhew, Stephen. The Pool Cue Book. Rocha, Tina, ed. LC 97-74026. (Illus.). 100p. 1998. 15.95 (0-9660794-0-X) Merrimack Pub.

Mayhew, Susan. A Dictionary of Geography. 2nd ed. LC 96-52361. (Oxford Paperback Reference Ser.). (Illus.). 466p. 1997. pap. 12.95 (0-19-280034-5) OUP.

— Minidictionary of Geography. LC 93-46664. (Oxford Minireference Ser.). (Illus.). 320p. 1994. pap. write for info. (0-19-211692-4) OUP.

Mayhew, Terry M., jt. ed. see Reith, Albrecht.

Mayhew, Wilbur W. Pictorial History of the 7th Bombardment Group/Wing 1918-1995, Vol. 1. LC 97-61932. (Illus.). 328p. 1998. 50.00 (0-9660462-0-X) Seventh Bomb Gp.

Mayhew, Y. R., jt. auth. see Rogers, G. F.

Mayhill, R. Thomas. Lancaster County, Pa. Deed Abstracts 1729 to 1770 & Oaths of Allegiance. enl. rev. ed. 277p. 1979. 24.00 (0-686-27817-8) Bookmark.

Mayho, Paul. Positive Careers: The Rights & Responsibilities of HIV Positive Health Care Workers. 160p. 1997. pap. 27.50 (0-304-33277-1); text 79.50 (0-304-33275-5) Continuum.

Mayhofer, C. M., jt. auth. see Abdularahameana.

Mayhoff, jt. ed. see Jan.

Mayhue. Healing Promise. 1997. pap. 15.99 (1-85792-302-2) Spring Arbor Dist.

— How to Interpret the Bible. 1997. pap. 10.99 (1-85792-254-9, Pub. by Christian Focus) Spring Arbor Dist.

Mayhue, Richard. The Biblical Pattern for Divine Healing. 1979. pap. 1.50 (0-88469-108-X) BMH Bks.

— Fight the Good Fight: Learning from Winners & Losers in the Bible. 1999. pap. text 10.99 (1-85792-470-3) Christian Focus.

— 1st & 2nd Thessalonians. 1999. pap. text 12.99 (1-85792-452-5) Christian Focus.

— Que Diria Jesus de Tu Iglesia? 128p. 1997. pap. 7.99 (0-8254-1473-3, Edit Portavoz) Kregel.

Mayhue, Richard L. Como Interpretar la Biblia Uno Mismo. Orig. Title: How to Interpret the Bible for Yourself. (SPA.). 152p. 1994. pap. 6.99 (0-8254-1471-7, Edit Portavoz) Kregel.

— How to Interpret the Bible for Yourself. (Orig.). 1986. pap. 5.99 (0-88469-178-0) BMH Bks.

— La Promesa de Sanidad. (SPA.). 256p. 1995. pap. 8.99 (0-8254-1472-5, Edit Portavoz) Kregel.

— Snatched Before the Storm! 1980. pap. 1.50 (0-88469-124-1) BMH Bks.

— What Would Jesus Say about Your Church? 10.99 (1-85792-150-X, Pub. by Christian Focus) Spring Arbor Dist.

Mayhue, Richard L., ed. see Master's Seminary Faculty Staff & MacArthur, John F., Jr.

Mayinger, F., et al. Convective Flow & Pool Boiling: Proceedings of the International Engineering Foundation 3rd Conference Held at Isree, Germany, May 18th-23rd. LC 99-12276. 1999. 155.00 (1-56032-826-6) Taylor & Francis.

Mayinger, Franz, ed. Optical Measurements: Techniques & Applications. LC 94-20066. 1994. 131.95 (0-387-56765-8) Spr-Verlag.

Maykovich, Minako, jt. auth. see Lee, Ivy.

Maykovich, Minako K., jt. auth. see Lee, Ivy.

An Asterisk (*) at the beginning of an entry indicates that the title is appearing for the first time.

Maykrantz, Scott Paul. GURPS Creatures of the Night: Sixty-Seven Original Horrors to Haunt Your Dreams. Pinsonneault, Susan, ed. (GURPS Ser.). (Illus.). 128p. 1993. pap. 19.95 (*1-55634-273-X*, Pub. by S Jackson Games) BookWorld.

Maykut, Pamela & Morehouse, Richard. Beginning Qualitative Research: A Philosophic & Practical Guide. LC 94-26385. (Teachers' Library). 194p. 1994. pap. 27.95 (*0-7507-0273-7*, Falmer Pr) Taylor & Francis.

Maylam, Paul. Rhodes, the Tswana, & the British: Colonialism, Collaboration, & Conflict in the Bechuanaland Protectorate, 1885-1899, 4. LC 79-8582. (Contributions in Comparative Colonial Studies: No. 4). (Illus.). 245p. 1980. 79.50 (*0-313-20885-9*, MTB/) Greenwood.

Maylam, Paul & Edwards, Iain. The People's City: African Life in Twentieth-Century Durban. LC 96-50944. 1997. 60.00 (*0-435-07402-4*); pap. 22.95 (*0-435-07401-6*) Heinemann.

Maylam, Paul & Edwards, Iaina, eds. A People's City: African Life in Twentieth-Century Durban. (Illus.). 320p. 1996. pap. write for info. (*0-86980-916-4*, Pub. by Univ Natal Pr) Intl Spec Bk.

Mayland, Daniel. Red Wine. LC 97-65386. 163p. (Orig.). 1997. pap. 11.95 (*0-9656585-9-7*) New American.

Mayland, H. Adventures with Discus. (Illus.). 256p. 1994. 35.95 (*0-7938-0081-1*, TS218) TFH Pubns.

Mayland, Hans J. & Bork, Dieter. South American Dwarf Cichlids. (Aqualog Bks.: Vol. 1). (Illus.). 190p. 1997. 59.10 (*3-931702-29-4*, Pub. by Verlag ACS) Hollywood.

***Mayland, Hans J. & Goebel, Manfred.** South American Cichlids, No. 4. (Aqualog Reference Bks.: Vol. 10). (Illus.). 240p. 1998. 79.10 (*3-931702-75-8*, Pub. by Verlag ACS) Hollywood.

Mayland, Paul F. Bank Operating Credit Risk: Assessing & Controlling Credit Risk in Bank Operating. 1993. text 62.50 (*1-55738-346-4*, Irwn Prfssnl) McGraw-Hill Prof.

Mayle, Jan. Standard Securities Calculation Methods: Fixed Income Securities Formulas for Analytic Measures, Vol. 2. 1994. write for info. (*0-318-72505-3*) Securities Industry.

Mayle, Paul D. Eureka Summit: Agreement in Principle & the Big Three at Tehran, 1943. LC 85-40879. (Illus.). 216p. 1987. 38.50 (*0-87413-295-9*) U Delaware Pr.

Mayle, Peter. Acquired Tastes. 256p. 1993. pap. 13.95 (*0-553-37183-5*) Bantam.
— Anything Considered. LC 96-5761. 352p. 1996. 23.00 (*0-679-44123-9*) Random.
— Anything Considered. 1997. pap. 12.00 (*0-679-76268-X*) Vin Bks.
— Chasing Cezanne. LC 97-71925. 295p. 1997. 23.00 (*0-679-45511-6*) Knopf.
— Chasing Cezanne. LC 98-11055. 304p. 1998. reprint ed. pap. 12.00 (*0-679-78120-X*) Vin Bks.
— Congratulations, You're Not Pregnant. 1981. 10.95 (*0-02-582540-2*) Macmillan.
— Divorce Can Happen to the Nicest People. 1980. 9.95 (*0-02-582500-3*) Macmillan.
— A Dog's Life. 1995. 20.00 (*0-679-44122-0*) Knopf.
— A Dog's Life. (Illus.). 1996. pap. 12.00 (*0-679-76267-1*) Random Hse Value.
— A Dog's Life. 1996. pap. 11.00 (*0-614-97643-X*) Vin Bks.
— A Dog's Life. large type ed. LC 95-8911. (Illus.). 205p. 1995. 23.95 (*0-7862-0485-0*) Thorndike Pr.
— Encore Provence: New Adventures in the South of France. LC 99-62335. (Illus.). 256p. 1999. 23.00 (*0-679-44124-7*) Knopf.

***Mayle, Peter.** Encore Provence: New Adventures in the South of France. (Departures Ser.). 240p. 2000. pap. 12.00 (*0-679-76269-8*) Vin Bks.
— Encore Provence: New Adventures in the South of France. large type ed. LC 98-32362. 256p. 1999. pap. 23.00 (*0-375-70683-6*) Knopf.

Mayle, Peter. Grown-Ups & Other Problems. 1983. 12.95 (*0 02 582550-X*) Macmillan.
— Hotel Pastis. 400p. 1994. pap. 13.00 (*0-679-75111-4*) Vin Bks.
— Hotel Pastis: A Novel of Provence. LC 93-14641. 1993. 23.00 (*0-679-40229-2*) Knopf.
— How to Be a Pregnant Father. (Illus.). 56p. 1986. pap. 12.00 (*0-8184-0399-3*) Carol Pub Group.
— Toujours Provence. 1992. pap. 12.00 (*0-679-73604-2*) Vin Bks.
— Toujours Provence. abr. ed. 1991. pap. write for info. incl. audio (*1-55927-183-3*, Pub. by Audio Renaissance) Lndmrk Audiobks.
— Toujours Provence. large type ed. 336p. 1991. reprint ed. lib. bdg. 22.95 (*1-56054-262-4*) Thorndike Pr.
— Up the Agency: The Funny Business of Advertising. 3rd ed. 1994. pap. 9.95 (*0-312-11911-9*) St Martin.
— What's Happening to Me? The Answers to Some of the World's Most Embarrassing Questions. LC 75-14410. (Illus.). 56p. (J). (gr. 3 up). 1975. 12.00 (*0-8184-0221-0*) Carol Pub Group.
— What's Happening to Me? The Answers to Some of the World's Most Embarrassing Questions. LC 75-14410. (Illus.). 188p. (J). (gr. 4-7). 1981. pap. 6.95 (*0-8184-0312-8*, L Stuart) Carol Pub Group.
— Where Did I Come From. (Illus.). 48p. (J). (gr. 3 up). 1973. 12.00 (*0-8184-0161-3*) Carol Pub Group.
— Where Did I Come From? (Illus.). 43p. (J). (gr. 1-4). 1986. pap. 9.95 (*0-8184-0253-9*) Carol Pub Group.

***Mayle, Peter.** Where Did I Come From? A Guide for Children & Parents, African-American Edition. LC 99-39697. (J). 1999. write for info. (*0-8184-0608-9*, L Stuart) Carol Pub Group.

Mayle, Peter. Where Did I Come From? Special 20th Anniversary Gift Edition. anniversary ed. (Illus.). 48p. (J). (ps-3). 1996. 13.95 (*0-8184-0581-3*, L Stuart) Carol Pub Group.
— A Year in Provence. 1990. 26.00 (*0-394-57230-0*) Knopf.
— A Year in Provence. LC 90-50623. (Illus.). 207p. 1991. pap. 11.00 (*0-679-73114-8*) Vin Bks.
— A Year in Provence & Toujours Provence, 2 vols., Set. 1993. pap., boxed set 23.00 (*0-679-74943-8*) Knopf.

Mayleas, Davidyne S. By Appointment Only. 448p. 1989. mass mkt. 4.50 (*0-380-75362-6*, Avon Bks) Morrow Avon.
— The Gardiner Women. 480p. (Orig.). 1993. mass mkt. 5.99 (*0-380-75690-0*, Avon Bks) Morrow Avon.
— Naked Call. 672p. (Orig.). 1991. mass mkt. 5.50 (*0-380-75688-9*, Avon Bks) Morrow Avon.
— The Woman Who Had Everything. 1987. mass mkt. 4.50 (*0-380-75327-8*, Avon Bks) Morrow Avon.

Maylin, George A., jt. auth. see Krook, Lennart.

***Maylone, Brandon.** Today's Witch. (Illus.). 100p. 2000. pap. 10.95 (*1-893774-05-8*, Allisone Pr) Star Rising.

Maylone, Nelson J. That Can't Be Right! Using Counterintuitive Math Problems. LC 98-86275. 144p. 1998. pap. text 34.95 (*1-56676-676-1*) Scarecrow.

Maylor, Elizabeth A., jt. ed. see Perfect, Timothy J.

***Maylor, Harvey.** Project Management. 2nd ed. (Illus.). 302p. 1999. pap. 57.50 (*0-273-63829-7*, Pub. by F T P-H) Trans-Atl Phila.

Maylunas, Andrei & Mironenko, Sergei. A Lifelong Passion: Nicholas & Alexandra: Their Own Story. Galy, Darya, tr. from RUS. (Illus.). 667p. 1999. text 35.00 (*0-7881-6079-6*) DIANE Pub.

Mayman. Infant Research: The Dawn of Awareness. (Psychoanalytic Inquiry Book Ser.: Vol. 1, No. 4). 1994. 20.00 (*0-88163-988-5*) Analytic Pr.

Mayman, Martin & Schlesinger, Herbert J., eds. Psychoanalytic Research: Three Approaches to the Experimental Study of Subliminal Processes. LC 73-2848. (Psychological Issues Monographs: 30, Vol. 8, No. 2). 116p. (C). 1975. 27.50 (*0-8236-4490-1*) Intl Univs Pr.

Maymon, Gilbert W., jt. auth. see Cave, William C.

Maymon, Giora. Some Engineering Applications in Random Vibrations & Random Structures. (Progress in Astronautics & Aeronautics Ser.: Vol. 178). 257p. 1998. 84.95 (*1-56347-258-9*, TA355) AIAA.

Maynadier, G. H. Wife of Bath's Tale: Its Sources & Analogues. 1972. 200.00 (*0-8490-1299-6*) Gordon Pr.

Maynadier, Gustavus H. The First American Novelist. LC 79-175703. (Select Bibliographies Reprint Ser.). 1977. reprint ed. 17.95 (*0-8369-6618-X*) Ayer.
— Wife of Bath's Tale: Its Sources & Analogues. LC 71-144526. (Grimm Library: No. 13). reprint ed. 27.50 (*0-404-53556-9*) AMS Pr.

Maynadier, Howard. The Arthur of the English Poets. 454p. (C). 1966. lib. bdg. 75.00 (*0-8383-0670-5*) M S G Haskell Hse.

Maynar-Moliner, Manuel, et al, eds. Percutaneous Revascularization Techniques. LC 92-49670. 1993. 149.00 (*0-86577-441-2*) Thieme Med Pubs.

Maynard. Stars & Planets. (Young Scientist Ser.). (Illus.). 32p. (J). (gr. 4-8). 1976. lib. bdg. 14.95 (*0-88110-313-6*) EDC.

Maynard. Survey Interview. text. write for info. (*0-471-35829-0*) Wiley.

Maynard, ed. see Arden.

Maynard, Alan & Tether, Philip, eds. Preventing Alcohol & Tobacco Problems: The Addiction Market: Consumption, Production & Policy Development, Vol. 1. (Illus.). 270p. 1990. text 77.95 (*0-566-05701-8*, Pub. by Avebry) Ashgate Pub Co.

Maynard, Alan, jt. ed. see Culyer, A. J.

Maynard, Amy C. Health Protection & Promotion Against Sickness & Disease: Index of New Information with Authors, Subjects & References. 150p. 1997. 47.50 (*0-7883-1376-2*); pap. 44.50 (*0-7883-1377-0*) ABBE Pubs Assn.

Maynard, Ann Marie Grizzaf, jt. auth. see John, Lizy Kurian.

Maynard, Arthur H. Understanding the Gospel of John. LC 91-37589. 100p. 1991. lib. bdg. 59.95 (*0-7734-9640-8*) E Mellen.

Maynard, Beth. Meditations for Lay Eucharistic Ministers. LC 98-55966. (Faithful Servants Ser.). 96p. 1999. pap. 6.95 (*0-8192-1770-0*) Morehouse Pub.

Maynard, Beth, jt. auth. see Episcopal Church Women Staff.

Maynard, Bill. Heart Soul & Spirit: Bold Strategies for Transforming Your Organization. 64p. (Orig.). 1996. pap. 9.99 (*0-9656552-0-2*) Effect Inst.
— Incredible Ned. LC 95-53753. (Illus.). 40p. (J). (ps-3). 1997. 15.95 (*0-399-23023-8*, G P Putnam) Peng Put Young Read.
— Incredible Ned, If You Could See What He Said, Vol. 1. 32p. 1999. pap. 5.99 (*0-698-11813-8*, PuffinBks) Peng Put Young Read.

***Maynard, Bill.** Pondfire. LC 99-20082. 96p. (J). (gr. 4-8). 2000. 14.99 (*0-399-23439-X*, G P Putnam) Peng Put Young Read.

Maynard, Bill. Quiet, Wyatt! LC 97-28183. (Illus.). 32p. (J). (ps-3). 1999. 15.95 (*0-399-23217-6*) Putnam Pub Group.
— Rock River. LC 97-42156. 104p. (J). (gr. 4-6). 1998. 15.99 (*0-399-23224-9*) Putnam Pub Group.
— Santa's Time Off. LC 97-2081. (Illus.). 32p. (J). (gr. k-12). 1997. 15.95 (*0-399-23138-2*, G P Putnam) Peng Put Young Read.
— Time Out for the Family, 1989. 1989. pap. 6.95 (*0-89137-119-2*) Quality Pubns.

Maynard, Caitlin & Maynard, Thane. Rain Forests & Reefs: A Kid's-Eye View of the Tropics. (Cincinnati Zoo Bks.). 64p. (J). 1997. pap. 9.95 (*0-531-15806-3*) Watts.

Maynard, Caitlin, et al. Rain Forests & Reefs: A Kid's-Eye View of the Tropics. LC 96-33974. (Cincinnati Zoo Bks.). (Illus.). 64p. (J). (gr. 3-8). 1996. lib. bdg. 24.00 (*0-531-11281-0*) Watts.

Maynard, Charles. Murmansk Venture. LC 79-115564. (Russia Observed Ser.). (Illus.). 1971. reprint ed. 23.95 (*0-405-03085-1*) Ayer.
— Waterfalls of Grand Teton National Park: A National Park Waterfall Guide. (Illus.). 70p. (Orig.). 1996. pap. text 5.95 (*1-887205-07-1*) Panther TN.
— Waterfalls of Yellowstone National Park: A National Park Waterfall Guide. 120p. 1996. pap. text 11.95 (*1-887205-06-3*) Panther TN.

Maynard, Charles, ed. see Beeson, D. R.

Maynard, Charles W. Where the Rhododendrons Grow: A History of Camping & Leisure Ministries in the Holston Conference. (Illus.). 130p. 1988. 14.95 (*0-932807-31-3*); pap. 9.95 (*0-932807-32-1*) Overmountain Pr.

Maynard, Charles W., ed. see Beeson, D. R.

Maynard, Charles W., ed. see Mathes, C. Hodge.

Maynard, Christopher. Aircraft. LC 98-49158. (Need for Speed Ser.). 32p. (YA). (gr. 5-8). 1999. 17.95 (*0-8225-2485-6*, Lerner Publctns) Lerner Pub.
— Aircraft. (Need for Speed Ser.). 32p. (YA). (gr. 5-10). 1999. pap. 7.95 (*0-8225-9855-8*, LernerSports) Lerner Pub.

***Maynard, Christopher.** Aircraft. (Illus.). (J). 1999. 13.30 (*0-606-18812-6*) Turtleback.

Maynard, Christopher. Amazing Animal Babies. LC 92-23736. (Eyewitness Juniors Ser.: No. 25). 32p. (J). (ps-3). 1993. pap. 9.99 (*0-679-83924-0*, Pub. by Knopf Bks Yng Read) Random.
— Amazing Animal Babies. (Eyewitness Juniors Ser.: No. 25). (J). (ps-3). 1993. 15.19 (*0-606-05272-0*, Pub. by Turtleback) Demco.
— The Best Book of Dinosaurs. LC 97-42426. 32p. (J). (ps-4). 1998. 12.95 (*0-7534-5116-6*) LKC.
— Cutaway Boats. (Cutaway Ser.). (Illus.). 32p. (J). (gr. 5 up). 1997. pap. 6.95 (*0-7460-2400-2*, Usborne) EDC.
— Cutaway Boats. (Cutaway Ser.). (Illus.). 32p. (J). (gr. 5 up). 1999. 14.95 (*0-88110-888-X*, Usborne) EDC.
— Cutaways. (Cutaway Ser.). (Illus.). 96p. (J). (gr. 5 up). 1997. 17.95 (*0-7460-2403-7*, Usborne) EDC.
— Days of the Knights: A Tale of Castles & Battles. LC 97-29396. (Eyewitness Readers). (Illus.). 32p. (J). (gr. 2-4). 1998. pap. 3.95 (*0-7894-2963-2*) DK Pub Inc.

***Maynard, Christopher.** Days of the Knights: A Tale of Castles & Battles. (Eyewitness Readers). 0048p. (J). (ps-4). 1999. 12.95 (*0-7894-4253-1*) DK Pub Inc.
— Extreme Machines. LC 99-43606. (Eyewitness Readers). (Illus.). 48p. (J). (gr. 2-4). 2000. 12.95 (*0-7894-5418-1*, D K Ink); pap. 3.95 (*0-7894-5417-3*, D K Ink) DK Pub Inc.
— Extreme Machines. (Illus.). (J). 2000. 9.40 (*0-606-18117-2*) Turtleback.
— Ghosts. (Informania Ser.). (Illus.). 92p. (J). (gr. 4-8). 2000. pap. 6.99 (*0-7636-1114-X*, Pub. by Candlewick Pr) Penguin Putnam.
— History News: Revolution. LC 99-28787. (Illus.). 32p. (J). (gr. 4-8). 1999. 16.99 (*0-7636-0491-7*) Candlewick Pr.

Maynard, Christopher. I Wonder Why Planes Have Wings & Other Questions about Transport. LC 92-42373. (Illus.). 32p. (J). (gr. 4-8). 1993. 11.95 (*1-85697-877-X*, Kingfisher) LKC.
— I Wonder Why Stars Twinkle & Other Questions about Space: And Other Questions about Space. LC 92-44259. (I Wonder Why Ser.). (Illus.). 32p. (J). (ps-3). 1993. 11.95 (*1-85697-881-8*, Kingfisher) LKC.
— Incredible Clothes. (Incredible Words & Pictures Ser.). (Illus.). 32p. (J). (ps-3). 1995. pap. 4.95 (*1-56458-958-7*) DK Pub Inc.

***Maynard, Christopher.** Informania: Ghosts. LC 99-11358. (Illus.). 92p. (J). (gr. 4-8). 1999. 16.00 (*0-7636-0758-4*) Candlewick Pr.
— Informania: Sharks. LC 97-16537. (Informania Ser.). (Illus.). 92p. (J). (gr. 3-7). 2000. pap. 7.99 (*0-7636-1043-7*) Candlewick Pr.

Maynard, Christopher. Jobs People Do. LC 96-44202. (Illus.). 32p. (J). 1997. 12.95 (*0-7894-1492-9*) DK Pub Inc.

***Maynard, Christopher.** Micromonsters: Life under the Microscope. LC 99-20401. (Eyewitness Readers). 48p. (J). (gr. 2-4). 1999. 3.95 (*0-7894-4756-8*); 12.95 (*0-7894-4757-6*, D K Ink) DK Pub Inc.

Maynard, Christopher. Pirates: Raiders of the High Seas. LC 98-20850. (Eyewitness Readers). 48p. (J). (gr. 2-4). Date not set. 3.95 (*0-7894-3443-1*) DK Pub Inc.
— Pirates: Raiders of the High Seas. LC 98-20850. (Eyewitness Readers). 48p. (J). (gr. 2-4). 1998. 12.95 (*0-7894-3768-6*) DK Pub Inc.

Maynard, Christopher. Questions & Answers about Explorers. LC 94-31067. (Questions & Answers about Ser.). (Illus.). 40p. (J). (gr. 4-7). 1995. pap. 8.95 (*1-85697-555-X*, Kingfisher) LKC.

Maynard, Christopher. Sharks. LC 97-16537. (Informania Ser.). (Illus.). 80p. (J). (gr. 4-8). 1997. 14.99 (*0-7636-0328-7*) Candlewick Pr.
— Stars & Planets. LC 78-17545. (Young Scientist Ser.). (Illus.). 32p. (J). (gr. 4-8). 1977. pap. 6.95 (*0-86020-094-9*) EDC.
— Why Did Grandpa Die? Questions Children Ask about Families. LC 97-14463. (Why Bks.). (J). 1997. write for info. (*0-7894-2055-4*) DK Pub Inc.
— Why Do Sunflowers Face the Sun? Questions Children Ask about Nature. (Why Bks.). (Illus.). 24p. (J). 10.99 (*0-590-24954-1*) Scholastic Inc.

Maynard, Christopher & Martin, Terry. Why Do We Laugh? Questions Children Ask about the Human Body. (Why Bks.). (Illus.). 24p. (J). 10.99 (*0-590-24955-X*) Scholastic Inc.
— Why Does Lightning Strike? Questions Children Ask about Weather. (Why Bks.). (Illus.). 24p. (J). 10.99 (*0-590-24945-2*) Scholastic Inc.

Maynard, Christopher & White, Terry. Why Are Zebras Black & White? Questions Children Ask about Colour. (Why Bks.). (Illus.). 24p. (J). 10.99 (*0-590-24946-0*) Scholastic Inc.

Maynard, Cooper, & Gale Staff, et al. Alabama Environmental Law Handbook. 3rd ed. 166p. 1995. pap. text 79.00 (*0-86587-453-0*) Gov Insts.

Maynard, D. W. Inside Plea Bargaining: The Language of Negotiation. LC 84-9809. (Illus.). 270p. (C). 1984. 54.50 (*0-306-41577-1*, Plenum Trade) Perseus Pubng.

Maynard, Dennis R. Forgiven, Healed, & Restored. LC 94-92276. 80p. 1994. pap. 8.00 (*1-885985-01-0*) Dionysus Pubns.
— The Money Book: A Christian Perspective. LC 94-92275. 64p. (Orig.). 1994. pap. 8.00 (*1-885985-00-2*) Dionysus Pubns.
— Those Episkopols. rev. ed. LC 94-92277. Orig. Title: Episcopalians: Following in the Way of Jesus. 70p. (Orig.). 1994. pap. 8.00 (*1-885985-02-9*) Dionysus Pubns.

Maynard, Donald & Baird, B. Joyce. A Handbook of SOPs for Good Clinical Practice. 271p. 1996. ring bd. 229.00 (*1-57491-009-4*) Interpharm.

Maynard, Donald & De Woskin, Robert. The GCP Harmonization Handbook. 476p. 1996. ring bd. 197.00 (*1-57491-013-2*) Interpharm.

Maynard, Donald N. & Hochmuth, George J. Knott's Handbook for Vegetable Growers. 4th ed. LC 96-33492. 600p. 1997. pap. 90.00 (*0-471-13151-2*) Wiley.

M

Maynard, Douglas G. Sulfur in the Environment. LC 97-52812. (Books in Soils, Plants, & the Environment). (Illus.). 384p. 1998. text 165.00 (*0-8247-8992-X*) Dekker.

Maynard, Edwin H. Keeping up with a Revolution: The Story of United Methodist Communications, Purdue, Joretta, ed. 216p. 1990. write for info. (*1-878946-01-3*) United Meth Comm.

Maynard, Frankie. A Tree! for Me! (Illus.). 60p. 1986. 15.00 (*0-912783-02-8*) Upton & Sons.
— A Tree! for Me! LC 86-51132. (Illus.). 68p. (J). 1986. 15.00 (*0-912783-07-9*) Upton & Sons.

Maynard, G. Letters from Turkey, 1939-1946. LC 94-69122. (Illus.). viii, 298p. 1994. pap. text 20.00 (*0-918986-96-6*) Orient Inst.

***Maynard, Gary.** Correction Officer. 13th ed. (Illus.). 368p. 2000. pap. text 12.95 (*0-02-863736-4*, Arco) Macmillan Gen Ref.

Maynard, Geoffrey. Economic Development & the Price Level. LC 72-85018. (Reprints of Economic Classics Ser.). (Illus.). viii, 295p. 1972. reprint ed. lib. bdg. 39.50 (*0-678-07016-4*) Kelley.

Maynard, Harold B. Methods-Time Measurement. LC 48-7173. (McGraw-Hill Industrial Organization & Management Ser.). (Illus.). 302p. reprint ed. pap. 93.70 (*0-608-11457-X*, 205540500019) Bks Demand.

Maynard, Herman B., Jr. & Mehrtens, Susan. The Fourth Wave: Business in the 21st Century. LC 93-2705. (Illus.). 236p. 1996. reprint ed. pap. 18.95 (*1-57675-002-7*) Berrett-Koehler.

Maynard, Isabelle. China Dreams: Growing up Jewish in Tientsin. LC 96-24321. (Singular Lives Ser.). (Illus.). 186p. 1996. 24.95 (*0-87745-562-7*); pap. 13.95 (*0-87745-571-6*) U of Iowa Pr.

Maynard, J. Barry. Geochemistry of Sedimentary Ore Deposits. (Illus.). 305p. 1983. 105.00 (*0-387-90783-1*) Spr-Verlag.

Maynard, Jacqui. I Know Where My Food Goes. LC 98-19629. (Illus.). 32p. (J). (gr. k-2). 1999. 9.99 (*0-7636-0505-0*) Candlewick Pr.

Maynard, James. Some Microeconomics of Higher Education: Economics of Scale. LC 76-139371. (Illus.). 202p. reprint ed. pap. 62.70 (*0-8357-3806-X*, 203653400003) Bks Demand.

Maynard, Janice. Tent for Two. 1997. mass mkt. 1.78 (*0-8217-5774-1*) Kensgtn Pub Corp.

Maynard, Jeff. Computer Programming Made Simple. LC 73-157667. xix, 300p. 1972. write for info. (*0-491-00882-1*) Virgin Bks.

Maynard, Jeff. Modular Programming Languages: Joint Modular Languages Conference, JML '97, Linz, Austria, March 19-21, 1997: Proceedings. LC 72-180278. 100 p. 1972. write for info. (*0-408-70287-7*) Buttrwrth-Heinemann.
— Niagara's Gold. LC 96-150087. 1996. pap. text 16.95 (*0-86417-766-6*, Pub. by Kangaroo Pr) Seven Hills Bk.

Maynard, Jim. Jim Maynard's Celestial Guide 2000: An Astrological Week-at-a-Glance Engagement Calendar: Pacific & Eastern Time. (Illus.). 176p. Date not set. spiral bd. 9.95 (*0-930356-39-X*) Quicksilver Prod.

***Maynard, Jim.** Jim Maynard's Celestial Guide 2001: An Astrological Week-at-a-Glance Engagement Calendar: Pacific & Eastern. (Illus.). 176p. 2001. spiral bd. 9.95 (*0-930356-44-6*) Quicksilver Prod.

Maynard, Jim. Jim Maynard's Celestial Influences 2000: An Almanac & Textbook of Astrology, Ephemeris & Calendar: Pacific Time. (Illus.). 40p. Date not set. pap. 9.95 (*0-930356-35-7*) Quicksilver Prod.
— Jim Maynard's Celestial Influences 2000: An Almanac & Textbook of Astrology, Ephemeris & Calendar: Eastern Time. (Illus.). 40p. Date not set. pap. 9.95 (*0-930356-34-9*) Quicksilver Prod.

***Maynard, Jim.** Jim Maynard's Celestial Influences 2001: An Almanac & Textbook of Astrology, Ephemeris & Calendar: Eastern Time. (Illus.). 40p. 2001. pap. 9.95 (*0-930356-40-3*) Quicksilver Prod.
— Jim Maynard's Celestial Influences 2001: An Almanac & Textbook of Astrology, Ephemeris & Calendar: Pacific Time. (Illus.). 40p. 2001. pap. 9.95 (*0-930356-41-1*) Quicksilver Prod.

Maynard, Jim. Jim Maynard's Pocket Astrologer, 2000: Eastern Time. (Illus.). 64p. 1999. pap. 4.95 (*0-930356-36-5*) Quicksilver Prod.

— Jim Maynard's Pocket Astrologer, 2000: Pacific Time. (Illus.). 64p. 1999. pap. 4.95 (*0-930356-37-3*) Quicksilver Prod.

***Maynard, Jim.** Jim Maynard's Pocket Astrologer 2001: Eastern Time. (Illus.). 64p. 2001. pap. 4.95 (*0-930356-42-X*) Quicksilver Prod.

— Jim Maynard's Pocket Astrologer 2001: Pacific Time. (Illus.). 64p. 2001. 4.95 (*0-930356-43-8*) Quicksilver Prod.

Maynard, Joan. Mud Pies. 8p. (J). (gr. 1). 1988. pap. text 2.50 (*1-882225-09-0*) Tott Pubns.

— Mud Puddles. 7p. (J). (gr. 1). 1989. pap. text 2.50 (*1-882225-06-6*) Tott Pubns.

Maynard, Joe. Granpa Odis. (Chapbook Ser.: Vol. 4). (Illus.). 6p. 1996. pap. 10.00 (*0-9652505-3-9*) Synaesthesia.

Maynard, John. Bennett & the Pathfinders. (Illus.). 256p. 1996. 24.95 (*1-85409-258-8*, Pub. by Arms & Armour) Sterling.

— Browning Re-Viewed: Review Essays, 1980-1995. LC 97-27271. (American University Studies IV: Vol. 186). XIV, 247p. (C). 1998. text 44.95 (*0-8204-3337-3*) P Lang Pubng.

— Russia in Flux. Guest, S. Haden, ed. LC 83-45812. reprint ed. 48.50 (*0-404-20173-3*) AMS Pr.

Maynard, John & Auslander Munich, Adrienne, eds. Victorian Literature & Culture, 1992-1993, Vol. 20. rev. ed. (Illus.). 1993. 57.50 (*0-404-64220-9*) AMS Pr.

— Victorian Literature & Culture, 1992-1993, Vol. 21. rev. ed. (Illus.). 1993. 52.25 (*0-404-64221-7*) AMS Pr.

Maynard, John & Munich, Adrienne A., eds. An Annual of Victorian Literature & Cultural History, Vol. 19: Victorian Literature & Culture, Vol. 19. (Browning Institute Studies Ser.). 1991. 57.50 (*0-404-64219-5*) AMS Pr.

— Victorian Literature & Culture, 1992-1993, Set. rev. ed. (Illus.). 1992. write for info. (*0-404-64200-4*) AMS Pr.

Maynard, John, ed. see Ritchie, Anne Thackeray.

Maynard, John A. Bakersfield: A Centennial Portrait. (Illus.). 134p. 1997. 34.95 (*1-882933-20-6*) Cherbo Pub Grp.

— Venice West: The Beat Generation in Southern California. LC 90-45114. 264p. (C). 1991. 22.95 (*0-8135-1653-6*) Rutgers U Pr.

— Venice West: The Beat Generation in Southern California. LC 90-45114. 264p. 1993. pap. 15.95 (*0-8135-1965-9*) Rutgers U Pr.

Maynard, John R. Browning's Youth. (Illus.). 512p. 1977. 42.50 (*0-674-08441-1*) HUP.

Maynard, John T. & Peters, Howard M. Understanding Chemical Patents: A Guide for the Inventor. 2nd ed. LC 91-24124. 183p. 1991. text 44.00 (*0-8412-1997-4*, Pub. by Am Chemical); pap. text 34.00 (*0-8412-1998-2*, Pub. by Am Chemical) OUP.

Maynard, Joseph E. Healing Hands: The Story of the Palmer Family - Discoverers & Developers of Chiropractic. 4th ed. LC 59-14319. 432p. 1992. 34.95 (*0-9630413-0-4*) Jonorm Pubns.

Maynard, Joyce. At Home in the World: A Memoir. LC 98-28066. (Illus.). 347p. 1998. text 25.00 (*0-312-19556-7*, Picador USA) St Martin.

***Maynard, Joyce.** At Home in the World: A Memoir. 384p. 1999. pap. 14.00 (*0-312-20229-6*, Picador USA) St Martin.

Maynard, Joyce. Camp-Out. LC 85-5504. (Illus.). 32p. (J). (ps-3). 1985. 12.95 (*0-15-214077-8*, Harcourt Child Bks) Harcourt.

— The New House. (Illus.). 32p. (J). (gr. k-3). 1987. 12.95 (*0-15-257042-X*) Harcourt.

— Where Love Goes. 1995. 23.00 (*0-614-15472-3*, Crown) Crown Pub Group.

Maynard, Joyce. Where Love Goes. 352p. 1993. pap. 13.00 (*0-679-77102-6*) Random.

Maynard, Joyce. Where Love Goes. large type ed. LC 95-50400. (Large Print Ser.). 432p. 1995. lib. bdg. 22.95 (*1-57490-031-5*, Beeler LP Bks) T T Beeler.

Maynard, Katherine K. Thomas Hardy's Tragic Poetry: The Lyrics & "The Dynasts" LC 91-15975. 247p. 1991. text 32.95 (*0-87745-344-6*) U of Iowa Pr.

Maynard, Kenneth. Lamb in Command. LC 86-198652. 199p. 1986. write for info. (*0-297-78790-X*, Pub. by Weidenfeld & Nicolson) Trafalgar.

Maynard, Kenneth. Lieutenant Lamb. 176p. 1984. 10.95 (*0-312-48371-6*) St Martin.

Maynard, Kimberly A. Healing Communities in Conflict: International Assistance in Complex Emergencies. LC 98-46125. 1999. 29.50 (*0-231-11278-5*) Col U Pr.

— Healing Communities in Conflict: International Assistance in Complex Emergencies. LC 98-46125. 1999. pap. write for info. (*0-231-11279-3*) Col U Pr.

Maynard, Kitty & Maynard, Lucian. The American Country Inn & Bed & Breakfast Cookbook, Vol. I. LC 87-10105. (Illus.). 528p. 1987. 24.95 (*0-934395-50-0*) Rutledge Hill Pr.

— The American Country Inn & Bed & Breakfast Cookbook, Vol. I. 2nd ed. Pitkin, Julie M., ed. LC 87-10105. (Illus.). 511p. 1990. reprint ed. pap. 17.95 (*1-55853-064-9*) Rutledge Hill Pr.

— The American Country Inn & Bed & Breakfast Cookbook, Vol. II. LC 87-10105. (Illus.). 628p. 1990. 24.95 (*1-55853-059-2*) Rutledge Hill Pr.

— The American Country Inn & Bed & Breakfast Cookbook, Vol. II. LC 87-10105. (Illus.). 640p. 1993. pap. 19.95 (*1-55853-218-8*) Rutledge Hill Pr.

Maynard, Kitty, et al. The All-New Diabetic Cookbook: A Complete Guide to Easy Meal Preparation & Enjoyable Eating for Healthy Living. LC 98-37923. (Illus.). 304p. 1998. pap. 19.95 (*1-55853-675-2*) Rutledge Hill Pr.

Maynard, Leonard A., et al. Animal Nutrition. 7th ed. (Illus.). (C). 1979. text 100.75 (*0-07-041049-6*) McGraw.

Maynard, Lucian, jt. auth. see Maynard, Kitty.

Maynard, Mack. Instructor's Manual. pap. 7.50 (*0-393-96192-3*) Norton.

Maynard, Margaret. Fashioned from Penury: Dress As Cultural Practice in Colonial Australia. LC 93-37953. (Studies in Australian History). (Illus.). 200p. (C). 1994. pap. write for info. (*0-521-45925-7*) Cambridge U Pr.

— Fashioned from Penury: Dress As Cultural Practice in Colonial Australia. LC 93-37953. (Studies in Australian History). (Illus.). 247p. (C). 1994. text 59.95 (*0-521-45310-0*) Cambridge U Pr.

Maynard, Mary. Houses with Stories: From Cottages to Castles, Landmarks to Literary Sites, 50 Tours of New England's Most Fascinating Homes. LC 93-24180. (Travel Guide Ser.). (Illus.). 1994. pap. 12.95 (*0-89909-370-1*) Yankee Bks.

— SIF Sociological Theory. 1989. pap. text. write for info. (*0-582-00427-6*) Addison-Wesley.

Maynard, Mary, ed. Science & the Construction of Women. LC 98-103996. 192p. 1997. 72.00 (*1-85728-786-X*, Pub. by UCL Pr Ltd); pap. 23.95 (*1-85728-787-8*, Pub. by UCL Pr Ltd) Taylor & Francis.

Maynard, Mary & Purvis, June, eds. (Hetero)sexual Politics. LC 95-14661. 1995. pap. 24.95 (*0-7484-0296-9*, Pub. by Tay Francis Ltd) Taylor & Francis.

— (Hetero) Sexual Politics. LC 95-14661. 1995. 75.00 (*0-7484-0295-0*, Pub. by Tay Francis Ltd) Taylor & Francis.

— New Frontiers in Women's Studies: Knowledge, Identity, & Nationalism. LC 96-10665. 1996. 79.95 (*0-7484-0287-X*); pap. 27.95 (*0-7484-0288-8*) Taylor & Francis.

— Researching Women's Lives from a Feminist Perspective. LC 93-38801. 1994. write for info. (*0-7484-0152-0*, Pub. by Tay Francis Ltd); pap. write for info. (*0-7484-0153-9*, Pub. by Tay Francis Ltd) Taylor & Francis.

Maynard, Mary, jt. ed. see Afshar, Haleh.

Maynard, Mary, jt. ed. see Hanmer, Jalna.

Maynard, Meredy. Dreamcatcher. 144p. (J). (gr. 5-7). 1995. pap. 7.50 (*1-896095-01-1*) Polstar Bk.

— True Blue Dream of Sky. LC 97-65827. 144p. (Orig.). (J). 1997. pap. 7.95 (*1-896095-23-2*) Polstar Bk.

Maynard, Michael. Games Men Play. 304p. 1996. 9.95 (*1-874509-22-0*, Pub. by X Pr) LPC InBook.

— A History of the Debate over 1 John 5, 7-8: A Tracing of the Longevity of the Comma Johanneum, with Evaluations of Arguments Against Its Authenticity. LC 95-67775. (Illus.). 382p. (Orig.). 1995. 31.60 (*1-886971-05-6*) Comma Pubns.

Maynard, Michael, jt. auth. see Leigh, Andrew.

Maynard, Michael L. & Maynard, Senko K. Listen & Learn 101 Japanese Idioms. (JPN.). 224p. 1995. pap. 29.95 incl. audio (*0-8442-8341-X*, 8341X, Passprt Bks) NTC Contemp Pub Co.

Maynard, Michael L., jt. auth. see Maynard, Senko K.

Maynard, Micheline. Collision Course: Inside the Battle for General Motors. 320p. 1995. 21.95 (*1-55972-313-0*, Birch Ln Pr) Carol Pub Group.

— The Global Manufacturing Vanguard: New Rules from the Industry Elite. LC 97-49414. 256p. 1998. 29.95 (*0-471-18023-8*) Wiley.

Maynard, Nan. And Then the Rain Stopped. large type ed. LC 98-2819. 193p. 1998. 18.95 (*0-7838-0117-3*, G K Hall Lrg Type) Mac Lib Ref.

— Between the Waters. large type ed. LC 98-23164. (Romance Ser.). 211p. 1998. pap. write for info. (*0-7540-3417-8*) Chivers N Amer.

— Between the Waters. large type ed. LC 98-23164. (Nightingale Ser.). 1998. pap. 18.95 (*0-7838-0247-1*, G K Hall & Co) Mac Lib Ref.

— The Dancing Willows. large type ed. 384p. 1995. 27.99 (*0-7089-3360-2*) Ulverscroft.

— Rise up My Love. large type ed. (General Ser.). 400p. 1993. 27.99 (*0-7089-2789-0*) Ulverscroft.

Maynard, P., ed. see University of Western Ontario Conference Staff.

***Maynard, Patrick.** The Engine of Visualization: Thinking about Photography. (Illus.). 2000. reprint ed. pap. 18.95 (*0-8014-8689-0*) Cornell U Pr.

Maynard, Patrick. The Engine of Visualization: Thinking Through Photography. LC 97-23981. (Illus.). 336p. 1997. 39.95 (*0-8014-3365-7*) Cornell U Pr.

Maynard, Patrick, jt. ed. see Feagin, Susan L.

***Maynard, Philip.** To Slake a Thirst: The Matt Talbot Way to Sobriety. LC 00-25512. 208p. (YA). 2000. pap. 12.95 (*0-8189-0843-2*, Saint Pauls) Alba.

Maynard, Rebecca A. Kids Having Kids: Economic Costs & Social Consequences of Teen Pregnancy. 300p. 1996. 24.50 (*0-87766-654-7*) Urban Inst.

Maynard-Reid, Pedrito U. Complete Evangelism: The Luke-Acts Model. LC 96-33203. 184p. (Orig.). 1997. pap. 14.99 (*0-8361-9045-9*) Herald Pr.

***Maynard-Reid, Pedrito U.** Diverse Worship: African-American, Caribbean & Hispanic Perspectives. LC 00-24894. 2000. pap. 15.99 (*0-8308-1579-1*) InterVarsity.

Maynard, Robert. GoodParents.com: What Every Good Parent Should Know about the Internet. LC 98-36925. (Illus.). 170p. 2000. pap. 19.95 (*1-57392-270-6*) Prometheus Bks.

Maynard, Robert, et al. Chemical Warfare Agents: Toxicology & Treatment. LC 95-44142. 252p. 1996. 152.95 (*0-471-95994-4*, Wiley-Interscience) Wiley.

Maynard, Robert C. GoodParents.com: What Every Good Parent Should Know about the Internet... Even If You Don't Know Beans about Computers! (Illus.). 170p. 1998. pap. 19.95 incl. cd-rom (*0-9659287-0-5*) Fidelis Gp.

***Maynard, Robert L. & Howard, Vyvyan.** Particulate Matter: Properties & Effects upon Health. LC 99-39157. (Illus.). 208p. 1999. 115.00 (*0-387-91588-5*) Spr-Verlag.

Maynard, Robert L., jt. auth. see Brimblecombe, Peter.

Maynard, Robert W. English to Spanish Vocabulary Conversion. 487p. (Orig.). (C). 1990. pap. 14.95 (*0-9626879-0-1*) Convocab Pub.

Maynard, Roger. Advanced Bowhunting Guide. (Illus.). 224p. (Orig.). 1984. pap. 14.95 (*0-88317-115-5*) Stoeger Pub Co.

— Hunting & Shooting Modern Bow. 1999. pap. 21.95 (*0-88317-215-1*) Stoeger Pub Co.

Maynard, Roy, ed. see Spenser, Edmund.

Maynard, Senko K. Discourse Modality: Subjectivity, Emotion & Voice in the Japanese Language. LC 92-36878. (Pragmatics & Beyond New Ser.: No. 24). x, 315p. 1993. 65.00 (*1-55619-292-4*) J Benjamins Pubng Co.

— Japanese Communication: Language & Thought in Context. LC 96-46386. (Illus.). 296p. 1997. text 46.00 (*0-8248-1799-0*); pap. text 23.95 (*0-8248-1878-4*) UH Pr.

— Japanese Conversation - Self-Contextualization Though Structure & Interactional Management. Freedle, Roy O., ed. (Advances in Discourse Processes Ser.: Vol. 35). 264p. (C). 1989. text 78.50 (*0-89391-509-2*) Ablx Pub.

— Principles of Japanese Discourse: A Handbook. LC 97-3091. 318p. (C). 1998. text 64.95 (*0-521-59095-7*); pap. text 25.95 (*0-521-59909-1*) Cambridge U Pr.

Maynard, Senko K. & Maynard, Michael L. One Hundred-One Japanese Idioms. (JPN & ENG., Illus.). 224p. 1993. pap. 7.95 (*0-8442-8496-3*, 84963, Natl Textbk Co) NTC Contemp Pub Co.

Maynard, Senko K., jt. auth. see Maynard, Michael L.

Maynard-Smith, John. Evolution & the Theory of Games. 226p. 1982. pap. text 24.95 (*0-521-28884-3*) Cambridge U Pr.

— The Theory of Evolution. 3rd ed. LC 93-20358. (Canto Book Ser.). (Illus.). 376p. 1993. pap. 14.95 (*0-521-45128-0*) Cambridge U Pr.

Maynard-Smith, John & Szathmary, Eors. The Major Transitions in Evolution. (Illus.). 360p. 1998. pap. text 29.95 (*0-19-850294-X*) OUP.

Maynard, Steven. Of Toronto the Gay. 1997. 24.95 (*0-226-51379-3*) U Ch Pr.

Maynard, Sue, jt. auth. see Richter, Judy.

Maynard, Thane. Ostriches. (Nature Books Ser.). (Illus.). 32p. (J). (gr. 2-6). 1996. lib. bdg. 22.79 (*1-56766-274-9*) Childs World.

— Working with Wildlife: A Guide to Careers in the Animal World LC 99-12300. 1999. 26.00 (*0-531-11538-0*) Watts.

***Maynard, Thane.** Working with Wildlife: A Guide to Careers in the Animal World. (Illus.). (YA). 2000. pap. 12.95 (*0-531-16415-2*) Watts.

Maynard, Thane, jt. auth. see Maynard, Caitlin.

Maynard, Theodore. Carven from the Laurel Tree, Essays. LC 67-23246. (Essay Index Reprint Ser.). 1977. 15.95 (*0-8369-0700-0*) Ayer.

— Il Mondo E' Troppo Piccolo: Vita Di Francesca Cabrini. Santi, M., tr. from ENG. (ITA.). (Orig.). (C). 1987. reprint ed. pap. text 7.00 (*0-9619397-0-2*) MSSH.

— Pillars of the Church. LC 76-136763. (Essay Index Reprint Ser.). 1977. 21.95 (*0-8369-1940-8*) Ayer.

Maynard, Trisha, ed. An Introduction to Primary Mentoring. LC 97-179493. (Children, Teachers & Learning Ser.). (Illus.). 128p. 1997. 65.00 (*0-304-70046-0*); pap. 22.95 (*0-304-70047-9*) Continuum.

Maynard, Trisha, jt. auth. see Furlong, John.

Maynard, Ursula. Performing Postmodernity. X, 92p. (C). 1995. text 36.95 (*0-8204-2661-X*) P Lang Pubng.

Maynard, Virginia, ed. see White, Anthony W.

Maynard, Winifred. Elizabethan Lyric Poetry & Its Music. (Illus.). 256p. 1986. 75.00 (*0-19-812844-4*) OUP.

Mayne, Harry. Conrad Ferdinand Meyer und Sein Werk. LC 76-100522. (GER.). reprint ed. 49.50 (*0-404-00597-7*) AMS Pr.

Mayne, Alan. The Imagined Slum: Newspaper Representations in the English Speaking World, 1870-1914. 256p. 1993. 59.00 (*0-7185-1389-4*, Pub. by Leicester U Pr) Cassell & Continuum.

— Imagined Slum Vol. 1: Newspaper Representations in the English Speaking World, 1870-1914. 1994. pap. 20.00 (*0-7185-2134-X*) St Martin.

Mayne, Alan J. From Politics Past to Politics Future: An Integrated Analysis of Current & Emergent Paradigms. LC 98-31077. 336p. 1999. 59.95 (*0-275-96151-6*, Praeger Pubs) Greenwood.

— Resources for the Future: An International Annotated Bibliography, 13. LC 92-35820. (Bibliographies & Indexes in Economics & Economic History Ser.: No. 13). 288p. 1993. lib. bdg. 79.50 (*0-313-28911-5*, GR8911) Greenwood.

Mayne, Cora. Romance at Perristone. large type ed. 1990. 27.99 (*0-7089-2127-2*) Ulverscroft.

— Romance in Norway. large type ed. (Linford Romance Library). 255p. 1984. pap. 16.99 (*0-7089-6179-7*) Ulverscroft.

— Romance on Lizard Island. large type ed. (Linford Romance Library). 215p. 1984. pap. 16.99 (*0-7089-6021-9*) Ulverscroft.

— Romantic Legacy. large type ed. (Linford Romance Library). 304p. 1984. pap. 16.99 (*0-7089-6008-1*) Ulverscroft.

— The Roylake Ruby. large type ed. 1991. 27.99 (*0-7089-2373-9*) Ulverscroft.

— So Sweet an Enemy. large type ed. 304p. 1996. 27.99 (*0-7089-3469-2*) Ulverscroft.

Mayne, D. Q., jt. auth. see Krener, A. J.

Mayne, D. Q., ed. see NATO Advanced Study Institute Staff.

***Mayne, Don.** Draw Your Own Cartoons. (Quick Starts for Kids! Ser.). (Illus.). 64p. (J). (gr. 2 up). 2000. pap. 8.95 (*1-885593-76-7*) Williamson Pub Co.

Mayne, Elizabeth. All That Matters: (March Madness) LC 95-7083. (Historical Ser.). 354p. 1995. per. 4.50 (*0-373-28859-X*, 1-28859-6) Harlequin Bks.

— Heart of the Hawk. LC 95-21592. 372p. 1995. per. 4.50 (*0-373-28891-3*) Harlequin Bks.

— The Highlander's Maiden. 1999. mass mkt. 4.99 (*0-373-29049-7*, Harlequin) Harlequin Bks.

— Lady of the Lake. 1997. per. 4.99 (*0-373-28980-4*, 1-28980-0) Harlequin Bks.

— Lord of the Isles. 1997. per. 4.99 (*0-373-28947-2*, 1-28947-9) Silhouette.

— Man of the Mist. (Historical Ser.). 1996. per. 4.50 (*0-373-28913-8*, 1-28913-1) Harlequin Bks.

— The Sheik & the Vixen. 1996. per. 3.99 (*0-373-07755-6*, 1-07755-1) Silhouette.

Mayne, Ethel C. Byron. LC 76-117883. (Select Bibliographies Reprint Ser.). 1977. reprint ed. 26.95 (*0-8369-5336-3*) Ayer.

— Byron. (BCL1-PR English Literature Ser.). 474p. 1992. reprint ed. lib. bdg. 99.00 (*0-7812-7480-X*) Rprt Serv.

— Byron. LC 72-108511. (Illus.). xvi, 474p. 1972. reprint ed. 22.00 (*0-403-01098-5*) Scholarly.

Mayne, Ethel C., tr. see Haller, Johannes.

Mayne, Gilles. Eroticism in Georges Bataille & Henry Miller. LC 93-85167. 206p. (Orig.). 1993. pap. 24.95 (*0-917786-93-9*) Summa Pubns.

Mayne, J., et al, eds. Advancing Public Policy Evaluation: Learning from International Experiences. LC 92-40625. 328p. 1992. 119.25 (*0-444-89810-7*) Taylor & Francis.

Mayne, John & Zapico-Goni, Eduardo, eds. Monitoring Performance in the Public Sector. LC 96-43358. 172p. 1997. text 32.95 (*1-56000-292-1*) Transaction Pubs.

Mayne, John M. Serwich: A Four Hundred Year Old Mystery. LC 96-65981. 199p. 1998. pap. 11.95 (*1-880451-30-1*) Rainbows End.

Mayne, John W., jt. auth. see Hopkins, Nigel J.

Mayne, Jonathan, ed. see Baudelaire, Charles.

Mayne, Jonathan, ed. see Leslie, C. R.

Mayne, Jonathan, ed. & tr. see Baudelaire, Charles.

Mayne, Judith. Cinema & Spectatorship. LC 92-24927. (Sightlines Ser.). 208p. (C). 1993. pap. 22.99 (*0-415-03416-7*) Routledge.

— Directed by Dorothy Arzner. LC 93-51496. 240p. 1995. 29.95 (*0-253-33716-X*); pap. 15.95 (*0-253-20896-3*) Ind U Pr.

***Mayne, Judith.** Framed: Lesbians, Feminists, & Media Culture. LC 00-8440. 2000. pap. 18.95 (*0-8166-3457-2*) U of Minn Pr.

Mayne, Judith. Kino & the Woman Question: Feminism & Soviet Silent Film. LC 88-36622. (Illus.). 221p. reprint ed. pap. 68.60 (*0-608-09855-8*, 206982000006) Bks Demand.

— The Woman at the Keyhole: Feminism & Women's Cinema. LC 90-34125. (Illus.). 270p. 1990. pap. 13.95 (*0-253-20606-5*, MB-606) Ind U Pr.

Mayne, Leger D. Social Entertainment of the Nineteenth Century (What Shall We Do Tonight?) 366p. 1996. pap. 35.00 (*0-87556-821-1*) Saifer.

Mayne, Lynette K. A Glimpse of Our Society Through Poetry. 1987. 39.00 (*0-7223-2072-8*, Pub. by A H S Ltd) St Mut.

Mayne, Marjaree. Mirror Murder. 276p. 1996. pap. 5.99 (*1-888701-10-2*) Jarrett Pr.

Mayne, P. W., jt. ed. see Robertson, P. K.

Mayne, Philip. Clinical Chemistry in Diagnosis & Treatment. 6th ed. (Illus.). 478p. 1994. pap. text 32.50 (*0-340-57647-2*, Pub. by E A) OUP.

Mayne, Philip & Day, Andrew P. A Workbook of Clinical Chemistry: Case Presentation & Data Interpretation. 224p. 1994. pap. text, student ed., wbk. ed. 19.95 (*0-340-57646-4*, Pub. by E A) OUP.

Mayne, R. W., ed. see American Society of Mechanical Engineers Staff.

***Mayne, Richard.** The Language of Sailing. 320p. 2000. pap. 29.95 (*1-85754-168-5*, Pub. by Carcanet Pr) Paul & Co Pubs.

Mayne, Richard, compiled by. Operation 'Nestegg: The Liberation of Jersey, 1945. (Illus.). 80p. (C). 1987. pap. 21.00 (*0-7855-2165-8*, Pub. by Picton) St Mut.

Mayne, Richard J., ed. Western Europe. fac. rev. ed. LC 85-29242. (Handbooks to the Modern World Ser.). 717p. 1986. pap. 200.00 (*0-7837-8613-1*, 205916800008) Bks Demand.

Mayne, Ruth. The International Dimensions of Work: Some Implications for the U. K. (Working Papers). 96p. 1998. pap. 15.95 (*0-85598-397-3*, Pub. by Oxfam Pub) Stylus Pub VA.

Mayne, Ruth, jt. ed. see Picciotto, Sol.

***Mayne, Rutherford.** Selected Plays of Rutherford Mayne. LC 99-49786. (Irish Drama Selections Ser.: Vol. 13). 300p. 2000. 49.95 (*0-8132-0978-1*); pap. 16.95 (*0-8132-0979-X*) Cath U Pr.

Mayne, Sallie, ed. & photos by see Walker, Michael L.

***Mayne, Seymour.** Passing of Octavio Paz: Bilingual Spanish/English Text/Poem. 2000. pap. 10.00 (*0-88962-696-0*) Mosaic.

Mayne, Seymour, ed. see Dor, Moshe.

Mayne, Seymour, ed. see Korn, Rachel.

Mayne, Seymour, ed. & intro. see A. M. Klein Symposium, University of Ottawa, 1974.

Mayne, Seymour, tr. see Harasymowicz, Jerzy.

Mayne, Seymour, tr. see Ravitch, Melech.

Mayne, Sharon. Heart Trouble. (Temptation Ser.: No. 390). 1992. per. 2.99 (*0-373-25490-3*, 1-25490-3) Harlequin Bks.

— Winner Takes All. (Temptation Ser.). 1993. per. 2.99 (*0-373-25535-7*, 1-25535-5) Harlequin Bks.

Mayne, Thom. Morphosis Connected Isolation. (Architectural Monographs: No. 23). 1993. 55.00 (*1-85490-150-8*) Academy Ed UK.

M

An Asterisk (*) at the beginning of an entry indicates that the title is appearing for the first time.

***Mayne, Thom.** Morphosis/Diamond Ranch High School: Source Books in Architecture. 272p. 2000. pap. 40.00 (*1-58093-079-4*, Pub. by Monacelli Pr) Penguin Putnam.

Mayne, Thom & Robins, Tony, contrib. by. Morphosis Buildings & Projects, Vol. 3. (Illus.). 320p. 1999. 55.00 (*0-8478-2074-2*, Pub. by Rizzoli Intl) St Martin.

***Mayne, Tracy J., et al.** Insider's Guide to Graduate Programs in Clinical & Counseling Psychology: 2000-2001 Edition. rev. ed. 342p. 2000. pap. text 22.95 (*1-57230-495-2*, CO495) Guilford Pubns.

Mayne, W. Fairy Tales of London Town, Vol. 2. (Illus.). (J). 1996. text 24.95 (*0-340-64860-0*, Pub. by Hodder & Stought Ltd) Trafalgar.

— Fox Gate. mass mkt. 7.95 (*0-340-65571-2*, Pub. by Hodder & Stought Ltd) Trafalgar.

Mayne, W. Harry. Fifty Years of Geophysical Ideas. 104p. (C). 1989. pap. 17.00 (*0-931830-73-7*, 305A) Soc Expl Geophys.

Mayne, William. The Book of Hob Stories. LC 96-52907. (Illus.). 96p. (J). (gr. 1-5). 1997. 17.99 (*0-7636-0390-2*) Candlewick Pr.

— Earthfasts. (J). (gr. 4-7). 1990. 20.25 (*0-8446-6430-8*) Peter Smith.

Mayne, William. Hob & the Goblins. LC 94-7029. (Illus.). 144p. (J). (gr. 4-7). 1994. 12.95 (*1-56458-713-4*) DK Pub Inc.

Mayne, William. Hob & the Peddler. LC 97-208970. 160p. (J). (gr. 3-6). 1997. 15.95 (*0-7894-2462-2*) DK Pub Inc.

— Lady Muck. LC 95-14009. (Illus.). 32p. (J). (gr. k-4). 1997. 15.95 (*0-395-75281-7*) HM.

— A Year & a Day. LC 99-34806. (Treasures Ser.). (Illus.). 96p. (YA). (gr. 3-7). 2000. 11.99 (*0-7636-0850-5*) Candlewick Pr.

— A Year & a Day. (J). (gr. 4-7). 1990. 19.25 (*0-8446-6431-6*) Peter Smith.

Mayne, Xavier, pseud. Imre: A Memorandum. LC 75-12337. (Homosexuality Ser.). 1975. reprint ed. 17.95 (*0-405-07388-7*) Ayer.

— The Intersexes: A History of Similsexualism As a Problem in Social Life. LC 75-12338. (Homosexuality Ser.). 1975. reprint ed. 48.95 (*0-405-07364-X*) Ayer.

Maynell, Everard. The Life of Francis Thompson. 1988. reprint ed. lib. bdg. 75.00 (*0-317-90165-6*) Rprt Serv.

Mayner, Blake A. At Peace with Honor: The Civil War Burials of Laurel Hill Cemetery - Philadelphia, Pennsylvania. LC 97-197619. (Illus.). 100p. (Orig.). 1997. pap. 10.00 (*0-9637745-2-2*) C W Hist.

Maynes, Charles W. & Williamson, Richard S., eds. U. S. Foreign Policy & the United Nations System. 304p. 1996. 27.50 (*0-393-03907-2*) Norton.

Maynes, Edwin S. Decision-making for Consumers: An Introduction to Consumer Economics. LC 75-17567. xi, 364p. 1976. write for info. (*0-02-378300-1*) Glencoe.

Maynes, Florence J., jt. auth. see Ross, John A.

Maynes, Judah L. Judah L. Magnes - Pioneer & Prophet on Two Continents: A Pictorial Biography. (Illus.). 56p. 1986. pap. 6.00 (*0-943376-06-8*) Magnes Mus.

Maynes, Mary J. Schooling for the People: Comparative Local Studies of Schooling History in France & Germany, 1750-1850. LC 84-10929. 272p. 1985. 49.75 (*0-8419-0966-0*) Holmes & Meier.

— Schooling in Western Europe: A Social History. LC 84-8847. 177p. (C). 1985. text 21.50 (*0-87395-978-7*) State U NY Pr.

— Taking the Hard Road: Life Course & Class Identity in Nineteenth-Century French & German Workers' Autobiographies. LC 94-27197. (Illus.). 300p. 1995. pap. text 19.95 (*0-8078-4497-7*); lib. bdg. 49.95 (*0-8078-2187-X*) U of NC Pr.

Maynes, Mary J., et al, eds. Gender, Kinship, Power: An Interdisciplinary & Comparative History. LC 95-33971. 480p. (C). 1995. pap. 20.99 (*0-415-91298-9*) Routledge.

Maynes, Mary J., jt. ed. see Joeres, Ruth-Ellen B.

Maynial, ed. see Flaubert, Gustave.

Maynooth Conference on the New Catechism, et al. Evangelising for the Third Millennium: The Maynooth Conference on the New Cathechism, May 1996. LC 97-226020. 259 p. 1997. write for info. (*1-85390-342-6*) Veritas Pubns.

Mayntz, Renate, et al. East European Academies in Transition. LC 98-21721. (Sociology of the Sciences Library). 162p. 1998. write for info. (*0-7923-5168-1*) Kluwer Academic.

Mayntz, Renate, ed. see Geiger, Theodor.

Mayo. Introduction to Computing for Engineers. 1991. student ed. 27.50 (*0-07-041140-9*) McGraw.

— Investments: An Introduction. 6th ed. (C). 1998. text 62.00 (*0-03-020994-3*) Harcourt Coll Pubs.

— Microsoft Word 97. LC 98-158672. (Quick Reference Guide Ser.). pap., spiral bd. 27.00 (*1-56243-455-1*, G-26) DDC Pub.

— Organic: Selected Experiments. 3rd ed. (C). 1998. pap. text 39.00 (*0-471-32863-4*) Wiley.

Mayo & Carey. Introduction to the Fine Arts. 2nd ed. 1991. pap. text 52.00 (*0-536-58050-2*) Pearson Custom.

***Mayo & Lank.** Power of Learning: Gaining Competitive Advantage. 288p. 2000. pap. 59.95 (*0-8464-5132-8*) Beekman Pubs.

***Mayo, et al.** Freeman Omnibus: Pastiches & Scholarship. (R. Austin Freeman Omnibus Edition Ser.: Vol. 11). 2000. 28.00 (*1-55246-170-X*) Battered Silicon.

Mayo, Amory D. Southern Women in the Recent Educational Movement in the South. fac. ed. Carter, Dan T. & Friedlander, Amy, eds. LC 78-1554. (Library of Southern Civilization). 333p. 1978. reprint ed. pap. 103.30 (*0-7837-7807-4*, 204756300007) Bks Demand.

***Mayo, Andrew.** Creating a Training & Development Strategy. 216p. 2000. pap. 44.99 (*0-8464-5022-4*) Beekman Pubs.

Mayo, Andrew. Managing Careers. 320p. (C). 1991. pap. 100.00 (*0-85292-481-X*, Pub. by IPM Hse) St Mut.

Mayo, Andrew & Lank, Elizabeth. The Power of Learning: A Guide to Gaining Competitive Advantage. 280p. (C). 1994. pap. 60.00 (*0-85292-565-4*, Pub. by IPM Hse) St Mut.

***Mayo, Barbara.** Fundamentals of Communication Workbook: UTPA Communication 1313. 2nd ed. 98p. (C). 1999. per., wbk. ed. 14.95 (*0-7872-6415-6*) Kendall-Hunt.

Mayo, Bernard. Jefferson Himself: The Personal Narrative of a Many-Sided American. LC 70-87871. (Illus.). 384p. 1970. reprint ed. pap. 18.95 (*0-8139-0310-6*) U Pr of Va.

— The Philosophy of Right & Wrong. 176p. 1986. 25.00 (*0-7102-0851-0*, 08510, Routledge Thoemms); pap. 13.95 (*0-7102-0859-6*, 08596, Routledge Thoemms) Routledge.

Mayo, Bernard, ed. Instructions to the British Ministers to the United States, 1791-1812. LC 70-75280. (Law, Politics & History Ser.). 1971. lib. bdg. 55.00 (*0-306-71303-9*) Da Capo.

Mayo, Bernard & Bear, James A., eds. Thomas Jefferson & His Unknown Brother. LC 80-25272. 59p. 1981. text 10.00 (*0-8139-0890-6*) U Pr of Va.

Mayo, Brad, jt. auth. see Hohl, Pat.

Mayo, C. & Henley, N. H., eds. Gender & Nonverbal Behavior. (Social Psychology Ser.). (Illus.). 288p. 1981. 64.00 (*0-387-90601-0*) Spr-Verlag.

Mayo, C. M. Sky over El Nido. LC 95-9961. 176p. 1995. 22.95 (*0-8203-1766-7*) U of Ga Pr.

— Sky over El Nido: Stories. 176p. 1999. pap. 12.95 (*0-8203-2119-2*) U of Ga Pr.

Mayo, C. M., ed. & tr. see Ansay, A. Manette, et al.

Mayo, Clark. Kurt Vonnegut: The Gospel from Outer Space: or Yes We Have No Nirvanas. LC 77-24460. (Milford Ser.: Popular Writers of Today Vol. 7). 64p. 1977. pap. 13.00 (*0-89370-211-0*) Millefleurs.

Mayo Clinic Department of Internal Medicine Staff & Prakash, Udaya B.S. Mayo Internal Medicine Board Review, 2000-2001. 1006p. pap. text 89.95 (*0-7817-2393-0*) Lppncott W & W.

Mayo Clinic Staff. Mayo Clinic Examinations in Neurology. 7th ed. LC 97-26131. (Illus.). 528p. (C). (gr. 13). 1997. text 62.95 (*0-8151-9319-X*, 26881) Mosby Inc.

— Mayo Clinic Heart Book. LC 93-25353. 368p. 1993. 26.00 (*0-688-09972-6*, Wm Morrow) Morrow Avon.

— The Mayo Clinic Williams - Sonoma Cookbook: Simple Solutions for Eating Well. LC 98-22188. (Illus.). 272p. (gr. 11). 1999. 29.95 (*0-7370-0008-2*) T-L Custom Pub.

Mayo, Dana W., et al. Microscale Organic Laboratory: With Multistep & Multiscale Syntheses. 4th ed. LC 99-30131. 688p. 2000. text 80.95 (*0-471-32185-0*) Wiley.

— Microscale Organic Laboratory with Selected Macroscale Experiments. 3rd ed. 800p. 1994. text 80.95 (*0-471-57505-4*) Wiley.

— Techniques of Microscale Organic Chemistry. LC 91-4412. 304p. 1991. pap. 49.95 (*0-471-62192-7*) Wiley.

***Mayo, David.** Physician-Assisted Suicide: Pro & Con. (Point/Counterpoint Ser.). 2000. 53.00 (*0-8476-8815-1*) Rowman.

Mayo, DeBarra. Runner's World Yoga, Bk. II. 180p. (Orig.). 1983. pap. 9.95 (*0-89037-274-8*) Anderson World.

Mayo, Debarra. Women's Bodybuilding for Beginners. 1984. pap. 2.95 (*0-02-499890-7*, Macmillan Coll) P-H.

Mayo, Deborah G. Error & the Growth of Experimental Knowledge. (Science & Its Conceptual Foundations Ser.). (Illus.). 456p. 1996. pap. text 29.95 (*0-226-51198-7*) U Ch Pr.

Mayo, Deborah G., et al, eds. Acceptable Evidence: Science & Values in Risk Management. (Environmental Ethics & Science Policy Ser.). (Illus.). 304p. 1994. reprint ed. pap. text 24.95 (*0-19-508929-4*) OUP.

Mayo, Debroah G. Error & the Growth of Experimental Knowledge. (Science & Its Conceptual Foundations Ser.). (Illus.). 456p. 1996. lib. bdg. 74.00 (*0-226-51197-9*) U Ch Pr.

Mayo, Diana, jt. auth. see Auld, Mary.

Mayo, Diana, jt. illus. see Auld, Mary.

Mayo, Diane. Murder at Bean & Beluga. (Illus.). 64p. 1983. pap. 5.95 (*0-932966-33-0*) Permanent Pr.

Mayo, Diane, et al. Wired for the Future. LC 98-8814. 280p. 1998. 38.00 (*0-8389-3491-9*) ALA.

Mayo, Donald H. Jung & Aesthetic Experience: The Unconscious As Source of Artistic Inspiration. (New Studies in Aesthetics: Vol. 25). 160p. (C). 1995. pap. text 29.95 (*0-8204-2724-1*) P Lang Pubng.

— 101 Things You Need to Know, 1. LC 98-201698. 1999. 10.00 (*1-56243-675-9*) DDC Pub.

Mayo, Dorothy O., jt. auth. see Whitcomb, Esther K.

Mayo, E. L. Collected Poems. Ray, David, ed. LC 80-84519. (New Letters Ser.). 272p. (Orig.). 1981. pap. text 20.00 (*0-938652-00-1*) New Letters MO.

Mayo, Edith, ed. American Material Culture: The Shapes of Things Around Us. LC 84-71338. 255p. 1984. 30.95 (*0-87972-303-3*); pap. 13.95 (*0-87972-304-1*) Bowling Green Univ Popular Press.

Mayo, Edith P. The Smithsonian Book of the First Ladies: Their Lives, Times, & Issues. (Illus.). 352p. (J). (gr. 6-9). 1995. 19.95 (*0-8050-1751-8*) H Holt & Co.

Mayo, Edith P. & Meringolo, Denise D. First Ladies: Political Role & Public Image. LC 94-14470. 1994. 8.95 (*0-929847-06-7*) Natl Mus Am.

Mayo, Edith P., et al. Mamie D. Eisenhower, Wife, Mother, First Lady: Her Impact & Influence on Her Time. LC 98-70448. (Eisenhower Seminar Ser.: No. 1). (Illus.). 1998. pap. 5.95 (*0-9663741-0-X*) Eisenhower Natl.

Mayo, Elton. The Human Problems of an Industrial Civilization. Stein, Leon, ed. LC 77-70515. 1977. reprint ed. lib. bdg. 28.95 (*0-405-10184-8*) Ayer.

— The Social Problems of an Industrial Civilization. Stein, Leon, ed. LC 77-70516. 1977. reprint ed. lib. bdg. 22.95 (*0-405-10185-6*) Ayer.

Mayo Foundation for Medical Education & Research. Pregnancy-Mayo Clinic. LC 94-7264. (Illus.). 750p. 1994. 33.00 (*0-688-11761-9*, Wm Morrow) Morrow Avon.

Mayo Foundation Staff, jt. ed. see Peterson, Ronald C.

***Mayo, Frank.** Boo! (Illus.). 16p. (J). (ps-3). 2000. pap. 2.99 (*0-375-80378-5*, Pub. by Random Bks Yng Read) Random.

Mayo, Gene. Your Stained Glass Workshop. (Illus.). 26p. 1996. pap. 12.95 (*0-936459-34-4*) Stained Glass.

Mayo, Georges, ed. International Continence Society, Annual Meeting, 7th, Portoroz, 1977. (Urologia Internationalis Ser.: Vol. 33, No. 5). (Illus.). 1978. pap. 34.00 (*3-8055-2974-0*) S Karger.

Mayo, Gretchen W. Big Trouble Tricky. (J). 1999. pap. 3.99 (*0-14-037781-6*, Viking) Viking Penguin.

— Earthmaker's Tales: North American Indian Stories about Earth Happenings. LC 88-20515. (Illus.). 96p. (J). (gr. 5 up). 1989. 12.95 (*0-8027-6839-3*); lib. bdg. 13.85 (*0-8027-6840-7*) Walker & Co.

— Meet Tricky Coyote! LC 92-12424. (Native American Trickster Tales Ser.). (Illus.). 35p. (J). (gr. 6-10). 1993. 12.95 (*0-8027-8198-5*); lib. bdg. 13.85 (*0-8027-8199-3*) Walker & Co.

— More Star Tales. (North American Indian Tales Ser.). (J). 1990. 11.15 (*0-606-04751-4*, Pub. by Turtleback) Demco.

— North American Indian Stories, 4 vols., Set. (Illus.). 256p. (J). (gr. 5 up). 1990. pap. 23.80 (*0-8027-7341-9*) Walker & Co.

— North American Indian Stories: Earthmaker's Tales. (Illus.). 48p. (J). (gr. 5 up). 1990. pap. 5.95 (*0-8027-7343-5*) Walker & Co.

— North American Indian Stories: More Earthmaker's Tales. (Illus.). 48p. (J). (gr. 5 up). 1990. pap. 5.95 (*0-8027-7344-3*) Walker & Co.

— North American Indian Stories: More Star Tales. LC 90-12786. (Illus.). 48p. (J). (gr. 4-7). 1990. pap. 5.95 (*0-8027-7347-8*) Walker & Co.

— North American Indian Stories: Star Tales. (Illus.). 48p. (J). (gr. 5 up). 1990. pap. 5.95 (*0-8027-7345-1*) Walker & Co.

— Star Tales: North American Indian Stories about the Stars. 96p. (J). (gr. 5 up). 1987. 12.95 (*0-8027-6672-2*); lib. bdg. 13.85 (*0-8027-6673-0*) Walker & Co.

— That Tricky Coyote! LC 92-12440. (Native American Trickster Tales Ser.). (Illus.). 32p. (J). (gr. 1-5). 1993. 12.95 (*0-8027-8200-0*); lib. bdg. 13.85 (*0-8027-8201-9*) Walker & Co.

Mayo, Gretchen W. Big Trouble for Tricky Rabbit! LC 93-29749. (Native American Trickster Tales Ser.). 48p. (J). (gr. 2-3). 1994. 12.95 (*0-8027-8275-2*); lib. bdg. 13.85 (*0-8027-8276-0*) Walker & Co.

— Here Comes Tricky Rabbit. LC 93-29763. (Native American Trickster Tales Ser.). 48p. (J). (gr. 2-3). 1994. 12.95 (*0-8027-8273-6*); lib. bdg. 13.85 (*0-8027-8274-4*) Walker & Co.

Mayo, Herbert B. Financial Institutions, Investments, & Management. 6th ed. 184p. (C). 1997. pap. text, student ed. 49.50 (*0-03-024409-9*) Dryden Pr.

— Financial Institutions, Investments, & Management: An Introduction. 6th ed. LC 97-65087. 720p. (C). 1997. text 77.00 (*0-03-024407-2*) Dryden Pr.

— Financial Institutions, Investments & Management: An Introduction, Test bank. 5th ed. (C). 1994. pap. text, teacher ed. 49.75 (*0-03-094818-5*) Dryden Pr.

— Investments. 5th ed. (C). 1996. pap. text, teacher ed. 42.00 (*0-03-019218-8*) Harcourt.

— Investments: An Introduction. 5th ed. (C). 1996. 94.50 (*0-03-024024-7*); text 104.50 (*0-03-017788-X*) Dryden Pr.

Mayo, Hope, ed. Descriptive Inventories of Manuscripts Microfilmed for the Hill Monastic Manuscript Library, Austrian Libraries, Vol. III: Herzogenburg. (Orig.). 1985. pap. 50.00 (*0-940250-03-9*) Hill Monastic.

Mayo, Hope, jt. ed. see Dupont, Inge.

Mayo, James M. The American Country Club: Its Origins & Development. LC 97-24553. (Illus.). 243p. 1998. 25.00 (*0-8135-2485-7*) Rutgers U Pr.

— The American Grocery Store: The Business Evolution of an Architectural Space, 150. LC 92-45072. (Contributions in American History Ser.: No. 150). 304p. 1993. 69.50 (*0-313-26520-8*, MGS, Greenwood Pr) Greenwood.

— War Memorials As Political Landscape: The American Experience & Beyond. LC 87-22328. 319p. 1988. 62.95 (*0-275-92812-8*, C2812, Praeger Pubs) Greenwood.

***Mayo, Jeff.** Astrology: A Key to Personality. 2000. pap. 25.95 (*0-85207-339-9*, Pub. by C W Daniel) Natl Bk Netwk.

Mayo, Jeff. Teach Yourself Astrology. 182p. 1995. pap. 7.95 (*0-8442-3906-2*, Teach Yrslf) NTC Contemp Pub Co.

— Teach Yourself Astrology. (Illus.). 224p. 1996. pap. 9.95 (*0-8442-3916-X*, Teach Yrslf) NTC Contemp Pub Co.

Mayo-Jefferies, Deborah. Equal Educational Opportunity for All Children: A Research Guide to Discrimination in Education, 1950-1992. LC 93-43237. Vol. 15. xiii, 89p. 1994. 35.00 (*0-89941-859-7*, 308050) W S Hein.

— Religious Freedom in the Education Process: A Research Guide to Religion in Education (1950-1992) LC 94-8623. (Legal Research Guides Ser.: Vol. 16). xv, 38p. 1994. 32.50 (*0-89941-871-6*, 308170) W S Hein.

Mayo, John & Collier, Simon. Mining in Chile's Norte Chico: Journal of Charles Lambert, 1825-1830. LC 98-29741. (Dellplain Latin American Studies: No. 36). 248p. 1998. text 55.00 (*0-8133-3584-1*, Pub. by Westview) HarpC.

Mayo, John, jt. auth. see Kaserman, David L.

Mayo, Jon. Computer Virus Pocket Reference. (Bigelow's Pocket Reference Ser.). 1998. pap. text 19.95 (*0-07-041159-X*) McGraw.

Mayo, Jon, jt. auth. see Accrocco, Joseph O.

Mayo, Jonathan L. Optical Disks. (Illus.). 208p. 1990. pap. 15.95 (*0-8306-3372-3*, 3372, Windcrest) TAB Bks.

— The Packet Radio Handbook. (Illus.). 224p. 1987. pap. 14.95 (*0-8306-2722-7*, NO. 2722) McGraw-Hill Prof.

— The Packet Radio Handbook. 2nd ed. (Illus.). 240p. 1989. pap. 16.95 (*0-8306-3222-0*) McGraw-Hill Prof.

— The Radio Amateur's Digital Communications Handbook. 1991. 22.95 (*0-07-155996-5*) McGraw.

— The Radio Amateur's Digital Communications Handbook. (Illus.). 224p. 1992. 22.95 (*0-8306-8362-3*, 3362); pap. 14.95 (*0-8306-3362-6*) McGraw-Hill Prof.

— Superconductivity - The Threshold of a New Technology. 1988. pap. 12.95 (*0-8306-9322-X*, 3022P) McGraw-Hill Prof.

Mayo, Jonathan L., jt. auth. see Traister, Robert J., Sr.

Mayo, Joseph & Mayo, Mary Ann. The Menopause Manager: Mapping Your Choices for Optimal Living. 1997. pap. 10.99 (*0-614-27367-6*, Plume) Dutton Plume.

Mayo, Joseph L., jt. auth. see Mayo, Mary Ann.

Mayo, Katherine. Justice to All: The Story of the Pennsylvania State Police. LC 70-154576. (Police in America Ser.). 1971. reprint ed. 24.95 (*0-405-03374-5*) Ayer.

***Mayo, Katherine.** Mother India. Sinha, Mrinalini, ed. LC 99-58162. 308p. 2000. text 49.50 (*0-472-09715-6*, 09715); pap. text 19.95 (*0-472-06715-X*, 06715) U of Mich Pr.

Mayo, Katherine. Mother India. LC 76-88906. 440p. 1970. reprint ed. lib. bdg. 75.00 (*0-8371-2309-7*, MAMO, Greenwood Pr) Greenwood.

Mayo, Katherine & Sinha, Mrinalini. Selections from Mother India. LC 99-931167. 298 p. 1998. write for info. (*81-85107-26-2*, Pub. by Kali for Women) S Asia.

Mayo, Kathleen & O'Donnell, Ruth, eds. The ADA Library Kit: Sample ADA-Related Documents to Help You Implement the Law. 132p. 1994. 22.99 (*0-8389-7765-0*) ASCLA.

Mayo, Kenneth F., Jr. Detective for Hire. 220p. mass mkt. 4.99 (*1-896329-23-3*) Picasso Publ.

Mayo, Kevin H. & Daragan, Vladimir A. Protein Dynamics Using NMR Relaxation. 300p. 1998. 48.00 (*1-86094-076-5*, Pub. by Imperial College) World Scientific Pub.

Mayo, L. R. The Design & Use of Wormgear Hobs. (Technical Papers: Vol. P19). (Illus.). 14p. 1932. pap. text 30.00 (*1-55589-149-7*) AGMA.

Mayo, Laurence S. John Endecott: A Biography. 1988. reprint ed. lib. bdg. 49.00 (*0-7812-0166-7*) Rprt Serv.

— John Endecott: A Biography. (Illus.). 1971. reprint ed. 49.00 (*0-403-01099-3*) Scholarly.

Mayo, Lawrence S. Jeffrey Amherst: A Biography. (Illus.). 344p. 1995. reprint ed. lib. bdg. 45.00 (*0-8328-4505-1*) Higginson Bk Co.

Mayo, Louise A. The Ambivalent Image: Nineteenth-Century America's Perception of the Jew. LC 87-45572. 224p. 1988. 32.50 (*0-8386-3318-8*) Fairleigh Dickinson.

Mayo, M. J., et al, eds. Superplasticity in Metals, Ceramics, & Intermetallics. (Symposium Proceedings Ser.: Vol. 196). 403p. 1990. text 17.50 (*1-55899-085-2*) Materials Res.

***Mayo, Margaret.** Brother Sun, Sister Moon: The Life & Story of St. Francis. LC 99-33140. (Illus.). 80p. (J). (gr. 5-9). 2000. 16.95 (*0-316-56466-4*) Little.

— Contrato Matrimonial. (Bianca Ser.: Vol. 227). (SPA.). 2000. mass mkt. 3.50 (*0-373-33577-6*, Harlequin) Harlequin Bks.

Mayo, Margaret. First Bible Stories. LC 97-36433. (Illus.). 96p. (J). (gr. k). 1998. 14.95 (*0-7641-5082-0*) Barron.

— An Impossible Situation. (Romance Ser.: No. 190). 1992. per. 2.89 (*0-373-03190-4*, 1-03190-5) Harlequin Bks.

— An Impossible Situation. large type ed. 1991. reprint ed. lib. bdg. 18.95 (*0-263-12565-3*) Thorndike Pr.

— Intrigue. (Romance Ser.). 1995. pap. 2.99 (*0-373-17216-8*, 1-17216-2) Harlequin Bks.

— Intrigue. large type ed. 1993. reprint ed. lib. bdg. 18.95 (*0-263-13185-8*) Mac Lib Ref.

— Las Leyes del Amor: (The Laws of Love) (Bianca Ser.: No. 132).Tr. of Love Laws. (SPA.). 1998. per. 3.50 (*0-373-33482-6*, 1-33482-0) Harlequin Bks.

— Matrimonio Prohibido (Forbidden Marriage) (Bianca Ser.). (SPA.). 1999. per. 3.50 (*0-373-33496-6*, 1-33496-0) Harlequin Bks.

***Mayo, Margaret.** Mutual Attraction. large type ed. 352p. 1999. 31.99 (*0-7505-1464-7*, Pub. by Mgna Lrg Print) Ulverscroft.

Mayo, Margaret. Our Fate: The Zodiac (1900) 154p. 1998. reprint ed. pap. 11.00 (*0-7661-0638-1*) Kessinger Pub.

— Our Fate & the Zodiac. 135p. 1996. reprint ed. spiral bd. 12.00 (*0-7873-0592-8*) Hlth Research.

— Reluctant Hostage. large type ed. 1992. lib. bdg. 18.95 (*0-263-13126-2*) Mac Lib Ref.

— Stormy Relationship. 1994. per. 2.99 (*0-373-11652-7*) Harlequin Bks.

Mayo, Margaret. When the World Was Young: Creation & Pourquois Tale. (Illus.). 80p. (J). (gr. k-5). 1996. pap. 19.95 (*0-689-80867-4*) S&S Bks Yung.

Mayo, Margaret. Wild Injustice. large type ed. 1995. 18.95 (*0-263-14041-5*) Thorndike Pr.

Mayo, Margaret E. Ancient Art. West, Rosalie A., ed. LC 98-8465. (Collections Handbooks Ser.). (Illus.). 96p. 1998. pap. 14.95 (*0-917046-51-X*) Va Mus Arts.

Mayo, Marjorie. Communities & Caring: The Mixed Economy of Welfare. LC 93-37356. 1994. text 49.95 (*0-312-12027-3*) St Martin.

***Mayo, Marjorie.** Cultures, Communities, Identities: Cultural Strategies for Participation & Empowerment. LC 00-33295. 2000. write for info. (*0-312-23770-7*) St Martin.

M

Mayo, Martha, ed. Comunidade: The Portuguese Community in Lowell, 1905-1930. LC 94-225266. (Illus.). 84p. (Orig.). 1994. pap. 8.95 (*0-9631604-2-7*) Lowell Hist Soc.

Mayo, Marti. Robert Helm, 1981-1993. LC 93-74800. 128p. 1995. pap. 25.00 (*0-941193-09-8*) U Houst Sarah.

Mayo, Marti, ed. Four Painters: Jones, Smith, Stack, Utterback. (Illus.). 28p. 1981. pap. 9.00 (*0-936080-04-3*) Cont Arts Museum.

Mayo, Marti, text. Robert Morris: Selected Works, 1970-1980. (Illus.). 60p. 1981. pap. 8.00 (*0-936080-06-X*) Cont Arts Museum.

Mayo, Marti & Ward, Elizabeth. Houston Area Exhibition, 1988. (Illus.). 28p. 1988. pap. 3.00 (*0-941193-03-9*) U Houst Sarah.

Mayo, Marti, jt. ed. see Schnabel, Julian.

Mayo, Martin. The Musician's Notebook: Manuscript Paper for Inspiration & Composition. 96p. 1998. 5.95 (*0-7624-0369-1*) Running Pr.

Mayo, Mary A. Parents' Guide to Sex Education. 208p. 1986. pap. 7.95 (*0-310-44581-7*, 11357P) Zondervan.

Mayo, Mary Ann & Mayo, Joseph L. The Menopause Manager: A Safe Path for a Natural Change. LC 97-20700. 352p. 1998. 19.99 (*0-8007-1740-6*) Revell.

***Mayo, Mary Ann & Mayo, Joseph L.** The Menopause Manager: A Safe Path for a Natural Change. 352p. 2000. pap. 14.99 (*0-8007-5733-5*) Revell.

Mayo, Mary Ann, jt. auth. see Mayo, Joseph.

Mayo, Mary E., ed. Sixteen Hundred Lines to Pilgrims of the National Society of the Sons & Daughters of the Pilgrims. 1048p. 1996. reprint ed. 75.00 (*0-8063-1499-0*) Genealog Pub.

Mayo, Michael. Flea Market Owners Manuals: How to Open & Operate a Flea Market. (Illus.). 72p. 1998. pap. 39.95 (*1-883103-09-6*) United NC.

Mayo, Michael R. The Stone Cocoon. Scott, Bernard, ed. (Illus.). 487p. 1997. 27.95 (*0-9660636-0-0*) M R Mayo.

Mayo, Mike. Horror Show: 999 Hair-Raising, Hellish, & Humorous Movies. LC 98-21515. (Videohound's Ser.). (Illus.). 524p. 1998. pap. 17.95 (*1-57859-047-7*) Visible Ink Pr.

***Mayo, Mike.** Videohound's DVD Guide. (Illus.). 2000. pap. 19.95 (*1-57859-115-5*) Visible Ink Pr.

Mayo, Mike. Videohound's Video Premieres: The Only Guide to Video Originals & Limited Releases. LC 97-970. (Illus.). 450p. 1997. pap. 17.95 (*0-7876-0825-4*) Visible Ink Pr.

Mayo, Mike, ed. Videohound's War Movies: Medieval to Modern Conflicts on Film. LC 99-40600. 638p. 1999. text 19.95 (*1-57859-089-2*) Visible Ink Pr.

Mayo, Morrow. Los Angeles. 1992. reprint ed. lib. bdg. 75.00 (*0-7812-5064-1*) Rprt Serv.

Mayo, Oliver. Agriculture: The Theory of Plant Breeding. 2nd ed. (Illus.). 320p. 1987. 55.00 (*0-19-854172-4*); pap. 29.95 (*0-19-854171-6*) OUP.

Mayo, Patricia T. Sugarless Baking Book. 1983. pap. 5.95 (*0-394-71429-6*) Random.

Mayo, Patrick. You're Entitled! Browne, Thomas P., ed. LC 89-80335. 144p. (Orig.). 1989. pap. 9.95 (*0-926991-00-0*) Linmar Assocs.

Mayo, Patty & Gajewski, Nancy. Transfer Activities: Thinking Skill Vocabulary Development. (Illus.). 202p. (YA). (gr. 5-12). 1987. pap. text 35.00 (*0-930599-13-6*) Thinking Pubns.

Mayo, Patty & Waldo, Pattii. Communicate. (Educational Game Activity Ser.). (J). (gr. 5-12). 1986. 47.00 (*0-930599-04-7*) Thinking Pubns.

— Communicate Expansion Cards. (Educational Game Activity Ser.). (YA). (gr. 5-12). 1988. 30.00 (*0-930599-22-5*) Thinking Pubns.

— Scripting: Social Communication for Adolescents. 2nd ed. 292p. (YA). (gr. 5-12). 1994. pap. 37.00 (*0-930599-08-X*) Thinking Pubns.

Mayo, Patty, et al. Communicate Junior. (Illus.). 60p. (J). (gr. 1-4). 1991. bds. 47.00 (*0-930599-68-3*) Thinking Pubns.

— Social Star: General Interaction Skills, Bk. 1. LC 92-39097. 485p. 1993. pap. 47.00 (*0-930599-79-9*) Thinking Pubns.

Mayo, Peg E. Heroes in the Seaweed: A Therapist's View of the Resilient Human Spirit. 408p. 1991. pap. 14.95 (*1-880797-02-X*) RiverVoice Pr.

Mayo, Peg Elliott. Blind Raftery: Seven Nights of a Wake. 2nd ed. (Illus.). 196p. 1999. pap. 25.00 (*1-880797-00-3*) RiverVoice Pr.

***Mayo, Peg Elliott.** Country Living & Other Excesses: Pleasure, Pain & Learning. (Illus.). 220p. 1999. pap. 22.00 (*1-880797-06-2*) RiverVoice Pr.

— An Enthusiastic Guide to Basketry: And a Celtic Myth, Iree the Basketmaker. (Illus.). 30p. 1999. pap. 15.00 (*1-880797-05-4*) RiverVoice Pr.

— Heroes in the Seaweed: A Therapist's View of the Resilient Human Spirit. 280p. 1999. pap. 25.00 (*1-880797-01-1*) RiverVoice Pr.

— Mister Gariety, Himself: A Tale of Some Incredulity. (Illus.). 258p. 1999. pap. 25.00 (*1-880797-04-6*) RiverVoice Pr.

— When a Friend Dies: Help in Decision Making & Grieving Animal Companions. (Illus.). 60p. 1999. pap. write for info. (*1-880797-03-8*) RiverVoice Pr.

Mayo, Peter. Gramsci, Freire, & Adult Education: Possibilities for Transformative Action. LC 98-30388. 1999. 59.95 (*1-85649-613-9*, Pub. by Zed Books); pap. 62.50 (*1-85649-614-7*, Pub. by Zed Books) St Martin.

Mayo, Peter J. The Morphology of Aspect in Seventeenth-Century Russian: Based on Texts of the Smutnoe Vremja. xi, 234p. (Orig.). 1985. pap. 22.95 (*0-89357-145-8*) Slavica.

***Mayo, Porter.** Medicine in the Athens of the West: The History & Influence of the Lexington-Fayette County Medical Society. LC 99-65231. (Illus.). 352p. 1999. 24.95 (*0-913383-64-3*) McClanahan Pub.

Mayo, Robert M. Introduction to Nuclear Concepts for Engineers. LC 98-42552. 376p. (C). 1998. text 45.00 (*0-89448-454-0*, 350019) Am Nuclear Soc.

Mayo, S. J., et al. The Genera of Araceae. (Illus.). xii, 370p. 1997. 140.00 (*1-900347-22-9*, Pub. by Royal Botanic Edinburgh) Balogh.

Mayo, S. T., jt. auth. see Kurtz, A. K.

Mayo, Sandra M. & Carey, Peter. Introduction to the Fine Arts: Dance Music. 408p. (C). 1990. pap. 52.00 (*0-536-57872-9*) Pearson Custom.

Mayo-Santana, Raul, jt. auth. see Negron-Portillo, Mariano.

***Mayo-Smith, I.** Trying to Walk the Way: Hopes, Memories & Fantasies. LC 99-25964. 154p. 1999. 12.95 (*1-56549-951-4*, Frog Bks) Kumarian Pr.

***Mayo-Smith, Ian.** The Children's Aviary. LC 98-42702. (Illus.). 42p. (J). (gr. 3 up). 1998. pap. 7.95 (*1-56549-950-6*, Frog Bks) Kumarian Pr.

Mayo-Smith, Ian. Poems, Essays & Comments for Everyone. LC 94-39164. 92p. (Orig.). 1994. pap. 9.95 (*1-56549-043-6*) Kumarian Pr.

— Reports That Get Results: Guidelines for Executives. fac. ed. LC 89-24716. (Illus.). 45p. 1990. pap. 30.00 (*0-7837-7582-2*, 204733500007) Bks Demand.

Mayo, Terry. Illustrated Rules of In-Line Hockey. (Illustrated Rules of the Game Ser.). (Illus.). 32p. (J). (gr. 1-4). 1996. lib. bdg. 21.27 (*1-884756-13-1*) Davidson Titles.

— The Illustrated Rules of In-Line Hockey. LC 95-35318. (Illustrated Sports Ser.). (Illus.). 32p. (Orig.). (J). (gr. 1-4). 1996. pap., per. 6.95 (*1-57102-064-0*, Ideals Child) Hambleton-Hill.

Mayo, Todd L. The Art & Science of Successful Investing: Your Complete Guide to Creating & Managing Wealth. LC 99-203433. (Illus.). 780p. 1999. pap. 24.95 (*0-9647700-5-9*) Capital Com Inc.

— The Joy of Self Employment: Entrepreneurship & Education in a Changing World. LC 96-95452. 400p. 1997. 27.95 (*0-9647700-4-0*) Capital Com Inc.

— Pathways to Success: Your Roadmap to Total Happiness & Achievement. LC 96-67933. 450p. (Orig.). 1996. pap. 14.95 (*0-9647700-1-6*) Capital Com Inc.

— Words to Live By: Thoughts on Living a Happy & Successful Life. LC 95-70414. 288p. 1995. pap. 9.95 (*0-9647700-0-8*) Capital Com Inc.

— Words to Live By: Thoughts on Living a Happy & Successful Life. deluxe rev. ed. LC 95-70414. 470p. 1996. pap. 15.95 (*0-9647700-2-4*) Capital Com Inc.

Mayo, Virginia. Remembering: The Story of a Soldier. (Illus.). 32p. (J). (gr. 2-4). 1997. 19.95 (*0-09-176687-7*, Pub. by Hutchnson) Trafalgar.

Mayo, Virginia, jt. ed. see Forrister, Brad.

***Mayo, Wendell.** B Horror: And Other Stories. unabridged ed. 144p. 1999. 23.00 (*0-942979-62-1*) Livingston AL.

— B. Horror: And Other Stories. unabridged ed. 144p. 1999. pap. 11.00 (*0-942979-61-3*) Livingston AL.

Mayo, Wendell. Centaur of the North. LC 96-16943. 140p. 1996. pap. 11.95 (*1-55885-165-8*) Arte Publico.

— In Lithuanian Wood. 208p. 1998. pap. 14.00 (*1-877727-87-3*) White Pine.

Mayo, William E. & Cwiakala, Martin. The FORTRAN 90 Workbook. (C). 1991. text 14.50 (*0-07-041148-4*) McGraw.

— Introduction to Computing for Engineers. (C). 1991. text 62.25 (*0-07-041139-5*) McGraw.

— Introduction to Computing for Engineers: The Fortran 90. (C). 1991. text, wbk. ed. 66.00 (*0-07-911192-0*) McGraw.

— Schaum's Outline of Programming with FORTRAN. (Schaum's Outline Ser.). (C). 1994. pap. text 14.95 (*0-07-041155-7*) McGraw.

Mayo, William E., ed. see Metallurgical Society of AIME Staff.

Mayo, William S. Kaloolah: or Journeyings to the Djebel Kumri: An Autobiography of Jonathan Romer. LC 72-2071. (Black Heritage Library Collection). 1977. reprint ed. 43.95 (*0-8369-9059-5*) Ayer.

Mayobre, Eduardo, ed. G-24: The Developing Countries in the International Financial System. LC 99-26297. 330p. 1999. lib. bdg. 45.00 (*1-55587-846-6*) L Rienner.

Mayoh, Brian, ed. Scandinavian Conference on Artificial Intelligence, '91: Proceedings of the SCAI '91, Roskilde, Denmark, 21-24 May, 1991. (Frontiers in Artificial Intelligence & Applications Ser.: Vol. 12). 350p. 1991. 66.00 (*90-5199-056-1*, Pub. by IOS Pr) IOS Press.

Mayoh, Brian H. Problem Solving with ADA. LC 81-14675. (Wiley Series in Computing). 243p. reprint ed. pap. 75.40 (*0-608-18444-6*, 203265800080) Bks Demand.

***Mayol, Jacques.** Homo Delphinus: The Dolphin Within Man. (Illus.). 2000. 120.00 (*1-928649-03-3*) Idelson Gnocchi Pub.

Mayol, Pierre, jt. auth. see Giard, Luce.

Mayon-White, Richard T., et al. Immunizing Children: A Practical Guide. LC 96-53160. 1997. write for info. (*1-85775-154-X*) Scovill Paterson.

Mayon-White, William M. Decision Support Systems: Experiences & Expectations: Proceedings of the IFIP TC-WG8.3 Working Conference on Decision Support Systems: Experiences & Expectations, Fontainebleau, France, 30 June-3 July 1992. LC 92-16588. (IFIP Transactions A: Computer Science & Technology Ser.: Vol. A-9). 324p. 1992. 131.50 (*0-444-89673-2*, North Holland) Elsevier.

Mayor, A. Hyatt. A. Hyatt Mayor: Selected Writings & a Bibliography. (Illus.). 200p. 1983. 7.95 (*0-87099-332-1*) Metro Mus Art.

— Prints & People: A Social History of Printed Pictures. LC 80-7817. (Illus.). 496p. 1980. pap. text 37.50 (*0-691-00326-2*, Pub. by Princeton U Pr) Cal Prin Full Svc.

Mayor, A. Hyatt, ed. Fifteenth & Sixteenth Century European Drawings. (Illus.). 1967. pap. 7.95 (*0-8079-0101-6*) October.

***Mayor, Adrienne.** The First Fossil Hunters: Palentology in Greek & Roman Times. 2000. 35.00 (*0-691-05863-6*, Pub. by Princeton U Pr) Cal Prin Full Svc.

Mayor, Alan. The Nashville Family Album: A Country Music Scrapbook. (Illus.). 272p. 1999. 27.50 (*0-312-24412-6*, Thomas Dunne) St Martin.

Mayor, Andreas, tr. see Proust, Marcel.

Mayor, Archer. Bellows Falls. 336p. 1998. mass mkt. 6.99 (*0-446-60630-8*, Pub. by Warner Bks) Little.

— Bellows Falls. large type ed. LC 97-48567. (Mystery Ser.). 394p. 1998. pap. 25.95 (*0-7838-8405-2*, G K Hall Lrg Type) Mac Lib Ref.

— Borderlines. 320p. 1991. mass mkt. 4.50 (*0-380-71600-3*, Avon Bks) Morrow Avon.

— Borderlines. 320p. 1994. mass mkt. 6.99 (*0-446-40443-8*, Pub. by Warner Bks) Little.

— Borderlines. large type ed. LC 91-2310. 398p. 1991. reprint ed. lib. bdg. 20.95 (*1-56054-162-8*) Thorndike Pr.

— The Dark Root. 400p. 1996. mass mkt. 5.99 (*0-446-40376-8*, Pub. by Warner Bks) Little.

— The Disposable Man. LC 98-19551. 304p. 1998. 22.00 (*0-89296-685-8*, Pub. by Mysterious Pr) Little.

— The Disposable Man. 336p. 1999. mass mkt. 6.50 (*0-446-60768-1*, Pub. by Warner Bks) Little.

— Fruits of the Poisonous Tree. 304p. 1995. mass mkt. 6.99 (*0-446-40374-1*, Pub. by Warner Bks) Little.

***Mayor, Archer.** The Marble Mask. 320p. 2000. 23.95 (*0-89296-723-4*) Mysterious Pr.

Mayor, Archer. Occam's Razor. LC 99-26221. 352p. 1999. 23.95 (*0-89296-682-3*, Pub. by Mysterious Pr) Little.

***Mayor, Archer.** Occam's Razor. 2000. mass mkt. 6.99 (*0-446-60887-4*) Warner Bks.

Mayor, Archer. Open Season. 320p. 1989. pap. 3.95 (*0-380-70756-X*, Avon Bks) Morrow Avon.

— Open Season. 320p. 1994. mass mkt. 6.99 (*0-446-40414-4*, Pub. by Warner Bks) Little.

— The Ragman's Memory. 368p. 1997. 6.50 (*0-446-40524-8*) Mysterious Pr.

— The Ragman's Memory. 1997. mass mkt. 6.50 (*0-446-60590-5*, Pub. by Warner Bks) Little.

— Scent of Evil. 416p. 1993. mass mkt. 6.50 (*0-446-40335-0*, Pub. by Warner Bks) Little.

— The Skeleton's Knee. 320p. 1993. 18.95 (*0-89296-470-7*) Mysterious Pr.

— The Skeleton's Knee. 320p. 1994. mass mkt. 6.50 (*0-446-40099-8*, Pub. by Warner Bks) Little.

— The Skeleton's Knee. large type ed. LC 94-5669. 579p. 1994. lib. bdg. 21.95 (*0-7862-0227-0*) Thorndike Pr.

Mayor, Barbara & Pugh, A. K., eds. Language, Communication & Education. 480p. (Orig.). (C). 1986. pap. text 16.95 (*0-7099-3590-0*, Pub. by C Helm) Routldge.

Mayor, David G., ed. The Saga of a Quiet Birdman: The Autobiography of Paul B. Jackson, Colonel USAF (Ret.) (Illus.). 320p. (Orig.). 1994. pap. 19.95 (*1-877633-20-8*) Luthers.

Mayor, F. M. The Rector's Daughter. large type ed. 1993. 39.95 (*0-7066-1030-X*, Pub. by Remploy Pr) St Mut.

Mayor, Federico. The New Page. (UNESCO Ser.). 128p. 1995. text 51.95 (*1-85521-652-3*, Pub. by Dartmth Pub) Ashgate Pub Co.

Mayor, Federico, et al. Patterns. Wiltshire, Rosemary et al, trs. from SPA. LC 93-74145. 95p. 1994. pap. 14.95 (*1-85610-034-0*, Pub. by Forest Bks) Dufour.

Mayor, Georges & Zingg, Ernst J. Urologic Surgery: Diagnosis, Techniques & Postoperative Treatment. LC 75-36660. 643p. reprint ed. pap. 199.40 (*0-608-30549-9*, 201647500004) Bks Demand.

Mayor, J. B. Classification of Shelley's Metre. LC 75-116796. (Studies in Shelley: No. 25). 1970. reprint ed. lib. bdg. 75.00 (*0-8383-1038-9*) M S G Haskell Hse.

Mayor, John E. Ricardi di Cirenscestria Speculum Historiale de Gestis Regum Angliae, 2 vols. (Rolls Ser.: No. 30). 1974. reprint ed. 110.00 (*0-8115-1058-1*); reprint ed. write for info. (*0-8115-1059-X*) Periodicals Srv.

Mayor, John E., ed. see Ascham, Roger.

Mayor, John E., ed. see Fisher, John.

Mayor, Joseph B. Chapters on English Metre. LC 73-100516. reprint ed. 29.50 (*0-404-04285-6*) AMS Pr.

— The Epistle of James. 3rd ed. LC 90-36539. 624p. 1990. reprint ed. pap. 21.99 (*0-8254-3255-3*, Kregel Class) Kregel.

— The Epistle of James. 3rd deluxe ed. LC 90-36539. 624p. 1990. reprint ed. lib. bdg. 27.99 (*0-8254-3256-1*, Kregel Class) Kregel.

Mayor la Guardia's Commission on the Harlem Riot. Complete Report of Mayor La Guardia's Commission on the Harlem Riot of March 19, 1935. LC 76-90204. (Mass Violence in America Ser.). 1977. reprint ed. 20.95 (*0-405-01328-0*) Ayer.

Mayor Marsan, Maricel. Rostro Cercano: (Antologia Poetica) LC 86-82717. (SPA., Illus.). 62p. 1986. pap. 8.00 (*0-935318-12-7*) Edins Hispamerica.

Mayor, Michael, jt. ed. see Duquennoy, Antoine.

Mayor, P. & Roberge, P. R. Computers in Corrosion Control, Vol. IV. (Illus.). 128p. 1994. pap. 30.00 (*1-877914-72-X*) NACE Intl.

Mayorga, Margaret, ed. Best Short Plays of 1957-58. LC 38-8006. 316p. 1958. 16.95 (*0-910278-84-9*) Boulevard.

Mayorga, Nancy. Hunger of the Soul. 144p. 1995. pap. 9.95 (*0-940698-00-5*) InrQuest.

Mayorga, R. V., ed. Robotics & Manufacturing. 465p. 1995. 150.00 (*0-88986-220-6*, 232) Acta Pr.

— Robotics & Manufacturing. 380p. 1996. 115.00 (*0-88986-209-5*, 247) Acta Pr.

— Robotics & Manufacturing. LC 97-18417. (Series on Robotics & Manufacturing). (Illus.). 407p. 1997. pap. 135.00 (*0-88986-227-3*) Acta Pr.

Mayorga, Roberto & Montt, Luis. Foreign Investment in Chile: The Legal Framework for Business, the Foreign Investment Regime in Chile, Environmental System in Chile, Documents. LC 95-4054. 1995. lib. bdg. 106.50 (*0-7923-3359-4*, Pub. by M Nijhoff) Kluwer Academic.

Mayorova, K. V. Teach Yourself Russian. 318p. (C). 1988. 19.95 incl. audio (*0-8285-3927-8*) Firebird NY.

Mayors Commission for Women of Philadelphia, et al. Guide to Women's History Resources in the Delaware Valley Area. (Illus.). 224p. (Orig.). 1983. pap. 23.95 (*0-8122-1168-5*) U of Pa Pr.

Mayott, Clarence W. & Milano, Geraldine B. Solid Modelling with Pro-Engineer. 336p. (C). 1993. ring bd. 40.95 (*0-8403-8729-6*) Kendall-Hunt.

Mayotte, Judy. Disposable People? The Plight of Refugees. LC 92-29489. 300p. 1992. 24.00 (*0-88344-839-4*) Orbis Bks.

***Mayotte, Raymond.** Corners. LC 00-190113. 204p. 2000. 25.00 (*0-7388-1532-2*); pap. 18.00 (*0-7388-1533-0*) Xlibris Corp.

Mayotte, Ricky A. The Complete Jesus: All the Sayings of Jesus Gathered from Ancient Sources & Compiled into a Single Volume for the First Time. LC 97-33149. 274p. 1998. reprint ed. pap. 15.00 (*1-883642-77-9*) Steerforth Pr.

Mayotte, Ricky A., ed. The Complete Jesus: All the Saying of Jesus Gathered from Ancient Sources & Complied into a Single Volume for the First Time. LC 97-33149. 320p. 1997. 25.00 (*1-883642-45-0*) Steerforth Pr.

Mayou, Richard, et al, eds. Treatment of Functional Somatic Symptoms. (Illus.). 466p. (C). 1995. text 89.50 (*0-19-262499-7*) OUP.

Mayoue, John C. Relationships in Turmoil: Emerging Rights & Duties of Spouses, Significant Others, & Persons Affected by Dissolutions. LC 98-9629. 1998. pap. write for info. (*1-57073-537-9*) Amer Bar Assn.

Mayper, Monica. Come & See: A Christmas Story. LC 93-45730. 32p. (J). (ps-3). 1999. 14.95 (*0-06-023526-8*) HarpC Child Bks.

— Come & See: A Christmas Story. LC 93-45730. (Illus.). 32p. (J). (ps-3). 1999. lib. bdg. 14.89 (*0-06-023527-6*) HarpC Child Bks.

— Oh Snow. LC 90-42088. (Illus.). 32p. (J). (ps-1). 1991. 14.95 (*0-06-024203-5*); lib. bdg. 14.89 (*0-06-024204-3*) HarpC Child Bks.

Mayr, Birgit. Das Japanische Malerportrat in der Spaten Edo-Zeit (ca. 1750-1868) (Europaische Hochschulschriften Ser.: Reihe 28, vol. 322). (Illus.). XII, 460p. 1998. pap. 73.95 (*3-631-32745-5*) P Lang Pubng.

Mayr, D. & Sussmann, G. Space, Time, & Mechanics. 260p. 1982. text 112.50 (*90-277-1525-4*, D Reidel) Kluwer Academic.

***Mayr, Diane.** The Everything Kids' Money Book. LC 99-56503. (Everything Kids' Ser.). 144p. (J). 2000. pap. 9.95 (*1-58062-322-0*) Adams Media.

Mayr, E., et al, eds. Lectures on Proof Verification & Approximation Algorithms, Vol. 136. LC 98-14448. (Lecture Notes in Computer Science Ser.: Vol. 1367). 470p. 1998. pap. 69.00 (*3-540-64201-3*) Spr-Verlag.

Mayr, Ernst. Evolutionary Synthesis: Perspectives on the Unification of Biology. (Illus.). 504p. 1998. pap. text 19.95 (*0-674-27226-9*) HUP.

— Systematics & the Orgin of Species from the Viewpoint of a Zoologistt: With a New Introduction. LC 99-36391. 368p. 1999. pap. text 17.95 (*0-674-86250-3*) HUP.

— This Is Biology: The Science of the Living World. LC 96-42192. (Illus.). 352p. 1997. 29.95 (*0-674-88468-X*) Belknap Pr.

— This Is Biology: The Science of the Living World. 1997. 29.95 (*0-614-28203-9*) HUP.

— This Is Biology: The Science of the Living World. 352p. 1998. pap. 15.95 (*0-674-88469-8*) HUP.

Mayr, Ernst W. Animal Species & Evolution. LC 63-9552. (Illus.). 811p. 1963. text 56.00 (*0-674-03750-2*) Belknap Pr.

— Evolution & the Diversity of Life: Selected Essays. (Illus.). 709p. 1976. 50.00 (*0-674-27104-1*) HUP.

— Evolution & the Diversity of Life: Selected Essays. 752p. 1997. pap. text 26.00 (*0-674-27105-X*) HUP.

— The Growth of Biological Thought: Diversity, Evolution & Inheritance. 992p. 1990. pap. text 22.95 (*0-674-36446-5*) Belknap Pr.

— One Long Argument: Charles Darwin & the Genesis of Modern Evolutionary Thought. (Illus.). 192p. (C). 1991. text 19.95 (*0-674-63905-7*) HUP.

— One Long Argument: Charles Darwin & the Genesis of Modern Evolutionary Thought. (Questions of Science Ser.). (Illus.). 224p. (C). 1993. pap. text 14.95 (*0-674-63906-5*) HUP.

— Populations, Species, & Evolution: An Abridgment of Animal Species & Evolution. abr. ed. LC 79-111486. 453p. 1970. pap. 18.50 (*0-674-69013-3*) Belknap Pr.

— Toward a New Philosophy of Biology: Observations of an Evolutionist. (Illus.). 640p. 1988. pap. text 18.95 (*0-674-89666-1*) HUP.

Mayr, Ernst W., ed. Graph-Theoretic Concepts in Computer Science: Eighteenth International Workshop, Wiesbaden-Naurod, Germany, June 18-20, 1992, Proceedings. LC 92-46173. (Lecture Notes in Computer Science Ser.: Vol. 657). 1993. 55.95 (*0-387-56402-0*) Spr-Verlag.

— The Species Problem. LC 73-17831. (Natural Sciences in America Ser.). (Illus.). 410p. 1974. reprint ed. 28.95 (*0-405-05749-0*) Ayer.

Mayr, Ernst W., et al, eds. STACS, '94: Eleventh Annual Symposium on Theoretical Aspects of Computer Science, Caen, France, February 24-26, 1994 Proceedings. LC 94-2919. (Lecture Notes in Computer Science Ser.: Vol. 775). xiv, 782p. 1994. 108.95 (*0-387-57785-8*) Spr-Verlag.

An Asterisk (*) at the beginning of an entry indicates that the title is appearing for the first time.

Mayr, Ernst W. & Kohler, Rolf. Edv-Abkuerzungen. 3rd ed. (GER & RUS.). 408p. 1981. 135.00 (*0-8288-0003-0*, F35420); 110.00 (*0-8288-1163-6*, M7981) Fr & Eur.

Mayr, Ernst W. & Provine, William B. The Evolutionary Synthesis: Perspectives on the Unification of Biology. LC 98-157613. (Illus.). 498p. 1980. 44.00 (*0-674-27225-0*) HUP.

Mayr, Ernst W. & Schmidt, G., eds. Graph-Theoretic Concepts in Computer Science. (Lecture Notes in Computer Science Ser.: Vol. 903). 414p. 1995. 68.00 (*3-540-59071-4*) Spr-Verlag.

Mayr, Ernst W. & Short, Lester L. Species Taxa of North American Birds: A Contribution to Comparative Systematics. (Publications of the Nuttall Ornithological Club: No. 9). (Illus.). 127p. 1970. 7.00 (*1-877973-19-X*, 9) Nuttall Ornith.

Mayr-Harting, Henry. The Coming of Christianity to Anglo-Saxon England. 3rd ed. 336p. 1991. 35.00 (*0-271-00806-7*); pap. 16.95 (*0-271-00769-9*) Pa St U Pr.

— Ottonian Book Illumination: An Historical Study. (Illus.). 500p. 1999. text 75.00 (*1-872501-74-5*) Gordon & Breach.

— Ottonian Book Illumination: An Historical Study. (Illus.). 544p. 1999. pap. text 38.00 (*1-872501-79-6*) Gordon & Breach.

Mayr-Harting, Henry, ed. St. Hugh of Lincoln. (Illus.). 144p. 1987. text 45.00 (*0-19-820120-6*) OUP.

Mayr-Harting, Henry & Moore, R. I., eds. Studies in Medieval History. (Illus.). 330p. 1985. 60.00 (*0-907628-68-0*) Hambledon Press.

Mayr-Harting, Ursula. Early Netherlandish Engravings. (Illus.). 40p. 1997. pap. 10.00 (*1-85444-105-1*, 1051, Pub. by Ashmolean Mus) A Schwartz & Co.

Mayr, Helmut. A Guide to Fossils. 256p. 1993. pap. text 19.95 (*0-691-02922-9*, Pub. by Princeton U Pr) Cal Prin Full Svc.

— A Guide to Fossils. Dinalay, D. & Windsor, A. G., trs. LC 92-15856. (Illus.). 256p. (C). 1993. 39.50 (*0-691-08789-X*, Pub. by Princeton U Pr) Cal Prin Full Svc.

Mayr, Hubert. Orchid Names & Their Meanings. Schmucker, M., tr. pap. 50.00 (*3-904144-07-3*) Gantner Verlag.

Mayr, Marlene, ed. Does the Church Really Want Religious Education? LC 87-35592. 267p. 1988. pap. 22.95 (*0-89135-062-4*) Religious Educ.

— Modern Masters of Religious Education. LC 82-25009. 323p. (Orig.). 1983. pap. 24.95 (*0-89135-033-0*) Religious Educ.

Mayr, Otto. Authority, Liberty & Automatic Machinery in Early Modern Europe. LC 85-15460. (Illus.). 288p. 1989. reprint ed. pap. text 17.95 (*0-8018-3939-4*) Johns Hopkins.

— The Deutsches Museum, Munich. (Illus.). 160p. 1990. 35.00 (*1-870248-29-5*) Scala Books.

Mayr, Otto, ed. The Clockwork Universe. 1980. lib. bdg. 55.00 (*0-88202-188-5*); write for info. (*0-686-77549-X*) Watson Pub Intl.

— Philosophers & Machines. LC 75-39528. 1975. pap. text 6.95 (*0-685-52444-2*) Watson Pub Intl.

Mayr, Otto & Post, Robert C., eds. Yankee Enterprise: The Rise of the American System of Manufactures. LC 81-607315. (Illus.). 236p. (Orig.). (C). 1982. pap. text 16.95 (*0-87474-631-0*, MAYEP) Smithsonian.

Mayr, Otto & Stephens, Carlene. American Clocks: Highlights from the Collections of the National Museum of American History. (Illus.). 48p. (Orig.). 1989. pap. 6.95 (*0-929847-03-2*) Natl Mus Am.

Mayr, P., ed. Surface Engineering: Papers Presented at the 1993 International Conference. (Illus.). 590p. 1993. 105.00 (*3-88355-189-9*, Pub. by DGM Metallurgy Info) IR Pubns.

Mayr-Pletschen, Heide. A Christmas Carol Book. (J). (gr. 3 up). 2.75 (*0-685-24603-5*) Merry Thoughts.

Mayr, Robert. Vocabularium Codicis Justiniani, 2 vols. 1965. reprint ed. write for info. (*0-318-72048-5*) G Olms Pubs.

— Vocabularium Codicis Justiniani, 2 vols. 1552p. 1986. reprint ed. write for info. (*3-487-00835-1*); reprint ed. write for info. (*0-318-70781-0*); reprint ed. write for info. (*0-318-70782-9*) G Olms Pubs.

Mayr, Troy & Sweeney, Anthony. Southern California Sport Climbing: The Guide. 216p. 1995. pap. 24.00 (*0-9647462-0-4*) Mobius Pubns.

— Williamson Rock: Southern California Sport Climbing. (Pocketguide Ser.). 78p. 1997. pap. 10.95 (*0-9647462-1-2*) Mobius Pubns.

Mayrand, Albert. Dictionnaire de Maximes et Locutions Latines Utilissees en Droit Quebecois. (FRE & LAT.). 235p. 1972. 39.95 (*0-7859-8020-2*, 2760107787) Fr & Eur.

Mayrhauser, Anneliese Von, see Von Mayrhauser, Anneliese.

Mayrhofer, H. & Poelt, J. Die Saxicolen Arten der Flechtengattung Rinodina in Europa. (Bibliotheca Lichenologica Ser.: No. 12). (GER., Illus.). 1979. lib. bdg. 30.00 (*3-7682-1237-8*) Lubrecht & Cramer.

Mayrhofer, Helmut. Monographie der Flechtengattung Thelenella. Wirth, Volkmar et al, eds. (Bibliotheca Lichenologica: Vol. 26). (GER., Illus.). 116p. 1987. 36.00 (*3-443-58005-X*, Pub. by Gebruder Borntraeger) Balogh.

Mayrhofer, Manfred. Kurzgefasstes Etymologisches Woerterbuch des Altindischen, 4 vols., Set. (GER & SAN.). 1976. 995.00 (*0-8288-5722-9*, M7529) Fr & Eur.

Mayrhofer, Michaela. Studien Uber die Saxicolen Arten der Flechtengattung Lecania in Europa Vol. II: Lecania S. Qtr. Wirth, Volkmar et al, eds. (Bibliotheca Lichenologica: Vol. 28). (GER., Illus.). 133p. 1988. text 36.00 (*3-443-58007-6*, Pub. by Gebruder Borntraeger) Balogh.

***Mayrhofer, Silvia.** Syntaktische und Semantische Funktionen des Adverbalen Syntagmas [A+SN] in Altitalienischen Texten. (Europaische Hochschulschriften Linguistik Ser.). 183p. 1999. 35.95 (*3-631-34739-1*) P Lang Pubng.

Mayrhofer, Wolfgang, jt. ed. see Golz, Reinhard.

Mayrocker, Friederike. Heiligenanstalt: Stories. Waldrop, Rosmarie, tr. from GER. LC 97-140211. (Dichten=Ser.: No. 1). 96p. 1994. pap. 8.00 (*0-930901-95-9*) Burning Deck.

— Night Train. Bjorklund, Beth, tr. from GER. & afterword by by. (Studies in Austrian Literature, Culture, & Thought. Translation Ser.). 126p. 1992. 17.00 (*0-929497-53-8*) Ariadne CA.

— With Each Clouded Peak. Waldrop, Rosmarie & Watts, Harriett, trs. from ENG. (Classics Ser.: No. 162). 86p. (Orig.). 1997. pap. 11.95 (*1-55713-277-1*) Sun & Moon CA.

Mays. Hydrosystems Engineering & Management. 1992. text, student ed. 30.00 (*0-07-041147-6*) McGraw.

— Juvenile Justice. LC 99-45949. 432p. 1999. pap. 41.25 (*0-07-040300-7*) McGraw.

— S.g. Contemporary Corrections. (Criminal Justice). (C). 1998. student ed. 13.50 (*0-534-54217-4*) Wadsworth Pub.

***Mays & Valentine Staff.** Virginia Environmental Law Handbook. 3rd ed. (State Environmental Law Ser.). 372p. 1998. pap. text 89.00 (*0-86587-651-7*) Gov Insts.

***Mays, Antje.** Legal Research on the Internet: A Compilation of Websites to Access United States Federal, State, Local & International Laws. LC 99-62273. (Legal Research Guide Ser.: Vol. 33). 58p. 1999. 45.00 (*1-57588-499-2*, 322910) W S Hein.

Mays, Belinda S., jt. auth. see Goudeaux, Phillip G.

Mays, Benjamin E. Born to Rebel: An Autobiography by Benjamin E. Mays. LC 86-19308. (Brown Thrasher Bks.). (Illus.). 440p. 1987. reprint ed. pap. 15.95 (*0-8203-0881-1*) U of Ga Pr.

— Negro's God As Reflected in His Literature. LC 69-16578. (Illus.). 269p. 1970. reprint ed. lib. bdg. 59.50 (*0-8371-1139-0*, MAG&) Greenwood.

Mays, Benjamin E. & Nicholson, Joseph W. Negro's Church. LC 70-83430. (Religion in America, Ser. 1). 1973. reprint ed. 35.95 (*0-405-00255-6*) Ayer.

Mays, Bruce & Maltbie, Cynthis. Arenas, Stages & Spaces: A Guide to Theatres in Chicago & Vicinity. (Illus.). 117p. (Orig.). 1982. pap. 6.95 (*0-941906-00-0*) Diversity Pr.

Mays, Buddy. Ancient Cities of the Southwest. LC 81-21732. 132p. 1990. pap. 10.95 (*0-87701-696-8*) Chronicle Bks.

— Guide to Western Wildlife. 2nd ed. LC 77-22043. (Illus.). (Orig.). 1988. pap. 8.95 (*0-87701-504-X*) Chronicle Bks.

Mays, Carl. Anatomy of a Leader. Crews, Judith, ed. (Power of One Ser.). (Illus.). 48p. 1997. pap. 5.95 (*1-880461-43-9*) Successories Inc.

— Hope for the World: Spiritual Values to Guide Our Lives. 96p. 1999. 9.95 (*1-879111-99-3*) Lincoln-Bradley.

— Prayers from the Heart. LC 95-75424. (Illus.). 128p. (Orig.). 1995. pap. 9.95 (*1-879111-49-7*) Lincoln-Bradley.

— A Strategy for Winning: Winning...in Business, in Sports, in Family, in Life. LC 90-62803. (Illus.). 272p. 1991. 21.95 (*1-879111-75-6*) Lincoln-Bradley.

— Winning Thoughts: A Very Special Gift Book. LC 94-78067. 96p. (Orig.). 1994. pap. 5.95 (*1-879111-23-3*) Lincoln-Bradley.

Mays, Carol. Holiday Gardens. (Illus.). 64p. 1998. pap. 10.95 (*1-57377-044-2*, 019884-02232-9) Easl Pubns.

— Holiday Helpers. (Illus.). 62p. 1998. pap. 10.95 (*1-57377-042-6*, 019884-02228-2) Easl Pubns.

Mays, David, ed. see Forrest, Thomas.

***Mays, Desiree'.** Opera Unveiled - 2000: The 2000 Santa Fe Opera Season. Fitzsimmons, Thomas, ed. LC 99-53616. (Illus.). 80p. 2000. pap. 12.95 (*0-942668-51-5*) Katydid Bks.

Mays, E. C., tr. see Kung, Guido.

Mays, Edith. Amherst Papers, 1756-1763: The Southern Sector: Dispatches from South Carolina, Virginia & His Majesty's Superintendent of Indian Affairs. LC 99-219955. 417p. 1999. pap. 33.50 (*0-7884-1131-4*, M097) Heritage Bk.

Mays, Elaine & Midgley, Jon. CompuCat. 85p. pap. text 7.95 (*0-9640463-1-8*) Compucat Ptrns.

***Mays, Elizabeth.** Handbook of Credit Scoring. 2000. 70.00 (*0-8144-0619-X*) AMACOM.

***Mays, Elizabeth, ed.** Credit Risk Modeling: Design & Application. 340p. 1999. 65.00 (*1-888998-38-5*, 98-38-5) Glenlake Pub.

Mays, Elizabeth & Klein, Robert. Credit Risk Modeling: Design & Application. (Glenlake Business Monographs). 257p. 1998. 65.00 (*1-57958-005-X*) Fitzroy Dearborn.

Mays, Elizabeth, jt. auth. see Cornyn, Anthony J.

Mays, Elizabeth, jt. ed. see Cornyn, Anthony G.

Mays, Frank Reese. And No Purple Heart. 301p. 1999. pap. 7.50 (*1-892614-16-2*, BWP-PH) Briarwood VA.

Mays, G. C., ed. Durability of Concrete Structures: Investigation, Repair, Protection. 264p. 1991. mass mkt. 76.50 (*0-419-15620-8*, E & FN Spon) Routledge.

Mays, G. C. & Hutchinson, A. R. Adhesives in Civil Engineering. (Illus.). 345p. (C). 1992. text 125.00 (*0-521-32677-X*) Cambridge U Pr.

Mays, G. C. & Smith, P. D., eds. Blast Effects of Buildings: Design of Buildings to Optimize Resistance to Blast Loading. 130p. 1995. 48.00 (*0-7277-2030-9*) Am Soc Civil Eng.

Mays, G. Larry. Privatization & the Provision of Correctional Services: Context & Consequences. Gray, Tara, ed. LC 95-81802. (ACJS - Anderson Monographs). 175p. (C). 1996. pap. 22.95 (*0-87084-552-7*) Anderson Pub Co.

Mays, G. Larry, ed. Setting the Jail Research Agenda for the 1990s: Proceedings from a Special Meeting. 84p. (C). 1999. reprint ed. pap. text 20.00 (*0-7881-7852-0*) DIANE Pub.

***Mays, G. Larry & Gregware, Peter R., eds.** Courts & Justice: A Reader. 2nd ed. 561p. (C). 1999. pap. 26.95 (*1-57766-072-2*) Waveland Pr.

Mays, G. Larry & Winfree, L. Thomas. Contemporary Corrections. LC 97-44689. (Criminal Justice Ser.). (C). 1997. 60.95 (*0-534-54216-6*) Wadsworth Pub.

Mays, G. Larry, jt. auth. see Champion, Dean J.

Mays, G. Larry, jt. auth. see Rogers, Joseph W.

Mays, G. Larry, jt. ed. see Thompson, Joel A.

Mays, Harriet A. Daring Hearts & Spirits Free: South Carolina Women in the United Methodist Tradition. LC 95-69617. (Illus.). 256p. 1995. 16.95 (*1-881576-53-1*) Providence Hse.

Mays, Harry B. The History of Main Street United Methodist Church, Greenwood, South Carolina. (Illus.). 224p. 1993. 19.95 (*1-881576-09-4*) Providence Hse.

Mays, Howard L. Raising Fishworms with Rabbits: A Profitable Combination... rev. ed. 1999. pap. 8.00 (*0-914116-10-X*) Shields.

Mays, J. C., intro. The Collected Poems of Denis Devlin. 366p. (C). 1989. 63.00 (*0-948268-50-6*, Pub. by Dedalus) St Mut.

Mays, J. C., jt. auth. see Coleridge, Samuel Taylor.

Mays, J. C., ed. see Devlin, Denis.

Mays, James L. Amos: A Commentary. LC 79-76885. (Old Testament Library). 176p. 1996. 21.00 (*0-664-20863-0*) Westminster John Knox.

— Hosea: A Commentary. LC 75-79618. (Old Testament Library). 202p. 1969. 29.95 (*0-664-20871-1*) Westminster John Knox.

— The Lord Reigns: A Theological Handbook of the Psalms. LC 94-10407. (Interpretation Ser.). 228p. (Orig.). 1994. pap. 22.95 (*0-664-25558-2*) Westminster John Knox.

— Micah: A Commentary. LC 76-2599. (Old Testament Library). 180p. 1976. 21.00 (*0-664-20817-7*) Westminster John Knox.

— Psalms. LC 93-32887. (Interpretation, A Bible Commentary for Teaching & Preaching Ser.). 432p. 1994. 31.00 (*0-8042-3115-X*) Westminster John Knox.

Mays, James L., ed. Harper's Bible Commentary. LC 88-45148. 1344p. 1988. 47.50 (*0-06-065541-0*, Pub. by Harper SF) HarpC.

— Interpreting the Gospels. LC 80-8057. 317p. reprint ed. pap. 98.30 (*0-608-17179-4*, 202787200056) Bks Demand.

Mays, James L. & Achtemeier, Paul J., eds. Interpreting the Prophets. LC 86-45223. 304p. 1987. pap. 24.00 (*0-8006-1932-3*, 1-1932, Fortress Pr) Augsburg Fortress.

***Mays, James L. & Gaventa, Beverly Roberts.** HarperCollins Bible Commentary. rev. ed. Society of Biblical Literature Staff, ed. LC 00-20818. 1184p. 2000. 49.50 (*0-06-065548-8*) HarpC.

Mays, James L., et al. Old Testament Interpretation: Past, Present & Future Essays in Honor of Gene M. Tucker. 400p. (Orig.). 1995. pap. 20.00 (*0-687-13871-X*) Dimen for Liv.

Mays, James L., ed. see Clements, Ronald E.

Mays, James L., ed. see Janzen, J. Gerald.

Mays, James L., ed. see Japhet, Sara.

Mays, James L., ed. see Limburg, James.

Mays, James L., ed. see Seitz, Christopher R.

Mays, Jeanne, jt. auth. see Mays, John.

Mays, Jimmy W., jt. ed. see Barth, Howard G.

Mays, John & Mays, Jeanne. Worth Remembering: Ten Year Family Diary. (Illus.). 274p. 1994. 20.00 (*1-880994-22-4*); pap. 20.00 (*1-880994-33-X*) Mt Olive Coll Pr.

Mays, John Barron. Crime & Its Treatment. 2nd ed. LC 76-357144. (Illus.). 173p. 1975. 4.50 (*0-582-48184-8*) Addison-Wesley.

— Crime & Its Treatment. 2nd ed. LC 76-357144. (Aspects of Modern Sociology: the Social Structure of Modern Britain Ser.). 183p. reprint ed. pap. 56.80 (*0-608-18379-2*, 202770800056) Bks Demand.

Mays, John Barron, ed. see Hall, Penelope.

Mays, John Bentley. In the Jaws of the Black Dogs: A Memoir of Depression. LC 99-22461. (Illus.). 256p. 1999. 24.00 (*0-06-019288-7*) HarpC.

Mays, June B. Women's Guide to Financial Self-Defense. LC 96-20081. 176p. (Orig.). 1997. mass mkt. 12.99 (*0-446-67264-5*, Pub. by Warner Bks) Little.

Mays, K. J. The Cinder Road. LC 97-90684. (Illus.). 65p. 1998. mass mkt. 8.95 (*0-533-12456-5*) Vantage.

Mays, Kay J. Recipe Revelation: KJ's Passed down Recipes Forwarded. LC 96-80325. (Illus.). 56p. 1997. 8.95 (*0-9656248-0-3*) K J Mays.

Mays, Ken. Harly Weaver & the Race across America. 128p. (YA). (gr. 6-12). 1994. pap. 9.99 (*0-88092-089-0*) Royal Fireworks.

Mays, Larry, ed. Gangs & Gang Behavior. LC 96-38332. (Criminal Justice). (Orig.). 1997. pap. text 48.95 (*0-8304-1457-6*) Thomson Learn.

Mays, Larry, jt. ed. see Thompson, Joel.

Mays, Larry W. Hydraulic Design Handbook. LC 99-20240. 1999. 125.00 (*0-07-041152-2*) McGraw.

— Optimal Control of Hydrosystems. LC 96-29981. (Illus.). 384p. 1997. text 160.00 (*0-8247-9830-9*) Dekker.

— Water Distribution Systems Handbook. LC 99-16987. (Engineering Handbook Ser.). 912p. 1999. 125.00 (*0-07-134213-3*) McGraw.

***Mays, Larry W.** Water Resources Engineering. 752p. (C). 2000. text. write for info. (*0-471-29783-6*) Wiley.

Mays, Larry W. Water Resources Handbook. 1568p. 1996. 140.00 (*0-07-041150-6*) McGraw.

Mays, Larry W., ed. Reliability Analysis of Water Distribution Systems. 544p. 1989. pap. text 39.00 (*0-87262-712-8*, 712) Am Soc Civil Eng.

Mays, Larry W. & Tung, Yeo-Koung. Hydrosystems Modeling for Engineering & Modeling. 544p. (C). 1991. 87.81 (*0-07-041146-8*) McGraw.

Mays, Larry W., jt. ed. see Chaudhry, M. Hanif.

Mays, Marianne. Exotic Shorthair Cats. 1999. 25.95 (*1-85279-036-9*) TFH Pubns.

***Mays, Marianne.** Factfinder Guide Cats. LC 99-29422. (Factfinder Guides Ser.). (Illus.). 160p. 2000. 12.98 (*1-57145-200-1*, Thunder Bay) Advantage Pubs.

Mays, Marianne. Moggies: A Book for Owners of Non-Pedigree Cats. (Illus.). 128p. 1997. 14.95 (*1-85279-024-5*, GB-011) TFH Pubns.

— Persian Cats. (Illus.). 160p. 1997. 19.95 (*0-7938-0489-2*, GB-005) TFH Pubns.

— Pet Owner's Guide to Rabbits. (Pet Owner's Guide Ser.). 80p. 1997. 8.00 (*0-948955-89-9*, Pub. by Ringpr Bks) Seven Hills Bk.

— The World of Cats. 1999. 12.99 (*0-517-16127-3*) Random Hse Value.

Mays, Marilyn E., ed. The Genetics Revolution: Programs & Issues for the Community College. (Illus.). 188p. 1998. pap. 24.00 (*0-87117-309-3*, 1420) Comm Coll Pr Am Assn Comm Coll.

Mays, Mark & Croake, James W. Treatment of Depression in Managed Care. Sauber, S. Richard, ed. LC 96-36748. (Mental Health Practice under Managed Health Care Ser.: Vol. 7). 256p. 1997. 27.95 (*0-87630-829-9*) Brunner-Mazel.

Mays, Melinda, jt. auth. see Grierson, Philip.

Mays, Michael, jt. ed. see Mackaman, Douglas P.

Mays, Nick. Bunnies as Pets. (Bunnies As Pets). 32p. pap. 1.79 (*0-87666-187-8*) TFH Pubns.

— Proper Care of Fancy Rats. (Illus.). 256p. 1993. 16.95 (*0-86622-340-1*, TW122) TFH Pubns.

— Your First Mouse. (Illus.). 32p. 1995. pap. text 2.29 (*0-7938-0179-6*, YF120) TFH Pubns.

Mays, Osceola & Govenar, Alan. Osceola: Memories of a Sharecropper's Daughter. LC 98-40411. (Illus.). 64p. (J). (gr. 3-7). 2000. 15.99 (*0-7868-0407-6*, Pub. by Disney Pr) Time Warner.

Mays, Osceola, et al. Osceola: Memories of a Sharecropper's Daughter. Govenar, Alan, ed. LC 98-40411. 64p. (J). (gr. 3-7). 2000. lib. bdg. 16.00 (*0-7868-2357-7*, Pub. by Disney Pr) Time Warner.

Mays, Patrick C. & Novitski, B. J. Construction Administration: An Architect's Guide to Surviving Information Overload. LC 96-37130. 168p. 1997. pap. text 69.95 incl. disk (*0-471-15419-9*) Wiley.

Mays, Renee H., jt. auth. see Forrest, Carol J.

Mays, Richard. Mays: Summary Case Procedure in the Sheriff Court. 1995. pap. write for info. (*0-406-04657-3*, MSCP1, MICHIE) LEXIS Pub.

Mays, Richard H. Environmental Law Forms Guide. 2nd ed. LC 94-32775. (Environmental Law Ser.). 1994. write for info. (*0-07-172542-3*) Shepards.

— Environmental Laws: Impact on Business Transactions: A Practice Guide with Forms. 538p. 1992. 98.00 (*0-87179-711-9*) BNA Books.

Mays, Robert E. Laboratory Experiences at USI. 60p. (C). 1995. pap. text 7.21 (*0-89917-468-X*) Tichenor Pub.

Mays, Sandra C. & Driscoll, Michael P. PetVet: Dog First Aid. (Illus.). 105p. (Orig.). 1995. pap. 16.95 (*1-878117-05-X*) Lagumo Corp.

Mays, Simon. The Archaeology of Human Bones. LC 97-15894. (Illus.). 256p. (C). 1998. 100.00 (*0-415-16621-7*); pap. 32.99 (*0-415-17407-4*) Routledge.

Mays, Spike, jt. auth. see Ketteridge, Christopher.

Mays, Sue. Easy Violin Tunes. (Tunebooks Ser.). (Illus.). 64p. (J). (gr. 1-4). 1996. pap. 10.95 (*0-7460-1996-3*, Usborne); lib. bdg. 18.95 (*0-88110-784-0*, Usborne) EDC.

Mays, Terry M. Historical Dictionary of Multinational Peacekeeping. (International Organizations Ser.: No. 9). 388p. 1996. 49.50 (*0-8108-3031-0*) Scarecrow.

— Historical Dictionary of the American Revolution. LC 98-24704. (Historical Dictionaries of War, Revolution, & Civil Unrest Ser.: No. 7). (Illus.). 800p. 1998. 125.00 (*0-8108-3404-9*) Scarecrow.

Mays, Terry M., jt. auth. see DeLancey, Mark W.

***Mays, Vernon.** Office & Work Spaces: Portfolios of 40 Designers. (Illus.). 192p. 1999. 50.00 (*1-56496-581-3*) Rockport Pubs.

Mays, Vickie M., et al, eds. Primary Prevention of AIDS. (Primary Prevention of Psychopathology Ser.: Vol. 13). (Illus.). 400p. (C). 1989. 49.95 (*0-8039-3600-1*) Sage.

Mays, W., tr. see Beth, E. W. & Piaget, J.

Mays, William E. Sublette Revisited: Stability & Change in a Rural Kansas Community After a Quarter of a Century. 142p. 1968. pap. 4.95 (*0-912598-03-4*) Florham.

Mays, Willie. Say Hey: The Autobiography of Willie Mays. (J). 1988. 9.60 (*0-606-04313-6*, Pub. by Turtleback) Demco.

Mays, Wolfe, jt. ed. see Brown, S. C.

Mayse, Susan. Awen: A Novel of Early Medieval Wales. LC 97-28782. (Illus.). 416p. 1997. 35.00 (*0-910055-37-8*) East Wash Univ.

— Earthquake: Surviving the Big One. (Illus.). 192p. 1992. pap. 8.95 (*1-55105-003-X*) Lone Pine.

Mayse, Susan W. Merlin's Web. 368p. 1989. mass mkt. 4.50 (*0-380-70624-5*, Avon Bks) Morrow Avon.

Mayshack, John L. 175 Sermon Outlines. (Sermon Outline Ser.). 60p. 1979. pap. 4.99 (*0-8010-6085-0*) Baker Bks.

Mayson, James. Street Food from Around the World. 1998. pap. text 16.95 (*0-7318-0589-5*) S&S Pub.

Mayson, Cedric. A Certain Sound: The Struggle for Liberation in South Africa. LC 85-13678. 160p. (Orig.). reprint ed. pap. 49.60 (*0-8357-8546-7*, 203488400091) Bks Demand.

***Mayson, Richard.** Port & the Douro. (Illus.). 320p. 2000. pap. 16.00 (*0-571-19522-9*) Faber & Faber.

M

Mayson, Richard. Portugal's Wines & Winemakers: Port Madeira & Regional Wines. (Illus.). 224p. 1997. 34.95 (*0-932664-80-6*, 6679) Wine Appreciation.

— Portugal's Wines & Winemakers: Port, Madeira & Regional Wines. 2nd rev. ed. (Illus.). 250p. 1999. 34.95 (*1-891267-01-9*) Wine Appreciation.

Mayson, Stephen. Making Sense of Law Firms: Strategy, Structure & Ownership. LC 98-128322. 566p. 1997. 84.00 (*1-85431-700-8*, Pub. by Blackstone Pr) Gaunt.

Mayson, Stephen W. Personal Management Skills. 112p. (C). 1992. 31.00 (*1-85431-166-2*, Pub. by Blackstone Pr) Gaunt.

Mayson, Stephen W. & Blake, Susan. Revenue Law, 1992-93. 13th ed. 606p. 1993. pap. 58.00 (*1-85431-226-X*, Pub. by Blackstone Pr) Gaunt.

Mayson, Stephen W., et al. Company Law. 10th ed. 709p. 1994. pap. 54.00 (*1-85431-270-7*, Pub. by Blackstone Pr) Gaunt.

— Company Law, 1992-93. 9th ed. 704p. 1993. pap. 58.00 (*1-85431-225-1*, Pub. by Blackstone Pr) Gaunt.

— Mayson, French & Ryan on Company Law. 13th ed. 709p. 1996. pap. 56.00 (*1-85431-549-8*, Pub. by Blackstone Pr) Gaunt.

— Mayson, French & Ryan on Company Law: 1997-98. 14th ed. 719p. 1998. pap. 56.00 (*1-85431-652-4*, Pub. by Blackstone Pr) Gaunt.

— Mayson, French & Ryan on Company Law, 1998-99. 15th ed. 745p. 1998. pap. 58.00 (*1-85431-758-X*) Gaunt.

***Mayson, Stephen W., et al.** Mayson, French & Ryan on Company Law 1999-2000. 16th ed. 771p. 1999. 49.00 (*1-85431-884-5*, 18417, Pub. by Blackstone Pr) Gaunt.

Mayson, Stephen W., jt. auth. see Blake, Susan.

***Maysonave, Sherry.** Casual Power: How to Power up Your Nonverbal Communication & Dress down for Success. (Illus.). 248p. 1999. 29.95 (*1-880092-48-4*, Pub. by Bright Bks TX) Partners Pubs Grp.

Maysonet. Intermediate Algebra. 312p. 1998. pap. text 25.15 (*0-536-01413-2*) Pearson Custom.

Mayss, Abla & Reed, Alan, Sr. European Business Litigation. LC 98-18644. (European Business Law Library: Vol. 3). 624p. 1998. text 114.95 (*1-85521-687-6*, KJE983.C66M39, Pub. by Ashgate Pub) Ashgate Pub Co.

Mayss, Abla J. Conflict of Laws. (Lecture Notes Ser.). 220p. 1995. pap. write for info. (*1-874241-55-4*, Pub. by Cavendish Pubng) Gaunt.

— Principles of Conflict of Laws. 3rd ed. LC 99-168454. (Principles of Law Ser.). xiii, 464 p. 1998. pap. 32.57 (*1-85941-460-5*, Pub. by Cavendish Pubng) Gaunt.

Mayss, Abla J. & Reed, Alan, Sr. European Business Litigation. LC 98-18644. (European Business Law Library). 1998. pap. 42.95 (*1-85521-691-4*) Ashgate Pub Co.

Maystre, Charles. Les Grands Pretres de Ptah de Memphis. (Orbis Biblicus et Orientalis Ser.: Vol. 113). (FRE.). 456p. 1992. text 96.75 (*3-7278-0794-6*, Pub. by Presses Univ Fribourg) Eisenbrauns.

Maystre, Daniel, ed. Selected Papers on Diffraction Gratings. LC 93-27724. (Milestone Ser.: Vol. MS 83/HC). 1993. 55.00 (*0-8194-1371-2*) SPIE.

— Selected Papers on Diffraction Gratings. LC 93-27724. (Milestone Ser.: Vol. MS83). 1993. pap. 45.00 (*0-8194-1370-4*) SPIE.

Maystre, Daniel, jt. ed. see Dainty, J. C.

Maytag Staff. Maytag Handbook of Good Cooking. Settel, Trudy, ed. (Illus.). (Orig.). 1985. pap. 3.95 (*0-932523-00-5*) Briarcliff Pr.

Mayton, William T., jt. auth. see Aman, Alfred C., Jr.

***Mayuga, Sylvia.** Insight Guide Phillipines. 11th ed. (Illus.). 2000. pap. 23.95 (*0-88729-753-6*, Insight Guides) Langenscheidt.

Mayumi, Kozo, ed. see Georgescu-Roegen, Nicholas & Leontief, Wassily.

Mayur, Rashmi, jt. ed. see Hernandez, Carlos.

Mayur, Rashmi, jt. ed. see Hernandez, Carols.

Mayura. Sanskrit Poems of Mayura. Quackenbos, George P., tr. LC 77-181072. (Columbia University. Indo-Iranian Ser.: No. 9). reprint ed. 39.50 (*0-404-50479-5*) AMS Pr.

Mayuranathan, P. V. The Flowering Plants of Madras City & Its Immediate Neighbourhood. 345p. 1981. 360.00 (*0-7855-3112-2*, Pub. by Intl Bk Distr) St Mut.

— Flowering Plants of Madras City & Its Immediate Neighbourhood. 345p. (C). 1981. text 350.00 (*0-89771-584-5*, Pub. by Intl Bk Distr) St Mut.

Maywald, Henry. Cabins, Crummios & Hacks (And Vans) Vol. 5: Northern North America. (Illus.). 96p. 1997. 33.95 (*1-882608-18-6*) H & M Prods.

— Classic Fitcars Vol. 10: North American Work Trains & Equipment. (Illus.). 64p. 1997. pap. 26.95 (*1-882608-17-8*) H & M Prods.

— Classic FRT Cars Vol. 8: 50 Ft. Boxcars. (Illus.). 64p. (Orig.). 1995. pap. 26.95 (*1-882608-11-9*, 4700) H & M Prods.

Maywald, Henry, ed. Classic Freight Cars Vol. 7: More 40 Ft. Boxcars. (Illus.). 64p. (Orig.). 1994. pap. text 24.95 (*1-882608-08-9*) H & M Prods.

Mayyasi, Kim A. Inside Cellular: An Operating Manual for Dealers, Carriers & Investors. LC 89-9687. iv, 197p. 1989. ring bd. 95.00 (*0-931790-88-3*) Brick Hse Pub.

Mayz, Eusebio, et al. Mercury Poisoning, No. 1. LC 72-13563. (Illus.). 220p. (C). 1972. text 29.50 (*0-8422-7072-8*) Irvington.

Maz, Veronica. Call Me Ruth. LC 94-80006. 98p. 1995. pap. 8.95 (*1-880451-12-3*) Rainbows End.

— Introducing Angel Faux Pearl. LC 94-80007. 97p. 1995. pap. 8.95 (*1-880451-11-5*) Rainbows End.

Maza, E. R. De la, see De la Maza, E. R.

Maza, L. M. De La, see De la Maza, L. M., ed.

Maza, Sara C. Private Lives & Public Affairs: The Causes Celebres of Prerevolutionary France. (Studies on the History of Society & Culture: Vol. 18). (Illus.). 354p. 1995. pap. 17.95 (*0-520-20163-9*, Pub. by U CA Pr) Cal Prin Full Svc.

Maza, Sarah. Private Lives & Public Affairs: The Causes Celebres of Prerevolutionary France. LC 93-4518. (Studies on the History of Society & Culture: No. 18). 354p. 1993. 45.00 (*0-520-08144-7*, Pub. by U CA Pr) Cal Prin Full Svc.

Mazabraud, Andre. Pathology of Bone Tumors: Personal Experience. LC 97-29696. (Illus.). 550p. 1998. 175.00 (*3-540-62751-0*) Spr-Verlag.

***Mazade, Leah.** Analysis of the President's Budgetary Proposals for Fiscal Year 1999. 61p. 1998. pap. 5.50 (*0-16-049518-0*, Congress) USGPO.

— Analysis of the President's Budgetary Proposals for Fiscal Year 2000. 101p. 1999. per. 8.50 (*0-16-049998-4*, Congress) USGPO.

Mazade, Leah, ed. see Pinkston, Elizabeth.

Mazaheri, J. H. Myth & Guilt - Consciousness in Balzac's la Femme de Trente Ans. LC 98-48616. (Studies in French Literature: Vol. 32). 128p. 1999. text 59.95 (*0-7734-8267-9*) E Mellen.

Mazaheri, John Hamayoun. La Satire Demystificatrice de la Bruyere Vol. 8: Essais sur les Caracteres ou les Moeur. (Sociocriticism Ser.). (FRE.). XVI, 132p. (C). 1995. text 42.95 (*0-8204-2873-6*) P Lang Pubng.

Mazal, ed. Aristaeneti. (GRE.). 1971. 59.50 (*3-519-01000-3*, T1000, Pub. by B G Teubner) U of Mich Pr.

Mazal-Cami, Charles. Twenty Thousand Words in Spanish, in Twenty Minutes! LC 91-91298. 198p. (Orig.). (C). 1991. pap. 14.95 (*0-9630572-2-7*) Palabra Pr.

Mazal-Cami, Charles, ed. 20,000 Words in Spanish, in 20 Minutes! 2nd ed. 198p. (Orig.). (C). 1995. pap. 14.95 (*0-9630572-3-5*) Palabra Pr.

Mazal, O., comment. Wiener "Hispana"-Handschrift. fac. ed. (Codices Selecti B Ser.: Vol. XLI). (GER.). 634p. 1974. reprint ed. lthr. 366.00 (*3-201-00831-1*, Pub. by Akademische Druck-und) Balogh.

Mazal, Otto, comment. Josua-Rolle. fac. limited ed. (Codices Selecti A Ser.: Vol. LXXVII). (GRE., Illus.). 90p. 1983. 1661.00 (*3-201-01240-8*, Pub. by Akademische Druck-und) Balogh.

Mazal, Otto, intro. Das Juengere Gebetbuch Karls V. fac. limited ed. (Codices Selecti A Ser.: Vol. XCVI). (GER.). 248p. 1993. 1430.00 (*3-201-01606-3*, Pub. by Akademische Druck-und) Balogh.

Mazalov, V. V., jt. auth. see Petrosjan, L. A.

Mazalov, V. V., jt. ed. see Petrosjan, L. A.

Mazalov, V. V., jt. ed. see Petrosjan, Leon A.

Mazanares, C. La Otra Cara del Paraiso: Verdad/Sectas.Tr. of Other Side of Paradise. (SPA.). 272p. 1995. 7.99 (*1-56063-462-6*, 498442) Editorial Unilit.

Mazancova, E., jt. auth. see Mazanec, K.

Mazanec, Josef A. & Grabler, Klaus. International City Tourism: Analysis & Strategy. LC 96-42574. (Cutting Edge of Tourism Ser.). (Illus.). 256p. 1997. 99.50 (*1-85567-392-4*) Bks Intl VA.

***Mazanec, Josef A. & Strasser, Helmut.** A Nonparametric Approach to Perceptions-Based Market Segmentation: Foundations. LC 00-32194. (Interdisciplinary Studies in Economics & Mangement). 2000. write for info. (*3-211-83473-7*) Spr-Verlag.

Mazanec, K. & Mazancova, E. Physical Metallurgy of Thermomechanical Treatment of Structural Steels. 130p. 1996. pap. 70.00 (*1-898326-43-6*, Pub. by CISP) Balogh.

Mazar, Amihai. Archeology of the Land of the Bible: 10,000-586 B.C.E. 608p. 1992. pap. 29.95 (*0-385-42590-2*) Doubleday.

Mazar, Amihai, jt. auth. see Kelm, George L.

Mazar, Benjamin. Biblical Israel: State & People. Ahituv, Shmuel, ed. 175p. 1992. 25.00 (*965-223-797-3*, Pub. by Magnes Pr) Gefen Bks.

Mazar, Hansan. Requiem for the Earth. LC 98-930694. 232p. 1998. pap. 12.00 (*0-19-577899-5*) OUP.

Mazar, Peter. Clip Art for Year A. (Illus.). 84p. 1992. pap. 25.00 (*0-929650-59-X*, CLIP/A) Liturgy Tr Pubns.

— School Year, Church Year. (Illus.). 180p. 2000. pap. 15.00 (*1-56854-240-2*, DECOR) Liturgy Tr Pubns.

— Take Me Home, Too. (Illus.). 128p. (Orig.). (J). (gr. 1-6). 1997. pap. 15.00 (*1-56854-180-5*, TKHOM2) Liturgy Tr Pubns.

— To Crown the Year: Decorating the Church Through the Seasons. LC 95-6923. (Illus.). 297p. 1995. pap. 19.00 (*1-56854-041-8*, CROWN) Liturgy Tr Pubns.

— Winter: Celebrating the Seaason in a Christian Home. (Illus.). 48p. (Orig.). 1996. pap. 15.00 (*1-56854-134-1*, WINTER) Liturgy Tr Pubns.

Mazar, Peter, et al, eds. A Lent Sourcebook, 2 vols., Set. (Orig.). 1991. pap. 28.00 (*0-929650-36-0*, 2/LENT) Liturgy Tr Pubns.

Mazar, Peter & Piercy, Robert. A Guide to the Lectionary for Masses with Children. 128p. (Orig.). 1994. pap. 8.95 (*1-56854-043-4*, G/LMC) Liturgy Tr Pubns.

Mazar, Peter, ed. see Hynes, Mary E.

Mazar, Sherif. Nostradamus. (SPA., Illus.). 1997. pap. 7.98 (*968-403-789-9*) Selector.

Mazarakis, Helen, ed. Controlling the Complement System for Novel Drug Development. (Biomedical Library). 1997. pap. write for info. (*1-57936-025-4*) IBC USA.

Mazarakis, Helen & Swart, Sarah, eds. Environmental Management Information Systems. (Environmental Library). 536p. 1996. pap. 995.00 (*1-57936-004-1*) IBC USA.

Mazareth, J. L., jt. ed. see Adams, Loyce M.

Mazari, Shehyar, ed. see Mazari, Sherbaz Khan.

Mazari, Sherbaz Khan. A Journey to Disillusionment. Mazari, Shehyar, ed. (Illus.). 650p. 2000. text 45.00 (*0-19-579076-6*) OUP.

Mazaris. Mazaris' Journey to Hades. (Arethusa Monographs: No. 5). xxxviii, 134p. (C). 1975. pap. 8.00 (*0-930881-02-8*) Dept Classics.

Mazarlik, Tom, jt. auth. see Zoffer, David.

Mazaroff, Stanley. Maryland Employment Law. 767p. 1990. 90.00 (*0-87473-658-7*, 64645-10, MICHIE) LEXIS Pub.

— Maryland Employment Law, 1998 Cumulative Supplement. 250p. 1998. write for info. (*0-327-00823-7*, 6464613) LEXIS Pub.

Mazarr, M. Light Forces & the Future of U. S. Military Strategy. (Association of the U. S. Army Book Ser.). (Illus.). 192p. 1990. 34.00 (*0-08-040565-7*, 3980M) Brasseys.

Mazarr, Michael J. North Korea & the Bomb: A Case Study in Nonproliferation. LC 94-34868. 290p. 1995. text 35.00 (*0-312-12443-0*) St Martin.

— North Korea & the Bomb: A Case Study in Nonproliferation. 290p. 1997. pap. 17.95 (*0-312-16455-6*) St Martin.

— Semper Fidel: America & Cuba, 1776-1988. 516p. 1997. reprint ed. text 30.00 (*0-7881-5132-0*) DIANE Pub.

Mazarr, Michael J. & Lennon, Alexander T., eds. Toward a Nuclear Peace: The Future of Nuclear Weapons. LC 93-28019. 227p. 1994. text 45.00 (*0-312-10404-9*) St Martin.

Mazarr, Michael J. & Ram Irez De La O., Rogelio. Mexico, 2005: The Challenge of the New Millennium. LC 98-41066. (Global Trends 2005 Ser.). 192p. (C). 1998. pap. text 21.95 (*0-89206-338-6*) CSIS.

Mazars, J., ed. Cracking & Damage - Strain Localization & Size Effects: Proceedings of the France - U. S. Workshop Held at the Laboratoire de Mechanique et Technolgie, ENS de Cachan, France, 6-9 September 1988. 552p. 1989. mass mkt. 171.95 (*1-85166-347-9*) Elsevier.

Mazas, J. F. Seventy-Five Melodious & Progressive Studies Bk. 1: Violin Opus 36. 44p. 1986. pap. 5.95 (*0-7935-3774-6*) H Leonard.

— Seventy-Five Melodious & Progressive Studies Bk. 3: Violin Opus 36. 52p. 1986. pap. 7.95 (*0-7935-3683-9*) H Leonard.

— Twelve Little Duets Opus 38 Bk. 1: For 2 Violins. 16p. 1986. pap. 7.95 (*0-7935-5450-0*) H Leonard.

Mazat, Alberta. Captivated by Love: Sharing & Enhancing Sexuality in Marriage. 112p. 1996. pap. 8.95 (*1-57847-002-1*) Genl Conf Svnth-day.

Mazauskas, Joan L. Mayday! Mayday! Eastern Airlines in a Tailspin! LC 89-84208. (Illus.). 352p. 1990. pap. 9.95 (*0-9623740-0-8*) Mazauskas Pubns.

Mazawi, Andre E., jt. auth. see Ichilov, Orit.

Mazda, F. F. Analytical Techniques in Telecommunications. LC 96-192448. (Illus.). 310p. 1996. pap. text 32.95 (*0-240-51451-3*, Focal) Buttrwrth-Heinemann.

— Electronics Engineer's Reference Book. 6th ed. LC 98-101702. 1008p. 1997. pap. text 100.00 (*0-7506-0809-9*, Newnes) Buttrwrth-Heinemann.

— Illustrated Dictionary of Telecommunications. LC 99-182429. (Illus.). 704p. 2000. pap. text 50.00 (*0-240-51544-7*, Focal) Buttrwrth-Heinemann.

— Integrated Circuits: Technology & Applications. LC 77-71418. 218p. reprint ed. pap. 62.20 (*0-608-18399-7*, 2030609) Bks Demand.

— Mobile Communications. (Illus.). 350p. 1996. pap. text 32.95 (*0-240-51458-0*, Focal) Buttrwrth-Heinemann.

— Power Electronics Handbook. 3rd ed. LC 98-134644. 448p. 1999. pap. text 54.95 (*0-7506-2926-6*) Buttrwrth-Heinemann.

— Telecommunications Engineer's Reference Book. (Illus.). 1000p. 1993. 135.00 (*0-7506-1162-6*) Buttrwrth-Heinemann.

Mazda, Fraidoon. Engineering Management. LC 97-22139. 1997. pap. text 72.95 (*0-201-17798-6*, Prentice Hall) P-H.

— Packet Communications. (Telecommunication Ser.). (Illus.). 254p. 1996. pap. text 32.95 (*0-240-51455-6*, Focal) Buttrwrth-Heinemann.

— Principles of Radio Communication. LC 96-213594. (Telecommunication Ser.). (Illus.). 270p. 2000. pap. text 32.95 (*0-240-51457-2*, Focal) Buttrwrth-Heinemann.

— Switching Systems & Applications. (Telecommunication Ser.). (Illus.). 288p. 1996. pap. text 32.95 (*0-240-51456-4*, Focal) Buttrwrth-Heinemann.

— Telecommunication Networks. (Telecommunication Ser.). (Illus.). 314p. 2000. pap. text 32.95 (*0-240-51454-8*, Focal) Buttrwrth-Heinemann.

— Telecommunication Transmission Principles. (Telecommunication Ser.). (Illus.). 342p. 1996. pap. text 32.95 (*0-240-51452-1*, Focal) Buttrwrth-Heinemann.

Mazda, Fraidoon, ed. Telecommunications Engineer's Reference Book. 2nd ed. LC 98-25186. (Illus.). 1216p. 1998. text 150.00 (*0-240-51491-2*, Newnes) Buttrwrth-Heinemann.

Mazda, Maideh. In a Persian Kitchen: Favorite Recipes from the Near East. LC 60-6926. (Illus.). 176p. 1960. pap. 12.95 (*0-8048-1619-0*) Tuttle Pubng.

Mazdiyasni, K. S., ed. Fiber-Reinforced Ceramic Composites: Materials, Processing & Technology. LC 89-70989. (Illus.). 515p. 1990. 139.00 (*0-8155-1233-3*) Noyes.

Maze, C. Norman Glossary: Glossaire Normand. (FRE.). 124p. 1984. pap. 39.95 (*0-8288-1716-2*, F52940) Fr & Eur.

Maze, Carol M. Mexican Microwave Cookery. Lark, Virginia & Medina, Robert C., eds. LC 84-72508. 116p. (Orig.). 1984. pap. text 6.00 (*0-933196-03-2*) Bilingue Pubns.

Maze, Deborah, jt. auth. see Lewis, C. S.

Maze, Dessie L., ed. see Michelson, Maureen R.

Maze, John, jt. auth. see White, Graham.

Maze, John R. Virginia Woolf: Feminism, Creativity & the Unconscious, 84. LC 97-5857. (Contributions to the Study of World Literature Ser.: Vol. 84). 232p. 1997. 55.00 (*0-313-30283-9*, Greenwood Pr) Greenwood.

Maze, Lori, ed. Insurance Settlement Handbook. 1990. ring bd. 129.00 (*0-938065-53-X*) James Pub Santa Ana.

Maze, Lori L., ed. California Causes of Action. 1998. write for info. (*1-58012-027-X*) James Pub Santa Ana.

Maze, Marilyn, et al. The Enhanced Guide for Occupational Exploration: Descriptions for the 2,500 Most Important Jobs. 2nd rev. ed. LC 91-8830. 608p. 1991. pap. 29.95 (*1-56370-207-X*, EGOE) JIST Works.

— The Enhanced Guide for Occupational Exploration: Descriptions for the 2,800 Most Important Jobs. 2nd ed. 704p. 1995. 44.95 (*1-56370-244-4*, J2444) JIST Works.

Maze-Sencier, Genevieve. Dictionnaire des Matechaux de France du Moyen Age a nos Jours. (FRE.). 452p. 1988. 115.00 (*0-7859-8637-5*, 226200546x) Fr & Eur.

***Maze, Stephanie.** Dancer. LC 96-21839. (I Want to Be ... Ser.). (Illus.). 48p. (J). (gr. 4-7). 2000. 16.00 (*0-7398-1104-5*) Raintree Steck-V.

— Fashion Designer. (I Want to Be ... Ser.). (Illus.). 48p. (J). (gr. 4-7). 2000. 27.11 (*0-7398-1970-4*) Raintree Steck-V.

— Firefighter. (I Want to Be ... Ser.). (J). 2000. 27.12 (*0-7398-1365-X*) Raintree Steck-V.

— I Want to Be... 1999. 71.92 (*0-7398-0997-0*) Raintree Steck-V.

— I Want to Be a Chef. (I Want to Be ... Ser.). (Illus.). 48p. (gr. 4-9). 1999. 27.12 (*0-8172-6373-X*) Raintree Steck-V.

Maze, Stephanie. I Want to Be a Dancer. LC 96-21839. (I Want to Be...Bks.). (Illus.). 48p. (J). (gr. 7). 1997. 16.00 (*0-15-201299-0*) Harcourt.

***Maze, Stephanie.** I Want to Be a Dancer. 48p. (J). 1999. pap. 9.00 (*0-15-202108-6*, Harcourt Child Bks) Harcourt.

— I Want to Be a Dancer. (Illus.). (J). 1999. 14.45 (*0-606-18176-8*) Turtleback.

Maze, Stephanie. I Want to Be a Fashion Designer. LC 98-38506. 48p. (J). (gr. 3-7). 2000. pap. 9.00 (*0-15-201938-3*, Harcourt Child Bks) Harcourt.

— I Want to Be a Fashion Designer. LC 98-38506. (Illus.). 48p. (J). (gr. 3-7). 2000. 18.00 (*0-15-201863-8*, Harcourt Child Bks) Harcourt.

***Maze, Stephanie.** I Want to Be a Fashion Designer. (I Want to Be Ser.). (Illus.). (J). 2000. 14.45 (*0-606-18177-6*) Turtleback.

Maze, Stephanie. I Want to Be a Firefighter. LC 98-8270. 47p. (J). (gr. 4-6). 1999. 18.00 (*0-15-201865-4*, Harcourt Child Bks); pap. 9.00 (*0-15-201937-5*, Harcourt Child Bks) Harcourt.

Maze, Stephanie. I Want to Be a Vet: Discover. 1997. 16.00 (*0-15-201871-9*) Harcourt.

Maze, Stephanie. I Want to Be an Astronaut. LC 96-17481. (I Want to Be ... Ser.). (Illus.). 48p. (gr. 4-9). 1999. 25.69 (*0-8172-4159-0*) Raintree Steck-V.

***Maze, Stephanie.** I Want to Be an Engineer. 48p. (J). 1999. pap. 9.00 (*0-15-202109-4*, Harcourt Child Bks) Harcourt.

— I Want to Be an Engineer. LC 96-26982. (Illus.). 48p. (gr. 4-9). 1999. 16.00 (*0-8172-4160-4*) Raintree Steck-V.

— I Want to Be an Engineer. (Illus.). (J). 1999. 14.45 (*0-606-18178-4*) Turtleback.

— I Want to Be an Environmentalist. LC 98-52397. (I Want to Be...Bks.). 48p. (J). (gr. 4-7). 2000. 18.00 (*0-15-201862-X*, Harcourt Child Bks) Harcourt.

— I Want to Be an Environmentalist. (I Want to Be... Ser.). 2000. 27.11 (*0-7398-3071-6*) Raintree Steck-V.

Maze, Stephanie. I Want to Be an Veterinarian. (I Want to Be ... Ser.). (Illus.). 48p. (gr. 4-9). 1999. 25.69 (*0-8172-6374-8*) Raintree Steck-V.

Maze, Stephanie, creator. I Want to Be a Chef. LC 98-3906. (Illus.). 48p. (J). 1999. 17.00 (*0-15-201864-6*); pap. 9.00 (*0-15-201936-7*) Harcourt.

***Maze, Stephanie, creator.** I Want to Be a Veterinarian. LC 96-215. (Illus.). 48p. (J). 1999. pap. 9.00 (*0-15-201965-0*) Harcourt.

Maze, Stephanie, creator. I Want to Be an Astronaut. LC 96-17481. (Illus.). 48p. (J). 1999. pap. 9.00 (*0-15-201966-9*) Harcourt.

Maze, Stephanie & Grace, Catherine O. I Want to Be an Astronaut. LC 96-17481. (I Want to Be...Bks.). (Illus.). 48p. (J). 1997. 16.00 (*0-15-201300-8*) Harcourt.

— I Want to Be an Engineer. LC 96-26982. (I Want to Be...Bks.). (Illus.). 48p. (J). (gr. 3-5). 1997. 16.00 (*0-15-201298-2*) Harcourt.

— I Want to Be an Environmentalist. LC 98-52397. (I Want to Be...Bks.). 48p. (gr. 4-7). 2000. pap. 9.00 (*0-15-201939-1*, Harcourt Child Bks) Harcourt.

Maze, Susan, et al. Neal-Schuman Authoritative Guide to Web Search Engines: Policies, Templates & Icons for Library Web Pages; Training Modules for Library Staff & Patrons. LC 97-14805. 178p. 1997. 55.00 (*1-55570-305-4*) Neal-Schuman.

Maze, T. H., jt. ed. see Maggio, Margk.

Mazel, Charles. Heave Ho: My Little Green Book of Seasickness. (J). 1992. pap. 7.95 (*0-07-041165-4*) McGraw.

— Heave Ho! My Little Green Book of Seasickness. (Illus.). xii, 116p. 1996. reprint ed. pap. 9.95 (*0-9641887-1-6*) Bernel Bks.

— Side Scan Sonar Record Interpretation. 146p. 1985. 48.95 (*0-932146-50-3*) Peninsula CA.

***Mazel, David.** American Literary Environmentalism. LC 99-43730. 240p. 2000. 40.00 (*0-8203-2180-X*) U of Ga Pr.

— A Century of Early Ecocriticism. LC 00-30216. 2001. pap. write for info. (*0-8203-2222-9*) U of Ga Pr.

Mazel, David. My Heart's World: Stories by David Mazel. Adam-Casimiro, Niki, ed. & illus. by. LC 84-62148. 144p. 1985. pap. 9.95 (*0-931762-02-2*) Phunn Pubs.

An Asterisk (*) at the beginning of an entry indicates that the title is appearing for the first time.

*Mazel, David. Pioneering Ascents: The Origins of Climbing. 255p. 1998. 14.00 (0-915746-83-2) Potomac Appalach.

Mazel, David, ed. Mountaineering Women: Stories by Early Climbers. LC 94-11260. (Illus.). 200p. 1994. pap. 14.95 (0-89096-617-6) Tex A&M Univ Pr.

— Mountaineering Women: Stories by Early Climbers. LC 94-11260. (Illus.). 200p. 1994. 27.50 (0-89096-616-8) Tex A&M Univ Pr.

Mazel, David & Blake, Robert. Southern Arizona Trails. 4th rev. ed. LC 97-42410. (Illus.). 268p. 1998. pap. 14.95 (0-89997-216-0) Wilderness Pr.

Mazel, Ella, selected by. Ahead of Her Time: A Sampler of the Life & Thought of Mary Wollstonecraft. (Women's Studies: No. 17). (Illus.). 136p. (Orig.). 1995. pap. 10.95 (0-9641887-3-2) Bernel Bks.

Mazel, Henry F. Murderously Incorrect. LC 98-93489. 208p. 1999. pap. 12.95 (0-9665899-0-4) Crime & Again.

*Mazel, Joe. Inventory Reduction Report 2000 Yearbook. Solomon, David, ed. (Illus.). 200p. 1999. pap. 199.00 (1-58673-016-9) IOMA.

— Supplier Selection & Management Report 2000 Yearbook. Solomon, David, ed. (Illus.). 200p. 1999. pap. 199.00 (1-58673-015-0) IOMA.

Mazel, Judy. Beverly Hills Diet. 1981. 10.95 (0-02-582600-X) Macmillan.

— The Beverly Hills Diet. 1994. reprint ed. lib. bdg. 29.95 (1-56849-542-0) Buccaneer Bks.

— The New Beverly Hills Diet: Born Again Skinny. 320p. (Orig.). 1996. 24.00 (1-55874-431-2, 4258) Health Comm.

— The New Beverly Hills Diet: Born Again Skinny. rev. ed. 250p. (Orig.). 1996. pap. 12.95 (1-55874-425-8, 4258) Health Comm.

— The New Beverly Hills Diet: Little Skinny Companion. LC 97-3330. 64p. 1997. pap. 4.95 (1-55874-476-2) Health Comm.

— The New Beverly Hills Diet: Recipes to Forever. LC 97-3323. 200p. 1997. pap. 9.95 (1-55874-475-4) Health Comm.

— The New Beverly Hills Diet Slim Kit, Set. unabridged ed. 40p. 1998. 24.95 incl. audio (1-55874-650-1) Health Comm.

*Mazel, Judy & Monaco, John E. Slim & Fit Kids: Raising Healthy Children in a Fast-Food World. LC 99-44490. 250p. 1999. pap. 12.95 (1-55874-729-X) Health Comm.

Mazelev, L. Ye. Borate Glasses: Thermochemical Processes in Glass Formation, Crystallo-Optics, Technology, Physicochemical Properties, & Structure of Glasses with the Composition B203-Li20-MeO. LC 60-8719. 159p. reprint ed. pap. 49.30 (0-8357-7349-3, 205579900038) Bks Demand.

Mazen, Barbara S. Pass the Cheese, Please! (Whole-Language Big Bks.). (Illus.). 16p. (Orig.). (J). (ps-2). 1994. pap. 16.95 (1-56784-057-4) Newbridge Educ.

Mazen, Thomas L., jt. auth. see Ratner, David L.

*Mazenko. Field Theory. 300p. (C). 2000. write for info. (0-471-32842-1) Wiley.

Mazenko. Nonequilibrium. 300p. (C). 2000. write for info. (0-471-32841-3) Wiley.

Mazenko, G., jt. ed. see Grinstein, G.

*Mazenko, Gene F. Equilibrium Statistical Mechanics. 640p. 2000. 105.00 (0-471-32839-1) Wiley.

Mazenod, Lucienne. Dictionnaire des Femmes Celebres. (FRE.). 940p. 1992. pap. 59.95 (0-7859-7803-8, 2221052927) Fr & Eur.

Mazepa, S. C. Mazepa the Cossack: Mazepa Hetman of the Ukraine. (Illus.). 250p. 19.95 (0-9636099-0-4) S C Mazepa.

Mazer. Anthology of Drama. 2nd ed. (C). 1996. pap. text, teacher ed. 28.00 (0-15-502169-9) Harcourt Coll Pubs.

Mazer, Ann. 101 Dalmatians. (J). 1996. pap. 3.95 (0-7868-4140-0, Pub. by Disney Pr) Little.

Mazer, Anne. The Accidental Witch. LC 94-44284. (Illus.). 128p. (J). (gr. 3-7). 1995. 13.89 (0-7868-2073-X, Pub. by Hyprn Child) Little.

*Mazer, Anne. Declaration of Independence. (Amazing Days of Abby Hayes Ser.: Vol. 2). (Illus.). 144p. (J). (gr. 3-7). 2000. pap. 4.50 (0-439-17876-2) Scholastic Inc.

— Every Cloud Has a Silver Lining. (Amazing Days of Abby Hayes Ser.). (Illus.). 144p. (J). (gr. 3-7). 2000. pap. 4.50 (0-439-14977-0) Scholastic Inc.

Mazer, Anne. The Fixits. LC 96-13599. (Illus.). 24p. (J). (ps-3). 1999. 12.99 (0-7868-0213-8, Pub. by Hyprn Child); lib. bdg. 13.89 (0-7868-2202-3, Pub. by Hyprn Child) Time Warner.

— Goldfish Charlie & the Case of the Missing Planet. LC 96-229092. (Illus.). 80p. (Orig.). (J). (gr. 1-4). 1996. pap. 2.95 (0-8167-4141-7) Troll Communs.

— A Kid in King Arthur's Court: Junior Novelization. LC 95-70037. (Illus.). 112p. (J). (gr. 2-6). 1995. pap. 4.95 (0-7868-4069-2, Pub. by Disney Pr) Time Warner.

*Mazer, Anne. The No-Nothings & Their Baby. (Illus.). 40p. (J). (ps-3). 2000. 15.95 (0-590-68049-8, Apple Classics) Scholastic Inc.

Mazer, Anne. 101 Dalmatians Junior Novelization. (Illus.). 96p. (J). (gr. 2-6). 1996. pap. 3.95 (0-7868-4101-X, Pub. by Disney Pr) Little.

— 101 Dalmatians: Special Collectors' Edition. LC 96-85929. 96p. (J). 1996. lib. bdg. 14.89 (0-7868-5045-0, Pub. by Disney Pr) Little.

— The Oxboy. 112p. (YA). (gr. 10 up). 1999. reprint ed. pap. 6.95 (0-89255-240-9) Persea Bks.

— The Salamander Room. LC 90-33301. (Illus.). 32p. (J). (ps-3). 1991. 17.00 (0-394-82945-X, Pub. by Knopf Bks Yng Read); lib. bdg. 17.99 (0-394-92945-4, Pub. by Knopf Bks Yng Read) Random.

— The Salamander Room. (Dragonfly Bks.). (Illus.). 32p. (J). (ps-3). 1994. pap. 6.99 (0-679-86187-4, Pub. by Knopf Bks Yng Read) Random.

Mazer, Anne. The Salamander Room. 1994. 12.19 (0-606-07075-3, Pub. by Turtleback) Demco.

Mazer, Anne. A Sliver of Glass & Other Uncommon Tales. LC 95-45992. (Illus.). 80p. (J). (gr. 4-7). 1996. 13.95 (0-7868-0197-2, Pub. by Hyprn Child); lib. bdg. 13.89 (0-7868-2165-5, Pub. by Hyprn Child) Little.

*Mazer, Anne, ed. A Walk in My World: International Short Stories about Youth. 224p. (YA). (gr. 8-12). 2000. pap. 8.95 (0-89255-249-2, Pub. by Persea Bks) Norton.

Mazer, Anne, ed. Working Days: Stories about Teenagers & Work. LC 96-50243. 224p. (YA). (gr. 7-12). 1997. 18.95 (0-89255-223-9); pap. 7.95 (0-89255-224-7) Persea Bks.

Mazer, Anne, ed. A Walk in My World: International Short Stories about Youth. 240p. 1998. 16.95 (0-89255-237-9) Persea Bks.

Mazer, Anne, intro. America Street: A Multicultural Anthology of Stories. (YA). 1993. 14.95 (0-89255-190-9); pap. 6.95 (0-89255-191-7) Persea Bks.

— Going Where I'm Coming From: Memoirs of American Youth. (YA). (gr. 6 up). 1995. 15.95 (0-89255-205-0); pap. 6.95 (0-89255-206-9) Persea Bks.

Mazer, Ben. White Cities. LC 95-75261. (Illus.). 52p. (Orig.). 1995. pap. 10.00 (0-9645516-0-8) B Matteau.

Mazer, Bill. Bill Mazer's Amazin' Baseball Book. 1990. 19.95 (0-8217-2947-0, Zebra Kensgtn) Kensgtn Pub Corp.

Mazer, Bill & Fischler, Stanley I. The Amazin' Bill Mazer's Football Trivia Book. 160p. (Orig.). 1981. mass mkt. 2.50 (0-446-91784-2, Pub. by Warner Bks) Little.

Mazer, Harry. The Dog in the Freezer. LC 96-44833. 160p. (J). (gr. 3-7). 1997. mass mkt. 16.00 (0-689-80753-8) S&S Childrens.

— The Dog in the Freezer. LC 96-44833. 176p. (J). (gr. 3-7). 1998. per. 4.50 (0-689-80754-6) S&S Childrens.

— The Girl of His Dreams. 1988. pap. 2.95 (0-380-70599-0, Avon Bks) Morrow Avon.

— Hey Kid! Does She Love Me? 176p. 1986. pap. 2.95 (0-380-70025-5, Avon Bks) Morrow Avon.

— I Love You, Stupid! 192p. (J). 1983. pap. 3.50 (0-380-61432-4, Avon Bks) Morrow Avon.

— The Island Keeper. 176p. (YA). (gr. k-12). 1982. mass mkt. 3.99 (0-440-94774-X, LLL BDD) BDD Bks Young Read.

— Island Keeper. 1981. 8.95 (0-440-03976-2) Dell.

Mazer, Harry. Island Keeper. (Laurel-Leaf Contemporary Fiction Ser.). (J). 1981. 9.09 (0-606-04114-1, Pub. by Turtleback) Demco.

Mazer, Harry. The Last Mission. LC 79-50674. 192p. (YA). (gr. 7 up). 1981. mass mkt. 4.99 (0-440-94797-9, LE) Dell.

Mazer, Harry. The Last Mission. 192p. (YA). (gr. 7 up). pap. 4.99 (0-8072-1366-7) Listening Lib.

Mazer, Harry. Last Mission. (Laurel-Leaf Historical Fiction Ser.). 1979. 9.60 (0-606-02154-X, Pub. by Turtleback) Demco.

— Snow Bound. 144p. (YA). (gr. 5 up). 1974. mass mkt. 4.99 (0-440-96134-3, LLL BDD) BDD Bks Young Read.

Mazer, Harry. Snow Bound. 144p. (YA). (gr. 7 up). pap. 4.99 (0-8072-1367-5) Listening Lib.

Mazer, Harry. Snow Bound. 1987. 19.50 (0-8446-6240-2) Peter Smith.

— Snow Bound. 1973. 9.60 (0-606-04924-X, Pub. by Turtleback) Demco.

— Twelve Shots: Outstanding Short Stories about Guns. (J). 1998. 10.09 (0-606-13880-3, Pub. by Turtleback) Demco.

— Twelve Shots: Stories about Guns. 1997. mass mkt. 15.95 (0-385-44698-5) Doubleday.

— When the Phone Rang. 192p. (YA). (gr. 7-9). 1986. pap. 4.50 (0-590-44773-4) Scholastic Inc.

— Who Eddie Leonard? (J). 1994. mass mkt. 4.99 (0-440-91034-X) BDD Bks Young Read.

Mazer, Harry. Who Is Eddie Leonard? (J). 1995. 9.09 (0-606-08379-0, Pub. by Turtleback) Demco.

*Mazer, Harry. The Wild Kid. (Illus.). 112p. (YA). (gr. 5-8). 2000. per. 4.50 (0-689-82289-8) Aladdin.

Mazer, Harry. The Wild Kid. LC 97-42578. 112p. (YA). (gr. 5-8). 1998. per. 15.00 (0-689-80751-1) S&S Childrens.

Mazer, Harry, ed. Twelve Shots: Outstanding Short Stories about Guns. 240p. (YA). 1998. mass mkt. 4.99 (0-440-22002-5) BDD Bks Young Read.

Mazer, Harvey, jt. ed. see Rako, Susan.

Mazer, Jeffrey A. Solar Cells: An Introduction to Crystalline Photovoltaic Technology. LC 96-34491. 240p. (C). 1996. text 145.00 (0-7923-9808-4) Kluwer Academic.

Mazer, Milton. People & Predicaments. (Illus.). 332p. 1976. 29.50 (0-674-66075-7) HUP.

Mazer, Norma F. After the Rain. LC 86-33270. 304p. (YA). (gr. 7 up). 1987. 16.00 (0-688-06867-7, Wm Morrow) Morrow Avon.

— After the Rain. large type ed. 408p. (YA). (gr. 7 up). 1989. 15.95 (0-8161-4807-4, G K Hall Lrg Type) Mac Lib Ref.

— Babyface. LC 90-6485. 176p. (YA). (gr. 7 up). 1991. mass mkt. 4.50 (0-380-75720-6, Avon Bks) Morrow Avon.

— Bright Days, Stupid Nights. (YA). 1993. pap. 3.50 (0-553-56253-3) Bantam.

— C My Name Is Cal. 144p. (YA). 1990. pap. 2.95 (0-685-49598-1, Point) Scholastic Inc.

— C, My Name Is Cal. 144p. (J). (gr. 4-6). 1991. pap. 2.95 (0-590-41832-7) Scholastic Inc.

— C, My Name Is Cal. (J). 1990. 8.05 (0-606-00333-9, Pub. by Turtleback) Demco.

— Crazy Fish. LC 98-10587. 192p. (YA). (gr. 5-9). 1998. 15.00 (0-688-16281-9, Wm Morrow) Morrow Avon.

— Crazy Fish. LC 98-10578. 160p. (J). (gr. 4-7). 1999. mass mkt. 4.50 (0-380-73189-4, Avon Bks) Morrow Avon.

— D, My Name Is Danita. 176p. (J). (gr. 4-6). 1991. 13.95 (0-590-43655-4) Scholastic Inc.

— Downtown. 208p. 1984. mass mkt. 4.50 (0-380-88534-4, Avon Bks) Morrow Avon.

*Mazer, Norma F. Girlhearts. (J). 2001. 15.95 (0-688-13350-9, Wm Morrow); lib. bdg. 15.89 (0-688-06866-9) Morrow Avon.

Mazer, Norma F. Missing Pieces. LC 94-39271. (Illus.). 208p. (YA). (gr. 7 up). 1995. 16.00 (0-688-13349-5, Wm Morrow) Morrow Avon.

— Missing Pieces. 144p. (YA). (gr. 7 up). 1996. mass mkt. 4.50 (0-380-72289-5, Avon Bks) Morrow Avon.

— Mrs. Fish, Ape, & Me, the Dump Queen. 144p. (J). (gr. 4 up). 1981. pap. 3.50 (0-380-69153-1, Avon Bks) Morrow Avon.

— Out of Control. LC 92-32516. 224p. (YA). (gr. 7 up). 1993. 16.00 (0-688-10208-5, Wm Morrow) Morrow Avon.

— Out of Control. LC 92-32516. 224p. (YA). (gr. 7 up). 1994. mass mkt. 4.99 (0-380-71347-0, Avon Bks) Morrow Avon.

— Silver. LC 88-18652. 272p. (YA). (gr. 7 up). 1988. 16.00 (0-688-06865-0, Wm Morrow) Morrow Avon.

— Silver. LC 88-18652. 208p. (YA). (gr. 7-12). 1989. mass mkt. 4.99 (0-380-75026-0, Avon Bks) Morrow Avon.

— Silver. (J). 1988. 9.60 (0-606-04325-X, Pub. by Turtleback) Demco.

— Solid Gold Kid: A Novel. (J). 1977. 9.09 (0-606-04328-4, Pub. by Turtleback) Demco.

— Someone to Love. 256p. (J). (gr. k-12). 1985. mass mkt. 3.25 (0-440-98062-3, LLL BDD) BDD Bks Young Read.

— Taking Terri Mueller. LC 81-65081. 192p. (YA). (gr. 7-12). 1981. mass mkt. 4.50 (0-380-79004-1, Avon Bks) Morrow Avon.

— Taking Terri Mueller. (Avon/Flare Bks.). (J). 1996. 10.25 (0-606-00593-5, Pub. by Turtleback) Demco.

— When She Was Good. LC 96-35532. 240p. (J). (gr. 7). 2000. 4.99 (0-590-13506-6) Scholastic Inc.

— When She Was Good. LC 96-35532. (Illus.). 240p. (YA). (gr. 7-12). 2000. pap. 4.99 (0-590-31990-6, Pub. by Scholastic Inc) Penguin Putnam.

Mazer, Norma F., et al. Courage: How We Face Challenges. (Target Ser.). 160p. (Orig.). (J). (ps-1). 1996. pap. text 11.95 (0-8167-4274-X) Troll Communs.

— When I Was Your Age: Original Stories about Growing Up, Vol. 2. Erlich, Amy, ed. LC 95-4820. (Illus.). 192p. (YA). (gr. 4-9). 1999. 16.99 (0-7636-0407-0, Pub. by Candlewick Pr) Penguin Putnam.

Mazer, Norma Fox. After the Rain. 1987. 9.60 (0-606-03541-9, Pub. by Turtleback) Demco.

Mazer, Norma Fox. After the Rain. LC 86-33270. 256p. (gr. 7-12). 1987. reprint ed. mass mkt. 4.99 (0-380-75025-2, Avon Bks) Morrow Avon.

— Babyface. 1991. 9.60 (0-606-04870-7, Pub. by Turtleback) Demco.

Mazer, Norma Fox. Bright Days, Stupid Nights. 1992. 9.09 (0-606-05172-4, Pub. by Turtleback) Demco.

— Downtown. 1984. 9.60 (0-606-03356-4, Pub. by Turtleback) Demco.

— Good Night, Maman. LC 98-49220. 192p. (J). (gr. 4-7). 1999. 16.00 (0-15-201468-3, Harcourt Child Bks) Harcourt.

— Missing Pieces. 1996. 9.60 (0-606-09620-5, Pub. by Turtleback) Demco.

Mazer, Norma Fox. Out of Control. LC 92-32516. 1993. 9.60 (0-606-06652-7, Pub. by Turtleback) Demco.

Mazer, Norma Fox. Victory at Last. 2002. write for info. (0-15-201462-4) Harcourt.

*Mazer, Renee. Not Too Scary Vocabulary, Vol. 1. abr. ed. (YA). (gr. 9 up). 1999. pap. Price not set. incl. audio (0-9664845-0-9, Pub. by High Score) Penton Overseas.

Mazer, Sharon. Professional Wrestling: Sport & Spectacle. LC 97-42266. (Performance Studies Ser.). (Illus.). 192p. 1998. 45.00 (1-57806-020-6); pap. 18.00 (1-57806-021-4) U Pr of Miss.

Mazer, Susan, et al. Sound Choices: Using Music to Design the Environments in Which You Live, Work & Heal. LC 99-31742. 240p. 1999. pap. 16.95 incl. audio compact disk (1-56170-569-1, 577) Hay House.

Mazer, William M. Electrical Accident Investigation Handbook: Includes 1983-96 Supplements. LC 82-72167. (Illus.). 1300p. (C). 1996. 290.00 (0-943890-03-9, NA) Electrodata.

— Electrical Accident Investigation Handbook: 1983 Supplement. LC 82-72167. (Illus.). 100p. 1983. ring bd. write for info. (0-943890-04-7) Electrodata.

— Electrical Accident Investigation Handbook: 1984 Supplement. LC 82-72167. (Illus.). 150p. 1984. ring bd. 45.00 (0-943890-05-5) Electrodata.

— Electrical Accident Investigation Handbook: 1985 Supplement. LC 82-72167. (Illus.). 175p. 1985. ring bd. 55.00 (0-943890-06-3) Electrodata.

— Electrical Accident Investigation Handbook: 1986 Supplement. LC 82-72167. (Illus.). 200p. 1987. ring bd. 60.00 (0-943890-07-1) Electrodata.

— Electrical Accident Investigation Handbook: 1996 Supplement. 350p. 1996. ring bd., suppl. ed. 70.00 (0-943890-10-1) Electrodata.

— The Electrical Accident Investigation Handbook, 1987: 1987 Supplement. 300p. (C). 1990. ring bd., suppl. ed. 65.00 (0-943890-08-X) Electrodata.

Mazerolle, jt. auth. see Piquero.

Mazerolle, Lorraine G., ed. Civil Remedies & Crime Prevention. (Crime Prevention Studies: No. 9). (Illus.). 220p. 1998. text 47.50 (1-881798-12-7, Criminal Justice) Willow Tree NY.

*Mazerolle, Lorraine Green & Roehl, Jan, eds. Civil Remedies & Crime Prevention. (Crime Prevention Studies: Vol. 9). (Illus.). 350p. 1999. reprint ed. pap. text 37.50 (1-881798-19-4, Pub. by Willow Tree NY) Lib Res.

Mazey, Mary E., et al. Her Space, Her Place: A Geography of Women. LC 83-22289. (Resource Publications in Geography). 90p. (C). 1983. pap. text 15.00 (0-89291-172-7) Assn Am Geographers.

Mazey, Sonia & Newman, Michael, eds. Mitterrand's France. 256p. 1987. lib. bdg. 67.50 (0-7099-4648-1, Pub. by C Helm) Routldge.

Mazey, Sonia & Richardson, Jeremy J., eds. Lobbying in the European Community. (Nuffield European Studies, New Ser.). (Illus.). 278p. 1993. text 55.00 (0-19-827789-X) OUP.

Mazey, Sonia, jt. ed. see Loughlin, John.

Mazey, Sonia, jt. ed. see Rhodes, Carolyn.

Mazgaj, Marian S. Visiting Home in Poland after 33 Years & World War II True Stories. 188p. 1996. pap. 14.95 (0-87012-561-3) McClain.

For over thirty-three years, Father Marian S. Mazgaj lived with joyful & often painful memories of his early years growing up in Poland. His experiences with the people of this colorful land are captured in the pages of the premier release of VISITING HOME IN POLAND AFTER 33 YEARS & WORLD WAR II TRUE STORIES. Join Father Mazgaj as he reminisces about his return trip to his homeland & the memories it stirred of a time when the world was filled with destruction & hate, yet reigned supreme with love & strength. This 188-page paperbound book is filled with stories relative to those who have experienced similar ordeals in their lifetime & those who wish to learn of the true times during this era.
Publisher Paid Annotation.

M

Mazgaj, Paul. The Action Francaise & Revolutionary Syndicalism. LC 79-4229. 293p. reprint ed. pap. 90.90 (0-8357-4422-1, 203724200008) Bks Demand.

*Mazgalev, Todor N. & Tchou, Patrick J., eds. Atrial-AV Nodal Electrophysiology: A View from the Millennium. (Illus.). 528p. 2000. 130.00 (0-87993-461-1) Futura Pub.

*Mazi, Zef. Albanian Phasebook. (ALB.). 1999. pap. 9.95 (0-7818-0791-3) Hippocrene Bks.

Mazia, V. G. & Shaposhnikova, T. O. The Life & Work of Jacques Hadamard. LC 97-36357. (History of Mathematics Ser.). 574p. 1998. text 79.00 (0-8218-0841-9) Am Math.

Mazian, Florence. Why Genocide? The Armenian & Jewish Experiences in Perspective. LC 89-15268. 306p. 1990. reprint ed. pap. 94.90 (0-608-00182-1, 206096400006) Bks Demand.

*Maziana, Peter, et al. Better Information Practices, Vol. 6. 144p. 2000. pap. 16.95 (0-85092-582-7, Pub. by Comm Sec) Stylus Pub VA.

Maziar, A., tr. see Trakl, Georg.

Maziarka, Cynthia, ed. see Hemingway, Ernest.

*Maziasz, Philip J., et al, eds. Gas Turbine Materials Technology: Conference Proceedings from ASM Materials Solutions, Rosemont, IL, 12-15 October 1998. LC 99-73476. 144p. 1999. 110.00 (0-87170-628-8, 06679G) ASM.

Maziasz, Robert L. & Hayes, John P. Layout Minimization of CMOS Cells. (C). 1991. text 106.50 (0-7923-9182-9) Kluwer Academic.

Mazidi, Janice, jt. auth. see Mazidi, Muhammad A.

Mazidi, Janice, jt. auth. see Mazidi, Muhammad Ali.

Mazidi, Muhammad A. 80x86 IBM PC & Compatible Computers: Assembly Language Programming, Vol. 1. 2nd ed. LC 97-41632. 384p. (C). 1997. text 78.00 (0-13-758483-0) P-H.

Mazidi, Muhammad A. & Mazidi, Janice. Introduction to the 8051 Microcontroller. (Illus.). 435p. (C). 1999. text 89.00 incl. disk (0-13-861022-3, Macmillan Coll) P-H.

*Mazidi, Muhammad Ali & Mazidi, Janice. 80x86 IBM PC & Compatible Computers: Assembly Language, Design & Interfacing. 3rd ed. 1024p. 2000. 106.00 (0-13-016568-9, Prentice Hall) P-H.

— 80x86 IBM PC & Compatible Computers: Design & Interfacing of Ibm Pc, Ps And Com. 3rd ed. 784p. 2000. 98.00 (0-13-016567-0, Prentice Hall) P-H.

Mazidi, Muhammed A. Design & Interfacing of IBM PC & Compatible Computers, Vol. 2. 2nd ed. LC 98-106946. 784p. (C). 1997. text 85.00 (0-13-758491-1) P-H.

Mazie, Sara M., jt. ed. see Hawley, Amos H.

Mazier, Jacques, et al. When Economic Crises Endure. Rosen, Myriam, tr. from FRE. LC 98-30972. 296p. (C). (gr. 13-13). 1998. text 66.95 (1-56324-568-X) M E Sharpe.

— When Economic Crises Endure. Rosen, Myriam, tr. from FRE. LC 98-30972. (Illus.). 296p. (gr. 13). 1998. pap. text 29.95 (1-56324-569-8) M E Sharpe.

Mazier, Patrick W., et al. Surgery of the Colon, Rectum & Anus. LC 93-40034. (Illus.). 992p. 1994. text 250.00 (0-7216-4689-1, W B Saunders Co) Harcrt Hlth Sci Grp.

Mazik, James M., jt. auth. see Parsons, Bonnie.

Mazin, Larry, et al. An Educator's Legal Guide to Stress-Free Discipline & School Safety. LC 98-151226. 311p. 1998. spiral bd. 59.00 (1-879639-59-9) Natl Educ Serv.

Mazingo, Christopher, jt. auth. see Ballantyne, Duncan.

Mazioun, Claude. The Art of Erotic Jewelry. 192p. 1996. 62.00 (88-7301-053-9, Pub. by Gremese Intl) Natl Bk Netwk.

Mazique, Mignon S., jt. auth. see Kaplan, Robert E.

Mazis. Current Readings: Marketing. 1998. 20.00 (0-07-428686-2) McGraw.

Mazis, Glen A. Emotion & Embodiment: Fragile Ontology. LC 93-3083. (Studies in Contemporary Continental Philosophy: Vol. 3). XIII, 335p. 1994. 39.95 (*0-8204-2171-5*) P Lang Pubng.

Mazja, W. G., jt. auth. see Gelman, I. W.

***Maz'kila, V. G., et al.** Mathematical Aspects of Boundary Element Methods: Dedicated to Vladimir Maz'ya on the Occasion of His 60th Birthday LC 99-38269. 312p. 1999. per. 69.95 (*1-58488-006-6*) CRC Pr.

Mazlakh, Serhifi & Shakhrai, Vasyl. On the Current Situation in the Ukraine. Potichnyj, Peter J., ed. LC 76-107976. 254p. reprint ed. pap. 78.80 (*0-608-13966-1*, 205563100029) Bks Demand.

Mazliak, Paul, ed. see Eleventh International Meeting on Plant Lipids Sta.

Mazlish, Anne, ed. The Tracy Log Book: A Month in Summer. (Illus.). 1997. 19.95 (*0-934745-22-6*); pap. 9.95 (*0-934745-25-0*) Acadia Pub Co.

Mazlish, Bruce. The Fourth Discontinuity: The Co-Evolution of Humans & Machines. LC 92-38075. (Illus.). 272p. 1993. 37.50 (*0-300-05411-4*) Yale U Pr.

— Fourth Discontinuity: The Co-Evolution of Humans & Machines. 1995. pap. 16.00 (*0-300-06512-4*) Yale U Pr.

— James & John Stuart Mill: Father & Son in the Nineteenth Century. 475p. (Orig.). 1988. pap. 29.95 (*0-88738-727-6*) Transaction Pubs.

— The Leader, the Led & the Psyche: Essays in Psychohistory. LC 90-35351. 333p. reprint ed. pap. 103.30 (*0-608-09088-3*, 206972200005) Bks Demand.

— A New Science: The Breakdown of Connections & the Birth of Sociology. LC 93-3773. 348p. 1993. reprint ed. pap. 18.95 (*0-271-01092-4*) Pa St U Pr.

— The Uncertain Sciences. LC 98-9716. 336p. 1998. 35.00 (*0-300-07477-8*) Yale U Pr.

Mazlish, Bruce, jt. auth. see Bronowski, Jacob.

Mazlish, Bruce, jt. ed. see Marx, Leo.

Mazlish, Bruce H. A New Science: The Breakdown of Connections & the Birth of Sociology. 352p. 1989. text 70.00 (*0-19-505846-1*) OUP.

Mazlish, Elaine, jt. auth. see Faber, Adele.

Mazloomi, Carolyn. Spirits of the Cloth: Contemporary African American Quilts. LC 97-44101. (Illus.). 192p. 1998. 40.00 (*0-609-60091-5*) C Potter.

Mazloomian, Kemba S. To Dine with the Blameless Ethiopians. 112p. 1995. pap. 10.95 (*1-870989-67-8*) Bahai.

Mazloum, Claude. Designer Jewellery: The World's Top Artists. 1994. 75.00 (*88-7301-021-0*, Pub. by Gremese Intl) Natl Bk Netwk.

— Jewelry & Gemstones: An Investor's & Connoisseur's Guide. 1994. 27.00 (*88-7301-005-9*, Pub. by Gremese Intl) Natl Bk Netwk.

***Mazloum, Claude.** Jewelry Design in the 21st Century. (Illus.). 200p. 1999. 60.00 (*88-7301-310-4*, Pub. by Gremese Intl) Natl Bk Netwk.

Mazloum, Claude. Jewelry Gem by Gem: Masters & Materials. 1996. 60.00 (*88-7301-070-9*, Pub. by Gremese Intl) Natl Bk Netwk.

Mazmanian, Daniel A. Third Parties in Presidential Elections. LC 74-281. (Studies in Presidential Selection). (Illus.). 175p. reprint ed. pap. 54.30 (*0-608-18058-0*, 202796900057) Bks Demand.

Mazmanian, Daniel A. & Kraft, Michael E., eds. Toward Sustainable Communities: Transition & Transformation in Enviromental Policy. LC 99-34658. (American & Comparative Environmental Policy Ser.). (Illus.). 308p. 1999. pap. 25.00 (*0-262-63194-6*) MIT Pr.

— Toward Sustainable Communities: Transition & Transformations in Environmental Policy. LC 99-34658. (American & Comparative Environmental Policy Ser.). (Illus.). 308p. 1999. pap. 60.00 (*0-262-13358-X*) MIT Pr.

Mazmanian, Daniel A. & Nienaber, Jeanne. Can Organizations Change? Environmental Protection, Citizen Participation, & the Army Corps of Engineers. LC 78-27767. 232p. reprint ed. pap. 72.00 (*0-8357-8823-7*, 203358900086) Bks Demand.

Mazmanian, Daniel A. & Trzyna, Thaddeus C. Issues & Alternatives: Reasons & Methods for Protecting California Farmlands. (California Farmlands Project Working Papers: No. 3). 24p. (Orig.). 1983. pap. 5.00 (*0-912102-64-0*) Cal Inst Public.

Mazmanian, Daniel A., et al. Breaking Political Gridlock: California's Experiment in Public-Private Cooperation for Hazardous Waste Policy. LC 88-15342. (Environmental Studies: No. 8). (Illus.). 104p. (Orig.). 1988. pap. 20.00 (*0-912102-86-1*) Cal Inst Public.

Mazmanian, Daniel A., jt. auth. see Sabatier, Paul A.

Mazo-Calf, Karyn, et al. Among Us: A Collection of Writings. (Illus.). 53p. (Orig.). 1989. pap. 7.00 (*0-929848-00-4*) Peace Ventures Pr.

Mazo-Calf, Karyn, jt. auth. see Shepherd-Hayes, Deborah.

Mazo, Chaim. Energizing Hanukkah Story for Children. rev. ed. (J). (gr. 2-7). 1998. pap. text 7.95 (*0-943706-27-0*) Pitspopany.

***Mazo, Gary.** And the Flames Did Not Consume Us: A Rabbi's Journey Through Communal Crisis. 2001. pap. write for info. (*0-933670-06-0*) Rising Star.

Mazo, Joseph H. American Modern Dance: The First Hundred Years. 1997. 25.00 (*0-02-864503-0*, Schirmer Books); 25.00 (*0-02-860283-8*, Schirmer Books) Mac Lib Ref.

— Prime Movers: The Makers of Modern Dance in America. 2nd ed. (Illus.). 384p. 1999. pap. 21.95 (*0-87127-211-3*) Princeton Bk Co.

Mazo, Judith F., et al, eds. Providing Health Care Benefits in Retirement. LC 94-13655. (Pensions Research Council Publications). 280p. (C). 1994. text 42.50 (*0-8122-3270-4*) U of Pa Pr.

Mazoff, C. D. Anxious Allegiances: Legitimizing Identity in the Early Canadian Long Poem. 184p. 1997. text 49.95 (*0-7735-1715-4*, Pub. by McG-Queens Univ Pr) CUP Services.

Mazollier, J., jt. auth. see Daumas, Eugene.

Mazon, Mauricio. The Zoot-Suit Riots: The Psychology of Symbolic Annihilation. (Mexican American Monographs: No. 8). (Illus.). 179p. 1984. reprint ed. pap. 10.95 (*0-292-79803-2*) U of Tex Pr.

Mazonowicz, Douglas. Cave Art. (Shorewood Art Programs for Education Ser.). 8p. (Orig.). 1984. pap. 57.50 (*0-88185-025-X*); 75.50 (*0-685-09477-4*) Shorewood Fine Art.

***Mazonson, Peter.** Cooking Without a Kitchen: The Coffeemaker Cookbook. Grohmann, Susan & Miller, Nancy, eds. (Illus.). 63p. 1999. pap. 7.95 (*0-9637062-1-7*, Pub. by MCB Pubns) Southwest Cookbk.

Mazor, Emanuel. Chemical & Isotopic Groundwater Hydrology: The Applied Approach. 2nd ed. LC 96-44786. (Books in Soils, Plants & the Environment). (Illus.). 432p. 1996. text 165.00 (*0-8247-9803-1*) Dekker.

Mazor, M., jt. ed. see Svehla, Gyula I.

Mazor, Michel. The Vanished City: Everyday Life in the Warsaw Ghetto. Jacobson, David, tr. from FRE. LC 92-62367. 208p. 1993. 24.00 (*0-941419-93-2*) Marsilio Pubs.

Mazor, Miriam & Simons, Harriet F. Infertility: Medical, Emotional & Social Considerations. 264p. 1984. pap. 22.95 (*0-89885-177-7*, Kluwer Acad Hman Sci) Kluwer Academic.

Mazor, Miriam, jt. auth. see Simons, Harriet F.

Mazor, Stanley & Langstraat, Patricia. A Guide to VHDL. LC 92-17444. 336p. (C). 1992. text 116.50 (*0-7923-9255-8*) Kluwer Academic.

— A Guide to VHDL. 2nd ed. LC 93-23132. 1993. text 115.50 (*0-7923-9387-2*) Kluwer Academic.

***Mazorlig, Tom.** Bearded Dragon. 1999. 12.95 (*0-7938-3020-6*) TFH Pubns.

***Mazorling, Tom.** Guide to Owning Tree Boas & Tree Pythons. (Illus.). 1999. pap. 9.95 (*0-7938-2065-0*) TFH Pubns.

Mazotti, Mary K. The Liguorian Know-Your-Bible Quiz Collection. LC 95-82114. 63 :p. (Orig.). 1996. pap. 3.95 (*0-89243-911-4*) Liguori Pubns.

Mazoue, Jo A. Queen of the Island. 280p. (Orig.). 1993. pap. 11.95 (*0-923568-30-1*) Wilderness Adventure Bks.

Mazour. World History: People & Nations. 1990. 58.50 (*0-15-373458-2*) Harcourt Schl Pubs.

Mazour, Anatole G. Finland Between East & West. LC 75-31771. (Illus.). 298p. 1975. reprint ed. lib. bdg. 35.00 (*0-8371-8495-9*, MAFEW, Greenwood Pr) Greenwood.

— Modern Russian Historiography. rev. ed. LC 75-16962. (Illus.). 224p. 1976. 57.95 (*0-8371-8285-9*, MRH/, Greenwood Pr) Greenwood.

— Rise & Fall of the Romanovs. (Anvil Ser.). 190p. (Orig.). 1960. reprint ed. pap. 11.50 (*0-685-07020-4*) Krieger.

— Women in Exile: Wives of the Decembrists. LC 74-22111. (Illus.). 134p. 1975. 15.00 (*0-910512-19-1*) Diplomatic IN.

***Mazower, Mark.** After the War Was Over: Reconstructing the Family, Nation & State in Greece, 1943-1960. LC 00-36680. (Modern Greek Studies). (Illus.). 352p. 2000. 65.00 (*0-691-05841-5*); pap. 19.95 (*0-691-05842-3*) Princeton U Pr.

— The Balkans: A Short History. 144p. 2000. 19.95 (*0-679-64087-8*) Modern Lib NY.

Mazower, Mark. The Dark Continent. 2000. pap. 16.00 (*0-679-75704-X*) Knopf.

— Dark Continent: Europe's Twentieth Century. LC 98-15886. (Borzoi Book Ser.). (Illus.). 512p. 1999. 30.00 (*0-679-43809-2*) Knopf.

— Greece & the Inter-War Economic Crisis. (Oxford Historical Monographs). 352p. 1991. 75.00 (*0-19-820205-9*) OUP.

— Inside Hitler's Greece: The Experience of Occupation, 1941-1944. 1995. pap. 19.00 (*0-300-06552-3*) Yale U Pr.

Mazower, Mark, ed. The Policing of Politics in the 20th Century: Historical Perspectives. LC 95-37154. 288p. 1997. 59.95 (*1-57181-873-1*) Berghahn Bks.

Mazoyer, B. M., ed. Pet Studies on Amino Acid Metabolism & Protein Synthesis. (Developments in Nuclear Medicine Ser.). 288p. (C). 1993. text 145.50 (*0-7923-2076-X*) Kluwer Academic.

Mazoyer, J, jt. auth. see Delorme, M.

Mazquiaran de Rodriguez, Mercedes, jt. ed. see Glenn, Kathleen M.

Mazraani, Nathalie. Aspects of Language Variation in Arabic Political Speech-Making. 288p. 1997. 75.00 (*0-7007-0673-9*, Pub. by Curzon Pr Ltd) Paul & Co Pubs.

Mazrui, A. A., ed. see UNESCO Staff.

Mazrui, Alamin M. & Shariff, Ibrahim N. The Swahili: Idiom & Identity of an African People. LC 93-9903. 1994. 45.95 (*0-86543-310-0*); pap. 14.95 (*0-86543-311-9*) Africa World.

Mazrui, Alamin M., jt. auth. see Mazrui, Ali A.

***Mazrui, Ali A.** Africa since 1935. Vol. 8. (UNESCO General History of Africa Ser.). 1072p. 1999. pap. 24.95 (*0-520-06703-7*, Pub. by U CA Pr) Cal Prin Full Svc.

Mazrui, Ali A. The African Condition. LC 79-9657. 192p. 1980. text 57.95 (*0-521-23265-1*); pap. text 17.95 (*0-521-29884-9*) Cambridge U Pr.

— Africa's International Relations: The Diplomacy of Dependency & Change. LC 77-595. 1979. pap. text 19.90 (*0-89158-671-7*) Westview.

— The Barrel of the Gun & the Barrel of Oil in the North-South Equation. 33p. 1978. pap. 21.95 (*0-87855-759-8*) Transaction Pubs.

— Black Reparations in a Conservative World: Racial Aspirations & Political Realities. (Studies on Global Africa). 225p. 1998. pap. 17.00 (*1-883058-05-8*, Studies Global) Global Pubns.

— Christianity & Islam in Africa's Political Experience: Piety, Passion, & Power. (Occasional Papers Ser.). iii, 28p. 1996. pap. 3.95 (*1-929218-03-6*) Georgetwn U Ctr Muslim.

— Cultural Forces in World Politics. LC 90-4869. 262p. (C). 1990. pap. 24.95 (*0-435-08047-4*, 08047) Heinemann.

— Cultural Forces in World Politics. 272p. 1989. text 27.95 (*0-8133-7443-X*) Westview.

— The Moving Cultural Frontier of World Order: From Monotheism to North-South Relations. 20p. 1982. pap. 14.95 (*0-911646-11-6*) Transaction Pubs.

— Towards a Pax Africana: A Study of Ideology & Ambition. LC 67-12232. (Nature of Human Society Ser.). 1993. lib. bdg. 22.00 (*0-226-51427-7*) U Ch Pr.

— Towards a Pax Africana: A Study of Ideology & Ambition. LC 67-12232. (Nature of Human Society Ser.). 299p. reprint ed. pap. 92.70 (*0-608-09478-1*, 205427800005) Bks Demand.

— The Trial of Christopher Okigbo. (African Writers Ser.). 145p. (C). 1971. pap. 8.95 (*0-435-90097-8*, 90097) Heinemann.

— The Trial of Cristopher Okigbo. LC 78-180662. 160p. 1972. 15.95 (*0-89388-024-8*) Okpaku Communications.

Mazrui, Ali A. & Kleban, Toby, eds. The Africans: A Reader. LC 85-28166. 366p. 1986. 29.95 (*0-275-92066-6*, C2066, Praeger Pubs); pap. 22.95 (*0-275-92073-9*, B2073, Praeger Pubs) Greenwood.

Mazrui, Ali A. & Kokole, Omari H. Political Values & Ideological Trends in Africa. 29p. 1992. 3.00 (*0-9633277-5-5*, Studies Global) Global Pubns.

Mazrui, Ali A. & Mazrui, Alamin M. The Political Culture of Language: Swahili, Society, & the State. (Studies on Global Africa). 320p. (C). 1996. reprint ed. pap. 17.00 (*1-883058-06-6*, Studies Global) Global Pubns.

— The Power of Babel: Language in the African Experience. LC 97-32844. 256p. 1998. pap. text 19.00 (*0-226-51429-3*); lib. bdg. 40.00 (*0-226-51428-5*) U Ch Pr.

Mazrui, Ali A. & Patel, Hasu H. Africa in World Affairs: The Next Thirty Years. LC 72-80184. 286p. (C). 1973. 25.00 (*0-89388-046-9*) Okpaku Communications.

Mazru'i, Shaykh Al-Amin bin Ali al, see Al-Amin bin Ali al Mazru'i, Shaykh.

Mazsu, Janos. The Social History of the Hungarian Intelligentsia in the "Long Nineteenth Century," 1825-1914. (Atlantic Studies on Society in Change: No. 89). 300p. 1996. 42.00 (*0-88033-362-6*, 465, Pub. by East Eur Monographs) Col U Pr.

Mazue, Amy G. Gender Bias & the State: Symbolic Reform at Work in Fifth Republic France. LC 95-44896. (Policy & Institutional Studies). 336p. (C). 1996. text 49.95 (*0-8229-3902-9*) U of Pittsburgh Pr.

Mazuka, Reiko. The Development of Language Processing Strategies: A Cross-Linguistic Study Between Japanese & English. LC 97-39707. 300p. 1998. write for info. (*0-8058-1296-2*) L Erlbaum Assocs.

Mazuka, Reiko & Nagai, Noriko, eds. Japanese Sentence Processing. 368p. 1995. text 89.95 (*0-8058-1125-7*) L Erlbaum Assocs.

Mazulli, L.A. The Nephilim: The Truth Is Here. LC 99-35509. 352p. 1999. pap. 12.99 (*0-310-22011-4*) HarpC.

Mazullo. Environmental Geology. (C). 2000. pap. text 55.50 (*0-03-015024-8*) Harcourt Coll Pubs.

Mazumdar, Dipak. Microeconomic Issues of Labor Markets in Developing Countries: Analysis & Policy Implications. (EDI Seminar Ser.: No. 40). 128p. 1989. pap. 22.00 (*0-8213-1183-2*, 11183) World Bank.

Mazumdar, J. Biofluid Mechanics. 200p. 1992. text 43.00 (*981-02-0927-4*) World Scientific Pub.

***Mazumdar, J.** An Introduction to Mathematical Physiology & Biology. 2nd ed. LC 99-10173. (Studies in Mathematical Biology: Vol. 15). 256p. (C). 1999. 74.95 (*0-521-64110-1*); pap. 29.95 (*0-521-64675-8*) Cambridge U Pr.

Mazumdar, Pauline M. Species & Specificity: An Interpretation of the History of Immunology. LC 93-31219. (Illus.). 473p. (C). 1995. text 69.95 (*0-521-43172-7*) Cambridge U Pr.

Mazumdar, Shudha. Memoirs of an Indian Woman. Forbes, Geraldine H., ed. & intro. by. LC 89-10272. (Foremother Legacies). 248p. (C). (gr. 13). 1989. 69.95 (*0-87332-520-6*, East Gate Bk) M E Sharpe.

Mazumdar, Shudha. Memoirs of an Indian Woman. Forbes, Geraldine, ed. & intro. by. LC 89-10272. (Foremother Legacies Ser.). 248p. (gr. 13). 1995. pap. 19.95 (*1-56324-552-3*, East Gate Bk) M E Sharpe.

— Ramayana. 542p. 1974. 12.95 (*0-318-37159-6*) Asia Bk Corp.

Mazumdar, Subash. Mahabharata Is Believable. LC 97-66792. 128p. 1997. 14.95 (*1-887750-60-6*) Rutledge Bks.

Mazumdar, Sucheta. Sugar & Society in China: Peasants, Technology & the World Market. LC 98-4763. (Harvard-Yenching Institute Monograph Ser.). (Illus.). 500p. 1998. 49.50 (*0-674-85408-X*) HUP.

Mazumdar, Vina, ed. Role of Rural Women in Development. 373p. 1979. 11.95 (*0-318-37072-7*) Asia Bk Corp.

— Symbols of Power. 373p. 1979. 19.95 (*0-318-37080-8*) Asia Bk Corp.

Mazumdar, Vina, jt. ed. see Kasturi, Leela.

Mazumdarm. Component Based Test Plans for System Relation. (Industrial Engineering Ser.). 1997. text. write for info. (*0-442-01437-6*, VNR) Wiley.

Mazumder, Bibhuti. In Search of the Meaning of Life. LC 97-76328. 128p. 1998. 17.95 (*1-56167-415-X*) Noble House.

Mazumder, J. & Kar, A. Theory & Application of Laser Chemical Vapor Deposition. (Lasers, Photonics, & Electro-Optics Ser.). (Illus.). 408p. (C). 1995. 95.00 (*0-306-44936-6*, Kluwer Plenum) Kluwer Academic.

Mazumder, Jyoti, et al, eds. Laser Processing, Surface Treatment & Film Deposition: Proceedings of the NATO Advanced Study Institute, Sesimbra, Portugal, July 3-16, 1994. (NATO ASI Series E: Applied Sciences). 960p. (C). 1996. text 423.00 (*0-7923-3901-0*) Kluwer Academic.

Mazumder, Jyoti & Mukherjee, K., eds. Lasers in Metallurgy: Proceedings of a Symposium. LC 81-85419. (Conference Proceedings Ser.). (Illus.). 309p. reprint ed. pap. 95.80 (*0-8357-7502-X*, 203260000080) Bks Demand.

Mazumder, Jyoti, ed. see Minerals, Metals & Materials Society Staff.

Mazumder, Pinaki & Chakraborty, Kanad. Testing & Testable Design of High-Density Random-Access Memories. LC 96-2750. (Frontiers in Electronic Testing Ser.). 424p. (C). 1996. text 153.50 (*0-7923-9782-7*) Kluwer Academic.

Mazumder, Pinaki, et al. Genetic Algorithms for Vision Design: Layout & Test Automation. LC 98-50400. 352p. 1998. 88.00 (*0-13-011566-5*) P-H.

Mazumder, Pinaki, jt. ed. see Lomax, Ronald J.

Mazumder, Pinaki, jt. ed. see Rajusuman, Rochit.

Mazur. Introduction to Physics: Calculus Based. 544p. 1999. 13.33 (*0-13-489469-3*) P-H.

Mazur, Allan. Global Social Problems. 240p. (C). 1990. pap. text 21.40 (*0-13-357013-4*) P-H.

— A Hazardous Inquiry: The Rashomon Effect at Love Canal. LC 97-44639. (Illus.). 272p. 1999. text 27.00 (*0-674-74833-6*) HUP.

Mazur, Allan & Robertson, Leon S. Biology & Social Behavior. LC 72-169236. 1972. 19.95 (*0-02-920450-X*) Free Pr.

Mazur, Amy G. Gender Bias & the State: Symbolic Reform at Work in Fifth Republic France. LC 95-44896. 336p. (C). 1996. pap. 22.95 (*0-8229-5601-2*) U of Pittsburgh Pr.

Mazur, Amy G., jt. ed. see Stetson, Dorothy M.

Mazur, B. W. Colloquial Polish. (Colloquials Ser.). 224p. 1983. pap. 14.95 (*0-7100-9030-7*, Routledge Thoemms); audio 14.95 (*0-7100-9387-X*, Routledge Thoemms) Routledge.

— Colloquial Polish, Set. (Colloquials Ser.). 282p. 1988. pap. 24.95 incl. audio (*0-415-00078-5*, A2583) Routledge.

Mazur, Barry. Deformation Theory of Galois Representations & Modular Forms. 300p. (C). 1998. 42.00 (*1-57146-043-8*) Intl Pr Boston.

Mazur, Barry & Stevens, Glenn, eds. P-Adic Monodromy & the Birch & Swinnerton-Dyer Conjecture, Vol. 165. LC 94-10073. 315p. 1994. 34.00 (*0-8218-5180-2*, CONM/165C) Am Math.

Mazur, Barry, jt. auth. see Artin, Michael.

Mazur, Barry, jt. auth. see Friedlander, Eric M.

Mazur, Barry, jt. auth. see Hirsch, Morris W.

Mazur, Cynthia S. & Bullis, Ronald K. Legal Guide for Day-to-Day Church Matters: A Handbook for Pastors & Church Members. LC 94-7401. 148p. (Orig.). 1994. pap. 6.95 (*0-8298-0990-2*) Pilgrim OH.

Mazur, Cynthia S., jt. auth. see Bullis, Ronald K.

Mazur, Dennis J. Medical Risk & the Right to an Informed Consent in Clinical Care & Clinical Research. LC 98-86506. 183p. 1998. pap. 48.00 (*0-924674-64-4*) Am Coll Phys Execs.

Mazur, Edward H. Minyans for a Prairie City: The Politics of Chicago Jewry, 1850-1940. LC 90-3294. (European Immigrants & American Society Ser.). 456p. 1990. reprint ed. text 30.00 (*0-8240-0297-0*) Garland.

Mazur, Elena, jt. auth. see Mazur, Ivan.

Mazur, Eric. Peer Instruction: A User's Manual. LC 96-20088. 253p. (C). 1996. pap. 24.20 (*0-13-565441-6*) P-H.

***Mazur, Eric Michael.** Americanization of Religious Minorities: Confronting the Constitutional Order. LC 99-24616. 196p. 1999. 38.00 (*0-8018-6220-5*) Johns Hopkins.

***Mazur, Eric Michael & McCarthy, Kate.** God in the Details: American Religion in Popular Culture. LC 00-35309. 2000. pap. write for info. (*0-415-92564-9*) Routledge.

Mazur, G. A., jt. auth. see Proctor, Thomas E.

Mazur, Gail. The Common. LC 94-33930. (Phoenix Poets Ser.). 86p. 1995. lib. bdg. 22.50 (*0-226-51438-2*) U Ch Pr.

— The Common. LC 94-33930. (Phoenix Poets Ser.). 86p. 1995. pap. 11.95 (*0-226-51439-0*) U Ch Pr.

— The Pose of Happiness. LC 85-45963. 96p. 1986. pap. 8.95 (*0-87923-616-7*) Godine.

***Mazur, Gail.** They Cant Take That Away from Me. 1999. lib. bdg. 26.00 (*0-226-51444-7*) U Ch Pr.

Mazur, Glen A. Digital Multimeter Principles. LC 98-211210. 1998. pap. text 15.96 (*0-8269-1488-8*) Am Technical.

***Mazur, Glen A.** Power Quality Measurement & Troubleshooting. (Illus.). 192p. 1999. pap. text 29.96 (*0-8269-1425-X*) Am Technical.

— Power Quality Measurement & Troubleshooting: Resource Guide. 192p. pap. 295.00 (*0-8269-1426-8*) Am Technical.

Mazur, Glen A. & Proctor, Thomas E. Troubleshooting Electrical/Electronic Systems: Instructor's Guide. (Illus.). 476p. 1994. teacher ed. 11.96 (*0-8269-1776-3*) Am Technical.

Mazur, Glen A. & Zurlis, Peter A. Electrical Principles & Practices. (Illus.). 460p. 1997. text 36.96 (*0-8269-1755-0*) Am Technical.

Mazur, Glen A., jt. auth. see Proctor, Thomas E.

Mazur, Glen A., jt. auth. see Rockis, Gary.

An Asterisk (*) at the beginning of an entry indicates that the title is appearing for the first time.

Mazur, Glenn, et al. Tutorials from the Eighth Symposium on QFD. (Illus.). 250p. 1996. pap. 150.00 (*1-889477-76-1*) QFD Inst.

— Tutorials from the Ninth Symposium on QFD. (Illus.). 300p. 1997. pap. 150.00 (*1-889477-77-X*) QFD Inst.

— Tutorials from the Seventh Symposium on QFD. (Illus.). 200p. 1995. pap. 150.00 (*1-889477-75-3*) QFD Inst.

— Tutorials from the Tenth Symposium on QFD. (Illus.). 375p. 1998. pap. 150.00 (*1-889477-78-8*) QFD Inst.

Mazur, Grace D. Silk. 220p. 1996. pap. 15.95 (*1-57129-028-1*) Brookline Bks.

— Trespass: A Novel. LC 98-50060. 1998. write for info. (*0-9666750-0-2*, Pub. by Nocturnum Pr) Consort Bk Sales.

Mazur, Ivan & Mazur, Elena. Neptune's Kingdom. Freedman, Stella, ed. (Ecology for Children Ser.: Vol. 1). (Illus.). 48p. (J). (gr. 2-6). 1998. 11.95 (*1-892316-03-X*) Rama Pr.

— Treasures of the North. Freedman, Stella, ed. (Ecology for Children Ser.: Vol. 2). (Illus.). 48p. (J). (gr. 2-6). 1998. 11.95 (*1-892316-04-8*) Rama Pr.

Mazur, James. Learning & Behavior. 4th ed. LC 97-12807. 433p. 1997. 73.00 (*0-13-857566-5*) P-H.

Mazur, Joan, jt. auth. see Bliss, Traci.

***Mazur, Joe.** Explorations in Calculus with a Computer Algebra System. 1998. 37.95 (*0-387-14249-5*) Spr-Verlag.

Mazur, Laura & Economist Intelligence Unit (Great Britain) Staff. Why You Need Public Relations LC 93-224956. (Special Report Ser.). xii, 300p. 1992. write for info. (*0-85058-595-3*) Economist Intell.

Mazur, Laura & Hogg, Annik. The Marketing Challenge. LC 93-15369. 298p. (C). 1993. 44.00 (*0-201-63191-1*) Addison-Wesley.

Mazur, Laurie A., ed. Beyond the Numbers: A Reader on Population & Consumption Issues. LC 94-75842. 1994. text 45.00 (*1-55963-298-4*); pap. text 22.00 (*1-55963-299-2*) Island Pr.

Mazur, Marcia L., et al. The Dinosaur Tamer & Other Stories for Children with Diabetes. LC 95-43126. 192p. (J). 1996. pap. 9.95 (*0-945448-58-9*, 4906-01) Am Diabetes.

Mazur, Mary F. How Do You Perceive the World? LC 95-79170. 65p. (J). 1995. 29.95 (*1-888024-00-3*) Ahead Desktop.

Mazur, Michael T. & Kurman, Robert J. Diagnosis of Endometrial Biopsies & Curetting: A Practical Approach. LC 94-10428. 1994. 158.00 (*3-540-94230-0*) Spr-Verlag.

— Diagnosis of Endometrial Biopsies & Curetting: A Practical Approach. LC 94-10428. (Illus.). 260p. 1995. 79.00 (*0-387-94230-0*) Spr-Verlag.

Mazur, P., jt. auth. see DeGroot, S. R.

Mazur, Robert E., ed. Breaking the Links: Development Theory & Practice in Southern Africa - a Festschrift for Ann W. Seidman. 321p. 1990. 45.00 (*0-86543-178-7*); pap. 14.95 (*0-86543-179-5*) Africa World.

Mazur, T., ed. Classical Analysis: Proceedings of 6th Symposium, Kazimierz Dolny, Poland, 23-29 September 1991. 400p. 1992. text 109.00 (*981-02-0983-5*) World Scientific Pub.

Mazur, Walter G. Lagniappe Something a Little Extra Special: Louisiana Cooking from the Kitchen of Chef Walter's Blue Bayou Inn. Hegeman, B. J., ed. LC 95-83544. (Illus.). 144p. (Orig.). 1995. write for info. (*0-942495-51-9*); pap. 14.95 (*0-942495-50-0*) Palmer Pubns Inc.

Mazuran, Cody. A Fine Finish: New Bindings for Award-Winning Quilts. White, Janet, ed. LC 96-16466. (Illus.). 56p. 1996. pap. 12.95 (*1-56477-160-1*, B271) Martingale & Co.

Mazure, A., et al, eds. A New Vision of an Old Cluster: Untangling Coma Berenices Marseille, France, 17-20 June, 1997. 250p. 1998. 78.00 (*981-02-3322-1*) World Scientific Pub.

Mazure, Caren. Erica Has a Problem: Epilepsy. LC 97-90137. (Illus.). 88p. (J). (ps-4). 1998. 11.95 (*0-533-12295-3*) Vantage.

Mazure, Carolyn M., ed. Does Stress Cause Psychiatric Illness? (Progress in Psychiatry Ser.: Vol. 46). 315p. 1994. text 39.50 (*0-88048-482-9*, 8482) Am Psychiatric.

***Mazure, Jeanne, ed.** Single Voice: Individual Performance Pieces. 72p. 1999. pap. text 12.95 (*0-646-32433-0*, Pub. by Aust Assn Teach) Calendar Islands.

Mazurek, et al. International Comparative Education. LC 99-41940. 421p. 1999. 62.00 (*0-205-26752-1*) P-H.

Mazurek, Jan. Making Microchips: Policy, Globalization, & Economic Restructuring in the Semiconductor Industry. LC 98-35601. (Urban & Industrial Environment Ser.). (Illus.). 261p. 1998. 30.00 (*0-262-13345-8*) MIT Pr.

Mazurek, Jan, jt. auth. see Davies, J. Clarence.

Mazurek, Kas & Winzer, Margret A., eds. Comparative Studies in Special Education. LC 94-212. 522p. 1994. text 55.95 (*1-56368-027-0*) Gallaudet Univ Pr.

Mazurek, Kas, jt. ed. see Kach, Nick.

Mazurek, Linda J. Forever Loved, My Lost & Found Faith. LC 98-92122. 224p. (Orig.). (C). 1998. pap. write for info. (*1-57579-122-6*) Pine Hill Pr.

Mazurik, Martin, jt. auth. see Polson, Eric.

Mazurin, Oleg V., et al. Handbook of Glass Data: Ternary Silicate Glasses, Part C. (Physical Sciences Data Ser.: Vol. 15C). 1110p. 1987. 591.50 (*0-444-42889-5*) Elsevier.

— Handbook of Glass Data Pt. A: Silica Glass & Binary Silicate Glasses. (Physical Sciences Data Ser.: Vol. 15). 670p. 1983. 367.50 (*0-444-42215-3*) Elsevier.

— Handbook of Glass Data, Part B: Single-Component & Binary Non-Silicate Oxide Glasses: Physical Sciences Data, Pt. 15B. 806p. 1985. 438.50 (*0-444-42484-9*) Elsevier.

— Handbook of Glass Data, Pt. D: Ternary Non-Silicate Glasses. (Physical Sciences Data Ser.: No. 15D). 992p. 1991. 487.25 (*0-444-88955-8*) Elsevier.

— Single-Component, Binary, & Ternary Oxide Glasses. LC 93-27810. (Handbook of Glass Data Ser., Pt. E, Physical Sciences Data Ser.: Vol. 15). 894p. 1993. 552.00 (*0-444-81635-6*) Elsevier.

Mazurkiewicz, A., ed. Mathematical Foundations of Computer Science, 1976. (Lecture Notes in Computer Science Ser.: Vol. 45). (Illus.). 1976. 33.95 (*0-387-07854-1*) Spr-Verlag.

Mazurkiewicz, A. & Winkowski, J., eds. CONCUR'97 - Concurrency Theory: Proceedings 8th International Conference, Warsaw, Poland, July 1-4, 1997. (Lecture Notes in Computer Science Ser.: Vol. 1243). viii, 421p. 1997. pap. 67.00 (*3-540-63141-0*) Spr-Verlag.

Mazurkiewicz, B. K. Design & Consruction of Dry Docks. (Illus.). 500p. (C). 1980. 75.00 (*0-87849-028-0*, Pub. by Trans T Pub); pap. 75.00 (*0-87849-036-1*, Pub. by Trans T Pub) Enfield Pubs NH.

— Offshore Platforms & Pipelines: Selected Contributions. (Series on Rock & Soil Mechanics: Vol. 13). 390p. 1987. text 70.00 (*0-87849-058-2*, Pub. by Trans T Pub) Enfield Pubs NH.

Mazurkiewicz, Ludwik. Human Geography in Eastern Europe & the Former Soviet Union. 256p. 1993. text 110.00 (*0-471-94719-9*) Wiley.

— Human Geography in Eastern Europe & the Soviet Union. LC 92-19942. 163p. 1992. text 53.95 (*0-470-21905-X*) Wiley.

Mazurowski, Jeff. Aurora & Boris Touch the Sky. (Illus.). 22p. (J). (gr. k-5). 1998. pap. 9.95 (*0-9662153-1-1*) My World Pr.

— The Christmas Boy. (Illus.). 40p. (YA). (gr. 3 up). 1996. mass mkt. 7.95 (*0-9662153-0-3*) My World Pr.

Mazursky, Alan D. & Dlugoss, Eileen B. The dBASE IV: A Practical Learning Guide. 448p. (C). 1990. teacher ed. 19.00 (*1-56118-347-4*); pap. text 30.95 (*1-56118-346-6*) Paradigm MN.

— Lotus 1-2-3: A Practical Learning Guide. 500p. (C). 1988. teacher ed. 14.00 (*1-56118-087-4*); pap. text 25.95 (*1-56118-086-6*) Paradigm MN.

— Lotus 1-2-3: Short Course. 208p. (C). pap. text 19.95 (*1-56118-089-0*) Paradigm MN.

***Mazursky, Paul.** Show Me the Magic: My Further Adventures with Woody, Fellini, Orson, Danny Kaye, Peter Sellers, Bette Midler, John Cassavetes, Natalie Wood, Stanley Kubrick, & My Bubbi & Zeda. LC 99-14008. (Illus.). 288p. 1999. 24.50 (*0-684-84735-3*) Simon & Schuster.

Mazursky, Paul & Capetanos, Leon. Tempest: A Screenplay. LC 82-81975. (Illus.). 1982. pap. 8.95 (*0-933826-41-9*) PAJ Pubns.

Mazuzan, George T. Warren R. Austin at the U. N., 1946-1953. LC 76-52990. 245p. reprint ed. pap. 76.00 (*0-7837-0504-2*, 204082800018) Bks Demand.

Mazuzan, George T., jt. ed. see Fausold, Martin L.

Maz'ya, V., et al, eds. Asymptotic Theory of Elliptic Boundary Value Problems in Singularly Perturbed Domains, 2 vols. Incl. Vol. I. Asymptotic Theory of Elliptic Boundary Value Problems in Singularly Perturbed Domains. 464p. 2000. 135.00 (*3-7643-6397-5*); Vol. II. Asymptotic Theory of Elliptic Boundary Value Problems in Singularly Perturbed Domains. LC 00-39812. 352p. 2000. 135.00 (*3-7643-6398-3*); 238.00 (*0-8176-2964-5*) Birkhauser.

Maz'ya, V., jt. auth. see Kozlov, Vladimir.

Maz'ya, V. G. Sobolev Spaces. Saposnikova, T. O., tr. from RUS. (Soviet Mathematics Ser.). (Illus.). 510p. 1985. 225.00 (*0-387-13589-8*) Spr-Verlag.

Maz'ya, V. G. & Nikol'skij, S. M. Analysis IV: Linear & Boundary Integral Equations. Gamkrelidze, R. V., ed. Bottcher, A. & Prossdorf, S., trs. from RUS. (Encyclopedia of Mathematical Sciences Ser.: Vol. 27). (Illus.). 248p. 1991. 108.95 (*0-387-51997-1*) Spr-Verlag.

Mazya, V. G., jt. auth. see Burago, Iurii D.

Maz'ya, V. G., jt. auth. see Kozlov, Vladimir.

Mazza, Antonino. The Way I Remember It, Vol. 1. (Essential Poets Ser.: No. 56). 64p. 1994. pap. 8.00 (*0-920717-74-8*) Guernica Editions.

Mazza, Antonino, tr. see Montale, Eugenio.

Mazza, Antonio, tr. & intro. see Duliani, Mario.

Mazza, Cris. Animal Acts. 163p. (Orig.). 1989. 18.95 (*0-932511-15-5*); pap. 8.95 (*0-932511-16-3*) Fiction Coll.

— Dog People. LC 96-54051. 200p. (Orig.). 1997. pap. 13.95 (*1-56689-055-1*) Coffee Hse.

— Exposed. LC 93-23689. 250p. (Orig.). 1994. pap. 11.95 (*1-56689-019-5*) Coffee Hse.

— Former Virgin. 120p. (Orig.). 1997. pap. 11.95 (*1-57366-033-7*) Fiction Coll.

— How to Leave a Country. LC 92-4005. 180p. (Orig.). 1992. pap. 11.95 (*0-918273-96-X*) Coffee Hse.

— Is It Sexual Harassment Yet? 1991. 18.95 (*0-932511-33-3*); pap. 8.95 (*0-932511-34-1*) Fiction Coll.

— Is It Sexual Harassment Yet? 2nd rev. ed. 224p. 1998. pap. 13.95 (*1-57366-041-8*) Fiction Coll.

— Your Name Here. LC 94-45779. 280p. (Orig.). 1995. pap. 12.95 (*1-56689-031-4*) Coffee Hse.

Mazza, Cris, et al, eds. Chick-Lit No. 2: No Chick Vics. 150p. (Orig.). 1996. pap. 11.95 (*1-57366-020-5*) Fiction Coll.

Mazza, Cris & De Shell, Jeffrey, eds. Chick-Lit: Postfeminist Fiction. 150p. (Orig.). 1995. pap. 11.95 (*1-57366-005-1*, Black Ice Bks) Fiction Coll.

Mazza, Cris & Orland, Ted. Revelation Countdown: Stories by Cris Mazza. (Black Ice Books Ser.). (Illus.). 151p. 1993. pap. 7.00 (*0-932511-73-2*) Fiction Coll.

Mazza, Debora, ed. The Oxford Color Italian Dictionary. 2nd rev. ed. 512p. 1999. pap. 9.95 (*0-19-860251-0*) OUP.

— The Oxford Italian Dictionary: Italian-English, English-Italian. LC 98-194788. (ENG & ITA.). 512p. 1997. mass mkt. 4.99 (*0-425-16012-2*) Berkley Pub.

***Mazza, Debora & Lexus (Firm).** The Oxford College Italian Dictionary. LC 98-49987. 380p. 2000. pap. 11.95 (*0-19-860282-0*) OUP.

Mazza, Debora, et al, eds. The Oxford Italian Desk Dictionary. LC 98-116332. (ENG & ITA.). 390p. (C). 1997. 15.95 (*0-19-860158-1*) OUP.

— The Pocket Oxford Italian Dictionary. LC 97-228867. 704p. 1997. pap. 11.95 (*0-19-860007-0*) OUP.

Mazza, Enrico. The Celebration of the Eucharist: The Origin of the Rite & the Development of Its Interpretation. O'Connell, Matthew J., tr. from ITA. LC 98-37348. 351p. 1998. pap. 39.95 (*0-8146-6170-X*, Pueblo Bks) Liturgical Pr.

— Eucharistic Prayers of the Roman Rites. 376p. 1992. pap. 19.50 (*0-8146-6078-9*, Pueblo Bks) Liturgical Pr.

— Mystagogy: A Theology of Liturgy in the Patristic Age. 228p. 1992. pap. 14.50 (*0-8146-6093-2*, Pueblo Bks) Liturgical Pr.

— The Origins of the Eucharistic Prayer. 376p. (Orig.). 1995. pap. text 34.95 (*0-8146-6119-X*, Pueblo Bks) Liturgical Pr.

Mazza, G. Anthocyanins of Food Crops. 384p. 1992. lib. bdg. 217.95 (*0-8493-0172-6*, QK898) CRC Pr.

— Functional Foods. LC 98-85171. 480p. 1998. 99.95 (*1-56676-487-4*) Technomic.

***Mazza, G. & Oomah, B. D., eds.** Herbs, Botanicals & Teas. LC 00-102584. 440p. 2000. text 99.95 (*1-56676-851-9*) Technomic.

Mazza, George J., jt. auth. see Brown, Cherie R.

***Mazza, Jacqueline.** Don't Disturb the Neighbors: U. S. & Democracy in Mexico. LC 00-32834. 2000. pap. write for info. (*0-415-92305-0*) Routledge.

***Mazza, Joan.** Dream Back Your Life: A Practical Guide to Dreams, Daydreams & Fantasies. 2000. pap. 13.95 (*0-399-52610-2*, Perigee Bks) Berkley Pub.

Mazza, Joan. Dreaming Your Real Self: A Personal Approach to Dream Interpretation. LC 97-40741. 256p. 1998. 13.00 (*0-399-52414-2*) Putnam Pub Group.

***Mazza, Joan.** From Dreams to Discovery. (Guided Journals). 144p. 2000. 14.99 (*1-58297-012-2*, Walking Stick Pr) F & W Pubns Inc.

— Things That Tick Me Off. (Guided Journals). 144p. 2000. 14.99 (*1-58297-020-3*, Walking Stick Pr) F & W Pubns Inc.

Mazza, Joseph J., ed. Manual of Clinical Hematology. 2nd ed. LC 94-26649. 382p. 1995. spiral bd. 35.95 (*0-316-55220-8*, Little Brwn Med Div) Lppncott W & W.

Mazza, Karen A., jt. compiled by see Franzosa, Susan D.

Mazza, L. & Rydin, Y. Urban Sustainability: Discourses, Networks & Policy Tools. (Progressin Planning Ser.: Vol. 47). 70p. 1997. pap. 69.00 (*0-08-043090-2*, Pergamon Pr) Elsevier.

Mazza, Michael J. The Truth Will Set You Free: A Presentation of the Catholic Faith for Young Adults Based on the Catechism of the Catholic Church. 85p. 1995. teacher ed. 20.00 (*0-9646214-1-X*) Veritas Pr SD.

— The Truth Will Set You Free: A Presentation of the Catholic Faith for Young Adults Based on the Catechism of the Catholic Church. LC 96-111561. (Illus.). 98p. (YA). (gr. 9-12). 1995. pap. 7.95 (*0-9646214-0-1*) Veritas Pr SD.

***Mazza, Nicholas.** Poetry Therapy: Interface of the Arts & Psychology. LC 99-29951. (Innovations in Psychology Ser.). 232p. 1999. boxed set 39.95 (*0-8493-0350-8*) CRC Pr.

— Poetry Therapy: Interface of the Arts & Psychology. LC 99-29951. (Innovations in Psychology Ser.). 1999. 39.95 (*1-57444-183-3*) CRC Pr.

Mazza, Patrick, jt. auth. see Dauncey, Guy.

Mazza, Samuele. Brahaus. LC 93-5515.Tr. of Reggi-Secolo. (ITA., Illus.). 192p. 1994. pap. 16.95 (*0-8118-0593-X*) Chronicle Bks.

— Cinderella's Revenge. Jensen, Jack, ed. (Illus.). 192p. 1994. pap. 16.95 (*0-8118-0681-2*) Chronicle Bks.

— In the Bag. 192p. 1997. pap. text 17.95 (*0-8118-1798-9*) Chronicle Bks.

— Magli: Storia E Immagini Di una Dinastia. (ENG & ITA., Illus.). 112p. 1997. 80.00 (*88-7813-739-1*, Pub. by Art Bks Intl) Partners Pubs Grp.

— Spectacles. (Illus.). 192p. 1996. pap. 16.95 (*0-8118-1367-3*) Chronicle Bks.

Mazza, Valentino Del, see Del Mazza, Valentino.

Mazza, Valerie. My Mud Puddle Ran Away. LC 98-66127. (Illus.). 34p. 1998. pap. 7.95 (*1-882792-63-7*) Proctor Pubns.

Mazza, Virginia S., jt. auth. see Clark, Madeline A.

Mazzaferri, E. L., jt. auth. see Bowen, J.

Mazzaferri, Ernest L. Advances in Endocrinology & Metabolism, Vol. 7. 300p. 1996. 64.95 (*0-8151-6153-0*) Mosby Inc.

— Endocrinology for Primary Care. 1999. text. write for info. (*0-7216-6044-4*, W B Saunders Co) Harcrt Hlth Sci Grp.

***Mazzaferri, Ernest L., ed.** 2001 Year Book of Endocrinology. (Illus.). 450p. 2001. write for info. (*0-323-01513-1*) Mosby Inc.

— 2002 Year Book of Endocrinology. (Illus.). 450p. 2002. write for info. (*0-323-01514-X*) Mosby Inc.

— 2000 Year Book of Endocrinology. (Illus.). 432p. 2000. 85.00 (*0-323-01502-6*) Mosby Inc.

Mazzaferri, Ernest L., jt. auth. see Marsh, Clay B.

Mazzaferri, Ernest L., ed. see Advances in Endocrinology & Metabolism Staff.

Mazzaferri, Ernest L., ed. see Samaan, Naguib A.

Mazzaferri, Frederick D. The Genre of the Book of Revelation from a Source-Critical Perspective. xix, 486p. (C). 1989. lib. bdg. 134.65 (*3-11-011518-2*) De Gruyter.

Mazzaferro, John F., jt. auth. see Dell'Acqua, Alexa A.

Mazzagatti, Frank A. & Lebowitz, Leon C., eds. Respiratory Care Pearls. LC 97-3043. (Pearls Ser.). (Illus.). 200p. 1997. pap. text 39.00 (*1-56053-204-1*) Hanley & Belfus.

Mazzagetti, Dominick A. Structuring Mortgage Banking Transactions. 620p. 1996. 155.00 (*0-7913-2596-2*) Warren Gorham & Lamont.

Mazzalongo, Michael, ed. Gay Rights or Wrongs: A Christian's Guide to Homosexual Issues & Ministry. LC 95-8743. 287p. 1996. pap. 13.99 (*0-89900-773-2*) College Pr Pub.

Mazzaoui, Maureen F. Textiles: Production, Trade & Demand. LC 96-52046. (Expanding World Ser.: No. 12). 350p. Date not set. text 107.95 (*0-86078-509-2*, Pub. by Variorum) Ashgate Pub Co.

Mazzaoui, Maureen F., jt. ed. see Blomquist, Thomas W.

Mazzaoui, Michel M. & Millward, William G., eds. Social & Cultural Selections from Contemporary Persian. LC 73-569. 128p. (C). 1973. text 15.00 (*0-88206-100-3*) Caravan Bks.

Mazzara, Richard A., tr. see Lispector, Clarice.

Mazzarella, Barbara. Bach Flower Remedies for Children: A Parents' Guide. LC 97-302. 192p. 1997. pap. 14.95 (*0-89281-649-X*) Inner Tradit.

Mazzarella, Mark, jt. auth. see Dimitrius, Jo-Ellan.

Mazzarella, Mimi. Alphabatty Animals & Funny Foods. LC 83-81449. (Illus.). 96p. (Orig.). (J). (gr. k-3). 1984. pap. 5.95 (*0-89709-045-4*) Liberty Pub.

***Mazzarella, Sharon R. & Pecora, Norma Odom, eds.** Growing up Girls: Popular Culture & the Construction of Identity. LC 98-9272. (Adolescent Cultures, School & Society Ser.: Vol. 9). 288p. 1999. pap. text 29.95 (*0-8204-4021-3*) P Lang Pubng.

Mazzarello, Paolo. The Hidden Structure: A Scientific Biography of Camillo Golgi. Buchtel, Henry A. & Badiani, Aldo, trs. from ITA. LC 99-22934. (Illus.). 446p. 1999. text 90.00 (*0-19-852444-7*) OUP.

***Mazzari, Caterina.** C'Eravamo Tanto Amati: Instructor's Guide. 250p. 2000. pap. 24.95 (*0-8425-2467-3*) Brigham.

Mazzarino. Catonis. (LAT.). 1982. 49.50 (*3-322-00198-9*, T1132, Pub. by B G Teubner) U of Mich Pr.

Mazzarins, Laimdota, tr. see Beck-Gernsheim, Elisabeth.

Mazzarins, Laimdota, tr. see Bolz, Norbert & Van Reijen, Willem.

Mazzarins, Laimdota, tr. see Press, Bernhard.

Mazzario, G. & Dorigato, A. Ev-Venetian Palazzi. 1998. 39.99 (*3-8228-7050-1*) Taschen Amer.

Mazzariol, Giuseppe & Dorigato, Attila. Venetian Palaces. (Illus.). 336p. 1998. 39.95 (*3-8228-7423-X*) Taschen Amer.

Mazzaro, Jerome. The Figure of Dante: An Essay on the Vita Nuova. LC 81-47146. (Princeton Essays in Literature Ser.). 173p. reprint ed. pap. 53.70 (*0-8357-4671-2*, 203761700008) Bks Demand.

— Postmodern American Poetry. fac. ed. LC 79-11119. 215p. 1980. reprint ed. pap. 66.70 (*0-7837-8079-6*, 204783200008) Bks Demand.

Mazzatinti, Guiseppe. Gli Archivi Della Storia d'Italia, 9 vols. in 5. xxxviii, 3498p. 1988. reprint ed. write for info. (*3-487-09043-0*) G Olms Pubs.

Mazzawi, Musa. Palestine & the Law: Guidelines for the Resolution of the Arab-Israel Conflict. LC 98-111964. 432p. 1997. 45.00 (*0-86372-222-9*, Pub. by Garnet-Ithaca) LPC InBook.

Mazze, Edward M., jt. auth. see Michman, Ronald D.

***Mazze, R. S. & International Diabetes Center Staff.** Staged Diabetes Management: A Systematic Approach to the Prevention, Detection & Treatment of Diabetes & Its Complications. LC 99-21829. 1999. write for info. (*1-885115-55-5*) IDC Pub.

Mazze, Roger, et al. Staged Diabetes Management: DecisionPaths. 1995. ring bd. write for info. (*1-885115-03-2*) IDC Pub.

Mazzei, Nicholas A. Shed for Your Salvation. 48p. (Orig.). (J). (gr. 7). 1996. pap. 3.50 (*0-9655903-0-5*) N A Mazzei.

Mazzei, Philip. The Constitutional Society of 1784. 49p. 1984. pap. 5.00 (*0-614-10132-8*) Am Inst Ital Stud.

— Istruzioni Per Essere Liberi Ed Eguali. 160p. 1984. pap. write for info. (*88-205-0481-2*) Am Inst Ital Stud.

— Researches on the United States. Sherman, Constance D., ed. & tr. by. LC 75-20037. (Illus.). 436p. reprint ed. 135.20 (*0-8357-9814-3*, 201696500004) Bks Demand.

— Scritti Scelti e Lettere, Set, Vols. I-III. (ITA.). 1984. write for info. (*0-614-10131-X*) Am Inst Ital Stud.

— Selected Writings & Correspondence Vol. I: Virginia's Agent During the American Revolution. xlviii, 585p. 1983. write for info. (*0-614-10128-X*) Am Inst Ital Stud.

— Selected Writings & Correspondence Vol. II: Agent for the King of Poland During the French Revolution. 802p. 1983. write for info. (*0-614-10129-8*) Am Inst Ital Stud.

— Selected Writings & Correspondence Vol. III: World Citizen. 623p. 1983. pap. write for info. (*0-614-10130-1*) Am Inst Ital Stud.

Mazzeno, Laurence W. The British Novel, 1680-1832: An Annotated Bibliography. LC 96-42524. (Magill Bibliographies Ser.). 264p. 1996. 40.00 (*0-8108-3249-6*) Scarecrow.

***Mazzeno, Laurence W.** Matthew Arnold's Critical Legacy. LC 99-38102. (Studies in English & American Literature). 256p. 1999. 55.00 (*1-57113-278-3*) Camden Hse.

Mazzeno, Laurence W. The Victorian Novel: An Annotated Bibliography. (Magill Bibliographies Ser.). 222p. 1989. 40.00 (*0-8108-2805-7*) Scarecrow.

— Victorian Poetry: An Annotated Bibliography. annot. ed. LC 95-5328. (Magill Bibliographies Ser.). 261p. 1995. 36.50 (*0-8108-3008-6*) Scarecrow.

Mazzeno, Laurence W., jt. ed. see Magill, Frank N.

Mazzeo, Guido. Abate Juan Andres, Literary Historian & Defender of Spanish & Medieval Hispano-Arab Learning, Literature & Culture, 1740-1917. 228p. 1965. 5.00 (*0-318-22340-6*) Hispanic Inst.

Mazzeo, Joseph A., jt. ed. see Henderson, Katherine U.

Mazzeo, Kelly, jt. auth. see Hartman, Rhona C.

Mazzeo, Rob. A Man's Viewpoint: Viewing Gender Issues Through Men's Eyes. LC 97-91253. (Illus.). 276p. 1998. pap. 17.95 (*0-9660666-0-X*) Viewpt Publ.

Mazzeo Zocchi, Judy. Circus or Not - Here We Come. LC 98-92883. (Adventures of Paulie & Sasha Ser.). (Illus.). 32p. (J). (gr. k-4). 1998. 15.95 (*1-891997-00-9*, THC 01, Treehse Ct) Dingles & Co.

***Mazzeo Zocchi, Judy.** Conflict. (Paulie & Sasha Ser.). (Illus.). 32p. (J). (gr. k-4). 2000. 15.95 (*1-891997-05-X*) Dingles & Co.

— Lord Zip's Bubble Mystery. (Lord Zip Ser.). (Illus.). 8p. (J). (ps). 2000. mass mkt. 4.99 (*1-891997-11-4*) Dingles & Co.

***Mazzilli-Blount, Tricia, ed.** Fashion & Print 2000: Image Makers Source of the Madison Avenue Handbook. 200p. 2000. pap. 59.95 (*0-87314-251-9*, Pub. by Peter Glenn) SCB Distributors.

— Film & Television 2000: Production Makers Source of the Madison Avenue Handbook. 400p. 2000. pap. 49.95 (*0-87314-276-4*, Pub. by Peter Glenn) SCB Distributors.

— Screen & Stage 2001: The National Casting Guide. 200p. 2000. pap. 22.95 (*0-87314-155-5*, Pub. by Peter Glenn) SCB Distributors.

***Mazzini, Anthony.** Poems of Misery & Love. 1999. pap. write for info. (*1-58235-310-7*) Watermrk Pr.

Mazzini, Giuseppe. The Living Thoughts of Mazzini Presented by Ignazio Silone. LC 79-138163. (Illus.). 130p. 1972. reprint ed. lib. bdg. 49.50 (*0-8371-5620-3*, MALI, Greenwood Pr) Greenwood.

Mazzio, Carla & Hillman, David, eds. Body in Parts: Discourses & Anatomies in Early Modern Europe. LC 97-1481. (Illus.). 376p. 1997. pap. 20.99 (*0-415-91694-1*) Routledge.

— Body in Parts: Discourses & Anatomies in Early Modern Europe. LC 97-1481. (Illus.). 376p. (C). 1997. 75.00 (*0-415-91693-3*) Routledge.

***Mazzio, Carla & Trevor, Douglas.** Historicism, Psychoanalysis & Making of Early Modern Culture: Cul.ture. LC 99-31717. (Culture Work Ser.). 2000. pap. 22.99 (*0-415-92053-1*) Routledge.

***Mazzio, Carla & Trevor, Douglas, eds.** Historicism, Psychoanalysis & Making of Early Modern Culture. LC 99-31717. (CultureWork Ser.). 432p. (C). 2000. text. write for info. (*0-415-92052-3*) Routledge.

Mazzio, Joann. Leaving Eldorado. LC 92-13853. 176p. (J). (gr. 5-9). 1993. 16.00 (*0-395-64381-3*) HM.

— The One Who Came Back. 208p. (J). (gr. 5-9). 1992. 16.00 (*0-395-59506-1*) HM.

Mazzio, Skip & Veca, Donna. Just Plane Crazy: Biography of Bobbi Trout. Osborne, Carol L. et al, eds. (Biography Ser.). (Illus.). 320p. 1987. 23.95 (*0-940997-01-0*); 37.95 (*0-940997-04-5*); pap. 19.95 (*0-940997-03-7*) Aviation Archives.

— Just Plane Crazy: Biography of Bobbi Trout, Set. Osborne, Carol L. et al, eds. (Biography Ser.). (Illus.). 320p. 1987. pap. 29.95 (*0-940997-05-3*) Aviation Archives.

***Mazziotta, John C., et al.** Brain Mapping: The Disorders. LC 99-67664. (Illus.). 614p. 2000. 199.95 (*0-12-481460-3*) Acad Pr.

Mazziotta, John C., jt. ed. see Toga, Arthur W.

Mazziotti, Maria. Luce d'Inverno: English & Italian Poetry. Scammacca, Nina & Scammacca, Nat, trs.Tr. of Winter Light. (Illus.). 67p. 1988. 15.00 (*0-89304-525-X*); pap. 7.50 (*0-89304-524-1*) Cross-Cultrl NY.

Mazzo, David J., ed. International Stability Testing. 332p. 1998. 219.00 (*1-57491-078-7*) Interpharm.

***Mazzocchi, Dorothy.** Organic Chemistry I: Laboratory Manual to Chemistry 233. 2nd ed. 166p. (C). 1999. spiral bd. 16.95 (*0-7872-6374-5*, 41637401) Kendall-Hunt.

Mazzocco, Angelo. Linguistic Theories in Dante & the Humanists: Studies of Language & Intellectual History in Late Medieval & Early Renaissance Italy. LC 93-21469. (Studies in Intellectual History: No. 38). xvi, 270p. 1993. 93.00 (*90-04-09702-3*) Brill Academic Pubs.

Mazzocco, Dennis W. Networks of Power: Corporate TV's Threat to Democracy. 200p. (Orig.). (C). 1994. pap. text 14.00 (*0-89608-472-8*); lib. bdg. 30.00 (*0-89608-473-6*) South End Pr.

Mazzola, Anthony T. & Zachary, Frank, eds. The Best Families: The Town & Country Social Directory, 1846-1996. LC 96-5529. (Illus.). 192p. 1996. 45.00 (*0-8109-3890-1*, Pub. by Abrams) Time Warner.

Mazzola, Claude J. Active Sound Absorption. LC 92-93587. (Illus.). 113p. (Orig.). (C). 1993. pap. text 49.50 (*0-9636316-0-8*) NAMLAK.

Mazzola, Claudio, jt. auth. see Capek-Habekovic, Romana.

Mazzola, Claudio, jt. auth. see Habekovic, Romana.

Mazzola, Claudio, jt. auth. see Olken, Ilene T.

Mazzola, Elizabeth. The Pathology of English Renaissance: Sacred Remains & Holy Ghosts. LC 98-25295. (Studies in the History of Christian Thought: Vol. 86). (Illus.). 168p. 1998. 64.00 (*90-04-11195-6*) Brill Academic Pubs.

Mazzola, Frank, Jr. Counting Is for the Birds. LC 95-25825. 32p. (J). (ps-3). 1997. pap. 6.95 (*0-88106-950-7*) Charlesbridge Pub.

— Counting Is for the Birds. LC 95-25825. (Illus.). 32p. (J). (ps-3). 1997. 16.95 (*0-88106-951-5*) Charlesbridge Pub.

— Counting Is for the Birds. (J). 1997. 12.15 (*0-606-13293-7*, Pub. by Turtleback) Demco.

Mazzola, Michael L. Proto-Romance & Sicilian. 142p. 1976. pap. 21.00 (*90-316-0088-1*, Pub. by B R Gruner) Humanities.

Mazzola, Michael L., ed. Issues & Theory in Romance Linguistics: Selected Papers from the Linguistic Symposium on Romance Languages XXIII. LC 93-36991. 544p. (C). 1994. 60.00 (*0-87840-243-8*) Georgetown U Pr.

Mazzola, Toni & Guten, Mimi. Wally Koala & Friends. unabridged ed. Cohen, Keri, ed. LC 93-94001. (Wally Koala Ser.). (Illus.). 24p. (J). (ps-3). 1993. 9.95 incl. audio (*1-883747-00-7*) WK Prods.

— Wally Koala & the Little Green Peach. Cohen, Keri, ed. LC 93-94002. (Wally Koala Ser.). (Illus.). 22p. (J). (ps-3). 1993. 9.95 (*1-883747-01-5*) WK Prods.

Mazzolani, F., ed. Testing of Metals for Structures: Proceedings of the International Rilem Workshop. (Rilem Proceedings Ser.: Vol. 12). (Illus.). 465p. (C). 1991. 150.00 (*0-419-15810-3*, E & FN Spon) Routledge.

Mazzolani, F. M. & Piluso, V. Theory & Design of Seismic Resistant Steel Frames. (Illus.). 450p. 1996. 150.00 (*0-419-18760-X*, E & FN Spon) Routledge.

Mazzolani, Federico M. Aluminium Alloy Structures. 2nd ed. (Illus.). 720p. (C). 1994. 165.00 (*0-419-17770-1*, E & FN Spon) Routledge.

***Mazzolani, Federico M.** Moment Resistant Connections of Steel Frames in Seismic Areas: Design & Reliability. LC 00-25172. 2000. write for info. (*0-415-23577-4*, Comedia) Routledge.

Mazzolani, Federico M., ed. Testing of Metals for Structures: Proceedings of the International Workshop. (Rilem Proceedings Ser.: No. 12). (Illus.). 500p. 1991. write for info. (*0-412-42650-1*, E & FN Spon) Routledge.

Mazzolani, Federico M. & Gioncu, Victor, eds. Behaviour of Steel Structures in Seismic Areas. (Illus.). 792p. (C). 1995. 200.00 (*0-419-19890-3*, E & FN Spon) Routledge.

Mazzoldi, Paolo. From Galileo's "Occhialino" to Optoelectronics. 750p. 1993. text 135.00 (*981-02-1332-8*) World Scientific Pub.

Mazzoldi, Paolo, jt. ed. see Draper, Clifton W.

***Mazzoleni, Donatella.** Places of Naples. (Illus.). 312p. 2000. text 95.00 (*0-8478-2216-8*) Rizzoli Intl.

Mazzoleni, Mario. A Catholic Priest Meets Sai Baba. Moevs, Christian, tr. from ITA. LC 93-86227. 294p. (Orig.). 1994. pap. 12.00 (*0-9629835-1-9*) Leela Pr.

Mazzoli, Marco. Credit, Investments & the Macroeconomy: A Few Open Issues. LC 97-14438. 230p. (C). 1998. text 57.95 (*0-521-58411-6*) Cambridge U Pr.

Mazzolini, Renato. Government Controlled Enterprises: International Strategic & Policy Decisions. LC 78-10961. 424p. reprint ed. pap. 131.50 (*0-8357-8892-X*, 203334900085) Bks Demand.

Mazzone, Domenico. Sculpturing. (Artist's Library). (Illus.). 64p. (Orig.). 1994. pap. 7.95 (*1-56010-124-5*, AL21) W Foster Pub.

Mazzone, Horace M. Handbook of Viruses Mass & Molecular Weight Determination. LC 98-2701. 224p. 1998. boxed set 149.95 (*0-8493-2625-7*) CRC Pr.

Mazzone, Jaures & Taylor, Robert G., eds. A Guide for Foreign Investors to the Brazilian Stock Market. 2nd ed. (Illus.). 68p. 1992. pap. 95.00 (*1-880506-01-7*) Intl Reports.

Mazzone, Kelly. A House for Hickory. LC 95-15319. (Illus.). 16p. (J). (ps-2). 1995. pap. text 4.95 (*1-57255-027-9*) Mondo Pubng.

Mazzone, Leo & Rosenthal, Jim. Pitching Like a Pro: A Guide for Young Pitchers & Their Coaches, Little League, Through High School. LC 98-43623. (Illus.). 112p. 1999. pap. 12.95 (*0-312-19946-5*) St Martin.

Mazzoni, A., ed. see European Skull Base Society Staff.

Mazzoni, Christina. Saint Hysteria: Neurosis, Mysticism, & Gender in European Culture. LC 96-13417. 248p. 1996. text 42.50 (*0-8014-3229-4*) Cornell U Pr.

Mazzoni, Cosimo M. A Legal Framework for Bioethics. LC 97-32491. (Nijhoff Law Specials Ser.). 256p. 1998. pap. text 81.00 (*90-411-0523-9*) Kluwer Academic.

***Mazzoni, Cristina, ed.** Angela of Foligno's Memorial. Cirignano, John, tr. from LAT. LC 99-39712. (Library of Medieval Women). 128p. 2000. pap. 19.95 (*0-85991-562-X*, DS Brewer) Boydell & Brewer.

Mazzoni, Giacopo, jt. auth. see Mazzoni, Jacopo.

Mazzoni, Giuliana & Nelson, Thomas O., eds. Metacognition & Cognitive Neuropsychology: Monitoring & Control Processes. LC 98-5819. 200p. 1998. write for info. (*0-8058-2662-9*) L Erlbaum Assocs.

Mazzoni, Jacopo & Mazzoni, Giacopo. On the Defense of the Comedy of Dante, Introduction & Summary. Montgomery, Robert L., tr. & pref. by. LC 83-3579. 157p. 1983. reprint ed. pap. 48.70 (*0-608-04509-8*, 206525400001) Bks Demand.

Mazzoni, Steve. Safety Considerations of Energy Saving Materials & Devices. 1978. 3.25 (*0-686-12080-9*, TR 78-6) Society Fire Protect.

Mazzoni, Tim L., Jr., jt. auth. see Campbell, Roald F.

Mazzoni, Wayne. The Athletic Recruiting & Scholarship Guide for High School Athletes & Parents. LC 99-172634. 111p. (YA). (gr. 9-12). 1998. pap. 19.95 (*0-9663557-0-9*) Mazz Mktg.

Mazzotta, Giuseppe. Dante's Vision & the Circle of Knowledge. 352p. 1992. text 49.50 (*0-691-06966-2*, Pub. by Princeton U Pr) Cal Prin Full Svc.

— The New Map of the World: The Poetic Philosophy of Giambattista Vico. LC 98-26421. 1999. 45.00 (*0-691-00180-4*, Pub. by Princeton U Pr) Cal Prin Full Svc.

— The World at Play in Boccaccio's Decameron. LC 85-43299. 297p. 1986. reprint ed. pap. 92.10 (*0-608-07808-5*, 205987500010) Bks Demand.

— The Worlds of Petrarch. LC 93-19793. (Monographs in Medieval & Renaissance Studies: Vol. 14). 248p. 1993. text 49.95 (*0-8223-1363-4*); pap. text 17.95 (*0-8223-1396-0*) Duke.

Mazzotta, Giuseppe & Spariosu, Mihai I., eds. Mimesis in Contemporary Theory-An Interdisciplinary Approach Vol. 1: The Literary & Philosophical Debate. LC 84-14494. (Cultura Ludens Ser.: No. 1:1). 1985. pap. 39.95 (*0-915027-14-3*) J Benjamins Pubng Co.

Mazzotta, Lawrence A. Education Profile: Omaha & the State. 34p. (Orig.). 1973. pap. 3.00 (*1-55719-056-9*) U NE CPAR.

Mazzotti, Jose A., ed. see Bueno, Raul & Schmidt, Friedhlem.

***Mazzucato, Mariana.** Firm Size, Innovation & Market Structure: The Evolution of Industry Concentration & Instability. LC 00-35347. (New Horizons in the Economics of Innovation Ser.). 2000. write for info. (*1-84064-346-3*) E Elgar.

Mazzucchelli, David, jt. auth. see Miller, Frank.

Mazzucchi-Ballard, Lois, jt. auth. see Torres, Hazel O.

Mazzucchi, Lois E., jt. auth. see Torres, Hazel O.

Mazzucelli, Colette. France & Germany at Maastricht: Politics & Negotiations to Create the European Union. LC 96-37688. (Contemporary Issues in European Politics Ser.: Vol. 3). (Illus.). 374p. 1997. text 61.00 (*0-8153-2195-3*, SS1084) Garland.

Mazzuchelli, Samuel. The Memoirs of Father Samuel Mazzuchelli, O. P. (American Biography Ser.). 329p. 1991. reprint ed. lib. bdg. 79.00 (*0-7812-8279-9*) Rprt Serv.

Mazzula, Jo. Al Packer: A Colorado Cannibal. 3.50 (*0-686-16037-1*) F&J Mazzulla.

Mazzull. Invest into Physical Geology: 1997. 2nd ed. (C). 1996. lab manual ed. 35.00 (*0-03-020294-9*) Harcourt Coll Pubs.

— Investigations into Physical. (C). 1996. pap. text, lab manual ed. 46.50 (*0-03-096542-X*) Harcourt Coll Pubs.

***Mazzullo, Dorobek.** Physical Geology. (Earth Science Ser.). 2002. 55.00 (*0-534-37731-9*) Brooks-Cole.

Mba, Nina E., jt. auth. see Johnson-Odim, Cheryl.

Mbabuike, Michael. Poems of Memory Trips. LC 98-60016. (Poetry Ser.). 96p. 1998. 19.95 (*1-889218-08-1*); pap. 6.95 (*1-889218-09-X*) Sungai Bks.

***Mbabuike, Michael C.** Once upon the Earth: An African Folktale. (Illus.). 50p. (YA). (gr. 3-12). 2000. 15.50 (*0-9678460-4-8*) Timbuktu.

— Remembering the Baobab. (Illus.). 80p. (J). (gr. 3-13). 2000. 15.50 (*0-9678460-5-6*) Timbuktu.

Mbach, Urs, jt. auth. see Hilton, Peter J.

Mbachu, Richard. African Tales in Igbo Proverbs. Ibe, Cyril, ed. (Illus.). 1997. mass mkt. write for info. (*0-9659547-0-6*) Omenala Net.

Mbaeyi, Paul M. British Military & Naval Forces in West African History 1807-1874. LC 77-23627. (Library of African Affairs). (Illus.). 263p. 1978. 21.95 (*0-88357-029-7*) NOK Pubs.

Mbaku, John M. Institutions & Reform in Africa: The Public Choice Perspective. LC 96-52631. 304p. 1997. 69.50 (*0-275-95879-5*, Praeger Pubs) Greenwood.

***Mbaku, John M.** Preparing Africa for the Twenty-First Century: Strategies for Peaceful Coexistence & Sustainable Development. LC 99-72656. 357p. 1999. 78.95 (*0-7546-1085-3*) Ashgate Pub Co.

Mbaku, John M., ed. Corruption & the Crisis of Institutional Reforms in Africa. LC 98-22547. (African Studies: Vol. 47). 360p. 1998. text 99.95 (*0-7734-8351-9*) E Mellen.

Mbaku, John M. & Ihonvbere, Julius O., eds. Multiparty Democracy & Political Change: Constraints to Democratization in Africa. LC 97-77172. (Illus.). 354p. 1998. text 72.95 (*1-84014-379-7*, Pub. by Ashgate Pub) Ashgate Pub Co.

Mbaku, John M., jt. ed. see Kimenyi, Mwangi S.

***Mbaku, John Mukum.** Bureaucratic & Political Corruption in Africa: The Public Choice Perspective. LC 99-32677. 240p. 2000. pap. 21.50 (*1-57524-120-X*) Krieger.

Mbalia, Doreatha D. John Edgar Wideman: Reclaiming the African Personality. LC 94-47088. 136p. 1995. 29.50 (*0-945636-78-4*) Susquehanna U Pr.

— Toni Morrison's Developing Class Consciousness. LC 90-50402. 144p. 1991. 32.50 (*0-945636-17-2*) Susquehanna U Pr.

***Mbanugo, Nwando.** The Spices of Our Sky - Ikuku Si Ike: A Collection of Poems from Igboland. 2000. pap. 9.95 (*1-930454-00-7*) Swan Scythe.

Mbarquez, Patricia C. The Street Is My Home: Youth & Violence in Caracas. LC 98-43805. 1999. 45.00 (*0-8047-3453-4*) Stanford U Pr.

***Mbatybas, Csaba.** Forest Genetics & Sustainability. LC 99-47044. (Forestry Sciences Ser.). 1999. write for info. (*0-7923-6011-7*) Kluwer Academic.

M'Baye, A. A., jt. ed. see Mun, J.

***M'Bayo, Ritchard Tamba, et al, eds.** Press & Politics in Africa. LC 00-36435. (African Studies: Vol. 53). 2000. pap. 99.95 (*0-7734-7684-9*) E Mellen.

***MBD Staff.** The U. K. Kitchen Furniture Market Development. LC 99-45594. 81p. 1999. pap. 560.00 (*1-894330-04-8*) AKTRIN.

Mbeki, Govan. Learning from Robben Island: Govan Mbeki's Prison Writings. LC 91-3198. 232p. 1991. pap. 15.95 (*0-8214-1007-5*); text 24.95 (*0-8214-1006-7*) Ohio U Pr.

— South Africa: The Peasant's Revolt. 1990. 16.50 (*0-8446-0791-6*) Peter Smith.

Mbele, Joseph L. Matengo Folk Tales. 1999. pap. 13.95 (*0-7414-0028-6*) Buy Books.

Mbella, Mokeba H., jt. auth. see Delancey, Mark W.

***Mbembe, Achille.** On the Postcolony. (Studies on the History of Society & Culture: Vol. 41). (Illus.). 292p. 2001. 45.00 (*0-520-20434-4*, Pub. by U CA Pr); pap. 16.95 (*0-520-20435-2*, Pub. by U CA Pr) Cal Prin Full Svc.

Mberi, Antar S. K. A Song Out of Harlem. LC 80-12500. (Vox Humana Ser.). 85p. 1980. 12.95 (*0-89603-018-0*); pap. 6.95 (*0-89603-021-0*) Humana.

MBG Publications Staff, ed. see Balarezo, Martin.

Mbhartrta, Anna & Ramakrishna Math Staff. Tarka-Sagngrahash With the Deipikea of Annarmbhartrta & Notes 2nd rev. ed. LC 98-907768. 196p. 1994. write for info. (*81-7120-674-3*, Pub. by Ramakrishna Math) Vedanta Pr.

Mbiba, Beacon. Urban Agriculture in Zimbabwe: Implications for Urban Management, Urban Economy, Urban Poverty, the Environment & Gender. LC 95-79656. 240p. 1995. 72.95 (*1-85628-857-9*, Pub. by Avebry) Ashgate Pub Co.

Mbilinyi, Marjorie, jt. auth. see Mascarenhas, Ophelia.

***Mbiock, Aristide & Weber, Roman.** Radiation in Enclosures: Elliptic Boundary Value Problem. LC 99-34218. (Scientific Computation Ser.). (Illus.). xiii, 211p. 1999. 59.95 (*3-540-66095-X*) Spr-Verlag.

Mbithi, Philip M. & Rasmusson, Rasmus. Self-Reliance in Kenya: The Case of Harambee. 177p. 1977. write for info. (*91-7106-121-5*, Pub. by Nordic Africa) Transaction Pubs.

Mbiti. Love & Marriage in Africa. 1974. pap. text. write for info. (*0-582-64122-5*, Pub. by Addison-Wesley) Longman.

Mbiti, John S. African Religions & Philosophy. 1970. reprint ed. pap. 6.50 (*0-385-03713-9*) Doubleday.

— African Religions & Philosophy. 2nd ed. LC 89-48596. 288p. (C). 1990. pap. 21.50 (*0-435-89591-5*, 89591) Heinemann.

— Afrikanische Religion und Weltanschauung. Feuser, W. F., tr. from ENG. (GER.). xvi, 375p. (C). 1974. 36.95 (*3-11-002498-5*) De Gruyter.

— Introduction to African Religion. 2nd rev. ed. (Illus.). 216p. (Orig.). (C). 1992. pap. 18.50 (*0-435-94002-3*, 94002) Heinemann.

MBKA Staff. Red Foley's Best Baseball Book Ever. 10th ed. (J). 1996. pap. 9.95 (*0-689-80811-9*) S&S Childrens.

Mbon, Friday M. Brotherhood of the Cross & Star: A New Religious Movement in Nigeria. (Studies in the Intercultural History of Christianity: Vol. 78). (Illus.). XI, 350p. 1992. pap. 52.80 (*3-631-44181-9*) P Lang Pubng.

Mboya, Tom. The Challenge of Nationhood. (African Writers Ser.). 278p. (C). 1970. pap. 9.95 (*0-435-90081-1*, 90081) Heinemann.

Mbuende, Kaire. Namibia, the Broken Shield: Anatomy of Imperialism & Revolution. 213p. (Orig.). 1986. 19.95 (*91-40-05156-0*, Pub. by Nordic Africa) Transaction Pubs.

Mbugua, Judy, ed. Our Time Has Come: African Christian Women Address the Issues of Today. LC 94-41369. (World Evangelical Fellowship Ser.). 154p. 1995. pap. 10.99 (*0-8010-2018-2*) Baker Bks.

***Mbugua, Judy & Kisuke, Connie.** Judy! A Second Chance: She Refused to Give Up. 161p. 1999. reprint ed. mass mkt. 9.99 (*1-85078-337-3*, Pub. by O M Pubng) OM Literature.

Mbugua, Kioi Wa. Inkishu: Myths & Legends of the Maasai. (African Art & Literature Ser.). (Illus.). 1995. pap. 15.95 (*9966-884-97-1*) Jacaranda.

Mbugua, Njeri S. Empowerment of Third World Woman Against AIDS: Special Reference to East & Central Africa. 29p. 1996. pap. 2.00 (*0-941934-74-8*) Indiana Africa.

Mbukanma, Jude O. Is It in the Bible? 134p. 1994. pap. 9.95 (*1-885417-02-0*) MET Pubng.

— Power in the Bread. 130p. 1994. pap. 7.95 (*1-885417-03-9*) MET Pubng.

Mbukanma, Jude O., ed. On the Eucharist: A Divine Appeal. rev. ed. 215p. 1994. reprint ed. pap. 11.95 (*1-885417-00-4*) MET Pubng.

Mbulu, Mba. Black Smart: Essays to Black People. 1996. pap. 10.00 (*1-883885-09-4*) ASET Pubns.

— The Black Studies Book: A Black Studies Guide for Teenagers & Adults. Sekou, Bomani, ed. 256p. (Orig.). 1997. pap. text 14.00 (*1-883885-11-6*) ASET Pubns.

— Not to Be: Essays about Integration. 105p. 1995. pap. 8.00 (*1-883885-10-8*) ASET Pubns.

Mbulu, Mba & Sekou, Bomani. Spotlight on Male Female Relations. 29p. 1993. pap. 4.00 (*1-883885-00-0*) ASET Pubns.

Mbulu, Mba & Sekou, Bomani, eds. Ten Lessons: An Introduction to Black History. 2nd ed. 225p. 1994. reprint ed. pap. 12.00 (*1-883885-06-X*) ASET Pubns.

Mburu, F. M. Ocular Needs in Africa. 147p. 1984. pap. 25.00 (*0-08-031299-3*, Pergamon Pr) Elsevier.

Mbuy-Beya, Bernadette, jt. ed. see Abraham, K. C.

Mbuyi, Dennis M. Beyond Policy & Language Choice: An Analysis of Texts in Four Instructional Contexts in East Africa. LC 87-6362. (Special Studies in Comparative Education: No. 18). 1987. pap. text 10.00 (*0-937033-08-1*) Grad Schl of Educ.

Mc Bride, Turtle. The Story of Sue & Ivan: An Economic Fairy Tale. (Illus.). 60p. (Orig.). 1997. pap. 5.95 (*1-891098-01-2*, 97-0701, Paper Tools) Think Publ.

Mc Bride, Will. I, Will Mc Bride. (ENG & GER., Illus.). 400p. 1997. 39.95 (*3-89508-452-2*, 810078) Konemann.

Mc Cain, Ted D. & Ekelund, Mark. Computer Networking for Educators. 2nd rev. ed. LC 99-236295. (Illus.). 186p. 1996. spiral bd. 30.95 (*1-56484-107-3*) Intl Society Tech Educ.

Mc Cormick. Reading Our History & Understanding Culture: A Sequenced Approach to Thinking, Reading & Writing. 602p. 1998. pap. text 38.00 (*0-205-26176-0*) Allyn.

An Asterisk (*) at the beginning of an entry indicates that the title is appearing for the first time.

Mc Cormick, jt. auth. see Knapp, Mary H.

Mc Cormick, Donald B., et al, eds. Vitamins & Coenzymes, Pt. L. (Methods in Enzymology Ser.: Vol. 282). (Illus.). 505p. 1997. text 99.95 (*0-12-182183-8*) Morgan Kaufmann.

Mc Cullough, L. E. Anyone Can Produce a Play with Kids: The Absolute Basics to Staging Your Own At-Home, In-School, Round-the Neighborhood Plays. LC 98-36282. 192p. (J). (gr. k-6). 1999. pap. 14.95 (*1-57525-151-5*) Smith & Kraus.

Mc Donald, Robert, jt. auth. see Dilts, Robert.

***Mc Fadden, Ted.** Hermes' Viper. 368p. 2000. pap. 19.95 (*1-892693-14-3*) Hughes Henshaw Pubs.

Mc Gowan Consultants Staff. Health Care Protocols: A Handbook for DD Nurses. (Illus.). 486p. 1998. pap. 49.95 (*1-928752-02-0*) Mc Gowan Pubns.

Mc Gowan, Jim, jt. auth. see Mc Gowan, Karen G.

Mc Gowan, Karen G. Drugs & Disabilities: Handle with Care. (Illus.). 344p. 1995. pap. 29.95 (*1-928752-01-2*) Mc Gowan Pubns.

Mc Gowan, Karen G. & Mc Gowan, Jim. Assessing Health Risk in Developmental Disabilities. (Illus.). 248p. 1995. pap. 29.95 (*1-928752-00-4*) Mc Gowan Pubns.

— Functional Life Planning. (Illus.). 174p. 1994. pap. 23.95 (*1-928752-04-7*) Mc Gowan Pubns.

— Practical Home Modification. (Illus.). 128p. 1993. pap. 19.95 (*1-928752-10-1*) Mc Gowan Pubns.

Mc Gowan, Karen G., ed. see Winters, Jody.

***Mc Kenna, Kristine, et al.** Forming: The Early Days of L. A. Punk. 2nd ed. (Illus.). 96p. 2000. reprint ed. pap. 20.00 (*1-889195-44-8*, Pub. by Smart Art Pr) Dist Art Pubs.

Mc Loughlin, Thomas. Contesting Ireland: Irish Voices Against England in the Eighteenth-Century. 240p. 1999. boxed set 55.00 (*1-85182-448-0*, Pub. by Four Cts Pr) Intl Spec Bk.

***Mc Loughlin, Thomas.** Contesting Ireland: Irish Voices Against England in the Eighteenth-Century. 240p. 1999. pap. 29.95 (*1-85182-449-9*, Pub. by Four Cts Pr) Intl Spec Bk.

Mc Nally, Louise, jt. ed. see Culicover, Peter.

MC Pub. Co. Staff. Candy Buyers Directory, 1998. Allured, Allen R., ed. 345p. 1998. pap. 55.00 (*0-944254-54-3*) MC Pub Co NJ.

— McCutcheon's Functional Materials: North American & International Edition. rev. ed. Allured, Michael, ed. LC 82-64457. 475p. 1998. 165.00 (*0-944254-60-8*) MC Pub Co NJ.

Mc-Quil. Radiographic Critique. 1995. 435.00 (*0-7216-4980-7*) Harcourt.

Mc., Tim. Today I Will Do One Thing: Daily Readings for Awareness & Hope. LC 95-1887. 400p. pap. 10.00 (*1-56838-083-6*) Hazelden.

McA. Mason, D. & Eakin, B. E. Calculation of Heating & Specific Gravity of Fuel Gases. (Research Bulletin Ser.: No. 32). iv, 18p. 1961. 3.50 (*1-58222-012-3*) Inst Gas Tech.

McA. Mason, D., et al. Investigation of Factors Affecting Gas Mantle Life. (One GT Technical Report Ser.: No. 6). vi, 33p. 1962. pap. 25.00 (*1-58222-029-8*) Inst Gas Tech.

McAlly, Mary, ed. We Sing Our Struggle: A Tribute to Us All. (Illus.). 82p. (Orig.). 1982. pap. 7.50 (*0-943594-03-0*) Cardinal Pr.

McAbee, Harold V., jt. auth. see Grunwald, Bernice B.

***McAdam, Christine.** Barney's Shapes. (Barney Ser.). (Illus.). 22p. (J). (ps-k). 1999. bds. 5.95 (*1-57064-651-1*, Barney Publ) Lyrick Pub.

McAdam, Don. Engineering Problem Solving & Design Graphics. 1999. spiral bd. write for info. (*0-201-89200-6*) Addison-Wesley.

McAdam, Doug. Political Process & Development of Black Insurgency,1930-70. 2nd ed. LC 99-32405. 304p. 1999. pap. text 14.00 (*0-226-55553-4*) U Ch Pr.

— Social Movements. (New Perspectives in Sociology Ser.). (C). 1996. text 39.95 (*0-8133-1653-7*); pap. text 14.95 (*0-8133-1654-5*) Westview.

McAdam, Doug, et al, eds. Comparative Perspectives on Social Movements: Political Opportunities, Mobilizing Structures, & Cultural Framings. (Cambridge Studies in Comparative Politics). (Illus.). 442p. (C). 1996. pap. text 20.95 (*0-521-48516-9*) Cambridge U Pr.

— Comparative Perspectives on Social Movements: Political Opportunities, Mobilizing Structures, & Cultural Framings. (Cambridge Studies in Comparative Politics). (Illus.). 440p. (C). 1996. text 64.95 (*0-521-48039-6*) Cambridge U Pr.

McAdam, Doug & Snow, David A., eds. Social Movements: Readings on Their Emergence, Mobilization & Dynamics. LC 96-19801. 557p. (C). 1997. pap. text. write for info. (*0-935732-86-1*) Roxbury Pub Co.

McAdam, Douglas. Freedom Summer. (Illus.). 368p. 1990. reprint ed. pap. 15.95 (*0-19-506472-0*) OUP.

— Political Process & the Development of Black Insurgency, 1930 to 1970. LC 82-2712. (Illus.). viii, 312p. (C). 1985. pap. text 12.95 (*0-226-55552-6*) U Ch Pr.

— Political Process & the Development of Black Insurgency, 1930 to 1970. LC 82-2712. (Illus.). viii, 304p. (C). 1993. 27.50 (*0-226-55551-8*) U Ch Pr.

McAdam, Douglas, et al. The Politics of Privacy: Planning for Personal Data Systems As Powerful Technologies. LC 80-13788. 212p. 1981. lib. bdg. 42.50 (*0-444-99074-7*, RPP/) Greenwood.

McAdam, Douglas, jt. auth. see Marx, Gary T.

McAdam, E. L., Jr., ed. see Johnson, Samuel.

McAdam, Ian. The Irony of Identity: Self & Imagination in the Drama of Christopher Marlowe. LC 98-36997. 288p. 1999. 43.50 (*0-87413-665-2*) U Delaware Pr.

McAdam, John M., jt. auth. see Scharer, Lawrence L.

McAdam, K., jt. auth. see Porter, J.

***McAdam, Maryln & McDermott, Ed.** Expanding Federal Work-Study & Community Service Opportunities. 61p. 1999. reprint ed. pap. text 20.00 (*0-7881-7992-6*) DIANE Pub.

McAdam, Peter, jt. auth. see Lee, Geoffrey.

McAdam, Peter, jt. ed. see Hallett, Andrew Hughes.

McAdam, R. History of Insects. (Illus.). 160p. 1995. pap. 20.00 (*0-87556-787-8*) Saifer.

McAdam, S. Asymptotic Prime Divisors. (Lecture Notes in Mathematics Ser.: Vol. 1023). 118p. 1983. 29.95 (*0-387-12722-4*) Spr-Verlag.

— Primes Associated to an Ideal. LC 89-27624. (Contemporary Mathematics Ser.: Vol. 102). 167p. 1989. pap. 37.00 (*0-8218-5108-X*, CONM/102) Am Math.

McAdam, Terry W. Doing Well by Doing Good: The Complete Guide to Careers in the Nonprofit Sector. 199p. 1991. 27.95 (*0-930807-21-9*, 600300) Fund Raising.

***McAdam, Winn.** Engineering Problem Solving & Design Graphics Autocad R14LT. (Illus.). 1999. pap. text. write for info. (*0-201-65460-1*) Addison-Wesley.

McAdams. The Person. 2nd ed. (C). 1994. pap. text, teacher ed. 35.00 (*0-15-501967-8*) Harcourt Coll Pubs.

— The Person. 3rd ed. (C). 1999. text. write for info. (*0-15-508066-0*) Harcourt Coll Pubs.

Mcadams, jt. auth. see Yopp.

McAdams- Pincus. Legal Environment of Business. 2nd ed. 1999. 58.00 (*0-07-230335-2*) McGraw.

McAdams, A. James. East Germany & Detente: Building Authority after the Wall. (Cambridge Russian, Soviet & Post-Soviet Studies: No. 49). 245p. 1985. text 69.95 (*0-521-26835-4*) Cambridge U Pr.

— Germany Divided: From the Wall to Reunification. LC 92-15654. (Studies in International History & Politics). 272p. 1993. text 45.00 (*0-691-07892-0*, Pub. by Princeton U Pr) Cal Prin Full Svc.

— Transitional Justice & the Rule of Law in New Democracies. LC 97-5313. (Title from the Helen Kellogg Institute for International Studies). 1997. pap. 20.00 (*0-268-04203-9*) U of Notre Dame Pr.

McAdams, Bob, jt. auth. see Gebert, Gordon G.

McAdams, C. Michael. Croatia: Myth & Reality: The Final Chapter. 3rd rev. ed. Wolterbeek, Kim S., ed. (Illus.). 154p. (Orig.). 1997. pap. 14.95 (*0-9633625-3-4*) CIS Monographs.

Mcadams, Christine. Barney's Colors. (Barney's Beginnings Ser.). (Illus.). (J). (ps-k). 1998. bds. 5.95 (*1-57064-310-5*) Lyrick Pub.

McAdams, Dan P. The Person: An Introduction to Personality Psychology. 2nd ed. (Illus.). 704p. (C). 1994. text 86.00 (*0-15-501274-6*) Harcourt Coll Pubs.

— Power, Intimacy, & the Life Story: Personological Inquiries into Identity. LC 88-5285. 336p. 1988. pap. text 25.00 (*0-89862-506-8*) Guilford Pubns.

— The Stories We Live By: Personal Myths & the Making of the Self. LC 96-49264. 336p. 1997. pap. text 18.95 (*1-57230-188-0*, 0188) Guilford Pubns.

McAdams, Dan P. & de St. Aubin, Ed, eds. Generativity & Adult Development: How & Why We Care for the Next Generation. LC 97-32831. 511p. 1998. 49.95 (*1-55798-470-0*) Am Psychol.

McAdams, Dan P., ed. see Ochberg, Richard L.

***McAdams, Donald R.** Fighting to Save Our Urban Schools-- & Winning! Lessons from Houston. LC 99-52194. 312p. 2000. pap. write for info. (*0-8077-3884-0*) Tchrs Coll.

— Fighting to Save Our Urban Schools... & Winning! Lessons from Houston. LC 99-52194. (Illus.). 312p. 2000. text 46.00 (*0-8077-3885-9*) Tchrs Coll.

McAdams, Elizabeth & Bayless, Raymond. The Case for Life After Death. LC 80-29289. 168p. 1981. text 28.95 (*0-88229-592-6*) Burnham Inc.

McAdams, Eric T., jt. auth. see Walsh, Deirdre M.

***McAdams, Janet.** The Island of Lost Luggage. LC 99-50807. (First Book Awards Ser.). 90p. 2000. 13.95 (*0-8165-2056-9*) U of Ariz Pr.

McAdams, Jerry L. The Reward Plan Advantage: A Manager's Guide to Improving Business Performance Through People. LC 96-461. (Business & Management Ser.). 270p. 1996. 32.95 (*0-7879-0232-2*) Jossey-Bass.

McAdams, Jerry L. & Hawk, Elizabeth J. Capitalizing on Human Assets: The Benchmark Study (Full Report) (Illus.). 144p. 1992. 100.00 (*1-57963-071-5*) Am Compensation.

— Capitalizing on Human Assets: The Benchmark Study (Summary Report) (Illus.). 1992. 25.00 (*1-57963-072-3*) Am Compensation.

— Organizational Performance & Rewards: 663 Experiences in Making the Link. (Illus.). 1994. 150.00 (*1-57963-073-1*) Am Compensation.

— Organizational Performance & Rewards: 663 Experiences in Making the Link (Executive Summary) (Illus.). 1994. 25.00 (*1-57963-074-X*) Am Compensation.

McAdams, Jerry L., jt. auth. see Mai, Robert P.

McAdams, Laurel D. & Skindzier, James J. Pennsylvania Continuing Education for Real Estate Salespersons & Brokers: Elective Course. 2nd ed. LC 95-137515. 88p. (C). 1994. pap. text 9.95 (*0-7931-0938-8*, 152008-01, Real Estate Ed) Dearborn.

— Pennsylvania Continuing Education for Real Estate Salespersons & Brokers: Required Course. 2nd ed. 112p. (C). 1994. pap. text 9.95 (*0-7931-1144-7*, 152004-02, Real Estate Ed) Dearborn.

McAdams, Mrs. Harry K. Kentucky Pioneer & Court Records: Abstracts of Early Wills, Deeds, & Marriages. 381p. 1999. reprint ed. pap. 35.00 (*0-8063-0217-8*, 3470, Pub. by Clearfield Co) ACCESS Pubs Network.

McAdams, Richard. Lessons from Abroad: How Other Countries Educate Their Children. LC 93-60192. 340p. 1998. text 39.95 (*0-87762-986-2*) Scarecrow.

McAdams, Richard, jt. auth. see Langlois, Donald.

***McAdams, Robert W., Jr. & Gallagher, Mary L.** State & Federal Prohibitions on Physician Referrals: A Guide to Compliance. LC 99-202067. 466p. 1998. 189.00 (*0-8342-1214-5*) Aspen Pub.

McAdams, Robert W., Jr., et al. Managed Care Contracts Manual. LC 95-47265. 492p. Date not set. ring bd. 269.00 (*0-8342-0813-X*) Aspen Pub.

McAdams, Stephen. Music & Psychology: A Mutual Regard, Vol. 2, No. 1. (Contemporary Music Review Ser.). viii, 320p. 1987. pap. text 74.00 (*3-7186-0382-9*) Gordon & Breach.

McAdams, Stephen & Deilege, I., eds. Music & the Cognitive Sciences: Proceedings from the "Symposium on Music & the Cognitive Sciences," 14-18 March 1988 Paris, France. (Contemporary Music Review Ser.: Vol. 4). x, 468p. 1989. pap. text 96.00 (*3-7186-4953-5*) Gordon & Breach.

McAdams, Tony. Law, Business & Society. 6th ed. 832p. 2000. 85.63 (*0-07-231401-X*) McGraw.

McAdams, Tony & Pincus, Laura B. The Legal Environment of Business: Ethical & Public Policy Contexts. 704p. (C). 1996. text 70.75 (*0-256-17051-7*, Irwn McGrw-H) McGrw-H Hghr Educ.

McAdams, Tony, et al. Law, Business & Society. 4th ed. LC 94-21204. (Legal Studies in Business). 876p. (C). 1994. text 70.75 (*0-256-14166-5*, Irwn McGrw-H) McGrw-H Hghr Educ.

— Law, Business & Society. 5th ed. LC 97-15193. (C). 1997. text. write for info. (*0-256-23690-9*, Irwn McGrw-H) McGrw-H Hghr Educ.

McAden, Ann S., jt. auth. see Saunders, Boyd.

McAden, Anthony E. Sing a Message to Freedom: The Freedom Man. Satchell, Alexis, ed. (Illus.). 50p. (Orig.). 1986. pap. 6.25 (*0-931841-07-0*) Satchells Pub.

McAdie, Alexander G. Making the Weather. LC 77-10233. reprint ed. 29.50 (*0-404-16213-4*) AMS Pr.

McAdoo, Caryl, jt. auth. see McAdoo, Ron.

McAdoo, David. The Dragon of Ord. LC 85-81417. (Books for Students by Students). 1985. lib. bdg. 15.95 (*0-933849-23-0*) Landmark Edns.

McAdoo, Harriette P. Black Families. 2nd ed. (Focus Editions Ser.: Vol. 41). 320p. 1988. pap. 26.00 (*0-8039-3180-8*); text 59.95 (*0-8039-3179-4*) Sage.

— Black Families. 3rd ed. 400p. 1996. 55.00 (*0-8039-5572-3*); pap. 25.95 (*0-8039-5573-1*) Sage.

— Family Ethnicity: Strength in Diversity. (Illus.). 320p. (C). 1993. text 55.00 (*0-8039-3736-9*); pap. text 26.95 (*0-8039-3737-7*) Sage.

***McAdoo, Harriette P.** Family Ethnicity: Strength in Diversity. 2nd ed. LC 98-40271. 1999. pap. write for info. (*0-7619-1857-4*) Sage.

— Family Ethnicity Strength in Diversity. 2nd ed. LC 98-40271. 3p. 1999. write for info. (*0-7619-1856-6*) Sage.

McAdoo, Harriette P. & McAdoo, John L. Black Children. (Focus Editions Ser.: Vol. 72). 1985. 59.95 (*0-8039-2461-5*); pap. 26.00 (*0-8039-2462-3*) Sage.

McAdoo, Henry R. Anglican Heritage: Theology & Spirituality. 127p. 1994. pap. 10.95 (*1-85311-045-0*, 814, Pub. by Canterbury Press Norwich) Morehouse Pub.

— First of Its Kind: Jeremy Taylor's Life of Christ: A Study in the Functioning of a Moral Theology. 1994. pap. 17.95 (*1-85311-083-3*, 6342, Pub. by Canterbury Press Norwich) Morehouse Pub.

— The Unity of Anglicanism: Catholic & Reformed. LC 82-62392. 88p. (Orig.). 1983. pap. 4.95 (*0-8192-1324-1*) Morehouse Pub.

McAdoo, Henry R. & Stevenson, Kenneth. The Mystery of the Eucharist in the Anglican Tradition. 206p. (Orig.). 1995. pap. 16.95 (*1-85311-113-9*, 851, Pub. by Canterbury Press Norwich) Morehouse Pub.

McAdoo, Joe. McAdoo about Nothing: Selections from "The Rusty Saber" (Illus.). 150p. 1997. pap. 8.95 (*0-9638648-1-5*) Barnabs Pub.

McAdoo, John L., jt. auth. see McAdoo, Harriette P.

***McAdoo, Ron & McAdoo, Caryl.** Texas Firehouse Cooks: Favorite Recipes. (Illus.). 250p. 2000. pap. 18.95 (*1-55622-790-6*, Rep of TX Pr) Wordware Pub.

McAdoo, William. Guarding a Great City. LC 73-154577. (Police in America Ser.). 1971. reprint ed. 24.95 (*0-405-03373-7*) Ayer.

— Pre-Civil War Black Nationalism. LC 83-60956. (Illus.). 96p. (Orig.). (C). 1983. 12.95 (*0-912135-01-8*); pap. 6.95 (*0-912135-00-X*) D Walker Pr.

***McAdory, Jerry.** Upward Bound to Higher Ground. 160p. 2000. pap. 9.99 (*1-930027-11-7*, 921-027, Pub. by Insght Pub) BookWorld.

***McAdow, Ron.** Antiquing in North Texas: A Guide to Antique Shops, Malls & Flea Markets. LC 99-26681. 1999. pap. 18.95 (*1-55622-694-2*) Wordware Pub.

McAdow, Ron. The Charles River: Exploring Nature & History on Foot & by Canoe. LC 91-21450. (Illus.). 224p. (Orig.). 1992. pap. 16.50 (*0-9625144-1-1*) Bliss Pub Co.

— The Concord, Sudbury, & Assabet Rivers: A Guide to Canoeing, Wildlife, & History. LC 90-38. (Illus.). 232p. (Orig.). 1990. pap. 16.50 (*0-9625144-0-3*) Bliss Pub Co.

***McAdow, Ron.** The Concord, Sudbury & Assabet Rivers: A Guide to Canoeing, Wildlife & History. 2nd rev. ed. (Illus.). 223p. 2000. pap. 18.00 (*0-9625144-4-6*) Bliss Pub Co.

McAdow, Ron. New England Time Line. 2nd ed. LC 92-80179. 96p. 1992. pap. write for info. (*1-880644-01-0*) Nutshell Bks.

— New England Time Line: A Concise Guide to the Region's History. (McAdow's Time Lines Ser.). 48p. 1991. pap. 4.95 (*1-880644-00-2*) Nutshell Bks.

McAdow, Ron, jt. auth. see Stier, Maggie.

***McAfee, Annalena.** Busy Baby. (Illus.). 18p. (J). 1998. pap. 9.99 (*1-58048-055-1*) Sandvik Pub.

McAfee, Annalena & Lewis, Anthony. All the Way to the Stars. (Illus.). 32p. (J). (ps-k). 1996. 18.95 (*1-85681-530-7*, Pub. by Julia MacRae) Trafalgar.

McAfee, B. The Phone Book System: Drum Yellow Pages. (Illus.). 40p. (Orig.). 1997. pap. 10.95 (*1-57424-043-9*) Centerstream Pub.

McAfee, Caleb. Money & the Christian: A Course in Biblical Economics. 192p. pap. 14.95 (*0-9656010-0-5*) Dimensn Four.

— Start Your Own Business. 300p. 1999. pap. 24.99 (*0-9656010-1-3*) Dake Pub.

Mcafee, Carol. The Climbing Tree. large type ed. 1991. 27.99 (*0-7089-2502-2*) Ulverscroft.

McAfee, Helen, ed. see Pepys, Samuel.

McAfee, Ila, jt. auth. see Lester, Katherine Morris.

McAfee, James W. Power to Live Through Nutrition. LC 80-82331. (Illus.). 196p. (Orig.). 1980. pap. 6.95 (*0-9604592-0-0*) Image Awareness.

McAfee, John P. On Rims of Empty Moons. LC 97-33405. 267p. 1997. 25.95 (*0-89672-386-0*) Tex Tech Univ Pr.

— Slow Walk in a Sad Rain. (Fresh Voices Ser.). 224p. 1994. mass mkt. 5.99 (*0-446-36500-9*) Warner Bks.

McAfee, Julie G., jt. auth. see Shipley, Kenneth G.

McAfee, Kathy. Storm Signals: Structural Adjustment & Development Alternatives in the Caribbean. 259p. 1991. 30.00 (*0-89608-421-3*); pap. 15.00 (*0-89608-420-5*) South End Pr.

McAfee, Michael J. Billy Yank: The Uniform of the Union Army, 1861-1865. LC 99-21377. (G.I. Ser.). (Illus.). 84p. (YA). (gr. 5 up). 1999. 19.95 (*0-7910-5368-7*) Chelsea Hse.

— Zouaves: The First & the Bravest. (Illus.). 124p. (C). 1994. pap. text 12.95 (*0-939631-80-6*) Thomas Publications.

McAfee, Michael J., jt. auth. see Langellier, John P.

***McAfee, Nohelle.** Habermas, Kristeva & Citizenship. LC 99-56445. 2000. write for info. (*0-8014-3706-7*) Cornell U Pr.

McAfee, Norman, tr. see Sartre, Jean-Paul.

McAfee, Oralie & Leong, Deborah J. Assess & Guide Young Child. 2nd ed. LC 96-32717. 283p. 1996. pap. text 41.00 (*0-205-26332-1*) Allyn.

***McAfee, Pat.** Irish Stone Walls: History, Building, Conservation. LC 97-212333. (Illus.). 176p. 2000. 24.95 (*0-86278-478-6*, Pub. by OBrien Pr) IPG Chicago.

McAfee, Patrick. Stone Buildings: Conservation, Repair, Building. LC 98-230929. 224p. 1998. 27.95 (*0-86278-577-4*) OBrien Pr.

McAfee, Paul C., jt. auth. see Long, Donlin M.

McAfee, Paul K. Bonner. large type ed. (Linford Western Library). 256p. 1993. pap. 16.99 (*0-7089-7439-2*, Linford) Ulverscroft.

***McAfee, Paul K.** Cabel. large type ed. 272p. 1999. pap. 18.99 (*0-7089-5474-X*, Linford) Ulverscroft.

McAfee, Paul K. The Dark Trail. large type ed. (Linford Western Large Print Ser.). 272p. 1998. pap. 17.99 (*0-7089-5279-8*, Linford) Ulverscroft.

McAfee, R. Bruce & Champagne, Paul J. Organizational Behavior: A Manager's View. LC 86-24745. (Illus.). 489p. (C). 1987. pap. text, teacher ed. write for info. (*0-314-35226-0*) West Pub.

McAfee, R. Bruce, jt. auth. see Champagne, Paul J.

McAfee, R. Preston & McMillan, John, eds. Incentives in Government Contracting. (Economic Council Research Ser.). 168p. 1989. pap. text 17.95 (*0-8020-6638-0*) U of Toronto Pr.

McAfee, Virginia T. A Season of the Heart. (Illus.). 96p. (Orig.). 1995. pap. 12.95 (*0-9647323-0-0*) Home Place Bks.

McAfee, W. R. The Cattlemen. 228p. 1989. 29.95 (*0-9623394-0-7*) Davis Mntn Pr.

— The Cattlemen. 270p. 1991. reprint ed. 27.95 (*0-9623394-1-5*) Davis Mntn Pr.

McAfee, W. R., ed. see Grigar, Rudy.

McAfee, Ward. A History of the World's Great Religions. 240p. (Orig.). (C). 1983. lib. bdg. 50.50 (*0-8191-3394-9*) U Pr of Amer.

***McAfee, Ward.** Never an Island A History of California. LC 98-46781. (West Coast Studies). 1999. write for info. (*0-89370-808-9*) Millefleurs.

McAfee, Ward M. Religion, Race, & Reconstruction: The Public School in the Politics of the 1870s. LC 97-37731. (SUNY Series, Religion & American Public Life). (Illus.). 320p. (C). 1998. text 65.50 (*0-7914-3847-3*); pap. text 21.95 (*0-7914-3848-1*) State U NY Pr.

McAffee, Michael, ed. Apple Access: Users' Guide to Apple Computer-Related Periodical Literature (Jan.-June 1984) (Apple Access of Semi-Annual Ser.: Vol. 1). (Illus.). 256p. (Orig.). 1985. pap. 19.95 (*0-931293-00-6*) Stony Point Pubns.

McAffee, R. Bruce & Champagne, Paul J. Effectively Managing Troublesome Employees. LC 93-49029. 200p. 1994. 59.95 (*0-89930-773-6*, Quorum Bks) Greenwood.

***McAffee, Thomas B.** Inherent Rights, the Written Constitution, & Popular Sovereignty: The Founders' Understanding. 95. LC 00-21049. (Contributions in Legal Studies: Vol. 95). 200p. 2000. 65.00 (*0-313-31507-8*) Greenwood.

McAinsh, T. F. Physics in Medicine & Biology. 2 vols., Vol. 1-2. 1986. 185.00 (*0-08-033930-1*, Pergamon Pr); 135.00 (*0-08-033931-X*, Pergamon Pr) Elsevier.

McAinsh, T. F., ed. Physics in Medicine & Biology Encyclopedia. 2 vols., Set. (Illus.). 650p. 1986. 447.00 (*0-08-026497-2*, Pub. by Pergamon Repr) Franklin.

McAlary, Florence & Cohen, Judith L. Tu Puedes Ser Biologa Marina. Yanez, Juan, tr. from ENG. (SPA., Illus.). 40p. (J). (gr. 4-7). 1992. pap. 6.00 (*1-880599-07-4*) Cascade Pass.

— You Can Be a Woman Marine Biologist. (Illus.). 40p. (Orig.). (J). (gr. 4-7). 1992. pap. 6.00 (*1-880599-06-6*) Cascade Pass.

M

McAlary, Florence & Katz, David A. You Can Be a Woman Marine Biologist. 40p. (Orig.). (J). (gr. 3-6). 1997. pap. 19.95 incl. cd-rom (*1-880599-21-X*) Cascade Pass.

McAlary, Mike. Cop Land: Based on the Screenplay by James Mangold. LC 97-18699. 256p. (J). 1997. pap. 11.45 (*0-7868-8252-2*, Pub. by Hyperion) Time Warner.

McAlary, Mike. Mark of a Murderer. 2000. pap. write for info. (*0-7868-8424-X*, Pub. by Disney Pr) Little.

— Sore Loser: A Mickey Donovan Mystery. 352p. 1998. 24.00 (*0-688-15610-X*, Wm Morrow) Morrow Avon.

McAlary, Mike, jt. auth. see Trimboli, Joseph.

McAleavey, David. The Forty Days. LC 75-328954. 40p. 1975. 3.50 (*0-87886-071-1*, Greenfld Rev Pr) Greenfld Rev Lit.

— Holding Obsidian. LC 84-52605. (Series Nine). 53p. 1985. pap. 7.00 (*0-931846-26-9*) Wash Writers Pub.

— Shrine, Shelter, Cave. LC 80-19572. 72p. 1980. 4.00 (*0-87886-110-6*, Greenfld Rev Pr) Greenfld Rev Lit.

McAleavey, David, ed. Evidence of Community: Writings from the Jenny McKean Moore Workshops at the George Washington University, Vol. M11. 1984. 7.00 (*1-888028-09-2*) GWU Ctr WAS.

— Washington & Washington Writing, Vol. M12. 1986. 7.00 (*1-888028-10-6*) GWU Ctr WAS.

McAleavy, Tony. Agricultural Change. (C). 1988. 40.00 (*0-7157-2769-9*) St Mut.

— The Arab-Israeli Conflict. (Cambridge History Program Ser.). (Illus.). 64p. (C). 1998. pap. 13.95 (*0-521-62953-5*) Cambridge U Pr.

— Medieval Britain: Conquest, Power & People. (Cambridge History Programme Ser.). (Illus.). 80p. (C). 1993. pap. 14.95 (*0-521-40708-7*) Cambridge U Pr.

— Modern World History: International Relations from 1914 to the Present. LC 96-227985. (Cambridge History Programme Ser.). (Illus.). 176p. (C). 1996. pap. 20.95 (*0-521-44575-2*) Cambridge U Pr.

— Superpower Rivalry: The Cold War, 1945-1991. LC 98-150068. (Cambridge History Program Ser.). (Illus.). 80p. (C). 1998. pap. 13.95 (*0-521-59739-0*) Cambridge U Pr.

McAleavy, Tony, jt. auth. see Kernaghan, Pamela.

McAleer, Dave. All Music Book of Hit Albums: The Top Ten U. S. & U. K. Album Charts from 1960 to the Present. (Illus.). 352p. 1996. pap. 22.95 (*0-87930-393-X*) Miller Freeman.

— Encyclopedia of Hits: The 1960's. 320p. 1996. pap. 19.95 (*0-7137-2609-1*, Pub. by Blandford Pr) Sterling.

***McAleer, Dave, compiled by.** The Book of Hit Singles: Top 20 Charts from 1954 to the Present Day. 3rd ed. (Illus.). 456p. 1999. pap. 24.95 (*0-87930-596-7*, Pub. by Miller Freeman) Publishers Group.

McAleer, E. C., ed. see Browning, Robert.

McAleer, Edward C., ed. see Browning, Robert.

McAleer, G. A Study in the Etymology of the Indian Place Name. 1977. 59.95 (*0-8490-2709-8*) Gordon Pr.

McAleer, J. Philip. A Pictorial History of St. Paul's Anglican Church, Halifax, Nova Scotia. LC 92-98603. (Illus.). 160p. 1993. pap. 16.95 (*0-929112-19-9*, Pub. by Tuns Pr) Baker & Taylor.

McAleer, J. Philip. Rochester Cathedral: An Architectural History of the Fabric to the Dissolution, 604-1540. (Illus.). 350p. 1999. text 65.00 (*0-8020-4222-8*) U of Toronto Pr.

McAleer, Jill, jt. auth. see Gunter, Barrie.

McAleer, Joe. Passion's Fortune: The History of Mills & Boon. (Illus.). 352p. 2000. text 35.00 (*0-19-820455-8*) OUP.

McAleer, Kevin. Dueling: The Cult of Honor in Fin-de-Siecle Germany. LC 94-4401. 288p. 1994. text 39.50 (*0-691-03462-1*, Pub. by Princeton U Pr); pap. text 14.95 (*0-691-01594-5*, Pub. by Princeton U Pr) Cal Prin Full Svc.

McAleer, M. J., jt. auth. see Mahendrarajah, S.

McAleer, Michael, jt. ed. see Oxley, Leslie.

McAleer, Neil. The Cosmic Mind-Boggling Book. 320p. (Orig.). 1989. mass mkt. 11.95 (*0-446-39046-1*, Pub. by Warner Bks) Little.

McAleese, Dermot. Economics for Management. 600p. 1997. pap. 40.00 (*0-13-371246-X*) P-H.

McAleese, Dermot, et al. Africa & the European Community after 1992. LC 92-43305. (EDI Seminar Report Ser.). 108p. 1993. pap. 22.00 (*0-8213-2368-7*, 12368) World Bank.

McAleese, Frank G. The Laser Experimenter's Handbook. (Illus.). 1979. 11.95 (*0-8306-9770-5*); pap. 10.95 (*0-8306-1123-1*, 1123) McGraw-Hill Prof.

McAleese, Mary. Love in Chaos: Spiritual Growth & the Search for Peace in Northern Ireland. LC 82-40254. 124p. 1998. reprint ed. pap. 11.95 (*0-8264-1137-1*) Continuum.

McAleese, Ray, ed. Hypertext: Theory into Practice. (Illus.). 156p. 1993. pap. text 24.95 (*1-871516-04-8*, Pub. by Intellect) Cromland.

— Hypertext: Theory into Practice. 2nd ed. 160p. 1998. pap. 24.95 (*1-871516-28-5*, Pub. by Intellect) Intl Spec Bk.

McAleese, Ray & Green, Catherine. Hypertext: State of the Art. (Illus.). 269p. 1995. write for info. (*1-871516-08-0*, Pub. by Intellect) Cromland.

McAleese, Ray, jt. ed. see Unwin, Derek.

***McAleese, Stuart.** Operational Aspects of Oil & Gas Well Testing. LC 00-22084. (Handbook of Petroleum Exploration & Production Ser.). 2000. write for info. (*0-444-50311-0*) Elsevier.

McAleese, Tama. Money: How to Get It, Keep It & Make It Grow. (Money & Power Ser.). 100p. 1997. text 19.95 (*0-7910-4471-8*) Chelsea Hse.

— Money & Power for Families. (Money & Power Ser.). 100p. 1997. text 14.95 (*0-7910-4468-8*) Chelsea Hse.

— Money & Power for Retirement. (Money & Power Ser.). 100p. 1997. text 14.95 (*0-7910-4470-X*) Chelsea Hse.

— Money & Power for Singles. (Money & Power Ser.). 100p. 1997. text 14.95 (*0-7910-4467-X*) Chelsea Hse.

— Money & Power Through Mutual Funds. (Money & Power Ser.). 100p. 1996. text 14.95 (*0-7910-4469-6*) Chelsea Hse.

— Winning the Money Game: No-Nonsense Answers for You & Your Money. 304p. 1998. pap. 16.99 (*1-889692-16-6*) Summit Finan.

McAlester, A. Lee. The Earth: An Introduction to the Geological & Geophysical Sciences. 1973. 29.95 (*0-685-03849-1*); teacher ed. 1.95 (*0-685-03850-5*) P-H.

McAlester, A. Lee & Hay, Edward A. Physical Geology: Principles & Perspectives. (Illus.). 448p. 1975. 26.95 (*0-685-03894-7*) P-H.

McAlester, Lee, jt. auth. see McAlester, Virginia.

McAlester, Virginia. A Field Guide to America's Historic Neighborhoods. 580p. 1998. pap. 29.95 (*0-375-70172-9*) Random.

McAlester, Virginia & McAlester, Lee. A Field Guide to American Houses. LC 82-48740. (Illus.). 525p. 1984. pap. 24.95 (*0-394-73969-8*) Knopf.

— A Field Guide to American Houses. LC 82-48740. (Illus.). 525p. 1984. 40.00 (*0-394-51032-1*) Knopf.

— A Field Guide to America's Historic Neighborhoods & Museum Houses: The Western States. LC 97-48419. (Illus.). 580p. 1998. 45.00 (*0-679-42569-1*) Knopf.

— Great American Houses & Their Architectural Styles. LC 94-11055. (Illus.). 348p. 1994. 65.00 (*1-55859-750-6*) Abbeville Pr.

McAlevey, Peter. Surviving As an Independent Film Producer: Based on the Acclaimed UCLA Course. LC 98-10916. (Illus.). 288p. 1998. 24.95 (*0-87951-861-8*, Pub. by Overlook Pr) Penguin Putnam.

McAlexander, Hubert H. Critical Essays on Peter Taylor. (Critical Essays on American Literature Ser.). 200p. 1993. 49.00 (*0-8161-7322-2*, Twyne) Mac Lib Ref.

— The Prodigal Daughter: A Biography of Sherwood Bonner. LC 98-40283. (Illus.). 272p. 1999. reprint ed. pap. text 20.00 (*1-57233-049-X*, Pub. by U of Tenn Pr) U Ch Pr.

McAlexander, Hubert H., ed. Conversations with Peter Taylor. LC 87-13679. (Literary Conversations Ser.). 178p. 1987. pap. 15.95 (*0-87805-325-5*); text 39.50 (*0-87805-324-7*) U Pr of Miss.

McAlexander, Hubert H., jt. auth. see Jacobs, Selby.

McAlexander, Patricia J., jt. auth. see Hayes, Christopher G.

McAlhone, Beryl & Stuart, David. Smile in the Mind. LC 96-172742. (Illus.). 240p. 1996. 69.95 (*0-7148-3328-2*, Pub. by Phaidon Press) Phaidon Pr.

— A Smile in the Mind: Witty Thinking in Graphic Design. LC 99-158556. (Illus.). 427p. 1998. pap. 35.00 (*0-7148-3812-8*) Phaidon Pr.

McAliley, Susan, jt. auth. see Tripp, Valerie.

***McAlindon, Harold R.** The Little Book of Big Ideas. LC 99-44288. 256p. 1999. pap. 10.95 (*1-58182-054-2*, Cumberland Hearthside) Cumberland Hse.

McAlindon, Thomas. Doctor Faustus: Divine in Show. (Twayne's Masterwork Studies: No. 134). 125p. 1994. 29.00 (*0-8057-4453-3*, Twyne); pap. 18.00 (*0-8057-8388-1*, Twyne) Mac Lib Ref.

— Shakespeare's Tragic Cosmos. 324p. 1996. pap. text 19.95 (*0-521-56605-3*) Cambridge U Pr.

McAlinn, Gerald P. Business Guide to Japan. LC 97-134831. 320p. 2000. pap. text 24.95 (*981-00-7077-2*) Buttrwrth-Heinemann.

McAliskey, Bernadette D. On the Irish Freedom Struggle. 16p. 1983. reprint ed. pap. 2.00 (*0-87348-478-9*) Pathfinder NY.

McAlister, Diane L. The Native American Crafts Directory: A Guide for Locating Craft Shops & Craft Suppliers. 2nd ed. LC 98-16036. 1998. 9.95 (*1-57067-058-7*) Book Pub Co.

McAlister, Elizabeth A. Zanj Nan Miwa - Angels in the Mirror: Haitian Vodou Music & Culture & the People... (Illus.). 96p. 1996. 28.95 incl. cd-rom (*1-55961-387-4*, Ellipsis Arts) Relaxtn Co.

McAlister, H., ed. Complementary Approaches to Double & Multiple Star Research. (ASP Conference Series Proceedings: Vol. 32). 598p. 1992. 34.00 (*0-937707-51-1*) Astron Soc Pacific.

McAlister, Jeffrey G., ed. see Richardson, Jessica.

McAlister, Joan M. Radionuclide Techniques in Medicine. LC 78-68348. (Techniques of Measurement in Medicine Ser.: No. 3). 239p. reprint ed. pap. 68.20 (*0-608-16499-2*, 2026349) Bks Demand.

McAlister, Katsy, jt. auth. see Crim, Lottie.

McAlister-Kizzier, Donna. Case Studies for Effective Business Instruction. unabridged ed. 242p. (C). 1999. pap. text 25.00 (*1-881530-14-0*) Delta Pi Epsilon.

McAlister, Leigh & Rothschild, Michael, eds. Advances in Consumer Research Vol. 20: Proceedings of the 1992 Conference. 719p. 1993. 59.00 (*0-915552-30-2*) Assn Consumer Res.

Mcalister, Leigh, jt. auth. see Kahn, Barbara E.

McAlister, Linda L. History of Feminist Philosophy in the United States. (C). (gr. 13). 1999. 65.00 (*0-415-91448-5*) Routledge.

— Hypatia's Daughters: Fifteen Hundred Years of Women Philosophers. LC 95-45598. (Hypatia Book). 336p. 1996. 49.95 (*0-253-33057-2*); pap. text 22.50 (*0-253-21060-7*) Ind U Pr.

McAlister, Linda L., tr. see Brentano, Franz.

McAlister, Linda L., tr. see Wittgenstein, Ludwig Josef Johann.

McAlister, Lyle N. Spain & Portugal in the New World, 1492-1700. LC 83-21745. (Europe & the World in the Age of Expansion Ser.: Vol. 3). (Illus.). 612p. 1984. pap. 19.95 (*0-8166-1218-8*) U of Minn Pr.

McAlister, Marcia. McAlister's Car Care Organizer. 12p. (Orig.). 1985. pap. 3.00 (*0-9615587-0-9*) M McAlister Enterps.

McAlister, Martha K., jt. auth. see McAlister, Wayne H.

McAlister, Micheal J. The Language of Visual Effects. (Illus.). 176p. 1993. 18.95 (*0-943728-47-9*) Lone Eagle Pub.

McAlister, Renee, jt. contrib. by see Brudet, Julie.

McAlister, Renee, jt. contrib. by see Brunet, Julie.

McAlister, Roy E. Precision Spark Injection (PSI) System. 1986. pap. 4.95 (*0-685-24740-6*) Research Analysts.

McAlister, Wayne H. & McAlister, Martha K. Aransas: A Naturalist's Guide. LC 94-41619. (Illus.). 400p. (Orig.). 1995. pap. 19.95 (*0-292-75172-9*); text 45.00 (*0-292-75171-0*) U of Tex Pr.

— Matagorda Island: A Naturalist's Guide. LC 92-13024. (Illus.). 380p. (Orig.). 1993. pap. 19.95 (*0-292-75151-6*) U of Tex Pr.

McAll. Under the Golden Dome. pap. text 3.95 (*0-9615319-0-8*) Colorado & West.

McAll, Christopher. Class, Ethnicity & Social Inequality. (McGill-Queen's Studies in Ethnic History). 304p. (C). 1990. text 44.95 (*0-7735-0716-7*, Pub. by McG-Queens Univ Pr) CUP Services.

— Class, Ethnicity & Social Inequality. (McGill-Queen's Studies in Ethnic History). 304p. (C). 1992. pap. 22.95 (*0-7735-0923-2*, Pub. by McG-Queens Univ Pr) CUP Services.

McAll, Frances. For God's Sake Doctor. 96p. (Orig.). 1984. pap. 3.95 (*0-901269-82-4*) Grosvenor USA.

McAll, Kenneth. A Guide to Healing the Family Tree. LC 96-69338. 232p. 1996. reprint ed. pap. 8.95 (*1-882972-64-3*, 3491) Queenship Pub.

— Healing the Haunted. LC 96-69422. 83p. 1996. reprint ed. pap. text 6.95 (*1-882972-76-7*, 3492) Queenship Pub.

***McAllen, Audrey E.** The Extra Lesson: Movement, Drawing & Painting Exercises to Help Children with Difficulties in Writing, Reading & Arithmetic. 5th rev. ed. (Illus.). viii, 230p. 1998. pap. 28.95 (*0-945803-34-6*, 00198) R Steiner Col.

McAllen, Audrey E. The Listening Ear: The Development of Speech As a Creative Influence in Education. (Learning Resources Ser.). (Illus.). 162p. 1989. pap. 14.95 (*1-869890-18-3*, 1477, Pub. by Hawthorn Press) Anthroposophic.

— Sleep: An Unobserved Element in Education. 68p. 1990. pap. 14.95 (*1-869890-03-5*, 619, Pub. by Hawthorn Press) Anthroposophic.

McAllen, Jack B. The Boss Should Be a Woman: How Women Can Manage Their Way to the Top & Compromise Nothing; How to Succeed Because You Are a Woman. LC 93-28066. (Illus.). 208p. 1993. pap. 12.95 (*0-931892-56-2*) B Dolphin Pub.

McAllen, John B. The Boss Should Be a Woman: How Women Can Manage Their Way to the Top & Compromise Nothing; How to Succeed Because You Are a Woman. 264p. 1992. pap. text 38.95 (*0-9634510-4-9*) Castlerock Pub.

McAllen, Margaret. The Heritage Sampler: Selections from the Rich & Colorful History of the Rio Grande Valley. 113p. 1991. text 13.95 (*0-935071-08-3*) Hidalgo Cty Hist Mus.

***McAllester, David A.** Automated Deduction - CADE-17: Proceedings of the 17th International Conference On Automated Deduction, Pittsburgh, PA., U. S. A., June 2000. International Conference on Automated Deduction Staff, ed. LC 00-41908. (Lecture Notes in Computer Science). 2000. pap. write for info. (*3-540-67664-3*) Spr-Verlag.

McAllester-Jones, Mary. Gaston Bachelard, Subversive Humanist: Texts & Readings. LC 90-50649. (Science & Literature Ser.). 192p. 1991. lib. bdg. 40.00 (*0-299-12790-7*) U of Wis Pr.

McAllester-Jones, Mary, tr. see Bachelard, Gaston.

McAllester, Mary, ed. The Philosophy & Poetics of Gaston Bachelard. LC 89-33901. (Current Continental Research Ser.: No. 011). 192p. (C). 1989. lib. bdg. 42.00 (*0-8191-7471-8*) U Pr of Amer.

McAllester, Melanie. The Lessons. LC 94-2770. 240p. 1994. pap. 9.95 (*0-933216-99-8*) Spinsters Ink.

Mcallis. Great War: God, Satan & You. 1992. pap. text 8.95 (*0-923417-23-0*) Shepherd Minst.

McAllis. Pack Your Bag, Jesus Is Coming. 1993. pap. 8.95 (*0-923417-42-7*) Shepherd Minst.

McAllister. The Nationwide Competition for Votes. 1992. text 42.50 (*0-86187-383-1*) St Martin.

— Pathways to Print: Conquering Color, Trapping, Designing for Production, 8 modules. (Complete Series for Desktop Publishing). (Illus.). 608p. (C). 1997. mass mkt. 55.95 (*0-8273-7926-9*) Delmar.

— Pathways to Print: Quality Assurance. (Illus.). 80p. (C). 1997. mass mkt. 19.95 (*0-8273-7924-2*) Delmar.

McAllister. Pathways to Print: Scanning & Image Manipulation. LC 96-34459. (Illus.). 64p. (C). 1996. pap. 19.95 (*0-8273-7917-X*) Delmar.

— Pathways to Print: The Business Side. LC 98-157800. (Illus.). 80p. (C). 1997. mass mkt. 19.95 (*0-8273-7923-4*) Delmar.

McAllister. Pathways to Print: Trapping. LC 97-15143. (Illus.). 80p. (C). 1997. mass mkt. 19.95 (*0-8273-7915-3*) Delmar.

McAllister, jt. auth. see Clarkson.

McAllister, jt. auth. see Field, A.

McAllister, Ray. Journey of Passion: Poems. LC 98-32057. 82p. 1999. pap. text 14.95 (*0-7734-3120-9*) E Mellen.

McAllister, A. S. Thomson: Descendants of John Thomson, Pioneer Scotch Covenanter: Genealogical Notes on All Known Descendants of John Thomson of Scotland, Ireland & Pennsylvania, with Biographical Sketches. (Illus.). 357p. 1993. reprint ed. pap. 59.50 (*0-8328-3423-8*); reprint ed. lib. bdg. 69.50 (*0-8328-3422-X*) Higginson Bk Co.

McAllister, Angela. The Acorn Sailor. LC 90-7774. (Illus.). (J). 1991. lib. bdg. write for info. (*0-531-08513-9*) Orchard Bks Watts.

— Clever Cowboy. LC 98-219515. (Illus.). 32p. (J). (ps-2). 1998. 15.95 (*0-7894-3491-1*) DK Pub Inc.

***McAllister, Angela.** The Clever Cowboy. 32p. (J). (gr. k-2). 2000. pap. text 5.95 (*0-7894-2659-5*, D K Ink) DK Pub Inc.

McAllister, Angela. The Honey Festival. LC 92-46079. (Illus.). (J). (gr. 1-8). 1999. pap. 13.99 (*0-8037-1240-5*, Dial Yng Read) Peng Put Young Read.

— Midnight at the Oasis. (Illus.). 32p. (J). (ps-2). 1995. 19.95 (*0-370-31884-6*, Pub. by Bodley Head) Trafalgar.

— Nesta, the Little Witch. (Illus.). 32p. (J). (ps-3). 1999. pap. 4.99 (*0-14-054266-3*, PuffinBks) Peng Put Young Read.

— X-Mas Wish. (Illus.). (J). 1999. pap. write for info. (*0-14-054430-5*) NAL.

Mcallister, Angela & Bloomfield, Michaela. The Whales' Tale. LC 92-173799. 32p. (J). 1990. 5.95 (*1-85406-053-8*) Aurum Pub.

McAllister, Angus. McAllister: Scottish Law of Leases. 208p. 1989. pap. 44.00 (*0-406-10589-8*, MICHIE) LEXIS Pub.

McAllister, Angus & Guthrie, T. G. McAllister & Guthrie: Scottish Property Law - an Introduction. 304p. 1992. pap. 44.00 (*0-406-00105-7*, MICHIE) LEXIS Pub.

McAllister, Anne. The Alexakis Bride. LC 95-22301. 187p. 1995. per. 3.25 (*0-373-11769-8*, 1-11769-6) Harlequin Bks.

***Mcallister, Anne.** Un Amor a Prueba. Vol. 211.Tr. of A Love on Trial. (SPA.). 2000. per. 3.50 (*0-373-33561-X*, 1-335611) Harlequin Bks.

McAllister, Anne. A Baby for Christmas. 1996. per. 3.50 (*0-373-11854-6*, 1-11854-6) Harlequin Bks.

— Un Bebe en Heritage. 1998. mass mkt. 3.50 (*0-373-34720-0*, 1-34720-2) Harlequin Bks.

— Call up the Wind. (Presents Ser.). 1994. per. 2.99 (*0-373-11620-9*, 1-11620-1) Harlequin Bks.

— The Cowboy & the Kid. (Desire Ser.: No. 1009). 1996. per. 3.50 (*0-373-76009-4*, 1-76009-9) Silhouette.

— The Cowboy Crashes a Wedding. (Desire Ser.). 1998. per. 3.75 (*0-373-76153-8*, 1-76153-5) Silhouette.

— A Cowboy for Christmas. 1992. per. 3.39 (*0-373-16466-1*, 1-16466-4) Harlequin Bks.

— Cowboy on the Run. 1999. per. 4.50 (*0-373-65029-9*, 1-65029-0) Harlequin Bks.

— Cowboy Pride. 1996. per. 3.50 (*0-373-76034-5*, 1-76034-7) Silhouette.

— The Cowboy Steals a Lady: Man of the Month. (Desire Ser.: No. 1117). 1998. per. 3.50 (*0-373-76117-1*, 1-76117-0) Silhouette.

— Cowboy's Don't Cry. (Desire Ser.). 1995. per. 3.25 (*0-373-05907-8*, 1-05907-0) Silhouette.

— Cowboys Don't Cry. large type ed. (Silhouette Romance Ser.). 1996. 19.95 (*0-373-59741-X*) Harlequin Bks.

— Cowboys Don't Quit. (Desire Ser.). 1995. per. 3.25 (*0-373-05944-2*, 1-05944-3) Silhouette.

— Cowboys Don't Stay. 1995. per. 3.25 (*0-373-05969-8*, 1-05969-0) Silhouette.

***McAllister, Anne.** A Cowboy's Gift. (Desire Ser.: Bk. 1329). 2000. mass mkt. 3.99 (*0-373-76329-8*, 1-76329-1) Silhouette.

— Cowboy's Secret. (Desire Ser.: Vol. 127). 2000. per. 3.99 (*0-373-76279-8*) Silhouette.

McAllister, Anne. A Cowboy's Tears. 1997. per. 3.99 (*0-373-24137-2*, 1-24137-1) Silhouette.

— Una Dama Muy Especial: A Very Special Lady.Tr. of A Very Special Lady. (SPA.). 1999. per. 3.50 (*0-373-35283-2*, 1-35283-0) Harlequin Bks.

— Dare to Trust. large type ed. (Lythway Ser.). 272p. 1991. 21.95 (*0-7451-1258-7*, G K Hall Lrg Type) Mac Lib Ref.

— Do You Take This Cowboy? The Seduction of Jake Tallman: Cowboys Don't Cry, 2 vols. in 1. (By Request 2's Ser.). 2000. pap. 4.99 (*0-373-21708-0*, 1-21708-2) Harlequin Bks.

— Dream Chasers. (American Romance Ser.). 1991. per. 3.29 (*0-373-15151-9*) Harlequin Bks.

— The Eight-Second Wedding. (American Romance Ser.). 1994. per. 3.50 (*0-373-16533-1*) Harlequin Bks.

— The Eight Second Wedding. (Promo Ser.). 1999. per. 4.50 (*0-373-21966-0*, 1-21966-6) Harlequin Bks.

— Finn's Twins! (Presents Ser.: No. 1890). 1997. per. 3.50 (*0-373-11890-2*, 1-11890-0) Harlequin Bks.

— Fletcher's Baby. (Presents Ser.: No. 1932). 1998. per. 3.50 (*0-373-11932-1*, 1-11932-0) Harlequin Bks.

— Gibson's Girl. (Presents Ser.: No. 2060). 1999. per. 3.75 (*0-373-12060-5*, 1-12060-9) Harlequin Bks.

— Gifts of the Spirit. 1996. pap. 4.99 (*0-614-16983-6*) Harlequin Bks.

— I Thee Wed. (American Romance Ser.: No. 387). 1991. pap. 3.25 (*0-373-16387-8*) Harlequin Bks.

Mcallister, Anne. Imagine. (American Romance Ser.: No. 341). 1990. per. 2.95 (*0-373-16341-X*) Harlequin Bks.

McAllister, Anne. Island Interlude. (Presents Ser.: No. 459). 1992. pap. 2.89 (*0-373-11459-1*, 1-11459-4) Harlequin Bks.

— Island Interlude. large type ed. 285p. 1992. reprint ed. 18.95 (*0-263-12840-7*) Thorndike Pr.

— Mackenzie's Baby. (American Romance Ser.). 1992. per. 3.39 (*0-373-16459-9*, 1-16459-9) Harlequin Bks.

— Mackenzie's Baby. (Born in the U. S. A. Ser.). 1997. mass mkt. 4.50 (*0-373-47195-5*, 1-47195-2) Harlequin Bks.

— Marry Sunshine. (Here Come the Grooms Ser.: No. 36). 1996. per. 3.99 (*0-373-30136-7*, 1-30136-5) Harlequin Bks.

— No Abandons Nunca (Don't Quit Ever) (SPA.). 1997. per. 3.50 (*0-373-35203-4*, 1-35203-8) Harlequin Bks.

— Un Novio Dificil, Vol. 161. (Silhouette Deseo Ser.). (SPA.). 156p. 1999. mass mkt. 3.50 (*0-373-35291-3*) Harlequin Bks.

— Un Play-Boy a Seduire. (Azur Ser.: No. 775). (FRE.). 1999. mass mkt. 3.99 (*0-373-34775-8*, 1-34775-6) Harlequin Bks.

An Asterisk (*) at the beginning of an entry indicates that the title is appearing for the first time.

Mcallister, Anne. The Playboy & the Nanny. 1998. per. 3.75 (*0-373-12005-2*, 1-12005-4, Mira Bks) Harlequin Bks.

***McAllister, Anne.** Rhys's Redemption. (Presents Ser.). 2000. mass mkt. 3.99 (*0-373-12126-1*, 1-12126-8) Harlequin Bks.

— Sentimientos Equivocados. (Bianca Ser.: Vol. 225). (SPA.). 2000. mass mkt. 3.50 (*0-373-33575-X*, Harlequin) Harlequin Bks.

McAllister, Anne. The Stardust Cowboy. (Desire Ser.: No. 1219). 1999. per. 3.75 (*0-373-76219-4*, 1-76219-4) Silhouette.

— Starstruck. (Men Made in America Ser.). 1994. pap. 3.99 (*0-373-45199-7*, 1-45199-6) Harlequin Bks.

— To Tame a Wolfe. 1994. per. 3.59 (*0-373-45172-5*) Harlequin Bks.

— Los Vaqueros No Lloran. (Silhouette Deseo Ser.: No. 147). 1996. per. 3.50 (*0-373-35147-X*, 1-35147-7) Harlequin Bks.

McAllister, Anne & Michaels, Kasey. Christmas Celebration: Gifts of the Spirit, to Marry at Christmas, 2 vols., Set. 1996. per. 4.99 (*0-373-15252-3*, 2-15252-8) Harlequin Bks.

***McAllister, Anne, et al.** Blood Brothers. (Desire Ser.: Bk. 1307). 2000. mass mkt. 3.99 (*0-373-76307-7*, 1-76307-7) Silhouette.

McAllister, Anne, jt. auth. see Bretton, Barbara.

McAllister, Becky. Justin. 32p. 1987. pap. 0.75 (*0-88144-101-5*) Christian Pub.

McAllister, Bill. History of Inverness. 200p. (C). 1989. pap. text 60.00 (*0-85976-369-2*, Pub. by J Donald) St Mut.

McAllister, Bruce. Dream Baby. 448p. 1994. pap. 13.95 (*0-312-89025-7*) Orb NYC.

— North American Horse Travel Guide. LC 94-180827. (Illus.). 312p. (Orig.). 1993. pap. 19.95 (*0-9638817-2-8*) Roundup Pr.

— North American Horse Travel Guide. 2nd ed. (Illus.). 444p. (Orig.). 1995. pap. 19.95 (*0-9638817-3-6*) Roundup Pr.

— North American Horse Travel Guide. 4th ed. (Illus.). 494p. (Orig.). 1996. pap. 22.95 (*0-9638817-4-4*) Roundup Pr.

McAllister, Bruce, jt. ed. see Harrison, Harry.

McAllister, Carol H., jt. auth. see Callison, William.

McAllister, Casey. Catch Me If You Can. 288p. (Orig.). 1993. mass mkt. 4.50 (*0-380-76571-3*, Avon Bks) Morrow Avon.

McAllister, D. E., ed. On Lampreys & Fishes: A Memorial Anthology in Honor of Vadim D. Vladykov. (Developments in Environmental Biology of Fishes Ser.). (C). 1988. text 177.50 (*90-6193-661-6*) Kluwer Academic.

McAllister, D. J. Chasing Shadows. LC 98-89496. 224p. 1999. 25.00 (*0-7388-0255-7*); pap. 18.00 (*0-7388-0256-5*) Xlibris Corp.

McAllister, David F. Ontic: A Knowledge Representation System for Mathematics. (Artificial Intelligence Ser.). 174p. 1989. 27.50 (*0-262-13235-4*) MIT Pr.

McAllister, Dawson. Como Saber Si Estas Verdaderamente Enamorado.Tr. of How to Know If You're Really in Love. (SPA.). 176p. 1996. 8.99 (*0-88113-382-5*, B008-3825) Caribe Betania.

— Discussion Manual for Student Relationships, Vol. 2. (Illus.). (J). (gr. 5-12). 1976. pap. 8.75 (*0-923417-07-9*) Shepherd Minst.

— Discussion Manual for Student Relationships, Vol. 3. (Illus.). (J). (gr. 5-12). 1978. pap. 8.75 (*0-923417-08-7*) Shepherd Minst.

Mcallister, Dawson. The Great War. 1991. pap. 9.99 (*0-923417-21-4*) Shepherd Minst.

McAllister, Dawson. How to Know If You're Really in Love. LC 93-40906. (YA). 1994. pap. 9.99 (*0-8499-3312-9*) Word Pub.

— Please Don't Tell My Parents. 176p. (YA). 1992. pap. 8.99 (*0-8499-3311-0*) Word Pub.

— Self Esteem & Loneliness. (Illus.). (J). (gr. 5-12). 1989. pap. 3.95 (*0-923417-02-8*) Shepherd Minst.

— Student Conference Follow-Up Manual. (Illus.). (J). (gr. 5-12). 1989. pap. 2.95 (*0-923417-10-9*) Shepherd Minst.

— Student Relationships, Vol. 1. (J). (gr. 5-12). 1981. pap., teacher ed. 6.95 (*0-923417-18-4*) Shepherd Minst.

— A Walk with Christ Through the Resurrection. (Illus.). (J). (gr. 5-12). 1981. pap. 8.95 (*0-923417-14-1*) Shepherd Minst.

— A Walk with Christ to the Cross. (Illus.). (J). (gr. 5-12). 1980. pap. 8.95 (*0-923417-09-5*) Shepherd Minst.

— Who Are You, Jesus? (Illus.). (J). (gr. 5-12). 1986. pap. 7.95 (*0-923417-05-2*) Shepherd Minst.

McAllister, Dawson & Altman, Tim. Preparing Your Teenager for Sexuality. Peterson, Wayne, ed. (Illus.). 1988. pap. 6.95 (*0-923417-00-1*) Shepherd Minst.

— You, God & Your Sexuality. Peterson, Wayne, ed. (Illus.). (J). (gr. 5-12). 1988. pap. 3.95 (*0-923417-01-X*) Shepherd Minst.

McAllister, Dawson & Kimmel, Tim. Student Relationships, Vol. 2. (J). (gr. 5-12). 1981. pap., teacher ed. 6.95 (*0-923417-04-4*) Shepherd Minst.

— A Walk with Christ to the Cross. (J). (gr. 5-12). 1981. pap., teacher ed. 5.95 (*0-923417-20-6*) Shepherd Minst.

McAllister, Dawson & May, Tom. Who Are You Jesus? (J). (gr. 5-12). 1986. pap., teacher ed. 7.95 (*0-923417-03-6*) Shepherd Minst.

McAllister, Dawson & McGee, Robert S. The Search for Significance. 1990. pap., student ed., wbk. ed. 10.99 (*0-923417-12-5*) Shepherd Minst.

McAllister, Dawson & Miller, John. Discussion Manual for Student Discipleship, Vol. 2. (Illus.). (J). (gr. 5-12). 1978. pap. 8.50 (*0-923417-16-8*) Shepherd Minst.

McAllister, Dawson & Miller, Rich. Who Are You, God? (Illus.). (J). (gr. 5-12). 1988. pap. 7.95 (*0-923417-11-7*) Shepherd Minst.

— Who Are You God? (J). (gr. 5-12). 1990. pap., teacher ed. 5.95 (*0-923417-13-3*) Shepherd Minst.

McAllister, Dawson & Sharp, Floyd. Handbook for Financial Faithfulness. (Illus.). (J). (gr. 5-12). 1974. pap. 6.95 (*0-923417-17-6*) Shepherd Minst.

McAllister, Dawson & Springle, Pat. Saving the Millennial Generation. LC 98-51359. 192p. 1999. pap. 12.99 (*0-7852-8296-3*) Nelson.

McAllister, Dawson & Webster, Dan. Discussion Manual for Student Discipleship, Vol. 1. (Illus.). (J). (gr. 5-12). 1975. pap. 8.50 (*0-923417-15-X*) Shepherd Minst.

— Discussion Manual for Student Relationships, Vol. 1. (Illus.). (J). (gr. 5-12). 1975. pap. 8.75 (*0-923417-06-0*) Shepherd Minst.

McAllister, Donald. Evaluation in Environmental Planning: Assessing Environmental, Social, Economic & Political Tradeoffs. 1982. pap. text 22.00 (*0-262-63087-7*) MIT Pr.

McAllister, Donald & Naas, Lucille, eds. Marriage Returns of Oxford County, Maine, Prior to 1892. rev. ed. 352p. 1993. 37.50 (*0-89725-141-5*, 1455) Picton Pr.

McAllister, E. W. Pipeline Rules of Thumb. 4th rev. ed. 616p. 1998. pap. 79.00 (*0-88415-671-0*, 5671) Gulf Pub.

McAllister, E. W., ed. Pipeline Rules of Thumb Handbook: A Manual of Quick, Accurate Solutions to Everyday Pipeline Problems. fac. ed. LC 87-24408. (Illus.). 456p. 1988. reprint ed. pap. 141.40 (*0-608-00979-2*, 206183300012) Bks Demand.

McAllister, Elizabeth. Peer Teaching & Collaborative Learning in the Language Arts. Lewis, Warren W., ed. (Illus.). 68p. 1990. pap. 15.95 (*0-927516-21-7*) ERIC-REC.

McAllister, Elizabeth A. Learning Together: Collaboration for Active Learning in the Elementary Language Arts. LC 94-12655. (TRIED (Teaching Resources in the ERIC Database) Ser.). (Illus.). 140p. (Orig.). (C). 1995. pap. 16.95 (*1-883790-12-3*, EDINFO Pr) Grayson Bernard Pubs.

— Learning Together: Collaborative Activities for Elementary Language Arts Students. LC 94-12655. (Teaching Resources in the ERIC Database, TRIED Ser.). 1994. 14.95 (*0-927516-42-X*) ERIC-REC.

McAllister, Elizabeth A. & Neubert, Gloria A. New Teachers Helping New Teachers: Preservice Peer Coaching. LC 94-49407. 132p. (Orig.). 1995. pap. 19.95 (*1-883790-14-X*, 100-1272, EDINFO Pr) Grayson Bernard Pubs.

McAllister, Fran, jt. auth. see McAllister, Frank.

McAllister, Frank. The Tooth Fairy Legend. LC 90-28136. (Illus.). 40p. (J). (gr. k-6). 1992. 12.95 (*0-915677-54-7*) Roundtable Pub.

McAllister, Frank & McAllister, Fran. The Tooth Fairy Legend. LC 76-9595. (J). (gr. k-4). 1976. 9.95 (*0-916864-01-4*) Block.

McAllister, Gary & Clark, Graham. Captain's Log - The Gary McAllister Story. (Illus.). 192p. 1996. 34.95 (*1-85158-790-X*, Pub. by Mainstream Pubng) Trafalgar.

McAllister, Greg & McAllister, Jim. Leading Questions: A Free Will Baptist Discipleship Manual. 145p. 1988. ring bd. 12.95 (*0-89265-133-4*) Randall Hse.

McAllister, Hayden. My Big Christmas Book. (J). 1988. 5.98 (*0-671-07565-9*) S&S Trade.

McAllister, Heather. Jilt Trip. LC 95-13945. (Temptation Ser.). 216p. 1995. per. 3.25 (*0-373-25643-4*, 1-25643-7) Harlequin Bks.

McAllister, Ian. The Great Bear Rainforest: Canada's Forgotten Coast. LC 98-230238. 1998. 40.00 (*1-57805-011-1*, Pub. by Sierra) Random.

— Sustaining Relief with Development: Strategic Issues for the Red Cross & Red Crescent. LC 93-75. 280p. (C). 1993. lib. bdg. 111.00 (*0-7923-2163-4*) Kluwer Academic.

McAllister, Ian, jt. auth. see Graetz, Brian.

McAllister, Ian, jt. auth. see Rose, Richard.

McAllister, J. Gray. McAllister Family Records: Compiled for the Descendants of Abraham Addams McAllister & His Wife Julia Ellen Stratton McAllister of Covington, Virginia. (Illus.). 88p. 1994. reprint ed. pap. 17.50 (*0-8328-4227-3*); reprint ed. lib. bdg. 27.50 (*0-8328-4226-5*) Higginson Bk Co.

McAllister, J. M. & Tandy, L. B. Genealogy of the Lewis & Kindred Families. (Illus.). 416p. 1989. reprint ed. pap. 62.00 (*0-8328-0770-2*); reprint ed. lib. bdg. 70.00 (*0-8328-0769-9*) Higginson Bk Co.

***McAllister, J. Murray Jason.** How to Make a Woman Horny! 75p. 1999. pap. 19.95 (*0-914094-29-7*) Symphony Pr.

McAllister, James A. The Government of Edward Schreyer: Democratic Socialism in Manitoba. 224p. 1984. pap. 27.95 (*0-7735-0437-0*, Pub. by McG-Queens Univ Pr) CUP Services.

— The Government of Edward Schreyer: Democratic Socialism in Manitoba. LC 85-160930. (Illus.). 224p. reprint ed. pap. 69.50 (*0-7837-6904-0*, 204673400003) Bks Demand.

McAllister, James W. Beauty & Revolution in Science. LC 96-3910. (Illus.). 248p. 1996. text 29.95 (*0-8014-3240-5*) Cornell U Pr.

— Beauty & Revolution in Science. 1999. pap. text 16.95 (*0-8014-8625-4*) Cornell U Pr.

***McAllister, Jim.** Salem: From Naumkeag to Witch City. (Town Memoirs Ser.). (Illus.). 128p. 2000. pap. 14.95 (*1-889833-14-2*, Commonwealth Eds) Memoirs Unltd.

McAllister, Jim, jt. auth. see McAllister, Greg.

***McAllister, John Meriwether & Tandy, Lura Boulton.** Genealogies of the Lewis & Kindred Families. 416p. 2000. reprint ed. pap. 42.50 (*0-8063-4990-5*, Pub. by Clearfield Co) ACCESS Pubs Network.

McAllister, Lee. Squaw Dance. Seginski, Jon, ed. 245p. 1991. write for info. (*1-879586-00-2*) TJE NV.

***McAllister, Leslie D., et al.** A Practical Approach to Neurooncology. 350p. 2000. pap. 47.50 (*0-7506-7180-7*) Buttrwrth-Heinemann.

McAllister, Lester G. & Tucker, William E. Journey in Faith: A History of the Christian Church. LC 75-11738. 512p. 1975. 18.99 (*0-8272-1703-X*) Chalice Pr.

McAllister, Lisa. Buffalo Gal. (Superromance Ser.: No. 810). 1998. per. 4.25 (*0-373-70810-6*, 1-70810-6) Harlequin Bks.

***McAllister, Lisa S.** Feather Edge Stoneware: Identification & Values. (Illus.). 96p. 2000. pap. 19.95 (*1-57432-193-5*) Collector Bks.

McAllister, Lisz. Yellow Ware Collecting, Bk. 2. 1996. pap. text 17.95 (*0-89145-741-0*, 4734) Collector Bks.

McAllister, Marcia. Steven Spielberg, Reading Level 2. (Reaching Your Goal Bks.: Set II). (Illus.). 24p. (J). (gr. 1-4). 1989. 10.95 (*0-685-58803-3*) Rourke Corp.

— With House in Hand: A Step-by-Step Planner for Home or Office. 5th ed. (Illus.). 54p. (Orig.). 1982. reprint ed. pap. 13.95 (*0-9615587-1-7*, Pub. by M McAllister Enterps) Wimmer Bk Dist.

***McAllister, Margaret.** Hold My Hand & Run. (Illus.). 160p. (J). (gr. 5-9). 2000. 15.99 (*0-525-46391-7*, Dutton Child) Peng Put Young Read.

McAllister, Marica. Steven Spielberg. (Reaching Your Goal Ser.: Set II). (Illus.). 24p. (J). (gr. 1-4). 1989. lib. bdg. 18.60 (*0-86592-427-9*) Rourke Enter.

McAllister, Mary C. McAllister. Descendants of Archibald McAllister of W. Pennsboro Township, Cumberland Co., Pa., 1730-1898. 105p. 1996. reprint ed. pap. 19.50 (*0-8328-5324-0*); reprint ed. lib. bdg. 29.50 (*0-8328-5323-2*) Higginson Bk Co.

McAllister, Mary L. & Alexander, Cynthia J. A Stake in the Future: Redefining the Canadian Mineral Industry. LC 97-175370. 248p. 1997. 75.00 (*0-7748-0603-6*) U of Wash Pr.

— A Stake in the Future: Redefining the Canadian Mineral Industry. 224p. 1997. pap. text 29.95 (*0-7748-0602-8*, HD9506) U of Wash Pr.

McAllister, Matthew P. The Commercialization of American Culture. 256p. 1995. 48.00 (*0-8039-5379-8*); pap. 22.95 (*0-8039-5380-1*) Sage.

McAllister, Pam, jt. auth. see Riley, Dick.

McAllister, Pam, jt. ed. see Riley, Dick.

McAllister, Pamela. The Charity's Guide to Charitable Contributions. LC 97-94744. (Law & Tax Guides for Charities Ser.). (Illus.). 140p. 1998. pap. 29.00 (*0-9661596-0-8*, 9701) Conlee Gibbs.

McAllister, Patricia. Fire Raven. 352p. 1997. mass mkt. 4.99 (*0-8217-5605-2*, Zebra Kensgtn) Kensgtn Pub Corp.

— Sea Raven. 352p. 1996. mass mkt. 4.99 (*0-8217-5236-7*, Zebra Kensgtn) Kensgtn Pub Corp.

— Snow Raven. 352p. 1998. pap. 4.99 (*0-8217-5887-X*, Zebra Kensgtn) Kensgtn Pub Corp.

McAllister, Patrick. Culture & the Common Place: Anthropological Essays in Honor of David Hammond-Tooke. (African Studies Special Issue 1997: Vol. 2). 400p. 1998. pap. 54.95 (*1-86814-326-0*, U Pr W Africa) Intl Scholars.

McAllister, Patrick A. & Wilmsen, Edwin, eds. The Politics of Differences: Ethnic Premises in a World of Power. LC 95-35762. 208p. 1996. pap. text 13.95 (*0-226-90017-7*) U Ch Pr.

McAllister, Patrick A., jt. ed. see Spiegel, Andrew D.

McAllister, Patrick A., jt. ed. see Wilmsen, Edwin N.

Mcallister, Richard. From EC to EU: A Historical & Political Survey. LC 96-24793. 256p. (C). 1997. 75.00 (*0-415-14265-2*); pap. 22.99 (*0-415-14266-0*) Routledge.

McAllister, Robin B. Illustration. (C). 1997. pap. 12.95 (*0-8273-7918-8*) Delmar.

— Legal & Ethical Issues in Presentation/Desktop Publishing. 1997. pap. 12.95 (*0-8273-7922-6*) Delmar.

— Page Layout. (C). 1997. pap. 12.95 (*0-8273-7920-X*) Delmar.

— Pathways to Print: Color. LC 98-157804. 80p. (C). 1997. mass mkt. 19.95 (*0-8273-7916-1*) Delmar.

— Pathways to Print: Design for Production. LC 96-29481. (Illus.). 80p. (C). 1996. mass mkt. 19.95 (*0-8273-7919-6*) Delmar.

— Pathways to Print: Introduction to Desktop Publishing. LC 96-34409. (Illus.). 80p. (C). 1996. mass mkt. 19.95 (*0-8273-7914-5*) Delmar.

— Pathways to Print: Type Management. LC 96-36056. (Illus.). 80p. (C). 1996. mass mkt. 19.95 (*0-8273-7921-8*) Delmar.

— Preparing Files for Output. (C). 1997. pap. 12.95 (*0-8273-7925-0*) Delmar.

McAllister, Samuel W. Society As I Have Found It. LC 75-1855. (Leisure Class in America Ser.). 1975. reprint ed. 34.95 (*0-405-06921-9*) Ayer.

— Society As I Have Found It. (American Biography Ser.). 469p. 1991. reprint ed. lib. bdg. 89.00 (*0-7812-8280-2*) Rprt Serv.

McAllister, Shawn R. Columbus in Black & White. (Illus.). 114p. (Orig.). 1993. pap. 5.95 (*0-9637286-0-1*) Remmington Pr.

McAllister, Ted V. Revolt Against Modernity: Leo Strauss, Eric Voegelin, & the Search for a Postliberal Order. LC 95-35016. (American Political Thought Ser.). (Illus.). 338p. (C). 1996. 35.00 (*0-7006-0740-4*) U Pr of KS.

— Revolt Against Modernity: Leo Strauss, Eric Voegelin, & the Search for a Postliberal Order. (American Political Thought Ser.). (Illus.). 338p. 1997. pap. 16.95 (*0-7006-0873-7*) U Pr of KS.

***McAllister, Troon, pseud.** The Foursome: A Novel. LC 99-54497. 304p. 2000. 23.95 (*0-385-49910-8*) Doubleday.

— The Green. LC 98-27469. 304p. 1999. 22.95 (*0-385-49459-9*) Doubleday.

***McAllister, Troon, pseud.** The Green. 304p. 2000. pap. 12.95 (*0-385-49460-2*, Main St Bks) Doubleday.

McAllister, V. L., jt. auth. see Sengupta, R. P.

McAllister, Warren A., jt. auth. see Clemens, Donald F.

***McAllister, William B.** Drug Diplomacy in Twentieth Century: International History. LC 99-18225. 304p. 1999. pap. 27.99 (*0-415-17990-4*); text. write for info. (*0-415-17989-0*) Routledge.

— Personal Income Tax Saving Handbook: How to Maximize Your Tax Refund & Keep More of Your Hard. 2000. pap. 6.95 (*0-9676087-1-6*) Interactive Sales & Mktg.

McAlmon, Robert. North America: Continent of Conjecture, An Archetype Edition. (Illus.). 44p. (Orig.). (C). 1983. reprint ed. pap. 10.00 (*0-932139-02-7*) Dark Child Pr.

— Village: As It Happened Through a Fifteen Year Period. Lorusso, Edward N., ed. & intro. by. LC 89-70638. 196p. 1990. reprint ed. pap. 60.80 (*0-608-04149-1*, 206488200011) Bks Demand.

McAlmon, Robert & Boyle, Kay. Being Geniuses Together, 1920-1930. LC 96-35087. (Illus.). 408p. 1997. reprint ed. pap. 15.95 (*0-8018-5584-5*) Johns Hopkins.

McAlmont, Trevor. Life's Absurd! Our Meaningful & Meaningless Life: A Collection of Thoughts, Ideas & Concerns. 37p. 1997. pap. 8.95 (*0-533-12448-4*) Vantage.

Mcaloon, Kenneth & Tretkoff, Carol. Optimization & Computational Logic. LC 96-23734. (Discrete Mathematics & Optimization Ser.). 560p. 1996. 84.95 (*0-471-11533-9*, Wiley-Interscience) Wiley.

***McAloone, T. C.** Industrial Application of Environmentally Conscious Design. 199p. 2000. 131.00 (*1-86058-239-7*) Prof Eng Pubng.

McAlpin, Anne. Pack It Up Vol. 1: A Book for the Contemporary Traveler. 3rd rev. ed. LC 90-82758. (Illus.). 89p. (Orig.). 1996. pap. 7.95 (*0-9627263-0-3*) Flying Cloud.

McAlpin, Jim L. Faded Tracks: Historical Novel of Ruben McNair's Family Prior to & During American Civil War. LC 96-95458. (Illus.). v, 218p. (Orig.). 1997. pap. 14.95 (*0-9658220-0-1*) HHI.

— Looking for Trouble: Another Historical Novel of Ruben McNair's Adventures after Civil War. Wilson, Rivers M., ed. (Historical Novels of Civil War & Aftermath: Vol. III). (Illus.). 1999. pap. write for info. (*0-9658220-2-8*) HHI.

— Neal's Homecoming: Sequel to Faded Tracks. (Historical Novels on Civil War & Aftermath Ser.). 250p. 1997. pap. 15.95 (*0-9658220-1-X*) HHI.

McAlpin, Jon, ed. Stopover in Kansas. (Illus.). 156p. 1995. pap. text 9.95 (*1-57166-014-3*) Quixote Pr IA.

McAlpin, Michelle B. Subject to Famine: Food Crises & Economic Change in Western India, 1860-1920. LC 82-61376. 304p. 1983. reprint ed. pap. 94.30 (*0-7837-9385-5*, 206012900004) Bks Demand.

McAlpine. Ruthless. 352p. 2000. 22.95 (*0-471-37247-1*) Wiley.

McAlpine, A., et al, eds. New Challenges for Teachers & Teacher Education. vi, 174p. 1988. 31.50 (*90-265-0884-0*) Swets.

***McAlpine, Alistair.** The New Machiavelli: The Art of Politics in Business. LC 98-21069. 256p. 1998. 24.95 (*0-471-29564-7*) Wiley.

— The New Machiavelli: The Art of Politics in Business. 224p. 1999. pap. 16.95 (*0-471-35095-8*) Wiley.

McAlpine, Alistair. Once a Jolly Bagman. (Illus.). 256p. 1997. 45.00 (*0-297-81737-X*) Weidenfeld & Nicolson.

McAlpine, Alistair & Giangrande, Cathy. Collecting & Display. (Illus.). 192p. 1998. 45.00 (*1-85029-956-0*, Pub. by Conran Octopus) Antique Collect.

McAlpine, Barbara, jt. auth. see Art Gallery California State University, Fullerton.

McAlpine, David & Book, Leon. Para Empezar: Interacciones & Exploraciones. 1995. pap. text, suppl. ed. write for info. (*0-07-044983-X*) McGraw.

— Para empezar: Interacciones & Exploracions. (C). 1995. student ed. 21.00 incl. audio (*0-07-911088-6*) McGraw.

McAlpine, David, et al. Para Empezar: Interacciones. (C). 1995. pap., wbk. ed., lab manual ed. 32.19 (*0-07-044980-5*) McGraw.

— Para Empezar: Interacciones & Exploracions. (C). 1995. pap. text, teacher ed. 42.81 (*0-07-044979-1*) McGraw.

— Para Empezar: Interacciones & Exploracions. 1995. write for info. incl. audio (*0-07-911087-8*) McGraw.

— Para Empezar - Interacciones: Beginning Spanish. 432p. (C). 1995. 56.25 (*0-07-044978-3*) McGraw.

McAlpine, Frank. Popular Poetic Pearls & Biographies of Poets. LC 74-15745. (Popular Culture in America Ser.). (Illus.). 384p. 1975. reprint ed. 33.95 (*0-405-06380-6*) Ayer.

McAlpine, Gordon. The Persistence of Memory. 176p. 1998. 29.95 (*0-7206-1047-8*, Pub. by P Owen Ltd) Dufour.

McAlpine, Gwen & Warren, Janice. Reader-Response Approaches to Teaching Literature. Walling, Donovan R., ed. LC 97-65155. (Fastback Ser.: Vol. 417). 40p. 1997. pap. 3.00 (*0-87367-617-3*) Phi Delta Kappa.

McAlpine, Helen. Japanese Tales & Legends. 1958. 18.05 (*0-606-01552-3*, Pub. by Turtleback) Demco.

McAlpine, Jan C. & LeDonne, Patricia, eds. The Greening of World Trade. (Illus.). 240p. (C). 1998. pap. text 40.00 (*0-7881-4451-0*) DIANE Pub.

McAlpine, Janet. Play Guide 2: Travel Through Time & Space. (Illus.). 1990. teacher ed. 10.00 (*1-879616-01-7*, 34892) Brio Scanditoy.

McAlpine, Janice, jt. ed. see Fee, Margery.

McAlpine, Jim, et al. Faces of Man No. 2: The Arts. Date not set. teacher ed. 8.95 (*0-910857-66-0*, 066-OAP) Educ Impress.

— Faces of Man No. 2: The Sciences, Date not set. teacher ed. 8.95 (*0-910857-67-9*, 067-9AP) Educ Impress.

M

— I Want to Be Like. Date not set. teacher ed. 7.95 (*1-56644-958-8*, 958-8AP) Educ Impress.

— Weekly Writing Activites for Intermediate Grades. Date not set. teacher ed. 9.95 (*1-56644-008-4*, 008-4AP) Educ Impress.

— Weekly Writing Activites for Middle Grades. Date not set. teacher ed. 9.95 (*1-56644-988-X*, 988-XAP) Educ Impress.

McAlpine, Joan. The Lady of Claremont House: Isabella Elder, Pioneer & Philanthropist. LC 98-146756. 206 p. 1997. write for info. (*1-874640-97-1*) Argyll Pubng.

McAlpine, Katherine. Muse Strikes Back: A Poetic Response by Women to Men. LC 97-25390. 360p. 1997. pap. text 15.95 (*1-885266-49-9*) Story Line.

McAlpine, Ken, jt. auth. see Tinley, Scott.

McAlpine, Monica E. Chaucer's Knight's Tale: An Annotated Bibliography, 1894-1984. (Chaucer Bibliographies Ser.). 496p. 1991. text 85.00 (*0-8020-5913-9*) U of Toronto Pr.

McAlpine, R. W. The Life & Times of Col. James Fisk, Jr. Bruchey, Stuart, ed. LC 80-1329. (Railroads Ser.). (Illus.). 1981. reprint ed. lib. bdg. 35.95 (*0-405-13803-2*) Ayer.

***McAlpine, Rachel.** Web Word Wizardry: A Net-Savvy Writing Guide. 144p. 2000. pap. 11.95 (*1-58008-223-8*) Ten Speed Pr.

McAlpine, Sophia. The Landscape Palimpsest. 79p. 1997. pap. 19.95 (*0-7326-1165-2*, Pub. by Monash Asia Inst) Intl Spec Bk.

McAlpine, T. S. The Process of Management. 1973. pap. 26.95 (*0-8464-0765-5*) Beekman Pubs.

— Profit Planning & Control. (Illus.). 164p. 1969. pap. 24.95 (*0-8464-1122-9*) Beekman Pubs.

McAlpine, Thomas H. By Word, Work & Wonder: Cases in Holistic Mission. 147p. 1995. pap. 15.95 (*0-912552-92-1*) MARC.

— Facing the Powers. 103p. 1991. pap. 3.95 (*0-912552-72-7*) MARC.

— Sleep, Divine & Human, in the Old Testament. (JSOTS Ser.: Vol. 38). 264p. 1987. pap. 24.50 (*0-905774-99-X*, Pub. by Sheffield Acad) CUP Services.

McAlpine, Trevor. The Partition Principle: Remapping Quebec after Separation. (Illus.). 80p. 1996. pap. 9.95 (*1-55022-291-0*, Pub. by ECW) Genl Dist Srvs.

Mcalpine, William, ed. Japanese Tales & Legends. (Oxford Myths & Legends Ser.). (Illus.). 218p. (YA). (gr. 5-12). 1989. pap. 12.95 (*0-19-274140-3*) OUP.

McAlvany, Donald S. The Coming Persecution of the Church. 64p. (Orig.). 1992. pap. 2.95 (*1-879366-36-3*) Hearthstone OK.

— Confronting Our Nation's Problems. 30p. (Orig.). 1994. pap. 2.95 (*1-879366-47-9*) Hearthstone OK.

— The Fourth Reich. 70p. (Orig.). 1994. pap. 2.95 (*1-879366-86-X*) Hearthstone OK.

***McAlvany, Donald S.** Storm Warning The Coming Persecution of Christians & Traditionalists in America. 1999. pap. 14.95 (*1-57558-048-9*) Hearthstone OK.

McAlvany, Donald S. Toward a New World Order: The Countdown to Armageddon. 250p. (Orig.). (C). 1990. pap. 8.95 (*0-9624517-9-7*) Hearthstone OK.

— Y2K Crisis: Preparing for the Coming Computer Crash. 1998. pap. text 22.50 (*0-9647861-9-2*) A N Inc Intl.

— Y2k Tidal Wave: Year 2000 Economic Survival, 1. 1999. pap. text 13.99 (*0-921714-54-8*) Fon3tier Res.

McAlvany, Donald S. & Hutchings, Noah W. Five Years to World Government & the Cashless Society. 60p. 1995. pap. 2.95 (*1-879366-91-6*) Hearthstone OK.

McAlvay, Nora & Chorpenning, Charlotte B. The Elves & the Shoemaker. (J). 1946. 6.00 (*0-87602-124-0*) Anchorage.

— Flibbertygibbet. (J). 1952. 6.00 (*0-87602-127-5*) Anchorage.

***McAmby, Geohn C.** Sesquicentennial. LC 00-90216. 2000. pap. 10.95 (*0-533-13500-1*) Vantage.

***McAmis, Herb.** The Cherokee. LC 99-23093. (Indian Nations Ser.). (Illus.). 48p. (ps-3). 2000. 25.69 (*0-8172-5456-0*) Raintree Steck-V.

McAnallen, Rachel & Frye, Ellen. Action Fractions. (Ms. Math Presents Ser.). 40p. (YA). 1993. 6.00 (*1-886915-02-4*) Koplow Games.

— Action Fractions with Hexadrons & Pattern Blocks. (Ms. Math Presents Ser.). 40p. (J). (gr. 2 up). 1995. 20.00 (*1-886915-00-8*) Koplow Games.

— Action Fractions with Hexahedron. (Ms. Math Presents Ser.). 40p. (YA). 1993. 8.50 (*1-886915-01-6*) Koplow Games.

McAnally, Brian, jt. auth. see Ferguson, Rick E.

McAnally, Don. Kisses, Dime-On Pins, Twins, Celebrities, & Humor Are My Life! (Illus.). 132p. 1991. pap. 14.95 (*0-9630282-0-0*) McAnally & Assocs.

— Thoroughbred Hookers I Have Known (Items to Make You Chuckle) 72p. 1991. pap. 5.95 (*0-9630282-1-9*) McAnally & Assocs.

McAnally, Kathleen. Letters from the Canyon (Grand Canyon) LC 95-78447. (Illus.). 32p. (Orig.). (J). (gr. 2-4). 1995. pap. 8.95 (*0-938216-52-X*) GCA.

McAnally, Mary E. The Absence of the Father & the Dance of Zygotes. Dochniak, Jim, ed. (U. S. A. Poetry Chapbook Ser.: No. 1). 20p. (C). 1982. pap. 1.95 (*0-937724-00-9*) Shadow Pr.

***McAnally, Niamh.** Loveonline.com: The Story of an Email Romance. 191p. 1999. pap. 8.00 (*0-9673237-1-1*) Keenore Pubg.

McAnally, Patricia L., et al. Language Learning Practices with Deaf Children. 2nd ed. LC 93-39470. 321p. (C). 1994. text 38.00 (*0-89079-597-5*, 6667) PRO-ED.

— Reading Practices with Deaf Learners. LC 98-49354. 1999. 38.00 (*0-89079-813-3*) PRO-ED.

McAnally, Sue, jt. auth. see Litherland, Janet.

McAnally, Tom. Questions & Answers about the United Methodist Church. 24p. (Orig.). 1995. pap. 2.25 (*0-687-01670-3*) Abingdon.

McAnaney, Kate D. I Wish... Dreams & Realities of Parenting a Special Needs Child. 96p. (Orig.). 1992. pap. 8.95 (*0-9632338-0-7*) United Cereb Palsy.

McAnaney, Pat. Dear Psychic: A New Perspective of Life's Everyday Problems. LC 92-31487. 167p. 1992. pap. 9.95 (*1-878217-07-0*) Victory Press.

McAnany, Emile G., ed. Communications in the Rural Third World: The Role of Information in Development. LC 79-21406. (Praeger Special Studies). 222p. 1980. 39.95 (*0-275-90519-5*, C0519, Praeger Pubs) Greenwood.

McAnany, Emile G., et al, eds. Communication & Social Structure: Critical Studies in Mass Media Research. 348p. 1981. 37.95 (*0-275-90679-5*, C0679, Praeger Pubs) Greenwood.

McAnany, Emile G. & Wilkinson, Kenton T., eds. Mass Media & Free Trade: NAFTA & the Cultural Industries. LC 96-10222. 1996. 45.00 (*0-292-75198-2*); pap. 24.95 (*0-292-75199-0*) U of Tex Pr.

McAnany, Emile G., jt. ed. see Atwood, Rita.

McAnany, Kathleen, jt. auth. see Schavitz, Peter.

McAnany, Patricia A. Living with the Ancestors: Kinship & Kingship in Ancient Maya Society. LC 94-5469. (Illus.). 248p. (C). 1995. text 30.00 (*0-292-75165-6*) U of Tex Pr.

***McAnany, Patricia A.** Living with the Ancestors: Kinship & Kingship in Ancient Maya Society. (Illus.). 229p. 2000. pap. 16.95 (*0-292-75236-9*) U of Tex Pr.

McAnarney, Elizabeth R., et al. Textbook of Adolescent Medicine. (Illus.). 1269p. 1992. text 152.00 (*0-7216-3077-4*, W B Saunders Co) Harcrt Hlth Sci Grp.

McAndless-Davis, Karen, jt. auth. see Cory, Jill.

McAndrew, Bill. Canadians & the Italian Campaign, 1943-1945. LC 96-940971. (Illus.). 168p. 1997. 50.00 (*2-920718-63-0*, Pub. by A4rt Global) Howell Pr VA.

McAndrew, Bill, et al. Liberation: The Canadians in Europe. (Illus.). 160p. 1996. 50.00 (*2-920718-59-2*, Pub. by A4rt Global) Howell Pr VA.

— Normandy, 1994: The Canadian Summer. (Illus.). 164p. 1996. 50.00 (*2-920718-55-X*, Pub. by A4rt Global) Howell Pr VA.

McAndrew, Bill, jt. auth. see Copp, Terry.

McAndrew, Brendan J., jt. auth. see Beveridge, Malcolm C. M.

McAndrew-Cazorla, Nathalie, jt. auth. see Williams, Stuart.

McAndrew, Elizabeth, jt. auth. see McCreedy, Dale.

McAndrew, Ian. On Poultry & Game. (gr. 13). 1990. mass mkt. 24.95 (*0-442-30274-6*) Chapman & Hall.

McAndrew, James. The Roswell Report: Case Closed. (Illus.). 231p. 1998. pap. text 45.00 (*0-7881-4832-X*) DIANE Pub.

— Roswell Report: Case Closed. LC 97-11361. 243p. 1997. per. 18.00 (*0-16-049018-9*) USGPO.

McAndrew, James & Weaver, Richard L. The Roswell Report: Fact vs. Fiction in the New Mexico Desert. LC 95-219411. (Illus.). 1995. pap. 52.00 (*0-16-048023-X*) AFH & MP.

McAndrew, James, jt. auth. see Weaver, Richard L.

McAndrew, Kelly, jt. auth. see Fluharty, Jeff.

McAndrew, Laura. Little Flower: A Story for Children. LC 98-46960. (Illus.). (J). 1999. 6.95 (*0-87868-714-9*, Child-Family Pr) Child Welfare.

McAndrew, Maura, ed. see Leone, Diana.

McAndrew, Phillip. The Fuse. 134p. 1998. pap. 6.95 (*0-9666013-0-0*) Nash Vegas.

McAndrew, Toni. Seasons of Myself. (Illus.). 21p. (Orig.). 1990. pap. 5.00 (*0-910147-86-8*) World Poetry Pr.

McAndrews, Anita. Conquistador's Lady. LC 90-30127. 240p. (Orig.). 1990. pap. 10.95 (*0-931832-48-9*) Fithian Pr.

McAndrews, Edward. Great Spirit: North American Indian Portraits. (Illus.). 104p. 1997. pap. 19.95 (*1-887694-10-2*) C Mautz Pubng.

McAndrews, J., et al. Key to the Quaternary Pollen & Spores of the Great Lakes Region. (Illus.). 68p. pap. 11.43 (*0-88854-149-X*) Brill Academic Pubs.

McAndrews, Laurence J. Broken Ground: John F. Kennedy & the Politics of Education. LC 91-14284. (Modern American History Ser.). 248p. 1991. text 20.00 (*0-8240-1897-4*) Garland.

McAndrews, Lynn. My Father Forgets. LC 90-91658. 110p. (Orig.). 1991. pap. 8.95 (*0-9626683-0-3*) Nrthrn Expressions.

McAnelly, James R. & McAnelly, Patricia L. Business Mathematics for College. LC 86-26670. (Illus.). 534p. (Orig.). (C). 1987. pap. text, teacher ed. 52.00 (*0-314-26207-5*) West Pub.

McAnelly, Patricia L., jt. auth. see McAnelly, James R.

McAnelly, Verla P., jt. auth. see Easley, Barbara P.

McAnelly, Verla P., ed. see Easley, Barbara P.

McAnelly, Verla P., jt. ed. see Easley, Barbara P.

***McAneny.** Frankenstein's Manager: Leadership's Missing Links. 200p. 2000. pap. 24.95 (*1-86076-149-6*, Pub. by Oak Tr) Midpt Trade.

McAneny, Daniel T. So You're "On Disability"...& You Think You Might Want to Get Back into Action: Thoughts & Stories That May Help Some People Who Are Receiving "Long Term Disability" Benefits. 124p. (Orig.). 1995. pap. 7.95 (*0-9646490-0-4*) D T McAneny.

McAniff, Edward. Strategic Concepts in Fire Fighting. (Illus.). 1994. 18.95 (*0-912212-02-0*) Fire Eng.

McAninch, Amy R. Teacher Thinking & the Case Method: Theory & Future Directions. LC 93-18207. 160p. (C). 1993. text 23.00 (*0-8077-3243-5*) Tchrs Coll.

McAninch, H. A. Motion Characteristics of Silent Chains. (Technical Papers: Vol. P215). (Illus.). 11p. 1940. pap. text 30.00 (*1-55589-453-4*) AGMA.

McAninch, Jack W. New Techniques in Reconstructive Urology. (Illus.). 160p. 1996. write for info. (*0-89640-281-9*) Igaku-Shoin.

— Smith's General Urology. 15th ed. (Illus.). 900p. (C). 1999. pap. 43.95 (*0-8385-8607-4*) Appleton & Lange.

— Traumatic & Reconstructive Urology. Zorab, Richard, ed. LC 95-10055. 640p. 1996. text 163.00 (*0-7216-3886-4*, W B Saunders Co) Harcrt Hlth Sci Grp.

McAninch, Jay B., jt. auth. see Selders, Arthur W.

McAninch, Sandra, compiled by. Sun Power: A Bibliography of United States Government Documents on Solar Energy. LC 80-29037. 944p. 1981. lib. bdg. 145.00 (*0-313-20992-8*, MSU/, Greenwood Pr) Greenwood.

McAninch, Walter H. The Builders Hardware Industry: A United States History 1830s to 1990s. LC 96-84506. (Illus.). 209p. (Orig.). 1996. pap. 22.00 (*0-9651989-0-1*) Ballard Locks.

McAninch, William S. & Fairey, W. Gaston. The Criminal Law of South Carolina. 3rd ed. LC 97-114543. 1996. text 109.95 (*0-943856-39-6*, 514) SC Bar CLE.

McAninch, William S., jt. auth. see Watson, Patricia S.

McAnulla, Charles. Children of God. (Illus.). 40p. (Orig.). 1995. pap. text 4.95 (*0-9649095-0-2*) C McAnulla.

McAnulla, Chuck. My Dodgers. (Illus.). 48p. (Orig.). 1995. pap. text 6.95 (*0-9649095-1-0*) C McAnulla.

***McAnulty.** Human Sexuality. 1998. text 57.00 (*0-205-19519-9*) Allyn.

***McAnulty & Burnette.** Exploring Human Sexuality: Making Healthy Decisions. 2000. pap. 22.00 (*0-205-31969-6*) Allyn.

McAnulty, Richard D., jt. ed. see Diamant, Louis.

McAra, Duncan. Sir James Gowans: Romantic Rationalist. 1977. 14.95 (*0-8464-0851-1*) Beekman Pubs.

***McArdle, Andrea & Erzen, Tanya.** Zero Tolerance: Quality of Life & the New Police Brutality in New York City. 2001. 55.00 (*0-8147-5632-8*) NYU Pr.

***Mcardle, Ann.** Decorating Essentials with Fabric & Pattern. (Illus.). 2000. pap. 22.00 (*1-56496-701-8*) Rockport Pubs.

— Decorating with Color & Texture. 2000. pap. 22.00 (*1-56496-702-6*) Rockport Pubs.

— Decorating with Fabric & Pattern. 2000. pap. 22.00 (*1-56496-703-4*) Rockport Pubs.

— East & West Style: A Design Guide for Blending Eastern & Western Elements at Home. (Illus.). 2000. pap. 25.00 (*1-56496-655-0*) Rockport Pubs.

— Elegant Interiors, 2000. pap. text 19.99 (*1-56496-611-9*) Rockport Pubs.

— Harmonious Interiors: A Design Guide for Using Feng Shui at Home, 2000. pap. text 24.99 (*1-56496-656-9*) Rockport Pubs.

— Minimal Interiors. (Interiors Ser.). (Illus.). 112p. 1999. pap. 19.99 (*1-56496-612-7*) Rockport Pubs.

— Natural Interiors, 1vol. 2000. pap. text 19.99 (*1-56496-609-7*) Rockport Pubs.

— Romantic Interiors. (Interiors Ser.). (Illus.). 112p. 1999. pap. 19.99 (*1-56496-610-0*) Rockport Pubs.

McArdle, Colin S., jt. ed. see Kerr, David J.

McArdle, Deborah A. California Marine Protected Areas. (Illus.). 282p. 1997. pap. text 13.00 (*1-888691-03-4*, T-039) U CA Calif Sea.

Mcardle, G. Developing Instructional Design: A Step-by-Step Guide to Success. Crisp, Michael, ed. LC 90-83479. (Fifty-Minute Ser.). (Illus.). 75p. (Orig.). 1991. pap. 10.95 (*1-56052-076-0*) Crisp Pubns.

McArdle, Geri. Conducting a Needs Analysis: A Fifty Minute Book. (Fifty-Minute Ser.). (Illus.). 112p. 1998. pap. 10.95 (*1-56052-423-5*) Crisp Pubns.

— Delivering Effective Training Sessions: Techniques for Productivity. Schneider, Sara, ed. LC 92-73847. (Fifty-Minute Ser.). 120p. (Orig.). 1993. pap. 10.95 (*1-56052-193-7*) Crisp Pubns.

— Managing Differences. Manber, Beverly, ed. LC 93-74234. 110p. (Orig.). 1995. pap. 12.95 (*1-56052-320-4*) Crisp Pubns.

***McArdle, Geri E.** Training Design & Delivery: A Single-Source Guide for Every Trainer, Training Manager, & Occasional Trainer. LC 98-68521. viii, 205 p. 1999. pap. 28.00 (*1-56286-099-2*) Am Soc Train & Devel.

McArdle, H. & Suggitt, G. Per Saecula, Pt. 1. 1974. pap. text 10.84 (*0-582-36727-1*, 72516) Longman.

— Per Saecula, Pt. 2. 1974. pap. text 10.84 (*0-582-36728-X*, 72517) Longman.

McArdle, J. Functional Morphology of the Hip & Thigh of the Lorisiformes. (Contributions to Primatology Ser.: Vol. 17). (Illus.). viii, 132p. 1981. pap. 28.00 (*3-8055-1767-X*) S Karger.

McArdle, J. L., et al. Treatment of Hazardous Waste Leachate: Unit Operations & Costs. LC 87-34715. (Pollution Technology Review Ser.: No. 151). (Illus.). 111p. 1988. 36.00 (*0-8155-1160-4*) Noyes.

McArdle, Jack. It's Me Again, Lord: Heart-to-Heart Chats Between God & Myself LC 98-215596. 144p. 1998. write for info. (*1-85607-242-8*) Intl Scholars.

— It's Really Very Simple: Uncomplicating the Message. 144p. (Orig.). 1994. pap. 9.95 (*1-85607-093-X*, Pub. by Columba Press) Whitecap Bks.

— One Hundred-Fifty More Stories for Preachers & Teachers. LC 92-82675. 96p. (Orig.). 1993. pap. 7.95 (*0-89622-540-2*) Twenty-Third.

— Stories for Reflection. 176p. (Orig.). 1996. pap. 14.95 (*1-85607-172-3*, Pub. by Columba Press) Whitecap Bks.

— Twelve Simple Words. 134p. (Orig.). 1994. pap. 7.95 (*1-85607-119-7*, Pub. by Columba Press) Whitecap Bks.

McArdle, John J. & Woodcock, Richard W., eds. Human Cognitive Abilities in Theory & Practice. LC 97-51455. 250p. 1998. 79.95 (*0-8058-2717-X*) L Erlbaum Assocs.

***McArdle, William D.** Sports & Exercise Nutrition. LC 98-42089. 749p. 1999. 49.95 (*0-683-30449-6*) Lppncott W & W.

McArdle, William D., et al. Essentials of Exercise Physiology. (Illus.). 563p. 1994. pap. text 47.95 (*0-8121-1724-7*) Lppncott W & W.

— Essentials of Exercise Physiology. 2nd ed. LC 99-48195. 679p. 2000. 52.95 (*0-683-30507-7*) Lppncott W & W.

— Exercise Physiology: Energy, Nutrition & Home Performance. 3rd ed. 853p. 1990. text 57.95 (*0-8121-1351-9*) Lppncott W & W.

— Exercise Physiology: Energy, Nutrition & Human Performance. 4th ed. (Illus.). 896p. 1996. 59.95 (*0-683-05731-6*) Lppncott W & W.

— Exercise Physiology Text & Study Guide Set. 1997. write for info. (*0-683-30051-2*) Lppncott W & W.

McArdle, William D., jt. auth. see Katch, Frank I.

McAreavey, John. The Canon Law of Marriage & the Family. 192p. 1997. pap. 29.50 (*1-85182-356-5*, Pub. by Four Cts Pr); boxed set 60.00 (*1-85182-342-5*, Pub. by Four Cts Pr) Intl Spec Bk.

McArielly, Verla P., jt. auth. see Easley, Barbara P.

McAroy, Hazel, jt. ed. see Powell, Alice.

McArt, Pat. Irish Almanac & Yearbook of Facts 1999. 1999. pap. text 14.95 (*0-9529596-3-1*) ArtCam Pubng.

McArt, Pat, et al, eds. Irish Almanac & Yearbook of Facts 1998. (Illus.). 450p. 1997. pap. 14.95 (*0-9529596-2-3*) Dufour.

McArt, Pat & Campbell, Donal. Irish Almanac & Yearbook of Facts, 1997. 318p. 1997. pap. 9.95 (*0-9529596-1-5*) Dufour.

McArthur. The Economics of Money & Banking. 4th ed. (C). 1995. pap. text, student ed. 21.95 (*0-673-52402-7*) Addson-Wesley Educ.

***McArthur.** No Mean City? The Image of Dublin in the Novels of Dermot Bolger, Roddy Doyle & Val Mulkerns. 2000. pap. 10.95 (*0-552-07583-3*, Pub. by Transworld Publishers Ltd) Trafalgar.

McArthur, ed. Trans Acetates. 4th ed. 1997. pap. text 177.00 (*0-673-54250-5*) S&S Trade.

McArthur, jt. auth. see Eakins.

***McArthur, Alex & Shepard, Tristram.** Textiles Technology for Key Stage 3 Course Guide: Pupils' Book. (Design & Make It Ser.). (Illus.). 144p. (YA). (gr. 6-9). 2000. pap. 22.50 (*0-7487-4431-2*, Pub. by S Thornes Pubs) Trans-Atl Phila.

— Textiles Technology for Key Stage 3 Course Guide: Teacher Support Pack. (Design & Make It Ser.). (Illus.). 223p. (YA). (gr. 6-9). 2000. pap. 99.50 (*0-7487-4432-0*, Pub. by S Thornes Pubs) Trans-Atl Phila.

— Textiles Technology for Key Stage 3 Course Guide: Teacher Support Pack CD-Rom. (Design & Make It Ser.). (Illus.). 144p. (YA). (gr. 6-9). 2000. audio compact disk 187.50 (*0-7487-5454-7*, Pub. by S Thornes Pubs) Trans-Atl Phila.

McArthur, Alex, et al. Design & Make It! Textile Technology. 144p. 1998. pap. 30.00 (*0-7487-2471-0*) St Mut.

McArthur, Alfred G. & Loveridge, John W. Economic Theory & Organization. LC 72-194559. 399p. 1972. write for info. (*0-00-460103-3*) Collins SF.

***McArthur, Andrew.** Over the Top with the Tartan Army: Active Service, 1992-97. 2000. pap. 14.94 (*0-946487-45-6*) Luath Pr Ltd.

***McArthur, Benjamin.** Actors & American Culture, 1880-1920. (Studies in Theatre History & Culture). (Illus.). 304p. 2000. reprint ed. pap. text 17.95 (*0-87745-710-7*) U of Iowa Pr.

McArthur, Bruce. Your Life: Why It Is the Way It Is & What You Can Do about It: An Exploration of the Universal Laws That Govern all of Us. 273p. (Orig.). 1993. pap. 12.95 (*0-87604-300-7*, 375) ARE Pr.

McArthur, Bruce, jt. auth. see McArthur, David.

McArthur, C. Operations Analysis in the United States Army Eighth Air Force in World War II. LC 90-829. (History of Mathematics Ser.: Vol. 4). 349p. 1990. text 36.00 (*0-8218-0158-9*, HMATH/4) Am Math.

McArthur, C. Dan & Womack, Larry. Outcome Management: Redesigning Your Business Systems to Achieve Your Vision. LC 95-5100. 242p. 1995. 24.95 (*0-527-76292-X*) Productivity Inc.

McArthur, Colin. The Big Heat. (BFI Film Classics Ser.). 80p. 1993. pap. 9.95 (*0-85170-342-9*, Pub. by British Film Inst) Ind U Pr.

McArthur, Colin & Barnard, Ian. A Director's Guide. (Waterlow Practitioner's Library). 144p. 1990. pap. 26.00 (*0-08-040121-X*, Pergamon Pr) Elsevier.

McArthur, Dalton R. The First Snowflake. (Illus.). 32p. (Orig.). (J). (ps-4). 1991. pap. 4.95 (*0-9626111-0-7*) McArthur UT.

McArthur, David & McArthur, Bruce. The Intelligent Heart: Transform Your Life with the Laws of Love. LC 97-2180. 224p. 1997. pap. 12.95 (*0-87604-389-9*, 459) ARE Pr.

McArthur, David J., et al. Untangling the Web: Applications of the Internet & Other Information Technologies to Higher Education. LC 98-3968. (Illus.). 114p. 1998. pap. 15.00 (*0-8330-2617-8*, MR-975-EDU) Rand Corp.

McArthur, David L. Alternative Approach. (Evaluation in Education & Human Services Ser.). 1987. lib. bdg. 133.00 (*0-89838-190-8*) Kluwer Academic.

***McArthur, Don.** How We Christians Can Save Society. LC 98-94061. 234p. 2000. 22.95 (*0-533-12965-6*) Vantage.

McArthur, Douglas. Information, Its Forms & Functions: The Elements of Semiology. LC 97-788. (Studies in Sociology: Vol. 13). 240p. 1997. text 89.95 (*0-7734-8675-5*) E Mellen.

McArthur, E. Durant, et al. Nutritive Quality & Mineral Content of Potential Desert Tortoise Food Plants. (Illus.). 36p. 1998. reprint ed. pap. 5.00 (*0-89904-546-4*, Wildlife Resrch Grp) Crumb Elbow Pub.

An Asterisk (*) at the beginning of an entry indicates that the title is appearing for the first time.

McArthur, Edith, jt. auth. see August, Diane.

McArthur, Edith K. Language Characteristics & Schooling in the U. S. A Changing Picture, 1979 & 1989. (Illus.). 67p. (Orig.). (C). 1994. pap. text 25.00 (*0-7881-0696-1*) DIANE Pub.

McArthur, Edwin. Flagstad: A Personal Memoir. LC 79-28361. (Music Reprint Ser.: 1980). (Illus.). 1980. reprint ed. lib. bdg. 39.50 (*0-306-76028-2*) Da Capo.

McArthur, Erna, tr. see Steiner, Rudolf.

McArthur, Harvey K. & Johnston, Robert M. They Also Taught in Parables: Rabbinic Parables from the First Centuries of the Christian Era. 176p. 1990. pap. 12.99 (*0-310-51581-5*) Zondervan.

McArthur, Hugh. Corrosion Prediction & Prevention in the Motor Vehicle. (Mechanical Engineering Ser.). 450p. 1988. text 81.95 (*0-470-20995-X*) P-H.

McArthur, Ian. Reading Japanese Signs: Deciphering Daily Life in Japan. (Illus.). 138p. 1994. pap. 10.00 (*4-7700-1671-9*) Kodansha.

McArthur, Janice & McGuire, Barbara E. Books on Wheels: Cooperative Learning Through Thematic Units. LC 98-15994. (Illus.). 160p. 1998. pap. 23.50 (*1-56308-535-6*) Libs Unl.

McArthur, John. High Performance Rowing. (Illus.). 160p. 1997. pap. 24.95 (*1-86126-039-3*, Pub. by Crolwood) Trafalgar.

McArthur, John F. Introduction to Biblical Counseling. (MacArthur Resource Library). 400p. 1994. 24.99 (*0-8499-1093-5*) Word Pub.

McArthur, Judith M. Creating the New Woman: The Rise of Southern Women's Progressive Culture in Texas, 1893-1918. LC 97-21067. (Women in American History Ser.). 216p. 1998. text 39.95 (*0-252-02376-5*) U of Ill Pr.

McArthur, Judith N. Creating the New Woman: The Rise of Southern Women's Progressive Culture in Texas, 1893-1918. LC 97-21067. (Women in American History Ser.). 216p. 1998. text 17.95 (*0-252-06679-0*) U of Ill Pr.

McArthur, Judith N. & Burton, Orville V. A Gentleman & an Officer: A Social & Military History of James B. Griffin's Civil War. (Illus.). 392p. 1996. pap. 15.95 (*0-19-509312-7*) OUP.

McArthur, Kent R. How to Be Happy, Healthy, Wealthy & Wise: The Guide to Taking Control of Your Life. LC 98-91289. (Illus.). 384p. 1999. pap. 24.95 (*0-9668078-0-4*) Life Plan Inst.

McArthur, Lewis. Oregon Geographic Names. 6th ed. 968p. 1992. pap. 19.95 (*0-87595-237-2*) Oregon Hist.

McArthur, Lewis L. Oregon Geographic Names. 6th ed. 920p. 1992. 29.95 (*0-87595-236-4*) Oregon Hist.

Mcarthur, Lewis L. & Gardiner, Cynthia B. The Railroad Stations of Oregon. LC 96-21275. 137p. 1996. pap. text 20.00 (*0-87595-261-5*) Oregon Hist.

McArthur, Loretta & Clark, Tim. Yoga Cards: Create Your Own Yoga Program. (Illus.). 24p. 1995. pap. 14.95 (*0-89087-740-8*) Celestial Arts.

McArthur, Lynne C. & Goldsberry, Yvonne. Approval & Monitoring of Narcotic Treatment Programs: A Guide on the Roles of Federal & State Agencies. (Illus.). 179p. (C). 1998. pap. text 35.00 (*0-7881-3950-9*) DIANE Pub.

McArthur, M. P. Tense Logic. 91p. 1976. text 106.00 (*90-277-0697-2*, D Reidel) Kluwer Academic.

McArthur, M. S. Report on Brunei in Nineteen Hundred Four. LC 87-11218. (Monographs in International Studies, Southeast Asia Ser.: No. 74). 297p. 1987. pap. text 15.00 (*0-89680-135-7*) Ohio U Pr.

McArthur, Margaret. Earth Magic: A Seasonal Guide. 1994. pap. 19.95 (*1-898307-01-6*, Pub. by Capall Bann Pubng) Holmes Pub.

McArthur, Margie. WiccaCraft for Families. (Illus.). 272p. (Orig.). 1994. pap. 14.95 (*0-919345-52-2*) Phoenix WA.

— Wisdom of the Elements: The Sacred Wheel of Earth, Air, Fire & Water. LC 98-24643. 176p. 1998. pap. 16.95 (*0-89594-936-9*) Crossing Pr.

McArthur, Mary P., jt. ed. see Peay, Cherilyn J.

McArthur, Meher. Gods & Goblins: Japanese Folk Paintings from Otsu. LC 99-70233. (Illus.). 64p. 1999. pap. 25.00 (*1-877921-16-5*) Pacific Asia.

McArthur, Micky. I'd Rather Be Wanted Than Had: The Memoirs of an Unrepentant Bank Robber. 272p. 1990. 24.95 (*0-7737-2340-4*) Genl Dist Srvs.

McArthur, Murray. Stolen Writings: Blake's "Milton", Joyce's "Ulysses", & the Nature of Influence. Litz, A. Walton, ed. LC 87-28566. (Studies in Modern Literature: No. 87). 188p. reprint ed. 58.30 (*0-8357-1846-8*, 207074200004) Bks Demand.

McArthur, Nancy. The Escape of the Plant That Ate Dirty Socks. (Plant That Ate Dirty Socks Ser.: Bk. 3). (J). (gr. 2-5). 1992. 9.09 (*0-606-00397-5*, Pub. by Turtleback) Demco.

McArthur, Nancy. The Escape of the Plant That Ate Dirty Socks, Bk. 3. (Plant That Ate Dirty Socks Ser.: Bk. 3). 128p. (J). (gr. 2-5). 1992. mass mkt. 3.99 (*0-380-76756-2*, Avon Bks) Morrow Avon.

McArthur, Nancy. How to Do Theatre Publicity. 1978. spiral bd. 30.00 (*0-9603940-0-1*) Good Ideas.

— More Adventures of the Plant That Ate Dirty Socks. (Plant That Ate Dirty Socks Ser.: No. 5). 128p. (J). (gr. 2-5). 1994. pap. 3.99 (*0-380-77663-4*, Avon Bks) Morrow Avon.

— More Adventures of the Plant That Ate Dirty Socks. LC 94-94095. (Plant That Ate Dirty Socks Ser.: Bk. 5). (J). (gr. 2-5). 1994. 9.09 (*0-606-06580-6*, Pub. by Turtleback) Demco.

McArthur, Nancy. The Mystery of the Plant That Ate Dirty Socks. (Plant That Ate Dirty Socks Ser.: No. 7). (J). (gr. 2-5). 1996. 9.09 (*0-606-09663-9*, Pub. by Turtleback) Demco.

— The Mystery of the Plant That Ate Dirty Socks, Bk. 7. (Plant That Ate Dirty Socks Ser.: Bk. 7). 160p. (J). (gr. 2-5). 1996. mass mkt. 3.99 (*0-380-78318-5*, Avon Bks) Morrow Avon.

McArthur, Nancy. The Plant That Ate Dirty Socks. (Plant That Ate Dirty Socks Ser.: Bk. 1). 52p. (J). (gr. 2-5). Date not set. pap. 5.60 (*0-87129-240-8*, P94) Dramatic Pub.

McArthur, Nancy. The Plant That Ate Dirty Socks. (Plant That Ate Dirty Socks Ser.: Bk. 1). 119p. (J). (gr. 2-5). pap. 4.50 (*0-8072-1494-9*) Listening Lib.

— The Plant That Ate Dirty Socks, Bk. 1. (Plant That Ate Dirty Socks Ser.: Bk. 1). 144p. (J). (gr. 2-5). 1988. mass mkt. 4.50 (*0-380-75493-2*, Avon Bks) Morrow Avon.

McArthur, Nancy. The Plant That Ate Dirty Socks Gets a Girlfriend. (Plant That Ate Dirty Socks Ser.: No. 8). (J). (gr. 2-5). 1997. pap. 3.99 (*0-614-28632-8*, Avon Bks) Morrow Avon.

— The Plant That Ate Dirty Socks Gets a Girlfriend. (Plant That Ate Dirty Socks Ser.: Bk. 8). (J). (gr. 2-5). 1997. 9.09 (*0-606-11756-3*, Pub. by Turtleback) Demco.

McArthur, Nancy. The Plant That Ate Dirty Socks Gets a Girlfriend, Bk. 8. (Plant That Ate Dirty Socks Ser.: Bk. 8). 144p. (J). (gr. 2-5). 1997. mass mkt. 3.99 (*0-380-78319-3*, Avon Bks) Morrow Avon.

— The Plant That Ate Dirty Socks Goes Hollywood, Vol. 9. (Plant That Ate Dirty Socks Ser.: Bk. 9). 144p. (J). (gr. 2-5). 1999. mass mkt. 3.99 (*0-380-79935-9*, Avon Bks) Morrow Avon.

McArthur, Nancy. The Plant that Ate Dirty Socks Goes Up in Space. (Plant That Ate Dirty Socks Ser.: No. 6). (J). (gr. 2-5). 1988. 9.60 (*0-606-03890-6*, Pub. by Turtleback) Demco.

— The Plant that Ate Dirty Socks Goes Up in Space. (Plant That Ate Dirty Socks Ser.: Bk. 6). (J). (gr. 2-5). 1995. 9.85 (*0-606-08022-8*) Turtleback.

McArthur, Nancy. The Plant that Ate Dirty Socks Goes Up in Space, Bk. 6. (Plant That Ate Dirty Socks Ser.: Bk. 6). 144p. (J). (gr. 2-5). 1995. mass mkt. 4.50 (*0-380-77664-2*, Avon Bks) Morrow Avon.

McArthur, Nancy. The Return of the Plant That Ate Dirty Socks. (Plant That Ate Dirty Socks Ser.: Bk. 2). (J). (gr. 2-5). 1990. 9.09 (*0-606-04525-2*, Pub. by Turtleback) Demco.

McArthur, Nancy. The Return of the Plant That Ate Dirty Socks, Bk. 2. (Plant That Ate Dirty Socks Ser.: Bk. 2). 128p. (J). (gr. 2-5). 1990. mass mkt. 3.99 (*0-380-75873-3*, Avon Bks) Morrow Avon.

McArthur, Nancy. The Secret of the Plant That Ate Dirty Socks. (Plant That Ate Dirty Socks Ser.: Bk. 4). 128p. (J). (gr. 2-5). 1993. pap. 3.99 (*0-380-76757-0*, Avon Bks) Morrow Avon.

McArthur, Nancy. The Secret of the Plant That Ate Dirty Socks. (Plant That Ate Dirty Socks Ser.: Bk. 4). (J). (gr. 2-5). 1993. 9.09 (*0-606-05588-6*, Pub. by Turtleback) Demco.

McArthur, Nancy, ed. The Plant That Ate Dirty Socks, Set. unabridged ed. (Plant That Ate Dirty Socks Ser.: Bk. 1). (J). (gr. 2-5). 1997. audio. write for info. (*0-8072-7751-7*, YA909SP) Listening Lib.

McArthur, Pete, jt. auth. see Guarnaccia, Steven.

McArthur, Robert, jt. auth. see Payne, Edmund C.

McArthur, Shirley D. Frank Lloyd Wright: American System Built Homes in Milwaukee. LC 83-61201. (Illus.). 186p. (Orig.). 1985. pap. text 20.00 (*0-9606072-1-8*) N Point Hist Soc.

— North Point Historic Districts - Milwaukee. LC 80-83990. (Illus.). 260p. (Orig.). 1981. pap. 25.00 (*0-9606072-0-X*) N Point Hist Soc.

McArthur, Shirley H. Raising Your Hearing-Impaired Child: Guideline for Parents. 256p. 1982. pap. 15.95 (*0-88200-150-7*) Alexander Graham.

McArthur, Simon, jt. auth. see Hall, C. Michael.

McArthur, Simon, jt. ed. see Hall, C. Michael.

McArthur, Thomas. The Oxford Companion to the English Language. (Illus.). 1216p. 1992. 55.00 (*0-19-214183-X*) OUP.

McArthur, Thomas & Wright, Alan J. ABC Airbus A340. (Illus.). 96p. 1999. pap. text 12.95 (*1-882663-43-8*) Plymouth VT.

McArthur, Tom. The English Languages. LC 97-42227. (Canto Book Ser.). (Illus.). 268p. (C). 1998. pap. 13.95 (*0-521-48582-7*) Cambridge U Pr.

— Living Words: Language, Lexicography & the Knowledge Revolution. 304p. 1999. 80.00 (*0-85989-611-0*, Pub. by Univ Exeter Pr); pap. 29.95 (*0-85989-620-X*, Pub. by Univ Exeter Pr) Northwestern U Pr.

McArthur, Tom, ed. The Concise Oxford Companion to the English Language. (Illus.). 1,072p. 1996. pap. 25.00 (*0-19-863136-7*) OUP.

McArthur, Victoria, ed. see Faber, Nancy & Faber, Randall.

***Mcarthur, Wenda.** Jumbo Gumbo: Songs, Poems & Stories for Children. (Illus.). 144p. (J). 1998. pap. 9.95 (*0-919926-99-1*, Pub. by Coteau) Genl Dist Srvs.

Mcarthur, Wenda, ed. Prairie Jungle: Songs, Poems & Stories for Children. LC 85-91257. (Illus.). 120p. (J). (ps-5). 1998. pap. 9.95 (*0-919926-45-2*, Pub. by Coteau) Genl Dist Srvs.

McArtor, Judith. Life . . . An Event! LC 89-90275. (Illus.). 80p. (Orig.). 1989. pap. 6.95 (*0-9623782-0-8*) Cynosure Self Discovery.

McArtot, Marion, jt. auth. see Goss, Louise.

McAsey, Ann. Get a Job: The Only Resume & Interview Guide You'll Ever Need. LC 98-65701. 110p. 1998. pap. 19.95 (*0-9663276-0-8*) River Rd Pr.

McAsey, Christopher. How to Live in Australia: A Guide for the Japanese. 176p. 1993. pap. 12.95 (*4-89684-756-3*, Pub. by Yohan Pubns) Weatherhill.

McAshan, Hildreth H. Competency-Based Education & Behavioral Objectives. LC 78-31160. (Illus.). 280p. 1979. 39.95 (*0-87778-132-X*) Educ Tech Pubns.

— Comprehensive Planning for School Administrators. (Orig.). (C). 1983. pap. text 11.95 (*0-89894-000-1*) Advocate Pub Group.

McAshan, M., ed. Supercollider 1. (Illus.). 840p. 1989. 155.00 (*0-306-43365-6*, Plenum Trade) Perseus Pubng.

— Supercollider 2. LC 90-49839. (Illus.). 790p. 1990. 155.00 (*0-306-43801-1*, Plenum Trade) Perseus Pubng.

McAskill, J. Dan & MacQuarrie, Kate. Nature Trails of Prince Edward Island. (Island Pathways Ser.). (Illus.). 152p. 1996. spiral bd. 14.95 (*0-921556-58-6*, Pub. by Gynergy-Ragweed) U of Toronto Pr.

McAskill, Jim. Plant Nutrient Facts for Hydroponics: How to Make Your Own Fully Formulated Plant Nutrient. Germann, Dennis, ed. (Plant Nutrient Facts for Hydroponics Ser.). (Illus.). 69p. 1998. pap. 24.95 (*0-9669557-0-6*) Foothill.

McAssey, E. V., jt. ed. see Cheung, F. B.

***MCatasney, Liam.** The Irish American Pub Quiz. LC 99-46001. 160p. 1999. pap. 9.95 (*0-7407-0339-0*) Andrews & McMeel.

— Irish American Pub Quiz. 160p. 2001. 5.98 (*1-56731-404-X*, MJF Bks) Fine Comms.

McAtee, Robert E. Facilitated Stretching. 2nd ed. LC 98-37474. 152p. 1999. pap. 16.95 (*0-7360-0066-6*) Human Kinetics.

McAtee, W. L., et al. Some Folk & Scientific Names for Plants; Vernacular Names for Texas Plants; Gleanings from the Dialect of Grant County, Indiana; A Sample of New Hampshire Dialect; A Word-List from Louisiana; Language Trends in Oil Field Jargon. (Publications of the American Dialect Society: No. 15). 95p. 1951. pap. text 9.55 (*0-8173-0615-3*) U of Ala Pr.

McAthie, Marylou, jt. auth. see Lindeman, Carol A.

McAtlee, Eric G. 175+ Uses for the Dremel Multipro & Cordless Multipro. (Illus.). 96p. (Orig.). 1989. pap. 5.15 (*0-9606512-1-7*) Dremel.

McAughey, Patricia. Calculated Risk. (Rainbow Romances Ser.). 160p. 1993. 14.95 (*0-7090-4919-6*) Parkwest Pubns.

— Calculated Risk. large type ed. (Romance Ser.). 272p. 1995. pap. 16.99 (*0-7089-7662-X*, Linford) Ulverscroft.

McAughtry, Sam. Belfast Stories. 157p. 1994. pap. 14.95 (*0-85640-520-5*, Pub. by Blackstaff Pr) Dufour.

McAughtry, Sam, et al. Touch & Go: A Novel. 233p. 1994. pap. 14.95 (*0-85640-503-5*, Pub. by Blackstaff Pr) Dufour.

McAulay, Alastair D. Optical Computer Architectures: The Application of Optical Concepts to Next Generation Computers. LC 90-42103. 560p. 1991. 135.00 (*0-471-63242-2*) Wiley.

McAulay, John D. Carbines of the Civil War, 1861-1865. 1981. 12.95 (*0-913150-45-2*) Pioneer Pr.

— Carbines of the U. S. Cavalry, 1861-1905. LC 95-80556. (Illus.). 144p. 1996. 35.00 (*0-917218-70-1*) A Mowbray.

— Civil War Breech Loading Rifles: A Survey of the Innovative Infantry Arms of the American Civil War. LC 87-60724. (Illus.). 144p. 1987. pap. 15.00 (*0-917218-29-9*) A Mowbray.

— Civil War Pistols. (Illus.). 166p. 1992. pap. 24.00 (*0-917218-72-8*) A Mowbray.

— Civil War Pistols. 2nd ed. (Illus.). 166p. 1992. 36.00 (*0-917218-55-8*) A Mowbray.

***McAulay, John D.** Civil War Small Arms of the U. S. Navy & Marine Corps. LC 99-74277. (Illus.). 183p. 1999. 39.00 (*0-917218-87-6*) A Mowbray.

McAulay, John D. & Coates, Jerry. Civil War Sharps Carbines & Rifles. (Illus.). 108p. (Orig.). 1996. pap. 12.95 (*0-939631-93-8*) Thomas Publications.

McAulay, Paul, jt. auth. see Acton, Lesley.

McAulay, Robert J., jt. auth. see Quatieri, Thomas F.

***McAuley.** Pasquale's Angel. 2000. 22.00 (*0-380-97253-0*) Morrow Avon.

— Red Dust. 2000. 22.00 (*0-380-97245-X*) Morrow Avon.

McAuley, Gay. Space in Performance: Making Meaning in the Theatre. LC 98-58101. (Theater: Theory - Text - Performance Ser.). (Illus.). 320p. 1999. text 44.50 (*0-472-11004-7*, 11004) U of Mich Pr.

McAuley, A., ed. Inorganic Reaction Mechanisms, Vols. 1-6. Incl. Vol. 1. 1969-70 Literature. LC 73-642977. 1971. 38.00 (*0-85186-255-1*); Vol. 3. 1972-73 Literature. LC 73-642977. 1974. 47.00 (*0-85186-275-6*); Vol. 4. 1973-74 Literature. LC 73-642977. 1976. 59.00 (*0-85186-285-3*); Vol. 5. 1975-76 Literature. LC 73-642977. 1977. 73.00 (*0-85186-295-0*); Vol. 6. LC 73-642977. 1979. 86.00 (*0-85186-305-1*); Vol. 2. 1970-71 Literature. LC 73-642977. 1972. 38.00 (*0-85186-265-9*); LC 73-642977. write for info. (*0-318-50472-3*) Am Chemical.

McAuley, Alastair. Economic Welfare in the Soviet Union: Poverty, Living Standards, & Inequality. LC 78-53290. 400p. 1979. 40.00 (*0-299-07640-7*) U of Wis Pr.

— Economic Welfare in the Soviet Union: Poverty, Living Standards, & Inequality. LC 78-53290. (Illus.). 411p. 1979. reprint ed. pap. 127.50 (*0-608-07011-4*, 206721800009) Bks Demand.

***McAuley, Charles.** Programming AutoCAD Using Object ARX. LC 99-48556. (Illus.). 678p. 2000. pap. 44.95 (*0-7668-0643-X*, AutoDesk Pr) Delmar.

McAuley, Collette. Children in Long Term Foster Care: Educational & Social Development. 206p. (C). 1996. 72.95 (*1-85972-252-0*, Pub. by Avebry) Ashgate Pub Co.

McAuley, Helen & Jackson, Peter. Educating Young Children: A Structural Approach. 144p. 1992. 27.50 (*1-85346-195-4*, Pub. by David Fulton) Taylor & Francis.

M'Cauley, I. H. Historical Sketch of Franklin County, PA. 294p. 1994. reprint ed. lib. bdg. 29.50 (*0-8328-3976-0*) Higginson Bk Co.

McAuley, Ian. Guide to Ethnic London. (C). 1990. pap. 100.00 (*0-902743-46-5*, Pub. by IMMEL Pubng) St Mut.

— Guide to Ethnic London. 1995. pap. 50.00 (*1-898162-20-4*, Pub. by IMMEL Pubng) St Mut.

— Passport's Guide to Ethnic London: A Complete Guide to the Many Faces & Cultures of London. 2nd ed. (Illus.). 224p. 1994. pap. 14.95 (*0-8442-9632-5*, 9604X, Passprt Bks) NTC Contemp Pub Co.

McAuley, James. Versification: A Short Introduction. 88p. 1996. reprint ed. pap. 10.95 (*0-87013-096-X*) Mich St U Pr.

McAuley, James J. After the Blizzard: Poems. LC 74-84571. (Breakthrough Bks). 72p. 1975. text 18.95 (*0-8262-0170-9*) U of Mo Pr.

McAuley, James W. The Politics of Identity. LC 94-161479. 204p. 1993. 66.95 (*1-85628-537-5*, Pub. by Avebry) Ashgate Pub Co.

McAuley, John. Hazardous Renaissance. 1978. pap. 3.00 (*0-916696-06-5*) Cross Country.

— Mattress Testing. 1979. pap. 3.00 (*0-916696-09-X*) Cross Country.

McAuley, John J., jt. auth. see Young, Philip K. Y.

McAuley, Karen. Golda Meir. (World Leaders Ser.). (Illus.). 112p. (YA). 1997. reprint ed. pap. text 15.00 (*0-7881-5079-0*) DIANE Pub.

McAuley, Kathleen A. Edgar Allan Poe Cottage. 36p. 1988. pap. text, teacher ed. 10.00 (*0-941980-23-5*) Bronx County.

McAuley, Marilyn M. God Hears Everything. LC 91-72357. 18p. (J). 1992. 4.99 (*1-55513-715-6*, Chariot Bks) Chariot Victor.

— God Made Fireflies. LC 91-72356. 18p. (J). 1992. 4.99 (*1-55513-716-4*, Chariot Bks) Chariot Victor.

McAuley, Marilyn M. & Gray, Alice. Mirror, Mirror. 144p. (Orig.). 1985. pap. 6.70 (*0-310-42951-X*, 11344P) Zondervan.

McAuley, Marilyn M., jt. auth. see Lockwood, Barbara.

McAuley, Mary. Bread & Justice: State & Society in Petrograd, 1917-1922. (Illus.). 480p. 1991. text 89.00 (*0-19-821982-2*) OUP.

McAuley, Mary. Russia's Politics of Uncertainty. (Illus.). 372p. (C). 1997. text 64.95 (*0-521-47452-3*); pap. text 24.95 (*0-521-47976-2*) Cambridge U Pr.

— Soviet Politics, Nineteen Seventeen to Nineteen Ninety-One. LC 92-7517. 140p. (C). 1992. pap. text 16.95 (*0-19-878067-2*) OUP.

McAuley, Milt. Guide to the Backbone Trail: Santa Monica Mountains. LC 90-83558. (Illus.). 144p. (Orig.). 1990. pap. 7.95 (*0-942568-23-0*) Canyon Pub Co.

— Hiking in Topanga State Park. 3rd rev. ed. LC 81-67940. (Illus.). 160p. 1991. pap. 7.95 (*0-942568-24-9*) Canyon Pub Co.

— Hiking Trails of Malibu Creek State Park. 2nd rev. ed. LC 82-74274. (Illus.). 160p. (Orig.). 1996. pap. 7.95 (*0-942568-29-X*) Canyon Pub Co.

— Hiking Trails of the Santa Monica Mountains. 6th ed. LC 80-67568. (Illus.). 368p. 1998. pap. 11.95 (*0-942568-28-1*) Canyon Pub Co.

— Wildflower Walks in the Santa Monica Mountains, Vol. 1. LC 87-72856. (Illus.). 128p. (Orig.). 1988. pap. 5.95 (*0-942568-16-8*) Canyon Pub Co.

— Wildflowers of the Santa Monica Mountains. 2nd ed. LC 84-73487. (Illus.). 576p. 1996. pap. 19.95 (*0-942568-27-3*) Canyon Pub Co.

***McAuley, Paul J.** Ancients of Days. LC 99-20951. (Confluence Trilogy Ser.: Vol. 2). 416p. 2000. mass mkt. 6.99 (*0-380-79297-4*, Avon Bks) Morrow Avon.

McAuley, Paul J. Ancients of Days: The Second Book of Confluence. LC 99-20951. 400p. 1999. 16.00 (*0-380-97516-5*, Eos) Morrow Avon.

— Child of the River: The First Book of Confluence. LC 98-11355. 320p. 1998. mass mkt. 14.00 (*0-380-97515-7*, Eos) Morrow Avon.

— Child of the River: The First Book of Confluence. LC 98-11355. 321p. 1999. mass mkt. 6.99 (*0-380-79296-6*, Avon Bks) Morrow Avon.

— Eternal Light. 432p. 1994. mass mkt. 4.99 (*0-380-76623-X*, Avon Bks) Morrow Avon.

— Eternal Light. 2000. 22.00 (*0-380-97227-1*, Avon Bks) Morrow Avon.

— Fairyland. 1997. mass mkt. 5.99 (*0-614-27713-2*, Avon Bks); mass mkt. 5.99 (*0-380-79429-2*, Avon Bks) Morrow Avon.

— The Invisible Country. LC 99-164521. 320p. 1998. pap. 13.50 (*0-380-79299-0*, Eos) Morrow Avon.

— Pasquale's Angel. 384p. 1997. mass mkt. 5.99 (*0-380-77820-3*, Avon Bks) Morrow Avon.

***McAuley, Paul J.** Shrine of Stars: The Third Book of Confluence. LC 00-29382. 384p. 2000. 18.00 (*0-380-97517-3*, Avon Bks) Morrow Avon.

McAuley, Paul J., jt. auth. see Acton, Lesley.

McAuley, R. J. & Elias, R. J. Bulletins of American Paleontology Vol. 98, No. 333: Latest Ordovician to Earliest Silurian Solitary Rugose Corals of the East-Central United States. 82p. 1990. 15.00 (*0-87710-414-X*) Paleo Res.

McAuley, Rob, jt. auth. see Miller, William.

McAuley, Skeet. Sign Language: Contemporary Southwest Native America. (Illus.). 80p. 1989. 44.95 (*0-89381-333-8*) Aperture.

McAuley, Susie. STATS for Those in the Know! LC 88-90536. 76p. (Orig.). 1988. pap. text. write for info. (*0-9619964-0-4*) S McAuley.

McAuley, Tanya, jt. auth. see Townsend, Charles E.

McAuley, William J. Applied Research in Gerontology. 258p. 1987. 99.00 (*0-471-29082-3*, VNR) Wiley.

***McAuliffe.** Growing up with Diabetes: What Kids with Diabetes Want Their Parents to Know. 128p. 1998. pap. 10.95 (*0-471-34731-0*) Wiley.

***McAuliffe, Alicia.** Growing up with Diabetes: What Kids with Diabetes Want Their Parents to Know. LC 98-230248. 128p. 1998. pap. 10.95 (*1-56561-150-0*) Wiley.

***McAuliffe, Angela T.** Between the Temple & the Cave: The Religious of the Poetry of E. J. Pratt. 256p. 2000. 65.00 (*0-7735-2057-0*, Pub. by McG-Queens Univ Pr) CUP Services.

McAuliffe, Bill. ATV Racing. LC 98-7055. (Motorsports Ser.). (J). 1998. 19.00 (*0-7368-0024-7*, Cpstone High Low) Capstone Pr.

***McAuliffe, Bill.** ATV Racing. 1999. 19.93 (*0-516-21468-3*) Capstone Pr.

McAuliffe, Bill. Black Widow Spiders. (Dangerous Animals Ser.). (Illus.). 48p. (J). (gr. 3-7). 1997. lib. bdg. 19.00 (*0-531-11469-4*, Rivr Front Bks) Capstone Pr.

— Black Widow Spiders. LC 97-8318. (Dangerous Creatures Ser.). (J). 1998. lib. bdg. write for info. (*1-56065-619-0*) Capstone Pr.

— Chief Joseph of the Nez Perce. (Read-&-Discover Biographies Ser.). (Illus.). 24p. (J). (gr. k-3). 1997. lib. bdg. 13.75 (*0-516-20900-0*) Childrens.

— Indiana: Facts & Symbols. LC 98-43102. 1999. 14.00 (*0-531-11802-9*) Capstone Pr.

— Indiana: Facts & Symbols. LC 98-43102. (States & Their Symbols Ser.). (J). 1999. write for info. (*0-7368-0218-5*) Capstone Pr.

— Minnesota: Facts & Symbols. LC 98-43014. 1999. 14.00 (*0-531-11803-7*) Capstone Pr.

— Minnesota Facts & Symbols. LC 98-43014. (States & Their Symbols Ser.). (J). 1999. write for info. (*0-7368-0219-3*) Capstone Pr.

***McAuliffe, Bill.** Motorsports. 1999. 59.79 (*0-516-29624-8*) Capstone Pr.

— Off-Road Truck Racing. 1999. 19.93 (*0-516-21470-5*) Capstone Pr.

McAuliffe, Bill. Offroad Truck Racing. LC 98-7246. (Motorsports Ser.). (J). 1998. 19.00 (*0-7368-0026-3*) Capstone Pr.

— South Carolina: Facts & Symbols. LC 98-43013. 1999. 14.00 (*0-531-11805-3*) Capstone Pr.

— South Carolina: Facts & Symbols. LC 98-43013. (States & Their Symbols Ser.). (J). 1999. write for info. (*0-7368-0220-7*) Capstone Pr.

— Virginia: Facts & Symbols. LC 98-10893. 1999. 14.00 (*0-531-11807-X*) Capstone Pr.

— Virginia Facts & Symbols. LC 98-10893. (States & Their Symbols Ser.). (J). 1999. write for info. (*0-7368-0221-5*) Capstone Pr.

McAuliffe, Bill, et al. Dangerous Animals. (Illus.). 48p. 21.26 (*0-7368-0459-5*, Capstone Bks) Capstone Pr.

***McAuliffe, Catherine & Perillo, Joseph M.** Corbin on Contracts Vol. 8: Conditions. rev. ed. 550p. 1999. write for info. (*0-327-04969-3*, 6332311) LEXIS Pub.

McAuliffe, Cathleen F., jt. auth. see Catalani, J. Christine.

McAuliffe, Daniel J. Arizona Civil Rules Handbook. 1120p. (C). 1993. pap. text 43.50 (*0-314-02418-2*) West Pub.

— Arizona Civil Rules Handbook: 1994-1995 Edition. 1125p. 1994. pap. text. write for info. (*0-314-05641-6*) West Pub.

— Arizona Civil Rules Handbook 1996 Edition. 1050p. 1996. pap. text. write for info. (*0-314-09312-5*) West Pub.

McAuliffe, Daniel J., jt. auth. see Androvich, Bob.

McAuliffe, Dennis. Bloodland: A Family Story of Oil, Greed & Murder on the Osage Reservation. LC 99-32256. Orig. Title: The Deaths of Sybil Bolton. 350p. 1999. pap. 13.95 (*1-57178-083-1*, Pub. by Coun Oak Bks) SPD-Small Pr Dist.

McAuliffe, Emily. Alabama Facts & Symbols. 1999. 15.00 (*0-531-12000-7*) Watts.

***McAuliffe, Emily.** Alabama Facts & Symbols LC 99-20044. (States & Their Symbols Ser.). 2000. write for info. (*0-7368-0374-2*, Hlltop Bks) Capstone Pr.

McAuliffe, Emily. Arizona. (States & Their Symbols Ser.). 1998. 14.00 (*0-531-11604-2*) Childrens.

— Arizona Facts & Symbols. LC 98-15808. (States & Their Symbols Ser.). 24p. (J). 1999. write for info. (*0-7368-0080-8*, Hlltop Bks) Capstone Pr.

— California & Its Emblems. LC 97-40419. (States & Their Emblems Ser.). (J). 1998. lib. bdg. write for info. (*1-56065-763-4*) Capstone Pr.

— California Facts & Symbols. (States & Their Symbols Ser.). 24p. (J). 1998. lib. bdg. 14.00 (*0-531-11548-8*) Watts.

— Colorado Facts & Symbols. LC 97-40418. (States & Their Emblems Ser.). (J). 1998. lib. bdg. write for info. (*1-56065-764-2*, Hlltop Bks) Capstone Pr.

— Colorado Facts & Symbols. (States & Their Symbols Ser.). 24p. (J). 1998. lib. bdg. 14.00 (*0-531-11549-6*) Watts.

— Connecticut: Facts & Symbols. LC 98-43045. 1999. 14.00 (*0-531-11800-2*) Capstone Pr.

Mcauliffe, Emily. Connecticut: Facts & Symbols. LC 98-43045. (States & Their Symbols Ser.). (J). 1999. write for info. (*0-7368-0214-2*, Hlltop Bks) Capstone Pr.

McAuliffe, Emily. Florida & Its Emblems. LC 97-40420. (States & Their Emblems Ser.). (J). 1998. lib. bdg. write for info. (*1-56065-765-0*) Capstone Pr.

— Florida Facts & Symbols. (States & Their Symbols Ser.). 24p. (J). 1998. lib. bdg. 13.75 (*0-531-11550-X*) Watts.

— Georgia: Facts & Symbols. LC 98-41523. 1999. 14.00 (*0-531-11801-0*) Capstone Pr.

Mcauliffe, Emily. Georgia: Facts & Symbols. LC 98-41523. (States & Their Symbols Ser.). (Illus.). (J). 1999. write for info. (*0-7368-0215-0*, Hlltop Bks) Capstone Pr.

McAuliffe, Emily. Hawaii Facts & Symbols. LC 99-19768. (States & Their Symbols Ser.). 2000. write for info. (*0-7368-0375-0*, Hlltop Bks) Capstone Pr.

— Hawaii Facts & Symbols. (States &Their Symbols Ser.). 1999. 15.00 (*0-531-12001-5*) Watts.

— Illinois & Its Emblems. LC 97-40686. (States & Their Emblems Ser.). (J). 1998. lib. bdg. write for info. (*1-56065-766-9*) Capstone Pr.

— Illinois Facts & Symbols. (States & Their Symbols Ser.). 24p. (J). 1998. lib. bdg. 14.00 (*0-531-11551-8*) Watts.

— Louisiana. (States & Their Symbols Ser.). 1998. 14.00 (*0-531-11605-0*) Childrens.

— Louisiana Facts & Symbols. LC 98-16600. (States & Their Symbols Ser.). 24p. (J). 1999. write for info. (*0-7368-0081-6*, Hlltop Bks) Capstone Pr.

***McAuliffe, Emily.** Maine Facts & Symbols. LC 99-25111. (States & Their Symbols Ser.). 1999. 14.60 (*0-7368-0376-9*) Capstone Pr.

McAuliffe, Emily. Maine Facts & Symbols. (States & Their Symbols Ser.). 1999. 15.00 (*0-531-12002-3*) Watts.

— Massachusetts. (States & Their Symbols Ser.). 1998. 14.00 (*0-531-11606-9*) Childrens.

— Massachusetts Facts & Symbols. LC 98-3674. (States & Their Symbols Ser.). 24p. (J). 1999. write for info. (*0-7368-0082-4*, Hlltop Bks) Capstone Pr.

***Mcauliffe, Emily.** Michigan Facts & Symbols. LC 98-15484. (States & Their Symbols Ser.). 24p. (J). 1999. write for info. (*0-7368-0083-2*, Hlltop Bks) Capstone Pr.

McAuliffe, Emily. Michigan Facts & Symbols. (J). 1998. 14.00 (*0-531-11607-7*) Childrens.

— Missouri Facts & Symbols. LC 99-25346. (States & Their Symbols Ser.). 2000. 14.60 (*0-7368-0377-7*, Hlltop Bks) Capstone Pr.

— Missouri Facts & Symbols. (States & Their Symbols Ser.). 1999. 15.00 (*0-531-12003-1*) Watts.

— Montana Facts & Symbols. 1999. 15.00 (*0-531-12004-X*) Watts.

***McAuliffe, Emily.** Nebraska Facts & Symbols. LC 98-7357. (States & Their Symbols Ser.). 24p. (J). 1999. write for info. (*0-7368-0084-0*) Capstone Pr.

— Nebraska Facts & Symbols. 1998. 14.00 (*0-531-11608-5*) Childrens.

McAuliffe, Emily. New Jersey Facts & Symbols. 1999. 15.00 (*0-531-12005-8*) Watts.

— New Mexico Facts & Symbols. (States & Their Symbols Ser.). 1999. 15.00 (*0-531-12006-6*) Watts.

— New York & Its Emblems. LC 97-40685. (States & Their Emblems Ser.). (J). 1998. lib. bdg. write for info. (*1-56065-767-7*, Hlltop Bks) Capstone Pr.

— New York Facts & Symbols. (States & Their Symbols Ser.). 24p. (J). 1998. lib. bdg. 14.00 (*0-531-11552-6*) Watts.

— North Carolina Facts & Symbols. (States & Their Symbols Ser.). 1999. 15.00 (*0-531-12007-4*) Watts.

— Ohio. (States & Their Symbols Ser.). (ps-3). 1998. 14.00 (*0-531-11609-3*) Orchard Books.

***McAuliffe, Emily.** Ohio Facts & Symbols. LC 98-7359. (States & Their Symbols Ser.). 24p. (J). 1999. write for info. (*0-7368-0085-9*) Capstone Pr.

McAuliffe, Emily. Oregon: Facts & Symbols. LC 98-41526. 1999. 14.00 (*0-531-11804-5*) Capstone Pr.

Mcauliffe, Emily. Oregon: Facts & Symbols. LC 98-41526. (States & Their Symbols Ser.). (J). 1999. write for info. (*0-7368-0216-9*, Hlltop Bks) Capstone Pr.

McAuliffe, Emily. Pennsylvania Facts & Symbols. LC 98-7360. (States & Their Symbols Ser.). (J). 1999. write for info. (*0-7368-0086-7*) Capstone Pr.

***McAuliffe, Emily.** Pennsylvania Facts & Symbols. LC 98-7360. (J). 1998. 14.00 (*0-531-11610-7*) Childrens.

McAuliffe, Emily. Piranhas. (Dangerous Animals Ser.). (Illus.). 48p. (J). (gr. 3-7). 1997. lib. bdg. 19.00 (*0-531-11471-6*, Rivr Front Bks) Capstone Pr.

— Piranhas. LC 97-8317. (Dangerous Creatures Ser.). (Illus.). 48p. (J). 1998. lib. bdg. write for info. (*1-56065-620-4*) Capstone Pr.

— States & Their Symbols, Vol. 14. (J). (ps-3). 1998. 196.00 (*0-531-19415-9*, Hlltop Bks) Capstone Pr.

— Tarantulas. (Dangerous Animals Ser.). (Illus.). 48p. (J). (gr. 3-7). 1997. lib. bdg. 19.00 (*0-531-11472-4*, Rivr Front Bks) Capstone Pr.

— Tarantulas. LC 97-8342. (Dangerous Creatures Ser.). (J). 1998. lib. bdg. 19.93 (*1-56065-621-2*) Capstone Pr.

— Texas Facts & Symbols. LC 97-46009. (States & Their Symbols Ser.). (J). 1998. lib. bdg. 14.00 (*1-56065-768-5*, Hlltop Bks) Capstone Pr.

— Texas Facts & Symbols. (States & Their Symbols Ser.). 24p. (J). 1998. lib. bdg. 13.75 (*0-531-11553-4*) Watts.

***McAuliffe, Emily.** Washington. (States & Their Symbols Ser.). 1998. 14.00 (*0-531-11611-5*) Childrens.

— Washington Facts & Symbols. LC 98-7358. (States & Their Symbols Ser.). 24p. (J). 1999. write for info. (*0-7368-0087-5*) Capstone Pr.

McAuliffe, Emily. Wisconsin: Facts & Symbols. LC 98-41527. 1999. 14.00 (*0-531-11806-1*) Capstone Pr.

— Wisconsin: Facts & Symbols. LC 98-41527. (States & Their Symbols Ser.). (J). 1999. write for info. (*0-7368-0217-7*) Capstone Pr.

McAuliffe, Emily, et al. States & Their Symbols. (Illus.). 24p. 454.10 (*0-7368-0559-1*, Bridgestone Bks) Capstone Pr.

McAuliffe, Garrett. Outcomes of a Group Career Planning Process. 1988. 3.00 (*0-318-40010-3*, OC 126) Ctr Educ Trng Employ.

***McAuliffe, Garrett & Eriksen, Karen.** Preparing Counselors: Creating Constructivist & Developmental Programs. Association for Counselor Education & Supervision Staff, ed. LC 00-25186. (Illus.). 2000. write for info. (*1-57864-100-4*) Donning Co.

McAuliffe, Jane D. Qur'anic Christians: An Analysis of Classical & Modern Exegesis. 352p. (C). 1991. text 69.95 (*0-521-36470-1*) Cambridge U Pr.

McAuliffe, Jane D., tr. The History of al-Tabari: Abbasid Authority Affirmed: The Early Years of Al-Mansur, Vol. XXVIII. LC 93-44496. (Series in Near Eastern Studies). 326p. (C). 1995. pap. text 24.95 (*0-7914-1896-0*) State U NY Pr.

— The History of al-Tabari: Abbasid Authority Affirmed: The Early Years of Al-Mansur, Vol. XXVIII. LC 93-44496. (Series in Near Eastern Studies). 326p. (C). 1995. text 64.50 (*0-7914-1895-2*) State U NY Pr.

***McAuliffe, Jane Dammen, ed.** Encyclopaedia of the Qur'an. 500p. 2000. 221.00 (*90-04-11465-3*) Brill Academic Pubs.

McAuliffe, Jody, ed. Plays, Movies, & Critics. LC 93-17308. (Illus.). 304p. 1993. text 49.95 (*0-8223-1404-5*); pap. text 17.95 (*0-8223-1418-5*) Duke.

***McAuliffe, Kevin.** Sayings of Generalissimo Giuliani. 2000. pap. 12.00 (*1-56649-163-0*) Welcome Rain.

McAuliffe, Mary B. & McAuliffe, Robert M. The Essentials of Chemical Dependency, Vol. I. LC 75-13362. 1975. 9.95 (*0-317-00368-2*) Am Chem Dep Soc.

McAuliffe, Mary B., jt. auth. see McAuliffe, Robert M.

***McAuliffe, Michelle M. & Black, Marsha W.** Busy Teacher's Guide: Art Lessons. (Illus.). 80p. (J). 1999. pap., teacher ed. 9.95 (*1-57690-471-7*, TCM2471) Tchr Create Mat.

— Busy Teacher's Guide: Art Lessons. Taggart, Mary Kaye, ed. (Illus.). 80p. 1999. pap., teacher ed. 9.95 (*1-57690-210-2*, TCM2210) Tchr Create Mat.

McAuliffe, Patricia. Fundamental Ethics: A Liberationist Approach. LC 93-11108. 320p. 1993. 35.00 (*0-87840-541-0*) Georgetown U Pr.

McAuliffe, Robert, ed. The Blackwell Encyclopedic Dictionary of Managerial Economics. LC 96-46009. 450p. 1997. 105.95 (*1-55786-965-0*) Blackwell Pubs.

— The Blackwell Encyclopedic Dictionary of Managerial Economics. (Blackwell Encyclopedia of Management Ser.). 240p. 1999. reprint ed. pap. 29.95 (*0-631-21483-6*) Blackwell Pubs.

McAuliffe, Robert M. & McAuliffe, Mary B. Diagnostic Manual: Essentials for the Diagnosis of Chemical Dependency, Vol. II. LC 75-13360. 1975. 6.95 (*0-317-00369-0*) Am Chem Dep Soc.

— Essentials of Chemical Dependency, Vol. III: Patient Work Book. 1986. 9.95 (*0-318-33040-7*) Am Chem Dep Soc.

McAuliffe, Robert M., jt. auth. see McAuliffe, Mary B.

***McAuliffe, Thomas.** Disarming the Debt Bomb: America's Huge Debt Is a Bomb That Is Exploding & Devatating the Lives of Millions. It Doesn't Have to Happen Though. There Is a Solution. (Illus.). 292p. 1999. pap. 14.95 (*0-929408-27-6*) Amer Eagle Pubns Inc.

McAuliffe, Thomas P. & Shamlin, Carolyn S. Critical Information Network: The Next Generation of Executive Information Systems. (Illus.). 130p. 1992. pap. 29.95 (*0-9633121-7-0*) McAuliffe & Co.

McAuliffe, William E. & Albert, Jeffrey. Clean Start: An Outpatient Program for Initiating Cocaine Recovery. LC 92-1528. (Substance Abuse Ser.). 234p. 1993. pap. text 20.95 (*0-89862-194-1*) Guilford Pubns.

McAulyfe, William E., jt. auth. see Zackon, Fred.

McAuslan, Ian & Walcot, Peter, eds. Greek Tragedy. LC 92-26819. (Greece & Rome Studies). 232p. 1993. text 60.00 (*0-19-920300-8*) OUP.

— Homer, Vol. IV. (Greecee & Rome Studies). 224p. 1998. text 55.00 (*0-19-920188-9*); pap. text 24.95 (*0-19-920187-0*) OUP.

— Virgil. (Greece & Rome Studies: No. I). 208p. 1990. 65.00 (*0-19-920166-8*) OUP.

McAuslan, Ian, jt. ed. see Walcot, Peter.

McAuslan, J. P., jt. ed. see Kanyeihamba, G. W.

McAuslan, Patrick. The Ideologies of Planning Law. (Urban & Regional Planning Ser.: Vol. 22). 1980. 125.00 (*0-08-023696-0*, Pub. by Pergamon Repr) Franklin.

McAuslan, Patrick, jt. auth. see Farvacque, Catherine.

McAuslane, Neil & Walker, Stuart R., eds. Improving the Regulatory Review Process: Assessing Performance & Setting Targets. LC 98-147056. (Centre for Medicines Research Workshop Ser.). 392p. 1998. 97.00 (*0-7923-8731-7*) Kluwer Academic.

McAveeney, David C. Kipling in Gloucester: The Writing of Captain Courageous. (Illus.). 108p. (Orig.). 1996. pap. 14.95 (*0-9625660-4-7*) Curious Traveller Pr.

Mcavera, Brian. Picasso's Women: Eight Monologues. 144p. 1998. pap. 16.95 (*1-870259-86-6*, Pub. by Oberon Bks Ltd) Consort Bk Sales.

McAvin, Margaret, ed. see Council of Educators in Landscape Architecture Sta.

McAvinn, Douglas, jt. auth. see Opie, Brenda.

McAvity, Helen. Everybody Has to Be Somebody. 1971. pap. 5.25 (*0-8222-0366-9*) Dramatists Play.

McAvity, Helen, jt. auth. see Howard, Eleanor H.

McAvoy, Brian R., ed. Caring for Asians in General Practice. (Oxford General Practice Ser.: No. 18). (Illus.). 344p. 1990. pap. 35.00 (*0-19-261733-8*) OUP.

McAvoy, Elaine A. Irresistible Love. (Serenade Serenata Ser.: No. 12). 192p. (Orig.). (J). (gr. 10-12). 1985. pap. 2.50 (*0-310-46612-1*, 15520P) Zondervan.

McAvoy, George E. And Then There Was One: A History of the Hotels of the Summit & the West Side of Mount Washington. 356p. 1988. pap. 18.50 (*0-9630647-0-3*) Crawford Pr.

— And Then There Was One: A History of the Hotels of the Summit & the West Side of Mount Washington. limited ed. 356p. 1988. 100.00 (*0-9630647-1-1*) Crawford Pr.

— A Citizen-Soldier Remembers 1942-1946: 149th Armored Signal Company of the 9th Armored Division. (Illus.). 238p. 1991. 25.00 (*0-9630647-2-X*) Crawford Pr.

McAvoy, Gregory E. Controlling Technocracy: Citizen Rationality & the NIMBY Syndrome. LC 99-18787. (American Governance & Public Policy Ser.). 160p. 1999. 55.00 (*0-87840-740-5*); pap. 18.95 (*0-87840-741-3*) Georgetown U Pr.

***McAvoy, Jane E.** The Satisfied Life. LC 99-54447. 2000. pap. 15.95 (*0-8298-1377-2*) Pilgrim OH.

McAvoy, Jane E., ed. Table Talk: Resources for the Communion Meal. 112p. (Orig.). 1993. pap. 8.99 (*0-8272-3632-8*) Chalice Pr.

McAvoy, Jim. Tom Hanks. LC 99-32042. (Galaxy of Superstars Ser.). (Illus.). 64p. (YA). (gr. 3-7). 1999. pap. 9.95 (*0-7910-5335-0*) Chelsea Hse.

— Tom Hanks. LC 99-32042. (Illus.). 64p. 1999. 17.95 (*0-7910-5235-4*) Chelsea Hse.

McAvoy, Joseph M. Nottoway River Survey Pt. 1: Clovis Settlement Patterns, Vol. 28. 171p. 1992. pap. 22.50 (*1-884626-01-7*) Notto Way.

McAvoy, Katherine T. Stories & Activities for Articulation Reinforcement, No. 803118. 128p. (gr. k-6). 1990. student ed. 19.50 (*0-86703-216-2*) Opportunities Learn.

McAvoy, Martin. The Profession of Ignorance: With Constant Reference to Socrates. LC 99-20590. 344p. 1999. 49.00 (*0-7618-1387-X*) U Pr of Amer.

McAvoy, Nelson. Teaching Soccer Fundamentals. LC 98-8163. (Illus.). 184p. 1998. pap. 14.95 (*0-88011-855-5*, PMCA0855) Human Kinetics.

***McAvoy, T., et al, eds.** Chemical Process Control, Mineral & Metal Processing, Vol. N. 542p. 1999. pap. 126.00 (*0-08-043225-5*) Elsevier.

— Fault Detection II, Aerospace, Marine Systems, Vol. P. 618p. 1999. pap. 126.00 (*0-08-042754-5*) Elsevier.

— Power Systems, Biotechnological Processes, Fault Detection, Vol. O. 606p. 1999. pap. 126.00 (*0-08-042753-7*) Elsevier.

McAvoy, Thomas T. Catholic Church in Indiana, 1789-1834. LC 41-6425. (Columbia University. Studies in the Social Sciences: No. 471). reprint ed. 27.50 (*0-404-51471-5*) AMS Pr.

McAvoy, Thomas T., ed. Roman Catholicism & the American Way of Life. LC 72-13177. (Essay Index Reprint Ser.). 1977. reprint ed. 18.95 (*0-8369-8167-7*) Ayer.

McAvoy, Thomas T. & Nye, Russel B. The Midwest: Myth or Reality? A Symposium. LC 61-10848. 104p. reprint ed. pap. 32.30 (*0-608-15459-8*, 202931100060) Bks Demand.

McAvoy, William C., compiled by. Twelfth Night, or, What You Will: A Bibliography to Supplement the New Variorum Edition of 1901. LC 84-6546. (New Variorum Edition of Shakespeare Ser.). vi, 57p. 1984. pap. text 10.00 (*0-87352-285-0*, Z125P) Modern Lang.

M'Caw & Co. Staff. A User's Guide to Patents. 1995. pap. text. write for info. (*0-406-01307-1*, UK, MICHIE) LEXIS Pub.

McBain, A. G. The Private Secretary. (C). 1982. pap. write for info. (*0-7219-0500-5*, Pub. by Scientific) St Mut.

McBain, Donald J., jt. auth. see Graves, Barbara F.

***McBain, Ed.** Barking at Butterflies & Other Stories. LC 00-25939. 275p. 2000. 22.95 (*0-7862-2536-X*) Five Star.

— Driving Lessons. /80p. 2000. 12.95 (*0-7867-0805-0*, Pub. by Carroll & Graf) Publishers Group.

— He Who Hesitates. 2000. mass mkt. 3.50 (*0-380-64198-4*) Morrow Avon.

— The Last Dance. 320p. 2000. reprint ed. per. 7.99 (*0-671-02570-8*) PB.

McBain, Ed, jt. auth. see Hunter, Evan.

McBain, Ed, pseud. Another Part of the City. 1987. mass mkt. 3.95 (*0-445-40584-8*, Pub. by Warner Bks) Little.

— Beauty & the Beast. 256p. 1988. mass mkt. 3.99 (*1-55817-662-4*, Pinncle Kensgtn) Kensgtn Pub Corp.

— The Big Bad City: A Novel of the 87th Precinct. LC 98-40890. 304p. 1999. 25.00 (*0-684-85512-7*) Simon & Schuster.

***McBain, Ed, pseud.** The Big Bad City: A Novel of the 87th Precinct. large type ed. LC 99-19335. 1999. 26.95 (*1-56895-714-9*, Compass) Wheeler Pub.

McBain, Ed, pseud. Big Man. 176p. 1991. mass mkt. 4.50 (*0-380-71123-0*, Avon Bks) Morrow Avon.

— Bread. (Eighty-Seventh Precinct Ser.). 224p. 1997. reprint ed. mass mkt. 5.99 (*0-446-60425-9*, Pub. by Warner Bks) Little.

— Bread: An 87th Precinct Mystery Novel. 176p. 1987. mass mkt. 4.50 (*0-380-70368-8*, Avon Bks) Morrow Avon.

— Calypso: A Novel. 208p. 1988. mass mkt. 4.99 (*0-380-70591-5*, Avon Bks) Morrow Avon.

— Cinderella. 272p. 1987. mass mkt. 3.95 (*0-445-40618-6*, Pub. by Warner Bks) Little.

— Cinderella. 272p. 1989. mass mkt. 4.99 (*0-445-40898-7*, Pub. by Warner Bks) Little.

***McBain, Ed, pseud.** Cop Hater: 87th Precinct Mystery. 224p. 1999. per. 6.99 (*0-671-77547-2*, Pocket Books) PB.

McBain, Ed, pseud. Death of a Nurse. 192p. 1991. mass mkt. 4.50 (*0-380-71125-7*, Avon Bks) Morrow Avon.

— Doll. (Eighty-Seventh Precinct Novel Ser.). 160p. 1986. mass mkt. 4.50 (*0-380-70082-4*, Avon Bks) Morrow Avon.

— Doll. 208p. 1997. reprint ed. mass mkt. 5.99 (*0-446-60146-2*, Pub. by Warner Bks) Little.

— Doors. 256p. 1988. pap. 3.50 (*0-380-70371-8*, Avon Bks) Morrow Avon.

— Doors. 288p. 1995. mass mkt. 5.99 (*0-446-60148-9*, Pub. by Warner Bks) Little.

— Downtown. 352p. 1993. reprint ed. mass mkt. 5.99 (*0-380-70761-6*, Avon Bks) Morrow Avon.

— Ed McBain: Three Complete 87th Precinct Novels. LC 92-7598. (Illus.). 528p. 1992. 13.99 (*0-517-06499-5*) Random Hse Value.

— Eight Black Horses: An 87th Precinct Novel. (Eighty-Seventh Precinct Novel Ser.). 256p. 1986. mass mkt. 4.99 (*0-380-70029-8*, Avon Bks) Morrow Avon.

— Eighty Million Eyes. 176p. 1987. mass mkt. 4.50 (*0-380-70367-X*, Avon Bks) Morrow Avon.

***McBain, Ed, pseud.** Eighty Million Eyes. large type ed. 229p. 2000. lib. bdg. 25.95 (*1-58547-011-2*) Ctr Point Pubg.

McBain, Ed, pseud. Eighty Million Eyes. 208p. 1997. reprint ed. mass mkt. 5.99 (*0-446-60386-4*, Pub. by Warner Bks) Little.

— The Eighty-Seventh Precinct Companion. (Orig.). 1995. pap. write for info. (*0-89296-989-X*, Mysterious Paperbk) Warner Bks.

— Even the Wicked. 128p. 1991. mass mkt. 3.99 (*0-380-71122-2*, Avon Bks) Morrow Avon.
— Gangs! 208p. 1989. reprint ed. pap. 3.50 (*0-380-70757-8*, Avon Bks) Morrow Avon.
— Gladly the Cross-Eyed Bear. LC 96-3492. 336p. 1998. mass mkt. 6.50 (*0-446-60494-1*, Pub. by Warner Bks) Little.
— Gladly the Cross-Eyed Bear. large type ed. LC 96-21105. 424p. 1996. 25.95 (*0-7838-1899-8*, G K Hall Lrg Type) Mac Lib Ref.
— Gladly the Cross-Eyed Bear. large type ed. LC 96-21105. 410p. 1998. pap. 23.95 (*0-7838-1900-5*, G K Hall Lrg Type) Mac Lib Ref.
— Guns. 224p. 1988. mass mkt. 3.99 (*0-380-70373-4*, Avon Bks) Morrow Avon.
McBain, Ed, pseud. Hail, Hail, the Gang's All Here: An 87th Precinct Mystery. LC 78-39799. 307p. (J). 1972. write for info. (*0-8161-6025-2*, G K Hall & Co) Mac Lib Ref.
McBain, Ed, pseud. Hail to the Chief: An 87th Precinct Mystery. 192p. 1997. mass mkt. 5.99 (*0-614-13859-0*) Warner Bks.
— Hail to the Chief: An 87th Precinct Mystery. 192p. 1997. reprint ed. mass mkt. 5.99 (*0-446-60405-4*, Pub. by Warner Bks) Little.
— He Who Hesitates. (Eighty-Seventh Precinct Novel Ser.). 160p. 1986. mass mkt. 4.50 (*0-380-70084-0*, Avon Bks) Morrow Avon.
— He Who Hesitates. 160p. 1996. reprint ed. mass mkt. 5.99 (*0-446-60147-0*, Pub. by Warner Bks) Little.
— The House That Jack Built. 256p. 1989. mass mkt. 4.99 (*0-445-40623-2*, Pub. by Warner Bks) Little.
— The House That Jack Built. large type ed. (General Ser.). 320p. 1989. lib. bdg. 20.95 (*0-8161-4758-2*, G K Hall Lrg Type) Mac Lib Ref.
— Ice. 320p. 1984. mass mkt. 5.99 (*0-380-67108-5*, Avon Bks) Morrow Avon.
— Ice. 336p. 1996. reprint ed. mass mkt. 5.99 (*0-446-60390-2*, Pub. by Warner Bks) Little.
— Jack & the Beanstalk. 256p. 1994. mass mkt. 5.99 (*0-446-60132-2*, Pub. by Warner Bks) Little.
— Killer's Choice: An 87th Precinct Mystery. (Eighty-Seventh Precinct Novel Ser.). 160p. 1986. mass mkt. 4.50 (*0-380-70083-2*, Avon Bks) Morrow Avon.
*__McBain, Ed, pseud.__ Killer's Wedge. large type ed. 232p. 2000. lib. bdg. 27.95 (*1-58547-032-5*) Ctr Point Pubg.
McBain, Ed, pseud. Kiss: A Novel of the 87th Precinct. 384p. 1992. mass mkt. 5.99 (*0-380-71382-9*, Avon Bks) Morrow Avon.
— The Last Best Hope. 291p. 1999. mass mkt. 7.50 (*0-446-60673-1*, Pub. by Warner Bks) Little.
— The Last Best Hope. large type ed. LC 98-27664. 383p. 1998. pap. 30.00 (*0-7862-1605-0*) Thorndike Pr.
— The Last Dance: A Novel of the 87th Precinct. LC 99-53534. 360p. 2000. 24.95 (*0-684-85513-5*) S&S Trade.
— Lightning: An 87th Precinct Novel. (Eighty-Seventh Precinct Novel Ser.). 304p. 1985. mass mkt. 4.95 (*0-380-69974-5*, Avon Bks) Morrow Avon.
— Long Time No See. 272p. 1987. mass mkt. 4.99 (*0-380-70369-6*, Avon Bks) Morrow Avon.
— Long Time No See. 304p. 1997. mass mkt. 5.99 (*0-446-60449-6*, Pub. by Warner Bks) Little.
— Lullaby: An 87th Precinct Novel. 352p. 1990. mass mkt. 5.99 (*0-380-70384-X*, Avon Bks) Morrow Avon.
— Mary, Mary. 384p. 1994. mass mkt. 5.99 (*0-446-60054-7*, Pub. by Warner Bks) Little.
McBain, Ed, pseud. McBain's Ladies: The Women of the 87th Precinct. LC 87-40389. 272p. 1988. 16.45 (*0-89296-284-4*, Pub. by Mysterious Pr) Little.
McBain, Ed, pseud. McBain's Ladies: The Women of the 87th Precinct. 1989. mass mkt. 4.95 (*0-445-40334-9*, Pub. by Warner Bks) Little.
— Mischief. 352p. 1994. mass mkt. 5.99 (*0-380-71384-5*, Avon Bks) Morrow Avon.
— The Mugger. 192p. 1996. mass mkt. 5.99 (*0-446-60143-8*, Pub. by Warner Bks) Little.
— Mugger. (Eighty-Seventh Precinct Novel Ser.). 160p. 1986. mass mkt. 3.50 (*0-380-70081-6*, Avon Bks) Morrow Avon.
— Nocturne. (87th Precinct Ser.). 1998. mass mkt. 188.73 (*0-446-16558-1*) Warner Bks.
— Nocturne. LC 96-42030. 352p. 1998. reprint ed. mass mkt. 6.99 (*0-446-60538-7*, Pub. by Warner Bks) Little.
— Poison. 256p. 1988. mass mkt. 4.99 (*0-380-70030-1*, Avon Bks) Morrow Avon.
— Puss in Boots. 1988. mass mkt. 4.95 (*0-445-40621-6*, Pub. by Warner Bks) Little.
— Puss in Boots. 224p. 1994. mass mkt. 5.99 (*0-446-60135-7*, Pub. by Warner Bks) Little.
— Romance. 352p. 1996. reprint ed. mass mkt. 6.50 (*0-446-60280-9*, Pub. by Warner Bks) Little.
— Rumpelstiltskin. 240p. 1994. mass mkt. 5.99 (*0-446-60130-6*, Pub. by Warner Bks) Little.
*__McBain, Ed, pseud.__ Running from Legs & Other Stories. LC 00-34747. (First Edition Mystery Ser.). 2000. write for info. (*0-7862-2671-4*) Five Star.
McBain, Ed, pseud. The Sentries. 304p. 1988. pap. 3.50 (*0-380-70489-7*, Avon Bks) Morrow Avon.
— The Sentries. 304p. 1995. mass mkt. 5.99 (*0-446-60145-4*, Pub. by Warner Bks) Little.
— Snow White & Rose Red. 256p. 1986. reprint ed. mass mkt. 4.99 (*0-445-40513-9*, Pub. by Warner Bks) Little.
— There Was a Little Girl. 352p. 1995. mass mkt. 6.50 (*0-446-60214-0*, Pub. by Warner Bks) Little.
— There Was a Little Girl. large type ed. 480p. 1995. 24.95 (*0-7838-1180-2*, G K Hall Lrg Type) Mac Lib Ref.
— There Was a Little Girl. large type ed. 424p. 1995. pap. 19.95 (*0-7838-1181-0*, G K Hall Lrg Type) Mac Lib Ref.
— Three Blind Mice. 1990. 18.95 (*0-685-36235-3*) Little.
— Three Blind Mice. 1991. mass mkt. 4.99 (*0-446-40035-1*, Pub. by Warner Bks) Little.
— Three Blind Mice: A Novel. large type ed. (General Ser.). 396p. 1991. lib. bdg. 21.95 (*0-8161-5169-5*, G K Hall Lrg Type) Mac Lib Ref.
— Tricks. 256p. 1989. reprint ed. mass mkt. 5.99 (*0-380-70383-1*, Avon Bks) Morrow Avon.
— Vanishing Ladies. 160p. 1991. reprint ed. mass mkt. 4.50 (*0-380-71121-4*, Avon Bks) Morrow Avon.
— Vespers. 352p. 1991. mass mkt. 5.99 (*0-380-70385-8*, Avon Bks) Morrow Avon.
— Where There's Smoke. 192p. 1987. pap. 3.50 (*0-380-70372-6*, Avon Bks) Morrow Avon.
— Where There's Smoke. 224p. 1997. mass mkt. 5.99 (*0-446-60483-6*, Pub. by Warner Bks) Little.
— Widows. 336p. 1992. reprint ed. mass mkt. 6.50 (*0-380-71383-7*, Avon Bks) Morrow Avon.
*__McBain, Ed, pseud, ed.__ The Best American Mystery Stories 1999. 352p. 1999. 27.50 (*0-395-93916-X*); pap. 13.00 (*0-395-93915-1*) HM.
McBain, Graham S. Butterworths Banking Law Handbook. 2nd ed. 730p. 1993. pap. 110.00 (*0-406-02005-1*, UK, MICHIE) LEXIS Pub.
McBain, Howard L. De Witt Clinton & the Origin of the Spoils System in New York. LC 07-36153. (Columbia University. Studies in the Social Sciences: No. 75). reprint ed. 27.50 (*0-404-51075-2*) AMS Pr.
— Prohibition Legal & Illegal. LC 72-67. (Select Bibliographies Reprint Ser.). 1977. reprint ed. 15.95 (*0-8369-9963-0*) Ayer.
McBain, J. The Merrick & the Neighbouring Hills. 340p. 1985. 30.00 (*0-7855-1040-0*, Pub. by Alloway Pub) St Mut.
McBaine, Robert. Sentence Combining Student Workbook with Exercises & Key. 135p. (Orig.). (YA). (gr. 8 up). 1984. pap. 9.90 (*0-89420-244-8*, 261000) Natl Book.
McBaine, Susan. Miniature Needlepoint Rugs for Dollhouses Charted for Easy Use. (Illus.). 40p. (Orig.). 1976. pap. 3.95 (*0-486-23388-X*) Dover.
McBane, Bruce N. Automotive Coatings. (Illus.). 62p. 1987. pap. 30.00 (*0-934010-11-0*) Fed Soc Coat Tech.
*__McBane, Susan.__ The Essential Book of Horse Tack & Equipment. 2000. 29.95 (*0-7153-0821-1*, Pub. by D & C Pub) Sterling.
McBane, Susan. Feeding Horses & Ponies: Overcoming Common Feeding Problems. (Illus.). 160p. 1996. 27.95 (*0-7153-0309-0*, Pub. by D & C Pub) Sterling.
*__McBane, Susan.__ Feeding Horses & Ponies: Overcoming Common Feeding Problems. 2000. pap. 19.95 (*0-7153-1007-0*) D & C Pub.
McBane, Susan. Fitness in the Horse. (Illus.). 160p. 1997. 35.00 (*1-85223-963-8*, Pub. by Crolwood) Trafalgar.
— Grooming. (Threshold Picture Guides Ser.). (Illus.). 24p. 1992. pap. 12.00 (*1-872082-29-7*, Pub. by Kenilworth Pr) Half Halt Pr.
— The Horse & the Bit. (Illus.). 144p. 1996. pap. 29.95 (*1-85223-900-X*, Pub. by Crolwood) Trafalgar.
— How to Cure Behavior Problems in Horses. 1991. pap. 15.00 (*0-87980-429-7*) Wilshire.
*__McBane, Susan.__ How Your Horse Works. (Illus.). 160p. 2000. 27.95 (*0-7153-0861-0*, Pub. by D & C Pub) Sterling.
McBane, Susan. Illustrated Encyclopedia of Horse Breeds. 256p. 1997. 19.98 (*0-7858-0604-0*) Bk Sales Inc.
— The Illustrated Guide to Horse Tack. Steege, Gwen, ed. LC 95-31204. (Illus.). 198p. 1996. 29.95 (*0-88266-879-X*, 879-X, Storey Pub) Storey Bks.
— Keeping Horses: The Working Owner's Guide to Saving Time & Money. 2nd ed. (Illus.). 192p. 1993. pap. 24.95 (*0-632-03443-2*) Blackwell Sci.
— Know Your Pony. (Illus.). 112p. 1996. pap. 10.95 (*0-7063-7423-1*, Pub. by WrLock) Sterling.
— The Outdoor Pony. (Threshold Picture Guides Ser.). (Illus.). 24p. 1992. pap. 12.00 (*1-872082-30-0*, Pub. by Kenilworth Pr) Half Halt Pr.
— Poor Richards Horse Keeper. 1993. 27.95 (*0-914327-52-6*) Breakthrgh NY.
— Tack & Clothing. (WLRS Ser.). (Illus.). 112p. 1996. pap. 10.95 (*0-7063-7427-4*, Pub. by WrLock) Sterling.
— Ward Lock Riding School: Modern Stable Management. (Illus.). 96p. 1998. pap. 10.95 (*0-7063-7699-4*, Pub. by WrLock) Sterling.
McBarnet, Gill. The Brave Little Turtle. (Illus.). 32p. (J). (gr. k-2). 1994. 8.95 (*0-9615102-8-5*) Ruwanga Trad.
— Fountain of Fire. (Illus.). 32p. (J). (gr. k-2). 1987. 8.95 (*0-9615102-3-4*) Ruwanga Trad.
— Gecko Hide & Seek. (Illus.). 24p. (J). (gr. k-2). 1993. 8.95 (*0-9615102-7-7*) Ruwanga Trad.
— Gift of Aloha. (Illus.). 32p. (J). (gr. k-2). 1996. 8.95 (*0-9615102-9-3*) Ruwanga Trad.
— The Goodnight Gecko. (Illus.). 32p. (J). (gr. k-2). 1991. 8.95 (*0-9615102-6-9*) Ruwanga Trad.
— The Pink Parrot. (Illus.). 40p. (J). (gr. k-2). 1986. 8.95 (*0-9615102-1-8*) Ruwanga Trad.
— The Shark Who Learned a Lesson. (Illus.). 32p. (J). (gr. k-2). 1990. 8.95 (*0-9615102-5-0*) Ruwanga Trad.
— The Whale Who Wanted to Be Small. (Illus.). 32p. (J). (gr. k-2). 1985. 8.95 (*0-9615102-0-X*) Ruwanga Trad.
— A Whale's Tale. (Illus.). 32p. (J). (gr. k-2). 1988. 8.95 (*0-9615102-4-2*) Ruwanga Trad.
— The Wonderful Journey. (Illus.). 32p. (J). (gr. k-2). 1986. 8.95 (*0-9615102-2-6*) Ruwanga Trad.
McBarron, Jan. Flavor Without Fat. 1999. pap. text 15.95 (*0-9622923-3-8*) Mossy Oak Pub.
— Flavor Without Fat: Cookbook for Healthy Living for the Entire Family. 312p. 1995. reprint ed. pap. 15.95 (*0-9649825-0-1*) Inst Healthy.
McBath, James H., jt. auth. see Dickens, Milton.
McBay, Marian Y. & Higgins, Raymond E. First Do No Harm: Leader's Guide. 1994. pap. 5.95 (*0-687-00264-8*) Abingdon.
*__McBean & Rovers.__ Statistical Procedures for Analysis of Environmental Monitoring Data & Risk Assessment, Vol. 3. LC 98-24799. 336p. (C). 1998. 80.00 (*0-13-675018-4*) P-H.
McBean, Edward A., et al, eds. Reliability in Water Resources Management. LC 79-64191. 1979. 30.00 (*0-918334-30-6*) WRP.
McBean, Edward A., et al. Solid Waste Landfill Engineering & Design. LC 94-10676. 544p. 1994. 89.00 (*0-13-079187-3*) P-H.
McBean, Edward A., ed. see Balek, Jaroslav, et al.
McBean, Edward A., jt. ed. see Unny, T. E.
McBean, Elanor. The Hidden Dangers in Polio Vaccine. 86p. 1993. reprint ed. spiral bd. 9.00 (*0-7873-0593-6*) Hlth Research.
— The Poisoned Needle. 230p. 1993. reprint ed. pap. 18.50 (*0-7873-0594-4*) Hlth Research.
McBean, G. A. & Hantel, M., eds. Interactions Between Global Climate Subsystems: The Legacy of Hann. LC 93-13345. (Geophysical Monograph Ser.: Vol. 75). 1993. 28.00 (*0-87590-466-1*) Am Geophysical.
McBeath, Gerald A. The Alaska State Constitution: A Reference Guide, 27. LC 96-18229. (Reference Guides to the State Constitutions of the United States). 288p. 1997. lib. bdg. 99.50 (*0-313-27778-8*) Greenwood.
— North Slope Borough Government & Policymaking. (ISER Reports: No. 51). (Illus.). 94p. 1981. pap. 7.50 (*0-88353-028-7*) U Alaska Inst Res.
— Wealth & Freedom: Taiwan's New Political Economy. LC 97-39118. (Illus.). 280p. 1998. text 68.95 (*1-84014-041-0*, Pub. by Ashgate Pub) Ashgate Pub Co.
McBeath, Gerald A. & Morehouse, Thomas A. Alaska Politics & Government. LC 93-5390. (Politics & Governments of the American States Ser.). (Illus.). xxx, 367p. 1994. text 55.00 (*0-8032-3120-2*); pap. text 22.00 (*0-8032-8149-8*) U of Nebr Pr.
McBeath, Gerald A. & Morehouse, Thomas A., eds. Alaska State Government & Politics. LC 86-51368. (Illus.). 357p. 1987. 27.00 (*0-912006-20-X*); pap. 17.00 (*0-912006-21-8*) U of Alaska Pr.
McBeath, Gordon. Practical Management Development: Strategies for Management Resourcing & Development in the 1990s. (Illus.). 350p. 1994. pap. text 31.95 (*0-631-19346-4*) Blackwell Pubs.
McBeath, Ron J., ed. Instructing & Evaluating in Higher Education: A Guidebook for Planning Learning Outcomes. LC 91-40486. (Illus.). 365p. (Orig.). 1992. pap. 39.95 (*0-87778-242-3*) Educ Tech Pubns.
*__McBeath, Simon.__ Competition Car Composites: A Practical Guide. (Illus.). 208p. 2000. 39.95 (*1-85960-624-5*, 129532AE, Pub. by J H Haynes & Co) Motorbooks Intl.
McBeath, Simon. Competition Car down Force - a Practical Guide. LC 97-76816. (Illus.). 192p. 1998. 39.95 (*0-85429-977-7*) Haynes Manuals.
*__McBeath, Simon.__ Competition Car Downforce: A Practical Handbook. 2nd ed. (Illus.). 208p. 2000. 39.95 (*1-85960-662-8*, 130740AE, Pub. by Haynes Manuals) Motorbooks Intl.
— Competition Car Preparation: A Practical Guide to Basic Principles. (Illus.). 208p. 1999. 39.95 (*1-85960-609-1*, 129512AE, Pub. by Haynes Manuals) Motorbooks Intl.
McBee. Dance Hall Days. text 30.00 (*0-8147-5620-4*) NYU Pr.
McBee, Alice F. From Utopia to Florence: The Story of a Transcendentalist Community in Northampton, Massachusetts, 1830-1852. LC 74-31281. (American Utopian Adventure Ser.). (Illus.). x, 97p. 1975. reprint ed. lib. bdg. 25.00 (*0-87991-027-5*) Porcupine Pr.
McBee, Jim. Exchange Server 5.5. LC 99-61307. (24seven Ser.). 688p. 1999. pap. 34.99 (*0-7821-2505-0*) Sybex.
*__McBee, May W.__ Mississippi County Court Records. LC 67-29601. 94p. 1999. reprint ed. pap. 16.50 (*0-8063-0218-6*) Clearfield Co.
McBee, May W. The Nachez Court Records, 1767-1805. 635p. 1994. pap. 47.50 (*0-8063-1452-4*, 3490) Clearfield Co.
McBee, Shar. To Lead Is to Serve: How to Attract Volunteers & Keep Them. 208p. 1994. pap. 14.95 (*0-9638560-0-6*) S McBee.
McBee, Susanna, et al. Downtown Development Handbook. 2nd ed. LC 92-60669. (Community Builders Handbook Ser.). 273p. 1992. 64.95 (*0-87420-732-0*, D13) Urban Land.
McBee, Wanda N. Get It Together. 300p. (Orig.). pap. text 29.95 (*0-317-91112-0*) W McBee.
McBeth. Challenge of Health Care in the 21St Century, No. 21. LC 99-35784. 158p. (C). 2000. pap. text 30.00 (*0-205-27618-0*, Macmillan Coll) P-H.
McBeth, Amy, compiled by. A Discography of 78 RPM Era Recordings of the Horn: Solo & Chamber Literature with Commentary, Vol. 74. LC 97-34709. (Discographies Ser.: Vol. 74). 232p. 1997. lib. bdg. 72.95 (*0-313-30444-0*, Greenwood Pr) Greenwood.
McBeth, Brenda G., et al. Alaska Resource Guide, 1997: African Americans in Alaska Resource Guide 1995. 8th ed. 48p. 1995. 14.95 (*0-9630369-4-7*) A Abraham.
McBeth, Brian S. British Oil Policy, 1919-1939. (Illus.). 190p. 1985. 35.00 (*0-7146-3229-5*, Pub. by F Cass Pubs) Intl Spec Bk.
*__McBeth, Brian S.__ Gunboats, Corruption, & Claims: Foreign Intervention in Venezuela, 1899-1908, 20. LC 00-35357. (Contributions in Latin American Studies: Vol. 20). 272p. 2001. 64.00 (*0-313-31356-3*, GM1356, Greenwood Pr) Greenwood.
McBeth, Brian S. Privatisation: A Strategic Report. 600p. 1996. ring bd. 765.00 (*1-85564-335-9*, Pub. by Euromoney) Am Educ Systs.
*__McBeth, Colin & Lynn, Heloise B.__ Applied Seismic Anisotropy: Theory, Background & Field Studies. LC 00-34434. (Geophysics Reprint Ser.). (Illus.). 2000. write for info. (*1-56080-095-X*) Soc Expl Geophys.
McBeth, H. Leon. English Baptist Literature on Religious Liberty to Sixteen Eighty Nine: Doctoral Dissertation. Gaustad, Edwin S., ed. LC 79-52575. (Baptist Tradition Ser.). 1980. lib. bdg. 42.95 (*0-405-12443-0*) Ayer.
— A Sourcebook for Baptist Heritage. LC 89-33091. 544p. 1990. 29.99 (*0-8054-6589-8*, 4265-89) Broadman.
McBeth, Kate. The Nez Perces since Lewis & Clark. (Idaho Yesterdays Ser.). (Illus.). 288p. (C). 1993. reprint ed. pap. 15.95 (*0-89301-160-6*) U of Idaho Pr.
McBeth, Leon. Baptist Heritage. LC 86-31667. 848p. 1987. 29.99 (*0-8054-6569-3*, 4265-69) Broadman.
McBeth, Liz, ed. The Joint Rolling Handbook. (Illus.). 64p. 1997. pap. 9.95 (*0-932551-23-8*) Quick Am Pub.
McBeth, Mark, jt. auth. see Clemons, Randall.
McBeth, Muhammad A. Combinatorial Number-Theory: A Treatise on Growth, Based on the Goodstein-Skolem Hierarchy, Including a Critique of Non-Constructive or First-Order Logic. LC 94-13953. 430p. 1994. text 109.95 (*0-7734-9085-X*) E Mellen.
McBeth, Robert W. & Ferguson, J. Robert. IBM Assembler: An Intuitive Approach. LC 86-32468. 789p. 1987. text 93.95 (*0-471-82424-0*) Wiley.
McBeth, Sally J., jt. auth. see Horne, Esther B.
*__McBeth, Tom E.__ Hit the Clock: Worker's Words of Wisdom. Gordon, Michelle A., ed. 93p. 1998. pap. 12.95 (*0-9655253-2-5*) Merging Worlds Publishers.
McBey, James. The Early Life of James McBey: An Autobiography. (Classics Ser.). 130p. 1994. pap. 11.95 (*0-86241-445-8*, Pub. by Canongate Books) Interlink Pub.
*__McBey, Shirley.__ Laying a Foundation for Tomorrow: Report on the Quality Education for Minorities (QEM) Network Initial Years, July 1, 1990-June 30, 1993. (Illus.). 57p. 1999. reprint ed. pap. text 15.00 (*0-7881-7892-X*) DIANE Pub.
McBirney, Alexander R. Igneous Petrology. 2nd ed. 520p. 1992. 57.50 (*0-86720-175-4*) Jones & Bartlett.
McBirney, Alexander R. & Williams, Howel. Volcanic History of Honduras. LC 79-627247. (University of California Publications in Social Welfare: vol. 85). 111p. reprint ed. pap. 34.50 (*0-608-16249-3*, 201500100093) Bks Demand.
McBirney, Alexander R. & Williams, Howell. Geology & Petrology of the Galapagos Islands. LC 79-98018. (Geological Society of America, Memoir Ser.: No. 118). 223p. reprint ed. pap. 69.20 (*0-608-13542-9*, 202546800044) Bks Demand.
McBirney, Alexander R., tr. see Fouque, Ferdinand A.
McBirney, Alexander R., tr. see Friedrich, Walter L.
McBirney, Connie A., jt. ed. see Taylor, Robert M., Jr.
McBirnie, William S. The Search for the Twelve Apostles. 312p. 1979. mass mkt. 5.99 (*0-8423-5839-0*) Tyndale Hse.
McBogg, Bruce. Ropeless Jumping: The Conversion of a Jogger. (Illus.). 71p. 1981. 3.45 (*0-686-32863-9*) B McBogg.
McBraney, S. Long Fall Short & Hairy Poems. (Illus.). (J). 1996. mass mkt. 8.95 (*0-340-66494-0*, Pub. by Hodder & Stought Ltd) Trafalgar.
McBratney, Sam. Adivina Cuanto Te Quiero.Tr. of Guess How Much I Love You. (SPA., Illus.). 32p. (Orig.). (J). (gr. 1-3). 1995. 15.95 (*84-88342-08-X*) Lectorum Pubns.
— The Caterpillow Fight. LC 95-32015. (Illus.). 24p. (J). (ps). 1996. 9.99 (*1-56402-804-6*) Candlewick Pr.
— The Caterpillow Fight. LC 95-32015. (Illus.). 24p. (J). (ps-1). 1997. reprint ed. pap. 3.29 (*0-7636-0124-1*) Candlewick Pr.
— The Chieftain's Daughter. 160p. (J). 1997. pap. 6.95 (*0-86278-338-0*) Irish Amer Bk.
— Dark at the Top of the Stairs. LC 94-48921. (Illus.). 32p. (J). (ps-2). 1996. 15.99 (*1-56402-640-X*) Candlewick Pr.
— Dark at the Top of the Stairs. LC 94-48921. (Illus.). 32p. (J). (ps-2). 1998. pap. 5.99 (*0-7636-0417-8*) Candlewick Pr.
*__McBratney, Sam.__ Devine Combien Je T'aime. 1998. pap. 16.95 (*2-211-03745-3*) Distribks Inc.
McBratney, Sam. The Ghastly Gertie Swindle: With the Ghosts of Hungryhouse Lane. (Illus.). 128p. (J). (gr. 3-6). 1995. 14.95 (*0-8050-2614-2*, Bks Young Read) H Holt & Co.
McBratney, Sam. Guess How Much I Love You. 32p. 15.99 (*0-8499-5904-7*) Tommy Nelson.
McBratney, Sam. Guess How Much I Love You: My Baby Book. LC 94-1599. (Illus.). 32p. (J). (ps-3). 1995. 15.99 (*1-56402-473-3*) Candlewick Pr.
McBratney, Sam. Guess How Much I Love You: My Baby Book. 1997. 191.88 (*0-7636-0332-5*) Candlewick Pr.
McBratney, Sam. Guess How Much I Love You: My Baby Book. (Illus.). (J). (ps-k). 1997. boxed set, bds. 13.99 (*0-7636-0331-7*) Candlewick Pr.
— Guess How Much I Love You: My Baby Book. (J). (ps up). 1998. 15.99 (*0-7636-0599-9*) Candlewick Pr.
— Guess How Much I Love You: My Baby Book. LC 94-1599. (Illus.). 16p. (J). (ps-k). 1998. 17.99 (*0-7636-0675-8*) Candlewick Pr.
— Guess How Much I Love You: My Baby Book. (CHI., Illus.). 40p. (J). (ps-1). 1996. write for info. (*1-85430-383-X*, Pub. by MAGI1 UK); write for info. (*1-85430-384-8*, Pub. by MAGI1 UK); write for info. (*1-85430-387-2*, Pub. by MAGI1 UK) Midpt Trade.
— Guess How Much I Love You: My Baby Book. LC 94-1599. (Illus.). 40p. (J). (ps up). 1996. reprint ed. 15.99 (*0-7636-0164-0*); reprint ed. bds. 6.99 (*0-7636-0013-X*) Candlewick Pr.
*__McBratney, Sam.__ I'm Not Your Friend. LC 00-32008. (Illus.). (J). 2001. write for info. (*0-06-029485-X*) HarpC Child Bks.

M

McBratney, Sam. I'm Sorry. (Illus.). 24p. (J). 1999. write for info. (0-7636-0981-1) Candlewick Pr.

— I'm Sorry. LC 99-60933. 40p. (J). (ps-2). 2000. 15.95 (0-06-028686-5) HarpC Child Bks.

— Just One. LC 97-10175. (Illus.). 24p. (J). (ps-1). 1997. pap. 3.99 (0-7636-0223-X) Candlewick Pr.

— Just One. 1997. 9.19 (0-606-12748-8, Pub. by Turtleback) Demco.

— Just You & Me. LC 97-16456. (Illus.). 32p. (J). (ps-1). 1998. 15.99 (0-7636-0436-4) Candlewick Pr.

*__McBratney, Sam.__ Just You & Me. LC 97-16456. (Illus.). 32p. (J). (ps-1). 2000. pap. 5.99 (0-7636-1078-X) Candlewick Pr.

— Once There Was a Hoodie. LC 00-23137. (Illus.). (J). 2001. write for info. (0-399-23581-7, G P Putnam) Peng Put Young Read.

McBrayer, James D., Jr. Escape! Memoir of a World War II Marine Who Broke Out of a Japanese POW Camp & Linked up with Chinese Communist Guerillas. LC 94-24528. (Illus.). 232p. 1995. lib. bdg. 29.95 (0-7864-0058-7) McFarland & Co.

McBrayer, W. David, jt. auth. see Goodwin, Charles D.

McBrayer, William D., jt. auth. see Goodwin, Charles D.

McBrayer, William D., ed. & intro. see Sharp, Granville.

M

McBrearty, Daniel. Electronics Calculations Data Handbook. LC 98-218556. 224p. 1999. pap. text 29.95 (0-7506-3744-7, Newnes) Buttrwrth-Heinemann.

McBrearty, James C. American Labor History & Comparative Labor Movements: A Selected Bibliography. LC 78-190624. 272p. reprint ed. pap. 84.40 (0-8357-5378-6, 202275000029) Bks Demand.

McBrearty, Kathleen. Caribbean Pink. large type ed. 1991. pap. 16.99 (0-7089-6983-6) Ulverscroft.

McBrearty, Robert Garner. A Night at the Y. LC 99-12912. 160p. 1999. pap. 12.00 (1-880284-36-7) J Daniel.

McBreen, James, ed. see Symposium on Advances in Battery Materials & Proce.

McBreen, James T., et al. Human Behavior: A Perspective for the Helping Professions. 4th ed. 240p. (C). 1995. pap. 49.00 (0-8013-1634-0, 77087) Longman.

McBreen, Joan. Poems Selected & New. 1998. pap. 13.95 (1-897648-86-3, Pub. by Salmon Poetry) Dufour.

— A Walled Garden in Moylough. (Irish Literature Ser.). 80p. 1995. pap. 10.95 (1-885266-07-3) Story Line.

*__McBreen, Joan.__ The White Page/An Bhileog Bh'an: Twentieth-Century Irish Women Poets. 312p. 2000. 34.95 (1-897648-40-5, Pub. by Salmon Poetry); pap. 19.95 (1-897648-57-X, Pub. by Salmon Poetry) Dufour.

McBreen, Joan. The Wind Beyond the Wall. 2nd ed. (Irish Literature Ser.). 64p. (Orig.). (C). 1990. pap. 8.95 (0-934257-33-7) Story Line.

McBriar, A. M. An Edwardian Mixed Doubles: The Bosanquets Versus the Webbs: A Study in British Social Policy 1890-1929. 418p. 1987. text 79.00 (0-19-820111-7) OUP.

— Fabian Socialism & English Politics, 1884-1918. LC 66-70570. 398p. reprint ed. pap. 113.50 (0-608-16877-7, 2027245) Bks Demand.

McBriarty, J. P. & Henry, N., III, eds. Performance of Protective Clothing, Vol. 4. (Special Technical Publication Ser.: No. STP 1133). (Illus.). 1025p. 1992. text 83.00 (0-8031-1430-3, STP1133) ASTM.

McBride. Developmental Writing II. 1997. pap. 20.50 (0-07-221375-2) McGraw.

— The Gambling Times Guide to Greyhound Racing. Date not set. pap. text 9.95 (0-8065-9995-2, Citadel Pr) Carol Pub Group.

McBride. A Guide to Help Desk Technology, Tools & Techniques. 376p. per. 46.95 (0-7600-7151-9, Pub. by Course Tech) Thomson Learn.

McBride. Internet for Windows Made Simple. 160p. Date not set. pap. text 19.95 (0-7506-2311-X) Buttrwrth-Heinemann.

— Internet for Windows 95 Made Simple. 160p. Date not set. pap. text 19.95 (0-7506-2835-9) Buttrwrth-Heinemann.

— Internet Resources Made Simple. 160p. Date not set. pap. text 19.95 (0-7506-2836-7) Buttrwrth-Heinemann.

— IT Core Skills. 160p. 1997. pap. text 19.99 (0-7506-3378-6) Buttrwrth-Heinemann.

— Microsoft Networking Made Simple. 160p. Date not set. pap. text 19.95 (0-7506-2837-5) Buttrwrth-Heinemann.

— MS Works for Windows 3.1 Made Simple. 160p. Date not set. pap. text 19.95 (0-7506-2065-X) Buttrwrth-Heinemann.

— Office 95 Made Simple. 160p. Date not set. pap. text 19.95 (0-7506-2625-9) Buttrwrth-Heinemann.

— Pascal Made Simple. 200p. Date not set. pap. text. write for info. (0-7506-3242-9) Buttrwrth-Heinemann.

— Searching for John Ford / LC 99-33994. 1999. text 27.95 (0-312-24232-8) St Martin.

— Windows 3.1 Made Simple. 160p. Date not set. pap. text 19.95 (0-7506-2072-2) Buttrwrth-Heinemann.

— Windows 95 Made Simple. 160p. Date not set. pap. text 19.95 (0-7506-2306-3) Buttrwrth-Heinemann.

— Works for Windows 95 Made Simple. 160p. Date not set. pap. text. write for info. (0-7506-3396-4) Buttrwrth-Heinemann.

McBride, jt. auth. see Tracy, Diane L.

*__McBride, Lela J.__ Opothleyaholo & the Loyal Muskogee: Their Flight to Kansas in the Civil War. LC 99-48305. (Illus.). 256p. 1999. lib. bdg. 39.95 (0-7864-0638-0) McFarland & Co.

*__McBride, Alfred.__ Celebrating Mass Vol. 1: A Guide for Understanding & Loving that Mass More Deeply. 1999. pap. 29.95 (0-87973-185-0) Our Sunday Visitor.

— Celebrating the Mass: A Guide for Understanding & Loving the Mass More Deeply. LC 99-74102. 64p. 1999. pap. 4.95 (0-87973-148-6) Our Sunday Visitor.

McBride, Alfred. Essentials of the Faith: A Guide to the Catechism of the Catholic Church. LC 93-87231. 224p. 1994. pap. 11.95 (0-87973-740-9, 740) Our Sunday Visitor.

— Father McBride's Family Catechesim. LC 97-69273. (Illus.). 228p. 1998. pap. 9.95 (0-87973-930-4) Our Sunday Visitor.

— Father McBride's Teen Catechism: Based on the Catechism of the Catholic Church. LC 84-60745. 192p. (YA). 1996. pap., student ed. 9.95 (0-87973-704-2, 704) Our Sunday Visitor.

— Father McBride's Teen Catechism: Based on the Catechism of the Catholic Church. 48p. 1997. pap., teacher ed. 5.95 (0-87973-712-3) Our Sunday Visitor.

— Images of Mary, 1. 200p. 1999. pap. text 10.95 (0-86716-330-5, B3305) St Anthony Mess Pr.

— Our Sunday Visitor's Popular Bible Study Series, 7 bks. Incl. Director's Guide. 24p. 1992. pap. 1.95 (0-87973-353-5); Human Face of Jesus: Luke. LC 91-62164. 216p. 1992. pap. 5.95 (0-87973-358-6); Second Coming of Jesus: Meditation & Commentary on the Book of Revelation. LC 92-61979. 180p. (Orig.). 1993. pap. 5.95 (0-87973-526-0, 526); 35.95 (0-87973-959-2) Our Sunday Visitor.

— A Retreat with Pope John XXIII: Opening the Windows to Wisdom. 168p. (Orig.). 1996. pap. 9.95 (0-86716-258-9, B2589) St Anthony Mess Pr.

— The Story of the Church: Peak Moments from Pentecost to the Year 2000. rev. ed. (Illus.). 168p. (YA). (gr. 7-12). 1996. pap. text 12.95 (0-86716-246-5) St Anthony Mess Pr.

McBride, Alfred & Praem, O. Invitation: A Catholic Learning Guide for Adults: The Search for God, Self & Church. rev. ed. (Illus.). 124p. 1994. per. 9.95 (0-918951-00-3) Paulist Natl Catholic.

*__McBride, Andrew.__ The Arizona Kid. large type ed. 240p. 1999. pap. 18.99 (0-7089-5497-9, Linford) Ulverscroft.

McBride, Angela B. & Austin, Joan K., eds. Psychiatric-Mental Health Nursing: Integrating the Behavioral & Biological Sciences. LC 95-10059. (Illus.). 471p. 1995. text 56.00 (0-7216-4038-9, W B Saunders Co) Harcrt Hlth Sci Grp.

McBride, Angus. The Zulu War. (Men-at-Arms Ser.: No. 57). (Illus.). 48p. pap. 12.95 (0-85045-256-2, 9009, Pub. by Ospry) Stackpole.

McBride, Anne. Why Does My Rabbit...? (Illus.). 208p. 1999. 24.95 (0-285-63440-2, Pub. by Souvenir Pr Ltd) IPG Chicago.

*__McBride, Anne.__ Why Does My Rabbit... ? 208p. 2000. pap. 14.95 (0-285-63550-6, Pub. by Souvenir Pr Ltd) IPG Chicago.

McBride, Annie. Rabbits & Hares. (Illus.). 128p. text 19.95 (0-905483-67-7, Pub. by Whittet Bks) Diamond Farm Bk.

McBride, Becan, jt. auth. see Garza.

McBride, Betty, ed. see Fisher, James N.

McBride, Bill. Book Collecting for Fun & Profit. 96p. 1998. pap. 9.95 (0-930313-05-4) McBride Pub.

— How to Beat the Dog Races. 1999. pap. 18.95 (0-9671282-0-X) S Potts Pubg.

McBride, Bunny. Molly Spotted Elk: A Penobscot in Paris. LC 95-6891. 384p. 1995. 24.95 (0-8061-2756-2) U of Okla Pr.

— Molly Spotted Elk: A Penobscot in Paris. LC 95-6891. (Illus.). 384p. 1997. pap. 13.95 (0-8061-2989-1) U of Okla Pr.

— Women of the Dawn. LC 99-20617. 160p. 1999. 22.00 (0-8032-3209-8) U of Nebr Pr.

McBride, Carolyn. Bobbing for Apples - with Success! Practical How-to's for Congregational Leaders. McBride, Christy, ed. LC 96-5061. (Illus.). 208p. (Orig.). 1996. pap. 11.95 (1-880292-09-2) LangMarc.

*__McBride, Carolyn.__ Making Magnificent Machines: Fun with Math, Science & Engineering. LC 99-34584. 1999. 22.00 (1-56976-102-7) Zephyr Pr AZ.

McBride, Charles C. Mission Failure & Survival. (Illus.). 192p. (Orig.). 1989. pap. 17.95 (0-89745-125-2) Sunflower U Pr.

McBride, Christy, ed. see Dungan, F. Alvin.

McBride, Christy, ed. see McBride, Carolyn.

McBride, David. Integrating the City of Medicine: Blacks in Philadelphia Health Care, 1910-1965. LC 88-15924. 320p. (C). 1989. 49.95 (0-87722-546-X) Temple U Pr.

McBride, David, et al, eds. Crosscurrents: African-Americans, Africa, & Germany in the Modern World. LC 97-41684. (GERM Ser.). 278p. 1998. 75.00 (1-57113-098-5) Camden Hse.

McBride, David N. & McBride, Jane N. Common Pleas Court Records of Highland County, Ohio 1805-1860. (Vital Records of Highland County, Ohio Ser.). 306p. 1984. lib. bdg. 32.50 (0-941000-02-8) S Ohio Genealog.

— Marriage Records of Highland County, Ohio, 1805-1880. (Vital Records of Highland County, Ohio Ser.). 416p. 1982. reprint ed. lib. bdg. 37.00 (0-941000-01-X) S Ohio Genealog.

— Records of the Recorder's Office of Highland County, Ohio, 1805-1850. (Vital Records of Highland County, Ohio Ser.). 570p. reprint ed. lib. bdg. 45.00 (0-941000-03-6) S Ohio Genealog.

McBride, Dean, ed. see Wolff, Hans W., Jr.

McBride, Deborah, jt. auth. see Berman, Richard L.

McBride, Denis. Impressions of a Life: Stories of Jesus. LC 93-36055. 224p. (Orig.). 1994. 15.95 (0-89243-642-5, Liguori Triumph) Liguori Pubns.

*__McBride, Denis.__ The Parables of Jesus. LC 99-25160. 1999. pap. 13.95 (0-7648-0511-8, Liguori Triumph) Liguori Pubns.

McBride, Dennis. How to Do Architectural Ink Renderings. (Illus.). 1980. 7.95 (0-910158-68-1) Art Dir.

— How to Make Visual Presentations. rev. ed. LC 85-7201. (Illus.). 80p. (C). 1981. pap. 6.95 (0-910158-86-X) Art Dir.

*__McBride, Dennis.__ Killing the Mockingbird. 176p. 2000. pap. 10.95 (1-882550-38-2, Pub. by Quiet Lion Pr) SPD-Small Pr Dist.

McBride, Dennis. Looking for Peoria: The Epicurean at Rest. (Orig.). 1995. pap. 9.95 (1-882550-13-7) Quiet Lion Pr.

McBride, Dennis, jt. auth. see Dunar, Andrew.

McBride, Dennis, jt. auth. see Dunar, Andrew J.

McBride, Don, jt. ed. see Bray, Donald E.

McBride, Donna, ed. see McDaniel, Nello & Thorn, George.

McBride, Douglas F. Learning Veterinary Terminology. LC 95-48284. (Illus.). 560p. (C). (gr. 13). 1996. pap. text 30.00 (0-8151-5960-9, 25550) Mosby Inc.

McBride, Duane C., jt. auth. see Inciardi, James A.

McBride, Dwight A., ed. James Baldwin Now. 1999. pap. text 19.50 (0-8147-5618-2) NYU Pr.

— James Baldwin Now. LC 99-6546. (Illus.). 356p. 1999. text 55.00 (0-8147-5617-4) NYU Pr.

McBride, Earle F. Sedimentary Petrology & History of the Haymond Formation (Pennsylvanian), Marathon Basin, Texas. (Reports of Investigations: RI 57). 101p. 1966. pap. 2.50 (0-686-29339-8) Bur Econ Geology.

*__McBride, Earvin, Jr.__ The Adventurous Cyborg. 2nd unabridged ed. (Amazing Sci-Fi & Adventure Heroes Ser.). (Illus.). 43p. (YA). (gr. 7-12). 2000. 4.95 (1-892511-06-1) E J MacBride.

McBride, Earvin, Jr. The American Blonds. unabridged ed. (Earvin MacBride's Fun Fun Lovable Cartoons Ser.). (Illus.). 123p. (J). (gr. 7-12). 2000. pap. 4.95 (1-892511-01-0) E J MacBride.

— Angel on My Shoulders. unabridged ed. (Illus.). 24p. (gr. 7-12). 2000. write for info. (1-892511-14-2) E J MacBride.

*__McBride, Earvin, Jr.__ The Blockheads from Planet Ecto. 2nd unabridged ed. (Earvin MacBride's Amazing Sci-Fi & Adventure Heroes Ser.). (Illus.). 41p. (YA). (gr. 7-12). 2000. pap. 4.95 (1-892511-10-X, Disposition Sketch) E J MacBride.

McBride, Earvin, Jr. The Bowdery Rodeo Cowboys of Texas. 2nd unabridged ed. (Earvin MacBride's Amazing Sci-Fi & Adventure Heroes Ser.). (Illus.). 329p. (J). (gr. 7-12). 2000. pap. 4.95 (1-892511-07-X) E J MacBride.

— Dumbball the Bodybuilder. unabridged ed. (Earvin MacBride's Fun Fun Lovable Cartoons Ser.). (Illus.). 123p. (YA). (gr. 7-12). 2000. pap. 4.95 (1-892511-02-9) E J MacBride.

— Earvin MacBride's Amazing Sci-Fi & Adventure Heroes, 7 vols. 2nd unabridged ed. (Illus.). (J). (gr. 7-12). 2000. pap. 25.95 (1-892511-05-3) E J MacBride.

— Earvin MacBride's Fun Fun Lovable Cartoons, 4 vols. unabridged ed. (Illus.). (J). (gr. 7-12). 2000. pap. 16.95 (1-892511-00-2) E J MacBride.

— The Eerie Adventures of Detective Omar Mendez. 2nd unabridged ed. (Earvin MacBride's Amazing Sci-Fi & Adventure Heroes Ser.). (Illus.). 329p. (J). (gr. 7-12). 2000. pap. 5.95 (1-892511-08-8) E J MacBride.

— The Joyous Adventures of Sam & Pam. unabridged ed. (Earvin MacBride's Fun Fun Lovable Cartoons Ser.). (Illus.). 123p. (J). (gr. 7-12). 2000. pap. 3.95 (1-892511-03-7) E J MacBride.

— The Mice. unabridged ed. (Earvin MacBride's Fun Fun Lovable Cartoons Ser.). (Illus.). 123p. (J). (gr. 7-12). 2000. pap. 3.95 (1-892511-04-5) E J MacBride.

— Neddy Buddy Basil. unabridged ed. (Illus.). 6p. (J). (gr. 7-12). 2000. pap. write for info. (1-892511-13-4) E J MacBride.

— Space-M. D. 3001. 2nd unabridged ed. (Earvin MacBride's Amazing Sci-Fi & Adventure Heroes Ser.). (Illus.). 329p. (J). (gr. 7-12). 2000. pap. 4.95 (1-892511-09-6) E J MacBride.

McBride, Elizabeth. Addresses by Worthy Matron & Worthy Patron. 44p. 1998. pap. 4.95 (0-88053-359-5, S 306) Macoy Pub.

McBride, Elizabeth, ed. Great Weekend Adventures: Favorite Getaways, Festivals & Events from the Editors of Wisconsin Trails. LC 96-60291. 184p. 1996. pap. 14.95 (0-915024-50-0) Trails Media.

McBride, Elizabeth, ed. see Apps, Jerry.

McBride, Elizabeth, ed. see Bell, Jeannette & Bell, Chet.

McBride, Elizabeth, ed. see Butler, Dori H.

McBride, Elizabeth, ed. see Getto, Dennis.

McBride, Elizabeth, ed. see McGrath, William C.

McBride, Elizabeth, ed. see Rath, Jay.

McBride, Elizabeth, ed. see Svob, Mike.

McBride, Ella A., ed. Roses from Heaven, 2 vols., Set. Incl. Vol. I. 1984. 25.00 (0-933731-00-0); Vol. II. 1992. pap., pap. 13.50 (0-933731-03-5); (Orig.). 1984. 33.00 (0-933731-02-7); Set pap. 27.00 (0-933731-05-1) Children of Mary.

McBride, Eve. Dandelions Help. 160p. pap. (0-9698752-5-8) Sh1oreline.

McBride, Francis R., compiled by. Iceland. 2nd rev. ed. LC 96-192755. (World Bibliographical Ser.: Vol. 37). 374p. 1996. lib. bdg. 99.00 (1-85109-237-4, DL331) ABC-CLIO.

McBride, Genevieve G. On Wisconsin Women: Working for Their Rights from Settlement to Suffrage. LC 93-846. (History of American Thought & Culture Ser.). (Illus.). 304p. (Orig.). (C). 1993. lib. bdg. 45.00 (0-299-14000-8) U of Wis Pr.

McBride, Gerald. A Collector's Guide to Cast Metal Bookends. LC 97-67660. (Illus.). 192p. 1997. pap. 34.95 (0-7643-0040-7) Schiffer.

McBride, Geraldine, ed. see Pirie, Inez.

McBride, Glenn & Westfall, Peggy. Shiftwork Safety & Performance: A Manual for Managers & Trainers. 270p. 1992. 99.50 (0-9638482-0-8) McBride Pubns.

McBride, Glenn N. Info-10 Series: 10 Minute Training Sessions for Shift Personnel, 3 vols. Incl. Info-10-1. (Illus.). 1996. ring bd. 65.00 (0-9638482-2-4); Info-10-2. (Illus.). 1996. ring bd. 65.00 (0-9638482-3-2); Info-10-3. (Illus.). 1996. ring bd. 65.00 (0-9638482-4-0); write for info. (0-9638482-5-9) McBride Pubns.

— Scheduling the 24-Hr. Operation: The Manual of Shift Scheduling - Planning, Implementation & Evaluation. (Illus.). 280p. 1996. ring bd. 99.50 (0-9638482-1-6) McBride Pubns.

— Supervising & the 12-Hour Schedule: A Manual for Shiftwork Supervisors. (Illus.). 120p. 1998. ring bd. 89.00 (0-9638482-7-5) McBride Pubns.

— The 12-Hour Schedule Lifestyle: The Guide for Shiftworkers & Their Families. (Illus.). 60p. 1998. 39.00 (0-9638482-8-3) McBride Pubns.

McBride, Glenn N. & Westfall, Peggy. The Book of Schedules: Schedule Templates & Analyses. 2nd rev. ed. 65p. 1995. ring bd. 45.00 (0-9638482-6-7) McBride Pubns.

McBride, Helen, et al. Kimono 1: Teacher's manual. 29.00 (0-8219-0874-X) EMC-Paradigm.

— Kimono 1: Textbook. 29.95 (0-8219-0872-3) EMC-Paradigm.

— Kimono 1: Workbook. 18.95 (0-8219-0873-1) EMC-Paradigm.

— Kimono 3: Teacher's manual. 39.00 (0-8219-1036-1) EMC-Paradigm.

— Kimono 3: Textbook. 34.95 (0-8219-1037-X) EMC-Paradigm.

— Kimono 3: Workbook. 20.95 (0-8219-1038-8) EMC-Paradigm.

— Kimono 2: Teacher's manual. 31.00 (0-8219-0710-7) EMC-Paradigm.

— Kimono 2: Textbook. 30.95 (0-8219-1039-6) EMC-Paradigm.

— Kimono 2: Workbook. 31.00 (0-8219-1040-X) EMC-Paradigm.

McBride, Henry. The Flow of Art: Essays & Criticisms. LC 97-60059. 1997. 35.00 (0-300-06996-0); pap. 16.00 (0-300-06997-9) Yale U Pr.

*__McBride, Henry, et al.__ An Eye on the Modern Century: The Selected Letters of Henry McBride. LC 00-28106. (Henry McBride Series in Modernism & Modernity). (Illus.). 368p. 2000. 35.00 (0-300-08326-2) Yale U Pr.

McBride, Henry, et al. Hadrian's Villa & Its Legacy. 462p. 1997. pap. 30.00 (0-300-06851-4) Yale U Pr.

— John Marin. LC 66-26650. (Museum of Modern Art Publications in Reprint). reprint ed. 17.95 (0-405-01520-8) Ayer.

McBride, Henry, jt. auth. see New York City Museum Of Modern Art Staff.

McBride, Herbert W. A Rifleman Went to War. 425p. 1987. reprint ed. 29.95 (0-935856-01-3) Lancer.

McBride, I. R. Scripture Politics: Ulster Presbyterians & Irish Radicalism in the Late Eighteenth Century. 286p. 1998. text 69.00 (0-19-820642-9) OUP.

McBride, Ian. The Siege of Derry in Ulster Protestant Mythology. 120p. 1997. boxed set 30.00 (1-85182-299-2, Pub. by Four Cts Pr) Intl Spec Bk.

McBride, Ian, jt. ed. see Claydon, Tony.

McBride, J. H. Firelands Pioneer: Third Series, Vol. VII. 1988. 22.00 (0-932535-06-2) Firelands Hist.

McBride, J. LeBron. Spiritual Crisis: Surviving Trauma to the Soul. LC 97-37273. (Illus.). 207p. 1998. 39.95 (0-7890-0135-7, Haworth Pastrl); pap. 19.95 (0-7890-0460-7, Haworth Pastrl) Haworth Pr.

McBride, J. R., jt. ed. see Miller, P.

McBride, Jack, ed. see United States Catholic Conference Staff.

McBride, James. Butler Co. Pioneer Biography: Sketches of the Lives of Some of the Early Settlers of Butler Co., 2 vols. in 1. (Illus.). 640p. 1997. reprint ed. lib. bdg. 65.00 (0-8328-6295-9) Higginson Bk Co.

McBride, James. Color of Water. pap. write for info. (1-57322-623-8, Riverhd Trade) Berkley Pub.

McBride, James. The Color of Water: A Black Man's Tribute to His White Mother. LC 95-37243. 228p. 1996. 23.95 (1-57322-022-1, Riverhead Books) Putnam Pub Group.

— The Color of Water: A Black Man's Tribute to His White Mother. LC 95-37243. 228p. (C). 1997. reprint ed. pap. 12.95 (1-57322-578-9) Berkley Pub.

— War, Battering, & Other Sports: The Gulf Between American Men & Women. LC 94-39404. (Religion/Society - Society/Religion Ser.). (Illus.). 240p. (C). 1995. pap. 49.95 (0-391-03882-6); text 17.50 (0-391-03881-8) Humanities.

McBride, James, jt. auth. see Jones, Quincy.

McBride, Jane N., jt. auth. see McBride, David N.

McBride, Jeffrey. Teach Yourself SQL Server: MCSE Exam Preparation Guide. 1997. pap. text 49.99 (0-672-31084-8) Sams.

McBride, Jere J. Quiet-Time Messages: Training for Believers. Rodriguez, Maria et al, trs. (ENG & SPA.). 375p. (Orig.). 1995. pap. 12.95 (0-9645310-0-3) LPC Pub.

McBride, Jim. The Clearing. 240p. (Orig.). 1996. pap. 10.95 (0-9650466-0-5) One Co Pubng.

— Horsethief Moon. (Illus.). 206p. (Orig.). 1997. pap. 10.95 (0-9650466-1-3) One Co Pubng.

McBride, Joseph. American Madness: The Life of Frank Capra. 1989. 29.95 (0-394-54417-X) Knopf.

— The Book of Movie Lists. LC 98-15254. 320p. 1999. pap. 11.95 (0-8092-2891-2, 289120, Contemporary Bks) NTC Contemp Pub Co.

— Frank Capra: The Catastrophe of Success. (Illus.). 768p. 1993. pap. 16.00 (0-671-79788-3, Touchstone) S&S Trade Pap.

An Asterisk (*) at the beginning of an entry indicates that the title is appearing for the first time.

***McBride, Joseph.** Frank Capra: The Catastrophe of Success. (Illus.). 784p. 2000. pap. 24.95 (0-312-26324-4) St Martin.

McBride, Joseph. Hawks on Hawks. LC 81-362. (Illus.). 172p. 1982. pap. 15.95 (0-520-04552-1, Pub. by U CA Pr) Cal Prin Full Svc.

— Orson Welles. 2nd expanded rev. ed. (Illus.). 320p. 1996. pap. 14.95 (0-306-80674-6) Da Capo.

— Steven Speilberg: A Biography. LC 99-10621. (Illus.). 544p. 1999. reprint ed. mass mkt. 16.95 (0-306-80900-1, Pub. by Da Capo) HarpC.

— Steven Spielberg: A Biography. LC 96-38053. 528p. 1997. 29.50 (0-684-81167-7) S&S Trade.

McBride, Joseph & Wilmington, Michael. John Ford. LC 75-19281. (Theatre, Film & the Performing Arts Ser.). (Illus.). 234p. 1975. pap. 11.95 (0-306-80016-0); lib. bdg. 29.50 (0-306-70750-0) Da Capo.

McBride, Jule. AKA Marriage: Big Apple Babies. large type ed. (American Romance Ser.: Vol. 733). 1998. per. 3.99 (0-373-16733-4, 1-16733-7) Harlequin Bks.

— The Baby & the Bodyguard. (American Romance Ser.). 1994. per. 3.50 (0-373-16562-5, 1-16562-0) Harlequin Bks.

— A Baby for the Boss. (Temptation Ser.: Bk. 761). 217p. 2000. per. 3.75 (0-373-25861-5, 1-25861-5) Harlequin Bks.

— The Baby Maker: More than Men. (Harlequin American Romance Ser.: No. 599). 1995. per. 3.50 (0-373-16599-4) Harlequin Bks.

— Baby Romeo: P. I. (American Romance Ser.). 1996. per. 3.75 (0-373-16636-2, 1-16636-2) Harlequin Bks.

— Baby Trap. (American Romance Ser.). 1994. per. 3.50 (0-373-16519-6, 1-16519-0) Harlequin Bks.

— Baby Trap. (Promo Ser.). 1999. per. 4.50 (0-373-21980-6, 1-21980-7) Harlequin Bks.

— La Belle Intrigante. (Horizon Ser.: Vol. 471). 1998. mass mkt. 3.50 (0-373-39471-3, 1-39471-7) Harlequin Bks.

— The Bounty Hunter's Baby. LC 96-3648. (American Romance Ser.). 248p. 1996. per. 3.75 (0-373-16617-6, 1-16617-2) Harlequin Bks.

— Bride of the Badlands. LC 95-6866. (American Romance Ser.). 249p. 1995. per. 3.50 (0-373-16577-3, 1-16577-8) Harlequin Bks.

— Cole in My Stocking. 1996. per. 3.75 (0-373-16658-3, 1-16658-6) Harlequin Bks.

— Diagnosis: Daddy. (American Romance Ser.). 246p. 1998. per. 3.99 (0-373-16725-3, 0-16725-4) Harlequin Bks.

***McBride, Jule.** Hitched by Christmas, No. 6. (Heart of the West Ser.). 1999. mass mkt. 4.50 (0-373-82590-0) Harlequin Bks.

McBride, Jule. How the West Was Wed. (Love & Laughter Ser.). 1998. per. 3.50 (0-373-44046-4, 1-44046-0) Harlequin Bks.

— Mission: Motherhood. 1997. per. 3.75 (0-373-16693-1, 1-16693-3) Harlequin Bks.

***McBride, Jule.** Prescription - Baby. (Maitland Maternity Ser.). 2000. mass mkt. 4.50 (0-373-65066-3, 1650662) Harlequin Bks.

McBride, Jule. Santa Slept Over: The/Little Matchmaker. 1998. per. 3.99 (0-373-16757-1, 1-16757-6, Mira Bks) Harlequin Bks.

— The Strong, Silent Type. (Intrigue Ser.: No. 519). 1999. per. 3.99 (0-373-22519-9, 1-22519-2, Harlequin) Harlequin Bks.

— Verdict: Parenthood. 1997. per. 3.75 (0-373-16699-0, 1-16699-0) Harlequin Bks.

— Wed to a Stranger? (Hidden Identity Ser.). 1997. per. 3.75 (0-373-22418-4, 1-22418-7) Harlequin Bks.

— Who's Been Sleeping in My Bed? (Love & Laughter Ser.: No. 23). 1997. per. 3.50 (0-373-44023-5, 1-44023-9) Harlequin Bks.

— Wild Card Wedding. (American Romance Ser.). 1993. per. 3.50 (0-373-16500-5, 1-16500-0) Harlequin Bks.

***McBride, Jule.** Wild Card Wedding. 2000. mass mkt. 4.50 (0-373-82246-4, 1-82246-9) Harlequin Bks.

McBride, Jule. The Wrong Wife? (American Romance Ser.). 1994. per. 3.50 (0-373-16546-3, 1-16546-3) Harlequin Bks.

— The Wrong Wife? (Promo Ser.). 1999. per. 4.50 (0-373-21963-6, 1-21963-3) Harlequin Bks.

McBride, Jule, et al. Bridal Showers: Jack & Jillian's Wedding; Raining Violets; She's the One!, 3 bks. in 1. (Promo Ser.). 1998. per. 5.99 (0-373-83350-4, 1-83350-8) Harlequin Bks.

McBride, Jule, jt. auth. see Jensen, Muriel.

McBride, Julie. Smoochin' Santa: Christmas Is for Kids - The Little Matchmaker. (American Romance Ser.: No. 753). 1998. per. 3.99 (0-373-16753-9, 1-16753-5) Harlequin Bks.

***McBride, June.** Catfish Jack LC 99-189735. 88 p. 1998. write for info. (1-55630-840-X) Brentwood Comm.

McBride, Karen H. & Luntz, Elizabeth D. Help! I Have HYPERSTUDIO. Now What Do I Do? A Multimedia Planning Resource for Teachers. 2nd rev. ed. (Illus.). 83p. 1995. spiral bd. 19.95 (0-9670850-0-4, 85004) McB Media.

McBride, Katharine, ed. see Cummings, E. E.

McBride, Kathleen. Tips for Working Parents: Creative Solutions to Everyday Problems. Burns, Deborah, ed. LC 88-62787. (Illus.). 144p. 1989. pap. 7.95 (0-88266-546-4, Storey Pub) Storey Bks.

McBride, Keith R. Organizing Corporations in California. 2nd ed. Briggs, Donald R., ed. LC 82-74145. 260p. 1996. ring bd. 76.00 (0-88124-989-0, BU-37761) Cont Ed Bar-CA.

McBride, Keith W. Organizing Corporations in California. 2nd ed. Briggs, Donald R., ed. LC 82-74145. 370p. 1997. ring bd. 65.00 (0-7626-0102-7, BU-37763) Cont Ed Bar-CA.

— Organizing Corporations in California - 5-99 Update. 2nd ed. Peyerwold, David, ed. LC 82-74145. 440p. 1999. ring bd. 77.00 (0-7626-0319-4, BU-37765) Cont Ed Bar-CA.

— Organizing Corporations in California - 5/98 Update. 2nd ed. Briggs, Donald R., ed. LC 82-74145. 290p. 1998. ring bd. 67.00 (0-7626-0229-5, BU-37764) Cont Ed Bar-CA.

McBride, Kirsten, ed. see Buterin, Leslie.

McBride, Kirsten, ed. see Dawes, Susan.

McBride, L. R. About Hawaii's Volcanoes. rev. ed. (Illus.). 48p. 1986. pap. 5.95 (0-912180-43-9) Petroglyph.

***McBride, L. R.** The Kahuna: Jersatile Mystics of Old Hawaii. 2nd rev. ed. 2000. pap. 9.95 (0-912180-51-X) Petroglyph.

McBride, L. R. Petroglyphs of Hawaii. rev. ed. 1996. pap. 7.95 (0-912180-49-8) Petroglyph.

— Practical Folk Medicine of Hawaii. (Illus.). 1975. pap. 8.95 (0-912180-27-7) Petroglyph.

McBride, Landy J. Textbook of Urinalysis & Body Fluids: A Clinical Approach. LC 97-38213. (Illus.). 352p. 1997. pap. text 37.00 (0-397-55231-9) Lppncott W & W.

***McBride, Laura Harrison.** Surviving Y2K & Beyond. (Unofficial Guides Ser.). 466p. 1999. pap. 15.95 (0-02-863678-3) Macmillan.

McBride, Lawrence W. The Greening of Dublin Castle: The Transformation of Bureaucratic & Judicial Personnel in Ireland, 1892-1922. LC 89-38830. (Illus.). 337p. 1991. text 44.95 (0-8132-0715-0) Cath U Pr.

***McBride, Lawrence W., ed.** Images, Icons, & the Irish Nationalist Imagination, 1870-1925. (Illus.). 202p. 1999. 55.00 (1-85182-493-6, Pub. by Four Cts Pr) Intl Spec Bk.

— The Reynolds Letters: An Irish Emigrant Family in Late Victorial Manchester. 96p. 1999. pap. 12.95 (1-85918-200-3, Pub. by Cork Univ) Intl Spec Bk.

McBride, Linda, jt. auth. see Bauer, Mark S.

McBride, M. Aloysius, ed. & compiled by see Cooke, Terence Cardinal.

McBride, M. M. Constance Bennett. 1976. lib. bdg. 59.95 (0-8490-1667-3) Gordon Pr.

— The Story of Dwight W. Morrow. 1972. 59.95 (0-8490-1131-0) Gordon Pr.

***McBride, Margaret.** Ulysses & the Metamorphosis of Stephen Dedalus. LC 00-35449. 2000. write for info. (0-8387-5446-5) Bucknell U Pr.

McBride, Mark. How to Marry a Beautiful Woman: Even if You're a Frog. (Illus.). 96p. 1996. pap. 8.95 (0-9652952-1-4) Doyle Studio.

— The Yonomicon: An Enlightened Tome of Yoyo Tricks. (Illus.). 144p. 1998. pap. 14.95 (0-941463-01-X) Magnolia FL.

***McBride, Mary.** Bandera's Bride. (Historical Ser.: Bk. 517). 2000. per. 4.99 (0-373-29117-5, 1-29117-8) Harlequin Bks.

— Bluer Than Velvet. (Intimate Moments Ser.: Vol. 1031). 2000. mass mkt. 4.50 (0-373-27101-8, 1-27101-4) Harlequin Bks.

McBride, Mary. Darling Jack. (Harlequin Historical Ser.: No. 323). 344p. 1996. per. 4.99 (0-373-28923-5, 1-28923-0) Harlequin Bks.

— Fly Away Home. (Historical Ser.). 1993. mass mkt. 3.99 (0-373-28789-5, 1-28789-5) Harlequin Bks.

— Forever & a Day. LC 95-21596. 296p. 1995. per. 4.50 (0-373-28894-8) Harlequin Bks.

— The Fourth of Forever. 1994. per. 3.99 (0-373-28821-2) Harlequin Bks.

— Grandma Knows Best, But No One Ever Listens! LC 87-1575. 132p. 1987. pap. 6.00 (0-88166-094-9) Meadowbrook.

— Grandma Knows Best, But No One Ever Listens! LC 87-1575. 110p. 1987. per. 7.00 (0-671-63622-7) S&S Trade.

— The Gunslinger. LC 95-7117. (Historical Ser.). 299p. 1995. per. 4.50 (0-373-28856-5, 1-28856-2) Harlequin Bks.

***McBride, Mary.** Just One Look. (Intimate Moments Ser.: No. 966). 1999. per. 4.25 (0-373-07966-4, 1-07966-4) Silhouette.

McBride, Mary. The Marriage Knot. (Historical Ser.: No. 465). 1999. per. 4.99 (0-373-29065-9, 1-29065-9, Harlequin) Harlequin Bks.

— Quicksilver's Catch. 1997. per. 4.99 (0-373-28975-8, 1-28975-0) Harlequin Bks.

— Storming Paradise: 10th Anniversary Promotion. anniversary ed. (Historical Ser.: Vol. 424). 1998. per. 4.99 (0-373-29024-1, 1-29024-6) Harlequin Bks.

— The Sugerman. (Historical Ser.). 1994. per. 3.99 (0-373-28837-9, 1-28837-2) Harlequin Bks.

McBride, Mary & McBride, Veronica. Don't Call Mommy at Work Today, Unless the Sitter Runs Away. Duffy, Helen, ed. (Illus.). 98p. 1991. reprint ed. pap. 5.95 (0-9627601-2-9) Bros Grinn.

— Empty Nest Symphony. (Illus.). 96p. 1991. reprint ed. pap. 5.95 (0-9627601-3-7) Bros Grinn.

— Grandma's Guide to a Happy Marriage. (Illus.). 84p. (Orig.). 1991. pap. 4.95 (0-9627601-1-0) Bros Grinn.

— Grandma's Guide to Child Care. Duffy, Helen, ed. (Illus.). 112p. (Orig.). 1990. pap. 4.95 (0 9627601 0 2) Bros Grinn.

— Grandpa Knows Best, but No One Ever Listens! Hilarious Helpful Hints for Grandpas. Duffy, Helen, ed. (Illus.). 75p. (Orig.). 1992. pap. 5.95 (0-9627601-4-5) Bros Grinn.

— Please Don't Call Me Collect on Mother's Day. Duffy, Helen, ed. (Illus.). 105p. (Orig.). 1995. pap. 5.95 (0-9627601-6-1) Bros Grinn.

— Take This Book & Call Me in the Morning! Duffy, Helen, ed. (Illus.). 104p. (Orig.). 1993. pap. 5.95 (0-9627601-5-3) Bros Grinn.

McBride, Mary M. & Whiteman, Paul. Jazz. LC 74-15753. (Popular Culture in America Ser.). (Illus.). 298p. 1978. reprint ed. 21.95 (0-405-06387-3) Ayer.

McBride, Mekeel. The Going under of the Evening Land. LC 82-71662. 1983. pap. 11.95 (0-915604-77-9) Carnegie-Mellon.

— Red Letter Days. LC 87-71457. (Poetry Ser.). 1988. pap. 11.95 (0-88748-065-9) Carnegie-Mellon.

— Red Letter Days. LC 87-71457. (Poetry Ser.). 1988. 20.95 (0-88748-064-0) Carnegie-Mellon.

— Wind of the White Dresses. LC 94-70465. (Poetry Ser.). 80p. 1995. 20.95 (0-88748-184-1); pap. 11.95 (0-88748-185-X) Carnegie-Mellon.

McBride-Mellinger, Maria. The Perfect Wedding. LC 96-19111. (Illus.). 336p. 1997. 40.00 (0-06-258663-7) Collins SF.

— The Wedding Dress. LC 93-17435. 1993. 40.00 (0-679-41884-9) Random.

McBride-Mellinger, Maria & Stites, William. Bridal Flowers: Arrangements for a Perfect Wedding. (Illus.). 96p. 1992. 25.95 (0-8212-1917-0, Pub. by Bulfinch Pr) Little.

***McBride, Michael B. & Baldwin, Marva.** Meeting National Standards with Handbells & Handchimes. (Illus.). 80p. 1999. pap. 24.95 (0-8108-3740-4) Scarecrow.

McBride, Murray B. Environmental Chemistry of Soils. (Illus.). 416p. (C). 1994. text 57.95 (0-19-507011-9) OUP.

McBride, Neal. Real Small Groups Don't Just Happen: Nurturing Relationships in Your Small Group. LC 98-16991. 1998. pap. write for info. (1-57683-103-5) NavPress.

McBride, Neal F. How to Build a Small-Groups Ministry. 200p. (Orig.). 1995. pap. 20.00 (0-89109-769-4) NavPress.

— How to Have Great Small Group Meetings: Dozens of Ideas You Can Use Right Now. LC 97-9828. 128p. (Orig.). 1997. pap. 7.00 (1-57683-021-7) NavPress.

— How to Lead Small Groups. LC 90-61778. 144p. 1990. pap. 7.00 (0-89109-303-6) NavPress.

McBride, P. K. Windows '98: Clear & Simple. LC 98-34955. 160p. 1998. pap. text 12.95 (0-7506-7114-9) Buttrwrth-Heinemann.

***McBride, P. K. & Grant, David.** Caterer & Hotelkeeper Guide to the Internet: Getting Your Business Online. 176p. 2000. pap. 28.95 (0-7506-4896-1) Buttrwrth-Heinemann.

McBride, Patricia. The Assertive Social Worker. LC 97-44525. 150p. 1998. pap. 29.95 (1-85742-421-2, Pub. by Arena) Ashgate Pub Co.

McBride, Peter. The Internet. (Clear & Simple Ser.). 160p. 1996. pap. text 10.95 (0-7506-9801-2, Digital DEC) Buttrwrth-Heinemann.

— Windows 95: Clear & Simple. (Clear & Simple Ser.). 150p. 1996. pap. text 10.95 (0-7506-9800-4, Digital DEC) Buttrwrth-Heinemann.

McBride, Philip J. Lectionary Index for the Catechism of the Catholic Church. 80p. (Orig.). 1994. pap. 15.00 (0-89390-325-6) Resource Pubns.

— The Word of the Lord, Year A: Reflections on the Sunday Readings. LC 95-60665. 160p. (Orig.). 1995. pap. 9.95 (0-89622-659-X) Twenty-Third.

McBride, R. Bruce, jt. auth. see Brearley, K.

McBride, R. Bruce, jt. auth. see Gordon, Gary R.

McBride, R. Bruce, jt. auth. see Thibault, Edward A.

***McBride, Regina.** The Selkie. 2000. write for info. (0-688-17092-7, Wm Morrow) Morrow Avon.

McBride, Regina. Yarrow Field. Iddings, Kathleen, ed. LC 90-60171. (American Bk.). 91p. (Orig.). 1990. per. 10.00 (0-931289-04-1) San Diego Poet Pr.

McBride, Rob, ed. Teacher Education Policy: Some Issues Arising from Research & Practice. 304p. 1996. 79.95 (0-7507-0487-X, Falmer Pr); pap. 34.95 (0-7507-0488-8, Falmer Pr) Taylor & Francis.

McBride, Robert. The Triumph of Ballet in Moliere's Theatre. LC 92-19477. 380p. 1992. text 99.95 (0-7734-9567-3) E Mellen.

McBride, Robert E., ed. Mexico & the United States. LC 81-5171. 312p. 1981. 11.95 (0-13-579565-6) Am Assembly.

McBride, Robert W. Cooking with Tofu: For Those Who Hate Tofu but Don't Know Any Better. LC 91-76659. 66p. 1991. pap. 7.95 (1-880197-01-4) Gylantic Pub.

McBride, Roger Lea. Little Town in the Ozarks. (Little House). (Illus.). (J). (gr. 3-6). 1996. 10.05 (0-606-09565-9, Pub. by Turtleback) Demco.

McBride, Roy, ed. My Heart Is a Glowing Sunset: My Voice Is a Warming Song. (Illus.). 177p. (Orig.). 1990. pap. 8.00 (0-927663-15-5) COMPAS.

***McBride, Sarah Davis & State Historical Society of Wisconsin Staff.** History Just Ahead: A Guide to Wisconsin's Historical Markers. LC 99-36990. 1999. 12.95 (0-87020-317-7, Pub. by State Hist Soc Wis) U of Wis Pr.

***McBride, Scott.** Landscaping with Wood: The Practical Guide to Building Outdoors. LC 98-44061. 1999. pap. text 19.95 (1-56158-194-1) Taunton.

— Young Butt Full. 160p. 2000. reprint ed. pap. 5.95 (1-930535-07-4) Star Dists.

McBride, Shannon. Writing Proposals for Contract Training. 67p. 39.95 (0-914951-76-9) LERN.

***McBride, Simon.** Private Ireland. (Illus.). 224p. 2000. text 35.00 (0-312-26111-X) St Martin.

McBride-Smith, Barbara. Greek Myths, Western Style. LC 98-27423. 1998. 14.95 (0-87483-524-0) August Hse.

McBride, Stephanie & Flynn, Roddy, eds. Here's Looking At You, Kid! Ireland Goes to The Pictures. LC 97-107515. 240p. 1997. pap. 15.95 (0-86327-556-7, Pub. by Wolfhound Press) Irish Amer Bk.

McBride, Stephanie G., jt. auth. see Bueford, Timothy W.

McBride, Stephen. Not Working: State, Unemployment, & Neo-Conservatism in Canada. (State & Economic Life Ser.: No. 16). 272p. (Orig.). 1992. text 50.00 (0-8020-5998-8); pap. text 19.95 (0-8020-6929-0) U of Toronto Pr.

***McBride, Susan.** And Then She Was Gone. LC 98-66690. 238p. 1999. pap. 14.95 (1-878044-61-3) Mayhaven Pub.

McBride, Tammy. The Mouldings Recipe Book: Recipes, Ideas, Instructions, Hints & Other Stuff. 20p. 1993. pap. write for info. (0-9639921-0-4) Mouldings.

— The Mouldings Recipe Book: Recipes, Ideas, Instructions, Hints & Other Stuff, Bk. 2. 2nd ed. (Illus.). 32p. pap. 1.50 (0-9639921-1-2) Mouldings.

McBride, Tracey. Frugal Luxuries: Simple Pleasures to Enhance Your Life & Comfort Your Soul. LC 96-40421. 288p. 1997. pap. 13.95 (0-553-37886-4) Bantam.

***McBride, Tracey.** Frugal Luxuries by the Seasons. 2000. pap. 14.95 (0-553-37995-X, Spectra) Bantam.

McBride, Travis & Sieber, Mary. Initiative & Referendum: Direct Democracy in the American States. (Illus.). 6p. 1980. pap. text 0.50 (0-915757-09-5) League Women Voters TX.

McBride, Vaughn. Echoes. 1988. 5.50 (0-87129-514-8, E25) Dramatic Pub.

— Pass My Imperfections Lightly By. 1991. 5.60 (0-87129-144-4, P69) Dramatic Pub.

McBride, Veronica, jt. auth. see McBride, Mary.

McBride, W. Blan, jt. auth. see Burton, James.

McBride, Walter J. Computer Troubleshooting & Maintenance. 306p. (C). 1988. pap. text 3.50 (0-15-512664-4) SCP.

McBride, Wesley D., jt. auth. see Jackson, Robert K.

McBride, William. Entertaining an Elephant: A Novel about Learning & Letting Go. 2nd ed. LC 96-90048. 116p. 1997. reprint ed. pap. 7.95 (0-9656254-0-0) Pearl St Pr.

— Gambling Times Guide to Greyhound Racing, 1990. (Illus.). (Orig.). 1984. pap. 9.95 (0-89746-007-3) Gambling Times.

McBride, William E. High Pressure Breathing Air Handbook. Lauer, Richard A. & Ballmann, Doug, eds. (Illus.). viii, 212p. 1996. 39.95 (0-9655986-0-8) Sub-Aquatics.

McBride, William L. Fundamental Change in Law & Society: Hart & Sartre on Revolution. LC 77-118280. (Studies in the Social Sciences: No. 6). (Orig.). 1971. pap. text 26.95 (3-10-800276-7) Mouton.

— Philosophical Reflections on the Changes in Eastern Europe. (Philosophy & the Global Context Ser.). 160p. 1998. 57.95 (0-8476-8797-X) Rowman.

— Sartre's Political Theory. LC 90-25291. (Studies in Continential Thought). 246p. Date not set. reprint ed. pap. 76.30 (0-608-20561-3, 205447500002) Bks Demand.

McBride, William L. Social & Political Philosophy. LC 92-44094. (Issues in Philosophy Ser.). 144p. (C). 1993. pap. text 16.95 (1-55778-220-2) Paragon Hse.

McBride, William L., ed. The Development & Meaning of Twentieth-Century Existentialism. LC 96-36702. (Sartre & Existentialism Ser.: Vol. 1). 400p. 1996. reprint ed. text 75.00 (0-8153-2491-X) Garland.

— Existentialist Background: Kierkegaard, Dostoevsky, Nietzsche, Jaspers, Heidegger. LC 96-36698. (Sartre & Existentialism Ser.: Vol. 2). 424p. 1996. reprint ed. text 80.00 (0-8153-2492-8) Garland.

— Existentialist Ethics: Issues in Existentialist Ethics. LC 96-46538. (Sartre & Existentialism Ser.: Vol. 5). 400p. 1996. reprint ed. text 77.00 (0-8153-2495-2) Garland.

— Existentialist Literature & Aesthetics. LC 96-48997. (Sartre & Existentialism Ser.: Vol. 7). 376p. 1996. reprint ed. text 75.00 (0-8153-2497-9) Garland.

— Existentialist Ontology & Human Consciousness. LC 96-44915. (Sartre & Existentialism Ser.: Vol. 4). 392p. 1996. reprint ed. text 73.00 (0 8153 2494 4) Garland.

— Existentialist Politics & Political Theory. LC 96-46537. (Sartre & Existentialism Ser.: Vol. 6). 376p. 1996. reprint ed. text 75.00 (0-8153-2496-0) Garland.

— Sartre's French Contemporaries & Enduring Influences: Camus, Merleau-Ponty, Debeauvoir & Enduring Influences. LC 96-48996. (Sartre & Existentialism Ser.: Vol. 8). 392p. 1996. reprint ed. text 73.00 (0-8153-2498-7) Garland.

— Sartre's Life, Times & Vision du Monde. LC 96-44914. (Sartre & Existentialism Ser.: Vol. 3). 392p. 1996. reprint ed. text 80.00 (0-8153-2493-6) Garland.

McBride, William L., ed. Sartre & Existentialism: Philosophy, Politics, Ethics, the Psyche, Literature & Aesthetics, 8 vols. 1996. 608.00 (0-8153-2440-5) Garland.

McBride, William L. & Raynova, Yvanka. Philosophical Reflections on the Changes in Eastern Europe. LC 98-35373. (Philosophy & the Global Context Ser.). 160p. 1998. pap. 16.95 (0-8476-8798-8) Rowman.

McBride, William L. & Schrag, Calvin O., eds. Phenomenology in a Pluralistic Context. LC 82-19609. (Selected Studies in Phenomenology & Existential Philosophy: No. 9). 317p. (C). 1984. text 74.50 (0-87395-730-X); pap. text 24.95 (0-87395-731-8) State U NY Pr.

McBride, William M. Mark Twain: A Bibliography of the Collections of the Mark Twain Memorial & the Stowe-Day Foundation. (Illus.). 512p. 1984. 60.00 (0-930313-00-3) McBride Pub.

***McBride, William M.** Technological Change & the United States Navy, 1865-1945. LC 00-9313. (Studies in the History of Technology). (Illus.). 344p. 2000. 42.50 (0-8018-6486-0) Johns Hopkins.

McBride, William M., ed. New Interpretations in Naval History: Selected Papers from the Thirteenth Naval History Symposium. LC 98-38020. 302p. 1998. 37.50 (1-55750-648-5) Naval Inst Pr.

M

— A Pocket Guide to the Identification of First Editions. 5th ed. 100p. 1995. pap. 9.95 (*0-930313-03-8*) McBride Pub.

McBride, William M. & Arledge, Amy A., eds. Points of Issue: A Compendium of Points of Issue of Books by 20th Century Authors. 3rd ed. 104p. 1996. pap. 12.95 (*0-930313-04-6*) McBride Pub.

McBrien, J. Lynn & Brandt, Ronald S. The Language of Learning: A Guide to Education Terms. LC 97-19649. viii, 115 p. (Orig.). 1997. pap. 13.95 (*0-87120-274-3*, 197155) ASCD.

McBrien, Judith P. City in a Garden: Parks & Plans. Kelly, Samantha L., ed. (Skyline: Pt. IV). (Illus.). 50p. 1996. 6.95 (*1-880005-06-9*) Perspectvs Intl.

McBrien, Judith P. Pocket Guide to Chicago Architecture. LC 96-38750. (Illus.). 120p. 1997. pap. 15.95 (*0-393-73013-1*) Norton.

McBrien, Marianne. The Emergency Department Technician. LC 94-71971. (Clinical Allied Healthcare Ser.). (Illus.). 540p. (C). 1995. spiral bd. 44.95 (*0-89262-432-9*) Career Pub.

— The Emergency Department Technician: Instructor's Guide. Cox, Kay, ed. (Clinical Allied Healthcare Ser.). (Illus.). 422p. (C). 1997. teacher ed., ring bd. 99.95 (*0-89262-440-X*) Career Pub.

McBrien, Philip J. Children's Catechumenate: A Catechist's Guide. LC 97-17869. (Celebrating the Sacraments Ser.). 104p. (Orig.). 1997. pap., teacher ed. 14.95 (*0-89390-413-9*) Resource Pubns.

— The Word of the Lord, Year B: Reflections to the Sunday Readings. LC 95-60665. 184p. (Orig.). 1996. pap. 9.95 (*0-89622-700-6*) Twenty-Third.

McBrien, Richard P. Catholicism: New Study Edition--Completely Revised & Updated. rev. ed. LC 93-21328. 1344p. 1994. pap., student ed. 38.00 (*0-06-065405-8*, Pub. by Harper SF) HarpC.

— Inside Catholicism: Rituals & Symbols Revealed. Roether, Barbara, ed. LC 95-16468. (Illus.). 112p. 1995. pap. 20.00 (*0-00-649052-2*, Pub. by Harper SF) HarpC.

— Lives of the Popes: The Pontiffs from St. Peter to John Paul II. LC 97-21897. 528p. 2000. pap. 18.00 (*0-06-065304-3*) HarpC.

— Lives of The Popes: The Pontiffs from St. Peter to John Paul II. LC 97-21897. (Illus.). 528p. 1997. 29.50 (*0-06-065303-5*) HarpC.

— Ministry: A Theological, Pastoral Handbook. LC 86-43011. 128p. 1988. pap. 12.00 (*0-06-065324-8*, Pub. by Harper SF) HarpC.

— Responses to 101 Questions on the Church. LC 95-26172. (Responses to 101 Questions Ser.). 176p. 1996. pap. 9.95 (*0-8091-3638-4*, 3638-4) Paulist Pr.

McBrien, Richard P., ed. The HarperCollins Encyclopedia of Catholicism. 1392p. 1995. 47.50 (*0-06-065338-8*, Pub. by Harper SF) HarpC.

McBrien, Vincent O. Introductory Analysis. LC 61-6044. (Century Mathematics Ser.). (Illus.). 1969. 42.00 (*0-89197-248-X*); pap. text 19.50 (*0-89197-804-6*) Irvington.

McBrien, William. Cole Porter: A Biography. LC 97-46116. (Illus.). 480p. 1998. 30.00 (*0-394-58235-7*) Knopf.

McBrien, William, jt. auth. see Barbera, Jack.

McBrier, E. M. Loucks: Genealogy of the Loucks Family, Beginning with Johann Dietrich Loucks & His Descendants in Direct Line to Joseph Louck, & All His Known & Traceable Descendants to Date. (Illus.). 317p. 1991. reprint ed. pap. 48.50 (*0-8328-1727-9*); reprint ed. lib. bdg. 58.50 (*0-8328-1726-0*) Higginson Bk Co.

McBrier, Page. Beatrice's Goat. LC 99-27018. (Illus.). (J). 1999. 17.00 (*0-689-82460-2*) S&S Childrens.

— The Best Things in Life Are Free, Right? (Party of Five Ser.: No. 4). 144p. (Orig.). (J). (gr. 3-7). 1984. pap. 1.95 (*0-671-00682-7*, Minstrel Bks) PB.

— Daphne Takes Charge. (Treehouse Times Ser.: No. 5). (J). 1990. pap. 2.95 (*0-380-75899-7*, Avon Bks) Morrow Avon.

— First Course: Trouble. (Treehouse Times Ser.: No. 4). 128p. (J). 1990. pap. 2.50 (*0-380-75783-4*, Avon Bks) Morrow Avon.

— The Great Rip-Off. (Treehouse Times Ser.: No. 8). 128p. (J). 1990. pap. 2.95 (*0-380-75902-0*, Avon Bks) Morrow Avon.

— The Kickball Crisis. (Treehouse Times Ser.: No. 2). 96p. (J). 1989. pap. 2.50 (*0-380-75781-8*, Avon Bks) Morrow Avon.

— The Press Mess. (Treehouse Times Ser.: No. 6). 128p. (Orig.). (J). (gr. 4-5). 1990. pap. 2.95 (*0-380-75900-4*, Avon Bks) Morrow Avon.

— Rats. (Treehouse Times Ser.: No. 7). 128p. (J). 1990. pap. 2.95 (*0-380-75901-2*, Avon Bks) Morrow Avon.

— Spaghetti Breath. (Treehouse Times Ser.: No. 3). 128p. (J). (gr. 4). 1989. pap. 2.50 (*0-380-75782-6*, Avon Bks) Morrow Avon.

— Stinky Business. (Treehouse Times Ser.: No. 9). 128p. (Orig.). (YA). 1991. pap. 2.95 (*0-380-76269-2*, Avon Bks) Morrow Avon.

— Under Twelve Not Allowed. (Treehouse Times Ser.: No. 1). 128p. (J). (gr. 4). 1989. pap. 2.50 (*0-380-75780-X*, Avon Bks) Morrow Avon.

McBrier, Vivian F. R. Nathaniel Dett: His Life & Works (1882-1943) (YA). 1990. 15.95 (*0-87498-092-5*) Assoc Pubs DC.

McBrierty, Vincent J. & Packer, Kenneth J. Nuclear Magnetic Resonance in Solid Polymers. LC 92-45158. (Solid State Science Ser.). (Illus.). 370p. (C). 1993. text 99.95 (*0-521-30140-8*) Cambridge U Pr.

McBrinn, Laurie, ed. see Gueson, Emerita T.

McBrinn, Laurie, ed. see Gueson, Emerita T. & Gerolamo, Frank A.

McBroom, Amanda. Amanda McBroom Songbook. Okun, Milton, ed. pap. 14.95 (*0-89524-583-3*) Cherry Lane.

McBroom, Bonell, Sr. Understanding the Book of Revelation. 128p. 1995. pap. text. write for info. (*0-9648274-0-9*) D E McBroom.

McBroom, Charlotte, ed. see McBroom, Gary.

*__McBroom, Gary.__ Pocket Guide to the Best of Los Angeles. deluxe ed. McBroom, Charlotte, ed. LC 99-66044. 224p. 2000. pap. 12.95 (*0-9674258-0-8*) GPS Advent.

McBroom, Michael. McBroom's Camera Bluebook: A Complete, Up-to-Date Price & Buyer's Guide for New & Used Cameras, Lenses & Accessories. 6th ed. (Illus.). 323p. 1999. pap. 29.95 (*1-58428-013-1*, Pub. by Amherst Media) IPG Chicago.

McBroom, Patricia A. The Third Sex: The New Professional Woman. rev. adapted ed. 288p. 1994. pap. 14.95 (*1-56924-908-3*) Marlowe & Co.

McBrown, Gertrude P. Picture Poetry Book. (Illus.). (J). 1990. 4.25 (*0-87498-007-0*) Assoc Pubs DC.

McBryde, Brenda. Hannah Robson. large type ed. 519p. write for info. (*0-7505-1088-9*, Pub. by Mgna Lrg Print) Ulverscroft.

McBryde, Jack. Half-Bred Thoroughbreds, 1919-1924. 60p. 1998. spiral bd. 34.95 (*1-893033-00-7*) Loshadt Publishing.

— The National Quarter Horses. LC 97-50619. Date not set. 99.95 (*1-879984-03-2*) Loshadt Publishing.

— The Postpublication National Quarter Horses. 274p. 1998. spiral bd. 99.95 (*1-893033-02-3*) Loshadt Publishing.

McBryde, Linda. The Mass Market Woman: Defining Yourself As a Person in a World That Defines You By. LC 98-96650. 224p. 1999. 19.95 (*1-893070-06-9*) Crowded Hour.

McBryde, Mary. The Irish Wolfhound Guide. LC 98-11599. 320p. 1998. 49.95 (*0-87605-169-7*) Howell Bks.

McBryde, W., intro. Erskine: An Institute of the Law of Scotland, 1871, 2 vols., Set. (Scottish Legal Classics Ser.). 1990. 220.00 (*0-406-17897-6*, MICHIE) LEXIS Pub.

McBurney. Research Methods. 5th ed. (Psychology Ser.). 2000. text 57.25 (*0-534-57762-8*) Wadsworth Pub.

— Research Methods with InfoTrac. 4th ed. (Psychology Ser.). 1998. 51.00 incl. cd-rom (*0-534-36352-0*) Brooks-Cole.

McBurney, C. B. Early Man in the Soviet Union, 1975. (Albert Reckitt Archaeological Lectures). 1976. 3.98 (*0-19-725731-3*) David Brown.

McBurney, Charles, ed. Reformed Presbyterian Ministers: 1950-1993. 225p. 1994. 25.00 (*1-884527-05-1*); pap. 15.00 (*1-884527-09-4*) Crown & Covenant.

McBurney, Charles B. The Haua Fteah (Cyrenaica) & the Stone Age of the South-East Mediterranean. LC 67-10257. 457p. reprint ed. pap. 130.30 (*0-608-12056-1*, 2024495) Bks Demand.

McBurney, Craig, jt. auth. see Baird, Bob.

McBurney, Donald H. Experimental Psychology. 289p. (C). 1983. mass mkt. 26.75 (*0-534-01319-8*) Brooks-Cole.

— Experimental Psychology. 2nd ed. 410p. (C). 1989. mass mkt. 53.50 (*0-534-12084-9*) Brooks-Cole.

— How to Think Like a Psychologist: Critical Thinking in Psychology. LC 95-25246. 111p. (C). 1995. pap. 14.40 (*0-02-378392-3*, Macmillan Coll) P-H.

— Research Methods. 3rd ed. LC 93-5651. 410p. 1993. mass mkt. 54.25 (*0-534-17646-1*) Brooks-Cole.

— Research Methods. 4th ed. LC 97-31135. (Psychology Ser.). (C). 1997. pap. 56.25 (*0-534-35510-2*) Brooks-Cole.

McBurney, Henrietta. Mark Catesby's Natural History of America: Watercolours from the Royal Library, Windsor Castle. LC 97-181018. 1997. 40.00 (*1-85894-039-7*, Pub. by Merrell Holberton) U of Wash Pr.

— Mark Catesby's Natural History of America: Watercolours from the Royal Library, Windsor Castle. (Illus.). 144p. 1997. 40.00 (*1-85894-038-9*, Pub. by Merrell Holberton) U of Wash Pr.

McBurney, Henrietta, et al. Mark Catesby's Natural History of America: Watercolours from the Royal Library, Windsor Castle. LC 97-3931. 1997. pap. write for info. (*0-89090-081-7*) Mus Fine TX.

McBurney, Jim. Technopoly. Kraven, Mae, ed. (Technology Education Ser.). (Illus.). 96p. (J). (gr. 4-5). 1991. text 19.95 (*0-9629471-0-5*) J McBurney.

McBurney, John T. Memoirs of John T. McBurney. (Wisdom of the Ages Ser.: Vol. 6). 50p. (Orig.). 1996. pap. 20.00 (*0-936390-12-3*) Dialog Pr.

McBurney, Louis. Counseling Christian Workers. (Resources for Christian Counseling Ser.). pap. 10.99 (*0-8499-3608-X*) Word Pub.

— Counseling Christian Workers. (Resources for Christian Counseling Ser.: Vol. 2). 291p. 18.99 (*0-8499-0586-9*) Word Pub.

McBurney, Margaret. True Newfoundlanders: Early Home & Families of Newfoundland & Labrador. LC 97-190989. (Illus.). 240p. 1997. 28.00 (*1-55046-199-0*, Pub. by Boston Mills) Genl Dist Srvs.

McBurney, Margaret & Byers, Mary. Tavern in the Town: Early Inns & Taverns of Ontario. (Illus.). 259p. 1987. 35.00 (*0-8020-5732-2*) U of Toronto Pr.

McBurney, Margaret, jt. auth. see Byers, Mary.

McBurney, Melissa & Ensor, Pat, eds. Key Guide to Electronic Resources: Engineering. LC 96-183178. (Key Guide Ser.). 196p. 1995. pap. 39.50 (*1-57387-008-0*) Info Today Inc.

McBurney, Meredith. Innovative Fundraising Ideas for Legal Services. LC 98-73168. 1998. write for info. (*1-57073-608-1*) Amer Bar Assn.

McBurney, Shirley. Memoirs of Shirley Mae Larsen. (Wisdom of the Ages Ser.: Vol. 5). 50p. (Orig.). 1996. pap. 20.00 (*0-936390-11-5*) Dialog Pr.

McBurney, Thelma Pierce. Thelma's Life of Poetry. 1998. pap. write for info. (*1-58235-081-7*) Watermrk Pr.

McBurney, Thomas R. Artistic Greatness: A Comparative Exploration of Michelangelo, Beethoven & Monet. LC 99-22009. (Illus.). 16p. 1999. 24.95 (*1-880090-78-3*) Galde Pr.

McBurney, Valerie, compiled by. Guide to Libraries in London. (Key Resources Ser.). (Illus.). 384p. 1995. pap. 75.00 (*0-7123-0821-0*, Pub. by SRIS) L Erlbaum Assocs.

McBurney, William H. A Check List of English Prose Fiction, 1700-1739. LC 60-13292. 164p. reprint ed. pap. 50.90 (*0-608-11263-1*, 200158500079) Bks Demand.

— Four Before Richardson: Selected English Novels, 1720-1727. LC 63-9095. (Illus.). 411p. reprint ed. pap. 127.50 (*0-608-16037-7*, 203313800084) Bks Demand.

McBurney, William H., ed. see Lillo, George.

McBurnie, Grant & Polack, Michael. Aunt Wilhelmina's Will. LC 93-6570. (Illus.). (J). 1994. write for info. (*0-383-03676-3*) SRA McGraw.

MCC Staff. Laser Compendium of Higher Education. 460p. 1997. pap. 39.95 (*0-7506-3678-5*) Buttrwrth-Heinemann.

Mccabe. Unit Operations of Chemical Engineering. 5th ed. 1993. 26.87 (*0-07-044845-0*) McGraw.

McCabe. Writing Effective Resumes: A Complete Guide. (CA - Career Development Ser.). 1992. mass mkt. 11.95 (*0-538-61750-0*) S-W Pub.

McCabe, jt. auth. see Moore.

McCabe, A. Language Games to Play with Your Child: Enhancing Communication fromn Infancy Through Late Childhood. (Illus.). 286p. (C). 1992. 24.95 (*0-306-44320-1*, Plen Insight) Perseus Pubng.

McCabe, A. & Peterson, C., eds. Developing Narrative Structure. 376p. (C). 1991. pap. 36.00 (*0-8058-0476-5*); text 75.00 (*0-8058-0475-7*) L Erlbaum Assocs.

McCabe, Alice S. Supplement to Gwinnett County, Georgia, Families, 1818-1968. 32p. (Orig.). 1988. pap. 5.00 (*0-914923-08-0*) Gwinnett Hist.

McCabe, Alice S., ed. Gwinnett County, Georgia, Families 1818-1968 with 1987 Supplement. 686p. 1988. reprint ed. 40.00 (*0-914923-02-1*) Gwinnett Hist.

— Gwinnett County, Georgia, Inferior Court Minutes for Ordinary Purposes, 1819-1861. 104p. 1987. pap. 10.00 (*0-914923-07-2*) Gwinnett Hist.

McCabe, Alice S. & Garrett, Franklin M. Gwinnett County, Georgia, Deaths 1818-1989. 810p. 1991. 60.00 (*0-914923-10-2*) Gwinnett Hist.

McCabe, Alice S., jt. auth. see Baughman, John W.

McCabe, Alice S., ed. see Cates, Donald W.

McCabe, Allyssa, et al. Chameleon Readers: Teaching Children to Appreciate all Kinds of Good Stories. LC 95-38739. 216p. (C). 1995. pap. 30.00 (*0-07-045016-1*) McGraw.

McCabe, Allyssa, jt. auth. see Mandell, Charlotte.

McCabe, Allyssa, jt. auth. see Peterson, Carole.

McCabe, Ann C. & Fairbanks, Eugene B. English Writing: Fifteen-Day Competency Review Text. Garnsey, Wayne H., ed. (Illus.). 160p. (Orig.). (YA). (gr. 7-12). 1992. pap. text 7.95 (*0-935487-56-5*) N & N Pub Co.

*__McCabe, Anne C.__ English Big 8 Review. Garnsey, Wayne & Stich, Paul, eds. 128p. 1999. pap. text 11.95 (*0-935487-67-0*) N & N Pub Co.

McCabe, Arva M. P. & Bush, Gregory. Miami: American Crossroad. 232p. (C). 1996. text 15.60 (*0-536-59693-X*) Pearson Custom.

McCabe, Bernard, ed. & intro. see Yeats, William Butler.

McCabe, Bob. Dark Knights & Holy Fools: The Art & Films of Terry Gilliam. (Illus.). 192p. 1999. 49.95 (*0-7893-0290-X*, Pub. by Universe); pap. 29.95 (*0-7893-0265-9*, Pub. by Universe) St Martin.

— Dark Secrets Within Child Protective Services. 216p. 1998. pap. 15.95 (*0-9665963-0-7*) Whispering Words.

— The Excorcist: Out of the Shadows. (Illus.). 190p. 1999. pap. text 19.95 (*0-7119-7509-4*, OP48103) Omnibus NY.

*__McCabe, Bob.__ Sean Connery: A Biography. (Illus.). 2000. 34.95 (*1-56025-290-1*, Thunders Mouth) Avalon NY.

McCabe, Brian F. One Atom to Another. LC 87-63148. 76p. (Orig.). 1988. pap. 10.95 (*0-948275-22-7*) Dufour.

McCabe, Brian F., et al, eds. Immunobiology in Otology, Rhinology & Laryngology. LC 92-10311. (Illus.). 407p. 1992. lib. bdg. 123.00 (*90-6299-083-5*, Pub. by Kugler) Kugler Pubns.

McCabe, Brian F., jt. ed. see Veldman, Jan E.

McCabe-Cardoza, Monica. A Woman's Guide to Martial Arts. 192p. 1998. pap. 13.95 (*0-87951-843-X*, Pub. by Overlook Pr) Penguin Putnam.

— A Woman's Guide to Martial Arts: How to Choose a Discipline & Get Started. 1996. 19.95 (*0-87951-670-4*, Pub. by Overlook Pr) Penguin Putnam.

McCabe, Charles R., ed. see Scripps, Edward W.

McCabe, Chuck. Uncle Rhythm's Cosmic Riff & Gig Guide: The First How-Not-to Book for a Career in Music. LC 93-60729. 164p. 1993. pap. 12.95 (*0-9636869-6-8*) Woodshed Prods.

McCabe, Colin, ed. TVEI: The Organisation of the Early Years. 68p. 1984. pap. 19.95 (*0-905028-62-7*, Pub. by Multilingual Matters) Taylor & Francis.

McCabe, Constance & McCabe, Neal. Baseball's Golden Age: The Photographs of Charles M. Conlon. (Illus.). 198p. 1997. reprint ed. pap. 19.98 (*0-8109-8177-7*, Pub. by Abrams) Time Warner.

McCabe, Constance, jt. auth. see McCabe, Neal.

McCabe, Cynthia J. Artistic Collaboration in the Twentieth Century. LC 84-3090. (Illus.). 224p. 1984. pap. 32.00 (*0-87474-687-6*, MCACP) Smithsonian.

McCabe, D. E. Ductile Fracture Toughness of Modified A 302 Grade B Plate Materials: Data Analysis. 90p. 1997. pap. 8.50 (*0-16-062806-7*) USGPO.

— Ductile Fracture Toughness of Modified A 302 Grade B Plate Materials: Data Records. 648p. 1997. per. 55.00 (*0-16-062818-0*) USGPO.

McCabe, David A. Standard Rate in American Trade Unions. LC 70-156435. (American Labor Ser., No. 2). 1971. reprint ed. 19.95 (*0-405-02932-2*) Ayer.

McCabe, David A., jt. auth. see Barnett, George E.

McCabe, David J., jt. auth. see Schmidt, Peter W.

McCabe, Deborah. Business Communication: Career Guide. 384p. (C). 1995. per. 46.95 (*0-7872-1625-9*, 41162501) Kendall-Hunt.

*__McCabe, Don.__ If It Is to Be, It Is up to Me: Helping Anyone (Children/Parents/Neighbors/Relatives/Friends) 1999. 19.95 (*1-56400-746-4*) AVKO Educ Res.

— If It Is to Be, It Is up to Us to Help: Helping Volunteers Become Reading/Spelling Tutors Not in One. 1998. pap. 12.95 (*1-56400-701-4*) AVKO Educ Res.

— Improving Reading/Spelling Skills Via Keyboarding: A Teacher's Manual to Accompany the Student Text: Individual. 24p. 1990. pap., teacher ed. 5.95 (*1-56400-404-X*) AVKO Educ Res.

— Individualized Keyboarding for Personal Typing & Computing. 90p. 1990. pap. 12.95 (*1-56400-401-5*) AVKO Educ Res.

— Let's Write Right: Manuscript & Cursive, Student Edition. 82p. 1995. pap., student ed. 12.95 (*1-56400-036-2*) AVKO Educ Res.

— Let's Write Right: Manuscript & Cursive Teacher Edition AVKO Sequential Handwriting. 164p. 1995. pap., teacher ed. 19.95 (*1-56400-030-3*) AVKO Educ Res.

McCabe, Don. The Patterns of English Spelling: The Teacher's Book of Word Lists Organized by Phonograms. 4th rev. unabridged ed. Orig. Title: The Basic Patterns of English Spelling. 894p. 1997. teacher ed., ring bd. 149.95 (*1-56400-201-2*, 200) AVKO Educ Res.

McCabe, Don. The Patterns of English Spelling Vol. 1: The Short Vowel - CVC Families. 86p. 1995. ring bd. 19.95 (*1-56400-221-7*) AVKO Educ Res.

— The Patterns of English Spelling Vol. 2: The Short Vowel - CVCC Families. 100p. 1995. ring bd. 19.95 (*1-56400-222-5*) AVKO Educ Res.

— The Patterns of English Spelling Vol. 3: The Long Vowels - CV, CVV, & CVCe. 1995. ring bd. 19.95 (*1-56400-223-3*) AVKO Educ Res.

— The Patterns of English Spelling Vol. 4: The Long Vowel - CVVC & Miscellaneous Relatives. 98p. 1995. ring bd. write for info. (*1-56400-224-1*) AVKO Educ Res.

— The Patterns of English Spelling Vol. 5: The -R & W-Controls & Miscellaneous Relatives. 106p. 1995. ring bd. 19.95 (*1-56400-225-X*) AVKO Educ Res.

— The Patterns of English Spelling Vol. 6: The Ending "UL" & "UR" Suffixes & Miscellaneous Relatives. 98p. 1995. ring bd. 19.95 (*1-56400-226-8*) AVKO Educ Res.

— The Patterns of English Spelling Vol. 8: The Advanced Suffixes. 102p. 1995. ring bd. 19.95 (*1-56400-228-4*) AVKO Educ Res.

— The Patterns of English Spelling Vol. 9: Advanced Phonic Patterns. 70p. 1995. ring bd. 19.95 (*1-56400-229-2*) AVKO Educ Res.

— The Patterns of English Spelling Vol. 10: Prefixes, Roots, Suffixes. 78p. 1995. ring bd. 19.95 (*1-56400-230-6*) AVKO Educ Res.

— The Patterns of English Spelling Vols. 1-5: The Teacher's Book of Basic Word Lists by Phonograms, 5 vols. 480p. 1995. ring bd. 79.95 (*1-56400-235-7*) AVKO Educ Res.

— Readings for Fluency: Practice Sentences to Help the Beginning Adult Reader. 72p. 1997. 12.95 (*1-56400-011-7*) AVKO Educ Res.

— Rimes & More Rhymes. 258p. 1994. pap. 29.95 (*1-56400-026-5*) AVKO Educ Res.

McCabe, Don. Sequential Spelling Examination Set. (Sequential Spelling Ser.: Vols. 1-7). 240p. 1995. ring bd. 79.95 (*1-56400-300-0*, 300) AVKO Educ Res.

— Sequential Spelling V. 36p. 1992. pap. text 12.95 (*1-56400-351-5*, 305) AVKO Educ Res.

— Sequential Spelling 5. 72p. 1995. pap. text 12.95 (*1-56400-350-7*) AVKO Educ Res.

— Sequential Spelling IV. 36p. 1992. pap. text 12.95 (*1-56400-341-8*, 304) AVKO Educ Res.

— Sequential Spelling 4. 72p. 1995. pap. text 12.95 (*1-56400-340-X*) AVKO Educ Res.

— Sequential Spelling I. 36p. 1992. pap. text 12.95 (*1-56400-311-6*, 301) AVKO Educ Res.

— Sequential Spelling 1. 72p. 1995. pap. text 12.95 (*1-56400-310-8*) AVKO Educ Res.

McCabe, Don. Sequential Spelling 1 for Adults Only. (Sequential Spelling for Adults Only Ser.). 28p. 1987. pap. 8.95 (*1-56400-393-0*) AVKO Educ Res.

McCabe, Don. Sequential Spelling 7. 72p. 1995. pap. text 12.95 (*1-56400-370-1*, 307) AVKO Educ Res.

— Sequential Spelling 6. 72p. 1995. pap. text 12.95 (*1-56400-362-0*, 306) AVKO Educ Res.

— Sequential Spelling III. 36p. 1992. pap. text 12.95 (*1-56400-331-0*, 303) AVKO Educ Res.

— Sequential Spelling 3. 72p. 1995. pap. text 12.95 (*1-56400-330-2*) AVKO Educ Res.

— Sequential Spelling II. 36p. 1992. pap. text 12.95 (*1-56400-321-3*, 302) AVKO Educ Res.

— Sequential Spelling 2. 72p. 1995. pap. text 12.95 (*1-56400-320-5*) AVKO Educ Res.

McCabe, Don. Sequential Spelling 2 for Adults Only. (Sequential Spelling for Adults Only Ser.). 48p. 1997. pap. write for info. (*1-56400-394-9*) AVKO Educ Res.

— Speech to Spelling: Spelling Dictation Sentences. 82p. 1997. ring bd. write for info. (*1-56400-060-5*) AVKO Educ Res.

McCabe, Don. Student Response Book for Sequential Spelling. (Sequential Spelling Ser.). 64p. 1993. pap., student ed. 12.95 (*1-56400-390-6*) AVKO Educ Res.

*__McCabe, Don.__ The Teaching of Reading: A Continuum from Kindergarten Through College: A Supplementary Textbook. 324p. 1999. text 39.95 (*1-56400-650-6*, 650, Pub. by AVKO Educ Res) Distributors.

An Asterisk (*) at the beginning of an entry indicates that the title is appearing for the first time.

McCabe, Don. To Teach a Dyslexic. unabridged ed. 288p. (Orig.). 1996. pap. 14.95 (1-56400-004-4, 663) AVKO Educ Res.

McCabe, Don. The Tricky Words: A Collection of Teacher-Directed Student Self-Corrected Exercise. 90p. 1997. 12.95 (1-56400-505-4) AVKO Educ Res.

— Word Families in Sentence Context: Completely Cross-Referenced to Volumes 1-5 of "The Patterns of English Spelling" 314p. 1996. ring bd. 39.95 (1-56400-424-4) AVKO Educ Res.

McCabe, Donald F. The Prose-Rhythm of Demosthenes. rev. ed. Connor, W. R., ed. LC 80-2658. (Monographs in Classical Studies). 203p. 1981. lib. bdg. 35.95 (0-405-14044-4) Ayer.

McCabe, Donald L. The Handbook of Basic Clinical Manipulation. LC 95-23661. (Clinical Handbook Ser.). (Illus.). 240p. 1996. 44.95 (1-85070-670-0) Prthnon Pub.

McCabe, Donna & Stroud, Mamie. Meet Me at the Loveless: A Southern Cafe's Cookbook. LC 98-43872. (Illus.). 208p. 1998. pap. 19.95 (1-888608-37-4) Cool Springs Pr.

McCabe, Douglas M. Corporate Nonunion Complaint Procedures & Systems: A Strategic Human Resources Management Analysis. LC 88-11758. 220p. 1988. 57.95 (0-275-93059-9, C3059, Praeger Pubs) Greenwood.

McCabe, Ed. Against Gravity. 1991. mass mkt. 15.95 (0-446-39239-1, Pub. by Warner Bks) Little.

McCabe, Ed. Oxygen Therapies. 142p. 12.00 incl. audio (1-879323-08-7) Sound Horizons AV.

McCabe, Ed. Oxygen Therapies: A New Way of Approaching Disease. (Energy Publications Alternatives). (Illus.). 224p. (Orig.). (C). 1988. pap. 12.00 (0-9620527-0-1) Energy Pubns.

McCabe, Edith, ed. see Ruchhoft, Robert H.

***McCabe, Edward R. & McCabe, Linda.** How to Succeed in Academics. 200p. 2000. 29.95 (0-12-481833-1) Morgan Kaufmann.

McCabe, Eugene. Cancer. (Adaptations Ser.). 1980. pap. 2.95 (0-912262-68-0) Proscenium.

— King of the Castle. LC 98-150810. 80p. 1997. pap. 14.95 (1-85235-192-6) Dufour.

— King of the Castle. 1978. pap. 2.95 (0-912262-50-8) Proscenium.

— King of the Castle. deluxe ed. 1978. 7.50 (0-912262-49-4) Proscenium.

— Pull Down a Horseman & Gale Day. 70p. 1979. pap. 12.95 (0-902996-96-7) Dufour.

***McCabe, Eugene.** Tales from the Poorhouse. LC 99-198448. 124p. 2000. 27.95 (1-85235-249-3, Pub. by Gallery Pr); pap. 18.95 (1-85235-248-5, Pub. by Gallery Pr) Dufour.

McCabe, George A. Catch the Vision on Prayer & Health. rev. ed. 250p. 1996. pap. 18.95 (0-929529-05-7) Vision Ministry Pr.

— Catch the Vision on Prayer in the Last Days. (Illus.). 152p. 1988. pap. 6.95 (0-929529-00-6) Vision Ministry Pr.

— Catch the Vision on Prayer in the Last Days: Advanced. 24p. 1988. pap. 4.00 (0-929529-03-0) Vision Ministry Pr.

— Catch the Vision on Prayer in the Last Days: Children's Prayer Book. 8p. (J). 1988. pap. 3.00 (0-929529-01-4) Vision Ministry Pr.

— Catch the Vision on Prayer in the Last Days: Double Eagle. 35p. 1988. pap. 5.00 (0-929529-04-9) Vision Ministry Pr.

— Catch the Vision on Prayer in the Last Days: Teen's Intercessory Prayer Book. 8p. (YA). 1988. pap. 3.00 (0-929529-02-2) Vision Ministry Pr.

— Fossilized in a Tangled Web of Worship. 100p. 1996. pap. 12.95 (0-929529-07-3) Vision Ministry Pr.

— Passover the Two Lambs. 136p. 1988. pap. 19.95 (0-929529-08-1) Vision Ministry Pr.

— The Two Sabbaths. 200p. 1996. pap. 12.95 (0-929529-06-5) Vision Ministry Pr.

McCabe, George P., jt. auth. see Moore, David S.

***McCabe, Gerard B.** Planning for A New Generation of Public Library Buildings. LC 99-32004. 184p. 2000. lib. bdg. 59.95 (0-313-30592-7) Greenwood.

McCabe, Gerard B., ed. Academic Libraries in Urban & Metropolitan Areas: A Management Handbook. LC 91-21182. (Library Management Collection). 288p. 1991. lib. bdg. 62.95 (0-313-27536-X, MLZ, Greenwood Pr) Greenwood.

— Operations Handbook for the Small Academic Library. LC 88-34811. (Library Management Collection). 360p. 1989. lib. bdg. 65.00 (0-313-26474-0, MOB/, Greenwood Pr) Greenwood.

— The Smaller Academic Library: A Management Handbook. LC 87-23655. (Library Management Collection). (Illus.). 391p. 1988. lib. bdg. 69.50 (0-313-25027-8, MMH/, Greenwood Pr) Greenwood.

McCabe, Gerard B. & Kreissman, Bernard, eds. Advances in Library Administration & Organization, Vol. 1. 148p. 1981. 78.50 (0-89232-213-6) Jai Pr.

— Advances in Library Administration & Organization, Vol. 2. 373p. 1983. 78.50 (0-89232-214-4) Jai Pr.

— Advances in Library Administration & Organization, Vol. 3. 320p. 1984. 78.50 (0-89232-386-8) Jai Pr.

— Advances in Library Administration & Organization, Vol. 4. 233p. 1985. 78.50 (0-89232-566-6) Jai Pr.

— Advances in Library Administration & Organization, Vol. 5. 307p. 1985. 78.50 (0-89232-674-3) Jai Pr.

— Advances in Library Administration & Organization, Vol. 6. 323p. 1987. 78.50 (0-89232-724-3) Jai Pr.

— Advances in Library Administration & Organization, Vol. 7. 287p. 1988. 78.50 (0-89232-817-7) Jai Pr.

— Advances in Library Administration & Organization, Vol. 9. 262p. 1991. 78.50 (1-55938-066-7) Jai Pr.

— Advances in Library Administration & Organization, Vol. 10. 298p. 1992. 78.50 (1-55938-460-3) Jai Pr.

— Advances in Library Administration & Organization, Vol. 11. 320p. 1993. 78.50 (1-55938-596-0) Jai Pr.

— Advances in Library Administration & Organization, Vol. 12. 282p. 1994. 78.50 (1-55938-846-3) Jai Pr.

— Advances in Library Administration & Organization: A Research Annual, Vol. 8. 302p. 1989. 78.50 (0-89232-967-X) Jai Pr.

McCabe, Gerard B. & Person, Ruth J., eds. Academic Libraries: Their Rationale & Role in American Higher Education, 84. LC 94-40319. (Contributions in Librarianship & Information Science Ser.: Vol. 84). 248p. 1995. 59.95 (0-313-28597-7, Greenwood Pr) Greenwood.

McCabe, Gerard B., jt. ed. see Head, John W.

McCabe, Gerard B., jt. ed. see Mech, Terrence F.

McCabe, Helen. Burning Heart. large type ed. (Linford Romance Library). 208p. 1997. pap. 16.99 (0-7089-5179-1) Ulverscroft.

— Dangerous Love. large type ed. (Linford Romance Library). 176p. 1998. pap. 17.99 (0-7089-5242-9) Ulverscroft.

— Dream of Love. large type ed. (Linford Romance Library). 208p. 1997. pap. 16.99 (0-7089-5018-3, Linford) Ulverscroft.

— Love's Treasure. large type ed. (Linford Romance Library). 192p. 1997. pap. 16.99 (0-7089-5084-1, Linford) Ulverscroft.

— Secret Summer. large type ed. (Linford Romance Library). 208p. 1997. pap. 16.99 (0-7089-5121-X, Linford) Ulverscroft.

— Tempestuous Sands. large type ed. (Linford Romance Library). 1995. pap. 16.99 (0-7089-7795-2, Linford) Ulverscroft.

— Tides of Love. large type ed. (Linford Romance library). 224p. 1996. pap. 16.99 (0-7089-7890-8, Linford) Ulverscroft.

— Wind of Change. large type ed. (Linford Romance Library). 192p. 1996. pap. 16.99 (0-7089-7927-0) Ulverscroft.

McCabe, Herbert. God Matters. 1990. pap. 17.95 (0-225-66491-7, 6346, Pub. by G Chapman) Morehouse Pub.

— God Matters. 250p. 1991. pap. 14.95 (0-87243-190-8) Templegate.

McCabe, Ian. A Diplomatic History of Ireland 1948-49: The Republic, the Commonwealth & NATO. 212p. 1991. 29.95 (0-7165-2461-9, Pub. by Irish Acad Pr) Intl Spec Bk.

— The Pillars of Eternity: Time & Providence in the Faerie Queene. 256p. 1989. 14.95 (0-7165-2428-7, Pub. by Irish Acad Pr) Intl Spec Bk.

McCabe, J. L. Algebra Word Prob. 1997. 4.95 (1-55708-486-6, MCR467) McDonald Pub Co.

— Basic Trigonometry. 1996. 4.95 (1-55708-489-0, MCR469) McDonald Pub Co.

— Everyday Algebra. rev. ed. (Illus.). 133p. 1987. reprint ed. pap. text 14.95 (0-942465-03-2, 2-038-778) Summertree Bks.

— Everyday Geometry. rev. ed. (Illus.). 140p. 1987. reprint ed. pap. text 14.95 (0-942465-02-4, 2-009-496) Summertree Bks.

— Everyday Mathematics, A Study Guide. (Illus.). 168p. (Orig.). (YA). 1988. pap. text 14.95 (0-942465-11-3, 2 323 279) Summertree Bks.

— Everyday Trigonometry. (Illus.). 60p. 1996. pap. text 9.95 (0-942465-19-9) Summertree Bks.

— Getting Started As a Contractor. Orig. Title: How to Get Started As a Contractor. (Illus.). 65p. 1986. reprint ed. pap. text 9.95 (0-942465-00-8, 1-929-072) Summertree Bks.

— Percents. 1993. 4.95 (1-55708-404-1, MCR458) McDonald Pub Co.

— Using Metric System. 1991. 4.95 (1-55708-354-1, R464) McDonald Pub Co.

— Word Problems - Addition, Subtraction, Multiplication, Division. 1989. 4.95 (1-55708-217-0, R461) McDonald Pub Co.

— Word Problems - Fractions-Decimals-Per-Con. 1989. 4.95 (1-55708-218-9, R462) McDonald Pub Co.

— Word Problems-Basic Oper. 1990. 4.95 (1-55708-243-X, R430) McDonald Pub Co.

— Word Problems Made Easy. Orig. Title: Word Problems Simplified. (Illus.). 127p. 1986. pap. text 14.95 (0-942465-01-6) Summertree Bks.

McCabe, J. L., ed. Basic Algebra. 1992. 4.95 (1-55708-338-X, MCR465) McDonald Pub Co.

— Basic Geometry. 1992. 4.95 (1-55708-339-8, MCR466) McDonald Pub Co.

McCabe, J. L. & Collins, Jim. The Survivors - A World War II Novel. 1997. pap. text. write for info. (0-942465-20-2) Summertree Bks.

McCabe, James. The Cloven Tongue, Kinsella & Tradition. 1995. pap. 13.95 (1-873790-82-1) Dufour.

— Language & Sentiment of Flowers. 1999. 14.95 (1-55709-384-9, Pub. by Applewood) Consort Bk Sales.

***McCabe, James.** The Neutral Heart. (Illus.). 192p. 2000. 54.50 (0-7165-2691-3, Pub. by Irish Acad Pr); pap. 24.50 (0-7165-2718-9, Pub. by Irish Acad Pr) Intl Spec Bk.

— The White Battlefield of Silence. LC 99-197289. 96p. 1999. 19.95 (1-901233-33-2, Pub. by Dedalus); pap. 12.95 (1-901233-32-4, Pub. by Dedalus) Dufour.

McCabe, James, jt. auth. see Murray, Stuart.

McCabe, James D., Jr. Behind the Scenes in Washington. LC 73-19158. (Politics & People Ser.). (Illus.). 548p. 1974. reprint ed. 41.95 (0-405-05880-2) Ayer.

— Great Fortunes & How They Were Made: Or, the Struggles & Triumphs of Our Selfmade Men. LC 70-37895. (Select Bibliographies Reprint Ser.). (Illus.). 1977. reprint ed. 44.95 (0-8369-6732-1) Ayer.

***McCabe, James D., Jr.** The Guerrillas. (Americana Series). 45p. 2000. reprint ed. pap. 4.95 (0-937657-56-5) Feedbk Theabks & Prospero.

McCabe, James D. History of the Grange Movement: Or the Farmer's War Against Monopolies. LC 68-18600. (Library of Early American Business & Industry: No. 37). 539p. 1969. reprint ed. 49.50 (0-678-00514-1) Kelley.

— Practical Network Analysis & Design. LC 97-34934. 450p. (C). 1997. text 54.95 (1-55860-498-7) Morgan Kaufmann.

McCabe, James D., jt. auth. see Authement, Eural.

McCabe, Janet, jt. auth. see Kochen, Cinda L.

***McCabe, Jay.** Of Bats & Rainbows, Vol. 1. 1999. pap. write for info. (1-58235-177-5) Watermrk Pr.

McCabe, John. Alan Rawsthorne: Portrait of a Composer. LC 98-24508. (Illus.). 340p. 1999. text 70.00 (0-19-816693-1) OUP.

— Babe: The Life & Times of Oliver Hardy. 1990. 16.95 (0-8065-1187-5, Citadel Pr) Carol Pub Group.

— Cagney. (Illus.). 464p. 1999. pap. 14.95 (0-7867-0580-9) Carroll & Graf.

— Cagney. LC 97-5067. (Illus.). 416p. 1997. 29.95 (0-679-44607-9) Knopf.

— The Comedy World of Stan Laurel: Centennial Edition. rev. ed. (Vintage Comedy Ser.). 288p. 1990. reprint ed. 29.95 (0-940410-23-0, Moonstone Pr); reprint ed. pap. 19.95 (0-940410-22-2, Moonstone Pr) Past Times.

— Plastic Surgery Hopscotch: A Resource Guide for Those Considering Cosmetic Surgery. Ingersoll, Miriam, ed. LC 93-74927. 384p. 1995. pap. 19.95 (1-884702-32-5) Carmania Bks.

— Surgery Electives: What to Know Before the Doctor Operates, 2nd Edition, with Internet Addresses. 2nd ed. Ingersoll, Miriam, ed. LC 95-71658. 400p. 1996. pap. 19.95 (1-884702-22-8) Carmania Bks.

— Vegetarian Reasoning. 300p. (Orig.). 1999. pap. 14.95 (1-884702-34-1) Carmania Bks.

McCabe, John L. Applying Algebra. (Applied Math Ser.). 90p. (YA). (gr. 8 up). 1994. pap., teacher ed., wbk. ed. 7.95 (0-931993-63-6, GP-063) Garlic Pr OR.

— The Budget Book. 2nd ed. 45p. (Orig.). 1987. pap. 3.95 (0-945326-06-8) Intrawest Pub.

— Metrics at Work. (Applied Math Ser.). 89p. (YA). (gr. 8-12). 1995. pap. 7.95 (0-931993-70-9, GP-070) Garlic Pr OR.

McCabe, Joseph. Biographical Dictionary of Modern Rationalists. 1977. lib. bdg. 75.95 (0-8490-1506-5) Gordon Pr.

— A Candid History of the Jesuits. 1977. lib. bdg. 59.95 (0-8490-1567-7) Gordon Pr.

— Crises in the History of the Papacy. 1977. lib. bdg. 59.95 (0-8490-1684-3) Gordon Pr.

— The Forgery of the Old Testament & Other Essays. LC 93-27365. (Freethought Library). 150p. 1993. pap. 14.95 (0-87975-850-3) Prometheus Bks.

— George Bernard Shaw. LC 74-30406. (George Bernard Shaw Ser.: No. 92). 1974. lib. bdg. 75.00 (0-8383-1749-9) M S G Haskell Hse.

— The Lies & Fallacies of the Encyclopedia Britannica: How Powerful & Shameless Clerical Forces Castrated a Famous Work of Reference. 46p. 1996. reprint ed. spiral bd. 7.00 (1-885395-64-7) Book Tree.

— The Myth of the Resurrection & Other Essays. LC 92-46038. (Freethought Library). 168p. (Orig.). (C). 1993. pap. 14.95 (0-87975-833-3) Prometheus Bks.

— Peter Abelard. LC 74-148889. (Select Bibliographies Reprint Ser.). 1977. reprint ed. 24.95 (0-8369-5655-9) Ayer.

— Spain in Revolt, 1814-1931. 1976. lib. bdg. 59.95 (0-8490-2642-3) Gordon Pr.

McCabe, Joseph, compiled by. A Biographical Dictionary of Modern Rationalists: 1920 Edition. 500p. 1998. 120.00 (1-85506-597-5) Thoemmes Pr.

McCabe, Joseph, tr. see Carrere, Jean.

McCabe, Joseph, tr. see Denis, Pierre.

McCabe, Joseph, tr. see Drews, Arthur.

McCabe, Joseph, tr. see Ferrer Y Guardia, Francisco.

McCabe, Joseph, tr. see Haeckel, Ernst.

McCabe, Joseph, tr. see Iorga, Nicolae.

McCabe, Joseph, tr. see Voltaire.

McCabe, Kendall K. The Path of the Phoenix. Sherer, Michael L., ed. (Orig.). 1986. pap. 7.75 (0-89536-818-8, 6827) CSS OH.

McCabe, Kevin & Heilbron, Alexandra, eds. The Lucy Maud Montgomery Album. (Illus.). 544p. 1999. text 40.00 (1-55041-386-4) Fitzhenry & W Ltd.

***McCabe, Larry.** Blues Band Rhythm Guitar. 168p. 1998. spiral bd. 22.95 incl. audio compact disk (0-7866-3465-0) Mel Bay.

McCabe, Larry. Blues, Boogie & Rock Guitar. 112p. 1997. spiral bd. 19.95 incl. audio compact disk (0-7866-2769-7, 93996BCD) Mel Bay.

***McCabe, Larry.** Country Lead Guitar. 96p. 1998. pap. 19.95 (0-7866-3449-9, 94079BCD) Mel Bay.

— Famous Blues Bass Lines. (Quick Guide Ser.). 32p. 2000. pap. 5.95 (0-7866-4832-5, 98429BCD) Mel Bay.

— Famous Blues Guitar Lines. (Quick Guide Ser.). 32p. 2000. pap. 5.95 (0-7866-4831-7, 98428BCD) Mel Bay.

— Famous Country Guitar Lines. (Quick Guide Ser.). 32p. 2000. pap. 5.95 (0-7866-4892-9, 98427BCD) Mel Bay.

— Famous Rock Guitar Lines. (Quick Guide Ser.). 32p. 2000. pap. 5.95 (0-7866-4833-3, 98430BCD) Mel Bay.

— 101 Amazing Jazz Bass Patterns. 48p. 2000. pap. 17.95 incl. audio compact disk (0-7866-3631-9, 97336BCD) Mel Bay.

— 101 Bad to the Bone Blues Guitar Rhythm Patterns. 48p. 1999. pap. 17.95 incl. audio compact disk (0-7866-4044-8, 97760BCD) Mel Bay.

— 101 Blues Guitar Turnaround Licks. 48p. 1997. pap. 17.95 incl. audio compact disk (0-7866-2778-6, 95860BCD) Mel Bay.

— 101 Blues Patterns for Bass Guitar. 40p. 1996. pap. 17.95 incl. cd-rom (0-7866-2559-7, 95330BCD) Mel Bay.

— 101 Dynamite Blues Guitar Fill-In Licks. 56p. 1998. pap. 17.95 incl. audio compact disk (0-7866-0855-2, 97014BCD) Mel Bay.

— 101 Dynamite Latin Bass Patterns. (SPA & ENG., Illus.). 32p. 1997. pap. 17.95 incl. audio compact disk (0-7866-2387-X, 9622813CD) Mel Bay.

— 101 Dynamite Rock Bass Patterns. (SPA & ENG.). 48p. 1997. pap. 17.95 incl. audio compact disk (0-7866-2388-8, 9622913CD) Mel Bay.

— 101 Dynamite Rock Guitar Rhythm Patterns. 40p. 1997. pap. 17.95 incl. audio compact disk (0-7866-2732-8, 96591BCD) Mel Bay.

— 101 Dynamite Rock Guitar Riffs. 56p. 1998. pap. 17.95 incl. audio compact disk (0-7866-3268-2, 97049BCD) Mel Bay.

— 101 Dynamite Slide Guitar Licks in Open E Tuning. 56p. 1999. 17.95 (0-7866-3502-9, 97223BCD) Mel Bay.

— 101 Fingerstyle Guitar Accompaniment Patterns. (SPA & ENG.). 56p. 1998. 17.95 (0-7866-2383-7, 96224BCD) Mel Bay.

— 101 Mississippi Delta Blues Fingerpicking Licks. 48p. 1997. pap. 17.95 incl. audio compact disk (0-7866-2400-0, 96241BCD) Mel Bay.

— 101 Nashville-Style Guitar Licks Book. 48p. 1996. pap. 15.95 incl. audio compact disk (0-7866-0408-5, 95447BCD) Mel Bay.

— 101 Red-Hot Swing Guitar Licks. 48p. 1999. pap. 17.95 incl. audio compact disk (0-7866-3630-0) Mel Bay.

— You Can Teach Yourself Song Writing. (You Can Teach Yourself Ser.). 120p. 1994. pap. 9.95 (1-56222-568-5, MB94823) Mel Bay.

***McCabe, Larry.** You Can Teach Yourself Song Writing. 120p. 1999. pap. 17.95 incl. audio compact disk (0-7866-5012-5, 94823BCD) Mel Bay.

***McCabe, Lianne.** Construct-O-Rama. (Three-D Diorama Ser.). (Illus.). 8p. (J). (ps-3). 1999. 9.98 (0-7651-0960-3) Smithmark.

— Dance-O-Rama. (Three-D Diorama Ser.). (Illus.). 8p. (J). (ps-3). 1999. 9.98 (0-7651-0959-X) Smithmark.

***McCabe, Lianne & Brook, Jasmine.** The Dreamcatcher: Keeping Hold of Your Dreams. LC 98-61389. (Illus.). 32p. (J). (gr. 4-7). 1999. 7.98 (0-7651-0949-2) Smithmark.

McCabe, Linda, jt. auth. see McCabe, Edward R.

McCabe, Margaret E. & Rhoades, Jacqueline. Cooperative Meeting Management. 40p. (Orig.). (YA). (gr. 8 up). 1986. pap. 3.95 (0-933935-03-X) ITA Pubns.

— How to Say What You Mean. 31p. (Orig.). 1986. pap. 3.95 (0-933935-05-6) ITA Pubns.

— The Nurturing Classroom: Developing Thinking Skills, Self-Esteem, Responsibility through Simple Cooperation. LC 85-80102. (Illus.). 363p. (Orig.). (ps up). 1989. pap. 26.00 (0-933935-09-9) ITA Pubns.

McCabe, Margaret E., jt. auth. see Rhoades, Jacqueline.

McCabe, Margot, jt. auth. see McCabe, Patrick.

McCabe, Marsha. Spinner: People & Culture in Southeastern Massachusetts, Vol. V. Thomas, Joseph D., ed. (Illus.). 192p. (Orig.). 1996. 39.95 (0-932027-31-8); pap. 19.95 (0-932027-30-X) Spinner Pubns.

McCabe, Marsha & Thomas, Joseph D. Not Just Anywhere: The Story of W. H. A. L. E. & New Bedford's Waterfront Historic District. Bennett, Arthur & Stites, Clara, eds. (Illus.). 128p. 1995. 37.95 (0-932027-29-6); pap. 16.95 (0-932027-28-8) Spinner Pubns.

McCabe, Marsha & Thomas, Joseph D., eds. Portuguese Spinner: An American Story. LC 97-62313. (Illus.). 287 p. (Orig.). 1998. pap. 29.95 (0-932027-39-3) Spinner Pubns.

— The Portuguese Spinner: An American Story. LC 97-62313. (Illus.). 250p. 1988. 45.00 (0-932027-38-5) Spinner Pubns.

McCabe, Marsha, ed. see Romaniello, Kerry D.

McCabe, Mary. Everwinding Times. 416p. (C). 1994. pap. write for info. (1-874640-55-6, Pub. by Argyll Pubng) St Mut.

McCabe, Mary C. Allen. Some Early Settlers, Being a History of Allen, Littler, Metcalfe, Shouse (And Other) Families. 68p. 1997. reprint ed. pap. 13.50 (0-8328-7237-7); reprint ed. lib. bdg. 23.50 (0-8328-7236-9) Higginson Bk Co.

McCabe, Mary M. Plato's Individuals. LC 93-42370. 360p. 1994. text 47.50 (0-691-07351-1, Pub. by Princeton U Pr) Cal Prin Full Svc.

McCabe, Mary M., jt. ed. see Gill, Christopher.

***McCabe, Mary Margaret.** Plato & His Predecessors: The Dramatisation of Reason. 296p. 2000. write for info. (0-521-65306-1) Cambridge U Pr.

— Plato's Individuals. 360p. (C). 1999. pap. text 18.95 (0-691-02939-3, Pub. by Princeton U Pr) Cal Prin Full Svc.

McCabe, Mary Margaret, jt. ed. see Gill, Christopher.

McCabe, Michael. Arizona: Studies. (Illus.). 48p. (J). (gr. 4-6). 2000. pap., student ed. 6.45 (0-911981-59-4) Cloud Pub.

— Arizona: Studies: Blackline Masters. (Illus.). 43p. 2000. teacher ed. 29.95 (0-911981-64-0) Cloud Pub.

— Arizona: Su Origen. (SPA., Illus.). 64p. (J). (gr. 4-6). 1994. pap. 17.50 (0-911981-54-3) Cloud Pub.

— Colorado: Grassroots. (Illus.). 48p. (J). (gr. 4-6). 2000. pap. text, student ed. 5.95 (0-911981-13-6) Cloud Pub.

— Colorado: Grassroots Blackline Masters. (Illus.). 33p. 2000. teacher ed. 39.95 (0-911981-18-7) Cloud Pub.

— Colorado: Su Origen. (SPA., Illus.). 64p. (J). (gr. 4-6). 2000. pap. text 15.95 (0-911981-72-1) Cloud Pub.

M

— New York City Tattoo: The Oral History of an Urban Art. (Illus.). 1997. pap. 25.00 (*0-614-28151-2*) Dist Art Pubs.

— New York City Tattoo: The Oral History of an Urban Art. 1997. pap. text 25.00 (*0-945367-20-1*) Hardy Marks Pubns.

McCabe, Michael & Brew, Virginia. Colorado: Grassroots. 20p. (J). (gr. 4-6). 2000. teacher ed. 9.95 (*0-911981-14-4*) Cloud Pub.

McCabe, Michael, jt. auth. see Brew, Virginia.

McCabe, Michael, jt. auth. see Stacy, Darryl.

McCabe, Neal & McCabe, Constance. Baseball's Golden Age: The Photographs of Charles M. Conlon. LC 93-187. (Illus.). 198p. 1993. 35.00 (*0-8109-3130-3*) Abrams.

McCabe, Neal, jt. auth. see McCabe, Constance.

McCabe, Neil & Burnett, Catherine. State Constitutional Criminal Procedure. LC 94-78748. 630p. 1994. pap. 60.00 (*0-916081-34-6*) J Marshall Pub Co.

McCabe, Patrick. Breakfast on Pluto. LC 99-161426. 224p. 1998. 22.00 (*0-06-019340-9*) HarpC.

— Breakfast On Pluto: A Novel. 224p. 1999. pap. 13.00 (*0-06-093158-2*) HarpC.

— The Butcher Boy. 240p. 1994. pap. 11.95 (*0-385-31237-7*) Doubleday.

— The Butcher Boy. LC 93-2831. 224p. 1993. 19.95 (*0-88064-147-9*) Fromm Intl Pub.

— Carn. LC 98-137474. 256p. 1997. pap. 11.95 (*0-385-31585-6*, Delta Trade) Dell.

— The Dead School. 304p. 1996. pap. 11.95 (*0-385-31423-X*, Delta Trade) Dell.

McCabe, Patrick. Mondo Desperado: A Serial Novel. LC 99-89331. 256p. 2000. 24.00 (*0-06-019461-8*) HarpC.

***McCabe, Patrick.** Mondo Desperado: A Serial Novel. LC 99-89331. 2000. pap. write for info. (*0-06-093258-9*) HarpC.

McCabe, Patrick & McCabe, Margot. The Adventures of Shay Mouse: The Mouse from Longford. LC 94-241439. 64p. (J). 1994. pap. 8.95 (*1-874597-13-8*) Dufour.

McCabe, Peter. Wasteland: A Novel. LC 93-2238. 258p. 1994. 20.00 (*0-684-19681-6*) S&S Trade.

McCabe, Peter J. & Parrish, J. Totman, eds. Controls on the Distribution & Quality of Cretaceous Coals. (Special Papers: No. 267). (Illus.). 1992. pap. 40.00 (*0-8137-2267-5*) Geol Soc.

McCabe, Peter J., et al. The Future of Energy Gases. (Illus.). 58p. (C). 1995. pap. text 30.00 (*0-7881-1651-7*) DIANE Pub.

McCabe, Peter J., jt. ed. see Shanley, Keith W.

McCabe, Philip M., et al, eds. Stress, Coping & Cardiovascular Disease. LC 99-23561. 250p. 1999. write for info. (*0-8058-3419-2*) L Erlbaum Assocs.

McCabe, R. K. The Accountant's Guide to Peer & Quality Review. LC 92-34946. 248p. 1993. 65.00 (*0-89930-685-3*, MGQ, Quorum Bks) Greenwood.

McCabe, Richard A. Joseph Hall: A Study in Satire & Meditation. (Illus.). 1982. 89.00 (*0-19-812807-X*) OUP.

McCabe, Richard A., jt. ed. see Erskine-Hill, Howard.

McCabe, Richard E. The Unique Wood Duck: Tableau of a Field Trip with Frank Bellrose & Scott Nielsen. LC 92-46903. (Illus.). 136p. 1993. pap. 24.95 (*0-8117-3099-9*) Stackpole.

McCabe, Rick. The Tao of Beach Glass. LC 99-174636. (Illus.). 52p. 1997. pap. 9.95 (*0-9657553-1-2*) Med Bear.

McCabe, Robert, et al. Metering Pump Handbook. 280p. 1984. 29.95 (*0-8311-1157-7*) Indus Pr.

McCabe, Robert K. International Herald Tribune Guide to Business Travel in Asia. (Illus.). 208p. 1993. pap. 14.95 (*0-8442-9625-2*, Natl Textbk Co) NTC Contemp Pub Co.

McCabe, Robert W., jt. auth. see Hegedus, L. Louis.

McCabe, S. L., jt. ed. see Schultz, A. E.

McCabe, Sandra. Monstergrams: Twelve Spooky Pop-Up Greeting Cards to Make Yourself. (Illus.). 24p. (J). (gr. k-5). 1999. pap. 5.95 (*0-8037-1647-8*, Dial Yng Read) Peng Put Young Read.

McCabe, Sara, ed. see Tuttle, Merlin D.

McCabe, Sarah, et al, eds. The Police, Public Order & Civil Liberties: Legacies of Miners' Strike. 256p. (C). 1988. lib. bdg. 45.00 (*0-415-00724-0*) Routledge.

McCabe, Sarah, et al. The Police, Public Order & Civil Liberties: Legacies of the Miners' Strike. LC 88-190050. 221p. reprint ed. pap. 68.60 (*0-608-20398-X*, 207165100002) Bks Demand.

McCabe, Scott, jt. auth. see Schuytema, Paul.

McCabe, Steven. Quality Improvement Techniques in Construction. (C). 1998. pap. text 54.95 (*0-582-30776-7*) Addison-Wesley.

McCabe, Steven J. Hand, Arm & Wrist. LC 99-49140. (Illus.). 288p. 2000. pap. 16.95 (*0-7373-0248-8*, 02488W) NTC Contemp Pub Co.

McCabe, Susan. Elizabeth Bishop: Her Poetics of Loss. LC 93-30390. 1994. 50.00 (*0-271-01047-9*); pap. 18.95 (*0-271-01048-7*) Pa St U Pr.

McCabe, Thomas R. Supervictim Syndrome: How to Break the Cycle. 64p. 1992. pap. 7.00 (*1-56246-008-0*, 3264, HazeldenJohnson Inst) Hazelden.

McCabe, Timothy L. Atlas of Adirondack Caterpillars. (Bulletin Ser.: Bulletin No. 470). (Illus.). 114p. (Orig.). (C). 1991. pap. text 19.95 (*1-55557-185-9*) NYS Museum.

McCabe, Vickie & Balzano, Gerald J., eds. Event Cognition: An Ecological Perspective. (Ecological Psychology Ser.). 304p. (C). 1986. text 59.95 (*0-89859-811-7*) L Erlbaum Assocs.

McCabe, Vinton. Homeopathy Healing, & You. LC 98-53852. 1999. pap. 14.95 (*0-312-19909-0*) St Martin.

— Practical Homeopathy: A Beginner's Guide. LC 99-26936. 594p. 2000. pap. 18.95 (*0-312-20669-0*) St Martin.

McCabe, Virginia, tr. see Reeves, Dale, ed.

McCabe, Warren L., et al. Unit Operations in Chemical Engineering. 5th ed. LC 92-36218. (McGraw-Hill Chemical Engineering Ser.). 1088p. (C). 1993. 87.81 (*0-07-044844-2*) McGraw.

McCabe, Wayne & Gordon, Kate. Newton. LC 98-87868. (Images of America Ser.). (Illus.). 128p. 1998. pap. 16.99 (*0-7524-1239-6*) Arcadia Publng.

McCabe, William H. An Introduction to the Jesuit Theater. LC 83-81114. (Original Studies Composed in English III: No. 6). xiv, 346p. 1983. pap. 19.00 (*0-912422-62-9*) Inst Jesuit.

McCadden, Charlene S. The Masterbuilder. (Illus.). 14p. (Orig.). 1988. pap. 3.00 (*0-9620794-0-5*) King Realm Pubns.

McCadden, Joseph F. The Flight from Women in the Fiction of Saul Bellow. LC 80-5641. viii, 291p. 1980. 13.00 (*0-8191-1309-3*) U Pr of Amer.

McCadden, Joseph J. Education in Pennsylvania, 1801-1835 & Its Debt to Robert Vaux. LC 78-89199. (American Education: Its Men, Institutions, & Ideas. Series 1). 1978. reprint ed. 19.95 (*0-405-01438-4*) Ayer.

***McCade, Jillian.** New Orleans Nocturne: A Novel. LC 00-190852. 2000. 25.00 (*0-7388-2031-8*); pap. 18.00 (*0-7388-2032-6*) Xlibris Corp.

McCaffer, Ronald, jt. auth. see Harris, Frank.

McCafferty, Barbara. Double Murder. LC 96-76490. 288p. 1996. 18.95 (*1-57566-084-9*, Knsington) Kensgtn Pub Corp.

McCafferty, Barbara Taylor. Double Cross. LC 98-65258. (Bert & Nan Tatum Mystery Ser.). 240p. 1998. mass mkt. 20.00 (*1-57566-338-4*) Kensgtn Pub Corp.

— Double Exposure. (Bert & Nan Tatum Mystery Ser.). 320p. 1998. mass mkt. 5.99 (*1-57566-343-0*) Kensgtn Pub Corp.

***McCafferty, Barbara Taylor.** Double Cross. (Bert & Nan Tatum Mystery Ser.). 2000. mass mkt. 5.99 (*1-57566-511-5*) Kensgtn Pub Corp.

— Double Dealer. 2000. 20.00 (*1-57566-507-7*, Knsington) Kensgtn Pub Corp.

McCafferty, Barbara Taylor & Herald, Beverly Taylor. Double Exposure. LC 96-80344. 288p. 1997. 18.95 (*1-57566-207-8*, Knsington) Kensgtn Pub Corp.

— Double Murder. 288p. 1997. mass mkt. 5.50 (*1-57566-212-4*, Knsington) Kensgtn Pub Corp.

McCafferty, Bonnie. Smiling Through the Apocalypse. 248p. 1992. pap. 14.95 (*0-9634142-0-8*) Loose Canons.

***McCafferty, Carla Killoug.** The Head Bone's Connected to the Neck Bone: The Wierd Wacky Won. 2001. text. write for info. (*0-374-32908-7*) FS&G.

McCafferty, Catherine. Dave the Dinotourist. (Illus.). 8p. (J). (ps-3). 1999. bds. 6.99 (*1-57151-603-4*) Picture Me Bks.

— Just Be Nice... And Say You're Sorry! (Super Shape Bks.). (Illus.). 24p. (J). 1998. pap. 3.29 (*0-307-10343-9*, 10343, Goldn Books) Gldn Bks Pub Co.

***McCafferty, Catherine.** Little Mermaid II: Return to the Sea. (Illus.). (J). 2000. pap. 3.29 (*0-307-13260-9*, Goldn Books) Gldn Bks Pub Co.

McCafferty, Catherine. Picture Me at My Party with Mickey & Friends. (Picture Me Disney Ser.). (Illus.). 8p. (J). (ps-3). 1997. bds. 6.99 (*1-57151-540-2*) Picture Me Bks.

— Picture Me Dancing with Minnie Mouse. (Picture Me Disney Ser.). (Illus.). 8p. (J). (ps-k). 1997. bds. 6.99 (*1-57151-538-0*) Picture Me Bks.

— Picture Me on Vacation with Mickey Mouse. (Picture Me Disney Ser.). (Illus.). 8p. (J). (ps-k). 1997. bds. 6.99 (*1-57151-539-9*) Picture Me Bks.

***McCafferty, Catherine.** Picture Me with My Grandpa. (Illus.). 10p. (J). (ps-1). 2000. bds. 6.99 (*1-57151-579-8*) Picture Me Bks.

McCafferty, Catherine. Pirate Candy Treasure. (Illus.). 10p. (J). (gr. k-2). 1998. bds. 6.99 (*1-57151-607-7*, Nibble Me Bks) Picture Me Bks.

— Quest for Camelot. LC 98-171648. 1998. write for info. (*0-7853-2383-X*) Pubns Intl Ltd.

***McCafferty, Catherine.** Scamp's School Daze. LC 97-80839. (Golden Super Shape Bks.). 24p. (J). 1998. pap. text 3.29 (*0-307-13313-3*, 13313, Goldn Books) Gldn Bks Pub Co.

McCafferty, Catherine. Where's My Pet Tarantula? (Illus.). 8p. (J). (ps-3). 1999. bds. 6.99 (*1-57151-604-2*) Picture Me Bks.

McCafferty, Catherine & Pinkney, Debbie. Tiny Treasury of Favorite Animal Stories. LC 99-161461. 1997. write for info. (*0-7853-2545-X*) Pubns Intl Ltd.

McCafferty, Donald N. Successful Field Service Management. LC 79-54842. 191p. reprint ed. pap. 59.30 (*0-608-12831-7*, 202356100033) Bks Demand.

McCafferty, E., ed. see Electrochemical Society Staff.

McCafferty, Jane. Director of the World & Other Stories. LC 92-11734. (Drue Heinz Literature Prize Ser.). 160p. (C). 1992. text 22.50 (*0-8229-3729-8*) U of Pittsburgh Pr.

— One Heart: A Novel. LC 98-49469. 304p. 1999. 24.00 (*0-06-019263-1*) HarpC.

***McCafferty, Jane.** One Heart: A Novel. 304p. 2000. pap. 13.00 (*0-06-109757-8*) HarpC.

McCafferty, Jeanne. Set to Music. 224p. 26.00 (*0-7278-5557-3*) Severn Hse.

McCafferty, Jeanne. Star Gazer. (Worldwide Library Mysteries). 1996. per. 4.99 (*0-373-26211-6*, 1-26211-2, Wrldwide Lib) Harlequin Bks.

— Star Gazer. large type ed. (Large Print Ser.). 416p. 1996. 27.99 (*0-7089-3591-5*) Ulverscroft.

McCafferty, Jim. Holt & the Cowboys. LC 93-16618. (Illus.). 40p. (J). (gr. 4-7). 1993. 12.95 (*0-88289-985-6*) Pelican.

McCafferty, John, et al, eds. Antibody Engineering: A Practical Approach. LC 95-49216. (Practical Approach Ser.: No. 169). (Illus.). 348p. 1996. text 95.00 (*0-19-963593-5*); pap. text 55.00 (*0-19-963592-7*) OUP.

***McCafferty, Keith.** L. L. Bean Hiking & Backpacking Handbook. LC 99-53860. 1999. pap. 18.95 (*1-55821-940-4*) Lyons Pr.

— L. L. Bean Outdoor Family Camping Handbook. LC 99-25718. (Illus.). 192p. 1999. pap. 18.95 (*1-55821-880-7*) Lyons Pr.

McCafferty, Lawrence. The Heart of the Mystery. LC 94-75863. (Art of Meditation Ser.). 152p. (Orig.). 1995. pap. 11.95 (*1-884884-04-0*) La Chevre dOr Pr.

McCafferty, Maureen. Let Go the Glass Voice: A Novel. unabridged ed. LC 97-71805. (Illus.). 128p. 1997. 19.95 (*0-942979-27-3*, 942979); pap. 9.95 (*0-942979-28-1*, 942979) Livingston U Pr.

McCafferty, Michael D. & Meyer, Steven M. Medical Malpractice: Bases of Liability. LC 84-23580. 494p. 1985. text 125.00 (*0-07-044837-X*) Shepards.

McCafferty, Nell. In the Eyes of the Law. 185p. 1987. reprint ed. pap. 8.95 (*0-905169-95-6*, Pub. by Poolbeg Pr) Dufour.

— Peggy Deery: A Derry Family at War. (Orig.). 1992. 25.00 (*0-946211-58-2*) St Mut.

McCafferty, Owen, jt. ed. see Sheridan, John.

McCafferty, Patrick W. The Fabulous HEXAGENIA. (Illus.). xi, 173p. (Orig.). 1996. pap. 16.95 (*0-9657542-0-0*) Cdr Creek.

McCafferty, Taylor. Bed Bugs. Chelius, Jane, ed. 256p. (Orig.). 1993. mass mkt. 5.50 (*0-671-75468-8*) PB.

— Funny Money. 304p. 2000. per. 5.99 (*0-671-00129-9*, Pocket Star Bks) PB.

— Hanky Panky. 1995. mass mkt. 5.50 (*0-671-51049-5*) PB.

— Pet Peeves. Chelius, Jane, ed. 224p. (Orig.). 1990. mass mkt. 4.99 (*0-671-72802-4*) PB.

— Ruffled Feathers. Chelius, Jane, ed. 224p. (Orig.). 1992. mass mkt. 4.50 (*0-671-72803-2*) PB.

— Thin Skins. 1994. mass mkt. 4.99 (*0-671-79977-0*) PB.

McCafferty, Thomas. All about Options: The Easy Way to Get Started. 2nd ed. LC 98-9546. (Illus.). 241p. 1998. pap. 16.95 (*0-07-045543-0*) McGraw.

McCafferty, Thomas A. In House Telemarketing: The Masterplan for Starting & Managing a Profitable. rev. ed. LC 94-114223. 1993. text 27.50 (*1-55738-529-7*, Irwn Prfssnl) McGraw-Hill Prof.

— Winning with Managed Futures: How to Select a Top Performing Commodity Trading Advisor. 250p. 1994. text 47.50 (*1-55738-587-4*, Irwn Prfssnl) McGraw-Hill Prof.

McCafferty, Thomas A. & Wasendorf, Robert R. All about Options: From the Inside Out. 212p. 1994. per. 19.95 (*1-55738-434-7*, Irwn Prfssnl) McGraw-Hill Prof.

McCafferty, Thomas A. & Wasendorf, Russell R. All about Futures: From the Inside Out. 272p. 1992. per. 19.95 (*1-55738-296-4*, Irwn Prfssnl) McGraw-Hill Prof.

— All about Series, Set. 1995. per. 72.00 (*0-7863-0553-3*, Irwn Prfssnl) McGraw-Hill Prof.

McCafferty, Thomas A., jt. auth. see Wasendorf, Russell R.

McCafferty, W. Patrick. Aquatic Entomology: The Fisherman's & Ecologists Illustrated Guide to Insects & Their Relatives. (Illus.). 464p. (C). 1983. pap. 50.00 (*0-86720-017-0*) Jones & Bartlett.

— Aquatic Entomology: The Fisherman's & Ecologists Illustrated Guide to Insects & Their Relatives. deluxe ed. (Illus.). 448p. (C). 1982. lthr. 300.00 (*0-86720-010-3*) Jones & Bartlett.

McCafferty, W. Patrick, jt. auth. see Randolph, Robert P.

McCaffery, A. R. & Wilson, I. D. Chromatography & Isolation of Insect Hormones & Pheromones. (Chromatographic Society Symposium Ser.). (Illus.). 390p. (C). 1990. text 120.00 (*0-306-43707-4*, Kluwer Plenum) Kluwer Academic.

***McCaffery, Bonnie L.** Fantasy Fabrics: Techniques for Layered Surface Design. LC 99-34070. (Illus.). 80p. (Orig.). 1999. pap. 21.95 (*1-56477-272-1*, B395, Pub. by Martingale & Co) F & W Pubns Inc.

McCaffery, Dan. Battlefields in the Air: Canadians in the Allied Bomber Command. LC 96-106567. (Illus.). 196p. 1998. 29.95 (*1-55028-491-6*, Pub. by J Lorimer) Formac Dist Ltd.

***McCaffery, Dan.** Hell Island: The 1942 Air Battle for Malta. (Illus.). 214p. 1999. 29.95 (*1-55028-625-0*, Pub. by J Lorimer) Seven Hills Bk.

McCaffery, Edward J. Taxing Women. LC 96-30188. 310p. 1997. 29.95 (*0-226-55557-7*) U Ch Pr.

— Taxing Women. 1999. pap. 18.00 (*0-226-55558-5*) U Ch Pr.

McCaffery, James, jt. auth. see Clark, Noreen.

***McCaffery, Janet & Lindemeyer, Nancy.** A Show of Hands: Needlepoint Designs by Janet McCaffery. (Illus.). 127p. 1999. reprint ed. text 27.00 (*0-7881-6715-4*) DIANE Pub.

McCaffery, Jerry L. Budgetmaster. 3rd ed. (Illus.). 262p. (Orig.). (C). 1995. wbk. ed. 15.00 (*0-9620262-1-2*) J McCaffery.

McCaffery, Jerry L., jt. auth. see Jones, L. R.

McCaffery, John. Blessed Padre Pio: The Friar of San Giovanni. 143p. 1999. reprint ed. 19.95 (*0-912141-79-4*) Roman Cath Bks.

McCaffery, Larry. The Metafictional Muse: The Works of Robert Coover, Donald Barthelme, & William H. Gass. LC 82-1872. 315p. 1982. pap. 97.70 (*0-608-05088-1*, 206564200005) Bks Demand.

— Some Other Frequency: Interviews with Innovative American Authors. (Penn Studies in Contemporary American Fiction). (Illus.). 344p. 1996. pap. 19.95 (*0-8122-1442-0*); text 39.95 (*0-8122-3201-1*) U of Pa Pr.

McCaffery, Larry, ed. Across the Wounded Galaxies: Interviews with Contemporary American Science Fiction Writers. (Illus.). 280p. 1990. text 29.95 (*0-252-01692-0*) U of Ill Pr.

McCaffery, Larry, ed. Across the Wounded Galaxies: Interviews with Contemporary American Science Fiction Writers. (Illus.). 300p. 1991. pap. 12.95 (*0-252-06140-3*) U of Ill Pr.

McCaffery, Larry, ed. After Yesterday's Crash: The Avant-Pop Anthology. LC 94-48772. 1995. 12.95 (*0-01-402485-3*, Penguin Bks) Viking Penguin.

— Avant-Pop: Fiction for a Daydream Nation. (Black Ice Bks.). (Illus.). 247p. 1993. pap. 9.00 (*0-932511-72-4*) Fiction Coll.

— Storming the Reality Studio: A Casebook of Cyberpunk & Postmodern Science Fiction. LC 91-14316. (Illus.). 344p. 1992. text 54.95 (*0-8223-1158-5*); pap. text 19.95 (*0-8223-1168-2*) Duke.

***McCaffery, Larry, et al, eds.** Federman - A to X-X-X-X: A Recyclopedic Narrative. (Illus.). 398p. 1998. pap. 27.50 (*1-879691-53-1*) SDSU Press.

— Federman - A to X-X-X-X: A Recyclopedic Narrative. limited ed. (Illus.). 398p. 1998. pap. 100.00 incl. cd-rom (*1-879691-57-4*) SDSU Press.

McCaffery, Larry & Gregory, Sinda, eds. Alive & Writing: Interviews with American Authors of the 1980s. LC 86-25075. (Illus.). 296p. (C). 1987. text 29.95 (*0-252-01385-9*); pap. text 14.95 (*0-252-06011-3*) U of Ill Pr.

McCaffery, Larry, jt. ed. see Jaffe, Harold.

McCaffery, Larry, jt. ed. see Jeffe, Harold.

McCaffery, Larry, jt. ed. see LeClair, Tom.

McCaffery, Laura H. Building an ESL Collection for Young Adults: A Bibliography of Recommended Fiction & Nonfiction for Schools & Public Libraries. LC 98-5271. 200p. 1998. 39.95 (*0-313-29937-4*, Greenwood Pr) Greenwood.

McCaffery, Lawrence F., ed. Postmodern Fiction: A Bio-Bibliographical Guide, 2. LC 85-17723. (Movements in the Arts Ser.: No. 2). 632p. 1986. lib. bdg. 95.00 (*0-313-24170-8*, MML/, Greenwood Pr) Greenwood.

McCaffery, M. A. Irish Trivia. 1990. 6.99 (*0-685-33412-0*) Random Hse Value.

McCaffery, Margo & Pasero, Christine. Pain: Clinical Manual. 2nd ed. (Illus.). 814p. 1999. text 39.95 (*0-8151-5609-X*, 29563) Mosby Inc.

McCaffery, Michael. Directing a Play. rev. ed. (Theater Manuals Ser.). (Illus.). 128p. 1995. reprint ed. pap. 14.95 (*0-7148-2513-1*, Pub. by Phaidon Press) Phaidon Pr.

— Official VisiBroker for Java Handbook. LC 98-87216. 1998. pap. text 39.99 (*0-672-31451-7*) Sams.

McCaffery, Peter. When Bosses Ruled Philadelphia: The Emergence of the Republican Machine, 1867-1933. LC 92-42467. (Illus.). 304p. 1993. 40.00 (*0-271-00923-3*) Pa St U Pr.

McCaffery, Robert M. Employee Benefits. (SWC-Management). 250p. (C). 1988. pap. 20.75 (*0-534-87197-6*) PWS Pubs.

McCaffery, Robert M. & Harvey, Richard A. Employee Benefits Basics: Developing the Benefits Component of Total Compensation. (Building Blocks Ser.: Vol. 11). (Illus.). 24p. (Orig.). 1993. pap. 24.95 (*1-57963-014-6*, A0031) Am Compensation.

McCaffery, Robert P. Islands of Deutschtum: German-Americans in Manchester, New Hampshire & Lawrence, Massachusetts, 1870-1942. LC 96-11905. (New German-American Studies - Neue Deutsch-Amerikanische Studien: Vol. 11). XI, 254p. (C). 1997. 55.95 (*0-8204-3338-1*) P Lang Pubng.

McCaffery-Saville, Susanne. PugSpotting: A True History of How Pugs Saved Civilization. (Illus.). 2000. pap. 26.99 (*0-9671399-0-2*) Cliocopia Pr.

McCaffery, Steve. The Cheat of Words. LC 96-177409. 100p. 1996. pap. 12.00 (*1-55022-279-1*, Pub. by ECW) Genl Dist Srvs.

— Intimate Distortions. 96p. 1979. write for info. (*0-88984-017-2*); pap. write for info. (*0-88984-081-4*) Porcup Quill.

— North of Intention. LC 86-63324. (Roof Bks.). 240p. (Orig.). 1987. pap. 120.95 (*0-937804-23-1*) Segue NYC.

— Theory of Sediment. 216p. 1991. pap. 14.95 (*0-88922-299-1*) Talonbks.

McCaffery, Steve & Nichol, B. P. Rational Geomancy: The Kids Of The Book-MacHine: The Collected Research Reports Of The Toronto Research Group, 1973-1982. 320p. 1992. pap. 21.95 (*0-88922-300-9*, Pub. by Talonbks) Genl Dist Srvs.

— Rational Geomancy, the Kids of the Book Machine: The Collected Research Reports of the Toronto Research Group, 1973-1982. (Illus.). 320p. (Orig.). 1993. pap. 16.95 (*0-317-05589-5*) Genl Dist Srvs.

McCaffery, Steve, jt. ed. see Rasula, Jed.

***McCaffety, Kerri W.** The Majesty of the French Quarter. LC 99-40865. (Illus.). 192p. 1999. 39.95 (*1-56554-414-5*) Pelican.

— Majesty of the French Quarter Postcard Book. (Illus.). 2000. pap. text 9.95 (*1-56554-739-X*) Pelican.

McCaffray, Susan P. The Politics of Industrialization in Tsarist Russia: The Association of Southern Coal & Steel Producers, 1874-1914. LC 95-37346. 320p. 1996. lib. bdg. 35.00 (*0-87580-204-4*) N Ill U Pr.

McCaffray, Susan P., ed. see Fenin, Aleksandr I.

McCaffree, Maryjane & Innis, Pauline B. Protocol: The Complete Handbook of Diplomatic Official & Social Usage. rev. ed. LC 85-71131. (Illus.). 414p. 1998. reprint ed. pap. text 20.00 (*0-941402-04-5*) Devon Pub.

McCaffree, R., ed. Critical Care in Internal Medicine. (Progress in Critical Care Medicine Ser.: Vol. 2). (Illus.). viii, 352p. 1985. 82.75 (*3-8055-3900-2*) S Karger.

McCaffrey. Marriage & Divorce, Vol. 1. 1996. 125.00 (*0-316-55342-5*) Little.

An Asterisk (*) at the beginning of an entry indicates that the title is appearing for the first time.

— Scotland 19th Century. LC 97-37239. 168p. 1998. text 49.95 (*0-312-21124-4*) St Martin.

McCaffrey, Anne. Acorna: The Unicorn Girl. 61st ed. 416p. 2000. mass mkt. 6.99 (*0-06-105789-4*, HarperPrism) HarpC.

McCaffrey, Anne. Acorna's Quest. pap. write for info. (*0-06-105375-9*) HarpC.

— Acorna's World. 320p. 2000. 24.00 (*0-06-105095-4*, Avon Bks) Morrow Avon.

McCaffrey, Anne. All the Weyrs of Pern. 448p. 1992. mass mkt. 6.99 (*0-345-36893-2*, Del Rey) Ballantine Pub Grp.

— Black Horses for the King. 240p. (YA). 1997. pap. 10.95 (*0-345-40881-0*, Del Rey) Ballantine Pub Grp.

— Black Horses for the King. (YA). 1998. mass mkt. 6.99 (*0-345-42257-0*, Del Rey) Ballantine Pub Grp.

— Black Horses for the King. LC 95-36366. 240p. (YA). (gr. 6 up). 1996. 17.00 (*0-15-227322-0*) Harcourt.

— The Chronicles of Pern: First Fall. 336p. 1994. mass mkt. 5.99 (*0-345-36899-1*, Del Rey) Ballantine Pub Grp.

— The Coelura. 176p. 1995. 3.95 (*0-8125-0297-3*, Pub. by Tor Bks) St Martin.

— Crisis on Doona. 1992. mass mkt. 6.99 (*0-441-23194-2*) Ace Bks.

— Crystal Line. 320p. 1993. mass mkt. 6.99 (*0-345-38491-1*, Del Rey) Ballantine Pub Grp.

— Crystal Singer. 320p. 1985. mass mkt. 5.99 (*0-345-32786-1*, Del Rey) Ballantine Pub Grp.

— Crystal Singer. 1982. 11.09 (*0-606-01372-5*, Pub. by Turtleback) Demco.

— Damia. 352p. 1993. mass mkt. 6.99 (*0-441-13556-0*) Ace Bks.

— Damia's Children. 336p. 1994. mass mkt. 6.99 (*0-441-00007-X*) Ace Bks.

— Damia's Children. (J). 1994. 12.09 (*0-606-05797-8*, Pub. by Turtleback) Demco.

— Decision at Doona. 256p. 1987. mass mkt. 5.99 (*0-345-35377-3*, Del Rey) Ballantine Pub Grp.

***McCaffrey, Anne.** Dinosaur Planet. large type ed. (Science Fiction Ser.). 2000. 25.95 (*0-7838-8853-8*, G K Hall Lrg Type) Mac Lib Ref.

McCaffrey, Anne. The Dinosaur Planet Survivors. 304p. 1984. mass mkt. 5.99 (*0-345-27246-3*, Del Rey) Ballantine Pub Grp.

— A Diversity of Dragons. (J). 1995. 19.95 (*0-689-31868-5*) Atheneum Yung Read.

— A Diversity of Dragons. LC 98-109159. (Illus.). 96p. (gr. 7-12). 1997. 30.00 (*0-06-105531-X*, HarperPrism) HarpC.

— The Dolphins of Pern. 1995. mass mkt. 6.99 (*0-345-36895-9*, Del Rey) Ballantine Pub Grp.

— Dragondrums. Vol. 3. 208p. 1997. mass mkt. 6.99 (*0-553-25855-9*, Spectra) Bantam.

McCaffrey, Anne. Dragondrums. (Harper Hall Trilogy Ser.). (J). 1980. 11.60 (*0-606-01413-6*, Pub. by Turtleback) Demco.

McCaffrey, Anne. Dragondrums. large type ed. LC 98-51971. 290p. 1999. 24.95 (*0-7838-8506-7*, G K Hall & Co) Mac Lib Ref.

— Dragonflight. 320p. 1986. mass mkt. 3.99 (*0-345-33546-5*, Del Rey) Ballantine Pub Grp.

— Dragonflight. 1997. pap. 12.95 (*0-345-41936-7*, Del Rey) Ballantine Pub Grp.

McCaffrey, Anne. Dragonflight. (Dragonriders of Pern Ser.). 1978. 12.09 (*0-606-01414-4*, Pub. by Turtleback) Demco.

— Dragonquest. (Dragonriders of Pern Ser.). 1978. 12.09 (*0-606-01416-0*, Pub. by Turtleback) Demco.

McCaffrey, Anne. Dragonquest, Vol. 2. 368p. 1986. mass mkt. 6.99 (*0-345-33508-2*, Del Rey) Ballantine Pub Grp.

— The Dragonriders of Pern. LC 87-91864. 832p. 1988. pap. 16.00 (*0-345-34024-8*, Del Rey) Ballantine Pub Grp.

— Dragonsdawn. (Dragonriders of Pern Ser.). 384p. 1989. mass mkt. 6.99 (*0-345-36286-1*, Del Rey) Ballantine Pub Grp.

— Dragonsdawn. 431p. 1988. 25.00 (*0-89366-213-5*) Ultramarine Pub.

***McCaffrey, Anne.** Dragonseye. 399p. 1998. mass mkt. 6.99 (*0-345-41879-4*, Del Rey) Ballantine Pub Grp.

McCaffrey, Anne. Dragonsinger. LC 76-40988. 276p. (J). (gr. 5-9). 1977. 18.00 (*0-689-30570-2*) Atheneum Yung Read.

— Dragonsinger. LC 00-1018. Vol. 2. 256p. 1997. mass mkt. 6.99 (*0-553-25854-0*, Spectra) Bantam.

McCaffrey, Anne. Dragonsinger. (Harper Hall Trilogy Ser.). (J). 1977. 11.60 (*0-606-01501-9*, Pub. by Turtleback) Demco.

— Dragonsinger. large type ed. LC 98-50792. (G. K. Hall Science Fiction Ser.). 1999. 24.95 (*0-7838-8499-0*, G K Hall Lrg Type) Mac Lib Ref.

McCaffrey, Anne. Dragonsong. 1994. mass mkt. 6.99 (*0-553-54176-5*) Bantam.

McCaffrey, Anne. Dragonsong. (Harper Hall Trilogy Ser.). 1977. 11.60 (*0-606-01138-2*, Pub. by Turtleback) Demco.

McCaffrey, Anne. Dragonsong. large type ed. 1995. pap. 49.50 (*0-614-09546-8*, L-34855-00) Am Printing Hse.

— Dragonsong. large type ed. (Harper Hall Trilogy Ser.). 192p. 1977. mass mkt. 6.99 (*0-553-25852-4*, Bantam Classics) Bantam.

— Dragonsong. large type ed. LC 97-43858. (YA). 1998. 23.95 (*0-7838-8422-2*, G K Hall Lrg Type) Mac Lib Ref.

— An Exchange of Gifts. LC 95-34092. (Illus.). (J). 1995. mass mkt. 12.95 (*0-451-45520-7*, ROC) NAL.

— Freedom's Challenge. 303p. 1999. reprint ed. mass mkt. 5.99 (*0-441-00625-6*) Ace Bks.

— Freedom's Choice. 1998. mass mkt. 6.99 (*0-441-00531-4*) Ace Bks.

— Freedom's Landing. 324p. 1996. mass mkt. 6.99 (*0-441-00338-9*) Ace Bks.

***McCaffrey, Anne.** Freedom's Landing. 1999. 12.34 (*0-606-15538-4*) Turtleback.

McCaffrey, Anne. Get off the Unicorn. 1987. mass mkt. 5.99 (*0-345-34935-0*) Ballantine Pub Grp.

— The Girl Who Heard Dragons. 416p. 1995. 5.99 (*0-8125-1099-2*, Pub. by Tor Bks) St Martin.

— Growing Bulbs. (NK Lawn & Garden Guides Ser.). (Illus.). 80p. (Orig.). 1995. pap. 7.95 (*0-380-77428-3*, Avon Bks) Morrow Avon.

— Icefalcon's Quest. 1999. mass mkt. 5.99 (*0-345-38824-0*, Del Rey) Ballantine Pub Grp.

***McCaffrey, Anne.** If Wishes Were Horses. LC 98-23917. 160p. 1998. pap. 14.95 (*0-451-45642-4*, ROC) NAL.

McCaffrey, Anne. Killashandra. 384p. 1986. mass mkt. 6.99 (*0-345-31600-2*, Ballantine) Ballantine Pub Grp.

— Killashandra. LC 85-6193. 303p. 1985. 25.00 (*0-89366-187-2*) Ultramarine Pub.

— The Lady. 1988. mass mkt. 5.99 (*0-345-35674-8*, Del Rey) Ballantine Pub Grp.

— The Lady. 461p. 1987. 25.00 (*0-89366-214-3*) Ultramarine Pub.

***McCaffrey, Anne.** Legends: Tsoutsouvas,&Sam, Vol. 4. 1999. audio 34.95 (*0-694-52113-2*) HarperAudio.

McCaffrey, Anne. Lyon's Pride. (Rowan Ser.: Vol. 4). 336p. 1995. mass mkt. 6.99 (*0-441-00141-6*) Ace Bks.

— The Masterharper of Pern. (Dragonriders of Pern Ser.). 422p. 1999. mass mkt. 6.99 (*0-345-42460-3*, Del Rey) Ballantine Pub Grp.

— Moreta, Dragonlady of Pern. 384p. 1984. mass mkt. 6.99 (*0-345-29873-X*, Del Rey) Ballantine Pub Grp.

McCaffrey, Anne. Moreta, Dragonlady of Pern. 1983. 12.09 (*0-606-03412-9*, Pub. by Turtleback) Demco.

McCaffrey, Anne. Moreta, Dragonlady of Pern. LC 83-4630. 286p. 1983. 25.00 (*0-89366-251-8*) Ultramarine Pub.

— Nerilka's Story. 208p. 1987. mass mkt. 5.99 (*0-345-33949-5*, Del Rey) Ballantine Pub Grp.

***McCaffrey, Anne.** Nimisha's Ship. LC 98-45500. 388p. 1999. 25.00 (*0-345-38825-9*, Del Rey) Ballantine Pub Grp.

— Nimisha's Ship. 2000. mass mkt. 6.99 (*0-345-43425-0*, Del Rey) Ballantine Pub Grp.

McCaffrey, Anne. No One Noticed the Cat. LC 96-22033. 128p. 1996. text 13.95 (*0-451-45578-9*, ROC) NAL.

— Pegasus in Flight. 304p. 1991. mass mkt. 5.99 (*0-345-36897-5*, Del Rey) Ballantine Pub Grp.

***McCaffrey, Anne.** Pegasus in Flight. 2000. mass mkt. 5.99 (*0-345-91643-3*, Del Rey) Ballantine Pub Grp.

McCaffrey, Anne. Pegasus in Flight. 1991. 11.09 (*0-606-01229-X*, Pub. by Turtleback) Demco.

***McCaffrey, Anne.** Pegasus in Space. 464p. 2000. 25.00 (*0-345-43466-8*, Del Rey) Ballantine Pub Grp.

McCaffrey, Anne. The Renegades of Pern. 352p. 1990. mass mkt. 6.99 (*0-345-36933-5*, Del Rey) Ballantine Pub Grp.

— The Renegades of Pern. 384p. 1989. text 25.00 (*0-89366-284-4*) Ultramarine Pub.

— Restoree. 1987. mass mkt. 5.99 (*0-345-35187-8*, Del Rey) Ballantine Pub Grp.

— The Rowan. (Rowan Ser.: Vol. 1). 1991. mass mkt. 6.99 (*0-441-73576-2*) Ace Bks.

— The Rowan. (Rowan Ser.: Vol. 1). 1991. 11.60 (*0-606-00996-5*, Pub. by Turtleback) Demco.

— The Ship Who Sang. 1985. mass mkt. 5.99 (*0-345-33431-0*) Ballantine Pub Grp.

— The Space Opera. 1996. pap. 5.99 (*0-88677-714-3*, Pub. by DAW Bks) Penguin Putnam.

— Tax & Marriage. 1995. 125.00 (*0-316-55336-0*, Aspen Law & Bus) Aspen Pub.

— Three Women. 1992. mass mkt. 5.99 (*0-8125-0587-5*, Pub. by Tor Bks) St Martin.

— To Ride Pegasus. 256p. 1986. mass mkt. 5.99 (*0-345-33603-8*, Del Rey) Ballantine Pub Grp.

***McCaffrey, Anne.** To Ride Pegasus. 2000. mass mkt. 6.99 (*0-345-91644-1*, Del Rey) Ballantine Pub Grp.

McCaffrey, Anne. To Ride Pegasus. 1973. 11.09 (*0-606-01228-1*, Pub. by Turtleback) Demco.

***McCaffrey, Anne.** The Tower & the Hive. (Rowan Ser.: Vol. 5). 315p. 2000. mass mkt. 6.99 (*0-441-00720-1*) Ace Bks.

McCaffrey, Anne. The Tower & the Hive. LC 98-51946. (Rowan Ser.: Vol. 5). 288p. (YA). 1999. 23.95 (*0-399-14501-X*, G P Putnam) Peng Put Young Read.

— Treaty at Doona. Nye, Jody L., ed. 352p. (Orig.). 1994. mass mkt. 5.99 (*0-441-00089-4*) Ace Bks.

McCaffrey, Anne. The Unicorn Girl. write for info. (*0-06-105541-7*) HarpC.

— The White Dragon. (Dragonriders of Pern Ser.). 1978. 12.09 (*0-606-01881-6*, Pub. by Turtleback) Demco.

— The White Dragon. abr. ed. 1988. audio 14.00 (*0-89845-228-7*, SWC 1596) HarperAudio.

McCaffrey, Anne. The White Dragon, Vol. 3. Vol. 3. 368p. 1986. mass mkt. 6.99 (*0-345-34167-8*, Del Rey) Ballantine Pub Grp.

— The Year of the Lucy. 320p. 1987. pap. 3.95 (*0-8125-8565-8*) Tor Bks.

***McCaffrey, Anne & Ball, Margaret.** Acorna's Quest. LC 97-51201. 304p. 1998. 23.00 (*0-06-105297-3*, HarperPrism) HarpC.

McCaffrey, Anne & Ball, Margaret. Acorna's Quest. 416p. 2000. mass mkt. 6.50 (*0-06-105790-8*, HarpTorch) Morrow Avon.

— Partnership. 336p. 1992. mass mkt. 5.99 (*0-671-72109-7*) Baen Bks.

McCaffrey, Anne & Betancourt, John, eds. Serve It Forth: Cooking with Anne McCaffrey. 1996. write for info. (*0-446-67141-X*) Warner Bks.

McCaffrey, Anne & Lackey, Mercedes. The Ship Who Searched. 320p. 1992. per. 5.99 (*0-671-72129-1*) Baen Bks.

— The Ship Who Searched. large type ed. LC 95-52488. 440p. 1996. pap. 20.95 (*0-7862-0645-4*) Thorndike Pr.

McCaffrey, Anne & Moon, Elizabeth. Generation Warriors. 1991. mass mkt. 5.99 (*0-671-72041-4*) Baen Bks.

— Sassinak. (Planet Pirate Ser.). 352p. 1990. mass mkt. 6.99 (*0-671-69863-X*) Baen Bks.

McCaffrey, Anne & Nye, Jody L. The Death of Sleep. (Orig.). 1990. mass mkt. 6.99 (*0-671-69884-2*) Baen Bks.

— The Ship Who Won. (Brain-Brawn Ser.). 336p. 1994. 21.00 (*0-671-87595-7*) Baen Bks.

— The Ship Who Won. 336p. 1995. mass mkt. 5.99 (*0-671-87657-0*) Baen Bks.

McCaffrey, Anne & Scarborough, Elizabeth A. Acorna's People. Date not set. pap. write for info. (*0-06-107345-8*, HarperPrism) HarpC.

McCaffrey, Anne & Scarborough, Elizabeth A. Acorna's People. LC 99-12850. 320p. 1999. 24.00 (*0-06-105094-6*) HarpC.

***McCaffrey, Anne & Scarborough, Elizabeth A.** Acorna's People. 416p. 2000. mass mkt. 6.99 (*0-06-105983-8*) HarpC.

McCaffrey, Anne & Scarborough, Elizabeth A. Power Lines. 1995. mass mkt. 6.99 (*0-345-38780-5*, Del Rey) Ballantine Pub Grp.

— Power Play. 1996. mass mkt. 5.99 (*0-345-38781-3*, Del Rey) Ballantine Pub Grp.

— The Powers That Be. 384p. 1994. mass mkt. 5.99 (*0-345-38779-1*, Del Rey) Ballantine Pub Grp.

McCaffrey, Anne & Stirling, S. M. The City Who Fought. LC 93-2651. 432p. 1993. 19.00 (*0-671-72166-6*) Baen Bks.

— The City Who Fought. (Brain-Brawn Ser.). 448p. 1994. per. 6.99 (*0-671-87599-X*) Baen Bks.

McCaffrey, Anne, et al. A Dragon Lover's Treasury of the Fantastic. 432p. 1995. reprint ed. 22.00 (*0-7278-4778-3*) Severn Hse.

— The Planet Pirates. 864p. (Orig.). 1993. pap. 15.00 (*0-671-72187-9*) Baen Bks.

McCaffrey, Anne, jt. auth. see Nye, Jody L.

McCaffrey, Barry. National Drug Control Strategy (1998) A Ten Year Plan, 1998-2007. (Illus.). 93p. (C). 1999. pap. text 25.00 (*0-7881-7154-2*) DIANE Pub.

McCaffrey, Barry M. Pulse Check: National Trends in Drug Abuse: Summer 1998. (Illus.). 55p. 1999. text 20.00 (*0-7881-7942-X*) DIANE Pub.

***McCaffrey, Barry R.** Investing in our Nation's Youth, National Youth Anti-Drug Media Campaign: Phase 2 (Final Report) 220p. 1999. per. 19.00 (*0-16-050059-1*) USGPO.

McCaffrey, Barry R. The National Drug Control Strategy, 1996. (Illus.). 101p. (Orig.). 1996. pap. text 35.00 (*0-7881-3196-6*) DIANE Pub.

— National Drug Control Strategy (1997) (Illus.). 70p. (Orig.). 1997. pap. text 30.00 (*0-7881-3994-0*) DIANE Pub.

***McCaffrey, Barry R., ed.** Investing in Our Nation's Youth: National Youth Anti-Drug Media Campaign Phase II (Final Report) (Illus.). 150p. 2000. pap. text 30.00 (*0-7881-8849-6*) DIANE Pub.

— The National Drug Control Strategy 1998: Budget Summary. (Illus.). 207p. (C). 1999. pap. text 30.00 (*0-7881-8258-7*) DIANE Pub.

McCaffrey, Barry R., ed. Reducing Drug Abuse in America. (Illus.). 52p. (C). 1998. pap. text 20.00 (*0-7881-7463-0*) DIANE Pub.

***McCaffrey, Barry R. & USGPO Staff.** The Destructive Impact of Drugs on the United States: How the Legalization of Drugs Would Jeapordize the Health & Safety of the American People & Our Nation LC 99-12485. 1999. pap. write for info. (*0-16-050091-5*) USGPO.

McCaffrey, Barry R., jt. ed. see Jaffe, Steven L.

McCaffrey, Carlyn S. Divorce & Separation Taxation under the 1984 Tax Law. LC 84-246453. (Illus.). 160p. 35.00 (*0-685-10780-9*) Harcourt.

McCaffrey, Dan. Billy Bishop: Canadian Hero. 218p. 1990. mass mkt. 5.95 (*0-88780-158-7*, Pub. by Formac Publ Co) Formac Dist Ltd.

McCaffrey, David P. The Politics of Nuclear Power: A History of the Shoreham Nuclear Power Plant. (Technology, Risk & Society Ser.). 276p. 1991. lib. bdg. 155.00 (*0-7923-1035-7*) Kluwer Academic.

McCaffrey, David P., ed. OSHA & the Politics of Health Regulation: Organizational & Political Changes in a Regulatory Agency. LC 82-11201. 210p. 1982. 42.50 (*0-306-41050-8*, Plenum Trade) Perseus Pubng.

McCaffrey, David P. & Hart, David W. Wall Street Polices Itself: How Securities Firms Manage the Legal Hazards of Competitive Pressures. LC 97-18732. (Illus.). 224p. 1998. 35.00 (*0-19-511187-7*) OUP.

McCaffrey, Donald W. Assault on Society: Satirical Literature to Film. LC 92-4040. (Illus.). 293p. 1992. 42.00 (*0-8108-2507-4*) Scarecrow.

— Assault on Society: Satirical Literature to Film. LC 92-4040. (Illus.). 293p. 1992. reprint ed. pap. 24.00 (*0-8108-2594-5*) Scarecrow.

— Three Classic Silent Screen Comedies, Starring Harold Lloyd. LC 74-4993. (Illus.). 264p. 1976. 35.00 (*0-8386-1455-8*) Fairleigh Dickinson.

McCaffrey, Donald W. & Jacobs, Christopher P., eds. Guide to the Silent Years of American Cinema. LC 99-10111. (Reference Guides to the World's Cinema Ser.). 384p. 1999. lib. bdg. 79.50 (*0-313-30345-2*) Greenwood.

***McCaffrey, Edna.** Octave Mirbeau's Literary & Intellectual Evolution as a French Writer, 1880-1914. LC 99-58809. (Studies in French Literature: Vol. 39). 260p. 2000. text 89.95 (*0-7734-7792-6*) E Mellen.

McCaffrey, Eileen, jt. auth. see Cassell, Jenna.

McCaffrey, Eugene. Heart of Love. 1998. 5.95 (*1-85390-398-1*) Ignatius Pr.

McCaffrey, Eugene V. & McCaffrey, Roger A. Players Choice. LC 86-19705. (Illus.). 240p. reprint ed. pap. 74.40 (*0-7837-1567-6*, 204185900024) Bks Demand.

McCaffrey, Hugh, tr. see Isaac Of Stella.

McCaffrey, James M. Army of Manifest Destiny: The American Soldier in the Mexican War, 1846-1848. (American Social Experience Ser.). (Illus.). 275p. (C). 1994. pap. text 19.50 (*0-8147-5505-4*) NYU Pr.

McCaffrey, James M., ed. Surrounded by Dangers of All Kinds: The Mexican War Letters of Lieutenant Theodore Laidley. LC 97-22086. (War & the Southwest Ser.: Vol. 6). (Illus.). 185p. 1997. 25.00 (*1-57441-034*2*) UNTX Pr.

McCaffrey, James M., jt. auth. see Kinney, John F.

***McCaffrey, Joseph A.** Cassies Ruler. LC 99-94086. 296p. 1999. pap. 6.50 (*0-9670299-0-2*, 101) Jamic Ltd.

— Confessional Matters. unabridged ed. LC 99-94085. (Illus.). 318p. 1999. pap. 6.50 (*0-9670299-1-0*, 102) Jamic Ltd.

McCaffrey, Judy B., ed. see Harris, Brenda.

McCaffrey, K., et al, eds. Fractures, Fluid Flow & Mineralization. 338p. 1999. 115.00 (*1-86239-034-7*) Geol Soc Pub Hse.

McCaffrey, Larry, jt. ed. see Jaffe, Harold.

McCaffrey, Lawrence J. The Irish Catholic Diaspora in America. LC 97-9729. 256p. 1997. pap. text 24.95 (*0-8132-0896-3*) Cath U Pr.

M

— The Irish Diaspora in America. LC 83-25280. 224p. 1984. reprint ed. pap. 69.50 (*0-7837-9102-X*, 204990400004) Bks Demand.

— The Irish Question: Two Centuries of Conflict. 2nd ed. LC 95-6860. 240p. 1995. pap. 18.00 (*0-8131-0855-1*) U Pr of Ky.

— Textures of Irish America. (Irish Studies). (Illus.). 300p. 1992. 39.95 (*0-8156-0267-7*) Syracuse U Pr.

— Textures of Irish America. (Irish Studies Ser.). 1998. pap. text 18.95 (*0-8156-0521-8*) Syracuse U Pr.

McCaffrey, Lawrence J., ed. Irish Nationalism & the American Contribution. LC 76-6354. (Irish Americans Ser.). 1976. 23.95 (*0-405-09347-0*) Ayer.

McCaffrey, Lawrence J., et al, eds. Ideas, Concepts, Doctrine: A History of Basic Thinking in the United States Air Force, 1907-1964. LC 79-7255. (Flight: Its First Seventy-Five Years Ser.). 1980. reprint ed. lib. bdg. 52.95 (*0-405-12166-0*) Ayer.

McCaffrey, Lawrence J., jt. ed. see Hachey, Thomas E.

McCaffrey, Margot K., tr. To the Chukchi Peninsula & to the Tlingit Indians, 1881-1882: Journals & Letters by Aurel & Arthur Krause. LC 92-47100. (Rasmuson Library Historical Translation Ser.: Vol. VIII). (ENG & GER., Illus.). xiii, 230p. 1993. pap. 17.50 (*0-912006-66-8*) U of Alaska Pr.

McCaffrey, Mark, tr. see Mansilla, Lucio V.

McCaffrey, Moira, et al. Wrapped in the Colours of the Earth: Cultural Heritage of the First Nations. (Illus.). 128p. 1992. pap. 49.95 (*0-7735-0968-2*, Pub. by McG-Queens Univ Pr) CUP Services.

McCaffrey, Patrick, jt. auth. see Flanagan, Richard W.

McCaffrey, Robert J. & Puente, Antonio E., eds. Handbook of Neuropsychological Assessment: A Biopsychosocial Perspective. (Critical Issues in Neuropsychology Ser.). (Illus.). 488p. (C). 1991. text 90.00 (*0-306-43940-9*, Kluwer Plenum) Kluwer Academic.

McCaffrey, Robert J., et al. The Practice of Forensic Neuropsychology: Meeting Challenges in the Courtroom. LC 96-37015. (Critical Issues in Neuropsychology Ser.). (Illus.). 235p. (C). 1996. text 47.00 (*0-306-45256-1*, Kluwer Plenum) Kluwer Academic.

McCaffrey, Roger A., jt. auth. see McCaffrey, Eugene V.

McCaffrey, Rosanne, ed. see Platou, Dode.

McCaffrey, Thomas V. Rhinologic Diagnosis & Treatment. (Illus.). 432p. 1996. text 79.00 (*0-86577-619-9*) Thieme Med Pubs.

McCaffrey, Thomas V., ed. Systemic Disease & the Nasal Airway. LC 92-49198. (Rhinology & Sinusology Ser.). 1993. 59.00 (*0-86577-466-8*) Thieme Med Pubs.

McCaffrey, Thomas V. & Kern, Eugene B. The Obstructed Nasal Airway: Evaluation & Treatment. 350p. 1997. text. write for info. (*0-7817-0193-7*) Lppncott W & W.

McCaffrey, Todd. Dragonholder: The Life & Dreams (So Far) of Anne McCaffrey. LC 99-31283. 128p. 1999. 19.95 (*0-345-42217-1*, Del Rey) Ballantine Pub Grp.

McCaffrey, Tony. My Bedtime Prayer. LC 97-16411. (Illus.). 32p. (J). 1997. 12.95 (*0-8294-0966-1*) Loyola Pr.

— Storytellers of God: Teacher's Toolbox. 1996. pap. text 19.95 (*1-55612-920-3*) Sheed Ward Ltd.

***McCafrey, Barry R.** Inter-Related Problems of Substance Abuse & Crime. 20p. 1999. pap. 2.50 (*0-16-050090-7*) USGPO.

***McCagg, Mary.** Chicken Run: Rocky & Ginger's Great Eggscape. (Illus.). (J). 2000. 9.99 (*0-525-46423-9*) Viking Penguin.

McCagg, William O., Jr. A History of Habsburg Jews, 1670-1918. LC 88-544. (Illus.). 304p. 1989. 32.50 (*0-253-33189 7*) Ind U Pr.

— A History of Habsburg Jews, 1670-1918. LC 88-544. (Illus.). 304p. 1992. pap. 14.95 (*0-253-20649-9*, MB-649) Ind U Pr.

— Jewish Nobles & Geniuses in Modern Hungary. LC 73-189944. (East European Monographs: No. 3). 256p. 1972. text 59.50 (*0-88033-092-9*, Pub. by East Eur Monographs) Col U Pr.

McCagg, William O. Stalin Embattled, Nineteen Forty-Three to Nineteen Forty-Eight. LC 77-28286. 424p. reprint ed. pap. 131.50 (*0-608-17738-5*, 20320340077) Bks Demand.

McCagg, William O. & Siegelbaum, Lewis H., eds. The Disabled in the Soviet Union: Past & Present, Theory & Practice. LC 89-40206. (Russian & East European Studies). 310p. 1989. text 49.95 (0-8229-3622-4) U of Pittsburgh Pr.

McCagg, William O., Jr. & Silver, Brian D., eds. Soviet Asian Ethnic Frontiers. LC 77-11796. (Policy Studies). (Illus.). 1979. 96.00 (0-08-024637-0, Pergamon Pr) Elsevier.

***McCaghy, Charles H., et al.** Deviant Behavior: Crime, Conflict & Interest Groups. 5th ed. LC 99-28128. 454p. (C). 1999. pap. text 44.00 (0-205-29616-5, Longwood Div) Allyn.

McCagney, Nancy. Nagarjuna & the Philosophy of Openness. LC 97-16697. 256p. 1997. 63.00 (0-8476-8626-4); pap. 23.95 (0-8476-8627-2) Rowman.

— Religion & Ecology. (Religion & Modernity Ser.). 288p. 1999. 59.95 (0-631-20583-7); pap. 25.95 (0-631-20584-5) Blackwell Pubs.

McCague, James. Rivers of America - The Cumberland. lib. bdg. 21.95 (0-8488-2005-3) Amereon Ltd.

McCahery, James R. What Evil Lurks. 256p. 1996. mass mkt. 4.99 (1-57566-001-6) Kensgtn Pub Corp.

McCahery, Joseph, et al, eds. Corporate Control & Accountability: Changing Structures & Dynamics of Regulation. (Illus.). 466p. 1995. pap. text 35.00 (0-19-825990-5) OUP.

— International Regulatory Competition & Coordination: Perspectives on Economic Regulation in Europe & the United States. LC 96-8697. (Illus.). 564p. 1997. text 115.00 (0-19-826035-0) OUP.

McCahill, Bob. Dialogue of Life: A Christian among Allah's Poor. LC 95-50915. 150p. (Orig.). 1996. pap. 13.00 (1-57075-066-1) Orbis Bks.

McCahill, Margaret E. & Lindbloom, Erik. Challenging Diagnoses in the Academy Collection: Quick Reference Guides for Family Physicians. LC 98-22561. (Academy Collection). 227p. 1998. pap. 29.95 (0-683-30423-2) Lppncott W & W.

McCahill, T. A. Biology Basic Facts. (Collins Gem Ser.). 1996. pap. 8.00 (0-00-470994-2) Collins.

McCaig, jt. auth. see Moon.

McCaig, Barbara. Alabama Biking Guide. Boyce, Chris, ed. (Illus.). 80p. (Orig.). 1989. pap. text 5.95 (0-935201-81-5) Affordable Adven.

— Dakota's Parks Guide. Boyce, Chris, ed. (Illus.). 120p. (Orig.). 1989. pap. text 5.95 (0-935201-82-3) Affordable Adven.

— Dining Out Milwaukee. 3rd rev. ed. Boyce, Chris, ed. 150p. 1988. pap. 4.95 (0-935201-42-4) Affordable Adven.

— Door Country Family Fun & Adventure Guide. Bussler, Rod, ed. 120p. (Orig.). 1987. pap. text 7.95 (0-935201-21-1) Affordable Adven.

— Illinois Biking Guide. Vanderboom, Gretchen, ed. 100p. (Orig.). 1989. pap. text 5.95 (0-935201-80-7) Affordable Adven.

— Minnesota Biking Guide. Vanderboom, Gretchen, ed. 100p. (Orig.). 1989. pap. text 5.95 (0-935201-78-5) Affordable Adven.

— New York Biking Guide. Vanderboom, Gretchen, ed. 100p. (Orig.). 1989. pap. text 5.95 (0-935201-83-1) Affordable Adven.

— Oregon Parks Guide. Boyce, Chris, ed. 100p. (Orig.). 1988. pap. text 5.95 (0-935201-41-6) Affordable Adven.

— Texas Parks Guide. Boyce, Chris, ed. 100p. (Orig.). 1988. pap. text 5.95 (0-935201-40-8) Affordable Adven.

— Wisconsin Biking Guide. Vanderboom, Cary, ed. (Illus.). 100p. (Orig.). 1989. pap. text 5.95 (0-935201-77-7) Affordable Adven.

McCaig, Barbara & Boyce. Maine State Parks. (Illus.). 100p. (Orig.). 1989. pap. text 5.95 (0-935201-64-5) Affordable Adven.

— Maryland State Parks. (Illus.). 100p. (Orig.). 1989. pap. text 5.95 (0-935201-63-7) Affordable Adven.

— Massachusetts State Park. (Illus.). 100p. (Orig.). 1989. pap. text 5.95 (0-935201-67-X) Affordable Adven.

— New Mexico State Parks. (Illus.). 100p. (Orig.). 1989. pap. text 5.95 (0-935201-66-1) Affordable Adven.

— North Carolina State Parks. (Illus.). 100p. (Orig.). 1989. pap. text 5.95 (0-935201-65-3) Affordable Adven.

— Wisconsin State Parks. (Illus.). 100p. (Orig.). 1989. pap. text 5.95 (0-935201-69-6) Affordable Adven.

McCaig, Barbara & Boyce, Chris. California Parks Guide. 130p. 1988. pap. 5.95 (0-935201-36-X) Affordable Adven.

McCaig, Barbara & Kangas, Race. Alabama State Parks. (Illus.). 100p. (Orig.). 1989. pap. text 5.95 (0-935201-62-9) Affordable Adven.

McCaig, Barbara & Soli, Lynn D. Illinois Parks & Forest Guide. LC 85-73788. (Illus.). 100p. (Orig.). 1986. pap. 7.95 (0-935201-06-8) Affordable Adven.

— Michigan Parks & Forest Guide. (Illus.). 100p. (Orig.). 1986. pap. 7.95 (0-935201-09-2) Affordable Adven.

— Milwaukee Family Fun & Adventure Guide. (Illus.). 67p. (Orig.). 1985. pap. 7.95 (0-935201-02-5) Affordable Adven.

— Milwaukee's Finest Fish Frys. LC 85-73789. (Illus.). 75p. 1986. pap. 3.95 (0-935201-07-6) Affordable Adven.

— Ohio Parks & Forest Guide. (Illus.). 100p. (Orig.). 1986. pap. 7.95 (0-935201-10-6) Affordable Adven.

McCaig, Barbara & Vanderboom, Raster. Minnesota State Parks. (Illus.). 100p. (Orig.). 1989. pap. text 5.95 (0-935201-68-8) Affordable Adven.

McCaig, Barbara, et al. Twin Cities Brunches. (Illus.). 80p. (Orig.). 1986. pap. 4.95 (0-935201-12-2) Affordable Adven.

McCaig, Barbara, jt. auth. see Soli, Lynn D.

McCaig, Barbara, ed. see Boyce, Chris.

McCaig, Barbara, ed. see Boyce, Chris & McCaig, Margie.

McCaig, Barbara, ed. see Jones, Penny.

McCaig, Barbara, ed. see Powers, William H.

McCaig, C. D., ed. Nerve Growth & Guidance. (Frontiers in Neurobiology Ser.: No. 2). 188p. (C). 1996. text 110.50 (1-85578-085-2, Pub. by Portland Pr Ltd) Ashgate Pub Co.

McCaig, Donald. An American Homeplace. LC 97-15051. (Virginia Bookshelf Ser.). 227p. 1997. reprint ed. pap. 14.95 (0-8139-1775-1) U Pr of Va.

— Eminent Dogs, Dangerous Men. LC 98-14735. 240p. 1998. reprint ed. pap. 14.95 (1-55821-670-7) Lyons Pr.

— Jacob's Ladder: A Story of Virginia During the War. LC 97-31165. 525p. 1998. 25.95 (0-393-04629-X) Norton.

— Jacob's Ladder: A Story of Virginia During the War. 527p. 1999. pap. 13.95 (0-14-028265-3) Viking Penguin.

— Nop's Hope. 240p. 1998. reprint ed. pap. 14.95 (1-55821-574-3) Lyons Pr.

— Nop's Trials. 336p. 1992. pap. 13.95 (1-55821-185-3) Lyons Pr.

McCaig, Isabel. A Learner's Dictionary of English Idioms. 224p. 1986. pap. text 10.50 (0-19-431254-2) OUP.

McCaig, Linda. Preliminary Estimates from the Drug Abuse Warning Network, 1995. 75p. 1998. pap. text 30.00 (0-7881-4034-5) DIANE Pub.

McCaig, Margie, jt. auth. see Boyce, Chris.

Mccain. Game of Science. 2nd ed. (Psychology Ser.). 1973. pap. 5.25 (0-8185-0093-X) Brooks-Cole.

— Game of Science. 3rd ed. (Psychology Ser.). 1977. mass mkt. 11.00 (0-8185-0247-9) Brooks-Cole.

McCain & Khalili. Transitions: A Guide to Understanding Intercultural Business Communication. rev. ed. 1997. pap. 34.95 (0-87393-624-8) Dame Pubns.

McCain, Becky R. Grandmother's Dreamcatcher. LC 98-4996. (Illus.). (J). (gr. k-3). 1998. 15.95 (0-8075-3031-X) A Whitman.

McCain, Charles H. Plugged in & Turned On: Planning, Coordinating, & Managing Computer-Supported Instruction. 216p. 1996. pap. 24.95 (0-8039-6432-3); text 55.95 (0-8039-6431-5) Corwin Pr.

***McCain, Donald V.** Creating Training Courses: When You're Not a Trainer. LC 99-72436. 96p. 1999. pap. 21.95 (1-56286-114-X) Am Soc Train & Devel.

***McCain, Gillian.** Religion. 36p. (Orig.). 1999. pap. 10.00 (0-935724-99-0, Pub. by Figures) SPD-Small Pr Dist.

McCain, Gillian. Tilt. 88p. 1996. pap. 10.00 (0-935724-75-3) Figures.

— Tilt. 88p. 1996. pap. text 10.00 (1-889097-04-7) Hard Pr MA.

McCain, Gillian, jt. ed. see McNeil, Legs.

McCain, J. D., ed. see Minerals, Metals & Materials Society Staff.

***McCain, J. Holly.** Star. LC 99-65317. 64p. 2000. pap. 9.95 (1-56315-223-1, Pub. by SterlingHse) Natl Bk Netwk.

***McCain, John.** Faith of My Fathers: A Family Memoir. 368p. 2000. pap. 14.00 (0-06-095786-7, Perennial) HarperTrade.

***McCain, John, ed.** Air Bag Safety. (Illus.). 180p. 1998. reprint ed. pap. text 35.00 (0-7881-7393-6) DIANE Pub.

— Airport Revenue Diversion: Hearing Before the Committee on Commerce, Science & Transportation, U. S. Senate. 171p. (C). 1999. reprint ed. pap. text 30.00 (0-7881-7272-7) DIANE Pub.

McCain, John, ed. Aviation Accident Investigations. 92p. 1999. reprint ed. pap. text 20.00 (0-7881-8045-2) DIANE Pub.

***McCain, John, ed.** International Aviation Relations: Congressional Hearing. 103p. (C). 1999. reprint ed. pap. text 25.00 (0-7881-7273-5) DIANE Pub.

— Internet Indecency: Congressional Hearing. 77p. 2000. reprint ed. pap. text 20.00 (0-7567-0158-9) DIANE Pub.

McCain, John & Salter, Mark. Faith of My Fathers. LC 99-13496. (Illus.). 349p. 1999. 25.00 (0-375-50191-6) Random.

— Faith of My Fathers: Family Memoir. large type ed. LC 99-34272. 560p. 1999. 25.00 (0-375-40847-9) Random Hse Lrg Prnt.

McCain, John C., jt. auth. see Sadiq, Muhammad.

McCain, Joseph P. Diagnostic & Operative Arthroscopy of the Temporomandibular Joint. (Illus.). 321p. (C). (gr. 13). 1996. text 149.00 (0-8016-6074-2, 06074) Mosby Inc.

McCain, Liliane Q. & Strauss, Larry. What Do You Mean You Don't Want to Go to College? Turning Crisis into Opportunity for You & Your Child. 160p. 1990. 17.95 (0-929923-16-2) Lowell Hse.

— What Do You Mean You Don't Want to Go to College? Turning Crisis into Opportunity for You & Your Child. 156p. 1991. pap. 9.95 (0-929923-36-7) Lowell Hse.

McCain, Marian Van Eyck, see Van Eyck McCain, Marian.

***McCain, Mary M. & Merrill, Martha.** Dictionary for School Library Media Specialists: A Practical & Comprehensive Guide. 2000. pap. 40.00 (1-56308-696-4) Libs Unl.

McCain, Mic. Inflation: Its Real Causes. LC 82-90210. 126p. (Orig.). 1982. pap. 6.95 (0-9608314-0-1) McCain Pub.

McCain, Mollie H. Collector's Encyclopedia of Pattern Glass. (Illus.). 544p. 1996. pap. 12.95 (0-89145-211-7, 1380) Collector Bks.

***McCain, Mollie H.** Collectors Encyclopedia of Pattern Glass. 2nd ed. (Illus.). 544p. 2000. pap. 17.95 (1-57432-176-5) Collector Bks.

McCain, Paul, ed. see Chytraeus, David & Melanchthon, Philip.

McCain, Paul M. County Court in North Carolina Before 1750. LC 70-115996. (Duke University. Trinity College Historical Society. Historical Papers: No. 31). reprint ed. 30.00 (0-404-51781-1) AMS Pr.

***McCain, Roger A.** Agent-Based Computer Simulation of Dichotomous Economic Growth. LC 99-47346. (Advances in Computational Economics Ser.). 1999. write for info. (0-7923-8688-4, Kluwer Plenum) Kluwer Academic.

McCain, Roger A. A Framework for Cognitive Economics. LC 91-44446. 336p. 1992. 65.00 (0-275-94142-6, C4142, Praeger Pubs) Greenwood.

McCain, Ron, jt. auth. see Garrett, Kyle.

McCain, Rych. Let's Get Rich! The Pre-Millionaire's Guide to Music & Business. Smith, Janeska, ed. (Illus.). 175p. (Orig.). 1984. pap. text 6.95 (0-9611904-1-8) Street Wise Pubns.

— Make It Go Right! 14p. 1990. 3.00 (0-9611904-2-6) Street Wise Pubns.

***McCain, Steven.** Simply Grace. 112p. 1999. pap. 7.99 (0-9673503-0-1) Grace Abound Pubg.

McCain, Ted D. E., jt. auth. see Jukes, Ian.

McCain, Thomas A. & Shyles, Leonard, eds. The One Thousand Hour War: Communication in the Gulf, 148. LC 93-12979. (Contributions in Military Studies Ser.: No. 148). 232p. 1993. 57.95 (0-313-28747-3, GM8747, Greenwood Pr) Greenwood.

McCain, W. Calvin. Pieces of Peace. LC 74-25235. 80p. 1983. reprint ed. pap. text 5.95 (0-931680-01-8) Dunbar Pub.

— Soul in the Opera House. LC 82-229693. 80p. 1982. pap. 5.00 (0-931680-02-6) Dunbar Pub.

McCain, William D., Jr. Properties of Petroleum Fluids. 2nd ed. 596p. 1990. 99.95 (0-87814-335-1) PennWell Bks.

McCain, William D. United States & the Republic of Panama. LC 72-111724. (American Imperialism: Viewpoints of United States Foreign Policy, 1898-1941 Ser.). 1970. reprint ed. 21.95 (0-405-02036-8) Ayer.

McCain, Zack. Elevator Industry Inspection Handbook. (Illus.). 102p. 1997. ring bd. 19.00 (1-886536-23-6) Elevator Wrld.

***McCain, Zack.** Elevator Maintenance Field Handbook. (Illus.). 72p. 1999. pap. 14.00 (1-886536-28-7) Elevator Wrld.

— Elevator Maintenance Manual. (Illus.). 258p. 1999. pap. 55.00 (1-886536-27-9) Elevator Wrld.

McCaine, Alexander H. Food Contaminations & Adulterations in America: Index of New Information. 160p. 1997. 47.50 (0-7883-1772-5); pap. 44.50 (0-7883-1773-3) ABBE Pubs Assn.

McCairen, Patricia C. Canyon Solitude: A Woman's Solo River Journey Through the Grand Canyon. LC 98-11518. (Illus.). 245p. 1998. pap. 14.95 (1-58005-007-7) Seal Pr WA.

McCaleb, Charles S. Surf, Sand & Streetcars: A Mobile History of Santa Cruz, California. LC 95-11081. 1995. reprint ed. write for info. (0-940283-06-9) Santa Cruz Hist.

***McCaleb, Gary.** Community: The Other Side of Self. LC 00-100805. 125p. 2000. 15.95 (0-89112-425-X) Abilene Christ U.

McCaleb, Robert S. The Encyclopedia of Popular Herbs: Your Guide to the 40 Most Useful Medicinal Plants. LC 99-37610. (Illus.). 208p. 1999. pap. 16.00 (0-7615-1600-X) Prima Pub.

McCaleb, Sudia P. Building Communities of Learners: A Collaboration Among Students, Teachers, Families & Community. 240p. 1994. pap. text 13.00 (0-312-09163-X) St Martin.

— Building Communities of Learners: A Collaboration among Teachers, Students, Families, & Community. 216p. 1995. pap. 17.50 (0-8058-8005-4) L Erlbaum Assocs.

McCaleb, Walter F. The Aaron Burr Conspiracy. 476p. 1966. reprint ed. 25.00 (0-87266-021-4) Argosy.

McCaleb, Walter F., ed. see Reagan, John H.

McCalep, George O., Jr. Breaking the Huddle. 140p. (Orig.). 1997. mass mkt. write for info. (0-9652262-1-2) Orman Pr.

— Faithful over a Few Things: Seven Critical Church Growth Principles. LC 96-92249. 121p. 1996. mass mkt. 19.95 (0-9652262-0-4) Orman Pr.

— Faithful over a Few Things: Seven Critical Church Growth Principles. 1997. student ed., spiral bd. 9.95 (0-9652262-4-7) Orman Pr.

— Growing up to the Head: 10 Growth Essentials to Becoming a Better Christian & Church Member. 140p. 1997. mass mkt. 19.95 (0-9652262-3-9) Orman Pr.

— Prophecy Blessings. 140p. 1997. mass mkt. write for info. (0-9652262-6-3) Orman Pr.

***McCalep, George O.** Sin in the House: Ten Crucial Church Problems with Cleansing Solutions. 221p. 1999. write for info. (1-891773-06-2) Orman Pr.

McCalep, George O., Jr. Stir up the Gift. Date not set. mass mkt. write for info. (0-9652262-7-1) Orman Pr.

McCall. Fundamental Statistics for Behavioral Sciences. 7th ed. 1997. pap. 15.50 (0-534-35367-3) Brooks-Cole.

— Fundamental Statistics for Behavioral Sciences. 8th ed. (Psychology Ser.). 2000. text 85.95 (0-534-57780-6) Wadsworth Pub.

— Identity in Northern Ireland. LC 98-30879. 256p. 1999. text 65.00 (0-312-21844-3) St Martin.

— Negotiation: Theory & Practice. (C). 1992. pap. text. write for info. (0-201-56510-2) Addison-Wesley.

McCall, Andrew. The Medieval Underworld. 1979. 22.00 (0-241-10018-6, H Hamilton) Viking Penguin.

McCall, Anne B. Larger Vision: Tower-Room Talks. LC 77-156686. (Essay Index Reprint Ser.). 1977. reprint ed. 20.95 (0-8369-2283-2) Ayer.

***McCall, B. J., et al.** Secrets, Vol. 5. (Best in Women's Sensual Fiction Ser.). 248p. 1999. pap. 12.99 (0-9648942-5-4) Red Sage.

McCall, Barbara A. The Apache. (Native American People Ser.: Set II). (Illus.). 32p. (J). (gr. 4-8). 1990. lib. bdg. 22.60 (0-86625-384-X) Rourke Pubns.

— Los Apache. Lazzarino, Luciano & Marcuse, Aida E., trs. from SPA. LC 92-12177. (Pueblos Americanos Nativos Ser.).Tr. of Apache. (Illus.). 32p. (J). (gr. 5-8). 1992. lib. bdg. 22.60 (0-86625-454-4) Rourke Pubns.

— The Cherokee. (Native American People Ser.: Set I). (Illus.). 32p. (J). (gr. 4-8). 1989. lib. bdg. 22.60 (0-86625-376-9) Rourke Pubns.

— Los Cheroqui. (Pueblos Americanos Nativos Ser.). (SPA.). 32p. (J). (gr. 5-8). 1990. lib. bdg. 21.27 (0-86625-456-0) Rourke Pubns.

— Daily Life. (Native American Culture Ser.). 64p. (J). (gr. 4-8). Date not set. lib. bdg. 25.27 (1-57103-534-6) Rourke Pr.

— Daily Life. LC 94-5528. (Native American Culture Ser.). (J). 1994. write for info. (0-86625-534-6) Rourke Pubns.

— The European Invasion. LC 94-5530. (Native American Culture Ser.). 64p. (J). (gr. 4-8). 1994. lib. bdg. 25.27 (0-86625-535-4) Rourke Pubns.

— The Iroquois. (Native American People Ser.: Set I). (Illus.). 32p. (J). (gr. 4-8). 1989. lib. bdg. 22.60 (0-86625-378-5) Rourke Pubns.

McCall, Bevode C., jt. auth. see Maddox, George L.

McCall, Bruce. Sit! The Dog Portraits of Thierry Poncelet. (Illus.). 96p. 1993. 19.95 (1-56305-380-2, 3380) Workman Pub.

— Thin Ice: Coming of Age in Canada. 249p. 1999. pap. 14.00 (0-679-76959-5) Vin Bks.

McCall, Bruce F. Survival: The Ten Rules for Success in Petroleum Marketing. 145p. 15.00 (0-685-65573-3) Mkters Assn of Am.

McCall, Carlos, ed. see Zorotovich, Betty.

***McCall, Carol.** Listen! There's a World Waiting to Be Heard! The Empowerment of Listening. LC 99-93677. 2000. 14.95 (0-533-13115-4) Vantage.

McCall, Catherine. Concepts of Person: An Analysis of Concepts of Person, Self & Human Being. 210p. 1990. text 83.95 (1-85628-039-X, Pub. by Avebry) Ashgate Pub Co.

McCall, Chester H. Sampling & Statistics Handbook for Research. LC 82-15290. (Illus.). 352p. 1982. reprint ed. pap. 109.20 (0-608-00119-8, 206088400006) Bks Demand.

McCall, Christina & Clarkson, Stephen. Trudeau & Our Times Vol. 2: The Heroic Delusion. 460p. 1996. 29.99 (0-7710-5417-3) McCland & Stewart.

McCall, Cicely. Looking Back from the Nineties: An Autobiography. LC 95-128656. viii, 127 p. 1994. write for info. (0-947893-32-6) Gliddon Bks.

McCall, Clare M. Captain John McCall, Seventeen Twenty-Six to Eighteen Twelve: His Ancestors & His Descendants. LC 85-18767. (Illus.). 185p. 1985. lib. bdg. 5.00 (0-88082-012-8) New Eng Hist.

McCall, Dan. Citizens of Somewhere Else: Nathaniel Hawthorne & Henry James. LC 98-36633. 240p. 1999. 25.00 (0-8014-3640-0) Cornell U Pr.

— The Silence of Bartleby. LC 89-627. 240p. 1989. pap. text 14.95 (0-8014-9593-8) Cornell U Pr.

McCall, David, ed. Acute Myocardial Infarction. (Contemporary Management in Internal Medicine Ser.: Vol. 2, No. 2). (Illus.). 213p. 1992. text 36.00 (0-443-08838-1) Church.

McCall, David & Rahimtoola, Shahbudin. Heart Failure. (Illus.). 415p. (gr. 13). 1995. text 91.95 (0-412-04441-2, Pub. by E A) OUP.

McCall, David E. Crimes Against Children: A Guide to Child Protection for Parents & Professionals. LC 95-68229. 200p. (Orig.). 1995. pap. 19.95 (1-884570-27-5) Research Triangle.

McCall, Dewitt C., III. California Artists, 1935-1956. McCall, Ruth, ed. LC 81-65529. (Illus.). 212p. 1981. lib. bdg. 50.00 (0-939370-02-6) DeRus Fine Art.

McCall, Diana. Touchstone. 416p. 1999. mass mkt. 5.99 (0-06-108702-5) HarpC.

***McCall, Dina.** White Orchid. large type ed. 256p. 1999. pap. 18.99 (0-7089-5582-7, Linford) Ulverscroft.

McCall, Dinah. Chase the Moon. 1. LC 98-51967. 1999. 26.95 (0-7862-1784-7) Thorndike Pr.

— Chase the Moon. LC 99-19117. 1999. 23.95 (1-56895-705-X) Wheeler Pub.

— Dream Catcher. mass mkt. write for info. (0-06-108435-2, Harp PBks) HarpC.

— Dream Catcher. 304p. 1996. mass mkt. 5.50 (0-06-108325-9) HarpC.

— Jackson Rule. 304p. 1996. mass mkt. 5.99 (0-06-108391-7, Harp PBks) HarpC.

***McCall, Dinah.** The Return. 384p. 2000. per. 6.50 (1-55166-584-0, Mira Bks) Harlequin Bks.

McCall, Dinah. Tallchief. 352p. 1997. mass mkt. 5.99 (0-06-108444-1) HarpC.

McCall, Donald D., jt. auth. see Andrews, J. W.

McCall, Douglas L. Film Cartoons: A Guide to 20th Century American Animated Features & Shorts. LC 98-26404. 267p. 1998. pap. 39.95 (0-7864-0584-8) McFarland & Co.

McCall, Edith. Abe & the Wild River. 184p. (J). (gr. 3-7). 1999. pap. 9.99 (0-88092-439-X, 439X) Royal Fireworks.

— Better Than a Brother. (Illus.). 1988. 13.95 (0-8027-6782-6); 14.85 (0-8027-6783-4) Walker & Co.

— Mississippi Steamboatman: The Story of Henry Miller Shreve. LC 85-13795. (Walker's American History Series for Young People). (Illus.). 115p. (J). (gr. 5-8). 1986. 11.95 (0-8027-6597-1) Walker & Co.

— Sometimes We Dance Alone. large type ed. LC 94-41433. 236p. 1995. 19.95 (0-7838-1190-X, G K Hall Lrg Type) Mac Lib Ref.

— Sometimes We Dance Alone: Your Next Years Can Be Your Best Years. LC 93-23419. 192p. 1994. 16.95 (0-9636620-0-7) Brett Bks.

McCall, Edward. Hawaiian Gecko. pap. 4.95 (0-930492-36-6) Hawaiian Serv.

McCall, Elizabeth B. Old Philadelphia Houses on Society Hill, 1750-1840. (Illus.). 17p. 1966. 22.50 (*0-8038-0194-7*) Archit CT.

McCall, Eva. Edge of Heaven. LC 97-40066. 256p. 1997. pap. 14.95 (*0-914875-27-2*, Historical Images) Bright Mtn Bks.

McCall, Francis X., Jr., jt. auth. see Keeler, Patricia A.

McCall, G. J. & De Mulder, E. F. Urban Geoscience. (AGID Special Publication Ser.: No. 20). 280p. 1996. 82.00 (*90-5410-643-3*, Pub. by A A Balkema); pap. 41.00 (*90-5410-647-6*, Pub. by A A Balkema) Ashgate Pub Co.

McCall, G. J. & Marker, B. R., eds. Earth Science Mapping for Planning, Development & Conservation. (C). 1989. lib. bdg. 289.00 (*0-86010-989-5*, Pub. by Graham & Trotman) Kluwer Academic.

McCall, G. J., jt. auth. see Stow, D. A.

McCall, Gene H. & Corder, John A. New World Vistas: Air & Space Power for the 21st Century (Summary) (Illus.). 90p. (Orig.). (C). 1996. pap. text 35.00 (*0-7881-3385-3*) DIANE Pub.

McCall, George A. Letters from the Frontiers: A Facsimile Reproduction of the 1868 Edition with an Introduction & Index by John K. Mahon. LC 74-22038. (Bicentennial Floridian Facsimile Ser.). (Illus.). 591p. reprint ed. pap. 183.30 (*0-7837-0596-4*, 204094400019) Bks Demand.

McCall, George J., jt. auth. see Weber, George H.

McCall, Grant, ed. see Young Nations Conference, Sidney, 1976 Staff.

McCall, Helen. French Beaded Flowers I: A Guide for Beginners. Spears, Therese, ed. (Illus.). 32p. (Orig.). 1993. pap. 14.95 (*0-932255-04-3*) Promenade Pub.

***McCall, Henrietta.** Egyptian Mummies. (Fast Forward Ser.). (Illus.). (J). 2000. 26.50 (*0-531-11877-0*); pap. 9.95 (*0-531-16443-8*) Watts.

McCall, Henrietta. Mesopotamian Myths. (Legendary Past Ser.). (Illus.). 80p. 1991. pap. 12.95 (*0-292-75130-3*) U of Tex Pr.

— Pyramid. LC 99-27869. (Fast Forward Ser.). 1999. 26.00 (*0-531-14584-0*) Watts.

— Pyramids.Tr. of Pyramide. 1999. pap. text 9.95 (*0-531-15435-1*) Watts.

McCall, Ian. Je, Il, & Vous: Narrator, Protagonist, & Narratee from "Jean Santeuil" to "A la Recherche" (Currents in Comparative Romance Languages & Literatures Ser.: Vol. 55). 261p. (C). 1998. text 48.95 (*0-8204-3703-4*) P Lang Pubng.

McCall, J. David. Inside the Lotus Add-in Toolkit. 1990. pap. 24.95 (*0-13-471772-4*) P-H.

McCall, J. L. & Steele, J. H., Jr., eds. Practical Applications of Quantitative Metallography - STP 839. LC 83-73230. 190p. 1984. text 34.00 (*0-8031-0220-8*, STP839) ASTM.

McCall, Jack. The Principal's Edge. LC 94-4121. (Illus.). 250p. 1994. 35.95 (*1-883001-08-0*) Eye On Educ.

McCall, James. Antitrust. 2nd ed. (Sum & Substance Ser.). 1984. 15.95 (*0-940366-00-2*) Sum & Substance.

McCall, James L., et al, eds. Metallography & Interpretation of Weld Microstructures: Proceedings of a Symposium Co-Sponsored by the International Metallographic Society, ASM International, & the American Welding Society. LC 87-71104. (Illus.). 399p. reprint ed. pap. 123.70 (*0-8357-4091-9*, 203685700005) Bks Demand.

McCall, James L. & Mueller, William M., eds. Metallographic Specimen Preparation: Optical & Electron Microscopy. LC 74-8391. (Illus.). 366p. 1974. reprint ed. pap. 113.50 (*0-608-05493-3*, 206596200006) Bks Demand.

McCall, James P. The Stallion: A Breeding Guide for Owners & Handlers. (Illus.). 288p. 1995. 29.95 (*0-87605-987-6*) Howell Bks.

McCall, Jim & McCall, Lynda. Horses Behavin' Badly: Training Solutions for Problem Behaviors. LC 97-41021. (Illus.). 144p. 1997. 23.95 (*0-939481-50-2*) Half Halt Pr.

McCall, Jody, ed. see Reuther, Ruth E.

McCall, John. How to Write Themes & Essays. 3rd ed. LC 97-80143. 138p. 1998. pap. 9.95 (*0-02-862184-0*, Arc) IDG Bks.

— Interactions with Ancestors in Everyday Life. 29p. 1989. 2.00 (*0-941934-54-3*) Indiana Africa.

— Statistics: A Guide for Therapists. (Skills for Practice Ser.). (Illus.). 288p. 1997. pap. text 39.50 (*0-7506-2104-4*) Buttrwrth-Heinemann.

***McCall, John C.** Dancing Histories: Heuristic Ethnography with the Ohafia Igbo. LC 99-59065. 208p. 2000. text 42.50 (*0-472-11070-5*, 11070) U of Mich Pr.

McCall, John J. The Economics of Information & Uncertainty. LC 81-15930. (Illus.). 346p. reprint ed. pap. 107.30 (*0-608-09469-2*, 205426900005) Bks Demand.

McCall, John J., ed. The Economics of Information & Uncertainty. LC 81-15930. (Conference Report - Universities - National Bureau Committee for Economic Research Ser.: No. 32). 346p. reprint ed. pap. 107.30 (*0-8357-3237-1*, 205713100011) Bks Demand.

McCall, John J., jt. auth. see DesJardins, Joseph R.

McCall, John J., jt. ed. see DesJardins, Joseph R.

McCall, John R. The Principal as Steward. LC 96-3417. 250p. 1997. 35.95 (*1-883001-32-3*) Eye On Educ.

McCall, Junietta B. Grief Education for Caregivers of the Elderly. LC 98-28105. (Illus.). 190p. 1999. 29.95 (*0-7890-0498-4*) Haworth Pr.

McCall, Karen. Cougar: Ghost of the Rockies. LC 92-3691. (Illus.). 160p. 1993. reprint ed. pap. 22.00 (*0-87156-463-7*, Pub. by Sierra) Random.

***McCall, Karen.** It's Your Money: Achieving Financial Well-Being. LC 99-87436. 2000. pap. 18.95 (*0-8118-2503-5*) Chronicle Bks.

McCall, Karen & Dutcher, Jim. Cougar: Ghost of the Rockies. 1996. 27.50 (*0-8446-6875-3*) Peter Smith.

McCall, Kenneth. Healing the Family Tree. 1989. pap. text 9.95 (*0-687-85480-6*) Abingdon.

McCall, Laura & Yacovone, Donald, eds. A Shared Experience: Women, Men, & the History of Gender. LC 98-6850. 330p. 1998. text 55.00 (*0-8147-9682-6*); pap. text 18.50 (*0-8147-9683-4*) NYU Pr.

McCall, Linda L., tr. see Waquet, Jean-Claude.

McCall, Lynda, jt. auth. see McCall, Jim.

McCall, Mark. The AS/400 Programmer's Handbook: A Toolbox of Examples for Every AS/400 Programmer. LC 98-219498. (Illus.). 400p. 1998. spiral bd. 59.00 (*1-883884-48-9*, 585) Midrange Comput.

***McCall, Mark.** The AS/400 Programmer's Handbook Vol. II: More Toolbox Examples for Every AS/400 Programmer. (Illus.). 400p. 2000. pap. 69.00 (*1-58347-012-3*, 5017, IBM) Midrange Comput.

McCall, Mark. 7 Client/Server Applications in Visual Basic. LC 97-207422. (Toolbox of Templates Ser.). (Illus.). 439p. (Orig.). 1997. pap. 99.00 incl. disk (*1-883884-42-X*, 569) Midrange Comput.

McCall, Mary E., ed. see Boldy, Duncan P.

McCall, Mary R. Secret Vows. Date not set. mass mkt. write for info. (*0-380-81785-3*) Morrow Avon.

Mccall, Mary R., jt. auth. see Schmittroth, Linda.

McCall, Maxine, ed. A Handful of Stars: Concepts on Preaching by Maurice Berquist & Gerald Marvel. LC 97-144872. (Orig.). 1996. pap. 10.95 (*0-87162-691-8*) Warner Pr.

McCall, Michael. Shania Twain: An Intimate Portrait of a Country Music Diva. 3rd ed. LC 99-24346. (Illus.). 192p. 1999. pap. 10.99 (*0-312-20673-9*) St Martin.

McCall, Michael, et al. Country Music Stars: The Legends & the New Breed. (Illus.). 192p. 1992. 19.95 (*1-56173-697-X*) Pubns Intl Ltd.

McCall, Michael K. Indigenous Technical Knowledge in Farming Systems of Eastern Africa: A Bibliography. (Bibliographies in Technology & Social Change Ser.: No. 9). 101p. (Orig.). (C). 1994. pap. 12.00 (*0-945271-34-4*) ISU-CIKARD.

McCall, Michal M., jt. ed. see Becker, Howard S.

McCall, Miles. The Power Parent: Taking Corporate Management Home. 208p. 1995. teacher ed. 89.95 (*0-9648995-0-7*) C M & Assocs.

McCall, Morgan W., Jr. High Flyers: Developing the Next Generation of Leaders. LC 97-11699. (Illus.). 254p. 1997. 27.95 (*0-87584-336-0*) Harvard Busn.

McCall, Morgan W. Whatever It Takes: The Realities of Managerial Decision Making. 2nd ed. 160p. 1989. pap. text 37.80 (*0-13-952136-4*) P-H.

McCall, Morgan W., Jr. & Kaplan, Robert K. Whatever It Takes: Decision Makers at Work. (Illus.). 144p. 1985. text 27.00 (*0-13-952086-4*) P-H.

McCall, Morgan W., Jr., et al. The Lessons of Experience: How Successful Executives Develop on the Job. LC 87-46405. 212p. 1988. 27.50 (*0-669-18095-5*) Free Pr.

McCall, Nancy & Mix, Lisa A., eds. Designing Archival Programs to Advance Knowledge in the Health Fields. LC 93-40454. 256p. 1994. text 40.00 (*0-8018-4761-3*) Johns Hopkins.

McCall, Nathan. Makes Me Wanna Holler: A Young Black Man in America. 1995. 12.00 (*0-614-32215-4*) Vin Bks.

— Makes Me Wanna Holler: A Young Black Man in America. LC 93-30654. 416p. 1995. pap. 13.00 (*0-679-74070-8*) Vin Bks.

— What's Going On? 192p. pap. 11.00 (*0-375-70150-8*) Vin Bks.

McCall, Paul, jt. auth. see Stockbridge, Grant.

McCall, Pearl D. Holland-Jackson Record, with Related Hoyle-Swofford History. (Illus.). 334p. 1997. reprint ed. pap. 51.00 (*0-8328-9182-7*); reprint ed. lib. bdg. 61.00 (*0-8328-9181-9*) Higginson Bk Co.

McCall-Perez, Fred. Physician Equity Groups & Other Emerging Entities: Competitive Organizational Choices for Physicians. LC 97-16015. 1997. write for info. (*0-7863-0960-1*, Irwn Prfssnl) McGraw-Hill Prof.

McCall, Peter & Lacy, Maryanne. An Invitation to Healing. (Illus.). 213p. 1985. pap. 10.00 (*0-936269-00-6*) Hse of Peace.

— Rise & Be Healed. 239p. (Orig.). 1992. pap. 15.00 (*0-936269-01-4*) Hse of Peace.

— What Is Healing Prayer All About? Answers to Most Frequently Asked Questions about Healing. (Illus.). 300p. 1998. pap. 15.00 (*0-936269-03-0*) Hse of Peace.

McCall, Peter L., jt. ed. see Tevesz, Michael J.

McCall, Raymond J. Phenomenological Psychology: An Introduction. LC 83-47764. 136p. 1983. pap. 13.95 (*0-299-09414-6*) U of Wis Pr.

***McCall, Renee M. & Craft, Diane H.** Moving with a Purpose: Developing Programs for Preschoolers of All Abilities. LC 99-88414. (Illus.). 248p. 2000. 22.00 (*0-88011-976-4*) Human Kinetics.

McCall, Richard D. The Way of the Warrior-Trader: The Financial Risk-Taker's Guide to Samurai Courage, Confidence, & Discipline. LC 96-40909. 240p. 1997. 24.95 (*0-7863-1163-0*, Irwn Prfssnl) McGraw-Hill Prof.

McCall, Robert B. Fundamental Statistics for Behavioral Science. 6th ed. (Statistics). 1994. pap., student ed. 19.75 (*0-534-51151-1*) Wadsworth Pub.

— Fundamental Statistics for Behavioral Sciences. 6th ed. 469p. 1994. pap. 54.75 (*0-534-51150-3*) Wadsworth Pub.

— Fundamental Statistics for Behaviorial Science. 7th ed. LC 97-20694. (Psychology). 1997. pap. 85.95 (*0-534-52371-4*) Brooks-Cole.

— Infants. (Illus.). 185p. 1979. 25.95 (*0-674-45265-8*) HUP.

McCall, Robert B., et al. High School Underachievers. (Individual Differences & Development Ser.: Vol. 1). (Illus.). 160p. (C). 1992. 48.00 (*0-8039-4604-X*); pap. 21.50 (*0-8039-4605-8*) Sage.

McCall, Ruth, ed. see McCall, Dewitt C., III.

McCall, Ruth E. Phlebotomy Exam Review. 240p. 1996. pap. text 29.95 (*0-397-55232-7*) Lppncott W & W.

McCall, Ruth E. & Tankersley, Cathee M. Phlebotomy Essentials. 2nd ed. LC 97-11637. 368p. 1997. pap. text 29.95 (*0-7817-9198-7*) Lppncott W & W.

McCall, Samuel W. Business of Congress. LC 11-13147. reprint ed. 34.50 (*0-404-04101-9*) AMS Pr.

— Thaddeus Stevens. Morse, John T., Jr., ed. LC 78-128951. (American Statesmen Ser.: No. 31). reprint ed. 45.00 (*0-404-50881-2*) AMS Pr.

— Thomas B. Reed. Morse, John T., Jr., ed. LC 74-128950. (American Statesmen Ser.: No. 35). reprint ed. 45.00 (*0-404-50885-5*) AMS Pr.

McCall, Smith A. The Best of the First Ten Years of the Samoyed Quarterly. deluxe ed. (Illus.). 480p. 1995. pap. 60.00 (*0-614-04548-7*) Donald R Hoflin.

McCall-Smith, Alexander, jt. auth. see Shuman, Daniel W.

McCall, Stephen, ed. see Arter, Christine, et al.

McCall, Storrs. A Model of the Universe: Space-Time, Probability, & Decision. (Clarendon Library of Logic & Philosophy). (Illus.). 344p. 1994. text 55.00 (*0-19-824053-8*) OUP.

— A Model of the Universe: Space-Time, Probability, & Decision. (Clarendon Library of Logic & Philosophy). (Illus.). 338p. 1996. pap. text 19.95 (*0-19-823622-0*) OUP.

McCall, Thomas. Beyond Ice, Beyond Death. LC 94-12713. 304p. (J). 1995. 21.45 (*0-7868-6022-7*, Pub. by Hyperion) Little.

McCall, Timothy B. Examining Your Doctor: A Patient's Guide to Avoiding Harmful Medical Care. 224p. 1995. 18.95 (*1-55972-282-7*, Birch Ln Pr) Carol Pub Group.

McCall, Vicki B., jt. auth. see Lowenkamp, William.

McCall, Virginia. Sunrise: A Support Program for Children of Divorced Parents. LC 92-26329. 160p. 1992. pap. 12.95 (*0-8091-3330-X*) Paulist Pr.

***McCall, Walt.** Seagrave 70th Anniversary Series Photo Archive. (Illus.). 128p. 1999. pap. 29.95 (*1-58388-001-1*, 129098AE, Pub. by Iconografix) Motorbooks Intl.

***McCall, Walt & Lee, Matt.** Classic Seagrave, 1935-1951. (Photo Archives Ser.). (Illus.). 128p. 2000. pap. 29.95 (*1-58388-034-8*, 130629AE, Pub. by Iconografix) Motorbooks Intl.

McCall, Walt & McPherson, Tom. Classic American Ambulances 1900-1979 Photo Archive. LC 98-75268. (Photo Archives Ser.). (Illus.). 128p. 1999. pap. 29.95 (*1-882256-94-8*) Iconografix.

***McCall, Walt & McPherson, Tom.** Classic American Funeral Vehicles, 1900-1980: Photo Archive. LC 99-76053. (Illus.). 128p. 2000. pap. 29.95 (*1-58388-016-X*, 129954AE, Pub. by Iconografix) Motorbooks Intl.

McCall, Walter M. 80 Years of Cadillac LaSalle. LC 92-26171. (Crestline Ser.). (Illus.). 448p. 1992. 44.95 (*0-87938-676-2*, Crestline Pub) MBI Pubg.

McCall, Wayne, ed. see Andree, Herb, et al.

***McCall, Wendell.** Concerto in Dead Flat. 2000. pap. 12.95 (*1-890208-52-3*) Poisoned Pen.

McCall, Wendell. Concerto in Dead Flat: A Chris Klick Novel. LC 99-61906. 277p. 1999. 23.95 (*1-890208-18-3*) Poisoned Pen.

McCall, William A. & Crabbs, Lelah M. McCall Crabbs: Standard Test Lessons in Reading. 3rd ed. 1979. pap. text, teacher ed. 1.50 (*0-8077-5552-4*) Tchrs Coll.

— McCall Crabbs Bk. C: Standard Test Lessons in Reading. 3rd ed. (J). (gr. 5-7). 1979. pap. text 2.95 (*0-8077-5544-3*) Tchrs Coll.

— McCall Crabbs Bk. D: Standard Test Lessons in Reading. 3rd ed. (J). (gr. 6-8). 1979. pap. text 2.95 (*0-8077-5546-X*) Tchrs Coll.

— McCall Crabbs Bk. A: Standard Test Lessons in Reading. 3rd ed. (J). (gr. 3 5). 1979. pap. text 2.95 (*0-8077-5540-0*) Tchrs Coll.

— McCall Crabbs Bk. B: Standard Test Lessons in Reading. 3rd ed. (J). (gr. 4-6). 1979. pap. text 2.95 (*0-8077-5542-7*) Tchrs Coll.

— McCall Crabbs Bk. E: Standard Test Lessons in Reading. 3rd ed. (YA). (gr. 7-12). 1979. pap. text 2.95 (*0-8077-5548-6*) Tchrs Coll.

— McCall Crabbs Bk. F: Standard Test Lessons in Reading, Bk. F. 3rd ed. 1979. pap. text 2.95 (*0-8077-5550-8*) Tchrs Coll.

McCall, William A. & Harby, Mary L. Test Lessons in Primary Reading. 2nd ed. (J). (gr. 2-3). 1980. teacher ed. 2.95 (*0-8077-5966-X*) Tchrs Coll.

— Test Lessons in Primary Reading. 2nd ed. (J). (gr. 2-3). 1980. pap. text 3.95 (*0-8077-5965-1*) Tchrs Coll.

McCall, William A., et al. Test Lessons in Reading Figurative Language. (gr. 9-12). 1980. teacher ed. 1.95 (*0-8077-5971-6*) Tchrs Coll.

— Test Lessons in Reading Figurative Language. (YA). (gr. 9-12). 1980. pap. text 7.95 (*0-8077-5970-8*) Tchrs Coll.

McCall, Yvonne, ed. see Daniel, Glenda.

McCall, Yvonne, ed. see Roman, Alex.

McCall, Yvonne, ed. see Thomson-Daniel, Glenda.

McCall, Yvonne, ed. see Thomson-Daniel, Glenda G. & Thomson, Gabriel.

McCalla. Development of Canadian Capitalism. 1990. pap. text. write for info. (*0-7730-4943-6*) Addison-Wesley.

McCalla, Arthur. A Romantic Historiosophy: The Philosophy of History of Pierre-Simon Ballanche. LC 97-49398. (Studies in Intellectual History). ix, 464p. 1998. 162.00 (*90-04-10967-6*) Brill Academic Pubs.

McCalla, Douglas. The Upper Canada Trade, 1834 to 72: A Study of the Buchanans' Business. LC 79-323032. 239p. reprint ed. pap. 74.10 (*0-8357-8361-8*, 203400600088) Bks Demand.

McCalla, Gary, jt. auth. see Logue, John.

McCalla, Gord & Greer, Jim, eds. Student Modelling: The Key to Individualized Knowledge-Based Instruction. LC 94-2917. (NATO ASI Series F: Computer & Systems Sciences, Special Programme AET: Vol. 125). 1994. 107.05 (*0-387-57510-3*) Spr-Verlag.

Mccalla, Gordon, jt. auth. see Canadian Society For Computational Studies Of Inte.

McCalla, James. Jazz: A Listener's Guide. (Illus.). 192p. 1982. 17.50 (*0-13-510172-7*) P-H.

***McCalla, James.** Jazz: A Listener's Guide. 3rd ed. LC 99-29445. 216p. 1999. pap. 28.00 (*0-13-014545-9*) P-H.

McCalla, Robert B. Uncertain Perceptions: U. S. Cold War Crisis Decision Making. 240p. (C). 1992. text 44.50 (*0-472-10228-1*, 10228) U of Mich Pr.

McCalla, Robert J. The Maritime Provinces Atlas. 2nd ed. (Illus.). 96p. 1991. 29.95 (*0-921921-05-5*, Pub. by Formac Publ Co) Formac Dist Ltd.

McCalla, Robert J. Water Transportation in Canada. 259p. 1994. 39.95 (*0-88780-247-8*, Pub. by Formac Publ Co) Formac Dist Ltd.

McCalla, William J. Fundamentals of Computer-Aided Circuit Simulation. (C). 1987. text 121.00 (*0-89838-248-3*) Kluwer Academic.

McCallen, A. J. Follow Me. 48p. (J). 1989. pap. 3.95 (*0-8146-1797-2*) Liturgical Pr.

McCallen, Brian. Golf Magazine's Top 100 Courses You Can Play. LC 99-21273. (Illus.). 304p. 1999. 49.50 (*0-8109-4134-1*, Pub. by Abrams) Time Warner.

— Golf Resorts of the World: The Best Places to Stay & Play: A Golf Magazine Book. LC 93-21854. (Illus.). 304p. 1993. 49.50 (*0-8109-3372-1*, Pub. by Abrams) Time Warner.

McCalley, Bruce W. Model T Ford. LC 93-80697. (Illus.). 614p. 1994. 39.95 (*0-87341-293-1*, TF01) Krause Pubns.

McCalley, John W. Nantucket Yesterday & Today. (Illus.). 192p. (Orig.). 1981. pap. 13.95 (*0-486-24059-2*) Dover.

McCalley, Russell W. Marketing Channel Development & Management. LC 92-15768. 300p. 1992. 62.95 (*0-89930-780-9*, MKB, Quorum Bks) Greenwood.

— Marketing Channel Management: An Instructor's Manual. 80p. 1996. pap., teacher ed. 5.95 (*0-275-95547-8*, Praeger Pubs) Greenwood.

— Marketing Channel Management: People, Products, Programs & Markets. LC 95-26517. 288p. 1996. text 38.00 (*0-275-95439-0*, Praeger Pubs) Greenwood.

McCalley, Stuart W. & Neeson, Francis J. Photographic Case Studies in Cardiopulmonary Disease: Diagnostic Tests for the Practitioner. (Photographic Case Studies). 1993. pap. text. write for info. (*0-9633775-6-6*) Clinical Comms.

McCalley, Vivian, jt. auth. see Leeder, Ellen L.

McCallion, Barry. Art Maxims in a Bronx Fedora. 1973. pap. 1.75 (*0-911856-06-4*) Abyss.

McCallion, H. Vibration of Linear Mechanical Systems. LC 73-181235. 316p. reprint ed. pap. 98.00 (*0-608-11647-5*, 200638000058) Bks Demand.

McCallion, Jean. Tough Roots. 78p. 1987. 9.95 (*0-920806-94-5*, Pub. by Penumbra Pr) U of Toronto Pr.

McCallion, Kenneth F. Shoreham & the Rise & Fall of the Nuclear Power Industry. LC 94-32930. 256p. 1995. 62.95 (*0-275-94299-6*, Praeger Pubs) Greenwood.

McCallion, Michael. The Voice Book: For Actors, Public Speakers, & Everyone Who Wants to Make Best Use of Their Voice. 256p. 1988. 45.00 (*0-87830-986-1*, Thtre Arts Bks) Routledge.

McCallion, Phillip, jt. auth. see Toseland, Ronald.

McCallion, Phillip, jt. auth. see Toseland, Ronald W.

McCallion, Russell, ed. see Kao, Richard T.

***McCallister.** Computer Technician Certification. (Illus.). 554p. 2000. pap. 19.95 (*0-02-863757-7*, Arco) Macmillan Gen Ref.

McCallister, Bill. Work Force Management: Life-Changing Roles & Goals for Today's Christian Manager. LC 97-191583. 1997. pap. 9.99 (*0-88965-133-7*, Pub. by Horizon Books) Chr Pubns.

McCallister, Cynthia A. Reconceptualizing Literacy Methods Instruction: To Build a House That Remembers Its Forest. LC 95-45394. (Counterpoints: Vol. 28). XIV, 249p. (C). 1998. pap. text 29.95 (*0-8204-3082-X*) P Lang Pubng.

McCallister, Linda. I Wish I'd Said That! LC 92-7586. 313p. 1997. pap. 5.99 (*0-471-17687-7*) Wiley.

— I Wish I'd Said That: How to Talk Your Way Out of Trouble & into Success. LC 92-7586. 313p. 1992. 29.95 (*0-471-55551-7*) Wiley.

***McCallister, Linda.** Say What You Mean, Get What You Want. LC 98-36255. (Business Basics Ser.). 313p. 1998. pap. 12.95 (*0-471-32118-4*) Wiley.

***McCallister, Ron.** Frontier Medicine: Practicioners, Practices & Remedies on America's First Frontier, Northeast Tennessee, 1770-1850. (Illus.). 167p. 1999. pap. 9.95 (*0-9678307-0-2*, Pub. by Rocky Mount) Overmountain Pr.

McCall's Needlework & Crafts Editors. Xmas at Home. 1986. 22.95 (*0-02-609160-7*) Macmillan.

McCallum. Michigan Proficiency Pratice. 2nd ed. 1996. text 12.53 (*0-17-556995-9*) S&S Trade.

— Unsolved Mysteries. 1992. pap. text, student ed. write for info. (*0-17-555897-3*) Addison-Wesley.

McCallum, Albert D. Prostitutes, Margarine & Handguns. viii, 216p. (Orig.). 1996. pap. 9.00 (*0-9651659-0-6*) Pragmatic Publns.

McCallum, Barbara. More Than Beans & Cornbread: Traditional West Virginia Cooking. LC 93-86404. (Illus.). 200p. 1993. pap. text 12.95 (*0-929521-81-1*) Pictorial Hist.

McCallum, Bennett T. International Monetary Economics. (Illus.). 280p. (C). 1996. text 52.95 (*0-19-509494-8*) OUP.

— Monetary Economics: Theory & Policy. 352p. 1988. 34.95 (*0-02-948981-4*) Free Pr.

M

McCallum, Bennett T. Monetary Economics: Theory & Practice. 356p. (C). 1989. 75.00 (*0-02-378471-7*, Macmillan Coll) P-H.

McCallum, Brian K. Breaking the Bread of Revelation, Vol. 1. 150p. (Orig.). (C). 1988. pap. text 6.95 (*0-9620883-0-7*) McCallum Ministries.

— Israel - God's Glory Vol. 3: Breaking the Bread of Revelation. 160p. (Orig.). 1990. pap. text 6.95 (*0-9620883-2-3*) McCallum Ministries.

— Ministering Spirits Sent Forth. Mackall, Phyllis, ed. 225p. 1997. pap. 8.95 (*0-9620883-3-1*) McCallum Ministries.

— Seven Letters to Seven Churches Vol. 2: Breaking the Bread of Revelation. 105p. (Orig.). 1989. pap. 6.95 (*0-9620883-1-5*) McCallum Ministries.

— You & All Your House. Mackall, Phyllis, ed. 70p. 1998. pap. 4.95 (*0-9620883-4-X*) McCallum Ministries.

McCallum, Chriss. How to Write for Publication: Your Practical Guide to Success. 3rd ed. (Illus.). 192p. 1995. pap. 19.95 (*1-85703-140-7*, Pub. by How To Bks) Trans-Atl Phila.

— Writing for Publication: How to Sell Your Work & Succeed as a Writer. 4th ed. (Successful Writing Ser.). (Illus.). 192p. 1997. pap. 22.50 (*1-85703-226-8*, Pub. by How To Bks) Trans-Atl Phila.

McCallum, Corrie. Expressions: Images & Poems. LC 97-41610. 1997. pap. 8.95 (*0-910326-24-X*) Carolina Art.

M

McCallum, D. S. C. I. I. Liability Insurance, No. 220. (C). 1981. suppl. ed. 230.00 (*0-7855-4287-6*, Pub. by Witherby & Co) St Mut.

McCallum, David. The Social Production of Merit: Education, Psychology & Politics in Australia, 1900-1950. 224p. 1990. 65.00 (*1-85000-859-0*, Falmer Pr); pap. 29.95 (*1-85000-864-7*, Falmer Pr) Taylor & Francis.

— The Social Production of Merit: Education, Psychology & Politics in Australia 1900-1950. 224p. 1990. 50.00 (*1-85000-922-8*, Falmer Pr); pap. 22.00 (*1-85000-923-6*, Falmer Pr) Taylor & Francis.

McCallum, David B., jt. auth. see Grana, John M.

McCallum, Dennis. Christianity: The Faith That Makes Sense. 1997. mass mkt. 4.99 (*0-8423-0535-1*) Tyndale Hse.

McCallum, Dennis, ed. The Death of Truth: Finding Your Way Through the Maze of Multiculturism, Inclusivism, & the New Postmodern Diversity. LC 95-45770. 288p. (Orig.). 1996. pap. 11.99 (*1-55661-724-0*) Bethany Hse.

McCallum, Donald F. Zenkoji & Its Icon: A Study in Medieval Japanese Religious Art. LC 93-41543. 352p. 1994. text 45.00 (*0-691-03203-3*, Pub. by Princeton U Pr) Cal Prin Full Svc.

McCallum, E. L. Object Lessons: How to Do Things with Fetishism. LC 98-13179. (Series in Psychoanalysis & Culture). 192p. (C). 1998. text 59.50 (*0-7914-3979-8*); pap. text 19.95 (*0-7914-3980-1*) State U NY Pr.

McCallum, Frances T., jt. auth. see McCallum, Henry D.

McCallum, George P. Idiom Drills:for Students Of Esl. 2nd ed. (College ESL). (J). 1982. mass mkt. 21.95 (*0-8384-2853-3*) Heinle & Heinle.

— One Hundred & One Word Games. 176p. 1980. pap. text 12.50 (*0-19-502742-6*) OUP.

McCallum, George P., adapted by. Seven Plays from American Literature. rev. ed. 1977. pap. 3.75 (*0-87789-062-5*); audio 39.50 (*0-87789-126-5*) ELS Educ Servs.

McCallum George P., George P. Michigan Proficiency Practice Tests. 2nd ed. 1996. pap. text 11.90 (*0-17-557000-0*) Addison-Wesley.

McCallum, H. J. Tibet: One Second to Live. unabridged ed. Tracy, Charles L., ed. Needham, Lesley, tr. (Illus.). 339p. (Orig.). 1995. pap. 17.50 (*0-9651610-0-5*, 001) H J McCallum.

***McCallum, Hamish, et al.** Population Parameters: Estimation for Ecological Models. (Illus.). 2000. pap. 79.00 (*0-86542-740-2*) Blackwell Sci.

McCallum, Henry D. & McCallum, Frances T. The Wire That Fenced the West. LC 65-11234. (Illus.). 1985. pap. 17.95 (*0-8061-1559-9*) U of Okla Pr.

***McCallum, Iain.** Blood Brothers: The Lives & Times of Hiram & Hudson Maxim. 1999. 36.95 (*1-86176-096-5*, Chatham Pubg) G Duckworth.

McCallum, Ian, jt. auth. see Sumner, Raymond.

McCallum, Jack. Dream Team: The Inside Story of the Nineteen Ninety-Two U. S. Olympic Basketball Team. 1992. 19.95 (*0-316-55370-0*) Little.

McCallum, James. History of Giles County, Tennessee. 125p. 1983. reprint ed. pap. 15.00 (*0-89308-326-7*, TN 27) Southern Hist Pr.

McCallum, James D. Eleazar Wheelock. LC 78-89200. (American Education: Its Men, Institutions, & Ideas. Series 1). 1975. reprint ed. 24.95 (*0-405-01439-2*) Ayer.

***McCallum, James T.** Irwin Toys: The Canadian Star Wars Connection. (Illus.). 120p. 2000. pap. 19.95 (*1-896522-38-6*) CN06.

McCallum, Jodi. Fun with Bible Friends. 1999. pap. text 2.49 (*0-7847-0760-X*) Standard Pub.

***McCallum, Jodi.** God Made Me! 1999. pap. 2.49 (*0-7847-0981-5*) Standard Pub.

McCallum, Jodi. Good Manners & the Golden Rule. 1999. pap. 2.49 (*0-7847-0885-1*) Standard Pub.

McCallum, Jodie. My Bible Pals Storybook: Learning with Friends from the Bible & Today. (My Bible Pals Ser.). 128p. (J). (ps-k). 1996. 9.99 (*0-7847-0529-1*, 02749) Standard Pub.

McCallum, John. The Complete Keys to Progress. Strossen, Randall J., ed. LC 93-80635. 288p. (Orig.). 1993. pap. 17.95 (*0-926888-01-3*) IronMind Enterprises.

— Unequal Beginnings: Agriculture & Economic Development in Quebec & Ontario until 1870. (State & Economic Life Ser.). 1980. pap. 15.95 (*0-8020-6362-4*) U of Toronto Pr.

— Unequal Beginnings: Agriculture & Economic Development in Quebec & Ontario until 1870. LC 80-501832. (State & Economic Life Ser.: No. 2). 159p. reprint ed. pap. 49.30 (*0-8357-4026-9*, 203671800005) Bks Demand.

McCallum, John & Geiselhart, Karin. Australia's New Aged: Issues for Young & Old. LC 97-129758. 160p. 1997. pap. 24.95 (*1-86448-218-4*, Pub. by Allen & Unwin Pty) Paul & Co Pubs.

McCallum, Karen T. & Granovetter, Pamela. The Copperfield Checklist of Mystery Authors. 2nd ed. (Copperfield Collections: Vol. 2). 160p. (Orig.). 1992. reprint ed. pap. 6.95 (*0-9617037-1-7*) Copperfld NY.

— A Shopping List of Mystery Classics. (Copperfield Collections: Vol. 1). 96p. (Orig.). 1986. pap. 6.95 (*0-9617037-0-9*) Copperfld NY.

McCallum, Karen T., ed. see Cohen, Larry.

McCallum, Kent. Old Sturbridge Village. Larkin, Jack, ed. LC 96-6909. (Illus.). 224p. 1996. 45.00 (*0-8109-3686-0*, Pub. by Abrams) Time Warner.

McCallum, Lawrence. Italian Horror Films of the 1960s: A Critical Catalog of 62 Chillers. LC 98-22473. 288p. 1998. lib. bdg. 45.00 (*0-7864-0435-3*) McFarland & Co.

***McCallum, Mary.** Greece. (Illus.). 1999. pap. write for info. (*960-540-039-1*) M Toumpis.

McCallum, Mary & Piper, William E., eds. Psychological Mindedness: A Contemporary Understanding. LC 97-2440. (Personality & Clinical Psychology Ser.). (Illus.). 375p. 1997. text. write for info. (*0-8058-1722-0*) L Erlbaum Assocs.

McCallum, Pat. Stepping Free of Limiting Patterns with Essence Repatterning. 135p. 1992. pap. 16.00 (*0-9634488-0-3*) Source Unltd.

McCallum, Peter, jt. auth. see Lang, Moshe.

McCallum, R. & Bracken, Bruce A. Nonverbal Assessment of Intelligence. (C). 1995. 32.95 (*0-205-15765-3*, Macmillan Coll) P-H.

McCallum, R. B. & Readman, Alison. British General Election of 1945. 311p. 1964. 35.00 (*0-7146-1566-8*, Pub. by F Cass Pubs) Intl Spec Bk.

McCallum, R. C. Australian Labour Law: Cases & Materials. boxed set. write for info. (*0-409-30781-5*, Austral, MICHIE) LEXIS Pub.

— Australian Labour Law: Cases & Materials. 3rd ed. 1994. pap. 138.00 (*0-409-30731-9*, Austral, MICHIE) LEXIS Pub.

McCallum, R. C., jt. ed. see Ronfeldt, Paul.

McCallum, R. I., jt. ed. see Jardine, F. M.

McCallum, Richard W. Gastrointestinal Pharmacology. LC 96-41245. 752p. 1996. text 170.00 (*0-397-51625-8*, Lippnctt) Lppncott W & W.

McCallum, Richard W. & Whitlow, Robert. Linking Mathematics & Language: Practical Classroom Activities. (The Pippin Teacher's Library Ser.). 140p. 1994. pap. 17.00 (*0-88751-038-8*, 00765) Heinemann.

McCallum, Richard W., jt. ed. see Chen, Jiande Z.

McCallum, Robyn. Ideologies of Identity in Adolescent Fiction: The Dialogic Construction of Subjectivity. Zipes, Jack D., ed. LC 98-37713. (Children's Literature & Culture Ser.: No. 8). 304p. 1999. 62.00 (*0-8153-2290-9*) Garland.

McCallum, Robyn, jt. auth. see Stephens, John.

McCallum, Rod, des. Plotting Sheets & Sight Forms for Yachtsmen. (C). 1989. 35.00 (*0-7855-5957-4*, Pub. by Laurie Norie & Wilson Ltd) St Mut.

McCallum, Ron, et al, eds. Employment Security. 1994. pap. 49.00 (*1-86287-146-9*, Pub. by Federation Pr) Gaunt.

***McCallum, Ronald.** Employer Controls over Private Life. (Frontline Ser.). 64p. 1999. pap. 9.95 (*0-86840-450-0*, Pub. by NSW U Pr) Intl Spec Bk.

McCallum, Ross A. Franchising: An Accounting, Auditing, & Income Tax Guide. 416p. 1993. 190.00 (*0-471-59119-X*) Wiley.

McCallum, Sally & Ertel, Monica, eds. Automated Systems for Access to Multilingual & Multiscript Library Materials: Proceedings of the Second IFLA Satellite Meeting, Madrid, August 18-19, 1993, 70. LC 95-130494. (IFLA Publications: vol. 70). 185p. 1994. 65.00 (*3-598-21797-8*) K G Saur Verlag.

McCallum, Scott. The Christian Life - An Owner's Manual: A Basic Guide to Spiritual Growth. LC 95-8344. 144p. 1995. pap. 8.99 (*0-8254-3194-8*, 95-027) Kregel.

McCallum, Shara. The Water Between Us. LC 99-6564. (Pitt Poetry Ser.). 96p. 1999. pap. 12.95 (*0-8229-5710-8*) U of Pittsburgh Pr.

McCallum, Sheila & Strong, Anne. Starting Work in Sales. 128p. (C). 1987. 80.00 (*0-946139-27-X*, Pub. by Elm Pubns) St Mut.

McCallum, Stephen E. Low, Low Tide & Collected Stories. LC 98-89475. 375p. 1998. text 25.00 (*0-7388-0277-8*); pap. text 15.00 (*0-7388-0278-6*) Xlibris Corp.

***McCallum, Steven, et al.** Essentials of Nonverbal Assessment. (Essentials of Psychological Assessment Ser.). 2000. pap. 29.95 (*0-471-38318-X*) Wiley.

McCallum, Taffy G. South Africa: Land of Hope. 2nd ed. 1990. 21.95 (*0-620-14195-6*) Fielden Bks.

McCallum, Taffy G., told to. White Woman Witch Doctor: Tales of the African Life of Rae Graham. LC 92-72451. 248p. 1992. 22.95 (*0-9633721-8-1*) Fielden Bks.

McCallum, Tammy H. Dared to Dream. (Scarlet Ser.). 1997. mass mkt. 3.99 (*1-85487-985-5*, Pub. by Scarlet Bks) London Brdge.

McCallum, Toshiko M. Containing Beauty: Japanese Bamboo Flower Baskets. LC 88-50730. (Illus.). 96p. 1988. 40.00 (*0-930741-15-3*); pap. 27.00 (*0-930741-16-1*) UCLA Fowler Mus.

McCallum, W. C. & Curry, S. H. Slow Potential Changes in the Human Brain. LC 93-26280. (NATO ASI Ser.: Vol. 254). (Illus.). 326p. (C). 1993. text 114.00 (*0-306-44596-4*, Kluwer Plenum) Kluwer Academic.

McCallum, William G., et al. Applied Calculus for Business, Life & Social Sciences. 504p. 1998. pap. 87.95 (*0-471-10876-6*) Wiley.

— Multivariable Calculus. LC 97-133524. 528p. 1997. pap. 75.95 (*0-471-31151-0*) Wiley.

McCallum, William G., et al. Multivariable Calculus & Mathematica. 528p. 1997. pap. text, student ed. 139.95 (*0-471-19757-2*) Wiley.

— Multivariable Calculus & Mathematica Student Version. 528p. 1997. pap. text 139.95 (*0-471-19756-4*) Wiley.

McCallum, William G., et al. Multivariable Calculus, Student Solutions Manual. 168p. 1997. pap. 25.95 (*0-471-17356-8*) Wiley.

McCally, David. The Everglades: An Environmental History. LC 99-18766. (Illus.). 288p. 1999. 39.95 (*0-8130-1648-7*) U Press Fla.

***McCally, David.** The Everglades: An Environmental History. 2000. reprint ed. pap. 19.95 (*0-8130-1827-7*) U Press Fla.

McCally, John F. Capitation for Physicians: How to Negotiate the Contract, Maximie Reimbursement, & Manage Financial Risk. LC 96-6446. (HFMA Management Ser.). (Illus.). 240p. 1996. text 45.00 (*0-7863-1006-5*, Irwn Prfssnl) McGraw-Hill Prof.

— Capitation for Physicians: Understanding & Negotiating Contracts to Maximize Reimbursement & Manage Financial Risk. 1996. text 40.00 (*0-7863-1149-5*, Irwn Prfssnl) McGraw-Hill Prof.

— The Gatekeeper: A Guide to Capitation for the Primary Care Physician. 200p. 1995. 40.00 (*1-55738-634-X*, Irwn Prfssnl) McGraw-Hill Prof.

McCally, Regina W. The Secret of Mojo: The Story of the Odessa, Texas, Permian High School Football Team. Baldwin, James, ed. LC 86-90445. 236p. 1986. 20.00 (*0-9619703-0-8*) R W McCally.

McCalman, Iain. An Oxford Companion to the Romantic Age: British Culture, 1776-1832. (Illus.). 800p. 1999. text 150.00 (*0-19-812297-7*) OUP.

— Radical Underworld: Prophets, Revolutionaries & Pornographers in London, 1795-1840. (Illus.). 358p. 1993. pap. text 19.95 (*0-19-812286-1*) OUP.

McCalman, Ian, ed. see Wedderburn, Robert.

McCalman, James. The Electronics Industry in Britain: Coping with Change. 176p. 1989. 59.95 (*0-415-00031-9*) Routledge.

— The Electronics Industry in Britain: Coping with Change. LC 89-139757. 189p. reprint ed. pap. 58.60 (*0-608-20361-0*, 207161400002) Bks Demand.

McCalman, James & Paton, Robert A. Change Management: A Guide to Effective Implementation. 256p. 1992. pap. 35.00 (*1-85396-155-8*, Pub. by P Chapman) Taylor & Francis.

McCalman, James, jt. auth. see Buchanan, David A.

McCalman, Janet. Journeyings: The Biography of a Middle-Class Generation 1920-1990. 480p. 1995. pap. 19.95 (*0-522-84675-0*, Pub. by Melbourne Univ Pr) Paul & Co Pubs.

— Sex & Suffering: Women's Health & a Women's Hospital. LC 99-20663. (Illus.). 420p. 1999. pap. 17.95 (*0-8018-6226-4*) Johns Hopkins.

***McCalman, Janet.** Sex & Suffering: Women's Health & a Women's Hospital: The Royal Women's Hospital, Melbourne, 1856-1996. 432p. 1999. 39.95 (*0-522-84837-0*, Pub. by Melbourne Univ Pr) Paul & Co Pubs.

McCalman, Janet. Struggletown: Public & Private Life in Richmond, 1900. 154p. (Orig.). 1994. pap. 24.95 (*0-522-84303-4*, Pub. by Melbourne Univ Pr) Paul & Co Pubs.

***McCalmly, Tre.** The Palm Decoder. 144p. 1999. pap. text 19.95 (*0-7641-1186-8*) Barron.

McCalpin, Deborah J., et al, eds. Health Media Review Index, Nineteen Eighty-Four to Nineteen Eighty-Six: A Guide to Reviews & Descriptions of Commercially Available Nonprint Material for the Medical, Mental, Allied Healthy Human Service, & Related Counseling Professions. LC 88-18452. 771p. 1988. 55.50 (*0-8108-2172-9*) Scarecrow.

McCalpin, James P. Neotectonic Deformation along the East Cache Fault Zone, Cache County, Utah. (Special Study of the Utah Geological Survey Ser.: Vol. 83, No. 5). (Illus.). 37p. (Orig.). 1994. pap. 5.00 (*1-55791-202-5*, SS83) Utah Geological Survey.

— Paleoseismology. (Illus.). 588p. (C). 1998. pap. text 49.95 (*0-12-481826-9*) Acad Pr.

— Quaternary Geology & Neotectonics of the West Flank of the Northern Sangre de Cristo Mountains, South-Central Colorado. Raese, Jon W. & Goldberg, J. H., eds. LC 82-17899. (Colorado School of Mines Quarterly Ser.: Vol. 77, No. 3). 97p. 1983. pap. text 12.00 (*0-686-82132-7*) Colo Sch Mines.

McCalpin, James P. & Nelson, Alan R., eds. Paleoseismology. (International Geophysics Ser.: Vol. 62). (Illus.). 588p. (C). 1996. text 89.95 (*0-12-481825-0*) Acad Pr.

McCamant, Kathryn M. & Durrett, Charles R. Cohousing. 2nd rev. ed. LC 93-17381. (Illus.). 288p. 1994. pap. 29.95 (*0-89815-539-8*) Ten Speed Pr.

***McCambridge, Michael.** ESPN Sports Century. limited ed. 288p. 1999. 100.00 (*0-7868-6633-0*, Pub. by Disney Pr) Time Warner.

McCambridge, Michael, ed. ESPN SportsCentury. LC 99-27715. 256p. 1999. text 40.00 (*0-7868-6471-0*, Pub. by Hyperion) Time Warner.

***McCamley, Nick.** Secret Cold War Nuclear Bunkers. 2000. 29.95 (*0-85052-746-5*, Pub. by Pen & Sword Bks Ltd) Combined Pub.

— Secret Underground Cities. (Illus.). 273p. 2000. pap. 27.95 (*0-85052-733-3*, Pub. by Leo Cooper) Combined Pub.

McCammant, Wallace. George Washington the Mason. 50p. 1998. reprint ed. pap. 9.95 (*0-7661-0259-9*) Kessinger Pub.

***McCammon.** Boston Terrier: The American Gentleman. (Illus.). 224p. 2000. 24.99 (*1-58245-154-0*) Howell Bks.

McCammon & Knox. Making Choices in Sexuality: Research & Application with InfoTrac. (Psychology Ser.). 1998. pap. 28.00 incl. cd-rom (*0-534-36353-9*) Brooks-Cole.

McCammon, A. L. Currencies of the Anglo Norman Isles. (Illus.). 1984. lib. bdg. 60.00 (*0-907605-13-3*) S J Durst.

McCammon, Chuck, ed. Air Sampling Instrument Selection Guide: Indoor Air Quality. 56p. 1998. pap. text 25.00 (*1-882417-27-5*, 9852) Am Conf Govt Indus Hygienist.

McCammon, Laura, jt. auth. see Norris, Joel.

McCammon, Robert R. Baal. Peters, Sally, ed. 1988. mass mkt. 6.99 (*0-671-73774-0*) PB.

— Bethany's Sin. Peters, Sally, ed. 1988. mass mkt. 5.99 (*0-671-73775-9*) PB.

— Blue World. Peters, Sally, ed. 464p. 1990. per. 6.99 (*0-671-69518-5*) PB.

— Boy's Life. large type ed. 644p. 1992. reprint ed. lib. bdg. 21.95 (*1-56054-326-4*) Thorndike Pr.

— Boy's Life. large type ed. 644p. 1992. reprint ed. 14.95 (*1-56054-938-6*) Thorndike Pr.

— Boy's Life. Peters, Sally, ed. 592p. 1992. reprint ed. mass mkt. 7.50 (*0-671-74305-8*) PB.

— Boy's Life & Gone South. LC 97-36491. 1998. 12.00 (*0-671-01883-3*) PB.

— Gone South. 400p. 1993. reprint ed. mass mkt. 6.99 (*0-671-74307-4*, Pocket Star Bks) PB.

— Mine. Grose, Bill, ed. 496p. 1991. reprint ed. per. 6.99 (*0-671-73944-1*) PB.

— Mystery Walk. Peters, Sally, ed. 432p. 1992. reprint ed. per. 10.99 (*0-671-76991-X*) PB.

— Night Boat. Peters, Sally, ed. 1988. mass mkt. 5.99 (*0-671-73281-1*) PB.

— Stinger. Peters, Sally, ed. 512p. 1988. per. 7.50 (*0-671-73776-7*) PB.

— Swan Song. Peters, Sally, ed. 956p. 1987. per. 7.99 (*0-671-74103-9*) PB.

— Usher's Passing. Peters, Sally, ed. 416p. 1992. reprint ed. mass mkt. 6.99 (*0-671-76992-8*) PB.

— The Wolf's Hour. 1990. mass mkt. 6.99 (*0-671-73142-4*) PB.

McCammon, Susan, et al. Making Choices in Sexuality: Research & Applications. LC 97-41780. 1997. pap. 30.25 (*0-534-35595-1*) Brooks-Cole.

McCampbell, B. Harrison. Problems in Roofing Design. (Illus.). 256p. 1991. pap. text 54.95 (*0-7506-9162-X*) Buttrwrth-Heinemann.

McCampbell, Coleman. Saga of a Frontier Seaport. 1993. reprint ed. lib. bdg. 75.00 (*0-7812-5945-2*) Rprt Serv.

McCampbell, Darlene, jt. selected by see Rochman, Hazel.

McCampbell, Darlene Z., jt. auth. see Rochman, Hazel.

McCampbell, Darlene Z., jt. ed. see Rochman, Hazel.

McCampbell, Darlene Z., jt. selected by see Rochman, Hazel.

McCampbell, Debbie L. Natural Bridges. LC 96-19007. 246p. 1997. 24.00 (*1-877946-79-6*) Permanent Pr.

McCampbell, Linda, jt. auth. see Rentfro, Anne R.

McCamy, James L. The Quality of the Environment. LC 72-80576. 1972. 19.95 (*0-02-920480-1*) Free Pr.

McCamy, Ronald. Out of a Kantian Chrysalis? A Maritainian Critique of Fr. Marechal, Vol. 182. LC 97-10691. (American University Studies: No. V). XV, 180p. (C). 1998. pap. text 24.95 (*0-8204-3722-0*) P Lang Pubng.

McCan, Robert L. World Economy & World Hunger: The Response of the Churches. 119p. (C). 1982. lib. bdg. 45.00 (*0-313-27078-3*, U7078) Greenwood.

McCance, Dawne. Posts: Re Addressing the Ethical. LC 95-33677. (SUNY Series in Postmodern Culture). 169p. (C). 1996. text 46.50 (*0-7914-3001-4*); pap. text 14.95 (*0-7914-3002-2*) State U NY Pr.

McCance, Dennis J. Human Tumor Viruses. LC 98-12185. (Illus.). 375p. 1998. 79.95 (*1-55581-130-2*) ASM Pr.

McCance, Kathryn L. Pathophysiology: A Physiological Approach. 2nd ed. 1696p. (C). (gr. 13). 1993. text, teacher ed. 34.00 (*0-8151-5749-5*, 24200) Mosby Inc.

McCance, Kathryn L. & Huether, Sue E. Pathophysiology: The Biological Basis for Disease in Adults & Children. 3rd ed. LC 97-22899. (Illus.). 1728p. (C). (gr. 13). 1997. text 66.00 (*0-8151-9481-1*, 29322) Mosby Inc.

***McCance, Kathryn L. & Huether, Sue E.** Pathophysiology: The Biological Basis for Disease in Adults & Children. 3rd ed. (Illus.). 400p. 1998. student ed. write for info. (*0-8151-3766-4*) Mosby Inc.

— Pathophysiology: The Biological Basis for Disease in Adults & Children, Includes Testbank. 3rd ed. (Illus.). 1998. teacher ed. write for info. (*1-55664-433-7*) Mosby Inc.

McCance, Kathryn L., jt. auth. see Heuther, Sue E.

McCance, Kathryn L., jt. auth. see Huether, Sue E.

McCance-Katz, Elinore F. & Kosten, Thomas R., eds. New Treatments for Chemical Addictions. (Review of Psychiatry Ser.). 211p. 1998. pap. text 31.00 (*0-88048-838-7*, 8838) Am Psychiatric.

McCance, M. E., jt. auth. see Widdows.

McCance, Robert M., Jr., ed. see Andreas, Barbara K., et al.

McCandless, Amy T. The Past in the Present: A History of Women's Higher Education in the Twentieth-Century South. LC 98-40089. 1999. write for info. (*0-8173-0945-4*) U of Ala Pr.

McCandless, Amy Thompson. The Past in the Present: Women's Higher Education in the Twentieth-Century American South LC 98-40089. 1999. 24.95 (*0-8173-0994-2*) U of Ala Pr.

McCandless, Barbara. Equal Before the Lens: Jno. Trlica's Photographs of Granger, Texas. LC 91-26693. (Charles & Elizabeth Prothro Texas Photography Ser.: No. 3). (Illus.). 208p. 1992. 34.50 (*0-89096-486-6*) Tex A&M Univ Pr.

An Asterisk (*) at the beginning of an entry indicates that the title is appearing for the first time.

McCandless, Bruce, 3rd, ed. see Casey, John L.

McCandless, D. W., ed. Cerebral Energy Metabolism & Metabolic Encephalopathy. 478p. 1985. 125.00 (*0-306-41797-9*, Plenum Trade) Perseus Pubng.

McCandless, David. Gender & Performance in Shakespeare's Problem Comedies. LC 97-3934. (Drama & Performance Studies Ser.). 1997. 27.95 (*0-253-33306-7*) Ind U Pr.

McCandless, George T., Jr. & Wallace, Neil. Introduction to Dynamic Macroeconomic Theory: An Overlapping Generations Approach. 372p. (C). 1992. 48.95 (*0-674-46111-8*) HUP.

McCandless, Janet & McCandless, Keith. 5-Minute Relaxation. (Illus.). 40p. 1999. pap. write for info. (*1-893975-00-2*) Vienna St Pubg.

McCandless, Jaquelyn, jt. auth. see Zimmerman, Jack.

McCandless, Kate, tr. see Murata Kyuzo.

McCandless, Keith. Relaxation Diet Plan. (Illus.). 60p. 1999. pap. 14.95 (*1-893975-01-0*) Vienna St Pubg.

McCandless, Keith, jt. auth. see McCandless, Janet.

McCandless, N. Jane & Cintron, Myrna, eds. Women: Contemporary Issues & Perspectives. (Studies in Social Sciences). 100p. (Orig.). 1993. pap. text 5.00 (*1-883199-01-8*) St U W Georgia.

McCandless, Perry & Foley, William E. Missouri: Then & Now. 48p. 1992. 3.50 (*0-8262-0830-4*) U of Mo Pr.

— Missouri: Then & Now. rev. ed. LC 90-32545. (Illus.). 328p. (J). (gr. 4). 1992. text 19.95 (*0-8262-0825-8*) U of Mo Pr.

McCandless, Peter. Moonlight, Magnolias, & Madness: Insanity in South Carolina from the Colonial to the Progressive Eras. LC 95-16641. (Illus.). 432p. (C). 1996. pap. text 19.95 (*0-8078-4558-2*); lib. bdg. 55.00 (*0-8078-2251-5*) U of NC Pr.

McCandless, Stanley. Method of Lighting the Stage. 4th ed. LC 56-10331. 1958. 14.95 (*0-87830-082-1*, Thtre Arts Bks) Routledge.

McCandless, Susan K., tr. see Namikoshi, Toru.

McCandless, W., jt. auth. see Campbell, B.

McCandlish, David B. McCandlish Family History. (Illus.). 1991. 50.00 (*0-9619300-0-4*) D McCandlish.

— McCandlish Family History. 3rd ed. (Illus.). 1993. 49.00 (*0-9619300-2-0*) D McCandlish.

***McCandlish, Earl A.** Crash Boat: Wartime Missions of the P-399, Guadalcanal to the Philippines. LC 99-69830. (Illus.). 248p. 2000. 24.95 (*0-9678042-0-5*, Bowsprit Pr) Tall Ships Bks.

McCandlish, L. E., et al, eds. Multicomponent Ultrafine Microstructures Vol. 132: Materials Research Society Symposium Proceedings. 243p. 1989. text 17.50 (*1-55899-005-4*) Materials Res.

McCandliss, Adam, jt. auth. see Brooks, Dierdre.

McCandliss, Bill & Watson, Albert. Problemoids: Level IV. 1988. pap., teacher ed. 15.00 (*0-89824-188-X*); pap., student ed. 4.99 (*0-89824-189-8*) Trillium Pr.

— Problemoids: Math Challenge, Grade 5. 1982. pap., student ed. 4.99 (*0-89824-033-6*) Trillium Pr.

— Problemoids: Math Challenge, Grade 5. 1984. pap., teacher ed. 10.00 (*0-89824-070-0*); pap., suppl. ed. 1.00 (*0-89824-069-7*) Trillium Pr.

— Problemoids: Math Challenge, Grade 5. 1986. pap., teacher ed. 15.00 (*0-89824-044-1*) Trillium Pr.

— Problemoids: Math Challenge, Grade 6. 1983. pap., teacher ed. 15.00 (*0-89824-039-5*); pap., student ed. 4.99 (*0-89824-038-7*); pap., student ed., suppl. ed. 1.00 (*0-89824-071-9*) Trillium Pr.

— Problemoids: Math Challenge, Grade 6, Cards. 1983. 10.00 (*0-89824-072-7*) Trillium Pr.

McCane, Byron R., et al. Building a Faith to Live By: Programs for Youth. LC 87-3689. 143p. 1987. reprint ed. pap. 44.40 (*0-608-00218-6*, 206101200006) Bks Demand.

McCane, M. E., jt. auth. see Widdows.

McCaney, Kevin, ed. see Eveland, Thomas.

McCanles, M. The Discourse of (Machiavelli's) "Il Principe" 154p. 1983. pap. 26.00 (*0-89003-149-5*) Undena Pubns.

McCanles, Michael. Jonsonian Discriminations: The Humanist Poet & the Praise of True Nobility. 352p. 1992. text 65.00 (*0-8020-5955-4*) U of Toronto Pr.

— The Text of Sidney's Arcadian World. LC 88-26742. 224p. (C). 1989. text 46.95 (*0-8223-0797-9*) Duke.

McCanless, Christel L. Faberge & His Works: An Annotated Bibliography of the First Century of His Art. LC 93-46653. (Illus.). 454p. 1994. 58.00 (*0-8108-2836-7*) Scarecrow.

McCanless, William, ed. see Benefiel, Robert.

McCanlies, Tim. Harlem. 192p. (Orig.). 1994. mass mkt. 4.95 (*0-87067-699-7*, BH699-7) Holloway.

McCann. Brazil & the United States. 1995. 24.95 (*0-8057-7921-3*, Twyne) Mac Lib Ref.

— Brazil & the United States. 1996. pap. 14.95 (*0-8057-9218-X*) Macmillan.

***McCann.** Morecambe & Wise. 2000. pap. 17.95 (*1-85702-911-9*, Pub. by Fourth Estate) Trafalgar.

McCann. War & an Irish Town. 2nd rev. ed. LC 93-36051. 176p. (C). 95.95 (*0-7453-0830-9*, Pub. by Pluto GBR); pap. 29.95 (*0-7453-0725-6*, Pub. by Pluto GBR) Stylus Pub VA.

McCann, jt. auth. see Stewin.

McCann, tr. see So Chong-Ju.

McCann, Al. We Hold These Truths. LC 98-183544. 1998. pap. 12.95 (*0-9635272-3-1*, BK103) Pillar TX.

McCann, Andrew. Cultural Politics in the 1790's: Literature, Radicalism & the Public Sphere. LC 98-22100. xi, 240 p. 1999. 59.95 (*0-333-73498-X*) St Martin.

McCann, Anna M. Roman Sarcophagi in The Metropolitan Museum of Art. LC 77-28089. (Illus.). 152p. 1978. 25.00 (*0-87099-173-6*) Metro Mus Art.

McCann, Anna M. & Bourgeois, Joanne. The Roman Port & Fishery of Cosa: A Center of Ancient Trade. LC 85-42693. (Illus.). 615p. reprint ed. pap. 190.70 (*0-608-06479-3*, 206677600009) Bks Demand.

McCann, Anna M. & Freed, Joann. Deep Water Archaeology: A Late-Roman Ship from Carthage & an Ancient Trade Route Near Skerki Bank off Northwest Sicily. (JRA Supplementary Ser.: No. 13). (Illus.). 160p. 1994. 64.50 (*1-887829-13-X*) Jour Roman Arch.

McCann, Anne G. Contemporary Mexican Cooking: Recipes from Great Texas Chiefs. (Illus.). 240p. 1996. 29.95 (*0-87719-273-1*, 9273) Gulf Pub.

McCann, Annes, ed. Fundamental Principles of Gas Turbines. (Illus.). 88p. 1980. pap. 14.00 (*0-88698-147-6*, 1.76010) PETEX.

McCann, Annes & Whalen, Bruce R. Basic Instrumentation Instructor's Guide. 3rd ed. (Illus.). 104p. (Orig.). 1984. pap. text, teacher ed. 15.00 (*0-88698-141-7*, 1.20037) PETEX.

— Basic Instrumentation Workbook. 3rd ed. 75p. (Orig.). 1984. pap. text 15.00 (*0-88698-142-5*, 1.20036) PETEX.

McCann, Annes, ed. see Diener, Dan.

McCann, Annes, jt. ed. see Reynolds, Jeanette.

McCann-Baker, Annes & Whalen, Bruce. Field Handling of Natural Gas Workbook. Leecraft, Jodie, ed. 46p. (Orig.). 1988. pap., wbk. ed. 18.00 (*0-88698-182-4*, 3.10046) PETEX.

McCann, Brian, jt. ed. see Robinson, Jeffrey.

McCann, C. Trees of India, a Popular Handbook. (C). 1988. text 85.00 (*0-7855-6005-X*, Pub. by Scientific) St Mut.

McCann, C., jt. auth. see Blatter, E.

***McCann, C. Dagan.** New York @ Night: A Personal Guide to New York's Nightlife. (Illus.). 2000. pap. 11.95 (*0-9660570-5-8*) Preserv Pubns.

McCann, Carole R. Birth Control Politics in the United States, 1916-1945. 256p. 1994. text 32.50 (*0-8014-2490-9*) Cornell U Pr.

***McCann, Carole R.** Birth Control, Politics in the United States, 1916-1945. 1999. pap. text 16.95 (*0-8014-8612-2*) Cornell U Pr.

***McCann, Carole R. & Pigeau, Ross.** The Human in Command: Exploring the Modern Military Experience. LC 99-89695. 428p. 2000. 165.00 (*0-306-46366-0*, Kluwer Plenum) Kluwer Academic.

McCann, Charles R. John Maynard Keynes: Critical Responses. LC 97-12924. 1632p. (C). 1998. 700.00 (*0-415-15193-7*) Routledge.

McCann, Charles R., Jr., ed. F. Y. Edgeworth: Writings in Probability, Statistics & Economics, 3 vols., Set. LC 95-44045. (Elgar Mini Ser.). (Illus.). 1664p. 1996. 575.00 (*1-85898-238-3*) E Elgar.

McCann, Charles R., jt. auth. see Perlman, Mark.

McCann, Charles R., Jr., jt. ed. see Perlman, Mark.

McCann, Cheryl, ed. see Host, Atley.

McCann, Chris. Master Pieces Vol. 1: The Art History of Jigsaw Puzzles. LC 98-35401. Orig. Title: Masterpieces. (Illus.). 256p. 1999. 39.95 (*1-888054-24-7*, 54247) Collectors Pr.

***McCann, Christina K.** Great Leaders! You've Got What It Takes! 82p. 1999. pap. text. write for info. (*0-9678082-0-0*) Dr C K McCann.

***McCann, Colum.** Everything in the Country Must: A Novella & Two Stories. LC 99-43614. 150p. 2000. 21.00 (*0-8050-6398-6*, Metropol Bks) H Holt & Co.

— Everything in This Country Must. 2001. pap. 10.00 (*0-8050-6402-8*) St Martin.

McCann, Colum. Fishing the Sloe-Black River: Stories. 196p. 1996. 22.00 (*0-8050-4106-0*) H Holt & Co.

— Fishing the Sloe-Black River: Stories. 1997. pap. 12.00 (*0-8050-4107-9*, Owl) H Holt & Co.

— Songdogs. LC 96-19572. 224p. 1996. pap. 12.00 (*0-312-14741-4*, Picador USA) St Martin.

— Songdogs: A Novel. 89p. 1995. 22.50 (*0-8050-4104-4*) H Holt & Co.

— This Side of Brightness: A Novel. LC 97-29721. 292p. 1998. 23.00 (*0-8050-5452-9*, Metropol Bks) H Holt & Co.

— This Side of Brightness: A Novel. 288p. 1999. pap. 12.00 (*0-8050-5453-7*, Owl) H Holt & Co.

— This Side of Brightness: A Novel. LC 98-47824. (Compass Press Large Print Book Ser.). 1998. write for info. (*1-56895-587-1*) Wheeler Pub.

McCann, D. M., et al, eds. Modern Geophysics in Engineering Geology. (Geological Society Engineering Geology Special Publication Ser.: No. 12). (Illus.). 352p. 1997. 132.00 (*1-897799-92-6*, Pub. by Geol Soc Pub Hse) AAPG.

***McCann, Daryl & Forbes, Debbie.** Wish You Weren't Here. 138p. 2000. pap. 14.95 (*0-7022-3103-7*, Pub. by Univ Queensland Pr) Intl Spec Bk.

McCann, David, jt. auth. see Henton, Darcy.

***McCann, David R.** Early Korean Literature: Selections & Introductions. 192p. 2000. text 49.50 (*0-231-11946-1*); pap. text 18.50 (*0-231-11947-X*) Col U Pr.

McCann, David R., ed. Korea Briefing: Toward Reunification. (Asia Society Briefings Ser.). 248p. (C). 1996. pap. 27.95 (*1-56324-886-7*, East Gate Bk) M E Sharpe.

McCann, David R., ed. Korea Briefing: Toward Reunification. (Asia Society Briefings Ser.). 248p. (gr. 13). 1996. 69.95 (*1-56324-885-9*, East Gate Bk) M E Sharpe.

McCann, David R. & Sallee, Hyunjae Y., trs. from KOR. Selected Poems by Kim Namjo. (East Asia Papers: No. 63). (C). 1993. 18.70 (*0-939657-05-8*, 63); pap. 11.90 (*0-939657-63-5*, 63) Cornell East Asia Pgm.

***McCann, David R. & Strauss, Barry S., eds.** The Korean War & the Peloponnesian War: A Comparative Study of War & Democracy. 388p. 2000. 77.95 (*0-7656-0694-1*, East Gate Bk) M E Sharpe.

McCann, David R., jt. ed. see Holst-Warhaft, Gail.

McCann, David R., tr. see Chongju, So.

McCann, Debbie. A House in Order. (Illus.). 120p. (Orig.). 1994. pap. 10.00 (*1-883968-03-8*) Blinking Yellow.

***McCann, Deiric.** Winning Business Proposals. rev. ed. 180p. 2000. pap. 19.95 incl. cd-rom (*1-86076-166-6*, Pub. by Oak Tr) Midpt Trade.

***McCann, Dennis.** Dennis McCann Takes You for a Ride: Stories from the Byways of Iowa, Minnesota, Wisconsin, Michigan & Illinois. LC 99-27608. (Illus.). 168p. 1999. pap. 15.95 (*0-942495-67-5*) Palmer Pubns Inc.

McCann, Dennis & Gay, Ben, III. The Art & Science of Resort Sales. rev. ed. 144p. (Orig.). 1990. pap. 14.95 (*0-942645-07-3*) Hampton Books.

McCann, Dennis P., et al, eds. On Moral Business: Classical Contemporary Resources for Ethics in Economic Life. LC 94-21941. 991p. (Orig.). 1995. pap. text 39.00 (*0-8028-0626-0*) Eerdmans.

McCann, Dennis P. & Strain, Charles R. Polity & Praxis: A Program for American Practical Theology. 176p. 1985. 21.00 (*0-86683-986-0*, AY8571) Harper SF.

— Polity & Praxis: A Program for American Practical Theology. 252p. (C). 1990. reprint ed. pap. text 26.50 (*0-8191-7847-0*) U Pr of Amer.

McCann, Dermott. Small States, Open Markets & the Organization of Business Interests. (Illus.). 216p. 1995. text 79.95 (*1-85521-513-6*, Pub. by Dartmth Pub) Ashgate Pub Co.

McCann, Dick. How to Influence Others at Work. 2nd ed. 152p. 1993. pap. text 36.95 (*0-7506-0990-7*) Buttrwrth-Heinemann.

McCann, Dick & Aesop. Aesop's Managament Fables. LC 97-123134. 144p. 1997. pap. text 24.95 (*0-7506-3341-7*) Buttrwrth-Heinemann.

McCann, E. Armitage. How to Make a Clipper Ship Model. LC 94-46480. (Illus.). 176p. 1995. pap. text 6.95 (*0-486-28580-4*) Dover.

***McCann, Eamonn.** Bloody Sunday in Derry: What Really Happened. 256p. 2000. pap. 19.95 (*0-86322-274-9*, Pub. by Brandon Bk Pubs) Irish Bks Media.

McCann, Eamonn. The Free Music of Ireland: A Guide to Pub Sessions. 176p. 1996. pap. 17.95 (*0-85640-578-7*, Pub. by Blackstaff Pr) Dufour.

McCann, Edna. Heritage Book Nineteen Eighty-Five. 1984. 5.95 (*0-02-582880-0*) Macmillan.

McCann, Eileen. The Two-Step: Dancing Toward Intimacy. LC 85-14764. (Illus.). 160p. 1985. pap. 12.95 (*0-8021-3032-1*, Grove) Grove-Atltic.

McCann, Forrest. Great Songs of the Church. LC 85-82565. 673p. 1986. 8.95 (*0-915547-90-2*) Abilene Christ U.

McCann, Forrest M. Hymns & History: An Annotated Survey of Sources. LC 96-78995. 600p. (Orig.). 1997. pap. 31.95 (*0-89112-058-0*) Abilene Christ U.

McCann, Frank D., jt. ed. see Conniff, Michael L.

McCann, Garth. Edward Abbey. LC 77-76321. (Western Writers Ser.: No. 29). 47p. 1977. pap. 4.95 (*0-88430-053-6*) Boise St U W Writ Ser.

McCann, Gary & Zich, Joanne, eds. Lawyer's Research Companion: A Concise Guide to Sources. LC 97-48602. 233p. 1998. pap. 26.95 (*1-57588-442-9*, 310830) W S Hein.

— Lawyer's Research Companion: A Concise Guide to Sources. LC 97-48602. Bk. 4. xv, 218p. 1998. 39.50 (*1-57588-418-6*, 310830) W S Hein.

McCann, Gerard. Theory & History: The Political Thought of E. P. Thompson. LC 97-61062. (Avebury Series in Philosophy). 208p. 1997. text 69.95 (*1-85972-675-5*, Pub. by Ashgate Pub) Ashgate Pub Co.

McCann, Graham. Cary Grant: A Class Apart. LC 96-38577. 352p. 1997. 26.50 (*0-231-10884-2*) Col U Pr.

— Cary Grant: A Class Apart. (Illus.). 352p. 1998. pap. 16.95 (*0-231-10993-8*) Col U Pr.

— Cary Grant: A Class Apart. 1998. pap. 18.00 (*0 231 10885 0*) Col U Pr.

— Marilyn Monroe: The Body in the Library. LC 87-26522. (Illus.). 220p. (C). 1988. pap. 14.95 (*0-8135-1303-0*) Rutgers U Pr.

***McCann, Graham.** Morecambe & Wise. (Illus.). 416p. 2000. 35.00 (*1-85702-735-3*, Pub. by Fourth Estate) Trafalgar.

McCann, Graham. Rebel Males: Clift, Brando, & Dean. LC 92-33768. (Illus.). 235p. (C). 1993. text 38.00 (*0-8135-1952-7*) Rutgers U Pr.

McCann, H. Gilman. Chemistry Transformed: The Shift from Phlogiston to Oxygen. LC 78-19173. (Modern Sociology Ser.). 1978. text 73.25 (*0-89391-004-X*) Ablx Pub.

McCann, Heather. Whispers in the Dark. (Intrigue Ser.). 1993. per. 2.99 (*0-373-22236-X*, 1-22236-3) Harlequin Bks.

McCann, Helen. The Coward Readalong. LC 94-79393. (Ten-Minute Mysteries Ser.). 32p. (YA). (gr. 6-12). 1994. pap. 12.95 incl. audio (*0-7854-1050-3*, 40756) Am Guidance.

— I Dare You. LC 94-79395. (Ten-Minute Mysteries Ser.). 32p. (YA). (gr. 6-12). 1994. pap. 2.95 (*0-7854-0843-6*, 40760) Am Guidance.

— I Dare You Readalong. LC 94-79395. (Ten-Minute Mysteries Ser.). 32p. 1994. pap. 12.95 incl. audio (*0-7854-1052-X*, 40762) Am Guidance.

McCann, Hugh J. The Works of Agency: On Human Action, Will, & Freedom. LC 98-28463. 272p. 1998. text 49.95 (*0-8014-3528-5*) Cornell U Pr.

— The Works of Agency: On Human Action, Will & Freedom. LC 98-28463. 272p. 1998. pap. 19.95 (*0-8014-8583-5*) Cornell U Pr.

McCann, I. Lisa & Pearlman, Laurie A. Psychological Trauma & the Adult Survivor: Theory, Therapy, & Transformation. LC 90-2336. (Psychosocial Stress Ser.: No. 21). 320p. 1990. text 43.95 (*0-87630-594-X*) Brunner-Mazel.

McCann, Ian. Bob Marley. (Complete Guides to the Music Of...Ser.). (Illus.). 130p. (Orig.). pap. 8.95 (*0-7119-3550-5*, OP 47384, Pub. by Omnibus Press) Omnibus NY.

— Bob Marley: In His Own Words. (In Their Own Words Ser.). (Illus.). 96p. 1997. pap. 15.95 (*0-7119-3080-5*, OP 47052) Omnibus NY.

McCann, J. Clinton, Jr. The Shape & the Shaping of the Psalter. (JSOTS Ser.: Vol. 159). 130p. 1993. 46.50 (*1-85075-396-2*, Pub. by Sheffield Acad) CUP Services.

McCann, J. Clinton. A Theological Introduction to the Book of Psalms: The Psalms As Torah. 224p. (Orig.). 1993. pap. 17.95 (*0-687-41468-7*) Abingdon.

McCann, J. E. Thomas Howell & the School at Llandaff. 260p. (C). 1989. 39.00 (*0-7855-6866-2*, Pub. by D Brown & Sons Ltd) St Mut.

McCann, J. G. He's Alright: Reflections of the Life & Legacy of Rev. Dr. Samuel Austin. LC 98-91771. 128p. 1998. pap. write for info. (*1-57502-910-3*, PO2507) Morris Pubng.

— Lift the Veil. 120p. 1998. pap. 12.00 (*1-57502-841-7*, PO2307) Morris Pubng.

McCann, James. From Poverty to Famine in Northeast Ethiopia: A Rural History, 1900-1935. LC 86-14680. (Ethnohistory Ser.). (Illus.). 256p. 1987. text 42.95 (*0-8122-8038-5*) U of Pa Pr.

McCann, James A., jt. auth. see Dominguez, Jorge I.

McCann, James C. Green Land, Brown Land, Black Land: An Environmental History of Africa, 1800-1990. LC 98-35565. 224p. 1999. 24.95 (*0-325-00096-4*) Greenwood.

— People of the Plow: An Agricultural History of Ethiopia. LC 94-37124. (Illus.). 304p. 1994. pap. text 24.95 (*0-299-14614-6*) U of Wis Pr.

— People of the Plow: An Agricultural History of Ethiopia. LC 94-37124. (Illus.). 304p. 1995. text 54.00 (*0-299-14610-3*) U of Wis Pr.

McCann, James M. Return to the River. 176p. 1995. pap. 11.95 (*0-9627530-1-7*) Ridgetop Pr.

McCann, James Z. Aftershock: The Loma Prieta Earthquake & Its Impact on San Benito County. Churchill, Adele, ed. LC 90-63594. (Illus.). 80p. (Orig.). 1990. pap. 14.95 (*0-9628177-0-8*) J Churchill.

McCann, Jan. Sarasota Chef du Jour: Chef Recipes from Popular Area Restaurants. 4th ed. (Illus.). 38p. (Orig.). 1995. pap. 19.00 (*0-9640198-3-3*) Strawbry Press.

— Sarasota's Chef du Jour: Chef Recipes. rev. ed. (Illus.). 232p. 1999. pap. 16.00 (*0-9640198-7-6*) Strawbry Press.

— Sarasota's Chef du Jour: Chef Recipes. 5th rev. ed. (Illus.). 210p. 1997. pap. 14.50 (*0-9640198-6-8*) Strawbry Press.

McCann, Janet. Dialogue with the Dogcatcher. 50p. (Orig.). 1987. 10.95 (*0-941720-52-7*); pap. 3.95 (*0-941720-53-5*) Slough Pr TX.

— How They Got Here. 22p. 1985. pap. 7.95 (*0-944754-09-0*) Pudding Hse Pubns.

— Looking for Buddha in the Barbed-Wire Garden. 62p. 1996. pap. 10.00 (*1-888105-08-9*) Avisson Pr.

— Wallace Steven Revisited. (Twayne's United States Authors Ser.). 1995. 32.00 (*0-8057-7644-3*, Twyne) Mac Lib Ref.

McCann, Janet, jt. ed. see Craig, David.

McCann, Janice. Fort Myers Chef du Jour: Chef Recipes from Popular Ft. Myers Area Restaurants. LC 96-233027. 152p. 1994. pap. 14.00 (*0-9640198-4-1*) Strawbry Press.

***McCann, Jennifer, et al.** Aquidneck Island: Our Shared Vision. (Aquidneck Island Partnership Coastal Management Report Ser.: No. 3304). (Illus.). 1999. pap. write for info. (*1-885454-33-3*) Coastal Res.

***McCann, Jesse Leon.** Scooby-Doo! And the Fantastic Puppet Factory. (Illus.). 32p. (J). (ps-3). 2000. mass mkt. 3.50 (*0-439-17254-3*) Scholastic Inc.

— Scooby-Doo! And the Weird Water Park. (Illus.). 32p. (J). (gr. 1-4). 2000. mass mkt. 3.50 (*0-439-17253-5*) Scholastic Inc.

— Scooby-Doo & the Alien Invaders! (Illus.). (J). 2000. pap. 3.50 (*0-439-17700-6*) Scholastic Inc.

— Scooby-Doo & the Eerie Ice Monster. (Illus.). (J). 2000. pap. 5.99 (*0-439-20667-7*) Scholastic Inc.

— Scooby Doo & the Halloween Hotel Haunt: A Glow in the Dark Mystery! (Illus.). 24p. (J). (gr. k-3). 1999. mass mkt. 5.99 (*0-439-11768-2*) Scholastic Inc.

McCann, Jessica. Faith Family & Business: The Story of Paul Carollo, Sr. & RCO Engineering, Inc. 90p. 1998. write for info. (*0-929690-39-7*) Herit Pubs AZ.

Mccann, Jim. How I Made My Business Bloom. 1999. pap. write for info. (*0-345-41676-7*) Ballantine Pub Grp.

McCann, Joachim. Monks in the Modern World: The Monks of Mount Angel Abbey. (Illus.). 105p. (Orig.). 1993. pap. 15.95 (*1-884563-00-7*) Canyon Creat.

McCann, John. Clay & Cob Buildings. (Album Ser.: No. 105). (Illus.). 32p. 4.75 (*0-7478-0280-7*, Pub. by Shire Pubns) Parkwest Pubns.

McCann, John A., jt. auth. see Safford, Edward L., Jr.

McCann, John D., jt. auth. see Hoyer, Frederick C., Jr.

McCann, John M. Expert Systems for a Scanner Data Environment: The Marketing Workbench Experience. (C). 1990. lib. bdg. 95.50 (*0-7923-9076-8*) Kluwer Academic.

McCann, John T. NetWare 4.1 Supervisor's Guide. 89p. 1995. pap. 34.95 (*1-55851-402-3*, M&T Bks) IDG Bks.

McCann, John T. Netware Supervisor's Guide 4.0. 1995. pap. 32.95 (*1-55851-284-5*, M&T Bks) IDG Bks.

McCann, John T., et al. Netware Supervisor's Guide. (Illus.). 510p. (Orig.). 1995. pap. 29.95 (*1-55851-111-3*, M&T Bks) IDG Bks.

***McCann, Joseph T.** Assessing Adolescents with the MACI: Using the Million Adolescent Clinical Inventory. LC 98-42307. 238p. 1999. 57.50 (*0-471-32619-4*) Wiley.

M

An Asterisk (*) at the beginning of an entry indicates that the title is appearing for the first time.

McCann, Joseph T. Malingering & Deception in Adolescents: Assessing Credibility in Clinical & Forensic Settings. LC 97-37671. 243p. 1997. 34.95 (*1-55798-460-3*, 431-7990) Am Psychol.

McCann, Joseph T. & Dyer, Frank J. Forensic Assessment with the Millon Inventories. LC 96-7349. (Illus.). 241p. 1996. lib. bdg. 36.00 (*1-57230-055-8*, 0055) Guilford Pubns.

McCann, Justin, tr. see Adam, Karl.

***McCann, Katherine D., ed.** Handbook of Latin American Studies, Vol. 57. 960p. 2001. 95.00 (*0-292-75243-1*) U of Tex Pr.

McCann, Kevin D. Jackson Diamonds: Professional Baseball in Jackson, Tennessee. (Illus.). 208p. 1999. pap. 16.95 (*0-9671251-0-3*) Three Star TN.

McCann, Lee. Nostradamus: The Man Who Saw Through Time. (Illus.). 421p. 1982. pap. 9.95 (*0-374-51754-1*) FS&G.

— Nostradamus: The Man Who Saw Through Time. (Illus.). 448p. 1994. reprint ed. 9.99 (*0-517-43693-0*) Random Hse Value.

McCann, Lee I., jt. auth. see Perlman, Baron.

McCann, Lucas J. Christianity: A Growing Experience. 1983. pap. 6.95 (*0-89137-429-9*) Quality Pubns.

McCann, Margaret, jt. auth. see Brewer, Richard.

McCann, Marilyn. Country Brushstrokes. (Illus.). 90p. 1996. pap. 16.95 (*1-86351-148-2*, Pub. by Sally Milner) Sterling.

McCann, Mary Ann. Days in Waiting: A Guide to Surviving Pregnancy Bedrest. 144p. 1999. pap. 11.95 (*0-9650848-1-7*, A Place to Remember) deRuyter-Nelson.

McCann, Mary E. Body Caged, Spirit Free: The Mary Ellen Mccann Story. LC 99-12612. 1999. pap. 15.95 (*0-936389-65-6*) Tudor Pubs.

McCann, Maurice, jt. auth. see Appleby, Derek.

McCann, May, et al, eds. Irish Travellers: Culture & Ethnicity. 2nd ed. LC 94-204665. 287p. 1996. reprint ed. pap. 17.95 (*0-85389-493-0*, Pub. by Inst Irish Studies) Irish Bks Media.

McCann, Michael. Artist Beware. 2nd ed. (Illus.). 576p. 1992. 29.95 (*1-55821-175-6*) Lyons Pr.

McCann, Michael C. Oregon Ducks Football: 100 Years of Glory. LC 95-79214. (Illus.). 160p. 1995. 28.95 (*0-9648244-7-7*) McCann Communs.

McCann, Michael J. & Thomas, Mason P., Jr. The Law & the Elderly in North Carolina. 2nd ed. 307p. (C). 1996. pap. text 24.00 (*1-56011-202-6*, 96.10) Institute Government.

McCann, Michael J., et al. Treatment of Opiate Addiction Using Methadone: A Counselor's Manual. 335p. (Orig.). (C). 1995. pap. text 55.00 (*0-7881-2534-6*) DIANE Pub.

McCann, Michael L. Eating to Win Beyond 2000 A. D. A Christian's Guide to Survival. McCann, Rita R., ed. (Illus.). 205p. 1998. pap. 15.00 (*0-9638195-1-8*) M L McCann.

— The Ultimate Secrets of Knowing God, Vol. 1. Cotton, Irene, ed. 95p. (C). 1993. pap. text 6.00 (*0-9638195-0-X*) M L McCann.

McCann, Michael W. Rights at Work: Pay Equity Reform & the Politics of Legal Mobilization. LC 93-21278. (Language & Legal Discourse Ser.). 372p. 1994. pap. text 18.95 (*0-226-55572-0*) U Ch Pr.

— Rights at Work: Pay Equity Reform & the Politics of Legal Mobilization. LC 93-21278. (Language & Legal Discourse Ser.). 372p. 1994. lib. bdg. 65.00 (*0-226-55571-2*) U Ch Pr.

— Taking Reform Seriously: Perspectives on Public Interest Liberalism. LC 86-47647. 348p. 1986. pap. 18.95 (*0-8014-9415-X*) Cornell U Pr.

McCann, Michael W. & Houseman, Gerald L. Judging the Constitution: Critical Essays on Judicial Lawmaking. (C). 1989. pap. text 25.50 (*0-673-39897-8*) Addson-Wesley Educ.

McCann, Mike. Give Me the Hudson or the Yukon. 1991. 10.95 (*0-9627530-0-9*) Ridgetop Pr.

McCann, Mike, jt. auth. see Albertyn, Chris.

***McCann, Nessan.** A Doctor's Odyssey: The Life of an Irish Physician. (Illus.). 200p. 1999. 29.50 (*1-85776-455-2*, Pub. by Book Guild Ltd) Trans-Atl Phila.

McCann, Peter D., jt. ed. see Scuderi, Giles R.

McCann, Philip. The Economics of Industrial Location: A Logistics-Costs Approach. LC 98-27154. (Advances in Spatial Science Ser.). (Illus.). xii, 228p. 1998. 79.95 (*3-540-64586-1*) Spr-Verlag.

McCann, Rebecca. Complete Cheerful Cherub. 514p. 1990. reprint ed. lib. bdg. 35.95 (*0-89966-662-0*) Buccaneer Bks.

McCann, Richard. Border Town. 1999. pap. write for info. (*0-14-010043-1*, Viking) Viking Penguin.

— A Dream of the Traveler. LC 76-17642. 68p. 1976. 3.50 (*0-87886-070-3*, Greenfld Rev Pr) Greenfld Rev Lit.

— Ghost Letters: Poems. LC 94-26245. (Orig.). 1994. pap. 9.95 (*1-882295-04-8*) Alice James Bks.

— Nights of 1990. (Illus.). 22p. 1994. pap. 6.00 (*1-879294-08-7*) Warm Spring Pr.

McCann, Richard, jt. ed. see Klein, Michael.

McCann, Rita R., ed. see McCann, Michael L.

McCann, Robert, et al. Advance Directives & End of Life Discussions - A Manual for Instructors. 11p. 1997. 80.00 (*1-892273-00-4*) U Rchstr Med & Dntstry.

McCann, Ron & Vitale, Joe. The Joy of Service! Bring Service Excellence to the World Through Your Work. (Illus.). 135p. (Orig.). 1989. pap. 10.95 (*0-9617549-2-3*) Awareness Pubns.

McCann, S. B. & Ford, D. C., eds. Geomorphology Sans Frontieres. LC 96-1061. (Publications: No. 6). (Illus.). 260p. 1996. 180.00 (*0-471-96600-2*) Wiley.

McCann, S. M., ed. Endocrinology. (People & Ideas Ser.). (Illus.). 484p. 1988. text 75.00 (*0-19-520718-1*) OUP.

McCann, S. M., et al, eds. Cytokines & the Brain: A Satellite Symposium to the Society for Neuroscience 27th Annual Meeting, New Orleans, La., October 1997. (Illus.). 100p. 1998. pap. 33.25 (*3-8055-6766-9*) S Karger.

McCann, S. M. & Weiner, R. I., eds. Integrative Neuroendocrinology: Molecular, Cellular & Clinical Aspects. (Illus.). viii, 244p. 1987. 156.75 (*3-8055-4467-7*) S Karger.

McCann, S. M., jt. ed. see Doerner, G.

McCann, Sally, jt. auth. see Morris, Mary.

McCann, Samuel M., et al, eds. Neuroimmunomodulation: Molecular Aspects, Integrative Systems, & Clinical Advances. LC 98-15845. (Annals of the New York Academy of Sciences Ser.: No. 840). 866p. 1998. 160.00 (*1-57331-072-7*); pap. 160.00 (*1-57331-073-5*) NY Acad Sci.

McCann, Sean. Growing Things. LC 89-51018. 138p. (Orig.). (J). 1989. pap. 6.95 (*1-85371-029-6*, Pub. by Poolbeg Pr) Dufour.

***McCann, Sean.** Gumshoe America: Hard Boiled Crime Fiction & the Rise & Fall of New Deal Liberalism. 360p. 2000. pap. 19.95 (*0-8223-2594-2*); lib. bdg. 59.95 (*0-8223-2580-2*) Duke.

McCann, Sean. Miniature Roses: Their Care & Cultivation. (Illus.). 144p. 1996. pap. 17.95 (*0-304-34799-X*, Pub. by Cassell) Sterling.

— The Rose: An Encyclopedia of North American Roses, Rosarians, & Rose Lore. LC 93-9589. (Illus.). 224p. 1993. 24.95 (*0-8117-1490-X*) Stackpole.

— The Wit of Oscar Wilde. (Illus.). 128p. 1998. pap. 9.95 (*0-86278-248-1*, Pub. by OBrien Pr) Irish Amer Bk.

— World of Brendan Behan. 1976. 20.95 (*0-8488-0572-0*) Amereon Ltd.

McCann, Steve. Karate Everyone. (Everyone Ser.). 128p. 1998. pap. text 21.95 (*0-88725-246-X*) Hunter Textbks.

McCann, T., et al. Healthy Start Initiative Vol. IV: A Community Driven Approach to Infant Mortality Reduction. LC 94-67194. (Illus.). 164p. 1996. pap. write for info. (*1-57285-035-3*) Nat Ctr Educ.

McCann, Thurma, et al. Healthy Start Initiative Vol. III: A Community Driven Approach to Infant Mortality Reduction. LC 95-72697. 120p. 1995. pap. write for info. (*1-57285-024-8*) Nat Ctr Educ.

***McCann, Timmothy B.** Always. 304p. 2000. pap. 13.00 (*0-380-80597-9*, Avon Bks) Morrow Avon.

— Until... 266p. 1999. pap. 12.00 (*0-380-80579-0*, Avon Bks) Morrow Avon.

***McCann, Timmothy B.** Until... 2000. mass mkt. 6.99 (*0-380-81371-8*) Morrow Avon.

McCann, Timothy J. West Sussex Probate Inventories, Fifteen Twenty-One to Eighteen Thirty-Four. 1981. 110.00 (*0-86260-005-7*) St Mut.

McCann, Tom. The Droll Troll: A View from under the Bridge. LC 94-34978. (Illus.). 124p. 1994. pap. 10.00 (*0-943389-15-1*) Snow Lion-SLG Bks.

McCann, William, ed. & intro. see Bierce, Ambrose.

McCann, Yvette, ed. see Wikholm, Marion.

McCann, Yvette, ed. & illus. see Reese, Mildred L. & Smith, Thelma D.

McCann, Yvette B. Eddie Pasghetti. Damerest, Nancy & Lea, Judy, eds. (Eddie Pasghetti Collection: Bk. 1). (Illus.). 64p. (J). (gr. 4 up). 1994. 14.95 (*0-9639486-5-2*) Rhyme Tyme.

McCann, Yvette B., ed. see Nabauns, Leroy.

McCann, Yvette B., ed. see Shields, Abby.

***McCanna, Laurie.** Friends of ED: Foundation LiveMotion. 275p. 2000. pap. 19.99 (*1-903450-02-0*) Wrox Pr Inc.

McCannon, Tricia. Beings of Light, Worlds in Transition. 1998. pap. 13.95 (*1-886932-02-6*) Hrzns Unltd.

— Dialogues with the Angels. 229p. (Orig.). 1996. pap. 13.95 (*1-886932-01-8*) Hrzns Unltd.

McCanse, Anne E., jt. auth. see Blake, Robert R.

McCant, James L. Introduction to Learning to Learn (Internal Processing) A Handbook to Develop Common Sense. LC 96-90184. 1996. 16.00 (*0-533-11935-9*) Vantage.

***McCant, Jerry W.** 2 Corinthians. (Readings Ser.). 200p. 1999. 57.50 (*1-84127-031-8*, Pub. by Sheffield Acad); pap. 23.75 (*1-84127-032-6*, Pub. by Sheffield Acad) CUP Services.

McCants, Anne E. The Dawn of Philanthropy: Orphan Care in Early Modern Amsterdam. LC 96-51239. 288p. 1997. text 36.95 (*0-252-02333-1*) U of Ill Pr.

McCants, David A. Patrick Henry, the Orator, 8. LC 90-33274. (Great American Orators: Critical Studies, Speeches & Sources: No. 8). 176p. 1990. lib. bdg. 52.95 (*0-313-26210-1*, MPX, Greenwood Pr) Greenwood.

McCants, Dorothea O., ed. They Came to Louisiana: Letters of a Catholic Mission, 1854-1882. LC 72-96258. (Illus.). 287p. reprint ed. 89.00 (*0-8357-9392-3*, 202099700020) Bks Demand.

McCants, Glynis. Glynis Has Your Number. 2nd ed. McCants, Gwen & DePollo, Daryl, eds. 135p. (Orig.). 1997. pap., wbk. ed. 24.95 (*0-9663580-0-7*) Glynis Number.

McCants, Gwen, ed. see McCants, Glynis.

McCants, Louise & Robert, Cavett. Retire to Fun & Freedom. 192p. 1990. mass mkt. 12.95 (*0-446-39139-5*, Pub. by Warner Bks) Little.

McCants, William D. Much Ado about Prom Night. LC 94-43349. 192p. (YA). (gr. 7 up). 1995. 11.00 (*0-15-200083-6*, Harcourt Child Bks); pap. 5.00 (*0-15-200081-X*, Harcourt Child Bks) Harcourt.

McCants, William R. War Patrols of the USS Flasher. Turner, Ginny, ed. 480p. 1994. 27.00 (*1-57087-054-3*) Prof Pr NC.

McCardell, John M., Jr. The Idea of a Southern Nation: Southern Nationalists & Southern Nationalism, 1830-1860. 432p. (C). 1981. pap. text 10.50 (*0-393-95203-7*) Norton.

McCardell, Lee. Ill-Starred General: Braddock of the Coldstream Guards. LC 57-14574. (Illus.). 347p. 1958. pap. 107.60 (*0-608-05162-4*, 201049300068) Bks Demand.

McCardell, Marion, ed. see Ellsworth, Barry A.

McCardle, Arthur W. & Boenau, A. Bruce, eds. East Germany: A New German Nation under Socialism? LC 84-7476. 284p. (Orig.). (C). 1984. pap. text 30.00 (*0-8191-3998-X*); lib. bdg. 55.50 (*0-8191-3997-1*) U Pr of Amer.

McCardle, Ciaran B., ed. Side Chain Liquid Crystal Polymers. (Illus.). 416p. 1989. 150.00 (*0-412-01761-X*, Chap & Hall NY) Chapman & Hall.

McCardle, Ellen S. Nonverbal Communication for Media, Library, & Information. Penland, Patrick R., ed. LC 73-90766. (Communications Science & Technology Ser.: No. 5). (Illus.). 111p. reprint ed. pap. 34.50 (*0-7837-0650-2*, 204098900019) Bks Demand.

McCardle, William H., jt. auth. see Lowry, Robert.

***McCarey, Gladys Taylor & Stearn, Jess.** The Physician Within You: Medicine for the Millenium. 295p. 2000. pap. 14.95 (*0-9658158-5-4*) Inkwell Prods.

McCarey-Laird, M. Martin. Lester Dent: The Man, His Craft & His Market. LC 94-76268. 120p. (Orig.). 1994. pap. 11.95 (*0-9641004-9-5*) Hidalgo Pubng.

McCarg, Barbara. Georgia Parks Guide. Boyer, Chris, ed. 100p. (Orig.). 1988. pap. text 4.95 (*0-935201-31-9*) Affordable Adven.

McCarg, Barbara, ed. see Boyer, Chris.

McCarg, Barbara, ed. see McCarg, Margie.

McCarg, Margie. Virginia Parks Guide. McCarg, Barbara & Boyer, Chris, eds. 100p. (Orig.). 1988. pap. text 5.95 (*0-935201-30-0*) Affordable Adven.

McCargar, David J., jt. ed. see Shrimpton, Gordon S.

McCargo, Duncan. Chamlong Srimuang & the New Thai Politics. LC 96-38565. 362p. 1998. text 49.95 (*0-312-16588-9*) St Martin.

***McCargo, Duncan.** Contemporary Japan. LC 99-16562. 2000. pap. 18.95 (*0-312-22742-6*); text 59.95 (*0-312-22741-8*) St Martin.

McCarl, Julia, jt. auth. see Schwiebert, Pat.

McCarl, Mary R. The Plowman's Tale: The c. 1532 & 1606 Editions of a Spurious Canterbury Tale. rev. ed. LC 96-37836. (Renaissance Imagination Ser.). 320p. 1997. text 72.00 (*0-8153-1711-5*) Garland.

McCarl, Robert. The District of Columbia Fire Fighter's Project: A Case Study in Occupational Folklore. LC 84-600291. (Smithsonian Folklore Studies: No. 4). 244p. reprint ed. pap. 75.70 (*0-608-14939-X*, 202568200045) Bks Demand.

McCarley, Becky. Herman's Magical Universe. LC 98-73920. (Illus.). 48p. (J). (gr. 2-6). 1999. bds. 16.95 (*1-57174-114-3*) Hampton Roads Pub Co.

McCarley, J. Britt, et al. The Atlanta Campaign: A Civil War Driving Tour of Atlanta-Area Battlefields with a Reader's Guide to the Atlanta Campaign. Rice, Bradley R. & Weldon, Jane P., eds. LC 88-18941. (Illus.). 112p. (Orig.). 1989. reprint ed. pap. 9.95 (*0-87797-160-9*) Cherokee.

McCarley, R. W., jt. auth. see Steriade, M.

McCarn, Ellen D. Ellen McCarn on English Smocking. (Illus.). 32p. (Orig.). 1986. pap. 9.95 (*0-9618066-0-5*) McCarn Enterp.

— Picture Smocking with Ellen McCarn. (Illus.). 48p. 1990. pap. 10.00 (*0-9618066-2-1*) McCarn Enterp.

McCarney. Real World of Ideology. 168p. 1993. 53.95 (*0-7512-0191-X*) Ashgate Pub Co.

— Rutledge Philosophy Guidebook to Hegel on History. LC 99-59383. 2000. pap. 12.99 (*0-415-11696-1*) Routledge.

McCarney, Joseph. Hegel on History: Routledge Philosophy Guidebook. LC 99-59383. (Routledge Philosophy Guidebooks Ser.). 216p. (C). 1999. 50.00 (*0-415-11695-3*) Routledge.

McCarney-Muldoon, Eileen & O'Brien, Mary B. Fun with Colors. LC 91-42672. (Illus.). 24p. (J). (ps). 1992. pap. 6.95 (*0-689-71610-9*) Aladdin.

— Fun with Numbers. LC 91-39592. (Illus.). 24p. (J). (ps). 1992. pap. 6.95 (*0-689-71609-5*) Aladdin.

McCarney, Patricia L. World Cities & the Environment. (C). 1999. pap. text. write for info. (*0-8133-8482-6*) Westview.

McCarney, Scott. Far Horizons. (Illus.). 1998. pap. 25.00 (*0-89822-123-4*) Visual Studies.

McCarney, Stephen B. Adaptive Behavior Intervention Manual. 316p. 1995. pap. 20.00 (*1-878372-08-4*) Hawthorne Educ Servs.

— The At Risk Student in Our Schools: A Model Intervention Program for the At Risk Student's Most Common Learning & Behavior Problems. 504p. 1994. pap. 36.00 (*1-878372-03-3*) Hawthorne Educ Servs.

— The Attention Deficit Disorders Intervention Manual. 404p. 1994. pap. 30.00 (*0-685-29445-5*) Hawthorne Educ Servs.

— Early Childhood Behavior Intervention Manual. 130p. (Orig.). 1992. pap. 20.00 (*1-878372-15-7*) Hawthorne Educ Servs.

— Emotional & Behavior Problem Scale IEP & Intervention Manual. 167p. 1989. pap. 25.00 (*0-685-29444-7*) Hawthorne Educ Servs.

— Emotional Behavior Disorder Intervention Manual. 202p. (Orig.). 1992. pap. 22.00 (*1-878372-10-6*) Hawthorne Educ Servs.

— The Student Teacher's Guide: Intervention Strategies for the Most Common Learning & Behavior Problems Encountered by Student Teachers in Our Schools. 470p. (Orig.). 1989. pap. 33.00 (*1-878372-12-2*) Hawthorne Educ Servs.

— The Transition Behavior Scale IEP & Intervention Manual. 230p. (Orig.). 1989. pap. 20.00 (*1-878372-14-9*) Hawthorne Educ Servs.

— Work Adjustment Intervention Manual. 171p. (Orig.). 1991. pap. 16.00 (*1-878372-16-5*) Hawthorne Educ Servs.

McCarney, Stephen B. & Bauer, Angela M. The Learning Disability Intervention Manual. rev. ed. 217p. 1989. reprint ed. pap. 25.00 (*1-878372-07-6*) Hawthorne Educ Servs.

— The Parent's Guide to Attention Deficit Disorders. 408p. 1995. pap. 20.00 (*1-878372-01-7*, 840) Hawthorne Educ Servs.

— Parent's Guide to Learning Disabilities. 200p. 1991. pap. 17.00 (*1-878372-05-X*) Hawthorne Educ Servs.

McCarney, Stephen B. & Tucci, Janet. Study Skills for Students in Our Schools. 206p. 1991. pap. 18.00 (*1-878372-04-1*) Hawthorne Educ Servs.

McCarney, Stephen B. & Wunderlich, Kathy C. Pre-Referral Intervention Manual: The Most Common Learning & Behavior Problems Encountered in the Educational Environment. 504p. (Orig.). 1993. pap. 33.00 (*1-878372-11-4*) Hawthorne Educ Servs.

McCarr, Dorothy. Multiple Meanings for the Young Adult. (C). 1995. pap. text 9.00 (*0-89079-670-X*, 6972) PRO-ED.

McCarr, Ken. The Kentucky Harness Horse. LC 75-3548. (Kentucky Bicentennial Bookshelf Ser.). (Illus.). 152p. 1978. 15.00 (*0-8131-0213-8*) U Pr of Ky.

***McCarraher, Eugene.** Christian Critics: Religion & the Impasse in Modern American Social Thought. 288p. 2000. 26.95 (*0-8014-3473-4*) Cornell U Pr.

McCarren, Felicia. Dance Pathologies: Performance, Poetics, Medicine. (Writing Science Ser.). (Illus.). 296p. 1998. pap. 19.95 (*0-8047-3524-7*) Stanford U Pr.

McCarren, Felicia, tr. see Labarthe, Phillippe L.

McCarren, Felicia, tr. see Serres, Michel.

McCarren, Felicia M. Dance Pathologies: Performance, Poetics, Medicine. LC 98-11386. (Writing Science Ser.). 296p. 1998. 49.50 (*0-8047-2989-1*) Stanford U Pr.

McCarren, Vincent & Moffat, Douglas, eds. A Guide to Editing Middle English. LC 97-36540. 352p. (C). 1998. text 49.50 (*0-472-10604-X*, 10604) U of Mich Pr.

McCarren, Vincent P., ed. see Michigan Papyri Staff.

McCarrick, J. Edward, jt. auth. see Stevens, Dale J.

McCarrick, Theodore, intro. Pope John Paul II: An American Celebration. (Illus.). 128p. 1994. pap. 17.95 (*0-9642957-0-9*) Jersey Photo Project.

***McCarrier, Andrea, et al.** Interactive Writing: Language & Literacy & How It All Comes Together. LC 99-45057. 1999. pap. text 30.00 (*0-325-00209-6*) Heinemann.

McCarriston, Linda. Eva-Mary. 80p. (C). 1994. reprint ed. pap. 10.95 (*0-8101-5008-5*, TriQuart) Northwestern U Pr.

***McCarriston, Linda.** Little River: New & Selected Poems. 2000. pap. 13.95 (*1-903392-01-2*, Pub. by Salmon Poetry) Dufour.

McCarriston, Linda. Talking Soft Dutch. LC 83-51718. 71p. (Orig.). 1984. 10.95 (*0-89672-116-7*); pap. 6.95 (*0-89672-115-9*) Tex Tech Univ Pr.

McCarroll, John. Before You Go to Asia: A Primer for Personal Adventure Without Spending a Lot of Money. (Illus.). 120p. (Orig.). 1988. pap. 8.95 (*0-929220-01-3*) Laurel CA.

— Cheap Eats San Francisco: Good Meals Under Six Dollars. (Illus.). 192p. (Orig.). 1989. pap. 8.95 (*0-929220-02-1*) Laurel CA.

McCarroll, Kathleen. A Treasure Trove of Fitly Words. 70p. 1996. pap. write for info. (*1-57502-262-1*, P0945) Morris Pubng.

McCarroll, Les, jt. auth. see MacIver, Dan.

McCarroll, Tolbert. Notes from the Song of Life: A Spiritual Companion. rev. ed. LC 77-7135. (Illus.). 144p. (Orig.). 1995. reprint ed. pap. 8.95 (*0-89087-200-7*) Celestial Arts.

McCarron, David A., jt. ed. see Bennett, William M.

McCarron, E. M., III, et al, eds. Solid-State Chemistry of Inorganic Materials II Vol. 547: Materials Research Society Symposium Proceedings. LC 99-13882. 539p. 1999. text 89.00 (*1-55899-453-X*) Materials Res.

McCarron, Kevin. The Coincidence of Opposites: William Golding's Later Fiction. LC 95-232809. 206 p. 1995. write for info. (*1-85075-506-X*) Sheffield Acad.

— William Golding. 1994. pap. 19.95 (*0-7463-0730-6*, Pub. by Northcote House) Trans-Atl Phila.

— William Golding. LC 94-140309. (Writers & Their Work Ser.). 95p. 1996. pap. text 15.00 (*0-7463-0735-7*, Pub. by Northcote House) U Pr of Miss.

McCarron, Paul. The Prints of Martin Lewis: A Catalogue Raisonne. LC 95-76596. (Illus.). 256p. 1995. 120.00 (*0-9628234-1-4*) M Hausberg.

McCarron, Richard. The Eucharistic Prayer at Sunday Mass. 154p. (J). 1997. pap. 11.00 (*1-56854-021-3*, EPSUN) Liturgy Tr Pubns.

McCarron, Richard E., et al. The Living Light Vol. 34, No. 1: Countdown to the Millennium: The Holy Spirit. Marthaler, Berard, ed. 96p. (C). 1997. pap. 8.95 (*1-57455-154-X*) US Catholic.

McCarron, Robert J., jt. auth. see Leavitt, Christine.

McCarron, Shane. Open Systems Standards. UniForum Staff, ed. (Illus.). 32p. (C). 1995. pap. text. write for info. (*0-936593-31-8*) UniForum.

McCarron, William E. Lesser Metaphysical Poets: A Bibliography, 1961-1980. LC 83-448. (Checklists in the Humanities & Education Ser.: No. 7). 64p. reprint ed. pap. 30.00 (*0-8357-6351-X*, 203562600096) Bks Demand.

McCarry, Charles. Double Eagle. large type ed. 1982. 27.99 (*0-7089-0812-8*) Ulverscroft.

— The Great Southwest. LC 78-21450. (Special Publications Series 15: No. 3). (Illus.). 1980. lib. bdg. 12.95 (*0-87044-288-0*) Natl Geog.

— The Last Supper. large type ed. 624p. 1986. 11.50 (*0-7089-8322-7*, Charnwood) Ulverscroft.

M

McCarry, Charles, ed. From the Field: A Collection of Writings from National Geographic. LC 97-14217. 458p. 1997. 25.00 (*0-7922-7012-6*) Natl Geog.
McCarry, Charles, jt. auth. see Haig, Alexander M., Jr.
McCarry, D. C., jt. ed. see Wightman, W. D.
McCarry, G. J., et al. The Law of Employment. 3rd ed. xxxiv, 618p. 1990. pap. 59.50 (*0-455-20965-0*, Pub. by LawBk Co) Gaunt.
McCarry, John. County Fairs. National Geographic Society Staff, ed. LC 97-11868. 1997. 30.00 (*0-7922-7091-6*) Natl Geog.
McCarson, Bonnie. Touch My Soul. (Illus.). 96p. 1997. pap. 15.00 (*1-880994-52-6*) Mt Olive Coll Pr.
McCarson, Bonnie & Burton, Bonnie B. Beneath the Surface. LC 93-81285. (Illus.). 93p. (Orig.). 1996. pap. 15.95 (*1-880994-30-5*) Mt Olive Coll Pr.
McCart, Alice, ed. Health Data Directory, 1997. 424p. 1996. pap. 365.00 (*1-881393-83-6*) Faulkner & Gray.
McCart, Dennie D. Memories of Edenbrook Farm: Twenty-One Years of Farm Life. (Illus.). 1984. pap. 7.95 (*0-8323-0432-8*) Binford Mort.
McCart, Gerald D., jt. auth. see Welch, Charles D.
McCart, Janet. Forgiving Rose: An Alaska Novel of Mystery, Friendship, & Romance. LC 98-85657. 224p. 1998. pap. 14.95 (*1-888125-31-4*) Publ Consult.
McCart, Linda. Changing Systems for Children & Families. Glass, Karen, ed. 60p. (Orig.). 1994. pap. text 15.00 (*1-55877-224-3*) Natl Governor.
— Developing Innovative Programs to Support Families. Glass, Karen, ed. 56p. (Orig.). 1992. pap. text 15.00 (*1-55877-147-6*) Natl Governor.
— Investing in Family Self-Sufficiency. Glass, Karen, ed. 51p. (Orig.). 1992. pap. text 15.00 (*1-55877-149-2*) Natl Governor.
McCart, Linda & Heller, Anne. Putting Families First. Glass, Karen, ed. 56p. (Orig.). 1993. pap. text 15.00 (*1-55877-211-1*) Natl Governor.
McCart, Neil. Atlantic Liners of the Cunard Line: From 1884 to the Present Day. 1990. 29.95 (*1-85260-065-9*, Pub. by P Stephens) Haynes Manuals.
McCart, Thomas K. The Matter & Manner of Praise: The Controversial Evolution of Hymnody in the Church of England, 1760-1820. LC 97-39136. (Drew Studies in Liturgy: No. 5). 176p. 1998. 49.50 (*0-8108-3450-2*) Scarecrow.
McCartan, Anne-Marie, jt. auth. see Cross, K. Patricia.
McCartan, Greg, intro. see Mandela, Nelson.
***McCarten, Anthony.** Spinners: A Novel. 272p. 2000. pap. 13.00 (*0-688-17904-5*, Perennial) HarperTrade.
McCarten, Anthony. Spinners: A Novel. LC 98-20792. 288p. 1999. 24.00 (*0-688-16303-3*, Wm Morrow) Morrow Avon.
***McCarten, James M.** Health Care Worker Classification. (Health Law & Business Ser.: No. 2700). 1999. pap. 95.00 (*1-55871-399-9*) BNA.
***McCarter.** Microsoft Publisher 2000 for Dummies. LC 99-61891. (For Dummies Ser.). 384p. 1999. pap. 19.99 (*0-7645-0525-4*) IDG Bks.
— Using Your First PC. LC 99-64851. (Cliffs Technology Extension Ser.). 128p. 1999. 8.99 (*0-7645-8519-3*) IDG Bks.
***McCarter, Andre, ed.** Anatomy of a Champion: John Wooden & the UCLA Championship Years. (Illus.). 192p. 2000. 29.95 (*1-58382-051-5*) Sports Pub.
McCarter-Cook, Barbara. God Loves Children Like You! (Orig.). (J). (ps-5). 1997. pap. 6.95 (*0-533-12105-1*) Vantage.
***McCarter, David.** David McCarter's Essential VB Tips & Techniques. LC 99-58974. 225p. 2000. pap. 27.95 (*1-893115-22-4*, Pub. by APress L P) Spr-Verlag.
McCarter, David. VB Tips & Tricks, Vol. 1. Thomas, Zane & Shields, James, eds. LC 97-71094. (Illus.). 160p. (Orig.). 1997. pap. 24.95 (*1-890422-00-2*) Mabry Sftware.
McCarter, Dwight & Schmidt, Ronald. Lost! A Ranger's Journal of Search & Rescue. LC 97-73123. (Illus.). 180p. 1998. pap. 14.95 (*0-9641734-1-7*) Graphicom Pr.
***McCarter, Jim.** Upgrading & Repairing Your PC. (Cliffs Notes Ser.). 128p. 1999. pap. text 8.99 (*0-7645-8531-2*) IDG Bks.
McCarter, Jim, et al. Microsoft Publisher 98 for Dummies. LC Z253.532.M53M4 1998. 384p. 1998. pap. 19.99 (*0-7645-0395-2*) IDG Bks.
McCarter, Joan, jt. ed. see Smith, Eric A.
***McCarter, John.** Recruit & Retain the Best: Key Solutions for HR Professionals. LC 99-89878. (Savvy CareerBuilder Ser.). 2000. pap. 14.95 (*1-57023-134-6*) Impact VA.
McCarter, John, jt. auth. see Schreyer, Ray.
McCarter, Kyle P., jt. auth. see Bozman, John.
McCarter, M. K., ed. see Society of Mining Engineers of AIME Staff.
McCarter, Margaret H. Rock Chalk Dreams: Adapted from "Cuddy's Baby" adapted ed. (Illus.). 96p. Date not set. pap. 14.95 (*0-9649023-0-3*) Hist Advent Prodn.
McCarter, P. Kyle. Ancient Inscriptions: Voices from the Biblical World. LC 96-43428. 1996. 39.95 (*1-880317-49-4*) Biblical Arch Soc.
McCarter, P. Kyle, Jr. Samuel I Vol. 8: A New Translation with Introduction & Commentary. LC 79-7201. (Anchor Bible Ser.). 504p. 1979. 40.00 (*0-385-06760-7*) Doubleday.
McCarter, P. Kyle, Jr., ed. Samuel II. LC 81-43919. (Anchor Bible Ser.: Vol. 9). (Illus.). 576p. 1984. 40.00 (*0-385-06808-5*, Anchor NY) Doubleday.
McCarter, P. Kyle, Jr., et al. Ancient Israel: A Short History from Abraham to the Roman Destruction of the Temple. Shanks, Hershel, ed. LC 88-42996. (Illus.). 267p. (C). 1988. reprint ed. 23.95 (*0-9613089-4-X*, 7H70) Biblical Arch Soc.
— Ancient Israel: A Short History from Abraham to the Roman Destruction of the Temple. Shanks, Hershal, ed. LC 88-42996. (Illus.). 267p. (C). 1998. reprint ed. pap. 16.95 (*1-880317-13-3*, 7H70P) Biblical Arch Soc.
McCarter, P. S., jt. auth. see Greaves, A.
McCarter, R. William. 1200 Art Appreciation SG. 176p. (C). 1995. pap. text, per. 20.95 (*0-7872-1099-4*) Kendall-Hunt.
McCarter, Rob. Life Is Good! LC 99-62258. 129p. 1999. reprint ed. pap. 11.95 (*0-937539-37-6*) Executive Bks.
— Optimistic Thinking: The Key to Success. 96p. 1994. pap. 9.95 (*1-57087-073-X*) Prof Pr NC.
McCarter, Robert. Fallingwater: Bear Run, Pennsylvania, 1935, Frank Lloyd Wright. LC 95-142736. (Architecture in Detail Ser.). (Illus.). 60p. (Orig.). (C). 1994. pap. 29.95 (*0-7148-2995-1*, Pub. by Phaidon Press) Phaidon Pr.
— Frank Lloyd Wright. (Architecture 3s Ser.). 368p. 1999. pap. 19.95 (*0-7148-3854-3*) Phaidon Pr.
— Frank Lloyd Wright. (Illus.). 320p. 1997. 79.95 (*0-7148-3148-4*, Pub. by Phaidon Press) Phaidon Pr.
— Unity Temple: Oak Park, Illinois, 1905: Frank Lloyd Wright. (Architecture in Detail Ser.). (Illus.). 60p. 1997. pap. 29.95 (*0-7148-3629-X*, Pub. by Phaidon Press) Phaidon Pr.
McCarter, Robert, ed. Abstract, 1988-89. (Illus.). 120p. (Orig.). (C). 1989. pap. write for info. (*0-9623829-0-6*) CUGSA.
— Abstract, 1989-90. (Illus.). 136p. (Orig.). 1990. pap. write for info. (*0-9623829-1-4*) CUGSA.
— Abstract, 1990-91. (Illus.). 128p. (Orig.). (C). 1991. pap. 19.95 (*0-9623829-2-2*) CUGSA.
— Frank Lloyd Wright: A Primer on Architectural Principles. LC 91-8534. (Illus.). 304p. (Orig.). 1991. pap. 29.95 (*0-910413-86-X*) Princeton Arch.
McCarter, Robert, et al, eds. Building Machines. (Pamphlet Architecture Ser.: Vol. 12). (Illus.). 64p. (Orig.). 1987. pap. 12.95 (*0-910413-40-1*) Princeton Arch.
McCarter, Robert L., jt. auth. see Johnson, Sandi.
McCarter, Steve. Guide to the Milwaukee Road in Montana. LC 92-23233. (Illus.). 112p. 1992. pap. 5.95 (*0-917298-27-6*) MT Hist Soc.
McCartey, W., Jr., jt. auth. see Hill, Levi L.
McCarthy. Balconies & Roof Gardens. pap. text. write for info. (*0-471-48959-X*) Wiley.
McCarthy. Better Writing: A Handbook for Teachers in All Disciplines. (C). 1992. pap. text. write for info. (*0-07-044317-3*) McGraw.
— Color Atlas of Surgery for the Removal of Melanoma, Vol. 40. (Illus.). 1991. write for info. (*0-8151-5859-9*) Mosby Inc.
— Community-based Corrections. 4th ed. (Criminal Justice Ser.). 2000. pap. text 46.25 (*0-534-51673-4*) Wadsworth Pub.
— Descriptive Writing. 64p. 1998. pap. 9.95 (*0-590-20932-9*, 893250Q) Scholastic Inc.
— Essentials of Safe Dentistry for the Medical Compromised Patient. 272p. 1989. text 46.00 (*0-7216-6233-1*, W B Saunders Co) Harcrt Hlth Sci Grp.
— Materials Characterization Applied to Utilization, Immobilization & Disposal of Solid Wastes. write for info. (*0-444-00870-5*) Elsevier.
— Nursing Assistance: Spanish Version. (SPA.). 1995. pap., wbk. ed. 13.60 (*0-8359-4947-8*) P-H.
— Nursing Assistant: Spanish Version. (SPA.). 304p. (C). 1995. pap. text 22.00 (*0-8359-4920-6*) P-H.
— Obstetrics & Gynaecology. 1998. pap. text 24.95 (*0-443-05244-1*) Church.
***McCarthy.** Operating Systems for Teams. (C). 1999. pap. text. write for info. (*0-201-60456-6*) Addison-Wesley.
McCarthy. Plastic Surgery, 8 vols., Set. 3rd ed. (Illus.). 6448p. 1989. text 995.00 (*0-7216-1514-7*, W B Saunders Co) Harcrt Hlth Sci Grp.
— Plastic Surgery, Vol. 1. 3rd ed. 1989. text 165.00 (*0-7216-2542-8*, W B Saunders Co) Harcrt Hlth Sci Grp.
— Plastic Surgery, Vol. 2. 3rd ed. 1989. text 165.00 (*0-7216-2543-6*, W B Saunders Co) Harcrt Hlth Sci Grp.
— Plastic Surgery, Vol. 3. 3rd ed. 1989. text 165.00 (*0-7216-2544-4*, W B Saunders Co) Harcrt Hlth Sci Grp.
— Plastic Surgery, Vol. 4. 3rd ed. 1989. text 165.00 (*0-7216-2545-2*, W B Saunders Co) Harcrt Hlth Sci Grp.
— Plastic Surgery, Vol. 5. 3rd ed. 1989. text 165.00 (*0-7216-2546-0*, W B Saunders Co) Harcrt Hlth Sci Grp.
— Plastic Surgery, Vol. 6. 3rd ed. 1989. text 165.00 (*0-7216-2547-9*, W B Saunders Co) Harcrt Hlth Sci Grp.
— Plastic Surgery, Vol. 7. 3rd ed. 1989. text 165.00 (*0-7216-2548-7*, W B Saunders Co) Harcrt Hlth Sci Grp.
— Plastic Surgery, Vol. 8. 3rd ed. 1989. text 165.00 (*0-7216-2549-5*, W B Saunders Co) Harcrt Hlth Sci Grp.
***McCarthy.** Practical Horse & Pony Nutrition. 2000. pap. 22.95 (*0-85131-697-2*, Pub. by J A Allen) Trafalgar.
— The Sea: Biological-Physical Interactions in the Ocean, Vol. 12. 500p. 110.00 (*0-471-18901-4*) Wiley.
McCarthy. Using Your 401(k) Plan Wisely. 88p. 1994. pap. 5.00 (*0-614-26855-9*, BLS-3329) CCH INC.
McCarthy & Cambron-McCabe, Nelda H. Public School Law. 2nd ed. 1987. text 40.95 (*0-205-10489-4*, H04898) Allyn.
McCarthy & Carr. Juvenile Law & Its Process: 1992 Supplement. 177p. 1992. pap. 6.50 (*0-87473-991-8*, 12301-10, MICHIE) LEXIS Pub.
McCarthy & Levy. Frommer's Greece on $45 a Day, 1995-1996. 1995. pap. 17.95 (*0-671-51167-X*) S&S Trade.
McCarthy & Mitchell. Get the Message. 1991. pap. text. write for info. (*0-582-86977-3*, Pub. by Addison-Wesley) Longman.
McCarthy & Sunsoft Inc. Staff. UNIX Security Audit. (C). 2001. pap. text 32.00 (*0-13-494998-6*) P-H.
McCarthy, jt. auth. see Gibaldi.
McCarthy, jt. auth. see Repp.
McCarthy, jt. ed. see Gathercole.
McCarthy, Albert J., jt. auth. see Hentoff, Nat.
McCarthy, Albert J., ed. see Hentoff, Nat.
McCarthy, Alice. Health 'n Me! Grade 3. (Illus.). 250p. 1996. teacher ed., ring bd. 38.00 (*1-57035-096-5*) Sopris.
McCarthy, Alice R. Health 'n Me! Grade 5: Teachers Manual. (Illus.). 444p. 1997. teacher ed., ring bd. 38.00 (*1-57035-101-5*, 91MAN5) Sopris.
— Health 'n Me! Grade 4: Teacher Guide. (Illus.). 434p. 1997. teacher ed., ring bd. 38.00 (*1-57035-100-7*, 91MAN4) Sopris.
— Health 'n Me! Grade 1: Teacher Guide. (Illus.). 358p. (J). (gr. 1). 1996. teacher ed., ring bd. 38.00 (*1-57035-098-1*, 91MAN1) Sopris.
— Health 'n Me! Grade 6: Teacher Guide. (Illus.). 492p. 1997. teacher ed., ring bd. 38.00 (*1-57035-102-3*, 91MAN6) Sopris.
— Health 'n Me! Grade 2: Teacher Guide. (Illus.). 378p. (J). (gr. 2). 1996. teacher ed., ring bd. 38.00 (*1-57035-097-3*, 91MAN2) Sopris.
— Health 'n Me! Kindergarten: Teacher Guide. (Illus.). 374p. (J). (gr. k). 1996. teacher ed., ring bd. 38.00 (*1-57035-099-X*, 91MANK) Sopris.
— Healthy Preschoolers: At School - At Home. 2nd ed. McCarthy, Jim, ed. LC 94-72479. (Illus.). 93p. 1995. pap. 7.98 (*0-9621645-2-6*) Bridge Commns Inc.
— Healthy Teens: Success in High School & Beyond. 2nd rev. ed. McCarthy, James et al, eds. LC 97-213198. 130p. (Orig.). 1997. pap. 5.95 (*0-9621645-4-2*, HT-2D) Bridge Commns Inc.
***McCarthy, Alice R., et al.** Healthy Teens: Facing the Challenges of Young Teens. 3rd ed. Raphael, Donna & McCarthy, David, eds. LC 99-90976. Orig. Title: Healthy Teens: Success in High School & Beyond. (Illus.). 247p. 2000. pap. 14.95 (*0-9621645-5-0*) Bridge Commns Inc.
McCarthy, Aline. Lose Weight & Keep Fit: The Complete Handbook for Healthier Living. 126p. 1990. pap. 19.95 (*0-7463-0571-0*, Pub. by How To Bks) Trans-Atl Phila.
McCarthy-Arnolds, Eileen, et al, eds. Africa, Human Rights, & the Global System: The Political Economy of Human Rights in a Changing World, 15. LC 93-1643. 288p. 1993. 57.95 (*0-313-29007-5*, Greenwood Pr) Greenwood.
McCarthy, Arthur M. & Nocito, James A. Spanish for Public Safety Personnel. 2nd rev. ed. (Illus.). 149p. 1996. pap. text 24.99 (*1-890431-00-1*) Anticipatory Lang Lrning.
— Spanish for Public Safety Personnel: Complete Package: Main Book, Pocket Book, 3 Audio Cassettes. LC 97-32873. (ENG & SPA.). 192p. 1998. pap. 70.00 incl. audio (*0-7506-7017-7*) Buttrwrth-Heinemann.
— Spanish for Public Safety Personnel: Pocket Book. LC 97-32873. (ENG & SPA.). 60p. 1998. pap. 29.95 incl. audio (*0-7506-7033-9*) Buttrwrth-Heinemann.
— Spanish for Public Safety Personnel Laminated Booklet. 2nd rev. ed. 60p. 1996. ring bd. 39.95 (*1-890431-02-8*) Anticipatory Lang Lrning.
— Spanish Grammar for Public Safety Personnel. 2nd rev. ed. (Illus.). 36p. 1996. pap. text 8.95 (*1-890431-01-X*) Anticipatory Lang Lrning.
McCarthy, B. Eugene. Thomas Gray: The Progress of a Poet. LC 96-25906. (Illus.). 280p. 1997. 42.50 (*0-8386-3715-9*) Fairleigh Dickinson.
McCarthy, B. G. The Female Pen: Women Writer's & Novelists, 1621-1818. LC 94-10446. 448p. (C). 1994. text 55.00 (*0-8147-5519-4*); pap. text 19.00 (*0-8147-5518-6*) NYU Pr.
McCarthy, Bairbre. Favourite Irish Legends: A Dual Language Book. 61p. (J). 1998. pap. 7.95 (*1-85635-186-6*) Irish Bks Media.
— Irish Leprechaun Stories. 93p. (J). (gr. 3 up). 1998. pap. 7.95 (*1-85635-229-3*) Irish Bks Media.
McCarthy, Barbara, tr. see Verkhovsky, Abbess V.
McCarthy, Barry & McCarthy, Emily. Couple's Sexual Awareness: Building Sexual Happiness. (Illus.). 304p. 1998. pap. 12.95 (*0-7867-0525-6*) Carroll & Graf.
— Male Sexual Awareness: Increasing Sexual Satisfaction. LC 97-45907. (Illus.). 304p. 1998. pap. 12.95 (*0-7867-0473-X*) Carroll & Graf.
McCarthy, Barry W. & McCarthy, Emily. Confronting the Victim Role: Healing from an Abusive Childhood. 222p. 1993. pap. 11.95 (*0-7867-0011-4*) Carroll & Graf.
— Female Sexual Awareness: Achieving Sexual Fulfillment. (Illus.). 320p. 1989. pap. 9.95 (*0-88184-479-9*) Carroll & Graf.
— Intimate Marriage: Developing a Life Partnership. (Illus.). 256p. 1992. pap. 10.95 (*0-88184-824-7*) Carroll & Graf.
— Sexual Awareness: 10th Anniversary Edition. 10th enl. rev. anniversary ed. LC 84-9502. (Illus.). 272p. 1993. pap. 11.95 (*0-7867-0015-7*) Carroll & Graf.
***McCarthy, Bart.** Whales of the Mystery Sea. 2000. pap. 18.00 (*0-7388-2095-4*) Xlibris Corp.
McCarthy, Belinda R. & Langworthy, Robert J., eds. Older Offenders: Perspectives in Criminology & Criminal Justice. LC 87-7147. 253p. 1988. 67.95 (*0-275-92734-2*, C2734, Praeger Pubs) Greenwood.
McCarthy, Belinda R. & McCarthy, Bernard J., Jr. Community-Based Corrections. 2nd ed. LC 90-47532. 431p. (C). 1991. mass mkt. 26.50 (*0-534-15510-3*) Wadsworth Pub.
— Community-Based Corrections. 3rd ed. LC 96-43363. (Criminal Justice Ser.). 458p. (C). 1996. 64.95 (*0-534-23124-1*) Wadsworth Pub.
McCarthy, Bernard J., Jr., jt. auth. see McCarthy, Belinda R.
McCarthy, Bernice. About Learning. McNamara, Mary, ed. (Illus.). 442p. 1996. 29.95 (*0-9608992-6-X*) About Learning.
— About Learning Paperback. McNamara, Mary, ed. (Illus.). 442p. 1996. 19.95 (*0-9608992-9-4*) About Learning.
— The 4Mat System: Teaching to Learning Styles with Right-Left Mode Techniques. 3rd rev. ed. LC 80-70421. (Illus.). 1987. 25.95 (*0-9608992-0-0*) About Learning.
McCarthy, Bernice & Morris, Susan. 4mat in Action: Sample Units for Grades K-6. 3rd ed. (Illus.). 1995. 22.95 (*0-9608992-4-3*) About Learning.
— 4mat in Action: Sample Units for Grades 7-12. 3rd ed. (Illus.). 1995. 22.95 (*0-9608992-5-1*) About Learning.
McCarthy, Betty. Utah. rev. ed. LC 89-35083. (America the Beautiful Ser.). (Illus.). 144p. (J). (gr. 5-8). 1989. lib. bdg. 28.00 (*0-516-00490-5*) Childrens.
***McCarthy, Bill.** The Our Father: Four Commentaries on the Lord's Prayer. (Illus.). 122p. 1999. pap. 8.95 (*1-891903-15-2*) St Andrew Prodns.
McCarthy, Bill & Mallowe, Mike. Vice Cop. 352p. 1993. mass mkt. 5.99 (*0-8217-4025-3*, Zebra Kensgtn) Kensgtn Pub Corp.
***McCarthy, Bill & Tibbets, James.** Mary in the Church Today: Official Catholic Teachings on the Mother of God Since Vatican II. (Illus.). 504p. 2000. pap. 14.95 (*1-891903-22-5*) St Andrew Prodns.
McCarthy, Bill, jt. auth. see Hagan, John.
McCarthy, Bobette. Happy Hiding Hippos. LC 92-32599. (Illus.). 32p. (J). (ps-1). 1994. text 13.95 (*0-02-765446-X*, Bradbury S&S) S&S Childrens.
***McCarthy, Bobette.** See You Later, Alligator. (Illus.). 30p. (J). (ps-1). 1999. reprint ed. text 15.00 (*0-7881-6645-X*) DIANE Pub.
McCarthy, Bridget-Beattie. Cultural Tourism: How the Arts Can Help Market Tourism Products; How Tourism Can Help Provide Markets for the Arts. (Illus.). 200p. (Orig.). 1992. pap. 59.00 (*0-9616696-7-5*) B B McCarthy.
— Where to Find the Oregon in Oregon: A Guide to Oregon's Local, Natural, & Cultural Resources. 8th rev. ed. (Illus.). 182p. 1994. pap. 10.95 (*0-9616696-6-7*) B B McCarthy.
— Where to Find the Oregon in Oregon, 1989-1990. 5th rev. ed. (Illus.). 128p. (Orig.). 1989. pap. 6.95 (*0-9616696-3-2*) B B McCarthy.
McCarthy, Brigid, tr. see Archimandrite I. Balan & Balan, Ioanichie.
McCarthy, C., jt. auth. see Evans, A.
McCarthy, Callum, jt. auth. see Davies, Duncan.
McCarthy, Cameron. The Uses of Culture: Education & the Limits of Ethnic Affiliation. LC 97-19763. (Critical Social Thought Ser.). 192p. (C). 1997. 70.00 (*0-415-91299-7*); pap. 19.99 (*0-415-91300-4*) Routledge.
***McCarthy, Cameron, et al, eds.** Sound Identities: Popular Music & the Cultural Politics of Education. LC 98-27792. (Counterpoints Ser.: Vol. 96). 504p. (C). 1999. pap. text 32.95 (*0-8204-4139-2*) P Lang Pubng.
McCarthy, Cameron & Crichlow, Warren, eds. Race, Identity & Representation in Education. (Critical Social Thought Ser.). 416p. (C). (gr. 13). 1993. pap. 20.99 (*0-415-90558-3*, A6869) Routledge.
McCarthy, Cameron, jt. auth. see Mahalingam, Ram.
***McCarthy, Candace.** Fireheart. (Zebra Splendor Historical Romances Ser.). 352p. 2000. mass mkt. 4.99 (*0-8217-6622-8*, Zebra Kensgtn) Kensgtn Pub Corp.
McCarthy, Candace. Irish Linen. 352p. 1996. mass mkt. 4.99 (*0-8217-5379-7*, Zebra Kensgtn) Kensgtn Pub Corp.
— Sweet Possession. 352p. 1999. mass mkt. 4.99 (*0-8217-6121-8*) Kensgtn Pub Corp.
— White Bear's Woman. 352p. 1998. mass mkt. 4.99 (*0-8217-5823-3*, Zebra Kensgtn) Kensgtn Pub Corp.
— Wild Innocence. 1999. mass mkt. 4.99 (*0-8217-6387-3*, Zebra Kensgtn) Kensgtn Pub Corp.
McCarthy, Candace, et al. Affairs of the Heart. 352p. 1999. mass mkt. 5.50 (*0-8217-6116-1*) Kensgtn Pub Corp.
McCarthy, Caritas. The Spirituality of Connelly. LC 86-21718. (Studies in Women & Religion: Vol. 19). 280p. 1986. lib. bdg. 89.93 (*0-88946-530-4*) E Mellen.
McCarthy, Carlton. Detailed Minutiae of Soldier Life in the Army of Northern Virginia, 1861-1865. LC 93-26190. (Illus.). xix, 224p. 1993. pap. 10.95 (*0-8032-8197-8*, Bison Books) U of Nebr Pr.
McCarthy, Carmel. The Scent of Jasmine: Reflections for Peace in Everyday Life. LC 95-30480. 216p. (Orig.). 1995. pap. 14.95 (*0-8146-2332-8*, Liturg Pr Bks) Liturgical Pr.
McCarthy, Carmel, ed. Saint Ephrem's Commentary on Tatian's "Diatessaron" An English Translation of Chester Beatty Syriac MS 709 with Introduction & Notes. LC 94-159657. (Journal of Semetic Studies Supplement: Suppl. No. 2). (Illus.). 388p. 1994. text 65.00 (*0-19-922163-4*) OUP.
McCarthy, Carol H. An Archaeological Sample Survey of the Middle Santa Cruz River Basin, Picacho Reservoir to Tucson, Arizona: A Class II Survey of the Proposed Tucson Aqueduct Phase A, Central Arizona Project. (Archaeological Ser.: No. 148). (Illus.). 78p. 1982. pap. 6.95 (*1-889747-20-3*) Ariz St Mus.
McCarthy, Carol J., jt. auth. see Kennedy, Joycee.
***McCarthy, Cathy.** Ojibwa. LC 00-39026. (Indian Nations Ser.). (Illus.). (J). 2000. pap. 25.69 (*0-8172-5460-9*) Raintree Steck V.
McCarthy, Charles. Doing Business in Ireland. 1987. ring bd. 195.00 (*0-8205-1111-0*) Bender.
McCarthy, Charles H. Lincoln's Plan of Reconstruction. LC 01-26549. reprint ed. 37.50 (*0-404-04105-1*) AMS Pr.
McCarthy, Christopher. Wind Towers, Academy Edition. 96p. 1999. pap. 25.00 (*0-471-98087-0*) Wiley.
McCarthy, Christopher J., jt. auth. see Matheny, Kenneth B.
McCarthy, Claire. Everyone's Children: A Pediatrician's Story of an Inner-City Practice. LC 97-28289. 1998. 22.50 (*0-684-81876-0*, Scribners Ref) Mac Lib Ref.

An Asterisk (*) at the beginning of an entry indicates that the title is appearing for the first time.

— Learning How the Heart Beats: The Making of a Pediatrician. 256p. 1997. pap. 12.95 (0-14-023156-0) Viking Penguin.

McCarthy, Claire F. & National Joint Committee for the Communication Nee. Communication Supports Checklist for Programs Serving Individuals with Severe Disabilities. LC 98-24169. 1998. 35.95 (1-55766-361-0) P H Brookes.

McCarthy, Clarence F., et al. The Federal Income Tax: Its Sources & Applications, 1985 Edition. 1985th ed. (Illus.). 912p. (C). 1984. pap. text 39.33 (0-13-309220-8) P-H.

— The Federal Income Tax, 1983: Its Sources & Applications. 32.95 (0-685-05834-4) P-H.

*McCarthy, Colin. Reptile. (Eyewitness Books). (Illus.). (J). (gr. 4-7). 2000. 19.99 (0-7894-6575-2) DK Pub Inc.

— Reptile. (Eyewitness Books). (J). (gr. 4-7). 2000. 15.95 (0-7894-5786-5) DK Pub Inc.

McCarthy, Colleen, jt. auth. see Ohlinger, John.

McCarthy, Colleen, ed. see Hujsak, Edward.

McCarthy, Colman. All of One Peace. LC 93-45521. 256p. (C). 1994. pap. text 16.00 (0-8135-2097-5) Rutgers U Pr.

McCarthy, Colman, jt. auth. see Regan, Tom.

*McCarthy, Conor. Modernization, Crisis & Culture in Ireland, 1969-1992. 288p. 2000. 55.00 (1-85182-475-8, Pub. by Four Cts Pr); pap. 27.50 (1-85182-479-0, Pub. by Four Cts Pr) Intl Spec Bk.

*McCarthy, Cormac. All the Pretty Horses. (Cliffs Notes Ser.). (Illus.). 2000. pap. 4.95 (0-7645-8551-7) IDG Bks.

McCarthy, Cormac. All the Pretty Horses. 1992. 27.50 (0-394-57474-5) Random.

— All the Pretty Horses. LC 92-50836. 320p. 2000. pap. 13.00 (0-679-74439-8) Vin Bks.

— Blood Meridian or the Evening Redness in the West. 1994. 25.00 (0-8446-6793-5) Peter Smith.

— Blood Meridian or the Evening Redness in the West. 1992. pap. 12.00 (0-679-72875-9) Vin Bks.

*McCarthy, Cormac. The Border Trilogy. 1999. 30.00 (0-676-79534-X) Everymns Lib.

McCarthy, Cormac. Child of God. 1994. 23.50 (0-8446-6750-1) Peter Smith.

— Child of God. LC 92-50587. 1993. pap. 11.00 (0-679-72874-0) Vin Bks.

— Cities of the Plain. LC 98-11583. (Border Trilogy Ser.: Vol.3). 259p. 1998. 24.00 (0-679-42390-7) Knopf.

— Cities of the Plain. (Border Trilogy Ser.). 292p. 1999. pap. 13.00 (0-679-74719-2) Vin Bks.

— Cities of the Plain. limited ed. 292p. 1998. boxed set 195.00 (1-890885-04-5) B E Trice.

— Crossing. 1995. pap. 7.00 (0-679-76086-5) Random.

— The Crossing. 1994. 27.50 (0-394-57475-3) Knopf.

— The Crossing. (Border Trilogy Ser.). 426p. 1995. pap. 13.00 (0-679-76084-9) Vin Bks.

— The Gardener's Son: A Screenplay. LC 96-13611. 128p. 1996. 22.00 (0-88001-481-4) HarpC.

— The Orchard Keeper. 1994. 24.00 (0-8446-6751-X) Peter Smith.

— The Orchard Keeper. LC 92-56360. 1993. pap. 12.00 (0-679-72872-4) Vin Bks.

— The Orchard Keeper. 1997. reprint ed. lib. bdg. 29.95 (1-56849-686-9) Buccaneer Bks.

— Outer Dark. 1994. 24.00 (0-8446-6749-8) Peter Smith.

— Outer Dark. LC 92-50588. 1993. pap. 12.00 (0-679-72873-2) Vin Bks.

— The Stonemason: A Play in Five Acts. LC 93-41252. 144p. 1994. 19.95 (0-88001-359-1) HarpC.

— The Stonemason: A Play in Five Acts. 1995. pap. 12.00 (0-679-76280-9) Random Hse Value.

— Suttree. 1994. 24.50 (0-8446-6792-7) Peter Smith.

— Suttree. 1992. pap. 13.00 (0-679-73632-8) Vin Bks.

McCarthy, Cornelius. The Under 40 Financial Planning Guide: From Graduation to Your First House. LC 96-75088. 398p. 1996. pap. 19.95 (1-56343-134-3) Silver Lake.

McCarthy, D. D. & Carter, W. E., eds. Variations in Earth Rotation. (Geophysical Monograph Ser.: Vol. 59/IUGG 9). 205p. 1990. 32.00 (0-87590-459-9) Am Geophysical.

McCarthy, Dan. Elementary 101 Dieting for Beginners: Electronic Weight Management. unabridged ed. 100p. 1997. pap. 12.00 (0-9666725-1-8) D F McCarthy.

McCarthy, Daniel F. The Pedestal. unabridged ed. 114p. 1998. pap. 18.00 (0-9666725-0-X) D F McCarthy.

McCarthy, David. Golden Age of Rock. 1990. 12.98 (1-55521-559-9) Bk Sales Inc.

— The Nude in American Painting, 1950-1980. LC 97-27042. (Illus.). 272p. (C). 1998. text 70.00 (0-521-59316-6) Cambridge U Pr.

— Nude in Contemporary Art. 1999. pap. 19.95 (1-888332-10-7) Lebhar Friedman.

*McCarthy, David. Pop. (Movements in Modern Art Ser.). (Illus.). 100p. 2000. 39.95 (0-521-79014-X); pap. 15.95 (0-521-79363-7) Cambridge U Pr.

McCarthy, David, ed. see McCarthy, Alice R., et al.

McCarthy, David A. Fear No More: A B-17 Navigator's Journey. LC 91-73262. (Illus.). 254p. (Orig.). 1991. pap. 12.95 (0-9624155-3-7) Cottage Wordsmiths.

McCarthy, David J., Jr. Local Government Law in a Nutshell. 3rd ed. (Nutshell Ser.). 435p. 1990. pap. text 17.50 (0-314-74486-X) West Pub.

McCarthy, David J., Jr., jt. auth. see Valente, William D.

McCarthy, David L. Full Speed, Full Torque Testing of a High Performance Marine Gearbox. (1985 Fall Technical Meeting Ser.: Vol. 85FTM14). 11p. 1985. pap. text 30.00 (1-55589-107-1) AGMA.

McCarthy, David F. Essentials of Soil Mechanics & Foundations: Basic Geotechnics. 5th ed. LC 97-14326. 730p. 1997. 90.67 (0-13-506932-7) P-H.

McCarthy, Dennis. The Loyalty Link: How Loyal Employees Create Loyal Customers. LC 96-46702. 198p. 1997. 19.95 (0-471-16389-9) Wiley.

McCarthy, Dennis D. & Pilkington, John D., eds. Time & the Earth's Rotation. (International Astronomical Union Symposia Ser.: No. 82). 1979. pap. text 70.50 (90-277-0893-2); lib. bdg. 104.50 (90-277-0892-4) Kluwer Academic.

McCarthy, Dennis M. Colonial Bureaucracy & Creating Underdevelopment: Tanganyika, 1919-1940. LC 80-28269. 164p. reprint ed. pap. 50.90 (0-608-00176-7, 206095800006) Bks Demand.

— International Business History: A Contextual & Case Approach. LC 92-31844. 304p. 1994. 69.50 (0-275-94413-1, C4413, Praeger Pubs); pap. 21.95 (0-275-94414-X, B4414, Praeger Pubs) Greenwood.

McCarthy, Dermot. A Poetics of Place: The Poetry of Ralph Gustafson. 352p. (C). 1990. text 55.00 (0-7735-0815-5, Pub. by McG-Queens Univ Pr) CUP Services.

— Ralph Gustafson & His Works. (Canadian Author Studies). 86p. (C). 1989. pap. text 9.95 (1-55022-009-8, Pub. by ECW) Genl Dist Srvs.

— Word, Woman & Place. 116p. 1987. pap. 6.95 (0-86492-051-2, Pub. by Goose Ln Edits) Genl Dist Srvs.

McCarthy, Desmond F. Reconstructing the Family in Contemporary American Fiction. 2nd ed. (Studies on Themes & Motifs in Literature: Vol. 6). VI, 166p. (C). 1998. reprint ed. pap. text 24.95 (0-8204-4266-6) P Lang Pubng.

McCarthy, Dianne, jt. auth. see Davison, Michael.

McCarthy, Donald G., ed. The Family Today & Tomorrow: The Church Addresses Her Future. LC 85-12245. 291p. 1985. pap. 17.95 (0-935372-17-2) NCBC.

— Moral Theology Today: Certitudes & Doubts. LC 84-11714. 355p. (Orig.). 1984. pap. 17.95 (0-935372-14-8) NCBC.

— The New Technologies of Birth & Death: Medical, Legal & Moral Dimensions. LC 80-83425. xvi, 196p. (Orig.). 1980. pap. 8.95 (0-935372-07-5) NCBC.

— Reproductive Technologies, Marriage & the Church: Proceedings of 1988 Bishops' Workshop. LC 88-28997. 318p. (Orig.). 1988. pap. 17.95 (0-935372-23-7) NCBC.

— Scarce Medical Resources & Justice: Proceedings of 1987 Bishops' Workshop. LC 87-18302. 308p. (Orig.). 1987. pap. 17.95 (0-935372-21-0) NCBC.

McCarthy, Donald G. & Leies, John A., eds. Human Sexuality & Personhood: Proceedings of the 1981 Bishops' Workshop. rev. ed. LC 90-14180. 280p. 1990. pap. text 9.95 (0-935372-28-8) NCBC.

McCarthy, Donald W. Fun with Math-E-Magic. Cooper, William H., ed. (Illus.). 65p. (J). (gr. 4-9). 1984. pap. 3.95 (0-914127-01-2) Univ Class.

— Fun with Science Magic. Cooper, William H., ed. LC 84-50893. (Illus.). 80p. (J). (gr. 4-9). 1984. pap. 5.27 (0-914127-15-2) Univ Class.

— More Fun with Math-E-Magic. LC 94-61919. (Illus.). 83p. (J). (gr. 5-8). 1995. pap. 7.33 (0-914127-45-4, M005) Univ Class.

— More Fun with Science Magic. LC 91-75095. (Illus.). 80p. (Orig.). (J). 1991. pap. 6.63 (0-914127-12-8) Univ Class.

McCarthy, Dorothea. The Language Development of the Preschool Child, Vol. 4. LC 74-141549. (University of Minnesota Institute of Child Welfare Monographs: No. 4). (Illus.). 174p. 1975. reprint ed. lib. bdg. 45.00 (0-8371-5896-6, CWML, Greenwood Pr) Greenwood.

McCarthy, E. Doyle. Knowledge As Culture: The New Sociology of Knowledge. LC 96-5489. 144p. (C). 1996. 75.00 (0-415-06496-1); pap. 18.99 (0-415-06497-X) Routledge.

McCarthy, E. Doyle, jt. ed. see Franks, David D.

McCarthy, E. Jerome & Perreault, William D. Basic Marketing: A Global-Managerial Approach. 12th ed. LC 95-34965. (Irwin Series in Marketing). 896p. (C). 1995. text 72.19 (0-256-13990-3, Irwn Prfssnl) McGraw-Hill Prof.

— Essentials of Marketing. 4th ed. (C). 1988. text 56.95 (0-256-06009-6, Irwn McGrw-H) McGrw-H Hghr Educ.

McCarthy, E. Jerome, Jr. & Perreault, William D. Essentials of Marketing: A Global-Managerial Approach. 6th ed. LC 93-29973. (Marketing Ser.). 576p. (C). 1993. text 63.95 (0-256-12746-8, Irwn McGrw-H) McGrw-H Hghr Educ.

McCarthy, E. Jerome & Perreault, William D. Essentials of Marketing: A Global Managerial Approach. 7th ed. 608p. (C). 1996. text 63.95 (0-256-18341-4, Irwn McGrw-H) McGrw-H Hghr Educ.

McCarthy, E. Jerome, jt. auth. see Perreault, William D., Jr.

*McCarthy, Ed. Champagne for Dummies. (For Dummies Ser.). 264p. 1999. pap. 16.99 (0-7645-5216-3) IDG Bks.

McCarthy, Ed. The Financial Advisor's Analytical Toolbox: Using Technology to Optimize Client Solutions. LC 96-50180. 336p. 1997. 55.00 (0-7863-1052-9, Irwn Prfssnl) McGraw-Hill Prof.

— Red Wine for Dummies. LC 96-77705. (For Dummies Ser.). 288p. 1996. pap. 12.99 (0-7645-5012-8, Dummies Tech) IDG Bks.

McCarthy, Ed & Ewing-Mulligan, Mary. White Wine for Dummies. LC 96-77704. (For Dummies Ser.). 304p. 1996. pap. 12.99 (0-7645-5011-X, Dummies Tech) IDG Bks.

— Wine Buying Companion for Dummies. LC 97-80185. (For Dummies Ser.). (Illus.). 432p. 1997. pap. 14.99 (0-7645-5043-8) IDG Bks.

— Wine for Dummies. 2nd ed. LC TP548.M465 1998. (For Dummies Ser.). 432p. 1998. pap. 19.99 (0-7645-5114-0) IDG Bks.

*McCarthy, Edward. Fast Forward MBA in Financial Planning. LC 98-13504. (Fast Forward MBA Ser.). 290p. 1998. pap. 14.95 (0-471-23829-5) Wiley.

McCarthy, Edward F. Differential Diagnosis in Pathology: Bone & Joint Disorders. LC 95-48167. (Illus.). 184p. 1996. 98.50 (0-89640-313-0) Igaku-Shoin.

McCarthy, Edward F. & Frassica, Frank J. Pathology of Bone & Joint Disorders: With Clinical & Radiographic Correlation. Ross, Alan, ed. LC 97-27845. (Illus.). 384p. (C). 1998. text 95.00 (0-7216-6336-2, W B Saunders Co) Harcrt Hlth Sci Grp.

McCarthy, Edward G. Farm Equipment: How Farmers Get All That Work Done. 2nd large type ed. (Illus.). 48p. (J). (gr. 1-5). 1998. reprint ed. pap. 4.98 (0-9664138-0-6) Ed D Bear.

McCarthy, Edward H. Speechwriting: A Professional Step-by-Step Guide for Executives. LC 89-83450. 121p. 1989. pap. 19.95 (0-930255-01-1) Exec Speaker Co.

McCarthy, Edward V. Working Press. LC 96-90547. 350p. (Orig.). 1997. pap. 14.95 (0-533-12094-2) Vantage.

McCarthy, Eithne, tr. see Michel, Marianne R.

McCarthy, Elizabeth. Flood Management. McClurg, Sue, ed. (Layperson's Guide Ser.). (Illus.). 20p. 1998. pap. 5.00 (1-893246-63-9) Water Educ.

— San Francisco Bay. McClurg, Sue, ed. (Layperson's Guide Ser.). (Illus.). 20p. 1997. pap. 5.00 (1-893246-59-0) Water Educ.

— Water Marketing & Transfer. McClurg, Sue, ed. (Layperson's Guide Ser.). (Illus.). 20p. 1996. pap. 5.00 (1-893246-55-8) Water Educ.

— Water Rights Law. McClurg, Sue, ed. (Layperson's Guide Ser.). (Illus.). 20p. 1995. pap. 5.00 (1-893246-53-1) Water Educ.

McCarthy, Elizabeth, ed. see Brickson, Betty.

McCarthy, Ellie, jt. auth. see Davis, Stan.

McCarthy, Elmarie & Budd, Stanley. European Community: A Guide Through the Maze. 6th ed. 1998. pap. 19.95 (0-7494-2117-7) Kogan Page Ltd.

McCarthy, Emily. Couple Sexual Awareness: Building Sexual Happiness. 1990. pap. text 9.95 (0-88184-592-2) Carroll & Graf.

McCarthy, Emily, jt. auth. see McCarthy, Barry.

McCarthy, Emily, jt. auth. see McCarthy, Barry W.

McCarthy, Eugene. Cool Reflections. 1997. pap. 56.95 (1-57553-595-5) Watermrk Pr.

— No-Fault Politics: Modern Presidents, the Press, & Reformers. LC 97-37297. 320p. 1998. 25.00 (0-8129-3016-9, Times Bks) Crown Pub Group.

— Triumph of the Innocent. LC 97-37297. 1997. 24.00 (0-679-45218-4) McKay.

McCarthy, Eugene & McGaughey, William. Nonfinancial Economics: The Case for Shorter Hours of Work. LC 88-28833. 244p. 1989. 55.00 (0-275-92514-5, C2514, Praeger Pubs) Greenwood.

McCarthy, Eugene, et al. Second Opinion Elective Surgery. LC 81-3471. 206p. 1981. 55.00 (0-86569-079-0, Auburn Hse) Greenwood.

McCarthy, Eugene J. An American Bestiary. LC 99-68856. (Illus.). 140p. 2000. pap. 16.95 (1-883477-33-6) Lone Oak MN.

*McCarthy, Eugene J. And Time Began. 1999. pap. text 10.00 (1-889324-07-8) EPM Pubns.

McCarthy, Eugene J. And Time Began. (Illus.). 1993. pap. 10.00 (0-9627860-6-3) Lone Oak MN.

— Complexities & Contraries: Essays of Mild Discontent. LC 81-48016. 192p. 1982. 10.95 (0-15-121202-3) Harcourt.

— Eugene J. McCarthy: Selected Poems. Howe, Ray, ed. LC 96-80114. 160p. 1997. lib. bdg. 14.95 (1-883477-15-8) Lone Oak MN.

— Gene McCarthy's Minnesota. (Illus.). 144p. 1982. 13.45 (0-86683-682-9) Harper SF.

— Ground Fog & Night. LC 78-11437. 64p. 1979. 8.95 (0-15-137261-6) Harcourt.

*McCarthy, Eugene J. Hard Years. rev. ed. LC 99-68859. 300p. 2000. pap. 24.95 (1-883477-38-7) Lone Oak MN.

McCarthy, Eugene J. Memories of a Native Son. 2nd rev. ed. Howe, Ray, ed. LC 99-68850. (Illus.). 196p. 2000. pap. 16.95 (1-883477-32-8) Lone Oak MN.

— Mr. Raccoon & His Friends. (Illus.). 100p. (J). 1992. reprint ed. 16.00 (0-89733-377-2); reprint ed. pap. 6.95 (0-89733-374-8) Academy Chi Pubs.

*McCarthy, Eugene J. 1968. rev. ed. LC 99-68858. 300p. 2000. pap. 24.95 (1-883477-37-9) Lone Oak MN.

McCarthy, Eugene J. Required Reading: A Decade of Political Wit & Wisdom. 256p. 1988. 17.95 (0-15-176880-3) Harcourt.

— The Ultimate Tyranny: The Majority over the Majority. LC 79-3530. 256p. 1980. 12.95 (0-15-192581-X) Harcourt.

— Up 'Til Now: A Memoir of the Decline of American Politics. 192p. 1987. 16.95 (0-15-193170-4) Harcourt.

McCarthy, Francis B. & Carr, James G. Juvenile Law & Its Processes. 2nd ed. (Contemporary Legal Education Ser.). 822p. 1989. text 50.00 (0-87473-435-5, 12301-10, MICHIE) LEXIS Pub.

*McCarthy, Fred. Awards & Recognition: Everything You Need to Know about the Value & Power of Effective Recognition & Award Giving. (Illus.). v, 96p. 2000. ring bd. 49.95 (0-914607-72-3, 1753) Master Tchr.

McCarthy, G. J., et al, eds. Fly Ash & Coal Conversion By-Products: Characterization, Utilization & Disposal III. (MRS Symposium Proceedings Ser.: Vol. 86). 1987. text 17.50 (0-931837-51-0) Materials Res.

McCarthy, Gary. Blood Brothers. 192p. 1999. pap. text 3.99 (0-8439-4585-0, Leisure Bks) Dorchester Pub Co.

— Cimarron River. 288p. 1998. mass mkt. 5.50 (0-553-56798-5) Bantam.

— Grand Canyon. 1996. mass mkt. 5.99 (0-7860-0272-7, Pinncle Kensgtn) Kensgtn Pub Corp.

— Grand Canyon. 1996. pap. 5.99 (0-614-98081-X, Onyx) NAL.

— Gunsmoke. 1998. mass mkt. 5.99 (0-425-16518-3) Berkley Pub.

— Gunsmoke No. 2: Dead Man's Witness. 272p. (Orig.). 1999. mass mkt. 5.99 (0-425-16775-5) Berkley Pub.

— Marshall Festus, Vol. 3. (Gunsmoke Ser.). 1999. mass mkt. 5.99 (0-425-16974-X) Berkley Pub.

— Mesa Verde. 384p. 1997. mass mkt. 5.99 (0-7860-0390-1, Pinncle Kensgtn) Kensgtn Pub Corp.

*McCarthy, Gary. The Mustangers. 192p. 1999. mass mkt. 3.99 (0-8439-4518-4, Leisure Bks) Dorchester Pub Co.

McCarthy, Gary. Powder River. 384p. (Orig.). 1998. mass mkt. 5.50 (0-8439-4408-0, Leisure Bks) Dorchester Pub Co.

— Sodbuster. 208p. 1998. mass mkt. 4.50 (0-8439-4467-6, Leisure Bks) Dorchester Pub Co.

— Wind River. rev. ed. 400p. 1998. mass mkt. 5.99 (0-8439-4377-7, Leisure Bks) Dorchester Pub Co.

— Yellowstone. 384p. 1998. pap. 5.99 (0-7860-0517-3, Pinncle Kensgtn) Kensgtn Pub Corp.

— Yosemite. 384p. 1995. mass mkt. 5.99 (0-8217-0144-4, Zebra Kensgtn) Kensgtn Pub Corp.

— Yosemite: A Sweeping Epic Novel of the American Wilderness in the Bestselling Tradition of James Michener... 476p. 1995. mass mkt. 5.99 (0-7860-0144-5, Pinncle Kensgtn) Kensgtn Pub Corp.

McCarthy, George. Marx & the Ancients. 356p. (C). 1990. lib. bdg. 51.00 (0-8476-7641-2) Rowman.

McCarthy, George D. Acquisitions & Mergers. LC 63-15017. 361p. reprint ed. pap. 112.00 (0-8357-5081-7, 201663200004) Bks Demand.

McCarthy, George E. Marx' Critique of Science & Positivism. 233p. (C). 1988. lib. bdg. 140.50 (90-277-2702-3, Pub. by Kluwer Academic) Kluwer Academic.

— Romancing Antiquity: German Critique of the Enlightenment from Weber to Habermas. LC 97-1989. 408p. 1997. 76.00 (0-8476-8528-4); pap. 29.95 (0-8476-8529-2) Rowman.

McCarthy, George E., ed. Dialectics & Decadence: Echoes of Antiquity in Marx & Nietzsche. LC 93-49607. 250p. (C). 1994. pap. text 23.95 (0-8476-7921-7); lib. bdg. 59.50 (0-8476-7920-9) Rowman.

— Marx & Aristotle: Nineteenth-Century German Social Theory & Classical Antiquity. 260p. (C). 1992. text 67.50 (0-8476-7713-3); pap. text 27.95 (0-8476-7714-1) Rowman.

McCarthy, George E. & Rhodes, Royal W. Eclipse of Justice: Ethics, Economics & the Lost Traditions of American Catholicism. LC 91-34527. 304p. reprint ed. pap. 94.30 (0-608-20276-2, 207153500012) Bks Demand.

McCarthy, Gerald D., jt. auth. see Ottensmeyer, Edward J.

McCarthy, Gillian T., ed. Physical Disability in Childhood. (Interdisciplinary Approach to Management Ser.). (Illus.). 594p. 1992. text 64.95 (0-443-04288-8) Church.

McCarthy, Gregory J. & Lauf, Robert J., eds. Fly Ash & Coal Conversion By-Products: Characterization, Utilization & Disposal, Vol. 43. LC 85-7248. 1985. text 17.50 (0-931837-08-1) Materials Res.

McCarthy, Gregory J., ed. see Materials Research Society Staff, et al.

McCarthy, Harold T. The Expatriate Perspective: American Novelists & the Idea of America. LC 72-418. 320p. 1973. 35.00 (0-8386-1150-8) Fairleigh Dickinson.

McCarthy, Helen. The Anime! Movie Guide. LC 96-49034. (Illus.). 288p. (Orig.). 1997. pap. 16.95 (0-87951-781-6, Pub. by Overlook Pr) Penguin Books.

— Hayao Miyazaki: Master of Japanese Animation. LC 99-43688. (Illus.). 240p. 1999. pap. 18.95 (1-880656-41-8, Pub. by Stone Bridge Pr) Consort Bk Sales.

McCarthy, Helen & Clements, Jonathan. The Erotic Anime Movie Guide. LC 99-10819. (Illus.). 192p. 1999. pap. 17.95 (0-87951-705-0, Pub. by Overlook Pr) Penguin Putnam.

McCarthy, Henry. Featherweight Boatbuilding. (Illus.). 96p. 1996. pap. 19.95 (0-937822-39-6) WoodenBoat Pubns.

McCarthy, Henry, ed. Complete Guide to Employing Persons With Disabilities. LC 84-43093. 1985. 15.00 (0-318-19037-0) Human Res Ctr.

McCarthy, Henry & Smart, Lana. Affirmative Action in Action: Strategies for Enchancing Employment Prospects of Qualified Handicapped Individuals. LC 79-90291. 40p. 1979. 3.75 (0-686-38808-9) Human Res Ctr.

McCarthy, I. E., jt. auth. see Weigold, Erich.

McCarthy, Ian E. Nuclear Reactions. 1970. pap. 120.00 (0-08-006629-1, Pub. by Pergamon Repr) Franklin.

McCarthy, Ian E. & Weigold, Erich. Electron-Atom Collisions. (Cambridge Monographs on Atomic, Molecular, & Chemical Physics: 5). (Illus.). 340p. (C). 1995. text 95.00 (0-521-41359-1) Cambridge U Pr.

McCarthy, J. E. & Tuite, Mick F., eds. Post-Transcriptional Control of Gene Expression. (NATO ASI Series H: Cell Biology: Vol. 49). xix, 652p. 1991. 238.95 (0-387-51774-X) Spr-Verlag.

*McCarthy, J. M. Geometric Design of Linkages. Marsden, J. E. et al, eds. (Interdisciplianry Applied Mathematics Eds: 4). 300p. 2000. text Spr-Verlag.

— Geometric Design of Linkages. Marsden, J. E. et al, eds. LC 99-87080. (Interdisciplinary Applied Mathematics Ser.: Vol. 11). 300p. 2000. 69.95 (0-387-98983-8) Spr-Verlag.

McCarthy, J. M., ed. Kinematics of Robot Manipulators. 200p. 1987. pap. text 25.00 (0-262-63105-9) MIT Pr.

McCarthy, J. Patrick, jt. auth. see Sheeran, Joan G.

McCarthy, J. Thomas. McCarthy on Trademarks & Unfair Competition. 3rd ed. LC 92-33247. (IP Ser.). 1992. ring bd. 625.00 (0-87632-900-8) West Group.

— McCarthy on Trademarks & Unfair Competition. 4th ed. LC 96-40294. 1996. write for info. (0-8366-1108-X) West Group.

An Asterisk (*) at the beginning of an entry indicates that the title is appearing for the first time.

M

McCarthy, Marianthy. Readings in English Bk. 3: Careers. (Readings in English Ser.). 105p. (gr. 9-12). 1987. pap. text. write for info. (0-13-756032-X, 18884) Prentice ESL.

***McCarthy, Marie.** Passing It On: Music & Irish Culture. 224p. 1999. 65.00 (1-85918-178-3); pap. 20.00 (1-85918-179-1) Cork Univ.

McCarthy, Marie, ed. Winds of Change: A Colloquium in Music Education with Charles Fowler & David J. Elliott. LC 94-6524. (State-of-the-Arts Ser.). 49p. 1994. pap. 10.95 (1-879903-19-9) Am for the Arts.

McCarthy, Marie, jt. auth. see Campbell, Patricia S.

McCarthy, Marie, ed. see Martin, Kathryn A., et al.

McCarthy, Martha M. How Can I Best Manage My Classroom? (Teachers Education Ser.: No. 2). (Orig.). 1980. pap. 1.50 (0-934402-05-1) BYLS Pr.

McCarthy, Martha M., et al. Public School Law. 4th ed. LC 96-53463. 514p. 1997. 84.00 (0-205-16676-8) Allyn.

McCarthy, Martha M., et al. Under Scrutiny: The Educational Administration Professoriate. 1988. 13.95 (0-922971-01-3) Univ Council Educ Admin.

McCarthy, Martin & Carty, Alistair. Building 3D Worlds in Java & VRML. LC 97-42083. 500p. (C). 1998. pap. text 49.95 (0-13-748625-1) P-H.

McCarthy, Mary. Birds of America. 1994. lib. bdg. 24.95 (1-56849-426-2) Buccaneer Bks.

— Birds of America. LC 75-147230. 344p. 1971. 11.95 (0-15-112770-0) Harcourt.

— Birds of America. 348p. 1992. pap. 10.95 (0-15-612630-3) Harcourt.

— Cannibals & Missionaries. LC 79-4869. 384p. 1979. 10.95 (0-15-115387-6, Harvest Bks) Harcourt.

— Cannibals & Missionaries. 384p. 1991. pap. 10.95 (0-15-615386-6) Harcourt.

— Cast a Cold Eye. LC 50-9761. 212p. 1950. 12.95 (0-15-115941-6) Harcourt.

— Cast a Cold Eye. LC 92-21660. 228p. 1992. pap. 10.95 (0-15-615444-7, Harvest Bks) Harcourt.

— A Charmed Life. LC 55-10153. 318p. 1955. 15.95 (0-15-116907-1) Harcourt.

— A Charmed Life. 324p. 1992. pap. 10.95 (0-15-616774-3, Harvest Bks) Harcourt.

— The Company She Keeps. 1994. lib. bdg. 24.95 (1-56849-400-9) Buccaneer Bks.

— The Company She Keeps. LC 60-3858. 324p. 1967. pap. 10.00 (0-15-620085-6, Harvest Bks) Harcourt.

— Crescendo LC 99-165773. 494p. 1998. write for info. (1-85371-857-2) Poolbeg Pr.

— The Group. (Modern Classic Ser.). 1989. 15.95 (0-15-137281-0) Harcourt.

— The Group. 492p. (C). 1991. pap. 13.00 (0-15-637208-8) Harcourt.

— The Group. 1980. mass mkt. 4.95 (0-380-52134-2, Avon Bks) Morrow Avon.

— The Group. 400p. 1991. reprint ed. lib. bdg. 28.95 (0-89966-856-9) Buccaneer Bks.

— Le Groupe. (FRE.). 1983. pap. 17.95 (0-7859-4181-9) Fr & Eur.

— The Groves of Academe. LC 92-21659. 312p. 1992. pap. 12.95 (0-15-637211-8, Harvest Bks) Harcourt.

***McCarthy, Mary.** The Groves of Academe. LC 99-51682. 330p. 2000. 27.95 (1-56000-455-X) Transaction Pubs.

McCarthy, Mary. How I Grew. 1987. 16.95 (0-15-142193-5) Harcourt.

— How I Grew. (Illus.). 278p. 1988. pap. 8.95 (0-15-642185-2) Harcourt.

***McCarthy, Mary.** How I Grew. LC 00-26118. 315p. 2000. 29.95 (0-7658-0775-0) Transaction Pubs.

McCarthy, Mary. Ideas & the Novel. LC 80-82344. 128p. 1980. 7.95 (0-15-143682-7) Harcourt.

— Intellectual Memoirs: New York, 1936-1938. 1992. 15.95 (0-15-144820-5) Harcourt.

***McCarthy, Mary.** Making Books by Hand: A Step-by-Step Guide, 2000. pap. text 16.99 (1-56496-675-5) Rockport Pubs.

McCarthy, Mary. The Mask of State: Watergate Portraits Including a Postscript on the Pardons. LC 74-26953. 183p. 1975. pap. 2.65 (0-15-657302-4, Harvest Bks) Harcourt.

— Memories of a Catholic Girlhood. LC 57-8842. (Illus.). 264p. 1972. reprint ed. pap. 12.00 (0-15-658650-9, Harvest Bks) Harcourt.

— Remember Me. LC 96-184713. 698p. 1996. pap. 12.95 (1-85371-610-3, Pub. by Poolbeg Pr) Dufour.

— The Seventeenth Degree. LC 74-1065. 451p. 1974. reprint ed. pap. 3.95 (0-15-680680-0, Harvest Bks) Harcourt.

— The Stones of Florence. LC 64-49015. 252p. 1963. pap. 11.00 (0-15-685080-X, Harvest Bks) Harcourt.

— The Stones of Florence. LC 59-10257. (Illus.). 138p. 1976. 49.95 (0-15-185079-8) Harcourt.

— The Stones of Florence. (Illus.). 288p. 1987. pap. 19.95 (0-15-685081-8, Harvest Bks); text 49.95 (0-317-64159-X, Harvest Bks) Harcourt.

— Venice Observed. LC 64-49016. 168p. 1963. pap. 11.00 (0-15-693521-X, Harvest Bks) Harcourt.

— The Writing on the Wall & Other Literary Essays. LC 70-100498. Orig. Title: Hanging by a Thread & Other Literary Essays. 213p. 1971. reprint ed. pap. 4.95 (0-15-698390-7, HB207, Harvest Bks) Harcourt.

McCarthy, Mary & Manna, Philip. Making Books by Hand: A Step-by-Step Guide. (Illus.). 108p. 1997. 24.99 (1-56496-328-4, Quarry Bks) Rockport Pubs.

McCarthy, Mary Ellen, jt. auth. see Cundiff, David.

McCarthy, Mary F., tr. see Ciria, Alberto.

McCarthy, Mary F., tr. see Ratzinger, Joseph C.

McCarthy, Mary F., tr. see Von Balthasar, Hans U.

McCarthy, Mary F., tr. see Von Speyr, Adrienne.

McCarthy, Mary J. Elk Grove: The Peony Village. Wagner, Roswita M., ed. (Illus.). 167p. 1981. pap. 6.95 (0-9605940-0-0) Elk Grove Vill.

— Fund-Raising Standards for Annual Giving & Campaign Reports: For Not-for-profit Organizations Other Than Educational Institutions. 60p. 1998. pap. 59.95 (0-89964-336-1) Coun Adv & Supp Ed.

— The Impact of FASB Standards 116 & 117 on Development Operations. 29p. 1995. 9.00 (0-89964-312-4, 25202) Coun Adv & Supp Ed.

McCarthy, Mary-Jane, et al. Reading & Learning Across the Disciplines. 424p. (C). 1992. mass mkt. 25.75 (0-534-12817-3) Wadsworth Pub.

— Reading & Learning Across the Disciplines. 2nd ed. 1996. 32.50 (0-534-25722-4) Wadsworth Pub.

McCarthy, Mary Pat, jt. auth. see Patel, Keyur.

McCarthy, Mary T. Cape May for All Seasons. gif. ed. LC 98-96789. (Illus.). 96p. 1998. pap. 24.95 (0-9668335-0-3) Preserv Media.

***McCarthy, Maureen.** Prelude to Passion: Journey to Love. (Illus.). 84p. 1999. pap. 7.95 (1-879007-36-3) St Bedes Pubns.

— Sneaking Through the Evening. 80p. 1999. pap. 14.95 (1-55017-216-6) Harbour Pub Co.

McCarthy, Maureen E. & Rosenberg, Gail S. Work Sharing Case Studies. LC 81-15943. 277p. 1981. pap. 14.00 (0-911558-88-8) W E Upjohn.

McCarthy, Maxine. Benin (Dahomey) LC 95-22472. (OIES Country Guide Ser.). Date not set. 20.00 (0-929851-65-X) Am Assn Coll Registrars.

McCarthy, Meladee & McCarty, Hanoch. Daily Journal of Kindness: A Year Long Guide for Creating Your Own Kindness Revolution. 390p. (Orig.). 1996. pap. 11.95 (1-55874-412-6, 4126) Health Comm.

McCarthy, Michael. Dark Continent: Africa As Seen by Americans, 75. LC 83-8878. (Contributions in Afro-American & African Studies: No. 75). (Illus.). 192p. 1983. 57.95 (0-313-23828-6, MDK/, Greenwood Pr) Greenwood.

— Discourse Analysis for Language Teachers. (Language Teaching Library). (Illus.). 223p. (C). 1991. pap. text 20.95 (0-521-36746-8) Cambridge U Pr.

— The Gothic Revival. LC 86-28119. 214p. 1987. 50.00 (0-300-03723-6) Yale U Pr.

— Language Teaching: A Scheme for Teacher Education Vocabulary. Widdowson, H. G. & Candlin, C. N., eds. (Illus.). 184p. 1990. pap. text 14.95 (0-19-437136-0) OUP.

***McCarthy, Michael.** Spoken Language & Applied Linguistics. LC 98-39755. 1998. write for info. (0-521-59213-5); pap. write for info. (0-521-59769-2) Cambridge U Pr.

McCarthy, Michael, ed. Cambridge Word Routes: English-French. (FRE., Illus.). 479p. (C). 1995. text 32.95 (0-521-45464-6); pap. text 21.95 (0-521-42583-2) Cambridge U Pr.

— Cambridge Word Routes: English-Italian. (ITA., Illus.). 480p. (C). 1995. text 32.95 (0-521-48025-6); pap. text 21.95 (0-521-42223-X) Cambridge U Pr.

— Cambridge Word Selector: English-Spanish. (SPA., Illus.). 476p. (C). 1994. pap. text 21.95 (0-521-42582-4) Cambridge U Pr.

— Cambridge Word Selector: English-Spanish. (SPA., Illus.). 476p. (C). 1995. text 32.95 (0-521-47311-X) Cambridge U Pr.

— The New Politics of Welfare: An Agenda for the 1990s. LC 89-12855. 274p. (Orig.). (C). 1989. pap. text 29.95 (0-925065-23-4) Lyceum IL.

McCarthy, Michael & Brooks, Catherine M. Medieval Pottery in Britain, A. D. 900-1600. (Illus.). 520p. 1992. 49.00 (0-7185-1254-5) St Martin.

McCarthy, Michael & O'Dell, Felicity A. Vocabulary in Use: Vocabulary Reference & Practice for Intermediate to Advanced Students. LC 96-44820. 297p. (C). 1997. pap. text, student ed. 22.95 (0-521-57768-3); pap. text, student ed. 18.95 (0-521-57700-4) Cambridge U Pr.

***McCarthy, Michael, et al.** Basic Vocabulary in Use. 176p. (C). 2000. pap. Price not set. (0-521-78865-X); pap. Price not set. (0-521-78864-1) Cambridge U Pr.

McCarthy, Michael, jt. auth. see Allen, Janis.

McCarthy, Michael, jt. auth. see Carter, Ronald.

McCarthy, Michael, jt. auth. see Galgay, Frank.

McCarthy, Michael, jt. auth. see Monnett, John H.

McCarthy, Michael H. The Crisis of Philosophy. LC 89-30040. (SUNY Series in Philosophy). 383p. (C). 1989. text 21.50 (0-7914-0152-9) State U NY Pr.

McCarthy, Michael J. Introducing Art History: A Guide for Teachers. LC 78-319686. (Ontario Institute for Studies in Education, Symposium Ser.: No. 33). 128p. reprint ed. pap. 39.70 (0-608-12568-7, 202397400035) Bks Demand.

— Magnetic Resonance Imaging for Food Research & Technology. LC 92-34008. 1992. text 69.95 (0-442-01021-4) Chapman & Hall.

***McCarthy, Michael P.** Baltimore: The Living City. 1999. 40.00 (0-938420-68-2) MD Hist.

McCarthy, Michael P. Typhoid & the Politics of Public Health in Nineteenth Century Philadelphia. LC 86-72881. (Memoirs Ser.: Vol. 179). (Illus.). 150p. (Orig.). (C). 1988. pap. 10.00 (0-87169-179-5, M179-MCM) Am Philos.

McCarthy, Michael R. Medieval Poetry in Britain, A. D. 900-1600. 1995. pap. 31.90 (0-7185-1271-5) Bks Intl VA.

McCarthy, Michael W. Thomas Edison & His Innovation Dream Team: A Brief History of America's Most Prolific Inventor & the Men Behind His Success. LC 99-73819. (Illus.). 112p. 1999. pap. 10.95 (0-9659638-4-5) Fin Literacy.

McCarthy, Michelle. Sex & Women with Learning Disabilities. LC 98-45896. 1999. pap. 28.95 (1-85302-730-8) Taylor & Francis.

***McCarthy, Mike.** Iron & Steamship Archaeology: Success & Failure of the SS Xantho. LC 00-35704. (Series in Underwater Archaeology). (Illus.). 2000. write for info. (0-306-46365-2) Plenum.

McCarthy, Miriam J., jt. auth. see Herman, David.

McCarthy, Muriel Q. David R. Williams: Pioneer Architect. LC 82-17002. (Illus.). 192p. 1984. 35.00 (0-87074-182-9) SMU Press.

McCarthy, Nan. Chat. 144p. 1998. pap. 6.00 (0-671-02339-X, Pocket Books) PB.

***McCarthy, Nan.** Chat: A Cybernovel. ed. 1998. per. 6.00 (0-671-03691-2, Pocket Books) PB.

McCarthy, Nan. Connect. 144p. 1998. pap. 6.00 (0-671-02340-3, Pocket Books) PB.

***McCarthy, Nan.** Connect: A Cybernovel. ed. 1998. per. 6.00 (0-671-03692-0, Pocket Books) PB.

McCarthy, Nan. Crash. LC 99-195318. 144p. 1998. pap. 6.00 (0-671-02341-1, Pocket Books) PB.

***McCarthy, Nan.** Crash: A Cybernovel. ed. 1998. per. 6.00 (0-671-03693-9, Pocket Books) PB.

McCarthy, Nancy. Chat: A Cybernovel. LC 96-172478. 136p. (C). 1996. pap. text 7.95 (0-201-88668-5) Peachpit Pr.

— Quark Design: A Step-by-Step Approach to Page Layout Software. (Illus.). 144p. (C). 1995. pap. text 34.95 (0-201-88376-7) Peachpit Pr.

McCarthy, Nancy W., ed. see Heideman, Carol.

McCarthy, P. Critical Essays on Finnegans Wake. (Critical Essays on British Literature Ser.). 250p. 1992. 49.00 (0-8161-8870-X, Hall Reference) Macmillan.

McCarthy, P. J. Introduction to Arithmetical Functions. (Universitext Ser.). (Illus.). 375p. 1985. 64.95 (0-387-96262-X) Spr-Verlag.

McCarthy, P. M., jt. auth. see Elix, J. A.

McCarthy, Padraig. A Wedding of Your Own. 108p. 1989. pap. 22.00 (0-86217-107-5, Pub. by Veritas Pubns) St Mut.

McCarthy, Pat. Classical Kata of Okinawan Karate. Lee, Mike, ed. LC 87-61100. (Japanese Arts Ser.). 256p. (Orig.). 1987. pap. 19.95 (0-89750-113-6, 453) Ohara Pubns.

***McCarthy, Pat.** Daniel Boone: Frontier Legend. LC 99-24578. (Historical American Biographies Ser.). (Illus.). 128p. (gr. 6 up). 2000. lib. bdg. 20.95 (0-7660-1256-5) Enslow Pubs.

— Thomas Paine: Revolutionary Patriot & Writer. LC 00-9261. (Historical American Biographies Ser.). 2001. write for info. (0-7660-1446-0) Enslow Pubs.

McCarthy, Pat, jt. auth. see Hestor, Harold.

McCarthy, Patricia. Passion & Folly: A Scriptural Foundation for Peace. LC 97-41222. ix, 128 p. 1998. pap. 11.95 (0-8146-2469-3) Liturgical Pr.

McCarthy, Patricia A., jt. auth. see Alpiner, Jerome G.

McCarthy, Patricia A., jt. ed. see Alpiner, Jerome G.

***McCarthy, Patrick.** After the Fall: Srebrenica Survivors in St. Louis. (Illus.). 156p. 2000. 24.95 (1-883982-36-7) U of Mo Pr.

McCarthy, Patrick. Ancient Okinawan Martial Arts, Vol. 1. LC 99-37846. 1999. pap. 14.95 (0-8048-2093-7) Tuttle Pubng.

— Ancient Okinawan Martial Arts, Vol. 2. LC 99-37846. 1999. pap. 14.95 (0-8048-3147-5) Tuttle Pubng.

— The Bible of Karate: The Bubishi. (Illus.). 248p. (Orig.). 1995. pap. 16.95 (0-8048-2015-5) Tuttle Pubng.

— Camus: "The Stranger" (Landmarks of World Literature Ser.). 128p. 1988. pap. text 11.95 (0-521-33851-4) Cambridge U Pr.

— The Crisis of the Italian State: From the Origins of the Cold War to the Fall of Berlusconi. LC 95-11890. (Illus.). 256p. 1995. text 35.00 (0-312-12667-0) St Martin.

McCarthy, Patrick. France-germany in the 21st Century. text. write for info. (0-312-22814-7) St Martin.

McCarthy, Patrick. Hierarchy & Flexibility in World Politics: Adaptation to Shifting Power Distributions in the United Nations Security Council & the International Monetary Fund. LC 98-35234. ix, 277p. 1998. text 68.95 (1-84014-471-8, Pub. by Ashgate Pub) Ashgate Pub Co.

***McCarthy, Patrick, ed.** Italy since 1945. (Short Oxford History of Italy Ser.). 235p. 2000. pap. 19.95 (0-19-873169-8); text 65.00 (0-19-873170-1) OUP.

McCarthy, Patrick & Jones, Erik, eds. Disintegration or Transformation? The Crisis of the State in Advanced Industrial Societies. LC 95-37477. 208p. 1995. text 55.00 (0-312-12199-7) St Martin.

McCarthy, Patrick, tr. see Nagamine, Shoshin.

McCarthy, Patrick A. Forests of Symbols: World, Text & Self in Malcolm Lowry's Fiction. LC 93-5337. 216p. 1994. 40.00 (0-8203-1609-1) U of Ga Pr.

— The Riddles of Finnegans Wake. LC 79-24075. 184p. 1970. 29.50 (0-8386-3005-7) Fairleigh Dickinson.

— Ulysses: Portals of Discovery. (Masterwork Studies: No. 41). 130p. 1989. 23.95 (0-8057-7976-0, MWS-41) Macmillan.

McCarthy, Patrick A., ed. The French Socialists in Power, 1981-1986, 174. LC 86-33569. (Contributions in Political Science Ser.: No. 174). 224p. 1987. 57.95 (0-313-25407-9, MFH/, Greenwood Pr) Greenwood.

— Malcolm Lowry's "La Mordida" LC 95-12606. xxiii, 400p. 1996. 75.00 (0-8203-1763-2) U of Ga Pr.

McCarthy, Patrick A., et al, eds. The Legacy of Olaf Stapledon: Critical Essays & an Unpublished Manuscript, 34. LC 88-25097. (Contributions to the Study of Science Fiction & Fantasy Ser.: No. 34). 140p. 1989. 49.95 (0-313-26114-8, MLC/, Greenwood Pr) Greenwood.

McCarthy, Patrick A. & Tiessen, Paul. Joyce/Lowry: Critical Perspectives. LC 96-43475. (Illus.). 216p. 1997. text 34.95 (0-8131-2002-0) U Pr of Ky.

McCarthy, Patrick D., jt. auth. see Spector, Robert.

McCarthy, Patrick M. Saxicolous Species of Porina Mull.Arg. (Trichotheliaceae) in the Western Hemisphere. Wirth, Volkmar et al, eds. (Bibliotheca Lichenologica: Vol. 52). (GER., Illus.). 132p. 1993. pap. 42.00 (3-443-58031-9, Pub. by Gebruder Borntraeger) Balogh.

***McCarthy, Pattie.** Choragus. 32p. 1998. 6.00 (0-937013-84-6, Pub. by Potes Poets) SPD-Small Pr Dist.

McCarthy, Paul. Postmodern Desire Learning from India. LC 94-904666. (C). 1995. 32.00 (81-85002-41-X, Pub. by Promilla) S Asia.

— "The Twisted Mind" Madness in Herman Melville's Fiction. LC 90-10754. 192p. (C). 1990. text 26.95 (0-87745-284-9) U of Iowa Pr.

McCarthy, Paul, ed. Bullying: From Backyard to Boardroom. LC 96-156168. 181p. (Orig.). 1996. pap. 12.95 (1-86429-049-8, Pub. by E J Dwyer) Morehouse Pub.

McCarthy, Paul & Schroeder, Roger. Woodcarving Illustrated Bk. 2: Eight Useful Projects You Can Carve Out of Wood. LC 85-10081. (Illus.). 256p. (Orig.). 1985. pap. 12.95 (0-8117-2285-6) Stackpole.

McCarthy, Paul, jt. auth. see Kelley, Mike.

McCarthy, Paul, jt. auth. see Schroeder, Roger.

McCarthy, Paul, ed. see Ahmed, Saleem.

McCarthy, Paul, ed. see Blackburn, Tom.

McCarthy, Paul, ed. see Brady, James P.

McCarthy, Paul, jt. ed. see Brennan, Matthew.

McCarthy, Paul, ed. see Camp, R. D.

McCarthy, Paul, ed. see Carroll, Gerry.

McCarthy, Paul, ed. see Coonts, Stephen.

McCarthy, Paul, ed. see Coyle, Harold.

McCarthy, Paul, ed. see Cussler, Clive.

McCarthy, Paul, ed. see Davis, Bart.

McCarthy, Paul, ed. see Dickson, Paul.

McCarthy, Paul, ed. see Edelman, Bernard.

McCarthy, Paul, ed. see Foss, Joe & Brennan, Matthew.

McCarthy, Paul, ed. see Galantin, I. J.

McCarthy, Paul, ed. see Goddard, Donald.

McCarthy, Paul, ed. see Hackworth, David H. & Sherman, Julie.

McCarthy, Paul, ed. see Hinshaw, Arned L.

McCarthy, Paul, ed. see Holtz, L.

McCarthy, Paul, ed. see Hynes, Samuel.

McCarthy, Paul, ed. see Joseph, Mark.

McCarthy, Paul, ed. see Kessler, Ronald.

McCarthy, Paul, ed. see Ketwig, John.

McCarthy, Paul, ed. see Krause, Moose & Singular, Stephen.

McCarthy, Paul, ed. see Krulak, Victor H.

McCarthy, Paul, ed. see Kurzman, Dan.

McCarthy, Paul, ed. see Lust, John B. & Tierra, Michael.

McCarthy, Paul, ed. see Marcinko, Richard & Weisman, John.

McCarthy, Paul, ed. see Marshall, Bryce & Williams, Paul.

McCarthy, Paul, ed. see Miller, F. D. & Kureth, E. C.

McCarthy, Paul, ed. see Miller, John G.

McCarthy, Paul, ed. see Norman, Geoffrey.

McCarthy, Paul, ed. see Peters, Ralph.

McCarthy, Paul, ed. see Ruggero, Ed.

McCarthy, Paul, ed. see Sasser, Charles W.

McCarthy, Paul, ed. see Sellers, Con.

McCarthy, Paul, ed. see Slap, Gail B. & Jablow, Martha M.

McCarthy, Paul, ed. see Stauth, Cameron.

McCarthy, Paul, ed. see Taylor, Charles D.

McCarthy, Paul, ed. see Wastermann, John.

McCarthy, Paul, ed. see Westermann, John.

McCarthy, Paul, ed. see Wilcox, Robert K.

McCarthy, Paul, ed. see Wilson, George C.

McCarthy, Paul, ed. see Zumbro, Ralph.

McCarthy, Paul, tr. see Tanizaki, Jun'ichiro.

McCarthy, Paul, tr. see Umehara, Takeshi.

McCarthy, Paul A. Operation Sea Angel: A Case Study. LC 93-42926. 1994. pap. 13.00 (0-8330-1492-7, MR-374-A) Rand Corp.

McCarthy, Paul A., jt. auth. see Childress, Michael T.

McCarthy, Paul J. Algebraic Extensions of Fields. ix, 166p. 1991. pap. 8.95 (0-486-66651-4) Dover.

McCarthy, Paul L. Childhood Illness: Knowing When to Call the Doctor. (Pediatrics Ser.). 32p. 1997. pap. text 2.95 (1-885274-29-7) Health InfoNet Inc.

McCarthy, Pearl. Leo Smith: A Biographical Sketch. LC 76-383510. 64p. reprint ed. pap. 30.00 (0-608-10857-X, 201427700089) Bks Demand.

McCarthy, Peggy & Loren, John. Breast Cancer? Let Me Check My Schedule! LC 97-16378. 288p. 1997. pap. 14.00 (0-465-00763-5) Basic.

McCarthy, Peggy, ed. see Loren, Jo An.

McCarthy, Peter, jt. auth. see Allen, Robert.

McCarthy, Philip J., jt. auth. see Stephen, Fredirick F.

McCarthy, Philip L. & Shklar, Gerald. Diseases of the Oral Mucosa. 2nd ed. LC 80-10335. (Illus.). 589p. reprint ed. pap. 182.60 (0-8357-8687-0, 205684400092) Bks Demand.

McCarthy, R. J., tr. see Al-Ghazali.

***McCarthy, Ralph F.** Adventure of Momotaro, the Peach Boy. 2000. 10.00 (4-7700-2098-8) Kodansha Intl.

McCarthy, Ralph F. Click-Clack Mountain. (Children's Classics Ser.). (Illus.). 48p. (J). 1994. 14.95 (4-7700-1850-9) Kodansha.

— Grandfather Cherry Blossom. LC 93-18301. (Children's Classics Ser.: Vol. 5). (Illus.). 48p. (J). 1993. 19.95 (4-7700-1759-6) Kodansha.

***McCarthy, Ralph F.** Kintaro, the Nature Boy. 2000. 10.00 (4-7700-2102-X) Kodansha Intl.

An Asterisk (*) at the beginning of an entry indicates that the title is appearing for the first time.

McCarthy, Ralph F. The Monkey & the Crab. (Children's Classics Ser.). (Illus.). 48p. (J). 1994. 14.95 (*4-7700-1844-4*) Kodansha.
— The Moon Princess. LC 93-18300. (Children's Classics Ser.: Vol. 2). (Illus.). 48p. (J). 1993. 19.95 (*4-7700-1756-1*) Kodansha.
***McCarthy, Ralph F.** Moon Princess. 2000. 10.00 (*4-7700-2099-6*) Kodansha Intl.
McCarthy, Ralph F. The Sparrow's Inn. (Children's Classics Ser.). (Illus.). 48p. (J). 1994. 14.95 (*4-7700-1849-5*) Kodansha.
— Urashima & the Kingdom Beneath the Sea. LC 93-18500. (Children's Classics Ser.). (Illus.). 48p. (J). 1994. 14.95 (*4-7700-1757-X*) Kodansha.
McCarthy, Ralph F. & Kasamatsu, Shiro. The Inch-High Samurai. LC 93-16310. (Children's Classics Ser.: No. 4). (Illus.). 48p. (J). 1993. 19.95 (*4-7700-1758-8*) Kodansha.
McCarthy, Ralph F., jt. auth. see Maurakami, Ryu.
McCarthy, Ralph F., tr. see Kusama, Yayoi.
McCarthy, Ralph F., tr. see Murakami, Mamiko.
McCarthy, Raymond G., ed. Drinking & Intoxication: Selected Readings in Social Attitudes & Controls. 1959. pap. 23.95 (*0-8084-0409-1*) NCUP.
— Drinking & Intoxication: Selected Readings in Social Attitudes & Controls. LC 59-5289. 1963. pap. 13.95 (*0-911290-28-1*) Rutgers Ctr Alcohol.
McCarthy, Rebecca, ed. see Hodler, Thomas W. & Schretter, Howard A.
***McCarthy, Richard C.** Designing Better Libraries: Selecting & Working with Building Professionals. 2nd ed. LC 99-35255. 132p. 1999. pap. 19.00 (*1-57950-044-7*) Highsmith Pr.
McCarthy, Rita, jt. auth. see Mather, Peter.
McCarthy, Rita E. & White, Olivia M. Eighteenth-Century English Pottery: Selections from the Collection of Harry A. Root. (Illus.). 48p. 1991. pap. 14.95 (*0-86559-093-1*) Art Inst Chi.
McCarthy, Robert A. Vinyl Plastics: A World View of the Industry & Market. LC 85-20410. (Series of Special Reports: No. 14). (Illus.). 392p. reprint ed. pap. 121.60 (*0-7837-0859-9*, 204116700019) Bks Demand.
McCarthy, Robert E. Secrets of Hollywood Special Effects. (Illus.). 224p. 1992. pap. 49.95 (*0-240-80108-3*, Focal) Buttrwrth-Heinemann.
— Special Effects Sourcebook. 96p. 1992. 39.95 (*0-240-80147-4*, Focal) Buttrwrth-Heinemann.
McCarthy, Robert L. Introduction to Health Care Delivery: A Primer for Pharmacists. LC 97-34805. 350p. 40.00 (*0-8342-0914-4*, 09144) Aspen Pub.
McCarthy, Robert V. Captive in the Wild. (Illus.). 120p. 1997. pap. text 9.95 (*0-9657494-0-1*) R V McCarthy.
McCarthy, Rockne M., et al. Confessing Christ & Doing Politics. Rogers, Lilian, tr. LC 80-71233. 100p. (Orig.). 1982. pap. 3.95 (*0-936456-02-7*) Ctr Pub Justice.
— Disestablishment a Second Time: Genuine Pluralism for American Schools. LC 82-9409. 183p. reprint ed. pap. 56.80 (*0-608-14504-1*, 202533500043) Bks Demand.
McCarthy, Roger E. Tears of the Lotus: Accounts of Tibetan Resistance to the Chinese Invasion, 1950-1962. LC 97-6131. 296p. 1997. lib. bdg. 49.95 (*0-7864-0331-4*) McFarland & Co.
McCarthy, Ronald & Sharp, Gene. Nonviolent Action: A Research Guide. LC 97-25316. (History Reference Ser.). 692p. 1997. text 109.00 (*0-8153-1577-5*, SS940) Garland.
McCarthy, Ronald M. & Kruegler, Christopher. Toward Research & Theory Building in the Study of Nonviolent Action. (Monograph Ser.). 35p. (Orig.). 1993. pap. 3.00 (*1-880813-08-4*) A Einstein Inst.
McCarthy, Rosaleen A. & Warrington, Elizabeth K. Cognitive Neuropsychology: A Clinical Introduction. 428p. 1990. text 89.95 (*0-12-481845-5*); pap. text 45.00 (*0-12-481846-3*) Acad Pr.
McCarthy, Ruth. By the Seat of Your Pants. 64p. 1994. pap. text, per. 9.95 (*0-7872-0054-9*) Kendall-Hunt.
— Lefton China. LC 97-80252. (Illus.). 180p. 1998. pap. 29.95 (*0-7643-0415-1*) Schiffer.
***McCarthy, Ruth.** More Lefton China. (Illus.). 176p. 1999. pap. 29.95 (*0-7643-1028-3*) Schiffer.
McCarthy, Samantha, jt. ed. see Bartholomew, Keith.
McCarthy, Samuel T. The MacCarthys of Munster, the History of a Great Irish Sept: A Facsimile Edition with an Extended Commentary Thereon by the MacCarthy Mor. (Illus.). 570p. 1997. 60.00 (*0-9654220-1-1*) Gryfons Pubs & Dist.
McCarthy, Scott. People of the Circle, People of the Four Directions. LC 99-43461. (Illus.). 720p. Date not set. 49.95 (*1-57733-014-5*) B Dolphin Pub.
McCarthy, Sharon, jt. ed. see Stern, Robert N.
McCarthy, Sharon M., jt. auth. see Yocom, John E.
McCarthy, Shaun P. The Function of Intelligence in Crisis Management. LC 97-6100. 311p. 1997. text 71.95 (*1-85521-935-2*, Pub. by Ashgate Pub) Ashgate Pub Co.
McCarthy, Sheila M., jt. auth. see Young, David W.
McCarthy, Sherri. Personal Filing Systems: Creating Information Retrieval Systems on Microcomputers. (Orig.). 1988. pap. text 22.40 (*0-8108-2428-0*) Med Lib Assn.
McCarthy, Shirley & Haseltine, Florence P. Magnetic Resonance of the Reproductive System. 180p. 1986. 68.95 (*0-316-55374-3*, Little Brwn Med Div) Lppncott W & W.
McCarthy, Stephen. Africa: The Challenge of Transformation. 256p. 1995. text 24.50 (*1-85043-820-X*, Pub. by I B T) St Martin.
McCarthy, Stephen, jt. auth. see Colclough, Christopher.
McCarthy, Steven. Black Angels, Red Blood. 1998. pap. 16.95 (*0-7022-2963-6*, Pub. by Univ Queensland Pr) Intl Spec Bk.
McCarthy, Susan. Ethnobotany & Medicinal Plants Bibliography: July 1991-July 1992. 134p. (Orig.). (C). 1993. pap. text 30.00 (*1-56806-620-1*) DIANE Pub.
McCarthy, Susan, jt. auth. see Cavanaugh, Michael.
McCarthy, Susan, jt. auth. see Mason, Jeffrey M.
McCarthy, Susan, jt. auth. see Masson, Jeffrey M.
McCarthy, Susanne. Bad Influence. (Presents Ser.: No. 103). 1999. pap. 3.75 (*0-373-18703-3*, 1-18703-8, Harlequin) Harlequin Bks.
— A Candle for the Devil. LC 95-6877. (Presents Ser.). 186p. 1995. per. 3.25 (*0-373-11748-5*, 1-11748-0) Harlequin Bks.
— Esposa de Otro Hombre: A Married Woman? (Bianca Ser.: Vol. 118).Tr. of Other Man's Wife. (SPA.). 1998. per. 3.50 (*0-373-33468-0*, 1-33468-9) Harlequin Bks.
— Forsaking All Others. 1996. per. 3.50 (*0-373-11850-3*, 1-11850-4) Harlequin Bks.
— Un Guardaespaldas Personal (A Personal Bodyguard) (Bianca Ser.: No. 130).Tr. of Personal Bodyguard. (SPA.). 1998. per. 3.50 (*0-373-33480-X*, 1-33480-4) Harlequin Bks.
— Love Is for the Lucky. large type ed. 1990. lib. bdg. 18.95 (*0-263-12347-2*) Mac Lib Ref.
***McCarthy, Susanne.** El Mejor Postor. (Harlequin Bianca Ser.: Vol.158).Tr. of Highest Bidder. (SPA.). 156p. 1999. per. 3.50 (*0-373-33508-3*, 1-33508-2) Harlequin Bks.
McCarthy, Susanne. Mundos de Ilusion. (Bianca Ser.). 1996. per. 3.50 (*0-373-33374-9*, 1-33374-9) Harlequin Bks.
— Nido de Amor (No Place for Love) (SPA.). 1996. per. 3.50 (*0-373-33381-1*, 1-33381-4) Harlequin Bks.
— No Place for Love. (Forbidden! Ser.). 1997. per. 3.50 (*0-373-11885-6*, 1-11885-0) Harlequin Bks.
— Pasion Ilicita: Forsaking All Others. (Bianca Ser.: No. 385). (SPA.). 1996. per. 3.50 (*0-373-33385-4*, 1-33385-5) Harlequin Bks.
— La Promesse Rompue. (Azur Ser.: No. 783). (FRE.). 1999. mass mkt. 3.99 (*0-373-34783-9*, 1-34783-0) Harlequin Bks.
— Satan's Contract. (Presents Ser.). 1995. per. 2.99 (*0-373-11717-5*, 1-11717-5) Harlequin Bks.
— Tangled Threads. large type ed. (Magna Large Print Ser.). 256p. 1996. 27.99 (*0-7505-1015-3*, Pub. by Mgna Lrg Print) Ulverscroft.
— La Tentation d'Une Femme Mariee. (Azur Ser.: Vol. 702). (FRE.). 1998. mass mkt. 3.50 (*0-373-34702-2*, 1-34702-0) Harlequin Bks.
— Trial by Love. large type ed. 231p. 1995. 11.50 (*0-7505-0830-2*, Pub. by Mgna Lrg Print) Ulverscroft.
McCarthy, T. L., jt. auth. see Bia, Fred.
McCarthy, Tara. Been There, Haven't Done That: A Virgin's Memoir. 224p. 1998. mass mkt. 10.99 (*0-446-67381-1*, Pub. by Warner Bks) Little.
— Expository Writing. (Teaching Writing Ser.). 48p. (J). (gr. 4-8). 1998. pap. 9.95 (*0-590-10387-3*) Scholastic Inc.
— The Middle Ages. (Illus.). (J). 1996. pap. 12.95 (*0-590-25103-1*) Scholastic Inc.
— Multicultural Fables & Fairy Tales: Stories & Activities & Promote Literacy. LC 94-226010. 112p. (gr. 1-8). 1993. pap. 14.95 (*0-590-49231-4*) Scholastic Inc.
— Multicultural Fables & Fairy Tales Stories & Activities & Promote Literacy. 1993. 20.15 (*0-606-06586-5*, Pub. by Turtleback) Demco.
— Multicultural Myths & Legends: Stories & Activities to Promote Cultural Awareness. LC 95-113153. (Illus.). 127p. (J). 1994. pap. text 15.95 (*0-590-49645-X*) Scholastic Inc.
— Narrative Writing. (Teaching Writing Ser.). 48p. (J). (gr. 4-8). 1998. pap. 9.95 (*0-590-20937-X*) Scholastic Inc.
***McCarthy, Tara.** Persuasive Writing, Vol. 4. (Illus.). (J). (gr. 4-7). 1998. mass mkt. 9.95 (*0-590-20934-5*) Scholastic Inc.
McCarthy, Tara. Teaching Genre. LC 97-112760. 111p. (J). 1996. pap. 14.95 (*0-590-60345-0*) Scholastic Inc.
***McCarthy, Tara.** Teaching Literary Elements with Short Stories: Ready-to-Use, High Interest Stories with Mini-Lessons. (Illus.). 96p. 2000. pap. 14.95 (*0-439-09843-2*) Scholastic Inc.
McCarthy, Tara. Teaching the Stories & Poems of Edgar Allan Poe. (Illus.). 1999. pap. text 12.95 (*0-590-66138-8*) Scholastic Inc.
McCarthy, Tara & Freeney, Lorraine. Big Night Out. LC 98-37532. 288p. 1999. pap. 14.95 (*0-312-19834-5*) St Martin.
McCarthy, Tara & Townsend, Donna. Conclusion. (Comprehension Skills Ser.). 1997. pap., student ed. 8.20 (*0-8114-7846-7*) Raintree Steck-V.
— Context. (Comprehension Skills Ser.). 1997. pap., student ed. 8.20 (*0-8114-7845-9*) Raintree Steck-V.
— Sequence. (Comprehension Skills Ser.). 1997. pap., student ed. 8.20 (*0-8114-7844-0*) Raintree Steck-V.
McCarthy, Tara, et al. Sequence. (Comprehension Skills Ser.). 1997. pap., student ed. 8.20 (*0-8114-7856-4*) Raintree Steck-V.
McCarthy, Tara, jt. auth. see Staton, Hilarie N.
McCarthy, Tara, jt. auth. see Ward-Beech, Linda.
***McCarthy, Ted.** November Wedding & Other Poems. LC 98-204407. 2000. pap. 13.95 (*1-901866-21-1*, Pub. by Lilliput Pr) Dufour.
McCarthy, Terence. An Introduction to Malory. Orig. Title: Reading the Morte Darthur. 192p. 1991. reprint ed. 75.00 (*0-85991-328-7*) Boydell & Brewer.
— An Introduction to Malory. Orig. Title: Reading the Morte Darthur. 192p. 1996. reprint ed. pap. 24.95 (*0-85991-325-2*) Boydell & Brewer.
McCarthy, Thomas. Asya & Christine. 217p. 1993. pap. 14.95 (*1-85371-175-6*, Pub. by Poolbeg Pr) Dufour.
— The Critical Theory of Jurgen Habermas. 1981. pap. text 23.00 (*0-262-63073-7*) MIT Pr.
— Gardens of Remembrance. LC 98-215102. 1997. pap. 16.95 (*1-874597-66-9*, Pub. by New Island Books) Dufour.
— Ideals & Illusions: On Reconstruction & Deconstruction in Contemporary Critical Theory. (Illus.). 264p. (C). 1993. pap. text 17.50 (*0-262-63145-8*) MIT Pr.
— The Lost Province. LC 97-179141. 76p. 1996. pap. 15.95 (*0-85646-276-4*, Pub. by Anvil Press) Dufour.
***McCarthy, Thomas.** Mr. Dineen's Careful Parade. 176p. 2000. pap. 22.95 (*0-85646-320-5*, Pub. by Anvil Press) Dufour.
McCarthy, Thomas. The Non-Aligned Storyteller. 64p. 1984. pap. 14.95 (*0-85646-123-7*, Pub. by Anvil Press) Dufour.
— Seven Winters in Paris. Date not set. pap. 14.95 (*0-85646-224-1*, Pub. by Anvil Press) Dufour.
***McCarthy, Thomas.** Transportation Economics: Theory & Practice: A Case Study Approach. 400p. 2000. 69.95 (*0-631-22180-8*) Blackwell Pubs.
McCarthy, Thomas, jt. auth. see Hoy, David.
McCarthy, Thomas, tr. see Habermas, Jurgen.
McCarthy, Thomas, tr. & intro. see Habermas, Jurgen.
McCarthy, Thomas J. Relationships of Sympathy: The Writer & the Reader in British Romanticism. LC 96-41036. (Nineteenth Century Ser.). 192p. 1997. text 74.95 (*1-85928-315-2*, Pub. by Scolar Pr) Ashgate Pub Co.
McCarthy, Tim. AutoCAD Express. (Illus.). xiii, 312p. (C). 1991. pap. 29.00 (*0-387-19590-4*, 3781) Spr-Verlag.
— AutoCAD Express. 2nd rev. ed. (Illus.). xvi, 335p. 1993. 49.95 (*0-387-19748-6*) Spr-Verlag.
— AutoCAD for Windows Express. 1994. pap. 39.00 (*3-540-19865-2*) Spr-Verlag.
— AutoCAD of Windows Express. (Illus.). 328p. 1994. 29.95 (*0-387-19865-2*) Spr-Verlag.
McCarthy, Tim J. AutoCAD Express NT: Covering Release 14. LC 98-13200. (Illus.). 293p. 1998. pap. 42.00 (*3-540-76155-1*) Spr-Verlag.
McCarthy, Timothy. Marx & the Proletariat: A Study in Social Theory, 18. LC 78-4025. (Contributions in Political Science Ser.: No. 18). 102p. 1978. 49.95 (*0-313-20412-8*, MPL/, Greenwood Pr) Greenwood.
McCarthy, Timothy G. Catholic Tradition: The Church in the 20th Century. 2nd ed. LC 97-36980. 1997. pap. 15.95 (*0-8294-0971-8*) Loyola Pr.
— Christianity & Humanism: From Their Biblical Foundations into the Third Millennium. LC 96-7998. (Illus.). 450p. (C). 1996. 26.95 (*0-8294-0913-0*) Loyola Pr.
McCarthy, Todd. Howard Hawks: The Grey Fox of Hollywood. LC 96-49075. (Illus.). 768p. 1997. 35.00 (*0-8021-1598-5*, Grove) Grove-Atltic.
***McCarthy, Todd.** Howard Hawks: The Grey Fox of Hollywood. 2000. pap. 17.50 (*0-8021-3740-7*, Grove) Grove-Atltic.
McCarthy, Tom. The King's Men. 256p. (C). pap. 15.95 (*0-7453-0414-1*, Pub. by Pluto GBR) Stylus Pub VA.
McCarthy, Tom, ed. see Blumenberg, Hans.
McCarthy, Tony. The Ancestral Album: Record Your Family Tree for Living Memory. (Illus.). 64p. (Orig.). 1994. pap. 9.95 (*1-874675-45-7*, Pub. by Lilliput Pr) Irish Bks Media.
— The Irish Roots Guide. 128p. (Orig.). 1991. pap. 9.95 (*0-946640-77-7*, Pub. by Lilliput Pr) Irish Bks Media.
McCarthy-Tucker, Sherri N. Coping with Special-Needs Classmates. LC 92-40662. (YA). (gr. 7-12). 1993. lib. bdg. 17.95 (*0-8239-1598-0*) Rosen Group.
McCarthy, Vincent A. The Phenomenology of Moods in Kierkegaard. 1978. pap. text 64.50 (*90-247-2008-7*) Kluwer Academic.
McCarthy, W. E., et al. Change in Trade Unions: The Development of UK Unions since 1960. 400p. (C). 1981. 65.00 (*0-7855-2148-8*) St Mut.
McCarthy, Wil. Bloom. 1999. mass mkt. 6.99 (*0-345-42465-4*, Del Rey) Ballantine Pub Grp.
***McCarthy, Wil.** The Collapsium. 336p. 2000. 24.95 (*0-345-40856-X*, Del Rey) Ballantine Pub Grp.
McCarthy, Wil. Murder in the Solid State. 256p. 1996. 22.95 (*0-312-85938-4*) Tor Bks.
McCarthy, Willard. Machine Tool Technology, No. 5. 5th ed. 1984. 35.72 (*0-02-671570-8*) Macmillan.
McCarthy, William. Bible, Church & God. 1990. 50.00 (*0-936128-46-1*) De Young Pr.
— Bible, Church & God. 2nd ed. LC 70-169211. (Atheist Viewpoint Ser.). (Illus.). 736p. 1972. reprint ed. 45.95 (*0-405-03805-4*) Ayer.
— A Police Administrator Looks at Police Corruption. (Criminal Justice Center Monographs). 1978. pap. text 3.50 (*0-318-37488-9*) John Jay Pr.
McCarthy, William & Kraft, Elizabeth, eds. The Poems of Anna Letitia Barbauld. LC 92-39712. (Illus.). 448p. 1994. 65.00 (*0-8203-1528-1*) U of Ga Pr.
McCarthy, William B., et al, eds. Jack in Two Worlds: Contemporary North American Tales & Their Tellers. LC 93-35592. (Publications of the American Folklore Society, Bibliographical & Special Ser.). (Illus.). xlvi, 290p. (C). 1994. pap. 19.95 (*0-8078-4443-8*); lib. bdg. 55.00 (*0-8078-2135-7*) U of NC Pr.
McCarthy, Williard J., jt. auth. see Repp, Victor E.
***McCarthy, Zoe.** Crumbled, Tumbled, Humbled - Saved: Fifteen Contemporary Christian Stories. LC 99-94286. (Illus.). 174p. 1999. pap. 11.95 (*0-9662499-1-7*) Holy Ghost Writ.
McCarthy, Zoe. Pearls in the Muddle: Twelve Christian Stories. LC 98-72101. (Illus.). 128p. 1998. pap. 9.95 (*0-9662499-0-9*) Holy Ghost Writ.
McCartin, James T. The Crazy Aunt & Other Stories. LC 87-26256. 1988. pap. 7.95 (*0-9617589-2-9*) Lincoln Springs Pr.
McCartin, Joseph A. Labor's Great War: The Struggle for Industrial Democracy & the Transformation of the American Workplace, 1912-1921. LC 97-9364. 328p. (gr. 13). 1998. pap. 19.95 (*0-8078-4679-1*); lib. bdg. 49.95 (*0-8078-2372-4*) U of NC Pr.
McCartin, Joseph A., ed. see Dubofsky, Melvyn.
McCartin, Joseph Anthony, jt. auth. see Dubofsky, Melvyn.
McCartne. Pratice Your Comprehension Skills 4. 1994. pap. text. write for info. (*0-582-87520-X*, Pub. by Addison-Wesley) Longman.
— Practice Your Comprehension Skills 3. 1994. pap. text. write for info. (*0-582-87519-6*, Pub. by Addison-Wesley) Longman.
— Practice Your Comprehension Skills 6. 1994. pap. text. write for info. (*0-582-87522-6*, Pub. by Addison-Wesley) Longman.
— Practice Your Conprehension Skills 5. 1994. pap. text. write for info. (*0-582-87521-8*, Pub. by Addison-Wesley) Longman.
McCartney. An Embassy to China: Being the Journal Kept by Lord Macartney During His Embassy to the Emperor Ch'ien-lung. LC 70-166618. xv, 241p. 1950. lib. bdg. 49.00 (*0-403-02250-9*) Scholarly.
McCartney, jt. auth. see Lennon.
McCartney, Bill. Stand in the Gap. 64p. 1997. pap. 2.99 (*0-8499-4047-8*) Word Pub.
McCartney, Bill & Diles, Dave. From Ashes to Glory. rev. ed. LC 95-3528. (Illus.). 320p. 1995. pap. 12.99 (*0-7852-7731-5*) Nelson.
McCartney, Bill & Halbrook, David. Sold Out: Becoming Man Enough to Make a Difference. LC 97-36710. 368p. 1997. 19.99 (*0-8499-1515-5*) Word Pub.
McCartney, Bill & McCartney, Lyndi. Sold Out to Each Other. LC 98-54740. xi, 252p. 1999. pap. 16.99 (*0-8499-4046-X*) Word Pub.
McCartney, Bill, et al. What Makes a Man? Twelve Promises That Will Change Your Life. LC 92-61235. 240p. 1992. 18.00 (*0-89109-707-4*) NavPress.
McCartney, Bruce L. Inland Navigation: Locks, Dams, & Channels. LC 98-13187. (ASCE Manuals & Reports on Engineering Practice Ser.). 400p. 1998. 79.00 (*0-7844-0320-1*) Am Soc Civil Eng.
McCartney, Dan G. Why Does It Have to Hurt? The Meaning of Christian Suffering. LC 97-48594. 140p. 1998. pap. 9.99 (*0-87552-386-2*) P & R Pubng.
McCartney, Donal. W. E. H. Lecky: Historian & Politician, 1838-1903. LC 93-238769. 272p. 1994. 39.95 (*1-874675-22-8*) Dufour.
***McCartney, Elspeth.** Speech/Language Therapists & Teachers Working Together, 1. 1999. pap. text 36.95 (*1-86156-124-5*) Whurr Pub.
McCartney, Eugene S. Recurrent Maladies in Scholarly Writing. LC 77-90361. 141p. (C). 1969. reprint ed. 50.00 (*0-87752-068-2*) Gordian.
***McCartney, Francesca.** Intuition Medicine: The Science of Energy, 9 vols. Mills, Edward, ed. (Illus.). 100p. 2000. pap. 20.00 (*0-9677861-1-8*) Intuition.
— Intuition Medicine - The Science of Energy, 9 vols., Set. Mills, Edward, ed. (Illus.). 100p. 2000. pap. 90.00 incl. audio (*0-9677861-0-X*) Intuition.
McCartney, George. Confused Roaring: Evelyn Waugh & the Modernist Tradition. LC 86-46166. 191p. 1987. pap. 59.30 (*0-608-05033-4*, 205969400004) Bks Demand.
McCartney, J. P., et al. Handbook of Transcranial Doppler. LC 96-13737. (Illus.). 92p. 1996. pap. 39.95 (*0-387-94693-4*) Spr-Verlag.
McCartney, Jenny. Grandma's Hospital. LC 92-29958. (Voyages Ser.). (Illus.). (J). 1993. 4.25 (*0-383-03570-8*) SRA McGraw.
McCartney, Joan M. The Other Side Makes Chocolate. (Illus.). 88p. (Orig.). 1981. pap. 2.95 (*0-9609788-0-1*) J M McCartney.
McCartney, John T. Black Power Ideologies: An Essay in African-American Political Thought. 256p. (C). 1992. 54.95 (*0-87722-914-7*) Temple U Pr.
— Black Power Ideologies: An Essay in African-American Political Thought. 256p. (C). 1993. pap. 22.95 (*1-56639-145-8*) Temple U Pr.
McCartney, Kathleen, ed. Child Care & Maternal Employment: A Social Ecology Approach. LC 85-644581. (New Directions for Child Development Ser.: No. CD 49). 1990. pap. 25.00 (*1-55542-805-3*) Jossey-Bass.
McCartney, Kathleen & Pillemer, Karl A., eds. Parent Child Relations Throughout Life. 304p. 1991. text 59.95 (*0-8058-0822-1*) L Erlbaum Assocs.
McCartney, Linda. Linda McCartney on Tour: 200 Meat-Free Dishes from Around the World. LC 98-17947. (Illus.). 192p. (gr. 8). 1998. 29.95 (*0-8212-2487-5*) Little.
— Linda McCartney's Home Cooking: Quick, Easy & Economical Dishes for Today. (Illus.). 176p. 1992. pap. 19.45 (*1-55970-160-9*, Pub. by Arcade Pub Inc) Time Warner.
— Linda McCartney's Home Cooking: Quick, Easy, & Economical Vegetarian Dishes for Today. (Illus.). 176p. 1990. 27.45 (*1-55970-097-1*, Pub. by Arcade Pub Inc) Time Warner.
— Linda McCartney's Sixties: Portrait of an Era. (Illus.). 175p. 1992. 60.00 (*0-8212-1959-6*, Pub. by Bulfinch Pr) Little.
— Linda McCartney's Sixties: Portrait of an Era, Vol. 1. (Illus.). 176p. 1993. pap. 29.95 (*0-8212-2056-X*, Pub. by Bulfinch Pr) Little.
***McCartney, Linda.** Linda McCartney's World of Vegetarian Cooking. (Illus.). 192p. 2001. pap. 19.95 (*0-8212-2696-7*) Bulfinch Pr.
McCartney, Linda. Linda's Kitchen: Simple & Inspiring Meatless Meals. 192p. 1997. pap. 19.95 (*0-8212-2393-3*, Pub. by Bulfinch Pr) Little.

M

An Asterisk (*) at the beginning of an entry indicates that the title is appearing for the first time.

— Linda's Kitchen: Simple & Inspiring Recipes for Meatless Meals. 192p. 1995. 29.95 (*0-8212-2123-X*, Pub. by Bulfinch Pr) Little.
— Performances. 120p. 1999. write for info. (*0-8212-2486-7*) Little.
— Roadworks. (Illus.). 176p. 1994. 55.00 (*0-8212-2172-8*, Pub. by Bulfinch Pr) Little.
— Roadworks. 1995. 50.00 (*0-614-96888-7*) Little.
— Wide Open. LC 98-75607. (Illus.). 100p. 1999. 22.50 (*0-8212-2596-0*, Pub. by Bulfinch Pr) Little.

McCartney, Lyndi, jt. auth. see McCartney, Bill.

McCartney, Martha W. James City County: Keystone of the Commonwealth. LC 97-3113. 1997. write for info. (*0-89865-999-X*) Donning Co.

McCartney, Nancy G., et al. Emerging Patterns of Plum Bayou Culture: Preliminary Investigations of the Toltec Mounds Research Project: Toltec Papers II. Rolingson, Martha A., ed. (Illus.). 99p. 1982. pap. 8.00 (*1-56349-042-0*, RS18) AR Archaeol.

McCartney, Paul. Liverpool Oratorio: Vocal Score. 1992. 19.95 (*0-7935-5369-5*) H Leonard.
— Paul McCartney, Composer-Artist. 1981. 12.95 (*0-671-43124-2*) S&S Trade.

*__McCartney, Paul.__ Paul McCartney's Paintings. (Illus.). 148p. 2000. 50.00 (*0-8212-2673-8*) Bulfinch Pr.

*__McCartney, Paul, et al.__ The Beatles Anthology. LC 00-23685. (Illus.). 368p. 2000. 60.00 (*0-8118-2684-8*) Chronicle Bks.

McCartney, Paul, jt. auth. see Lennon, John.

McCartney, Rae. The Crossing: A Study Guide. Friedland, J. & Kessler, R., eds. (Novel-Ties Ser.). (J). (gr. 5-7). 1994. pap. text, student ed. 15.95 (*1-56982-066-X*) Lrn Links.

McCartney, Ronald L. Escape to Reality: A Roadmap to the Coming Age. LC 96-71302. 144p. 1996. pap. 10.95 (*1-889902-01-2*) Prtnrshp Bk Servs.

McCartney, Scott. Defying the Gods: Inside the New Frontiers of Organ Transplants. LC 93-38976. 298p. 1994. 22.00 (*0-02-582820-7*) Macmillan.
— ENIAC: The Triumphs & Tragedies of the World's First Computer. LC 98-54845. (Illus.). 262p. 1999. 23.00 (*0-8027-1348-3*) Walker & Co.

*__McCartney, Scott.__ Eniac: The Triumphs & Tragedies of the World's First Computer. 2001. pap. 12.95 (*0-425-17644-4*) Berkley Pub.

McCartney, Scott, jt. auth. see Bartimus, Tad.

McCartney, Susan. Mastering Flash Photography: A Course in Basic to Advanced Lighting Techniques. LC 97-18999. (Illus.). 144p. 1997. pap. 24.95 (*0-8174-4545-5*, Amphoto) Watsn-Guptill.

*__McCartney, Susan.__ Mastering the Basics of Photography. (Illus.). 192p. 2000. pap. 19.95 (*1-58115-054-7*, Pub. by Allworth Pr) Watsn-Guptill.

McCartney, Susan. Nature & Wildlife Photography: A Practical Guide to How to Shoot & Sell. LC 93-71919. (Illus.). 256p. (Orig.). 1994. pap. 18.95 (*1-880559-12-9*) Allworth Pr.
— Travel Photography. 2nd ed. LC 98-72762. (Illus.), 360p. (Orig.). 1999. pap. 22.95 (*1-58115-011-3*) Allworth Pr.
— Travel Photography: A Complete Guide to How to Shoot & Sell. LC 91-77926. (Illus.). 384p. 1992. pap. 22.95 (*1-880559-00-5*) Allworth Pr.

McCartney, William. The Jungleers: A History of the 41st Infantry Division. (Divisional Ser.). (Illus.). 208p. 1988. reprint ed. 49.95 (*0-89839-120-2*) Battery Pr.

McCartney, Wilma M. Ring the Doorbell with Your Elbow: A Cookbook of "Portables" rev. ed. LC 80-84349. (Illus.). 136p. 1981. pap. 8.95 (*0-933050-07-0*) New Eng Pr VT.

McCartor, Robert & Tyner, George. Eye of the Storm. (Instant Doctor Ser.: Vol. 1). (Illus.). viii, 208p. 1986. 24.95 (*0-89672-141-8*) Tex Tech Univ Pr.

McCarty. Motivating Your Audience: Speaking from the Heart. 164p. (C). 1998. pap. text 14.95 (*0-205-26894-3*) P-H.
— Nobel Laureates. 2000. 29.95 (*0-07-135614-2*) McGraw.
— Suki. LC 99-46685. (Illus.). 32p. (ps up). 2000. 15.95 (*0-8050-5953-9*) H Holt & Co.
— Sweet & Natural: More Than 120 Naturally Sweet & Dairy-Free Desserts. LC 98-47977. 272p. 1999. text 29.95 (*0-312-20029-3*) St Martin.

McCarty, ed. I'm Dollars Sense. 7th ed. 1997. text 11.00 (*0-673-55195-4*) P-H.

McCarty, ed. Introduction to Dollars & Senses: Study Guide. 8th ed. (C). 1997. pap. text, student ed. 22.50 (*0-673-98071-5*) Addison-Wesley.

McCarty, Bankie, ed. see Johnson, G. W.

McCarty, Bert. Best Management Practices for Florida Golf Courses: Greens Construction, Water, Fertilizing, Cultural Practices & Pest Management. (Illus.). 184p. 1995. pap. 16.00 (*0-916287-06-8*) Univ Fla Food.

*__McCarty, Bill.__ Learning Debian GNU/Linux. Stone, Mark, ed. (Illus.). 400p. 1999. pap. 34.95 incl. cd-rom (*1-56592-705-2*) OReilly & Assocs.
— Learning Red Hat Linux. Stone, Mark, ed. (Illus.). 400p. 1999. pap. 32.95 incl. cd-rom (*1-56592-627-7*) OReilly & Assocs.
— RHCE Study Guide. 2000. pap. 49.99 (*0-7821-2793-2*) Sybex.

McCarty, Bill. Visual C++ Core Language Little Black Book. LC 99-17357. 1999. pap. text 24.99 (*1-57610-389-7*) Coriolis Grp.
— Visual Developer SQL & Java Database Programming. 10th ed. LC 98-123578. (CTI Coriolis Ser.). (Illus.). 500p. (C). 1997. pap., mass mkt. 39.99 incl. cd-rom (*1-57610-176-2*) Coriolis Grp.

McCarty, Bill & Gilbert, Steve. Object-Oriented Programming in Java. LC 97-9501. (Mitchell Waite Signature Ser.). 1000p. 1997. 59.99 incl. cd-rom (*1-57169-086-7*) Mac USA.

McCarty, Burke. The Suppressed Truth about the Assassination of Abraham Lincoln. 1972. 250.00 (*0-87968-169-1*) Gordon Pr.
— The Suppressed Truth about the Assassination of Abraham Lincoln. 255p. 1960. reprint ed. spiral bd. 28.00 (*0-686-29301-0*) A-albionic Res.
— The Suppressed Truth about the Assassination of Abraham Lincoln. 272p. 1993. reprint ed. spiral bd. 16.50 (*0-7873-0595-2*) Hlth Research.

McCarty, C. Barry. Parables & Miracles: Blueprints for 30 Messages Built upon God's Word. (Sermon Starters Ser.). 64p. 1999. 5.99 (*0-7847-0933-5*, 23011) Standard Pub.
— A Parliamentary Guide for Church Leaders. 1990. pap. 9.99 (*0-8054-3116-0*, 4231-16) Broadman.

McCarty, Cara. Information Art: Diagramming Microchips. (Illus.). 48p. 1991. pap. 14.95 (*0-87070-310-2*) Mus of Modern Art.
— Mario Bellini, Designer. (Illus.). 80p. (Orig.). 1987. pap. 9.95 (*0-87070-224-6*, 0-8109-6014-1) Mus of Modern Art.
— Mario des Bellini. (Illus.). 80p. 1990. pap. 12.95 (*0-8109-6014-1*, Pub. by Abrams) Time Warner.

McCarty, Cara & McQuaid, Matilda. Structure & Surface: Contemporary Japanese Textiles. LC 98-67047. (Illus.). 104p. 1999. 24.95 (*0-8109-6190-3*, Pub. by Abrams) Time Warner.

*__McCarty, Cara & McQuaid, Matilda.__ Structure & Surface: Contemporary Japanese Textiles. LC 98-67047. 104p. 1998. 24.95 (*0-87070-076-6*, Pub. by Mus of Modern Art) Abrams.

McCarty, Cara, jt. auth. see Nunley, John W.

McCarty, Cheryll S., see Maum, Ima G., pseud.

McCarty, Christopher. Confessions in Verse. 40p. 1998. pap. 8.00 (*0-8059-4363-3*) Dorrance.

McCarty, Christopher. Public Opinion in Ghana, 1997. ii, 128p. 1997. pap. 15.00 (*1-879720-80-9*) Intl Fndt Elect.

McCarty, Clifford. Bogey: The Films of Humphrey Bogart. (Illus.). 1970. pap. 16.95 (*0-8065-0001-8*, Citadel Pr) Carol Pub Group.

Mccarty, Clifford. The Complete Films of Humphrey Bogart. (Illus.). 192p. 1985. pap. 16.95 (*0-8065-0955-4*, Citadel Pr) Carol Pub Group.

McCarty, Clifford. Film Composers in America: A Filmography, 1911-1970. 2nd ed. LC 98-42710. 552p. 2000. text 75.00 (*0-19-511473-6*) OUP.
— Published Screenplays: A Checklist. LC 73-138656. (Serif Series: Bibliographies & Checklists: No. 18). 141p. reprint ed. pap. 43.80 (*0-8357-5574-6*, 203520100093) Bks Demand.

*__McCarty, Clinton.__ The Reins of Power: Racial Change & Challenge in a Southern County. (Illus.). 450p. 1999. 34.95 (*1-889574-06-6*) Sentry Press.

McCarty, Collin. For You, Just Because You're Very Special to Me. LC 91-73570. (Illus.). 64p. 1991. pap. 8.95 (*0-88396-347-7*) Blue Mtn Art.

McCarty, Craig. Rinkside: A Family's Story of Courage & Inspiration. 1998. 14.95 (*1-892049-09-0*) Benchmark Press.

McCarty, Daniel J. Arthritis & Allied Conditions: A Textbook of Rheumatology, 2 vols. 12th ed. LC 91-33513. (Illus.). 2151p. 1992. text 198.50 (*0-8121-1430-2*) Lppncott W & W.

McCarty, Darlene. Glory from the Honeycomb. 84p. 1999. pap. 7.95 (*1-58169-019-3*) Genesis Comm Inc.

McCarty, Dennis, jt. auth. see Argerion, Milton.

McCarty, Diane. Bassett Hounds. (Illus.). 1997. pap. 9.95 (*0-7938-2381-1*, KW-069S) TFH Pubns.
— Collies: AKC Rank #29. (Illus.). 1997. pap. 9.95 (*0-7938-2307-2*, KW-078S) TFH Pubns.
— English Springer Spaniels, AKC Rank No. 21. (Illus.). 1996. pap. 9.95 (*0-7938-2387-0*, KW081S) TFH Pubns.
— German Shorthaired Pointers, AKC Rank No. 29. (KW Dog Ser.). (Illus.). 1996. pap. 9.95 (*0-7938-2361-7*, KW086S) TFH Pubns.
— Great Danes: AKC Rank #32. (Illus.). 1997. pap. 9.95 (*0-7938-2313-7*, KW-082S) TFH Pubns.
— Labrador Retrievers. 1998. pap. text 9.95 (*0-7938-2315-3*, KW040S) TFH Pubns.
— Lhasa Apsos: AKC Rank #33. (Illus.). 1997. pap. 9.95 (*0-7938-2316-1*, KW-076S) TFH Pubns.

McCarty, Diane, contrib. by. Great Danes. 158p. 9.95 (*0-86622-735-0*) TFH Pubns.

McCarty, Donald E. & Hooper, Glynn. The Fine Art of Fault Locating. (ABC of the Telephone Ser.: Vol. 16). (Illus.). 90p. 1989. spiral bd. 28.95 (*1-56016-063-2*) ABC TeleTraining.

McCarty, Donald J. New Perspectives on Teacher Education. LC 73-1852. (Jossey-Bass Higher Education Ser.). 271p. reprint ed. pap. 84.10 (*0-608-14789-3*, 202566200045) Bks Demand.

McCarty, Donald J., et al. The School Managers: Power & Conflict in American Public Education, 8. LC 70-105975. (Illus.). 281p. 1971. 65.00 (*0-8371-3299-1*, MSM/, Greenwood Pr) Greenwood.

*__McCarty, Donald L.__ Impotence & Prostate Solutions. LC 00-130307. (Illus.). 160p. 2000. write for info. (*1-57197-214-5*, Pub. by Pentland Pr) Assoc Pubs Grp.

McCarty, Dwight G. History of Palo Alto County. (Illus.). 201p. 1997. reprint ed. lib. bdg. 29.50 (*0-8328-6697-0*) Higginson Bk Co.
— Psychology for the Lawyer. (Historical Foundations of Forensic Psychiatry & Psychology Ser.). 1980. lib. bdg. 59.50 (*0-306-76068-1*) Da Capo.

McCarty, F. William & Bagby, John W. Irwin's Legal & Regulatory Environment of Business. 3rd ed. LC 95-24860. 864p. (C). 1995. text 70.75 (*0-256-14071-5*, Irwn Prfssnl) McGraw-Hill Prof.

McCarty, Florence. To Catch a Star. (Illus.). iv, 220p. (Orig.). 1996. pap. 15.95 (*0-943640-03-2*) High Valley Pr.

McCarty, George. Topology: An Introduction with Application to Topological Groups. (Illus.). 288p. 1999. reprint ed. pap. text 9.95 (*0-486-65633-0*) Dover.

McCarty-Gould, Colleen. Crisis & Chaos: Life with the Combat Veteran. LC 98-34038. 189p. 1998. pap. 18.95 (*1-56072-617-2*, Nova Kroshka Bks) Nova Sci Pubs.

McCarty, Hanoch & McCarty, Meladee. Acts of Kindness: How to Make a Gentle Difference. LC 93-47019. 235p. (Orig.). 1994. pap. 10.00 (*1-55874-295-6*, 2956) Health Comm.

McCarty, Hanoch, jt. auth. see McCarthy, Meladee.

McCarty, Hanoch, jt. auth. see Simon, Sidney.

McCarty, Harold H., et al. The Measurement of Association in Industrial Geography. LC 81-23752. 143p. 1982. reprint ed. lib. bdg. 65.00 (*0-313-23442-6*, MCME, Greenwood Pr) Greenwood.

McCarty, J. W., tr. see Wyrick, D.

*__McCarty, James A., ed.__ Home Buyer's Guide: Financing & Evaluating Prospective Homes. (Illus.). 72p. 1998. reprint ed. pap. 8.00 (*0-935817-34-4*, 50) NRAES.

*__McCarty, James M.__ The Impact of New Technology & Organizational Stress on Public Safety Decision Making. LC 98-53714. (Criminology Studies: Vol. 5). 186p. 1999. 79.95 (*0-7734-8168-0*) E Mellen.

McCarty, Jeannette H. Flowers & Fantasies in the Garden: A Guide for Gardeners & Stories for Romantics. Shea, Jim, ed. LC 92-63257. (Illus.). 186p. (Orig.). 1993. pap. text 16.95 (*0-9635434-0-7*) J H McCarty.

McCarty, Jerry, et al. Missouri Challenge: The Real Golfer's Guide. (Illus.). 109p. (Orig.). 1993. per. 7.95 (*0-9651906-0-9*) Lily Pubns.

McCarty, John. The Complete Films of John Huston. 1990. pap. 15.95 (*0-8065-1190-7*, Citadel Pr) Carol Pub Group.
— The Films of Mel Gibson. LC 97-20555. (Illus.). 240p. 1997. pap. 21.95 (*0-8065-1918-5*) Carol Pub Group.
— Movie Psychos & Madmen: Ninety Years of Mad Movies, Maniacs, & Murderous Deeds. LC 92-37552. (Illus.). Date not set. pap. 16.95 (*0-8065-1392-6*, Citadel Pr) Carol Pub Group.
— The Official Splatter Movie Guide. 1989. pap. 10.95 (*0-312-02958-6*) St Martin.
— Sleaze Merchants: Adventures in Exploitation Filmmaking. 3rd ed. 1995. pap. 16.95 (*0-312-11893-7*) St Martin.
— Tell Me When to Look! Modern Horror Films from The Curse of Frankenstein to Today. (Illus.). 256p. Date not set. pap. 19.95 (*0-8065-1849-9*, Citadel Pr) Carol Pub Group.
— Thrillers: Seven Decades of Classic Film Suspense. (Illus.). 256p. 1992. pap. 17.95 (*0-8065-1339-X*, Citadel Pr) Carol Pub Group.

McCarty, John L. Maverick Town: The Story of Old Tascosa. LC 87-5946. (Illus.). 320p. 1988. pap. 15.95 (*0-8061-2089-4*) U of Okla Pr.

McCarty, Kieran. A Frontier Documentary: Sonora & Tucson, 1821-1856. LC 97-4576. 1997. text 29.95 (*0-8165-1715-0*) U of Ariz Pr.

McCarty, Kim, jt. auth. see Lempert, David H.

*__McCarty, L. B.__ Best Golf Course Management Practices. 720p. 2000. 90.00 (*0-13-088359-X*) P-H.

McCarty, Leah. The Board's from Bedford County, Virginia to Breckinridge & Meade Counties of Kentucky. 2nd rev. ed. LC 96-80179. (Illus.). 316p. 1996. spiral bd. 25.00 (*0-9655475-0-7*) L McCarty.

McCarty, Lyle, compiled by. 459th Bomb Group "Coffee Tower" LC 97-60397. (Illus.). 224p. Date not set. 49.95 (*1-56311-365-1*) Turner Pub KY.

McCarty, Maclyn. The Transforming Principle: Discovering That Genes Are Made of DNA. LC 84-20544. (Illus.). 288p. 1986. pap. 9.95 (*0-393-30450-7*) Norton.

McCarty, Marilu H. Dollars & Sense. 6th ed. (C). 1991. text 46.00 (*0-673-46323-0*) Addson-Wesley Educ.
— Dollars & Sense: An Introduction to Economics. 7th ed. 372p. (C). 1997. text 68.00 (*0-673-46806-2*); pap. text, student ed. 29.00 (*0-673-46807-0*) Addson-Wesley Educ.
— Dollars & Sense: An Introduction to Economics. 8th ed. LC 95-49761. (C). 1996. pap. write for info. (*0-673-98070-7*) HarpC.
— Dollars & Sense: Study Guide. 6th ed. (C). 1991. 19.33 (*0-673-46324-9*) Addson-Wesley Educ.
— Introductory Macroeconomics. (C). 1988. pap. text 38.66 (*0-673-18432-3*) Addson-Wesley Educ.
— Introductory Microeconomics. (C). 1988. pap. text 40.33 (*0-673-18433-1*) Addson-Wesley Educ.
— Money & Banking: Financial Institutions & Economic Policy. (Economics Ser.). (Illus.). 544p. (C). 1982. text 31.25 (*0-201-05098-6*) Addison-Wesley.

McCarty, Marilu H. & Galambos, Eva C. Supply & Demand for College Graduates in the South, 1985. 1978. pap. text 2.50 (*0-686-23907-5*) S Regional Ed.

McCarty, Martha. Don't Stop with the Want Ads: Conducting a Successful Job Search. Jensen, Jill, ed. LC 97-70156. (How-To Book Ser.). 128p. 1998. pap. 12.95 (*1-884926-76-2*, HGJ) Amer Media.

McCarty, Maxine. Togo. LC 95-22468. (Oles Country Guide Ser.). 1996. 24.00 (*0-929851-67-6*) Am Assn Coll Registrars.

McCarty, Maxine R., et al. The Educational System of Spain. (ECE Presents Ser.: Vol. 97A). (Illus.). 118p. (Orig.). 1997. pap. text 25.00 (*1-883971-06-3*) Educ Credential.

McCarty, Meladee, jt. auth. see McCarty, Hanoch.

McCarty, Meredith. American Macrobiotic Cuisine. LC 85-16481. (Illus.). 110p. 1986. pap. 11.95 (*0-934947-02-3*) Turning Pubns.
— American Macrobiotic Cuisine: A Macrobiotic Celebration of America's Ethnic Cooking. LC 95-20784. (Illus.). 126p. 1996. pap. 12.95 (*0-89529-711-6*, Avery) Penguin Putnam.
— Fresh from a Vegetarian Kitchen. (Illus.). 262p. (Orig.). 1995. pap. 16.95 (*0-312-11795-7*, St Martin Griffin) St Martin.
— Fresh from a Vegetarian Kitchen. (Illus.). 262p. (Orig.). 1989. pap. 14.95 (*0-934947-03-1*) Turning Pubns.

*__McCarty, Michele.__ Deciding. LC 99-178776. 344 p. 1999. write for info. (*0-15-950429-5*) Harcourt.

McCarty, Michelle, ed. see Shen-Lang, Zhen.

McCarty, Michelle, ed. see Shen-Lang, Zhen & O'Connor, Sifu R.

*__McCarty, Millie, et al.__ The Pathfinder: A Quick Reference & Intervention Guide for Pastors & Counselors. 200p. 1999. 59.95 (*1-929643-09-8*) Ambris Publ.

McCarty, Nolan M., et al. Income Redistribution & the Realignment of American Politics. LC 97-160789. (Studies on Understanding Economic Inequality). 68p. (Orig.). 1997. pap. 9.95 (*0-8447-7078-7*, AEI Pr) Am Enterprise.

McCarty, Oseola. Oseola McCarty's Simple Wisdom for Rich Living. LC 96-76509. 112p. 1996. 9.95 (*1-56352-341-8*) Longstreet.

McCarty, Patrick, jt. auth. see Yamamoto, Shizuko.

McCarty, Perry L. & Roberts, P. V., eds. Contaminants in the Subsurface Environment: Proceedings of the International Symposium on Processes Governing the Movement & Fate of Contaminants in the Subsurface Environment, Held at Stanford University, California, U. S. A., 23-26 July 1989. (Water Science & Technology Ser.: Vol. 22). (Illus.). 118p. 1990. pap. 79.25 (*0-08-040768-4*, Pergamon Pr) Elsevier.

McCarty, Peter. Little Bunny on the Move. LC 98-29787. 32p. (J). (ps-1). 2000. 14.95 (*0-8050-4620-8*) H Holt & Co.

*__McCarty, Peter.__ Untitled Picture Book. 2001. text 16.95 (*0-8050-6352-8*) St Martin.

McCarty, Raymond. Trumpet in the Twilight of Time. LC 80-53734. (Illus.). 144p. (Orig.). 1981. 10.95 (*0-938310-00-3*); pap. 6.95 (*0-938310-01-1*) Volunteer Pubns.

McCarty, Richard, et al, eds. Stress: Molecular Genetic & Neurobiological Advances, 2 vols. 985p. 1996. text 162.00 (*90-5702-520-5*, ECU208, Harwood Acad Pubs) Gordon & Breach.

McCarty, Robert. Tips for Raising Teens: A Primer for Parents. LC 98-21716. 128p. 1998. pap. 8.95 (*0-8091-3818-2*) Paulist Pr.

McCarty, Robert J. Survival in Youth Ministry. LC 95-109780. 80p. 1994. pap. 6.95 (*0-88489-317-0*) St Marys.
— Teen to Teen: Responding to Peers in Crisis. (Illus.). 104p. (YA). 1996. spiral bd. 22.95 (*0-88489-353-7*) St Marys.

McCarty, Shaun. Partners in the Divine Dance . . . Praying with Our Three Person'd God. (Illumination Bks.). 88p. 1996. pap. 4.95 (*0-8091-3655-4*, 3655-4) Paulist Pr.

McCarty, Susan, ed. see Allen, George.

McCarty, Timothy P., et al. Fresh & Processed Potatoes: Competitive Conditions Affecting the U. S. & Canadian Industries. (Illus.). 316p. (C). 1998. pap. text 50.00 (*0-7881-4875-3*) DIANE Pub.

McCarty, William. History of the American War of 1812. 2nd ed. LC 75-126242. (Select Bibliographies Reprint Ser.). 1977. reprint ed. 20.95 (*0-8369-5469-6*) Ayer.

McCarty, William B. Official Netscape Guide to the Navigator 5 Source Code. 500p. 1998. pap. 49.99 (*1-57610-292-0*) Coriolis Grp.

McCarus, Ernest N. The Development of Arab-American Identity. 232p. 1994. text 49.50 (*0-472-10439-X*, 10439) U of Mich Pr.
— Kurdish-English Dictionary. x, 194p. 1967. 16.00 (*0-916798-64-X*) UM Dept NES.

McCarus, Ernest N. & Abdulla, Jamal. Kurdish Basic Course: Dialect of Sulaimania, Iraq. viii, 482p. 1967. pap. text 20.00 (*0-916798-60-7*) UM Dept NES.

McCarus, Ernest N., et al. Contemporary Arabic Readers: Essays, Vol. 2. 1997. 19.95 (*0-86685-363-4*) Intl Bk Ctr.
— Contemporary Arabic Readers: Formal Arabic, Vol. 3. 1987. pap. 19.95 (*0-86685-364-2*) Intl Bk Ctr.
— Contemporary Arabic Readers: Modern Arabic Poetry, 2 Pts., Vol. 5. 1987. 24.95 (*0-86685-366-9*) Intl Bk Ctr.
— Contemporary Arabic Readers: Newspaper Arabic, Vol. 1. 1992. pap. 19.95 (*0-86685-362-6*) Intl Bk Ctr.
— Contemporary Arabic Readers: Short Stories, Vol. 4. 1992. pap. 19.95 (*0-86685-365-0*) Intl Bk Ctr.
— Modern Standard Arabic: Intermediate Level, 3 vols. as a set. Set. 1971. 16.00 (*0-916798-09-7*) UM Dept NES.

McCarus, Ernest N., jt. auth. see Rammuny, Raji M.

McCarus, Ernest N., jt. ed. see Abdulla, Jamal.

McCarver, Aaron, jt. auth. see Morris, Gilbert.

McCarver, Sam. The Case of Cabin 13. 256p. 1999. mass mkt. 5.99 (*0-451-19690-2*) NAL.

*__McCarver, Sam.__ The Case of Cabin 13: A John Darnell Mystery. large type ed. LC 00-21299. (Mystery Ser.). 2000. 26.95 (*0-7862-2487-8*) Thorndike Pr.
— Case of Compartment 7. 2000. mass mkt. 5.99 (*0-451-19959-6*, Sig) NAL.

*__McCarver-Snyder, Bernadette.__ Have You Ever Seen an Ant Who Can't? Creepy, Crawly Stings & Wings from God's "Buggy" World. LC 99-30179. (Illus.). 72p. 1999. pap. 7.95 (*0-87793-693-5*) Ave Maria.

McCarver, Tim & Peary, Danny. The Perfect Season: Why 1998 Was Baseball's Greatest Year. LC 99-13423. 224p. 1999. 19.95 (*0-375-50330-7*) Villard Books.
— Tim McCarver's Baseball for Brain Surgeons & Other Fans: Understanding & Interpreting the Game so You Can Watch It Like a Pro. 344p. 1999. pap. 12.95 (*0-375-75340-0*) Random.
— Tim McCarver's Baseball for Brain Surgeons & Other Fans: Understanding & Interpreting the Game so You Can Watch It Like a Pro. LC 97-49301. 344p. 1998. 23.00 (*0-375-50085-5*) Villard Books.

McCarvill, Barbara J., ed. see Formhals, Hugh.

McCary. Human Sexuality. 2nd ed. (Physical Education Ser.). 1979. pap. 13.00 (*0-534-25250-8*) Wadsworth Pub.
— Human Sexuality. 3rd ed. (Physical Education Ser.). 1978. pap. 16.00 (*0-534-25249-4*); pap., student ed. 4.00 (*0-534-25247-8*) Wadsworth Pub.
— Human Sexuality. 3rd ed. (Physical Education Ser.). 1979. pap., teacher ed. 2.50 (*0-534-25252-4*) Wadsworth Pub.
McCary, Ben C. Indians in Seventeenth Century Virginia. 102p. 1995. pap. 12.00 (*0-8063-4541-1*) Clearfield Co.
McCary, Ben C. Indians in Seventeenth Century Virginia. (Illus.). 93p. 1980. reprint ed. pap. 6.95 (*0-8139-0142-1*) U Pr of Va.
— John Smith's Map of Virginia: With a Brief Account of Its History. LC 81-138846. (Jamestown Three Hundred Fiftieth Anniversary Historical Booklets Ser.: No. 3). 26p. reprint ed. pap. 30.00 (*0-7837-3568-5*, 204342600009) Bks Demand.
McCary, Ben C., jt. auth. see Hranicky, W. Jack.
***McCary, Stephen C.** Calvary Road: Companion Study Guide. 26p. 2000. pap. 3.25 (*0-87508-634-9*) Chr Lit.
McCasey, Tracy, ed. see Forrest, Jan.
McCash, June H. The Jekyll Island Cottage Colony. LC 96-54871. 352p. 1998. 45.00 (*0-8203-1928-7*) U of Ga Pr.
McCash, June H., ed. The Cultural Patronage of Medieval Women. LC 94-13063. (Illus.). 352p. 1995. pap. 25.00 (*0-8203-1702-0*) U of Ga Pr.
McCaskey, J. P. Lincoln Literary Collection. LC 71-108586. (Granger Index Reprint Ser.). 1977. 29.95 (*0-8369-6114-5*) Ayer.
McCaskey, John P. Christmas in Song, Sketch & Story: Nearly Three Hundred Christmas Songs, Hymns & Carols. 1980. lib. bdg. 67.95 (*0-8490-3175-3*) Gordon Pr.
McCaskie, T. C. State & Society in Pre-Colonial Asante. (African Studies: No. 79). (Illus.). 514p. (C). 1995. text 85.00 (*0-521-41009-6*) Cambridge U Pr.
McCaskie, T. C., jt. ed. see Henige, David.
McCaskill, Agnes, tr. see Aliotta, Antonio.
McCaskill, Barbara, jt. ed. see Miller, Suzanne M.
McCaskill, Don. Development or Domestication? Indigenous Peoples of Southeast Asia. LC 97-946086. (Illus.). 662p. 1998. pap. text 27.95 (*974-7100-33-9*) U of Wash Pr.
***McCaskill, Mary & Gilliam, Dona.** Mozart for Flute. 112p. 1998. pap. 12.95 (*0-7866-3309-3*, 97063) Mel Bay.
McCaskill, Mizzy. Children's Tinwhistle Method. 32p. 1994. pap. 5.95 (*0-7866-0154-X*, 95305) Mel Bay.
— French Pieces for Flute & Piano. 76p. 1994. pap. 9.95 (*0-7866-0159-0*, 95295) Mel Bay.
— Sacred Solos for the Flute, Vol. 1. 64p. 1984. pap. 23.95 incl. audio compact disk (*0-7866-1390-4*, 94014CDP) Mel Bay.
— Sacred Solos for the Flute, Vol. 2. 64p. 1989. pap. 23.95 incl. audio compact disk (*0-7866-1391-2*, 94246CDP) Mel Bay.
***McCaskill, Mizzy & Gilliam, Dona.** Antiquities of Scottish Music for Flute & Whistle. 112p. 2000. pap. 14.95 (*0-7866-4950-X*, 98267) Mel Bay.
— Childrens Tinwhistle Method. 32p. 2000. pap. 14.95 incl. audio compact disk (*0-7866-5677-8*, 95305BCD) Mel Bay.
— Complete Irish Flute: Beginning Level. 192p. 1997. spiral bd. 34.95 incl. audio compact disk (*0-7866-2930-4*, 96332CDP) Mel Bay.
McCaskill, Mizzy & Gilliam, Dona. Complete Irish Flute Book. (Complete Bks.). 192p. 1997. pap. 19.95 (*0-7866-2549-X*, MB96332) Mel Bay.
— Complete Irish Tin Whistle Book. (Complete Bks.). 144p. 1996. pap. 19.95 (*0-7866-2318-7*, MB96191) Mel Bay.
McCaskill, Mizzy & Gilliam, Dona. Complete Irish Tinwhistle. 144p. 1996. 32.95 incl. audio compact disk (*0-7866-2363-2*, 96191CDP) Mel Bay.
McCaskill, Mizzy & Gilliam, Dona. Flute Handbook. (Building Excellence Ser.). 56p. 1987. pap. 7.95 (*0-87166-414-3*, 94110); 9.98 (*0-87166-415-1*, 94110C) Mel Bay.
— Flute Handbook. (Building Excellence Ser.). 1993. 16.95 incl. audio (*0-87166-416-X*, 94110P) Mel Bay.
— The Flutist's Companion: A Comprehensive Method. 112p. 1983. spiral bd. 9.95 (*0-87166-764-9*, 93886) Mel Bay.
McCaskill, Mizzy & Gilliam, Dona. French Pieces for Clarinet & Piano. 72p. 1994. pap. 9.95 (*0-7866-0161-2*, 95296) Mel Bay.
McCaskill, Mizzy & Gilliam, Dona. Fun with the Fife. (Fun Bks.). 32p. 1992. pap. 4.95 (*1-56222-448-4*, 94811) Mel Bay.
***McCaskill, Mizzy & Gilliam, Dona.** Fun with the Fife. 32p. 1998. pap. 19.95 incl. audio compact disk (*0-7866-4284-X*, 94811CDP) Mel Bay.
McCaskill, Mizzy & Gilliam, Dona. Fun with the Melody Flute. (Fun Bks.). 1992. audio 9.98 (*1-56222-451-4*, 94812C) Mel Bay.
— Fun with the Melody Flute. (Fun Bks.). 1993. 13.95 incl. audio (*0-7866-1117-0*, 94812P) Mel Bay.
— Fun with the Melody Flute. (Fun Bks.). 32p. 1993. pap. 4.95 (*1-56222-450-6*, 94812) Mel Bay.
— Indispensable Scales, Exercs. 80p. 1994. pap. 9.95 (*0-7866-0038-1*, 95163) Mel Bay.
***McCaskill, Mizzy & Gilliam, Dona.** Noels for Flute & Piano. 64p. 1998. pap. 10.95 (*0-7866-4506-7*, 98259) Mel Bay.
— Scottish Flute Collection for Flute & Piano. 80p. 1999. pap. 11.95 (*0-7866-4507-5*, 98260) Mel Bay.
— Solo Pieces for the Advanced Flutist. 64p. 1995. pap. 8.95 (*1-56222-841-2*, 95005) Mel Bay.
— You Can Teach Yourself Tinwhistle. 80p. 1994. pap. 9.95 (*0-7866-0210-4*) Mel Bay.
— You Can Teach Yourself Tinwhistle. 80p. 1999. pap. 17.95 incl. audio compact disk (*0-7866-4896-1*, 95361BCD) Mel Bay.
McCaskill, Mizzy, jt. auth. see Gilliam, Dana.
McCaskill, Mizzy, jt. auth. see Gilliam, Dona.
McCasland, David. Oswald Chambers: Abandoned to God: The Life Story of the Author of My Upmost for His Highest. LC 98-43187. (Illus.). 336p. 1998. pap. 14.99 (*1-57293-050-0*) Discovery Hse Pubs.
— Pinstripe Parables: Searching Stories about Things That Matter Most to a Man. 144p. 1995. 12.99 (*0-929239-91-1*) Discovery Hse Pubs.
McCasland, David, jt. auth. see Irwin, Bill.
McCasland, Selby V. By the Finger of God: Demon Possession & Exorcism in Early Christianity in the Light of Modern Views of Mental Illness. LC 79-8111. reprint ed. 37.50 (*0-404-18425-1*) AMS Pr.
McCaslin. Creative Drama in the Classroom & Beyond. 7th ed. LC 99-13629. 460p. (C). 1999. pap. 65.00 (*0-8013-3073-4*) Longman.
McCaslin, Dan E. Stone Anchors in Antiquity: Coastal Settlements & Maritime Trade-Routes in the Eastern Mediterranean ca. 1600-1050 B. C. (Studies in Mediterranean Archaeology: Vol. LXI). (Illus.). 157p. (Orig.). 1980. pap. 52.50 (*91-85058-96-3*, Pub. by P Astroms) Coronet Bks.
McCaslin, Mary J. Royal Bayreuth: A Collector's Guide. (Illus.). 150p. 1994. 42.95 (*0-915410-97-4*); pap. 34.95 (*0-915410-96-6*) Antique Pubns.
***McCaslin, Mary M. & Good, Thomas L.** Listening in Classrooms. 232p. 2000. pap. text 17.00 (*0-7881-9030-X*) DIANE Pub.
McCaslin, Mary M., et al. Listening in Classrooms. LC 95-41088. (Illus.). 224p. (C). 1997. pap. 43.00 (*0-673-46881-X*) Addson-Wesley Educ.
McCaslin, Matthew. Matthew McCaslin: Ausstellungen = Exhibitions: Sprengel Museum Hannover, Stadtische Ausstellungs. (Reihe Cantz Ser.). (Illus.). 1994. pap. text 14.95 (*3-89322-270-7*, Pub. by Edition Cantz) Dist Art Pubs.
McCaslin, Nellie. Angel of the Battlefield. LC 93-2604. 20p. (J). 1993. pap. 5.00 (*0-88734-430-5*) Players Pr.
— The Bailiff's Wonderful Coat. LC 96-21292. 55p. (Orig.). (J). (gr. 1-6). 1996. pap. 5.00 (*0-88734-453-4*) Players Pr.
— Bluebonnets. LC 93-5271. 18p. (J). 1993. pap. 5.00 (*0-88734-439-9*) Players Pr.
— Borrowed Trouble. LC 96-2533. (Orig.). 1996. pap. 5.00 (*0-88734-451-8*) Players Pr.
— Brave New Banner. 20p. (J). 1993. pap. 5.00 (*0-88734-436-4*) Players Pr.
— Christmas Fiesta. LC 96-19458. 55p. (Orig.). (J). (gr. k-6). 1996. pap. 5.00 (*0-88734-400-3*) Players Pr.
— The Christmas Lamb. LC 96-25050. 55p. (Orig.). (J). (gr. k-5). 1996. pap. 5.00 (*0-88734-479-8*) Players Pr.
— Clever Marya & the Czar. (Illus.). 55p. (Orig.). 1996. pap. 5.00 (*0-88734-446-1*) Players Pr.
— The Coins of Lin Foo. (Illus.). 55p. (Orig.). 1996. pap. 5.00 (*0-88734-448-8*) Players Pr.
— Cold Face - Warm Heart. LC 93-5273. 20p. (J). 1993. pap. 5.00 (*0-88734-440-2*) Players Pr.
— Creative Drama in the Classroom. 5th ed. 448p. (C). 1990. text 43.95 (*0-8013-0380-X*, 78160) Longman.
— Creative Drama in the Classroom. 5th rev. ed. LC 89-63227. (Illus.). 520p. 1990. pap. 29.00 (*0-88734-604-9*) Players Pr.
— Creative Drama in the Intermediate Grades. LC 89-63228. (Illus.). 346p. 1990. pap. 29.00 (*0-88734-605-7*) Players Pr.
— Creative Drama in the Primary Grades. LC 89-63229. (Illus.). 276p. 1990. pap. 29.00 (*0-88734-606-5*) Players Pr.
— The Crowning of Arthur. 55p. (Orig.). 1996. pap. 5.00 (*0-88734-450-X*) Players Pr.
— Daring, Darling Dolly. LC 93-14392. 20p. 1993. pap. 5.00 (*0-88734-435-6*) Players Pr.
— A Gift of Music. 55p. (Orig.). (J). (gr. 1-6). 1996. pap. 5.00 (*0-88734-455-0*) Players Pr.
— Historical Guide to Children's Theatre in America. LC 85-12684. 365p. 1987. lib. bdg. 85.00 (*0-313-24466-9*, Greenwood Pr) Greenwood.
— Humai's Secret. LC 96-9625. 55p. (Orig.). (J). (gr. 1-6). 1996. pap. 5.00 (*0-88734-427-5*) Players Pr.
— Johnny Appleseed. LC 96-4974. (J). 1996. pap. 5.00 (*0-88734-447-X*) Players Pr.
— The Last Horizon: Playscript. LC 93-5270. 24p. (J). 1993. pap. 5.00 (*0-88734-431-3*) Players Pr.
— The Lazy Ones. LC 96-31747. 55p. (Orig.). (YA). (gr. 6-12). 1996. pap. 5.00 (*0-88734-454-2*) Players Pr.
— Leading Lady: Playscript. LC 93-14391. 20p. 1993. pap. 5.00 (*0-88734-432-1*) Players Pr.
— The Legend of Minna Lamourrie. LC 93-2603. 20p. (J). 1993. pap. 5.00 (*0-88734-438-0*) Players Pr.
— Legends in Action: Ten Plays of Ten Lands. LC 93-22161. (J). Date not set. pap. 20.00 (*0-88734-633-2*) Players Pr.
— Little Snow Girl. 33p. 1963. pap. 3.50 (*0-87129-070-7*, L66) Dramatic Pub.
— The Little Squire of Flanders. 55p. (Orig.). 1996. pap. 5.00 (*0-88734-476-3*) Players Pr.
— Maelduin of Arran. LC 96-32005. 55p. (Orig.). (YA). (gr. 6-12). 1996. pap. 5.00 (*0-88734-480-1*) Players Pr.
— Mercy in Moccasins: Playscript. LC 93-14393. 16p. 1993. pap. 5.00 (*0-88734-441-0*) Players Pr.
— A Miracle in the Christmas City: Playscript. LC 93-2602. 16p. (J). 1993. pap. 5.00 (*0-88734-437-2*) Players Pr.
— Paul Bunyan: Lumberjack. LC 96-30034. 55p. (Orig.). (J). (gr. 1-6). 1996. pap. 5.00 (*0-88734-477-1*) Players Pr.
— Pioneers in Petticoats. (Illus.). 205p. 1993. 20.00 (*0-88734-625-1*) Players Pr.
— Prelude to Fame. LC 93-14390. 24p. (Orig.). 1993. pap. 5.00 (*0-88734-433-X*) Players Pr.
— The Rabbit Who Wanted Red Wings. 28p. 1963. reprint ed. pap. 3.50 (*0-87129-023-5*, R44) Dramatic Pub.
— Shows on a Shoestring. 106p. 1979. 9.95 (*0-679-20952-2*) New Plays Inc.
— A Straight Shooter (Playscript) LC 93-5252. 16p. (J). 1993. pap. 5.00 (*0-88734-429-1*) Players Pr.
— Theatre for Children in the United States: A History. Landes, William-Alan, ed. LC 96-47570. (Illus.). 425p. (Orig.). 1997. pap. 40.00 (*0-88734-677-4*) Players Pr.
— Three Meals a Day. 55p. (J). (gr. 1-7). 1996. pap. 5.00 (*0-88734-445-3*) Players Pr.
McCaslin, Nellie. The Tinker of Toledo. 55p. (Orig.). 1996. pap. 5.00 (*0-88734-456-9*) Players Pr.
McCaslin, Nellie. Too Many Cooks. LC 93-5250. 20p. (J). 1993. pap. 5.00 (*0-88734-434-8*) Players Pr.
— Travelers from Olympus. 55p. (Orig.). 1996. pap. 5.00 (*0-88734-475-5*) Players Pr.
— Who Laughs Last? (Illus.). 50p. (Orig.). 1996. pap. 5.00 (*0-88734-449-6*) Players Pr.
— Wisely Chosen. LC 96-27212. 55p. (Orig.). (J). (gr. k-6). 1996. pap. 5.00 (*0-88734-478-X*) Players Pr.
McCaslin, Richard B. Portraits of Conflict: A Photographic History of North Carolina in the Civil War. LC 97-1757. 1997. 75.00 (*1-55728-454-7*) U of Ark Pr.
— Portraits of Conflict Vol. 4: A Photographic History of South Carolina in the Civil War. LC 94-5238. (Illus.). 416p. 1995. 75.00 (*1-55728-363-X*) U of Ark Pr.
— Tainted Breeze: The Great Hanging at Gainesville, Texas 1862. (Illus.). 256p. 1997. pap. 13.95 (*0-8071-2219-X*) La State U Pr.
McCaslin, Richard B., compiled by. Andrew Johnson: A Bibliography, 17. LC 92-31761. (Bibliographies of the Presidents of the United States Ser.: No. 17). 352p. 1992. lib. bdg. 79.50 (*0-313-28175-0*, AP17, Greenwood Pr) Greenwood.
***McCaslin, Susan.** Flying Wounded. LC 99-86327. (Contemporary Poetry Ser.). 2000. pap. write for info. (*0-8130-1797-1*) U Press Fla.
— Flying Wounded. 2000. 24.95 (*0-8130-1796-3*) U Press Fla.
McCaslin, Susan. Thinking about God. (Illus.). 24p. (J). (ps-4). 1994. 7.95 (*0-89622-615-8*) Twenty-Third.
McCathern, Gerald. Horns. 250p. 1997. 24.95 (*0-9656946-0-7*) Outlaw Bks TX.
— Quarantined. 200p. 1998. 24.95 (*0-9656946-1-5*) Outlaw Bks TX.
McCaughan, Edward J. Reinventing Revolution: The Renovation of Left Discourse in Cuba & Mexico. 224p. 1998. pap. text 24.00 (*0-8133-3547-7*, Pub. by Westview) HarpC.
McCaughan, Edward J., jt. auth. see Jonas, Suzanne.
McCaughan, Jill A., jt. ed. see Kaminski, John P.
McCaughan, Michael. The Birth of the Titanic. (Illus.). 192p. 1999. 29.95 (*0-7735-1864-9*, Pub. by McG-Queens Univ Pr) CUP Services.
McCaughan, Nano & McDougall, Kay, eds. Group Work: A Guide for Teachers & Practitioners. 1978. 23.00 (*0-7855-0559-8*, Pub. by Natl Inst Soc Work) St Mut.
McCaughan, Nano & Palmer, Barry. Systems Thinking for Harassed Managers. 144p. 1994. pap. text 27.00 (*1-85575-055-4*, Pub. by H Karnac Bks Ltd) Other Pr LLC.
McCaughan, Richard. Socks on a Rooster - Louisiana's Earl K. Long. 1967. 20.00 (*0-87511-081-9*) Claitors.
McCaughey, jt. auth. see Battifora.
McCaughey, Bobbi. Celebrating the Wonder of Motherhood: Intimate Moments with Bobbi McCaughey & Her Children. (Illus.). 128p. 1999. 15.99 (*0-7852-7048-5*) Nelson.
McCaughey, Bobbi, jt. auth. see McCaughey, Kenny.
McCaughey, Davis. Tradition & Dissent. 288p. 1998. pap. 24.95 (*0-522-84764-1*, Pub. by Melbourne Univ Pr) Paul & Co Pubs.
McCaughey, Donald G., Jr. Graphic Design for Corrugated Packaging. LC 94-7885. (Illus.). 296p. 1995. 96.00 (*1-885067-00-3*) Jelmar Pub.
McCaughey, Elizabeth P. From Loyalist to Founding Father. 1980. text 67.00 (*0-231-04506-9*) Col U Pr.
McCaughey, Kenny & McCaughey, Bobbi. Seven from Heaven. LC 98-33949. (Illus.). 288p. 1998. 22.99 (*0-7852-7049-3*) Nelson.
McCaughey, Martha. Real Knockouts: The Physical Feminism of Women's Self-Defense. LC 97-4774. 280p. 1997. text 45.00 (*0-8147-5512-7*); pap. text 19.00 (*0-8147-5577-1*) NYU Pr.
McCaughey, Patrick. Woods: Bryan Nash Gill. LC 63-62002. (Illus.). 8p. Date not set. 3.00 (*0-614-10433-5*) W Benton Mus.
McCaughey, Patrick, ed. Australian Paintings of the Heidelberg School: The Jack Manton Collection. (Illus.). 160p. 1980. text 65.00 (*0-19-550592-1*) OUP.
***McCaughey, Patrick, et al.** Henry Moore & the Heroic: A Centenary Tribute. LC 98-75234. 79 p. 1999. write for info. (*0-930606-87-6*) Yale Ctr Brit Art.
McCaughey, Robert A. International Studies & Academic Enterprise. 1984. text 61.50 (*0-231-05054-2*) Col U Pr.
— Josiah Quincy, 1772 to 1864: The Last Federalist. LC 73-89506. (Historical Studies: No. 90). 288p. 1974. 20.00 (*0-674-48375-8*) HUP.
McCaughey, William. Anesthetic Pharmacology & Physiology. LC 97-9202. 1997. text 160.00 (*0-443-05203-4*) Church.
McCaughranara, Tom. In Search of the Liberty Tree. 2nd ed. (Illus.). 223p. (YA). (gr. 7-12). 1994. reprint ed. 13.95 (*0-947962-84-0*, Pub. by Anvil Books Ltd) Irish Bks Media.
***McCaughrean.** Never Let Go. 1998. pap. text 11.95 (*0-340-68291-4*, Pub. by Hodder & Stought Ltd) Trafalgar.
— Princess Stories. (J). 2000. pap. 22.95 (*0-385-40783-1*, Pub. by Transworld Publishers Ltd) Trafalgar.
— Too Big. (J). 2000. pap. 6.95 (*0-552-54618-6*, Pub. by Transworld Publishers Ltd) Trafalgar.
***McCaughrean, Geraldine.** Beauty & the Beast. LC 00-8023. (Picture Bks.). 32p. (J). (ps-3). 2000. 15.95 (*1-57505-491-4*, Carolrhoda) Lerner Pub.
McCaughrean, Geraldine. The Bronze Cauldron: Myths & Legends of the World. LC 97-72081. (Illus.). 144p. (J). (gr. 5-9). 1998. per. 19.95 (*0-689-81758-4*) S&S Childrens.
— Casting the Gods Adrift. (Flashbacks Ser.: No. 12). (Illus.). (J). (gr. 3-6). 1998. reprint ed. pap. 5.95 (*0-7136-4655-1*, Pub. by A & C Blk) Midpt Trade.
— El Cid. (Oxford Illustrated Classics Ser.). (Illus.). 128p. (J). (gr. 4 up). 1997. pap. 14.95 (*0-19-274169-1*) OUP.
***McCaughrean, Geraldine.** God's Kingdom: Stories from the New Testament. LC 98-68536. (Illus.). 128p. (J). (gr. 3-7). 2000. per. 20.00 (*0-689-82488-2*) McElderry Bks.
McCaughrean, Geraldine. God's People: Stories from the Old Testament. LC 97-2191. (Illus.). 128p. (J). (gr. 4-7). 1997. 19.95 (*0-689-81366-X*) McElderry Bks.
— God's People: Stories from the Old Testament. (Illus.). (J). 1997. write for info. (*0-614-29305-7*) S&S Childrens.
— Greek Gods & Goddesses. LC 97-75538. (Illus.). 112p. (J). (gr. 4-7). 1998. per. 20.00 (*0-689-82084-4*) S&S Childrens.
— Greek Myths. LC 92-61748. (Illus.). 96p. (J). (gr. 4-7). 1993. 20.00 (*0-689-50583-3*) McElderry Bks.
— Lovesong. 424p. 1997. pap. 17.95 (*1-86066-040-1*, Pub. by R Cohen Bks) Trafalgar.
***McCaughrean, Geraldine.** My First Oxford Book of Stories. (Illus.). 96p. 2000. 19.95 (*0-19-278115-4*) OUP.
— Nochebuena. (SPA.). 1997. pap. 13.95 (*84-261-3012-7*) Juventud Edit.
McCaughrean, Geraldine. The Nutcracker 28p. (YA). 1999. 17.95 (*0-19-279969-X*) OUP.
— The Odyssey. (Illus.). 100p. (J). (gr. 4 up). 1993. 14.95 (*1-56288-433-6*) Checkerboard.
***McCaughrean, Geraldine.** One Thousand & One Arabian Nights. (Oxford Story Collections). (Illus.). 288p. (YA). 2000. pap. 12.95 (*0-19-275013-5*) OUP.
McCaughrean, Geraldine. A Pack of Lies. large type ed. 320p. (J). (gr. 3 up). 1990. 16.95 (*0-7451-1154-8*, G K Hall Lrg Type) Mac Lib Ref.
— The Pirate's Son. LC 97-45650. 224p. (YA). (gr. 5-9). 1998. 16.95 (*0-590-20344-4*, Pub. by Scholastic) Scholastic Inc.
***McCaughrean, Geraldine.** The Pirate's Son. 304p. (gr. 5-9). 1999. mass mkt. 4.99 (*0-590-20348-7*) Scholastic Inc.
McCaughrean, Geraldine. Polvo de Oro (Gold Dust) (SPA., Illus.). (YA). 1995. pap. 6.99 (*968-16-4720-3*, Pub. by Fondo) Continental Bk.
— Una Sarta de Mentiras (A Pack of Lies) De Leon, Jorge G., tr. (SPA., Illus.). 227p. (YA). 1992. pap. 6.99 (*968-16-3915-4*, Pub. by Fondo) Continental Bk.
— The Silver Treasure: Myths & Legends of the World. LC 96-76845. (Illus.). 144p. (J). (gr. 4-7). 1997. per. 19.95 (*0-689-81322-8*) S&S Childrens.
McCaughrean, Geraldine. The Stones Are Hatching. LC 99-39895. 240p. (gr. 5 up). mass mkt. 5.95 (*0-06-447218-3*) HarpC.
— The Stones Are Hatching. LC 99-39895. (Illus.). 240p. (YA). (gr. 7-12). 2000. 15.95 (*0-06-028765-9*); lib. bdg. 15.89 (*0-06-028766-7*) HarpC Child Bks.
McCaughrean, Geraldine. The Story of the Nativity. LC 99-159347. (Illus.). 16p. (J). 1998. 17.95 (*0-385-32631-9*) Doubleday.
— Unicorns! Unicorns! LC 97-5296. (Illus.). 32p. (J). (gr. k-3). 1997. lib. bdg. 15.95 (*0-8234-1319-5*) Holiday.
***McCaughrean, Geraldine & Chichester-Clark, Emma.** Roman Myths. LC 00-28357. 2001. write for info. (*0-689-83822-0*) McElderry Bks.
***McCaughrean, Geraldine & Holland, Heather.** How the Reindeer Got Their Antlers. LC 99-49961. (Illus.). 32p. (J). (gr. k-3). 2000. 16.95 (*0-8234-1562-7*) Holiday.
McCaughrean, Geraldine & Windham, Sophie. Unicorns! Unicorns! (Illus.). 32p. 1997. 19.95 (*0-385-25673-6*) Bantam.
McCaughrean, Geraldine, ed. see Chaucer, Geoffrey.
McCaughren, Tom. The Children of the Forge. 138p. 1996. pap. 8.95 (*0-947962-69-7*) Dufour.
— In Search of the Liberty Tree. 224p. 1997. pap. 8.95 (*0-947962-89-1*) Dufour.
— The Legend of the Corrib King. 106p. 1993. pap. 8.95 (*0-947962-60-3*) Dufour.
— The Legend of the Golden Key. 144p. 1993. pap. 8.95 (*0-947962-36-0*) Dufour.
— The Legend of the Phantom Highwayman. 112p. 1993. pap. 8.95 (*0-947962-58-1*) Dufour.
— Rainbows of the Moon. 160p. (YA). (gr. 9-12). 1989. pap. 7.95 (*0-947962-51-4*, Pub. by Childrens Pr) Irish Bks Media.
— Ride a Pale Horse. LC 99-195130. 144p. (YA). (gr. 4 up). 1998. 13.95 (*1-901737-08-X*, Pub. by Anvil Books Ltd) Irish Bks Media.
— Run Swift, Run Free. 1987. pap. 9.95 (*0-86327-106-5*) Dufour.
— Run Swift, Run Free. 191p. (J). (ps-8). 1987. 14.95 (*0-86327-111-1*); pap. 7.95 (*0-685-25877-7*) Dufour.
— Run to the Wild Wood. 160p. 1997. 10.95 (*0-86327-492-7*, Pub. by Wolfhound Press) Irish Amer Bk.
— The Silent Sea. (Illus.). 111p. (Orig.). (YA). 1988. reprint ed. pap. 7.95 (*0-947962-20-4*, Pub. by Childrens Pr) Irish Bks Media.
McCaul, Robert L. The Black Struggle for Public Schooling in Nineteenth-Century Illinois. LC 86-26004. 208p. 1987. text 26.95 (*0-8093-1335-9*) S Ill U Pr.
McCauley. On the Job, Vol. 1. (C). 1984. pap. text. write for info. (*0-7730-4322-5*) Addison-Wes.

M

An Asterisk (*) at the beginning of an entry indicates that the title is appearing for the first time.

McCauley, Adam. My Friend Chicken. LC 98-36187. (Illus.). 28p. (J). 1999. 9.95 (0-8118-2327-X) Chronicle Bks.

McCauley, Anna K. Miles from Home. 108p. 1984. pap. 3.95 (0-9612430-0-7) A K L M Pubns.

McCauley, Anne. Nineteenth-Century French Caricatures & Comic Illustrations. (Illus.). 40p. 1986. pap. 6.00 (0-935213-02-3) J S Blanton Mus.

McCauley, Anne, jt. auth. see Haworth-Booth, Mark.

McCauley, Barbara. Algo en Comun. (Deseo Ser.). 1996. per. 3.50 (0-373-35152-6, 1-35152-7) Harlequin Bks.

— Blackhawk's Sweet Revenge: Secrets! (Desire Ser.: Bk. 1230). 1999. per. 3.75 (0-373-76230-5, 1-76230-1) Silhouette.

***McCauley, Barbara.** Callan's Proposition: Secrets. 2000. per. 3.99 (0-373-76290-9) Silhouette.

McCauley, Barbara. Camino de la Felicidad: The Nanny & the Reluctant Rancher. (Deseo Ser.: Vol. 124).Tr. of Way to Happiness. 1998. per. 3.50 (0-373-35254-9, 1-35254-1) Harlequin Bks.

— Courtship in Granite Ridge. (Desire Ser.: No. 1128). 1998. per. 3.75 (0-373-76128-7, 1-76128-7) Silhouette.

***McCauley, Barbara.** Gabriel's Honor. (Intimate Moments Ser.). 2000. mass mkt. 4.50 (0-373-27094-1, 1-27094-1) Silhouette.

McCauley, Barbara. Her Kind of Man. (Desire Ser.). 1993. pap. 2.89 (0-373-05771-7, 5-05771-6) Silhouette.

— Killian's Passion: Secrets! (Desire Ser.: No. 1242). 1999. mass mkt. 3.75 (0-373-76242-9, 1-76242-6) Silhouette.

— Man from Cougar Pass. (Desire Ser.: No. 698). 1992. per. 2.89 (0-373-05698-2, 5-05698-1) Harlequin Bks.

— A Man Like Cade. (Desire Ser.). 1994. per. 2.99 (0-373-05832-2, 5-05832-6) Silhouette.

— Mas Que Amigos: Courtship in Granite Ridge. (Deseo Ser.: No. 139).Tr. of More Than Friends. 1999. mass mkt. 3.50 (0-373-35269-7, 1-35269-9) Harlequin Bks.

— Mi Estilo de Hombre. Orig. Title: Her Kind of Man. (SPA.). 1996. per. 3.50 (0-373-35133-X) Harlequin Bks.

— Midnight Bridge. (Desire Ser.). 1996. per. 3.50 (0-373-76028-0, 1-76028-9) Silhouette.

— The Nanny & the Reluctant Rancher. 1997. per. 3.50 (0-373-76066-3, 1-76066-9) Silhouette.

— Nightfire. large type ed. (Silhouette Romance Ser.). 1995. 18.95 (0-373-59632-4) Thorndike Pr.

— Novia de Medianoche: Midnight Bride. (Deseo Ser.).Tr. of Midnight Bride. (SPA.). 1997. per. 3.50 (0-373-35209-3, 1-35209-5) Harlequin Bks.

***McCauley, Barbara.** Una Novia Especial: (A Special Bride) (Deseo Ser.: No. 151).Tr. of A Special Bride. (SPA.). 1999. per. 3.50 (0-373-35281-6, 1-35281-4) Harlequin Bks.

— Una Pequena Mentira (One Small Lie) (Deseo Ser.). (SPA.). 2000. mass mkt. 3.50 (0-373-35360-X, 1-35360-6) Harlequin Bks.

McCauley, Barbara. Secret Baby Santos. (Desire Ser.: No. 1236). 1999. per. 3.75 (0-373-76236-4, 1-76236-8) Silhouette.

— Seduction of the Reluctant Bride. 1998. per. 3.75 (0-373-76144-9, 1-76144-4) Silhouette.

— Small Mercies. LC 98-29013. 144p. 1998. 20.00 (1-890932-04-3); pap. 13.50 (1-890932-05-1) Sherman Asher Pub.

— Le Testament D'Amour. (Rouge Passion Ser.: No. 523). (FRE.). 1999. mass mkt. 3.99 (0-373-37523-9, 1-37523-7) Harlequin Bks.

— Texas Heat. (Desire Ser.). 1995. mass mkt. 3.25 (0-373-05917-5, 1-05917-9) Silhouette.

— Texas Heat. large type ed. (Silhouette Romance Ser.). 1996. 19.95 (0-373-59747-9) Thorndike Pr.

— Texas Pride. 1995. per. 3.25 (0-373-05971-X, 1-05971-6) Silhouette.

— Texas Temptation. (Desire Ser.). 1995. per. 3.25 (0-373-05948-5, 1-05948-4) Silhouette.

— Whitehorn's Woman. (Desire Ser.). 1993. mass mkt. 2.99 (0-373-05803-9, 5-05803-7) Silhouette.

McCauley, Carole S. The Honesty Tree. LC 84-25905. 224p. (Orig.). 1986. pap. 6.95 (0-9603628-6-X) Frog in Well.

— Pregnancy after Thirty-Five. 224p. 1987. pap. 3.95 (0-317-59883-X) PB.

McCauley, Clark, ed. Terrorism Research & Public Policy. 168p. 1991. 39.50 (0-7146-3429-8, Pub. by F Cass Pubs) Intl Spec Bk.

McCauley, Cleyburn L. A Brief Bible Outline. Foley, Lucy, ed. (Illus.). 245p. (Orig.). 1995. pap. text 15.95 (0-910531-21-8) Wolcotts.

— Messiah. Foley, Lucy, ed. 198p. (Orig.). 1995. pap. text 9.95 (0-910531-20-X) Wolcotts.

McCauley, Cynthia D. The Center for Creative Leadership Handbook of Leadership Development. LC 98-19684. 512p. 1998. 65.00 (0-7879-0950-5) Jossey-Bass.

— Effective School Principals: Competencies for Meeting the Demands of Educational Reform. (Technical Reports: No. 146G). 52p. pap. 7.50 (0-912879-43-2) Ctr Creat Leader.

***McCauley, Cynthia D. & Martineau, Jennifer W.** Reaching Your Development Goals. (Ideas into Action Guidebook Ser.). 27p. 1998. pap. text 6.95 (1-882197-37-2) Ctr Creat Leader.

***McCauley, Dana.** Noodles Express: Fast & Easy Meals in 15 to 45 Minutes. (Illus.). 160p. 1999. pap. 14.95 (1-55209-396-4) Firefly Bks Ltd.

McCauley, Dana, jt. auth. see Archbold, Rick,

McCauley, Daniel & McCauley, Kathryn. Decorative Arts of the Amish of Lancaster County. LC 88-81264. (Illus.). 175p. 1988. 29.95 (0-934672-66-0); pap. 19.95 (0-934672-69-5) Good Bks PA.

McCauley, Deborah V. Appalachian Mountain Religion: A History. LC 94-18247. 584p. 1995. 49.95 (0-252-02129-0); 24.95 (0-252-06414-3) U of Ill Pr.

McCauley, George. Aces. 78p. (Orig.). 1991. pap. 8.95 (0-9622889-2-6) Something More.

— Night Air Dancing. 80p. (Orig.). 1990. pap. 8.95 (0-9622889-1-8) Something More.

— No Bright Shield. 80p. (Orig.). 1989. pap. text 8.95 (0-9622889-0-X) Something More.

McCauley, Georgia. Child Labor: Exploited & Abused Youth at Work. Barnitz, Laura A., ed. 34p. 1998. pap. 6.00 (0-9663709-1-0) Youth Advocate.

McCauley, James E. A Stove-Up Cowboy's Story. LC 65-4439. (Illus.). 100p. 1965. reprint ed. 9.95 (0-87074-093-8) SMU Press.

***McCauley, James F.** Steam Distribution Systems Deskbook. LC 99-52402. 405p. 2000. 82.00 (0-88173-303-2) Fairmont Pr.

— Steam Distribution Systems Deskbook. 424p. 2000. 82.00 (0-13-026769-4) P-H.

McCauley, James F. The Steam Trap Handbook. LC 95-13399. 322p. 1995. 79.00 (0-88173-187-0) Fairmont Pr.

McCauley, James R., jt. auth. see Buchanan, Rex.

McCauley, James W. & Weiss, Volker, eds. Materials Characterization for Systems Performance & Reliability. LC 85-19118. (Sagamore Army Materials Research Conference Proceedings Ser.: Vol. 31). 618p. 1986. 135.00 (0-306-42095-3, Plenum Trade) Perseus Pubng.

McCauley, Jane R. Phoenix Baby Resource Guide. 2nd rev. ed. (Illus.). 300p. pap. 9.95 (0-9637868-1-4) AZ Baby Res.

McCauley, Jane R. Wonderful Animals of Australia: A National Geographic Pop-Up Book. (Pop-Up Bks.). (Illus.). 12p. (YA). (ps up). 16.00 (0-87044-809-9, Pub. by Natl Geog) Publishers Group.

McCauley, Jane R. & National Geographic Society Staff. Field Guide of Birds in North America. 2nd ed. LC 86-33249. (Illus.). 464p. 1993. pap. 21.00 (0-87044-692-4) Natl Geog.

McCauley, John. Harley Teaches. (Illus.). 34p. (J). (gr. k-6). 1998. text 12.95 (0-9664005-7-7) Amer Health.

McCauley, Joseph L. Chaos, Dynamics, & Fractals: An Algorithmic Approach to Deterministic Chaos. (Nonlinear Science Ser.: No. 2). (Illus.). 347p. (C). 1994. pap. text 33.95 (0-521-46747-0) Cambridge U Pr.

— Classical Mechanics: Transformations, Flows, Integrable & Chaotic Dynamics. (Illus.). 487p. (C). 1997. text 90.00 (0-521-48132-5); pap. text 42.95 (0-521-57882-5) Cambridge U Pr.

McCauley, Kathryn, jt. auth. see McCauley, Daniel.

McCauley, Kirby, ed. see Hammett, Dashiell.

McCauley, Leo P., tr. see Cyril of Jerusalem.

McCauley, Leo P., tr. see St. Gregory Nazianzen & St. Ambrose.

McCauley, Lucy, ed. Traveler's Tales Spain. (Travelers' Tales Guides Ser.). 495p. 1995. pap. 17.95 (1-885211-07-4) Thomson Learn.

— Women in the Wild: True Stories of Adventure & Connection. (Travelers' Tales Guides). 307p. 1998. pap. 17.95 (1-885211-21-X) Trvlers Tale.

***McCauley, Lucy, et al, eds.** A Woman's Path: Women's Best Spiritual Travel Writing. LC 00-21839. 252p. 2000. pap. 16.95 (1-885211-48-1) Trvlers Tale.

***McCauley, Mark.** Color Therapy at Home: Real-Life Solutions for Adding Color to Your Life. 2000. 35.00 (1-56496-625-9) Rockport Pubs.

McCauley, Mark. Interior Design for Idiots. 168p. (Orig.). 1995. pap. 5.95 (1-56245-186-3) Great Quotations.

— Let's Talk Decorating: Professional's Guide to Smart Design. Caton, Patrick, ed. 168p. (Orig.). 1996. pap. 5.95 (1-56245-226-6) Great Quotations.

McCauley, Marlene. Adventures with a Saint: Kateri Tekawitha, "Lily of the Mohawks" McCauley, R. Allan, ed. (Illus.). 208p. (Orig.). 1992. pap. text 8.00 (0-9633633-0-1) Grace House Pub.

McCauley, Martin. The Companion to Russia since 1914. LC 97-14166. (Longman Companions to History Ser.). 376p. (C). 1997. pap. text 27.50 (0-582-27639-X) Longman.

McCauley, Martin. Gorbachev PIP Series. LC 97-38886. (Profiles in Power Ser.). 360p. (C). 1998. 80.00 (0-582-21597-8) Longman.

— The Origins of the Cold War, 1941-1948. 2nd ed. LC 95-9846. (Seminar Studies in History). 168p. (C). 1995. pap. 15.93 (0-582-27659-4) Longman.

— Russia, America & the Cold War, 1949-1991. LC 98-3445. (Seminar Studies in History). 168p. (C). 1998. pap. 15.73 (0-582-27936-4) Longman.

— Russia since 1914: Longman Companion. LC 97-14166. (Longman Companions to History Ser.). (C). 1998. text 76.00 (0-582-27640-3) Longman.

— Russia's Leading Commercial Banks. LC 94-70632. 178p. 69.00 (0-9639807-0-X) CEBIS.

— The Soviet Union, 1917-1991. 2nd ed. LC 92-25942. (Longman History of Russia Ser.). 440p. (C). 1995. pap. 48.00 (0-582-01323-2, 79637) Addson-Wesley Educ.

— The Soviet Union Since 1917. LC 80-71827. (History of Russia Ser.). (Illus.). 290p. (C). 1989. pap. text 24.33 (0-582-48980-6, 73426) Longman.

— Stalin & Stalinism. 2nd ed. LC 95-10104. (Seminar Studies in History). 160p. (C). 1995. pap. 15.93 (0-582-27658-6) Longman.

— Who's Who in Russia since 1900. LC 96-42009. (Illus.). 268p. (C). 1997. 75.00 (0-415-13897-3); pap. 18.99 (0-415-13898-1) Routledge.

McCauley, Martin, ed. The Soviet Union after Brezhnev. LC 83-12956. (Illus.). 160p. (C). 1983. 19.95 (0-8419-0918-0); pap. 15.00 (0-8419-0919-9) Holmes & Meier.

McCauley, Martin & Carter, Stephen, eds. Leadership & Succession in the Soviet Union, Eastern Europe & China. LC 85-2370. 270p. (Orig.). (gr. 13). 1986. pap. text 31.95 (0-87332-347-5) M E Sharpe.

McCauley, Michael. Jim Thompson: Sleep with the Devil. 1991. 19.45 (0-89296-392-1, Pub. by Mysterious Pr) Little.

McCauley, P. Remuneration Policy. 1996. pap. 129.00 (1-85953-092-3, Pub. by Tech Comm) St Mut.

McCauley, R. Allan, ed. see McCauley, Marlene.

McCauley, R. W. Marxist Ideology & Soviet Criminal Law. 319p. 1980. 44.00 (0-389-20099-9, 06873) B&N Imports.

McCauley, Ray. Holy Spirit. 192p. 1998. pap. 11.99 (1-57794-025-3) Harrison Hse.

***McCauley, Rebecca.** Assessment of Childhood Language Disorders. 560p. 2000. write for info. (0-8058-2561-4); pap. write for info. (0-8058-2562-2) L Erlbaum Assocs.

McCauley, Robert N. The Euro & the Dollar. LC 97-40211. (Essays in International Finance: Vol. 205). 1997. pap. 10.00 (0-88165-112-5) Princeton U Int Finan Econ.

McCauley, Robert N., et al. Dodging Bullets: Changing U. S. Corporate Capital Structure in the 1980s & 1990s. LC 99-32604. (Illus.). 352p. 1999. 34.95 (0-262-13351-2) MIT Pr.

McCauley, Ronald A. Corrosion of Ceramics. LC 94-37778. (Corrosion Technology Ser.: Vol. 7). (Illus.). 320p. 1994. text 145.00 (0-8247-9448-6) Dekker.

McCauley, Rosemarie. Mini Sims Temporaries: Modern Office Simulations, 2 vols. 232p. (Orig.). 1979. teacher ed. write for info. (0-672-97168-2) Macmillan.

— Mini Sims Temporaries: Modern Office Simulations, 2 vols., 1. 232p. (Orig.). 1979. pap. text. write for info. (0-672-97167-4) Macmillan.

— Mini Sims Temporaries: Modern Office Simulations, 2 vols., 2. 232p. (Orig.). 1979. pap. text. write for info. (0-672-97424-X) Macmillan.

McCauley, Rosemarie & Slocum, Keith. Business Spelling & Word Power. 2nd ed. 336p. (C). 1983. teacher ed. write for info. (0-672-97976-4); pap. text. write for info. (0-672-97975-6) Macmillan.

McCauley, Rosemarie & Slocum, Keith. Business Spelling & Word Power. 3rd ed. 1991. text 25.96 (0-02-678291-X) Glencoe.

***McCauley, Ruth.** This Place in All Its Seasons: The Henry Fonda Home in Nebraska. LC 99-89018. 2000. 15.95 (1-886225-56-7) Dageforde Pub.

McCauley, Stephen. The Easy Way Out. Rosenman, Jane, ed. LC 92-42590. 304p. 1993. reprint ed. per. 14.00 (0-671-78738-1, WSP) PB.

— The Man of the House. 1996. per. 14.00 (0-671-00225-2) PB.

— The Man of the House: A Novel. 320p. 1996. 22.00 (0-684-81053-0) S&S Trade.

— Object Affection. 316p. 1991. mass mkt. 14.00 (0-671-74350-3) S&S Trade.

— The Object of My Affection. 1998. per. 6.99 (0-671-02066-8) PB.

McCauley, William. The Turning Over. LC 97-30147. 1999. pap. 16.00 (1-57962-058-2) Permanent Pr.

McCaull, Charlene. The Weekend Galley. (Illus.). 56p. 1984. pap. 6.95 (0-916669-01-7) Alcyone Pubns.

McCaull, Julian. The Hinge: A Novel on the Mind of War. LC 84-70570. 361p. 1984. 16.95 (0-916669-00-9) Alcyone Pubns.

— Train No. 8. LC 87-30756. 1989. 22.95 (0-87949-279-1) Ashley Bks.

***McCaulley, Paul.** The Dangers of Neo-Fundamentalism. 72p. 1999. reprint ed. pap. 5.00 (0-9673318-0-3) Aviatn Missn.

McCausland, et al. Speech Through Pictures. 1973. text 2.50 (0-686-09390-9) Expression.

McCausland, Clare. An Element of Love. Mobium Corporation Staff & Ineman, K., eds. (Illus.). 140p. (Orig.). 1981. pap. 10.00 (0-9607400-0-7) Childrens Memorial.

McCausland, Cynthia & McCausland, Robert, eds. Index to the Illustrated History of Kennebec County Maine. 265p. (Orig.). 1996. pap. 39.50 (0-89725-267-5, 1551) Picton Pr.

McCausland, Cynthia MacAlman, jt. tr. see McCausland, Robert R.

McCausland, Elizabeth. George Inness. LC 76-42705. reprint ed. 26.00 (0-404-15365-8) AMS Pr.

— Life & Work of Edward Lamson Henry N. A. LC 74-100614. (Library of American Art). (Illus.). 1970. reprint ed. lib. bdg. 55.00 (0-306-71866-9) Da Capo.

McCausland, Jeffrey D. Conventional Arms Control & European Security. (Adelphi Papers). 65p. 1996. pap. text 24.95 (0-19-829241-4) OUP.

McCausland, M. A., jt. auth. see Calvert, Jack M.

McCausland, Robert, jt. ed. see McCausland, Cynthia.

McCausland, Robert R. & McCausland, Cynthia MacAlman, trs. The Diary of Martha Ballard, 1785-1812: MGS Special Pub. No. 10. LC 92-67980. 992p. 1998. 65.00 (0-929539-62-1, 1335) Picton Pr.

Mccausland, Ruth. Washington's Westport. LC 98-4381. 1998. write for info. (1-57864-033-4) Donning Co.

McCauslin, Mark. AIDS. LC 94-27798. (Update Ser.). (J). 1995. lib. bdg. 13.95 (0-89686-812-5, Crstwood Hse) Silver Burdett Pr.

— The Homeless. LC 93-24106. (Update Ser.). 48p. (J). 1994. pap. 4.95 (0-382-24757-4) Silver Burdett Pr.

McCave. Census. 1998. 16.98 (0-8050-5379-4) H Holt & Co.

***McCave & Sinclair Staff.** Statistics. 8th ed. LC 99-39266. (Illus.). 848p. 1999. text 91.00 incl. disk (0-13-022329-8) P-H.

Mccave, Marta E. Counting Heads, & More. LC 97-51643. 64p. (J). (gr. 5-8). 1998. 22.40 (0-7613-3017-8) TFC Bks NY.

McCavitt, William E. Radio & Television: A Selected, Annotated Bibliography Supplement One: 1977-1981. LC 82-5743. 167p. 1982. 25.00 (0-8108-1556-7) Scarecrow.

McCavoy, Paul W. Explaining Metal Price. 1988. lib. bdg. 95.50 (0-89838-293-9) Kluwer Academic.

McCaw, Herbert. Eleven Angels: General Rappaport's Journal - Judas. LC 98-84870. 1998. mass mkt., per. 19.95 (1-889131-26-1) CasAnanda.

McCaw, J. Emory. The Witch of Black Hawk Tower: A Frontier Woman. LC 98-90114. (Illus.). 146p. 1998. pap. 7.95 (0-9657052-1-8) Vinco Pubns.

— The Witch of Bute: A Guardian Angel. (Illus.). 152p. (Orig.). 1997. pap. 7.95 (0-9657052-0-X) Vinco Pubns.

McCaw, John B. & Arnold, Phillip G. Lower Extremity Reconstruction. LC 87-82108. (Illus.). 246p. 1987. text 163.50 (0-939789-04-3) Lppncott W & W.

McCaw, Larry. See You Sunday! Sixty-Two Pastor's Letters to Children. 1992. pap. 3.95 (1-55673-512-X, 9304) CSS OH.

McCaw, Mabel. What Is Loving? (Good Little Books for Good Little Children). (Illus.). 12p. (J). (ps). 1987. 3.25 (0-8378-5208-0) Gibson.

McCaw, Neil. George Eliot & Victorian Historiography: Imagining the National. text 65.00 (0-312-23413-9) St Martin.

McCawley. Syntactic Phenomena English. 2nd ed. LC 97-11825. 840p. 1998. lib. bdg. 110.00 (0-226-55627-1) U Ch Pr.

McCawley, Chris. The First Thing in the Field. LC 82-12061. (Kestrel Chapbks.). 32p. (Orig.). 1982. pap. 3.00 (0-914974-33-5) Holmgangers.

McCawley, Cynthia D. & Brutus, Stephane. Management Development Through Job Experiences: An Annotated Bibliography. LC 97-23154. 116p. 1998. pap. text 20.00 (1-882197-32-1) Ctr Creat Leader.

McCawley, James D. Adverbs, Vowels & Other Objects of Wonder. LC 78-11608. xii, 304p. 1985. pap. text 10.00 (0-226-55616-6) U Ch Pr.

— Adverbs, Vowels & Other Objects of Wonder. LC 78-11608. 1995. lib. bdg. 20.00 (0-226-55615-8) U Ch Pr.

— Adverbs, Vowels & Other Objects of Wonder. LC 78-11608. 315p. reprint ed. pap. 97.70 (0-608-09471-4, 205427100005) Bks Demand.

***McCawley, James D.** Against Virtue Syntax & Semantics. 1999. pap. text 20.00 (0-226-55609-3); lib. bdg. 52.00 (0-226-55608-5) U Ch Pr.

McCawley, James D. The Eater's Guide to Chinese Characters. LC 83-14535. (Illus.). vi, 296p. 1984. lib. bdg. 17.00 (0-226-55590-9) U Ch Pr.

— The Eater's Guide to Chinese Characters. LC 83-14535. (Illus.). vi, 296p. 1992. pap. 5.95 (0-226-55591-7) U Ch Pr.

— Everything That Linguists Have Always Wanted to Know about Logic but Were Ashamed to Ask. LC 80-345. (Illus.). 528p. 1996. pap. text 22.95 (0-226-55618-2) U Ch Pr.

— Everything That Linguists Have Always Wanted to Know about Logic but Were Ashamed to Ask. LC 80-345. (Illus.). 528p. 2000. lib. bdg. 12.50 (0-226-55617-4) U Ch Pr.

— Everything That Linguists Have Always Wanted to Know about Logic but Were Ashamed to Ask. LC 80-345. (Illus.). 524p. reprint ed. pap. 162.50 (0-608-09019-0, 206965400005) Bks Demand.

— Everything That Linguists Have Always Wanted to Know about Logic but Were Ashamed to Ask. 2nd ed. LC 92-30744. 656p. (C). 1993. pap. text 37.00 (0-226-55611-5); lib. bdg. 100.00 (0-226-55610-7) U Ch Pr.

— Syntactic Phenomena English. 2nd ed. LC 97-11825. 840p. 1998. pap. text 50.00 (0-226-55629-8) U Ch Pr.

— The Syntactic Phenomena of English, Vol. 1. (Illus.). 416p. 1988. pap. text 22.50 (0-226-55624-7) U Ch Pr.

— The Syntactic Phenomena of English, Vol. 1. (Illus.). 416p. 1993. lib. bdg. 60.00 (0-226-55623-9) U Ch Pr.

— Syntactic Phenomena of English, Vol. 2. (Illus.). 466p. 1988. pap. text 22.50 (0-226-55626-3) U Ch Pr.

— Syntactic Phenomena of English, Vol. 2. (Illus.). 464p. 1993. lib. bdg. 60.00 (0-226-55625-5) U Ch Pr.

— Thirty Million Theories of Grammar. LC 82-40319. 232p. (C). 1996. 27.95 (0-226-55619-0) U Ch Pr.

McCawley, Patrick. Selected Civil War Bibliography. LC 97-183475. (Illus.). 44p. 1997. pap. text 2.00 (1-880067-42-0) SC Dept of Arch & Hist.

McCawley, Patrick J. Artificial Limbs for Confederate Soldiers. Brimelow, Judith M., ed. 40p. 1992. pap. 2.00 (1-880067-15-3) SC Dept of Arch & Hist.

— Guide to Civil War Records in the South Carolina Department of Archives & History. Andrews, Judith M., ed. LC 94-621658. 84p. 1994. pap. 5.00 (1-880067-23-4) SC Dept of Arch & Hist.

McCawley, Robert N., ed. The Churchlands & Their Critics. LC 96-161357. (Philosophers & Their Critics Ser.). (Illus.). 320p. (C). 1996. 58.95 (0-631-18968-8); pap. 28.95 (0-631-18969-6) Blackwell Pubs.

McCawley, Rosemary, jt. auth. see Dobrot, Nancy L.

McCawley, William. The First Angelinos: The Gabrielino Indians of Los Angeles. Vane, Sylvia B. & Lawton, Harry, eds. LC 95-43042. 304p. 1996. 49.95 (0-9651016-1-4); pap. 34.95 (0-9651016-0-6) Malki-Ballena.

McCay. Oyster Wars & Public Trust: Property, Law & Ecology in New Jersey History. LC 97-33776. 304p. 1998. 45.00 (0-8165-1804-1) U of Ariz Pr.

McCay, Bill. Plague of Perfection. (Spider-Man Super-Thriller Ser.: No. 2). 1996. mass mkt. 4.99 (0-671-00320-8) PB.

— Reconnaissance. (Stargate Ser.). 304p. 1998. mass mkt. 5.99 (0-451-45663-7, ROC) NAL.

— Resistance, 5. 1999. mass mkt. 5.99 (0-451-45664-5, ROC) NAL.

— Stargate: Rebellion. 272p. 1995. mass mkt. 4.99 (0-451-45502-9, ROC) NAL.

An Asterisk (*) at the beginning of an entry indicates that the title is appearing for the first time.

— Stargate: Retaliation. 1996. mass mkt. 5.99 (0-614-20519-0, ROC) NAL.

— Stargate 3: Retribution. 1997. mass mkt. 5.99 (0-451-45556-8, ROC) NAL.

— Stargate 2. 1996. mass mkt. 5.99 (0-451-45516-9) NAL.

— Young Indiana Jones & the Mask of the Madman. (Young Indiana Jones Ser.: No. 18). (J). (gr. 4-6). 1998. pap. 3.99 (0-679-87907-2, Bullseye Bks) Random Bks Yng Read.

McCay, Bill, jt. auth. see Lee, Stan.

McCay, Bonnie J. & Acheson, James M., eds. The Question of the Commons: The Culture & Ecology of Communal Resources. LC 87-19833. (Arizona Studies in Human Ecology). 439p. (C). 1990. reprint ed. pap. text 21.95 (0-8165-1205-1) U of Ariz Pr.

McCay, Clive M. & McCay, Jeanette B. The Cornell Bread Book: Fifty-Four Recipes for Nutritious Loaves, Rolls & Coffee Cakes. rev. ed. (Illus.). 52p. 1980. reprint ed. pap. 2.95 (0-486-23995-0) Dover.

McCay, James T. The Management of Time. 1986. 14.95 (0-13-548909-1, Reward) P-H.

McCay, Jeanette B. Clive McCay, Nutrition Pioneer: Biographical Memoirs by His Wife. LC 94-10013. 1994. 24.95 (1-881539-04-0) Tabby Hse Bks.

McCay, Jeanette B., jt. auth. see McCay, Clive M.

McCay, Mary A. Ellen Gilchrist. LC 97-20635. 1997. 32.00 (0-8057-4029-5) Macmillan.

— Rachel Carson. (Twayne's United States Authors Ser.). 160p. 1993. 21.95 (0-8057-3988-2, Twyne) Mac Lib Ref.

McCay, T. D. & Roux, J. A., eds. Combustion Diagnostics by Nonintrusive Methods. PAAS92. LC 84-12425. (Illus.). 347p. 1984. 75.95 (0-915928-86-8, V-92) AIAA.

McCay, T. D., jt. ed. see Roux, J. A.

McCay, W. A. & Flood, E. L. The Chains of Command. Stern, David, ed. (Star Trek: The Next Generation Ser.: No. 21). 288p. (Orig.). 1992. mass mkt. 5.50 (0-671-74264-7) PB.

McCay, William. The Lost Temple of Zorro. (The Mask of Zorro Ser.). (J). (gr. 3-6). 1999. pap. 4.50 (0-671-51971-9) PB.

— The Secret Swordsman. (Zorro Ser.: No. 3). 160p. (J). (gr. 4-7). 1999. pap. 3.99 (0-671-51969-7, Minstrel Bks) PB.

— The Treasure of Don Diego. (Zorro Ser.: No. 1). (Orig.). (J). (gr. 3-7). 1998. pap. 4.50 (0-671-51968-9, Minstrel Bks) PB.

— Young Indiana Jones & the Circle of Death. LC 89-43390. (Young Indiana Jones Ser.: No. 3). 112p. (J). (gr. 4-6). 1990. pap. 2.95 (0-679-80578-8) Random Bks Yng Read.

— Young Indiana Jones & the Plantation Treasure. LC 89-43388. (Young Indiana Jones Ser.: No. 1). 112p. (J). (gr. 4-6). 1990. pap. 3.99 (0-679-80579-6) Random Bks Yng Read.

McCay, William, ed. see Lewis, C. Jonathan.

McCay, Winsor. The Complete Little Nemo, Vol. 4. Marschall, Richard, ed. (Illus.). 96p. 1990. 35.00 (1-56097-045-6) Fantagraph Bks.

— Dreams of the Rarebit Fiend. (Illus.). 62p. 1973. reprint ed. pap. 4.95 (0-486-21347-1) Dover.

— Little Nemo in the Palace of Ice, & Further Adventures. LC 75-19834. (Illus.). 32p. (Orig.). 1976. pap. 8.95 (0-486-23234-4) Dover.

***McCay, Winsor.** Little Nemo, 1905-1914. (Illus.). 2000. 39.99 (3-8228-6300-9) Taschen Amer.

***McCay, Winsor.** Little Nemo in Slumberland: Birthday Book. 50p. 2000. reprint ed. text 18.00 (0-7881-9048-2) DIANE Pub.

McCellan. Young Hegelians & Karl Marx. 184p. 1993. 61.95 (0-7512-0178-2) Ashgate Pub Co.

McCelland, Doug. Blackface to Blacklist: Al Jolson, Larry Parks, & "The Jolson Story" LC 86-29797. (Illus.). 298p. 1987. 37.00 (0-8108-1965-1) Scarecrow.

McCelland, Robert W., et al, eds. Macro Case Studies in Social Work. 160p. 1998. pap. 24.95 (0-87304-296-4) Manticore Pubs.

MccGwire, Michael. Military Objectives in Soviet Foreign Policy. LC 86-24932. 530p. 1987. 49.95 (0-8157-5552-X); pap. 19.95 (0-8157-5551-1) Brookings.

— Perestroika & Soviet National Security. LC 87-17657. 481p. 1991. 44.95 (0-8157-5554-6); pap. 19.95 (0-8157-5553-8) Brookings.

McChesney, Debbie. Once upon a Child: Writing Your Child's Special Story. (Illus.). 1995. 19.95 (1-56145-100-2) Peachtree Pubs.

McChesney, Fred & Rubin, Paul. The Role of Economists in Modern Antitrust. LC 97-24260. 190p. 1998. 134.95 (0-471-97074-3) Wiley.

McChesney, Fred S. Money for Nothing: Politicians, Rent Extraction, & Political Extortion. LC 96-47873. (Illus.). 216p. 1997. 36.50 (0-674-58330-2) HUP.

McChesney, Fred S. & Shughart, William F., II, eds. The Causes & Consequences of Antitrust: The Public-Choice Perspective. (Illus.). 392p. 1994. pap. text 32.95 (0-226-55635-2) U Ch Pr.

— The Causes & Consequences of Antitrust: The Public-Choice Perspective. (Illus.). 392p. 1995. lib. bdg. 66.00 (0-226-55634-4) U Ch Pr.

McChesney, Fred S., jt. auth. see Goetz, Charles J.

McChesney, J. Meghan, jt. auth. see Gust, John.

McChesney, James. Picture Oregon: Portraits of the University of Oregon. (Illus.). 1994. 59.95 (0-87114-287-2) U of Oreg Bks.

McChesney, Lea S., jt. auth. see Wade, Edwin L.

McChesney, Malcolm. Thermodynamics of Electrical Processes. LC 75-166417. 286p. reprint ed. pap. 88.70 (0-608-11574-6, 201614700098) Bks Demand.

McChesney, R. D. Central Asia: Foundations of Change. LC 96-42976. (Leon B. Poullada Memorial Lecture Ser.: Vol. 2). (Illus.). 160p. 1996. text 35.00 (0-87850-077-4) Darwin Pr.

— War in Central Asia: Four Hundred Years in the History of a Muslim Shrine, 1480-1889. 347p. 1991. text 67.50 (0-691-05584-X, Pub. by Princeton U Pr) Cal Prin Full Svc.

McChesney, Randal A. Stepping Stones: Early Childhood Teacher's Guide, Year 2. Hawn, C. Michael, ed. (Stepping Stones Ser.). (Illus.). 64p. (Orig.). 1996. reprint ed. pap. text, teacher ed. 22.95 (1-929187-06-8, CGBK57, Pub. by Choristers) Lorenz Corp.

***McChesney, Robert.** Rich Media, Poor Democracy: Communication Politics in Dubious Times. 2000. reprint ed. pap. 17.95 (1-56584-634-6, Pub. by New Press NY) Norton.

McChesney, Robert, jt. ed. see Solomon, William.

McChesney, Robert D., ed. see Muhammad, Fayz.

McChesney, Robert W. Corporate Media & the Threat to Democracy. LC 96-37525. (Open Media Pamphlet Ser.: Vol. 1). 80p. (Orig.). 1997. pap. 5.95 (1-888363-47-9) Seven Stories.

***McChesney, Robert W.** Rich Media, Poor Democracy: Communication Politics in Dubious Times. LC 98-58055. (History of Communication Ser.). 424p. 1999. 32.95 (0-252-02448-6) U of Ill Pr.

McChesney, Robert W. Telecommunications, Mass Media & Democracy: The Battle for the Control of U. S. Broadcasting, 1928-1935. 416p. 1995. reprint ed. pap. text 22.00 (0-19-509394-1) OUP.

McChesney, Robert W., et al, eds. Capitalism & the Information Age: The Political Economy of the Global Communication Revolution. 224p. 1997. 38.00 (0-85345-988-6, Pub. by Monthly Rev) NYU Pr.

— Capitalism & the Information Age: The Political Economy of the Global Communication Revolution. 224p. 1997. pap. 16.00 (0-85345-989-4, Pub. by Monthly Rev) NYU Pr.

***McChesney, Robert W. & Nichols, John.** It's the Media, Stupid: Unleash the democracy. LC 00-20252. (Open Media Pamphlet Ser.: No. 17). 128p. 2000. pap. 10.00 (1-58322-029-1) Seven Stories.

McChesney, Robert W., jt. auth. see Herman, Edward S.

McChesney, Robert W., ed. see Berry, William E.

McChesney, Stephen E. The Denture Wearer's Cookbook: Full, Partial & Flippers. (Illus.). 128p. (Orig.). 1996. pap. 13.95 (0-9636339-7-X) Spec Pubns.

McCheyne, Robert M. The Basket of Fragments. 1996. pap. 9.99 (0-906731-03-8, Pub. by Christian Focus) Spring Arbor Dist.

— Comfort in Sorrow. large type ed. 5.99 (1-85792-012-0, Pub. by Christian Focus) Spring Arbor Dist.

— From the Preacher's Heart. 27.99 (1-85792-025-2, Pub. by Christian Focus) Spring Arbor Dist.

— God Makes a Path. 1997. pap. text 11.99 (1-898787-51-4) Emerald House Group Inc.

— Mensajes Biblicos. (SPA.). 284p. 1988. reprint ed. pap. 6.50 (0-85151-541-X) Banner of Truth.

— Seven Churches of Asia. 5.99 (0-614-11464-0, Pub. by Christian Focus); 5.99 (0-906731-51-8, Pub. by Christian Focus) Spring Arbor Dist.

McChirstian, Douglas C. The U. S. Army in the West, 1870-1880: Uniforms. LC 94-48216. (Illus.). 316p. 1995. 36.95 (0-8061-2705-8) U of Okla Pr.

McChristal, James. Pikes Peak: Legends of America's Mountain. 1999. pap. 12.00 (0-9670867-0-1) Sierra Grande.

McChristian, Douglas C., ed. Garrison Tangles in the Friendless Tenth: The Journal of First Lieutenant John Bigelow, Jr., Fort Davis, Texas. (Guidon Monographs). (Illus.). 1985. 15.95 (0-8488-0238-1, J M C & Co) Amereon Ltd.

McChristian, Sarah. Smart Is As Smart Does: Emotional Self Help for Young People. LC 97-68827. 50p. (Orig.). (YA). (gr. 7-12). 1997. pap. 12.95 (1-882792-49-1) Proctor Pubns.

McClafferty, Carla K. Forgiving God: A Woman's Struggle to Understand When God Answers No. LC 95-16722. 128p. 1995. 12.99 (0-929239-97-0) Discovery Hse Pubs.

McClafferty, Karen, ed. Challenges of Urban Education: Sociological Perspectives for the Next Century. LC 99-24397. (C). 2000. pap. text 19.95 (0-7914-4434-1) State U NY Pr.

— Challenges of Urban Education: Sociological Perspectives for the Next Century. LC 99-24397. (C). 2000. text 59.50 (0-7914-4433-3) State U NY Pr.

McClain, Alva J. Bible Truths. 1981. pap. 1.75 (0-88469-013-X) BMH Bks.

— Daniel's Prophecy of the Seventy Weeks. pap. 7.99 (0-88469-076-8) BMH Bks.

— Freemasonry & Christianity. 1979. pap. 1.25 (0-88469-012-1) BMH Bks.

— The Greatness of the Kingdom. 18.99 (0-88469-011-3) BMH Bks.

— The Inspiration of the Bible. 1980. pap. 1.50 (0-88469-115-2) BMH Bks.

— The Jewish Problem. 1979. pap. 1.00 (0-88469-014-8) BMH Bks.

— Law & Grace. pap. 3.95 (0-88469-001-6) BMH Bks.

— The "Problems" of Verbal Inspiration. 1968. pap. 0.75 (0-88469-116-0) BMH Bks.

— Romans Outlined & Summarized. 1979. pap. 3.50 (0-88469-015-6) BMH Bks.

— Romans, the Gospel of God's Grace. 1979. 12.99 (0-88469-080-6) BMH Bks.

McClain, Bebe F. Super Eight Filmaking from Scratch. (Illus.). 1978. pap. 19.95 (0-13-876110-8) P-H.

McClain, Brenda, jt. auth. see Hemphill, Bethni.

McClain, Buzz, jt. auth. see Strauss, Annette.

McClain, C., jt. auth. see Kazanis, B.

McClain, Carol S., ed. Women As Healers: Cross-Cultural Perspectives. LC 88-16896. 272p. (C). 1989. pap. text 17.00 (0-8135-1370-7) Rutgers U Pr.

McClain, Charles J. In Search of Equality: The Chinese Struggle Against Discrimination in Nineteenth-Century America. LC 93-4942. 385p. (C). 1996. pap. 14.95 (0-520-20514-6, Pub. by U CA Pr) Cal Prin Full Svc.

— The Mass Internment of Japanese Americans & the Quest for Legal Redress. LC 94-22630. (Asian Americans & the Law Ser.: No. 3). (Illus.). 485p. 1994. text 88.00 (0-8153-1866-9) Garland.

McClain, Charles J., ed. Asian Indians, Filipinos, Other Asian Communities & the Law. LC 94-22629. (Asian Americans & the Law Ser.: No. 4). (Illus.). 424p. 1994. text 77.00 (0-8153-1851-0) Garland.

— Chinese Immigrants & American Law. LC 94-26787. (Asian Americans & the Law Ser.: No. 1). (Illus.). 479p. 1994. text 88.00 (0-8153-1849-9) Garland.

— Japanese Immigrants & American Law: The Alien Land Laws & Other Issues. LC 94-29033. (Asian Americans & the Law Ser.: No. 2). (Illus.). 448p. 1994. text 77.00 (0-8153-1850-2) Garland.

McClain, Cindy, ed. Mission Friends Planbook. (Illus.). 39p. (Orig.). 1995. pap. text 2.95 (1-56309-134-8, W958106) Womans Mission Union.

McClain, Cindy, jt. auth. see Burdeshaw, Jane.

McClain, Cindy, ed. see Bishop, Gary.

McClain, Cindy, ed. see Burns, Kathy.

McClain, Cindy, ed. see DeLoach, Sylvia.

McClain, Cindy, ed. see Faughn, Jackie & McQueen, Marcia.

McClain, Cindy, ed. see House, Janie.

McClain, Cindy, ed. see Kent, Renee.

McClain, Cindy, ed. see Martin, Sara H.

McClain, Cindy, ed. see McCoy, Leighann.

McClain, Cindy, ed. see McCullough, Mary F.

McClain, Cindy, ed. see Strawn, Kathy.

McClain, Clifford H. Fluid Flow in Pipes: A Clear-Sut Summary of Modern Theory in the Flow of Liquids & Gases Through Piping & Ducts, with Practical Applications & Detailed Worked-Out Examples. 2nd ed. LC 63-2059. 132p. reprint ed. pap. 41.00 (0-608-11588-6, 200191000008) Bks Demand.

McClain, Dan & Chatham, Hugh H., Jr. The Art of the Creel. LC 97-74370. (Illus.). 200p. 1997. 85.00 (0-9659172-7-4) Blue Heron MT.

McClain, Ellen Jaffe. No Big Deal. (J). 1997. 10.09 (0-606-11685-0, Pub. by Turtleback) Demco.

McClain, Ernest G. Myth of Invariance: The Origin of the Gods, Mathematics & Music from the Rg Veda to Plato. LC 76-28411. (Illus.). 216p. 1985. pap. 8.95 (0-89254-012-5) Nicolas-Hays.

— Pythagorean Plato: Prelude to the Song Itself. LC 77-13355. (Illus.). 192p. (Orig.). 1984. pap. 8.95 (0-89254-010-9) Nicolas-Hays.

McClain, Florence W. A Practical Guide to Past Life Regression. LC 84-45285. 160p. (Orig.). 1999. pap. 7.95 (0-87542-510-0) Llewellyn Pubns.

— The Truth about Past Life Regression. (Truth About Ser.). (Illus.). 64p. (Orig.). 1986. mass mkt. 1.99 (0-87542-359-0) Llewellyn Pubns.

— La Verdad Sobre la Regresion a las Vidas Pasadas (The Truth about Past Life Regression) (Truth About Ser.). (SPA.). 64p. 1999. mass mkt. 1.99 (1-56718-880-X) Llewellyn Pubns.

McClain, Francis L. Quitting for Good: A Christ-Centered Approach to Nicotine Dependency. 224p. 1995. pap. text 12.95 (0-8054-9844-3, LifeWy Press) LifeWay Christian.

McClain, Gary, jt. auth. see LeVert, Suzanne.

McClain, George D. Claiming All Things for God: A Guide to Prayer, Discernment & Ritual for Social Change. LC 97-50249. 176p. 1998. pap. 12.95 (0-687-00489-6) Abingdon.

McClain, Heidi, jt. auth. see Denegar, Cynthia.

***McClain, Jackie R.** Guide to Legal Issues: For Human Resource Professionals in Colleges & Universities. Edeburn, Melissa, ed. (Illus.). 135p. 2000. 54.99 (1-878240-76-5) Coll & U Personnel.

— Violence on Campus: How to Minimize Its Risk & Impact. Wilson, Elizabeth A., ed. 30p. 1998. pap. 14.95 (1-878240-67-6) Coll & U Personnel.

***McClain, James L., ed.** Osaka, the Merchant's Capital of Early Modern Japan. LC 98-45675. (Illus.). 295p. 1999. 49.95 (0-8014-3630-3) Cornell U Pr.

McClain, James L., et al, eds. Edo & Paris: Urban Life & the State in the Early Modern Era. (Illus.). 512p. 1994. text 52.50 (0-8014-2987-0) Cornell U Pr.

— Edo & Paris: Urban Life & the State in the Early Modern Era. (Illus.). 512p. 1996. pap. 22.50 (0-8014-8183-X) Cornell U Pr.

***McClain, Jennifer Christiansen, ed.** Wishes & Wonders: Crochet. LC 99-75969. (Illus.). 160p. 2000. 19.96 (1-57367-112-6) Hse White Birches.

McClain, Jerry. Happy Days & Dark Nights. LC 96-171671. 171p. 1996. pap. text 10.99 (0-9641058-1-0) Western Front.

***McClain, La Vonda J.** Never Say Never. 2000. pap. 7.95 (0-533-13310-6) Vantage.

McClain, Lamar. The God of the Valley: Moving from Tragedy to Triumph. LC 92-60933. 76p. (Orig.). 1992. pap. text 4.95 (1-880679-01-9) Mtn MD.

McClain, Leanita. A Foot in Each World: Articles & Essays. Page, Clarence, ed. 181p. 1986. 29.95 (0-8101-0741-4); pap. 12.95 (0-8101-0742-2) Northwestern U Pr.

McClain, Leanita & Page, Clarence. What Killed Leanita McClain? Essays on Living in Both Black & White Worlds. 224p. 1995. 21.95 (1-879360-38-1) Noble Pr.

McClain, Margaret S. Bellboy: A Muletrain Journey. LC 89-61681. (Illus.). 154p. (J). (gr. 5 up). 1990. 17.95 (0-9622468-1-6) NM Pub Co.

McClain, Maria T., ed. Making Commissions Work: A Handbook for Parish Religious Education Boards/Commissions. 104p. (Orig.). 1996. pap. 15.00 (1-55833-151-4) Natl Cath Educ.

McClain, Mary. Baby's Pockets. (Illus.). 8p. (J). (ps). 1981. pap. 3.95 (0-671-43204-4) Litle Simon.

***McClain, Maureen E. & Polsky, Jeffrey D.** Preparing for Trial - Action Guide - Spring 1999. Compton, Linda A., ed. 88p. 1999. ring bd. 58.00 (0-7626-0330-5, CP-11135) Cont Ed Bar-CA.

McClain, Maureen E., et al. Wrongful Termination Claims: What Plaintiffs & Defendants Have to Know. LC 98-150890. (Litigation Course Handbook Ser.). 944p. 1998. 129.00 (0-87224-423-7) PLI.

McClain, Molly. Writing Great Essays. LC 98-30613. (Schaum's Quick Guides). (Illus.). 108p. 1998. pap. 10.95 (0-07-047170-3) McGraw.

McClain, Paula D. Agenda Setting, Public Policy, & Minority Group Influence. (Orig.). 1989. pap. 15.00 (0-944285-19-8) Pol Studies.

McClain, Paula D., ed. Minority Group Influence: Agenda Setting, Formulation, & Public Policy, 333. LC 93-7707. (Contributions in Political Science Ser.: No. 333). 232p. 1993. 62.95 (0-313-29036-9, GM9036, Greenwood Pr) Greenwood.

***McClain, Paula D. & Stewart, Joseph.** Can We All Get Along? Racial & Ethnic Minorities in American Politics. 2nd ed. LC 99-18281. (Dilemmas in American Politics Ser.). 272p. 1999. pap. 17.00 (0-8133-6835-9, Pub. by Westview) HarpC.

McClain, Paula D., jt. auth. see Rose, Harold M.

McClain, Paula D., jt. ed. see Karnig, Albert K.

McClain Printing Co., Staff, ed. see Clagg, Sam E.

McClain Printing Co., Staff, ed. see Long, Roy C.

***McClain-Ruelle, Leslie & Buss, Kathleen.** Creating a Classroom Newspaper. LC 00-40925. 2000. write for info. (0-87207-274-6) Intl Reading.

McClain, S. Navajo Weapon. Kristiansson, Jan, ed. LC 94-72306. (Illus.). 336p. 1994. 29.95 (1-883862-07-8) Bks Beyond Brdrs.

McClain, T. Davina, jt. auth. see Gaisser, Julia Haig.

***McClain, Tee.** I'm Bored Mom. 1999. pap. 9.00 (0-9700191-0-6) Angelic.

McClain, Timothy A., et al. Community Flood Mitigation Planning Guide Book. (Illus.). 167p. 1996. reprint ed. pap. text 30.00 (0-7881-3499-X) DIANE Pub.

McClain-Watson, Teresa. Plenty Good Room. LC 97-23995. (Discoveries Ser.: No. 1). 272p. 1997. pap. 14.00 (0-940242-74-5) Fjord Pr.

McClain, William B. Black People in the Methodist Church: Whither Thou Goest? 160p. (Orig.). 1985. pap. 10.95 (0-687-03588-0) Abingdon.

— Come Sunday: The Liturgy of Zion. 1990. 12.95 (0-687-08884-4) Abingdon.

McClain, William H. Between Real & Ideal: Course of Otto Ludwig's Development As a Narrative Writer. LC 72-181951. (North Carolina. University. Studies in the Germanic Languages & Literatures: No. 40). reprint ed. 27.00 (0-404-50940-1) AMS Pr.

McClain, Yoko M. Families: Japan & America. (Illus.). 101p. 1997. pap. 19.95 (4-590-00938-2, Pub. by Hokuseido Pr) Book East.

— Japan & America: One Woman's View. (Illus.). 98p. 1997. pap. 19.95 (4-590-00894-7, Pub. by Hokuseido Pr) Book East.

McClaine, L. S. Games for Learning: A Curriculum Supplement for Children. 145p. (Orig.). (J). (gr. k-8). 1998. pap. text 12.95 (1-890537-03-9) Nutmeg Pubns.

— History Activities for Fun & Learning. 40p. (J). (gr. k-8). 1998. pap. 3.95 (1-890537-04-7) Nutmeg Pubns.

— My Book about Me: My Homeschool Yearbook. (Illus.). 26p. (Orig.). (J). (gr. 1-6). 1995. pap. text 2.95 (1-890537-02-0) Nutmeg Pubns.

— Physical Education for Homeschoolers: An Easy to Use, Low Equipment Cost Program for Homeschooling Families. (Illus.). 153p. (Orig.). 1994. pap. text 12.95 (1-890537-00-4) Nutmeg Pubns.

— Typing for Kids! Learning to Type on Typewriters & Computer Keyboards. (Illus.). 32p. (Orig.). (J). (gr. 2-8). 1996. pap. text 5.95 (1-890537-01-2) Nutmeg Pubns.

***McClaine, Lee.** Ignatz Witzi Watzi. (Illus.). 30p. 1999. pap. 19.50 (1-892343-06-1) Oak Tree Pub.

McClam, jt. auth. see Woodside.

McClam, Tricia, jt. auth. see Woodside, Marianne.

McClamrock, Ron. Existential Cognition: Computational Minds in the World. LC 93-48967. (Illus.). 216p. 1995. 28.95 (0-226-55641-7) U Ch Pr.

McClanahan. Chimp. (Wild Baby Animals Ser.). 16p. 1999. 4.99 (0-7681-0187-5, McClanahan Book) Learn Horizon.

— Database Systems 11 for Windows NT. (ITCP-US Computer Science Ser.). 1997. pap. 42.99 (1-85032-870-6) ITCP.

— Elephant. (Wild Baby Animals Ser.). (J). 1999. 4.99 (0-7681-0188-3, McClanahan Book) Learn Horizon.

***McClanahan.** First Mazes: Bible Stories. 48p. 1999. pap. 3.99 (0-7681-0113-1, McClanahan Book) Learn Horizon.

McClanahan. Fox. 16p. (J). 1999. 4.99 (0-7681-0189-1, McClanahan Book) Learn Horizon.

— Pre-GED Intrepretive Literature & Arts Exercise Book. (YA - Adult Education Ser.). 1996. pap. 6.95 (0-538-63996-2) S-W Pub.

— Pre-GED Math Exercise Book. (YA - Adult Education Ser.). 1996. pap. 6.95 (0-538-63997-0) S-W Pub.

— Pre-GED Science Exercies Book. (YA - Adult Education Ser.). 1996. pap. 6.95 (0-538-63995-4) S-W Pub.

— Pre-GED Social Studies Exercise Book. (YA - Adult Education Ser.). 1996. pap. 6.95 (0-538-63994-6) S-W Pub.

M

— Pre-GED Writing Exercise Book. (YA - Adult Education Ser.). 1996. pap. 6.95 (0-538-63993-8) S-W Pub.

— Tiger. (J). 1999. 4.99 (0-7681-0190-5, McClanahan Book) Learn Horizon.

***McClanahan, Alexandra J.** Growing Up Native in Alaska. LC 00-100761. (ENG.). 389p. 2000. per. 20.00 (1-57833-114-5) Todd Commns.

McClanahan, Alexandra J. Our Stories, Our Lives. (Illus.). 243p. (Orig.). 1986. pap. 15.95 (0-938227-01-7) CIRI Found.

McClanahan, Arthur L. Be Filled: Sermons on the Beatitudes. LC 96-16084. (Protestant Pulpit Axchange Ser.). 96p. 1996. pap. 8.95 (0-687-06134-2) Abingdon.

McClanahan, Betty J. Simply Tennessee. LC 95-78262. 128p. 1995. pap. 12.95 (0-913383-40-6) McClanahan Pub.

McClanahan Book Co., Inc. Staff. Cursive Writing. 32p. 1997. pap., wbk. ed. 2.25 (1-56293-915-7, McClanahan Book) Learn Horizon.

— Fractions. (High Q Ser.). 1997. pap., wbk. ed. 2.25 (1-56293-919-X, McClanahan Book) Learn Horizon.

— Tricky Puppies: Math. (Flap Bks.). (Illus.). (J). (ps-3). 1994. 4.95 (1-56293-435-X, McClanahan Book) Learn Horizon.

— Vocabulary. 1997. pap., wbk. ed. 2.25 (1-56293-918-1, McClanahan Book) Learn Horizon.

McClanahan Book Co., Inc. Staff, jt. auth. see James, Kari.

McClanahan Book Co., Inc. Staff, jt. auth. see Moerbeek, Kees.

McClanahan Book Co., Inc. Staff, jt. auth. see Murray, Thelma.

M

***McClanahan Book Company Staff.** First Dot-to-Dots: Dino-Mite Dinosaurs. 48p. 1999. pap. text 3.99 (0-7681-0111-5, McClanahan Book) Learn Horizon.

McClanahan Book Company Staff. Mother Goose Rhymes. (I-See-You-Bks.). (Illus.). 8p. (J). 1997. 3.50 (1-56293-983-1, McClanahan Book) Learn Horizon.

— My Big Reading & Math Book: K-1 Advanced. (High Q Ser.). (Illus.). 160p. (J). (gr. k-2). 1997. mass mkt. 9.99 (0-7681-0017-8, McClanahan Book) Learn Horizon.

— My Big Reading & Math Book: K-1 Beginning. (High Q Ser.). (Illus.). 160p. (J). (gr. k-2). 1997. mass mkt. 9.99 (0-7681-0016-X, McClanahan Book) Learn Horizon.

Mcclanahan Book Company Staff. My Big Reading & Math Books: Preschool - Advanced. 1997. pap. text 9.99 (0-7681-0015-1, McClanahan Book) Learn Horizon.

McClanahan Book Company Staff. The World Sticker Book, 8 vols. (Active Learning Bks.). (Illus.). 96p. (J). (gr. 2-6). 1998. pap. 8.99 (1-56293-941-6, McClanahan Book) Learn Horizon.

McClanahan Books Staff. Addition. (J). (gr. k-1). 1997. pap. text, wbk. ed. 2.25 (1-56293-958-0, McClanahan Book) Learn Horizon.

— All about Me. 32p. (J). 1997. pap. text, wbk. ed. 2.25 (1-56293-945-9, McClanahan Book) Learn Horizon.

— Get Ready to Read. (J). 1997. pap. text, wbk. ed. 2.25 (1-56293-948-3, McClanahan Book) Learn Horizon.

— Key Words to Reading. (J). (gr. k-1). 1997. pap. text, wbk. ed. 2.25 (1-56293-964-5, McClanahan Book) Learn Horizon.

— Phonics, Consonants. (J). (gr. k-1). 1997. pap. text, wbk. ed. 2.25 (1-56293-966-1, McClanahan Book) Learn Horizon.

McClanahan, Clarence. European Romanticism: Literary Societies, Poets, & Poetry. LC 89-12632. (American University Studies: Comparative Literature: Ser. III, Vol. 31). 245p. (C). 1990. text 48.95 (0-8204-1167-1) P Lang Pubng.

McClanahan, David. Developing Client/Server Applications. 1999. pap. 49.95 incl. audio compact disk (1-55851-479-1, M&T Bks) IDG Bks.

— Powerbuilder 4.0: Developer's Guide. 1995. pap. 44.95 incl. disk (1-55851-417-1, M&T Bks) IDG Bks.

— Powerbuilder 6: A Developer's Guide. LC 97-46340. 1024p. 1998. pap. 59.99 (1-55851-581-X, M&T Bks) IDG Bks.

McClanahan, Ed. Congress of Wonders. 176p. 1997. pap. 13.50 (1-887178-56-2, Pub. by Counterpt DC) HarpC.

— Famous People I Have Known. rev. ed. LC 97-74433. 232p. 1997. pap. 13.50 (0-917788-58-3) Gnomon Pr.

— My Vita, If You Will: The Uncollected Ed McClanahan. Marksbury, Tom, ed. LC 98-34792. 256p. 1998. pap. 13.50 (1-887178-77-5, Pub. by Counterpt DC) HarpC.

— The Natural Man. LC 93-77697. 240p. 1993. reprint ed. pap. 13.50 (0-917788-56-7) Gnomon Pr.

McClanahan, Elaine & Wicks, Carolyn. Future Force - Kids That Want to, Can & Do! A Teacher's Handbook for Using TQM in the Classroom. (Illus.). 158p. 1995. reprint ed. pap. text 19.95 (0-9646935-0-X) Pact Pubng.

McClanahan, Kay, tr. see ChiWhan Yoo.

McClanahan, R. S. American Democracy. LC 94-78148. 300p. 1995. per. 18.95 (1-57258-003-8) Teach Servs.

McClanahan, Rebecca. The Intersection of X & Y: Poems. LC 96-11192. 62p. (Orig.). 1996. pap. 9.95 (0-914278-70-3) Copper Beech.

***McClanahan, Rebecca.** Naked As Eve: Poems. 63p. 2000. pap. 11.00 (0-914278-78-9) Copper Beech.

McClanahan, Rebecca. One Word Deep: Lectures & Readings. (Writers-in-Residence Ser.). 112p. 1993. pap. 7.00 (0-912592-34-6) Ashland Poetry.

McClanahan, Rebecca. Word Painting: A Guide to Writing More Descriptively. LC 98-48002. 256p. 1999. 18.99 (0-89879-861-2, 10598, Wrtrs Digest Bks) F & W Pubns Inc.

***McClanahan, Rebecca.** Word Painting: A Guide to Writing More Descriptively. 256p. 2000. pap. 14.99 (1-58297-025-4, Wrtrs Digest Bks) F & W Pubns Inc.

McClanahan Staff. First Numbers. (I Can Learn Ser.). (Illus.). 24p. (J). (ps-2). 1994. 1.95 (1-56293-514-3, McClanahan Book) Learn Horizon.

— First Words: First Words. (I Can Learn Ser.). (Illus.). 24p. (J). (ps-2). 1994. 1.95 (1-56293-509-7, McClanahan Book) Learn Horizon.

— Little Red Riding Hood. (I Can Learn Ser.). (Illus.). 24p. (J). (ps-2). 1994. 1.95 (1-56293-513-5, McClanahan Book) Learn Horizon.

— Old MacDonald's Farm. (I Can Learn Ser.). (Illus.). 24p. (J). (ps-2). 1994. 1.95 (1-56293-512-7, McClanahan Book) Learn Horizon.

— Shapes & Sizes. (I Can Learn Ser.). (Illus.). 24p. (J). (ps-2). 1994. 1.95 (1-56293-510-0, McClanahan Book) Learn Horizon.

McClanahan, Tim & Young, Truman P. East African Ecosystems & Their Conservation. (Illus.). 480p. 1996. text 75.00 (0-19-510817-5) OUP.

McClanahan, Tim R., et al, eds. Coral Reefs of the Indian Ocean: Their Ecology & Conservation. LC 99-40236. (Illus.). 544p. 2000. text 85.00 (0-19-512596-7) OUP.

Mclananhan Book Company Staff. My Big Reading & Math Books: Preschool - Beginning. (Illus.). 160p. 1997. pap. text 9.99 (0-7681-0013-5, McClanahan Book) Learn Horizon.

McClane, A. J. McClane's Field Guide to Freshwater Fishes of North America. LC 77-11967. (Illus.). 232p. 1995. pap. 15.95 (0-8050-0194-8, Owl) H Holt & Co.

— McClane's Field Guide to Saltwater Fishes of North America. LC 77-14417. (Illus.). 304p. 1995. pap. 15.95 (0-8050-0733-4, Owl) H Holt & Co.

— McClane's Field Guide to Saltwater Fishes of North America: A Project of the Gamefish Research Association. 1978. pap. 13.95 (0-03-021121-2) Holt R&W.

— McClane's New Standard Fishing Encyclopedia & International Angling Guide. rev. ed. LC 74-6108. (Illus.). 88p. 1995. 75.00 (0-8050-1117-X) H Holt & Co.

— McClane's Secrets of Successful Fishing. LC 78-24367. (Owl Bks.). (Illus.). 288p. 1995. pap. 11.95 (0-8050-0707-5, Owl) H Holt & Co.

— North American Fish Cookery. 1995. 27.95 (0-8050-1065-3) H Holt & Co.

— The Practical Fly Fisherman. 240p. 1983. pap. 7.95 (0-13-689380-5, Reward) P-H.

McClane, B., et al. Microbial Pathogenesis. (Integrated Medical Sciences Ser.). (C). 1998. pap. 22.95 (1-889325-27-9) Fence Crk Pubng.

McClane, Debra, jt. auth. see McClane, Patrick.

McClane, Kenneth A. Take Five: Collected Poems, 109. LC 87-23699. (Contributions in Afro-American & African Studies: No. 109). 296p. 1988. 55.00 (0-313-25761-2, MTA/, Greenwood Pr) Greenwood.

— Walls: Essays, 1985-1990. LC 90-22624. (African American Life Ser.). 122p. 1991. 14.95 (0-8143-2134-8) Wayne St U Pr.

McClane, Patricia, jt. auth. see Flynn, Patricia.

McClane, Patrick & McClane, Debra. James Gamble Rogers II: Residential Architecture in Winter Park, Florida. (Illus.). 104p. 1995. text 19.95 (1-885066-04-X) Four-G Pubs.

McClaney, Eula. God I Listened. 277p. 1988. write for info. (0-9621422-0-4) McClaney.

McClannahan, Lynn E. & Krantz, Patricia J. Activity Schedules for Children with Autism: A Guide for Parents & Professionals. LC 98-49913. (Topics in Autism Ser.). (Illus.). 200p. 1998. pap. 14.95 (0-933149-93-X) Woodbine House.

McClaran, Don, jt. auth. see Moore, Greg.

McClaran, Jeanne L., ed. see Stopke, Judy & Staley, Chip.

McClaran, Mitchel P. & Van Devender, Thomas R. The Desert Grassland. (Illus.). 346p. 1997. pap. 19.95 (0-8165-1823-8) U of Ariz Pr.

McClaran, Mitchel P. & Van Devender, Thomas R., eds. The Desert Grassland. LC 95-327. (Illus.). 346p. 1995. 42.00 (0-8165-1580-8) U of Ariz Pr.

McClard, Judy & Wall, Nomi, compiled by. Come with Us: Children Speak for Themselves. (Illus.). 120p. (J). pap. 5.95 (0-88961-045-2, Pub. by Womens Pr) LPC InBook.

McClard, Megan. Harriet Tubman: Slavery & the Underground Railroad. (History of the Civil War Ser.). (Illus.). 160p. (YA). (gr. 5 up). 1990. pap. 7.95 (0-382-24047-2) Silver Burdett Pr.

McClard, Megan & Ypsilantis, George. Hiawatha. Furstinger, Nancy, ed. (Alvin Joseph's Biography of the American Indians Ser.). (Illus.). 138p. (J). (gr. 5-7). 1989. pap. 7.95 (0-382-09757-2, Silver Pr NJ); lib. bdg. 12.95 (0-382-09568-5, Silver Pr NJ) Silver Burdett Pr.

McClarin, Elizabeth A., jt. auth. see Bonham, Christine E.

***McClarnand, Elaine & Goodson, Steve, eds.** The Impact of the Cold War on American Popular Culture. (State University of West Georgia Studies in Social Science). 103p. 1999. pap. text. write for info. (1-883199-11-5) St U W Georgia.

McClary, Andrew. Toys with Nine Lives: A Social History of American Toys. LC 96-21550. (Illus.). ix, 258p. 1997. lib. bdg. 35.00 (0-208-02386-0, Linnet Bks) Shoe String.

McClary, Ben H. Samuel Lorenzo Knapp & Early American Biography. 30p. 1985. reprint ed. pap. 4.50 (0-912296-80-1) Am Antiquarian.

McClary, Ben H., ed. The Lovingood Papers, 1965. LC 63-22059. 77p. reprint ed. pap. 30.00 (0-8357-6544-X, 203590700097) Bks Demand.

— The Lovingood Papers, 1964. LC 63-22059. 51p. reprint ed. pap. 30.00 (0-8357-6543-1, 203590600097) Bks Demand.

McClary, Ben H., ed. see Irving, Washington.

McClary, Cheryl & Ray, Keith. Wellness & the Liberal Arts. 140p. (C). 1996. pap. text, per. 21.95 (0-7872-2679-3) Kendall-Hunt.

— Wellness & the Liberal Arts: Preliminary Edition. 92p. (C). 1994. spiral bd. 11.95 (0-8403-9362-8) Kendall-Hunt.

McClary, Clebe & Barker, Diane. Living Proof. 230p. 1978. pap. 12.95 (0-9649666-2-X) C McClary Evang.

McClary, D. C., jt. auth. see Lumpkin, T. A.

McClary, Deanna & Jenkins, Jerry. Commitment to Love. 220p. 1989. pap. 19.95 (0-9640666-0-2) C McClary Evang.

***McClary, Susan.** Conventional Wisdom: The Content of Musical Form. LC 99-29428. (Ernest Bloch Lectures Ser.). 284p. 2000. 24.95 (0-520-22106-0, Pub. by U CA Pr) Cal Prin Full Svc.

McClary, Susan. Feminine Endings: Music, Gender & Sexuality. (Illus.). 224p. (Orig.). (C). 1991. pap. 17.95 (0-8166-1899-2) U of Minn Pr.

— Georges Bizet: "Carmen" (Cambridge Opera Handbooks Ser.). (Illus.). 175p. (C). 1992. pap. text 19.95 (0-521-39897-5) Cambridge U Pr.

McClary, Susan, jt. ed. see Leppert, Richard D.

McClaskey, Marilyn H. What Kind of Name Is Juan? Rosen, Roger, ed. (Flipside Fiction Ser.). (YA). (gr. 7-12). 1989. lib. bdg. 12.95 (0-8239-0830-5) Rosen Group.

McClatchey, Kenneth D. Clinical Laboratory Medicine. (Illus.). 1920p. 1994. 95.00 (0-683-05755-3) Lppncott W & W.

McClatchey, Kenneth D., contrib. by. Fine-Needle Aspiration Biopsy (FNAB) Techniques: Approved Guideline, 1996. 1996. 75.00 (1-56238-305-1, GP20-A) NCCLS.

McClatchey, Kenneth D., et al. Clinical Laboratory Medicine: Self-Assessment & Review. LC 96-47824. 341p. 1997. pap. 32.00 (0-683-05757-X) Lppncott W & W.

***McClatchey, Will.** Introductory Ethnobotany. 200p. (C). 1999. pap. text 39.95 (0-7872-6210-2, 41621001) Kendall-Hunt.

McClatchie, Stephen. Analyzing Wagner's Operas: Alfred Lorenz & German Nationalist Ideology. LC 98-28637. (Eastman Studies in Music: Vol. 11, 1071-9989). (Illus.). 416p. 1998. 95.00 (1-58046-023-2) Univ Rochester Pr.

***McClatchy, J. D.** On Wings of Song: Poems about Birds. 2000. 12.50 (0-375-40749-9) Knopf.

McClatchy, J. D. Stars Principal. 80p. 1986. pap. 9.95 (0-02-070030-X) Macmillan.

— Ten Commandments. LC 97-49451. 96p. 1998. 22.00 (0-375-40137-7) Knopf.

— Ten Commandments. 1999. pap. 15.00 (0-375-70134-6) Knopf.

— Twenty Questions. LC 97-49622. xii, 200 p. 1998. 24.00 (0-231-11172-X) Col U Pr.

— Twenty Questions. 1999. pap. text 15.00 (0-231-11173-8) Col U Pr.

McClatchy, J. D., ed. Poets on Painters: Essays on the Art of Painting by Twentieth-Century Poets. (Illus.). 228p. 1988. pap. 17.95 (0-520-06971-4, Pub. by U CA Pr) Cal Prin Full Svc.

— Vintage Book of Contemporary American Poetry. LC 90-50119. 400p. (Orig.). 1990. pap. 16.00 (0-679-72858-9) Vin Bks.

***McClatchy, J. D., ed.** The Voice of the Poet: Elizabeth Bishop. 2000. pap. 15.95 incl. audio (0-375-40964-5) Random AudioBks.

McClatchy, J. D., ed. Vintage Book of Contemporary World Poetry. 672p. 1996. pap. 15.00 (0-679-74115-1) Vin Bks.

McClatchy, J. D., jt. ed. see Hollander, John.

McClatchy, J. D., ed. see Longfellow, Henry Wadsworth.

McClatchy, James, ed. see Zall, Terald A.

McClatchy, Kenneth D. Papanicolaou Technique: Approved Guideline, (1994) 1994. 85.00 (1-56238-238-1, GP15-A) NCCLS.

McClatchy, Valentine S. Four Anti-Japanese Pamphlets: An Original Anthology. Daniels, Roger, ed. LC 78-7080. (Asian Experience in North America Ser.). 1979. lib. bdg. 23.95 (0-405-11282-3) Ayer.

***McClaughlin, Trevor, ed.** Irish Women in Colonial Australia. (Illus.). 248p. 1999. pap. 24.95 (1-86448-715-1, Pub. by Allen & Unwin Pty) Paul & Co Pubs.

McClaughry, C. C. McClaughry. Genealogy of the MacClaughry Family: A Scoto-Irish Family from Galloway, Scotland, Appearing in Ireland about 1600, & Emigrants to N.Y. in 1765. 459p. 1991. reprint ed. pap. 71.00 (0-8328-1994-8); reprint ed. lib. bdg. 81.00 (0-8328-1993-X) Higginson Bk Co.

McClaughry, Charles C. Beach. Genealogy of the Beach Family of Ct., with Portions of the Genealogies of the Allied Families of Demmond, Walker, Gooding & Carpenter. 246p. 1997. reprint ed. lib. bdg. 48.50 (0-8328-7434-5) Higginson Bk Co.

— Beach Genealogy of the Beach Family of Ct., with Portions of the Genealogies of the Allied Families of Demmond, Walker, Gooding & Carpenter. 246p. 1997. reprint ed. pap. 38.50 (0-8328-7435-3) Higginson Bk Co.

McClaurin, Irma. Women of Belize: Gender & Change in Central America. LC 95-52269. (Illus.). 240p. (C). 1996. text 48.00 (0-8135-2307-9); pap. text 16.95 (0-8135-2308-7) Rutgers U Pr.

McClave. First Course in Business. 7th ed. 1998. pap. text, student ed. 32.70 (0-13-746116-X) P-H.

— Instructors Notes Statistics. 7th ed. 1997. pap. text. write for info. (0-13-494931-5) P-H.

McClave. Statistics for Business & Economics. 7th ed. LC 97-13248. 1067p. (C). 1997. 96.00 (0-13-840232-9, Prentice Hall) P-H.

McClave. Statistics for Business & Economics. 7th annot. ed. 1997. text, teacher ed. write for info. (0-13-840265-5) P-H.

McClave, jt. auth. see Boudreau, Nancy S.

McClave, jt. auth. see Scheaffer.

McClave, James T. & Scheaffer, Richard L. Statistics for Engineers. 480p. (C). 1982. pap. 30.75 (0-87872-298-X, 6950) PWS Pubs.

McClave, James T. & Sincich, Terry. A First Course in Statistics. 6th ed. LC 96-34853. 1996. text 78.00 (0-13-579277-0) P-H.

***McClave, James T. & Sincich, Terry.** A First Course in Statistics. 7th ed. LC 99-47176. 2000. write for info. (0-13-014360-X) P-H.

— Statistics 8th ed. LC 99-39266. 2000. pap. write for info. (0-13-022574-6) P-H.

McClave, James T., et al. First Course in Business Statistics. 7th ed. LC 97-44372. 7186p. 1998. 91.00 (0-13-836446-X) P-H.

***McClave, James T., et al.** Statistics for Business & Economics. 8th ed. 1000p. 2000. 91.00 (0-13-027293-0, Prentice Hall) P-H.

McClave, James T., jt. auth. see Schaeffer.

McClave, James T., jt. auth. see Scheaffer, Richard L.

McClay, Gail C. Past, Present, & Future: Perspectives in American Education. (Illus.). 663p. 1995. 55.00 (0-911541-34-9) Gregory Pub.

McClay, Jodi. Learning Centers. LC 96-159854. 1997. pap. text 8.95 (1-55734-891-X) Tchr Create Mat.

— The Multi-Age Classroom: Professional Guide. (Professional's Guide Ser.). 80p. 1997. pap. 9.95 (1-55734-881-2) Tchr Create Mat.

McClay, John B. & Matthews, Wendy L. Corpus Juris Humorous - In Brief: A Compilation of Outrageous, Unusual, Infamous & Witty Judicial Opinions from 1256 A.D. to the Present. 288p. 1994. 9.95 (0-9631488-1-8) Mac-Mat.

McClay, Ken, ed. Thrust Tectonics. (Illus.). 428p. (C). (gr. 13). 1992. pap. text 58.95 (0-412-43900-X, A8208) Chapman & Hall.

McClay, Kenneth. The Mapping of Geological Structures. 2nd ed. (Geological Society of London Professional Handbook Ser.). 2000. pap. text 20.00 (0-471-96635-5) Wiley.

McClay, Kenneth R. The Mapping of Geological Structures. (Geological Society of London Professional Handbook Ser.: No. 1572). 168p. 1991. pap. 59.95 (0-471-93243-4) Wiley.

***McClay, Laura A.** Angels & Ashes. LC 99-48640. 2000. write for info. (1-56492-284-7) Laredo.

McClay, Michael. I Love Lucy: The Complete Picture History of the Most Popular TV Show Ever. (Illus.). 320p. 1995. 34.95 (0-446-51750-X, Pub. by Warner Bks) Little.

— I Love Lucy: The Complete Picture History of the Most Popular TV Show Ever. (Illus.). 320p. 1998. mass mkt. 19.99 (0-446-67420-6, Pub. by Warner Bks) Little.

McClay, Robert E., ed. Career Guide to the Safety Profession. (Illus.). 68p. (YA). (gr. 10 up). 1997. pap. write for info. (1-885581-10-6, 3327) ASSE.

McClay, Wilfred M. The Masterless: Self & Society in Modern America. LC 93-9673. 380p. (C). 1994. pap. 22.50 (0-8078-4419-5); lib. bdg. 59.95 (0-8078-2117-9) U of NC Pr.

***McClay, Wilfred M.** A Student's Guide to American History. LC 00-101236. 75p. (C). 2000. text 5.95 (1-882926-45-5) ISI Books.

McClean. Education & Empire: Naval Tradition & England's Elite Society. 224p. 1999. text 59.50 (1-86064-295-0, Pub. by I B T) St Martin.

McClean, Andrew, compiled by. Security, Arms Control, & Conflict Reduction in East Asia & the Pacific, 19. LC 93-18142. (Bibliographies & Indexes in Law & Political Science Ser.: No. 19). 576p. 1993. lib. bdg. 115.00 (0-313-27539-4, MNB, Greenwood Pr) Greenwood.

McClean, Cheryl, ed. see Butherus, Cindy.

McClean, David. International Judicial Assistance. LC 92-5648. 422p. 1992. text 125.00 (0-19-825224-2) OUP.

McClean, J. R. The Origin of Weight. (Illus.). 1979. pap. 5.00 (0-916710-46-7) Obol Intl.

McClean, Mary. Creating Jobs by Creating New Businesses: The Role of Business Incubators. 72p. (Orig.). 1985. pap. 20.00 (0-317-04904-6) Natl Coun Econ Dev.

— Establishing & Operating Private Sector Development Organizations. Kailo, Andrea, ed. 72p. (Orig.). 1984. pap. 20.00 (0-317-04824-4) Natl Coun Econ Dev.

— Private Sector Development Organizations: A Directory. 84p. (Orig.). 1987. pap. 20.00 (0-317-04816-3) Natl Coun Econ Dev.

— Special Improvement Districts: Business Self-Help. Murphy, Jenny, ed. 52p. (Orig.). 1988. pap. 18.00 (0-317-04850-3) Natl Coun Econ Dev.

McClean, Mary, ed. see Nutter, David.

McClean, Mervyn, jt. auth. see Firth, Raymond.

McClean, R. J. Teach Yourself Swedish. (Teach Yourself Ser.). 1992. 15.95 (0-8288-8406-4) Fr & Eur.

— Teach Yourself Swedish. 2nd ed. (ENG & SWE., Illus.). 324p. 1995. pap. 15.95 (0-8442-3702-7, Teach Yrslf) NTC Contemp Pub Co.

— Teach Yourself Swedish Audio Pack: A Complete Course for Beginners. 2nd ed. (SWE.). 322p. 1994. pap. 14.95 incl. audio (0-8442-3839-2, Teach Yrslf) NTC Contemp Pub Co.

***McClean, Shilo T.** The Digital What? A Filmmaker's Non-Technical Guide to Digital Effects. 132p. 2000. 12.95 (1-879505-55-X, Pub. by Silman James Pr) SCB Distributors.

***McClean, Vernon.** Solutions for the New Millennium: Race, Class & Gender. 300p. (C). 1999. per. 45.00 (0-7872-6088-6) Kendall-Hunt.

McClean, Vernon & Lyles, Lois. Solutions to Problems of Race, Class & Gender. 464p. (C). 1993. per. 32.95 (0-8403-8785-7) Kendall-Hunt.

McClean, Will, jt. auth. see Singman, Jeffrey L.

McClean, William J., ed. see Bowman, Ron.

An Asterisk (*) at the beginning of an entry indicates that the title is appearing for the first time.

McClear, Johanna, jt. auth. see Appleman, Diane.

***McClear, Preston.** Awful Roy. (Illus.). 50p. (J). (gr. k-5). 1999. 16.95 (*1-929084-08-0*); pap. 12.95 (*1-929084-09-9*) Malibu Bks Chldn.

— The Boy under the Bed. (Illus.). 50p. (J). (gr. k-5). 1999. 16.95 (*1-929084-02-1*); pap. 12.95 (*1-929084-03-X*) Malibu Bks Chldn.

— Frannie & Pickles. (Illus.). 29p. (J). (gr. k-5). 1999. 16.95 (*1-929084-04-8*); pap. 12.95 (*1-929084-05-6*) Malibu Bks Chldn.

— Old Man Brown & His Magic Bike. (Illus.). 30p. (J). (gr. k-5). 1999. 16.95 (*1-929084-06-4*); pap. 12.95 (*1-929084-07-2*) Malibu Bks Chldn.

— The Sailor & the Sea Witch. (Illus.). 31p. (J). (gr. k-5). 1999. 16.95 (*1-929084-00-5*); pap. 12.95 (*1-929084-01-3*) Malibu Bks Chldn.

McClearen, H. Addison & Sheetz, S. Owen. St. Thaddeus of Aiken: A Church & Its City. LC 94-7187. (Illus.). 308p. 1994. 37.50 (*0-87152-481-3*) Reprint.

McClearn, Gerald E., jt. ed. see Plomin, Robert.

McCleary, Dick. The Logic of Imaginative Education: Research Understanding. (Advances in Contemporary Educational Thought Ser.). 192p. (C). 1993. text 43.00 (*0-8077-3302-4*); pap. text 18.95 (*0-8077-3301-6*) Tchrs Coll.

***McCleary, Jim, et al.** Don't Lose Your Destiny. LC 00-131593. 183p. 2000. pap. 9.95 (*0-9679693-4-4*) Yes! Enter.

McCleary, Joan, ed. see McCleary, John.

McCleary, John. Geometry from a Differential Viewpoint. (Illus.). 320p. (C). 1995. text 64.95 (*0-521-41430-X*); pap. text 25.95 (*0-521-42480-1*) Cambridge U Pr.

— Glossary of Printing & Publishing Terms, Spanish-English/English-Spanish. (ENG & SPA.). 202p. 1997. pap. 75.00 (*0-7859-9642-7*) Fr & Eur.

— The HIP Dictionary. McCleary, Joan, ed. (Illus.). Date not set. pap. 4.75 (*0-9668687-2-2*) Slow Limbo.

— The Hippie Dictionary: And Cultural Encyclopedia of the 1960's & 70's. 300p. 1999. pap. 25.00 (*0-9668687-1-4*) Slow Limbo.

— The Peninsula People Book. LC 96-93128. (Illus.). 124p. 1998. pap. 25.00 (*0-9668687-0-6*) Slow Limbo.

— A User's Guide to Spectral Sequences. 2nd ed. (Studies in Advanced Mathematics: Vol. 58). (Illus.). 450p. (C). 2000. write for info. (*0-521-56141-8*); pap. write for info. (*0-521-56759-9*) Cambridge U Pr.

McCleary, John, ed. Higher Homotopy Structures in Topology & Mathematical Physics: Proceedings of an International Conference, June 13-15, 1996 at Vassar College, Poughkeepsie, New York, to Honor the Sixtieth Birthday of Jim Stasheff. LC 98-38823. (Contemporary Mathematics Ser.: Vol. 227). 321p. 1998. pap. 69.00 (*0-8218-0913-X*) Am Math.

McCleary, John, jt. ed. see Rowe, David.

McCleary, Kathy & Handley, Gord. The Antique Mystique: Guide to Southern Ontario. LC 97-210198. (Illus.). 120p. 1994. pap. 19.95 (*1-55046-089-7*, Pub. by Boston Mills) Genl Dist Srvs.

McCleary, Linda, jt. ed. see Richard, Ginger.

McCleary, Marguerite D. With Magee & Me. Ciano, Jim, ed. (Illus.). 50p. (Orig.). 1997. pap. 12.95 (*1-888672-17-X*) J Ciano Pubng.

McCleary, Rachel M. Dictating Democracy: Guatemala & the End of Violent Revolution LC 99-24402. 1999. 49.95 (*0-8130-1726-2*) U Press Fla.

— The Ethics of Intervention: The United States & Nicaragua, 1978-1979. (Pew Case Studies in International Affairs). 52p. (C). 1988. pap. text 3.50 (*1-56927-347-2*) Geo U Inst Dplmcy.

— New International Economic Order. (Pew Case Studies in International Affairs). 81p. (C). 1988. pap. text 3.50 (*1-56927-149-6*) Geo U Inst Dplmcy.

McCleary, Richard. Dangerous Men: The Sociology of Parole. 2nd ed. 182p. (C). 1992. pap. 19.90 (*0-911577-24-6*, Criminal Justice) Willow Tree NY.

McCleary, Richard C., jt. auth. see Sartre, Jean-Paul.

McCleary, Richard C., tr. see Merleau-Ponty, Maurice.

McCleary, Rita W. Conversing with Uncertainty: Practicing Psychotherapy in a Hospital Setting. (Relational Perspectives Book Ser.: Vol. 1). 160p. 1992. text 29.95 (*0-88163-148-5*) Analytic Pr.

McCleary, Sheila C., jt. auth. see Scott, Janet M.

McCleary, Timothy P. The Stars We Know: Crow Indian Astronomy & Lifeways. LC 97-205606. (Illus.). 127p. (C). 1996. pap. text 10.95 (*0-88133-924-5*) Waveland Pr.

McCleery, Alistair, ed. Landscape & Light: Essays by Neil M. Gunn. 264p. 1987. text 30.00 (*0-08-035060-7*, Pub. by Aberdeen U Pr); pap. text 19.95 (*0-08-035061-5*, Pub. by Aberdeen U Pr) Macmillan.

McCleery, Patsy R. Josephine's Story: A True Story about a Special Whooping Crane. LC 97-91119. (Illus.). 112p. (J). (gr. 1-12). 1997. pap. 9.95 (*0-9661485-3-3*) Sunny Days Bks.

McCleery, Peter R. & Rankin, Judy. A Woman's Guide to Better Golf. (Illus.). 208p. 1995. 24.95 (*0-8092-3406-8*, 340680, Contemporary Bks) NTC Contemp Pub Co.

— A Woman's Guide to Better Golf. (Illus.). 208p. 1996. pap. 15.95 (*0-8092-3126-3*, 312630, Contemporary Bks) NTC Contemp Pub Co.

McCleery, William. Wolf Story. LC 87-25977. (Illus.). 82p. (J). (gr. 1-6). 1988. reprint ed. lib. bdg. 16.50 (*0-208-02191-4*, Linnet Bks) Shoe String.

McClell. Hallelujah Yippie Kie Yay. 1996. pap. 7.00 (*0-7601-0465-4*) Brentwood Music.

McClellan, Alan, jt. auth. see Geary, David.

McClellan, Alan, jt. auth. see Geary, David M.

McClellan, Alan, jt. auth. see Jackson, Jerry R.

McClellan, Andrew. Inventing the Louvre: Art, Politics, & The Origins of the Modern Museum in Eighteenth-century Paris LC 99-14254. 298p. 1999. pap. 18.95 (*0-520-22176-1*, Pub. by U CA Pr) Cal Prin Full Svc.

McClellan, B. Edward. Moral Education in America: Schools & the Shaping of Character from Colonial Times to the Present. LC 99-13652. 2. 160p. 1999. pap. 21.95 (*0-8077-3820-4*); text 46.00 (*0-8077-3821-2*) Tchrs Coll.

McClellan, B. Edward & Reese, William J., eds. The Social History of American Education. LC 87-5893. 381p. 1988. pap. text 15.95 (*0-252-01462-6*) U of Ill Pr.

McClellan, Bill. Evidence of Murder. 352p. (Orig.). 1993. mass mkt. 6.99 (*0-451-40347-9*, Onyx) NAL.

— Slogging Towards the Millennium. Holdener, Marie & Anderson, Cindi, eds. (Illus.). 250p. 1997. 50.00 (*0-9661397-0-4*); pap. 12.00 (*0-9661397-1-2*) Pulitzer Pub Co.

McClellan, Billy A. To the Sea Again. Waters, Bette & Sallemi, Ann, eds. 245p. 1998. text 29.95 (*0-9665584-1-3*) Bluwaters Pr.

McClellan, Bob. Order on the Court: Lon Kruger & the Revitalization of Florida Gator Basketball. 176p. 1995. 35.00 (*0-9648680-0-8*) Heritage Spts.

McClellan, Carole & Vogler, Lawrence. An Archaeological Assessment of Luke Air Force Range Located in Southwestern Arizona. (Archaeological Ser.: No. 113). (Illus.). 142p. 1977. pap. 6.95 (*1-889747-04-1*) Ariz St Mus.

McClellan, Dave. Crosspoint Scripts Collection. 333p. 1997. 79.00 (*0-930921-10-0*, CPC1) Comm Res OH.

***McClellan, Dennis.** Millennium Aptitude Test: Entrance Exam for the 21st Century. 200p. 2000. pap. 15.95 (*0-9673439-0-9*) InSync Commn.

McClellan, Diane, jt. auth. see Katz, Lilian.

McClellan, Doris. Baxter Badger's Home. LC 95-9774. (Illus.). 32p. (J). (gr. k up). 1995. 15.95 (*1-885777-03-5*) Hendrick-Long.

McClellan, Douglas, et al, frwds. Albert Stewart: The Artist, Teacher & Friend. (Illus.). 125p. 1966. 30.00 (*0-915478-05-6*) Williamson Gallery.

McClellan, E. P., Jr. The Ghosts of Castle Pinckney: A Charlestonian's True Tales of His Boyhood on a Harbor Island. LC 98-65031. (Illus.). 106p. 1998. 19.95 (*1-886391-18-1*); pap. 12.95 (*1-886391-19-X*) Narwhal Pr.

McClellan, Edwin. Two Japanese Novelists: Soseki & Toson. LC 76-81223. 180p. reprint ed. pap. 55.80 (*0-608-10965-7*, 200727600063) Bks Demand.

— Woman in the Crested Kimono: The Life of Shibue Io & Her Family Drawn from Mori Ogai's Shibue Chusai. 200p. 1985. pap. 12.00 (*0-300-04618-9*) Yale U Pr.

McClellan, Edwin, tr. see Natsume Soseki, pseud.

McClellan, Edwin, tr. see Shiga Naoya.

McClellan, Edwin, tr. see Washburn, Dennis & Tansman, Alan, eds.

McClellan, Edwin, tr. see Yoshikawa, Eiji.

McClellan, Edwin, tr. & intro. see Natsume Soseki, pseud.

McClellan, Elisabeth. Historic Dress in America Sixteen Seven to Eighteen Seventy, 2 Vols., Set. LC 70-81515. (Illus.). 1972. reprint ed. 82.95 (*0-88143-077-3*) Ayer.

— Historic Dress in America Sixteen Seven to Eighteen Seventy, 2 Vols., Vol. 1. LC 70-81515. (Illus.). 1988. reprint ed. 38.95 (*0-88143-075-7*) Ayer.

— Historic Dress in America Sixteen Seven to Eighteen Seventy, 2 Vols., Vol. 2. LC 70-81515. (Illus.). 1988. reprint ed. 44.95 (*0-88143-076-5*) Ayer.

McClellan, Frank M. Medical Malpractice: Law, Tactics, & Ethics. 296p. (C). 1993. text 69.95 (*1-56639-065-6*) Temple U Pr.

McClellan, George B. The Armies of Europe: The Military Systems of England, France, Russia, Prussia, Austria, & Sardinia. 1976. lib. bdg. 59.95 (*0-8490-1450-6*) Gordon Pr.

— The Civil War Papers of George B. McClellan: Selected Correspondence 1860-1865. Sears, Stephen W., ed. 669p. 1992. reprint ed. pap. 17.95 (*0-306-80471-9*) Da Capo.

— Report of the Organization & Campaigns of the Army of the Potomac: To Which Is Added an Account of the Campaign in Western Virginia, with Plans of Battle-Fields. LC 78-109629. (Select Bibliographies Reprint Ser.). 1977. 35.95 (*0-8369-5238-3*) Ayer.

McClellan, George M. Old Greenbottom Inn & Other Stories. LC 74-144654. reprint ed. 35.00 (*0-404-00199-8*) AMS Pr.

— Path of Dreams. LC 70-152925. (Black Heritage Library Collection). 1977. 19.95 (*0-8369-8769-1*) Ayer.

— Poems of George Marion M'Clellan. LC 79-133159. (Black Heritage Library Collection). 1977. 12.00 (*0-8369-8714-4*) Ayer.

McClellan, Hassell H. Managing One-Bank Holding Companies. LC 81-4351. 314p. 1981. 42.95 (*0-275-90680-9*, C0680, Praeger Pubs) Greenwood.

McClellan, Helen R. God Speaks His Heart: A Spiritual Message. LC 96-61138. 130p. (Orig.). 1996. pap. 15.95 (*0-9653155-3-3*, 84333) Stuart Victor.

McClellan, Henry B. Campaigns of Stuart's Cavalry. 504p. 1993. 9.98 (*1-55521-971-3*) Bk Sales Inc.

— I Rode with Jeb Stuart: The Life & Campaigns of Major General J. E. B. Stuart. LC 96-14586. 1996. pap. write for info. (*0-253-21099-2*) Ind U Pr.

— I Rode with Jeb Stuart: The Life & Campaigns of Major General J.E.B. Stuart. (Illus.). 475p. 1994. reprint ed. pap. 15.95 (*0-306-80605-3*) Da Capo.

McClellan, James. Joseph Story & the American Constitution: A Study in Political & Legal Thought. LC 75-160499. (Illus.). 448p. 1990. 32.50 (*0-8061-0971-8*) U of Okla Pr.

— Joseph Story & the American Constitution: A Study in Political & Legal Thought. LC 75-160499. (Illus.). 448p. 1990. reprint ed. pap. 17.95 (*0-8061-2290-0*) U of Okla Pr.

— Liberty, Order & Justice: An Introduction to the Constitutional Principles of American Government. LC 89-10544. 1989. 16.95 (*0-940973-08-1*); pap. write for info. (*0-940973-09-X*) James River.

***McClellan, James.** Liberty, Order & Justice: An Introduction to the Constitutional Principles of American Government. 2nd rev. ed. LC 99-46334. 2001. 25.00 (*0-86597-255-9*); pap. 15.00 (*0-86597-256-7*) Liberty Fund.

McClellan, James E., III. Colonialism & Science: Saint Domingue in the Old Regime. (Illus.). 416p. 1992. text 58.00 (*0-8018-4270-0*) Johns Hopkins.

***McClellan, James E., III.** Science & Technology in World History: An Introduction. LC 98-28898. viii, 404 p. 1999. pap. 18.95 (*0-8018-5869-0*) Johns Hopkins.

McClellan, James E., III & Dorn, Harold. Science & Technology in World History: An Introduction. LC 98-28898. (Illus.). 424p. 1999. 55.00 (*0-8018-5868-2*) Johns Hopkins.

McClellan, James F. Science Reorganized. 1985. text 84.00 (*0-231-05996-5*) Col U Pr.

McClellan, James H., et al. Computer-Based Exercises for Signal Processing Using Matlab5. LC 97-41449. 404p. (C). 1997. pap. 25.00 (*0-13-789009-5*) P-H.

McClellan, Janet. Chimney Rock Blues: A Tru North Mystery. LC 98-44754. (Tru North Mysteries Ser.). 240p. 1999. pap. 11.95 (*1-56280-233-X*) Naiad Pr.

— K. C. Bomber: A Tru North Mystery. LC 96-45484. 208p. (Orig.). 1997. pap. 11.95 (*1-56280-157-0*) Naiad Pr.

— Penn Valley Phoenix: A True North Mystery. LC 97-40427. 240p. (Orig.). 1998. pap. 11.95 (*1-56280-200-3*) Naiad Pr.

— River Quay. LC 98-13233. (Tru North Mystery Ser.: No. 3). 208p. 1998. pap. 11.95 (*1-56280-212-7*) Naiad Pr.

— Windrow Garden. 256p. 1998. pap. 11.95 (*1-56280-216-X*) Naiad Pr.

McClellan, Jim R. Great Moments in American History, Vol. I. (Illus.). 384p. (Orig.). (C). 1994. text 14.95 (*1-56134-114-2*, Dshkn McG-Hill) McGrw-H Hghr Educ.

— Great Moments in American History, Vol. II. (Illus.). 464p. (Orig.). (C). 1995. text 14.95 (*1-56134-115-0*, Dshkn McG-Hill) McGrw-H Hghr Educ.

McClellan, Keith. Prayer Therapy. LC 89-82664. (Illus.). 76p. (Orig.). 1990. pap. 4.95 (*0-87029-225-0*, 20206-9) Abbey.

— The Sunday Game: At the Dawn of Professional Football. LC 98-24175. (Ohio History & Culture Ser.). 503p. 1998. 39.95 (*1-884836-35-6*); pap. 19.95 (*1-884836-36-4*) U Akron Pr.

McClellan, Keith & Corneil, Wayne, eds. Alcohol in Employment Settings: The Results of the WHO-ILO International Review. LC 87-35998. (Employee Assistance Quarterly Ser.: Vol. 3, No. 2). (Illus.). 119p. 1988. text 39.95 (*0-86656-713-5*) Haworth Pr.

McClellan, Keith & Miller, Richard E., eds. EAPs & the Information Revolution: The Dark Side of Megatrends. LC 86-33519. (Employee Assistance Quarterly Ser.: Vol. 2, No. 2). 106p. 1987. text 39.95 (*0-86656-606-6*) Haworth Pr.

McClellan, Maggie. Artist's Express: Secrets of the Obedient Brush. (Illus.). 117p. 1990. pap. 21.50 (*0-9623952-0-X*) DAVCO.

McClellan, Marian, jt. auth. see McClellan, Sherman.

McClellan, Marian A. Seeds of Stillness: Opening to the Self. LC 93-5439. (Illus.). 64p. (Orig.). 1994. pap. 8.50 (*1-56474-074-9*) Fithian Pr.

McClellan, Mark & Kessler, Daniel, eds. A Global Analysis of Technological Change in Health Care: Heart Attack. (Illus.). (C). text. write for info. (*0-472-11128-0*) U of Mich Pr.

McClellan, Mary E. Felt-Silk-Straw Handmade Hats: Tools & Processes, Vol. III. (Illus.). 23p. 1978. pap. 4.00 (*0-910302-04-9*) Bucks Co Hist.

Mcclellan-Mccle. Historic Moments in American History, Vol. 2. 2nd ed. 384p. 1999. pap. 22.50 (*0-07-228383-1*) McGraw.

McClellan, Melanie, ed. see McClellan, Michael.

McClellan, Michael. Applying Manufacturing Execution Systems. LC 97-204570. 1997. lib. bdg. 42.50 (*1-57444-135-3*) St Lucie Pr.

— In Plane View. McClellan, Melanie, ed. 249p. 1998. pap. 6.95 (*1-57502-845-X*, PO2316) Morris Pubng.

— Monasticism of Egypt: Images & Stories of the Desert Fathers. 112p. 1998. 17.95 (*977-424-463-X*, Pub. by Am Univ Cairo Pr) Col U Pr.

McClellan, Pam. Don't Be a Slave to Housework. 176p. 1995. pap. 10.99 (*1-55870-356-X*, Betrwy Bks) F & W Pubns Inc.

McClellan, Phyllis I. The Artillerymen of Historic Fort Monroe, Virginia. (Illus.). 264p. (Orig.). 1992. pap. text 20.00 (*1-55613-529-7*) Heritage Bk.

— Silent Sentinel on the Potomac, Fort McNair, 1791-1991. (Illus.). 280p. (Orig.). 1993. pap. text 24.00 (*1-55613-848-2*) Heritage Bk.

McClellan, Robert W. & Usher, Carolyn E. Claiming a Frontier: Ministry & Older People. LC 77-85413. 1977. 10.00 (*0-88474-040-4*, 05741-X) Free Pr.

McClellan, Roby, ed. The New Jersey Guide to Nursing Homes: And Other Care Facilities for the Elderly. LC 97-77548. 252p. 1997. pap. 19.95 (*0-9661654-0-3*) Guide Inc.

McClellan, Roger O. Tobacco-Specific N-Nitrosomes: Recent Advances. LC 97-102975. 85p. 1996. boxed set 64.95 (*0-8493-1156-X*) CRC Pr.

McClellan, Roger O. & Henderson, Rogene F. Concepts in Inhalation Toxicology. 2nd ed. LC 95-13914. 648p. 1995. 136.00 (*1-56032-368-X*) Hemisp Pub.

McClellan, Sam & Monte, Tom. Integrative Acupressure: A Hands-On Guide to Balancing the Body's Structure & Energy for Health & Healing. LC 98-3034. (Illus.). 256p. 1998. pap. 15.95 (*0-399-52441-X*) Putnam Pub Group.

McClellan, Sherman & McClellan, Marian. Patterns for Profit. 2nd ed. 54p. 1989. reprint ed. pap. 50.00 (*1-879192-07-1*) Fndtn Study Cycles.

McClellan, Tim, ed. see Biasiotto, Judd.

McClellan, Val J. This Is Our Land, Vol. 1. LC 77-151749. (Illus.). 902p. 1977. 17.95 (*0-533-02248-7*, 77-151749) Western Pubs NC.

— This Is Our Land, Vol. 2. LC 77-151749. (Illus.). 927p. 1979. 17.95 (*0-9602218-0-8*) Western Pubs NC.

McClellan, William S. Smuggling in the American Colonies at the Outbreak of the Revolution: With Special Reference to the West Indies Trade. xx, 105p. 1997. reprint ed. pap. 15.00 (*0-7884-0639-6*, M111) Heritage Bk.

McClellan, Woodford. Revolutionary Exiles: The Russians in the First International & the Paris Commune. (Illus.). 266p. 1979. 42.50 (*0-7146-3115-9*, Pub. by F Cass Pubs) Intl Spec Bk.

— Russia. 4th ed. LC 97-14284. 356p. (C). 1997. pap. text 54.00 (*0-13-646613-3*) P-H.

***McClelland.** Adobe InDesign for Dummies. (For Dummies Ser.). 408p. 1999. pap. 19.99 (*0-7645-0599-8*) IDG Bks.

— CorelDRAW 9 for Dummies. LC 99-63119. (For Dummies Ser.). 384p. 1999. pap. 19.99 (*0-7645-0523-8*) IDG Bks.

McClelland. Embers of War 1945-1946. (Illus.). 196p. 1997. text 55.00 (*1-86064-312-4*, Pub. by I B T) St Martin.

***McClelland.** Photoshop Studio Secrets. 2nd ed. LC 98-75152. (Illus.). 368p. 1999. pap. 49.99 (*0-7645-3271-5*) IDG Bks.

McClelland. Seeing Statistics. (Career Education Ser.). 1999. 43.95 (*0-534-34982-X*) Brooks-Cole.

McClelland & Wilson. Impossible with Men. 1997. pap. 8.99 (*1-898787-84-0*) Emerald House Group Inc.

McClelland, jt. auth. see King.

***McClelland & Stewart Staff.** Time Passages 1980. 1999. pap. 15.95 (*1-894455-40-1*) Stewart Hse.

— Time Passages 1985. 1999. pap. 15.95 (*1-894455-45-2*) Stewart Hse.

— Time Passages 1984. 1999. pap. 15.95 (*1-894455-44-4*) Stewart Hse.

— Time Passages 1989. 1999. pap. 15.95 (*1-894455-49-5*) Stewart Hse.

— Time Passages 1987. 1999. pap. 15.95 (*1-894455-47-9*) Stewart Hse.

— Time Passages 1986. 1999. pap. 15.95 (*1-894455-46-0*) Stewart Hse.

— Time Passages 1983. 1999. pap. 15.95 (*1-894455-43-6*) Stewart Hse.

— Time Passages 1982. 1999. pap. 15.95 (*1-894455-42-8*) Stewart Hse.

— Time Passages 1950. 1999. pap. 15.95 (*1-894455-10-X*) Stewart Hse.

— Time Passages 1958. 1999. pap. 15.95 (*1-894455-18-5*) Stewart Hse.

— Time Passages 1955. 1999. pap. 15.95 (*1-894455-15-0*) Stewart Hse.

— Time Passages 1954. 1999. pap. 15.95 (*1-894455-14-2*) Stewart Hse.

— Time Passages 1959. 1999. pap. 15.95 (*1-894455-19-3*) Stewart Hse.

— Time Passages 1951. 1999. pap. 15.95 (*1-894455-11-8*) Stewart Hse.

— Time Passages 1956. 1999. pap. 15.95 (*1-894455-16-9*) Stewart Hse.

— Time Passages 1953. 1999. pap. 15.95 (*1-894455-13-4*) Stewart Hse.

— Time Passages 1952. 1999. pap. 15.95 (*1-894455-12-6*) Stewart Hse.

— Time Passages 1940. 1999. pap. 15.95 (*1-894455-00-2*) Stewart Hse.

— Time Passages 1948. 1999. pap. 15.95 (*1-894455-08-8*) Stewart Hse.

— Time Passages 1945. 1999. pap. 15.95 (*1-894455-05-3*) Stewart Hse.

— Time Passages 1944. 1999. pap. 15.95 (*1-894455-04-5*) Stewart Hse.

— Time Passages 1949. 1999. pap. 15.95 (*1-894455-09-6*) Stewart Hse.

— Time Passages 1947. 1999. pap. 15.95 (*1-894455-07-X*) Stewart Hse.

— Time Passages 1946. 1999. pap. 15.95 (*1-894455-06-1*) Stewart Hse.

— Time Passages 1943. 1999. pap. 15.95 (*1-894455-03-7*) Stewart Hse.

— Time Passages 1942. 1999. pap. 15.95 (*1-894455-02-9*) Stewart Hse.

— Time Passages 1990. 1999. pap. 15.95 (*1-894455-50-9*) Stewart Hse.

— Time Passages 1998. 1999. pap. 15.95 (*1-894455-58-4*) Stewart Hse.

— Time Passages 1995. 1999. pap. 15.95 (*1-894455-55-X*) Stewart Hse.

— Time Passages 1994. 1999. pap. 15.95 (*1-894455-54-1*) Stewart Hse.

— Time Passages 1991. 1999. pap. 15.95 (*1-894455-51-7*) Stewart Hse.

— Time Passages 1997. 1999. pap. 15.95 (*1-894455-57-6*) Stewart Hse.

— Time Passages 1996. 1999. pap. 15.95 (*1-894455-56-8*) Stewart Hse.

— Time Passages 1993. 1999. pap. 15.95 (*1-894455-53-3*) Stewart Hse.

— Time Passages 1992. 1999. pap. 15.95 (*1-894455-52-5*) Stewart Hse.

— Time Passages 1970. 1999. pap. 15.95 (*1-894455-30-4*) Stewart Hse.
— Time Passages 1978. 1999. pap. 15.95 (*1-894455-38-X*) Stewart Hse.
— Time Passages 1975. 1999. pap. 15.95 (*1-894455-35-5*) Stewart Hse.
— Time Passages 1974. 1999. pap. 15.95 (*1-894455-34-7*) Stewart Hse.
— Time Passages 1979. 1999. pap. 15.95 (*1-894455-39-8*) Stewart Hse.
— Time Passages 1971. 1999. pap. 15.95 (*1-894455-31-2*) Stewart Hse.
— Time Passages 1977. 1999. pap. 15.95 (*1-894455-37-1*) Stewart Hse.
— Time Passages 1976. 1999. pap. 15.95 (*1-894455-36-3*) Stewart Hse.
— Time Passages 1973. 1999. pap. 15.95 (*1-894455-33-9*) Stewart Hse.
— Time Passages 1972. 1999. pap. 15.95 (*1-894455-32-0*) Stewart Hse.
— Time Passages 1965. 1999. pap. 15.95 (*1-894455-25-8*) Stewart Hse.
— Time Passages 1964. 1999. pap. 15.95 (*1-894455-24-X*) Stewart Hse.
— Time Passages 1969. 1999. pap. 15.95 (*1-894455-29-0*) Stewart Hse.
— Time Passages 1961. 1999. pap. 15.95 (*1-894455-21-5*) Stewart Hse.
— Time Passages 1966. 1999. pap. 15.95 (*1-894455-26-6*) Stewart Hse.
— Time Passages 1963. 1999. pap. 15.95 (*1-894455-23-1*) Stewart Hse.
— Time Passages 1962. 1999. pap. 15.95 (*1-894455-22-3*) Stewart Hse.
— Time Passages 1941. 1999. pap. 15.95 (*1-894455-01-0*) Stewart Hse.
— Time Passages 1957. 1999. pap. 15.95 (*1-894455-17-7*) Stewart Hse.
— Time Passages 1960. 1999. pap. 15.95 (*1-894455-20-7*) Stewart Hse.
— Time Passages 1967. 1999. pap. 15.95 (*1-894455-27-4*) Stewart Hse.
— Time Passages 1968. 1999. pap. 15.95 (*1-894455-28-2*) Stewart Hse.
— Time Passages 1981. 1999. pap. 15.95 (*1-894455-41-X*) Stewart Hse.
— Time Passages 1988. 1999. pap. 15.95 (*1-894455-48-7*) Stewart Hse.

McClelland & Stewart Staff, ed. The 1999 Canadian Encyclopedia World Edition. (Illus.). 1999. pap. text 19.99 (*0-7710-2041-4*) McCland & Stewart.

McClelland, Alan & Varma, Ved P., eds. The Needs of Teachers. LC 95-26740. (Education Ser.). (Illus.). 160p. 1996. pap. 25.95 (*0-304-33335-2*) Continuum.

McClelland, Alan M., jt. auth. see Ough, R.

McClelland, Allen. Virginian & Ohio Story. (Illus.). 104p. 1983. pap. 19.95 (*0-911868-47-X*, C47) Carstens Pubns.

McClelland, Atha F. Heavenly Ways of Earths Graduates. 160p. (Orig.). 1994. pap. 10.00 (*0-9636435-4-1*) M A P.

McClelland, Averil E. The Education of Women in the United States: A Guide to Theory, Teaching, & Research. LC 92-14495. (Source Books on Education: Vol. 23). 248p. 1992. text 43.00 (*0-8240-4842-3*, SS551) Garland.

McClelland, Ben W. New American Rhetoric. LC 92-15012. 658p. (C). 1993. pap. text 48.00 (*0-673-38605-8*) Addson-Wesley Educ.

McClelland, Ben W. & Donovan, Timothy R., eds. Perspectives on Research & Scholarship in Composition. LC 85-15401. ix, 266p. 1985. pap. 19.75 (*0-87352-145-5*, J304P); lib. bdg. 37.50 (*0-87352-144-7*, J304C) Modern Lang.

McClelland, Bramlette & Reifel, Michael, eds. Planning & Design of Fixed Offshore Platforms. LC 84-27078. (Illus.). 1056p. 1985. text 125.95 (*0-442-25223-4*, VNR) Wiley.

McClelland, Bruce. The Marchen Cycle. LC 80-10183. (Illus.). 50p. 1980. pap. 6.00 (*0-930794-25-7*) Station Hill Pr.

McClelland, Bruce, tr. Tristia: Poems by Osip Mandelstam. LC 86-32305. (Illus.). 120p. 1987. 16.95 (*0-88268-041-2*) Station Hill Pr.

McClelland, C. Ivor, ed. see Gacy, John W.

McClelland, Carol. Dragon Fire. 2000. pap. 7.95 (*0-533-13554-0*) Vantage.

McClelland, Carol L. Nature's Wisdom: A Powerfully Insightful Guide for Exploring Life's Changes. (Illus.). 80p. 1993. pap. 28.95 (*0-9635123-3-1*) Transition Dyn.
— The Seasons of Change: Using Nature's Wisdom to Grow Through Life's Inevitable Ups & Downs. LC 97-53277. (Illus.). 320p. 1998. pap. 14.95 (*1-57324-078-8*) Conari Press.

McClelland, Charles E. Certain Arrangements. (YA). (gr. 6-12). 1998. pap. 6.00 (*0-87602-356-1*) Anchorage.
— The German Experience of Professionalization: Modern Learned Professions & Their Organizations from the Early Nineteenth Century to the Hitler Era. 265p. (C). 1991. text 80.00 (*0-521-39457-0*) Cambridge U Pr.
— The German Historians & England: A Study in Nineteenth-Century Views. LC 79-154514. 311p. reprint ed. pap. 88.70 (*0-608-30135-3*, 2013895) Bks Demand.

McClelland, Clive W., III. The Interrelations of Syntax, Narrative Structure & Prosody in a Berber Language. LC 00-22281. (Studies in Linguistics & Semiotics: 8). 400p. 2000. pap. text 99.95 (*0-7734-7740-3*) E Mellen.

McClelland, D. E., et al, eds. Gravitational Astronomy: Instrument Design & Astrophysical Prospects. 468p. (C). 1991. text 104.00 (*981-02-0688-7*) World Scientific Pub.

McClelland, David C. Achievement Motive. LC 75-34465. (Illus.). 42.50 (*0-8290-1167-6*) Irvington.
— The Achieving Society: With a New Introduction. 520p. (C). 50.50 (*0-8290-0870-5*) Irvington.
— Human Motivation. 688p. 1988. pap. text 44.95 (*0-521-36951-7*) Cambridge U Pr.
— Motives, Personality & Society. LC 84-2033. (Centennial Psychology Ser.). 502p. 1984. 65.00 (*0-275-91224-8*, C1224, Praeger Pubs) Greenwood.
— Personality. rev. ed. 672p. reprint ed. text. write for info. (*0-318-53722-2*) Irvington.
— Power: The Inner Experience. LC 75-35603. (Illus.). 441p. 1979. 39.50 (*0-8290-0686-9*); pap. text 24.95 (*0-8290-0101-8*) Irvington.
— The Roots of Consciousness. enl. ed. (Illus.). text. write for info. (*0-8290-0124-7*) Irvington.
— Some Social Consequences of Achievement Motivation. (Reprint Series in Social Sciences). (C). 1993. reprint ed. pap. text 2.30 (*0-8290-2669-X*, S-457) Irvington.

McClelland, David C., ed. Development of Social Maturity. 260p. 1982. 32.50 (*0-8290-0089-5*) Irvington.
— Development of Social Maturity. 260p. 1984. pap. text 12.95 (*0-8290-1556-6*) Irvington.
— Education for Values. 220p. 1982. 32.50 (*0-8290-0090-9*) Irvington.
— Education for Values. 220p. 1984. pap. text 12.95 (*0-8290-1557-4*) Irvington.

McClelland, Deke. CorelDRAW 7 for Dummies. LC 97-70369. (For Dummies Ser.). (Illus.). 412p. 1997. pap. 19.99 (*0-7645-0124-0*) IDG Bks.

McClelland, Deke. CorelDraw 8 for Dummies. LC 97-81453. (For Dummies Ser.). 432p. 1998. pap. 19.99 (*0-7645-0317-0*) IDG Bks.
— FreeHand 8 Bible. (Bible Ser.). 700p. 1998. pap. text 39.99 (*0-7645-3234-0*) IDG Bks.

McClelland, Deke. Mac Multimedia & CD-ROMS for Dummies. 400p. 1995. pap. 19.99 (*1-56884-910-9*) IDG Bks.
— Mac Multimedia & CD-ROMs for Dummies, Interactive Multimedia Value Pack. LC 95-77669. 416p. 1995. pap. 29.99 (*1-56884-911-7*); pap. 29.99 (*1-56884-912-5*) IDG Bks.
— MacWorld Freehand 4.0 Bible. LC 94-75904. 700p. 1994. pap. 29.95 (*1-56884-170-1*) IDG Bks.
— MacWorld Photoshop 5 Bible. (Bible Ser.). (Illus.). 960p. 1998. pap. text 49.99 incl. cd-rom (*0-7645-3231-6*) IDG Bks.
— MacWorld Photoshop 3.0 Bible. 2nd ed. LC 94-79605. 894p. 1994. pap. 39.95 (*1-56884-158-2*) IDG Bks.
— MacWorld Photoshop 2.5 Bible. (Illus.). 650p. 1993. pap. 29.95 (*1-56884-022-5*) IDG Bks.
— MW Freehand 5 Bible. 2nd ed. 784p. 1995. pap. 29.99 (*1-56884-492-1*) IDG Bks.
— PageMaker 5 for Windows for Dummies. LC 94-77746. 416p. 1994. pap. 19.95 (*1-56884-160-4*) IDG Bks.
— Painting on the Macintosh: A Non-Artist's Guide to Superpaint, Pixelpaint, Painter, & Many More. rev. ed. (Desktop Publishing Library). 1993. pap. 25.00 (*1-55623-910-6*, Irwn Prfssnl) McGraw-Hill Prof.
— Painting on the PC: A Non-Artist's Guide to Popular Painting Programs. rev. ed. 1993. pap. 25.00 (*1-55623-912-2*, Irwn Prfssnl) McGraw-Hill Prof.
— Photoshop 5 for Macs for Dummies. (For Dummies Ser.). (Illus.). 400p. 1998. pap. 19.99 (*0-7645-0391-X*) IDG Bks.
— Photoshop 5 for Windows for Dummies. LC 98-85679. (For Dummies Ser.). (Illus.). 400p. 1998. pap. 19.99 (*0-7645-0392-8*) IDG Bks.
— Photoshop 4 for Macs for Dummies. 2nd ed. LC 96-77699. 384p. 1996. pap. 19.99 (*0-7645-0039-2*) IDG Bks.

McClelland, Deke. Photoshop 4 for Windows for Dummies. LC 96-80227. (Illus.). 384p. 1997. pap. 19.99 (*0-7645-0102-X*) IDG Bks.
— Photoshop 4 for Windows 95 Bible. 912p. 1997. pap. 49.99 (*0-7645-4032-7*) IDG Bks.

McClelland, Deke. Photoshop 4 Studio Secrets. LC 97-74339. 256p. 1997. pap. 49.99 (*0-7645-4028-9*) IDG Bks.
— Photoshop 3 for Macs for Dummies. 376p. 1995. pap. 19.99 (*1-56884-208-2*) IDG Bks.

McClelland, Deke. Photoshop "X" for Dummies. (For Dummies Ser.). (Illus.). 424p. 2000. pap. 19.99 (*0-7645-0704-4*) IDG Bks.

McClelland, Deke. Photoshop X for Windows Bible. (Bible Ser.). (Illus.). 960p. 1998. pap. text 49.99 incl. cd-rom (*0-7645-3232-4*) IDG Bks.

McClelland, Deke. Photoshop 5 Bible: Gold Edition. (Bible Ser.). 1024p. 1999. pap. 59.99 (*0-7645-3372-X*) IDG Bks.

McClelland, Deke. QR/Photoshop 3 for Macs for Dummies. 224p. 1995. spiral bd. 9.99 (*1-56884-968-0*) IDG Bks.
— Real World Illustrator Eight. 2nd ed. LC 99-193701. 860p. (C). 1998. pap. text 34.99 (*0-201-35387-3*, Pub. by Peachpit Pr) Addison-Wesley.
— Real World Illustrator 7. LC 97-205175. (Illus.). 816p. (C). 1997. pap. text 29.95 (*0-201-69612-6*, Pub. by Peachpit Pr) Addison-Wesley.

McClelland, Deke. Web Design Studio Secrets. 2nd ed. (Illus.). 288p. 2000. pap. text 49.99 (*0-7645-3455-6*) IDG Bks.

McClelland, Deke & Cohen, Sandee. Real World Illustrator 9. 896p. 2000. pap. text 39.99 (*0-201-70405-6*) Peachpit Pr.

McClelland, Deke & Danuloff, Craig. Desktop Publishing - Type & Graphics: A Comprehensive Handbook. 1987. pap. 29.95 (*0-15-625298-8*, Harvest Bks) Harcourt.
— Mastering Adobe Illustrator PC. 300p. 1989. pap. 28.00 (*1-55623-158-X*, Irwn Prfssnl) McGraw-Hill Prof.

McClelland, Deke & Eismann, Katrin. Real World Digital Photography. 400p. (C). 1999. pap. text 44.99 (*0-201-35402-0*) Addison-Wesley.
— Web Design Studio Secrets. LC TK5105.888.M3747. (Secrets Ser.). (Illus.). 336p. 1998. pap. 49.99 incl. cd-rom (*0-7645-3171-9*) IDG Bks.

McClelland, Donald, jt. ed. see Tweeten, Luther G.

McClelland, Donna, jt. auth. see Donnan, Christopher B.

McClelland, Doug. Blackface to Blacklist: Al Jolson, Larry Parks, & "The Jolson Story" (Illus.). 308p. 1998. reprint ed. pap. 19.95 (*0-8108-3530-4*) Scarecrow.
— Eleanor Parker, Woman of a Thousand Faces: A Bio-Bibliography & Filmography. LC 89-10292. (Illus.). 291p. 1989. 34.50 (*0-8108-2242-3*) Scarecrow.
— Forties Film Talk: Oral Histories of Hollywood, with 120 Lobby Posters. LC 92-54087. 469p. 1992. lib. bdg. 55.00 (*0-89950-672-0*) McFarland & Co.

McClelland, Elizabeth. The Cosmic Rhthyms: Public Sculpture of Athena Tacha. Rabson, Caroline, ed. LC 98-92198. (Women's Ser.). (Illus.). 96p. 1998. pap. 25.00 (*1-893023-57-5*) Ohio Artists.
— Small Animals of America Coloring Book. (Illus.). (J). (gr. k-3). 1981. pap. 2.95 (*0-486-24217-X*) Dover.

McClelland, Elizabeth & Hinson, Tom. The Art of La Wilson. (Women's Ser.). 55p. 1994. pap. text 20.00 (*1-893023-51-6*) Ohio Artists.
— The Art of Mary Lou Ferbert. (Women's Ser.). 64p. 1993. pap. text 20.00 (*1-893023-50-8*) Ohio Artists.

McClelland, Elizabeth & Jean, William M. The Art of Shirley Aley-Campbell. (Women's Ser.). 1995. pap. text 20.00 (*1-893023-53-2*) Ohio Artists.

McClelland, Elizabeth & Kurtz, Robert. The Art of Gloria Plevin. (Women's Ser.). 1998. pap. text 20.00 (*1-893023-55-9*) Ohio Artists.

McClelland, Elizabeth A. Pagemaker 6.5 for Windows for Dummies. 3rd ed. LC 97-70370. 408p. 1997. pap. 19.99 (*0-7645-0126-7*) IDG Bks.

McClelland, Fleming, jt. ed. see Tarr, Rodger L.

McClelland, G. E., et al, eds. Practical Aspects of International Management & Processing. LC 95-73104. (Illus.). 124p. (Orig.). 1996. pap. 49.00 (*0-87335-143-6*, 143-6) SMM&E Inc.

McClelland, Gordon, jt. auth. see Lovoos, Janice.

McClelland, Gordon T. Emil Kosa, Jr. (Illus.). 71p. 1990. 27.50 (*0-914589-06-7*) Hillcrest Pr.
— George Post. (Illus.). 82p. 1992. 27.50 (*0-914589-08-3*) Hillcrest Pr.

McClelland, Gordon T. & Last, Jay T. California Orange Box Labels. (Illus.). 133p. 1984. 35.00 (*0-914589-01-6*) Hillcrest Pr.
— Fruit Box Labels: An Illustrated Price Guide to Citrus Labels. (Illus.). 144p. (C). 1995. 35.00 (*0-914589-09-1*) Hillcrest Pr.

McClelland, Gordon T. & Zornes, Milford. Milford Zornes. (Illus.). 70p. 1992. 27.50 (*0-914589-07-5*) Hillcrest Pr.

McClelland, I. L. Pathos Dramatico en el Teatro Espanol de 1750 a 1808, 2 vols. Cenoz, Guillermina & Huerta, Fernando, trs. (SPA.). 784p. 1998. 99.95 (*0-85323-128-1*, Pub. by Liverpool Univ Pr); pap. 44.95 (*0-85323-138-9*, Pub. by Liverpool Univ Pr) Intl Spec Bk.

McClelland, Ivy L. Benito Jeronimo Feijoo. LC 68-17230. (Twayne's World Authors Ser.). 1969. lib. bdg. 20.95 (*0-8057-2308-0*) Irvington.
— Diego de Torres Villarroel. LC 76-6548. (Twayne's World Authors Ser.). 162p. (C). 1976. lib. bdg. 20.95 (*0-317-38185-7*) Irvington.
— Spanish Drama of Pathos, 1750-1808, Vol. 2. LC 70-504666. 300p. reprint ed. pap. 93.00 (*0-8357-3767-5*, 203649600002) Bks Demand.
— Spanish Drama of Pathos, 1750-1808 Vol. 1: High Tragedy. LC 70-504666. 360p. reprint ed. pap. 111.60 (*0-7837-0039-3*, 203649600001) Bks Demand.
— Tirso de Molina. LC 76-28272. (Liverpool Studies in Spanish Literature 3rd Ser.). reprint ed. 50.00 (*0-404-15033-0*) AMS Pr.

McClelland, J. B. & Gibson, B. F. New Vistas in Physics with High-Energy Pion Beams: Preconference Workshop. 180p. 1993. text 95.00 (*981-02-1275-5*) World Scientific Pub.

McClelland, Jame C. Autocrats & Academics: Education, Culture, & Society in Tsarist Russia. LC 79-12504. (Illus.). 1979. 14.00 (*0-226-55661-1*) U Ch Pr.

McClelland, James. The Ambassador Book of Great Hymn Stories. 2nd ed. 160p. 1997. pap. 9.99 (*0-907927-99-8*) Emerald House Group Inc.

McClelland, James C. Autocrats & Academics: Education, Culture & Society in Tsarist Russia. LC 79-12504. 164p. reprint ed. pap. 50.90 (*0-608-09472-2*, 205427200005) Bks Demand.

McClelland, James L. & Rumelhart, David E. Explorations in Parallel Distributed Processing: A Handbook of Models, Programs & Exercises MAC. 368p. 1989. pap. text 47.50 (*0-262-63129-6*) MIT Pr.

McClelland, James L. & Siegler, Robert S. Mechanisms of Cognitive Development: Behavioral & Neural Perspectives. LC 00-33163. (Carnegie Mellon Symposia on Cognition Ser.). 2000. pap. write for info. (*0-8058-3276-9*) L Erlbaum Assocs.

McClelland, James L. & Siegler, Robert S., eds. Mechanisms of Cognitive Development: Behavioral & Neural Perspectives. (A Volume in the Carnegie mellon Symposia on Cognition Series). 510p. 2000. write for info. (*0-8058-3275-0*) L Erlbaum Assocs.

McClelland, James L., jt. ed. see Inui, Toshio.

McClelland, Jim. Guardian Guide to the Internet. 1999. pap. 15.95 (*1-85702-665-9*, Pub. by Fourth Estate) Trafalgar.

McClelland, Jim, ed. see McClelland, Mike.

McClelland, John. The Bravest of Bears. (Illus.). 32p. (J). (ps-1). 1994. bds. 12.95 (*0-86264-389-9*) Andersen Pr.
— A History of Western Political Thought. LC 96-170920. 824p. (C). 1996. 80.00 (*0-415-11961-8*) Routledge.

McClelland, John, Jr. Window to the Past: The Washington State Historical Society's First Century. LC 92-13738. 196p. 1992. pap. 29.00 (*0-917048-69-5*) Wash St Hist Soc.
— Wobbly War: The Centralia Story. LC 87-51095. (Illus.). 256p. 1987. 15.00 (*0-917048-62-8*) Wash St Hist Soc.

McClelland, John S. History of Western Political Thought. LC 96-170920. 824p. (C). 1998. pap. 29.99 (*0-415-11962-6*) Routledge.

McClelland, Joseph C. & Di Gangi, Mario, trs. Early Writings: Creed, Scripture, Church. LC 94-18802. (Peter Martyr Library, Series 1: Vol. 1). 244p. 1995. 40.00 (*0-940474-32-8*, SCJP) Truman St Univ.

McClelland, Judy A. Some Only Dream: Journal of an Earthwatcher. 60p. 1998. pap. 14.95 (*1-58244-011-5*) Rutledge Bks.

McClelland, Keith, jt. ed. see Kaye, Harvey J.

McClelland, L. & Hale, P. English Grammar Through Guided Writing: Parts of Speech. 192p. 1979. pap. text 26.20 (*0-13-281089-1*) P-H.

McClelland, L., et al. English Sounds & Spelling. 144p. (C). 1979. pap. text 29.00 (*0-13-282954-1*) P-H.

McClelland, Linda F. Building the National Parks: Historic Landscape Design & Construction. LC 97-12664. (Illus.). 384p. 1997. text 59.95 (*0-8018-5582-9*) Johns Hopkins.
— Building the National Parks: The Historic Landscape Design & Construction. LC 97-12664. (Illus.). 384p. 1997. pap. 29.95 (*0-8018-5583-7*) Johns Hopkins.
— Presenting Nature: The Historic Landscape Design of the National Park Service, 1916 to 1942. (Illus.). 314p. 1997. reprint ed. pap. text 45.00 (*0-7881-4716-1*) DIANE Pub.

McClelland, Linda Flint. Presenting Nature: The Historic Landscape Design of the National Park Service, 1916 To 1942. 326p. 1995. per. 27.00 (*0-16-045136-1*) USGPO.

McClelland, Lindsay, et al. Global Volcanism (1975-1985) 672p. 1989. text 42.00 (*0-13-357203-X*) Am Geophysical.

McClelland, Lucille A., ed. see Hogan, Judy.

McClelland, Maria G. The Sisters of Mercy, Popular Politics & the Growth of the Roman Catholic Community in Hull, 1855-1930. LC 99-53144. 368p. 2000. 99.95 (*0-7734-7856-6*) E Mellen.

McClelland, Michael. Expression Genetics: Differential Display. Pardee, Arthur B. et al, eds. LC 99-17654. (Biotechniques Update Ser.). (Illus.). 520p. 1999. 44.95 (*1-881299-31-7*, BioTechniques) Eaton Pub Co.

McClelland, Michael & Pardee, Arthur B., eds. Expression Genetics: Accelerated & High-Throughput Methods. LC 99-34993. (Update Ser.). (Illus.). 400p. 1999. pap. 36.95 (*1-881299-24-4*) Eaton Pub Co.

McClelland, Micki, ed. Haiku-Sine: 217 Tiny Food Poems by Texans Who Love to Eat & Feed Their Head. (Illus.). 256p. 2000. pap. 9.95 (*0-9665716-3-0*) Lazywood Pr.

McClelland, Mike. Bank Fishing Secrets. (Illus.). 144p. 1996. pap. 19.95 (*0-9622571-6-8*) Fishing Enterprises.
— Bank Fishing Secrets. McClelland, Jim & Hoyme, Neal, eds. (Illus.). 144p. 1996. write for info. (*0-9622571-2-5*); lib. bdg. write for info. (*0-9622571-4-1*) Fishing Enterprises.
— Walleye Trouble Shooting. (Illus.). 224p. (Orig.). 1996. 14.95 (*0-9622571-8-4*); pap. 17.95 (*0-9622571-9-2*); lib. bdg. 14.95 (*0-9622571-7-6*) Fishing Enterprises.

Mcclelland, Mike, jt. auth. see Murray, Jeff.

McClelland, Nina I. & Evans, Joe L., eds. Individual Onsite Wastewater Systems, Vol. 7: Proceedings of the Seventh National Conference, 1980. LC 76-50983. (Illus.). 355p. 1981. 30.00 (*0-940006-00-6*) Natl Sanit Foun.

McClelland, Peter. A Confidential Guide to Introductory Macroeconomics: Lettes from an Economics Professor to His Son. 210p. (C). 1997. per. 32.95 (*0-7872-4175-X*, 41417501) Kendall-Hunt.

McClelland, Peter D. Causal Explanation & Model Building in History, Economics, & the New Economic History. LC 74-25372. (Illus.). 296p. 1975. text 45.00 (*0-8014-0929-2*) Cornell U Pr.
— Sowing Modernity: America's First Agricultural Revolution. LC 97-9030. (Illus.). 384p. 1996. text 45.00 (*0-8014-3326-6*) Cornell U Pr.

McClelland, Ralph A. The Law of Corporate Mortgage Bond Issues. Reams, Bernard D., Jr., ed. LC 38-7784. (Historical Reprints in Jurisprudence & Classical Legal Literature Ser.). xiii, 1077p. 1983. reprint ed. lib. bdg. 87.50 (*0-89941-251-3*, 303230) W S Hein.

McClelland, Robert W. Architects of Worship. 1990. pap. 20.95 (*1-55673-216-3*) CSS OH.

McClelland, Robert W., jt. ed. see Austin, Carol D.

McClelland, Robyn. Bibliography: Social Networks, Social Planning & Community Needs, No. 1135. 1976. 5.00 (*0-686-20409-3*, Sage Prdcls Pr) Sage.

McClelland, Samuel B. Organizational Needs Assessment: Design, Facilitation & Analysis. LC 95-14606. 336p. 1995. 69.50 (*0-89930-950-X*, Quorum Bks) Greenwood.

McClelland, Sharon. Clinical Manual for Nursing Assistants. LC 84-11985. 440p. (C). 1985. pap. 33.75 (*0-86720-365-X*) Jones & Bartlett.

McClelland, Stephen. Surface Mount Technology: The Future for Electronics Assembly. (Illus.). 200p. 1987. pap. 173.00 (*0-387-17430-3*) Spr-Verlag.

McClelland, Stephen, ed. Intelcom '94: The Outlook for Mediterranean Communications. 1994. write for info. (*0-89006-811-9*) Artech Hse.

McClelland, Susan. If There's Anything I Can Do... An Easy Guide to Showing You Care. 2nd rev. ed. 176p. 2000. 18.95 (*0-937404-47-0*) Triad Pub FL.

McClelland, V. Alan. Christian Education in Pluralist Society. 224p. (C). 1988. lib. bdg. 47.50 (*0-415-00540-X*, A1841) Routledge.

An Asterisk (*) at the beginning of an entry indicates that the title is appearing for the first time.

McClelland, V. Alan & Varma, Ved P., eds. The Needs of Teachers. LC 95-26740. (Education Ser.). (Illus.). 160p. 1996. text 70.00 (*0-304-33334-4*) Continuum.

McClelland, Vincent A., ed. Christian Education in a Pluralist Society. LC 88-11401. 249p. reprint ed. pap. 77.20 (*0-608-20362-9*, 207161500002) Bks Demand.

McClelland, W. Robert. Fire in the Hole. 1991. pap. 8.25 (*1-55673-315-1*, 9136) CSS OH.

McClelland, Whitney. 1997 Viewers Guide to the PGA Tour. (Illus.). 240p. 1996. pap. 24.95 (*0-9631259-5-8*) Golfguide.

— The 1996 Viewers Guide to the PGA Tour. (Illus.). 240p. 1995. pap. 24.95 (*0-9631259-4-X*) Golfguide.

— 1993 Viewer's Guide to Professional Golf. 1992. pap. 24.95 (*0-9631259-1-5*) Golfguide.

— The Viewer's Guide to Professional Golf, 1993. 1992. pap. 24.95 (*0-9631259-0-7*) Golfguide.

— The Viewer's Guide to Professional Golf, 1993. (Illus.). 192p. 1993. write for info. (*0-9631259-2-3*) Golfguide.

— The Viewer's Guide to Professional Golf, 1995. 1994. pap. 24.95 (*0-9631259-3-1*) Golfguide.

McClelland, William C., jt. auth. see Stowell, Harold H.

McClellanville Arts Council Staff. The McClellanville Coast Cookbook: Recipes, Oral Histories, Poetry, Prose, Prints, Photographs & Paintings. 1992. pap. 17.95 (*1-882966-00-7*) McClellanville Arts.

McClellen, James H., et al. DSP First: A Multimedia Approach. LC 97-36447. 523p. 1997. 96.00 (*0-13-243171-8*) P-H.

McClement. The Day Tecumseh Died Postponed. 1979. 8.95 (*0-385-11280-7*) Doubleday.

McClement, Fred. The Strange Case of Ambrose Small. LC 75-301595. 158p. 1974. write for info. (*0-7710-5498-X*) McCland & Stewart.

McClements, David J. Food Emulsions Principles, Practices & Techniques. LC 98-217132. (Contemporary Food Science Ser.). 392p. 1998. boxed set 109.95 (*0-8493-8008-1*) CRC Pr.

***McClements, Richard.** Death Poem. LC 99-68404. 404p. 2000. pap. 17.95 (*0-88739-323-3*) Creat Arts Bk.

McClenaghan, Leroy R. & Gaines, Michael S. Reproduction in Marginal Populations of the Hispid Cotton Rat (Sigmodon hispidus) (Occasional Papers: No. 74). 16p. 1978. pap. 1.00 (*0-317-04888-0*) U KS Nat Hist Mus.

McClenaghan, Robert, jt. auth. see Allin, Craig W.

McClenaghan, Robert, jt. auth. see Knight, Jeffrey A.

McClenaghan, W. Magruders American Government. 1993. 36.47 (*0-13-544560-4*) P-H.

***McClenaghan, William A.** 2000 Magruder's American Government. (gr. 9-12). 1999. student ed. 73.80 (*0-13-050016-X*) P-H.

McClenahan, Kelly L., jt. ed. see Belous, Richard S.

McClenahan, Pat & Jaqua, Ida. Cool Cooking for Kids. LC 75-32841. (J). (ps-k). 1976. pap. 10.99 (*0-8224-1614-X*) Fearon Teacher Aids.

McClenathan, DayAnn K., jt. ed. see Monson, Dianne L.

McClenathan, J. C., et al. Centennial History of the Borough of Connellsville, 1806-1906. (Illus.). 564p. 1995. reprint ed. lib. bdg. 59.00 (*0-8328-5106-X*) Higginson Bk Co.

McClendon. Wild Days. LC 89-62912. 1989. pap. 12.95 (*0-916990-23-0*) META Pubns.

McClendon, Bruce W. Customer Service in Local Government: Challenges for Planners & City Managers. LC 91-75139. 226p. 1992. pap. 38.95 (*0-918286-75-1*, Planners Press) Am Plan Assn.

McClendon, Bruce W. & Catanese, Anthony J. Planners on Planning: Leading Planners Offer Real-Life Lessons on What Works, What Doesn't & Why. LC 96-10091. (Public Administration Ser.). 1996. 30.95 (*0-7879-0285-3*) Jossey-Bass.

McClendon, Bruce W. & Quay, Ray. Mastering Change: Winning Strategies for Effective City Planning. LC 87-70796. (Illus.). 282p. 1988. pap. 29.95 (*0-918286-48-4*, Planners Press) Am Plan Assn.

McClendon, Charles B. The Imperial Abbey of Farfa. LC 86-3466. Vol. 36. 318p. 1987. 47.50 (*0-300-03333-8*) Yale U Pr.

McClendon, Charles B., et al. Rome & the Provinces: Studies in the Transformation of Art & Architecture in the Mediterranean World. LC 86-18234. (Illus.). 83p. (Orig.). 1986. pap. 13.00 (*0-89467-043-3*) Yale Art Gallery.

***McClendon, Clarence E.** The X Blessing: Unveiling God'sStrategy for a Marked Generation. LC 99-47715. 192p. 2000. pap. 10.99 (*0-7852-6902-9*) Nelson.

McClendon, Dennis E. Lady Be Good. 204p. 20.95 (*0-8488-2612-4*) Amereon Ltd.

McClendon, Dennis E. & Richards, Wallace F. The Legend of Colin Kelly: America's First Hero of WWII. (Illus.). 72p. 1994. pap. 8.95 (*0-929521-92-7*) Pictorial Hist.

McClendon, Gerrard O. The African-American Guide to Better English Vol. 3: A Speaking & Writing Survival Manual for African-Americans. 3rd rev. ed. LC 93-80308. (Illus.). 112p. (Orig.). 1997. pap. 10.00 (*0-9639329-0-X*) Positive People.

McClendon, James W., Jr. Doctrine: Systematic Theology, Vol. 2. 496p. (Orig.). 1994. pap. 24.95 (*0-687-11021-1*) Abingdon.

McClendon, James W. Ethic: Systematic Theology, Vol. 1. 384p. 1988. pap. 19.95 (*0-687-12016-0*) Abingdon.

McClendon, James W., Jr. Making Gospel Sense: To a Troubled Church. LC 95-180872. 176p. 1995. pap. 14.95 (*0-8298-1072-2*) Pilgrim OH.

McClendon, James W., Jr., ed. see American Academy of Religion Staff.

McClendon, Joseph, III, jt. auth. see Robbins, Anthony.

McClendon, Lise. The Bluejay Shaman. (Mystery Ser.). 1996. per. 4.99 (*0-373-26213-2*, Wrldwide Lib) Harlequin Bks.

***McClendon, Lise.** Nordic Nights. (Mystery Ser.: Bk. 364). 2000. mass mkt. 5.99 (*0-373-26364-3*, 1-26364-9, Wrldwide Lib) Harlequin Bks.

McClendon, Lise. Nordic Nights. LC 99-34869. (Alix Thorssen Mystery Ser.). 292p. 1999. 23.95 (*0-8027-3340-9*) Walker & Co.

— Painted Truth: An Alix Thorssen Mystery. 1996. per. 4.99 (*0-373-26222-1*, 1-26222-9, Wrldwide Lib) Harlequin Bks.

— Painted Truth: An Alix Thorssen Mystery. LC 95-34117. 252p. 1995. 22.95 (*0-8027-3271-2*) Walker & Co.

McClendon, Marion W. & Grelle, June R. Cee Vee, Our Home on the Range. 500p. 1991. text 58.50 (*0-9629112-0-8*) Cee Vee Hist.

McClendon, McKee J. Multiple Regression Causal Analysis. LC 93-86171. 358p. (C). 1994. boxed set 55.00 (*0-87581-384-4*, MR) F E Peacock Pubs.

McClendon, Muriel C. The Quiet Reformation: Magistrates & the Emergence of Protestantism in Tudor Norwich. LC 98-37996. 1999. 55.00 (*0-8047-3513-1*) Stanford U Pr.

***McClendon, Muriel C., et al.** Protestant Identities: Religion, Society & Self-Fashioning in Post-Reformation England LC 99-37228. 2000. 55.00 (*0-8047-3611-1*) Stanford U Pr.

McClendon, Patience. Under a Tyler Moon. (Illus.). 50p. (Orig.). 1988. pap. write for info. (*0-941402-06-1*) Devon Pub.

McClendon, R. Earl. Autonomy of the Air Arm. Orig. Title: The Question of Autonomy for the United States Air Arm, 1907-1945. (Illus.). 199p. 1996. reprint ed. pap. 14.00 (*0-16-045510-3*) AFH & MP.

McClendon, Ray. Dr. Laura: A Mother in America: Christian Insights about America's Best-Known Mom. LC 99-17557. 200p. 1999. pap. 12.99 (*1-56476-772-8*, Victor Bks) Chariot Victor.

McClendon, Ruth, jt. auth. see Kadis, Leslie B.

McClendon, Stewart & Goodman, Rosabel E., eds. International Commercial Arbitration in New York. 326p. 1986. lib. bdg. 35.00 (*0-941320-41-3*) Transnatl Pubs.

McClendon, Theodore. How to Find a Good Black Man: Find Yourself. 2nd rev. ed. LC 94-74085. 96p. 1997. pap. 10.00 (*0-9639329-1-8*) Positive People.

McClendon, W. A. Recollections of War Times. 209p. (Orig.). 1997. reprint ed. pap. 20.00 (*1-885480-20-2*) Pioneer Pubng.

McClendon, William H. Straight Ahead: Essays on the Struggle of Blacks in America 1934-1994. Chrisman, Robert, ed. & pref. by. (Illus.). 227p. (Orig.). 1995. pap. 19.95 (*0-933296-16-9*) Black Scholar Pr.

McClendon, Yvonne D. PreNuptial Bliss: What Every Woman Should Know Before Planning a Wedding. LC 98-91273. 112p. 1998. pap. 10.99 (*0-9663013-0-7*) McSterling Pubg.

***McClennen, Crane.** 2000 Supplement to Arizona Courtroom Evidence Manual. 2000. pap. 30.00 (*0-9677819-1-4*) Archangl Pubng AZ.

McClennen, Edward F. Rationality & Dynamic Choice: Foundational Explorations. 325p. (C). 1990. text 69.95 (*0-521-36047-1*) Cambridge U Pr.

***McClennen, Joan C. & Gunther, John.** A Professional's Guide to Understanding Gay & Lesbian Domestic Violence: Understanding Practice Interventions. LC 99-45504. (Symposium Ser.: Vol. 56). 356p. 1999. text 99.95 (*0-7734-7892-2*) E Mellen.

McClenney, Byron N. Management for Productivity. LC 80-134596. 128p. reprint ed. pap. 39.70 (*0-608-17104-2*, 202729400055) Bks Demand.

McClenney, Earl H., Jr. How to Supervise Black, Minorities & Women: A Guide for White & Asian Males. 200p. (Orig.). 1996. pap. text 10.95 (*0-9618835-3-7*) First Assocs Pub.

— How to Survive When You're the Only Black in the Office: What They Can't Teach You at White Business Schools. 212p. (Orig.). 1988. pap. 9.95 (*0-9618835-0-2*) First Assocs Pub.

***McClenney, Earl H., Jr** Root Little Pig or Die Poor Hog: Old Folks' Sayings & Stories. 60p. 1999. pap. 9.95 (*0-9618835-4-5*) First Assocs Pub.

McClenney, Kay, et al. Building Communities Through Strategic Planning: A Guidebook for Community Colleges. 79p. 1991. 10.00 (*0-87117-230-5*, 1324) Comm Coll Pr Am Assn Comm Coll.

McClenon, James. Wondrous Events: Foundations of Religious Belief. LC 94-20228. (Illus.). 296p. (Orig.). (C). 1994. text 42.50 (*0-8122-3074-4*); pap. text 18.95 (*0-8122-1355-6*) U of Pa Pr.

***McCleod, Chris.** City of Skies. 288p. 2000. pap. 17.95 (*1-86368-268-6*, Pub. by Fremantle Arts) Intl Spec Bk.

McClernan, James. Change Your Mind, Change Your Weight. LC 85-24890. 254p. 1986. pap. 10.95 (*0-932090-15-X*) Health Plus.

— Hugs from the Refrigerator. LC 93-24657. 192p. (Orig.). 1994. pap. 12.00 (*0-933701-61-6*) Westport Pubs.

McCleskey, Dale. Family & Friends: Facilitator's Guide: Helping the Person You Care about in Recovery. LC 95-230649. (Life Support Group Ser.). 64p. 1995. write for info. (*0-8054-9871-0*) Broadman.

McCleskey, Dale W., jt. auth. see Springle, Pat.

McCleskey, F. David, Jr. Crane Operation & Preventive Maintenance. (Illus.). 104p. 1983. pap. text 20.00 (*0-934114-43-9*, BK-101) Marine Educ.

McCleskey, Kendra, jt. auth. see Molnar, Gwen.

McClester, Cedric. Kwanzaa: Everything You Always Wanted to Know but Didn't Know Where to Ask. (Illus.). 64p. pap. 5.95 (*0-936073-08-X*) Gumbs & Thomas.

McClester, Cedric. Kwanzaa: Everything You Always Wanted to Know but Didn't Know Where to Ask. LC 99-462611. (Illus.). 1997. write for info. (*0-936073-24-1*) Gumbs & Thomas.

McClester, Cedric. Kwanzaa: Everything You Always Wanted to Know but Didn't Know Where to Ask. LC 98-148305. 1998. pap. 6.00 (*0-936073-21-7*) Gumbs & Thomas.

McCleverty, J. A., jt. ed. see Pombeiro, A. J.

McCleverty, Jon A. Chemistry of the First-row Transition Metals. LC 98-51828. (Oxford Chemistry Primers Ser.: 71). (Illus.). 96p. 1999. pap. text 12.95 (*0-19-850151-X*) OUP.

McClew, Polly. Legal Office Administration. LC 89-78038. (C). 1994. pap. text 24.95 (*0-8273-3975-5*) Delmar.

McClincy, William D. Instructional Methods in Emergency Services: A Resource Text Designed for EMS, Fire, & Rescue Instructors. LC 94-37817. 352p. 1994. pap. text 58.00 (*0-89303-541-6*) P-H.

McClinn, Patricia. Not a Family Man. (Special Edition Ser.). 1994. per. 3.50 (*0-373-09864-2*, 5-09864-5) Silhouette.

McClinte, Paige. Buyer Beware: Step-by-Step Guide for the First Time Home Buyer. LC 94-65053. 320p. (Orig.). 1998. 29.95 (*1-884573-01-0*); pap. 19.95 (*1-884573-18-5*) S-By-S Pubns.

— In Search of Success: Step-by-Step Guide for the Entrepreneur. LC 94-65051. 320p. (Orig.). 1998. 29.95 (*1-884573-03-7*); pap. 19.95 (*1-884573-16-9*) S-By-S Pubns.

— Life Styles of the Fittest: Step-by-Step Guide to Living Longer & Healthier. LC 94-65055. 320p. (Orig.). 1999. 29.95 (*1-884573-21-5*); pap. 19.95 (*1-884573-20-7*) S-By-S Pubns.

— Yes, There Is Life after Bankruptcy: Step-by-Step Guide to Getting Your Life Back on Track. LC 94-65049. 320p. (Orig.). 1998. 29.95 (*1-884573-05-3*); pap. 19.95 (*1-884573-14-2*) S-By-S Pubns.

McClintic, Rick. Adweek Major Medica Directory 1998. annuals 1000p. 1997. pap. 295.00 (*1-891204-07-6*) Adweek Direct.

McClintic, Rick, ed. Marketers Collide to Media, 98-99: Media Trends, Rates & Demographics. 304p. 1998. pap. 75.00 (*1-891204-10-6*) Adweek Direct.

McClintick, David. Stealing from the Rich: The Home Stake Oil Swindle. LC 77-22103. 336p. 1977. 10.00 (*0-87131-240-9*) M Evans.

McClintick, Malcolm. Death of an Old Flame. 208p. 1989. pap. 3.50 (*0-380-70817-5*, Avon Bks) Morrow Avon.

— The Key. 256p. 1990. pap. 3.50 (*0-380-70819-1*, Avon Bks) Morrow Avon.

— Mary's Grave. 224p. 1990. pap. 3.50 (*0-380-70818-3*, Avon Bks) Morrow Avon.

McClintock. Little Princess Picture Book. LC 97-43631. (Illus.). 40p. (J). (ps-3). pap. 4.95 (*0-06-443539-3*) HarpC Child Bks.

McClintock, Walter. The Old North Trail: Life, Legends & Religion of the Blackfeet Indians. LC 99-31857. (Illus.). 539p. 1999. pap. 16.95 (*0-8032-8258-3*, Bison Books) U of Nebr Pr.

McClintock, Alexander, ed. The Convergence of Machine & Human Nature: A Critique of the Computer Metaphor of Mind & Artificial Intelligence. 160p. 1995. 67.95 (*1-85628-997-4*, Pub. by Avebry) Ashgate Pub Co.

McClintock, Ann, jt. auth. see Ellis, Richard.

McClintock, Anne. Imperial Leather: Race, Gender & Sexuality in the Colonial Conquest. LC 94-7593. 400p. (C). (gr. 13). 1995. 85.00 (*0-415-90889-2*); pap. 23.99 (*0-415-90890-6*) Routledge.

— Sex Workers & Sex Work, Vol. 11, No. 4. 1994. pap. 8.00 (*0-8223-6412-3*) Duke.

McClintock, Anne, et al, eds. Dangerous Liaisons: Gender, Nation, & Postcolonial Perspectives. LC 96-51991. (Cultural Politics Ser.: Vol. 11). 560p. (C). 1997. pap. 24.95 (*0-8166-2649-9*) U of Minn Pr.

— Queer Transexions of Race, Nation & Gender: Social Text Special Issue, Vol. 15. (Illus.). 425p. 1997. pap. text 19.00 (*0-8223-6452-2*) Duke.

***McClintock, Barbara.** Animal Fables from Aesop. (Illus.). 48p. (YA). (gr. 1 up). 2000. reprint ed. pap. 15.95 (*1-56792-144-2*) Godine.

McClintock, Barbara. The Discovery & Character of Transposable Elements: The Collected Papers (1938-1984) of Barbara McClintock. (Genes Cells & Organisms Ser.). (Illus.). 650p. 1987. text 95.00 (*0-8240-1391-3*) Garland.

— The Fantastic Drawings of Danielle. LC 94-48842. (Illus.). 32p. (J). (ps-3). 1996. 17.00 (*0-395-73980-2*) HM.

***McClintock, Barbara.** Molly & the Magic Wishbone. LC 98-31789. (J). 2000. 16.00 (*0-374-34999-1*) FS&G.

— Princess & the Goblin. 40p. (J). (ps-3). 2002. 14.95 (*0-06-028228-2*) HarpC Child Bks.

McClintock, Cynthia. Peasant Cooperatives & Political Change in Peru. LC 80-8563. 437p. 1981. reprint ed. pap. 135.50 (*0-7837-9386-3*, 206013000004) Bks Demand.

— Revolutionary Movements in Latin America: El Salvador's FMLN & Peru's Shining Path. LC 98-13334. (Illus.). 416p. 1998. 37.50 (*1-878379-77-1*); pap. 19.95 (*1-878379-76-3*) US Inst Peace.

McClintock, Cynthia & Lowenthal, Abraham F., eds. The Peruvian Experiment Reconsidered. LC 82-61377. 464p. 1983. reprint ed. pap. 143.90 (*0-608-03322-7*, 206403400008) Bks Demand.

McClintock, Dalene & Holmes, Carolyn. Communication Skillbook 3: New Worlds in English. (Communication Skillbooks Ser.). 64p. 1994. pap. text 9.25 (*0-8325-0656-7*, Natl Textbk Co) NTC Contemp Pub Co.

McClintock, David, tr. see Bernhard, Thomas.

***McClintock, Elizabeth.** The Trees of Golden Gate Park & San Francisco. Turner, Richard G., Jr., ed. (Illus.). 150p. 2000. pap. 16.95 (*1-890771-28-7*) Heyday Bks.

McClintock, Elizabeth, et al. A Flora of the San Bruno Mountains. (Special Publications: No. 8). 192p. (Orig.). 1990. pap. 14.95 (*0-317-99709-2*) Calif Native.

McClintock, Elizabeth, jt. auth. see Fuller, Thomas C.

***McClintock, Evie.** Room for Change: Empowering Possibilities for Therapists & Clients. LC 98-31393. 306p. 1998. pap. text 31.00 (*0-205-28438-8*) Allyn.

McClintock, F. A. & Argon, A. S. Mechanical Behavior of Materials: Proceedings. 1966. text 44.75 (*0-201-04545-1*) Addison-Wesley.

McClintock, Frank A. & Argon, A. S. Mechanical Behavior of Materials. 784p. (C). 1993. reprint ed. text 138.00 (*1-878907-71-9*) TechBooks.

McClintock, Grant & Crockett, Michael. Flywater. LC 94-25931. (Illus.). 144p. 1994. 39.95 (*1-55821-339-2*) Lyons Pr.

McClintock, Grant, et al. Watermark. LC 98-26268. (Illus.). 148p. 1998. mass mkt. 39.95 (*1-55821-779-7*) Lyons Pr.

McClintock, James. Mormon Settlement in Arizona. LC 78-134397. reprint ed. 54.00 (*0-404-08439-7*) AMS Pr.

McClintock, James, jt. auth. see Nybakken, James W.

McClintock, James C. & Caroline, Nancy L. Workbook for Emergency Care in the Streets. 3rd ed. 1987. 17.50 (*0-316-55437-5*, Little Brwn Med Div) Lppncott W & W.

McClintock, James I. Jack London's Strong Truths. rev. ed. LC 97-16852. (Red Cedar Classics Ser.: No. 2). Orig. Title: White Logic: Jack London's Short Stories. 220p. 1997. reprint ed. pap. 16.95 (*0-87013-471-X*) Mich St U Pr.

— Nature's Kindred Spirits: Aldo Leopold, Joseph Wood Krutch, Edward Abbey, Annie Dillard, & Gary Snyder. LC 93-38110. (Illus.). 198p. reprint ed. pap. 61.40 (*0-608-07017-3*, 206722400009) Bks Demand.

***McClintock, John.** Pioneer Days in the Black Hills: Accurate History & Facts Related by One of the Early Day Pioneers. LC 99-55842. (Illus.). 368p. 2000. pap. text 17.95 (*0-8061-3191-8*) U of Okla Pr.

McClintock, John & Strong, James. Cyclopaedia of Biblical, Theological, & Ecclesiastical Literature: Cyclopaedia of Biblical Literature, Vol. 1[00ad]10. 250.00 (*0-405-00020-0*, 11917) Ayer.

***McClintock, Karen A.** Sexual Shame: An Urgent Call to Healing. 2000. pap. 16.00 (*0-8006-3238-9*, Fortress Pr) Augsburg Fortress.

McClintock, Lorene. The McClintock Piano Course: A New Experience in Learning, 11 vols., Set. 2198p. (YA). 1992. spiral bd., boxed set 388.00 (*1-880556-70-7*) McClintock Ent.

McClintock, Marian, jt. auth. see Bracy, Jane.

McClintock, Mike. Alternative Housebuilding. LC 88-38140. (Popular Science Ser.). (Illus.). 384p. 1989. pap. 19.95 (*0-8069-6995-4*) Sterling.

— Fly Went By. LC 58-9018. (Illus.). (J). (gr. 1-3). 1958. lib. bdg. 11.99 (*0-394-90003-0*) Beginner.

— A Fly Went By. LC 58-9018. (Illus.). (J). (gr. 1-3). 1958. 7.99 (*0-394-80003-6*) Beginner.

— Lalique for Collectors. 1986. pap. 17.50 (*0-684-14101-9*, Scribners Ref) Mac Lib Ref.

— Mike McClintock's Home Sense Care & Repair Almanac. (Orig.). 1989. pap. 14.60 (*0-318-41624-7*) McGraw-Hill Prof.

— Mike McClintock's Home Sense Care & Repair Almanac. (Illus.). 416p. (Orig.). 1989. 28.95 (*0-8306-0449-9*); pap. 19.95 (*0-8306-0349-2*) McGraw-Hill Prof.

— Stop That Ball! LC 59-9741. (Illus.). (J). (gr. 1-2). 1959. 7.99 (*0-394-80010-9*) Beginner.

McClintock, Mike, ed. see Groff, David M.

McClintock, Mike, ed. see Wagner, John D.

McClintock, P. V., jt. ed. see Moss, Frank.

McClintock, R. Princess & the Goblin. 40p. (J). (ps-3). 2000. pap. 4.95 (*0-06-443538-5*) HarpC Child Bks.

McClintock, Robert. God's Healing Leaves. 102p. 1998. pap. 9.95 (*1-883012-82-1*) Remnant Pubns.

McClintock, Robert O., ed. Computing & Education: The Second Frontier. LC 88-18577. (Special Issues from the Teachers College Record Ser.). (Illus.). 112p. reprint ed. pap. 34.80 (*0-608-08643-6*, 206916600003) Bks Demand.

McClintock, Thomas. Threads & Knots. LC 97-49876. (New Perspectives in Philosophical Scholarship Ser.: Vol. 10). XV, 128p. (C). 1999. text 38.95 (*0-8204-4029-9*) P Lang Pubng.

McClintock, Thomas L. Skepticism & the Basis of Morality, Vol. 6. (New Perspectives in Philosophical Scholarship Ser.). XIV, 204p. (C). 1995. text 48.95 (*0-8204-2761-6*) P Lang Pubng.

McClintock, Walter. Four Days in a Medicine Lodge. 21p. 1986. reprint ed. pap. 10.00 (*0-8466-0097-8*, S-97, Shorey Pubns) Shoreys Bkstore.

— Old Indian Trails. 416p. 1992. pap. 15.00 (*0-395-61155-5*) HM.

— The Old North Trail: Life, Legends & Religion of the Blackfeet Indians. LC 92-16001. (Illus.). xxiv, 539p. (C). 1992. reprint ed. pap. 14.95 (*0-8032-8188-9*, Bison Books) U of Nebr Pr.

— The Tragedy of the Blackfoot. (Illus.). 53p. 1970. reprint ed. pap. 5.00 (*0-916561-63-1*) Southwest Mus.

McClintock, William. Coca-Cola Trays. LC 96-33783. (Illus.). 144p. (gr. 10-13). 1996. pap. write for info. (*0-7643-0043-1*) Schiffer.

***McClintock, William.** Coca-Cola Trays. 2nd rev. ed. LC 99-56135. (Illus.). 144p. 2000. pap. 12.95 (*0-7643-0984-6*) Schiffer.

***McClinton, Calvin A.** The Work of Vinnette Carroll, an African American Theatre Artist. LC 99-36641. (Studies in Theatre Arts: Vol. 8). 360p. 1999. text 99.95 (*0-7734-7940-6*) E Mellen.

McClinton, Joe, tr. see Courtillot, Vincent.

M

An Asterisk (*) at the beginning of an entry indicates that the title is appearing for the first time.

M

***McClinton, Sandra.** Lyrical Aviators: Traveling America's Airways in a Small Place. LC 97-62092. (Illus.). 232p. 2000. 29.95 (0-9659300-0-9, Pub. by Whistling Swan) ACCESS Pubs Network.

McClish, Glen, jt. auth. see Walker, Jeffrey.

McClish, Jerry. A Gallery of Marine Art. (Illus.). 144p. 1999. 29.99 (1-56496-418-3) Rockport Pubs.

McClister, M. T. Victims Choice. 2nd ed. LC 99-21986. 1999. text 22.95 (0-312-20618-6) St Martin.

McClister, M. T. & Midgley, Amy. The Veterinary Receptionist's Handbook. LC 95-61831. 264p. 1995. pap. 39.95 (0-935078-56-8) Veterinary Med.

***McClister, Michael.** Body Man. 2000. text 23.95 (0-312-26562-X) St Martin.

McCloghrie, Keith, jt. auth. see Rose, Marshall T.

McClone, Melissa. Fiance for the Night. 1999. per. 3.50 (0-373-52090-5, 1-52090-7) Silhouette.

***McClone, Melissa.** If the Ring Fits... (Romance Ser.: Vol. 145). 2000. mass mkt. 3.50 (0-373-19431-5) Silhouette.

— The Wedding Lullaby. (Romance Ser.: Bk. 1485). 2000. mass mkt. 3.50 (0-373-19485-4, 1-19485-1) Silhouette.

***McClory, Robert.** Faithful Dissenters: Stories of Men & Women Who Loved & Changed the Church. (Illus.). 180p. 2000. pap. 16.00 (1-57075-322-9) Orbis Bks.

McClory, Robert. Power & the Papacy: The People & Politics Behind the Doctrine of Infallibility. LC 97-10772. 256p. (Orig.). 1997. 25.00 (0-7648-0141-4, Liguori Triumph) Liguori Pubns.

— Turning Point: The Inside Story of the Papal Birth Control Commission, & How Humanae Vitae Changed the Life of Patty Crowley & the Future of the Church. (Illus.). 192p. 1995. 19.95 (0-8245-1458-0) Crossroad NY.

— Turning Point: The Inside Story of the Papal Birth Control Commission, & How "Humane Vitae" Changed the Life of Patty Crowley & the Future of the Church. 224p. 1997. pap. 15.95 (0-8245-1613-3) Crossroad NY.

McCloskey. Making Connections 1: 1996 Version, No. 1. (Adult ESL Ser.). 168p. (Orig.). (J). 1996. mass mkt., student ed. 31.95 (0-8384-7008-4); mass mkt., wbk. ed. 7.50 (0-8384-7000-9) Heinle & Heinle.

— Making Connections 3. (Secondary ESL Ser.). (J). 1995. mass mkt., suppl. ed. 104.95 (0-8384-3844-X) Heinle & Heinle.

— Making Connections 3. (Adult ESL Ser.). (J). 1996. mass mkt., student ed. 24.95 (0-8384-7010-6) Heinle & Heinle.

— Making Connections 3, No. 3. (Secondary ESL Ser.). (J). 1995. mass mkt., teacher ed. 29.95 (0-8384-3845-8); mass mkt., wbk. ed. 8.50 (0-8384-4243-9) Heinle & Heinle.

— Making Connections 3: Activity Masters. (Secondary ESL Ser.). (J). 1995. mass mkt., suppl. ed. 25.95 (0-8384-4342-7) Heinle & Heinle.

— Making Connections 2. (Secondary ESL Ser.). (J). 1994. suppl. ed. 25.95 incl. audio (0-8384-3838-5) Heinle & Heinle.

— Making Connections 2. (Adult ESL Ser.). (J). 1996. mass mkt., student ed. 24.95 (0-8384-7011-4) Heinle & Heinle.

— Making Connections 2: Activity Masters. (Secondary ESL Ser.). (J). 1994. pap., suppl. ed. 11.75 (0-8384-4341-9) Heinle & Heinle.

— Making Connections 2: 1996 Version, Bk. 2. (Adult ESL Ser.). (J). 1996. mass mkt., wbk. ed. 7.50 (0-8384-7040-8) Heinle & Heinle.

— Making Connections 2: 1996 Version, No. 2. (Adult ESL Ser.). (J). 1996. mass mkt., teacher ed. 29.95 (0-8384-7041-6) Heinle & Heinle.

— Making Connections 2: 1996 Version, No. 2. (Adult ESL Ser.). 184p. (J). 1997. pap., student ed. 31.95 (0-8384-7012-2) Heinle & Heinle.

— Making Connections 1-student Text Paper. (Adult ESL). (J). 1996. mass mkt., student ed. 24.95 (0-8384-7009-2) Heinle & Heinle.

— Making Connections 1-workbook. (Secondary ESL). (J). 1994. text, wbk. ed. 8.95 (0-8384-3831-8) Heinle & Heinle.

— Making Connections 2-workbook. (Secondary ESL). (J). 1994. mass mkt., wbk. ed. 8.95 (0-8384-3840-7) Heinle & Heinle.

— Tee-Making Connections 1-'96 Version, No. 1. (Adult Esl Ser.). (J). 1996. mass mkt., teacher ed. 29.95 (0-8384-7001-7) Heinle & Heinle.

— Texas Correllations to Essent Elements. (Secondary ESL Ser.). 1997. text. write for info. (0-8384-7583-3) Heinle & Heinle.

— Trans-Making Connections 1996, No. 1. (Global ESL/ELT Ser.). (J). 1996. text 104.95 (0-8384-7002-5) Heinle & Heinle.

— Trans-Making Connections 1996, No. 2. (Adult ESL Ser.). (J). 1996. text 104.95 (0-8384-7014-9) Heinle & Heinle.

— Voices In Lit Bronze-std Ed Paperback. (Adult ESL). (J). 1996. mass mkt., student ed. 27.95 (0-8384-7029-7) Heinle & Heinle.

— Voices In Lit Silver-stdt Ed Paper. (Adult ESL). (J). 1996. mass mkt., student ed. 32.95 (0-8384-7018-1) Heinle & Heinle.

— Voices in Literature Book 3-Bronze, Bk. 3. (Global ESL/ELT Ser.). (J). 1996. mass mkt., suppl. ed. 25.95 (0-8384-2284-5) Heinle & Heinle.

— Voices in Literature Book 3-Bronze, Bk. 3. (Global ESL/ELT Ser.). (J). 1996. mass mkt., teacher ed. 15.95 (0-8384-2285-3) Heinle & Heinle.

— Voices in Literature Gold: 1996 Version. (Adult ESL Ser.). (J). 1996. pap., student ed. 41.95 (0-8384-7035-1); mass mkt., teacher ed. 15.95 (0-8384-7033-5) Heinle & Heinle.

— Voices in Literature Silver. (Adult ESL Ser.). (J). 1996. mass mkt. 23.95 (0-8384-7023-8) Heinle & Heinle.

— Voices in Literature Silver: 1996 Version. (Adult ESL Ser.). (J). 1996. pap., student ed. 41.95 (0-8384-7019-X); mass mkt., teacher ed. 15.95 (0-8384-7020-3) Heinle & Heinle.

***McCloskey & Stack.** Voices in Lit Gold-Texas. 2000. pap., teacher ed. 17.00 (0-8384-1526-1) Heinle & Heinle.

— Voices in Lit Gold-Texas Assessment. 2000. pap. 35.00 (0-8384-1527-X) Heinle & Heinle.

McCloskey & Stack, Lydia. Making Connections 3. (Secondary ESL Ser.). (J). 1995. suppl. ed. 18.00 incl. audio (0-8384-3843-1) Heinle & Heinle.

— Voices in Literature, Bk. 1. (J). 1992. pap. 27.25 (0-8384-2258-6) Heinle & Heinle.

— Voices in Literature, Bk. 2. (J). 1994. 27.25 (0-8384-2259-4) Heinle & Heinle.

— Voices in Literature, Bk. 2. (J). 1995. pap., teacher ed. 11.25 (0-8384-2261-6) Heinle & Heinle.

McCloskey, et al. Pals: Tllc Activ Black. 80p. 1996. pap. text 39.69 (0-201-85320-5) Addison-Wesley.

McCloskey, Amanda H. & Luehrs, John. State Initiatives to Improve Rural Health Care. Glass, Karen, ed. 129p. (Orig.). 1990. pap. text 15.00 (1-55877-081-X) Natl Governor.

McCloskey, Barbara. George Grosz & the Communist Party: Art & Radicalism in Crisis, 1918 to 1936. LC 96-14405. 272p. 1997. text 39.50 (0-691-02725-0, Pub. by Princeton U Pr) Cal Prin Full Svc.

***McCloskey, Deirdre N.** Crossing: A Memoir. LC 99-19450. 280p. 1999. 25.00 (0-226-55668-9) U Ch Pr.

— Economical Writing. 98p. (C). 1999. pap. 8.95 (1-57766-063-3) Waveland Pr.

— How to be Human: Though an Economist. (Illus.). 300p. (C). 2000. pap. 16.95 (0-472-06744-3, 06744); text 59.50 (0-472-09744-X, 09744) U of Mich Pr.

McCloskey, Deirdre N. The Rhetoric of Economics. 2nd ed. LC 97-37740. (Rhetoric of the Human Sciences Ser.). 248p. 1998. pap. 19.95 (0-299-15814-4); text 34.95 (0-299-15810-1) U of Wis Pr.

McCloskey, Deirdre N. The Vices of Economists: The Virtues of the Bourgeoisie. (Illus.). 120p. 1997. pap. 14.95 (90-5356-233-8, Pub. by Amsterdam U Pr) U of Mich Pr.

McCloskey, Dierdre. The Value of Culture: On the Relationship Between Economics & the Arts. Klamer, Arjo, ed. LC 97-144735. (C). 1997. text 54.50 (90-5356-219-2, Pub. by Amsterdam U Pr) U of Mich Pr.

— The Vices of Economists: The Virtues of the Bourgeoisie. LC 97-143404. (C). 1996. 24.95 (90-5356-244-3, Pub. by Amsterdam U Pr) U of Mich Pr.

McCloskey, Dierdre, jt. auth. see Klammer, Arjo.

McCloskey, Donald N. Economic Maturity & Entrepreneurial Decline: British Iron & Steel, 1870-1913. LC 72-92131. (Economic Studies: No. 142). 192p. 1973. 12.00 (0-674-22875-8) HUP.

— Enterprise & Trade in Victorian Britain: Essays in Historical Economics. (Modern Revivals in Economic History Ser.). 232p. 1993. reprint ed. text 61.95 (0-7512-0176-6, Pub. by Gregg Revivals) Ashgate Pub Co.

— If You're So Smart: The Narrative of Economic Expertise. LC 90-33041. 190p. 1990. 21.95 (0-226-55670-0) U Ch Pr.

— If You're So Smart: The Narrative of Economic Expertise. LC 90-33041. ix, 190p. 1992. pap. text 14.95 (0-226-55671-9) U Ch Pr.

— Knowledge & Persuasion in Economics. LC 93-12078. (Illus.). 463p. (C). 1994. text 64.95 (0-521-43475-0) Cambridge U Pr.

McCloskey, Donald N. Knowledge & Persuasion in Economics. LC 93-12078. (Illus.). 463p. (C). 1994. pap. text 19.95 (0-521-43603-6) Cambridge U Pr.

McCloskey, Donald N., ed. Second Thoughts: Myths & Morals of U. S. Economic History. 224p. 1995. pap. 17.95 (0-19-510118-9) OUP.

— Second Thoughts: The Uses of Economic History. 224p. 1993. text 55.00 (0-19-506633-2) OUP.

McCloskey, Donald N. & Hersh, George K., Jr., eds. A Bibliography of Historical Economics to 1980. 517p. 1991. text 80.00 (0-521-40327-8) Cambridge U Pr.

McCloskey, Donald N., jt. ed. see Floud, Roderick.

McCloskey, Donald N., ed. see Mathematical Social Science Board Conference on th.

McCloskey, Ellen D., jt. auth. see Ehrlich, Ruth A.

McCloskey, Gary N., jt. ed. see Provenzo, Eugene F., Jr.

McCloskey, James. Transformational Syntax & Model Theoretic Semantics. (Synthese Language Library: No. 9). 1979. pap. text 54.00 (90-277-1026-0); lib. bdg. 100.50 (90-277-1025-2) Kluwer Academic.

McCloskey, Jenny. Your Sexual Health: What Every Teen Should Know about Sex. LC 92-35228. 336p. 1993. 15.95 (1-879904-08-X) Halo Bks.

McCloskey, Joanne, jt. auth. see Johnson, Alice R.

McCloskey, Joanne, jt. auth. see Johnson, Joyce Y.

McCloskey, Joanne C. Toward an Educational Model of Nursing Effectiveness. Kalisch, Philip & Kalisch, Beatrice, eds. LC 83-9288. (Studies in Nursing Management: No. 11). 187p. 1983. reprint ed. pap. 58.00 (0-8357-1490-X, 207002500063) Bks Demand.

McCloskey, Joanne C. & Grace, Helen K. Current Issues in Nursing. 5th ed. (Illus.). 736p. (C). (gr. 13). 1997. pap. text 39.00 (0-8151-8594-4, 28840) Mosby Inc.

McCloskey, Joanne C., et al. Nursing Interventions Classification (NIC) 2nd ed. Bulechek, Gloria M., ed. (Illus.). 768p. (C). (gr. 13). 1995. pap. text 37.95 (0-8151-6302-9, 26018) Mosby Inc.

McCloskey, Joanne C., jt. auth. see Bulechek, Gloria M.

McCloskey, John W. America's Federal Gold Coinage, 1793-1933 No. 8: Handbook. 36p. 1989. pap. 9.50 (0-685-72021-7); boxed set 30.00 incl. sl. (0-685-72022-5) Am Numismatic.

— America's Silver Coinage, 1794-1891: Handbook, No. 6. 38p. 1986. pap. 6.00 (0-685-72023-3) Am Numismatic.

— America's Silver Coinage, 1794-1891: Handbook, Vol. 6. 38p. 1986. boxed set 25.00 incl. sl. (0-685-72024-1) Am Numismatic.

McCloskey, Kevin. Mrs. Fitz's Flamingos. LC 90-2278. (Illus.). (J). (ps-3). 1992. lib. bdg. 13.93 (0-688-10475-4) Lothrop.

McCloskey, Larry & Collett, Dennis. TQM: A Basic Text: A Primer Guide to Total Quality Management. 150p. 1993. pap. write for info. (1-879364-35-2) GOAL-QPC.

***McCloskey, Mabel M.** Some Descendants of John Endecott, Governor, Massachusetts Bay Colony. fac. ed. 286p. 1999. reprint ed. 52.50 (0-8328-9900-3) Higginson Bk Co.

McCloskey, Margot. Etiqueta para Profesionales. (SPA.). 240p. 1995. pap. write for info. (0-929441-71-0) Pubns Puertorriquenas.

McCloskey, Mark. The Secret Documents of America. 1976. pap. 1.50 (0-88031-032-4) Invisible-Red Hill.

McCloskey, Mark, tr. see Herbert, George.

McCloskey, Marsha. Katie's Alaphabet Quilt. (Illus.). 34p. 1999. pap. 12.95 (0-9635422-6-5) Feathered Star.

— Marsha McCloskey's Block Party: A Quilter's Extravaganza of 120 Rotary-Cut Block Patterns. LC 98-25353. (Illus.). 256p. 1998. text 29.95 (0-87596-756-6) Rodale Pr Inc.

***McCloskey, Marsha.** Marsha McCloskey's Block Party: A Quilter's Extravaganza of 120 Rotary-Cut Block Patterns. (Illus.). 256p. 2000. pap. 18.95 (1-57954-266-2) Rodale Pr Inc.

— Quilts for Katie Rose. (Illus.). 56p. 1999. pap. 15.95 (0-9635422-7-3) Feathered Star.

McCloskey, Marsha & Moore, Linda. Make Your Own Outdoor Flags & Banners. LC 97-119603. (Illus.). 24p. (Orig.). 1999. pap. 6.95 (0-9635422-5-7, FSP6) Feathered Star.

McCloskey, Marsha R. Christmas Quilts. 72p. 1990. pap. 6.95 (0-486-26406-8) Dover.

— Feathered Star Quilts. (Illus.). 128p. (Orig.). 1995. pap. 22.95 (0-9635422-3-0) Feathered Star.

— Feathered Star Sampler. 24p. 1994. pap. 7.95 (0-9635422-2-2) Feathered Star.

— On to Square Two. (Illus.). 80p. 1996. pap. text 8.95 (0-486-29476-5) Dover.

— One Hundred Pieced Patterns for Eight Inch Quilt Blocks. 64p. 1993. pap. 11.95 (0-9635422-0-6) Feathered Star.

— Quick Classic Quilts. 176p. 1996. pap. 19.95 (0-8487-1465-2) Oxmoor Hse.

— Rotary Cutting Companion for Feathered Star Quilts. 24p. 1995. pap. 6.95 (0-9635422-4-9) Feathered Star.

— Wall Quilts. (Illus.). 84p. 1990. pap. 5.95 (0-486-26370-3) Dover.

McCloskey, Marsha R., jt. auth. see Martin, Nancy.

McCloskey, Mary A. Kant's Aesthetic. LC 86-14479. 184p. (C). 1987. pap. text 21.95 (0-88706-423-X) State U NY Pr.

McCloskey, Mary J., ed. see Thompson, E. Joe, Sr. & Thompson, Jack L.

McCloskey, Mary J., ed. see Thompson, E. J. & Thompson, Jack L.

McCloskey, Mary L. & Stack, Lydia. Voices in Literature: Integrated Language & Literature for ESL, Gold, Silver, & Bronze. (J). 1995. pap. 41.95 (0-8384-2283-7) Heinle & Heinle.

McCloskey, Mary Lou & Stack, Lydia. Voices in Literature: Bronze (Beginning) Student's Journal. 1996. student ed. 7.25 (0-8384-7032-7) Heinle & Heinle.

— Voices in Literature: Silver (Intermediate) Student's Journal. 1996. student ed. 7.25 (0-8384-7024-6) Heinle & Heinle.

McCloskey, Michael. The Formative Years of the Missionary College of Santa Cruz of Queretaro: 1683-1733. (Monograph Ser.). 1955. 25.00 (0-88382-051-X) AAFH.

***Mccloskey, Moya.** Quercus: Statistics for Bioscientists: A Student Guidebook. 160p. 2000. pap. text 24.95 (0-340-67768-6) OUP.

***McCloskey, Moya & Robertson, Chris.** Business Statistics: A Multimedia Guide. (Illus.). 256p. 2000. pap. text 50.00 (0-340-71927-3, Pub. by E A) OUP.

McCloskey-Padgett, Patty, et al. The Real Mother Goose Book of American Rhymes. LC 94-48663. 128p. (J). 1995. 8.95 (0-590-50955-1) Scholastic Inc.

McCloskey, Pat. Day by Day with Followers of Francis & Clare. Orig. Title: Franciscan Saint of the Day. 170p. 1999. pap. 8.95 (0-86716-336-4, B3364) St Anthony Mess Pr.

McCloskey, Patrick. Friars Minor in China. (History Ser.). 336p. 1995. 28.00 (1-57659-002-X) Franciscan Inst.

McCloskey, Patrick & Schoenberg, Ronald. Criminal Law Deskbook. 1984. 205.00 (0-8205-1217-6) Bender.

McCloskey, Paul N., Jr. The Taking of Hill 610: And Other Essays on Friendship. 220p. 1992. 12.95 (0-9635186-0-7) Eaglet Bks.

McCloskey, Richard G., jt. auth. see Beavis, Bill.

McCloskey, Robert. Abran Paso a los Patitos: Make Way for Ducklings. (Picture Puffin Ser.). 1997. 10.19 (0-606-11017-8, Pub. by Turtleback) Demco.

— Abran Paso a los Patitos: Make Way for Ducklings. (SPA., Illus.). 68p. (J). 1996. 15.99 (0-670-86830-2) Viking Penguin.

— Abran Paso a los Patitos: Make Way for Ducklings. (J). 1997. pap. 5.99 (0-14-056182-X) Viking Penguin.

— Blueberries for Sal. LC 48-4955. (Illus.). 56p. (J). (ps-1). 1948. 16.99 (0-670-17591-9, Viking Child) Peng Put Young Read.

— Blueberries for Sal. LC 48-4955. (Picture Puffin Ser.). (Illus.). (J). (ps-1). 1976. pap. 5.99 (0-14-050169-X, PuffinBks) Peng Put Young Read.

— Blueberries for Sal. (Picture Puffin Ser.). (Illus.). (J). 1976. 10.19 (0-606-01675-9, Pub. by Turtleback) Demco.

— Burt Dow: Deep-Water Man. LC 68-364. (Illus.). 64p. (J). (gr. 4-6). 1963. 18.99 (0-670-19748-3, Viking Child) Peng Put Young Read.

— Burt Dow, Deep-Water Man. (Illus.). 64p. (J). (ps-3). 1989. pap. 5.99 (0-14-050978-X, PuffinBks) Peng Put Young Read.

— Burt Dow, Deep-Water Man: A Tale of the Sea in the Classic Tradition. (Picture Puffin Ser.). (J). 1989. 11.19 (0-606-04004-8, Pub. by Turtleback) Demco.

***McCloskey, Robert.** Centerburg Tales. (gr. 4-7). 1999. pap. 13.50 (0-8085-8462-6) Econo-Clad Bks.

McCloskey, Robert. Centerburg Tales. LC 51-10675. (Illus.). 192p. (J). (gr. 4-6). 1951. 16.99 (0-670-20977-5, Viking Child) Peng Put Young Read.

— Centerburg Tales. (Illus.). (J). (gr. 1-3). 1977. pap. 5.99 (0-14-031072-X, PuffinBks) Peng Put Young Read.

— Centerburg Tales. 1979. 10.09 (0-606-01090-4, Pub. by Turtleback) Demco.

— Homer Price. LC 43-16001. (Illus.). (J). (gr. 4-7). 1943. 15.99 (0-670-37729-5, Viking Child) Peng Put Young Read.

— Homer Price. (Storybooks Ser.). (Illus.). (J). (gr. 3-7). 1976. pap. 4.99 (0-14-030927-6, PuffinBks) Peng Put Young Read.

— Homer Price. (J). 1987. pap. 2.25 (0-590-09049-6) Scholastic Inc.

— Homer Price. (J). 1976. 9.09 (0-606-03532-X, Pub. by Turtleback) Demco.

— Homer Price. large type ed. (J). (gr. 4-6). reprint ed. 10.00 (0-89064-072-6) NAVH.

— Lentil. (Illus.). (J). (gr. k-3). 1940. 16.99 (0-670-42357-2, Viking Child) Peng Put Young Read.

— Lentil. (J). (ps-3). 1978. pap. 5.99 (0-14-050287-4, PuffinBks) Peng Put Young Read.

McCloskey, Robert. Lentil. (Picture Puffin Ser.). (Illus.). (J). 1978. 10.19 (0-606-02156-6, Pub. by Turtleback) Demco.

McCloskey, Robert. Make Way for Ducklings. (Illus.). (J). (gr. k-3). 1941. 16.99 (0-670-45149-5, Viking Child) Peng Put Young Read.

***McCloskey, Robert.** Make Way for Ducklings. 76p. (J). (ps-3). 1999. pap. 6.99 (0-14-056434-9, PuffinBks) Peng Put Young Read.

McCloskey, Robert. Make Way for Ducklings. (Picture Puffin Ser.). (J). 1976. 10.19 (0-606-03886-8, Pub. by Turtleback) Demco.

— One Morning in Maine. (Illus.). (J). (gr. k-3). 1952. 17.99 (0-670-52627-4, Viking Child) Peng Put Young Read.

— One Morning in Maine. LC no-na6604. (Picture Puffin Ser.). (J). (ps-3). 1976. pap. 5.99 (0-14-050174-6, PuffinBks) Peng Put Young Read.

— One Morning in Maine. (Picture Puffin Ser.). (Illus.). (J). 1976. 10.19 (0-606-04247-4, Pub. by Turtleback) Demco.

— Time of Wonder. (Illus.). 64p. (J). (gr. k-3). 1989. pap. 5.99 (0-14-050201-7, PuffinBks) Peng Put Young Read.

— Time of Wonder. LC 76-54741. (J). 1985. 11.19 (0-606-03977-5, Pub. by Turtleback) Demco.

McCloskey, Robert G. American Supreme Court. LC 60-14235. (Chicago History of American Civilization Ser.). 265p. 1996. pap. text 10.95 (0-226-55675-1, CHAC13) U Ch Pr.

— The American Supreme Court. Levinson, Sanford, ed. LC 94-10905. 286p. 1994. pap. text 13.00 (0-226-55678-6) U Ch Pr.

— The American Supreme Court. 2nd ed. Levinson, Sanford, ed. LC 94-10905. 286p. 1994. lib. bdg. 45.00 (0-226-55677-8) U Ch Pr.

— The Modern Supreme Court. LC 70-173408. 388p. reprint ed. pap. 120.30 (0-7837-6079-5, 205912500007) Bks Demand.

***McCloskey, Robert G. & Levinson, Sanford.** The American Supreme Court. 3rd ed. LC 00-30214. (Chicago History of American Civilization Ser.). 2000. pap. write for info. (0-226-55680-8) U Ch Pr.

McCloskey, Seosamh. Irish Language Books: A Reader's Guide. rev. ed. 72p. 1996. pap. 9.95 (0-9635738-2-9) Irish Bks NY.

McCloskey, Susan. Patty & Pop's Picnic: Big Book. large type ed. (Little Books & Big Bks.). (Illus.). 8p. (J). (ps-1). 1998. pap. text 19.89 (0-8215-0863-6) Sadlier.

McCloskey, Susan, jt. auth. see Davidson, Wilma.

***McCloskey, Walter.** Risking Elizabeth. 306p. 1998. mass mkt. 6.99 (0-425-16413-6) Berkley Pub.

McCloskey, Walter. Risking Elizabeth. LC 96-44984. 1997. 21.50 (0-684-82434-5) S&S Trade.

***McCloskey, William.** Breakers. 352p. 2000. 24.95 (1-58574-084-5) Lyons Pr.

— Highliners: The Classic Novel about the Commercial Fishermen of Alaska. (Illus.). 416p. 2000. pap. 16.95 (1-58574-028-4) Lyons Pr.

McCloskey, William. Highliners: The Classic Novel of Alaska & Its Fishermen. 416p. 1995. pap. 16.95 (1-55821-375-9) Lyons Pr.

— Their Father's Work: Casting Nets with the World's Fishermen. LC 97-49595. (Illus.). 352p. 1998. 24.95 (0-07-045347-0) Intl Marine.

McClosky. Ideologies in Conflict. 1994. 24.95 (0-02-920511-5) S&S Trade.

McClosky, Herbert. Consensus & Ideology in American Politics. (Reprint Series in Social Sciences). (C). 1993. reprint ed. pap. text 5.00 (0-8290-3149-9, P-403) Irvington.

McClosky, Herbert & Brill, Alida. Dimensions of Tolerance: What Americans Believe about Civil Liberties. LC 82-72959. 525p. 1983. 45.00 (0-87154-591-8) Russell Sage.

— Dimensions of Tolerance: What Americans Believe about Civil Liberties. 512p. (C). 1986. pap. 17.95 (0-87154-592-6) Russell Sage.

An Asterisk (*) at the beginning of an entry indicates that the title is appearing for the first time.

McClosky, Herbert & Zaller, John R. The American Ethos: Public Attitudes Toward Capitalism & Democracy. LC 84-12793. (Twentieth Century Fund Study). 360p. 1988. pap. 19.50 (*0-674-02331-5*) HUP.

McClosky, Marylou, et al. TLLC Systems. 1996. pap. text, wbk. ed. 441.00 (*0-201-59321-1*) Addison-Wesley.

McClosky, Robert. Blueberries for Sal. (Illus.). (J). 1993. pap. 9.99 incl. audio (*0-14-095110-5*, PuffinBks) Peng Put Young Read.

— Make Way for Ducklings. (Illus.). (J). 1993. pap. 9.99 incl. audio (*0-14-095118-0*, PuffinBks) Peng Put Young Read.

McClothlin, Bruce. High Performance Through Understanding Systems, 10 vols. (Learning-a-Living Library). (Illus.). 64p. (YA). (gr. 7-12). 1996. lib. bdg. 16.95 (*0-8239-2210-3*) Rosen Group.

McCloud, Aminah B. African American Islam. LC 94-18313. 200p. (gr. 13). 1994. pap. 18.99 (*0-415-90786-1*, B0638) Routledge.

— African American Islam. LC 94-18313. 200p. (C). 1995. 70.00 (*0-415-90785-3*, B0634) Routledge.

McCloud, Barry. Definite Country: The Ultimate Encyclopedia of Country Music & Its Performers. LC 94-28400. 1995. pap. 40.00 (*0-399-51890-8*, Perigee Bks); pap. 20.00 (*0-399-52144-5*, Perigee Bks) Berkley Pub.

McCloud, Bill. What Should We Tell Our Children about Vietnam? LC 89-40218. 144p. 1989. 19.95 (*0-8061-2229-3*) U of Okla Pr.

***McCloud, Bill.** What Should We Tell Our Children about Vietnam? LC 89-40218. (Illus.). 176p. 2000. pap. text 12.95 (*0-8061-3240-X*) U of Okla Pr.

McCloud, Caron, ed. see McCloud, Shiloh.

McCloud, Cleveland & McCloud, Rudolph. You & Your Used Automobile: Things You Should Know & Do Before & After You Purchase a Used Automobile. 16p. 1997. pap. 7.00 (*0-8059-4096-0*) Dorrance.

McCloud, Cornie B. Cumberland Gap's Hillbilly Preacher: Hugh Vancel. LC 95-69283. 128p. 1995. pap. 11.95 (*1-881576-55-8*) Providence Hse.

McCloud, Donald G. Southeast Asia: Tradition & Modernity in the Contemporary World. 2nd ed. LC 95-5014. 360p. (C). 1995. pap. 32.00 (*0-8133-1896-3*, Pub. by Westview) HarpC.

McCloud, Frederick T. Amina, see Amina McCloud, Frederick T.

Mccloud, Kevin. Decorative Style Most Original: The Most Original & Comprehensive Sourcebook of Styles, Treatments, Techniques & Materials. 352p. 1990. 40.00 (*0-671-69142-2*) S&S Trade.

McCloud, Kevin. Grand Designs: Designing & Building Your Own Home. (Illus.). 192p. 1999. 34.95 (*0-7522-1373-3*) Trans-Atl Phila.

— Lighting Style: The Complete Visual Sourcebook for Every Room in Your House. LC 94-13676. 144p. 1995. 25.00 (*0-671-88706-8*) S&S Trade.

***McCloud, Kevin & Blake, Fanny.** Grand Designs: Building Your Dream Home. (Illus.). 192p. 1999. 34.95 (*0-7522-1355-5*, Pub. by Channel Four) Trans-Atl Phila.

McCloud, Kevin & Crockett, Michael. Kevin McCloud's Complete Book of Paint & Decorative Techniques. LC 96-33205. 1997. 40.00 (*0-684-87434-2*) S&S Trade.

McCloud, Mac, jt. auth. see Barrett, R.

***McCloud, Melody T.** The Health Diary for Women of Color: Your Personal Log. 66p. 1999. pap. 9.95 (*0-9643554-1-8*) New Life GA.

McCloud, Melody T. Medical Bloopers!! Amusing & Amazing Stories of Health Care Workers. (Illus.). 72p. (Orig.). 1994. pap. 6.95 (*0-9643554-0-X*) New Life GA.

McCloud, Rudolph, jt. auth. see McCloud, Cleveland.

McCloud, Scot. Zot!, Bk. 3. 1998. pap. 19.95 (*0-87816-429-4*) Kitchen Sink.

— Zot!, Bk. 3. 1998. 34.95 (*0-87816-527-4*) Kitchen Sink.

***McCloud, Scott.** Reinventing Comics: How Imagination & Technology Are Revolutionizing an Art Form. 256p. 2000. pap. 22.95 (*0-06-095350-0*, Perennial) HarperTrade.

McCloud, Scott. Understanding Comics. (Illus.). 224p. 1999. pap. 19.95 (*1-56389-557-9*, Pub. by DC Comics) Diamond Comic Distributors Inc.

— Understanding Comics. 2nd deluxe limited ed. Martin, Mark, ed. (Illus.). 224p. (J). (gr. 4 up). 1993. 34.95 (*0-87816-245-3*) Kitchen Sink.

— Understanding Comics. 2nd ed. (Illus.). 244p. (J). (gr. 4 up). 1998. reprint ed. pap. 22.95 (*0-87816-243-7*) Kitchen Sink.

— Understanding Comics: The Invisible Art. 224p. 1994. pap. 22.50 (*0-06-097625-X*) HarpC.

— Zot!, Bk. 1. Garnier, Catherine, ed. (Illus.). 288p. 1997. pap. 34.95 (*0-87816-427-8*) Kitchen Sink.

— Zot!, Bk. 1. deluxe ed. Garnier, Catherine, ed. 288p. 1997. 55.00 (*0-87816-525-8*) Kitchen Sink.

— Zot!, Bk. 2. 176p. 1998. 34.95 (*0-87816-526-6*); pap. 19.95 (*0-87816-428-6*) Kitchen Sink.

***McCloud, Shiloh.** Color of Woman: A Coloring Book & Journal. 4th rev. ed. McCloud, Caron, ed. (Illus.). 130p. 1999. spiral bd. 25.00 (*0-9674214-0-3*, Tribe Diynah) Color of Woman.

— Heart Wings: A Book about Real Friendship. (Coloring Books & Journals: Vol. 3). (Illus.). 120p. 2000. spiral bd. 18.00 (*0-9674214-2-X*, Tribe Diynah) Color of Woman.

— She Moves to Her Own Rythem: A Guided Exploration. 4th rev. ed. McCloud, Caron, ed. (Coloring Books & Journals: Vol. 2). (Illus.). 130p. 1999. pap. 25.00 (*0-9674214-1-1*, Tribe Diynah) Color of Woman.

***McCloud, Susan E.** The Last Suspect. LC 98-70865. 236p. 1998. write for info. (*1-57008-419-X*) Bookcraft Inc.

McCloud, Susan Evans. Black Stars over Mexico. 1985. pap. text 9.95 (*1-890558-02-8*) Granite UT.

***McCloud, Susan Evans.** Brigham Young: An Inspiring Personal Biography. 1999. 17.95 (*1-57734-241-0*, 01113380) Covenant Comms.

McCloud, Susan Evans. Mormon Girls Bk. 1: Something Lost, Something Gained. 1995. pap. 6.95 (*0-88494-993-1*) Bookcraft Inc.

— Mormon Girls Bk. 2: The Giving Heart. 1995. pap. 5.95 (*0-88494-994-X*) Bookcraft Inc.

— Mormon Girls Bk. 3: The Angels Sing. 1995. pap. 5.95 (*0-88494-995-8*) Bookcraft Inc.

— Mormon Girls Bk. 4: New Friends. 1996. pap. 5.95 (*1-57008-282-0*) Bookcraft Inc.

— Mormon Girls Bk. 5: A Lesson Learned. 1996. pap. 5.95 (*1-57008-283-9*) Bookcraft Inc.

— Mormon Girls Bk. 6: The Little Stranger. 1996. pap. 5.95 (*1-57008-284-7*) Bookcraft Inc.

— Mothers: Praising the Daughters of God. 24p. 1996. pap. 3.95 (*1-55503-912-X*, 01112244) Covenant Comms.

— Murder by the Sea. LC 97-71249. 192p. 1997. pap. 9.95 (*1-57008-314-2*) Bookcraft Inc.

— Out of the Shadows. LC 98-74083. 1998. 16.95 (*1-57008-571-4*) Bookcraft Inc.

— Sunset Across India. 1997. pap. 9.95 (*1-57008-350-9*) Bookcraft Inc.

— Sunset Across the Rockies. LC 97-74689. ix, 196 p. 1997. 15.95 (*1-57008-341-X*) Bookcraft Inc.

— Sunset Across the Waters. 1996. 14.95 (*1-57008-285-5*) Bookcraft Inc.

— Treasures of Womanhood: Timeless Words of Faith & Inspiration. LC 99-30485. 1999. 14.95 (*1-57734-447-2*, 01113976) Covenant Comms.

— Voices from the Dust. LC 95-83704. 1996. pap. 10.95 (*1-57008-226-X*) Bookcraft Inc.

McCloud, Susan Evans, ed. A. A. Seagull. (J). 1989. pap. 4.95 (*0-88494-721-1*) Bookcraft Inc.

McCloud, Tom, jt. auth. see Benner, Bob.

McCloughlin, Moira. Museums & the Representation of Native Canadians: Negotiating the Borders of Culture. LC 99-12896. 1999. 69.00 (*0-8153-2988-1*) Garland.

McCloughry, R. K., ed. see Hayek, Friedrich A.

McClow, Arnold H. From Saybrook & Lyons Farms to Hillside: A Pictorial History. LC 97-17345. 1997. write for info. (*1-57864-002-4*); pap. write for info. (*1-57864-003-2*) Donning Co.

McCloy, A. Coastwalk. 1996. text 35.00 (*0-340-65739-1*, Pub. by Hodder & Stought Ltd) Trafalgar.

McCloy, Andrew. In & Around London. Smith, Roger, ed. (Twenty-Five Walks Ser.). (Illus.). 112p. 1997. pap. 16.95 (*0-11-495797-5*, Pub. by Statnry Office) Seven Hills Bk.

McCloy, Charles H. & Young, Norma D. Tests & Measurements in Health & Physical Education. 3rd ed. (Illus.). 1979. reprint ed. text 29.50 (*0-89197-448-2*) Irvington.

McCloy, Helen. Mr. Splitfoot. large type ed. (Keating's Choice Ser.). 287p. 1992. 24.95 (*1-85089-493-0*, Pub. by ISIS Lrg Prnt) Transaction Pubs.

McCloy, James F. & Miller, Ray, Jr. The Jersey Devil. (Illus.). 121p. 1987. pap. 10.95 (*0-912608-11-0*) Mid Atlantic.

— Phantom of the Pines: More Tales of the Jersey Devil. LC 98-13684. 1998. pap. 11.95 (*0-912608-95-1*) Mid Atlantic.

McCloy, Keith. Resource Management: Information Systems. LC 94-159198. 542p. 1995. 126.00 (*0-7484-0119-9*); pap. 54.95 (*0-7484-0120-2*) Taylor & Francis.

McCloy, Kristin. Some Girls. 1995. pap. 11.95 (*0-452-27273-4*, Plume) Dutton Plume.

— Velocity. 272p. 1990. pap. 7.95 (*0-671-68920-7*, WSP) PB.

McCloy, Shelby T. French Inventions of the Eighteenth Century. LC 52-5903. 255p. reprint ed. pap. 79.10 (*0-608-11460-X*, 200028400025) Bks Demand.

— Government Assistance in Eighteenth Century France. LC 77-23743. (Perspectives in European History Ser.: No. 14). xi, 496p. 1977. reprint ed. lib. bdg. 49.50 (*0-87991-621-4*) Porcupine Pr.

— Humanitarianism in 18th Century. LC 72-5476. (World History Ser.: No. 48). 1972. reprint ed. lib. bdg. 75.00 (*0-8383-1600-X*) M S G Haskell Hse.

— The Negro in France. LC 72-5545. (Studies in Black History & Culture: No. 54). 1972. reprint ed. lib. bdg. 75.00 (*0-8383-1601-8*) M S G Haskell Hse.

McClsokey, et al. Making Connections 3: Text, No. 3. (Secondary ESL Ser.). 160p. (J). 1995. mass mkt. 31.95 (*0-8384-3841-5*) Heinle & Heinle.

McCluggage, Denise. By Brooks Too Broad for Leaping: Selections from Autoweek. (Illus.). 284p. 1994. pap. 17.95 (*0-9642309-0-9*) Fulcorte Pr.

— Centered Skier. anniversary ed. (Illus.). 186p. 1999. reprint ed. pap. 16.95 (*0-9632484-4-8*) Tempest Bk.

McCluggage, Robert W., ed. Selected Papers in Illinois History, 1982. LC 85-14310. 1984. pap. 7.50 (*0-912226-15-3*) Ill St Hist Soc.

— Selected Papers in Illinois History, 1983. LC 86-116885. 1985. pap. 7.50 (*0-912226-17-X*) Ill St Hist Soc.

McCluhan, Michael, ed. see Owl, Michael W.

McClun, Diana & Nownes, Laura. Quilts Galore! Quiltmaking Styles & Techniques. LC 90-42209. (Illus.). 192p. 1990. pap. 24.95 (*0-8442-2621-1*, Quilt Dgst Pr) NTC Contemp Pub Co.

— Quilts, Quilts & More Quilts! Nadel, Harold, ed. LC 93-28345. (Illus.). 160p. (Orig.). 1995. pap. 23.95 (*0-914881-67-1*, 10081) C & T Pub.

— Quilts! Quilts!! Quilts!!! The Complete Guide to Quiltmaking. LC 88-18563. (Illus.). 160p. 1989. pap. 21.95 (*0-8442-2616-5*, Quilt Dgst Pr) NTC Contemp Pub Co.

— Quilts! Quilts!! Quilts!!! The Complete Guide to Quiltmaking. LC 98-227910. (Illus.). 64p. 1997. pap., teacher ed. 9.95 (*0-8442-2618-1*, Quilt Dgst Pr) NTC Contemp Pub Co.

McClun, Diana, jt. auth. see Nownes, Laura.

McClun, Diana & Nownes, Laura. Quilts! Quilts!! Quilts!!! The Complete Guide to Quiltmaking. 2nd ed. LC 97-2537. (Illus.). 160p. 1997. pap. 24.95 (*0-8442-2617-3*, Quilt Dgst Pr) NTC Contemp Pub Co.

McClung, David & Schaerer, Peter. The Avalanche Handbook. 2nd ed. LC 93-2027. (Illus.). 256p. 1993. pap. 19.95 (*0-89886-364-3*) Mountaineers.

McClung, Emily. Ecologia y Cultura en Mesoamerica. 2nd ed. 120p. 1984. pap. 2.50 (*968-837-113-0*, UN015) UPLAAP.

McClung, Emily & Rattray, Evelyn C. Teotihuacan: Nuevos Datos, Nuevas Sintesis, Nuevos Problemas. 526p. 1987. pap. 13.71 (*968-837-968-9*, UN016) UPLAAP.

McClung, Floyd. Basic Discipleship. LC 92-14863. 190p. (Orig.). 1992. reprint ed. pap. 9.99 (*0-8308-1319-5*, 1319) InterVarsity.

McClung, Floyd, Jr. El Corazon Paternal de Dios. Guerra, Francisco B., tr. from ENG.Tr. of Father Heart of God. 96p. 1988. reprint ed. pap. 7.99 (*0-88113-027-3*) Caribe Betania.

— The Father Heart of God. LC 85-61075. (Orig.). 1985. pap., student ed. 7.99 (*0-89081-491-0*) Harvest Hse.

McClung, Floyd. Learning to Love People You Don't Like: How to Develop Love & Unity in Every Relationship. 120p. 1992. pap. 7.99 (*0-927545-19-5*) YWAM Pub.

— Light the Window. 1999. pap. 8.99 (*1-57658-150-0*) YWAM Pub.

— Living on the Devil's Doorstep: A Family's Trail of Compassion from Kabul to Amsterdam. (International Adventures Ser.). 196p. 1988. pap. 8.99 (*0-927545-45-4*) YWAM Pub.

— Lordship: Basic Discipleship. (Christian Basics Bible Studies: No. 15). 64p. (Orig.). 1996. pap., wbk. ed. 4.99 (*0-8308-2015-9*, 2015) InterVarsity.

— O Imensuravel Amor de Deus.Tr. of Father Heart of God. (POR.). 96p. 1991. pap. 5.95 (*0-8297-1649-1*) Vida Pubs.

McClung, Frank. Clamoring Voices. 469p. mass mkt. 6.99 (*1-55197-385-5*) Picasso Publ.

McClung, Gavin. Astrology Plus Insight. LC 83-72571. 136p. 1984. 15.00 (*0-86690-259-7*, M2427-014) Am Fed Astrologers.

McClung, Gordon W., jt. auth. see Reidenbach, R. Eric.

***McClung, Grant.** Globalbeliever.Com: Connecting to God's Work in Your World. 2000. pap. 12.99 (*0-87148-373-4*) Pathway Pr.

McClung, Jean. Effects of High Altitude on Human Birth: Observations on Mothers, Placentas, & the Newborn in Two Peruvian Populations. LC 72-91629. 168p. 1969. 17.95 (*0-674-24065-0*) HUP.

— Mischief & Mercy: Tales of the Saints. LC 93-2487. (Illus.). 224p. (YA). (gr. 7 up). 1993. pap. 10.95 (*1-883672-02-3*) Tricycle Pr.

McClung, Karen S., ed. GFWC Centennial Cookbook. (Illus.). 384p. 1988. write for info. (*0-318-64786-9*) Bright America.

McClung, L. Grant, Jr., ed. Azusa Street & Beyond. LC 86-70742. 245p. 1986. pap. 8.99 (*0-88270-607-1*) Bridge-Logos.

McClung, Leland S. The Anaerobic Bacteria: Their Activities in Nature & Disease, 4 vols., Vol. P1V1. LC 82-10085. 760p. 1982. reprint ed. pap. 200.00 (*0-8357-5421-9*, 202707200006) Bks Demand.

— The Anaerobic Bacteria: Their Activities in Nature & Disease, 4 vols., Vol. P1V2. LC 82-10085. 757p. 1982. reprint ed. pap. 200.00 (*0-8357-6274-2*, 202707200007) Bks Demand.

— The Anaerobic Bacteria: Their Activities in Nature & Disease, 4 vols., Vol. P1V3. LC 82-10085. 792p. 1982. reprint ed. pap. 200.00 (*0-8357-6275-0*, 202707200003) Bks Demand.

— The Anaerobic Bacteria: Their Activities in Nature & Disease, 4 vols., Vol. P1V4. LC 82-10085. 732p. 1982. reprint ed. pap. 200.00 (*0-8357-6276-9*, 202707200004) Bks Demand.

— The Anaerobic Bacteria: Their Activities in Nature & Disease, Vol. P1V5. LC 82-10085. 865p. 1982. reprint ed. pap. 200.00 (*0-8357-5418-9*, 202707200005) Bks Demand.

— The Anaerobic Bacteria: Their Activities in Nature & Disease, Vol. P2V1. LC 82-10085. 1066p. 1982. reprint ed. pap. 200.00 (*0-8357-5419-7*, 202707200001) Bks Demand.

— The Anaerobic Bacteria: Their Activities in Nature & Disease, Vol. P2V2. LC 82-10085. 349p. 1982. reprint ed. pap. 108.20 (*0-8357-5420-0*, 202707200002) Bks Demand.

McClung, Liz, ed. see Unknown Critic Staff.

McClung, Nellie L. In Times Like These. LC 70-163829. (Social History of Canada Ser.). 160p. 1972. pap. 12.95 (*0-8020-6125-7*) U of Toronto Pr.

— Purple Springs. 2nd ed. (Illus.). 400p. 1992. text 40.00 (*0-8020-5924-4*); pap. text 19.95 (*0-8020-6864-2*) U of Toronto Pr.

McClung, Patricia, jt. ed. see Stephenson, Christie.

McClung, Patricia A. Digital Collections Inventory Report. 64p. 1996. pap. 20.00 (*1-887334-48-3*) Coun Lib & Info.

McClung, Patricia A., ed. Selection of Library Materials in the Humanities, Social Sciences, & Sciences. LC 85-20084. 1985. 20.00 (*0-8389-3305-X*) ALA.

McClung, Paul. Papa Jack: Cowman from the Wichitas. LC 76-19071. 249p. reprint ed. 77.20 (*0-8357-9738-4*, 201623800002) Bks Demand.

McClung, Paul J. & Carpenter, Scott. Texas Criminal Jury Charges. 2nd rev. ed. 550p. 1997. pap. write for info. (*1-58012-003-2*) James Pub Santa Ana.

McClung, Paul J. & Carpenter, W. Scott. Texas Criminal Jury Charges. 2nd ed. 1998. pap. 99.00 (*1-58012-022-9*) James Pub Santa Ana.

McClung, Paul J., et al. Texas Criminal Lawyers Handbook. 2nd rev. ed. 450p. 1997. pap. write for info. (*1-58012-002-4*) James Pub Santa Ana.

McClung, R. C., ed. see Symposium on Advances in Fatigue Crack Closure Measurement & Analysis Staff, et al.

***McClung, Robert.** The True Adventures of Grizzly Adams. LC 85-8886. (Illus.). 208p. (J). (gr. 5-9). 1998. pap. 4.95 (*0-688-16370-X*, Wm Morrow) Morrow Avon.

McClung, Robert M. Animals That Build Their Homes. (J). 1976. pap. write for info. (*0-87044-198-1*) Natl Geog.

— Black Jack: Last of the Big Alligators. LC 91-14387. (Animal Life Cycle Ser.). (Illus.). 64p. (J). (gr. 3-7). 1991. reprint ed. lib. bdg. 16.50 (*0-208-02326-7*, Linnet Bks) Shoe String.

— Last of the Wild: Vanished & Vanishing Giants of the Animal World. LC 96-35814. (Illus.). xii, 292p. (YA). (gr. 6 up). 1997. lib. bdg. 27.50 (*0-208-02452-2*, Linnet Bks) Shoe String.

— Lost Wild America: The Story of Our Extinct & Vanishing Wildlife. enl. rev. ed. LC 93-15657. (Illus.). xvi, 277p. (YA). (gr. 6-12). 1993. lib. bdg. 29.50 (*0-208-02359-3*, Linnet Bks) Shoe String.

— Samson: Last of the California Grizzlies. LC 91-33350. (Animal Life Cycle Ser.). (Illus.). 96p. (J). (gr. 3-6). 1992. reprint ed. lib. bdg. 16.50 (*0-208-02327-5*, Linnet Bks) Shoe String.

— Shag: Last of the Plains Buffalo. LC 91-7508. (Animal Life Cycle Ser.). (Illus.). 96p. (J). (gr. 3-7). 1991. reprint ed. lib. bdg. 16.50 (*0-208-02313-5*, Linnet Bks) Shoe String.

— Snakes: Their Place in the Sun. (Illus.). 64p. (J). (gr. 2-4). 1995. 14.95 (*0-8050-1718-6*, Bks Young Read) H Holt & Co.

***McClung, William A.** Landscapes of Desire: Anglo Mythologies of Los Angeles LC 99-23426. 316p. 2000. 35.00 (*0-520-21827-2*, Pub. by U CA Pr) Cal Prin Full Svc.

McClure. Block Post. 1991. pap. text 50.00 (*0-340-55041-4*, Pub. by E A) Routldge.

***McClure & Teyber.** Child & Adolescent Psychopathology. (C). 2002. text 32.00 (*0-534-36596-5*) Wadsworth Pub.

McClure, Abbot, jt. auth. see Eberlein, Harold D.

McClure, Alexander K. Abraham Lincoln & Men of War-Times: Some Personal Recollections of War & Politics During the Lincoln Administration. LC 96-22221. (Illus.). 496p. 1996. pap. 19.95 (*0-8032-8228-1*, Bison Books) U of Nebr Pr.

— Colonel Alexander K. McClure's Recollections of Half a Century. LC 76-172762. reprint ed. 62.75 (*0-404-00086-X*) AMS Pr.

— Our Presidents & How We Make Them. LC 79-130559. (Select Bibliographies Reprint Ser.). 1977. reprint ed. 28.95 (*0-8369-5532-3*) Ayer.

McClure, Alexander K., ed. The Annals of the Civil War. LC 94-11563. (Illus.). 808p. 1994. reprint ed. pap. 21.50 (*0-306-80606-1*) Da Capo.

***McClure, Alexander W.** Authors of the English Version of the Holy Bible. 250p. 1999. pap. 50.00 (*1-57074-443-2*) Greyden Pr.

McClure, Amy A. Sunrises & Songs: Reading & Writing Poetry in an Elementary Classroom. LC 89-19919. (Illus.). 261p. (Orig.). (C). (gr. 1). 1990. pap. text 23.50 (*0-435-08507-7*, 08507) Heinemann.

McClure, Amy A. & Kristo, Janice V., eds. Books That Invite Talk, Wonder, & Play. LC 95-52945. 335p. 1996. pap. 19.95 (*0-8141-0370-7*) NCTE.

— Inviting Children's Responses to Literature: Guides to 57 Notable Books. 145p. (Orig.). 1994. pap. 12.95 (*0-8141-2379-1*) NCTE.

McClure, Arthur F. Memories of Splendor: The Midwestern World of William Inge. LC 89-62833. (Illus.). 85p. 1989. pap. 10.95 (*0-87726-038-9*) Kansas St Hist.

— The Truman Administration & the Problems of Postwar Labor, 1945-1948. LC 68-57718. 267p. 1975. 35.00 (*0-8386-6999-9*) Fairleigh Dickinson.

McClure, Arthur F., et al, eds. Ronald Reagan: His First Career, a Bibliography of the Movie Years. LC 88-7198. (Studies in American History: Vol. 1). 240p. 1988. lib. bdg. 89.95 (*0-88946-098-1*) E Mellen.

McClure, Arthur F. & Rice, C. David, eds. A Bibliographical Guide to the Works of William Inge 1913-1973. LC 91-30669. (Studies in American Literature: Vol. 14). 180p. 1991. lib. bdg. 79.95 (*0-7734-9688-2*) E Mellen.

McClure, Arthur F., et al. Education for Work: The Historical Evolution of Vocational & Distributive Education in America. LC 83-49203. 168p. 1985. 29.50 (*0-8386-3205-X*) Fairleigh Dickinson.

McClure, Arthur F., jt. auth. see Lynn, Naomi B.

McClure, Barbara, ed. see Titus, Jack.

McClure, Bud A. Putting a New Spin on Groups: The Science of Chaos. LC 98-13600. 300p. 1998. 59.95 (*0-8058-2904-0*); pap. write for info. (*0-8058-2905-9*) L Erlbaum Assocs.

McClure, Carma. Software Reuse Techniques. LC 97-10629. 350p. (C). 1997. 59.00 (*0-13-661000-5*) P-H.

McClure, Carma L. CASE Software Automation. 304p. 1988. text 57.80 (*0-13-119330-9*) P-H.

McClure, Carma L., jt. auth. see Martin, James.

McClure, Carol A. Prayer of St. Francis. 1.25 (*0-687-02774-8*) Abingdon.

McClure, Carol A. & Ramsey, Wes. Early Easter Morning. 1.25 (*0-687-07235-2*) Abingdon.

M

McClure, Charles E., Jr. Vertical Fiscal Imbalance & the Assignment of Taxing Powers in Australia. LC 93-2405. (Essays in Public Policy Ser.: No. 40). 1993. pap. text 5.00 (*0-8179-5452-X*) Hoover Inst Pr.

McClure, Charles M., et al. Planning & Role Setting for Public Libraries: A Manual of Options & Procedures. LC 87-11445. 140p. 1987. pap. text 25.00 (*0-8389-3341-6*) ALA.

McClure, Charles M., jt. auth. see Harman, Keith.

McClure, Charles R. Information for Academic Library Decision Making: The Case for Organizational Information Management, 31. LC 79-8412. (Contributions in Librarianship & Information Science Ser.: No. 31). (Illus.). 227p. 1980. 55.00 (*0-313-21398-4*, MCA/) Greenwood.

— Libraries & the Internet. 500p. 1994. pap. 35.00 (*0-88736-824-7*) Mecklermedia.

McClure, Charles R., ed. Planning for Library Services: A Guide to Utilizing Planning Methods for Library Management. LC 82-896. (Journal of Library Administration: Vol. 2, Nos. 3-4). 250p. 1982. 49.95 (*0-917724-84-4*) Haworth Pr.

— State Library Services & Issues: Facing Future Challenges. LC 85-2287. 320p. 1986. text 73.25 (*0-89391-317-0*) Ablx Pub.

McClure, Charles R., et al, eds. United States Government Information Policies: Views & Perspectives. LC 88-35081. (Information Management, Policies & Services Ser.: Vol. 5). 352p. (C). 1989. text 73.25 (*0-89391-563-7*) Ablx Pub.

McClure, Charles R. & Bertot, John C. Linking People to the Global Networked Society. 109p. (Orig.). 1998. pap. 25.00 (*0-937597-45-7*, IR-105) ERIC Clear.

McClure, Charles R. & Hernon, Peter. Academic Library Use of NTIS: Suggestions for Services & Core Collections. LC 86-228871. 72p. (Orig.). 1986. pap. 12.00 (*0-934213-04-6*) Natl Tech Info.

— Library & Information Science Research: Perspectives & Strategies for Improvement. LC 90-25018. (Information Management, Policies, & Services Ser.: Vol. 18). 416p. (C). 1991. pap. 42.50 (*0-89391-732-X*); text 78.50 (*0-89391-731-1*) Ablx Pub.

McClure, Charles R. & Hernon, Peter, eds. United States Scientific & Technical Information Policies: Views & Perspectives. LC 89-278. (Information Management, Policies & Services Ser.: Vol. 8). 336p. (C). 1989. text 73.25 (*0-89391-571-8*) Ablx Pub.

McClure, Charles R. & Lopata, Cynthia. Assessing the Academic Networked Environment: Strategies & Options. LC 97-201736. 135p. 1996. 15.00 (*0-918006-28-7*) ARL.

McClure, Charles R. & Powell, Ronald R. Basic Research Methods for Librarians. 2nd ed. (Information Management, Policies & Services Ser.: Vol. 10). 208p. (C). 1991. text 73.25 (*0-89391-688-9*) Ablx Pub.

McClure, Charles R., et al. Internet Costs & Cost Models for Public Libraries: Final Report. (Illus.). 47p. (C). 1996. pap. text 20.00 (*0-7881-3182-6*) DIANE Pub.

— Linking the U. S. National Technical Information Service with Academic & Public Libraries. LC 86-8067. 320p. 1986. text 73.25 (*0-89391-377-4*) Ablx Pub.

— National Research & Education Network (NREN) Research & Policy Perspectives. Hernon, Peter, ed. (Information Management, Policies & Services Ser.). 760p. (C). 1991. pap. 125.00 (*0-89391-813-X*) Ablx Pub.

— Public Libraries & the Internet: Study Results, Poicy Issues, & Recommendations. (Illus.). 62p. (Orig.). (C). 1994. pap. text 20.00 (*0-7881-1391-7*) DIANE Pub.

McClure, Charles R., jt. auth. see Hernon, Peter.

McClure, Charles R., jt. auth. see Moen, William E.

McClure, Charles R., ed. see Eisenberg, Michael B. & Berkowitz, Robert.

McClure, Charles R., ed. see Eisenberg, Michael B. & Berkowitz, Robert E.

McClure, Charles R., ed. see Eisenberg, Michael B., et al.

McClure, Charles R., ed. see Harman, Keith.

McClure, Charles R., ed. see Harris, Roma.

McClure, Charles R., ed. see Hernon, Peter.

McClure, Charles R., jt. ed. see Hernon, Peter.

McClure, Charles R., ed. see Hernon, Peter, et al.

McClure, Charles R., ed. see Robbins, Jane, et al.

McClure, Charlotte S. Gertrude Atherton. LC 76-45133. (Western Writers Ser.: No. 23). 47p. 1976. pap. 4.95 (*0-88430-022-6*) Boise St U W Writ Ser.

McClure, Charlotte S., jt. ed. see Fowlkes, Diane L.

McClure, Cole R., Jr., jt. ed. see Hatheway, Allen W.

McClure, Cynthia Rowland. The Monster Within: Overcoming Eating Disorders. 192p. 1998. mass mkt. 5.99 (*0-8007-8652-1*, Spire) Revell.

McClure, Diane K., ed. Probate Court Records, Cook County, Illinois, 1872-1873. 92p. 1992. pap. 12.00 (*1-881125-13-0*) Chi Geneal Soc.

McClure, Doug. TV or Not TV. 32p. 1997. pap. 3.25 (*0-87440-052-X*) Bakers Plays.

McClure, Doug, adapted by. A Midsummer Night's Dream: Adapted for the Modern Stage. 64p. 1997. pap. 5.00 (*0-87440-043-0*) Bakers Plays.

McClure, Elliot. Bird Banding. (Illus.). 340p. (Orig.). 1984. pap. 15.00 (*0-910286-65-5*) Boxwood.

— Whistling Wings: Dove Chronicles. 1991. 9.95 (*0-940168-19-7*) Boxwood.

McClure, Evelyn S. Sebastopol's Historic Cemetery: A Serindipitous Guide to the Pioneers & Citizens Residing Therein. (Illus.). 207p. 1999. pap. 19.95 (*0-9647746-1-5*) Belle View Pr.

McClure, F. Daniel, jt. auth. see Gordon, Michael.

McClure, Faith H. Child & Adolescent Therapy. LC 95-79404. (C). 1995. text 60.50 (*0-15-501453-6*, Pub. by Harcourt Coll Pubs) Harcourt.

McClure, Floyd A. The Bamboos. (Illus.). 368p. (C). 1993. reprint ed. pap. text 18.95 (*1-56098-323-X*) Smithsonian.

— The Bamboos, a Fresh Perspective. LC SB0317.. (Illus.). 365p. reprint ed. pap. 113.20 (*0-8357-4130-3*, 205706500005) Bks Demand.

McClure, Gerry S. Heaven on Earth's Little Book of Angels. (Illus.). 18p. 10.00 (*0-9641174-0-1*) Heaven On Erth.

McClure, Gillian. The Christmas Donkey. LC 92-56506. 32p. (J). (ps-3). 1993. 15.00 (*0-374-31261-3*) FS&G.

— The Christmas Donkey. LC 92-56506. (Illus.). 32p. (J). (ps-3). 1995. pap. 5.95 (*0-374-41191-3*) FS&G.

McClure, Gillian. Christmas Donkey. LC 92-56506. 1995. 11.15 (*0-606-09146-7*, Pub. by Turtleback) Demco.

— Selkie. LC 98-55143. (Illus.). 32p. (J). (gr. k-3). 1999. 16.00 (*0-374-36709-4*) FS&G.

McClure, Grace. The Bassett Women. LC 85-7143. (Illus.). 270p. 1985. 25.00 (*0-8040-0876-0*); pap. 9.95 (*0-8040-0877-9*) Swallow.

McClure, Gregory L., ed. Computerized Quantitative Infrared Analysis. LC 86-26534. (Special Technical Publication Ser.: No. 934). (Illus.). viii, 186p. 1987. text 37.00 (*0-8031-0929-6*, STP934) ASTM.

McClure, H. Elliott. Inago - Children of Rice. LC 92-74250. 1993. pap. 17.95 (*0-87212-259-X*) Libra.

***McClure, Hugh M.** Medevac. 288p. 2000. pap. 16.95 (*1-893162-14-1*) Erica Hse.

McClure, J. Derrick. Scots & Its Literature. LC 95-43671. (Varieties of English Around the World General Ser.: Vol. 14). vi, 218p. 1995. 52.00 (*1-55619-445-5*) J Benjamins Pubng Co.

— Why Scots Matters. 1989. 40.00 (*0-7855-3909-3*, Pub. by Saltire Soc) St Mut.

— Why Scots Matters. 1993. pap. 28.00 (*0-85411-071-2*, Pub. by Saltire Soc) St Mut.

McClure, J. Derrick, ed. Scotland & the Lowland Tongue: Studies in the Language & Literature of Lowland Scotland in Honour of David Donald Murison. 248p. 1983. text 38.00 (*0-08-028482-5*, Pergamon Pr) Elsevier.

McClure, James. The Artful Egg. 1986. 5.95 (*0-07-544541-7*) McGraw.

McClure, James. Basic Principles of General Chemistry. 156p. (C). 1993. text 23.20 (*0-536-58485-0*) Pearson Custom.

McClure, James. The Blood of an Englishman. large type ed. 498p. 1982. 27.99 (*0-7089-0744-X*) Ulverscroft.

— Cop World: Policing the Streets of San Diego. LC 85-217205. 1984. write for info. (*0-333-30688-0*) Macmillan.

— The Song Dog. 1991. 17.45 (*0-89296-274-7*, Pub. by Mysterious Pr) Little.

McClure, Janet. Light Techniques That Trigger Transformation. Harben, Lillian, ed. 147p. (Orig.). 1989. pap. 11.95 (*0-929385-00-4*) Light Tech Pubng.

— Prelude to Ascension. 850p. 1996. pap. 29.95 (*0-929385-54-3*) Light Tech Pubng.

— Sanat Kumara: Training a Planetary Logos. 179p. 1990. pap. 11.95 (*0-929385-17-9*) Light Tech Pubng.

— Scopes of Dimensions. 176p. (Orig.). 1989. pap. 11.95 (*0-929385-09-8*) Light Tech Pubng.

— The Source Adventure. Harben, Lillian, ed. 157p. (Orig.). 1988. pap. 11.95 (*0-929385-06-3*) Light Tech Pubng.

McClure, Janet & Harben, Lillian. Aha! The Realization Book. 217p. (Orig.). 1995. reprint ed. pap. 11.95 (*0-929385-61-6*) Light Tech Pubng.

McClure, Jim. Stainless Steel Bar from Brazil, India, Japan, & Spain: An International Trade Investigation. (Illus.). 229p. (Orig.). (C). 1995. pap. text 50.00 (*0-7881-2368-8*) DIANE Pub.

McClure, Joanna. Hard Edge. (Morning Coffee Chapbook Ser.). 15p. (Orig.). 1987. pap. 15.00 (*0-918273-35-8*) Coffee Hse.

— Wolf Eyes. unabridged ed. 48p. 1998. pap. 8.95 (*0-9661037-0-X*) Bearthm Pr.

McClure, John. Explanations, Accounts & Illusions: A Critical Analysis. (European Monographs in Social Psychology). 196p. (C). 1991. text 54.95 (*0-521-38532-6*) Cambridge U Pr.

McClure, John A. Kipling & Conrad: The Colonial Fiction. LC 81-4117. 195p. (C). 1981. 28.00 (*0-674-50529-8*) HUP.

— Late Imperial Romance. LC 93-42312. (Haymarket Ser.). 300p. (C). 1994. pap. 19.00 (*0-86091-612-X*, Pub. by Verso) Norton.

McClure, John R. God's Plan of Redemption. Cagle, J. C., ed. 138p. (Orig.). 1990. pap. 3.95 (*0-934942-84-6*, 149) White Wing Pub.

— God's Plan of Redemption Leader's Guide. Cagle, J. C., ed. (Orig.). 1990. teacher ed. 2.95 (*0-934942-85-4*, 231) White Wing Pub.

McClure, John S. Best Advice for Preaching. LC 97-46146. 1998. pap. text 14.00 (*0-8006-2997-3*, 1-2997, Fortress Pr) Augsburg Fortress.

— The Roundtable Pulpit: Where Leadership & Preaching Meet. LC 95-3956. 144p. 1995. pap. 14.95 (*0-687-01142-6*) Abingdon.

McClure, John S. & Ramsay, Nancy J., eds. Telling the Truth: Preaching Against Sexual & Domestic Violence. LC 98-36258. 176p. 1999. pap. 15.95 (*0-8298-1282-2*) Pilgrim OH.

***McClure, Judy W.** Healers & Researchers: Physicians, Biologists, Social Scientists. LC 99-13010. (Remarkable Women, Past & Present Ser.). (Illus.). 80p. (gr. 4-7). 2000. lib. bdg. 28.55 (*0-8172-5734-9*) Raintree Steck-V.

— Theoreticians & Builders: Mathematicians, Physical Scientists, Inventors. LC 00-27839. (Remarkable Women Ser.). (Illus.). 2000. write for info. (*0-8172-5728-4*) Raintree Steck-V.

McClure, Julie B. Road to a Dream: The Art of Jesse Barnes. (Illus.). 187p. 1998. 89.95 (*0-9668129-2-1*) J Barnes Fine Art.

McClure, Kathy. Quick Basic for Technology Students. (C). 2001. pap. 40.00 (*0-13-610875-X*, Macmillan Coll) P-H.

McClure, Ken. Chameleon. large type ed. (Large Print Ser.). 544p. 1996. 27.99 (*0-7089-3592-3*) Ulverscroft.

***McClure, Ken.** Resurrection. 352p. 2000. 24.00 (*0-684-86943-8*) S&S Trade.

— Tangled Web. 288p. 2000. 24.50 (*0-7432-0508-1*) S&S Trade.

McClure, Kenneth. Reflections of a Bexley Boy. (Illus.). 227p. 1996. pap. text 19.95 (*0-9660309-0-7*, 1) North Stream Pub.

McClure, Kevin. Putting it Together: A Conversation Management Text. 240p. (C). 1995. pap. text 26.27 (*0-13-128174-7*) P-H.

McClure, Kirstie M. Judging Rights: Lockean Politics & the Limits of Consent. 320p. 1996. text 37.50 (*0-8014-3111-5*) Cornell U Pr.

McClure, Laura. Spoken Like a Woman: Speech & Gender in Athenian Drama. LC 98-55157. 331p. 1999. 39.50 (*0-691-01730-1*, Pub. by Princeton U Pr) Cal Prin Full Svc.

McClure, Laura, jt. auth. see Lardinois, A. P.

McClure, Lewis. The Mc Clure Press. limited ed. (Illus.). 32p. 1984. 95.00 (*0-915998-21-1*) Lime Rock Pr.

***McClure, Lynne.** Anger & Conflict in the Workplace: Nine Management Skills Everyone Needs. 2000. 15.95 (*1-57023-138-9*) Impact VA.

McClure, Lynne, jt. auth. see Arnold, William E.

McClure, Lynne F. Risky Business: Managing Employee Violence in the Workplace. LC 96-4070. 224p. 1996. 39.95 (*0-7890-0075-X*); pap. 19.95 (*0-7890-0100-4*) Haworth Pr.

McClure, Mabel B. Abernathy. The Abernathys, the Alexanders, the Forneys, the Sims. 48p. 1997. reprint ed. pap. 10.00 (*0-8328-7195-8*); reprint ed. lib. bdg. 20.00 (*0-8328-7194-X*) Higginson Bk Co.

McClure, Mac. Chicken by Request. (Illus.). 200p. 1998. pap. 15.00 (*0-9660819-2-7*, 6990) Cooking With Grannie.

McClure, Mae. Cooking with Grannie Mae. unabridged ed. (Illus.). 364p. 1996. mass mkt. 18.00 (*0-9660819-1-9*, 5975) Cooking With Grannie.

— Grannie Mae's Christmas Cooky Book. unabridged ed. (Illus.). 341p. 1995. mass mkt. 15.00 (*0-9660819-0-0*, 5682) Cooking With Grannie.

McClure, Margaret. A Civilized Community: The History of Social Welfare. LC 99-181271. (Illus.). 256p. 1998. pap. 29.95 (*1-86940-183-2*, Pub. by Auckland Univ) Paul & Co Pubs.

McClure, Margaret L., et al. Magnet Hospitals: Attraction & Retention of Professional Nurses. 150p. (Orig.). (C). 1983. pap. 16.25 (*1-55810-070-9*, G-160, Am Acad Nursing) Am Nurses Pub.

McClure, Marilyn, et al, trs. This Old Man: Este Viejito. (Singing Your Way to English & Spanish Ser.). (ENG & SPA., Illus.). 32p. (J). (ps-2). 1997. pap. 9.95 incl. audio (*0-9632621-9-X*) High Haven Mus.

McClure, Marilyn, tr. see Barchas, Sarah.

McClure, Marilyn, tr. see Barchas, Sarah, ed.

McClure, Michael. Antechamber & Other Poems. LC 77-25300. 1978. pap. 2.95 (*0-8112-0682-3*, NDP455, Pub. by New Directions) Norton.

— Camping Wyoming. LC 99-93832. (Illus.). 375p. 1999. pap. 14.95 (*1-928786-00-6*) Wig Raf Pubg.

— Fragments of Perseus. LC 83-2134. 1983. pap. 6.25 (*0-8112-0867-2*, NDP554, Pub. by New Directions) Norton.

— General Gorgeous. 1982. pap. 5.25 (*0-8222-0436-3*) Dramatists Play.

— Gorf. LC 76-14932. (Illus.). 1976. pap. 1.95 (*0-8112-0612-2*, NDP416, Pub. by New Directions) Norton.

— Huge Dreams. LC 98-47393. 184p. 1999. pap. 16.95 (*0-14-058917-1*) Viking Penguin.

— Lie, Sit, Stand, Be Still. limited ed. (Illus.). 52p. 1995. text 5000.00 (*0-910457-37-9*) Arion Pr.

— The Mad Cub. 230p. 1996. pap. 10.95 (*1-56201-087-5*) FoxRock.

— McClure: Selected Poems. (J). 1999. pap. write for info. (*0-14-058705-5*) NAL.

— Rain Mirror: New Poems. LC 99-20709. 112p. 1999. pap. 13.95 (*0-8112-1426-5*, Pub. by New Directions) Norton.

— Rebel Lions. LC 90-48705. 128p. (Orig.). 1991. pap. 10.95 (*0-8112-1164-9*, NDP712, Pub. by New Directions) Norton.

— Simple Eyes & Other Poems. LC 93-46673. 144p. (Orig.). 1994. pap. 10.95 (*0-8112-1265-3*, NDP780, Pub. by New Directions) Norton.

— Touching the Edge: Dharma Devotions from the Hummingbird Sangha. LC 98-39898. 128p. (C). 1999. pap. 16.00 (*1-57062-440-2*, Pub. by Shambhala Pubns) Random.

McClure, Michael, jt. auth. see Murray, Terry.

McClure, Michael R. Acorn Alone. Robertson, Jon, ed. LC 94-6638. (Illus.). 32p. (J). 1994. 14.95 (*0-87604-326-0*, 401) ARE Pr.

McClure, Nancee. Clip & Copy Art: Creative Curriculum Cutouts. (Illus.). (J). (gr. k-8). 1989. 13.99 (*0-86653-487-3*, GA1086) Good Apple.

— Clip & Copy Art: Holidays, Seasons & Events. (Illus.). (J). (gr. k-8). 1989. 13.99 (*0-86653-486-5*, GA1085) Good Apple.

— Creative Egg Carton Crafts. (Early Childhood Paper Craft Ser.). (Illus.). 64p. (J). (ps-2). 1989. student ed. 7.99 (*0-86653-471-7*, GA1077) Good Apple.

— The Good Apple Book of Reproducible Patterns. 352p. 1991. 25.99 (*0-86653-622-1*, GA1341) Good Apple.

McClure, Nancee & Rhodes, Janis. Free & Inexpensive Arts & Crafts to Make & Use. 112p. (J). (gr. 2-6). 1987. student ed. 12.99 (*0-86653-387-7*, GA 1003) Good Apple.

McClure, Nancee, jt. auth. see Daniel, Becky.

McClure, Norman E., ed. Sixteenth-Century English Poetry. LC 73-139767. (Granger Index Reprint Ser.). 1977. 36.95 (*0-8369-6221-4*) Ayer.

McClure, Pat. Country Lovin' (Illus.). 40p. 1985. pap. 7.50 (*0-941284-29-8*) J Shaw Studio.

— Sweet, Soft, & Country. (Illus.). 32p. 1984. pap. 6.50 (*0-941284-25-5*) J Shaw Studio.

McClure, Patricia. And You Think You Have Problems: Teen Dilemmas. Bird, Tate, ed. LC 90-70582. (Illus.). 150p. (J). (gr. 8-9). 1990. 13.95 (*0-914127-73-X*) Univ Class.

— Getting to the Heart of It: Stories about My Friends & Me. 3rd ed. Bard, Tate, ed. (Illus.). 110p. (J). (gr. 4-6). 1985. 13.27 (*0-914127-99-3*) Univ Class.

McClure, Patricia & West Virginia Writers, Inc. Staff. Beyond the Magpie: A Selection of Winning Entries from Four Years - 1987, 1988, 1989, 1990 - of the West Virginia Writers, Inc. Annual Awards Competition. Carper, Helen, ed. (Illus.). 148p. (Orig.). 1991. pap. 9.40 (*0-941092-23-2*) Mtn St Pr.

McClure, Patricia S. Handbook for Elementary Counselors: How to Start a Program. (Illus.). 94p. 1993. pap. text 9.95 (*0-9660309-1-5*, 2) North Stream Pub.

McClure, Patrick V. Our Body . . . God's Temple: A Study of Nutrition from a Biblical Perspective. (Illus.). 224p. (Orig.). 1995. pap. text 12.95 (*0-9646792-0-5*) P McClure.

McClure, Paul. Early Marriages in Bath Co., KY: Bonds 1811-1850 & Returns 1811-1852. LC 94-178654. 209p. 1994. pap. text 31.00 (*1-55613-952-7*) Heritage Bk.

— The New Entrepreneur's Guidebook: Leading Your Venture to Business Success. Christopher, Bill, ed. LC 97-68248. (Management Library: No. 10). 96p. 1997. pap. 12.95 (*1-56052-441-3*) Crisp Pubns.

— Washington Information Directory. 1997. 148.61 (*0-87187-908-5*) Congr Quarterly.

McClure, Paul & Gardner, Will, eds. Federal Regulatory Directory. 8th ed. viii, 760p. 1997. pap. text 240.00 (*1-57979-241-3*) DIANE Pub.

McClure, Paul A. The Humorous Musings of a School Principal. LC 97-74592. (Illus.). 200p. 1997. pap. 12.95 (*0-942936-32-9*) Lincoln-Herndon Pr.

McClure, Paul L., jt. auth. see Philpott-Jones, Pamela.

***McClure, Paula.** The Mood Spa Weight-Loss Plan: You Can Now Control Your Weight, Stress & Moods. (Mood Spa System Ser.). 132p. 2000. pap. 19.95 (*0-9677527-0-1*) Mood Spa.

McClure, Peggy J. & Boyd, Arrie F. Basic Chemistry: An Introductory Approach - a Self-Teaching Textbook - Workbook. 640p. (C). 1994. pap. text, per. 65.95 (*0-8403-8849-7*) Kendall-Hunt.

***McClure, Rhonda R.** The Complete Idiot's Guide to Online Genealogy. (Complete Idiot's Guides (computers) Ser.). 352p. 1999. pap. 16.95 (*0-02-863635-X*) Macmillan.

McClure, Rhyder. Fast Access-Wordperfect Library. 320p. 1989. pap. 39.95 incl. disk (*0-685-28296-1*) P-H.

McClure, Robert, jt. auth. see Deneen, Sally.

McClure, Robert C., et al. Cat Anatomy: An Atlas, Text, & Dissection Guide. LC 73-3094. 248p. reprint ed. pap. 76.90 (*0-608-16683-9*, 205619000055) Bks Demand.

McClure, Robert D., jt. auth. see Fowler, Linda L.

McClure, Robert J. The Discovery of the North-West Passage by H.M.S. Investigator: 1850-54. Osborn, Sherard, ed. LC 74-5853. reprint ed. 32.50 (*0-404-11660-4*) AMS Pr.

***McClure, Ron.** Classic Wooden Yachts of the Northwest. (Illus.). 160p. 2000. pap. 22.95 (*1-57061-230-7*) Sasquatch Bks.

McClure, Ronale, ed. see Thomas, D.

***McClure, Ronnie C., et al.** Guide to Charitable Giving Strategies, Vol. 1. 1999. ring bd. 79.00 (*0-7646-0726-X*) Prctnrs Pub Co.

McClure, Ruth K. Coram's Children: The London Foundling Hospital in the Eighteenth Century. LC 80-21375. (Illus.). 322p. (C). 1981. 50.00 (*0-300-02465-7*) Yale U Pr.

McClure, Samuel S. My Autobiography. (American Biography Ser.). 266p. 1991. reprint ed. lib. bdg. 69.00 (*0-7812-8281-0*) Rprt Serv.

McClure, Sandy. Christie Whitman for the People: A Political Biography. LC 95-43777. (Illus.). 282p. 1996. 25.95 (*1-57392-014-2*) Prometheus Bks.

McClure, Sharon. Endless Inspiration: How to Have It Right Now. unabridged ed. (Illus.). xii, 80p. (Orig.). 1997. pap. 19.95 (*1-890214-03-5*) Images In Words.

McClure, Steve. Nippon Pop: Sounds from the Land of the Rising Sun. (Illus.). 162p. 1998. pap. 26.95 (*0-8048-2107-0*) Tuttle Pubng.

McClure, Stuart, jt. auth. see Scambray, Joel.

McClure, Susan. Companion Planting. LC 93-44918. (Rodale's Successful Organic Gardening Ser.). 1994. text 24.95 (*0-87596-615-2*) Rodale Pr Inc.

— Culinary Gardens: From Design to Palate. LC 97-11850. (Illus.). 224p. 1997. 37.95 (*1-55591-311-3*) Fulcrum Pub.

— The Free-Spirited Garden: Gorgeous Gardens That Flourish Naturally. LC 97-49846. (Illus.). 144p. 1999. pap. 18.95 (*0-8118-2112-9*) Chronicle Bks.

***McClure, Susan.** The Gardener's Guide to Water Management. LC 99-49810. (Illus.). 128p. 2000. pap. 11.95 (*0-7611-1778-4*) Workman Pub.

McClure, Susan. Midwest Gardener's Book of Lists. LC 97-47321. 1998. pap. text 17.95 (*0-87833-985-X*) Taylor Pub.

— Midwest Landscape Design. LC 98-43757. 1999. 34.95 (*0-87833-218-9*) Taylor Pub.

— Preserving Summer's Bounty: A Quick & Easy Guide to Freezing, Canning, Preserving, & Drying What You Grow. 384p. 1998. pap. 14.95 (*0-87596-979-8*) Rodale Pr Inc.

An Asterisk (*) at the beginning of an entry indicates that the title is appearing for the first time.

McClure, Susan & Burrell, C. Colston. 365 Down-to-Earth Gardening Hints & Tips LC 97-69450. 216 p. 1997. write for info. (0-7853-2436-4) Pubns Intl Ltd.

McClure, Susan A. Companion Planting. LC 93-44918. (Rodale's Successful Organic Gardening Ser.). 1994. pap. 14.95 (0-87596-616-0) Rodale Pr Inc.

— Easy-Care Perennial Gardens: Ready-to-Use Plans for Your Beds & Borders. LC 96-19375. (Illus.). 160p. 1997. text 27.95 (0-87596-778-7) Rodale Pr Inc.

— The Harvest Gardener: Growing for Maximum Yield, Prime Flavor, & Garden-Fresh Storage. Steege, Gwen, ed. LC 92-53951. (Illus.). 288p. 1993. 24.95 (0-88266-798-X, Garden Way Pub); pap. 17.95 (0-88266-797-1, Garden Way Pub) Storey Bks.

— The Herb Gardener: A Guide for All Seasons. 240p. 1996. 29.95 (0-88266-910-9) Storey Bks.

— The Herb Gardener: A Guide for All Seasons. (Illus.). 240p. 1997. pap. 21.95 (0-88266-873-0) Storey Bks.

— Smith & Hawken Seeds & Propagation. LC 97-5745. (Hands-On Gardener Ser.). (Illus.). 128p. 1997. pap. 10.95 (0-7611-0733-9, 10733) Workman Pub.

McClure, Susan A., ed. Preserving Summer's Bounty: A Quick & Easy Guide to Freezing, Canning, Preserving & Drying What You Grow. (Illus.). 372p. 1995. text 26.95 (0-87596-648-9) Rodale Pr Inc.

McClure, Susan A., text. Perennials. LC 92-45809. (Rodale's Successful Organic Gardening Ser.). (Illus.). 1993. pap. 14.95 (0-87596-560-1); text 24.95 (0-87596-559-8) Rodale Pr Inc.

McClure, Susan A. & Hynes, Erin. Low-Maintenance Landscaping. (Successful Organic Gardening Ser.). (Illus.). 160p. 1994. pap. 14.95 (0-87596-614-4); text 24.95 (0-87596-613-6) Rodale Pr Inc.

McClure, Susan A., et al. Cleveland Garden Handbook: Expert Local Advice on Growing a Beautiful Lawn & Garden in Northeast Ohio. 2nd rev. ed. (Illus.). 264p. 1995. pap. 12.95 (1-886228-00-0) Gray & Co Pubs.

McClure, Susan A., jt. auth. see Buscher, Fred K.

McClure, Teyber. Casebook in Child & Adolescent Psychopathology. (Psychology Ser.). 2000. pap. text 25.00 (0-534-52940-2) Brooks-Cole.

McClure, Thomas A., ed. see Lipinsky, Edward S.

McClure, Tony Mack. Cherokee Proud: A Guide for Tracing & Honoring Your Cherokee Ancestors. 2nd ed. 336p. 1999. 29.95 (0-9655722-3-4); pap. 22.95 (0-9655722-2-6) Chu Nan Nee.
Greatest aid yet to either confirm or dispel those old family stories about great grandma being a Cherokee Indian. Includes comprehensive listings & sources of original data for all Cherokee census rolls dating back to 1817 & explanations of their contents. Lists scores of bibliographical sources which include references to Cherokee surnames & addresses of all archives known to house important historical records pertaining to the cherokee people. Detailed information on recognition & enrollment requirements for all individual in all federal & state recognized Cherokee tribes, as well as important ways to honor Cherokee ancestors. Traditional dress illustrations & brief Cherokee history with maps. This is the "bible" for anyone attempting to establish their Cherokee ancestry. To order: Chu-Nan-Nee Books, P.O. Box 127, Somerville, TN 38068. 901-465-9426. www.cherokeeproud.com. ***Publisher Paid Annotation.***

McClure, Vimala. The Path of Parenting: Twelve Principles to Guide You on Your Journey of Parenthood. LC 99-22342. 272p. 1999. pap. 14.00 (1-57731-078-0, Pub. by New Wrld Lib) Publishers Group.

— The Tao of Motherhood. 2nd rev. ed. LC 96-47177. (Illus.). 176p. 1997. pap. 12.95 (1-57731-014-4) New Wrld Lib.

— A Woman's Guide to Tantra Yoga. 2nd ed. LC 96-54836. Orig. Title: Some Still Want the Moon: A Woman's Guide to Tantra Yoga. (Illus.). 240p. 1997. pap. 14.00 (1-57731-017-9) New Wrld Lib.

***McClure, Vimala Schneider.** Infant Massage: A Handbook for Loving Parents. 3rd rev. ed. LC 00-39754. 2000. pap. 14.95 (0-553-38056-7) Bantam.

McClure, W., jt. auth. see Wildermuth, K.

McClure, W. F. Near-Infrared Spectroscopy. 350p. 1997. text. write for info. incl. disk (0-471-18613-9) Wiley.

McClure, W. Fred. Near-Infrared Spectrometry: Learning the Fundamentals. 350p. 1996. 115.00 (1-56081-690-2, Wiley-VCH) Wiley.

McClure, W. K. Italy in North Africa. 434p. 1986. 350.00 (0-7855-3023-1, Pub. by Darf Pubs Ltd) St Mut.

— Italy in North Africa. 434p. (C). 1990. 140.00 (1-85077-092-1, Pub. by Darf Pubs Ltd) St Mut.

McClure, Wallace. International Executive Agreements: Democratic Procedure under the Constitution of the United States. LC 41-10428. reprint ed. 34.50 (0-404-04106-X) AMS Pr.

McClure, Wallace M. New American Commercial Policy As Evidenced by Section 317 of the Tariff Act of 1922. LC 70-82240. (Columbia University. Studies in the Social Sciences: No. 255). reprint ed. 37.50 (0-404-51255-0) AMS Pr.

***McClurg, Sue.** Water & the Shaping of California. (Illus.). 176p. 2000. pap. 35.00 (1-890771-33-3) Heyday Bks.

McClurg, Sue, ed. see Mayer, Jim.

McClurg, Bob. Mustang, the Next Generation. LC 94-70071. (Illus.). 208p. 1994. 39.95 (0-9640895-0-5) Bolder Ventures.

***McClurg, David R.** Adventure of Caving: A Practical Guide for Advanced & Beginning Cavers. (Orig.). 1998. 20.00 (0-937757-01-2) D & J Pr TX.

***McClurg, Patricia, ed.** Prairie to Mountain Explorer User's Guide. 64p. 1999. pap. text, teacher ed. 55.00 incl. cd-rom (0-941570-19-3) U of Wyoming.

McClurg, R. S. The Rummager's Handbook: Finding, Buying, Cleaning, Fixing, Using & Selling Secondhand Treasures. LC 94-47930. (Illus.). 160p. 1995. pap. 12.95 (0-88266-894-3, Storey Pub) Storey Bks.

McClurg, Sue. The American River. (Layperson's Guide Ser.). (Illus.). 20p. 1995. pap. 5.00 (1-893246-52-3) Water Educ.

McClurg, Sue, ed. see Blanton, Melissa.

McClurg, Sue, ed. see Brickson, Betty.

McClurg, Sue, ed. see Brickson, Betty, et al.

McClurg, Sue, ed. see Klionsky, Lisa C.

McClurg, Sue, ed. see Mahoney, Laura.

McClurg, Sue, ed. see Mayer, Jim.

McClurg, Sue, ed. see McCarthy, Elizabeth.

McClurg, Sue, ed. see Newcom, Josh.

McClurg, Sue, ed. see Totten, Glenn.

McClurken, James. Fish in the Lakes, Wild Rice & Game in Abundance: Testimony on Behalf of Mille Lacs Ojibwe Hu. LC 99-88247. 2000. 34.95 (0-87013-492-2) Mich St U Pr.

McClurken, James M. Gah-Baeh-Jhagwah-Buk, the Way It Happened: A Visual Culture History of the Little Traverse Bay Bands of Odawa. Caltrider, Suzanne, ed. (Illus.). 130p. (Orig.). 1991. 22.95 (0-944311-06-7); pap. 16.95 (0-944311-05-9) MSU Museum.

McCluskey. Advising Managing & Operating. 276p. (C). 1998. pap. text 39.80 (0-536-01473-6) Pearson Custom.

— Criminal Appeals. 286p. 1993. pap. 49.00 (0-406-12134-6, MICHIE) LEXIS Pub.

McCluskey, ed. Success Broadcast Station Management. 356p. 1999. pap. text 33.00 (0-536-02649-1) P-H.

***McCluskey, Audrey Thomas.** Mary McLeod Bethune: Building A Better World. LC 99-43292. 1999. 39.95 (0-253-33626-0) Ind U Pr.

McCluskey, F. Patrick, et al. High Temperature Electronics. LC 96-36956. 352p. 1996. boxed set 89.95 (0-8493-9623-9) CRC Pr.

McCluskey, James, ed. Antigen Processing - Recognition. 248p. 1991. lib. bdg. 195.00 (0-8493-6932-0, RB52) CRC Pr.

***McCluskey, James J.** Starting a Student Non Commerical Radio Station. LC 99-163994. 256p. (C). 1998. text 34.50 (0-536-01067-6) Pearson Custom.

McCluskey, John A., Jr., ed. The City of Refuge: The Collected Stories of Rudolph Fisher. 240p. 1991. pap. 16.95 (0-8262-0786-3) U of Mo Pr.

McCluskey, John A., ed. see Ceasor, Frank, Sr. & Gaines, Edith M.

McCluskey, John A., Jr., jt. ed. see Johnson, Charles.

McCluskey, John A., ed. see Johnston, Brenda A. & Pruitt, Pamela.

McCluskey, John A., ed. see Johnston, Brenda A., et al.

McCluskey, John A., ed. see Pruitt, Pamela, et al.

McCluskey, John A., ed. see Shepard, Mary L. & Gaines, Edith M.

McCluskey, John A., ed. see Shepard, Mary, et al.

***McCluskey, John William.** The Complete Book of Wedding Toasts: Hundreds of Toasts for the Ceremony & All the Events That Lead up to It. Frevert, Lois E., ed. 138p. 2000. pap. 15.00 (0-9677332-0-0) Arden Bk.

McCluskey, Karen C., ed. Notes from a Traveling Childhood: Readings for Internationally Mobile Parents & Children. (Illus.). x, 122p. (Orig.). 1994. pap. 5.95 (0-9658538-1-0) Foreign Serv Youth.

McCluskey, Kathleen A. Reverberations: Sound & Structure in the Novels of Virginia Woolf. LC 85-21015. (Studies in Modern Literature: No. 54). (Illus.). 156p. reprint ed. pap. 48.40 (0-8357-1710-0, 207050800097) Bks Demand.

McCluskey, Lord. Appeals in Scottish Criminal Cases. 1991. pap. 49.00 (0-406-12135-4, UK, MICHIE) LEXIS Pub.

McCluskey, Martha T., jt. ed. see Fineman, Martha A.

McCluskey, Patrick, jt. auth. see Pecht, Michael G.

McCluskey, Robert T. & Andres, Giuseppe A., eds. Immunologically Mediated Renal Diseases: Criteria for Diagnosis & Treatment. LC 78-10283. (Immunology Ser.: No. 10). 123p. reprint ed. pap. 38.20 (0-7837-0792-4, 204110600019) Bks Demand.

McCluskey, Stephen C. Astronomies & Cultures in Early Medieval Europe. LC 97-6557. (Illus.). 250p. (C). 1998. text 54.95 (0-521-58361-6) Cambridge U Pr.

***McCluskey, Stephen C.** Astronomies & Cultures in Early Medieval Europe. (Illus.). 252p. (C). 2000. pap. write for info. (0-521-77852-2) Cambridge U Pr.

McCluskey, William, ed. Property Tax: An International Comparative Review. 2nd ed. LC HJ4113.P758 1999. 482p. 1999. text 86.95 (1-85972-517-1) Ashgate Pub Co.

McCluskey, William J. Comparative Property Tax Systems. 196p. 1991. text 82.95 (1-85628-133-7, Pub. by Avebry) Ashgate Pub Co.

McCluskey, William J. & Adair, Alistair S. Computer Assisted Mass Appraisal: An International Review of Comparative Property Tax Systems. LC 97-71714. (Illus.). 384p. 1997. text 83.95 (1-85972-089-7, Pub. by Ashgate Pub) Ashgate Pub Co.

McCluskie, Tom. Anatomy of the Titanic. LC 98-36577. (Illus.). 144p. 1998. 15.98 (1-57145-160-9, Thunder Bay) Advantage Pubs.

McCluskie, Tom, et al. Titanic & Her Sisters: Olympic & Britannic. LC 99-29273. (Illus.). 512p. 1999. 24.98 (1-57145-175-7, Thunder Bay) Advantage Pubs.

McCluskoy, Jim, jt. auth. see Bradley, John.

McClusky, Mark, ed. see Ruzich, Christian.

McClusky, Pamela. African Art: From Crocodiles to Convertibles in the Collection of the Seattle Art Museum. LC 87-61752. (Illus.). 32p. 1987. pap. 4.95 (0-932216-24-2) Seattle Art.

— Praise Poems: The Katherine White Collection. LC 83-51840. (Illus.). 122p. 1984. 34.95 (0-932216-16-1); pap. 22.95 (0-932216-15-3) Seattle Art.

— Praise Poems: The Katherine White Collection. LC 83-51840. (Illus.). xiv, 122p. 1993. pap. 20.00 (0-226-73446-3, 73446-3) U Ch Pr.

— Praise Poems: The Katherine White Collection. LC 83-51840. (Illus.). xiv, 134p. 1997. 54.00 (0-226-73445-5, 73445-5) U Ch Pr.

McClusky, William & Moss, Peter. The Uniform Business Rate: A Practical Guide. 180p. 1992. 66.00 (1-85190-149-3, Pub. by Tolley Pubng) St Mut.

***McClutcheon, George Barr.** Brewster's Millions. LC 99-30003. 1999. pap. text 12.95 (0-253-21349-5) Ind U Pr.

McClyde, James O., ed. Not-for-Profit-Hospitals: Conversion Issues Prompt Increased State Oversight. 51p. (C). 1999. reprint ed. pap. text 20.00 (0-7881-7719-2) DIANE Pub.

McClymer. American Stories, Vol. 2. LC 98-89230. (C). 1998. pap. 21.00 (0-15-507941-7, Pub. by Harcourt Coll Pubs) Harcourt.

McClymer, John F. American Stories. (C). 1997. pap. text 21.00 (0-15-503818-4, Pub. by Harcourt Coll Pubs) Harcourt.

— War & Welfare: Social Engineering in America, 1890-1925, 84. LC 79-54060. (Contributions in American History Ser.: No. 84). 248p. 1980. 59.95 (0-313-21129-9, MWW/, Greenwood Pr) Greenwood.

McClymer, John F., jt. auth. see Estus, Charles W., Sr.

***McClymer, Kelly.** Fairy Tale Bride. (Once Upon a Wedding Ser.). 2000. mass mkt. 5.50 (0-8217-6699-6, Zebra Kensgtn) Kensgtn Pub Corp.

McClymond, Michael J. Encounters with God: An Approach to the Theology of Jonathan Edwards. LC 97-9358. (Religion in America Ser.). 208p. 1998. text 39.95 (0-19-511822-7) OUP.

McClymond, Michael J., jt. ed. see Freedman, David Noel.

McClymonds, Marita P., jt. ed. see Bauman, Thomas.

McClymonds, Marita P., ed. see Cannabich, Christian.

***McClymont, David & Armstrong, Mark.** Lonely Planet Melbourne. 3rd ed. (Travel Guides Ser.). (Illus.). 200p. 2000. pap. 14.95 (1-86450-124-3) Lonely Planet.

McClymont, Diane. Books. Young, Richard, ed. LC 91-20532. (First Technology Library). (Illus.). 32p. (J). (gr. 3-5). 1991. lib. bdg. 15.93 (1-56074-010-8) Garrett Ed Corp.

— Water. Young, Richard, ed. LC 91-20536. (First Technology Library). (Illus.). 32p. (J). (gr. 3-5). 1991. lib. bdg. 15.93 (1-56074-006-X) Garrett Ed Corp.

***McClymont, Mary & Golub, Stephen.** Many Roads to Justice: The Law Related Work of Ford Foundation Grantees Around the World. LC 99-88905. 2000. write for info. (0-916584-54-2) Ford Found.

McClymont, Mary, et al. Health Visiting & the Elderly People. 2nd ed. (Illus.). 340p. 1991. pap. text 42.00 (0-443-04228-4) Church.

McClynomt, W. G. The Exploration of New Zealand. LC 86-318. (Illus.). 136p. 1986. reprint ed. lib. bdg. 55.00 (0-313-25167-3, MCEX, Greenwood Pr) Greenwood.

McCoard, Barbara, jt. auth. see Bradway, Katherine.

***McCobb, Paul.** Fifties Furniture by Paul Mccobb. (Illus.). 112p. 2000. 39.95 (0-7643-1139-5) Schiffer.

McCoid, Catherine H. Carrying Capacities of Nation-States. LC 84-152784. (Cross-Cultural Research Ser.). 1984. 22.00 (0-317-07533-0) HRAFP.

McCoin, John M. Adult Foster Homes: Their Managers & Residents. LC 82-6083. 232p. 1983. 35.95 (0-89885-087-8, Kluwer Acad Hman Sci) Kluwer Academic.

McCold, Paul, ed. Restorative Justice: An Annotated Bibliography--1997. LC 97-210419. 185p. (Orig.). 1997. text 20.00 (1-881798-11-9, Criminal Justice) Willow Tree NY.

McCold, Sheridan. Hollywood Lovers: The Taunchy Revelations of Tinseltown's Rich, Famous & Beautiful People. (Illus.). 224p. 1998. pap. 22.95 (0-7528-1035-9, Pub. by Orion Pubng Grp) Trafalgar.

McCole, C. John. Lucifer at Large. LC 68-16949. (Essay Index Reprint Ser.). 1977. reprint ed. 19.95 (0-8369-0643-8) Ayer.

— Lucifer at Large. LC 68-57457. (Studies in Fiction: No. 34). 1969. reprint ed. lib. bdg. 75.00 (0-8383-0595-4) M S G Haskell Hse.

McCole, John. Walter Benjamin & the Antinomies of Tradition. LC 92-21431. 352p. 1993. text 49.95 (0-8014-2465-8); pap. text 19.95 (0-8014-9711-6) Cornell U Pr.

McColgan, Aileen. The Case for Taking the Date Out of Rape. (Pandora Soap Box Ser.). 128p. 1996. pap. 11.95 (0-04-440977-X, Pub. by Rivers Oram) NYU Pr.

— Just Wages for Women. LC 97-12929. (Oxford Monographs on Labour Law). (Illus.). 486p. 1998. text 89.00 (0-19-826588-3) OUP.

***McColgan, Aileen.** Women under the Law: The False Promise of Human Rights. 315p. 2000. pap. 31.50 (0-582-29451-7, Pub. by Addison-Wesley) Gaunt.

McColgan, Aileen, ed. The Future of Labour Law. LC 95-52249. 320p. (C). 1996. text 110.00 (1-85567-405-X) Bks Intl VA.

McColgan, Kristin P. & Durham, Charles W., eds. Arenas of Conflict: Milton & the Unfettered Mind. LC 96-31256. 296p. 1997. 44.50 (0-945636-93-8) Susquehanna U Pr.

McColgan, Kristin P., jt. ed. see Durham, Charles W.

***McColgan, M. L.** 101 Superstitions of Golf. (Illus.). 103p. 2000. write for info. (0-9666893-1-3) Ultra Clb Clean.

McColgan, Michael. Open Your Hearts. LC 95-72818. 126p. (Orig.). 1996. pap. text 5.95 (1-882972-62-7, 3479) Queenship Pub.

McColgan, Mike L. 101 Sins of Golf. (Illus.). 101p. 1998. write for info. (0-9666893-0-5) Ultra Clb Clean.

McColl, Amy, ed. Images in Libraries, Museums & Archives. 119p. 1995. pap. text 18.00 (2-88449-221-6) Gordon & Breach.

McColl, Arch, III & McColloch, Mike. Erisman's Reversible Errors in Texas Criminal Cases, 2 vols., Vols. 1 & 2. 3rd ed. 1981. ring bd. 185.00 (1-878337-16-5) Knowles Pub Inc.

McColl, Duncan. The Magic of Mind Power: Awareness Techniques for the Creative Mind. 177p. 1999. reprint ed. pap. 14.50 (1-899836-29-2, Pub. by Crown Hse) LPC Group.

McColl, Duncan. Precision Therapy: A Professional Manual of Fast & Effective Hypnoanalysis Techniques. 224p. 1995. pap. text 81.95 (1-85398-069-2, Pub. by Ashgrove Pr) Words Distrib.

McColl, Duncan. Precision Therapy: A Professional Manual of Fast & Effective Hypnoanalysis Techniques. 270p. 1998. pap. 25.00 (1-899836-18-7, Pub. by Crown Hse) LPC Group.

***McColl, G.** England: The Alf Ramsey Years. 1998. pap. text 35.00 (0-233-99331-2, Pub. by Andre Deutsch) Trafalgar.

— Scotland in the World Cup. 1998. text 35.00 (0-233-99330-4) Andre Deutsch.

McColl, J., jt. ed. see Bowman, A.

***McColl, John Hope.** Multivariate Probability & Stochastic Processes. (Arnold Texts in Statistics). (Illus.). 288p. 2000. pap. text 34.95 (0-340-71996-6) OUP.

***McColl, Mary Ann.** Introduction to Disability & Handicap. 204p. 1998. pap. 49.75 (0-7020-2221-7) W B Saunders.

McColl, Michael W. The Frugal Romantic: Affordable Romantic Getaways in Northern California. (Illus.). 250p. (Orig.). Date not set. pap. 12.95 (0-9633512-2-2) Insider Pubns.

— The Worldwide Guide to Cheap Airfares: How to Travel the World Without Breaking the Bank. 6th rev. ed. LC 94-77556. (Illus.). 250p. 1996. pap. 14.95 (0-9633512-3-0) Insider Pubns.

McColl, Nancy & Paskowitz, Karen. Bilingual ABC's: A Spanish-English Alphabet Book. (ENG & SPA.). 112p. (J). (gr. k-1). 11.99 (0-86653-904-2, FE0904) Fearon Teacher Aids.

McColl, Sandra. Music Criticism in Vienna, 1896-1897: Critically Moving Forms. (Oxford Monographs on Music). (Illus.). 260p. 1996. text 69.00 (0-19-816564-1) OUP.

McCollam, C. Harold. The Brick & Tile Industry in Stark County, 1809-1976: A History. LC 76-17281. 351p. reprint ed. pap. 108.90 (0-8357-7400-7, 202492500038) Bks Demand.

McCollam, Dan, jt. auth. see Betts, Keith.

McCollam, Pat, jt. auth. see Brownstead, Frank.

McCollester, Charles J., ed. Fighter with a Heart: Writings of Charles Owen Rice, Pittsburgh Labor Priest. (Illus.). 242p. 1996. pap. 19.95 (0-8229-5619-5); text 49.95 (0-8229-3966-5) U of Pittsburgh Pr.

***McColley.** Pecking Order. LC 93-17768. 224p. (YA). (gr. 12 up). 2000. pap. 4.95 (0-06-440516-8) HarpC Child Bks.

McColley. A Perfect Game. 1996. pap. 3.99 (0-689-80896-8) S&S Bks Yung.

— Winners & Losers. (J). 1998. 16.00 (0-689-80270-6) Aladdin.

McColley, Diane K. A Gust for Paradise: Milton's Eden & the Visual Arts. LC 92-13654. (Illus.). 356p. 1993. text 49.95 (0-252-01828-1) U of Ill Pr.

— Poetry & Music in Seventeenth-Century England. LC 97 7581. (Illus.). 330p. (C). 1998. text 59.95 (0-521-59363-8) Cambridge U Pr.

McColley, Grant. Milton's Technique of Source Adaptation. 50p. (C). 1938. reprint ed. pap. 39.95 (0-8383-0053-7) M S G Haskell Hse.

McColley, Grant, tr. see Campanella, Tommaso.

***McColley, Kevin.** The Other Side. LC 00-29161. 384p. 2000. 24.00 (0-684-85762-6) S&S Trade.

McColley, Kevin. Praying to a Laughing God: A Novel. LC 97-48720. 336p. 1998. 23.50 (0-684-83761-7) S&S Trade.

— Switch. LC 96-30917. 240p. (J). 1997. mass mkt. 4.50 (0-689-81527-1) Atheneum Yung Read.

— Switch. LC 96-30917. 224p. (J). (gr. 7 up). 1997. 16.00 (0-689-81122-5) S&S Childrens.

— Switch, a Mystery. LC 96-30917. 1997. 9.60 (0-606-11962-0, Pub. by Turtleback) Demco.

McColley, P. D., jt. auth. see Lopushinsky, Cochran W.

McCollister, John. The Bucs: The Story of the Pittsburgh Pirates. LC 97-53243. (Illus.). 240p. 1998. 39.95 (1-886110-40-9) Addax Pubng.

***McCollister, John.** The Tigers & Their Den: The Official Story of the Detroit Tigers. LC 99-27437. (Illus.). 240p. 1999. 39.95 (1-886110-81-6, Pub. by Addax Pubng) Midpt Trade.

McCollister, John C. The Christian Book of Why. 360p. 1986. pap. 16.95 (0-8246-0317-6) Jonathan David.

— The Christian Book of Why. LC 99-29269. 2000. 7.99 (0-517-20582-3) Random Hse Value.

McColloch, Mark & Gilmore, Peter, afterword by. Them & Us. 1995. pap. 6.00 (0-916180-20-4) United Elec R&M.

McColloch, Mark D. White Collar Workers in Transition: The Boom Years, 1940-1970, 15. LC 83-5546. (Contributions in Labor History Ser.: No. 15). 193p. 1983. 49.95 (0-313-23785-9, MCW/, Greenwood Pr) Greenwood.

McColloch, Mark D., jt. auth. see Filippelli, Ronald L.

M

McColloch, Mike, jt. auth. see McColl, Arch, III.
McCollom, Marion, jt. ed. see Gillette, Jonathon.
McCollough. Dermabrasion & Chemical Peel. 85.00 (*0-86577-284-3*) Thieme Med Pubs.
McCollough, et al. Native Peoples of the Great Plains. 240p. (C). 1997. pap. text 70.95 (*0-7872-3801-5*, 41380101) Kendall-Hunt.
McCollough, Allison P. A Gathering of Angels: A Through Z. LC 97-76031. (Illus.). 32p. 1998. pap. 12.95 (*0-9661492-0-3*) Oaks Pub Co.
— Southern XYZ's: Alabama Edition. LC 97-75765. (Illus.). 34p. 1998. pap. 12.95 (*0-9661492-1-1*) Oaks Pub Co.
McCollough, C. R., jt. ed. see Faulkner, Charles H.
***McCollough, Charles.** Faith Made Visible: Shaping the Human Spirit in Sculpture & Word. 2000. pap. 22.95 (*0-8298-1378-0*) Pilgrim OH.
***McCollough, David.** Wars of the Irish Kings: A Thousand Years of Struggle, from the Age of Myth Through the Reign of Queen Elizabeth I. (Illus.). 400p. 2000. 35.00 (*0-8129-3233-1*) Crown Pub Group.
McCollough, Dennis M., jt. auth. see Gershman, Karen.
McCollough, E. Gaylon. Before & after. 496p. 1994. 19.95 (*0-9637600-0-9*); pap. 14.95 (*0-9637600-1-7*) McCollough Pub.
— Nasal Plastic Surgery. LC 93-26436. (Illus.). 400p. 1994. text 152.00 (*0-7216-4067-2*, W B Saunders Co) Harcrt Hlth Sci Grp.
McCollough, Jeannie. Ezra: Leader of Moral Restoration. 88p. 1999. pap. 12.99 (*0-8341-1801-7*) Beacon Hill.
McCollough, Jennifer. Compliance Sourcebook: A Manual for Implementing & Managing the Compliance Program. 100p. (C). 1996. 203.00 (*0-89982-437-4*) Am Bankers.
McCollough, L. E. Plays of the Wild West: Grades K-3. LC 97-14729. (Plays for Young Actors Ser.: No. 1). 160p. (J). (gr. 1-5). 1997. pap. 14.95 (*1-57525-104-3*) Smith & Kraus.
McCollough, Thomas E. The Moral Imagination & Public Life: Raising the Ethical Question. LC 91-6821. (Chatham House Studies in Political Thinking). 192p. (C). 1991. pap. text 19.95 (*0-934540-85-3*, Chatham House Pub) Seven Bridges.
McCollum, Allan. Allan McCollum. (Illus.). 68p. 1988. 35.00 (*3-88375-100-6*, Pub. by Walther Konig) Dist Art Pubs.
McCollum, Allan & Lawson, Thomas. Allan McCollum. (Illus.). 64p. 1993. pap. 25.00 (*0-932183-14-X*) ART Pr NY.
McCollum, Ann, jt. auth. see Calder, Judith.
McCollum, Audrey. Two Women, Two Worlds: Friendship Swept by Winds of Change. LC 98-93628. (Illus.). 224p. 1999. pap. 16.00 (*0-9666896-0-7*) Hillwinds Pr.
McCollum, Audrey T. The Trauma of Moving: Psychological Issues for Women. (Library of Social Research: Vol. 182). 312p. (C). 1990. text 59.95 (*0-8039-3699-0*); pap. text 26.00 (*0-8039-3700-8*) Sage.
McCollum, Bill, ed. FBI Murder Investigation in Haiti: Hearing Before the Committee on the Judiciary, U. S. House of Representatives. 111p. (C). 1998. pap. text 35.00 (*0-7881-7019-8*) DIANE Pub.
***McCollum, Bill, ed.** Federal Prison Industries, Incorporated: Congressional Hearings. (Illus.). 165p. 2000. pap. text 25.00 (*0-7567-0060-4*) DIANE Pub.
McCollum, Bill, ed. Nature, Extent, & Proliferation of Federal Law Enforcement: Hearing Before the Committee on the Judiciary, U. S. House of Representatives. (Illus.). 199p. 1998. reprint ed. pap. text 40.00 (*0-7881-4234-8*) DIANE Pub.
— Violent Youth Predator Act of 1996 & Balanced Juvenile Justice & Crime Prevention Act of 1996. 385p. 1999. reprint ed. pap. text 40.00 (*0-7881-8065-7*) DIANE Pub.
McCollum, Duncan O. Japanese Rifles of World War II. (Illus.). 64p. (Orig.). 1996. pap. 18.95 (*1-880677-11-3*) Excalibur AZ.
***McCollum, Eric E. & Trepper, Terry S.** Family Solutions for Substance Abuse: Clinical & Counseling Approaches. LC 00-40765. 2000. write for info. (*0-7890-0623-5*, Haworth Clinical) Haworth Pr.
McCollum, Harriet L. What Makes a Master? 114p. 1996. reprint ed. spiral bd. 14.00 (*0-7873-0596-0*) Hlth Research.
— What Makes a Master? Being & Outline of the Law of Life & the Process of Its Development & Unfoldment Towards Self Conscious Awareness & Mastery of Destiny (1932) 114p. 1996. reprint ed. pap. 12.95 (*1-56459-841-1*) Kessinger Pub.
McCollum, James K. Is Communism Dead Forever? LC 98-39211. 180p. 1998. 42.00 (*0-7618-1259-8*); pap. 24.50 (*0-7618-1260-1*) U Pr of Amer.
McCollum, Jerry, et al. Georgia Wildlife Viewing Guide. LC 96-775. (Illus.). 132p. (Orig.). 1996. pap. 12.95 (*0-9644522-1-9*) GA Wildlife Fed.
McCollum, John H., jt. ed. see Holsoe, Svend E.
McCollum, Malcolm, jt. auth. see McCollum, Nancy.
McCollum, Michael. Thunderstrike! A Novel. LC 98-85972. 325p. 1998. 25.00 (*0-7388-0010-4*); pap. 15.00 (*0-7388-0033-3*) Xlibris Corp.
McCollum, Michele D., et al, eds. Proceedings of the Third International Workshop on Transducers for Sonics & Ultrasonics. LC 92-62615. 420p. 1992. text 119.95 (*0-87762-993-5*) Technomic.
McCollum, Nancy & McCollum, Malcolm. Humanities II SG. 134p. (C). 1996. pap. text, student ed., per. 17.95 (*0-7872-2173-2*, 41217301) Kendall-Hunt.
McCollum, Oscar, Jr. Marble Vol. 1: A Town Built on Dreams. (Illus.). 352p. 1992. 42.00 (*0-913582-55-7*, 0248) Sundance.
— Marble Vol. 2: A Town Built on Dreams. (Illus.). 352p. 1993. 42.00 (*0-913582-56-5*, 0249) Sundance.
***McCollum, Pam.** Lessons Learned, Lessons Shared: Texas Immigrant Education Collaborative. 60p. 1999. pap. 24.95 (*1-878550-66-7*) Inter Dev Res Assn.
McCollum, Rocky. The Prime Mover, Opus III: The String Model Universe Where Strings Are Everything. 2nd ed. (Illus.). 500p. 1988. reprint ed. pap. 10.00 (*0-317-91063-9*) KIVA Pub.
— The Prime Mover, Opus III: The String Model Universe, Where Strings Are Everything. 3rd ed. (Illus.). 500p. (C). 1988. reprint ed. pap. 10.00 (*0-317-91116-3*) KIVA Pub.
McCollum, Rocky & Slick, Gandalf. The Higher Self. (Illus.). 170p. (Orig.). 1988. pap. 8.95 (*0-317-91064-7*) KIVA Pub.
McCollum, Sean. Australia. LC 97-18774. (Globe-Trotter's Club Ser.). 48p. (J). (gr. 1-4). 1999. lib. bdg. 22.60 (*1-57505-104-4*, Carolrhoda) Lerner Pub.
— Kenya. LC 97-16447. (Globe-Trotters Club Ser.). 48p. (J). (gr. 3-5). 1999. lib. bdg. 22.60 (*1-57505-105-2*, Carolrhoda) Lerner Pub.
Mccollum, Sean. Poland. LC 98-8831. (Globe-Trotters Club Ser.). 48p. (J). (gr. 3-5). 1999. lib. bdg. 22.60 (*1-57505-106-0*, Carolrhoda) Lerner Pub.
McCollum, Sean. Poland. (Ticket to . . . Ser.). (Illus.). 48p. (J). (gr. 1-3). 1999. lib. bdg. 16.95 (*1-57505-131-1*) Lerner Pub.
— A Ticket to Australia. LC 98-22573. 48p. (J). (gr. k-2). 1999. lib. bdg. 22.60 (*1-57505-129-X*, Carolrhoda) Lerner Pub.
— A Ticket to Kenya. LC 98-36632. 48p. (J). (gr. k-2). 1999. lib. bdg. 22.60 (*1-57505-130-3*, Carolrhoda) Lerner Pub.
McCollum, Susan & Risley, Teena. Plant Basics: A Manual for the Care of Indoor Plants. 86p. 1994. pap. 14.95 (*0-9644264-0-4*) McCollum Risley.
McCollum, Thomas C., 3rd. Tainted Blood: A Frightening Possibility. 368p. 1996. 25.00 (*1-880404-11-7*, Shoji Bks) Bkwrights.
McCollum, Vashti C. One Woman's Fight. 4th ed. (Illus.). 240p. 1993. reprint ed. pap. 15.00 (*1-877733-08-3*) Freedom Rel Found.
McColly, Michael. Narratives of ESL Students: The World Is Round. 1996. mass mkt. write for info. (*0-614-19906-9*) R Dean Pr.
McColm, I. J. Ceramic Hardness. (Illus.). 336p. (C). 1989. 95.00 (*0-306-43287-0*, Plenum Trade) Perseus Pubng.
— Dictionary of Ceramic Science & Engineering. 2nd ed. (Illus.). 396p. (C). 1994. 85.00 (*0-306-44542-5*, Plenum Trade) Perseus Pubng.
McColm, I. J. & Clark, N. J. The Forming, Shaping & Working of High-Performance Ceramics. 320p. 1988. mass mkt. 151.95 (*0-412-01271-5*, Chap & Hall NY) Chapman & Hall.
McColm, Michelle. Adoption Reunions: A Book for Adoptees, Birthparents & Adoptive Families. 175p. (Orig.). 1993. pap. 15.95 (*0-929005-41-4*, Pub. by Sec Story Pr) LPC InBook.
McColm, R. Bruce. El Salvador: Peaceful Revolution or Armed Struggle? (Perspectives on Freedom Ser.: No. 1). (Illus.). 47p. 1982. pap. 9.50 (*0-932088-03-1*) Freedom Hse.
— To License a Journalist? A Landmark Decision in the Schmidt Case. LC 86-18407. 1986. 13.50 (*0-932088-09-0*) Freedom Hse.
McColm, R. Bruce, ed. Freedom in the World: Political Rights & Civil Liberties, 1989-1990. (Illus.). 336p. (C). 1990. pap. text 23.25 (*0-932088-56-2*) Freedom Hse.
McColm, R. Bruce, ed. see Chalidze, Valerii & Schifter, Richard.
***McColman, Carl.** The Aspiring Mystic: Practical Steps for Spiritual Seekers. 192p. 2000. pap. 9.95 (*1-58062-416-2*) Adams Media.
— Embracing Jesus & the Goddess: A Radical Call for Spiritual Sanity. 2000. 21.95 (*1-86204-849-5*) Element MA.
McColman, Carl. Spirituality: Where Body & Soul Encounter the Sacred. 256p. (Orig.). 1997. pap. 14.95 (*1-880823-16-0*) N Star Pubns.
McColman, John, ed. Scanner Master Metro D. C.-Virginia Guide. 3rd ed. (Frequency Guide Ser.: No. 6). (Illus.). 350p. 1991. 29.95 (*0-685-51888-4*) Scanner Master.
McColman, John, jt. auth. see Burke, Lynne.
***McComac, Jack.** Design of Reinforced Concrete. 4th ed. LC 97-37841. (Illus.). 726p. (C). 1998. text 76.95 (*0-321-01462-6*) Addson-Wesley Educ.
McComas, Alan J. Skeletal Muscle: Form & Function. LC 95-24525. (Illus.). 416p. 1996. text 59.00 (*0-87322-780-8*, BMCC0780) Human Kinetics.
McComas, Annette P. Kansas & Me: Memories of a Jewish Childhood. Kravetz, Nathan, ed. LC 94-40787. (Studies in Judaica & the Holocaust: No. 10). 152p. 1995. pap. 19.00 (*0-8095-1408-7*) Millefleurs.
McComas, Dan, jt. auth. see Kremer, John.
McComas, Donna C. & Satterwhite, Marilyn L. Modern Business Correspondence. 1993. teacher ed. 21.79 (*0-02-803013-3*) Glencoe.
McComas, Donna C. & Satterwhite, Marilyn L. Modern Business Correspondence. 6th ed. 320p. 1993. text, wbk. ed. 41.59 (*0-02-803012-5*) Glencoe.
McComas, Edward W. The Complete Chevrolet V-8 Engine Code Pocket Guide, 1955-1991: The Lime Book. 3rd ed. LC 95-79828. 79p. 1997. pap. 7.95 (*0-9649292-2-8*) AME Pubng.
McComas, Henry C. Psychology of Religious Sects. LC 70-172763. reprint ed. 37.50 (*0-404-04107-8*) AMS Pr.
McComas, J. Francis. Graveside Companion. 1962. 12.95 (*0-8392-1040-X*) Astor-Honor.
McComas, Katherine, jt. auth. see Shanahan, James.
McComas, Paul. Twenty Questions: A Collection of Short & Very Short Stories. LC 97-26225. 160p. (Orig.). 1998. pap. 10.95 (*1-56474-238-5*) Fithian Pr.
McComas, Steve. Lake Smarts: The First Lake Maintenance Handbook. Reeder, Rachel, ed. (Illus.). 228p. (Orig.). 1993. pap. 21.95 (*1-880686-11-2*) Terrene Inst.
McComas, Stuart T., ed. Thermodynamics Exam File. LC 84-24688. (Exam File Ser.). 250p. (C). 1985. pap. 18.50 (*0-910554-49-8*) Engineering.
McComas, Terence. Pearl Harbor Fact & Reference Book: Everything to Know about Dec. 7, 1941. 132p. 1991. pap. 9.95 (*0-935180-02-8*) Mutual Pub HI.
McComas, Tom. TM's 3-Rail Illustrated Price Guide. (Illus.). 1996. pap. 14.95 (*0-937522-26-0*) TM Bks Video.
***McComas, Tom & Krone, Chuck.** MTH Electric Trains Illustrated Price & Rarity Guide: 1999 Edition. (Illus.). 192p. 1999. pap. 19.95 (*0-937522-93-7*, Pub. by TM Bks Video) Motorbooks Intl.
— TM's Lionel Illustrated Price & Rarity Guide, 1901-1969: 2000 Edition, Vol. 1. (Illus.). 232p. 2000. pap. 19.95 (*0-937522-91-0*, Pub. by TM Bks Video) Motorbooks Intl.
— TM's Lionel Illustrated Price & Rarity Guide, 1970-2000: 2000 Edition, Vol. 2. (Illus.). 232p. 1999. pap. 19.95 (*0-937522-92-9*, Pub. by TM Bks Video) Motorbooks Intl.
***McComas, William F.** The Nature of Science in Science Education: Rationales & Strategies. LC 98-20973. (Science & Technology Education Library). 15p. 1998. write for info. (*0-7923-5080-4*) Kluwer Academic.
McComas, William F., ed. Investigating Evolutionary Biology in the Laboratory. 1994. 8.00 (*0-941212-15-7*) Natl Assn Bio Tchrs.
McComb. Annual Editions: World History. 5th ed. 1997. pap. text 11.10 (*0-697-39293-7*) McGraw.
— Annual Editions: World History, Vol. 2. 5th ed. 1997. pap. text 11.10 (*0-697-39294-5*) McGraw.
— World History. 4th annot. ed. 1996. teacher ed. (*0-697-32793-0*, WCB McGr Hill) McGrw-H Hghr Educ.
McComb, Arthur J., ed. Eutropic Shallow Estuaries & Lagoons. LC 94-37997. 252p. 1995. boxed set 199.95 (*0-8493-6839-1*) CRC Pr.
McComb, Carol. Country & Blues Guitar for the Musically Hopeless. (Illus.). 106p. (Orig.). pap., boxed set 13.95 incl. audio (*0-932592-12-0*) Klutz.
McComb, Colin. Complete Book of Elves. (Illus.). 1993. 19.95 (*1-56076-376-0*, Pub. by TSR Inc) Random.
— Faces of Evil: The Fiends. 1997. 18.95 (*0-7869-0684-7*, Pub. by TSR Inc) Random.
— Hellbound: The Blood War. 1996. 25.00 (*0-7869-0407-0*, Pub. by TSR Inc) Random.
— On Hallowed Ground. 1996. 25.00 (*0-7869-0430-5*, Pub. by TSR Inc) Random.
— Well of Worlds: Planetscape Adventure. 1994. 15.00 (*1-56076-893-2*) TSR Inc.
McComb, Colin, jt. auth. see Cook, Monte.
***McComb, David.** World History, Vol. 2. 6th ed. (Annual Editions Ser.). 240p. (C). 1999. pap. 16.56 (*0-07-233954-3*) McGrw-H Hghr Educ.
— World History, Vol.1. 6th ed. (Annual Editions Ser.). 240p. (C). 1999. pap. 16.56 (*0-07-233948-9*) McGrw-H Hghr Educ.
Mccomb, David, jt. auth. see Salvant, J.
McComb, David G. Annual Editions Vol. 1: World History. (C). 1987. per. write for info. (*0-87967-708-2*) Brown & Benchmark.
— Annual Editions Vol. II: World History. (C). 1987. per. write for info. (*0-87967-736-8*) Brown & Benchmark.
— Galveston: A History. LC 85-20956. (Illus.). 293p. 1986. 32.50 (*0-292-72049-1*); pap. 15.95 (*0-292-72053-X*) U of Tex Pr.
***McComb, David G.** Galveston: A History & a Guide. (Illus.). 64p. 2000. pap. 7.95 (*0-87611-178-9*) Tex St Hist Assn.
McComb, David G. Sports: An Illustrated History. LC 98-15133. (Oxford Illustrated Histories Ser.). (Illus.). 144p. (YA). (gr. 7-12). 1999. 29.95 (*0-19-510097-2*) OUP.
— Texas: A Modern History. LC 89-31666. (Illus.). 208p. 1989. pap. 16.95 (*0-292-74665-2*) U of Tex Pr.
— Texas : An Illustrated History. (Oxford Illustrated Histories Ser.). (Illus.). 144p. (YA). (gr. 5 up). 1995. 25.00 (*0-19-509246-5*) OUP.
McComb, F. Wilson. The MG. (Album Ser.: No. 152). (Illus.). 32p. pap. 6.25 (*0-7478-0421-4*, Pub. by Shire Pubns) Parkwest Pubns.
— MGA: 1500, Twin Cam, 1600. (Expert Histories Ser.). (Illus.). 144p. 2000. pap. 19.95 (*1-84176-012-9*, 130038AE, Pub. by Ospry) Motorbooks Intl.
— MGB: MGB Roadster & GT, MCG, MGB V8. (Expert Histories Ser.). (Illus.). 144p. 2000. pap. 19.95 (*1-84176-013-7*, 130039AE, Pub. by Ospry) Motorbooks Intl.
McComb, Gordon. Fantastic Lost Inventions You Can Build. (Illus.). 320p. 1992. pap. 17.95 (*0-8306-3421-5*, 3421) McGraw-Hill Prof.
— Gordon McComb's Gadgeteers Gold. (Illus.). 400p. 1990. 29.95 (*0-8306-8360-7*, 3360) McGraw-Hill Prof.
— Gordon McComb's Gadgeteer's Goldmine! (Illus.). 400p. 1990. pap. 21.95 (*0-8306-3360-X*) McGraw-Hill Prof.
— Gordon McComb's Gadgeteer's Goldmine! Fifty-Five Space-Age Projects. 400p. 1990. pap. 24.95 (*0-07-155983-3*) McGraw.
— Illustrated Guide To VCR Repair. (Illus.). 350p. 1998. pap. 24.95 (*0-07-045596-1*) McGraw.
— Is This Thing On? Sound Systems for Your Business, School, & Auditorium. rev. ed. LC 97-155110. Orig. Title: Installing & Maintaining Sound Systems. (Illus.). 124p. (C). 1996. reprint ed. pap. 19.95 (*0-7906-1081-7*) Prompt Publns.
— The JavaScript Sourcebook: Create Interactive Java Programs for the... LC 96-2977. 752p. 1996. pap. 44.95 incl. cd-rom (*0-471-16185-3*) Wiley.
— The Laser Cookbook: 88 Practical Projects. 304p. 1988. pap. 24.95 (*0-07-155335-5*) McGraw.
— The Laser Cookbook: 99 Practical Projects. (Illus.). 304p. 1988. 25.95 (*0-8306-9090-5*, 3090); pap. 19.95 (*0-8306-9390-4*, 3090) McGraw-Hill Prof.
— Lasers, Ray Guns, & Light Cannons! Projects from the Wizard's Workbench. LC 97-989. (Illus.). 432p. 1997. pap. 21.95 (*0-07-045035-8*) McGraw.
— Model Building & Finishing Guide. (Illus.). 128p. (Orig.). 1989. pap. write for info. (*0-938545-05-1*) Jennings & Keefe.
***McComb, Gordon.** Robot Builder's Bonanza. 2nd ed. (Illus.). 425p. 2000. pap. text 24.95 (*0-07-136296-7*) McGraw.
McComb, Gordon. Robot Builder's Bonanza: 99 Inexpensive Robotics Projects. (Illus.). 326p. pap. 17.95 (*0-8306-2800-2*) McGraw.
— Robot Builder's Bonanza: 99 Inexpensive Robotics Projects. 336p. 1987. pap. 18.95 (*0-07-157146-9*) McGraw.
— Security Systems for Your Home & Automobile. (Illus.). 130p. 1994. pap. 19.95 (*0-7906-1054-X*) Prompt Publns.
— Troubleshooting & Repairing VCRs. (Illus.). 432p. 1988. 26.95 (*0-8306-0060-4*, 2960) McGraw-Hill Prof.
— Troubleshooting & Repairing VCRs. 2nd ed. (Illus.). 352p. 1991. 29.95 (*0-8306-7777-1*, 3777); pap. 19.95 (*0-8306-3777-X*) McGraw-Hill Prof.
— Troubleshooting & Repairing VCRs. 3rd ed. LC 95-3221. (Illus.). 400p. 1995. pap. 22.95 (*0-07-155017-8*) McGraw.
— Troubleshooting & Repairing VCRs. 3rd ed. LC 95-3221. 432p. 1995. 34.95 (*0-07-155016-X*) McGraw-Hill Prof.
— Using Javascript: Special Edition. LC 96-68041. 864p. 1996. pap. text 49.99 incl. cd-rom (*0-7897-0789-6*) Que.
— The Video Book: Creating an Integrated Home Entertainment System with Your TV, VCR, & the Latest Video Components. rev. ed. (Illus.). 192p. (C). 1992. reprint ed. pap. 19.95 (*0-7906-1030-2*) Prompt Publns.
— Web Commerce Cookbook. LC 97-35771. 416p. 1997. pap., pap. text 44.99 incl. cd-rom (*0-471-19663-0*) Wiley.
— Web Programming Languages Sourcebook. LC 97-3988. 624p. 1997. pap. text 49.95 incl. cd-rom (*0-471-17576-5*) Wiley.
McComb, Gordon & Cook, J. Compact Disc Player Maintenance & Repair Service Manual. 256p. 1987. pap. 19.95 (*0-07-157051-9*) McGraw.
McComb, Gordon & Cook, John. Compact Disc Player Maintenance & Repair Manual. 256p. 1987. 19.95 (*0-8306-0190-2*, 2790H); pap. 15.95 (*0-8306-2790-1*) McGraw-Hill Prof.
McComb, Gordon & Van Buren, Christopher. PC World You Can Do It with DOS. (You Can Do It Ser.). 214p. 1992. 19.95 (*1-878058-38-X*) IDG Bks.
McComb, Gordon, et al. Using Corel WordPerfect X. 1997. 39.99 (*0-7897-1300-4*) Que.
McComb, Gordon, jt. auth. see Goodman, Danny.
McComb, Gordon, jt. auth. see Rathbone, Andy.
McComb, H. G., Jr., jt. auth. see Noor, A. K.
McComb, Henry G., ed. The National Municipal Gazetteer: New York, 1991 Volume. (Illus.). 600p. (Orig.). 1990. pap. 95.00 (*1-878684-01-9*) Target Exchange.
— The National Municipal Gazetteer: New York, 1992 Volume. 3rd ed. (Illus.). 529p. 1992. pap. 95.00 (*1-878684-02-7*) Target Exchange.
— The National Municipal Gazetteer: New York, 1993 Volume. 4th ed. (Illus.). 525p. 1993. pap. 95.00 (*1-878684-03-5*) Target Exchange.
— The National Municipal Gazetteer: New York, 1994 Volume. 5th rev. ed. (Illus.). 525p. (C). 1994. pap. 95.00 (*1-878684-04-3*) Target Exchange.
— The National Municipal Gazetteer: New York, 1995 Volume. (Illus.). 525p. (C). 1995. pap. 95.00 (*1-878864-05-X*) Target Exchange.
— The National Municipal Gazetteer: New York, 1996 Volume. 7th ed. (Illus.). 550p. 1996. pap. 95.00 (*1-878684-06-X*) Target Exchange.
— The National Municipal Gazetteer: New York, 1997 Volume. 8th unabridged ed. (Illus.). 550p. 1997. pap. 95.00 (*1-878684-08-6*) Target Exchange.
***McComb, Henry G., ed.** The National Municipal Gazetteer Vol. 10: New York 1999 Volume. 10th ed. (Illus.). 650p. 1999. pap. 95.00 incl. cd-rom (*1-878684-09-4*) Target Exchange.
***McComb, John C.** I Love You: Transforming Your Life with Love. 2000. pap. 21.95 (*0-9671671-0-8*) LoveU Unl.
McComb, Samuel. The Power of Self-Suggestion. 1991. lib. bdg. 69.95 (*0-8490-4542-8*) Gordon Pr.
— The Power of Self-Suggestion. 53p. 1996. reprint ed. spiral bd. 10.00 (*0-7873-1241-X*) Hlth Research.
— Power of Self Suggestion (1916) 60p. 1998. reprint ed. pap. 7.95 (*0-7661-0668-3*) Kessinger Pub.
McComb, Thomas L. Scar. (Illus.). 138p. 1993. pap. text. write for info. (*1-883517-00-1*) Alef Bet Comns.
McComb, W. D. The Physics of Fluid Turbulence. (Oxford Engineering Science Ser.: No. 25). (Illus.). 600p. 1992. reprint ed. pap. text 65.00 (*0-19-856256-X*) OUP.
McComb, William David. Dynamics & Relativity. LC 99-24781. (Illus.). 392p. 2000. pap. text 45.00 (*0-19-850112-9*) OUP.
McCombe, A. W., jt. auth. see Hawke, M. F.
McCombe, Pamela A., jt. auth. see Pender, Michael P.
McComber, Diane & Holsing, James J., eds. Society of Wine Educators Resource Manual. 82p. (Orig.). 1993. pap. text 45.00 (*0-614-13713-6*) Soc Wine Educators.
McCombie, C., jt. ed. see McKinley, I. G.
McCombie, J. S. & Thirlwall, A. P. Economic Growth & the Balance of Payments Constraint. LC 93-1788. 1993. text 85.00 (*0-312-10183-X*) St Martin.

An Asterisk (*) at the beginning of an entry indicates that the title is appearing for the first time.

McCombie, S. L. The Rape Crisis Intervention Handbook: A Guide for Victim Care. LC 80-14191. (Illus.). 250p. 1980. 47.50 (0-306-40401-X, Kluwer Plenum) Kluwer Academic.

McCombs, Barbara, et al. The Sun's Joules: The Energy Education Program Guide. (Illus.). 67p. (gr. 8-12). 1997. spiral bd. 59.95 (1-888573-05-8, 552201) Learning Team.

McCombs, Barbara L. & Brannan, Linda. Accepting Criticism - Role Playing. (Skills for Job Success Ser.). (Illus.). 52p. (Orig.). 1990. pap. 39.95 (1-56119-055-1) Educ Pr MD.

— Adjusting to a New Boss. (Skills for Job Success Ser.). (Illus.). 32p. (Orig.). (YA). (gr. 7-12). 1990. teacher ed. 1.95 (1-56119-026-8); disk 39.95 (1-56119-113-2) Educ Pr MD.

— Adjusting to a New Boss. (Skills for Job Success Ser.). (Illus.). 32p. (Orig.). 1990. pap., student ed. 5.95 (1-56119-025-X) Educ Pr MD.

— Adjusting to a New Boss, Set. (Skills for Job Success Ser.). (Illus.). 32p. (Orig.). (YA). (gr. 7-12). 1990. teacher ed. 54.95 (1-56119-071-3) Educ Pr MD.

— Asking for Help - Role Playing. (Skills for Job Success Ser.). (Illus.). 52p. (Orig.). 1990. pap., teacher ed. 39.95 (1-56119-056-X) Educ Pr MD.

— Consideration for Co-Worker Rights. (Skills for Job Success Ser.). (Illus.). 32p. (Orig.). (YA). (gr. 7-12). 1990. teacher ed. 1.95 (1-56119-010-1); disk 39.95 (1-56119-105-1) Educ Pr MD.

— Consideration for Co-Worker Rights. (Skills for Job Success Ser.). (Illus.). 32p. (Orig.). 1990. pap., student ed. 5.95 (1-56119-009-8) Educ Pr MD.

— Consideration for Co-Worker Rights, Set. (Skills for Job Success Ser.). (Illus.). 32p. (Orig.). (YA). (gr. 7-12). 1990. teacher ed., student ed. 54.95 (1-56119-063-2) Educ Pr MD.

— Do. (Skills for Job Success Ser.). (Illus.). 32p. (Orig.). 1990. teacher ed. 1.95 (1-56119-006-3); disk 39.95 (1-56119-103-5) Educ Pr MD.

— Do. (Skills for Job Success Ser.). (Illus.). 32p. (Orig.). 1990. pap., student ed. 5.95 (1-56119-005-5) Educ Pr MD.

— Do, Set. (Skills for Job Success Ser.). (Illus.). 32p. (Orig.). 1990. teacher ed. 54.95 (1-56119-061-6) Educ Pr MD.

— Done on Time. (Skills for Job Success Ser.). (Illus.). 32p. (Orig.). 1990. teacher ed. 1.95 (1-56119-048-9); disk 39.95 (1-56119-124-8) Educ Pr MD.

— Done on Time. (Skills for Job Success Ser.). (Illus.). 32p. (Orig.). 1990. pap., student ed. 5.95 (1-56119-047-0) Educ Pr MD.

— Done on Time, Set. (Skills for Job Success Ser.). (Illus.). 32p. (Orig.). 1990. teacher ed., student ed. 54.95 (1-56119-082-9) Educ Pr MD.

— Good Grooming Habits. (Skills for Job Success Ser.). (Illus.). 32p. (Orig.). (YA). (gr. 7-12). 1990. teacher ed. 1.95 (1-56119-044-6); disk 39.95 (1-56119-122-1) Educ Pr MD.

— Good Grooming Habits. (Skills for Job Success Ser.). (Illus.). 32p. (Orig.). 1990. pap., student ed. 5.95 (1-56119-043-8) Educ Pr MD.

— Good Grooming Habits, Set. (Skills for Job Success Ser.). (Illus.). 32p. (Orig.). (YA). (gr. 7-12). 1990. teacher ed., student ed. 54.95 (1-56119-080-2) Educ Pr MD.

— Help, Please! (Skills for Job Success Ser.). (Illus.). 32p. (Orig.). (YA). (gr. 7-12). 1990. teacher ed. 1.95 (1-56119-038-1); disk 39.95 (1-56119-119-1) Educ Pr MD.

— Help, Please! (Skills for Job Success Ser.). (Illus.). 32p. (Orig.). 1990. pap., student ed. 5.95 (1-56119-037-3) Educ Pr MD.

— Help, Please!, Set. (Skills for Job Success Ser.). (Illus.). 32p. (Orig.). (YA). (gr. 7-12). 1990. 54.95 (1-56119-077-2) Educ Pr MD.

— How Does It Work? (Skills for Job Success Ser.). (Illus.). 32p. (Orig.). (YA). (gr. 7-12). 1990. teacher ed. 1.95 (1-56119-034-9); disk 39.95 (1-56119-117-5) Educ Pr MD.

— How Does It Work? (Skills for Job Success Ser.). (Illus.). 32p. (Orig.). 1990. pap., student ed. 5.95 (1-56119-033-0) Educ Pr MD.

— How Does It Work?, Set. (Skills for Job Success Ser.). (Illus.). 32p. (Orig.). (YA). (gr. 7-12). 1990. 54.95 (1-56119-075-6) Educ Pr MD.

— How Should I Do It? (Skills for Job Success Ser.). (Illus.). 32p. (Orig.). (YA). (gr. 7-12). 1990. teacher ed. 1.95 (1-56119-022-5); disk 39.95 (1-56119-111-6) Educ Pr MD.

— How Should I Do It? (Skills for Job Success Ser.). (Illus.). 32p. (Orig.). 1990. pap., student ed. 5.95 (1-56119-021-7) Educ Pr MD.

— How Should I Do It?, Set. (Skills for Job Success Ser.). (Illus.). 32p. (Orig.). (YA). (gr. 7-12). 1990. 54.95 (1-56119-069-1) Educ Pr MD.

— Keep Calm! (Skills for Job Success Ser.). (Illus.). 32p. (Orig.). (YA). (gr. 7-12). 1990. teacher ed. 1.95 (1-56119-024-1); disk 39.95 (1-56119-112-4) Educ Pr MD.

— Keep Calm! (Skills for Job Success Ser.). (Illus.). 32p. (Orig.). 1990. pap., student ed. 5.95 (1-56119-023-3) Educ Pr MD.

— Keep Calm!, Set. (Skills for Job Success Ser.). (Illus.). 32p. (Orig.). (YA). (gr. 7-12). 1990. teacher ed. 54.95 (1-56119-070-5) Educ Pr MD.

— Late for Work. (Skills for Job Success Ser.). (Illus.). 32p. (Orig.). 1990. pap., student ed. 5.95 (1-56119-013-6) Educ Pr MD.

— Late Work. (Skills for Job Success Ser.). (Illus.). 32p. (Orig.). (YA). (gr. 7-12). 1990. teacher ed. 1.95 (1-56119-014-4); disk 39.95 (1-56119-107-8) Educ Pr MD.

— Late Work, Set. (Skills for Job Success Ser.). (Illus.). 32p. (Orig.). (YA). (gr. 7-12). 1990. teacher ed., student ed. 54.95 (1-56119-065-9) Educ Pr MD.

— Leaving Early. (Skills for Job Success Ser.). (Illus.). 32p. (Orig.). (YA). (gr. 7-12). 1990. teacher ed. 1.95 (1-56119-040-3); disk 39.95 (1-56119-120-5) Educ Pr MD.

— Leaving Early. (Skills for Job Success Ser.). (Illus.). 32p. (Orig.). 1990. pap., student ed. 5.95 (1-56119-039-X) Educ Pr MD.

— Leaving Early, Set. (Skills for Job Success Ser.). (Illus.). 32p. (Orig.). (YA). (gr. 7-12). 1990. teacher ed. 54.95 (1-56119-078-0) Educ Pr MD.

— Making the Best Use of Time. (Skills for Job Success Ser.). (Illus.). 32p. (Orig.). 1990. teacher ed. 1.95 (1-56119-030-6); disk 39.95 (1-56119-115-9) Educ Pr MD.

— Making the Best Use of Time. (Skills for Job Success Ser.). (Illus.). 32p. (Orig.). 1990. pap., student ed. 5.95 (1-56119-029-2) Educ Pr MD.

— Making the Best Use of Time, Set. (Skills for Job Success Ser.). (Illus.). 32p. (Orig.). 1990. teacher ed., student ed. 54.95 (1-56119-073-X) Educ Pr MD.

— May I Try It? (Skills for Job Success Ser.). (Illus.). 32p. (Orig.). (YA). (gr. 7-12). 1990. teacher ed. 1.95 (1-56119-054-3); disk 39.95 (1-56119-127-2) Educ Pr MD.

— May I Try It? (Skills for Job Success Ser.). (Illus.). 32p. (Orig.). 1990. pap., student ed. 5.95 (1-56119-053-5) Educ Pr MD.

— May I Try It?, Set. (Skills for Job Success Ser.). (Illus.). 32p. (Orig.). (YA). (gr. 7-12). 1990. teacher ed. 54.95 (1-56119-085-3) Educ Pr MD.

— Neatness Counts. (Skills for Job Success Ser.). (Illus.). 32p. (Orig.). (YA). (gr. 7-12). 1990. teacher ed. 1.95 (1-56119-046-2); disk 39.95 (1-56119-123-X) Educ Pr MD.

— Neatness Counts. (Skills for Job Success Ser.). (Illus.). 32p. (Orig.). 1990. pap., student ed. 5.95 (1-56119-045-4) Educ Pr MD.

— Neatness Counts, Set. (Skills for Job Success Ser.). (Illus.). 32p. (Orig.). (YA). (gr. 7-12). 1990. teacher ed. 54.95 (1-56119-081-0) Educ Pr MD.

— Notice & Think. (Skills for Job Success Ser.). (Illus.). 32p. (Orig.). (YA). (gr. 7-12). 1990. teacher ed. 1.95 (1-56119-002-0); disk 39.95 (1-56119-101-9) Educ Pr MD.

— Notice & Think. (Skills for Job Success Ser.). (Illus.). 32p. (Orig.). 1990. pap., student ed. 5.95 (1-56119-001-2) Educ Pr MD.

— Notice & Think, Set. (Skills for Job Success Ser.). (Illus.). 32p. (Orig.). (YA). (gr. 7-12). 1990. teacher ed., wbk. ed. 54.95 (1-56119-059-4) Educ Pr MD.

— On the Job Training. (Skills for Job Success Ser.). (Illus.). (Orig.). 1990. pap. 49.95 (1-56119-057-8) Educ Pr MD.

— Respect for Property. (Skills for Job Success Ser.). (Illus.). 32p. (Orig.). (YA). (gr. 7-12). 1990. teacher ed. 1.95 (1-56119-028-4); teacher ed., student ed. 54.95 (1-56119-072-1); disk 39.95 (1-56119-114-0) Educ Pr MD.

— Respect for Property. (Skills for Job Success Ser.). (Illus.). 32p. (Orig.). 1990. pap., student ed. 5.95 (1-56119-027-6) Educ Pr MD.

— Say. (Skills for Job Success Ser.). (Illus.). 32p. (Orig.). (YA). (gr. 7-12). 1990. teacher ed. 1.95 (1-56119-004-7); disk 39.95 (1-56119-102-7) Educ Pr MD.

— Say. (Skills for Job Success Ser.). (Illus.). 32p. (Orig.). 1990. pap., student ed. 5.95 (1-56119-003-9) Educ Pr MD.

— Say, Set. (Skills for Job Success Ser.). (Illus.). 32p. (Orig.). (YA). (gr. 7-12). 1990. teacher ed., student ed. 54.95 (1-56119-060-8) Educ Pr MD.

— Social Skills for Job Success: Teacher's Guide. (Skills for Job Success Ser.). 150p. (Orig.). 1990. ring bd. 19.95 (1-56119-058-6) Educ Pr MD.

— Taking Breaks. (Skills for Job Success Ser.). (Illus.). 32p. (Orig.). (YA). (gr. 7-12). 1990. teacher ed. 1.95 (1-56119-042-X); disk 39.95 (1-56119-121-3) Educ Pr MD.

— Taking Breaks. (Skills for Job Success Ser.). (Illus.). 32p. (Orig.). 1990. pap., student ed. 5.95 (1-56119-041-1) Educ Pr MD.

— Taking Breaks, Set. (Skills for Job Success Ser.). (Illus.). 32p. (Orig.). (YA). (gr. 7-12). 1990. teacher ed., student ed. 54.95 (1-56119-079-9) Educ Pr MD.

— Too Much Talking. (Skills for Job Success Ser.). (Illus.). 32p. (Orig.). (YA). (gr. 7-12). 1990. teacher ed. 1.95 (1-56119-012-8); teacher ed., student ed. 54.95 (1-56119-064-0); disk 39.95 (1-56119-106-X) Educ Pr MD.

— Too Much Talking. (Skills for Job Success Ser.). (Illus.). 32p. (Orig.). 1990. pap., student ed. 5.95 (1-56119-011-X) Educ Pr MD.

— What Should I Do? (Skills for Job Success Ser.). (Illus.). 32p. (Orig.). (YA). (gr. 7-12). 1990. teacher ed. 1.95 (1-56119-032-2); disk 39.95 (1-56119-116-7) Educ Pr MD.

— What Should I Do? (Skills for Job Success Ser.). (Illus.). 32p. (Orig.). 1990. pap., student ed. 5.95 (1-56119-031-4) Educ Pr MD.

— What Should I Do?, Set. (Skills for Job Success Ser.). (Illus.). 32p. (Orig.). (YA). (gr. 7-12). 1990. teacher ed., wbk. ed. 54.95 (1-56119-074-8) Educ Pr MD.

— What's Next? (Skills for Job Success Ser.). (Illus.). 32p. (Orig.). (YA). (gr. 7-12). 1990. teacher ed. 1.95 (1-56119-020-9); teacher ed., wbk. ed. 54.95 (1-56119-068-3); disk 39.95 (1-56119-110-8) Educ Pr MD.

— What's Next? (Skills for Job Success Ser.). (Illus.). 32p. (Orig.). 1990. pap., student ed. 5.95 (1-56119-019-5) Educ Pr MD.

— What's the Proper Way? (Skills for Job Success Ser.). (Illus.). 32p. (Orig.). (YA). (gr. 7-12). 1990. teacher ed. 1.95 (1-56119-018-7); teacher ed., wbk. ed. 54.95 (1-56119-067-5); disk 39.95 (1-56119-109-4) Educ Pr MD.

— What's the Proper Way? (Skills for Job Success Ser.). (Illus.). 32p. (Orig.). 1990. pap., student ed. 5.95 (1-56119-017-9) Educ Pr MD.

— Which Tools to Use? (Skills for Job Success Ser.). (Illus.). 32p. (Orig.). (YA). (gr. 7-12). 1990. teacher ed. 1.95 (1-56119-050-0); teacher ed., wbk. ed. 54.95 (1-56119-083-7); disk 39.95 (1-56119-125-6) Educ Pr MD.

— Which Tools to Use? (Skills for Job Success Ser.). (Illus.). 32p. (Orig.). 1990. pap., student ed. 5.95 (1-56119-049-7) Educ Pr MD.

— Which Way Is Right? (Skills for Job Success Ser.). (Illus.). 32p. (Orig.). (YA). (gr. 7-12). 1990. teacher ed. 1.95 (1-56119-052-7); teacher ed., wbk. ed. 54.95 (1-56119-084-5); disk 39.95 (1-56119-126-4) Educ Pr MD.

— Which Way Is Right? (Skills for Job Success Ser.). (Illus.). 32p. (Orig.). 1990. pap., student ed. 5.95 (1-56119-051-9) Educ Pr MD.

— Who Can Help? (Skills for Job Success Ser.). (Illus.). 32p. (Orig.). (YA). (gr. 7-12). 1990. teacher ed. 1.95 (1-56119-036-5); teacher ed., wbk. ed. 54.95 (1-56119-076-4); disk 39.95 (1-56119-118-3) Educ Pr MD.

— Who Can Help? (Skills for Job Success Ser.). (Illus.). 32p. (Orig.). 1990. pap., student ed. 5.95 (1-56119-035-7) Educ Pr MD.

— Will You Do Me a Favor? (Skills for Job Success Ser.). (Illus.). 32p. (Orig.). (YA). (gr. 7-12). 1990. teacher ed. 1.95 (1-56119-016-0); disk 39.95 (1-56119-108-6) Educ Pr MD.

— Will You Do Me a Favor? (Skills for Job Success Ser.). (Illus.). 32p. (Orig.). 1990. pap., student ed. 5.95 (1-56119-015-2) Educ Pr MD.

— Will You Do Me a Favor?, Set. (Skills for Job Success Ser.). (Illus.). 32p. (Orig.). (YA). (gr. 7-12). 1990. teacher ed., wbk. ed. 54.95 (1-56119-066-7) Educ Pr MD.

— Working Too Slowly. (Skills for Job Success Ser.). (Illus.). 32p. (Orig.). (YA). (gr. 7-12). 1990. teacher ed. 1.95 (1-56119-008-X); disk 39.95 (1-56119-104-3) Educ Pr MD.

McCombs, Barbara L. & Pope, James E. Motivating Hard to Reach Students. LC 94-8336. (Psychology in the Classroom Ser.). 123p. (Orig.). 1994. pap. text 17.95 (1-55798-220-1) Am Psychol.

McCombs, Barbara L. & Whisler, Jo S. The Learner-Centered Classroom & School: Strategies for Increasing Student Motivation & Achievement. LC 96-52661. (Jossey-Bass Education Ser.). 1997. 29.95 (0-7879-0836-3) Jossey-Bass.

McCombs, Barbara L., jt. ed. see Lambert, Nadine M.

McCombs, Betsy & Wayne, Ellen K., eds. Graduate Law Study Program: Student Guide to Graduate Law Study Programs Offered Throughout the World. 14th ed. LC 81-643006. 157p. 1986. 19.00 (0-942598-02-4) Jt Comm Law Study.

— Graduate Law Study Programs, Nineteen Eighty-Two: Student Guide to Graduate Law Programs Offered Throughout the World. 13th rev. ed. LC 81-643006. 157p. 1982. pap. 13.00 (0-942598-01-6) Jt Comm Law Study.

— Summer Law Study Programs, 1988: Student Guide to Summer Law Study Programs Offered Throughout the World. 9th rev. ed. LC 80-645058. 1988. pap. 17.50 (0-318-35051-3) Jt Comm Law Study.

***McCombs, David.** Detecting the World: Capturing Physical Measurements with C++ 344p. 1999. pap. 44.95 incl. disk (0-87930-559-2) C M P Books.

***McCombs, Davis.** Ultima Thule. LC 99-52548. (Yale Series of Younger Poets). 72p. 2000. 19.00 (0-300-08316-5) Yale U Pr.

— Ultima Thule. LC 99-52548. (Yale Series of Younger Poets: Vol. 94). 72p. 2000. pap. 12.00 (0-300-08317-3) Yale U Pr.

McCombs, Donald & Worth, Fred L. World War II: 4,139 Strange & Fascinating Facts. 672p. 1994. 12.99 (0-517-42286-7) Crown Pub Group.

McCombs, Gillian M., ed. Access Services: The Convergence of Reference & Technical Services. LC 91-35637. (Reference Librarian Ser.: No. 34). 178p. 1991. lib. bdg. 59.95 (1-56024-170-5) Haworth Pr.

McCombs, Judith. Against Nature: Wilderness Poems. (American Dust Ser.: No. 9). 1979. 7.95 (0-913218-83-9); pap. 2.95 (0-913218-84-7) Dustbooks.

— Territories, Here & Elsewhere. 1996. pap. 6.00 (0-932412-10-6) Mayapple Pr.

McCombs, Judith & Palmer, Carole L. Margaret Atwood: A Reference Guide. (Reference Guides to Literature Ser.). 300p. 1991. 65.00 (0-8161-8940-4, Hall Reference) Macmillan.

McCombs, M., jt. ed. see Protess, D.

McCombs, Maxwell, et al. Contemporary Public Opinion: Issues & the News. (Communication Textbook Series, Journalism Subseries). 128p. 1991. pap. 14.95 (0-8058-1102-8) L Erlbaum Assocs.

McCombs, Maxwell, jt. ed. see Reynolds, Amy.

McCombs, Maxwell E., et al. Communication & Democracy: Exploring the Intellectual Frontiers in Agenda-Setting Theory. LC 97-12616. 1997. 59.95 (0-8058-2554-1); pap. 29.95 (0-8058-2555-X) L Erlbaum Assocs.

McCombs, Philip A., jt. auth. see Klose, Kevin.

McCombs, Robert P. Fundamentals of Internal Medicine: A Physiologic & Clinical Approach to Disease. 4th ed. LC 74-115098. (Illus.). 939p. reprint ed. pap. 200.00 (0-608-15504-7, 202973800064) Bks Demand.

McCombs, Rufe & Zacharias, Karen S. Benched: Judge Rufe McCombs. LC 97-38821. 1997. 29.95 (0-86554-570-7, MUP/H426) Mercer Univ Pr.

McComish, Charles D. & Lambert, Rebecca T. History of Colusa & Glenn Counties, California. (Illus.). 1074p. 1993. reprint ed. lib. bdg. 105.00 (0-8328-3233-2) Higginson Bk Co.

McComish, William A. The Epigones: A Study of the Theology of the Synod of Dort, with Special Reference to Giovanni Diodati. LC 87-11073. (Princeton Theological Monographs: No. 13). (Orig.). 1989. pap. 15.00 (0-915138-62-X) Pickwick.

***McComiskey, Bruce.** Teaching Composition as a Social Process. LC 99-6774. 180p. 2000. pap. 19.95 (0-87421-283-9) Utah St U Pr.

McComiskey, Thomas E., ed. The Minor Prophets: An Exegetical & Expository Commentary (Obadiah-Habakkuk), 2. LC 91-38388. 420p. (C). 1993. 44.99 (0-8010-6307-8) Baker Bks.

— The Minor Prophets Vol. 1: An Exegetical & Expository Commentary (Hosea, Joel & Amos), 1. LC 91-38388. 520p. (gr. 13). 1992. 44.99 (0-8010-6285-3) Baker Bks.

McComiskey, Thomas Edward, ed. The Minor Prophets, 3. 1468p. 1996. 115.00 (0-8010-1124-8) Baker Bks.

— The Minor Prophets: An Exegetical & Expository Commentary (Zephaniah-Malachi), 3. LC 91-38388. 528p. (C). 1998. 44.99 (0-8010-2055-7) Baker Bks.

McCommons, Richard E., et al. Guide to Architecture Schools in North America LC 88-12765. xxvi, 274 p. 1989. 14.95 (0-935437-31-2) Info Dynamics.

McConachie, Bruce A. Melodramatic Formations: American Theatre & Society, 1820-1870. LC 91-44085. (Studies in Theatre History & Culture). (Illus.). 334p. 1992. text 42.95 (0-87745-359-4); pap. text 16.95 (0-87745-360-8) U of Iowa Pr.

McConachie, Bruce A. & Friedman, Daniel P., eds. Theatre for Working-Class Audiences in the United States, 1830-1980, 14. LC 84-19773. (Contributions in Drama & Theatre Studies: No. 14). (Illus.). 265p. 1985. 65.00 (0-313-24629-7, MTU/) Greenwood.

McConachie, Bruce A., jt. ed. see Postlewait, Thomas.

***McConachie, Dorothy.** Our Texas Heritage: Traditions & Recipes. (Illus.). 250p. 2000. pap. 18.95 (1-55622-785-X, Rep of TX Pr) Wordware Pub.

McConachie, Helen. Parents & Young Mentally Handicapped Children: A Review of Research Issues. 276p. 1986. text 29.95 (0-914797-28-X) Brookline Bks.

McConachie, Helen, jt. ed. see Zinkin, Pam.

McConagha, Glenn L. Blackburn College, 1837-1987: An Anecdotal & Analytical History of the Private College. Hamlin, Griffith A., ed. (Illus.). 531p. (C). 1988. 20.00 (0-9621555-0-0) Blackburn Univ.

McConaghy, June. Children Learning Through Literature: A Teacher Researcher Study. LC 89-71089. (Illus.). 80p. (Orig.). (C). 1990. pap. text 15.00 (0-435-08515-8, 08515) Heinemann.

McConaghy, N. Sexual Behavior: Problems & Management. (Applied Clinical Psychology Ser.). (Illus.). 426p. (C). 1993. 75.00 (0-306-44177-2, Plenum Trade) Perseus Pubng.

***McConal, Patrick M.** Over the Wall: The Men Behind the 1934 Death House Escape. LC 99-54607. 2000. write for info. (1-57168-365-8, Eakin Pr) Sunbelt Media.

McConathy, Donald R., et al, eds. Civil Space in the Clinton Era, 32nd Goddard Memorial Symposium, March 1-2, 1994, Crystal City, Virginia, & Partners in Space . . . 2001 41st Annual Meeting: 41st Annual Meeting, 32nd Goddard Memorial Symposium, Crystal City, VA, Mar. 1-2, 1994. (Science & Technology Ser.: Vol. 85). (Illus.). 292p. 1995. pap. 50.00 (0-87703-398-6, Am Astronaut Soc) Univelt Inc.

McConathy, Donald R. & Korn, Paula, eds. Civil Space in the Clinton Era, 32nd Goddard Memorial Symposium, March 1-2, 1994, Crystal City, Virginia, & Partners in Space . . . 2001 41st Annual Meeting: 41st Annual Meeting, 32nd Goddard Memorial Symposium, Crystal City, VA, Mar. 1-2, 1994. (Science & Technology Ser.: Vol. 85). (Illus.). 292p. 1995. 70.00 (0-87703-397-8, Am Astronaut Soc) Univelt Inc.

McConaughy, Mark A., ed. Rench: A Stratified Site in the Central Illinois River Valley. (Reports of Investigations: No. 49). (Illus.). 430p. 1993. pap. 20.00 (0-89792-143-7) Ill St Museum.

McConaughy, Stephanie H. & Achenbach, Thomas M. Manual for the Semistructured Clinical Interview for Children & Adolescents. 228p. (Orig.). 1994. pap. 25.00 (0-938565-32-X) U of VT Psych.

McConaughy, Stephanie H., jt. auth. see Achenbach, Thomas M.

McConchie, Lyn, jt. auth. see Norton, Andre.

McConchie, R. W. Lexicography & Physicke: The Record of Sixteenth-Century English Medical Terminology. LC 97-12359. (Oxford Studies in Lexicography). 460p. 1997. text 100.00 (0-19-823630-1) OUP.

McConduit, Denise W. D. J. & the Jazz Fest. LC 96-46639. (Illus.). 32p. (J). 1997. 14.95 (1-56554-239-8) Pelican.

— D. J. & the Zulu Parade. LC 94-12210. (Illus.). 32p. (J). (ps-3). 1994. 14.95 (1-56554-063-8) Pelican.

Mccone & Cubillos. Sempre Adelante. (College Spanish Ser.). (SPA.). (C). 1995. mass mkt. 34.95 (0-8384-6522-6) Heinle & Heinle.

***McConeghy, Howard.** Art & Soul. (Illus.). 168p. 2000. pap. 18.50 (0-88214-383-2, Pub. by Spring Pubns) Continuum.

McConell, ed. Algebra, Vol. 1. (C). 1994. text 25.31 (0-673-45870-9) Addison-Wesley.

McConell, John H. The Shrine Circus: The Mystic Shriners Yankee Circus in Egypt. 325p. 1998. 29.95 (0-9636019-2-X, Astley & Ricketts) McConnell-Simmons.

McConica, Carol M., jt. ed. see Blewer, Robert S.

M

An Asterisk (*) at the beginning of an entry indicates that the title is appearing for the first time.

McConica, James K. The History of the University of Oxford Vol. III: The Collegiate University, Vol. 3. (Illus.). 800p. 1986. text 135.00 (*0-19-951013-X*) OUP.

***McConkey, Dale & Lawler, Peter Augustine.** Social Structures, Social Capital, & Personal Freedom. LC 99-43105. 200p. 2000. write for info. (*0-275-96476-0*, Praeger Pubs) Greenwood.

McConkey, Dale, jt. ed. see Lawler, Peter Augustine.

McConkey, Dale D. How Staff Managers Make Things Happen: Productivity Through MBO. LC 83-60030. 1983. 15.95 (*0-912164-09-3*) Masterco Pr.

McConkey, Edwin H. Human Genetics: Molecular Revolution. 336p. (C). 1993. 55.00 (*0-86720-854-6*) Jones & Bartlett.

McConkey, Edwin H., ed. Protein Synthesis. LC 75-155743. 400p. reprint ed. pap. 124.00 (*0-608-09995-3*, 202711200002) Bks Demand.

— Protein Synthesis, Vol. 1. LC 74-155743. 314p. 1971. reprint ed. pap. 97.40 (*0-7837-0017-2*, 202711200001) Bks Demand.

McConkey, Gladys, ed. Plasma Studies at Cornell University. 64p. 1988. write for info. (*0-918531-01-2*) Cornell Coll Eng.

McConkey, James. Court of Memory. (Nonpareil Bks.: Vol. 71). 288p. 1993. pap. 14.95 (*0-87923-983-2*) Godine.

— The Oxford Book of Memory. 1996. 30.00 (*0-614-96853-4*) OUP.

— Stories from My Life with Other Animals. 192p. 1993. 19.95 (*0-87923-967-0*) Godine.

***McConkey, James.** To a Distant Island. 196p. 2000. reprint ed. pap. 14.95 (*0-9664913-5-1*, Pub. by Paul Dry Bks) IPG Chicago.

McConkey, James, ed. The Anatomy of Memory: An Anthology. 528p. (C). 1996. 35.00 (*0-19-507841-1*) OUP.

— Chekhov & Our Age. 237p. 1985. 24.95 (*0-86731-078-2*); pap. 8.95 (*0-86731-081-2*) Cornell CIS RDC.

McConkey, Kenneth. Edwardian Portraits: Images of an Age of Opulence. (Illus.). 264p. 1987. 49.50 (*1-85149-060-4*) Antique Collect.

— A Free Spirit: Irish Art, 1860-1960. (Illus.). 228p. 1990. 59.50 (*1-85149-127-9*) Antique Collect.

— Impressionism in Britain. LC 94-41771. 224p. 1995. 50.00 (*0-300-06334-2*) Yale U Pr.

— Sir John Lavery. (Illus.). 256p. 1995. 50.00 (*0-86241-440-7*, Pub. by Canongate Books) Interlink Pub.

McConkey, Kevin M. & Sheehan, Peter W. Hypnosis, Memory & Behavior in Criminal Investigation. LC 95-14251. (Clinical & Experimental Hypnosis Ser.). 240p. 1995. lib. bdg. 40.00 (*1-57230-008-6*) Guilford Pubns.

McConkey, Kevin M., jt. auth. see Sheehan, Peter W.

McConkey, Kevin M., jt. ed. see Lynn, Steven J.

McConkey, Lois. Sea & Cedar: How the Northwest Coast Indians Lived. (How They Lived Ser.). (Illus.). 40p. (J). (ps-3). 1991. pap. 7.95 (*0-88894-371-7*) Firefly Bks Ltd.

McConkey, Roy, jt. ed. see O'Toole, Brian.

McConkey, Wilfred J. Haute As in Oat: A Pronunciation Guide to European Wines & Cuisines. 184p. 1989. pap. 7.95 (*0-8191-6824-6*) Madison Bks UPA.

McConkie, Bruce R. Doctrinal New Testament Commentary, 1. 1965. 21.95 (*0-88494-137-X*) Bookcraft Inc.

— Doctrinal New Testament Commentary, 2. 1971. 17.95 (*0-88494-216-3*) Bookcraft Inc.

— Doctrinal New Testament Commentary, 3. 1972. 17.95 (*0-88494-250-3*) Bookcraft Inc.

— Doctrinal New Testament Commentary, 3 vols., Set. 1998. pap. 34.95 (*1-57008-559-5*) Bookcraft Inc.

— The Messiah Series, 6 titles, Set. 3234p. 1990. pap. 41.95 (*0-87579-401-7*) Deseret Bk.

— Mormon Doctrine. 1958. 25.95 (*0-88494-062-4*) Bookcraft Inc.

— Mormon Doctrine. 1979. pap. 9.95 (*0-88494-446-8*) Bookcraft Inc.

— The Mortal Messiah: From Bethlehem to Calvary, Bk. 2. LC 79-19606. (Messiah Ser.). 424p. 1990. reprint ed. pap. 9.95 (*0-87579-404-1*) Deseret Bk.

— The Mortal Messiah: From Bethlehem to Calvary, Bk. 3. LC 79-19606. (Messiah Ser.). 486p. 1990. reprint ed. pap. 10.95 (*0-87579-405-X*) Deseret Bk.

— The Promised Messiah: The First Coming of Christ. LC 78-3478. (Messiah Ser.). 636p. 1990. reprint ed. pap. 11.95 (*0-87579-402-5*) Deseret Bk.

— The Purifying Power of Gethsemane & the Seven Deadly Heresies. LC 97-78185. (Classic Talk Ser.). 51 p. 1998. write for info. (*0-87579-883-7*) Deseret Bk.

McConkie, Joseph F. Answers: Straightforward Answers to Tough Gospel Questions. LC 97-41267. 1998. write for info. (*1-57345-355-2*) Deseret Bk.

— Gospel Symbolism. 14.95 (*0-88494-568-5*) Bookcraft Inc.

— Here We Stand. 1995. 14.95 (*1-57345-045-6*) Deseret Bk.

— Sons & Daughters of God. 1994. 14.95 (*0-88494-936-2*) Bookcraft Inc.

McConkie, Joseph F. & Millet, Robert L. Doctrinal Commentary on the Book of Mormon, 2 vols., 2. 1988. 14.95 (*0-88494-655-X*) Bookcraft Inc.

— Doctrinal Commentary on the Book of Mormon, 4 vols., Vol. 1. 1987. 21.95 (*0-88494-632-0*) Bookcraft Inc.

— Doctrinal Commentary on the Book of Mormon, Vol. 4. 1991. 21.95 (*0-88494-807-2*) Bookcraft Inc.

— The Holy Ghost. 1989. 12.95 (*0-88494-707-6*) Bookcraft Inc.

— Joseph Smith the Choice Seer. 1996. 19.95 (*1-57008-269-3*) Bookcraft Inc.

— The Life Beyond. 1986. 13.95 (*0-88494-601-0*) Bookcraft Inc.

— Sustaining & Defending the Faith. 1998. pap. 8.95 (*1-57008-437-8*) Bookcraft Inc.

McConkie, Joseph F., et al. Doctrinal Commentary on the Book of Mormon, Vol. 4. 1992. 21.95 (*0-88494-818-8*) Bookcraft Inc.

McConkie, Mark L. The Father of the Prophet. 1993. 12.95 (*0-88494-887-0*) Bookcraft Inc.

— Sermons & Writings of Bruce R. McConkie. 1998. 21.95 (*1-57008-523-4*) Bookcraft Inc.

McConn, Rita, ed. The Role of Chemical Mediators in the Pathophysiology of Acute Illness & Injury. LC 81-40742. (Illus.). 407p. 1982. reprint ed. pap. 126.20 (*0-608-00608-4*, 206119500007) Bks Demand.

McConnachie, Brian. Blowing Smoke: The Wild & Whimsical World of Cigars. (Illus.). 144p. 1997. 15.95 (*1-57243-229-2*) Triumph Bks.

McConnachie, John. Barthian Theology. LC 72-2493. (Select Bibliographies Reprint Ser.). 1977. reprint ed. 21.95 (*0-8369-6861-1*) Ayer.

McConnaughey, Bayard H. & McConnaughey, Evelyn. Pacific Coast. Elliott, Charles, ed. LC 84-48673. (Audubon Society Nature Guides Ser.). (Illus.). 633p. 1985. pap. 19.95 (*0-394-73130-1*) Knopf.

McConnaughey, Evelyn. Sea Vegetables: Harvesting Guide & Cookbook, Vol. 1. LC 85-18828. (Illus.). 244p. 1985. pap. 9.95 (*0-87961-151-0*) Naturegraph.

McConnaughey, Evelyn, jt. auth. see McConnaughey, Bayard H.

McConnaughhay, JoDee. Be Brave, Anna! God Helps When I'm Afraid. Caldwell, Lise, ed. LC 98-61310. (Happy Day Bks.). (Illus.). 24p. (J). (ps-2). 1999. pap. 1.99 (*0-7847-0895-9*, 04268) Standard Pub.

***McConnaughhay, JoDee.** Can God See Me? Stewart, Jennifer, ed. (Illus.). 24p. (J). (ps-2). 2000. pap. 1.99 (*0-7847-1104-6*, 04309) Standard Pub.

— Don't Do That, Dexter! Ring, Laura, ed. LC 99-70914. (Illus.). 24p. (J). (ps-1). 1999. pap. 1.99 (*0-7847-1049-X*, 04279, Bean Sprouts) Standard Pub.

— Keep Trying, Travis! Stewart, Jennifer, ed. (Illus.). 24p. (J). (ps-2). 2000. pap. 1.99 (*0-7847-1105-4*, 04310) Standard Pub.

McConnaughhay, JoDee. Molly Wants More! God Gives Me What I Need. Caldwell, Lise, ed. LC 98-61311. (Illus.). 24p. (J). (ps-2). 1999. pap. 1.99 (*0-7847-0896-7*, 04269) Standard Pub.

***McConnaughhay, JoDee.** Tell the Truth, Tyler! Ring, Laura, ed. LC 99-70915. (Illus.). 24p. (ps-1). 1999. pap. 1.99 (*0-7847-1048-1*, 04278, Bean Sprouts) Standard Pub.

McConnaughy, Holly P., ed. O Christmas Tree! (Illus.). 64p. 1996. 4.98 (*0-614-29844-X*) DoveTail Bks.

McConnaughy, James, intro. Antique Silver from Local Collections. LC 89-63657. (Illus.). 64p. (Orig.). 1989. pap. 10.00 (*0-614-30233-1*) Okla City Art.

McConnaughy, James, jt. ed. see Langstaff, Bard.

McConnel. Swallowing & Pharyngology. 2001. 65.00 (*1-56593-742-2*, M3256) Thomson Learn.

McConnel, Bridget. The Story Of Antique Needlework Tools LC 98-51410. (Illus.). 250p. 1999. 59.95 (*0-7643-0710-X*) Schiffer.

— The Story of the Thimble: An Illustrated Guide for Collectors. LC 97-23818. (Illus.). 160p. 1997. 49.95 (*0-7643-0311-2*) Schiffer.

McConnel, Charles R. The Health Care Supervisor on Professional Nursing Management. (Health Care Supervisor Ser.). 236p. 1993. pap. 40.00 (*0-8342-0369-3*) Aspen Pub.

McConnel, Frances, ed. One Step Closer: New Poetry by Women of the West Coast. 1976. pap. 3.95 (*0-915242-09-5*) Pygmalion Pr.

McConnel, John L. Western Characters: Or, Types of Border Life in the Western States. LC 75-110. (Mid-American Frontier Ser.). (Illus.). 1975. reprint ed. 33.95 (*0-405-06877-8*) Ayer.

McConnel, Patricia. Eye of the Beholder: Deer Hunting Through the Eyes of a Born-Again Pagan. (Chapbook Ser.). 32p. 1994. pap. 5.95 (*1-884106-02-1*) Jumping Cholla.

— Eye of the Beholder: Deer Hunting Through the Eyes of a Born-Again Pagan. (Illus.). 28p. 1998. reprint ed. pap. 4.00 (*0-9643253-1-4*) Logoria.

— Sing Soft, Sing Loud. 272p. 1995. pap. 12.00 (*0-9643253-0-6*) Logoria.

McConnell. Algebra: Student Manual (Hardcover Book) (C). 1997. teacher ed. 75.00 (*0-673-67581-5*) Addison-Wesley.

McConnell. Algebra School Mathematics Project. 24.11 (*0-673-45263-8*, Scott Frsmn) Addson-Wesley Educ.

McConnell. Computer Graphics Companion. (ITCP-UK Computer Science Ser.). 1998. mass mkt. 29.99 (*1-85032-337-2*) ITCP.

— Cpsq Sel Chapters from Microec. 14th ed. 1998. pap. text 23.50 (*0-07-230701-3*) McGraw.

— Economics. 14th ed. 540p. 1998. pap., student ed. 24.06 (*0-07-289837-2*) McGraw.

Mcconnell. Macroeconomics. 2nd ed. 1998. 47.00 (*0-07-229579-1*) McGraw.

McConnell. Macroeconomics. 14th ed. 1998. pap., student ed. 17.19 (*0-07-289839-9*) McGraw.

Mcconnell. Microeconomics. 2nd ed. 1998. 47.00 (*0-07-229580-5*) McGraw.

McConnell. Microeconomics. 14th ed. 1998. pap., student ed. 17.19 (*0-07-289838-0*) McGraw.

McConnell, ed. Algebra, Vol. 2. (C). 1994. text 25.31 (*0-673-45871-7*) Addson-Wesley Educ.

McConnell, A. J. Applications of Tensor Analysis. 318p. 1957. pap. 10.95 (*0-486-60373-3*) Dover.

McConnell, Allan. State Policy Formation & the Origin of the Poll Tax. 256p. 1995. text 77.95 (*1-85521-488-1*, Pub. by Dartmth Pub) Ashgate Pub Co.

McConnell, Amanda, jt. auth. see Suzuki, David.

***McConnell, Anita.** Barometers. (Album Ser.: Vol. 220). (Illus.). 32p. 1999. pap. 6.25 (*0-7478-0240-8*, Pub. by Shire Pubns) Parkwest Pubns.

McConnell, Anita. Instrument Makers to the World. 1999. pap. 50.00 (*1-85072-096-7*, Pub. by W Sessions) St Mut.

***McConnell, Anita.** King of the Clinicals: The Life & Times of J. J. Hicks (1835-1916) 160p. 1999. pap. 24.00 (*1-85072-204-8*, Pub. by W Sessions) St Mut.

McConnell, Anita. The World Beneath Us. LC 84-1654. (World of Science Ser.). (Illus.). 64p. 1985. reprint ed. pap. 30.00 (*0-7837-9921-7*, 206064800006) Bks Demand.

McConnell, Anita, ed. see Wallis, Helen.

McConnell, Ashley. The Courts of Sorcery. 224p. 1997. mass mkt. 5.99 (*0-441-00393-1*) Ace Bks.

***McConnell, Ashley.** The First Amendment. (Stargate Ser.: Vol. 1). (Illus.). 2000. mass mkt. 5.99 (*0-451-45777-3*, ROC) NAL.

McConnell, Ashley. The Fountains of Mirlacca. 208p. (Orig.). 1995. mass mkt. 4.99 (*0-441-00206-4*) Ace Bks.

— Highlander: Scimitar. 224p. 1996. reprint ed. mass mkt. 5.99 (*0-446-60284-1*, Pub. by Warner Bks) Little.

— The Iterant Exorcist. 208p. (Orig.). 1996. mass mkt. 5.99 (*0-441-00312-5*) Ace Bks.

— Quantum Leap: Prelude. 1994. mass mkt. 5.99 (*1-57297-134-7*) Blvd Books.

— Quantum Leap: The Novel. 1992. mass mkt. 5.99 (*1-57297-094-4*) Blvd Books.

— Quantum Leap: The Wall. 256p. 1994. mass mkt. 4.99 (*0-441-00015-0*) Ace Bks.

— Quantum Leap: The Wall. 1994. mass mkt. 5.99 (*1-57297-216-5*) Blvd Books.

— Quantum Leap: Too Close for Comfort. 272p. (Orig.). 1993. mass mkt. 4.99 (*0-441-69323-7*) Ace Bks.

— Random Measures. (Quantum Leap Ser.). 1995. mass mkt. 5.99 (*1-57297-095-2*) Blvd Books.

— Stargate SG-1: The Price You Pay. (Stargate Ser.). 199p. 1999. mass mkt. 5.99 (*0-451-45726-9*, ROC) NAL.

— Stargate SG-1. (Stargate Ser.). 1998. mass mkt. 5.99 (*0-451-45725-0*, ROC) NAL.

— Too Close for Comfort. (Quantum Leap Ser.: No. 2). 1994. mass mkt. 5.99 (*1-57297-157-6*) Blvd Books.

McConnell, B. D., ed. see Spring Lubrication Symposium (1972, Boston).

McConnell, Brian. The Possessed: True Stories of Demonic Possession. (Illus.). 448p. 1997. mass mkt. 13.95 (*0-7472-4720-X*, Pub. by Headline Bk Pub) Trafalgar.

McConnell, C. Douglas, ed. The Holy Spirit & Mission Dynamics. LC 97-28933. (Evangelical Missiological Society Ser.). 1997. 8.95 (*0-87808-379-0*) William Carey Lib.

McConnell, Campbell R. Economics. 15th ed. 2001. 67.50 (*0-07-234036-3*) McGraw.

— Economics Concepts: A Programmed Approach. 7th ed. 1984. pap. text. write for info. (*0-07-044937-6*) McGraw.

— Macroeconomics. 15th ed. 2001. 45.74 (*0-07-234089-4*) McGraw.

— Microeconomics. 15th ed. 2001. 47.50 (*0-07-234037-1*) McGraw.

McConnell, Campbell R. & Brue, S. L. Contemporary Labor Economics. 4th ed. 688p. (C). 1994. text 63.44 (*0-07-045657-7*) McGraw.

McConnell, Campbell R. & Brue, Stanley L. Contemporary Labor Economics. 5th ed. LC 98-29110. 672p. 1998. 80.00 (*0-07-046040-X*) McGraw.

— Economics: Principles, Problems & Policies. 12th ed. (C). 1993. pap. text, student ed. 21.25 (*0-07-045590-2*) McGraw.

— Economics: Principles, Problems, & Policies. 14th ed. LC 98-23775. 1998. 66.50 (*0-07-047094-4*) McGraw.

— Economics Principles, Problems, & Policies. 13th ed. LC 95-13487. (C). 1995. text 92.50 (*0-07-046814-1*) McGraw.

— Macroeconomics. 13th ed. (C). 1995. pap. text 67.50 (*0-07-046819-2*) McGraw.

— Macroeconomics: Principles, Problems, & Policies. 14th ed. LC 98-19045. 1998. 60.50 (*0-07-289841-0*) McGraw.

— Microeconomics. 13th ed. (C). 1995. text 67.50 (*0-07-046820-6*) McGraw.

McConnell, Campbell R. & Brue, Stanley L. Microeconomics: Principles, Problems, & Policies. 14th ed. LC 98-7747. 1998. 47.50 (*0-07-289840-2*) McGraw.

***McConnell, Campbell R. & Brue, Stanley L.** Microeconomics: Principles, Problems, & Policies. 14th ed. LC 98-7747. (Illus.). 1999. write for info. (*0-07-366216-X*) McGrw-H Hghr Educ.

McConnell, Carol. This Is My Life. 128p. (Orig.). 1996. pap. 15.95 (*1-886094-29-2*) Chicago Spectrum.

McConnell, Catherine S. High on a Windy Hill. (Illus.). 466p. 1995. 34.95 (*1-57072-041-X*) Overmountain Pr.

McConnell, Cecilio. Comentario Sobre los Himnos Que Cantamos: Commentary on the Hymns We Sing. (SPA.). 368p. 1985. pap. 11.50 (*0-311-32433-9*) Casa Bautista.

McConnell, Cecilio, compiled by. Concordancia Basica de la Biblica RVA.Tr. of Concordance of the RVA Bible. (SPA.). 238p. 1997. pap. text 9.99 (*0-311-42101-6*, Edit Mundo) Casa Bautista.

***McConnell, Cecilio & McConnell, Maria.** Dedito y Sus Hermanos Aprenden de Dios.Tr. of Digit & His Brothers Learn about God. (SPA.). 144p. 1998. pap. text 7.50 (*0-311-44009-6*) Casa Bautista.

McConnell, Cecilio & McConnell, Mary. Objetos Que Ensenan de Dios: Objects That Teach about God. (SPA.). 96p. 1986. pap. 7.99 (*0-311-44007-X*) Casa Bautista.

McConnell, Charles N. Audel Plumbers Maintenance/ Troubleshooting Pocket Manual. LC 96-79618. (Illus.). 288p. 1996. pap. 14.95 (*0-02-861385-6*, Aude IN) IDG Bks.

— Home Plumbing Handbook. 4th ed. 224p. 1993. pap. 17.00 (*0-02-079651-X*, Aude IN) IDG Bks.

— Pipefitters & Welders Pocket Manual. LC 96-79620. 320p. 1996. per. 14.95 (*0-02-034624-7*, Aude IN) IDG Bks.

McConnell, Charles R. Case Studies in Health Care Supervision. LC 98-20876. 176p. 1998. 28.00 (*0-8342-1133-5*, 11335) Aspen Pub.

— The Effective Health Care Supervisor. 3rd ed. LC 93-10915. 470p. 1993. 55.00 (*0-8342-0377-4*, 20377) Aspen Pub.

— The Effective Health Care Supervisor. 4th ed. LC 97-9705. 528p. 1997. 39.00 (*0-8342-0986-1*) Aspen Pub.

— The Health Care Manager's Guide to Performance Appraisal. LC 92-17876. 240p. 1992. text 70.00 (*0-8342-0348-0*, 20348) Aspen Pub.

McConnell, Charles R., ed. The Health Care Supervisor on Career Development. LC 93-195. (Health Care Supervisor Ser.). 238p. 1993. pap. 40.00 (*0-8342-0364-2*) Aspen Pub.

— The Health Care Supervisor on Effective Communication. (Health Care Supervisor Ser.). 228p. 1993. pap. 42.00 (*0-8342-0365-0*) Aspen Pub.

— The Health Care Supervisor on Effective Employee Relations. (Health Care Supervisor Ser.). 240p. 1993. pap. 40.00 (*0-8342-0366-9*) Aspen Pub.

— The Health Care Supervisor on Law. (Health Care Supervisor Ser.). 238p. 1993. pap. 40.00 (*0-8342-0367-7*) Aspen Pub.

— The Health Care Supervisor on Productivity. LC 93-9324. (Health Care Supervisor Ser.). 240p. 1993. pap. 40.00 (*0-8342-0368-5*) Aspen Pub.

— Health Care Supervisor Series. 1993. pap. 192.00 (*0-8342-0370-7*) Aspen Pub.

McConnell, Charles R., jt. auth. see Liebler, Joan G.

McConnell, Charles R., jt. auth. see Phillips, Richard L.

McConnell, Chris. A Nation of Amor. LC 93-36291. 187p. 1994. 22.00 (*1-877946-40-0*) Permanent Pr.

McConnell, Christine, jt. auth. see Webster, Alec.

***McConnell, Curt.** Coast-to-Coast Auto Races of the Early 1900s: Three Contests That Changed the World. LC 00-40054. (Illus.). 2000. write for info. (*0-7680-0604-X*) Soc Auto Engineers.

— Coast to Coast by Automobile: The Pioneering Trips, 1899-1908. LC 99-26742. 351p. 2000. 45.00 (*0-8047-3380-5*) Stanford U Pr.

McConnell, Curt. Great Cars of the Great Plains. LC 94-3860. (Illus.). xiv, 271p. (YA). 1995. text 50.00 (*0-8032-3163-6*) U of Nebr Pr.

McConnell, D. R. A Different Gospel: Biblical & Historical Insights into the Word of Faith Movement. rev. ed. 226p. 1995. pap. 12.95 (*1-56563-132-3*) Hendrickson MA.

McConnell, David. Encounters with the Environment: Readings on Environmental. 240p. (C). 1997. per. 52.95 (*0-7872-4165-2*, 41416501) Kendall-Hunt.

***McConnell, David.** Implementing Computer Supported Cooperative Learning. 2nd ed. 256p. 2000. pap. 32.50 (*0-7494-3135-0*, Pub. by Kogan Page Ltd) Stylus Pub VA.

McConnell, David. Importing Diversity: Inside Japan's Jet Program. LC 99-38465. 417p. 1999. 50.00 (*0-520-21635-0*, Pub. by U CA Pr) Cal Prin Full Svc.

— Importing Diversity: Inside Japan's Jet Program. LC 99-38465. 417p. 2000. pap. 19.95 (*0-520-21636-9*, Pub. by U CA Pr) Cal Prin Full Svc.

McConnell, David, jt. auth. see Parker, Lois.

McConnell, David B. Explore Michigan A to Z. McConnell, Stella M., ed. LC 93-17430. (Illus.). 48p. (Orig.). (J). (gr. 3-4). 1993. pap. 7.95 (*0-910726-55-8*) Hillsdale Educ.

— Forging the Peninsulas. (Illus.). 410p. 1995. 39.95 (*0-910726-83-3*) Hillsdale Educ.

— Michigan's Story. LC 95-493. (Illus.). 256p. (J). 1995. 29.95 (*0-910726-85-X*); pap. 21.95 (*0-910726-84-1*) Hillsdale Educ.

— Our Michigan Adventure. McConnell, Stella M., ed. LC 98-155043. (Illus.). 282p. (J). (gr. 3-4). 1998. 30.95 (*0-910726-35-3*, 35-3) Hillsdale Educ.

McConnell, David B. & Thomas, Steven. Michigan Government & You. LC 91-32794. (Illus.). 323p. (Orig.). 1991. pap. 26.95 (*0-910726-47-7*) Hillsdale Educ.

McConnell, Donald. Economic Virtues in the United States. LC 73-2520. (Big Business; Economic Power in a Free Society Ser.). 1973. reprint ed. 12.95 (*0-405-05100-X*) Ayer.

McConnell, Donald K., Jr. Public Company Auditor Changes & Big Eight Firms: Disagreements & Other Issues. Farmer, Richard, ed. LC 83-5953. (Research for Business Decisions Ser.: No. 62). 330p. reprint ed. pap. 102.30 (*0-8357-1425-X*, 207040600088) Bks Demand.

McConnell, Donna. Lively Little Logs. Reikes, Ursula G., ed. LC 93-8014. (Illus.). 72p. 1993. pap. 17.95 (*1-56477-027-3*, B157) Martingale & Co.

McConnell, Donna F. Fun with Miniature Log Cabin Blocks: Featuring 20 Charming Quilts. Barnes, Christine, ed. LC 98-18128. (Illus.). 96p. 1998. pap. 21.95 (*1-56477-230-6*, B340, That Patchwrk Pl) Martingale & Co.

McConnell, Doug & Emory, Jerry. Bay Area Backroads. (Illus.). 166p. 1999. pap. 16.95 (*0-8118-2091-2*) Chronicle Bks.

McConnell, Douglas J. & Dillon, John L. Farm Management for Asia: A Systems Appproach. LC 98-211971. (Farm Systems Management Ser.: No. 13). 385p. 1998. pap. 43.00 (*92-5-104077-X*, F4077X, Pub. by FAO) Bernan Associates.

McConnell, Edwina A. Clinical Considerations in Perioperative Nursing. LC 64-4347. 1987. text 24.95 (*0-397-54494-4*, Lippncott) Lppncott W & W.

An Asterisk (*) at the beginning of an entry indicates that the title is appearing for the first time.

McConnell, Edwina A. & Lewis, LuVerne W. Lippincott's State Board Review for NCLEX-RN. 4th ed. 1989. text 24.50 (*0-397-54722-6*, Lippncott) Lppncott W & W.

McConnell, Edwina A. & Zimmerman, Mary F. Care of Patients with Urologic Problems. (Illus.). 309p. 1982. text 22.50 (*0-397-54402-2*, 64-03430, Lippncott) Lppncott W & W.

McConnell, Elizabeth Huffmaster & Moriarty, Laura J. American Prisons: An Annotated Bibliography, 1. LC 98-25566. (Bibliographies of the History of Crime & Criminal Justice: Vol. 1). 344p. 1998. lib. bdg. 75.00 (*0-313-30616-8*, Greenwood Pr) Greenwood.

McConnell-Falk, Judith, jt. ed. see Bolin, Francis S.

McConnell, Fiona. The Biodiversity Convention - a Negotiating History: A Personal Account of Negotiating the United Nations Convention on Biological Diversity, & After. LC 96-9257. (International Environmental Law & Policy Ser.). 223p. 1996. 175.00 (*90-411-0917-X*) Kluwer Law Intl.

McConnell, Francis J. Borden Parker Bowne, His Life & Philosophy. LC 75-3077. reprint ed. 27.50 (*0-404-59078-0*) AMS Pr.

McConnell, Francis J., ed. A Basis for the Peace to Come: Proceedings of the National Study Conference of the Churches on a Just & Durable Peace, 1st, Ohio Wesleyan University, 1942. 1977. 12.95 (*0-8369-7277-5*, 8076) Ayer.

McConnell, Frank. Liar's Poker: A Harry Garnish/Bridget O'Toole Mystery. LC 92-43525. 234p. 1993. 19.95 (*0-8027-3229-1*) Walker & Co.

McConnell, Frank, ed. The Bible & the Narrative Tradition. 160p. 1991. reprint ed. pap. text 19.95 (*0-19-507002-X*) OUP.

McConnell, Frank D. The Confessional Imagination: A Reading of Wordsworth's Prelude. LC 73-19333. 224p. reprint ed. pap. 69.50 (*0-608-07398-9*, 206762500009) Bks Demand.

— Four Postwar American Novelists: Bellow, Mailer, Barth & Pynchon. LC 76-25638. 1978. reprint ed. pap. text 5.50 (*0-226-55685-9*, P800) U Ch Pr.

— The Spoken Seen: Film & the Romantic Imagination. LC 75-11342. 214p. reprint ed. pap. 66.40 (*0-608-15003-7*, 202588600046) Bks Demand.

McConnell, Frank D., ed. see Byron, George Gordon.

McConnell, Freeman, ed. see National Symposium on Deafness in Childhood Staff.

McConnell, G. Accents. 1985. pap. text, student ed. 38.28 (*0-201-14914-1*) Addison-Wesley.

— Accents, Level 1. 1986. pap. text, wbk. ed. 12.96 (*0-201-14916-8*) Addison-Wesley.

— Accents, Level 2. 1985. pap. text, student ed. 38.28 (*0-201-14921-4*) Addison-Wesley.

— Promenades 1. 1981. text 22.20 (*0-201-18671-3*); pap. text 12.16 (*0-201-18672-1*) Addison-Wesley.

— Promenades 2. 1982. pap. text 22.20 (*0-201-18681-0*); pap. text 12.16 (*0-201-18682-9*) Addison-Wesley.

— Vive le Francais, Level 1. 1978. text 22.20 (*0-201-14700-9*) Addison-Wesley.

Mcconnell, G. Vive le Francais: Level 3, Level 3. (FRE.). 1979. pap. text, student ed. 28.12 (*0-201-14714-9*) Addison-Wesley.

McConnell, G. Vive Le Francais Level 1: Cahier D'Activities. (FRE.). 1978. pap. text 10.04 (*0-201-14701-7*) Addison-Wesley.

— Vive le Francais Level 2. 1978. text 22.20 (*0-201-14707-6*) Addison-Wesley.

— Vive Le Francais Level 3. (FRE.). 1979. pap. text 12.16 (*0-201-14715-7*) Addison-Wesley.

McConnell, Gerald. Assemblage: Three Dimensional Picture Making. (Illus.). 96p. 1976. pap. 21.95 (*0-442-25264-1*) Madison Square.

McConnell, Gerald, ed. California Graphic Design. LC 96-76797. (Illus.). 244p. 1997. 49.95 (*0-942604-56-3*) Madison Square.

McConnell-Ginet, Sally, et al, eds. Women & Language in Literature & Society. LC 80-20816. 352p. 1980. 75.00 (*0-275-90520-9*, C0520, Praeger Pubs) Greenwood.

McConnell-Ginet, Sally, jt. auth. see Chierchia, Gennaro.

McConnell-Ginet, Sally, jt. ed. see Kramsch, Claire.

McConnell, Grant. The Spirit of Private Government. (Reprint Series in Social Sciences). (C). 1993. reprint ed. pap. text 5.00 (*0-8290-2738-6*, PS-196) Irvington.

McConnell, H. H. Five Years a Cavalryman. LC 75-133525. (Select Bibliographies Reprint Ser.). 1977. reprint ed. 20.95 (*0-8369-5557-9*) Ayer.

— Five Years a Cavalryman: Or, Sketches of Regular Army Life on the Texas Frontier, 1866-1871. LC 95-25718. (Western Frontier Library: Vol. 62). 320p. (Orig.). 1996. pap. 12.95 (*0-8061-2817-8*) U of Okla Pr.

McConnell, Harry W. & Snyder, Peter J., eds. Psychiatric Comorbidity in Epilepsy: Basic Mechanisms, Diagnosis, & Treatment. 416p. 1998. text 56.00 (*0-88048-853-0*, 8853) Am Psychiatric.

McConnell, I. & Oldstone, Michael B. Bunyaviridae. (Current Topics in Microbiology & Immunology Ser.: Vol. 169). (Illus.). x, 256p. 1991. 120.00 (*0-387-53061-4*) Spr-Verlag.

McConnell, Imogene, jt. auth. see McLane, Bobbie J.

McConnell, Inez B. The Taming of the Wilderness in Northern New York: Wm. C. Pierrepont's 1826 Journal. (The/Piereepont Journals). 86p. 1993. pap. 10.00 (*1-886303-03-7*) Write to Print.

***McConnell, J. C. & Robson, James C.** Noncommutative Noetherian Rings. LC 00-34990. (Graduate Studies in Mathematics). (Illus.). 616p. 2001. reprint ed. 72.00 (*0-8218-2169-5*) Am Math.

McConnell, J. R., jt. auth. see Gaiduk, V. I.

McConnell, J. W. Field Lysimeter Investigations: Low-level Waste Data Base Development Program for Fiscal Year 1996, Annual Report. 55p. 1997. pap. 6.00 (*0-16-062859-8*) USGPO.

— Low-Level Waste Data Base Development Program. 448p. 1998. per. 35.00 (*0-16-062954-3*) USGPO.

McConnell, James. Guide to Safe Stairways, Walkways, & Railings. (Illus.). 20p. 1978. pap. text 8.00 (*0-88698-153-0*, 1.50010) PETEX.

McConnell, James. Ambrose Bierce: Great American Short Stories II. LC 94-75024. (Classic Short Stories Ser.). 80p. 1994. pap. 5.95 (*0-7854-0582-8*, 40023) Am Guidance.

— Anton Chekhov: Great Short Stories from Around the World I. LC 94-75341. (Classic Short Stories Ser.). 80p. 1994. pap. 5.95 (*0-7854-0648-4*, 40062) Am Guidance.

— Arthur Conan Doyle: Great British & Irish Short Stories I. LC 94-75351. (Classic Short Stories Ser.). 80p. 1994. pap. 5.95 (*0-7854-0633-6*, 40041) Am Guidance.

— E. M. Forster: Great British & Irish Short Stories I. LC 94-75356. (Classic Short Stories Ser.). 80p. 1994. pap. 5.95 (*0-7854-0634-4*, 40046) Am Guidance.

— Edgar Allan Poe: Great American Short Stories I. LC 94-75016. (Classic Short Stories Ser.). 80p. 1994. pap. 5.95 (*0-7854-0577-1*, 40005) Am Guidance.

— Edith Wharton: Great American Short Stories II. LC 94-75026. (Classic Short Stories Ser.). 80p. 1994. pap. 5.95 (*0-7854-0591-7*, 40025) Am Guidance.

— Frank R. Stockton: Great American Short Stories II. LC 94-75028. (Classic Short Stories Ser.). 80p. 1994. pap. 5.95 (*0-7854-0590-9*, 40027) Am Guidance.

— Guy de Maupassant: Great Short Stories from Around the World I. LC 94-75350. (Classic Short Stories Ser.). 80p. 1994. pap. 5.95 (*0-7854-0652-2*, 40061) Am Guidance.

— H. G. Wells: Great British & Irish Short Stories I. LC 94-75358. (Classic Short Stories Ser.). 80p. 1994. pap. 5.95 (*0-7854-0642-5*, 40048) Am Guidance.

— James Joyce: Great British & Irish Short Stories I. LC 94-75360. (Classic Short Stories Ser.). 80p. 1994. pap. 5.95 (*0-7854-0637-9*, 40050) Am Guidance.

— John Galsworthy: Great British & Irish Short Stories I. LC 94-75359. (Classic Short Stories Ser.). 80p. 1994. pap. 5.95 (*0-7854-0635-2*, 40049) Am Guidance.

— Katherine Mansfield: Great British & Irish Short Stories I. LC 94-75354. (Classic Short Stories Ser.). 80p. 1994. pap. 5.95 (*0-7854-0639-5*, 40044) Am Guidance.

— Leo Tolstoy: Great Short Stories from Around the World I. LC 94-75342. (Classic Short Stories Ser.). 80p. 1994. pap. 5.95 (*0-7854-0655-7*, 40063) Am Guidance.

— Nathaniel Hawthorne: Great American Short Stories I. LC 94-75013. (Classic Short Stories Ser.). 80p. 1994. pap. 5.95 (*0-7854-0624-7*, 40002) Am Guidance.

— Robert Louis Stevenson: Great British & Irish Short Stories I. LC 94-75357. (Classic Short Stories Ser.). 80p. 1994. pap. 5.95 (*0-7854-0641-7*, 40047) Am Guidance.

— Saki: Great British & Irish Short Stories I. LC 94-75352. (Classic Short Stories Ser.). 80p. 1994. pap. 5.95 (*0-7854-0640-9*, 40042) Am Guidance.

— Selma Lagerlof: Great Short Stories from Around the World I. LC 94-75343. (Classic Short Stories Ser.). 80p. 1994. pap. 5.95 (*0-7854-0651-4*, 40064) Am Guidance.

— Thomas Hardy: Great British & Irish Short Stories I. LC 94-75355. (Classic Short Stories Ser.). 80p. 1994. pap. 5.95 (*0-7854-0636-0*, 40045) Am Guidance.

McConnell, James V. Understanding Human Behavior: An Introduction to Psychology. 6th ed. 768p. (C). 1989. wbk. ed. 12.95 (*0-318-43181-5*); text 29.95 (*0-318-43180-7*) Harcourt Coll Pubs.

— Vive le Francais: Cahier D'Activites, Level 2. 1978. pap. text 10.04 (*0-201-14708-4*) Addison-Wesley.

McConnell, James V. & Gorenflo, Daniel W., eds. Classic Readings in Psychology. LC 89-7620. (C). 1989. 13.00 (*0-03-027614-4*) Harcourt Coll Pubs.

McConnell, James V. & Philipchalk, Ronald P. Understanding Human Behavior. 7th ed. 750p. (C). 1991. text. write for info. (*0-318-69127-2*) Harcourt Coll Pubs.

McConnell, James V., jt. auth. see Philipchalk, Ronald P.

McConnell, Jane L., jt. auth. see O'Mara, Peggy.

McConnell, Jean S. A Farm at Shwando. (Illus.). 1993. pap. 10.95 (*0-9627860-7-1*) Lone Oak MN.

— The Janes' Addiction. Howe, Ray, ed. LC 95-81510. 170p. (Orig.). 1996. pap. 9.95 (*1-883477-11-5*) Lone Oak MN.

McConnell, Jenny, jt. auth. see Grelsamer, Ronald P.

McConnell, Joan. A Vocabulary Analysis of Gadda's "Pasticciaccio" LC 73-81570. (Romance Monographs: No. 2). 1973. 24.00 (*84-399-0685-4*) Romance.

McConnell, Joanne, ed. see Perlstein, Scott.

McConnell, John D. Benign Prostatic Hyperplasia 8: Diagnosis & Treatment, Clinical Practice Guideline. 241p. 1994. per. 13.00 (*0-16-061528-3*) USGPO.

— Benign Prostatic Hyperplasia 8: Diagnosis & Treatment Reference for Clinicians. 13p. 1994. pap. 23.00 (*0-16-061529-1*) USGPO.

McConnell, John D., jt. auth. see Chapple, Christopher R.

***McConnell, John H.** Auditing Your Human Resources Department: A Step-by-Step Guide. LC 00-36232. 2000. 99.95 (*0-8144-7076-9*) AMACOM.

— Hunting Heads: How to Find & Keep the Best People. 250p. 2000. 24.95 (*0-938721-76-3*, Pub. by Kiplinger Bks) Natl Bk Netwk.

McConnell, John H. A Ring, a Horse & a Clown: An Eight Generation History of the Hannefords. (Illus.). 348p. (C). 1992. 29.95 (*0-9636019-0-3*, Astley & Ricketts) McConnell-Simmons.

McConnell, John S. Analysis & Control of Variation: Control Chart Techniques for TQC Practitioners. 4th rev. ed. (Illus.). 144p. 1987. pap. 30.00 (*0-9588324-2-0*, Pub. by Delaware Grp) Am Overseas Bk Co.

— Safer Than a Known Way. 2nd rev. ed. (Illus.). 266p. 1988. 50.00 (*0-9588324-3-9*, Pub. by Delaware Grp) Am Overseas Bk Co.

— The Seven Tools of TQC. 4th ed. (Illus.). 176p. 1986. pap. 35.00 (*0-9588324-0-4*, Pub. by Delaware Grp) Am Overseas Bk Co.

McConnell, Judy. Sports-a-Thon: A Fund Raising Event in a Box. (Illus.). 40p. 1998. text 149.00 (*0-9664415-0-8*) Triple Step.

McConnell, Judy G., jt. auth. see Underhill, Robert M.

McConnell, Kathleen. Salvation: A Comparative Analysis of Differing Theological Traditions. LC 94-17139. (Catholic Scholars Press Ser.). 350p. 1997. text 74.95 (*1-883255-67-8*, Cath Scholar Pr); pap. text 54.95 (*1-883255-66-X*) Intl Scholars.

***McConnell, Kathleen & Ryser, Gail.** Practical Ideas That Really Work for Students with Autism Spectrum Disorders. LC 00-32803. 2000. write for info. (*0-89079-858-3*) PRO-ED.

***McConnell, Kathleen, et al.** Practical Ideas That Really Work for Students with ADHD. LC 99-41748. (Illus.). 2000. pap. write for info. (*0-89079-837-0*) PRO-ED.

McConnell, Keith. The AnimAlphabet Encyclopedia. 5th ed. (NaturEncyclopedia Ser.). (Illus.). 48p. (J). (gr. 4 up). 1982. pap. 5.95 (*0-916144-97-6*, Naturencyclop) Stemmer Hse.

McConnell, Keith A. Dinosaurs from A to Z. (NaturEncyclopedia Ser.). (Illus.). 40p. (Orig.). (J). (gr. 2 up). 1988. pap. 5.95 (*0-88045-095-9*) Stemmer Hse.

— The ReptAlphabet Encyclopedia. (NaturEncyclopedia Ser.). (Illus.). 48p. (Orig.). (J). (gr. 4 up). 1984. pap. 5.95 (*0-88045-045-2*) Stemmer Hse.

— The Sealphabet Encyclopedia. 5th ed. (NaturEncyclopedia Library). (Illus.). 48p. (Orig.). (J). (gr. 4 up). 1982. pap. 6.95 (*0-88045-016-9*, Intl Design) Stemmer Hse.

McConnell, Kenneth G. Vibration Testing: Theory & Practice. LC 95-16398. 624p. 1995. 140.00 (*0-471-30435-2*) Wiley.

***McConnell, Kenneth R., et al.** Fax. 3rd ed. LC 99-23716. 460p. 1999. 85.00 (*0-89006-944-1*) Artech Hse.

McConnell, Kenneth R., et al. Fax: Digital Facsimile Technology & Applications. (Artech House Telecom Management Library). 234p. 1989. text 60.00 (*0-89006-310-9*) Artech Hse.

McConnell, Kevin. Collecting Art Deco. LC 90-62902. (Illus.). 144p. 1990. 49.95 (*0-88740-279-8*) Schiffer.

— Heintz Art Metal. LC 90-64023. (Illus.). 128p. 1991. pap. 19.95 (*0-88740-298-4*) Schiffer.

— More Roycroft Art Metal. LC 95-69727. (Illus.). 160p. (Orig.). 1995. pap. 19.95 (*0-88740-848-6*) Schiffer.

— Redware: America's Folk Art Pottery. 2nd rev. ed. LC 98-89250. (Illus.). 96p. (Orig.). 1999. pap. 12.95 (*0-7643-0767-3*) Schiffer.

— Redware, America's Folk Art Pottery. LC 88-64156. (Illus.). 96p. 1989. pap. 12.95 (*0-88740-159-7*) Schiffer.

— Roycraft Art Metal. rev. ed. LC 89-63420. (Illus.). 144p. 1989. pap. 16.95 (*0-88740-694-7*) Schiffer.

— Roycroft Art Metal. 3rd rev. ed. LC 99-60154. (Illus.). 144p. 1999. pap. 16.95 (*0-7643-0851-3*) Schiffer.

— Spongeware & Spatterware. 2nd rev. ed. LC 98-89266. (Illus.). 128p. 1999. pap. 16.95 (*0-7643-0768-1*) Schiffer.

***McConnell, Kym.** Tibet Overland: A Route & Planning Guide for Mountain Bikers & Other Overlanders. 2000. pap. 19.95 (*1-873756-41-0*, Pub. by Trailblazer) Seven Hills Bk.

McConnell, Louise. Dictionary of Shakespeare. 2000. pap. 15.95 (*1-901659-39-9*, Pub. by P Collin) IPG Chicago.

McConnell, Malcolm. Inside Hanoi's Secret Archives. 1995. 25.00 (*0-671-87118-8*) S&S Trade.

— Into the Mouth of the Cat: The Story of Lance Sijan, Hero of Vietnam. LC 97-49705. 255p. 1997. reprint ed. lib. bdg. 30.00 (*0-7351-0013-6*) Replica Bks.

McConnell, Malcolm, jt. auth. see Ballard, Robert Duane.

McConnell, Malcolm, jt. auth. see Kantoff, Philip.

McConnell, Malcolm, jt. auth. see Mendez, Antonio J.

McConnell, Malcolm, jt. auth. see Zuyev, Alexander.

McConnell, Maria, jt. auth. see McConnell, Cecilio.

McConnell, Marian. Emergence, a Novel. 184p. 1999. 19.95 (*0-939748-49-5*); pap. 10.95 (*0-939748-48-7*) Cave Bks MO.

McConnell, Marie-Antoinette, tr. see Rougeyron, Andre.

McConnell, Mark K. Risk a Thousand, Make a Million? How to Trade Stock Index Futures. (Illus.). 34p. (Orig.). 1989. pap. 6.95 (*0-9622816-0-3*) Capital Growth.

***McConnell, Mark L. & Ryan, James M., eds.** The Fifth Compton Symposium. LC 00-101590. (AIP Conference Proceedings Ser.: Vol. 510). (Illus.). xx, 840p. 2000. 195.00 (*1-56396-932-7*, Pub. by Am Inst Physics) Spr-Verlag.

McConnell, Mary, jt. auth. see McConnell, Cecilio.

McConnell, Mary Jo. Dear Mrs. Bartlett: Letters from the Field. LC 98-50064. 232p. 1999. pap. text 16.95 (*0-9666750-1-0*, Pub. by Nocturnum Pr) Consort Bk Sales.

McConnell, Mary M. Outdoor Adventures with Kids. LC 95-44971. 230p. 1996. pap. 12.95 (*0-87833-849-7*) Taylor Pub.

McConnell, Michael, jt. auth. see Golden, Renny.

McConnell, Michael N. A Country Between: The Upper Ohio Valley & Its Peoples, 1724-1774. LC 91-42867. (Illus.). xiii, 359p. 1992. text 55.00 (*0-8032-3142-3*) U of Nebr Pr.

— A Country Between: The Upper Ohio Valley & Its Peoples, 1724-1774. LC 91-42867. (Illus.). xxi, 359p. 1992. pap. 20.00 (*0-8032-8238-9*, Bison Books) U of Nebr Pr.

Mcconnell, Mick. Lax: The Los Angeles Experiment: Architecture Design. 112p. 1994. pap. 25.00 (*0-930829-36-0*) Lumen Inc.

McConnell, Missy. Plain Jane Vanilla. (Illus.). 48p. (J). 1980. 24.00 (*0-88014-018-6*) Mosaic Pr OH.

***McConnell, Mitch & Biden, Joe, eds.** Proceedings of the Senate Task Force on Economic Sanctions. (Illus.). 192p. 2000. reprint ed. pap. text 35.00 (*0-7881-8505-5*) DIANE Pub.

McConnell, Molly C. Advent: Prepare Ye the Way of the Lord. large type ed. (Illus.). 1987. pap. 9.95 (*0-8027-2598-8*) Walker & Co.

McConnell, Nelie D. At the Miranda. 1981. 40.00 (*0-7223-1436-1*, Pub. by A H S Ltd) St Mut.

McConnell, Pam & Ayres, Kate. You Are Not Alone Vol. 1: A Practical Guide for Managing Diabetes. (Illus.). 32p. 1997. spiral bd. 14.95 (*0-9658282-0-4*) You Are Not.

McConnell, Patricia B. The Cautious Canine: How to Help Dogs Conquer Their Fears. 29p. 1998. pap. 5.00 (*1-891767-00-3*) Dogs Bst Frnd.

— Dogs Best Friend's Beginning Family Dog Training. 2nd ed. 67p. 1996. reprint ed. pap. 10.00 (*1-891767-03-8*) Dogs Bst Frnd.

— How to Be the Leader of the Pack & Have Your Dog Love You for It! 2nd ed. (How to Booklets from Dogs Best Friend Ser.). 12p. 1996. reprint ed. pap. 3.00 (*1-891767-02-X*) Dogs Bst Frnd.

***McConnell, Patricia B.** I'll Be Home Soon! How to Prevent & Treat Separation Anxiety. (How to Booklets from Dogs Best Friend Ser.). 37p. 2000. pap. 7.00 (*1-891767-05-4*) Dogs Bst Frnd.

McConnell, Patricia B. & Scidmore, Brenda K. Dog's Best Friend's Puppy Primer. 2nd ed. 64p. 1996. reprint ed. pap. 10.00 (*1-891767-01-1*) Dogs Bst Frnd.

McConnell, Paul, ed. Making a Difference: Measuring the Impact of Information on Development: Proceedings of a Workshop Held in Ottawa, Canada 10-12 July 1995. LC 97-701287. iv, 254p. 1995. pap. 19.95 (*0-88936-783-3*, Pub. by IDRC Bks) Stylus Pub VA.

McConnell, R., et al, eds. The Genetics & Epidemiology of Inflammatory Bowel Disease. (Frontiers of Gastrointestinal Research Ser.: Vol. 11). (Illus.). viii, 180p. 1986. 123.50 (*3-8055-4265-8*) S Karger.

McConnell, R. A. Introduction to Parapsychology in the Context of Science. LC 82-99945. (Illus.). xiv, 337p. 1983. pap. 12.00 (*0-9610232-3-6*) McConnell.

***McConnell, R. A.** Joyride to Infinity. 440p. 2000. 25.00 (*1-878465-35-X*) Scott-Townsend Pubs.

McConnell, R. A. Parapsychology in Retrospect: My Search for the Unicorn. LC 86-90590. (Illus.). 240p. (Orig.). 1987. pap. 15.00 (*0-9610232-4-4*) McConnell.

McConnell, R. A., ed. Encounters with Parapsychology. LC 81-90032. (Illus.). ix, 235p. 1982. pap. 9.00 (*0-9610232-1-X*) McConnell.

— Parapsychology & Self-Deception in Science. LC 81-90464. (Illus.). vii, 150p. 1983. pap. 7.00 (*0-9610232-2-8*) McConnell.

McConnell, R. A., jt. auth. see Schmeidler, Gertrude R.

McConnell, R. D. & Noufi, Rommel, eds. Science & Technology of Thin Film Superconductors 2. (Illus.). 656p. (C). 1990. text 174.00 (*0-306-43803-8*, Kluwer Plenum) Kluwer Academic.

McConnell, R. D. & Wolf, Stuart A., eds. Science & Technology of Thin Film Superconductors. (Illus.). 572p. (C). 1989. text 162.00 (*0-306-43215-3*, Kluwer Plenum) Kluwer Academic.

McConnell, Rachel, jt. ed. see Brodie, David A.

McConnell, Richard E. The Debt Penalty. LC 91-91155. 120p. 1991. 24.95 (*0-9630852-0-4*) R E McConnell.

***McConnell, Ro.** Land of Waters: The South American Rainforest & Savannah. (Illus.). 328p. 2000. 32.50 (*1-85776-458-7*, Pub. by Book Guild Ltd) Trans-Atl Phila.

McConnell, Robert. Baby Boid. (Illus.). 48p. (J). (gr. 2-5). 1991. pap. 7.95 (*0-929141-11-3*) Napoleon Publ.

— Boid & the Bullies. (Illus.). 48p. 1990. pap. 7.95 (*0-929141-04-0*) Napoleon Publ.

— Davenport Dumpling. (Illus.). 48p. (J). (gr. 2-6). 1991. pap. text 7.95 (*0-929141-08-3*) Napoleon Publ.

— Emonde et Scie. Warnant-Cote, M. A., tr. (FRE., Illus.). 48p. (Orig.). 1991. pap. 14.95 (*0-929141-05-9*) Napoleon Publ.

McConnell, Robert. Far Out in the New Age. The Subversion of Science by Cultural Communism. LC 94-76288. (Illus.). iv, 200p. (Orig.). 1995. pap. 24.00 (*0-9610232-6-0*) McConnell.

McConnell, Robert. Fraises en Deconfiture.Tr. of Strawberry Jam. (FRE., Illus.). 48p. (Orig.). 1990. pap. 12.95 (*0-929141-06-7*) Napoleon Publ.

McConnell, Robert. Gentle Expeditions: A Guide to Ethical Mountain Adventure. (Illus.). 128p. 1996. pap. 10.00 (*0-930410-67-X*) Amer Alpine Club.

McConnell, Robert. Nip & Tuck. (Illus.). 48p. 1990. 12.95 (*0-929141-01-6*) Napoleon Publ.

— Nip & Tuck: Teacher's Resource Package, Grades 1-3. 1995. pap. text, teacher ed. 8.95 (*0-929141-46-6*) Napoleon Publ.

— Norbert Nipkin. (J). 1994. audio 7.95 (*0-929141-24-5*) Napoleon Publ.

— Norbert Nipkin & the Magic Riddle Stone. (Illus.). 48p. 1990. 14.95 (*0-929141-03-2*) Napoleon Publ.

— Norbert Nipkin & the Magic Riddle Stone. (Illus.). (J). 1995. audio 7.95 (*0-929141-25-3*) Napoleon Publ.

— Norbert Nipkin et la Pierre aux Enigmes.Tr. of Norbert Nipkin & the Magic Riddle Stone. (FRE., Illus.). 48p. (Orig.). 1990. pap. 15.95 (*0-929141-07-5*) Napoleon Publ.

— Sarah's Secret. (Illus.). 24p. 1991. pap. text 8.95 (*0-929141-12-1*) Napoleon Publ.

— Sarah's Secret: Teachers' Resource Package. Sidorchuk, Ruth, ed. (J). (gr. 2-3). 1998. 8.95 (*0-929141-57-1*) Napoleon Publ.

— The Strawberry Jam. (Illus.). 48p. 1990. 12.95 (*0-929141-02-4*) Napoleon Publ.

McConnell, Robert, jt. auth. see Gamble, Judi.

McConnell, Robert D., ed. Future Generation of Photovoltaic Technologies: First NREL Conference. (AIP Conference Proceedings: Vol. 404). (Illus.). 464p. 1997. 115.00 (*1-56396-704-9*) Am Inst Physics.

M

Mcconnell, Robert L. Environmental Issues: Measuring, Analyzing & Evaluating. LC 98-15739. 205p. (gr. 1). 1998. pap. text 28.60 (*0-13-095270-2*) P-H.

McConnell, Robert R., ed. see Technical Association of the Pulp & Paper Industry.

***McConnell, Robin.** Inside the All Blacks LC 98-225371. 279 p. 1998. write for info. (*1-86950-274-4*) HarpC.

McConnell, Roland C. Negro Troops of Antebellum Louisiana: A History of the Battalion of Free Men of Color. LC 68-15430. (Louisiana State University Studies: No. 13). 158p. reprint ed. pap. 49.00 (*0-608-30718-1*, 200716400062) Bks Demand.

***McConnell, Sarah & Lynam, P. J.** Virtually Global? Creating an Adaptive International Model to Accelerate Performance. 63p. 2000. 8.00 (*0-9701465-0-7*) Virtual Pubns.

McConnell, Scott. Leftward Journey: The Education of Vietnamese Students in France, 1919-1939. 220p. 1988. 44.95 (*0-88738-238-X*) Transaction Pubs.

McConnell, Scott R., jt. auth. see Walker, Hill M.

McConnell, Seamus, ed. Wile Big Derry Phrasebook. (Illus.). 100p. 1996. pap. 7.95 (*0-946451-36-2*, Pub. by Guildhall Pr) Irish Bks Media.

***McConnell, Stacy A., ed.** American Revolution Primary Sources. LC 99-46940. 200p. (J). 2000. text 42.00 (*0-7876-3790-4*) Gale.

McConnell, Stacy A. & Hall, Linda D., eds. Industry Reference Handbooks: Entertainment. (Dun & Bradstreet & Gale Industry Reference Handbooks Ser.). 600p. 1999. 99.00 (*0-7876-3773-4*, GML00299-113537, Gale Res Intl) Gale.

McConnell, Stacy A., ed. see Knight, Judson.

McConnell, Stacy A., ed. see Schmittroth, Linda.

McConnell, Stacy A., ed. see Schmittroth, Linda & Rosteck, Mary Kay.

McConnell, Stella M., ed. see McConnell, David B.

***McConnell, Steve M.** After the Gold Rush: Creating a True Profession of Software Engineering. LC 99-47009. 1999. pap. text 24.99 (*0-7356-0877-6*) Microsoft.

McConnell, Steve M. Code Complete: A Practical Handbook of Software Construction. LC 92-41059. (Code Ser.). 880p. 1993. pap. 35.00 (*1-55615-484-4*) Microsoft.

— Rapid Development: Taming Wild Software Schedules. LC 96-21517. (Code Ser.). 648p. 1996. pap. text 35.00 (*1-55615-900-5*) Microsoft.

***McConnell, Steve M.** Software Estimation: The Black Art Demystified. 2000. pap. 24.99 (*0-7356-0535-1*) Microsoft.

McConnell, Steve M. Software Project Survival Guide: How to Be Sure Your First Important Project Isn't Your Last. LC 97-37923. 288p. 1997. pap. text 24.99 (*1-57231-621-7*) Microsoft.

McConnell, Stuart. Glorious Contentment: The Grand Army of the Republic, 1865-1900. LC 91-50793. (Illus.). 332p. (C). 1997. pap. 17.95 (*0-8078-4628-7*) U of NC Pr.

McConnell, Sylvia, tr. see Warnant-Cote, Marie-Andree.

McConnell, T. R., jt. auth. see Mortimer, Kenneth P.

McConnell, Terrance. Gratitude. LC 92-25292. 288p. (C). 1993. 59.95 (*1-56639-038-9*) Temple U Pr.

***McConnell, Terrance C.** Inalienable Rights: The Limits of Consent in Medicine & the Law. LC 99-41540. 240p. 2000. write for info. (*0-19-513462-1*) OUP.

McConnell, Terrence. Moral Issues in Health Care. 2nd ed. LC 96-19413. (Philosophy Ser.). 320p. (C). 1996. 31.95 (*0-534-24744-X*) Wadsworth Pub.

***McConnell, Terry & Sprouse, Harry W.** Great Communication with Video Production in School Libraries. (Professional Growth Ser.). 280p. 2000. pap. 39.95 (*0-938865-95-1*) Linworth Pub.

McConnell, Thomas G. Conversations with General Grant: An Informal Biography. LC 89-29620. (Illus.). 248p. (Orig.). 1990. 19.95 (*1-878332-11-2*); pap. 9.95 (*1-878332-10-4*) Walnut VA.

***Mcconnell, Vicki C. & Ritchie, Branson W.** Calculations for Veterinary Professionals. LC 99-47112. 2000. pap. 24.95 (*0-8138-0879-0*) Iowa St U Pr.

McConnell, Virginia A. Arsenic under the Elms: Murder in Victorian New Haven. LC 99-19261. 288p. 1999. 26.95 (*0-275-96297-0*, Praeger Pubs) Greenwood.

McConnell, W. H. William R. McIntyre: Paladin of the Common Law. 240p. 34.95 (*0-88629-341-3*, Pub. by McG-Queens Univ Pr) CUP Services.

McConnell, William F. Remember Reno: A Biographer of Major General Jesse Lee Reno. LC 96-16506. (Illus.). 113p. 1996. 19.95 (*1-57249-020-9*) White Mane Pub.

McConnell, William J. Frontier Law: A Story of Vigilante Days. LC 78-156027. (Illus.). reprint ed. 39.50 (*0-404-09177-6*) AMS Pr.

McConnell, Winder. Kudrun. LC 92-16058. (Medvl Ser.: Vol. 73). xxii, 182p. 1992. 65.00 (*1-879751-12-7*) Camden Hse.

— Lament of the Nibelungen. (Medvl Ser.). xxiii, 220p. 1994. 60.00 (*1-879751-73-9*) Camden Hse.

— The Wate Figure in Medieval Tradition. (Stanford German Studies: Vol. 13). 129p. 1978. pap. 23.00 (*3-261-03058-5*) P Lang Pubng.

McConnell, Winder, ed. A Companion to the Nibelungenlied. LC 98-21818. (Studies in German Literature, Linguistics & Culture). 240p. 1998. 65.00 (*1-57113-151-5*) Camden Hse.

McConnen, Harold L. Destruction. 128p. 1988. pap. write for info. (*0-318-64421-5*) Talking Leaf Pubs.

Mcconnell. Brookdale Economics & Concepts. 1998. 77.58 (*0-07-397140-5*) McGraw.

McConney, Anne. Lenten Journal. 112p. 2000. pap. 9.95 (*0-8192-1787-5*, 5980) Morehouse Pub.

— Our December Hearts: Meditations for Advent & Christmas. LC 99-31259. 112p. 1999. pap. 10.95 (*0-8192-1786-7*, 5979) Morehouse Pub.

McConnor, Vincent. Limbo. 288p. 1988. mass mkt. 3.95 (*0-445-40677-1*, Pub. by Mysterious Pr) Little.

McConochie, Jean A. Secret among the Ruins. (Readers Ser.). 1984. pap. text 2.25 (*0-88345-575-7*) Prentice ESL.

— Twentieth Century American Short Stories. (J). 1975. pap. 17.95 (*0-8384-3233-6*) Heinle & Heinle.

— Twentieth-Century American Short Stories, Vol. 1. 2nd rev. ed. 160p. (J). 1995. mass mkt. 26.95 (*0-8384-4851-8*); mass mkt. 26.95 (*0-8384-4850-X*) Heinle & Heinle.

— 20th Century American Short Stories: Anthology. LC 94-43027. 224p. (J). 1995. mass mkt. 33.95 (*0-8384-6146-8*) Heinle & Heinle.

McConochie, Jean A., ed. see Barkman, Bruce.

McConochie, Jean A., ed. see Bernkopf, Michael.

McConochie, Jean A., ed. see Emanuel, James A.

McConochie, Jean A., ed. see Gabriel, Gary.

McConochie, Jean A., ed. see Gogan, Robert.

McConochie, Jean A., ed. see Kearney, Mary A. & Kearney, Edward.

McConochie, Jean A., ed. see Messec, Jerry.

McConochie, Jean A., ed. see Winer, Lisa.

McConochie, Jean A., ed. see Winer, Lise.

McConvell, Patrick. Archaeology & Linguistics: Aboriginal Australia in Global Perspective. LC P35.5.A8A73 1997. (Illus.). 476p. 1998. text (*0-19-553728-9*) OUP.

McConvell, Patrick & Evans, Nicholas, eds. Archaeology & Linguistics: Aboriginal Australia in Global Perspective. (Illus.). 476p. 1998. pap. text 55.00 (*0-19-550670-7*) OUP.

McConville, Brendan J. These Daring Disturbers of the Public Peace: The Struggle for Property & Power in Early New Jersey. LC 99-12574. (Illus.). 318p. 1999. 45.00 (*0-8014-3389-4*) Cornell U Pr.

McConville, Bridget & Sharma, Rajendra. Allergies. LC 98-52354. (Your Child Ser.). 128p. 1999. pap. 9.95 (*1-86204-499-6*, Pub. by Element MA) Penguin Putnam.

***McConville, Brigid.** My Secret Life: Sexual Revelations from Long-Term Lovers. 192p. 1998. pap. 13.00 (*0-7225-3662-3*, Pub. by Thorsons MD) Natl Bk Netwk.

McConville, J. & Sheldrake, John. Urban Transport: An Annotated International Bibliography. LC 96-32816. 416p. 1997. 150.00 (*0-7201-2335-6*) Continuum.

McConville, J. Gordon. Chronicles. 288p. 1993. pap. 25.00 (*0-7152-0527-7*) St Mut.

— Ezra, Nehemiah. 212p. 1993. pap. 35.00 (*0-7152-0532-3*) St Mut.

— Grace in the End: A Study of Deuteronomic Theology. 176p. 1993. pap. 18.99 (*0-310-51421-5*) Zondervan.

— Judgment & Promise: An Interpretation of the Book of Jeremiah. 208p. 1993. pap. 17.95 (*0-931464-81-1*) Eisenbrauns.

— Law & Theology in Deuteronomy. (Journal for the Study of the Old Testament Supplement Ser.: Vol. 33). 214p. 1985. 50.00 (*0-905774-78-7*, Pub. by Sheffield Acad); pap. 14.95 (*0-905774-79-5*, Pub. by Sheffield Acad) CUP Services.

— Teach Yourself Old Testament. (Illus.). 176p. 1996. pap., student ed. 12.95 (*0-8442-3114-2*, Teach Yrslf) NTC Contemp Pub Co.

McConville, J. Gordon & Millar, J. G. Time & Place in Deuteronomy. LC 95-126648. (Journal for the Study of the Old Testament Supplement Ser.: Vol. 179). 155p. 1995. 52.50 (*1-85075-494-2*, Pub. by Sheffield Acad) CUP Services.

McConville, J. Gordon, jt. ed. see Knoppers, Gary N.

***McConville, James.** Economic of Maritime Transport Theory & Practice. 430p. 1999. pap. 90.00 (*1-85609-162-7*, Pub. by Witherby & Co) St Mut.

McConville, James. Transport Regulation Matters. LC 96-44707. 192p. 1997. 89.50 (*1-85567-386-X*) Bks Intl VA.

McConville, James & Rickaby, Glenys. Shipping Business & Maritime Economics: An Annotated International Bibliography. annot. ed. LC 94-23314. 512p. 1995. 140.00 (*0-7201-2180-9*) Continuum.

McConville, James & Sheldracke, John, eds. Transport in Transition: Aspects of British & European Experience. LC 94-73136. 211p. (C). 1995. text 72.95 (*1-85628-664-9*, Pub. by Avebry) Ashgate Pub Co.

McConville, John G. International Construction Costs & Reference Data Yearbook. 416p. 1995. 120.00 (*0-471-11810-9*) Wiley.

— Managing Construction Purchasing. 300p. 1993. 62.95 (*0-87629-316-X*, 67302) R S Means.

McConville, Mark. Adolescence: Psychotherapy & the Emergent Self. (Gestalt Institute of Cleveland Book Ser.). 296p. 1995. 34.50 (*0-88163-291-0*) Analytic Pr.

McConville, Michael & Bridges, Lee, eds. Criminal Justice in Crisis. LC 94-5165. (Law in Its Social Setting Ser.). 352p. 1994. 90.00 (*1-85898-003-8*) E Elgar.

McConville, Michael, et al. Standing Accused: The Organization & Practices of Criminal Defence Lawyers in Britain. (Oxford Monographs on Criminal Law & Justice). 328p. 1994. 59.00 (*0-19-825868-2*) OUP.

McConville, Sean, jt. auth. see Fairweather, Leslie.

McConville, Sean, jt. ed. see Gottfredson, Stephen D.

McConville Stensrud, Mary. Mount St. Helens Ash Potpourri: Yakima's Story. 341p. 1985. 15.00 (*0-614-30201-3*) Mary M Stensrud.

***McConway, K. J., et al.** Statistical Modelling Using Genstat. (An Arnold Publication). 384p. 1999. pap. text 50.00 (*0-340-75985-2*, Pub. by E A) OUP.

McConway, Kevin, ed. Studying Health & Disease. LC 93-43194. (Health & Disease Ser.: Bk. 2). 132p. 1994. pap. 32.95 (*0-335-19252-1*) OpUniv Pr.

McConway, Kevin, ed. see Hand, D. J. & Daly, F.

McCooey, David. Artful Histories: Modern Australian Autobiography. 245p. (C). 1996. text 69.95 (*0-521-56101-9*) Cambridge U Pr.

McCoog, Thomas M. The Society of Jesus in Ireland, Scotland & England, 1541-1588: "Our Way of Proceeding" LC 96-2790. (Studies in Medieval & Reformation Thought). xxii, 318p. 1996. 114.50 (*90-04-10482-8*) Brill Academic Pubs.

McCoog, Thomas M., ed. The Reckoned Expense: Edmund Campion & the Early English Jesuits: Essays in Celebration of the First Centenary of Campion Hall, Oxford, 1896-1996. 364p. 1996. 75.00 (*0-85115-590-1*) Boydell & Brewer.

McCook, Henry C. The Latimers. 1993. reprint ed. lib. bdg. 89.00 (*0-7812-5486-8*) Rprt Serv.

McCook, Kathleen D. & American Library Association Staff. Women of Color in Librarianship: An Oral History. LC 98-42843. 1998. write for info. (*0-8389-7993-9*) ALA.

***McCook, Kathleen D., et al.** Libraries: Global Reach, Local Touch. LC 98-4397. 256p. 1998. 42.00 (*0-8389-0738-5*) ALA.

***McCook, Kathleen de la Pedna.** A Place at the Table: Participating in Community Building. LC 00-38050. 2000. pap. write for info. (*0-8389-0788-1*) ALA.

McCook, Kathleen de la Pena, et al, eds. Developing Readers' Advisory Services: Concepts & Commitments. LC 93-22853. 120p. 1993. pap. 38.50 (*1-55570-163-9*) Neal-Schuman.

McCook, Kathleen De La Pena, see De La Pena McCook, Kathleen.

McCook, Kathleen de la Pena, jt. ed. see Immroth, Barbara.

McCool, Audrey C. Inflight Catering Management. LC 94-42490. 426p. 1995. 64.95 (*0-471-04253-6*) Wiley.

McCool, Audrey C., et al. Dimensions of Noncommercial Foodservice Management. 392p. 1994. text 48.95 (*0-442-01358-2*, VNR) Wiley.

McCool, Daniel C. Command of the Waters: Iron Triangles, Federal Water Development, & Indian Water. 321p. 1994. reprint ed. pap. 17.95 (*0-8165-1502-6*) U of Ariz Pr.

McCool, Daniel C., ed. Public PolicyTheories, Models & Concepts: An Anthology. LC 94-22744. 352p. 1994. pap. text 51.00 (*0-13-737867-X*) P-H.

McCool, Daniel C., jt. auth. see Clarke, Jeanne N.

McCool, Daniel C., jt. ed. see Goodman, Doug.

McCool, Gerald. The Neo-Thomists. LC 94-42271. (Orig.). (C). 1994. pap. 20.00 (*0-87462-601-3*) Marquette.

McCool, Gerald A. From Unity to Pluralism: The Internal Evolution of Thomism. LC 89-80460. 248p. 1992. reprint ed. pap. 19.95 (*0-8232-1242-4*) Fordham.

— Nineteenth Century Scholasticism: The Search for a Unitary Method. 2nd ed. LC 89-85007. 301p. 1989. pap. 19.95 (*0-8232-1257-2*) Fordham.

McCool, Gerald A., ed. The Universe As Journey: Conversations with W. Norris Clarke, S.J. LC 88-80357. 183p. (C). 1988. text 37.50 (*0-8232-1208-4*) Fordham.

Mccool, Kenneth B. Aviation Meteorology Unscrambled: For VFR & IFR Operations - Certificates & Ratings. 6th ed. LC 95-79659. (Illus.). 695p. (C). 1996. pap. text 44.00 (*0-9621387-9-7*) K B McCool.

McCool, Martha H. & Woodruff, Sandra. My Doctor Says I Have a Little Diabetes: A Guide to Understanding & Controlling Type 2 Non-Insulin-Dependent Diabetes. LC 98-51136. 144p. 1999. pap. 9.95 (*0-89529-860-0*, Avery) Penguin Putnam.

McCool, Samuel, jt. auth. see Cornesky, Robert.

McCool, Samuel A., jt. auth. see Cornesky, Robert A.

McCool, Stephen F. & Cole, David N., eds. Limits of Acceptable Change & Related Planning Processes: Progress & Future Directions: Proceedings. (Illus.). 84p. 1999. reprint ed. pap. text 20.00 (*0-7881-8034-7*) DIANE Pub.

McCool, Stephen F. & Watson, Alan E. Linking Tourism, the Environment, & Sustainability. (Illus.). 95p. (C). 1997. reprint ed. pap. text 30.00 (*0-7881-3862-6*) DIANE Pub.

McCool, Thomas J. The Commodity Exchange Act: Legal & Regulatory Issues Remain. 81p. 1998. pap. text 20.00 (*0-7881-3832-4*) DIANE Pub.

— Federal Housing Finance Board: Actions Needed to Improve Regulatory Oversight. 112p. 1999. pap. text 30.00 (*0-7881-7834-2*) DIANE Pub.

McCool, Thomas J., et al, eds. Bank & Thrift Regulation: Implementation of FDICA's Prompt Regulatory Action Provisions. (Illus.). 72p. (Orig.). (C). 1997. pap. text 30.00 (*0-7881-4061-2*) DIANE Pub.

McCool, Thomas J., ed. see Trop, Cecile O.

McCoole, Sinead. Hazel: A Life of Lady Lavery 1880-1935. LC 95-235680. 240p. 1997. 53.95 (*1-874675-84-8*); pap. 32.95 (*1-874675-55-4*) Dufour.

McCoppin. Tradition & Reality. 1994. 34.00 (*0-443-04217-9*) Harcourt.

***McCord.** Criminal Law & Procedure. 2nd ed. (Paralegal Ser.). (C). 2000. pap. 47.25 (*0-7668-1965-5*) Delmar.

McCord. Gilbert Estate & Gift Tax. 15th ed. 1993. pap. 18.95 (*0-15-900019-X*) Harcourt.

McCord, A. The Visual Dictionary of Prehistoric Life. LC 94-30705. (Eyewitness Visual Dictionaries Ser.). (Illus.). 64p. (J). (gr. 4 up). 1995. 15.95 (*1-56458-859-9*) DK Pub Inc.

McCord Adams, Marilyn. Horrendous Evils & the Goodness of God. LC 98-31382. 1999. 22.95 (*0-8014-3611-7*) Cornell U Pr.

McCord, Anne. Dinosaurs. (Picture History Ser.). (Illus.). (J). (gr. 3-7). 1977. pap. 6.95 (*0-7460-1469-4*, Usborne); lib. bdg. 14.95 (*0-88110-680-1*, Usborne) EDC.

— Prehistoric Mammals. (Picture History Ser.). (Illus.). 32p. (J). (gr. 3-7). 1985. pap. 6.95 (*0-86020-128-7*, Usborne) EDC.

McCord, Blanche. The Expanding Light Cookbook: Vegetarian Favorites from California's Premier Yoga. 2nd ed. (Illus.). 199p. 1999. pap. 12.95 (*1-56589-128-7*) Crystal Clarity.

McCord, Bruce E. Designing Pneumatic Control Circuits: Efficient Techniques for Practical Application. LC 83-2103. (Fluid Power & Control Ser.: No. 2). (Illus.). 176p. reprint ed. pap. 54.60 (*0-7837-0940-4*, 204124500019) Bks Demand.

McCord, Carey P. A Blind Hog's Acorns. 320p. 1998. pap. text 29.00 (*1-882417-31-3*, 9854) Am Conf Govt Indus Hygienist.

McCord, Charles L., jt. auth. see Kneer, Marian E.

McCord, Christopher K., ed. Nielsen Theory & Dynamical Systems: AMS-IMS-SIAM Joint Summer Research Conference on Nielsen Theory & Dynamical Systems. LC 93-26685. (Contemporary Mathematics Ser.: No. 152). 350p. 1993. pap. 52.00 (*0-8218-5181-0*, CONM/152) Am Math.

McCord, Christopher K., et al. The Integral Manifolds of the Three Body Problem. LC 97-47115. (Memoirs of the American Mathematical Society Ser.). 92p. 1998. pap. 40.00 (*0-8218-0692-0*) Am Math.

McCord, Clinton D., Jr., et al, eds. Oculoplastic Surgery. 3rd ed. LC 94-11199. (Illus.). 672p. 1994. text 144.00 (*0-7817-0192-9*) Lppncott W & W.

McCord, Clinton D., Jr., et al. Eyelid Surgery: Principles & Techniques. LC 95-12660. (Illus.). 480p. 1995. text 153.00 (*0-7817-0293-3*) Lppncott W & W.

McCord, David. All Day Long: Fifty Rhymes of the Never Was & Always Is. (J). (gr. 4-7). 1992. mass mkt. 6.95 (*0-316-55532-0*) Little.

— As Built with Second Thoughts, Reforming What Was Old. pap. 2.00 (*0-89073-099-7*, 221) Boston Public Lib.

— Bad Bunny Blues. 66p. 1995. 5.00 (*1-887151-04-4*) Andromeda CA.

***McCord, David.** Every Time I Climb a Tree. (Illus.). 24p. (J). (ps-3). 1999. pap. 5.95 (*0-316-15885-2*) Little.

McCord, David. Harvard: A Living Portrait. Patrick, James B., ed. (College Ser.). 144p. 1982. 35.00 (*0-940078-02-3*) Foremost Pubs.

— One at a Time. (Illus.). (J). (gr. 4 up). 1986. 18.95 (*0-316-55516-9*) Little.

— The World Owes Me Lunch. 112p. 1993. pap. 6.00 (*1-887151-02-8*) Andromeda CA.

McCord, David & Cleveland, William. The Armstrongs of South Carolina: African American Magicians. (Illus.). 40p. 1989. pap. 16.95 (*0-685-26487-4*) Dreamkeeper Pr.

— Black & Red: The Historical Meeting of Africans & Native Americans. (Illus.). (Orig.). 1989. pap. 16.95 (*0-685-26486-6*) Dreamkeeper Pr.

McCord, David, et al. Art & Education. 1966. 5.00 (*0-89073-024-5*, 106) Boston Public Lib.

McCord, David T. In Sight of Sever, Essays from Harvard. LC 63-19143. 298p. reprint ed. pap. 92.40 (*0-7837-2298-2*, 205738600004) Bks Demand.

McCord, Edward A. The Power of the Gun: The Emergence of Modern Chinese Warlordism. LC 92-31375. 384p. 1993. 50.00 (*0-520-08128-5*, Pub. by U CA Pr) Cal Prin Full Svc.

McCord, Gary. Golf for Dummies. 2nd ed. LC 99-62290. (For Dummies Ser.). (Illus.). 416p. 1999. pap. 19.99 (*0-7645-5146-9*) IDG Bks.

McCord, Gary. Golf for Dummies: A Reference for the Rest of Us. abr. ed. 1997. audio 12.00 (*0-694-51852-2*, CPN 10116) HarperAudio.

McCord, Gary. Golf for Dummies: Mini Edition. 1999. 4.95 (*0-7624-0633-X*) Running Pr.

— Just a Range Ball in a Box of Titleists: On & Off the Tour with Gary McCord. 224p. 1998. pap. 12.00 (*0-425-16164-1*) Berkley Pub.

McCord, Gary & Huggan, John. Golf for Dummies. (For Dummies Ser.). (Illus.). 360p. 1996. pap. 19.99 (*1-56884-857-9*) IDG Bks.

McCord, Grace D., jt. auth. see Long, John.

McCord, Howard. The Duke of Chemical Birds. (Bloody Twin Press Ser.). (Illus.). 32p. (Orig.). 1989. pap. 30.00 (*1-886350-36-1*) Bloody Twin Pr.

— The Man Who Walked to the Moon. LC 97-15513. 128p. 1997. 18.00 (*0-929701-51-8*) McPherson & Co.

— Mirrors. (Illus.). 1973. pap. 5.00 (*0-685-37097-6*) Stone-Marrow Pr.

— The Wisdom of Silenus & Other Essays. 136p. 1996. pap. 11.95 (*1-879934-35-3*) St Andrews NC.

McCord, Hugo. From Heaven or from Men. 1970. pap. 2.75 (*0-88027-033-0*) Firm Foun Pub.

McCord, J. & Laub, J. H. Contemporary Masters in Criminology. (Plenum Series in Crime & Justice). (Illus.). 426p. (C). 1995. 70.00 (*0-306-44960-9*, Kluwer Plenum) Kluwer Academic.

Mccord, James T., jt. auth. see Selker, John S.

McCord, James W. The Litigation Paralegal: A Systems Approach. 3rd ed. (Paralegal Ser.). (C). 1997. pap. 19.25 (*0-314-20702-3*) Brooks-Cole.

McCord, James W. A Piece of Tape: The Watergate Story: Fact & Fiction. LC 74-79864. xvi, 329 p. 1974. write for info. (*0-914286-00-5*) McCord Pubns.

McCord, James W. & McCord, Sandra L. Criminal Law & Procedure for the Paralegal: A Systems Approach. LC 94-13488. 628p. (C). 1994. mass mkt. 45.00 (*0-314-03917-1*) West Pub.

McCord, Joan, ed. Coercion & Punishment in Long-Term Perspectives. (Illus.). 408p. (C). 1995. text 64.95 (*0-521-45069-1*) Cambridge U Pr.

— Coercion & Punishment in Long-Term Perspectives. (Illus.). 408p. (C). 1998. pap. text 21.95 (*0-521-64567-0*) Cambridge U Pr.

— Facts, Frameworks, & Forecasts. (Advances in Criminological Theory Ser.: Vol. 3). 224p. (C). 1991. text 44.95 (*0-88738-363-7*) Transaction Pubs.

— Violence & Childhood in the Inner City. (Criminology Ser.). (Illus.). 348p. (C). 1997. pap. text 19.95 (*0-521-58720-4*) Cambridge U Pr.

McCord, Joan & Tremblay, Richard E., eds. Preventing Antisocial Behavior: Interventions from Birth Through Adolescence. LC 92-1444. 391p. 1992. lib. bdg. 49.00 (*0-89862-882-2*) Guilford Pubns.

McCord, Joan, jt. auth. see McCord, William J.

McCord, Joe M., ed. Advances in Molecular & Cell Biology Vol. 25: Oxyradicals in Medical Biology. 1998. 128.50 (*0-7623-0379-4*) Jai Pr.

McCord, John. Blind Eagles. 256p. 1998. 22.00 (*0-938313-23-1*) E B Houchin.

McCord, John S. California Eagles No. 4. 256p. (Orig.). 1995. mass mkt. 4.99 (*0-515-11725-0*, Jove) Berkley Pub.

— Kansas Gambler. 1997. mass mkt. 4.99 (*0-425-15719-9*) Berkley Pub.

— Montana Horseman No. 1. 256p. (Orig.). 1995. mass mkt. 4.99 (*0-515-11532-0*, Jove) Berkley Pub.

— Texas Comebacker No. 2. 256p. (Orig.). 1995. mass mkt. 4.99 (*0-515-11585-1*, Jove) Berkley Pub.

— Walking Hawk: A Novel of Frontier Justice. 1998. mass mkt. 5.99 (*0-425-16220-6*) Berkley Pub.

— Wyoming Giant No. 3. 256p. 1995. mass mkt. 4.99 (*0-515-11651-3*, Jove) Berkley Pub.

*__McCord, Jonas.__ Class of '61. 2000. 24.95 (*1-56649-153-3*) Welcome Rain.

McCord, Margaret. The Calling of Katie Makanya: A Memoir of South Africa. LC 96-45147. (Illus.). 252p. 1997. 24.95 (*0-471-17890-X*) Wiley.

*__McCord, Margaret.__ The Calling of Katie Makanya: A Memoir of South Africa. 272p. 1998. pap. 14.95 (*0-471-24691-3*) Wiley.

McCord, Mark. Clodrow's Adventure: A Book about Frienship. LC 96-83704. (Illus.). 8p. (J). (ps). 1996. 8.99 (*0-7814-0292-1*) Chariot Victor.

— Rattlebang: The Picture Book. LC 96-20231. (Illus.). 32p. (J). (ps-2). 1996. 14.99 (*0-7814-0290-5*) Chariot Victor.

— Rattlebang Helps: A Book about Helpfulness. LC 96-83705. (Illus.). 8p. (J). (ps). 1996. 8.99 (*0-7814-0293-X*) Chariot Victor.

McCord, Marvin, ed. see Kaufman, John P.

McCord, Monty. Cars of the State Police & Highway Patrol. LC 94-74170. (Illus.). 304p. 1995. pap. 16.95 (*0-87341-319-9*, CSP01) Krause Pubns.

— Law Enforcement Memorabilia: Price & Identification Guide. LC 98-87373. (Illus.). 192p. 1999. per. 19.95 (*0-87341-697-X*) Krause Pubns.

— Police Cars: A Photographic History. LC 91-61303. (Illus.). 304p. 1991. pap. 14.95 (*0-87341-171-4*, PC01) Krause Pubns.

McCord, Norman. The Anti-Corn League. (Modern Revivals in History Ser.). 224p. 1993. 61.95 (*0-7512-0147-2*, Pub. by Gregg Revivals) Ashgate Pub Co.

McCord, Norman. English History, 1815-1906. (Short Oxford History of the Modern World Ser.). (Illus.). 538p. 1991. pap. text 24.00 (*0-19-822858-9*) OUP.

*__McCord, Norman & Thompson, Richard.__ The Northern Counties from A. D. 1000. LC 97-38880. (Regional History of England Ser.). 480p. (C). 1998. pap. text 42.19 (*0-582-49334-X*) Addison-Wesley.

— Northern Counties from Ad 1000. LC 97-38880. (Regional History of England Ser.). 480p. 1998. 98.00 (*0-582-49333-1*) Longman.

McCord, Peter J., ed. The Voice of the Shepherdess. LC 96-6982. 94p. (Orig.). 1996. pap. 10.95 (*1-55612-819-3*) Sheed & Ward WI.

McCord, Richard. The Chain Gang: One Newspaper vs. the Gannett Empire. (Illus.). 304p. (C). 1996. 24.95 (*0-8262-1064-3*) U of Mo Pr.

*__McCord, Robert.__ Best Advice Ever for Golfers. (Illus.). 192p. 2000. 12.95 (*0-7407-1010-9*) Andrews & McMeel.

McCord, Robert. The Golf 100: Ranking the Greatest Golfers of All Time. LC 99-39415. (Illus.). 320p. 1999. pap. 27.50 (*0-8065-2066-3*, Citadel Pr) Carol Pub Group.

*__McCord, Robert, ed.__ The Quotable Golfer. (Illus.). 256p. 2000. 20.00 (*1-55821-998-6*) Lyons Pr.

McCord, Robert R. The Best 499 Public Golf Courses in the United States, Canada, Mexico & the Caribbean: The Best Public Golf Courses in the United States, Canada, Mexico & the Caribbean. LC 97-143761. 1996. pap. 21.95 (*0-679-76903-X*) Random.

— Golf: An Album of Its History. LC 98-17974. (Illus.). 144p. 1998. 35.00 (*1-58080-063-7*) Burford Bks.

— The Golf Book of Days: Fascinating Golf Facts & Stories for Every Day of the Year. LC 94-44302. 1995. 18.95 (*1-55972-292-4*, Birch Ln Pr) Carol Pub Group.

— The Golf Connoisseur. LC 95-46950. 176p. 1995. pap. 14.95 (*1-55821-397-X*) Burford Bks.

— Golf Insults. 1995. pap. write for info. (*0-8092-3399-1*) NTC Contemp Pub Co.

McCord, Sandra L., jt. auth. see McCord, James W.

McCord, Shirley, compiled by. Travel Accounts of Indiana, 1679-1961. 331p. 1970. 13.50 (*1-885323-24-7*) IN Hist Bureau.

McCord, Sue. The Storybook Journey: Pathways to Literature Through Story & Play. LC 95-1304. 1995. pap. text 32.00 (*0-13-183997-7*, Merrill Pub Co) Macmillan.

McCord, William C. The People vs. Judas Iscariot. LC 98-47230. (Worship & Drama Ser.). 108p. 1999. pap. 10.50 (*0-7880-1311-4*) CSS OH.

McCord, William J. The Dawn of the Pacific Century: Implications for Three Worlds of Development. 224p. 1990. 39.95 (*0-88738-367-X*) Transaction Pubs.

— The Dawn of the Pacific Century: Implications for Three Worlds of Development. 222p. 1996. pap. text 24.95 (*1-56000-886-5*) Transaction Pubs.

McCord, William J. & McCord, Joan. Origins of Crime: A New Evaluation of the Cambridge-Sommerville Youth Study. LC 69-14939. (Criminology, Law Enforcement, & Social Problems Ser.: No. 49). (C). 1969. reprint ed. 30.00 (*0-87585-049-9*); reprint ed. pap. 12.00 (*0-87585-908-9*) Patterson Smith.

McCord, William J., jt. auth. see Moine, Donald J.

McCord, Wilson, Jr. Biology for Beginners. 192p. 1995. pap. 11.00 (*0-86316-194-4*) Writers & Readers.

McCordick, David. Scottish Literature: An Anthology, Vol. 1. 1256p. 1994. pap. 60.00 (*1-84017-020-4*) St Mut.

— Scottish Literature: An Anthology, Vol. 2. 1242p. 1994. pap. 60.00 (*1-84017-021-2*) St Mut.

McCordick, David, ed. The Civil War Letters of Private Henry Kauffman, (1862-1865) The Harmony Boys Are All Well. LC 91-34380. (Illus.). 124p. 1991. lib. bdg. 59.95 (*0-7734-9684-X*) E Mellen.

McCordick, David D., ed. Scottish Literature: An Anthology, Vol. I. XX, 1256p. (C). 1996. text 55.95 (*0-8204-2880-9*) P Lang Pubng.

— Scottish Literature: An Anthology, Vol. 2. XXV, 1241p. (C). 1997. 55.95 (*0-8204-3399-3*) P Lang Pubng.

McCorduck, Ed. Understanding American Football: The Simplest, Clearest, & Most Detailed Guide for Spectators. LC 97-50063. (Illus.). 320p. 1998. pap. 14.95 (*0-8442-0572-9*, 05729) NTC Contemp Pub Co.

McCorduck, Pamela. Machines Who Think. LC 79-13809. (Illus.). 375p. 1981. pap. text 12.00 (*0-7167-1135-4*) W H Freeman.

McCorduck, Pamela & Ramsey, Nancy. The Futures of Women: Scenarios for the 21st Century. LC 96-46351. 384p. 1997. mass mkt. 14.99 (*0-446-67337-4*, Pub. by Warner Bks) Little.

McCorduck, Pamela, jt. auth. see Feigenbaum, Edward A.

McCorison, Marcus A. Additions & Corrections to Vermont Imprints. 1985. 3.50 (*0-912296-72-0*) Am Antiquarian.

McCorison, Marcus A., compiled by. Additions & Corrections to Vermont Imprints, 1778-1820, 1. (Orig.). 1968. pap. 5.00 (*0-912296-35-6*) Am Antiquarian.

— Additions & Corrections to Vermont Imprints, 1778-1820, 2. (Orig.). 1968. pap. 3.00 (*0-912296-36-4*) Am Antiquarian.

*__McCorkell-Robertson, Deborah.__ Tender Trap. 160p. 2000. pap. 9.99 (*1-930027-02-8*) Insight Intl.

McCorkle, Beth. The Gurdjieff Years, 1929-1949: Recollections of Louise March. 106p. (Orig.). 1990. pap. write for info. (*0-9626729-0-4*) Work Study Assn.

— The Kramurg. (Illus.). 32p. (Orig.). (J). (gr. 1-8). 1991. pap. write for info. (*0-9626729-1-2*) Work Study Assn.

McCorkle, Chester O. & Archibald, Sandra O. Management & Leadership in Higher Education. LC 82-48073. (Jossey-Bass Series in Higher Education). (Illus.). 264p. reprint ed. pap. 81.90 (*0-8357-4908-8*, 203783800009) Bks Demand.

McCorkle, Constance M. Farmer Innovation in Niger. (Studies in Technology & Social Change: Vol. 21). 52p. (Orig.). (C). 1994. pap. text 7.00 (*0-945271-33-6*) ISU-CIKARD.

McCorkle, Constance M., ed. The Social Sciences in International Agricultural Research: Lessons from the CRSPs. LC 89-32083. 300p. 1989. lib. bdg. 44.00 (*1-55587-133-X*) L Rienner.

McCorkle, Constance M., et al. Ethnoveterinary Research & Development. (IT Studies in Indigenous Knowledge & Development). 450p. 1996. pap. 29.95 (*1-85339-326-6*, Pub. by Intermed Tech) Stylus Pub VA.

McCorkle, Constance M., jt. auth. see Mathias-Mundy, Evelyn.

*__McCorkle, Dennis F.__ Midi Orchestrator's Handbook. (Illus.). 64p. 1999. pap. 14.95 (*0-8256-1616-6*) Music Sales.

McCorkle, James. The Still Performance: Writing, Self, & Interconnection in Five Postmodern American Poets. LC 88-35305. 225p. 1989. text 35.00 (*0-8139-1196-6*) U Pr of Va.

McCorkle, James, ed. Conversant Essays: Contemporary Poets & Poetry. LC 89-32152. 598p. (C). 1990. 45.00 (*0-8143-2099-6*); pap. text 21.95 (*0-8143-2100-3*) Wayne St U Pr.

McCorkle, Jill. Carolina Moon. LC 96-1611. 276p. 1996. 18.95 (*1-56512-136-8*) Algonquin Bks.

— Carolina Moon. 272p. 1997. pap. 12.00 (*0-449-91280-9*) Fawcett.

— The Cheer Leader. (Front Porch PB Ser.). 288p. 1992. pap. 8.95 (*1-56512-001-9*, 72001) Algonquin Bks.

McCorkle, Jill. Crash Diet: Stories by Jill McCorkle. 272p. 1992. 16.95 (*0-945575-75-0*) Algonquin Bks.

McCorkle, Jill. Ferris Beach. 288p. 1991. mass mkt. 5.99 (*0-449-21996-8*) Fawcett.

— Ferris Beach. 1991. 11.09 (*0-606-00857-8*, Pub. by Turtleback) Demco.

— Final Vinyl Days: And Other Stories. LC 97-50540. 224p. 1998. 18.95 (*1-56512-204-6*) Algonquin Bks.

— Final Vinyl Days: And Other Stories. 1999. pap. 12.95 (*0-449-00574-7*) Fawcett.

— July 7th. (Front Porch PB Ser.). 400p. 1992. pap. 9.95 (*1-56512-002-7*, 72002) Algonquin Bks.

McCorkle, John. Three Years with Quantrell. Barton, D. S., ed. LC 67-6851. (American Biography Ser.: No. 32). 1970. lib. bdg. 75.00 (*0-8383-1107-5*) M S G Haskell Hse.

McCorkle, John & Barton, O. S. Three Years with Quantrill: A True Story, Told by His Scout John McCorkle. LC 92-54158. (Western Frontier Library: Vol. 60). (Illus.). 240p. 1998. pap. 9.95 (*0-8061-3056-3*) U of Okla Pr.

McCorkle, Llyod, jt. auth. see MacNamara, Donal E.

McCorkle, Richard C., jt. auth. see Miethe, Terance D.

McCorkle, Richard C., jt. auth. see Miethe, Terence D.

McCorkle, Ruth & Grant, Marcia, eds. Pocket Companion for Cancer Nursing. LC 94-6847. (Illus.). 537p. 1994. pap. text 38.95 (*0-7216-5410-X*, W B Saunders Co) Harcrt Hlth Sci Grp.

McCorkle, Ruth, et al. Cancer Nursing: A Comprehensive Textbook. 2nd ed. (Illus.). 1487p. 1996. text 150.00 (*0-7216-5668-4*, W B Saunders Co) Harcrt Hlth Sci Grp.

McCorkle, Suzanne, jt. auth. see Witt, Stephanie L.

*__McCormac.__ Reinforced Concrete. 4th ed. 736p. 1998. text 105.95 incl. disk (*0-471-36383-9*) Wiley.

McCormac. Reinforced Concrete Professional Company. 4th ed. 1998. text 25.00 (*0-471-36391-X*) Wiley.

— Reinforced Concrete Solution Manual. 4th ed. 1998. pap. text 25.00 (*0-471-36395-2*) Wiley.

— Solutions Manual to Accompany Structural Steel Design. 2nd ed. (C). 1997. pap. text 10.67 (*0-06-501628-9*) Addison-Wesley.

— Structure Analysis Instructor Solutions. 2nd ed. 1997. pap. text 39.71 (*0-471-36409-6*) Wiley.

*__McCormac.__ Surveying. 4th ed. 432p. 1999. pap. 99.95 incl. disk (*0-471-36657-9*) Wiley.

McCormac, B. M., ed. see Summer Advanced Study Institute Staff.

McCormac, Billy M., ed. Atmospheres of Earth & the Planets. LC 75-4954. (Astrophysics & Space Science Library: No. 51). 430p. 1975. lib. bdg. 216.50 (*90-277-0575-5*) Kluwer Academic.

— Magnetospheric Particles & Fields. (Astrophysics & Space Science Library: No. 58). 1976. lib. bdg. 141.50 (*90-277-0702-2*) Kluwer Academic.

— Weather & Climate Responses to Solar Variations. LC 82-73247. 636p. reprint ed. pap. 197.20 (*0-608-17114-X*, 202729700055) Bks Demand.

McCormac, Billy M. & Seliga, Thomas A., eds. Solar-Terrestrial Influences on Weather & Climate. 1979. text 160.50 (*90-277-0978-5*) Kluwer Academic.

McCormac, Billy M., ed. see Advanced Study Institute Staff.

McCormac, Billy M., ed. see Advanced Study Institute Symposium Staff & ESRO Symposium Staff.

McCormac, Billy M., ed. see Advanced Summer Institute Staff.

McCormac, Billy M., ed. see Summer Advanced Study Institute Staff.

McCormac, Eugene I. James K. Polk Vol. 1: A Political Biography: To the Prelude of War 1795-1845. Speirs, Katherine E., ed. LC 95-75148. (Signature Ser.). (Illus.). 384p. 1995. reprint ed. 32.50 (*0-945707-09-6*) Amer Political.

— James K. Polk Vol. 2: A Political Biography: To the End of a Career 1845-1849. Speirs, Katherine E., ed. LC 95-75148. (Signature Ser.). (Illus.). 384p. 1995. reprint ed. 32.50 (*0-945707-10-X*) Amer Political.

— White Servitude in Maryland, 1634-1820. LC 78-63901. (Johns Hopkins University. Studies in the Social Sciences. Thirtieth Ser. 1912: 3-4). reprint ed. 29.50 (*0-404-61154-0*) AMS Pr.

McCormac, Jack. Structural Steel Design. 5th ed. (C). 1997. text. write for info. (*0-673-98235-1*) Addison-Wesley.

McCormac, Jack C. Design of Reinforced Concrete. 2nd ed. 624p. (C). 1989. student ed. write for info. (*0-318-59890-6*) Addson-Wesley Educ.

McCormac, Jack C. Design of Reinforced Concrete: Solutions Manual. 4th ed. write for info. (*0-321-00255-5*) Addson-Wesley Educ.

— Design Reinforced Concrete. 5th ed. 768p. (C). 2000. write for info. (*0-471-39576-5*) Wiley.

— Structural Analysis: A Classical & Matrix Approach. 2nd ed. (Illus.). 624p. 1997. 102.95 incl. disk (*0-471-36411-8*) Wiley.

McCormac, Jack C. Structural Steel Design. 4th ed. 740p. (C). 1997. 105.00 (*0-06-500060-9*) Addson-Wesley Educ.

McCormac, Jack C. Structural Steel Design: ASD Method. 4th ed. write for info. (*0-06-500065-X*) HarpC.

— Structural Steel Design: Lrfd Design Reinforced. 1997. pap. text 122.67 (*0-321-00920-7*) Addison-Wesley.

— Surveying Fundamentals. 2nd ed. 592p. 1991. 96.95 incl. disk (*0-471-36407-X*) Wiley.

McCormac, Jack C. & Nelson, James K. Structural Analysis: A Classical & Matrix Approach. 2nd ed. LC 96-23304. 614p. (C). 1997. text. write for info. (*0-673-99753-7*) Addson-Wesley Educ.

McCormac, John W. Ohio Civil Rules Practice with Electronic Forms. 2nd ed. 587p. 1992. 85.00 (*0-87084-596-9*) Anderson Pub Co.

— Wrongful Death in Ohio with Forms. 194p. 1991. 37.50 (*0-87084-560-8*) Anderson Pub Co.

McCormac, John W., et al. Anderson's Ohio Civil Practice with Electronic Forms, 7 vols., 8 bks., Set. 1975. 475.00 (*0-87084-594-2*) Anderson Pub Co.

McCormac, Richard & Yamamura, Whitney. How to Look Forward to Money Decisions. 120p. 1998. pap. 31.95 (*1-56226-398-6*) CAT Pub.

McCormac, Ruairi. Snapshot. 345p. 1995. pap. 25.00 (*1-898162-30-1*, Pub. by IMMEL Pubng) St Mut.

McCormack. Crow's Request. 1998. pap. write for info. (*0-8050-5433-2*) H Holt & Co.

*__McCormack.__ George Elliot & Intoxication. LC 99-33013. 2000. text 59.95 (*0-312-22711-6*) St Martin.

McCormack. Self-Defense in Intern Law. LC 96-22889. 380p. 1996. text 49.95 (*0-312-16279-0*) St Martin.

— STP Analysis of Motor Control. (C). pap. text 49.00 (*0-12-785063-5*) Acad Pr.

McCormack, A. Ross. Reformers, Rebels, & Revolutionaries: The Western Canadian Radical Movement, 1899-1919. (Reprints in Canadian History Ser.). 256p. 1992. pap. text 18.95 (*0-8020-7682-3*) U of Toronto Pr.

— Reformers, Rebels, & Revolutionaries: The Western Canadian Radical Movement, 1899-1919. LC 77-4338. 246p. reprint ed. pap. 76.30 (*0-608-12881-3*, 202364600033) Bks Demand.

McCormack, Alan. Inventor's Workshop. LC 80-84185. (Crafts Workshop Ser.). (J). (gr. 3-8). 1981. pap. 11.99 (*0-8224-9783-2*) Fearon Teacher Aids.

McCormack, Alan J. The Great Bone Mysteries. (Illus.). 198p. (Orig.). 1990. pap. text 19.95 (*1-885041-05-5*) Idea Factory.

McCormack, Alfred. History of Special Branch, M.I.S., in World War II. 84p. 1994. pap. 20.80 (*0-89412-231-2*) Aegean Park Pr.

McCormack, Allen, ed. Adweek Client/Brand Directory 1998. annuals 1000p. 1997. pap. 295.00 (*1-891204-08-4*) Adweek Direct.

*__McCormack, Allen E.__ Stern's Performing Arts Directory 2000. 1999. pap. 65.00 (*0-930036-31-X*) Dance Mag Inc.

McCormack, Allison, jt. auth. see Davis, William S.

McCormack, Barbara, jt. auth. see Borland, Deedee.

McCormack, Bill & Cooper, Bob. Without Fear or Favour. 1999. text 19.95 (*0-7737-3168-7*) Genl Dist Srvs.

McCormack, Brenda. Conducting a Survey: The SPSS Workbook. (Illus.). 192p. 1997. pap., wbk. ed. 21.99 (*1-86152-137-5*) Thomson Learn.

McCormack, Brenda, jt. ed. see Gregoriadis, Gregory.

*__McCormack, Bridget.__ Perceptions of St. Patrick in Eighteenth-Century Ireland. (Maynooth History Studies Ser.). (Illus.). 136p. 1999. 55.00 (*1-85182-457-X*, Pub. by Four Cts Pr) Intl Spec Bk.

McCormack Brown, Kelli, jt. auth. see Edlin, Gordon.

McCormack, Bruce L. Karl Barth's Critically Realistic Dialectical Theology: Its Genesis & Development, 1909-1936. 520p. 1997. reprint ed. pap. text 26.00 (*0-19-826956-0*) OUP.

McCormack, Cathy. Financial Management for Musicians. LC 99-62531. 200p. 1999. pap. text 39.95 (*0-87288-713-8*) Intertec Pub.

McCormack, Christine E. Little Books from A to Z. 1998. pap. 9.95 (*0-673-57727-9*, GoodYrBooks) Addson-Wesley Educ.

— Little Books 1,2,3. 1998. pap. text 9.95 (*0-673-58659-6*) Addson-Wesley Educ.

McCormack, Colette. After the Famine. (J). 1996. pap. 7.95 (*1-85594-142-2*, Pub. by Attic Press) Intl Spec Bk.

McCormack, Colin & Jones, David. Building a Web-Based Education System. LC 97-33992. 464p. 1997. pap., pap. text 49.99 incl. cd-rom (*0-471-19162-0*) Wiley.

McCormack, David R. Rico, 2 vols., Vols. 1 & 2. 1988. ring bd. 185.00 (*1-878337-18-1*) Knowles Pub Inc.

McCormack, Derek. Dark Rides. LC 95-933383. (Illus.). 104p. 1996. pap. 9.95 (*1-896356-06-0*, 610551, Pub. by Gutter Pr) Dist Art Pubs.

*__McCormack, Don.__ Alameda 2000. (Illus.). 1999. pap. 13.95 (*1-929365-00-4*, Pub. by McCormacks Guides) Bookpeople.

— Contra Costa/Solano 2000. (Illus.). 1999. pap. 13.95 (*1-929365-01-2*, Pub. by McCormacks Guides) Bookpeople.

— Los Angeles 2000. (Illus.). 1999. pap. 13.95 (*1-929365-02-0*, Pub. by McCormacks Guides) Bookpeople.

— Marin, Napa & Sonoma 2000. (Illus.). 1999. pap. 13.95 (*1-929365-03-9*, Pub. by McCormacks Guides) Bookpeople.

*__McCormack, Don, ed.__ Greater Sacramento 2000. (Illus.). 1999. pap. 13.95 (*1-929365-06-3*, Pub. by McCormacks Guides) Bookpeople.

— Orange County 2000. (Illus.). 1999. pap. 13.95 (*1-929365-04-7*, Pub. by McCormacks Guides) Bookpeople.

— Riverside/San Bernardino 2000. (Illus.). 1999. pap. 13.95 (*1-929365-05-5*, Pub. by McCormacks Guides) Bookpeople.

— San Diego 2000. (Illus.). 1999. pap. 13.95 (*1-929365-07-1*, Pub. by McCormacks Guides) Bookpeople.

— San Francisco & San Mateo 2000. (Illus.). 1999. pap. 13.95 (*1-929365-08-X*, Pub. by McCormacks Guides) Bookpeople.

— Santa Barbara & Ventura 2000. (Illus.). 1999. pap. 13.95 (*1-929365-09-8*, Pub. by McCormacks Guides) Bookpeople.

— Santa Clara 2000. (Illus.). 1999. pap. 13.95 (*1-929365-10-1*, Pub. by McCormacks Guides) Bookpeople.

McCormack, Edward. Jim Buckels: Metaphysical Landscapes. Lee, Marshall, ed. (Illus.). 96p. 1996. 57.00 (*0-940577-06-2*) Intl Archive Art.

— Jim Buckels: Metaphysical Landscapes. deluxe ed. Lee, Marshall, ed. (Illus.). 96p. 1996. write for info. (*0-940577-07-0*) Intl Archive Art.

McCormack, Erliss. Cairn Terriers. 1997. pap. 9.95 (*0-7938-2383-8*, KW-1695) TFH Pubns.

McCormack, Frank. Never Lose: A Decade of Sports & Politics in Sacramento. LC 89-80370. 200p. (Orig.). 1989. pap. 16.95 (*0-9622140-9-4*) First Ink Pub Hse.

McCormack, Gavan. Chang Tso-lin in Northeast China, 1911-1928: China, Japan, & the Manchurian Idea. LC 76-48028. (Illus.). x, 334p. 1977. 47.50 (*0-8047-0945-9*) Stanford U Pr.

— The Emptiness of Japanese Affluence. LC 96-4391. (Japan in the Modern World Ser.). (Illus.). 332p. (C). (gr. 13). 1996. pap. 26.95 (*1-56324-712-7*, East Gate Bk) M E Sharpe.

— The Emptiness of Japanese Affluence. LC 96-4391. (Japan in the Modern World Ser.). (Illus.). 332p. (C). (gr. 13-13). 1996. 64.95 (*1-56324-711-9*, East Gate Bk) M E Sharpe.

McCormack, Gavan & Gittings, John, eds. The Crisis in Korea. 190p. 1977. pap. 22.50 (*0-85124-187-5*, Pub. by Spkesman) Coronet Bks.

M

McCormack, Gavan & Sugimoto, Yoshio, eds. Democracy in Contemporary Japan. LC 86-17744. 272p. (gr. 13). 1986. pap. text 42.95 (0-87332-398-X) M E Sharpe.

McCormack, Gavan & Sugimoto, Yoshio, eds. Democracy in Contemporary Japan. LC 86-17744. 272p. 1986. reprint ed. pap. 84.40 (0-7837-9951-9, 206067800006) Bks Demand.

McCormack, Gavan, jt. auth. see Halliday, Jon.

McCormack, Gavan, jt. auth. see Nelson, Hank.

McCormack, Ian, contrib. by. Are You Going to Heaven with Ian McCormack. 1996. 19.95 incl. VHS (1-890553-04-2, CV 605 VSN) Double Vision.

McCormack, J., et al. X Tool Kit: Intrinsics & Athena Widgets. 300p. (Orig.). 1990. pap. 29.95 (0-929306-04-X) Silicon Pr.

McCormack, James G. & Cobbold, Peter H., eds. Cellular Calcium: A Practical Approach. (Practical Approach Ser.). (Illus.). 448p. 1991. 85.00 (0-19-963131-X); pap. text 55.00 (0-19-963130-1) OUP.

McCormack, Jeri. When It Came Time. LC 98-203861. 1998. pap. 13.95 (1-897648-05-7, Pub. by Salmon Poetry) Dufour.

McCormack, Jerusha H. John Gray: Poet, Dandy, & Priest. LC 90-50906. (Illus.). 332p. reprint ed. pap. 103.00 (0-608-09089-1, 206972300005) Bks Demand.

McCormack, Jerusha H. The Man Who Was Dorian Gray. text 24.95 (0-312-23278-0) St Martin.

M

***McCormack, Joe.** Webmaster's Gurv Pack. (Illus.). i, 146p. 1999. vinyl bd. 35.00 (0-9672273-1-3, TCHPUB#1) MnetWeb.

McCormack, Joe, jt. auth. see Neal, Tim.

McCormack, John. Fields & Pastures New: My First Year as a Country Vet. 288p. 1997. pap. 12.00 (0-449-22536-4) Fawcett.

— A Friend of the Flock: Tales of a Country Veterinarian. 1998. pap. 12.95 (0-449-00331-0) Fawcett.

— The Hero of the Herd: More Tales from a Country Veterinarian. LC 99-23442. 272p. 1999. 23.00 (0-609-60373-6, Crown) Crown Pub Group.

Mccormack, John. Self Made in America: Plain Talk for Plain People about Extraordinary Success. 1990. 19.95 (0-201-55099-7) Addison-Wesley.

McCormack, John & Legge, David R. Self-Made in America: Plain Talk for Plain People about the Meaning of Success. (Illus.). 240p. 1992. pap. 12.00 (0-201-60823-5) Addison-Wesley.

McCormack, John A. Deathblow. LC 87-91069. 1988. 18.95 (0-87212-207-7) Libra.

McCormack, Kathleen. Magic for Lovers: How to Use Magical & Astrological Techniques to Locate Your Ideal Lover. (Illus.). 176p. 1987. pap. 6.95 (0-85030-468-7) Aqrn Pr.

— Tarot Decoder. (Illus.). 144p. 1998. 19.95 (0-7641-0677-5) Barron.

McCormack, Kelli, ed. see Stone, Scott C.

McCormack, Kenneth A. Broken Promise. 99p. (C). 1989. text 45.00 (1-872795-65-X, Pub. by Pentland Pr) St Mut.

McCormack, M. D., jt. auth. see Tatham, Robert H.

***McCormack, Mark H.** Getting Results for Dummies. 384p. 1999. pap. 19.99 (0-7645-5205-8) IDG Bks.

McCormack, Mark H. Hit the Ground Running: The Insider's Guide to Executive Travel. 268p. pap. 14.00 (1-878843-09-5) Intl Merc OH.

— On Communicating. 224p. 1999. pap. 14.00 (0-7871-1838-9, NewStar Pr) NewStar Media.

— On Managing. Set. abr. ed. 1996. audio. write for info. (0-7871-1004-3, Dove Audio) NewStar Media.

***McCormack, Mark H.** Staying Street Smart in the Internet Age. LC 00-36788. 272p. 2000. 24.95 (0-670-89306-4, Viking) Viking Penguin.

McCormack, Mark H. The Terrible Truth about Lawyers: What I Should Have Learned at Yale Law School. 1988. mass mkt. 4.95 (0-380-70652-0, Avon Bks) Morrow Avon.

— What They Don't Teach You at Harvard Business School: Notes from a Street-Smart Executive. 272p. 1984. pap. 15.95 (0-553-34583-4) Bantam.

— What They Still Don't Teach You at Harvard Business School: Selling More, Managing Better, & Getting the Job Done in the '90s. 320p. 1990. pap. 15.95 (0-553-34961-9) Bantam.

— The World of Professional Golf, 1989: Presented by ICI. (Illus.). 556p. 1989. 24.95 (0-9615344-5-1) Intl Merc OH.

— The World of Professional Golf, 1990. (Illus.). 1990. 24.95 (0-9615344-8-6) Intl Merc OH.

— The World of Professional Golf, 1991. (Illus.). 596p. 1991. 24.95 (1-878843-01-X) Intl Merc OH.

— The World of Professional Golf, 1992. 1992. 24.95 (0-87884-303-5) Unicorn Ent.

— The World of Professional Golf, 1994. (Illus.). 640p. 1994. 29.95 (1-878843-06-0) Intl Merc OH.

— The World of Professional Golf, 1994. 1993. 29.95 (0-87884-306-X) Unicorn Ent.

— The World of Professional Golf, 1995. (Illus.). 640p. 1995. 29.95 (1-878843-12-5) Intl Merc OH.

— The World of Professional Golf, 1996. (Illus.). 672p. 1996. 29.95 (1-878843-15-X) Intl Merc OH.

— The World of Professional Golf, 1997. (Illus.). 704p. 1997. 29.95 (1-878843-17-6) Intl Merc OH.

— The World of Professional Golf, 1998. (Illus.). 702p. 1998. 29.95 (1-878843-20-6) Intl Merc OH.

— The World of Professional Golf 1999. (Illus.). 720p. 1999. 29.95 (1-878843-24-9) Intl Merc OH.

***McCormack, Mark H.** The World of Professional Golf, 2000. (Illus.). 736p. 2000. 29.95 (1-878843-28-1) Intl Merc OH.

McCormack, Michael, ed. see Cox, Arthur B., Jr.

McCormack, Michael K., ed. Prevention of Mental Retardation & Other Developmental Disabilities. LC 80-24771. (Pediatric Habilitation Ser.: No. 1). (Illus.). 680p. reprint ed. pap. 200.00 (0-7837-0831-9, 204114500019) Bks Demand.

McCormack, Mike. Crowe's Requiem: A Novel. 232p. 1999. 25.00 (0-8050-5370-0) H Holt & Co.

— Getting It in the Head. LC 97-43465. 232p. 1998. 23.00 (0-8050-5371-9) H Holt & Co.

— Getting It in the Head. 1999. pap. write for info. (0-8050-5434-0) H Holt & Co.

McCormack, Nancy. Death: Words of Comfort. 82p. 1986. 35.00 (0-7223-2029-9, Pub. by A H S Ltd) St Mut.

McCormack, Nancy, ed. see Kirby, Jackie M.

McCormack, Nell J. Creative Quantity Cooking. 3rd ed. LC 89-186. 369p. 1989. 115.00 (0-8342-0058-9) Aspen Pub.

McCormack, P. D., et al, eds. Terrestrial Space Radiation & Its Biological Effects. (NATO ASI Series A, Life Sciences: Vol. 154). (Illus.). 850p. 1988. 175.00 (0-306-43020-7, Plenum Trade) Perseus Pubng.

***McCormack, Patricia A.** Fostering Student Self-Esteem in the Catholic Elementary School. 100p. 1999. pap. 13.00 (1-55833-225-1) Natl Cath Educ.

McCormack, Patrick J. Minnesota's Programs for Troubled Gamblers. (Illus.). 61p. (Orig.). (C). 1995. pap. text 25.00 (0-7881-2121-9) DIANE Pub.

McCormack, Peggy. The Rule of Money: Gender, Class & Exchange Economics in the Fiction of Henry James. LC 89-20489. (Studies in Modern Literature: No. 116). 131p. (C). 1990. reprint ed. 40.70 (0-8357-2059-4, 207074300004) Bks Demand.

***McCormack, Peggy, ed.** Questioning the Master: Gender & Sexuality in Henry James's Writings. LC 99-33518. 232p. 2000. 39.50 (0-87413-712-8) U Delaware Pr.

***McCormack, Percival, ed.** Vortex Physics. 1999. 74.95 (0-12-482260-6) Morgan Kaufmann.

McCormack, Pete. Shelby. LC 93-27527. 267p. 1994. 22.00 (1-877946-47-8) Permanent Pr.

McCormack, Robert, jt. auth. see Ward, Richard H.

***McCormack, Stuart C.** Intellectual Property Law of Canada. 580p. 1999. ring bd. 225.00 (1-57823-070-5) Juris Pubng.

McCormack, Thelma, jt. auth. see Crum, Gary.

McCormack, Thomas J., tr. see Cumont, Franz.

McCormack, Thomas P. The AIDS Benefits Handbook: Everything You Need to Know to Get Social Security, Welfare, Medicaid, Medicare, Food Stamps, Housing, Drugs, & Other Benefits. 240p. (C). 1990. 37.50 (0-300-04736-3); pap. 14.00 (0-300-04721-5) Yale U Pr.

McCormack, Thomas W. Canadian Demand for Household Furniture & Trends. 6th ed. (Illus.). 55p. 1998. spiral bd. 450.00 (0-921577-87-7) AKTRIN.

— Employment & Wages in the American Furniture Industry. 3rd ed. LC 98-24199. (Illus.). 59p. 1998. spiral bd. 410.00 (0-921577-83-4) AKTRIN.

***McCormack, Thomas W.** Employment & Wages in the Canadian Furniture Industry. (Illus.). 55p. 1999. pap. text 450.00 (1-894330-01-3) AKTRIN.

McCormack, Thomas W. & Aktrin Research Institute Staff. Canadian Demand for Office Furniture & Trends. 4th ed. LC 98-13243. (Illus.). 67p. 1999. spiral bd. 450.00 (0-921577-78-8) AKTRIN.

— Financial Health of the American Furniture Industry. 3rd ed. LC 99-20538. 6p. 1999. spiral bd. 450.00 (0-921577-92-3) AKTRIN.

***McCormack, Thomas W., et al.** The Financial Health of the Canadian Furniture Industry. 4th ed. 2000. write for info. (1-894330-10-2) Aktrin Resrch.

McCormack, Timothy L. & Simpson, Gerry J. The Law of War Crimes: National & International Approaches. LC 96-22730. 1997. 175.00 (90-411-0273-6) Kluwer Law Intl.

McCormack, Timothy L., jt. auth. see Durham, Helen.

McCormack, Tom. American Roulette. 1969. pap. 3.25 (0-8222-0036-8) Dramatists Play.

McCormack, Vincent & O'Hara, Joe. Enduring Inequality: Religious Discrimination in Employment in Northern Ireland. 79p. (C). 1990. pap. text 35.00 (0-946088-37-3, Pub. by NCCL) St Mut.

McCormack, Vincent F. Developing Microcomputer Models for Cost Analysis & Decision Making. (C). 1993. pap. text 29.50 (0-07-044772-1) McGraw.

McCormack, W. J. The Dublin Paper War of 1786-1788: A Bibliographical & Critical Inquiry. 166p. 1993. 39.50 (0-7165-2505-4, Pub. by Irish Acad Pr) Intl Spec Bk.

***McCormack, W. J.** Fool of the Family: A Life of J. M. Synge. LC 00-34878. 2000. write for info. (0-8147-5652-2) NYU Pr.

— From Burke to Beckett. 448p. 1994. pap. 29.95 (0-902561-94-4, Pub. by Cork Univ) Stylus Pub VA.

McCormack, W. J. The Pamphlet Debate on the Union Between Great Britain & Ireland, 1797-1800. 144p. 1996. 39.50 (0-7165-2568-2, Pub. by Irish Acad Pr) Intl Spec Bk.

— Sheridan le Fanu. (Illus.). 336p. 1999. pap. 22.95 (0-7509-1489-0, Pub. by Sutton Pub Ltd) Intl Pubs Mktg.

— Sheridan le Fanu & Victorian Ireland. 2nd ed. LC 92-188554. vi, 324 p. 1991. write for info. (0-946640-69-6) Lilliput Pr.

McCormack, W. J., ed. Irish Poetry: An Interpretive Anthology from Before Swift to Yeats & After. LC 99-33575. 384p. 1999. 28.95 (0-8147-5628-X) NYU Pr.

McCormack, W. J. & Stead, Alistair, eds. James Joyce & Modern Literature. 224p. 1982. 29.50 (0-7100-9058-7, Routledge Thoemms) Routledge.

McCormack, W. J., ed. see Trollope, Anthony.

McCormack, W. J., ed. & intro. see Le Fanu, Joseph Sheridan.

McCormack, W. J., ed. & intro. see Trollope, Anthony.

McCormack, William. Life on Homicide: True Cases from the Files of William McCormack. (Illus.). 240p. 1998. 22.95 (0-7737-3072-9) Stoddart Publ.

McCormack, William C. Kannada: A Cultural Introduction to the Spoken Styles of the Language. LC 66-13804. 218p. 1966. reprint ed. pap. 67.60 (0-608-01865-1, 206251700003) Bks Demand.

McCormack, William C. & Wurm, Stephen A. Approaches to Language: Anthropological Issues. (World Anthropology Ser.). xiv, 674p. 1978. 107.70 (90-279-7660-0) Mouton.

McCormack, William C. & Wurm, Stephen A., eds. Language & Society. (World Anthropology Ser.). 771p. 1979. text 103.85 (90-279-7800-X) Mouton.

McCormack, William J. The Blackwell Companion to Modern Irish Culture. LC 98-5572. (Illus.). 686p. 1998. 99.95 (0-631-16525-8) Blackwell Pubs.

***McCormack, Win, et al, eds.** Tin House, Vol. 2. (Tin House Literary Quarterly Ser.). (Illus.). 224p. 1999. pap. 9.95 (0-9673846-1-3) McCormack Comm.

McCormally, Timothy J., ed. see Tax Executives Institute, Inc. Staff.

McCormich, Colin, jt. auth. see Sabbionet, Anna M.

McCormick. Chi Cerca Trova. 1987. pap. text. write for info. (0-582-87313-4, Pub. by Addison-Wesley) Longman.

— Comparative Politics in Transition. (C). 1994. pap. text, teacher ed. 28.00 (0-534-18901-6) Harcourt Coll Pubs.

— Comparative Politics in Transition. 2nd ed. LC 97-74861. (C). 1997. pap. text 53.00 (0-15-505326-4, Pub. by Harcourt Coll Pubs) Harcourt.

— Drillbook for Readwrite & Realtime. 160p. 1997. pap. text 16.20 (0-13-621954-3) P-H.

— Instr. Students Have Literacy. 3rd ed. LC 98-45924. 601p. 1999. 72.00 (0-13-896028-3) P-H.

***McCormick.** Manicuring for the Salon & Spa. LC 99-46252. 1999. 29.95 (1-56253-460-2) Thomson Learn.

McCormick. Notebook for Realwrite & Realtime. 272p. 1997. pap. text 11.60 (0-13-621947-0) P-H.

***McCormick.** Parents Guide Best Family videos. 1999. pap., student ed. write for info. (0-312-24575-0) St Martin.

McCormick. The Parents Guide to the Best Family Videos. LC 99-23458. 288p. 1999. pap. 11.95 (1-58238-054-6, Whitman Coin) St Martin.

McCormick & Fritz. Damages. 2nd ed. 1952. text 30.00 (0-88277-356-9) Foundation Pr.

McCormick & Rushman. Deductive Interpretation of Progressed Horoscopes. LC 77-10369. 120p. 1977. 11.00 (0-86690-127-2, M1306-014) Am Fed Astrologers.

McCormick, jt. auth. see Knapp.

McCormick, jt. auth. see Renfrew.

McCormick, Adele V. & McCormick, Marlena D. Horse Sense & the Human Heart: What Horses Can Teach Us about Trust, Bonding, Creativity & Spirituality. LC 97-35476. (Illus.). 200p. 1997. pap. 10.95 (1-55874-523-8) Health Comm.

McCormick, Albert E. American Society: Readings in Social Behavior. 2nd ed. 336p. (C). 1995. text 64.00 (0-536-58820-1) Pearson Custom.

McCormick, Albert E., ed. American Society: Readings in Social Behavior. 3rd ed. 204p. (C). 1998. pap. text 36.00 (0-536-00741-1) S&S Trade.

***McCormick, Alexander C.** Credit Production & Progress Toward the Bachelor's Degree: An Analysis of Post Secondary Transcripts for Beginning Students at 4-Year Institutions. 81p. 1999. pap. 7.00 (0-16-049927-5) USGPO.

— Descriptive Summary of 1992-93 Bachelor's Degree Recipients 1 Year Later, with An Essay on Time to Degree. 141p. 1996. pap. 11.00 (0-16-048748-X) USGPO.

— Life after College: A Descriptive Summary of 1992-93 Bachelor's Degree Recipients in 1997 : with an Essay on Participation in Graduate & First-professional Education. LC 99-227863. (Illus.). 131p. 1999. write for info. (0-16-050066-4) USGPO.

— Transfer Behavior among Beginning Postsecondary Students: 1989-94. LC 97-189283. 89p. 1997. per. 10.00 (0-16-049061-8) USGPO.

McCormick, Allen, ed. Germans in America: Aspects of German-American Relations in the Nineteenth Century. LC 82-61910. (Studies on Society in Change: No. 27). 1983. text 64.50 (0-88033-025-2, Pub. by East Eur Monographs) Col U Pr.

McCormick, Andrew, tr. see Aikema, Bernard.

McCormick, Andrew, tr. see Grijzenhout, Frans & Van Veen, Henk, eds.

McCormick, Anita L. The Industrial Revolution in American History. LC 97-23479. (In American History Ser.). (Illus.). 128p. (YA). (gr. 6 up). 1998. lib. bdg. 20.95 (0-89490-985-1) Enslow Pubs.

— The Internet: Surfing the Issues. LC 98-12673. (Issues in Focus Ser.). (Illus.). 128p. (YA). (gr. 6 up). 1998. lib. bdg. 20.95 (0-89490-956-8) Enslow Pubs.

— Native Americans & the Reservation in American History. LC 96-12266. (In American History Ser.). (Illus.). 128p. (YA). (gr. 5 up). 1996. lib. bdg. 20.95 (0-89490-769-7) Enslow Pubs.

— Shortwave Radio Listening for Beginners. 200p. 1993. 19.95 (0-07-044990-2); pap. 19.95 (0-07-044991-0) McGraw.

— Shortwave Radio Listening for Beginners. LC 92-41603. 1993. 18.95 (0-8306-4136-X); pap. 10.60 (0-8306-4135-1) McGraw-Hill Prof.

— Space Exploration. LC 93-1830. (Overview Ser.). (Illus.). 100p. (YA). (gr. 4 up). 1994. lib. bdg. 22.45 (1-56006-149-9) Lucent Bks.

***McCormick, Anita Louise.** The Vietnam Antiwar Movement in American History. LC 99-37118. (In American History Ser.). (Illus.). 128p. (J). (gr. 5 up). 2000. lib. bdg. 20.95 (0-7660-1295-6) Enslow Pubs.

McCormick, Anne. World at Home. LC 70-121486. (Essay Index Reprint Ser.). 1977. 23.95 (0-8369-1985-8) Ayer.

McCormick, Anne E., jt. ed. see Quinn, Patricia O.

McCormick, B. J. The World Economy: Patterns of Growth & Change. LC 88-14639. 256p. (Orig.). (C). 1988. pap. text 38.50 (0-389-20801-9, N8359); lib. bdg. 75.50 (0-389-20800-0, N8358) B&N Imports.

McCormick, Barnes W. Aerodynamics, Aeronautics & Fight Mechanics. 2nd ed. LC 94-22312. 672p. 1994. text 105.95 (0-471-57506-2) Wiley.

McCormick, Barnes W., Jr. Aerodynamics of Vistol Flight. unabridged ed. LC 98-48730. 328p. 1999. pap. 11.95 (0-486-40460-9) Dover.

McCormick, Barnes W. & Papadakis, M. P. Aircraft Accident Reconstruction & Litigation. rev. ed. LC 98-41473. (Illus.). 802p. 1998. kivar 115.00 (0-913875-67-8, 5155) Lawyers & Judges.

McCormick, Barnes W. & Papadakis, Myron P. Aircraft Accident Reconstruction & Litigation. LC 98-41473. (Illus.). 693p. 1998. 115.00 (0-913875-15-5, 5155-N) Lawyers & Judges.

McCormick, Barrett L. & Unger, Jonathan, eds. China after Socialism: In the Footsteps of Eastern Europe or East Asia? LC 95-31601. (Socialism & Social Movements Ser.). (Illus.). 224p. (C). 1995. text 79.95 (1-56324-666-X) M E Sharpe.

— China after Socialism: In the Footsteps of Eastern Europe or East Asia? LC 95-31601. (Socialism & Social Movements Ser.). (Illus.). 232p. (C). (gr. 13). 1995. pap. text 29.95 (1-56324-667-8) M E Sharpe.

McCormick, Barrett L., jt. ed. see Friedman, Edward.

McCormick, Barry. Paediatric Audiology: Zero to Five Years. 2nd ed. 458p. 1993. 55.00 (1-56593-239-0, 0558) Singular Publishing.

McCormick, Barry, ed. The Medical Practitioners' Guide to Paediatric Audiology. (Illus.). 146p. (C). 1995. pap. text 30.95 (0-521-45988-5) Cambridge U Pr.

McCormick, Barry, et al. Cochlear Implants for Young Children: The Nottingham Approach to Assessment & Habilitation. (Illus.). 302p. (Orig.). (C). 1994. pap. text 59.95 (1-56593-372-9, 0720) Singular Publishing.

***McCormick, Blaine.** Ben Franklin's 12 Rules of Management: The Founding Father of American Business Solves Your Toughest Problems. LC 99-87362. (Illus.). 200p. 2000. pap. 14.95 (1-891984-14-4, Pub. by Entrepreneur) Natl Bk Netwk.

McCormick, Bob. The Story of Tahoe Tessie: The Original Lake Tahoe Monster. 5th rev. ed. (Illus.). (J). (gr. 1-4). 1990. pap. 5.95 (0-9626792-6-7) Tahoe Tourist.

McCormick, Bret, jt. auth. see Steinfeld, Adam.

McCormick, Brian & McCormick, Kevin. Japanese Companies - British Factories. 336p. 1996. 77.95 (1-85972-358-6, Pub. by Avebry) Ashgate Pub Co.

McCormick, C. A., ed. see Pirandello, Luigi.

McCormick Calkins, Lucy & Bellino, Lydia. Raising Lifelong Learners: A Parent's Guide. LC 97-18548. 320p. 1997. 24.00 (0-201-12749-0) Addison-Wesley.

McCormick, Carlo. Anton Van Dalen - "The Memory Cabinet" (Illus.). 32p. (Orig.). 1988. pap. 15.00 (0-913263-24-9) Exit Art.

— The Strange Case of T. L. Art by Tony Labat & Fiction by Carlo McCormick. 56p. 1995. 15.00 (0-9631095-4-5) Artspace Bks.

McCormick, Carlo, et al. Joshua Neustein. (Illus.). 47p. (Orig.). 1987. pap. 15.00 (0-913263-18-4) Exit Art.

McCormick, Carlynn L. & Chamberlin, J. Allen. Psychiatry: Help or Betrayal?: An Authoritative Text on the History & Development of Psychiatry. 1991. pap. 12.95 (0-9631117-0-1) Gavilan Hills.

***McCormick, Carol.** Your Special Gift: A Child's Guide to the Facts of Life. 32p. (J). (gr. 4-8). 1999. pap. 5.98 (0-9675368-0-4) Celestial.

McCormick, Catherine. British-American - American-British Dictionary & Phrasebook: Hippocrene Dictionary & Phrasebook. 160p. (Orig.). 1996. pap. 11.95 (0-7818-0450-7) Hippocrene Bks.

***McCormick, Charles, ed.** Stimuli-Responsive Water-Soluble Polymers. (Illus.). 306p. 2000. text 115.00 (0-8412-3725-5) Am Chemical.

McCormick, Charles H. Leisler's Rebellion. (Outstanding Studies in Early American History). 417p. 1989. reprint ed. 25.00 (0-8240-6190-X) Garland.

— Run for the Kitchen. (Illus.). 272p. 1998. pap. 16.95 (0-9666401-0-1) Run for the Kitchen.

— Seeing Reds: Federal Surveillance of Radicals in the Pittsburgh Mill District, 1917-1921. LC 97-21173. (Illus.). 360p. 1998. text. write for info. (0-8229-3998-3) U of Pittsburgh Pr.

— This Nest of Vipers: McCarthyism & Higher Education in the Mundel Affair, 1951-52. LC 88-29592. (Illus.). 248p. 1989. text 24.95 (0-252-01614-9) U of Ill Pr.

McCormick, Charles T. & Aaron, Richard I. Evidence: Adaptable to Courses Utilizing Materials by McCormick. LC 87-114969. (Legalines Ser.). 318p. 12.95 (0-685-18530-3) Harcourt.

McCormick, Charles T., et al. Author's Suggestions for the Use of Cases & Materials on Federal Courts. 9th ed. (University Casebook Ser.). 44p. (C). 1992. pap. text. write for info. (1-56662-054-6) Foundation Pr.

— Cases & Materials on Federal Courts. 9th ed. LC 92-5649. (University Casebook Ser.). 1992. text 42.95 (0-88277-991-5) Foundation Pr.

— Evidence, Cases & Materials. 7th ed. LC 92-5652. (American Casebook Ser.). 932p. (C). 1992. text 49.00 (0-314-00426-2) West Pub.

McCormick, Christine B., ed. S/G Educational Psychology. (C). 1997. pap. text, student ed. 19.69 (0-673-99862-2) Addison-Wesley.

McCormick, Christine E. & Mason, Jana M. Little Books, Ages 4-6, 80p. 1989. pap. 8.95 (0-673-38878-6, GoodYrBooks) Addson-Wesley Educ.

McCormick, Christy, ed. see Kondaks, Tony.

An Asterisk (*) at the beginning of an entry indicates that the title is appearing for the first time.

McCormick, D. B., jt. ed. see Edmondson, D. E.

***McCormick, Dan H., et al.** Creating Foundations for American Schools. LC 00-41608. 2000. write for info. (*0-8342-1837-2*) Aspen Pub.

McCormick, David. The Downsized Warrior. LC 97-21219. 1997. text 25.00 (*0-8147-5584-4*) NYU Pr.

McCormick, David A., jt. auth. see Huguenard, John.

McCormick, Dell J. Paul Bunyan Swings His Axe. LC 36-33409. (Illus.). (J). (gr. 4-6). 1936. 15.95 (*0-87004-093-6*) Caxton.

— Tall Timber Tales: More Paul Bunyan Stories. LC 39-20778. (Illus.). (J). (gr. 4-6). 1939. 11.95 (*0-87004-094-4*) Caxton.

McCormick, Donald. 17F the Life of Ian Fleming. 232p. 1994. 35.00 (*0-7206-0888-0*, Pub. by P Owen Ltd) Dufour.

McCormick, Donald B., ed. Annual Review of Nutrition, Vol. 15. 1995. text 48.00 (*0-8243-2815-9*) Annual Reviews.

— Annual Review of Nutrition, Vol. 16. 1996. text 53.00 (*0-8243-2816-7*) Annual Reviews.

— Annual Review of Nutrition, Vol. 17. 1997. text 60.00 (*0-8243-2817-5*) Annual Reviews.

— Annual Review of Nutrition, Vol. 18. 1998. text 60.00 (*0-8243-2818-3*) Annual Reviews.

— Vitamins & Hormones, Vol. 42. 372p. 1985. text 167.00 (*0-12-709842-9*) Acad Pr.

***McCormick, Donald B., et al, eds.** Annual Review of Nutrition, Vol. 19. 600p. 1999. 60.00 (*0-8243-2819-1*) Annual Reviews.

McCormick, Donald B., jt. ed. see Aurbach, Gerald D.

McCormick, Donald D., ed. Vitamins & Hormones, Vol. 40. (Serial Publication Ser.). 1983. text 167.00 (*0-12-709840-2*) Acad Pr.

McCormick, Donald M., jt. ed. see Aurbach, Gerald D.

McCormick, Donna, jt. auth. see Katz, Jeffrey.

McCormick, E. Allen. Theodor Storm's Novellen: Essays on Literary Technique. LC 64-64253. (North Carolina. University. Studies in the Germanic Languages & Literatures: No. 47). reprint ed. 27.00 (*0-404-50947-9*) AMS Pr.

McCormick, E. Allen, jt. auth. see Ryder, Frank G.

McCormick, E. Allen, ed. see Kielkopf, Charles F.

McCormick, Edward A., tr. see Lessing, Gotthold Ephraim.

McCormick, Elaine, ed. Gilded Glory: Portrait of Georgian Court College. (Illus.). Date not set. pap. 25.00 (*0-9660586-1-5*) Aerial Perspect.

McCormick, Elizabeth W. Change for the Better: A Life-Enhancing Self-Help Psychotherapy Programme. (Illus.). 256p. 1996. pap. 25.95 (*0-304-33530-4*) Continuum.

— The Heart Attack Recovery Book: A Look at the Emotional & Practical Problems Encountered During Rehabilitation, for Patients & Their Families. 1991. pap. 9.95 (*0-904575-37-3*) Sigo Pr.

— Living on the Edge: Breaking Through Instead of Breaking Down. LC 97-7503. 160p. 1997. pap. 15.95 (*1-85230-966-0*, Pub. by Element MA) Penguin Putnam.

***McCormick, Elizabeth Wilde & Wellings, Nigel, eds.** Transpersonal Psychotherapy: Theory & Practice. 224p. 2000. 74.95 (*0-8264-4845-3*); pap. write for info. (*0-304-70678-7*) Continuum.

McCormick, Ellen R. Our Good Teachers: What the Real Experts Are Saying about Education. 96p. 1995. pap. 8.95 (*0-9629972-5-0*) Meredith VA.

McCormick, Ellen R., jt. auth. see Oliver, Carolyn C.

McCormick, Eric Hall. An Absurd Ambition: Autobiographical Writings. McEldowney, Dennis, ed. 232p. 1997. pap. 24.95 (*1-86940-156-5*, Pub. by Auckland Univ) Paul & Co Pubs.

— Portrait of Frances Hodgkins. (Illus.). 1981. 34.95 (*0-19-647991-6*) OUP.

McCormick, Ernest J. & IlGen, Daniel. Industrial & Organizational Psychology. 8th ed. (Illus.). 480p. (C). 1984. text 54.00 (*0-13-463092-0*) P-H.

McCormick, Ernest J., jt. auth. see Sanders, Mark S.

McCormick, Floyd G. The Power of Positive Teaching. LC 92-42276. 336p. 1994. 39.50 (*0-89464-831-4*) Krieger.

***McCormick, Frank.** International Trade Issues. 80p. 2000. write for info. (*1-58692-027-8*) Copyright Mgmt.

McCormick, Frank G. Sir John Vanbrugh: A Reference Guide. LC 92-13099. (Reference Bks.). 200p. 1992. 50.00 (*0-8161-8990-0*, Hall Reference) Macmillan.

— Sir John Vanbrugh: The Playwright As Architect. (Illus.). 224p. 1991. 37.50 (*0-271-00723-0*) Pa St U Pr.

***McCormick, Gail J.** Living with Multiple Chemical Sensitivity: Narratives of Coping. 256p. 2000. pap. 35.00 (*0-7864-0887-1*) McFarland & Co.

McCormick, Gail J. Our Proud Past, Vol. I. rev. ed. 186p. 1993. 18.95 (*0-9635889-1-5*) G McCormick Pub.

McCormick, Garth P., jt. auth. see Fiacco, A. V.

McCormick, Gary E. One of the Many Roses. 80p. (Orig.). 1991. pap. 9.50 (*0-9630037-0-4*) GEM MI.

McCormick, Gene H. Uncompromising Chess: The Games of Viktor Kupreichik. 66p. (Orig.). 1986. pap. 6.00 (*0-931462-58-4*) Chess Ent.

McCormick, Gene H. & Soltis, Andrew. The United States Chess Championship, 1845-1996. 2nd ed. LC 96-35534. (Illus.). 247p. 1997. lib. bdg. 45.00 (*0-7864-0248-2*) McFarland & Co.

McCormick, George C. Kitchel, John Kitchel & Esther Peck, Their Ancestors, Descendants & Some Kindred Families. (Illus.). 136p. 1997. reprint ed. pap. 21.00 (*0-8328-9441-9*); reprint ed. lib. bdg. 31.00 (*0-8328-9440-0*) Higginson Bk Co.

McCormick, Gordon H. & Bissell, Michael E., eds. Strategic Dimensions of Economic Behavior. LC 84-13292. 288p. 1984. 45.00 (*0-275-91225-6*, C1225, Praeger Pubs) Greenwood.

McCormick, Harold J. Two Years Behind the Mast: An American Landlubber at Sea in World War Two. (Illus.). 147p. (Orig.). 1991. pap. 16.00 (*0-89745-138-4*) Sunflower U Pr.

McCormick, Harold W., et al. Shadows in the Sea: The Sharks, Skates & Rays, Fully Updated Edition. LC 96-32190. (Illus.). 432p. 1996. pap. text 18.95 (*1-55821-518-2*) Lyons Pr.

McCormick, Harvey L. Medicare & Medicaid Claims & Procedures, 2 vols. LC 86-9150. 1440p. 1986. text. write for info. (*0-314-97401-6*) West Pub.

— Social Security Claims & Procedure, Vol. 1. 4th ed. 549p. 1991. pap. write for info. (*0-318-67297-9*) West Pub.

— Social Security Claims & Procedure, Vol. 2. 4th ed. 706p. 1991. pap. write for info. (*0-318-67298-7*) West Pub.

— Social Security Claims & Procedure, Vols. 1 & 2. 4th ed. LC 99-162425. 1991. text. write for info. (*0-314-77340-1*) West Pub.

***McCormick, Henrietta H.** McCormick Genealogies & Reminiscences. fac. rev. ed. (Illus.). 211p. 1999. reprint ed. 43.00 (*0-8328-9960-7*); reprint ed. pap. 33.00 (*0-8328-9961-5*) Higginson Bk Co.

McCormick, Hugh D. Confederate Son. 260p. 1993. 17.95 (*0-9636351-0-7*) Shenandoah Univ.

McCormick, Ian. The Routledge Anthology of Lesbian & Gay Writing: The Seventeenth & Eighteenth Century. LC 96-1605. 272p. (C). 1997. 90.00 (*0-415-13953-8*) Routledge.

***McCormick, Ian.** Sexual Outcasts, 1750-1850, 4 vols. LC 99-31733. 860p. 2000. write for info. (*0-415-20146-2*) Routledge.

McCormick, Ian, ed. The Routledge Anthology of Lesbian & Gay Writing: The Seventeenth & Eighteenth Century. LC 96-1605. 272p. (C). 1997. pap. 25.99 (*0-415-13954-6*) Routledge.

McCormick, J. Frank, jt. ed. see Kormondy, Edward J.

McCormick, J. Michael & Thiruvathukal, John V. Elements of Oceanography. 464p. 1993. per. 50.95 (*0-8403-8625-7*) Kendall-Hunt.

— Elements of Oceanography. 2nd ed. 448p. (C). 1981. text 68.50 (*0-03-057806-X*, Pub. by SCP) Harcourt.

McCormick, James, jt. auth. see Skrabanek, Petr.

McCormick, James, ed. see Hymers, Lewis.

McCormick, James, jt. ed. see McDowell, Eleanor.

McCormick, James B. Eighteenth Century Microscopes: Synopsis of History & Workbook. (History of Microscopy Ser.). (Illus.). 88p. 1987. 26.00 (*0-940095-01-7*) Sci Heritage Ltd.

McCormick, James B. & Bracegirdle, Brian. The Microscopic Photographs of J. B. Dancer. (Illus.). 288p. 1993. 50.00 (*0-940095-10-6*) Sci Heritage Ltd.

McCormick, James C. The Stone Bruise. LC 93-70998. 442p. 1993. 23.00 (*1-880909-11-1*) Baskerville.

McCormick, James M. American Foreign Policy & Process. 3rd rev. ed. LC 97-66352. 630p. (C). 1997. pap. text 50.00 (*0-87581-410-7*, AFP3) F E Peacock Pubs.

McCormick, James M., jt. ed. see Wittkopf, Eugene R.

McCormick, James R. Jerusalem & the Holy Land: The First Ecumenical Pilgrim's Guide. LC 96-72180. (Illus.). 208p. 1997. pap. 12.95 (*0-9649401-3-2*) Rhodes & Easton.

McCormick, James R., jt. auth. see Choy, Penelope.

McCormick, Jami S., jt. auth. see Poland, Scott.

McCormick, Janice, jt. ed. see Frommer, Judith G.

***McCormick, Jean M.** Talk Sports Like a Pro: 99 Secrets to Becoming a Sports Goddess. LC 99-34873. 1999. pap. 13.95 (*0-399-52534-3*, Perigee Bks) Berkley Pub.

McCormick, Jerusha H. Wilde the Irishman. LC 97-80783. 256p. 1998. 30.00 (*0-300-07296-1*) Yale U Pr.

McCormick, Joe. Up on Plane. 136p. 1998. pap. 7.95 (*0-9659288-0-2*) Great Horned.

McCormick, Joe & McKenney, Tom C. Holy Spirit Baptism. (Illus.). 23p. (Orig.). 1982. pap. 3.95 (*0-934527-02-4*) Words Living Mins.

McCormick, John. Acid Earth: The Politics of Acid Pollution. 3rd ed. 224p. 1997. 60.00 (*1-85383-302-9*, Pub. by Escan Pubns); pap. 26.00 (*1-85383-298-7*, Pub. by Escan Pubns) Island Pr.

***McCormick, John.** American & European Literary Imagination. LC 99-45931. 256p. 2000. pap. 24.95 (*0-7658-0635-5*) Transaction Pubs.

McCormick, John. British Politics & Environment. 1990. 20.00 (*1-85383-090-9*, Pub. by Escan Pubns) Island Pr.

— Bullfighting: Art, Technique, & Spanish Society. LC 97-28425. 276p. 1997. text 32.95 (*1-56000-345-6*) Transaction Pubs.

***McCormick, John.** Bullfighting: Art, Technique & Spanish Society. 282p. 2000. pap. 24.95 (*0-7658-0657-6*) Transaction Pubs.

McCormick, John. Careers in Conservation. 112p. (Orig.). 1989. pap. 17.95 (*0-8464-1402-3*) Beekman Pubs.

— Catastrophe & Imagination: English & American Writings from 1870 to 1950. LC 97-43285. 327p. 1998. pap. text 24.95 (*1-56000-975-6*) Transaction Pubs.

— Comparative Politics in Transition. LC 94-23386. 476p. (C). 1994. text 51.50 (*0-534-18900-8*) Harcourt.

— Deductive Interpretation of Natal Horoscope. 76p. 1976. 9.50 (*0-86690-126-4*, M1305-014) Am Fed Astrologers.

— Dion Boucicault (1820-1890) (Theatre in Focus Ser.). 1987. pap. write for info. incl. sl. (*0-85964-194-5*) Chadwyck-Healey.

— The European Union: Politics & Policies. Hoffman, Stanley, ed. (New Europe Ser.). 346p. (C). 1996. pap. 34.00 (*0-8133-2233-2*, Pub. by Westview) HarpC.

— Fiction as Knowledge: The Modern Post-Romantic Novel. LC 98-34564. 184p. 1999. pap. 19.95 (*0-7658-0480-8*) Transaction Pubs.

— Melodrama Theatres of the French Boulevard. (Theatre in Focus Ser.). (Illus.). 120p. 1982. pap. write for info. incl. sl. (*0-85964-117-1*) Chadwyck-Healey.

— The Right Kind of War. large type ed. LC 92-44777. (General Ser.). 548p. 1993. reprint ed. lib. bdg. 18.95 (*1-56054-663-8*) Thorndike Pr.

— The Right Kind of War: A Novel. LC 92-19546. 333p. 1992. 24.95 (*1-55750-574-8*) Naval Inst Pr.

***McCormick, John.** Seagoing: Essay-Memoirs. 123p. 2000. 29.95 (*0-7658-0021-7*) Transaction Pubs.

McCormick, John. Understanding the European Union: A Concise Introduction. LC 99-13585. (European Union Series). 256p. 1999. pap. 22.95 (*0-312-22166-5*); text 59.95 (*0-312-22165-7*) St Martin.

McCormick, John & McCormick, Nancy. Baby Doll & Friends. LC 90-60247. (Illus.). (Orig.). (J). (ps-2). 1991. pap. 10.00 (*0-614-10787-3*) MV Assocs MI.

McCormick, John & Pratasik, Bennie. Popular Puppet Theatre in Europe, 1800-1914. LC 97-16552. (Illus.). 272p. (C). 1998. text 80.00 (*0-521-45413-1*) Cambridge U Pr.

***McCormick, John A.** Fantastic Fax Modems: Communicate with Your PC, Mac, or LAN. (Illus.). 301p. 1999. reprint ed. pap. text 15.00 (*0-7881-6511-9*) DIANE Pub.

McCormick, John F. St. Thomas & the Life of Learning. (Aquinas Lectures). 1937. 15.00 (*0-87462-101-1*) Marquette.

McCormick, John P. Carl Schmitt's Critique of Liberalism: Against Politics As Technology. (Modern European Philosophy Ser.). 352p. (C). 1999. pap. 18.95 (*0-521-66457-8*) Cambridge U Pr.

McCormick, John S. The European Union: Politics & Policies. 2nd ed. LC 99-19924. (New Europe Ser.). 352p. 1999. pap. 25.00 (*0-8133-9032-X*, Pub. by Westview) HarpC.

***McCormick, John S.** A Gathering Place: An Illustrated History of Salt Lake City. LC 99-41904. (Illus.). 303p. 2000. text 39.95 (*1-56085-132-5*) Signature Bks.

McCormick, John S. & Sillito, John R., eds. A World We Thought We Knew: New Readings in Utah History. (Illus.). 540p. 1995. pap. 24.95 (*0-87480-484-1*); text 65.00 (*0-87480-483-3*) U of Utah Pr.

McCormick, John S., jt. auth. see McCormick, Nancy D.

McCormick, John W. Project Factors & Influences Integral to the Development of Fire Protection Solutions. 1984. 4.35 (*0-318-03821-8*, TR84-4) Society Fire Protect.

McCormick, Jon. Automobile Sales & Leasing: The Complete How to Book for Auto Sales Professionals. 182p. 1997. pap. 21.95 (*1-57002-066-3*) Univ Publng Hse.

— The Automobile Sales Manager's Complete Success Formula: A Current Guide to Managing a Profitable Car Dealership. 330p. 1994. pap. 24.95 (*1-57002-004-3*) Univ Publng Hse.

***McCormick, Kathleen.** The Garden Lover's Guide to the West Coast. LC 00-8109. (Garden Lover's Guide to the United States Ser.). (Illus.). 192p. 2000. pap. 21.95 (*1-56898-166-X*) Princeton Arch.

McCormick, Kathleen A. The Culture of Reading & the Teaching of English. LC 93-28179. 1994. text 24.95 (*0-7190-3245-8*, Pub. by Manchester Univ Pr) St Martin.

— Ulysses, "Wandering Rocks," & the Reader: Multiple Pleasures in Reading. LC 90-21975. (Studies in British Literature: Vol. 12). 196p. 1991. lib. bdg. 79.95 (*0-88946-493-6*) E Mellen.

McCormick, Kathleen A. & Flatter, Charles H. Learning to Live Drug Free: A Curriculum Model for Prevention. (Illus.). 182p. (Orig.). (C). 1994. pap. text 30.00 (*0-7881-0450-0*) DIANE Pub.

McCormick, Kathleen A. & Steinberg, Erwin R. Approaches to Teaching Joyce's "Ulysses" LC 93-736. (Approaches to World Literature Ser.: No. 44). xii, 178p. 1993. pap. 18.00 (*0-87352-712-7*, AP44P); lib. bdg. 37.50 (*0-87352-711-9*, AP44C) Modern Lang.

McCormick, Kathleen A., et al. Reading Texts: Reading, Responding, Writing. LC 86-82150. 320p. (C). 1987. pap. text 32.36 (*0-669-09564-8*) HM Trade Div.

McCormick, Kathleen A., jt. auth. see Diokno, Ananias.

McCormick, Kathleen A., jt. auth. see Saba, Virginia K.

McCormick, Kathleen Ann, jt. auth. see Saba, Virginia K.

McCormick, Keith M. & Stamschror, Robert P. A Companion Way: Mentoring Youth in Searching Faith. (Illus.). 72p. 1992. spiral bd. 15.95 (*0-88489-283-2*) St Marys.

McCormick, Kelly, jt. auth. see Clarke, Stevens H.

***McCormick, Kevin.** Engineers in Japan & Britain: Education Training & Employment. LC 99-14505. (Nissan Institute/Routledge Japanese Studies Ser.). 1998. text. write for info. (*0-415-16181-9*) Routledge.

McCormick, Kevin, jt. auth. see McCormick, Brian.

McCormick, L. J. McCormick Family Record & Biography. (Illus.). 490p. 1989. reprint ed. pap. 73.50 (*0-8328-0861-X*); reprint ed. lib. bdg. 81.50 (*0-8328-0860-1*) Higginson Bk Co.

McCormick, Larry, et al. Living with Long Island's South Shore. LC 83-20670. (Living with the Shore Ser.). (Illus.). 167p. (C). 1984. pap. 16.95 (*0-8223-0502-X*); text 39.95 (*0-8223-0501-1*) Duke.

***McCormick, Leander.** Fishing Round the World. (Blue Water Classics Ser.). 308p. 2000. lthr. 65.00 (*1-56416-184-6*) Derrydale Pr.

McCormick, Linda, et al. Supporting Children with Communication Difficulties. 3rd ed. Orig. Title: Early Language Intervention: Supporting Children with Communication Difficulties in Inclusive Settings. (Illus.). 512p. (C). 1996. pap. text 62.00 (*0-02-379272-8*, Macmillan Coll) P-H.

McCormick, Linda, jt. auth. see Stodden, Norma J.

McCormick, Love, ed. see Caine, Dona & Caine, Michael.

McCormick, M. Diane, ed. see Bergsten, Martha C.

McCormick, M. Patrick, jt. ed. see Hobbs, Peter V.

McCormick, Maggie. Book of Home Sewing. LC 96-71660. (Illus.). 160p. 1997. 27.95 (*0-670-87364-0*) Viking Penguin.

***McCormick, Maggie.** Dead Good Read: Classic Tales of Mystery & Horror. 1999. 16.99 (*1-84100-265-8*) Quadrillion Pubng.

— Spooky Stories: Super-Scary Tales to Chill Your Spine. (J). 1999. 16.99 (*1-84100-266-6*) Quadrillion Pubng.

— Terror Trail: Tales of Mystery & the Unexplained from Around the World. 1999. 16.99 (*1-84100-267-4*) Quadrillion Pubng.

McCormick, Malachi. A Collection of English Proverbs. (Proverbs of the World Ser.). (Illus.). 60p. 1981. pap. text 20.00 (*0-943984-03-3*) Stone St Pr.

— A Collection of Irish Proverbs. (Proverbs of the World Ser.). (Illus.). 60p. 1981. pap. text 20.00 (*0-943984-00-9*) Stone St Pr.

— A Collection of Yiddish Proverbs. (Proverbs of the World Ser.). (Illus.). 60p. 1982. pap. text 20.00 (*0-943984-02-5*) Stone St Pr.

McCormick, Malachi. Colum Cille Vol. 1: His Life & Tiimes (521 AD-597 AD) (Illus.). 80p. (C). 1997. pap. 24.00 (*0-943984-65-3*) Stone St Pr.

McCormick, Malachi. Dark Secrets: Cooking with Stout - Porter. 40p. 1988. 10.00 (*0-943984-34-3*) Stone St Pr.

— Herself Long Ago: Six Irish Women, 1000 Years Ago, Bk. 1. 96p. 1990. write for info. (*0-943984-38-6*) Stone St Pr.

— Herself Long Ago: Six Irish Women, 1000 Years Ago, Bk. 2. 96p. 1990. write for info. (*0-943984-39-4*) Stone St Pr.

— Herself Long Ago: Six Irish Women, 1000 Years Ago, Bk. 3. 96p. 1990. write for info. (*0-943984-40-8*) Stone St Pr.

— Herself Long Ago: Six Irish Women, 1000 Years Ago, 3 vols., Set. 96p. 1990. boxed set 28.00 (*0-943984-37-8*) Stone St Pr.

— How to Make a Decent Cup of Tea. 24p. 1986. 4.00 (*0-943984-27-0*) Stone St Pr.

— How to Make a Perfect Cup of Coffee. 24p. 1992. 4.00 (*0-943984-55-6*) Stone St Pr.

— In Praise of Irish Breakfasts: A Frying Paean! 42p. 1991. 15.00 (*0-943984-42-4*) Stone St Pr.

— Irish Bread & Cake: Classic Recipes. 28p. 1981. pap. text 9.00 (*0-943984-01-7*) Stone St Pr.

— Irish Festive Fare. (Irish Traditional Cooking Ser.). 32p. 1984. 10.00 (*0-943984-14-9*) Stone St Pr.

— Irish Traditional Cooking, 3 Vols., Set. 92p. 1984. boxed set 28.00 (*0-943984-20-3*) Stone St Pr.

— Irish Traditional Soups. (Irish Traditional Cooking Ser.). 32p. 1984. 9.00 (*0-943984-19-X*) Stone St Pr.

— Listening to the River: Family Biography. 60p. 1989. 24.00 (*0-943984-35-1*) Stone St Pr.

— Love of Frog: Ranaphilia, 3 vols., 3. 96p. 1993. 35.00 (*0-318-70248-7*) Stone St Pr.

— Love of Frog: Ranaphilia, 3 vols., Vol. 1. (Special Paste Paper Miniature Collections Ser.). 84p. 1993. write for info. (*0-943984-57-2*) Stone St Pr.

— Love of Frog: Ranaphilia, 3 vols., Vol. 2. (Special Paste Paper Miniature Collections Ser.). 84p. 1993. write for info. (*0-943984-58-0*) Stone St Pr.

— Love of Frog: Ranaphilia, 3 vols., Vol. 3. (Special Paste Paper Miniature Collections Ser.). 84p. 1993. write for info. (*0-943984-59-9*) Stone St Pr.

— The Sacred Tree: Early Irish Nature Poetry, Bk. 1. 96p. 1992. write for info. (*0-943984-50-5*) Stone St Pr.

— The Sacred Tree: Early Irish Nature Poetry, Bk. 2. 96p. 1992. write for info. (*0-943984-51-3*) Stone St Pr.

— The Sacred Tree: Early Irish Nature Poetry, Bk. 3. 96p. 1992. write for info. (*0-943984-52-1*) Stone St Pr.

— The Sacred Tree: Early Irish Nature Poetry, 3 vols., Set. 96p. 1992. boxed set 28.00 (*0-943984-49-1*) Stone St Pr.

McCormick, Malachi, ed. Cat Folk Tales, 5 vols., 1. 120p. 1987. write for info. (*0-943984-29-7*) Stone St Pr.

— Cat Folk Tales, 5 vols., 2. 120p. 1987. write for info. (*0-943984-30-0*) Stone St Pr.

— Cat Folk Tales, 5 vols., 3. 120p. 1987. write for info. (*0-943984-31-9*) Stone St Pr.

— Cat Folk Tales, 5 vols., 4. 120p. 1987. write for info. (*0-943984-32-7*) Stone St Pr.

— Cat Folk Tales, 5 vols., 5. 120p. 1987. write for info. (*0-943984-33-5*) Stone St Pr.

— Cat Folk Tales: Five Handmade Books, 5 vols., Set. 120p. 1987. boxed set 24.00 (*0-943984-28-9*) Stone St Pr.

— Collected Nursery Rhymes: Four Handmade Books. 80p. (J). 1985. boxed set 24.00 (*0-943984-21-1*) Stone St Pr.

— A Collection of African Proverbs. 60p. 1992. 20.00 (*0-943984-53-X*) Stone St Pr.

— Deer's Cry: St. Patrick's Breast Plate. (ENG & IRI., Illus.). 24p. (Orig.). 1982. pap. text 8.00 (*0-943984-05-X*) Stone St Pr.

— The Love of Irish Women. 32p. 1984. 9.00 (*0-943984-15-7*) Stone St Pr.

— Other Cats: Six Handmade Books of Poems about Cats. (Illus.). 120p. 1983. pap., boxed set 24.00 (*0-943984-06-8*) Stone St Pr.

— The Pleasures of Irish Nature Poetry. 32p. 1984. 10.00 (*0-943984-18-1*) Stone St Pr.

— We Cats Three, 3 vols. 84p. 1991. boxed set 24.00 (*0-943984-43-2*) Stone St Pr.

— We Cats Three, 3 vols., 1. 84p. 1991. write for info. (*0-943984-44-0*) Stone St Pr.

— We Cats Three, 3 vols., 2. 84p. 1991. write for info. (*0-943984-45-9*) Stone St Pr.

— We Cats Three, 3 vols., 3. 84p. 1991. write for info. (*0-943984-46-7*) Stone St Pr.

***McCormick, Malachi, ed.** Consolations Vol. 1: c. 1500 AD, Anonymous. 24p. 2000. pap. 10.00 (*0-943984-71-8*) Stone St Pr.

M

An Asterisk (*) at the beginning of an entry indicates that the title is appearing for the first time.

McCormick, Malachi, ed. Hail to the Herring: Sixteenth Century Poem. 20p. 1984. 7.00 (*0-943984-16-5*) Stone St Pr.

***McCormick, Malachi, ed.** The Irish Harp: In Poetry & Story, 3 vols. (Illus.). 96p. (C). 1999. pap. 28.00 (*0-943984-67-X*) Stone St Pr.

McCormick, Malachi, ed. Irish Poetry Set: Love, Nature, Monastic Poetry Collection, 3 vols., Set. 96p. 1986. 28.00 (*0-943984-24-6*) Stone St Pr.

— Not Sweet (The Snoring Poem) 24p. 1986. 7.00 (*0-943984-26-2*) Stone St Pr.

— Old Irish Monastic Prayer-Poetry. (Irish Poetry Ser.). 32p. 1986. 9.00 (*0-943984-23-8*) Stone St Pr.

— Pangur Bawn the Cat: Ninth Century. (Miniatures Ser.). 24p. 1991. pap. 7.00 (*0-943984-48-3*) Stone St Pr.

McCormick, Malachi, ed. see Berkeley, George.

McCormick, Malachi, ed. see Hoffman, Marilynn.

McCormick, Malachi, ed. see Provisional Government of Ireland Staff.

McCormick, Malachi, ed. & tr. see Bhaird, Laoiseach Mac An.

McCormick, Malachi, ed. & tr. see Bhaird, Laoiseach Macan.

McCormick, Malachi, ed. & tr. see O'Connell, Eileen Dubh.

McCormick, Malachi, ed. & tr. see O'Heffernan, Mahon.

McCormick, Margaret. World Evolution: Our Future in the Twenty-First Century. LC 91-91572. 240p. 1991. pap. 12.95 (*0-9631930-3-1*) Channel CA.

McCormick, Marie C. & Siegel, Joanna E., eds. Prenatal Care: Effectiveness & Implementation. (Illus.). 300p. (C). 1999. pap. 67.95 (*0-521-66196-X*) Cambridge U Pr.

McCormick, Marjorie J. Mothers in the English Novel: From Stereotype & Archetype. LC 91-249241. (Gender & Genre in Literature Ser.: Vol. 1). 232p. 1991. text 15.00 (*0-8240-7131-X*, H1302) Garland.

McCormick, Mark, jt. auth. see Barber, Steve.

McCormick, Mark, jt. auth. see Starr, V. Hale.

McCormick, Mark, ed. see Cook, J. Sue & Fontaine, Karen L.

McCormick, Mark, ed. see Maas, Meridean, et al.

McCormick, Mark, ed. see Wilson, Holly S.

McCormick, Marlena D., jt. auth. see McCormick, Adele V.

McCormick, Mary J. Enduring Values in a Changing Society. LC 75-18288. 208p. reprint ed. pap. 64.50 (*0-608-18327-X*, 203160300075) Bks Demand.

McCormick, Michael. Across the Pond. 1993. 10.95 (*0-533-10579-X*) Vantage.

McCormick, Michael, jt. auth. see Sillick, Ardis.

McCormick, Michael E., ed. Anchoring Systems. 1979. 36.00 (*0-08-022694-9*, Pergamon Pr) Elsevier.

— Port & Ocean Engineering under Arctic Conditions: Selected Papers from the 3rd International Conference. 1977. pap. 29.00 (*0-08-021421-5*, Pergamon Pr) Elsevier.

McCormick, Michael E. & Kim, Young C., eds. Utilization of Ocean Waves - Wave to Energy Conversion. 212p. 1987. 26.00 (*0-87262-624-5*) Am Soc Civil Eng.

McCormick, Michael J., jt. auth. see Perkinson, Gary.

McCormick, Nancy, jt. auth. see McCormick, John.

McCormick, Nancy D. & McCormick, John S. Saltair. LC 85-665. (Bonneville Bks.). (Illus.). 117p. (Orig.). reprint ed. pap. 36.30 (*0-8357-4375-6*, 203720500007) Bks Demand.

McCormick, Naomi B. Sexual Salvation: Affirming Women's Sexual Rights & Pleasures. LC 94-6378. 304p. 1994. 35.00 (*0-275-94359-3*, Praeger Pubs) Greenwood.

McCormick, Norman J. Reliability & Risk Analysis: Methods & Nuclear Power Applications. LC 81-2758. 1981. text 100.00 (*0-12-482360-2*) Acad Pr.

McCormick, Norman J., jt. ed. see Williams, M. M.

McCormick, Norman J., jt. ed. see Williams, M. R.

McCormick, P., ed. Developing & Applying End of Arm Tooling. 264p. 1986. 11.50 (*0-87263-211-3*) SME.

McCormick, Patrick M. & Lovill, J. E., eds. Space Observations of Aerosols & Ozone: Proceedings of the Topical Meeting of the COSPAR Interdisciplinary Scientific Commission A (Meetings A1 & A2) of the COSPAR 24th Plenary Meeting held in Ottawa, Canada, 16 May-2 June, 1982, Vol. 2/5. (Illus.). 120p. 1983. pap. 50.00 (*0-08-030427-3*, Pergamon Pr) Elsevier.

McCormick, Patrick T. Sin As Addiction. 1989. pap. 7.95 (*0-8091-3064-5*) Paulist Pr.

McCormick, Patrick T., jt. auth. see Conners, Russell B., Jr.

***McCormick, Patty.** Cut. 2000. 16.95 (*1-886910-61-8*, Front Street) Front Str.

McCormick, Patty. Pieces of an American Quilt: Quilts, Patterns, Photos & Behind the Scene Stories from the Movie. Aneloski, Elizabeth, ed. LC 96-33759. (Illus.). 96p. (Orig.). 1996. pap. 19.95 (*1-57120-012-6*, 10136) C & T Pub.

McCormick, Peggy. Making a Home in Stillwater. LC 88-83680. (Illus.). 96p. 1989. pap. 14.95 (*0-934188-28-9*) Evans Pubns.

McCormick, Peggy, jt. auth. see Gardiner, Joanna.

McCormick, Penny, jt. auth. see McCormick, Tom.

McCormick, Penny, jt. ed. see McCormick, Tom.

McCormick, Peter. Canada's Courts. LC 94-187321. 222p. pap. 19.95 (*1-55028-434-7*, Pub. by J Lorimer) Formac Dist Ltd.

McCormick, Peter & Elliston, Frederick A., eds. Husserl: Shorter Works. LC 80-53178. 440p. (C). 1982. text 22.00 (*0-268-01703-4*) U of Notre Dame Pr.

McCormick, Peter, jt. auth. see Greene, Ian.

McCormick, Peter, jt. ed. see Dziemidok, Bohdan.

McCormick, Peter, tr. see Marcel, Gabriel.

McCormick, Peter J. Fictions, Philosophies, & the Problems of Poetics. LC 88-47783. 384p. 1988. 49.95 (*0-8014-2204-3*); pap. text 19.95 (*0-8014-9519-9*) Cornell U Pr.

— Modernity, Aesthetics, & the Bounds of Art. LC 89-71309. (Illus.). 368p. 1990. 49.95 (*0-8014-2452-6*) Cornell U Pr.

— Modernity, Aesthetics & the Bounds of Art. LC 89-71309. 367p. reprint ed. pap. 113.80 (*0-608-20921-X*, 207202000003) Bks Demand.

McCormick, Peter J., ed. Starmaking: Realism, Anti-Realism, & Irrealism. LC 95-48929. (Representation & Mind Ser.). (Illus.). 238p. (C). 1996. 32.00 (*0-262-13320-2*, Bradford Bks) MIT Pr.

McCormick, R. J., et al. Costs for Hazardous Waste Incineration: Capital, Operation & Maintenance, Retrofit. LC 85-16839. (Pollution Technology Review Ser.: No. 123). (Illus.). 274p. 1986. 39.00 (*0-8155-1047-0*) Noyes.

McCormick, Rachael L., jt. ed. see Paratore, Jeanne R.

McCormick, Richard A. Ambiguity in Moral Choice. (Pere Marquette Lectures). 1977. pap. 15.00 (*0-87462-505-X*) Marquette.

— Corrective Vision: Explorations in Moral Theology. LC 93-21332. 248p. (Orig.). 1994. pap. 15.95 (*1-55612-601-8*) Sheed & Ward WI.

— The Critical Calling: Reflections on Moral Dilemmas since Vatican II. LC 89-7622. 434p. (Orig.). 1989. reprint ed. pap. 134.60 (*0-608-07915-4*, 205985500011) Bks Demand.

— How Brave a New World? Dilemmas in Bioethics. LC 84-25840. (Studies in Ethics). 477p. reprint ed. pap. 147.90 (*0-608-07020-3*, 206722700009) Bks Demand.

McCormick, Richard A. & Curran, Charles E. Readings in Moral Theology No. 6: Dissent in the Church. 560p. 1988. pap. 14.95 (*0-8091-2930-2*) Paulist Pr.

McCormick, Richard A., jt. auth. see Curran, Charles E.

McCormick, Richard A., jt. ed. see Curran, Charles A.

McCormick, Richard A., jt. ed. see Curran, Charles E.

McCormick, Richard L. The Party Period & Public Policy: American Politics from the Age of Jackson to the Progressive Era. 384p. (C). 1988. reprint ed. pap. text 23.95 (*0-19-504784-2*) OUP.

— Public Life in Industrial America, 1877-1917. 2nd expanded rev. ed. (New American History Ser.). 26p. (C). 1997. reprint ed. pap. 5.00 (*0-87229-091-3*) Am Hist Assn.

McCormick, Richard L., jt. auth. see Link, Arthur S.

McCormick, Richard P. New Jersey from Colony to State, 1609-1789. (Classics Ser.). (Illus.). 191p. 1988. pap. 12.95 (*0-911020-02-0*) NJ Hist Soc.

— The Presidential Game: The Origins of American Presidential Politics. 288p. 1984. pap. text 21.95 (*0-19-503455-4*) OUP.

McCormick, Richard P. & Schlatter, Richard, eds. The Selected Speeches of Mason Gross. 160p. 1980. 34.95 (*0-87855-388-6*) Transaction Pubs.

McCormick, Richard S., jt. ed. see Curran, Charles E.

McCormick, Richard W. Politics of the Self: Feminism & the Postmodern in West German Literature & Film. LC 90-47160. (Illus.). 274p. 1991. reprint ed. pap. 85.00 (*0-608-02571-2*, 206321600004) Bks Demand.

McCormick, Robert. The Concept of Happiness in the Spanish Poetry of the Eighteenth Century. LC 80-68000. (Coleccion de Estudios Hispanicos - Hispanic Studies Collection). 206p. (Orig.). 1980. pap. 19.95 (*0-89729-264-2*) Ediciones.

— Freedom of the Press. LC 77-125705. (American Journalists Ser.). 1976. reprint ed. 14.95 (*0-405-01686-7*) Ayer.

— Realwrite Realtime Computerized. LC 97-5143. 256p. 1997. pap. text 42.00 (*0-13-490004-9*) P-H.

***McCormick, Robert.** Rose Petals. 1999. pap. write for info. (*1-58235-034-5*) Watermrk Pr.

McCormick, Robert, et al. Sports Law. (Illus.). 672p. (C). 1999. ring bd. 68.00 (*1-879581-69-8*) Lupus Pubns.

McCormick, Robert, jt. ed. see Cross, Anita.

McCormick, Robert E. Managerial Economics. 714p. 1992. 95.00 (*0-13-544750-X*) P-H.

McCormick, Robert E. & Tollison, Robert D. Politicians, Legislation, & the Economy: An Inquiry into the Interest-Group Theory of Government. (Rochester Studies in Economics & Policy Issues). 160p. 1981. lib. bdg. 111.00 (*0-89838-058-8*) Kluwer Academic.

McCormick, Robert L. A Variety of Poems. (Orig.). 1996. pap. write for info. (*1-57553-291-3*) Watermrk Pr.

— A Variety of Poems, No. 2. (Orig.). 1997. pap. write for info. (*1-57553-511-4*) Watermrk Pr.

***McCormick, Robert W.** Around Worthington. (Images of America Ser.). 1999. pap. 18.99 (*0-7385-0028-3*) Arcadia Publng.

McCormick, Robert W., jt. auth. see McCormick, Virginia E.

McCormick, Rosemary, tr. see Trottier, Maxine.

McCormick, Rosie. All Kinds of Animals. (Fun Finding Out Ser.). (Illus.). 32p. (J). (ps-1). 1997. pap. 9.95 (*0-7534-5071-2*, Kingfisher) LKC.

— La Selva Tropical. (Biblioteca de Descubrimentos Ser.).Tr. of World of the Rain Forest. (SPA., Illus.). (J). (gr. 3-6). 1997. 11.95 (*0-915741-86-5*, SY7078) C D Stampley Ent.

— Things That Go. (Fun Finding Out Ser.). (Illus.). 32p. (J). (ps-1). 1997. pap. 9.95 (*0-7534-5072-0*) LKC.

McCormick, Rosie. World of the Rainforest. (Launch Pad Library). (Illus.). 32p. (J). (gr. k-4). 1997. 11.95 (*0-915741-79-2*) C D Stampley Ent.

McCormick, Rosie & Lewis, Anthony. Me & My Body. LC 97-39705. (Fun Finding Out Ser.). (Illus.). 32p. (J). (ps-3). 1998. 12.95 (*0-7534-5126-3*) LKC.

Mccormick, Rosie & Lewis, Anthony. Me & My Body. LC 97-39705. (Fun Finding Out Ser.). (J). (ps-1). 1998. pap. 9.95 (*0-7534-5127-1*) LKC.

McCormick, Rosie & Lewis, Anthony. Me & My World. LC 97-39704. (Fun Finding Out Ser.). (J). (ps-1). 1998. pap. 9.95 (*0-7534-5129-8*) LKC.

McCormick, Ross. For Sale by Owner - A Practical Guide for Selling Your Home. 110p. 1991. pap. 18.95 (*0-9630593-0-0*); lib. bdg. write for info. (*0-9630593-1-9*) Gt Falls North.

McCormick, Roy C. Coverages Applicable. Kowatch, Diana, ed. LC 99-164413. 329p. 1998. pap. text 59.50 (*1-56461-255-4*, 30040) Rough Notes.

McCormick, S., jt. ed. see Mandel, Jan.

McCormick, S. P., jt. auth. see Petroski, R. J.

***McCormick, Samuel.** Passionately Yours... A Collection of Love Letters to My Beloved. (Illus.). 70p. 1999. pap. 9.95 (*0-7414-0021-9*) Buy Books.

McCormick, Sandra, jt. ed. see Neuman, Susan B.

McCormick, Scott, Jr. Behold the Man: Re-Reading Gospels, Re-Humanizing Jesus. LC 81-22226. 216p. (C). 1994. 19.95 (*0-8264-0680-7*) Continuum.

***McCormick, Scott, Jr.** Cafe Philadelphia: A Guidebook to Philadelphia Coffee Culture. rev. ed. 64p. 1999. 10.95 (*0-9649295-1-1*, Pub. by Caffe Philadelphia) Koen Bk Distributors.

McCormick, Shawn H. The Angolan Economy: Prospects for Growth in a Postwar Economy. LC 94-11211. (Significant Issues Ser.). 88p. (Orig.). (C). 1994. pap. 8.95 (*0-89206-187-1*) CSIS.

McCormick Spice Company Staff. Cooking with Old Bay. (Collector's Ser.: Vol. 27). 64p. (Orig.). 1989. pap. 3.95 (*0-942320-34-4*) Am Cooking.

McCormick Spice Staff. More Cooking with Old Bay. (Collector's Ser.). (Illus.). 64p. 1996. per. 3.95 (*0-942320-58-1*) Am Cooking.

McCormick, Stephen F. Multigrid Methods. (Lecture Notes in Pure & Applied Mathematics Ser.: Vol. 110). (Illus.). 672p. 1988. pap. text 199.00 (*0-8247-7979-7*) Dekker.

— Multilevel Adaptive Methods for Partial Differential Equations. LC 89-22034. (Frontiers in Applied Mathematics Ser.: No. 6). ix, 162p. 1989. pap. 33.00 (*0-89871-247-5*) Soc Indus-Appl Math.

— Multilevel Projection Methods for Partial Differential Equations. LC 91-39536. (CBMS-NSF Regional Conference Series in Applied Mathematics: No. 62). vi, 114p. (C). 1992. pap. text 26.00 (*0-89871-292-0*) Soc Indus-Appl Math.

McCormick, Stephen F., ed. Multigrid Methods. LC 87-60444. (Frontiers in Applied Mathematics Ser.: No. 3). xvii, 282p. 1987. text 51.00 (*0-89871-214-9*) Soc Indus-Appl Math.

McCormick, Steve, ed. see D'yakonov, Eugene G.

McCormick, Susan, ed. Administration & Finance Report. (ASTC Science Center Survey Report Ser.). (Illus.). 78p. 1989. pap. 15.00 (*0-685-29593-1*) AST Ctrs.

— Education Report & Directory. (ASTC Science Center Survey Report Ser.). (Illus.). 100p. 1988. pap. 20.00 (*0-685-29592-3*) AST Ctrs.

McCormick, Susan, jt. ed. see Bridal, Tessa.

McCormick, Terrence C. Stressed Vowel Phonology of the Urkunden of St. Gallen in the First Half of the Fourteenth Century: German Language & Literature, Vol. 189. (European University Studies: Ser. 1). 272p. 1977. pap. 44.00 (*3-261-02926-9*) P Lang Pubng.

McCormick, Thelma, ed. Impact of the '60s: The Decade of Dissent. (Studies in Communications: Vol. 1). 1985p. 1980. 73.25 (*0-89232-146-6*) Jai Pr.

— Studies in Communications, Vol. 2: Culture, Code & Content Analysis. 192p. 1982. 73.25 (*0-89232-305-1*) Jai Pr.

— Studies in Communications, Vol. 4: Censorship & Libel: The Chilling Effect. 166p. 1990. 73.25 (*0-89232-761-8*) Jai Pr.

— Studies in Communications, Vol. 5. LC 97-17990. 171p. 1995. 73.25 (*1-55938-235-X*) Jai Pr.

— Studies in Communications, Vol. 6. Date not set. 73.25 (*0-7623-0052-3*) Jai Pr.

— Studies in Communications Vol. 3: News & Knowledge. 232p. 1986. 73.25 (*0-89232-363-9*) Jai Pr.

McCormick, Theresa. Creating the Nonsexist Classroom. 224p. (C). 1994. text 37.00 (*0-8077-3348-2*); pap. text 16.95 (*0-8077-3347-4*) Tchrs Coll.

McCormick, Thomas. Charles-Louis Clerisseau & the Genesis of Neoclassicism: The Birth of Neoclassicism. (Illus.). 300p. 1991. 42.00 (*0-262-13262-1*) MIT Pr.

McCormick, Thomas & LaFeber, Walter, eds. Behind the Throne: Servants of Power to Imperial Presidents, 1898-1968. LC 93-18754. 288p. (C). 1993. text 47.95 (*0-299-13740-6*) U of Wis Pr.

McCormick, Thomas C. Carson - McCormick Family Memorials. (Illus.). 158p. 1997. reprint ed. pap. 26.00 (*0-8328-7863-4*); reprint ed. lib. bdg. 36.00 (*0-8328-7862-6*) Higginson Bk Co.

McCormick, Thomas J. America's Half-Century: United States Foreign Policy in the Cold War & After. 2nd rev. ed. LC 94-34698. (American Moment Ser.). 312p. 1995. text 38.95 (*0-8018-5010-X*); pap. text 14.95 (*0-8018-5011-8*) Johns Hopkins.

— China Market: America's Quest for Informal Empire, 1893-1901. 252p. 1990. pap. text 9.95 (*0-929587-24-3*, Elephant Paperbacks) I R Dee.

McCormick, Thomas J., Jr. A Partial Edition of les Fais des Rommains with a Study of Its Style. LC 94-48863. 264p. 1995. text 89.95 (*0-7734-2918-2*) E Mellen.

McCormick, Thomas J. Ruins as Architecture: Architecture as Ruins. Morgan, William, ed. LC 99-28590. (F. L. Morgan Art & Architecture Ser.). (Illus.). 64p. (Orig.). 1998. pap. 12.50 (*0-87233-117-2*) Bauhan.

McCormick, Thomas W. Theories of Reading in Dialogue: An Interdisciplinary Study. LC 88-20821. 410p. (Orig.). (C). 1988. pap. text 33.00 (*0-8191-7169-7*); lib. bdg. 62.00 (*0-8191-7168-9*) U Pr of Amer.

McCormick, Tiffany, ed. see Gallagher, Steve.

***McCormick, Todd.** The Ephemeral Mind of the Climber. (Illus.). 158p. 1999. pap. 10.95 (*0-7392-0261-8*, PO3332) Morris Pubng.

McCormick, Tom & McCormick, Penny. Nursing Home Ministry. 128p. 1987. pap. 9.95 (*0-310-34571-5*, 18418P) Zondervan.

McCormick, Tom & McCormick, Penny, eds. Nursing Home Ministry: A Manual. (Orig.). 1982. pap. text 6.95 (*0-934688-08-7*) Great Comm Pubns.

McCormick, Twila, et al. Words of Wisdom. 155p. 1998. mass mkt. 10.00 (*0-9666551-0-9*) Edwyna E Boyington.

***McCormick, Virginia E.** Educational Architecture in Ohio: From One-Room Schools & Carnegie Libraries to Community Education Villages. LC 00-36877. (Illus.). 2000. write for info. (*0-87338-666-3*) Kent St U Pr.

— New Englanders on the Ohio Frontier: Migration & Settlement of Worthington, Ohio. 1999. pap. 19.00 (*0-87338-652-3*) Kent St U Pr.

McCormick, Virginia E. & McCormick, Robert W. New Englanders on the Ohio Frontier: Migration & Settlement of Worthington, Ohio. LC 97-36189. 1998. 39.00 (*0-87338-586-1*) Kent St U Pr.

McCormick-Watson, Jan. Essential English Legal System. Bourne, Nicholas, ed. (Essential Law Ser.). 206p. 1995. pap. write for info. (*1-85941-127-4*, Pub. by Cavendish Pubng) Gaunt.

McCormick, Wendy. Daddy, Will You Miss Me? LC 97-45012. (Illus.). 32p. (J). (ps-1). 1999. lib. bdg. 16.00 (*0-689-81898-X*) S&S Childrens.

***McCormick, Wendy.** The Night You Were Born. (Illus.). 32p. (J). (ps-2). 2000. 15.95 (*1-56145-225-4*) Peachtree Pubs.

McCormick, Wynne. Meet Me at the Wall. LC 93-9364. 189p. (Orig.). 1995. pap. 7.95 (*1-886825-00-9*) Stetson Pub.

McCormley, Jane H. Celebrate with Soup. (Illus.). 80p. 1990. pap. 3.95 (*0-936369-27-2*) Son-Rise Pubns.

McCormmach, Russell K. Historical Studies in the Physical Sciences, Vol. 5. LC 77-75220. (Illus.). 197p. 1975. pap. 61.10 (*0-8357-8899-7*, 203339400085) Bks Demand.

— Night Thoughts of a Classical Physicist. LC 81-6674. (Illus.). 29.95p. 1982. 31.00 (*0-674-62460-2*) HUP.

— Night Thoughts of a Classical Physicist. (Illus.). 232p. 1991. pap. text 14.50 (*0-674-62461-0*, MCCNIX) HUP.

McCormmach, Russell K., ed. Historical Studies in the Physical Sciences, Vol. 6. LC 77-75220. 564p. 1975. reprint ed. pap. 174.90 (*0-7837-9387-1*, 206013100006) Bks Demand.

— Historical Studies in the Physical Sciences, Vol. 7. LC 77-75220. 526p. 1976. pap. 163.10 (*0-7837-0043-1*, 204027800007) Bks Demand.

McCormmach, Russell K. & Jungnickel, Christa. Cavendish. LC 95-79391. (Memoirs Ser.: Vol. 220). (Illus.). 600p. 1996. 32.00 (*0-87169-220-1*, M220-mcr) Am Philos.

— Intellectual Mastery of Nature Vol. 1: Theoretical Physics from Ohm to Einstein: The Torch of Mathem. LC 85-16507. xxviii, 378p. 1999. pap. text 22.50 (*0-226-41582-1*) U Ch Pr.

— Intellectual Mastery of Nature Vol. 2: Theoretical Physics from Ohm to Einstein: The Now Mighty Theo Physics, 1870-1925. LC 85-28920. (Illus.). xx, 456p. 1990. pap. text 24.00 (*0-226-41585-6*) U Ch Pr.

— Intellectual Mastery of Nature Vol. 2: Theoretical Physics from Ohm to Einstein: The Now Mighty Theoretical Physics, 1870-1925. LC 85-28920. (Illus.). 456p. 1996. 78.00 (*0-226-41584-8*) U Ch Pr.

McCormmach, Russell K., ed. see Jungnickel, Christa.

McCormmach, Russell K., jt. ed. see Pyenson, Lewis.

McCornack & Jarett. Advanced Programming Tips for the HP-41. (Illus.). 340p. (Orig.). 1987. pap. text 9.95 (*0-9612174-6-4*, 491) Interfab Corp.

***McCorquodale, Charles.** The Renaissance: European Painting, 1400-1600. (Illus.). 304p. 2000. 84.95 (*0-9684749-8-5*, Pub. by NDE Pub) IPG Chicago.

McCorquodale, D. & Pidgeon, Monica, eds. Nicholas Grimshaw & Partners. (Illus.). 24p. 1997. pap. 39.95 incl. cd-rom (*1-901033-00-7*, Pub. by Art Bks Intl) Partners Pubs Grp.

McCorquodale, Duncan, et al, eds. Occupational Hazard: Critical Writing on Recent British Art. (Illus.). 256p. 1997. pap. 24.95 (*0-9521773-8-2*, Pub. by Black Dog Pubg) RAM Publications.

McCorquodale, Duncan & Stallabrass, Julian, eds. Ground Control: Technology & Utopia. (Illus.). 290p. 1997. pap. 24.95 (*0-9521773-2-3*, Pub. by Black Dog Pubg) RAM Publications.

McCorquodale, Robert, ed. Self-Determination in International Law. LC 99-28312. (Library of Essays in International Law). 610p. 2000. text 166.95 (*1-84014-099-2*) Ashgate Pub Co.

McCorquodale, Robert & Orosz, Nicholas, eds. Tibet: The Position of International Law. (Illus.). 238p. 1995. pap. 25.00 (*0-906026-34-2*, Pub. by Serindia) Weatherhill.

McCorquodale, Robert, jt. auth. see Dixon, Martin.

McCorquodale, Robert, jt. ed. see Dixon, Martin.

McCorrisken, Walter. Hairy Knees & Heather Hills. 128p. pap. 9.95 (*1-874744-34-3*, Pub. by Birlinn Ltd) Dufour.

— A Wee Dribble of Dross. 64p. pap. 7.95 (*1-874744-12-2*, Pub. by Birlinn Ltd) Dufour.

***McCorry.** Building a Microsoft Exchange 2000 Infrastructure. 2000. pap. 44.95 (*1-55558-245-1*, Digital DEC) Buttrwrth-Heinemann.

McCorry, Frank. Preventing Substance Abuse: A Comprehensive Program for Catholic Education. 111p. 1990. pap. 6.00 (*1-55833-040-2*) Natl Cath Educ.

An Asterisk (*) at the beginning of an entry indicates that the title is appearing for the first time.

McCorry, Kieran. Connecting Microsoft Exchange Server. LC 99-35808. 416p. 1999. pap. text 34.95 (*1-55558-204-4*, Digital DEC) Buttrwrth-Heinemann.
McCort, Dennis. States of Unconsciousness in Three Tales by C. F. Meyer. LC 87-47786. 136p. 1988. 28.50 (*0-8387-5130-X*) Bucknell U Pr.
McCorvey, Norma & Thomas, Gary. Won by Love: Norma McCorvey, Jane Roe of "Roe vs. Wade," Speaks Out Against Abortion As She Shares Her New Conviction for Life. LC 97-29645. (Illus.). 256p. 1998. 19.99 (*0-7852-7237-2*, J Thoma Bks) Nelson.
McCorvie, Mary R., jt. auth. see Wagner, Mark J.
McCorvie, Mary R., jt. ed. see Wagner, Mark J.
McCory, David L. Technology Education: Industrial Arts in Transition, A Review & Synthesis of the Research. 4th ed. 69p. 1987. 7.00 (*0-318-35275-3*, IN 325) Ctr Educ Trng Employ.
McCory, J. R., jt. auth. see Jacobs, G.
McCosh, F. W. Boussingault. 1984. text 179.50 (*90-277-1682-X*) Kluwer Academic.
McCosh, James. Development: What It Can Do & What It Cannot Do. LC 75-3252. reprint ed. 29.50 (*0-404-59240-6*) AMS Pr.
— The Development Hypothesis: Is It Sufficient. LC 75-3251. reprint ed. 29.50 (*0-404-59239-2*) AMS Pr.
— First & Fundamental Truths: Being a Treatise on Metaphysics. LC 75-3255. reprint ed. 37.50 (*0-404-59242-2*) AMS Pr.
— Ideas in Nature Overlooked by Dr. Tyndall. LC 75-3256. reprint ed. 32.50 (*0-404-59243-0*) AMS Pr.
— The Intuitions of the Mind Inductively Investigated. 3rd ed. LC 75-3257. reprint ed. 45.00 (*0-404-59244-9*) AMS Pr.
— The Method of the Divine Government Physical & Moral: 1887 Edition. 576p. 1996. reprint ed. 85.00 (*1-85506-196-1*) Bks Intl VA.
— Our Moral Nature. LC 75-3260. reprint ed. 32.50 (*0-404-59247-3*) AMS Pr.
— The Prevailing Types of Philosophy: Can They Logically Reach Reality? LC 75-3262. reprint ed. 35.00 (*0-404-59248-1*) AMS Pr.
— Psychology: The Cognitive Powers. LC 75-3263. reprint ed. 34.50 (*0-404-59249-X*) AMS Pr.
— Psychology: The Motive Powers-Emotions, Conscience, Will. LC 75-3264. reprint ed. 36.00 (*0-404-59250-3*) AMS Pr.
— Realistic Philosophy Defended in a Philosophic Series. 2 vols. LC 75-3265. reprint ed. 75.00 (*0-404-59251-1*) AMS Pr.
— The Scottish Philosophy, Bibliographical, Expository, Critical, from Hutcheson to Hamilton. ix, 481p. 1966. reprint ed. 89.70 (*0-685-66492-9*, 05101276); reprint ed. write for info. (*0-318-71927-4*) G Olms Pubs.
— The Scottish Philosophy, Bibliographical, Expository, Critical, from Hutcheson to Hamilton (1875 Edition) LC 75-3266. (Philosophy in America Ser.). 496p. 1980. reprint ed. 69.50 (*0-404-59254-6*) AMS Pr.
— The Scottish Philosophy, Biographical, Expository, Critical: From Hutcheson to Hamilton (1875 Edition) 494p. 1996. reprint ed. 58.00 (*1-85506-079-5*) Bks Intl VA.
— The Supernatural in Relation to the Natural. LC 75-3267. reprint ed. 38.00 (*0-404-59255-4*) AMS Pr.
McCoshan, Andrew, jt. auth. see Bennett, Robert J.
McCosker, John E. The History of Steinhart Aquarium: A Very Fishy Tale LC 99-27480. 1999. write for info. (*1-57864-073-3*) Donning Co.
McCosker, John E., jt. auth. see Ellis, Richard.
McCosker, Karen, jt. ed. see Albery, Nicholas.
***McCoubrey, H. & Morris, Justin.** Regional Peacekeeping in the Post-Cold War Era. LC 99-57394. (Illus.). 272p. 2000. write for info. (*90-411-1317-7*) Kluwer Law Intl.
McCoubrey, Hilaire. The Development of Naturalist Legal Theory. 224p. 1987. 59.95 (*0-7099-4669-4*, Pub. by C Helm) Routldge.
— International Humanitarian Law. 240p. 1990. text 91.95 (*1-85521-040-1*, Pub. by Dartmth Pub) Ashgate Pub Co.
— International Humanitarian Law: Modern Developments in the Limitation of Warfare. 2nd ed. LC 98-18639. 326p. 1998. text 110.95 (*1-84014-012-7*, KZ6471.M38, Pub. by Ashgate Pub) Ashgate Pub Co.
— The Obligation to Obey in Legal Theory. LC 96-8163. 240p. 1997. text 78.95 (*1-85521-825-9*, Pub. by Dartmth Pub) Ashgate Pub Co.
McCoubrey, Hilaire & White, N. D. International Law & Armed Conflict. 350p. 1992. 87.95 (*1-85521-229-3*, Pub. by Dartmth Pub) Ashgate Pub Co.
McCoubrey, Hilaire & White, Nigel D. The Blue Helmets: Legal Regulation of United Nations Military Operations. LC 96-30776. (Illus.). 240p. 1996. text 76.95 (*1-85521-626-4*, Pub. by Dartmth Pub) Ashgate Pub Co.
— International Organizations & Civil Wars. LC 94-21208. 250p. 1995. 87.95 (*1-85521-468-7*, Pub. by Dartmth Pub) Ashgate Pub Co.
— Textbook on Jurisprudence. 270p. 1993. pap. 36.00 (*1-85431-265-0*, Pub. by Blackstone Pr) Gaunt.
— Textbook on Jurisprudence. 2nd ed. 299p. 1996. pap. 36.00 (*1-85431-582-X*, Pub. by Blackstone Pr) Gaunt.
***McCoubrey, Hilaire & White, Nigel D.** Textbook on Jurisprudence. 3rd ed. 335p. 1999. 34.00 (*1-85431-896-9*, Pub. by Blackstone Pr) Gaunt.
McCoubrey, John W. American Tradition in Painting, Revised Edition. rev. ed. LC 99-38868. 1999. pap. text 17.50 (*0-8122-1694-6*) U of Pa Pr.
McCoubrey, John W., ed. American Art, 1700-1960: Sources & Documents. (Orig.). (C). 1965. pap. text 31.60 (*0-13-024521-6*) P-H.
Mccourt. Preparator's Guide to Biology. 1988. 12.18 (*0-07-553862-8*) McGraw.
McCourt, Aimee, jt. auth. see McCourt, Lisa.
McCourt, Frank. Angela's Ashes: A Memoir. (YA). 1998. per. write for info. (*0-684-86993-4*) S&S Trade.
***McCourt, Frank.** Angela's Ashes: A Memoir. 464p. (YA). 1999. per. 7.99 (*0-684-87215-3*); per. 14.00 (*0-684-87217-X*) S&S Trade.
McCourt, Frank. Angela's Ashes: A Memoir. 364p. (YA). 1997. per. 6.99 (*0-684-84313-7*) S&S Trade Pap.
— Angela's Ashes: A Memoir. LC 96-5335. 368p. (YA). 1999. per. 14.00 (*0-684-84267-X*, Touchstone) S&S Trade Pap.
— Angela's Ashes: A Memoir. 368p. (YA). 1996. 23.00 (*0-684-87435-0*) Scribner.
— Angela's Ashes: A Memoir. large type ed. LC 96-50228. (Large Print Bks.). (YA). 1997. 25.95 (*1-56895-396-8*) Wheeler Pub.
***McCourt, Frank.** Angela's Ashes: A Memoir. large type ed. LC 99-87544. 1999. pap. 11.95 (*1-56895-963-X*) Wheeler Pub.
— Die Asche Meiner Mutler. 1999. pap. 22.00 (*3-442-72307-8*) W Goldmann.
— Les Cendre's D'angela. 1999. pap. 18.95 (*2-290-50008-9*) Distribks Inc.
McCourt, Frank. Las Cenizas de Angela.Tr. of Angela's Ashes. (SPA.). 400p. 1999. per. 12.00 (*0-684-85933-5*) S&S Trade.
***McCourt, Frank.** 'Tis: A Memoir. 480p. 2000. per. 8.99 (*0-7432-0098-5*) S&S Trade.
McCourt, Frank. 'Tis: A Memoir. LC 99-31280. 368p. 1999. 26.00 (*0-684-84878-3*) Scribner.
***McCourt, Frank.** 'Tis: A Memoir. large type ed. LC 99-31280. 608p. 1999. 26.00 (*0-684-86449-5*) Scribner.
McCourt, Frederick R., et al. Nonequilibrium Phenomena in Polyatomic Gases Vol. 1: Dilute Gases. (International Series of Monographs on Chemistry: No. 18). (Illus.). 596p. 1990. text 115.00 (*0-19-855631-4*) OUP.
— Nonequilibrium Phenomena in Polyatomic Gases Vol. 2: Cross Sections, Scattering, & Rarefied Gases. (International Series of Monographs on Chemistry: No. 19). (Illus.). 346p. 1991. text 80.00 (*0-19-855648-9*) OUP.
McCourt, James. Delancey's Way. LC 98-51915. 384p. 2000. 25.00 (*0-375-40311-6*) Knopf.
***McCourt, John.** The Years of Bloom: James Joyce in Trieste, 1904-1920. 2000. 29.95 (*0-299-16980-4*) U of Wis Pr.
McCourt, Kathleen. Working-Class Women & Grass-Roots Politics. LC 76-26340. 262p. reprint ed. pap. 81.30 (*0-608-10732-8*, 201762800007) Bks Demand.
McCourt, Lisa. The Braids Girl. LC 97-30377. (Chicken Soup for Little Souls Ser.). (Illus.). 32p. (J). (ps-3). 1998. 14.95 (*1-55874-554-8*) Health Comm.
***McCourt, Lisa.** Candy Counting: Delicious Ways to Add & Subtract. (Illus.). 32p. (J). (ps-3). 2000. pap. 5.95 (*0-8167-6330-5*) Troll Communs.
McCourt, Lisa. Candy Counting Book. LC 99-21929. 32p. (J). (gr. k-3). 1999. 15.95 (*0-8167-6329-1*) BrdgeWater.
— Chicken Soul for Little Souls Collection, 3 vols., Set. LC 97-16921. (J). 1997. boxed set 44.85 (*1-55874-509-2*) Health Comm.
— Chicken Soup for Little Souls: A Dog of My Own. LC 97-30906. (Illus.). 32p. (J). (ps-3). 1998. 14.95 (*1-55874-555-6*) Health Comm.
— Chicken Soup for Little Souls: The Best-Ever Bike Race. LC 97-30378. (Illus.). (J). 1998. write for info. (*1-55874-556-4*) Health Comm.
— Chicken Soup for Little Souls: The Best Night Out with Dad. (Illus.). 32p. (J). (ps-3). 1997. 14.95 (*1-55874-508-4*) Health Comm.
— Chicken Soup for Little Souls: The Goodness Gorillas. LC 97-19959. (Illus.). 32p. (J). (ps-3). 1997. 14.95 (*1-55874-505-X*) Health Comm.
— Chicken Soup for Little Souls: The Never-Forgotten Doll. (Illus.). 32p. (J). (ps-3). 1997. 14.95 (*1-55874-507-6*) Health Comm.
***McCourt, Lisa.** Chicken Soup for the Little Souls: 3 Colorful Stories to Warm the Hearts of Children. (Chicken Soup for Little Souls Ser.). (Illus.). (J). 2000. pap. 12.95 (*1-55874-812-1*) Health Comm.
McCourt, Lisa. Deadly Snakes: Level 2. LC 98-230242. (Planet Reader Picture Bks.: Level 2). (Illus.). 32p. (J). (gr. k-3). 1998. pap. 2.95 (*0-8167-4382-7*) Troll Communs.
— Della Splatnuk, Birthday Girl. LC 98-49908. (Chicken Soup for Little Souls Ser.). 1999. 14.95 (*1-55874-600-5*) Health Comm.
***McCourt, Lisa.** Hairy 'n' Weird. (Weird in the Wild Ser.). (Illus.). 32p. (J). (gr. k-3). 2000. pap. 7.95 (*0-7373-0404-9*, 04049W, Pub. by Lowell Hse Juvenile) NTC Contemp Pub Co.
McCourt, Lisa. I Love You, Stinky Face. LC 97-10017. (Illus.). 32p. (J). (ps-3). 1997. 15.95 (*0-8167-4392-4*) BrdgeWater.
— I Love You, Stinky Face. (Illus.). 32p. (J). (ps-2). 1997. pap. 5.95 (*0-8167-4459-9*) Troll Communs.
— I Miss You, Stinky Face. LC 98-31230. (Illus.). 32p. (J). 1999. 15.95 (*0-8167-5647-3*) BrdgeWater.
***McCourt, Lisa.** I Miss You, Stinky Face. 1999. 5.95 (*0-8167-5648-1*) Bridgewater Pub.
— It's Time for School, Stinky Face. (Illus.). 32p. (J). (ps-2). 2000. 15.95 (*0-8167-6961-3*) BrdgeWater.
McCourt, Lisa. Love You Until... LC 98-32045. (Illus.). 32p. (J). (gr. k-2). 1999. 16.95 (*0-8091-6658-5*) Paulist Pr.
***McCourt, Lisa.** Mysterious Science. (Brain Builders Ser.). 48p. (J). 2000. pap. 7.95 (*0-7373-0465-0*, 04650W, Pub. by Lowell Hse Juvenile) NTC Contemp Pub Co.
McCourt, Lisa. The New Kid & the Cookie Thief. LC 98-5111. (Illus.). 32p. (J). 1998. 14.95 (*1-55874-588-2*) Health Comm.
***McCourt, Lisa.** 101 Ways to Raise a Happy Baby. LC 99-23464. (Illus.). 160p. 1999. pap. 13.95 (*0-7373-0270-4*, 02704W) NTC Contemp Pub Co.
— 101 Ways to Raise a Happy Toddler. 2000. pap. 13.95 (*0-7373-0473-1*, Pub. by Lowell Hse) NTC Contemp Pub Co.
McCourt, Lisa. The Rain Forest Counts. LC 97-9995. (Illus.). 32p. (J). (ps-3). 1997. 15.95 (*0-8167-4388-6*) BrdgeWater.
— The Rainforest Counts. (Illus.). 32p. (J). (ps-3). 1997. pap. 5.95 (*0-8167-4458-0*) Troll Communs.
— Raptors! Level 2. (Planet Reader Picture Bks.). (Illus.). 32p. (J). (gr. k-3). 1998. pap. 2.95 (*0-8167-4381-9*) Troll Communs.
***McCourt, Lisa.** Wet 'n' Weird. (Weird in the Wild Ser.). (Illus.). 32p. (J). (gr. k-3). 2000. pap. 7.95 (*0-7373-0405-7*, 04057W, Pub. by Lowell Hse Juvenile) NTC Contemp Pub Co.
— What's Inside My Body? (Brain Builders Ser.). 48p. (J). 2000. pap. 7.95 (*0-7373-0463-4*, 04634W, Pub. by Lowell Hse Juvenile) NTC Contemp Pub Co.
***McCourt, Lisa & McCourt, Aimee.** Tips to Help You Deal, Feel & Be Real. LC 99-76530. (Attitude: How to Be the Coolest Ser.). (Illus.). 96p. (J). (gr. 3-7). 2000. pap. 6.95 (*0-7373-0336-0*, 03360W, Pub. by Lowell Hse Juvenile) NTC Contemp Pub Co.
McCourt, Lisa, jt. auth. see Nathan, Cheryl.
McCourt, Malachy. A Monk Swimming: A Memoir. 304p. 1998. write for info. (*0-7868-6431-1*) Hyperion.
— A Monk Swimming: A Memoir. LC 97-46720. (Illus.). 320p. 1998. 23.95 (*0-7868-6398-6*, Pub. by Hyperion) Time Warner.
— A Monk Swimming: A Memoir. large type ed. LC 98-39410. (Large Print Book Ser.). 1998. 26.95 (*1-56895-671-1*) Wheeler Pub.
— A Monk Swimming: A Memoir. 304p. 1999. reprint ed. pap. 14.00 (*0-7868-8414-2*, Pub. by Disney Pr) Time Warner.
***McCourt, Malachy.** Singing My Him Song. 304p. 2000. 25.00 (*0-06-019593-2*) HarpC.
— Singing My Him Song. 2001. pap. write for info. (*0-06-095548-1*, Perennial) HarperTrade.
— Singing My Him Song. large type ed. 405p. 2000. 25.00 (*0-06-019721-8*) HarpC.
McCourt, Malachy, frwd. Through Irish Eyes: A Visual Companion to Angela Mccourt's Ireland. LC 98-60825. 64p. 1998. write for info. (*0-86278-591-X*) OBrien Pr.
McCourt-Perring, C., jt. auth. see Youll, P. J.
McCourt, Tom. Conflicting Communication Interests in America: The Case of National Public Radio. LC 99-22136. 224p. 1999. 55.00 (*0-275-96358-6*, Praeger Pubs) Greenwood.
McCourtney, Lorena. Betrayed. 290p. 1996. pap. 9.99 (*0-88070-756-9*, Palisades OR) Multnomah Pubs.
— Canyon. LC 98-215128. 1998. pap. 9.99 (*1-57673-287-8*, Palisades OR) Multnomah Pubs.
— Dear Silver. LC 97-5494. 286p. 1997. pap. 9.99 (*1-57673-110-3*, Palisades OR) Multnomah Pubs.
— Escape. LC 96-41679. 256p. 1996. pap. 9.99 (*1-57673-012-3*, Palisades OR) Multnomah Pubs.
— Forgotten. LC 97-32393. 1998. pap. 9.99 (*1-57673-222-3*, Palisades OR) Multnomah Pubs.
— Searching for Stardust. LC 99-21997. 352p. 1999. pap. 6.99 (*1-57673-414-5*) Multnomah Pubs.
McCowan. Venous Access Management. (C). 1998. text 125.00 (*0-443-07786-X*) Church.
***McCowan, C. N.** Secondary Ferrite Number Reference Materials Gage Calibration & Assignment of Values. 88p. 2000. pap. 7.00 (*0-16-059125-2*) USGPO.
McCowan, Ray R. Winter Moon I. 48p. 1999. pap. 8.00 (*0-8059-4534-2*) Dorrance.
McCowen, Michael W. Rio Oro. LC 94-69824. 208p. (Orig.). 1995. pap. 11.95 (*0-9644823-0-4*) Capitan Pub.
McCown, Ada C. Congressional Conference Committee. LC 76-181952. (Columbia University. Studies in the Social Sciences: No. 290). reprint ed. 20.00 (*0-404-51290-9*) AMS Pr.
***McCown, Clint.** War Memorials. 240p. 2000. 23.95 (*1-55597-312-4*) Graywolf.
McCown, Donald E., et al. Nippur II: The North Temple & Sounding E: Excavations of the Joint Expedition to Nippur of the American Schools of Oriental Research & the Oriental Institute of the University of Chicago. LC 77-74719. (Oriental Institute Publications: No. 97). (Illus.). 1978. lib. bdg. 60.00 (*0-918986-04-4*) Orient Inst.
McCown, Edna, tr. see Hackl, Erich.
McCown, Edna, tr. see Hasler, Eveline.
McCown, Edna, tr. see Hurlimann, Thomas.
McCown, Edna, tr. see Mettler, Felix.
McCown, Joe. Availability: Gabriel Marcel & the Phenomenology of Human Openness. LC 77-22358. (American Academy of Religion. Studies in Religion: No. 14). 94p. reprint ed. pap. 30.00 (*0-7837-5481-7*, 204524600005) Bks Demand.
McCown, Marjorie. Death by Design. LC 98-83079. 182p. 2000. pap. 13.95 (*0-88739-244-X*) Creat Arts Bk.
McCown, Rick R., et al. Educational Psychology: A Learning-Centered Approach to Classroom Practice. 2nd ed. 144p. 1995. pap. text, student ed. 21.00 (*0-205-17586-4*, H7586-4) Allyn.
— Educational Psychology: A Learning-Centered Approach to Classroom Practice. 2nd ed. 192p. (C). 1995. teacher ed. write for info. (*0-205-17587-2*, H7587-2) Allyn.
— Educational Psychology: A Learning-Centered Approach to Classroom Practice Assessment Package. 2nd ed. (C). 1995. write for info. (*0-205-17632-1*, H7632-6) Allyn.
— Educational Psychology: A Learning-Centered Approach to Classroom Practice Examination Copy. 2nd ed. 592p. (C). 1995. write for info. (*0-205-17599-6*, H7599-7) Allyn.
McCown, T. D., jt. auth. see Heizer, R. F.
McCown, William & Associates Staff, jt. auth. see Johnson, Judith.
McCown, William G., et al, eds. The Impulsive Client: Theory, Research, & Treatment. LC 93-11911. (Illus.). 434p. 1993. text 49.95 (*1-55798-208-2*) Am Psychol.
McCown, William G. & Chamberlain, Linda L. Best Possible Odds: Contemporary Treatment Strategies for Gambling Disorders. LC 99-16055. 272p. 2000. 45.00 (*0-471-18969-3*) Wiley.
McCown, William G., et al. Therapy with Treatment Resistant Families: A Consultation-Crisis Intervention Model. LC 93-35618. 328p. 1993. pap. 19.95 (*1-56024-245-0*) Haworth Pr.
— Therapy with Treatment Resistant Families: A Consultation-Crisis Intervention Model. LC 93-35618. 328p. 1993. 59.95 (*1-56024-244-2*) Haworth Pr.
***McCoy, Adam D.** A Collection of Poems. 2000. pap. write for info. (*1-58235-399-9*) Watermrk Pr.
McCoy, Alexandra. Political Affiliations of American Economic Elites: Wayne County, Michigan, 1844-1860 As a Test Case. (Nineteenth Century American Political & Social History Ser.). 291p. 1989. reprint ed. 20.00 (*0-8240-4069-4*) Garland.
***McCoy, Alfred W.** Closer Than Brothers: Manhood at the Philippine Military Academy. LC 99-20239. (Illus.). 416p. 1999. 40.00 (*0-300-07765-3*) Yale U Pr.
McCoy, Alfred W. The Politics of Heroin: CIA Complicity in the Global Drug Trade. LC 90-47398. (Illus.). 654p. 1991. pap. 24.95 (*1-55652-125-1*, Lawrence Hill) Chicago Review.
McCoy, Alfred W., ed. Southeast Asia under Japanese Occupation: Transition & Transformation. LC 80-610. (Monographs: No. 22). (Illus.). 250p. 1980. pap. 14.00 (*0-938692-08-9*) Yale U SE Asia.
***McCoy, Angel.** Defenders. (Hunter Ser.). 2000. pap. text 14.95 (*1-56504-740-0*) White Wolf.
McCoy, Angel. Kithbook: Pooka. (Changeling: The Dreaming Ser.). (Illus.). 96p. 1999. pap. 15.00 (*1-56504-729-X*, 7054) White Wolf.
— Kithbook: Satyrs. (Changeling: The Dreaming Ser.). (Illus.). 1998. pap. 15.00 (*1-56504-728-1*, 7053) White Wolf.
McCoy, Barbara. A Christmas Death. 1979. pap. 2.00 (*0-913719-39-0*, High Coo Pr) Brooks Books.
McCoy, Barry & Wu, Tai T. The Two-Dimensional Ising Model. LC 72-188972. (Illus.). 438p. 1973. 44.50 (*0-674-91440-6*) HUP.
McCoy, Betsy. Cosmetic Plastic Surgery. Osborn, John M., ed. LC 92-62104. (Illus.). 176p. 1993. 24.95 (*0-9633816-0-1*) Paradise Sacramento.
McCoy, Betty S. Miracles & Other Happenings. (Illus.). 80p. 1993. pap. write for info. (*0-935648-42-9*) Halldin Pub.
McCoy, Beverly. Threads of Silver, Cords of Gold. LC 99-70984. 300p. 2000. pap. 10.95 (*1-881636-21-6*) Windsor Hse Pub Grp.
McCoy, Bill W., III. Introduction to Commercial Real Estate Sales. LC 94-41135. 1995. pap. text 59.00 (*0-7931-1407-1*, 1520-3801, Real Estate Ed) Dearborn.
***McCoy, Bob.** Quack: Tales of Medical Fraud from the Museum of Questionable Medical Devices. LC 99-59928. (Illus.). 240p. 2000. pap. 19.95 (*1-891661-10-8*, Pub. by Snta Monica) IPG Chicago.
McCoy, C. T. Sturgeon: A Genealogical History of the Sturgeons of North America. (Illus.). 239p. 1991. reprint ed. pap. 38.00 (*0-8328-1792-9*); reprint ed. lib. bdg. 48.00 (*0-8328-1791-0*) Higginson Bk Co.
McCoy, Candace. Politics & Plea Bargaining: Victims' Rights in California. LC 92-46518. (Law in Social Context Ser.). 248p. (Orig.). (C). 1993. text 39.95 (*0-8122-3190-2*); pap. text 19.95 (*0-8122-1433-1*) U of Pa Pr.
— Teacher's Manual to Accompany Criminal Justice: Introductory Cases & Materials. 5th ed. 300p. 1993. pap. text write for info. (*1-56662-127-5*) Foundation Pr.
McCoy, Candace, ed. see McCoy, John C.
McCoy, Carl L. Queens of Hearts & Souls: The Story of the Miss Black Athens-Clarke County Teen Pageant, 1975-1997. (Illus.). 81p. 1998. lib. bdg. 10.00 (*0-9664030-1-0*) CKG Concepts.
McCoy, Carol P. Managing a Small HRD Department: You Can Do More Than You Think. LC 92-43607. (Management Ser.). 302p. 1993. 39.95 (*1-55542-529-1*) Jossey-Bass.
McCoy, Carol Prescott, ed. see American Society for Training and Development Staff.
McCoy, Charles A. Polk & the Presidency. LC 72-10451. (American Biography Ser.: No. 32). 1973. reprint ed. lib. bdg. 75.00 (*0-8383-1686-7*) M S G Haskell Hse.
McCoy, Charles N. On the Intelligibility of Political Philosophy: Essays of Charles N. R. McCoy. Schall, James V. & Schrems, John J., eds. LC 88-31601. 318p. 1989. reprint ed. pap. 98.60 (*0-7837-9109-7*, 204991100004) Bks Demand.
— The Structure of Political Thought: A Study in the History of Political Ideas. LC 74-25996. 323p. 1978. reprint ed. lib. bdg. 52.50 (*0-8371-7880-0*, MCPT, Greenwood Pr) Greenwood.
McCoy, Charles S. Management of Values: The Ethical Difference in Corporate Policy & Performance. LC 84-16487. (Business & Public Policy Ser.). 394p. 1989. text 29.95 (*0-88730-431-1*, HarpBusn) HarpInfo.
McCoy, Charles S., ed. see Pomeroy, Richard M.
McCoy, Charlie. All-American Harp Solos, 1 vol. (Learn to Play Ser.). 1998. pap. text 17.95 (*0-7119-6680-X*) Music Sales.
— Learn to Play All-American Harp, 1 vol. (Learn to Play Ser.). 1998. pap. text 17.95 (*0-7119-5641-3*) Music Sales.
McCoy, Clyde B., et al, eds. Intervening with Drug-Involved Youth. LC 96-10052. 272p. 1996. 47.00 (*0-8039-7371-3*); pap. 19.95 (*0-8039-7372-1*) Sage.

McCoy, Clyde B. & Inciardi, James A. Sex, Drugs, & the Continuing Spread of AIDS. LC 94-13908. (Illus.). 181p. (Orig.). (C). 1995. pap. text. write for info. (0-935732-64-0) Roxbury Pub Co.

McCoy, David B. The Geometry of Blue. 112p. 1995. pap. 12.00 (0-945568-17-7) Spare Change Pr.

McCoy, Deborah. The Elegant Wedding & the Budget-Savvy Bride: How to Have the Wedding of Your Dreams for Half the Price. LC 98-29062. (Illus.). 244p. 1999. pap. 19.95 (0-452-27850-3, Plume) Dutton Plume.

— Weddings A-Z. LC 99-29438. 156p. 1999. text 19.95 (1-56170-652-3) Hay House.

***McCoy, Deborah.** Weddings A-Z. (Illus.). 156p. 2001. pap. 11.95 (1-56170-790-2, L473) Hay House.

McCoy, Deborah. The World's Most Unforgettable Weddings: Love, Lust, Money & Madness. LC 99-22611. (Illus.). 224p. 1999. 19.95 (1-55972-466-8, Birch Ln Pr) Carol Pub Group.

McCoy, Dell A. Artistic Reflections of Women. 1986. 19.50 (0-913582-41-7) Sundance.

McCoy, Dell A. & Collman, Russ. The RGS Story Vol. 6: Rico to Dolores. (Illus.). 480p. 1997. 72.00 (0-913582-63-8, 0256) Sundance.

McCoy, Dell A. & Cook, W. George. The RGS Story Vol. 7: Dolores & McPhee. Collman, Russ, ed. (Illus.). 496p. 1998. 72.00 (0-913582-66-2, 0259) Sundance.

McCoy, Donald. Calvin Coolidge: The Quiet President. Speirs, Katherine E., ed. LC 98-74526. (Signature Ser.). (Illus.). 472p. 1999. reprint ed. 35.00 (0-945707-23-1) Amer Political.

McCoy, Donald R. Calvin Coolidge: The Quiet President. LC 67-11629. xvi, 472p. 1988. reprint ed. pap. 14.95 (0-7006-0351-4) U Pr of KS.

— Landon of Kansas. LC 65-16190. (Illus.). 631p. reprint ed. pap. 195.70 (0-8357-3807-8, 203653500003) Bks Demand.

— The National Archives: America's Ministry of Documents, 1934-1968. LC 78-2314. 447p. reprint ed. pap. 138.60 (0-7837-3757-2, 204357400010) Bks Demand.

— The Presidency of Harry S. Truman. LC 84-3624. (American Presidency Ser.). xii, 356p. 1984. 29.95 (0-7006-0252-6); pap. 15.95 (0-7006-0255-0) U Pr of KS.

McCoy, Doyle. Oklahoma Wildflowers. (Illus.). 206p. 1987. 19.95 (0-9619985-0-4); pap. 16.95 (0-9619985-1-2) McCoy Pub Co.

— Roadside Flowers of Oklahoma, Vol. 1. (Illus.). 116p. 1976. reprint ed. pap. 10.00 (0-9619985-2-0) McCoy Pub Co.

— Roadside Flowers of Oklahoma, Vol. 2. (Illus.). 60p. 1978. reprint ed. pap. 5.00 (0-9619985-3-9) McCoy Pub Co.

— Roadside Trees & Shrubs of Oklahoma. LC 80-5944. (Illus.). 180p. 1981. pap. 12.95 (0-8061-1556-4) U of Okla Pr.

McCoy, Drew R. Elusive Republic: Political Economy in Jeffersonian America. 278p. (C). 1996. pap. text 14.95 (0-8078-4616-3) U of NC Pr.

— The Elusive Republic: Political Economy in Jeffersonian America. LC 79-20952. 278p. reprint ed. pap. 86.20 (0-7837-6859-1, 204668800003) Bks Demand.

— The Last of the Fathers: James Madison & the Republican Legacy. (Illus.). 384p. (C). 1989. 47.95 (0-521-36407-8) Cambridge U Pr.

— The Last of the Fathers: James Madison & the Republican Legacy. (Illus.). 406p. (C). 1991. pap. text 19.95 (0-521-40772-9) Cambridge U Pr.

McCoy, Duff. Savage Blood. (Cutter Ser.: No. 3). 1991. mass mkt. 3.50 (1-55817-482-6, Pinncle Kensgtn) Kensgtn Pub Corp.

McCoy, E. Sue, jt. auth. see Grinder, Alison L.

McCoy, E. W. & Chongpeepien, T., eds. Bivalve Mollusc Culture Research in Thailand. (ICLARM Technical Reports: No. 19). 170p. 1988. per. write for info. (971-10-2243-5, Pub. by ICLARM) Intl Spec Bk.

McCoy, Earl D., jt. auth. see Shrader-Frechette, Kristin S.

McCoy, Edain. Astral Projection for Beginners. LC 98-51538. (For Beginners Ser.). (Illus.). 256p. 1999. 7.95 (1-56718-625-4) Llewellyn Pubns.

***McCoy, Edain.** Bewitchments: Love Magick for Modern Romance. LC 99-89968. (Illus.). 264p. 2000. pap. 14.95 (1-56718-700-5) Llewellyn Pubns.

McCoy, Edain. Celtic Myth & Magick: Harness the Power of the Gods & Goddesses. LC 95-1369. (World Religion & Magic Ser.). (Illus.). 464p. 1999. pap. 19.95 (1-56718-661-0) Llewellyn Pubns.

— Celtic Women's Spirituality: Accessing the Cauldron of Life. LC 97-45110. (Illus.). 352p. (Orig.). 1999. pap. 16.95 (1-56718-672-6, K672-6) Llewellyn Pubns.

— Entering the Summerland: Customs & Rituals of Transition into the Afterlife. LC 96-9052. (Illus.). 256p. (Orig.). 1999. pap. 17.95 (1-56718-665-3, K-665-3) Llewellyn Pubns.

— How to Do Automatic Writing. LC 94-35157. (How to Ser.). (Illus.). 288p. 1994. mass mkt. 3.99 (1-56718-662-9) Llewellyn Pubns.

— Inside a Witches' Coven. LC 96-39501. (Modern Witchcraft Ser.). (Illus.). 224p. (Orig.). 1997. pap. 9.95 (1-56718-666-1) Llewellyn Pubns.

— Lady of the Night: A Handbook of Moon Magick & Rituals. LC 95-32399. (Llewellyn's Modern Witchcraft Ser.). (Illus.). 256p. 1999. pap. 14.95 (1-56718-660-2) Llewellyn Pubns.

— Making Magick: What It Is & How It Works. LC 97-20979. (Illus.). 336p. (Orig.). 1997. pap. 14.95 (1-56718-670-X, K670-X) Llewellyn Pubns.

— Mountain Magick: Folk Wisdom from the Heart of Appalachia. LC 97-17470. (Illus.). 240p. 1997. reprint ed. pap. 14.95 (1-56718-671-8) Llewellyn Pubns.

— The Sabbats: A New Approach to Living the Old Ways. LC 94-29602. (Illus.). 368p. 1999. pap. 14.95 (1-56718-663-7) Llewellyn Pubns.

— A Witch's Guide to Faery Folk: Reclaiming Our Working Relationship with Invisible Helpers. LC 93-50837. (Illus.). 384p. 1999. reprint ed. pap. 14.95 (0-87542-733-2) Llewellyn Pubns.

— Witta: An Irish Pagan Tradition. LC 93-26366. (Llewellyn's New World Magic Ser.). (Illus.). 272p. 1999. pap. 12.95 (0-87542-732-4) Llewellyn Pubns.

McCoy, Edain, et al. Llewellyn's 1996 Magical Almanac. (Illus.). 368p. (Orig.). 1995. pap. text 6.95 (1-56718-914-8) Llewellyn Pubns.

McCoy, Edward, ed. Commercial Cockle Farming in Southern Thailand. (ICLARM Translations Ser.: No. 7). 13p. 1986. pap. 2.00 (971-10-2220-6, Pub. by ICLARM) Intl Spec Bk.

McCoy, Elin. Cards for Kids: Games, Tricks & Amazing Facts. LC 91-11373. (Illus.). 160p. (J). (gr. 1-7). 1991. text, lib. bdg. 13.95 (0-02-765461-3, Mac Bks Young Read) S&S Childrens.

— What to Do When Kids Are Mean to Your Child. LC 97-2464. (What to Do Parenting Guides Ser.). (Illus.). 96p. (J). 1997. 12.95 (0-89577-984-6, Pub. by RD Assn) Penguin Putnam.

***McCoy, Elizabeth L., ed.** In Nomine Liber Castellorum: The Book of Tethers. 128p. 1999. pap. 19.95 (1-55634-365-5, Pub. by S Jackson Games) BookWorld.

McCoy, Elizabeth L. & Milliken, Walter. Gurps I. O. U. Welcome to Illuminati University! Butler, Lillian, ed. (Illus.). 128p. 2000. pap. 19.95 (1-55634-206-3, 6072, Pub. by S Jackson Games) BookWorld.

***McCoy, Elizabeth L. & Milliken, Walter.** Gurps in Nomine. Jackson, Steve, ed. 224p. 2000. pap. 24.95 (1-55634-400-7, Pub. by S Jackson Games) BookWorld.

McCoy, Elizabeth L., ed. see Edelstein, David S.

McCoy, Esther. Case Study Houses, 1945-1962. 2nd ed. LC 77-14499. (Illus.). 1977. reprint ed. pap. 24.50 (0-912158-71-9) Hennessey.

— Craig Ellwood: Architecture. (California Architecture & Architects Ser.: Vol. 9). (Illus.). 155p. 1997. reprint ed. pap. 39.95 (0-940512-02-5) Hennessey.

— Vienna to Los Angeles: Two Journeys. LC 78-54270. (Illus.). 1979. 17.50 (0-931228-01-8); pap. 10.95 (0-931228-02-6) Arts & Arch.

McCoy, Esther & Makinson, Randall L. Five California Architects. 2nd ed. 200p. 1987. reprint ed. pap. 22.50 (0-275-71720-8) Hennessey.

McCoy, Eugene B. Climbing up the Mountain: The Musical Life & Times of Dr. Mattie Moss Clark. LC 94-35097. 1994. write for info. (0-917143-32-9) Sparrow TN.

McCoy, F. N. Researching & Writing in History: A Practical Handbook for Student. 1974. pap. 13.95 (0-520-02621-7, Pub. by U CA Pr) Cal Prin Full Svc.

— Robert Baillie & the Second Scots Reformation. LC 73-76110. 256p. reprint ed. pap. 79.40 (0-608-15826-7, 203130700074) Bks Demand.

McCoy, Florence T. Grand Manners: The Golden Rule Manners Book. 4th rev. ed. (Illus.). i, 37p. (J). (gr. k-12). 1997. reprint ed. pap. 6.00 (0-9670652-1-6, 100-1) Louisiana Images.

***McCoy, Floyd & Heiken, Grant.** Volcanic Hazards & Disasters in Human Antiquity. LC 99-462015. (Special Paper Ser.). 2000. write for info. (0-8137-2345-0) Geol Soc.

McCoy, Garnett. David Smith. text. write for info. (0-8054-3130-6) H Holt & Co.

McCoy, Garnett, intro. The Card Catalog of the Oral History Collections of the Archives of American Art. LC 83-27098. 343p. 1984. lib. bdg. 75.00 (0-8420-2216-3) Scholarly Res Inc.

McCoy, Gerard. Hong Kong Cases 1993, Vol. 2. 672p. 1994. write for info. (0-409-99710-2, ASIA, MICHIE) LEXIS Pub.

McCoy, Gerard, jt. auth. see Bruce, Andrew.

McCoy, Gerard, jt. auth. see Clark, David.

McCoy, Glenn. Duplex: The First Collection. LC 97-74518. 1998. pap. 9.95 (0-8362-5185-7) Andrews & McMeel.

— Pot Shots: Scribblings by an Unabashed Clinton Basher. Alexander, Wesley, ed. (Illus.). 144p. 1998. pap. 12.95 (0-9662637-0-7) Stormfield Pr.

***McCoy, Glenn.** Pot Shots 2 Vol. 2: More Scribblings by an Unabashed Clinton Basher. rev. ed. Alexander, Wesley, ed. (Illus.). 100p. 1999. pap. 12.95 (0-9662637-1-5) Stormfield Pr.

***McCoy, Hayes F.** The Element Encyclopedia of Fairytales, Myths, & Legends. (Illus.). (gr. 4-7). 2000. 21.95 (1-84207-011-8) Element MA.

McCoy, Henry B. The Carpenter-Wier Family of Upper South Carolina & Other Ancestors, Including Benson, Beryy, Blassingame, Caldwell, Maxwell, Richey, Sloan, Stewart, Wilson. (Illus.). 326p. 1993. reprint ed. pap. 51.00 (0-8328-3110-7); reprint ed. lib. bdg. 61.00 (0-8328-3109-3) Higginson Bk Co.

***McCoy, Henry D., II.** American & International Aquaculture Law: Aquaculture Law, Business & Finance. Oliver, Julia M., ed. LC 00-44652. (American & International Aquaculture Law Ser.: Vol. 1). 476p. 2000. 175.00 (0-9701312-5-9) Supranatl Pub.

McCoy, Horace. Adieu la Vie, Adieu l'Amour (Demian Il Fera Nuit) (FRE.). 306p. 1987. pap. 11.95 (0-7859-4513-X, 207037887X) Fr & Eur.

— I Should Have Stayed Home. (Midnight Classics Ser.). 113p. 1996. reprint ed. pap. 11.99 (1-85242-402-8) Serpents Tail.

— J'Aurais du Rester Chez Nous. (FRE.). 1982. pap. 10.95 (0-7859-4173-8) Fr & Eur.

— Kiss Tomorrow Goodbye. LC 96-68817. 250p. (Orig.). (C). 1997. reprint ed. pap. text 11.99 (1-85242-433-8, Midnght Classics) Serpents Tail.

— No Pockets in a Shroud. (Midnight Classics Ser.). 160p. 1998. pap. 11.99 (1-85242-434-6) Serpents Tail.

— On Acheve Bien les Chevaux. (FRE.). 1977. pap. 10.95 (0-7859-4086-3) Fr & Eur.

— Le Scalpel. (FRE.). 1984. pap. 11.95 (0-7859-4203-3) Fr & Eur.

— Le Scalpel. 1995. reprint ed. lib. bdg. 24.95 (1-56849-583-8) Buccaneer Bks.

— They Shoot Horses, Don't They? 1993. reprint ed. lib. bdg. 29.95 (1-56849-241-3) Buccaneer Bks.

— They Shoot Horses, Don't They? 2nd ed. (Midnight Classics Ser.). 132p. 1995. pap. 9.99 (1-85242-401-X) Serpents Tail.

McCoy, Horace, et al. Crime Novels Vol. I: American Noir of the 1930s & '40s. Polito, Robert, ed. LC 97-2485. 990p. 1997. 35.00 (1-883011-46-9, Pub. by Library of America) Penguin Putnam.

McCoy, Isabelle, jt. auth. see Graham, Leland.

McCoy, J. H. & Sarhan, M. E. Livestock & Meat Marketing. 3rd ed. (Illus.). 688p. 1988. text 99.95 (0-442-20488-4, VNR) Wiley.

McCoy, J. J. The Hunt for the Whooping Cranes: A Natural History Detective Story. 2nd rev. ed. LC 96-22081. (Illus.). 224p. 1996. reprint ed. pap. 16.95 (0-8397-3500-6) Eriksson.

***McCoy, Jack & Sellers, Keith.** Racing's Real McCoy: Sharing the Road with the Pioneers of the Wild West. (Illus.). 250p. 1999. 29.95 (1-929055-45-5) Veracity Bks.

McCoy, James C. Darby's Rainbow. LC 88-70551. (Illus.). 32p. (J). (ps-3). 1990. pap. 3.95 (0-943864-52-6) Davenport.

McCoy, James C., et al. Comic Tales Anthology, No. 2. 2nd ed. LC 88-70551. (Illus.). 100p. (YA). (gr. 7-12). 1988. pap. 6.95 (0-943864-53-4) Davenport.

McCoy, James W. Chemical Analysis of Industrial Water. (Illus.). 1969. 75.00 (0-8206-0017-2) Chem Pub.

— Chemical Treatment of Cooling Water. 2nd ed. (Illus.). 1983. 80.00 (0-8206-0298-1) Chem Pub.

— Industrial Chemical Cleaning. (Illus.). 1984. 80.00 (0-8206-0305-8) Chem Pub.

McCoy, Janetta Mitchell. Assessing Quality in the Work Environment. (Publications in Architecture & Urban Planning Ser.: Vol. R95-5). 131p. 1995. pap. 12.50 (1-886437-02-5) U of Wis Ctr Arch-Urban.

***McCoy, Jennifer.** Political Learning & Redemocratization in Latin America: Do Politicians Learn from Crises? LC 99-47546. 1999. pap. 200p. 21.95 (1-57454-066-1, Pub. by U Miami N-S Ctr) L Rienner.

McCoy, Jennifer, et al, eds. Venezuelan Democracy under Stress. LC 94-40527. 300p. (C). 1995. pap. 23.95 (1-56000-770-2, Pub. by U Miami N-S Ctr) L Rienner.

McCoy, John. Spore: A Star Guide to Extraterrestrial Worlds. (Illus.). 128p. 1999. 29.95 (0-9667382-0-9) Penterion.

Mccoy, John B. Bottomline Banking: Meeting the Challenges for Survival & Success. LC 97-139601. 354p. 1996. per. 24.95 (0-7863-1112-6, Irwn Prfssnl) McGraw-Hill Prof.

McCoy, John B., et al. Bottomline Banking: A Strategic Vision. LC 94-139273. 368p. 1993. text 37.50 (1-55738-389-8, Irwn Prfssnl) McGraw-Hill Prof.

McCoy, John C. John McCoy's Comprehensive Guitar Method Bk. I: Beginner Through Intermediate for Group or Individual Study. McCoy, Candace & Gleason, Jeff, eds. (Illus.). 152p. Date not set. pap. 15.00 (0-9671045-0-5) McCoy Music.

McCoy, Jonni. Frugal Families: Making the Most of Your Hard Earned Money. 237p. 1998. pap. 9.99 (1-888306-50-5, Full Quart Pr) Holly Hall.

— Miserly Moms: Living on One Income in a Two Income Economy. 2nd ed. 256p. 1996. pap. 9.99 (1-888306-14-9, Full Quart Pr) Holly Hall.

McCoy, Judy. Rap Music in the 1980s: A Reference Guide. 275p. 1992. 34.50 (0-8108-2649-6) Scarecrow.

McCoy, K. Byron. White vs. Reliable Realtors, Inc. Real Estate Fraud & Breach of Contract. 128p. 1989. pap. 22.95 (1-55681-192-6, FBA0192) Natl Inst Trial Ad.

— White vs. Reliable Realtors, Inc., et al (Pretrial Casefile) 100p. 1993. pap. 22.95 (1-55681-380-5) Natl Inst Trial Ad.

McCoy, K. Byron, jt. auth. see Lucas, Richard H.

McCoy, Karen, jt. auth. see Spiller, Jan.

McCoy, Karen K. Bon Odori Dancer. LC 98-12050. (Illus.). 32p. (J). (gr. k-4). 1998. 14.95 (1-879965-16-X) Polychrome Pub.

McCoy, Kathleen. Solo Parenting: Your Essential Guide. 1987. pap. 7.95 (0-317-56843-4, Plume) Dutton Plume.

— Understanding Your Teenager's Depression: Issues & Insights for Every Parent. 352p. (Orig.). 1994. pap. 13.95 (0-399-51856-8, Perigee Bks) Berkley Pub.

McCoy, Kathleen M. Teaching Special Learners in the General Education Classroom: Methods & Techniques. 2nd rev. ed. Orig. Title: Teaching Mainstreamed Students. 496p. 1995. text 54.00 (0-89108-238-7) Love Pub Co.

McCoy, Kathy. Monroeville: Literary Capital of Alabama. LC 98-87570. (Images of America Ser.). (Illus.). 128p. 1998. pap. 18.99 (0-7524-1212-4) Arcadia Publng.

McCoy, Kathy & Wibbelsman, Charles. Growing & Changing: A Handbook for Preteens. LC 86-17059. (Illus.). 192p. 1987. pap. 13.00 (0-399-51280-2, Perigee Bks) Berkley Pub.

— Life Happens: A Teenager's Guide to Friends, Failure, Sexuality, Love, Rejection, Addiction, Peer Pressure, Families, Loss, Depression, Change & Other Challenges of Living. LC 95-9647. 224p. (Orig.). (YA). 1996. pap. 11.00 (0-399-51987-4, Perigee Bks) Berkley Pub.

— The New Teenage Body Book. rev. ed. (Illus.). 288p. (YA). (gr. 9-12). 1992. pap. 15.95 (0-399-51725-1, Body Pr-Perigee) Berkley Pub.

— The Teenage Body Book. rev. ed. (YA). 1999. pap. 17.95 (0-399-52535-1, Perigee Bks) Berkley Pub.

McCoy, Katie, jt. auth. see Haines, Stephen.

McCoy, Keith. Melodic Whistles in the Columbia River Gorge. Duncan, Charles T., ed. (Illus.). 136p. 1995. pap. 12.95 (0-9618402-3-4) Pahto Pubns.

McCoy, Kirby. VMS Files Systems Internals. rev. ed. (VAX-VMS Ser.). (Illus.). 460p. (Orig.). 1990. pap. text 59.95 (1-55558-056-4, Digital DEC) Buttrwrth-Heinemann.

McCoy, Leah P. Elementary Math Flipper No. 1. 39p. (J). (gr. 4 up). 1989. 6.75 (1-878383-13-2) C Lee Pubns.

McCoy, Leighann. The Incredible Journey of Gina GA: Member Book for Older Girls in Action. McClain, Cindy, ed. 40p. (Orig.). (J). (gr. 5-6). 1995. pap. text 1.95 (1-56309-126-7, W957113) Womans Mission Union.

McCoy, Lew. Lew McCoy on Antennas. LC 94-69519. (Illus.). 128p. (Orig.). 1995. pap. 15.95 (0-943016-08-8) CQ Commns Inc.

McCoy, Lewistine, tr. see Kirkpatrick, Dow, ed.

McCoy, Linda J., jt. auth. see Sundbye, Nita.

McCoy, Linda P. Twenty Something & Breast Cancer: Images in Healing. Keitlen, Tomi & Swearenger, Marsha, eds. LC 95-76050. (Illus.). 160p. (Orig.). 1995. pap. 13.95 (1-886966-02-8) In Print.

McCoy, Lisa, ed. see Ennis, Judith.

McCoy, Lisa, ed. see Kaster, Bill.

McCoy, Lisa, ed. see Leonard, Lorenzo D.

McCoy, Lisa, ed. see Russell, Steven J.

McCoy, Lois, et al. The Byte Brothers Input an Investigation. (Illus.). (J). 2000. mass mkt. 2.25 (0-380-85571-2, 85571, Avon Bks) Morrow Avon.

McCoy, Mary V., et al. Cross-Cultural Orientation: A Guide for Leaders & Educators. rev. ed. Fantini, Alvino E., ed. (International Exchange Ser.). 230p. 1984. ring bd. 30.00 (0-936141-01-8) Experiment Pr.

McCoy, Maureen. Walking after Midnight. 1987. pap. 5.95 (0-685-18036-0) PB.

McCoy, Max. Indiana Jones & the Dinosaur Eggs, Vol. 10. 240p. 1996. mass mkt. 5.50 (0-553-56193-6) Bantam.

— Indiana Jones & the Hollow Earth, No. 11. 288p. 1997. mass mkt. 5.50 (0-553-56195-2) Bantam.

— Indiana Jones & the Philosopher's Stone. 256p. 1995. mass mkt. 4.99 (0-553-56196-0) Bantam.

— Indiana Jones & the Secret of the Sphinx. 204p. 1999. mass mkt. 5.50 (0-553-56197-9) Bantam.

***McCoy, Max.** Jesse: A Novel of the Outlaw. 256p. 1999. mass mkt. 4.99 (0-553-57178-8) BDD Bks Young Read.

***McCoy, Melanie & DiGeorgio-Lutz, JoAnn, eds.** The Woman-Centered University: Interdisciplinary Perspectives. LC 99-34905. 192p. 1999. 54.00 (0-7618-1459-0); pap. 26.50 (0-7618-1460-4) U Pr of Amer.

***McCoy, Michael.** Cycling the Great Divide: From Canada to Mexico on America's Premier Long-Distance Mountain Bike Route. (Illus.). 224p. 2000. pap. 14.95 (0-89886-698-7) Mountaineers.

McCoy, Michael. Montana: Off the Beaten Path: A Guide to Unique Places. 3rd ed. LC 98-33899. (Illus.). 160p. 1998. pap. 12.95 (0-7627-0271-0) Globe Pequot.

***McCoy, Michael.** Montana - Off the Beaten Path: A Guide to Unique Places. 4th ed. (Illus.). 2000. pap. 12.95 (0-7627-0760-7) Globe Pequot.

McCoy, Michael. Mountain Bike Adventures in the Four Corners Region. LC 90-40743. (Illus.). 224p. (Orig.). 1990. pap. 12.95 (0-89886-251-5) Mountaineers.

— Mountain Bike Adventures in the Northern Rockies. LC 89-3007. (Illus.). 224p. (Orig.). 1989. pap. 10.95 (0-89886-190-X) Mountaineers.

***McCoy, Michael.** Mountain Bike! Southern Utah: A Guide to the Classic Trails. LC 00-39444. (Illus.). 2000. pap. 15.95 (0-89732-314-9) Menasha Ridge.

McCoy, Michael. The Wild West: A Traveler's Guide. 2nd rev. ed. LC 97-35442. (Discover Historic America Ser.). (Illus.). 384p. 1998. pap. 17.95 (0-7627-0115-3) Globe Pequot.

— Wyoming: Off the Beaten Path: A Guide to Unique Places. 2nd ed. LC 98-51174. (Off the Beaten Path Ser.). (Illus.). 160p. 1999. pap. text 12.95 (0-7627-0425-X) Globe Pequot.

***McCoy, Michael Dalton.** Domestic Policy Narratives & International Relations Theory: Chinese Ecological Agriculture as a Case Study. LC 99-57989. 282p. 2000. 64.00 (0-7618-1598-8); pap. 37.50 (0-7618-1599-6) U Pr of Amer.

McCoy, Michael L. Baptism: For You & Your Baby. 26p. (Orig.). 1990. pap. 2.00 (0-8100-0340-6, 15N0527) Northwest Pub.

— A Christian Perspective on Creation vs. Evolution. LC 97-107743. (Christian Perspective Book Studies). 1996. pap. 4.99 (0-570-09648-0, 20-2587) Concordia.

— A Christian Perspective on Homosexuality. LC 97-118932. (Christian Perspective Book Studies). 1996. pap. 5.50 (0-570-09647-2, 20-2586) Concordia.

McCoy, Michaelandre. The Antitruth: A Fascinating Encounter Leading to a Re-examination of Beliefs & an Understanding of Higher Truths. 150p. 1996. pap. 12.95 (0-931761-47-6) Beckham Pubns.

***McCoy, Michelle & Utterback, Ann S.** Sound & Look Professional on Television & the Internet: How to Improve Your On-Camera Presence. 180p. 2000. pap. 18.95 (1-56625-154-0) Bonus Books.

McCoy, Mike. Journey to the Northern Rockies. LC 98-17599. (Illus.). 352p. 1998. pap. 19.95 (0-7627-0187-0) Globe Pequot.

***McCoy-Miller, Judith.** The Journey of Yung Lee: From China to America. LC 99-41982. (Immigrants Chronicles Ser.). 132p. (J). 2000. pap. 5.99 (0-7814-3285-5) Chariot Victor.

***McCoy, Nancy.** Butterflies Do Not Sleep in Hot Tubs: A Lawyer's Tortured Search for Truth. 232p. 1999. 18.95 (0-9645102-3-5, Pub. by Cyprss Pub) Sunbelt Media.

An Asterisk (*) at the beginning of an entry indicates that the title is appearing for the first time.

McCoy, Neal H. & Janusz, Gerald. Introduction to Modern Algebra. 5th ed. 288p. (C). 1992. text 55.63 (*0-697-08570-8*, WCB McGr Hill) McGrw-H Hghr Educ.

McCoy, Neal H. & Janusz, Gerald J. Introduction to Modern Algebra. 4th ed. 288p. 1987. text 55.63 (*0-697-06865-X*, WCB McGr Hill) McGrw-H Hghr Educ.

McCoy, Paul B. Leaving Tracks. 128p. 1998. pap. 7.95 (*1-56167-466-4*) Am Literary Pr.

McCoy, Peggy, jt. contrib. by see Rocke, Jennifer.

McCoy, Peter. Choosing Small Trees: Creative Planting. LC 99-55191. (Care Manual Ser.). (Illus.). 128p. 1999. 19.95 (*1-57145-647-3*, Laurel Glen Pub) Advantage Pubs.

***McCoy, Quincy.** No Static: A Guide to Creative Radio Programming. 273p. 1999. 39.95 (*0-87930-594-0*) Miller Freeman.

McCoy, R. A. & Ntantu, I. Topological Properties of Spaces of Continuous Functions. (Lecture Notes in Mathematics Ser.: Vol. 1315). 124p. 1988. 30.95 (*0-387-19302-2*) Spr-Verlag.

McCoy, Ralph. Children's Puzzle Packet. rev. ed. Sladkey, Sandra, ed. (H. I. S. Songs for Children Ser.). (Illus.). 18p. (J). (gr. 1-5). 1994. pap. 1.95 (*1-885819-06-4*) His Songs.

— Halloween Harvest Handbook: A Positive Alternative. rev. ed. Gruszewski, Ellen & Sladkey, Sandra, eds. (Illus.). 20p. 1994. pap. 3.00 (*1-885819-00-5*) His Songs.

— Poster Song Book. rev. ed. Sladkey, Sandra, ed. (Illus.). 60p. (J). (gr. 1-5). 1994. pap. 23.95 (*1-885819-05-6*) His Songs.

— Teacher's Resource Manual. rev. ed. Gruszewski, Ellen & Sladkey, Sandra, eds. (H. I. S. Songs for Children Ser.). (Illus.). 45p. 1994. pap., teacher ed. 7.95 (*1-885819-04-8*) His Songs.

McCoy, Ralph E. Freedom of the Press: A Bibliocyclopedia. Ten Year Supplement (1967-1977) LC 78-16573. 544p. 1979. 46.95 (*0-8093-0844-4*) S Ill U Pr.

— Freedom of the Press: An Annotated Bibliography. LC 67-10032. 576p. 1968. 46.95 (*0-8093-0335-3*) S Ill U Pr.

— Freedom of the Press: An Annotated Bibliography: Second Supplement, 1978-1992. LC 92-8395. 576p. (C). 1993. 102.00 (*0-8093-1583-1*) S Ill U Pr.

McCoy, Ramelle & Morand, Martin J., eds. Short-Time Compensation: A Formula for Work Sharing. LC 83-13265. 223p. 1984. 31.00 (*0-08-030148-7*, 29/59/4) Work in Amer.

McCoy, Ray, ed. see Krishnamurti, J. & Bohm, David.

McCoy, Rick, jt. auth. see Cooper, Nic.

McCoy, Riley, ed. see McCoy, Suzy.

McCoy, Robert, jt. compiled by see Hinkle, James C.

McCoy, Robert L. Modern Exterior Ballistics: The Launch & Flight Dynamics of Symmetric Projectiles. (Illus.). 328p. 1999. 95.00 (*0-7643-0720-7*) Schiffer.

McCoy, Ron. Kiowa Memories: Images from Indian Territory, 1880. (Illus.). 67p. 1987. 35.00 (*0-317-67928-7*) Morning Star Gal.

— People of the Plateau. (Plateau Ser.). 32p. 1993. pap. 6.95 (*0-89734-117-1*) Mus Northern Ariz.

McCoy, Ron, ed. The Best of Deming. LC 95-230960. 175p. 1996. reprint ed. pap. 6.00 (*0-945320-37-X*) Stat Process Contrl.

McCoy, Ronald. Archaeoastronomy. (Plateau Ser.). (Illus.). 32p. 1992. pap. 6.95 (*0-89734-109-0*) Mus Northern Ariz.

— Summoning the Gods: Sandpainting of the Native American Southwest. (Plateau Ser.: PL 59: 1). (Illus.). 32p. 1988. pap. 5.95 (*0-89734-059-0*) Mus Northern Ariz.

McCoy, Sandy. Something Happened to Me: Helping a Child to Become a Sexual Abuse Survivor. 18p. (J). (ps-2). 1993. 4.95 (*1-882811-01-1*) Skyline Pubns.

McCoy, Sharon. Friendship Bracelets, Rings & Other Things. (Fifty Nifty Ser.). (Illus.). 64p. (J). (gr. 3-7). 1994. pap. 4.95 (*1-56565-130-8*, 01308W, Pub. by Lowell Hse) NTC Contemp Pub Co.

McCoy, Sharon & Ghaffari, Michelle. 50 Nifty Super Friendship Crafts. LC 97-14876. (Fifty Nifty Super Ser.). (Illus.). 80p. (J). 1997. pap. 6.95 (*1-56565-728-4*, 07284W, Pub. by Lowell Hse Juvenile) NTC Contemp Pub Co.

McCoy, Sharon, et al. The Ultimate Best Friends Book. LC 99-73103. (Illus.). 80p. (J). (gr. 3-6). 1999. pap. 6.95 (*0-7373-0225-9*, 02259W) NTC Contemp Pub Co.

McCoy, Sondra Van Meter, see Van Meter McCoy, Sondra.

McCoy, Stanton P. As Straight As an Arrow. LC 98-72302. 196p. 1998. pap. 9.95 (*0-9644644-1-1*) DC Publ.

McCoy, Suzy. Babysitting a Ghost Town. McCoy, Riley, ed. (Travels with Riley Ser.: Vol. 1). (Illus.). 175p. 1998. pap. 10.95 (*1-893944-00-X*) S McCoy.

McCoy, Theresa. Getting Ready for Adoption. 26p. (J). (gr. 1-7). 1993. student ed. 8.95 (*0-9639685-0-5*) Adoption Wrld.

McCoy, Thomas A., ed. What It Costs - 1997. (Illus.). 44p. 1997. pap. text 37.95 (*1-56461-226-0*, 30182) Rough Notes.

McCoy, Thomas J. Compensation & Motivation: Maximizing Employee Performance with Behavior-Based Incentive Plans. 320p. 1992. 65.00 (*0-8144-5029-6*) AMACOM.

— Creating an "Open Book" Organization: Where Employees Think & Act Like Business Partners. LC 95-52017. 320p. 1996. 55.00 (*0-8144-0293-3*) AMACOM.

McCoy, Thomas S. Voices of Difference: Studies in Critical Philosophy & Mass Communication. Good, Leslie T., ed. LC 93-357. (Communication Series: Critical Studies in Communication). 288p. (C). 1993. text 57.50 (*1-881303-55-1*); pap. text 23.95 (*1-881303-56-X*) Hampton Pr NJ.

McCoy-Thompson, M., et al. Healthy Start Initiative Vol. II: A Community Driven Approach to Infant Mortality Reduction. LC 94-61353. (Illus.). 108p. 1994. pap. write for info. (*1-57285-008-6*) Nat Ctr Educ.

McCoy-Thompson, Steven, jt. ed. see Pu, S. C.

***McCoy, Thorunn.** Poems for a Friend: Kind Thoughts. LC 00-35019. 2000. write for info. (*0-8249-4176-4*) Ideals.

— Poems for Christmas: Joyous Thoughts. Kea, Elizabeth, ed. LC 00-27772. 2000. 9.95 (*0-8249-4193-4*) Ideals.

McCoy, Tom. The Wish Peddler. 22p. 1983. pap. 3.50 (*0-87129-678-0*, W54) Dramatic Pub.

McCoy, Toni, jt. auth. see Mahley, Mary J.

McCoy, W. U. Performing & Visual Arts Writing & Reviewing. 182p. (Orig.). (C). 1992. pap. text 24.00 (*0-8191-8774-7*) U Pr of Amer.

McCoy, William & McGeary, Mitchell. Every Little Thing: The Definitive Guide to Beatles Recording Variations, Rare Mixes & Other Musical Oddities, 1958-1986. Schultheiss, Thomas, ed. LC 89-92321. (Rock & Roll Reference Ser.: No. 20). (Illus.). 380p. 1990. 37.50 (*1-56075-004-9*) Popular Culture.

McCoyd, Ed. To Live & Dream: The Incredible Story of George Foreman. unabridged ed. (Illus.). 96p. (Orig.). (J). (gr. 5-9). 1997. pap. 6.99 (*0-9654118-0-X*) New Street.

McCracen. Pulp: Reading Popular Fiction. LC 98-221676. 256p. 1998. text 22.95 (*0-7190-4759-5*, Pub. by Manchester Univ Pr) St Martin.

McCrachen, Betsy. Farm Journal's Homemade Pickles & Relishes. LC 76-14048. 128p. (Orig.). 1976. pap. 3.95 (*0-89795-018-6*) Farm Journal.

McCrackan, William D. The New Palestine: An Authoritative Account of Palestine Since the Great War; the Problems, Political, Economic & Racial, That Confront the British Administration. Davis, Moshe, ed. LC 77-70722. (America & the Holy Land Ser.). (Illus.). 1977. reprint ed. lib. bdg. 47.95 (*0-405-10266-6*) Ayer.

McCracken. Bibliography of Women Artists & Designers in Europe since 1800, Vol. 2. LC 97-39199. 1998. 100.00 (*0-7838-0087-8*) Mac Lib Ref.

— Gender & Human Nature. LC 96-76122. (C). 1996. text 47.50 (*0-15-502495-7*) Harcourt.

McCracken. Hating Tradition Properly. pap. text 20.00 (*0-85315-901-7*) Lawrence & Wishart.

McCracken. Pulp: Reading Popular Fiction. LC 98-221676. 256p. 1998. text 69.95 (*0-7190-4758-7*, Pub. by Manchester Univ Pr) St Martin.

McCracken & Sutherland. Deaf Ability, Not Disability. 1991. 24.95 (*1-85359-080-0*, Pub. by Multilingual Matters); pap. 59.00 (*1-85359-081-9*, Pub. by Multilingual Matters) Taylor & Francis.

McCracken, jt. auth. see Orten.

McCracken, Aliza. The Dance of Love: A Personal Collection of Artwork & Poetry. (Illus.). 64p. 1998. 29.95 (*0-9667291-0-2*) Grace Pubg Grp.

***McCracken, Anne & Semel, Mary.** A Broken Heart Still Beats: After Your Child Dies. 328p. 2000. pap. 15.00 (*1-56838-556-0*) Hazelden.

McCracken, Anne, jt. auth. see Semel, Mary.

***McCracken, C. J. & Tipton, I. C., eds.** Berkeley's Principles & Dialogues: Background Source Materials. LC 99-59435. (Cambridge Philosophical Texts in Context Ser.). 312p. (C). 2000. 59.95 (*0-521-49681-0*); pap. 22.95 (*0-521-49806-6*) Cambridge U Pr.

McCracken, Catherine. Status, Management & Commercialization of the American Black Bear (Ursus Americanus) LC 95-6971. 1995. pap. 16.00 (*0-89164-143-2*) World Wildlife Fund.

McCracken County Genelogical-Historical Society, I. History & Families, McCracken County, Kentucky. LC 89-50044. 376p. 1989. 49.95 (*0-938021-36-2*) Turner Pub KY.

McCracken, D. P. & McCracken, E. M. The Way to Kirstenbosch. (Annals of Kirstenbosch Botanic Gardens Ser.: Vol. 18). 125p. 1988. 15.00 (*0-620-11648-X*, Pub. by Natl Botanical Inst) Balogh.

McCracken, Daniel D. A Guide to NOMAD for Applications Development. LC 80-66545. pap. 18.00 (*0-201-04624-5*); pap. text. write for info. (*0-318-50142-2*) Addison-Wesley.

— Guide to PL-M Programming for Microcomputer Applications. 1978. pap. text 20.76 (*0-201-04575-3*) Addison-Wesley.

— A Second Course in Computer Science with Pascal. LC 86-32586. (Illus.). 432p. (C). 1987. text 73.95 (*0-471-01062-6*) Wiley.

McCracken, Daniel D. & Golden, Donald G. A Simplified Guide to Structured COBAL Programming. 2nd ed. LC 87-34608. 656p. 1988. pap. 73.95 (*0-471-88658-0*) Wiley.

McCracken, Daniel D. & Salmon, William I. Computing for Engineers & Scientists with FORTRAN 77. 2nd ed. LC 88-17208. 752p. 1988. pap. 75.95 (*0-471-62552-3*) Wiley.

— A Second Course on Computer Science with MODULA-2. LC 87-14230. 496p. (C). 1987. pap. 77.95 (*0-471-63111-6*) Wiley.

McCracken, Daniel D., jt. auth. see Dorn, William S.

McCracken, Dave. Advanced Dredging Techniques, Vol. 2, Pt. 1: Finding & Recovering Paystreaks. (Illus.). 176p. (Orig.). (C). 1983. pap. 7.95 (*0-9636015-4-7*) New Era CA.

— Advanced Dredging Techniques, Vol. 2, Pt. 2: Succeeding at a Gold Dredging Venture. (Illus.). 164p. (Orig.). (C). 1983. pap. 7.95 (*0-9636015-5-5*) New Era CA.

— Gold Mining in the Nineteen-Eighties. rev. ed. (Illus.). 260p. (Orig.). (C). 1988. reprint ed. pap. text 15.95 (*0-317-90481-7*) Keene Engr Co Inc.

— Gold Mining in the 21st Century: The Complete Book of Modern Gold Mining Procedures. (Illus.). 279p. 1993. pap. 19.95 (*0-9636015-0-4*) New Era CA.

McCracken, David. The Scandal of the Gospels: Jesus, Story & Offense. 216p. 1994. text 55.00 (*0-19-508428-4*) OUP.

McCracken, David, ed. see Godwin, William.

McCracken, Donal P. Gardens of Empire: Botanical Institutions of the Victorian British Empire. LC 96-35962. (Illus.). 256p. 1997. 55.00 (*0-7185-0109-8*) Bks Intl VA.

McCracken, Donald L. A Production System Version of the Hearsay-II Speech Understanding System. Stone, Harold, ed. LC 81-7459. (Computer Science: Artificial Intelligence Ser.: No. 2). 151p. 1981. reprint ed. pap. 46.90 (*0-8357-1197-8*, 207004400063) Bks Demand.

McCracken, Donna. No More Litter: How to Train Your Cat to Use the Toilet. (Illus.). 64p. (Orig.). 1991. pap. 7.95 (*0-9629301-0-5*) Purr Pubns.

McCracken, E. M., jt. auth. see McCracken, D. P.

McCracken, Edward R., jt. auth. see Lewis, Delano E.

McCracken, Elizabeth. The Giant's House: A Romance. 272p. 1996. 19.95 (*0-385-31433-7*, Dial Pr) Dell.

— The Giant's House: A Romance. 1997. pap. 12.00 (*0-614-27273-4*, Avon Bks) Morrow Avon.

— Giant's House: A Romance. LC 95-52433. 290p. 1997. pap. 12.50 (*0-380-73020-0*, Avon Bks) Morrow Avon.

— The Giant's House: A Romance. large type ed. LC 96-34449. (Basic Ser.). 424p. 1996. 24.95 (*0-7862-0891-0*) Thorndike Pr.

— Here's Your Hat, What's. 224p. 1997. pap. 12.00 (*0-380-73079-0*, Avon Bks) Morrow Avon.

McCracken, Ellen. New Latina Narrative: The Feminine Space of Postmodern Ethnicity. LC 98-25528. 1999. 40.00 (*0-8165-1940-4*); pap. 19.95 (*0-8165-1941-2*) U of Ariz Pr.

***McCracken, Ellen, ed.** Fray Angelico Chavez: Poet, Priest & Artist. LC 99-50726. 2000. 24.95 (*0-8263-2007-4*) U of NM Pr.

McCracken-Flesher, Caroline, jt. ed. see Spilka, Mark.

McCracken, Floyd. Southwest Corner Stories: Seventy-Five Years of Memories. LC 98-85273. (Illus.). 176p. (Orig.). 1993. pap. 8.95 (*0-9637445-7-7*) Shasta Valley.

McCracken, G. E., tr. City of God Against the Pagans, 7 vols, 1. (Loeb Classical Library: No. 411-417). 490p. 1957. 18.95 (*0-674-99452-3*) HUP.

McCracken, George E. Penn's Colony: Genealogical & Historical Materials Relating to the Settlement of Pennsylvania, Vol. 2. xviii, 660p. 1996. pap. 44.00 (*0-7884-0397-4*, M121) Heritage Bk.

McCracken, Grant. Big Hair: A Journey into the Transformation of Self. LC 95-47536. 218p. 1996. pap. 16.95 (*0-87951-657-7*, Pub. by Overlook Pr) Penguin Putnam.

— Culture & Consumption: New Approaches to the Symbolic Character of Consumer Goods & Activities. LC 87-45394. (Illus.). 190p. 1990. pap. 14.95 (*0-253-20628-6*, MB-628) Ind U Pr.

— The Long Interview. (Qualitative Research Methods Ser.: Vol. 13). 96p. (C). 1988. text 24.00 (*0-8039-3352-5*); pap. text 10.50 (*0-8039-3353-3*) Sage.

McCracken, J. L., ed. see Irish Conference of Historians Staff.

***McCracken, James.** Secrets: The Wallace Family. 360p. 1998. pap. 8.95 (*0-9667853-0-4*) JaMarque Pubg.

McCracken, James. Securitization Issue 5: Asset-Backed & Mortgage-Backed Securities. 227p. 1998. ring bd. write for info. (*0-327-00724-9*, 8239013) LEXIS Pub.

McCracken, Janet B. Valuing Diversity: The Primary Years. LC 93-84576. (Illus.). 104p. 1993. pap. text 5.00 (*0-935989-55-2*, 238) Natl Assn Child Ed.

McCracken, Janet B., ed. Reducing Stress in Young Children's Lives. LC 86-62564. (Illus.). 170p. 1986. pap. 7.00 (*0-935989-03-X*, NAEYC 216) Natl Assn Child Ed.

McCracken, Janet B., jt. auth. see Jalongo, Mary R.

McCracken, Janet B., ed. see Brown, Audrey & Gross, Toby.

McCracken, Janet B., jt. ed. see Johnson, Julienne.

McCracken, Jim. Fish & Seafood. 93p. 1994. write for info. (*1-57215-004-1*) World Pubns.

McCracken, K. J., et al, eds. Energy Metabolism of Farm Animals. LC SF94.6.S95 1997. (A CAB International Publication). (Illus.). 480p. (C). 1998. text 100.00 (*0-85199-276-5*) OUP.

McCracken, Karen H. Connie Hagar: The Life History of a Texas Birdwatcher. LC 85-40748. 312p. 1988. pap. 14.95 (*0-89096-406-8*) Tex A&M Univ Pr.

McCracken, Kathleen. The Constancy of Objects. 96p. 1988. 9.95 (*0-920806-98-8*, Pub. by Penumbra Pr) U of Toronto Pr.

— Radical Vision: Paul Durcan. 1997. 49.95 (*1-85224-345-7*, Pub. by Bloodaxe Bks); pap. 23.95 (*1-85224-346-5*, Pub. by Bloodaxe Bks) Dufour.

McCracken, Kevin, jt. auth. see Curson, Peter.

***McCracken, Kristin.** Jennifer Love Hewitt. (High Interest Bks.). (Illus.). (J). 2000. 19.00 (*0-516-23321-1*) Childrens.

— Jennifer Love Hewitt. LC 00-24228. (High Interest Bks.). (Illus.). 48p. (J). (gr. 4-7). 2000. pap. write for info. (*0-516-23521-4*) Childrens.

— Leonardo DiCaprio. (Illus.). (J). 2000. 19.00 (*0-516-23323-8*) Childrens.

— Leonardo DiCaprio. (High Interest Bks.). (Illus.). 48p. (J). (gr. 4-7). 2000. pap. 6.95 (*0-516-23523-0*) Childrens.

— Prince William. (High Interest Bks.). (Illus.). (J). 2000. 19.00 (*0-516-23325-4*) Childrens.

— Prince William. LC 00-24227. (High Interest Bks.). (Illus.). 48p. (J). (gr. 4-7). 2000. pap. write for info. (*0-516-23525-7*) Childrens.

McCracken, L. J., ed. & intro. see Porter, Francis K.

McCracken, Marlene J. & McCracken, Robert A. Animals. rev. ed. (Themes Ser.). (Illus.). 92p. (J). (gr. k-4). 1985. pap. 12.00 (*0-920541-12-7*) Peguis Pubs Ltd.

— Celebrations. rev. ed. (Themes Ser.). (Illus.). 76p. (J). (gr. k-4). 1986. pap. 12.00 (*0-920541-72-0*) Peguis Pubs Ltd.

— Fall. (Themes Ser.). (Illus.). 96p. (J). (gr. k-4). 1987. pap. 12.00 (*0-920541-16-X*) Peguis Pubs Ltd.

— Fantasy. 4th ed. (Themes Ser.). (Illus.). 48p. (Orig.). (J). (gr. k-4). 1992. pap. 12.00 (*0-920541-02-X*) Peguis Pubs Ltd.

— Halloween. rev. ed. (Themes Ser.). (Illus.). 84p. (J). (gr. k-4). 1984. pap. 12.00 (*0-920541-76-3*) Peguis Pubs Ltd.

— Myself. rev. ed. (Themes Ser.). (Illus.). 92p. 1984. pap. 12.00 (*0-920541-78-X*) Peguis Pubs Ltd.

— Reading Is only the Tiger's Tail. 12th rev. ed. 248p. (J). (gr. k-4). 1987. reprint ed. text, teacher ed. 15.00 (*0-920541-13-5*) Peguis Pubs Ltd.

— The Sea & Other Water. rev. ed. (Themes Ser.). (Illus.). 80p. (J). (gr. k-4). 1985. pap. 12.00 (*0-920541-80-1*) Peguis Pubs Ltd.

— Spelling Through Phonics. 2nd rev. ed. (Illus.). 175p. (J). (gr. 1-3). 1996. pap., teacher ed. 18.00 (*1-895411-86-6*) Peguis Pubs Ltd.

— Spring. rev. ed. (Themes Ser.). (Illus.). 92p. (J). (gr. k-4). 1987. pap. 12.00 (*0-920541-14-3*) Peguis Pubs Ltd.

— Stories, Songs & Poetry to Teach Reading & Writing Stories, Songs & Poetry to Teach. rev. ed. (Illus.). 160p. (J). (gr. k-4). 1987. text, teacher ed. 15.00 (*0-920541-35-6*) Peguis Pubs Ltd.

— Tiger Cub Chants & Poems, 8 vols., Set. rev. ed. (Tiger Cub Bks.). (Illus.). 128p. (J). (gr. k-3). 1988. pap. 20.00 (*0-920541-66-6*) Peguis Pubs Ltd.

— Tiger Cub Readers, 8 vols., Set. rev. ed. (Tiger Cub Bks.). (Illus.). 128p. (J). (gr. k-1). 1988. pap. 20.00 (*0-920541-62-3*) Peguis Pubs Ltd.

— Tiger Cub Songs, 8 vols., Set. rev. ed. (Tiger Cub Bks.). (Illus.). 16p. (J). (gr. k-2). 1988. pap. 20.00 (*0-920541-68-2*) Peguis Pubs Ltd.

— Tiger Cub Stories, 8 vols., Set. rev. ed. (Tiger Cub Bks.). (Illus.). 128p. (J). (gr. k-2). 1988. pap. 20.00 (*0-920541-64-X*) Peguis Pubs Ltd.

— Winter. rev. ed. (Themes Ser.). (Illus.). 72p. (J). (gr. k-4). 1987. pap. 12.00 (*0-920541-10-0*) Peguis Pubs Ltd.

McCracken, Marlene J., jt. auth. see McCracken, Robert A.

McCracken, Mary J. The Great Dane Handbook. LC 95-38576. (Illus.). 240p. 1995. 27.95 (*0-940269-08-2*) OTR Pubns.

***McCracken, Michael K.** Memories from the Rain. 1999. pap. write for info. (*1-58235-386-7*) Watermrk Pr.

McCracken, Nancy M. & Appleby, Bruce C., eds. Gender Issues in the Teaching of English. LC 92-11979. 228p. (J). 1992. pap. text 25.00 (*0-86709-310-2*, 0310, Pub. by Boynton Cook Pubs) Heinemann.

McCracken, Paul W., et al. Consumer Installment Credit & Public Policy. LC 65-4634. (Michigan Business Studies: Vol. 17, No. 1). 260p. reprint ed. pap. 80.60 (*0-608-13532-1*, 202208300024) Bks Demand.

— On Key Economic Issues. LC 84-70039. (AEI Studies: No. 399). 56p. reprint ed. pap. 30.00 (*0-8357-4518-X*, 203737700008) Bks Demand.

McCracken, Peggy. The Romance of Adultery: Queenship & Sexual Transgression in Old French Narratives. LC 97-49185. (Illus.). 240p. (C). 1998. text 39.95 (*0-8122-3432-4*) U of Pa Pr.

McCracken, Philip. Philip McCracken. Tacoma Art Museum Staff, ed. LC 80-51071. (Illus.). 136p. 1980. 20.00 (*0-295-95771-9*) U of Wash Pr.

McCracken, Philip G. Your Retirement Money: How to Make It Last. 263p. (Orig.). 1992. pap. 17.95 (*0-9633349-0-5*) B&G Pub.

McCracken, Robert A. & McCracken, Marlene J. Reading, Writing & Language: A Practical Guide for Primary Teachers. 2nd ed. (Illus.). 296p. 1995. teacher ed. 17.00 (*1-895411-70-X*) Peguis Pubs Ltd.

— Stories, Songs, & Poetry for Teaching Reading & Writing: Literacy Through Language. 176p. (C). 1986. pap. text 16.95 (*0-8077-2856-X*) Tchrs Coll.

McCracken, Robert A., jt. auth. see McCracken, Marlene J.

McCracken, Robert D. Beatty: Frontier Oasis. (Illus.). 128p. (Orig.). 1996. pap. 12.95 (*1-878138-55-3*) Nye Cty Pr.

— The Fallacies of Women's Liberation. LC 72-89863. (Illus.). 150p. (C). 1972. pap. 5.95 (*0-88310-000-2*) Publishers Consult.

— A History of Amargosa Valley, Nevada. 152p. 1996. 16.95 (*1-878138-56-1*) Nye Cty Pr.

— A History of Beatty, Nevada. 208p. 1996. 16.95 (*1-878138-54-5*) Nye Cty Pr.

— A History of Pahrump, Nevada. 192p. 1996. 16.95 (*1-878138-51-0*) Nye Cty Pr.

— A History of Tonopah, Nevada. 248p. 1996. 16.95 (*1-878138-52-9*) Nye Cty Pr.

— Las Vegas: The Great American Playground. (Illus.). 128p. 1996. pap. 10.95 (*0-9639119-8-8*) Marion Street.

— Las Vegas: The Great American Playground. 2nd expanded rev. ed. LC 97-3272. (Illus.). 160p. 1997. pap. 15.95 (*0-87417-301-9*) U of Nev Pr.

— The Modern Pioneers of the Amargosa Valley. (Illus.). 112p. (Orig.). 1996. pap. 12.95 (*1-878138-58-8*) Nye Cty Pr.

— Pahrump: A Valley Waiting to Become a City. (Illus.). 96p. (Orig.). 1996. pap. 12.95 (*1-878138-53-7*) Nye Cty Pr.

— Tonopah: The Greatest, the Richest, & the Best Mining Camp in the World. (Illus.). 96p. (Orig.). 1996. pap. 12.95 (*1-878138-50-2*) Nye Cty Pr.

McCracken, Robert D., jt. auth. see Howerton, Jeanne S.

McCracken, Ronnie. God's Ravens Still Fly. 151p. 1996. pap. 8.99 (*1-898787-78-6*) Emerald House Group Inc.

McCracken, Scott, ed. see Ledger, Sally & Kee Yong Lim.

McCracken, Sheelagh. McCracken: The Banker's Remedy of Set-Off. 1997. write for info. (*0-406-99613-X*, MBRS1, MICHIE) LEXIS Pub.

M

McCracken, Sheelagh, jt. auth. see Everett, Dianne.
McCracken, Sheelagh, jt. ed. see Sheedy, Elizabeth.
McCracken, Stanley G., jt. auth. see Corrigan, Patrick W.
McCracken, Susan. For the Call of a Friend. LC 97-18695. 313p. 1997. 12.50 (*0-944350-41-0*) Friends United.
— For the Gift of a Friend: Sequel to "For the Love of a Friend" 192p. 1995. pap. 11.00 (*0-944350-35-6*) Friends United.
— For the Love of a Friend. LC 94-7130. 168p. 1994. 10.00 (*0-944350-29-1*) Friends United.
***McCracken, Thomas O.** New Atlas of Human Anatomy. (Illus.). 240p. 2000. 24.98 (*1-58663-097-0*) M Friedman Pub Grp Inc.
McCracken, Thomas O. & Kainer, Robert A. Spurgeon's Color Atlas of Large Animal Anatomy: The Essentials. LC 99-20525. 160p. 1999. text 69.00 (*0-683-30673-1*) Lppncott W & W.
McCracken, Thomas O., jt. auth. see Kainer, Robert A.
McCracken, Thomas O., jt. auth. see Twietmeyer, T. Alan.
McCracken, Ursula E., ed. see Zeri, Federico & Packard, Elisabeth.
McCracken, Wendy & Laoide-Kemp, Siobhan, eds. Audiology in Education. 450p. 1997. 90.00 (*1-56593-911-5*, 1804) Singular Publishing.
McCracken, William D. Rise of the Swiss Republic. 2nd ed. LC 75-130235. reprint ed. 57.50 (*0-404-04109-4*) AMS Pr.
Mccrady, Barbara S. & Epstein, Elizabeth E., eds. Addictions: A Sourcebook for Professionals. LC RC564.M327 1999. (Illus.). 672p. 1999. text 65.00 (*0-19-511489-2*) OUP.
McCrady, Barbara S. & Miller, William R. Research on Alcoholics Anonymous: Opportunities & Alternatives. LC 92-63233. 440p. (Orig.). (C). 1993. pap. 25.95 (*0-911290-24-9*, BBK-139) Rutgers Ctr Alcohol.
McCrady, Edward. History of South Carolina, Sixteen Seventy to Seventeen Eighty-Three, 4 vols. LC 69-18185. reprint ed. 306.00 (*0-404-04120-5*) AMS Pr.
McCrady, Edward, III, ed. Seen & Unseen: A Biologist Views the Universe. 1990. pap. 14.95 (*0-918769-16-7*) Univ South Pr.
McCrady, Edward, jt. auth. see Feduccia, Alan.
McCrady, Ellen, ed. Literature Supplement to the Abbey Newsletter: References & Publications Collected, 1992-1997. 39p. 1998. spiral bd. write for info. (*0-9622071-5-2*) Abbey Pubns.
— North American Permanent Papers - 1998: A Guide to Permanent Papers Available in the U. S. & Canada. 60p. 1998. pap. 19.50 (*0-9622071-4-4*) Abbey Pubns.
McCrady, Ellen R. North American Permanent Papers. 52p. (Orig.). 1995. pap. 19.50 (*0-9622071-3-6*) Abbey Pubns.
McCrady, Ellen R., ed. see Laursen, Per M.
McCrae, Alister. Scots in Burma: Golden Times in a Golden Land. (Illus.). 120p. (C). 1995. pap. 25.00 (*1-870838-50-5*, Pub. by Kiscadale) Weatherhill.
McCrae, Barry, et al, eds. Specialist Mathematics: Core. 192p. (C). 1993. pap. 24.95 (*0-522-84578-9*, Pub. by Melbourne Univ Pr) Paul & Co Pubs.
Mccrae, Gordon, jt. auth. see James, Stuart.
McCrae, Ian. Global Economics: Seeking a Christian Ethic, a Workbook for Beginners. LC 92-42908. 1993. pap. 7.95 (*0-377-00253-4*) Friendship Pr.
McCrae, Jody. Lake of Dreams. large type ed. 244p. 1992. reprint ed. 13.95 (*1-56054-409-0*) Thorndike Pr.
McCrae, Linda R. Latina Vivit! A Guide to Lively Latin Classes. 2nd ed. LC 96-135973. (ENG & LAT., Illus.). 149p. (Orig.). 1995. reprint ed. pap. text 20.00 (*0-86516-273-5*) Bolchazy-Carducci.
McCrae, Lori M., jt. auth. see Benson, Judith.
McCrae, Lori M., jt. auth. see Horne, Constance.
McCrae, Malcolm A., et al, eds. Molecular Aspects of Host-Pathogen Interactions. (Society for General Microbiology Symposium Ser.: Vol. 55). 372p. (C). 1997. text 115.00 (*0-521-59215-1*) Cambridge U Pr.
McCrae, Marya. Surviving Sexual Abuse. (Master's Touch Bible Study Ser.). 1994. pap. 4.50 (*0-570-09521-2*, 20-2462) Concordia.
McCrae, Robert R. & Costa, Paul. Personality in Adulthood. LC 89-78494. 198p. 1990. pap. text 21.00 (*0-89862-528-9*) Guilford Pubns.
McCrae, William. Basic Organic Reactions. LC 72-75486. (Illus.). 230p. reprint ed. pap. 71.30 (*0-8357-8814-8*, 203334100085) Bks Demand.
McCraig, Linda F. & McLemorel, Thomas. Plan & Operation of the National Hospital Ambulatory Medical Care Survey. LC 94-12448. (Vital & Health Statistics, Series 1, Programs & Collection Procedures: No. 34). 1994. 6.00 (*0-8406-0493-9*) Natl Ctr Health Stats.
McCraig, William, tr. see Rosselli, Carlo.
***McCraken, Donal P.** Macbride's Brigade: Irish Commandos in the Anglo-Boer War. (Illus.). 224p. 1999. 29.95 (*1-85182-499-5*, Pub. by Four Cts Pr) Intl Spec Bk.
McCraney, Leah, jt. auth. see Barnwell, Thomas.
McCranie, James R. & Wilson, Larry D. A New Hylid Frog of the Genus Plectrohyla from a Cloud Forest in Honduras. (Occasional Papers: No. 92). 7p. 1981. 1.00 (*0-317-04882-1*) U KS Nat Hist Mus.
McCrank, Lawrence. Historical Information Science: An Emerging Unidiscipline. 1500p. 2000. 149.95 (*1-57387-071-4*) Info Today Inc.
McCrank, Lawrence J. Education for Rare Book Librarianship: A Reexamination of Trends & Problems. LC 80-622854. (University of Illinois, Graduate School of Library Science Occasional Papers: No. 144). (Illus.). 98p. reprint ed. pap. 30.40 (*0-7837-1175-1*, 204170300022) Bks Demand.
— Medieval Frontier History in New Catalonia. LC 96-1437. (Collected Studies: CS528). (Illus.). 1996. text 101.95 (*0-86078-582-3*, Pub. by Variorum) Ashgate Pub Co.
McCrank, Lawrence J., compiled by. Mt. Angel Abbey: A Centennial History of the Benedictine Community & Its Library, 1882-1982. LC 83-10536. 224p. 1983. pap. 20.00 (*0-8420-2212-0*) Scholarly Res Inc.
McCrank, Lawrence J., ed. Archives & Library Administration: Divergent Tradition & Common Concerns. LC 86-19405. (Journal of Library Administration: Vol. 7, Nos. 2-3). 176p. 1986. text 49.95 (*0-86656-590-6*) Haworth Pr.
— Bibliographical Foundations of French Historical Studies. LC 91-25540. (Primary Sources & Original Works: Vol. 1, Nos. 1-2). (Illus.). 245p. 1992. 49.95 (*1-56024-150-0*) Haworth Pr.
— Bibliographical Foundations of French Historical Studies. LC 91-25540. (Primary Sources & Original Works: Vol. 1, Nos. 1-2). 245p. 1996. pap. 24.95 (*0-7890-6042-6*) Haworth Pr.
— Discovery in the Archives of Spain & Portugal: Quincentenary Essays, 1492-1992. LC 93-50115. (Primary Sources & Original Works: Vol. 2, Nos. 1-4). (Illus.). 590p. 1994. 119.95 (*1-56024-643-X*) Haworth Pr.
McCraois, Cormac. The Battle Below Giltspur. 128p. 1997. pap. 6.95 (*0-86327-356-4*, Pub. by Wolfhound Press) Irish Amer Bk.
McCraren, Joseph P., ed. The Aquaculture of Striped Bass. 1985. 6.50 (*0-943676-16-9*) MD Sea Grant Col.
McCrary, Crystal, jt. auth. see Ewing, Rita.
McCrary, Jim. And/Or & Or & Or. 1991. pap. 5.00 (*0-938979-41-8*) EG Bksellers.
— Coon Creek. 20p. (Orig.). 1972. ring bd. 1.00 (*0-685-30031-5*) Cottonwood KS.
— West of Mass. Moritz, John & Dillon, Curtis, eds. (Illus.). 76p. (Orig.). 1992. pap. 8.00 (*1-881175-01-4*) Tansy Pr.
McCrary, Joan C. Good Morning, Sun! A Novel of Transformation. 154p. (Orig.). 1989. pap. 9.95 (*0-9623541-0-4*) Redite Pr.
McCrary, Joan C., ed. see Cramer, Malinda E.
McCrary, Peyton. Abraham Lincoln & Reconstruction: The Louisiana Experiment. LC 78-51181. 441p. reprint ed. pap. 136.80 (*0-7837-1404-1*, 204175800023) Bks Demand.
McCrary, Sharie. Love, Lust, & Handcuffs: Understanding the Sex Abuser. LC 92-45167. 166p. (Orig.). 1993. pap. 8.95 (*1-880489-03-1*) Hoopuka Pr.
McCrary, Susan N. El Ultimo Godo' & the Dynamics of the Urdrama. 116p. 1990. 27.50 (*0-916379-36-1*) Scripta.
McCrary, William C. & Madrigal, Jose A. Studies in Honor of Everett W. Hesse. LC 80-53824. 208p. (Orig.). reprint ed. pap. 64.50 (*0-608-16684-7*, 202706200053) Bks Demand.
McCravey, Janice B., jt. auth. see Browning, James A.
McCraw, David R. Du Fu's Laments from the South. LC 92-24973. 296p. (C). 1992. pap. text 21.00 (*0-8248-1455-X*) UH Pr.
McCraw, John B. & Arnold, Phillip G. Head & Neck Reconstruction. LC 87-82109. (McGraw & Arnold's Atlas of Muscle & Musculocutaneous Flaps Ser.). (Illus.). 262p. 1988. text 163.50 (*0-939789-02-7*) Lppncott W & W.
— McCraw & Arnold's Atlas of Muscle & Musculocutaneour Flaps. LC 86-82307. (Illus.). 748p. 1986. text 291.50 (*0-939789-00-0*) Lppncott W & W.
McCraw, Thomas K. America Vs. Japan: A Comparative Study. 1988. text 35.00 (*0-07-103255-X*); pap. text 19.95 (*0-07-103254-1*) McGraw.
***McCraw, Thomas K.** American Business, 1920-2000: How It Worked. Franklin, John H. & Eisenstadt, A. S., eds. LC 99-86083. (American History Ser.). 300p. 2000. pap. text 15.95 (*0-88295-985-9*) Harlan Davidson.
McCraw, Thomas K. Prophets of Regulation. (Illus.). 416p. 1986. pap. text 16.50 (*0-674-71608-6*) Belknap Pr.
— Prophets of Regulation: Charles Francis Adams, Louis D. Brandeis, James M. Landis, Alfred E. Kahn. LC 84-296. 416p. 1984. 32.00 (*0-674-71607-8*) Belknap Pr.
— Regulation in Perspective: Historical Essays. 1982. text 18.50 (*0-07-103281-9*); pap. text 14.95 (*0-07-103282-7*) McGraw.
McCraw, Thomas K., ed. Creating Modern Capitalism: How Entrepreneurs, Companies, & Countries Triumphed in Three Industrial Revolutions. LC 97-15334. (Illus.). 800p. 1998. 59.95 (*0-674-17555-7*); pap. 29.95 (*0-674-17556-5*) HUP.
McCraw, Thomas K., intro. The Essential Alfred Chandler: Essays Toward a Historical Theory of Big Business. 538p. 1991. pap. 19.95 (*0-87584-306-9*) Harvard Busn.
McCraw, Thomas K. & Cruikshank, Jeffrey L., eds. The Intellectual Venture Capitalist: John H. McArthur & the Work of the Harvard Business School, 1980-1995. 400p. 1999. 35.00 (*0-87584-900-8*) Harvard Busn.
***McCray, Billy Q. & Roe, Jon.** Between These Walls: Working for the People. (Illus.). 180p. 1999. pap. write for info. (*0-9677092-1-0*) McCray Pubn.
***McCray, Carrie Allen.** Freedom's Child: The Life of a Confederate General's Black Daughter. LC 97-32659. (Illus.). 288p. 1999. 23.95 (*1-56512-186-4*, 72186) Algonquin Bks.
McCray, Carrie Allen. Freedom's Child: The Life of a Confederate General's Black Daughter. 1999. pap. 12.95 (*0-14-028252-1*) Viking Penguin.
McCray, Debbie, jt. auth. see Holt, Jerry.
McCray, James. Church Choir Director's Guide to Success. 172p. (C). 1997. pap. text 12.95 (*0-9648071-1-4*) Snta Barb Music.
McCray, James A. & Cahill, Thomas. Electronic Circuit Analysis for Scientists. LC 72-8986. (Illus.). 308p. reprint ed. pap. 95.50 (*0-608-10050-1*, 201246200081) Bks Demand.
McCray, Jan. El Amor Que Toda Mujer Necesita. 1998. pap. text 8.99 (*0-88113-510-0*) Caribe Betania.
— How to Delight the Heart of God. LC 99-24450. 299p. 1999. pap. 11.99 (*0-8007-9273-4*) Chosen Bks.
— The Love Every Woman Needs: Intimacy with Jesus. LC 97-13496. 256p. 1997. pap. 12.99 (*0-8007-9253-X*) Chosen Bks.
McCray, Janet H. Once upon a Summertime: A Personal Memoir of Summer Cottage Days in Door County, Wisconsin During the Mid-Twentieth Century. (Illus.). 120p. 1998. pap. 12.95 (*0-9666023-0-7*) Hough House.
McCray, K., ed. Criteria, Guidelines, Practices, Procedures & Standards of the Ground Water Industry. 40p. 1988. 6.25 (*1-56034-065-7*, K454) Natl Grnd Water.
McCray, Marilyn. Electroworks. LC 79-67569. (Illus.). 1979. pap. text 10.00 (*0-935398-01-5*) G Eastman Hse.
***McCray, Patrick.** Glassmaking in Renaissance Venice: The Fragile Craft. LC 99-31647. 280p. 1999. text 78.95 (*0-7546-0050-5*, Pub. by Ashgate Pub) Ashgate Pub Co.
McCray, Patrick & Kingery, W. David, eds. The Prehistory & History of Glassmaking Technology. (Ceramics & Civilization Ser.: Vol. 8). (Illus.). 360p. 1998. 95.00 (*1-57498-041-6*, CC08) Am Ceramic.
McCray, Philip R. The McCrays of America. 2nd ed. (Illus.). xiv, 441p. (Orig.). 1993. pap. 43.00 (*1-55613-829-6*) Heritage Bk.
McCray, Richard & Wang, Zhenri, eds. Supernovae & Supernova Remnants: IAU Colloquium 145. (Illus.). 449p. (C). 1996. text 85.00 (*0-521-46080-8*) Cambridge U Pr.
***McCray, Sandra & Hartman, Diane.** The Patients' Book: How to Survive in Today's Medical System. 150p. 2000. pap. 12.00 (*0-9678647-3-9*) Colorado Hlth.
McCray, Walter A. Black Folks & Christian Liberty: Be Christian, Be Black, Be Culturally & Socially Free. 2nd ed. (Black Light Fellowship Ser.). 210p. (Orig.). 1987. pap. 10.00 (*0-933176-08-2*) Black Light Fellow.
— The Black Presence in the Bible Vol. 1: Discovering the Black & African Identity of Biblical Persons & Nations. LC 90-80108. (Illus.). 208p. (C). 1995. pap. 19.95 (*0-933176-12-0*) Black Light Fellow.
— The Black Presence in the Bible Vol. 1: Discovering the Black & African Identity of Biblical Persons & Nations. 2nd ed. 210p. 1995. reprint ed. pap., teacher ed. 14.95 (*0-933176-23-6*) Black Light Fellow.
— The Black Presence in the Bible Vol. 2: The Table of Nations, Genesis 10:1-32 - With Emphasis on the Hamitic Genealogical Line from a Black Perspective. 2nd ed. 212p. 1995. reprint ed. pap. 14.95 (*0-933176-24-4*) Black Light Fellow.
— The Black Presence in the Bible & the Table of Nations Vol. 2: (Genesis 10: 1-32), with Emphasis on the Hamitic Genealogical Line from a Black Perspective. LC 90-83436. (Illus.). 210p. (Orig.). (C). 1995. pap. 19.95 (*0-933176-13-9*) Black Light Fellow.
— The Black Young Adult Test (Christian Version) How Mature Are You? LC 94-96612. 48p. (Orig.). (YA). (gr. 11 up). 1995. pap. 2.99 (*0-933176-15-5*) Black Light Fellow.
— The Black Young Adult Test (General Version) How Mature Are You? LC 94-96611. 48p. (Orig.). 1995. pap. 2.99 (*0-933176-16-3*) Black Light Fellow.
— Black Young Adults - How to Reach Them, What to Teach Them: Strengthening the Black Church & Community by Educating Black Young Adults. 2nd ed. LC 92-72415. 144p. (gr. 12 up). 1992. reprint ed. pap. 8.95 (*0-933176-09-0*) Black Light Fellow.
— Get Grown & Keep Growing! The Self-Help Adult Maturity Handbook. 160p. (Orig.). 1997. pap. 5.95 (*1-889303-00-3*) Yama Twenty-first.
— How to Stick Together During Times of Tension: Directives for Christian Black Unity. LC 83-70288. 170p. (Orig.). (C). 1983. pap. 7.50 (*0-933176-03-1*); boxed set 11.95 (*0-933176-04-X*) Black Light Fellow.
— A Rationale for Black Christian Literature. 2nd ed. LC 92-72557. 56p. (C). 1992. reprint ed. pap. 4.95 (*0-933176-14-7*) Black Light Fellow.
McCrea, Adriana. Constant Minds: Political Virtue & the Lipsian Paradigm in England, 1584-1650. LC 97-226191. (Illus.). 348p. 1997. text 65.00 (*0-8020-0666-3*) U of Toronto Pr.
McCrea, Barbara, et al. The Rough Guide to South Africa. 2nd ed. (Illus.). 736p. 1999. 19.95 (*1-85828-460-0*, Pub. by Rough Guides) Penguin Putnam.
McCrea, Barbara P., jt. auth. see Rossi, Ernest E.
McCrea, Brian. Addison & Steele Are Dead: The English Department, Its Canon, & the Professionalization of Literary Criticism. LC 88-40600. 280p. 1990. 40.00 (*0-87413-366-1*) U Delaware Pr.
— Impotent Fathers: Patriarchy & Demographic Crisis in the Eighteenth-Century Novel. LC 97-24000. 248p. 1998. 39.50 (*0-87413-656-3*) U Delaware Pr.
McCrea, Frances B. Minutes to Midnight: Nuclear Weapons Protest in America. (Violence, Cooperation, & Peace Ser.). 240p. (C). 1989. text 55.00 (*0-8039-3417-3*); pap. text 24.95 (*0-8039-3418-1*) Sage.
McCrea, Henry V. Red Dirt & Isinglass: A Wartime Biography of a Confederate Soldier. 578p. 1992. 31.95 (*0-9646766-0-5*) Chipola Pr.
Mccrea, Maria. Preschool Lessons about Jesus. Date not set. pap. text 8.95 (*0-86653-767-8*) Good Apple.
McCrea, Nancy. Developing High Impact Projects Downtown: Managing the Development Process to Minimize Risk. Murphy, Jenny, ed. 48p. (Orig.). 1988. pap. 18.00 (*0-317-04837-6*) Natl Coun Econ Dev.
— Incubator Resource Kit. 130p. (Orig.). 1988. pap. 35.00 (*0-317-04899-6*) Natl Coun Econ Dev.
— Minority Enterprise Development. Murphy, Jenny, ed. 46p. (Orig.). 1989. pap. 21.50 (*0-317-04808-2*) Natl Coun Econ Dev.
McCrea, Nancy, ed. see Gillen, Lori.
McCrea, Ross, jt. ed. see Pinkerton, John.
***McCrea, Steve.** Boni Finds Clean Air: A Video Story about an Ecological Board. unabridged ed. Parra, Ale, tr. (Talk Video Story Book Ser.). (Illus.). 1999. pap. 10.00 (*1-879857-72-3*, Talk Intl Bks) SFEAA.
McCrea, Steve. The NGV (Natural Gas Vehicle) Activity Book. (Illus.). 20p. (J). 1995. pap. text 4.00 (*1-57074-246-4*) Greyden Pr.
— Preparing for the Post-Petroleum Era: What Policy Analysts & Administrators Need to Know about Alternative Fuel Vehicles. 12p. 1995. pap. text 5.00 (*1-57074-249-9*) Greyden Pr.
— A Speculative Investor's Guide to the Electric Vehicle Industry. (Illus.). 40p. 1995. pap. text 13.00 (*1-57074-263-4*) Greyden Pr.
— Where's My AFV? (Alternative Fuel Vehicle?) (Illus.). 1995. pap. text. write for info. (*1-57074-251-0*) Greyden Pr.
— Why Wait for Detroit? Drive an Electric Car Today! Minner, R., ed. (Illus.). 163p. 1995. 25.00 (*1-57074-236-7*) Greyden Pr.
McCrea, Steve, ed. see Denning, Jenna.
McCrea, Steve, ed. see Yuzenas, Abby.
McCrea, W. A. & Findley, L. J. Syncope & Related Disorders. (Neurological Disease & Therapy Ser.). Date not set. write for info. (*0-8247-9497-4*) Dekker.
McCreadie, Marsha. The Casting Couch & Other Front Row Seats: Women in Films of the 1970s & 1980s. LC 89-72131. 208p. 1990. 55.00 (*0-275-92912-4*, C2912, Praeger Pubs) Greenwood.
— Women on Film: The Critical Eye. LC 82-13221. 156p. 1983. 49.95 (*0-275-91042-3*, C1042, Praeger Pubs) Greenwood.
— The Women Who Write the Movies: From Frances Marion to Nora Ephron. LC 94-18113. (Illus.). 256p. 1995. 19.95 (*1-55972-251-7*, Birch Ln Pr) Carol Pub Group.
***McCreadie, Mary.** Canoeing Canada's Northwest Territories: A Paddler's Guide. LC 96-111868. (Illus.). 194p. 1999. pap. 19.95 (*1-895465-09-5*) CNR Canoe.
McCready. Business Mathematics. 3rd ed. (Math). 1978. 14.00 (*0-534-00570-5*) Brooks-Cole.
— Business Mathematics 2nd. 2nd ed. (Math). 1973. 8.75 (*0-534-00239-0*) Brooks-Cole.
— Solving Bus Prob W Calc 4. 4th ed. (Math). 1972. 8.75 (*0-534-00107-6*) Brooks-Cole.
McCready, Benjamin W. On the Influence of Trades, Professions & Occupations in the United States in the Production of Disease. LC 78-180583. (Medicine & Society in America Ser.). 144p. 1980. reprint ed. 19.95 (*0-405-03960-3*) Ayer.
McCready, Douglas. Jesus Christ for the Modern World: The Christology of the Catholic Tubingen School. LC 90-33275. (American University Studies: Theology & Religion: Ser. VII, Vol. 77). X, 353p. (C). 1991. text 52.95 (*0-8204-1337-2*) P Lang Pubng.
McCready, Jack. Furred & Feathered Wildgame from Bullet to Table. 2nd ed. Bolkey, Lorna & Roberts, Pat H., eds. LC 93-60865. (Illus.). 144p. 1993. reprint ed. pap. 9.95 (*1-56664-031-8*) WorldComm.
McCready, Karen. Art Deco & Modernist Ceramics. LC 94-61467. (Illus.). 192p. 1995. 45.00 (*0-500-01669-0*, Pub. by Thames Hudson) Norton.
— Art Deco & Modernist Ceramics. LC 94-61467. (Illus.). 192p. 1996. pap. 24.95 (*0-500-27825-3*, Pub. by Thames Hudson) Norton.
McCready, Richard R. Business Mathematics. 4th ed. LC 81-19308. (Math). 1982. mass mkt. 21.50 (*0-534-01075-X*) PWS Pubs.
— Business Mathematics. 5th ed. (Math). 301p. (YA). (gr. 11-12). 1986. mass mkt. 33.00 (*0-534-05730-6*) PWS Pubs.
— Chess. LC 81-83687. 64p. 1981. 24.00 (*0-88014-035-6*) Mosaic Pr OH.
— Lrng Bus Math With Elec Calc. (Math). 1975. mass mkt. 12.75 (*0-534-00396-6*) PWS Pubs.
— Office Machines: Electronic Calculators. 6th ed. LC 82-21337. (Math). 248p. 1983. mass mkt. 19.50 (*0-534-01285-X*) PWS Pubs.
McCready, Sam. Lucille Lortel: A Bio-Bibliography, 42. LC 93-23892. (Bio-Bibliographies in the Performing Arts Ser.: No. 42). 304p. 1993. lib. bdg. 69.50 (*0-313-27605-6*, MUC/, Greenwood Pr) Greenwood.
— A William Butler Yeats Encyclopedia. LC 96-50288. 512p. 1997. lib. bdg. 95.00 (*0-313-28371-0*, Greenwood Pr) Greenwood.
McCreaner, A., jt. auth. see Green, J.
McCreary, Alf. Spirit of the Age: The Story of "Old Bushmills" 232p. 1983. 25.00 (*0-8159-6837-X*) Devin.
McCreary, David. Rolling Around Puget Sound: Thirty-Six Places You Can Skate in Snohomish, King & Pierce Counties. 96p. 1994. pap. write for info. (*0-9642001-0-4*) McCreary Direct.
McCreary, Don R. Japanese-U. S. Business Negotiations: A Cross-Cultural Study. LC 86-554. 130p. 1986. 55.00 (*0-275-92006-2*, C2006, Praeger Pubs) Greenwood.
McCreary, Donald R., jt. auth. see Sadava, Stanley W.
McCreary, Edward, jt. auth. see Zeckendorf, William.
McCreary, Eugene. Madame President. 501p. 1998. pap. 14.95 (*0-9659308-0-7*) Erica Hse.
McCreary, Jane. Trim-a-tree Story Of Christmas. 1999. 6.99 (*1-57866-079-3*) Arrowood Pr.
***McCreary, Jenn.** Stigmata Errata. 22p. 1999. pap. 6.00 (*0-937013-99-4*, Pub. by Potes Poets) SPD-Small Pr Dist.
***McCreary, Jennifer.** Four O'Clock Pocket Chiming. 28p. 2000. write for info. (*0-9667655-4-0*, Pub. by Beautifulswimmer) SPD-Small Pr Dist.
***McCreary, Lew.** Minus Man. LC 99-43716. 256p. 1999. reprint ed. pap. 12.00 (*0-8021-3674-5*, Pub. by Grove-Atltic) Publishers Group.
McCreary, Mallory, ed. see McCreary, Susan A.
McCreary, Paul. The Maze Book. (Ann Arbor Educational Ser.). (Illus.). (J). (gr. 2-4). 1979. pap. 8.00 (*0-87879-712-2*, Ann Arbor Div) Acad Therapy.

An Asterisk (*) at the beginning of an entry indicates that the title is appearing for the first time.

— Perceptual Activities: A Multitude of Perceptual Actitivies, Level 2-Advanced, Consumerable (Coloring) Edition. 1972. student ed. 12.00 (*0-87879-711-4*, Ann Arbor Div) Acad Therapy.

— Perceptual Activities: A Multitude of Reusable Perceptual Activities, Level 1-Primary. 1972. 12.00 (*0-87879-708-4*, Ann Arbor Div) Acad Therapy.

— Perceptual Activities, Level 1 - Primary: A Multitude of Perceptual Activities. rev. ed. 62p. (J). (gr. 2-4). 1976. 12.00 (*0-87879-710-6*, Ann Arbor Div) Acad Therapy.

— Perceptual Activities, Level 2 - Elementary. 1994. 12.00 (*0-87879-709-2*) Acad Therapy.

*McCreary, Rosemary.** Container Gardens. (Time Life How to Ser.). (Illus.). 144p. 2001. pap. 16.95 (*0-7370-0624-2*) Time-Life Educ.

McCreary, Scott T., jt. auth. see Sorensen, Jens C.

McCreary, Susan A. Cupid's Cuisine, the Foods of Love. LC 85-22279. (Illus.). 160p. 1985. pap. 9.95 (*0-9608428-4-5*) Straw Patchwork.

— Parsley, Sage, Rosemary & Mine: An Herbal Faire. LC 91-37719. (Illus.). 160p. (Orig.). 1991. pap. 14.95 (*0-9608428-5-3*) Straw Patchwork.

— A Strawberry Serendipity: Unexpected Discoveries. McCreary, Mallory, ed. LC 95-68715. (Illus.). 160p. (Orig.). 1995. pap. 14.95 (*0-9608428-6-1*) Straw Patchwork.

— Sugarplum Visions: Old Christmases Made New. LC 83-18300. (Illus.). 160p. 1983. pap. 12.95 (*0-9608428-3-7*) Straw Patchwork.

— With a Spot of Tea: The Niceties of Tea. McCreary, Mallory, ed. LC 97-69422. (Illus.). 160p. (Orig.). 1997. pap. 14.95 (*0-9608428-7-X*) Straw Patchwork.

McCreary, W. Burgess. One Thousand Bible Drill Questions. 1980. pap. 3.95 (*0-87162-263-7*, WP#D5899) Warner Pr.

McCreath, D., jt. ed. see Kaiser, P. K.

McCreddan, Lyn. James McAuley. (Australian Writers Ser.). 128p. 1993. pap. 19.95 (*0-19-553349-6*) OUP.

McCredden, Lyn, jt. auth. see Lucas, Rosemary.

McCredie, James R., et al. Samothrace: Excavations Conducted by the Institute of Fine Arts of New York University Vol. 7, Pt. 1: The Rotunda of Arsinoe. Lehmann, Karl, ed. LC 58-8985. (Bollingen Ser.: Vol. 60). 466p. 1958. reprint ed. pap. 144.50 (*0-608-04572-1*, 206534200007) Bks Demand.

— Samothrace: Excavations Conducted by the Institute of Fine Arts of New York University Vol. 7, Pt. 2: The Rotunda of Arsinoe. Lehmann, Karl, ed. LC 58-8985. (Bollingen Ser.: Vol. 60). 108p. 1992. reprint ed. pap. 33.50 (*0-608-04573-X*, 206534200008) Bks Demand.

McCredie, L. Wills, Probate & the Administration of the Estates of Deceased Persons in Victoria. 2nd ed. 280p. 1989. 76.00 (*0-409-49474-7*, AT, MICHIE); pap. 60.00 (*0-409-49475-5*, AT, MICHIE) LEXIS Pub.

McCree. John Sjolander: Poet of Cedar Bayou. (Illus.). 192p. 1988. 10.95 (*0-89015-569-0*) Sunbelt Media.

— Leisure & Play in Therapy. 1998. pap. text 36.00 (*0-12-784562-3*) Acad Pr.

McCree, Suesetta T. Leisure & Play in Therapy: Theory, Goals & Activities. 140p. 1993. pap. text 38.00 (*0-7616-4281-1*) Commun Skill.

McCreede, Jess. Big Horn Massacre. 1991. mass mkt. 3.99 (*1-55817-569-5*, Pinncle Kensgtn) Kensgtn Pub Corp.

— Blue Sky, Night Thunder: The Utes of Colorado. 416p. 19.95 (*1-879915-08-1*) Affil Writers America.

— Colorado Ambush. 1989. mass mkt. 2.95 (*1-55817-186-X*, Pinncle Kensgtn) Kensgtn Pub Corp.

— Gold Rush Revenge. 352p. 1992. mass mkt. 3.99 (*1-55817-643-8*, Pinncle Kensgtn) Kensgtn Pub Corp.

— Mountain Man's Blood. 1990. mass mkt. 2.95 (*1-55817-326-9*, Pinncle Kensgtn) Kensgtn Pub Corp.

— Mountain Men on the Santa Fe Trail. 1992. mass mkt. 3.99 (*1-55817-594-6*, Pinncle Kensgtn) Kensgtn Pub Corp.

***McCreedy.** Structures. 2000. 10.95 (*0-07-135251-1*) McGraw.

— Water. 2000. 10.95 (*0-07-135250-3*) McGraw.

McCreedy, Dale. Expladora del Espacio. (National Science Partnership para Girl Scouts y Museos de Ciencia Ser.). Orig. Title: Space Explorer. (ENG & SPA., Illus.). 50p. 1997. pap. 8.00 (*1-889939-05-6*) Franklin PA.

— Motores. (National Science Partnership para Girl Scouts y Museos de Ciencia Ser.). Orig. Title: Movers. (ENG & SPA., Illus.). 33p. 1997. pap. 8.00 (*1-889939-03-X*) Franklin PA.

— Movers. (National Science Partnership for Girl Scouts & Science Museums Ser.). (Illus.). 38p. (Orig.). 1995. pap. 8.00 (*0-9625622-1-1*) Franklin PA.

— Space Explorer. (National Science Partnership for Girl Scouts & Science Museums Ser.). (Illus.). 56p. (Orig.). 1995. pap. 8.00 (*0-9625622-5-4*) Franklin PA.

McCreedy, Dale & Andrews, Julia. Maravillas del Agua. Orig. Title: Water Wonders. (ENG & SPA., Illus.). 69p. 1997. pap. 8.00 (*1-889939-06-4*) Franklin PA.

— Water Wonders. (National Science Partnership for Girl Scouts & Science Museums Ser.). (Illus.). 72p. (Orig.). 1995. pap. 8.00 (*0-9625622-6-2*) Franklin PA.

McCreedy, Dale & Kuhn, Jean N. Maravillas de la Ciencia. (National Science Partnership para Girl Scouts y Museos de Ciencia Ser.). Orig. Title: Science Wonders. (ENG & SPA., Illus.). 37p. 1997. pap. 8.00 (*1-889939-04-8*) Franklin PA.

— Science Wonders. (National Science Partnership for Girl Scouts & Science Museums Ser.). (Illus.). 40p. (Orig.). 1995. pap. 8.00 (*0-9625622-4-6*) Franklin PA.

McCreedy, Dale & McAndrew, Elizabeth. Observations del Tiempo Meteorologico. (National Science Partnership para Girl Scouts y Museos de Ciencia Ser.). Orig. Title: Weather Watch. (ENG & SPA., Illus.). 60p. 1997. pap. 8.00 (*1-889939-07-2*) Franklin PA.

— Weather Watch. (National Science Partnership for Girl Scouts & Science Museums Ser.). (Illus.). 63p. (Orig.). 1995. pap. 8.00 (*0-9625622-7-0*) Franklin PA.

McCreedy, Dale & Tabachnick, Kate. NSP Training Handbook: Science Sampler. (National Science Partnership for Girl Scouts & Science Museums Ser.). (Illus.). 32p. 1996. pap. 8.00 (*1-889939-01-3*) Franklin PA.

— Science in the Worlds. (National Science Partnership for Girl Scouts & Science Museums Ser.). (Illus.). 80p. (Orig.). 1995. pap. 8.00 (*0-9625622-2-X*) Franklin PA.

McCreedy, Dale, et al. Detective Cientifica. (National Science Partnership para Girl Scouts y Museos de Ciencia Ser.). Orig. Title: Science Sleuth. (ENG & SPA., Illus.). 66p. 1997. pap. 8.00 (*1-889939-08-0*) Franklin PA.

— NSP Training Handbook: Movers, Space Explorer, Science Wonder. (National Science Partnership for Girl Scouts & Science Museums Ser.). (Illus.). 52p. 1996. pap. 12.00 (*1-889939-00-5*) Franklin PA.

— NSP Training Handbook: Water Wonders, Weather Watch, Science Sleuth, Science in the Worlds. (National Science Partnership for Girl Scouts & Science Museums Ser.). (Illus.). 68p. 1996. pap. 12.00 (*1-889939-02-1*) Franklin PA.

— Science Sleuth. (National Science Partnership for Girl Scouts & Science Museums Ser.). (Illus.). 72p. (Orig.). 1995. pap. 8.00 (*0-9625622-3-8*) Franklin PA.

McCreedy, Dale, jt. auth. see Tabachnick, Kate.

McCreery, Charles, jt. auth. see Green, Celia.

McCreery, Cindy. Ports of the World: Prints of Ports from the National Maritime Museum, 1700-1850. 176p. 1999. 70.00 (*0-85667-505-9*, Pub. by P Wilson) Antique Collect.

McCreery, David. Development & the State in Reforma Guatemala, 1871-1885. LC 81-22545. (Papers in International Studies: Latin America Ser.: No. 10). 128p. (Orig.). reprint ed. pap. 39.70 (*0-7837-6472-3*, 204647600001) Bks Demand.

— Rural Guatemala, 1760-1940. LC 93-27405. xii, 450p. 1994. 49.50 (*0-8047-2318-4*) Stanford U Pr.

Mccreery, David. Rural Guatemala, 1760-1940. 1996. pap. text 18.95 (*0-8047-2792-9*) Stanford U Pr.

***McCreery, David.** The Sweat of Their Brow: A History of Work in Latin America. (Latin American Realities Ser.). (Illus.). 224p. 2000. text 61.95 (*0-7656-0207-5*) M E Sharpe.

McCreery, Elaine. Worship in the Primary School. (Roehampton Teaching Studies). 144p. 1993. pap. 29.00 (*1-85346-233-0*, Pub. by David Fulton) Taylor & Francis.

***McCreery, John.** Japanese Consumer Behaviour: From Worker Bees to Wary Shoppers. LC 99-49175. (Consumasian Ser.). (Illus.). 216p. 2000. text 37.00 (*0-8248-2315-X*); pap. text 19.95 (*0-8248-2316-8*) UH Pr.

McCreery, Kathleen, jt. auth. see Stourac, Richard.

***McCreery, Patrick.** Out Front. 150p. 2000. pap. 12.00 (*0-8223-6476-X*) Duke.

McCreery, Patrick, jt. ed. see Krupat, Kitty.

***McCreery, Richard L.** Raman Spectroscopy for Chemical Analysis. LC 99-86491. 448p. 2000. 99.95 (*0-471-25287-5*) Wiley.

McCreesh, Thomas P. Biblical Sound & Sense: Poetic Sound Patterns in Proverbs 10-29. (JSOT Supplement Ser.: No. 128). 164p. (C). 1991. 52.50 (*1-85075-326-1*, Pub. by Sheffield Acad) CUP Services.

***McCreesh, Thomas P.** Proverbs. (Berit Olam (The Everlasting Covenant) Ser.). 2000. 0.00 (*0-8146-5071-6*) Liturgical Pr.

McCreight, Brenda. Recognizing & Managing Children with Fetal Alcohol Syndrome - Fetal Alcohol Effects: A Guidebook. LC 97-9039. 1997. pap. 16.95 (*0-87868-607-X*) Child Welfare.

McCreight, Dan J., et al. Short Staple Yarn Manufacturing. LC 97-68959. 552p. 1997. 75.00 (*0-89089-853-7*) Carolina Acad Pr.

***McCreight, Dan J., et al.** Short Staple Yarn Spinner's Handbook. LC 99-66995. 1999. spiral bd. 40.00 (*0-89089-897-9*) Carolina Acad Pr.

McCreight, John L. Making Membership Meaningful. LC 93-73487. 1994. pap. 6.95 (*1-55673-582-0*, 7981) CSS OH.

McCreight, Robert G. The Psalms Were Made for Lent: Six Sermons & Worship Services. LC 95-39883. 66p. (Orig.). 1996. pap. 7.95 (*0-7880-0565-0*) CSS OH.

McCreight, Tim. Boxes & Lockets: Metalsmithing Techniques. (Illus.). 144p. text. write for info. (*90-5703-682-7*, Pub. by Craftsman House) Gordon & Breach.

McCreight, Tim. The Complete Metalsmith: An Illustrated Handbook. rev. ed. LC 81-66573. (Illus.). 208p. (Orig.). 1991. spiral bd. 14.95 (*0-87192-240-1*) Davis Mass.

— Custom Knifemaking: Ten Projects from a Master Craftsman. LC 85-2844. (Illus.). 224p. (Orig.). 1985. pap. 17.95 (*0-8117-2175-2*) Stackpole.

— Design Language. 192p. (C). 1997. 8.95 (*0-9615984-6-8*) Brynmorgen.

— Jewelry: Fundamentals of Metalsmithing. (Illus.). 144p. 1997. 29.99 (*1-880140-29-2*) GUILDcom.

***McCreight, Tim.** Jewelry: Fundamentals of Metalsmithing. (Illus.). 144p. 1998. text. write for info. (*90-5703-162-0*, Harwood Acad Pubs) Gordon & Breach.

McCreight, Tim. The Metalsmith's Book of Boxes & Lockets. (Illus.). 1999. 29.99 (*0-9658248-9-6*) GUILDcom.

— Practical Jewelry Rendering. (Illus.). 96p. (C). 1993. pap. text 24.95 (*0-9615984-1-7*) Brynmorgen.

McCreight, Tim, ed. Metals Technic: A Collection of Techniques for Metalsmiths. 151p. 1997. pap. 17.95 (*0-9615984-7-6*) Brynmorgen.

***McCreight, Tim & Bsullak, Nicole.** Color on Metal: 50 Exceptional Works from Jewelers & Metal Artists. (Illus.). 128p. 2001. 27.99 (*1-893164-06-3*, Pub. by GUILDcom) F & W Pubns Inc.

McCrery, Nigel. Silent Witness. LC 98-16364. 320p. 1998. 23.95 (*0-312-18178-7*, Thomas Dunne) St Martin.

***McCrery, Nigel.** Silent Witness. large type ed. 344p. 1999. 31.99 (*0-7089-9116-5*) Ulverscroft.

McCrery, Nigel. The Spider's Web. LC 98-51199. 1999. text 22.95 (*0-312-20017-X*) St Martin.

McCrickard-Benas, Mary A. Dancing with God Through the Evening of Life. 1996. write for info. (*0-9648448-2-6*) CMJ Marian Pubs.

McCrickard, Eleanor F., jt. auth. see Gianturco, Carolyn.

McCrickard, Francis. The Boy & the Book: A Story of Early Christian Ireland. 104p. 1989. pap. 30.00 (*1-85390-018-4*, Pub. by Veritas Pubns) St Mut.

— Faith Questions: Helping Young Adults Develop Their Faith. 126p. 1989. pap. 30.00 (*1-85390-097-4*, Pub. by Veritas Pubns) St Mut.

McCrie, Robert D. Security Letter Source Book, 1993. 450p. 1992. pap. 84.95 (*0-9609820-4-3*) Buttrwrth-Heinemann.

McCrie, Robert D., ed. Security Letter Source Book: A Reference Directory of Leading Services. 6th ed. (Orig.). 1997. pap. write for info. (*0-614-30062-2*) Security Let.

— Security Letter Source Book, 1993. abr. ed. 416p. 1990. pap. 75.00 (*0-9609820-3-5*) Security Let.

McCrie, Thomas. The Early Years of John Calvin: A Fragment, 1509-1536. LC 83-45622. reprint ed. 32.50 (*0-404-19840-6*) AMS Pr.

— History of the Progress & Suppression of the Reformation in Italy. LC 72-1006. reprint ed. 47.50 (*0-404-04118-3*) AMS Pr.

— Life of John Knox. LC 83-45584. (Illus.). reprint ed. 57.50 (*0-404-19902-X*) AMS Pr.

***McCright, Grady E.** Engineering Economy. 2nd ed. 178p. 1999. pap. text 13.00 (*0-536-02411-1*) Pearson Custom.

McCright, Grady E. & Powell, James H. Jessie Evans: Lincoln County Badman. LC 83-20902. (Early West Ser.). (Illus.). 239p. 1983. 21.95 (*0-932702-28-7*); pap. 10.95 (*0-932702-30-9*) Creative Texas.

McCrillis, Neal R. The British Conservative Party in the Age of Universal Suffrage: Popular Conservatism, 1918-1929. LC 97-17141. 314p. 1998. text 45.00 (*0-8142-0771-5*, MCCCON) Ohio St U Pr.

McCrimmon, Barbara. Richard Garnett: The Scholar As Librarian. LC 89-297. (ACRL Publications in Librarianship: No. 46). (Illus.). 224p. 1989. reprint ed. pap. 69.50 (*0-7837-9685-4*, 206041400005) Bks Demand.

McCrimmon, Ian. Big Bang Theory - or Rotating Universe? (C). 1992. text 25.00 (*0-9514698-7-8*, Pub. by Cosmatom) St Mut.

— The Body & the Spirit. (C). 1992. text 40.00 (*0-9514698-6-X*, Pub. by Cosmatom) St Mut.

— Flying Saucers: The Alternation of Space & Time. (C). 1992. text 25.00 (*1-874686-02-5*, Pub. by Cosmatom) St Mut.

— Imaginary Time: Journeys in Space Faster Than Light. (C). 1992. text 19.00 (*1-874686-03-3*, Pub. by Cosmatom) St Mut.

— Mass & Antimass (Positive & Negative Mass) in Five Dimensions. (C). 1992. text 19.00 (*1-874686-01-7*, Pub. by Cosmatom) St Mut.

— The Nature of the Fifth Dimension: De Revolutionibus Orbium Rotantium. 512p. (C). 1990. text 195.00 (*0-9514698-0-0*, Pub. by Cosmatom) St Mut.

— Proof of God. (C). 1992. text 19.00 (*0-9514698-5-1*, Pub. by Cosmatom) St Mut.

— The Strange Case of the Disapparing Antiproton. (C). 1992. text 19.00 (*0-9514698-9-4*, Pub. by Cosmatom) St Mut.

— TCP Invariance & Charge Quantization: Anti-Hydrogen & the Fifth Dimension. (C). 1992. pap. 35.00 (*0-9514698-8-6*, Pub. by Cosmatom) St Mut.

— Twelve Questions for Theologians. (C). 1992. text 59.95 (*0-9514698-1-9*, Pub. by Cosmatom) St Mut.

— Twenty Questions for Scientists. (C). 1992. text 40.00 (*0-9514698-2-7*, Pub. by Cosmatom) St Mut.

— The Unity in the Trinity. (C). 1992. text 30.00 (*0-9514698-4-3*, Pub. by Cosmatom) St Mut.

— A Whirling Mass of Space - Time. (C). 1992. text 60.00 (*1-874686-00-9*, Pub. by Cosmatom) St Mut.

McCrimmon, James M. Writing with a Purpose. 6th ed. 1976. text 10.95 (*0-685-42615-7*) HM.

McCrimmon, Mitch. Unleash the Enterpreneur Within: How to Make Everyone an Enterpreneur & Stay Efficient. LC 95-223594. 240p. 1995. 29.95 (*0-273-61456-8*, Pub. by F T P-H) Natl Bk Netwk.

McCrindle, J. W. Ancient India: As Described by in Classical Literature Being a Collection of Greek & Latin. 246p. 1974. 25.00 (*1-55528-085-4*, Pub. by Today Tomorrow) Scholarly Pubns.

— Ancient India: As Described by Ktesias the Knidian. reprint ed. 25.00 (*1-55528-062-5*, Pub. by Today Tomorrow) Scholarly Pubns.

— Ancient India: As Described by Megasthenes & Arriyan. 315p. 1972. reprint ed. 30.00 (*0-88065-158-X*) Scholarly Pubns.

— Ancient India: As Described by Ptolemy. Jain, Ramachandra, ed. 450p. 1985. 25.00 (*1-55528-034-X*, Pub. by Today Tomorrow) Scholarly Pubns.

— Ancient India: As Desribed by Arrian Q. Curtius, Diodorus, Plutarch & Justin in "Invasion of India by Alexander the Great" 470p. 1973. reprint ed. 25.00 (*0-88065-159-8*) Scholarly Pubns.

***McCrindle, John W.** Ancient India as Described by Megasthenes & Arrian. 2nd ed. (Illus.). 2000. reprint ed. 29.50 (*81-215-0948-3*, Pub. by M Manoharial) S Asia.

— Ancient India as Described by Ptolemy. 2nd ed. 2000. reprint ed. 37.50 (*81-215-0945-9*, Pub. by M Manoharial) S Asia.

McCrindle, John W. Ancient India As Described in Classical Literature. 247p. reprint ed. text 28.50 (*0-685-13414-8*) Coronet Bks.

McCririe, Philip G., jt. auth. see Alperin, Barry J.

McCrohan, Donna. Archie & Edith, Mike & Gloria: The Tumultuous History of "All in the Family" LC 87-42743. (Illus.). 280p. 1988. pap. 7.95 (*0-89480-527-4*, 1527) Workman Pub.

— The Honeymooners' Companion. LC 77-93033. (Illus.). 224p. 1978. pap. 7.95 (*0-89480-022-1*, 175) Workman Pub.

McCrone. Housing Policy in Britain & Europe. 256p. 1995. 79.00 (*1-85728-410-0*, Pub. by UCL Pr Ltd); pap. 29.95 (*1-85728-411-9*, Pub. by UCL Pr Ltd) Taylor & Francis.

McCrone, David. Sociological Revolution: From the Enlightenment to the Global Age. LC 98-23813. (International Library of Sociology Ser.). 248p. (C). (gr. 13). 1998. 85.00 (*0-415-02920-1*) Routledge.

— The Sociology of Nationalism: Tomorrow's Ancestors. LC 98-9523. (International Library of Sociology Ser.). 224p. (C). 1998. 75.00 (*0-415-11459-4*); pap. 24.99 (*0-415-11460-8*) Routledge.

McCrone, David, et al. Scotland the Brand: The Heritage Industry. 160p. 1995. pap. 22.00 (*0-7486-0615-7*, Pub. by Edinburgh U Pr) Col U Pr.

McCrone, David, jt. ed. see Brown, Alice.

Mccrone, David, jt. ed. see Kendrick, Stephen.

McCrone, Gavin. Scotland's Future: An Essay on the Economics of Nationalism. LC 71-92501. 111p. 1969. 24.95 (*0-678-06252-8*) Kelley.

McCrone, Guy. Aunt Bel. 240p. 1994. pap. 13.95 (*1-873631-39-1*, Pub. by B&W Pub) Firebird Dist.

— The Hayburn Family. 244p. 1996. pap. 16.95 (*1-873631-58-8*, Pub. by B&W Pub) Firebird Dist.

— Wax Fruit: Antimacassar City, The Philistines, The Puritans. 618p. 1993. pap. 19.95 (*1-873631-21-9*, Pub. by B&W Pub) Firebird Dist.

McCrone, Ian. Make Money Freelance News Writing. 1997. pap. text 15.95 (*0-86417-788-7*) Seven Hills Bk.

McCrone, John. The Ape That Spoke. 288p. 1992. pap. 10.00 (*0-380-71399-3*, Avon Bks) Morrow Avon.

McCrone, Kathleen E. Playing the Game: Sport & the Physical Emancipation of English Women, 1870-1914. LC 87-32038. (Illus.). 336p. 1988. 37.50 (*0-8131-1641-4*) U Pr of Ky.

— Sport & the Physical Emancipation of English Women, 1870-1914. LC 88-733. (Illus.). 320p. reprint ed. pap. 99.20 (*0-608-20363-7*, 207161600002) Bks Demand.

***McCrone, Walter.** Judgment Day for the Shroud of Turin. LC 98-51679. (Illus.). 365p. 1999. 34.95 (*1-57392-679-5*) Prometheus Bks.

McCrone, Walter, et al, eds. Scientific Detection of Fakery in Art, Vol. 3315. LC 98-227309. 112p. 1998. 48.00 (*0-8194-2755-1*) SPIE.

McCrone, Walter C. Asbestos Identification. LC 86-61873. (Illus.). 1987. 59.50 (*0-904962-11-3*) Microscope Pubns.

— Judgement Day for the Turin Shroud. LC 96-94693. (Illus.). 1996. 36.00 (*0-904962-15-6*) Microscope Pubns.

McCrone, Walter C., et al. Polarized Light Microscopy. 8th ed. LC 78-61047. (Illus.). 1979. 39.50 (*0-250-40262-9*) Microscope Pubns.

McCrorey, Dolores, jt. auth. see McCrorey, Helen.

McCrorey, Helen & McCrorey, Dolores. The Business of Family Day Care. LC 87-61785. 128p. (Orig.). 1988. pap. 12.95 (*0-915677-35-0*) Roundtable Pub.

McCrorie, Edward. Needle Man. (Chestnut Hills Ser.). (Illus.). 80p. 1998. pap. 10.00 (*0-932616-64-X*) Brick Hse Bks.

McCrorie, Edward, tr. see Virgil.

McCrory, DL Grace... It's Amazing - LDR. 48p. 1997. pap., teacher ed. 5.35 (*1-56212-255-X*) CRC Pubns.

— Grandmother's Tale. (Illus.). (J). 1995. 13.95 (*1-85430-045-8*); 13.95 (*1-85430-047-4*); 13.95 (*1-85430-048-2*); 13.95 (*1-85430-049-0*); 13.95 (*1-85430-051-2*) Magi Pubns.

McCrory, C. Elizabeth, ed. see Wolff, James A., et al.

McCrory, Clint. Geometry & Topology: Manifold, Varieties & Knots. Shifrin, Theodore, ed. (Lecture Notes in Pure & Applied Mathematics Ser.: Vol. 105). (Illus.). 368p. 1986. pap. text 155.00 (*0-8247-7621-6*) Dekker.

McCrory, David E. Liquor Licenses: A Guide to California Retail Alcoholic Beverage Licensing. LC 86-83036. (Illus.). 186p. (Orig.). 1987. pap. 29.95 (*0-9617755-0-5*) Full Ct Pr CA.

McCrory, Elliot S., ed. Accelerator Instrumentation. LC 91-55347. (AIP Conference Proceedings Ser., Subseries: Particle & Fields: No. 229, 44). 304p. 1991. lib. bdg. 85.00 (*0-88318-832-5*) Am Inst Physics.

McCrory, K. C., ed. see Bendis, Brian Michael.

McCrory, Martin & Moulder, Robert. French Revolution for Beginners. 12.95 (*0-318-00805-X*) Writers & Readers.

— French Revolution for Beginners. (Illus.). 192p. pap. 7.95 (*0-86316-015-8*) Writers & Readers.

McCrory, R. H. Lock, Stock & Barrel. 1992. reprint ed. 8.95 (*0-913150-68-1*) Pioneer Pr.

— Make Muzzleloader Accessories Top. 1971. 6.00 (*0-913150-67-3*) Pioneer Pr.

— The Modern Kentucky Rifle. 1990. reprint ed. 8.95 (*0-913150-66-5*) Pioneer Pr.

McCrory, Rosemary & Ourth, John. Art-Favorite All-Time Projects. 64p. (J). (gr. k-6). Date not set. 8.99 (*0-916456-53-6*, GA111) Good Apple.

McCrory, Wallace W. Developmental Nephrology. LC 72-75399. (Commonwealth Fund Publications). (Illus.). 230p. 1972. 35.95 (*0-674-20275-9*) HUP.

M

McCroskey, Alfred. Bibles for Russia. LC 98-65159. (Illus.). 150p. 1998. pap. 10.00 (*1-57502-731-3*, PO2043) Morris Pubng.

McCroskey, Jack. Answering the Phone for Colorado's Future: Should Technology & Markets or Bureaucracy & Controls Take the Call? 10p. 1987. pap. text 8.00 (*1-57655-021-4*) Independ Inst.

— How to Cut Fares to the New Airport. (Issue Papers: No. 16-93). 7p. 1993. pap. text 8.00 (*1-57655-071-0*) Independ Inst.

McCroskey, Jack & Hall, Lowell. The Tourism Tax: Are the Taxpayers Being Taken for a Ride? (Issue Papers: No. 19-93). 8p. 1993. pap. text 8.00 (*1-57655-069-9*) Independ Inst.

McCroskey, Jacquelyn & Meezan, William. Family Preservation & Family Functioning. LC 97-8593. 400p. 1997. pap. 16.95 (*0-87868-614-2*) Child Welfare.

McCroskey, Jacquelyn D. & Einbinder, Susan, eds. Universities & Communities: Remaking Professional & Interprofessional Education for the Next Century. LC 97-33000. 336p. 1998. 65.00 (*0-275-95849-3*, Praeger Pubs) Greenwood.

McCroskey, James C. An Introduction to Rhetorical Communication: Instructor's Manual with Tests. 7th ed. (C). 1997. pap. text, teacher ed. write for info. (*0-205-27298-3*, T7298-7) Allyn.

— Maclopedia: The Macintosh Hardware & Software Compendium. 1990. pap. 24.95 (*0-13-541947-6*) P-H.

McCroskey, James C., et al, eds. Communication & Personality: Trait Perspectives. LC 98-3065. (Communication Ser.). 336p. (C). 1998. text 69.50 (*1-57273-179-6*); pap. text 26.50 (*1-57273-180-X*) Hampton Pr NJ.

McCroskey, James C. & Daly, John A., eds. Personality & Interpersonal Communication. (Series in Interpersonal Communication: Vol. 6). 288p. 1987. text 52.00 (*0-8039-2645-6*); pap. text 24.50 (*0-8039-2646-4*) Sage.

McCroskey, James C. & Richmond, Virginia P. Fundamentals of Human Communication: An Interpersonal Perspective. LC 96-136829. (Illus.). 324p. (C). 1995. pap. text 25.95 (*0-88133-855-9*) Waveland Pr.

— Workbook to Accompany Fundamentals of Human Communication: An Interpersonal Perspective. 331p. (C). 1995. pap. text 18.95 (*0-88133-856-7*) Waveland Pr.

McCroskey, James C. & Richmond, Virginia P., eds. Quiet Children & the Classroom Teacher. 2nd ed. 60p. 1991. pap. 9.50 (*0-927516-27-6*) Natl Comm Assn.

McCroskey, James C., jt. auth. see Richmond, Virginia P.

McCroskey, James C., jt. ed. see Daly, John A.

McCroskey, James C., jt. ed. see Richmond, Virginia P.

McCroskey, Mona L., ed. Summer Sojourn to the Grand Canyon: The 1898 Diary of Zella Dysart. LC 96-75066. (Illus.). 108p. (Orig.). 1996. pap. 9.95 (*0-9651067-0-5*) HollyBear Pr.

McCroskey, Mona L., jt. compiled by see Shaw, Harley G.

McCrosky, Marilyn. Cataloging Nonbook Materials with AACR2R & MARC: A Guide for the School Library Media Specialist. 75p. 1994. 20.00 (*0-8389-7736-7*) ALA.

McCrossan, Hugh M. Revenue Law. 420p. 1996. pap. 125.00 (*0-7510-0785-4*, Pub. by HLT Pubns) St Mut.

***McCrossan, John Anthony.** Books & Reading in the Lives of Notable Americans: A Biographical Sourcebook. LC 99-45598. 288p. 2000. 49.95 (*0-313-30376-2*) Greenwood.

McCrossan, T. J. Bodily Healing & the Atonement. 1982. pap. 5.95 (*0-89276-505-4*) Faith Lib Pubns.

***McCrossen, Alexis.** Holy Day, Holiday: The American Sunday. LC 99-55042. (Illus.). 240p. 2000. 35.00 (*0-8014-3417-3*) Cornell U Pr.

McCrossin, G. Michael. Broken Rainbows: Growing Faith in a Changing World. LC 96-53402. 192p. (Orig.). 1997. pap. 10.95 (*1-55612-913-0*, LI1913) Sheed & Ward WI.

McCrosskey, jt. auth. see Richmond.

McCrudden, Christopher. Anti-Discrimination Law 2nd Series. 185.95 (*0-7546-2011-5*) Ashgate Pub Co.

McCrudden, Christopher, ed. Anti-Discrimination Law. (International Library of Essays in Law & Legal Theory). 484p. (C). 1991. lib. bdg. 150.00 (*0-8147-5466-X*) NYU Pr.

— Regulation & Deregulation: Policy & Practice in the Utilities & Financial Services Industries. (Law Colloguium Ser.). 450p. 1999. text 100.00 (*0-19-826881-5*) OUP.

McCrudden, Christopher & Chambers, Gerald, eds. Individual Rights & the Law in Britain. 724p. 1995. pap. text 38.00 (*0-19-826022-9*) OUP.

McCrudden, Christopher, jt. ed. see Baldwin, Robert.

McCrudden, John & Avenoso, Ellen, eds. The Long Island Job Source. 80p. (Orig.). 1989. pap. 4.95 (*0-9623212-0-6*) LIU SC.

— The Long Island Job Source. rev. ed. 125p. (Orig.). 1990. pap. text 4.95 (*0-9623212-1-4*) LIU SC.

McCrum, Carolyn, jt. auth. see Aylmer, Ursula.

McCrum, Elizabeth. Fabric & Form: Irish Fashion since 1950. LC 98-111593. (Illus.). 160p. 1997. pap. 30.95 (*0-7509-1286-3*, Pub. by Sutton Pub Ltd) Intl Pubs Mktg.

McCrum, I., jt. auth. see Cahill, S. J.

***McCrum, Mark.** The Craic. 1999. pap. 15.95 (*0-7538-0836-6*, Pub. by Phoenix Hse) Trafalgar.

McCrum, N. G. Anelastic & Dielectric Effects in Polymeric Solids. xv, 617p. 1991. pap. 15.95 (*0-486-66752-9*) Dover.

McCrum, N. G., et al. Principles of Polymer Engineering. 2nd ed. LC 97-12589. (Illus.). 462p. 1997. text 95.00 (*0-19-856527-5*); pap. text 44.95 (*0-19-856526-7*) OUP.

McCrum, R. C. Dear Mom: World War II Remembered in a Sailor's Letters. LC 94-61069. (Illus.). 210p. 1994. pap. 19.95 (*0-89101-083-1*) U Maine Pr.

McCrum, Robert. My Year Off: Recovering Life after a Stroke. LC 99-27259. 256p. 1999. pap. 13.00 (*0-7679-0400-1*) Bantam.

— My Year Off: Rediscovering Life after a Stroke. LC 98-29629. 224p. 1998. 23.95 (*0-393-04656-7*) Norton.

— My Year Off: Rediscovering Life after a Stroke. large type ed. LC 99-18677. 285p. 1999. write for info. (*0-7838-8584-9*, G K Hall & Co) Mac Lib Ref.

McCrum, Robert, et al. The Story of English. rev. ed. (Illus.). 384p. 1993. pap. 24.95 (*0-14-015405-1*, Penguin Bks) Viking Penguin.

McCrumb, Sharyn. The Ballad of Frankie Silver. large type ed. LC 98-34895. (Large Print Book Ser.). 1998. 26.95 (*1-56895-656-8*) Wheeler Pub.

***McCrumb, Sharyn.** The Ballad of Frankie Silver. 416p. 1999. reprint ed. mass mkt. 7.50 (*0-451-19739-9*, Sig) NAL.

McCrumb, Sharyn. Bimbos of the Death Sun. 212p. 1997. mass mkt. 5.99 (*0-345-41215-X*) Ballantine Pub Grp.

— Foggy Mountain Breakdown & Other Stories. 1998. pap. 6.99 (*0-345-41494-2*) Ballantine Pub Grp.

— Foggy Mountain Breakdown & Other Stories. large type ed. LC 97-38875. 428p. 1998. 27.95 (*0-7838-8360-9*, G K Hall & Co) Mac Lib Ref.

— The Hangman's Beautiful Daughter: A Novel of Suspense. 288p. 1992. text 19.00 (*0-684-19407-4*, Scribners Ref) Mac Lib Ref.

— The Hangman's Beautiful Daughter: A Novel of Suspense. 384p. 1993. mass mkt. 7.50 (*0-451-40370-3*, Onyx) NAL.

McCrumb, Sharyn. The Hangman's Beautiful Daughter: A Novel of Suspense. 1992. 12.09 (*0-606-06147-9*, Pub. by Turtleback) Demco.

McCrumb, Sharyn. The Hangman's Beautiful Daughter: A Novel of Suspense. large type ed. LC 96-41032. 1996. lib. bdg. 23.95 (*1-57490-069-2*, Beeler LP Bks) T T Beeler.

— Highland Laddie Gone. (Mysteries Around the World Promotion Ser.). 1999. mass mkt. 5.99 (*0-345-36036-2*) Ivy Books.

— If Ever I Return, Pretty Peggy-O. 1991. mass mkt. 6.99 (*0-345-36906-8*) Ballantine Pub Grp.

— If Ever I Return, Pretty Peggy-O. 1998. mass mkt. 6.99 (*0-345-91352-3*) Ballantine Pub Grp.

— If I'd Killed Him When I Met Him... Date not set. pap. write for info. (*0-449-22537-2*) Fawcett.

— If I'd Killed Him When I Met Him... 288p. 1996. mass mkt. 6.50 (*0-449-14998-6*) Fawcett.

— If I'd Killed Him When I Met Him... large type ed. LC 97-24406. (Wheeler Large Print Book Ser.). 1997. pap. 23.95 (*1-56895-472-7*) Wheeler Pub.

***McCrumb, Sharyn.** Lovely in Her Bones. 1999. 5.99 (*0-345-91574-7*) Ballantine Pub Grp.

— Lovely in Her Bones. large type ed. LC 00-22871. 2000. pap. 22.95 (*1-56895-859-5*) Wheeler Pub.

McCrumb, Sharyn. Lovely in Her Bones. 224p. 1999. reprint ed. mass mkt. 5.99 (*0-345-36035-4*) Ballantine Pub Grp.

— MacPherson's Lament. (Elizabeth MacPherson Ser.). 1993. mass mkt. 6.99 (*0-345-38474-1*) Ballantine Pub Grp.

***McCrumb, Sharyn.** Missing Susan. 2000. mass mkt. 6.99 (*0-345-91578-X*) Ballantine Pub Grp.

McCrumb, Sharyn. Missing Susan. large type ed. LC 92-46703. (General Ser.). 408p. 1993. pap. 18.95 (*0-8161-5566-6*, G K Hall Lrg Type) Mac Lib Ref.

— Missing Susan. 1992. reprint ed. mass mkt. 5.99 (*0-345-37945-4*) Ballantine Pub Grp.

— Official Code of Georgia. annot. ed. write for info. (*0-614-05934-8*, MICHIE) LEXIS Pub.

— Paying the Piper. 1999. mass mkt. 5.99 (*0-345-34518-5*) Ballantine Pub Grp.

***McCrumb, Sharyn.** Paying the Piper. 1999. 5.99 (*0-345-91576-3*) Ballantine Pub Grp.

— The PMS Outlaws. Vol. 9. 304p. 2000. 24.00 (*0-345-38231-5*, Ballantine) Ballantine Pub Grp.

McCrumb, Sharyn. The Rosewood Casket. 303p. 1998. text 24.00 (*0-7881-5352-8*) DIANE Pub.

— The Rosewood Casket. 432p. 1997. mass mkt. 7.50 (*0-451-18471-8*, Sig) NAL.

— She Walks These Hills. 447p. 1995. mass mkt. 7.50 (*0-451-18472-6*, Sig) NAL.

— She Walks These Hills. 320p. 1994. 21.00 (*0-684-19556-9*) S&S Trade.

— She Walks These Hills. large type ed. LC 96-31684. (Large Print Bks.). 1996. 24.95 (*1-56895-357-7*, Compass) Wheeler Pub.

— Sick of Shadows. LC 84-90802. 240p. 1999. mass mkt. 5.99 (*0-345-35653-5*) Ballantine Pub Grp.

***McCrumb, Sharyn.** Sick of Shadows. 1999. 5.99 (*0-345-91573-9*) Ballantine Pub Grp.

— Sick of Shadows. large type ed. LC 99-57454. (Basic Ser.). 344p. 2000. 29.95 (*0-7862-2370-7*) Thorndike Pr.

— Songcatcher. 2001. 24.95 (*0-525-94488-5*, Dutt) Dutton Plume.

McCrumb, Sharyn. The Windsor Knot. 1992. mass mkt. 5.99 (*0-345-36427-9*) Ballantine Pub Grp.

***McCrumb, Sharyn.** The Windsor Knot. 2000. mass mkt. 6.50 (*0-345-91577-1*) Ballantine Pub Grp.

McCrumb, Sharyn. Zombies of the Gene Pool. 1993. mass mkt. 5.99 (*0-345-37914-4*) Ballantine Pub Grp.

McCrumb, Sharyn, ed. Malice Domestic Vol. 7: An Anthology of Original Traditional Mystery Stories. 256p. 1998. mass mkt. 5.99 (*0-380-79406-3*, Avon Bks) Morrow Avon.

McCrumb, Sharyn & Helper, Mona W. Our Separate Days. LC 89-10584. (Illus.). 114p. (Orig.). 1989. reprint ed. pap. 9.95 (*0-926487-01-9*) Rowan Mtn Pr.

McCrummen, Pat, jt. ed. see Unmacht, Robert.

McCrystle, Michael J., jt. auth. see Poland, James M.

McCuaig, Katherine. The Weariness, the Fever & the Fret: The Campaign Against Tuberculosis in Canada, 1900-1950. pap. 24.95 (*0-7735-1875-4*) McG-Queens Univ Pr.

— The Weariness, the Fever & the Fret: The Campaign Against Tuberculosis in Canada, 1900-1950. (Illus.). 416p. 55.00 (*0-7735-1833-9*) McG-Queens Univ Pr.

McCuaig, William. Carlo Sigonio: The Changing World of the Late Renaissance. LC 89-30402. 394p. 1989. reprint ed. pap. 122.20 (*0-608-06473-4*, 206677000009) Bks Demand.

McCuaig, William, tr. see Chabod, Federico.

McCuaig, William, tr. see Frugoni, Chiara.

McCuaig, William, tr. see Gobetti, Piero.

McCuan, Walter R., jt. ed. see Markley, Oliver W.

McCubbin. Mediapractice: A Media Skills Book. 1991. pap. text. write for info. (*0-582-87133-6*, Pub. by Addison-Wesley) Longman.

McCubbin, Bob. Roots of Lesbian & Gay Oppression: A Marxist View. 1993. pap. 7.95 (*0-89567-116-6*) World View Forum.

McCubbin, Chris. GURPS Magic Items 1: Sorcerous Shops Stocked With a Multitude of Mighty Magics. Blankenship, Loyd, ed. (Illus.). 128p. 1997. pap. 19.95 (*1-55634-190-3*, Pub. by S Jackson Games) BookWorld.

McCubbin, Chris. Wing Commander Armada Playtesters' Guide. (Illus.). 96p. (Orig.). 1994. pap. 14.95 (*0-929373-23-5*) Origin Syst.

McCubbin, Chris, et al. GURP'S Martial Arts Adventures: Hard-Hitting Scenarios for GURPS Martial Arts. Koke, Jeff & Stephens, Monica, eds. (Illus.). 128p. 1992. pap., suppl. ed. 19.95 (*1-55634-249-7*, 6127) S Jackson Games.

— The Wing Commander Confederation Handbook. LC 99-207580. (Illus.). 128p. 1999. pap. 19.95 (*0-06-107553-1*) HarpC.

McCubbin, Chris, jt. auth. see Jackson, Steve, Games Staff.

McCubbin, Chris, ed. see Pulver, David.

McCubbin, Hamilton I. Resiliency in African-American Families. LC 98-9024. (Resiliency in Families Ser.). 357p. 1998. 65.00 (*0-7619-1392-0*); pap. 29.95 (*0-7619-1393-9*) Sage.

— Resiliency in Native American & Immigrant Families. LC 98-9023. (Resiliency in Families Ser.). 454p. 1998. 67.50 (*0-7619-1398-X*); pap. 33.95 (*0-7619-1399-8*) Sage.

— Stress, Coping, & Health in Families: Sense of Coherence & Resiliency. LC 98-9082. (Resiliency in Families Ser.). 336p. 1998. 36.00 (*0-7619-1396-3*); pap. 17.99 (*0-7619-1397-1*) Sage.

***McCubbin, Hamilton I., et al, eds.** The Dynamics of Resilient Families. LC 99-6191. (Resiliency in Families Ser.: Vol. 4). 279p. 1999. 74.95 (*0-7619-1390-4*) Sage.

McCubbin, Hamilton I., et al, eds. Family Assessment: Resiliency, Coping & Adaptation - Inventories for Research & Practice. LC 95-61517. 700p. (C). 1996. text 50.00 (*0-9639334-5-0*) U of Wis CEFM.

— Family Assessment: Resiliency, Coping & Adaptation Inventories for Research & Practice. 400p. (Orig.). (C). 1995. pap. text 40.00 (*0-9639334-1-8*) U of Wis CEFM.

— Resiliency in Ethnic Minority Families: African American Families, Vol. 2. LC 94-61816. 350p. (Orig.). (C). 1995. pap. text 30.00 (*0-9639334-3-4*) U of Wis CEFM.

— Resiliency in Ethnic Minority Families: Native & Immigrant American Families, Vol. 1. 453p. (Orig.). 1994. pap. text 30.00 (*0-9639334-2-6*) U of Wis CEFM.

— Sense of Coherence & Resiliency: Stress, Coping, & Health. LC 94-60612. (Resiliency & Families Ser.). 300p. (Orig.). (C). 1994. pap. write for info. (*0-9639334-0-X*) U of Wis CEFM.

— Social Stress & the Family: Advances & Developments in Family Stress Therapy & Research. LC 83-190. (Marriage & Family Review Ser.: Vol. 6, Nos. 1-2). 231p. 1983. text 49.95 (*0-86656-163-3*) Haworth Pr.

McCubbin, Hamilton I. & Figley, Charles R., eds. Stress & the Family Vol. I: Coping with Normative Transitions. LC 83-6048. (Psychosocial Stress Ser.: No. 2). 296p. 1983. text 35.95 (*0-87630-321-1*) Brunner-Mazel.

McCubbin, Hamilton I., et al. Family Stress, Coping & Social Support. (Illus.). 294p. 1982. pap. 36.95 (*0-398-06275-7*) C C Thomas.

— Family Stress, Coping & Social Support. (Illus.). 294p. (C). 1982. text 48.95 (*0-398-04692-1*) C C Thomas.

— Family Types & Strengths. 228p. (Orig.). 1988. pap. text. write for info. (*0-8087-7607-X*) Pearson Custom.

McCubbin, Hamilton I., jt. ed. see Figley, Charles R.

McCubbin, Jack H. & Fuqua, Marjorie V. The Unborn Baby Book. (Illus.). 128p. (Orig.). 1985. pap. 7.95 (*0-9615085-7-4*) Tex Med Pr.

McCubbin, Jack H. & McCubbin, Marjorie F. The Unborn Baby Book. 2nd ed. LC 85-51698. (Illus.). 144p. (Orig.). 1986. pap. 7.95 (*0-9615085-8-2*) Tex Med Pr.

McCubbin, Marjorie F., jt. auth. see McCubbin, Jack H.

McCubbin, Virginia. Oklahoma City Secrets: A Resource Guide for the Home & Garden. (Illus.). 224p. (Orig.). 1993. pap. 12.95 (*1-883554-02-0*) City Secrets.

McCubbins, Frank. Animals Tails: Fifty True Stories of Birds & Animals. (Illus.). 278p. 1997. pap. 12.00 (*1-57502-620-1*, PO1772) Morris Pubng.

McCubbins, Mathew D., ed. Under the Watchful Eye: Managing Presidential Campaigns in the Television Era. LC 92-24570. 193p. 1992. 21.95 (*0-87187-752-X*) Congr Quarterly.

McCubbins, Mathew D., jt. auth. see Cox, Gary W.

McCubbins, Mathew D., jt. auth. see Drake, Paul W.

McCubbins, Mathew D., jt. auth. see Kiewiet, D. Roderick.

McCubbins, Mathew D., jt. auth. see Lupia, Arthur.

McCubbins, Mathew D., jt. ed. see Cowhey, Peter F.

McCubbrey, Donald J. Accounting Information Systems. (C). 1996. text. write for info. (*0-03-098412-2*) Harcourt Coll Pubs.

McCubbrey, Dorie. Dr. Dorie's Don't Diet Book: A New Life Free of the Weight Loss Games. LC 98-91449. 216p. 1998. pap. 14.95 (*0-9664188-3-2*) Postve Pthways.

***McCudden, James Thomas Byford.** Flying Fury: Five Years in the Royal Flying Corps. LC 00-36359. (Greenhill Military Ser.). (Illus.). (J). 2000. pap. write for info. (*1-85367-406-0*) Stackpole.

McCue. Equine Reproduction. 1999. pap. text. write for info. (*0-7216-7686-3*, W B Saunders Co) Harcrt Hlth Sci Grp.

***McCue.** PowerPoint 97 for Windows for Dummies Quick Reference. LC T385.M377999 1998. (Illus.). 224p. 1998. spiral bd. 12.99 (*0-7645-0494-0*) IDG Bks.

McCue. Private Practice. 1991. 32.95 (*0-316-55531-2*, Little Brwn Med Div) Lppncott W & W.

McCue, Andrew G. Baseball by the Books: A History & Complete Bibliography of Baseball Fiction. 176p. 1991. ring bd. write for info. (*0-697-12764-8*) Brown & Benchmark.

McCue, C. F., et al, eds. Performance Testing of Lubricants for Automotive Engines & Transmissions. (Illus.). 811p. 1974. 99.00 (*0-85334-468-X*) Elsevier.

***McCue, Camille.** Cliffs Notes on Exploring the World with Yahoo!, Vol. 1. 128p. 1999. pap. text 8.99 (*0-7645-8525-8*, CPG Pr) IDG Bks.

— Finding What You Want on the Web. (Illus.). 128p. 2000. pap. 8.99 (*0-7645-8636-X*, CPG Pr) IDG Bks.

— PowerPoint 2000 for Windows for Dummies. LC 98-88741. (Windows for Dummies Ser.). (Illus.). 224p. 1999. spiral bd. 12.99 (*0-7645-0451-7*) IDG Bks.

McCue, Clifford P., jt. auth. see Gianakis, Gerasimos A.

McCue, Dick. Bunny's Numbers. (Animal Shape Board Bks.). (Illus.). 24p. (J). (ps). 1984. pap. 2.95 (*0-671-50944-6*) Litle Simon.

***McCue, Dick.** Bunny's Numbers. (Illus.). 14p. (J). (ps-3). 2000. 4.99 (*0-689-83086-6*) S&S Childrens.

— Ducky's Seasons. (Illus.). 14p. (J). (ps-3). 2000. pap. 4.99 (*0-689-83087-4*) Litle Simon.

McCue, Dick. Raccoon's Hide & Seek. (Animal Shape Board Bks.). (Illus.). 12p. (J). (ps). 1985. 2.95 (*0-671-55854-4*) Litle Simon.

McCue, Dick & McCue, Lisa. Puppy's Day. (Animal Shape Board Bks.). (J). (ps). 1984. pap. 2.95 (*0-671-50945-4*) Litle Simon.

***McCue, Donna & Donovan, Stacey.** Your Fate Is in Your Hands: Using the Principles of Palmistry to Change Your Life. LC 99-55093. 272p. 2000. per. 13.95 (*0-671-03877-X*, PB Trade Paper) PB.

McCue, Edward R. & Talaske, Richard H., eds. Acoustical Design of Music Education Facilities. LC 90-83693. (Illus.). 236p. 1990. pap. 26.00 (*0-88318-810-4*) Acoustical Soc Am.

McCue, Frances. The Stenographer's Breakfast. LC 91-41839. (Barnard New Women Poets Ser.). 96p. 1992. pap. 12.00 (*0-8070-6817-9*) Beacon Pr.

***McCue, Gary.** Trekking in Tibet: A Traveler's Guide. 2nd ed. (Illus.). 304p. 1999. pap. 18.95 (*0-89886-662-6*) Mountaineers.

McCue, George, ed. Music in American Society, 1776-1976. LC 76-24527. (Illus.). 201p. 1976. text 39.95 (*0-87855-209-X*); pap. text 24.95 (*0-87855-634-6*) Transaction Pubs.

McCue, George & Peters, Frank. A Guide to the Architecture of St. Louis. LC 88-9998. (Illus.). 248p. (C). 1989. pap. 19.95 (*0-8262-0679-4*) U of Mo Pr.

***McCue, Gerrie.** The Heel of the Loaf. LC 00-190715. 263p. 2000. 25.00 (*0-7388-1946-8*); pap. 18.00 (*0-7388-1947-6*) Xlibris Corp.

McCue, Greg S. Dark Knights: The New Comics in Context. LC 92-36707. 154p. (C). 49.95 (*0-7453-0662-4*, Pub. by Pluto GBR) Stylus Pub VA.

McCue, Greg S. & Bloom, Clive. Dark Knights: The New Comics in Context. LC 92-36707. 192p. (C). 1993. pap. 16.95 (*0-7453-0663-2*, Pub. by Pluto GBR) Stylus Pub VA.

McCue, Helga P., jt. auth. see Garrett, Agnes.

McCue, Helga P., jt. ed. see Garret, Agnes.

McCue, Helga P., jt. ed. see Garrett, Agnes.

McCue, Jack D., et al. Geriatric Drug Handbook for Long-Term Care. LC 92-23440. (Illus.). 216p. 1992. pap. 29.00 (*0-683-05793-6*) Lppncott W & W.

McCue, Janice H. Online Searching in Public Libraries: A Comparative Study of Performance. LC 88-18482. 288p. 1988. 29.00 (*0-8108-2171-0*) Scarecrow.

McCue, Jim. Edmund Burke & Our Present Discontents. LC 98-101780. 208p. 1997. 29.95 (*1-870626-17-6*, Pub. by Claridge Pr) Paul & Co Pubs.

McCue, Kathleen. How to Help Children Through a Parent's Serious Illness: Supportive, Practical Advice. 3rd ed. (Illus.). 240p. 1996. pap. 12.95 (*0-312-14619-1*) St Martin.

McCue, Kathleen & Bonn, Ron. How to Help Children Through a Parent's Serious Illness: Supportive Practical Advice from a Leading Child Life Specialist. 221p. 1999. reprint ed. text 19.00 (*0-7881-6160-1*) DIANE Pub.

McCue, Lisa. Babe: Fuzzytail World. LC 98-66711. (Illus.). 1998. 5.99 (*0-679-89441-1*) Random.

— Christmas Stories & Poems. LC 94-18344. (Illus.). 32p. (J). (gr. k-3). 1996. pap. 2.95 (*0-8167-3514-X*) Troll Communs.

— Christmas Stories & Poems. LC 94-18344. (Illus.). 32p. (J). (gr. k-3). 1997. lib. bdg. 16.65 (*0-8167-3597-2*) Troll Communs.

— Corduroy Goes to the Doctor. (Corduroy Ser.). (Illus.). (J). (gr. k-1). 1987. pap. 3.99 (*0-670-81495-4*, Viking Child) Peng Put Young Read.

An Asterisk (*) at the beginning of an entry indicates that the title is appearing for the first time.

— Corduroy on the Go. (Corduroy Ser.). (Illus.). (J). (gr. k-1). 1987. pap. 3.99 (*0-670-81497-0*, Viking Child) Peng Put Young Read.
— Corduroy Playtime Activity Book. (Corduroy Ser.). (Illus.). 16p. (J). (gr. k-1). 1998. 7.99 (*0-670-88028-0*) Viking Penguin.
— Corduroy's Busy Street. (Corduroy Ser.). (Illus.). (J). (gr. k-1). 1987. pap. 3.99 (*0-670-81496-2*, Viking Child) Peng Put Young Read.
— Corduroy's Busy Street & Corduroy Goes to the Doctor, 2 cass., Set. (Corduroy Ser.). (Illus.). (J). (gr. k-1). 1989. reprint ed. pap. 15.95 incl. audio (*0-87499-133-1*) Live Oak Media.
— Corduroy's Christmas. LC 92-241114. (Corduroy Ser.). (Illus.). 16p. (J). (ps-k). 1992. 10.99 (*0-670-84477-2*, Viking Child) Peng Put Young Read.
— Fuzzytail Bunny. (Chunky Shape Bks.). (Illus.). 22p. (J). (ps). 1992. 3.99 (*0-679-81721-2*, Pub. by Random Bks Yng Read) Random.
— Fuzzytail Friends Lift-&-Look Animal Book. LC 96-68920. (Great Big Flap Book Ser.). 1997. 11.99 (*0-679-88131-X*) Random.
— Jingle Bell Mice. LC 97-223901. 1997. pap. 3.50 (*0-8167-4380-0*) Troll Communs.
— Kittens Love. LC 89-61137. (Illus.). 24p. (J). (ps-1). 1990. 4.95 (*0-394-82876-3*) Random Bks Yng Read.
— Kittens Love. 24p. (J). 1999. 1.99 (*0-679-89400-4*, Pub. by Random Bks Yng Read); lib. bdg. 7.99 (*0-679-99400-9*, Pub. by Random Bks Yng Read) Random.
— The Little Chick. LC 85-63658. (Board Bks.). (Illus.). 7p. (J). (ps). 1986. 4.99 (*0-394-88017-X*, Pub. by Random Bks Yng Read) Random.
— Mama Loves. LC 98-23375. (J). 1999. 7.99 (*0-679-89462-4*); lib. bdg. 11.99 (*0-679-99462-9*) Random.
— Puppies Love. 24p. (J). 1999. 1.99 (*0-679-89470-5*) Random.
— Puppies Love. (J). 1999. lib. bdg. 7.99 (*0-679-99470-X*, Pub. by Random Bks Yng Read) Random.
McCue, Lisa. Ducky's Seasons. (Animal Shape Board Bks.). 24p. (J). (ps-2). 1983. pap. 2.95 (*0-671-45491-9*) Litle Simon.
— Kitten's Christmas. (Animal Shape Board Bks.). 24p. (J). (ps-3). 1985. pap. 2.95 (*0-671-55851-X*) Litle Simon.
— My First Mother Goose. 20p. (J). (gr. k-3). 1999. bds. 11.99 (*1-57584-254-8*, RD Childrens) Rdrs Digest.
McCue, Lisa, jt. auth. see McCue, Dick.
McCue, Lois. Learning Letters Through All Five Senses: A Language Development Activity Book. (Illus.). 76p. (Orig.). 1983. pap. 12.95 (*0-87659-106-3*) Gryphon Hse.
McCue, Margaret. Domestic Violence: A Reference Handbook. (Contemporary World Issues Ser.). 273p. 1995. lib. bdg. 39.50 (*0-87436-762-X*) ABC-CLIO.
McCue, Mary C., jt. auth. see Zoglman, Marie.
McCue, Noelle B. Moonlight Dream. (Desire Ser.). 1993. per. 2.99 (*0-373-05815-2*, 5-05815-1) Silhouette.
— Moonlight Miracle. (Desire Ser.: No. 694). 1992. per. 2.79 (*0-373-05694-X*, 5-05694-0) Harlequin Bks.
— Sueno de Luna llena (Full Moon Dream), Vol. 202. (Silhouette Deseo Ser.).Tr. of Full Moon Dream. (SPA.). 1997. per. 3.50 (*0-373-35202-6*, 1-35202-0) Harlequin Bks.
McCue, Noelle B. & Reisser, Anne N. A Valentine Sampler: Only the Present; The Face of Love, 2 bks. in 1. 368p. 1994. pap. text, mass mkt. 4.99 (*0-8439-3571-5*) Dorchester Pub Co.
McCue, Noelle B., jt. auth. see Delton, Judy.
McCue, Sarah. Internet - Force or Farce? Results of an Internet Marketing Study. 90p. 1998. pap. text 15.00 (*1-886641-01-3*) MI Small Busn.
— Trade Secrets: The Export Answer Book. 2nd ed. 1998. pap. text 25.00 (*1-886641-03-X*) MI Small Busn.
McCue, Sarah S. & Clowes, Julie. Trade Secrets: Answers to the Most Commonly Asked Exporting Questions. LC 94-37338. 200p. 1994. pap. 14.95 (*1-886641-00-5*) MI Small Busn.
McCue, Susan, ed. Specialty & Minor Crops Handbook. 2nd ed. (Illus.). 184p. 1998. pap. 35.00 (*1-879906-38-4*, 3346) ANR Pubns CA.
McCue, William P. How to Run for Public Office & Win: A Step by Step Guide. LC 95-61435. (Illus.). 92p. (Orig.). 1995. pap. 25.00 (*1-887818-00-6*) Europa Publns.
McCuen. Readings for Writers. 1994. 288.00 (*0-15-502555-4*) Harcourt Coll Pubs.
McCuen & Winkler. From Idea to Essay. 8th ed. LC 97-41771. 702p. 1997. pap. text 47.00 (*0-205-26907-9*) P-H.
McCuen, Anne K. Abstracts of Some Greenville, South Carolina, Records Concerning Black People, Free & Slave, 1791-1861, Vol. 1. LC 89-21121. 240p. 1991. 25.00 (*0-87152-440-6*) Reprint.
McCuen, Brooks, jt. auth. see Madreperla, Steven A.
McCuen, Gary E. Ecocide & Genocide in the Vanishing Forest: The Rainforest & Native People. (Ideas in Conflict Ser.). (Illus.). 133p. (YA). (gr. 7-12). 1993. lib. bdg. 15.95 (*0-86596-087-9*) G E M.
— Militarism & Global Ecology. (Ideas in Conflict Ser.). (Illus.). 134p. (YA). (gr. 7-12). 1993. lib. bdg. 15.95 (*0-86596-086-0*) G E M.
— Toxic Nightmare: Ecocide in the U. S. S. R. & Eastern Europe. Swanson, Ronald P., ed. (Ideas in Conflict Ser.). (Illus.). 134p. (YA). (gr. 7-12). 1993. lib. bdg. 15.95 (*0-86596-090-9*) G E M.
McCuen, Gary E., ed. Abortion, Violence & Extremism. (Ideas in Conflict Ser.). (Illus.). 174p. (YA). (gr. 7-12). 1997. lib. bdg. 15.95 (*0-86596-139-5*) G E M.
— Biological Terrorism & Weapons of Mass Destruction. (Ideas in Conflict Ser.). (Illus.). 174p. (YA). (gr. 9-12). 1999. text 13.95 (*0-86596-177-8*) G E M.
— Born Hooked: Poisoned in the Womb. rev. ed. (Ideas in Conflict Ser.). (Illus.). 159p. (YA). (gr. 7-12). 1994. lib. bdg. 15.95 (*0-86596-091-7*) G E M.
— Children of Violence in America. (Ideas in Conflict Ser.). (Illus.). 164p. (YA). (gr. 7-12). 1995. lib. bdg. 15.95 (*0-86596-095-X*) G E M.
— Cloning, Science & Society. (Ideas in Conflict Ser.). (Illus.). 144p. (YA). (gr. 7-12). 1998. lib. bdg. 15.95 (*0-86596-143-3*) G E M.
— The Conservative Agenda. (Ideas in Conflict Ser.). (Illus.). 167p. (YA). (gr. 7-12). 1996. lib. bdg. 15.95 (*0-86596-138-7*) G E M.
— The Death Penalty & the Disadvantaged. (Ideas in Conflict Ser.). (Illus.). 176p. (YA). (gr. 7-12). 1997. lib. bdg. 15.95 (*0-86596-140-9*) G E M.
— Doctor Assisted Suicide: And the Euthanasia Movement. 2nd rev. ed. (Ideas in Conflict Ser.). (Illus.). 178p. (YA). (gr. 8-12). 1999. text 15.95 (*0-86596-178-6*) G E M.
— Ending War Against the Earth. (Ideas in Conflict Ser.). (Illus.). 176p. (YA). (gr. 7-12). 1991. 15.95 (*0-86596-081-X*) G E M.
— Foreign Intervention & Global Security. (Ideas in Conflict Ser.). 155p. (YA). (gr. 7-12). 1995. lib. bdg. 15.95 (*0-86596-097-6*) G E M.
— Health Care & Human Values. (Ideas in Conflict Ser.). (Illus.). 180p. (YA). (gr. 7-12). 1993. lib. bdg. 15.95 (*0-86596-088-7*) G E M.
— Homosexuality & Gay Rights. (Ideas in Conflict Ser.). (Illus.). 165p. (YA). (gr. 7-12). 1994. lib. bdg. 15.95 (*0-86596-094-1*) G E M.
— Human Experimentation: When Research Is Evil. (Ideas in Conflict Ser.). (Illus.). 176p. (YA). (gr. 7-12). 1998. lib. bdg. 15.95 (*0-86596-144-1*) G E M.
— Illiteracy in America. LC 87-9151. (Ideas in Conflict Ser.). (Illus.). 152p. (YA). (gr. 7-12). 1988. lib. bdg. 15.95 (*0-86596-067-4*) G E M.
— The International Drug Trade. LC 88-62174. (Ideas in Conflict Ser.). (Illus.). 160p. (YA). (gr. 7-12). 1989. lib. bdg. 15.95 (*0-86596-071-2*) G E M.
— The Issues of Immigration: Melting Pot or Boiling Point? (Ideas in Conflict Ser.). (Illus.). 182p. (YA). (gr. 7-12). 1997. lib. bdg. 15.95 (*0-86596-141-7*) G E M.
— Manipulating Life: Debating the Genetic Revolution. (Ideas in Conflict Ser.). (Illus.). 136p. (YA). (gr. 7-12). 1985. lib. bdg. 15.95 (*0-86596-054-2*) G E M.
— The Militia Movement & Hate Groups in America. (Ideas in Conflict Ser.). (Illus.). 176p. (YA). (gr. 7-12). 1996. lib. bdg. 15.95 (*0-86596-135-2*) G E M.
— Modern Slavery & the Global Economy. (Ideas in Conflict Ser.). (Illus.). 176p. (YA). (gr. 7-12). 1998. lib. bdg. 15.95 (*0-86596-145-X*) G E M.
— The Nicaraguan Revolution. (Ideas in Conflict Ser.). (Illus.). 184p. (YA). (gr. 7-12). 1986. lib. bdg. 15.95 (*0-86596-058-5*) G E M.
— Nuclear Winter. (Ideas in Conflict Ser.). (Illus.). 140p. (YA). (gr. 7-12). 1987. lib. bdg. 15.95 (*0-86596-062-3*) G E M.
— Political Murder in Central America: Death Squads & U. S. Policies. (Ideas in Conflict Ser.). (Illus.). 136p. (YA). (gr. 7-12). 1985. lib. bdg. 15.95 (*0-86596-050-X*) G E M.
— Poor & Minority Health Care. LC 87-91953. (Ideas in Conflict Ser.). (Illus.). 202p. (YA). (gr. 7-12). 1988. lib. bdg. 15.95 (*0-86596-065-8*) G E M.
— Population & Human Survival. (Ideas in Conflict Ser.). (Illus.). 158p. (YA). (gr. 7-12). 1993. lib. bdg. 15.95 (*0-86596-089-5*) G E M.
— Protecting Water Quality. (Ideas in Conflict Ser.). 180p. (YA). (gr. 7-12). 1986. lib. bdg. 15.95 (*0-86596-056-9*) G E M.
— Secret Democracy: Civil Liberties vs. the National Security State. (Ideas in Conflict Ser.). (Illus.). 167p. (YA). (gr. 7-12). 1990. 15.95 (*0-86596-074-7*) G E M.
— Tobacco: People, Profits & Public Health. (Ideas in Conflict Ser.). (Illus.). 188p. (YA). (gr. 7-12). 1997. lib. bdg. 15.95 (*0-86596-142-5*) G E M.
— Transforming the Warfare State: Global Militarism & Economic Conversion. (Ideas in Conflict Ser.). (Illus.). 155p. (YA). (gr. 7-12). 1992. lib. bdg. 15.95 (*0-86596-083-6*) G E M.
— Treating the Mentally Disabled. (Ideas in Conflict Ser.). (Illus.). 140p. (YA). (gr. 7-12). 1988. lib. bdg. 15.95 (*0-86596-066-6*) G E M.
McCuen, Jo R. Readings for Writers. 8th ed. (C). 1994. pap. text, teacher ed. 33.75 (*0-15-502170-2*) Harcourt Coll Pubs.
— Rewriting Writing. 2nd ed. (C). 1990. pap. text, teacher ed. 3.75 (*0-15-576720-8*) Harcourt Coll Pubs.
McCuen, Jo R. & Winkler, Anthony C. Reading, Writing, & the Humanities. 750p. (C). 1991. pap. text 36.50 (*0-15-575512-9*, Pub. by Harcourt Coll Pubs) Harcourt.
— Readings for Writers. 9th ed. LC 97-71822. 880p. (C). 1997. pap. text 35.50 (*0-15-503844-3*, Pub. by Harcourt Coll Pubs) Harcourt.
— Rewriting Writing: A Rhetoric & Reader. 2nd ed. 733p. (C). 1990. teacher ed. write for info. (*0-318-67028-3*); pap. text 43.00 (*0-15-576719-4*, Pub. by Harcourt Coll Pubs) Harcourt.
— Rewriting Writing: A Rhetoric, Reader & Handbook. 2nd ed. 835p. (C). 1990. teacher ed. write for info. (*0-318-67021-6*); text 46.00 (*0-15-576721-6*, Pub. by Harcourt Coll Pubs) Harcourt.
McCuen, Jo R., jt. auth. see Wilkler, Anthony C.
McCuen, Jo R., jt. auth. see Winkler, Anthony.
McCuen, Jo R., jt. auth. see Winkler, Anthony C.
McCuen, Jo-Ray. Designs for Writing: A Brief Rhetorical Reader. 704p. (C). 1996. 23.00 (*0-02-428610-9*, Macmillan Coll) P-H.
McCuen, Jo Ray, jt. auth. see Winkler, Anthony C.
McCuen, JoRay, jt. auth. see Winkler, Anthony.
McCuen, Marnie, ed. Fat & Famine: Hunger & Debt in the Global Economy. (Ideas in Conflict Ser.). (Illus.). 128p. 2000. text 15.95 (*0-86596-183-2*) G E M.
— The Genocide Reader: The Politics of Ethnicity & Extermination. (Ideas in Conflict Ser.). (Illus.). 176p. 2000. text 15.95 (*0-86596-184-0*) G E M.
— Redesigning Creation: Debating the Genetic Revolution. (Ideas in Conflict Ser.). (Illus.). 152p. 2000. text 15.95 (*0-86596-185-9*) G E M.
— The World Environment & the Global Economy. (Ideas in Conflict Ser.). (Illus.). 182p. (YA). (gr. 9-12). 1999. text 15.95 (*0-86596-179-4*) G E M.
McCuen, R. H. & Hromadka, T. V., eds. Computational Hydrology '87: Proceedings of the First International Conference, Anaheim, CA, U.S.A., July 1987. LC 87-81446. (Illus.). 268p. (Orig.). 1987. pap. text 24.00 (*0-914055-06-2*) Lighthouse Pubns.
McCuen, Richard H. FORTRAN Programming for Civil Engineers. 1975. pap. 36.25 (*0-13-329417-X*) P-H.
— Hydrologic Analysis & Design. 2nd ed. LC 97-44779. 814p. (C). 1997. 105.00 (*0-13-134958-9*) P-H.
— Probability, Statistics & Reliability for Engineers. LC 96-41741. 528p. 1997. boxed set 84.95 (*0-8493-2690-7*) CRC Pr.
McCuen, Richard H., ed. The Elements of Academic Research. LC 96-7958. (Illus.). 296p. 1996. 30.00 (*0-7844-0171-3*) Am Soc Civil Eng.
McCuen, Richard H., et al. Dynamic Communication for Engineers. LC 93-9395. 192p. 1993. 31.00 (*0-87262-856-6*) Am Soc Civil Eng.
McCuen, Richard H., jt. auth. see Ayyub, Bilal M.
McCuistion, Dennis. The Prevention & Collection of Problem Loans. 1988. per. 42.50 (*1-55520-041-9*, Irwn Prfssnl) McGraw-Hill Prof.
McCuistion, Patrick J., jt. auth. see Marrelli, Richard S.
McCulla, L. Cleaves, 2nd. How to Buy Stocks Factory Direct & Save. LC 95-83533. 108p. (Orig.). 1996. pap. 19.95 (*0-9649420-0-3*) Finan Indep.
McCulla, Patricia C. Bahamas: Major World Nations. (Major World Nations Ser.). (Illus.). 144p. (YA). (gr. 5 up). 1999. lib. bdg. 19.95 (*0-7910-4755-5*) Chelsea Hse.
McCulla, Patricia E. Tanzania: Major World Nations. (Major World Nations Ser.). (Illus.). 144p. (YA). (gr. 5 up). 1999. lib. bdg. 19.95 (*0-7910-4768-7*) Chelsea Hse.
McCullagh, C. Behan. The Truth of History. LC 97-8185. 344p. (C). 1997. 75.00 (*0-415-17110-5*); pap. 25.99 (*0-415-17111-3*) Routledge.
McCullagh, Ciaran. Crime in Ireland: A Sociological Introduction. LC 96-133730. 172p. 1996. 39.95 (*1-85918-096-5*, Pub. by Cork Univ); pap. 22.50 (*1-85918-034-5*, Pub. by Cork Univ) Stylus Pub VA.
McCullagh, James C. The Complete Bicycle Fitness Book. 320p. 1985. mass mkt. 10.95 (*0-446-38363-5*, Pub. by Warner Bks) Little.
McCullagh, P. S., jt. auth. see Hammond, R.
McCullagh, Peter. Tensor Methods in Statistics. (Monographs on Statistics & Applied Probability). 288p. 1987. ring bd. 52.95 (*0-412-27480-9*, Chap & Hall CRC) CRC Pr.
McCullagh, Peter & Nelder, J. A. Generalized Linear Model. 2nd ed. LC 99-13896. (Monographs on Statistics & Applied Probability). 532p. (gr. 13). 1989. boxed set 78.95 (*0-412-31760-5*, A3827, Chap & Hall CRC) CRC Pr.
McCullagh, Peter J. The Foetus As Transplant Donor: Scientific, Social, & Ethical Perspectives. LC 86-18971. (Wiley Medical Publication). 221p. 1987. reprint ed. pap. 68.60 (*0-608-01628-4*, 206221300002) Bks Demand.
McCullagh, Suzanne F. & Giles, Laura. Italian Drawings before 1600 in the Art Institute of Chicago: A Catalogue of the Collection. LC 97-3932. (Illus.). 456p. 1997. 125.00 (*0-86559-147-4*) Art Inst Chi.
McCullagh, Suzanne F. & Giles, Laura M. Italian Drawings Before 1600 in the Art Institute of Chicago: A Catalog of the Collection. LC 97-3932. (Illus.). 496p. 1997. text 125.00 (*0-691-01748-4*, Pub. by Princeton U Pr) Cal Prin Full Svc.
McCullagh, Suzanne F., jt. auth. see Joachim, Harold.
McCullar, Michael. Restoring Texas: Raiford Stripling's Life & Architecture. LC 85-40052. (Illus.). 176p. 1985. 29.95 (*0-89096-254-5*) Tex A&M Univ Pr.
McCullar, Scott. Dewey Decimal System Defeats Truman! Library Cartoons. (Illus.). 95p. 1998. pap. 22.95 (*0-7864-0521-X*) McFarland & Co.
McCullem, Emily, ed. see Dunster, Julian.
McCullen, Carl L. Church Worker's Manual, Vol. 1. (Orig.). Date not set. pap. write for info. (*1-887939-26-1*, Go & Compel) VisionQuest Media.
McCullen, Dan. Lest We Forget: A POW Memoir of World War II. (Illus.). 208p. 1997. 22.95 (*1-56474-191-5*) Fithian Pr.
McCullen, Sean. The Centurion's Empire. LC 98-10257. 384p. 1998. text 24.95 (*0-312-85131-6*) St Martin.
— Souls in the Great Machine. 2nd ed. LC 99-21934. 448p. 1999. text 27.95 (*0-312-87055-8*) St Martin.
McCullen, Wendy H. Biology III Laboratory Manual. Mayer, Laurence P., ed. (Illus.). 144p. 1997. pap. text, lab manual ed. 14.60 (*1-889766-04-6*) Columbus State Bks.
McCullers, Carson. Ballad of the Sad Cafe. 1976. 18.95 (*0-8488-0573-9*) Amereon Ltd.
— The Ballad of the Sad Cafe. 1963. pap. 5.25 (*0-8222-0092-9*) Dramatists Play.
— The Ballad of the Sad Cafe & Other Stories. 160p. 1971. mass mkt. 5.99 (*0-553-27254-3*, Bantam Classics) Bantam.
— Ballad of the Sad Cafe & Other Stories. (J). 1969. 10.60 (*0-606-01508-6*, Pub. by Turtleback) Demco.
— The Clock Without Hands. 256p. 1998. pap. 12.00 (*0-395-92973-3*) HM.
— Collected Short Stories, 001. 1973. 9.95 (*0-395-07982-9*) HM.
— The Collected Stories of Carson McCullers. 416p. 1998. pap. 15.00 (*0-395-92505-3*) HM.
— El Corazon Es Un Cazador Soitario. 1998. pap. 9.95 (*84-322-1510-4*) Continental Bk.
— The Heart Is a Lonely Hunter. 320p. 1983. mass mkt. 5.99 (*0-553-26963-1*, Bantam Classics) Bantam.
— The Heart Is a Lonely Hunter. 1994. mass mkt. 6.99 (*0-553-54173-0*) Bantam.
— The Heart Is a Lonely Hunter. 1994. lib. bdg. 19.95 (*1-56849-462-9*) Buccaneer Bks.
***McCullers, Carson.** The Heart Is a Lonely Hunter. 320p. 2000. pap. 12.00 (*0-618-08474-6*, Mariner Bks) HM.
McCullers, Carson. The Heart Is a Lonely Hunter. 448p. 1993. 17.95 (*0-679-42474-1*) Modern Lib NY.
— The Heart Is a Lonely Hunter. 1953. 11.09 (*0-606-00786-5*, Pub. by Turtleback) Demco.
***McCullers, Carson.** The Heart Is a Lonely Hunter. large type ed. LC 99-40365. (Perennial Bestsellers Ser.). 1999. 27.95 (*0-7838-8773-6*, G K Hall & Co) Mac Lib Ref.
McCullers, Carson. The Member of the Wedding. 160p. (YA). (gr. 9-12). 1979. mass mkt. 5.99 (*0-553-25051-5*) Bantam.
— The Member of the Wedding. LC 51-10532. 1963. pap. 7.95 (*0-8112-0093-0*, NDP153, Pub. by New Directions) Norton.
McCullers, Carson. The Member of the Wedding. 1950. 9.60 (*0-606-01060-2*, Pub. by Turtleback) Demco.
— Reflections in a Golden Eye. 160p. 2000. pap. 10.00 (*0-618-08475-4*, Mariner Bks) HM.
McCullers, Carson. The Square Root of Wonderful. LC 90-47728. 169p. 1990. reprint ed. 34.95 (*0-87797-188-9*) Cherokee.
McCullers, Carson & Dews, C. L. Barney. Illumination & Night Glare: The Unfinished Autobiography of Carson McCullers. LC 99-19805. (Studies in American Autobiography). (Illus.). 280p. 1999. text 24.95 (*0-299-16440-3*) U of Wis Pr.
McCullers, Jamey, jt. auth. see Robinson, Bryan.
McCullers, Michael, jt. auth. see Meyers, Mike.
McCulley, Denny. Denny McCulley's Guide to Moving: For Senior Citizens & Anyone Making a Major Move. 112p. 1994. write for info. (*0-9639628-0-9*) Sr Concerns.
McCulley, Doug, jt. auth. see Hess, Karol.
***McCulley, Fred & Clark, Sushannah.** Wildlife in the Bluegrass: With Excerts from a Raven Run Diary. (Illus.). 250p. 2000. pap. 24.95 (*0-9648814-1-1*) Quiet Woods.
McCulley, Johnston. Black Star. reprint ed. lib. bdg. 22.95 (*0-89190-995-8*, Rivercity Pr) Amereon Ltd.
— Black Star's Campaign. reprint ed. lib. bdg. 22.95 (*0-89190-996-6*, Rivercity Pr) Amereon Ltd.
— Black Star's Return. reprint ed. lib. bdg. 22.95 (*0-89190-997-4*, Rivercity Pr) Amereon Ltd.
— The Mark of Z: The Original Zorro. 1976. reprint ed. lib. bdg. 24.95 (*0-89190-999-0*, Rivercity Pr) Amereon Ltd.
— The Mark of Zorro. 288p. 1997. mass mkt. 4.99 (*0-8125-4007-7*, Pub. by Forge NYC) St Martin.
***McCulley, Johnston.** The Mark of Zorro. 1998. 10.09 (*0-606-13597-9*, Pub. by Turtleback) Demco.
McCulley, Johnston. The Mark of Zorro. 1990. reprint ed. lib. bdg. 25.95 (*0-89968-541-2*) Buccaneer Bks.
***McCulley, Johnston.** Zorro Vol. 1: The Masters. (Zorro Ser.: No. 1). (Illus.). 128p. 2000. per. 15.00 (*1-891729-20-9*, Z-1) Pulp Advents.
McCulley, Murriell. Evangelism. (Discovery Ser.). 72p. 1999. pap. text. write for info. (*1-891110-03-9*) Africa Theolog Trng.
***McCulley, Murriell.** L'Evangelisation. (Discovery Ser.).Tr. of Evangelism. (FRE.). 76p. 1999. pap. text. write for info. (*2-912377-04-8*, Editions SAFT) Africa Theolog Trng.
McCulley, Richard T. The Social Safety Net Reexamined: FDR to Reagan. (Policy Research Project Report: No. 86). 240p. 1992. reprint ed. pap. 12.00 (*0-89940-693-9*) LBJ Sch Pub Aff.
McCulley, Richard T., jt. auth. see Redford, Emmette S.
***McCullin, Don.** India. (Illus.). 130p. 2000. 50.00 (*0-224-05089-3*, Pub. by Jonathan Cape) Trafalgar.
McCullin, Donald. Sleeping with Ghosts: A Life's Work in Photography. (Illus.). 208p. 1996. 45.00 (*0-89381-659-0*) Aperture.
McCulloch, Alan. The Encyclopedia of Australian Art. rev. ed. LC 94-20404. (Illus.). 880p. (C). 1994. text 75.00 (*0-8248-1688-9*) UH Pr.
McCulloch, B. Jan, ed. Old, Female, & Rural: What Is the Reality? 97p. 1998. pap. 14.95 (*0-7890-0671-5*) Haworth Pr.
— Old, Female & Rural: What Is the Reality? LC 98-44956. 97p. 1998. 39.95 (*0-7890-0664-2*) Haworth Pr.
McCulloch, Charles E., jt. auth. see Searle, Shayle R.
McCulloch, Chris, jt. auth. see Hyland, Greg.
McCulloch, Ellen. Birds in Your Garden. (Illus.). 96p. pap. 16.95 (*1-86447-050-X*) Hyland Hse.
McCulloch, Gary. Educational Reconstruction: The 1944 Education Act & the Twenty-First Century. LC 94-21265. (Woburn Education Ser.). 230p. 1994. 35.00 (*0-7130-0191-7*, Pub. by Woburn Pr); pap. 19.50 (*0-7130-4019-X*, Pub. by Woburn Pr) Intl Spec Bk.
— Philosophers & Kings: Education for Leadership in Twentieth-Century England. 173p. (C). 1991. text 59.95 (*0-521-39175-X*) Cambridge U Pr.
— Schools for the People: The Theory & Practice of Working Class Secondary Education. LC 97-39367. 202p. 1998. 95.00 (*0-335-19788-4*); pap. 32.95 (*0-335-19787-6*) OpUniv Pr.

M

An Asterisk (*) at the beginning of an entry indicates that the title is appearing for the first time.

***McCulloch, Gary & Richardson, William.** Historical Research in Educational Settings. LC 00-36726. (Doing Qualitative Research in Educational Settings Ser.). 2000. pap. write for info. (*0-335-20254-3*, Pub. by OpUniv Pr) Taylor & Francis.

***McCulloch, Gary, et al.** Politics of Professionalism. 176p. 2000. 74.95 (*0-304-70296-X*); pap. 24.95 (*0-304-70297-8*) Continuum.

— Politics of Professionalism: Teachers & the Curriculum. 2000. pap. 24.95 (*0-8264-4798-8*) Continuum.

McCulloch, Gary, jt. ed. see Helsby, Gill.

McCulloch, Gary F. & Boxer, Judy. Mental Health Promotion: Policy, Practice & Partnerships. (Illus.). 256p. 1997. pap. 31.00 (*0-7020-1981-X*) W B Saunders.

McCulloch, Graham. Workshop Shortcuts: Tips, Tricks, Jigs & Aids for Woodworkers. LC 93-44539. (Illus.). 224p. 1994. pap. 17.95 (*0-8069-0650-2*) Sterling.

McCulloch, Gregory. The Game of the Name: Introducing Logic, Language & Mind. 336p. 1989. text 75.00 (*0-19-875087-0*); pap. text 22.00 (*0-19-875086-2*) OUP.

— The Mind & Its World. LC 97-33896. (Problems of Philosophy Series: Their Past & Present). 264p. (C). 1995. pap. 24.99 (*0-415-12205-8*, C0419) Routledge.

— The Mind & Its World. LC 94-33896. (Problems of Philosophy Series: Their Past & Present). 264p. (C). (gr. 13). 1995. 75.00 (*0-415-09330-9*, C0418) Routledge.

— Using Sartre: An Analytical Introduction to Early Sartrean Themes. LC 93-33903. 160p. (C). 1994. pap. 22.99 (*0-415-10954-X*, B3955) Routledge.

McCulloch, Hugh. Men & Measures of Half a Century. LC 77-87404. (American Scene Ser.). 1969. reprint ed. lib. bdg. 65.00 (*0-306-71548-1*) Da Capo.

McCulloch, Iain & Shalaby, Shalaby W., eds. Tailored Polymeric Materials for Controlled Delivery Systems. LC 98-25962. (ACS Symposium Ser.: No. 709). (Illus.). 336p. 1998. text 120.00 (*0-8412-3585-6*) OUP.

McCulloch, Ian. Childforever: A Novel. 208p. 1997. pap. 15.95 (*1-55128-035-3*) Dist Art Pubs.

— The Efficiency of Killers. 72p. 1988. 9.95 (*0-920806-97-X*, Pub. by Penumbra Pr) U of Toronto Pr.

— Moon of Hunger. 48p. 1982. 5.95 (*0-920806-33-3*, Pub. by Penumbra Pr) U of Toronto Pr.

McCulloch, J. R. Classical Writings on Economics, 6 vols., Set. 1996. 650.00 (*1-85196-252-2*, Pub. by Pickering & Chatto) Ashgate Pub Co.

— Collected Works of J. R. McCulloch, 8 vols., Set. 4000p. (C). (gr. 13). 1995. text, boxed set 745.00 (*0-415-11352-0*, C0433) Routledge.

McCulloch, J. R., jt. auth. see Ricardo, David.

McCulloch, James A. A Medical Greek & Latin Workbook. 2nd ed. 212p. 1984. pap., spiral bd. 33.95 (*0-398-04905-X*) C C Thomas.

McCulloch, James A., ed. Arctic & Global Change: Proceedings of the Symposium on the Arctic & Global Change. (Illus.). 156p. (Orig.). 1990. pap. 25.00 (*0-9623610-1-1*) Climate Inst.

Mcculloch, Janet. Infection Control, Science, Management & Practice. 1999. pap. text 29.95 (*1-86156-053-2*) Singular Publishing.

McCulloch, Jim. How to Tell if You're a Real Race Fan: A Guidebook for Stock Car Fans. (Illus.). 80p. (Orig.). 1996. pap. 6.95 (*0-9651107-2-9*) StoneBrook.

***McCulloch, Jock.** Black Peril, White Virtue: Sexual Crime in Southern Rhodesia, 1902-1935. LC 99-55755. 272p. 2000. 35.00 (*0-253-33728-3*) Ind U Pr.

McCulloch, Jock. Colonial Psychiatry & 'The African Mind' 195p. (C). 1995. text 59.95 (*0-521-45330-5*) Cambridge U Pr.

McCulloch, John. Principles of Microsurgery for Lumbar Disc Disease. LC 86-42896. (Illus.). 317p. reprint ed. pap. 98.30 (*0-608-09633-4*, 205440900001) Bks Demand.

McCulloch, John A. Microsurgery of the Spine. 600p. 1998. text 165.00 (*0-397-51861-7*) Lppncott W & W.

— Principles of Microsurgery for Lumbar Disc Disease. 317p. 1989. text 126.00 (*0-88167-487-7*) Lppncott W & W.

McCulloch, John A. & Young, Paul H. Essentials of Spinal Microsurgery. LC 97-43644. 1998. write for info. (*0-7817-1607-1*) Lppncott W & W.

Mcculloch, John A., et al. Macnab's Backache. 3rd ed. LC 96-21766. (Illus.). 795p. 1997. 75.00 (*0-683-05797-9*) Lppncott W & W.

McCulloch, John A., jt. auth. see Macnab, Ian.

McCulloch, John R. The Literature of Political Economy: A Classified Catalogue of Select Publications in the Different Departments of the Science, with Historical, Critical & Biographical Notices. LC 86-7486. (Reprints of Economic Classics Ser.). xiii, 407p. 1991. reprint ed. lib. bdg. 57.50 (*0-678-01457-4*) Kelley.

— The Principles of Political Economy: With Some Inquiries Respecting Their Application. 5th ed. LC 65-19651. (Reprints of Economic Classics Ser.). xxiv, 518p. 1965. reprint ed. 49.50 (*0-678-00097-2*) Kelley.

— A Treatise on the Circumstances Which Determine the Rate of Wages & the Conditions of the Labouring Classes. LC 64-56231. (Reprints of Economic Classics Ser.). x, 114p. 1967. reprint ed. 29.50 (*0-678-00005-0*) Kelley.

— A Treatise on the Principles & Practical Influence of Taxation & the Funding System. 2nd ed. LC 67-28411. (Reprints of Economic Classics Ser.). xvi, 552p. 1968. reprint ed. 57.50 (*0-678-00331-9*) Kelley.

— Treatises & Essays on Subjects Connected with Economical Policy: With Biographical Sketches of Quesnay, Adam Smith & Ricardo. LC 67-20088. (Reprints of Economic Classics Ser.). vii, 487p. 1967. reprint ed. 57.50 (*0-678-00255-X*) Kelley.

McCulloch, John R., et al. Letters of John Ramsay McCulloch to David Ricardo. 1979. 17.95 (*0-405-10625-4*) Ayer.

McCulloch, Joseph M., et al, eds. Wound Healing: Alternatives in Management. 2nd ed. LC 94-1175. (Contemporary Perspectives in Rehabilitation Ser.). (Illus.). 442p. 1994. 39.95 (*0-8036-5966-0*) Davis Co.

McCulloch, Margery. Edwin Muir: Poet, Critic & Novelist. (Modern Scottish Writers Ser.). 144p. 1994. pap. 28.00 (*0-7486-0406-5*, Pub. by Edinburgh U Pr) Col U Pr.

McCulloch, Merran. Peoples of Sierra Leone. LC 67-4643. (Ethnographic Survey of Africa: Western Africa Ser.: Pt. 2). 121p. reprint ed. pap. 37.60 (*0-8357-6961-5*, 203902100009) Bks Demand.

McCulloch, Myrna T. America's Spelling & Reading with Riggs Series: Supplements to The Writing Road to Reading. Huneger, R. J., ed. (Illus.). 1993. write for info. (*0-318-66814-9*); 6.50 incl. audio (*0-924277-07-6*); 26.50 (*0-685-74194-X*); student ed. 17.50 incl. audio (*0-924277-08-4*); boxed set 20.00 (*0-924277-06-8*); pap., teacher ed. 43.50 (*0-924277-02-5*); pap., teacher ed., student ed. 12.95 (*0-924277-09-2*) K & M Pub.

McCulloch, Myrna T., ed. The Writing & Spelling Road to Reading & Thinking: A Neurolinguistic Approach to Cognitive Development & English. 300p. (C). 1999. teacher ed. 74.50 (*0-924277-21-1*) K & M Pub.

McCulloch, Myrna T. & Madsen, Sharon, eds. Spelling & Usage Vocabulary Builder. large type ed. (Illus.). 478p. (J). (gr. k-2). 1993. reprint ed. 26.50 (*0-924277-04-1*) K & M Pub.

McCulloch, Patty. Take Ten for Prayer. LC 99-28629. 1999. pap. 6.95 (*0-87793-679-X*) Ave Maria.

McCulloch, Peter & Kingsnorth, Andrew, eds. Management of Gastrointestinal Cancer. 416p. 1996. 128.00 (*0-7279-1071-X*, Pub. by BMJ Pub) Login Brothers Bk Co.

McCulloch, Rachel. Research & Development As a Determinant of U. S. International Competitiveness. LC 78-63432. (Committee on Changing International Realities Ser.). 60p. 1978. 3.00 (*0-89068-044-2*) Natl Planning.

— Unexpected Real Consequences of Floating Exchange Rates. LC 83-10857. (Essays in International Finance Ser.: No. 153). 28p. 1983. pap. text 10.00 (*0-88165-060-9*) Princeton U Int Finan Econ.

McCulloch, Richard. Destiny of Angels. (Illus.). 314p. 1986. 20.00 (*0-9608928-1-8*) Towncourt Ent.

— The Ideal & Destiny. LC 82-82103. 534p. 1982. 20.00 (*0-9608928-0-X*) Towncourt Ent.

— The Nordish Quest. 108p. 1989. pap. 5.00 (*0-9608928-2-6*) Towncourt Ent.

— The Racial Compact: A Call for Racial Rights, Preservation & Independence. 135p. (Orig.). 1994. pap. 7.95 (*0-9608928-3-4*) Towncourt Ent.

McCulloch, Robert, ed. see Antelman, Gordon.

***McCulloch, Ron.** Baseball Roots: The Fascinating Birth of America's Game & the Amazing Players That Were Its Champions. (Illus.). 380p. 2000. pap. 14.95 (*1-894020-71-5*) Warwick Publ.

McCulloch, Ron. How Baseball Began: The Long Overdue Truth about the Birth of Baseball. (Illus.). 144p. (Orig.). 1995. pap. 18.95 (*1-895629-44-6*) Warwick Publ.

***McCulloch, Ron, ed.** The Warwick Encyclopedia of Early Baseball. 16p. 1998. pap. 49.95 incl. cd-rom (*1-895629-87-X*) Warwick Publ.

McCulloch, Rook, ed. W. S. McCulloch, 4 vols. 1392p. 1989. pap. text 84.00 (*0-685-25893-9*) Intersystems Pubns.

McCulloch, Ros & Mathieson, Margaret. English 16-19: Entitlement at "A" Level. 160p. 1993. pap. 32.00 (*1-85346-214-4*, Pub. by David Fulton) Taylor & Francis.

— Moral Education Through English 11-16. 144p. 1995. pap. 24.95 (*1-85346-276-4*, Pub. by David Fulton) Taylor & Francis.

***McCulloch, Susan.** Contemporary Aboriginal Art: A Guide to the Rebirth of an Ancient Culture. LC 99-34262. 1999. text 39.00 (*0-8248-2268-4*) UH Pr.

McCulloch, W. Bengali Household Tales. LC 78-63211. (Folktale Ser.). reprint ed. 28.00 (*0-404-16146-4*) AMS Pr.

McCulloch, Warren S. Embodiments of Mind. 432p. 1988. pap. text 21.00 (*0-262-63114-8*, Bradford Bks) MIT Pr.

McCulloch, Wendell., jt. auth. see Ball, Donald A.

McCulloch, Wendell H., Jr., jt. auth. see Ball, Donald A.

McCulloch, William & Laing, Evelyn. New Ordinary Cause Rules. 216p. 1995. pap. 47.00 (*1-85811-027-0*, Pub. by CLT Prof) Gaunt.

McCulloch, William, et al. Ordinary Cause Rules. 2nd rev. ed. 224p. 1998. pap. 53.00 (*1-85811-175-7*, Pub. by CLT Prof) Gaunt.

McCulloch, William F., ed. see Hubbert, William T.

McCulloch-Williams, Martha. Dishes & Beverages of the Old South. LC 88-2981. 344p. 1988. reprint ed. 16.95 (*0-87049-580-1*) U of Tenn Pr.

McCulloch, Winifred. A Short History of the American Teilhard Association. 1979. pap. 3.00 (*0-89012-013-7*) Am Teilhard.

— Teilhard de Chardin & the Piltdown Hoax. (Teilhard Studies: No. 33). 1996. pap. write for info. (*0-89012-075-7*) Am Teilhard.

McCulloch, Yolanda. A Portrait's Lifelines. 40p. 1998. pap. 7.00 (*0-8059-4305-6*) Dorrance.

McCullogh, Dale R., ed. Metapopulations & Wildlife Conservation. 432p. (C). 1996. text 58.00 (*1-55963-457-X*); pap. text 29.95 (*1-55963-458-8*) Island Pr.

McCullogh, T. H., jt. ed. see Naeser, N. D.

McCulloh, Douglas. Chance Encounters: The LA Project. LC 99-178680. (Illus.). 220p. 1998. pap. 38.00 (*0-9666936-0-4*); pap. 45.00 (*0-9666936-1-2*) Geographics CA.

McCulloh, Elisha. The Shoebox Plague. LC 98-92175. 200p. 1998. pap. 15.00 (*0-9667307-0-4*) Lamp-post Pr.

McCulloh, Gerald O. Ministerial Education in the American Methodist Movement. LC 80-69028. (Informed Ministry Series, Two Hundred Years of American Methodist Thought: 200 Years of American Methodist Thought). 342p. (Orig.). 1980. pap. 3.95 (*0-938162-00-4*) United Meth Educ.

McCulloh, Gerald W. Christ's Person & Life-Work in the Theology of Albrecht Ritschi: With Special Attention to Munus Triplex. 234p. (Orig.). (C). 1990. lib. bdg. 49.00 (*0-8191-7885-3*) U Pr of Amer.

McCulloh, James H. Researches on America: Being an Attempt to Settle Some Points Relative to the Aborigines of America. (LC History-America-E). 230p. 1999. reprint ed. lib. bdg. 79.00 (*0-7812-4348-3*) Rprt Serv.

***McCulloh, James H.** Researches, Philosophical & Antiquarian, Concerning the Aboriginal History of America. (LC History-America-E). 535p. 1999. reprint ed. lib. bdg. 119.00 (*0-7812-4349-1*) Rprt Serv.

McCulloh, Judith, jt. ed. see Malone, Bill C.

McCulloh, William E. Longus. LC 77-99541. (Twayne's World Authors Ser.). 1970. lib. bdg. 20.95 (*0-8057-2540-7*) Irvington.

Mc'Cullough. Fortunes Favor. 1999. pap. 12.98 (*0-671-04439-7*) PB.

McCullough. Theatre Praxis: Teaching Drama Through Practice. LC 98-16916. 256p. 1998. pap. 19.95 (*0-312-21611-4*); text 55.00 (*0-312-21610-6*) St Martin.

McCullough, Ashley M. A Critical Analysis of the Fuel Management Program for Schools: Selected New Jersey Cities Compared with Nation-Wide Practice. LC 72-177019. (Columbia University. Teachers College. Contributions to Education Ser.: No. 713). reprint ed. 37.50 (*0-404-55713-9*) AMS Pr.

***McCullough, Barry.** Stop! Break Free from the Tyranny of the Urgent: A Novel Approach to Self Help. 250p. 1999. pap. 17.95 (*1-898256-43-8*, Pub. by Collins Press) Dufour.

McCullough, Bob. My Greatest Day in Baseball, 1946-1997: Baseball's Greatest Share Their Triumphs. LC 98-10673. 273p. 1998. pap. text 22.95 (*0-87833-989-2*) Taylor Pub.

***McCullough, Bob.** My Greatest Day in NASCAR. LC 99-55496. (Illus.). 320p. 2000. text 24.95 (*0-312-25254-4*, Thomas Dunne) St Martin.

McCullough, Bob & Jaffe, Miles. New York Running Guide. LC 98-6094. (City Running Guide Ser.). (Illus.). 168p. 1998. pap. 16.95 (*0-88011-765-6*, PMCC0765) Human Kinetics.

McCullough, Bonnie. 21 Ways Make Home Life. unabridged ed. 1988. audio 9.95 (*0-07-044968-6*) HarperAudio.

McCullough, Bonnie R. Bonnie's Household Budget Book: The Essential Guide for Getting Control of Your Money. 4th rev. ed. LC 95-36219. 64p. 1995. pap. 10.95 (*0-312-14098-3*, St Martin Griffin) St Martin.

— Bonnie's Household Organizer: The Essential Guide for Getting Control of Your Home. rev. ed. (Illus.). 192p. 1983. pap. 8.95 (*0-312-08795-0*) St Martin.

McCullough, Bonnie Runyan & Mon, Susan. 401 Ways to Get Your Kids to Work at Home. (Illus.). 224p. 1981. pap. 11.95 (*0-312-30147-2*) St Martin.

McCullough, Bruce. Representative English Novelists: Defoe to Conrad. LC 72-5807. (Essay Index Reprint Ser.). 1977. reprint ed. 27.95 (*0-8369-7298-8*) Ayer.

McCullough, Burton V. Letters of Credit. 1987. ring bd. 215.00 (*0-8205-1387-3*) Bender.

McCullough, Carol. Oracle 8 Bible. LC 98-70265. 1176p. 1998. pap. 49.99 (*0-7645-3198-0*) IDG Bks.

***McCullough, Carol.** Oracle 8i for Dummies. rev. ed. (For Dummies (Computers) Ser.). (Illus.). 400p. 1999. pap. 24.99 incl. cd-rom (*0-7645-0570-X*) IDG Bks.

McCullough, Carol. Oracles for Dummies. LC 97-80356. 384p. 1997. pap. 29.99 incl. cd-rom (*0-7645-0239-5*) IDG Bks.

***McCullough, Charlotte.** Managed Care & Privatization Child Welfare Tracking Project. 1999. pap. 14.95 (*0-87868-773-4*, CWLA Pr) Child Welfare.

McCullough, Christopher J. Managing Your Anxiety: Regaining Control When You Feel Stressed, Helpless & Alone. Mann, Robert W., ed. 320p. 1994. reprint ed. mass mkt. 6.50 (*0-425-14295-7*) Berkley Pub.

McCullough, Colleen. Caesar: Let the Dice Fly. LC 90-37080. (Illus.). 752p. 1997. 27.50 (*0-688-09372-8*, Wm Morrow) Morrow Avon.

— Caesar: Let the Dice Fly. (Masters of Rome Ser.: Vol. 5). 672p. 1999. pap. 16.50 (*0-380-71085-4*, Avon Bks) Morrow Avon.

— Caesar's Women. 960p. 1997. mass mkt. 7.99 (*0-380-71084-6*, Avon Bks) Morrow Avon.

— Cesar. Orig. Title: Caesar. 1999. 34.95 (*84-08-02795-6*) Planeta.

— Creed for Third Millen. 464p. 1986. mass mkt. 6.99 (*0-380-70134-0*, Avon Bks) Morrow Avon.

— First Man in Rome Co. 1104p. 1991. mass mkt. 7.99 (*0-380-71081-1*, Avon Bks) Morrow Avon.

— Fortune's Favorites. 1072p. 1994. mass mkt. 7.99 (*0-380-71083-8*, Avon Bks) Morrow Avon.

— The Grass Crown. 1104p. 1992. mass mkt. 6.99 (*0-380-71082-X*, Avon Bks) Morrow Avon.

— An Indecent Obsession. 336p. 1982. mass mkt. 6.99 (*0-380-60376-4*, Avon Bks) Morrow Avon.

— Ladies of Missalonghi. 192p. 1988. mass mkt. 5.99 (*0-380-70458-7*, Avon Bks) Morrow Avon.

***McCullough, Colleen.** Morgan's Run: A Novel. 608p. 2000. 28.00 (*0-684-85329-9*) S&S Trade.

McCullough, Colleen. Una Obsesion Indecente. (SPA.). 320p. 1992. pap. 4.95 (*1-56780-235-4*) La Costa Pr.

— The Thorn Birds. 1998. lib. bdg. 49.95 (*1-56849-697-4*) Buccaneer Bks.

— The Thorn Birds. 1978. 12.09 (*0-606-01301-6*, Pub. by Turtleback) Demco.

— Thorn Birds. 704p. 1978. mass mkt. 6.99 (*0-380-01817-9*, Avon Bks) Morrow Avon.

— The Thorn Birds: A Novel. LC 97-50349. 704p. 1998. 11.99 (*0-517-20165-8*) Random Hse Value.

***McCullough, Colleen.** Three Complete Novels. LC 98-19504. 768p. 1999. 13.99 (*0-517-20166-6*) Random Hse Value.

McCullough, Colleen. Tim. 288p. 1990. mass mkt. 6.99 (*0-380-71196-6*, Avon Bks) Morrow Avon.

— Tovismadarak. Goncz, Arpad & Borbas, Margit, trs. from ENG.Tr. of Thorn Birds. (HUN.). 568p. 1984. 20.00 (*0-935484-11-6*) Universe Pub Co.

McCullough, Cynthia W. My Husband Said He Needed More Space, So I Locked Him Outside: Reflections on Life by Women. LC 98-2626. 112p. 1998. per. 10.00 (*0-684-84189-4*, Fireside) S&S Trade Pap.

***McCullough, Dale R.** Kangaroos of Outback Australia: Comparative Ecology & Behavior of Three Co-Occuring Species. (Illus.). 2000. 50.00 (*0-231-11916-X*) Col U Pr.

— Kangaroos of Outback Australia: Comparative Ecology & Behavior of Three Co-Occuring Species. 2000. pap. text 30.00 (*0-231-11917-8*) Col U Pr.

McCullough, Dale R. The Tule Elk: Its History, Behavior, & Ecology. LC 75-626287. (University of California Publications in Social Welfare: No. 88). (Illus.). 219p. reprint ed. pap. 67.90 (*0-608-18065-3*, 202905300058) Bks Demand.

McCullough, Darryl & Miller, Andy. Symmetric Automorphisms of Free Products. LC 96-12850. (Memoirs of the American Mathematical Society Ser.: No. 582). 97p. 1996. pap. 35.00 (*0-8218-0459-6*, MEMO/122/582) Am Math.

McCullough, David. Brave Companions: Portraits in History. 256p. 1992. per. 12.00 (*0-671-79276-8*) S&S Trade Pap.

— The Great Bridge. 640p. 1983. pap. 16.00 (*0-671-45711-X*) S&S Trade Pap.

— The Johnstown Flood. 1990. 26.75 (*0-8446-6292-5*) Peter Smith.

— The Johnstown Flood. 304p. 1987. pap. 12.00 (*0-671-20714-8*) S&S Trade Pap.

— Mornings on Horseback. 1994. 28.00 (*0-8446-6732-3*) Peter Smith.

— Mornings on Horseback. 446p. 1982. pap. 15.00 (*0-671-44754-8*, Touchstone) S&S Trade Pap.

— The Path Between the Seas: The Creation of the Panama Canal, 1870-1914. 700p. 1977. 14.95 (*0-685-75146-5*, SS09-4) Am Soc Civil Eng.

— The Path Between the Seas: The Creation of the Panama Canal, 1870-1914. (Illus.). 698p. 1978. pap. 16.00 (*0-671-24409-4*, Touchstone) S&S Trade Pap.

— Truman. (Illus.). 1120p. 1992. 32.00 (*0-671-45654-7*) S&S Trade.

— Truman. (Illus.). 1120p. 1993. per. 18.00 (*0-671-86920-5*) S&S Trade Pap.

— Truman. (Reading Group Guides Ser.). 1996. pap. write for info. (*0-684-00445-3*, Touchstone) S&S Trade Pap.

McCullough, David. Truman. abr. ed. 1992. audio. write for info. (*0-671-79887-1*, Pub. by S&S Audio) Lndmrk Audiobks.

McCullough, David & Miller, Arthur. Homeomorphisms of 3-Manifolds with Compressible Boundary. LC 86-3387. (Memoirs of the AMS Ser.: No. 61/344). 100p. 1986. pap. 21.00 (*0-8218-2346-9*, MEMO/61/344) Am Math.

McCullough, David, ed. see Shapiro, Michael E. & Hassrick, Peter H.

McCullough, David G., ed. see Sulzberger, C. L.

McCullough, David W. Three Score & Ten: A History of Christ School 1900-1970 - Arden NC. LC 96-61366. (Illus.). 302p. 1996. 24.95 (*1-56664-104-7*) WorldComm.

McCullough, David Willis. Chronicles of the Barbarians: Firsthand Accounts of Pillage & Conquest, from the Ancient World to the Fall of Constantinople. LC 98-20314. 392p. 1998. 35.00 (*0-8129-3082-7*, Times Bks) Crown Pub Group.

McCullough, Dennis J., tr. Kids Coping with War: How Young People React to Military Conflict. (Illus.). 112p. (J). 1991. pap. 6.95 (*0-933879-37-7*) Alegra Hse Pubs.

***McCullough, Donald W.** Say Please, Say Thank You: The Respect We Owe One Another. LC 98-22401. 288p. 1998. 21.95 (*0-399-14439-0*, G P Putnam) Peng Put Young Read.

McCullough, Donald W. Say Please, Say Thank You: The Respect We Owe One Another. LC 99-10425. 1999. 26.95 (*0-7838-8551-2*) Thorndike Pr.

***McCullough, Donald W.** Say Please, Say Thank You: The Respect We Owe One Another. 1999. reprint ed. pap. 14.00 (*0-399-52538-6*, Perigee Bks) Berkley Pub.

McCullough, Donald W. The Trivialization of God: The Dangerous Illusion of a Manageable Deity. LC 95-14409. 176p. 1995. 16.00 (*0-89109-909-3*) NavPress.

McCullough, Duane K. Spirit of Atlantis Version 3: The Treasure Adventure. rev. ed. LC 88-92585. (Illus.). 132p. (C). 1994. reprint ed. pap. 20.00 (*0-9621605-3-9*) D K McCullough.

***McCullough, Edo.** Good Old Coney Island: A Sentimental Journey into the Past: The Most Rambunctious, Scandalous, Rapscallion, Splendiferous, Pugnacious, Spectacular, Illustrious, Prodigious, Frolicsome Island on Earth. LC 99-34320. (Illus.). 372p. 2000. reprint ed. pap. 19.95 (*0-8232-1997-6*, Pub. by Fordham) BookMasters.

McCullough, Edo. World's Fair Midways: An Affectionate Account of American Amusement Areas from the Crystal Palace to the Crystal Ball. LC 75-22828. (America in Two Centuries Ser.). (Illus.). 1976. reprint ed. 18.95 (*0-405-07700-9*) Ayer.

McCullough, Edward E. How the First World War Began. 256p. 1999. 57.99 (*1-55164-141-0*) Consort Bk Sales.

— How the First World War Began: The Triple Entente & the Coming of the Great War of 1914-1918. 1. 256p. 1999. pap. 28.99 (*1-55164-140-2*) Consort Bk Sales.

McCullough, Edwin C. Optical Radiations in Medicine. (AAPM Reports: No. 3). 28p. (Orig.). 1997. pap. 10.00 (*1-888340-06-1*) AAPM.

McCullough, Eileen. More Than Blarney: The Irish Influence in Appalachia. LC 96-61512. (Illus.). 179p. 1997. pap. 14.95 (*1-888715-00-6*) Wolfhnd Pr.

McCullough, Elizabeth. A Square Peg: An Ulster Childhood. (Illus.). 192p. 1998. pap. 12.95 (*1-86023-065-2*, Pub. by Martello Bks) Irish Amer Bk.

McCullough, Fran. Living Low-Carb: The Complete Guide to Long-Term Low-Carb Dieting. LC 99-57132. 384p. (gr. 8). 2000. 25.95 (*0-316-55768-4*) Little.

***McCullough, Fran.** The Low-Carb Cookbook: The Complete Guide to the Healthy Low-Carbohydrate Lifestyle - With over 250 Recipes. (Illus.). 2001. mass mkt. 7.99 (*0-7868-8991-8*) Hyperion.

***McCullough, Fran & Hamlin, Suzanne.** The Best American Recipes 2000: The Year's Top Picks from Books, Magazines, Newspapers & the Internet. (Illus.). 304p. 2000. 26.00 (*0-618-00996-5*) HM.

***McCullough, Fran & Hamlin, Suzanne, eds.** The Best American Recipes 1999: The Year's Top 100 from Books, Magazines, Newspapers & More. (Illus.). 300p. 1999. 26.00 (*0-395-96647-7*) HM.

McCullough, Frances. Great Food Without Fuss: Simple Recipes from the Best Cooks. 88p. 1995. pap. 14.95 (*0-8050-3001-8*) H Holt & Co.

McCullough, Frances, ed. Earth, Air, Fire & Water. rev. ed. LC 88-45854. (Charlotte Zolotow Bk.). 160p. (YA). (gr. 7 up). 1989. 13.95 (*0-06-024207-8*) HarpC Child Bks.

— Love Is Like the Lion's Tooth. LC 77-25659. 96p. (YA). (gr. 7 up). 1984. 12.95 (*0-06-024138-1*) HarpC Child Bks.

McCullough, Frances & Witt, Barbara. Great Entertaining Without Fuss. 1995. 25.00 (*0-614-15467-7*) Villard Books.

— Great Food Without Fuss: Simple Recipes from the Best Cooks. LC 92-8473. 352p. 1995. 25.00 (*0-8050-2230-9*) H Holt & Co.

McCullough, Frances, jt. ed. see Hughes, Ted.

McCullough, Frances, ed. see Plath, Sylvia.

McCullough, Frances M. The Low-Carb Cookbook: The Complete Guide to the Healthy Low Carbohydrate Lifestyle - With over 250 Delicious Recipes, Everything You Need to Know about Stocking the Pantry, & Sources for the Best Prepared Foods & Ingredients. LC 96-49343. (Illus.). 400p. 1997. 22.95 (*0-7868-6273-4*, Pub. by Hyperion) Time Warner.

McCullough, Grace A. Speech Improvement Work & Practice Book. text 3.50 (*0-686-00149-4*) Expression.

McCullough, Grace C. Backward Glances. LC 98-90060. 1998. 14.95 (*0-533-12696-7*) Vantage.

McCullough, Helen C. Brocade by Night: 'Kokin Wakashu' & the Court Style in Japanese Classical Poetry. LC 84-50637. 608p. 1985. 67.50 (*0-8047-1246-8*) Stanford U Pr.

— Bungo Manual: Selected Reference Materials for Students of Classical Japanese. (Cornell East Asia Ser.: No. 48). 108p. 1993. reprint ed. pap. 10.20 (*0-939657-48-1*) Cornell East Asia Pgm.

McCullough, Helen C., ed. Classical Japanese Prose: An Anthology. LC 89-78331. (Illus.). 596p. 1990. 67.50 (*0-8047-1628-5*); pap. 22.50 (*0-8047-1960-8*) Stanford U Pr.

McCullough, Helen C., tr. from JPN. Kokin Wakashu: The First Imperial Anthology of Japanese Poetry: With "Tosa Nikki" & "Shinsen Waka" LC 84-50756. 400p. 1985. 57.50 (*0-8047-1258-1*) Stanford U Pr.

— The Tale of the Heike. LC 87-18001. (Illus.). 504p. 1988. pap. 18.95 (*0-8047-1803-2*) Stanford U Pr.

— Tales of Ise: Lyrical Episodes from Tenth-Century Japan. 277p. 1968. 39.50 (*0-8047-0653-0*) Stanford U Pr.

— Yoshitsune: A Fifteenth Century Japanese Chronicle. viii, 367p. 1966. 42.50 (*0-8047-0270-5*) Stanford U Pr.

McCullough, Helen C., tr. Genji & Heike: Selections from the 'Tale of Genji' & 'The Tale of Heike' LC 93-20623. x, 490p. 1994. 69.50 (*0-8047-2257-9*); pap. 19.95 (*0-8047-2258-7*) Stanford U Pr.

— Okagami, the Great Mirror: Fujiwara Michinaga, 966-1027 & His Time. LC 90-21410. (Michigan Classics in Japanese Studies: No. 4). x, 381p. 1991. reprint ed. pap. 12.95 (*0-939512-50-5*) U MI Japan.

McCullough, Helen C., jt. tr. see McCullough, William H.

McCullough, Ian. Little Irish Songbook: Words & Music to 27 Classic Irish Songs. 60p. 1992. 7.95 (*0-8118-0187-X*) Chronicle Bks.

McCullough, Ian, jt. auth. see Wallace, Martin.

McCullough, J. Golf in the Year 2000: Or, What We Are Coming To. LC 98-25220. (Illus.). 160p. 1998. 14.95 (*1-55853-664-7*) Rutledge Hill Pr.

McCullough, J. & Scott, D. Experimental Thermodynamics Vol. 1: Calorimetry of Non-Reacting Systems. 1968. 272.00 (*0-08-020831-2*, Pub. by Pergamon Repr) Franklin.

McCullough, Jack W. Living Pictures of the New York Stage. LC 83-16754. (Theater & Dramatic Studies: No. 13). (Illus.). 212p. reprint ed. pap. 65.80 (*0-8357-1479-9*, 207056100001) Bks Demand.

McCullough, Jacqueline E. Daily Moments with God: In Quietness & Confidence. 109p. 1996. pap. 9.99 (*1-56229-473-3*) Pneuma Life Pub.

McCullough, James A., et al. Analysis of Health Indicators for California's Minority Populations. (Illus.). 92p. (C). 1998. reprint ed. pap. text 20.00 (*0-7881-4319-0*) DIANE Pub.

***McCullough, James P., Jr.** Treatment for Chronic Depression: Cognitive Behavioral Analysis System of Psychotherapy (CBASP) 300p. 1999. lib. bdg. 35.00 (*1-57230-527-4*, CO527) Guilford Pubns.

McCullough, Jeffrey. Transfusion Medicine: A Practical Guide. LC 97-29682. (Illus.). 528p. 1997. pap. text 45.00 (*0-07-045113-3*) McGraw-Hill HPD.

McCullough, Joseph B., ed. see Garland, Hamlin.

McCullough, Joseph B., ed. see Twain, Mark, pseud.

McCullough, Karen M. The Ruin Islanders: Early Thule Culture Pioneers in the Eastern High Arctic. (Mercury Ser.: ASC No. 141). (Illus.). 368p. 1994. pap. 24.95 (*0-660-10793-7*, Pub. by CN Mus Civilization) U of Wash Pr.

McCullough, Kate. Regions of Identity: The Construction of America in Women's Fiction, 1885-1914. LC 98-36884. 1999. 45.00 (*0-8047-3307-4*) Stanford U Pr.

McCullough, Kathleen. Concrete Poetry: An Annotated International Bibliography, with an Index of Poets & Poems. LC 87-50085. xviii, 1010p. 1989. 125.00 (*0-87875-332-X*) Whitston Pub.

McCullough, Ken. Sycamore - Oriole. Boyer, Dale K., ed. LC 91-71532. (Ahsahta Press Modern & Contemporary Poets of the West Ser.). 60p. (Orig.). 1991. pap. 6.95 (*0-916272-50-8*) Ahsahta Pr.

McCullough, Ken, jt. tr. see Oeur, U. Sam.

McCullough, Kenneth C. Monoclonal Antibodies in Biotechnology: Theoretical & Practical Aspects. Spier, Raymond E., ed. (Cambridge Studies in Biotechnology: No. 8). (Illus.). 399p. (C). 1990. text 115.00 (*0-521-25890-1*) Cambridge U Pr.

McCullough, L. E. The Complete Irish Tin Whistle Tutor. (Illus.). 80p. 1987. pap. 9.95 (*0-8256-0311-0*, OK64923, Oak) Music Sales.

***McCullough, L. E.** The Complete Irish Tin Whistle Tutor. rev. ed. 74p. 1999. pap. text 17.95 (*0-8256-0340-4*, OK65006) Music Sales.

McCullough, L. E. Ice Babies in Oz: Original Character Monologues. LC 95-2289. (Monologue Audition Ser.). 80p. 1995. pap. 8.95 (*1-880399-82-2*) Smith & Kraus.

— Learn to Play Irish Tinwhistle. (Homespun Tapes Ser.). 1996. VHS 19.95 (*0-7935-6867-6*) H Leonard.

***McCullough, L. E.** Now I Get It! Thirty-Six Ten-Minute Skits about Science, Math, Language & Social Studies for Fun & Learning. 256p. (J). (gr. k-2). 2000. pap., teacher ed. 16.95 (*1-57525-161-2*) Smith & Kraus.

McCullough, L. E. Plays of America from American Folklore for Children, K-6. LC 96-6172. (Young Actors Ser.). 176p. (Orig.). (J). (gr. k-6). 1996. pap. 14.95 (*1-57525-038-1*) Smith & Kraus.

— Plays of America from American Folklore for Young Actors, 7-12. 176p. (Orig.). (YA). (gr. 7-12). 1996. pap. 14.95 (*1-57525-040-3*) Smith & Kraus.

***McCullough, L. E.** Plays of Ancient Israel. 192p. (J). (gr. k-2). 2000. pap. 15.95 (*1-57525-252-X*) Smith & Kraus.

McCullough, L. E. Plays of Exploration & Discovery. LC 99-30020. 128p. (J). (gr. 4-6). 1999. pap. 14.95 (*1-57525-113-2*) Smith & Kraus.

— Plays of Fairy Tales for Grades K-3. LC 97-32881. (Plays for Young Actors Ser.). 224p. (Orig.). (J). (gr. k-3). 1998. pap. 14.95 (*1-57525-109-4*) Smith & Kraus.

***McCullough, L. E.** Plays of Israel Reborn. 192p. (J). (gr. k-3). 2000. 15.95 (*1-57525-253-8*) Smith & Kraus.

McCullough, L. E. Plays of Mythology. LC 97-32882. 224p. (YA). (gr. 4-6). 1997. pap. 14.95 (*1-57525-110-8*) Smith & Kraus.

— Plays of People at Work. 128p. (J). (gr. k-3). 1998. pap. 14.95 (*1-57525-140-X*) Smith & Kraus.

— The Plays of the Songs of Christmas. LC 96-22834. (Young Actors Ser.). 128p. 1996. pap. 19.95 (*1-57525-062-4*) Smith & Kraus.

— Plays of the Wild West: Grades 4-6, Vol. II. (Plays for Young Actors Ser.). (Illus.). 160p. (Orig.). (J). (gr. 4-6). 1997. pap. 14.95 (*1-57525-105-1*) Smith & Kraus.

— Saint Patrick Was a Cajun. (Illus.). 93p. 1998. pap. 15.95 (*1-900428-46-6*, OS10512, Pub. by Ossian) Music Sales.

— Stories of the Songs of Christmas: For Children of All Ages. LC 97-2681. 160p. 1997. pap. 8.95 (*1-57525-116-7*) Smith & Kraus.

McCullough, Laura, jt. auth. see Phillips, Vicki.

McCullough, Laurence B. John Gregory & the Invention of Professional Medical Ethics & Profession of Medicine. LC 97-49822. (Philosophy & Medicine Ser.). 347p. 1998. write for info. (*0-7923-4917-2*) Kluwer Academic.

McCullough, Laurence B., et al, eds. Surgical Ethics. 416p. 1998. text 52.50 (*0-19-510347-5*) OUP.

McCullough, Laurence B. & Chervenak, Frank A. Ethics in Obstetrics & Gynecology. LC 93-6426. (Illus.). 296p. (C). 1994. text 41.50 (*0-19-506005-9*) OUP.

McCullough, Laurence B., jt. auth. see Gregory, John.

McCullough, Lawrence B. Leibniz on Individuals & Individuation: The Persistence of Premodern Ideas in Modern Philosophy. LC 95-46629. (Philosophical Studies in Contemporary Culture: Vol. 3). 232p. (C). 1996. text 140.00 (*0-7923-3864-2*) Kluwer Academic.

McCullough, Lawrence B. & Wilson, Nancy L., eds. Long-Term Care Decisions: Ethical & Conceptual Dimensions. LC 94-37416. (Illus.). 304p. 1995. text 40.00 (*0-8018-4993-4*) Johns Hopkins.

McCullough, Leigh, jt. ed. see Soldz, Stephen.

McCullough, Malcolm. Abstracting Craft: The Practiced Digital Hand. (Illus.). 329p. (C). 1997. 41.50 (*0-262-13326-1*) MIT Pr.

— Abstracting Craft: The Practiced Digital Hand. LC 96-28356. (Illus.). 309p. 1998. pap. text 17.50 (*0-262-63189-X*) MIT Pr.

— The Electronic Design Studio: Architectural Knowledge & the Media in Computer Era. (Illus.). 516p. 1990. 70.00 (*0-262-13254-0*) MIT Pr.

McCullough, Malcolm, jt. auth. see Mitchell, William J.

McCullough, Mamie. Mama's Rules for Livin' LC 95-838606. (Illus.). 160p. 1996. pap. 6.99 (*1-56292-085-5*, HB-085) Honor Bks OK.

— Rules for Success. 160p. 1998. pap. 6.99 (*1-57757-012-X*) Honor Bks OK.

McCullough, Marshall E. Total Mixed Rations & Supercows. rev. ed. (Illus.). 63p. (C). 1994. pap. text 4.00 (*0-932147-22-4*, Hoards Dairyman) Hoard & Sons Co.

McCullough, Mary F. Brown Eyes, Blue Eyes. LC 86-195585. (Illus.). 32p. (J). (gr. k-3). 1986. pap. text 3.95 (*0-936625-04-X*, N868113, New Hope) Womans Mission Union.

— The City: Sights, Sounds, & Smells. McClain, Cindy, ed. (Illus.). 32p. (J). (ps). 1991. pap. text 3.95 (*0-936625-96-1*, N918102, New Hope) Womans Mission Union.

McCullough, Mary K., jt. auth. see President's Institute on the Catholic Character of Loyola Marymount University Staff.

McCullough, Mary W. Black & White Women As Friends: Building Cross-Race Friendships. LC 98-20701. (Communication Ser.). 256p. (C). 1998. text 49.50 (*1-57273-112-5*); pap. text 21.95 (*1-57273-113-3*) Hampton Pr NJ.

McCullough, Michael E., et al, eds. Forgiveness: Theory, Research & Practice. LC 99-47188. 330p. 1999. lib. bdg. 40.00 (*1-57230-510-X*, CO510) Guilford Pubns.

McCullough, Michael G., et al. To Forgive Is Human: How to Put Your Past in the Past. LC 96-46371. 240p. 1997. pap. 13.99 (*0-8308-1683-6*, 1683) InterVarsity.

McCullough, Myrna. America's Spelling & Reading with Riggs Series. (Illus.). 1993. pap. write for info. (*0-924277-10-6*) K & M Pub.

McCullough, Nance. Equal vs. Unequal. (Illus.). 23p. 1980. pap. 3.50 (*0-936916-00-1*) NAMAC.

— Love Formulas: The Works! (Illus.). 85p. 1980. pap. 4.40 (*0-936916-01-X*) NAMAC.

— Love Formulas: The Works. rev. ed. (Illus.). 85p. 1981. pap. 8.45 (*0-936916-02-8*, Pub. by NAMAC) New Leaf Dist.

***McCullough, Nance.** Solor Returns: Formulas & Analyses. (Illus.). 184p. 1999. pap. 12.95 (*0-936916-03-6*, Pub. by NAMAC) New Leaf Dist.

McCullough, Peter E. Sermons at Court: Politics & Religion in Elizabethan & Jacobean Preaching. LC 97-8761. (Cambridge Studies in Early Modern British History). (Illus.). 256p. (C). 1998. text 64.95 (*0-521-59046-9*) Cambridge U Pr.

McCullough, R. L. Concepts of Fiber-Resin Composites. LC 76-150245. (Monographs & Textbooks in Material Science: No. 2). (Illus.). 126p. reprint ed. pap. 39.10 (*0-8357-6071-5*, 203455100090) Bks Demand.

McCullough, Rita I., ed. Sources: An Annotated Bibliography of Women's Issues. 320p. (Orig.). 1991. pap. 24.95 (*1-879198-28-2*) Knwldg Ideas & Trnds.

McCullough, Robert. The Landscape of Community: A History of Communal Forests in New England. LC 94-35541. (Illus.). 423p. 1995. text 55.00 (*0-87451-696-X*) U Pr of New Eng.

McCullough, Robert J. & Everard, Kenneth. Bank Reconciliation Projects. 3rd ed. 1987. 13.04 (*0-02-830530-2*) Glencoe.

McCullough, Roy L., jt. auth. see Whitney, James M.

McCullough, Sally, jt. auth. see Lindsay, Jeanne W.

McCullough, Sandra, ed. Older Residents' Legal Rights: Supported Accommodation in New South Wales. 546p. 1992. pap. 64.00 (*1-86287-090-X*, Pub. by Federation Pr) Gaunt.

McCullough, Stacy. Your Special Baby: REAL Lamaze Prepared Childbirth. expanded ed. LC 95-94033. (Illus.). 80p. 1995. pap. 11.95 (*0-9643837-0-5*, YSB95) Luckenbooth.

McCullough, Susan M., jt. auth. see Fortunato, Nancymarie.

McCullough, Virginia, ed. see Malter, Rick & Malter, Rosalie.

McCullough, Virginia, ed. see Miles, Linda L.

McCullough, Virginia E. Testing & Your Child: What You Should Know about 150 of the Most Common Medical, Educational, & Psychological Tests. 334p. 1998. pap. text 12.00 (*0-7881-5691-8*) DIANE Pub.

McCullough, Virginia E., jt. auth. see Cukier, Daniel.

McCullough, W. S., ed. The Seed of Wisdom: Essays in Honour of T. J. Meek. LC DS0057.M35. 212p. reprint ed. pap. 65.80 (*0-608-11795-1*, 201430200089) Bks Demand.

McCullough, W. W. Sticky Fingers: A Close Look at America's Fastest-growing Crime. LC 80-69696. 158p. reprint ed. pap. 49.00 (*0-608-12852-X*, 202359100033) Bks Demand.

McCullough, William E. Listen to the Howl of the Wolf. LC 95-4128. 160p. (J). (gr. 6-7). 1996. 14.95 (*1-57168-026-8*, Eakin Pr) Sunbelt Media.

McCullough, William H. & McCullough, Helen C., trs. from JPN. A Tale of Flowering Fortunes: Annals of Japanese Aristocratic Life in the Heian Period, 2 vols., Set. LC 78-66183. (Illus.). 930p. 1980. 95.00 (*0-8047-1039-2*) Stanford U Pr.

McCullough, William H., jt. ed. see Shively, Donald H.

McCullough, William S. The History & Literature of the Palestinian Jews from Cyrus to Herod, 550 B. C. to 4 B. C. LC 74-80889. 266p. reprint ed. pap. 82.50 (*0-608-15663-9*, 203193300077) Bks Demand.

McCullum, Emily, jt. ed. see Harding, Lee E.

McCullum, Richard E., jt. auth. see Levine, Howard.

McCullum, Rodney J., jt. auth. see Sturdivant, Margaret H.

***McCullum, Sharyn.** Live Work & Play Around the World. 160p. 2000. per. 9.00 (*0-7432-0068-3*) Simon & Schuster.

McCullum, Sharyn. Live, Work & Play in Australia. 144p. pap. 10.95 (*0-86417-773-9*, Pub. by Kangaroo Pr) Seven Hills Bk.

McCully, Brian J. & Robinson, Grace I. The Legal Research Workbook. 224p. (C). 1995. pap. 21.95 (*0-87084-556-X*) Anderson Pub Co.

— The Legal Research Workbook: California Supplement. 88p. (C). 1995. pap. text 5.00 (*0-87084-555-1*) Anderson Pub Co.

McCully, C. B., ed. The Poet's Voice & Craft. 200p. 1995. pap. 25.00 (*1-85754-020-4*, Pub. by Carcanet Pr) Paul & Co Pubs.

McCully, C. B. & Anderson, J. J., eds. English Historical Metrics. LC 95-49017. 269p. (C). 1996. text 64.95 (*0-521-55464-0*) Cambridge U Pr.

McCully, Chris. Not Only I. LC 97-131679. 1997. pap. 14.95 (*1-85754-255-X*, Pub. by Carcanet Pr) Paul & Co Pubs.

McCully, Emily Arnold. The Ballot Box Battle. LC 95-38095. (Illus.). (J). (gr. 1-4). 1996. 17.00 (*0-679-87938-2*) Knopf.

— The Ballot Box Battle. (J). (gr. k-3). 1998. pap. 6.99 (*0-679-89312-1*, Pub. by Random Bks Yng Read) Random.

— Beautiful Warrior: The Legend of the Nun's Kung Fu. LC 97-3823. 40p. (J). (ps-3). 1998. 16.95 (*0-590-37487-7*) Scholastic Inc.

— The Bobbin Girl. LC 95-6997. (Illus.). 40p. (J). (gr. 1-4). 1996. 15.99 (*0-8037-1827-6*, Dial Yng Read) Peng Put Young Read.

— The Bobbin Girl. (J). (gr. 1-4). 1999. pap. 5.99 (*0-14-056186-2*) Viking Penguin.

— First Snow. LC 84-43244. (Illus.). 32p. (J). (ps-1). 1985. 12.95 (*0-06-024128-4*) HarpC Child Bks.

***McCully, Emily Arnold.** Four Hungry Kittens. LC 99-88779. (Illus.). (J). 2001. write for info. (*0-8037-2505-1*) Peng Put Young Read.

McCully, Emily Arnold. The Grandma Mix-up. (I Can Read Bks.). (Illus.). 64p. (J). (gr. 1-3). 1988. 11.95 (*0-06-024201-9*); lib. bdg. 15.89 (*0-06-024202-7*) HarpC Child Bks.

— The Grandma Mix-up. (I Can Read Bks.). (Illus.). 64p. (J). (gr. 1-3). 1991. pap. 3.95 (*0-06-444150-4*, HarpTrophy) HarpC Child Bks.

— Grandmas at Bat. (I Can Read Bks.). (Illus.). 64p. (J). (gr. 1-3). 1995. pap. 3.95 (*0-06-444193-8*, HarpTrophy) HarpC Child Bks.

— Grandmas at Bat. (I Can Read Bks.). (J). (gr. 1-3). 1995. 8.95 (*0-606-09346-X*, Pub. by Turtleback) Demco.

— Grandmas at the Lake. (I Can Read Bks.). (Illus.). 64p. (J). (gr. 1-3). 1990. 10.95 (*0-06-024126-8*) HarpC Child Bks.

— Grandmas at the Lake. (I Can Read Bks.). (Illus.). 64p. (J). (gr. 1-3). 1994. pap. 3.95 (*0-06-444177-6*, HarpTrophy) HarpC Child Bks.

— Grandmas at the Lake. (I Can Read Bks.). (J). (gr. 1-3). 1994. 8.95 (*0-606-06423-0*, Pub. by Turtleback) Demco.

McCully, Emily Arnold. Historical Fiction. 64p. (gr. k-3). pap. 3.95 (*0-06-444278-0*) HarpC.

McCully, Emily Arnold. Hurry! LC 97-45564. 32p. (J). (gr. 1-5). 2000. 16.00 (*0-15-201579-5*, Harcourt Child Bks) Harcourt.

McCully, Emily Arnold. McCully Historical Fiction. (I Can Read Bks.). (Illus.). 64p. (ps-3). 14.95 (*0-06-028728-4*) HarpC.

— McCully Historical Fiction. (I Can Read Bks.). (Illus.). 64p. (ps-3). 14.89 (*0-06-028729-2*) HarpC Child Bks.

McCully, Emily Arnold. Mirette on the High Wire. (Illus.). 32p. (J). (ps-3). 1992. 15.95 (*0-399-22130-1*, G P Putnam) Peng Put Young Read.

— Mirette on the High Wire. LC 91-36324. (Illus.). 32p. (J). (ps-3). 1997. pap. 5.99 (*0-698-11443-4*, PapStar) Peng Put Young Read.

McCully, Emily Arnold. Mirette on the High Wire. LC 91-36324. (J). 1997. 11.15 (*0-606-11628-1*, Pub. by Turtleback) Demco.

— Monk Camps Out. LC 99-23237. (Illus.). 32p. (J). (ps-4). 2000. 15.95 (*0-439-09976-5*, A A Levine) Scholastic Inc.

— Mouse Practice. (YA). (ps up). 1999. write for info. (*0-439-07055-4*) Scholastic Inc.

McCully, Emily Arnold. Mouse Practice. LC 98-18522. (J). 1999. pap. 16.95 (*0-590-68267-9*) Scholastic Inc.

— Mouse Practice. LC 98-18522. 32p. (J). (ps-4). 1999. 15.95 (*0-590-68220-2*) Scholastic Inc.

— My Real Family. LC 92-46290. (Illus.). 32p. (J). (ps-3). 1994. 14.00 (*0-15-277698-2*, Harcourt Child Bks) Harcourt.

— My Real Family. 32p. (C). 1999. pap. 6.00 (*0-15-201957-X*, Voyager Bks) Harcourt.

— New Baby. LC 87-45294. (Illus.). 32p. (J). (ps-1). 1988. 12.95 (*0-06-024130-6*) HarpC Child Bks.

— An Outlaw Thanksgiving. LC 97-29553. (Illus.). (J). (gr. k-3). 1998. 15.99 (*0-8037-2197-8*, Dial Yng Read) Peng Put Young Read.

***McCully, Emily Arnold.** Outlaw Thanksgiving. (Illus.). 40p. (J). (gr. k-3). 2000. pap. 6.99 (*0-14-056768-2*, PuffinBks) Peng Put Young Read.

McCully, Emily Arnold. Picnic. (Illus.). (J). (ps-1). 1984. 12.95 (*0-06-024099-7*, 622997); lib. bdg. 16.89 (*0-06-024100-4*) HarpC Child Bks.

— The Pirate Queen. LC 94-5389. (Illus.). 32p. (J). (ps-3). 1995. 16.95 (*0-399-22657-5*, G P Putnam) Peng Put Young Read.

— The Pirate Queen. (Illus.). 32p. (J). (gr. k-3). 1998. pap. 6.99 (*0-698-11629-1*, PapStar) Peng Put Young Read.

— The Pirate Queen. 1998. 12.19 (*0-606-13709-2*, Pub. by Turtleback) Demco.

— Popcorn at the Palace. LC 96-17592. (Illus.). 40p. (J). (gr. k-3). 1997. 16.00 (*0-15-277699-0*, Harcourt Child Bks) Harcourt.

— School. (Illus.). (J). (ps-1). 1987. 12.95 (*0-06-024132-2*, 622645) HarpC Child Bks.

— School. LC 87-156. (Illus.). 32p. (J). (ps-2). 1987. lib. bdg. 15.89 (*0-06-024133-0*) HarpC Child Bks.

An Asterisk (*) at the beginning of an entry indicates that the title is appearing for the first time.

— School. LC 87-156. (Trophy Picture Bk.). (Illus.). 32p. (J). (ps-1). 1990. pap. 5.95 (*0-06-443233-5*, HarpTrophy) HarpC Child Bks.

— School. 1987. 10.15 (*0-606-04793-X*, Pub. by Turtleback) Demco.

— Speak up, Blanche! LC 90-36945. (Illus.). 32p. (J). (gr. k-3). 1991. 15.00 (*0-06-024227-2*); lib. bdg. 14.89 (*0-06-024228-0*) HarpC Child Bks.

— Starring Mirette & Bellini. LC 95-34115. (Illus.). 32p. (J). 1997. 15.99 (*0-399-22636-2*, G P Putnam) Peng Put Young Read.

***McCully, Emily Arnold.** Starring Mirette & Bellini. (Illus.). 32p. (J). (ps-3). 2000. pap. 6.99 (*0-698-11822-7*) Putnam Pub Group.

— The Trick-or-Treat Grandmas. (Illus.). 48p. (J). (gr. k-3). 14.95 (*0-06-028730-6*) HarpC.

— The Trick-or-Treat Grandmas. (Illus.). 48p. (J). (gr. k-3). 14.89 (*0-06-028731-4*) HarpC Child Bks.

— The Trick-or-treat Grandmas. 48p. pap. 3.95 (*0-06-444277-2*) HarpC.

McCully, Emily Arnold. Zaza's Big Break. (J). 1997. pap. 5.00 (*0-15-201569-8*, Harcourt Child Bks) Harcourt.

— Zaza's Big Break. LC 88-36836. (Illus.). 32p. (J). (ps-3). 1989. 12.95 (*0-06-024223-X*) HarpC Child Bks.

McCully, Johnston. The Scarlet Scourge. reprint ed. lib. bdg. 22.95 (*0-89190-998-2*, Rivercity Pr) Amereon Ltd.

***McCully, Kilmer.** Heart Revolution: The Vitamin B Breakthrough that Lowers Homocysteine Levels, Cuts Your Risk of Heart Disease, & Protects Your HealthMcCully,&Kilmer. 1999. audio 18.00 (*0-694-52087-X*) HarperAudio.

***McCully, Kilmer & McCully, Martha.** The Heart Revolution: The B Vitamin Breakthrough That Lowers Homocysteine, Cuts Your Risk of Heart Disease & Protects Your Health. 234p. 2000. text 24.00 (*0-7881-6865-7*) DIANE Pub.

McCully, Kilmer S. The Heart Revolution: The Medical Breakthrough That Cuts Your Risk of Heart Disease. LC 98-43944. 256p. 1999. 24.00 (*0-06-019237-2*) HarpC.

— The Homocysteine Revolution. rev. ed. 272p. 1999. pap. 14.95 (*0-87983-975-9*, Keats Publng) NTC Contemp Pub Co.

— The Homocysteine Revolution: Medicine for the New Millennium. LC 96-29882. 250p. (Orig.). 1997. pap. 14.95 (*0-87983-767-5*, Keats Publng) NTC Contemp Pub Co.

***McCully, Kilmer S. & McCully, Martha.** The Heart Revolution: The Extraordinary Discovery That Finally Laid the Cholesterol Myth to Rest & Put Good Food Back on the Table. LC 99-56348. 288p. 2000. pap. 13.00 (*0-06-092973-1*, Perennial) HarperTrade.

***McCully, Marilyn.** Ceramics by Picasso, 2 vols. (Illus.). 800p. 1999. 395.00 (*2-913355-01-3*, Pub. by Images Modernes) Ursus Bks.

McCully, Marilyn, ed. Picasso: The Early Years, 1892-1906. 1997. 60.00 (*0-614-28054-0*) Yale U Pr.

McCully, Marilyn, ed. Picasso: The Early Years, 1892-1906. (Illus.). 430p. 1997. 65.00 (*0-300-07166-3*) Yale U Pr.

McCully, Marilyn, ed. A Picasso Anthology: Documents, Criticism, Reminiscences. LC 82-47632. (Illus.). 288p. 1982. pap. 16.95 (*0-691-00348-3*, Pub. by Princeton U Pr) Cal Prin Full Svc.

McCully, Martha, jt. auth. see McCully, Kilmer.

McCully, Martha, jt. auth. see McCully, Kilmer S.

McCully, Patrick. Silenced Rivers: The Ecology & Politics of Large Dams. 320p. 1996. text 65.00 (*1-85649-435-7*, Pub. by Zed Books); text 25.00 (*1-85649-436-5*, Pub. by Zed Books) St Martin.

McCully, Robert S. The Enigma of Symbols in Fairy Tales: Zimmer's Dialogue Renewed. LC 90-22128. (Studies in Comparative Literature: Vol. 14). 102p. 1991. lib. bdg. 59.95 (*0-88946-498-7*) E Mellen.

McCully, Roland C. Testing Program: Up with Math. 2nd ed. Jacobs, Erika, ed. 139p. 1995. pap. text, teacher ed. 15.95 (*0-918272-25-4*, 117) Jacobs.

— Up with Math: Basic Skills Step by Step. 2nd rev. ed. Jacobs, Russell F., ed. (Illus.). 292p. (YA). (gr. 5-12). 1994. pap. text 12.95 (*0-918272-22-X*, 115) Jacobs.

McCully, Roland C. & Jacobs, Russell F. Answer Key for Up with Math. 2nd ed. Jacobs, Erika, ed. 28p. (Orig.). (J). 1994. pap. text, teacher ed. 3.50 (*0-918272-23-8*, 116) Jacobs.

***McCumber, David.** The Cowboy Way: Seasons of a Montana Ranch. LC 98-46861. 352p. 1999. 24.00 (*0-380-97341-3*, Avon Bks) Morrow Avon.

— The Cowboy Way: Seasons of a Montana Ranch. 352p. 2000. pap. 14.00 (*0-380-78841-1*, Avon Bks) Morrow Avon.

McCumber, David. Playing Off the Rail. LC 95-6955. 384p. 1997. pap. 12.50 (*0-380-72923-7*, Avon Bks) Morrow Avon.

***McCumber, David.** X-Rated. 2000. mass mkt. 6.50 (*0-7860-1113-0*, Pinncle Kensgtn) Kensgtn Pub Corp.

McCumber, Dennis. Guitar Styles Funk. (National Guitar Workshop Arts Ser.). 1997. pap. 14.95 incl. audio compact disk (*0-88284-851-8*, 17843) Alfred Pub.

McCumber, John. The Company of Words: Hegel, Language, & Systematic Philosophy. (Studies in Phenomenology & Existential Philosophy). 400p. (Orig.). 1993. 59.95 (*0-8101-1055-5*); pap. 24.95 (*0-8101-1082-2*) Northwestern U Pr.

— Metaphysics & Oppression: Heidegger's Challenge to Western Philosophy. LC 98-45926. (Studies in Continental Thought). (Illus.). 525p. 1999. pap. 24.95 (*0-253-21316-9*); text 49.95 (*0-253-33473-X*) Ind U Pr.

***McCumber, John.** Philosophy & Freedom: Derrida, Rorty, Habermas, Foucault. LC 99-43396. (Studies in Continental Thought). 256p. 2000. pap. 18.95 (*0-253-21363-0*); lib. bdg. 39.95 (*0-253-33697-X*) Ind U Pr.

McCumber, John. Poetic Interaction: Language, Freedom, Reason. LC 88-19831. 504p. 1989. lib. bdg. 72.00 (*0-226-55703-0*) U Ch Pr.

— Poetic Interaction: Language, Freedom, Reason. LC 88-19831. 504p. 1997. pap. text 30.00 (*0-226-55704-9*) U Ch Pr.

***McCumber, John.** Time in the Ditch: American Philosophy & the McCarthy Era. 2000. 29.95 (*0-8101-1809-2*) Northwestern U Pr.

McCumber, John, jt. ed. see Comay, Rebecca.

McCumber, W. E. All Our Days. 48p. 1989. pap. 3.99 (*0-8341-1320-1*) Beacon Hill.

— The Bible Speaks to Me about My Beliefs. 88p. 1989. pap. 7.99 (*0-8341-1285-X*) Beacon Hill.

— Everybody into the Field! The Power of Sunday School to Transform Lives Through Evangelism. 120p. 1995. pap., pap. text 8.99 (*0-8341-1547-6*) Beacon Hill.

— The God of New Beginnings: Brief Insights from Genesis & Exodus. 144p. 1991. pap. 9.99 (*0-8341-1365-1*) Beacon Hill.

— Love Conquers All: Essays on Holy Living. 100p. (Orig.). 1993. pap. 7.99 (*0-8341-1455-0*) Beacon Hill.

— Prayer & Fasting. 36p. 1990. pap. 3.25 (*0-8341-1379-1*) Beacon Hill.

— Questions of Jesus. LC 98-25253. 108p. 1998. 9.99 (*0-8341-1704-5*) Nazarene.

— Take a Bible Break. 116p. 1986. pap. 7.99 (*0-8341-1080-6*) Beacon Hill.

McCumber, W. E. Was It Not I? And Other Questions God Asks. LC 94-200293. 196p. 1994. pap. 12.99 (*0-8341-1485-2*) Beacon Hill.

McCumber, W. E., ed. Holiness Preachers & Preaching, vol. 5. (Great Holiness Classic Ser.: Vol. 5). 408p. 1989. 34.99 (*0-8341-1289-2*) Beacon Hill.

***McCumsey, Robert, ed.** California Missions Measured Drawings of the Historic American Building Survey. 346p. 1999. pap. 49.95 (*0-9673772-1-8*, HABS 011) Learning Widows.

McCune, Allison & Spears, Tomye B. Rationalizations for Women Who Do Too Much: While Running with the Wolves. LC 94-168041. 1994. pap. 5.95 (*1-55850-380-3*) Adams Media.

McCune, Bob. Gambling Times Guide to Football Handicapping. (Illus.). (Orig.). 1984. pap. 5.95 (*0-89746-022-7*) Gambling Times.

McCune, Bonnie F. & Nelson, Charleszine T. Recruiting & Managing Volunteers in Libraries: A-How-to-Do-It Manual for Librarians. (How-to-Do-It Manuals Ser.: Vol. 51). (Illus.). 174p. (Orig.). 1995. pap. 45.00 (*1-55570-204-X*) Neal-Schuman.

McCune, Bruce & Geiser, Linda. Macrolichens of the Pacific Northwest. LC 97-3549. (Illus.). 400p. (Orig.). 1997. pap. 25.95 (*0-87071-394-9*) Oreg St U Pr.

McCune, Bruce & Goward, Trevor. Macrolichens of the Northern Rocky Mountains. (Illus.). 200p. (Orig.). 1995. pap. 24.95 (*0-916422-82-8*) Mad River.

McCune, Bunny & Traunstein, Deb. Girls to Women, Women to Girls. LC 98-35798. (Illus.). 208p. 1998. pap. 14.95 (*0-89087-881-1*) Celestial Arts.

McCune, David, tr. see Vedung, Evert.

McCune, Dianne. Gifted Goes Thinking. (Illus.). 96p. 2000. pap. 11.95 (*1-880505-41-X*, CLC0225) Pieces of Lrning.

McCune, Dianne, et al. The Welcome Back to School Book. (Illus.). 112p. (J). (gr. k-4). 1987. pap. 12.99 (*0-86653-383-4*, GA1001) Good Apple.

McCune, Don. Trail to the Klondike. LC 97-735. (Illus.). 128p. 1997. 35.00 (*0-87422-143-9*); pap. 19.95 (*0-87422-144-7*) Wash St U Pr.

McCune, Donald L. Fertilizers for Tropical & Subtropical Agriculture. Thompson, Marie K., ed. LC 82-11908. (Special Publications: No. SP-2). (Illus.). 30p. (Orig.). 1982. pap. text 4.00 (*0-88090-040-7*) Intl Fertilizer.

McCune, Donald L., ed. IFDC Annual Report, 1978. (Circular Ser.: No. S-2). (Illus.). 22p. (Orig.). 1979. pap. write for info. (*0-88090-028-8*) Intl Fertilizer.

— IFDC Annual Report, 1979. (Circular Ser.: No. S-3). (Illus.). 64p. (Orig.). 1980. pap. write for info. (*0-88090-029-6*) Intl Fertilizer.

McCune, George M. Korea Today. LC 81-20290. 372p. 1982. reprint ed. lib. bdg. 75.00 (*0-313-23446-9*, MCKT, Greenwood Pr) Greenwood.

McCune, Kelly. One Bowl: One-Pot Meals from Around the World. LC 96-33956. (Illus.). 108p. 1996. pap. 14.95 (*0-8118-1111-5*) Chronicle Bks.

***McCune, Michael.** Integrating Linux & Windows. 400p. 2000. 39.99 (*0-13-030670-3*) P-H.

McCune, Robert. The World's Best Golf Jokes. 96p. 1998. pap. 6.95 (*0-00-638332-7*, Pub. by HarpC) Trafalgar.

***McCune, S. L., et al.** How to Prepare for the EXCET. 2nd ed. LC 99-42038. 400p. 1999. pap. 14.95 (*0-7641-0771-2*) Barron.

McCune, Sandra, et al. Algebra. LC 96-54296. (Barron's College Review Ser.). 496p. 1997. pap. text 11.95 (*0-8120-9746-7*) Barron.

***McCune, Sandra L., et al.** How to Prepare for the TASP - Texas Academic Skills Program. 3rd ed. LC 98-33374. 790p. (YA). 1999. pap. 16.95 (*0-7641-0479-9*) Barron.

McCune, Shannon. Intelligence on the Economic Collapse of Japan in 1945. LC 89-16677. 124p. (C). 1989. lib. bdg. 44.50 (*0-8191-7560-9*) U Pr of Amer.

McCune, Shannon, et al. The American Society for Professional Geographers: Papers Presented on the Occasion of the Fiftieth Anniversary of Its Founding. LC 93-18849. (Occasional Publications of the Association of American Geographers: No. 3). 1993. 5.00 (*0-89291-211-1*) Assn Am Geographers.

McCune, Shannon B. Geographical Aspects of Agricultural Changes in the Ryukyu Islands. LC 75-11729. (University of Florida Monographs: Social Sciences: No. 54). 94p. reprint ed. pap. 30.00 (*0-7837-5090-0*, 204478900004) Bks Demand.

McCune, Shirley, jt. auth. see Milanovich, Norma J.

McCune, Shirley D., et al. Growing Free: Ways to Help Children Overcome Sex-Role Stereotypes. Cohen, Monroe D. & Martin, Lucy P., eds. 34p. (C). 1976. pap. 2.00 (*0-87173-002-2*) ACEI.

McCune, W., et al, eds. Automated Deduction - CADE-14: 14th International Conference on Automated Deduction, Townsville, North Queensland, Australia, July 13-17, 1997, Proceedings. LC 97-20663. (Lecture Notes in Artificial Intelligence: No. 1249). xiv, 462p. 1997. pap. 76.00 (*3-540-63104-6*) Spr-Verlag.

McCune, W. & Padmanabhan, R. Automated Deduction in Equational Logic & Cubic Curves, Vol. 1095. LC 96-26660. (Lecture Notes in Computer Science Ser.). (Illus.). x, 231p. 1996. pap. 43.00 (*3-540-61398-6*) Spr-Verlag.

McCune, Wesley. Who's Behind Our Farm Policy? LC 75-14699. 374p. 1975. reprint ed. lib. bdg. 69.50 (*0-8371-8238-7*, MCWB, Greenwood Pr) Greenwood.

***McCuniff, Mara.** Vampire Memoirs. 432p. 2000. mass mkt. 5.99 (*0-7860-1124-6*, Pinncle Kensgtn) Kensgtn Pub Corp.

McCunn, Donald H. How to Make Sewing Patterns. LC 77-85078. (Illus.). 192p. (C). 1977. pap. 16.95 (*0-932538-00-2*) Design Ent SF.

McCunn, J. C., ed. see Stubbs, George.

McCunn, Ruthanne L. Chinese Proverbs. (Little Bks.). (Illus.). 60p. 1992. 7.95 (*0-8118-0083-0*) Chronicle Bks.

— Pie-Biter. Yeung, Ellen L. & Mlawer, Teresa, trs. from CHI. LC 97-27586. (Illus.). 32p. (J). (gr. k-4). 1998. 15.95 (*1-885008-07-4*) Shens Bks.

— Sole Survivor: A Story of Record Endurance at Sea. LC 99-14163. (Illus.). 240p. (gr. 8-12). 1999. pap. 12.00 (*0-8070-7139-0*) Beacon Pr.

McCunn, Ruthanne Lum. Chinese American Portraits: Personal Histories 1828-1988. (Illus.). 176p. 1996. pap. 18.95 (*0-295-97552-0*) U of Wash Pr.

***McCunn, Ruthanne Lum.** The Moon Pearl. LC 00-8738. 336p. 2000. 24.00 (*0-8070-8348-8*) Beacon Pr.

McCunn, Ruthanne Lum. Thousand Pieces of Gold: A Biographical Novel. Hooks, Tisha, ed. LC 88-47881. (Blue Streak Ser.). 308p. (YA). 1981. pap. 13.00 (*0-8070-8317-8*) Beacon Pr.

***McCunn, Ruthanne Lum.** Wooden Fish Songs. LC 00-29788. 384p. 2000. pap. 14.00 (*0-8070-6229-4*) Beacon Pr.

McCunney, Michelle. Mario's Mayan Journey. LC 95-39407. (Illus.). (J). (gr. 2-6). 1996. pap. 4.95 (*1-57255-203-4*) Mondo Pubng.

McCunney, Robert J. A Manager's Guide to Occupational Health Services. LC 98-179273. viii, 47 p. 1996. 27.00 (*1-883595-06-1*) OEM Health.

— Medical Center Occupational Health & Safety. LC 99-14496. 429p. 1999. text. write for info. (*0-7817-2198-9*) Lppncott W & W.

McCunney, Robert J. & Brandt-Rauf, Paul W., eds. A Practical Approach to Occupational & Environmental Medicine. 2nd rev. ed. LC 94-11269. Orig. Title: Handbook of Occupational Medicine. 856p. 1994. reprint ed. pap. text 65.00 (*0-316-55534-7*, Little Brwn Med Div) Lppncott W & W.

McCunney, Robert J. & Mauderly, Joe L., eds. Particle Overload in the Rat Lung & Lung Cancer - Implications for Human Risk Assessment: Proceedings of MIT Conference Held March 29-30, 1995. LC 95-47904. 320p. 1996. 89.95 (*1-56032-543-7*) Hemisp Pub.

McCunney, Robert J. & Rountree, Paul P. Occupational & Environmental Medicine Self-Assessment & Review. LC 98-5990. 150p. 1998. pap. text 49.95 (*0-7817-1612-8*) Lppncott W & W.

McCurdy. Public Administration: A Bibliographic Guide to the Literature. (Public Administration & Public Policy Ser.: Vol. 29). (Illus.). 328p. 1986. text 95.00 (*0-8247-7518-X*) Dekker.

McCurdy, Bob. Carving Faces. LC 97-4284. (Illus.). 1996. pap. 15.00 (*0-940473-36-4*) Wm Caxton.

***McCurdy, Charles W.** The Anti-Rent Era in New York Law & Politics, 1839-1865. (Studies in Legal History). 496p. 2001. 49.95 (*0-8078-2590-5*) U of NC Pr.

McCurdy, David, jt. auth. see Spradley, James.

McCurdy, David W. & Spradley, James P., eds. Issues in Cultural Anthropology: Selected Readings. 390p. 1987. reprint ed. pap. text 20.95 (*0-88133-298-4*) Waveland Pr.

McCurdy, David W., jt. auth. see Spradley, James P.

McCurdy, Dwight R. Park Management. LC 84-27653. 272p. 1985. 41.95 (*0-8093-1226-3*); pap. 31.95 (*0-8093-1202-6*) S Ill U Pr.

McCurdy, Dwight R., et al. How to Choose Your Tree: A Guide to Parklike Landscaping in Illinois, Indiana, & Ohio. LC 74-156791. (Illus.). 255p. 1972. 14.95 (*0-8093-0514-3*) S Ill U Pr.

McCurdy, Garvin. Ramble, after Action: A Rite of Passage, a Poetic Exploration of Things Thought Known. 200p. pap. 15.00 (*0-9641979-1-X*) Info Age Handyman.

— Salt on the Windowpane: Doggered, Counterpoint & Main Theme from the New England Seacoast. rev. ed. (Illus.). 90p. 1994. 11.00 (*0-9641979-0-1*) Info Age Handyman.

McCurdy, Goward E., jt. auth. see Launius, Roger D.

McCurdy, Howard E. Inside NASA: High Technology & Organizational Change in the American Space Program. LC 92-18753. (New Series in NASA History). (Illus.). 240p. 1993. text 38.50 (*0-8018-4452-5*) Johns Hopkins.

— Inside NASA: High Technology & Organizational Change in the American Space Program. (New Series in NASA History). 232p. 1994. reprint ed. pap. text 14.95 (*0-8018-4975-6*) Johns Hopkins.

— Space & the American Imagination. LC 97-16. (Smithsonian History of Aviation Ser.). (Illus.). 294p. 1997. 29.95 (*1-56098-764-2*) Smithsonian.

— Space & the American Imagination. (American History & Culture Ser.). (Illus.). 416p. 1999. pap. 17.95 (*1-56098-445-7*) Smithsonian.

— The Space Station Decision: Incremental Politics & Technological Choice. LC 90-30831. (New Series in NASA History). (Illus.). 320p. 1990. text 45.00 (*0-8018-4004-X*) Johns Hopkins.

McCurdy, Howard E., jt. auth. see Launius, Roger D.

McCurdy, J. Cosmetic Surgery of the Asian Face. (American Academy of Facial Plastic & Reconstructive Surgery Monograph). (Illus.). 160p. 1990. text 85.00 (*0-86577-329-7*) Thieme Med Pubs.

***McCurdy, Karen & Jones, Elizabeth.** Supporting Families: Lessons from the Field. LC 00-8120. 2000. pap. write for info. (*0-7619-0679-7*) Sage.

***McCurdy, Kay & Gregory, Kay.** Blood Bank Regulations: A to Z. 2nd ed. LC 99-222813. 160p. 1999. 100.00 (*1-56395-106-1*, AABB Pr) Am Assn Blood.

McCurdy, Kay & Gregory, Kay, eds. Blood Bank Regulations A-Z: A Handbook. LC 98-138828. 1997. pap. text 79.00 (*1-56395-085-5*) Am Assn Blood.

McCurdy, Kay & Wilkenson, Susan L., eds. CLIA & Transfusion Medicine: A Guide to Total Compliance. 1996. ring bd. 109.00 (*1-56395-053-7*, PC97-PR9603) Am Assn Blood.

***McCurdy, Leslie.** Attributes & Atonement: The Holy Love of God in the Theology of P. T. Forsyth. (Biblical & Theological Monographs). xi, 327p. 1999. reprint ed. pap. 40.00 (*0-85364-833-6*, Pub. by Paternoster Pub) OM Literature.

***McCurdy, Michael.** The Algonquian Year: The Year According to the Full Moon. LC 99-87157. 2000. 15.00 (*0-618-00705-9*) HM.

McCurdy, Michael. Hannah's Farm: Seasons on an Early American Homestead. LC 87-29631. (Illus.). 32p. (J). (gr. k-3). 1988. lib. bdg. 15.95 (*0-8234-0700-4*) Holiday.

— The Sailor's Alphabet. LC 97-20647. 32p. 1998. 16.00 (*0-395-84167-4*) HM.

— Trapped by the Ice! Shackleton's Amazing Antarctic Adventure. LC 97-6976. (Illus.). 40p. (J). (gr. 1-5). 1997. 16.95 (*0-8027-8438-0*); lib. bdg. 17.85 (*0-8027-8439-9*) Walker & Co.

McCurdy, Michael. American Fairy Tales: From Rip Van Winkle to the Rootabaga Stories. LC 95-49143. 160p. (J). 1996. 22.45 (*0-7868-0207-3*, Pub. by Hyprn Child); lib. bdg. 22.89 (*0-7868-2171-X*, Pub. by Hyprn Child) Little.

McCurdy, Michael & Peich, Michael. The First Ten: A Penmaen Press Bibliography. LC 78-52650. (Illus.). 1978. 22.50 (*0-915778-20-3*) Penmaen Pr.

McCurdy, Michael, ed. & illus. see Douglass, Frederick.

McCurdy, Nan. Voice of the Seas & Hills. 65p. (Orig.). 1983. pap. 10.00 (*0-9655169-0-3*) Bard Pub Co.

— Voice of the Seasons. LC 97-228394. 160p. (Orig.). 1996. pap. 12.00 (*0-9655169-1-1*) Bard Pub Co.

McCurdy, Sheryl, jt. ed. see Hodgson, Dorothy L.

McCurley & Davis. Alabama Real Estate Handbook: Land Laws of Alabama, 1991 Supplement. 5th ed. 95p. 1992. write for info. (*0-87473-838-5*, 64683-10, MICHIE) LEXIS Pub.

McCurley, Foster R. Wrestling with the Word: Christian Preaching from the Hebrew Bible. LC 96-23. 256p. 1996. pap. 20.00 (*1-56338-142-7*) TPI PA.

McCurley, Foster R. & Weitzman, Alan. Making Sense Out of Sorrow: A Journey of Faith. LC 95-6281. 96p. (Orig.). 1995. pap. 8.00 (*1-56338-113-3*) TPI PA.

McCurley, K. S., et al, eds. Advances in Cryptology, 1981-1997: Electronic Proceedings of the CRYPTO & Conferences, 1981-1997. LC 99-15829. (Lecture Notes in Computer Science Ser.: Vol. 1440). xii, 320p. 1999. pap. 106.00 incl. cd-rom (*3-540-65069-5*) Spr-Verlag.

***McCurley, Marian F.** NIST International & Academic Activities for FY 1997/1998. 86p. 1999. pap. 8.75 (*0-16-058873-1*) USGPO.

***McCurley, Marie Huggins.** The Easy Way to Plan a Church Conference. LC 99-93626. 96p. 1999. pap. 16.95 (*0-9670200-0-X*) TKK Pub.

McCurley, Robert L., Jr. Alabama Real Estate Handbook, 1984. 4th ed. 1983. text. write for info. (*0-87473-600-5*, 64680-10, MICHIE) LEXIS Pub.

McCurley, Robert L., Jr. & Davis, Penny A. Real Estate Handbook: Land Laws of Alabama. 6th ed. LC 96-78223. 814p. 1996. 95.00 (*1-55834-412-8*, 64682-11, MICHIE) LEXIS Pub.

McCurley, Steve. Building Understanding & Collaboration: Creative Synergistic Relationships Between Staff & Volunteers. (Changing The Paradigm Organizational Effectiveness Ser.: Vol. 4). 18p. 1996. pap. write for info. (*1-58534-013-8*) Points of Light.

— Recruiting Volunteers for Difficult or Long-Term Positions. 1991. pap. 8.00 (*0-911029-30-3*) Heritage Arts.

McCurley, Steve & Lynch, Rick. Volunteer Management: Mobilizing All the Resources of the Community. 236p. (Orig.). 1996. pap. 25.00 (*0-911029-45-1*) Heritage Arts.

McCurley, Steve & Vineyard, Sue. Measuring Up: Assessment Tools for Volunteer Programs. 72p. (Orig.). 1997. pap. 17.95 (*0-911029-48-6*) Heritage Arts.

— One Hundred & One Ideas for Volunteer Programs. (Brainstorm Ser.). (Illus.). 72p. (Orig.). 1986. pap. text 11.95 (*0-911029-04-4*) Heritage Arts.

McCurley, Steve, jt. auth. see Vineyard, Sue.

McCurley, T. Mark. Awake the Hornet. LC 99-90477. 344p. 1999. 25.00 (*0-7388-0436-3*); pap. 18.00 (*0-7388-0437-1*) Xlibris Corp.

***McCurley, T. Mark.** Destiny's Child. LC 99-91108. 253p. 1999. 25.00 (*0-7388-0614-5*); pap. 18.00 (*0-7388-0615-3*) Xlibris Corp.

McCurn, Lucy. Lucy in the Sky . . . Poems by Lucy McCurn. 108p. (J). (gr. 4-8). 1997. spiral bd. 5.95 (*1-887480-23-4*) Wrds Lght Intl.

McCurnin, Dennis M. Clinical Textbook for Veterinary Technicians. 4th ed. Kaszczuk, Selma, ed. LC 97-17014. (Illus.). 928p. 1998. text 62.50 (*0-7216-2196-1*, W B Saunders Co) Harcrt Hlth Sci Grp.

M

An Asterisk (*) at the beginning of an entry indicates that the title is appearing for the first time.

— Veterinary Practice Management. LC 65-9467. 401p. 1988. text 64.00 (0-397-50782-8, Lippnctt) Lppncott W & W.

McCurnin, Dennis M. & Poffenbarger. Small Animal Physical Diagnosis & Clinical Procedures. (Illus.). 244p. 1990. text 54.00 (0-7216-5931-4, W B Saunders Co) Harcrt Hlth Sci Grp.

***McCurrach, David.** The Allowance Workbook: For Kids & Their Parents. (Illus.). 16p. 2000. pap., wbk. ed. 2.95 (0-9677671-1-3) Kids Money Pr.

— Kids' Allowances: How Much, How Often & How Come - A Guide for Parents, 2 bks., Set. LC 99-91813. (Illus.). xvi, 97p. 2000. pap. 8.95 (0-9677671-0-5) Kids Money Pr.

***McCurrach, Ian.** Drama for People with Learning Disabilities. LC 98-49772. (Special Talents, Special Needs Ser.). 1999. pap. 29.95 (1-85302-561-5) Jessica Kingsley.

McCurry, Dan C., et al, eds. The Labor of Women in the Production of Cotton. LC 74-30616. (American Farmers & the Rise of Agribusiness Ser.). (Illus.). 1975. reprint ed. 28.95 (0-405-06761-5) Ayer.

McCurry, Dan C. & Rubenstein, Richard E., eds. American Farmers & the Rise of Agribusiness: Seeds of Struggle, 46 bks., Set. 1975. 1674.00 (0-405-06760-7) Ayer.

— Bankers & Beef: An Original Press Anthology. LC 74-30618. (American Farmers & the Rise of Agribusiness Ser.). (Illus.). 1975. reprint ed. 33.95 (0-405-06763-1) Ayer.

— Cannery Captives: Women Workers in the Produce Processing Industry (an Original Press Anthology) LC 74-30623. (American Farmers & the Rise of Agribusiness Ser.). (Illus.). 1975. 46.95 (0-405-06770-4) Ayer.

— Children in the Fields: An Original Anthology. LC 74-30624. (American Farmers & the Rise of Agribusiness Ser.). (Illus.). 294 p. 1975. 29.95 (0-405-06775-5) Ayer.

— The Farmer-Labor Party-History, Platform & Programs: An Original Press Anthology. LC 74-30628. (American Farmers & the Rise of Agribusiness Ser.). 1975. 19.95 (0-405-06790-9) Ayer.

— Grange Melodies. LC 74-30647. (American Farmers & the Rise of Agribusiness Ser.). 1975. reprint ed. 26.95 (0-405-06819-0) Ayer.

— Land Speculation - New England's Old Problem: An Original Arno Press Anthology. LC 74-30640. (American Farmers & the Rise of Agribusiness Ser.). 1975. 19.95 (0-405-06808-5) Ayer.

— The National Nonpartisan League Debate: An Original Anthology. LC 74-30645. (American Farmers & the Rise of Agribusiness Ser.). (Illus.). 1975. 29.95 (0-405-06815-8) Ayer.

McCurry, Dan C., ed. see Bivins, Frank J.

McCurry, Dan C., ed. see Brinton, J. W.

McCurry, Dan C., ed. see Caldwell, Erskine & Bourke-White, Margaret.

McCurry, Dan C., ed. see Commission on Country Life, Jr.

McCurry, Dan C., ed. see Cooperative Central Exchange Staff.

McCurry, Dan C., ed. see Dies, Edward J.

McCurry, Dan C., ed. see Education & Labor Committee.

McCurry, Dan C., ed. see Federal Trade Commission.

McCurry, Dan C., ed. see Hill, John, Jr.

McCurry, Dan C., ed. see Howe, Frederic C.

McCurry, Dan C., ed. see Kerr, William H.

McCurry, Dan C., ed. see Kinney, J. P.

McCurry, Dan C., ed. see Lord, Russell.

McCurry, Dan C., ed. see Loucks, Henry L.

McCurry, Dan C., ed. see Murphy, Jerre C.

McCurry, Dan C., ed. see Rochester, Anne.

McCurry, Dan C., ed. see Russell, Charles E.

McCurry, Dan C., ed. see Simonsen, Sigurd J.

McCurry, Dan C., ed. see Todes, Charlotte.

McCurry, Dan C., ed. see U. S. Department of Labor, Bureau of Statistics St.

McCurry, Dan C., ed. see Wallace, Henry C.

McCurry, Dan C., ed. see Watson, Thomas E.

McCurry, Dan C., ed. see White, Roland A.

McCurry, Dan C., ed. see Whitney, Caspar.

McCurry, Don. Esperanza para los Musulmanes.Tr. of Bringing New Life to Muslims. (ENG & SPA.). 468p. 1996. 10.99 (0-7899-0171-4, 498681) Editorial Unilit.

McCurry, Leta. Commercial Real Estate: An Intro to Marketing Investment Properties. 336p. (C). 1990. text 42.80 (0-13-151465-2) P-H.

McCurry, Margaret. Margaret McCurry: Constructing Twenty-Five Short Stories. LC 99-53960. (Illus.). 192p. 2000. pap. 40.00 (1-58093-046-8, Pub. by Monacelli Pr) Penguin Putnam.

***McCurry, Meryl Alyse.** The Sea Monster's Darkest Night. (Illus.). 34p. (J). (ps-7). 1999. pap. 7.99 (1-881524-67-1, Prof Busn) Milligan Bks.

***McCurry, Miya Lynn.** The Foods. (Illus.). 34p. (J). (ps-7). 1999. pap. 7.99 (1-881524-66-3, Prof Busn) Milligan Bks.

McCurry, Stephanie. Masters of Small Worlds: Yeoman Households, Gender Relations & the Political Culture of the Antebellum South Carolina Low Country. 344p. 1995. text 60.00 (0-19-507236-7) OUP.

— Masters of Small Worlds: Yeoman Households, Gender Relations, & the Political Culture of the Antebellum South Carolina Low Country. (Illus.). 344p. 1997. reprint ed. pap. 19.95 (0-19-511795-6) OUP.

McCurry, Steve. Portraits. (Contemporary Artists Ser.). 1999. 16.95 (0-7148-3839-X) Phaidon Press.

***McCurry, Steve.** South Southeast. (Illus.). 160p. 2000. 59.95 (0-7148-3938-8) Phaidon Pr.

McCurry, Tom, ed. see Rued, Tim.

McCurtie, Francis E. Jane's Fighting Ships of World War II. (Illus.). 320p. 1994. 29.99 (0-517-67963-9) Random Hse Value.

***McCurtin, Peter.** Drumfire - Buffalo War, 2 vols. in 1. (Sundance Ser.). 384p. 2000. pap. 5.50 (0-8439-4701-2, Leisure Bks) Dorchester Pub Co.

McCurtin, Peter. Hangman's Knot - Apache War, 1. (Sundance Ser.). 368p. 1999. mass mkt. 5.50 (0-8439-4561-3) Dorchester Pub Co.

***McCurtin, Peter.** The Marauders - Day of the Halfbreeds, 2 vols. in 1. (Sundance Ser.: Vols. 3 & 5). 368p. 1999. mass mkt. 5.50 (0-8439-4521-4, Leisure Bks) Dorchester Pub Co.

McCurtin, Peter. Los Olvidados. large type ed. (Linford Western Library). 1989. pap. 16.99 (0-7089-6763-9, Linford) Ulverscroft.

— Sundance: Hangman's Knot. large type ed. (Linford Western Library). 256p. 1989. pap. 16.99 (0-7089-6718-3, Linford) Ulverscroft.

— Sundance: Iron Men. large type ed. (Linford Western Library). 272p. 1988. pap. 16.99 (0-7089-6530-X, Linford) Ulverscroft.

— Sundance: The Cage. large type ed. (Linford Western Library). 368p. 1992. pap. 16.99 (0-7089-7299-3) Ulverscroft.

McCurty, Darlene M. I'm Special Too. 1992. 6.95 (0-913543-27-6) African Am Imag.

McCusker, Brian. The Quest for Quarks. LC 83-7459. (Illus.). 164p. 1984. text 20.95 (0-521-24850-7) Cambridge U Pr.

McCusker, G. Games & Full Abstraction for a Functional Metalanguage with Recursive Types. Van Rijsbergen, C. J., ed. LC 98-18047. (Distinguished Dissertations Ser.). xiii, 189p. 1998. 89.95 (3-540-76255-8) Spr-Verlag.

McCusker, Honor. Fifty Years of Music in Boston. 1937. 3.00 (0-89073-104-7, 182) Boston Public Lib.

McCusker, Honor C. John Bale: Dramatist & Antiquary. LC 79-148890. (Select Bibliographies Reprint Ser.). 1977. reprint ed. 19.95 (0-8369-5678-8) Ayer.

***McCusker, John J.** Bothwell Boy. (Illus.). 62p. 1998. pap. 0.00 (0-9511204-9-2) Kinmor.

McCusker, John J. Essays in the Economic History of the Atlantic World. LC 97-5386. (Illus.). 426p. (C). 1997. write for info. (0-415-16841-4) Routledge.

— How Much Is That in Real Money? Addenda et Corrigenda. 7p. 1997. pap. 2.00 (0-944026-78-8) Am Antiquarian.

— Money & Exchange in Europe & America, 1600-1775: A Handbook. (Institute of Early American History & Culture Ser.). xiii, 367p. 1992. pap. 37.50 (0-8078-4367-9) U of NC Pr.

— Rum & the American Revolution, 2 vols., Set. (Outstanding Studies in Early American History). 1396p. 1989. reprint ed. 75.00 (0-8240-6191-8) Garland.

McCusker, John J. & Menard, Russell R. The Economy of British America, 1607-1789. rev. ed. LC 91-50283. (Institute of Early American History & Culture Ser.). xxiv, 513p. (C). 1991. reprint ed. pap. 32.50 (0-8078-4351-2) U of NC Pr.

McCusker, P. Vantage Points. 1991. pap. 8.99 (0-00-528638-7) Lillenas.

***McCusker, Paul.** Annison's Risk LC 99-36357. (Illus.). (J). 1999. 6.99 (1-56179-809-6) Tommy Nelson.

— Arin's Judgement, Vol. 2. LC 99-14247. (Passages Ser.). 1999. pap. 6.99 (1-56179-774-X) Tommy Nelson.

McCusker, Paul. Behind the Locked Door. LC 93-1749. (Adventures in Odyssey Ser.: No. 4). 84p. (J). (gr. 3-7). 1993. pap. 5.99 (1-56179-133-4) Focus Family.

McCusker, Paul. A Carnival of Secrets. LC 97-10868. (Adventures in Odyssey Ser.: Bk. 12). 120p. (J). (gr. 3-7). 1997. pap. 5.99 (1-56179-546-1) Focus Family.

McCusker, Paul. Catacombs. LC 96-40211. 296p. 1997. pap. 10.99 (0-8423-0378-2) Tyndale Hse.

Mccusker, Paul. Catacombs: A Story of Persecution, Faith, & Survival. 63p. 1985. 8.99 (0-8341-9320-5) Lillenas.

McCusker, Paul. Danger Lies Ahead. LC 95-7714. (Adventures in Odyssey Ser.: No. 7). (J). 1995. pap. 5.99 (1-56179-369-8) Focus Family.

— Dark Passage. LC 96-7655. (Adventures in Odyssey Ser.: Vol. 9). (J). (gr. 4-7). 1996. pap. 5.99 (1-56179-474-0) Focus Family.

— Dear Diary. 1998. pap. 6.99 (0-8341-9772-3) Nazarene.

***McCusker, Paul.** Draven's Defiance. (Passages Ser.: Vol. 5). 208p. (J). (gr. 5-9). 2000. pap. 6.99 (1-56179-844-4) Tommy Nelson.

Mccusker, Paul. Epiphany: A Christmas Story. LC 98-28854. 128p. 1998. 12.99 (0-310-22545-0) Zondervan.

McCusker, Paul. Family Outings. 1988. 8.99 (0-8341-9080-X, MP-643) Lillenas.

— Fathers Anonymous. 1995. pap. 8.99 (0-8341-9341-8, MP-755) Nazarene.

***McCusker, Paul.** Fendar's Legacy. LC 99-86121. (Passages Ser.: Vol. 6). 208p. (J). (gr. 5-9). 2000. pap. 6.99 (1-56179-845-2) Tommy Nelson.

McCusker, Paul. Freedom Run, Vol. 10. LC 96-25908. (Adventures in Odyssey Ser.: Bk. 10). 1996. pap. 5.99 (1-56179-475-9) Focus Family.

***McCusker, Paul.** Glennall's Betrayal. LC 99-34006. (Illus.). 208p. (J). 1999. 6.99 (1-56179-808-8) Tommy Nelson.

McCusker, Paul. High Flyer with a Flat Tire. (Adventures in Odyssey Ser.: No. 2). (J). (gr. 4-7). 1991. pap. 5.99 (1-56179-100-8) Focus Family.

— The King's Quest. LC 93-42883. (Adventures in Odyssey Ser.: No. 6). 150p. 1994. pap. 5.99 (1-56179-167-9) Focus Family.

— Lights Out at Camp What-a-Nut. (Adventures in Odyssey Ser.: No. 5). 150p. (J). (gr. 3-7). 1993. pap. 5.99 (1-56179-134-2) Focus Family.

— Memory's Gate. LC 96-17155. (Time Twists Ser.: No. 3). 144p. (YA). 1996. pap. text 5.99 (0-7459-3613-X) Lion USA.

— Pap's Place: A Two-Act Play about Family & Change. 1993. 8.99 (0-685-72852-8, MP-688); pap. 8.99 (0-8341-9855-X); pap. text 8.99 (0-00-543972-8) Lillenas.

— Play Writing: A Study in Choices & Challenges. LC 97-171168. 1995. pap. 14.99 (0-8341-9353-1, MP-760) Nazarene.

— Point of No Return. LC 95-19068. (Adventures in Odyssey Ser.: No. 8). (J). (gr. 3-7). 1995. pap. 5.99 (1-56179-401-5) Focus Family.

— Radio Scripts, Vol. 3. (Adventures in Odyssey Ser.). 1999. pap. 19.99 (0-8341-9839-8) Lillenas.

— The Secret Cave of Robinwood. (Adventures in Odyssey Ser.: No. 3). (J). (gr. 4-7). 1991. pap. 5.99 (1-56179-102-4) Focus Family.

— Snapshots & Portraits: A Two-Act Play about the Family. 59p. 1989. 8.99 (0-8341-9298-5, MP-652) Lillenas.

— A Strange Journey Back. (Adventures in Odyssey Ser.: No. 1). (J). (gr. 4-7). 1991. pap. 5.99 (1-56179-101-6) Focus Family.

— Stranger in the Mist. (Time Twists Ser.: No. 2). 144p. (YA). 1996. pap. text 5.99 (0-7459-3612-1) Lion USA.

— The Stranger's Message. LC 96-54640. (Adventures in Odyssey Ser.: Bk. 11). (J). (gr. 3-7). 1997. pap. 5.99 (1-56179-537-2) Focus Family.

— Sudden Switch. LC 96-19911. (Time Twists Ser.: No. 1). 144p. (YA). 1996. pap. text 5.99 (0-7459-3611-3) Lion USA.

— Vantage Points. 1986. 8.99 (0-685-68718-X, MP-636) Lillenas.

***McCusker, Paul.** Voice & Protector. LC 99-14208. (J). 1999. 6.99 (1-56179-773-1) Tommy Nelson.

McCusker, Paul. A Work in Progress: A Full-Length Play about Christian Identity, Evangelism, & Refrigerator Magnets. 52p. 1991. 8.99 (0-8341-9735-9, MP-669) Nazarene.

McCusker, Paul, jt. auth. see Bolte, Chuck.

McCusker, Penny. Happily Ever after. 1997. mass mkt. 1.78 (0-8217-5775-X) Kensgtn Pub Corp.

McCuskey, Dee D. Ketchum Cooks Vol. 1: A Centennial Celebration. (Illus.). 276p. 1995. 19.95 (0-9651469-0-1) Ketchum Cooks.

McCuskey, Dorothy. Bronson Alcott, Teacher. LC 71-89201. (American Education: Its Men, Institutions, & Ideas. Series 1). 1977. reprint ed. 21.95 (0-405-01440-6) Ayer.

***McCuskey, R. S. & Earnest, D. L.** Hepatic & Gastrointestinal Toxicology, 13 vols. (Comprehensive Toxicology Ser.: Vol. 9). 750p. 1999. 200.50 (0-08-042974-2) Elsevier.

McCuskey, W. H. Hervey. A Tree of Four Ancient Stocks: Fourfold Family History (Hervey, Huey, McCombs, McCuskey) (Illus.). 84p. 1997. reprint ed. pap. 15.50 (0-8328-9106-1); reprint ed. lib. bdg. 25.50 (0-8328-9105-3) Higginson Bk Co.

McCutchan, Ann. Marcel Moyse: Voice of the Flute. LC 93-33357. (Illus.). 344p. 1994. 29.95 (0-931340-68-3, Amadeus Pr) Timber.

— The Muse That Sings: Composers Speak about the Creative Process. LC 98-47028. (Illus.). 288p. 1999. 35.00 (0-19-512707-2) OUP.

McCutchan, Betty. Already Ours Every Day of the Year: 366 Devotional Moments. LC 99-70373. 224p. 1999. pap. 18.95 (1-57736-146-6) Providence Hse.

McCutchan, Philip. Assignment Argentina. large type ed. 239p. 1996. pap. 18.99 (1-85389-603-9, Dales) Ulverscroft.

— Assignment Gaolbreak. large type ed. 240p. 1994. pap. 18.99 (1-85389-474-5, Dales) Ulverscroft.

— Assignment London. large type ed. (Dales Ser.). 325p. 1994. pap. 18.99 (1-85389-432-X, Dales) Ulverscroft.

— The Bright Red Businessmen. large type ed. (Dales Large Print Ser.). 381p. 1996. pap. 18.99 (1-85389-610-1, Dales) Ulverscroft.

— Call for Simon Shard. large type ed. 1976. 27.99 (0-85456-499-3) Ulverscroft.

***McCutchan, Philip.** Cameron in the Gap. large type ed. LC 99-14885. 253p. 1999. pap. 22.95 (0-7862-1964-5) Mac Lib Ref.

McCutchan, Philip. Cameron's Chase. large type ed. LC 95-17590. (General Ser.). 1996. pap. 20.95 (0-7862-0473-7) Thorndike Pr.

— Cameron's Raid. large type ed. 257p. 1996. pap. 19.95 (0-7862-0472-9) Thorndike Pr.

— Coach North. large type ed. 1977. 27.99 (0-85456-535-3) Ulverscroft.

— Convoy East. LC 97-11291. 1997. pap. 11.95 (0-312-15499-2) St Martin.

— Convoy North. 192p. 1996. pap. 8.95 (0-312-14298-6) St Martin.

— Convoy of Fear. LC 97-11289. 192p. 1997. pap. 11.95 (0-312-16607-9) St Martin.

— Corpse. large type ed. 317p. 1992. 27.99 (0-7505-0309-2) Ulverscroft.

— The First Command. large type ed. LC 98-29773. 352p. 1999. 30.00 (0-7862-1589-5) Thorndike Pr.

— Greenfly. large type ed. (Magna Large Print Ser.). 332p. 1997. 27.99 (0-7505-1052-8) Ulverscroft.

— Halfhyde & the Admiral. large type ed. (Lythway Ser.). 288p. 1991. 21.95 (0-7451-1259-5, G K Hall Lrg Type) Mac Lib Ref.

— Halfhyde Goes to War. large type ed. (Dales Large Print Ser.). 304p. 1998. pap. 19.99 (1-85389-834-1, Dales) Ulverscroft.

McCutchan, Philip. Halfhyde to the Narrows LC 77-376036. 180p. (J). 1977. write for info. (0-297-77321-6, Pub. by Weidenfeld & Nicolson) Trafalgar.

— Halfhyde to the Narrows. 336p. 2000. 31.99 (0-7505-1539-2) Ulverscroft.

McCutchan, Philip. Halfhyde's Island. large type ed. 1978. 27.99 (0-7089-0159-X) Ulverscroft.

— Hartinger's Mouse. large type ed. 1978. 27.99 (0-7089-0143-3) Ulverscroft.

— Lieutenant Cameron RNVR. large type ed. LC 95-11465. 256p. 1995. pap. 20.95 (0-7862-0474-5) Thorndike Pr.

— The Logan File. large type ed. (Magna Large Print Ser.). 336p. 1996. 27.99 (0-7505-1051-X, Pub. by Mgna Lrg Print) Ulverscroft.

— The Negative Man. large type ed. (Dales Large Print Ser.). 274p. 1997. pap. 18.99 (1-85389-683-7) Ulverscroft.

— The New Lieutenant. LC 97-10026. 1997. text 20.95 (0-312-15604-9) St Martin.

— The New Lieutenant. large type ed. LC 97-13095. 266p. 1997. pap. 20.95 (0-7862-1127-X) Thorndike Pr.

***McCutchan, Philip.** Ogilvie at War. LC 00-28685. 2000. write for info. (0-7862-2567-X) Thorndike Pr.

McCutchan, Philip. Shard Calls the Tune. large type ed. 320p. 1994. 27.99 (0-7505-0537-0, Pub. by Mgna Lrg Print) Ulverscroft.

— Soldier of the Queen. large type ed. LC 98-44364. Date not set. 30.00 (0-7862-1667-0) Thorndike Pr.

McCutchan, Philip, told to. The First Command. LC 98-29773. 315 p. 1999. write for info. (0-7540-3472-0) Chivers N Amer.

***McCutchan, Philip D.** Cameron's Convoy. large type ed. LC 98-55239. 1999. 30.00 (0-7862-1821-5) Thorndike Pr.

McCutchan, Philip D. Captain at Arms. large type ed. LC 99-16582. 409p. 1999. 22.95 (0-7862-2094-5) Mac Lib Ref.

— Honour & Empire. 224p. 1999. 25.00 (0-7278-2293-4, Pub. by Severn Hse) Chivers N Amer.

***McCutchan, Philip D.** Honour & Empire. large type ed. LC 99-49109. (General Ser.). 2000. pap. 23.95 (0-7862-2303-0) Thorndike Pr.

McCutchan, Philip D. Ogilvie at War. 1999. 25.00 (0-7278-5471-2, Pub. by Severn Hse) Chivers N Amer.

McCutchan, Robert. Hymn Tune Names: Their Sources & Significance. reprint ed. 49.00 (0-403-03608-9) Scholarly.

***McCutchan, Stephen P.** Experiencing the Psalms: Weaving the Psalms into Your Ministry & Faith. LC 99-38656. 192p. 2000. pap. 20.00 (1-57312-283-1) Smyth & Helwys.

McCutchen, Ann A., ed. The NESFA Index to the Science Fiction Magazines & Original Anthologies, 1977-1978. vi, 74p. 1983. pap. 7.00 (0-915368-17-X) New Eng SF Assoc.

— The NESFA Index to the Science Fiction Magazines & Original Anthologies, 1979-80. (Index Ser.). viii, 90p. 1982. pap. 7.00 (0-915368-09-9) New Eng SF Assoc.

— The NESFA Index to the Science Fiction Magazines & Original Anthologies, 1981. (Index Ser.). (Illus.). vi, 60p. 1982. pap. 5.00 (0-915368-10-2) New Eng SF Assoc.

— The NESFA Index to the Science Fiction Magazines & Original Anthologies, 1982. vi, 64p. 1983. pap. 12.00 (0-915368-21-8) New Eng SF Assoc.

McCutchen, G. Calvin, Sr. & Chappelle, T. Oscar, Sr. Guidebook for Church Workers: Pointers for Pastors, Officers, Boards, Auxiliaries & Special Committees. rev. ed. Smith, Marvin L., ed. LC 90-81708. 50p. 1990. pap. text 6.00 (0-9625115-3-6) Campbell Rd Pr.

McCutchen, Heather. Alabama Rain. 1995. 5.50 (0-87129-566-0, A62) Dramatic Pub.

McCutcheon. Exploring Health Careers. 2nd ed. 96p. 1998. pap. text, teacher ed. 14.00 (0-8273-8534-X); mass mkt. 41.95 (0-8273-8533-1) Delmar.

— Water Quality Modeling Vol. 2: Biochem - Geochem Cycles - Rivers. 1995. 195.00 (0-8493-6972-X) CRC Pr.

***McCutcheon, et al.** Communication Applications: Teacher Edition. (Speech & Journalism Ser.). (C). 2000. text 79.00 (0-538-42919-4) Sth-Wstrn College.

McCutcheon, Allan L. Latent Class Analysis. (Quantitative Applications in the Social Sciences Ser.: Vol. 64). 88p. 1987. pap. 10.95 (0-8039-2752-5) Sage.

McCutcheon, Andrew H. & Gleason, Michael P. Sarge Reynolds: In the Time of His Life. (Illus.). vi, 180p. (Orig.). 1996. pap. 9.95 (0-9655584-0-1) Gleason Pub.

McCutcheon, Gail. Curriculum Decision Making. (C). 1995. pap. text. write for info. (0-8013-0940-9) Addison-Wesley.

— Developing the Curriculum. LC 94-8965. 256p. (C). 1995. pap. text 33.50 (0-8013-0949-2) Longman.

McCutcheon, George B. Beverly of Graustark. 1976. lib. bdg. 16.25 (0-89968-057-7, Lghtyr Pr) Buccaneer Bks.

— Brewster's Millions. 1976. lib. bdg. 19.95 (0-89968-058-5, Lghtyr Pr) Buccaneer Bks.

— Castle Craneycrow. 1976. lib. bdg. 17.25 (0-89968-059-3, Lghtyr Pr) Buccaneer Bks.

— The Daughter of Anderson Crow. 1976. lib. bdg. 15.75 (0-89968-060-7, Lghtyr Pr) Buccaneer Bks.

— Graustark. 1976. lib. bdg. 19.95 (0-89968-061-5, Lghtyr Pr) Buccaneer Bks.

— Graustark: The Story of a Love Behind a Throne. LC 72-145159. 1971. reprint ed. 18.00 (0-403-01087-X) Scholarly.

— Jane Cable. 1976. lib. bdg. 15.25 (0-89968-062-3, Lghtyr Pr) Buccaneer Bks.

— Nedra. 1976. lib. bdg. 15.75 (0-89968-063-1, Lghtyr Pr) Buccaneer Bks.

— Prince of Graustark. 1976. 23.95 (0-8488-0289-6) Amereon Ltd.

***McCutcheon, George Barr.** Brewster's Millions. LC 99-30003. 1999. 25.00 (0-253-33632-5) Ind U Pr.

McCutcheon, Gregory K. & Carlson, Kimberly S. A Year of Change. 1999. 250p. 1998. pap. 22.95 (0-9667789-0-1) Delaney Pubg.

M

McCutcheon, Ian E., jt. ed. see Hall, Walter A.

McCutcheon, James M. China & America: A Bibliography of Interactions, Foreign & Domestic. LC 74-190449. 85p. (Orig.). reprint ed. pap. 30.00 (*0-8357-8678-1*, 205683500092) Bks Demand.

***McCutcheon, Janette.** RMS Queen Mary: Transatlantic Masterpiece. (Illus.). 96p. 2000. pap. 24.99 (*0-7524-1716-9*, Pub. by Tempus Pubng) Arcadia Publng.

McCutcheon, John T. John McCutcheon: Stone by Stone. 104p. 1995. otabind 14.95 (*0-7935-3874-2*, 00698970) H Leonard.

McCutcheon, John T., et al. John McCutcheon's Book. LC 83-46027. (Classics of Modern American Humor Ser.). reprint ed. 64.50 (*0-404-19937-2*) AMS Pr.

McCutcheon, Lynn. Getting Something Out of Applied Psychology. 236p. (C). 1990. pap. text 28.57 (*0-929655-79-6*) CAT Pub.

— Psychological & Educational Testing: The User Friendly Text Book. 144p. 1998. pap. text 24.95 (*1-56226-389-7*) CAT Pub.

McCutcheon, Lynn E. Rhythm & Blues. (Illus.). 1971. 10.95 (*0-87948-028-9*) Beatty.

***McCutcheon, Marc.** The Beast in You: Activities & Questions to Explore Evolution. LC 99-20855. (Illus.). 96p. (J). (gr. 2-7). 1999. pap. 10.95 (*1-885593-36-8*) Williamson Pub Co.

M

McCutcheon, Marc. Descriptionary: A Thematic Dictionary. 496p. 1992. lib. bdg. 40.00 (*0-8160-2487-1*) Facts on File.

***McCutcheon, Marc.** Descriptionary: A Thematic Dictionary. 2nd ed. LC 99-89026. (Writer's Library Ser.). 576p. 2000. 45.95 (*0-8160-4105-9*, Checkmark); pap. 19.95 (*0-8160-4106-7*, Checkmark) Facts on File.

— Facts on File Student's Thesaurus. 2nd ed. LC 99-30711. 512p. 2000. 40.00 (*0-8160-4058-3*) Facts on File.

McCutcheon, Marc. Grandfather's Christmas Camp. (Illus.). 32p. (J). (gr. k-3). 1995. 15.95 (*0-395-69626-7*, Clarion Bks) HM.

— Grandfather's Christmas Camp. LC 94-15589. (Illus.). 32p. (J). (gr. k-3). 1997. pap. 5.95 (*0-395-86629-4*, Clarion Bks) HM.

— The Writer's Digest Sourcebook for Building Believable Characters. 288p. 1996. 17.99 (*0-89879-683-0*, Wrtrs Digest Bks) F & W Pubns Inc.

***McCutcheon, Marc.** The Writer's Digest Sourcebook for Building Believable Characters. 304p. 2000. pap. 14.99 (*1-58297-027-0*, Wrtrs Digest Bks) F & W Pubns Inc.

McCutcheon, Marc. Writer's Guide to Everyday Life from Prohibition Through World War II. (Writer's Guide to Everyday Life Ser.). 272p. 1995. 18.99 (*0-89879-697-0*, Wrtrs Digest Bks) F & W Pubns Inc.

— The Writer's Guide to Everyday Life in the 1800's. (Illus.). 320p. 1993. 18.99 (*0-89879-541-9*, Wrtrs Digest Bks) F & W Pubns Inc.

***McCutcheon, Marc, ed.** Webster's Thesaurus. (Webster's Ser.). (Illus.). 704p. 1999. 9.98 (*0-7651-1071-7*) Smithmark.

***McCutcheon, Mark.** Damn! Why Didn't I Write That? How Ordinary People Are Raking in $100,000 or More Writing Niche Books & How You Can Too! Mettee, Stephen B., ed. 212p. (Orig.). 2000. pap. 14.95 (*1-884956-17-3*, Pub. by Quill Driver) Amer West Books.

McCutcheon, Mark. Roget's Superthesaurus. 2nd rev. ed. 672p. 1998. pap. 19.99 (*0-89879-775-6*, Wrtrs Digest Bks) F & W Pubns Inc.

McCutcheon, Maureen. Exploring Health Careers. LC 92-14924. 317p. (C). 1993. mass mkt. 43.95 (*0-8273-4897-5*) Delmar.

— Exploring Health Careers. rev. ed. 133p. 1993. text, teacher ed. 12.75 (*0-8273-4898-3*) Delmar.

McCutcheon, Meredith A. Guitar & Vihuela: An Annotated Bibliography of the Literature on Their History. LC 85-17437. (Illus.). 1985. lib. bdg. 64.00 (*0-918728-28-2*) Pendragon NY.

McCutcheon, Pam. Chasing Baby. (American Romance Ser.). 1996. per. 3.75 (*0-373-16647-8*, 1-16647-9) Harlequin Bks.

— Here Comes the . . . Baby. (American Romance Ser.). 1998. per. 3.99 (*0-373-16722-9*, 1-16722-0) Harlequin Bks.

— A Little Something Extra. LC 96-3369. (American Romance Ser.). 248p. 1996. per. 3.50 (*0-373-16614-1*, 1-16614-9) Harlequin Bks.

— Quicksilver. 368p. (Orig.). 1996. mass mkt. 4.99 (*0-505-52141-5*, Love Spell) Dorchester Pub Co.

— A Reluctant Rogue. 1997. mass mkt. 3.75 (*0-373-16696-6*, 1-16696-6) Harlequin Bks.

— Writing the Fiction Synopsis: A Step by Step Approach. Clough, Judy, ed. 172p. 1998. 18.95 (*0-9654371-1-6*) Gryphon Bks Writers.

McCutcheon, Paul, jt. auth. see Byrne, Raymond.

***McCutcheon, Randall.** Elemental Methods in Ergodic Ramsey Theory. LC 99-88663. (Lecture Notes in Mathematics Ser.). vii, 160p. 2000. pap. 36.80 (*3-540-66809-8*) Spr-Verlag.

McCutcheon, Randall, et al. Communication Matters. LC 93-10452. (J). 1993. mass mkt. 42.25 (*0-314-01390-3*) West Pub.

McCutcheon, Randall, jt. auth. see Bergelson, V.

McCutcheon, Randall J. Get off My Brain: A Survival Guide for Lazy* Students (*Bored, Frustrated, & Otherwise Sick of School) rev. ed. LC 97-39354. (Illus.). 112p. (YA). (gr. 10 up). 1998. pap. 12.95 (*1-57542-037-6*) Free Spirit Pub.

McCutcheon, Russell, jt. ed. see Braun, Willi.

***McCutcheon, Russell T.** Critics Not Caretakers: Redescribing the Public Study of Religion. (C). 2001. pap. text 22.95 (*0-7914-4944-0*) State U NY Pr.

— Critics Not Caretakers: Redescribing the Public Study of Religion. (C). 2001. text 68.50 (*0-7914-4943-2*) State U NY Pr.

McCutcheon, Russell T. Manufacturing Religion: The Discourse of Sui Generis Religion & the Politics of Nostalgia. LC 96-22755. (Illus.). 272p. 1997. text 35.00 (*0-19-510503-6*) OUP.

McCutcheon, Russell T., ed. The Insider/Outsider Problem in the Study of Religion: A Reader. LC 98-4479. 432p. 1999. 85.00 (*0-304-70177-7*, Pub. by Cassell); pap. 35.00 (*0-304-70178-5*, Pub. by Cassell) Cassell.

McCutcheon, Sean. Electric Rivers: The Story of the James Bay Project. LC 91-72981. (Illus.). 194p. 1992. text 47.99 (*1-895431-19-0*, Pub. by Black Rose); pap. text 18.99 (*1-895431-18-2*, Pub. by Black Rose) Consort Bk Sales.

McCutcheon, Steve C. Water Quality Modeling Vol. 1: River Transport & Surface Exchange. (Illus.). 553p. 1990. lib. bdg. 249.00 (*0-8493-6971-1*, TD370) CRC Pr.

McCutcheon, Susan & Rosegg, Peter. Natural Childbirth the Bradley Way. rev. ed. LC 96-333. (Illus.). 256p. 1996. pap. 17.95 (*0-452-27659-4*, Plume) Dutton Plume.

— Natural Childbirth the Bradley Way. rev. ed. 256p. 1999. pap. 16.95 (*0-452-27658-6*, Plume) Dutton Plume.

McCutcheon, Vincent. Essays on Contemporary Issues: A Challenge for Today's Church. LC 98-66723. 115p. 1998. pap. 12.95 (*0-9647473-3-2*) Russell Cnslt.

McCutcheon, W. A. The Industrial Archaeology of Northern Ireland. LC 81-72046. (Illus.). 640p. 1984. 90.00 (*0-8386-3125-8*) Fairleigh Dickinson.

***McCutchion & Bhowmik.** Patuas & Patua Art in Bengal. 1999. 88.00 (*81-7102-061-5*, Pub. by Firma KLM) S Asia.

McCutchion, David. Brick Temples of Bengal: From the Archives of David McCutchion. Michell, George, ed. LC 82-3872. (Illus.). 465p. 1983. reprint ed. pap. 144.20 (*0-608-02524-0*, 206316800004) Bks Demand.

McCutecheon, J. J. Introduction to the Math of Science. 1986. pap. text 59.95 (*0-7506-0388-7*) Buttrwrth-Heinemann.

***McDade, Arthur.** The Natural Arches of the Big South Fork: A Guide to Selected Landforms. LC 99-6687. (Outdoor Tennessee Ser.). (Illus.). 144p. 2000. pap. 12.95 (*1-57233-074-0*) U of Tenn Pr.

McDade, Arthur, ed. see Kephart, Horace, et al.

McDade, Barbara E., jt. ed. see Spring, Anita.

McDade, Christina. Apples in the Sky. LC 89-84590. 108p. (Orig.). 1989. pap. 3.95 (*0-939810-12-3*) Jordan Valley.

***McDade, Joseph E., ed.** National Symposium on Medical & Public Health: Response to Bioterrorism. (Illus.). 76p. 2000. pap. text 25.00 (*0-7881-8531-4*) DIANE Pub.

— Tracking Trends & Analyzing New & Reemerging Infectious Disease Issues Around the World. (Illus.). 734p. (C). 2000. pap. text 30.00 (*0-7881-8606-X*) DIANE Pub.

McDade, Lucinda A., et al. La Selva: Ecology & Natural History of a Neotropical Rainforest. LC 93-1776. (Illus.). 498p. 1994. pap. text 34.00 (*0-226-03952-8*); lib. bdg. 90.00 (*0-226-03950-1*) U Ch Pr.

McDade, Paul, ed. see Wines, E. C.

McDade, Sharon A. Higher Education Leadership: Enhancing Skills through Professional Development Programs. Fife, Jonathan D., ed. LC 88-70150. (ASHE-ERIC Higher Education Reports: No. 87-5). 145p. (Orig.). 1988. pap. 24.00 (*0-913317-40-3*) GWU Grad Schl E&HD.

McDade, Sharon A. & Lewis, Phyllis H., eds. Developing Administrative Excellence: Creating a Culture of Leadership. LC 85-644752. (New Directions for Higher Education Ser.: No. HE 87). 110p. (Orig.). 1994. pap. 22.00 (*0-7879-9986-5*) Jossey-Bass.

McDade, Sharon A., jt. auth. see Green, Madeleine F.

McDaid, Hugh. Smart Weapons: The Top Secret History of Remote Controlled Weapons. 208p. 1998. pap. 29.95 (*1-56649-287-4*) Welcome Rain.

McDaid, Pearl, jt. ed. see Fisher, Ronald A.

McDalton, Magdalena. Qaltayak Aquiyaryugyaaquq.Tr. of Qaltayak Wants to Play Outside. (ESK., Illus.). 8p. (J). (gr. k-3). 1998. pap. text 6.00 (*1-58084-037-X*) Lower Kuskokwim.

McDalton, Magdalena, et al. Agay'am Egalerkun Uyangqallra. large type ed. (ESK., Illus.). 12p. (J). (gr. k-3). 1998. pap. text 6.00 (*1-58084-015-9*) Lower Kuskokwim.

— I Want to Take It Home. large type ed. (Illus.). 8p. (J). (gr. k-3). 1999. pap. text 6.00 (*1-58084-101-5*) Lower Kuskokwim.

— Kaviaq Kayangussulria. large type ed. (ESK., Illus.). 16p. (J). (gr. k-3). 1997. pap. text 6.00 (*1-58084-006-X*) Lower Kuskokwim.

— Ut'rucugaqa (I Want to Take It Home) large type ed. (ESK., Illus.). 8p. (J). (gr. k-3). 1999. pap. text 6.00 (*1-58084-148-1*) Lower Kuskokwim.

— Ut'rucugyaaqaqa (I Want to Take It Home) large type ed. (ESK., Illus.). 8p. (J). (gr. k-3). 1999. pap. text 6.00 (*1-58084-102-3*) Lower Kuskokwim.

***McDanel, Ralph Clipman.** The Virginia Constitutional Convention of 1901-1902. v, 167p. 1999. 52.00 (*1-56169-546-7*) Gaunt.

McDaniel. Atomic Collisions. 1411p. 1993. text 395.00 (*0-471-30441-7*) Wiley.

McDaniel. Floral Design & Arranging. 3rd ed. 1996. text, teacher ed. write for info. (*0-13-507898-9*) Allyn.

McDaniel. Introduction to Business. 3rd ed. LC 99-48395. 1999. pap. 79.95 (*0-324-01571-2*) Thomson Learn.

— Media Guide. Date not set. write for info. (*0-314-08703-6*) West Pub.

— Understanding Education Measurement. 1993. teacher ed. 9.06 (*0-697-21056-1*, WCB McGr Hill) McGrw-H Hghr Educ.

— Writing about Art. (C). Date not set. pap. text. write for info. (*0-15-507173-4*) Harcourt Coll Pubs.

McDaniel & Gates. Contemporary Marketing Research. 3rd ed. 1996. 62.20 (*0-314-08608-0*) Sth-Wstrn College.

***McDaniel & Gates.** Contemporary Marketing Research. 5th ed. 2001. pap. 68.57 (*0-324-06797-6*) Sth-Wstrn College.

— Investigacion de Mercados Contemporanea. 4th ed. 1999. pap. 92.95 (*968-7529-57-1*) Thomson Learn.

— Marketing Research & Exercise. 3rd ed. 1995. 60.20 (*0-314-08609-9*) Sth-Wstrn College.

McDaniel, jt. auth. see Gitman.

McDaniel, Antonio. Swing Low, Sweet Chariot: The Mortality Cost of Colonizing Liberia in the Nineteenth Century. (Illus.). 213p. 1995. 34.00 (*0-226-55724-3*) U Ch Pr.

McDaniel, Arlo. The Sea Resembling Glass. (Illus.). 198p. (Orig.). 1996. pap. write for info. (*1-57502-338-5*, PO1121) Morris Pubng.

McDaniel, Audrey. Greatest of These Is Love. LC 64-23538. (Illus.). 1972. 9.50 (*0-8378-1713-7*) Gibson.

— Hope for Every Heart. large type ed. (Large Print Inspirational Ser.). 1987. pap. 5.95 (*0-8027-2584-8*) Walker & Co.

— Touched by the Master: Reflections on My Life & Mission LC 74-83777. (C. R. Gibson Gift Books.). 88p. 1975. write for info. (*0-8378-1770-6*) Gibson.

McDaniel, Becky B. Katie Can. LC 87-5190. (Rookie Readers Ser.). (Illus.). 32p. (J). (ps-2). 1987. lib. bdg. 17.00 (*0-516-02082-X*) Childrens.

— Katie Couldn't. LC 85-11666. (Rookie Readers Ser.). (Illus.). 32p. (J). (ps-2). 1985. pap. 4.95 (*0-516-42069-0*); lib. bdg. 17.00 (*0-516-02069-2*) Childrens.

— Katie Did It. LC 83-7260. (Rookie Readers Ser.). (Illus.). 32p. (J). (ps-2). 1983. pap. 4.95 (*0-516-42043-7*); lib. bdg. 17.00 (*0-516-02043-9*) Childrens.

— Larry & the Cookie. LC 92-37871. (Rookie Readers Ser.). (Illus.). 32p. (J). (ps-2). 1993. lib. bdg. 17.00 (*0-516-02014-5*) Childrens.

McDaniel, Bonnie. In the Eye of the Storm. (Illus.). 120p. 1999. 32.50 (*0-9653869-4-5*) Castle Pacific.

— In the Eye of the Storm: A Celebration of Family & the Real Purpose of Home. (Illus.). 110p. 1999. 29.50 (*0-9671858-9-0*, Pub. by Art Good Living) Wash Bk Distrib.

McDaniel, Burt. Seize the Day: A Declaration of the Coming Revival. 165p. (Orig.). 1996. pap. 10.00 (*1-57502-289-3*, PO998) Morris Pubng.

***McDaniel, Cammie.** Children Surviving in a World of Violence: 35 Lessons for Students in Grades 5-9. (J). (gr. 5-9). 2000. pap. 19.95 (*1-57543-083-5*) Mar Co Prods.

McDaniel, Cammie. Situational Problem Solving: 44 Conflict-Resolution Role-Play Situations for Grades 5-9. 1995. 7.95 (*1-884063-68-3*) Mar Co Prods.

McDaniel, Carl, Jr. & Darden. Marketing. 768p. 1986. teacher ed. write for info. (*0-318-61505-3*, H0517-6); write for info. (*0-318-61506-1*, H0518-4); write for info. (*0-318-61508-8*, H1313-9); trans. write for info. (*0-318-61507-X*, H05192) P-H.

McDaniel, Carl & Gates, Roger. Marketing Research Essentials. 2nd ed. LC 97-12978. (SC - Marketing Research Ser.). 512p. 1997. pap. 79.95 (*0-538-87669-7*) Thomson Learn.

McDaniel, Carl, Jr. & Gates, Roger H. Contemp Marketing Research 2e. 2nd ed. Leyh, ed. LC 92-17896. (SWC-Marketing). 750p. (C). 1992. text 64.00 (*0-314-01026-2*) West Pub.

— Contemporary Marketing Research. 3rd ed. LC 92-17896. 800p. (C). 1995. pap. 68.50 (*0-314-06122-3*) West Pub.

— Marketing Research Essentials. LC 94-20227. (SWC-Marketing). 550p. (C). 1995. pap. 50.25 (*0-314-04283-0*) West Pub.

McDaniel, Carl, Jr., et al. Principles of Marketing. 2nd ed. (C). 1994. mass mkt. 54.75 (*0-538-82982-6*, SB61BA) S-W Pub.

McDaniel, Carl D. & Gates, Roger H. Contemporary Marketing Research. 4th ed. LC 98-7413. 1998. write for info. (*0-324-00603-9*); pap. 96.95 (*0-538-88507-6*) Sth-Wstrn College.

***McDaniel, Carl D. & Gates, Roger H.** Marketing Research Essentials. LC 00-36524. 2001. write for info. incl. disk (*0-324-03713-9*) Sth-Wstrn College.

McDaniel, Carl N. & Gowdy, John M. Paradise for Sale. LC 99-12829. 208p. 2000. 45.00 (*0-520-21864-7*, Pub. by U CA Pr) Cal Prin Full Svc.

— Paradise for Sale: Back to Sustainability. LC 99-12829. 208p. 2000. pap. 17.95 (*0-520-22229-6*, Pub. by U CA Pr) Cal Prin Full Svc.

McDaniel, Charlotte. Health Care Benefits Problem Solver for Human Resource Professionals & Managers. 302p. 1994. 125.95 (*0-471-00658-0*) Wiley.

McDaniel, Colleen, jt. auth. see McDaniel, Jack.

McDaniel, Dana, et al, eds. Methods for Assessing Children's Syntax. LC 96-33915. (Language, Speech & Communication Ser.). (Illus.). 408p. 1996. 49.50 (*0-262-13325-3*, Bradford Bks) MIT Pr.

— Methods for Assessing Children's Syntax. (Language, Speech, & Communication Ser.). (Illus.). 408p. 1998. pap. text 20.00 (*0-262-63190-3*, Bradford Bks) MIT Pr.

McDaniel, Danielle. How to Teach Clay the Clay Lady Way. (Illus.). 68p. (Orig.). 1996. spiral bd. 14.95 (*0-9654074-0-3*) Clay Ladys Hse.

McDaniel, Danny L. A Chef's Salad of Poems & Other Ramblings. 100p. (Orig.). 1997. pap. 13.00 (*1-57502-389-X*, P01225) Morris Pubng.

McDaniel, David. The Bride of Film Book Reference Guide. (Illus.). 56p. (Orig.). 1991. pap. 8.00 (*0-88734-901-3*) Players Pr.

— The Final Affair: A "Man from U.N.C.L.E" Novel. 176p. 1984. 14.00 (*0-935892-03-6*) Extequer.

McDaniel, David B. Paradox 5.0 for Windows at a Glance. (At a Glance Ser.). 136p. (Orig.). 1995. pap. 15.95 (*1-55622-456-7*) Wordware Pub.

McDaniel, Deborah. Foster Care in the 1980s. 174p. 1981. pap. 16.75 (*0-08-028096-X*, Pergamon Pr) Elsevier.

McDaniel, Dennis K. John Ogden: Abolitionist & Leader in Southern Education. LC 97-42359. (Transactions Ser.: Vol. 87, Pt. 6). (Illus.). 100p. 1997. pap. 15.00 (*0-87169-876-5*, T876-mcd) Am Philos.

McDaniel, Denzil. Enniskillen: The Remembrance Day Bombing. LC 98-128877. (Illus.). 192p. 1998. pap. 14.95 (*0-86327-611-3*, Pub. by Wolfhound Press) Irish Amer Bk.

McDaniel, Don. Body Fat: A Loser's Manual. (Illus.). 185p. (Orig.). 1992. pap. 12.95 (*0-9624378-2-4*) Life Fitness.

— Weightshaping - Body Sculpting & Human Performance: An Instructional Manual. (Illus.). 131p. 1998. pap. 14.95 (*0-9624378-5-9*) Life Fitness.

McDaniel, Doreen L., ed. see McDaniel, Melvyn C.

McDaniel, Douglas E. United States Technology Export Control: An Assessment. LC 91-45608. 304p. 1993. 62.95 (*0-275-94164-7*, C4164, Praeger Pubs) Greenwood.

McDaniel, Drew. Fundamental Communication Electronic. 192p. (C). 1995. pap. text, spiral bd. 21.95 (*0-7872-0594-X*) Kendall-Hunt.

— Fundamentals of Communication Electronics. 3rd ed. 216p. (C). 1998. spiral bd. 33.95 (*0-7872-5125-9*, 41512501) Kendall-Hunt.

McDaniel, Drew O. Broadcasting in the Malay World: Radio, Television, & Video in Brunei, Indonesia, Malaysia, & Singapore. LC 93-46297. (Communication & Information Science Ser.). 352p. 1994. pap. 39.50 (*1-56750-071-4*); text 78.50 (*1-56750-070-6*) Ablx Pub.

McDaniel, Dwight. Understanding the Dispensation. 125p. 1993. pap. text 9.95 (*1-883866-00-6*) Clarion Pub.

McDaniel, E. & Lawrence, C. Levels of Cognitive Complexity: An Approach to the Measurement of Thinking. (Recent Research in Psychology Ser.). (Illus.). xii, 97p. 1990. 58.95 (*0-387-97301-X*) Spr-Verlag.

McDaniel, Earl W. Atomic Collisions - Electron & Photon Projectiles. LC 89-5427. 736p. 1989. 239.00 (*0-471-85307-0*) Wiley.

McDaniel, Earl W., et al. Atomic Collisions: Heavy Particle Projectiles. LC 92-26121. 712p. 1993. 239.00 (*0-471-85308-9*) Wiley.

McDaniel, Edmond, jt. auth. see McDaniel, Wilfred.

McDaniel, Edwin B., ed. Second Asian Regional Workshop on Injectable Contraceptives. (Illus.). 93p. 1982. pap. 5.00 (*0-942716-04-3*) World Neigh.

McDaniel, Effie. Taste of Louisiana: Cajun - Creole Recipes. 2nd ed. Millang, Theresa, ed. 163p. 1989. write for info. (*0-9624584-0-6*) id Pub.

McDaniel, Ellen. A Guide to Eos & Unity Computing. 214p. (C). 1996. pap. text, ring bd. 17.95 (*0-7872-2648-3*) Kendall-Hunt.

— Guide to EOS & Unity Computing, 1997-1998. 2nd ed. 224p. (C). 1997. spiral bd. 16.95 (*0-7872-4250-0*) Kendall-Hunt.

McDaniel, Ernest. Understanding Educational Measurement. 384p. (C). 1993. text. write for info. (*0-697-13208-0*) Brown & Benchmark.

***McDaniel, Garry L.** Managing the Business: How Successful Managers Align Management Systems with Business Strategy. LC 99-44758. (Studies on Industrial Productivity). 1999. write for info. (*0-8153-3691-8*) Garland.

McDaniel, Gary L. Floral Design & Arrangement. 3rd ed. LC 95-23087. 290p. 1995. 98.00 (*0-13-230608-5*) P-H.

McDaniel, George, compiled by. IBM Dictionary of Computing. 10th ed. LC 93-20948. 1994. pap. 24.95 (*0-07-031489-6*) McGraw.

McDaniel, George W. Smith Wildman Brookhart: Iowa's Renegade Republican. LC 95-12116. (Illus.). 320p. 1995. text 39.95 (*0-8138-2107-X*) Iowa St U Pr.

McDaniel, George W. & Pearce, John N., eds. Images of Brookland: The History & Architecture of a Washington Suburb, Vol. M10. 1982. 7.00 (*1-888028-08-4*) GWU Ctr WAS.

McDaniel, Gerald. Aindreas: The Messenger, Louisville, Kentucky 1855. 293p. pap. 14.95 (*0-9673667-1-2*) VanMeter Pubg.

— Aindreas: The Messenger, Louisville, Kentucky 1855. 293p. 2000. 24.95 (*0-9673667-3-9*) VanMeter Pubg.

McDaniel-Hayko, Penny. War Baby. LC 96-94604. v, 124p. (Orig.). 1996. pap. 9.95 (*0-9653811-3-7*) Hasor-Plenny.

McDaniel, Herman. Computer Snafus. LC 98-23482. 248p. 1998. 22.95 (*0-9663993-0-7*) Chicora.

McDaniel, Ivan G. Realizing Eternal Selfhood. 297p. 1981. 10.95 (*0-932785-41-7*) Philos Pub.

McDaniel, J. The Lesbian Couples Guide. LC 95-14601. 288p. 1995. pap. 14.00 (*0-06-095021-8*) HarpC.

McDaniel, J. R. Making Automation Work: Successful Strategies for Managing New Technology. rev. ed. LC 92-27799. (Series in Entrepreneurship). 232p. 1992. text 20.00 (*0-8153-0997-X*) Garland.

McDaniel, Jack & McDaniel, Colleen. Pooches & Small Fry: Parenting Skills for Dogs (& Kids!) Luther, Luana, ed. LC 94-69540. (Parenting Skills for Dogs & Kids Ser.). (Illus.). 174p. 1995. pap. 14.95 (*0-944875-37-8*) Doral Pub.

McDaniel, Jan. Come Home Forever. 400p. (Orig.). 1997. mass mkt. 3.99 (*1-85487-717-8*, Pub. by Scarlet Bks) London Brdge.

— Dance until Morning: Opposites Attract. (Scarlet Ser.). 1998. mass mkt. 3.99 (*1-85487-573-6*, Pub. by Scarlet Bks) London Brdge.

— Keepsakes. (Scarlet Ser.). (Orig.). 1997. mass mkt. 3.99 (*1-85487-967-7*, Pub. by Scarlet Bks) London Brdge.

An Asterisk (*) at the beginning of an entry indicates that the title is appearing for the first time.

— A Sentimental Notion. large type ed. 185p. 1995. pap. 20.95 (*0-7838-1517-4*, G K Hall Lrg Type) Mac Lib Ref.

— Two for Tea. LC 96-97023. 192p. 1996. 18.95 (*0-8034-9179-4*, Avalon Bks) Bouregy.

***McDaniel, Jan.** Women Yes You Can! Wealth Thru Real Estate Investments. unabridged ed. LC 99-97021. (Illus.). 194p. 2000. pap. 20.00 (*0-9674682-0-5*) J McDaniel.

***McDaniel, Jay.** Living from the Center: Spirituality in an Age of Consumerism. 2000. pap. 24.99 (*0-8272-2130-4*) Chalice Pr.

McDaniel, Jay B. Earth, Sky, Gods, & Mortals: Developing an Ecological Spirituality. LC 89-51581. 228p. (Orig.). (C). 1990. pap. 14.95 (*0-89622-412-0*) Twenty-Third.

— With Roots & Wings: Christianity in an Age of Ecology & Dialogue. LC 95-500359. (Ecology & Justice Ser.). 280p. (Orig.). 1995. pap. 17.00 (*1-57075-001-7*) Orbis Bks.

McDaniel, Jay B., jt. auth. see Pinches, Charles.

McDaniel, Jay B., jt. ed. see Pinches, Charles R.

McDaniel, Jeffrey. Alibi School. LC 95-2002. 80p. (Orig.). 1995. pap. 8.95 (*0-916397-38-6*) Manic D Pr.

Mcdaniel, Jeffrey. Forgiveness Parade. LC 98-25399. 144p. 1998. pap. 11.95 (*0-916397-55-6*) Manic D Pr.

McDaniel, Jodi, ed. see Dykes, Mary Ann.

***McDaniel, John M.** The American Wild Turkey: Hunting Tactics & Techniques. LC 00-20389. (Illus.). 2000. write for info. (*1-58574-037-3*) Lyons Pr.

McDaniel, John M. Spring Turkey Hunting: The Serious Hunter's Guide. LC 85-27723. (Illus.). 224p. 1986. 21.95 (*0-8117-1688-0*) Stackpole.

McDaniel, Joshua, jt. auth. see Starrett, Robert A.

McDaniel, Judith. Just Say Yes: A Novel. LC 91-310. 176p. 1991. pap. 10.95 (*0-932379-96-6*); lib. bdg. 22.95 (*0-932379-97-4*) Firebrand Bks.

— Metamorphosis: Reflections on Recovery. LC 89-80611. 80p. 1989. pap. 7.95 (*0-932379-61-3*); lib. bdg. 16.95 (*0-932379-62-1*) Firebrand Bks.

— Sanctuary, A Journey. LC 87-7398. 176p. (Orig.). 1987. pap. 7.95 (*0-932379-23-0*); lib. bdg. 16.95 (*0-932379-24-9*) Firebrand Bks.

— Yes I Said Yes I Will. 256p. (Orig.). 1996. pap. 11.95 (*1-56280-138-4*) Naiad Pr.

McDaniel, Judith, ed. I Change, I Change: Poems by Barbara Deming. LC 95-26693. 150p. 1996. 12.95 (*0-934678-72-3*); pap. 9.95 (*0-934678-79-0*) New Victoria Pubs.

McDaniel, Judith, ed. see Bielawski, Jill & Weinert, Jerry.

McDaniel, Julie A., jt. auth. see Ohles, Judith K.

McDaniel, June. The Madness of the Saints: Ecstatic Religion in Bengal. LC 88-35657. (Illus.). 346p. 1989. pap. text 19.95 (*0-226-55723-5*) U Ch Pr.

McDaniel, June. The Madness of the Saints: Ecstatic Religion in Bengal. LC 88-35657. (Illus.). 352p. 1996. lib. bdg. 54.00 (*0-226-55722-7*) U Ch Pr.

***McDaniel, Karell.** Spiritual Agriculture: Such Is the Kingdom of God. (YA). 1999. pap. write for info. (*0-7392-0399-1*, PO3625) Morris Pubng.

McDaniel, Katy, jt. auth. see Crutsinger, Carla.

McDaniel, Keith E., ed. The Geospatial Technology Report, 1998: A Survey of Fifty Utility Companies Implementing Geospatial Information Technologies. Orig. Title: AM/FM/GIS Project Status Report. (Illus.). 48p. 1998. pap. write for info. (*0-9644786-2-5*) GITA.

***McDaniel, Kristyne.** Building Visual FoxPro Frameworks. Anderson, Bill, ed. 400p. 2000. pap. 49.95 (*1-930919-02-6*) Hentzenwerke.

McDaniel, L. L., et al, eds. American Type Culture Collection Catalogue of Plant Viruses & Antisera. 7th ed. 84p. 1993. pap. text. write for info. (*0-930009-48-7*) ATCC.

McDaniel, Laraine. Within the Law. (Intrigue Ser.). 1994. per. 2.99 (*0-373-22272-6*, 1-22272-8) Harlequin Bks.

McDaniel, Loraine. One Foot in Heaven. (American Romance Ser.). 1993. per. 3.50 (*0-373-16499-8*, 1-16499-5) Harlequin Bks.

McDaniel, Lorna. The Big Drum Ritual of Carriacou: Praisesongs in Rememory of Flight. LC 98-13515. 192p. 1998. 39.95 (*0-8130-1607-X*) U Press Fla.

McDaniel, Lurlene. All the Days of Her Life. (One Last Wish Ser.: No. 10). 192p. (YA). 1994. mass mkt. 4.50 (*0-553-56264-9*) Bantam.

— All the Days of her Life. (One Last Wish Ser.). 1994. 9.60 (*0-606-07970-X*, Pub. by Turtleback) Demco.

***McDaniel, Lurlene.** Angel of Hope. LC 99-46450. 240p. (YA). (gr. 7-12). 2000. 4.99 (*0-553-57148-6*, Starfire BDD) BDD Bks Young Read.

— Angel of Hope. (Illus.). (J). 2000. 10.34 (*0-606-17991-7*) Turtleback.

McDaniel, Lurlene. Angel of Mercy. LC 99-23983. 211p. (J). (gr. 7-12). 1999. 8.95 (*0-553-57145-1*) BDD Bks Young Read.

***McDaniel, Lurlene.** Angel of Mercy. (Illus.). (J). 1999. 14.30 (*0-606-17992-5*) Turtleback.

McDaniel, Lurlene. Angels Watching Over. (J). 1996. mass mkt. 6.99 (*0-553-54262-1*) BDD Bks Young Read.

— Angels Watching over Me. 176p. (J). (gr. 7-12). 1996. mass mkt. 4.99 (*0-553-56724-1*) Bantam.

McDaniel, Lurlene. Angels Watching over Me. (J). 1996. 10.09 (*0-606-11044-5*, Pub. by Turtleback) Demco.

McDaniel, Lurlene. Baby Alicia Is Dying. 192p. (YA). 1993. mass mkt. 4.99 (*0-553-29605-1*) Bantam.

Mcdaniel, Lurlene. Baby Alicia is Dying. 1993. 9.60 (*0-606-05131-7*, Pub. by Turtleback) Demco.

***McDaniel, Lurlene.** Dawn Rochelle: Four Novels. 576p. (J). (gr. 5 up). 2000. mass mkt. 6.99 (*0-553-57095-1*, Starfire BDD) BDD Bks Young Read.

— Dawn Rochelle: Four Novels. (Illus.). (J). 2000. 12.34 (*0-606-17994-1*) Turtleback.

McDaniel, Lurlene. Don't Die, My Love. (J). 1995. mass mkt. 4.99 (*0-553-54205-2*) BDD Bks Young Read.

— Don't Die, My Love. 256p. (YA). 1995. mass mkt. 4.99 (*0-553-56715-2*) Bantam.

McDaniel, Lurlene. Don't Die, My Love. 1995. 9.60 (*0-606-07440-6*, Pub. by Turtleback) Demco.

McDaniel, Lurlene. Eternal Flame, No. 13. (Serenade Serenata Ser.). 1985. pap. 2.50 (*0-310-46642-3*, 15523P) Zondervan.

— For Better, for Worse, Forever. 224p. (YA). 1997. mass mkt. 4.50 (*0-553-57088-9*) BDD Bks Young Read.

— For Better, for Worse, Forever. (J). (gr. 7). 1997. 4.50 (*0-614-29177-1*, Starfire BDD) BDD Bks Young Read.

— For Better, for Worse, Forever. 1997. 9.60 (*0-606-11342-8*, Pub. by Turtleback) Demco.

— Girl Death Left Behind. LC 98-27641. 192p. (YA). (gr. 6-12). 1999. mass mkt. 4.99 (*0-553-57091-9*) BDD Bks Young Read.

— Goodbye Doesn't Mean Forever. 208p. (YA). (gr. 7 up). 1989. mass mkt. 4.99 (*0-553-28007-4*, Starfire BDD) BDD Bks Young Read.

— Happily Ever After. 176p. (YA). 1992. mass mkt. 4.99 (*0-553-29056-8*) Bantam.

— Hold Fast the Dream, No. 20. (Serenade Serenata Ser.). 1985. pap. 2.50 (*0-310-46802-7*, 15539P) Zondervan.

— I Want to Live. (J). 1995. mass mkt. 4.99 (*0-553-54220-6*) BDD Bks Young Read.

— I Want to Live. 128p. (YA). 1995. mass mkt. 4.50 (*0-553-56766-7*) Bantam.

— I Want to Live. (J). 1995. 9.60 (*0-606-08553-X*, Pub. by Turtleback) Demco.

— I'll Be Seeing You. 208p. (YA). (gr. 7 up). 1996. mass mkt. 4.99 (*0-553-56718-7*, Starfire BDD) BDD Bks Young Read.

McDaniel, Lurlene. I'll Be Seeing You. 1996. 9.60 (*0-606-09451-2*, Pub. by Turtleback) Demco.

McDaniel, Lurlene. The Legacy: Making Wishes Come True. (One Last Wish Ser.: No. 7). 224p. (YA). 1993. mass mkt. 4.50 (*0-553-56134-0*) Bantam.

— Legacy: Making Wishes Come True. (One Last Wish Ser.). (J). 1993. 9.60 (*0-606-05422-7*, Pub. by Turtleback) Demco.

— Let Him Live. (One Last Wish Ser.: No. 6). 192p. (YA). 1993. mass mkt. 4.50 (*0-553-56067-0*) Bantam.

— Let Him Live. (One Last Wish Ser.). (J). 1993. 9.09 (*0-606-02706-8*, Pub. by Turtleback) Demco.

— Lifted up by Angels. 240p. (Orig.). (YA). (gr. 7 up). 1997. mass mkt. 4.99 (*0-553-57112-5*) BDD Bks Young Read.

McDaniel, Lurlene. Lifted up by Angels. (Orig.). 1997. 10.09 (*0-606-13569-3*, Pub. by Turtleback) Demco.

McDaniel, Lurlene. Love's Full Circle. (Serenade Serenata Ser.: No. 33). 1986. pap. 1.49 (*0-310-47302-0*) Zondervan.

— Mother, Help. (One Last Wish Ser.: No. 3). (J). 1997. mass mkt. 4.99 (*0-553-54280-X*) BDD Bks Young Read.

— Mother, Help Me Live. (One Last Wish Ser.). 1992. 9.09 (*0-606-00704-0*, Pub. by Turtleback) Demco.

— Mother, Help Me Live: One Last Wish. 176p. (YA). 1992. mass mkt. 4.50 (*0-553-29811-9*) Bantam.

— Mourning Song. (One Last Wish Ser.). 1992. 9.09 (*0-606-00496-3*, Pub. by Turtleback) Demco.

— Mourning Song, No. 2. 192p. (YA). 1992. mass mkt. 4.50 (*0-553-29810-0*) Bantam.

— No Time to Cry. 160p. (YA). (gr. 5). 1996. mass mkt. 4.99 (*0-553-57079-X*) Bantam.

— No Time to Cry. (J). 1996. 9.09 (*0-606-09697-3*, Pub. by Turtleback) Demco.

— Now I Lay Me down to Sleep. 160p. (YA). 1991. mass mkt. 4.50 (*0-553-28897-0*) Bantam.

— Now I Lay Me Down to Sleep. (J). 1995. 9.60 (*0-606-07960-2*) Turtleback.

— One Last Wish: Omnibus, 3 vols. in 1. 448p. (YA). 1998. mass mkt. 6.99 (*0-553-57142-7*) BDD Bks Young Read.

— One Last Wish: Time to Die, No. 1. 192p. (YA). 1992. mass mkt. 4.50 (*0-553-29809-7*) Bantam.

— Please Don't Die. 192p. (YA). (gr. 10 up). 1993. mass mkt. 4.50 (*0-553-56262-2*) Bantam.

— Please Don't Die. 1993. 9.60 (*0-606-07972-6*, Pub. by Turtleback) Demco.

— Reach for Tomorrow. LC 98-31794. (One Last Wish Ser.). 171p. (YA). (gr. 8-10). 1999. mass mkt. 4.50 (*0-553-57109-5*) BDD Bks Young Read.

— Saving Jessica. (J). 1995. mass mkt. 4.99 (*0-553-54234-6*) BDD Bks Young Read.

— Saving Jessica. (Seasonal Inspiration Ser.: No. 3). 208p. (YA). 1996. mass mkt. 4.99 (*0-553-56721-7*) Bantam.

Mcdaniel, Lurlene. Saving Jessica. 1996. 9.60 (*0-606-09820-8*, Pub. by Turtleback) Demco.

McDaniel, Lurlene. A Season for Goodbye. (One Last Wish Ser.: No. 11). 192p. (J). (gr. 7 up). 1995. mass mkt. 4.50 (*0-553-56265-7*) Bantam.

— Season for Goodbye. (J). 1994. mass mkt. 4.50 (*0-553-54177-3*) BDD Bks Young Read.

— Season for Goodbye. (One Last Wish Ser.). 1995. 9.85 (*0-606-07971-8*) Turtleback.

— She Died Too Young. (One Last Wish Ser.: No. 9). 192p. (YA). 1994. mass mkt. 4.50 (*0-553-56263-0*) Bantam.

— She Died Too Young. (One Last Wish Ser.). 1994. 9.09 (*0-606-07973-4*) Turtleback.

— Six Months to Live. (J). 1995. mass mkt. 4.99 (*0-553-54211-7*) BDD Bks Young Read.

— Six Months to Live. 144p. (YA). (gr. 7 up). 1995. mass mkt. 4.99 (*0-553-56760-8*, Starfire BDD) BDD Bks Young Read.

— Sixteen & Dying. (One Last Wish Ser.: No. 5). 176p. (YA). 1992. mass mkt. 4.50 (*0-553-29932-8*) Bantam.

— Sixteen & Dying. (One Last Wish Ser.). 1992. 9.09 (*0-606-00713-X*, Pub. by Turtleback) Demco.

— So Much to Live For. 160p. (YA). 1995. mass mkt. 4.50 (*0-553-56763-2*) Bantam.

— So Much to Live For. 1996. 9.60 (*0-606-08609-9*, Pub. by Turtleback) Demco.

— Someone Dies. (J). 1997. mass mkt. 4.99 (*0-553-54281-8*) BDD Bks Young Read.

— Someone Dies, Someone Lives. (One Last Wish Ser.: No. 4). 192p. (YA). 1992. mass mkt. 4.50 (*0-553-29842-9*) Bantam.

— Someone Dies, Someone Lives. (One Last Wish Ser.). 1992. 9.09 (*0-606-00707-5*, Pub. by Turtleback) Demco.

— Somewhere Between Life & Death. 160p. (YA). (gr. 5 up). 1990. mass mkt. 4.99 (*0-553-28349-9*, Starfire BDD) BDD Bks Young Read.

McDaniel, Lurlene. Somewhere Between Life & Death. 1991. 9.60 (*0-606-04804-9*, Pub. by Turtleback) Demco.

— Starry, Starry Nigh: Three Holiday Stories. (Illus.). 272p. (J). 2000. mass mkt. 4.99 (*0-553-57106-0*, Starfire BDD) BDD Bks Young Read.

McDaniel, Lurlene. Starry, Starry Night: Three Holiday Stories. LC 98-13372. 272p. (YA). (gr. 7 up). 1998. 8.95 (*0-553-57130-3*) Bantam.

— Til Death Do Us Part. 224p. (YA). 1997. mass mkt. 4.99 (*0-553-57085-4*) BDD Bks Young Read.

— Till Death Do Us Part. (J). (gr. 7). 1997. 4.50 (*0-614-29176-3*, Starfire BDD) BDD Bks Young Read.

McDaniel, Lurlene. Till Death Do Us Part. 1997. 9.60 (*0-606-11990-6*, Pub. by Turtleback) Demco.

McDaniel, Lurlene. Time to Die. (One Last Wish Ser.). 1992. 9.09 (*0-606-00492-0*, Pub. by Turtleback) Demco.

— Time to Let Go. 176p. (YA). (gr. 5 up). 1990. mass mkt. 4.99 (*0-553-28350-2*, Starfire BDD) BDD Bks Young Read.

— Time to Let Go. (J). 1991. 9.60 (*0-606-08308-1*, Pub. by Turtleback) Demco.

— Too Young to Die. 176p. (YA). (gr. 7 up). 1989. mass mkt. 4.99 (*0-553-28008-2*, Starfire BDD) BDD Bks Young Read.

McDaniel, Lurlene. Too Young to Die. (J). 1989. 9.60 (*0-606-04349-7*, Pub. by Turtleback) Demco.

McDaniel, Lurlene. Until Angels Close My Eyes. 176p. (YA). (gr. 7 up). 1998. mass mkt. 4.99 (*0-553-57115-X*, Starfire BDD) BDD Bks Young Read.

— Until Angels Close My Eyes. 1998. 10.09 (*0-606-13884-6*, Pub. by Turtleback) Demco.

— When Happily Ever after Ends. (Bantam Starfire Bks.). 1992. 9.09 (*0-606-00431-9*, Pub. by Turtleback) Demco.

McDaniel, Lynda. Longstreet Highroad Guide to the North Carolina Mountains, 5 vols. LC 97-76535. (Illus.). 308p. 1998. pap. 18.95 (*1-56352-463-5*) Longstreet.

McDaniel, Lynn. Conversational Journeys: And the Word of God. unabridged ed. 186p. 1996. pap. 7.95 (*0-89137-469-8*, 74698) Quality Pubns.

McDaniel, M. A. & Pressley, M., eds. Imagery & Related Mnemonic Processes. (Illus.). 440p. 1987. 139.95 (*0-387-96427-4*) Spr-Verlag.

McDaniel, M. A., jt. ed. see Cornoldi, C.

***McDaniel, Melissa.** Arizona, 5 vols. , Set. LC 00-22486. (Celebrate the States Ser.). (Illus.). 144p. (J). 2000. 35.64 (*0-7614-0647-6*, Benchmark NY) Marshall Cavendish.

McDaniel, Melissa. Ernest Hemingway: The Writer Who Suffered from Depression. LC 95-41554. (Great Achievers Ser.). (Illus.). 120p. (YA). (gr. 5 up). 1995. lib. bdg. 19.95 (*0-7910-2420-2*) Chelsea Hse.

***McDaniel, Melissa.** North Dakota. (Celebrate the States Ser.). (Illus.). (J). 2001. 35.64 (*0-7614-1069-4*, Benchmark NY) Marshall Cavendish.

McDaniel, Melissa. The Sac & Fox Indians. LC 94-44785. (Illus.). 80p. (J). (gr. 4-7). 1995. pap. 7.95 (*0-7910-2034-7*) Chelsea Hse.

***McDaniel, Melissa.** Spike Lee: On His Own Terms. (Book Report Biographies). (Illus.). 112p. (YA). (gr. 6-8). 1999. pap. text 6.95 (*0-531-15935-3*) Watts.

McDaniel, Melissa. Stephen Hawking: The Physicist Who Has Lou Gehrig's Disease. (Great Achievers Ser.). (Illus.). 120p. (YA). (gr. 5 up). 1994. lib. bdg. 19.95 (*0-7910-2078-9*) Chelsea Hse.

McDaniel, Melvyn C. The Best in Mousetrap Cars. 3rd ed. (Illus.). 74p. (YA). (gr. 4 up). 1997. pap. 12.50 (*0-9653457-2-6*) Adexell Pub.

— Great Pranks Using Mousetraps: Can Your Mousetrap Do This? 4th ed. (Illus.). xi, 70p. 1995. reprint ed. pap. 12.50 (*0-9653457-0-X*) Adexell Pub.

— Mousetrap Science Is Fun. 4th rev. ed. McDaniel, Doreen L., ed. (Illus.). 212p. (YA). (gr. 4 up). 1997. pap. 29.95 (*0-9653457-1-8*) Adexell Pub.

McDaniel, Nello. Artists' Projects. Conger, Shelley, ed. 64p. (Orig.). (C). 1994. pap. text. write for info. (*1-884345-02-6*) ARTS Action.

McDaniel, Nello & Thorn, George. Arts Boards: Creating a New Community Equation. rev. ed. Carlisle, Barbara & Conger, Shelley, eds. 104p. (C). 1994. pap. text 12.00 (*1-884345-03-4*) ARTS Action.

— The Quiet Crisis in the Arts. rev. ed. Rockwell, Mark & McBride, Donna, eds. 48p. (C). 1993. pap. text 6.00 (*1-884345-01-8*) ARTS Action.

— Toward a New Arts Order: Process, Power, Change. Block, Sharon, ed. 88p. (Orig.). (C). 1993. pap. text 10.00 (*1-884345-00-X*) ARTS Action.

McDaniel, Paul D., Jr. & Schmitt, Paul J. The Comprehensive Guide to Soviet Orders & Medals. LC 97-70605. (RUS., Illus.). 409p. 1997. 95.00 (*0-9656289-0-6*) Hist Resch LLC.

McDaniel, Paul R. & Ault, Hugh J. Introduction to United States International Taxation. 3rd rev. ed. (Series on International Taxation). 226p. 1989. 80.00 (*90-6544-423-8*) Kluwer Law Intl.

— Introduction to United States International Taxation. 4th ed. LC 98-5148. 1998. 95.00 (*90-411-0619-7*) Kluwer Law Intl.

McDaniel, Paul R. & Surrey, Stanley S. International Aspects of Tax Expenditures: A Comparative Study. LC 84-12575. (Series on International Taxation: No. 5). 1985. 214.00 (*90-6544-163-8*) Kluwer Law Intl.

McDaniel, Paul R., et al. Federal Income Taxation: Cases & Materials. 3rd ed. Simmons, Daniel L., ed. (University Casebook Ser.). 1291p. 1994. text 47.00 (*1-56662-170-4*) Foundation Pr.

— Federal Income Taxation, Cases & Materials: 1996 Supplement. 3rd ed. (University Casebook Ser.). 47p. 1996. pap. text. write for info. (*1-56662-392-8*) Foundation Pr.

— Federal Income Taxation of Business Organizations. (University Casebook Ser.). 1102p. 1990. text 43.75 (*0-88277-843-9*) Foundation Pr.

— Federal Income Taxation of Business Organizations. 2nd ed. LC 96-45034. (University Casebook Ser.). 1182p. 1996. write for info. (*1-56662-349-9*) Foundation Pr.

— Federal Income Taxation of Business Organizations: 1994 Supplement. (University Casebook Ser.). 140p. 1994. pap. text 8.95 (*1-56662-179-8*) Foundation Pr.

— Federal Income Taxation of Business Organizations: 1997 Supplement. 2nd ed. (University Casebook Ser.). 64p. 1997. pap. text. write for info. (*1-56662-560-2*) Foundation Pr.

— Federal Income Taxation of Corporations. LC 96-39881. (University Casebook Ser.). 816p. (C). 1996. text. write for info. (*1-56662-493-2*) Foundation Pr.

— Federal Income Taxation of Corporations, 1997 Supplement To. (University Casebook Ser.). 52p. 1997. pap. text. write for info. (*1-56662-561-0*) Foundation Pr.

— Federal Income Taxation of Partnerships & S Corporations. (University Casebook Ser.). 326p. 1990. text 28.75 (*0-88277-825-0*) Foundation Pr.

— Federal Income Taxation of Partnerships & S Corporations. 2nd ed. LC 96-39883. (University Casebook Ser.). 454p. (C). 1996. text. write for info. (*1-56662-484-3*) Foundation Pr.

— Federal Income Taxation of Partnerships & S Corporations: 1994 Supplement. (University Casebook Ser.). 82p. 1994. pap. text 5.95 (*1-56662-178-X*) Foundation Pr.

— Federal Income Taxation of Partnerships & S Corporations, 1997 Supplement To. 2nd ed. (University Casebook Ser.). 35p. 1997. pap. text. write for info. (*1-56662-503-3*) Foundation Pr.

— 1998 Supplement to Federal Income Taxation of Corporations. 86p. 1998. pap. text. write for info. (*1-56662-666-8*) Foundation Pr.

— 1998 Supplement to Federal Income Taxation of Business Organizations. 2nd ed. (University Casebook Ser.). 134p. (C). 1998. pap. text. write for info. (*1-56662-668-4*) Foundation Pr.

— 1998 Supplement to Federal Income Taxation & Partnerships & S Corporations. 2nd ed. (University Casebook Ser.). 82p. 1998. pap. text. write for info. (*1-56662-669-2*) Foundation Pr.

— 1995 Supplement to Federal Income Taxation, Cases & Materials, Suppl. 1. 3rd ed. (University Casebook Ser.). 31p. 1995. pap. text 4.95 (*1-56662-274-3*) Foundation Pr.

— 1995 Supplement to Federal Income Taxation of Partnerships & S Corporations, Suppl. 5. (University Casebook Ser.). 100p. 1995. pap. text 6.50 (*1-56662-267-0*) Foundation Pr.

— 1995 Supplement to Federal Income Taxation of Business Organizations, Suppl. 5. (University Casebook Ser.). 169p. 1995. pap. text 9.50 (*1-56662-266-2*) Foundation Pr.

— 1997 Supplement to Federal Income Taxation, Cases & Materials. 3rd ed. (University Casebook Ser.). 101p. 1997. pap. text. write for info. (*1-56662-507-6*) Foundation Pr.

McDaniel, Paul R., jt. auth. see Surrey, Stanley S.

McDaniel, Pete, jt. auth. see Woods, Earl.

McDaniel, Randy. A Blacksmithing Primer: A Course in Basic & Intermediate Blacksmithing. (Illus.). 174p. 1998. pap., spiral bd. 20.00 (*0-9662589-0-8*) Dragonfly Ent.

McDaniel, Rebecca. Scared Speechless: Public Speaking Step by Step. (C). 1994. text 44.00 (*0-8039-5173-6*); pap. text 18.50 (*0-8039-5174-4*) Sage.

McDaniel, Rebecca, jt. auth. see Hansen, Barbara.

McDaniel, Richard. The Drawing Book: Materials & Techniques for Today's Artist. (Materials & Techniques for Today's Artist Ser.). (Illus.). 176p. 1995. 35.00 (*0-8230-1392-8*) Watsn-Guptill.

— Hudson River Drawings. LC 94-7378. (Illus.). 111p. 1994. pap. 9.95 (*0-935796-48-7*) Purple Mnt Pr.

— Landscape: A Comprehensive Guide to Drawing & Painting Nature. LC 97-9185. (Illus.). 176p. 1997. 35.00 (*0-8230-2592-6*) Watsn-Guptill.

McDaniel, Robert, et al. PC Magazine Webmaster's Ultimate Resource Guide. LC 97-159624. 576p. 1996. 34.99 (*1-56276-435-7*, Ziff-Davis Pr) Que.

McDaniel, Robert A. The Shuster Mission & the Persian Constitutional Revolution. LC 72-96696. (Studies in Middle Eastern History: No. 1). 1974. 30.00 (*0-88297-004-6*) Bibliotheca.

***McDaniel, Robert Cecil.** The 1920 Population Census of Sabine County, Texas. 285p. 2000. pap. 20.00 (*1-887745-12-2*) Dogwood TX.

McDaniel, Robert E. Eternal Success Through Internal Assurance, 1 Vol., Vol. 1. (Illus.). 12p. (Orig.). 1989. pap. 3.95 (*0-685-31086-8*) Zanni Pubs.

— Fourth Estate. (Orig.). 1992. pap. 9.95 (*0-9623475-6-6*) Zanni Pubs.

— Jud Troy Syndrome: How to Build a Barn or Succeed at Anything. (Illus.). 6p. (Orig.). (C). 1989. pap. 3.95 (*0-9623475-2-3*) Zanni Pubs.

M

An Asterisk (*) at the beginning of an entry indicates that the title is appearing for the first time.

— Syndromic Living. 153p. (Orig.). 1989. pap. 9.95 (0-9623475-0-7) Zanni Pubs.

***McDaniel, Robert S.** Essentially Soap: The Elegant Art of Handmade Soap Making, Scenting, Coloring & Shaping. (Illus.). 128p. 2000. pap. 19.95 (0-87341-832-8) Krause Pubns.

McDaniel, Ruth E. The Exciting World of Creative Writing. (Illus.). 136p. (YA). (gr. 7-10). 1995. pap. text 8.00 (1-930092-70-9, CLP49910) Christian Liberty.

— The Exciting World of Creative Writing: Test Booklet. 1995. 1.00 (1-930092-71-7) Christian Liberty.

McDaniel, S., et al. Family-Oriented Primary Care. (Illus.). 400p. 1997. 60.00 (0-387-97056-8) Spr-Verlag.

McDaniel, S. T., jt. auth. see Lee, D.

McDaniel, Sandy & Bielen, Peggy. Project Self-Esteem: A Parent-Involvement Program for Children Grades K-6. rev. ed. Lovelady, Janet, ed. LC 89-84056. (Creative Teaching & Parenting Ser.). (Illus.). 408p. (J). (gr. k-6). 1990. reprint ed. pap. 39.95 (0-915190-59-1, JP9059-1) Jalmar Pr.

McDaniel, Sandy S. Recipes from Parenting. (Orig.). 1990. pap. 12.50 (0-9626359-0-1) S McDaniel Enter.

McDaniel, Stanley V. The Case for the Face: Scientists Examine the Evidence for Alien Artifacts on Mars. LC 98-84516. (Illus.). 220p. 1998. pap. 17.95 (0-932813-59-3) Adventures Unltd.

— The McDaniel Report: On the Failure of Executive, Congressional, & Scientific Responsibility in Investigating Possible Evidence of Artificial Structures on the Surface of Mars & in Setting Mission Priorities for NASA's Mars Exploration Program. (Illus.). 174p. (Orig.). (C). 1994. pap. 20.00 (1-55643-088-4) North Atlantic.

— The Philosophical Etymology of Hobbit. 24p. (Orig.). 1995. pap. 3.50 (1-881799-10-7) Am Tolkien Soc.

McDaniel, Susan. Counseling Families with Chronic Illness. 100p. 1995. pap. text 17.95 (1-55620-144-3, 72670) Am Coun Assn.

McDaniel, Susan H., et al. Medical Family Therapy: Psychosocial Treatment of Families with Health Problems. LC 92-11151. 352p. 1992. 38.00 (0-465-04437-9, Pub. by Basic) HarpC.

— The Shared Experience of Illness: Stories of Patients, Families, & Their Therapists. LC 97-2010. 1997. 42.00 (0-465-09737-5, Pub. by Basic) HarpC.

***McDaniel, Suzanne H., et al.** At Home in South Carolina. rev. ed. LC 99-39952. 2000. write for info. (1-928930-00-X) Ed Developmental.

— At Home in South Carolina: Resource Manual Sampler. 2nd ed. LC 99-41343. 2000. pap. write for info. (1-928930-02-6) Ed Developmental.

***McDaniel, Sylvia.** Rancher Takes a Wife. (Ballad Romances Ser.). 2000. mass mkt. 5.50 (0-8217-6666-X) Kensgtn Pub Corp.

— Scarlet Bride. 2000. mass mkt. 4.99 (0-8217-6478-0, Zebra Kensgtn) Kensgtn Pub Corp.

***McDaniel, T. C.** Disease Reprieve: Living into the Golden Years. LC 99-91005. 1999. 25.00 (0-7388-0572-6); pap. 18.00 (0-7388-0573-4) Xlibris Corp.

McDaniel, Terry W. & Victora, Randall, eds. Handbook of Magneto-Optical Data Recording: Materials, Subsystems, Techniques. 940p. 1997. 195.00 (0-8155-1391-7) Noyes.

***McDaniel, Thomas R.** Dr. Luke's Prescriptions for Spiritual Healing. 120p. 1999. pap. 12.00 (0-9654806-6-6) Magnus Pr.

McDaniel, Thomas R. Improving Student Behavior: Essays on Classroom Management & Motivation. LC 86-28228. 148p. (Orig.). 1987. pap. text 18.00 (0-8191-6065-2); lib. bdg. 40.50 (0-8191-6064-4) U Pr of Amer.

McDaniel, Tim. The Agony of the Russian Idea. 212p. 1996. pap. text 14.95 (0-691-00248-7, Pub. by Princeton U Pr) Cal Prin Full Svc.

— The Agony of the Russian Idea. LC 95-53191. 210p. (C). 1996. text 24.95 (0-691-02786-2, Pub. by Princeton U Pr) Cal Prin Full Svc.

— Autocracy, Modernization & Revolution in Russia & Iran. 256p. 1991. text 49.50 (0-691-03147-9, Pub. by Princeton U Pr) Cal Prin Full Svc.

— Autocracy, Modernization, & Revolution in Russia & Iran. 256p. 1991. pap. text 17.95 (0-691-02482-0, Pub. by Princeton U Pr) Cal Prin Full Svc.

***McDaniel, Toby.** Heroes, Honchos & Humdingers: A Newspaper Columnist Looks Back 30 Years. LC 99-96117. (Illus.). vi, 438p. 1999. pap. 9.95 (0-9675600-0-4, 2000) St Jrnl-Reg.

McDaniel, Wilfred & McDaniel, Edmond. Alaska Gold: Life on the New Frontier, 1899-1906. Kunkel, Jeff, ed. (Illus.). 160p. 1997. 34.95 (0-942087-14-3) Scottwall Assocs.

McDaniel, William, jt. auth. see Shiffer, Scott W.

McDaniel, William H. The History of Beech: Fifty Years of Excellence. rev. ed. LC 32-1640. (Illus.). 604p. reprint ed. write for info. (0-911978-00-3) McCormick-Armstrong.

McDaniel, Wilma E. Junkyard Sculpture. Meyer, Maggi H., ed. 28p. 1984. pap. 3.00 (0-915727-09-9) im-Press.

— The Last Dust Storm. LC 95-9865. 104p. 1995. 20.00 (1-882413-17-2); pap. 12.00 (1-882413-16-4) Hanging Loose.

— A Primer for Buford. 1990. 15.00 (0-914610-88-0); pap. 9.00 (0-914610-87-2) Hanging Loose.

— A Prince Albert Wind. 1994. 10.95 (0-9636829-1-1); pap. 7.95 (0-9636829-2-X) Mother Road.

— Sister Vayda's Song. 1982. pap. 10.00 (0-914610-27-9) Hanging Loose.

— Sleepin in a Truck. 48p. 1998. pap. 6.00 (1-890887-03-X) Mille Grazie.

— Tollbridge. 32p. 1980. 3.00 (0-936556-01-3) Contact Two.

— Vito & Zona. (Dog River Review Poetry Ser.). 40p. (Orig.). 1993. pap. 4.00 (0-916155-21-8) Trout Creek.

McDaniels, Dwight. The Dangers of Drifting. 25p. 1999. pap. text 12.95 (1-883866-15-4) Clarion Pub.

— I Am Invinsible Through Christ. 25p. 1999. pap. text 12.95 (1-883866-16-2) Clarion Pub.

McDaniels, Abigail. Althea. 1995. pap. 4.99 (0-8217-5170-0) NAL.

— Dead Voices. 256p. 1994. mass mkt. 4.50 (0-8217-4695-2, Zebra Kensgtn) Kensgtn Pub Corp.

— Playmates. 256p. 1993. mass mkt. 4.50 (0-8217-4296-5, Zebra Kensgtn) Kensgtn Pub Corp.

— The Uprising. 320p. 1994. mass mkt. 4.50 (0-8217-4501-8, Zebra Kensgtn) Kensgtn Pub Corp.

McDaniels, Carl. The Changing Workplace: Career Counseling Strategies for the 1990s & Beyond. LC 88-46081. (Management Ser.). 280p. 1989. text 32.95 (1-55542-146-6) Jossey-Bass.

— Developing a Professional Vitae or Resume. 3rd rev. ed. LC 96-41900. (Illus.). 108p. 1997. pap. 10.95 (0-89434-178-2, F137) Ferguson.

McDaniels, Carl & Gysbers, Norman C. Counseling for Career Development: Theories, Resources, & Practice. LC 91-25851. (Management Ser.). 485p. 1992. text 40.95 (1-55542-399-X) Jossey-Bass.

McDaniels, David K. The Sun: Our Future Energy Source. 360p. (C). 1991. reprint ed. lib. bdg. 44.50 (0-89464-594-3) Krieger.

McDaniels, Mike. The Pro 3-4: Winning Football with a Multipurpose Defense. 228p. (C). 1986. text 27.95 (0-13-711433-8) P-H.

McDaniels, Nawah, ed. see McDaniels, Pellom, III.

McDaniels, Pellom, III. My Own Harlem. McDaniels, Nawah, ed. LC 98-129906. (Illus.). 66p. 1997. pap. write for info. (0-9661814-0-9) P McDaniels.

***McDaniels, Pellom, III.** My Own Harlem. 2nd ed. LC 98-43009. 80p. 1998. pap. 12.95 (1-886110-67-0, Pub. by Addax Pubng) Midpt Trade.

McDaniels, Pellom, III. So You Want to Be a Pro. LC 99-26141. (Illus.). 224p. (YA). 1999. pap. 14.95 (1-886110-77-8, Pub. by Addax Pubng) Midpt Trade.

McDaniels, Preston, jt. auth. see Milligan, Bryce.

McDaniels, William. Abdul & the Designer Tennis Shoes. (YA). 1990. pap. 6.95 (0-913543-15-2) African Am Imag.

McDannel, Wally. Fly Till You Die: 452nd Bomb Wing. LC 93-60956. (Illus.). 134p. 1994. 49.95 (1-56311-112-8) Turner Pub KY.

McDannell, Colleen. The Christian Home in Victorian America, 1840-1900. LC 85-42947. (Religion in North America Ser.). (Illus.). 216p. 1994. pap. 14.95 (0-253-20882-3) Ind U Pr.

— Heaven: A History. 1995. pap. 18.00 (0-300-04858-0) Yale U Pr.

— Material Christianity: Religion & Popular Culture in America. (Illus.). 384p. 1996. pap. 24.95 (0-300-07499-9) Yale U Pr.

— Material Christianity: Religion & Popular Culture in America. LC 95-18066. (Illus.). 384p. 1998. 40.00 (0-300-06440-3) Yale U Pr.

***McDannold, Thomas A.** California's Chinese Heritage: A Legacy of Places. LC 99-95593. (Illus.). 224p. 2000. pap. 27.95 (0-9623048-9-1) Heritage West.

McDarby, Nancy. The Collegeville Bible Handbook. LC 96-40325. 352p. 1997. pap. 19.95 (0-8146-2376-X) Liturgical Pr.

McDarby, Nancy, ed. see Lazarev, Viktor Nikitich.

McDargh, Eileen. Work for a Living & Still Be Free to Live. 5th rev. ed. LC 85-1846. 260p. 1997. pap. 14.95 (1-885221-54-1) BookPartners.

McDargh, John. Psychoanalytic Object Relations Theory & the Study of Religion: On Faith & the Imaging of God. 296p. (C). 1983. pap. text 25.00 (0-8191-3511-9); lib. bdg. 53.00 (0-8191-3510-0) U Pr of Amer.

***McDaris, Catfish.** Bitchslapped. (Illus.). 32p. 2000. pap. 3.95 (1-930935-09-9, Pick Pocket Pr) Phony Lid Pubns.

***McDarrah, Timothy S.** The Photography Encyclopedia. 1998. 80.00 (0-02-865025-5, Schirmer Books) Mac Lib Ref.

***McDavid, Cathy.** The Attraction Fear. 2000. pap. 5.99 (1-929613-45-8, Kismet MI) Avid MI.

McDavid, Cathy. Wild Notion. 256p. 1998. pap. 12.00 (0-9655340-3-0) Neighbrhd Pr Pubng.

***McDavid, Cathy, ed.** 'Tis the Season: A Holiday Anthology. (Illus.). 1999. pap. 14.99 (1-893108-58-9) Neighbrhd Pr Pubng.

McDavid, Edmund R., III. God's Guarantee: Are You Covered? 250p. (Orig.). 1999. write for info. (0-9630447-2-9); pap. write for info. (0-9630447-3-7) Hope AL.

— Let God Speak: Let Us Listen. 382p. 1991. 14.95 (0-9630447-0-2); pap. 10.95 (0-9630447-1-0) Hope AL.

McDavid, Mary C., jt. ed. see Krogh, Peter F.

McDavid, Mimi. Grief & Loss Take Us on a Journey. (Illus.). 10p. 1998. pap. text 6.95 (0-9662513-0-X) Prospect Home Care.

McDavid, R. I., jt. auth. see Harder, K. B.

McDavid, Raven I., Jr. Needed Research in American English. (Publications of the American Dialect Society: No. 71). iv, 76p. (Orig.). 1984. pap. 7.60 (0-8173-0238-7) U of Ala Pr.

McDavid, Raven I. & Green, Donald C. The Structure of American English Workbook. LC PE2811.F672. 147p. reprint ed. pap., wbk. ed. 45.60 (0-608-30126-4, 201251300081) Bks Demand.

McDavid, Raven I., Jr. & O'Cain, Raymond K. Linguistic Atlas of the Middle & South Atlantic States: Fascicles 1 & 2, 1. LC 79-24748. (Illus.). 1994. pap. text 15.00 (0-226-55742-1) U Ch Pr.

— Linguistic Atlas of the Middle & South Atlantic States: Fascicles 1 & 2, 2. LC 79-24748. (Illus.). 128p. 1980. pap. text 18.00 (0-226-55744-8) U Ch Pr.

McDavid, Raven I., Jr. & Walton, Gerald W. Dialect Labels in the Merriam Third; Some Southern Farm Terms in Faulkner's Go down Moses. (Publications of the American Dialect Society: No. 47). 42p. 1967. pap. 4.25 (0-8173-0647-1) U of Ala Pr.

McDavid, Raven I., jt. auth. see Kurath, Hans.

McDavid, Raven I., Jr., jt. ed. see Blair, Walter.

McDavid, Virginia, ed. see Jaffe, Hilda.

***McDean, Craig, photos by.** I Love Fast Cars. (Illus.). 64p. 1999. 40.00 (1-57687-059-6, pwerHse Bks) pwerHse Cultrl.

McDean, Gleen. Gilding Book: A Complete Guide to Easy Gilding. 96p. 1998. pap. 33.00 (0-85532-876-2, Pub. by Srch Pr) St Mut.

McDean, Glenn. Gilding Ball: A Complete Guide to Easy Guilding. (Illus.). 96p. 1996. 19.95 (0-8230-2083-5) Watsn-Guptill.

— The Gilding Kit: A Complete Guide to Easy Gilding. (Illus.). 1996. 35.00 (0-8230-2084-3) Watsn-Guptill.

McDermid. Russian Women at Work, 1880-1930. LC 97-51648. (C). 1998. text 63.75 (0-582-27987-9, Pub. by Addison-Wesley); pap. text 23.44 (0-582-27986-0, Pub. by Addison-Wesley) Longman.

McDermid, J. A., jt. ed. see Ghezzi, C.

***McDermid, Jane & Hillyar, Anna.** Midwives of the Revolution: Female Bolsheviks & Women Workers in 1917. LC 99-21962. 304p. 1999. text 42.95 (0-8214-1289-2) Ohio U Pr.

McDermid, John A., ed. Software Engineer's Reference Book. 1993. lib. bdg. 89.95 (0-8493-7766-8, QA76) CRC Pr.

McDermid, Patt. Steppingstones: Ways to Better Reading. LC 92-33024. 379p. (C). 1993. pap. text 34.95 (1-55934-163-7, 1163) Mayfield Pub.

— Steppingstones, Instructor's Manual: Ways to Better Reading. LC 92-33024. (C). 1993. pap. text, teacher ed. write for info. (1-55934-164-5, 1164) Mayfield Pub.

McDermid, Patt C. Mountainhouse: A Novella. LC 81-83724. 137p. (Orig.). 1981. pap. 9.95 (0-912288-17-5) Perivale Pr.

***McDermid, Terry Z.** Matters of the Heart. LC 99-90716. 192p. 1999. 18.95 (0-8034-9373-8, Avalon Bks) Bouregy.

McDermid, Terry Z. The Romantic Doctor. LC 98-96334. 192p. 1998. lib. bdg. 18.95 (0-8034-9314-2, Avalon Bks) Bouregy.

— A Tapestry of Reading: Introducing Literary Genres, Grades 4-6. (Illus.). 130p. (Orig.). 1994. pap. 10.95 (0-673-36090-3, GoodYrBooks) Addson-Wesley Educ.

***McDermid, Terry Zahniser.** Love's Healing Power. LC 99-90978. 192p. 1999. 18.95 (0-8034-9383-5, Avalon Bks) Bouregy.

McDermid, Val. Blue Genes: A Kate Brannigan Mystery. LC 96-25146. 304p. 1997. 21.50 (0-684-83398-0, Scribner Pap Fic) S&S Trade Pap.

***McDermid, Val.** Booked for Murder. 2nd ed. (Lindsay Gordon Mystery Ser.). 260p. 2000. pap. 12.00 (1-883523-37-0, Pub. by Spinsters Ink) Words Distrib.

McDermid, Val. Clean Break: A Kate Brannigan Mystery. LC 95-959. 288p. 1995. 19.50 (0-684-80461-1) S&S Trade.

— Clean Break: A Kate Brannigan Mystery. large type ed. (General Ser.). 443p. 1996. pap. 21.95 (0-7862-0603-9) Thorndike Pr.

— Common Murder. 2nd ed. LC 95-23565. 264p. 1995. pap. 10.95 (1-883523-08-7) Spinsters Ink.

— Conferences Are Murder: A Lindsay Gordon Mystery. LC 98-55437. (Lindsay Gordon Mystery Ser.: Vol. 4). (Illus.). 264p. 1999. pap. 12.00 (1-883523-30-3) Spinsters Ink.

— Crack Down. 288p. 1994. 20.00 (0-684-19756-1, Scribners Ref) Mac Lib Ref.

— Dead Beat. large type ed. LC 96-47135. 1997. pap. 20.95 (0-7862-0929-1) Thorndike Pr.

— Deadline for Murder: A Lindsay Gordon Mystery. 2nd ed. LC 97-636. (Lindsay Gordon Mystery Ser.). 264p. (Orig.). 1997. pap. 10.95 (1-883523-17-6) Spinsters Ink.

— Kickback. large type ed. LC 94-24141. 328p. 1995. lib. bdg. 19.95 (0-7862-0360-9) Thorndike Pr.

***McDermid, Val.** A Place of Execution. 416p. 2000. 24.95 (0-312-26632-4, Minotaur) St Martin.

— Report for Murder. 224p. 25.00 (0-7278-5554-9) Severn Hse.

McDermid, Val. Report for Murder. 2nd ed. LC 97-50509. 264p. 1998. pap. 10.95 (1-883523-24-9) Spinsters Ink.

— The Wire in the Blood. limited ed. xii, 372p. 1998. 50.00 (1-890208-21-3) Poisoned Pen.

McDermot. Sega Mega Drive Games Secret. 1994. pap. 12.95 (1-55958-542-0) Prima Pub.

McDermot, Murtagh & Lunatic, Humphrey. Gulliveriana, No. 1: A Trip to the Moon. LC 73-13332. 220p. 1970. reprint ed. 50.00 (0-8201-1084-1) Schol Facsimiles.

McDermott. Brain Injury Pathway. (C). 1998. pap. text 75.00 (0-12-785065-1) Acad Pr.

— College Reading Extracts. 3rd ed. 104p. (C). 1999. pap. text 16.00 (0-536-01213-X) Pearson Custom.

Mcdermott. Coyote. 1994. 14.95 (0-15-200811-X, Harcourt Child Bks) Harcourt.

McDermott. Critical Paths. 1998. teacher ed. 75.00 (0-7616-2470-8) Harcourt.

Mcdermott. Cultural Introduction to Philosophy, Vol. 2. 1988. 9.95 (0-07-557117-X) McGraw.

— A Hopkins Chronology. LC 96-24546. 192p. 1997. text 49.95 (0-312-16167-0) St Martin.

McDermott. Medicine Made Memorable. (C). 1998. pap. text 28.00 (0-443-05195-X) Church.

— Psychology. 3rd ed. 316p. (C). 1998. pap. text 27.75 (0-536-01547-3) Pearson Custom.

— Spinal Cord Injury Pathway. (C). 1998. pap. text 75.00 (0-12-785067-8) Acad Pr.

— Stroke Recovery Pathway. (C). 1998. pap. text 75.00 (0-12-785068-6) Acad Pr.

McDermott, A. C., ed. An Eleventh-Century Buddhist Logic of 'Exists' Ratnakirti's Ksanabhangasiddih Vyatirekatmika. (Foundations of Language Supplementary Ser.: No. 11). 88p. 1969. text 112.00 (90-277-0081-8) Kluwer Academic.

McDermott, A. Charlene, ed. Godfrey of Fontaine's Abridgement of Boethius of Dacia's Modi Significandi Sive Quaestiones Super Priscianum Maiorem. (Studies in the History of Language Sciences: No. 22). ix, 237p. 1980. 59.00 (90-272-4503-7, SIHOL 22) J Benjamins Pubng Co.

McDermott, Alice. At Weddings & Wakes. 224p. 1998. pap. 12.95 (0-385-31985-1) Delacorte.

— At Weddings & Wakes. large type ed. LC 92-31035. (General Ser.). 320p. 1993. 20.95 (0-8161-5570-4, G K Hall Lrg Type) Mac Lib Ref.

— A Bigamist's Daughter. 304p. 1999. pap. 12.95 (0-385-33329-3, Delta Trade) Dell.

— Charming Billy. 256p. 1999. pap. 12.95 (0-385-33334-X, Delta Trade) Dell.

— Charming Billy. LC 97-77089. 280p. 1997. text 22.00 (0-374-12080-3) FS&G.

— Charming Billy. LC 98-44849. 1998. 25.95 (1-56895-685-1) Wheeler Pub.

McDermott, Alice. Charming Billy. aut. ed. text. write for info. (0-374-91390-0) FS&G.

— Happiest of Mothers. 2000. text. write for info. (0-374-16809-1) FS&G.

McDermott, Alice. That Night. 192p. 1999. pap. 12.95 (0-385-33330-7, Delta Trade) Dell.

McDermott, Annella, tr. see Abeles, Marc.

McDermott, Annella, tr. see Xitu, Uanhenga.

McDermott, Anthony. Egypt from Nasser to Mubarak: A Flawed Revolution. 320p. 1988. text 39.50 (0-7099-1736-8) Routledge.

***McDermott, Anthony.** The New Politics of Financing the UN. LC 99-23353. 1999. text 65.00 (0-312-22224-6) St Martin.

McDermott, Anthony, et al, eds. The Multinational Force in Beirut, 1982-1984. (Illus.). 293p. 1991. 49.95 (0-8130-1051-9) U Press Fla.

McDermott, Betty. Violin Pieces Country Style. (Illus.). 72p. 1977. pap. 12.95 (0-8256-2164-X, AM32426) Music Sales.

McDermott, Bobbye L., ed. How to Get Lost & Found in Fiji. 4th rev. ed. (Australia, California, Cook Islands, Fiji, Hawaii, Japan, London, New Zealand, & Tahiti Ser.). (Illus.). 208p. 1984. pap. 9.95 (0-912273-08-9) Orafa Pub Co.

McDermott, Bobbye L., jt. auth. see McDermott, John W.

McDermott, Bobbye L., ed. see McDermott, John W.

McDermott, Bobbye L., jt. ed. see McDermott, John W.

McDermott, Brian C. Word Becomes Flesh: Dimensions of Christology. (New Theology Studies). 302p. 1993. pap. 24.95 (0-8146-5015-5, M Glazier) Liturgical Pr.

McDermott, Catherine. The Design Museum Book of 20th Century Design. LC 97-43594. (Illus.). 400p. 1998. 65.00 (0-87951-852-9, Pub. by Overlook Pr) Penguin Putnam.

— English Eccentrics: The Textile Designs of Helen Littman. (Illus.). 120p. (C). 1993. pap. 19.95 (0-7148-2915-3, Pub. by Phaidon Press) Phaidon Pr.

***McDermott, Catherine.** Gianni Versace. 80p. 2000. 14.95 (1-85868-880-9, Pub. by Carlton Bks Ltd) Natl Bk Netwk.

— Matthew Hilton: Furniture for Our Time. (Illus.). 80p. 2000. pap. 33.00 (0-85331-807-7) Lund Humphries.

— Twentieth Century Design. (Illus.). 2000. pap. text 21.95 (1-58567-029-4, Pub. by Overlook Pr) Penguin Putnam.

— Vivienne Westwood. 1999. text 14.95 (1-85868-753-5, Pub. by Carlton Bks Ltd) Natl Bk Netwk.

***McDermott, Catherine, ed.** The Product Book. (D & AD Mastercraft Ser.). (Illus.). 176p. 1999. 55.00 (2-88046-394-7, Rotovision) Watsn-Guptill.

***McDermott, Catherine & Ehrman, Edwina.** Vivienne Westwood: A London Fashion. (Illus.). 90p. 2000. 29.95 (0-85667-525-3, Pub. by P Wilson) Antique Collect.

McDermott, Charlene, intro. Comparative Philosophy: Selected Essays. 566p. (Orig.). (C). 1983. pap. text 34.00 (0-8191-3487-2) U Pr of Amer.

McDermott, Charles, ed. see Merulo, Claudio.

McDermott, David & McGough, Peter, photos by. McDermott & McGough: A History of Photography. (Illus.). 144p. 1998. text 100.00 (0-9657280-2-1, 810081) Arena Editions.

McDermott, David, jt. auth. see Davies, Rex.

McDermott, Dennis & Grimm, Jacob W. The Golden Goose. LC 99-34513. (Illus.). 32p. (J). (ps-3). 2000. 15.95 (0-688-11402-4, Wm Morrow); 15.89 (0-688-11403-2, Wm Morrow) Morrow Avon.

***McDermott, Diane & Snyder, C. R.** Making Hope Happen: A Workbook for Turning Possibilities into Reality. 168p. 1999. pap. 14.95 (1-57224-167-5) New Harbinger.

***McDermott, Diane & Synder, C. R.** The Great Big Book of Hope: Help Your Children Achieve Their Dreams. (Illus.). 250p. 2000. pap. 15.95 (1-57224-212-4, Pub. by New Harbinger) Publishers Group.

McDermott, Drew V., jt. auth. see Hendler, James.

McDermott, E. Patrick & Berkeley, Arthur E. Alternative Dispute Resolution in the Workplace: Concepts & Techniques for Human Resource Executives & Their Counsel. LC 96-2211. 208p. 1996. 57.95 (1-56720-055-9, Quorum Bks) Greenwood.

McDermott, Ed, jt. auth. see McAdam, Maryln.

McDermott, Edwin J. Distinctive Qualities of the Catholic School. LC 97-207110. (NCEA Keynote Ser.). 82p. 1997. pap. 8.00 (1-55833-041-0) Natl Cath Educ.

An Asterisk (*) at the beginning of an entry indicates that the title is appearing for the first time.

McDermott, Emily A. Euripides' Medea: The Incarnation of Disorder. LC 88-17905. 166p. 1989. lib. bdg. 35.00 *(0-271-00647-1)* Pa St U Pr.

McDermott, Frank. Health Education. 3rd ed. 1999. 32.69 *(0-07-231957-7)* McGraw.

McDermott, Gerald. Anansi the Spider: A Tale from the Ashanti. (J). 1992. pap. write for info. *(0-03-080236-9)* H Holt & Co.

— Anansi the Spider: A Tale from the Ashanti. (J). 1986. 11.15 *(0-606-00366-5,* Pub. by Turtleback) Demco.

— Arrow to the Sun: A Pueblo Indian Tale. LC 73-16172. (Illus.). 48p. (J). (ps-3). 1974. 16.99 *(0-670-13369-8,* Viking Child) Peng Put Young Read.

McDermott, Gerald. Arrow to the Sun: A Pueblo Indian Tale. (Picture Puffin Ser.). 1977. 11.19 *(0-606-01088-2,* Pub. by Turtleback) Demco.

McDermott, Gerald. Coyote: A Trickster Tale from the American Southwest. LC 92-32979. (Illus.). 32p. 1999. pap. 6.00 *(0-15-201958-8)* Harcourt.

— Coyote: A Trickster Tale from the Southwest. abr. ed. LC 92-32979. (Illus.). 32p. (J). (ps-3). 1994. 14.95 *(0-15-220724-4)* Harcourt.

— Coyote: Un Cuento Folclorico Del Sudoeste De Estados Unidos. 1995. 11.20 *(0-606-09168-8,* Pub. by Turtleback) Demco.

— Coyote: Un Cuento Folklorico del Sudoeste de Estados Unidos. Marcuse, Aida E., tr. LC 95-731. (SPA., Illus.). 32p. (J). (ps-3). 1995. pap. 6.00 *(0-15-200032-1,* Voyager Bks) Harcourt.

— Flecha al Sol. unabridged ed.Tr. of Arrow to the Sun. (SPA.). (J). (gr. k-3). 1997. pap. 15.95 incl. audio *(0-87499-411-X)* Live Oak Media.

— Flecha al Sol, 4 bks., Set.Tr. of Arrow to the Sun. (SPA.). (J). (gr. k-3). 1997. pap., teacher ed. 33.95 incl. audio *(0-87499-413-6)* Live Oak Media.

— Flecha Al Sol: Un Cuento de los Indios Pueblo. (Picture Puffin Ser.). (SPA., Illus.). (J). 1991. 10.19 *(0-606-01988-X,* Pub. by Turtleback) Demco.

— Flecha al Sol: Un Cuento do los Indios Pueblo.Tr. of Arrow to the Sun: A Pueblo Indian Tale. (SPA., Illus.). 48p. (J). (ps-3). 1991. pap. 5.99 *(0-14-054364-3,* PuffinBks) Peng Put Young Read.

— Flecha al Sol (Arrow to the Sun) unabridged ed. (ENG & SPA.). (J). (gr. k-3). 1997. 22.95 incl. audio *(0-87499-412-8)* Live Oak Media.

***McDermott, Gerald.** Fox & the Stone. (Green Light Reader Ser.). (Illus.). (J). 1999. 9.44 *(0-606-18172-5)* Turtleback.

— Fox & the Stork. (Illus.). (J). 1999. 9.40 *(0-606-18173-3)* Turtleback.

McDermott, Gerald. The Light of the World: The Story of the Nativity, Bk. 2. LC 97-41484. (J). 1999. 17.00 *(0-689-80707-4)* S&S Childrens.

— The Magic Tree. (J). 1995. 15.95 *(0-8050-3080-8)* H Holt & Co.

— The Magic Tree: A Tale from the Congo. LC 72-76567. 41p. 1973. write for info. *(0-03-086716-9)* Holt R&W.

— Musicians of the Sun. (J). 1997. write for info. *(0-614-29297-2)* S&S Childrens.

— Musicians of the Sun. LC 93-44050. (J). 1994. 14.95 *(0-590-47337-9,* Blue Sky Press) Scholastic Inc.

— Papagayo: The Mischief Maker. LC 91-4036. (Illus.). 32p. (J). (ps-3). 1992. pap. 8.00 *(0-15-259464-7,* Harcourt Child Bks) Harcourt.

— Papagayo: The Mischief Maker. LC 91-4036. (Illus.). 32p. (J). (ps-3). 1992. 16.95 *(0-15-259465-5,* Harcourt Child Bks) Harcourt.

McDermott, Gerald. Papagayo, the Mischief Maker. (Voyager Bks.). 1992. 13.20 *(0-606-01023-8,* Pub. by Turtleback) Demco.

McDermott, Gerald. Raven: A Trickster Tale from the Pacific Northwest. LC 91-14563. (Illus.). 32p. (J). (ps-3). 1993. 16.00 *(0-15-265661-8,* Harcourt Child Bks) Harcourt.

— The Stonecutter. (Illus.). (J). (gr. 1-3). 1978. pap. 5.99 *(0-14-050289-0,* PuffinBks) Peng Put Young Read

— Stonecutter: A Japanese Folk Tale. (J). 1975. 11.19 *(0-606-02280-5,* Pub. by Turtleback) Demco.

— Untitled McDermott Myth Omnibus. (J). Date not set. 16.00 *(0-689-80711-2)* S&S Childrens.

— Untitled McDermott Mythworks # 3. (J). Date not set. 16.00 *(0-689-80709-0)* S&S Childrens.

— Untitled McDermott Mythworks #2. (J). Date not set. 16.00 *(0-689-80708-2)* S&S Childrens.

— Untitled McDermott Mythworks #4. (J). Date not set. 16.00 *(0-689-80710-4)* S&S Childrens.

— Zomo the Rabbit: A Trickster Tale from West Africa. LC 91-14558. (Illus.). 32p. (J). (ps-3). 1992. 14.95 *(0-15-299967-1,* Harcourt Child Bks) Harcourt.

— Zomo the Rabbit: A Trickster Tale from West Africa. LC 91-14558. (Illus.). 32p. (J). (ps-3). 1996. pap. 22.00 *(0-15-201011-4)* Harcourt.

— Zomo the Rabbit: A Trickster Tale from West Africa. abr. ed. LC 91-14558. (Illus.). 32p. (J). (ps-3). 1996. pap. 6.00 *(0-15-201010-6,* Voyager Bks) Harcourt.

McDermott, Gerald. Jabuti the Tortoise: A Trickster Tale from the Amazon. LC 94-23290. 1995. lib. bdg. 14.95 *(0-15-292874-X)* Harcourt.

McDermott, Gerald. Anansi the Spider: A Tale from the Ashanti. LC 76-150028. 48p. (J). (ps-2). 1995. pap. 5.95 *(0-8050-0311-8,* Bks Young Read) H Holt & Co.

McDermott, Gerald. Anansi the Spider: A Tale from the Ashanti. LC 76-150028. 48p. (J). (ps-3). 1995. lib. bdg. 15.95 *(0-8050-0310-X,* Bks Young Read) H Holt & Co.

McDermott, Gerald, retold by. Musicians of the Sun, No. 1. LC 96-19891. (Illus.). 40p. (J). (gr. k-4). 1997. per. 17.00 *(0-689-80706-6)* S&S Childrens.

McDermott, Gerald & Fintel, William A. Dear God, It's Cancer: A Medical & Spiritual Guide for Patients & their Families. rev. ed. LC 97-11438. 272p. 1997. pap. 12.99 *(0-8499-4041-9)* Word Pub.

***McDermott, Gerald R.** Can Evangelicals Learn from World Religions? Jesus, Revelation & Religious Traditions. 240p. 2000. pap. 14.99 *(0-8308-2274-7)* InterVarsity.

— Jonathan Edwards Confronts the Gods: Christian Theology, Enlightenment Religion & Non-Christian Faiths. LC 99-26834. (Religion in America Ser.). 264p. 2000. text 45.00 *(0-19-513274-2)* OUP.

McDermott, Gerald R. One Holy & Happy Society: The Public Theology of Jonathan Edwards. 256p. 1992. 35.00 *(0-271-00850-4)* Pa St U Pr.

— Seeing God: Twelve Reliable Signs of True Spirituality. LC 95-25286. 288p. (Orig.). 1995. pap. 11.99 *(0-8308-1616-X,* 1616) InterVarsity.

— Zomo the Rabbit: A Trickster Tale from West Africa. LC 91-14558. (J). 1996. 11.20 *(0-606-10107-1,* Pub. by Turtleback) Demco.

McDermott, Henry J. Handbook of Ventilation for Contaminant Control. 2nd ed. 1991. 56.95 *(0-7506-9221-9)* Buttrwrth-Heinemann.

McDermott, Hubert, ed. Vertue Rewarded: or The Irish Princess: A New Novel. 107p. 1994. lib. bdg. 42.00 *(0-86140-305-3,* Pub. by Smyth) B&N Imports.

McDermott, Ian & O'Connor, Joseph. Practical NLP for Managers. 200p. 1996. 61.95 *(0-566-07671-3,* Pub. by Gower) Ashgate Pub Co.

McDermott, Ignatius D., et al. Intervention Instruction Inc. Level 2M DUI Risk Reduction Education & Treatment Program: Program Description & Operations Procedures. 107p. (Orig.). 1995. pap. 9.95 *(0-9654994-0-5)* Intervention Instruct Inc.

McDermott, J., jt. auth. see Dougherty, J.

McDermott, J. Cynthia, ed. Beyond the Silence: Listening for Democracy. LC 98-30141. 146p. 1998. pap. text 17.50 *(0-325-00072-7)* Heinemann.

McDermott, J. P. Why Women & Power Don't Mix: The Perils of Feminism. 1996. 18.95 *(0-9654987-0-0)* Patriarchic Pub Co.

McDermott, James. Maker, Lover & Keeper. 112p. (C). 1988. 35.00 *(0-85597-454-0,* Pub. by McCrimmon Pub) St Mut.

McDermott, James & Phillips, John. Administering Usenet News Servers: A Comprehensive Guide to Planning, Building & Managing. LC 97-3462. 320p. (C). 1997. pap. text 39.95 *(0-201-41967-X)* Addison-Wesley.

McDermott, James M., et al, eds. Statistical Agencies: Adherence to Guidelines & Coordination of Budgets. (Illus.). 56p. 1997. reprint ed. pap. text 30.00 *(0-7881-4107-4)* DIANE Pub.

McDermott, James M., et al. Cooperative Purchasing: Effects Are Likely to Vary among Governments & Businesses. (Illus.). 114p. (C). 1999. pap. text 30.00 *(0-7881-4367-0)* DIANE Pub.

McDermott, James P. Development in the Early Buddhist Concept of Kamma-Karma. 1984. 14.50 *(0-8364-2542-1,* Pub. by M Manoharial) S Asia.

***McDermott, Jeanne.** Babyface: A Story of Heart & Bones. LC 99-87649. 225p. (C). 2000. 22.95 *(1-890627-15-1)* Woodbine House.

McDermott, John. The Crisis in the Working Class: And Some Arguments for a New Labor Movement. LC 80-51437. 255p. (Orig.). 1980. 30.00 *(0-89608-015-3)* South End Pr.

— The Crisis in the Working Class: Some Arguments for a New Labor Movement. LC 80-51437. 255p. (Orig.). 1980. pap. 6.00 *(0-89608-014-5)* South End Pr.

McDermott, John, et al. Hendrix: Setting the Record Straight. (Orig.). 1992. mass mkt. 15.99 *(0-446-39431-9,* Pub. by Warner Bks) Little.

McDermott, John, jt. auth. see MacKinnon, John.

McDermott, John, jt. ed. see Connolly, Michael B.

McDermott, John D. A Guide to the Indian Wars of the West. LC 98-16048. (Illus.). xxv, 211p. 1998. pap. 16.95 *(0-8032-8246-X)* U of Nebr Pr.

McDermott, John E. The Diabetic Foot. 70p. 1995. pap. 35.00 *(0 89203-119-0)* Amer Acad Ortho Surg.

McDermott, John F. Before Mark Twain: A Sampler of Old, Old Times on the Mississippi. LC 97-42246. 1998. pap. 14.95 *(0-8093-2191-2)* S Ill U Pr.

— Seth Eastman, Pictorial Historian of the Indian. LC 61-15145. (Illus.). 302p. reprint ed. pap. 93.70 *(0-608-16139-X,* 200584600055) Bks Demand.

McDermott, John F., ed. The French in the Mississippi Valley. LC 65-11736. (Illus.). 299p. reprint ed. pap. 92.70 *(0-608-10906-1,* 202021300016) Bks Demand.

— Frenchmen & French Ways in the Mississippi Valley. LC 68-24622. (Illus.). 320p. reprint ed. 99.20 *(0-8357-9677-9,* 201494100093) Bks Demand.

— Research Opportunities in American Cultural History. LC 77-22111. 205p. 1977. reprint ed. lib. bdg. 55.00 *(0-8371-9754-6,* MCRO, Greenwood Pr) Greenwood.

— Travelers on the Western Frontier. LC 77-100375. (Illus.). 363p. reprint ed. 112.60 *(0-8357-9700-7,* 201492000093) Bks Demand.

McDermott, John F., Jr., et al, eds. People & Cultures of Hawaii: A Psychocultural Profile. LC 80-11959. 252p. 1980. pap. 11.95 *(0-8248-0706-5)* UH Pr.

McDermott, John F. & Harrison, Saul I., eds. Psychiatric Treatment of the Child. LC 76-45569. 839p. 1977. 75.00 *(0-87668-289-1)* Aronson.

McDermott, John F., Jr., jt. ed. see Harrison, Saul I.

McDermott, John J. What Are They Saying about the Formation of Israel? 144p. 1998. pap. 10.95 *(0-8091-3838-7)* Paulist Pr.

McDermott, John J., ed. see Bradbeer, Wilma.

McDermott, John J., ed. see Dewey, John.

McDermott, John J., ed. see James, William.

McDermott, John M. The Bible on Human Suffering. 155p. (C). 1996. pap. 60.00 *(0-85439-363-3,* Pub. by St Paul Pubns) St Mut.

McDermott, John T., ed. Legal Aspects of Investment & Trade with the Republic of China, No. 1. 94p. 1991. 6.00 *(0-925153-13-3,* 102) Occasional Papers.

McDermott, John W. How to Get Lost & Found in Australia. 2nd ed. McDermott, Bobbye L. & Suga, Roger, eds. (Australia, California, Cook Islands, Fiji, Hawaii, Japan, London, New Zealand, & Tahiti Ser.). (Illus.). 304p. 1984. pap. 9.95 *(0-912273-07-0)* Orafa Pub Co.

— How to Get Lost & Found in California & Other Lovely Places. McDermott, Bobbye L., ed. (Australia, California, Cook Islands, Fiji, Hawaii, Japan, London, New Zealand, & Tahiti Ser.). (Illus.). 308p. 1982. pap. 9.95 *(0-912273-05-4)* Orafa Pub Co.

— How to Get Lost & Found in New Japan. McDermott, Bobbye L., ed. (Australia, California, Cook Islands, Fiji, Hawaii, Japan, London, New Zealand, & Tahiti Ser.). (Illus.). 286p. 1984. pap. 9.95 *(0-912273-06-2)* Orafa Pub Co.

— How to Get Lost & Found in Tahiti. 2nd ed. McDermott, Bobbye L., ed. LC 86-62292. (Australia, California, Cook Islands, Fiji, Hawaii, Japan, London, New Zealand, & Tahiti Ser.). (Illus.). 272p. 1986. reprint ed. pap. 9.95 *(0-912273-13-5)* Orafa Pub Co.

— Kelleys of the Outrigger. McDermott, Bobbye L., ed. (Illus.). 304p. 1990. 19.95 *(0-912273-18-6)*; write for info. *(0-912273-20-8)*; pap. 10.95 *(0-912273-19-4)* Orafa Pub Co.

McDermott, John W. & McDermott, Bobbye L. How to Get Lost & Found in Our Hawaii. LC 85-61324. (Australia, California, Cook Islands, Fiji, Hawaii, Japan, London, New Zealand, & Tahiti Ser.). Orig. Title: Our Hawaii: What We Tell Friends To Do In Our Islands. (Illus.). 296p. (Orig.). 1986. pap. 9.95 *(0-912273-12-7)* Orafa Pub Co.

— How to Get Lost & Found in the Cook Islands. 2nd ed. LC 86-62293. (Australia, California, Cook Islands, Fiji, Hawaii, Japan, London, New Zealand, & Tahiti Ser.). (Illus.). 236p. 1987. reprint ed. pap. 9.95 *(0-912273-15-1)* Orafa Pub Co.

— How to Get Lost & Found in Upgraded New Zealand. LC 86-62291. (Australia, California, Cook Islands, Fiji, Hawaii, Japan, London, New Zealand, & Tahiti Ser.). (Illus.). 320p. 1987. reprint ed. pap. 9.95 *(0-912273-11-9)* Orafa Pub Co.

McDermott, John W. & McDermott, Bobbye L., eds. How to Get Lost & Found in London. (Australia, California, Cook Islands, Fiji, Hawaii, Japan, London, New Zealand, & Tahiti Ser.). (Illus.). 336p. 1988. pap. 9.95 *(0-912273-17-8)* Orafa Pub Co.

McDermott, Joseph P., ed. State & Court Ritual in China. LC 97-19297. (University of Cambridge Oriental Publications: No. 54). 448p. (C). 1998. text 79.95 *(0-521-62157-7)* Cambridge U Pr.

***McDermott, Kathleen.** Timex: A Company & Its Community 1854-1998. unabridged ed. LC 97-61156. (Illus.). 248p. 1998. 29.95 *(0-9675087-0-3)* TIMEX Corp.

McDermott, Kathleen, jt. auth. see Allen, David G.

McDermott, Kathleen, jt. auth. see King, Roy.

McDermott, Kathryn A. Controlling Public Education: Localism Versus Equity. LC 99-24853. (Studies in Government & Public Policy). 200p. 1999. pap. 17.95 *(0-7006-0972-5)* U Pr of KS.

***McDermott, Kathryn A.** Controlling Public Education: Localism Versus Equity. LC 99-24853. (Studies in Government & Public Policy). 200p. 1999. 40.00 *(0-7006-0971-7)* U Pr of KS.

McDermott, Kevin. The Czech Red Unions, 1918-1929. (East European Monographs: No. 239). 350p. 1988. text 72.00 *(0-88033-136-4,* Pub. by East Eur Monographs) Col U Pr.

— A Master of the Sultan. 148p. 1997. pap. 7.95 *(1-85371-706-1,* Pub. by Poolbeg Pr) Dufour.

***McDermott, Kevin & Morison, John, eds.** Politics & Society under the Bolsheviks: Selected Papers from the 5th World Congress of Central & East European Studies, Warsaw, 1995. LC 99-23351. 302p. 1999. text 79.95 *(0-312-22593-8)* St Martin.

McDermott, Kim. All Work All Play: Career Education Activities. LC 95-79473. (Career Education Activities Ser.). (Illus.). 36p. (Orig.). (YA). (gr. 7-12). 1995. pap. 8.95 *(1-884063-70-5)* Mar Co Prods.

McDermott, Lillian C. Tutorials in Introductory Physics: Preliminary Edition. 224p. (C). 1997. pap. text 10.00 *(0-13-954637-5)* P-H.

McDermott, Lillian C. Tutorials in Introductory Physics & Homework Manual Package. 1997. pap. 20.00 *(0-13-956640-6,* Prentice Hall) P-H.

McDermott, Lillian C. & Physics Education Group Staff. Physics by Inquiry: An Introduction to Physics & the Physical Sciences, 2 vols., Vol. 2. Incl. Vol. 1. Physics by Inquiry: An Introduction to Physics & the Physical Sciences. LC 95-40316. 400p. 1995. pap. 40.95 *(0-471-14440-1)*; Vol. 2. Physics by Inquiry: An Introduction to Physics & the Physical Sciences. LC 95-40316. 464p. 1995. pap. 40.95 *(0-471-14441-X,* Wiley-Interscience); LC 95-40316. 1995. Set pap. text 52.95 *(0-471-54870-7)* Wiley.

McDermott, Lois. Psychology: Lectures 226p. (C). 1994. text 34.00 *(0-536-58655-1)* Pearson Custom.

— Psychology: Lectures & Study Guide. 2nd ed. 286p. (C). 1995. text 34.20 *(0-536-59077-X)* Pearson Custom.

***McDermott, Lynda, et al.** World Class Teams: Working Across Borders. LC 98-15211. 336p. 1998. 29.95 *(0-471-29265-6,* VNR) Wiley.

McDermott, M. Hubert. Novel & Romance: The Odyssey to Tom Jones. 192p. 1989. text 53.50 *(0-389-29869-7,* N8427) B&N Imports.

McDermott, Margaret H., jt. auth. see Reams, Bernard D., Jr.

McDermott, Margaret H., jt. ed. see Reams, Bernard D., Jr.

McDermott, Marianne. 1995-96 Greeting Card Industry Directory: A Comprehensive Guide to the Products & Services of the Greeting Card Industry. 8th ed. Albertson, Mila, ed. 276p. (Orig.). 1995. pap. 75.00 *(0-938369-25-3)* Greeting Card Assn.

— 1995-96 Directory of Greeting Card Sales Representatives. 3rd ed. Albertson, Mila, ed. 124p. 1995. pap. 95.00 *(0-938369-24-5)* Greeting Card Assn.

McDermott, Mary A., jt. auth. see Solari-Twadell, Phyllis A.

***McDermott, Mary Kay.** Bridesmaid's Survival Guide: A Hilarious Handbook to Womanhood's Most Dubious Distinction. LC 00-20288. (Illus.). 144p. 2000. pap. 12.95 *(0-14-029460-0)* Viking Penguin.

McDermott, Michael. Stories of the Fire: Personal Growth Through Firewalking. LC 94-219748. 179p. (Orig.). (C). 1994. 9.95 *(0-9640871-0-3)* Frog & Latte.

McDermott, Michael, jt. auth. see Bisyak, Steven.

McDermott, Michael, jt. auth. see Sirkin, Arlene F.

McDermott, Michael C. & Tagart, James H. The Essence of International Business. LC 92-45582. 192p. (C). 1993. pap. text 19.95 *(0-13-288077-6)* P-H.

McDermott, Michael T., ed. Endocrine Secrets: Questions You Will Be Asked on Rounds, in the Clinic, on Oral Exams. 2nd ed. LC 97-81435. (Secrets Ser.). (Illus.). 350p. 1998. pap. text 36.00 *(1-56053-268-8)* Hanley & Belfus.

McDermott, Mustafa Y. Muslim Nursery Rhymes. 40p. (J). 1996. pap. 3.50 *(0-614-21030-5,* 1588) Kazi Pubns.

***McDermott, Nancie.** The Curry Book: Memorable Flavors & Irresistibly Simple Recipes from Around the World. (Illus.). 272p. 1999. pap. 15.00 *(0-618-00202-2)* HM.

McDermott, Nancie. Real Thai: The Best of Thailand's Regional Cooking. 208p. 1992. pap. 11.95 *(0-8118-0017-2)* Chronicle Bks.

— Real Vegetarian Thai. LC 96-37096. 1997. pap. 11.95 *(0-8118-1151-4)* Chronicle Bks.

McDermott, Patrice. Politics & Scholarship: Feminist Academic Journals & the Production of Knowledge. LC 93-31206. 208p. (C). 1994. text 36.95 *(0-252-02078-2)*; pap. text 14.95 *(0-252-06369-4)* U of Ill Pr.

McDermott, Patricia, jt. ed. see Briskin, Linda.

McDermott, Patricia, jt. ed. see Fudge, Judy.

McDermott, Patrick. Solving the Year 2000 Crisis. LC 98-2923. 222p. 1998. 59.00 *(0-89006-725-2)* Artech Hse.

McDermott, Patti. Como Hablar Con Su Esposo, Esposa. 1997. pap. text 12.98 *(968-890-165-2)* Edit Diana.

— How to Talk to Your Husband - How to Talk to Your Wife. 208p. 1994. pap. write for info. *(0-8092-3682-6)* NTC Contemp Pub Co.

— Sisters & Brothers: Resolving Your Adult Sibling Relationships. 240p. 1993. pap. 14.95 *(1-56565-083-2,* Legcy) Lowell Hse.

McDermott, Paul A. ASCA: National Profiles in Youth Psychopathology. 64p. 1993. pap. 34.95 *(0-9638072-3-4)* Ed & Psych.

McDermott, Peter, jt. ed. see Rowlinson, Steve.

***McDermott, Rachel Fell.** Mother of My Heart, Daughter of My Dreams: Kali & Uma in the Devotional Poetry of Bengal. LC 99-89433. (Illus.). 432p. 2001. text 60.00 *(0-19-513435-4)* OUP.

— Singing to the Goddess: Poems to Kali & Uma from Bengal. LC 99-88189. (Illus.). 304p. 2000. text 45.00 *(0-19-513433-8)* OUP.

***McDermott, Rachell Fell.** Singing to the Goddess: Poems to Kali & Uma from Bengal. LC 99-88189. (Illus.). 304p. 2000. pap. 19.95 *(0-19-513434-6)* OUP.

***McDermott, Richard E.** Code Blue: A Tale of Romance, Murder, Mystery, Intrigue & Managed Care. Stocks, Kevin & Ogden, Joan, eds. (Illus.). 336p. 2000. pap. 28.00 *(0-9675072-0-0)* Traemus Bks.

***McDermott, Richard E., et al.** Code Blue: A Tale of Romance, Murder, Mystery, Intrigue & Managed Care. (Illus.). 370p. (C). 1999. pap. 27.00 *(0-9675072-1-9)* Traemus Bks.

McDermott, Richard J., ed. see Edwards, Robert D. & Magee, John.

McDermott, Richard J., ed. see Laura, Ronald S. & Dutton, Kenneth R.

McDermott, Richard J., ed. & illus. see Magee, John.

McDermott, Richard T. Legal Aspects of Corporate Finance. 1995. write for info. *(0-8205-2917-6)* Bender.

***McDermott, Richard T.** Legal Aspects of Corporate Finance. 3rd ed. LC 99-462254. (Analysis & Skills Ser.). 2000. write for info. *(0-8205-4372-1)* Bender.

McDermott, Robert J. & Sarvela, Paul D. Health Education Evaluation & Measurement: A Practitioners Perspective. 2nd ed. (Illus.). 384p. 1999. 32.69 *(0-697-22322-1)* McGrw-H Hghr Educ.

McDermott, Robert J., jt. auth. see Sarvela, Paul.

McDermott, Robin E., et al. The Basics of FMEA. LC 96-209109. 76p. 1996. pap. 7.95 *(0-527-76320-9)* Productivity Inc.

— The Basics of Mistake Proofing. 66p. 1997. pap. 7.95 *(0-527-76327-6)* Productivity Inc.

Employee-Driven Quality: Releasing the Creative Spirit of Your Organization Through Suggestion Systems. LC 93-11078. 243p. 1993. 31.00 *(0-527-91670-6)* Productivity Inc.

— Tools of Continuous Improvement. (Illus.). 40p. (C). 1993. student ed. 20.00 *(1-882307-13-5)* Res Engineering.

McDermott, Rosalie, jt. auth. see Modugno, Carolyn.

McDermott, Rose. Political Psychology. (Analytical Perspectives on Politics Ser.). (Illus.). (C). text. write for info. *(0-472-09701-6)*; pap. text. write for info. *(0-472-06701-X)* U of Mich Pr.

M

McDermott, Rose. Risk Taking in International Politics: Prospect Theory in American Foreign Policy. LC 97-21113. 256p. (C). 1998. text 42.50 (*0-472-10867-0*, 10867) U of Mich Pr.

McDermott, Sean & Woulfe, Richard. Compulsory Purchase & Compensation in Ireland: Law & Practice. 1992. boxed set 104.00 (*1-85475-102-6*, IE, MICHIE) LEXIS Pub.

***McDermott, Shawn Michael.** Exposing Religious Strongholds in the Church: Pulling off the Masks. LC 99-91620. 1999. 25.00 (*0-7388-1136-X*); pap. 18.00 (*0-7388-1137-8*) Xlibris Corp.

McDermott, Shirley F., ed. see Kirkham, Lester D.

McDermott, Shirley F., ed. see Kirkhart, Lester D.

McDermott, Stella. Metaphysics of Raw Foods. 78p. 1996. reprint ed. spiral bd. 11.50 (*0-7873-0597-9*) Hlth Research.

— Metaphysics of Raw Foods (1919) 80p. 1996. reprint ed. pap. 9.95 (*1-56459-860-8*) Kessinger Pub.

McDermott, Thomas J. McDermott's Handbook of Ohio Real Estate Law. 2nd ed. 304p. 1980. 15.00 (*0-614-05898-8*, MICHIE); pap. 15.00 (*0-87473-130-5*, MICHIE) LEXIS Pub.

McDermott, Thomas V. Son of a Rail. (Illus.). 193p. 1998. pap. 12.95 (*0-9641688-1-2*) Uncommon Buffalo.

McDermott, Timothy, ed. see Aquinas, Thomas, Saint.

McDermott, Timothy, tr. & selected by see Aquinas, Thomas, Saint.

McDermott, Tom. Wireless Digital Communications: Design & Theory. 336p. 1997. pap. 39.99 incl. disk (*0-9644707-2-1*, TK5103) Tucson Amat Pack Rad.

Mcdermott, Will. Official Guide to Urza's Destiny. (Magic the Gathering Ser.). 1999. pap. 11.99 (*0-7869-1400-9*, Pub. by TSR Inc) Random.

***Mcdermott, Will.** Official Guide to Urza's Legacy. (Magic the Gathering Ser.). 1999. pap. 11.99 (*0-7869-1353-3*, Pub. by TSR Inc) Random.

Mcdermott, Will. Official Guide to Urza's Saga. 1998. pap. 16.99 (*0-7869-1302-9*, Pub. by TSR Inc) Random.

McDermott, Will & Emery Staff, jt. auth. see American Psychological Association Staff.

***McDermott, William V.** Doctors Afield & Afar. LC 99-50053. 2000. write for info. (*0-87233-126-1*) Bauhan.

McDermott, William V. A Surgeon in Combat: European Theatre - World War II - Omaha Beach to Ebensee, 1943-1945. LC 97-3025. (Illus.). 332p. 1998. 27.50 (*0-87233-120-2*) Bauhan.

McDermottl. Crossing Borders. (Business Technology Ser.). 1998. text 29.95 (*0-442-02589-0*, VNR) Wiley.

McDermut, W. E. & Trautmann, William E., eds. Founding Convention of the IWW: Proceedings. 2nd ed. LC 70-85538. Orig. Title: Proceedings of the First Convention of the Industrial Workers of the World: Officially Approved, Stenographically Reported. 616p. 1969. lib. bdg. 70.00 (*0-87348-013-9*) Pathfinder NY.

McDevitt, Arthur S. Inscriptions from Thessaly. (GER.). 159p. 1970. write for info. (*0-318-70444-7*); write for info. (*0-318-72104-X*) G Olms Pubs.

McDevitt, ARthur S. Inscriptions from Thessaly. 159p. 1970. write for info. (*0-318-70972-4*) G Olms Pubs.

McDevitt, Arthur S. Inscriptions from Thessaly: An Analytical Handlist & Bibliography. 159p. 1970. 37.70 (*0-685-66493-7*, 05102705) G Olms Pubs.

McDevitt, Brian P. Evidence of An Ancient Greek Navigation System. LC 95-80461. 100p. 1995. pap. 25.00 (*1-888032-04-9*); lib. bdg. 35.00 (*1-888032-05-7*) Lib Sales NJ.

— A Historian's Thematic Study of Western Civilization, Pt. 1. 60p. (C). 1994. student ed. 15.00 (*1-888032-02-2*) Lib Sales NJ.

— A Historian's Thematic Study of Western Civilization, Pt. 2. 60p. (C). 1994. student ed. 15.00 (*1-888032-03-0*) Lib Sales NJ.

— The Irish Librists. 125p. 1988. pap. 15.00 (*1-888032-06-5*); lib. bdg. 25.00 (*1-888032-00-6*) Lib Sales NJ.

— The Irish Librists & the Scrolls of Aristotle. 115p. 1993. pap. 15.00 (*1-888032-07-3*); lib. bdg. 25.00 (*1-888032-01-4*) Lib Sales NJ.

— The Irish Librists & the Vatican Library Mystery. unabridged ed. 125p. (Orig.). 1997. lib. bdg. 25.00 (*1-888032-09-X*) Lib Sales NJ.

McDevitt, Chas. Skiffle: The Definitive Inside Story. (Illus.). 294p. 1999. 33.95 (*1-86105-140-9*, Pub. by Robson Bks) Parkwest Pubns.

McDevitt, Howard. Howie Houses. 20p. 1993. pap. 5.95 (*1-883612-00-4*) Bks Unltd.

McDevitt, J., jt. auth. see Levin, J.

McDevitt, Jack. Ancient Shores (MM) Ancient Shores (MM) 384p. 1996. mass mkt. 5.99 (*0-06-105426-7*, HarperPrism) HarpC.

McDevitt, Jack. Deep Six. Date not set. mass mkt. write for info. (*0-06-102006-0*, HarperPrism) HarpC.

— Deep Six. Date not set. write for info. (*0-06-105124-1*) HarperTrade.

McDevitt, Jack. The Engines of God. LC 94-7131. 432p. 1994. 21.95 (*0-441-00077-0*) Ace Bks.

— The Engines of God. 432p. 1995. mass mkt. 6.99 (*0-441-00284-6*) Ace Bks.

— Eternity Road. 416p. 1998. mass mkt. 5.99 (*0-06-105427-5*, HarperPrism) HarpC.

— Far As the Eye Can See. Date not set. mass mkt. 5.99 (*0-06-102005-2*) HarpC.

***McDevitt, Jack.** Hello Out There. 600p. 2000. pap. 20.00 (*1-892065-23-1*); pap. write for info. (*1-892065-22-3*) Meisha Merlin.

McDevitt, Jack. Infinity Beach. LC 99-40569. 448p. 2000. 25.00 (*0-06-105123-3*) HarpC.

— Moonfall. LC 98-147774. 480p. 1998. 24.00 (*0-06-105036-9*, HarperPrism) HarpC.

— Moonfall. 560p. 1999. mass mkt. 6.50 (*0-06-105112-8*, HarperPrism) HarpC.

— Standard Candles: The Best Short Fiction of Jack McDevitt. 250p. 1996. 25.00 (*0-9648320-4-6*) Tachyon Pubns.

— A Talent for War. 320p. 1989. reprint ed. mass mkt. 5.99 (*0-441-79553-6*) Ace Bks.

McDevitt, Jack, jt. auth. see Sgarzi, Judith M.

McDevitt, John B. The Collected Works of John B. McDevitt. LC 95-61727. (Illus.). 1324p. (Orig.). (C). 1995. text 80.00 (*0-9631546-2-1*) TNL Pr.

McDevitt, John B. & Settlage, Calvin F., eds. Separation-Individuation: Essays in Honor of Margaret S. Mahler. LC 78-143378. 520p. 1971. 77.50 (*0-8236-6065-6*) Intl Univs Pr.

McDevitt, Matthew. Joseph McKenna. LC 73-21874. (American Constitutional & Legal History Ser.). 250p. 1974. reprint ed. lib. bdg. 32.50 (*0-306-70632-6*) Da Capo.

McDevitt, Maureen K. The Old World & America - Answer Key. LC 98-90276. 71p. 1998. pap. 10.00 (*0-89555-620-0*, 1550) TAN Bks Pubs.

— Our Pioneers & Patriots - Answer Key. LC 96-61306. 90p. (J). (gr. 5-8). 1997. pap., student ed. 10.00 (*0-89555-606-5*, 1529) TAN Bks Pubs.

McDevitt, S. C., jt. ed. see Carey, W. B.

McDevitt, Sean C., jt. auth. see Carey, William B.

McDevitt, Sean C., jt. ed. see Carey, William B.

McDevitt, Thomas M. World Population Profile: 1996. 190p. 1996. per. 14.00 (*0-16-048732-3*) USGPO.

***McDevitt, Thomas M.** World Population Profile 1996. (Illus.). 182p. (C). 1999. reprint ed. pap. text 30.00 (*0-7881-8265-X*) DIANE Pub.

McDevitt, Thomas M., et al. Trends in Adolescent Fertility & Contraceptive Use in the Developing World. (Illus.). 81p. 1997. pap. text 25.00 (*0-7881-4706-4*) DIANE Pub.

McDevitt, Tom. Health America. 615p. 1992. pap., teacher ed. 37.56 (*0-933046-06-5*) Little Red Hen.

— Health America, Chapter 26 Supplement. 1995. pap. 8.95 (*0-933046-07-3*) Little Red Hen.

— Mike O'Garry's Pocket: Selected Short Stories. 1986. pap. 6.00 (*0-933046-04-9*) Little Red Hen.

— No Slouch. LC 78-70914. 1979. 8.95 (*0-933046-00-6*) Little Red Hen.

— Smoking - Is It a Sin? 80p. (Orig.). 1981. pap. 5.00 (*0-933046-03-0*) Little Red Hen.

McDiarmid. Tadpoles. LC 99-17655. 1999. 70.00 (*0-226-55762-6*) U Ch Pr.

McDiarmid, D. R. & Gattinger, R., eds. Instruments & Analysis Techniques for Space Physics: Proceedings of Workshop VI of the COSPAR 24th plenary meeting held in Ottawa, Canada, 16 May-2 June, 1982, Vol. 2/7. (Illus.). 200p. 1983. pap. 55.00 (*0-08-030431-1*, Pergamon Pr) Elsevier.

McDiarmid, Finley. Letters to My Wife. LC 97-28200. 1997. 19.95 (*0-87770-472-4*); pap. 14.95 (*0-87770-609-3*) Ye Galleon.

McDiarmid, G. Williamson. Kathy: A Case of Innovative Mathematics Teaching in a Multicultural Classroom. Kleinfeld, Judith, ed. (Teaching Cases in Cross-Cultural Education Ser.: No. 9). (Orig.). (C). 1992. pap. text 7.50 (*1-877962-24-4*) Univ AK Ctr CCS.

McDiarmid, Jim. Kuta. Coolidge, Joe, tr.Tr. of Boiling, Freezing & Thawing. (ESK., Illus.). 16p. (J). (gr. k-3). 1998. pap. text 6.00 (*1-58084-045-0*) Lower Kuskokwim.

McDiarmid, Lucy. Auden's Apologies for Poetry. LC 89-10660. 196p. 1990. reprint ed. pap. 60.80 (*0-608-07632-5*, 205994800010) Bks Demand.

McDiarmid, Lucy, jt. ed. see DiBattista, Maria.

McDiarmid, Lucy, ed. see Gregory, Lady.

***McDiarmid, Mac.** Triumph: The Legend. (Legends Ser.). (Illus.). 80p. 1998. 7.98 (*0-7651-0849-6*) Smithmark.

— Ultimate Harley Davidson: An Encyclopedia of the Definitive Motorbike from Classic to Custom. (Illus.). 256p. 2000. 35.00 (*0-7548-0487-9*, Lorenz Bks) Anness Pub.

McDiarmid, Orville J. Unskilled Labor for Development: Its Economic Cost. LC 76-47398. 219p. reprint ed. pap. 67.90 (*0-7837-4276-2*, 204396800012) Bks Demand.

McDiarmid, Susan. Making Plant Places: Original Craft Projects for Making Containers, Hangers, Boxes, Baskets & Stands. LC 99-50033. (Illus.). 314p. 2000. pap. 24.95 (*0-88179-172-5*, Pub. by Hartley & Marks) Andrews & McMeel.

McDiarmid, Susan, jt. auth. see Rosenbluth, Vera.

McDiarmid, Susan, jt. auth. see Turner, Edward R.

McDicken. Diagnostic Ultrasonics. 4th ed. 1998. text 105.00 (*0-443-05465-7*, W B Saunders Co) Harcrt Hlth Sci Grp.

McDicken, W. N. Diagnostic Ultrasonics: Principles & Use of Instruments. 3rd ed. (Illus.). 367p. 1990. text 105.00 (*0-443-04132-6*) Church.

McDill, Edward L. & Rigsby, Leo C. Structure & Process in Secondary Schools: The Academic Impact of Educational Climates. LC 73-8123. 224p. reprint ed. pap. 69.50 (*0-608-18671-6*, 202586100046) Bks Demand.

McDill, Linda, jt. auth. see McDill, S. R.

McDill, S. R. & McDill, Linda. Dangerous Marriage: Breaking the Cycle of Domestic Violence. 192p. (Orig.). (C). (gr. 13). 1998. mass mkt. 5.99 (*0-8007-8654-8*, Shattered and B, Spire) Revell.

McDill, S. Rutherford. Parenting the Prodigal. LC 96-22680. 120p. 1996. pap. 7.99 (*0-8361-9042-4*) Herald Pr.

McDill, Wayne. The Message in Your Emotions: Tracing Emotional Pain to Victorious Living. 272p. 1996. pap. 11.99 (*0-8054-6275-9*, 4262-75) Broadman.

***McDill, Wayne.** The 12 Essential Skills for Great Preaching. 1998. pap. text 11.99 (*0-8054-1876-8*) Broadman.

McDill, Wayne V. The Moment of Truth: A Guide to Effective Sermon Delivery. LC 99-12003. 128p. 1999. pap. 19.99 (*0-8054-1827-X*) Broadman.

McDirmit, Evan & McDirmit, Marilynn. Milk, Meat & Strong Meat of the Bible: Deep Spiritual Nutrition. (Illus.). 416p. (Orig.). (C). 1995. pap. 12.95 (*0-9623953-2-3*) Eagle Pubn Co.

McDirmit, Marilynn. Devotional Diary: An Inspiring Journey Through the Psalms. (Illus.). 136p. (Orig.). 1986. pap. 5.00 (*0-9623953-0-7*) Eagle Pubn Co.

— Reincarnation - A Biblical Doctrine? Whose Time Has Come for the Evangelical Christian. 118p. (Orig.). (C). 1990. pap. 9.95 (*0-9623953-1-5*) Eagle Pubn Co.

McDirmit, Marilynn, jt. auth. see McDirmit, Evan.

***McDivitt, Carl B.** Flowers for Kasia. LC 00-190559. 2000. 25.00 (*0-7388-1826-7*); pap. 18.00 (*0-7388-1827-5*) Xlibris Corp.

McDivitt, James M. & Manners, Gerald. Minerals & Men: An Exploration of the World of Minerals & Metals, Including Some of the Major Problems That Are Posed. 2nd ed. LC 73-8138. xiii, 175p. 1974. pap. 15.95 (*0-8018-1827-3*) Resources Future.

McDivitt, John D., jt. auth. see Fessenden, Ralph J.

McDivitt, Robert W., jt. ed. see Hoogstraten, Barth.

McDohough, Mark G., jt. auth. see Jones, Rodney W.

McDonagh. Green Management: A Reader. 1998. pap. 21.99 (*1-86152-451-X*) Thomson Learn.

McDonagh. Renegotiating Rural Development. 69.95 (*1-84014-996-5*) Ashgate Pub Co.

McDonagh, Barbara S. Makana Aloha: Gift of Love. LC TXU 635-646. 24p. (J). (gr. k-8). 1994. 12.95 (*0-9643781-0-8*) Liko Pubng.

— Na Momi Ho'omana'o: Pearls to Remember, Vol. 2. Teves, Harold H., ed. (Illus.). 49p. (YA). (gr. 4 up). 1997. 21.95 (*0-9643781-1-6*) Liko Pubng.

McDonagh, Bernard. Belgium & Luxembourg. 8th ed. (Blue Guide Ser.). (Illus.). 448p. 1993. pap. 24.95 (*0-393-30989-4*) Norton.

— Blue Guide to Turkey. 2nd rev. ed. (Blue Guide Ser.). (Illus.). 736p. 1995. pap. 27.50 (*0-393-31195-3*, Norton Paperbks) Norton.

McDonagh, Bernard & Robertson, Ian. Cyprus. 4th ed. (Blue Guide Ser.). (Illus.). 256p. 1998. pap. 19.95 (*0-393-31798-6*, Norton Paperbks) Norton.

McDonagh, Edward W. Chelation Can Cure: How to Reverse Heart Disease, Diabetes, Stroke, High Blood Pressure & Poor Circulation Without Drugs or Surgery. 225p. (Orig.). 1983. pap. 9.95 (*0-912815-00-0*) Platinum Pen Pubs.

McDonagh, Francis, tr. see Amin, Samir.

McDonagh, Francis, tr. see Casaldaliga, Pedro & Vigil, Jose M.

McDonagh, Francis, tr. see Mesters, Carlos.

McDonagh, Francis, tr. see Sobrino, Jon.

McDonagh, J. Plasma Fibronectin: Structure & Functions. (Hematology Ser.: Vol. 5). (Illus.). 288p. 1985. text 150.00 (*0-8247-7384-5*) Dekker.

Mcdonagh, Joe. Opening Night. LC 98-54259. 1999. pap. 5.00 (*0-88734-820-3*) Players Pr.

McDonagh, Josephine. De Quincey's Disciplines. LC 93-39460. 220p. 1994. text 45.00 (*0-19-811285-8*, Clarendon Pr) OUP.

— George Eliot. Armstrong, Isobel & Loughrey, Bryan, eds. (Writers & Their Work Ser.). 1997. pap. 17.00 (*0-7463-0799-3*, Pub. by Northcote House) U Pr of Miss.

McDonagh, Kathryn J., ed. Patient-Centered Hospital Care: Reform from Within. LC 93-14569. 222p. 1993. text 44.00 (*1-56793-002-6*, 0936) Health Admin Pr.

McDonagh, Maitland. Broken Mirrors - Broken Minds: The Dark Dreams of Dario Angento. LC 93-45770. 1994. 18.95 (*0-8065-1514-7*, Citadel Pr) Carol Pub Group.

— Filmmaking on the Fringe: The Good, the Bad & the Deviant Directors. LC 94-20342. (Illus.). 256p. 1994. pap. 18.95 (*0-8065-1557-0*, Citadel Pr) Carol Pub Group.

McDonagh, Margaret. Full Circle. large type ed. (Linford Romance Library). 400p. 1997. pap. 16.99 (*0-7089-5085-X*, Linford) Ulverscroft.

— Hidden Love. large type ed. (Linford Romance Library). 416p. 1997. pap. 16.99 (*0-7089-5037-X*) Ulverscroft.

McDonagh, Margaret. Shadows of the Past. large type ed. 208p. pap. 18.99 (*0-7089-5440-5*) Ulverscroft.

McDonagh, Margaret. Sweet Revenge. large type ed. (Linford Romance Large Print Ser.). 176p. 1998. pap. 17.99 (*0-7089-5259-3*, Linford) Ulverscroft.

***McDonagh, Margaret.** Web of Deceit. large type ed. 208p. 1999. pap. 18.99 (*0-7089-5471-5*, Linford) Ulverscroft.

Mcdonagh, Martin. Beauty Queen of Leenane. 1996. pap. 11.95 (*0-413-70730-X*, Methuen Drama) Methn.

McDonagh, Martin. The Beauty Queen of Leenane. 1998. pap. 5.25 (*0-8222-1664-7*) Dramatists Play.

Mcdonagh, Martin. Beauty Queen of Leenane & Other Plays. LC 98-8798. 1998. pap. 13.00 (*0-375-70487-6*) Villard Books.

McDonagh, Martin. The Cripple of Inishmaan. 1998. pap. 5.25 (*0-8222-1663-9*) Dramatists Play.

— The Cripple of Inishmaan. LC 98-26267. 1998. pap. 11.00 (*0-375-70523-6*) Vin Bks.

— Lonesome West. 1998. pap. 5.25 (*0-8222-1666-3*) Dramatists Play.

— A Skull in Connemara. 1998. pap. 5.25 (*0-8222-1665-5*) Dramatists Play.

McDonagh, P. F., ed. Microvascular Perfusion & Transport in Health & Disease. (Illus.). x, 254p. 1986. 209.75 (*3-8055-4394-8*) S Karger.

McDonagh, Sean. The Greening of the Church. LC 90-33049. 1990. pap. 17.00 (*0-88344-694-4*) Orbis Bks.

— Passion for the Earth. LC 95-141327. (Ecology & Justice Ser.). 175p. reprint ed. pap. 54.30 (*0-608-20242-8*, 207150100012) Bks Demand.

Mcdonald. Loss in Pregnancy: Guidelnes for Pregnancy. (C). 1996. pap. text 30.00 (*0-7020-1742-6*) Harcourt.

Mcdonald, jt. auth. see Salomone.

McDonald, Margaret. Colossians & Ephesians. (Sacra Pagina Ser.: No. 17). 2000. 39.95 (*0-8146-5819-9*, M Glazier) Liturgical Pr.

McDonald, A. Water Resources: Issues & Strategies. 1988. pap. 50.95 (*0-582-30121-1*, Pub. by Addison-Wesley) Longman.

McDonald, A. G., ed. Selective Studies in Health & Social Services. (OMEGA Special Issue Ser.: Vol. 9, No. 5). 104p. 1981. pap. 35.00 (*0-08-023620-0*, Pergamon Pr) Elsevier.

McDonald, Agnes. Quickest Door, Smallest Room. 94p. Date not set. pap. 8.95 (*1-879934-04-3*) St Andrews NC.

McDonald, Agnes, ed. Journey Proud: Southern Women's Personal Writings. 156p. 1994. pap. 10.95 (*0-932112-36-6*) Carolina Wren.

McDonald, Alan T., jt. auth. see Fox, Robert W.

McDonald, Alexander H. Ab Urbe Condita, Vol. V, Bks. XXXI-XXXV. (Oxford Classical Texts Ser.). 356p. 1965. text 45.00 (*0-19-814646-9*) OUP.

McDonald, Alice, ed. To Touch the Future: The Educators' Book of Quotations. LC 86-82570. 179p. (Orig.). 1986. pap. 8.95 (*0-935680-31-4*) Kentucke Imprints.

McDonald, Alvis E. A Multiplicity-Independent, Global Iteration for Meromorphic Functions. LC 73-130610. 116p. 1969. 19.00 (*0-403-04516-9*) Scholarly.

McDonald, Amy, ed. see Null, Gary.

Mcdonald, Andrew. Howard Fast: A Critical Companion. LC 95-50458. (Critical Companions to Popular Contemporary Writers Ser.). 224p. 1996. 29.95 (*0-313-29493-3*, Greenwood Pr) Greenwood.

McDonald, Ann. All about Weller Price Guide. 2000. 3rd rev. ed. 20p. 1999. pap. 4.95 (*1-57080-060-X*) Antique Pubns.

McDonald, Ann L. Communicating with Legal Databases: Terms & Abbreviations for the Legal Researcher. 206p. 1987. pap. 82.50 (*0-918212-95-2*) Neal-Schuman.

McDonald, Archie. The Japanese Experience in Butte County, California. 176p. 1993. 12.50 (*0-614-05680-2*) Assn NC Records.

— When the Corn Grows Tall in Texas. (Illus.). 96p. (J). (gr. 4-5). 1991. 12.95 (*0-89015-808-8*) Sunbelt Media.

McDonald, Archie P. Helpful Cooking Hints for Househusbands of Uppity Women. 1997. pap. 14.95 (*0-935014-13-6*) E-Heart Pr.

McDonald, Archie P. Historic Texas: An Illustrated Chronicle of Texas History. Dean, Oida & Dean, R. G., eds. (Illus.). 248p. 1996. 59.95 (*0-9654999-0-1*) Hist Pub Network.

— Nacogdoches, Texas: A Pictorial History. LC 96-31218. 1996. write for info. (*0-89865-975-2*) Donning Co.

— The Old Stone Fort. v, 41p. 1981. pap. 7.95 (*0-87611-057-X*) Tex St Hist Assn.

— Republic of Texas. (Texas History Ser.). (Illus.). 40p. (C). 1981. pap. text 8.95 (*0-89641-073-0*) American Pr.

— Texas: All Hail the Mighty State. 288p. 1983. pap. 16.95 (*0-89015-389-2*) Sunbelt Media.

— The Trail to San Jacinto. (Texas History Ser.). (Illus.). 45p. 1982. pap. text 9.95 (*0-89641-074-9*) American Pr.

— William Barrett Travis: A Biography. Eakin, Edwin M., ed. (Illus.). 216p. 1989. 18.95 (*0-89015-656-5*, Eakin Pr) Sunbelt Media.

McDonald, Archie P., ed. Shooting Stars: Heroes & Heroines of Western Film. LC 85-45988. (Illus.). 287p. reprint ed. pap. 89.00 (*0-8357-3957-0*, 205705300004) Bks Demand.

McDonald, Archie P., jt. auth. see Blake, Roy M.

McDonald, Archie P., jt. auth. see Nance, Joseph M.

McDonald, Archie P., jt. auth. see Procter, Ben.

McDonald, Archie P., ed. see Hotchkiss, Jedediah.

McDonald, Arlys L. & Hixon, Donald L. Ned Rorem: A Bio-Bibliography, 23. LC 89-2139. (Bio-Bibliographies in Music Ser.: No. 23). 294p. 1989. lib. bdg. 49.95 (*0-313-25565-2*, MNR/, Greenwood Pr) Greenwood.

McDonald, Art, jt. auth. see Pond, Doreen.

***McDonald, Arthur S.** This Date in New York Yankee Hating: Going Negative on Baseball's Most Despised Team. LC 98-92314. (Illus.). viii, 408p. 1999. pap. 19.95 (*0-9669841-0-2*, HY-1) W D Maharg.

McDonald, Arthur W., jt. ed. see Fitzsimmons, Linda.

McDonald, B., jt. ed. see Przbylski, R.

***McDonald, B. J.** Color of Nature... Birds. 12p. 2000. pap. 6.95 (*0-9652041-3-8*) Pack-O-Fun.

— Cross-Stitch Christmas Keepsakes. (Illus.). 16p. 2000. pap. 6.95 (*0-9652041-4-6*) Pack-O-Fun.

McDonald, Barbara A. Intergenerational Transfer of Cognitive Skills Vol. 1: Programs, Policies & Research Issues. Orasanu, Judith M. et al, eds. (Cognition & Literacy Ser.). 224p. 1992. text 73.25 (*0-89391-736-2*) Ablx Pub.

McDonald, Barbara A., jt. auth. see Sticht, Thomas G.

McDonald, Barrie C., jt. ed. see Jopling, Alan V.

McDonald, Ben, ed. see DeBraak, LaRonna.

McDonald, Ben, ed. see Johnson, George G., Jr.

McDonald, Benjamin R. The Vietnam Book List. 2nd ed. LC 89-81201. 180p. 1990. ring bd. 29.95 (*0-685-37770-9*) Biblio Unlimited.

— The Vietnam Book List. 3rd ed. 1991. pap. 23.95 (*0-9626437-3-4*) Biblio Unlimited.

McDonald, Benjamin R., compiled by. The Vietnam Book List. 164p. 1990. 34.95 (*0-685-35161-0*); ring bd. 19.95 (*0-9626437-0-X*) Biblio Unlimited.

McDonald, Bernadette, jt. auth. see Templeman, Ian.

McDonald, Bernard R. Finite Rings with Identity. LC 74-19018. (Pure & Applied Mathematics Ser.: Vol. 28). 443p. reprint ed. pap. 137.40 (*0-608-08958-3*, 206959300005) Bks Demand.

An Asterisk (*) at the beginning of an entry indicates that the title is appearing for the first time.

— Geometric Algebra over Local Rings. LC 76-41623. (Pure & Applied Mathematics Ser.: Vol. 36). 439p. reprint ed. pap. 136.10 (*0-608-08959-1*, 206959400005) Bks Demand.
— Linear Algebra over Commutative Rings. (Pure & Applied Mathematics Ser.: Vol. 87). (Illus.). 568p. 1984. text 175.00 (*0-8247-7122-2*) Dekker.
— R-Linear Endomorphisms of R(n) Preserving Invariants. LC 83-15648. (Memoirs Ser.: No. 46/287). 67p. 1983. pap. 17.00 (*0-8218-2287-X*, MEMO/46/287) Am Math.
McDonald, Bernard R., ed. see Ring Theory Conference Staff.
McDonald, Bill. Dakota Incarnate: A Collection of Short Stories. LC 98-89712. (Minnesota Voices Project Ser.: Vol. 92). 204p. 1999. pap. 12.95 (*0-89823-196-5*, Pub. by New Rivers Pr) Consort Bk Sales.
— The Nunda Irish: A Story of Irish Immigrants: the Joys & Sorrows of Their Life in America & Dakota. (Illus.). 275p. (Orig.). 1991. pap. 10.00 (*0-9629033-0-2*) Farmstead MN.
***McDonald, Bob.** The Catholic Family Vol. I: Image & Likeness of God: Family Life. (Catholic Family Ser.: Vol. 1). 240p. 1999. pap. 9.95 (*1-57918-118-X*, 3781) Queenship Pub.
— The Catholic Family Vol. II: Image & Likeness of God: Family Values. (Catholic Family Ser.: Vol. 2). 240p. 2000. pap. 9.95 (*1-57918-119-8*, 3782) Queenship Pub.
McDonald, Bob, jt. auth. see Hutcheson, Don.
McDonald, Boyd, ed. Cream: True Homosexual Experiences from S. T. H., Vol. 7. 2nd ed. (Illus.). 176p. 1994. pap. 14.95 (*0-943595-55-X*) Leyland Pubns.
— Flesh: True Homosexual Experiences from S. T. H. Writers, Vol. 2. (Illus.). 192p. (Orig.). 1997. reprint ed. pap. 14.95 (*0-917342-91-7*) Gay Sunshine.
— Meat: True Homosexual Experiences from S. T. H., Vol. 1. (STH Ser.). (Illus.). 192p. 1994. reprint ed. pap. 14.95 (*0-917342-78-X*) Gay Sunshine.
— Sex Vol. 3: True Homosexual Experiences from S. T. H. Writers. (Illus.). 192p. (Orig.). 1996. reprint ed. pap. 14.95 (*0-917342-98-4*) Gay Sunshine.
***McDonald, Boyd, ed.** Wads: True Homosexual Experiences from STH Writers, Vol. 6. (Illus.). 192p. 2000. reprint ed. pap. 14.95 (*0-917342-11-9*) Leyland Pubns.
***McDonald, Brian.** My Father's Gun: One Family, Three Badges: One Hundred Years in the NYPD. LC 98-51156. 312p. 2000. pap. 12.95 (*0-452-27924-0*, Plume) Dutton Plume.
McDonald, Brian & Purcell, Gordon. Lost in Space. (Illus.). 72p. (J). (gr. 3 up). 1998. pap. 7.95 (*1-56971-341-3*) Dark Horse Comics.
McDonald, Bridget, tr. see Nancy, Jean-Luc.
McDonald, Brix. Riding on the Wind. LC 97-77039. 243p. (YA). (gr. 5-10). 1998. pap. 5.95 (*0-9661306-0-X*) Avenue Publng.
McDonald, C., ed. Computer Science '98: Proceedings of the 21st Australasian Computer Science Conference ACSC'98. 250p. 1998. pap. 79.95 (*981-3083-90-5*) Spr-Verlag.
— Database Systems: Proceedings of the 9th Australasian Database Converence - ADC'98. 250p. 1998. pap. 59.95 (*981-3083-91-3*) Spr-Verlag.
McDonald, C. F., ed. see American Society of Mechanical Engineers Staff.
McDonald, C. J. Enzymes in Molecular Biology: Essential Data. LC 96-35031. (Bios Essential Data Ser.). 144p. 1997. pap. 40.00 (*0-471-94842-X*) Wiley.
McDonald, C. J., ed. Buying Equipment & Programs for Home or Office. (M.D. Computing: Benchmark Papers). (Illus.). 205p. 1987. 54.00 (*0-387-96455-X*) Spr-Verlag.
— Tutorials. (M.D. Computing: Benchmark Papers). 1987. 49.00 (*0-387-96505-X*) Spr-Verlag.
McDonald, Cal. The Leaves of Autumn. 143p. 1998. pap. 7.95 (*0-9662740-0-8*) Peace Arch Bks.
McDonald, Camille. R-r-rhubarb: From Soup to Nuts. 34p. (Orig.). 1988. pap. 5.00 (*0-9625416-0-5*) Cynthia Promos.
McDonald, Cathy M. & Whitney, Stephen R. Nature Walks in & Around Seattle: All-Season Exploring in Parks, Forests & Wetlands. 2nd ed. LC 97-25271. (Illus.). 208p. 1997. pap. text 14.95 (*0-89886-525-5*) Mountaineers.
McDonald, Charles J. Immunomodulatory & Cytotoxic Agents in Dermatology. LC 96-45655. (Basic & Clinical Dermatology Ser.: Vol. 13). (Illus.). 425p. 1997. text 175.00 (*0-8247-9406-0*) Dekker.
McDonald, Christie. The Proustian Fabric: Associations of Memory. LC 90-21940. xiv, 247p. 1991. text 45.00 (*0-8032-3150-4*) U of Nebr Pr.
McDonald, Christie & Wihl, Gary, eds. Transformations in Personhood & Culture: The Languages of History, Aesthetics, & Ethics. LC 93-23859. (Literature & Philosophy Ser.). 224p. (C). 1994. 40.00 (*0-271-01010-X*); pap. 18.95 (*0-271-01011-8*) Pa St U Pr.
McDonald, Christie, ed. see Derrida, Jacques.
McDonald, Claudette M., jt. auth. see McDonald, Patrick J.
McDonald, Clement J. Action-Orientated Decisions in Ambulatory Medicine. LC 80-20451. (Illus.). 394p. reprint ed. pap. 122.20 (*0-8357-5086-8*, 203300300082) Bks Demand.
McDonald, Cleveland & McDonald, Philip M. Creating a Successful Christian Marriage. 4th ed. LC 93-29180. 360p. 1994. 34.99 (*0-8010-6310-8*) Baker Bks.
McDonald, Clif, jt. auth. see Townsend, David.
McDonald, Coleman. Guide to Owning a Himalayan Cat. LC 99-26493. (Illus.). 64p. 1999. 19.95 (*0-7910-5463-2*) Chelsea Hse.
— Guide to Owning a Himalayan Cat. (Illus.). 64p. 1997. 6.95 (*0-7938-2170-3*, RE-403) TFH Pubns.
McDonald, Colin. Advertising Reach & Frequency: Maximizing Advertising Results Through Effective Frequency. 2nd ed. LC 95-18555. (Illus.). 176p. 1995. 49.95 (*0-8442-3506-7*) NTC Contemp Pub Co.
— Small Enterprise Development in Mini Island Economics: The Case of Tobago. LC 99-16154. (European University Studies: Vol. 2486, No. 5). (Illus.). XV, 309p. 1999. pap. 56.95 (*0-8204-4352-2*) P Lang Pubng.
McDonald, Colleen. What If Nobody Forgave & Other Stories of Principle LC 99-30341. 1999. write for info. (*1-55896-386-3*, Skinner Hse Bks) Unitarian Univ.
McDonald, Cornelia P. A Woman's Civil War: A Diary with Reminiscences of the War, from March 1862. Gwin, Minrose C., ed. LC 91-32345. (Studies in American Autobiography). (Illus.). 314p. (Orig.). (C). 1992. pap. 18.95 (*0-299-13264-1*) U of Wis Pr.
McDonald, Corry. The Dilemma of Wilderness: Protecting Our Forests. LC 86-5839. 120p. (Orig.). 1987. pap. 10.95 (*0-86534-088-9*) Sunstone Pr.
— Wilderness: A New Mexico Legacy. LC 84-26691. (Illus.). 128p. (Orig.). 1985. pap. 15.95 (*0-86534-056-0*) Sunstone Pr.
McDonald, Craig, ed. Johannes de Irlandia's Meroure of Wyssdome III. 250p. 1991. pap. text 50.00 (*0-08-037001-2*, Pub. by Aberdeen U Pr) Macmillan.
McDonald, D. Coinage of Aphrodisias. (Illus.). 200p. 1992. lib. bdg. 75.00 (*0-901405-30-2*) S J Durst.
McDonald, D. & Brown, M. Indicators of Aggressive Behavior. (Research & Public Policy Ser.: Vol. 8). 1999. pap. 60.00 (*0-642-24036-1*, Pub. by Aust Inst Criminology) St Mut.
McDonald, D., jt. ed. see Biles, D.
McDonald, D. D. & Bolc, Leonard, eds. Natural Language Generation Systems. (Symbolic Computation - Artificial Intelligence Ser.). (Illus.). 389p. 1988. 72.95 (*0-387-96691-9*) Spr-Verlag.
McDonald, D. G. & Hodgdon, J. A. Psychological Effects of Aerobic Fitness Training: Research & Theory. xi, 224p. 1991. 58.95 (*0-387-97603-5*) Spr-Verlag.
***McDonald, Dale.** United States Catholic Elemenatry & Secondary Schools, 1998-1999: The Annual Statistical Report on Schools, Enrollment & Staffing. (Illus.). 55p. 1998. pap. 16.00 (*1-55833-208-1*) Natl Cath Educ.
McDonald, Dale, ed. Catholic Schools & School Choice Partners for Justice: Proceeding of the NCEA Symposium. 182p. pap. 13.00 (*1-55833-234-0*) Natl Cath Educ.
McDonald, Dale, ed. see Drahmann, Theodore, et al.
McDonald, Daniel. Quantum Retirement: Waltzing in Cosmic Babylon. (Illus.). 150p. 1997. pap. write for info. (*0-9659311-0-2*) Gulf Coast AL.
McDonald, Daniel & Goodman, Richard A. Precision Woods & Long Iron Shots. LC 97-47390. (Precision Golf Ser.). (Illus.). 144p. 1998. pap. text 16.95 (*0-88011-766-4*, PMCD0766) Human Kinetics.
McDonald, Daniel L. The Language of Argument. 7th ed. LC 92-23334. 368p. (C). 1997. pap. 39.00 (*0-06-500583-X*) Addson-Wesley Educ.
McDonald, Daniel L. & Burton, Larry W. The Language of Argument. 9th ed. LC 98-13713. (Illus.). 400p. (C). 1998. pap. text 38.00 (*0-321-01937-7*) Addson-Wesley Educ.
McDonald, Daniel L., ed. see Addison, Joseph & Steele, Richard.
McDonald, Daniel M. The Origins of Metrology. (Illus.). 143p. 1992. 27.00 (*0-9519420-0-X*) David Brown.
McDonald, Darlinda, ed. see Fischer-Furey, Norma.
McDonald, David. Legislative Options for Cannabis in Australia LC 96-132275. (Monograph Series). xviii, 110 p. 1994. write for info. (*0-644-35086-5*) AGPS Pr.
— National Police Custody Survey. LC 98-201071. 64p. 1999. pap. 25.00 (*0-642-24038-8*, Pub. by Aust Inst Criminology) Advent Bks Div.
***McDonald, David A.** On Borders: Perspectives on International Migration in Southern Africa. 2000. text 45.00 (*0-312-23268-3*) St Martin.
McDonald, David A. & Surdam, Ronald C., eds. Clastic Diagenesis. LC 84-70676. (American Association of Petroleum Geologists. Memoir Ser.: No. 37). 444p. 1984. pap. 137.70 (*0-608-05611-1*, 206606900006) Bks Demand.
McDonald, David A., jt. auth. see Schmidt, Volkmar.
McDonald, David M. United Government & Foreign Policy in Russia, 1900-1914. 280p. (C). 1992. 52.00 (*0-674-92239-5*) HUP.
McDonald, David R. Masters' Theses in Anthropology: A Bibliography of Theses from United States Colleges & Universities. LC 77-7867. (Bibliographies Ser.). 460p. 1977. 15.00 (*0-87536-217-6*) HRAFP.
McDonald, David R., jt. auth. see Mail, Patricia D.
McDonald, David R., ed. see Matovina, Timothy M. & Navarro, Jose A.
McDonald, David R., ed. see Navarro, Jose A.
McDonald, Deirdre, ed. see Hyatt, James A.
McDonald, Deirdre, ed. see National Association of College & University Busin.
***McDonald, Donald.** How We Kept the Flag Flying: The Story of the Siege of Ladysmith. 304p. 1999. 80.00 (*1-86227-089-9*, Pub. by Spellmnt Pubs) St Mut.
McDonald, Donald F., Jr., ed. Advanced Skills & Knowledge of Cost Engineering, Vol. 1. 102p. 1989. pap. 32.50 (*0-930284-39-9*) AACE Intl.
— Skills & Knowledge of Cost Engineering. 3rd rev. ed. 164p. 1992. pap. 32.50 (*0-930284-50-X*) AACE Intl.
McDonald, Donogh, jt. ed. see Lipchitz, Leslie.
McDonald, Dorothy C. & Simons, Gene M. Musical Growth & Development: Birth Through Six. 304p. 1989. 12.00 (*0-02-871347-8*, Schirmer Books) Mac Lib Ref.
McDonald, Dorothy T. Music in Our Lives: The Early Years. LC 79-51509. 68p. 1979. pap. text 4.00 (*0-912674-65-2*, NAEYC #107) Natl Assn Child Ed.
McDonald, Doug S. Home on the Range: The Complete Practice Guide for the Golf Range. LC 96-94083. (Illus.). 200p. (Orig.). 1996. pap. 15.95 (*0-9628642-9-3*) Golf Eighties.
McDonald, Doug S., jt. ed. see Brislin, Joann.
McDonald, Douglas. Camels in Nevada. (Illus.). 32p. 1983. pap. 4.95 (*0-913814-56-3*) Nevada Pubns.
— A Catalogue of Nevada Checks, 1860-1933. (Illus.). 128p. 1993. 19.50 (*1-879767-02-3*) Castenholz Sons.
— Julia Bulette & the Red Light Ladies of Nevada. (Illus.). 32p. 1980. pap. 4.95 (*0-913814-55-5*) Nevada Pubns.
— Nevada Lost Mines & Buried Treasures. (Illus.). 128p. 1981. pap. 7.95 (*0-913814-37-7*) Nevada Pubns.
— Virginia City & the Silver Region of the Comstock Lode. (Illus.). 128p. 1982. 29.95 (*0-913814-50-4*); pap. 14.95 (*0-913814-47-4*) Nevada Pubns.
McDonald, Douglas & Goldtown. Bodie Boomtown of California. (Illus.). 48p. 1988. pap. 5.95 (*0-913814-88-1*) Nevada Pubns.
McDonald, Douglas & McDonald, Gina. History of the Weaverville Joss House & the Chinese of Trinity County, California. (Illus.). 32p. 1986. pap. 2.95 (*0-932151-02-7*) Gypsyfoot Ent.
McDonald, Douglas C. Punishment Without Walls: Community Service Sentences in New York City. 278p. 1989. pap. text 16.95 (*0-8135-1469-X*) Rutgers U Pr.
McDonald, Douglas C., ed. Day Fines in American Courts: The Staten Island & Milwaukee Experiments. (Illus.). 95p. (Orig.). (C). 1995. pap. text 25.00 (*0-7881-1900-1*) DIANE Pub.
— Private Prisons & the Public Interest. LC 90-30616. (Crime, Law & Deviance Ser.). 235p. (C). 1990. text 40.00 (*0-8135-1574-2*) Rutgers U Pr.
McDonald, Douglas C. & Carlson, Kenneth E. Sentencing in the Federal Courts: Does Race Matter?: The Transition to Sentencing Guidelines, 1986-90. (Illus.). 229p. (Orig.). (C). 1994. pap. text 50.00 (*0-7881-1472-7*) DIANE Pub.
McDonald, Dugan. Who Is Jesus? 163p. (Orig.). 1989. pap. 6.95 (*0-685-27181-1*) Bible Key Pubns.
McDonald, Duncan, jt. auth. see Kessler, Lauren.
McDonald, Earl. Closing the Loop. 64p. 1997. pap. 8.00 (*1-877603-42-2*) Pecan Grove.
McDonald, Edward, jt. auth. see Sayre, Henry.
McDonald, Eileen M., jt. auth. see Adger, Hoover, Jr.
McDonald, Elizabeth. Am I the Only One Who's Crazy? 212p. (Orig.). 1995. pap. text 5.95 (*1-879331-53-5*, Classc Pub) Marciel Pub & Print.
— Make It, Break It. 1999. pap. 3.95 (*0-14-054278-7*) NAL.
— Wildflowers of the Wallum. 71p. (C). 1990. 33.00 (*0-908175-16-7*, Pub. by Boolarong Pubns) St Mut.
McDonald, Ellen S., jt. auth. see McDonald, Forrest.
McDonald, Elvin. Northeast Gardening: The Diverse Art & Special Considerations of Gardening in the Northeast. 160p. 1990. text 35.00 (*0-02-583125-9*) Macmillan.
— The 100 Best Perennials. 1997. pap. 14.00 (*0-679-76028-8*) Random.
— Recycling for the Soul. 1997. 18.95 (*0-02-861012-1*) Macmillan.
— Smith & Hawken 100 Orchids for the American Gardener. LC 98-11201. 272p. 1998. pap. 17.95 (*0-7611-1071-2*) Workman Pub.
McDonald, Elvin, jt. auth. see Asbury, Greg.
***McDonald, Emma & Hershman, Dyan.** ABC's of Effective Parent Communication. 150p. 2000. pap. write for info. (*0-9667145-2-0*) Inspiring Teachers Pubg.
McDonald, Emma S., jt. auth. see Hershman, Dyan M.
***McDonald, Erroll.** The Great Negro Plot: An Urban Historical. (Illus.). 2001. 19.95 (*1-58234-099-4*) Bloomsbury Pubg.
McDonald, Eugene T., ed. Treating Cerebral Palsy: For Clinicians by Clinicians. LC 86-22568. (For Clinicians by Clinicians Ser.). (Illus.). 312p. 1987. pap. text 31.00 (*0-89079-141-4*, 1412) PRO-ED.
McDonald, Eugene T. & Chance, B., Jr. Cerebral Palsy. 1964. pap. text 25.67 (*0-13-122812-9*) P-H.
McDonald, Eugene T. & Gallagher, Diane L., eds. Facilitating Social-Emotional Development in Multiply Handicapped Children. 285p. (Orig.). (C). 1985. pap. text. write for info. (*0-9613558-0-8*) Home Merciful SFCC.
McDonald, Eva. John Ruskin's Wife. large type ed. (Lythway Ser.). 256p. 1991. 21.95 (*0-7451-1300-1*, G K Hall Lrg Type) Mac Lib Ref.
— The Rebel Bride. large type ed. LC 97-18109. 233p. 1997. pap. 21.95 (*0-7838-8274-2*, G K Hall Lrg Type) Mac Lib Ref.
McDonald, Eve. Chateau of Nightingales. large type ed. 1989. 22.95 (*0-7451-0933-0*, G K Hall Lrg Type) Mac Lib Ref.
McDonald, Ewen & Engsberg, Juliana. Binocular: In Stillness & Motion. (Illus.). 112p. 1995. pap. 14.95 (*0-646-22593-6*) Dist Art Pubs.
McDonald, Ewen, et al. Masterpieces of the Twentieth Century: The Beyeler Collection. LC 98-175470. 231p. 1996. write for info. (*0-7310-9480-8*) NSW.
McDonald, F. & Ireland, A. J. Diagnosis of the Orthodontic Patient. (Illus.). 278p. 1998. pap. text 49.50 (*0-19-262889-5*) OUP.
***Mcdonald, Fiona.** Women in a Changing World, 1945-2000. (Other Half of History Ser.). 48p. (YA). 2000. 17.95 (*0-87226-572-2*, P Bedrick Books) NTC Contemp Pub Co.
McDonald, Forrest. Alexander Hamilton: A Biography. (Illus.). 480p. 1982. pap. 16.95 (*0-393-30048-X*) Norton.
— The American Presidency: An Intellectual History. LC 93-30235. 524p. (Orig.). (C). 1994. 29.95 (*0-7006-0652-1*) U Pr of KS.
— The American Presidency: An Intellectual History. LC 93-30235. 524p. (Orig.). (C). 1995. pap. 17.95 (*0-7006-0749-8*) U Pr of KS.
— E Pluribus Unum: The Formation of the American Republic, 1776-1790. LC 79-4130. 1979. reprint ed. 12.00 (*0-913966-58-4*); reprint ed. pap. 5.00 (*0-913966-59-2*) Liberty Fund.
— Liberty's Five Flags. Cahill, George F., ed. (Flag Plaza Standard Ser.: Special Edition: Vol. 4). (Illus.). 12p. (Orig.). 1988. pap. 2.50 (*0-934021-06-6*) Natl Flag Foun.
— Novus Ordo Seclorum: The Intellectual Origins of the Constitution. LC 85-13544. xiv, 362p. 1985. 29.95 (*0-7006-0284-4*); pap. 14.95 (*0-7006-0311-5*) U Pr of KS.
— The Presidency of George Washington. LC 73-11344. (American Presidency Ser.). xiv, 210p. 1974. 29.95 (*0-7006-0110-4*); pap. 12.95 (*0-7006-0359-X*) U Pr of KS.
— The Presidency of Thomas Jefferson. LC 76-803. (American Presidency Ser.). xii, 204p. 1976. 29.95 (*0-7006-0147-3*); pap. 12.95 (*0-7006-0330-1*) U Pr of KS.
***McDonald, Forrest.** States' Rights & the Union: Imperium in Imperio, 1776-1876. LC 00-39242. (American Political Thought Ser.). 2000. 29.95 (*0-7006-1040-5*) U Pr of KS.
McDonald, Forrest. We the People: The Economic Origins of the Constitution. 455p. (C). 1992. pap. text 24.95 (*1-56000-574-2*) Transaction Pubs.
— We the People: The Economic Origins of the Constitution. LC 73-22298. (Publication of the American History Research Center, Madison, Wisconsin Ser.). 448p. reprint ed. pap. 138.90 (*0-608-09474-9*, 205427400005) Bks Demand.
McDonald, Forrest & McDonald, Ellen S. Requiem: Variations on Eighteenth-Century Themes. LC 88-14033. xii, 220p. 1988. 25.00 (*0-7006-0370-0*) U Pr of KS.
McDonald, Forrest, et al. Derailing the Constitution: The Undermining of American Federalism. McLean, Edward B., ed. LC 94-73312. 1997. pap. text 12.95 (*1-882926-06-4*) ISI Books.
McDonald, Frances B. Censorship & Intellectual Freedom: A Survey of School Librarians' Attitudes & Moral Reasoning. LC 93-29500. 237p. 1993. 31.00 (*0-8108-2680-1*) Scarecrow.
McDonald, Frank. Provenance. large type ed. 656p. 1983. 11.50 (*0-7089-8158-5*, Charnwood) Ulverscroft.
McDonald, Frank & Dearden, Stephen. European Economic Integration. 2nd ed. 320p. (C). 1995. pap. text 29.25 (*0-582-25141-9*, 76763) Addison-Wesley.
McDonald, Frank & Dearden, Steven. European Economic Integration. 3rd ed. LC 98-27076. 1998. pap. write for info. (*0-582-30917-4*) Longman.
McDonald, Frank & Doyle, Peigin. Ireland's Earthen Houses. LC 97-189614. (Illus.). 32p. 1997. pap. 11.95 (*1-899047-28-X*, Pub. by A A Farmar) Irish Bks Media.
***McDonald, Fraser, et al.** Local Anaesthesia in Dentistry. (Illus.). 128p. 2000. pap. text 32.00 (*0-7236-1063-0*, Pub. by John Wright) Buttrwrth-Heinemann.
McDonald, Fred & Marshall, Jeremy, eds. Questions of English. (Illus.). 208p. 1995. 19.95 (*0-19-869230-7*) OUP.
McDonald, G., et al, eds. Early Life Stage Mortality Syndrome in Fishes of the Great Lakes & Baltic Sea. LC 98-71305. (Symposium Ser.: Vol. 21). (Illus.). 187p. 1998. pap. 46.00 (*1-888569-08-5*, 540.21P) Am Fisheries Soc.
McDonald, G. J., jt. auth. see White, J. J.
McDonald, G. W. & Canadian Mineral Processors Staff. Proceedings of the International Symposium on Gold Metallurgy. Salter, R. S. et al, eds. (Proceedings of Metallurgical Society of Canadian Institute of Mining & Metallurgy Ser.: Vol. 1). 408p. 1987. 127.25 (*0-08-035882-9*, Pergamon Pr) Elsevier.
McDonald, Gabrielle. New Zealand's Secret Heroes: Don Stott & the "Z" Special Unit. LC 93-120100. xvi, 168 p. 1991. write for info. (*0-7900-0216-7*) Reed Pubng.
***McDonald, Gabrielle Kirk & Swaak-Goldman, Olivia.** Substantive & Procedural Aspects of International Criminal Law: The Experience of International & National Courts: Materials. LC 99-30899. 1999. write for info. (*90-411-1134-4*) Kluwer Law Intl.
***McDonald, Gabrielle Kirk & Swaak-Goldman, Olivia, eds.** Substantive & Procedural Aspects of International Criminal Law: The Experience of International & National Courts, Vols. I & II. 3408p. 2000. text 742.00 (*90-411-1135-2*) Kluwer Law Intl.
McDonald, Gail. Learning to Be Modern: Pound, Eliot & the American University. 256p. 1993. text 55.00 (*0-19-811980-1*) OUP.
***McDonald, Geoff & Lane, Marcus, eds.** Securing the Wet Tropics? 252p. 2000. pap. 39.95 (*1-86287-349-6*, Pub. by Federation Pr) Gaunt.
McDonald, George. Bed & Breakfast: Mid-Atlantic. 144p. 1996. 16.95 (*0-02-860880-1*) Prntice Hall Bks.
— Bed & Breakfast: New England. (Illus.). 144p. 1996. 16.95 (*0-02-860881-X*) Prntice Hall Bks.
— Born to Shop: France. 400p. 1996. 14.95 (*0-02-860710-4*) Macmillan.
— Born to Shop: Italy. 7th ed. (Frommer's Complete Guides Ser.). (Illus.). 288p. 1997. 14.95 (*0-02-860715-5*) Macmillan.
— Born to Shop: Mexico. 288p. 1996. 13.95 (*0-02-860711-2*) Macmillan.
— Born to Shop: New England. 3rd ed. (Frommer's Cape Cod, Martha's Vineyard & Nantucket Ser.). (Illus.). 288p. 1997. 14.95 (*0-02-860714-7*) Macmillan.
— Born to Shop: Paris. 7th ed. (Frommer's Complete City Guides Ser.). (Illus.). 288p. 1997. 14.95 (*0-02-860713-9*, Pub. by Macmillan) S&S Trade.
— China. (Thomas Cook Illustrated Guides Ser.). (Illus.). 192p. (Orig.). 1996. pap. 12.95 (*0-8442-9051-3*, 90513, Passprt Bks) NTC Contemp Pub Co.

M

An Asterisk (*) at the beginning of an entry indicates that the title is appearing for the first time.

*__McDonald, George.__ China. 2nd ed. (Illustrated Travel Guides Ser.). (Illus.). (Orig.). 2000. pap. 14.95 (*0-658-01077-8*, Passprt Bks) NTC Contemp Pub Co.

McDonald, George. Complete Hostel Vacation Guide to England. 272p. 1996. 14.95 (*0-02-860701-5*) Macmillan.

*__McDonald, George.__ Essential Amsterdam. 3rd ed. (AAA Essential Guides Ser.). 128p. 2000. pap. 8.95 (*0-658-00634-7*, 006347, Passprt Bks) NTC Contemp Pub Co.

McDonald, George. Frommer's Amsterdam by Night. (Illus.). 1996. 12.95 (*0-02-861137-3*) Macmillan.

— Frommer's Barcelona, Madrid & Seville. 1997. 14.95 (*0-02-861159-4*, P-H Travel) Prntice Hall Bks.

— Frommer's Berlin from Fifty Dollars a Day 1996. 3rd rev. ed. (Illus.). 240p. 1995. 14.95 (*0-02-860633-7*) Macmillan.

— Frommer's California from $60 a Day. (Frommer's Travel Guides Ser.). (Illus.). 624p. 1997. 18.95 (*0-02-861237-X*, P-H Travel) Prntice Hall Bks.

— Frommer's Canada. 9th ed. (Frommer's Comprehensive Travel Guide Ser.). 816p. 1996. 19.95 (*0-02-860707-4*, P-H Travel) Prntice Hall Bks.

— Frommer's Cape Cod, Nantucket & Martha's Vineyard. (Illus.). 272p. 1996. pap. 14.95 (*0-02-860896-8*) Macmillan.

— Frommer's Caribbean Hideaways. 7th ed. (Illus.). 384p. 1995. 15.95 (*0-02-860647-7*) Macmillan.

— Frommer's Chicago by Night. (Illus.). 176p. 1996. 12.95 (*0-02-861131-4*) Macmillan.

— Frommer's Chicago '97. (Frommer's Travel Guides Ser.). 1997. 13.95 (*0-02-861151-9*, P-H Travel) Prntice Hall Bks.

— Frommer's Cruises, 1995-1996. (Illus.). 420p. 1994. pap. 19.00 (*0-671-88482-4*) Prntice Hall Bks.

— Frommer's Israel. 432p. 1996. 16.95 (*0-02-860860-7*) Macmillan.

— Frommer's Israel from $45 a Day. 16th ed. 432p. 1996. 16.95 (*0-02-860716-3*, P-H Travel) Prntice Hall Bks.

— Frommer's Las Vegas by Night. (By Night Guides Ser.). (Illus.). 176p. 1996. pap. 12.95 (*0-02-861427-5*) Macmillan.

— Frommer's London by Night. (Illus.). 176p. 1996. 12.95 (*0-02-861210-8*, P-H Travel) Prntice Hall Bks.

— Frommer's London From $60 a Day. 4th ed. (Frommer's Dollar-A-Day Guides Ser.). 288p. 1996. 14.95 (*0-02-861245-0*) Macmillan.

— Frommer's Los Angeles by Night. (Illus.). 176p. 1996. 12.95 (*0-02-861127-6*) Macmillan.

— Frommer's Miami by Night. (Illus.). 176p. 1996. 12.95 (*0-02-861138-1*) Macmillan.

— Frommer's Montana & Wyoming. 416p. 1996. 15.95 (*0-02-860685-X*) Macmillan.

— Frommer's New England '97. (Frommer's Travel Guides Ser.). (Illus.). 1997. 18.95 (*0-02-861149-7*, P-H Travel) Prntice Hall Bks.

— Frommer's New York by Night. (Illus.). 176p. 1996. 12.95 (*0-02-861130-6*) Macmillan.

— Frommer's Nova Scotia, New Brunswick, Prince Edward Island. 240p. 1996. 14.95 (*0-02-860861-5*, P-H Travel) Prntice Hall Bks.

— Frommer's Paris by Night. 176p. 1996. 12.95 (*0-02-861128-4*) Macmillan.

— Frommer's Portable New Orleans. (Frommer's Portable Guides Ser.). (Illus.). 176p. 1996. pap. 9.95 (*0-02-861423-2*) Macmillan.

— Frommer's San Francisco by Night. (Illus.). 176p. 1996. 12.95 (*0-02-861129-2*) Macmillan.

— Frommer's 25 Best Beach Vacations: Carolinas & Georgia. (Illus.). 288p. 1996. 14.95 (*0-02-860661-2*, P-H Travel) Prntice Hall Bks.

— Frommer's Utah. 320p. 1996. 15.95 (*0-02-860478-4*) Macmillan.

— Frommer's Virginia. 3rd ed. 304p. 1996. 14.95 (*0-02-860704-X*) Macmillan.

— Frommer's Walking Tours: London. 2nd ed. 176p. 1995. 12.95 (*0-02-860468-7*) Macmillan.

— Frommer's Walking Tours: New York City. 2nd ed. 176p. 1995. 12.95 (*0-02-860470-9*) Macmillan.

— Frommer's Walking Tours: San Francisco. 2nd ed. 176p. 1995. 12.95 (*0-02-860472-5*) Macmillan.

— Frommer's Walking Tours: Tokyo. 176p. 1995. 12.95 (*0-02-860466-0*, Pub. by Macmillan) S&S Trade.

— Frommer's Walt Disney World & Orlando, 1996. 304p. 1995. 13.95 (*0-02-860649-3*) Macmillan.

— Frommer's Washington & Oregon. 6th ed. (Frommer's Complete Guides Ser.). (Illus.). 480p. 1996. 16.95 (*0-02-860705-8*, Pub. by Macmillan) S&S Trade.

— Greek Islands Guide. (Illus.). 416p. (Orig.). 1997. pap. 16.95 (*1-883323-40-1*) Open Rd Pub.

McDonald, George & Balliett, Will. Irreverent Guides to Amsterdam. 224p. 1995. 12.95 (*0-02-860882-8*) Macmillan.

— Irreverent Guides to Paris. 224p. 1995. 12.95 (*0-02-860686-8*) Macmillan.

— Irreverent Guides to Santa Fe. 224p. 1996. 12.95 (*0-02-860883-6*) Macmillan.

— Irreverent Guides to Washington, DC. 224p. 1996. 12.95 (*0-02-860884-4*) Macmillan.

McDonald, George & Groff, Donald. Frommer's 25 Best Beach Vacations: New York & Washington. LC 96-76211. 288p. 1996. 14.95 (*0-02-860662-0*, P-H Travel) Prntice Hall Bks.

McDonald, George & Hatch, Susan. Frommer's 25 Best Beach Vacations: New England. (Illus.). 288p. 1996. 14.95 (*0-02-860660-4*) Macmillan.

McDonald, George, et al. Frommer's Great Beach Vacations: California. 288p. 1995. 14.95 (*0-02-860498-9*) Macmillan.

— Frommer's Great Beach Vacations: Florida. (Illus.). 288p. 1995. 14.95 (*0-02-860496-2*) Macmillan.

— Frommer's Great Beach Vacations: Hawaii. (Illus.). 288p. 1995. 14.95 (*0-02-860497-0*) Macmillan.

— Frommer's Irreverent Guide: New York. (Illus.). 224p. 1995. 12.95 (*0-02-860653-1*) Macmillan.

— Frommer's Irreverent Guide to Chicago: Chicago. (Illus.). 224p. 1996. 12.95 (*0-02-860687-6*) Macmillan.

McDonald, George, jt. auth. see Wood, Katie.

McDonald, George A., et al. Atlas of Hematology. 5th ed. (Illus.). 296p. 1989. text 110.00 (*0-443-02560-6*) Church.

McDonald, Gerald. Training & Careers for the Professional Musician. 112p. 1979. 35.00 (*0-905418-03-4*, Pub. by Gresham Bks) St Mut.

McDonald, Gerald D., et al. A Checklist of American Newspaper Carriers' Addresses, 1720-1820. LC 89-18226. (Illus.). 248p. 1999. 30.00 (*0-944026-16-8*) Am Antiquarian.

— The Complete Films of Charlie Chaplin. rev. ed. (Illus.). 224p. 1988. reprint ed. pap. 15.95 (*0-8065-1095-1*, Citadel Pr) Carol Pub Group.

McDonald, Giles N., jt. ed. see Jordan, Darryl F.

McDonald, Gina, jt. auth. see McDonald, Douglas.

McDonald, Glenn, jt. auth. see Johnson, Ben C.

McDonald, Gordon. Restaurando Su Vida Desecha.Tr. of Rebuilding Your Broken World. (SPA.). 220p. 1990. pap. 7.99 (*1-56063-009-4*, 498458) Editorial Unilit.

McDonald, Gordon, jt. ed. see Wood, Chris.

McDonald, Grace. History of the Irish in Wisconsin in the Nineteenth Century. LC 76-6355. (Irish Americans Ser.). (Illus.). 1976. reprint ed. 29.95 (*0-405-09348-9*) Ayer.

McDonald, Gregory. The Brave. LC 97-23051. 1999. mass mkt. 11.00 (*0-684-84424-9*, Scribner Pap Fic) S&S Trade Pap.

— Carioca Fletch. LC 85-16378. 288p. (Orig.). 1988. mass mkt. 4.99 (*0-446-34899-6*) Warner Bks.

— Confess, Fletch. 272p. 1976. mass mkt. 4.99 (*0-380-00814-9*, Avon Bks) Morrow Avon.

— The Education of Gregory McDonald: Writings about America, 1966-1973. 256p. (Orig.). 1985. mass mkt. 7.95 (*0-446-38214-0*, Pub. by Warner Bks) Little.

— Fletch. 256p. 1976. mass mkt. 4.99 (*0-380-00645-6*, Avon Bks) Morrow Avon.

— Fletch Reflected. 288p. 1995. mass mkt. 6.50 (*0-515-11676-9*, Jove) Berkley Pub.

— Fletch, Too. large type ed. LC 86-23181. (Basic Ser.). 327p. 1993. reprint ed. lib. bdg. 22.95 (*0-89621-769-8*) Thorndike Pr.

— Fletch Won. large type ed. LC 85-24497. 383p. 1993. reprint ed. lib. bdg. 22.95 (*0-89621-677-2*) Thorndike Pr.

— Fletch's Fortune. 1988. mass mkt. 4.99 (*0-380-37978-3*, Avon Bks) Morrow Avon.

— Flynn. 1977p. 1977. pap. 3.95 (*0-380-01764-4*, Avon Bks) Morrow Avon.

— Flynn's In. LC 83-63161. ("Flynn" Ser.). 1987. 45.00 (*0-89296-086-8*, Pub. by Mysterious Pr) Little.

— Last Laughs: The 1986 Mystery Writers of America Anthology. (Illus.). 208p. 1986. 16.95 (*0-89296-246-1*, Pub. by Mysterious Pr) Little.

— Running Scared. 1964. 12.95 (*0-8392-1095-7*) Astor-Honor.

— Safekeeping. LC 85-16708. 1987. 45.00 (*0-89296-140-6*, Pub. by Mysterious Pr) Little.

— Skylar. 1997. mass mkt. 5.99 (*0-380-72524-X*, Avon Bks) Morrow Avon.

— Skylar in Yankeeland. 256p. 1998. mass mkt. 5.99 (*0-380-72525-8*, Avon Bks) Morrow Avon.

— Son of Fletch. 272p. 1994. mass mkt. 5.99 (*0-515-11470-7*, Jove) Berkley Pub.

— Son of Fletch. large type ed. LC 93-33295. 323p. 1993. lib. bdg. 22.95 (*0-7862-0079-0*) Thorndike Pr.

McDonald, Hamish. The Polyester Prince: The Rise of Dhirubhai Ambani. (Illus.). 296p. 1999. pap. 15.95 (*1-86448-468-3*, Pub. by Allen & Unwin Pty) IPG Chicago.

McDonald, Hamish, jt. auth. see Ball, Desmond.

*__McDonald, Helen.__ Erotic Ambiguities: The Female Nude in Art. LC 00-32184. 2000. pap. write for info. (*0-415-17099-0*) Routledge.

McDonald, Hemprova G. New Concepts in Blood Formation Cell Generation in Malignant & Benign Tissues: Adult & Embryonic Tissues from Humans & Animals in Chronic Ischemic Conditions, Acute Rhuematic Fever & Coronary Occlusion with Myocardial Infarction. LC 89-90849. (Cardiac Muscle Ser.: Vol. II). (Illus.). 117p. (C). 1995. 90.00 (*0-9627824-1-6*) Diagnostic & Cell.

McDonald, Henry. Normative Basis of Culture: A Philosophical Inquiry. LC 85-23795. xii, 241p. 1986. text 35.00 (*0-8071-1280-1*) La State U Pr.

McDonald, Howard. Voices in the Big Sky! The History of Montana Broadcasting. 160p. (Orig.). 1996. pap. 12.95 (*1-57502-109-9*) Morris Pubng.

McDonald, Hugh C. Appointment in Dallas: The Final Solution to the Assassination of JFK. (Illus.). 210p. (Orig.). 1975. mass mkt. 3.99 (*0-8217-3893-3*, Zebra Kensgtn) Kensgtn Pub Corp.

McDonald, Hugh J. & Lappe, Robert J. Ionography: Electrophoresis in Stabilized Media. LC QD0561.M1455. 278p. reprint ed. pap. 86.20 (*0-608-30431-X*, 201192800080) Bks Demand.

McDonald, Hugh J., tr. see Singh, Rajendra.

McDonald, Hugh P. Political Philosophy & Ideology: A Critique of Political Essentialism. LC 96-46101. 440p. 1996. 64.50 (*0-7618-0594-X*); pap. 39.50 (*0-7618-0595-8*) U Pr of Amer.

McDonald, I. A., ed. see Kruger, F. J. & Ferrar, A. A.

*__McDonald, Ian.__ Bruno the Bandit. (Illus.). 152p. 1999. pap. 12.95 (*0-9660676-7-3*) Plan Nine Publ.

McDonald, Ian. Essequibo. 68p. (C). 1992. pap. 10.95 (*0-934257-90-6*) Story Line.

— The Hummingbird Tree. 2nd ed. (Caribbean Writers Ser.). 182p. (C). 1992. pap. 9.95 (*0-435-98934-0*, 98934) Heinemann.

McDonald, Ian & Brown, Stewart, eds. The Heinemann Book of Caribbean Poetry. (Caribbean Writers Ser.). 236p. (C). 1992. pap. 11.95 (*0-435-98817-4*, 98817) Heinemann.

McDonald, Ian & Lyttleton, David. Kling Klang Klatch. (Illus.). 80p. (Orig.). 1992. pap. 11.95 (*1-878574-41-8*) Dark Horse Comics.

McDonald, Ian R., jt. auth. see Hansen, J. P.

McDonald, Irene M., jt. auth. see Whitty, Mike.

McDonald, Irene M., ed. see Whitty, Mike.

McDonald, J. The Magic Story. 1984. pap. 6.95 (*0-912576-09-X*) R Collier.

McDonald, J. C. Fundamentals of Digital Switching. 2nd ed. LC 89-72201. (Illus.). 508p. (C). 1990. 89.50 (*0-306-43347-8*, Plen Insight) Perseus Pubng.

McDonald, J. C., ed. Epidemiology of Work Related Diseases. 500p. 1995. text 88.00 (*0-7279-0856-1*, Pub. by BMJ Pub) Login Brothers Bk Co.

McDonald, J. I. Biblical Interpretation & Christian Ethics. LC 93-16555. (New Studies in Christian Ethics: No. 2). 319p. (C). 1994. text 64.95 (*0-521-43059-3*) Cambridge U Pr.

McDonald, J. I. & Shaw, W. A. Gospel of Matthew. (C). 1988. 45.00 (*0-7157-2154-2*) St Mut.

McDonald, J. I., jt. auth. see Chilton, Bruce D.

McDonald, J. Ian. Christian Values: Theory & Practice in Christian Ethics Today. 192p. pap. 29.95 (*0-567-29282-7*, Pub. by T & T Clark) Bks Intl VA.

McDonald, J. K., ed. see Barrett, Alan J.

McDonald, J. Ken, jt. auth. see Barrett, Alan J.

McDonald, James, ed. see Hester, William.

McDonald, James H., jt. ed. see Dubinskas, Franks A.

McDonald, James I. The Crucible of Christian Morality. LC 97-50236. (Religion in the First Christian Centuries Ser.). 256p. (C). 1998. 75.00 (*0-415-11858-1*); pap. 24.99 (*0-415-11859-X*) Routledge.

McDonald, James J., Jr. Mental & Emotional Injuries in Employment Litigation with 1998 Supplement. Kulick, Francine B., ed. LC 94-15827. 500p. 1994. text 125.00 (*0-87179-832-8*) BNA Books.

— Mental & Emotional Injuries in Employment Litigation, 1998 Supplement. 219p. pap. 55.00 (*1-57018-117-9*, 1117-PR8) BNA Books.

McDonald, James P. John Demjanjuk. (Illus.). 200p. (Orig.). (C). 1990. pap. 8.95 (*0-915597-79-9*) Amana Bks.

McDonald, James R. The European Scene: A Geographic Perspective. 2nd ed. LC 96-43933. 375p. (C). 1996. 75.00 (*0-13-368614-0*) P-H.

McDonald/Eampoler, Susan. GIS in Practice. LC 99-27278. (C). 2001. pap. text 49.95 (*1-56690-192-8*) Thomson Learn.

McDonald, Jane, jt. auth. see Flannery, Linda.

McDonald, Jane E. A Pocket Guide to Physical Examination & Nutritional Assessment. (Illus.). 156p. 1994. pap. text 29.00 (*0-920513-21-2*, Pub. by Saulnders) Saunders.

McDonald, Janet. Project Girl. LC 98-23281. 256p. 1999. 23.00 (*0-374-23757-3*) FS&G.

*__McDonald, Janet.__ Project Girl. LC 99-86211. 231p. 2000. pap. 15.95 (*0-520-22345-4*, Pub. by U CA Pr) Cal Prin Full Svc.

— Spelling Bee. 2001. text. write for info. (*0-374-37140-7*) FS&G.

McDonald, Jean, jt. auth. see Clarke, Marianne.

McDonald, Jeanne, jt. auth. see Brow, Fred.

McDonald, Jeanne P., ed. Voices from the Valley: Selections from the Knoxville Writers' Guild. 239p. (Orig.). 1994. pap. text 14.95 (*0-9643178-0-X*) Knoxville Writ.

McDonald, Jerry N. & Woodward, Susan L. Indian Mounds of the Atlantic Coast: A Guide to Sites from Maine to Florida. LC 87-90428. (Illus.). ix, 162p. (Orig.). 1987. pap. 14.95 (*0-939923-03-3*) M & W Pub Co.

McDonald, Jerry N., jt. auth. see Woodward, Susan L.

McDonald, Jesse. Toulouse-Lautrec. 48p. 1994. 5.98 (*0-7858-0209-6*) Bk Sales Inc.

McDonald, Jim. Control Room Volume: Workbook & Postings. 4th rev. ed. (Radio Broadcaster's Bigbook Ser.: No. 2). 100p. 1998. ring bd., wbk. ed. 129.00 (*0-938023-16-0*) Wind River Inst Pr.

— The Translator Big Book: Licensee Manual & Site Book, 2. Incl. Radio Broadcaster's Big Book: Public File Workbook. (Illus.). 100p. 1999. student ed., ring bd. 129.00 (*0-938023-17-9*); Translator Big Book No. 2: Licensee Manual, TV & FM Translators. (Illus.). 100p. student ed. 99.00 (*0-938023-18-7*) Wind River Inst Pr.

McDonald, Jimmie. The Kathryn Kuhlman I Knew That Believed in Miracles. 196p. (Orig.). 1996. pap. 10.99 (*1-56043-272-1*, Treasure Hse) Destiny Image.

McDonald, Joanna. Dubious Assets. large type ed. (Black Satin Romance Ser.). 528p. 1996. 27.99 (*1-86110-009-4*) Ulverscroft.

— The Faces of Manassas: Rare Photographs of Soldiers Who Fought at Bull Run. LC 98-66452. (Illus.). 72p. 1998. pap. 15.00 (*1-888967-01-3*) Rank & File.

*__McDonald, Joanna, ed.__ The Faces of D-Day. 70p. 2000. pap. 15.00 (*1-888967-05-6*) Rank & File.

— The Liberation of Pointe du Hoc: The 2nd Rangers at Normandy, June 6, 1944. 200p. 2000. pap. write for info. (*1-888967-06-4*) Rank & File.

McDonald, JoAnna M. Give Them the Bayonet: A Guide to the Battle for Henry Hill, July 21, 1861. LC 98-56449. 1998. pap. 6.95 (*1-57249-107-8*, Burd St Pr) White Mane Pub.

*__McDonald, JoAnna M.__ Goodbye Boys! Goodbye! A Walking Guide to the High Water Mark, Gettysburg, July 2-3, 1863. LC 99-13311. 64p. 1998. pap. 6.95 (*1-57249-104-3*, Burd St Pr) White Mane Pub.

— We Shall Meet Again: The First Battle of Manassas (Bull Run), July 18-21, 1861. (Illus.). 224p. 2000. pap. 13.95 (*0-19-513938-0*) OUP.

— We Shall Meet Again: The First Battle of Manassas (Bull Run), July 18-21, 1861. LC 98-44741. 224p. 1998. 27.95 (*1-57249-108-6*, Burd St Pr) White Mane Pub.

— We're Going in There... A Guide to the Battles for Little Round Top-Valley of Death-Devil's Den. LC 99-19712. 75p. 1999. pap. 6.95 (*1-57249-119-1*, Burd St Pr) White Mane Pub.

McDonald, JoAnna M. The World Will Long Remember: A Guide to the Battle of Gettysburg. LC 96-9807. (Illus.). 240p. 1997. 29.95 (*1-57249-000-4*) White Mane Pub.

— The World Will Long Remember: A Guide to the Battle of Gettysburg. LC 96-9807. 183p. 1998. pap. 14.95 (*1-57249-127-2*) White Mane Pub.

McDonald, JoAnna M., ed. The Faces of Gettysburg: Photographs from the Gettysburg National Military Park Archives. (Illus.). 70p. (Orig.). 1997. pap. 15.00 (*1-888967-00-5*) Rank & File.

— The Faces of Irish Civil War Soldiers. (Illus.). 60p. 1999. pap. 15.00 (*1-888967-03-X*) Rank & File.

*__McDonald, Joe.__ African Wildlife. 1999. 10.95 (*1-57717-129-2*) Todtri Prods.

McDonald, Joe. Designing Wildlife Photographs: Professional Field Techniques for Composing Great Pictures. LC 94-16283. (Illus.). 144p. 1994. pap. 24.95 (*0-8174-3781-9*) Watsn-Guptill.

— Navy Poems. (Limited Chapbook Ser.). 1998. pap. text 10.00 (*1-56439-073-X*, Pub. by Ridgeway) Partners Pubs Grp.

— The New Complete Guide to Wildlife Photography: How to Get Close & Capture Animals on Film. LC 98-18559. 160p. 1998. pap. 24.95 (*0-8174-5009-2*, Amphoto) Watsn-Guptill.

— Photographing on Safari: A Field Guide to Wildlife Photography in East Africa. LC 96-17751. (Illus.). 144p. 1996. pap. 19.95 (*0-8174-5440-3*, Amphoto) Watsn-Guptill.

McDonald, John. House of Eternity: The Tomb of Nefertari. LC 96-24123. (Conservation & Cultural Heritage Ser.). (Illus.). 120p. 1996. pap. 24.95 (*0-89236-415-7*, Pub. by J P Getty Trust) OUP.

— Jeffrey Smart: Paintings of the '70s & '80s. (Illus.). 180p. 1991. text 37.00 (*976-8097-01-9*) Gordon & Breach.

*__McDonald, John.__ The Maine Dictionary. (Illus.). 128p. (C). 2000. pap. 12.95 (*1-58066-057-6*, Covered Brdge Pr) Douglas Charles Ltd.

McDonald, John. The Message of a Master: A Classic Tale of Wealth, Wisdom, & the Secret of Success. Dieter, Katherine & Allen, Marc, eds. LC 91-38486. 96p. 1993. reprint ed. pap. 8.95 (*0-931432-95-2*) New Wrld Lib.

— Production Efficiency in Domesday England, 1086. LC 97-12877. (Explorations in Economic History Ser.). 256p. (C). 1998. 85.00 (*0-415-16187-8*) Routledge.

— The Sacraments in the Christian Life. (C). 1988. 39.00 (*0-85439-226-2*, Pub. by St Paul Pubns) St Mut.

— Strategy in Poker, Business & War. rev. ed. (Illus.). 128p. 1996. pap. 11.00 (*0-393-31457-X*, Norton Paperbks) Norton.

*__McDonald, John, et al, eds.__ Evidence Based Gastroenterology & Hepatology. (Illus.). 557p. 1999. text 152.95 (*0-7279-1182-1*) BMJ Pub.

McDonald, John & Snooks, Graeme D. Domesday Economy: A New Approach to Anglo-Norman History. (Illus.). 208p. 1986. 58.00 (*0-19-828524-8*) OUP.

McDonald, John, et al. The Origins of Angling: And a New Printing of "The Treatise of Fishing with an Angle" 3rd ed. LC 97-4452. (Illus.). 288p. 1997. reprint ed. 40.00 (*1-55821-587-5*) Lyons Pr.

— Real Justice Training Manual: Coordinating Family Group Conferences. LC 96-116467. 128p. (Orig.). (C). 1995. pap. text 25.00 (*0-9633887-2-X*) Pipers Pr.

McDonald, John, jt. auth. see Diamond, Louise.

McDonald, John A., ed. Lung Growth & Development. LC 96-52512. (Lung Biology in Health & Disease Ser.: Vol. 100). (Illus.). 768p. 1997. text 215.00 (*0-8247-9772-8*) Dekker.

McDonald, John A., jt. ed. see Ebrom, Daniel A.

*__McDonald, John D., et al.__ Automating a Distribution Cooperative from A to Z: A Primer on Employing Technology. LC 99-51725. 1999. write for info. (*0-917599-28-4*) Natl Rural.

McDonald, John F. Employment Location & Industrial Land Use in Metropolitan Chicago. 224p. (Orig.). 1984. pap. text 7.80 (*0-87563-242-4*) Stipes.

— Fundamentals of Urban Economics. LC 96-16026. 545p. (C). 1996. 58.60 (*0-02-378852-6*, Macmillan Coll) P-H.

McDonald, John F., ed. Transposable Elements & Evolution. LC 93-17743. (Contemporary Issues in Genetics & Evolution Ser.: Vol. 1). 350p. (C). 1993. text 250.00 (*0-7923-2338-6*) Kluwer Academic.

*__McDonald, John F., et al.__ Economics of Urban Highway Congestion & Pricing. LC 99-44505. 1999. text 105.00 (*0-7923-8631-0*) Kluwer Academic.

McDonald, John F., jt. ed. see Mills, Edwin S.

McDonald, John S., jt. auth. see Bonica, John J.

McDonald, John W. Aircraft Yearbook 3-View Drawings 1903-1946. LC 98-82256. (Illus.). 276p. 1999. pap. 35.00 (*0-9669996-0-6*) J W Mc Donald.

McDonald, John W., Jr. The North-South Dialogue & the United Nations. 26p. (Orig.). (C). 1985. reprint ed. pap. text 11.50 (*0-8191-5058-4*) U Pr of Amer.

McDonald, Joseph. The Wildlife Photographer's Field Manual. (Illus.). 200p. 1991. pap. 14.95 (*0-936262-07-9*) Amherst Media.

McDonald, Joseph & Micikas, Basney. Academic Libraries: The Dimensions of Their Effectiveness, 32. LC 93-14464. (New Directions in Information Management Ser.). 208p. 1994. 52.95 (*0-313-27269-7*, Greenwood Pr) Greenwood.

An Asterisk (*) at the beginning of an entry indicates that the title is appearing for the first time.

McDonald, Joseph P. School Reform Behind the Scenes: How Atlas Is Shaping the Future of Education. LC 99-17328. (Series on School Reform). viii, 151 p. 1999. write for info. (0-8077-3860-3) Tchrs Coll.
— Teaching: Making Sense of an Uncertain Craft. (Professional Development & Practice Ser.). 160p. (C). 1992. pap. text 15.95 (0-8077-3167-6) Tchrs Coll.
McDonald, Joseph P., et al. Graduation by Exhibition: Assessing Genuine Achievement. LC 92-46613. 1993. pap. 10.95 (0-87120-204-2) ASCD.
***McDonald, Joyce.** Comfort Creek. 1998. 9.09 (0-606-13289-9, Pub. by Turtleback) Demco.
— Shadow People. LC 00-24307. (Illus.). 2000. 15.95 (0-385-32662-9) Delacorte.
McDonald, Joyce. The Stuff of Our Forebears: Willa Cather's Southern Heritage. LC 97-40646. 144p. 1998. text 29.95 (0-8173-0920-9) U of Ala Pr.
— Swallowing Stones. 256p. (YA). (gr. 7-12). 1999. mass mkt. 4.50 (0-440-22672-4) BDD Bks Young Read.
— Swallowing Stones. LC 97-1402. 256p. (YA). (gr. 7). 1997. 15.95 (0-385-32309-3) Delacorte.
McDonald, Julie. Amalie's Story. rev. ed. LC 71-128605. 256p. 1985. 7.95 (0-930942-08-6) Sutherland IA.
— The Ballad of Bishop Hill. LC 85-90372. 1986. 7.95 (0-930942-02-7) Sutherland IA.
— The Heather & the Rose. LC 86-90362. 1987. 7.95 (0-930942-07-8) Sutherland IA.
— Nils Discovers America Adventures: Adventures with Erik. 96p. (J). (gr. 2-6). 1990. pap. 8.95 (0-941016-74-9) Penfield.
— Reaching. LC 88-61287. 202p. (Orig.). 1988. pap. 7.95 (0-930942-12-4) Sutherland IA.
— Scottish Proverbs. Zug, John & Liffring-Zug, Joan, eds. (Illus.). 30p. (Orig.). 1987. pap. 10.95 (0-941016-42-0) Penfield.
— Young Rakes. Bergren, Anne B. & Joy, Melissa M., eds. 140p. (Orig.). 1991. pap. 9.95 (1-878326-01-5) East Hall Pr.
McDonald, Julie, ed. German Proverbs. 1988. pap. 10.95 (0-941016-41-2) Penfield.
McDonald, Julie J. Delectably Danish: Recipes & Reflections. LC 82-81568. (Illus.). 64p. 1982. pap. 8.95 (0-941016-04-8) Penfield.
— Savory Scottish Recipes. (Illus.). 140p. 1996. spiral bd. 6.95 (1-57216-026-8) Penfield.
McDonald, Julie J., ed. Scandinavian Proverbs: Foldk Wisdom from Denmark, Finland, Iceland, Norway & Sweden. 30p. 1993. pap. 10.95 (0-941016-27-7) Penfield.
McDonald, Julie Jensen. Definitely Danish: History, Culture Recipes. 64p. 1994. pap. 12.95 (0-941016-94-3) Penfield.
McDonald, Julie Jensen & Bourret, Joan Liffring-Zug. Grant Wood's Little Sister Nan: An American Icon. (Illus.). 130p. 1999. pap. 16.95 (1-57216-038-1) Penfield.
McDonald, Julie M. Contemporary Moral Issues in a Diverse Society. LC 97-36695. (Philosophy Ser.). (C). 1997. pap. 52.95 (0-534-51321-2) Wadsworth Pub.
McDonald, Karen. And It Was Good: A Book of Verse. 68p. 1997. pap. 9.95 (1-880451-22-0) Rainbows End.
McDonald, Kathleen. How to Meditate: A Practical Guide. rev. ed. Courtin, Robina, ed. LC 88-51646. 224p. 1994. pap. 14.95 (0-86171-009-6) Wisdom MA.
McDonald, Kathleen, jt. auth. see Eternal Quest Staff.
***McDonald, Kathryn M., et al.** An Evaluation of Beta-Blockers, Calcium Antagonists, Nitrates & Alternative Therapies for Stable Angina. (Evidence Report - Technology Assessment Ser.: No. 10). 128p. 2000. pap. write for info. (1-58763-006-0) Agency Healthcare.
McDonald, Kathy, ed. BASIC Programming One: Course Code 303-2. rev. ed. (Illus.). 78p. (gr. 5). 1989. reprint ed. pap. text 9.95 (0-917531-90-6) CES Compu-Tech.
***McDonald, Kathy & Sirull, Beth.** Creating Your Life Collage: Strategies for Solving the Work/Life Dilemma. LC 99-42375. 336p. 2000. pap. 15.00 (0-609-80410-3, SEL027000, Three Riv Pr) Crown Pub Group.
McDonald, Kathy, ed. see Broadie, Kim, et al.
McDonald, Kathy J., jt. ed. see Schmidt, Wyman C.
***McDonald, Kay L.** Beyond the Vision. 2000. 25.95 (0-7862-2304-9) Five Star.
McDonald, Kay L. Brightwood Expedition. 1999. 26.95 (0-7862-1782-0) Thorndike Pr.
— The Brightwood Expedition. LC 75-25793. 342p. 1976. lib. bdg. 14.95 (0-87140-605-5) Trilogy OR.
— The Vision Is Fulfilled. 343p. 1983. 14.95 (0-8027-4019-7) Trilogy OR.
— The Vision Is Fulfilled. 383p. 1995. reprint ed. pap. 9.95 (1-883273-05-6) Trilogy OR.
— Vision of the Eagle. 2nd ed. LC 93-94065. 312p. 1993. reprint ed. 24.95 (1-883273-00-5) Trilogy OR.
— Vision of the Eagle: A Novel. large type ed. LC 97-40434. 1997. 24.95 (0-7862-1255-1) Thorndike Pr.
McDonald, Keiko, ed. Ugetsu. LC 92-8419. (Films in Print Ser.: Vol. 17). (Illus.). 200p. (C). 1992. 37.00 (0-8135-1861-X); pap. 17.00 (0-8135-1862-8) Rutgers U Pr.
McDonald, Keiko & Rimer, J. Thomas, eds. Nara Encounters. LC 97-2452. (Illus.). 112p. 1997. pap. 19.95 (0-8348-0387-9) Weatherhill.
McDonald, Keiko I. Cinema East: A Critical Study of Major Japanese Films. LC 81-65870. (Illus.). 280p. 1983. 45.00 (0-8386-3094-4) Fairleigh Dickinson.
***McDonald, Keiko I.** From Book to Screen: Modern Japanese Literature in Films. LC 99-10679. (Illus.). 368p. 2000. 62.95 (0-7656-0387-X, East Gate Bk); pap. 25.95 (0-7656-0388-8, East Gate Bk) M E Sharpe.
McDonald, Keiko J. Japanese Classical Theater in Films. LC 92-54669. (Illus.). 360p. 1994. 48.50 (0-8386-3502-4) Fairleigh Dickinson.
McDonald, Kelley, ed. see Levine, Toby Kleban.
McDonald, Kenneth. The Monstrous Trick 1998. write for info. (0-9695634-2-6) A1PEC.
***McDonald, Kenneth.** The Quick Python Book. LC 99-38928. (Illus.). 422p. 1999. pap. 39.95 (1-884777-74-0) Manning Pubns.
McDonald, Kent A., et al. Wood Decks: Materials, Construction, & Finishing. (Illus.). 100p. (Orig.). 1996. pap. 19.95 (0-935018-77-8, 7298) Forest Prod.
McDonald, Kevin. Struggles for Subjectivity: Identity, Action & Youth Experience. LC 99-33082. (Cultural Social Studies). (Illus.). 272p. 2000. 64.95 (0-521-66279-6); pap. 22.95 (0-521-66446-2) Cambridge U Pr.
***McDonald, Kim.** Life in Outer Space. LC 00-31075. (Space Explorer Ser.). (Illus.). (J). 2000. write for info. (0-7398-2213-6) Raintree Steck-V.
— Life in Outer Space: The Search for Extraterrestrials. (Space Explorer Ser.). (Illus.). (J). 2000. pap. 8.95 (0-7398-2223-3) Raintree Steck-V.
McDonald, Kyle C. & Ulaby, Fawaaz T. Modeling Microwave Backscatter from Discontinuous Tree Canopies. LC G 0070.. (Technical Reports: No. 026511-2-T). 377p. reprint ed. pap. 116.90 (0-7837-1390-8, 20415710021) Bks Demand.
McDonald, L. Racial Equality. Haiman, Franklyn S., ed. (To Protect These Rights Ser.). 168p. 1991. pap. 12.95 (0-8442-6004-5, Natl Textbk Co) NTC Contemp Pub Co.
McDonald, L. E., ed. Veterinary Endocrinology & Reproduction. 4th ed. LC 88-9015. (Illus.). 571p. 1989. text 58.00 (0-8121-1134-6) Lppncott W & W.
***McDonald, Laughlin.** The Rights of Racial Minorities. (American Civil Liberties Union Handbooks Ser.). 1998. 14.09 (0-606-13741-6, Pub. by Turtleback) Demco.
McDonald, Laughlin & Powell, John A. The Rights of Racial Minorities: The Basic ACLU Guide to Racial Minority Rights. rev. ed. LC 93-15756. (American Civil Liberties Union Handbook Ser.). 288p. (C). 1993. pap. 9.95 (0-8093-1888-1) S Ill U Pr.
— The Rights of Racial Minorities: The Basic ACLU Guide to Racial Minority Rights. 2nd rev. ed. LC 93-15756. (American Civil Liberties Union Handbook Ser.). 344p. (C). 1993. 34.95 (0-8093-1899-7) S Ill U Pr.
McDonald, Laurie, jt. illus. see Knake, James.
McDonald, Laurie A. From Lydia B's Galley. LC 91-91299. (Illus.). 125p. (Orig.). 1991. pap. 9.95 (0-9630977-0-9) Mtn View Ent.
McDonald, Lawrence P. We Hold These Truths: A Reverent Review of the U. S. Constitution. 1992. pap. 12.50 (0-9632809-1-0) L McDonald Mem.
McDonald, Lee C. Western Political Theory: From Its Origins to the Present, 3 vols. Incl. Vol. 1. Ancient & Medieval. 228p. (C). 1970. pap. text 34.00 (0-15-595297-8, Pub. by Harcourt Coll Pubs); Vol. 2. From Machiavelli to Burke. 297p. (C). 1970. pap. text 34.00 (0-15-595298-6, Pub. by Harcourt Coll Pubs); Vol. 3. Nineteenth & Twentieth Centuries. 239p. (C). 1970. pap. text 34.00 (0-15-595299-4, Pub. by Harcourt Coll Pubs); (C). 1970. pap. text. write for info. (0-318-52978-5) Harcourt Coll Pubs.
McDonald, Lee M. Formation of the Christian Biblical Canon. expanded rev. ed. 340p. 1995. pap. 19.95 (1-56563-052-1) Hendrickson MA.
McDonald, Lee M., jt. auth. see Porter, Stanley E.
***McDonald, Lee Martin & Porter, Stanley, eds.** Early Christianity & Its Sacred Literature. (Illus.). 2000. 39.95 (1-56563-266-4) Hendrickson MA.
McDonald, Linda. Bones to Biscuits. LC 77-1236. 1977. pap. 6.95 (0-916198-03-0) Oaklawn Pr.
— Everything You Need to Know about Babies. LC 77-21017. (Illus.). 1978. pap. 12.95 (0-916198-04-9) Oaklawn Pr.
— Instant Baby Food. LC 75-27760. (Illus.). 113p. 1975. 8.95 (0-916198-02-2); pap. 6.95 (0-916198-01-4) Oaklawn Pr.
— The Joy of Breastfeeding. LC 77-18536. (Illus.). 1978. pap. 8.95 (0-916198-07-3) Oaklawn Pr.
McDonald, Linda & Cullens, Carol, eds. California Historical Landmarks. rev. ed. (Illus.). 350p. 1996. pap. text 11.95 (0-941925-19-6) Cal Parks Rec.
McDonald, Linda, jt. auth. see Criswell, Ann.
McDonald, Linda, jt. auth. see Steves, Renie.
McDonald, Linda, ed. see Criswell, Ann.
McDonald, Lisa A. Modeling Environmental Policy. Martin, Wade E., ed. LC 96-51423. (Natural Resource Management & Policy Ser.). 216p. (C). 1997. lib. bdg. 115.50 (0-7923-9855-6) Kluwer Academic.
McDonald, Lois, jt. auth. see White, Thelma B.
McDonald, Lois H. Elsie Hamburger: I Never Look Back. LC 88-92825. (Illus.). 212p. 1989. pap. 11.75 (0-9621992-1-4) Paradise Fact & Folklore.
McDonald, Lorna. Cattle Country. 250p. (C). 1990. 90.00 (0-685-67404-5, Pub. by Boolarong Pubns) St Mut.
— Gladstone: The City That Waited. 464p. (C). 1990. 90.00 (0-9599124-1-X, Pub. by Boolarong Pubns) St Mut.
— Magic Ships: The Life Story of Colin Archer. (Illus.). xi, 175p. 1997. pap. 24.95 (1-875998-26-8, Pub. by Central Queensland) Accents Pubns.
***McDonald, Lorna.** Over Earth & Ocean: The Archers of Ttolderodden & Gracemere. 412p. 2000. pap. 39.95 (0-7022-3145-2, Pub. by Univ Queensland Pr) Intl Spec Bk.
McDonald, Lucile. Alaska Steam: A Pictorial of the Alaska Steamship Company. Chapman, Jean & Rennick, Penny, eds. LC 84-216730. (Alaska Geographic Ser.: Vol. 11, No. 4). (Illus.). 160p. (Orig.). 1984. pap. 19.95 (0-88240-268-4) Alaska Geog Soc.
— Search for the Northwest Passage. LC 58-11860. (Illus.). 142p. (gr. 4-9). 1958. 8.95 (0-8323-0029-2); pap. 6.95 (0-8323-0253-8) Binford Mort.
— Swan among the Indians: Life of James Swan, 1818-1900. LC 72-85230. (Illus.). 280p. 1972. 14.95 (0-8323-0066-7) Binford Mort.
McDonald, Lucile & McDonald, Richard. A Foot in the Door: The Reminiscences of Lucile McDonald. (Illus.). 296p. (Orig.). 1995. pap. 19.95 (0-87422-120-X) Wash St U Pr.
McDonald, Lyle. The Ketogenic Diet: A Complete Guide for the Dieter & Practitioner. Volk, Elzi, ed. Date not set. pap. 29.95 (0-9671456-0-0) L McDonald.
McDonald, Lyman L., et al, eds. Estimation & Analysis of Insect Populations. (Lecture Notes in Statistics Ser.: Vol. 55). (Illus.). xiv, 492p. 1989. 96.95 (0-387-96998-5) Spr-Verlag.
McDonald, Lynn. The Early Origins of the Social Sciences. 408p. 1993. 65.00 (0-7735-1124-5, Pub. by McG-Queens Univ Pr) CUP Services.
— The Early Origins of the Social Sciences. 408p. 1995. pap. 22.95 (0-7735-1408-2, Pub. by McG-Queens Univ Pr) CUP Services.
McDonald, Lynn, ed. Women Theorists on Society & Politics. LC 98-205528. 336p. 1998. 54.95 (0-88920-290-7) W Laurier U Pr.
***McDonald, Lynn, ed.** Women Theorists on Society & Politics. LC 98-205528. 326p. 1999. pap. 34.95 (0-88920-316-4) Wilfrid Laurier.
McDonald, M., tr. see Ichikawa, T.
McDonald, M. B. & Copeland, L. O. Seed Science & Technology Laboratory Manual. LC 88-83562. (Illus.). 240p. (C). 1989. pap. text 26.95 (0-8138-0190-7) Iowa St U Pr.
— Seed Science & Technology Laboratory Manual. (C). 1992. pap. 90.00 (81-7233-038-3, Pub. by Scientific Pubs) St Mut.
McDonald, M. B., Jr. & Pardee, W. D., eds. The Role of Seed Certification in the Seed Industry. (Special Publication Ser.: Vol. 10). 46p. 1985. 12.00 (0-89118-521-6) Crop Sci Soc Am.
McDonald, M. H. & Leppard, J. W. La Auditoria de Marketing (The Marketing Audit) (SPA.). 285p. 1994. pap. 30.50 (84-7978-173-4, Pub. by Ediciones Diaz) IBD Ltd.
McDonald, M. V., tr. The History of al-Tabari Vol. 7: The Foundation of the Community - Muhammad at Al-Madina, A. D. 622-626, Hijrah-4 A. H. LC 87-12940. (SUNY Series in Near Eastern Studies). 182p. (C). 1987. text 59.50 (0-88706-344-6); pap. text 20.95 (0-88706-345-4) State U NY Pr.
McDonald, M. V., jt. ed. see Watt, W. Montgomery.
McDonald, M. V., tr. see Al-Tabari.
McDonald, M. W., jt. auth. see Maslin, B. R.
McDonald, Malcolm. Key Account Selection Matrix. Date not set. audio compact disk 370.00 (0-7506-4904-6) Buttrwrth-Heinemann.
— Marketing Portfolio Planner. Date not set. audio compact disk 340.00 (0-7506-4893-7) Buttrwrth-Heinemann.
— Portfolio Management Using the Directional Policy Matrix. Date not set. audio compact disk 65.95 (0-7506-4891-0) Buttrwrth-Heinemann.
McDonald, Malcolm & Dunbar, Ian. Market Segmentation: How to Do It. How to Profit from It. 2nd ed. (Illus.). 376p. 1998. pap. 64.50 (0-333-73369-X, Pub. by Macmillan) Trans-Atl Phila.
***McDonald, Malcolm & Keegan, Warren J.** Marketing Plans That Work. 2nd ed. 2001. pap. 21.95 (0-7506-7307-9) Buttrwrth-Heinemann.
McDonald, Malcolm & Leppard, John W. Marketing by Matrix: 100 Practical Ways to Improve Your Strategic & Tactical Marketing. LC 92-161964. (Illus.). 174p. 1992. reprint ed. pap. 54.00 (0-608-07967-7, 206793900012) Bks Demand.
***McDonald, Malcolm & Morris, Peter.** Marketing Plan in Color: A Pictorial Guide for Managers. 4th ed. (Illus.). 96p. 2000. pap. 24.95 (0-7506-4759-0) Buttrwrth-Heinemann.
***McDonald, Malcolm, et al.** Key Customers: How to Manage Them Profitably. 320p. 2000. pap. 37.95 (0-7506-4615-2) Buttrwrth-Heinemann.
McDonald, Malcolm B., ed. Marketing Strategies: New Approaches New Techniques. (Best of Long Range Planning Ser.: No. 2). 250p. 1995. text 57.50 (0-08-042572-0, Pergamon Pr) Elsevier.
McDonald, Malcolm B. & Tideman, Chrsitopher C. Retail Marketing Plans: How to Prepare Them, How to Use Them. 220p. 1997. pap. text 26.95 (0-7506-2021-8) Buttrwrth-Heinemann.
McDonald, Malcolm B., jt. auth. see Dunbar, Ian.
Mcdonald, Malcolm H. Marketing Plans: How to Prepare Them: How to Use Them. 3rd ed. (Professional Development Ser.). 360p. 1999. pap. text 39.95 (0-7506-2213-X) Buttrwrth-Heinemann.
McDonald, Malcolm H. & Keegan, Warren J. Marketing Plans That Work: Targeting Growth & Profitability. LC 97-7401. 240p. 1997. pap. text 19.95 (0-7506-9828-4) Buttrwrth-Heinemann.
McDonald, Malcolm H. & Morris, Peter. Pocket Guide to Selling Services & Products. 96p. 1995. pap. text 15.95 (0-7506-2641-0) Buttrwrth-Heinemann.
McDonald, Malcolm H., jt. auth. see De Chernatony, Leslie.
McDonald, Malcolm H. B. Marketing Plans: How to Prepare Them, How to Use Them. 4th ed. 578p. 2000. pap. text 44.95 (0-7506-4116-9) Buttrwrth-Heinemann.
McDonald, Mandy. Gender Planning in Development Agencies. (Gender & Development Ser.). (Illus.). 232p. (C). 1994. text 45.00 (0-85598-262-4, Pub. by Oxfam Pub) Stylus Pub VA.
***McDonald-Mann, Dana & Buron, Raoul J.** Giving Feedback to Subordinates. 28p. 1999. pap. text 6.95 (1-882197-39-9) Ctr Creat Leader.
McDonald, Marc. Hotel, Restaurant & Public House Law: Registrations, Licenses & Names. xxix, 441p. 1992. pap. write for info. (1-85475-105-0, IE, MICHIE); pap. text 92.00 (0-85475-105-X, IE, MICHIE) LEXIS Pub.
McDonald, Margaret M., ed. Towards Excellence: Case Studies of Good School Libraries. LC 85-44387. (Illus.). 104p. reprint ed. pap. 32.30 (0-7837-5328-4, 204506800005) Bks Demand.
McDonald, Marge. Simple Wisdom of Faith. (Illus.). 96p. 1999. 8.95 (1-56352-556-9) Longstreet.
***McDonald, Marge & Lenz, Richard.** Simple Wisdom of Aging. LC 99-61771. (Illus.). 96p. 1999. 8.95 (1-56352-572-0) Longstreet.
— Simple Wisdom of Friendship. LC 99-61770. (Illus.). 96p. 1999. 8.95 (1-56352-573-9) Longstreet.
McDonald, Marge & Lenz, Richard. Simple Wisdom of Living. (Illus.). 96p. 1999. 8.95 (1-56352-560-7) Longstreet.
— Simple Wisdom of Love. (Illus.). 96p. 1999. 8.95 (1-56352-555-0) Longstreet.
***McDonald, Marge & Lenz, Richard.** Simple Wisdom of Marriage. LC 99-61773. (Illus.). 96p. 1999. 8.95 (1-56352-574-7) Longstreet.
— Simple Wisdom of Parenting. LC 99-61772. (Illus.). 96p. 1999. 8.95 (1-56352-571-2) Longstreet.
McDonald, Marge & Lenz, Richard. Simple Wisdom of Success. (Illus.). 96p. 1999. 8.95 (1-56352-541-0) Longstreet.
McDonald, Marge, ed. see Pfeifer, Diane.
McDonald, Marianne. Ancient Sun, Modern Light. (Illus.). 288p. 1991. text 44.00 (0-231-07654-1) Col U Pr.
— Mythology of the Zodiac: Tales of the Constellations. (Illus.). 120p. 2000. 19.98 (1-56799-581-0, Friedman-Fairfax) M Friedman Pub Grp Inc.
Mcdonald, Marie. Ka Lei. (Illus.). 1995. pap. text 24.95 (0-914916-32-7) Ku Paa.
McDonald, Marilyn, ed. BookNotes: The Booklover's Organizer. 178p. (Orig.). 1994. pap. 12.95 (0-943097-02-9) Jackson Creek Pr.
McDonald, Marjorie. Not by the Color of Their Skin: The Impact of Racial Differences on the Child's Development. LC 73-134334. Orig. Title: Integration & Skin Color. 242p. 1971. 37.50 (0-8236-3690-9); pap. 24.95 (0-8236-8166-1, 23690) Intl Univs Pr.
McDonald, Mark & Milne, George. Cases in Sport Marketing. LC 98-42614. 1998. 24.00 (0-7637-0863-1) Jones & Bartlett.
McDonald, Mark, jt. auth. see Farquhar, Bobby.
***McDonald, Mary.** Art of the Hymn. 2000. 6.95 (5-550-01045-3) Nairi.
***McDonald, Mary & NLN Staff.** Evaluating Critical Thinking in the Classroom. (Illus.). 256p. (C). 2000. pap. text 40.00 (0-7637-1174-8) JB Pubns.
McDonald, Mary, jt. auth. see Pollard, Neil.
McDonald, Mary A. Blue Whales. LC 97-38098. (Illus.). 32p. 1998. lib. bdg. 22.79 (1-56766-472-5) Childs World.
— Boas. (Nature Books Ser.). (Illus.). 32p. (J). (gr. 2-6). 1996. lib. bdg. 22.79 (1-56766-212-9) Childs World.
— Chickens. LC 96-46192. (Nature Books Ser.). (Illus.). 32p. (J). (gr. 2-6). 1997. lib. bdg. 22.79 (1-56766-374-5) Childs World.
— Cobras. LC 95-46573. (Nature Books Ser.). (Illus.). 32p. (J). (gr. 2-6). 1996. lib. bdg. 22.79 (1-56766-265-X) Childs World.
— Cows. LC 96-46139. (Nature Books Ser.). (Illus.). 32p. (J). (gr. 2-6). 1997. lib. bdg. 22.79 (1-56766-375-3) Childs World.
— Ducks. LC 96-46138. (Nature Books Ser.). (Illus.). 32p. (J). (gr. 2-6). 1997. lib. bdg. 22.79 (1-56766-376-1) Childs World.
— Flying Squirrels. LC 93-9118. (Nature Books Ser.). (Illus.). 32p. (J). (gr. 2-6). 1994. lib. bdg. 22.79 (1-56766-058-4) Childs World.
— Foxes. LC 97-38096. (Nature Books Ser.). (Illus.). 32p. (J). (gr. 2-6). 1998. lib. bdg. 22.79 (1-56766-479-2) Childs World.
— Garter Snakes. (Illus.). 48p. (J). (gr. 3-7). 1995. 19.00 (0-516-35295-4) Childrens.
— Garter Snakes. LC 97-40607. (Illus.). 32p. (J). 1998. lib. bdg. 22.79 (1-56766-500-4) Childs World.
— Grizzlies. (Nature Books Ser.). (Illus.). 32p. (J). (gr. 2-6). 1996. lib. bdg. 22.79 (1-56766-213-7) Childs World.
— Horses. LC 96-46191. (Nature Books Ser.). (Illus.). 32p. (J). (gr. 2-6). 1997. lib. bdg. 22.79 (1-56766-377-X) Childs World.
— Jupiter. LC 93-3595. (Vision Bks.). (Illus.). 32p. (J). (gr. 2-6). 1994. lib. bdg. 22.79 (1-56766-022-3); lib. bdg. 22.79 (1-56766-041-X) Childs World.
— Jupiter. LC 96-47044. (Our Universe Ser.). 32p. (J). (gr. 2-6). 1997. lib. bdg. 22.79 (1-56766-390-7) Childs World.
— Leopards. LC 95-30899. (Nature Books Ser.). (Illus.). 32p. (J). (gr. 2-6). 1995. lib. bdg. 22.79 (1-56766-211-0) Childs World.
— Manatees. LC 97-38097. (Nature Books Ser.). (Illus.). 32p. (J). (gr. 2-6). 1998. lib. bdg. 22.79 (1-56766-475-X) Childs World.
— Pythons. (Illus.). 48p. (J). (gr. 3-7). 1995. lib. bdg. 19.00 (0-516-35296-2) Childrens.
— Rattlesnakes. (Illus.). 48p. (J). (gr. 3-7). 1995. lib. bdg. 19.00 (0-516-35294-6) Childrens.
— Starting & Running Your Own Horse Business. LC 96-49470. 160p. (Orig.). 1997. pap. 19.95 (0-88266-960-5) Storey Bks.
— Sunflowers. (Nature Books Ser.). (Illus.). 32p. (J). (gr. 2-6). 1996. lib. bdg. 22.79 (1-56766-272-2) Childs World.
— Woodpeckers. LC 95-46109. (Nature Books Ser.). (Illus.). 32p. (J). (gr. 2-6). 1996. lib. bdg. 22.79 (1-56766-218-8) Childs World.

M

McDonald, Mary Ann. Anacondas. LC 97-44645. (Illus.). 32p. (J). 1998. lib. bdg. 22.79 (*1-56766-494-6*) Childs World.
— Bees. LC 98-49134. (Illus.). 32p. (J). 1999. lib. bdg. write for info. (*1-56766-611-6*) Childs World.
— Chimpanzees. LC 97-44646. (Illus.). 32p. (J). 1998. lib. bdg. 22.79 (*1-56766-497-0*) Childs World.
— Doves. LC 98-42058. (J). 1999. lib. bdg. 22.79 (*1-56766-593-4*) Childs World.
— Grasshoppers. LC 97-44644. (Illus.). 32p. (J). 1998. lib. bdg. 22.79 (*1-56766-505-5*) Childs World.
— Jays. LC 98-42059. (Illus.). 32p. (J). 1999. lib. bdg. 22.79 (*1-56766-591-8*) Childs World.
— Lemurs. LC 97-44649. (Illus.). 32p. (J). 1998. lib. bdg. 22.79 (*1-56766-495-4*) Childs World.
***McDonald, Mary Ann.** Mosquitoes. LC 98-49135. (Illus.). 32p. (J). 1999. lib. bdg. write for info. (*1-56766-635-3*) Childs World.
McDonald, Mary Ann. Out of the Past Amish Traditon & Faith. 1998. pap. text 12.98 (*1-880908-45-X*) Todtri Prods.
— Reindeer. LC 97-44647. (Illus.). 32p. (J). 1998. lib. bdg. 22.79 (*1-56766-491-1*) Childs World.
— Toucans. LC 97-44648. (Illus.). 32p. (J). 1998. lib. bdg. 22.79 (*1-56766-496-2*) Childs World.
McDonald, Mary F., tr. see Lactantius.
McDonald, Mary G., jt. ed. see Birrell, Susan.
McDonald, Maryon, ed. Gender, Drink & Drugs. 224p. 1994. 49.50 (*0-85496-719-2*, Pub. by Berg Pubs); pap. 19.50 (*0-85496-867-9*, Pub. by Berg Pubs) NYU Pr.
McDonald, Megan. Bedbugs. LC 99-10184. (Illus.). 32p. (J). (ps-1). 1999. 15.95 (*0-531-30193-1*); lib. bdg. 16.99 (*0-531-33193-8*) Orchard Bks Watts.
— Beezy. LC 96-53866. (Illus.). 48p. (J). (gr. 1-4). 1997. 13.95 (*0-531-30046-3*) Orchard Bks Watts.
***McDonald, Megan.** Beezy. LC 96-53866. (Illus.). 48p. (J). (gr. 1-4). 2000. pap. 4.95 (*0-531-07162-6*) Orchard Bks Watts.
— Beezy & Funnybone. LC 99-24698. (Illus.). 48p. (J). (gr. 1-4). 2000. 14.95 (*0-531-30211-3*); pap. 4.95 (*0-531-07161-8*); lib. bdg. 15.99 (*0-531-33211-X*) Orchard Bks Watts.
— Beezy at Bat. LC 97-35015. (Illus.). 48p. (J). (gr. 1-4). 1998. lib. bdg. write for info. (*0-531-33085-0*) Orchard Bks Watts.
***McDonald, Megan.** Beezy at Bat. LC 97-35015. (Illus.). 48p. (J). (gr. 1-4). 2000. pap. 4.95 (*0-531-07164-2*) Orchard Bks Watts.
Mcdonald, Megan. Beezy at Bat. LC 97-35015. (Illus.). 48p. (J). (gr. 1-4). 1998. 13.95 (*0-531-30085-4*) Orchard Bks Watts.
McDonald, Megan. Beezy Magic. LC 97-24006. (Illus.). 48p. (J). (gr. k-2). 1998. 13.95 (*0-531-30064-1*); lib. bdg. 14.99 (*0-531-33064-8*) Orchard Bks Watts.
***McDonald, Megan.** Beezy Magic. LC 97-24006. (Illus.). 48p. (J). (gr. 1-4). 2000. pap. 4.95 (*0-531-07163-4*) Orchard Bks Watts.
— Beezy Magic. (Illus.). (J). 2000. 10.40 (*0-606-18331-0*) Turtleback.
McDonald, Megan. The Bone Keeper. LC 98-3680. (Illus.). 32p. (J). (gr. k-3). 1999. 16.95 (*0-7894-2559-9*, D K Ink) DK Pub Inc.
— The Bridge to Nowhere. LC 92-50844. 160p. (J). (gr. 6 up). 1993. 15.95 (*0-531-05478-0*); lib. bdg. 16.99 (*0-531-08628-3*) Orchard Bks Watts.
— The Great Pumpkin Switch. LC 91-39660. (Illus.). 32p. (J). (ps-2). 1996. pap. 5.95 (*0-531-07065-4*) Orchard Bks Watts.
— The Great Pumpkin Switch. LC 91-39660. (J). 1995. 11.15 (*0-606-09359-1*, Pub. by Turtleback) Demco.
— Insects Are My Life. LC 94-21960. (Illus.). 32p. (J). (ps-2). 1995. 15.95 (*0-531-06874-9*); lib. bdg. 16.99 (*0-531-08724-7*) Orchard Bks Watts.
— Insects Are My Life. LC 94-21960. (Illus.). 32p. (J). (ps-2). 1997. pap. 6.95 (*0-531-07093-X*) Orchard Bks Watts.
— Insects Are My Life. 1997. 11.15 (*0-606-13518-9*, Pub. by Turtleback) Demco.
— Is This a House for Hermit Crab? LC 89-35653. (Illus.). 32p. (J). (ps-1). 1990. 15.95 (*0-531-05855-7*) Orchard Bks Watts.
— Is This a House for Hermit Crab? LC 89-35653. (Illus.). 32p. (J). (ps-1). 1993. pap. 5.95 (*0-531-07041-7*) Orchard Bks Watts.
McDonald, Megan. Is This a House for Hermit Crab? (J). 1993. 12.15 (*0-606-05887-7*, Pub. by Turtleback) Demco.
McDonald, Megan. Judy Moody. LC 99-13464. (Illus.). 160p. (J). (gr. 1-4). 2000. 15.99 (*0-7636-0685-5*) Candlewick Pr.
***McDonald, Megan.** Judy Moody Gets Famous. LC 00-24200. (Illus.). (J). 2001. write for info. (*0-7636-0849-1*) Candlewick Pr.
McDonald, Megan. My House Has Stars. LC 95-53798. (Illus.). 32p. (J). (gr. k-3). 1996. lib. bdg. 17.99 (*0-531-08879-0*) Orchard Bks Watts.
— My House Has Stars. LC 95-53798. (Illus.). 32p. (J). (ps-3). 1996. 16.95 (*0-531-09529-0*) Orchard Bks Watts.
— The Potato Man. LC 90-7758. (Illus.). 32p. (J). (ps-2). 1991. 15.95 (*0-531-05914-6*) Orchard Bks Watts.
— The Potato Man. LC 90-7758. (Illus.). 32p. (J). (ps-3). 1991. lib. bdg. 16.99 (*0-531-08514-7*) Orchard Bks Watts.
— The Potato Man. LC 90-7758. (Illus.). 32p. (J). (ps-2). 1994. pap. 5.95 (*0-531-07053-0*) Orchard Bks Watts.
— Potato Man. 1994. 11.15 (*0-606-08847-4*, Pub. by Turtleback) Demco.
***McDonald, Megan.** Shadows in the Glasshouse. LC 00-29336. (History Mysteries Ser.). (Illus.). (J). 2000. pap. write for info. (*1-58485-092-2*) Pleasant Co.
McDonald, Megan. Tundra Mouse: A Storyknife Tale. LC 96-53221. (Illus.). 32p. (J). (ps-2). 1997. 15.95 (*0-531-30047-1*); lib. bdg. 16.99 (*0-531-33047-8*) Orchard Bks Watts.
— Whoo-oo Is It? LC 91-18494. (Illus.). 32p. (J). (ps-1). 1992. lib. bdg. 16.99 (*0-531-08574-0*) Orchard Bks Watts.
— Whoo-oo Is It? LC 91-18494. (Illus.). 32p. (J). (ps-1). 1997. pap. 5.95 (*0-531-07094-8*) Orchard Bks Watts.
***McDonald, Megan & Payne, Tom.** Ant & Honey Bee. LC 00-37888. 2001. write for info. (*0-7636-1265-0*) Candlewick Pr.
***McDonald, Megan & Wallace, Andrea.** Lucky Star. LC 99-24652. (Road to Reading Ser.). 2000. 3.99 (*0-307-26329-0*, Whitman Coin) St Martin.
McDonald, Michael. The Quiz of Enchantment. Vigil, Arnold, ed. LC 91-67865. (Illus.). 136p. (Orig.). 1992. pap. 3.95 (*0-937206-23-7*) New Mexico Mag.
McDonald, Michael, jt. auth. see Adkison, Peter.
McDonald, Michael, jt. auth. see Golvan, Colin.
McDonald, Michael, ed. see Sym, John.
McDonald, Michael J., jt. auth. see Wheeler, William B.
McDonald, Mike, ed. see Gonzales, Rod & Faurot, Chip.
McDonald, Mike R. Government Student Loan Survival Manual, Vol. I. (Illus.). 131p. 1996. pap. text 79.95 (*0-9661077-8-0*) New Dawn TX.
McDonald, Nancy, ed. see Volden, Jon.
McDonald, Nancy A., ed. Poetry: A Collection of Poems Written by Medical Students 1992-1996. 79p. (Orig.). 1996. pap. text 8.95 (*0-925664-03-0*) NE Ohio Univs.
McDonald, Neelan. The International Business Management Decision Simulation. LC 98-50563. 1999. pap. text 15.16 (*0-256-26687-5*, Irwn McGrw-H) McGrw-H Hghr Educ.
***McDonald, Neil.** Caro-Kann Main Line. 2001. pap. 19.95 (*1-85744-227-X*, Pub. by Everyman Chess) Globe Pequot.
McDonald, Neil. The Dutch Leningrad. 1997. text 19.95 (*1-901259-03-X*) S&S Trade.
***McDonald, Neil.** French Winawer. 2000. pap. 19.95 (*1-85744-276-8*, Pub. by Everyman Chess) Globe Pequot.
McDonald, Neil. King's Gambit. (Batsford Chess Openings Ser.). (Illus.). 190p. 1998. pap. text 19.95 (*0-7134-8451-9*, Pub. by B T B) Branford.
— Planning. 88p. 1995. pap. 12.00 (*0-8050-3897-3*, Pub. by Batsford Chess) H Holt & Co.
— Positional Sacrifices. 128p. 1995. pap. 15.95 (*1-85744-110-9*, Pub. by Cadgn Bks) Macmillan.
— Practical Endgame Play. 160p. 1996. pap. 17.95 (*1-85744-176-1*, Pub. by Cadgn Bks) Macmillan.
***McDonald, Neil.** Sveshnikov Sicilian: Tournament. (Chess Bks.). (Illus.). 144p. 1999. pap. text 15.95 (*0-7134-8581-7*) B T B.
McDonald, Neil. Winning with the Kalashnikov. (Batsford Chess Library). 1995. pap. 20.00 (*0-8050-3907-4*) H Holt & Co.
McDonald, Neil, jt. auth. see Speelman, Jon.
McDonald, Neil R., intro. Pacific Basin Nuclear Conference, 9th, 1994: Nuclear Energy, Science & Technology, Pacific Partnership, 2 vols., Set. (National Conference Publication Ser.: No. 94-6). (Illus.). 1087p. (Orig.). 1994. pap. 105.50 (*0-85825-602-9*, Pub. by Inst Engrs Aust-EA Bks) Accents Pubns.
McDonald, Nicholas G. The Connecticut Valley in the Age of Dinosaurs: A Guide to the Geologic Literature 1681-1995. (State Geological & Natural History Survey Bulletin: Vol. 116). (Illus.). 242p. (Orig.). (C). 1996. pap. 34.95 (*0-942081-10-2*); text 49.95 (*0-942081-09-9*) CT DEP CGNHS.
McDonald, Nick, et al, eds. Applications of Psychology to the Aviation System, Proceedings: Conference on the European Association for Aviation Psychology (EAAP) (21st), Vol. 1. LC 94-72786. 352p. 1995. 91.95 (*0-291-39818-9*, Pub. by Avebury Technical) Ashgate Pub Co.
***McDonald, Nola L.** Nineteen Hundred: The Magic Year. (Illus.). 64p. 1999. pap. 9.95 (*1-928547-03-6*, QuickWorks) Q W Inc.
McDonald, Nora M. & Weibel, Ruth E. Principles of Flat Pattern Design. (Illus.). 320p. 1988. pap. text. write for info. (*0-318-62257-2*) P-H.
McDonald, Olin T., jt. auth. see Cobb, John T.
McDonald, Olivia & McDonald, Ronald. God's Gifts Are for Sharing. (Illus.). 90p. 1997. pap. 9.95 (*0-9665064-0-5*) O R Ent.
McDonald, P. Tire Imprint Identification: Practical Aspects of Criminal Forensic Investigation Ser. 448p. 1989. 45.00 (*0-444-01456-X*, CRC Reprint) Franklin.
McDonald, P. I., jt. auth. see O'Reilly, F. D.
McDonald, Patricia. Forgiveness Generates Internal Vital Energy. (Illus.). 72p. 1999. pap. 10.00 (*0-8059-4685-3*) Dorrance.
McDonald, Patricia, ed. see Beach, Lynn.
McDonald, Patricia, ed. see Peusner, Stella.
McDonald, Patricia, ed. see Stine, R. L., pseud.
McDonald, Patricia A. & Haney, Margaret. Counseling the Older Adult: A Training Manual in Clinical Gerontology. 2nd ed. LC 97-28413. 1997. pap. 27.95 (*0-7879-3941-2*) Jossey-Bass.
McDonald, Patrick. Make 'Em Talk: Principles of Military Interrogation. 80p. 1993. pap. 16.00 (*0-87364-728-9*) Paladin Pr.
McDonald, Patrick D. & Bouvier, Edouard S., eds. Solid Phase Extraction Applications Guide & Bibliography: A Resource for Sample Preparation Methods Development. 6th ed. LC 95-60173. (Illus.). 646p. (Orig.). (C). 1995. pap. text 75.00 (*1-879732-06-8*) Waters MA.
McDonald, Patrick H. Continuum Mechanics. LC 94-23728. 1995. mass mkt. 79.95 (*0-534-93984-8*) PWS Pubs.
McDonald, Patrick J. & McDonald, Claudette M. Marital Spirituality: The Search for the Hidden Ground of Love. LC 99-39713. 208p. 1999. pap. 14.95 (*0-8091-3891-3*) Paulist Pr.
— Out of the Ashes: A Handbook for Starting Over. LC 96-44805. 144p. (Orig.). 1997. pap. 7.95 (*0-8091-3695-3*) Paulist Pr.
— The Soul of a Marriage. LC 94-44929. 160p. (Orig.). 1995. pap. 9.95 (*0-8091-3555-8*) Paulist Pr.
— Soul Work: A Workbook for Couples. 88p. (Orig.). 1995. pap. 10.95 (*0-8091-3558-2*) Paulist Pr.
McDonald, Paul. How to Start Your Own Silk Screening Business & Make up to $1,000,000. (Illus.). 170p. (Orig.). 1997. pap. 16.95 (*1-890585-00-9*) Pauls Bkshelf.
— Your Goldmine Is Your Gold Mind: You Can Brainstorm & Strike It Rich. (Illus.). 60p. 1997. pap. 7.95 (*1-890585-01-7*) Pauls Bkshelf.
McDonald, Paula, et al. Crossing the Border Fast & Easy: How to Get in - & Out! - of Baja, Mexico, Without the Hassle. LC 92-90310. (Illus.). 208p. (Orig.). 1992. pap. 6.95 (*0-9633517-0-2*) Borderline Assocs.
McDonald-Pavelka, Mary. Monkeys of the Mesquite: The Social Life of the American Snow Monkey. 128p. (C). 1995. pap. text, per. 14.95 (*0-8403-8986-8*) Kendall-Hunt.
McDonald, Penny, jt. auth. see Marcus, Susan A.
McDonald, Peter. Adam's Dream. 64p. 1996. pap. 15.95 (*1-85224-333-3*, Pub. by Bloodaxe Bks) Dufour.
— Biting the Wax. LC 89-82484. 64p. 1990. pap. 11.95 (*1-85224-077-6*, Pub. by Bloodaxe Bks) Dufour.
— Louis MacNeice: The Poet in His Contexts. 252p. 1991. text 65.00 (*0-19-811766-3*) OUP.
***McDonald, Peter.** Mistaken Identities. 240p. 2000. pap. 24.95 (*0-19-818687-8*) OUP.
McDonald, Peter. Mistaken Identities: Poetry & Northern Ireland. 236p. 1997. text 65.00 (*0-19-818422-0*) OUP.
— Tire Imprint Evidence. (Practical Aspects of Criminal & Forensic Investigations Ser.). 248p. 1992. boxed set 83.95 (*0-8493-9515-1*, HV8097) CRC Pr.
McDonald, Peter, ed. The Literature of Soil Science. LC 93-27394. (Literature of the Agricultural Sciences Ser.). (Illus.). 456p. 1994. text 72.50 (*0-8014-2921-8*) Cornell U Pr.
McDonald, Peter & Lassoie, James P., eds. The Literature of Forestry & Agroforestry. LC 95-39328. (Literature of the Agricultural Sciences Ser.). (Illus.). 445p. 1996. text 79.95 (*0-8014-3181-6*) Cornell U Pr.
McDonald, Peter, ed. see MacNeice, Louis.
McDonald, Peter C. Grieving: A Healing Process. 24p. (Orig.). 1985. pap. 2.00 (*0-89486-318-5*, 5350B) Hazelden.
McDonald, Peter D. British Literary Culture & Publishing Practice, 1880-1914. (Studies in Publishing & Printing History). 242p. (C). 1997. text 64.95 (*0-521-57149-9*) Cambridge U Pr.
McDonald, Philip M., jt. auth. see McDonald, Cleveland.
McDonald, Philip R. Factors Influencing Fuel Oil Growth. Bruchey, Stuart, ed. LC 78-22700. (Energy in the American Economy Ser.). (Illus.). 1979. lib. bdg. 35.95 (*0-405-12002-8*) Ayer.
McDonald, Phyllis P. Cloning & Genetic Engineering: Social & Legal Implications. 82p. 1978. student ed. 18.90 (*1-877960-02-0*, 2-505) Kemtec Educ.
McDonald, R. Colour Physics for Industry. 2nd ed. 1996. pap. 95.00 (*0-7855-2801-6*, Pub. by Textile Inst) St Mut.
— Tales from a Tall Islander. 80p. 1994. pap. 7.95 (*0-947962-88-3*) Dufour.
McDonald, R. Michael, jt. auth. see Boone, Donna L.
McDonald, R. Robin. Black Widow: The True Story of the Hilley Poisonings. LC 85-12676. 409p. 1986. 18.95 (*0-88282-020-6*) New Horizon NJ.
— Secrets Never Lie: The Death of Sara Tokars - A Southern Tragedy of Money, Murder & Innocence Betrayed. 544p. 1998. mass mkt. 6.99 (*0-380-77752-5*, Avon Bks) Morrow Avon.
McDonald, Ralph E. & Avery, David R., eds. Dentistry for the Child & Adolescent. 6th ed. LC 93-20508. (Illus.). 928p. (C). (gr. 13). 1993. text 70.00 (*0-8016-6705-4*, 06705) Mosby Inc.
McDonald, Ralph J. A Down-Home Gallery of American Wildlife. (Illus.). 101p. 1980. 39.95 (*0-9605428-1-7*) Countryside Studio.
— A Down-Home Gallery of American Wildlife. deluxe limited ed. (Illus.). 101p. 1980. 95.00 (*0-9605428-0-9*) Countryside Studio.
McDonald, Ric, et al. Mississauga: City of Excellence. LC 97-21428. 304p. 1997. 39.00 (*1-885352-64-6*); pap. text. write for info. (*1-885352-65-4*) Community Comm.
***McDonald, Richard.** A Universal Tao, the Way of the Heart. 96p. 1999. pap. 24.00 (*0-9667354-0-4*, Pub. by Blue Star Coun) ACCESS Pubs Network.
McDonald, Richard, jt. auth. see McDonald, Lucile.
McDonald, Richard, ed. see Taylor, Lyn P.
McDonald, Richard E. & Min, David B., eds. Food Lipids & Health. LC 96-18488. (IFT Basic Symposium Ser.: Vol. 11). (Illus.). 480p. 1996. text 150.00 (*0-8247-9712-4*) Dekker.
McDonald, Richard E. & Mossoba, Magdi M. New Techniques & Applications in Lipid Analysis. LC 97-3204. 1997. 105.00 (*0-935315-80-2*) Am Oil Chemists.
McDonald, Robert. Art of the States: Works from a Santa Barbara Collection. LC 84-51013. (Illus.). 76p. (Orig.). 1984. pap. 15.00 (*0-89951-053-1*) Santa Barb Mus Art.
— The Carolyn & Jack Farris Collection: Selected Contemporary Works. LC 82-81520. (Illus.). 68p. 1982. 13.50 (*0-934418-13-6*) Mus Contemp Art.
— A Contemporary Collection on Loan from the Rothschild Bank AG, Zurich. LC 82-84588. (Illus.). 72p. 1983. 13.50 (*0-934418-16-0*) Mus Contemp Art.
— Craig Kauffman: A Comprehensive Survey 1957-1980. LC 80-70807. (Illus.). 95p. 1980. pap. 12.00 (*0-934418-09-8*) Mus Contemp Art.
— D. J. Hall: Selected Works 1974-1985. De Alcuaz, Marie & Ianco-Starrels, Josine, eds. LC 85-82100. (Illus.). 32p. (Orig.). 1986. pap. 12.00 (*0-936429-00-3*) LA Municipal Art.
McDonald, Robert, ed. Ground Time. LC 98-71704. (Illus.). 120p. 1999. 40.00 (*1-881529-50-9*) Custom & Limited.
— Sense of Place. 24p. (Orig.). 1987. 15.00 (*0-9602974-8-0*) USC Fisher Gallery.
McDonald, Robert & Kauffman, Craig, contrib. by. Craig Kauffman: A Comprehensive Survey, 1957-1980. LC 80-70807. (Illus.). 96p. 1981. pap. 15.00 (*0-911291-06-7*, Pub. by Fellows Cont Art) RAM Publications.
McDonald, Robert, jt. auth. see Adler, Sebastian.
McDonald, Robert, ed. see Buelteman, Robert.
McDonald, Robert A. Adjustment of School Organization to Various Population Groups. LC 70-177021. (Columbia University. Teachers College. Contributions to Education Ser.: No. 75). reprint ed. 37.50 (*0-404-55075-4*) AMS Pr.
— Corona Between the Sun & the Earth: The First NRO Reconnaissance Eye in Space. LC 97-7944. 1997. 50.00 (*1-57083-041-X*) ASP & RS.
— Making Vancouver, 1863-1913. LC 96-162574. (Illus.). 336p. 1996. 49.95 (*0-7748-0555-2*, F1089) U of Wash Pr.
— Making Vancouver, 1863-1913. (Illus.). 336p. 1997. pap. 25.95 (*0-7748-0570-6*, F1087) U of Wash Pr.
McDonald, Robert C. Introduction to General Chemistry: Laboratory Manual. 2nd ed. 112p. (C). 1995. pap. text, spiral bd., lab manual ed. 18.95 (*0-7872-1877-4*, 41187701) Kendall-Hunt.
McDonald, Robert J. & Frew, David. Home Port Erie: Voices of Silent Images. (Illus.). 318p. 1997. 31.95 (*1-883658-33-0*, 0428) Erie Cnty Hist.
McDonald, Robert K. The Altar Boy. LC 98-93215. 288p. 1998. pap. 13.95 (*0-9665753-9-3*) Finbar Pr.
McDonald, Robert L., ed. The Critical Response to Erskine Caldwell, 28. LC 97-16239. (Critical Responses in Arts & Letters Ser.: Vol. 28). 336p. 1997. lib. bdg. 72.95 (*0-313-30072-0*, Greenwood Pr) Greenwood.
McDonald, Robert L., ed. see Caldwell, Erskine.
McDonald, Rochelle L. How to Pinch a Penny Till It Screams: Hundreds of Simple & Practical Money Saving Tips. LC 93-8827. 240p. 1994. pap. 9.95 (*0-89529-529-6*, Avery) Penguin Putnam.
McDonald, Roderick A. Economy & Material Culture of Slaves: Goods & Chattels on the Sugar Plantations of Jamaica & Louisiana. LC 93-392. (Illus.). 400p. (C). 1993. text 57.50 (*0-8071-1794-3*) La State U Pr.
McDonald, Roderick P. Factor Analysis & Related Methods. 272p. (C). 1985. text 39.95 (*0-89859-388-3*) L Erlbaum Assocs.
— Test Theory: A Unified Treatment. LC 99-24196. 504p. 1999. 69.95 (*0-8058-3075-8*) L Erlbaum Assocs.
***McDonald, Roger.** Mr. Darwin's Shooter. LC 98-36819. 365p. 1999. 25.00 (*0-87113-733-X*, Atlntc Mnthly) Grove-Atltic.
— Mr. Darwin's Shooter. 384p. 2000. pap. 13.95 (*0-14-028859-7*, Penguin Bks) Viking Penguin.
McDonald, Roger. 1915. (Paperbacks Ser.). 434p. (YA). (gr. 10 up). 1989. reprint ed. pap. 16.95 (*0-7022-2134-1*, Pub. by Univ Queensland Pr) Intl Spec Bk.
McDonald, Ron. Leadership among Friends. 1995. pap. 4.00 (*0-87574-320-X*) Pendle Hill.
McDonald, Ronald, jt. auth. see Hallwood, C. Paul.
McDonald, Ronald, jt. auth. see McDonald, Olivia.
McDonald, Ronald L. The Complete Hamburger: The History, Business, & Culinary Pleasures of America's Favorite Sandwich. LC 96-40491. (Illus.). 176p. 1997. 18.95 (*1-55972-407-2*, Birch Ln Pr) Carol Pub Group.
McDonald, Roxanna. Illustrated Building Glossary. LC 98-55391. (Illus.). 208p. 1998. pap. 24.95 (*0-7506-3643-2*, Architectural Pr) Buttrwrth-Heinemann.
McDonald, Roy W. McDonald Texas Civil Practice, 1981-1990, 5 vols. Elliott, Frank W., ed. LC 80-28736. 337.00 (*0-8321-0051-X*) West Group.
McDonald, Russ. Shakespeare & Jonson - Jonson & Shakespeare. LC 87-19158. 249p. 1988. reprint ed. pap. 77.20 (*0-7837-8894-0*, 204960500001) Bks Demand.
— Shakespeare in Context: A Documentary Companion. 373p. 1996. pap. text 16.95 (*0-312-10075-2*) St Martin.
McDonald, Russ, ed. Shakespeare Reread: The Texts in New Contexts. (Illus.). 296p. 1994. pap. text 16.95 (*0-8014-8144-9*) Cornell U Pr.
***McDonald, Russ, ed.** Titus Andronicus. (Shakespeare Ser.). 176p. 2000. pap. 5.95 (*0-14-071491-X*) Pelican.
McDonald, S., tr. see Ichikawa, T.
McDonald, Scott, jt. auth. see Hellweg, Paul.
McDonald, Scott D. Where in Moscow. 6th ed. 1996. pap. 10.00 (*1-880100-31-2*) Russian Info Srvs.
— Where in St. Petersburg. 3rd ed. 174p. 1995. pap. 13.50 (*1-880100-29-0*) Russian Info Srvs.
McDonald, Scott D., ed. Where in St. Petersburg. 4th ed. 128p. 1996. pap. 10.00 (*1-880100-32-0*) Russian Info Srvs.
McDonald, Scott L., jt. auth. see Bailey, Bruce H.
McDonald, Sharen. A Gentleman & a Scholar. (Illus.). 192p. (*1-896754-02-3*) Shloreline.
McDonald, Sharon. Portfolio & Its Use: A Road Map for Assessment. (Illus.). 120p. 1997. pap. 19.95 (*0-942388-20-8*) So Early Chldhood Assn.
McDonald, Sharon, jt. auth. see Rivers, Lynn.
Mcdonald, Sky E. Communication Disorders Following Traumatic Brain Injury: Management of Cognitive, Language, & Motor Impairments. (Brain Damage, Behaviour & Cognition Ser.). 352p. 1999. 59.95 (*0-86377-724-4*) L Erlbaum Assocs.

M

An Asterisk (*) at the beginning of an entry indicates that the title is appearing for the first time.

McDonald, Stephen. European Economic Integration. (C). 1992. text 62.95 (*0-582-08226-9*) Addison-Wesley.

— European Economic Integration: Longman Economics Series. (C). 1992. pap. text 49.00 (*0-582-08225-0*) Addison-Wesley.

McDonald, Stephen & Salomone, William. Reading-Based Writing. LC 95-33217. (C). 1995. pap. 29.50 (*0-534-20094-X*) Wadsworth Pub.

McDonald, Stephen, jt. auth. see Salomone, William.

***McDonald, Stephen E.** Baker 30. 170p. 1999. 10.95 (*0-9677056-0-6*, Pub. by SM & Assocs) Partners-West.

— Bitteroot. LC 99-492270. 240p. 1999. pap. 12.95 (*0-7392-0310-X*, PO3452) Morris Pubng.

McDonald, Stephen L. Federal Tax Treatment of Income from Oil & Gas. LC 79-29702. (Brookings Institution, National Committee on Government Finance, Studies of Government Finance). (Illus.). xv, 163p. 1980. reprint ed. lib. bdg. 65.00 (*0-313-22289-4*, MCFT, Greenwood Pr) Greenwood.

— The Leasing of Federal Lands for Fossil Fuels Production. LC 78-23437. 184p. 1979. 21.95 (*0-8018-2194-0*) Resources Future.

— Petroleum Conservation in the United States: An Economic Analysis. LC 71-149242. (Resources for the Future Ser.). (Illus.). 279p. 1971. 22.50 (*0-8018-1261-5*, Pub. by Resources Future) Johns Hopkins.

McDonald, Stephen L. & Mohammadioun, Mina, eds. The Role of Natural Gas in Environmental Policy. (Illus.). 63p. (Orig.). (C). 1994. pap. text 25.00 (*0-7881-0274-5*) DIANE Pub.

McDonald, Steve. Historic Aircraft. 128p. 10.99 (*1-57215-251-6*, JG2516) World Pubns.

***McDonald, Steve.** A Sailor's Adventures: A Novel. 2000. pap. 7.95 (*0-533-13387-4*) Vantage.

McDonald, Steven. Event Horizon. 1997. mass mkt. 6.99 (*0-8125-4006-9*, Pub. by Tor Bks) St Martin.

McDonald, Steven E. Supernova. 1999. mass mkt. 5.99 (*0-8125-8406-6*, Pub. by Tor Bks) St Martin.

McDonald, Stuart W. Case Studies in Clinical Anatomy. 74p. (gr. 13). 1995. 20.00 (*0-7234-2202-8*, QM23) Mosby Inc.

McDonald, Susan. Kissing Games: A Study in Folklore. 1978. 3.00 (*0-916750-32-9*) Dayton Labs.

McDonald, Susan & Gerrick, David J. Folklore of Kissing Games. 84p. (Orig.). 1981. pap. 3.00 (*0-685-01374-X*) Dayton Labs.

McDonald, Susan, ed. see Blair, Laurence R. & Blair, Mary E.

McDonald, Susan, ed. see Wallace, William G.

McDonald, Susie, ed. see Nimersheim, Jack.

McDonald, Susie, ed. see O'Diear, James.

McDonald, T. David. The Technological Transformation of China. (Illus.). 191p. 1996. pap. text 30.00 (*0-7881-3062-5*) DIANE Pub.

— The Technological Transformation of China. (Illus.). 221p. 1990. per. 5.50 (*0-16-001720-3*, S/N 008-020-01172-0) USGPO.

McDonald, T. E. & Margolis, L. Synopsis of the Parasites of Fishes of Canada (1978-1993) (Canadian Special Publication of Fisheries & Aquatic Sciences Ser.). (FRE & ENG.). 265p. (Orig.). 1995. pap., suppl. ed. 45.00 (*0-660-15902-3*, Pub. by NRC Res Pr) Accents Pubns.

McDonald, T. F. Connective Tissues in Arterial & Pulmonary Disease. Chandler, A. B., ed. (Illus.). 355p. 1981. 106.00 (*0-387-90623-1*) Spr-Verlag.

McDonald-Taylor, Margaret. Dictionary of Marks N - E: Ceramics, Metalwork, Furniture, Tapestry. (Illus.). 336p. 1993. pap. 22.95 (*0-7126-5303-1*, Pub. by Barrie & Jenkins) Trafalgar.

McDonald, Terrence J., ed. The Historic Turn in the Human Sciences. LC 96-18773. 1996. pap. 24.95 (*0-472-06632-3*, Pub. by Amsterdam U Pr) U of Mich Pr.

— The Historic Turn in the Human Sciences. LC 96-18773. 432p. 1996. text 65.00 (*0-472-09632-X*, 09632) U of Mich Pr.

McDonald, Terrence J. & Ward, Sally K., eds. The Politics of Urban Fiscal Policy. LC 84-13431. (New Approaches to Social Science History Ser.: No. 5). 176p. 1984. reprint ed. pap. 54.60 (*0-608-01503-2*, 205954700001) Bks Demand.

McDonald, Terrence J., ed. see Riordan, William L.

McDonald, Theresa. Achill Island. 386p. 25.00 (*0-9519974-1-6*) IAS.

McDonald, Thomas D., et al, eds. Rural Criminal Justice: Conditions, Constraints, & Challenges. 254p. (C). 1995. pap. text 16.50 (*1-879215-29-2*) Sheffield WI.

McDonald, Thomas P., et al. Assessing the Long-Term Effects of Foster Care: A Research Synthesis. LC 96-26102. 1996. pap. 12.95 (*0-87868-603-7*) Child Welfare.

McDonald, Tom. Business of Portrait Photography: A Professional's Guide to Successful Marketing & Managing. (Illus.). 192p. 1996. 35.00 (*0-8174-3616-2*, Amphoto) Watsn-Guptill.

McDonald, Travis C. Understanding Old Buildings: Architectural Investigation. 12p. 1994. pap. 1.75 (*0-16-061665-4*) USGPO.

***McDonald, Trevor.** Trevor McDonald Favourite Poems. large type ed. 320p. 1999. 31.99 (*0-7089-9052-5*) Ulverscroft.

***McDonald, Trevy.** Time Will Tell. Ramsey, Erica, ed. LC 99-90200. 328p. 1999. pap. 14.95 (*0-9670712-0-8*) Reyomi Pubg.

McDonald, Trevy A. & Ford-Ahmed, T. Nature of a Sistuh: Black Women's Lived Experiences in Contemporary Culture. LC 98-88954. 335p. 1998. pap. 25.95 (*0-89089-859-6*) Carolina Acad Pr.

McDonald, Vincent R., ed. The Caribbean Economies. LC 72-8622. 196p. 1972. pap. text 11.95 (*0-8422-0258-7*) Irvington.

McDonald, Vincent R., jt. ed. see Hogan, Lloyd.

McDonald, W. N. History of the Laurel Brigade. 1969. reprint ed. 49.95 (*0-87948-018-1*) Beatty.

***McDonald-Walker, Suzanne.** Bikers: Culture, Politics & Power. (Illus.). 160p. 2000. 65.00 (*1-85973-351-4*, Pub. by Berg Pubs); pap. 19.50 (*1-85973-356-5*, Pub. by Berg Pubs) NYU Pr.

***McDonald, Walt.** All Occasions. 118p. 2000. 24.95 (*0-268-02005-1*); pap. 12.95 (*0-268-02006-X*) U of Notre Dame Pr.

McDonald, Walt. Blessings the Body Gave. LC 98-29035. 96p. 1998. pap. 14.00 (*0-8142-5004-1*, MCDBX); text 35.00 (*0-8142-0804-5*, MCDBLE) Ohio St U Pr.

McDonald, Walter. After the Noise of Saigon. LC 87-20582. 104p. (Orig.). (C). 1988. lib. bdg. 18.50 (*0-87023-600-8*) U of Mass Pr.

— Anything, Anything. LC 79-26383. 54p. (Orig.). 1980. pap. 4.25 (*0-934332-22-3*) LEpervier Pr.

— A Band of Brothers. LC 89-36088. xvi, 144p. (C). 1989. 16.50 (*0-89672-208-2*); pap. 9.00 (*0-89672-209-0*) Tex Tech Univ Pr.

— Burning the Fence. LC 80-54792. 58p. (Orig.). 1981. 7.95 (*0-89672-088-8*); pap. 4.95 (*0-89672-087-X*) Tex Tech Univ Pr.

— Counting Survivors. LC 94-43044. 80p. 1995. pap. 10.95 (*0-8229-5555-5*); text 24.95 (*0-8229-3874-X*) U of Pittsburgh Pr.

— The Digs in Escondido Canyon. xii, 52p. 1991. 16.95 (*0-89672-258-9*) Tex Tech Univ Pr.

— Rafting the Brazos. LC 88-28073. (Texas Poets Ser.: No. 1). 120p. 1988. pap. 6.95 (*0-929398-04-1*) UNTX Pr.

— Some Ethical Questions of Peace & War: With Special Reference to Ireland. LC 98-230761. 1999. pap. text 19.95 (*1-900621-18-5*) Univ Coll Dublin Pr.

***McDonald, Walter.** Whatever the Wind Delivers: Celebrating West Texas & the Near Southwest. LC 99-16608. 1999. 24.95 (*0-89672-427-1*) Tex Tech Univ Pr.

McDonald, Walter. Where Skies Are Not Cloudy. LC 93-14496. (Texas Poets Ser.: Vol. 4). 84p. 1993. pap. 10.95 (*0-929398-60-2*) UNTX Pr.

McDonald, Walter & Williams, Miller. Caliban in Blue. 51p. (Orig.). 1976. 4.50 (*0-89672-054-3*); pap. 2.25 (*0-89672-053-5*) Tex Tech Univ Pr.

McDonald, Wil, jt. auth. see Duren, Lista.

McDonald, William. Letters to the Thessalonians. rev. ed. 1982. pap. 6.00 (*0-937396-43-5*) Walterick Pubs.

***McDonald, William.** Modern Faith Healing Scripturally Considered. 64p. 1999. pap. 5.99 (*0-88019-398-0*) Schmul Pub Co.

McDonald, William, jt. ed. see Carson, Chris.

McDonald, William, tr. see Kierkegaard, Soren.

McDonald, William A. & Thomas, Carol G. Progress into the Past: The Rediscovery of Mycenaean Civilization. 2nd ed. LC 89-45196. (Illus.). 558p. Date not set. reprint ed. pap. 173.00 (*0-608-20562-1*, 205447600002) Bks Demand.

McDonald, William A. & Wilkie, Nancy C., eds. Excavations at Nichoria in Southwest Greece Vol. The Bronze Age Occupation, Vol. 2. (Illus.). 1000p. (C). 1992. text 155.95 (*0-8166-1935-2*) U of Minn Pr.

McDonald, William C. Arthur & Tristan: On the Intersection of Legends in German Medieval Literature. LC 91-40230. 308p. 1991. lib. bdg. 99.95 (*0-7734-9448-0*) E Mellen.

— Ritual Illumination: Poems. Schultz, Patricia, ed. LC 90-41266. (Mellen Poetry Ser.: Vol. 12). 72p. 1990. lib. bdg. 24.95 (*0-88946-836-2*) E Mellen.

— The Tristan Story in German Literature of the Late Middle Ages & Early Renaissance: Tradition & Innovation. LC 90-41478. (Studies in German Language & Literature: Vol. 5). 250p. 1990. lib. bdg. 89.95 (*0-88946-075-2*) E Mellen.

McDonald, William C., ed. Fifteenth Century Studies, Vol. 22. 300p. 1996. pap. 60.00 (*1-57113-048-9*) Camden Hse.

McDonald, William C. & DuBruck, Edelgard E., eds. Fifteenth Century Studies: The Uses of Walgard Benjamin, Vol. 25. (LCGERM Ser.). 300p. 2000. 75.00 (*1-57113-077-2*) Camden Hse.

McDonald, William C. & Plail, William, eds. Fifteenth-Century Studies, Vol. 23. viii, 292p. 1997. pap. 85.00 (*1-57113-135-3*) Camden Hse.

— Fifteenth-Century Studies, Vol. 24. (Illus.). 300p. 1998. pap. 65.00 (*1-57113-266-X*) Camden Hse.

McDonald, William C., jt. auth. see Harris, Joel Chandler.

McDonald, William C., ed. see Classen, Albrecht.

McDonald, William C., jt. ed. see Classen, Albrecht.

McDonald, William C., jt. ed. see DuBruck, Edelgard E.

McDonald, William E. The Sons of Jacob: Thomas Mann, Freud, & Joseph & His Brothers. (Studies in German Literature, Linguistics, & Culture). 250p. 1999. 55.00 (*1-57113-258-9*) Camden Hse.

— Thomas Mann's "Joseph & His Brothers" Writing, Performance & the Politics of Loyalty. LC 98-32148. (Studies in German Literature, Linguistics & Culture). 250p. 1999. 55.00 (*1-57113-154-X*) Camden Hse.

McDonald, William F., ed. Criminal Justice & the Victim. LC 75-42754. (Sage Criminal Justice System Annuals Ser.: No. 6). 288p. reprint ed. pap. 89.30 (*0-8357-8496-7*, 203477100091) Bks Demand.

— The Defense Counsel. LC 83-4564. (Sage Criminal Justice System Annuals Ser.: No. 18). 312p. 1983. reprint ed. pap. 96.80 (*0-608-01491-5*, 205953500001) Bks Demand.

— The Prosecutor. LC 79-14388. (Sage Criminal Justice System Annuals Ser.: No. 11). 279p. 1979. reprint ed. pap. 86.50 (*0-608-01504-0*, 205954800001) Bks Demand.

McDonald, William J. Cases in Strategic Marketing Management: An Integrated Approach. LC 97-41735. 352p. (C). 1997. pap. text 53.00 (*0-02-379424-0*) Macmillan.

— Direct Marketing: An Integrated Approach. 1997. 83.50 (*0-07-561743-9*) McGraw.

— Direct Marketing: An Integrated Approach. LC 97-27343. (Irwin-McGraw-Hill Series in Marketing). 1997. 58.50 (*0-256-19783-0*, Irwn Prfssnl) McGraw-Hill Prof.

— The General Council: Special Studies in Doctrinal & Historical Background. LC 62-20329. 192p. reprint ed. pap. 59.60 (*0-608-10667-4*, 200522300051); reprint ed. pap. 54.80 (*0-608-30256-2*, 2005223); reprint ed. pap. 54.80 (*0-608-30302-X*, 2005223) Bks Demand.

— The Social Value of Property According to St. Thomas Aquinas: A Study in Social Philosophy. 1972. 59.95 (*0-8490-1068-3*) Gordon Pr.

McDonald, William L. Dallas Rediscovered. 1988. 14.95 (*0-932018-01-7*) Dallas His Soc.

— Nashville Ratt. (Illus.). 32p. (J). 1995. 2.95 (*0-9647114-0-0*) Two Starz Prods.

McDonald, William N. History of the Laurel Brigade. 449p. 1988. reprint ed. 30.00 (*0-942211-59-6*) Olde Soldier Bks.

McDonald, William P. Gracious Voices: Shouts & Whispers for God Seekers. LC 96-86581. (Christian Initiation Ser.). 160p. 1997. pap. 18.95 (*0-88177-178-3*, DR178) Discipleship Res.

***McDonald, William V.** You Are Free to Worry No More. 1999. pap. 10.95 (*1-891341-06-5*) HaKesher.

McDonald, Winnie P. & Peters, Bonnie H. Our Union County Families. (Illus.). 420p. 1993. lib. bdg. 50.00 (*0-9636662-0-7*) Peters McDonald.

McDonald, Winnie P., jt. auth. see Peters, Bonnie H.

McDonaugh, Chris, jt. ed. see MacClancy, Jeremy.

***McDonell, Chris.** Hockey All-Stars: The NHL Honor Roll. (Illus.). 248p. 2000. 40.00 (*1-55209-542-8*) Firefly Bks Ltd.

McDonell, Chris. Hockey's Greatest Stars: Legends & Young Lions. (Illus.). 190p. 1999. 35.00 (*1-55209-332-8*) Firefly Bks Ltd.

McDonell, Edwin D. Document Imaging Technology: How Automated Solutions Are Revolutionizing the Way Organizations & People Work. 300p. 1992. text 55.00 (*1-55738-336-7*, Irwn Prfssnl) McGraw-Hill Prof.

***McDonell, J. M.** Half Crazy: A Novel. 2000. pap. text 12.95 (*1-893224-04-X*) New Millenn Enter.

McDonell, J. M. Half Crazy: A Novel, Vol. 1. LC 94-33348. 1995. 19.95 (*0-316-55560-6*) Little.

***McDonell, J. M.** Out of Darkness: Collected Writings on Depression, Despair & Melancholy. LC 00-33954. 2000. write for info. (*1-893224-15-5*, New Millenn Pr) New Millenn Enter.

McDonell, James. Stained Glass Craft Made Simple: Step-by-Step Instructions Using the Modern Copper-Foil Method. (Illus.). 32p. 1985. pap. 3.95 (*0-486-24963-8*) Dover.

McDonell, Katherine M., ed. see Lindsay, William A.

McDonnall, Denis L. & Monroe, John G. Kerr on the Law of Fraud & Mistake: Including Misrepresentation Generally, Undue Influence, Fiduciary Relationship, Constructive & Imputed Notice, Etc. 7th ed. (Legal Reprint Ser.). (Illus.). liv, 738p. 1986. reprint ed. 65.00 (*0-421-35540-9*) W S Hein.

McDonnel & Kissel. In-Situ Impact Detection Techniques, Interplanetary Dust & Future, Vol. 12. Masson, ed. (Advances in Space Research Ser.: Vol. 17). 222p. 1995. pap. write for info. (*0-08-042661-1*, Pergamon Pr) Elsevier.

McDonnel, Anna. Bill Mack. (Illus.). 166p. (C). 1989. write for info. (*0-318-65799-6*) Maresa Editions.

McDonnel, Flora. Quiero a los Animales (I Love Animals) (SPA.). 28p. (J). (gr. 1-3). 1996. 12.99 (*968-16-4933-8*, Pub. by Fondo) Continental Bk.

McDonnell. Cosmic Dust. (Advances in Space Research Ser.: Vol. 6). 1988. pap. 56.00 (*0-08-036642-2*, Pergamon Pr) Elsevier.

***McDonnell.** Festival & Special Event Management. 1999. pap. 43.95 (*0-471-33934-2*) Wiley.

McDonnell. International GIS Dictionary. 2nd ed. 200p. (C). 2000. pap. 19.95 (*0-471-32194-X*) Wiley.

McDonnell, Chris. For the Love of Hockey: Hockey Stars' Personal Stories. (Illus.). 200p. 1997. 45.00 (*1-55209-170-8*) Firefly Bks Ltd.

McDonnell, Christine. Los Amigos Primero (Friends First) Bracho, Coral & Uribe, Marcelo, trs. (SPA., Illus.). 216p. (J). (gr. 5-6). 1994. pap. 5.99 (*968-16-4466-2*, Pub. by Fondo) Continental Bk.

— It's a Deal, Dogboy. LC 98-3845. (Illus.). 92p. (J). (gr. 2-4). 1998. 14.99 (*0-670-83264-2*) Viking Penguin.

— Trouble Times 2. (J). 1999. pap. 3.95 (*0-14-034393-8*, Viking) Viking Penguin.

***McDonnell, David, ed.** Bond 'James Bond', Vol. 2. (Starlog Movie Ser.: No. 9). 1999. pap. 9.99 (*0-934551-94-4*, Pub. by Starlog Grp Inc) Kable News Co Inc.

— Dinosaur. (Mega Movie Series Presents: No. 1). 2000. pap. 9.99 (*0-88013-023-7*, Pub. by Starlog Grp Inc) Kable News Co Inc.

— Dinosaurs. (Starlog Movie Magic Ser.: No. 1). 2000. pap. 6.99 (*0-88013-010-5*, Pub. by Starlog Grp Inc) Kable News Co Inc.

McDonnell, David, ed. Starlog Movie Hits No. 4: Wing Commander. 1999. pap. 5.99 (*0-934551-68-5*) Starlog Grp Inc.

***McDonnell, David, ed.** Starlog Movie Series Presents Battlefield Earth, Vol. 11. 2000. pap. (*0-88013-004-0*, Pub. by Starlog Grp Inc) Kable News Co Inc.

McDonnell, David, ed. Starlog's 100 Years of Animation. 2000. pap. 9.99 (*0-934551-80-4*, Pub. by Starlog Grp Inc) Kable News Co Inc.

— Starlog's 100 Years of Comics. (Illus.). 1999. pap. 9.99 (*0-934551-79-0*, Pub. by Starlog Grp Inc) Kable News Co Inc.

— Starlog's 100 Years of Science-Fiction. 1999. pap. 9.99 (*0-934551-81-2*, Pub. by Starlog Grp Inc) Kable News Co Inc.

McDonnell, Ed, jt. ed. see Link, David.

McDonnell, Eugene E., ed. A Source Book in APL: Papers by Adin D. Falkoff & Kenneth E. Iverson. 144p. (Orig.). 1981. pap. 15.00 (*0-917326-10-5*) APL Pr.

***McDonnell, Evelyn & Powers, Ann, eds.** Rock She Wrote: Women Write about Rock, Pop & Rap. LC 99-32192. 496p. 1999. pap. 16.95 (*0-8154-1018-2*) Cooper Sq.

McDonnell, Evelyn, jt. ed. see Kelly, Karen.

McDonnell, Flora. Flora McDonnell's ABC. LC 96-8418. (Illus.). 40p. (J). (ps-1). 1997. 16.99 (*0-7636-0118-7*) Candlewick Pr.

— I Love Animals. LC 93-2463. (Illus.). 32p. (J). (ps up). 1994. 14.95 (*1-56402-387-7*) Candlewick Pr.

— I Love Animals. LC 93-2463. (Illus.). (J). (ps-3). 1996. pap. 5.99 (*1-56402-672-8*) Candlewick Pr.

— I Love Animals: Big Book. LC 93-2463. (J). (ps-3). 1996. pap. 19.99 (*1-56402-662-0*) Candlewick Pr.

— I Love Boats. LC 94-4861. (Illus.). 32p. (J). (ps up). 1995. 15.95 (*1-56402-539-X*) Candlewick Pr.

— Splash! LC 98-12384. (Illus.). 32p. (J). (ps-1). 1999. 16.99 (*0-7636-0481-X*, Pub. by Candlewick Pr) Penguin Putnam.

McDonnell, Frances. Emigrants from Ireland to America, 1735-1743: A Transcription of the Report of the Irish House of Commons into Enforced Emigration to America. 142p. 1992. 18.50 (*0-8063-1331-5*, 3510) Genealog Pub.

***McDonnell, Frances.** Highland Jacobites 1745. 115p. 1999. pap. 15.00 (*0-8063-4935-2*) Clearfield Co.

— Jacobites of Perthshire, 1745. 78p. pap. 12.00 (*0-8063-4838-0*) Clearfield Co.

McDonnell, Frances. Jacobites of 1715 & 1745, North East Scotland, 2 vols. in 1. 96p. 2000. reprint ed. pap. 14.50 (*0-8063-4685-X*, 9234) Clearfield Co.

McDonnell-Garvey, Maire. Mid-Connaught: The Ancient Territory of Sliabh Lugha. LC 96-106178. (Illus.). 208p. (Orig.). 1995. pap. 17.95 (*1-873437-12-9*, Pub. by Drumlin Pubns Ltd) Irish Bks Media.

McDonnell, Ginny & Mogard, Sue. Creative Thinking. 1994. 6.95 (*1-55708-417-3*, MCR899); 6.95 (*1-55708-423-8*, MCC921) McDonald Pub Co.

— Graph It. 1994. 4.95 (*1-55708-427-0*, MCR290) McDonald Pub Co.

McDonnell, Ginny, jt. auth. see Mogard, Sue.

McDonnell, Greg. Heartland. (Illus.). 176p. 1993. 50.00 (*1-55046-064-1*, Pub. by Boston Mills) Genl Dist Srvs.

— Passing Trains. (Illus.). 160p. 1996. 50.00 (*1-55046-183-4*, Pub. by Boston Mills) Genl Dist Srvs.

— Signatures in Steel. Hudson, Noel, ed. (Illus.). 208p. 1991. 50.00 (*0-7737-2554-7*, Pub. by Boston Mills) Genl Dist Srvs.

— Signatures in Steel. (Illus.). 208p. 1995. 50.00 (*1-55046-162-1*, Pub. by Boston Mills) Genl Dist Srvs.

— U-Boats: General Electric's Diesel Locomotives. LC 97-137999. (Illus.). 192p. 1996. 50.00 (*1-55046-112-5*, Pub. by Boston Mills) Genl Dist Srvs.

— Wheat Kings. LC 98-230642. (Illus.). 120p. 1998. 29.95 (*1-55046-249-0*, Pub. by Boston Mills) Genl Dist Srvs.

McDonnell, Helen M., jt. ed. see Neumann, Bonnie H.

McDonnell, J. A., et al, eds. Hypervelocity Impacts in Space & Planetology: Proceedings of the BO.5 Symposium of COSPAR Scientific Commission B Which Was Held During the Thirty-First COSPAR Scientific Assembly, Birmingham, UK, 14-21 July 1996. 232p. 1997. pap. 100.50 (*0-08-043305-7*, Pergamon Pr) Elsevier.

McDonnell, J. J., jt. ed. see Kendall, C.

McDonnell, James & Trampiets, Frances. Communicating Faith in a Technological Age. 256p. (C). 1996. pap. 39.95 (*0-85439-314-5*, Pub. by St Paul Pubns) St Mut.

McDonnell, James, ed. see DeGiacomo, F. P.

McDonnell, James A., ed. Cosmic Dust. LC 77-2895. (Illus.). 713p. reprint ed. pap. 200.00 (*0-608-17603-6*, 203045300069) Bks Demand.

McDonnell, Jane. Living to Tell the Tale: A Guide to Writing Memoir. LC 97-34341. 164p. 1998. pap. 12.95 (*0-14-026530-9*) Viking Penguin.

McDonnell, Janet. Animal Builders. LC 96-30062. (Nature Books Ser.). (Illus.). 32p. (J). (gr. 2-6). 1997. lib. bdg. 22.79 (*1-56766-399-0*) Childs World.

— Animal Communication. LC 96-30061. (Illus.). 32p. (J). (gr. k-2). 1997. lib. bdg. 22.79 (*1-56766-401-6*) Childs World.

— Animal Migration. LC 96-30060. (Nature Books Ser.). (Illus.). 32p. (J). (gr. 2-6). 1997. lib. bdg. 22.79 (*1-56766-402-4*) Childs World.

— Celebrating Earth Day. (Circle the Year with Holidays Ser.). (Illus.). 32p. (J). (ps-2). 1994. pap. 3.95 (*0-516-40689-2*) Childrens.

— The Child's World of Success. rev. ed. (Child's World of Values Ser.). (Illus.). 24p. (J). (ps-2). 1996. lib. bdg. 18.50 (*1-56766-294-3*) Childs World.

— The Child's World of Thankfulness. rev. ed. (Child's World of Values Ser.). (Illus.). 24p. (J). (ps-2). 1996. lib. bdg. 18.50 (*1-56766-295-1*) Childs World.

— Christmas in Other Lands. LC 93-7632. (Circle the Year with Holidays Ser.). (Illus.). 32p. (J). (ps-2). 1993. pap. 3.95 (*0-516-40682-5*) Childrens.

— The Fourth of July. LC 94-4827. (Circle the Year with Holidays Ser.). (Illus.). 32p. (J). (gr. 1-2). 1994. pap. 3.95 (*0-516-40694-9*) Childrens.

— Sharing Hanukkah. LC 93-13250. (Circle the Year with Holidays Ser.). (Illus.). 32p. (J). (ps-2). 1993. pap. 3.95 (*0-516-40685-X*) Childrens.

M

An Asterisk (*) at the beginning of an entry indicates that the title is appearing for the first time.

— Thankfulness. LC 88-2657. (Values to Live By Ser.). (ENG & SPA., Illus.). 32p. (J). (ps-2). 1988. lib. bdg. 21.36 (0-89565-375-3) Childs World.

***McDonnell, Janet A.** After Desert Storm: The United States Army & the Reconstruction of Kuwait. 314p. 1999. per. 21.00 (0-16-049770-1) USGPO.

McDonnell, Janet A. The Dispossession of the American Indian, 1887-1934. LC 90-44508. (Illus.). 176p. 1991. 24.95 (0-253-33628-7) Ind U Pr.

— Response to the Loma Prieta Earthquake. (Illus.). 91p. (Orig.). (C). 1995. pap. text 30.00 (0-7881-2582-6) DIANE Pub.

— Supporting the Troops: The United States Army Corps of Engineers in the Persian Gulf War. 260p. 1996. per. 18.00 (0-16-042689-8) USGPO.

McDonnell, Jeffrey J., et al, eds. Watershed Restoration Management: Physical, Chemical, & Biological Considerations: New York City Water Supply Studies. LC 96-85384. (Technical Publications: No. 96-2). (Illus.). 174p. (Orig.). 1996. pap. 25.00 (1-882132-38-6, TPS96-1) Am Water Resources.

McDonnell, Jeffrey J., ed. see American Water Resources Association Staff.

McDonnell, John, et al. Transition Programs for Students with Moderate - Severe Disabilities. 448p. 1995. pap. 81.95 (0-534-34080-6) Brooks-Cole.

McDonnell, John, jt. ed. see McGwire, Michael.

McDonnell, John J. The Concept of an Atom from Democritus to John Dalton. LC 91-40434. 144p. 1992. lib. bdg. 69.95 (0-7734-9649-1) E Mellen.

— An Introduction to Persons with Severe Disabilities: Educational & Social Issues. LC 94-32871. 352p. 1995. 68.00 (0-205-15090-X) Allyn.

— The World Council of Churches & the Catholic Church. (Toronto Studies in Theology: Vol. 21). 479p. 1985. lib. bdg. 109.95 (0-88946-765-X) E Mellen.

McDonnell, John R. & Reynolds, Robert G., eds. Evolutionary Programming IV: Proceedings of the Fourth Annual Conference on Evolutionary Programming, March 1-3 1995, San Diego, CA. LC 95-240. 827p. 1995. 77.00 (0-262-13317-2, Bradford Bks) MIT Pr.

McDonnell, Joseph. Five Hundred Years of the Art of the Book in Ireland: 1500 to the Present. LC 97-224812. (Illus.). 176p. 1997. 125.00 (0-903162-98-9, Pub. by Merrell Holberton) U of Wash Pr.

McDonnell, Judith, jt. ed. see Litoff, Judy B.

***McDonnell, Julian B.** Uniform Commercial Code 1998 Revised Article 9: Text, Comments & Analysis. LC 99-20266. 1999. write for info. (0-8205-3869-8) Bender.

McDonnell, Jullian B. & Coleman, Elizabeth. Commercial & Consumer Warranties: Drafting, Performing & Litigating, 3 vols. 1987. ring bd. 660.00 (0-8205-2385-2) Bender.

McDonnell, Kathleen. Kidculture: Children, Adults & Popular Culture. 184p. 1994. pap. 14.95 (0-929005-64-3, Pub. by Sec Story Pr) LPC InBook.

***McDonnell, Kathleen.** The Nordlings. 207p. (YA). (gr. 5-9). 2000. pap. 6.95 (1-896764-23-1, Pub. by Sec Story Pr) Orca Bk Pubs.

McDonnell, Kathleen. Not an Easy Choice: A Feminist Re-Examines Abortion. 192p. pap. 9.95 (0-88961-089-4, Pub. by Womens Pr) LPC InBook.

McDonnell, Kathleen, ed. Adverse Effects: Women & the Pharmaceutical Industry. 220p. reprint ed. pap. 12.95 (0-88961-108-4, Pub. by Womens Pr) LPC InBook.

McDonnell, Ken, et al. EBRIs Databook on Employer Benefits: What Is the Promise? 4th ed. LC 97-30519. 556p. 1997. pap. text 99.00 (0-86643-089-X) Empl Benefit Res Inst.

***McDonnell, Ken, et al.** Health Benefits Databook LC 99-41519. 1999. write for info. (0-86643-094-6) Empl Benefit Res Inst.

McDonnell, Kevin, jt. auth. see Freeman, John.

McDonnell, Kevin, jt. auth. see Freeman, John M.

McDonnell, Kilian. The Baptism of Jesus in the Jordan: The Trinitarian & Cosmic Order of Salvation. LC 96-8000. 272p. 1996. pap. 24.95 (0-8146-5307-3, M Glazier) Liturgical Pr.

— John Calvin, the Church & the Eucharist. LC 65-17149. 420p. reprint ed. pap. 130.20 (0-608-30469-7, 201057200069) Bks Demand.

McDonnell, Kilian, ed. Open the Windows: The Popes & Charismatic Renewal. LC 88-83044. xxvii, 67p. (Orig.). 1989. pap. 5.95 (0-937779-06-7) Greenlawn Pr.

— Toward a New Pentecost, for a New Evangelization: Malines Document I. 2nd ed. LC 92-46910. 80p. 1993. pap. text 5.95 (0-8146-5846-6, M Glazier) Liturgical Pr.

McDonnell, Kilian & Montague, George T. Christian Initiation & Baptism in the Holy Spirit. 368p. (C). 1991. pap. 14.95 (0-8146-5009-0, M Glazier) Liturgical Pr.

— Fanning the Flame: What Does Baptism in the Holy Spirit Have to Do with Christian Initiation? 30p. (Orig.). 1991. pap. text 1.95 (0-8146-5013-9) Liturgical Pr.

McDonnell, L. P. Portable Power Tools. 2nd ed. (Construction & Building Trades Ser.). 1978. teacher ed. 13.50 (0-8273-1101-X); mass mkt. 25.75 (0-8273-1100-1) Delmar.

McDonnell, L. P. & Kaumeheiwa, A. I. The Use of Hand Woodworking Tools. 2nd ed. LC 76-48504. 301p. (C). 1978. teacher ed. 13.50 (0-8273-1099-4); pap. text 25.75 (0-8273-1098-6) Delmar.

McDonnell, Lawrence. October Revolution: A BBC Correspondent's Eye-Witness Account of the Storming of the Russian Parliament. LC 96-138798. (Illus.). 200p. (C). 1997. pap. 16.95 (1-873376-07-3, Pub. by Spellmnt Pubs) St Mut.

McDonnell, Leo & Ball, John. Blueprint Reading & Sketching for Carpenters: Residential. LC 80-66027. (Blueprint Reading Ser.). (Illus.). 151p. (C). 1981. teacher ed. 13.50 (0-8273-1355-1); pap. text 36.95 (0-8273-1354-3) Delmar.

***McDonnell, Leslie.** The London Scottish in the Great War. 2000. 34.95 (0-85052-713-9, Pub. by Pen & Sword Bks Ltd) Combined Pub.

McDonnell, Lorraine M. Policymakers' Views of Student Assessment. LC 94-12141. ix, 48p. 1994. pap. 7.50 (0-8330-1542-7, MR-348) Rand Corp.

***McDonnell, Lorraine M.** Rediscovering the Democratic Purposes of Education. LC 00-26689. 304p. 2000. text 40.00 (0-7006-1026-X); pap. text. write for info. (0-7006-1027-8) U Pr of KS.

McDonnell, Lorraine M., ed. see Committee on Goals 2000 & the Inclusion of Student.

McDonnell, Margaret H. Marge! (Illus.). 192p. (Orig.). 1997. pap. write for info. (1-885527-10-1) Feather Fables.

McDonnell, Mark J. & Pickett, Steward T., eds. Humans as Components of Ecosystems: The Ecology of Subtle Human Effects & Populated Areas. LC 93-10444. 1993. 59.95 (0-387-94062-6) Spr-Verlag.

— Humans as Components of Ecosystems: The Ecology of Subtle Human Effects & Populated Areas. (Illus.). 386p. 1997. pap. text 42.95 (0-387-98243-4) Spr-Verlag.

McDonnell, Mary A. Village Streets. 64p. 1991. pap. 10.00 (0-9632201-0-1) Zeugpress.

McDonnell, Nancy A., jt. auth. see Alderson, Wayne T.

McDonnell, Patricia. Marsden Hartley: An American Modern. LC 97-13221. (Illus.). 86p. 1997. pap. 22.95 (1-885116-04-7) Weisman Art.

McDonnell, Patricia, et al. Charles Biederman. LC 99-24230. 1999. write for info. (1-885116-09-8) Weisman Art.

McDonnell, Patrick. Cats & Dogs: Mutts II. LC 97-71625. (Illus.). 128p. (Orig.). 1997. pap. 9.95 (0-8362-3732-3) Andrews & McMeel.

— More Stuff. LC 98-85338. (Mutts Ser.: Vol. III). (Illus.). 128p. 1998. pap. 9.95 (0-8362-6823-7) Andrews & McMeel.

— Mutts. (Illus.). 127p. (Orig.). 1996. pap. 9.95 (0-8362-1025-5) Andrews & McMeel.

***McDonnell, Patrick.** Mutt's Sundays. 144p. 1999. pap. 12.95 (0-7407-0010-3) Andrews & McMeel.

— Our Mutts, Vol. 5. (Illus.). 2000. pap. 9.95 (0-7407-0456-7); pap. 59.70 (0-7407-1285-3) Andrews & McMeel.

McDonnell, Patrick. Yesh! Mutts IV. 1999. pap. 9.95 (0-8362-8286-8) Andrews & McMeel.

McDonnell, Patrick, et al. Krazy Kat: The Art of George Herriman. (Illus.). 224p. 1986. pap. 14.95 (0-8109-2313-0, Pub. by Abrams) Time Warner.

— Krazy Kat: The Comic Art of George Herriman. (Illus.). 224p. 1999. 19.98 (0-8109-8152-1, Pub. by Abrams) Time Warner.

McDonnell, Peter J., jt. auth. see Thompson, Frank B.

McDonnell, Porter. Introduction to Map Projections. 2nd ed. 198p. 1991. pap. 51.00 (0-910845-39-5, 462) Landmark Ent.

McDonnell, Rachael & Kemp, Karen A. International Gls Dictionary. 112p. 1996. pap. 34.95 (0-470-23607-8) Wiley.

McDonnell, Rachel A., jt. auth. see Burrough, Peter A.

***McDonnell, Rea.** Experiencing Scripture: How God Comes Close in Spirit & Sacrament LC 99-38553. 2000. write for info. (0-8198-2346-5) Pauline Bks.

McDonnell, Rea. When God Comes Close: A Journey Through Scripture. rev. ed. LC 94-1614. 172p. 1994. pap. 5.25 (0-8198-8271-2) Pauline Bks.

McDonnell, Rea & Callahan, Rachel. Wholing the Heart: Good News for Those Who Grew up in Troubled Families. 2nd rev. ed. 120p. 1998. pap. 10.95 (1-888461-07-1) Islewest Pub.

McDonnell, Rea, jt. auth. see Callahan, Rachel.

McDonnell, Robert, ed. see Kleeman, Mary.

McDonnell, Robert W., jt. auth. see Partington, Paul G.

McDonnell, Rose Anita, et al. New Progress in Mathematics, Grade 8, Workbook. rev. ed. (New Progress in Mathematics Ser.: Vol. 2). (Illus.). 208p. (YA). (gr. 8-9). 1993. pap., wbk. ed. 9.75 (0-8215-1728-7) Sadlier.

— New Progress in Mathematics, Grade 8, Workbook, Teacher's Edition. rev. ed. (New Progress in Mathematics Ser.: Vol. 2). (Illus.). 208p. 1993. pap., teacher ed., wbk. ed. 13.95 (0-8215-1758-9) Sadlier.

— New Progress in Mathematics, Grade 8, Student Test Booklet, Free Response. rev. ed. (New Progress in Mathematics Ser.: Vol. 2). (Illus.). 44p. (YA). (gr. 8-9). 1994. pap. write for info. (0-8215-1748-1) Sadlier.

— New Progress in Mathematics, Grade 8, Student Test Booklet, Standardized. rev. ed. (New Progress in Mathematics Ser.: Vol. 2). (Illus.). 44p. (YA). (gr. 8-9). 1994. pap. 35.73 (0-8215-1768-6) Sadlier.

— New Progress in Mathematics, Grade 8, Student Text: An Innovative Approach Including Two Options: Pre-Algebra, Algebra. rev. ed. (New Progress in Mathematics Ser.: Vol. 2). (Illus.). 578p. (YA). (gr. 8-9). 1996. pap. text 40.50 (0-8215-1708-2) Sadlier.

— New Progress in Mathematics, Grade 8, Teacher's Edition: An Innovative Approach Including Two Options: Pre-Algebra, Algebra. rev. ed. (New Progress in Mathematics Ser.: Vol. 2). (Illus.). 704p. 1996. pap., teacher ed. 67.50 (0-8215-1718-X) Sadlier.

— New Progress in Mathematics, Grade 7, Workbook, Teacher's Edition. rev. ed. (New Progress in Mathematics Ser.: Vol. 2). (Illus.). 176p. 1994. pap., teacher ed., wbk. ed. 13.95 (0-8215-1757-0) Sadlier.

— New Progress in Mathematics, Grade 7, Workbook. rev. ed. (New Progress in Mathematics Ser.: Vol. 2). (Illus.). 178p. (YA). (gr. 7-8). 1993. pap., wbk. ed. 9.75 (0-8215-1727-9) Sadlier.

— New Progress in Mathematics, Grade 7, Student Test Booklet, Free Response. rev. ed. (New Progress in Mathematics Ser.: Vol. 2). (Illus.). 44p. (YA). (gr. 7-8). 1994. pap. write for info. (0-8215-1747-3) Sadlier.

— New Progress in Mathematics, Grade 7, Student Test Booklet, Standardized. rev. ed. (New Progress in Mathematics Ser.: Vol. 2). (Illus.). 44p. (YA). (gr. 7-8). 1994. pap. 35.73 (0-8215-1767-8) Sadlier.

— New Progress in Mathematics, Grade 7, Student Text: With Pre-Algebra Readiness. rev. ed. (New Progress in Mathematics Ser.: Vol. 2). (Illus.). 516p. (YA). (gr. 7-8). 1996. text 40.50 (0-8215-1707-4) Sadlier.

— New Progress in Mathematics, Grade 7, Teacher's Edition: With Pre-Algebra Readiness. rev. ed. (New Progress in Mathematics Ser.: Vol. 2). (Illus.). 632p. 1996. pap., teacher ed. 67.50 (0-8215-1717-1) Sadlier.

— Progress in Mathematics, Grade 5, Skills Update Practice Book. (Progress in Mathematics Ser.: Vol. 7). (Illus.). 32p. (J). (gr. 5-6). 2000. pap. 1.95 (0-8215-2645-6) Sadlier.

— Progress in Mathematics, Grade 5, Skills Update Practice Book, Teacher's Edition. (Progress in Mathematics Ser.: Vol. 7). (Illus.). 32p. 2000. pap., teacher ed. 3.00 (0-8215-2655-3) Sadlier.

— Progress in Mathematics, Grade 5, Student Text. (Progress in Mathematics Ser.: Vol. 7). (Illus.). 516p. (J). (gr. 5-6). 2000. text 39.12 (0-8215-2605-7) Sadlier.

— Progress in Mathematics, Grade 5, Student Test Booklet. (Progress in Mathematics Ser.: Vol. 7). (Illus.). 32p. (J). (gr. 5-6). 2000. pap. write for info. (0-8215-2665-0) Sadlier.

— Progress in Mathematics, Grade 5, Teacher's Edition. (Progress in Mathematics Ser.: Vol. 7). (Illus.). 646p. 2000. teacher ed., spiral bd. 67.50 (0-8215-2615-4) Sadlier.

— Progress in Mathematics, Grade 5, Workbook. (Progress in Mathematics Ser.: Vol. 7). (Illus.). 160p. (J). (gr. 5-6). 2000. pap., wbk. ed. 9.60 (0-8215-2625-1) Sadlier.

— Progress in Mathematics, Grade 5, Workbook, Teacher's Edition. (Progress in Mathematics Ser.: Vol. 7). (Illus.). 160p. 2000. pap., teacher ed., wbk. ed. 10.59 (0-8215-2635-9) Sadlier.

— Progress in Mathematics, Grade 4, Skills Update Practice Book. (Progress in Mathematics Ser.: Vol. 7). (Illus.). 32p. (J). (gr. 4-5). 2000. pap. 1.95 (0-8215-2644-8) Sadlier.

— Progress in Mathematics, Grade 4, Skills Update Practice Book, Teacher's Edition. (Progress in Mathematics Ser.: Vol. 7). (Illus.). 32p. 2000. pap., teacher ed. 3.00 (0-8215-2654-5) Sadlier.

— Progress in Mathematics, Grade 4, Student Text. (Progress in Mathematics Ser.: Vol. 7). (Illus.). 520p. (J). (gr. 4-5). 2000. text 38.40 (0-8215-2604-9) Sadlier.

— Progress in Mathematics, Grade 4, Student Test Booklet. (Progress in Mathematics Ser.: Vol. 7). (Illus.). 32p. (J). (gr. 4-5). 2000. pap. write for info. (0-8215-2664-2) Sadlier.

— Progress in Mathematics, Grade 4, Teacher's Edition. (Progress in Mathematics Ser.: Vol. 7). (Illus.). 640p. 2000. teacher ed., spiral bd. 67.50 (0-8215-2614-6) Sadlier.

— Progress in Mathematics, Grade 4, Workbook. (Progress in Mathematics Ser.: Vol. 7). (Illus.). 160p. (J). (gr. 4-5). 2000. pap., wbk. ed. 9.60 (0-8215-2624-3) Sadlier.

— Progress in Mathematics, Grade 4, Workbook, Teacher's Edition. (Progress in Mathematics Ser.: Vol. 7). (Illus.). 160p. 2000. pap., teacher ed., wbk. ed. 10.59 (0-8215-2634-0) Sadlier.

— Progress in Mathematics, Grade K, Student Text. (Progress in Mathematics Ser.: Vol. 7). (Illus.). 320p. (J). (gr. k-1). 2000. pap. text 16.35 (0-8215-2600-6) Sadlier.

— Progress in Mathematics, Grade K, Teacher's Edition. (Progress in Mathematics Ser.: Vol. 7). (Illus.). 464p. 2000. teacher ed., spiral bd. 61.50 (0-8215-2610-3) Sadlier.

— Progress in Mathematics, Grade K, Workbook. (Progress in Mathematics Ser.: Vol. 7). (Illus.). 128p. (J). (gr. k). 2000. pap. text, wbk. ed. 7.50 (0-8215-2620-0) Sadlier.

— Progress in Mathematics, Grade K, Workbook, Teacher's Edition. (Progress in Mathematics Ser.: Vol. 7). (Illus.). 128p. 2000. pap., teacher ed., wbk. ed. 8.49 (0-8215-2630-8) Sadlier.

— Progress in Mathematics, Grade 1, Skills Update Practice Book. (Progress in Mathematics Ser.: Vol. 7). (Illus.). 32p. (J). 2000. pap. 1.95 (0-8215-2641-3) Sadlier.

— Progress in Mathematics, Grade 1, Skills Update Practice Book, Teacher's Edition. (Progress in Mathematics Ser.: Vol. 7). (Illus.). 32p. 2000. pap., teacher ed. 3.00 (0-8215-2651-0) Sadlier.

— Progress in Mathematics, Grade 1, Student Text. (Progress in Mathematics Ser.: Vol. 7). (Illus.). 506p. (J). (gr. 1-2). 2000. pap. text 21.12 (0-8215-2601-4) Sadlier.

— Progress in Mathematics, Grade 1, Student Test Booklet with Answer Booklet. (Progress in Mathematics Ser.: Vol. 7). (Illus.). 32p. (J). (gr. 1-2). 2000. pap. write for info. (0-8215-2661-8) Sadlier.

— Progress in Mathematics, Grade 1, Teacher's Edition. (Progress in Mathematics Ser.: Vol. 7). (Illus.). 496p. 2000. teacher ed., spiral bd. 61.50 (0-8215-2611-1) Sadlier.

— Progress in Mathematics, Grade 1, Workbook. (Progress in Mathematics Ser.: Vol. 7). (Illus.). 160p. (J). 2000. pap., wbk. ed. 7.50 (0-8215-2621-9) Sadlier.

— Progress in Mathematics, Grade 1, Workbook, Teacher's Edition. (Progress in Mathematics Ser.: Vol. 7). (Illus.). 160p. 2000. pap., teacher ed., wbk. ed. 8.49 (0-8215-2631-6) Sadlier.

— Progress in Mathematics, Grade 6, Skills Update Practice Book. (Progress in Mathematics Ser.: Vol. 7). (Illus.). 32p. (YA). (gr. 6-7). 2000. pap. 1.95 (0-8215-2646-4) Sadlier.

— Progress in Mathematics, Grade 6, Skills Update Practice Booklet, Teacher's Edition. (Progress in Mathematics Ser.: Vol. 7). (Illus.). 32p. 2000. pap., teacher ed. 3.00 (0-8215-2656-1) Sadlier.

— Progress in Mathematics, Grade 6, Student Text. (Progress in Mathematics Ser.: Vol. 7). (Illus.). 546p. (YA). (gr. 6-7). 2000. text 39.96 (0-8215-2606-5) Sadlier.

— Progress in Mathematics, Grade 6, Student Test Book. (Progress in Mathematics Ser.: Vol. 7). (Illus.). 32p. (YA). (gr. 6-7). 2000. pap. write for info. (0-8215-2666-9) Sadlier.

— Progress in Mathematics, Grade 6, Teacher's Edition. (Progress in Mathematics Ser.: Vol. 7). (Illus.). 672p. 2000. teacher ed., spiral bd. 69.00 (0-8215-2616-2) Sadlier.

— Progress in Mathematics, Grade 6, Workbook. (Progress in Mathematics Ser.: Vol. 7). (Illus.). 176p. (YA). (gr. 6-7). 2000. pap., wbk. ed. 9.60 (0-8215-2626-X) Sadlier.

— Progress in Mathematics, Grade 6, Workbook, Teacher's Edition, (Progress in Mathematics Ser.: Vol. 7). (Illus.). 176p. 2000. pap., teacher ed., wbk. ed. 10.59 (0-8215-2636-7) Sadlier.

— Progress in Mathematics, Grade 3, Skills Update Practice Book. (Progress in Mathematics Ser.: Vol. 7). (Illus.). 32p. (J). (gr. 3-4). 2000. pap. 1.95 (0-8215-2643-X) Sadlier.

— Progress in Mathematics, Grade 3, Skills Update Practice Book, Teacher's Edition. (Progress in Mathematics Ser.: Vol. 7). (Illus.). 32p. 2000. pap., teacher ed. 3.00 (0-8215-2653-7) Sadlier.

— Progress in Mathematics, Grade 3, Student Text. (Progress in Mathematics Ser.: Vol. 7). (Illus.). 500p. (J). (gr. 3-4). 2000. text 38.40 (0-8215-2603-0) Sadlier.

— Progress in Mathematics, Grade 3, Student Test Booklet. (Progress in Mathematics Ser.: Vol. 7). (Illus.). 32p. (J). (gr. 3-4). 2000. pap. write for info. (0-8215-2663-4) Sadlier.

— Progress in Mathematics, Grade 3, Teacher's Edition. (Progress in Mathematics Ser.: Vol. 7). (Illus.). 640p. 2000. teacher ed., spiral bd. 67.50 (0-8215-2613-8) Sadlier.

— Progress in Mathematics, Grade 3, Workbook. (Progress in Mathematics Ser.: Vol. 7). (Illus.). 160p. (J). (gr. 3-4). 2000. pap., wbk. ed. 9.60 (0-8215-2623-5) Sadlier.

— Progress in Mathematics, Grade 3, Workbook, Teacher's Edition. (Progress in Mathematics Ser.: Vol. 7). (Illus.). 160p. 2000. pap., teacher ed., wbk. ed. 10.59 (0-8215-2633-2) Sadlier.

— Progress in Mathematics, Grade 2, Skills Update Practice Book. (Progress in Mathematics Ser.: Vol. 7). (Illus.). 32p. (J). (gr. 2-3). 2000. pap. 1.95 (0-8215-2642-1) Sadlier.

— Progress in Mathematics, Grade 2, Skills Update Practice Book, Teacher's Edition. (Progress in Mathematics Ser.: Vol. 7). (Illus.). 32p. 2000. pap., teacher ed. 3.00 (0-8215-2652-9) Sadlier.

— Progress in Mathematics, Grade 2, Student Text. (Progress in Mathematics Ser.: Vol. 7). (Illus.). 496p. (J). (gr. 2-3). 2000. pap. text 21.12 (0-8215-2602-2) Sadlier.

— Progress in Mathematics, Grade 2, Student Test Booklet. (Progress in Mathematics Ser.: Vol. 7). (Illus.). 32p. (J). (gr. 2-3). 2000. pap. 29.47 (0-8215-2662-6) Sadlier.

— Progress in Mathematics, Grade 2, Teacher's Manual. (Progress in Mathematics Ser.: Vol. 7). (Illus.). 640p. 2000. teacher ed., spiral bd. 61.50 (0-8215-2612-X) Sadlier.

— Progress in Mathematics, Grade 2, Workbook. (Progress in Mathematics Ser.: Vol. 7). (Illus.). 160p. (J). (gr. 2-3). 2000. pap., wbk. ed. 7.50 (0-8215-2622-7) Sadlier.

— Progress in Mathematics, Grade 2, Workbook, Teacher's Edition. (Progress in Mathematics Ser.: Vol. 7). (Illus.). 160p. 2000. pap., teacher ed., wbk. ed. 8.49 (0-8215-2632-4) Sadlier.

McDonnell, S. N. & Brown, David. This Is Old Mac Calling All the Team: The Story of James S. McDonnell & McDonnell Douglas. (Illus.). 121p. 1999. 29.95 (0-9670989-0-4) S N McDonnell.

***McDonnell, Sharon.** Everything Internet Book. LC 98-27124. (Everything Ser.). xxi, 281p. 1999. pap. text 12.95 (1-58062-073-6) Adams Media.

McDonnell, Sharon. Unofficial Guide to Finding the Perfect Job. (Unofficial Guides Ser.). 416p. 1999. pap. text 14.95 (0-02-863536-1, Arco) Macmillan Gen Ref.

— You're Hired. 1995. pap. 12.00 (0-671-50053-8) S&S Trade.

— You're Hired! Secrets to a Successful Job Search. LC 99-60768. (Illus.). 264p. 1999. pap. 12.95 (0-02-862509-9, Arc) IDG Bks.

— You're Hired! Secrets to Successful Job Interviews. LC 95-40390. 224p. 1995. 12.95 (0-02-860347-8, Arco) Macmillan Gen Ref.

— You're Hired! Secrets to Successful Job Interviews. 2nd ed. LC 97-81091. 224p. 1998. 12.95 (0-02-862510-2, Arc) IDG Bks.

McDonnell, Sue. Understanding Horse Behavior: Your Guide to Horse Health Care & Management. 1999. pap. text 14.95 (1-58150-017-3) Blood-Horse.

McDonnell, Thomas. Pinpointing Student Behavioral Problems. (Orig.). 1988. pap. 9.95 (1-55804-950-9) Info Res Cons.

— RATS: (Rapid Assessment & Treatment Strategies for Human Resource Personnel) (Orig.). 1989. pap. 9.95 (0-931821-97-5) Info Res Cons.

McDonnell, Thomas P., ed. Classic Catholic Poetry. LC 88-60924. 144p. 1988. 13.95 (0-87973-494-9, 494) Our Sunday Visitor.

McDonnell, Thomas P., ed. see Merton, Thomas.

McDonnell, Vincent. The Knock Airport Mystery. 1993. pap. 7.95 (1-85371-305-8, Pub. by Poolbeg Pr) Dufour.

An Asterisk (*) at the beginning of an entry indicates that the title is appearing for the first time.

McDonnell-Wieczorek, Colleen. Go to College but Don't Go to Class: The Guide to Alternate Methods of Earning College Credits. 200p. (Orig.). 1994. pap. 19.95 (*1-885097-02-6*) NAOACS.
— The Guide for Adults Thinking about Going to College. 120p. (Orig.). 1994. pap. 12.95 (*1-885097-01-8*) NAOACS.
McDonnough, jt. auth. see Saidoff.
McDonogh, Gary, ed. Conflict in Catalonia: Images of an Urban Society. LC 86-956. (University of Florida Social Sciences Monographs: No. 71). 112p. (Orig.). 1985. pap. 19.95 (*0-8130-0821-2*) U Press Fla.
McDonogh, Gary, jt. auth. see Rotenberg, Robert.
McDonogh, Gary W. Black & Catholic in Savannah, Georgia. LC 93-15389. (Illus.). 360p. (Orig.). (C). 1993. 45.00 (*0-87049-810-X*); pap. 19.95 (*0-87049-811-8*) U of Tenn Pr.
— Good Families of Barcelona: A Social History of Power in the Industrial Era. LC 86-5607. 279p. 1986. reprint ed. pap. 86.50 (*0-608-02868-1*, 206393200007) Bks Demand.
McDonogh, Gary W., ed. The Florida Negro: A Federal Writers' Project Legacy. LC 92-28493. 184p. 1993. text 35.00 (*0-87805-588-6*) U Pr of Miss.
McDonough, Alex. Scorpio Six: Dragon Claw. 176p. (Orig.). 1993. mass mkt. 4.99 (*0-441-75514-3*) Ace Bks.
***McDonough, Andrew L.** Labview: Data Acquisition & Analysis for the Movement Sciences. LC 00-37491. 256p. 2000. spiral bd. 64.00 (*0-13-012847-3*, Brady Emerg Care) P-H.
McDonough, Ann. The Golden Stage: Dramatic Activities for Older Adults. 63p. 1998. pap., teacher ed. 12.95 (*0-87129-854-6*, G99) Dramatic Pub.
McDonough, Ann, compiled by. New Monologues for Mature Actors. 190p. 1996. pap. 19.95 (*0-87129-715-9*, N44) Dramatic Pub.
McDonough, Ann, compiled by. Short Stuff: Ten- to Twenty-Minute Plays for Mature Actors. 269p. 1998. pap. 19.95 (*0-87129-851-1*, SC8) Dramatic Pub.
***McDonough, Ann & Brown, Kent R., eds.** A Grand Entrance: Scenes & Monologues for Mature Actors. 356p. 2000. pap. 18.95 (*0-87129-933-X*, G68) Dramatic Pub.
McDonough, Barbara. Meet Me at the Fair: A "Choose Your Own Adventure" That Lets You Explore the Exciting Treasures of the 1904 St. Louis World's Fair. (Illus.). 64p. (Orig.). (J). (gr. 4-6). 1988. pap. 4.50 (*0-931821-43-6*) Info Res Cons.
McDonough, Brenna, jt. auth. see Wolfe, John Leslie.
McDonough, Brian P., ed. Talking Health with Dr. Brian McDonough. LC 94-6020. (Health, Society, & Policy Ser.). 288p. (C). 1994. 39.95 (*1-56639-207-1*) Temple U Pr.
McDonough, C. J., ed. see Hugh Primus.
McDonough, Carla J. Staging Masculinity: Male Identity in Contemporary American Drama. LC 96-44555. 192p. 1996. lib. bdg. 32.50 (*0-7864-0268-7*) McFarland & Co.
McDonough, Connie. Am I on the Right Plane? Transcendental Airlines Puts You on a Different Plane. Chandler, Patricia M., ed. (Illus.). 201p. (Orig.). 1991. pap. 7.95 (*0-9630660-0-5*) Hagall.
McDonough, D. Annotated Mergers & Acquisitions Law of Australia. 3rd ed. 470p. 1993. pap. 70.00 (*0-455-21182-5*, Pub. by LawBk Co) Gaunt.
McDonough, Dan, et al. 3-Step Approach to Better Jumping: Intermediate Program. unabridged ed. (Illus.). 36p. 1997. pap. 5.95 (*1-891200-04-6*) Performance Conditioning.
***McDonough, Daniel J.** Christopher Gadsden & Henry Laurens: The Parallel Lives of Two American Patriots. LC 00-25820. 2000. 52.50 (*1-57591-039-X*) Susquehanna U Pr.
McDonough, Dennis, ed. see Adamson, Bruce C.
McDonough, Dennis, ed. see Adamson, Bruce Campbell.
McDonough, Elizabeth, jt. ed. see Fleming, David L.
***McDonough, Frank.** Conflict, Communism & Fascism: European History, 1890-1945. (Cambridge Perspectives in History Ser.). 160p. 2000. pap. Price not set. (*0-521-77796-8*) Cambridge U Pr.
McDonough, Frank. Hitler & Nazi Germany. (Perspectives in History Ser.). (Illus.). vii, 152p. (C). 1999. pap. 11.95 (*0-521-59502-9*) Cambridge U Pr.
— Neville Chamberlain, Appeasement & the Road to War. LC 97-15519. (New Frontiers in History Ser.). 224p. 1998. pap. 27.95 (*0-7190-4832-X*, Pub. by Manchester Univ Pr); text 69.95 (*0-7190-4831-1*, Pub. by Manchester Univ Pr) St Martin.
— The Origins of the First & Second World Wars. (Perspectives in History Ser.). 128p. (C). 1998. pap. 13.95 (*0-521-56861-7*) Cambridge U Pr.
McDonough, Gerald M. The Hogles. LC 88-23045. 539p. 1988. 22.50 (*0-914740-33-4*) Western Epics.
— An Improbable Journey: The Life & Times of Eugene Jelesnik. LC 97-13244. 1997. 25.95 (*1-57345-269-6*) Deseret Bk.
McDonough, Hanna & Bartha, Christina. Putting Children First: A Guide for Parents Breaking Up. 192p. 1999. pap. 15.95 (*0-8020-8064-2*); text 45.00 (*0-8020-4217-1*) U of Toronto Pr.
McDonough, Ian & Conn, Stewart, eds. The Ice Horses: The Second Shore Poets Anthology. 64p. 1990. pap. 21.00 (*1-898218-85-4*) St Mut.
McDonough, Irene R. History of the Public Library in Vigo County, 1816-1975. LC 77-18403. (Illus.). 203p. 1977. 6.00 (*0-9601522-1-0*) Vigo Cnty Pub Lib.
McDonough, J., jt. auth. see Young, N.
McDonough, James L. Chattanooga: A Death Grip on the Confederacy. LC 83-23582. 318p. 1984. pap. 17.95 (*0-87049-630-1*) U of Tenn Pr.
— Shiloh-in Hell Before Night. LC 76-18864. (Illus.). 272p. 1977. 34.00 (*0-87049-199-7*); pap. 17.95 (*0-87049-232-2*) U of Tenn Pr.
— Stones River: Bloody Winter in Tennessee. LC 80-11580. 286p. 1980. pap. 17.95 (*0-87049-373-6*) U of Tenn Pr.
— War in Kentucky: From Shiloh to Perryville. LC 94-4508. (Illus.). 408p. (C). 1994. 34.00 (*0-87049-847-9*) U of Tenn Pr.
— War in Kentucky: From Shiloh to Perryville. LC 94-4508. (Illus.). 408p. 1996. pap. 17.95 (*0-87049-935-1*) U of Tenn Pr.
McDonough, James L. & Connelly, Thomas L. Five Tragic Hours: The Battle of Franklin. LC 83-3449. (Illus.). 232p. 1983. pap. 17.95 (*0-87049-397-3*) U of Tenn Pr.
McDonough, James L. & Gardner, Richard S. The Skyriders: History of the 327-401 Glider Infantry. LC 80-67956. (Airborne Ser.: No. 11). (Illus.). 176p. 1980. 29.95 (*0-89839-034-6*) Battery Pr.
McDonough, James R. Platoon Leader. LC 84-24839. (Illus.). 208p. 1996. pap. 14.00 (*0-89141-606-4*) Presidio Pr.
McDonough, Jerome. Addict: A Tragic Portrayal of the Horrors of Drug & Alcohol Abuse. (Illus.). 47p. (YA). (gr. 7-12). 1985. pap. 4.00 (*0-88680-241-5*) I E Clark.
— Alky: A Tragedy in One Act. 40p. (YA). (gr. 7-12). 1991. pap. 3.25 (*0-88680-354-3*) I E Clark.
— Asylum: A One-Act Play. (Illus.). 40p. 1975. pap. 3.25 (*0-88680-008-0*) I E Clark.
— Asylum: Director's Script. (Illus.). 40p. 1975. pap. 10.00 (*0-88680-009-9*) I E Clark.
— B. A. T. S. A Comedy in 2-Acts. (Illus.). 56p. 1988. pap. 4.00 (*0-88680-289-X*) I E Clark.
— Blues: An Ensemble Play in One Act. 28p. (Orig.). 1990. pap. 3.50 (*0-88680-323-3*) I E Clark.
— Butterfly: A Tragedy in One Act Based on Madame Butterfly. (Illus.). 22p. 1993. pap. 3.25 (*0-88680-390-X*) I E Clark.
— C. C.'s Power & Light Company. 28p. (Orig.). 1996. pap. 2.50 (*1-57514-172-8*, 3073) Encore Perform Pub.
— Carol-A Christmas: A One-Act Play. 1989. pap. 3.00 (*0-88680-312-8*) I E Clark.
— Carriers: A Tragedy in One Act. 34p. (YA). (gr. 7-12). 1992. pap. 3.50 (*0-88680-370-5*) I E Clark.
— A Christmas Carol: One-Act Adaptation of Dickens' Novel. (Illus.). 34p. 1976. pap. 3.25 (*0-88680-024-2*) I E Clark.
— Dolls: A Tragedy in One-Act. 28p. 1988. pap. 4.00 (*0-88680-298-9*) I E Clark.
— Eden: A Frightening Drama. 38p. 1978. pap. 3.50 (*0-88680-044-7*) I E Clark.
— Fables: A Play in One Act. (Illus.). 40p. 1974. pap. 3.25 (*0-88680-047-1*) I E Clark.
— Fables: Director's Script. (Illus.). 40p. 1974. pap. 10.00 (*0-88680-048-X*) I E Clark.
— Fine Arts Under-Graduate Housing. (Illus.). 36p. 1986. pap. 4.25 (*0-88680-281-4*) I E Clark.
— GrEEKS. 1997. pap. 3.00 (*1-57514-333-X*, 3108) Encore Perform Pub.
— GrEEKS: A Campus Disaster. 1998. pap. 3.00 (*1-57514-274-0*, 3108) Encore Perform Pub.
— Hoods: One-Act Drama about Teen Gangs. 22p. (YA). (gr. 7-12). 1992. pap. 3.25 (*0-88680-369-1*) I E Clark.
— It's Sad, So Sad When an Elf Goes Bad: A Christmas Parable in One-Act. (Illus.). 24p. (J). (gr. k-6). 1979. pap. 3.25 (*0-88680-100-1*) I E Clark.
— Juvie: A Drama Set in a Juvenile Detention Center. (Illus.). 32p. (YA). (gr. 7-12). 1982. pap. 4.00 (*0-88680-103-6*) I E Clark.
— Limbo: A One-Act Drama. 28p. (YA). (gr. 7 up). 1984. pap. 3.25 (*0-88680-219-9*) I E Clark.
— Mirrors: A Reflection in One-Act. (Illus.). 32p. (YA). (gr. 7 up). 1987. pap. 3.25 (*0-88680-278-4*) I E Clark.
— The Nearest Star: A Christmas Musical in One-Act. 28p. 1981. pap. 3.25 (*0-88680-137-0*) I E Clark.
— Not Even A Mouse: A Chris Mouse Tale. (Illus.). 20p. (Orig.). (J). (gr. k-9). 1984. pap. 3.00 (*0-88680-220-2*) I E Clark.
— O, Little Town: One-Act Christmas Drama. (Illus.). 27p. 1978. pap. 3.25 (*0-88680-144-3*) I E Clark.
— Plots: A Funereal Comedy in One-Act. 24p. 1981. pap. 3.25 (*0-88680-154-0*) I E Clark.
— Posadas: A Bilingual Play. Alderete, Betty, tr. from SPA. (Illus.). 26p. 1994. pap. 3.25 (*0-88680-398-5*) I E Clark.
— Postlude, a Play for the Moment. 32p. 1998. pap. 3.25 (*0-87440-067-8*) Bakers Plays.
— Requiem: A One-Act Drama. (Illus.). 41p. 1977. pap. 3.25 (*0-88680-163-X*) I E Clark.
— Requiem: Director's Script. (Illus.). 41p. 1977. pap. 10.00 (*0-88680-164-8*) I E Clark.
— Reunion: A Comedy with Drama in 2 Acts. 30p. (J). 1997. pap. 4.00 (*0-88680-446-9*) I E Clark.
— Roomers: A One-Act Comedy. 36p. 1983. pap. 3.25 (*0-88680-165-6*) I E Clark.
— Splits: A One-Act Play about Children of Divorce. (Illus.). 17p. 1996. pap. 3.25 (*0-88680-422-1*) I E Clark.
— Stages: A Theatre Piece in One-Act. (Illus.). 52p. 1979. pap. 3.25 (*0-88680-183-4*) I E Clark.
— Stages: Director's Script. (Illus.). 52p. 1979. pap. 10.00 (*0-88680-184-2*) I E Clark.
— Turners: A Drama in 2-Acts. 40p. (YA). (gr. 7-12). 1989. pap. 4.00 (*0-88680-320-9*) I E Clark.
— Twinderella: En Espanol, Gemelarela. Alderette, Betty, tr. (ENG & SPA., Illus.). 39p. 1996. pap. 3.25 (*0-88680-433-7*) I E Clark.
***McDonough, Jerome.** Users: An Ongoing Tragedy. (Young Adult Awareness Plays Ser.). 32p. (YA). 1999. pap. 4.00 (*0-88680-459-0*) I E Clark.
McDonough, Jerome, jt. auth. see Brinsley, Richard.
McDonough, Jo & McDonough, Steven. Research Methods for English Language Teachers. LC 96-35143. (Illus.). 272p. 1997. pap. text 19.95 (*0-340-61472-2*) OUP.
McDonough, Jo & Shaw, Christopher. Materials & Methods in ELT: A Teachers Guide. (Applied Language Studies). 288p. 1993. pap. 25.95 (*0-631-18003-6*) Blackwell Pubs.
***McDonough, John, ed.** Encyclopedia of Advertising. 3 vols. (Illus.). 2500p. 1999. 300.00 (*1-57958-172-2*) Fitzroy Dearborn.
***McDonough, John E.** Experiencing Politics: A Legislator's Stories of Government & Health Care. LC 99-56844. Vol. 2. (Illus.). 336p. 2000. 50.00 (*0-520-22410-8*, Pub. by U CA Pr); pap. 19.95 (*0-520-22411-6*, Pub. by U CA Pr) Cal Prin Full Svc.
McDonough, John E. Interests, Ideas, & Deregulation: The Fate of Hospital Rate Setting. LC 97-32100. 296p. 1997. text 42.50 (*0-472-10888-3*, 10888) U of Mich Pr.
McDonough, John J., jt. auth. see Culbert, Samuel A.
McDonough, John J., ed. see French, Benjamin B.
McDonough, John J., ed. see French, Francis O.
McDonough, Kathleen, jt. auth. see Fox, Micheal.
McDonough, Kathleen L. School Survival Skills: Student Syllabus. 1985. audio 36.25 (*0-89420-245-6*, 340000) Natl Book.
— School Survival Skills: Student Syllabus. (Illus.). 64p. (YA). (gr. 8 up). 1985. pap. 8.95 (*0-89420-246-4*, 340025) Natl Book.
McDonough, Kevin. A Tabloid History of the World. LC 97-225831. (Illus.). 176p. (J). 1997. pap. 9.70 (*0-7868-8223-9*, Pub. by Hyperion) Time Warner.
McDonough, Kris P. Who Are They? LC 99-90269. (Illus.). 32p. (J). (gr. k-6). 1999. 14.95 (*1-893849-01-5*); pap. 7.99 (*1-893849-00-7*) McMyr Pubg.
McDonough, Kristin & Langstaff, Eleanor. Access Information: Research in Social Sciences & Humanities. 300p. 1991. pap. text 29.95 (*0-8403-6739-2*) Kendall-Hunt.
McDonough, Larry, et al. MapView User's Guide. LC 93-10349. 1993. pap. 9.00 (*0-8330-1363-7*, MR-160-AF/A) Rand Corp.
McDonough, Lynn, jt. auth. see Woodland, Leanne.
McDonough, Maitland. The 50 Most Erotic Films of All Times. (Illus.). 256p. 1995. pap. 19.95 (*0-8065-1697-6*, Citadel Pr) Carol Pub Group.
McDonough, Marjorie. Emergency! CE Booklet. 32p. pap. text 35.95 (*0-7817-1896-1*) Lppncott W & W.
McDonough, Mark G., jt. auth. see Harrison, Michael M.
McDonough, Mark K., jt. auth. see DePetrillo, Paolo B.
McDonough, Martin. Calculus: CLEP & AP Subject Examination. (Scholarship Exam Ser.). 1978. pap. 8.95 (*0-668-03802-0*, ARCO) Macmillan.
***McDonough, Mary E.** God's Plan of Redemption. 1999. pap. text. write for info. (*0-7363-0718-4*) Living Stream Ministry.
Mcdonough, Michael. Malaparte: A House Like Me. LC 99-24603. 200p. 1999. 50.00 (*0-609-60378-7*) Crown Pub Group.
McDonough, Michael, et al, eds. Technological Powers & the Person: Nuclear Energy & Reproduction Technology: Proceedings of the 1983 Bishops' Workshop. LC 84-1933. (Illus.). 500p. (Orig.). 1983. pap. 15.95 (*0-935372-12-1*) NCBC.
McDonough, Patricia A. Without Keys: My 15 Weeks with the Street People. LC 96-216387. (Illus.). 427p. 1996. pap. 24.00 (*0-9653467-0-6*); lib. bdg. 42.00 (*0-9653467-1-4*) Terra Sancta.
McDonough, Patricia M. Choosing Colleges: How Social Class & Schools Structure Opportunity. LC 96-47380. 174p. (C). 1997. text 50.50 (*0-7914-3477-X*); pap. text 16.95 (*0-7914-3478-8*) State U NY Pr.
McDonough, Peter. Men Astutely Trained: A History of the Jesuits in the American Century. 618p. 1991. text 29.95 (*0-02-920527-1*) Free Pr.
— Power & Ideology in Brazil. LC 81-47147. 360p. 1981. reprint ed. pap. 111.60 (*0-608-02996-3*, 206322200004) Bks Demand.
McDonough, Peter, et al. The Cultural Dynamics of Democratization in Spain. LC 98-15273. (Illus.). 288p. 1998. text 39.95 (*0-8014-3516-1*) Cornell U Pr.
McDonough, Peter W., ed. Seismic Design Guide for Natural Gas Distributors. LC 95-23678. (Monograph Ser.: No. 9). 104p. 1995. 26.00 (*0-7844-0105-5*) Am Soc Civil Eng.
McDonough, R. P., jt. auth. see Brallier, Jess M.
McDonough, Richard. The Argument of the "Tractatus" Its Relevance to Contemporary Theories of Logic, Language, Mind, & Philosophical Truth. LC 85-9916. (SUNY Series in Logic & Language). 311p. (C). 1986. pap. text 21.95 (*0-88706-153-2*) State U NY Pr.
McDonough, Robert E. No Other World. (Cleveland Poets Ser.: No. 44). 64p. (Orig.). 1988. pap. 6.00 (*0-914946-72-2*) Cleveland St Univ Poetry Ctr.
McDonough, Robert N. & Whalen, A. D. Detection of Signals in Noise. 2nd ed. LC 94-24910. (Illus.). 495p. 1995. text 92.00 (*0-12-744852-7*) Acad Pr.
McDonough, Robert N., jt. auth. see Curlander, John C.
McDonough, Sheila. Gandhi's Responses to Islam. (C). 1994. 14.00 (*81-246-0035-X*, Pub. by DK Pubs Ind) S Asia.
McDonough, Steven. Strategy & Skill in Learning a Foreign Language. LC 95-5125. 160p. 1995. pap. 18.95 (*0-340-59109-9*) OUP.
McDonough, Steven, jt. auth. see McDonough, Jo.
McDonough, Steven H. Psychology in Foreign Language Teaching. 2nd ed. (Illus.). 192p. 1987. pap. text 16.95 (*0-04-418006-3*) Routledge.
McDonough, Sue, jt. ed. see Angers, Trent.
McDonough, Sue, ed. see Angers, W. Thomas.
McDonough, Suzanne, jt. auth. see Garfield, Gary.
McDonough, Suzanne, jt. auth. see Garfield, Gary M.
McDonough, T., et al. Situationism: Art Politics Urbanism. 180p. 1997. pap. 32.00 (*84-89698-14-7*) Dist Art Pubs.
McDonough, Thomas R. The Architects of Hyperspace. 272p. 1987. pap. 2.95 (*0-380-75144-5*, Avon Bks) Morrow Avon.
McDonough, Tom, ed. see Rirdan, Daniel.
McDonough, W. F., jt. auth. see Hilst, Robert Dirk van der.
***McDonough, Will.** The NFL Century: The Complete Story of the National Football League, 1920-2000. LC 99-23696. (Illus.). 320p. 1999. 19.98 (*0-7651-1062-8*) Smithmark.
***McDonough, William.** Cradle to Cradle. 2000. text. write for info. (*0-86547-587-3*) N Point Pr.
McDonough, William, tr. see Donghi, Antonio.
McDonough, William, tr. see Schroer, Silvia.
McDonough, Yona. Between "Yes & I Do" Resolving Conflicts & Relieving Anxiety During Your Engagement. LC 97-49857. 208p. 1998. pap. text 12.00 (*0-8065-1967-3*, Citadel Pr) Carol Pub Group.
***McDonough, Yona.** The Doll with the Yellow Star. 2000. text (*0-8050-6337-4*) H Holt & Co.
— She's Got the Whole World in Her Hands. 2001. text (*0-8050-6338-2*) H Holt & Co.
McDonough, Yona Z. Eve & Her Sisters: Women of the Old Testament. LC 93-9378. (Illus.). 32p. (J). (gr. k up). 1994. 15.00 (*0-688-12512-3*, Grenwillow Bks) HarpC Child Bks.
***McDonough, Yona Zeldis.** The Barbie Chronicles: A Living Doll Turns Forty. LC 99-15725. 240p. 1999. per. 13.00 (*0-684-86275-1*, Touchstone) S&S Trade Pap.
— The Doll House Magic. LC 00-22432. (Illus.). 64p. (gr. 2-4). 2001. text 14.95 (*0-8050-6464-8*) H Holt & Co.
— Sisters in Strength: American Women Who Made a Difference. LC 99-31779. (Illus.). 48p. (J). 2000. 17.95 (*0-8050-6102-9*) H Holt & Co.
McDoom, Omar, jt. auth. see Martinot, Eric.
McDorman, Kathryne S. Ngaio Marsh. (Twayne's English Authors Ser.: No. 481). 190p. (C). 1991. 22.95 (*0-8057-6999-4*, Twyne) Mac Lib Ref.
McDorman, Ted L., jt. auth. see Bolla, Alexander J.
McDougal. Tess of the d'Urbervilles. (J). Date not set. pap. 13.32 (*0-395-78404-2*) HM.
— West with the Night. Date not set. text 15.96 (*0-395-77502-7*) HM.
— Writer's Craft: Grade 10. Date not set. text. write for info. (*0-395-73037-6*) HM.
— Writer's Craft: Grade 11. Date not set. text. write for info. (*0-395-73038-4*) HM.
— Writer's Craft: Grade 12. Date not set. text. write for info. (*0-395-73039-2*) HM.
— Writer's Craft: Grade 6. Date not set. text. write for info. (*0-395-73033-3*) HM.
— Writer's Craft: Grade 7. Date not set. text. write for info. (*0-395-73034-1*) HM.
— Writer's Craft: Grade 8. Date not set. text. write for info. (*0-395-73035-X*) HM.
— Writer's Craft: Grade 9. Date not set. text. write for info. (*0-395-73036-8*) HM.
***McDougal, Alan.** Mastering SWAPS Markets: A Step-By-Step Guide to Products, Applications & Risks. 208p. 1999. pap. 59.95 (*0-273-62588-8*) F T P-H.
McDougal, Charles. The Kulunga Rai: A Study in Kinship & Marriage Exchange. 1979. 70.00 (*0-7855-0315-3*, Pub. by Ratna Pustak Bhandar) St Mut.
— The Kulunge Rai: A Study in Kinship & Marriage Exchange. 1979. 60.00 (*0-7855-0229-7*, Pub. by Ratna Pustak Bhandar) St Mut.
— The Kulunge Rai: A Study in Kinship & Marriage Exchange. 170p. (C). 1989. 90.00 (*0-89771-125-4*, Pub. by Ratna Pustak Bhandar) St Mut.
McDougal, Dennis. Angel of Darkness. 1991. 19.95 (*0-446-51538-8*) Warner Bks.
— Angel of Darkness. (Illus.). 416p. 1992. mass mkt. 7.50 (*0-446-36302-2*, Pub. by Warner Bks) Little.
— Mother's Day. 1995. mass mkt. 5.99 (*0-449-14930-7*) Fawcett.
***McDougal, Dennis.** The Yosemite Murders. (Illus.). 2000. mass mkt. 6.99 (*0-345-43834-5*) Ballantine Pub Grp.
McDougal, Harold. All Things Are Possible: Hearing from the Heroes of Faith. 1997. pap. text 8.99 (*1-884369-32-4*) McDougal Pubng.
— Fundamentos de la Fe Christiena (Principles of Christian Faith) Una Serie de Estudios Biblicos para Sentar Bases. Nigh, Kepler, tr. (SPA.). 344p. 1998. pap. 13.99 (*1-884369-21-9*, Serenity Bks) McDougal Pubng.
— Laying Biblical Foundations. LC 99-180276. 162p. 1997. pap. 8.99 (*1-884369-03-0*) McDougal Pubng.
— Principles of the Christian Faith: A Biblical Study Series for Laying Foundations in Spirit Filled for Believers. 3rd rev. ed. 339p. 1997. pap. 13.99 (*1-884369-66-9*) McDougal Pubng.
— Speaking in Tongues: Understanding the Uses & Abuses of This Supernatural Phenomenon. 4th rev. ed. (Master Keys Ser.). 140p. 1997. pap. 7.99 (*1-884369-07-3*) McDougal Pubng.
— Who We Are in Christ: Experiencing Our True Potential Through Understanding Jesus Christ & His Work Through Us. (Master Keys Ser.). 1997. pap. 8.99 (*1-884369-08-1*) McDougal Pubng.
McDougal, Harold, ed. see Brown, Les.
McDougal, Harold, ed. see Heflin, Ruth W.
McDougal, Harold, ed. see Heflin, Ruth Ward.
McDougal, Harold, ed. see Heflin, Wallace H.
McDougal, Harold, ed. see Kirchner, Jerry.
McDougal, Harold, ed. see Pendry, Pattie.
McDougal, Jim & Wilkie, Curtis. Arkansas Mischief. LC 98-24342. 352p. 1998. 25.00 (*0-8050-5808-7*) H Holt & Co.
McDougal-Littell Staff. Daily Science Workout. (J). (gr. 1). 1994. pap., teacher ed. 26.64 (*0-395-68805-1*) HM.

M

An Asterisk (*) at the beginning of an entry indicates that the title is appearing for the first time.

— Daily Science Workout. (J). (gr. 2). 1994. pap., teacher ed. 26.64 (*0-395-68806-X*) HM.

— Daily Science Workout. (J). (gr. 3). 1994. pap., teacher ed. 26.64 (*0-395-68807-8*) HM.

— Daily Science Workout. (J). (gr. 4). 1994. pap., teacher ed. 26.64 (*0-395-68808-6*) HM.

— Daily Science Workout. (J). (gr. 5). 1994. pap., teacher ed. 26.64 (*0-395-68809-4*) HM.

— Daily Science Workout. (J). (gr. 6). 1994. pap., teacher ed. 26.64 (*0-395-68810-8*) HM.

McDougal-Littell Staff. Handwriting Connections. 6th ed. (Illus.). pap. 7.25 (*0-8123-7706-0*) McDougal-Littell.

McDougal, Luther L., 3rd & Felix, Robert L. Casenote Law Outlines Conflicts of Law. Goldenberg, Norman S. & Tenen, Peter, eds. (Law Outlines Ser.). (Orig.). (C). 1996. pap. text. write for info. (*0-87457-186-3*, 5070) Casenotes Pub.

McDougal, Luther L., 3rd, et al. American Conflicts Law, Cases & Materials. 3rd ed. (Michie Contemporary Legal Education Ser.). 250p. 1998. pap., teacher ed. 54.00 (*0-327-00483-5*, 1205710) LEXIS Pub.

McDougal, Luther L., III, et al. American Conflicts Laws: Cases & Materials. 3rd rev. ed. LC 98-85490. (Michie Contemporary Legal Education Ser.). 900p. (C). 1998. text 52.00 (*0-327-00188-7*, 12054-11) LEXIS Pub.

McDougal, Marianne, jt. auth. see Dowling, Barbara T.

McDougal, Myers S., & Associates Staff, et al. Studies in World Public Order. 1986. lib. bdg. 277.50 (*0-89838-900-3*) Kluwer Academic.

McDougal, Myres S. & Burke, William T. The Public Order of the Oceans: A Contemporary International Law of the Sea. LC 86-14171. (New Haven Studies in International Law & World Public Order: No. 5). 1987. lib. bdg. 316.50 (*0-89838-901-1*) Kluwer Academic.

McDougal, Myres S. & Reisman, W. Michael. International Law Essays: A Supplement to International Law in Contemporary Perspective. (University Casebook Ser.). reprint ed. pap. text 22.50 (*0-88277-484-0*) Foundation Pr.

McDougal, Myres S., et al. The Interpretation of Agreements & World Public Order: Principles of Content & Procedure. LC 93-39683. (New Haven Studies in International Law & World Public Order). 536p. 1994. lib. bdg. 200.00 (*0-7923-2569-9*) Kluwer Academic.

McDougal, Russel W. Mirror of Mind. LC 76-17152. 1977. pap. 8.95 (*0-917694-01-5*) Open Window.

***McDougal, Scarlett.** Have a Nice Life 1 - Start Here. (Illus.). (J). 2000. pap. 4.99 (*0-14-131020-0*, PuffinBks) Peng Put Young Read.

— Have a Nice Life 2. (Illus.). (J). 2000. pap. 4.99 (*0-14-131021-9*, PuffinBks) Peng Put Young Read.

McDougal, Stan. World's Greatest Golf Jokes. 176p. 1990. 4.98 (*0-89009-600-7*) Bk Sales Inc.

— World's Greatest Golf Jokes. (Illus.). 1983. pap. 4.95 (*0-8065-0831-0*, Citadel Pr) Carol Pub Group.

McDougal, Stan, ed. World's Greatest Golf Jokes. (Illus.). 180p. 1991. pap. 4.95 (*0-8216-2502-0*, Carol Paperbacks) Carol Pub Group.

McDougal, Stuart Y. Dante among the Moderns. LC 85-4804. (Illus.). 189p. reprint ed. pap. 58.60 (*0-608-06006-2*, 206633400008) Bks Demand.

— Made into Movies: From Literature to Films. 528p. (C). 1985. pap. text 43.50 (*0-03-063804-6*, Pub. by Harcourt Coll Pubs) Harcourt.

McDougal, W. S., et al. Manual of Burns. LC 78-18210. (Comprehensive Manuals of Surgical Specialties Ser.). (Illus.). 1978. 107.00 (*0-387-90319-4*) Spr-Verlag.

McDougal, W. Scott & Skerrett, Pat. Prostate Disease: A Massachusetts General Hospital Book. LC 95-15175. (Illus.). 368p. 1996. pap. 14.00 (*0-8129-2319-7*, Times Bks) Crown Pub Group.

McDougald, Charles C. The Marcos File. 356p. 1987. 22.95 (*0-940777-05-3*) SF Pubs.

McDougald, Dana. 100 More Research Topic Guides for Students. LC 99-17855. (Professional Guides in School Librarianship Ser.). 240p. 1999. 39.95 (*0-313-30852-7*) Greenwood.

McDougald, Dana & Bowie, Melvin M. Information Services for Secondary Schools. LC 96-29275. (Greenwood Professional Guides In School Librarianship Ser.). 144p. 1997. 35.00 (*0-313-29820-3*) Greenwood.

McDougald, Larry R. Handbook of Poultry Parasitology. Long, Peter L., ed. LC 83-2141. 250p. 1985. 29.50 (*0-03-062489-4*, Praeger Pubs) Greenwood.

McDougall & Reidelbach, Maria. Completely Mad: A History of the Comic Book & Magazine. (Illus.). 288p. 1999. reprint ed. 17.98 (*1-56731-127-X*, MJF Bks) Fine Comms.

McDougall, Allan K. John P. Robarts: His Life & Government. (Ontario Economic Council Research Studies). 352p. 1986. text 30.00 (*0-8020-3426-8*) U of Toronto Pr.

McDougall, Angus & Hampton, Veita J. Picture Editing & Layout: A Guide to Better Visual Communication. LC 89-51942. (Illus.). 300p. 1990. text 27.50 (*0-9625137-0-9*) Viscom Pr.

McDougall, Anne, jt. auth. see Roberts-Phelps, Graham.

McDougall, Anne, jt. auth. see Squires, David.

McDougall, Betsey, ed. see Burke, Marcus.

McDougall, Bonnie S. Mao Zedong's "Talks at the Yan'an Conference on Literature & Art" A Translation of the 1943 Text with Commentary. LC 80-18443. (Michigan Monographs in Chinese Studies: No. 39). 112p. 1980. pap. text 15.00 (*0-89264-039-1*) Ctr Chinese Studies.

McDougall, Bonnie S., jt. auth. see Louie, Kam.

McDougall, Bonnie S., tr. see Anyi, Wang.

McDougall, Bonnie S., tr. see Bei Dao.

McDougall, Bonnie S., tr. see Tao, Pei.

McDougall, Bryce. My Child Is Gay: How Parents React When They Hear the News. 189p. 1998. pap. 12.95 (*1-86448-658-9*) IPG Chicago.

McDougall, Carl. Early Days of a Better Nation. 220p. 1999. text 34.95 (*1-85410-640-6*, Pub. by Aurum Pr) London Brdge.

McDougall, Colin. Execution. 233p. 1988. pap. 5.95 (*0-7715-9280-9*) Genl Dist Srvs.

McDougall, Derek. The International Politics of the New Asia Pacific. LC 97-13573. 260p. 1997. 55.00 (*1-55587-723-0*); pap. 19.95 (*1-55587-728-1*) L Rienner.

McDougall, Dorothy. Madeleine de Scudery: Her Romantic Life & Death. LC 72-80149. (Illus.). 1972. reprint ed. 26.95 (*0-405-08764-0*, Pub. by Blom Pubns) Ayer.

McDougall, Douglas, jt. auth. see Haylock, Derek.

McDougall, Duncan. Annals of Astoria: The Headquarters Log of the Pacific Fur Company on the Columbia River, 1811-1813. Jones, Robert F., ed. xv, 210p. 1999. 30.00 (*0-8232-1763-9*) Fordham.

McDougall, E. Ann, ed. Sustainable Agriculture in Africa. LC 89-81235. (Comparative Studies in African-Caribbean Literature Ser.). 345p. (C). 1990. 45.00 (*0-86543-147-7*); pap. 14.95 (*0-86543-148-5*) Africa World.

McDougall, Elizabeth, ed. Pedro Cano: Jornadas. LC 88-60324. (Illus.). 77p. (Orig.). (C). 1988. text 20.00 (*0-685-37293-6*) Meadows Mus.

McDougall, Elizabeth, ed. see Sullivan, Edward J.

McDougall, Elspeth M., jt. ed. see Clayman, Ralph V.

***McDougall, Fiona.** Tibetan Journal. (Illus.). 144p. 2000. 14.95 (*0-89087-982-6*) Celestial Arts.

McDougall, Frances H. Shahmah in Pursuit of Freedom. LC 71-154082. (Black Heritage Library Collection). 1977. 34.95 (*0-8369-8793-4*) Ayer.

McDougall, Garry. Heritage Walks in New South Wales. (Illus.). 160p. (Orig.). 1993. pap. 9.95 (*0-86417-383-0*, Pub. by Kangaroo Pr) Seven Hills Bk.

McDougall, Harold A. Black Baltimore: A New Theory of Community. LC 92-32548. 288p. 1993. 49.95 (*1-56639-037-0*) Temple U Pr.

— Black Baltimore: A New Theory of Community. LC 92-32548. 288p. 1993. pap. 22.95 (*1-56639-193-8*) Temple U Pr.

McDougall, Harriette. Sketches of Our Life at Sarawak. (Illus.). 296p. 1992. reprint ed. text 45.00 (*0-19-588583-X*) OUP.

McDougall, I. Ross. Thyroid Disease in Clinical Practice. (Illus.). 344p. 1992. text 88.50 (*0-19-520936-2*) OUP.

McDougall, Ian. Geochronology & Thermochronology by the 40ar/39ar Method. 2nd ed. LC 98-29075. (Illus.). 288p. 1999. text 90.00 (*0-19-510920-1*) OUP.

McDougall, Jain, ed. Diodorus Siculus - Lexicon in Diodorum Siculum, 2 vols., Set. (Alpha-Omega, Reihe A Ser.: Bd. LXIV). 1780p. 1983. write for info. incl. 3.5 hd (*3-487-07324-2*) G Olms Pubs.

McDougall, Jo. From Darkening Porches: Poems by Jo McDougall. LC 95-36191. 72p. 1996. pap. 12.00 (*1-55728-408-3*) U of Ark Pr.

— From Darkening Porches: Poems by Jo McDougall. 2nd ed. LC 95-36191. 72p. 1996. 20.00 (*1-55728-407-5*) U of Ark Pr.

— Towns Facing Railroads. 64p. 1991. pap. 12.00 (*1-55728-199-8*) U of Ark Pr.

***McDougall, Jo.** The Woman in the Next Booth: Poems. 64p. 2000. reprint ed. pap. 12.95 (*1-886157-26-X*) BkMk.

McDougall, John. Canadian Pacific: A Brief History. LC 68-23392. 212p. reprint ed. pap. 65.80 (*0-608-12240-8*, 202383300034) Bks Demand.

— The New McDougall Cookbook. 1997. pap. 13.95 (*0-452-27465-6*, Plume) Dutton Plume.

McDougall, John & McDougall, Mary. The McDougall Quick & Easy Cookbook: Over 300 Delicious Low-Fat Recipes You Can Prepare in Fifteen Minutes or Less. 336p. 1999. pap. 19.95 (*0-452-27696-9*, Plume) Dutton Plume.

Mcdougall, John A. The McDougall Program. 448p. 1998. pap. 15.95 (*0-452-27266-1*, Plume) Dutton Plume.

McDougall, John A. The McDougall Program: Twelve Days to Dynamic Health. 448p. 1991. reprint ed. pap. 14.95 (*0-452-26639-4*, Plume) Dutton Plume.

— The McDougall Program for a Healthy Heart: A Life-Saving Approach to Preventing & Treating Heart Disease. (Illus.). 430p. 1998. text 25.00 (*0-7881-5356-0*) DIANE Pub.

— The McDougall Program for a Healthy Heart: A Life-Saving Approach to Preventing & Treating Heart Disease. large type ed. LC 96-46142. (Spec-Hall Ser.). 1997. lib. bdg. 25.95 (*0-7838-2013-5*, G K Hall Lrg Type) Mac Lib Ref.

— The McDougall Program for Maximum Weight Loss. 336p. 1995. pap. 13.95 (*0-452-27380-3*, Plume) Dutton Plume.

***McDougall, John A.** McDougall Program for Women: What Every Woman Needs to Know to Be Healthy for Life. 2000. pap. 14.95 (*0-452-27697-7*) NAL.

McDougall, John A. McDougall's Medicine: A Challenging Second Opinion. LC 85-21686. 298p. 1986. pap. 12.95 (*0-8329-0448-1*) New Win Pub.

McDougall, John A. & McDougall, Mary. The McDougall Quick & Easy Cookbook: Over 300 Quick & Easy Recipes for Delicious Low-Fat Meals. 1997. 25.95 (*0-614-27971-2*) NAL.

McDougall, John A. & McDougall, Mary A. The McDougall Plan. LC 83-19412. (Illus.). 352p. 1985. pap. 11.95 (*0-8329-0392-2*) New Win Pub.

McDougall, John N. The Politics & Economics of Eric Kierans: A Man for All Canadas. 320p. 1993. 55.00 (*0-7735-1122-9*, Pub. by McG-Queens Univ Pr) CUP Services.

McDougall, Joyce. The Many Faces of Eros: A Psychoanalytic Exploration of Human Sexuality. 256p. 1995. 30.00 (*0-393-70215-4*) Norton.

— Plea for a Measure of Abnormality. LC 92-29739. 493p. 1992. reprint ed. pap. text 39.95 (*0-87630-701-2*) Brunner-Mazel.

— Theaters of the Body: A Psychoanalytic View of Psychosomatic Illness. (C). 1989. 22.95 (*0-393-70082-8*) Norton.

— Theaters of the Mind: Illusion & Truth on the Psychoanalytic Stage. LC 91-20628. 320p. 1991. pap. text 28.95 (*0-87630-648-2*) Brunner-Mazel.

McDougall, Kay. Simple Task-Centered Exercises As an Aid to Social Work Training. 1977. 30.00 (*0-7855-0996-8*, Pub. by Natl Inst Soc Work) St Mut.

McDougall, Kay, jt. ed. see McCaughan, Nano.

McDougall, Kristin A., jt. auth. see Dunne, George C.

McDougall, Kristin A., jt. ed. see Howell, David G.

McDougall, Len. The Complete Tracker. LC 96-37815. (Illus.). 240p. (Orig.). 1997. pap. 14.95 (*1-55821-458-5*, 14585) Lyons Pr.

***McDougall, Len.** The Complete Tracker: The Tracks, Signs & Habits of North American Wildlife. 288p. 1999. 7.98 (*1-56731-326-4*, MJF Bks) Fine Comms.

McDougall, Len. Made for the Outdoors. (Illus.). 224p. 1995. pap. 12.95 (*1-55821-329-5*) Lyons Pr.

***McDougall, Len.** The Outdoors Almanac. LC 99-28384. (Illus.). 208p. 1999. pap. 16.95 (*1-58080-035-1*) Burford Bks.

— Outward Bound Wilderness Survival Handbook. (Illus.). 2001. pap. 14.95 (*1-58574-159-0*) Lyons Pr.

McDougall, Len. Practical Outdoor Survival: A Modern Approach. (Illus.). 148p. 1993. pap. 11.95 (*1-55821-228-0*) Lyons Pr.

***McDougall, Len.** The Snowshoe Handbook. 160p. 2000. pap. 12.95 (*1-58080-083-1*) Burford Bks.

McDougall, M. T. The Daiquiri Tree: A Higher Power Novel. 208p. (Orig.). 1993. pap. 10.95 (*0-9610330-7-X*) J Tabler-Bks.

McDougall, Marina, jt. ed. see Bellows, Andy Masaki.

McDougall, Marion G. Fugitive Slaves, 1619-1865. LC 75-154083. (Black Heritage Library Collection). 1977. 17.95 (*0-8369-8794-2*) Ayer.

McDougall, Mary, jt. auth. see McDougall, John.

McDougall, Mary, jt. auth. see McDougall, John A.

McDougall, Mary A. The McDougall Health-Supporting Cookbook, Vol. 1. LC 85-5056. 122p. (Orig.). 1985. pap. 9.95 (*0-8329-0393-0*) New Win Pub.

— The McDougall Health-Supporting Cookbook, Vol. II. LC 86-5606. (Orig.). 1986. pap. 9.95 (*0-8329-0422-8*) New Win Pub.

McDougall, Mary A., jt. auth. see DeRoche, Frederick W.

McDougall, Mary A., jt. auth. see McDougall, John A.

McDougall, Mary L. The Working Class in Modern Europe. (Problems in European Civilization Ser.). 176p. (C). 1975. pap. text 18.36 (*0-669-92833-X*) HM Trade Div.

McDougall, Nancy & Roper, Janet. Creative Coaching a Support Group for Children with ADHD. (Illus.). 300p. 1997. ring bd. 34.95 (*1-889636-06-1*) Youthlight.

McDougall, Richard, tr. Herculine Barbin: Being the Recently Discovered Memoirs of a Nineteenth-Century French Hermaphodite. 1980. pap. 10.36 (*0-394-73862-4*) Pantheon.

McDougall, Richard & Mauro, Jim. Solaris Internals: Architecture & Techniques Core Kernel Components, 1. 800p. 2000. 59.00 (*0-13-022496-0*) P-H.

McDougall, Richard, et al. Resource Management. LC 99-41140. 332p. (C). 1999. pap. text 42.00 (*0-13-025855-5*) P-H.

McDougall, Richard, tr. & intro. see Monnier, Adrienne.

McDougall, Ruth B. Tell Me a Story. LC 85-17214. (Illus.). 152p. (Orig.). 1985. pap. 7.95 (*0-89407-070-3*) Strawberry Hill.

McDougall, Scott. Candytown. (Sticker Stories Ser.). (Illus.). 16p. (J). (ps-1). 1998. mass mkt. 4.99 (*0-448-41860-6*, G & D) Peng Put Young Read.

McDougall, Scott. Peek-a-Boo Gingerbread House. LC 96-78084. (Lift & Look Board Book Ser.). 12p. (J). (ps up). 1997. bds. 4.95 (*0-448-41622-0*, G & D) Peng Put Young Read.

— The Sticker Gingerbread House. (Books & Stuff Ser.). 16p. (Orig.). (J). (gr. 1-5). 1996. pap. 7.95 (*0-448-40955-0*, G & D) Peng Put Young Read.

McDougall, Sean, jt. ed. see Catterall, Peter.

McDougall, Walter A. The Heavens & the Earth: A Political History of the Space Age. LC 97-16786. (Illus.). 580p. 1997. reprint ed. pap. 19.95 (*0-8018-5748-1*) Johns Hopkins.

***McDougall, Walter A.** Most Interesting Empire. 2000. 35.00 (*0-06-019789-7*); pap. 18.00 (*0-06-095755-7*) HarpC.

McDougall, Walter A. Promised Land, Crusader State. 288p. 1998. pap. 14.00 (*0-395-90132-4*) HM.

— Promised Land, Crusader State: The American Encounter with the World since 1776. LC 96-35467. 286p. 1997. 26.00 (*0-395-83085-0*) HM.

McDougall, William. The Group Mind. 2nd ed. LC 73-2976. (Classics in Psychology Ser.). 1976. reprint ed. 29.95 (*0-405-05148-4*) Ayer.

McDougall, William. An Introduction to Social Psychology. 451p. 100.00 (*1-85506-693-9*) Thoemmes Pr.

McDougall, William. Is America Safe for Democracy? Grob, Gerald N., ed. LC 76-46088. (Anti-Movements in America Ser.). 1977. lib. bdg. 19.95 (*0-405-09961-4*) Ayer.

— Religion & the Sciences of Life: With Other Essays on Allied Topics. LC 70-39108. (Essay Index Reprint Ser.). 1977. reprint ed. 23.95 (*0-8369-2700-1*) Ayer.

McDougall, William, jt. auth. see Hose, Charles.

McDouglas, Charles C. The Buddha, the Gold, & the Myth: How Marcos Looted the Central Bank. LC 97-69003. viii, 265p. 1998. pap. 14.95 (*0-940777-03-7*) SF Pubs.

McDouglas, Myres S. & Feliciano, Florentino P. The International Law of War: Transnational Coercion & World Public Order. LC 93-41147. (New Haven Studies in International Law & World Public Order: Vol. 9). 1994. lib. bdg. 314.00 (*0-7923-2584-2*) Kluwer Academic.

McDougle, Valli T., contrib. by. Promise & Perils of Biotechnology: Genetic Testing. 1996. pap., teacher ed. 70.00 (*0-87969-494-7*) Cold Spring Harbor.

McDow, George, Jr. Booms & Mushrooms: The Saga of Susanvile & the McDow Boys from 1910 to 1930. (Illus.). 171p. 1988. pap. 12.95 (*0-938373-05-6*) Lahontan Images.

— Maggie Greeno: The Life of Margaret Ann Wallace Greeno. LC 95-215243. (Illus.). 272p. (Orig.). 1995. pap. 18.95 (*0-938373-15-3*) Lahontan Images.

McDow, Malcolm & Reid, Alvin L. Firefall: How God Has Shaped History Through Revivals. LC 97-15830. 384p. 1997. pap. text 17.99 (*0-8054-1241-7*) Broadman.

McDow, Stephen R. Atmospheric Organic Aerosols. Date not set. 75.00 (*1-56670-129-5*) Lewis Pubs.

McDowall. Thomas Hardy. 1972. 59.95 (*0-8490-1197-3*) Gordon Pr.

McDowall, Arthur, tr. see Flausbert, Gustave.

McDowall, Arthur S. Ruminations. LC 68-22925. (Essay Index Reprint Ser.). 1977. 17.95 (*0-8369-0646-2*) Ayer.

McDowall, David. Britain in Close-Up. LC 92-18031. 1993. pap. text. write for info. (*0-582-06461-9*) Longman.

— The Kurds: A Nation Denied. (Illus.). 200p. pap. 17.95 (*1-873194-15-3*, Pub. by Minority Rts Pubns) Paul & Co Pubs.

— The Kurds: A Nation Denied. (Illus.). 200p. 1992. text 49.95 (*1-873194-30-7*, Pub. by Minority Rts Pubns) Paul & Co Pubs.

— A Modern History of the Kurds. 472p. 1996. 45.00 (*1-85043-653-3*, Pub. by I B T) St Martin.

***McDowall, David.** Modern History of the Kurds. rev. ed. 1999. pap. 19.95 (*1-86064-535-6*, Pub. by I B T) St Martin.

McDowall, David. Palestine & Israel: The Uprising & Beyond. (Illus.). 335p. 1991. reprint ed. pap. 16.95 (*0-520-07653-2*, Pub. by U CA Pr) Cal Prin Full Svc.

— The Palestinians: The Road to Nationhood. 224p. pap. 19.95 (*1-873194-90-0*, Pub. by Minority Rts Pubns) Paul & Co Pubs.

— The Palestinians: The Road to Nationhood. (Illus.). 224p. 1995. 24.95 (*1-873194-70-6*, Pub. by Minority Rts Pubns) Paul & Co Pubs.

McDowall, David, et al. Interrupted Time Series Analysis. (Quantitative Applications in the Social Sciences Ser.: Vol. 21). (Illus.). 96p. 1980. pap. 10.95 (*0-8039-1493-8*) Sage.

McDowall, Duncan. Steel at the Sault: Francis H. Clergue, Sir James Dunn, & the Algoma Steel Corporation, 1901-1956. 352p. 1988. pap. text 18.95 (*0-8020-6736-0*) U of Toronto Pr.

— Steel at the Sault: Francis H. Clergue, Sir James Dunn, & the Algoma Steel Corporation, 1901-1956. LC 85-115719. (Illus.). 348p. reprint ed. pap. 107.90 (*0-8357-3768-3*, 203649700003) Bks Demand.

McDowall, Duncan, jt. ed. see Marchildon, Gregory P.

McDowall, Frances & McDowall, Nicolas. The Dream Song of Olaf Asteson: A Fragment of a Norwegian Folk Epic C. 400 A.D. 84p. 1993. 95.00 (*0-907664-38-5*, Pub. by Old Stiles) St Mut.

— Robin Tanner & the Old Stile Press. limited ed. 120p. 1993. pap. 200.00 (*0-907664-35-0*, Pub. by Old Stiles) St Mut.

McDowall, Nicolas. A Wall in Wales. 1963. 70.00 (*0-907664-27-X*, Pub. by Old Stiles) St Mut.

McDowall, Nicolas, jt. auth. see McDowall, Frances.

McDowall, R. J. The Whiskies of Scotland. 4th rev. ed. LC 87-21962. (Illus.). 184p. 1987. pap. 11.95 (*0-941533-06-9*, NAB) I R Dee.

McDowall, William. Burns in Dumfriesshire. 3rd ed. LC 74-144516. reprint ed. 29.50 (*0-404-08518-0*) AMS Pr.

McDowell. Con Todo Mi Amor Papa.Tr. of Love you, Dad. (SPA.). 131p. 1992. pap. write for info. (*0-614-27016-2*) Editorial Unilit.

— Jean Paul Gaultier. 2000. 35.00 (*0-8478-2163-3*, Pub. by Rizzoli Intl) St Martin.

— Juvenile Delinquency: The/United States & the United Kingdom. LC 98-43701. 1999. text 59.95 (*0-312-22204-1*) St Martin.

— La Mejor Forma de Resolver, Conflictos. (Serie Enfoque a la Familia - Focus on the Family Ser.).Tr. of Resolving Conflicts. (SPA.). 27p. 1995. pap. write for info. (*0-614-27079-0*) Editorial Unilit.

McDowell & Hart. Listening Plus. 1992. pap. text. write for info. (*0-17-556150-8*) Addison-Wesley.

McDowell, A.G. Village Life in Ancient Egypt: Laundry Lists & Love Songs. LC 98-47423. (Illus.). 298p. 1999. text 70.00 (*0-19-814998-0*) OUP.

McDowell, Banks. The Crisis in Insurance Regulation. LC 93-11891. 192p. 1994. 59.95 (*0-89930-853-8*, Quorum Bks) Greenwood.

— Deregulation & Competition in the Insurance Industry. LC 88-32391. 158p. 1989. 65.00 (*0-89930-381-1*, MDT/, Quorum Bks) Greenwood.

— Ethical Conduct & the Professional's Dilemma: Choosing Between Service & Success. LC 91-18. 208p. 1991. 52.95 (*0-89930-596-2*, MTJ, Quorum Bks) Greenwood.

***McDowell, Banks.** Ethics & Excuses: The Crisis in Professional Responsibility. LC 99-462239. 184p. 2000. 59.95 (*1-56720-386-8*, Quorum Bks) Greenwood.

McDowell, Bart. Inside the Vatican. Kogod, Charles M. & Newhouse, Elizabeth L., eds. (Illus.). 1991. 41.95 (*0-87044-858-7*) Natl Geog.

— Inside the Vatican. Kogod, Charles M. & Newhouse, Elizabeth L., eds. (Illus.). 232p. 1993. 34.50 (*0-87044-857-9*) Natl Geog.

McDowell, Bert, Jr. From Pilot to Poet. (Illus.). 160p. (Orig.). 1990. pap. 14.95 (*0-89745-137-6*) Sunflower U Pr.

McDowell, Betty L., jt. auth. see McDowell, W. Jack.

***McDowell, Bruce A. & Zaka, Anees.** Muslims & Christians at the Table: Promoting Biblical Understanding among North American Muslims. LC 99-45496. 342p. 1999. pap. 14.99 (*0-87552-473-7*) P & R Pubng.

McDowell, Bruce D., ed. see National Research Council Staff.

McDowell, C. Forest. The Sanctuary Garden. LC 98-12770. 192p. 1998. per. 14.00 (*0-684-84637-3*) S&S Trade Pap.

McDowell, C. Forrest. Leisure Wellness Series. Incl. Assessing Your Leisurestyle & Formulating Strategies. 1983. 2.25 (*0-942064-06-2*); Concepts & Principles. 1.50 (*0-942064-02-X*); Coping Strategies & Managing Stress. 1983. 1.75 (*0-942064-07-0*); Identity & Social Roles. 1983. 1.75 (*0-942064-04-6*); Intimate Relationships. 1983. 1.00 (*0-942064-03-8*); Introduction. 1983. 2.25 (*0-942064-01-1*); Managing Attitudes, Affirmation & Assertion. 1983. 2.00 (*0-942064-08-9*); Managing Economics, Time & Cultural Forces. 1983. 1.75 (*0-942064-09-7*); Strategies for Fitness. 1983. 1.50 (*0-942064-05-4*); 1983. 12.95 (*0-942064-00-3*); 1983. write for info. (*0-318-57603-1*) Cortesia Pr.

***McDowell, C. Forrest & Clark-McDowell, Tricia.** Home Composting Made Easy. (Illus.). 32p. 1998. pap. 2.95 (*0-942064-74-7*) Cortesia Pr.

McDowell, Carol J. History of the Band Program at Jackson High School: Jackson, Missouri, 1920-1998. LC 98-91658. (Illus.). 256p. 1999. pap. 29.95 (*0-934426-86-4*) NAPSAC Reprods.

McDowell, Caroline J. Judd. Philip Judd & His Descendants. 291p. 1997. reprint ed. pap. 44.00 (*0-8328-9365-X*); reprint ed. lib. bdg. 54.00 (*0-8328-9364-1*) Higginson Bk Co.

McDowell, Charles P. Criminal Justice in the Community. 2nd ed. LC 92-70235. (Illus.). 482p. (C). 1993. pap. 35.95 (*0-87084-559-4*) Anderson Pub Co.

McDowell, Charles P., ed. see Andrews, Paul M.

McDowell, Charlie, jt. auth. see Pohl, Ira.

McDowell, Christopher. A Tamil Asylum Diaspora: Sri Lankan Migration, Settlement & Politics in Switzerland. LC 96-18377. (Refugee & Forced Migration Studies: Vol. 1). (Illus.). 288p. 1996. 59.95 (*1-57181-917-7*) Berghahn Bks.

McDowell, Christopher, ed. Understanding Impoverishment: The Consequences of Development-Induced Displacement. LC 96-42. (Refugee & Forced Migration Studies: Vol. 2). 208p. 1996. 55.00 (*1-57181-916-9*); pap. 18.95 (*1-57181-927-4*) Berghahn Bks.

***McDowell, Cindy Secrest.** Southern Style Christmas. 48p. 1999. 15.99 (*0-87788-781-0*, H Shaw Pubs) Waterbrook Pr.

***McDowell, Colin.** Fashion Today. (Illus.). 2000. 69.95 (*0-7148-3897-7*) Phaidon Pr.

McDowell, Colin. Hats: Status, Style, & Glamour. LC 96-61426. (Illus.). 224p. 1997. pap. 27.50 (*0-500-27944-6*, Pub. by Thames Hudson) Norton.

***McDowell, Colin.** Jean Paul Gaultier. (Illus.). 2001. 19.95 (*0-670-89230-0*, Viking Studio) Studio Bks.

McDowell, Colin. The Man of Fashion: Peacock Males & Perfect Gentlemen. LC 97-60245. (Illus.). 208p. 1997. 50.00 (*0-500-01797-2*, Pub. by Thames Hudson) Norton.

***McDowell, Colin.** Manolo Blahnik. 208p. 2000. 50.00 (*0-06-019684-X*, HarpCollins) HarperTrade.

McDowell, Colin. Shoes: Fashion & Fantasy. LC 93-61542. (Illus.). 224p. 1994. pap. 24.95 (*0-500-27755-9*, Pub. by Thames Hudson) Norton.

McDowell, Danny B., jt. auth. see Mills, Larry W.

McDowell, David. Palestine & Israel: The Uprising & Beyond. 1990. 40.00 (*0-520-06902-1*, Pub. by U CA Pr) Cal Prin Full Svc.

McDowell, David L. & Ellis, Rod, eds. Advances in Multiaxial Fatigue STP 1191. LC 93-11048. (Special Technical Publication Ser.). (Illus.). 465p. 1993. text 108.00 (*0-8031-1862-7*, STP1191) ASTM.

McDowell, David L., ed. see ASTM Committee E-8 on Fatigue & Fracture.

McDowell, David L., jt. ed. see Miller, Keith J.

***McDowell, David M.** Substance Abuse: From Principles to Practice. LC 99-13996. 250p. 1999. pap. 24.95 (*0-87630-889-2*) Brunner-Mazel.

McDowell, Deborah, ed. see Larsen, Nella.

McDowell, Deborah E. The Changing Same: Black Women's Literature, Criticism, & Theory. LC 94-10663. 224p. 1995. 39.95 (*0-253-33629-5*); pap. 14.95 (*0-253-20926-9*) Ind U Pr.

— Leaving Pipe Shop. LC 96-48173. 1997. 22.50 (*0-684-81449-8*) S&S Trade.

— Leaving Pipe Shop: Memories of Kin. 288p. 1998. pap. 13.00 (*0-393-31843-5*) Norton.

McDowell, Deborah E., ed. see Douglass, Frederick.

McDowell, Dottie. Mom's Check-Up. 104p. 1994. pap. 14.95 (*1-57326-019-3*) Core Ministries.

McDowell, Dottie & McDowell, Josh. The Right Choices Bible. LC 98-23019. (Illus.). (J). 1998. 16.99 (*0-8423-3907-8*) Tyndale Hse.

McDowell, Douglas S. Affirmative Action after the Johnson Decision: Practical Guidance for Planning & Compliance. 166p. 1988. 25.00 (*0-916559-14-9*) EPF.

— Alternative Dispute Resolution Techniques: Options & Guidelines to Meet Your Company's Needs. xviii, 114 p. (Orig.). 1993. pap. 25.00 (*0-916559-43-2*) EPF.

— Can an Educated Workforce Be a "Business Necessity"? 33p. 1991. pap. 10.00 (*0-614-06155-5*, 2025-PP-4040) EPF.

— "Disparate Impact" & "Business Necessity" An Assessment & Guidelines for the Civil Rights Debate. 68p. 1991. pap. 10.00 (*0-614-06158-X*, 2029-PP-4040) EPF.

McDowell, Douglas S., ed. The Civil Rights Act of 1991: Legislative History, 2 vols., Set. 1467p. (Orig.). 1992. pap. 120.00 (*0-916559-40-8*) EPF.

McDowell, Duncan. The Light: Brazilian Traction, Light & Power Co. Ltd., 1899-1945. (Illus.). 495p. (C). 1988. text 39.95 (*0-8020-5783-7*) U of Toronto Pr.

McDowell, Earl E. Interviewing Practices for Technical Writers. (Technical Communications Ser.). 251p. 1991. pap. text 28.47 (*0-89503-072-1*) Baywood Pub.

McDowell, Eleanor & McCormick, James, eds. Environment Scotland: Prospects for Sustainability. LC 98-74135. 5p. (C). 1999. text 65.95 (*1-84014-899-3*, Pub. by Ashgate Pub) Ashgate Pub Co.

McDowell, Elizabeth M., ed. Lung Carcinomas. LC 86-33361. (Current Problems in Tumor Pathology Ser.). (Illus.). 410p. 1987. text 72.00 (*0-443-03165-7*) Church.

McDowell, Elizabeth M. & Beals, Theodore F. Biopsy Pathology of the Bronchi. (Illus.). 410p. 1987. text 115.00 (*0-03-012119-1*, W B Saunders Co) Harcrt Hlth Sci Grp.

McDowell, Elizabeth V. Educational & Emotional Adjustments of Stuttering Children. LC 74-177022. (Columbia University. Teachers College. Contributions to Education Ser.: No. 314). reprint ed. 37.50 (*0-404-55314-1*) AMS Pr.

McDowell, Ernest. P-47 Thunderbolt. LC 99-189653. (Illus.). 64p. 1998. pap. 9.95 (*0-89747-393-0*, 6076) Squad Sig Pubns.

***McDowell, Ernest.** Seaplanes. (Illus.). 2000. 34.95 (*1-57427-111-3*) Howell Pr VA.

McDowell, Ernest R. Checkertails: The 325th Fighter Group in WWII. (Fighter Groups - Squadrons Ser.). (Illus.). 80p. 1994. pap. 12.95 (*0-89747-316-7*) Squad Sig Pubns.

— Flying Scoreboards: Aircraft Mission & Kill Markings. (Aircraft Specials Ser.). (Illus.). 64p. 1993. pap. 11.95 (*0-89747-305-1*) Squad Sig Pubns.

— FR-1 Fireball "Mini" in Action. (Mini in Action Ser.). (Illus.). 50p. 1995. pap. 5.95 (*0-89747-344-2*) Squad Sig Pubns.

McDowell, Eugene E., jt. auth. see Stillion, Judith M.

McDowell, Fletcher H., jt. ed. see Blass, John P.

McDowell, Frederick P. Caroline Gordon. LC 66-64592. (University of Minnesota Pamphlets on American Writers Ser.: No. 59). 48p. (Orig.). reprint ed. pap. 30.00 (*0-7837-2874-3*, 205758100006) Bks Demand.

— Ellen Glasgow & the Ironic Art of Fiction. LC 60-9551. 304p. reprint ed. pap. 94.30 (*0-7837-7026-X*, 204684100004) Bks Demand.

McDowell, Frederick P., ed. E. M. Forster: An Annotated Bibliography of Writings about Him. LC 73-18797. (Annotated Secondary Bibliography Series on English Literature in Transition, 1880-1920). 924p. 1976. 55.00 (*0-87580-046-7*) N Ill U Pr.

— Poet As Critic. LC 67-12675. 127p. reprint ed. 39.40 (*0-8357-9466-0*, 201476700093) Bks Demand.

McDowell, Gary L. Equity & the Constitution: The Supreme Court, Equitable Relief, & Public Policy. LC 81-16006. 196p. 1982. 24.00 (*0-226-55814-2*) U Ch Pr.

McDowell, Gary L. & Noble, Sharon L., eds. Reason & Republicanism: Thomas Jefferson's Legacy of Liberty. LC 97-8235. 350p. 1997. 68.50 (*0-8476-8520-9*); pap. 26.95 (*0-8476-8521-7*) Rowman.

McDowell, Gary L., jt. auth. see Hickock, Eugene, Jr.

McDowell, Gary L., jt. ed. see Sheehan, Colleen A.

McDowell, George L. & Sokolik, Merle, trs. from GEC. The Data of Euclid: Translated from the Text of Menge. LC 93-60045. (Illus.). 228p. (C). 1993. 40.00 (*0-9635924-1-6*); pap. 25.00 (*0-9635924-0-8*) Union Square.

***McDowell, Hilary.** On the Way to Bethlehem: Reflections on Christmas for Every Day in Advent. Halverson, Holly, ed. 160p. 2000. pap. 13.00 (*0-8358-0920-X*) Upper Room Bks.

McDowell, Hilary. Some Day I'm Going to Fly. 128p. 1995. pap. 6.95 (*0-687-85005-3*) Intl Pubs Mktg.

McDowell, Ian. Merlin's Gift. 256p. (Orig.). 1997. mass mkt. 5.99 (*0-380-78197-2*, Avon Bks) Morrow Avon.

— Mordred's Curse. 304p. (Orig.). 1996. mass mkt. 5.99 (*0-380-78195-6*, Avon Bks) Morrow Avon.

— The Reuters Handbook for Journalists. LC 92-5673. 192p. 1992. pap. 49.95 (*0-7506-0551-0*) Buttrwrth-Heinemann.

McDowell, Ian & Newell, Claire. Measuring Health: A Guide to Rating Scales & Questionnaires. 2nd ed. (Illus.). 544p. (C). 1996. text 62.50 (*0-19-510371-8*) OUP.

McDowell, J. Cristianismo (Christianity) Historia O Farsa (Hoax Or History?) (SPA.). 2.49 (*0-685-74923-1*, 498056) Editorial Unilit.

— Estudio de las Sectas.Tr. of Understanding the Cults. (SPA.). 168p. 1989. pap. 8.99 (*0-8297-0996-7*) Vida Pubs.

— Evidencia Que Exige un Veredicto.Tr. of Evidence That Demands a Verdict. 382p. 1982. pap. 13.99 (*0-8297-1370-0*) Vida Pubs.

— La Mejor Forma de Resolver, Conflictos. (Serie Enfoque a la Familia - Focus on the Family Ser.).Tr. of Resolving Conflicts. (SPA.). 87p. 1991. pap. 1.99 (*1-56063-131-7*, 497408) Editorial Unilit.

McDowell, Jack. Sports Illustrated Backpacking. 1989. pap. 9.95 (*1-56800-064-2*, Pub. by Sports Illus Bks) Natl Bk Netwk.

McDowell, Jack, jt. auth. see Ketels, Hank.

McDowell, Jack C. Power of Purpose: Your Pathway to Dynamic Living, Wealth, & Personal Success. LC 94-10904. 1993. pap. 14.95 (*0-9625485-1-0*) Epiphany GA.

McDowell, Jennifer, ed. Black Politics: A Study & Annotated Bibliography of the Mississippi Freedom Democratic Party. LC 68-58320. 1971. pap. 10.95 (*0-930142-02-0*) Merlin Pr.

McDowell, Jennifer, jt. auth. see Loventhal, Milton.

McDowell, Jim. Jose Narvaez the Forgotten Explorer: Including His Narrative of a Voyage on the Northwest Coast in 1788. LC 97-6599. (Spain in the West Ser.: Vol. XV). (Illus.). 192p. 1997. 32.50 (*0-87062-265-X*) A H Clark.

— Peace Conspiracy: Yishiro Fujimura: Warrior-Businessman. 264p. (Orig.). 1993. pap. write for info. (*0-9635944-0-0*) McBo Corp Pubs.

Mcdowell, Joan R. & Gordon, Derek, eds. Diabetes Caring for Patients in the Community. LC 96-25833. 273p. 1996. text 29.95 (*0-443-05295-6*) Church.

McDowell, John. Mind & World. LC 93-44418. 208p. (C). 1994. text 33.50 (*0-674-57609-8*, MCDMIN) HUP.

— Mind & World. LC 96-22268. 224p. 1996. pap. 17.50 (*0-674-57610-1*) HUP.

McDowell, John, tr. Theaetetus. (Clarendon Plato Ser.). 272p. 1977. pap. text 26.00 (*0-19-872083-1*) OUP.

McDowell, John & Hostetler, Bob. The Love Killer. LC 93-25122. (Powerlink Chronicle Ser.: Vol. 2). (YA). (gr. 6 up). 1993. pap. 9.99 (*0-8499-3509-1*) Word Pub.

McDowell, John, ed. see Evans, Gareth.

McDowell, John, jt. ed. see Evans, Gareth.

McDowell, John, ed. see Thompson, Stith.

***McDowell, John B.** Catholic Schools, Public Education & American Culture. 160p. 2000. pap. 9.95 (*0-87973-397-7*) Our Sunday Visitor.

McDowell, John H. Meaning, Knowledge, & Reality. LC 98-19801. 448p. 1999. text 39.95 (*0-674-55777-8*) HUP.

— Mind, Value & Reality. LC 97-38090. 384p. 1998. 35.00 (*0-674-57613-6*) HUP.

***McDowell, John H.** Poetry & Violence on Mexico's Costa Chica. LC 99-51010. (Music in American Life Ser.). (Illus.). 248p. 2000. text 39.95 (*0-252-02588-1*) U of Ill Pr.

McDowell, John H. Sayings of the Ancestors: The Spiritual Life of the Sibundoy Indians. LC 89-5435. 216p. 1989. 28.00 (*0-8131-1671-6*) U Pr of Ky.

— So Wise Were Our Elders: Mythic Narratives from the Kamsa. LC 93-5083. 296p. 1994. text 38.00 (*0-8131-1826-3*) U Pr of Ky.

McDowell, John M., jt. auth. see Greenwood, Michael J.

McDowell, Josh. El Amor Siempre Tiene Razon.Tr. of Love Is Always Right. (SPA.). 192p. 1997. pap. 11.99 (*0-311-46155-7*) Casa Bautista.

— El Anduvo Entre Nosotros.Tr. of He Walked among Us. (SPA.). 1995. 15.99 (*1-56063-372-7*, 498471) Editorial Unilit.

— Bien Plus Qu'un Charpentier. Cosson, Annie, ed. Flammanc, Solveng, tr. Orig. Title: More Than a Carpenter. 128p. 1982. mass mkt. 6.95 (*0-8297-1248-8*) Vida Pubs.

— Building Your Self-Image. 220p. 1986. 5.99 (*0-8423-1395-8*) Tyndale Hse.

— Christianity: Hoax or History. 96p. 1989. pap. 3.99 (*0-8423-0367-7*) Tyndale Hse.

— Como Preparar a Su Hijo, Decir No, Presiones Sexuales.Tr. of How to Help Your Child Say No to Sexual Pressure. (SPA.). 1990. pap. 5.99 (*0-945792-39-5*, 498403) Editorial Unilit.

— Como Prepararse para la Persecucion Que Se Avecina.Tr. of Coming Persecution. (SPA.). 208p. 1990. pap. 5.50 (*1-56063-439-1*, 494029) Editorial Unilit.

— Con Todo Mi Amor, Papa.Tr. of Love, Dad. (SPA.). 1990. pap. 5.99 (*1-56063-020-5*, 490225) Editorial Unilit.

***McDowell, Josh.** Conflicts with Others. LC 00-24467. (Friendship 911 Ser.). (Illus.). 64p. (gr. 8-12). 2000. pap. write for info. (*0-8499-3795-7*) Word Pub.

McDowell, Josh. El Cristianismo: Historia o Farsa? (Serie Guia de Bolsillo - Pocket Guides Ser.).Tr. of Christianity: Hoax or History?. (SPA.). 94p. 1995. 2.79 (*1-56063-024-8*, 498056) Editorial Unilit.

***McDowell, Josh.** Disconnected Generation: Saving Our Youth from Self-Destruction. 2000. pap. write for info. (*0-8499-4077-X*) Word Pub.

— Divorce of Parents. LC 00-23365. (Friendship 911 Ser.). (Illus.). 64p. (gr. 8-12). 2000. pap. write for info. (*0-8499-3794-9*) Word Pub.

McDowell, Josh. Don't Check Your Brain's Door. 1992. pap. text 9.99 incl. VHS (*0-8499-8371-1*, 7034) Word Pub.

— En Defensa del Cristianismo I.Tr. of Ready Defense I. (SPA.). 110p. 1995. 10.99 (*0-7899-0057-2*, 497515) Editorial Unilit.

McDowell, Josh. En Defensa del Cristianismo II.Tr. of Ready Defense II. 9.99 (*0-7899-0511-6*, 497516) Editorial Unilit.

McDowell, Josh. Escapa del Laberinto Moral. (Right from Wrong Ser.).Tr. of Out of the Moral Maze. (SPA.). 176p. 1996. pap., student ed., wbk. ed. 13.50 (*0-311-11084-3*) Casa Bautista.

— Escepticos Que Demandan un Veredicto. (Serie Guia de Bolsillo - Pocket Guides Ser.).Tr. of Skeptics Who Demanded a Verdict. (SPA.). 130p. 1995. 2.79 (*1-56063-266-6*, 498063) Editorial Unilit.

Evidence That Demands a Verdict, Vol. 1. rev. ed. LC 78-75041. 408p. 1979. pap. 16.99 (*0-8407-4378-5*) Nelson.

— Evidence That Demands a Verdict, Vol. II. rev. ed. LC 81-65403. 425p. 1992. 16.99 (*0-8407-4379-3*) Nelson.

— Evidence That Demands a Verdict - Chinese Edition. Han, Paul et al, trs. (CHI.). 544p. 1998. pap. 15.00 (*1-56582-011-8*) Christ Renew Min.

— The Father Connection: 10 Qualities of the Heart That Empower Your Children to Make Right Choices. 208p. 1996. pap. text 11.99 (*0-8054-6094-2*, 4260-94) Broadman.

***McDowell, Josh.** Finding True Love. LC 00-23363. (Friendship 911 Ser.). (Illus.). 64p. (gr. 8-12). 2000. pap. write for info. (*0-8499-3793-0*) Word Pub.

— Friendship 911. (Illus.). 156p. (gr. 8-12). 2000. pap. 12.99 (*0-8499-3789-2*) Word Pub.

— Friendship 911 Leaders Guide. (Illus.). 2000. 7.99 (*0-8499-3790-6*) Word Pub.

— God's Will, God's Best. 160p. (J). (gr. 7-12). 2000. pap. 10.99 (*0-7642-2328-3*) Bethany Hse.

McDowell, Josh. Hablemos del Sexo! (Serie Realidades - Realities Ser.).Tr. of Talking It Over. (SPA.). 32p. pap. 1.99 (*0-7899-0246-X*, 498149) Editorial Unilit.

— His Image... My Image. LC 84-70488. 168p. 1985. pap. 10.99 (*0-8407-4445-5*) Nelson.

— How to Be a Hero to Your Kids. 1993. pap. 10.99 (*0-8499-3826-0*) Word Pub.

— How To Help Your Child Say "No" to Sexual Pressure. 160p. 1987. pap. 10.99 (*0-8499-3093-6*) Word Pub.

— Josh McDowell's Counseling Youth in Crisis Resource. 1996. teacher ed. 199.99 incl. audio (*0-8499-1153-2*) Word Pub.

***McDowell, Josh.** Knowing God's Will. LC 00-23364. (Friendship 911 Ser.). (Illus.). 64p. (gr. 8-12). 2000. pap. write for info. (*0-8499-3798-1*) Word Pub.

— Libre para Decidir y Elegir lo Bueno: Edicion para Jovenes. (Es bueno Es Malo Ser.).Tr. of Setting You Free to Make Right Choices. (SPA.). 144p. (J). 1996. pap., student ed., wbk. ed. 11.95 (*0-311-11085-1*, Edit Mundo) Casa Bautista.

McDowell, Josh. Libre para Decidir y Elegir lo Bueno: Guia para el Lider. (Right from Wrong Ser.).Tr. of Setting You Free to Make Right Choices. (SPA.). 48p. 1996. pap., teacher ed. 6.95 (*0-311-11086-X*) Casa Bautista.

M

— Lo Que Deseo Mis Padres Sepan de Sexualidad.Tr. of What I Wish Parents Knew about Sexuality. (SPA.). 1994. pap. 5.99 (*0-8423-6523-0*, 498401) Editorial Unilit.

— Lo Que Deseo Que Mis Padres Sepan Acerca de Mi Sexualidad: Los Jovenes Hablan. Bruchez, Dardo, tr. from ENG. (SPA.). 210p. (Orig.). 1988. pap. 4.95 (*0-945792-03-4*) Editorial Unilit.

— Mas Que un Carpintero.Tr. of More Than a Carpenter. 1997. mass mkt. 3.99 (*0-7899-0356-3*, 497678) Editorial Unilit.

McDowell, Josh. More Than a Carpenter. 128p. 1977. mass mkt. 4.99 (*0-8423-4552-3*) Tyndale Hse.

— My Friend Is Struggling With-- Death of a Loved One. LC 00-24466. (Friendship 911 Ser.). (Illus.). 64p. (gr. 8-12). 2000. pap. write for info. (*0-8499-3791-4*) Word Pub.

McDowell, Josh. New Evidence That Demands a Verdict, Vol. 1. rev. ed. LC 99-47181. 800p. 1999. 29.99 (*0-7852-4219-8*) Nelson.

McDowell, Josh. La Nueva Tolerancia.Tr. of New Tolerance. write for info. (*0-7899-0604-X*, 497781) Editorial Unilit.

McDowell, Josh. Out of the Moral Maze: Workbook for College Students (Leader's Guide Included) 176p. (C). 1995. pap., teacher ed., wbk. ed. 11.95 (*0-8054-9832-X*, 7800-07) Broadman.

***McDowell, Josh.** El Padre Que Yo Quiero Ser. de Smith, Josie, tr.Tr. of Father Connection. (SPA.). 176p. 1998. pap. text 10.99 (*0-311-46157-3*, Edit Mundo) Casa Bautista.

— Past Sexual Abuse. (Friendship 911 Ser.). (Illus.). 64p. (gr. 8-12). 2000. pap. write for info. (*0-8499-3797-3*) Word Pub.

— Por Que Decir No al Sexo?Tr. of Why Say No to Sex?. (SPA.). 4.99 (*0-7899-0213-3*, 495030) Editorial Unilit.

McDowell, Josh. Por Que Esperar? Lo Que de Necesita Saber Sobre de Crisis Sexual.Tr. of Why Wait? What You Need to Know about the Teen Sexuality Crisis. (SPA.). 495p. 1987. pap. 12.99 (*0-945792-48-4*, 498402) Editorial Unilit.

— A Ready Defense. LC 92-41360. 496p. (Orig.). 1992. reprint ed. pap. 19.99 (*0-8407-4419-6*) Nelson.

— The Secret of Loving. (Living Bks.). 333p. 1986. reprint ed. mass mkt. 5.99 (*0-8423-5845-5*) Tyndale Hse.

— El Secreto de Amar & de Ser Amado. Araujo, Juan S., tr. from ENG.Tr. of Secret of Loving. (SPA.). 272p. (C). 1988. pap. 9.99 (*0-88113-271-3*) Caribe Betania.

— See Yourself As God Sees You. LC 99-22146. 1999. pap. text 12.99 (*0-8423-1832-1*) Tyndale Hse.

— Setting You Free to Make Right Choices: Leader's Guide. 48p. 1995. pap., teacher ed. 5.95 (*0-8054-9829-X*, 7800-10) Broadman.

— Setting You Free to Make Right Choices: Workbook for Junior High & High School Students. 144p. (YA). (gr. 7-12). 1995. pap., wbk. ed. 9.95 (*0-8054-9828-1*, 7800-08) Broadman.

McDowell, Josh. Sexo, Culpa y Perdon. (Serie Guia de Bolsillo - Pocket Guides Ser.).Tr. of Sex, Guilt & Forgiveness. (SPA.). 2.79 (*0-7899-0012-2*, 498065) Editorial Unilit.

— Sigue la Verdad y Triunfa: Guia del Lider - Ninos. (Es bueno Es Malo Ser.).Tr. of Truth Works Leader's Guide: Older & Younger Children. (SPA.). 128p. (J). (gr. 1-6). 1997. pap., teacher ed. 12.95 (*0-311-11089-4*, Edit Mundo) Casa Bautista.

— Sigue la Verdad y Triunfa: Ninos Mayores. (Right from Wrong Ser.).Tr. of Truth Works. (SPA.). 40p. Date not set. pap. 5.95 (*0-311-11087-8*) Casa Bautista.

McDowell, Josh. Sigue la Verdad y Triunfa: Ninos Menores. (Right from Wrong Ser.).Tr. of Truth Works: Making Right Choices, Younger Children Ed.. (SPA.). 40p. 1997. pap. 5.50 (*0-311-11088-6*) Casa Bautista.

— Skeptics Who Demanded a Verdict. 96p. 1989. pap. 3.99 (*0-8423-5925-7*) Tyndale Hse.

— Thirteen Things You Gotta Know to Keep Your Love Life Alive & Well. 1994. pap. 6.99 (*0-8499-3534-2*) Word Pub.

M

*McDowell, Josh. Thoughts of Suicide. (Friendship 911 Ser.). (Illus.). 64p. (gr. 8-12). 2000. pap. 3.99 (0-8499-3792-2) Word Pub.
— Los Tres Caras del Amor.Tr. of Givers, Takers & Other Kinds of Lovers. (SPA.). 4.50 (0-7899-0461-6, 495026) Editorial Unilit.
McDowell, Josh. Truth Matters: For You & Tomorrow's Generation. 208p. 1995. pap., wbk. ed. 13.95 (0-8054-9834-6, 7800-05) Broadman.
— Truth Matters: For You & Tomorrow's Generation Leader's Guide. 64p. 1995. pap., teacher ed. 6.95 (0-8054-9833-8, 7800-06) Broadman.
— Truth Works - Making Right Choices: Leader's Guide. 128p. 1995. pap., teacher ed. 12.95 (0-8054-9827-3, 7800-13) Broadman.
— Truth Works - Making Right Choices: Workbook for Children. 32p. (J). (gr. 1-3). 1995. pap., wbk. ed. 4.95 (0-8054-9831-1, 7800-12) Broadman.
— Truth Works - Making Right Choices: Workbook for Children. 32p. (J). (gr. 4-6). 1995. pap., wbk. ed. 4.95 (0-8054-9830-3, 7800-11) Broadman.
— Under Siege. (Powerlink Chronicle Ser.: No. 1). 192p. (J). 1992. pap. 8.99 (0-8499-3363-3) Word Pub.
*McDowell, Josh. Unplanned Pregnancy. (Friendship 911 Ser.). (Illus.). 64p. (gr. 8-12). 2000. pap. 3.99 (0-8499-3796-5) Word Pub.
— La Verdad Si Impora: Edicion para Adultos. (Es bueno Es Malo Ser.).Tr. of Truth Matters. (SPA.). 208p. 1995. reprint ed. pap., student ed., wbk. ed. 13.95 (0-311-11082-7, Edit Mundo) Casa Bautista.
McDowell, Josh. La Verdad Si Importa: Guia del Lider. (Right from Wrong Ser.).Tr. of Truth Matters. (SPA.). 60p. 1996. pap., teacher ed. 6.95 (0-311-11083-5) Casa Bautista.
— Vote of Intolerance. 1998. pap. 12.99 (0-8423-7816-2) Tyndale Hse.
McDowell, Josh. Won by One Video Curriculum. 1993. pap., teacher ed. 8.99 (0-8499-8080-1, 7142) Word Pub.
McDowell, Josh & Day, Dick. Why Wait? What You Need to Know About the Teen Sexuality Crisis. LC 87-194. 1987. pap. 14.99 (0-8407-4282-7) Nelson.
McDowell, Josh & Giesler, Norm. Love Is Always Right. 196p. 1996. pap. 12.99 (0-8499-3965-8) Word Pub.
McDowell, Josh & Hostetler, Bob. Don't Check Your Brains at the Door. (YA). (gr. 7 up). 1992. pap. 9.99 (0-8499-3234-3) Word Pub.
— Es Bueno o es Malo: Lo Que Usted Necesita Saber para Ayuder los Jovenes a Tomar Decisiones Correctas. (Right from Wrong Ser.).Tr. of Right from Wrong: What You Need to Know to Make Right Choices. (SPA.). 352p. 1996. 13.50 (0-311-11081-9) Casa Bautista.
— Handbook on Counseling Youth. 544p. 1996. pap. 18.99 (0-8499-3236-X) Word Pub.
— Josh McDowell's One Year Book of Family Devotions: A daily Devotional for Passing Biblical Values to the Next Generation. LC 97-17460. 383p. 1997. pap. 11.99 (0-8423-4302-4) Tyndale Hse.
— Josh McDowell's One Year Book of Youth Devotions: A Daily Adventure to Making Right Choices. LC 97-17458. 366p. (YA). (gr. 5-10). 1997. pap. 11.99 (0-8423-4301-6) Tyndale Hse.
— The New Tolerance. LC 98-27048. 1998. pap. 9.99 (0-8423-7088-9) Tyndale Hse.
— No Dejes Tu Cerebro en la Puerta.Tr. of Don't Check Your Brains at the Door. (SPA.). 208p. 1993. 9.99 (0-88113-197-0, B008-1970) Caribe Betania.
— Right from Wrong: What You Need to Know to Help Youth Make the Right Choices. LC 94-27539. 336p. 1994. pap. 14.99 (0-8499-3604-7) Word Pub.
— Right from Wrong: What You Need to Know to Help Youth Make the Right Choices. LC 94-27539. 1994. 19.99 (0-8499-1079-X) Word Pub.
— Thirteen Things You Gotta Know: To Make It As a Christian. LC 92-33490. (YA). 1992. pap. 6.99 (0-8499-3413-3) Word Pub.
— The Truth Slayers: A Battle of Right from Wrong. LC 94-47961. 192p. (J). 1995. pap. 10.99 (0-8499-3662-4) Word Pub.
McDowell, Josh & Jones, Bill. The Teenage Q & A Book. 160p. 1990. pap. 9.99 (0-8499-3232-7) Word Pub.
McDowell, Josh & Klein, Chuck. Sitiados!Tr. of Under Siege!. (SPA.). 208p. 1997. 9.99 (0-88113-303-5, B008-3035) Caribe Betania.
McDowell, Josh & Lewis, Paul. Givers, Takers & Other Kinds of Lovers. 119p. 1981. mass mkt. 4.99 (0-8423-1031-2) Tyndale Hse.
— Los Tres Caras del Amor, No. 26.Tr. of Givers, Takers & Other Kinds of Lovers. 96p. 1983. 6.99 (0-88113-289-6) Caribe Betania.
McDowell, Josh & Stewart, Don. Answers. 256p. (Orig.). 1986. mass mkt. 5.99 (0-8423-0021-X) Tyndale Hse.
— Answers to Tough Questions Skeptics Ask about the Christian Faith. LC 80-67432. 198p. 1980. pap. 10.99 (0-8407-4464-1, 402776) Nelson.
— Demonios, Brujeria y Ocultismo. (Serie Guia de Bolsillo - Pocket Guides Ser.).Tr. of Demons, Witches & the Occult. (SPA.). 84p. 1989. pap. 2.79 (0-945792-72-7, 498045) Editorial Unilit.
— Handbook of Today's Religions. 576p. 1983. 29.99 (0-8407-3501-4) Nelson.
— Reasons Skeptics Should Consider Christianity. (Living Bks.). 256p. 1986. mass mkt. 4.99 (0-8423-5287-2) Tyndale Hse.
— Respuestas a Preguntas Dificles.Tr. of Answers to Tough Questions. (SPA.). 216p. 1986. pap. 7.99 (0-8297-0689-5) Vida Pubs.
*McDowell, Josh & Stewart, Ed. Finding True Love: Interactive Discovery Book: Devotional & Journal for Youth. LC 00-24465. 144p. (YA). 2000. pap. 8.99 (0-8499-4080-X) Word Pub.
— Handling Conflicts: Interactive Discovery Book: Devotional & Journal for Youth. LC 00-24464. (YA). 2000. pap. 8.99 (0-8499-3788-4) Word Pub.
McDowell, Josh & Stewart, Ed. Vote of Intolerance. LC 97-11014. 400p. 1997. 19.99 (0-8423-3905-1) Tyndale Hse.
McDowell, Josh, et al. The Topsy-Turvy Kingdom. LC 96-18987. (Illus.). 48p. (J). 1996. 12.99 (0-8423-7218-0) Tyndale Hse.
McDowell, Josh, jt. auth. see McDowell, Dottie.
*McDowell, Joyce. Monitoring Inventory: Stocking the Shelves Workbook II. Woodburg, Debbie & Bosarge, Charlotte, eds. LC 99-69617. (Retailing Smarts Ser.). (Illus.). 80p. 2000. pap. 7.95 (1-56052-576-2) Crisp Pubns.
— Protecting Company Assets: Preventing Loss. Woodbury, Debbie, ed. LC 99-80075. (Retailing Smarts Ser.: Vol. 9). (Illus.). 80p. 2000. pap., wbk. ed. 7.95 (1-56052-574-6) Crisp Pubns.
— Protecting Company Assets: Promoting Safety. Woodbury, Debbie, ed. LC 99-80076. (Retailing Smarts Ser.: Vol. 10). (Illus.). 80p. 2000. pap., wbk. ed. 7.95 (1-56052-575-4) Crisp Pubns.
McDowell, Judith H., tr. see Rousseau, Jean-Jacques.
*McDowell, Katharine Sherwood Bonner. A Sherwood Bonner Sampler, 1869-1884: What a Bright, Educated, Witty, Lively, Snappy Young Woman Can Say on a Variety of Topics. Gowdy, Anne Razey, ed. LC 99-50682. 560p. 2000. text 42.00 (1-57233-067-8, Pub. by U of Tenn Pr) U Ch Pr.
McDowell, Kevin. Creative Job Search. 2nd rev. ed. (Illus.). 143p. 1999. pap. 15.95 (0-9670505-0-2, ES-90550-5) MN Dept Eco Sec.
McDowell, L. R. Minerals for Grazing Ruminants in Tropical Regions. 3rd ed. LC 97-20222. (Bulletin Ser.). 1997. write for info. (0-916287-23-8) Univ Fla Food.
McDowell, Lee R. Minerals in Animal & Human Nutrition: Comparative Aspects to Human Nutrition. Cunha, Tony J., ed. (Animal Feeding & Nutrition Ser.). (Illus.). 524p. (C). 1992. text 104.00 (0-12-483369-1) Acad Pr.
*McDowell, Lee R. Vitamins in Animal & Human Nutrition. 2nd ed. LC 00-27082. 809p. 2000. 89.95 (0-8138-2630-6) Iowa St U Pr.
McDowell, Lee R. Vitamins in Animal Nutrition: Comparative Aspects to Human Nutrition. Cunha, Tony J., ed. (Animal Feeding & Nutrition Ser.). 486p. 1989. text 100.00 (0-12-483372-1) Acad Pr.
McDowell, Lee R., ed. Nutrition of Grazing Ruminants in Warm Climates. (Animal Feeding & Nutrition Ser.). 1985. text 125.00 (0-12-483370-5) Acad Pr.
*McDowell, Lena M. Public Elementary & Secondary Education Statistics: School Year 1997-98. 17p. 1998. pap. 2.00 (0-16-049487-7) USGPO.
McDowell, Linda. Capital Culture: Gender at Work in the City. LC 97-7780. (Studies in Urban & Social Change). (Illus.). 256p. (C). 1997. text 62.95 (0-631-20530-6) Blackwell Pubs.
McDowell, Linda. Capital Culture: Gender at Work in the City. LC 97-7780. (Studies in Urban & Social Change). (Illus.). 256p. (C). 1997. pap. text 26.95 (0-631-20531-4) Blackwell Pubs.
McDowell, Linda. Gender, Identity & Place: Understanding Feminist Geographies LC 98-45467. 1999. pap. 19.95 (0-8166-3394-0) U of Minn Pr.
*McDowell, Linda. Gender, Identity & Place: Understanding Feminist Geographies LC 98-45467. 1999. write for info. (0-8166-3393-2) U of Minn Pr.
McDowell, Linda, ed. Undoing Place? A Geographical Reader. (Arnold Publications). (Illus.). 360p. 1997. pap. text 29.95 (0-340-67746-5) OUP.
Mcdowell, Linda, ed. Undoing Place? A Geographical Reader. (Arnold Publications). (Illus.). 360p. 1997. text 75.00 (0-340-67747-3) OUP.
McDowell, Linda & Sharp, Joanne P. Geography & Gender: A Glossary. LC 98-36481. (Arnold Publications). 384p. 1999. text 65.00 (0-340-70659-7) OUP.
*McDowell, Linda & Sharp, Joanne P., eds. A Feminist Glossary of Human Geography. (An Arnold Publication). 384p. 2000. pap. 24.95 (0-340-74143-0, Pub. by E A) OUP.
McDowell, Linda & Sharp, Joanne P., eds. Space, Gender, Knowledge: Feminist Readings. (Arnold Publications). (Illus.). 480p. 1997. text 60.00 (0-340-70019-X); pap. text 29.95 (0-340-67792-9) OUP.
McDowell, Linda, jt. auth. see Allen, John.
McDowell, Lisa, et al. 500 Tips for Research Students. 128p. 1997. pap. 19.95 (0-7494-1767-6, Kogan Pg Educ) Stylus Pub VA.
McDowell, Lucinda S. Quilts from Heaven: Finding Parables in the Patchwork of Life. gif. ed. LC 98-31315. (Illus.). 160p. 1999. 17.00 (0-8054-1099-6) Broadman.
McDowell, Lucinda S., ed. Women's Spiritual Passages: Celebrating Faith after 40. LC 95-44698. 240p. 1996. pap. 9.99 (0-87788-456-0, H Shaw Pubs) Waterbrook Pr.
McDowell, M. Math Workbook for FDSER 3D Answer. 1997. pap. 9.95 (0-442-31830-8, VNR) Wiley.
McDowell, M. C. & Crawford, H. W. Math Workbook for Foodservice/Lodging. (Hospitality, Travel & Tourism Ser.). 265p. 1988. pap. 39.95 (0-471-28875-6, VNR) Wiley.
McDowell, Marcia A. Signature Bets: A Guide to Recognizing Roulette Advantage Play. (Illus.). 60p. (C). Date not set. pap. text 19.95 (0-9648090-1-X) Cndlelight NV.
— Techniques of Casino Surveillance. (Illus.). 196p. (C). 1995. pap. text 32.50 (0-9648090-0-1) Cndlelight NV.
— Techniques of Casino Surveillance. 2nd rev. ed. (Illus.). 228p. 1998. spiral bd. 31.95 (0-9648090-4-4) Cndlelight NV.
*McDowell, Margaret. Poems from the Heart. 1999. pap. write for info. (1-58235-078-7) Watermrk Pr.
McDowell, Margaret B. Carson McCullers. (United States Authors Ser.: No. 354). 160p. 1980. 20.95 (0-8057-7297-9, Twyne) Mac Lib Ref.
— Edith Wharton. rev. ed. (Twayne's United States Authors Ser.). 168p. 1990. 32.00 (0-8057-7618-4, TUSAS 265) Macmillan.
McDowell, Marion, jt. frwd. see Eastin, Delaine.
McDowell, Marsha, jt. ed. see Dewhurst, C. Kurt.
McDowell, Martin R., jt. auth. see Bransden, Brian H.
McDowell, Michael. Toplin. (Illus.). 186p. 1985. lib. bdg. 22.50 (0-910489-11-4) Scream Pr.
McDowell, Michael S. Anonymous Sender. LC 96-3535. 349p. 1996. 22.95 (0-8420-2589-8) Scholarly Res Inc.
McDowell, Mildred. The Little People. LC 72-133255. (Story & Its Verse Ser.). (Illus.). 44p. (J). (gr. 1-2). 1971. 2.50 (0-87884-002-8) Unicorn Ent.
— The Squirrel & the Frog. LC 76-133256. (Story & Its Verse Ser.). (Illus.). 44p. (J). (gr. 1-2). 1971. 2.50 (0-87884-007-9) Unicorn Ent.
McDowell, Milton C. & Crawford, Hollie W. Math Workbook for Foodservice-Lodging. 3rd ed. (Illus.). 288p. 1988. pap. 44.95 (0-442-21872-9, VNR) Wiley.
McDowell, Nancy. The Mundugumor: From the Field Notes of Margaret Mead & Reo Fortune. LC 90-24915. (Series in Ethnographic Inquiry). (Illus.). 352p. (C). 1991. text 50.00 (1-56098-062-1) Smithsonian.
McDowell, Nicholas. Hemingway. (Life & Works Ser.). (Illus.). 112p. (YA). (gr. 7 up). 1989. lib. bdg. 25.27 (0-86592-298-5) Rourke Enter.
— Life & Works, 3 bks., Set. (Illus.). 448p. (J). (gr. 7 up). 1989. lib. bdg. 75.80 (0-86592-295-0) Rourke Enter.
— Life & Works, 4 bks., Set I, Reading Level 8. (Illus.). 448p. (J). (gr. 7 up). 1989. 59.80 (0-685-58807-6) Rourke Corp.
McDowell, Paula. The Women of Grub Street: Press, Politics, & Gender in the London Literary Marketplace 1678-1730. LC 97-44996. (Illus.). 360p. 1998. text 89.00 (0-19-818395-X); pap. text 24.95 (0-19-818449-2) OUP.
McDowell, Peggy & Meyer, Richard. The Revival Styles in American Memorial Art. LC 93-72851. (Illus.). 212p. 1994. 49.95 (0-87972-633-4); pap. 22.95 (0-87972-634-2) Bowling Green Univ Popular Press.
McDowell, Philip. Choosing & Using Four Bit Microcontrollers. LC 93-15660. 276p. 1993. text 75.00 (0-8247-9153-3) Dekker.
— Choosing & Using 4 Bit Microcontrollers. LC 94-152787. (Illus.). 268p. 1994. pap. 83.10 (0-608-04995-6, 206561300004) Bks Demand.
McDowell, R. B. Crisis & Decline: The Fate of the Southern Unionists. LC 98-120834. 240p. 1998. 34.95 (1-874675-92-9, Pub. by Lilliput Pr) Dufour.
— Land & Learning: Two Irish Clubs. 176p. 1993. 31.95 (1-874675-14-7) Dufour.
McDowell, R. Bruce. A Study of Colt Conversions & Other Percussion Revolvers. LC 97-176689. (Illus.). 464p. 1997. 39.95 (0-87341-446-2, FCOL) Krause Pubns.
McDowell, R. E. Dairying with Improved Breeds in Warm Climates. LC 93-81317. (Illus.). 10p. (C). 1994. pap. text 19.00 (1-880762-05-6) Kinnic Pubs.
— A Partnership for Humans & Animals. vii, 95p. 1991. pap. text 10.00 (1-880762-03-X) Kinnic Pubs.
McDowell, R. E., et al. Potential Commercial Dairying with Buffalo. (Illus.). 78p. (Orig.). 1995. pap. 10.00 (1-880762-07-2) Kinnic Pubs.
McDowell, Richard E. Simple Secrets of Home Mortgages: What 90,000,000 Homeowners Need to Know about Refinancing. (Illus.). 144p. (Orig.). 1997. pap. 16.95 (0-9656885-1-8) Smple Secrets Hme Mrtgages.
McDowell, Robert. The Diviners: A Book Length Poem. 90p. 1995. pap. 10.00 (1-885266-10-3, Pub. by Peterloo Poets) Story Line.
*McDowell, Robert, ed. Cowboy Poetry Matters: From Abilene to the Mainstream: Contemporary Cowboy Writing. LC 99-89819. 128p. 2000. pap. 17.95 (1-885266-89-8, Pub. by Story Line) Consort Bk Sales.
McDowell, Robert, ed. Poetry after Modernism. (New Criticism Ser.). 378p. 1991. 24.95 (0-934257-36-1) Story Line.
— Poetry after Modernism. 2nd rev. ed. LC 97-2209. 288p. 1998. pap. 17.95 (1-885266-34-0) Story Line.
McDowell, Robert, jt. auth. see Gross, Harvey.
McDowell, Robert, jt. auth. see Jarman, Mark.
McDowell, Robert, jt. auth. see Lavitt, Edward.
McDowell, Robert, tr. see Pavel, Ota.
McDowell, Robert B. Ireland in the Age of Imperialism & Revolution, 1760-1801. 750p. 1991. reprint ed. pap. text 45.00 (0-19-822167-3) OUP.
— The Irish Administration, 1801-1914. LC 75-35336. 328p. 1976. reprint ed. lib. bdg. 69.50 (0-8371-8561-0, MCIA, Greenwood Pr) Greenwood.
McDowell, Robert B., ed. see Burke, Edmund.
McDowell, Robert E. & Lavitt, Edward, eds. Third World Voices for Children. LC 71-169091. (Odarkai Book Ser.). (Illus.). 156p. (J). (gr. 5-9). 1981. 7.95 (0-89388-020-5, Odakai) Okpaku Communications.
McDowell, Ruth B. Pattern on Pattern: Spectacular Quilts from Simple Traditional Blocks. LC 90-29178. (Illus.). 160p. 1991. pap. 24.95 (0-8442-2631-9, Quilt Dgst Pr) NTC Contemp Pub Co.
— Piecing: Expanding the Basics. Lanzarotti, Sally, ed. LC 97-43176. (Illus.). 160p. 1998. pap. 27.95 (1-57120-041-X, 10166) C & T Pub.
— Ruth B. McDowell: Art & Inspirations. Aneloski, Elizabeth, ed. LC 96-10010. (Art & Inspirations Ser.: No. 1). (Illus.). 144p. (Orig.). 1996. pap. 29.95 (1-57120-015-0, 10139) C & T Pub.
— Symmetry: A Design System for Quiltmakers. Kuhn, Barbara K. & Nadel, Harold, eds. LC 93-40036. (Illus.). 144p. (Orig.). 1995. pap. 21.95 (0-914881-78-7, 10098) C & T Pub.
*McDowell, Sean & Willey, Ray. Josh McDowell's Youth Ministry Handbook: Making the Connection. LC 00-39921. 200p. 2000. pap. write for info. (0-8499-4209-8) Word Pub.
McDowell, Stephen & Beliles, Mark. In God We Trust: Tour Guide Featuring America's Landmarks of Liberty. enl. rev. ed. 256p. 1998. pap. 13.95 (1-887456-07-4) Providence Found.
Mcdowell, Stephen D. Globalization, Liberalization & Policy Change: A Political Economy of India's Communications Sector. LC 96-22553. (International Political Economy Ser.). 267p. 1997. text 49.95 (0-312-16280-4) St Martin.
McDowell, Stephen K. & Beliles, Mark A. Liberating the Nations: Biblical Principles of Government, Education, Economics, & Politics. 215p. 1993. pap. 12.95 (1-887456-01-5) Providence Found.
McDowell, Stephen K., jt. auth. see Beliles, Mark A.
*McDowell, Steve. Windows NT Kernel Debugging. Denn, Robert, ed. (Illus.). 300p. 2000. pap. 34.95 (1-56592-546-7) OReilly & Assocs.
*McDowell, Steve & Race, Phil. 500 Computing Tips for Trainers. 160p. 1999. pap. 25.00 (0-7494-2675-6, Kogan Pg Educ) Stylus Pub VA.
McDowell, Steve, jt. auth. see Race, Phil.
McDowell, Steven & Seyer, Martin D. USB Explained. LC 98-3619. 384p. 1998. pap. text 34.95 (0-13-081153-X) P-H.
*McDowell, Steven Dale. Chasing the Minnesota Moon. LC 99-91450. 1999. 25.00 (0-7388-0800-8); pap. 18.00 (0-7388-0801-6) Xlibris Corp.
*McDowell, Susan & Ray, Brian, eds. The Home Education Movement in Context, Practice & Theory: A Special Issue of the Peabody Journal of Education. 292p. 2000. pap. write for info. (0-8058-9757-7) L Erlbaum Assocs.
McDowell, Terry, ed. see Lee, Betsy.
*McDowell, Thelma. Leader's Guide: Light for the Journey: A Fresh Focus on Doctrine. 169p. 1999. pap., teacher ed. 14.95 (0-911866-47-7) LifeSprings Res.
McDowell, Vera. When Your Ox Is in the Ditch: Genealogical How-To Letters. LC 95-78281. 161p. 1996. pap. 19.95 (0-8063-1484-2, 3515) Genealog Pub.
McDowell, W. H. The History of BBC Broadcasting in Scotland, 1923-1983. 376p. 1993. text 79.00 (0-7486-0376-X, Pub. by Edinburgh U Pr) Col U Pr.
McDowell, W. J. The Incomparable Book. 13p. 1988. pap. 1.00 (0-85151-543-6) Banner of Truth.
McDowell, W. Jack & McDowell, Betty L. Liquid Scintillation Alpha Spectrometry. LC 93-8546. 160p. 1993. lib. bdg. 89.95 (0-8493-5288-6) CRC Pr.
McDowelle, James O., jt. auth. see Miller, Patricia S.
McDuell, Bob, et al, eds. Science: On Course for GCSE, NEAB Edition. 192p. 1998. pap., teacher ed. 48.00 (0-7487-3670-0, Pub. by S Thornes Pubs) Trans-Atl Phila.
— Science: On Course for GCSE, SEG Edition. 192p. 1998. pap., teacher ed. 48.00 (0-7487-3671-9, Pub. by S Thornes Pubs); pap., student ed. 24.00 (0-7487-3668-9, Pub. by S Thornes Pubs) Trans-Atl Phila.
— Science: On Course for GCSE, Universal Edition. 192p. 1998. pap., teacher ed. 48.00 (0-7487-3669-7, Pub. by S Thornes Pubs); pap., student ed. 24.00 (0-7487-3666-2, Pub. by S Thornes Pubs) Trans-Atl Phila.
McDuff, David, ed. Ice Around Our Lips. LC 88-51313. 208p. 1988. pap. 19.95 (1-85224-011-3, Pub. by Bloodaxe Bks) Dufour.
McDuff, David, jt. auth. see Gunnarsson, Olafur.
McDuff, David, ed. see Turgenev, Ivan Sergeevich.
McDuff, David, ed. & intro. see Babel, Isaac.
McDuff, David, tr. see Agren, Gosta.
McDuff, David, tr. see Bely, Andrei.
McDuff, David, tr. see Carpelan, Bo.
McDuff, David, tr. see Forsstrom, Tua.
McDuff, David, tr. see Ratushinskaya, Irina.
McDuff, David, tr. see Ratushinskaya, Irina.
McDuff, David, tr. see Sodergran, Edith.
McDuff, David, tr. see Tsvetaeva, Marina I.
McDuff, David, tr. see Tuominen, Mirjam, et al.
McDuff, David, tr. & intro. see Dostoyevsky, Fyodor.
McDuff, David, tr. & intro. see Tolstoy, Leo.
McDuff, Dusa & Salamon, Dietmar. Introduction to Symplectic Topology. 2nd ed. LC 98-26275. (Oxford Mathematical Monographs). (Illus.). 496p. 1999. pap. text 65.00 (0-19-850451-9) OUP.
— J-Holomorphic Curves & Quantum Cohomology. LC 94-25414. (University Lectures: Vol. 6). 207p. 1994. pap. 24.00 (0-8218-0332-8, ULECT/6) Am Math.
McDuff, Judith, tr. see Yeh, Ning.
McDuffee, Franklin. Church Records of Rochester, New Hampshire. 52p. 1984. pap. 6.50 (0-912606-21-5) Hunterdon Hse.
— Church Records of Rochester, NH. 1986. reprint ed. pap. 6.50 (0-935207-61-9) Danbury Hse Bks.
— History of Rochester, New Hampshire from 1722 to 1890, Vol. One. Hayward, Silvanus, ed. (Illus.). 378p. 1988. reprint ed. lib. bdg. 39.50 (0-8328-0069-4, NH0051) Higginson Bk Co.
— History of Rochester, New Hampshire, from 1722 to 1890, Vol. Two. Hayward, Silvanus, ed. (Illus.). 327p. 1988. reprint ed. lib. bdg. 33.50 (0-8328-0070-8, NH0052) Higginson Bk Co.
McDuffie, Dwayne. Prince: Alter Ego. Clark, Margaret, ed. 32p. 1991. pap. 2.00 (1-56389-058-5, Piranha Pr) DC Comics.
McDuffie, Harriet E. Transitions. 416p. 1994. per. 47.95 (0-8403-9019-X, 40901901) Kendall-Hunt.
McDuffie, Helen H., et al, eds. Human Sustainability in Agriculture: Health, Safety, Environment. 656p. 1995. lib. bdg. 129.95 (0-87371-617-5, L617) Lewis Pubs.

An Asterisk (*) at the beginning of an entry indicates that the title is appearing for the first time.

***McDuffie, Jerome.** AP U. S. History Text Prep. (Illus.). 2000. pap. text 29.95 incl. cd-rom (*0-87891-332-7*) Res & Educ.

McDuffie, Jerome, et al. AP United States History with Software. LC 97-168910. 640p. 1999. pap. 29.95 incl. disk (*0-87891-098-0*) Res & Educ.

McDuffie, Merrilee T. QuickCalc Med Dosage Calculations. LC 93-39298. 273p. (C). 1994. spiral bd. 37.60 (*0-8053-1366-4*) Benjamin-Cummings.

McDuffie, Norton G. Bioreactor Design Fundamentals. 152p. 1991. text 84.95 (*0-7506-9107-7*) Buttrwrth-Heinemann.

McDuffy, Dennis J. Sacrificial Lambs Vol. 1: Alcohol's Human Road Kill. LC 96-94232. (Illus.). 224p. (Orig.). 1996. pap. 14.95 (*0-9651625-0-8*) D McDuffy.

McDugal, Stuart Y., jt. auth. see Horton, Andrew.

McDugal, Stuart Y., jt. ed. see Horton, Andrew.

McDunn, Mark, jt. auth. see Severson, Paul.

McDyer, James. The Island of the Setting Sun. 1989. pap. 15.00 (*0-86217-227-6*, Pub. by Veritas Pubns) St Mut.

McDysan, David. ATM: Theory & Applications. LC 94-16750. (Illus.). 608p. 1994. 65.00 (*0-07-060362-6*) McGraw.

***McDysan, David.** QOS & Traffic Management in IP & ATM Networks. LC 99-53277. 480p. 1999. pap. 55.00 (*0-07-134959-6*) McGraw-Hill Prof.

— VPN Applications Guide: Real Solutions for Enterprise Networks. LC 00-24456. 320p. 2000. pap. 44.99 (*0-471-37175-0*) Wiley.

McDysan, David & Spohn, Darren. ATM Theory & Application: Signature Edition. LC 98-28203. 1011p. 1998. pap. 69.99 (*0-07-045346-2*) McGraw.

— Hands-On ATM. LC 97-46059. (Computer Communications Ser.). (Illus.). 656p. 1998. pap. 49.95 (*0-07-045047-1*) McGraw.

***McEachern.** Contemporary Introduction to Microeconomics. 5th ed. 1999. pap. 18.50 (*0-538-88852-0*) Thomson Learn.

— Economics. 5th ed. 1999. pap. 21.25 (*0-538-88850-4*) Thomson Learn.

McEachern. Economics: A Contemporary Approach. 4th ed. LC 96-21299. (HB - Economics Ser.). 1996. mass mkt. 71.95 (*0-538-85514-2*) S-W Pub.

— Economics: A Contemporary Introduction. 3rd ed. (HB - Economics Ser.). (C). 1994. mass mkt., student ed. 19.00 (*0-538-82853-6*) S-W Pub.

— Economics: A Contemporary Introduction. 4th ed. (HB - Economics Ser.). 1996. mass mkt., student ed. 24.95 (*0-538-85517-7*) S-W Pub.

***McEachern.** Macro-Economia. 4th ed. 1999. pap. 62.95 (*968-7529-51-2*) Thomson Learn.

McEachern. Macroeconomics: A Contemporary Introduction. 3rd ed. (HB - Economics Ser.). (C). 1994. mass mkt., student ed. 16.00 (*0-538-82854-4*) S-W Pub.

— Macroeconomics: A Contemporary Introduction. 4th ed. (HB - Economics Ser.). 1996. mass mkt., student ed. 20.95 (*0-538-85522-3*) S-W Pub.

— Macroeconomics Split - Economics: A Contemporary Introduction. 3rd ed. (HB - Economics Ser.). (C). 1994. mass mkt. 40.00 (*0-538-82851-X*) S-W Pub.

***McEachern.** Micro-Economia. 4th ed. 1999. pap. 64.95 (*968-7529-50-4*) Thomson Learn.

McEachern. Microeconomics: A Contemporary Introduction. 4th ed. (HB - Economics Ser.). 1996. mass mkt., student ed. 20.95 (*0-538-85523-1*) S-W Pub.

— Microeconomics: Contemporary Introduction. 4th ed. LC 96-18536. (HB - Economics Ser.). 1996. mass mkt. 48.95 (*0-538-85516-9*) S-W Pub.

— Microeconomics Split - Economics: Contemporary Introductions. 3rd ed. (HB - Economics Ser.). (C). 1994. mass mkt. 40.00 (*0-538-82852-8*) S-W Pub.

— Microsplit - Economics: A Contemporary Introduction. 3rd ed. (HB - Economics Ser.). (C). 1994. mass mkt., student ed. 16.00 (*0-538-82855-2*) S-W Pub.

***McEachern.** SG Macroeconmics: Contempory Introduction. 5th ed. (SWC-Economics Ser.). 1999. pap. 18.50 (*0-538-88851-2*) Sth-Wstrn College.

***McEachern & Lunn.** Web Tutor on Webct to Accompany Macroeconomics. 5th ed. 1999. pap. 19.00 (*0-534-76542-4*) Wadsworth Pub.

— Web Tutor on Webct to Accompany Microeconomics. 5th ed. 1999. pap. 19.00 (*0-534-76536-X*) Wadsworth Pub.

McEachern, A. W. Organizational Illusions. LC 84-51382. (Illus.). 200p. 1984. 25.00 (*0-930237-00-5*); pap. 12.50 (*0-930237-01-3*) Shale Bks.

***McEachern, Claire.** Henry IV, Pt. 1. (Shakespeare Ser.: Pt. 1). 144p. 2000. pap. 3.95 (*0-14-071456-1*) Penguin Putnam.

— Henry IV, Pt. 2. (Shakespeare Ser.: Pt. 2). 144p. 2000. pap. 4.95 (*0-14-071457-X*) Penguin Putnam.

McEachern, Claire. The Poetics of English Nationhood, 1590-1612. (Cambridge Studies in Renaissance Literature & Culture: No. 13). (Illus.). 250p. (C). 1996. text 59.95 (*0-521-57031-X*) Cambridge U Pr.

***McEachern, Claire, ed.** Henry V. (Pelican Shakespeare Ser.). 144p. 1999. pap. 4.95 (*0-14-071458-8*, Penguin Bks) Viking Penguin.

McEachern, Claire & Shuger, Debora, eds. Religion & Culture in Renaissance England. (Illus.). 304p. (C). 1997. text 59.95 (*0-521-58425-6*) Cambridge U Pr.

McEachern, Doug. A Class Against Itself: Power & the Nationalisation of the British Steel Industry. LC 79-41766. 239p. reprint ed. pap. 68.20 (*0-608-15752-X*, 2031689) Bks Demand.

McEachern, Doug, jt. auth. see Doyle, Timothy.

McEachern, Douglas. Economics: A Contemporary Introduction. 3rd ed. (C). 1994. mass mkt. 68.50 (*0-538-82849-8*, HB83CA) S-W Pub.

— The Expanding State: Class & Economy in Europe since 1945. LC 90-31758. 241p. 1990. text 45.00 (*0-312-04652-9*) St Martin.

McEachern, J. Edward & Veatch, Reggi, eds. CQI Annual, 1995: Innovations & Breakthrough Improvements: Applying Continuous Improvement to Integrated Delivery Systems. (Illus.). 124p. (Orig.). 1995. pap. text 25.00 (*0-915963-12-4*) Capitol Publns.

McEachern, John & Towle, Edward. Ecological Guidelines for Island Development. 65p. 1974. 7.50 (*0-318-14613-4*) Isl Resources.

***McEachern, Leslie.** The Angelica Home Kitchen. 2000. pap. 24.95 (*1-55970-510-8*, Pub. by Arcade Pub Inc) Time Warner.

McEachern, Michael. A Color Guide to Corn Snakes Captive-Bred in the U. S. 48p. 1992. pap. text 8.50 (*1-882770-15-3*) Adv Vivarium.

McEachern, Patricia A. Deprivation & Power: The Emergence of Anorexia Nervosa in Nineteenth Century French Literature, 162. LC 97-32017. (Contributions in Women's Studies: Vol. 162). 216p. 1998. 59.95 (*0-313-30518-8*, Greenwood Pr) Greenwood.

McEachern, Tim & O'Keefe, Bob. Re-Wiring: Uniting Management & the Web. LC 97-17565. (Illus.). 278p. 1997. 29.95 (*0-471-17556-0*) Wiley.

McEachern, Trudy, ed. see Andrel, Vika.

***McEachern, William A.** Economics: A Contemporary Introduction. 5th ed. LC 99-11640. 816p. 1999. 92.95 incl. cd-rom (*0-538-88846-6*) Sth-Wstrn College.

McEachern, William A. Macro Economics. (SWC-Economics). 832p. (C). 1988. mass mkt. 37.75 (*0-538-08845-1*, H85) S-W Pub.

***McEachern, William A.** Macroeconomics: A Contemporary Intro. 5th ed. LC 99-11638. 530p. 1999. pap. text 64.95 (*0-538-88847-4*) Thomson Learn.

McEachern, William A. Macroeconomics: A Contemporary Introduction. 4th ed. LC 96-18535. 1996. mass mkt. 48.95 (*0-538-85515-0*) S-W Pub.

— Micro Economics. (SWC-Economics). 832p. (C). 1988. pap. 37.75 (*0-538-08840-0*, H84) S-W Pub.

McEachern, William A., jt. auth. see Lile, Laird A.

McEachin, James. Farewell to the Mockingbirds. LC 97-65746. 512p. 1997. 27.00 (*0-9656661-9-0*) Rharl Pub.

***McEachin, James.** The Heroin Factor. 340p. 1999. 25.00 (*0-9656661-4-X*) Rharl Pub.

— Say Goodnight to the Boys in Blue. LC 98-68156. 281p. 2000. 25.00 (*0-9656661-5-8*) Rharl Pub.

McEachin, James. Tell Me a Tale: A Novel of the Old South. 288p. 1997. mass mkt. 6.99 (*0-425-15689-3*) Berkley Pub.

McEachin, John, et al. A Work in Progress: Behavior Management Strategies & a Curriculum for Intensive Behavioral Treatment of Autism. 400p. 1999. pap. 42.95 (*0-9665266-0-0*) DRL Bk.

McEachin, Tom, jt. auth. see Hundley, Rod.

Mceachran, John D. & Fechhelm, Janice D. Fishes of the Gulf of Mexico Vol. 1: Myxiniformes to Gasterosteiformes. LC 98-4605. (Illus.). 1120p. 1998. 125.00 (*0-292-75206-7*) U of Tex Pr.

***McEachron.** Self in the World. 2000. 38.75 (*0-07-239077-8*) McGraw.

McEachron, D. L., ed. Functional Mapping in Biology & Medicine: Computer Assisted Autoradiography. (Experimental Biology & Medicine Ser.: Vol. 11). (Illus.). viii, 280p. 1986. 225.25 (*3-8055-4325-5*) S Karger.

McEachron-Hirsch, Gail, ed. Student Self-Esteem: Integrating the Self. LC 93-60638. 440p. 1995. text 39.95 (*1-56676-031-3*) Scarecrow.

McEathron, Margaret & Holmes, Fenwicke. I Am Two Men. LC 80-15442. 1983. pap. 14.95 (*0-87949-190-6*) Ashley Bks.

McEathron, Scott R. & Hill, Sharon, compiled by. The Sphere of the Cartographer: Descriptive Exhibit Catalog. (American Geographical Society Collection Special Publication: No. 5). (Illus.). vi, 30p. (Orig.). 1996. pap. 3.00 (*1-879281-18-X*) G Meir Lib.

McEdward, Larry R., ed. Ecology of Marine Invertebrate Larvae. 480p. 1995. boxed set 139.95 (*0-8493-8046-4*, 8046) CRC Pr.

McElderry, Bruce R., Jr. Thomas Wolfe. (United States Authors Ser.: No. 50). 208p. 1965. 32.00 (*0-8057-0833-2*) Macmillan.

McElderry, Bruce R., Jr., ed. see Shelley, Percy Bysshe.

McElderry, Hillary. Multiplication Tables & Coloring Book. 1993. pap. 8.50 (*0-906212-85-5*, Pub. by Tarquin Pubns) Parkwest Pubns.

McElderry, Margaret K., jt. auth. see Graham, Harriet.

McElderry, Mona. Beneath Her Gentle Wings. LC 95-68928. (Illus.). 20p. (Orig.). (J). (ps-4). 1995. pap. 8.95 (*0-9641573-2-2*) Sisu Pr.

— Out of the Bulrushes: A Tale of Romanian Adoptions. 184p. (Orig.). 1995. pap. 16.95 (*0-9641573-1-4*) Sisu Pr.

— To Seek His Fortune. LC 96-66997. (Illus.). 64p. 1994. 10.00 (*0-9641573-0-6*) Sisu Pr.

McEldowney, Dennis, ed. see McCormick, Eric Hall.

McEldowney, Eugene. A Kind of Homecoming. large type ed. (Magna Large Print Ser.). 283p. 1996. 27.99 (*0-7505-0936-8*, Pub. by Mgna Lrg Print) Ulverscroft.

— A Stone of the Heart. large type ed. (Magna Large Print Ser.). (Illus.). 356p. 1996. 27.99 (*0-7505-0937-6*) Ulverscroft.

McEldowney, J. & O'Higgins, R., eds. The Common Law Tradition: Essays in Legal History Irish. 220p. 1989. 39.50 (*0-7165-2397-3*, Pub. by Irish Acad Pr) Intl Spec Bk.

McEldowney, John F. Environment & the Law. LC 97-112568. (C). 1996. pap. text. write for info. (*0-582-22712-7*, Pub. by Addison-Wesley) Longman.

McEldowney, John S., Jr. History of Wetzel County. (Illus.). 187p. 1997. reprint ed. lib. bdg. 26.50 (*0-8328-6956-2*) Higginson Bk Co.

McEldowney, Sharron, et al. Pollution. LC 92-36776. (C). 1993. pap. text 52.50 (*0-582-08655-8*) Longman.

McEleavy, Peter, jt. auth. see Beaumont, Paul.

McElfish, James M., Jr. Almanac of Enforceable State Laws to Control Nonpoint Source Water Pollution. LC 99-208753. (Research Report Ser.). 293p. 1998. 30.00 incl. 5.25 hd (*0-911937-81-1*) Environ Law Inst.

McElfish, James M., Jr. & Beier, Ann E. Environmental Regulation of Coal Mining: SMCRA's Second Decade. 282p. 1990. pap. 28.00 (*0-911937-35-8*) Environ Law Inst.

McElfresh, Beth. Chuck Wagon Cookbook. LC 60-8068. 75p. 1960. pap. 7.95 (*0-8040-0042-5*) Swallow.

McElfresh, Earl B. Antietam Battlefield. (Civil War Watercolor Map Ser.). (Illus.). 1994. 9.95 (*0-7834-1671-7*) McElfresh Map.

— The Battlefield of Saratoga, New York, 1777. (American Battlefields Watercolor Map Ser.). (Illus.). 1997. 19.95 (*1-885294-15-8*) McElfresh Map.

— Chancellorsville (Includes Fredericksburg & Salem Church), Spotsylvania County, Virginia, 1863. (Civil War Watercolor Map Ser.). (Illus.). 1996. 9.95 (*1-885294-10-7*) McElfresh Map.

— Little Big Horn Battlefield Montana Territory, 1876. (American Battlefields Watercolor Map Ser.). (Illus.). 1996. 9.95 (*1-885294-09-3*) McElfresh Map.

— Maps & Mapmakers of the Civil War. LC 99-28098. (Illus.). 272p. 1999. 55.00 (*0-8109-3430-2*, Pub. by Abrams) Time Warner.

— Santiago de Cuba, Cuba, 1898. (World Battlefield Water Color Map Ser.). 1998. 14.95 (*1-885294-16-6*) McElfresh Map.

McElfresh, Earl B. Second & Third Day Battlefield Gettysburg 1863. LC 95-680010. 1994. pap. 8.95 (*1-885294-06-9*) McElfresh Map.

McElfresh, Lynn E. Can You Feel the Thunder? LC 98-36609. 144p. (J). (gr. 5-9). 1999. 16.00 (*0-689-82324-X*) S&S Trade.

McElfresh, Patricia M. Scottsdale: Jewel in the Desert. LC 84-19605. (Illus.). 136p. 1988. 22.95 (*0-89781-105-4*) Am Historical Pr.

McElhaney, Jacquelyn M. Pauline Periwinkle & Progressive Reform in Dallas. LC 97-32344. (Centennial Series of the Association of Former Students: Vol. 73). (Illus.). 224p. 1998. 29.95 (*0-89096-800-4*) Tex A&M Univ Pr.

McElhaney, James. The Art of Cross-Examination. unabridged ed. P. E. G. Staff, ed. (McElhaney's Master Advocate Ser.). 184p. 1998. pap. 95.00 incl. audio (*0-943380-85-5*) PEG MN.

— Expert Witnesses: The Art & the Law. unabridged ed. P. E. G. Staff, ed. (McElhaney's Master Advocate Ser.). 38p. 1998. pap. 95.00 incl. audio (*0-943380-84-7*) PEG MN.

McElhaney, James, jt. auth. see Tigar, Michael E.

McElhaney, James W., intro. Clarence Darrow's Summation in People vs. Henry Sweet (1926) Murder/Darrows Attack on Prejudice. (Classics of the Courtroom: Vol. XXII). 42p. 1992. pap. 10.00 (*0-943380-28-6*) PEG MN.

— Daniel K. Webb's Direct Examination of Oliver North & Summation in U. S. vs. John M. Poindexter. (Classics of the Courtroom: Vol. XIX). 348p. 1991. pap. 15.00 (*0-943380-25-1*) PEG MN.

— Highlights from the Direct & Cross-Examination of Richard Hauptmann in The State of New Jersey vs. Hauptmann: The Lindbergh Kidnapping Trial. (Classics of the Courtroom: Vol. XIV). 326p. 1988. pap. 15.00 (*0-943380-20-0*) PEG MN.

— Joseph M. Jamail's Summation in Pennzoil Company vs. Texaco, Inc. (Classics of the Courtroom: Vol. XXIV). 55p. 1992. pap. 10.00 (*0-943380-30-8*) PEG MN.

— Ulysses in Court The Litigation Surrounding the First Publication of James Joyce's Novel in the United States (Irving Younger Speech) (Classics of the Courtroom: Vol. XVI). 68p. 1988. pap. 10.00 (*0-943380-22-7*) PEG MN.

— Vincent Fuller's Summation in U. S. vs. Hinckley. (Classics of the Courtroom: Vol. XII). 54p. 1988. pap. 10.00 (*0-943380-18-9*) PEG MN.

McElhaney, Sandra J., jt. auth. see Gullotta, Thomas P.

McElhearn, Kirk, tr. see Javary, Cyrille.

***McElheny.** James Watson & the DNA Revolution. 2000. pap. 25.00 (*0-7382-0341-6*, Pub. by Perseus Pubng) HarpC.

McElheny, Kenneth R., jt. ed. see Moffett, James.

***McElheny, Victor K.** Insisting on the Impossible: The Life of Edwin Land. 544p. 1999. pap. text 22.50 (*0-7382-0190-1*, Pub. by Perseus Pubng) HarpC.

— Insisting on the Impossible: The Life of Edwin Land, Inventor of Instant Photography. 510p. 2000. reprint ed. text 30.00 (*0-7881-9203-5*) DIANE Pub.

McElheny, Victor K. & Abrahamson, Seymour, eds. Assessing Chemical Mutagens: The Risk to Humans. LC 79-998. (Banbury Reports: No. 1). (Illus.). 367p. 1979. 44.00 (*0-87969-200-6*) Cold Spring Harbor.

McElheran, Brock. Conducting Technique for Beginners & Professionals. 2nd rev. ed. (Illus.). 148p. 1989. pap. text 11.95 (*0-19-385830-4*) OUP.

— Music Reading by Intervals: A Modern Sight-Reading & Ear-Training Method. LC 98-73279. (Illus.). 140p. (C). 1998. spiral bd. 14.95 (*0-9658910-0-3*, BRM-1) Brichtmark Music.

— V-Bombs & Weathermaps: Reminiscences of World War II. LC 96-128124. (Illus.). 224p. 1995. 32.95 (*0-7735-1330-2*, Pub. by McG-Queens Univ Pr) CUP Services.

McElherne, Linda N. Jump Starters: Quick Classroom Activities That Develop Self-Esteem, Creativity, & Cooperation. LC 98-30998. (Illus.). 184p. 1998. pap. 21.95 (*1-57542-050-3*) Free Spirit Pub.

McElherton, Paul, jt. auth. see Mirams, Mike.

McElhiney, Annette B., jt. ed. see St. Joan, Jacqueline.

McElhinney, Camillus P., jt. auth. see McFarlane, Robert.

McElhinny, M. W. & Valencio, D. A. Paleoreconstruction of the Continents. (Geodynamics Ser.: Vol. 2). 194p. 1981. 20.00 (*0-87590-511-0*) Am Geophysical.

***McElhinny, Michael W.** Paleomagnetism. 2nd ed. 400p. 1999. 69.95 (*0-12-483355-1*) Acad Pr.

McElhinny, Michael W., et al. Global Reconstruction & the Geomagnetic Field During the Palaeozoic. 1981. text 118.00 (*90-277-1231-X*) Kluwer Academic.

McElhinny, Michael W., jt. ed. see Lock, J.

McElhone, Alice P. & Butler, Edward B. Mail It! High Impact Business Mail: From Design to Delivery. (Pitney Bowes Best Practices Guide Ser.). (Illus.). 250p. (Orig.). 1996. pap. 29.95 (*0-9647121-0-5*) Benchmark CT.

McElhone, Keven. Mechanical Music. (Album Ser.: No. 333). (Illus.). 32p. 1997. pap. 6.25 (*0-7478-0354-4*, Pub. by Shire Pubns) Parkwest Pubns.

Mceliece. Introduction to Discrete Mathematics. 1989. 26.87 (*0-07-557048-3*) McGraw.

McEliece, Robert J. Finite Fields for Computer Scientists & Engineers. 1986. reprint ed. text 89.00 (*0-89838-191-6*) Kluwer Academic.

— Introduction to Discrete Math. (C). 1989. text 61.74 (*0-07-557015-7*) McGraw.

McEliece, Robert J. & Ash, Robert B. Introduction to Discrete Mathematics. 500p. (C). 1988. text 27.50 (*0-317-58264-X*) Random.

McEligot, D. M., ed. Gas Turbine Heat Transfer - 1993. (HTD Ser.: Vol. 242). 68p. 1993. 30.00 (*0-7918-1155-7*, G00799) ASME.

***McEligot, Mace B.** Angelica with Simplified Celtic: With Stained Glass Angel. (Illus.). 12p. 1999. pap. 9.95 (*0-9647921-3-3*) Mace Motif.

McEligot, Mace B. Magic Star - 6 Inspirations. (Illus.). 22p. (Orig.). 1995. pap. 10.00 (*0-9647921-0-9*) Mace Motif.

— Magic Star 8 Innovations. (Illus.). 52p. 1997. reprint ed. pap. 16.95 (*0-9647921-1-7*) Mace Motif.

***McEligot, Mace B.** Simplified Celtic: Easy Interlocking Designs for Quarter Inch Bias Tape. (Illus.). 16p. 1998. pap. 9.95 (*0-9647921-2-5*) Mace Motif.

McElhennery, John G., et al, eds. United Methodism in America: A Compact History. 160p. (Orig.). 1992. pap. 10.95 (*0-687-43170-0*) Abingdon.

McElhenney, John G. John Wesley. 4th ed. 36p. 1996. reprint ed. pap. 2.00 (*1-880927-20-9*) Gen Comm Arch.

McElligott, Anthony. Contested City: Municipal Politics & the Rise of Nazism in Altona, 1917-1937. LC 98-19712. (Social History, Popular Culture, & Politics in Germany Ser.). (Illus.). 352p. (C). 1998. text 59.50 (*0-472-10929-4*, 10929) U of Mich Pr.

McElligott, Anthony, jt. ed. see Kirk, Tim.

McElligott, David, jt. auth. see Cofer, Rebecca.

McElligott, Ken. Bartending & Cocktail Serving: A Complete Course. LC 94-96224. (Illus.). 120p. 1994. ring bd. 29.95 (*0-9618067-0-2*) McElligott Ent.

McElligott, Mary E., ed. Transactions of the Illinois State Historical Society: Selected Papers from the Seventh Annual History Symposium & the Eighth Annual History Symposium. LC 89-28563. 90p. 1989. pap. 12.50 (*0-912226-25-0*) Ill St Hist Soc.

McElligott, Mary E. & O'Neal, Patrick H., eds. Transactions of the Illinois State Historical Society: Selected Papers from the Fifth & Sixth Illinois History Symposium of the Illinois State Historical Society. LC 89-28563. 132p. (Orig.). 1988. pap. text 12.50 (*0-912226-21-8*) Ill St Hist Soc.

McElligott, Matthew. The Truth about Cousin Ernie's Head. LC 95-21743. (Illus.). 32p. (J). (gr. k-3). 1996. mass mkt. 15.00 (*0-689-80179-3*) S&S Bks Yung.

— Uncle Frank's Pit. LC 97-27303. 32p. (J). (gr. k-3). 1998. 15.99 (*0-670-87737-9*, Viking Child) Peng Put Young Read.

McElligott, P. Observations on the Gaelic Language. 1996. reprint ed. pap. 10.00 (*0-89979-085-2*) British Am Bks.

McElligott, Robert, jt. auth. see Synnott, Thomas.

McElligott, Tom. The Story of Handball: The Game, The Players, The History. 176p. 1997. pap. 6.95 (*0-86327-034-4*, Pub. by Wolfhound Press) Irish Amer Bk.

Mcellquham, K. The Adaptable Apple. (Illus.). 150p. 1997. spiral bd. 9.95 (*1-57166-092-5*) Hearts N Tummies.

McElmeel, Sharron L. ABCs of an Author-Illustrator Visit. LC 94-11471. (Professional Growth Ser.). 100p. 1994. student ed., ring bd. 29.95 (*0-938865-33-1*) Linworth Pub.

— An Author a Month (for Dimes) (Illus.). xiv, 185p. (Orig.). 1993. pap. text 23.50 (*0-87287-952-6*) Teacher Ideas Pr.

— An Author a Month (for Nickels) (Illus.). xiv, 172p. 1990. pap. text 24.00 (*0-87287-827-9*) Teacher Ideas Pr.

— An Author a Month (for Pennies) (Illus.). xviii, 224p. 1988. pap. text 24.50 (*0-87287-661-6*) Teacher Ideas Pr.

— Authors for Children: A Calendar. 1992. pap. 10.00 (*0-931510-43-0*) Hi Willow.

— Bookpeople: A Multicultural Album. LC 92-13252. (Illus.). xvii, 170p. 1992. pap. text 23.50 (*0-87287-953-4*) Teacher Ideas Pr.

— Bookpeople: A Second Album. (Illus.). xv, 200p. 1990. pap. text 20.00 (*0-87287-721-3*) Teacher Ideas Pr.

— Educator's Companion to Children's Literature Vol. 1: Mysteries, Animal Tales, Books of Humor, Adventure Stories, & Historical Fiction. LC 95-11608. (Illus.). xv, 153p. 1995. pap. text 23.50 (*1-56308-329-9*) Libs Unl.

— Educator's Companion to Children's Literature Vol. 2: Folklore, Contemporary Realistic Fiction, Fantasy, Biographies, & Tales from Here & There. (Illus.). 200p. 1996. pap. text 24.00 (*1-56308-330-2*) Libs Unl.

— Great New Nonfiction Reads. (Illus.). xvi, 225p. 1995. pap. text 21.00 (*1-56308-228-4*) Libs Unl.

— The Latest & Greatest Read-Alouds. (Illus.). xv, 210p. 1994. pap. text 18.50 (*1-56308-140-7*) Libs Unl.

M

— Literature Frameworks: From Apples to Zoos. LC 96-43888. (Professional Growth Ser.). 278p. 1996. pap. 29.95 (0-938865-53-6) Linworth Pub.

***McElmeel, Sharron L.** 100 Most Popular Children's Authors: Biographical Sketches & Bibliographies. LC 98-41942. (Popular Authors Ser.). 495p. (YA). (gr. 6-9). 1999. 48.00 (1-56308-646-8) Teacher Ideas Pr.

McElmeel, Sharron L. 100 Most Popular Picture Book Authors & Illustrators: Biographical Sketches & Bibliographies. (Popular Authors Ser.). 575p. 2000. 49.00 (1-56308-647-6) Libs Unl.

Mcelmeel, Sharron L. The Poet Tree. LC 93-20268. (Illus.). xvi, 186p. 1993. pap. text 23.50 (1-56308-102-4) Teacher Ideas Pr.

McElmeel, Sharron L. Research Strategies for Moving Beyond Reporting. LC 96-34558. (Professional Growth Ser.). 181p. 1996. pap. 29.95 (0-938865-54-4) Linworth Pub.

***McElmeel, Sharron L.** Shoptalk: Ideas for Elementary School Librarians & Technology Specialists. 2nd ed. LC 99-58605. 1999. write for info. (0-938865-94-3) Linworth Pub.

— Tips: Ideas for Secondary School Librarians & Technology Specialists. 2nd ed. LC 99-89594. (Professional Growth Ser.). 2000. write for info. (0-938865-93-5) Linworth Pub.

McElmeel, Sharron L. & Simpson, Carol M. Internet for Schools. 2nd rev. ed. LC 97-6448. (Professional Growth Ser.). 150p. 1997. pap. 29.95 (0-938865-59-5) Linworth Pub.

***McElmeel, Sharron L. & Smallwood, Carol.** World Wide Web Almanac: Making Curriculum Connections to Special Days, Weeks & Months. LC 99-41399. (Professional Growth Ser.). 227p. 1999. 36.95 (0-938865-78-1) Linworth Pub.

McElmeel, Sharron L., jt. auth. see Simpson, Carol M.

McElmurray, Karen Salyer. Strange Birds in the Tree of Heaven: A Novel. LC 99-22047. 320p. 1999. 25.00 (1-892514-24-9) Hill St Pr.

McElmurray, Mary A., jt. auth. see Kino Learning Center Staff.

McElmurry, Beverly J. Annual Review of Women's Health, Vol. I. 350p. 1993. pap. 31.95 (0-88737-598-7) Natl League Nurse.

— Annual Review of Women's Health, Vol. II. 1995. pap. 37.95 (0-88737-636-3) Natl League Nurse.

***McElmurry, Beverly J., ed.** Introduction to Primary Health Care in Urban Communities. LC 98-52867. (National League for Nursing Ser.). 266p. 1999. 30.00 (0-7637-1010-5) Jones & Bartlett.

McElmurry, Beverly J., et al, eds. Primary Health Care in Urban Communities. 1997. 25.95 (0-88737-734-3, 14-7343, NLN Pr) Natl League Nurse.

— Women's Health & Development: Global Perspective. 400p. 1993. 55.00 (0-86720-799-X) Jones & Bartlett.

McElmurry, Beverly J., jt. auth. see Parker, Randy S.

***McElmurry, Jill.** Mad About Plaid. LC 99-28800. (Illus.). 40p. (J). (gr. k-5). 2000. 14.95 (0-688-16951-1); lib. bdg. 14.89 (0-688-16952-X, Wm Morrow) Morrow Avon.

McElmurry, Mary A. Appreciating. (Illus.). 64p. (J). (gr. 2-8). 1983. student ed. 8.99 (0-9607366-1-1, GA 493) Good Apple.

— Belonging. (Illus.). 64p. (J). (gr. 2-8). 1983. student ed. 8.99 (0-9607366-0-3, GA 492) Good Apple.

— Caring. 64p. (J). (gr. 4-8). 1981. 8.99 (0-86653-052-5, GA275) Good Apple.

— Cooperating. (Illus.). 64p. (J). (gr. 3-8). 1985. student ed. 8.99 (0-86653-334-6, GA 680) Good Apple.

— Feelings. 80p. (J). (gr. 3-8). 1981. 10.99 (0-86653-027-4, GA 276) Good Apple.

McElnay, James C., jt. ed. see D'Arcy, Patrick F.

***McElrath.** Critical Essays on Charles Chesnutt. LC 99-34852. 1999. 47.00 (0-7838-0055-X) Mac Lib Ref.

— Unsafe Haven. 28.95 (0-7453-1317-5) Pluto GBR.

***McElrath.** Unsafe Haven. LC 99-46659. 2000. 95.95 (0-7453-1322-1) Pluto GBR.

McElrath, Buckskin J. The Cowboy Stuntman. Keltgen-Pierson, Jaciel, ed. 165p. 1997. pap. 9.95 (0-9624593-5-6) Rushmore Hse Pub.

McElrath, Clifford. On Santa Cruz Island. 128p. (Orig.). 1993. pap. 12.95 (0-9634635-3-5) Caractacus.

McElrath, Damian. Biography of Dan Anderson. LC 98-35225. (Pioneers Ser.). xxi, 171p. 1999. 19.95 (1-56838-310-X) Hazelden.

— Biography of Patrick Butler. LC 98-35226. (Pioneers Ser.). 1998. 19.95 (1-56838-309-6) Hazelden.

— Franciscan Christology. (Franciscan Sources Ser.). vii, 240p. 1980. pap. 18.00 (1-57659-040-2) Franciscan Inst.

— Haz a Spiritual Odyssey. 28.00 (0-89486-451-3, 5004 A) Hazelden.

McElrath, Damian & Hazelden Foundation Staff. Further Reflections on Hazelden's Spiritual Odyssey. LC 98-35227. xiv, 134p. 1999. 19.95 (1-56838-308-8) Hazelden.

McElrath, Damian, jt. auth. see Pittman, Bill.

McElrath, Hugh T., jt. auth. see Eskew, Harry.

McElrath, J. Frank Norris Revisited. (Twayne's United States Authors Ser.). 150p. 1992. 32.00 (0-8057-3965-3) Macmillan.

McElrath, Joseph R., Jr. Frank Norris: A Descriptive Bibliography. LC 92-7198. (Series in Bibliography). (Illus.). 120p. (C). 1992. text 120.00 (0-8229-3712-3) U of Pittsburgh Pr.

— Walden Notes. (Cliffs Notes Ser.). 80p. 1964. pap. 4.95 (0-8220-1358-4, Cliff) IDG Bks.

McElrath, Joseph R., Jr., et al, eds. John Steinbeck: The Contemporary Reviews. (American Critical Archives Ser.: No. 8). 586p. (C). 1996. text 115.00 (0-521-41038-X) Cambridge U Pr.

McElrath, Joseph R. & Burgess, Douglas K. The Apprenticeship Writings of Frank Norris, 1896-1898. LC 96-83741. (Memoirs Ser.: Vol. 219). (Illus.). 276p. 1996. 20.00 (0-87169-219-8, M219-MCJ) Am Philos.

McElrath, Joseph R., Jr., ed. see Chestnut, Charles W.

McElrath, Karen, jt. ed. see Inciardi, James A.

McElrath, Roger G. & Slowinski, Betty J. Employee Financial Participation: An International Survey, Supplement, 1990-1998. (Multinational Industrial Relations Ser.: Vol. 12). (Illus.). 150p. 1998. pap., suppl. ed. 25.00 (1-891496-15-8) J M Olin.

McElrath, Ruth G., tr. see McElrath, William N.

McElrath, William N. Mi Primer Diccionario Biblico. McElrath, Ruth G., tr. from ENG.Tr. of Bible Dictionary for Young Readers. (SPA., Illus.). 128p. (J). (gr. 4-6). 1975. reprint ed. pap. 7.99 (0-311-03656-2) Casa Bautista.

— Mi Primer Diccionario Biblico: My First Bible Dictionary. (SPA.). 122p. 1978. pap. 7.95 (0-8288-5252-9, S37577) Fr & Eur.

— Ways We Worship. LC 96-39694. (Illus.). 224p. (J). (gr. 3 up). 1997. 16.95 (0-8120-6625-1) Barron.

McElreath, Brent, ed. see Ernst, Jeri.

McElreath, Brent, ed. see Stewart, Branner.

McElreath, Mark. Systematic & Ethical Public Relations Campaigns. 2nd ed. 464p. (C). 1997. per. write for info. (0-07-114584-2) McGraw.

McElreath, Mark P. Introduction to Public Relations & Advertising 4th ed. 530p. (C). 1995. text 83.00 (0-536-58686-1) Pearson Custom.

McElreath, Mark P. Managing Systematic & Ethical Public Relations. 2nd ed. LC 96-86355. 464p. (C). 1996. text. write for info. (0-697-28882-X) Brown & Benchmark.

***McEleavey, Ken, ed.** The Genetic Basis of Male Infertility. LC 99-39566. (Results & Problems in Cell Differentiation Ser.: Vol. 28). (Illus.). 280p. 1999. 165.00 (3-540-66264-2) Spr-Verlag.

McElreavy, Tim, jt. auth. see Medvedow, Jill.

McElrey, Onyria H. WNW Spanish/English Dictionary of Computer Technical Terms. 1997. 10.95 (0-02-861046-6) Macmillan.

McElroy. Jesus Forgives Peter: Mark 14:10-52; Luke 22:61. (Arch Bks.). 24p. (Orig.). (J). (gr. k-4). 1985. pap. 1.99 (0-570-06192-X, 59-1293) Concordia.

— Texas Civil Pre-Trial Procedure, 1998 Supplements, Vols. 24, 25 & 26. 600p. 1998. suppl. ed. write for info. (0-327-00544-0, 6898712) LEXIS Pub.

McElroy & Tye, eds. Thermal Insulation Performance - STP 718. 566p. 1981. 43.00 (0-8031-0794-3, STP718) ASTM.

***McElroy, Alan.** Blood & Sutures. Vol. 2. (Illus.). 96p. 1999. pap. 9.95 (1-58240-113-6) Image Comics.

— Curse of the Spawn. (Spawn Ser.: Vol. 3). (Illus.). 96p. (J). 2000. pap. 9.95 (1-58240-134-9) Image Comics.

— Curse of the Spawn Vol. 4: Lost Values. (Illus.). 96p. 2000. pap. 9.95 (1-58240-162-4, Pub. by Image Comics) Midpt Trade.

— Curse of The Spawn, Book 1: Sacrifice of The Soul, 1. 1999. pap. text 9.95 (1-58240-096-2) Image Comics.

— Spawn Blood & Sutures. 1999. pap. text 4.95 (1-58240-114-4) Image Comics.

McElroy, Ann & Townsend, Patricia K. Medical Anthropology in Ecological Perspective. 3rd ed. (C). 1996. pap. 36.00 (0-8133-8610-1, Pub. by Westview) HarpC.

***McElroy, B. Roland.** The Great Mizzariddle. Smith, Donald A., ed. (Illus.). 32p. (J). (ps-6). 1999. pap. 12.95 (0-9673917-0-9) McElroy Assocs.

McElroy, Bernard. Shakespeare's Mature Tragedies. LC 72-5389. 266p. reprint ed. pap. 82.50 (0-7837-4326-2, 204403000012) Bks Demand.

McElroy, Bonnie. Damodara Coloring Book. large type ed. (Illus.). 32p. (J). (gr. k-5). 1992. pap. 4.95 (0-945475-27-6, 1201, Pub. by Mandala Pub Grp) Words Distrib.

— Gopal Coloring Book. large type ed. (Illus.). 32p. (J). 1992. pap. 4.95 (0-945475-26-8, 1200, Pub. by Mandala Pub Grp) Words Distrib.

— Jagannath Coloring Book. large type ed. (Illus.). 32p. (J). 1992. pap. 4.95 (0-945475-29-2, 1203, Pub. by Mandala Pub Grp) Words Distrib.

— Krsna Coloring Book. large type ed. (Illus.). 32p. (J). 1992. pap. 4.95 (0-945475-28-4, 1202, Pub. by Mandala Pub Grp) Words Distrib.

— Nimai Coloring Book. large type ed. (Illus.). 32p. (J). 1992. pap. 4.95 (0-945475-30-6, 1204, Pub. by Mandala Pub Grp) Words Distrib.

***McElroy, Carolyn.** Preventing & Detecting Managed Care Fraud. Youngstrom, Nina, ed. 100p. 1998. pap. 93.00 (0-929156-36-6) Atlantic Info Services Inc.

McElroy, Charles H. & Lienhart, David A., eds. Rock for Erosion Control. LC 92-44625. (ASTM Special Technical Publication Ser.: No. 1177). (Illus.). 150p. 1993. 46.00 (0-8031-1489-3, STP1177) ASTM.

McElroy, Colleen. Jesus & Fat Tuesday & Other Stories. LC 87-70508. 216p. 1987. pap. 8.95 (0-88739-023-4) Creat Arts Bk.

— Winters Without Snow. LC 79-92501. 81p. 1980. pap. 5.95 (0-918408-17-2) Ishmael Reed.

McElroy, Colleen, jt. intro. see Cady, Jack.

McElroy, Colleen J. Driving under the Cardboard Pines: And Other Stories. 224p. (Orig.). 1989. pap. 10.95 (0-88739-073-0) Creat Arts Bk.

— A Long Way from St. Louie. LC 96-53099. 200p. (Orig.). 1997. pap. 13.95 (1-56689-059-4) Coffee Hse.

— Over the Lip of the World: Among the Storytellers of Madagascar. LC 99-14595. (Illus.). 350p. 1999. 24.95 (0-295-97824-4) U of Wash Pr.

— Queen of the Ebony Isles. LC 84-7494. (Wesleyan Poetry Ser.). (Illus.). 100p. 1984. pap. 12.95 (0-8195-6101-0, Wesleyan Univ Pr) U Pr of New Eng.

— Travelling Music: Poems. LC 98-35751. 88p. 1998. pap. 13.95 (1-885266-65-0) Story Line.

— What Madness Brought Me Here: New & Selected Poems, 1968-1988. LC 89-37803. (Wesleyan Poetry Ser.). 118p. 1990. pap. 13.95 (0-8195-1188-9, Wesleyan Univ Pr) U Pr of New Eng.

McElroy, D. L. & Kimpflen, J. F., eds. Insulation Materials, Testing & Applications STP 1030. LC 89-17743. (Special Technical Publication (STP) Ser.). (Illus.). 800p. 1990. text 95.00 (0-8031-1278-5, STP1030) ASTM.

McElroy, D. P. Fundamentals of Petroleum Maps. LC 86-22920. 144p. 1987. reprint ed. pap. 44.70 (0-608-01572-5, 206199200001) Bks Demand.

McElroy, Davis D. Existentialism & Modern Literature: An Essay in Existential Criticism. LC 68-8067. (Illus.). 58p. 1969. reprint ed. lib. bdg. 49.50 (0-8371-0179-4, MCEL, Greenwood Pr) Greenwood.

— Scotland's Age of Improvement: A Survey of Eighteenth-Century Literary Clubs & Societies. LC 73-9172. 183p. reprint ed. pap. 56.80 (0-8357-4567-8, 203747700008) Bks Demand.

McElroy, Dorothy E. & Earp, Charles A. The History & Roster of the First Christian Church (Disciples of Christ) of Baltimore, Maryland, 1810-1996. LC 97-160177. vii, 129p. (Orig.). 1996. pap. 22.00 (0-7884-0576-4, M117) Heritage Bk.

McElroy, Elam E. Applied Business Statistics: An Elementary Approach. 2nd ed. 1979. student ed. 9.95 (0-8162-5536-9); text 26.95 (0-8162-5535-0); teacher ed. 6.00 (0-8162-5537-7) Holden-Day.

McElroy, Frank E., jt. auth. see Konikow, Robert B.

McElroy, Frank E., ed. see National Safety Council Staff.

McElroy, G. Mark. Coaching the No-Huddle Offense. (Illus.). 135p. 1998. pap. 16.95 (1-57167-204-4) Coaches Choice.

McElroy, Guy C. & Gates, Henry Louis, Jr. Facing History: The Black Image in American Art, 1710-1940. (Illus.). 190p. 1991. 50.00 (0-938491-39-3) Chronicle Bks.

McElroy, Guy C., Jr. & Gates, Henry Louis, Jr. Facing History: The Black Image in American Art, 1710-1940. (Illus.). 190p. 1991. pap. 24.95 (0-938491-38-5) Chronicle Bks.

McElroy, J. M. McElroy: The Scotch-Irish McElroys in America, 1717-1900 A.D. 183p. 1992. reprint ed. pap. 28.00 (0-8328-2687-1); reprint ed. lib. bdg. 38.00 (0-8328-2686-3) Higginson Bk Co.

***McElroy, James.** Management Communications. 66p. 2000. write for info. (1-58692-030-8) Copyright Mgmt.

***McElroy, James T.** We've Got Spirit: The Life & Times of America's Greatest Cheerleading Team. (Illus.). 2000. pap. 12.95 (0-425-17356-9) Berkley Pub.

McElroy, James T. We've Got Spirit: The Life & Times of America's Greatest Cheerleading Team. LC 98-37655. (Illus.). 304p. 1999. 20.00 (0-684-84967-4) Simon & Schuster.

McElroy, Jerome E., et al. Community Policing in New York: The CPOP Research. (Illus.). 216p. (C). 1992. 48.00 (0-8039-4789-5); pap. 22.50 (0-8039-4790-9) Sage.

McElroy, Jerome L. & Caines, Joseph E. Consumer Expenditure Patterns: A Survey of St. Thomas, U. S. V. I., 1975-1976. LC 79-22424. 118p. reprint ed. pap. 36.60 (0-7837-5062-5, 204475200004) Bks Demand.

McElroy, Jerome L. & De Albuquerque, Klaus. An Integrated Sustainable Ecotourism for Small Caribbean Islands. Conway, Dennis, ed. (Series on Environment & Development). 49p. (Orig.). 1992. pap. 2.00 (1-881157-09-1) In Ctr Global.

McElroy, John. Andersonville: A Story of Rebel Military Prisons. (Illus.). 664p. 1993. reprint ed. pap. text 38.00 (1-55613-851-2) Heritage Bk.

— This Was Andersonville. (Illus.). 1957. 29.95 (0-8392-1117-1) Astor-Honor.

McElroy, John H. American Beliefs: What Keeps a Big Country & a Diverse People United. LC 98-45603. (Illus.). 288p. 1999. 25.00 (1-56663-231-5) I R Dee.

— Finding Freedom: America's Distinctive Cultural Formation. LC 88-26547. (Illus.). 208p. (C). 1989. 26.95 (0-8093-1515-7) S Ill U Pr.

McElroy, John H. & Heacock, E. Larry, eds. Space Applications at the Crossroads, 21st Goddard Memorial Symposium, Mar. 24-25, 1983, Greenbelt, MD. (Science & Technology Ser.: Vol. 55). (Illus.). 308p. 1983. 45.00 (0-87703-186-X, Am Astronaut Soc); pap. 35.00 (0-87703-187-8, Am Astronaut Soc) Univelt Inc.

McElroy, John H., ed. see Whitman, Walt.

***McElroy, John Harmon.** American Beliefs: What Keeps a Big Country & a Diverse People United. (Illus.). 272p. 2000. reprint ed. pap. 14.95 (1-56663-314-1, Pub. by I R Dee) Natl Bk Netwk.

McElroy, Joseph. Women & Men. LC 92-29481. 1192p. 1993. reprint ed. pap. 15.95 (1-56478-023-6) Dalkey Arch.

McElroy, Keith. Early Peruvian Photography: A Critical Case Study. LC 84-16119. (Studies in Photography: No. 7). (Illus.). 216p. reprint ed. pap. 67.00 (0-8357-1583-3, 207056200001) Bks Demand.

McElroy, Linda S., jt. ed. see Gilmore, Donald Y.

***McElroy, Lisa Tucker.** Meet My Grandmother: She's a Deep Sea Explorer. LC 00-23091. (Grandmothers at Work Ser.). (Illus.). 2000. lib. bdg. write for info. (0-7613-1720-1) Millbrook Pr.

— Meet My Grandmother: She's A Supreme Court Justice. LC 99-31130. (J). (gr. 3-5). 1999. 22.90 (0-7613-1566-7) Millbrook Pr.

— Meet My Grandmother: She's a United States Senator. (Grandmothers at Work Ser.). 32p. (J). (gr. 2-4). 2000. 22.90 (0-7613-1721-X) Millbrook Pr.

— Meet My Grandmother: She's a United States Senator. (Grandmothers at Work Ser.). (Illus.). (J). 2000. pap. 7.95 (0-7613-1432-6) Millbrook Pr.

— Meeting Grandmother: She's a Supreme Court Justice. (Grandmother at Work Ser.). (Illus.). (J). 2000. pap. text 7.95 (0-7613-1386-9) Millbrook Pr.

McElroy, Lorie J. Voices of the Holocaust. LC 97-33195. (J). 1997. write for info. (0-7876-1747-4, UXL); 68.25 (0-7876-1748-2, UXL) Gale.

McElroy, Lorie J. Women's Voices. (Women's Reference Library). 350p. 1996. text 63.00 (0-7876-0663-4, UXL) Gale.

McElroy, Lorie J. Women's Voices: A Documentary History of Women in America. LC 96-29247. 1996. write for info. (0-7876-0664-2, UXL); write for info. (0-7876-0665-0, UXL) Gale.

McElroy, Margaret D., jt. ed. see Rassi, Judith A.

McElroy, Martin P., jt. ed. see Meyer, Katharine M.

McElroy, Mary L., et al. Business Application Software: An IBM PC Lab Manual. (C). 1986. pap. text 12.95 (0-938188-34-8) Mitchell Pub.

McElroy, Mary M. Construction Industry Forms, 1. 2nd ed. LC 95-51320. (Construction Law Library). 720p. 1996. boxed set 150.00 (0-471-14263-8) Wiley.

McElroy, Michael B. Macroeconomy. 1995. text 87.00 (0-02-378801-1, Macmillan Coll) P-H.

McElroy, Michael B., et al, eds. Energizing China: Reconciling Environmental Protection & Economic Growth. LC 98-22687. 576p. 1999. 25.00 (0-674-25329-9) HUP.

McElroy, Nan & Ohlman-Roberge, Melissa. The Actor's Guide Southeast: An Introductory Guide to the Southeast Regional Film & Television Market. LC 97-222649. Orig. Title: Acting in Atlanta. 90p. (Orig.). 1997. pap. (1-885436-10-6) Twoworkingactors.

***McElroy, Nan & Ohlman-Roberge, Melissa, eds.** The Actor's Guide Southeast Industry Directory 2000. 55p. 2000. pap. (1-885436-00-9) Twoworkingactors.

McElroy, Onyria H. Spanish-English/English-Spanish Medical Dictionary, Vol. 1. 2nd ed. (SPA.). 560p. 1996. pap. text 29.95 (0-316-55448-0) Lppncott W & W.

McElroy, Onyria H., jt. auth. see Grabb, Lolita L.

McElroy, Paul S. New Beginnings. (Charming Petites Ser.). 80p. 1992. 4.95 (0-88088-737-0) Peter Pauper.

McElroy, Phyllis, jt. auth. see Slawson, Millie.

McElroy, Richard L. William McKinley & Our America: A Pictorial History. (Illus.). 232p. 1996. 40.00 (0-9634712-0-1); pap. 24.95 (0-9634712-1-X) Stark Cnty Hist.

McElroy, Robert. Christ above Culture: The Answer to Farrakhanism. LC 97-61846. 184p. 1997. pap. 12.95 (0-9660529-0-0) Union Grove Pr.

McElroy, Robert C. Automotive Engine Electronics. (Illus.). 112p. 1990. 13.95 (0-929603-37-0) Accuracy Pub Co.

McElroy, Robert M. Jefferson Davis: The Unreal & the Real, 2 vols., Set. (History - United States Ser.). 1993. reprint ed. lib. bdg. 180.00 (0-7812-4900-7) Rprt Serv.

— Levi Parsons Morton: Banker, Diplomat & Statesman. LC 75-2646. (Wall Street & the Security Market Ser.). (Illus.). 1975. reprint ed. 33.95 (0-405-06971-5) Ayer.

McElroy, Robert W. Morality & American Foreign Policy: The Role of Ethics in International Affairs. (Illus.). 244p. 1992. pap. text 16.95 (0-691-00078-6, Pub. by Princeton U Pr) Cal Prin Full Svc.

— The Search for an American Public Theology: The Contribution of John Courtney Murray. 1989. pap. 10.95 (0-8091-3051-3) Paulist Pr.

McElroy, Ross, ed. see Grodsky, Emanual.

McElroy, Roxanne. That Perfect Stitch: The Secrets to Fine Hand Quilting. LC 97-15389. (Illus.). 160p. 1997. pap. 24.95 (0-8442-2652-1, Quilt Dgst Pr) NTC Contemp Pub Co.

McElroy, Sharon. Quiet Dreams from the Heart. 300p. (J). 1998. pap. 12.50 (1-878431-16-1) Artist Profile Pub.

McElroy, Susan C. Animals As Guides for the Soul: Stories of Life-Changing Encounters. 1998. pap. 23.00 (0-345-42404-2) Ballantine Pub Grp.

— Animals As Guides for the Soul: Stories of Life-Changing Encounters. LC 98-29805. 291p. (YA). (gr. 7 up). 1998. 23.95 (0-345-42403-4) Ballantine Pub Grp.

— Animals As Teachers & Healers. large type ed. LC 97-97061. (Illus.). 272p. 1998. pap. 12.00 (0-345-42117-5) Ballantine Pub Grp.

— Animals As Teachers & Healers: True Stories & Reflections. large type ed. LC 97-15102. 324p. 1997. 24.95 (0-7862-1187-3) Thorndike Pr.

McElroy, Thomas P., Jr. The New Handbook of Attracting Birds. (Illus.). 258p. 1985. pap. 9.95 (0-393-30280-6) Norton.

McElroy, Tom, jt. compiled by see North State Cooperative Library System Staff.

McElroy, Walter, tr. see Corbiere, Tristan.

***McElroy, Wendy.** Queen Silver: The Godless Girl. LC 99-45067. (Women's Studies). 300p. 1999. 28.95 (1-57392-755-4) Prometheus Bks.

McElroy, Wendy. The Reasonable Woman: A Guide to Intellectual Survival. LC 97-51477. 313p. 1998. pap. 17.95 (1-57392-208-0) Prometheus Bks.

— Sexual Correctness: The Gender-Feminist Attack on Women. LC 96-25691. 200p. 1996. lib. bdg. 32.50 (0-7864-0226-1) McFarland & Co.

— A Woman's Right to Pornography. 1997. pap. 12.95 (0-614-27687-X, St Martin Griffin) St Martin.

McElroy, Wendy, compiled by. Liberty, 1881-1908: A Comprehensive Index. LC 82-1383. 162p. 1982. 30.00 (0-9602574-2-X) M E Coughlin.

McElroy, Wendy, ed. Freedom, Feminism & the State. 250p. 1991. pap. 19.95 (0-945999-67-4, 8029); lib. bdg. 49.95 (0-945999-68-2, 8056) Independent Inst.

McElroy, William. Fences & Retaining Walls. 400p. (Orig.). 1990. pap. 23.25 (0-934041-53-9) Craftsman.

— Painter's Handbook. 320p. (Orig.). 1987. pap. 21.25 (0-934041-28-8) Craftsman.

An Asterisk (*) at the beginning of an entry indicates that the title is appearing for the first time.

McElroy, William C. Forms Library for the Professional Construction Contractor. 288p. (C). 1993. text 40.00 (*0-13-174558-1*) P-H.

McElroy, William D., ed. see Light & Life Symposium Staff.

McElroy, William D., ed. see Symposium on the Chemical Basis of Heredity Staff.

***McElvain, Frank C.** A History of the McElvain-McIlvaine Family Line: The Notes of Frank C. McElvain, 1948. LC 99-74085. (Illus.). 550p. 1999. 58.00 (*0-9672293-0-8*) S MacElvaine.

McElvaine, R. Eve's Seed. 432p. 2000. 27.95 (*0-07-135528-6*) McGraw.

McElvaine, Robert. The Depression & New Deal: A History in Documents. LC 99-36644. (Pages from History Ser.). (Illus.). 192p. (YA). 2000. 30.00 (*0-19-510493-5*) OUP.

McElvaine, Robert S. The Great Depression: America, 1929-1941. 1993. pap. 16.00 (*0-8129-2327-8*) Random.

McElvaine, Robert S., ed. Down & Out in the Great Depression: Letters from the Forgotten Man. LC 82-7022. (Illus.). xvii, 251p. 1983. pap. 14.95 (*0-8078-4099-8*) U of NC Pr.

McElvaney, Leigh F., ed. Proceedings of the Sixth Southeastern Safety & Health Conference & Exhibition, 1992. 227p. 1993. 40.00 (*0-9624647-7-5*) GA Tech Rsch Inst.

— Proceedings of the Southeastern Safety & Health Conference & Exhibition, 1993. 318p. 1993. 40.00 (*0-9624647-8-3*) GA Tech Rsch Inst.

McElvaney, William K. Eating & Drinking at the Welcome Table: The Holy Supper for All People. LC 98-31360. 120p. 1998. pap. 12.99 (*0-8272-0812-X*) Chalice Pr.

— Good News Is Bad News Is Good News. LC 79-22032. 144p. (Orig.). reprint ed. pap. 44.70 (*0-8357-2685-1*, 204022100015) Bks Demand.

— Preaching from Camelot to Covenant. LC 89-14948. 144p. 1989. pap. 10.95 (*0-687-33842-5*) Abingdon.

McElveen, Floyd C. The Beautiful Side of Death. (Orig.). 1988. 4.95 (*0-9620963-0-X*) Inst Rel Rsch.

— The Compelling Christ. 2nd rev. ed. (Illus.). 80p. 1996. mass mkt. 1.95 (*0-9620963-6-9*) Inst Rel Rsch.

— The Disney Boycott. LC 98-72678. 64p. 1998. pap. 4.99 (*1-56384-154-1*) Huntington Hse.

— Evidence You Never Knew Existed: Reasons to Trust Jesus & the Bible. Orig. Title: The Compelling Christ. (RUS.). 1996. 1.95 (*0-9620963-7-7*) Inst Rel Rsch.

— God's Word: Final, Infallible & Forever. 2nd ed. 386p. (Orig.). 1985. pap. 4.95 (*0-9620963-4-2*) Inst Rel Rsch.

— The Mormon Illusion: What the Bible Says about the Latter-Day Saints. rev. ed. LC 96-3420. 224p. 1997. pap. 10.99 (*0-8254-3192-1*) Kregel.

***McElveen, Steven.** Fear of Permanence. LC 00-100563. 50p. 2000. pap. 8.95 (*0-9673030-1-X*, bksm002) Nettle Pr.

McElvoy, Anne, jt. auth. see Wolf, Markus.

McElwain, Kenneth & McElwain, Shawna. Shiny Shoes. LC 97-69239. (Illus.). 32p. (J). (gr. 3-8). 1998. pap. 6.95 (*1-57197-087-8*) Pentland Pr.

McElwain, Shawna, jt. auth. see McElwain, Kenneth.

McElwain, Wilbur J. Cumberland County, PA, Cemetery Records Collected by Jeremiah Zeamer. 266p. (Orig.). 1994. pap. text 36.00 (*0-7884-0075-4*) Heritage Bk.

— A Documentary & Genealogical History of the Family of Andrew: McElwain & Mary Mickey of Cumberland County, Pennsylvania. LC 97-190252. xi, 367p. 1997. pap. 30.00 (*0-7884-0682-5*, M118) Heritage Bk.

— Genealogical Data Abstracted from History of Middle Spring Presbyterian Church, Middle Spring, Pennsylvania, 1738-1900. vi, 180p. (Orig.). 1992. pap. text 27.50 (*1-55613-722-2*) Heritage Bk.

— United States Direct Tax of 1798 Tax List for Washington County, Pennsylvania. LC 98-107766. xxii, 285p. 1997. pap. 32.00 (*0-7884-0743-0*, M119) Heritage Bk.

***McElwain, Wilbur J.** United States Direct Tax of 1798: Tax Lists for City of Philadelphia, PA; Upper Delaware, Lower Delaware, High Street, Chestnut, Walnut & Dock Wards. LC 99-230467. 281p. 1999. pap. 45.00 (*0-7884-1194-2*, M122) Heritage Bk.

McElwain, Wilbur J. United States Direct Tax of 1798: Tax Lists for Cumberland Co., PA. (Illus.). 231p. (Orig.). 1995. pap. text 33.00 (*0-7884-0118-1*) Heritage Bk.

McElwain, Wilbur J., ed. Genealogical Data Abstracted from History of the Big Spring Presbyterian Church. 130p. (Orig.). 1992. pap. 27.50 (*1-55613-707-9*) Heritage Bk.

***McElwee, B. G.** Cherokee County, Alabama. (Images of America Ser.). (Illus.). 128p. 2000. pap. 18.99 (*0-7385-0587-0*) Arcadia Publng.

McElwee, B. G. Floyd County, GA. LC 98-87451. (Images of America Ser.). (Illus.). 128p. 1998. pap. 18.99 (*0-7524-0966-2*) Arcadia Publng.

McElwee, David A., et al, eds. Media Resource Guide. 5th ed. (Illus.). 108p. 1987. pap. 10.00 (*0-910755-05-1*) Foun Am Comm.

McElwee, William L. Argyll & Sutherland Highlanders. LC 72-170400. (Men-at-arms Ser.). 40p. 1972. write for info. (*0-85045-085-3*) Ospry.

— Britain's Locust Years: Nineteen Eighteen to Nineteen Forty. LC 78-25900. 292p. 1979. reprint ed. lib. bdg. 65.00 (*0-313-21162-0*, MCBL, Greenwood Pr) Greenwood.

— The Reign of Charles V, 1516-1558. LC 83-45657. reprint ed. 36.00 (*0-404-19807-4*) AMS Pr.

— The Wisest Fool in Christendom. LC 74-7449. (Illus.). 296p. 1974. reprint ed. lib. bdg. 35.00 (*0-8371-7522-4*, MCWF, Greenwood Pr) Greenwood.

McElya, Lisa C. Dallas Party & Event Planners Sourcebook: To Throw an Unforgettable Party or Special Event, Here's What You Need, & Where To Find It! McElya, Shirley, ed. (Orig.). 1988. 19.95 (*0-929708-02-4*) Applause TX.

McElya, Shirley, ed. see McElya, Lisa C.

***McEnally, Julie.** Julie & Laurie McEnally's Complete Book of Fishing Baits & Rigs. (Illus.). 80p. 1998. pap. 9.95 (*0-646-24873-1*) F Amato Pubns.

***McEnally, Julie & McEnally, Laurie.** Bluewater Fishing Guide. (Illus.). 88p. 1998. pap. 22.95 (*1-86513-006-0*, Pub. by AFN AUS) F Amato Pubns.

McEnally, Laurie, jt. auth. see McEnally, Julie.

McEnanay, Frank, jt. auth. see Hemstock, Gillian.

McEnaney, B., et al, eds. Characterisation of Porous Solids IV. (Special Publication Ser.: Vol. 213). 718p. 1998. 160.00 (*0-85404-782-4*) Spr-Verlag.

***McEnaney, Frank & Hemstock, Gillian.** Luminosity. 1999. pap. write for info. (*0-679-31004-5*) Random.

***McEnaney, Laura.** Civil Defense Begins at Home: Militarization Meets Everyday Life in the Fifties. LC 99-87365. (Politics & Society in Twentieth-Century America Ser.). (Illus.). 240p. 2000. 29.95 (*0-691-00138-3*, Pub. by Princeton U Pr) Cal Prin Full Svc.

McEneaney, Karen, jt. auth. see McEneaney, Terry.

McEneaney, Terry & McEneaney, Karen. Birds of Yellowstone. (Illus.). 171p. (Orig.). 1988. pap. 14.95 (*0-911797-44-0*) Roberts Rinehart.

McEneny, John J. Albany: Capital City on the Hudson. LC 98-74147. (Illus.). 268p. 1998. 29.95 (*0-9654754-9-2*) Am Historical Pr.

McEnerney, Barbara, ed. see Arroyo, Stephen.

McEnerney, John, tr. see Cyril of Alexandria, St.

McEnerney, John I., tr. see Cyril.

McEnery, Anthony Mark, jt. ed. see Botley, Simon.

Mcenery, E. C. The Life & Times of Darryl Sutter: Wit, Wisdom & Tougher Love. (Illus.). 128p. 1999. pap. 12.95 (*1-57098-288-0*) Roberts Rinehart.

McEnery, John H. Epilogue in Burma, 1945-48. 200p. (C). 1991. 85.00 (*0-946771-84-7*, Pub. by Spellmnt Pubs) St Mut.

***McEnery, M. J. & Refausse, Raymond, eds.** Christ Church Deeds. 400p. 1999. boxed set 45.00 (*1-85182-470-7*, Pub. by Four Cts Pr) Intl Spec Bk.

McEnery, Thomas. California Cavalier: The Journal of Captain Thomas Fallon. (Illus.). 112p. 1985. reprint ed. lib. bdg. 9.95 (*0-914139-05-3*) Hist San Jose.

McEnery, Tom. The New City State: Change & Renewal in America's Cities. LC 94-66090. (Illus.). 342p. 1994. 24.95 (*1-879373-40-8*) Roberts Rinehart.

McEnery, Tony & Paice, Chris, eds. IRSG, '92: Proceedings of the BCS 14th Information Retrieval Colloquium, University of Lancaster, 13-14 April 1992. LC 93-7747. (Workshops in Computing Ser.). 1993. 69.00 (*0-387-19808-3*) Spr-Verlag.

McEnery, Tony & Wilson, Andrew. Corpus Linguistics. (Edinburgh Textbooks in Empirical Linguistics Ser.). 256p. 1996. 70.00 (*0-7486-0808-7*, Pub. by Edinburgh U Pr); pap. 24.50 (*0-7486-0482-0*, Pub. by Edinburgh U Pr) Col U Pr.

McEniry, John H. A Marine Dive-Bomber Pilot at Guadalcanal. LC 86-16053. (Illus.). 195p. 1987. reprint ed. pap. 60.50 (*0-608-01674-8*, 206233000002) Bks Demand.

McEno, John, et al. Cannabis Ecology: A Compendium of Diseases & Pests. rev. ed. LC 98-89322. 1998. pap. 50.00 (*1-893553-03-5*) AMRITA Pr.

McEnroe Consulting Staff. Web for Economic Development. 32p. 1999. 79.95 (*0-7872-5759-1*, 41575901) Kendall-Hunt.

***McEnroe, Patrick & Bodo, Peter.** Tennis for Dummies. (For Dummies Ser.). (Illus.). 408p. 1998. pap. 19.99 (*0-7645-5087-X*) IDG Bks.

McEnroe, Richard. The Invisible Dirty Old Man. unabridged ed. (Illus.). 48p. 1999. pap. 9.95 (*1-893992-50-0*) Red Giant Prods.

— Skinner. Cover, Arthur B., ed. Date not set. pap. write for info. (*1-893475-20-4*) Alexander Pubg.

McEnroe, Robert E. The Silver Whistle. 1950. pap. 5.25 (*0-8222-1028-2*) Dramatists Play.

McEnroe, Tim, et al. Ethical Standards for Drug Abuse Counselors. rev. ed. 1995. 21.95 (*1-55691-165-3*) Learning Pubns.

***McEntarffer, Robert.** How to Prepare for the Advanced Placement Exam, AP: Psychology. 320p. 2000. pap. 14.95 (*0-7641-0959-6*) Barron.

McEntee, Art, et al. Computerized Accounting: Tutorial & Applications. LC 92-33453. 1992. write for info. (*0-07-017739-2*) Glencoe.

***McEntee, Grace H.** 52 Carolina Weekends: Great Getaways & Adventures for Every Season. LC 99-59312. (52 Weekends Ser.). (Illus.). 192p. 2000. pap. 14.95 (*0-658-00174-4*, 001744) NTC Contemp Pub Co.

McEntee, Grace H. The Island, the Ox, You & Me. (Illus.). 27p. (Orig.). 1986. pap. 3.95 (*0-917012-82-8*) RI Pubns Soc.

McEntee, Kenneth. Reproductive Pathology of Domestic Mammals. 401p. 1990. text 125.00 (*0-12-483375-6*) Acad Pr.

McEntee, Margaret, ed. Resources for Catechists & Chaplains. 216p. (Orig.). 1994. pap. 12.95 (*1-85607-108-1*, Pub. by Columba Press) Whitecap Bks.

McEntee, Margaret A. Fluids & Electrolytes. (NSNA Review Ser.). (Illus.). 224p. (C). 1996. pap. 31.95 (*0-8273-7641-3*) Delmar.

McEntee, Phil, jt. auth. see Francey, David.

McEntee, Sean. Lectionary for Masses with Children, Cycle C. 192p. (Orig.). (J). (gr. 2-8). 1988. pap. text 19.95 (*0-89622-385-X*) Twenty-Third.

McEnteer, James. Fighting Words: Independent Journalists in Texas. LC 91-32797. (Illus.). 238p. 1992. 24.95 (*0-292-72474-8*) U of Tex Pr.

McEntire, Frank. Dreams & Shields: Spiritual Dimensions in Contemporary Art. (Illus.). 130p. (Orig.). 1992. pap. 17.95 (*0-942291-01-8*) Salt Lake Art Ctr.

McEntire, Mark. The Blood of Abel: The Violent Plot in the Hebrews Bible. LC 98-33339. 192p. 1999. 35.00 (*0-86554-628-2*); pap. 18.00 (*0-86554-629-0*) Mercer Univ Pr.

McEntire, Mark H. The Function of Sacrifice in Chronicles, Ezra, & Nehemiah. LC 93-2688. (Biblical Press Ser.: Vol. 8). 140p. 1993. text 69.95 (*0-7734-2362-1*) E Mellen.

McEntire, Patricia. Mommy I'm Hungry: How to Feed Your Child Nutritiously. LC 81-68292. 168p. 1982. pap. 3.00 (*0-917982-11-8*, Cougar Books) Capitol Enquiry.

***McEntire, Reba.** Comfort from a Country Quilt. LC 99-21644. (Illus.). 192p. 1999. 19.95 (*0-553-10794-1*, Fanfare) Bantam.

— Comfort from a Country Quilt: Finding New Inspiration & Strength from Old-Fashioned Values. 192p. 2000. pap. 9.95 (*0-553-38094-X*, Spectra) Bantam.

— Comfort from a Country Quilt: Finding New Inspiration & Strength from Old-Fashioned Values. large type ed. LC 00-26168. (Biography Ser.). 185p. 2000. 29.95 (*0-7862-2502-5*, MML06500-171902) Thorndike Pr.

McEntire, Reba. Starting Over. 56p. 1996. per. 14.95 (*0-7935-6192-2*) H Leonard.

McEntire, Reba & Carter, Tom. Reba: My Story. 352p. 1995. mass mkt. 6.50 (*0-553-57238-5*) Bantam.

McEntire, Sandra. The Doctrine of Compunction in Medieval England: Holy Tears. LC 90-22127. (Studies in Medieval Literature: Vol. 8). 200p. 1991. lib. bdg. 79.95 (*0-88946-225-9*) E Mellen.

McEntire, Sandra J., ed. Margery Kempe: A Book of Essays. LC 92-6437. 280p. 1992. text 20.00 (*0-8153-0378-5*) Garland.

McEntire, Sandra J. & Salisbury, Joyce E., eds. Julian of Norwich: A Book of Essays. LC 98-12955. (Medieval Casebks.: Vol. 21). 368p. 1998. text 70.00 (*0-8153-2529-0*, H2034) Garland.

McEntire, Walter F. Was Christopher Columbus a Jew? 1976. lib. bdg. 59.95 (*0-8490-1278-3*) Gordon Pr.

McEntyre, John G. Land Survey Systems. (Illus.). 537p. 1986. reprint ed. 60.00 (*0-910845-27-1*, 511) Landmark Ent.

— Workbook for Land Survey Systems. (Illus.). 186p. 1990. pap., wbk. ed. 50.00 (*0-910845-41-7*) Landmark Ent.

McEntyre, Marilyn C., ed. Where Icarus Falls. 1998. pap. 14.95 (*0-9655497-3-9*) SB Review Pubns.

— Word Tastings. 1998. pap. 14.95 (*0-9655497-4-7*) SB Review Pubns.

McEntyre, Marilyn C., jt. auth. see Hawkins, Anne H.

***McEntyre, Marilyn Chandler.** In Quiet Light: Poems on Vermeer's Women. 2000. 20.00 (*0-8028-3879-0*) Eerdmans.

McEntyre, Marilyn Chandler, jt. ed. see Hawkins, Anne Hunsaker.

McEntyre, Robert L. Top 200 "Meds" for the Surgical Patient. 263p. 1991. pap. 19.95 (*0-942219-23-6*) Quality Med Pub.

***Mcenzie, H.** The Way Things Were. 1999. 29.95 (*0-7472-2112-X*, Pub. by Headline Bk Pub) Trafalgar.

McErlain, Jeff. Basix Rock Guitar Techniques. 1997. pap. 7.95 (*0-88284-760-0*); pap. 9.95 incl. audio compact disk (*0-88284-761-9*) Alfred Pub.

— Technique - Metal. (Alfred Handy Guide Ser.). 1993. pap. 4.50 (*0-88284-620-5*, 4443) Alfred Pub.

McErlean, J. M. Napolean & Pozzo Di Borgo in Corsica & after, 1764-1821: Not Quite a Vendetta. LC 95-48785. (Studies in French Civilization: Vol. 10). 328p. 1996. text 99.95 (*0-7734-8853-7*) E Mellen.

McErlean, Jennifer. Philosophies of Science. LC 99-41580. (Philosophy Ser.). 243p. 1999. pap. text 55.95 (*0-534-55163-7*) Wadsworth Pub.

McEuen, Caroline K., ed. see Gittinger, Mattiebelle.

McEuen, James. Snake Country. LC 89-51582. 64p. (Orig.). 1990. pap. 8.00 (*0-915380-26-9*) Word Works.

McEuen, Melissa A. Seeing America: Women Photographers Between the Wars. LC 99-17219. (Illus.). 360p. 1999. 29.95 (*0-8131-2132-9*) U Pr of Ky.

Mcevay. Managing Human Resources. 4th ed. 1995. student ed. 26.56 (*0-07-011237-1*) McGraw.

McEvedy, Colin. The New Penguin Atlas of Medieval History. enl. rev. ed. (Illus.). 128p. 1992. pap. 13.95 (*0-14-051249-7*, Penguin Bks) Viking Penguin.

— The Penguin Atlas of African History. 2nd ed. (Illus.). 144p. 1995. pap. 15.95 (*0-14-051321-3*, Penguin Bks) Viking Penguin.

— The Penguin Atlas of Ancient History. 1986. pap. 12.95 (*0-14-051151-2*, Penguin Bks) Viking Penguin.

— The Penguin Atlas of Modern History. 1986. pap. 12.95 (*0-14-051153-9*, Penguin Bks) Viking Penguin.

— The Penguin Atlas of Recent History. 1986. pap. 12.95 (*0-14-051154-7*, Penguin Bks) Viking Penguin.

— The Penguin Historical Atlas of the Pacific. LC 98-9434. (Illus.). 120p. 1998. pap. 16.95 (*0-14-025428-5*) Viking Penguin.

McEvenue, Sean. Interpretation & Bible: Essays on Truth in Literature. 187p. (Orig.). 1994. pap. text 12.95 (*0-8146-5036-8*, M Glazier) Liturgical Pr.

— Interpreting the Pentateuch. (Old Testament Message Ser.: No. 4). 194p. (Orig.). 1990. pap. 14.95 (*0-8146-5654-4*, M Glazier) Liturgical Pr.

McEvenue, Sean E. & Meyer, Ben F., eds. Lonergan's Hermeneutics: Its Development & Application. LC 88-28383. 313p. 1989. 44.95 (*0-8132-0670-7*) Cath U Pr.

***McEver, Jimmie, et al.** Exhalt: An Interdiction Model for Exploring Halt Capabilities. xvii, 80p. 2000. pap. 12.00 (*0-8330-2829-4*) Rand Corp.

McEvers, Joan, jt. auth. see March, Marion D.

McEvey, Shane F., ed. see Paterson, Hugh E.

McEvilley, Thomas. Art & Discontent: Theory at the Millennium. LC 90-48316. 1993. pap. 12.00 (*0-929701-31-3*) McPherson & Co.

— Art & Otherness: Crisis in Cultural Identity. LC 92-7120. 176p. 1992. 20.00 (*0-929701-21-6*) McPherson & Co.

— Art & Otherness: Crisis in Cultural Identity. LC 92-7120. 174p. 1995. reprint ed. pap. 12.00 (*0-929701-48-8*) McPherson & Co.

— Capacity: The History, the World, & the Self in Contemporary Art & Criticism. (Critical Voices in Art, Theory, & Culture Ser.: Vol. 1). 170p. 1996. pap. 18.95 (*90-5701-041-0*, Pub. by G & B) Dist Art Pubs.

— Capacity: The History, the World & the Self in Contemporary Art & Criticism. (Critical Visions in Art, Theory & Culture Ser.: Vol. 1). 160p. 1996. 35.00 (*90-5701-051-8*, Pub. by G & B) Dist Art Pubs.

— Ingeborg Luscher: Brightness/Stillness. Longhauser, Elsa, ed. LC 94-74308. (Illus.). 10p. 1995. pap. 10.00 (*1-58442-030-8*) Galleries at Moore.

— James Croak. (Illus.). 144p. 1999. 45.00 (*0-8109-6379-5*, Pub. by Abrams) Time Warner.

— Joe Overstreet: (Re)Call & Response. Piche, Thomas E., Jr., ed. (Illus.). 48p. 1996. pap. text 12.00 (*0-914407-19-8*) Everson Mus.

— North of Yesterday. LC 86-33250. 288p. 1987. 20.00 (*0-914232-86-X*); pap. 12.00 (*0-914232-85-1*) McPherson & Co.

— Pat Steir. LC 94-30546. (Illus.). 176p. 1995. 49.50 (*0-8109-4459-6*, Pub. by Abrams) Time Warner.

***McEvilley, Thomas.** Sculpture in the Age of Doubt. LC 98-74535. (Aesthetics Today Ser.). (Illus.). 448p. 1999. pap. 24.95 (*1-58115-023-7*) Allworth Pr.

McEvilley, Thomas. Soil & Sky: Mel Chin at the Fabric Workshop. (Illus.). 32p. 1993. pap. 15.00 (*0-9619760-3-9*) Fabric Workshop Inc.

McEvilley, Thomas, contrib. by. Julian Schnabel Fox Farm Paintings. (Illus.). 38p. 1989. pap. write for info. (*1-878283-02-2*) PaceWildenstein.

McEvilley, Thomas, et al. Allocations: Art for a Natural & Artificial Environment. (Illus.). 1992. 55.00 (*90-800914-2-1*) Dist Art Pubs.

— An Artist's Body: Performances, 1969-1998. (Illus.). 468p. 1998. 75.00 (*88-8158-175-2*, Pub. by Charta) Dist Art Pubs.

— Fusion: West African Artists at the Venice Biennale. (Focus on African Art Ser.). (Illus.). 96p. 1993. pap. 19.95 (*3-7913-1327-4*, Pub. by Prestel) te Neues.

— James Croak: Twenty-Year Servey. (Illus.). 144p. 1998. 49.95 (*1-885163-06-1*) Virginia Beach Ctr.

— Lucas Samaras: Objects & Subjects, 1969-1986. (Illus.). 224p. 1988. 65.00 (*0-89659-803-9*) Abbeville Pr.

— Too Late for Goya: Works by Francesc Torres. (ENG & SPA., Illus.). 124p. (Orig.). 1993. pap. 40.00 (*1-879286-07-6*) Ariz St U Art Mus.

McEvilley, Thomas, jt. auth. see Howard, Richard.

McEvily, A. J., jt. auth. see Tetelman, A. S.

McEvily, A. J., jt. ed. see Iida, K.

McEvoy. Early Intervention Methods. (C). 1999. text 52.00 (*0-15-502491-4*) Harcourt Coll Pubs.

McEvoy, Alan W. When Disaster Strikes: Preparing Schools for Bus Accidents, Murders, Suicides, Tornados & Other Community Catastrophes. rev. ed. 1998. pap. 6.95 (*1-55691-155-6*) Learning Pubns.

***McEvoy, Alan W., et al, abrs.** If He Is Raped: A Guidebook for Parents, Mates & Friends. 112p. 1999. pap. 11.95 (*1-55691-150-5*) Learning Pubns.

— If He Is Raped: A Guidebook for Parents, Partners, Spouse & Friends. 32p. 1999. pap. 13.50 (*1-55691-166-1*) Learning Pubns.

McEvoy, Alan W. & Brookings, Jeff D. Helping Battered Women: A Volunteer's Handbook. 2nd ed. 1990. pap. 11.95 (*1-55691-067-3*, 673) Learning Pubns.

— If She Is Raped: A Book for Husbands, Fathers & Male Friends. 2nd abr. ed. 1990. pap. 12.95 (*1-55691-061-4*, 614) Learning Pubns.

— If She Is Raped: A Book for Husbands, Fathers & Male Friends. 2nd unabridged ed. 176p. 1990. pap. 12.95 (*1-55691-062-2*, 622) Learning Pubns.

McEvoy, Alan W. & Erickson, Edsel L. Abused Children: The Educator's Guide to Prevention & Intervention. 1994. pap. 19.95 (*1-55691-052-5*, 525) Learning Pubns.

— Youth & Exploitation: A Process Leading to Running Away, Violence, Substance Abuse & Suicide. 1990. pap. 12.95 (*1-55691-042-8*, 428) Learning Pubns.

McEvoy, Alan W. & McEvoy, Marcia. Preventing Youth Suicide: A Handbook for Educators & Human Service Professionals. 1994. pap. 22.95 (*1-55691-056-8*, 568) Learning Pubns.

McEvoy, Arthur F. The Fisherman's Problem: Ecology & Law in California Fisheries, 1850-1980. (Illus.). 388p. (C). 1990. pap. text 20.95 (*0-521-38586-5*) Cambridge U Pr.

— The Fisherman's Problem: Ecology & Law in the California Fisheries, 1850-1980. (Studies in Environment & History). (Illus.). 392p. 1986. text 74.95 (*0-521-32427-0*) Cambridge U Pr.

***McEvoy, Christine M. & Grasso, Joseph A.** Massachusetts Suppression Matters: A Guide to Search, Seizure, & Massachusetts Law. 360p. 1999. 95.00 (*0-327-01658-2*, 6453010) LEXIS Pub.

McEvoy, Colleen A. Career Focus: One Day at a Time. 369p. 1992. pap. text 8.95 (*0-9633810-0-8*) C A McEvoy.

McEvoy, Donald W. The Police & Their Many Publics. LC 76-6851. 154p. reprint ed. pap. 47.80 (*0-608-15229-3*, 202749400055) Bks Demand.

McEvoy, Gerald K., ed. AHFS Drug Information, 1999. 40th rev. ed. 3300p. 1999. pap. text 155.00 (*1-879907-91-7*) Am Soc Hlth-Syst.

***McEvoy, Gerald K., ed.** AHFS Drug Information, 2000. 42nd rev. ed. LC 59-7620. 3600p. 2000. pap. text 150.00 (*1-58528-004-6*) Am Soc Hlth-Syst.

M

An Asterisk (*) at the beginning of an entry indicates that the title is appearing for the first time.

McEvoy, Gerald K., ed. AHFS Drug Information, 1997. 39th rev. ed. 2900p. 1997. pap. text 132.00 (*1-879907-69-0*) Am Soc Hlth-Syst.

— AHFS Drug Information, 1998. 40th rev. ed. 3000p. 1998. pap. text 139.00 (*1-879907-76-3*) Am Soc Hlth-Syst.

McEvoy, Greg. Alfie's Long Winter. unabridged ed. LC 99-476008. (Illus.). 32p. (J). (ps-3). 1996. 13.95 (*0-7737-2910-0*) STDK.

— The Ice Cream King. (Illus.). 32p. (J). (gr. k-3). 1999. pap. 7.95 (*0-7737-6024-5*) Genl Dist Srvs.

McEvoy, Greg. The Ice Cream King. LC 98-226147. (Illus.). 32p. (J). (gr. k up). 1998. 13.95 (*0-7737-3069-9*) STDK.

McEvoy, H. K. Knife-Throwing. 7.95 (*0-685-63762-X*) Wehman.

McEvoy, Hallie I. Showing for Beginners. LC 96-30498. (Illus.). 176p. 1996. pap. 16.95 (*1-55821-500-X*) Lyons Pr.

McEvoy, Harry K. Knife & Tomahawk Throwing. (Illus.). 28p. 1983. pap. 3.95 (*0-940362-10-4*) Knife World.

— Knife & Tomahawk Throwing: The Art of the Experts. LC 88-50409. (Illus.). 152p. 1988. pap. 8.95 (*0-8048-1542-9*) Tuttle Pubng.

— Knife Throwing: A Practical Guide. LC 72-91550. (Illus.). 112p. 1973. pap. 6.95 (*0-8048-1099-0*) Tuttle Pubng.

— Scagel: The Man & His Knives. (Illus.). 28p. 1985. pap. 3.95 (*0-940362-09-0*) Knife World.

McEvoy, Hubert, compiled by. Prayers from the Psalms: With Other Prayers from Scripture. 2nd unabridged ed. (Marian Ser.: Vol. 7). 152p. 1995. 13.95 (*0-940147-39-4*) Source Bks CA.

McEvoy, ion, ed. see Alarcon, Francisco X.

McEvoy, J. D. Winning Secrets of a Poker Master. 32p. 1997. pap. 7.95 (*0-934650-11-X*) Sunnyside.

McEvoy, J. P. Introducing Quantum Theory. LC 96-60308. (Illus.). 176p. 1996. pap. 9.95 (*1-874166-37-4*, Pub. by Totem Bks) Natl Bk Netwk.

McEvoy, J. P. & Zarate, Oscar. Introducing Stephen Hawking. LC 95-60967. (Illus.). 176p. pap. 9.95 (*1-874166-25-0*, Pub. by Totem Bks) Natl Bk Netwk.

***McEvoy, James.** Robert Grosseteste. (Great Medieval Thinkers). 224p. 2000. pap. 18.95 (*0-19-511450-7*); text 39.95 (*0-19-511449-3*) OUP.

McEvoy, James. Robert Grosseteste, Exegete & Philosopher. LC 94-5847. (Collected Studies: No. CS 446). 205p. 1994. 101.95 (*0-86078-433-9*, Pub. by Variorum) Ashgate Pub Co.

McEvoy, James E., ed. Catalysts for the Control of Automotive Pollutants. LC 75-20298. (Advances in Chemistry Ser.: No. 143). 199p. 1975. 27.95 (*0-8412-0219-2*) Am Chemical.

— Catalysts for the Control of Automotive Pollutants: A Symposium. LC 75-20298. (Advances in Chemistry Ser.: No. 143). (Illus.). 207p. reprint ed. pap. 64.20 (*0-608-04356-7*, 206513700001) Bks Demand.

— Partnerships in Chemical Research & Education. LC 91-32420. (ACS Symposium Ser.: No. 478). (Illus.). 250p. 1992. text 55.00 (*0-8412-2173-1*, Pub. by Am Chemical) OUP.

***McEvoy, John.** Great Horse Racing Mysteries: True Tales from the Track. 256p. 2000. 24.95 (*1-58150-052-1*, Pub. by Blood-Horse) IPG Chicago.

McEvoy, John. Through the Pages of Daily Racing Form. (Illus.). 102p. 1995. pap. 19.95 (*0-9648493-4-8*) Daily Racing.

McEvoy, John G. & Schwartz, A. Truman, eds. Motion Toward Perfection: The Achievement of Joseph Priestley, 1733-1804. (Orig.). 1990. pap. 7.00 (*1-55896-010-4*, Skinner Hse Bks) Unitarian Univ.

McEvoy, Joseph P. Reading the Building Code: A Short Hermeneutic. 89p. (C). 1991. pap. text 20.00 (*0-89801-020-9*) NE Univ Pub.

McEvoy, Joseph P., jt. ed. see Keefe, Richard S. E.

McEvoy, Kathleen, jt. ed. see Resnick, Robert J.

McEvoy, Ken, jt. auth. see Frantzen, Trond.

McEvoy, M. External Components. (Mitchell's Building Ser.). (C). 1996. pap. text 49.95 (*0-582-21255-3*) Addison-Wesley.

McEvoy, Marcia, jt. auth. see McEvoy, Alan W.

***McEvoy, Marian.** Steps to Style. 2000. 35.00 (*0-06-019673-4*) HarpC.

McEvoy, Nion, ed. see Blumer, Bob.

McEvoy, Nion, ed. see Saeks, Diane D.

McEvoy, Nion, ed. see Sansweet, Stephen J.

McEvoy, Nion, ed. see Welsh, Pat.

McEvoy, Nion, ed. see Zwaerepoel, Jean-Pierre.

McEvoy, Patrick. Educating the Future GP: The Course Organizer's Handbook. 2nd ed. LC 98-27318. 1998. write for info. (*1-85775-281-3*, Radcliffe Med Pr) Scovill Paterson.

McEvoy, R. C., jt. ed. see Ginsberg-Fellner, F.

***McEvoy, Sean.** Shakespeare: Basics. LC 99-46914. 304p. (C). 2000. text. write for info. (*0-415-21288-X*) Routledge.

— Shakespeare: Basics. LC 99-46914. (Illus.). 277p. (C). 2000. pap. write for info. (*0-415-21289-8*) Routledge.

***McEvoy, Seth.** Microsoft Windows Media Player Handbook. 336p. 2000. pap. 29.99 (*0-7356-1178-5*) Microsoft.

***McEvoy, Thomas J. & Natural Resource, Agriculture Staff.** Introduction to Forest Ecology & Silviculture. 2nd ed. LC 00-30490. (Illus.). 2000. pap. write for info. (*0-935817-55-7*) NRAES.

— Using Fertilizers in the Culture of Christmas Trees. rev. ed. LC 00-41140. 2000. pap. write for info. (*0-935817-56-5*) NRAES.

McEvoy, Tom. Tournament Poker. LC 94-80002. (Illus.). 312p. (Orig.). 1995. pap. 39.95 (*1-884466-05-2*) Poker Plus.

***McEvoy, Tom & Cloutier, T. J.** Championship Hold'em: Limit Hold'em Cash Game Strategies & Tournment Tactics. Smith, Dana, ed. (Illus.). 320p. 2000. pap. 39.95 (*1-884466-00-1*) Poker Plus.

McEvoy, Tom, jt. auth. see Cloutier, T. J.

McEwan. The Art of Classroom Managemt: Effective Practices for Building Equitable. LC 99-12027. 233p. 1999. pap. text 37.00 (*0-13-079975-0*) P-H.

— The Heart of Cool. LC 98-36614. (J). 1999. per. 15.00 (*0-689-82177-8*); per. 3.99 (*0-689-82178-6*) S&S Childrens.

McEwan, Angela, tr. see Miranda, Veronica.

McEwan, Barbara. Agricultural Crisis in America. LC 99-52004. (Contemporary World Issues Ser.). 270p. 1999. lib. bdg. 45.00 (*0-87436-737-9*) ABC-CLIO.

— White House Landscapes: Horticultural Achievements of American Presidents. 224p. 1992. 24.95 (*0-8027-1192-8*) Walker & Co.

McEwan, Barbara, ed. Practicing Judicious Discipline: An Educator's Guide to a Democratic Classroom. 2nd ed. 128p. (C). 1994. pap. text 14.95 (*1-880192-09-8*) Caddo Gap Pr.

***McEwan, Barbara, ed.** Practicing Judicious Discipline: An Educator's Guide to a Democratic Classroom. 3rd rev. ed. 224p. 1999. pap. 24.95 (*1-880192-29-2*) Caddo Gap Pr.

McEwan, Barbara, et al. On Being the Boss. LC 94-68539. (Quick Read Ser.). (Illus.). 98p. (Orig.). 1995. pap. 13.95 (*1-56052-309-3*) Crisp Pubns.

McEwan, Barbara, jt. ed. see Butchart, Ronald E.

McEwan, Bennett W. & Solomon, David. Teach Yourself Transact SQL in 21 Days. LC 96-72164. 548p. 1997. 35.00 (*0-672-31045-7*) Sams.

McEwan, Bonnie G., ed. The Spanish Missions of la Florida. LC 93-7937. (Illus.). 488p. 1993. 49.95 (*0-8130-1231-7*) U Press Fla.

McEwan, Bonnie G., jt. auth. see Hann, John H.

McEwan, Calvin W., et al. Soundings at Tell Fakhariyah. LC 57-11216. (Oriental Institute Publications: No. 79). (Illus.). 104p. 1958. lib. bdg. 48.00 (*0-226-62180-4*, OIP79) U Ch Pr.

***McEwan, Cheryl.** Gender, Geography & Empire: Victorian Women Travellers in Africa. 256p. 2000. text 78.95 (*1-84014-252-9*, Pub. by Ashgate Pub) Ashgate Pub Co.

McEwan, Colin, et al. Patagonia: Natural History, Prehistory, & Ethnography at the Uttermost End of the Earth. LC 97-18348. 200p. 1998. pap. text 24.95 (*0-691-05849-0*, Pub. by Princeton U Pr) Cal Prin Full Svc.

McEwan, Dorothea. Women Experiencing Church: A Documentation of Alienation. 278p. 1992. pap. 15.95 (*0-85244-187-8*, 976, Pub. by Gra1cewing) Morehouse Pub.

McEwan, Dorothea, jt. auth. see Isherwood, Lisa.

McEwan, Dorothea, jt. ed. see Isherwood, Lisa.

McEwan, Elaine K. The ABCs of School Success: Preparing Your Young Child. LC 95-18060. (Guides for Parents & Educators Ser.). 240p. 1995. pap. 8.99 (*0-87788-635-0*, H Shaw Pubs) Waterbrook Pr.

— The ADHD Intervention Checklist. 16p. 1997. pap. 19.95 (*0-8039-6668-7*) Corwin Pr.

— Angry Parents, Failing Schools: What's Wrong with the Public Schools & What You Can Do about It. LC 98-23773. 304p. 1998. pap. 12.99 (*0-87788-019-0*, H Shaw Pubs) Waterbrook Pr.

— Attention Deficit Disorder. LC 95-18443. (Guides for Parents & Educators Ser.). 312p. 1995. pap. 11.99 (*0-87788-056-5*, H Shaw Pubs) Waterbrook Pr.

— The Dog Ate It: Conquering Homework Hassles. 96p. 1996. pap. 6.99 (*0-87788-389-0*, H Shaw Pubs) Waterbrook Pr.

— How to Deal with Parents Who Are Angry, Troubled, Afraid or Just Plain Crazy. LC 97-45277. 104p. 1998. pap. 18.95 (*0-8039-6525-7*) Corwin Pr.

— How to Deal with Parents Who Are Angry, Troubled, Afraid or Just Plain Crazy. LC 97-45277. 104p. 1998. lib. bdg. 43.95 (*0-8039-6524-9*) Corwin Pr.

— How to Raise a Reader. LC 99-22613. 208p. 1999. pap. 9.99 (*0-8010-1184-1*) Baker Bks.

— I Didn't Do It: Coping with Dishonesty in Children. 96p. 1996. pap. 6.99 (*0-87788-177-4*, H Shaw Pubs) Waterbrook Pr.

— Leading Your Team to Excellence: How to Make Quality Decisions. LC 95-17300. (Illus.). 192p. 1996. 61.95 (*0-8039-6520-6*); pap. 27.95 (*0-8039-6521-4*) Corwin Pr.

— Managing Attention & Learning Disorders: Survival Skills for Adults with Learning or Attention Difficulties. LC 97-2831. 186p. 1997. pap. 11.99 (*0-87788-181-2*, H Shaw Pubs) Waterbrook Pr.

— "Mom, He Hit Me!" What to Do about Sibling Rivalry. 96p. 1996. pap. 6.99 (*0-87788-556-7*, H Shaw Pubs) Waterbrook Pr.

— Murphy's Mansion. Norton, LoraBeth, ed. LC 94-7136. (Josh McIntire Ser.). 96p. (J). (gr. 3-6). 1994. pap. 4.99 (*0-7814-0160-7*, Chariot Bks) Chariot Victor.

— "Nobody Likes Me" Helping Your Child Make Friends. 96p. 1996. pap. 6.99 (*0-87788-590-7*, H Shaw Pubs) Waterbrook Pr.

— The Principal's Guide to Attention Deficit Hyperactivity Disorder. 240p. 1997. 65.95 (*0-8039-6531-1*); pap. 29.95 (*0-8039-6532-X*) Corwin Pr.

— The Principal's Guide to Raising Reading Achievement. LC 98-8874. 120p. 1998. 55.95 (*0-8039-6627-X*); pap. 24.95 (*0-8039-6628-8*) Corwin Pr.

— Seven Steps to Effective Instructional Leadership. LC 97-35718. (Illus.). 192p. 1997. 61.95 (*0-8039-6665-2*); pap. 27.95 (*0-8039-6666-0*) Corwin Pr.

— Solving School Problems: Kindergarten Through Middle School. 336p. (Orig.). 1992. pap. 10.99 (*0-87788-640-7*, H Shaw Pubs) Waterbrook Pr.

— Ten Traits of Highly Successful Schools: How Can You Tell If Your School Is a Good One? LC 99-32775. 160p. 1999. pap. 12.99 (*0-87788-840-X*, H Shaw Pubs) Waterbrook Pr.

— Underground Hero. LC 92-27104. 96p. (J). (gr. 3-6). 1993. pap. 4.99 (*0-7814-0113-5*, Chariot Bks) Chariot Victor.

— When Kids Say No to School: Helping Children at Risk of Failure, Refusal, Or Dropping Out. LC 98-23002. 114p. 1998. pap. 9.99 (*0-87788-406-4*, H Shaw Pubs) Waterbrook Pr.

***McEwan, Elaine K. & Damer, Mary.** Managing Unmanageable Students: Practical Solutions for Administrators. LC 99-50495. (Illus.). 192p. (C). 1999. pap. 32.95 (*0-8039-6787-X*); lib. bdg. 69.95 (*0-8039-6786-1*) Corwin Pr.

McEwan, Elaine K., jt. auth. see Kottler, Jeffrey A.

McEwan, G. J. The Late Babylonian Tablets in the Royal Ontario Museum, Two. (Illus.). 128p. pap. 20.00 (*0-88854-282-8*) Brill Academic Pubs.

McEwan, Gilbert J., ed. Late Babylonian Texts in the Ashmolean Museum. (OXECT Ser.). (Illus.). 136p. 1985. pap. text 39.95 (*0-19-815459-3*) OUP.

McEwan, Gilbert J., ed. Texts from Hellenistic Babylonia in the Ashmolean Museum. (Oxford Editions of Cuneiform Texts Ser.). (Illus.). 1982. pap. 49.95 (*0-19-815457-7*) OUP.

McEwan, Glenn H. Introduction to Computer Systems. 2nd ed. 1999. text 32.95 (*0-07-044351-3*); text. write for info. (*0-07-044352-1*) McGraw.

McEwan, Gordon F., jt. ed. see Isbell, William H.

McEwan, Hunter & Egan, Kieran, eds. Narrative in Teaching, Learning & Research. (Critical Issues in Curriculum Ser.). 256p. (C). 1995. text 44.00 (*0-8077-3400-4*); pap. text 21.95 (*0-8077-3399-7*) Tchrs Coll.

McEwan, Ian. Amsterdam: A Novel. LC 98-41401. 208p. 1998. 21.00 (*0-385-49423-8*, N A Talese) Doubleday.

***McEwan, Ian.** Amsterdam: A Novel. 193p. 1999. pap. 12.00 (*0-385-49424-6*, Anchor NY) Doubleday.

— Amsterdam: A Novel. large type ed. LC 98-53487. 1999. 28.95 (*0-7862-1796-0*) Mac Lib Ref.

McEwan, Ian. Black Dogs. 176p. 1998. pap. 14.00 (*0-385-49432-7*, Anchor NY) Doubleday.

— The Cement Garden. 1994. pap. 11.00 (*0-679-75018-5*) Villard Books.

— A Child in Time. LC 99-46225. 272p. 1999. pap. 14.00 (*0-385-49752-0*, Anchor NY) Doubleday.

McEwan, Ian. A Child in Time. large type ed. 21.95 (*1-85695-342-4*, Pub. by ISIS Lrg Prnt) Transaction Pubs.

McEwan, Ian. The Comfort of Strangers. 1994. pap. 10.00 (*0-679-74984-5*) Vin Bks.

***McEwan, Ian.** The Daydreamer. 160p. 2000. pap. 10.00 (*0-385-49805-5*, Anchor NY) Doubleday.

McEwan, Ian. The Daydreamer. LC 93-44476. (Illus.). 208p. (J). (gr. 3 up). 1994. 15.95 (*0-06-024426-7*) HarpC Child Bks.

— The Daydreamer. LC 93-44476. (Trophy Bk.). (Illus.). 208p. (J). (gr. 4-7). 1996. mass mkt. 5.95 (*0-06-440576-1*, HarpTrophy) HarpC Child Bks.

— Daydreamer. 1996. 11.05 (*0-606-09184-X*, Pub. by Turtleback) Demco.

— Enduring Love: A Novel. LC 97-23029. 262p. 1998. pap. 12.95 (*0-385-49414-9*) Doubleday.

— Enduring Love: A Novel. large type ed. LC 98-13542. (Basic Ser.). 375p. 1998. 27.95 (*0-7862-1447-3*) Thorndike Pr.

— First Love, Last Rites. 1994. pap. 12.00 (*0-679-75019-3*) Knopf.

— In Between the Sheets, And Other Stories. 1994. pap. 11.00 (*0-679-74983-7*) Vin Bks.

— The Innocent. 288p. 1995. mass mkt. 6.99 (*0-553-56554-0*) Bantam.

— The Innocent. 288p. 1998. pap. 14.00 (*0-385-49433-5*, Anchor NY) Doubleday.

McEwan, Janet M., ed. Writing for Our Lives, Vol. 5, No. 1. 80p. (Orig.). 1996. pap. 6.00 (*0-9633743-8-9*) Running Deer.

— Writing for Our Lives, Vol. 5, No. 2. 92p. (Orig.). 1996. pap. 6.00 (*0-9633743-9-7*) Running Deer.

— Writing for Our Lives, Vol. 6, No. 1. 80p. (Orig.). 1997. pap. 8.00 (*1-890882-00-3*) Running Deer.

— Writing for Our Lives, Vol. 6, No. 2. (Illus.). 84p. (Orig.). 1997. pap. 8.00 (*1-890882-01-1*) Running Deer.

— Writing for Our Lives, Vol. 7, No. 1. 84p. (Orig.). 1998. pap. 8.00 (*1-890882-02-X*) Running Deer.

***McEwan, Janet M., ed.** Writing for Our Lives, Vol. 7, No. 2. 80p. (Orig.). 1998. pap. 8.00 (*1-890882-03-8*) Running Deer.

— Writing for Our Lives, Vol. 8. 94p. (Orig.). 1999. pap. 8.00 (*1-890882-04-6*) Running Deer.

McEwan, Janet M., ed. Writing for Our Lives Vol. 1, No. 1: Creative Expressions in Writing by Women. 64p. 1992. per. 4.00 (*0-9633743-0-3*) Running Deer.

— Writing for Our Lives Vol. 1, No. 2: Creative Expressions in Writing by Women. 80p. 1992. per. 4.00 (*0-9633743-1-1*) Running Deer.

— Writing for Our Lives Vol. 2, No. 1: Creative Expressions in Writing by Women. 80p. 1993. per. 6.00 (*0-9633743-2-X*) Running Deer.

— Writing for Our Lives Vol. 2, No. 2: Creative Expressions in Writing by Women. 80p. 1993. per. 6.00 (*0-9633743-3-8*) Running Deer.

— Writing for Our Lives Vol. 3, No. 1: Creative Expressions in Writing by Women. 80p. 1994. per. 6.00 (*0-9633743-4-6*) Running Deer.

— Writing for Our Lives Vol. 3, No. 2: Creative Expressions in Writing by Women. 80p. 1994. per. 6.00 (*0-9633743-5-4*) Running Deer.

— Writing for Our Lives Vol. 4, No. 1: Creative Expressions in Writing by Women. 80p. 1995. per. 6.00 (*0-9633743-6-2*) Running Deer.

— Writing for Our Lives Vol. 4, No. 2: Creative Expressions in Writing by Women. 80p. 1995. per. 6.00 (*0-9633743-7-0*) Running Deer.

McEwan, Jean R., ed. Current Issues in Cardiology. 245p. 1997. pap. text 53.00 (*0-7279-1010-8*, Pub. by BMJ Pub) Login Brothers Bk Co.

***McEwan, John.** Out of the Depths of Hell: A Soldier's Story of Life & Death in Japanese Hands. 1999. write for info. (*0-85052-668-X*) Pen & Sword Bks Ltd.

McEwan, John, jt. auth. see Glendinning, Eric.

McEwan, Neil. Perspectives in British Historical Fiction Today. LC 86-7200. 200p. 1987. 25.00 (*0-89341-547-2*, Longwood Academic) Hollowbrook.

McEwan, Patrick J., jt. auth. see Levin, Henry M.

McEwan, Peter J. Dictionary of Scottish Art & Architecture. (Illus.). 626p. 1995. 99.50 (*1-85149-134-1*) Antique Collect.

McEwan, Peter J., ed. International Conference on Social Science & Medicine, 6th, Amsterdam, 1979: Second Special Conference Issue. 80p. 1981. pap. 17.25 (*0-08-026763-7*, Pergamon Pr) Elsevier.

— Second Special Conference Issue. 144p. 1983. pap. 22.00 (*0-08-027937-6*, Pergamon Pr) Elsevier.

— Social Science & Medicine: Seventh International Conference Background Papers. (Journal of Social Science & Medicine Ser.: Vol. 15A, No. 3). 100p. 1981. pap. 18.00 (*0-08-028130-3*, Pergamon Pr) Elsevier.

— Some Case Studies in Latin America. 88p. 1983. pap. 25.00 (*0-08-030843-0*, 27, Pergamon Pr) Elsevier.

McEwan, Robert J. Woodbridge. (Images of America Ser.). 1997. pap. 16.99 (*0-7524-0803-8*) Arcadia Publng.

***McEwan, Robert J. & Troeger, Virginia B.** Woodbridge, Vol. 2. (Images of America Ser.). 1999. pap. 18.99 (*0-7524-1304-X*) Arcadia Publng.

McEwan, Vera. Education Law. 212p. 1996. pap. 53.00 (*1-85811-075-0*, Pub. by CLT Prof) Gaunt.

McEwen. Heteroatom Chemistry: An International Journal of Main Group Elements. 1999. write for info. (*0-471-15516-0*) Wiley.

— Rubber Stamping. 128p. 1995. 12.98 (*0-7858-0358-0*) Bk Sales Inc.

McEwen, jt. auth. see Merritt.

McEwen, Alastair, tr. see Baricco, Alessandro.

McEwen, Alastair, tr. see Eco, Umberto.

McEwen, Alex. Public Policy in a Divided Society: Schooling, Culture & Identity in Northern Ireland. LC LC93.G7M336 1999. 160p. (C). 1999. text 56.95 (*1-84014-316-9*, Pub. by Ashgate Pub) Ashgate Pub Co.

McEwen, Alex & Robinson, Earl. Evangelical Beliefs & Educational Values. LC 95-77882. 176p. 1995. 61.95 (*1-85628-671-1*, Pub. by Avebry) Ashgate Pub Co.

McEwen, Annie Laurie, jt. auth. see Wunderlich, F. C.

***McEwen, Bruce S., ed.** The Endocrine System, Vol. 4. (Handbook of Physiology Ser.). (Illus.). 592p. 2000. text 150.00 (*0-19-511252-0*) OUP.

McEwen, Bruce S. & Schmeck, Harold M., Jr. The Hostage Brain. LC 94-67849. (Illus.). 323p. pap. 19.95 (*0-87470-056-6*) Rockefeller.

— The Hostage Brain. LC 94-67849. (Illus.). 323p. 1994. text 39.95 (*0-87470-054-X*) Rockefeller.

McEwen, Charles, jt. ed. see Larsen, Barbara.

McEwen, Charles N., jt. ed. see Merritt, Charles, Jr.

McEwen, Christian, ed. Jo's Girls: Tomboy Tales of High Adventure, True Grit, & Real Life. LC 96-47124. 352p. 1997. pap. 19.00 (*0-8070-6211-1*) Beacon Pr.

***McEwen, Christian & Statman, Mark, eds.** The Alphabet of the Trees: A Guide to Nature Writing. (Illus.). 320p. 2000. pap. 19.95 (*0-915924-63-3*) Tchrs & Writers Coll.

McEwen, Colleen M., ed. see Cox, Bobbi & Flanagan, Beth.

McEwen, Craig A., jt. auth. see Rogers, Nancy H.

McEwen, Currier. The Japanese Iris. LC 89-24974. (Illus.). 167p. 1990. 29.95 (*0-87451-512-2*) U Pr of New Eng.

— The Siberian Iris. LC 95-14643. (Illus.). 242p. 1996. 39.95 (*0-88192-329-X*) Timber.

McEwen, Evelyn, ed. Age: The Unrecognised Discrimination. (C). 1989. 49.00 (*0-86242-094-6*, Pub. by Age Concern Eng) St Mut.

McEwen, Gerald & Wenninger, John, eds. CTFA International Cosmetic Ingredient Dictionary & Handbook. 7th ed. LC 97-66873. 2608p. 1997. 750.00 (*1-882621-20-4*, 8077) Cosmetic T&FA.

McEwen, Gilbert D. The Oracle of the Coffee House: John Dunton's Athenian Mercury. LC 78-171109. (Huntington Library Publications). 265p. 1972. reprint ed. pap. 82.20 (*0-608-03171-2*, 206362400007) Bks Demand.

McEwen, Indra K. Socrates' Ancestor: An Essay on Architectural Beginnings. LC 93-21863. (Illus.). 206p. 1993. pap. text 18.00 (*0-262-63148-2*) MIT Pr.

McEwen, Indra K., tr. see Perrault, Claude.

McEwen, Irene R., ed. Occupational & Physical Therapy in Educational Environments. 1995. 39.95 (*1-56024-777-0*) Haworth Pr.

McEwen, J. Thomas & Weisburd, David, eds. Crime Mapping & Crime Prevention. (Crime Prevention Studies: Vol. 8). (Illus.). 300p. 1997. text 47.50 (*1-881798-08-9*, Criminal Justice) Willow Tree NY.

McEwen, J. Thomas, jt. ed. see Weisburd, David.

McEwen, James, et al. Oxford Textbook of Public Health, 3 vols., Set. 3rd ed. (Illus.). 1,646p. 1997. text 475.00 (*0-19-262553-5*) OUP.

McEwen, John. Escape. 200p. 1997. 19.95 (*1-889587-52-4*) Pure Play Pub.

— Glenkiln. (Illus.). 96p. 1995. 34.95 (*0-86241-324-9*, Pub. by Canongate Books) Interlink Pub.

— John Bellany. (Illus.). 232p. 1995. 60.00 (*1-85158-632-6*, Pub. by Mainstream Pubng) Trafalgar.

An Asterisk (*) at the beginning of an entry indicates that the title is appearing for the first time.

— Patrick Procktor. LC 97-39673. (Illus.). 96p. 1997. text 43.95 (1-85928-322-5, Pub. by Ashgate Pub) Ashgate Pub Co.

— Patrick Procktor. limited ed. LC 97-39673. (Illus.). 96p. 1997. text 425.95 (1-85928-323-3, Pub. by Ashgate Pub) Ashgate Pub Co.

— Paula Rego. 2nd ed. LC 99-215820. (Illus.). 288p. 1997. pap. 39.95 (0-7148-3622-2, Pub. by Phaidon Press) Phaidon Pr.

McEwen, Katharine, jt. auth. see Root, Phyllis.

McEwen, Katharine, jt. auth. see Rowan, Kate.

McEwen, Lee R. The Sylvia Factor: The Aftermath of World War II. LC 98-75446. (Illus.). 256p. 1999. 26.95 (1-57736-130-X) Providence Hse.

McEwen, Melanie. Community Based Nursing: An Introduction. Eoyang, Thomas, ed. LC 97-41326. 608p. (C). 1998. pap. 27.95 (0-7216-6109-2, W B Saunders Co) Harcrt Hlth Sci Grp.

McEwen, Peter, jt. ed. see Haskell, Peter T.

McEwen, R. F. Heartwood & Other Poems. (Illus.). 113p. (Orig.). 1995. pap. 10.95 (0-9635559-5-2) Slow Tempo.

McEwen, Susan, jt. ed. see MacLaughlin, Dawn.

McEwen, Tom. National Data Collection on Police Use of Force. 100p. (Orig.). (C). 1996. pap. text 30.00 (0-7881-3719-0) DIANE Pub.

McEwen, W. E. & Berlin, K. Darrell, eds. Organophosphorous Stereochemistry, 2 pts. Incl. Pt. 1. Origins of (P3&4) Compounds. 387p. 1975. 77.00 (0-12-787031-8); Pt. 2. P(5) Compounds. 1975. 70.00 (0-12-787032-6); (Benchmark Papers in Organic Chemistry: Vols. 3 & 4). 1975. write for info. (0-318-50321-2) Acad Pr.

McEwen, William J., jt. auth. see Tompson, James D.

McEwin, C. Kenneth. Focus on Interscholastic Sports & the Middle School. Romano, Louis G., ed. (Illus.). 18p. 1981. pap. text 3.00 (0-918449-03-0) MI Middle Educ.

McEwin, C. Kenneth & Scales, Peter C. Growing Pains: The Making of America's Middle School Teachers. 112p. (C). 1994. pap. text 15.00 (1-56090-083-0) Natl Middle Schl.

— Growing Pains: The Making of America's Middle School Teachers. 98p. 1994. reprint ed. pap. 7.00 (1-57482-708-1) Search Inst.

McEwin, C. Kenneth, et al. America's Middle Schools: Practices & Progress: a 25 Year Perspective. LC 96-10806. 1996. pap. write for info. (1-56090-102-0) Natl Middle Schl.

McEwing, Mary C., ed. see Griffin, Ricky.

McEwing, Mary C., ed. see Griffin & Pustav.

McEwing, Mary D., ed. see Barney, Jay.

McFadden. Science Plus: Technology & Society. 97th ed. 1997. text, teacher ed. 114.50 (0-03-095091-0) Holt R&W.

— Science Plus, 1997: Technology & Society. 97th ed. 1997. text, teacher ed. 114.50 (0-03-095094-5); text, student ed. 62.50 (0-03-095093-7) Holt R&W.

McFadden, Alneer A. & Burk, Janelle M. The Fritter Tree & the Honey Pond. (Illus.). 168p. 1985. 13.95 (0-9615736-0-0) Milestone Pr.

***McFadden, Bernice.** Sugar. LC 99-35589. 240p. 2000. 22.95 (0-525-94531-8, Dutt) Dutton Plume.

***McFadden, Bernice L.** Sugar. 2001. reprint ed. pap. 13.00 (0-452-28220-9, Plume) Dutton Plume.

— The Warmest December. LC 00-43043. 2001. write for info. (0-525-94564-4) NAL.

McFadden, Billie. The New Boxer. (Illus.). 256p. 1989. 25.95 (0-87605-062-3) Howell Bks.

McFadden, Carol H. Biology: An Exploration of Life. (C). 1995. pap. text, teacher ed., suppl. ed. write for info. (0-393-96772-7) Norton.

McFadden, Carol H. & Keeton, William T. Biology: An Exploration of Life. LC 93-1530. (Illus.). (C). 1995. pap. text, student ed. write for info. (0-393-95947-3) Norton.

— Biology: An Exploration of Life. LC 93-1530. (Illus.). (C). 1995. pap. text, student ed. write for info. (0-393-95718-7) Norton.

— Biology: An Exploration of Life. (Illus.). (C). 1995. text. write for info. (0-393-96692-5) Norton.

— Biology: An Exploration of Life. 4th ed. LC 93-1530. (Illus.). 700p. (C). 1995. 90.50 (0-393-95716-0) Norton.

McFadden, Carol H., jt. auth. see Keeton, William T.

***McFadden, Charles J.** Dignity of Life: Moral Values in a Changing Society. 1999. pap. text. write for info. (0-87973-891-X) Our Sunday Visitor.

***McFadden, Christine.** Essential Kitchen: Basic Tools, Recipes & Tips for Equipping a Classic Kitchen. (Illus.). 144p. 2000. text 29.95 (0-8478-2263-X) Rizzoli Intl.

— Ultimate Encyclopedia of Chocolate: With over 200 Recipes. (Ultimate Cookbook Ser.). (Illus.). 256p. 1997. 19.98 (0-7651-9476-7) Smithmark.

McFadden, Christine & Michaud, Michael. Cool Green Leaves & Red Hot Peppers. (Illus.). 208p. 1999. 29.95 (1-58062-161-9) Adams Media.

McFadden, Christine & Zelman, Kathleen M. A Harvest of Healing Foods. LC 97-47105. 144p. 1998. pap. 16.95 (0-8092-2926-9, 292690, Contemporary Bks) NTC Contemp Pub Co.

McFadden, Cyra. Rain or Shine: A Family Memoir. LC 97-39943. (Illus.). 178p. 1998. pap. 10.00 (0-8032-8241-9) U of Nebr Pr.

McFadden, D., ed. Neural Mechanisms in Behavior: A Texas Symposium. (Illus.). 350p. 1980. 102.00 (0-387-90468-9) Spr-Verlag.

McFadden, D. L., jt. ed. see Engle, R. F.

McFadden, David. Gypsy Guitar. LC 88-110777. 112p. 1993. pap. 12.95 (0-88922-250-9) Genl Dist Srvs.

— An Innocent in Ireland: Curious Rambles & Singular Encounters. LC 95-167850. 320p. (Orig.). 1995. pap. 16.95 (0-7710-5527-7) McCland & Stewart.

***McFadden, David.** An Innocent in Scotland: More Curious Rambles & Singular Encounters. LC 99-234591. 358p. 1999. pap. 17.95 (0-7710-5528-5) McCland & Stewart.

— McFadden's Funnies, Vol. 101. (Illus.). 36p. 1999. 2.95 (0-9675254-0-3) D McFadden.

McFadden, David. My Body Was Eaten by Dogs: Selected Poems. Bowering, George, ed. & intro. by. 120p. 1981. 12.95 (0-916696-19-7); pap. 6.95 (0-916696-18-9) Cross Country.

— A New Romance. 1979. pap. 3.00 (0-916696-10-3) Cross Country.

— The Saladmaker. rev. ed. 1977. reprint ed. pap. 2.00 (0-916696-03-0) Cross Country.

McFadden, David A. & Phillips, Calvin. Investigating the Fireground. LC 82-1290. (Illus.). 288p. 1982. pap. 16.95 (0-89303-074-0) P-H.

McFadden, David A., jt. auth. see Phillipps, Calvin C.

McFadden, David R. & Adams, Henry (Brooks). Hair. LC 80-67094. (Exhibition Catalogue Ser.). (Illus.). 32p. (Orig.). 1980. pap. 6.95 (0-910503-31-1) Cooper-Hewitt Museum.

McFadden, David W. Great Lakes Suite. 416p. 1997. pap. 26.95 (0-88922-382-3, Pub. by Talonbks) Genl Dist Srvs.

— There'll Be Another. LC 96-106092. 125p. 1995. pap. 11.95 (0-88922-361-0) Genl Dist Srvs.

McFadden, Dennis & Rosenblatt, Paul. Manchester: A Neighborhood Sketchbook. (Illus.). 48p. 1998. pap. 5.00 (0-88039-035-2) Mus Art Carnegie.

McFadden, Dennis, jt. auth. see Cleary, Richard.

McFadden, E. & Rogers, Dawn, eds. Children's Christmas Party. (Illus.). 56p. (Orig.). (J). (gr. 3-6). 1994. pap. 4.99 (0-9640168-1-8) Pirate Writings.

McFadden, E. R. Exercise Induced Asthma. LC 98-56648. (Lung Biology in Health & Disease Ser.). (Illus.). 410p. 1999. text 175.00 (0-8247-9904-6) Dekker.

***McFadden, Ed.** Relocating to Washington D. C. & Surrounding Areas. (Relocating Ser.). 400p. 2000. pap. 16.95 (0-7615-2569-6) Prima Pub.

McFadden, Edward J., III, ed. The Best of Pirate Writings No. 1: Tales of Fantasy, Mystery & Science Fiction. (Best of Pirate Writings Ser.). (Illus.). 224p. 1998. pap. 12.99 (1-890096-04-0) Padwolf Pub.

McFadden, Edward J. & Piccirilli, Tom, eds. Year 1: A Time of Change. 98p. (Orig.). 1996. pap. 9.99 (0-9640168-4-2) Pirate Writings.

McFadden, Eleanor. Management of Data in Clinical Trials. LC 97-1251. (Probability & Statistics Ser.). 232p. 1997. 74.95 (0-471-30316-X) Wiley.

McFadden, Faith A. Acts of Faith: A Memoir. 274p. (Orig.). 1994. pap. 14.95 (0-89870-527-4) Ignatius Pr.

McFadden, Fred. Database Management. 4th ed. (C). 1994. pap. text. write for info. (0-8053-6039-5) Addison-Wesley.

— Modern Database Management Casebook. 4th ed. 96p. (C). 1994. pap. text 19.00 (0-8053-6048-4) Addison-Wesley.

McFadden, Fred R. Modern Database Management. 5th ed. LC 98-4120. 656p. (C). 1998. 83.00 (0-8053-6054-9, Prentice Hall) P-H.

McFadden, Fred R. & Hoffer, Jeffrey A. Modern Database Management. 4th ed. LC 93-31795. (C). 1994. text 61.95 (0-8053-6047-6) Benjamin-Cummings.

***McFadden, Fred R. & Hoffer, Jeffrey A.** Modern Database Management: Oracle Edition. 5th ed. 656p. 1999. 94.00 (0-201-38372-1) Addison-Wesley.

McFadden, Frederick R., Jr., ed. & intro. see Whibley, Charles.

McFadden, George. Dryden, the Public Writer, 1660-1685. LC 77-85551. 319p. reprint ed. pap. 98.90 (0-8357-3422-6, 203967900013) Bks Demand.

McFadden, Gerald. Federal Sentencing Manual, 2 vols. 1989. ring bd. 270.00 (0-8205-1471-3) Bender.

McFadden, Hugh, ed. see Jordan, John.

McFadden, Jenny, jt. auth. see McFadden, Judith.

McFadden, John, ed. Transcultural Counseling. 2nd ed. LC 98-29306. 416p. 1999. pap. text 40.95 (1-55620-208-3) Am Coun Assn.

McFadden, John, tr. see Erdozain, Placido.

***McFadden, John J.** Executive Compensation. 5th ed. 415p. (C). 2000. 48.00 (1-57996-023-5) Amer College.

McFadden, John J., ed. Financial Planning 2000. LC 97-70789. 350p. (Orig.). (C). 1997. pap. text 42.00 (0-943590-91-4) Amer College.

McFadden, John J., jt. auth. see Beam, Burton T.

***McFadden, John Joe.** Quantum Evolution: The New Science of Life. (Illus.). 352p. 2000. 27.95 (0-393-05041-6) Norton.

McFadden, Johnjoe, ed. Molecular Biology of the Mycobacteria. (Surrey Seminars in Molecular Microbiology Ser.). 233p. 1990. text 104.00 (0-12-483378-0) Acad Pr.

McFadden, Judith & McFadden, Jenny. Find Your Natural Weight the NECTAR Way. LC 94-68732. (Illus.). 192p. (Orig.). 1994. pap. 12.00 (0-944337-24-4, 244) New View Pubns.

McFadden, K. & SeniorNet Staff. SeniorNet Official Guide to the Web, 1997. 1997. pap. 29.99 (0-614-28474-0, Lycos Pr) Que.

McFadden, Kathleen, jt. auth. see Johnson, Eugenia.

McFadden, Kevin, see Pike, Christopher, pseud.

McFadden, Louis T. Federal Reserve Corporation. 1973. 59.95 (0-8490-0157-9) Gordon Pr.

McFadden, Margaret, ed. Ready Reference, Women's Issues. LC 96-48989. (Illus.). 1154p. 1997. lib. bdg. 315.00 (0-89356-765-5) Salem Pr.

McFadden, Margaret H. Golden Cables of Sympathy: The Transatlantic Sources of Nineteenth-Century Feminism. LC 98-49993. (Illus.). 272p. 1999. 29.95 (0-8131-2117-5) U Pr of Ky.

McFadden, Maria, ed. see Canavan, Francis.

McFadden, Marlene. Tell Me No Secrets. large type ed. (Dales Large Print Ser.). 1995. pap. 18.99 (1-85389-553-9, Dales) Ulverscroft.

***McFadden, Marlene E.** After the Storm. large type ed. 224p. 1999. pap. 20.99 (1-85389-816-3) Ulverscroft.

McFadden, Marlene E. Be Kind to the Stranger. large type ed. (Dales Large Print Ser.). 240p. 1998. pap. 19.99 (1-85389-815-5, Dales) Ulverscroft.

***McFadden, Marlene E.** Never to Let Go. large type ed. LC 99-22228. 1999. pap. 19.95 (0-7838-8656-X, G K Hall Lrg Type) Mac Lib Ref.

McFadden, Marlene E. A Promise to Keep. large type ed. LC 97-94871. (Nightingale Ser.). 143p. 1998. pap. 18.95 (0-7838-8411-7, G K Hall & Co) Mac Lib Ref.

— Return to Hardath. large type ed. (Dales Large Print Ser.). 1995. pap. 18.99 (1-85389-551-2, Dales) Ulverscroft.

— When Shannon Came Home. (Rainbow Romances Ser.). 160p. 1994. 14.95 (0-7090-5432-7, 919) Parkwest Pubns.

McFadden, Mary Ann. Eye of the Blackbird. LC 96-86567. (Intro Ser.). 80p. 1997. pap. 12.95 (1-884800-12-2) Four Way Bks.

***McFadden, Michael, et al.** Color of Ojai: The Light & Spirit. (Illus.). 112p. 2000. 34.95 (1-891901-08-7) M McFadden Photo.

McFadden, Michael, jt. auth. see Giddings, Patricia.

McFadden, Nickie. Judgments in Family Court: Here We Go Round the Mulberry Bush. unabridged ed. LC 97-185705. (Illus.). 401p. (Orig.). 1997. pap. 19.95 (0-9657441-0-8) McFadden Pub.

Mcfadden, Patrick. Electing Justice: The Law & Ethics of Judicial Election Campaigns. LC 90-82507. (Studies of the Justice System). 224p. (Orig.). 1990. pap. 6.00 (0-938870-44-0) Am Judicature.

McFadden, Roy. After Seymour's Funeral. 61p. 1990. pap. 13.95 (0-85640-434-9, Pub. by Blackstaff Pr) Dufour.

— Letters to the Hinterland. (C). 1986. pap. 15.00 (0-948268-15-8, Pub. by Dedalus) St Mut.

McFadden, S. Little Book of Native American Wisdom. 48p. 1994. text 5.95 (1-85230-566-5, Pub. by Element MA) Penguin Putnam.

McFadden, S. Michele, ed. see Stockton, Elizabeth L.

McFadden, Sarah & Simon, Joan, eds. Carnegie International, 1988. LC 88-30021. (Illus.). 202p. 1988. pap. 22.95 (0-88039-019-0) Mus Art Carnegie.

McFadden, Scott. Algebra Warm-Ups. 1997. text 11.95 (0-86651-344-2) Seymour Pubns.

— Math Warm-Ups. 96p. (J). (gr. 4-6). 1997. pap. text 11.95 (0-86651-612-3) Seymour Pubns.

— Math Warm-Ups. (J). (gr. 7-9). 1997. pap. text 11.50 (0-86651-107-5) Seymour Pubns.

McFadden, Steven. Teach Us to Number Our Days: Inspirational Thoughts on Wisdom & Aging. 1996. pap. 11.95 (1-85230-803-6, Pub. by Element MA) Penguin Putnam.

McFadden, Steven S., jt. auth. see Groh, Trauger M.

McFadden, Susan, tr. see Yang, Xiguang.

McFadden, Susan H., jt. auth. see Magai, Carol.

McFadden, Susan H., ed. see Kimble, Melvin.

McFadden, Susan H., jt. ed. see Magai, Carol.

***McFadden, T. J.** Landing Party. 368p. 1999. mass mkt. 5.50 (0-8439-4627-X, Leisure Bks) Dorchester Pub Co.

McFadden, Terry T. & Bennett, F. Lawrence. Construction in Cold Regions: A Guide for Planners, Engineers, Contractors & Managers. LC 91-10317. (Series of Practical Construction Guides: No. 1344). 640p. 1991. 130.00 (0-471-52503-0) Wiley.

McFadden, Terry T., jt. auth. see Freitag, Dean R.

McFadden, Tim. Whole Human Race. 1994. pap. 12.95 (0-9669655-0-7) Grace Hse.

McFadden, William. Techniques of Combined Gas Chromatography - Mass Spectrometry: Applications in Organic Analysis. LC 87-35344. 482p. (C). 1988. reprint ed. lib. bdg. 70.00 (0-89464-280-4) Krieger.

McFadden, William C., ed. Georgetown at Two Hundred: Faculty Reflections on the University's Future. LC 90-32745. 353p. (Orig.). 1990. 24.95 (0-87840-502-X); pap. 14.95 (0-87840-503-8) Georgetown U Pr.

McFaddin, Michelle A. Oil & Gas Field Waste Regulations Handbook. LC 95-45608. 1995. 99.95 (0-87814-461-7) PennWell Bks.

McFaddin, T. Adam. Saved Sexy? Cool: Help for the Contemporary Woman. 72p. 1998. pap. 7.95 (0-9667167-0-1) Hrvst Ent.

— Supernaturally Attractive: When There's More to You Than What Meets the Eye. 180p. 1996. pap. 12.00 (0-9667167-1-X) Hrvst Ent.

McFaddin, Terri. God Made Me Beauty-Full: Building Self-Esteem in African American Women. LC 97-65701. (Illus.). 200p. (Orig.). 1997. pap. 12.00 (1-884743-05-6) Quiet Time Pubng.

Mcfaden, H. H., jt. auth. see Akhiezer, N. I.

McFaden, H. H., tr. see Aizenberg, L. A. & Yuzhakov, A. P.

McFaden, H. H., tr. see Akhiezer, N. I.

McFaden, H. H., tr. see Berezanskii, Yu.

McFaden, H. H., tr. see Egorychev, G. P.

McFaden, H. H., tr. see Monakhov, V. N.

McFaden, H. H., tr. see Reshtenyak, Y.

McFaden, H. H., tr. see Shevchenko, V. N.

McFaden, H. H., tr. see Skorokhod, A. V.

McFaden, Michael. The Love Knot: A Comedy in One Act. (Illus.). 32p. 1975. pap. 3.25 (0-88680-118-4) I E Clark.

McFadyean, Melanie, et al. Thatcher's Reign: A Bad Case of the Blues. (Illus.). 144p. 1985. pap. 7.95 (0-7011-2857-7, Pub. by Chatto & Windus) Random House.

***McFadyen, Alistair I.** Bound to Sin: Abuse, the Holocaust & the Christian Doctrine of Sin. LC 99-58733. (Cambridge Studies in Christian Doctrine: Vol. 6). 259p. 2000. write for info. (0-521-43286-3); pap. write for info. (0-521-43868-3) Cambridge U Pr.

McFadyen, Alistair I. The Call to Personhood: A Christian Theory of the Individual in Social Relationships. 339p. (C). 1990. text 80.00 (0-521-38471-0) Cambridge U Pr.

McFadyen, Deidre, jt. ed. see Rosen, Fred.

McFadyen, John E. The Prayers of the Bible. LC 95-83608. (Bible Study Ser.: Pulpit Legends Collection). 375p. 1996. 14.99 (0-89957-213-8) AMG Pubs.

— The Prayers of the Bible. (Classic Library). 350p. 1996. reprint ed. 15.99 (0-529-10483-0, POTB) World Publng.

McFadyen, Philip. Open Door on John. LC 99-210355. 144p. 1998. pap. text 11.95 (0-281-05147-X) Abingdon.

McFadyen, Phillip. Corinthian Columns: Parish Preparation for Lambeth 1998. 48p. 1998. pap. text 5.95 (1-85311-196-1, 6032, Pub. by Canterbury Press Norwich) Morehouse Pub.

McFadyen, Stuart, et al, eds. Cultural Development in an Open Economy. iv, 300p. (C). 1995. pap. 24.95 (0-9698983-0-4) W Laurier U Pr.

McFague, Sallie. The Body of God: An Ecological Theology. LC 93-6584. 288p. 1993. pap. 18.00 (0-8006-2735-0, 1-2735) Augsburg Fortress.

***McFague, Sallie.** Life Abundant: Rethinking Theology & Economy for a Planet in Peril. 2000. pap. 16.00 (0-8006-3269-9, Fortress Pr) Augsburg Fortress.

McFague, Sallie. Metaphorical Theology: Models of God in Religious Language. LC 82-7246. 240p. (C). 1982. pap. 17.00 (0-8006-1687-1, 1-1687, Fortress Pr) Augsburg Fortress.

— Models of God: Theology for an Ecological, Nuclear Age. LC 86-46435. 240p. 1987. pap. 17.00 (0-8006-2051-8, 1-2051, Fortress Pr) Augsburg Fortress.

— Super, Natural Christians: How We Should Love Nature. LC 96-50992. 200p. 1997. pap. text 16.00 (0-8006-3076-9, 1-3076, Fortress Pr) Augsburg Fortress.

McFall, Gardner. The Pilot's Daughter. 79p. (Orig.). 1996. 18.95 (1-56809-028-5); pap. 12.50 (1-56809-029-3) Time Being Bks.

McFall, Gardner, ed. see Swenson, May.

McFall, Kathleen, jt. auth. see Hays, Clark.

McFall, Lynne. Dancer with Bruised Knees: A Novel. 224p. 1996. pap. 11.95 (0-8118-1259-6) Chronicle Bks.

— Happiness. (Studies in Moral Philosophy: Vol. 1). XII, 129p. (C). 1989. text 27.50 (0-8204-0711-9) P Lang Pubng.

McFall, Nancy, ed. see Brady, John C., II.

McFall, Pat. Index to Conway County, Arkansas, Deed Books A & B, 1825-1843. 50p. 1989. pap. 14.00 (0-941765-48-2) Arkansas Res.

McFall, Robert J. Railway Monopoly & Rate Regulation. LC 79-76704. (Columbia University. Studies in the Social Sciences: No. 164). reprint ed. 20.00 (0-404-51164-3) AMS Pr.

McFall, Sheryl. Greed, Teases, Love. 40p. 1996. 8.00 (0-8059-3972-5) Dorrance.

McFall, Snowden. Fired Up! How to Succeed by Making Your Dreams Come True. LC 96-77532. 1997. write for info. (0-938716-32-8) Markowski Intl.

McFall, Snowden. Fired Up! How to Succeed by Making Your Dreams Come True! LC 98-91562. 288p. 1998. pap. 12.95 (1-892372-01-0) Nrth Brdge Pr.

***McFall, Timothy M.** Close That Door & Keep the Devil Out. 112p. 1999. pap. 9.95 (0-9672308-0-2) T McFall Min.

McFalls, Laurence H. Communism's Collapse, Democracy's Demise? The Cultural Context & Consequences of the East German Revolution. LC 94-20535. (C). 1995. text 42.50 (0-8147-5521-6) NYU Pr.

McFann, Cathy. Nuclear Meditations. (Fastbook 1985 Ser.). 20p. 1985. 6.00 (0-911051-16-3) Plain View.

McFann, Jane. Be Mine. 208p. (J). (gr. 7 up). 1994. pap. 3.25 (0-590-46690-9) Scholastic Inc.

— Deathtrap & Dinosaur. 224p. (Orig.). 1989. pap. 2.75 (0-380-75624-2, Avon Bks) Morrow Avon.

— Free the Conroy Seven. 160p. (Orig.). 1993. mass mkt. 3.50 (0-380-76401-6, Avon Bks) Morrow Avon.

— Hide & Seek. 176p. (J). (gr. 7-9). 1995. mass mkt. 3.99 (0-590-60387-6) Scholastic Inc.

Mcfann, Jane. Hide & Seek. 1995. 9.09 (0-606-07643-3, Pub. by Turtleback) Demco.

McFann, Jane. Maybe by Then I'll Understand. 192p. (Orig.). 1987. pap. 2.50 (0-380-75221-2, Avon Bks) Morrow Avon.

— No Time for Rabbits. 176p. 1991. pap. 2.95 (0-380-76085-1, Avon Bks) Morrow Avon.

— Nothing More, Nothing Less. 176p. (Orig.). (YA). (gr. 5 up). 1993. pap. 3.50 (0-380-76636-1, Avon Bks) Morrow Avon.

McFann, Julia B. We Can Play. (Illus.). 13p. (Orig.). (J). (gr. 1). 1993. pap. text. write for info. (1-882225-15-5) Tott Pubns.

McFarlan, Donald, ed. & intro. see Stevenson, Robert Louis.

McFarlan, F. Warren. The Information Systems Research Challenge. 1984. pap. text 35.00 (0-07-103257-6) McGraw.

McFarlan, F. Warren, et al. Corporate Informational Systems Management: Text & Cases. 4th ed. LC 95-39279. 704p. (C). 1995. text 73.25 (0-256-18116-0, Irwn McGrw-H) McGrw-H Hghr Educ.

***McFarland.** Animal Behavior: Psychobiology, Ethology & Evolution. 3rd ed. 600p. (C). 1998. pap. 55.00 (0-582-32732-6) Longman.

McFarland. Animal Behaviour Problems. 1989. pap. text. write for info. (0-582-46820-5, Pub. by Addison-Wesley) Longman.

M

— Quick Reference: Lab & Diagnostic Tests. (Nursing Education Ser.). 1995. 23.95 (*0-8273-6169-6*) Delmar.

McFarland, Ken, ed. see Maxwell, Randy.

McFarland, Alan R. & Bishop, Wayne S. Union Authorization Cards & the NLRB: A Study of Congressional Intent, Administrative Policy, & Judicial Review. LC 70-78136. (Labor Relations & Public Policy Ser.: No. 2). 112p. reprint ed. pap. 34.80 (*0-8357-3160-X*, 203942300012) Bks Demand.

McFarland, Andrew S. Cooperative Pluralism: The National Coal Policy Experiment. LC 93-8156. (Studies in Government & Public Policy). 192p. 1993. 29.95 (*0-7006-0617-3*); pap. 14.95 (*0-7006-0618-1*) U Pr of KS.

McFarland, Andrew S., jt. ed. see Costain, Anne N.

McFarland, Barbara. Brief Therapy & Eating Disorders: A Practical Guide to Solution-Focused Work with Clients. LC 94-38947. (Social & Behavioral Sciences-Health Ser.). 284p. 1995. 34.95 (*0-7879-0053-2*) Jossey-Bass.

McFarland, Barbara & Erb, Ann M. Abstinence in Action: Food Planning for Compulsive Eaters. 140p. 1989. pap. 16.95 (*0-89486-538-2*, 5045A) Hazelden.

McFarland, Barbara & Watson-Rouslin, Virginia. My Mother Was Right: How Today's Women Reconcile with Their Mothers. LC 97-24510. 248p. 1997. mass mkt. 24.50 (*0-7879-0875-4*) Jossey-Bass.

McFarland, Carl, jt. auth. see Cummings, Homer.

McFarland, D. Michael, jt. auth. see Srinivasan, A.V.

McFarland, Dalton E. Managerial Innovation Change in the Metropolitan Hospital. LC 79-14551. (Praeger Special Studies). 322p. 1979. 69.50 (*0-275-90390-7*, C0390, Praeger Pubs) Greenwood.

McFarland, Dalton E., jt. ed. see Wickert, Frederic R.

McFarland, Daniel M. Historical Dictionary of Upper Volta. LC 77-14987. (African Historical Dictionaries Ser.: No. 14). (Illus.). 239p. 1978. 29.00 (*0-8108-1088-3*) Scarecrow.

Mcfarland, Daniel M. & Rupley, Lawrence. Historical Dictionary of Burkina Faso (Former Upper Volta) 2nd ed. LC 97-30169. (African Historical Dictionaries Ser.: No. 74). (Illus.). 360p. 1998. 90.00 (*0-8108-3405-7*) Scarecrow.

McFarland, Daniel M., jt. auth. see Owusu-Ansah, David.

McFarland, David. Dictionnaire du Comportement Animal. (FRE.). 1013p. 1990. pap. 55.00 (*0-7859-7802-X*, 2221052811) Fr & Eur.

McFarland, David J. Animal Behavior. 576p. 1985. text 43.25 (*0-8053-6790-X*) Benjamin-Cummings.

— Animal Behaviour: Psychobiology, Ethology, & Evolution. 2nd ed. LC 92-16276. (C). 1993. pap. text 58.13 (*0-582-06721-9*) Longman.

McFarland, David J. & Bosser, Thomas. Intelligent Behavior in Animals & Robots. LC 92-40583. (Bradford Series in Complex Adaptive Systems). (Illus.). 328p. (C). 1993. 47.50 (*0-262-13293-1*, Bradford Bks) MIT Pr.

McFarland, Dennis. A Face at the Window. 320p. 1998. pap. 13.00 (*0-7679-0130-4*) Broadway BDD.

— A Face at the Window. large type ed. LC 97-17232. (Cloak & Dagger Ser.). 524p. 1997. 25.95 (*0-7862-1153-9*) Thorndike Pr.

— The Music Room. 288p. 1991. reprint ed. pap. 12.00 (*0-380-71456-6*, Avon Bks) Morrow Avon.

***McFarland, Dennis.** Singing Boy. 2001. pap. text 26.00 (*0-8050-6608-X*) St Martin.

— Singing Boy. 2002. pap. text 14.00 (*0-8050-6609-8*) St Martin.

McFarland, Douglas & Keppel, William. Minnesota Civil Practice: 1999 Cumulative Supplement. 2nd ed. 350p. 1999. pap. write for info. (*0-327-01362-1*, 8174119) LEXIS Pub.

McFarland, Douglas D. Computer-Aided Exercises on Civil Procedure. 3rd ed. 210p. 1993. reprint ed. pap. text 19.50 (*0-314-86711-2*) West Pub.

McFarland, Douglas D. & Keppel, William J. Minnesota Civil Practice, 4 Vols. 3rd ed. 314.00 (*0-327-12453-9*) LEXIS Pub.

— Minnesota Civil Practice, 4 vols. 3rd ed. Incl. Vol. 1. Minnesota Civil Practice. 3rd ed. 1999. (*0-327-04994-4*); Vol. 2. Minnesota Civil Practice. 3rd ed. 1999. (*0-327-04995-2*); Vol. 3. Minnesota Civil Practice. 3rd ed. 1999. (*0-327-04996-0*); Vol. 4. Minnesota Civil Practice. 3rd ed. 1999. (*0-327-04997-9*); 700p. 1999. write for info. (*0-327-04998-7*) LEXIS Pub.

McFarland, Douglas D. & Keppel, William J. Minnesota Civil Practice, No. 98:2. 480p. 1998. pap. write for info. (*0-327-00717-6*, 8174118) LEXIS Pub.

— Minnesota Civil Practice, 4 vols., Set. 2nd ed. 2560p. 1994. 295.00 (*0-86678-858-1*, 81736-10, MICHIE) LEXIS Pub.

McFarland, Douglas D., jt. auth. see Keppel, William J.

McFarland, Douglas D., jt. auth. see Park, Roger C.

McFarland, Elaine W. Ireland & Scotland in the Age of Revolution. (Illus.). 256p. 1995. 60.00 (*0-7486-0539-8*, Pub. by Edinburgh U Pr) Col U Pr.

— Protestants First: Orangeism in 19th Century Scotland. (Illus.). 224p. 1992. pap. 28.00 (*0-7486-0216-X*, Pub. by Edinburgh U Pr) Col U Pr.

McFarland, Elizabeth F. Forever Frontier: The Gila Cliff Dwellings. LC 67-63242. (Illus.). 68p. 1967. pap. 2.50 (*0-9615359-0-3*) Crest Pr Inc.

McFarland, Ella M. Climb 'Til Your Dream Comes True: The Educational Journey of a Black Single Mother. 150p. 1997. pap. write for info. (*1-57502-581-7*, PO1669) Morris Pubng.

McFarland, Ella Mae G. Climb 'Til Your Dreams Come True: The Educational Journey of a Black Single Mother; Suggestions for Welfare Reform. (Illus.). 136p. 1999. pap. 13.00 (*0-8059-4664-0*) Dorrance.

McFarland, Ernest W. The Ernest W. McFarland Papers: The United States Senate Years, 1940-1952. McMillan, James E., ed. LC 94-74978. (Illus.). 510p. 1995. 29.95 (*0-927579-06-5*) Sharlot Hall Mus Pr.

Mcfarland, Ernie. Einstein's Special Relativity: Discover It for Yourself. rev. ed. (Illus.). 88p. 1997. pap. text 8.95 (*1-895579-23-6*) Trifolium Inc.

McFarland, Floyd B. Economic Philosophy & American Problems: Classical Mechanism, Marxist Dialectic, & Cultural Evolution. 256p. (C). 1991. text 54.50 (*0-8476-7670-6*) Rowman.

McFarland, Gail. The Best for Last. 288p. 1998. pap. 4.99 (*0-7860-0561-0*) Kensgtn Pub Corp.

— Summer Wind. 288p. 1997. mass mkt. 4.99 (*0-7860-0436-3*, Pinncle Kensgtn) Kensgtn Pub Corp.

McFarland, Gail A. When Love Calls, 1. (Arabesque Ser.). 1999. mass mkt. 4.99 (*1-58314-031-X*) BET Bks.

McFarland, George B. Thai-English Dictionary. xxi, 1060p. 1944. 45.00 (*0-8047-0383-3*) Stanford U Pr.

McFarland, Gerald W. The "Counterfeit" Man: The True Story of the Boorn-Colvin Murder Case. LC 92-43533. (Illus.). 264p. (C). 1993. reprint ed. pap. 17.95 (*0-87023-837-X*) U of Mass Pr.

***McFarland, Gerald W.** A Scattered People: An American Family Moves West. LC 99-57801. (Illus.). 304p. 2000. pap. 16.95 (*1-56663-297-8*, Pub. by I R Dee) Natl Bk Netwk.

McFarland, Gerald W., ed. Mugwumps, Morals, & Politics, 1884-1920. LC 74-21242. 292p. 1975. 32.50 (*0-87023-175-8*) U of Mass Pr.

McFarland, Gertrude K. Nursing Diagnosis & Process in Psychiatric Mental Health Nursing. 3rd ed. LC 96-41727. 480p. 1996. pap. text 23.95 (*0-397-55317-X*) Lppncott W & W.

McFarland, Gertrude K. & McFarlane, Elizabeth A. Nursing Diagnosis & Intervention. 3rd ed. LC 97-223430. (Illus.). 896p. (C). (gr. 13). 1996. pap. text 38.00 (*0-8151-7026-2*, 27464) Mosby Inc.

McFarland, Gertrude K. & Thomas, Mary D., eds. Psychiatric Mental Health Nursing: Application of the Nursing Process. LC 90-5958. (Illus.). 1070p. 1991. reprint ed. pap. 200.00 (*0-608-07311-3*, 206753900009) Bks Demand.

McFarland, Gertrude K. & Wasli, Evelyn L. Nursing Diagnoses & Process in Psychiatric-Mental Health Nursing. LC 64-5161. 308p. 1986. text 17.95 (*0-397-54598-3*, Lippnett) Lppncott W & W.

McFarland, Gertrude K., et al. Nursing Leadership & Management: Contemporary Strategies. LC 83-16724. 349p. (C). 1989. text 34.95 (*0-8273-4309-4*) Delmar.

McFarland, H. N., et al, eds. Applied Toxicology of Petroleum Hydrocarbons. LC 84-60312. (Advances in Modern Environmental Toxicology Ser.: Vol. 6). (Illus.). 287p. 1984. text 65.00 (*0-911131-07-8*) Specialist Journals.

McFarland, Ian A. Listening to the Least: Doing Theology from the Outside In. LC 98-36234. 160p. 1998. pap. 15.95 (*0-8298-1283-0*) Pilgrim OH.

McFarland-Icke, Bronwyn Rebekah. Nurses in Nazi Germany: Moral Choice in History. LC 99-18151. 335p. 1999. 35.00 (*0-691-00665-2*, Pub. by Princeton U Pr) Cal Prin Full Svc.

McFarland, J. W. Sulfonyl Isocyanates & Sulfonyl Isothiocyanates, Vol. 1I. (Sulfur Reports). 54p. 1981. pap. text 85.00 (*3-7186-0255-5*) Gordon & Breach.

McFarland, Jeannie. Advanced Pattern Book: For Pine Needle Raffia Basketry. rev. ed. (Illus.). 64p. (C). 1993. reprint ed. pap. 11.00 (*0-9618828-1-6*) Baskets & Bullets.

— Pine Needle Raffia Basketry. rev. ed. (Illus.). 48p. 1996. reprint ed. pap. 9.00 (*0-9618828-0-8*) Baskets & Bullets.

McFarland, Jeffery, jt. auth. see Tolman, Ruth.

McFarland, Joe S. Coaching Pitchers. 2nd ed. LC 89-37721. (Illus.). 152p. 1990. pap. 20.95 (*0-88011-368-5*, PMCF0368) Human Kinetics.

McFarland, John R. The Strange Calling. LC 99-20557. 224p. 1999. 22.00 (*1-57312-273-4*) Smyth & Helwys.

McFarland-Johnson, Jeffrey. The Perfect ABC Songbook. (Illus.). 55p. (J). (ps-1). 1998. spiral bd. 24.95 incl. audio compact disk (*1-892397-03-X*); spiral bd. 19.95 incl. audio (*1-892397-04-8*) JohnSong.

McFarland-Johnson, Jeffrey, ed. The Perfect ABC Songbook. (Illus.). 55p. (J). (ps-1). 1998. spiral bd. 10.00 (*1-892397-00-5*) JohnSong.

McFarland, Joseph F. Twentieth Century History of the City of Washington & Washington County, Pennsylvania. (Illus.). 1369p. 1993. reprint ed. lib. bdg. 139.00 (*0-8328-3113-1*) Higginson Bk Co.

McFarland, Judy L. Aging Without Growing Old. LC 96-62079. 416p. 1997. pap. 15.95 (*1-888848-08-1*) Western Front.

McFarland, K. T. Allegheny County, Pennsylvania Achives, Vol. 3. 174p. 1990. 19.95 (*1-55856-067-X*, 132) Closson Pr.

— Allegheny County, Pennsylvania Archives, Vol. 2. 136p. 1990. 19.95 (*1-55856-065-3*, 131) Closson Pr.

— Allegheny County, Pennsylvania Archives, Vol. 4. 157p. 1991. 19.95 (*1-55856-068-8*, 140) Closson Pr.

— Allegheny County, Pennsylvania Archives, Vol. 5. 117p. 1991. 19.95 (*1-55856-069-6*, 141) Closson Pr.

— Allegheny County, Pennsylvania Archives, Vol. 6. 167p. 1991. 19.95 (*1-55856-060-2*, 142) Closson Pr.

— Allegheny County, Pennsylvania Archives Vol. 8: Partition Dockets 4-7, 1873-1884. 127p. 1994. text 19.95 (*1-55856-166-8*, 151) Closson Pr.

— Allegheny County, Pennsylvania Archives Vol. 9: Will Book 6, 1845-1850, Abstracts. LC 96-71598. 149p. 1997. 19.95 (*1-55856-246-X*, 152) Closson Pr.

— Allegheny County, Pennsylvania Archives Vol. 10: Will Book 7, 1850-1854, Abstracts. LC 96-71598. 128p. 1997. 19.95 (*1-55856-247-8*, 160) Closson Pr.

— Allegheny County, Pennsylvania Archives Vol. 11: Will Book 8, 1854-1858, Abstracts. LC 96-71598. 114p. 1997. 19.95 (*1-55856-248-6*, 161) Closson Pr.

— Allegheny County, Pennsylvania Archives Vol. 12: Will Book 9, 1857-1861, Abstracts. LC 96-71598. 118p. 1997. 19.95 (*1-55856-249-4*, 162) Closson Pr.

— Allegheny County, Pennsylvnaia Archives, Vol. 1. 185p. 1990. 19.95 (*1-55856-052-1*, 130) Closson Pr.

— Early West Virginia Wills, Vol. 1. 167p. 1993. pap. text 14.95 (*1-55856-156-0*, 483) Closson Pr.

— Hollidaysburg Records: Marriages, Deaths, & Petitions from Weekly Newspapers of Hollidaysburg, Huntingdon-Blair Counties, PA, 1836-1852. LC 94-238757. 129p. 1994. per. 12.95 (*1-55856-167-6*, 105) Closson Pr.

— Inscriptions from Chartiers Cemetery, Pittsburgh, PA, Vol. I. 118p. 1988. pap. text 11.95 (*0-933227-76-0*, 460) Closson Pr.

— Inscriptions from Chartiers Cemetery, Pittsburgh, PA, Vol. II. 248p. 1988. pap. text 16.95 (*0-933227-78-7*, 461) Closson Pr.

— Inscriptions from Highwood Cemetery, Allegheny (Now Pittsburgh), PA, Vol. I. 138p. 1988. pap. text 11.95 (*0-933227-74-4*, 457) Closson Pr.

— Inscriptions from Highwood Cemetery, Allegheny (Now Pittsburgh), PA, Vol. II. 229p. 1988. pap. text 16.95 (*1-55856-003-3*, 458) Closson Pr.

— Will Abstracts of Brooke County, (West) Virginia, 1797-1850. 88p. 1986. per. 9.50 (*0-933227-26-4*, 503) Closson Pr.

McFarland, Kathleen & Larkin, Judy. Colleen Marie. (Illus.). 56p. (Orig.). (J). (ps). 1985. pap. write for info. (*0-9621691-1-0*, TX 1-705-162) B Bumpers Inc.

— Meet Colleen Marie. (Illus.). 22p. (Orig.). (J). (ps). 1985. pap. write for info. (*0-9621691-0-2*, TX 1-650-724) B Bumpers Inc.

McFarland, Kenneth. Let's Get Acquainted. LC 86-30397. (Outreach Ser.). 32p. 1987. pap. 0.99 (*0-8163-0691-5*) Pacific Pr Pub Assn.

McFarland, Kenneth, jt. auth. see Holland, Kenneth J.

McFarland, Kenneth, ed. see Hill, Roland J.

McFarland, Kenneth T. Bedford County, PA Archives Vol. 6: Bedford Records, Births, Marriages & Partitions 1850-1870. 227p. 1994. pap. 16.00 (*1-55856-158-7*, 299) Closson Pr.

McFarland, Kenneth T., ed. Union Dale Cemeteries, Vol. 2. 112p. 1985. per. 11.95 (*0-933227-25-6*, 450) Closson Pr.

— Union Dale Cemetery, Vol. I. 109p. 1986. per. 11.95 (*0-933227-24-8*, 449) Closson Pr.

McFarland, Lee J. SimPleat. 41p. 1988. pap. 6.00 (*1-883763-03-7*) Kideko Hse.

— Swimsuits: Drafting & Design. 80p. 1989. pap. 12.00 (*1-883763-00-2*) Kideko Hse.

McFarland, Lynne J. Twenty-First Century Leadership: Dialogues with 100 Top Leaders. 1998. pap. text 15.95 (*0-9648466-5-9*) Leadrship Pr.

McFarland, Lynne J., et al. 21st Century Leadership: Dialogues with One-Hundred Top Leaders. 336p. 1993. pap. 15.95 (*0-9636018-1-4*) Leadrship Pr.

— 21st Century Leadership: Dialogues with One-Hundred Top Leaders. 372p. 1997. 21.95 (*0-9636018-0-6*) Leadrship Pr.

— Twenty-First Century Leadership: Dialogues with 100 Top Leaders. 1998. 21.95 (*0-9648466-4-0*) Leadrship Pr.

McFarland, Martha. The Super, Stupendous, & Tremendously Terrific Show-&-Tell Day. LC 98-60021. (Illus.). 32p. (J). (gr. k-3). 1998. 12.95 (*0-9662431-6-1*) Viewpoint NC.

***McFarland, Marvin W.** Papers of Wilbur & Orville Wright, Including the Chanute-Wright Papers: 1899-1905, Vol. 1. (Illus.). 2000. 99.95 (*0-07-136376-9*) McGraw.

McFarland, Marvin W., ed. Papers of Wilbur & Orville Wright, 2 vols., 1. LC 79-169428. (Literature & History of Aviation Ser.). 1979. reprint ed. 54.95 (*0-405-03814-3*) Ayer.

— Papers of Wilbur & Orville Wright, 2 vols., Set. LC 79-169428. (Literature & History of Aviation Ser.). 1979. reprint ed. 160.00 (*0-405-03771-6*) Ayer.

— Papers of Wilbur & Orville Wright, 2 vols., Vol. 2. LC 79-169428. (Literature & History of Aviation Ser.). 1979. reprint ed. 54.95 (*0-405-03815-1*) Ayer.

McFarland, Matthew, jt. auth. see Grove, Heather.

McFarland, Michael J. The Biosolids Engineering. 1999. 99.95 (*0-07-047178-9*) McGraw.

***McFarland, Michael J., et al.** Practice Problems for the P. E. Examination in Environmental Engineering. 2nd ed. Anderson, William, ed. LC 99-23154. 120p. 1999. 69.95 (*1-883767-30-X*) Am Acad Environ.

McFarland, Minnie B. & Olsen, Afton S. A Young & Ardent Eye: The Story of Minnie Bullack McFarland. 106p. (Orig.). pap. text 25.00 (*0-9629578-6-0*) Intl Long WA.

McFarland, Norman. Delivered from Death Unto Life. 70p. 1974. pap. 0.25 (*1-881909-06-9*) Advent Christ Gen Conf.

McFarland, P. J. Angel Standing By: The Life of Jewel. LC 98-44407. 128p. 1998. pap. 11.99 (*0-312-19827-2*) St Martin.

McFarland, Peggy A. & Carter, Cheryl J. Becoming Women of Strength. LC 94-28283. 1994. pap. 9.95 (*1-55503-708-9*, 019411) Covenant Comms.

McFarland, Philip. The Brave Bostonians: Hutchinson, Quincy, Franklin, & the Coming of the American Revolution. 301p. 1999. mass mkt. 16.00 (*0-8133-3652-X*, Pub. by Perseus Pubng) HarpC.

McFarland, Phoenix. The Complete Book of Magical Names. LC 95-79695. (Illus.). 304p. (Orig.). 1996. pap. 19.95 (*1-56718-251-8*) Llewellyn Pubns.

McFarland, Randy, ed. see Chevchuc, Carol L.

McFarland, Rhoda. Cocaine. (Drug Abuse Prevention Library). 64p. (gr. 7 up). 1997. pap. 6.95 (*1-56838-164-6*, 1756 A) Hazelden.

— Cocaine. rev. ed. (Drug Abuse Prevention Library). (Illus.). 64p. (YA). (gr. 7-12). 1997. lib. bdg. 17.95 (*0-8239-2564-1*) Rosen Group.

— Coping with Sexism. (Coping Ser.). (YA). (gr. 7-12). 1990. lib. bdg. 17.95 (*0-8239-1175-6*, D1175-6) Rosen Group.

— Coping with Substance Abuse. rev. ed. Rosen, Ruth C., ed. (Coping Ser.). 144p. (YA). (gr. 7-12). 1990. lib. bdg. 17.95 (*0-8239-1135-7*) Rosen Group.

— Drugs & Your Brothers & Sisters. 3rd rev. ed. (Drug Abuse Prevention Library). (Illus.). 64p. (YA). (gr. 7-12). 1997. lib. bdg. 17.95 (*0-8239-2582-X*) Rosen Group.

— Drugs & Your Parents. (Drug Abuse Prevention Library). 64p. (gr. 7-12). 1997. pap. 6.95 (*1-56838-171-9*, 1763 A) Hazelden.

— Drugs & Your Parents. rev. ed. (Drug Abuse Prevention Library). (Illus.). 64p. (YA). (gr. 7-12). 1997. lib. bdg. 17.95 (*0-8239-2603-6*) Rosen Group.

— Working Together Against Sexual Harassment, Set. (Library of Social Activism). (Illus.). 64p. (YA). (gr. 7-12). 1996. lib. bdg. 16.95 (*0-8239-1775-4*) Rosen Group.

— The World of Work. Rosen, Ruth C., ed. (Life Skills Library). (Illus.). 48p. (YA). (gr. 7-12). 1993. lib. bdg. 14.95 (*0-8239-1467-4*) Rosen Group.

McFarland, Ron. David Wagoner. LC 89-60062. (Western Writers Ser.: No. 88). (Illus.). 55p. (Orig.). 1989. pap. 4.95 (*0-88430-087-0*) Boise St U W Writ Ser.

— The Haunting Familiarity of Things. 56p. (Orig.). 1993. pap. 7.50 (*1-880286-12-2*) Singular Speech Pr.

— Norman Maclean. LC 93-70135. (Western Writers Ser.: No. 107). (Illus.). 55p. 1993. pap. 4.95 (*0-88430-106-0*) Boise St U W Writ Ser.

***McFarland, Ron.** Stranger in Town: New & Selected Poems. LC 00-131798. 136p. 2000. pap. 10.00 (*1-881090-38-8*) Confluence Pr.

McFarland, Ron. Tess Gallagher. LC 95-75727. (Western Writers Ser.: No. 120). (Illus.). 55p. (C). 1995. pap. 4.95 (*0-88430-119-2*) Boise St U W Writ Ser.

McFarland, Ron, et al, eds. Deep Down Things: Poems of the Inland Pacific Northwest. LC 90-24601. 220p. 1991. 20.00 (*0-87422-081-5*); pap. 14.95 (*0-87422-078-5*) Wash St U Pr.

McFarland, Ron, ed. see Maclean, Norman F.

***McFarland, Ronald E.** Understanding James Welch. LC 00-8544. (Understanding Modern European & Latin Ser.). 224p. 2000. write for info. (*1-57003-349-8*) U of SC Pr.

McFarland, Ronald E. The World of David Wagoner. LC 96-44322. 225p. 1997. text 35.00 (*0-89301-200-9*) U of Idaho Pr.

McFarland, Sara, ed. see Speckmann, Doreen.

McFarland, Stephen L. America's Pursuit of Precision Bombing, 1910-1945. (Smithsonian History of Aviation Ser.). (Illus.). 312p. 1997. pap. text 19.95 (*1-56098-784-7*) Smithsonian.

— Concise History of the United States Air Force. LC 97-221675. 88p. 1997. pap. 5.00 (*0-16-049208-4*) USGPO.

— Conquering the Night: Army Air Forces Night Fighters at War. 47p. 1998. pap. 2.75 (*0-16-049672-1*) USGPO.

McFarland, Stephen L. & Newton, Wesley P. To Command the Sky: The Battle for Air Superiority over Germany, 1942-1944. LC 91-9712. (History of Aviation Ser.). (Illus.). 344p. (C). 1991. 40.00 (*1-56098-069-9*) Smithsonian.

McFarland, Stephen L., et al. Interservice Rivalry: The U. S. Military in Transition. (Illus.). 51p. (Orig.). (C). 1997. pap. text 30.00 (*0-7881-3849-9*) DIANE Pub.

McFarland, Thom. The Great Transfiguration of Bucky Muckleroy. LC 98-65633. 192p. 1999. pap. text 14.95 (*1-57197-112-2*) Pentland Pr.

McFarland, Thomas. The Mask of Keats: The Endeavour of a Poet. 264p. 2000. text 49.95 (*0-19-818645-2*) OUP.

— Originality & Imagination. LC 84-47949. 247p. reprint ed. pap. 76.60 (*0-608-07397-0*, 206762400009) Bks Demand.

— Paradoxes of Freedom: The Romantic Mystique of a Transcendence. (Illus.). 158p. 1996. text 45.00 (*0-19-812181-4*) OUP.

McFarland, Thomas. Romantic Cruxes: The English Essayists & the Spirit of the Age. 140p. 1988. text 45.00 (*0-19-812895-9*) OUP.

McFarland, Thomas. Romanticism & the Forms of Ruin: Wordsworth, Coleridge & Modalities of Fragmentation. LC 80-7546. 467p. 1981. reprint ed. pap. 144.80 (*0-608-02513-5*, 206315700004) Bks Demand.

— Romanticism & the Heritage of Rousseau. 356p. 1995. text 55.00 (*0-19-818287-2*) OUP.

— Shakespeare's Pastoral Comedy. LC 72-81325. 228p. reprint ed. pap. 70.70 (*0-7837-3752-1*, 204356900010) Bks Demand.

— Shapes of Culture. LC 86-14670. 201p. 1987. text 27.95 (*0-87745-162-1*) U of Iowa Pr.

— William Wordsworth: Intensity & Achievement. 192p. 1992. 49.95 (*0-19-811253-X*) OUP.

McFarland, Thomas D. & Parker, Reese. Expert Systems in Education & Training. LC 89-38713. (Illus.). 280p. 1990. 37.95 (*0-87778-210-5*) Educ Tech Pubns.

McFarland, Tracy E. Your Cat's Life: Your Complete Guide to Raising Your Pet from Kitten to Companion. 224p. 1998. per. 15.00 (*0-7615-1361-2*) Prima Pub.

McFarland, Twilah S. & Pugh, Barbara S. Cemeteries of Phelps County Missouri Vol. I: Rolla & Miller Townships. (Illus.). x, 163p. 1989. pap. 40.00 (*1-893474-08-9*) Phelps Cnty Gene.

An Asterisk (*) at the beginning of an entry indicates that the title is appearing for the first time.

McFarlane. AutoCAD Database Connectivity. LC 99-26737. (Illus.). 288p. (C). 1999. pap. text 44.95 (0-7668-1640-0) Delmar.

McFarlane, A. G., jt. auth. see Pang, G. K.

McFarlane, Adrian A. A Grammar of Fear & Evil: A Husserlian-Wittgensteinian Hermeneutic. LC 95-34835. (Studies in European Thought: Vol. 9). XIII, 214p. (C). 1997. pap. 34.95 (0-8204-3046-3) P Lang Pubng.

McFarlane, Alexander C., jt. ed. see Yehuda, Rachel.

McFarlane, Annette. Pig Keeping on a Small Scale. 1996. pap. 14.95 (0-86417-790-9, Pub. by Kangaroo Pr) Seven Hills Bk.

***McFarlane, Annette.** Successful Gardening in Warm Climates. 1998. pap. 21.95 (0-86417-868-9, Pub. by Kangaroo Pr) Seven Hills Bk.

McFarlane, Anthony. BRITSH IN AMER 1480 1815. LC 94-6450. (Studies in Modern History). (C). 1994. text 68.95 (0-582-20950-1, 76702, Pub. by Addison-Wesley) Longman.

— Colombia Before Independence: Economy, Society, & Politics under Bourbon Rule. LC 92-42299. (Cambridge Latin American Studies: No. 75). (Illus.). 415p. (C). 1993. text 74.95 (0-521-41641-8) Cambridge U Pr.

***McFarlane, Arlene.** I Hate Celery Soup. Wise, Noreen, ed. (Book-a-Day Collection). 32p. (YA). (ps up). 2000. pap. 5.95 (1-58584-428-4) Huckleberry CT.

— My Auntie Bean, She Is a Scream. Wise, Noreen, ed. (Lemonade Collection). (Illus.). 64p. (J). (ps-2). 2000. pap. 5.95 (1-58584-258-3) Huckleberry CT.

— My Name Is Not Magilla Gorilla. Wise, Noreen, ed. (Lemonade Collection). (Illus.). 48p. (J). (ps up). 2000. pap. 5.95 (1-58584-210-9) Huckleberry CT.

McFarlane, Bob. Advancing with AutoCAD LT. 176p. 1997. pap. 49.95 (0-470-24437-2) Wiley.

— Assignments in AutoCAD. LC 97-219411. 174p. 1997. pap. 49.95 (0-470-24415-1) Wiley.

— Beginning AutoCad. 200p. 1997. pap. 49.95 (0-470-24429-1) Wiley.

— Beginning Autocad R13 for Windows. LC 97-121039. 288p. (gr. 13). 1996. pap. text 24.95 (0-340-64572-5) Chapman & Hall.

— Introducing 3D AutoCad. 191p. 1997. pap. 49.95 (0-470-24434-8) Wiley.

— Progressing with AutoCAD. 186p. 1997. pap. 49.95 (0-470-24436-4) Wiley.

— Starting with AutoCAD LT. 266p. 1997. pap. 49.95 (0-470-24438-0) Wiley.

McFarlane, Brian. An Autobiography of British Cinema: By the Actors & Filmakers Who Made It. (Illus.). 656p. 1998. pap. 26.95 (0-413-70520-X, Methuen Drama) Methn.

— Best of It Happened in Hockey. 384p. 1998. 19.95 (0-7737-3046-X) Stoddart Publ.

***McFarlane, Brian.** The Blackhawks. 256p. 2000. 19.95 (0-7737-3252-7) Stoddart Publ.

McFarlane, Brian. Brian McFarlane's History of Hockey. (Illus.). 299p. 1997. 34.95 (1-57167-145-5) Sports Pub.

***McFarlane, Brian.** The Bruins: Brian McFarlane's Original Six. large type ed. (Original Six Ser.: Vol. 5). (Illus.). 256p. (J). (gr. 3-7). 1999. text 19.95 (0-7737-3189-X, Pub. by Stoddart Publ) Genl Dist Srvs.

McFarlane, Brian. The Habs. (Original Six Ser.). (Illus.). 208p. (J). (gr. 3-6). 1999. pap. 13.95 (0-7737-5919-0, Pub. by Stoddart Publ) Genl Dist Srvs.

— The Habs. LC 97-135973. (Original Six Ser.: Vol. 2). (Illus.). 208p. (J). (ps-1). 1999. 19.95 (0-7737-2981-X, Pub. by Stoddart Publ) Genl Dist Srvs.

— Hockey for Kids: Heroes, Tips, & Facts. LC 96-12618. (Illus.). (J). (gr. 4-7). 1996. reprint ed. mass mkt. 5.95 (0-688-15027-6, Wm Morrow) Morrow Avon.

— Hockey for Kids; Heroes, Tips, & Facts. (J). 1996. 11.15 (0-606-11464-5, Pub. by Turtleback) Demco.

***McFarlane, Brian.** Lance Comfort. LC 99-42907. (British Film Directors Ser.). 1999. pap. 19.95 (0-7190-5484-2); text 79.95 (0-7190-5483-4, Pub. by Manchester Univ Pr) St Martin.

— The Leafs. (Original Six Ser.). 208p. (J). (gr. 3-7). 1999. reprint ed. pap. 13.95 (0-7737-5843-7, Pub. by Stoddart Publ) Genl Dist Srvs.

McFarlane, Brian. Novel to Film: An Introduction to the Theory of Adaptation. (Illus.). 288p. (C). 1996. text 70.00 (0-19-871151-4) OUP.

— Novel to Film: An Introduction to the Theory of Adaptation. (Illus.). 288p. 1996. pap. text 21.00 (0-19-871150-6) OUP.

— The Rangers. LC 98-102820. (Original Six Ser.). (Illus.). 240p. (J). (gr. 3-7). 1999. 19.95 (0-7737-3047-8, Pub. by Stoddart Publ); pap. 13.95 (0-7737-6007-5, Pub. by Stoddart Publ) Genl Dist Srvs.

— The Red Wings: Brian McFarlane's Original Six. (Original Six Ser.: Vol. 4). (Illus.). 240p. (J). (gr. 3-7). 1999. 19.95 (0-7737-3116-4, Pub. by Stoddart Publ) Genl Dist Srvs.

***McFarlane, Brian.** The Red Wings: Brian McFarlane's Original Six. (Original Six Ser.: Vol. 4). (Illus.). 224p. (J). (gr. 3-7). 1999. pap. 13.95 (0-7737-6062-8, Pub. by Stoddart Publ) Genl Dist Srvs.

— Stanley Cup Fever: More Than A Century Of Hockey Greatness. rev. large type ed. (Illus.). 304p. 1999. pap. 22.95 (0-7737-6058-X, Pub. by Stoddart Publ) Genl Dist Srvs.

McFarlane, Brian. Stanley Cup Fever: One Hundred Years of Hockey Greatness. 271p. 1992. pap. 15.95 (0-7737-5554-3) Genl Dist Srvs.

***McFarlane, Brian.** The Ultimate Hockey Quiz Book. (Illus.). 160p. 2000. pap. 9.95 (1-55209-543-6) Firefly Bks Ltd.

McFarlane, Brian. The Youngest Goalie. (Warwick Young Adult Sports Ser.). 208p. (YA). (gr. 5-9). 1997. pap. 8.95 (1-895629-95-0) Warwick Publ.

McFarlane, Brian, ed. Sixty Voices: Celebrities Recall the Golden Age of British Cinema. (Illus.). 272p. (C). 1993. 60.00 (0-85170-353-4, Pub. by British Film Inst); pap. 29.95 (0-85170-349-6, Pub. by British Film Inst) Ind U Pr.

***McFarlane, Brian, et al, eds.** The Oxford Companion to Australian Film. (Illus.). 608p. 2000. text 65.00 (0-19-553797-1) OUP.

McFarlane, Brian, told to. Clancy: The King's Story. (Illus.). 220p. 1997. pap. 17.95 (1-55022-332-1, Pub. by ECW) LPC InBook.

McFarlane, Brian & Mayer, Geoff. New Australian Cinema: Sources & Parallels in British & American Film. (Illus.). 273p. (C). 1992. text 59.95 (0-521-38363-3); pap. text 20.95 (0-521-38768-X) Cambridge U Pr.

McFarlane, Bruce. Yugoslavia. (Marxist Regimes Ser.). 220p. 1988. text 49.00 (0-86187-452-8); text 17.50 (0-86187-453-6) St Martin.

McFarlane, Bruce, jt. auth. see Wheelwright, Edward.

McFarlane, C., jt. auth. see Hayward, Arthur L.

McFarlane, Cameron. Sodomite in Fiction & Satire, 1660-1750. LC 97-35684. 192p. 1997. pap. 17.50 (0-231-10895-8) Col U Pr.

McFarlane, Cameron. Sodomite in Fiction & Satire, 1660-1750. LC 97-35684. 192p. 1997. lib. bdg. 47.50 (0-231-10894-X) Col U Pr.

McFarlane, Craig, jt. ed. see Trapp, Stefan.

McFarlane, Deborah R. & Meier, Kenneth J. The Politics of Fertility Control: Family Planning & Abortion Policies in the American States. LC 99-50685. (Illus.). 308p. 2000. pap. text 24.95 (1-889119-39-3, Pub. by Seven Bridges) Stylus Pub VA.

McFarlane, Donna. Division of Surgery. large type ed. 224p. 11.95 (0-88961-193-9, Pub. by Womens Pr); 16.95 (0-88961-220-X, Pub. by Womens Pr) LPC InBook.

McFarlane, E. & Saywell, J. If: Questions for the Soul. LC 99-191124. 144p. 1998. 9.95 (0-679-45636-8) Villard Books.

McFarlane, Elizabeth A., jt. auth. see McFarland, Gertrude K.

McFarlane, Evelyn. If: Questions for the Game of Life. Rosenthal, David, ed. 129p. 1995. 9.95 (0-679-44535-8) Villard Books.

McFarlane, Evelyn & Saywell, James. If 3: Questions for the Game of Love. LC 97-6646. 129p. 1997. 9.95 (0-679-45637-6) Vin Bks.

— If2: More Questions for the Game of Life. 1996. 9.95 (0-614-20692-8) Villard Books.

McFarlane, Evelyn, jt. auth. see Saywel, James.

McFarlane, Evelyn, jt. auth. see Saywell, James.

McFarlane, G. Copyright Through Cases. 352p. 1986. pap. 30.00 (0-08-039208-3, Pergamon Pr) Elsevier.

— Customs & Excise Cases. (Criminal Law Library). 384p. 1988. 100.00 (0-08-039245-8, Pergamon Pr) Elsevier.

— A Practical Introduction to Copyright. 2nd ed. (Waterlow Practitioner's Library). 448p. 1990. reprint ed. pap. 59.95 (0-08-033074-6, Pergamon Pr) Elsevier.

McFarlane, Gavin. McFarlane's Customs Law Handbook, 1989-90. 320p. (C). 1990. 275.00 (1-85431-057-7) St Mut.

— McFarlane's Customs Law Handbook, 1990-1991. 494p. (C). 1991. 64.00 (1-85431-147-6, Pub. by Blackstone Pr) Gaunt.

— VAT. (C). 1991. text 22.00 (1-85431-134-4, Pub. by Blackstone Pr) Gaunt.

McFarlane, Graham. Christ & the Spirit: The Doctrine of the Incarnation According to Edward Irving. x, 204p. 1996. pap. text 25.00 (0-85364-694-5) Paternoster Pub.

— Edward Irving. (Devotional Library). 1996. 11.90 (0-7152-0719-9, Pub. by St Andrew) St Mut.

***McFarlane, Graham.** Why Do You Believe What You Believe about the Holy Spirit. 200p. 1998. reprint ed. pap. 14.99 (0-85364-886-7, Pub. by Paternoster Pub) OM Literature.

McFarlane, Graham, jt. auth. see Donnan, Hastings.

McFarlane, I. D., ed. Acta Conventus Neo-Latini Sanctandreani: Proceedings of the Fifth International Congress, 1982, at St. Andrews. (Medieval & Renaissance Texts & Studies: Vol. 38). (Illus.). 656p. 1986. 60.00 (0-86698-070-9, MR38) MRTS.

— Entry of Henri II into Paris, 1549. LC 81-18925. (Renaissance Triumphs & Magnificences, Medieval & Renaissance Texts & Studies: Vol. 7). (Illus.). 208p. 1982. 30.00 (0-86698-013-X, MR7) MRTS.

McFarlane, I. D. & Maclean, Ian. Montaigne: Essays in Memory of Richard Sayce. (Illus.). 1982. 55.00 (0-19-815769-X) OUP.

McFarlane, I D., jt. ed. see Smith, Pauline M.

***McFarlane, Ian.** The Encyclopedia of Australian Rock & Pop. (Illus.). 736p. 2000. pap. 24.95 (1-86448-768-2, Pub. by Allen & Unwin Pty) IPG Chicago.

McFarlane, Ian G. Molecular Basis of Autoimmune Hepatitis. (Molecular Biology Intelligence Unit Ser.). 197p. 1996. 99.00 (1-57059-339-6) Landes Bioscience.

McFarlane, James. Ibsen & Meaning: Studies, Essays & Prefaces, 1953-87. 396p. 1988. pap. 25.00 (1-870041-07-0, Pub. by Norvik Pr) Dufour.

McFarlane, James, ed. The Cambridge Companion to Ibsen. (Cambridge Companions to Literature Ser.). (Illus.). 297p. (C). 1994. pap. text 19.95 (0-521-42321-X) Cambridge U Pr.

McFarlane, James & Naess, Harald S., eds. Selected Letters: 1879-1998, Vol. 1. LC 89-81771. (Norvik Press Series A: No. 7). 300p. (Orig.). 1990. pap. 35.00 (1-870041-13-5, Pub. by Norvik Pr) Dufour.

McFarlane, James, tr. see Hamsun, Knut.

McFarlane, James, tr. see Ibsen, Henrik.

McFarlane, James, tr. & intro. see Obstfelder, Sigbjorn.

McFarlane, James R. Traction in Franklin County Vermont - St. Albans Street Railway St. Albans & Swanton Traction Company: St. Albans Street Railway, St. Albans & Swanton Traction Company. Harris, Marion, ed. LC 94-14087. (Illus.). 48p. 1994. pap. 16.50 (0-933449-21-6) Transport Trails.

McFarlane, James R., jt. auth. see Benedict, Roy G.

McFarlane, James W., tr. see Hamsun, Knut.

***McFarlane, Jessie.** Housewife's Adventure with God: The Story of Jessie McFarlane & 'Prayer Chain Ministries' 2000. pap. text 7.99 (1-85792-165-8) Christian Focus.

McFarlane, Judith & Parker, Barbara J. Abuse During Pregnancy: A Protocol for Prevention & Intervention. Damus, Karla & Freda, Margaret C., eds. LC 94-34250. 1994. write for info. (0-86525-059-6) March of Dimes.

McFarlane, Judith, jt. auth. see Anderson, Elizabeth T.

McFarlane, Judith M. The Clinical Handbook of Family Nursing. LC 85-31446. 562p. 1989. pap. text 34.95 (0-8273-4304-3) Delmar.

McFarlane, Judith M., jt. auth. see Anderson, Elizabeth T.

McFarlane, Judith M., jt. auth. see Whitson, Betty J.

McFarlane, K. B. England in the Fifteenth Century: Collected Essays. 307p. (C). 1982. 55.00 (0-9506882-5-8); pap. 20.00 (0-907628-01-X) Hambledon Press.

McFarlane, Leslie. The Ghost of the Hardy Boys. LC 97-14798. 212p. 1997. reprint ed. pap. 12.95 (1-55709-466-7) Applewood.

McFarlane, Lewis R., jt. auth. see Weil, Leon J.

McFarlane, M. J., ed. Laterites - Some Aspects of Current Research: Proceedings of the Laterite Workshop, 1st International Geomorphological Conference, 1985. (Annals of Geomorphology Ser.: Suppl. 64). (Illus.). 180p. 1987. pap. text 68.60 (3-443-21064-3, Pub. by Gebruder Borntraeger) Balogh.

McFarlane, Marilyn. Best Places to Stay in the Pacific Northwest. 5th rev. ed. (Illus.). 600p. 1998. pap. 18.00 (0-395-76339-8) HM.

***McFarlane, Marilyn.** Best Places to Stay in the Pacific Northwest. 6th ed. (Illus.). 491p. 2000. pap. 19.00 (0-618-00535-8) HM.

McFarlane, Marilyn. Quick Escapes in the Pacific Northwest: 32 Weekend Trips from Portland, Seattle, & Vancouver, B.C. 4th ed. Cunningham, Christine, ed. LC 99-24575. (Quick Escapes Ser.). 336p. 1999. pap. text 14.95 (0-7627-0468-3) Globe Pequot.

— Sacred Myths: Stories of World Religions. LC 96-221221. (Illus.). 102p. (J). (gr. 4 up). 1996. 26.95 (0-9638327-7-8) Sibyl Pubns.

McFarlane, Marilyn, jt. auth. see Osmont, Kelly.

McFarlane, Marilyn, ed. see Osmont, Kelly.

McFarlane, Nancy. Hawaii Revised Statues Annotated 1998 Advance Legislative Service Pamphlets, 4 vols. 2500p. 1998. pap. 79.50 (0-327-06092-1, 42135-12, MICHIE) LEXIS Pub.

McFarlane, Nancy, ed. Hawaii Revised Statutes Annotated, 1998 Advance Legislative Service Pamphlet, No. 1. annot. ed. 550p. 1998. pap. write for info. (0-327-06093-X, 42136-12, MICHIE) LEXIS Pub.

— Hawaii Revised Statutes Annotated, 1998 Advance Legislative Service Pamphlet, No. 2. annot. ed. 700p. 1998. pap. write for info. (0-327-06096-4, 42137-12, MICHIE) LEXIS Pub.

McFarlane, Nigel. Instant JavaScript. 400p. 1998. pap. 24.95 (1-86100-127-4) Wrox Pr Inc.

***McFarlane, Nigel, et al.** Professional JavaScript. (Professional Ser.). 1200p. 1999. pap. 49.99 (1-86100-270-X) Wrox Pr Inc.

McFarlane, Peter. Barnaby the Barbarian. 1998. pap. text 5.95 (0-207-19620-6) HarpC.

— Max the Man Mountain. 1998. pap. 5.95 (0-207-19116-6) HarpC.

— Soula the Ruler. 1999. pap. text 5.95 (0-207-19054-2) HarpC.

McFarlane, R. Modelling with AutoCAD Release 14: For Windows 95 & Windows NT. LC 99-167905. 256p. 1998. pap. 44.95 (0-470-32898-3) Halsted Pr.

McFarlane, Robert. Advancing with AutoCad R13 for Windows. 166p. 1997. pap. 49.95 (0-470-23752-X) Wiley.

— Beginning AutoCAD. (Mechanical Engineering Ser.). 1994. pap. text 21.95 (0-340-58571-4, VNR) Wiley.

— Beginning AutoCAD R13 for Windows. 275p. 1997. pap. 49.95 (0-470-23736-8) Wiley.

— Beginning AutoCAD R14: For Windows NT & Windows 95. 2nd ed. 256p. (C). 1998. pap. 49.95 (0-470-32364-7) Wiley.

— Modeling with AutoCAD: Release 13 for Windows. LC 97-167017. 248p. 1997. pap. 49.95 (0-470-23737-6) Wiley.

— Solid Modeling with AutoCad. 212p. 1997. pap. 49.95 (0-470-23735-X) Wiley.

— 3D Draughting Using AutoCAD. 172p. 1996. pap., pap. text 99.00 incl. disk (0-470-23732-5) Wiley.

McFarlane, Robert & McElhinney, Camillus P. Using AutoLISP with AutoCAD. LC 98-48450. 184p. 1998. 39.95 (0-470-32899-1) Halsted Pr.

McFarlane, Robert W. A Stillness in the Pines: The Ecology of the Red-Cockaded Woodpecker. 1994. pap. 10.95 (0-393-31167-8) Norton.

McFarlane, Robert W., jt. ed. see Esch, Gerald W.

McFarlane, Rodger & Bashe, Phillip. The Complete Bedside Companion: No-Nonsense Advice on Caring for the Seriously Ill. LC 97-43746. 480p. 1998. 26.50 (0-684-80143-4) S&S Trade.

— The Complete Bedside Companion: No-Nonsense Advice on Caring for the Seriously Ill. 544p. 1999. pap. 15.00 (0-684-84319-6, Fireside) S&S Trade Pap.

***McFarlane, Ronn.** Scottish Lute. 160p. 1998. pap. 14.95 (0-7866-2917-7, 96693); pap. 29.95 incl. audio compact disk (0-7866-2919-3, 96693CDP) Mel Bay.

McFarlane, Sheryl. Eagle Dreams. (Illus.). 32p. (J). (gr. k-3). 1998. pap. 6.95 (1-55143-125-4) Orca Bk Pubs.

McFarlane, Sheryl. Jessie's Island. (Illus.). 32p. (J). (gr. 1-4). 1992. pap. 6.95 (0-920501-76-1) Orca Bk Pubs.

McFarlane, Sheryl. Waiting for the Whales. (Illus.). 32p. (J). (gr. k-3). 1998. pap. 6.95 (0-920501-96-6) Orca Bk Pubs.

McFarlane, Stewart. The Complete Book of T'ai Chi. (DK Living Ser.). 120p. 1999. pap. text 13.95 (0-7894-4259-0) DK Pub Inc.

McFarlane, Todd. Spawn, Vol. I. (Illus.). 116p. (YA). 1995. pap. 9.95 (1-887279-01-6) Image Comics.

— Spawn, Vol. 1. 5th rev. ed. (Illus.). 120p. 1997. pap. 9.95 (1-887279-50-4) Image Comics.

— Spawn, Vol. III. Orzechowski, Tom, ed. (Illus.). 96p. (YA). pap. 9.95 (1-887279-35-0) Image Comics.

— Spawn, Vol. 3. 2nd rev. ed. Orzechowski, Tom, ed. (Illus.). 100p. 1997. pap. 9.95 (1-887279-54-7) Image Comics.

— Spawn, Vol. 6. (Illus.). 120p. 1998. pap. 9.95 (1-58240-001-6) Image Comics.

***McFarlane, Todd.** Spawn, Vol. 10. Vol. 10. (Illus.). 120p. (J). 2000. pap. 9.95 (1-58240-131-4) Image Comics.

McFarlane, Todd. Spawn: Betrayal of Blood. 1999. pap. text 9.95 (1-58240-021-0) Image Comics.

— Spawn Vol. V: The Hunt. (Illus.). 128p. 1997. pap. 9.95 (1-887279-71-7) Image Comics.

***McFarlane, Todd.** Spawn Vol. 11: Crossroads. Vol. 11. (Illus.). 96p. (J). 2000. pap. 9.95 (1-58240-132-2, Pub. by Image Comics) Midpt Trade.

McFarlane, Todd. Spawn Collected Edition No. VII: Deadman's Touch, 7. (Spawn Ser.). (Illus.). 96p. 1998. pap. 9.95 (1-58240-020-2) Image Comics.

— Spider-Man: Torment. (Spiderman Ser.). (Illus.). 128p. 1992. pap. 15.95 (0-87135-805-0) Marvel Entrprs.

***McFarlane, Todd.** Urban Jungle, 9. 1999. pap. text 9.95 (1-58240-111-X) Image Comics.

McFarlane, Todd, et al. Spawn, Vol. II. 2nd ed. Orzechowski, Tom, ed. (Illus.). 1996. reprint ed. pap. 9.95 (1-887279-38-5) Image Comics.

— Spawn TPB, No. II. Orzechowski, Tom, ed. (Illus.). 128p. (Orig.). (YA). pap. text 9.95 (1-887279-18-0) Image Comics.

McFarlane, Todd, jt. auth. see Michelinie, David.

McFarlane, Todd, ed. see Holguin, Brian.

McFarlane, William, ed. see Green, John L., Jr.

McFarlane, William R., ed. Family Therapy in Schizophrenia. LC 82-11742. (Guilford Family Therapy Ser.). 355p. 1983. lib. bdg. 42.00 (0-89862-042-2) Guilford Pubns.

McFarlene, Stewart. The Complete Book of T'ai Chi. LC 96-33596. 120p. 1997. 22.95 (0-7894-1476-7) DK Pub Inc.

Mcfarlin. Industrial Organizational Psychology. 1992. text 63.12 (0-07-042446-2) McGraw.

McFarlin. International Management. LC 97-12977. (Miscellaneous/Catalogs Ser.). 1997. mass mkt. 87.95 (0-538-87872-X) S-W Pub.

***McFarlin, Dean B. & Sweeney, Paul D.** House of Mirrors: The Untold Truth about Narcissistic Leaders - And How to Survive Them. 2000. pap. 24.95 (0-7494-2724-8) Kogan Page Ltd.

McFarquhar, Helena. General Principles of Law. LC 86-27432. (Longman Exam Guides Ser.). 256p. 1987. reprint ed. pap. 79.40 (0-608-03590-4, 206441300009) Bks Demand.

McFate, Katherine, et al, eds. Poverty, Inequality, & the Future of Social Policy: Western States in the New World Order. 704p. 1995. 70.00 (0-87154-510-1) Russell Sage.

— Poverty, Inequality, & the Future of Social Policy: Western States in the New World Order. 756p. (C). 1996. reprint ed. pap. text 24.95 (0-87154-593-4) Russell Sage.

McFatter, jt. auth. see Gibson.

McFatter, Janice, jt. auth. see Gibson, Dauhrice.

McFaul, Michael. Post-Communist Party Politics. LC 93-7396. (Significant Issues Series - Creating the Post-Communist Order: Vol. 15, No. 3). 151p. (C). 1993. pap. text 9.95 (0-89206-208-8) CSIS.

— Russia's 1996 Presidential Election: The End of Polarized Politics, Vol. 442. LC 97-9350. (Publication Ser.: No. 442). 169p. 1997. pap. 17.95 (0-8179-9502-1) Hoover Inst Pr.

— Understanding Russia's 1993 Parlimentary Elections: Implications for U. S. Foreign Policy. LC 94-10757. (Essays in Public Policy Ser.: No. 49). 1994. pap. text 5.00 (0-8179-5542-9) Hoover Inst Pr.

McFaul, Michael, ed. Can the Russian Military-Industrial Complex Be Privatized? 60p. (Orig.). 1993. pap. 6.00 (0-935371-29-X) CFISAC.

McFaul, Michael & Markov, Sergei. The Troubled Birth of Russian Democracy: Parties, Personalities, & Programs. (Publication Ser.: Vol. 415). 384p. (C). 1993. 39.95 (0-8179-9231-6) Hoover Inst Pr.

— The Troubled Birth of Russian Democracy: Partics, Personalities & Programs. (Publication Ser.: Vol. 415). 384p. (C). 1993. pap. 24.95 (0-8179-9232-4) Hoover Inst Pr.

McFeat, Tom, ed. Indians of the North Pacific Coast. LC 88-20675. 286p. 1967. pap. 10.95 (0-295-74095-7) U of Wash Pr.

McFedries, Paul. The Complete Idiot's Guide to Creating an HTML Web Page. 336p. 1996. 24.99 incl. disk (0-7897-0722-5) Que.

— The Complete Idiot's Guide to Creating an HTML Web Page. 2nd ed. 320p. 1997. 24.99 (0-7897-1146-X) Que.

M

***McFedries, Paul.** The Complete Idiot's Guide to Creating an HTML Web Page. 4th ed. LC 99-65790. (Illus.). 350p. 1999. 19.99 (*0-7897-2256-9*) Que.

McFedries, Paul. The Complete Idiot's Guide to Creating an HTML 4 Web Page. 3rd ed. 408p. 1997. pap. 24.99 (*0-7897-1490-6*) Que.

***McFedries, Paul.** Complete Idiot's Guide to Microsoft Windows Millennium. (Illus.). 400p. 2000. pap. 16.99 (*0-7897-2407-3*) Que.

McFedries, Paul. Complete Idiot's Guide to More Windows 98. LC 98-85582. (Complete Idiot's Guides). 1998. pap. 19.99 (*0-7897-1739-5*) Que.

— The Complete Idiot's Guide to Windows 95. 2nd ed. LC 97-65009. 416p. 1997. 19.99 (*0-7897-1161-3*) Que.

— The Complete Idiot's Guide to Windows 98. LC 97-75459. 408p. 1998. pap. 14.99 (*0-7897-1493-0*) Que.

— Complete Idiot's Guide to WordPerfect. 2nd ed. LC 94-71430. 347p. 1994. 16.95 (*1-56761-499-X*, Alpha Ref) Macmillan Gen Ref.

— The Complete Idiot's Guide to WordPerfect for Windows 6.1. 2nd ed. (Illus.). 350p. (Orig.). 1994. 16.95 (*1-56761-543-0*, Alpha Ref) Macmillan Gen Ref.

— Excel 5.0 Super Book. 1172p. 1993. 39.95 (*0-672-30385-X*) Sams.

— Paul McFedries' Windows 95 Unleashed: Professional Reference Edition. LC 96-72006. 1648p. 1997. 59.99 (*0-672-31039-2*) Sams.

— Paul McFedries' Windows 98 Unleashed, Professional Reforence Edition. LC 97-69136. 1440p. 1998. 54.99 (*0-672-31224-7*) Macmillan.

— Unofficial Guide to Windows 98. 1999. pap. text 17.99 (*0-7897-1912-6*) Que.

— Visual Basic Applications for Office 2000 Unleashed. LC 98-89206. (Sams Unleashed Series). (Illus.). 1114p. 1999. pap. 39.99 incl. cd-rom (*0-672-31567-X*) Sams.

— Visual Basic for Application Unleashed. LC 96-72008. 1008p. 1997. 49.99 (*0-672-31046-5*) Sams.

— Windows 95 Unleashed: MCSE Edition. 850p. 1997. 59.99 (*0-672-31187-9*) Sams.

***McFedries, Paul.** Windows 2000 Professional. (Complete Idiot's Guides Ser.). 1999. pap. 19.99 (*0-7897-2129-5*) Que.

McFedries, Paul. Windows 98 Unleashed. LC 97-69860. 1090p. 1998. 34.99 (*0-672-31235-2*) Macmillan.

McFedries, Paul & Wempen, Faithe. The Complete Idiot's Guide Windows 95. LC 94-71081. (Illus.). 385p. (Orig.). 1995. 19.99 (*1-56761-495-7*, Alpha Ref) Macmillan Gen Ref.

McFee, ed. Cultural Diversity & the Structure & Practice of Art Education. 1998. pap. 22.00 (*0-937652-76-8*, 279) Natl Art Ed.

McFee, Graham. Education, Sport & Leisure: Connections & Controversies. pap. text 17.95 (*3-89124-442-8*) Meyer & Meyer.

McFee, Graham. Understanding Dance. LC 91-44620. 352p. (C). 1992. pap. 25.99 (*0-415-07810-5*) Routledge.

McFee, June K. & Degge, Rogena M. Art, Culture, & Environment: A Catalyst for Teaching. 416p. (C). 1992. per. 31.95 (*0-8403-7418-6*) Kendall-Hunt.

McFee, Malcolm. Modern Blackfeet: Montanans on a Reservation. (Illus.). 134p. 1984. reprint ed. pap. text 10.50 (*0-88133-043-4*) Waveland Pr.

McFee, Michael. Colander. LC 95-67963. (Poetry Ser.). (C). 1996. pap. 11.95 (*0-614-96386-9*); pap. 11.95 (*0-88748-224-4*) Carnegie-Mellon.

— Plain Air. LC 83-9109. (University of Central Florida Contemporary Poetry Ser.). 65p. 1983. 14.95 (*0-8130-0774-7*) U Press Fla.

— Sad Girl Sitting on a Running Board. LC 91-72899. 80p. (Orig.). 1991. pap. 12.50 (*0-917788-49-4*) Gnomon Pr.

— Vanishing Acts. LC 89-80713. 64p. (Orig.). 1989. pap. 12.50 (*0-917788-38-9*) Gnomon Pr.

McFee, Michael, ed. The Language They Speak Is Things to Eat: Fourteen Contemporary North Carolina Poets. LC 94-4239. (Illus.). 270p. 1994. 29.95 (*0-8078-2172-1*); pap. 14.95 (*0-8078-4483-7*) U of NC Pr.

***McFee, Michael, ed.** This Is Where We Live: Short Stories by 25 Contemporary North Carolina Writers. 304p. 2000. 29.95 (*0-8078-2583-2*) U of NC Pr.

McFee, Michael, ed. The Spectator Reader. LC 85-61379. (Illus.). 224p. (Orig.). 1985. pap. 7.95 (*0-9614785-1-9*) Spectator Publ.

McFee, Michael, jt. auth. see Matheson, Elizabeth.

McFee, Michele A. Limestone Locks & Overgrowth: The Rise & Descent of the Chenango Canal. rev. ed. LC 93-40966. (Illus.). 240p. (Orig.). 1993. pap. 25.00 (*0-935796-44-4*) Purple Mnt Pr.

— A Long Haul: The Story of the New York State Barge Canal. LC 98-26211. (Illus.). 221p. 1998. reprint ed. pap. 25.00 (*0-935796-99-1*) Purple Mnt Pr.

McFee, William. Swallowing the Anchor. LC 70-128275. (Essay Index Reprint Ser.). 1977. 21.95 (*0-8369-1986-6*) Ayer.

McFee, William W. & Kelly, J. Michael, eds. Carbon Forms & Functions in Forest Soils: Proceedings: North American Forest Soils Conference (8th: 1993: Gainesville, FL) LC 94-35401. 594p. 1995. 70.00 (*0-89118-818-5*) Soil Sci Soc Am.

McFeeley, Daniel, jt. auth. see Schlessinger, Laura.

McFeeley, Daniel, jt. illus. see Schlessinger, Laura.

McFeeley, William. Civil War. 1999. pap. write for info. (*0-14-008392-8*, Viking) Viking Penguin.

— Civil War: As Seen. 1999. text 16.00 (*0-670-80834-2*) Viking Penguin.

***McFeeley, William.** Proximity to Death. 208p. 2000. reprint ed. pap. 13.95 (*0-393-32104-5*) Norton.

***McFeely, Eliza.** Zuni & the American Imagination. (Illus.). 288p. 2001. 26.00 (*0-8090-2707-0*) Hill & Wang.

McFeely, Mary D., ed. The Women's Annual: 1984-1985, No. 5. (Reference Publications, Women's Studies Annual). 184p. (C). 1985. 55.00 (*0-8161-8717-7*, Hall Reference); 39.95 (*0-8161-8741-X*, Hall Reference) Macmillan.

McFeely, Mary D., et al. Civil War Memoirs: Memoirs of Ulysses S. Grant & William T. Sherman, 2 vols. (Library of America Ser.). (Illus.). 2335p. 1990. boxed set 70.00 (*0-940450-69-0*, Pub. by Library of America) Penguin Putnam.

McFeely, Mary D., ed. see Grant, Ulysses S.

***McFeely, Mary Drake.** Can She Bake a Cherry Pie? American Women & the Kitchen in the Twentieth Century. 192p. 2000. 24.95 (*1-55849-250-X*) U of Mass Pr.

McFeely, William S. Frederick Douglass. (Illus.). 480p. 1995. pap. 14.95 (*0-393-31376-X*, Norton Paperbks) Norton.

— Grant: A Biography. Speirs, Katherine E., ed. LC 96-85992. (Signature Ser.). (Illus.). 492p. 1996. 35.00 (*0-945707-15-0*) Amer Political.

— Grant: A Biography. (Illus.). 608p. 1982. pap. 18.95 (*0-393-30046-3*) Norton.

— Proximity to Death. LC 99-31293. 224p. 1999. text 23.95 (*0-393-04819-5*) Norton.

— Sapelo's People. LC 93-45968. 1994. 18.95 (*0-393-03643-X*) Norton.

— Sapelo's People: A Long Walk into Freedom. 208p. 1995. pap. 11.00 (*0-393-31377-8*, Norton Paperbks) Norton.

— Yankee Stepfather: General O. O. Howard & the Freedmen. 1994. pap. 10.95 (*0-393-31178-3*) Norton.

McFeely, William S., jt. auth. see Sherman, William T.

McFeely, William S., ed. see Douglass, Frederick.

McFeely, William S., ed. see Grant, Ulysses S.

McFerran, Douglas. IRA Man: Talking with the Rebels. LC 97-8862. 200p. 1997. 22.95 (*0-275-95591-5*, Praeger Pubs) Greenwood.

McFerran, Douglass D. Symbolic Logic: A Conceptual Approach. 2nd ed. 68p. 1993. per. 21.95 (*0-8403-8354-1*) Kendall-Hunt.

— Thinking Clearly. 124p. 1993. per. 27.95 (*0-8403-9015-7*) Kendall-Hunt.

McFerran, J. B. & McNulty, M. S., eds. Acute Virus Infections of Poultry. (Current Topics in Veterinary Medicine & Animal Science Ser.). 1986. text 175.00 (*0-89838-809-0*) Kluwer Academic.

— Virus Infections of Birds. (Virus Infections of Vertebrates Ser.: Vol. 4). 640p. 1993. 289.00 (*0-444-89899-9*) Elsevier.

McFerran, J. B., jt. ed. see McNulty, M. S.

***McFerran, Tanya A.** A Dictionary of Nursing. 3rd ed. LC 97-42622. 1998. pap. write for info. (*0-19-280072-8*) OUP.

— Minidictionary for Nurses. 4th ed. LC 98-24055. 1998. write for info. (*0-19-860204-9*) OUP.

McFerren, Martha. Contours for Ritual. Poems. LC 87-12486. 64p. 1988. pap. 6.95 (*0-8071-1422-7*) La State U Pr.

— Contours for Ritual. Poems. LC 87-12486. 64p. 1988. text 15.95 (*0-8071-1421-9*) La State U Pr.

— Delusions of a Popular Mind. Cassin, Maxine, ed. (Journal Press Bks.: Louisiana Legacy). (Illus.). 80p. 1983. pap. 12.00 (*0-938498-04-5*) New Orleans Poetry.

— Get Me out of Here. 72p. 1984. 7.95 (*0-931694-29-9*) Wampeter Pr.

— Women in Cars: Poems. (Winner of the 1992 Marianne Moore Poetry Prize Ser.). 65p. (Orig.). 1992. pap. 9.95 (*0-9627460-6-1*) Helicon Nine Eds.

McFerren, Robert & McFerren, Tracie. Laurel & Hardy in "Big Quizness" Trivia & Film Facts on the Boys. Jones, JoAnn, ed. LC 97-97019. (Illus.). 394p. 1999. pap. 25.00 (*0-9660323-0-6*) Plumtree Pub.

McFerren, Tracie, jt. auth. see McFerren, Robert.

McFerrin, John B. Caldwell & Company: A Southern Financial Empire. LC 75-100905. 312p. 1984. reprint ed. 22.95 (*0-8265-1148-1*) Vanderbilt U Pr.

McFerrin, Linda W. The Impossibility of Redemption Was Something We Hadn't Figured on. 64p. 1990. pap. 9.95 (*0-917658-27-2*) BPW & P.

— Namako: Sea Cucumber. LC 98-21156. 256p. (YA). 1998. pap. 14.95 (*1-56689-075-6*) Coffee Hse.

***McFerrin, Linda Watanabe.** The Hand of Buddha. 192p. 2000. pap. 13.95 (*1-56689-104-3*, Pub. by Coffee Hse) Consort Bk Sales.

McFerson, Hazel M. The Racial Dimension of American Overseas Colonial Policy, 33. LC 97-2233. (Contributions in Comparative Colonial Studies: Vol. 33). 208p. 1997. 55.00 (*0-313-28996-4*, Greenwood Pr) Greenwood.

***McFerson, Hazel M., ed.** Mixed Blessing: Impact of the American Colonial Experience on Politics & Society in the Philippines. Vol. 41. 2001. write for info. (*0-313-30791-1*) Greenwood.

McFeters, G. A., ed. Drinking Water Microbiology. (Contemporary Bioscience Ser.). (Illus.). 528p. 1990. 102.00 (*0-387-97162-9*, 3531) Spr-Verlag.

McFetridge, D. G. Government Support of Scientific Research & Development: An Economic Analysis. LC 77-371187. (Ontario Economic Council Research Studies: No. 8). (Illus.). 104p. reprint ed. pap. 32.30 (*0-8357-3995-3*, 203669500005) Bks Demand.

McField, R. C. The Missles at Jarmah. Costa, Gwen, ed. LC 90-43990. 1991. pap. 14.95 (*0-87949-310-0*) Ashley Bks.

McFredries, Paul. The Complete Idiot's Guide to Access. LC 93-74246. 300p. 1994. 14.95 (*1-56761-457-4*, Alpha Ref) Macmillan Gen Ref.

— The Complete Idiot's Guide to WordPerfect for Windows 95. (Illus.). 375p. (Orig.). 1996. 19.99 (*0-7897-0452-8*) Que.

McFree, Faridi. Peace on Earth Begins with You: Simple Steps Each of Us Can Take to Bring Harmony to Our World. LC 97-22827. (Illus.). 112p. (Orig.). 1997. pap. 9.95 (*0-688-15651-7*, Wm Morrow) Morrow Avon.

MCG Foundation Staff. Cooking Right for Life: Tasty Recipes for Your Health. LC 90-45806. 1990. pap., spiral bd. 12.95 (*0-87197-289-1*) Favorite Recipes.

McGaa Eagle Man, Ed. Native Wisdom: Perceptions of the Natural Way. Diotte, Sharon, ed. (Illus.). 260p. (Orig.). 1995. pap. 15.00 (*0-9645173-1-0*) Four Dir Pub.

McGaa, Ed. Eagle Vision: Return of the Hoop. LC 99-199291. (Illus.). 311p. 1998. pap. 18.00 (*0-9645173-6-1*) Four Dir Pub.

— Mother Earth Spirituality: Native American Paths to Healing Ourselves & Our World. LC 89-46149. (Illus.). 256p. (Orig.). 1990. pap. 17.00 (*0-06-250596-3*, Pub. by Harper SF) HarpC.

McGaa, Ed & Man, Eagle. Rainbow Tribe: Ordinary People Journeying on the Red Road. LC 91-55325. 272p. (gr. 7). 1992. pap. 17.00 (*0-06-250611-0*, Pub. by Harper SF) HarpC.

McGaffey, G. W. Genealogical History of the McGaffey Family, Including Also the Fellows, Ethridge & Sherman Families. (Illus.). 145p. 1991. lib. bdg. 33.50 (*0-8328-1965-4*) Higginson Bk Co.

— Genealogical History of the McGaffey Family, Including Also the Fellows, Ethridge & Sherman Families. (Illus.). 145p. 1991. reprint ed. pap. 23.50 (*0-8328-1966-2*) Higginson Bk Co.

McGaffey, Jere. McGaffey Legal Forms with Tax Analysis, 1977-1990, 6 vols. LC 77-12085. 495.00 (*0-317-11955-9*) West Group.

McGaffey, Jere D. Buying, Selling & Merging Businesses. 2nd ed. LC 89-84075. 579p. 1989. text 99.00 (*0-8318-0519-6*, B519) Am Law Inst.

McGaffey, L. Honduras, 6 vols. , Set. LC 98-54908. (Cultures of the World Ser.). (Illus.). 128p. (YA). (gr. 5-9). 1999. lib. bdg. 35.64 (*0-7614-0955-6*) Marshall Cavendish.

McGaghie, W., et al. Competency-Based Curriculum Development in Medical Education: An Introduction. (Public Health Papers: No. 68). 91p. 1978. pap. text 9.00 (*92-4-130068-X*, 1110068) World Health.

McGaha, Agnes. Stair-Step Wit. McGaha, Michael, ed. (Took Modern Poetry in English Ser.: No. 10). (Illus.). 28p. (Orig.). 1991. pap. 5.00 (*1-879457-18-0*) Norton Coker Pr.

McGaha, Michael. Cervantes & the Renaissance. 246p. 1980. 16.50 (*0-936388-00-5*) Juan de la Cuesta.

— Coat of Many Cultures: The Joseph Story in Spanish Literature, 1200-1492. LC 95-51234. 464p. 1996. 34.95 (*0-8276-0570-6*) JPS Phila.

McGaha, Michael, tr. from SPA. The Story of Joseph in Spanish: Golden Age Drama. LC 97-36306. 344p. 1998. 47.50 (*0-8387-5380-9*) Bucknell U Pr.

McGaha, Michael, jt. ed. see Casa, Frank.

McGaha, Michael, ed. see McGaha, Agnes.

McGaha, Michael, ed. & tr. see Gomez, Antonio E.

McGaha, Michael D. & Casa, Frank P., eds. Editing the Comedia, II. LC 81-50963. (Michigan Romance Studies: Vol. 11). 162p. 1991. pap. 15.00 (*0-939730-10-3*) Mich Romance.

McGaha, Michael D., tr. see Mira de Amescua, Antonio.

McGahan. Praise. LC 98-17596. 288p. 1998. pap. 13.95 (*0-312-18754-8*) St Martin.

McGahan, Andrew. 1988. LC 96-44519. 314p. 1996. 22.95 (*0-312-15043-1*) St Martin.

— 1988. 320p. 1998. pap. 12.95 (*0-312-18032-2*, 837237) St Martin.

McGahan, John P. Diagnostic Ultrasound: A Logical Approach. 1,312p. 320.00 incl. cd-rom (*0-7817-1565-2*) Lppncott W & W.

McGahan, John P., ed. Controversies in Ultrasound. (Clinics in Diagnostic Ultrasound Ser.: Vol. 20). (Illus.). 371p. 1986. pap. text 59.95 (*0-443-08492-0*) Church.

McGahan, John P. & Goldberg, Barry B. Diagnostic Ultrasound: A Logical Approach. 1200p. 1997. write for info. (*0-397-58473-3*) Lppncott W & W.

McGahan, John P. & Goldberg, Barry B., eds. Diagnostic Ultrasound: A Logical Approach. LC 97-2677. (Illus.). 1200p. 1997. text 195.00 (*0-397-51614-2*) Lppncott W & W.

McGahan, John P. & Porto, Manuel. Diagnostic Obstetrical Ultrasound. (Illus.). 640p. 1994. text 105.00 (*0-397-51320-8*) Lppncott W & W.

McGahan, Peter. Crime & Policing in Maritime Canada. 246p. 1988. 19.95 (*0-86492-085-7*, Pub. by Goose Ln Edits); pap. 12.95 (*0-86492-081-4*, Pub. by Goose Ln Edits) Genl Dist Srvs.

— Killers, Thieves, Tramps & Sinners. 192p. 1989. pap. 12.95 (*0-86492-114-4*, Pub. by Goose Ln Edits) Genl Dist Srvs.

McGahan, William A., jt. auth. see Tompkins, Harland G.

McGahee, John. Louie the Lobster. LC 96-86374. 1996. mass mkt., spiral bd. 9.95 (*1-889131-04-0*) CasAnanda.

— A Marblous Story. LC 96-86374. 1996. mass mkt., spiral bd. 9.95 (*1-889131-05-9*) CasAnanda.

— A New Name for Nero. LC 96-86364. 1996. mass mkt., spiral bd. 9.95 (*1-889131-03-2*) CasAnanda.

— Terrapin Tom. LC 96-86359. 1996. mass mkt., spiral bd. 9.95 (*1-889131-06-7*) CasAnanda.

McGahee, Susan H. & Edmonds, Mary W. South Carolina's Historic Cemeteries: A Preservation Handbook. Andrews, Judith M., ed. (Illus.). 50p. 1997. pap. 10.00 (*1-880067-43-9*) SC Dept of Arch & Hist.

McGahern, John. Amongst Women. 192p. 1991. reprint ed. pap. 12.95 (*0-14-009255-2*, Penguin Bks) Viking Penguin.

— The Collected Stories. LC 93-43483. 408p. 1994. pap. 13.00 (*0-679-74401-0*) Vin Bks.

— High Ground. 156p. 1993. pap. 10.00 (*0-14-017708-6*, Penguin Bks) Viking Penguin.

McGahey, Jeanne. Homecoming with Reflections. (QRL Poetry Bks.: Vols. XXVIII-XXIX). 1989. 20.00 (*0-614-06426-0*) Quarterly Rev.

McGahey, Robert. The Orphic Moment: Shaman to Poet-Thinker in Plato, Nietzsche, & Mallarme. LC 93-46495. (SUNY Series, The Margins of Literature). 209p. (C). 1994. text 59.50 (*0-7914-1941-X*); pap. text 19.95 (*0-7914-1942-8*) State U NY Pr.

McGahran, Kathleen, jt. auth. see Shillinglaw, Gordon.

McGahren, Eugene D. & Wilson, William G. Pediatrics Recall. LC 96-29736. (Recall Ser.). 456p. 1997. pap. 27.00 (*0-683-05855-X*) Lppncott W & W.

McGaivl, Stephen, jt. ed. see Littlejohns, Andrew.

McGalliard, Emily, ed. see Hurwitz, Laura.

McGambley, Casimir, tr. & pref. see Saint Gregory of Nyssa.

McGann, Anthony J., jt. auth. see Kitschelt, Herbert.

McGann, Catherine, tr. see Calle, Mireille, ed.

McGann, James G. The Competition for Dollars, Scholars & Influence in the Public Policy Research Industry. 216p. (C). 1995. pap. text 27.50 (*0-8191-9751-3*); lib. bdg. 51.00 (*0-8191-9750-5*) U Pr of Amer.

***McGann, James G.** Think Tanks & Civil Societies: Catalysts for Ideas & Action. (Illus.). 2000. 59.95 (*0-7658-0032-2*) Transaction Pubs.

McGann, Jerome. The Poetics of Sensibility: A Revolution in Literary Style. 228p. 1998. reprint ed. pap. text 19.95 (*0-19-818478-6*) OUP.

McGann, Jerome, ed. Historical Studies & Literary Criticism. LC 85-40374. 312p. 1985. text 35.00 (*0-299-10280-7*) U of Wis Pr.

McGann, Jerome J. The Beauty of Inflections: Literary Investigations in Historical Method & Theory. 364p. 1988. pap. text 21.00 (*0-19-811750-7*) OUP.

— Black Riders: The Visible Language of Modernism. LC 92-29109. (Illus.). 192p. (C). 1993. text 39.50 (*0-691-06985-9*, Pub. by Princeton U Pr) Cal Prin Full Svc.

— Byron. (Oxford Authors Ser.). 1,108p. 1986. pap. text 23.95 (*0-19-281349-8*) OUP.

— A Critique of Modern Textual Criticism. LC 82-20151. 144p. (C). 1983. 12.50 (*0-226-55851-7*) U Ch Pr.

— A Critique of Modern Textual Criticism. LC 82-20151. 144p. (C). 1985. pap. text 6.50 (*0-226-55852-5*) U Ch Pr.

— A Critique of Modern Textual Criticism. LC 92-14702. 160p. (C). 1992. reprint ed. pap. text 14.50 (*0-8139-1418-3*) U Pr of Va.

***McGann, Jerome J.** Dante Gabriel Rossetti & the Game That Must Be Lost. LC 99-53380. 304p. 2000. 30.00 (*0-300-08023-9*) Yale U Pr.

McGann, Jerome J. Fiery Dust: Byron's Poetic Development. LC 68-53392. 1993. lib. bdg. 22.00 (*0-226-55844-4*) U Ch Pr.

— The Poetics of Sensibility: A Revolution in Literary Style. 232p. (C). 1996. text 39.95 (*0-19-818370-4*) OUP.

— The Romantic Ideology: A Critical Investigation. LC 82-17494. 184p. (C). 1983. 15.00 (*0-226-55849-5*) U Ch Pr.

— The Romantic Ideology: A Critical Investigation. LC 82-17494. 184p. (C). 1985. pap. text 16.00 (*0-226-55850-9*) U Ch Pr.

— Social Values & Poetic Acts: The Historical Judgment of Literary Work. LC 87-14649. 296p. 1988. 43.00 (*0-674-81495-9*) HUP.

— Swinburne: An Experiment in Criticism. LC 72-77598. 352p. (C). 1972. lib. bdg. 22.00 (*0-226-55846-0*) U Ch Pr.

— The Textual Condition. (Illus.). 210p. 1991. text 42.50 (*0-691-06931-X*, Pub. by Princeton U Pr) Cal Prin Full Svc.

— Textual Criticism & Literary Interpretation. LC 84-16174. (Illus.). 240p. 1985. pap. text 10.95 (*0-226-55843-6*) U Ch Pr.

— Textual Criticism & Literary Interpretation. LC 84-16174. (Illus.). 250p. 1985. lib. bdg. 26.50 (*0-226-55842-8*) U Ch Pr.

— Towards a Literature of Knowledge. 152p. 1998. 29.95 (*0-226-55839-8*) U Ch Pr.

McGann, Jerome J., ed. The New Oxford Book of Romantic Period Verse. LC 93-32333. (Illus.). 860p. 1994. reprint ed. pap. 18.95 (*0-19-282329-9*) OUP.

— Victorian Connections, Vol. 5. LC 89-30993. (Virginia Victorian Studies). 214p. 1989. text 35.00 (*0-8139-1218-0*) U Pr of Va.

McGann, Jerome J. & Riess, Daniel M., eds. Letitia Elizabeth Landon: Selected Writings. LC 98-219517. (Broadview Literary Texts Ser.). 400p. (C). 1997. pap. 14.95 (*1-55111-135-7*) Broadview Pr.

McGann, Jerome J., ed. see Byron, George Gordon.

McGann, Jerome J., ed. & intro. see Byron, George Gordon.

McGann, John, jt. auth. see Breslin, Jud.

McGann, Leonard D. Out of the Angel's Hand. LC 93-90560. 204p. 1993. pap. 5.95 (*0-9636783-0-2*) Bell Pub NC.

McGann, Michelle. Complete Idiot's Guide to Golf. 336p. 1997. 18.95 (*0-02-861760-6*) Macmillan Gen Ref.

McGann, Patrick E., et al. Illinois Practice Guide: Personal Injury. 2nd ed. LC 96-120593. 1100p. 1995. text. write for info. (*0-7620-0033-3*) West Group.

McGann, Terry, jt. auth. see Silva, Michael.

McGann, Thomas F., tr. see Romero, Jose L.

McGannon, A. & Rosst, Michael A. Keynote. (Illus.). 1995. audio 68.40 (*0-582-10225-1*) Longman.

McGannon, A., et al. Keynote Plus. (Illus.). 1994. teacher ed. 14.95 (*0-582-10234-0*); audio 55.00 (*0-582-10229-4*) Longman.

An Asterisk (*) at the beginning of an entry indicates that the title is appearing for the first time.

McGannon, Michael. The Urban Warrior's Book of Solutions: Staying Healthy, Fit & Sane in the Business Jungle. 240p. 1995. 22.00 (*0-273-61307-3*) F T P-H.

McGannon, Thomas. Study Guide for the Actuarial Exam 110: Probability & Statistics. 200p. (C). 1996. ring bd. 13.95 (*0-87563-671-3*) Stipes.

— Study Guide for the Actuarial Exam 100: Calculus & Linear Algebra. 276p. (C). 1996. ring bd. 18.95 (*0-87563-670-5*) Stipes.

***McGannon, Thomas.** Study Guide for the Course 1 Exam of the Society of Actuaries. 200p. (C). 2000. ring bd. 19.95 (*0-87563-962-3*) Stipes.

McGarey, Donald. Laboratory Manual for Health Microbiology. 156p. (C). 1996. pap. text, ring bd. 25.95 (*0-7872-2450-2*, 41245001) Kendall-Hunt.

McGarey, Gladys T. Physician Within You: Alternative Medicine for the Millennium. LC 96-29513. 250p. 1997. pap. 12.95 (*1-55874-454-1*) Health Comm.

McGarey, Gladys T., jt. auth. see Curns, Eileen B.

McGarey, William A. Edgar Cayce Remedies. 288p. 1983. mass mkt. 6.99 (*0-553-27427-9*) Bantam.

— Heal Arthritis: Physically, Mentally, Spiritually - The Edgar Cayce Approach. LC 97-31083. 168p. 1998. pap. 12.95 (*0-87604-399-6*, 513) ARE Pr.

— Healing Miracles. 1996. mass mkt. 5.99 (*0-312-95948-6*) St Martin.

— In Search of Healing: Whole-Body Healing Through the Mind-Body-Spirit Connection. 256p. (Orig.). 1996. pap. 12.00 (*0-399-51989-0*, Perigee Bks) Berkley Pub.

— Jesus, a Closer Walk: Reflections on John 14-17 from the Edgar Cayce Readings. LC 98-12303. 176p. 1998. pap. 9.95 (*0-87604-409-7*) ARE Pr.

— The Oil That Heals: A Physician's Successes with Castor Oil. 248p. (Orig.). 1993. pap. 12.95 (*0-87604-308-2*, 381) ARE Pr.

McGarey, William A., jt. auth. see Carter, Mary E.

***McGarigal, K., et al, eds.** Multivariate Statistics for Wildlife & Ecology Research. LC 99-16036. (Illus.). 312p. 2000. 79.95 (*0-387-98891-2*) Spr-Verlag.

***McGarigal, Kevin, et al.** Multivariate Statistics for Wildlife & Ecology Research. LC 99-16036. (Illus.). 312p. 2000. pap. 39.95 (*0-387-98642-1*) Spr-Verlag.

McGarigle, Bob. Nantasket Beach Branch, NY, NH & HRR. (Illus.). 76p. 1981. 12.00 (*0-910506-21-3*) De Vito.

McGarity, Arthur, jt. ed. see ReVelle, Charles S.

***McGarity, Carroll B.** Looking Back with Papaw's Little Gentleman. (Illus.). vi, 235p. 2000. 24.95 (*0-615-11826-7*) Look Back Pub.

McGarity, Thomas, jt. auth. see Hadden, Susan.

McGarity, Thomas O. Reinventing Rationality: The Role of Regulatory Analysis in the Federal Bureaucracy. (Illus.). 410p. (C). 1991. text 85.00 (*0-521-40256-5*) Cambridge U Pr.

McGarity, Thomas O. & Shapiro, Sidney A. Workers at Risk: The Failed Promise of the Occupational Safety & Health Administration. LC 92-1753. 376p. 1993. 69.50 (*0-275-94281-3*, C4281, Praeger Pubs) Greenwood.

McGarity, Thomas O., jt. auth. see Bonine, John E.

McGarr, Arthur, ed. Induced Seismicity. LC 93-30034. 1993. 34.50 (*0-8176-2918-1*) Birkhauser.

McGarr, Nancy S., jt. auth. see Hargrove, Patricia M.

McGarrah, Meg. Help Yourself: A Guide to Organizing a Phobia Self-Help Group. 100p. 1990. pap. write for info. (*0-935943-01-3*) Anxiety Disorders.

McGarrah, Robert E. Manufacturing for the Security of the United States: Reviving Competitiveness & Reducing Deficits. LC 89-28942. 200p. 1990. 59.95 (*0-89930-427-3*, MDG/, Quorum Bks) Greenwood.

***McGarrahan, Margaret.** Nessie's Cape Cod Vacation. LC 99-96597. (Illus.). 58p. (J). (gr. 1-3). 2000. pap. 12.50 (*0-9672639-0-5*) Smith Lane Pubs.

McGarrahan, Peggy. Transcending AIDS: Nurses & HIV Patients in New York City. LC 93-26279. (Studies in Health, Illness, & Caregiving). 200p. (Orig.). (C). 1994. text 35.00 (*0-8122-3203-8*); pap. text 14.95 (*0-8122-1418-8*) U of Pa Pr.

McGarrell, Ann, tr. see Bevilacqua, Alberto.

McGarrell, Edmund F. Juvenile Correctional Reform: Two Decades of Policy & Procedural Change. LC 87-24499. (SUNY Series in Critical Issues in Criminal Justice). (Illus.). 219p. (C). 1988. text 64.50 (*0-88706-759-X*); pap. text 21.95 (*0-88706-760-3*) State U NY Pr.

***McGarrell, Edmund F.** Targeting Firearms Violence Through Directed Police Patrol. 2000. pap. 7.00 (*1-55813-068-3*) Hudson Instit IN.

McGarrell, Edmund F., jt. auth. see Thurman, Quint C.

McGarrigle, Stephen. The Complete Who's Who of Irish International Football 1945-96. (Illus.). 208p. 1997. 39.95 (*1-85158-894-9*, Pub. by Mainstream Pubng) Trafalgar.

McGarrity, Mark. White Rush - Green Fire. 464p. 1992. mass mkt. 4.99 (*0-380-71097-8*, Avon Bks) Morrow Avon.

McGarrity, Michael. Hermit's Peak. LC 99-22960. 320p. 1999. 22.50 (*0-684-85078-8*) Scribner.

***McGarrity, Michael.** Hermit's Peak. 368p. 2000. reprint ed. mass mkt. 6.99 (*0-671-02147-8*, Pocket Books) PB.

— The Judas Judge: A Kevin Kerney Novel. LC 99-89181. 288p. 2000. 23.95 (*0-525-94547-4*, Dutt) Dutton Plume.

McGarrity, Michael. Mexican Hat. LC 96-35735. 304p. 1997. 22.95 (*0-393-04063-1*) Norton.

— Mexican Hat. (Kevin Kerney Novels Ser.). 300p. 1998. mass mkt. 6.50 (*0-671-00253-8*, Pocket Books) PB.

— Serpent Gate. 338p. 1999. mass mkt. 6.50 (*0-671-02146-X*, Pocket Star Bks) PB.

— Serpent Gate. LC 97-51142. 314p. 1998. 22.00 (*0-684-85076-1*) S&S Trade.

— Tularosa. LC 95-36128. 304p. 1996. 25.00 (*0-393-03922-6*) Norton.

— Tularosa. 336p. 1997. per. 6.50 (*0-671-00252-X*) PB.

— Tularosa. 1998. 3.99 (*0-671-02373-X*, Pocket Books) PB.

— Tularosa. large type ed. LC 96-3428. 1996. pap. 22.95 (*1-56895-372-0*, Compass) Wheeler Pub.

Mcgarry. Management Information Systems. 296p. 1998. pap. text 26.30 (*0-536-01633-X*) Pearson Custom.

McGarry, Annie. Laurel & Hardy. (Illus.). 80p. 1992. 10.98 (*1-55521-792-3*, Chrtwell) Bk Sales Inc.

McGarry, Betty. Practical Guide to Florida Retirement. 2nd ed. LC 88-31220. 250p. 1989. pap. 9.95 (*0-910923-61-2*) Pineapple Pr.

McGarry Carlson, Ellen, jt. auth. see Hern, Katie.

McGarry, Carmen R. Magnificent Mile: A History of Hillsboro Beach. (Illus.). 248p. 1997. 24.95 (*0-9641216-3-8*) RitAmelia Pr.

McGarry, Christin, tr. see Dubost, Thierry.

McGarry, Daniel, tr. see John of Salisbury.

McGarry, Daniel D., tr. see John of Salisbury.

McGarry, Deborah B. Fine Kettles of Fish: A Treasury of Seafood Chowders, Bisques, Soups & Stews. LC 97-66603. (Illus.). 288p. (Orig.). 1998. pap. 15.00 (*1-883684-15-3*) Peninsula MA.

McGarry, Dorothy. Directory of Catalogers in the Special Libraries Association. LC 89-111094. (Illus.). 96p. reprint ed. pap. 30.00 (*0-7837-1182-4*, 204171100023) Bks Demand.

***McGarry, Feargal.** Irish Politics & the Spanish Civil War. 240p. 2000. 65.00 (*1-85918-239-9*, Pub. by Cork Univ); pap. 25.00 (*1-85918-240-2*, Pub. by Cork Univ) Stylus Pub VA.

***McGarry, G. W. & Browning, G. G.** Ent: Colour Guide. Picture Tests. LC 99-36938. 1999. text. write for info. (*0-443-06235-8*, W B Saunders Co) Harcrt Hlth Sci Grp.

McGarry, Jean. Airs of Providence. LC 85-8905. (Poetry & Fiction Ser.). 144p. 1985. 16.95 (*0-8018-2909-7*) Johns Hopkins.

— The Courage of Girls. LC 91-23149. (Fiction Ser.). 250p. 1992. 22.95 (*0-8135-1771-0*) Rutgers U Pr.

— Gallagher's Travels. LC 97-7002. (Poetry & Fiction Ser.). 224p. 1997. 22.95 (*0-8018-5634-5*) Johns Hopkins.

— Home at Last. LC 93-45676. (Poetry & Fiction Ser.). 123p. 1994. 32.50 (*0-8018-4852-0*); pap. 12.95 (*0-8018-4853-9*) Johns Hopkins.

— The Red Coat. limited ed. (Illus.). 24p. 1990. 35.00 (*0-9623585-0-9*) Flockophobic Pr.

— The Very Rich Hours. LC 86-46290. (Johns Hopkins Poetry & Fiction Ser.). 144p. 1987. 16.95 (*0-8018-3504-6*) Johns Hopkins.

McGarry, Jean, et al. Mogana Inc. limited ed. (Illus.). 40p. 1992. 38.00 (*1-880392-01-1*) Flockophobic Pr.

McGarry, John & O'Leary, Brendan. Explaining Northern Ireland: Broken Images. (Illus.). 352p. (C). 1995. 75.95 (*0-631-18348-5*); pap. 29.95 (*0-631-18349-3*) Blackwell Pubs.

***McGarry, John & O'Leary, Brendan.** Policing Northern Ireland: Proposals for a New Start. LC 99-196638. (Orig.). 1999. pap. 22.95 (*0-85640-648-1*, Pub. by Blackstaff Pr) Dufour.

McGarry, John & O'Leary, Brendan, eds. The Politics of Ethnic Conflict Regulation: Case Studies of Protracted Ethnic Conflicts. LC 92-45848. 336p. (C). 1993. pap. 25.99 (*0-415-09931-5*, B2390) Routledge.

McGarry, Kaye B. A New Beginning: A Survival Guide for Parents of College Freshmen. LC 97-91212. (Illus.). 40p. 1998. pap. 9.95 (*0-9661201-0-8*) Survival College.

McGarry, M. Frances. Allegorical & Metaphorical Language in the Autos Sacramentales of Calderon. LC 79-94165. (Catholic University of America. Studies in Romance Languages & Literatures: No. 16). reprint ed. 37.50 (*0-404-50316-0*) AMS Pr.

McGarry, M. Shawn. A Woman's Book of Faith: 2000 Years of Inspirational Writings by & for Women. LC 97-26535. (Illus.). 176p. 1997. 15.95 (*1-55972-435-8*, Birch Ln Pr) Carol Pub Group.

McGarry, Megan. A Hundred Dead Roses. LC 93-71166. 256p. (Orig.). 1993. pap. 12.95 (*0-9636057-0-4*) Eros Bks.

McGarry, Molly. Becoming Visible. LC 97-49124. 282p. 1998. 34.95 (*0-670-86401-3*) Viking Penguin.

McGarry-Morris, Mary. A Dangerous Woman. 370p. 1994. pap. 10.95 (*0-14-023669-4*, Penguin Bks) Viking Penguin.

— Vanished. 246p. 1989. pap. 12.00 (*0-671-67943-0*, WSP) PB.

McGarry, Patricia A., ed. Managing the Prosecutor's Office: With Appendix of Sample Forms. 324p. (Orig.). 1987. pap. 25.00 (*0-910397-12-0*) NCDA.

McGarry, Richard. Marker Magic: The Rendering Problem Solver for Designers. 146p. 1992. 44.95 (*0-471-28434-3*, VNR) Wiley.

McGarry, Richard G. The Subtle Slant: A Cross-Linguistic Discourse Analysis Model for Evaluating Interethnic Conflict in the Press. (Illus.). 196p. 1994. 35.00 (*0-9635752-1-X*) Pkway Pubs.

McGarry, Richard M. Marker Magic. LC 92-6773. (Illus.). 192p. 1993. text 39.95 (*0-442-00769-8*, VNR) Wiley.

— Tracing File for Interior & Architectural Rendering. (Illus.). 280p. 1988. pap. 44.95 (*0-442-20530-9*, VNR) Wiley.

McGarry, Susan H. A Brush with Reality: Detailing the West in Contemporary Art. 64p. 1998. pap. 15.00 (*0-9657377-1-3*) Desert Cab.

McGarry, Thomas, jt. auth. see Rumler, John.

McGarry, Thomas W., jt. auth. see Baldwin, R. E.

***McGartland, Grace.** Thunderbolt Thinking: A How-To Guide for Strategic Innovators. 2nd rev. ed. 2000. pap. text. write for info. (*1-885167-42-3*) Bard Press.

McGartland, Grace. Thunderbolt Thinking: Transform Your Insights & Options into Powerful Business Results. LC 96-172745. 256p. 1993. 26.95 (*0-9632785-1-7*); pap. 16.95 (*0-9632785-0-9*) Bernard-Davis.

— Thunderbolt Thinking: Transform Your Insights & Options into Powerful Business Results. (Illus.). 256p. 1994. pap. text 16.95 (*0-7737-5657-4*) Stoddart Publ.

McGartland, Martin. Dead Man Running: The True Story of a Secret Agent's Escape from the IRA & the M15. 222p. 2000. pap. 16.95 (*0-8038-2005-4*, Pub. by Hastings) Midpt Trade.

***McGartland, Martin.** Fifty Dead Men Walking: The Heroic True Story of an Undercover Agent Inside the IRA. 252p. 2001. pap. 16.95 (*0-8038-2010-0*, Pub. by Hastings) Midpt Trade.

McGartland, Martin. Fifty Dead Men Walking: The Terrifying True Story of a Secret Agent Inside the IRA. (Illus.). 304p. 1997. 27.95 (*1-85782-178-5*, Pub. by Blake Publng) Seven Hills Bk.

McGarty, Craig & Haslan, S. Alexander, eds. The Message of Social Psychology: Perspectives on Mind in Society. LC 96-16494. 368p. 1996. 66.95 (*0-631-19779-6*); pap. 28.95 (*0-631-19781-8*) Blackwell Pubs.

McGarty, Raymond. Impasse: Resistance & Addiction Treatment: Combining Brief, Strategic & Twelve Step Approaches. 110p. (Orig.). (C). 1993. pap. text 10.00 (*0-9638389-0-3*) Addiction Therap.

McGarty, Terrence B. Business Plans That Win Venture Capital. LC 88-27609. 368p. 1989. 201.95 (*0-471-50180-8*) Wiley.

***McGarva, Andrew.** Country Pottery. 160p. 2000. pap. 59.95 (*0-7136-4813-9*, Pub. by A & C Blk) Midpt Trade.

McGarvey, Brian & Swallow, Derek. Microteaching in Teacher Education & Training. (New Patterns of Learning Ser.). 320p. 1986. 37.50 (*0-7099-4613-9*, Pub. by C Helm) Routldge.

McGarvey, Carol. Family Reunion Potluck: For When the Whole Gang Gets Together. (Wooden Spoon Cookbook Ser.). (Illus.). 117p. 1992. spiral bd. 8.50 (*1-882835-23-9*) STA-Kris.

— Fruits of the Season. (Wooden Spoon Cookbook Ser.). (Illus.). 108p. 1992. spiral bd. 8.50 (*1-882835-25-5*) STA-Kris.

— Hand-Picked Apple Recipes. 113p. 1992. spiral bd. 7.50 (*1-882835-20-4*) STA-Kris.

McGarvey, Carol, et al. The "Des Moines Register" Cookbook. LC 95-13459. (Bur Oak Original Ser.). (Illus.). 308p. (Orig.). 1995. pap. 14.95 (*0-87745-515-5*) U of Iowa Pr.

McGarvey, Charles L., III. Physical Therapy for the Cancer Patient. LC 90-32270. (Clinics in Physical Therapy Ser.). (Illus.). 202p. 1990. reprint ed. pap. 62.70 (*0-7837-9592-0*, 206034800005) Bks Demand.

McGarvey, Charles L., III, ed. Physical Therapy for the Cancer Patient. (Clinics in Physical Therapy Ser.). (Illus.). 188p. 1990. text 49.95 (*0-443-08667-2*) Church.

McGarvey, J. W. A Guide to Bible Study. 2nd ed. 1996. reprint ed. pap. 3.50 (*1-56794-106-0*, C-2420) Star Bible.

McGarvey, Judith T. My Grandmother's Family: The Strocks from Andrew County, Missouri. (Illus.). 174p. 1986. 16.00 (*0-932619-00-2*) JD McG Pubns.

***McGarvey, Robert.** How to Dotcom: A Step-by-Step Guide to E-Commerce. 300p. 2000. pap. 18.95 (*1-891984-18-7*, Pub. by Entrepreneur) Natl Bk Netwk.

McGarvey, Tracy. You Don't Dance to the Juke Box: The Bar Book. Richardson, Francis, ed. (Illus.). 300p. (Orig.). 1990. pap. 10.00 (*0-9627146-0-7*) Trac Pub Serv.

***McGarvie, Richard E.** Democracy: Choosing Australia's Republic. 250p. 2000. 24.95 (*0-522-84808-7*, Pub. by Melbourne Univ Pr) Paul & Co Pubs.

McGary, Howard. Race & Social Justice. LC 98-23968. 240p. 1998. 54.95 (*0-631-20720-1*); pap. 24.95 (*0-631-20721-X*) Blackwell Pubs.

McGary, Howard & Lawson, Bill E. Between Slavery & Freedom: Philosophy & American Slavery. LC 92-7738. (Blacks in the Diaspora Ser.). 176p. 1993. 35.00 (*0-253-33272-9*); pap. text 14.95 (*0-253-20745-2*, MB-745) Ind U Pr.

McGary, Jane, ed. see Herbert, Belle.

McGary, Jane, ed. see Jacobson, Steven A.

McGary, Jane, ed. see Kaplan, Lawrence D.

McGary, Jane, ed. see North American Rock Gardening Society Staff.

McGary, Jane, ed. see Thompson, Chad.

McGary, Kay. To Live Is to Learn. LC 98-94018. 1999. 10.95 (*0-533-12939-7*) Vantage.

McGary, Mary J., ed. see Sapir, Edward.

McGary, Ruth W. The Healthy Homestyle Cookbook. LC 93-1898. (Illus.). 192p. 1993. pap. 12.50 (*0-945448-29-5*, 00295Q, Pub. by Am Diabetes) NTC Contemp Pub Co.

***McGatch, Milton.** Eschatology & Christian Nurture: Themes in Anglo-Saxon & Medieval Religious Life. LC 00-20059. 2000. 101.95 (*0-86078-827-X*, Pub. by Ashgate Pub) Ashgate Pub Co.

McGath, Gary D., jt. auth. see Wagner, Jane.

McGatlin, Ron. The Basileia Letters, Vol. 1. LC 99-185557. 161p. 1998. pap. 6.95 (*0-9654546-2-2*) Basileia Pub.

— Overcoming Life on a Small Planet: Heaven Style Living for Earthlings. Orig. Title: Kingdom Freedom I. (Illus.). 166p. 1996. pap. 12.95 (*0-9654546-0-6*) Basileia Pub.

— The Seventh Millennium: Restoration of a Small Planet. LC 99-171894. 207p. 1998. pap. 7.95 (*0-9654546-1-4*) Basileia Pub.

McGaugh, James L., et al, eds. Brain Organization & Memory: Cells, Systems & Circuits. (Illus.). 432p. 1992. pap. text 60.00 (*0-19-507712-1*) OUP.

— Plasticity in the Central Nervous System: Learning & Memory. 272p. 1995. text 39.95 (*0-8058-1573-2*) L Erlbaum Assocs.

McGaugh, James L. & Frederickson, R. C., eds. Peripheral Signaling of the Brain: Its Role in Neural-Immune Interactions, Learning & Memory. Felton, D. L., tr. (Nueronal Control of Bodily Function Ser.: Vol. 6). (Illus.). 550p. 1991. text 98.00 (*0-88937-035-4*) Hogrefe & Huber Pubs.

McGaugh, Lawrence. Vacuum Cantos. 1969. pap. 1.50 (*0-685-04679-6*) Oyez.

McGaughey, Douglas R. Christianity for the Third Millennium: Faith in an Age of Fundamentalism & Skepticism. LC 98-13902. 220p. 1998. pap. 54.95 (*1-57309-288-6*) Intl Scholars.

— Christianity for the Third Millennium: Faith in an Age of Fundamentalism & Skepticism. LC 98-13902. 220p. 1998. 74.95 (*1-57309-289-4*) Intl Scholars.

— Strangers & Pilgrims: On the Role of Aporiai in Theology. LC 97-19225. (Theologische Bibliiothek Toepelmann Ser.: Vol. 81). xii, 537p. (C). 1997. lib. bdg. 132.00 (*3-11-015493-5*) De Gruyter.

McGaughey, Mark. Marriage: A Powerful Partnership. 49p. (Orig.). 1996. teacher ed. 9.00 (*1-888220-02-3*) Reality Living.

— Marriage: A Powerful Partnership. 49p. (Orig.). 1996. student ed. 9.00 (*1-888220-03-1*) Reality Living.

McGaughey, Neil. And Then There Were Ten. LC 94-44395. 1995. 21.00 (*0-684-19760-X*) S&S Trade.

— Best Money Murder Can Buy: A Stokes Moran Mystery. 256p. 1996. 21.00 (*0-684-19761-8*) S&S Trade.

— A Corpse by Any Other Name: A Stokes Moran Mystery. LC 97-37234. 208p. 1998. 22.00 (*0-684-19762-6*) S&S Trade.

— Otherwise Known As Murder. LC 94-1527. 224p. 1994. text 20.00 (*0-684-19674-3*, Scribners Ref) Mac Lib Ref.

McGaughey, R. H. Molly of the Shakers: A Story of Love...& Tragedy. 126p. Date not set. 19.95 (*1-56311-087-3*) Turner Pub KY.

McGaughey, Stephen E. & Gregersen, Hans M. Investment Policies & Financing Mechanisms for Sustainable Forestry Development. 132p. 1988. 14.50 (*0-940602-26-1*) IADB.

McGaughey, Stephen E. & Gregersen, Hans M., eds. Forest-Based Development in Latin America. 216p. 1983. 14.50 (*0-940602-07-5*) IADB.

McGaughey, William, Jr. A Shorter Workweek in the 1980's. LC 80-54666. 320p. (Orig.). 1981. pap. 6.95 (*0-9605630-0-8*) Thistlerose.

— A U. S. - Mexico - Canada Free-Trade Agreement: Do We Just Say No? 230p. (Orig.). 1992. pap. 11.95 (*0-9605630-2-4*) Thistlerose.

McGaughey, William, jt. auth. see McCarthy, Eugene.

McGauley, Nancy, jt. auth. see Heiman, Barbara.

McGaulley, Michael T. Selling 101: Essential Selling Skills For Business Owners & Non-Sales People. 1997. pap. text 9.95 (*1-55850-705-1*) Adams Media.

McGausher, Katherine. Expressions. 16p. 1998. 9.95 (*1-885206-53-4*) Cader Pubng.

McGauvran, Mary, ed. see Blewett, Mary H. & McKenna, Christine.

McGavic, Adrian D. From McGuffock to McGaffick to McGavock, McGavic & McGavick: A Scotch-Irish American Genealogy. LC 88-90779. (Illus.). 585p. (C). 1988. 39.60 (*0-9620628-0-4*) McGavic Geneal Pubns.

McGavick, Phyllis A., jt. auth. see Hernan, Frances.

***McGavin, George.** Insects, Spiders & Other Terrestrial Arthropods. LC 99-53252. (Illus.). 256p. 2000. pap. 18.95 (*0-7894-5337-1*) DK Pub Inc.

***McGavin, George C.** Bugs of the World. 192p. 1999. pap. text 19.95 (*0-7137-2786-1*) Blandford Pr.

McGavin, George C. Bugs of the World. (Of the World Ser.). (Illus.). 192p. 1993. 29.95 (*0-8160-2737-4*) Facts on File.

— Insects. (Science Nature Guides Ser.). (Illus.). 80p. (J). (gr. 1-8). 1998. reprint ed. 12.95 (*1-57145-378-4*, Silver Dolph) Advantage Pubs.

McGavin, Gregor, ed. see Martin, Jim.

***McGavin, John J.** Chaucer & Dissimilarity: Literary Companions in Chaucer & Other Late-Medieval Writing. LC 99-47453. 2000. 39.50 (*0-8386-3814-7*) Fairleigh Dickinson.

McGavin, M. Donald & Thompson, Samuel W. Specimen Dissection & Photography: For the Pathologist, Anatomist & Biologist. (Illus.). 300p. (C). 1988. text 72.95 (*0-398-05451-7*) C C Thomas.

McGavin, M. Donald, jt. auth. see Carlton, William W.

McGavin, P. A. Economic Security in Melanesia: Key Issues for Managing Contract Stability & Mineral Resources Development in Papua New Guinea, Solomon Islands, & Vanuatu. LC 93-23306. (Research Report Ser.: No. 16). 112p. (C). 1994. pap. text 8.00 (*0-86638-159-7*) EW Ctr HI.

— Wages & Whitlam: The Wages Policy of the Whitlam Government. 280p. (C). 1987. 45.00 (*0-19-554732-2*) OUP.

McGavin, P. A. & Australian National University Staff. Pacific 2010: Urbanisation in Polynesia. LC 98-197170. (Pacific Policy Papers). viii, 84p. 1997. write for info. (*0-7315-2364-4*) ANU Res Sch.

McGavin, P. A. & Millett, John. Industrialization in Papua New Guinea: Unrealized Potential? (Economic Reports: No. 5). 45p. 1993. pap. text 10.00 (*0-86638-156-2*) EW Ctr HI.

McGavok, Catalina J. de, see de McGavock, Catalina J.

McGavran, Donald. The Bridges of God: A Study in the Strategy of Missions. 176p. 1996. reprint ed. pap. 16.00 (*1-881266-08-7*) Fuller Seminary.

McGavran, Donald A. The Bridges of God: A Study in the Strategy of Missions. LC 55-3682. 194p. reprint ed. pap. 60.20 (*0-7837-1951-5*, 204216800001) Bks Demand.

— The Satnami Story: A Thrilling Drama of Religious Change. LC 89-39652. 192p. (Orig.). 1990. pap. 8.95 (*0-87808-225-5*, WCL225-5) William Carey Lib.

M

An Asterisk (*) at the beginning of an entry indicates that the title is appearing for the first time.

— Understanding Church Growth. 3rd ed. (Orig.). 1990. pap. 18.00 (*0-8028-0463-2*) Eerdmans.

McGavran, Donald A., ed. Church Growth Bulletin: Second Consolidated Volume (Sept. 1969 -July 1975) LC 77-5192. 1977. pap. text 8.95 (*0-87808-702-8*) William Carey Lib.

McGavran, Donald A., jt. auth. see Hunter, George G., III.

McGavran, Donald A., jt. auth. see Montgomery, James H.

McGavran, James H., ed. Literature & the Child: Romantic Continuations, Postmodern Contestations. LC 99-24458. (Illus.). 280p. 1999. text 32.95 (*0-87745-690-9*) U of Iowa Pr.

McGavran, S. B. Brief History of Harrison County. (Illus.). 56p. 1997. reprint ed. pap. 11.00 (*0-8328-6324-6*) Higginson Bk Co.

McGaw, Barry. Making Schools More Effective. (C). 1993. pap. 70.00 (*0-86431-135-4*, Pub. by Aust Council Educ Res) Stylus Pub VA.

McGaw, Charles J. Acting is Believing. 7th ed. (C). 1995. text 51.50 (*0-15-501584-2*, Pub. by Harcourt Coll Pubs) Harcourt.

McGaw, David, jt. auth. see Environmental Resource Center Staff.

McGaw, Francis A. John Hyde. LC 86-70507. (Men of Faith Ser.). 64p. 1986. reprint ed. mass mkt. 4.99 (*0-87123-909-4*) Bethany Hse.

McGaw, Francis A., et al. Praying Hyde. pap. 4.99 (*1-56632-009-7*) Revival Lit.

McGaw, Judith A. Most Wonderful Machine: Mechanization & Social Change in Berkshire Paper Making, 1801-1885. (Illus.). 457p. 1987. pap. text 19.95 (*0-691-00625-3*, Pub. by Princeton U Pr) Cal Prin Full Svc.

McGaw, Judith A., ed. Early American Technology: Making & Doing Things from the Colonial Era to 1850. LC 94-4913. (Institute of Early American History & Culture Ser.). (Illus.). 500p. 1994. text 55.00 (*0-8078-2173-X*); pap. text 22.50 (*0-8078-4484-5*) U of NC Pr.

McGaw, Laurie, jt. auth. see Tanaka, Shelley.

McGaw, Martha M. Stevenson in Hawaii. LC 77-13757. (Illus.). 182p. 1978. reprint ed. lib. bdg. 49.75 (*0-8371-9864-X*, MCSH, Greenwood Pr) Greenwood.

McGaw, Nancy, ed. see Wray, Vicki.

McGaw, Robert A. The Vanderbilt Campus: A Pictorial History. LC 78-9913. (Illus.). 160p. 1979. 24.95 (*0-8265-1210-0*) Vanderbilt U Pr.

McGeachie, J. Smooth Muscle Regeneration: A Review & Experimental Study. (Monographs in Developmental Biology: Vol. 9). (Illus.). vii, 90p. 1975. 48.00 (*3-8055-2058-1*) S Karger.

McGeagh, Robert. Juan de Onate's Colony in the Wilderness: An Early History of the American Southwest. Smith, James C., Jr., ed. LC 90-49998. (Illus.). 64p. (Orig.). 1990. pap. 8.95 (*0-86534-153-2*) Sunstone Pr.

McGean, Betsy, jt. ed. see Poffenberger, Mark.

McGear, Reba & Simms, Jo P. Telephone Triage & Management: A Nursing Process Approach. (Illus.). 174p. 1988. pap. text 52.00 (*0-7216-2406-5*, W B Saunders Co) Harcrt Hlth Sci Grp.

McGearhart, Susea, jt. auth. see Ashcraft, Tami O.

McGeary. Emblem Books at the University of Illinois: A Bibliographic Catalog. 1993. 135.00 (*0-8161-0533-2*, G K Hall & Co) Mac Lib Ref.

McGeary. Physical Geology. 3rd ed. 1997. 47.50 (*0-697-38185-4*, WCB McGr Hill) McGrw-H Hghr Educ.

McGeary, jt. auth. see Plummer.

McGeary, David & Plummer, Charles C. Physical Geology: Earth Revealed. 2nd ed. 540p. (C). 1994. text 40.00 (*0-697-24675-2*, WCB McGr Hill) McGrw-H Hghr Educ.

— Physical Geology: Earth Revealed. 3rd ed. LC 97-11483. 560p. (C). 1997. per. write for info. (*0-697-37649-4*, WCB McGr Hill) McGrw-H Hghr Educ.

— Physical Geology with Interactive Plate Tectonics. 7th ed. 560p. (C). 1995. pap., per. write for info. incl. cd-rom (*0-697-26676-1*, WCB McGr Hill); text, student ed. write for info. (*0-697-28732-7*, WCB McGr Hill) McGrw-H Hghr Educ.

— Physical Geology with Interactive Plate Tectonics. 7th ed. 240p. (C). 1995. text, student ed. 21.87 (*0-697-26678-8*, WCB McGr Hill) McGrw-H Hghr Educ.

***McGeary, David, et al.** Physical Geology: Earth Revealed. 4th ed. LC 00-33937. 2001. write for info. (*0-07-366183-X*) McGraw.

McGeary, David, jt. auth. see Plummer, Charles C.

McGeary, Michael G., jt. ed. see Lynn, Laurence E., Jr.

McGeary, Mitchell, jt. auth. see McCoy, William.

McGeary, Thomas. The Music of Harry Partch: A Descriptive Catalog. LC 91-70674. (I.S.A.M. Monographs: No. 31). (Illus.). xiv, 186p. (Orig.). 1991. pap. 20.00 (*0-914678-34-5*) Inst Am Music.

McGeary, Thomas, ed. see Partch, Harry.

McGeary, Thomas, ed. & intro. see Partch, Harry.

McGechan, Justice. The Principles of the Law of Evidence. 7th ed. 445p. 1984. pap. 63.00 (*0-409-70174-2*, NZ, MICHIE) LEXIS Pub.

McGee. Nicolo Paganini. 49.95 (*1-85928-400-0*) Ashgate Pub Co.

McGee. Physical Diagnosis. 2001. pap. text Price not set. (*0-7216-8693-1*, W B Saunders Co) Harcrt Hlth Sci Grp.

Mcgee. Psychology. Date not set. pap. text, teacher ed. write for info. (*0-314-79143-4*); pap. text, student ed. 17.75 (*0-314-79144-2*) West Pub.

McGee & Thomas. Competitive Groups. (Pergamon Strategic Management Ser.). 1996. text. write for info. (*0-08-037273-2*, Pergamon Pr) Elsevier.

— Competitive Groups. (Technology, Innovation, Entrepreneurship, & Competitive Strategy Ser.: Vol. 1). 1997. pap. write for info. (*0-08-037307-0*) Elsevier.

McGee, Adolph P. How to Correct Your Own Credit, Vol. 1. (Illus.). 50p. (Orig.). 1984. student ed. 24.95 (*0-685-25238-8*) A&J Consult.

— How to Correct Your Own Credit: A Workbook to Correct Your Credit. rev. ed. 1990. write for info. (*0-9621957-0-7*) A&J Consult.

***McGee, Andrea Lins, ed.** War Child: Morazan, El Salvador 1981 Poetry. x, 60p. 2000. pap. 14.99 (*0-9678800-0-9*) ReDe Arte.

McGee, Andrew. Company Law. 180p. (C). 1990. pap. 40.00 (*1-85352-762-9*, Pub. by HLT Pubns) St Mut.

— The Financial Services Ombudsmen. 69p. 1992. 55.00 (*1-85190-169-8*, Pub. by Tolley Pubng) St Mut.

— Limitation Periods, Vol. 1. 2nd ed. 1994. 176.00 (*0-421-48560-4*, Pub. by Sweet & Maxwll) Gaunt.

— The Single Market in Insurance: Breaking down the Barriers. LC 98-3168. (European Business Law Library). 160p. 1998. pap. 29.95 (*1-85521-570-5*, KJE2301.M39, Pub. by Ashgate Pub); text 68.95 (*1-85521-563-2*, KJE2301.M39, Pub. by Ashgate Pub) Ashgate Pub Co.

McGee, Andrew & Williams, Christina. The Business of Company Law: An Introduction for Students. 416p. 1996. text 82.00 (*0-19-876304-2*); pap. text 32.00 (*0-19-876305-0*) OUP.

McGee, Anne, ed. see Sabine, Elizabeth.

McGee, Art. How to Value Players for Rotisserie Baseball. LC 97-184129. 140p. 1997. pap. 15.95 (*1-886094-64-0*) Chicago Spectrum.

McGee, Arthus. The Elizabethan Hamlet. LC 87-13271. 208p. 1987. 32.50 (*0-300-03988-3*) Yale U Pr.

McGee Banks, Cheryl A., jt. ed. see Banks, James A.

McGee, Barbara. Counting Sheep. (Illus.). 24p. (J). (gr. k-3). 1991. 12.95 (*1-55037-157-6*, Pub. by Annick); pap. 4.95 (*1-55037-160-6*, Pub. by Annick) Firefly Bks Ltd.

McGee, Barbara, ed. see Wassung, Keith.

McGee, Bob. Ebbets Field. Date not set. write for info. (*0-393-03964-1*) Norton.

***McGee, Bobby.** Letters to Colleen. (Illus.). 170p. 1999. pap. 14.95 (*1-930499-02-7*) Bobbysez Pub.

— Magical Golf. (Illus.). 170p. 2000. 21.95 (*1-930499-03-5*) Bobbysez Pub.

— Magical Life. (Illus.). 170p. 2000. pap. 15.95 (*1-930499-07-8*) Bobbysez Pub.

— Magical Life Workbook. (Illus.). 50p. 2000. pap., wbk. ed. 13.95 (*1-930499-08-6*) Bobbysez Pub.

— Magical Running. (Illus.). 170p. 2000. pap. 15.95 (*1-930499-00-0*) Bobbysez Pub.

— Magical Running Workbook. (Illus.). 50p. 2000. pap., wbk. ed. 13.95 (*1-930499-01-9*) Bobbysez Pub.

— Magical Work. (Illus.). 170p. 2000. 19.95 (*1-930499-05-1*) Bobbysez Pub.

— Magical Work: The Workbook. (Illus.). 50p. 2000. pap., wbk. ed. 13.95 (*1-930499-06-X*) Bobbysez Pub.

McGee, Brenda. Felita. Friedland, Joyce & Kessler, Rikki, eds. (Novel-Ties Ser.). (J). (gr. 2-4). 1991. pap. text, student ed. 15.95 (*0-88122-567-3*) Lrn Links.

McGee, Brenda H. Global Geography: Research Activities for All Seasons. (Illus.). 48p. (YA). (gr. 9 up). 1994. 6.99 (*0-86653-793-7*, GA1487) Good Apple.

— Old Yeller: A Study Guide. Friedland, Joyce & Kessler, Rikki, eds. (Novel-Ties Ser.). 21p. (J). (gr. 5-7). 1990. pap. text 15.95 (*0-88122-415-4*) Lrn Links.

— Rascal: A Study Guide. Friedland, Joyce & Kessler, Rikki, eds. (Novel-Ties Ser.). 26p. (J). (gr. 5-7). 1990. pap. text 15.95 (*0-88122-416-2*) Lrn Links.

— Robin Hood of Sherwood Forest: A Study Guide. Friedland, J. & Kessler, R., eds. (Novel-Ties Ser.). (J). (gr. 3-5). 1993. pap. text, student ed. 15.95 (*0-88122-909-1*) Lrn Links.

McGee, C. E. The Elizabethan Theatre Vol. X: Papers Given at the International Conference on Elizabethan Theatre Held at the University of Waterloo, Ontario, in July 1983, Vol. X. (Illus.). 154p. 1988. 38.00 (*0-88835-022-8*) P D Meany.

McGee, C. E., ed. The Elizabethan Theatre Vol. XII: Papers Given at the Twelfth International Conference on Elizabethan Theatre Held at the University of Waterloo in July 1987, Vol. XII. (Illus.). 215p. 1993. 38.00 (*0-88835-036-8*) P D Meany.

McGee, C. E., jt. ed. see Magnusson, A. L.

McGee, Charles T. Heart Frauds: The Misapplication of High Technology in Heart Disease. Zirschky, Martha, ed. (Illus.). 263p. (Orig.). 1993. pap. 11.95 (*0-9636979-4-3*) MediPress.

***McGee, Charles T.** Heart Frauds: Uncovering the Biggest Health Scam in History. LC 00-25780. 2000. pap. write for info. (*0-941599-56-6*, HlthWise Pubns) Piccadilly Bks.

McGee, Charlie. Winning Secrets of a Master Sports Bettor - Baseball. 32p. 1997. pap. 7.95 (*0-934650-21-7*) Sunnyside.

McGee, Charmayne. So Sings the Blue Deer. LC 93-26580. 160p. (J). (gr. 3-7). 1994. 14.95 (*0-689-31888-X*) Atheneum Yung Read.

McGee-Cooper, Ann & Trammell, Duane. Time Management for Unmanageable People. LC 93-47683. 272p. 1994. pap. 14.95 (*0-553-37071-5*) Bantam.

McGee-Cooper, Ann, et al. You Don't Have to Go Home from Work Exhausted! 288p. 1992. pap. 14.95 (*0-553-37061-8*) Bantam.

McGee, D. C. Soybean Diseases: A Reference Source for Seed Technologists. 1993. 34.00 (*0-89054-141-8*) Am Phytopathol Soc.

McGee, David, jt. auth. see Perkins, Carl.

McGee, Denis C. Maize Diseases: A Reference Source for Seed Technologists. LC 88-70647. (Illus.). 160p. (Orig.). 1988. pap. text 34.00 (*0-89054-090-X*) Am Phytopathol Soc.

McGee, Denis C., ed. Plant Pathogens & the Worldwide Movement of Seeds. LC 97-75237. (Illus.). 109p. 1997. pap. 39.00 (*0-89054-185-X*) Am Phytopathol Soc.

McGee, Deron, jt. auth. see Schaffer, John.

McGee, E. S. & Geological Survey (U.S.). Acid Rain & Our Nation's Capital: A Guide to Effects on Buildings & Monuments. LC 97-122142. 35 p. 1995. write for info. (*0-16-048068-X*) USGPO.

McGee, Eddie. The Emergency Handbook. Arico, Diane, ed. (Corgi Bks.). (Illus.). 176p. (J). (gr. 8-12). 1985. reprint ed. pap. 4.95 (*0-671-60483-X*); reprint ed. lib. bdg. 9.79 (*0-671-60484-8*) S&S Trade.

— No Need to Die. 1996. pap. 18.95 (*0-901764-41-8*, 93228) P H Crompton.

***McGee, Elder K.** C. O. G. I. C. Unsanctioned Issues. 335p. (Orig.). 1999. pap. 14.95 (*1-881524-59-0*, Pub. by Milligan Bks) Baker & Taylor.

McGee, Elizabeth A. & Blank, Susan. A Stitch in Time: Helping Young Mothers Complete High School. 70p. 1989. pap. 8.00 (*0-89492-068-5*) Acad Educ Dev.

McGee, Frank. UCI: The First Twenty-Five Years. Cronin, Barbara, ed. (Illus.). 155p. 1992. text 24.95 (*0-9634697-0-3*) U CA Alumni.

McGee, G. Kay, jt. auth. see McGee, Norman T.

McGee, Gary. Systematic Theology: A Pentecostal Perspective. Horton, Stanley M. et al, eds. LC 93-23568. (Logion Press Ser.). 704p. 1994. text 34.99 (*0-88243-319-9*, 02-0319) Gospel Pub.

McGee, Gary B. This Gospel Shall Be Preached Vol. 2: A History & Theology of Assemblies of God Foreign Missions since 1959. LC 86-80015. 358p. 1989. kivar 12.95 (*0-88243-673-2*, 02-0673) Gospel Pub.

McGee, Gary B., ed. How Sweet the Sound! God's Grace for Suffering Christians. LC 94-75922. 112p. 1994. pap. 7.95 (*0-88243-315-6*, 02-0315) Gospel Pub.

McGee, Gary B., jt. auth. see Burgess, Stanley M.

McGee, Gary B., jt. ed. see Aker, Benny C.

McGee, Glenn. The Perfect Baby: A Pragmatic Approach to Genetics. LC 96-31064. 176p. 1997. 52.50 (*0-8476-8343-5*); pap. 14.95 (*0-8476-8344-3*) Rowman.

***McGee, Glenn.** The Perfect Baby: Parenthood in the New World of Cloning & Genetics. 2nd ed. LC 00-21041. 176p. 2000. 57.00 (*0-8476-9758-4*) Rowman.

— The Perfect Baby: Parenthood in the New World of Cloning & Genetics. 2nd ed. LC 00-21041. 176p. 2000. pap. 16.95 (*0-8476-9759-2*) Rowman.

McGee, Glenn, ed. The Human Cloning Debate. LC 98-18451. (Illus.). 270p. 1998. pap. 16.95 (*0-9653774-8-2*) Berkeley Hills.

— Pragmatic Bioethics. LC 98-25317. (Vanderbilt Library of American Philosophy). 344p. 1999. lib. bdg. 49.95 (*0-8265-1320-4*) Vanderbilt U Pr.

McGee, Glenn, ed. see Wilmut, Ian & Kaplan, Arthur.

McGee, Gloria, et al. Black, Beautiful & Recovering. (Orig.). 1985. pap. 2.00 (*0-89486-280-4*, 1219B) Hazelden.

McGee, Hannah. Quality of Life Following Renal Failure: Psychosocial Challenges Accompanying High Technology Medicine. 1994. pap. write for info. (*3-7186-5522-5*) Gordon & Breach.

McGee, Hannah M. & Bradley, Clare, eds. Quality of Life Following Renal Failure: Psychosocial Challenges Accompanying High Technology Medicine. 312p. 1994. text 59.00 (*3-7186-5501-2*) Gordon & Breach.

McGee, Harold. On Food & Cooking. 1997. per. 21.00 (*0-684-84328-5*) S&S Trade.

McGee, Harold. Six MicMac Stories. 51p. 1992. pap. 5.95 (*0-919680-35-6*) Nimbus Publ.

McGee, Harold & Whitehead, Ruth H. The Micmac. (Illus.). 64p. 1991. pap. 7.95 (*0-920852-21-1*) Nimbus Publ.

McGee, Harold J. The Curious Cook. (Illus.). 336p. 1992. reprint ed. pap. 15.95 (*0-02-009801-4*) Macmillan.

— On Food & Cooking: The Science & Lore of the Kitchen. (Illus.). 672p. 1984. 45.00 (*0-684-18132-0*, Scribners Ref) Mac Lib Ref.

***McGee, Heather D.** Blue Jean Clouded. LC 99-69450. (Illus.). 273p. 2000. pap. 12.95 (*1-930437-00-5*) Eves Eye Pr.

***McGee, Heather D., et al.** Automobilia: Modern Women in the Automotive Stratosphere. LC 99-69452. (Illus.). 400p. 2000. pap. 18.95 (*1-930437-02-1*) Eves Eye Pr.

McGee, J. Amos/Obadiah. (Thru the Bible Commentary Ser.). 1997. pap. text 6.97 (*0-7852-0556-X*) Nelson.

McGee, J. Ecclesiastes, Song of Solomon. (Thru The Bible Commentary Ser.). 1997. pap. 6.97 (*0-7852-0489-X*) Nelson.

— Exodus. (Thru the Bible Commentary Ser.). 1997. pap. text 6.97 (*0-7852-0300-1*) Nelson.

— I & II Chronicles. (Thru The Bible Commentary Ser.). 1997. pap. 5.97 (*0-7852-0413-X*) Nelson.

— I & II Samuel. (Thru the Bible Commentary Ser.). 1997. pap. 6.97 (*0-7852-0380-X*) Nelson.

— I Corinthians. (Thru the Bible Commentary Ser.: Vol. 44). 1997. pap. 6.97 (*0-7852-0735-X*) Nelson.

McGee, J. Joshua/Judges. (Thru the Bible Commentary Ser.). 1997. pap. text 6.97 (*0-7852-0363-X*) Nelson.

McGee, J. Leviticus. (Thru the Bible Commentary Ser.: Vol. 1). 1997. pap. text 6.97 (*0-7852-0315-X*) Nelson.

Mcgee, J. Leviticus. (Thru the Bible Commentary Ser.: Vol. 2). 1997. pap. text 6.97 (*0-7852-0329-X*) Nelson.

McGee, J. Matthew, Pt. II. (Thru the Bible Commentary Ser.: Vol. 35). 1997. pap. text 6.97 (*0-7852-0640-X*) Nelson.

— Revelation, Pt. I. (Thru the Bible Commentary Ser.: Vol. 58). 1997. pap. 6.97 (*0-7852-0895-X*) Nelson.

— Ruth. (Thru the Bible Commentary Ser.). 1997. pap. text 6.97 (*0-7852-0377-X*) Nelson.

Mcgee, J. II Peter. (Thru the Bible Commentary Ser.). 1997. pap. 6.97 (*0-7852-0864-X*) Nelson.

McGee, J. Zechariah. (Thru the Bible Commentary Ser.: Vol. 32). 1997. pap. text 5.97 (*0-7852-0606-X*) Nelson.

— Zephaniah/Haggai. (Thru The Bible Commentary Ser.: Vol. 31). 1997. pap. 5.97 (*0-7852-0590-X*) Nelson.

McGee, J. hVernon. Nahum/Habakkuk. 1997. pap. 6.97 (*0-7852-0587-X*) Nelson.

McGee, J. J. & Menolascino, F. J. Beyond Gentle Teaching: A Nonaversive Approach to Helping Those in Need. (Illus.). 244p. (C). 1991. 42.00 (*0-306-43856-9*, Plenum Trade) Perseus Pubng.

McGee, J. Ve. Thru the Bible S-S, 5 vols. 1998. 124.97 (*0-7852-0041-X*) Nelson.

McGee, J. Vernon. Acts, Pt. 1. (Thru the Bible Commentary Ser.: Vol. 40). 1997. pap. 6.97 (*0-7852-0699-X*) Nelson.

— Acts, Pt. II. (Thru the Bible Commentary Ser.: Vol. 41). 1997. pap. 6.97 (*0-7852-0704-X*) Nelson.

— Daniel. (Thru the Bible Commentary Ser.: Vol. 26). 1997. pap. 6.97 (*0-7852-0539-X*) Nelson.

***McGee, J. Vernon.** David: A Man after God's Own Heart. LC 99-87431. 2000. 14.99 (*0-7852-6821-9*) Nelson.

McGee, J. Vernon. Doctrine for Difficult Days. 288p. 1996. 19.99 (*0-7852-7353-0*) Nelson.

— Ephesians. (Thru the Bible Commentary Ser.: Vol. 47). 1997. pap. 6.97 (*0-7852-0766-X*) Nelson.

— Exodus, Vol. 2. (Thru the Bible Commentary Ser.: Vol. 5). 1997. pap. 6.97 (*0-7852-0301-X*) Nelson.

— Ezekiel. (Thru the Bible Commentary: Bk. 25). 1997. pap. 6.97 (*0-7852-0525-X*) Nelson.

McGee, J. Vernon. I & II John/Jude. (Thru The Bible Commentary Ser.). 1997. pap. text 6.97 (*0-7852-0881-X*) Nelson.

McGee, J. Vernon. I & II Kings. (Thru the Bible Commentary: Vol. 13). 1997. pap. 6.97 (*0-7852-0394-X*) Nelson.

— I & II Thessalonians. (Thru the Bible Commentary Ser.: Vol. 49). 1997. pap. 6.97 (*0-7852-0797-X*) Nelson.

— I & II Timothy, Titus, Philemon. (Thru the Bible Commentary Ser.: Vol. 50). 1997. pap. 6.97 (*0-7852-0802-X*) Nelson.

— I John. (Thru the Bible Commentary Ser.: Vol. 56). 1997. pap. 6.97 (*0-7852-0878-X*) Nelson.

— I Peter. (Thru the Bible Commentary Ser.: Vol. 54). 1997. pap. 6.97 (*0-7852-0850-X*) Nelson.

— Galatians. (Thru the Bible Commentary Ser.: Vol. 46). 1997. pap. 6.97 (*0-7852-0752-X*) Nelson.

— Genesis. (Thru the Bible Commentary Ser.: Vol. 1). 1997. pap. 6.97 (*0-7852-0279-X*) Nelson.

— Genesis. (Thru the Bible Commentary Ser.: Vol. 2). 1997. pap. 6.97 (*0-7852-0282-X*) Nelson.

— Genesis. (Thru the Bible Commentary: Vol. 3). 1997. pap. 6.97 (*0-7852-0296-X*) Nelson.

— Hebrews, Pt. I. (Thru the Bible Commentary Ser.: Vol. 51). 1997. pap. 6.97 (*0-7852-0816-X*) Nelson.

— Hebrews, Pt. II. (Thru the Bible Commentary Ser.: Vol. 52). 1997. pap. 6.97 (*0-7852-0833-X*) Nelson.

— Hosea/Joel. (Thru the Bible Commentary Ser.: Vol. 27). 1997. pap. 6.97 (*0-7852-0542-X*) Nelson.

— Isaiah, Pt. I. (Thru the Bible Commentary Ser.: Vol. 22). 1998. pap. text 6.97 (*0-7852-0492-X*) Nelson.

— Isaiah, Pt. II. (Thru the Bible Commentary: Vol. 23). 1997. pap. 6.97 (*0-7852-0508-X*) Nelson.

— James. (Thru the Bible Commentary Ser.: Vol. 53). 1997. pap. 6.97 (*0-7852-0847-X*) Nelson.

— Jeremiah/Lamentations. (Thru the Bible Commentary). 1997. pap. 6.97 (*0-7852-0511-X*) Nelson.

— Jesus: Centerpiece of Scripture. LC 95-10597. 240p. 1996. 14.99 (*0-7852-7603-3*) Nelson.

— Job. (Thru the Bible Commentary: Vol. 16). 1997. pap. 6.97 (*0-7852-0430-X*) Nelson.

— John, Pt. 1. (Thru the Bible Commentary: Vol. 38). 1997. pap. 6.97 (*0-7852-0671-X*) Nelson.

— John, Pt. 2. (Thru the Bible Commentary: Vol. 39). 1997. pap. 6.97 (*0-7852-0685-X*) Nelson.

— Jonah/Micah. (Thru the Bible Commentary: Bk. 29). 1997. pap. 6.97 (*0-7852-0573-X*) Nelson.

— Love, Liberation & the Law. LC 95-154353. 1995. 15.99 (*0-7852-7828-1*) Nelson.

Mcgee, J Vernon. Luke. (Thru the Bible Commentary Ser.: Vol. 37). 1997. pap. 6.97 (*0-7852-0668-X*) Nelson.

McGee, J. Vernon. Malachi. (Thru the Bible Commentary Ser.: Vol. 33). 1997. pap. 6.97 (*0-7852-0623-X*) Nelson.

— Mark. (Thru the Bible Commentary Ser.: Vol. 36). 1997. pap. 6.97 (*0-7852-0654-X*) Nelson.

***McGee, J. Vernon.** Marriage & Divorce. LC 97-36461. 240p. 1998. 16.99 (*0-7852-7454-5*) Nelson.

McGee, J. Vernon. Matthew, Pt. 1. (Thru the Bible Commentary Ser.: Vol. 34). 1997. pap. 6.97 (*0-7852-0637-X*) Nelson.

Mcgee, J. Vernon. More Real Characters. LC 96-50886. 240p. 1997. 14.99 (*0-7852-7172-4*) Nelson.

McGee, J. Vernon. Numbers. (Thru the Bible Commentary: Vol. 8). 1997. pap. 6.97 (*0-7852-0332-X*) Nelson.

— On Prophecy: Man's Fascination with the Future. LC 93-38942. 1993. 15.99 (*0-8407-6798-6*) Nelson.

— Philippians/Colossians. (Thru the Bible Commentary Ser.: Vol. 48). 1997. pap. 6.97 (*0-7852-0783-X*) Nelson.

— Proverbs. (Thru the Bible Commentary Ser.: Vol. 20). 1997. pap. 6.97 (*0-7852-0475-X*) Nelson.

— Psalms, Pt. I. (Thru the Bible Commentary Ser.: Vol. 17). 1997. pap. 6.97 (*0-7852-0444-X*) Nelson.

— Psalms, Pt. II. (Thru the Bible Commentary Ser.: Vol. 18). 1997. pap. 6.97 (*0-7852-0458-X*) Nelson.

— Psalms, Pt. III. (Thru the Bible Commentary Ser.: Vol. 19). 1997. pap. 6.97 (*0-7852-0461-X*) Nelson.

— Real Characters. LC 94-48154. 256p. 1995. 14.99 (*0-7852-7732-3*) Nelson.

An Asterisk (*) at the beginning of an entry indicates that the title is appearing for the first time.

— Revelation, Pt. III. (Thru the Bible Commentary Ser.: Vol. 60). 1997. pap. 6.97 (0-7852-0914-X) Nelson.
— Romans, Pt. 1. (Thru the Bible Commentary Ser.: Vol. 42). 1997. pap. 6.97 (0-7852-0718-X) Nelson.
— Romans, Pt. II. (Thru the Bible Commentary Ser.: Vol. 43). 1997. pap. 5.97 (0-7852-0721-X) Nelson.
— II Corinthians. (Thru The Bible Commentary Ser.: Vol. 45). 1997. pap. 6.97 (0-7852-0749-X) Nelson.
— Thru the Bible, 5 vols. Incl. Thru the Bible with J. Vernon McGee Vol. 1: Genesis- Deuteronomy., 5 vols. LC 81-3930. 640p. 1983. 34.99 (0-8407-4973-2); Thru the Bible with J. Vernon McGee Vol. 2: Joshua-Psalms., 5 vols. LC 81-3930. 896p. 1983. 34.99 (0-8407-4974-0); Thru the Bible with J. Vernon McGee Vol. 3: Proverbs-Malachi., 5 vols. LC 81-3930. 1040p. 1983. 34.99 (0-8407-4975-9); Thru the Bible with J. Vernon McGee Vol. 4: Matthew-Romans., 5 vols. LC 81-3930. 768p. 1983. 34.99 (0-8407-4976-7); Thru the Bible with J. Vernon McGee Vol. 5: Corinthians-Revelation., 5 vols. LC 81-3930. 1088p. 1983. 34.99 (0-8407-4977-5); LC 81-3930. 1984. 174.99 (0-8407-4957-0) Nelson.
— Thru the Bible Commentary: Deuteronomy, Vol. 9. (Thru the Bible Commentary Ser.). 1997. pap. text 6.97 (0-7852-0346-X) Nelson.
— Thru the Bible Topical Index. (Thru The Bible Commentary Ser.). 352p. 1998. pap. 34.99 (0-7852-1253-1) Nelson.
— Who Is God? LC 99-37463. 192p. 1999. 14.99 (0-7852-6934-7) Nelson.
McGee, James & Duffy, Brian. Main Justice: The Men & Women Who Enforce the Nation's Criminal Laws & Guard Its Liberties. 384p. 1996. 25.00 (0-684-81135-9) Simon & Schuster.
McGee, James & Prusak, Laurence. Managing Information Strategically: Increase Your Company's Competitiveness & Efficiency by Using Information As a Strategic Tool. LC 92-37939. (Ernst & Young Information Management Ser.). 272p. 1993. 39.95 (0-471-57544-5) Wiley.
McGee, James, et al. Kings, Saints & Parliament: A Sourcebook for Western Civilization, 1050-1715. 2nd ed. 272p. (C). 1995. spiral bd. 27.95 (0-8403-9070-X) Kendall-Hunt.
McGee, James, jt. ed. see Polak, Julia.
McGee, James O., et al, eds. The Oxford Textbook of Pathology Vol. 1: General Principles of Pathology, Vol. 1. (Illus.). 918p. 1992. pap. text 85.00 (0-19-261972-1) OUP.
— The Oxford Textbook of Pathology Vol. 2: Pathology of Systems, 2 bks., Vol. 2, Pts. 1 & 2. (Illus.). 1992. pap. text 160.00 (0-19-261974-8) OUP.
McGee, James O., jt. ed. see Herrington, C. S.
McGee, James S. The Godly Man in Stuart England: Anglicans, Puritans, & the Two Tables, 1620-1670. LC 75-43325. (Yale Historical Publications: Miscellany: No. 110). 319p. reprint ed. pap. 98.90 (0-8357-8147-X, 203382000087) Bks Demand.
McGee, James S., ed. see Bunyan, John.
McGee, Jeffrey E. Cooperative Strategy & New Venture Performance: The Role of Managerial Experience. rev. ed. LC 93-39453. (Studies in Entrepreneurship). 240p. 1994. text 15.00 (0-8153-1673-9) Garland.
***McGee, Jerry.** Whiskey Riley. unabridged large type ed. LC 99-65949. 300p. 1999. pap. write for info. (0-9672772-0-5) EsJay Pr.
Mcgee, Jim. Terror's Price. 1999. write for info. (0-375-50123-1) Random.
McGee, Joe. God Knows How to Raise Your Kids: Even If You Don't. LC 99-175838. 1998. pap. text 12.99 (1-57794-032-6) Harrison Hse.
McGee, John. Industrial Organization. (Illus.). 656p. (C). 1988. text 45.00 (0-13-464207-4) P-H.
McGee, John S. The Robinson-Patman Act & Effective Competition. Bruchey, Stuart & Carosso, Vincent P., eds. LC 78-18968. (Small Business Enterprise in America Ser.). (Illus.). 1979. lib. bdg. 56.95 (0-405-11472-9) Ayer.
***McGee, Joyce.** Thoughts from Within. 32p. 2000. pap. 7.00 (0-8059-4849-X) Dorrance.
McGee, Larry. Aquarium Maintenance Guide: Freshwater. (Illus.). 32p. (Orig.). 1996. pap. 2.95 (0-9652059-0-8) Aquarium Attract.
McGee, Lea M. & Richgels. Literacy's Beginnings: Supporting Young Readers & Writers. 3rd ed. LC 99-40038. 396p. 1999. pap. text 51.00 (0-205-29931-8, Longwood Div) Allyn.
McGee, Lea M., jt. auth. see Tompkins, Gail E.
McGee, Lee & Troeger, Thomas H. Wrestling with the Patriarchs: Retrieving Women's Voices in Preaching. (Preacher's Library). 144p. 1996. pap. 13.95 (0-687-00621-X) Abingdon.
McGee, Leo & Boone, Robert S., eds. The Black Rural Landowner - Endangered Species: Social, Political, & Economic Implications, 44. LC 78-69538. (Contributions in Afro-American & African Studies: No. 44). (Illus.). 200p. 1979. 47.95 (0-313-20609-0, MCB/) Greenwood.
McGee, Leo & Neufeldt, Harvey G., compiled by. Education of the Black Adult in the United States: An Annotated Bibliography, 4. LC 84-19785. (Bibliographies & Indexes in Afro-American & African Studies: No. 4). 108p. 1985. lib. bdg. 49.95 (0-313-23473-6, MBA/) Greenwood.
McGee, Leo, jt. ed. see Neufeldt, Harvey G.
McGee, Lynn. Bonanza: Collection of Poems. 36p. 1997. pap. 8.00 (0-9624178-6-6) Slapering Hol.
McGee, M. W. Ambosia Dancing at Mary's. Lomax, Joseph F. & Whitebird, J., eds. (Illus.). 1977. pap. 15.00 (0-930324-02-1) Wings Pr.
***McGee, Marcus.** An Essay on Niggers & Squirrels. 14p. 2000. pap. 4.95 (0-9673123-1-0, Pegasus Books) Marcus McGee Med.
— Four Stories. LC 99-90734. 216p. (C). 1999. pap. 14.95 (0-9673123-0-2, Pegasus Books) Marcus McGee Med.
— Legal Thriller. 430p. 2000. 27.99 (0-9673123-3-7, Pegasus Books) Marcus McGee Med.
McGee, Marie. Millersburg Glass. Measell, James, ed. (Illus.). 128p. 1995. pap. 29.95 (1-57080-005-7) Antique Pubns.
McGee, Mark. Human Spatial Abilities: Sources of Sex Difference. 145p. 1979. 55.00 (0-275-90391-5, C0391, Praeger Pubs) Greenwood.
***McGee, Mark.** R-War: On Human Relationships. (Illus.). 190p. 2000. write for info. (0-9651323-0-7) Mentor Inst.
McGee, Mark G. & Wilson, David W. Psychology: Science & Application. (Illus.). 666p. (C). 1984. text 60.00 (0-314-77927-2) West Pub.
McGee, Mark T. Beyond Ballyhoo: Motion Picture Promotion & Gimmicks. LC 89-42731. (Illus.). 253p. 1989. lib. bdg. 37.50 (0-89950-435-3) McFarland & Co.
— Faster & Furiouser: The Revised & Fattened Fable of American International Pictures. LC 95-39083. (Illus.). 360p. 1995. lib. bdg. 45.00 (0-7864-0137-0) McFarland & Co.
McGee, Mark Thomas. Roger Corman: The Best of the Cheap Acts. LC 87-46389. (Illus.). 261p. 1997. pap. 20.00 (0-7864-0477-9) McFarland & Co.
McGee, Marni. The Alphabet Between. LC 91-25489. (Illus.). 32p. 1997. text, lib. bdg. 14.95 (0-689-31753-0) Atheneum Yung Read.
— The Forest Child. LC 92-37148. (Illus.). 40p. (J). (ps-2). 1994. 15.00 (0-671-86608-7, Green Tiger S&S) S&S Childrens.
— Forest Child. LC 92-37148. (Illus.). 40p. (J). (ps-3). 1999. pap. 5.99 (0-689-82578-1, 076714005990) S&S Childrens.
— Jack Takes the Cake, Level 2. (Planet Reader Picture Bks.). (Illus.). 32p. (J). (gr. k-3). 1998. pap. 2.95 (0-8167-4435-1) Troll Communs.
— The Sleepy Men. LC 98-19971. (Illus.). (J). 2001. per. 16.00 (0-689-82378-9) S&S Childrens.
McGee, Marsha G., jt. ed. see Johnson, Christopher J.
***McGee, Marty.** Traditional Musicians of the Central Blue Ridge: Old Time, Early Country, Folk & Bluegrass Label Recording Artists, with Discographies. (Illus.). 245p. 2000. pap. 25.00 (0-7864-0876-6) McFarland & Co.
McGee, Marty & Tellington-Jones, Linda. Llama Handling & Training: The Team Approach. LC 92-60582. (Illus.). 200p. (Orig.). 1992. pap. text 24.75 (0-9633002-0-2) Zephyr Farm.
McGee, Marty, jt. auth. see Presnell, Don.
McGee, Mary, jt. ed. see Leslie, Julia.
McGee, Mary P., jt. auth. see Pace, Ruth.
McGee, May L., tr. see Bustamante, Cecilia.
McGee, Michael V. Stark Drama: Crime & ... Punishment? (Illus.). 20p. 1992. pap. 3.25 (0-88680-375-6) I E Clark.
McGee, Michelle, jt. auth. see Graham, Mary.
McGee, Norman T. Tennessee Land Entries of the First Surveyor's District, 6 vols., Set. (Illus.). 1685p. (Orig.). 1998. write for info. (0-9622403-8-9) Lilac Hill Pubns.
— Tennessee Land Entries of the First Surveyor's District: Entry Book G, 1813-1815. (Illus.). 270p. (Orig.). 1997. write for info. (0-9622403-5-4) Lilac Hill Pubns.
— Tennessee Land Entries of the First Surveyor's District: Entry Book H, 1815-1817. (Illus.). 330p. (Orig.). 1998. write for info. (0-9622403-6-2) Lilac Hill Pubns.
— Tennessee Land Entries of the First Surveyor's District: Entry Book I, 1817-1823. (Illus.). 400p. (Orig.). 1998. write for info. (0-9622403-7-0) Lilac Hill Pubns.
— Tennessee Land Entries of the First Surveyor's District: Entry Books C & D, 1809-1811. (Illus.). 275p. (Orig.). 1996. write for info. (0-9622403-3-8) Lilac Hill Pubns.
— Tennessee Land Entries of the First Surveyor's District: Entry Books E & F, 1811-1913. (Illus.). 360p. (Orig.). 1997. write for info. (0-9622403-4-6) Lilac Hill Pubns.
— Tennessee Land Entries of the First Surveyor's District: Entry Books A1, A2, & B, 1807-1809. (Illus.). 380p. (Orig.). 1996. write for info. (0-9622403-2-X) Lilac Hill Pubns.
McGee, Norman T. & McGee, G. Kay. United States Census of Putnam County Tennessee, 1870. LC 89-80386. (Illus.). 170p. (Orig.). 1989. pap. 25.00 (0-9622403-1-1) Lilac Hill Pubns.
McGee, O. D., jt. ed. see Herrington, C. S.
McGee, P. Tristan. Development of the Regional Policy of the European Communities. (C). 1982. 40.00 (0-7855-3852-6, Pub. by Oxford Polytechnic) St Mut.
— Local Government & the Regional Policy of the European Communities: Overview. (C). 1982. 29.00 (0-7855-3851-8, Pub. by Oxford Polytechnic) St Mut.
McGee, Patrick. Cinema, Theory, & Political Responsibility in Contemporary Culture. (Literature, Culture, Theory Ser.: Vol. 24). 252p. (C). 1997. text 64.95 (0-521-58130-3); pap. text 20.95 (0-521-58908-8) Cambridge U Pr.
— Ishmael Reed-Ends of Race. LC 96-25156. 180p. 1997. text 39.95 (0-312-16256-1) St Martin.
— Paperspace: Style As Ideology in Joyce's "Ulysses" LC 87-19074. 253p. 1988. reprint ed. pap. 78.50 (0-608-02686-7, 206333900004) Bks Demand.
— Telling the Other: The Question of Value in Modern & Postcolonial Writing. LC 91-48247. 232p. 1992. text 42.50 (0-8014-2749-5); pap. text 15.95 (0-8014-8027-2) Cornell U Pr.
McGee, Paul. Models of Nursing in Practice: A Pattern for Practical Care. (Illus.). 152p. 1998. pap. 22.95 (0-7487-3343-4, Pub. by S Thornes Pubs) Trans-Atl Phila.
McGee, Paula. Teaching Transcultural Care: A Guide for Teachers of Nursing & Health Care. LC 92-22885. 1992. 38.25 (1-56593-065-7, 0379) Singular Publishing.
McGee, Paula, jt. auth. see Casteldine, George.
McGee, Peter. Kayak Routes of the Pacific Northwest Coast. LC 97-52684. (Illus.). 288p. 1998. pap. 14.95 (0-89886-579-4) Mountaineers.
McGee, R. Harley. Getting It Right: Regional Development in Canada. 360p. 1992. 60.00 (0-7735-0921-6, Pub. by McG-Queens Univ Pr) CUP Services.
***McGee, R. Jon & Warms, Richard L.** Anthropological Theory: An Introductory History. 2nd ed. LC 99-17966. viii, 599p. 1999. pap. text 50.95 (0-7674-1166-8, 1166-8) Mayfield Pub.
McGee, Reece. Academic Janus: The Private College & Its Faculty. LC 70-149913. (Jossey-Bass Higher Education Ser.). 288p. reprint ed. pap. 89.30 (0-8357-9293-5, 201381900087) Bks Demand.
McGee, Reece J., jt. auth. see Caplow, Theodore.
McGee, Robert, et al. Breaking the Cycle of Hurtful Family Experiences. 224p. 1994. pap. text 12.95 (0-8054-9981-4, LifeWy Press) LifeWay Christian.
McGee, Robert S. La Busqueda de Significado: The Search for Significance. Duffer, Hiran & De Duffer, Beatriz L., trs. from ENG. (SPA.). 174p. (Orig.). 1992. pap. 6.99 (0-311-46129-8) Casa Bautista.
— Father Hunger. 280p. 1993. pap. 12.99 (0-89283-818-3, Vine Bks) Servant.
— The Search for Freedom: Demolishing the Strongholds That Diminish Your Faith, Hope, & Confidence in God. 220p. (Orig.). 1995. pap. 12.99 (0-89283-862-0, Vine Bks) Servant.
— The Search for Significance. LC 98-10096. (Orig.). 1998. 14.99 (0-8499-4091-5) Word Pub.
— Search for Significance. 224p. 1992. pap. text 12.95 (0-8054-9990-3, LifeWy Press) LifeWay Christian.
McGee, Robert S. Search for Significance. 1998. pap. text 17.99 (0-8499-4092-3) Word Pub.
McGee, Robert S. Search for Significance. rev. ed. 200p. 1990. pap. 9.99 (0-685-62305-X) Rapha Pub.
— The Search for Significance Small Group Leader's Guide. 58p. 1990. pap. 5.00 (0-945276-09-5) Rapha Pub.
— The Search for Significance (With Workbook) rev. ed. 479p. (Orig.). 1990. pap., wbk. ed. 16.99 (0-945276-07-9) Rapha Pub.
McGee, Robert S. & Jones, Johnny. Search for Significance Leaders Guide. 1993. pap. text 6.95 (0-8054-9989-X) Broadman.
McGee, Robert S. & Mountcastle, William D. Conquering Eating Disorders: A Christ-Centered 12-Step Process. 224p. 1993. pap. text 12.95 (0-8054-9977-6, LifeWy Press) LifeWay Christian.
McGee, Robert S. & Mountcastle, William D. Rapha's Twelve-Step Program for Overcoming Eating Disorders. 1990. pap. 15.99 (0-945276-19-2) Rapha Pub.
McGee, Robert S. & Springle, Pat. Getting Unstuck. 1992. pap. 14.99 (0-945276-32-X) Rapha Pub.
McGee, Robert S., et al. Conquering Chemical Dependency: A Christ Centered 12-Step Process. 224p. 1994. pap. text 12.95 (0-8054-9983-0, LifeWy Press) LifeWay Christian.
McGee, Robert S., et al. Rapha's Twelve-Step Program for Overcoming Chemical Dependency. 302p. 1990. pap. 14.99 (0-945276-10-9) Rapha Pub.
— Your Parents & You Small Group Leader's Guide. 85p. 1990. pap. 5.00 (0-945276-15-X) Rapha Pub.
McGee, Robert S., jt. auth. see McAllister, Dawson.
McGee, Robert W. Accounting & Tax Aspects for Computer Software Manufactures. LC 87-15140. 176p. 1987. 57.95 (0-275-92273-1, C2273, Praeger Pubs) Greenwood.
— Accounting for Data Processing Costs. LC 87-24933. 208p. 1988. 59.95 (0-89930-214-9, MGA/, Quorum Bks) Greenwood.
— Commentaries on Law & Public Policy: 1997 Yearbook. (Yearbook Ser.). 300p. 1998. 30.00 (0-9648794-2-5) Dumont Inst.
— A Model Program for Schools of Professional Accountancy. LC 86-28226. 206p. (Orig.). 1987. pap. text 22.50 (0-8191-6095-4) U Pr of Amer.
— A Trade Policy for Free Societies: The Case Against Protectionism. LC 93-42760. 216p. 1994. 59.95 (0-89930-898-8, Quorum Bks) Greenwood.
McGee, Robert W., ed. Business Ethics & Common Sense. LC 92-9568. 320p. 1992. 59.95 (0-89930-728-0, MNN, Quorum Bks) Greenwood.
— Commentaries on Law & Economics: 1997 Yearbook. (Yearbook Ser.). 300p. 1998. 30.00 (0-9648794-1-7) Dumont Inst.
— Commentaries on Law & Economics: 1998 Yearbook. (Yearbook Ser.). 300p. 1999. 30.00 (0-9648794-5-X) Dumont Inst.
— Commentaries on Law & Public Policy: 1998 Yearbook. (Yearbook Ser.). 300p. 1999. 30.00 (0-9648794-6-8) Dumont Inst.
— Commentaries on the Law of Accounting & Finance: 1997 Yearbook. (Yearbook Ser.). 300p. 1998. 30.00 (0-9648794-0-9) Dumont Inst.
— Commentaries on the Law of Accounting & Finance: 1998 Yearbook. (Yearbook Ser.). 300p. 1999. 30.00 (0-9648794-4-1) Dumont Inst.
— Commentaries on the Supreme Court: 1997 Term. (Yearbook Ser.). 300p. 1998. 30.00 (0-9648794-3-3) Dumont Inst.
— Commentaries on the Supreme Court: 1998 Term. (Yearbook Ser.). 300p. 1999. 30.00 (0-9648794-7-6) Dumont Inst.
— The Economics & Politics of Eastern Europe. 300p. 1998. 25.00 (0-9648794-9-2) Dumont Inst.
— The Ethics of Tax Evasion. LC 98-73007. 300p. 1998. 25.00 (0-9648794-8-4) Dumont Inst.
— Insider Trading: Law, Economics & Ethics. 1999. 25.00 (1-892736-01-2) Dumont Inst.
— The Market Solution to Economic Development in Eastern Europe. LC 92-16214. 332p. 1992. lib. bdg. 99.95 (0-7734-9545-2) E Mellen.
— Palestine & Israel: Conflict & Change. 1998. 25.00 (1-892736-00-4) Dumont Inst.
McGee, Robert W., jt. auth. see Georges, Walter.
McGee, Robert W., jt. ed. see Greaves, Bettina B.
McGee, Rose F., jt. ed. see Clark, Jane C.
McGee, S., jt. auth. see Taylor, Maurice C.
McGee, S. W., jt. ed. see Bewley, James G.
***McGee, Samuel.** Building Successful Schools from Within. 225p. 1999. pap. text 29.95 (0-9700155-0-X) Quantum Mktg.
— Procedural Manual for Classroom Teachers: A Practical Guide for Improving Job Performance. 87p. 1992. pap. text 19.95 (0-9700155-1-8) Quantum Mktg.
McGee, Sharon J., jt. ed. see Addison, Joanne.
***McGee, Sherry.** Apple Jaleel - Pass It On. (Applekid's Chapter Bks.). (Illus.). 12p. (J). (gr. k-7). 2000. pap. 4.99 (0-9673591-3-9) Apple Bk Ctr.
— Apple Mack - How I Learned to Learn. (Applekid's Chapter Bks.). (Illus.). 12p. (J). (gr. k-7). 2000. pap. 4.99 (0-9673591-5-5) Apple Bk Ctr.
— Apple Neil - An Apple a Day. (Applekid's Chapter Bks.). (Illus.). 12p. (J). (gr. k-7). 2000. pap. 4.99 (0-9673591-4-7) Apple Bk Ctr.
— Applekid's Chapter Books: AppleJack "Everywhere I Go" (Illus.). 12p. (J). (gr. 1-6). 1999. pap. 4.99 (0-9673591-2-0) Apple Bk Ctr.
— Applekid's Chapter Books: AppleLonia "I Like to Read" (Illus.). 12p. (J). (gr. k-6). 1999. pap. 4.99 (0-9673591-0-4) Apple Bk Ctr.
***McGee, Sherry & Kelsey, Kim.** Applekid's Chapter Books: AppleJill "The World Is Science" (Illus.). 12p. (J). (gr. 1-6). 1999. pap. 4.99 (0-9673591-1-2) Apple Bk Ctr.
McGee, Sherwood W., ed. see National Powder Metallurgy Conference Staff.
McGee, Terence, jt. auth. see Armstrong, Warwick.
McGee, Teresa R. The Comforter: Stories of Loss & Rebirth. LC 96-12528. 144p. 1997. pap. 14.95 (0-8245-1567-6) Crossroad NY.
McGee, Therese. Real Grandmas Don't Bake Cookies Anymore. Conn, Carmelita J., ed. LC 88-23949. (Illus.). 96p. (Orig.). 1988. pap. text 8.00 (0-943663-00-8) San Joaquin Eagle.
McGee, Thomas D. Principles & Methods of Temperature Measurement. LC 87-22926. 608p. 1988. 175.00 (0-471-62767-4) Wiley.
McGee, Timothy, ed. Taking a Stand: Essays in Honour of John Beckwith. 320p. 1995. text 65.00 (0-8020-0583-7) U of Toronto Pr.
McGee, Timothy J. Medieval & Renaissance Music: A Performer's Guide. LC 86-149637. (Illus.). 303p. reprint ed. pap. 94.00 (0-8357-6363-3, 203571700069) Bks Demand.
— Medieval & Renaissance Music: A Performer's Guide. (Illus.). 304p. 1988. reprint ed. pap. 18.95 (0-8020-6729-8) U of Toronto Pr.
— Medieval Instrumental Dances. LC 88-45498. (Music: Scholarship & Performance Ser.). (Illus.). 192p. 1990. spiral bd. 29.95 (0-253-33353-9) Ind U Pr.
— The Music of Canada. LC 84-27318. 257p. (C). 1985. pap. text 22.25 (0-393-95376-9) Norton.
McGee, Timothy J. & Rosenfield, Randall A. The Sound of Medieval Song: Ornamentation & Vocal Style According to the Treatises. (Oxford Monographs on Music). (Illus.). 216p. 1998. text 68.00 (0-19-816619-2) OUP.
McGee, Timothy J., jt. auth. see Eastman, Sheila J.
McGee, Tom. Betty Grable: The Girl with the Million Dollar Legs. LC 94-31145. 400p. 1995. pap. 19.95 (1-879511-18-5, Vestal Pr) Madison Bks UPA.
McGee, Tom, ed. see Ceolin, David.
McGee, Vann. Truth, Vagueness, & Paradox: An Essay on the Logic of Truth. LC 89-27742. 246p. (C). 1990. 39.95 (0-87220-087-6) Hackett Pub.
McGee, Vern W., tr. see Bakhtin, Mikhail M.
McGee, Vernon. Ezra, Nehemiah, Esther. (Thru the Bible Commentary Ser.). 1997. pap. text 6.97 (0-7852-0427-X) Nelson.
McGee, W. J. & Governors in the White House Conference Staff, eds. Proceedings of the Governors in the White House Conference, Washington, D.C., May 13-15, 1908. LC 72-2855. (Use & Abuse of America's Natural Resources Ser.). 1972. 35.95 (0-405-04519-0) Ayer.
***McGee, Wanda.** Invisible Currents: Nature's Lessons for the Mind & Heart. LC 99-50201. (Illus.). 96p. 1999. pap. 12.95 (0-917917-13-8) Miles River.
McGee, Warren & Nixon, Ron, photos by. The Northern Pacific Railway. 2nd ed. (Illus.). 1996. 49.95 (0-915370-10-7) NW Short Line.
***McGee, William L.** The Amphians Are Coming: Emergence of the 'Gator Navy & Its Revolutionary New Landing Craft in World War II, 3 vols. unabridged ed. (Amphibious Operations in the South Pacific in WW II: Vol. 1). (Illus.). 300p. 2000. pap. write for info. (0-9701678-6-5, BMC Comuns) BMC CA.
McGee, William L. Bluejacket Odyssey: Guadalcanal to Bikini Atoll, Naval Armed Guard in the Pacific. LC 97-61096. Vol. 3. (Illus.). 544p. 1997. 35.00 (1-889901-05-9) Glencannon Pr.
McGee, Willie, jt. auth. see Morris, John.
McGeehan, Charles, tr. see Schierbeek, Bert.
***McGeehan, Jane Rasp, ed.** Transformations: Leadership for Brain-Compatible Learning. rev. ed. 276p. 1999. pap. text 24.95 (1-878631-54-3, Pub. by S Kovalik) Bks Educators.
McGeehan, John. Barron's Regents Exams & Answers: U. S. History & Government. 1996. pap. 5.95 (0-8120-3344-2) Barron.

M

An Asterisk (*) at the beginning of an entry indicates that the title is appearing for the first time.

— Barron's Regents Power Pack: U. S. History & Government. 2nd ed. 1995. pap., student ed. 15.95 (*0-8120-8274-5*) Barron.

McGeehan, John & Gall, Morris. Let's Review: U. S. History & Government. 2nd ed. LC 94-29829. (Review Course Ser.). 1995. pap. 12.95 (*0-8120-1962-8*) Barron.

***McGeehan, John & Gall, Morris.** Let's Review: U. S. History & Government. 3rd ed. LC 00-31243. (Review Course Ser.). 2001. write for info. (*0-7641-1346-1*) Barron.

McGeehan, Michael, et al. World Wide Web Database Developer's Guide with Microsoft SQL Server 6.5. 600p. 1999. 49.99 (*1-57521-178-5*) Sams.

McGeehan, P. J., ed. Advances in Powder Metallurgy - 1990, 3 vols. LC 90-42924. (Illus.). 1712p. 1990. text 100.00 (*1-878954-00-8*) Metal Powder.

— Advances in Powder Metallurgy, 1990, Vol. 1. LC 90-42924. (Illus.). 624p. 1990. text 57.50 (*1-878954-01-6*) Metal Powder.

— Advances in Powder Metallurgy, 1990, Vol. 2. LC 90-42924. (Illus.). 576p. 1990. text 57.50 (*1-878954-02-4*) Metal Powder.

— Advances in Powder Metallurgy, 1990, Vol. 3. LC 90-42924. (Illus.). 512p. 1990. text 57.50 (*1-878954-03-2*) Metal Powder.

McGeehee, jt. auth. see Horton.

McGeehee, Ralph W. Deadly Deceits: My Twenty-Five Years in the CIA. 1990. pap. 9.95 (*0-941781-06-2*) IMA NYC.

M

McGeeney, John, jt. auth. see Grote, Jim.

McGeer, Edith G., et al, eds. Kainic Acid As a Tool in Neurobiology. LC 78-55812. 283p. 1978. reprint ed. pap. 87.80 (*0-608-00322-0*, 206103900007) Bks Demand.

McGeer, Eric. Sowing the Dragon's Teeth: Byzantine Warfare in the Tenth Century. LC 94-29133. 405p. 1996. 40.00 (*0-88402-224-2*, Dumbarton Rsch Lib) Dumbarton Oaks.

McGeer, Gerald G. Conquest of Poverty: A Challenge to the Money Power Bankers. 1979. lib. bdg. 59.95 (*0-8490-2901-5*) Gordon Pr.

McGeer, P. L., et al. Molecular Neurobiology of the Mammalian Brain. 2nd ed. LC 86-25333. (Illus.). 800p. (C). 1987. pap. text 49.50 (*0-306-42511-4*, Kluwer Plenum) Kluwer Academic.

— Molecular Neurobiology of the Mammalian Brain. 2nd ed. LC 86-25333. (Illus.). 800p. (C). 1987. 95.00 (*0-306-42329-4*, Plenum Trade) Perseus Pubng.

McGeer, Patrick C. & Brayton, Robert K. Integrating Functional & Temporal Domains in Logic Design: The False Path Problem & Its Implications. 1991. text 95.00 (*0-7923-9163-2*) Kluwer Academic.

McGehee & Kraft. MS SQL Server 7.0 Professional Reference. 1997. 59.99 (*1-56205-779-0*) New Riders Pub.

McGehee, Brad. MCSE Training Guide: SQL Server 6.5 Administration. LC 98-129914. (MCSE Training Guides). 1997. pap. text 49.99 (*1-56205-726-X*) New Riders Pub.

***McGehee, Brad & Kraft, Robert A.** Practical Microsoft SQL Server 7. 750p. 1999. pap. 29.99 (*0-7897-2147-3*) S&S Trade.

McGehee, Brad M. Using Microsoft SQL Server 7. LC 98-85911. 1998. pap. 29.99 (*0-7897-1628-3*) Que.

McGehee, Fielding, III, jt. ed. see Moore, Rebecca.

McGehee, Fielding M., 3rd. A Streak of Scarlet: Remembrances of Hilliary Moore. 230p. 1997. pap. 12.00 (*0-9663764-0-4*) Reivers Pr.

McGehee, Fielding M., III, jt. ed. see Moore, Rebecca.

McGehee, Jack. The Plaintiff's Case: From Voir Dire to Verdict. 1997. 85.00 (*1-891216-51-1*); pap. 65.00 (*1-891216-50-3*) TX Trial Lawyers.

McGehee, Linda. Creating Texture with Textiles! LC 98-84108. (Illus.). 128p. 1998. pap. 21.95 (*0-87341-657-0*, TWT) Krause Pubns.

***McGehee, Linda.** Simply Sensational Bags: How to Stitch & Embellish Handbags, Totes & Satchels. LC 00-100067. (Illus.). 128p. 2000. pap. 21.95 (*0-87341-848-4*, HTS) Krause Pubns.

McGehee, Linda F. A Companion Project Book: For Texture with Textiles. (Illus.). 40p. 1994. pap. text 14.95 (*0-9637160-1-8*) Ghees.

— More Texture with Textiles. 52p. 1993. pap. text 14.95 (*0-9637160-0-X*) Ghees.

McGehee, Liz, ed. Folded Fabric Fun. LC 97-46557. (Illus.). 30p. 1997. reprint ed. pap. 11.95 (*0-943574-69-2*) Martingale & Co.

McGehee, Liz, ed. see Kimball, Jeana.

McGehee, Liz, ed. see Thomas, Donna L.

McGehee, Lucius P. Due Process of Law under the Federal Constitution. (Studies in Constitutional Law). x, 452p. 1981. reprint ed. 48.50 (*0-8377-0837-0*, Rothman) W S Hein.

McGehee, Minnie L., ed. River Boat Echoes: Batteaux in Virginia. (Illus.). viii, 77p. (Orig.). 1995. pap. 10.00 (*1-888838-02-7*) VA Canals & Navigat.

McGehee, Nicole. Regret Not a Moment. 528p. 1994. mass mkt. 5.99 (*0-446-60071-7*, Pub. by Warner Bks) Little.

McGehee, O. C., jt. auth. see Graham, C. C.

***McGehee, O. Carruth.** An Introduction to Complex Analysis. 448p. 2000. 84.95 (*0-471-33233-X*) Wiley.

McGehee, Peggy L., jt. auth. see Horton, Andrew M.

McGehee, Peter. Boys Like Us. (Stonewall Inn Editions Ser.). 176p. 1992. pap. 9.95 (*0-312-06913-8*) St Martin.

— Sweetheart. (Stonewall Inn Editions Ser.). 224p. 1993. pap. 8.95 (*0-312-09399-3*) St Martin.

***McGehee, Ralph W.** Deadly Deceits: My 25 Years in the CIA. 1999. pap. text 12.95 (*1-876175-19-2*) Ocean Pr NJ.

McGehee, Robin, jt. auth. see Taylor, Robert.

McGehee, Robin A., jt. auth. see Taylor, Robert A.

McGehee, Scott, tr. see Barakat, Halim.

McGehee, Sharon, jt. auth. see Anderson, Chris.

McGeoch, A. J. Collected Poems. 125p. 1986. 30.00 (*0-905075-22-6*, Pub. by Wilfion Bks) Dufour.

McGeoch, C. C., jt. ed. see Goodrich, M. T.

McGeoch, Catherine C., jt. ed. see Johnson, David S.

McGeoch, Ian. The Princely Sailor: Mountbatten of Burma. LC 96-42448. (Illus.). 288p. 1996. 29.95 (*1-85753-161-2*, Pub. by Brasseys) Brasseys.

McGeoch, Lyle A. & Sleator, Daniel D., eds. On-Line Algorithms. LC 91-43417. (DIMACS Series in Doscrete Mathematics & Theoretical Computer Science: Vol. 7). 179p. 1992. text 32.00 (*0-8218-6596-X*, DIMACS/7C) Am Math.

McGeorge, Bundy & Kissinger, Henry A. The Dimensions of Diplomacy. Johnson, E. A., ed. LC 64-25072. 150p. reprint ed. pap. 46.50 (*0-608-14748-6*, 202585800046) Bks Demand.

McGeorge, Constance W. Boomer Goes to School. (Illus.). 32p. (J). (ps-1). 1996. 13.95 (*0-8118-1117-4*) Chronicle Bks.

— Boomer Goes to School. (Illus.). 32p. (J). (ps-1). 1998. pap. 5.95 (*0-8118-2020-3*) Chronicle Bks.

— Waltz of the Scarecrows. LC 97-1347. (Illus.). (J). (ps-2). 1998. 14.95 (*0-8118-1727-X*) Chronicle Bks.

***McGeorge, Constance W.** Boomer Va a la Escuela. (SPA.). 32p. (gr. k-2). 1999. pap. 6.95 (*0-8118-2472-1*) Chronicle Bks.

— Boomer Va a la Escuela. (Illus.). (J). 1999. 12.40 (*0-606-18040-0*) Turtleback.

McGeorge, Constance W. Boomer's Big Day. LC 93-27273. (Illus.). 32p. (J). 1994. 13.95 (*0-8118-0526-3*) Chronicle Bks.

— Boomer's Big Day. (Illus.). 32p. (J). (ps-1). 1996. pap. 5.95 (*0-8118-1492-0*) Chronicle Bks.

— Boomer's Big Surprise. LC 98-8434. (Boomer Ser.). (Illus.). 32p. (J). (ps-1). 1999. 14.95 (*0-8118-1977-9*) Chronicle Bks.

— Snow Riders. LC 94-47214. (Illus.). 32p. (J). 1995. 13.95 (*0-8118-0873-4*) Chronicle Bks.

— Snow Riders. (Illus.). 32p. (J). (ps-1). 1999. pap. 6.95 (*0-8118-2464-0*) Chronicle Bks.

McGeorge, Deborah M. The Job Seekers Guide to Success. LC 97-92983. 160p. (Orig.). 1997. pap. 13.50 (*1-57502-462-4*, PO1382) Morris Pubng.

McGeorge, H. David. Marine Auxiliary Machinery. 7th ed. LC 95-3360. (Illus.). 572p. 1995. 84.95 (*0-7506-1843-4*, Focal) Buttrwrth-Heinemann.

— Marine Electrical Equipment & Practice. 2nd ed. 160p. 1993. pap. 39.95 (*0-7506-1647-4*) Buttrwrth-Heinemann.

McGeorge, P. J., jt. auth. see Hallager, B. P.

McGeorge, W. D. & Palmer, Angela. Construction Management: New Developments. LC 97-10428. 1997. pap. 49.95 (*0-632-04258-3*) Blackwell Sci.

McGeown. Physiology. 1996. pap. text 22.95 (*0-443-05196-8*, W B Saunders Co) Harcrt Hlth Sci Grp.

McGeown, Mary G. Clinical Management of Electrolyte Disorders. 1983. text 135.00 (*0-89838-559-8*) Kluwer Academic.

McGeown, Mary G., ed. Clinical Management of Renal Transplantation. (Developments in Nephrology Ser.). 400p. (C). 1992. text 255.50 (*0-7923-1604-5*) Kluwer Academic.

McGerr, Rosemarie P. Chaucer's Open Books: Resistance to Closure in Medieval Discourse. LC 97-48787. (Illus.). 256p. 1998. 49.95 (*0-8130-1572-3*) U Press Fla.

McGerr, Rosemarie P., ed. The Pilgrimage of the Soul: A Critical Edition of the Middle English Dream Vision, Vol. I. (Medieval Texts Ser.: Vol. 16). 250p. 1990. text 20.00 (*0-8240-6617-0*) Garland.

McGervey, John D. Quantum Mechanics: Concepts & Applications. (Illus.). 408p. 1995. text 58.00 (*0-12-483545-7*) Acad Pr.

McGetrick, Mike. The Scrambler's Dozen. pap. 16.00 (*0-06-273685-X*) HarpC.

— The Scrambler's Dozen: The 12 Shots Every Golfer Needs to Score Like the Pros. LC 99-55095. 224p. 2000. 25.00 (*0-06-270246-7*) HarpC.

McGettigan, Anthony. Journey to Deep Freedom: Toward Abundance in All Things: Guidebook for the Ascending Human Consciousness. 124p. (Orig.). 1995. pap. 12.50 (*1-887873-00-7*) A McGettigan.

McGettigan, Barbara & Henderson, Frances. Managing Your Career in Nursing. 2nd ed. LC 95-102019. 1994. 24.95 (*0-88737-629-0*) Natl League Nurse.

McGettigan, Barbara O., jt. auth. see Henderson, Frances C.

***McGettigan, Donal.** Current Account & External Sustainability in the Baltics, Russia & Other Countries of the Former Soviet Union. LC 00-24645. (Occasional Paper Ser.). 2000. write for info. (*1-55775-826-3*) Intl Monetary.

McGettigan, James P. Complete Book of Drills for Winning Soccer. (Illus.). 264p. (C). 1980. text 27.95 (*0-13-156356-4*, Parker Publishing Co) P-H.

— Soccer Drills for Individual & Team Play. 240p. (C). 1986. text 27.95 (*0-13-815309-4*, Parker Publishing Co) P-H.

— Soccer Drills for Individual & Team Play. 240p. (C). 1989. pap. text 14.95 (*0-13-815366-3*) P-H.

***McGettigan, Timothy.** Utopia on Wheels: Blundering down the Road to Reality. LC 99-16475. 160p. 1999. pap. 26.50 (*0-7618-1465-5*) U Pr of Amer.

McGhee. Excimer Lasers in Ophthalmology. LC 97-166783. 453p. 1997. text 165.00 incl. audio (*0-7506-9785-7*, M3574) Buttrwrth-Heinemann.

— Introduction to Statistics. Date not set. pap. text, student ed. 19.50 (*0-314-87246-9*) West Pub.

McGhee. Quick & Fun Learning Activities for 1 Year Olds. (Illus.). 80p. 1996. pap. 8.95 (*1-55734-554-6*) Tchr Create Mat.

McGhee, A. Improvisation for Saxophone: The Scale Mode Approach. 136p. 1986. per. 12.95 (*0-7935-5426-8*, 50449860) H Leonard.

McGhee, Alison. Rainlight. LC 97-33039. 200p. 1998. 22.95 (*1-57601-006-6*) McGhee.

***McGhee, Alison.** Shadow Baby. LC 99-47315. 240p. 2000. 23.00 (*0-609-60632-8*) Harmony Bks.

McGhee-Anderson, Kathleen, jt. auth. see Hall, Monica.

***McGhee, Colin.** Rustic Birdhouses & Feeders. LC 99-86943. 144p. 2000. pap. 18.95 (*1-58017-137-0*) Storey Bks.

McGhee, Colin, jt. auth. see Reeve, Simon.

***McGhee, Fi.** Barn. 1999. 24.95 (*1-86154-003-5*) Booth-Clibborn.

McGhee, Fletcher. Awesome - The Power of Prayer. LC 97-67136. 112p. (Orig.). 1997. pap. 12.95 (*1-57197-076-2*) Pentland Pr.

— Bermuda Triangle. LC 97-91222. 149p. 1998. 15.95 (*0-533-12599-5*) Vantage.

— Devil's Ditch: Ol'Whitey & the Shivaree. 128p. 1999. pap. 13.00 (*0-8059-4612-8*) Dorrance.

***McGhee, Fletcher & Wolf, Jared.** Night of the Carnival. 209p. 1999. pap. write for info. (*0-7541-1066-4*, Pub. by Minerva Pr) Unity Dist.

***McGhee, George.** Theoretical Morphology: The Concept & Its Applications. LC 98-8660. (Perspectives in Paleobiology & Earth Ser.). 316p. 1998. pap. 29.95 (*0-231-10617-3*); lib. bdg. 55.00 (*0-231-10616-5*) Col U Pr.

McGhee, George C. International Community: A Goal for a New World Order. LC 92-10570. (Miller Center Series on a New World Order: Vol. 1). 1992. 42.50 (*0-8191-8538-8*); pap. 21.50 (*0-8191-8539-6*) U Pr of Amer.

— On the Front Line in the Cold War: An Ambassador Reports. LC 96-21321. 240p. 1997. 57.95 (*0-275-95649-0*, Praeger Pubs) Greenwood.

McGhee, George C., ed. Diplomacy for the Future. LC 87-3455. 118p. (Orig.). 1987. pap. text 13.00 (*0-8191-6488-7*); lib. bdg. 35.50 (*0-8191-6487-9*) U Pr of Amer.

McGhee, George C., et al, eds. National Interest & Global Goals. LC 89-36331. (Exxon Education Foundation Series on Rhetoric & Political Discourse: Vol. 16). 224p. 1989. pap. text 24.00 (*0-8191-7543-9*, Pub. by White Miller Center); lib. bdg. 46.00 (*0-8191-7542-0*, Pub. by White Miller Center) U Pr of Amer.

McGhee, George R., Jr. The Late Devonian Mass Extinctions: The Frasnian-Famennian Crisis. LC 95-38419. (Critical Moments in Paleobiology & Earth History Ser.). (Illus.). 378p. (C). 1996. 58.00 (*0-231-07504-9*); pap. 30.50 (*0-231-07505-7*) Col U Pr.

McGhee, J., et al, eds. Knowledge-Based Systems for Industrial Control. (Control Engineering Ser.: No. 44). 356p. 1990. 95.00 (*0-86341-221-1*, CE044) INSPEC Inc.

McGhee, Janice, jt. auth. see Watson, Lesley.

McGhee, Jerry R., jt. ed. see Kiyono, Hiroshi.

McGhee, Jery R., jt. ed. see Kiyono, Hiroshi.

McGhee, Jim. True Lies. LC 93-9537. (American University Studies: Theatre Arts: Ser. XXVI, Vol. 18). VII, 224p. (C). 1993. text 42.95 (*0-8204-2052-2*) P Lang Pubng.

McGhee, Ken. GaAs Reliability Workshop Proceedings. 105p. 1998. pap. 10.00 (*0-7908-0065-9*) Elec Ind Assn.

McGhee, Laura, et al. Three Novellas. Miller, Philip, ed. 178p. (Orig.). 1993. pap. 10.00 (*0-939391-17-1*) B Woodley Pr.

McGhee, Lucy K. Historical Records of Old Crab Orchard: Lincoln Co., Stanford. 117p. 1997. reprint ed. pap. 17.00 (*0-8328-6730-6*) Higginson Bk Co.

McGhee, Marla. Quick & Fun Learning Activities for 4-Year-Olds. LC 97-116793. 80p. 1997. pap. 6.95 (*1-55734-557-0*) Tchr Create Mat.

***McGhee, Michael.** Transformations of Mind: Philosophy As Spiritual Practice. LC 99-34667. 301p. (C). 2000. pap. 22.95 (*0-521-77753-4*); text 59.95 (*0-521-77169-2*) Cambridge U Pr.

McGhee, Michael, ed. Philosophy, Religion, & the Spiritual Life. LC 92-5707. (Royal Institute of Philosophy Supplements Ser.: No. 32). 261p. (C). 1992. pap. text 22.95 (*0-521-42196-9*) Cambridge U Pr.

McGhee, Michael, jt. auth. see Hammond, Robert H.

***McGhee, Millie.** Secrets Uncovered: J. Edgar Hoover - Passing for White? (Illus.). 252p. 2000. pap. 16.95 (*0-9701822-0-1*, Pub. by A Morris) Talion Pub.

McGhee, Paul. Health, Healing & Amuse System. 3rd ed. 304p. 1999. per. 20.00 (*0-7872-5797-4*, 41579701) Kendall-Hunt.

McGhee, Paul E. Health, Healing & the Amuse System: Humor As Survival Training. 2nd ed. 272p. 1996. per. 20.00 (*0-7872-2847-8*, 41284701) Kendall-Hunt.

— Humor & Children's Development: A Guide to Practical Applications. LC 88-37931. (Journal of Children in Contemporary Society: Vol. 20, Nos. 1-2). 280p. 1989. text 49.95 (*0-86656-681-3*) Haworth Pr.

McGhee, Paul E. & Chapman, Antony J., eds. Children's Humour. LC 79-40648. 336p. reprint ed. pap. 104.20 (*0-608-15934-4*, 203092700072) Bks Demand.

McGhee, Paul E. & Goldstein, Jeffrey H., eds. Handbook of Humor Research: Applied Studies, Vol. 2. (Illus.). 215p. 1983. 75.95 (*0-387-90853-6*) Spr-Verlag.

McGhee, Paul E., jt. ed. see Goldstein, Jeffrey H.

***McGhee, Quentin & Jones, Francis.** Hermeneutics. (Discovery Ser.). 98p. 1999. pap. text. write for info. (*1-891110-01-2*, ATTS Pubns) Africa Theolog Trng.

McGhee, Quentin & Kirigi, James. Homiletics 2. (FRE.). pap. text 5.00 (*2-912377-02-1*, Editions SAFT) Africa Theolog Trng.

McGhee, Quentin & Kirigi, James. Homiletics 2. (Discovery Ser.). 94p. 1999. pap. text. write for info. (*1-891110-05-5*) Africa Theolog Trng.

***McGhee, Quentin & Kirigi, James.** Homile'tique I. rev. ed. (Discovery Ser.).Tr. of Homiletics I. (FRE.). 166p. (C). 1999. pap. text 6.20i (*2-912377-06-4*, Editions SAFT) Africa Theolog Trng.

McGhee, Quentin & Kirigi, James. Homiletique 1. (Discovery Ser.).Tr. of Homiletics 1. (FRE.). 166p. 1999. pap. text 5.00i (*2-912377-01-3*, Editions SAFT) Africa Theolog Trng.

McGhee, Richard D. Guilty Pleasures: William Wordsworth's Poetry of Psychoanalysis. LC 92-81065. x, 351p. 1993. 49.50 (*0-87875-431-8*) Whitston Pub.

***McGhee, Richard D.** John Wayne: Actor, Artist, Hero. LC 89-43658. (Illus.). 399p. 1999. per. 25.00 (*0-7864-0752-2*, McFarland Cls) McFarland & Co.

McGhee, Richard D. Marriage, Duty, & Desire in Victorian Poetry & Drama. LC 80-11962. x, 318p. (C). 1980. 35.00 (*0-7006-0203-8*) U Pr of KS.

McGhee, Robert. Ancient Canada. (Illus.). 175p. 1992. 29.95 (*0-660-10795-3*, Pub. by CN Mus Civilization) U of Wash Pr.

— Ancient People of the Arctic. LC 97-102960. (Illus.). 272p. 1996. 35.95 (*0-7748-0553-6*) U of Wash Pr.

— Beluga Hunters: An Archaeological Reconstruction of the History & Culture of the Mackenzie Delta Kittegaryumiut. (Mercury Ser.: ASC No. 139). (Illus.). 142p. 1988. pap. 10.00 (*0-660-10784-8*, Pub. by CN Mus Civilization) U of Wash Pr.

— Canada Rediscovered. (Mercury Ser.). (Illus.). 176p. 1992. 29.95 (*0-660-12919-1*, Pub. by CN Mus Civilization) U of Wash Pr.

— Canadian Arctic Prehistory. (Canadian Prehistory Ser.). (Illus.). 136p. 1990. pap. 16.95 (*0-660-02477-2*, Pub. by CN Mus Civilization) U of Wash Pr.

McGhee, Robert, jt. auth. see Gordon, Kate.

McGhee, Robin. Offshore Investment Planning & Advice. 250p. 1996. pap. 120.00 (*0-85297-402-7*, Pub. by Chartered Bank) St Mut.

Mcghee, Robin. Offshore Practice & Administration. 300p. 1997. pap., wbk. ed. 120.00 (*0-85297-428-0*, Pub. by Chartered Bank) St Mut.

McGhee, Stephen, ed. see Meehan, Tim.

McGhee, Terrence. Water Supply & Sewerage. 6th ed. (Water Resources & Environmental Engineering Ser.). 704p. (C). 1991. 93.75 (*0-07-060938-1*); pap. text, teacher ed. 21.25 (*0-07-060939-X*) McGraw.

McGhie, Andrew. Psychology As Applied to Nursing. 8th ed. LC 83-7753. (Illus.). 329p. 1986. pap. text 26.00 (*0-443-02836-2*) Church.

McGhie, Andrew R., jt. auth. see Sloan, Gilbert J.

McGhie, Anna E. The Miracle Hand Around the World. 1989. pap. 8.99 (*0-88019-251-8*) Schmul Pub Co.

McGibbon, Barry. Managing Your Move to Object Technology: Guidelines & Strategies for a Smooth Transition. (Managing Object Technology Ser.: No. 2). 290p. 1995. pap. 34.95 (*0-13-242009-0*) Cambridge U Pr.

McGibbon, Ian. New Zealand & the Korean War: Combat Operations, Vol. II. (Illus.). 592p. 1997. 85.00 (*0-19-558343-4*) OUP.

***McGibbon, Ian, ed.** The Oxford Companion to New Zealand Military History. (Illus.). 720p. 2000. text 75.00 (*0-19-558376-0*) OUP.

McGibbon, Ian, ed. Undiplomatic Dialogue: Letters Between Carl Berendsen & Alister McIntosh, 1943-1952. (Auckland University Press Book). 328p. 1994. 29.95 (*1-86940-095-X*) OUP.

McGibbon, Phyllis, jt. auth. see Allen, Lynne.

McGibbon, Rob. The Backstreet Boys: Offical Biography. (Illus.). 128p. (Orig.). 1997. pap. 17.95 (*0-7522-2406-9*, Pub. by Boxtree) Trans-Atl Phila.

— Backstreet Boys: On the Road. (Illus.). 64p. (Orig.). 1999. pap. 19.95 (*1-891696-09-2*) BainBridgeBooks.

— Spice Power: The Inside Story of the Spice Girls. (Orig.). 1998. pap. 9.95 (*84-08-02335-7*) Planeta.

McGibbon, Rob, jt. auth. see McGibbon, Robin.

McGibbon, Robin. New Kids on the Block: The Whole Story by Their Friends. 1990. pap. 6.95 (*0-380-76344-3*, Avon Bks) Morrow Avon.

McGibbon, Robin & McGibbon, Rob. Simply Mick: Mick Hucknall of Simply Red - The Inside Story. (Illus.). 224p. 1994. pap. 15.95 (*0-297-81370-6*) Trafalgar.

McGiffen, Milt, Jr. & Neff, Michael W., eds. Weed Management in Horticultural Crops. (Illus.). 139p. 1997. pap. 29.95 (*0-9615027-8-9*) Am Soc Horticult.

McGiffen-Newkirk, Dawn. Homeowners' Planner: Decorating-Remodeling-Building. (Illus.). 38p. 1996. reprint ed. pap. text 7.95 (*0-9646730-1-0*) L D L Pubng.

McGiffert, Arthur C. Jonathan Edwards. LC 75-3134. (Philosophy in America Ser.). reprint ed. 45.00 (*0-404-59143-4*) AMS Pr.

McGiffert, Arthur C., Jr. Public Prayers. LC 83-83269. (Studies in Ministry & Parish Life). 44p. 1984. pap. 4.50 (*0-913552-24-0*) Exploration Pr.

McGiffert, Michael, ed. God's Plot: Puritan Spirituality in Thomas Shepard's Cambridge. rev. ed. LC 94-2899. 256p. 1994. pap. text 17.95 (*0-87023-915-5*); lib. bdg. 40.00 (*0-87023-926-0*) U of Mass Pr.

McGiffin, Heather & Brownley, Nancie, eds. Animals in Education. 160p. (Orig.). (gr. 9-12). 1980. pap. 9.95 (*0-937712-00-0*) Inst Study Animal.

McGiffin, Lee. Iron Scouts of the Confederacy. (Illus.). 158p. (YA). (gr. 7-12). 1993. pap. text 6.00 (*1-930092-19-9*, CLP29675) Christian Liberty.

McGiffin, Robert F. Furniture Care & Conservation. 3rd rev. ed. LC 89-6610. (American Association for State & Local History Book Ser.). (Illus.). 258p. 1992. reprint ed. pap. 22.95 (*0-942063-22-8*) AltaMira Pr.

Mcgill. Introduction to Dynamics. (Illus.). 600p. 1997. text. write for info. (*0-412-73180-0*, Chap & Hall NY) Chapman & Hall.

An Asterisk (*) at the beginning of an entry indicates that the title is appearing for the first time.

— Statics. (Illus.). 600p. 1997. text. write for info. (*0-412-73190-8*, Chap & Hall NY) Chapman & Hall.
***McGill & Wilmott.** Annotated Consumer Credit Code. 1999. pap. 60.00 (*0-455-21599-5*, 18157, Pub. by LBC Info Servs) Gaunt.
McGill, jt. auth. see Adler, A.
McGill, jt. auth. see Norheim.
McGill, A. The McGills: Celts, Ulstermen, & American Pioneers: History, Heraldry, & Tradition. (Illus.). 345p. 1989. reprint ed. pap. 52.00 (*0-8328-0863-6*); reprint ed. lib. bdg. 60.00 (*0-8328-0862-8*) Higginson Bk Co.
***McGill, Alice.** In the Hollow of Your Hand: Slave Lullabies. 2000. 18.00 (*0-618-10445-3*) HM.
— Miles' Song. LC 99-43157. 224p. (YA). (gr. 5-9). 2000. 15.00 (*0-395-97938-2*) HM.
McGill, Alice. Molly Bannaky. LC 96-3000. (Illus.). 32p. (J). (ps-3). 1999. 16.00 (*0-395-72287-X*) HM.
McGill, Allyson. Latin Grammar. 1977. pap. text 4.95 (*0-8120-5056-8*) Barron.
— The Swedish Americans. LC 96-36783. (Immigrant Experience Ser.). 120p. (YA). (gr. 5 up). 1997. 19.95 (*0-7910-4551-X*); pap. 9.95 (*0-7910-4552-8*) Chelsea Hse.
***McGill, Allyson F.** Encyclopedia of Gothic Literature. 2000. lib. bdg. 65.00 (*0-87436-996-7*) ABC-CLIO.
McGill, Ann. The Aumoniers: Craftsmen & Artists - A Family Memoir. LC 99-206623. (Illus.). 1998. 30.00 (*0-9666710-0-7*) Highlands Bks.
McGill, Ann & Wilson, Glynis. Mending Your Broken Heart: A Survival Kit. (Life Line Ser.). 128p. (Orig.). 1994. pap. 14.95 (*1-55059-091-X*) Temeron Bks.
McGill, Ann M. Hiring the Best. LC 93-4. 112p. 1993. pap. 10.95 (*1-55623-865-7*, Irwn Prfssnl) McGraw-Hill Prof.
— Supervising the Difficult Employee. LC 94-2845. (Business Skills Express Ser.). 120p. 1994. text 10.00 (*0-7863-0219-4*, Irwn Prfssnl) McGraw-Hill Prof.
McGill, D., jt. auth. see MacDonald, R.
McGill, Dan. Beneficiary in Life Insurance. 2nd ed. (C). 1956. 10.50 (*0-256-00662-8*, Irwn McGrw-H) McGrw-H Hghr Educ.
— Employer Guarantee of Pension Benefits. (C). 1974. 6.50 (*0-256-01704-2*, Irwn McGrw-H) McGrw-H Hghr Educ.
— Financing the Civil Service Retirement System. (C). 1979. 13.50 (*0-256-02250-X*, Irwn McGrw-H) McGrw-H Hghr Educ.
— Guaranty Fund for Private Pension Obligations. (C). 1970. 9.95 (*0-256-00659-8*, Irwn McGrw-H) McGrw-H Hghr Educ.
McGill, Dan M., ed. Social Security & Private Pension Plans: Competitive or Complementary? 200p. (C). 1977. text 20.95 (*0-256-01968-1*, Irwn McGrw-H) McGrw-H Hghr Educ.
— Social Security & Private Pension Plans: Competitive or Complementary?: A Compilation of Papers Presented at the 1976 Symposium for Institutional Members of the Pension Research Council of the Wharton School, University of Pennsylvania. LC 76-49315. (Ralph H. Blanchard Memorial Endowment Ser.: Vol. 1). 195p. 1977. reprint ed. pap. 60.50 (*0-608-05660-X*, 205971400007) Bks Demand.
McGill, Dan M. & Grubbs, Donald S. Fundamentals of Private Pensions. LC 88-10341. 813p. 1989. reprint ed. pap. 200.00 (*0-608-03638-2*, 206446400009) Bks Demand.
McGill, Dan M., et al. Fundamentals of Private Pensions. 7th rev. ed. LC 96-15518. (Pension Research Council Publications). (Illus.). 768p. 1996. text 79.95 (*0-8122-3380-8*) U of Pa Pr.
McGill, Daniel J. Forty Nights: Creation Centered Night Prayer. LC 93-21386. 288p. (Orig.). 1994. pap. 12.95 (*0-8091-3437-3*) Paulist Pr.
McGill, David. The Kid from Matata: Memories of a Postwar Pakeha Childhood. 112p. (C). 1988. 60.00 (*1-86934-011-6*, Pub. by Grantham Hse) St Mut.
McGill, David J. & King, Wilton W. Engineering Mechanics: An Introduction to Dynamics. 2nd ed. 608p. (C). 1989. text 60.95 (*0-534-91786-0*) PWS Pubs.
— Engineering Mechanics: An Introduction to Dynamics. 3rd ed. LC 94-33846. 608p. 1994. mass mkt. 111.95 (*0-534-93399-8*) PWS Pubs.
McGill, David J. & King, Wilton W. Engineering Mechanics: An Introduction to Statics. 3rd ed. LC 94-37333. 1216p. (C). 1994. 127.95 (*0-534-93405-6*) PWS Pubs.
McGill, David J. & King, Wilton W. Engineering Mechanics: Statics. 2nd ed. 600p. (C). 1989. text 63.95 (*0-534-91788-7*) PWS Pubs.
McGill, David J. & King, Wilton W. Engineering Mechanics: Statics. 3rd ed. LC 94-33845. 600p. 1994. pap. 111.95 (*0-534-93393-9*) PWS Pubs.
McGill, Dott. The Ol' Cookbook. (Illus.). 240p. (Orig.). 1992. pap. 13.95 (*0-935069-13-5*) White Oak Pr.
McGill, Fiona, et al. Statistics: Complete Advanced Level Mathematics. (Illus.). 552p. (YA). (gr. 11 up). 1999. pap. 43.50 (*0-7487-3560-7*, Pub. by S Thornes Pubs) Trans-Atl Phila.
McGill, Frances. Go Not Gently: Letters from a Patient with Amyotrophic Lateral Sclerosis. Kutscher, Lillian G., ed. LC 79-48047. (Foundation of Thanatology Ser.). 1980. lib. bdg. 20.95 (*0-405-12643-3*) Ayer.
McGill-Franzen, Anne. Shaping the Preschool Agenda: Early Literacy, Public Policy, & Professional Beliefs. LC 91-34722. (SUNY Series, Literacy, Culture, & Learning: Theory & Practice). (Illus.). 227p. (C). 1992. text 64.50 (*0-7914-1195-8*); pap. text 21.95 (*0-7914-1196-6*) State U NY Pr.
Mcgill, G. Building on the Past: A Guide to the Archaeology & Development Process. LC 94-79769. (Illus.). 392p. (C). 1995. 90.00 (*0-419-17690-X*, E & FN Spon) Routledge.
Mcgill, Gordon. Stallion. 1991. pap. 3.95 (*1-55773-449-6*, MICHIE) LEXIS Pub.
McGill, Guy, ed. see Durlacher, James V.
McGill, Ian & Beaty, Liz. Action Learning: A Guide for Professional, Management & Educational Development. 2nd rev. ed. LC 95-222645. 237p. 1995. pap. 29.95 (*0-7494-1534-7*, Kogan Pg Educ) Stylus Pub VA.
McGill, Ian, jt. auth. see Brockbank, Anne.
McGill, Ian, jt. ed. see Weil, Susan W.
McGill, John & Baker, Dave. Tim Couch: A Passion for the Game. 192p. 1999. pap. 14.95 (*1-58382-037-X*, Pub. by Sports Masters) Partners-West.
McGill, John K., jt. auth. see Blair, W. Charles.
McGill, Joyce. Unforgivable. 1997. per. 3.99 (*0-373-48349-X*, 1-48349-4) Harlequin Bks.
McGill, Kevin, jt. auth. see Dunn, George, Jr.
McGill, L. Jerome, jt. auth. see Norheim, Carol.
Mcgill, Leonard. Chiropractor's Health Book. LC 96-23966. 1997. pap. 16.00 (*0-517-88818-1*, Crown) Crown Pub Group.
McGill, Lyndon. Mating Game: What Every Woman Should Know. LC 91-91486. (Illus.). 208p. 1992. pap. 12.95 (*0-9631771-0-9*) Sundial Pr.
McGill, M., ed. Bibliotheca Susanna: A Used Book Sales Record. 3rd ed. 322p. 1993. 49.95 (*0-9623826-0-4*) Chinook OR.
McGill, Marci. Sun Through the Window. LC 95-79862. (Illus.). 64p. (J). (gr. 1-4). 1996. pap. 9.95 (*1-56397-454-1*) Boyds Mills Pr.
McGill, Mary M. Stories to Invite Faith-Sharing: Experiencing the Lord Through the Seasons. LC 92-37. (Illus.). 144p. (Orig.). 1992. pap. 8.95 (*0-89390-230-6*) Resource Pubns.
McGill, Marylyn E., jt. auth. see Cleveland, William C.
McGill, Meredith, ed. see Blair, W. Charles & McGill, John K.
McGill, Michael & Slocum, John W. The Smarter Organization: How to Build a Business That Learns & Adapts to Marketplace Needs. 304p. 1994. 34.95 (*0-471-59846-1*) Wiley.
McGill, Michael, jt. auth. see Van Houweling, Douglas.
McGill, Michael E. Organization Development for Operating Managers. LC 76-50051. 189p. reprint ed. pap. 58.60 (*0-608-12404-4*, 205213900040) Bks Demand.
McGill, Nancy L. & Nichols, Trudy. Disney's The Hunchback of Notre Dame. (Look & Find Ser.). (Illus.). 24p. (J). (gr. k-6). 1996. lib. bdg. 14.95 (*1-56674-179-3*, HTS Bks) Forest Hse.
McGill, Nancy L., et al. Disney's The Hunchback of Notre Dame. LC 97-161949. (J). 1996. write for info. (*0-7853-1644-2*) Pubns Intl Ltd.
McGill, Nicole. Kindred Spirits: Family Legends & Childhood Memories. LC 97-68985. (Illus.). 66p. 1997. pap. write for info. (*1-57502-559-0*, PO1621) Morris Pubng.
McGill, Ormond. Chalk Talks! The Magical Art of Drawing with Chalk. LC 95-1952. (Illus.). 80p. (J). (gr. 3-6). 1995. lib. bdg. 24.90 (*1-56294-669-2*) Millbrook Pr.
— Grieve No More, Beloved: The Book of Delight. 115p. 1995. 14.95 (*1-899836-00-4*, Pub. by Crown Hse) LPC Group.
— Hypnotism & Meditation. England, Diane L. & Mignosa, Charles, eds. 99p. (Orig.). (C). 1981. audio 14.95 (*0-930298-08-X*) Westwood Pub Co.
— Hypnotism & Mysticism of India. 2nd ed. (Illus.). 208p. (C). 1979. reprint ed. text 22.50 (*0-930298-01-2*) Westwood Pub Co.
— The New Encyclopedia of Stage Hypnotism. (Illus.). 608p. 1999. reprint ed. 55.00 (*1-899836-02-0*, Pub. by Crown Hse) LPC Group.
— Professional Stage Hypnotism. (Illus.). 203p. 1994. reprint ed. pap. 14.95 (*0-930298-03-9*) Westwood Pub Co.
— The Search for Cosmic Consciousness: The Book Einstein Would Have Loved. 120p. 1998. pap. 19.95 (*0-912559-52-7*) Creativity Unltd Pr.
— Seeing the Unseen: A Past Life Revealed Through Hypnotic Regression. 257p. 1997. pap. 19.95 (*1-899836-05-5*, Pub. by Crown Hse) LPC Group.
McGill, Ormond & Stockwell, Shelley. Everything You Ever Wanted to Know about Everything. LC 97-199049. (Illus.). 1998. pap. 14.95 (*0-912559-29-2*) Creativity Unltd Pr.
McGill, Ormond, jt. auth. see Silver, Tom.
McGill, Ralph. The South & the Southerner. LC 92-6038. (Brown Thrasher Bks.). 328p. 1992. reprint ed. pap. 15.95 (*0-8203-1443-9*) U of Ga Pr.
— Southern Encounters: Southerners of Note in Ralph McGill's South. Logue, Calvin M., ed. LC 83-953. 344p. 1982. 23.50 (*0-86554-050-0*, MUP-H048) Mercer Univ Pr.
McGill, Robert. Moving to the Country. LC 86-50758. (Illus.). 187p. (Orig.). (C). 1987. pap. 8.95 (*0-935069-17-8*) White Oak Pr.
McGill, Ronald. Institutional Development: A Third World City Management Perspective. LC 96-2598. 256p. 1996. text 59.95 (*0-312-15819-X*) St Martin.
McGill, T. C., et al, eds. Growth & Optical Properties of Wide-Gap II - VI Low-Dimensional Semoconductors. (NATO ASI Series B, Physics: Vol. 200). (Illus.). 372p. 1989. 89.50 (*0-306-43221-8*, Plenum Trade) Perseus Pubng.
McGill University, Graduate Studies & Research Sta. McGill University Thesis Directory Vol. 1: 1881-1959. Spitzer, Frank & Silvester, Elizabeth, eds. LC 78-317433. 776p. reprint ed. pap. 200.00 (*0-7837-1166-2*, 204169500022) Bks Demand.
— McGill University Thesis Directory Vol. 2: 1960-1973. rev. ed. Spitzer, Frank & Silvester, Elizabeth, eds. LC 78-317433. 871p. reprint ed. pap. 200.00 (*0-7837-4724-1*, 204169500002) Bks Demand.
McGill, Vivian J. Schopenhauer. LC 77-159487. (Studies in Philosophy: No. 40). 1971. lib. bdg. 75.00 (*0-8383-1258-6*) M S G Haskell Hse.
Mcgill, W. B. Environmental Impacts of Soil Component Interactions Vol. II: Toxic Metals, Other Inorganics, & Microbial Activities. LC 95-4071. 304p. 1995. lib. bdg. 95.00 (*0-87371-915-8*, L915) Lewis Pubs.
Mcgill, W. J. La Jolla Cancer Research Foundation: The Miracle on Torrey Pines Mesa. LC 95-81189. (Illus.). 224p. 1995. write for info. (*0-9647206-0-4*) La Jolla Cancer Res.
McGill, William A., ed. see Wilcox, Frank N.
McGill, William J., Jr. Maria Theresa. LC 85-17856. (Twayne's Rulers & Statesmen of the World Ser.). 169p. (C). 1972. lib. bdg. 17.95 (*0-8290-1738-0*) Irvington.
McGill, William J. The Rock Springs Chronicles. LC 98-45195. 192p. 1999. pap. 12.95 (*1-56474-299-7*) Fithian Pr.
McGillem, C. D., jt. auth. see Cooper, G. R.
McGillem, Clare D. & Cooper, George R. Continuous & Discrete Signal & System Analysis. 3rd ed. (Illus.). 108p. (C). 1995. pap. text. write for info. (*0-03-051022-8*) OUP.
McGillem, Clare D. & McLauchlan, William P. Hermes Bound: The Policy & Technology of Telecommunications. LC 77-86267. (Science & Society: Series in Science, Technology, & Human Values: Vol. 2). (Illus.). 304p. 1978. pap. 8.95 (*0-931682-03-7*) Purdue U Pubns.
McGillem, Clare D., jt. auth. see Cooper, George R.
***McGillick, Paul.** Alex Popov - Buildings & Projects. (Illus.). 144p. 2001. 79.00 (*3-932565-18-5*) Edition A Menges.
McGillicuddy, Dan, tr. see Redonnet, Marie.
McGilligan. Tender Comrades. 800p. 1999. pap. 19.95 (*0-312-20031-5*) St Martin.
McGilligan, Pat. Backstory 2: Interviews with Screenwriters of the 1940s & 1950s. LC 85-28949. (Illus.). 1997. pap. 19.95 (*0-520-20908-7*, Pub. by U CA Pr) Cal Prin Full Svc.
— Backstory 3: Interviews with Screenwriters of the 1960s. LC 96-44753. (Illus.). 418p. 1997. 45.00 (*0-520-20426-3*, Pub. by U CA Pr); pap. 24.95 (*0-520-20427-1*, Pub. by U CA Pr) Cal Prin Full Svc.
McGilligan, Pat, ed. Ed Elson: I Told You I Was Serious. 1985. pap. 2.00 (*0-685-10176-2*) Quixote.
McGilligan, Pat, ed. see Riskin, Robert.
***McGilligan, Patrick.** Alfred Hitchcock. 2001. write for info. (*0-06-039322-X*, ReganBks) HarperTrade.
— Alfred Hitchcock. 2001. pap. write for info. (*0-06-098827-4*, ReganBks) HarperTrade.
McGilligan, Patrick. Cagney: The Actor As Auteur. (Quality Paperbacks Ser.). (Illus.). 1980. reprint ed. pap. 6.95 (*0-306-80120-5*) Da Capo.
***McGilligan, Patrick.** Clint Eastwood. 1999. 29.95 (*0-00-255528-X*, Pub. by HarpC) Trafalgar.
— Clint's World. write for info. (*0-393-04657-5*) Norton.
— Film Crazy. LC 00-25482. 288p. 2000. text 23.95 (*0-312-26131-4*) St Martin.
McGilligan, Patrick. Fritz Lang: The Nature of the Beast. LC 96-30622. (Illus.). 480p. 1997. text 30.00 (*0-312-13247-6*) St Martin.
— Fritz Lang: The Nature of the Beast. 560p. 1998. pap. 19.95 (*0-312-19454-4*) St Martin.
— Jack's Life: A Biography of Jack Nicholson. 512p. 1996. pap. 14.00 (*0-393-31378-6*, Norton Paperbks) Norton.
McGilligan, Patrick, ed. Backstory: Interviews with Screenwriters of Hollywood's Golden Age. (Illus.). 1997. pap. 18.95 (*0-520-05689-2*, Pub. by U CA Pr) Cal Prin Full Svc.
McGilligan, Patrick & Buhle, Paul. Tender Comrades: A Backstory of the Hollywood Blacklist. LC 97-16178. 800p. 1997. text 35.00 (*0-312-17046-7*) St Martin.
McGilligan, Patrick, ed. see Riskin, Robert.
McGillion, Frank. The Opening Eye. 1991. pap. 10.95 (*0-904575-03-9*) Sigo Pr.
McGillis, Daniel. Community Mediation Programs: Developments & Challenges. (Illus.). 99p. (C). 1999. pap. text 20.00 (*0-7881-7670-6*) DIANE Pub.
McGillis, K. A., jt. auth. see Presley, M. W.
McGillis, Roderick. Literary Theory & Children's Literature. 1996. 22.95 (*0-8057-7810-1*, Twyne) Mac Lib Ref.
— A Little Princess. 1996. 29.00 (*0-8057-8818-2*, Twyne) Mac Lib Ref.
— A Little Princess. (Illus.). 144p. 1996. pap. 18.00 (*0-8057-8819-0*, Twyne) Mac Lib Ref.
— The Nimble Reader: Literary Theory & Children's Literature. LC 95-36099. 1996. 30.00 (*0-8057-9033-0*, Hall Reference) Macmillan.
McGillis, Roderick, ed. For the Childlike: George MacDonald's Fantasies for Children. LC 92-8991. (Children's Literature Association Ser.). 242p. 1992. 31.00 (*0-8108-2459-0*) Scarecrow.
***McGillis, Roderick, ed.** Voices of the Other: Children's Literature & the Postcolonial Context. (Children's Literature & Culture Ser.: Vol. 10). 250p. 1999. 55.00 (*0-8153-3284-X*, H2126) Garland.
McGillivray. America at the Polls, 1960-1996: Kennedy to Clinton - A Handbook of Presidential Election Statistics. LC 99-225764. 925p. 1998. 200.00 (*1-56802-322-7*) Congr Quarterly.
McGillivray, Alan. Teaching Scottish Literature: Curriculum & Classroom Applications. 192p. 1997. pap. 35.00 (*0-7486-0930-X*, Pub. by Edinburgh U Pr) Col U Pr.
McGillivray, Alice V. Congressional & Gubernatorial Primaries, 1991-1992: A Handbook of Election Statistics. LC 93-11872. 265p. (C). (gr. 11). 1993. text 142.00 (*0-87187-906-9*) Congr Quarterly.
— Congressional & Gubernatorial Primaries 1993-1994: A Handbook of Election Statistics. LC 93-11872. 352p. (YA). (gr. 11). 1995. text 142.00 (*0-87187-899-2*) Congr Quarterly.
— Presidential Primaries & Caucuses, 1992: A Handbook of Election Statistics. LC 92-33506. 294p. (YA). 1993. text 142.00 (*0-87187-890-9*) Congr Quarterly.
McGillivray, Alice V. & Scammon, Richard M. America at the Polls: Harding to Eisenhower; A Handbook of Presidential Statistics. 937p. (C). 1998. text 350.00 (*1-56802-376-6*) Congr Quarterly.
McGillivray, Alice V. & Scammon, Richard M., eds. America at the Polls: A Handbook of American Presidential Election Statistics Vol. 2: Kennedy to Clinton, 1960-1992. LC 94-30937. 937p. (YA). 1994. text 200.00 (*1-56802-058-9*) Congr Quarterly.
McGillivray, Alice V., jt. auth. see Cook, Rhodes.
McGillivray, Alice V., jt. auth. see Scammon, Richard A.
McGillivray, Alice V., jt. auth. see Scammon, Richard M.
McGillivray, Alice V., ed. see Scammon, Richard A.
McGillivray, Anne. Governing Childhood. LC 96-32163. (Issues in Law & Society Ser.). (Illus.). 272p. 1997. pap. 28.95 (*1-85521-840-2*, Pub. by Dartmth Pub); text 78.95 (*1-85521-833-X*, Pub. by Dartmth Pub) Ashgate Pub Co.
McGillivray, D. J. & Makinson, R. O. Grevillea: Proteaceae. (Miegunyah Press Ser.: No. 1:9). 480p. 1993. 225.00 (*0-522-84439-1*, Pub. by Melbourne Univ Pr) Paul & Co Pubs.
McGillivray, David. Doing Rude Things: History of the British Sex Film. (Illus.). 141p. 1995. pap. 19.95 (*0-9517012-2-3*, Pub. by Sun Tavern Flds) AK Pr Dist.
McGillivray, David & Zerlin, Walter. They Came from Mars & Landed Outside the Farndale Avenue Church Hall in Time for the Townswomen's Guild's Coffee Morning: A Comedy. LC 88-215463. 46 p. 1988. write for info. (*0-573-01665-8*) S French Trade.
McGillivray, E. J. & Parkington, M. Insurance Law. (C). 1988. 1110.00 (*0-7855-4130-6*, Pub. by Witherby & Co) St Mut.
McGillivray, Mark & Morrissey, Oliver, eds. Evaluating Economic Liberalization. LC 93-47023. (Case Studies in Economic Development: Vol. 4). 240p. 1999. text 79.95 (*0-312-22569-5*) St Martin.
McGillivray, Mark & Smith, Gary, eds. Australia & Asia. 256p. 1998. pap. text 35.00 (*0-19-553905-2*) OUP.
McGillivray, Murray. Memorization in the Transmission of the Middle English Romances. LC 90-3313. (Albert Bates Lord Studies in Oral Tradition: Vol. 5). 152p. 1990. text 10.00 (*0-8240-3423-6*, 1275) Garland.
McGilloway, Olly. Greyhood. 148p. 1988. pap. 12.95 (*0-85640-401-2*, Pub. by Blackstaff Pr) Dufour.
— McGilloway's Ireland. (Illus.). 288p. 1995. pap. 29.00 (*0-85640-540-X*, Pub. by Blackstaff Pr) Dufour.
McGilly, Frank. An Introduction to Canada's Public Social Services: Understanding Income & Health Programs. 2nd ed. LC 98-205027. 327p. 1998. pap. text 29.95 (*0-19-541232-X*) OUP.
McGilly, Kate, ed. Classroom Lessons: Integrating Cognitive Theory & Classroom Practice. (Illus.). 333p. 1994. 47.50 (*0-262-13300-8*, Bradford Bks) MIT Pr.
— Classroom Lessons: Integrating Cognitive Theory & Classroom Practice. (Illus.). 333p. 1996. reprint ed. pap. text 21.50 (*0-262-63168-7*, Bradford Bks) MIT Pr.
McGilp, Jacqueline & Michael, Maureen. The Home-School Connection: Guidelines for Working with Parents. 86p. 1994. pap. text 17.50 (*0-435-08820-3*, 08820) Heinemann.
McGilton, Henry. Postscript by Example. (C). 1993. pap. text. write for info. (*0-201-59481-1*) Addison-Wesley.
McGilton, Henry & Compione, Mary. PostScript by Example. LC 92-19743. 640p. (C). 1992. pap. text 36.95 (*0-201-63228-4*) Addison-Wesley.
McGilvary, Daniel. A Half Century Among the Siamese & the Lao: An Autobiography. LC 77-87044. reprint ed. 33.00 (*0-404-16838-8*) AMS Pr.
***McGilvary, Marion.** Aphrodisiac. (Illus.). 96p. 2000. 16.95 (*1 85626 322-3*, Pub. by Cathie Kyle) Trafalgar.
McGilvary, Tony, jt. auth. see Webber, Marlene.
***McGilvery, Carole.** New Guide to Massage: A Guide to Massage Techniques for Health, Relaxation & Vitality. (Illus.). 96p. 1998. 16.95 (*1-85967-194-2*, Lorenz Bks) Anness Pub.
McGilvery, Laurence, ed. Artforum, 1962-1968: A Cumulative Index to the First Six Volumes. LC 65-8747. 1970. pap. 10.00 (*0-910938-18-0*); lib. bdg. 12.00 (*0-910938-19-9*) McGilvery.
McGilvery, Lynette, ed. An Index to the Paperback Little Magazines. 1980. pap. 7.95 (*0-910938-64-4*) McGilvery.
McGilvery, R. W. & Pogell, B. M., eds. Fructose-One, Six-Diphosphates & Its Role in Gluconeogenesis. 1964. 12.50 (*0-934454-40-X*) Lubrecht & Cramer.
McGilvray, Barbara, tr. see Verri, Pietro.
McGilvray, Dennis. Symbolic Heat: Gender, Health & Worship Among the Tamils of South India & Sri Lanka. LC 97-75689. 1998. pap. 15.00 (*0-944142-87-7*) Grantha.
McGilvray, Ian, tr. see Petrucciolі, Sandro.
McGilvray, James. Chomsky. LC 99-11074. (Key Contemporary Thinkers Ser.). 1999. 54.95 (*0-7456-1887-1*); pap. 21.95 (*0-7456-1888-X*) Blackwell Pubs.
McGilvray, James A. Tense, Reference & Worldmaking. 392p. 1991. 65.00 (*0-7735-0871-6*, Pub. by McG-Queens Univ Pr) CUP Services.
***McGimpsey, David.** Imagining Baseball: America's Pastime & Popular Culture. LC 99-43397. 208p. 2000. 29.95 (*0-253-33696-1*) Ind U Pr.
McGimpsey, David. Lardcake. LC 96-178003. 80p. 1996. pap. 12.00 (*1-55022-278-3*, Pub. by ECW) Genl Dist Srvs.
McGimpsey, Kevin & Neach, David. Golf Memorabilia. (Illus.). 176p. 1999. 34.95 (*0-85667-507-5*, Pub. by P Wilson) Antique Collect.

M

An Asterisk (*) at the beginning of an entry indicates that the title is appearing for the first time.

McGimsey, Charles R., III. Mariana Mesa: Seven Prehistoric Settlements in West-Central New Mexico. LC 79-57109. (Peabody Museum Papers: Vol. 72). (Illus.). 298p. 1980. pap. 25.00 (*0-87365-198-7*) Peabody Harvard.

McGimsey, Charles R., jt. ed. see Wiant, Michael D.

McGimsey, Robert H. Sweet Little Jesus Boy: A Soliloquy. 32p. 1973. pap. 2.95 (*0-911336-53-2*) Sci of Mind.

McGin, Colin, et al. A Universe of Consciousness: How Matter Becomes Imagination. 288p. 2000. 27.50 (*0-465-01376-7*, Pub. by Basic) HarpC.

Mcginely, Mary Christine. The Words of a Woman. LC 98-52332. 160p. 1999. 16.00 (*0-609-60411-2*) Random Hse Value.

McGing, B. C. The Foreign Policy of Mithridates VI Eupator, King of Pontus. (Mnemosyne Ser.: Supplement 89). ix, 204p. 1986. pap. 64.00 (*90-04-07591-7*) Brill Academic Pubs.

McGing, Brian C., ed. see Parke, H. W.

McGinity, James W. Aqueous Polymeric Coatings for Pharmaceutical Dosage Forms. 2nd ed. LC 96-43038. (Drugs & the Pharmaceutical Sciences Ser.: Vol. 79). (Illus.). 600p. 1996. text 199.00 (*0-8247-9773-6*) Dekker.

McGinley, Carol. Allyn's Embarrassing & Mysterious Irish Adventures. (Illus.). 192p. (J). (gr. 4-6). 1999. pap. 7.95 (*1-892671-00-X*) AGA Pub.

McGinley, Gerald & Waye, Vicki. Evidence Handbook. 270p. 1994. pap. 29.00 (*0-455-21264-3*, Pub. by LawBk Co) Gaunt.

McGinley, Gerald, jt. auth. see Waye, Vicki.

McGinley, Jerry. Joaquin Strikes Back. LC 97-32555. 158p. (YA). (gr. 5-10). 1998. 18.95 (*0-936389-58-3*) Tudor Pubs.

— Waupaca County: Seven A. M. 46p. 1986. 20.00 (*0-9616222-0-2*); pap. 5.50 (*0-9616222-1-0*) Indian Crossing Bks.

***McGinley, John W.** Lust & Spirituality: Episodic Ruminations Concerning Ontotheology & the Esoteric in Plato. unabridged ed. 46p. 2000. pap. 5.00 (*0-9679316-1-4*) Golem Enter.

McGinley, John W. Miasma: "Haecceitas" in Scotus, the Esoteric in Plato, & 'Other Related Matters' LC 96-28882. 226p. 1996. lib. bdg. 36.50 (*0-7618-0453-6*) U Pr of Amer.

— Shame! An Other Guide for the Perplexed. LC 93-18431. 310p. (Orig.). (C). 1993. pap. text 27.50 (*0-8191-9094-2*); lib. bdg. 49.50 (*0-8191-9093-4*) U Pr of Amer.

***McGinley, John W.** The Walking, Talking, Wounded: Episodic Ruminations on Things Jewish, Things Greek & Things Human. 153p. 2000. 5.00 (*0-9679316-0-6*) Golem Enter.

***McGinley, Marjorie M.** Casey's Journey. LC 00-190024. 192p. 2000. 18.95 (*0-8034-9421-1*, Avalon Bks) Bouregy.

— Footloose Conroy. LC 99-90724. 192p. 1999. 18.95 (*0-8034-9381-9*, Avalon Bks) Bouregy.

McGinley, Marjorie M. John Crust & Snuffling Pig. LC 97-97120. 192p. 1998. lib. bdg. 18.95 (*0-8034-9281-2*, Avalon Bks) Bouregy.

***McGinley, Marjorie M.** Rattlesnake Gulch. LC 98-96852. 192p. 1999. lib. bdg. 18.95 (*0-8034-9341-X*, Avalon Bks) Bouregy.

***McGinley, Matthew Douglas.** Confessions of a Reformed Road Warrior. LC 99-95504. (Illus.). 374p. 1999. pap. 18.40 (*0-9675082-0-7*) A Class.

McGinley, Patton H. Shielding Techniques for Radiation Oncology Facilities. LC 97-36743. 1998. text 62.95 (*0-944838-81-2*) Med Physics Pub.

McGinley, Phyllis. The Most Wonderful Doll in the World. 64p. (J). (gr. 2-5). 1990. 10.95 (*0-590-43476-4*) Scholastic Inc.

— The Most Wonderful Doll in the World. 64p. (J). (ps-3). 1992. 3.95 (*0-590-43477-2*, Blue Ribbon Bks) Scholastic Inc.

— Most Wonderful Doll in the World. (Blue Ribbon Bks.). (J). 1978. 9.15 (*0-606-02762-9*, Pub. by Turtleback) Demco.

— Year without a Santa Claus. (Illus.). (J). (gr. k-3). 1957. 12.95 (*0-397-30399-8*) HarpC Child Bks.

— Year without a Santa Claus. (Illus.). (J). (gr. k-3). 1981. lib. bdg. 14.89 (*0-397-31969-X*) HarpC Child Bks.

McGinley, Ronald J. Systematics of the Colletidae Based on Mature Larvae with Phenetic Analysis of Apoid Larvae (Hymenoptera, Apoidea) LC 80-15362. (University of California Publications in Social Welfare: No. 91). (Illus.). 333p. reprint ed. pap. 103.30 (*0-608-18315-6*, 203158700075) Bks Demand.

***McGinley, Sarah.** A Moment with God for Sunday School Teachers: Prayers for Every Sunday School Teacher. 64p. 2000. pap. 5.00 (*0-687-09004-0*) Dimen for Liv.

***McGinley, Sharon.** The Friendly Beasts. LC 99-33704. 24p. (J). 2000. 15.89 (*0-688-17422-1*, Grenwillow Bks) HarpC Child Bks.

— The Friendly Beasts: A Christmas Carol. LC 99-33704. 24p. (J). 2000. 15.95 (*0-688-17421-3*, Grenwillow Bks) HarpC Child Bks.

McGinley, Theresa K., ed. A Commemorative History of the North Harris Montgomery Community College District. 152p. 1998. write for info. (*0-9654999-7-9*) Hist Pub Network.

McGinley, Tod. Mulligan's Name Was Ambrose. Simmons, Chere & Schipper, Eileen, eds. (Illus.). 128p. 1998. pap. 9.95 (*0-9664987-0-4*) T C McGinley.

***McGinley, Voyce.** Mallet Mayhem. 64p. 1999. pap. 9.95 (*0-7866-0566-9*, 95498) Mel Bay.

***McGinn.** Mysterious Flame: New SubTitle. 256p. 2000. pap. 14.00 (*0-465-01423-2*) HarpC.

McGinn, Anne P. Charting a New Course for Oceans, Vol. 145. Peterson, Jane A., ed. 80p. 1999. pap. 5.00 (*1-878071-47-5*) Worldwatch Inst.

— Rocking the Boat: Conserving Fisheries & Protecting Jobs. Peterson, Jane A., ed. LC 98-60965. 90p. 1998. pap. 5.00 (*1-878071-44-0*) Worldwatch Inst.

***McGinn, Bernard.** Antichrist: Two Thousand Years of the Human Fascination with Evil. (Illus.). 369p. 2000. reprint ed. 27.00 (*0-7881-9320-1*) DIANE Pub.

— Antichrist: 2000 Years of the Human Fascination with Evil. LC 99-45369. 2000. pap. 16.50 (*0-231-11977-1*) Col U Pr.

McGinn, Bernard. Apolcalypticism in the Western Tradition. (Collected Studies). 336p. 1994. 109.95 (*0-86078-396-0*, Pub. by Variorum) Ashgate Pub Co.

— The Doctors of the Church: Thirty-Three Men & Women Who Shaped Christianity. LC 99-22090. 192p. 1999. pap. 17.95 (*0-8245-1771-7*, Crsrd) Crossroad NY.

***McGinn, Bernard.** Encyclopedia of Apocalypticism, 3 vols. 2000. pap. text 119.95 (*0-8264-1252-1*) Continuum.

McGinn, Bernard. The Flowering of Mysticism. LC 97-52986. (Presence of God Ser.: No. 3). 242p. 1998. 60.00 (*0-8245-1742-3*, Herdr & Herdr); pap. 24.95 (*0-8245-1743-1*, Herdr & Herdr) Crossroad NY.

— The Foundations of Mysticism: Origins to the Fifth Century. 496p. 1994. reprint ed. pap. 24.95 (*0-8245-1404-1*) Crossroad NY.

— The Growth of Mysticism: From Gregory the Great Through the 12th Century, Vol. 2. (Presence of God Ser.). 1996. pap. text 24.95 (*0-8245-1628-1*) Crossroad NY.

— Visions of the End: Apocalyptic Traditions in the Middle Ages. LC 99-180823. 397p. 1998. pap. 18.50 (*0-231-11257-2*) Col U Pr.

***McGinn, Bernard, ed.** Apocalypticism in Western History & Culture. (Encyclopedia of Apocalypticism Ser. : Vol. 2). 544p. 2000. pap. text 39.95 (*0-8264-1254-8*) Continuum.

McGinn, Bernard, ed. Three Treatises on Man: A Cistercian Anthropology. LC 77-184906. (Cistercian Fathers Ser.: No. 24). 1977. 13.95 (*0-87907-024-2*) Cistercian Pubns.

McGinn, Bernard, tr. Apocalyptic Spirituality. LC 79-90834. (Classics of Western Spirituality Ser.). 352p. 1979. pap. 21.95 (*0-8091-2242-1*) Paulist Pr.

McGinn, Bernard & Eliade, Mircea. The Galabrian Abbot: Joachim of Flora in the History of Western Thought. 1985. write for info. (*0-317-18119-X*) Macmillan.

McGinn, Bernard & Idel, Moshe, eds. Mystical Union in Judaism, Christianity & Islam: An Ecumenical Dialogue. 264p. 1996. pap. 24.95 (*0-8264-0882-6*) Continuum.

McGinn, Bernard & Otten, Willemien, eds. Eriugena: East & West. LC 93-42514. (Conferences in Medieval Studies: Vol. 5). (C). 1994. text 46.00 (*0-268-00929-5*) U of Notre Dame Pr.

McGinn, Bernard, et al. Meister Eckhart: Teacher & Preacher. (Classics of Western Spirituality Ser.: Vol. 52). 448p. 1986. pap. 22.95 (*0-8091-2827-6*) Paulist Pr.

McGinn, Bernard, jt. ed. see Emmerson, Richard K.

McGinn, Bernard, jt. tr. see Colledge, Edmund.

Mcginn, Bernard L., ed. Meister Eckhart & the Beguine Mystics: Hadewijch of Brabant, Mechthild of Magdeburg, & Marguerite Porete. LC 77-18605. (Illus.). 160p. 1996. pap. 15.95 (*0-8264-0929-6*) Continuum.

McGinn, Colin. The Character of Mind: An Introduction to the Philosophy of Mind. 2nd ed. LC 96-35172. 186p. 1997. pap. text 16.95 (*0-19-875208-3*) OUP.

— The Character of Mind: An Introduction to the Philosophy of Mind. 2nd ed. LC 96-35172. 186p. (C). 1997. text 65.00 (*0-19-875209-1*) OUP.

— Ethics, Evil, & Fiction. LC 97-4157. 196p. (C). 1997. text 29.95 (*0-19-823716-2*) OUP.

— Ethics, Evil & Fiction. 196p. 1999. pap. text 16.95 (*0-19-823877-0*) OUP.

— Knowledge & Reality: Selected Essays. LC 98-49342. 338p. 1999. text 58.00 (*0-19-823823-1*) OUP.

— Minds & Bodies: Philosophers & Their Ideas. LC 96-27353. (Philosophy of Mind Ser.). 272p. 1997. 39.95 (*0-19-511355-1*) OUP.

— Moral Literacy: or How to Do the Right Thing. 110p. (C). 1993. pap. text 8.95 (*0-87220-196-1*); lib. bdg. 29.95 (*0-87220-197-X*) Hackett Pub.

— The Mysterious Flame: Conscious Minds in a Material World. 256p. 1999. 24.00 (*0-465-01422-4*, Pub. by Basic) HarpC.

***McGinn, Colin.** Philosophy from the Inside. 2000. 26.00 (*0-06-019792-7*); pap. 15.00 (*0-06-095760-3*) HarpC.

McGinn, Colin. The Problem of Consciousness: Essays Towards a Resolution. 216p. 1993. pap. 27.95 (*0-631-18803-7*) Blackwell Pubs.

— Problems in Philosophy: The Limits of Inquiry. LC 93-14752. 208p. 1993. pap. 25.95 (*1-55786-475-6*) Blackwell Pubs.

— The Subjective View: Secondary Qualities & Indexical Thoughts. 170p. 1983. pap. text 22.00 (*0-19-824695-1*) OUP.

***McGinn, Daniel.** For Lori. (Pale Ale Poets Ser.). 49p. 1999. pap. 4.95 (*1-929250-05-3*) FarStarFire Pr.

McGinn, Elinor M. At Hard Labor: Inmate Labor at the Colorado State Penitentiary, 1871-1940. LC 92-34581. (American University Studies: History: Ser. IX, Vol. 137). (Illus.). XIV, 172p. (C). 1993. text 39.95 (*0-8204-2097-2*) P Lang Pubng.

McGinn, Florence. Blood Trail: Poems of the Heart. 108p. 2000. pap. 12.00 (*0-938631-34-9*) Pennywhistle Pr.

McGinn, Joe. Inside Lotus Script: A Complete Guide to Notes Programming. LC 97-40461. (Illus.). 350p. 1997. pap. 43.95 incl. cd-rom (*1-884777-48-1*) Manning Pubns.

McGinn, John G., jt. auth. see Tedstrom, John.

McGinn, Joseph C. Lawyers: A Client's Manual. 1977. 11.95 (*0-13-526814-1*); pap. 5.95 (*0-13-526806-0*) P-H.

— Lawyers: A Client's Manual. 3rd ed. 1977. audio 215.00 (*0-13-530444-X*) P-H.

McGinn, Kerry A. The Informed Woman's Guide to Breast Health: Breast Changes That Are Not Cancer. rev. ed. Bull, David C., ed. (Illus.). 200p. (Orig.). 1992. pap. 13.95 (*0-923521-24-0*) Bull Pub.

— Women's Cancers: How to Prevent Them, How to Treat Them, How to Beat Them. 2nd ed. LC 97-20482. (Illus.). 512p. 1998. pap. 19.95 (*0-89793-223-4*) Hunter Hse.

McGinn, Kerry A. & Haylock, P. J. Women's Cancers: How to Prevent Them, How to Treat Them, How to Beat Them. 2nd ed. LC 97-20482. (Illus.). 512p. 1998. 29.95 (*0-89793-224-2*) Hunter Hse.

McGinn, Kerry A., jt. auth. see Mullen, Barbara D.

McGinn, Lata K. & Sanderson, William C. Treatment of Obsessive Compulsive Disorder. LC 98-54404. 9200p. 1999. 40.00 (*0-7657-0211-8*) Aronson.

McGinn, Linda R. Dancing in the Storm: Hope in the Midst of Chaos. LC 98-49636. 208p. (C). (gr. 13). 1999. pap. 12.99 (*0-8007-5696-7*) Revell.

— Resource Guide for Women's Ministries. LC 89-71084. 176p. (Orig.). 1990. pap. 8.99 (*0-8054-3005-9*, 4230-05) Broadman.

McGinn, Linda R. & Hollingsworth, T. R. Investing Your Life in Things That Matter. LC 94-21476. 192p. 1996. pap. 10.99 (*0-8054-6147-7*, 4261-47) Broadman.

McGinn, Marie & Wittgenstein, Ludwig Josef Johann. Routledge Philosophy Guidebook to Wittgenstein & the Philosophical Investigations. LC 96-27227. (Philosophy Guidebooks Ser.). 232p. (C). 1997. 60.00 (*0-415-11190-0*); pap. 12.99 (*0-415-11191-9*) Routledge.

McGinn, Mary, jt. auth. see Moody, Kim.

McGinn, Matt. Fry the Little Fishes. 1994. pap. 9.95 (*0-7145-0992-2*) Riverrun NY.

McGinn, Noel F. Crossing Lines: Research & Policy Networks for Developing Country Education. LC 95-53002. 208p. 1996. 57.95 (*0-275-95511-7*, Praeger Pubs) Greenwood.

***McGinn, Noel F.** Toward International Cooperation in Education for the Integration of the Americas. LC 99-39273. (Trends for a Common Future Ser.). 1999. lib. bdg. write for info. (*0-8270-4003-2*) OAS.

McGinn, Noel F. & Borden, Allison M. Framing Questions, Constructing Answers: Linking Research with Education Policy for Developing Countries. LC 94-21886. (Harvard Studies in International Development: Harvard Institute for International Development: Vol. 8). 1994. pap. text 15.00 (*0-674-31715-7*, MCGFRA) HUP.

***McGinn, Noel F. & Epstein, Erwin H., eds.** Comparative Perspectives, Vol. 8.1, Pt. 1. viii, 497p. 1999. pap. 58.95 (*3-631-31500-7*) P Lang Pubng.

McGinn, Noel F. & Epstein, Erwin H., eds. Comparative Perspectives on the Role of Education in Democratization Pt. 1: Transitional States & States of Transition. LC 99-23283. (Comparative Studies: Vol. 8). (Illus.). VIII, 497p. 1999. pap. text 56.95 (*0-8204-3261-X*) P Lang Pubng.

McGinn, Noel F., et al. Education & Development in Korea. (East Asian Monographs: No. 90). 311p. 1980. 16.50 (*0-674-23810-9*) HUP.

McGinn, Noel F., jt. auth. see Reimers, Fernando.

McGinn, Noel F., jt. ed. see Cummings, William.

McGinn, Noel F., jt. ed. see Epstein, Erwin H.

McGinn, P. J., jt. ed. see Balachandran, U.

McGinn, Richard. Studies in Austronesian Linguistics. LC 87-11242. (Monographs in International Studies, Southeast Asia Ser.: No. 76). 516p. 1986. pap. text 20.00 (*0-89680-137-3*) Ohio U Pr.

McGinn, Robert E. Science, Technology & Society. 304p. (C). 1990. pap. text 36.67 (*0-13-794736-4*) P-H.

McGinn, Sheila E. & Gale, Aaron M., compiled by. Bibliographies for Biblical Research: The Book of Revelation. LC 93-30864. (New Testament Ser.: Vol. XXI). 532p. 1997. text 119.95 (*0-7734-2438-5*, Mellen Biblical Pr) E Mellen.

McGinn, Thomas A. Prostitution, Sexuality, & the Law in Ancient Rome. 432p. 1998. text 55.00 (*0-19-508785-2*) OUP.

McGinn, Thomas A. Roman Prostitution. (Illus.). (C). text. write for info. (*0-472-10603-1*) U of Mich Pr.

McGinness, Frederick J. Right Thinking & Sacred Oratory in Counter-Reformation Rome. LC 95-3104. 368p. 1995. text 52.50 (*0-691-03426-5*, Pub. by Princeton U Pr) Cal Prin Full Svc.

McGinness, Joe. Son of Alyandabu. 1991. pap. 16.95 (*0-7022-2335-2*, Pub. by Univ Queensland Pr) Intl Spec Bk.

McGinness, John F. History of Lycoming County Pennsylvania. (Illus.). 1268p. 1996. 88.00 (*0-7884-0428-8*, M123) Heritage Bk.

***McGinness, Ryan.** Installationview. 2000. pap. 29.95 (*0-9664100-9-2*) Razorfish Studios.

McGinnies, Elliott. Social Psychology A to Z. 356p. 1993. pap. text 32.50 (*0-89876-210-3*) Gardner Pr.

McGinnies, William G. Discovering the Desert: The Legacy of the Carnegie Desert Botanical Laboratory. LC 81-1554. 276p. (C). 1981. pap. 16.00 (*0-8165-0728-7*) U of Ariz Pr.

McGinnies, William G., et al, eds. Food, Fiber & the Arid Land. LC 75-152038. 447p. reprint ed. pap. 138.60 (*0-608-15195-5*, 202738400055) Bks Demand.

McGinnies, William G., jt. ed. see Bishay, Adli.

Mcginnis. Rippon's Medical Mycology. 4th ed. 2001. text. write for info. (*0-7216-4684-0*) Harcourt.

McGinnis, et al, eds. Texas Employment Laws & Regulations: How to Comply. 148p. 1995. pap. 75.00 (*0-685-67824-5*) Amer CC Pubs.

McGinnis, Michael. Polycentric Games & Institutions: Readings from the Workshop in Political Theory & Policy Analysis. (Institutional Analysis Ser.). 448p. 1999. text 69.50 (*0-472-09714-8*, 09714); pap. text 24.95 (*0-472-06714-1*, 06714) U of Mich Pr.

McGinnis, Michael, ed. Polycentricity & Local Public Economies: Readings from the Workshop in Political Theory & Policy Analysis. LC 99-48673. 424p. 1999. text 69.50 (*0-472-11038-1*, 11038) U of Mich Pr.

McGinnis, Alan L. Bringing Out the Best in People: How to Enjoy Helping Others Excel. LC 84-28400. 192p. 1985. pap. 6.99 (*0-8066-2151-6*, 10-0922, Augsburg) Augsburg Fortress.

— Confidence: How to Succeed at Being Yourself. LC 87-1470. 192p. (Orig.). 1987. pap. 6.99 (*0-8066-2262-8*, 10-1639, Augsburg) Augsburg Fortress.

— The Power of Optimism. 1993. pap. 5.50 (*0-685-67757-5*, Harp PBks) HarpC.

McGinnis, Allen R. The Rest of Your Life. Thompson, Nancy V., ed. LC 85-23731. 175p. 1986. 10.00 (*0-9616042-0-4*) J & N Pubs.

McGinnis, Bruce. Reflections in Dark Glass: The Life & Times of John Wesley Hardin. LC 95-26599. 180p. 1996. 24.95 (*1-57441-008-3*) UNTX Pr.

McGinnis, Carol. Virginia Genealogy: Sources & Resources. 505p. 1998. 35.00 (*0-8063-1379-X*, 3526) Genealog Pub.

— West Virginia Genealogy, Sources & Resources. 135p. 1998. reprint ed. 20.00 (*0-8063-1230-0*, 3527) Genealog Pub.

McGinnis, Christopher. 202 Tips Even the Best Business Travelers May Not Know: MCI Special Edition. 1994. per. 11.00 (*0-7863-0339-5*, Irwn Prfssnl) McGraw-Hill Prof.

McGinnis, Christopher J. Two Hundred Two Tips Even the Best Business Travelers May Not Know. LC 94-2846. 160p. 1994. text 12.95 (*1-55623-966-1*, Irwn Prfssnl) McGraw-Hill Prof.

— The Unofficial Business Traveler's Pocket Guide: 249 Tips Even the Best Business Traveler May Not Know. LC 98-13844. (Illus.). 188p. 1998. pap. 10.95 (*0-07-045380-2*) McGraw.

McGinnis, Claude, compiled by. Expert's Guide to Excellent Wines: More Than 600 Highly-Rated Wines for 10 Dollars or Under. (Illus.). 200p. (Orig.). 1993. pap. 9.95 (*0-8128-8554-6*, Scrbrough Hse) Madison Bks UPA.

***McGinnis, Diane.** Bimbo: A Friend for Kindsay Lane. (Illus.). 28p. (J). 1999. 14.99 (*1-57921-190-9*) WinePress Pub.

McGinnis, Ellen & Goldstein, Arnold P. Skillstreaming in Early Childhood: Teaching Prosocial Skills to the Preschool & Kindergarten Child. LC 90-60925. (Illus.). 200p. (Orig.). 1990. pap. text 15.95 (*0-87822-320-7*, 4423) Res Press.

— Skillstreaming in Early Childhood: Teaching Prosocial Skills to the Preschool & Kindergarten Child-Program Forms. LC 90-60925. 76p. (Orig.). 1990. pap. text 13.95 (*0-87822-321-5*, 4424) Res Press.

— Skillstreaming the Elementary School Child: New Strategies & Perspectives for Teaching Prosocial Skills. 2nd rev. ed. LC 97-66999. 352p. (Orig.). 1997. pap. text 17.95 (*0-87822-372-X*) Res Press.

— Skillstreaming the Elementary School Child: New Strategies & Perspectives for Teaching Prosocial Skills - Program Forms. 60p. (Orig.). 1997. pap. text 14.95 (*0-87822-374-6*) Res Press.

— Skillstreaming the Elementary School Child: New Strategies & Perspectives for Teaching Prosocial Skills-Student Manual. LC 97-67000. 80p. (Orig.). 1997. pap. text, student ed. 12.95 (*0-87822-373-8*) Res Press.

McGinnis, Ellen, jt. auth. see Goldstein, Arnold P.

McGinnis, Esther, jt. auth. see Davis, Edith.

McGinnis, Evan. Web Based Network Management. (C). 1999. text 48.96 (*0-13-955113-1*, Macmillan Coll) P-H.

McGinnis, Evan & Perkins, David. Understanding SNMP MIBS. LC 97-135656. 528p. (C). 1996. 68.00 (*0-13-437708-7*) P-H.

McGinnis, Gary D., jt. ed. see Biermann, Christopher J.

McGinnis, Helen. Hiking Mississippi: A Trail Guide. LC 94-12156. (Illus.). 256p. 1994. pap. 15.95 (*0-87805-664-5*); text 35.00 (*0-87805-704-8*) U Pr of Miss.

McGinnis, Helen J. Carnegie's Dinosaurs. LC 82-70212. (Illus.). 120p. (Orig.). 1984. pap. 15.95 (*0-911239-00-6*) Carnegie Mus.

McGinnis, James. Call to Peace: 52 Reflections on the Family Pledge of Nonviolence. LC 98-65962. 144p. 1998. pap. 4.95 (*0-7648-0215-1*) Liguori Pubns.

McGinnis, James, et al, eds. Partners in Peacemaking: Family Workshop Models Guidebook for Leaders. LC 85-159853. 170p. 1984. pap. text 10.75 (*0-912765-08-9*) Inst Peace.

McGinnis, James & McGinnis, Kathleen. As We Teach & Learn Module 6: Recognizing Our Catholic Identity: Social Justice, 10 modules. Ristau, Karen & Haney, Regina, eds. 46p. 1997. pap. 64.00 (*1-55833-157-3*) Natl Cath Educ.

McGinnis, James, et al. Educating for Peace & Justice: A Manual for Teachers, 3 vols., Set. rev. ed. LC 83-145843. (Illus.). 1985. pap. text 37.00 (*0-912765-09-7*) Inst Peace.

— Educating for Peace & Justice: Global Dimensions, Vol. II. rev. ed. LC 83-145843. (Illus.). 324p. 1984. pap. text 14.25 (*0-912765-11-9*) Inst Peace.

— Educating for Peace & Justice: National Dimensions, Vol. I. rev. ed. LC 85-160342. (Illus.). 300p. 1985. pap. text 14.25 (*0-912765-12-7*) Inst Peace.

— Educating for Peace & Justice: Religious Dimensions, Vol. III. rev. ed. LC 83-145843. (Illus.). 243p. 1984. pap. text 14.25 (*0-912765-10-0*) Inst Peace.

— Global Family Puppets. LC 85-159827. (Illus.). 28p. 1984. pap. text 4.00 (*0-912765-14-3*) Inst Peace.

— Puppets for Peace. LC 85-159843. (Illus.). 44p. 1984. pap. text 5.00 (*0-912765-13-5*) Inst Peace.

McGinnis, James B. Solidarity with the People of Nicaragua. LC 84-27202. (Illus.). 176p. (Orig.). reprint ed. pap. 54.60 (*0-8357-8547-5*, 203488600091) Bks Demand.

McGinnis, Janice D., ed. see Jackson, Mary P.

McGinnis, Jeanne, jt. auth. see Eagen, Jane.

McGinnis, John, ed. Changing Times - Changing Styles: The Ruth Stoever Fleming Collection of Southern California Art. LC 85-5011. (Illus.). 80p. 1985. pap. 10.00 (*0-9614891-1-1*) Newport Mesa Sch.

McGinnis, Kathleen. Family Activities Guide. 1989. pap. 7.95 (*0-685-28773-4*) Baptist Peace.

McGinnis, Kathleen, jt. auth. see McGinnis, James.

McGinnis Kay, Carol & Kaufman, Natalie Hevener. "G" Is for Grafton: The World of Kinsey Millhone. LC 97-27861. 352p. 1997. 25.00 (*0-8050-5446-4*) H Holt & Co.

McGinnis, Ken, jt. auth. see Berdan, David.

McGinnis, L., ed. Dry Valley Drilling Project. (Antarctic Research Ser.: Vol. 33). (Illus.). 480p. 1981. 39.00 (*0-87590-152-2*) Am Geophysical.

McGinnis, Lila S. If Daddy Only Knew Me. LC 95-3135. (Albert Whitman Concept Bks.). (Illus.). 32p. (J). (ps-2). 1995. lib. bdg. 14.95 (*0-8075-3537-0*) A Whitman.

— The Twenty-Four Hour Genie. LC 89-77786. (Illus.). 80p. (J). (gr. 2-4). 1995. 12.95 (*0-8050-1303-2*, Redfeather BYR); pap. 4.95 (*0-8050-1845-X*, Redfeather BYR) H Holt & Co.

McGinnis, Linda. The Art of Hairdressing Success. 202p. 1995. pap. text 21.95 (*1-886203-64-4*) Pubs Paradigm.

McGinnis, Mark W. Elders of the Faiths: Interviews & Portraits. LC 96-16553. (Illus.). 72p. (Orig.). 1996. pap., per. 4.95 (*0-944287-15-8*) Ex Machina.

–Lakota & Dakota Animal Wisdom Stories. (Illus.). 24p. (J). 1994. pap. 11.98 (*1-877976-14-8*, 406-0016) Tipi Pr.

LAKOTA & DAKOTA ANIMAL WISDOM STORIES is a compilation of twelve traditional, northern plains Native American stories retold by Dakota storyteller, Pamela Greenhill Kaizen & are accompanied by twelve full-color illustrations by South Dakota artist & educator Mark W. McGinnis. Leonard R. Bruguier, a descendant of the Yankton chiefs, War Eagle & Struck by the Ree, presents the introduction. The stories use animal characters to deal with the themes of compassion, greed, generosity, protection, survival, hard work, laziness, bravery, foolishness, trickery, & others. They range from simple humor as in THE FROG & THE TURTLE BROTHERS, where two close friends decide to jump in the lake rather than catch colds by getting wet in the rain, to the rich & complex story of THE CRANE, which weaves a tale of compassion & caring for one's neighbors. The animal characters give insightful guidance on human morals & ethics, & give a glimpse into the wonderful wit & wisdom of the Lakota & Dakota people. Mark McGinnis' paintings interpret a critical instant from each story, translating the oral moment to a visual expression of color, texture & shapes. This book is well suited to be read to younger children, to be read by older children, or for adults who enjoy new perspectives into Native American culture. Available for $11.98 plus $3.00 S/H from Tipi Press, St. Joseph's Indian School, Chamberlain, SD 57326; 605-734-3300.
Publisher Paid Annotation.

McGinnis, Mary. Listening for Cactus. LC 96-30940. 96p. (Orig.). 1996. pap. 14.00 (*0-9644196-4-5*) Sherman Asher Pub.

McGinnis, Mary, jt. auth. see Sanders, Jo.

McGinnis, Michael. Polycentric Governance & Development: Readings from the Workshop in Political Theory & Policy Analysis. LC 99-24422. 448p. 1999. text 69.50 (*0-472-11039-X*, 11039); pap. text 24.95 (*0-472-08623-5*, 08623) U of Mich Pr.

McGinnis, Michael, ed. Polycentricity & Local Public Economies: Readings from the Workshop in Political Theory & Policy Analysis. LC 99-48673. 424p. 1999. pap. text 24.95 (*0-472-08622-7*, 08622) U of Mich Pr.

McGinnis, Michael A. & Vallopra, Rafeekh Mele. Purchasing & Supplier Involvement: New Product Development & Production/Operations Process Development & Improvement. LC 98-198504. 1998. write for info. (*0-945968-31-0*) Ctr Advanced Purchasing.

McGinnis, Michael R. Current Topics in Medical Mycology, Vol. 2. (Illus.). 385p. 1987. 196.00 (*0-387-96543-2*) Spr-Verlag.

— Laboratory Handbook of Medical Mycology. 1980. text 104.00 (*0-12-482850-7*) Acad Pr.

McGinnis, Michael R., ed. Current Topics in Medical Mycology, Vol. 1. (Illus.). 360p. 1985. 132.00 (*0-387-96095-3*) Spr-Verlag.

McGinnis, Michael R. & Borgers, M., eds. Current Topics in Medical Mycology. (Illus.). 448p. 1989. 232.00 (*0-387-96941-1*, 2540) Spr-Verlag.

McGinnis, Michael V. Bioregionalism. LC 98-20210. 1998. 100.00 (*0-415-15444-8*); pap. 22.99 (*0-415-15445-6*) Routledge.

McGinnis, Patrick E. Oklahoma's Depression Radicals: Ira M. Finley & the Veterans of Industry of America. LC 90-19401. (Recent American History Ser.: Vol. 3). VI, 196p. (C). 1991. text 36.95 (*0-8204-1295-3*) P Lang Pubng.

McGinnis, Peter M. Biomechanics of Sport & Exercise. LC 96-45731. 416p. (C). 1999. text 49.00 (*0-87322-955-X*, BMCG0955) Human Kinetics.

McGinnis, Ralph Y. Quotations from Abraham Lincoln. LC 77-24595. (Illus.). 144p. 1978. text 41.95 (*0-88229-316-8*) Burnham Inc.

McGinnis, Ralph Y. & Smith, Calvin. Abraham Lincoln & the Western Territories. LC 92-2743. 1993. text 31.95 (*0-8304-1247-6*) Burnham Inc.

McGinnis, Rebecca, jt. auth. see Sino-American Conference on Contemporary China Staff.

McGinnis, Richard, ed. see Ansah, Godfred T.

McGinnis, Richard G. Learning CADKey. (C). 1991. 28.75 (*0-07-044791-8*) McGraw.

McGinnis, Ruth. The Good Life: A Return to Simple Principles of Healthy Living. LC 98-122583. 256p. 1998. pap. 12.99 (*0-7852-7150-3*, J Thoma Bks) Nelson.

McGinnis, Samuel M. Freshwater Fishes of California. LC 83-5113. (California Natural History Guides Ser.: No. 49). (Illus.). 316p. 1984. pap. 14.95 (*0-520-04891-1*, Pub. by U CA Pr) Cal Prin Full Svc.

McGinnis, Scott, ed. Pathways to Advanced Skills Vol. 2: Chinese Pedagogy: An Emerging Field. LC 97-142168. 328p. (Orig.). 1996. pap. 20.95 (*0-87415-313-1*, PA02) Foreign Lang.

McGinnis, Scott, et al. Let's Play Games in Japanese. 178p. Date not set. 20.95 (*0-8442-8414-9*) NTC Contemp Pub Co.

McGinnis, Scott, jt. auth. see Walker, Galal.

McGinnis, Scott, jt. auth. see Yao, Tao-chung.

McGinnis, Terri. The Well Cat Book: The Classic Comprehensive Handbook of Cat Care. LC 95-25789. (Illus.). 336p. 1996. pap. 16.95 (*0-679-77000-3*) Random.

— The Well Dog Book: The Classic, Comprehensive Handbook of Dog Care. (Illus.). 288p. 1996. pap. 15.00 (*0-679-77001-1*) Random.

McGinnis, Wendy J. Selected Economic & Demographic Data for Counties of the Interior Columbia River Basin. (Illus.). 84p. 1997. pap. text 25.00 (*0-7881-4697-1*) DIANE Pub.

— Selected Economic & Demographic Data for Counties of the Interior Columbia River Basin. (Illus.). 88p. 1997. reprint ed. 17.00 (*0-89904-573-1*, Research Cent); reprint ed. pap. 12.00 (*0-89904-574-X*, Research Cent) Crumb Elbow Pub.

McGinnis, Wendy J. & Christensen, Harriet H. Interior Columbia River Basin: The Patterns of Population, Employment, & Income Change. (Illus.). 318p. 1997. reprint ed. 10.00 (*0-89904-565-0*, Research Cent); reprint ed. pap. 6.00 (*0-89904-566-9*, Research Cent) Crumb Elbow Pub.

McGinnis, William. Whitewater Rafting. LC 74-24280. (Illus.). 1978. pap. 12.95 (*0-8129-6301-6*, Times Bks) Crown Pub Group.

McGinnis, William N. School Administrative & Supervisory Organizations in Cities of 20,000 to 50,000 Population. LC 71-177024. (Columbia University. Teachers College. Contributions to Education Ser.: No. 392). reprint ed. 37.50 (*0-404-55392-3*) AMS Pr.

McGinniss, Alan L. The Friendship Factor: How to Get Closer to the People You Care for. LC 79-50076. 192p. 1979. pap. 6.99 (*0-8066-1711-X*, 10-2411, Augsburg) Augsburg Fortress.

Mcginniss, Cheryl Folkins, tr. see Vicente, Gil.

McGinniss, James. The Grass Poems. (Illus.). 47p. 1997. pap. 3.00 (*1-57141-035-X*) Runaway Spoon.

McGinniss, Joe. Blind Faith. 1989. mass mkt. 6.99 (*0-451-16218-8*, Sig) NAL.

— Cruel Doubt. Rubenstein, Julie, ed. 512p. 1992. reprint ed. mass mkt. 6.99 (*0-671-77539-1*) PB.

— Fatal Vision. 1984. mass mkt. 7.99 (*0-451-16566-7*, Sig) NAL.

— Going to Extremes. 228p. 1989. pap. 12.95 (*0-452-26301-8*, Plume) Dutton Plume.

— The Last Brother. 1994. pap. 6.99 (*0-671-89452-8*) PB.

— The Miracle of Castel Di Sangro. LC GV943.6.C35M35 1999. 416p. (gr. 8). 1999. 25.00 (*0-316-55736-6*) Little.

***McGinniss, Joe.** The Miracle of Castel di Sangro. 2000. pap. write for info. (*0-316-56603-9*) Back Bay Pr.

— The Miracle of Castel di Sangro. LC 99-58210. 416p. 2000. pap. 14.95 (*0-7679-0599-7*) Broadway BDD.

— The Miracle of Castel di Sangro. 1998. write for info. (*0-316-56615-2*) Little.

McGinniss, Joe. The Miracle of Castel di Sangro. 1999. write for info. (*0-316-56229-7*) Little.

— The Selling of the President. 288p. (C). 1988. pap. 13.95 (*0-14-011240-5*) Viking Penguin.

McGinnity, Frances, jt. auth. see O'Connell, Philip J.

McGinnity, Gerard. Celebrating with Mary: Reflections for Personal Prayer & Parish Devotions. 92p. (Orig.). 1987. pap. 7.95 (*0-86217-289-6*, Pub. by Veritas Pubns) St Mut.

McGinty. Prelude & Fugue in C Major: Bach Flute Choir. 1990. 10.00 (*0-685-32130-4*, 77193) Hansen Ed Mus.

McGinty & Jackson. Current Therapy in Orthopaedics. 1991. write for info. (*1-55664-040-4*) Mosby Inc.

McGinty, jt. auth. see Bach.

McGinty, A. B. Staying Healthy: Eating Right. LC 96-44287. (Library of Healthy Living). (J). (gr. k-3). 1997. lib. bdg. 17.27 (*0-8239-5136-7*, PowerKids) Rosen Group.

— Staying Healthy: Let's Exercise. LC 96-47208. (Library of Healthy Living). (J). (gr. k-3). 1997. lib. bdg. 17.27 (*0-8239-5137-5*, PowerKids) Rosen Group.

McGinty, Alice B. Detector Dogs: Sniffing Out Trouble. LC 97-53114. (Dogs Helping People Ser.). 24p. (J). (gr. k-4). 1999. 11.95 (*0-8239-5217-7*, PowerKids) Rosen Group.

— Guide Dogs: Seeing for People Who Can't. LC 97-44840. (Dogs Helping People Ser.). 24p. (J). (gr. k-4). 1999. 17.26 (*0-8239-5215-0*, PowerKids) Rosen Group.

— Police Dogs: Helping to Fight Crime. LC 97-52013. (Dogs Helping People Ser.). 24p. (J). (gr. k-4). 1999. 15.93 (*0-8239-5218-5*, PowerKids) Rosen Group.

— Sheep-Herding Dogs: Rounding up the Herd. LC 97-52011. (Dogs Helping People Ser.). 24p. (J). (gr. k-4). 1999. 17.26 (*0-8239-5219-3*, PowerKids) Rosen Group.

— Sled Dogs: Speeding Through Snow. LC 97-45034. (Dogs Helping People Ser.). 24p. (J). (gr. k-4). 1999. 15.93 (*0-8239-5216-9*, PowerKids) Rosen Group.

— Staying Healthy: Dental Care. LC 96-37360. (Library of Healthy Living). 24p. (J). (gr. k-3). 1997. lib. bdg. 17.27 (*0-8239-5139-1*, PowerKids) Rosen Group.

— Staying Healthy: Dental Care. Franklin Watts Ltd. Staff, ed. (Staying Healthy Ser.). (Illus.). 24p. (J). (gr. k-4). 1999. pap. 5.95 (*0-531-11661-1*) Watts.

— Staying Healthy: Good Hygiene. LC 96-53252. (Library of Healthy Living). (J). (gr. k-3). 1997. lib. bdg. 17.27 (*0-8239-5141-3*, PowerKids) Rosen Group.

— Staying Healthy: Let's Exercise. Franklin Watts Ltd. Staff, ed. (Staying Healthy Ser.). (Illus.). 24p. (J). (gr. k-4). 1999. pap. 5.95 (*0-531-11659-X*) Watts.

— Staying Healthy: Personal Safety. LC 96-39985. (Library of Healthy Living). (J). (gr. k-3). 1997. lib. bdg. 17.27 (*0-8239-5140-5*, PowerKids) Rosen Group.

— Staying Healthy: Personal Safety. Franklin Watts Ltd. Staff, ed. (Staying Healthy Ser.). (Illus.). 24p. (J). (gr. k-4). 1999. pap. 5.95 (*0-531-11662-X*) Watts.

— Staying Healthy: Sleep & Rest. LC 96-37359. (Library of Healthy Living). (J). (gr. k-3). 1997. lib. bdg. 17.27 (*0-8239-5138-3*, PowerKids) Rosen Group.

— Staying Healthy: Sleep & Rest. Franklin Watts Ltd. Staff, ed. (Staying Healthy Ser.). (Illus.). 24p. (J). (gr. k-4). 1999. pap. 5.95 (*0-531-11660-3*) Watts.

McGinty, Alice B. & Franklin Watts Ltd. Staff. Staying Healthy: Good Hygiene. (Staying Healthy Ser.). (Illus.). 24p. (J). (gr. k-4). 1999. pap. 5.95 (*0-531-11663-8*) Watts.

McGinty, Alice B. & Watts, Franklin. Staying Healthy: Eating Right. (Staying Healthy Ser.). (Illus.). 24p. (J). (gr. k-4). 1999. pap. text 5.95 (*0-531-11658-1*) Watts.

McGinty, Brian. Strong Wine: The Life & Legend of Agoston Haraszthy. LC 97-48454. 579p. 1998. 65.00 (*0-8047-3145-4*); pap. 24.95 (*0-8047-3146-2*) Stanford U Pr.

***McGinty, Charles P.** Preacher's Kid: A Journey from Pious Fundamentalism to Pragmatic Humanism. (Illus.). 484p. 1999. pap. 19.95 (*0-934426-89-9*) NAPSAC Reprods.

***McGinty, Jacqueline F.** Advancing from the Ventral Striatum to the Extended Amygdala: Implications for Neuropsychiatry & Drug Abuse: In Honor of Lennart Heimer LC 99-34750. (Annals of the New York Academy of Science Ser.). 1999. write for info. (*1-57331-179-0*) NY Acad Sci.

McGinty, Jacqueline F., ed. Advancing from the Ventral Striatum to the Extended Amygdala: Implications for Neuropsychiatry & Drug Abuse. LC 99-34750. 350p. 1999. text 140.00 (*1-57331-178-2*) NY Acad Sci.

McGinty, Jean & Fish, John. Further Education in the Market-Place: Equity, Opportunity & Individual Learning. LC 93-7346. 1994. pap. write for info. (*0-415-10041-0*) Routledge.

— Learning Support for Young People in Transition: Leaving School for Further Education & Work. 112p. 1992. 123.00 (*0-335-09766-9*); pap. 34.95 (*0-335-09765-0*) OpUniv Pr.

McGinty, John B., et al, eds. Operative Arthroscopy. 2nd ed. LC 95 15899. (Illus.). 1376p. 1995. text 270.00 (*0-7817-0294-1*) Lppncott W & W.

McGinty, Kevin J. The Fundamentals of Capital Markets Products. Behr, Joan H., ed. LC 88-32944. (Illus.). 48p. (Orig.). 1988. pap. text 17.00 (*0-936742-61-5*, 31071) Robt Morris Assocs.

Mcginty, Linda, ed. see Dancyger, Ruth.

McGinty, Martha E., tr. see Foucher De Chartres.

McGinty, Michael J. Medicare Reimbursement & the Quality of Hospital Care. 137p. (Orig.). (C). 1994. pap. text 40.00 (*0-7881-1053-5*) DIANE Pub.

McGinty, Park. Interpretation & Dionysos: Method in the Study of a God. (Religion & Reason Ser.: No. 16). 1978. 76.15 (*90-279-7844-1*) Mouton.

McGinty, Patricia. Dirges to Dance by. Galvin, Suzanne & LaRue, James, eds. (Chapbook Ser.: No. 9). 23p. 1982. pap. 3.00 (*0-932884-08-3*) Red Herring.

McGinty, Sarah M. College Application Essay. LC 97-68121. (Illus.). 160p. 1997. pap. text 12.95 (*0-87447-575-9*) College Bd.

***McGinty, Sarah Myers.** Power Talk: Using Language to Build Authority & Influence. 224p. 2001. 24.95 (*0-446-52537-5*) Warner Bks.

McGinty, Stephen. Gatekeepers of Knowledge: Journal Editors in the Sciences & the Social Sciences. LC 99-12703. 160p. 1999. 55.00 (*0-89789-664-5*, Bergin & Garvey) Greenwood.

McGinty, Sue. Resilience, Gender & Success at School. (Adolescent Cultures, School, & Society Ser.: Vol. 1). (Illus.). XIII, 183p. (C). 1999. pap. text 29.95 (*0-8204-3706-9*) P Lang Pubng.

McGirk, Jan S. Exploring Rural Spain. (Exploring Rural Europe Ser.). (Illus.). 168p. 1992. pap. 12.95 (*0-8442-9462-4*, Passprt Bks) NTC Contemp Pub Co.

McGirr, Nancy, jt. ed. see Franklin, Kristine L.

McGirr, Randall D. Learning How to Read New Testament Greek: With People Just Like You. 420p. (Orig.). 1992. pap. 24.95 (*0-9631877-0-8*) Context Script.

— Learning How to Use New Testament Reference Books: With People Just Like You. (Illus.). 290p. 1993. pap. 19.95 (*0-9631877-1-6*) Context Script.

McGirt, James E. Avenging the Maine, a Drunken A. B. & Other Poems. LC 73-133160. (Black Heritage Library Collection). 1977. 13.95 (*0-8369-8715-2*) Ayer.

— The Triumphs of Ephraim. LC 79-39093. (Black Heritage Library Collection). 1977. reprint ed. 22.95 (*0-8369-9031-5*) Ayer.

McGiverin, Rolland H., ed. Educational & Psychological Tests in the Academic Library. LC 90-4052. (Behavioral & Social Sciences Librarian Ser.: Vol. 8, Nos. 3-4). 94p. 1990. text 29.95 (*0-86656-915-4*) Haworth Pr.

***McGivering, Jill.** Macao Remembers. LC 99-36869. (Illus.). 248p. 1999. text 27.00 (*0-19-591735-9*) OUP.

McGivern, Diane O., jt. ed. see Mezey, Mathy D.

McGivern, Ed. Fast & Fancy Revolver Shooting. LC 84-62402. 1975. 19.95 (*0-8329-0557-7*, Winchester Pr) New Win Pub.

McGivern, Gene. Here's Johnny Orr. LC 92-24569. (Illus.). 312p. 1992. pap. 19.95 (*0-8138-1291-7*) Iowa St U Pr.

McGivern, Joseph. Interrupt-Driven PC System Design. 300p. 1998. mass mkt. 34.95 (*0-929392-50-7*) Annabooks.

McGivern, Justin. Broccoli-Flavored Bubble Gum. (Publish-a-Book Ser.). (Illus.). (J). (gr. k-7). 1997. pap. 5.95 (*0-8172-7210-0*) Raintree Steck-V.

McGivern, Mary A. Not by Bread Alone: Recipes & Reflections for Christian Cooks. LC 98-70832. 160p. 1998. pap. 12.95 (*0-87946-181-0*, 271) ACTA Pubns.

McGivern, William P. Odds Against Tomorrow. 208p. 1996. mass mkt. 4.95 (*0-7867-0339-3*) Carroll & Graf.

McGivney, Annette. Backpacker's Leave No Trace: A Practical Guide to the New Wilderness Ethic. LC 97-46839. (Illus.). 192p. 1998. pap. 10.95 (*0-89886-524-7*) Mountaineers.

***McGivney, Glen P. & Carr, Alan B.** McCracken's Removable Partial Prosthodontics. 10th ed. LC 99-37063. (Illus.). 576p. (C). 1999. text. write for info. (*0-323-00678-7*) Mosby Inc.

McGivney, Glenn P. & Castleberry. McCracken's Removable Partial Prosthodontics, No. 9. 9th ed. (Illus.). 544p. (C). (gr. 13). 1994. text 79.00 (*0-8016-7964-8*, 07964) Mosby Inc.

McGivney, Joseph H., jt. auth. see McGivney, Shawn A.

McGivney, Shawn A. & McGivney, Joseph H. Eternally Young: A Guide to Aging Well. LC 89-85373. (Illus.). (Orig.). 1989. pap. text 9.95 (*0-9623941-0-6*) Ageless Pub.

McGlade, J. M. Advanced Ecological Theory: Principles & Applications. LC 98-34024. (Illus.). 1999. pap. 69.00 (*0-86542-734-8*) Blackwell Sci.

McGlade, Shirley. Daddy, Where Are You? large type ed. (Illus.). 400p. 1993. 27.99 (*0-7089-8701-X*) Ulverscroft.

McGlade, William G. Oil & Gas Geology of the Amity & Claysville Quadrangles, Pennsylvania. (Mineral Resource Reports: No. 54). (Illus.). 131p. 1984. reprint ed. pap. 30.15 (*0-8182-0022-7*) Commonweal PA.

McGladre & Pullen. Mandated Benefits: A Practical Guide to Cost-Effective Compliance. LC 96-216135. 688p. 1995. pap. 106.00 (*1-56706-085-4*) Panel Pubs.

McGladrey. Mandated Benefits: 1997 Compliance Guide. LC 97-118902. 688p. 1996. 125.00 (*1-56706-403-5*) Panel Pubs.

McGladrey & Pullan. The Americans with Disabilities Act: A Practical Guide to Cost-Effective Compliance. 160p. 69.00 (*1-878375-92-X*) Panel Pubs.

McGladrey & Pullen Staff, jt. auth. see Harrop, David.

McGlaffery. E. T. A. Hoffman. LC 97-8269. 1997. 32.00 (*0-8057-4619-6*, Twyne) Mac Lib Ref.

McGlamry, E. Dalton, et al. Comprehensive Textbook of Foot Surgery, Set, Vols. 1 & 2. 2nd ed. (Illus.). 1840p. 1992. text 325.00 (*0-683-05857-6*) Lppncott W & W

McGlashan, Alan. Gravity & Levity: The Philosophy of Paradox. LC 96-173470. 213p. 1949. pap. 16.95 (*3-85630-548-3*) Continuum.

— The Savage & Beautiful Country: The Secret Life of the Mind. 208p. 1995. pap. 15.95 (*3-85630-517-3*) Continuum.

McGlashan, Charles F. History of the Donner Party: A Tragedy of the Sierra. 2nd rev. ed. Hinkle, George H. & Hinkle, Bliss M., eds. (Illus.). lvii, 261p. 1947. 29.50 (*0-8047-0366-3*); pap. 11.95 (*0-8047-0367-1*) Stanford U Pr.

McGlashan, Don, jt. auth. see Dadson, Philip.

McGlashan, J. E., ed. Modern Trends in Sludge Management, No. 115. (Water Science & Technology Ser.: Vol. 15). (Illus.). 254p. 1983. pap. 44.00 (*0-08-030416-8*, Pergamon Pr) Elsevier.

McGlashan, M. L., jt. ed. see Beynon, John H.

McGlashan, M. Nona. O Days of Wind & Moon. LC 97-11702. (Illus.). 128p. (Orig.). 1997. pap. 10.95 (*1-56474-232-6*) Fithian Pr.

McGlashan, N. D., ed. Health Problems in Australia & New Zealand. 180p. 1980. pap. 24.00 (*0-08-026103-5*, Pergamon Pr) Elsevier.

McGlashan, Neil & Blunden, John R., eds. Geographic Aspects of Health. 1983. text 132.00 (*0-12-483780-8*) Acad Pr.

McGlashan, Paul, jt. auth. see Beveridge, Tony.

McGlashan, Thomas H. The Borderline: Current Empirical Research. LC 85-6102. (Progress in Psychiatry Ser.). (Illus.). 128p. reprint ed. pap. 39.70 (*0-608-06651-6*, 206684800009) Bks Demand.

McGlashhan, C. F. Feher Sierrak. Gaal, Violetta, tr. (HUN.). 174p. (Orig.). 1996. pap. 25.00 (*0-9637584-2-X*) Violetta Gaal.

McGlashlan, Lara, tr. see Chraibi, Driss.

McGlasman, Zena B., ed. see Kearney, Patrick J.

M

*McGlasson, Paul G. Canon & Proclamation: Sermons for Our Times. LC 00-41728. 2000. pap. write for info. (0-8028-4731-5) Eerdmans.

McGlathery, James M. Wagner's Operas & Desire. LC 96-42507. (North American Studies in Nineteenth-Century German Literature: Vol. 22). 312p. (C). 1998. text 52.95 (0-8204-3693-3) P Lang Pubng.

McGlathery, James M., ed. Music & German Literature: Studies on Their Relationship since the Middle Ages. (GERM Ser.: Vol. 66). (Illus.). 400p. 1992. 75.00 (1-879751-03-8) Camden Hse.

McGlathery, James M., et al, eds. The Brothers Grimm & Folktale. (Illus.). 280p. 1991. pap. text 15.95 (0-252-06191-8) U of Ill Pr.

McGlathery, James M., et al. Grimms' Fairy Tales: A History of Criticism on a Popular Classic. LC 93-37093. (LCGERM Ser.). 144p. 1994. 50.00 (1-879751-90-9) Camden Hse.

McGlathrey, James, ed. German Source Readings in the Arts & Sciences. 1974. spiral bd. 16.80 (0-87563-083-9) Stipes.

*McGleenan, T., et al, eds. Genetics & Insurance. LC 99-40700. 144p. 1999. 85.00 (0-387-91595-8) Spr-Verlag.

Mcglen, Nancy E. & O'Connor, Karen. Women, Politics & American Society. 2nd ed. LC 97-31497. 310p. (C). 1998. pap. text 38.80 (0-13-639097-8) P-H.

McGlen, Nancy E. & Sarkees, Meredith R. The Status of Women in Foreign Policy. Hoepli-Phalon, Nancy L., ed. LC 95-61285. (Headline Ser.: No. 307). (Illus.). 72p. (Orig.). 1995. pap. 5.95 (0-87124-165-X) Foreign Policy.

— Women in Foreign Policy: The Insiders. LC 92-41704. 464p. (C). 1993. pap. 19.99 (0-415-90512-5, A6488) Routledge.

McGlenen, Edward W. Boston Marriages from 1700 to 1809, 2 vols. 1180p. 1997. reprint ed. pap. 85.00 (0-8063-4808-9) Clearfield Co.

McGlew, Jackie & Chesterfield, Trevor. South Africa's Cricket Captains: From Melville to Wessels. 292p. 1999. pap. 21.95 (1-86812-544-0) Menasha Ridge.

McGlew, James F. Tyranny & Political Culture in Ancient Greece. LC 93-15653. 232p. 1993. text 39.95 (0-8014-2787-8) Cornell U Pr.

— Tyranny & Political Culture in Ancient Greece. 248p. 1996. pap. text 15.95 (0-8014-8387-5) Cornell U Pr.

McGlew, Polly A. Young Lawyer's Handbook - Legal Administration Office: What They Don't Teach You in Law School. 154p. (C). 1990. pap. text 19.95 (1-885477-06-6) Fut Horizons.

McGlew, Polly A., jt. auth. see Bilz, Reed K.

McGlinchey, Charles. The Last of the Name. LC 86-1161. (Illus.). 144p. 1993. reprint ed. pap. 12.95 (0-85640-361-X, Pub. by Blackstaff Pr) Dufour.

McGlinchy. Technical Guide to Alternative Fuels. (Automotive Technology Ser.). 1996. pap. 36.95 (0-8273-7170-5, VNR) Wiley.

*McGlinn, Jeanne M. Ann Rinaldi: Historian & Storyteller, No. 2. LC 99-53130. (Studies in Young Adult Literature : Vol. 2). 112p. 2000. 23.50 (0-8108-3678-5) Scarecrow.

McGlinn, Judith, compiled by. Mrs. Boone's Wild Game Cookbook. (Illus.). 176p. (Orig.). 1991. pap. 12.95 (1-879094-08-8) Momentum Bks.

McGlohan, Loomis, jt. auth. see Kuralt, Charles.

McGlohan, Loonis, jt. auth. see Kuralt, Charles.

*McGloin, Joe. Graduating into Life: The Next Steps to Making Your Hopes & Dreams Come True. 1999. 7.99 (0-88486-241-0, Inspirational Pr) Arrowood Pr.

McGloin, Joseph. Listen, Lord: Prayer for Plodders. (Illus.). 115p. (Orig.). 1987. pap. 2.95 (0-8199-0915-7, Frncscn Herld) Franciscan Pr.

*McGlone, Bill, et al. Archaeoastronomy of Southeast Colorado & the Oklahoma Panhandle. (Illus.). 140p. 1999. pap. 19.95 (0-9641333-1-8) Mithras.

McGlone, Bill, et al. Petroglyphs of Southeast Colorado & the Oklahoma Panhandle. (Illus.). 118p. (Orig.). 1994. pap. 14.95 (0-9641333-0-X) Mithras.

McGlone, John, ed. Antietam: The Maryland Campaign of 1862. (Civil War Regiments Ser.: Vol. 5, No. 3). 1997. pap. text 12.00 (1-882810-53-8) Savas Pub.

McGlone, John, et al. To Live & Die in Dixie: How the South Formed a Nation. 1998. pap. text 16.95 (1-889332-17-8) So Herit Pr.

McGlone, John, ed. see Ellis, Billy.

McGlone, John, ed. see Segars, J. H.

McGlone, Mary. Compartiendo la Fe en el Hemisferio. Ruiz, Guadalupe, tr. (Illus.). 352p. (C). 1997. pap. 19.95 (1-57455-125-6) US Catholic.

McGlone, Mary M. Sharing Faith Across the Hemisphere. LC 97-125356. (Illus.). 302p. (Orig.). (C). 1997. pap. 19.95 (1-57455-015-2) US Catholic.

— Sharing Faith Across the Hemisphere. LC 97-125356. (Illus.). 316p. (Orig.). reprint ed. pap. 98.00 (0-608-20184-7, 207144300012) Bks Demand.

McGlone, Mary T. The Bare-Bones Guide to Genealogy: How to Researching & Recording Your Family History. LC 97-30026. (Bare-Bones Guides Ser.). 102p. 1997. pap. 9.95 (0-87576-213-1) Pilot Bks.

McGlone, Randall K. Guts & Glory. Tobias, Eric, ed. 224p. (Orig.). 1992. pap. 4.99 (0-671-76062-9) PB.

McGlone, William R., et al. Ancient American Inscriptions: Plowmarks or History? LC 93-72155. (Illus.). 415p. (Orig.). (C). 1993. pap. 19.95 (1-884810-00-4) Early Sites.

McGlothin, Bruce. Great Grooming for Guys. Rosen, Ruth C., ed. (Life Skills Library). (Illus.). 48p. (YA). (gr. 7-12). 1993. lib. bdg. 14.95 (0-8239-1468-2) Rosen Group.

*McGlothin, Victor. Autumn Leaves: Love So Deep. 1999. pap. 15.00 (0-9667243-1-3) Well Done Bks.

McGlothin, Victor. In Spite Of. (Illus.). 247p. 1998. pap. 12.00 (0-9667243-0-5) Well Done Bks.

*McGlothlin, Bruce. Choosing a Career in Transportation. rev. ed. (World of Work Ser.). (Illus.). 64p. (YA). (gr. 7-12). 1999. 16.95 (0-8239-2998-1) Rosen Group.

McGlothlin, Bruce. Search & Succeed: A Guide to Using the Classifieds. LC 93-47545. (Life Skills Library). (Illus.). 48p. (YA). (gr. 7-12). 1994. lib. bdg. 14.95 (0-8239-1695-2) Rosen Group.

— Traveling Light: An Self-Exploration Book for Adolescents. (Illus.). 68p. 1992. pap. text 8.95 (1-57543-049-5) Mar Co Prods.

McGlothlin, Chris A. World's Fair Spoons Vol. I: The World's Columbian Exposition. LC 85-70480. (Illus.). 1985. 35.00 (0-9614824-0-0) Fla Rare Coin.

McGlothlin, Christopher. Atarron. 360p. 1994. pap. 5.95 (0-9639383-0-4) Delacroix Pubng.

*McGloughlin, Stephen. Multimedia: Concepts & Practice. 608p. 2000. 73.33 (0-13-018830-1) Prntice Hall Bks.

McGlynn. Dynamics of Fitness. 4th ed. 1995. teacher ed. 12.81 (0-697-25622-7, WCB McGr Hill) McGrw-H Hghr Educ.

— Dynamics of Fitness. 6th ed. 2001. pap. 13.50 (0-07-235409-7) McGraw.

McGlynn, jt. auth. see Moran-McGlynn.

McGlynn, Betty H. & Murray, Mary. Jo Mora: Artist & Writer. (Illus.). 64p. 1998. pap. 24.95 (1-891586-01-7) Monterey Mus.

*McGlynn, Carole. The Ultimate Gardening Book: Over 1,000 Inspirational Ideas & Practical Tips to Transform Your Garden. (Illus.). 448p. 1999. pap. 24.95 (1-85585-738-3, Pub. by Collins & Br) Sterling.

McGlynn, Cathy, jt. auth. see Stewart, Bonnie.

McGlynn, Clare. Legal Feminisms: Theory & Practice. LC 97-41408. 242p. 1998. text 77.95 (1-85521-927-1, Pub. by Ashgate Pub) Ashgate Pub Co.

McGlynn, Edward M. & Hatcher, Richard G., eds. Gangs & Guns, Drugs & Death. 1998. 14.95 (0-268-01035-8); pap. 14.95 (0-268-01034-X) U of Notre Dame Pr.

McGlynn, Elizabeth A., ed. Exploring Policy Issues in Managed Care: Six Illustrative Case Studies, 2 vols. 267p. 2001. 38.00 (0-8330-2600-3, Pub. by Rand Corp) Natl Bk Netwk.

— Exploring Policy Issues in Managed Care Vol. 2: Six Illustrative Case Studies, 2 vols. (Illus.). 2001. pap. 25.00 (0-8330-2631-3, Pub. by Rand Corp) Natl Bk Netwk.

McGlynn, Elizabeth A., et al. Health Information Systems: Design Issues & Analytic Applications. (Illus.). 500p. 1998. 55.00 (0-8330-2599-6, MR-967-HF, Pub. by Rand Corp) Natl Bk Netwk.

— Health Information Systems: Design Issues & Analytic Applications. (Illus.). 350p. 1998. pap. 40.00 (0-8330-2630-5, MR-967-HF) Rand Corp.

— Medical Record Abstraction Form & Guidelines for Assessing the Appropriateness of Hysterectomy. LC 93-4601. 1993. pap. 9.00 (0-8330-1394-7, MR-239-HF) Rand Corp.

— Medical Record Abstraction Form & Guidelines for Assessing the Quality of Prenatal Care. LC 93-4622. 1993. pap. 9.00 (0-8330-1393-9, MR-238-HF) Rand Corp.

McGlynn, Elizabeth A., jt. auth. see Haaga, John G.

McGlynn, Frank, Jr. & Drescher, Seymour, eds. The Meaning of Freedom: Economics, Politics, & Culture after Slavery. LC 91-26606. (Latin American Ser.). (Illus.). 352p. 1992. pap. 19.95 (0-8229-5479-6); text 49.95 (0-8229-3695-X) U of Pittsburgh Pr.

McGlynn, George. Dynamics of Fitness. 4th ed. 368p. (C). 1997. per. write for info. (0-07-114976-7) McGraw.

Mcglynn, George. Dynamics of Fitness. 5th ed. LC 98-17043. 256p. 1998. pap. 17.50 (0-697-29576-1) McGraw.

McGlynn, George. Dynamics of Fitness: A Practical Approach. 4th ed. LC 95-187422. 368p. (C). 1995. text. write for info. (0-697-24651-5) Brown & Benchmark.

— Fitness Made Easy. 304p. 1990. text. write for info. (0-697-11015-X) Brown & Benchmark.

McGlynn, George, jt. auth. see Moran, Gary T.

McGlynn, George H., jt. auth. see Moran, Gary T.

McGlynn, John, jt. ed. see Stewart, Frank.

McGlynn, John H., jt. auth. see Kumar, Ann.

McGlynn, John H., tr. see Frederick, William H., ed.

McGlynn, John H., tr. see Marahimin, Ismail.

McGlynn, John H., tr. see Pane, Armijn.

McGlynn, R. P., ed. see Harvey, J. H., et al.

McGlynn, Sean. The Invasion of England, 1216: Warfare in the Early Thirteenth Century. (Illus.). 192p. 1998. 36.95 (0-7509-1016-X, Pub. by Sutton Pub Ltd) Intl Pubs Mktg.

McGlynn, Terrence D. Montana Tech: Eighteen Ninety-Three to Nineteen Eighty-Four. (Illus.). 112p. 1984. 14.95 (0-930609-00-X) Montana Tech.

McGlynn, Thomas J. & Metcalf, Harry L., eds. Diagnosis & Treatment of Anxiety Disorders: A Physician's Handbook. 2nd ed. 144p. 1991. spiral bd. 18.50 (0-88048-523-X, 8523) Am Psychiatric.

McGoffee, Michael & Gard, Diane. One in a Billion. (Illus.). 29p. (J). (gr. 3-5). 1996. 14.95 (1-887578-04-8) SpanPr.

McGoldrick. Video Technology for Personal Computers. 1996. text 50.00 (0-07-045018-8) McGraw.

McGoldrick, Ann & Copper, Cary. Early Retirement. 1989. text 78.95 (0-566-05244-X, Pub. by Gower) Ashgate Pub Co.

McGoldrick, Dominic. The Human Rights Committee: Its Role in the Development of the International Covenant on Civil & Political Rights. (Oxford Monographs in International Law). 640p. 1994. reprint ed. pap. text 39.95 (0-19-825894-1) OUP.

— International Relations of the European Communities. LC 96-43836. (European Law Ser.). xvii, 249p. (C). 1997. pap. text 29.00 (0-582-28857-6, 15708) Gaunt.

McGoldrick, James, jt. auth. see McGoldrick, Nikoo.

McGoldrick, James E. Baptist Successionism: A Crucial Question in Baptist History. LC 93-5931. (American Theological Library Association Monograph: No. 32). 190p. 1994. 31.00 (0-8108-2726-3) Scarecrow.

*McGoldrick, James E. Baptist Successionism: A Crucial Question in Baptist History. 192p. 2000. reprint ed. pap. 26.95 (0-8108-3681-5) Scarecrow.

McGoldrick, James E. Luther's Scottish Connection. LC 88-46054. 128p. 1989. 28.50 (0-8386-3357-9) Fairleigh Dickinson.

McGoldrick, Jim, jt. ed. see Stewart, Jim.

McGoldrick, Joseph D. Law & Practice of Municipal Home Rule, 1916-1930. LC 33-22314. reprint ed. 29.50 (0-404-04128-0) AMS Pr.

McGoldrick, Kathryn E., ed. Ambulatory Anesthesiology: A Problem-Oriented Approach. LC 94-1854. (Illus.). 808p. 1994. 89.00 (0-683-05875-4) Lppncott W & W.

— Anesthesia for Ophthalmic & Otolaryngologic Surgery. (Illus.). 336p. 1991. text 69.00 (0-7216-2837-0, W B Saunders Co) Harcrt Hlth Sci Grp.

McGoldrick, Linda C. Nora S. Unwin: Artist & Wood Engraver. LC 89-208. (Illus.). 208p. 1990. pap. 27.50 (0-87233-097-4) Bauhan.

McGoldrick, May. Beauty of the Mist. 384p. 1997. mass mkt. 5.99 (0-451-40714-8, Onyx) NAL.

— Flame. 1998. mass mkt. 5.99 (0-451-40807-1, Topaz) NAL.

*McGoldrick, May. Highland Treasure: The Dreamer. 2000. mass mkt. 5.99 (0-451-19718-6, Onyx) NAL.

— Highland Treasure: The Enchantress. 2000. mass mkt. 5.99 (0-451-19719-4, Onyx) NAL.

McGoldrick, May. Intended. 384p. 1998. mass mkt. 5.99 (0-451-40806-3, Onyx) NAL.

— The Thistle & the Rose. 384p. 1995. mass mkt. 4.99 (0-451-40626-5) NAL.

McGoldrick, Monica. Women in Families: A Framework for Family Therapy. 1991. pap. 20.95 (0-393-30776-X) Norton.

— You Can Go Home Again: Reconnecting with Your Family. (Illus.). 336p. 1997. pap. 15.95 (0-393-31650-5) Norton.

— You Can Go Home Again: Reconnecting with Your Family. (Illus.). 331p. 1998. reprint ed. lib. bdg. 32.95 (0-7351-0020-9) Replica Bks.

McGoldrick, Monica, ed. Re-Visioning Family Therapy: Race, Culture & Gender in Clinical Practice. LC 98-6174. 444p. 1998. lib. bdg. 44.00 (1-57230-027-2, C0027) Guilford Pubns.

McGoldrick, Monica, et al, eds. Ethnicity & Family Therapy. 2nd ed. LC 96-7923. 717p. 1996. lib. bdg. 59.00 (0-89862-959-4) Guilford Pubns.

McGoldrick, Monica & Gerson, Randy. Genograms: Assessment & Intervention. 2nd ed. LC 99-17993. (Illus.). 234p. 1999. pap. 17.00 (0-393-70294-4) Norton.

McGoldrick, Monica, jt. ed. see Walsh, Froma.

*McGoldrick, Nikoo & McGoldrick, James. Marriage of Minds: Collaborative Fiction Writing. LC 00-26784. 160p. 2000. pap. 12.95 (0-325-00232-0) Heinemann.

McGoldrick, Peter & Davies, Gary, eds. International Retailing: Trends & Strategies. 208p. 2000. pap. write for info. (0-273-61183-6) F T P H.

McGoldrick, Peter, jt. auth. see Thonpson, Mark.

McGoldrick, Peter J. Retailing of Financial Services. LC 94-7269. 1994. write for info. (0-07-707613-3) McGraw.

McGoldrick, Terence A. The Sweet & Gentle Struggle: Francis de Dales on the Necessity of Spiritual Friendship. LC 96-8817. 558p. 1996. lib. bdg. 59.50 (0-7618-0416-1) U Pr of Amer.

McGonagall, William. Collected Poems. 172p. pap. 17.95 (1-874744-01-7, Pub. by Birlinn Ltd) Dufour.

Mcgonagall, William. Mcgonagall: A Selection. LC 99-164629. 1998. pap. text 9.95 (1-874744-11-4, Pub. by Birlinn Ltd) Dufour.

*McGonagall, William. The Tay Bridge Disaster & Other Poetic Gems. 64p. 2000. pap. 12.95 (0-914061-84-4) Orchises Pr.

McGonagall, William. The World's Worst Poet. 128p. (Orig.). 1979. pap. 6.95 (0-87243-088-X) Templegate.

McGonagill, Grady. Overcoming Barriers to Education Restructuring: A Call for System Literacy. 40p. 1993. pap. 2.50 (0-87652-194-4) Am Assn Sch Admin.

McGonagle, Cindy. Garden Notes: From the Nature Devas. (Illus.). 94p. 1993. pap. 12.95 (0-9640243-0-6) Botanic Reprod.

— Queen D's Fairy Recipe Book. Alder, Debora, ed. (Illus.). 92p. 1994. pap. 13.25 (0-9640243-1-4) Botanic Reprod.

McGonagle, Declan & Warhol, Andy. After the Party: Andy Warhol: Works 1956-1986. (Illus.). 80p. pap. 30.00 (0-85331-716-X, Pub. by Lund Humphries) Antique Collect.

McGonagle, Dorothy. The Dolls of Jules Nicolas Steiner. LC 89-121889. (Illus.). 240p. 1988. 39.95 (0-87588-312-5, 3594) Hobby Hse.

McGonagle, Dorothy A. A Celebration of American Dolls. LC 98-185503. 144p. 1999. 29.95 (0-87588-479-2) Hobby Hse.

McGonagle, John, jt. auth. see Vella, Carolyn, Jr.

McGonagle, John J. & Vella, Carolyn M. The Internet Age of Competitive Intelligence. LC 98-27835. 240p. 1999. 59.95 (1-56720-204-7, Quorum Bks) Greenwood.

McGonagle, John J., Jr. & Vella, Carolyn M. A New Archetype for Competitive Intelligence. LC 95-50744. 240p. 1996. 59.95 (0-89930-973-9, Quorum Bks) Greenwood.

— Outsmarting the Competition: Practical Approaches to Finding & Using Competitive Information. LC 92-46122. 1993. 25.00 (0-07-707755-5) McGraw.

McGonagle, John J. & Vella, Carolyn M. Protecting Your Company Against Competitive Intelligence. LC 97-13402. 176p. 1998. 55.00 (1-56720-117-2, Quorum Bks) Greenwood.

McGonagle, John J., Jr., jt. auth. see Vella, Carolyn M.

McGonagle, Sara R. Mid-Level Practitioners: Their Role in Providing Quality Health Care. (Working Paper Ser.: No. 64). 42p. 1992. pap. 5.50 (0-89940-546-0) LBJ Sch Pub Aff.

McGonegal, Brian L. & Enger, David C. The Microgolf Primer: Raise Golf Acres in Yards. LC 97-222644. 87p. 1997. pap. 24.95 (0-9658430-0-9) Microgolf Pr.

McGonigle, Chris. Surviving Your Spouse's Chronic Illness: A Compassionate Guide. LC 98-23240. 256p. 1999. pap. 13.95 (0-8050-5573-8, Owl) H Holt & Co.

McGonigle, La Dean. Quiet Waters of Inspiration: In Verse. 140p. (Orig.). 1997. pap. 9.95 (1-57502-384-9, P01219) Morris Pubng.

McGonigle, Thomas. The Corpse Dream of N. Petkov. LC 86-72661. 134p. 1987. 20.00 (0-916583-19-8) Dalkey Arch.

— Going to Patchogue. LC 91-13068. (Illus.). 220p. 1992. 19.95 (0-916583-87-2) Dalkey Arch.

— In Patchogue. 32p. (Orig.). 1985. pap. 10.00 (0-916351-00-9) Adrift Edns.

McGonigle, Thomas D. & Quigley, James F. A History of the Christian Tradition Vol. 1: From Its Jewish Origins to the Reformation. 224p. 1988. pap. 16.95 (0-8091-2964-7) Paulist Pr.

— A History of the Christian Tradition Vol. 2: From the Reformation to the Present. 304p. 1996. pap. 17.95 (0-8091-3648-1, 3648-1) Paulist Pr.

McGonnagle, Warren J. International Advances in Nondestructive Testing. (International Advances in Nondestructive Ser.: Vol. 16). iv, 400p. 1991. text 209.00 (2-88124-497-1) Gordon & Breach.

— Nondestructive Testing. 2nd ed. (Illus.). xiv, 456p. 1971. text 252.00 (0-677-00500-8) Gordon & Breach.

McGonnagle, Warren J., ed. Automated Nondestructive Testing: Proceedings of a Topical Seminar. (Nondestructive Testing Monographs & Tracts: Vol. 4). xii, 284p. 1986. pap. text 249.00 (2-88124-056-9) Gordon & Breach.

— Internation Advances in Nondestructive Testing, Vol. 17. 400p. 1994. text 182.00 (2-88124-582-X) Gordon & Breach.

— International Advances in Nondestructive Testing, Vol. 10. 1984. text 283.00 (2-88124-101-8) Gordon & Breach.

— International Advances in Nondestructive Testing, Vol. 11. viii, 376p. 1985. text 198.00 (2-88124-034-8) Gordon & Breach.

— International Advances in Nondestructive Testing, Vol. 12. viii, 372p. 1986. text 192.00 (2-88124-182-4) Gordon & Breach.

— International Advances in Nondestructive Testing, Vol. 14. viii, 366p. 1989. text 182.00 (2-88124-327-4) Gordon & Breach.

— International Advances in Nondestructive Testing, Vol. 15. vii, 394p. 1990. text 165.00 (2-88124-445-9) Gordon & Breach.

McGoodwin, James R. Crisis in the World's Fisheries: People, Problems, & Policies. LC 90-37484. 247p. 1991. 39.50 (0-8047-1790-7) Stanford U Pr.

— Crisis in the World's Fisheries: People, Problems, & Policies. xii, 235p. 1994. pap. 14.95 (0-8047-2371-0) Stanford U Pr.

McGoodwin, James R., jt. ed. see Dyer, Christopher L.

McGoogan, Kenneth. Canada's Undeclared War: Fighting Words from the Literary Trenches. 277p. 1991. pap. 18.95 (1-55059-032-4) Temeron Bks.

McGoon, Cliff, ed. see International Association of Business Communicator.

McGoon, Dwight C. Parkinson's Handbook. 1994. pap. 12.95 (0-393-31143-0) Norton.

McGorian, Gladys. The Prince Regent's Silver Bell. 256p. 1987. 16.95 (0-8027-0954-0) Walker & Co.

McGormack, jt. auth. see Lone.

*McGorman, Evan. Life in the Foreign Legion: How to Join & What to Expect When You Get There. 250p. 2000. 22.95 (1-55571-532-X, Pub. by PSI Resch) Midpt Trade.

McGoron, Ted. Computers & What You Absolutely Need to Know about Them. 61p. (YA). (gr. 7-12). 1995. pap. 6.95 (1-57515-047-6) PPI Pubng.

*McGoron, Ted J. Fun Things You Can Do with a Catheter: Enduring a Prostatectomy. LC 99-91493. 1999. 25.00 (0-7388-0838-5); pap. 18.00 (0-7388-0839-3) Xlibris Corp.

McGorray, David, ed. see McGorray, Judy.

McGorray, Judy. Christmas Gift. 46p. (Orig.). 1996. pap. text 8.00 (1-888200-13-8) JayMac Commun.

— Cookbook for Planning an Eagle Court of Honor. (Illus.). 110p. 1997. ring bd. 25.00 (1-888200-15-4) JayMac Commun.

— Covenant. Meyers, Del & McGorray, David, eds. 26p. (Orig.). 1996. pap. text 10.00 (1-888200-11-1) JayMac Commun.

— Cradle of the Savior. 31p. (Orig.). 1996. pap. text 8.00 (1-888200-09-X) JayMac Commun.

*McGorray, Judy. Dawn Patrol. McGorray, David et al, eds. (Illus.). 209p. 1999. spiral bd. 15.00 (1-888200-20-0) JayMac Commun.

McGorray, Judy. Friends in Passing. Meyers, Del et al, eds. (Illus.). 107p. 1998. spiral bd. 10.00 (1-888200-17-0) JayMac Commun.

— Identity. Meyers, Del & McGorray, David, eds. 36p. (Orig.). 1997. pap. text 10.00 (1-888200-12-X) JayMac Commun.

— Joseph's Cantata. 25p. 1989. pap. text 10.00 (1-888200-05-7) JayMac Commun.

— Morning Exercises. 113p. 1993. pap. text 10.00 (1-888200-00-6) JayMac Commun.

An Asterisk (*) at the beginning of an entry indicates that the title is appearing for the first time.

— On the Road to Bethlehem. unabridged ed. Meyers, Del & McGorray, David, eds. 43p. 1997. spiral bd. 10.00 (*1-888200-16-2*) JayMac Commun.

— Questions. (Illus.). 31p. (Orig.). 1996. pap. text 8.00 (*1-888200-10-3*) JayMac Commun.

— Star Search. 25p. 1993. pap. text 8.00 (*1-888200-04-9*) JayMac Commun.

— Thoughts for Scouts Own. 35p. (YA). (gr. 6-12). 1997. pap. text 4.00 (*1-888200-08-1*) JayMac Commun.

— Thursday's Child. 129p. 1997. pap. text 10.00 (*1-888200-07-3*) JayMac Commun.

— Trial. 67p. 1995. pap. text 10.00 (*1-888200-02-2*) JayMac Commun.

— What Is the Gift? Poetry & a Little Prose. 94p. 1994. pap. text 10.00 (*1-888200-01-4*) JayMac Commun.

— A Winter's Tale. 19p. (Orig.). 1995. pap. text 8.00 (*1-888200-06-5*) JayMac Commun.

— Witness. 47p. 1994. pap. text 10.00 (*1-888200-03-0*) JayMac Commun.

McGorrin, Robert J., ed. see American Chemical Society Staff.

McGorry, Patrick D. & Jackson, Henry J., eds. The Recognition & Management of Early Psychosis: A Preventive Approach. LC 98-25807. (Illus.). 400p. (C). 1999. text 90.00 (*0-521-55383-0*) Cambridge U Pr.

McGorry, Patrick D., jt. auth. see Perris, Carlo.

McGough, Barry M. Georgia Divorce. LC 79-91143. (Practice Systems Library Manual). 1134p. ring bd. 120.00 (*0-317-00582-0*) West Group.

— Georgia Divorce. LC 79-91143. (Practice Systems Library Manual). 1134p. 1993. suppl. ed. 60.00 (*0-317-03208-9*) West Group.

McGough, Edward M. Beyond the Far Ridge: Pioneering in the Rocky Mountain High Country. LC 91-32596. (Illus.). 208p. (Orig.). 1992. pap. 10.95 (*0-931271-15-0*) Hi Plains Pr.

— Echoes from the West. LC 98-24077. 1999. pap. 14.95 (*0-931271-48-7*) Hi Plains Pr.

McGough, James P., tr. & selected by see Hsiao-t'ung Fei.

McGough, Lucy S. Child Witnesses: Fragile Voices in the American Legal System. LC 93-49769. (Illus.). 352p. 1994. 37.50 (*0-300-05748-2*) Yale U Pr.

— Child Witnesses: Fragile Voices in the American Legal System. (Illus.). 352p. 1996. pap. 19.00 (*0-300-06857-3*) Yale U Pr.

— Louisiana Children's Code Handbook LC 98-159679. (West's Louisiana Deskbks.). 1005 p. 1998. write for info. (*0-314-23268-0*) West Pub.

McGough, Michael R. Gettysburg Battlefield Tour Book. (Illus.). 32p. 1987. pap. 3.50 (*0-939631-06-7*) Thomas Publications.

— Hey, Mr. McRay! 160p. (Orig.). (YA). (gr. 7-12). 1999. pap. 10.00 (*0-9639450-3-3*) Joy Ent.

McGough, Peter, jt. photos by see McDermott, David.

Mcgough, Robert C. & Finch, Curtis R. Administering & Supervising Occupational Education. (Illus.). 302p. (C). 1991. reprint ed. pap. text 23.95 (*0-88133-640-8*) Waveland Pr.

McGough, Roger. Great Smile Robbery. (Illus.). 80p. (J). (gr. 3-6). 1984. pap. 7.95 (*0-14-031437-7*, Pub. by Pnguin Bks Ltd) Trafalgar.

— An Imaginary Menagerie. (YA). (gr. 7 up). 1990. pap. 7.95 (*0-14-032790-8*, Pub. by Pnguin Bks Ltd) Trafalgar.

— Nailing the Shadow. (Illus.). (J). (gr. 3). 1989. pap. 7.95 (*0-14-032390-2*, Pub. by Pnguin Bks Ltd) Trafalgar.

— Pillow Talk. (Illus.). 80p. (YA). (gr. 7 up). 1992. pap. 7.95 (*0-14-032504-2*, Pub. by Pnguin Bks Ltd) Trafalgar.

— Sky in the Pie. 1985. pap. 7.95 (*0-14-031612-4*, Pub. by Pnguin Bks Ltd) Trafalgar.

— Stowaways. (J). (gr. 3-6). 1988. pap. 7.95 (*0-14-031649-3*, Pub. by Pnguin Bks Ltd) Trafalgar.

— Summer with Monika. (J). pap. 14.95 (*0-14-058648-2*, Pub. by Pnguin Bks Ltd) Trafalgar.

McGough, Roger. Until I Met Dudley: How Every Day Things Really Work. LC 96-47900. (Illus.). 32p. (J). (gr. 1-5). 1997. 15.95 (*0-8027-8623-5*); lib. bdg. 16.85 (*0-8027-8624-3*) Walker & Co.

McGough, Roger & Prater, John. The Kite & Caitlin. (Illus.). 32p. (J). (gr. k-3). 1997. 19.95 (*0-370-32371-8*, Pub. by Bodley Head) Trafalgar.

McGough, Roger, jt. auth. see Henri, Adrian.

McGough, Roger, jt. auth. see Rosen, Michael.

McGough, Wallace D. The Adventures of Walter Ant Bk. I: The Unknown. 56p. (J). pap. 9.95 (*0-9645180-0-7*) Fam Val Pub.

— The Adventures of Walter Ant Bk. 1: The Unknown. (Illus.). 56p. (J). 1995. 11.95 (*0-9645180-1-5*) Fam Val Pub.

McGouldrick, Paul F. New England Textiles in the Nineteenth Century: Profits & Investment. LC 68-14267. (Economic Studies: No. 131). (Illus.). 1990. 20.00 (*0-674-61400-3*) HUP.

McGoun, Elton G., jt. auth. see Frankfurter, George M.

McGoun, William E. Prehistoric Peoples of South Florida. LC 92-40833. 152p. 1993. pap. text 19.95 (*0-8173-0686-2*) U of Ala Pr.

— Southeast Florida Pioneers: The Palm & Treasure Coasts. LC 98-20285. (Illus.). 192p. 1998. 16.95 (*1-56164-157-X*) Pineapple Pr.

McGoveran, David, jt. auth. see Date, C. J.

***McGovern.** Cracker to Be Somebody. 2000. mass mkt. write for info. (*0-312-96998-8*) St Martin.

— The Third Freedom. 2001. write for info. (*0-684-85334-5*) Simon & Schuster.

McGovern & Lawrence. Contracts & Sales: Cases & Problems. 1986. teacher ed. 56.00 (*0-8205-2881-1*) Bender.

***McGovern, et al.** Cracker. LC 98-50900. 256p. 1999. text 22.95 (*0-312-20086-2*) St Martin.

***Mcgovern, Adam, ed.** Musichound World: The Essential Album Guide. (Illus.). 1096p. 1999. pap. text 26.95 incl. cd-rom (*1-57859-039-6*) Visible Ink Pr.

McGovern, Ann. Adventures of the Shark Lady: Eugene Clark Around the World. (Illus.). 96p. (gr. 3-7). 1999. pap. 4.50 (*0-590-45712-8*) Scholastic Inc.

— The Defenders. 128p. (Orig.). (J). (gr. 4-7). 1987. pap. 2.95 (*0-590-43866-2*) Scholastic Inc.

— If You Grew up with Abraham Lincoln. (Illus.). 80p. (J). (gr. 4-7). 1992. pap. 5.99 (*0-590-45154-5*) Scholastic Inc.

— If You Grew up with Abraham Lincoln. 1992. 11.19 (*0-606-03408-0*, Pub. by Turtleback) Demco.

— If You Lived in Colonial Times. (J). 1964. 11.19 (*0-606-01131-5*, Pub. by Turtleback) Demco.

— If You Lived in Colonial Times. (Illus.). 80p. (J). (gr. 2-5). 1992. pap. 4.95 (*0-590-45160-X*) Scholastic Inc.

***McGovern, Ann.** If You Lived 100 Years Ago. (Illus.). 80p. (gr. 2-5). 1999. pap. 5.99 (*0-590-96001-6*) Scholastic Inc.

McGovern, Ann. If You Lived with the Sioux Indians. (J). 1972. 10.15 (*0-606-01132-3*, Pub. by Turtleback) Demco.

— If You Sailed on the Mayflower. (J). 1991. 11.19 (*0-606-00679-6*, Pub. by Turtleback) Demco.

McGovern, Ann. If You Sailed on the Mayflower in 1620. LC 74-124182. (Illus.). 80p. (J). (ps-3). 1991. pap. 5.99 (*0-590-45161-8*) Scholastic Inc.

McGovern, Ann. The Lady in the Box. LC 97-13633. (Illus.). 40p. (YA). (ps up). 1997. 14.95 (*1-890515-01-9*, Pub. by Turtle Bks) Publishers Group.

***McGovern, Ann.** The Lady in the Box. (Illus.). 40p. (YA). (ps up). 1999. pap. 7.95 (*1-890515-15-9*, Pub. by Turtle Bks) Publishers Group.

McGovern, Ann. Nicholas Bentley Stoningpot III. LC 91-77614. (Illus.). 32p. (J). (ps-3). 1992. lib. bdg. 14.95 (*1-56397-104-6*) Boyds Mills Pr.

— Nicholas Bentley Stoningpot III. 1997. 11.19 (*0-606-12782-8*, Pub. by Turtleback) Demco.

— The Pilgrim's 1st Thanksgiving. (Illus.). 48p. (J). (gr. k-5). 1984. pap. 2.50 (*0-590-40617-5*) Scholastic Inc.

— Pilgrims' First Thanksgiving. 32p. (J). (ps-3). 1993. pap. 3.95 (*0-590-46188-5*) Scholastic Inc.

— The Pilgrims' First Thanksgiving. 1993. 9.15 (*0-606-05973-3*, Pub. by Turtleback) Demco.

— Playing with Penguins & Other Adventures in Antarctica. LC 92-4646. 48p. (J). (gr. 4-7). 1995. pap. 4.95 (*0-590-44175-2*) Scholastic Inc.

McGovern, Ann. Playing with Penguins & Other Adventures in Antarctica. (J). 1994. 10.15 (*0-606-08023-6*, Pub. by Turtleback) Demco.

McGovern, Ann. Robin Hood of Sherwood Forest. LC 68-11066. 128p. (J). (gr. 4-7). 1991. pap. 3.50 (*0-590-45441-2*) Scholastic Inc.

McGovern, Ann. Robin Hood of Sherwood Forest. (J). 1968. 8.60 (*0-606-03260-6*, Pub. by Turtleback) Demco.

McGovern, Ann. The Secret Soldier: The Story of Deborah Sampson. 64p. (J). (gr. 4-7). 1990. pap. 2.99 (*0-590-43052-1*) Scholastic Inc.

McGovern, Ann. Secret Soldier: The Story of Deborah Sampson. (Scholastic Biography Ser.). (J). 1975. 8.19 (*0-606-03123-5*, Pub. by Turtleback) Demco.

McGovern, Ann. La Senora de la Caja de Carton. Peluffo, Ana Luisa, tr.Tr. of Lady in the Box. (SPA., Illus.). 40p. (YA). (ps up). 1997. 14.95 (*1-890515-02-7*, Pub. by Turtle Bks) Publishers Group.

***McGovern, Ann.** La Senora de la Caja de Carton.Tr. of Lady in the Box. (SPA., Illus.). 40p. (YA). (ps up). 1999. pap. 7.95 (*1-890515-16-7*, Pub. by Turtle Bks) Publishers Group.

McGovern, Ann. Shark Lady: True Adventures of Eugenie Clark. 1978. 8.60 (*0-606-03913-9*, Pub. by Turtleback) Demco.

— Sharks. 1976. 10.15 (*0-606-01065-3*, Pub. by Turtleback) Demco.

— Stone Soup. LC 86-10098. (Illus.). 32p. (J). (ps-3). 1986. pap. text 2.99 (*0-590-41602-2*) Scholastic Inc.

— Too Much Noise, 001. 48p. (J). (gr. k-3). 1967. 16.00 (*0-395-18110-0*) HM.

— Too Much Noise. (Illus.). 48p. (J). (gr. k-3). 1992. pap. 6.95 (*0-395-62985-3*, Sandpiper) HM.

— Too Much Noise. (Illus.). 48p. (J). (gr. k-3). 1967. pap. 1.95 (*0-590-02435-3*) Scholastic Inc.

— Too Much Noise. 1967. 12.15 (*0-606-01435-7*, Pub. by Turtleback) Demco.

— Wanted Dead or Alive: The True Story of Harriet Tubman. (Illus.). 64p. (J). (ps-3). 1991. 3.95 (*0-590-44212-0*) Scholastic Inc.

McGovern, Ann & Aesop. Aesop's Fables. (J). 1963. 9.19 (*0-606-03705-5*, Pub. by Turtleback) Demco.

McGovern, Ann, jt. auth. see Brookes, Diane.

McGovern, Arthur F., jt. auth. see Cavanagh, Gerald F.

McGovern, Barbara. Anne Finch & Her Poetry: A Critical Biography. LC 91-23862. 264p. 1992. 50.00 (*0-8203-1410-2*) U of Ga Pr.

McGovern, Bernie, ed. see Marth, Del & Martin, Martha J.

McGovern, Brian. Competitive Obedience for Winners. (Illus.). 144p. 1995. 24.95 (*1-86054-035-X*, Pub. by Ringpr Bks) Seven Hills Bk.

McGovern, Carolyn, ed. The Changing Landscape of Indexing: Proceedings of the 26th Annual Meeting of the American Society of Indexers. 59p. 1994. pap. text 25.00 (*0-936547-23-5*) Am Soc Index.

McGovern, Constance M. Masters of Madness: Social Origins of the American Psychiatric Profession. LC 85-40491. 278p. reprint ed. pap. 86.20 (*0-608-09090-5*, 206972400005) Bks Demand.

McGovern, Dan. The Campo Indian Landfill War: The Fight for Gold in California's Garbage. LC 95-5857. (Illus.). 352p. 1995. 26.95 (*0-8061-2755-4*) U of Okla Pr.

McGovern, Dave. The Complete Guide to Racewalking Technique & Training. (Illus.). xiv, 226p. 1998. pap. 17.95 (*0-9662176-0-8*) Wrld Class Pubns.

McGovern, Don, et al. Reading: Student's Book. LC 94-19762. (Series English for Academic Study). 1994. 9.75 (*0-01-397872-1*) P-H Intl.

McGovern, Don, jt. auth. see White, Ron.

McGovern, Edythe M. & Muller, Helen D. They're Never Too Young for Books: A Guide to Children's Books Ages 1-8. LC 93-33855. 342p. 1994. pap. 15.95 (*0-87975-858-9*) Prometheus Bks.

McGovern, Elizabeth. Math. 1997. 4.95 (*1-55708-574-9*, MCJ801) McDonald Pub Co.

McGovern, Frances. Written on the Hills: The Making of the Akron Landscape. (Ohio History & Culture Ser.). (Illus.). 241p. 1996. 39.95 (*1-884836-21-6*); pap. 19.95 (*1-884836-22-4*) U Akron Pr.

McGovern, Frances E., jt. auth. see Baldwin, Scott.

McGovern, G. S., et al. Vietnam: Four American Perspectives - Lectures by George S. McGovern, William C. Westmoreland, Edward N. Luttwak, & Thomas J. McCormick. Hearden, Patrick J., ed. LC 89-24267. 128p. 1990. 19.95 (*1-55753-002-5*); pap. 14.95 (*1-55753-003-3*) Purdue U Pr.

McGovern, Gail, jt. auth. see Rubin, Rhea J.

McGovern, George. Terry: My Daughter's Life & Death Struggle with Alcoholism. LC 97-11886. 224p. 1997. pap. 11.95 (*0-452-27823-6*, Plume) Dutton Plume.

— Terry: My Daughter's Life & Death Struggle with Alcoholism. 1999. pap. write for info. (*0-452-27833-3*, Plume) Dutton Plume.

McGovern, George S. Food & Popuation: The World in Crises. 1976. 27.95 (*0-405-06663-5*, 1752) Ayer.

McGovern, Ian, ed. Marketing: A Southeast Asian Perspective. LC 95-40594. 1997. write for info. (*0-201-88910-2*) Addison-Wesley.

McGovern, J. B. Among the Head-Hunters of Formosa. 220p. 1997. reprint ed. 30.00 (*957-638-421-4*) Oriental Bk Store.

McGovern, James A. The Essence of Engineering Thermodynamics. LC 95-40396. (Essence of Engineering Ser.). (C). 1996. pap. text 19.95 (*0-13-518192-5*) P-H.

***McGovern, James I.** Aura of Purgatory: A Novel. LC 99-50838. 224p. 2000. pap. 14.95 (*1-56474-339-X*) Fithian Pr.

McGovern, James R. Anatomy of a Lynching: The Killing of Claude Neal. LC 81-17140. (Illus.). 170p. (C). 1992. pap. 14.95 (*0-8071-1766-8*) La State U Pr.

— And a Time for Hope: Americans in the Great Depression. LC 99-41959. 368p. 2000. write for info. (*0-275-96786-7*, Praeger Pubs) Greenwood.

McGovern, James R. Black Eagle: General Daniel "Chappie" James, Jr. LC 84-8. (Illus.). 213p. 1985. reprint ed. pap. 66.10 (*0-608-01675-6*, 206233100002) Bks Demand.

— Yankee Family. LC 75-4470. 191p. 1978. pap. text 24.95 (*0-87855-674-5*) Transaction Pubs.

McGovern, Jean, jt. auth. see McGovern, John.

McGovern, Jimmy & Holliday, Liz. Cracker: One Day a Lemming Will Fly. 1999. mass mkt. 5.99 (*0-312-96817-5*) St Martin.

McGovern, Jimy, jt. auth. see Holliday, Liz.

McGovern, John & McGovern, Jean. First Class in Banking: Elementary English for Bank Counter Staff. LC 97-39368. 1998. 9.63 (*0-13-074386-0*) P-H.

McGovern, John, jt. ed. see Starck, Patricia.

McGovern, John P., jt. auth. see DuPont, Robert L.

McGovern, John T. Diogenes Discovers Us. LC 67-26758. (Essay Index Reprint Ser.). 1977. 21.95 (*0-8369-0647-0*) Ayer.

McGovern, Kathy. Creating Fun: Recreation, Sports & Hobbies. Coffey, Kathy, ed. LC 98-159711. (Crossings : Vol. 4). 72p. (YA). 1998. pap. 3.95 (*1-889108-38-3*) Liv Good News.

McGovern, Margaret & Witcher, Sarah. Altschul's Psychiatric & Mental Health Nursing. 7th ed. (Nurses' Aids Ser.). (Illus.). 383p. 1995. pap. text 16.95 (*0-7020-1412-5*, Pub. by W B Saunders) Saunders.

***McGovern, Michael H.** The Quotable Athlete: Words of Wisdom from Mark McGwire, Michael Jordan, Mia Hamm, Bonnie Blair. (Illus.). 2000. 14.95 (*0-07-136062-X*) McGraw.

McGovern, Michael H., jt. auth. see Probst, Katherine N.

McGovern, Mick, jt. auth. see O'Mahoney, Bernard.

McGovern, Mike. Eat Drink & Be Kinky: A Feast of Wit & Fabulous Recipes for Fans of Kinky Friedman. LC 99-39144. 208p. 1999. per. 12.00 (*0-684-85674-3*) S&S Trade Pap.

McGovern, Noel & Benik Staff, et al. Rhode Island Environmental Law Handbook. 2nd ed. 205p. 1994. pap. text 89.00 (*0-86587-424-7*) Gov Insts.

McGovern, P. E. Late Bronze Palestinian Pendants: Innovation in a Cosmopolitan Age. (Journal for the Study of the Old Testament Supplement Monographs Ser.: Vol. 1). 184p. 1987. 57.50 (*0-905774-90-6*, Pub. by Sheffield Acad) CUP Services.

McGovern, Pat. Here Come the Clowns. Doheny, Marilyn, ed. 8p. 1995. pap. 12.95 (*0-945169-15-9*) Doheny Pubns.

McGovern, Patrick. HRM, Technical Workers & the Multinational Corporation. LC 97-52285. 176p. (C). 1998. 85.00 (*0-415-18487-8*) Routledge.

McGovern, Patrick, ed. The Origins & Ancient History of Wine, Vol. 11. (Food & Nutrition in History & Anthropology Ser.). 409p. 1996. text 55.00 (*2-88124-577-3*) Gordon & Breach.

McGovern, Patrick, et al, eds. The Origins & Ancient History of Wine. (Food & Nutrition in History & Anthropology Ser.: Vol. II). 409p. 1996. pap. text 45.00 (*90-5699-552-9*, ECU38) Gordon & Breach.

McGovern, Patrick E., et al. The Late Bronze Age & Early Iron Ages of Central Jordan: The Baq'ah Valley Project, 1977-1981. (University Museum Monographs: No. 65). (Illus.). xxxii, 365p. 1987. text 95.00 (*0-685-67660-9*) U Museum Pubns.

McGovern, Patrick E., jt. auth. see James, Frances W.

McGovern, Petronella, jt. auth. see Hodge, Ivan.

McGovern, R., jt. ed. see Thompson, J.

McGovern, Robert. A Feast of Flesh & Other Occasions. 63p. 1971. pap. 6.00 (*0-912592-08-7*) Ashland Poetry.

— A Poetry Ritual for Grammar Schools. 42p. 1974. pap. 2.50 (*0-912592-23-0*) Ashland Poetry.

McGovern, Robert, et al, eds. Eighty on the Eighties: A Decade's History in Verse. LC 90-83622. 131p. 1990. pap. 8.00 (*0-912592-28-1*) Ashland Poetry.

McGovern, Robert & Haven, Stephen, eds. And What Rough Beast: Poems at the End of the Century. LC 98-74622. 1999. pap. 12.00 (*0-912592-41-9*) Ashland Poetry.

McGovern, Robert & Haven, Stephen H., eds. Scarecrow Poetry: The Muse in Post-Middle Age. LC 94-71673. 178p. (Orig.). 1994. pap. 19.00 (*0-912592-36-2*) Ashland Poetry.

McGovern, Robert & Snyder, Richard, eds. Our Only Hope Is Humor: Some Public Poems. 88p. (C). 1972. pap. 5.00 (*0-912592-13-3*) Ashland Poetry.

— Seventy on the Seventies: A Decade's History in Verse. 100p. 1981. pap. 7.00 (*0-912592-24-9*) Ashland Poetry.

McGovern, Robert, jt. auth. see McNamee, John P.

McGovern, Robert, ed. see Snyder, Richard.

McGovern, Robert B. Spreader's Handbook. LC 98-96128. 243p. 1998. 185.00 (*0-9664037-0-3*, 001) R B McGovern.

McGovern, Roger, jt. auth. see Gunderson, Ted L.

McGovern, Roxanne, ed. Picture Me Having Trick or Treat Fun. (Illus.). 8p. (J). (ps-k). 1998. bds. 6.99 (*1-57151-548-8*) Picture Me Bks.

McGovern, Seana. Education, Modern Development, & Indigenous Knowledge: An Analysis of Academic Knowledge Production. LC 98-46206. (Garland Reference Library of Social Science). viii, 213 p. 1999. write for info. (*0-8153-2840-0*) Garland.

McGovern, Stephen J. The Politics of Downtown Development. LC 97-53074. (Illus.). 342p. (C). 1998. 44.95 (*0-8131-2052-7*) U Pr of Ky.

McGovern, Terrence J., jt. ed. see Coffey, Thomas F.

McGovern, Thomas. Bearing Witness (to AIDS) (Illus.). 132p. 1999. 19.95 (*0-923183-24-8*, Pub. by ART Pr NY) Dist Art Pubs.

— Priestly Celibacy Today. 176p. 1997. pap. 30.00 (*1-85182-352-2*, Pub. by Four Cts Pr) Intl Spec Bk.

— Priestly Celibacy Today. 248p. 1998. pap. 12.95 (*1-890177-07-5*) Midwest Theol.

McGovern, Thomas V., ed. Handbook for Enhancing Undergraduate Education in Psychology. LC 93-7081. 273p. 1993. pap. text 19.95 (*1-55798-196-5*) Am Psychol.

***McGovern, Timothy Michael.** Dickens in Galdos. LC 98-53780. (Comparative Cultures & Literatures Ser.: Vol. 12). 176p. (C). 2000. 44.95 (*0-8204-4290-9*) P Lang Pubng.

McGovern, Todd M., jt. auth. see Hawkins, Jason.

McGovern, V. J., ed. see International Pigment Cell Conference Staff.

McGovern, Vincent J. Malignant Melanoma: Clinical & Histological Diagnosis. LC 76-3793. (Wiley Medical Publications). 192p. reprint ed. pap. 59.60 (*0-608-13853-3*, 205598800042) Bks Demand.

McGovern, William M. Completely Prime Maximal Ideals & Quantization. LC 93-48292. (Memoirs of the American Mathematical Society Ser.: No. 519). 67p. 1994. pap. 29.00 (*0-8218-2580-1*, MEMO/108/519) Am Math.

— From Luther to Hitler: The History of Fascist-Nazi Political Philosophy. LC 75-180412. reprint ed. 58.50 (*0-404-56137-3*) AMS Pr.

— Introduction to Mahayana Buddhism. LC 70-149665. reprint ed. 34.50 (*0-404-04129-9*) AMS Pr.

— Introduction to Mahayana Buddhism: With Special Reference to Chinese & Japanese Phases. (C). 1997. 27.00 (*81-215-0766-9*, Pub. by M Manoharial) Coronet Bks.

— A Manual of Buddhist Philosophy. LC 78-70097. reprint ed. 27.50 (*0-404-17346-2*) AMS Pr.

McGovern, William M., Jr. Wills, Trusts & Estates. LC 96-233490. (Law Outlines Ser.). 210p. (Orig.). 1995. pap. text. write for info. (*0-87457-183-9*, 5220) Casenotes Pub.

McGovern, William M., Jr., et al. Hornbook on Wills, Trusts & Estates-Including Taxation & Future Interests. (Hornbook Ser.). 996p. (C). 1988. reprint ed. student ed. 42.00 (*0-314-36114-6*) West Pub.

McGovern, William M., jt. auth. see Collingwood, David H.

McGowan. Coloring the News. 2005. 25.00 (*0-684-82740-9*) S&S Trade.

***McGowan.** Dragon Seekers. 2000. pap. 25.00 (*0-7382-0282-7*, Pub. by Perseus Pubng) HarpC.

McGowan. Grammar & Writing for Job & Personal Use. (YA - Adult Education Ser.). 1992. pap. 9.95 (*0-538-70479-9*) S-W Pub.

Mcgowan. Improving Basic Grammar & Writing. 1993. pap. 6.95 (*0-7854-1366-9*) Am Guidance.

McGowan. Improving Basic Grammar & Writing Skills. (YA - Adult Education Ser.). 1993. pap. 5.95 (*0-538-70772-0*) S-W Pub.

— New Technologies in Retailing: Card Readers, Scanners, & Monitors. 162p. 1998. 3150.00 (*1-56965-092-6*, G-226) BCC.

— Reading for Daily Living. (YA - Adult Education Ser.). 1993. pap. 5.95 (*0-538-70771-2*) S-W Pub.

— Reading for Employment. (YA - Adult Education Ser.). 1993. pap. 5.95 (*0-538-70770-4*) S-W Pub.

— Reading for Job & Personal Use. (YA - Adult Education Ser.). 1992. pap. 9.95 (*0-538-70477-2*) S-W Pub.

— Writing for Employment. (YA - Adult Education Ser.). 1993. pap. 5.95 (*0-538-70773-9*) S-W Pub.

McGowan, A., ed. Women Elders in the Kirk? 1995. 6.99 (*1-871676-30-4*, Pub. by Christian Focus) Spring Arbor Dist.

McGowan, A. T. The Federal Theology of Thomas L. Boston. (Rutherford Studies in Historical Theology). xix, 228p. 1997. pap. text 30.00 (*0-946068-59-3*, Pub. by Rutherford Hse) OM Literature.

***McGowan, Alan.** HMS Victory: Her Construction, Career & Restoration. (Illus.). 256p. 2000. 59.95 (*1-55750-387-7*) Naval Inst Pr.

McGowan, Allan. Sailing Ships: Pop-Up Book. (Illus.). 1997. 22.95 (*1-888443-04-9*, Pop-Up Pr) Intervisual Bks.

***McGowan, Andrew.** Ascetic Eucharists: Food & Drink in Early Christian Ritual Meals. LC 98-42962. 326p. 1999. text 80.00 (*0-19-826972-2*) OUP.

McGowan, Andy. A New Birth. 1996. 4.99 (*1-85792-241-7*, Pub. by Christian Focus) Spring Arbor Dist.

McGowan, Bob & Farren, Richard. Fishing the Big Bend: Inshore Saltwater. LC 93-60545. (Big Bend Ser.: Vol. II). (Illus.). 117p. (Orig.). 1993. pap. 11.95 (*0-9632059-1-9*) Woodland Prods.

McGowan, Bonnie R. Charlie & the Fox: A Program about Family Alcoholism. LC 95-77888. (Illus.). 32p. (Orig.). (J). (gr. 2-5). 1995. pap. 7.95 (*1-884063-66-7*) Mar Co Prods.

— Eddie & His Dad. LC 96-79865. (Illus.). 40p. (Orig.). (J). (gr. 1-6). 1997. pap. 8.95 (*1-57543-018-5*) Mar Co Prods.

— Sophie & Her Uncle: A Program about Abuse in the Family. (Illus.). 30p. (Orig.). (J). (gr. k-6). 1993. pap. 6.95 (*1-884063-54-3*) Mar Co Prods.

McGowan, Brenda. Trends in Employee Counseling Programs. (Studies in Productivity: Highlights of the Literature Ser.: No. 37). 55p. 1984. pap. 55.00 (*0-08-032361-8*, PS37) Work in Amer.

McGowan, Brenda G. & Blumenthal, Karen L. Why Punish the Children? A Study of Children of Women Prisoners. 124p. 1978. 6.50 (*0-318-15376-9*) Natl Coun Crime.

McGowan, Charlotte. Final Report of the Excavation of Cal.F:5:1 (CA-SDI-12,809) (Illus.). 670p. (C). 1997. pap. text 68.75 (*1-55567-837-8*) Coyote Press.

McGowan, Chris. In the Beginning: A Scientist Shows Why the Creationists Are Wrong. LC 83-62997. (Illus.). 208p. 1984. pap. 19.95 (*0-87975-240-8*) Prometheus Bks.

— T-Rex to Go: Build Your Own from Chicken Bones. LC 98-37526. (Illus.). 208p. (Orig.). (gr. 4-7). 1999. pap. 14.00 (*0-06-095281-4*) HarpC.

McGowan, Chris & Pessanha, Ricardo. The Brazilian Sound: Samba, Bossa Nova & the Popular Music of Brazil. LC 96-52587. 256p. 1998. 59.95 (*1-56639-544-5*); pap. 24.95 (*1-56639-545-3*) Temple U Pr.

McGowan, Christopher. Diatoms to Dinosaurs: The Size & Scale of Living Things. (Illus.). 272p. 1994. 27.50 (*1-55963-304-2*) Island Pr.

— Dinosaurs, Spitfires & Sea Dragons. LC 90-41552. (Illus.). 384p. 1991. text 29.95 (*0-674-20769-6*, MCGDIN) HUP.

— Dinosaurs, Spitfires & Sea Dragons. (Illus.). 384p. 1992. pap. text 14.95 (*0-674-20770-X*) HUP.

— Discover Dinosaurs: A Royal Ontario Museum Book. (Illus.). 96p. (J). (gr. 3-7). 1993. pap. 10.95 (*1-55074-048-2*) Addison-Wesley.

— Make Your Own Dinosaur out of Chicken Bones: Foolproof Instructions for Budding Paleontologists. LC 97-186864. (Illus.). 160p. (J). (gr. 4-7). 1997. pap. 13.00 (*0-06-095226-1*) HarpC.

***McGowan, Christopher.** A Practical Guide to Vertebrate Mechanics. LC 98-29462. (Illus.). 320p. (C). 1999. text 90.00 (*0-521-57194-4*); pap. text 39.95 (*0-521-57673-3*) Cambridge U Pr.

McGowan, Christopher. Raptor & the Lamb: Predators & Prey in the Living World. LC 96-53506. 272p. 1997. 25.00 (*0-8050-4298-9*) H Holt & Co.

McGowan, Clement L., jt. auth. see Marca, David A.

McGowan, Cynthia C. Robinson Crusoe Notes. (Cliffs Notes Ser.). 56p. (Orig.). 1976. pap. text 4.95 (*0-8220-1150-6*, Cliff) IDG Bks.

— Walden Two Notes. (Cliffs Notes Ser.). 60p. (gr. 10-12). 1979. pap. 4.95 (*0-8220-1361-4*, Cliff) IDG Bks.

— Who's Afraid of Virginia Woolf? Notes. (Cliffs Notes Ser.). 56p. (Orig.). 1979. pap. text 4.95 (*0-8220-1383-5*, Cliff) IDG Bks.

McGowan, Daniel. Constructive Awareness: Alexander Technique & the Spiritual Quest. 128p. (Orig.). 1997. pap. 11.95 (*0-943914-85-X*) Larson Pubns.

McGowan, Daniel & Ellis, Marc. Remembering Deir Yassin. 150p. 1998. pap. 15.00 (*1-56656-291-0*) Interlink Pub.

McGowan, Danny & Alexander, F. M., eds. Alexander Technique: Original Writings of F. M. Alexander - Constructive Conscious Control. abr. ed. LC 96-76393. 160p. (Orig.). 1997. pap. 14.95 (*0-943914-78-7*) Larson Pubns.

***McGowan, Dave.** Derailing Democracy: The America the Media Don't Want You to See. LC 99-54185. 240p. 2000. pap. 16.95 (*1-56751-184-8*, Pub. by Common Courage); lib. bdg. 29.95 (*1-56751-185-6*, Pub. by Common Courage) LPC InBook.

McGowan, Diane & Schrooten, Mark. Math Play! 80 Ways to Count & Learn. Williamson, Susan, ed. LC 96-37806. (Little Hands Ser.: Vol. 6). (Illus.). 141p. (Orig.). (J). (ps-1). 1997. pap. 12.95 (*1-885593-08-2*) Williamson Pub Co.

McGowan, Don. What Is Wrong with Jung? LC 93-38952. 219p. 1994. 30.95 (*0-87975-859-7*) Prometheus Bks.

McGowan, E. M. Horses & Ponies, A Photo-Fact Book. (Illus.). (Orig.). (J). 1988. pap. 1.95 (*0-942025-26-1*) Kidsbks.

***McGowan, F.** Kept Woman. 1999. pap. 13.95 (*0-575-60242-2*, Pub. by V Gollancz) Trafalgar.

McGowan, F., ed. European Energy Policies in a Changing Environment, Vol. 1. LC 96-225294. viii, 183p. 1996. pap. 59.00 (*3-7908-0951-9*) Spr-Verlag.

McGowan, Francis. Struggle for Power in Europe: Competition & Regulation in the EC Electricity Industry. 1993. pap. text 22.25 (*0-905031-67-9*, Pub. by Royal Inst Intl Affairs) Brookings.

McGowan, Gary, jt. auth. see Hansen, Joyce.

McGowan, Gordon. The Skipper & the Eagle. LC 99-191902. (Illus.). 1998. 25.00 (*0-930248-09-0*) Sea Hist Pr.

McGowan, Hugh B. The Tabernacle: God's Perfect Plan of Salvation to All Mankind. 2nd rev. ed. (Illus.). 152p. 1997. reprint ed. pap. text 7.95 (*0-9657661-0-1*) Impact Minist.

McGowan, Ian, ed. The Restoration & Eighteenth Century (Sixteen Sixty to Seventeen Ninety-Eight), Vol. 3. LC 89-70174. (St. Martin's Anthologies of English Literature Ser.: Vol. No. 3). 612p. 1990. text 20.00 (*0-312-04477-1*) St Martin.

McGowan, J. Butterworth's Student Companions - Marketing Law. 2nd ed. 100p. 1996. pap. write for info. (*0-409-31124-3*, MICHIE) LEXIS Pub.

McGowan, Jack. Magnificent Places: Oregon Coast. (Illus.). 95p. 1996. pap. text 19.95 (*1-55868-250-3*) Gr Arts Ctr Pub.

— Magnificent Places: Oregon Coast. 1997. 27.95 (*1-55868-291-0*) Gr Arts Ctr Pub.

McGowan, James. Station Master on the Underground Railroad: The Life & Letters of Thomas Garrett. LC 77-84816. (Illus.). 181p. 1977. 7.95 (*0-916178-00-5*) Whimsie Pr.

McGowan, James, tr. & notes see Baudelaire, Charles.

McGowan, James A. Freedom on the River: A Personal History of the World's First All-Disabled Rowing Regatta. Anderson, Lesley C., ed. LC 96-94864. (Illus.). 120p. (Orig.). 1997. pap. write for info. (*0-913911-13-5*) Akashic Pr.

— Hear Today! Here to Stay! A Personal History of Rhythm & Blues. LC 83-61178. (Illus.). 196p. (Orig.). 1983. pap. 7.95 (*0-913911-00-3*) Akashic Pr.

McGowan, James W., ed. The Excited State in Chemical Physics, Vol. 1. LC 74-6240. (Advances in Chemical Physics Ser.: No. 28). 502p. reprint ed. pap. 155.70 (*0-7837-3455-7*, 205778100001) Bks Demand.

McGowan, Joanne, jt. auth. see Fusco, Ann.

McGowan, John. Hannah Arendt: An Introduction. LC 97-15017. 1998. pap. 17.95 (*0-8166-3070-4*) U of Minn Pr.

— Postmodernism & Its Critics. LC 90-55758. 320p. 1991. text 47.50 (*0-8014-2494-1*); pap. text 15.95 (*0-8014-9738-8*) Cornell U Pr.

McGowan, John, jt. ed. see Calhoun, Craig.

McGowan, John C. & Mellors, Alan. Molecular Volumes in Chemistry & Biology: Applications Including Partitioning Toxicity. LC 86-10520. 259p. 1986. text 65.95 (*0-470-20353-6*) P-H.

McGowan, John J. Direct Digital Control: A Guide to Distributed Building Automation. LC 94-32120. 486p. 1994. 78.00 (*0-88173-166-8*) Fairmont Pr.

— Networking for Building Automation & Control Systems. (Illus.). 484p. 79.00 (*0-88173-077-7*, 0205) Fairmont Pr.

McGowan, John J., jt. auth. see Payne, F. William.

McGowan, Karen G. Solving Mealtime Problems. (Illus.). 158p. 1995. pap. 22.95 (*1-928752-11-X*) Mc Gowan Pubns.

***McGowan, Karen Green.** Drugs & Disabilities: Handle with Care. 2nd ed. (Illus.). 564p. 2000. pap. 49.95 (*1-928752-17-9*) Mc Gowan Pubns.

McGowan, Kate, ed. Year's Work in Critical & Cultural Studies. 384p. (C). 1997. text 95.00 (*0-631-20523-3*) Blackwell Pubs.

— The Year's Work in Critical & Cultural Theory, 1993: 1993, vol. 3. (Year's Work in Critical & Cultural Theory Ser.). 504p. 1996. 79.00 (*0-631-18861-4*) Blackwell Pubs.

McGowan, Kate, jt. ed. see Easthope, Anthony.

McGowan, Kate, jt. ed. see Easthope, Antony.

McGowan, Kate, jt. ed. see Kitson, Peter J.

McGowan, Kate, jt. ed. see Kitson, Peter.

McGowan, Kathleen, jt. auth. see McGuire, Terrance P.

***McGowan, Keith.** Hazardous Waste. LC 00-9233. (Overview Ser.). (Illus.). (J). 2000. write for info. (*1-56006-699-7*) Lucent Bks.

McGowan, Keith. Sexual Harassment. LC 98-14683. (Overview Ser.). (Illus.). 112p. (YA). (gr. 5 up). 1998. lib. bdg. 23.70 (*1-56006-507-9*) Lucent Bks.

McGowan, Kimberly. Bearings - Plain, Ball & Roller: U. S. Manufacturers & Selected Distributors: 1992 Competitive Analysis. 1993. pap. text 2400.00 (*1-878218-38-7*) World Info Tech.

***McGowan, Kimberly.** Cable Distribution & Interconnection Systems for Telephone Wire Centers: U. S. Markets, Competitors & Customers: 1999-2004 Analysis & Forecasts. 52p. 1999. pap. text 3900.00 (*1-929904-00-2*) World Info Tech.

McGowan, Kimberly. A Competitive Analysis of Electronic Wire & Cable End-Use Markets - Copper Vs. Fiber: 1993-1998 Analysis & Forecasts. 74p. 1994. pap. text 1900.00 (*1-878218-46-8*) World Info Tech.

— Electronic Filters: U. S. Markets, Applications & Competitors, 1991-1997 Analysis. (Illus.). 162p. 1992. pap. text 1595.00 (*1-878218-33-6*) World Info Tech.

— Electronic Wire & Cable - U.S. Markets & Opportunities: 1993-1998 Analysis & Forecasts. 76p. 1994. pap. text 2400.00 (*1-878218-43-3*) World Info Tech.

— Gaskets, Packings & Mechanical Seals: U. S. Markets, Competitors, & Opportunities: 1994-1999 Analysis & Forecasts. 100p. 1995. pap. text 1900.00 (*1-878218-53-0*) World Info Tech.

— Gaskets, Packings, & Mechanical Seals: 1998 U. S. Competitive Analysis & Forecasts. 161p. 1998. pap. text 2400.00 (*1-878218-87-5*) World Info Tech.

— Gaskets, Packings & Mechanical Seals - U. S. Markets, Competitors & Opportunities: 1991-1997 Analysis. (Illus.). 110p. 1992. pap. text 1295.00 (*1-878218-29-8*) World Info Tech.

— Telecommunications Outside Plant - U.S. Markets, Customers, & Competitors: 1994-1999 Analysis & Forecasts. 258p. 1994. pap. text 2400.00 (*1-878218-49-2*) World Info Tech.

***McGowan, Kimberly.** Telecommunications Outside Plant Cable - RBOCs Purchase Profiles: 1999-2004 Analysis & Forecasts. 45p. 2000. pap. text 2500.00 (*1-929904-06-1*) World Info Tech.

— Telecommunications Outside Plant Products: Copper vs. Fiber: 1999-2004 Analysis & Forecasts. 75p. 1999. pap. text 3900.00 (*1-878218-98-0*) World Info Tech.

McGowan, Kimberly. U. S. & Canadian Electrical & Electronic Wire & Cable Manufacturers, 1993: Competitive Analysis. 600p. 1993. pap. text 2400.00 (*1-878218-39-5*) World Info Tech.

— U. S. Communication Cable Manufacturers: 1998 Competitive Analysis & Forecasts. 172p. 1998. pap. text 3900.00 (*1-878218-91-3*) World Info Tech.

***McGowan, Kimberly.** U. S. Communications Cable Manufacturers: 1999 Competitive Analysis & Forecasts. 204p. 1999. pap. text 3900.00 (*1-878218-99-9*) World Info Tech.

— The U. S. Fire Alarm Cable Market: 2000-2004 Analysis & Forecasts. 12p. 2000. pap. text 1900.00 (*1-929904-07-X*) World Info Tech.

McGowan, Kimberly & O'Brien, Kimberly. Cable Distribution & Interconnection Systems for Telephone Wire Center Modernization - U. S. Markets, Competitors, & Customers: 1997-2002 Analysis & Forecasts. 100p. 1997. pap. text 2900.00 (*1-878218-76-X*) World Info Tech.

McGowan, Lee, jt. auth. see Cini, Michelle.

McGowan, M., jt. auth. see Chinere, David S.

McGowan, Marcia P., jt. ed. see Boschetto, Sandra M.

McGowan, Margaret, jt. ed. see Craig, George.

***McGowan, Margaret M.** The Vision of Rome in Late Renaissance France. (Illus.). 320p. 2000. 45.00 (*0-300-08535-4*) Yale U Pr.

McGowan, Marie, ed. see Ashton, Tia, et al.

McGowan, Mark, ed. see Ashton, Tia, et al.

McGowan, Mark, ed. see Ashton, Tita, et al.

McGowan, Mark, ed. see Kocher, Paul, et al.

McGowan, Mark G. Waning Of The Green: Catholics, The Irish, & Identity In Toronto, 1887-1922. (Illus.). 416p. 1998. text 55.00 (*0-7735-1789-8*) McG-Queens Univ Pr.

***McGowan, Mark G.** Waning Of The Green: Catholics, The Irish, & Identity In Toronto, 1887-1922. 440p. 1999. pap. 27.95 (*0-7735-1790-1*) McG-Queens Univ Pr.

McGowan, Martha. Literature: Experience & Meaning. 1105p. (C). 1988. pap. text 3.00 (*0-15-551085-1*) Harcourt Coll Pubs.

McGowan, Mary. The Girl Without a Country. 197p. 1985. 9.95 (*0-930061-03-9*) Interspace Bks.

— Mollie O'Leary. 117p. 1990. pap. 9.95 (*0-930061-51-9*) Interspace Bks.

McGowan, Mary, jt. auth. see Harbison, Elizabeth M.

McGowan, Mary, ed. see Slappey, Mary M.

McGowan, Mary P. Heart Fitness for Life: The Essential Guide for Preventing & Reversing Heart Disease. (Illus.). 336p. 1999. pap. 13.95 (*0-19-512909-1*) OUP.

McGowan, Mary P. & Chopra, J. McGowan. Heart Fitness for Life: The Essential Guide for Preventing & Reversing Heart Disease. LC 97-29834. (Illus.). 336p. 1997. 25.00 (*0-19-511624-0*) OUP.

McGowan, Maryrose. Specifying Interiors: A Guide to Construction & FF&E for Commercial Interiors Projects. LC 95-24631. (Illus.). 368p. 1996. 69.95 (*0-471-10619-4*) Wiley.

McGowan, Maurine. Heart Songs. LC TX2641211. 112p. (Orig.). 1989. lib. bdg. 15.00 (*0-9657234-0-2*, 89-001) W & M Pub.

— Love & Friendship Treasures. 22p. (Orig.). 1997. mass mkt. 8.00 (*0-9657234-1-0*, 97-001) W & M Pub.

— A Touch of Grace. 26p. (Orig.). 1997. mass mkt. 8.00 (*0-9657234-2-9*, 97-002) W & M Pub.

McGowan, Meredith, jt. auth. see McGowan, Thomas.

McGowan, Meredith, jt. auth. see McGowan, Tom.

McGowan, Michael. The Bread of Life: The Eucharist. 189p. 1998. mass mkt. 5.95 (*0-8189-0814-9*) Alba.

***McGowan, Michael.** The Canonical Status of Catholic Health Care Facilities in the Province of New Brunswick in Light of Recent Provincial Government Legislation. LC 00-32874. (Canadian Studies: Vol. 26). 380p. 2000. 99.95 (*0-7734-7683-0*) E Mellen.

McGowan, Pat, jt. ed. see Kegley, Charles W., Jr.

McGowan, Phillip, jt. compiled by see Dekker, Rene W.

***McGowan, Pierre.** The Gullah Mailman. LC 99-75820. (Illus.). 144p. 2000. 19.95 (*1-57197-199-8*, Pub. by Pentland Pr) Assoc Pubs Grp.

***McGowan Publications Staff, prod.** Health & Wellness Reference Guide. (Illus.). 568p. 1998. pap. 59.95 (*1-928752-20-9*) Mc Gowan Pubns.

McGowan, Richard. Business, Politics, & Cigarettes: Multiple Levels, Multiple Agendas. LC 95-7279. 184p. 1995. 55.00 (*0-89930-964-X*, Quorum Bks) Greenwood.

— Government Regulation of the Alcohol Industry: The Search for Revenue & the Common Good. LC 96-40913. 192p. 1997. 59.95 (*1-56720-034-6*, Quorum Bks) Greenwood.

— A Harlot of Venus. (Orig.). 1996. mass mkt. 5.95 (*1-56333-425-9*) Masquerade.

— State Lotteries & Legalized Gambling: Painless Revenue or Painful Mirage. LC 94-15884. 192p. 1994. 57.95 (*0-89930-859-7*, Quorum Bks) Greenwood.

McGowan, Robert & Ottensmeyer, Edward J., eds. Differing Perspectives on Economic Development. (Orig.). 1989. pap. 15.00 (*0-944285-10-4*) Pol Studies.

— Technology & Economic Development. 192p. (Orig.). 1987. pap. 15.00 (*0-918592-91-7*) Pol Studies.

McGowan, Robert P., jt. auth. see Stevens, John M.

***McGowan, Siobhan.** Teen Keepsakes. (Keepsakes Ser.). (Illus.). 128p. 2000. 25.00 (*1-929180-19-5*, Creating Keepsakes) Porchswing Pub.

McGowan, Siobhan, jt. auth. see Bearnson, Lisa.

McGowan, Siobhan, jt. auth. see Higgins, Becky.

McGowan, Siobhan, tr. see Brami, Elisabeth.

***McGowan, Slobhan.** Wedding Keepsakes. (Keepsakes Ser.). (Illus.). 128p. 2000. 25.00 (*1-929180-17-9*, Creating Keepsakes); pap. 19.95 (*1-929180-18-7*, Creating Keepsakes) Porchswing Pub.

McGowan, Spencer. The Do-It-Yourself Guide to Investment Information: Where to Find What You Need to Know. 450p. 1992. per. 29.95 (*1-55738-453-3*, Irwn Prfssnl) McGraw-Hill Prof.

McGowan, Susan & Miller, Amelia F. Family & Landscape: Deerfield Homelots from 1671. LC 96-70838. (Illus.). 224p. 1996. 60.00 (*1-882374-01-0*); pap. 40.00 (*1-882374-03-7*) Pocumtuck Valley Mem.

McGowan, Thomas & McGowan, Meredith. Telling America's Story: Teaching American History Through Children's Literature. (Illus.). 116p. (Orig.). 1989. pap. text 17.95 (*0-931205-41-7*) Jenson Pubns.

McGowan, Todd. The Feminine No. ring bd. write for info. (*0-7914-4874-6*) State U NY Pr.

McGowan, Tom & McGowan, Meredith. Children, Literature & Social Studies: Activities for the Intermediate Grades. (Illus.). 218p. (J). (gr. 4-6). 1986. spiral bd. 21.95 (*0-938594-06-0*) Spec Lit Pr.

— Integrating the Primary Curriculum: Social Studies & Children's Literature. Champlin, John, ed. (Library & Literature Ser.). (Illus.). 86p. 1988. pap. 20.95 (*0-938594-11-7*) Spec Lit Pr.

McGowan, Whitman. Contents May Have Shifted. (Illus.). 52p. (Orig.). 1994. pap. 6.00 (*1-880298-07-4*) Viridiana.

***McGowan, William.** Poems, Cartoons, Revelations, by Codger. 1999. pap. write for info. (*1-58235-168-6*) Watermrk Pr.

McGowan, Wynema. Beyond the River. 304p. 1997. mass mkt. 5.99 (*0-7860-0420-7*, Pinncle Kensgtn) Kensgtn Pub Corp.

— Catching Fire. 352p. 1997. mass mkt. 5.50 (*0-7860-0462-2*, Pinncle Kensgtn) Kensgtn Pub Corp.

— Catching Rainbows. 384p. 1996. mass mkt. 4.99 (*0-7860-0281-6*, Pinncle Kensgtn) Kensgtn Pub Corp.

Mcgowan, Wynema. Dare to Dream. 384p. 1998. mass mkt. 5.99 (*0-7860-0599-8*, Pinncle Kensgtn) Kensgtn Pub Corp.

McGowan, Wynema. Dare to Love. 384p. 1998. pap. 5.99 (*0-7860-0518-1*, Pinncle Kensgtn) Kensgtn Pub Corp.

— The Irishman. 400p. 1995. mass mkt. 4.99 (*0-8217-0120-7*, Zebra Kensgtn) Kensgtn Pub Corp.

— While the Rivers Run. 304p. 1996. mass mkt. 5.99 (*0-7860-0340-5*, Pinncle Kensgtn) Kensgtn Pub Corp.

Mcgowen. The Beginnings of Science. 18.98 (*0-8050-5403-0*) H Holt & Co.

McGowen, et al. Criminal & Civil Tax Fraud: 1989 Supplement. 1989. pap. write for info. (*0-930273-92-3*, 64659-10, MICHIE) LEXIS Pub.

Mcgowen, jt. see Demarios.

McGowen, jt. see DeMarios.

Mcgowen, jt. auth. see Demarois.

McGowen, Al. Extraction of Free Gold: Virgin Placer Gold. (Illus.). 64p. 1973. pap. 7.95 (*0-941620-26-3*) Carson Ent.

McGowen, Carolyn S. Teaching Literature by Women Authors. Lewis, Warren W., ed. LC 93-34695. 224p. (Orig.). 1993. pap. 16.95 (*0-927516-38-1*) ERIC-REC.

McGowen, Charles H. In Six Days. 2nd ed. 108p. 1986. reprint ed. pap. 3.95 (*0-936369-03-5*) Son-Rise Pubns.

McGowen, Darrell. Recovery of Damages for Crimes & Intentional Wrongs. LC 92-75760. 500p. 1993. 95.00 (*0-915544-24-5*) Lawpress CA.

McGowen, Darrell, et al. Criminal & Civil Tax Fraud: Law, Practice, Procedure, with 1992 Cumulative Supplements, 2 vols. 1986. write for info. (*0-930273-20-6*, MICHIE); write for info. (*0-930273-21-4*, MICHIE) LEXIS Pub.

— Criminal Tax Fraud, 3 vols., Set. 1994. 295.00 (*1-55834-133-1*, 64655-11, MICHIE) LEXIS Pub.

McGowen, Drusilla. Traveling the Way. 152p. (YA). (gr. 7-10). 1977. 7.65 (*0-7399-0129-X*, 2445) Rod & Staff.

McGowen, J. H. Gum Hollow Fan Delta, Nueces Bay, Texas. (Reports of Investigations: RI 69). (Illus.). 91p. 1971. reprint ed. pap. 5.50 (*0-318-03627-4*) Bur Econ Geology.

McGowen, J. H. & Groat, C. G. Van Horn Sandstone, West Texas: An Alluvial Fan Model for Mineral Exploration. (Reports of Investigations: RI 72). (Illus.). 57p. 1982. reprint ed. pap. 2.50 (*0-318-03173-6*) Bur Econ Geology.

McGowen, J. H., et al. Depositional Framework of the Lower Dockum Group (Triassic), Texas Panhandle. (Reports of Investigations: RI 97). (Illus.). 60p. 1979. pap. 2.00 (*0-318-03233-3*) Bur Econ Geology.

An Asterisk (*) at the beginning of an entry indicates that the title is appearing for the first time.

— Geochemistry of Bottom Sediments, Matagorda Bay System, Texas. (Geological Circular Ser.: GC 79-2). (Illus.). 64p. 1979. pap. 1.50 (0-686-29329-0) Bur Econ Geology.

McGowen, J. H., jt. auth. see Morton, R. A.

McGowen, Lee W. Another Path to Follow, Vol. 2. 70p. 1995. pap. 10.50 (1-56770-328-3) S Scheewe Pubns.

McGowen, Louis H. Johnston. (Images of America Ser.). 1997. pap. 16.99 (0-7524-0587-X) Arcadia Publng.

***McGowen, Louis H. & Johnston Historical Society Staff.** Johnston, Vol. 2. (Images of America Ser.). 1999. pap. 18.99 (0-7524-1253-1) Arcadia Publng.

McGowen, M. K. & Lopez, C. M. Depositional Systems in the Nacatoch Formation (Upper Cretaceous), Northeast Texas & Southwest Arkansas. (Reports of Investigations: RI 137). (Illus.). 59p. 1983. pap. 2.00 (0-318-03297-X) Bur Econ Geology.

McGowen, Mary K., jt. ed. see Keller, Margaret A.

McGowen, Mercedes, jt. auth. see Garrison, Catherine.

***McGowen, Sheena M.** The Beveled Mirrors of Poetry. Sinclair, Brian, ed. (Illus.). 70p. 2000. per. 11.99 (0-9676599-0-6) Word Quest Pub.

McGowen, Stanley S. Horse Sweat & Powder Smoke: The First Texas Cavalry in the Civil War. LC 99-24705. (Illus.). 1999. 29.95 (0-89096-903-5) Tex A&M Univ Pr.

McGowen, Thomas, ed. see Bujold, Edward J.

McGowen, Tom. Adventures in Archaeology. LC 97-9755. (Scientific American Sourcebooks Ser.). 96p. (YA). (gr. 5 up). 1997. 22.40 (0-8050-4688-7) TFC Bks NY.

— African-Americans in the Old West. LC 97-26583. (Cornerstones to Freedom Ser.). (Illus.). 32p. (J). (gr. 4-6). 1998. 19.50 (0-516-20835-7) Childrens.

Mcgowen, Tom. African-Americans in the Old West. (Cornerstones to Freedom Ser.). (Illus.). 32p. (J). (gr. 4-6). 1999. pap. text 5.95 (0-516-26348-X) Childrens.

McGowen, Tom. The Battle for Iwo Jima. LC 98-3491. (Cornerstones to Freedom Ser.). 30p. 1999. lib. bdg. 5.95 (0-516-26458-3) Childrens.

— The Battle for Iwo Jima. LC 98-3491. (Cornerstones to Freedom Ser.). 32p. (J). (gr. 4-6). 1999. 19.50 (0-516-21141-2) Childrens.

***McGowen, Tom.** The Battle of Midway. LC 00-30330. (Cornerstones of Freedom Ser.). (Illus.). 2001. write for info. (0-516-22005-5) Childrens.

McGowen, Tom. The Beginnings of Science. LC 97-51923. 80p. (J). (gr. 5-8). 1998. lib. bdg. 25.90 (0-7613-3016-X) Millbrook Pr.

— The Black Death. LC 95-2122. (First Bks.). 64p. (J). (gr. 4-6). 1995. lib. bdg. 22.00 (0-531-20199-6) Watts.

— Digging up the Past: Wonders of Archaeology. (J). 1996. pap. 8.95 (0-8050-4687-9) H Holt & Co.

— Germany's Lightning War: Panzer Divisions of World War II. LC 98-44009. (Military Might Ser.). (Illus.). 64p. 1999. lib. bdg. 23.90 (0-7613-1511-X) TFC Bks NY.

***McGowen, Tom.** Giant Stones & Earth Mounds. LC 00-25687. (Illus.). (J). 2000. write for info. (0-7613-1372-9) Millbrook Pr.

McGowen, Tom. Korean War. (First Bks.). (J). 1992. 11.15 (0-606-05400-6, Pub. by Turtleback) Demco.

— The Korean War. large type ed. (First Bks.). (Illus.). 64p. (J). (gr. 5-8). 1993. pap. 6.95 (0-531-15655-9) Watts.

— 1900-1919. (Yearbooks in Science Ser.). (Illus.). 80p. (J). (gr. 5-8). 1995. lib. bdg. 20.40 (0-8050-3431-5) TFC Bks NY.

— 1960-1969. (Yearbooks in Science Ser.). (Illus.). 80p. (J). (gr. 5-8). 1995. lib. bdg. 20.40 (0-8050-3436-6) TFC Bks NY.

***McGowen, Tom.** Robespierre & the French Revolution in World History. LC 99-41656. (In World History Ser.). (Illus.). 128p. (gr. 5 up). 2000. lib. bdg. 20.95 (0-7660-1397-9) Enslow Pubs.

— Sink the Bismarck: Germany's Super-Battleship of World War II. LC 98-48500. (Military Might Ser.). (Illus.). 64 p. 1999. lib. bdg. 23.90 (0-7613-1510-1) TFC Bks NY.

McGowen, Tom. World War I. (First Bks.). (J). 1993. 11.15 (0-606-05711-0, Pub. by Turtleback) Demco.

— World War I. large type ed. LC 92-28329. (First Bks.). (Illus.). 64p. (J). 1993. pap. 6.95 (0-531-15660-5) Watts.

— World War II. (First Bks.). (J). 1993. 11.15 (0-606-05712-9, Pub. by Turtleback) Demco.

— World War II. large type ed. (First Bks.). (Illus.). 64p. (J). (gr. 5-8). 1993. pap. 6.95 (0-531-15661-3) Watts.

McGowin, Diana F. Living in the Labyrinth. large type ed. 1994. 36.95 (0-7862-9976-2, G K Hall Lrg Type) Mac Lib Ref.

— Living in the Labyrinth: A Personal Journey Through the Maze of Alzheimer's. large type ed. LC 93-33820. 247p. 1994. lib. bdg. 20.95 (0-7862-0066-9) Thorndike Pr.

— Living in the Labyrinth: A Personal Journey Through the Maze of Alzheimer's. large type ed. LC 93-33820. 247p. 1995. lib. bdg. 13.95 (0-7862-0067-7) Thorndike Pr.

— Living in the Labyrinth: A Personal Journey Through the Maze of Alzheimer's. rev. ed. 176p. 1994. pap. 11.95 (0-385-31318-7, Delta Trade) Dell.

McGown, A., et al, eds. Performance of Reinforced Soil Structures. 485p. 1991. text 200.00 (0-7277-1637-9, Pub. by T Telford) RCH.

McGown, Alan, jt. ed. see Jarrett, Peter M.

McGown, Carl, ed. Science of Coaching Volleyball. LC 93-24319. (Science of Coaching Ser.). (Illus.). 184p. 1993. pap. 14.95 (0-87322-572-4, PMCG0572) Human Kinetics.

***McGown, Carl, et al.** Coaching Volleyball: Building a Winning Team. LC 00-32296. (Illus.). 2000. write for info. (0-205-30958-5) Allyn.

McGown, Jill. Murder . . . Now & Then. 407p. 1993. pap. 13.95 (0-330-33243-0, Pub. by Pan) Trans-Atl Phila.

— Murder at the Old Vicarage. (Mysteries Around the World Promotion Ser.). 1991. mass mkt. 5.99 (0-449-21819-8) Ivy Books.

— The Murders of Mrs. Austin & Mrs. Beale. 1994. reprint ed. mass mkt. 5.99 (0-449-22162-8, Crest) Fawcett.

— The Other Woman. large type ed. 477p. write for info. (0-7505-1065-X, Pub. by Mgna Lrg Print) Ulverscroft.

— A Perfect Match. 192p. 1990. mass mkt. 5.99 (0-449-21820-1, Crest) Fawcett.

***McGown, Jill.** Picture of Innocence. LC 97-45816. 336p. 1998. 22.00 (0-449-00250-0) Fawcett.

McGown, Jill. Picture of Innocence. 1999. mass mkt. 6.99 (0-449-00251-9, Crest) Fawcett.

— Picture of Innocence. large type ed. Date not set. 30.00 (0-7862-1670-0) Thorndike Pr.

— Plots & Errors. LC 99-14226. 1999. 22.95 (0-345-43313-0) Ballantine Pub Grp.

***McGown, Jill.** Plots & Errors. 384p. 2000. mass mkt. 6.99 (0-449-00253-5) Fawcett.

McGown, Jill. A Shred of Evidence. 1997. mass mkt. 5.99 (0-449-22499-6) Ballantine Pub Grp.

— Verdict Unsafe. 1998. mass mkt. 5.99 (0-449-22501-1, Crest) Fawcett.

— Verdict Unsafe. large type ed. (Myst-Hall Ser.). 522p. 1997. lib. bdg. 23.95 (0-7838-8287-4, G K Hall Lrg Type) Mac Lib Ref.

McGown, Linda B. & Bockris, John O. How to Obtain Abundant Clean Energy. LC 79-24468. 276p. 1980. 45.00 (0-306-40399-4, Plenum Trade) Perseus Pubng.

McGown, Linda B., jt. ed. see Warner, Isiah M.

McGowran, T. Newhaven on Forth: Port of Grace. (Illus.). 248p. (C). 1996. pap. 30.00 (0-85976-130-4, Pub. by J Donald) St Mut.

McGrade, A. S., ed. Richard Hooker & the Construction of Christian Community. LC 96-40326. (Medieval & Renaissance Texts & Studies: Vol. 165). 440p. 1997. 32.00 (0-86698-206-X, MR165) MRTS.

***McGrade, A. S., et al, eds.** The Cambridge Translations of Medieval Philosophical Texts: Ethics & Political Philosophy. LC 99-87118. 608p. (C). 2000. pap. 29.95 (0-521-28082-6) Cambridge U Pr.

— The Cambridge Translations of Medieval Philosophical Texts: Ethics & Political Philosophy, Vol. 2. LC 99-87118. 608p. (C). 2000. 85.00 (0-521-23625-8) Cambridge U Pr.

McGrade, A. S., ed. see Hooker, Richard.

McGrade, A. S., ed. see William of Ockham.

McGrade, Arthur S., ed. see Ockham, William.

McGrade, Bernard J., tr. see Heinzmann, Josef.

McGrade, Ferrer, jt. auth. see Wuillmier, Sandra.

***McGrade, Michael.** The Invisible Crown: A Story of Dorothy Von Flue, Wife of the Patron Saint of Switzerland. 148p. 1999. 26.95 (1-901157-76-8) St Austin.

McGrady. A Guide to Organizing Unions. 160p. 1989. pap. 40.00 (0-409-80953-5, MICHIE) LEXIS Pub.

McGrady, Donald. Mateo Aleman. LC 67-25196. (Twayne World Authors Ser.). 1968. lib. bdg. 20.95 (0-8057-2028-6) Irvington.

McGrady, Donald, ed. see de Vega, Lope.

McGrady, Donald, ed. see Tamariz, Cristobal de.

McGrady, John F. Sailing the Dream: The Querencia Chronicles. LC TXu775-43. (Illus.). 384p. 1999. pap. 19.95 (1-929317-99-9) Coco Info.

McGrady, L. J. How to Publish Your Genealogy. 3rd ed. LC 83-91302. (Illus.). 80p. 1984. pap. 6.75 (0-318-00804-1) L J McGrady.

McGrady, Mike, jt. auth. see Lovelace, Linda.

McGrady, Patrick, jt. auth. see Pritikin, Nathan.

McGrady, Richard. Music & Musicians in Early 19th Century Cornwall. 176p. 1991. pap. text 21.95 (0-85989-359-6, Pub. by Univ Exeter Pr) Northwestern U Pr.

McGrady, Sean. Dead Letter. Chelius, Jane, ed. 240p. (Orig.). 1992. mass mkt. 4.99 (0-671-74267-1) PB.

— Sealed with a Kiss. Chelius, Jane, ed. 256p. (Orig.). 1995. mass mkt. 5.50 (0-671-86941-8) PB.

— Town Without a Zip. 1997. per. 5.99 (0-671-86942-6) S&S Trade.

McGrady, Thomas. Beyond the Black Ocean: A Story of Social Revolution. LC 75-154450. (Utopian Literature Ser.). 1976. reprint ed. 25.95 (0-405-03532-2) Ayer.

***McGrail, Anna.** Infertility: The Last Secret. 1999. pap. 24.95 (0-7475-4396-8, Pub. by Blmsbury Pub) Trafalgar.

McGrail, Anna. Mrs. Einstein: A Novel. LC 98-14264. 320p. 1998. 24.95 (0-393-04611-7) Norton.

— Your Newborn & You: A National Childbirth Trust Guide. LC 94-10364. (Illus.). 254p. 1997. pap. 12.95 (1-55561-125-7) Fisher Bks.

McGrail, Janet, et al. Looking at Schools: Instruments & Processes for School Analysis. 140p. 1991. reprint ed. pap. 23.95 (1-56602-038-7) Research Better.

McGrail, Janet, jt. auth. see Wilson, Bruce L.

***McGrail, Mary Ann.** Tyranny in Shakespeare. LC 99-45933. (Applications of Political Theory Ser.: Vol. 135). 208p. 2000. 59.95 (0-7391-0082-3) Lxngtn Bks.

McGrail, Sean, ed. see Johnstone, Paul.

McGrain, Eleanore, jt. auth. see Bronstein, Leona B.

McGrain, John W. From Pig Iron to Cotton Duck: A History of Manufacturing Villages in Baltimore County, Vol. 1. (Baltimore County Heritage Publications). (Illus.). 350p. 1985. 25.00 (0-937076-01-5) Baltimore Co Pub Lib.

McGrain, Mark. Music Notation. 207p. 1990. pap. 16.95 (0-7935-0847-9, 50449399, Berklee Pr) H Leonard.

McGran, John. World's Greatest Sports Brawls. LC 97-76257. (Illus.). 144p. 1998. pap. 12.95 (1-56352-476-7) Longstreet.

McGran, John, jt. auth. see Zullo, Allan.

McGranaghan, Edmund. The Life's Work of a Minor Poet: Collected Fiction, Journalism, & Poetry of Edmund McGranaghan. McKinley, Sarah, ed. & intro. by. LC 83-80303. (Illus.). 254p. (Orig.). 1983. pap. 12.50 (0-912681-00-4) Fidelio Pr.

McGranahan, Carole, jt. auth. see Forbes, Ann.

McGrane, Angela, jt. auth. see Smailes, Joanne.

McGrane, Bernard. Beyond Anthropology: Society & the Other. 176p. (C). 1992. pap. 18.50 (0-231-06685-6) Col U Pr.

— The Un-TV & the Ten MPH Car: Experiments in Personal Freedom & Everyday Life. LC 93-87106. (Illus.). 350p. (Orig.). 1994. pap. 17.50 (1-878020-05-6) Small Pr CA.

McGrane, Bernard, jt. auth. see Bell, Inge.

McGrane, Helen F., jt. auth. see Cochrane, Barbara T.

McGrane, Michael F., jt. auth. see Fischer, Kay-Laurel.

McGrane, Reginald C. Panic of 1837: Some Financial Problems of the Jacksonian Era. 1993. pap. text 1.95 (0-226-55858-4, P202) U Ch Pr.

Mcgrata, Jinks. Enameling - First Steps. 96p. 1994. 12.98 (0-7858-0033-6) Bk Sales Inc.

McGrath. Bookman's Price Index, Vol. 51. 1995. 290.00 (0-8103-9148-1) Gale.

— Bookmans Price Index: Bookman's Price Cumulative Index to Vols. 47-54. 900p. 1998. 280.00 (0-7876-2214-1, GML00198-111729) Visible Ink Pr.

— Bookman's Price Index: Cumulative Index to Vols. 13-19. 1890p. 1996. 290.00 (0-7876-0866-1) Gale.

— Bookman's Price Index: Cumulative Index to Vols. 20-26. 1896p. 1995. 290.00 (0-7876-0562-X) Gale.

— Lotus 1-2-3 at Work: The Joy of Lotus. 1990. pap. 5.00 incl. 3.5 hd (0-13-633835-6) Macmillan USA.

Mcgrath. Point - Counterpoint. (C). 1998. pap. text 40.50 (0-15-503983-0) Harcourt.

McGrath, ed. Introductory Statistics: Study Guide. (C). 1997. pap. text, student ed. 25.00 (0-673-99424-4) Addison-Wesley.

McGrath & Noble. Different Kids, Same Classroom. 1993. pap. text. write for info. (0-582-90982-1, Pub. by Addison-Wesley) Longman.

***McGrath, Janet.** Building Strategies for College Reading: Text with Thematic Reader. 3rd ed. 496p. 2000. pap. 40.00 (0-13-085043-8, Prentice Hall) P-H.

McGrath, Alice, jt. auth. see Tegner, Bruce.

McGrath, Alice, ed. see Tegner, Bruce.

McGrath, Alister. Beyond the Quiet Time: Practical Evangelical Spirituality. LC 96-7030. 116p. (gr. 10). 1996. pap. 7.99 (0-8010-5708-6) Baker Bks.

— Christian Spirituality: An Introduction. LC 98-33147. 350p. 1999. 64.95 (0-631-21280-9); pap. 26.95 (0-631-21281-7) Blackwell Pubs.

— Evangelicalism & the Future of Christianity. 195p. 1994. pap. text 24.00 (0-340-60809-9, Pub. by Hodder & Stought Ltd) Lubrecht & Cramer.

— Explaining Your Faith. 2nd ed. LC 96-9239. 160p. (gr. 10). 1996. pap. 9.99 (0-8010-5728-0) Baker Bks.

— "I Believe" Exploring the Apostles' Creed. LC 98-18081. 120p. 1998. reprint ed. pap. 7.99 (0-8308-1946-0, 1946) InterVarsity.

— J. I. Packer: A Biography. LC 97-38734. (Illus.). 352p. 1998. 19.99 (0-8010-1157-4) Baker Bks.

***McGrath, Alister.** The J. I. Packer Collection. 288p. 2000. pap. 16.99 (0-8308-2287-9) InterVarsity.

— A Passion for Truth: The Intellectual Coherence of Evangelicalism. 1999. pap. text 15.99 (0-8308-1591-0) InterVarsity.

McGrath, Alister. Reformation Thought: An Introduction. 3rd ed. LC 99-25163. 320p. 1999. text 64.95 (0-631-21520-4); pap. text 32.95 (0-631-21521-2) Blackwell Pubs.

***McGrath, Alister.** The Unknown God: Searching for Spiritual Fulfilment. LC 99-28295. (Illus.). 128p. 1999. 18.00 (0-8028-3864-2) Eerdmans.

McGrath, Alister E. The Blackwell Encyclopedia of Modern Christian Thought. 720p. 1995. pap. 33.95 (0-631-19896-2) Blackwell Pubs.

— Christian Theology: An Introduction. 2nd ed. LC 95-42641. (Illus.). 544p. (C). 1996. pap. 34.95 (0-631-19849-0) Blackwell Pubs.

— Evangelicalism & the Future of Christianity. 209p. 1995. 17.99 (0-8308-1694-1, 1694) InterVarsity.

— Foundations of Dialogue in Science & Religion. LC 98-9207. 288p. 1998. 62.95 (0-631-20853-4) Blackwell Pubs.

— Foundations of Dialogue in Science & Religion. LC 98-9207. 288p. 1999. pap. 29.95 (0-631-20854-2) Blackwell Pubs.

— The Genesis of Doctrine: A Study in the Foundation of Doctrinal Criticism. LC 96-37765. 276p. 1997. pap. 25.00 (0-8028-4316-6) Eerdmans.

— The Genesis of Doctrine: A Study in the Foundation of Doctrinal Criticism. 266p. (C). 1995. reprint ed. pap. 25.00 (1-57383-072-0) Regent College.

— Historical Theology: An Introduction to the History of Christian Thought. 450p. 1998. 62.95 (0-631-20843-7); pap. 34.95 (0-631-20844-5) Blackwell Pubs.

— Intellectuals Don't Need God & Other Modern Myths: Christian Apologetics for Today. 224p. 1993. pap. 15.99 (0-310-59091-4) Zondervan.

— An Introduction to Christianity. LC 96-23776. 416p. (C). 1997. text 66.95 (0-631-20195-5); pap. text 34.95 (0-631-20196-3) Blackwell Pubs.

— Iustitia Dei: A History of the Christian Doctrine of Justification. 2nd expanded rev. ed. LC 97-45969. 546p. (C). 1999. text 85.00 (0-521-62426-6); pap. text 29.95 (0-521-62481-9) Cambridge U Pr.

***McGrath, Alister E.** The Journey: A Pilgrim in the Lands of the Spirit. LC 99-36568. 160p. 2000. 17.95 (0-385-49588-9) Doubleday.

McGrath, Alister E. Justification by Faith: An Introduction. 160p. 1988. 12.95 (0-310-21140-9, 10017) Zondervan.

— A Life of John Calvin: A Study in the Shaping of Western Culture. (Illus.). 320p. 1993. reprint ed. pap. 28.95 (0-631-18947-5) Blackwell Pubs.

— Luther's Theology of the Cross. 208p. 1990. pap. 28.95 (0-631-17549-0) Blackwell Pubs.

— The Mystery of the Cross. 160p. 1988. 11.95 (0-310-29980-2, 18406) Zondervan.

— The Mystery of the Cross. 1990. pap. 8.99 (0-310-29981-0) Zondervan.

— The NIV Bible Companion: A Basic Commentary on the Old & New Testaments. LC 96-51874. 400p. 1997. 24.99 (0-310-20547-6) Zondervan.

— A Passion for Truth: The Intellectual Coherence of Evangelicalism. 195p. 1995. pap. 24.00 (0-614-97984-6, Pub. by Hodder & Stought Ltd) Lubrecht & Cramer.

— A Passion for Truth: The Intellectual Coherence of Evangelicalism. LC 96-822. 283p. 1996. pap. 21.99 (0-8308-1866-9, 1866) InterVarsity.

— Reformation Thought: An Introduction. 2nd ed. LC 92-12336. 272p. (Orig.). 1993. pap. 30.95 (0-631-18651-4) Blackwell Pubs.

McGrath, Alister E. The Renewal of Anglicanism. LC 93-35681. 172p. 1993. pap. 12.95 (0-8192-1603-8) Morehouse Pub.

McGrath, Alister E. Science & Christianity: An Introduction. LC 98-23477. 256p. 1998. 59.95 (0-631-20841-0); pap. 29.95 (0-631-20842-9) Blackwell Pubs.

— Studies in Doctrine. LC 96-53076. 480p. 1997. 24.99 (0-310-21326-6) Zondervan.

***McGrath, Alister E.** T.F. Torrance: An Intellectual Biography. 320p. 1999. 49.95 (0-567-08683-6) T&T Clark Pubs.

McGrath, Alister E. Understanding Jesus: Who Jesus Christ Is & Why He Matters. 192p. (Orig.). 1987. reprint ed. 12.95 (0-310-29810-5, 18404) Zondervan.

— Understanding the Trinity. 160p. 1988. 11.95 (0-310-29680-3, 18405) Zondervan.

***McGrath, Alister E., ed.** Christian Literature. 2000. 64.95 (0-631-21605-7); pap. 29.95 (0-631-21606-5) Blackwell Pubs.

McGrath, Alister E., ed. The Christian Theology Reader. 544p. 1995. pap. 33.95 (0-631-19585-8) Blackwell Pubs.

McGrath, Alister E. & Lewis, Donald, eds. Doing Theology for the People of God. LC 96-8. 300p. (Orig.). 1996. pap. 22.99 (0-8308-1870-7, 1870) InterVarsity.

McGrath, Allen. Destruction of Pakistan's Democracy. 322p. 1999. pap. text 10.00 (0-19-579001-4) OUP.

McGrath, Ann. Contested Ground: Australian Aborigines Under the British Crown. 448p. 1996. pap. 29.95 (1-86373-646-8, Pub. by Allen & Unwin Pty) Paul & Co Pubs.

McGrath, Anne F. Bookman's Price Index, Vol. 50. 930p. 1995. 290.00 (0-8103-9147-3) Gale.

— Bookman's Price Index, Vol. 55. 930p. 1997. 290.00 (0-7876-0052-0, 00108702) Gale.

— Bookman's Price Index: Cumulative Index to Vols. 1-6. 2000p. 1997. 290.00 (0-7876-1577-3) Gale.

— Bookman's Price Index Vol. 52: A Guide to the Values of Rare & Other Out of Print Books. 940p. 1996. 290.00 (0-8103-6444-1) Gale.

— Bookman's Price Index Vol. 53: A Guide to the Values of Rare & Other Out of Print Books. 1996. 290.00 (0-8103-6445-X) Gale.

McGrath, Anne F., ed. Bookman's Price Index: CUM Index, Vol. 537-46. 1000p. 1993. 290.00 (0-8103-9554-1) Gale.

***McGrath Avery, Pat.** The Aged Tree Stands Proud: I See New Beauty Found. 1999. pap. 10.95 (0-9663276-1-6) River Rd Pr.

McGrath, Barbara B. The Baseball Counting Book. LC 97-36610. (Illus.). 32p. (J). (ps-3). 1999. 15.95 (0-88106-332-0); pap. 6.95 (0-88106-333-9) Charlesbridge Pub.

— El Libro de Contar de los Chocolates Marca "M&M" Mlawer, Teresa, tr. from ENG. LC 96-945. (SPA., Illus.). 32p. (J). (ps-3). 1996. pap. 6.95 (0-88106-903-5) Charlesbridge Pub.

— The "M & M's" Brand Chocolate Candies Counting Book. (Illus.). 32p. (J). (ps-3). 1994. 15.95 (0-88106-854-3); pap. 6.95 (0-88106-853-5) Charlesbridge Pub.

— More "M&M's" Brand Chocolate Candies Math. LC 97-29345. (Illus.). 32p. (J). (gr. 3-7). 1998. 15.95 (0-88106-993-0) Charlesbridge Pub.

— More "M&M's" Brand Chocolate Candies Math. LC 97-29345. (Illus.). 32p. (J). (gr. 3 up). 1998. pap. 6.95 (0-88106-994-9) Charlesbridge Pub.

— Pepperidge Farm Goldfish Counting Board Book. (Illus.). 12p. (J). (ps-k). 1998. bds. 4.95 (1-893017-50-8) Jennings Pond.

McGrath, Barbara Barbieri. The Cheerios Counting Book. LC 97-52819. (Illus.). 32p. (J). (ps-k). 1998. pap. 4.95 (0-590-68357-8, Pub. by Scholastic Inc) Penguin Putnam.

***McGrath, Barbara Barbieri.** The Cheerios Counting Book. LC 97-52819. (Illus.). 32p. (J). (ps-1). 1998. bds. 10.95 (0-590-00321-6, Pub. by Scholastic Inc) Penguin Putnam.

— The Cheerios Counting Book: 1, 2, 3. (Illus.). 14p. (J). (ps-k). 2000. 6.99 (0-590-68358-6, Cartwheel) Scholastic Inc.

— Contar Cheerios! (SPA.). 32p. (ps-k). 2000. pap. 4.95 (0-439-14979-7) Scholastic Inc.

McGrath, Barbara Barbieri. Hershey's Kisses: Counting Board Book, 1. 1998. 4.95 (0-9662445-0-8) Corp Board.

***McGrath, Barbara Barbieri.** Kellogg's Froot Loops Counting Fun Book. (Illus.). 16p. (J). (ps-k). 2000. bds. 5.99 (0-694-01506-7, HarpFestival) HarpC Child Bks.

McGrath, Barbara Barbieri. El Libro de Contar de Los Chocolates Marca M&M. 1996. 12.15 (0-606-10413-5, Pub. by Turtleback) Demco.

— The "M & M's" Brand Chocolate Candies Counting Book. LC 95-72220. (Illus.). 10p. (J). (ps-k). 1997. bds. 4.95 (0-88106-948-5) Charlesbridge Pub.

McGrath, Barbara Barbieri. M & M's Brand Counting Book. 1994. 12.15 (0-606-07028-1, Pub. by Turtleback) Demco.

M

— Necco's Sweethearts Be My Valentine Book. 10p. (J). (ps up). 2000. bds. 5.99 (*0-694-01534-2*, HarpFestival) HarpC Child Bks.

— Pepperidge Farm Goldfish Counting Fun Book. 16p. (J). (ps-1). 2000. bds. 5.99 (*0-694-01504-0*, HarpFestival) HarpC Child Bks.

— The Pepperidge Farm Goldfish Fun Book. (Illus.). 16p. (ps-k). 1999. 5.99 (*0-694-01450-8*) HarpC Child Bks.

— Skittles Riddles Math. LC 00-38372. (Illus.). 2001. write for info. (*1-57091-413-3*) Charlesbridge Pub.

McGrath, Bob. Oops! Excuse Me, Please: And Other Mannerly Tales. LC 97-45015. (Barron's Educational Ser.). (Illus.). 32p. (J). (ps-2). 1998. 5.95 (*0-7641-5083-9*) Barron.

— Uh Oh! Gotta Go! Potty Tales from Toddlers. LC 96-1527. (Illus.). 34p. (J). 1996. 5.95 (*0-8120-6564-6*) Barron.

McGrath, Brian J. Duck Calls & Other Game Calls. LC 88-90614. (Illus.). 1988. 100.00 (*0-9620155-0-4*) T B Reel.

McGrath, Brian J., jt. auth. see Gard, Ronald J.

McGrath, Brian J., ed. see Kelly, Mary K.

McGrath, Brian J., ed. see Vernon, Steven K. & Stewart, Frank M., III.

McGrath, Cambell, et al. Aristophanes Vol. 2: Wasps, Lysistrata, Frogs, the Sexual Congress. (Penn Greek Drama Ser.). 1999. pap. 17.95 (*0-8122-1684-9*) U of Pa Pr.

McGrath, Campbell. American Noise: Poems. 1994. pap. 11.00 (*0-88001-374-5*) HarpC.

McGrath, Campbell. Capitalism. LC 89-24962. (Wesleyan New Poets Ser.). 64p. 1990. pap. 12.95 (*0-8195-1195-1*, Wesleyan Univ Pr) U Pr of New Eng.

— Road Atlas: Prose & Other Poems. LC 98-37078. 96p. 1999. 23.00 (*0-88001-668-X*) HarpC.

— Spring Comes To Chicago. LC 96-17162. 96p. 1996. pap. 12.95 (*0-88001-484-9*) HarpC.

McGrath, Carmelita. Poems on Land & on Water. 80p. 1992. pap. 7.15 (*1-895387-11-6*) Creative Bk Pub.

***McGrath, Carmelita.** Stranger Things Have Happened. 160p. 1999. pap. 10.35 (*1-894294-10-6*, Pub. by Creative Bk Pub) Genl Dist Srvs.

McGrath, Carmelita. To the New World. LC 97-199969. 72p. 1996. pap. 9.95 (*1-895387-77-9*) Creative Bk Pub.

— Walking to Shenak. 164p. 1994. pap. 9.95 (*1-895387-32-9*) Creative Bk Pub.

McGrath, Carmelita, ed. Signatures: Newfoundland Women Artists & Writers. 68p. 1996. pap. 16.95 (*1-895387-66-3*) Creative Bk Pub.

McGrath, Carmelita, et al, eds. Their Lives & Times: Women in Newfoundland & Labrador. 372p. 1994. pap. 15.95 (*1-895387-42-6*) Creative Bk Pub.

McGrath, Carol R., et al. Road Trip. 80p. 1993. pap. text 12.95 (*0-944459-71-4*) ECS Lrn Systs.

***McGrath, Catherine B.** IESC's Approach to Assessing Import & Reporting Results. 8p. 1999. pap. 10.00 (*0-929556-20-8*) Ind Sector.

***McGrath, Charles & New York Times Book Review Staff, eds.** Books of the Century: A Hundred Years of Authors, Ideas & Literature. (Illus.). 672p. 2000. reprint ed. pap. 20.00 (*0-609-80688-2*, Three Riv Pr) Crown Pub Group.

McGrath, Cindy. Rejoice in Remembering. 8.00 (*0-945905-20-3*) Family Hstory Pubns.

McGrath, Connell. With Words. 32p. 1991. pap. 4.00 (*1-879645-04-1*) Garlic MA.

McGrath, Cynthia, jt. ed. see Boyd, Susan.

McGrath, Daniel F. Bookman's Price Index, Vol. 30. 944p. 1985. 290.00 (*0-8103-0643-3*) Gale.

— Bookman's Price Index, Vol. 35. 1250p. 1987. 290.00 (*0-8103-1806-7*) Gale.

— Bookman's Price Index, Vol. 38. 1989. 290.00 (*0-8103-1811-3*) Gale.

— Bookman's Price Index, Vol. 42. 1991. 290.00 (*0-8103-1815-6*) Gale.

— Bookman's Price Index, Vol. 43. 1991. 290.00 (*0-8103-1816-4*) Gale.

— Bookman's Price Index, Vol. 44. 1992. 290.00 (*0-8103-7493-5*) Gale.

— Bookman's Price Index, Vol. 45. 1992. 290.00 (*0-8103-7494-3*) Gale.

— Bookman's Price Index, Vol. 48. 1994. 290.00 (*0-8103-5602-3*, 004148) Gale.

— Bookman's Price Index, Vol. 49. 1994. 290.00 (*0-8103-5603-1*, 004149) Gale.

— Bookman's Price Index, Vol. 39, Vol. 39. 1000p. 1989. 290.00 (*0-8103-1812-1*) Gale.

McGrath, Daniel F., ed. Bookman's Price Index, Vol. 26. 896p. 1984. 290.00 (*0-8103-0639-5*) Gale.

— Bookman's Price Index, Vol. 27. 920p. 1984. 290.00 (*0-8103-0640-9*) Gale.

— Bookman's Price Index, Vol. 28. 880p. 1984. 290.00 (*0-8103-0641-7*) Gale.

— Bookman's Price Index, Vol. 29. 992p. 1985. 290.00 (*0-8103-0642-5*) Gale.

— Bookman's Price Index, Vol. 31. 1020p. 1985. 290.00 (*0-8103-0636-0*) Gale.

— Bookman's Price Index, Vol. 33. 1000p. 1986. 290.00 (*0-8103-1804-0*) Gale.

— Bookman's Price Index, Vol. 34. 1232p. 1987. 290.00 (*0-8103-1805-9*) Gale.

— Bookman's Price Index, Vol. 37. 1000p. 1988. 290.00 (*0-8103-1808-3*) Gale.

— Bookman's Price Index, Vol. 40. 1000p. 1990. 290.00 (*0-8103-1813-X*) Gale.

— Bookman's Price Index, Vol. 41. 1990. 290.00 (*0-8103-1814-8*) Gale.

— Bookman's Price Index: A Guide to the Values of Rare & Other Out-of-Print Books, 25 vols. Incl. Vol. 1. LC 64-8723. 2008p. 1964. 280.00 (*0-8103-0601-8*); Vol. 2. LC 64-8723. 1314p. 1967. 280.00 (*0-8103-0602-6*); Vol. 3. LC 64-8723. 1098p. 1968. 280.00 (*0-8103-0603-4*); Vol. 4. LC 64-8723. 1032p. 1969. 280.00 (*0-8103-0604-2*); Vol. 5. LC 64-8723. 1032p. 1971. 280.00 (*0-8103-0605-0*); Vol. 6. LC 64-8723. 706p. 1973. 280.00 (*0-8103-0606-9*); Vol. 7. LC 64-8723. 678p. 1973. 280.00 (*0-8103-0607-7*); Vol. 8. LC 64-8723. 676p. 1974. 280.00 (*0-8103-0608-5*); Vol. 9. LC 64-8723. 730p. 1974. 280.00 (*0-8103-0609-3*); Vol. 10. LC 64-8723. 750p. 1975. 280.00 (*0-8103-0635-2*); Vol. 11. LC 64-8723. 804p. 1976. 280.00 (*0-8103-0611-5*); Vol. 12. LC 64-8723. 808p. 1977. 280.00 (*0-8103-0612-3*); Vol. 13. LC 64-8723. 768p. 1978. 280.00 (*0-8103-0613-1*); Vol. 14. LC 64-8723. 768p. 1978. 280.00 (*0-8103-0614-X*); Vol. 15. LC 64-8723. 760p. 1979. 280.00 (*0-8103-0615-8*); Vol. 16. LC 64-8723. 736p. 1979. 280.00 (*0-8103-0616-6*); Vol. 17. LC 64-8723. 768p. 1979. 280.00 (*0-8103-0617-4*); Vol. 18. LC 64-8723. 792p. 1980. 280.00 (*0-8103-0618-2*); Vol. 19. LC 64-8723. 808p. 1980. 280.00 (*0-8103-0619-0*); Vol. 20. LC 64-8723. 872p. 1980. 280.00 (*0-8103-0620-4*); Vol. 21. LC 64-8723. 792p. 1981. 280.00 (*0-8103-0621-2*); Vol. 22. LC 64-8723. 880p. 1981. 280.00 (*0-8103-0622-0*); Vol. 23. LC 64-8723. 792p. 1983. 280.00 (*0-8103-0623-9*); Vol. 24. LC 64-8723. 792p. 1983. 280.00 (*0-8103-0624-7*); Vol. 25. LC 64-8723. 776p. 1983. 280.00 (*0-8103-0638-7*); LC 64-8723. 280.00 (*0-318-52353-1*) Gale.

— Bookman's Price Index, Vol. 36, Vol. 36. 1000p. 1988. 290.00 (*0-8103-1807-5*) Gale.

McGrath, Delia M. Rainbows . . . & Roses. (Illus.). 200p. (Orig.). 1986. pap. 10.00 (*0-9617794-0-3*) Laurel Pub TX.

McGrath, Dennis J. & Smith, Dane. Professor Wellstone Goes to Washington: The Inside Story of a Grassroots U. S. Senate Campaign. LC 94-41361. (Illus.). 328p. 1995. 24.95 (*0-8166-2662-6*); pap. 17.95 (*0-8166-2663-4*) U of Minn Pr.

McGrath, Donald, tr. see Kolbowski, Silvia, et al.

McGrath, Eamonn. Charnel House. 240p. 1990. pap. 14.95 (*0-85640-447-0*, Pub. by Blackstaff Pr) Dufour.

— The Fish in the Stone. 236p. 1994. pap. 14.95 (*0-85640-524-8*, Pub. by Blackstaff Pr) Dufour.

— Honour Thy Father. 256p. 1990. pap. 14.95 (*0-85640-433-0*, Pub. by Blackstaff Pr) Dufour.

McGrath, Eileen. Death of an Infant. 1997. pap. 3.95 (*0-7829-0753-9*, 661-010 12501) T More.

— Kids Get Stressed Too: Understanding What's Going on & How to Help, Vol. 1. 1999. pap. 6.95 (*0-88347-406-9*) T More.

— Limited Life, Lasting Love: Siblings Grieve Too. 40p. 1997. pap. 3.95 (*0-7829-0880-2*) T More.

— Miscarriage. 1997. pap. 3.95 (*0-7829-0752-0*, 661-009 12500) T More.

McGrath, Elizabeth. Rubens' Subjects from History, 2 vols., Pt. XIII. (Illus.). 752p. 1997. 225.00 (*0-905203-69-0*, Pub. by Harvey Miller) Gordon & Breach.

McGrath, Ellen, et al, eds. Women & Depression: Risk Factors & Treatment Issues: Final Report of the American Psychological Association's National Task Force on Women & Depression. LC 90-14448. 137p. 1990. reprint ed. pap. 42.50 (*0-608-04561-6*, 206530000001) Bks Demand.

McGrath, Elsie H., ed. Journey of Faith Cycle A: Participant Book. (Cycle A Ser.). 64p. 1995. pap. 1.95 (*0-89243-559-3*) Liguori Pubns.

McGrath, Elsie H., jt. auth. see Craghan, John.

***McGrath, F. C.** Brian Friel's (Post) Colonial Drama: Language, Illusion, & Politics. LC 99-47935. (Illus.). 312p. 1999. 34.95 (*0-8156-2813-7*) Syracuse U Pr.

McGrath, F. C. The Sensible Spirit: Walter Pater & the Modernist Paradigm. LC 85-29503. 320p. 1986. 49.95 (*0-8130-0829-8*) U Press Fla.

McGrath, Fergal. The Consecration of Learning: Lectures on Newman's Idea of a University. LC 62-22015. 351p. reprint ed. pap. 108.90 (*0-7837-0454-2*, 204077700018) Bks Demand.

McGrath, Francis. John Henry Newman: Universal Revelation. LC 98-134182. 192p. 1998. text 30.00 (*0-86554-603-7*, H455) Mercer Univ Pr.

— John Henry Newman: Universal Revelation. 176p. 1996. 60.00 (*0-86012-273-5*, Pub. by Srch Pr) St Mut.

McGrath, Franklin. History of One Hundred Twenty-Seventh New York Volunteers. 1976. 26.95 (*0-8488-1558-0*) Amereon Ltd.

McGrath, G. & Davidson, I. Limitation of Actions Handbook - NSW. 372p. 1996. pap. write for info. (*0-409-31115-4*, MICHIE) LEXIS Pub.

McGrath, Gai M., jt. auth. see Earp, Martin K.

McGrath, Gail. Workbook for Voice & Articulation for the Electronic Media. 141p. (C). 1993. student ed. 22.21 (*1-56870-070-9*) RonJon Pub.

McGrath, George B. Issues Management: Anticipation & Influence. (Strategic Communicator Ser.). 132p. 1998. 185.00 (*1-888015-12-8*) IABC.

Mcgrath, Gerald & Meana, Janet. Fashion Buckles: Common to Classic. LC 96-71099. (Illus.). 184p. 1997. pap. 29.95 (*0-7643-0215-9*) Schiffer.

McGrath, H. G. & Charles, M. E., eds. Origin & Refining of Petroleum. LC 73-164409. (Advances in Chemistry Ser.: No. 103). 1971. 24.95 (*0-8412-0120-X*) Am Chemical.

McGrath-Hadwen, Eileen & Society of Photo-Optical Instrumentation Engineers Staff. Wireless Technologies & Services for Cellular & Personal Communication Services: Proceedings: 25-26 October 1995, Philadelphia, Pennsylvania. LC 95-70383. viii, 308p. 1996. write for info. (*0-8194-1966-4*) SPIE.

McGrath, Ian, jt. ed. see Howard, Ron.

McGrath, J. J., ed. Advances in Biological Heat & Mass Transfer - 1992. (HTD Ser.: Vol. 231). 152p. 1992. 45.00 (*0-7918-1111-5*, G00755) ASME.

McGrath, Jack. Lotus 1-2-3 at Work: The Joy of Lotus. 1990. pap. 44.95 (*0-13-635327-4*) P-H.

— Using the 1-2-3 Solver. (Illus.). (Orig.). 1991. pap. 44.95 (*0-13-635335-5*) Brady Pub.

McGrath, Jacqueline O., ed. see Weihrouch, James W.

McGrath, James. Behind My Eyes: A Visit, Vol. 1. Benny, Louis M., ed. (Illus.). 65p. (Orig.). 1989. pap. 11.95 (*1-877608-00-9*) Rinky Inc.

***McGrath, James, et al.** Value Growers: Achieving Competitive Advantage Through Long-Term Growth & Profits. (Illus.). 272p. 2000. 27.95 (*0-07-136440-4*) McGraw.

McGrath, James, tr. see Gottfried & Theoderic Monks.

McGrath, James, tr. see Hoffsummer, William.

McGrath, James, tr. see Martini, Carlo M.

McGrath, James E., ed. Anionic Polymerization. LC 81-14911. (Symposium Ser.: No. 166). 594p. 1981. 63.95 (*0-8412-0643-0*) Am Chemical.

— Anionic Polymerization: Kinetics, Mechanisms, & Synthesis. LC 81-14911. (ACS Symposium Ser.: No. 166). (Illus.). 607p. 1981. reprint ed. pap. 188.20 (*0-608-03246-8*, 206376500007) Bks Demand.

— Ring-Opening Polymerization: Kinetics, Mechanisms, & Synthesis: Developed from a Symposium. LC 85-13352. (ACS Symposium Ser.: No. 286). (Illus.). 408p. 1985. reprint ed. pap. 126.50 (*0-608-04339-7*, 206511900001) Bks Demand.

McGrath, Jane L. Building Strategies for College Reading: A Text with Thematic Reader. 2nd ed. LC 97-14473. 468p. 1997. pap. text 41.00 (*0-13-262304-8*) P-H.

McGrath, Jill. The Rune of Salt Air. Warren, Shirley, ed. (Illus.). 36p. 1991. pap. 5.00 (*1-877801-16-X*) Still Waters.

McGrath, Jim, jt. auth. see Doughty, Carolyn.

McGrath, Jinks. Jewelry-Making Techniques: A Comprehensive Visual Guide to Traditional & Contemporary Techniques. LC 94-74910. (The Encyclopedia of Art Ser.). (Illus.). 176p. 1995. 24.95 (*1-56138-526-3*) Running Pr.

McGrath, Jinks, jt. auth. see Tolland, Susan.

McGrath, John. A Good Night Out: Popular Theatre: Audience, Class & Form. 144p. (Orig.). 1996. pap. 20.95 (*1-85459-370-6*, Pub. by N Hern Bks) Theatre Comm.

— Six Pack: Plays for Scotland. 1996. pap. 26.00 (*0-7486-6201-4*, Pub. by Polygon) Subterranean Co.

— Yobbo Nowt. 72p. (Orig.). 1981. pap. 6.95 (*0-904383-76-8*, NO. 4135) Routledge.

McGrath, John A. Baron Friedrich von Hugel & the Debate on Historical Christianity 1902-1905. LC 93-396. 380p. 1993. 99.95 (*0-7734-9817-6*) E Mellen.

***McGrath, John T.** The French in Early Florida: In the Eye of the Hurricane. LC 99-56332. (Illus.). 2000. write for info. (*0-8130-1784-X*) U Press Fla.

McGrath, Joseph E., ed. Social Psychology of Time: New Perspectives. (Focus Editions Ser.: Vol. 91). 320p. (C). 1988. text 59.95 (*0-8039-2766-5*); pap. text 26.00 (*0-8039-2767-3*) Sage.

— The Social Psychology of Time: New Perspectives. LC 87-37700. (Sage Focus Editions Ser.: Vol. 91). 271p. 1988. reprint ed. pap. 84.10 (*0-608-03009-0*, 206345900006) Bks Demand.

McGrath, Joseph E. & Hollingshead, Andrea B. Groups Interacting with Technology: Ideas, Evidence, Issues & an Agenda. LC 93-34627. (Library of Social Research: Vol. 194). (C). 1993. text 59.95 (*0-8039-4897-2*); pap. text 26.00 (*0-8039-4898-0*) Sage.

McGrath, Joseph E. & Kelly, Janice R. Time & Human Interaction: Toward a Social Psychology of Time. LC 86-396. (Illus.). 191p. 1986. reprint ed. pap. 59.30 (*0-608-07586-8*, 205990100010) Bks Demand.

McGrath, Joseph E., et al. Judgment Calls in Research. LC 82-16732. (Studying Organizations Ser.: No. 2). 128p. 1982. reprint ed. pap. 39.70 (*0-608-01162-2*, 205946200001) Bks Demand.

McGrath, Joseph E., jt. auth. see Brinberg, David.

McGrath, Joseph E., jt. auth. see Kelly, Janice R.

McGrath, Kate. Trademark: Legal Care for Your Business & Product Name, 1. 4th ed. LC 99-17558. 1999. pap. text 34.95 (*0-87337-519-X*) Nolo com.

Mcgrath, Kevin, jt. auth. see Kaplan, David.

McGrath, Kevin P. & Kaplan, David, eds. Protein-Based Materials. LC 96-28021. (Bioengineering of Materials Ser.). 330p. 1997. 79.95 (*0-8176-3848-2*) Birkhauser.

***McGrath, Kimberley A., ed.** World of Biology. LC 98-53855. 942p. (YA). (gr. 9 up). 1998. 85.00 (*0-7876-3044-6*) Gale.

***McGrath, Kimberley A. & Travers, Bridget, eds.** World of Invention. 2nd ed. LC 99-192310. 1043p. 1998. 85.00 (*0-7876-2759-3*) Gale.

McGrath, Kristina. House Work: A Novel. LC 94-13257. 192p. 1994. 19.95 (*1-882593-07-3*) Bridge Wrks.

McGrath, Laura J. I Am...by Mac! 2nd rev. ed. (Illus.). 18p. (J). (ps-3). 1996. pap. 4.95 (*0-9645696-1-2*) Mac & Co.

McGrath, Laura Marie & Simek, Robert W. Wedding Planner. (Illus.). 177p. 1998. pap. 11.95 (*1-890565-04-0*) Wedding & Bridal.

— Wedding Planner Kit with Video. (Illus.). 177p. 1998. pap. 24.95 (*1-890565-01-6*) Wedding & Bridal.

McGrath, Leslie, jt. auth. see Rafkin, Louise.

McGrath, Leueen, jt. auth. see Kaufman, George S.

McGrath, Madeleine S. These Women? Women Religious in the History of Australia: The Sisters of Mercy, Parramatta 1888-1988. 312p. 1990. 37.95 (*0-86840-299-0*, Pub. by New South Wales Univ Pr) Intl Spec Bk.

McGrath, Manda. East of Singapore. large type ed. (Large Print Ser.). 352p. 1997. 27.99 (*0-7089-3669-5*) Ulverscroft.

— Footlights. large type ed. (Ulverscroft Large Print Ser.). 352p. 1997. 27.99 (*0-7089-3739-X*) Ulverscroft.

— The Last Ditch. large type ed. (Ulverscroft Large Print Ser.). 448p. 1997. 27.99 (*0-7089-3761-6*) Ulverscroft.

***McGrath, Manda.** Wise Virgin. large type ed. 368p. 1999. 31.90 (*0-7089-4061-7*) Ulverscroft.

McGrath, Margaret. Etienne Gilson: A Bibliography/Une Bibliographie. xxviii, 124p. pap. text 17.71 (*0-88844-703-5*) Brill Academic Pubs.

McGrath, Marjory L. My Hair Is in the Outbox. 116p. (Orig.). 1995. pap. 7.95 (*0-9649200-0-X*) M&C Pubng.

McGrath, Mary. Trespassing Stoplights & Attitudes. (Illus.). 44p. (Orig.). 1980. pap. 5.00 (*0-930012-43-7*) J Mudfoot.

McGrath, Mary Z. Teachers Today: A Guide to Surviving Creatively. LC 95-9037. (Illus.). 128p. 1995. 45.95 (*0-8039-6336-X*); pap. 19.95 (*0-8039-6229-0*) Corwin Pr.

McGrath, Meggan. My Grapes. LC 93-24057. (Illus.). 48p. (Orig.). (J). 1993. pap. 16.95 (*0-938586-99-8*) Pfeifer-Hamilton.

McGrath, Melanie. Motel Nirvana. 1996. 22.00 (*0-614-96868-2*, Picador USA) St Martin.

***McGrath, Michael.** The Catholic Church & Catholic Schools in Northern Ireland: The Price of Faith. LC 99-31405. 336p. 2000. 49.50 (*0-7165-2651-4*, Pub. by Irish Acad Pr) Intl Spec Bk.

***McGrath, Michael E.** Product Strategy for High Technology Companies. 2nd ed. (Illus.). 320p. 2000. 49.95 (*0-07-136246-0*) McGraw.

McGrath, Michael E. Product Strategy for High-Technology Companies: How to Achieve Growth, Competitive Advantage, & Increased Profits. LC 94-27340. 284p. 1994. text 42.50 (*0-7863-0146-5*, Irwn Prfssnl) McGraw-Hill Prof.

McGrath, Michael E., ed. Setting the Pace in Product Development: A Guide to Product & Cycle-Time Excellence. rev. ed. 240p. 1996. pap. text 18.95 (*0-7506-9789-X*) Buttrwrth-Heinemann.

McGrath, Michael J., ed. Liberalism & the Modern Polity: Essays in Contemporary Political Theory. LC 78-2583. (Political Science Ser.: No. 5). 319p. reprint ed. pap. 98.90 (*0-8357-6190-8*, 203455000090) Bks Demand.

McGrath, Michael J., jt. ed. see Barber, Benjamin R.

McGrath, Morag. Multi-Disciplinary Teamwork: Community Mental Handicap Teams. (Care in the Community Studies). 217p. 1991. text 57.95 (*1-85628-152-3*, Pub. by Avebry) Ashgate Pub Co.

McGrath, Morag, jt. auth. see Hadley, Roger.

McGrath, Norman. Photographing Buildings Inside & Out. 2nd enl. rev. ed. LC 92-42306. (Illus.). 208p. 1993. text 27.50 (*0-8230-4016-X*, Whitney Lib) Watsn-Guptill.

McGrath, Pam. Hungry Ants: A Ready to Count Book. LC 98-27254. (Illus.). 24p. (J). 1998. 8.95 (*1-887714-26-X*) Summerhse Pr.

McGrath, Pamela. A Question of Choice: Bioethical Reflections on a Spiritual Response to the Technological Imperative. LC 97-74821. (Series in Philosophy). 256p. 1997. text 73.95 (*1-84014-166-2*, Pub. by Ashgate Pub) Ashgate Pub Co.

McGrath, Patricia A. Pain in Children: Nature, Assessment & Treatment. LC 89-11009. 466p. 1989. lib. bdg. 52.00 (*0-89862-390-1*) Guilford Pubns.

McGrath, Patricia L. The Unfinished Assignment: Equal Education for Women. 1976. pap. write for info. (*0-916468-06-2*) Worldwatch Inst.

McGrath, Patrick. Asylum. 1998. pap. 12.00 (*0-679-78138-2*) Vin Bks.

— Asylum. large type ed. LC 97-9694. 1997. 24.95 (*1-56895-439-5*) Wheeler Pub.

— Dr. Haggard's Disease. 1994. pap. 11.00 (*0-679-75261-7*) Random.

— The Grotesque: A Novel. LC 96-60779. 1997. pap. 11.00 (*0-679-77621-4*) Random.

— The Lewis & Clark Expedition. LC 84-40381. (Turning Points in American History Ser.). 64p. (J). (gr. 5 up). 1984. lib. bdg. 14.95 (*0-382-06828-9*) Silver Burdett Pr.

— The Lewis & Clark Expedition. LC 84-40381. (Turning Points in American History Ser.). (Illus.). 64p. (YA). (gr. 5 up). 1984. pap. 7.95 (*0-382-09899-4*) Silver Burdett Pr.

***McGrath, Patrick.** Martha Peake: A Novel of the Revolution. 400p. 2000. 24.95 (*0-375-50081-2*) Random.

McGrath, Patrick. Spider. LC 91-50095. (Vintage Contemporaries Ser.). 224p. 1991. pap. 13.00 (*0-679-73630-1*) Vin Bks.

McGrath, Patrick & Axelson, John A. Accessing Awareness & Developing Knowledge: Foundations for Skill in a Multicultural Society. 2nd ed. (Counseling Ser.). 265p. 1993. pap., student ed. 18.25 (*0-534-19903-8*) Brooks-Cole.

— Accessing Awareness & Developing Knowledge: Foundations for Skill in a Multicultural Society. 3rd ed. LC 98-16305. (Illus.). 244p. 1999. 27.95 (*0-534-34495-X*) Brooks-Cole.

McGrath, Patrick, et al. The Body. (Illus.). 212p. 1991. pap. 20.00 (*0-941548-23-6*) Ren Soc U Chi.

McGrath, Patrick, ed. see Browne, John.

McGrath, Patrick J. John Garfield: The Illustrated Career in Films & on Stage. LC 92-56666. (Illus.). 286p. 1993. lib. bdg. 39.95 (*0-89950-867-7*) McFarland & Co.

McGrath, Patrick J. & Finley, G. Allen, eds. Chronic & Recurrent Pain in Children & Adolescents. LC 99-23564. (Progress in Pain Research & Management Ser.: Vol. 13). (Illus.). 288p. 1999. 67.00 (*0-931092-27-2*) Intl Assn Study Pain.

McGrath, Patrick J., jt. ed. see Anand, K. J. S.

McGrath, Patrick J., jt. ed. see Finley, G. Allen.

McGrath, Paul. Ooh Ahh Paul McGrath: The Black Pearl of Inchicore. (Illus.). 208p. 1994. pap. write for info. (*1-85158-648-2*) Trafalgar.

McGrath, Paul & Dervan, Cathal. Ooh Aah Paul McGrath: The Black Pearl of Inchicore. (Illus.). 237p. 1995. 29.95 (*1-85158-647-4*, Pub. by Mainstream Pubng) Trafalgar.

McGrath, Paul, ed. & illus. see Zaslau, Stanley.

McGrath, Paul L., ed. see Zaslau, Stanley.

McGrath, Paul L., ed. & illus. see Zaslau, Stanley.

McGrath, Philomena & Mills, P. Atlas of Sectional Anatomy. 2nd ed. (Illus.). viii, 238p. 1985. 71.50 (*3-8055-4060-4*) S Karger.

McGrath, Rae. Landmines: Legacy of Conflict: a Manual for Development Workers. (Illus.). 86p. (C). 1998. reprint ed. pap. text 35.00 (*0-7881-3280-6*) DIANE Pub.

— Landmines: Legacy of Conflict: A Manual for Development Workers; Practical Handbooks. (Practical Handbooks). (Illus.). 96p. (C). 1994. pap. 12.95 (*0-85598-264-0*, Pub. by Oxfam Pub) Stylus Pub VA.

— Landmines & Unexploded Ordnance: A Resource Book. LC 99-52952. 300p. 2000. 79.95 (*0-7453-1264-0*, Pub. by Pluto GBR); pap. 27.95 (*0-7453-1259-4*, Pub. by Pluto GBR) Stylus Pub VA.

McGrath, Ray I. Great Lakes Stories: Ashore after Fifty Years. LC 96-85704. (Illus.). 256p. (Orig.). 1996. pap. 12.95 (*0-9652747-0-5*) Border Pub.

McGrath, Raymond, ed. see Cady, Barbara.

McGrath, Richard. California Criminal Law Workbook. 6th ed. 390p. (C). 1997. 33.95 (*0-7872-3949-6*, 41394901) Kendall-Hunt.

***McGrath, Rita Gunther & MacMillan, Ian C.** Entrepreneurial Mindset: Strategies for Continuously Creating Opportunity in an Age of Uncertainty. 2000. 29.95 (*0-87584-834-6*) Harvard Busn.

McGrath, Robert E. Understanding Statistics. LC 96-557. 436p. (C). 1997. 83.00 (*0-673-99058-3*) Addson-Wesley Educ.

McGrath, Robert E., jt. auth. see Yeager, Nancy J.

***McGrath, Robert L.** Gods in Granite: The Art of the White Mountains of New Hampshire. (Illus.). 246p. 2000. 49.95 (*0-8156-0663-X*) Syracuse U Pr.

McGrath, Robert L. A Wild Sort of Beauty: Public Places & Private Visions. Gilborn, Alice W., ed. (Illus.). 48p. 1992. pap. 10.00 (*0-910020-43-4*) Adirondack Mus.

***Mcgrath, Robin.** Escaped Domestics. 72p. (YA). (gr. 7 up). 1999. pap. 9.95 (*1-895387-94-9*) Creative Bk Pub.

McGrath, Robin. Trouble & Desire. 160p. 1996. pap. 9.55 (*1-895387-59-0*) Creative Bk Pub.

McGrath, Roger D. Gunfighters, Highwaymen, & Vigilantes: Violence on the Frontier. LC 83-6886. (Illus.). 288p. (C). 1984. pap. 16.95 (*0-520-06026-1*, Pub. by U CA Pr) Cal Prin Full Svc.

McGrath, Roland, jt. auth. see Stallman, Richard M.

McGrath, Sally V., ed. see Barchowsky, Nan J.

McGrath, Scott, jt. auth. see Wissolik, Richard D.

McGrath, Sean. XML by Example: A Webmaster's Guide. LC 98-7398. (Charles Goldfarb Series on Open Information). 528p. (C). 1998. pap. text 39.95 (*0-13-960162-7*) P-H.

***McGrath, Sean.** Xml Processing with Python. 450p. 2000. pap. 44.99 (*0-13-021119-2*) P-H.

McGrath, Sheena. Women's Mysteries in the Northern Tradition. (Orig.). 1997. pap. 21.95 (*1-86163-004-2*, Pub. by Capall Bann Pubng) Holmes Pub.

McGrath, Simon, jt. auth. see King, Kenneth.

McGrath-Sullivan, Karen, ed. see Kearney, Patrick J.

McGrath, Susan. Los Animales Hacen Cosas Asombrosas. Sanz, Maria T. & Larios S, Maia, trs. (Explora y Aprende Ser.). (SPA., Illus.). (YA). (gr. 3-8). 1994. 15.00 (*0-915741-52-0*) C D Stampley Ent.

— La Fisica Es Diversion. Sanz, Maria T. & Martin, Berta, trs. (Explora y Aprende Ser.). (SPA., Illus.). (YA). (gr. 3-8). 1995. 15.00 (*0-915741-45-8*) C D Stampley Ent.

— Your World of Pets. Crump, Donald J., ed. LC 85-7288. (Books for World Explorers Series 6: No. 4). (Illus.). 104p. (J). (gr. 3-8). 1985. lib. bdg. 8.95 (*0-87044-522-7*) Natl Geog.

McGrath, Terri. Profiles 1998. (Illus.). 700p. 1998. reprint ed. ring bd. 1245.00 (*1-877750-68-9*) Integrated Circuit.

McGrath, Thomas. Death Song. Hamill, Sam, ed. LC 90-85091. 128p. (Orig.). 1991. 19.00 (*1-55659-035-0*); pap. 10.00 (*1-55659-036-9*) Copper Canyon.

— Letter to an Imaginary Friend, Pts. I-IV. LC 97-33929. 1997. 35.00 (*1-55659-077-6*); pap. text 20.00 (*1-55659-078-4*) Copper Canyon.

— Letters to Tomasito: Poems. Perlman, James, ed. 1977. pap. 2.00 (*0-930100-01-8*) Holy Cow.

— The Movie at the End of the World: Collected Poems. LC 72-91918. 188p. 1972. reprint ed. pap. text 14.95 (*0-8040-0606-7*) Swallow.

— Politics, Interdenominational Relations & Education in the Public Ministry of Bishop James Doyle of Kildare & Leighlin, 1786-1834: A Study of Politics Interdenominational Relations & Education. LC 99-191730. 368p. 1999. boxed set 55.00 (*1-85182-372-7*, Pub. by Four Cts Pr) Intl Spec Bk.

— Religious Renewal & Reform in the Pastoral Ministry of Bishop James Doyle of Kildare & Leighlin, 1786-1834. 352p. 1999. boxed set 55.00 (*1-85182-371-9*, Pub. by Four Cts Pr) Intl Spec Bk.

— Selected Poems, 1938-1988. Hamill, Sam, ed. LC 87-172648. 208p. 1988. pap. 10.00 (*1-55659-012-1*) Copper Canyon.

McGrath, Thomas, et al. Voyages to the Inland Sea, Vol 3. Judson, John, ed. LC 73-78705. 83p. 1973. 10.00 (*0-917540-03-4*); pap. 7.00 (*0-917540-12-3*) Ctr Cont Poetry.

McGrath, Thomas, jt. ed. see Nolan, William.

McGrath, Thomas B., ed. Architectural Sketches of the Spanish Era Forts of Guam: From the Holdings of the Servicio Historico Militar, Madrid. Driver, Marjorie G. & Brunal-Perry, Omaira, trs. LC 95-621264. (Educational Ser.: No. 17). 62p. 1994. 20.00 (*1-878453-18-1*) Univ Guam MAR Ctr.

McGrath, Thomas B., ed. Architectural Sketches of the Spanish Era Forts of Guam: From the Holdings of the Servicio Historico Militar, Madrid. Driver, Marjorie G. & Brunal-Perry, Omaira, trs. (Educational Ser.: No. 17). 320p. 1994. pap. 10.00 (*0-614-07000-7*) Univ Guam MAR Ctr.

McGrath, Thomas B., et al, eds. Evolving Issues in the Pacific: Educational Challenges for the 21st Century. LC 95-175110. (Educational Ser.: No. 16). 143p. 1994. reprint ed. 10.00 (*1-878453-16-5*) Univ Guam MAR Ctr.

***McGrath, Tom.** MTV: The Making of a Revolution. (Illus.). 208p. 1999. reprint ed. text 23.00 (*0-7881-6664-6*) DIANE Pub.

— Raising Faith-Filled Kids: Ordinary Opportunities to Nurture Spirituality at Home. LC 00-35408. 2000. pap. 12.95 (*0-8294-1425-8*) Loyola Pr.

McGrath, Tom. Stress Therapy. LC 96-79961. (Illus.). 96p. 1997. pap. 4.95 (*0-87029-301-X*, 20153) Abbey.

— Voyages of the Damn Foole. LC 96-52300. (Illus.). 186p. 1997. 17.95 (*0-07-045089-7*) McGraw.

McGrath, William. A Devotional Study of the Sermon on the Mount. 1991. pap. 3.00 (*0-935409-00-9*) Amish Mennonite.

— Separation Throughout Church History. 4th rev. ed. 72p. 1990. pap. 2.00 (*0-935409-01-7*) Amish Mennonite.

— Why We Are Conscientious Objectors to War. 1991. pap. 1.50 (*0-935409-02-5*) Amish Mennonite.

McGrath, William C. Great Wisconsin Walks Vol. 1: 45 Strolls, Rambles, Hikes & Treks. McBride, Elizabeth, ed. LC 97-60828. (Illus.). 176p. (Orig.). 1997. pap. 16.95 (*0-915024-55-1*) Trails Media.

— Stride & Glide: A Guide to Wisconsin's Best Cross-Country Ski Trails. LC 94-71147. (Illus.). 112p. 1994. pap. 12.95 (*0-9640613-0-9*) Palmer Pubns Inc.

McGrath, William J. Dionysian Art & Populist Politics in Austria. LC 73-86908. 279p. reprint ed. pap. 86.50 (*0-8357-8096-1*, 203382100087) Bks Demand.

McGrath, William R., ed. Amish Folk Remedies for Plain & Fancy Ailments. 104p. 1988. pap. 9.95 (*0-9617405-8-2*) S Schupp.

— God Given Herbs. 97p. 1988. 6.99 (*0-9617405-9-0*) S Schupp.

***McGrath, Wm. Chad.** Great Minnesota Walks: 49 Strolls, Rambles, Hikes & Treks. Stoga, Stan, ed. LC 99-72896. (Illus.). 182p. 1999. pap. 16.95 (*0-915024-75-6*) Trails Media.

McGravie, Anne V. Wrens. 85p. 1997. pap. 5.60 (*0-87129-772-8*, W82) Dramatic Pub.

McGravie, Anne V., et al. The Radiance of a Thousand Suns: The Hiroshima Project. LC 99-475818. 102p. 1998. pap. 5.60 (*0-87129-792-2*, R62) Dramatic Pub.

McGraw, jt. auth. see Pope.

***McGraw, Allison, ed.** Power Washer's Guidebook. (Illus.). 241p. 1999. pap. 30.00 (*0-944352-31-6*) Cleaning Cons.

McGraw, Betty R., jt. ed. see Ungar, Steven.

McGraw, Cameron. Piano Duet Repertoire: Music Originally Written for 1 Piano, Four Hands. LC 80-8097. 384p. 1981. 49.95 (*0-253-14766-2*) Ind U Pr.

McGraw, Charles G., jt. auth. see Garland, Mark A.

***McGraw, Dan.** First & Last Seasons: A Father, a Son & Sunday Afternoon Football. 304p. 2000. 23.95 (*0-385-49833-0*) Doubleday.

McGraw, Eloise. The Moorchild. LC 95-34107. 240p. (J). (gr. 4-7). 1996. lib. bdg. 16.00 (*0-689-80654-X*) McElderry Bks.

— The Moorchild. 256p. (J). (gr. 4-7). 1998. per. 4.50 (*0-689-82033-X*) S&S Childrens.

***McGraw, Eloise.** The Moorchild. 1998. 9.60 (*0-606-13621-5*, Pub. by Turtleback) Demco.

McGraw, Eloise. Tangled Webb. LC 92-27911. 160p. (YA). (gr. 5 up). 1993. 13.95 (*0-689-50573-6*) McElderry Bks.

McGraw, Eloise, jt. illus. see Baum, L. Frank.

McGraw, Eloise J. The Golden Goblet. LC 85-43415. (Newbery Library). 248p. (J). (gr. 4-7). 1986. pap. 4.99 (*0-14-030335-9*, PuffinBks) Peng Put Young Read.

McGraw, Eloise J. Mara, Daughter of the Nile. LC 85-567. 280p. (J). (gr. 5-9). 1985. pap. 4.99 (*0-14-031929-8*, PuffinBks) Peng Put Young Read.

— The Moccasin Trail. (Newbery Library). 256p. (J). (gr. 5-9). 1986. pap. 4.99 (*0-14-032170-5*, PuffinBks) Peng Put Young Read.

— Moccasin Trail. (Puffin Newbery Library). (J). 1986. 10.09 (*0-606-01321-0*, Pub. by Turtleback) Demco.

— Sawdust in His Shoes. 1994. reprint ed. lib. bdg. 27.95 (*1-56849-310-X*) Buccaneer Bks.

McGraw, Eloise J., jt. auth. see Baum, L. Frank.

McGraw, Eloise Jarvis. The Golden Goblet. 1986. 10.09 (*0-606-01587-6*, Pub. by Turtleback) Demco.

McGraw, Eloise Jarvis, et al. Merry Go Round in Oz. (Illus.). 313p. (J). (gr. 3 up). 1989. 24.95 (*0-929605-06-3*) Books of Wonder.

McGraw, Eloise Jarvis, et al. Merry Go Round in Oz. (Illus.). 313p. (J). (gr. 3-10). 1996. reprint ed. pap. 12.95 (*0-929605-60-8*) Books of Wonder.

McGraw, Eric. Population: The Human Race. 145p. 1990. pap. 14.95 (*1-85219-032-9*, Pub. by Bishopsgte Pr) Intl Spec Bk.

— Population Growth. (World Issues Ser.). (Illus.). 48p. (YA). (gr. 5 up). 1987. lib. bdg. 18.60 (*0-317-60380-9*) Rourke Corp.

— Population Growth. (World Issues Ser.: Set II). (Illus.). 48p. (J). (gr. 5 up). 1988. lib. bdg. 25.27 (*0-86592-276-4*) Rourke Enter.

***McGraw, Gary & Felten, Edward W.** JAVA Security (1997) Hostile Applets, Holes & Antidotes. 192p. 2000. reprint ed. pap. text 20.00 (*0-7881-9196-9*) DIANE Pub.

— Securing Java: Getting down to Business with Mobile Code. 2nd ed. LC 98-49151. 324p. 1999. pap. 34.99 (*0-471-31952-X*) Wiley.

McGraw, Gary, jt. auth. see Voas, Jeffrey.

***McGraw, Gerald & McPeek, George.** Empowered: Discovering the Dynamics of Holy Living. 368p. 2000. pap. 14.99 (*0-87509-788-X*) Chr Pubns.

***McGraw-Hill Staff, ed.** McGraw-Hill Yearbook of Science & Technology. (Illus.). 450p. 2000. 125.00 (*0-07-135867-6*) McGraw.

***McGraw-Hill Book Company Staff.** Alien Encounter. (J). (gr. 4). 1999. 19.95 (*1-57768-314-5*) MG-Hill OH.

McGraw-Hill Book Company Staff. Civil Engineer's Solutions Suite. 1998. 99.95 (*0-07-852885-2*) McGraw.

***McGraw-Hill Book Company Staff.** Foggy Mchammer's Treehouse: Math. 1999. 14.95 (*1-57768-322-6*) MG-Hill OH.

— Freezing Frenzy: Math. (J). (gr. 3). 1999. 19.95 (*1-57768-333-1*) MG-Hill OH.

McGraw Hill Book Company Staff. Hurst's The Heart. 1998. 195.00 incl. cd-rom (*0-07-864185-3*) McGraw.

***McGraw-Hill Book Company Staff.** Meet Mudflat Joe Math. 1999. 19.95 (*1-57768-315-3*) MG-Hill OH.

McGraw-Hill Book Company Staff. The Merck Manual of Medical Information: Home Edition. Berkow, Robert, ed. 1999. cd-rom 39.95 (*0-07-864285-X*) McGraw.

***McGraw-Hill Book Company Staff.** Network Nightmare Language Arts. (J). (gr. 4). 1999. 19.95 (*1-57768-334-X*) MG-Hill OH.

— Nubby's Quiz Show: Math. 1999. 14.95 (*1-57768-321-8*) MG-Hill OH.

— Science Navigator 4.0: Single User. 1998. 150.00 (*0-07-853110-1*) McGraw.

***McGraw-Hill Book Company Staff, ed.** Ancient Times. (Illus.). 32p. (J). (ps-3). 2000. pap. 9.95 incl. cd-rom (*1-57768-760-4*) MG-Hill OH.

— Bugs. (Fact Finders Ser.). (Illus.). (J). 2000. pap. 9.95 (*1-57768-763-9*) MG-Hill OH.

— Building Profiles: In the Construction Industry. (Illus.). 448p. 1999. 74.95 (*0-07-134985-5*) McGraw.

— Children's Fact Finder. (Fact Finders Ser.). (Illus.). (J). 2000. pap. 24.95 (*1-57768-769-8*) MG-Hill OH.

— Children's Picture Bible. (Illus.). (J). 2000. pap. 14.95 (*1-57768-774-4*) MG-Hill OH.

— Dinosaurs. (Fact Finders Ser.). (Illus.). (J). 2000. pap. 9.95 (*1-57768-765-5*) MG-Hill OH.

— Earth. (Fact Finders Ser.). (Illus.). (J). 2000. pap. 9.95 (*1-57768-762-0*) MG-Hill OH.

— Language Arts Grade 5. (Spectrum Ser.). (Illus.). (J). 2000. pap. 7.95 (*1-57768-475-3*) MG-Hill OH.

— Language Arts Grade 4. (Spectrum Ser.). (Illus.). (J). 2000. pap. 7.95 (*1-57768-474-5*) MG-Hill OH.

— Language Arts Grade 6. (Spectrum Ser.). (Illus.). (J). 2000. pap. 7.95 (*1-57768-476-1*) MG-Hill OH.

— Language Arts Grade 3. (Spectrum Ser.). (Illus.). 208p. (J). 2000. pap. 7.95 (*1-57768-473-7*) MG-Hill OH.

— Language Arts Grade 2. (Spectrum Ser.). (Illus.). (J). 2000. pap. 7.95 (*1-57768-472-9*) MG-Hill OH.

— My World of Knowledge. (Young Learner's Ser.). (Illus.). (J). 2000. pap. 12.95 (*1-57768-770-1*) MG-Hill OH.

— Outer Space. (Fact Finders Ser.). (Illus.). (J). 2000. pap. 9.95 (*1-57768-764-7*) MG-Hill OH.

— Sea. (Fact Finders Ser.). (Illus.). (J). 2000. pap. 9.95 (*1-57768-767-1*) MG-Hill OH.

— Weather. (Fact Finders Ser.). (Illus.). (J). 2000. pap. 9.95 (*1-57768-766-3*) MG-Hill OH.

— Young Learner's Dictionary. (Young Learner's Ser.). (Illus.). (J). 2000. pap. 6.95 (*1-57768-771-X*) MG-Hill OH.

— Young Learner's Encyclopedia. (Young Learner's Ser.). (Illus.). (J). 2000. pap. 6.95 (*1-57768-772-8*) MG-Hill OH.

— Young Learner's U. S. & World Atlas. (Young Learner's Ser.). (Illus.). (Orig.). (J). 2000. pap. 6.95 (*1-57768-773-6*) MG-Hill OH.

McGraw-Hill Book Company Staff, jt. auth. see McPartland, Joseph F.

McGraw-Hill, College Division Staff. Author's Guide to Manuscript Preparation. (C). 1991. pap. text 9.68 (*0-07-046733-1*) McGraw.

McGraw-Hill Editors. Dictionary of Astronomy. LC 97-5934. (Illus.). 200p. 1997. pap. 12.95 (*0-07-052434-3*) McGraw.

— Dictionary of Electronics & Computer Science. 592p. 1985. 59.50 (*0-07-045416-7*) McGraw.

— Dictionary of Engineering. LC 97-8928. (Illus.). 420p. 1997. pap. 17.95 (*0-07-052435-1*) McGraw.

— Dictionary of Geology & Mineralogy. LC 97-324. (Illus.). 380p. 1997. pap. 16.95 (*0-07-052432-7*) McGraw.

— Dictionary of Mathematics. LC 97-5933. (Illus.). 250p. 1997. pap. 19.95 (*0-07-052433-5*) McGraw.

***McGraw-Hill Editors.** Distance Learning Faculty Guide: Connect with English. 48p. 1998. pap. 13.75 (*0-07-292755-0*) McGrw-H Hghr Educ.

— Elements Explorer: Good Periodic. 1997. 325.00 (*0-07-853092-X*, McGrw-H College) McGrw-H Hghr Educ.

McGraw-Hill Editors. Healthnet. 3rd ed. 60p. 1999. pap. 9.38 (*0-07-234591-8*) McGraw.

***McGraw-Hill Editors.** Iso 9000 Regular Company Direction North. 1999. write for info. (*0-07-135906-0*, McGrw-H College) McGrw-H Hghr Educ.

McGraw-Hill Editors. McGraw-Hill Encyclopedia of World Drama, 5 vols., Vol. 99. 2nd ed. LC 83-9919. (Illus.). 2900p. 1984. 450.00 (*0-07-079169-4*) McGraw.

— Meteorology Source Book. (Science Reference Ser.). (Illus.). 450p. 1989. 64.95 (*0-07-045511-2*) McGraw.

— Nuclear & Practice Physics Source Book. (Science Reference Ser.). 529p. 1988. 64.95 (*0-07-045509-0*) McGraw.

***McGraw-Hill Editors.** The U. S. Industry & Trade Outlook 2000: The McGraw-Hill Companies & the U. S. Department of Commerce/International Trade Administration. 2nd ed. 780p. 1999. pap. 69.95 (*0-07-135245-7*) Datapro Res.

McGraw-Hill Editors, ed. Clinical Vignettes for USMLE. (Illus.). 287p. 1999. pap. 24.95 (*0-07-135558-8*) McGraw.

— Get Fit Stay Fit. 2nd ed. 272p. 2000. pap. 16.56 (*0-07-232906-8*) McGraw.

McGraw-Hill Editors, jt. auth. see Wcb-Sdorow.

McGraw-Hill Encyclopedia of Science & Technology E. McGraw-Hill 1999 Yearbook of Science & Technology. (Illus.). 500p. 1998. 125.00 (*0-07-052625-7*) McGraw.

McGraw-Hill Inc Staff. Pre-Test Clinical Vignettes for USMLE Step I. LC 99-13440. 304p. 1999. 24.95 (*0-07-135133-7*) McGraw-Hill HPD.

McGraw Hill Publishing Company Staff. The Kitchen & Bath Sourcebook. 400p. 1998. 29.95 (*0-07-607110-3*) McGraw.

***McGraw-Hill Publishing Staff.** Basic Skills Curriculum, Grade 4: Making Children More Successful. rev. ed. (Illus.). 650p. (J). (gr. 3-4). 1999. pap. 19.95 (*1-57768-184-3*) MG-Hill OH.

— Basic Skills Curriculum, Grade 1: Making Children More Successful. rev. ed. (Illus.). 650p. (J). (ps-2). 1999. pap. 19.95 (*1-57768-181-9*) MG-Hill OH.

— Basic Skills Curriculum, Grade 3: Making Children More Sucessful. rev. ed. (Illus.). 650p. (J). (gr. 2-3). 1999. pap. 19.95 (*1-57768-183-5*) MG-Hill OH.

— Basic Skills Curriculum, Grade 2: Making Children More Successful. rev. ed. (Illus.). 650p. (J). (gr. 1-2). 1999. pap. 19.95 (*1-57768-182-7*) McGraw.

McGraw-Hill Publishing Staff. Engineering Universe. 1999. 695.00 (*0-07-134783-6*) McGraw.

***McGraw-Hill Publishing Staff.** McGraw-Hill 2000 Yearbook of Science & Technology. (Illus.). 1999. write for info. (*0-07-052771-7*) McGraw.

McGraw-Hill Publishing Staff. Modern China. LC 98-44545. 192p. 1998. pap. 13.75 (*0-07-292826-3*) McGraw.

***McGraw-Hill Staff.** Bible Stories. (CD-ROM Factfinders Ser.). 2000. pap. text 9.95 incl. cd-rom (*1-57768-761-2*) MG-Hill OH.

— Children's Fact Finder. (Fact Finders Ser.). (Illus.). 336p. (ps-3). 2000. pap. 24.95 (*1-57768-768-X*) MG-Hill OH.

— Defeat Dirty D: Grade 3 Math. 1999. pap. 19.95 (*1-57768-313-7*) MG-Hill OH.

McGraw Hill Staff. Diccionario de las Ciencias de la Vida. (SPA.). 940p. 1990. 125.00 (*0-7859-6236-0*, 8476006195) Fr & Eur.

— Diccionario de Terminos Cientificos, Vol. 1. (SPA.). 336p. 1987. 39.95 (*0-7859-6013-9*, 8439506651) Fr & Eur.

— Diccionario de Terminos Cientificos, Vol. 2. (SPA.). 312p. 1988. 39.95 (*0-7859-6470-3*) Fr & Eur.

— Diccionario de Terminos Cientificos, Vol. 3. (SPA.). 312p. 1988. 39.95 (*0-7859-6014-7*, 8439506678) Fr & Eur.

— Diccionario de Terminos Cientificos, Vol. 4. (SPA.). 320p. 1988. 39.95 (*0-7859-6015-5*, 8439506686) Fr & Eur.

— Diccionario de Terminos Cientificos, Vol. 5. (SPA.). 320p. 1988. 39.95 (*0-7859-6016-3*, 8439506694) Fr & Eur.

— Diccionario de Terminos Cientificos, Vol. 6. (SPA.). 320p. 1988. 39.95 (*0-7859-6017-1*, 8439506708) Fr & Eur.

McGraw-Hill Staff. Dictionary of Bioscience. LC 96-46183. (Mcgraw-Hill Dictionary Ser.). (Illus.). 656p. 1996. pap. 17.95 (*0-07-052430-0*) McGraw.

— Dictionary of Chemistry. LC 96-46184. (McGraw-Hill Dictionary Ser.). 416p. 1996. pap. 16.95 (*0-07-052428-9*) McGraw.

— Energy Systems Handbook. 310p. 1999. pap. 39.95 (*0-07-014019-7*) McGraw.

***McGraw-Hill Staff.** Fahrenheit's Fabulous Fortune: Grade 8+ Physical Science. 1999. sl. 14.95 (*1-57768-009-X*) MG-Hill OH.

— Magic Apple House: Grade K-2 Basic Skills Builder. 1999. pap. 19.95 (*1-57768-302-1*) MG-Hill OH.

McGraw-Hill Staff. McGraw-Hill Dictionary of Earth Science. (Mcgraw-Hill Dictionary Ser.). 480p. 1996. pap. 17.95 (*0-07-052427-0*) McGraw.

— McGraw-Hill Dictionary of Physics. 2nd ed. LC 96-46186. (Mcgraw-Hill Dictionary Ser.). 656p. 1996. pap. 16.95 (*0-07-052429-7*) McGraw.

McGraw Hill Staff. McGraw-Hill Dictionary of Scientific & Technical Terms: English-Arabic, 4 vols., Set. 1985. 295.00 (*0-86685-562-9*) Intl Bk Ctr.

McGraw-Hill Staff. McGraw-Hill Encyclopedia of Science & Technology, 20 vols. 8th ed. LC 96-52375. (Illus.). 15108p. (YA). (gr. 9). 1997. 1995.00 (*0-07-911504-7*) McGraw.

— McGraw-Hill Multimedia Encyclopedia of Science & Technology: Release 1.1. 1996. 1300.00 (*0-07-852753-8*) McGraw.

— Mechanical Engineering Solutions. 24p. 1998. 99.95 (*0-07-913724-5*) McGraw.

***McGraw-Hill Staff.** Mosquito Island: Grade 6+ Life Science. 1999. pap. 14.95 (*1-57768-002-2*) MG-Hill OH.

— Mummy Mystery: Language Arts. (J). (gr. 5). 1999. 19.95 (*1-57768-335-8*) MG-Hill OH.

McGraw Hill Staff. Natural Approch Theory & Practice. 1997. VHS 25.94 (*0-07-079620-3*) McGraw.

McGraw Hill Staff. New Look at Authentic Metals '95. 1997. VHS 25.94 (*0-07-079476-6*) McGraw.

***McGraw-Hill Staff.** Phonics: Grades K-1. 1999. sl. 19.95 (*1-57768-036-7*) MG-Hill OH.

— Phonics: Grades 2-3. 1999. pap. 19.95 (*1-57768-037-5*) MG-Hill OH.

— Scoring High: Grade 3-5. 1999. pap. 19.95 (*1-57768-306-4*) MG-Hill OH.

— Scoring High: Grade 6-8. 1999. pap. 19.95 (*1-57768-307-2*) MG-Hill OH.

— Spelling: Grades 1-3. 1999. pap. 19.95 (*1-57768-300-5*) MG-Hill OH.

— Spelling: Grades 4-6. 1999. pap. 19.95 (*1-57768-301-3*) MG-Hill OH.

M

McGraw-Hill Staff, ed. Marks' Electronic Standard Handbook for Mechanical Engineers. 1995. 150.00 incl. cd-rom (*0-07-005368-5*) McGraw.

Mcgraw-Hill Staff, ed. Modern Brazil. LC 98-12374. 168p. 1998. pap. 13.75 (*0-07-289122-X*) McGraw.

McGraw-Hill Staff, jt. auth. see Goldstein, Herman.

McGraw, James A., jt. auth. see Walsh, William M.

McGraw, John J. My Thirty Years in Baseball. LC 95-14325. (Illus.). xxiii, 311p. (C). 1995. pap. 12.95 (*0-8032-8139-0*, Bison Books) U of Nebr Pr.

— My Thirty Years in Baseball. LC 74-15746. (Popular Culture in America Ser.). (Illus.). 314p. 1975. reprint ed. 28.95 (*0-405-06381-4*) Ayer.

McGraw, Karen. User-Centered Requirements: The Scenario-Based Engineering Process. Harbison, Karan, ed. LC 96-31004. 384p. 1997. pap. 45.00 (*0-8058-2065-5*) L Erlbaum Assocs.

— User-Centered Requirements: The Scenario-Based Engineering Process. Harbison, Karan, ed. LC 96-31004. 384p. 1997. 79.95 (*0-8058-2064-7*) L Erlbaum Assocs.

***McGraw, Kathleen D.** The Employee Assistance Program Management Yearbook. 304p. 1998. spiral bd. 189.00 (*1-882364-25-2*, Amer Busn Pub) Hlth Res Pub.

McGraw, Kathleen M., jt. ed. see Lodge, Milton.

McGraw, Lora G. Guiding Strabismus Therapy. Corngold, Sally M., ed. (Illus.). 90p. (C). 1991. lib. bdg. 15.00 (*0-929780-02-7*) VisionExtension.

McGraw, Lora G., jt. auth. see Getz, Donald J.

McGraw, M. Loretta, jt. auth. see Lydon, William T.

McGraw, Marci. How to Make a Living with Horses. 119p. 1998. pap. 19.95 (*0-9673023-0-7*, 1-A) Wild Horse Arts.

McGraw, Marjie. Absolutely Alabama. 128p. 1997. pap. 6.95 (*1-887654-34-8*) Premium Pr TN.

— Great American Country Music. Armour, Joan, ed. LC 95-78962. 128p. 1997. pap. 6.95 (*1-887654-03-8*) Premium Pr TN.

McGraw, Mary Jo. Creative Rubber Stamping Techniques. LC 98-14960. (Illus.). 128p. 1998. pap. 22.99 (*0-89134-878-6*, North Lght Bks) F & W Pubns Inc.

***McGraw, Mary Jo.** Greeting Card Magic with Rubber Stamps. (Illus.). 128p. 2000. pap. 22.99 (*0-89134-979-0*, North Lght Bks) F & W Pubns Inc.

McGraw, Mary Jo. Making Greeting Cards with Rubber Stamps. LC 96-32192. (Illus.). 128p. 1997. pap. 21.99 (*0-89134-713-5*, North Lght Bks) F & W Pubns Inc.

McGraw, Mike. How Do You Spell Customer Service? Cash: Stories to Inspire Excellence in Client Service. LC 98-86664. 160p. 1998. 14.95 (*1-890394-31-9*, Sage Creek) Rhodes & Easton.

McGraw, Milena. After Dunkirk. 468p. 1999. pap. 13.00 (*0-395-97780-0*) HM.

— After Dunkirk: A Novel. LC 97-49148. 480p. 1998. 24.00 (*0-395-86885-8*) HM.

McGraw, Myrtle B. Growth: A Study of Johnny & Jimmie. LC 74-21422. (Classics in Child Development Ser.). 372p. 1975. reprint ed. 35.95 (*0-405-06471-3*) Ayer.

— The Neuromuscular Maturation of the Human Infant. (Classics in Developmental Medicine Ser.: No. 4). (Illus.). 117p. (C). 1991. text 19.95 (*0-521-41329-X*, Pub. by Mc Keith Pr) Cambridge U Pr.

McGraw, Nanci. Organized for Success! 95 Tips for Taking Control of Your Time, Your Space, & Your Life. Scanlon, Kelly, ed. LC 95-74769. (Self-Study Sourcebook Ser.). (Illus.). 188p. 1996. pap. 15.95 (*1-878542-79-6*, 13-0012) SkillPath Pubns.

— Speak up & Stand Out: How to Make Effective Presentations. Scanlon, Kelly, ed. LC 97-66334. (Self-Study Sourcebook Ser.). (Illus.). 153p. 1997. pap. 15.95 (*1-57294-070-0*, 13-0024) SkillPath Pubns.

McGraw, Phillip C. Life Strategies: Doing What Works, Doing What Matters. LC 98-46748. 304p. 1999. 21.95 (*0-7868-6548-2*, Pub. by Hyperion) Time Warner.

— Life Strategies: Doing What Works, Doing What Matters. 304p. 2000. pap. 11.95 (*0-7868-8459-2*, Pub. by Hyperion) Time Warner.

— Life Strategies: Doing What Works, Doing What Matters. large type ed. LC 99-32482. 1999. pap. 30.00 (*0-7838-8576-4*) Mac Lib Ref.

— The Life Strategies Workbook: Exercises & Self-Tests to Help You Change Your Life. (Illus.). 224p. 2000. pap., wbk. ed. 12.95 (*0-7868-8514-9*, Pub. by Hyperion) Time Warner.

***McGraw, Phillip C.** Relationship Rescue. large type ed. (Core Ser.). 459p. 2000. 29.95 (*0-7838-9089-3*, G K Hall Lrg Type) Mac Lib Ref.

— Relationship Rescue: A Seven-Step Strategy for Reconnecting with Your Partner. LC 99-57559. 272p. 2000. 22.95 (*0-7868-6631-4*, Pub. by Hyperion) Time Warner.

— Relationship Rescue: A Seven Step Strategy for Reconnecting with Your Partner. 2001. pap. 13.95 (*0-7868-8598-X*, Pub. by Hyperion) Time Warner.

— The Relationship Rescue Workbook: Exercises & Self-Tests to Help You Reconnect with Your Partner. 2000. pap. 13.95 (*0-7868-8604-8*, Pub. by Hyperion) Time Warner.

McGraw, Robert. Learning to Laugh at Work: The Power of Humor in the Workplace. Scanlon, Kelly & Guthrie, Jane D., eds. LC 95-70451. (Illus.). 70p. 1995. pap. 12.95 (*1-878542-40-0*, 12-0014) SkillPath Pubns.

— The Rogue & the Horse. (Illus.). 32p. (Orig.). (J). (ps-3). 1993. pap. 5.95 (*0-9633385-0-1*) Imagin Pr.

— The Technical Writer's Guide. Guthrie, Jane D. & Scanlon, Kelly, eds. LC 95-72618. 134p. (Orig.). 1996. pap. 15.95 (*1-57294-012-3*, 13-0007) SkillPath Pubns.

McGraw, Sheila. Dolls Kids Can Make. (Illus.). 72p. (YA). (gr. 6 up). 1995. pap. 9.95 (*1-895565-74-X*); lib. bdg. 19.95 (*1-895565-75-8*) Firefly Bks Ltd.

— Gifts Kids Can Make. (Illus.). 96p. (J). 1994. pap. 9.95 (*1-895565-35-9*); lib. bdg. 19.95 (*1-895565-36-7*) Firefly Bks Ltd.

— Je T'Aimera Toujours. (FRE., Illus.). 32p. (J). (ps-3). 1988. pap. 4.95 (*0-920668-49-6*) Firefly Bks Ltd.

— Painting & Decorating Furniture. (Illus.). 304p. 1997. 40.00 (*1-55209-137-6*) Firefly Bks Ltd.

— Painting & Decorating Furniture. (Illus.). 304p. 1997. reprint ed. pap. 29.95 (*1-55209-380-8*) Firefly Bks Ltd.

— Papier Mache for Kids. (Illus.). 72p. (J). (gr. k-7). 1991. 17.95 (*0-920668-92-5*) Firefly Bks Ltd.

— Papier Mache for Kids. (Illus.). 72p. (J). (gr. 5-7). 1991. pap. 9.95 (*0-920668-93-3*) Firefly Bks Ltd.

— Papier-Mache Today. (Illus.). 144p. (Orig.). 1990. pap. 19.95 (*0-920668-85-2*) Firefly Bks Ltd.

***McGraw, Sheila.** Pussycats Everywhere! (Illus.). 32p. (J). (gr. k-3). 2000. pap. 6.95 (*1-55209-348-4*); lib. bdg. 19.95 (*1-55209-346-8*) Firefly Bks Ltd.

McGraw, Shirley. Arkansas, Lonoke County: A Pictorial History. LC 98-49206. 1998. write for info. (*1-57864-058-X*) Donning Co.

McGray, Brian E. Handling Trophy Game: A How-to Field Guide for Hunters & Anglers. (Illus.). 72p. 1995. pap. 9.95 (*1-886975-00-0*) Goose Hse Pubns.

— How to Carve a Duck Decoy: A Step-by-Step Guide for Beginners. 32p. 1991. pap. 3.95 (*0-486-26735-0*) Dover.

— Pattern Book for Carving Fish: 18 Patterns & Instructions for Carving, Texturing & Painting Fresh & Saltwater Game Fish. McGray, Meredith A., ed. (Illus.). 96p. 1995. pap. 14.95 (*1-886975-01-9*) Goose Hse Pubns.

— Pattern Book for Carving Fish: 18 Patterns & Instructions for Carving, Texturing & Painting Fresh & Saltwater Game Fish. 2nd rev. ed. McGray, Meredith A., ed. LC 97-94065. (Illus.). 96p. 1998. per. 14.95 (*1-886975-03-5*) Goose Hse Pubns.

— Taxidermist's Journal: A Collection of True-Life Hunting & Fishing Stories. McGray, Meredith A., ed. (Illus.). 108p. (Orig.). 1996. pap. 11.95 (*1-886975-02-7*) Goose Hse Pubns.

McGray, Meredith A., ed. see McGray, Brian E.

McGrayne, Sharon B. Blue Genes & Polyester Plants: 365 More Surprising Scientific Facts, Breakthroughs, & Discoveries. LC 96-33303. 256p. (Orig.). 1997. pap. 14.95 (*0-471-14575-0*) Wiley.

— Blue Genes & Polyester Plants: 365 More Surprising Scientific Facts, Breakthroughs, & Discoveries. (Orig.). 1997. pap. 14.95 (*0-614-27638-1*) Wiley.

— Nobel Prize Women in Science: Their Lives, Struggles & Momentous Discoveries. (Illus.). 368p. 1992. 26.95 (*1-55972-146-4*, Birch Ln Pr) Carol Pub Group.

— Nobel Prize Women in Science: Their Lives, Struggles & Momentous Discoveries. rev. ed. LC 98-39490. (Illus.). xi, 451p. 1998. pap. 19.95 (*0-8065-2025-6*, Citadel Pr) Carol Pub Group.

***McGrayne, Sharon B.** Nobel Prize Women in Science: Their Lives, Struggles & Momentous Discoveries. 2nd rev. ed. (Illus.). xi, 451p. 1998. pap. 19.95 (*0-9702256-0-1*) Birch Tree.

McGrayne, Sharon Bertsch, jt. auth. see Mielczarek, Eugenie Vorborger.

McGreal, Ian, ed. Great Literature of the Eastern World. LC 95-26313. (Literary Criticsm Ser.). 576p. 1996. 50.00 (*0-06-270104-5*, Harper Ref) HarpC.

McGreal, Ian P. Great Thinkers Weste. LC 91-38362. 592p. 1992. 47.00 (*0-06-270026-X*, Harper Ref) HarpC.

McGreal, Jerrie & McGreal, Margery. Something to Think About. LC 98-210104. (Illus.). 123p. (Orig.). 1997. pap. 14.95 (*0-9656734-1-3*) CHOD.

McGreal, Margery, jt. auth. see McGreal, Jerrie.

McGreal, Margery J. Kids in Focus: Raising Happy Healthy Children. (Illus.). viii, 173p. (Orig.). 1997. pap. text. write for info. (*0-9656734-0-5*) CHOD.

***Mcgreal, Pat.** Veils. 96p. 1999. 24.95 (*1-56389-355-X*, Vertigo) DC Comics.

— Veils. (Illus.). 96p. 1999. pap. text 14.95 (*1-56389-561-7*, Pub. by DC Comics) Time Warner.

McGreal, Stanley, jt. auth. see Berry, Jim.

Mcgreal, Stanley, jt. ed. see Berry, James.

McGreal, Thomas L., jt. auth. see Danielson, Charlotte.

McGreal, Wilfred. At the Fountain of Elijah: The Carmelite Tradition. LC 99-20784. (Traditions of Christian Spirituality Ser.). 144p. 1999. pap. 13.00 (*1-57075-292-3*) Orbis Bks.

McGreal, Wilfrid. John of the Cross. Vardy, Peter, ed. LC 96-52494. (Great Christian Thinkers Ser.). 96p. 1997. reprint ed. pap. 9.00 (*0-7648-0114-7*, Liguori Triumph) Liguori Pubns.

McGreavy, C., ed. Polymer Reactor Engineering. LC 93-21352. 1993. write for info. (*0-7514-0083-1*, Pub. by B Acad & Prof) Routldge.

— Polymer Reactor Engineering. LC 93-21352. 1994. 95.00 (*1-56081-595-7*, Wiley-VCH) Wiley.

McGreevey, Thomas. Richard Aldington. LC 74-1231. (Twayne's English Authors Ser.). (C). 1974. lib. bdg. 20.95 (*0-8290-2404-2*) Irvington.

— Richard Aldington. LC 74-1231. (English Biography Ser.: No. 31). 1974. lib. bdg. 53.00 (*0-8383-1785-5*) M S G Haskell Hse.

— Thomas Stearns Eliot: A Study. LC 74-164026. (Studies in T. S. Eliot: No. 11). 1971. reprint ed. lib. bdg. 75.00 (*0-8383-1327-2*) M S G Haskell Hse.

McGreevey, Tom & Yeck, Joanne L. Our Movie Heritage. LC 97-3737. (Illus.). 208p. (C). 1997. 45.00 (*0-8135-2431-8*) Rutgers U Pr.

McGreevy. Thinking on One's Own. Date not set. write for info. (*0-393-04760-1*) Norton.

McGreevy, Ann. My Book of Things & Stuff: An Interest Questionnaire for Young Children. 1982. pap. 14.95 (*0-936386-17-7*) Creative Learning.

McGreevy, John T. Parish Boundaries: The Catholic Encounter with Race in the Twentieth-Century Urban North. LC 95-36746. (Historical Studies of Urban America). (Illus.). 362p. 1996. 27.50 (*0-226-55873-8*) U Ch Pr.

— Parish Boundaries: The Catholic Encounter with Race in the Twentieth-Century Urban North. (Historical Studies of Urban America). (Illus.). 362p. 1998. pap. text 17.00 (*0-226-55874-6*) U Ch Pr.

***McGreevy, Joyce.** Gardening by Heart: The Extraordinary Gift of an Ordinary Garden. LC 99-49546. (Illus.). 224p. 2000. 19.00 (*1-57805-051-0*, Pub. by Sierra) Random.

McGreevy, Joyce. The Wind Eagle: Big Book. (Wonders! Ser.: Level 2). (Illus.). 16p. (Orig.). (J). (gr. 2-4). 1992. pap. text 29.95 (*1-56334-178-6*) Hampton-Brown.

— The Wind Eagle: Small Book. (Wonders! Ser.: Level 2). (Illus.). 16p. (Orig.). (J). (gr. 2-4). 1992. pap. text 6.00 (*1-56334-179-4*) Hampton-Brown.

McGreevy, Linda. Ernest Mauer: To Arrest, Seduce, & Deceive: A Retrospective, 1926-1996. (Illus.). 15p. 1998. pap. 3.00 (*1-886845-05-0*) Penin Fine Arts.

McGreevy, Linda F. The Life & Works of Otto Dix: German Critical Realist. LC 81-1895. (Studies in the Fine Arts: The Avant-Garde: No. 12). (Illus.). 164p. reprint ed. pap. 50.90 (*0-8357-1165-X*, 207023500065) Bks Demand.

McGreevy, Mary. Coastings: A California Poetry Souvenir. Date not set. write for info. (*0-614-13296-7*) M McGreevy.

— Dreams & Illusions. 20p. 1996. pap. write for info. (*1-883331-02-1*) Anderie Poetry.

McGreevy, Mary & Rosenbaum, Dora. To a Sailor: Poems. (Illus.). 58p. (Orig.). 1989. pap. 10.00 (*0-685-28888-9*) M McGreevy.

McGreevy, Michael. Death Is Only a Horizon: Thoughts in Time of Bereavement. (Illus.). 16p. 1990. reprint ed. pap. text 1.95 (*0-89243-446-5*) Liguori Pubns.

McGreevy-Nichols, Susan & Scheff, Helene. Building Dances: A Guide to Putting Movements Together. LC 95-8141. (Illus.). 128p. 1995. pap. text 28.00 (*0-87322-573-2*, BMCG0573) Human Kinetics.

McGreevy, Patrick. Imagining Niagara: The Meaning & Making of Niagara Falls. LC 93-35720. (Illus.). 208p. 1994. lib. bdg. 30.00 (*0-87023-916-3*) U of Mass Pr.

— The Wall of Mirrors: Nationalism & Perceptions of the Border at Niagara Falls. (Borderlands Monographs: No. 5). 1-18p. (C). 1991. pap. text 5.00 (*0-9625055-4-4*) Canadian-Amer Ctr.

***McGreevy, Paul.** Cats. LC 99-39358. (Little Guides Ser.). (Illus.). 320p. 1999. pap. 14.95 (*1-875137-65-3*) Weldon Owen.

— Dogs. LC 99-39360. (Little Guides Ser.). 320p. 1999. pap. 14.95 (*1-875137-63-7*) Weldon Owen.

McGreevy, Paul. Why Does My Horse . . . ? (Illus.). 256p. 1996. 16.95 (*1-57076-067-5*) Trafalgar.

McGreevy, Susan B. & Gorman, R. C. Maria: The Legend, the Legacy. LC 81-14512. (Illus.). 32p. (Orig.). 1982. 4.50 (*0-86534-005-6*) Sunstone Pr.

***McGreevy, Susan Brown.** Indian Basketry Artists of the Southwest: Deep Roots, New Growth. (Indian Artists Convocation Ser.). (Illus.). 100p. 2000. pap. 30.00 (*0-933452-67-5*) Schol Am Res.

McGreevy, Susan Brown, ed. Washington Matthews: Studies of Navajo Culture, 1880-1894. LC 97-13901. 279p. 1996. 70.00 (*0-8263-1631-X*) U of NM Pr.

McGreevy, William J., jt. auth. see Brown, Sandra.

McGregor. Fundamental Techniques of Plastic Surgery & Their Surgical Applications. 9th ed. 1995. pap. text 72.95 (*0-443-05028-7*, M3572) Church.

— Membrane Separation in Biotechnology. (Bioprocess Technology Ser.: Vol. 1). (Illus.). 408p. 1986. text 180.00 (*0-8247-7465-5*) Dekker.

McGregor. Shared Vision. 45.00 (*1-85894-086-9*) Merrell Holberton.

McGregor, et al. Bairns: Scot Child Photo. LC 99-189753. (Photography Ser.). (Illus.). 152p. (Orig.). 1999. pap. 19.95 (*0-948636-65-3*, 6653) A Schwartz & Co.

McGregor, A. M., ed. Immunology of Endocrine Diseases. (Immunology & Medicine Ser.). 1986. text 127.50 (*0-85200-963-1*) Kluwer Academic.

McGregor, Adrian. Greg Chappell. 1991. pap. 16.95 (*0-7022-2342-5*, Pub. by Univ Queensland Pr) Intl Spec Bk.

— King Wally: The Story of Wally Lewis. (Illus.). 247p. 1988. pap. 14.95 (*0-7022-2037-X*, Pub. by Univ Queensland Pr) Intl Spec Bk.

— Wally Lewis: The Last Emperor. 1993. pap. 18.95 (*0-7022-2493-6*, Pub. by Univ Queensland Pr) Intl Spec Bk.

McGregor, Alan D., tr. see Lister, Graham, et al.

***McGregor, Alasdair & Chester, Quentin.** The Kimberley: Horizons of Stone. (Illus.). 208p. 2000. 39.95 (*1-86436-533-1*, Pub. by New Holland) BHB Intl.

McGregor, Andrew, et al. Commercial Management Companies in the Agricultural Development of the Pacific Islands. LC 92-16884. (Research Report Ser.: No. 15). 56p. 1992. pap. text 6.00 (*0-86638-151-1*) EW Ctr HI.

McGregor, Andrew, jt. auth. see Sturton, Mark.

McGregor, Bede & Norris, Thomas, eds. The Beauty of Christ: An Introduction to the Theology of Hans Urs von Balthasar. 296p. 49.95 (*0-567-09697-1*, Pub. by T & T Clark) Bks Intl VA.

***McGregor, Catrine.** Acting Across America: In Film & Television. (Illus.). 160p. 1999. pap. text 12.95 (*0-9672377-0-X*) Harvest UT.

McGregor, Colin, et al. Fundamentals of University Mathematics. LC 99-474270. 250p. 1995. 29.95 (*1-898563-09-8*, Pub. by Horwood Pub) Paul & Co Pubs.

McGregor, Craig. Headliners: 14 Social Portraits. 1991. pap. 14.95 (*0-7022-2344-1*, Pub. by Univ Queensland Pr) Intl Spec Bk.

— Real Lies. LC 87-10770. 126p. (Orig.). 1987. pap. 14.95 (*0-7022-2088-4*, Pub. by Univ Queensland Pr) Intl Spec Bk.

McGregor, Craig, ed. Bob Dylan: The Early Years: A Retrospective. (Quality Paperbacks Ser.). (Illus.). 424p. 1990. reprint ed. pap. 13.95 (*0-306-80416-6*) Da Capo.

***McGregor, D. B., et al, eds.** The Use of Short- & Medium-Term Tests for Carcinogens & Data on Genetic Effects in Carcinogenic Hazard Evaluation. LC 99-229301. (IARC Scientific Publications: 146). 536p. 1999. pap. text 69.00 (*92-832-2146-X*) OUP.

McGregor, D. I., ed. see Kettle.

McGregor, Deborah K. From Midwives to Medicine: The Birth of American Gynecology. LC 98-6811. (Illus.). 272p. (C). 1998. text 55.00 (*0-8135-2571-3*); pap. text 23.00 (*0-8135-2572-1*) Rutgers U Pr.

McGregor, Denise. Mama Drama: Making Your Peace With the One Woman Who Can Push Your Buttons, Make You Cry & Drive You Crazy. LC 98-12781. 224p. 1998. text 21.95 (*0-312-18627-4*) St Martin.

— Mama Drama: Making Your Peace With the One Woman Who Can Push Your Buttons, Make You Cry & Drive You Crazy. 1999. pap. 12.95 (*0-312-20421-3*, St Martins Paperbacks) St Martin.

McGregor, Diana, et al. Fizzle, Bubble, Pop & WOW! Simple Science Experiments for Young Children. 63p. (J). (ps-4). 1992. pap. 12.00 (*0-9638539-0-2*) Exper First Pr.

McGregor, Don. Sabre: 20th Anniversary. anniversary ed. (Illus.). 48p. 1998. pap. 12.95 (*1-58240-059-8*) Image Comics.

— The Variable Syndrome: A Science Fiction Story. 144p. 1981. pap. 10.00 (*0-934882-05-3*) Fictioneer Bks.

— Zorro: The Lady Wears Red. (Illus.). 96p. 1998. pap. 12.95 (*1-58240-061-X*) Image Comics.

McGregor, Douglas. The Human Side of Enterprise: 25th Anniversary Printing. 256p. (C). 1985. 40.94 (*0-07-045098-6*) McGraw.

McGregor, Duncan F. & Thompson, Donald A., eds. Geomorphology & Land Management in a Changing Environment. LC 94-24604. (British Geomorphological Research Group Symposia Ser.). 356p. 1995. 210.00 (*0-471-95511-6*) Wiley.

McGregor, Duncan F. M., et al, eds. Resource Sustainability & Caribbean Development. LC 98-194126. 408p. 1998. write for info. (*976-640-067-9*) UWI Fac Law.

McGregor, Fiona & Denny, Charlotte. Live & Work in Australia & New Zealand. (Live & Work Abroad Guides Ser.). 336p. (Orig.). 1997. pap. 16.95 (*1-85458-115-5*, Pub. by Vac Wrk Pubns) Seven Hills Bk.

— Live & Work in Australia & New Zealand. 2nd ed. (Live & Work Ser.). 356p. (Orig.). 1999. pap. 19.95 (*1-85458-213-5*, Pub. by Vac Wrk Pubns) Seven Hills Bk.

McGregor, Frances M., jt. auth. see McGregor, Ian A.

McGregor, G., ed. see Harris, Robert.

McGregor, Gaile. EcCentric Visions: ReConstructing Australia. LC 94-232749. 360p. (C). 1994. pap. 29.95 (*0-88920-229-X*) W Laurier U Pr.

***McGregor, Gaile.** Inclusive Schooling Practices. 1999. pap. 24.95 (*1-55766-395-5*) P H Brookes.

McGregor, Gaile. The Noble Savage in the New World Garden: Notes Toward a Syntactics of Place. LC 87-72549. 357p. (C). 1988. 34.95 (*0-87972-416-1*); pap. 17.95 (*0-87972-417-X*) Bowling Green Univ Popular Press.

— The Wacousta Syndrome: Explorations in the Canadian Langscape (sic) 488p. 1985. pap. 20.95 (*0-8020-6570-8*); text 47.50 (*0-8020-2554-4*) U of Toronto Pr.

Mcgregor, Glenn R., jt. auth. see Nieuwolt, Simon.

McGregor, Gordon. A Church College in the Twenty-First Century. (C). 1989. 59.00 (*1-85072-080-0*, Pub. by W Sessions); pap. 39.00 (*1-85072-079-7*, Pub. by W Sessions) St Mut.

McGregor, Gordon D. The Broken Pot Restored: Le Jeu de la Feuillee of Adam de la Halle. LC 90-84433. (Edward C. Armstrong Monographs on Medieval Literature: No. 6). 185p. (Orig.). 1991. pap. 14.95 (*0-917058-76-3*) French Forum.

McGregor, Graham, et al, eds. Dirty Silence: Aspects of Language & Literature in New Zealand. (Illus.). 200p. 1992. pap. 26.95 (*0-19-558227-6*) OUP.

McGregor, Gregor I. Massachusetts Environmental Law: 1996 Edition. LC 90-63090. 1400p. 1996. ring bd. 125.00 (*1-57589-014-3*, 96-09-14-SP) Mass CLE.

McGregor, Gregor L. Environmental Law & Enforcement. 256p. 1994. lib. bdg. 75.00 (*0-87371-745-7*, L745) Lewis Pubs.

McGregor, H. McGregor on Damages. (C). 1988. 1125.00 (*0-7855-4080-6*, Pub. by Witherby & Co) St Mut.

McGregor, H. C., tr. see Cicero, Marcus Tullius.

***McGregor, H. R.** Schrodinger's Baby. LC 99-21647. 286p. 1999. 22.00 (*0-688-16893-0*, Wm Morrow) Morrow Avon.

McGregor, Heather. A Guide to Glenwood Canyon. 2nd rev. ed. (Illus.). 32p. (Orig.). 1993. pap. 5.00 (*0-9634382-1-2*) Pika Pub.

McGregor, Ian A. Fundamental Techniques of Plastic Surgery & Their Surgical Applications. 8th ed. (Illus.). 235p. 1989. pap. text 49.95 (*0-443-03353-6*) Church.

— Fundamental Techniques of Plastic Surgery & Their Surgical Applications. 8th ed. LC 88-20320. (Illus.). 247p. 1989. reprint ed. pap. 76.60 (*0-7837-9744-3*, 206047200005) Bks Demand.

McGregor, Ian A. & McGregor, Frances M. Cancer of the Face & Mouth: Pathology & Management for Surgeons. (Illus.). 624p. 1986. text 215.00 (*0-443-02455-3*) Church.

***McGregor, Iona.** Getting Married in Scotland. (Past in Action Ser.). 96p. 1999. pap. 8.95 (*1-901663-29-9*, Pub. by Natl Mus Scotland) A Schwartz & Co.

McGregor, Iona & Kidd, Dorothy I. Bairns: Scottish Children in Photographs. LC 99-189753. (Photography Ser.). (Illus.). 152p. 1995. 29.95 (*0-948636-61-0*, 610, Pub. by Ashmolean Mus) A Schwartz & Co.

McGregor, James H. The Image of Antiquity in Boccaccio's Filocolo, Filostrato & Teseida. LC 89-32667. (Studies in Italian Culture: Literature in History: Vol. 1). 202p. (C). 1991. text 44.95 (*0-8204-0985-5*) P Lang Pubng.

***McGregor, James H., ed.** Approaches to Teaching Boccaccio's Decameron. (Approaches to Teaching World Literature Ser.: Vol. 69). 200p. 2000. 37.50 (*0-87352-761-5*); pap. 18.00 (*0-87352-762-3*) Modern Lang.

McGregor, James H., et al, eds. Renaissance Naples: A Documentary History: c.1400-1600. (Documentary History of Naples Ser.: Vol. 3). (Illus.). 300p. pap. 25.00 (*0-934977-51-8*) Italica Pr.

McGregor, James H., tr. & intro. see Guicciardini, Luigi.

McGregor, James L., jt. auth. see Berg, Paul.

McGregor, Jeffrey P., jt. auth. see Barnett, Donald L.

McGregor, Jim. I Love Me Enough to Let Me Go. 2nd ed. 69p. 1989. reprint ed. pap. text 7.95 (*0-9633662-0-3*) Willeo Pub.

— I Love You Enough to Let You Go. 2nd ed. 96p. 1992. reprint ed. pap. text 9.95 (*0-940549-05-0*) Willeo Pub.

— Simple C. LC 97-21933. 240p. (C). 1997. pap. text 40.00 (*0-201-40385-4*) Addison-Wesley.

— The Tao of Recovery: A Quiet Path to Wellness. Brand, Nancy, ed. LC 97-5279. (Illus.). 169p. 1997. lib. bdg. 26.95 (*0-89334-267-X*, Humanics Trade) Humanics Ltd.

McGregor, JoAnn. Staking Their Claim: Land Disputes in Southern Mozambique. (LTC Paper Ser.: Vol. 158). (Illus.). iv, 26p. (C). 1997. pap. 4.00 (*0-934519-76-5*, LTC158) U of Wis Land.

McGregor, John C. The Pool & Irving Villages: A Study of Hopewell Occupation in the Illinois River Valley. LC 58-5605. (Illus.). 244p. reprint ed. 75.70 (*0-8357-9694-9*, 201586400097) Bks Demand.

McGregor, John D. A Practical Guide to Testing Object-Oriented Software. (C). Date not set. pap. text. write for info. (*0-201-32564-0*) Addison-Wesley.

McGregor, Ken. David Larwill. (Illus.). 204p. 1998. pap. text 80.00 (*90-5703-781-5*) Gordon & Breach.

McGregor, Kim. Warriors of Truth: Adult Survivors Healing from Childhood Sexual Abuse. LC 96-170538. 280p. 1994. pap. 29.95 (*0-908569-84-X*, Pub. by Univ Otago Pr) Intl Spec Bk.

McGregor, L., jt. ed. see Wochert, G.

McGregor, Lani. Bertil Vallien at Bullseye Glass: Photodocumentary & Exhibition Catalog. (Illus.). 50p. 1997. write for info. (*0-9634551-3-3*) Bullseye Glass.

McGregor-Lowndes, M., et al, eds. Legal Issues for Non-Profit Associations. LC 96-170375. 224p. 1996. pap. 85.00 (*0-455-21401-8*, Pub. by Cavendish Pubng) Gaunt.

McGregor-Lowndes, Myles & Davidson, Alan. The Internet for Lawyers. 237p. 1996. pap. 31.50 (*0-455-21487-5*, Pub. by LawBk Co) Gaunt.

McGregor, Lynn, et al. Learning Through Drama: Schools Council Drama Teaching Project. 224p. 1977. pap. text 15.00 (*0-435-18565-9*, 18565) Heinemann.

McGregor, M. E. Making Sense of Algebra: Cognitive Processes: Influencing Comprehension. 139p. (C). 1991. pap. 100.00 (*0-7300-1282-4*, ECT403, Pub. by Deakin Univ) St Mut.

McGregor, M. J., jt. ed. see Dent, J. B.

McGregor, Malcolm, jt. auth. see Mollo, Andrew.

McGregor, Maxine. Chris McGregor & the Brotherhood of Breath. 1995. pap. 17.00 (*0-917453-32-8*) Bamberger.

McGregor, Merideth. Cowgirl. 32p. (J). 1992. 14.95 (*0-8027-8170-5*); lib. bdg. 15.85 (*0-8027-8171-3*) Walker & Co.

McGregor, P. K. Playback & Studies of Animal Communication. (NATO ASI Ser.: Vol. 228). (Illus.). 248p. (C). 1992. text 95.00 (*0-306-44205-1*, Kluwer Plenum) Kluwer Academic.

McGregor, Pat. Web Browsing with Netcom Cruiser 2.0, Vol. 3. 1995. pap. text 24.95 (*0-7615-0240-8*) Prima Pub.

McGregor, Peter. Lending. 247p. 1990. pap. 125.00 (*0-85297-352-7*, Pub. by Chartered Bank) St Mut.

McGregor, R., ed. McGregor's Who Owns Whom, 1993: The Southern African Edition. 1100p. (C). 1993. lib. bdg. 480.00 (*1-85333-908-3*) Kluwer Academic.

McGregor, R. C. An Outline of Hindi Grammar. (ENG & HIN.). 1991. 29.95 (*0-8288-8467-6*, F29977) Fr & Eur.

McGregor, R. M., jt. auth. see Corlett, M.

McGregor, R. R. Herbal Birth Control: A Brief History with Ancient & Modern Herbal Recipes. (Illus.). 64p. (Orig.). 1993. pap. 10.00 (*0-9636602-0-9*) Cloud Chief.

McGregor, R. S. Outline of Hindi Grammar: With Exercises. 3rd ed. (Illus.). 336p. 1995. pap. text 29.95 (*0-19-870008-3*) OUP.

— Outline of Hindi Grammar: With Exercises. 3rd ed. (Illus.). 320p. 1996. pap. 49.95 incl. audio (*0-19-870009-1*); text 70.00 (*0-19-870007-5*) OUP.

McGregor, R. S., ed. Devotional Literature in South Asia: Current Research, 1985-1988. (University of Cambridge Oriental Publications: No. 46). 338p. (C). 1992. text 109.95 (*0-521-41311-7*) Cambridge U Pr.

— The Oxford Hindi-English Dictionary. (HIN.). 1,104p. 1997. reprint ed. pap. text 25.00 (*0-19-864339-X*) OUP.

McGregor, Rae. Jane Mander: The Story of a New Zealand Writer. LC 98-216378. (Illus.). 176p. 1998. pap. 34.95 (*1-877133-37-X*, Pub. by Univ Otago Pr) Intl Spec Bk.

McGregor, Richard. Japan Swings: Politics, Culture & Sex in the New Japan. 336p. (Orig.). 1997. pap. 14.95 (*1-86448-077-7*, Pub. by Allen & Unwin Pty) IPG Chicago.

McGregor, Rob. Practical C++ 900p. 1999. pap. 29.99 (*0-7897-2144-9*) Que.

McGregor, Rob, jt. auth. see Norton, Peter.

McGregor, Rob R. Audition & Performance Preparation for Trumpet. (Orchestral Literature Studies: Vol. III). 160p. 1993. pap. 18.95 (*0-9630856-2-X*) Balquhidder.

— Audition & Performance Preparation for Trumpet: Orchestral Literature Studies. 128p. (C). 1996. pap. text 17.00 (*0-9630856-7-0*) Balquhidder.

— Audition & Performance Preparation for Trumpet Vol. 1: Orchestral Literature Studies. 128p. 1992. pap. text 17.95 (*0-9630856-0-3*) Balquhidder.

— Audition & Performance Preparation for Trumpet Vol. 2: Orchestral Literature Studies. 112p. 1992. pap. text 17.95 (*0-9630856-1-1*) Balquhidder.

McGregor, Rob R., jt. auth. see Stewart, Harry E.

McGregor, Robert & Meiers, Marion. Telling the Whole Story. (C). 1991. 65.00 (*0-86431-082-X*, Pub. by Aust Council Educ Res) St Mut.

McGregor, Robert, jt. auth. see Toews, Bea.

McGregor, Robert, jt. auth. see Towes, Bea.

Mcgregor, Robert K. A Wider View of the Universe: Henry Thoreau's Study of Nature. LC 96-45799. 264p. 1997. 16.95 (*0-252-06620-0*) U of Ill Pr.

***McGregor, Robert Kuhn & Lewis, Ethan.** Conundrums for the Long Weekend: England, Dorothy L. Sayers & Lord Peter Wimsey. LC 00-36876. 2000. pap. write for info. (*0-87338-665-5*) Kent St U Pr.

McGregor, Ronald J. Buying a Business: Tips for the First-Time Buyer. Keppler, Kay, ed. LC 92-82770. (Small Business & Entrepreneurship Ser.). 152p. (Orig.). 1993. pap. 15.95 (*1-56052-166-X*) Crisp Pubns.

McGregor, Ronald L., jt. auth. see Fitch, Henry S.

McGregor, Russell. Imagined Destinies: Aboriginal Australians & the Doomed Race Theory, 1880-1939. 256p. 1998. pap. 29.95 (*0-522-84762-5*, Pub. by Melbourne Univ Pr) Paul & Co Pubs.

McGregor, Tom. Elizabeth. 1998. mass mkt. 5.99 (*0-380-80417-4*, Avon Bks) Morrow Avon.

***McGregor, Tom.** The Making of C S Forester's Horatio Hornblower. 136p. 1999. pap. 22.00 (*0-06-107357-1*) HarpC.

— Oliver Twist: The Official Companion. (Illus.). 160p. 2000. 19.95 (*1-85227-837-4*) Virgin Pubng.

— This Life: The Companion Guide. 128p. 1998. pap. 19.95 (*0-14-027432-4*, Pub. by Pnguin Bks Ltd) Trafalgar.

McGregor, Tony L. Victory Week. LC 98-3142. 40p. (J). 1998. lib. bdg. 22.95 (*0-9634016-9-6*, Deaf Life Pr) MSM Prods.

Mcgregor, Trish. The Everything Astrology Book. LC 98-17890. (Illus.). 320p. 1998. pap. 12.95 (*1-58062-062-0*) Adams Media.

McGregor, Trish. Power Tarot. LC 97-46843. 288p. 1998. per. 12.00 (*0-684-84185-1*) S&S Trade.

***McGregor, Wes & Then, Danny Shem-Shin.** Facilities Management & the Business of Space. LC 99-51848. 272p. 1999. 80.00 (*0-470-38170-1*) Wiley.

McGregor, William. A Functional Grammar of Gooniyandi. LC 89-17877. (Studies in Language Companion Ser.: No. 22). xx, 618p. 1990. 133.00 (*90-272-3025-0*) J Benjamins Pubng Co.

McGregor, William, jt. ed. see Chappell, Hilary.

McGregor, William B. Semiotic Grammar. LC 97-7029. (Oxford Studies in Lexicography & Lexicology). (Illus.). 448p. (C). 1997. 100.00 (*0-19-823688-3*) OUP.

McGregory, Jerrilyn. Wiregrass Country. LC 96-32423. (Folklife in the South Ser.). (Illus.). 224p. 1997. 45.00 (*0-87805-925-3*); pap. 18.00 (*0-87805-926-1*) U Pr of Miss.

McGrew. Gombe: Wild Chimpanzees in the West. (C). 1999. pap. text 20.50 (*0-15-503817-6*, Pub. by Harcourt Coll Pubs) Harcourt.

McGrew, Annette, ed. see McGrew, Chuck.

McGrew, Anthony, ed. The Transformation of Democracy? Democratic Politics in the New World Order. LC 97-572. (Illus.). 288p. 1997. 57.95 (*0-7456-1816-2*, Pub. by Polity Pr); pap. 23.95 (*0-7456-1817-0*, Pub. by Polity Pr) Blackwell Pubs.

McGrew, Anthony & Brook, Christopher, eds. Asia Pacific in the New World Order. 347p. 1998. pap. 24.99 (*0-415-17272-1*) Routledge.

— Asia Pacific in the New World Order. LC 98-136122. (The Open University Pacific Studies Course: Vol. 1). 320p. (C). 1998. 75.00 (*0-415-17271-3*) Routledge.

McGrew, Anthony & Lewis, Paul. Global Politics: Globalization & the Nation State. (Illus.). (C). 1992. pap. text 31.95 (*0-7456-0756-X*) Blackwell Pubs.

McGrew, Anthony, jt. ed. see Held, David.

***McGrew, Chandler.** A Certain Slant of Light. LC 99-91601. 1999. 25.00 (*0-7388-0932-2*); pap. 18.00 (*0-7388-0933-0*) Xlibris Corp.

McGrew, Chuck. Don't Look Back: Terror Is Never Far Behind. McGrew, Annette, ed. (Illus.). 160p. (Orig.). 1995. pap. 19.00 (*0-9641674-0-9*) Mind Ventures.

McGrew, D. R. Traffic Accident Investigation & Physical Evidence. (Illus.). 132p. 1975. pap., spiral bd. 29.95 (*0-398-03503-2*) C C Thomas.

***McGrew, Edith L.** Today's Virtuous Woman. 30p. 1999. pap. 10.00 (*0-9679132-0-9*) E L McGrew.

McGrew, J. Chapman, Jr. & Monroe, Charles B. An Introduction to Statistical Problem Solving in Geography. 400p. (C). 1993. text. write for info. (*0-697-12682-X*) Brown & Benchmark.

— An Introduction to Statistical Problem Solving in Geography. 400p. (C). 1993. text 18.75 (*0-697-17233-3*) Brown & Benchmark.

***McGrew, J. Chapman, Jr. & Monroe, Charles B.** An Introduction to Statistical Problem Solving in Geography 2nd ed. LC 99-15121. 2000. write for info. (*0-697-22971-8*) McGrw-H Hghr Educ.

McGrew, J. R., et al. The American Wine Society Presents "Growing Wine Grapes" Reichwage, Randall J., ed. (Illus.). 96p. (Orig.). 1993. pap. 10.95 (*0-9619072-0-7*) G W Kent.

McGrew, James. Gas Daily's Guide to FERC's Regulation of Natural Gas. LC 97-165990. viii, 146 p. 1997. write for info. (*0-935453-80-6*) Pasha Pubns.

McGrew, John. Uncommon Remedies for America's Ills: Futuring for the New Millennium. LC 96-92648. 160p. (Orig.). 1997. pap. 13.50 (*0-936544-08-2*) New Vista.

McGrew, John F. Navigating Career Change. LC 80-80788. (Illus.). 124p. 1980. pap. 5.00 (*0-936544-00-7*) New Vista.

McGrew, Julia H. & Thomas, George, eds. Sturlunga Saga, Vol. 2: Shorter Sagas of the Icelanders, Vol. 2. LC 71-120536. (Library of Scandinavian Literature). (Illus.). 1974. pap. text 11.75 (*0-8290-2035-7*); lib. bdg. 49.00 (*0-8057-3365-5*) Irvington.

McGrew, Julia H. & Thomas, George R., eds. Sturlunga Saga, Vol. 1: The Saga of Hvamm-Sturla & the Sage of the Icelanders, Vol. 1. LC 71-120536. (Library of Scandinavian Literature). (Illus.). 1970. pap. text 9.75 (*0-8290-2036-5*); lib. bdg. 49.00 (*0-8057-3364-7*) Irvington.

McGrew, Kelly. Virtual Private Networks. 450p. 1999. pap. 55.00 (*0-07-047173-8*) McGraw.

McGrew, Kevin S. Clinical Interpretation of the Woodcock-Johnson Tests of Cognitive Ability. rev. ed. LC 93-31670. 288p. (C). 1994. 68.00 (*0-205-14801-8*, Longwood Div) Allyn.

— Clinical Interpretation of the Woodcock-Johnson Tests of Cognitive Ability. rev. ed. LC 93-31670. (C). 1994. write for info. (*0-205-14701-1*) Allyn.

***McGrew, Kevin S. & Flanagan, Dawn P.** The Intelligence Test Desk Reference (ITDR) Gf-Gc Cross-Battery Assessment. LC 97-27414. 352p. (C). 1998. 58.00 (*0-205-19857-0*) Allyn.

McGrew, Larry, ed. see Banks, Peter M. & Kraybill, William G.

McGrew, Larry, ed. see Clark, Orlo H. & Duh, Quan-Yang.

McGrew, Larry, ed. see Enlow, Donald H. & Hans, Mark G.

McGrew, Larry, ed. see Fonseca, Raymond J. & Walker, Robert V.

McGrew, Larry, ed. see Gordis, Leon.

McGrew, Larry, ed. see Johnson, Jonas T. & Yu, Victor Y.

McGrew, Larry, ed. see Kaban, Leonard B., et al.

McGrew, Larry, ed. see Liebert, Peter S.

McGrew, Larry, ed. see Marks, Malcolm W. & Marks, Charles.

McGrew, Larry, ed. see Myers, Eugene N.

McGrew, Larry, ed. see Nanda, Ravindra.

McGrew, Larry, ed. see Silver, Carl E.

McGrew, Larry, ed. see Suen, James Y. & Myers, Eugene N.

McGrew, Larry, ed. see Tardy, Eugene, Jr.

McGrew, Mac. American Metal Typefaces of the Twentieth Century. 2nd ed. (Illus.). 400p. 1993. 75.00 (*0-938768-34-4*); pap. 49.95 (*0-938768-39-5*) Oak Knoll.

McGrew, Milt. Exploring the Power of AutoCAD. 1990. pap. 32.50 (*0-8273-3694-2*) Delmar.

— The Powers of AutoCAD. (CAD/CAM Ser.). 1990. pap., teacher ed. 16.00 (*0-8273-3695-0*) Delmar.

McGrew, Richard. The America You May Never See! A Tribute to the Millennium. large type ed. LC 99-7759. (Illus.). 32p. 1999. pap. 11.95 (*0-9669386-0-7*) McGrew Multimedia.

McGrew, Roderick E. Paul I of Russia, 1754-1801. (Illus.). 424p. 1992. 85.00 (*0-19-822567-9*) OUP.

McGrew, Timothy. The Foundations of Knowledge. 154p. (Orig.). (C). 1995. pap. text 22.95 (*0-8226-3043-5*); lib. bdg. 48.50 (*0-8226-3042-7*) Rowman.

McGrew, William C. Chimpanzee Material Culture: Implications for Human Evolution. (Illus.). 293p. (C). 1992. text 80.00 (*0-521-41303-6*); pap. text 29.95 (*0-521-42371-6*) Cambridge U Pr.

McGrew, William C., et al, eds. Great Ape Societies. (Illus.). 348p. (C). 1996. text 69.95 (*0-521-55494-2*) Cambridge U Pr.

— Great Ape Societies. (Illus.). 348p. (C). 1996. pap. text 26.95 (*0-521-55536-1*) Cambridge U Pr.

McGrew, William W. Land & Revolution in Modern Greece, 1800-1881: The Transition in the Tenure & Exploitation of Land from Ottoman Rule to Independence. LC 84-27789. (Illus.). 355p. 1986. 35.00 (*0-87338-316-8*) Kent St U Pr.

McGriff. Beginners Guide to List Processing. (C). 1999. 14.20 (*0-8359-0450-4*) P-H.

— Intra-racial Prejudice. 2nd ed. 1999. pap. 8.00 (*0-07-232998-X*) McGraw.

— Intraracial Prejudice. 1996. 8.74 (*0-07-046517-7*) McGraw.

McGriff, Duane, et al. A Beginner's Guide to List Processing: The Other Side of Logo. (Illus.). 128p. 1986. pap. text 15.00 (*0-13-071705-3*) P-H.

McGriff, E. Carver. Hope for Tomorrow: What Jesus Would Say Today. LC 98-49096. 180p. 1999. pap. 15.50 (*0-7880-1323-8*) CSS OH.

— Hope for Tomorrow: What Jesus Would Say Today - Sermon Prep Version. LC 98-49096. 1999. pap. 15.50 (*0-7880-1325-4*) CSS OH.

— Lectionary Preaching Workbook. 1998. pap., wbk. ed. 42.95 incl. disk (*0-7880-1216-9*) CSS OH.

— Lectionary Preaching Workbook. LC 98-6062. (Series VI). (Illus.). 292p. 1998. pap., wbk. ed. 42.95 (*0-7880-1213-4*) CSS OH.

***McGriff, E. Carver.** Lectionary Preaching Workbook. LC 98-6062. (Series VI). 336p. 1999. pap., wbk. ed. 46.50 (*0-7880-1367-X*) CSS OH.

— Lectionary Preaching Workbook: Series VI, Cycle C. LC 98-6062. 364p. 2000. pap. 55.50 (*0-7880-1701-2*); disk 55.50 (*0-7880-1702-0*) CSS OH.

McGriff, E. Carver. Times of Refreshing Cycle B: Sermons for Lent-Easter: First Lesson Texts. LC 96-6867. 111p. 1996. pap. 10.75 (*0-7880-0773-4*) CSS OH.

***McGriff, Michelle.** Majestic Secret. 197p. 1999. pap. 14.95 (*0-7414-0333-1*) Buy Books.

McGrindell, Andrew L. A Guide to Insurance Accounting. 293p. 1981. 230.00 (*0-948691-02-6*, Pub. by Witherby & Co) St Mut.

McGrinder, Michael. Heathen Piper. LC 78-59774. (Scene Award Ser.). 104p. 1979. pap. 8.00 (*0-912292-56-3*) Smith.

McGrloughlin, Stephen. Multimedia on the Web. LC 96-70682. 193p. 1997. 58.00 (*1-57576-648-5*) Sams.

McGroarty, Daniel. Break These Chains: The Battle for School Choice. LC 96-280. 288p. 1996. 23.95 (*0-7615-0507-5*) Prima Pub.

McGroarty, John S., et al, eds. History of Los Angeles County: With Selected Biography of Actors & Witnesses in the Period of the County's Greatest Growth & Achievement, 3 vols. (Illus.). 1591p. 1997. reprint ed. lib. bdg. 149.50 (*0-8328-6609-1*) Higginson Bk Co.

McGroarty, Mary E. & Faltis, Christian J., eds. Languages in School & Society: Policy & Pedagogy. (Contributions to the Sociology of Language Ser.: No. 58). x, 570p. (C). 1991. lib. bdg. 175.40 (*0-89925-716-X*) Mouton.

McGroarty, Michael J. Free Landscape Plants: How to Grow Your Own Landscape Plants from Scratch. (Illus.). 136p. (Orig.). 1996. pap. 9.95 (*0-9649563-0-6*) Leprechn OH.

McGroarty, Stephen. Spanish: 2000 Daily Phrases. 1999. pap. 9.95 (*0-609-80430-8*) Liv Lang.

McGroarty, Stephen, jt. auth. see Danesi, Marcel.

McGrory, Arlene A. Mouton's Impossible Dream. LC 98-47275. (Illus.). 32p. (J). (ps-3). 2000. 16.00 (*0-15-202195-7*, Gulliver Bks) Harcourt.

***McGrory, Brian.** The Incumbent. 352p. 2000. 24.95 (*0-7434-0350-9*) PB.

McGrory, Dan, jt. auth. see Bhatia, Shyam.

McGrotha, Bill. Seminoles! The First Forty Years. LC 87-51238. (Illus.). 256p. 1987. 20.95 (*0-9613040-1-4*) Talla Dem.

***McGruder, Aaron.** Because I Know You Don't Read the Newspaper. (Illus.). 128p. (J). 2000. pap. 9.95 (*0-7407-0609-8*) Andrews & McMeel.

McGruder, Deorsey E. Picture Yourself More Independent. McGruder, Vera E., ed. (Illus.). 46p. (Orig.). 1996. pap. 14.95 (*0-9658837-0-1*) Windchime.

McGruder, Vera E., ed. see McGruder, Deorsey E.

McGuane. Hearts of Oak. Date not set. write for info. (*0-393-04749-0*) Norton.

McGuane, Thomas. The Bushwhacked Piano. 1994. pap. 11.00 (*0-394-25886-X*) Random.

— The Bushwhacked Piano. LC 84-40014. (Vintage Contemporaries Ser.). 224p. 1984. pap. 13.00 (*0-394-72642-1*) Vin Bks.

— Cutting Horse. 1991. 29.95 (*0-9627181-7-3*) NCHA.

— Fishing. 1999. pap. write for info. (*0-679-77757-1*) Vin Bks.

— In the Crazies: Book & Portfolio. deluxe limited ed. (Illus.). 112p. 1984. 1500.00 (*0-916947-02-5*) Winn Bks.

— Keep the Change. 1994. pap. 11.00 (*0-394-25889-4*) Random.

— Keep the Change. LC 90-50115. (Vintage Contemporaries Ser.). 240p. 1990. pap. 12.00 (*0-679-73033-8*) Vin Bks.

— Live Water. LC 96-159320. (Illus.). 133p. 1996. 50.00 (*1-886967-02-4*) Meadow Run Pr.

— The Longest Silence: A Life in Fishing. LC 99-27199. 320p. 1999. 25.00 (*0-679-45485-3*) Knopf.

— Ninety-Two in the Shade. LC 94-42801. 197p. 1995. pap. 12.00 (*0-679-75289-7*) Random.

— Nobody's Angel. (Vintage Contemporaries Ser.). 1986. pap. 14.00 (*0-394-74738-0*) Vin Bks.

— Nothing but Blue Skies. 1994. pap. 14.00 (*0-679-74778-8*) Random.

— Panama. 175p. 1995. pap. 11.00 (*0-679-75291-9*) Random.

— Some Horses. LC 98-56057. (Illus.). 176p. 1999. 20.00 (*1-55821-891-2*) Lyons Pr.

— Something to Be Desired. 1994. pap. 10.00 (*0-394-25887-8*) Random.

— Something to Be Desired. (Vintage Contemporaries Ser.). 1985. pap. 12.00 (*0-394-73156-5*) Vin Bks.

— Sons. deluxe ed. 1993. 75.00 (*0-935716-58-0*) Lord John.

— The Sporting Club. 1994. lib. bdg. 24.95 (*1-56849-401-7*) Buccaneer Bks.

— The Sporting Club. 224p. 1996. pap. 12.00 (*0-679-75290-0*) Random.

— To Skin a Cat. 1994. pap. 10.00 (*0-394-25888-6*) Random.

— To Skin a Cat: Stories. LC 87-40093. (Vintage Contemporaries Ser.). 224p. 1987. pap. 12.00 (*0-394-75521-9*) Vin Bks.

McGuane, Thomas, et al. Fiction, Flyfishing & the Search for Innocence: Short Stories on Flyfishing. limited aut. ed. LC 92-72296. (Sporting Life Ser.). (Illus.). 192p. 1994. 150.00 (*0-913559-20-2*) Birch Brook Pr.

— Silent Seasons. 4th ed. Chatham, Russell, ed. & illus. by. LC 88-72163. 240p. 1996. reprint ed. 24.95 (*0-944439-76-4*) Clark City Pr.

— Silent Seasons: Twenty-One Fishing Stories. Chatham, Russell, ed. & illus. by. LC 88-72163. 240p. (Orig.). 1988. pap. 14.95 (*0-944439-05-5*) Clark City Pr.

McGuarr, Lynn, et al. Tasmania. 2nd ed. (Illus.). 288p. 1999. pap. 16.95 (*0-86442-727-1*) Lonely Planet.

McGucken, William. Biodegradable: Detergents & the Environment. LC 90-29035. (Environmental History Ser.: No. 12). (Illus.). 160p. 1991. 39.95 (*0-89096-479-3*) Tex A&M Univ Pr.

*McGucken, William.** Lake Erie Rehabilitated: Controlling Cultural Eutrophication, 1960s-1990s. LC 99-53826. (Technology & the Environment Ser.). 2000. pap. 29.95 (*1-884836-58-5*) U Akron Pr.

McGucken, William. Nineteenth-Century Spectroscopy: Development of the Understanding of Spectra, 1802-1897. LC 74-94886. 249p. reprint ed. pap. 77.20 (*0-608-30476-X*, 201186800078) Bks Demand.

— Scientists, Society & State: The Social Relations of Science Movement in Great Britain, 1931-1947. LC 83-8320. 395p. 1984. reprint ed. pap. 122.50 (*0-608-04448-2*, 206498000012) Bks Demand.

McGuckian, M. & Archer, Nuala. Two Women, Two Shores. (New Poets Ser.: Vol. 16). 64p. 1989. pap. 5.95 (*0-932616-19-4*) Brick Hse Bks.

McGuckian, Medbh. Captain Lavender. LC 94-61972. 83p. 1995. 15.95 (*0-916390-67-5*); pap. 9.95 (*0-916390-66-7*) Wake Forest.

— The Flower Master & Other Poems. 58p. 1993. pap. 12.95 (*1-85235-124-1*) Dufour.

— The Flower Master & Other Poems. 58p. 1993. 21.00 (*1-85235-125-X*, Pub. by Gallery Pr) Dufour.

— Marconi's Cottage. LC 91-67446. 112p. 1992. pap. 8.95 (*0-916390-51-9*) Wake Forest.

— On Ballycastle Beach. LC 87-40624. 59p. 1988. pap. 6.95 (*0-916390-30-6*) Wake Forest.

— Selected Poems. 96p. (Orig.). 1997. 17.95 (*0-916390-78-0*); pap. 11.95 (*0-916390-77-2*) Wake Forest.

*McGuckian, Medbh.** Shelmalier. 1998. pap. text. write for info. (*0-916390-86-1*) Wake Forest.

McGuckian, Medbh. Venus & the Rain. 56p. 1994. pap. 12.95 (*1-85235-143-8*) Dufour.

McGuckin, Frank, ed. Terrorism in the United States. LC 97-3423. (Reference Shelf Ser.: 69). 131p. 1997. pap. 25.00 (*0-8242-0914-1*) Wilson.

— Violence in American Society. LC 97-51741. (Reference Shelf Ser.: 70). 1997. pap. 25.00 (*0-8242-0941-9*) Wilson.

— Volunteerism. LC 98-35206. 177p. 1998. write for info. (*0-8242-0944-3*) Wilson.

McGuckin, Henry E. Memoirs of a Wobbly. LC 87-80042. (First Person Ser.: No. 2). (Illus.). 96p. (Orig.). 1987. pap. 8.00 (*0-88286-157-3*) C H Kerr.

McGuckin, John A. At the Lighting of the Lamps: Hymns of the Ancient Church. LC 97-37690. 120p. 1997. pap. 9.95 (*0-8192-1717-4*) Morehouse Pub.

— St. Cyril of Alexandria: The Christological Controversey: Its History, Theology, & Texts. LC 94-11851. (Supplements to Vigiliae Christianae Ser.: Vol. 23). xiii, 430p. 1994. 191.50 (*90-04-09990-5*) Brill Academic Pubs.

— The Transfiguration of Christ in Scripture & Tradition. LC 86-23892. (Studies in Bible & Early Christianity: Vol. 9). 352p. 1986. lib. bdg. 99.95 (*0-88946-609-2*) E Mellen.

McGuckin, John A., tr. see St. Cyril of Alexandria.

McGuckin, Paul, tr. see St. Symeon.

McGuerty, David & Lester, Kent. Complete Guide to Contracting Your Home. 3rd ed. LC 97-853. (Illus.). 320p. 1997. pap. 18.99 (*1-55870-465-5*, Betrwy Bks) F & W Pubns Inc.

McGuff, Francis & Kador, John. Developing Analytical Database Applications. 640p. (C). 1998. pap. text 54.00 (*0-13-082430-5*) P-H.

McGuffee, Julie, jt. ed. see Stull, Katherine.

McGuffee, Michael. The Day The Earth Was Silent. LC 96-77103. (Illus.). 32p. (J). (gr. 3-6). 1996. 14.95 (*0-9634637-1-3*); pap. 7.95 (*0-9634637-2-1*) Inquir Voices.

McGuffee, Michael, ed. Homeplay: Joyful Learning for Children & Adults, Series I, 20 vols. Incl. Vol. 1. Tub Time. Allred, Debbie. Flores, Barbara, tr. (Illus.). 12p. (Orig.). (J). (ps-1). 1996. pap. 3.00 (*1-57518-085-5*); Vol. 2. Who's in the Box? Tolar, Jude. Flores, Barbara, tr. (Illus.). 12p. (Orig.). (J). (ps-1). 1996. pap. 3.00 (*1-57518-086-3*); Vol. 3. Hiding from the Hunter. Hartman, Holly. Flores, Barbara, tr. (Illus.). 12p. (Orig.). (J). (ps-1). 1996. pap. 3.00 (*1-57518-130-4*); Vol. 4. More Than Boxes. Tolar, Jude. (Illus.). 12p. (Orig.). (J). (ps-1). 1996. pap. 3.00 (*1-57518-088-X*); Vol. 5. Nice Shot! McGuffee, Michael. Flores, Barbara, tr. (Illus.). 12p. (Orig.). (J). (ps-1). 1996. pap. 3.00 (*1-57518-089-8*); Vol. 6. Jungle Socks. Ahern, Kathleen. Flores, Barbara, tr. (Illus.). 12p. (Orig.). (J). (ps-1). 1996. pap. 3.00 (*1-57518-090-1*); Vol. 7. Weather Dance. Hartman, Holly. Flores, Barbara, tr. (Illus.). 12p. (Orig.). (J). (ps-1). 1996. pap. 3.00 (*1-57518-091-X*); Vol. 8. Secret Pet. Hartman, Holly. Flores, Barbara, tr. (Illus.). 12p. (Orig.). (J). (ps-1). 1996. pap. 3.00 (*1-57518-092-8*); Vol. 9. Boat Builder. Hartman, Holly. Flores, Barbara, tr. (Illus.). 12p. (Orig.). (J). (ps-1). 1996. pap. 3.00 (*1-57518-093-6*); Vol. 10. Paper Play. Hartman, Holly. Flores, Barbara, tr. (Illus.). 12p. (Orig.). (J). (ps-1). 1996. pap. 3.00 (*1-57518-094-4*); Vol. 11. Grandma Always Listens. Alberts, Joye. Flores, Barbara, tr. (Illus.). 12p. (Orig.). (J). (ps-1). 1996. pap. 3.00 (*1-57518-095-2*); Vol. 12. Music Makers. Rains, Andrea. Flores, Barbara, tr. (Illus.). 12p. (Orig.). (J). (ps-1). 1996. pap. 3.00 (*1-57518-096-0*); Vol. 13. Goop. Hartman, Holly. Flores, Barbara, tr. (Illus.). 12p. (Orig.). (J). (ps-1). 1996. pap. 3.00 (*1-57518-097-9*); Vol. 14. Follow Your Feet. Baze, Kurt. Flores, Barbara, tr. (Illus.). 12p. (Orig.). (J). (ps-1). 1996. pap. 3.00 (*1-57518-098-7*); Vol. 15. What Good Is a Line? Hartman, Holly. Flores, Barbara, tr. (Illus.). 12p. (Orig.). (J). (ps-1). 1996. pap. 3.00 (*1-57518-099-5*); Vol. 16. We Can Build. Rains, Andrea. Flores, Barbara, tr. (Illus.). 12p. (Orig.). (J). (ps-1). 1996. pap. 3.00 (*1-57518-125-8*); Vol. 17. Sidewalk Art. Tolar, Jude. Flores, Barbara, tr. (Illus.). 12p. (Orig.). (J). (ps-1). 1996. pap. 3.00 (*1-57518-126-6*); Vol. 18. Grandpa's Secret Potion. Hartman, Holly. Flores, Barbara, tr. (Illus.). 12p. (Orig.). (J). (ps-1). 1996. pap. 3.00 (*1-57518-127-4*); Vol. 19. Fort for Fun. Hartman, Holly. Flores, Barbara, tr. (Illus.). 12p. (Orig.). (J). (ps-1). 1996. pap. 3.00 (*1-57518-128-2*); Vol. 20. Are You a Collector? Hartman, Holly. Flores, Barbara, tr. (Illus.). 12p. (Orig.). (J). (ps-1). 1996. pap. 3.00 (*1-57518-129-0*); 49.95 (*1-57518-084-7*) Arborlake.

McGuffey, Verne. Differences in the Activities of Teachers in Rural One-Teacher Schools & of Grade Teachers in Cities. LC 79-177026. (Columbia University. Teachers College. Contributions to Education Ser.: No. 346). reprint ed. 37.50 (*0-404-55346-X*) AMS Pr.

McGuffey, William H. McGuffey Eclectic Readers: Primer Through 6th Edition, 7 vols. 1997. 59.95 (*0-471-29428-4*) Wiley.

McGuffey, William H. McGuffey Readers, 9 vols., Set. 1973. lib. bdg. 2500.00 (*0-8490-0571-X*) Gordon Pr.

McGuffey, William H. McGuffey's Eclectic Primer. rev. ed. 64p. 1997. 9.95 (*0-471-28888-8*, VNR) Wiley.

McGuffey, William H. McGuffeys Eclectic Spelling Book. 1997. 9.95 (*0-317-64211-1*, VNR) Wiley.

— McGuffey's Eclectic Spelling Book. rev. ed. 144p. 1997. 9.95 (*0-471-28943-4*, VNR); text 9.95 (*0-442-26446-1*, VNR) Wiley.

McGuffey, William H. McGuffey's Fifth Eclectic Reader. rev. ed. 352p. (J). 1997. 12.95 (*0-471-28892-6*, VNR) Wiley.

— McGuffey's First Eclectic Reader. 96p. 1997. 9.95 (*0-471-28889-6*, VNR) Wiley.

— McGuffey's Fourth Eclectic Reader. rev. ed. 256p. (J). 1997. 10.95 (*0-471-28984-1*, VNR) Wiley.

McGuffey, William H. McGuffey's Illustrated Address Book. 1980. text 15.95 (*0-442-21257-7*, VNR) Wiley.

— McGuffey's New High School Reader. 1974. 250.00 (*0-87968-147-0*) Gordon Pr.

McGuffey, William H. McGuffey's Second Eclectic Reader. rev. ed. 160p. 1997. 9.95 (*0-471-28890-X*, VNR) Wiley.

— McGuffey's Sixth Eclectic Reader. 480p. (J). 1997. 12.95 (*0-471-28893-4*, VNR) Wiley.

— McGuffey's Third Eclectic Reader. rev. ed. 208p. (J). 1997. 10.95 (*0-471-28891-8*, VNR) Wiley.

McGuffey, William H. The Moore McGuffey Readers, 1836-43: First Reader for Young Children. Moore, Raymond S. et al, eds. (Illus.). 167p. (J). (gr. 1-3). 1984. text 16.95 (*0-913717-01-0*) Moore Fnd.

— The Original McGuffey's Eclectic Series, 8 vols., 1982. reprint ed. teacher ed., boxed set 109.99 (*0-88062-029-3*) Mott Media.

— The Original McGuffey's Eclectic Series, 7 Vols. (J). (gr. k-12). 1982. reprint ed. 99.99 (*0-88062-014-5*) Mott Media.

McGuffie, K. & Henderson-Sellers, A. Climate Modelling Primer 2e +c. 2nd ed. LC 96-12815. 268p. 1997. pap. 80.00 (*0-471-95558-2*) Wiley.

McGuffie, T. H. The Siege of Gibraltar, 1779-1783. LC 64-25508. (Illus.). 1965. 15.95 (*0-8023-1074-5*) Dufour.

McGuffin, Gary. Where Rivers Run. (Illus.). 241p. 1996. pap. text 14.50 (*0-7737-5352-4*, Pub. by Boston Mills) Genl Dist Srvs.

McGuffin, Gary & McGuffin, Joanie. Paddle Your Own Canoe. (Illus.). 240p. 1999. 29.95 (*1-55046-214-8*, Pub. by Boston Mills) Genl Dist Srvs.

— Superior: Journeys on an Inland Sea. (Illus.). 160p. 1997. 40.00 (*1-55046-067-6*, Pub. by Boston Mills) Genl Dist Srvs.

— Where Rivers Run: A Six Thousand Mile Exploration of Canada by Canoe. (Illus.). 272p. 1989. 23.95 (*0-913276-54-5*) Stone Wall Pr.

— Where Rivers Run: Travel & Adventure. (Illus.). 242p. 1999. pap. 18.95 (*1-55046-314-4*) Boston Mills.

*McGuffin, Jo A.** The Nurse's Guide to Successful Management. LC 98-43530. 1999. spiral bd. 29.95 (*0-323-00388-5*) Mosby Inc.

McGuffin, Joanie, jt. auth. see McGuffin, Gary.

*McGuffin, John.** In Praise of Poteen. (Illus.). 126p. 1999. pap. 16.95 (*0-86281-768-4*, Pub. by Appletree Pr) Irish Bks Media.

McGugan, Peter M. Priorganize! The Working from Home Wealth Plan. (Illus.). 128p. (Orig.). 1997. pap. 12.95 (*0-614-29793-1*) Potentls Pr.

— When Something Changes Everything: How to Recover from the Zero Zone of Loss & Change. (Illus.). 200p. (Orig.). 1991. pap. text 12.95 (*0-9694312-1-X*) Potentls Pr.

McGuigan. Managerial Economics. 8th ed. LC 98-21497. (HT - Managerial Economics Ser.). (C). 1998. pap. 90.95 (*0-538-88106-2*) S-W Pub.

— Managerial Economics. 8th ed. (HT - Managerial Economics Ser.). (C). 1998. pap., student ed. 22.95 (*0-538-88107-0*) S-W Pub.

Mcguigan. Stress Encyclopedia. LC 98-28926. 276p. 1998. pap. text 46.00 (*0-205-17876-6*) Allyn.

*McGuigan, et al.** Managerial Economics: Applications, Strategy & Tactics. 9th ed. (SWC-Business Statistics Ser.). (C). 2001. text, student ed. 19.75 (*0-324-05882-9*) Sth-Wstrn College.

McGuigan, jt. auth. see Moyer.

McGuigan, Amanda, jt. auth. see McGuigan, Dermot.

McGuigan, Christine. Imbalance: An Experimental Collection of Micro Stories & Poetry. 64p. 1998. per. 9.95 (*1-891571-00-1*) Easy Break.

McGuigan, Dermot & Jacobson, Beverly. Y2K & Y-O-U: The Sane Person's Home Preparation Guide. LC 98-53059. (Real Goods Solar Living Books Ser.). (Illus.). 160p. 1999. pap. 15.95 (*1-890132-26-8*) Chelsea Green Pub.

McGuigan, Dermot & McGuigan, Amanda. Heat Pumps: An Efficient Heating & Cooling Alternative. LC 81-7185. (Illus.). 208p. 1983. pap. 6.95 (*0-88266-255-4*, Garden Way Pub) Storey Bks.

McGuigan, F. J. Biological Psychology: A Cybernetic Science. LC 93-35572. 599p. (C). 1993. text 51.00 (*0-13-146655-0*) P-H.

McGuigan, F. J. & Ban, Thomas A., eds. Critical Issues in Psychology, Psychiatry & Physiology: A Memorial to W. Horsley Gantt. (Monographs in Psychobiology: Vol. 2). xviii, 380p. 1987. text 108.00 (*2-88124-137-9*) Gordon & Breach.

McGuigan, Frank J. Cognitive Psychophysiology: Principles of Covert Behavior. LC 78-18542. (Century Psychology Ser.). 1978. 34.95 (*0-13-139519-X*) P-H.

— Cognitive Psychophysiology: Principles of Covert Behavior. LC 78-18542. (Century Psychology Ser.). 544p. reprint ed. pap. 168.70 (*0-8357-3403-X*, 203966000013) Bks Demand.

— Experimental Psychology Methods of Research. 7th ed. LC 96-22933. 480p. (C). 1996. 79.00 (*0-13-398884-8*) P-H.

— Psychophysiological Measurement of Covert Behavior: A Guide for the Laboratory. LC 79-18482. (Illus.). 143p. reprint ed. pap. 44.40 (*0-8357-4208-3*, 203698500003) Bks Demand.

McGuigan, Frank J., ed. Thinking: Studies of Covert Language Processes. LC 66-15745. (Century Psychology Ser.). (Illus.). 1966. pap. text 19.95 (*0-89197-450-4*) Irvington.

McGuigan, Frank J., et al, eds. Stress & Tension Control, Vol. 2. 420p. 1985. 85.00 (*0-306-41815-0*, Plenum Trade) Perseus Pubng.

— Stress & Tension Control Vol. 3: Stress Management. (Illus.). 298p. (C). 1989. 114.00 (*0-306-43327-3*, Plenum Trade) Perseus Pubng.

McGuigan, James R. Managerial Economics. 6th ed. Date not set. pap. text, student ed. 20.50 (*0-314-01814-X*) West Pub.

— Managerial Economics. 6th ed. (HT - Managerial Economics Ser.). 1993. pap. 16.00 (*0-314-02278-3*) West Pub.

— Managerial Economics. 7th ed. Date not set. pap. text, teacher ed. write for info. (*0-314-07888-6*) West Pub.

— Managerial Economics. 7th ed. 1996. pap., student ed. 21.00 (*0-314-06516-4*) West Pub.

McGuigan, James R. & Moyer, R. Charles. Managerial Economics. 6th ed. Schiller, ed. LC 92-18132. 650p. (C). 1993. text 61.50 (*0-314-01220-6*) West Pub.

McGuigan, James R., et al. Managerial Economics. 7th ed. LC 95-36052. 700p. (C). 1995. pap. 67.00 (*0-314-06433-8*) West Pub.

McGuigan, Jim. Cultural Populism. LC 92-248. 304p. (C). 1992. pap. 24.99 (*0-415-06295-0*, A7754) Routledge.

— Culture & the Public Sphere. 240p. (C). 1996. 75.00 (*0-415-11262-1*); pap. 22.99 (*0-415-11263-X*) Routledge.

*McGuigan, Jim.** Modernity & Postmodern Culture. LC 99-33227. 1999. write for info. (*0-03-351996-X*) Open Univ TX.

McGuigan, Jim & Gray, Ann, eds. Studying Culture: An Introductory Reader. LC 93-7215. 256p. 1993. 60.00 (*0-340-58793-8*, B2562, Pub. by E A) St Martin.

— Studying Culture: An Introductory Reader. LC 93-7215. 256p. 1995. pap. text 16.95 (*0-340-55628-5*, Pub. by E A) St Martin.

McGuigan, Jim, jt. ed. see Gray, Ann.

McGuigan, K., ed. Flexible Manufacturing for Small to Medium Enterprises. 200p. 1988. 142.95 (*0-387-50077-4*) Spr-Verlag.

McGuigan, Mary A. Cloud Dancer. LC 93-5562. 128p. (J). (gr. 6-8). 1994. pap. 14.95 (*0-684-19632-8*) Scribner.

— Where You Belong. LC 96-32026. 192p. (J). (gr. 5-9). 1998. per. 4.50 (*0-689-82318-5*) Aladdin.

— Where You Belong. LC 96-32026. 176p. (J). (gr. 7 up). 1997. 16.00 (*0-689-81250-7*) S&S Childrens.

McGuigan, Patrick B. & Weyrich, Dawn M. Ninth Justice: The Fight for Bork. LC 89-23661. 340p. (C). 1990. pap. 14.95 (*0-942522-15-X*) Free Congr Res.

McGuigan, Tiffany. Cheers to You: The Ultimate Guide to Becoming a Cheerleader. 1996. pap. text 9.95 (*0-9647867-5-3*) St Simons Pr.

McGuiggan, Jim. The God of the Towel: Knowing the Tender Heart of God. LC 96-43931. 272p. 1997. 15.99 (*1-878990-63-2*) Howard Pub LA.

— The Irish Papers: Lessons from Life. 45p. (Orig.). 1992. pap. 2.95 (*0-940999-92-7*, C2251) Star Bible.

— Jesus, Hero of Thy Soul: Impressions Left by the Savior's Touch. LC 98-9380. 288p. 1998. 15.99 (*1-878990-87-X*) Howard Pub LA.

— The Reign of God. 120p. (Orig.). 1992. pap. 6.95 (*0-940999-88-9*, C2226) Star Bible.

— Where the Spirit of the Lord Is . . . LC 99-11020. 270p. 1999. 15.99 (*1-58229-011-3*) Howard Pub LA.

McGuin, Roger. Byrd's Eye View. 1999. pap. 22.95 (*0-965-93672-6*) NAL.

McGuiness, Brian. Coffee on the Wing Beam: Memories of the P2V Neptune. LC 98-91665. (Illus.). 240p. 1998. pap., per. 11.95 (*0-9665556-0-0*) Knights Red.

McGuiness, Brian & Von Wright, George H., eds. Ludwig Wittgenstein: Cambridge Letters: Correspondence with Russell, Keynes, Moore, Ramsey & Graffi. LC 94-40727. 352p. (C). 1996. text 55.95 (*0-631-19015-5*) Blackwell Pubs.

McGuiness, Brian & Von Wright, George H., eds. Ludwig Wittgenstein: Cambridge Letters: Correspondence with Russell, Keynes, Moore, Ramsey & Graffi. LC 94-40727. 352p. 1997. pap. text 31.95 (*0-631-20758-9*) Blackwell Pubs.

*McGuiness, Daniel.** Holding Patterns: Temporary Poetics in Contemporary Poetry. (C). 2001. pap. text 15.95 (*0-7914-4954-8*) State U NY Pr.

— Holding Patterns: Temporary Poetics in Contemporary Poetry. (C). 2001. text 47.50 (*0-7914-4953-X*) State U NY Pr.

McGuiness, Frank. Frank McGuiness Plays 1 Plays 1: The Factory Girls; Observe the Sons of Ulster Marching Towards... 336p. (Orig.). 1996. pap. 17.00 (*0-571-17740-9*) Faber & Faber.

McGuiness, Jeffrey C. & Williams, Robert E. Guard Unions & the Problem of Divided Loyalties: Supplement to the NLRB & the Appropriate Bargaining Unit. LC 89-84149. 76p. 1989. pap. 15.00 (*0-89546-076-9*) U PA Ctr Hum Res.

McGuiness, John. Teachers, Pupils & Behavior: A Managerial Approach. Best, Ron & Lang, Peter J., eds. (Studies in Pastoral Care, Personal & Social Education). (Illus.). 176p. 1994. text 90.00 (*0-304-32784-0*); pap. text 31.95 (*0-304-32785-9*) Continuum.

McGuiness, Kenneth C., jt. auth. see Potter, Edward E.

McGuiness, Mary, ed. Myers-Briggs Type Indicator: Australian Perspectives. (C). 1992. 75.00 (*0-86431-128-1*, Pub. by Aust Council Educ Res) St Mut.

McGuiness, Victoria. Very Simple Spanish. (SPA.). pap. write for info. (*1-86034-002-4*, 92990, Pub. by Global Bks) Midpt Trade.

McGuinn, Dana. Six Cups! Six Bowls! Six Spoons! Humorous Hints from a Formerly Frazzled Mom on How to Get Your House in Order & Keep It That Way. (Illus.). 48p. 1993. VHS 18.95 (*1-880163-07-1*) Dana McGuinn.

McGuinn, Dana, jt. auth. see Johnson, Joe A.

McGuinn, Doug. Cold Toes & Busted TVs. LC 95-111964. 128p. (Orig.). 1994. pap. 8.95 (*0-89754-097-2*) Dan River Pr.

*McGuinn-Freeman, Charlotte.** Place Last Seen: A Novel. LC 99-55047. 294p. 2000. text 23.00 (*0-312-24227-1*, Picador USA) St Martin.

McGuinn, Jack & McNamee, Tom. The Towery Report on DuPage County, IL. (Towery Report on New American Communities Ser.). (Illus.). 128p. 1995. pap. 9.50 (*1-881096-19-X*) Towery Pub.

McGuinn, Nicholas, ed. see Stevenson, Robert Louis.

McGuinn, Rex. Landing in Minneapolis. 64p. (Orig.). Date not set. pap. 8.95 (*1-879934-06-X*) St Andrews NC.

— Landing in Minneapolis. 72p. (Orig.). 1993. pap. 8.95 (*1-879934-19-1*) St Andrews NC.

*McGuinn, Taro.** East Timor: Island in Turmoil. LC 97-13683. (World in Conflict Ser.). (J). (gr. 9 up). 1998. lib. bdg. 25.26 (*0-8225-3555-6*) Lerner Pub.

McGuinn, William F., jt. auth. see Bazelon, Bruce S.

McGuinn, Young C., jt. auth. see Theodore, Louis.

McGuinne, Dermot. Irish Type Design: A History of Printing Types in the Irish Character. (Illus.). 224p. 1992. 39.50 (*0-7165-2463-5*, Pub. by Irish Acad Pr) Intl Spec Bk.

McGuinnes, Annelise, tr. see Pierson, Caryl K.

McGuinnes, Celia & Whelan, Leo. Report on the Australian Royal Commission on Aboriginal & Torres Strait Islander Deaths in Custody. Minnesota Lawyers International Human Rights Commi, ed. 32p. (Orig.). 1988. pap. 3.00 (*0-929293-18-5*) MN Advocates.

McGuinness. Flatnessisgod. 1999. pap. 24.50 (*1-887128-34-4*, Pub. by Soft Skull Pr); pap. 30.00 incl. cd-rom (*1-887128-36-0*, Pub. by Soft Skull Pr) Consort Bk Sales.

McGuinness & McGuinness. Reading Reflex. 1997. pap. text 30.00 (*0-13-095751-8*) P-H.

McGuinness, Arthur E. George Fitzmaurice. (Irish Writers Ser.). 96p. 1975. 8.50 (*0-8387-7870-4*); pap. 1.95 (*0-8387-7980-8*) Bucknell U Pr.

— Seamus Heaney: Poet & Critic. LC 92-43156. (Irish Studies: Vol. 3). XII, 199p. (C). 1994. text 39.95 (*0-8204-2065-4*) P Lang Pubng.

McGuinness, B. F., ed. see Wittgenstein, Ludwig Josef Johann.

McGuinness, B. F., tr. see Wittgenstein, Ludwig Josef Johann.

*McGuinness, Bill.** Cash Rules: Learn & Manage the 7 Cash-Flow Drivers for Your Company's Success. 300p. 2000. 34.95 (*0-938721-75-5*, Pub. by Kiplinger Bks) Natl Bk Netwk.

McGuinness, Brian, ed. Wittgenstein & His Times. (Wittgenstein Studies). 128p. 1998. pap. 15.00 (*1-85506-585-1*) Thoemmes Pr.

McGuinness, Brian & Oliveri, Gianluigi, eds. The Philosophy of Michael Dummett. LC 94-9709. (Synthese Library: Vol. 239). 402p. (C). 1994. lib. bdg. 166.50 (*0-7923-2804-3*, Pub. by Kluwer Academic) Kluwer Academic.

McGuinness, Brian, ed. see Frege, Gottlob.

McGuinness, Brian F., ed. Ernst Mach: Knowledge & Error. Foulkes, Paul, tr. from GER. LC 73-75641. (Vienna Circle Collection: Vol. 3). 432p. 1975. pap. text 120.50 (*90-277-0282-9*, D Reidel); lib. bdg. 175.00 (*90-277-0281-0*, D Reidel) Kluwer Academic.

— Friedrich Waismann: Philosophical Papers. Kaal, Hans, tr. from GER. (Vienna Circle Collection: No. 8). 212p. 1977. pap. text 73.50 (*90-277-0713-8*, D Reidel); lib. bdg. 104.50 (*90-277-0712-X*, D Reidel) Kluwer Academic.

— Hans Hahn Empiricism, Logic & Mathematics: Philosophical Papers. Kaal, Hans, tr. from GER. (Vienna Circle Collection: No. 13). 160p. 1980. lib. bdg. 80.00 (*90-277-1065-1*, D Reidel) Kluwer Academic.

— Hans Hahn Empiricism, Logic & Mathematics: Philosophical Papers. Kaal, Hans, tr. from GER. (Vienna Circle Collection: No. 13). 160p. 1980. pap. text 51.50 (*90-277-1066-X*, D Reidel) Kluwer Academic.

— The Infinite in Mathematics. (Vienna Circle Collection: No. 9). 252p. 1978. lib. bdg. 117.50 (*90-277-0847-9*, D Reidel) Kluwer Academic.

— Moritz Schlick. 156p. 1985. text 88.00 (*90-277-2096-7*, D Reidel) Kluwer Academic.

An Asterisk (*) at the beginning of an entry indicates that the title is appearing for the first time.

— Unified Science. 328p. (C). 1987. text 234.00 (*90-277-2484-9*, D Reidel) Kluwer Academic.
— Wittgenstein & His Times. LC 81-52670. 128p. (C). 1998. 18.00 (*0-226-55881-9*) U Ch Pr.
McGuinness, Brian F., ed. see Boltzmann, Ludwig.
McGuinness, Carmen. Reading Reflex: The Foolproof Phono-Graphix Method for Teaching Your Child to Read. LC 97-33967. (Illus.). 368p. 1999. per. 15.00 (*0-684-85367-1*, Fireside) S&S Trade Pap.
***McGuinness, Carmen & McGuinness, Geoffrey.** How to Increase Your Child's Verbal Intelligence: The Language Wise Method. 269p. 2000. 35.00 (*0-300-08318-1*); pap. 16.95 (*0-300-08320-3*) Yale U Pr.
McGuinness, Carmen & McGuinness, Geoffrey. Reading Reflex. LC 97-33967. 320p. 1998. pap. 30.00 (*0-684-83966-0*) Free Pr.
McGuinness, Diane. Why Our Children Can't Read & What We Can Do about It: A Scientific Revolution in Reading. LC 96-24112. 400p. 1997. 25.00 (*0-684-83161-9*) Free Pr.
— Why Our Children Can't Read & What We Can Do about It: A Scientific Revolution in Reading. 400p. 1999. per. 16.00 (*0-684-85356-6*, Touchstone) S&S Trade Pap.
McGuinness, Diane, jt. auth. see DK Publishing Staff.
McGuinness, Doreen. Nursery Rhymes. (My Big Little Fat Bks.). 20p. (J). (ps). 1996. bds. 3.49 (*1-85854-402-5*) Brimax Bks.
***McGuinness, Francis, et al.** Clinical Imaging in Non-Pulmonary Tuberculosis. LC 99-35196. (Illus.). 175p. 1999. 99.00 (*3-540-65940-4*) Spr-Verlag.
McGuinness, Frank. Booterstown. LC 94-234620. 86p. 1994. pap. 14.95 (*1-85235-135-7*) Dufour.
***McGuinness, Frank.** Dolly Wests Kitchen. 96p. 2000. pap. write for info. (*0-571-20370-1*) Faber & Faber.
McGuinness, Frank. Observe the Sons of Ulster Marching Towards the Somme. 72p. (Orig.). 1986. pap. 9.95 (*0-571-14611-2*) Faber & Faber.
***McGuinness, Frank.** Sea with No Ships. 74p. 2000. 27.95 (*1-85235-252-3*, Pub. by Gallery Pr); pap. 16.95 (*1-85235-251-5*, Pub. by Gallery Pr) Dufour.
McGuinness, Frank & Friel, Brian. Dancing at Lughnasa. (Illus.). 144p. 1998. pap. 13.95 (*0-571-19606-3*) Faber & Faber.
McGuinness, Geoffrey, jt. auth. see McGuinness, Carmen.
McGuinness, Jamie. Trekking in Langtang, Helambu & Gosainkund. 1998. pap. text 14.95 (*1-873756-13-5*, Pub. by Trailblazer) Seven Hills Bk.
— Trekking in the Everest Region. 2nd ed. 1996. pap. text 14.95 (*1-873756-08-9*, Pub. by Trailblazer) Seven Hills Bk.
— Trekking in the Everest Region. 3rd ed. (Illus.). 256p. 1998. pap. 15.95 (*1-873756-17-8*, Pub. by Trailblazer) Seven Hills Bk.
McGuinness, John. Counselling in Schools: New Perspectives. LC 97-2324. (Studies in Pastoral Care, Personal & Social Education). 128p. 1998. 69.95 (*0-304-33354-9*); pap. 24.95 (*0-304-33356-5*) Continuum.
***McGuinness, Justin.** Footprint Morocco Handbook. 2nd ed. (Footprint Handbooks Ser.). (Illus.). 544p. 1999. pap. 17.95 (*0-8442-2132-5*, 21325) NTC Contemp Pub Co.
McGuinness, Justin. Tunisia Handbook with Libya. 2nd ed. (Footprint Handbooks Ser.). 512p. 1999. pap. 19.95 (*0-8442-2192-9*, 21929) NTC Contemp Pub Co.
McGuinness, Kenneth C. How to Take a Case Before the National Labor Relations Board. 4th rev. ed. LC 74-32565. 557p. reprint ed. pap. 172.70 (*0-608-16707-X*, 202679700052) Bks Demand.
McGuinness, Marci Lynn. Baltimore & Ohio Railroad. LC 98-87774. (Images of America Ser.). (Illus.). 128p. 1998. pap. 16.99 (*0-7524-1310-4*) Arcadia Publng.
McGuinness, Mary. Weave Me a Dream. 1996. pap. 1.78 (*0-8217-5558-7*) Kensgtn Pub Corp.
McGuinness, Mary C. The Time of Your Life. (Impact Ser.). 16p. 1996. 1.95 (*1-55612-852-5*, LL1852) Sheed & Ward WI.
McGuinness, Mary C. & Kleissler, Thomas A. Beginnings Human & World Issues. (Impact Ser.). 16p. 1996. pap. text 1.95 (*1-55612-865-7*, LL1865) Sheed & Ward WI.
McGuinness, Nora A. The Literary Universe of Jack B. Yeats. LC 90-2536. 288p. 1992. text 45.95 (*0-8132-0737-1*) Cath U Pr.
McGuinness, Patrick. Maurice Maeterlinck & the Making of Modern Theatre. LC 99-40052. 240p. 2000. text 70.00 (*0-19-815977-3*) OUP.
— Selected Writings: T. E. Hulme. LC 99-206995. 192p. 1998. pap. 19.95 (*1-85754-362-9*, Pub. by Carcanet Pr) Paul & Co Pubs.
McGuinness, Patrick, ed. see Plowert, Jacques.
***McGuinness, Paul.** A Guide to the Equity Markets of Hong Kong. LC 99-33006. 256p. 2000. pap. 28.95 (*0-19-592076-7*) OUP.
McGuinness, Peter J., jt. auth. see Shapiro, Irving.
McGuire. Esthetics in Comprehensive Denistry. 1997. text. write for info. (*0-7216-6011-8*, W B Saunders Co) Harcrt Hlth Sci Grp.
— Inside the U. S. Supreme Court. 2001. pap. 17.50 (*0-07-233731-1*) McGraw.
— Introduction to Criminology. LC 98-43712. 1999. pap. 58.95 (*0-534-53784-7*) Brooks-Cole.
— Monitoring Active Volcanoes: Strategies, Procedure & Techniques. 352p. 1994. 99.00 (*1-85728-036-9*, Pub. by UCL Pr Ltd) Taylor & Francis.
— Religion: The Social Context. 5th ed. (Sociology-Upper Level Ser.). 2001. pap. 31.00 (*0-534-54126-7*) Wadsworth Pub.
McGuire & Dalton, Joe. The Omega Missile, Vol. 1. 304p. 1998. pap. 6.99 (*0-312-96660-1*, Pub. by Tor Bks) St Martin.
McGuire, et al. Fear, 3 bks., Set. (Emotional Literacy Ser.). 1995. pap. 19.95 (*1-56844-023-5*) Enchante Pub.
McGuire, jt. auth. see Campbell, J.
McGuire, jt. auth. see Harvey, Wendy.
McGuire, jt. auth. see Neutens, James.
McGuire, Alistair, et al, eds. Providing Health Care: The Economics of Alternative Systems of Finance & Delivery. (Illus.). 312p. 1991. 75.00 (*0-19-828322-9*) OUP.
***McGuire, Anne.** Burnin' Rubber: Behind the Scenes in Stock Car Racing. (Illus.). (J). 2000. 14.40 (*0-606-18280-2*) Turtleback.
— History of NASCAR. (Race Car Legends Ser.). (Illus.). 64p. (gr. 4-7). 1999. pap. 7.95 (*0-7910-5680-5*) Chelsea Hse.
***McGuire, Anne.** History of NASCAR. (Illus.). (J). 2000. 14.45 (*0-606-18034-6*) Turtleback.
McGuire, Anne, ed. see Riebel, Jim.
McGuire, Anne, jt. ed. see Turner, John D.
***McGuire, B. G., et al, eds.** The Archaeology of Geological Catastrophes. (Geological Society Special Publication Ser.: No. 171). 440p. 2000. 132.00 (*1-86239-062-2*, Pub. by Geol Soc Pub Hse) AAPG.
McGuire, Barbara A. Foundations in Polymer Clay Design. LC 99-61264. 144p. 1999. pap. 21.95 (*0-87341-800-X*) Krause Pubns.
McGuire, Barbara E., jt. auth. see McArthur, Janice.
McGuire, Beverly, ed. see Lavielle, Gail.
McGuire, Beverly, ed. see Nesheim, Gisela.
***McGuire, Bill.** Apocalypse: A Natural History of Global Disasters. (Illus.). 2000. pap. 19.95 (*0-304-35209-8*) Continuum.
McGuire, Bill & Wheeler, Leslie. American Cultural Leaders: From Colonial Times to the Present. Ludwig, Richard et al, eds. LC 93-36284. 550p. 1993. lib. bdg. 65.00 (*0-87436-673-9*) ABC-CLIO.
— American Social Leaders: From Colonial Times to Present. Gerstle, Gary & McPherson, James M., eds. LC 93-3991. 500p. 1993. lib. bdg. 65.00 (*0-87436-633-X*) ABC-CLIO.
McGuire, Bob. The Gate, Vol. 1. 1997. mass mkt. 5.99 (*0-312-96278-9*) St Martin.
— Line. 1996. mass mkt. 6.50 (*0-312-95874-9*) St Martin.
— The Line. 1996. mass mkt. 5.99 (*0-614-20523-9*, St Martins Paperbacks) St Martin.
McGuire, Brenda & McGuire, John. Golf at the Water's Edge: Scotland's Seaside Links. LC 96-39206. (Illus.). 128p. 1997. bds. 17.95 (*0-7892-0323-5*) Abbeville Pr.
McGuire, Brian P. The Cistercians in Denmark: Their Attitudes, Roles, & Functions in Medieval Society. (Cistercian Studies: No. 35). 1982. 35.00 (*0-87907-835-9*) Cistercian Pubns.
— The Difficult Saint: Bernard of Clairvaux & His Tradition. (Cistercian Studies: No. 126). 302p. 1991. 32.95 (*0-87907-626-7*); pap. 13.95 (*0-87907-726-3*) Cistercian Pubns.
— Friendship & Community: The Monastic Experience, 350-1250. 1988. pap. 52.95 (*0-87907-985-1*) Cistercian Pubns.
McGuire, Brian P., tr. from FRE. Jean Gerson: Early Works. LC 98-19127. (Classics of Western Spirituality Ser.: Vol. 95). 480p. 1998. 34.95 (*0-8091-0498-9*); pap. 24.95 (*0-8091-3820-4*) Paulist Pr.
McGuire, C. B. Rational Investment Behavior in the Face of Floods. LC 79-135090. 151p. 1969. 29.00 (*0-403-04517-7*) Scholarly.
McGuire, C. J., ed. see Paxton, Lisa & Paxton, Cecil.
McGuire, Carl, jt. auth. see El Mallakh, Ragaei E.
McGuire, Charles. The Legal Environment of Business. 3rd ed. 616p. (C). 1998. per. 49.95 (*0-7872-4558-5*, 41455801) Kendall-Hunt.
***McGuire, Charles & Abitz, Diana.** Best Advice Ever for Teachers. 192p. 2000. 12.95 (*0-7407-1011-7*) Andrews & McMeel.
McGuire, Christine. Until Death Do Us Part. 1997. mass mkt. 6.50 (*0-671-53618-4*) PB.
— Until Justice Is Done. 1995. per. 6.50 (*0-671-53052-6*) PB.
***McGuire, Christine.** Until Me Meet Again. 1999. per. 6.99 (*0-671-02435-3*) PB.
McGuire, Christine. Until Proven Guilty. Rubenstein, Julie, ed. 384p. 1995. per. 6.50 (*0-671-75012-7*) PB.
— Until the Bough Breaks. 1998. mass mkt. 6.50 (*0-671-53619-2*) PB.
McGuire, Christine & Norton, Carla. Perfect Victim. 384p. 1989. mass mkt. 6.99 (*0-440-20442-9*) Dell.
McGuire, Christine, jt. auth. see Grimshaw, Roger.
McGuire, Christine H., et al. Handbook of Health Professions Education. LC 83-48160. (Jossey-Bass Higher Education Ser.). (Illus.). 571p. reprint ed. pap. 177.10 (*0-8357-4910-X*, 203784000009) Bks Demand.
McGuire, Deborah, et al. Cancer Pain Management. 2nd ed. (Nursing Ser.). 400p. 1995. 49.95 (*0-86720-725-6*) Jones & Bartlett.
McGuire, Deborah, ed. see Caruth, Jeannette.
McGuire, Deborah K. & McGuire, Donald E. Linking Parents to Play Therapy. LC 98-4117. 1998. 40.00 (*0-7657-0169-3*) Aronson.
McGuire, Diane K., ed. Beatrix Farrand's Plant Book for Dumbarton Oaks. LC 80-12169. (Illus.). 1980. pap. 15.00 (*0-88402-102-5*) Dumbarton Oaks.
McGuire, Diane K. & Fern, Lois, eds. Beatrix Jones Farrand, Fifty Years of American Landscape Architecture. LC 82-2439. (Colloquium on the History of Landscape Architecture Ser.: Vol. 8). (Illus.). 232p. 1982. 24.00 (*0-88402-106-8*) Dumbarton Oaks.
McGuire, Donald E., jt. auth. see McGuire, Deborah K.
McGuire, Donald T. Acts of Silence. LC 97-184907. (Altertumswissenschaftliche Texte und Studien: Bd. 33). (GER.). 256p. 1997. 50.00 (*3-487-10334-6*) G Olms Pubs.
McGuire, Ed. Guitar Fingerboard Harmony. 112p. 1976. pap. 14.95 (*1-56222-042-X*, 93398) Mel Bay.
McGuire, Edward, jt. ed. see Kursh, Elroy D.
McGuire, Eugene, ed. Software Process Improvement: Concepts & Practices. LC 98-55194. 200p. 1999. pap. text 49.95 (*1-878289-54-3*) Idea Group Pub.
McGuire, Eugene, jt. ed. see Larsen, Tor J.
McGuire, Francis A., ed. Computer Technology & the Aged: Implications & Applications for Activity Programs. LC 85-21999. (Activities, Adaptation & Aging Ser.: Vol. 8, No. 1). 119p. 1986. text 3.95 (*0-86656-481-0*) Haworth Pr.
McGuire, Francis A., et al, eds. Therapeutic Humor with the Elderly. LC 92-43465. (Activities, Adaptation & Aging Ser.: No. 17(1)). (Illus.). 116p. 1993. lib. bdg. 39.95 (*1-56024-310-4*) Haworth Pr.
McGuire, Francis A., et al. Leisure & Aging: Ulyssean Living in Later Life. 286p. 1995. text 15.00 (*1-57167-014-9*) Sagamore Pub.
McGuire, Francis G. Helicopters, 1948-1998: A Contemporary History. McKinnis, Marilyn F., ed. (Illus.). 254p. 1998. 45.00 (*0-9630326-5-8*) Helicopter Assn Intl.
McGuire, Frederick L. Psychology Aweigh! A History of Clinical Psychology in the United States Navy, 1900-1988. LC 90-279. 249p. 1990. 19.95 (*1-55798-086-1*) Am Psychol.
McGuire, G, jt. auth. see Miller, H.
McGuire, G. C., jt. auth. see Enns, Richard H.
McGuire, Gary. Microscopic & Surface Analysis. (C). 2001. pap. text 14.95 (*0-13-123217-7*) P-H.
— We're All Mad, You Know. Roberts, Craig, ed. & intro. by. (Illus.). 219p. (Orig.). 1996. pap. 11.95 (*0-9652385-0-4*) M Lee Pr.
McGuire, Gary E., ed. Characterization of Semiconductor Materials: Principles & Methods, Vol. 1. LC 89-30273. (Illus.). 330p. 1989. 109.00 (*0-8155-1200-7*) Noyes.
— Semiconductor Materials & Process Technology Handbook: For Very Large Scale Integration (VLSI) & Ultra Large Scale Integration (ULSI) LC 87-31529. (Illus.). 675p. 1988. 145.00 (*0-8155-1150-7*) Noyes.
McGuire, Gary E., jt. auth. see Holloway, Paul H.
McGuire, Gayle. Belfry Bat the Scaredy Cat. (Illus.). 24p. (J). (ps-3). 1997. 12.95 (*0-929005-95-3*, Pub. by Sec Story Pr); pap. 5.95 (*0-929005-93-7*, Pub. by Sec Story Pr) LPC InBook.
McGuire, George, jt. auth. see Enns, Richard H.
McGuire, J. & Harrison, Bruce. Employee Discipline & Discharge Policies. Vol. E1. text 82.00 (*0-8205-2409-3*) Bender.
McGuire, J. E. Tradition & Innovation: Newton's Metaphysics of Nature. LC 95-30104. (University of Western Ontario Series in Philosophy of Science: Vol. 5). 304p. (C). 1995. lib. bdg. 144.00 (*0-7923-3617-8*, Pub. by Kluwer Academic) Kluwer Academic.
McGuire, J. H. Electron Correlation Dynamics in Atomic Collisions. LC 96-44743. (Cambridge Monographs on Atomic, Molecular, & Chemical Physics Ser.: No. 8). (Illus.). 302p. (C). 1997. text 90.00 (*0-521-48020-5*) Cambridge U Pr.
McGuire, J. J., jt. ed. see Rustum, Y.
McGuire, J. T. Pumps for Chemical Processing. (Illus.). 304p. 1990. text 145.00 (*0-8247-8324-7*) Dekker.
McGuire, J. V., et al. Bridges: A Self-Esteem Activity Book for Students in Grades 4-6. LC 94-30011. (Illus.). 192p. (J). (gr. 4-6). 1994. pap. text 33.00 (*0-205-16504-4*, Longwood Div) Allyn.
McGuire, J. Victor. No Negatives: A Positive Guide to Successful Leadership. Prado, Jan, ed. 130p. (Orig.). (YA). (gr. 9-12). 1989. pap., student ed. 7.95 (*0-685-26846-2*) Spice Life CO.
— Takiya & Thunderheard's Life Garden. (Illus.). 38p. (J). (gr. 2-4). 1997. 16.95 (*0-9623300-6-X*) Spice Life CO.
McGuire, Jack B. Uncle Earl Deserved Better. LC 96-105077. (Illus.). 329p. (Orig.). 1995. pap. text 20.00 (*1-888042-00-1*) Good Readng.
McGuire, Jacqueline & Richman, Naomi. Pre-School Behavior Checklist (PBCL) 1988. 16.00 (*0-87879-639-8*); teacher ed., ring bd. 55.00 (*0-87879-638-X*); 6.00 (*0-685-44973-4*) Acad Therapy.
McGuire, James, ed. What Works: Reducing Reoffending - Guidelines from Research & Practice. LC 94-44564. (Offender Rehabilitation Ser.). 250p. 1999. pap. text 46.50 (*0-471-95686-4*) Wiley.
McGuire, James & Priestley, Philip. Life after School: A Social Skills Curriculum. (Illus.). 239p. 1981. pap. text 21.00 (*0-08-025193-5*, Pergamon Pr) Elsevier.
— Offending Behavior: Skills & Stratagems for Going Straight. LC 84-18395. 256p. 1985. text 32.50 (*0-312-58208-0*) St Martin.
***McGuire, James, et al.** Behaviour, Crime & Legal Processes: A Guide for Forensic Practitioners. LC 00-43283. 2000. pap. write for info. (*0-471-99869-9*) Wiley.
McGuire, James B. Getting Out of the Gray Areas of Christianity. Esarey, Victoria & Gauldin, Gloria, eds. 40p. 1997. pap. 7.00 (*0-9664498-0-0*) Berean Eternal.
McGuire, James B., jt. auth. see Clark, David R.
McGuire, James E. & Lee, Jasper S. Advertising & Display: Promotion in Agribusiness. (Career Preparation for Agriculture-Agribusiness Ser.). (Illus.). 1979. text 19.43 (*0-07-045129-X*) McGraw.
***McGuire, James E. & Tuchanska, Barbara.** Science Unfettered: A Philosophical Study in Sociohistorical Ontology. (Series in Continental Thought : No. 28). 472p. (C). 2000. pap. text 29.95 (*0-8214-1351-1*) Ohio U Pr.
— Science Unfettered: A Philosophical Study in Sociohistorical Ontology. (Series in Continental Thought : Vol. 28). 472p. (C). 2000. text 65.00 (*0-8214-1350-3*) Ohio U Pr.
McGuire, James E., jt. auth. see Bogen, James.
McGuire, James L., jt. auth. see Sholtzhauer, Tammi L.
McGuire, James P. Greek Texans. 2nd ed. (Texians & the Texans Ser.). (Illus.). 26p. 1984. pap. 4.95 (*0-86701-007-X*) U of Tex Inst Tex Culture.
— Hermann Lungkwitz: Romantic Landscapist on the Texas Frontier. (Illus.). 245p. 1983. 35.00 (*0-292-73026-8*) U of Tex Pr.
Mcguire, James W. Peronism Without Peron: Unions, Parties, & Democracy in Argentina. LC 96-41942. 1997. 49.50 (*0-8047-2831-3*) Stanford U Pr.
— Peronism Without Peron: Unions, Parties, & Democracy in Argentina. 1999. pap. text 22.95 (*0-8047-3655-3*) Stanford U Pr.
McGuire, Jean F. AIDS & the Construction of Meaning: Research=Care. (Health Care Policy in the United States Ser.). 250p. 1998. 60.00 (*0-8153-3130-4*) Garland.
McGuire, Jerry. Flagpole Dance. LC 90-6487. (Contemporary Poets Ser.). 80p. (Orig.). 1990. 15.00 (*0-89924-033-X*); pap. 8.00 (*0-89924-070-4*) Lynx Hse.
McGuire, Jerry, jt. ed. see Myrsiades, Kostas.
McGuire, Jerry L. Write Like a Pro! A Guide for Freelance Writers. (Illus.). 224p. (Orig.). (C). 1992. pap. 22.95 (*0-9632004-0-2*) LeRoy & Co.
— Writing for Magazines - Like a Pro! (Illus.). 220p. 1995. pap. text 23.95 (*0-9632004-1-0*) LeRoy & Co.
McGuire, Jim, photos by. Rusty Wolfe: Introducing Lacquer. (Illus.). 60p. 1998. pap. 30.00 (*0-9665446-0-9*) Finer Things.
McGuire, John. Basketry: The Nantucket Tradition. LC 89-83931. (Illus.). 144p. 1990. 24.95 (*0-937274-50-X*) Lark Books.
***McGuire, John.** Basketry: The Nantucket Tradition. 2000. pap. 17.95 (*1-887374-52-3*, Pub. by Lark Books) Sterling.
McGuire, John. Basketry: The Shaker Tradition. LC 87-83653. (Illus.). 144p. 1990. 24.95 (*0-937274-46-1*) Lark Books.
McGuire, John, et al. Politics of Violence: From Ayodhya to Behrampada. LC 96-35431. (Studies on Contemporary South Asia). 1996. 44.00 (*0-8039-9351-X*) Sage.
McGuire, John, jt. auth. see McGuire, Brenda.
McGuire, John E. Old New England Splint Baskets & How to Make Them. LC 85-61526. (Illus.). 100p. (Orig.). 1985. pap. 14.95 (*0-88740-045-0*) Schiffer.
McGuire, John E., jt. auth. see Freeman, Chester D.
McGuire, Judith. Diary of a Southern Refugee During the War. 29.99 (*0-87377-171-0*) GAM Pubns.
McGuire, Judith S. & Popkin, Barry M. Helping Women Improve Nutrition in the Developing World: Beating the Zero Sum Game. (Technical Papers: No. 114). 102p. 1990. pap. 22.00 (*0-8213-1415-7*, 11415) World Bank.
McGuire, Judith W. Diary of a Southern Refugee, During the War. LC 72-2614. (American Women Ser.: Images & Realities). 364p. 1974. reprint ed. 32.95 (*0-405-04468-2*) Ayer.
— Diary of a Southern Refugee During the War, by a Lady of Virginia. LC 95-519. xiv, 355p. 1995. pap. 12.00 (*0-8032-8223-0*, Bison Books) U of Nebr Pr.
McGuire, Kelly. Culture Change along the Eastern Sierra Nevada/Cascade Front Vol. IV: Secret Valley. fac. ed. (Far Western Anthropological Research Group, Inc. Ser.). (Illus.). 319p. (C). 1997. reprint ed. pap. text 33.75 (*1-55567-722-3*) Coyote Press.
— Culture Change along the Eastern Sierra Nevada/Cascade Front Vol. VI: Fort Sage Uplands & Spanish Springs Valley. fac. ed. (Far Western Anthropological Research Group, Inc. Ser.). 191p. (C). 1997. reprint ed. pap. text 20.63 (*1-55567-720-7*) Coyote Press.
McGuire, Kelly R. Test Excavations at CA-FRE-61, Fresno County, California. (Anthropology Occasional Papers in Anthropology: No. 5). (Illus.). 138p. (Orig.). (C). 1995. pap. 10.00 (*0-9632633-4-X*) CSU Bakerfld Mus.
McGuire, Kelly R. & Garfinkel, Alan P. Archaeological Investigations in the Southern Sierra Nevada: The Bear Mountain Segment of the Pacific Crest Trail. (Illus.). 319p. (C). 1980. reprint ed. pap. text 33.75 (*1-55567-430-5*) Coyote Press.
McGuire, Kenneth B. State of the Art in Community-Based Education in the American Community College. Harlacher, Ervin L., ed. LC 88-151056. 83p. reprint ed. pap. 30.00 (*0-7837-2482-9*, 204263800005) Bks Demand.
McGuire, Kevin. Building Outdoor Play Structures. LC 94-13704. (Illus.). 144p. 1994. 27.95 (*0-8069-0808-4*) Sterling.
— Wood on Wheels: Making Toys That Rock & Roll, Wiggle & Shake. LC 94-37136. (Illus.). 144p. 1995. pap. 16.95 (*0-8069-1286-3*) Lark Books.
— Woodworking for Kids: Forty Fabulous, Fun & Useful Things for Kids to Me. (Illus.). 160p. (J). 1994. pap. 14.95 (*0-8069-0430-5*) Sterling.
McGuire, Kevin T. The Supreme Court Bar: Legal Elites in the Washington Community. LC 93-3074. (Constitutionalism & Democracy Ser.). 320p. (C). 1993. text 40.00 (*0-8139-1449-3*) U Pr of Va.
McGuire, Kim. The Isish Wedding Book: Everything You Need to Plan a Wedding. (Illus.). 192p. 1995. pap. 18.95 (*0-86327-376-9*) Dufour.
McGuire, Kristen West. The Glory to Be Revealed in You: A Spiritual Companion to Pregnancy. LC 94-40880. 156p. 1994. pap. 8.95 (*0-8189-0721-5*) Alba.
McGuire, Leslie. The Bouncing-Quitely Lessons: Winnie the Pooh. (Comes to Life Bks.). 16p. (J). (ps-2). 1995. write for info. (*1-57234-053-3*) YES Ent.
— Busy Firefighter. LC 94-1402. (Random House Pictureback Ser.). (Illus.). (J). (gr. 4 up). 1996. pap. 3.25 (*0-679-85438-X*) Random.
***McGuire, Leslie.** Circles at the Circus: My First Book of Shapes. 16p. (J). 1999. reprint ed. 5.95 (*1-892374-20-X*) Weldon Owen.

M

M

McGuire, Leslie. Comes to Life Storyplayer (Phase 2) & Micky Mouse: The Eagle's Treasure. (Comes to Life Bks.). 16p. (J). (ps-2). 1995. write for info. (*1-57234-054-1*) YES Ent.

— Death & Illness. (The Family Ser.). (Illus.). 64p. (J). (gr. 7 up). 1990. lib. bdg. 17.95 (*0-86593-079-1*) Rourke Corp.

— Disney's Hercules. Stiener, Jeanette, ed. (Magic Touch Talking Bks.). (Illus.). (J). (ps-2). 1997. 19.99 (*1-888208-33-3*) Hasbro.

— The Eagle's Treasure: Mickey Mouse. (Comes to Life Bks.). 16p. (J). (ps-2). 1995. write for info. (*1-57234-052-5*) YES Ent.

— Good Night, Little Bear. (Little Hugs Bk.). (Illus.). 18p. (J). (gr. k-3). 1996. bds. 10.99 (*1-57584-014-6*, Pub. by Rdrs Digest) Random.

***McGuire, Leslie.** I Get Dressed: A Fun Sticker Book. (Illus.). 20p. (J). 1999. reprint ed. 7.95 (*1-892374-22-6*) Weldon Owen.

McGuire, Leslie. Jurassic Park: Guide to the Lost World. Sahler, John, ed. (Magic Touch Talking Bks.). (Illus.). (J). (ps-2). 1997. 19.99 (*1-888208-32-5*) Hasbro.

***McGuire, Leslie.** My Rattle Book. (Illus.). 12p. (J). 1999. 5.95 (*1-892374-14-5*) Weldon Owen.

McGuire, Leslie. Napoleon Bonaparte. (World Leaders Past & Present Ser.). (Illus.). 120p. (YA). (gr. 5 up). 1987. lib. bdg. 19.95 (*0-87754-554-5*) Chelsea Hse.

— Nightmares in the Mist. LC 92-46876. (Illus.). 40p. (J). (gr. k-4). 1994. 14.95 (*1-56844-003-0*) Enchante Pub.

— Nightmares in the Mist. 2nd rev. ed. Hoy, Gudrun & Martin, Bobi, eds. (Emotional Literacy Ser.). (Illus.). 40p. (J). (gr. k-5). 1996. 14.95 (*1-56844-103-7*) Enchante Pub.

— Sammy Saves the Day. (Play Along Ser.). 16p. (J). (ps-2). 1995. write for info. (*1-57234-060-6*) YES Ent.

— Suicide. (Troubled Society Ser.). (Illus.). 64p. (YA). (gr. 7 up). 1990. lib. bdg. 17.95 (*0-86593-069-4*) Rourke Corp.

***McGuire, Leslie.** Tucker over the Top. (Illus.). 40p. (J). (ps up). 2000. 7.99 (*0-525-46465-4*, Dutton Child) Peng Put Young Read.

McGuire, Leslie. Victims. LC 91-11041. (Women Today Ser.). 64p. (J). (gr. 5-7). 1991. lib. bdg. 17.95 (*0-86593-120-8*) Rourke Corp.

***McGuire, Leslie & Brunelle, Lynn.** Animal Singalong. (Illus.). 12p. (J). 1999. 5.95 (*1-892374-16-1*) Weldon Owen.

McGuire, Leslie, jt. auth. see Fisher-Price Staff.

McGuire, Lillian H. Uprooted & Transplanted: From Africa to America. LC 98-90757. 264p. 2000. 24.95 (*0-533-12916-8*) Vantage.

***McGuire, Linda.** Australian Services: Marketing & Management. 400p. 1999. 99.95 (*0-7329-5068-6*, Pub. by Macmill Educ); pap. 49.95 (*0-7329-5067-8*, Pub. by Macmill Educ) Paul & Co Pubs.

McGuire, Linda A. Scherenschnitte - Crossing America. (Illus.). 145p. 1998. spiral bd. 45.00 (*0-9670423-0-5*) Collect Choice Antiques.

McGuire, Lloyd H. Birth or Guthrie: Oklahoma's Run of 1889 & Life of Guthrie in 1889 (With Follow-up Through the 20th Century) LC 98-92266. (Illus.). 364p. 1998. mass mkt. 21.00 (*0-9671023-0-8*) L McGuire.

McGuire, M. & Townsend, C., eds. Periodontal Disease Management. (Orig.). 100p. (Orig.). 1994. pap. 65.00 (*0-9624699-5-5*) Amer Acad Periodontology.

McGuire, M. T., ed. The St. Kitts Vervet. (Contributions to Primatology Ser.: Vol. 1). 202p. 1974. 48.75 (*3-8055-1692-4*) S Karger.

***McGuire, Mark & Gormley, Michael S.** Moments in the Sun: Baseball's Briefly Famous. LC 99-11100. (Illus.). 247p. 1999. pap. 28.50 (*0-7864-0549-X*) McFarland & Co.

***McGuire, Mark & Gormley, Michael Sean.** The 100 Greatest Baseball Players of the 20th Century Ranked. (Illus.). 215p. 2000. pap. 30.00 (*0-7864-0914-2*) McFarland & Co.

McGuire, Martin C. Secrecy & the Arms Race: A Theory of the Accumulation of Strategic Weapons & How Secrecy Affects It. LC 65-22062. (Economic Studies: No. 125). (Illus.). 1990. 16.50 (*0-674-79665-9*) HUP.

McGuire, Mary. Polymer Claywork. (New Crafts Ser.). (Illus.). 96p. 1996. 15.95 (*1-85967-298-1*, Lorenz Bks) Anness Pub.

***McGuire, Mary, et al.** The Internet Handbook for Writers, Researchers & Journalists: 2000/2001 Edition. LC 99-56397. (Illus.). 242p. 2000. pap. text 19.95 (*1-57230-550-9*, C0550) Guilford Pubns.

McGuire, Mary, ed. see Eckhart, Frank.

McGuire, Meredith B. Religion: The Social Context. 2nd ed. 301p. (C). 1986. pap. write for info. (*0-534-07242-9*) Wadsworth Pub.

— Religion: The Social Context. 3rd ed. 340p. (C). 1991. mass mkt. 25.25 (*0-534-16968-6*) Wadsworth Pub.

— Religion: The Social Context. 4th ed. (C). 1996. pap. 44.95 (*0-534-50572-4*) Wadsworth Pub.

Mcguire, Meredith B. & Kantor, Debra. Ritual Healing in Suburban America. 335p. (C). 1988. text 45.00 (*0-8135-1312-X*); pap. text 18.00 (*0-8135-1313-8*) Rutgers U Pr.

McGuire, Meredith B., jt. auth. see Freund, Peter E.

Mcguire, Michael. The Ice Forest. LC 90-60883. 96p. (Orig.). 1990. pap. 9.95 (*0-910395-59-4*) Marlboro Pr.

***McGuire, Michael.** Plays by Michael McGuire. 198p. 1999. pap. 11.95 (*0-88145-160-6*) Broadway Play.

McGuire, Michael & Troisi, Alfonso. Darwinian Psychiatry. LC 98-2504. (Illus.). 360p. (C). 1998. text 45.00 (*0-19-511673-9*) OUP.

McGuire, Michael, jt. auth. see Hartman, Bob.

McGuire, Michael J. & Suffet, Irwin H., eds. Treatment of Water by Granular Activated Carbon. LC 82-22662. (Advances in Chemistry Ser.: No. 202). 600p. 1983. lib. bdg. 68.95 (*0-8412-0665-1*, Pub. by Am Chemical) OUP.

— Treatment of Water by Granular Activated Carbon. LC 82-22662. (Advances in Chemistry Ser.: Vol. 202). 616p. 1983. reprint ed. pap. 191.00 (*0-608-03506-8*, 206422500008) Bks Demand.

McGuire, Michael T. The Neurotransmitter Revolution: Serotonin, Social Behavior, & the Law. Masters, Roger D., ed. LC 92-49968. 272p. (C). 1993. 41.95 (*0-8093-1792-3*); pap. 21.95 (*0-8093-1801-6*) S Ill U Pr.

***McGuire, Mick.** The Games Guide: 101 Warm-Up Games for Coaches & Sports Leaders. 120p. 1999. pap. 38.00 (*1-897676-91-3*, Pub. by Nottingham Univ Pr) St Mut.

McGuire, Mike, jt. auth. see Hartman, Bob.

McGuire, Molly. Forever Yours. (American Romance Ser.: No. 436). 1992. per. 3.39 (*0-373-16436-X*, 1-16436-7) Harlequin Bks.

— My Prince Charming. (American Romance Ser.). 1993. per. 3.39 (*0-373-16484-X*, 1-16484-7) Harlequin Bks.

***McGuire, Nina.** Thomas Alva Edison: America's Amazing Inventor. (Illus.). 72p. 1999. pap. 14.95 (*1-892629-04-6*) Tail Tours.

McGuire, Nina. An Uncommon Guide to Florida: A Resident's Guide to the Real Florida. 2nd ed. LC 98-228161. (Illus.). 224p. 1997. pap. 16.95 (*0-9631241-9-6*) Tail Tours.

McGuire, Nina & Sammons, Sandra W. Jacqueline Cochran, America's Fearless Aviator. LC 97-141342. (Southern Pioneer Ser.). (Illus.). 72p. (Orig.). (J). (gr. 4 up). 1997. pap. 14.95 (*0-9631241-6-1*) Tail Tours.

McGuire, Nina, jt. auth. see Sammons, Sandra W.

McGuire, Nina L., ed. see Hall, Maggi S.

McGuire, O. R., ed. see Beck, James M.

McGuire, Patricia D. Lullaby of Broadway: A Biography of Al Dubin. (Illus.). 256p. 1983. 14.95 (*0-8065-0871-X*, Citadel Pr) Carol Pub Group.

McGuire, Patrick. Hungarian Texans. 312p. 1993. 23.95 (*0-86701-041-X*); pap. 14.95 (*0-86701-048-7*) U of Tex Inst Tex Culture.

McGuire, Patrick & McQuarie, Donald, eds. From the Left Bank to the Mainstream: Historical Debates & Contemporary Research in Marxist Sociology. LC 93-81354. 318p. (Orig.). 1994. text 37.95 (*1-882289-14-5*); pap. text 34.95 (*1-882289-13-7*) Gen Hall.

McGuire, Patrick L. Red Stars: Political Aspects of Soviet Science Fiction. LC 84-28099. (Studies in Speculative Fiction: No. 7). 170p. reprint ed. pap. 52.70 (*0-8357-1579-5*, 207050900097) Bks Demand.

McGuire, Paul. Breakthrough Manual. 320p. (Orig.). 1992. pap. 9.99 (*0-88270-658-6*) Bridge-Logos.

— Countdown to Armageddon, Vol. 1. 1999. pap. 12.99 (*0-88419-656-9*) Creation House.

— From Earthquakes to Global Unity: The End Times Have Begun. LC 95-78183. 224p. 1996. pap. 10.99 (*1-56384-107-X*) Huntington Hse.

***McGuire, Paul.** Heal Your Past & Change Your Marriage. LC 00-23251. 224p. 2000. pap. write for info. (*0-88419-689-5*) Creation House.

McGuire, Paula. AIDS. LC 97-22366. (Preteen Pressures Ser.). (YA). 1998. 24.26 (*0-8172-5025-5*) Raintree Steck-V.

— Alcohol. LC 97-22371. (Preteen Pressures Ser.). 1998. lib. bdg. 24.26 (*0-8172-5026-3*) Raintree Steck-V.

McGuire, Paula, ed. Nobel Prize Winners: Supplement, 1987-1991. LC 92-12197. 143p. 35.00 (*0-8242-0834-X*) Wilson.

McGuire-Pertusati. Toward a Second Dimension: A Sociology Reader. 2nd ed. 454p. (C). 1998. per. 53.95 (*0-7872-5098-8*, 41509801) Kendall-Hunt.

McGuire, Peter J. & Putzell, Sara M. A Guide to Technical Writing. 415p. (C). 1988. pap. text, teacher ed. 2.50 (*0-15-530328-7*) Harcourt Coll Pubs.

McGuire, Philip. He, Too, Spoke for Democracy: Judge Hastie, World War II, & the Black Soldier, 110. LC 87-24943. (Contributions in Afro-American & African Studies: No. 110). 171p. 1988. 55.00 (*0-313-26115-6*, MHD/, Greenwood Pr) Greenwood.

McGuire, Philip C. Shakespeare: The Jacobean Plays. LC 93-42847. (English Dramatists Ser.). 1994. text 39.95 (*0-312-10628-9*) St Martin.

McGuire, Philip C. & Samuelson, David A., eds. Shakespeare: The Theatrical Dimension. LC 77-78320. (Studies in the Renaissance: No. 3). 1979. lib. bdg. 34.50 (*0-404-16002-6*) AMS Pr.

McGuire, Phillip, compiled by. Taps for a Jim Crow Army: Letters from Black Soldiers in World War II. LC 93-1718. 320p. 1993. reprint ed. pap. 19.00 (*0-8131-0822-5*) U Pr of Ky.

McGuire, Randall H. Rancho Punta de Agua. (Archaeological Ser.: Vol. 57). (Illus.). 113p. 1977. 6.95 (*1-889747-24-6*) Ariz St Mus.

McGuire, Randall H., ed. Ethnology of the Indians of Northwest Mexico. LC 91-33940. (Spanish Borderlands Sourcebooks Ser.: Vol. 6). 512p. 1992. text 25.00 (*0-8240-0833-2*) Garland.

McGuire, Randall H. & Villalpando, Maria E. An Archaeological Survey of the Altar Valley, Sonora, Mexico. (Archaeological Ser.: No. 184). (Illus.). 222p. 1993. pap. 19.95 (*1-889747-49-1*) Ariz St Mus.

McGuire, Raymond, jt. auth. see Heyl, Monica.

McGuire, Richard. The Orange Book. LC 94-15031. 1994. 10.19 (*0-606-06640-3*, Pub. by Turtleback) Demco.

McGuire, Richard L. Passionate Attention: An Introduction to Literary Study. (C). 1973. pap. text 11.25 (*0-393-09324-7*) Norton.

Mcguire, Rick, jt. auth. see Fox, James.

***McGuire, Roxanne.** Channeling. (Complete Guides Ser.). (Illus.). 128p. 1999. pap. 6.95 (*965-494-095-7*, Pub. by Astrolog Pub) Assoc Pubs Grp.

McGuire, Sean, ed. see Woelfl, Genevieve.

McGuire, Steve, jt. ed. see Ackland, Len.

McGuire, Steven, jt. auth. see Hocking, Brian.

McGuire, Steven, jt. ed. see Ackland, Len.

McGuire, Sumiye O. & Davis, Lester A. Foreign Direct Investment in the U. S. An Update (1993): Review & Analysis of Current Developments. (Illus.). 275p. (Orig.). (C). 1994. pap. text 75.00 (*0-7881-0610-4*) DIANE Pub.

McGuire, Terrance P. & McGowan, Kathleen. Care for the Caregiver: A Guide for Staff in the Helping Professions. LC 90-62085. 54p. (Orig.). (C). 1991. pap. 8.95 (*1-55612-400-7*) Sheed & Ward WI.

McGuire, Therese J. & Naimark, Dana W., eds. State & Local Government Finance for the 1990's: A Case Study of Arizona. 500p. (C). 1991. pap. text. write for info. (*1-879286-01-7*) AZ Bd Regents.

McGuire, Thomas. Tooth Fitness: Your Guide to Healthy Teeth. (Illus.). 367p. 1998. pap. text 17.00 (*0-7881-5507-5*) DIANE Pub.

McGuire, Thomas, et al, eds. Indian Water in the New West. LC 93-15609. 241p. 1993. 38.00 (*0-8165-1392-9*) U of Ariz Pr.

***McGuire, Thomas J.** Battle of Paoli. LC 99-86679. 2000. write for info. (*0-8117-0198-0*) Stackpole.

McGuire, Thomas J. The Surprise of Germantown: Or, the Battle of Cliveden, October 4th, 1777. (Illus.). 121p. (C). 1995. pap. text 11.95 (*0-939631-77-6*) Thomas Publications.

McGuire, Thomas R. Mixed-Bloods, Apaches, & Cattle Barons: Documents for a History of the Livestock Economy on the White Mountain Reservation, Arizona. (Archaeological Ser.: Vol. 142). (Illus.). 227p. 1980. 13.95 (*1-889747-56-4*) Ariz St Mus.

— Politics & Ethnicity on the Rio Yaqui: Potam Revisited. LC 86-11445. (PROFMEX Ser.). 186p. 1986. 28.50 (*0-8165-0893-3*) U of Ariz Pr.

McGuire, Thomas R., jt. auth. see Gregory, David A.

***McGuire, Tim.** Gold of Cortes. 288p. 2000. mass mkt. 4.50 (*0-8439-4729-2*, Leisure Bks) Dorchester Pub Co.

— Nobility. 288p. 1999. mass mkt. 4.50 (*0-8439-4526-5*, Leisure Bks) Dorchester Pub Co.

McGuire-Turcotte, Casey A. How Honu the Turtle Got His Shell. (Publish-a-Book Ser.). (Illus.). 30p. (J). (gr. 1-6). 1991. lib. bdg. 22.83 (*0-8172-2783-0*) Raintree Steck-V.

McGuire, Virginia C. Voices under Water. 40p. (Orig.). 1997. pap. 8.00 (*1-886361-02-9*) Blue Light Pr.

McGuire, W. C., et al, eds. Volcano Instability on the Earth & Other Planets. (Geological Society Special Publications Classics Ser.: No. 110). (Illus.). viii, 390p. 1996. 125.00 (*1-897799-60-8*, 349, Pub. by Geol Soc Pub Hse) AAPG.

McGuire, W. J., jt. ed. see Firth, C.

McGuire, William. Poetry's Catbird Seat: The Consultantship in Poetry in the English Language at the Library of Congress, 1937-1987. LC 87-33876. 512p. 1988. 21.00 (*0-685-48152-2*, 030-000-00204-1) Lib Congress.

— Ralph Norton & the Norton Gallery of Art. (Illus.). 47p. 1994. pap. 8.00 (*0-943411-26-2*) Norton Gal Art.

McGuire, William, ed. see Burnham, John C.

McGuire, William, ed. see Freud, Sigmund.

McGuire, William, ed. see Freud, Sigmund & Jung, C. G.

McGuire, William, ed. see Jung, C. G.

McGuire, William C., II. After the Liberators: A Father's Last Mission, a Son's Lifelong Journey. LC 99-32505. (Illus.). 200p. 1999. pap. 16.95 (*1-887905-19-7*) Pkway Pubs.

McGuire, William D. 50 Urgent Things You Need to Do Before the Millennium: Protect Yourself, Your Family & Your Finances from the Upcoming Computer Crisis! LC 99-24076. 128p. 1999. mass mkt. 9.99 (*0-446-67566-0*, Pub. by Warner Bks) Little.

***McGuire, William J.** ALM for Credit Unions. 162p. 1999. pap. 179.00 (*1-889394-47-5*) Credit Union Execs.

McGuire, William J. Constructing Social Psychology: Creative & Critical Processes. LC 98-24906. 300p. 1999. pap. text 24.95 (*0-521-64672-3*) Cambridge U Pr.

— Constructing Social Psychology: Creative & Critical Processes. LC 98-24906. (Illus.). 448p. (C). 1999. text 59.95 (*0-521-64107-1*) Cambridge U Pr.

McGuire, William J., jt. ed. see Iyengar, Shanto.

McGuire, William L., ed. Hormones, Receptors, & Breast Cancer. LC 77-90595. (Progress in Cancer Research & Therapy Ser.: Vol. 10). 383p. 1978. 82.50 (*0-89004-261-6*) Lppncott W & W.

— Hormones, Receptors, & Breast Cancer. fac. ed. LC 77-90595. (Progress in Cancer Research & Therapy Ser.: No. 10). (Illus.). 383p. pap. 118.80 (*0-7837-7170-3*, 204712700005) Bks Demand.

McGuire, William L., et al, eds. Progesterone Receptors in Normal & Neoplastic Tissues. fac. ed. LC 77-72065. (Progress in Cancer Research & Therapy Ser.: No. 4). (Illus.). 357p. pap. 110.70 (*0-7837-7353-6*, 204716200005) Bks Demand.

McGuire, William L., jt. ed. see Hansen, Heine H.

McGuire, William L., jt. ed. see Henderson, I. Craig.

McGuire, William L., jt. ed. see Lepor, Herbert.

McGuire, William P. & Rowinsky, Erick K., eds. Paclitaxel in Cancer Treatment, No. 8. LC 95-2352. (Basic & Clinical Oncology Ser.: Vol. 8). (Illus.). 368p. 1995. text 145.00 (*0-8247-9307-2*) Dekker.

McGuire, William P., jt. auth. see Gershenson, David M.

McGuire, William T. & Anderson, H. The U. S. Healthcare Dilemma: Mirrors & Chains. LC 98-47752. 216p. 1999. 39.95 (*0-86569-275-0*, Auburn Hse) Greenwood.

***McGuire Worley, Sam.** Emerson, Thoreau & the Role of the Cultural Critic. (C). 2000. pap. text 18.95 (*0-7914-4826-6*) State U NY Pr.

— Emerson, Thoreau & the Role of the Cultural Critic. (C). 2000. text 57.50 (*0-7914-4825-8*) State U NY Pr.

***McGuire's Irish Pub Staff.** McGuire's Irish Pub Postcard Book. (Illus.). 30p. 1999. pap. text 9.95 (*1-56554-692-X*) Pelican.

McGuirk. Critical Essays on Robert Burns. large type ed. LC 98-30504. (Critical Essays Ser.). 316p. 1998. 49.00 (*0-7838-0045-2*, G K Hall Lrg Type) Mac Lib Ref.

McGuirk, Bernard. Latin American Literature: Symptoms, Risks, & Strategies of Poststructuralist Criticism. LC 96-17603. 272p. (C). 1997. 90.00 (*0-415-07755-9*) Routledge.

McGuirk, Bernard & De Oliveira, Solange R., eds. Brazil & the Discovery of America: Narrative, History, Fiction, 1492-1992. LC 95-49119. 1996. write for info. (*0-7734-8804-9*) E Mellen.

McGuirk, Bernard & Millington, Mark I., eds. Inequality & Difference in Hispanic & Latin American Cultures: Critical Theoretical Approaches. LC 94-47533. 184p. 1995. text 79.95 (*0-7734-9476-6*) E Mellen.

McGuirk, Bernard, jt. ed. see Cardwell, Richard A.

McGuirk, Carol, ed. see Burns, Robert.

McGuirk, Frank D., et al. Blueprints for Managed Care: Mental Healthcare Concepts & Structure. (Illus.). 79p. (C). 1996. reprint ed. pap. text 25.00 (*0-7881-3691-7*) DIANE Pub.

McGuirk, Frank D., jt. ed. see Sanchez, A. Marie.

McGuirk, James F., jt. auth. see Hall, Betty L.

McGuirk, Leslie. Tucker Flips! LC 99-19806. (Illus.). 32p. (J). (ps-3). 1999. 9.99 (*0-525-46259-7*, Dutton Child) Peng Put Young Read.

***McGuirk, Leslie.** Tucker off His Rocker. LC 99-48163. (Illus.). 40p. (ps-3). 2000. 7.99 (*0-525-46398-4*, Dutton Child) Peng Put Young Read.

McGuirk, Martin. Realistic Track Plans for O Gauge Toy Trains. LC 97-213018. (Illus.). 80p. (Orig.). 1997. pap. 16.95 (*0-89778-434-0*, 10-8215, Kalmbach Books) Kalmbach.

McGuirk, Martin J. New Haven Railroad along the Shoreline: The Thoroughfare from New York City to Boston. LC 99-162124. (Golden Years of Railroading Ser.). (Illus.). 128p. 1998. pap. 18.95 (*0-89024-344-1*, 01088, Kalmbach Books) Kalmbach.

McGuirk, Marty. N Scale Model Railroading: Getting Started in the Hobby. 1999. pap. text 18.95 (*0-89024-347-6*) Kalmbach.

McGuirk, Russell. Colloquial Arabic of Egypt. 320p. 1986. pap. 14.95 (*0-7100-9936-3*, A2559, Routledge Thoemms) Routledge.

— Colloquial Arabic of Egypt. 320p. 1988. 34.99 incl. audio (*0-415-00072-6*, Routledge Thoemms) Routledge.

— Colloquial Arabic of Egypt: Hermeneutics As Method, Philosophy, & Critique. 201p. 1986. pap. 14.95 (*0-415-05172-X*, Pub. by Tavistock) Routldge.

McGuirk, Stephanie, ed. see Allbritton, Cliff.

McGuirl, Thomas & Spezzano, Remy. God, Honor, Fatherland: A Photo History of Panzergrenadier Division Grossdeutschland on the Eastern Front 1942-1944. (Illus.). 226p. 1997. 49.95 (*0-9657584-0-0*, RZM BK-001) RZM Imports.

McGuirl, Thomas, jt. auth. see Feist, Uwe.

McGuirl, Thomas, jt. auth. see Williamson, Gordon.

McGuirt, Curtis R., ed. see Caron, D. Phillip.

McGuirt, Curtis R., ed. & intro. see Caron, D. Phillip.

McGuirt, Ronald T. Family Secrets: A History of the Lives & Appetites of the Family of Annie Pauline Walters & James William Crenshaw. (Illus.). xii, 508p. 1997. write for info. (*1-890644-11-0*) Union Cnty.

McGunnigle, William C. Cognitive-Behavioral Coaching Strategies for Children & Families. LC 98-4118. 1999. 25.00 (*0-7657-0172-3*) Aronson.

McGurk. Elizabethan Conquest of Ireland. LC 96-51934. 340p. 1997. 74.95 (*0-7190-4959-8*, Pub. by Manchester Univ Pr) St Martin.

McGurk, Harry, jt. ed. see Dickerson, John W. T.

McGurk, Holly G. The Eulogy as a Literary Form. 264p. 1999. 69.95 (*1-57309-380-7*) Intl Scholars.

McGurk, Jeanette. You Can Too: A Guide to Homestyle Cajun Cooking. 2nd ed. (Illus.). 170p. (C). 1989. reprint ed. pap. 9.95 (*0-9624251-0-9*) Cajun Pantry.

McGurk, John. The Tudor Monarchies, 1485-1603. LC 99-230078. (Perspectives in History Ser.). iv, 124p. (C). 1999. pap. 11.95 (*0-521-59665-3*) Cambridge U Pr.

McGurk, P., ed. The Chronicle of John of Worcester Vol. III: The Annals from 1067 to 1140, Vol. 3. (Medieval Texts Ser.). (Illus.). 408p. 1998. text 105.00 (*0-19-820702-6*) OUP.

McGurk, Patrick. Gospel Books & Early Latin Manuscripts. LC 98-5422. (Variorum Collected Studies Ser.: Vol. 606). (Illus.). 250p. 1998. text 103.95 (*0-86078-684-6*, BS2552.A3M373, Pub. by Ashgate Pub) Ashgate Pub Co.

McGurk, Patrick, jt. ed. see Darlington, R. R.

***McGurk, Steve.** Poems from the Heartland. 2000. pap. 10.95 (*0-533-13283-5*) Vantage.

McGurn, Barrett. America's Court: The Supreme Court & the People. LC 97-25254. (Illus.). 208p. 1997. 27.95 (*1-55591-263-X*) Fulcrum Pub.

— The Pilgrim's Guide to Rome: For the Millennial Jubilee Year 2000. LC 98-29027. (Illus.). 205p. 1999. 19.95 (*0-670-87627-5*) Viking Penguin.

McGurn, James, jt. auth. see Davidson, Alan.

McGurn, Jim, jt. auth. see Davidson, Alan.

McGurn, Larry. The Printer. 68p. 1981. pap. 3.50 (*0-939391-00-7*) B Woodley Pr.

McGurn, Patrick S. Confidential Proxy Voting. 118p. 1989. pap. 35.00 (*0-931035-73-2*) IRRC Inc DC.

McGurn, William, ed. Terrorist or Freedom Fighter? The Cost of Confusion. (C). 1990. 35.00 (*0-907967-83-3*, Pub. by Inst Euro Def & Strat) St Mut.

McGurrin, James. Bourke Cockran: A Free Lance in American Politics. LC 74-172219. (Right Wing Individualist Tradition in America Ser.). 1972. reprint ed. 28.95 (*0-405-00428-1*) Ayer.

An Asterisk (*) at the beginning of an entry indicates that the title is appearing for the first time.

McGurrin, Joseph, et al. Interstate Fisheries of the Atlantic Coast. Hamer, Paul, ed. LC 91-71535. (Illus.). 120p. (Orig.). 1991. pap. 9.95 (*0-9630072-0-3*) Atlan States MFC.

McGurrin, Martin C. Pathological Gambling: Conceptual, Diagnostic, & Treatment Issues. Smith, Harold H., Jr., ed. LC 91-50928. (Practitioner's Resource Ser.). 96p. 1992. pap. 16.45 (*0-943158-69-9*, PGCBP, Prof Resc Pr) Pro Resource.

McGurty, Mark, jt. ed. see Kimbrough, S. T., Jr.

McGushin, Patrick, ed. The Histories, Vol. I, Bks. i-ii. (Clarendon Ancient History Ser.). 286p. 1992. pap. text 29.95 (*0-19-872140-4*) OUP.

— Sallust: Bellum Catilinae. (Bristol Latin Texts Ser.). (LAT.). 205p. 1980. pap. 20.95 (*0-906515-19-X*, Pub. by Brist Class Pr) Focus Pub-R Pullins.

McGuy, Bruce. Even Santa Cries Sometimes. 64p. 1994. pap. 7.95 (*0-9642311-0-7*) Santas Publng.

— Even Santa Laughs Sometimes: A Collection of Humorous & Heart Warming Letters to Santa. (Santa Collection). (Illus.). (Orig.). 1995. pap. 7.95 (*0-9642311-1-5*) Santas Publng.

— What Color Is Santa. (Illus.). 64p. 1997. pap. 7.95 (*0-9642311-2-3*) Santas Publng.

McGwire, Michael & McDonnell, John, eds. Soviet Naval Influence: Domestic & Foreign Dimensions. LC 75-23982. (Special Studies). 698p. 1977. 95.00 (*0-275-90271-4*, C0271, Praeger Pubs) Greenwood.

***McGwire, Scarlett.** Censorship: Changing Attitudes, 1900-2000. LC 99-17832. (Twentieth Century Issues Ser.). 64p. 2000. 27.12 (*0-8172-5574-5*) Raintree Steck-V.

McHaffie. Life, Death & Decisions: Doctors & Nurses Reflect. LC 97-142928. 304p. 1997. pap. text 37.50 (*1-898507-55-4*) Buttrwrth-Heinemann.

McHaffie, jt. auth. see Cline.

***McHaffie-Gow, Bertha.** What Makes the Ladybug? (Illus.). 40p. (J). 2000. pap. 15.59 (*1-55212-340-5*) Trafford Pub.

***McHaffie, Natalie.** C-Growl: The Daring Little Airplane. (Illus.). 32p. (J). 1999. write for info. (*1-55125-015-2*) Vanwell Publ.

McHale. Normandale Community College Introductory Algebra Package. rev. ed. (C). 1995. 51.00 (*0-201-89516-1*, 15887) Addison-Wesley.

McHale, Anna E., ed. Phase Equilibria Diagrams Annual, 1993. 227p. 1993. pap. 63.00 (*0-944904-62-9*, PHAN93) Am Ceramic.

McHale, Anna E., et al, eds. Phase Diagrams for Ceramists Vol. X: Borides, Carbides & Nitrides. 475p. 1994. 150.00 (*0-944904-74-2*, PH10) Am Ceramic.

McHale, Anna E. & Roth, Robert S., eds. Phase Equilibria Diagrams XII: Oxides, Vol. 12. (Illus.). 398p. 1996. 150.00 (*1-57498-014-9*, PH12) Am Ceramic.

Mchale, Anna E., ed. see American Ceramic Society Staff.

McHale, Barbara, jt. auth. see Bartlett, Janet.

McHale, Barbara B., jt. auth. see Kerr, Thomas J.

McHale, Brian. Constructing Postmodernism. LC 92-16210. 320p. (C). 1993. pap. 25.99 (*0-415-06014-1*, A6018) Routledge.

— Post Modernist Fiction. 300p. 1987. 42.50 (*0-416-36390-3*, A0751) Routledge.

— Post Modernist Fiction. 300p. (C). 1987. pap. 25.99 (*0-415-04513-4*, A0755) Routledge.

McHale, D., tr. see Azencott, R. & Dacunha-Castelle, D.

McHale, D., tr. see Dacunha-Castelle, D. & Duflo, M.

McHale, Des. The Book of Kerryman Jokes. 50p. 1990. pap. 4.95 (*0-85342-466-7*) Dufour.

McHale, Elizabeth, ed. see Abraham, Doc & Abraham, Katy.

McHale, Elizabeth, ed. see Lutzen, Karl F. & Stevens, Mark.

McHale, Elizabeth, ed. see McRaven, Charles.

McHale, Frank, compiled by. Pieces That Have Won Prizes: Also Many Encore Pieces; Enlarged Edition. LC 79-39381. (Granger Index Reprint Ser.). 1977. reprint ed. 21.95 (*0-8369-6346-6*) Ayer.

McHale, Gillian. Don't Bug Me! Thatch, Nancy R., ed. LC 97-18802. (Books for Students by Students). (Illus.). 32p. (J). (gr. 3-5). 1997. lib. bdg. 15.95 (*0-933849-65-6*) Landmark Edns.

— The First Day. (Publish-a-Book Ser.). (Illus.). (J). (gr. 1-6). 1996. lib. bdg. 22.83 (*0-8172-4429-8*) Raintree Steck-V.

McHale, Hank. Actual Experiences of a CEO: How to Make Continuous Improvement in Manufacturing Succeed for Your Company. 160p. 1995. 24.00 (*0-87389-329-8*, H0886) ASQ Qual Pr.

McHale, James & Coburn, George. Contracting with the Federal Government. Vol. G7. text 82.00 (*0-8205-2402-6*) Bender.

***McHale, Jean, et al.** Law & Nursing. 2nd ed. (Illus.). 256p. 2000. pap. text 35.00 (*0-7506-4806-6*) Buttrwrth-Heinemann.

McHale, Jean V., et al. Health Care Law: Text, Cases, & Materials. LC 97-135153. 963 p. 1997. write for info. (*0-421-51180-X*) Sweet & Maxwell.

McHale, Jean V., jt. auth. see Tingle, John.

McHale, Jeanne L. Molecular Spectroscopy. LC 98-4506. 463p. 1998. 91.00 (*0-13-229063-4*) P-H.

McHale, John. The Expendable Ikon. 67p. 1984. 13.95 (*0-914782-54-1*) Buffalo Fine-Albrght-Knox.

McHale, John & McHale, Magda C. Basic Human Needs: A Framework for Action. LC 77-17100. (Illus.). 249p. 1978. 32.95 (*0-87855-272-3*) Transaction Pubs.

McHale, John E., Jr. Dr. Samuel A. Mudd & the Lincoln Assassination. LC 94-24551. (People in Focus Ser.). (Illus.). (YA). (gr. 5 up). 1995. 13.95 (*0-87518-629-7*, Dillon Silver Burdett); pap. 7.95 (*0-382-24963-1*, Dillon Silver Burdett) Silver Burdett Pr.

McHale, Kathryn. Comparative Psychology & Hygiene of the Overweight Child. LC 72-177027. (Columbia University. Teachers College. Contributions to Education Ser.: No. 221). reprint ed. 37.50 (*0-404-55221-8*) AMS Pr.

McHale, Magda C., jt. auth. see McHale, John.

McHale, Mark. The Magic of Losing Weight. (Illus.). iii, 130p. 1998. pap. 19.95 (*0-9664458-0-5*) BAM Enter.

McHale, Mary C., jt. auth. see McHale, Thomas R.

Mchale, Michael. Embedding PROLOG in Visual Basic & Delphi. 1998. pap. text 49.95 (*0-387-98427-5*) Spr-Verlag.

McHale, Michael J., jt. auth. see Romano, John F.

McHale, Thomas J. Applied Trigonometry. 416p. (C). 1984. pap. text 37.00 (*0-201-04723-3*) Addison-Wesley.

McHale, Thomas J. Applied Trigonometry with Math Anxiety. (C). 1997. 42.00 (*0-201-31220-4*) Addison-Wesley.

Mchale, Thomas J. Basic Mathematics: Programmed. 1992. pap. text. write for info. (*0-201-05696-8*) Addison-Wesley.

McHale, Thomas J. & Witzke, Paul T. Advanced Algebra. (Milwaukee Area Technical College Mathematics Ser.). 1972. pap. text 32.76 (*0-201-04633-4*) Addison-Wesley.

McHale, Thomas J. & Witzke, Paul T. Applied Algebra I. 463p. (C). 1979. pap. text 76.00 (*0-201-04767-5*) Addison-Wesley.

McHale, Thomas J. & Witzke, Paul T. Arithmetic Module Series: One Volume Non-Programmed Edition. 400p. (C). 1976. pap. text. write for info. (*0-201-04757-8*); student ed. write for info. (*0-318-50126-0*) Addison-Wesley.

— Arithmetic Modules. 125p. (C). 1975. pap. text 18.25 (*0-201-04751-9*); pap. text 33.53 (*0-201-04753-5*); pap. text 28.00 (*0-201-04754-3*); pap. text 15.16 (*0-201-04756-X*) Addison-Wesley.

— Basic Algebra. (Milwaukee Area Technical College Mathematics Ser.). 1971. pap. text 41.95 (*0-201-04625-3*) Addison-Wesley.

— Calculation & Calculators. 419p. (C). 1977. pap. text 76.00 (*0-201-04771-3*) Addison-Wesley.

— Technical Mathematics I. 680p. (C). 1988. pap. text 76.00 (*0-201-15408-0*) Addison-Wesley.

— Technical Mathematics II. (Illus.). 688p. (C). 1988. pap. text 67.00 (*0-201-15409-9*) Addison-Wesley.

— Test Booklet Calculus Milwaukee. 1977. pap. text, student ed. 5.50 (*0-201-04772-1*) Addison-Wesley.

McHale, Thomas J., et al. Applied Algebra II. 444p. (C). 1980. pap. text 76.00 (*0-201-04775-6*) Addison-Wesley.

— Intermediate Algebra: Programmed. LC 86-10918. 700p. 1986. pap. text 76.00 (*0-201-15880-9*) Addison-Wesley.

— Introduction to Algebra. 2nd ed. LC 85-11848. 528p. (C). 1986. pap. text 11.25 (*0-201-15888-4*) Addison-Wesley.

— Introductory Algebra: Programmed. 544p. (C). 1977. text. write for info. (*0-201-04747-0*) Addison-Wesley.

— Introductory Algebra: Programmed. 2nd ed. LC 85-11848. 560p. (C). 1986. pap. text 76.00 (*0-201-15887-6*) Addison-Wesley.

McHale, Thomas R. Pacific Rim Energy Demand & Capital Requirements in the 1990s. 20p. 1992. pap. 10.00 (*0-918714-32-X*) Intl Res Ctr Energy.

— Saudi Oil Policy & the Changing World Energy Balance. 20p. 1986. pap. 10.00 (*0-918714-09-5*) Intl Res Ctr Energy.

McHale, Thomas R. & McHale, Mary C. Early American-Philippine Trade: The Journal of Nathaniel Bowditch in Manila, 1796. (Monographs: No. 2). viii, 63p. 1962. 4.75 (*0-938692-16-X*) Yale U SE Asia.

McHale, Vincent & Skowronski, Sharon, eds. Political Parties of Europe, 2 vols. LC 82-15408. (Greenwood Encyclopedia of the World's Political Parties Ser.). (Illus.). 1400p. 1983. lib. bdg. 195.00 (*0-313-21405-0*, MPP/) Greenwood.

— Political Parties of Europe, 2 vols., Vol. 1. LC 82-15408. (Greenwood Encyclopedia of the World's Political Parties Ser.). (Illus.). xix, 700p. 1983. lib. bdg. 125.00 (*0-313-23804-9*, MPP/01) Greenwood.

— Political Parties of Europe, 2 vols., Vol. 2. LC 82-15408. (Greenwood Encyclopedia of the World's Political Parties Ser.). (Illus.). 1297p. 1983. lib. bdg. 100.00 (*0-313-23805-7*, MPP/02) Greenwood.

Mchallam, Andrew, jt. ed. see Frost, Gerald.

McHam, Sarah Blake, ed. Looking at Italian Renaissance Sculpture. LC 97-14906. (Illus.). 304p. (C). 1998. text 75.00 (*0-521-47366-7*) Cambridge U Pr.

— Looking at Italian Renaissance Sculpture. LC 97-14906. (Illus.). 304p. (C). 2000. pap. text 27.95 (*0-521-47921-5*) Cambridge U Pr.

***McHaney-Danner, Ruth.** What I Learned from God While Quilting. 2000. pap. text 8.99 (*1-57748-852-0*) Barbour Pub.

McHaney, Larry J., jt. auth. see Bernhardt, L. Jerry, Jr.

McHaney, Pearl A., ed. Eudora Welty: Writers' Reflections upon First Reading Welty. limited ed. LC 98-75334. 1999. 200.00 (*1-892514-17-6*) Hill St Pr.

McHaney, Pearl A., jt. auth. see Burger, Nash K.

McHaney, Pearl A., ed. see Morris, Willie, et al.

McHaney, Pearl A., ed. see Welty, Eudora.

McHaney, Roger. Computer Simulation: A Practical Perspective. (Illus.). 314p. (C). 1991. text 59.00 (*0-12-484140-6*) Acad Pr.

Mchaney, Thomas & Millgate, Michael. Santuary: Carbon Typescript. (William Faulkner Manuscripts). 384p. 1987. text 55.00 (*0-8240-6811-4*) Garland.

McHaney, Thomas, ed. see Faulkner, William.

McHann, Marjorie, ed. What Every Home Health Nurse Needs to Know: A Book of Readings. 200p. 1994. pap. 40.00 (*0-9640767-0-5*) Cnslts in Care.

McHann, Marjorie, ed. What Every Home Health Nurse Needs to Know 2: A Book of Readings. 200p. 1998. pap. 40.00 (*0-9640767-2-1*) Cnslts in Care.

McHardy, A. K., ed. Clerical Poll-Taxes of the Diocese of Lincoln, 1377-81. (Publications of the Lincoln Record Society: No. 81). (Illus.). 296p. (C). 1992. 45.00 (*0-901503-54-1*, Lincoln Record Soc) Boydell & Brewer.

— Royal Writs Addressed to John Buchingham, Bishop of Lincoln, 1363-1398: Lincoln Register 12B: A Calendar. LC 98-216875. 232p. 1997. 55.00 (*0-907239-58-7*, Canterbury & York Soc) Boydell & Brewer.

***McHardy, John.** Don't Pay for a Promise! A Survivor's Guide to Swindles & Deceptive Practices. LC 99-91858. 2000. 25.00 (*0-7388-1334-6*); pap. 18.00 (*0-7388-1335-4*) Xlibris Corp.

McHardy, John & Ludwig, Frank, eds. Electrochemistry of Semiconductors & Electronics: Processes & Devices. LC 91-46659. (Illus.). 359p. 1992. 98.00 (*0-8155-1301-1*) Noyes.

McHardy, John & Sawan, Samuel P., eds. Supercritical Fluid Cleaning: Fundamentals, Technology, & Applications. LC 97-44663. (Illus.). 290p. 1998. 109.00 (*0-8155-1416-6*, Noyes Pubns) Noyes.

McHardy, K. C., et al. Illustrated Cases in Acute Clinical Medicine. LC 93-14398. (Illus.). 1994. pap. text 29.00 (*0-443-04697-2*) Church.

— Illustrated Signs in Clinical Medicine. (Illus.). 168p. 1997. pap. write for info. (*0-443-05545-9*) Church.

***McHardy, Louis W., ed.** Family Violence/Legislative Update. 4th ed. 97p. (C). 1999. pap. text 20.00 (*0-7881-8547-0*) DIANE Pub.

McHardy, Louis W., ed. Family Violence/Legislative Update, Vol. 1. 100p. (C). 1999. reprint ed. pap. text 20.00 (*0-7881-4352-2*) DIANE Pub.

— Family Violence/Legislative Update, Vol. 2. 96p. (C). 1999. reprint ed. text 20.00 (*0-7881-4366-2*) DIANE Pub.

***McHardy, Stuart.** Druidesses: The Quest for the Nine Maidens. 256p. 2000. pap. 19.95 (*0-946487-66-9*) Luath Pr Ltd.

— Edinburgh & Leith Pub Guide. (Illus.). 125p. 2000. pap. 9.95 (*0-946487-80-4*, Pub. by Luath Pr Ltd) Midpt Trade.

— Scotland: Myth, Legend & Folklore. 160p. 2000. 14.95 (*0-946487-69-3*) Luath Pr Ltd.

McHardy, Stuart, ed. see Telfer, Glen.

McHarg, Ian L. Design With Nature. (Series in Sustainable Design). 208p. 1995. pap. 49.95 (*0-471-11460-X*) Wiley.

— A Quest for Life: An Autobiography. LC 95-50489. (Illus.). 448p. 1996. 34.95 (*0-471-08628-2*) Wiley.

McHarg, Ian L. & Steiner, Friederick R. To Heal the Earth: Selected Writings of Ian McHarg. LC 98-3337. 310p. 1998. text 34.95 (*1-55963-573-8*) Island Pr.

McHargue, Carl, ed. Synthesis & Properties of Advanced Materials. LC 96-41137. 304p. (C). 1996. text 191.50 (*0-7923-9816-5*) Kluwer Academic.

McHargue, Carl J., et al, eds. Structure-Property Relationships in Surface-Modified Ceramics. (C). 1989. text 255.50 (*0-7923-0310-5*) Kluwer Academic.

McHargue, George. Beastie. 1992. 17.95 (*0-385-30721-7*) Doubleday.

McHargue, Georgess. Meet the Werewolf. LC 75-34046. (Illus.). 80p. (J). (gr. 2-5). 1976. 11.95 (*0-397-31662-3*) HarpC Child Bks.

— Meet the Witches. LC 83-48446. (Eerie Ser.). (Illus.). 128p. (J). (gr. 4-7). 1984. 11.95 (*0-397-32071-X*); lib. bdg. 11.89 (*0-397-32072-8*) HarpC Child Bks.

McHarris, Steve, ed. see Westfall, Douglas P.

McHarris, W., ed. Exotic Nuclear Spectroscopy. (Illus.). 668p. 1991. 145.00 (*0-306-43882-8*, Plenum Trade) Perseus Pubng.

McHarry, Hugh, compiled by. General & Everyname Index to the History of Hancock Co., IL (1880) 60p. (Orig.). 1989. pap. 6.50 (*0-9623531-0-8*) H McHarry.

McHattie, Andrew. The Investor's Guide to Warrants: Capitalize on the Fastest Growing Sector of the Stock Market, 2E. LC 95-218650. 334p. 1996. 45.00 (*0-273-61241-7*) F T P-H.

McHattie, Grace. Going Live! Cat Book. (Illus.). 94p. (YA). 1992. pap. 3.95 (*0-563-20880-5*, Pub. by BBC) Parkwest Pubns.

McHattie, Grace, ed. see Neilson, M.

McHatton, Jon. The Shepherding Flock: The Church Beyond 2000 A. D. 128p. 1999. pap. 8.95 (*0-89228-131-6*) Impact Christian.

McHatton, Robert J. Total Telemarketing: Complete Guide to Increasing Sales & Profits. LC 87-21547. 246p. 1988. 49.95 (*0-471-62754-2*); pap. 16.95 (*0-471-62755-0*) Wiley.

McHedlidze, G. A. Fossil Cetacea of the Caucasus. Rao, P. M., tr. (Russian Translation Ser.: No. 68). (Illus.). 150p. (C). 1989. text 91.00 (*90-6191-933-9*, Pub. by A A Balkema) Ashgate Pub Co.

— General Features of the Paleobiological Evolution of Cetacea. Chakravarty, R., tr. from RUS. (ENG.). 180p. (C). 1984. text 97.00 (*90-6191-438-8*, Pub. by A A Balkema) Ashgate Pub Co.

Mchedlishvili, G. I., et al, eds. Brain Edema: A Pathogenetic Analysis. 365p. (C). 1986. 120.00 (*963-05-4378-8*, Pub. by Akade Kiado) St Mut.

Mchedlishvili, G. I., et al. Brain Blood Supply. 320p. (C). 1977. 54.00 (*963-05-1130-4*, Pub. by Akade Kiado) St Mut.

— Regulation of Cerebral Circulation: Proceedings of the 4th Tbilisi Symposium on Cerebral Circulation, Tbilist, 19-21 April, 1978. 266p. (C). 1979. 60.00 (*963-05-2209-8*, Pub. by Akade Kiado) St Mut.

Mchedlishvili, George I. Arterial Behavior & Blood Circulation of the Brain. Bevan, John A., tr. from RUS. (Illus.). 354p. (C). 1986. text 132.00 (*0-306-10985-9*, Kluwer Plenum) Kluwer Academic.

Mchedlishvili, Georgii I. Vascular Mechanisms of the Brain. LC 70-141241. (RUS.). 127p. reprint ed. pap. 39.40 (*0-608-30228-7*, 202068400018) Bks Demand.

McHees, Nectaria, tr. see Vladimirov, Artemy.

McHeffey, Timothy. Juggling the Journey Vol. 1: 35 Unchanging Keys to Effective Living (at Work & Home) LC 96-75596. 160p. (Orig.). 1996. pap. 12.95 (*0-9651133-0-2*) IBE Pubng.

Mchels, Greg, ed. Governments of Missouri, 1985. (Governments of Your State Ser.). 1984. 120.00 (*1-55507-059-0*); text 150.00 (*0-317-38121-0*) Municipal Analysis.

McHenry. Adobe: Build It Yourself. 2nd rev. ed. LC 85-8432. (Illus.). 158p. 1985. pap. 23.95 (*0-8165-0948-4*) U of Ariz Pr.

— Adobe & Rammed Earth Buildings: Design & Construction. LC 89-5053. (Illus.). 217p. 1989. reprint ed. pap. 27.50 (*0-8165-1124-1*) U of Ariz Pr.

McHenry & Baker Harris Staff. 101 Classic Homes of the Twenties: Floor Plans & Photographs. LC 99-15551. 107p. 1999. text 9.95 (*0-486-40731-4*) Dover.

McHenry County Illinois Genealogical Society Staff, jt. auth. see Sullivan, Gary L.

McHenry, Dean E., Jr. Limited Choices: The Political Struggle for Socialism in Tanzania. LC 94-14623. 288p. 1994. lib. bdg. 49.95 (*1-55587-429-0*) L Rienner.

McHenry, Dean E. The Third Force in Canada: The Cooperative Commonwealth Federation,1932-1948. LC 76-2061. 351p. 1976. reprint ed. lib. bdg. 75.00 (*0-8371-8767-2*, MCTF, Greenwood Pr) Greenwood.

— Ujamaa Villages in Tanzania: A Bibliography. 69p. 1981. write for info. (*91-7106-187-8*, Pub. by Nordic Africa) Transaction Pubs.

McHenry, Dean E., Jr., jt. auth. see Manzo, Kate.

McHenry, Deni M. Donald Baechler. (Illus.). 14p. (Orig.). 1993. pap. 5.00 (*0-914489-12-7*) Univ Miss-KC Art.

McHenry, Donald. United States Firms in South Africa. (African Humanities Ser.). 74p. (Orig.). 1975. pap. text 4.00 (*0-941934-15-2*) Indiana Africa.

McHenry, Ellen J. Little Tropical Fish Coloring Book. (Illus.). (J). (gr. k-3). 1994. pap. 1.00 (*0-486-27951-0*) Dover.

— Music Activity Book. 1996. pap. 2.95 (*0-486-29079-4*) Dover.

McHenry, Harry I. Nondestructive Characterization of Reactor Pressure Vessel Steels: A Feasibility Study. 104p. 1998. per. 12.00 (*0-16-056741-6*) USGPO.

McHenry, Harry I. & Potter, John M., eds. Fatigue & Fracture Testing of Weldments, STP 1058. LC 90-251. (Special Technical Publication (STP) Ser.). (Illus.). 299p. 1990. text 69.00 (*0-8031-1277-7*, STP1058) ASTM.

McHenry, Hugh L. A Laboratory Manual for Computer Literacy. 138p. 1996. spiral bd. 22.95 (*0-7872-2081-7*) Kendall-Hunt.

— Manual for Computer Literacy. 200p. (C). 1995. spiral bd. 14.95 (*0-7872-1048-X*) Kendall-Hunt.

McHenry, James. Sidelight on History. LC 75-140875. (Eyewitness Accounts of the American Revolution Ser.). 1971. reprint ed. 15.95 (*0-405-01225-X*) Ayer.

McHenry, Janet. Caught in the Act. 48p. (J). 1996. mass mkt. 3.99 (*0-7814-0256-5*) Lion USA.

— Mission Impossible. 48p. (J). 1996. mass mkt. 3.99 (*0-7814-0255-7*) Chariot Victor.

McHenry, Janet H. And the Winner Is.... Reck, Sue, ed. LC 94-6636. (Golden Rule Duo Ser.). 48p. (J). (gr. 2-4). 1994. pap. 3.99 (*0-7814-0170-4*, Chariot Bks) Chariot Victor.

— Mystery at the Fairgrounds. LC 96-50884. (Annie Shepard Mysteries Ser.). (J). 1997. pap. 4.99 (*1-56476-566-0*) Chariot Victor.

— Mystery at the Old Stamp Mill, Vol. 3. LC 96-51183. (Annie Shepard Mysteries Ser.: Vol. 3). 129p. (J). (gr. 3-7). 1997. pap. 4.99 (*0-7814-1547-0*) Chariot Victor.

— Secret of the Locked Trunk. LC 96-49818. (Annie Shepard Mysteries Ser.). (J). 1997. pap. 4.99 (*1-56476-567-9*) Chariot Victor.

— Time Out! (Golden Rule Duo Ser.). (Illus.). 48p. (Orig.). (J). (gr. 2-5). 1995. pap. 2.99 (*0-7814-0173-9*) Chariot Victor.

— Trick 'n Trouble. Reck, Sue, ed. LC 94-6635. (Golden Rule Duo Ser.). 48p. (J). (gr. 2-4). 1994. pap. 3.99 (*0-7814-0171-2*, Chariot Bks) Chariot Victor.

McHenry, Jeffrey J., jt. auth. see McKenna, D. Douglas.

McHenry, Keith, jt. auth. see Butler, C. T. Lawrence.

McHenry, Lauren, ed. see Burns, John.

McHenry, Lawrence C., Jr. Garrison's History of Neurology. (Illus.). 568p. 1969. 92.95 (*0-398-01261-X*); pap. 65.95 (*0-398-06276-5*) C C Thomas.

McHenry, Leemon B. Whitehead & Bradley: A Comparative Analysis. LC 91-12725. (SUNY Series in Philosophy). 213p. (C). 1991. pap. text 21.95 (*0-7914-0916-3*) State U NY Pr.

— Whitehead & Bradley: A Comparative Analysis. LC 91-12725. (SUNY Series in Philosophy). 213p. (C). 1991. text 64.50 (*0-7914-0915-5*) State U NY Pr.

***McHenry, Mary.** The Emotional Feeling of a Poet. 1999. pap. write for info. (*1-58235-042-6*) Watermrk Pr.

McHenry, Paul G., Jr. The Adobe Story: A Global Treasure. (Illus.). 124p. 2000. pap. 18.95 (*0-8263-1921-1*) U of NM Pr.

***McHenry, Paul T., III.** Code Name: Antidote. LC 99-87462. 336p. 2000. pap. 12.99 (*0-8054-2083-5*) Broadman.

McHenry, Petei. The History of Valley Center, California: The Homestead Years, 1860-1900. (Illus.). 150p. 1997. 50.00 (*0-9660789-0-X*) GP Mkting.

— The History of Valley Center, California: The Homestead Years, 1860-1900, Vol. 1. rev. ed. (Illus.). 175p. 1998. pap. 14.95 (*0-9660789-1-8*) GP Mkting.

McHenry, Poke, pseud & Smith, Vic. Early Poke: A Great Southern Humorist Looks at Life's Pitfalls & Pinnacles. (Illus.). 352p. 1994. 23.95 (*0-9630463-4-9*) S & D.

***McHenry, Raymond.** McHenry's Quips, Quotes & Other Notes. 2000. 17.97 (*1-56563-462-4*) Hendrickson MA.

M

McHenry, Raymond. Something to Think About: Motivational & Inspirational Anecdotes. 434p. 1998. 19.95 (*1-56563-360-1*) Hendrickson MA.

McHenry, Robert. Encyclopedia Britannica, 32 vols. 1997th ed. LC 95-62057. (Illus.). 1996. 995.00 (*0-85229-633-9*) Ency Brit Inc.

McHenry, Robert, ed. Encyclopedia Britannica, 1998, 32 vols., Set. 15th rev. ed. (Illus.). 1997. 8.95 (*0-85229-663-0*) Ency Brit Inc.

— Famous American Women: A Biographical Dictionary from Colonial Times to the Present. 1984. 25.75 (*0-8446-6096-5*) Peter Smith.

— Famous American Women: A Biographical Dictionary from Colonial Times to the Present. (Americana Ser.). 482p. 1983. reprint ed. pap. 13.95 (*0-486-24523-3*) Dover.

— Webster's American Military Biographies. 1990. 25.75 (*0-8446-6143-0*) Peter Smith.

— Webster's American Military Biographies. LC 84-8004. 548p. 1984. reprint ed. pap. 14.95 (*0-486-24758-9*) Dover.

McHenry, Robert, ed. see Fujimura, Thomas H.

McHenry, Robert D., ed. The New Encyclopedia Britannica. (Illus.). 31919p. 1994. 1599.00 (*0-85229-571-5*) Ency Brit Inc.

McHenry, Robert W., ed. Contexts No. 3: Absalom & Achitophel. LC 84-24160. (Contexts Ser.: No. 3). (Illus.). xiii, 283p. (C). 1986. lib. bdg. 39.50 (*0-208-01845-X*, Archon Bks) Shoe String.

McHenry, Roy C. & Roper, Walter F. Smith & Wesson Hand Guns. 1994. reprint ed. 32.00 (*1-879356-35-X*) Wolfe Pub Co.

McHenry, Ruth W., ed. Ends & Means: The National Conference on Continuing Education in Nursing, 1970. LC 70-157408. (Notes & Essays Ser.: No. 69). 1971. pap. 2.50 (*0-87060-041-9*, NES 69) Syracuse U Cont Ed.

***McHenry, Sherene.** Career & Self-Exploration Guide. 126p. (C). 1999. pap. text 33.95 (*0-7872-6308-7*, 41630801) Kendall-Hunt.

McHenry, Sherry, jt. auth. see L'Abate, Luciano.

McHeyman, Josiah. States & Illegal Practices. 1999. pap. text 22.50 (*1-85973-262-3*) Berg Pubs.

McHeyman, Josiah, ed. States & Illegal Practices. 288p. 1999. 65.00 (*1-85973-257-7*, Pub. by Berg Pubs) NYU Pr.

M'Cheyne, R. M. Sermons of R. M. M'Cheyne. 1985. reprint ed. pap. 7.50 (*0-85151-165-1*) Banner of Truth.

McHoes, Ann, jt. auth. see Flynn, Ida M.

Mchombo, Sam A., ed. Theoretical Aspects of Bantu Grammar. LC 93-29496. (CSLI Lecture Notes Ser.: No. 38). 1993. 69.95 (*0-937073-73-3*); pap. 24.95 (*0-937073-72-5*) CSLI.

McHorney, Chris, jt. auth. see Bates, Brian.

McHose, Allen I. Teachers Dictation Manual. (Eastman School of Music Ser.). 29.95 (*0-89197-437-7*); pap. text 12.95 (*0-89197-960-3*) Irvington.

McHose, Andre. Manufacturing Development Applications: Guidelines for Attaining Quality & Productivity. 1993. 29.95 (*0-89806-122-9*, DEVAPP) Eng Mgmt Pr.

— Manufacturing Development Applications: Guidelines for Attaining Quality & Productivity. 275p. 1992. 45.00 (*1-55623-572-0*, Irwn Prfssnl) McGraw-Hill Prof.

McHoul, A. W. & Grace, Wendy. A Foucault Primer: Discourse, Power & the Subject. LC 97-5385. 1997. text 40.00 (*0-8147-5523-2*); pap. text 14.00 (*0-8147-5480-5*) NYU Pr.

McHoul, Alec. Semiotic Investigations: Towards an Effective Semiotics. LC 95-43854. (Stages Ser.). (Illus.). xxiii, 250p. 1996. text 45.00 (*0-8032-3191-1*) U of Nebr Pr.

McHoul, Alec & Grace, Wendy. A Foucault Primer: Discourse, Power & the Subject. (Interpretations Ser.). 136p. 1993. pap. 19.95 (*0-522-84577-0*, Pub. by Melbourne Univ Pr) Paul & Co Pubs.

McHoul, Alec & Wills, David. Writing Pynchon: Strategies in Fictional Analysis. 256p. 1990. 29.95 (*0-252-01700-5*) U of Ill Pr.

McHoul, Lilian. Wild Flowers of Marin: A Layman's Handbook. LC 79-51455. (Illus.). 1979. pap. 4.95 (*0-912908-08-4*) Tamal Land.

McHoy, Peter. The American Practical Gardening Encyclopedia: The Complete Step-by-Step Guide to Successful Gardening, from Designing, Planning & Planting, to Year-Round Maintenance Tasks. (Illus.). 256p. 1997. 30.00 (*1-85967-354-6*, Lorenz Bks) Anness Pub.

— Best Plants for Your Garden. LC 98-5058. (Illus.). 256p. 1998. 12.99 (*1-57145-137-4*, Thunder Bay) Advantage Pubs.

Mchoy, Peter. Cats. 1988. 6.98 (*1-55521-218-2*) Bk Sales Inc.

***McHoy, Peter.** Complete Garden Planner. (Practical Handbook Ser.). (Illus.). 2000. pap. 14.95 (*0-7548-0560-3*, Lorenz Bks) Anness Pub.

McHoy, Peter. Complete Guide to Gardening: Practical Handbook. 1999. pap. text 12.95 (*0-7548-0001-6*, Lorenz Bks) Anness Pub.

***McHoy, Peter.** Complete Houseplant Bible: The Essential Guide to Successful Indoor Gardening. (Illus.). 2000. pap. 14.95 (*0-7548-0469-0*, Lorenz Bks) Anness Pub.

— Design Solutions for Small Gardens. LC 99-57135. (Garden Factfile Ser.). (Illus.). 112p. (gr. 8). 2000. spiral bd. 12.95 (*0-7370-0607-2*) T-L Custom Pub.

— Essential Rose Garden. 96p. 2000. pap. 14.95 (*0-7548-0557-3*) Anness Pub.

McHoy, Peter. The Essential Rose Garden: The Complete Guide to Growing, Caring For & Maintaining Roses. 1998. 9.98 (*1-84038-071-3*) Hermes Hse.

— Garden Ornaments & Statuary. (Gardening by Design Ser.). (Illus.). 80p. 1987. 14.95 (*0-88162-243-5*, Pub. by WrLock) Sterling.

***McHoy, Peter.** Gardening Book: A Practical Guide to Creating a Beautiful Garden, from Design & Planting. (Illus.). 256p. 2000. pap. 19.95 (*0-7548-0594-8*, Lorenz Bks) Anness Pub.

— Gardening Handbook. (Illus.). 2000. pap. 8.95 (*1-55285-079-X*) Carlton Bks Ltd.

McHoy, Peter. Gardening Through the Year. (Illus.). 160p. 1995. 15.98 (*0-8317-3869-3*) Smithmark.

***McHoy, Peter.** Growing Roses & How to Arrange & Use Them. 2000. pap. 19.95 (*1-84215-025-1*) Anness Pub.

McHoy, Peter. Houseplant Identifier: Practical Handbook. 1999. pap. text 9.95 (*0-7548-0005-9*, Lorenz Bks) Anness Pub.

— Low-Maintenance Gardening: Beautiful Gardens in Half-An-Hour a Week. 1998. pap. text 12.95 (*1-85967-698-7*, Lorenz Bks) Anness Pub.

***McHoy, Peter.** Making the Most of a Small Garden. 160p. 2000. pap. 14.95 (*1-84215-051-0*) Anness Pub.

— Plan a Perfect Garden: Garden Design Made Simple, from Planning & Planting to Creating Special Gardens. (Illus.). 2000. 14.95 (*0-7548-0039-3*, Lorenz Bks) Anness Pub.

— Practical Garden Companion: How to Design, Plan & Create the Perfect Garden. (Illus.). 2000. 40.00 (*1-85967-922-6*, Lorenz Bks) Anness Pub.

— Practical Garden Companion: How to Design, Plan & Create the Perfect Garden. (Illus.). 2000. 40.00 (*1-84038-351-8*) Hermes Hse.

McHoy, Peter. Pruning: A Practical Guide. (Illus.). 240p. 1993. 35.00 (*1-55859-634-8*) Abbeville Pr.

— Pruning: The Complete Guide to Perfect Pruning. (Illus.). 96p. 1997. pap. 12.95 (*1-85967-463-1*, Lorenz Bks) Anness Pub.

***McHoy, Peter.** Rock & Water Garden. (Illus.). 2000. pap. 12.95 (*0-7548-0289-2*, Lorenz Bks) Anness Pub.

— Sensonal Flower Garden: A Practical Guide to Gardening Throughout the Year. (Illus.). 2000. pap. 12.95 (*0-7548-0287-6*, Lorenz Bks) Anness Pub.

— Sensonal Kitchen Garden: A Practical Guide to Gardening Throughout the Year. (Illus.). 2000. pap. 12.95 (*0-7548-0288-4*, Lorenz Bks) Anness Pub.

McHoy, Peter. Spring Bulbs. (The New Plant Library). (Illus.). 64p. 1998. 9.95 (*1-85967-596-4*, Lorenz Bks) Anness Pub.

— The Ultimate Garden Planner. (Illus.). 256p. 1998. 24.95 (*1-85967-577-8*, Lorenz Bks) Anness Pub.

***McHoy, Peter.** Weekend Gardener: Successful Garden Maintenance in Just Half an Hour a Week. (Illus.). 2000. 14.95 (*0-7548-0040-7*, Lorenz Bks) Anness Pub.

McHoy, Peter, et al. Practical Small Gardening: The Complete Step-by-Step Guide to Planning, Planting & Maintaining a Small Garden. (Illus.). 192p. 1997. pap. 16.95 (*1-85967-384-8*, Lorenz Bks) Anness Pub.

McHoy, Peter, ed. see Mikolajski, Andrew.

McHugh. Employee Labor Relations. (Nutshell Ser.). Date not set. pap. text. write for info. (*0-314-06581-4*) West Pub.

McHugh, et al. The Wellness Workbook: An Interactive Text. 2nd ed. 240p. (C). 1997. spiral bd. 38.95 (*0-7872-4182-2*, 41418201) Kendall-Hunt.

***McHugh, A. Rose.** Rebecca Lobo. LC 00-38430. (Illus.). (J). 2000. lib. bdg. write for info. (*1-56766-831-3*) Childs World.

McHugh, Bryan. An Exchange of Quivers. 32p. 1990. pap. 9.00 (*0-916258-21-1*) Left Hand Bks.

McHugh, Cathy L. Mill Family: The Labor System in the Southern Cotton Textile Industry. (Illus.). 160p. 1988. text 60.00 (*0-19-504299-9*) OUP.

McHugh, Christopher. Western Art, 1600-1800. LC 94-29041. (Art & Artists Ser.). (Illus.). 64p. (J). (gr. 5-10). 1994. lib. bdg. 24.26 (*1-56847-218-8*) Raintree Steck-V.

McHugh, Christopher M., ed. The 1995 Bankruptcy Yearbook & Almanac. 5th ed. 622p. 1995. pap. 175.00 (*0-9628991-4-3*) New Gen Research.

— The 1999 Bankruptcy Yearbook & Almanac. 472p. 1999. pap. 195.00 (*0-9628991-8-6*) New Gen Research.

— The 1997 Bankruptcy Yearbook & Almanac. 554p. 1997. pap. 195.00 (*0-9628991-6-X*) New Gen Research.

— The 1996 Bankruptcy Yearbook & Almanac. 6th ed. 624p. 1996. pap. 195.00 (*0-9628991-5-1*) New Gen Research.

McHugh, Connie K. Matthew Traveled Around the World. (Illus.). 32p. (Orig.). (J). (ps-4). 1997. pap. 12.95 incl. audio (*0-9657351-3-3*, Pub. by Music Fantasy) Penton Overseas.

***McHugh, David.** The Life & Times of Mr. Rip-Off. 184p. 1999. pap. 15.00 (*0-8059-4770-1*) Dorrance.

McHugh, Denise. Discover George Mason: Home, State, & Country: A Sampler of Lesson Plans, Activities, & Resources for Teachers of Students in Grades 3 Through 6. rev. ed. (Illus.). vi, 101p. 1993. pap. 9.50 (*1-884085-02-4*) Bd Regents.

— George Mason, Planter & Patriot: A Sampler of Lesson Plans Exploring Primary Sources for Teachers of Students in Grades 7 Through 12. (Illus.). viii, 200p. (Orig.). 1992. pap. 14.00 (*1-884085-00-8*) Bd Regents.

***Mchugh, Dick.** Insiders' Guide to the Great Smoky Mountains. (Illus.). 466p. 2000. pap. text 19.95 (*1-57380-106-2*) IPBI.

McHugh, Donald. Table Attendant Training. LC 83-720057. (Series 925). 1983. student ed. 7.00 (*0-8064-0401-9*) Bergwall.

***McHugh, Evan.** National Geographic Traveler: Sydney. LC 99-40370. 272p. 1999. per. 22.95 (*0-7922-7435-0*) Natl Geog.

***McHugh, Fenton.** First Cast: Celebrities Go Fishing for the Country's First Network Television Fishing Shows. Miller, Catherine, ed. LC 99-95449. (Illus.). 136p. 1998. pap. 12.95 (*0-9672918-0-1*) Ocean Seven Pubg.

McHugh, Fiona, adapted by. The Anne of Green Gables Storybook: Based on the Kevin Sullivan film of Lucy Maud Montgomery's classic novel. LC 87-214308. (Illus.). 80p. (J). (gr. 3 up). 1987. 19.95 (*0-920668-43-7*); pap. 9.95 (*0-920668-42-9*) Firefly Bks Ltd.

McHugh, Florence, tr. see Chan, Ts'ao.

***McHugh, Frances Y.** Emerald Mountain. large type ed. LC 99-42432. (Thorndike Candlelight Romance Ser.). 181p. 1999. 19.95 (*0-7862-2198-4*) Thorndike Pr.

McHugh, Frances Y. The Ghost Wore Black. large type ed. (Linford Mystery Library). 1991. pap. 16.99 (*0-7089-7031-1*) Ulverscroft.

***McHugh, Frances Y.** High on a Hill. large type ed. LC 99-58078. (Paperback Ser.). 2000. pap. 23.95 (*0-7838-8938-0*, G K Hall Lrg Type) Mac Lib Ref.

— The Hyacinth Spell. LC 00-42571. 2000. write for info. (*0-7862-2797-4*) Thorndike Pr.

McHugh, Frances Y. Vow of Love. large type ed. (Dales Romance Ser.). 211p. 1992. pap. 18.99 (*1-85389-331-5*) Ulverscroft.

McHugh, Francis P., et al, eds. Things Old & New: Catholic Social Teaching Revisited. LC 92-27123. 436p. (Orig.). (C). 1993. pap. text 37.50 (*0-8191-8902-2*) U Pr of Amer.

— Things Old & New: Catholic Social Teaching Revisited. LC 92-27123. 436p. (Orig.). (C). 1993. lib. bdg. 72.50 (*0-8191-8901-4*) U Pr of Amer.

McHugh, Francis P., jt. ed. see Frowen, Stephen F.

McHugh, Gerald A., jt. auth. see Litvin, S. Gerald.

McHugh, Gretchen. The Hungry Hiker's Book of Good Cooking. (Illus.). 288p. 1982. pap. 20.00 (*0-394-70774-5*) Knopf.

McHugh, Harry. The Road to Vinegar Hill: A 1798 Love Story. 360p. 1998. pap. 12.95 (*1-85635-207-2*, Pub. by Mercier Pr) Irish Amer Bk.

McHugh, Heather. Broken English: Poetry & Partiality. rev. ed. LC 93-13612. (Illus.). 162p. 1999. pap. 14.95 (*0-8195-6272-6*, Wesleyan Univ Pr) U Pr of New Eng.

— Dangers. 1977. 5.95 (*0-685-53924-5*) HM.

— The Father of the Predicaments. LC 99-14234. 86p. 1999. 19.95 (*0-8195-6375-7*, Wesleyan Univ Pr) U Pr of New Eng.

— Hinge & Sign: Poems, 1968-1993. LC 93-35917. (Wesleyan Poetry Ser.). 237p. 1994. pap. 15.95 (*0-8195-1216-8*, Wesleyan Univ Pr) U Pr of New Eng.

— Shades. LC 87-21179. (Wesleyan Poetry Ser.). 83p. 1988. pap. 12.95 (*0-8195-1137-4*, Wesleyan Univ Pr) U Pr of New Eng.

— To the Quick. LC 85-29504. (Wesleyan Poetry Ser.). 69p. 1987. pap. 12.95 (*0-8195-6162-2*, Wesleyan Univ Pr) U Pr of New Eng.

McHugh, Hugh. Construction: Interior Renovations for Business & Contractors. 144p. 1997. pap. 29.95 (*1-56167-204-1*) Am Literary Pr.

McHugh, Isabel, tr. see Chan, Ts'ao.

McHugh, Jack, jt. auth. see Van Valkenberg, Philip.

McHugh, James, jt. auth. see Nickels, William.

McHugh, James F., et al, eds. Damages in Massachusetts Litigation, 1996 Supplement. LC 93-77116. 1200p. 1996. ring bd., suppl. ed. 95.00 (*1-57589-032-1*, 96-05.58-SP) Mass CLE.

McHugh, James F., et al. Damages in Massachusetts Litigation. LC 93-77116. 404p. 1993. ring bd. 95.00 (*0-944490-37-9*) Mass CLE.

McHugh, James M., jt. auth. see Nickels, William G.

McHugh, James N. Hantu Hantu: An Account of Ghost Belief in Modern Malaya. 2nd ed. LC 77-87031. (Illus.). reprint ed. 29.50 (*0-404-16839-6*) AMS Pr.

McHugh, Jeanne. Alexander Holley & the Makers of Steel. LC 79-27414. (Johns Hopkins Studies in the History of Technology; New Ser.: No. 4). 416p. reprint ed. pap. 129.00 (*0-7837-2199-4*, 204253700004) Bks Demand.

McHugh, Joan C. Feast of Faith: Confessions of a Eucharistic Pilgrim. Romb, Anselm W., ed. & pref. by. (Illus.). 256p. (Orig.). 1994. pap. 12.00 (*0-9640417-0-7*) Witness Min.

McHugh, Joan C., ed. My Daily Eucharist. 384p. (Orig.). 1995. pap. text 10.00 (*0-9640417-3-1*) Witness Min.

— My Daily Eucharist, Vol. II. 392p. (Orig.). 1997. pap. 12.00 (*0-9640417-5-8*) Witness Min.

***McHugh, Joan Carter.** Eucharist: God among Us. McHugh, Thomas J. & Schanz, Anne Richards, eds. (Illus.). 160p. 1999. pap. 24.95 (*1-892835-01-0*) Witness Min.

McHugh, Joan Carter, et al. Eucharist, God Among Us: Essays & Images of the Eucharist in Sacred History. (Illus.). 144p. Date not set. 39.95 (*1-892835-04-5*) Witness Min.

McHugh, Joe. Better Than Money: Tales to Treasure for a Lifetime. LC 91-70909. (Illus.). 125p. (J). (gr. 1-8). 1991. 11.95 (*0-9619943-1-2*) Catalpa Pr.

— Ruff Tales: High Octane Stories from the Ruff Creek General Store. LC 87-92243. (Illus.). 144p. 1988. 11.95 (*0-9619943-0-4*) Catalpa Pr.

— Visitor from the Past: An Audio Adventure in Ten Thrilling Episodes, 5 cass., Set. (Illus.). 40p. (YA). (gr. 6-11). 1993. teacher ed. 55.00 incl. audio (*0-9619943-2-0*) Catalpa Pr.

McHugh, John, tr. see De Vaux, Roland.

McHugh, Joy Jackson. The Most Beautiful Tree in the Forest. Reid, Pamela J., ed. LC 96-77926. (Illus.). 32p. (J). (ps-6). 1997. 14.95 (*0-9654485-0-9*) Kinder Hse.

McHugh, Kathleen Anne. American Domesticity: From How-to Manual to Hollywood Melodrama. LC 98-25603. (Illus.). 248p. 1999. text 49.95 (*0-19-512261-5*) OUP.

McHugh, Kenna. Breaking into Film: Making Your Career Search a Blockbuster. 240p. 1998. pap. 14.95 (*0-7689-0123-5*) Petersons.

McHugh, Kevin. Regulation of the Capital Markets. LC 99-491065. 196p. 1998. 93.50 (*1-901657-13-2*); pap. 63.75 (*1-901657-12-4*) Gaunt.

McHugh, Kieran. Imaging in Paediatrics: A Casebook. (Illus.). 232p. 1997. text 69.50 (*0-19-262776-7*) OUP.

McHugh, Mark & Krukonis, Val J. Supercritical Fluid Extraction. 2nd ed. (Chemical Engineering Ser.). (Illus.). 608p. 1994. text 120.00 (*0-7506-9244-8*) Buttrwrth-Heinemann.

***McHugh, Mary.** Special Siblings. 256p. 2000. pap. write for info. (*0-7868-8536-X*) Disney Pr.

McHugh, Mary. Special Siblings: Growing up with Someone with a Disability. LC 98-21165. 238p. (YA). 1999. 23.45 (*0-7868-6285-8*, Pub. by Hyperion) Time Warner.

Mchugh, Maureen E. Shaking Your Family Tree Workbook: A Basic Guide to Tracing Your Family's Genealogy. 64p. (Orig.). 1990. pap. 9.95 (*0-89909-309-4*, 80-551-7) Yankee Bks.

McHugh, Maureen F. China Mountain Zhang. 320p. 1997. text 13.95 (*0-312-86098-6*) St Martin.

— China Mountain Zhang. 320p. 1993. mass mkt. 3.99 (*0-8125-0892-0*, Pub. by Tor Bks) St Martin.

— Half the Day is Night. 320p. 1996. mass mkt. 5.99 (*0-8125-2410-1*, Pub. by Tor Bks) St Martin.

— The Mission Child. LC 98-8774. 400p. 1998. 20.00 (*0-380-97456-8*, Eos) Morrow Avon.

***McHugh, Maureen F.** Mission Child. LC 98-8774. 384p. 1999. mass mkt. 6.99 (*0-380-79122-6*, Avon Bks) Morrow Avon.

***McHugh, Michael J.** The American People & Nation. 1998. teacher ed. 4.00 (*1-930092-83-0*) Christian Liberty.

— The American People & Nation. (Illus.). 88p. (J). (gr. k-1). 1998. pap. text 6.00 (*1-930092-82-2*, CLP79915) Christian Liberty.

— Beautiful Stories for Children. (Illus.). 190p. (J). (gr. 2-4). 1992. pap. text 7.00 (*1-930092-31-8*, CLP29620) Christian Liberty.

— Class Lesson Planner. (Illus.). 124p. 1994. pap. text 7.95 (*1-930092-13-X*, CLP89920) Christian Liberty.

— Enjoying Christian Literature: Answer Key. 1993. 1.50 (*1-930092-43-1*) Christian Liberty.

— Enjoying Christian Literature: Test Booklet. 1993. 1.50 (*1-930092-44-X*) Christian Liberty.

— Exploring Christian Literature: Answer Key. 1994. 1.50 (*1-930092-49-0*) Christian Liberty.

— Exploring Christian Literature: Test Booklet. 1994. 1.50 (*1-930092-50-4*) Christian Liberty.

— George B. McClellan: The Disposable Patriot. (Illus.). 212p. (YA). (gr. 7-12). 1998. pap. text 6.00 (*1-930092-15-6*, CLP29585) Christian Liberty.

— History for Little Pilgrims. 1998. teacher ed. 5.00 (*1-930092-85-7*) Christian Liberty.

— History for Little Pilgrims. (Illus.). 122p. (J). (gr. 1). 1998. pap. text 9.50 (*1-930092-84-9*, CLP79900) Christian Liberty.

— History for Little Pilgrims: Coloring Book. 1998. 3.00 (*1-930092-86-5*) Christian Liberty.

— Our Nation under God. 1996. teacher ed. 4.00 (*1-930092-88-1*) Christian Liberty.

— Our Nation under God. (Illus.). 154p. (J). (gr. 2-3). 1996. pap. text 7.95 (*1-930092-87-3*, CLP79920) Christian Liberty.

— Our Nation under God: Test Booklet. 1996. 1.95 (*1-930092-89-X*) Christian Liberty.

— Saint Patrick: Pioneer Missionary to Ireland. (Illus.). 152p. (YA). (gr. 6-12). 1999. pap. text 8.00 (*1-930092-14-8*, CLP29665) Christian Liberty.

— Studying Christian Literature: Answer Key. 1993. 1.50 (*1-930092-46-6*) Christian Liberty.

— Studying Christian Literature: Test Booklet. 1993. 1.50 (*1-930092-47-4*) Christian Liberty.

— Studying God's Word Book A. (Studying God's Word Ser.: Vol. 1). (Illus.). 152p. (J). (gr. k-1). 1996. pap. text 7.00 (*1-930092-56-3*, CLP19500) Christian Liberty.

— Studying God's Word Book B. (Studying God's Word Ser.: Vol. 2). (Illus.). 102p. (J). (gr. 1-2). 1995. pap. text 7.00 (*1-930092-57-1*, CLP19515) Christian Liberty.

— Writing with Power: Handwriting. (Christian Liberty Academy Handwriting Program Ser.). (Illus.). 60p. 1990. pap. text 5.50 (*1-930367-41-4*, CLP 39940) Christian Liberty.

McHugh, Michael J., ed. Enjoying Christian Literature. (Illus.). 184p. (YA). (gr. 7-12). 1993. pap. text 7.00 (*1-930092-42-3*, CLP29670) Christian Liberty.

— Exploring Christian Literature. (Illus.). 216p. (YA). (gr. 7-12). 1994. pap. text 8.00 (*1-930092-48-2*, CLP29695) Christian Liberty.

— Family Worship Hymnal. 240p. (YA). (gr. 7-12). 1999. pap. text 9.95 (*1-930092-81-4*) Christian Liberty.

— Studying Christian Literature. (Illus.). 248p. (YA). (gr. 7-12). 1993. pap. text 7.00 (*1-930092-45-8*, CLP29690) Christian Liberty.

***McHugh, Michael J. & Arwine, David K.** Our Father's World. 1999. teacher ed. 5.95 (*1-930092-06-7*) Christian Liberty.

— Our Father's World. (Illus.). 112p. (J). (gr. 1-2). 1999. pap. text 8.95 (*1-930092-05-9*) Christian Liberty.

— Our Father's World: Test Booklet. 1999. 2.95 (*1-930092-07-5*) Christian Liberty.

McHugh, Michael J. & Bachman, Frank P. The Story of Inventions. (Illus.). 354p. (J). (gr. 5-7). 1992. pap. text 8.00 (*1-930092-40-7*, CLP29660) Christian Liberty.

— The Story of Inventions: Answer Key. 1992. 1.00 (*1-930092-41-5*) Christian Liberty.

McHugh, Michael J. & Montgomery, D. H. Exploring American History. (Illus.). 360p. (J). (gr. 4-6). 1992. pap. text 5.95 (*1-930092-96-2*, CLP79950) Christian Liberty.

An Asterisk (*) at the beginning of an entry indicates that the title is appearing for the first time.

— Exploring American History: Answer Key. (J). 1992. 1.00 (1-930092-97-0) Christian Liberty.
*McHugh, Michael J., et al. A Child's Story of America. (Illus.). 202p. (J). (gr. 3-5). 1998. pap. text 8.95 (1-930092-93-8, CLP79945) Christian Liberty.
— A Child's Story of America: Answer Key. (J). 1998. 1.00 (1-930092-94-6, CLP79945) Christian Liberty.
— A Child's Story of America: Test Booklet. 1998. 1.00 (1-930092-95-4) Christian Liberty.
McHugh, Michael J., ed. see Abbott, Jacob.
McHugh, Michael J., ed. see Bailey, Carolyn Sherwin.
McHugh, Michael J., ed. see Green, William H.
McHugh, Michael J., ed. see Henty, G. A.
McHugh, Michael J., jt. ed. see Lindstrom, Paul D.
McHugh, Michael J., ed. see Moes, Garry J.
McHugh, Michael J., ed. see Morrison, J. A.
McHugh, Michael J., ed. see Pumphrey, Margaret B.
McHugh, Michael J., ed. see Wayland, John W.
McHugh, Michael J., ed. see Williamson, Mary L.
McHugh, Michael P., tr. see Ambrose.
McHugh, Ned. Drogheda Before the Famine: Urban Poverty in the Shadow of Privilege 1826-45. LC 99-176120. (Maynooth Studies in Local History). 80p. 1998. pap. 9.95 (0-7165-2709-X) Intl Spec Bk.
McHugh, Neil. Holymen of the Blue Nile: The Making of an Arab Islamic Community in the Nilotic Sudan, 1500-1850. (Islam & Society in Africa Ser.). 240p. 1993. 54.95 (0-8101-1069-5) Northwestern U Pr.
McHugh, P. E., ed. Frontiers & Engineering Materials. (Key Engineering Materials Ser.: Nos. 118-119). (Illus.). 376p. 1996. text 183.00 (0-87849-723-4, Pub. by Trans T Pub) Enfield Pubs NH.
McHugh, Patrick, et al. Beyond Business Process Reengineering: Moving Towards the Holonic Enterprise. 224p. 1997. pap. 45.00 (0-471-97481-1) Wiley.
— Beyond Business Process Reengineering: Towards the Holonic Enterprise. LC 94-30745. 224p. 1995. 89.95 (0-471-95087-4) Wiley.
Mchugh, Paul R. Perspectives of Psychiatry. 2nd ed. LC 98-26808. 375p. 1998. pap. text 16.95 (0-8018-6046-6) Johns Hopkins.
McHugh, Paul R. & McKusick, Victor A., eds. Genes, Brain, & Behavior. LC 90-8978. (Association for Research in Nervous & Mental Disease Research Publications: Vol. 69). (Illus.). 251p. 1991. reprint ed. pap. 77.90 (0-608-07186-2, 206741100009) Bks Demand.
McHugh, Paul R. & Slavney, Phillip R. The Perspectives of Psychiatry. LC 83-6157. 176p. 1986. reprint ed. pap. text 13.95 (0-8018-3302-7) Johns Hopkins.
— The Perspectives of Psychiatry. 2nd ed. LC 98-26808. (Illus.). 375p. 1998. 35.00 (0-8018-6045-8) Johns Hopkins.
McHugh, Paul R., jt. auth. see Slavney, Phillip R.
McHugh, Peter, jt. ed. see Blum, Alan.
McHugh, Roger, ed. Jack B. Yeats: A Centenary Gathering. 1971. 8.95 (0-685-20029-9, Pub. by Smyth) Dufour.
McHugh, Roland. Annotations to Finnegans Wake. LC 79-18419. 640p. reprint ed. pap. 198.40 (0-8357-7881-9, 203629900002) Bks Demand.
— Annotations to Finnegans Wake. rev. ed. LC 90-23512. 640p. 1991. pap. text 29.95 (0-8018-4190-9) Johns Hopkins.
— Annotations to Finnegans Wake. 2nd rev. ed. LC 90-23512. 640p. 1991. 75.00 (0-8018-4226-3) Johns Hopkins.
McHugh, Sean, ed. Illness Behavior: A Multidisciplinary Model. LC 87-2530. 442p. 1987. 85.00 (0-306-42486-X, Plenum Trade) Perseus Pubng.
McHugh, Thomas J., ed. see McHugh, Joan Carter.
McHugh, Thomas K., jt. auth. see Greenwald, Martin L.
McHugh, Tom. Flying Saucers Are Everywhere. LC 95-7389. (Illus.). 135p. 1995. pap. 12.95 (0-87975-982-8) Prometheus Bks.
— The Time of the Buffalo. LC 78-24261. (Illus.). xxiv, 383p. 1979. reprint ed. pap. 18.95 (0-8032-8105-6, Bison Books) U of Nebr Pr.
McHugh, Vincent. I Am Thinking of My Darling. LC 90-25933. 308p. 1991. reprint ed. pap. 9.95 (1-878274-05-8) Yarrow Pr.
— I Am Thinking of My Darling: An Adventure Story. Reginald, R. & Melville, Douglas, eds. LC 77-84254. (Lost Race & Adult Fantasy Ser.). 1978. reprint ed. lib. bdg. 28.95 (0-405-10998-9) Ayer.
McHugh, William D., jt. auth. see Granath, Lars.
*McHughen, Alan. Pandora's Picnic Basket: The Potential & Hazards of Genetically Modified Foods. (Illus.). 288p. 2000. 24.95 (0-19-850674-0) OUP.
Mchutchison, Meg, jt. auth. see Roche, Judith.
MCI Staff. MCI Directory of Management Information, 1998. LC 99-219125. 161p. 1999. text 95.00 (0-7506-3812-5) Buttrwrth-Heinemann.
McIan, Peter. Using Your Portable Studio: Techniques for Musicians. LC 96-154312. (Illus.). 128p. (Orig.). 1996. pap. 24.95 (0-8256-1437-6, AM92232) Omnibus NY.
McIan, Peter & Wichman, Larry. The Musician's Guide to Home Recording: How to Make Great Recordings at Home. rev. ed. 320p. 1994. pap. 24.95 (0-8256-1378-7, AM91470) Omnibus NY.
McIlhaney, Joe S., Jr. & McIlhaney, Marion. Sex: What You Don't Know Can Kill You. rev. adapted ed. LC 96-43362. 128p. (gr. 12). 1997. pap. 8.99 (0-8010-5737-X, Sexuality and S) Baker Bks.
McIlhaney, Joe S., Jr. & Nethery, Susan. 1,001 Health-Care Questions Women Ask. 3rd ed. LC 98-3257. (Illus.). 576p. (C). (gr. 13). 1998. pap. 19.99 (0-8010-5810-4) Baker Bks.
McIlhaney, Marion, jt. auth. see McIlhaney, Joe S., Jr.
McIlhany, Hugh M. Kinney. Some Virginia Families, Being Genealogies of the Kinney, Stribling, Trout, McIlhany . . . And Other Families of Virginia. 274p. 1997. reprint ed. pap. 35.00 (0-8328-9435-4); reprint ed. lib. bdg. 45.00 (0-8328-9434-6) Higginson Bk Co.
McIlhenny, E. A. Alligator's Life History. LC 76-6228. 1976. write for info. (0-916984-01-X) SSAR.
McIlhenny, Edward A. The Wild Turkey & Its Hunting. (Illus.). 245p. 1984. reprint ed. 24.95 (0-685-62740-3) Real Turkeys Pubs.
McIlhenny, Edward A., ed. Befo' de War Spirituals: Words & Melodies. LC 72-1724. reprint ed. 37.50 (0-404-08325-0) AMS Pr.
McIlhenny, Janet A. Special Bites. (Illus.). vi, 112p. (Orig.). 1996. pap. 12.95 (0-9657631-0-2, 6126) J A McIlhenny.
McIlhenny, Paul & Hunter, Barbara. The Tabasco Cookbook: 125 Years of America's Favorite Pepper Sauce. LC 92-5520. 144p. 1993. 15.00 (0-517-58965-6) C Potter.
McIlhenny, Robyn. Our Baby. LC 92-27268. (Voyages Ser.). (Illus.). (J). 1993. 3.75 (0-383-03646-1) SRA McGraw.
McIlhiney, David B. A Gentleman in Every Slum: Church of England Missions in East London, 1837-1914. (Princeton Theological Monographs: No. 16). x, 141p. (Orig.). 1988. pap. 10.00 (0-915138-95-6) Pickwick.
McIlhon, John J. Fifty Days Plus Forever: Daily Reflections for the Easter Season. 163p. 1990. pap. 5.95 (0-8146-1958-4) Liturgical Pr.
— Forty Days Plus Three: Daily Reflections for Lent & Holy Week. 135p. 1989. pap. 5.95 (0-8146-1769-7) Liturgical Pr.
— A Little Out of the Ordinary: Daily Reflections for Ordinary Time. LC 93-40564. 216p. (Orig.). 1994. pap. 11.95 (0-8146-2274-7) Liturgical Pr.
— O Marvellous Exchange: Daily Reflections for Christmas & Epiphany. 80p. (Orig.). 1992. pap. 5.95 (0-8146-2013-2) Liturgical Pr.
McIllvaney, H. McIllvanney on Racing. 1992. 24.95 (0-09-158430-2, Pub. by Random) Trafalgar.
McIllwain, Linda P. Women on the Outside Looking In. LC 84-90611. 96p. (Orig.). 1985. pap. 5.95 (0-930555-03-1) Wings Bks.
McIlnay, Dennis P. Foundations & Higher Education: Dollars, Donors & Scholars. 206p. 1991. 29.50 (0-914746-28-6) G Kurian.
— How Foundations Work: What Grant Seekers Need to Know about the Many Faces of Foundations. LC 98-9762. 1998. 28.95 (0-7879-4011-9) Jossey-Bass.
McIlraith, Sheila, jt. ed. see Biswas, Gautam.
McIlrath, T. J., ed. see American Institute of Physics.
McIlroy, Brian, jt. ed. see Loiselle, Andre.
McIlroy, Christopher. All My Relations. LC 93-23006. (Flannery O'Connor Award for Short Fiction Ser.). 200p. 1994. 19.95 (0-8203-1602-4) U of Ga Pr.
McIlroy, Kenneth, jt. ed. see Stoltzfus, Joel M.
McIlvaine, Charles & MacAdam, Robert K. One Thousand American Fungi. LC 72-91857. (Illus.). 1973. reprint ed. pap. 15.00 (0-87110-094-0) Ultramarine Pub.
McIlvaine, Eileen, et al, eds. P. G. Wodehouse: A Comprehensive Bibliography & Checklist. (Illus.). 489p. (Orig.). 1991. lib. bdg. 135.00 (0-87008-125-X) JAS Heineman.
McIlvaine, Eileen, et al. P. G. Wodehouse: A Comprehensive Bibliography & Checklist. (Wodehouse Monographs: No. 2). (Illus.). 544p. (Orig.). 1995. 135.00 (0-87008-101-2) JAS Heineman.
McIlvaine, Paul. Dead Towns of Sunbury & Dorchester. 3rd ed. LC 75-26008. 1976. 5.95 (0-9600410-3-6) P McIlvaine.
McIlvane, William J., jt. auth. see Soraci, Sal.
McILvanney, Hugh. McIlvanney on Boxing. 320p. 1997. 35.00 (1-85158-732-2, Pub. by Mainstream Pubng) Trafalgar.
McIlvanney, Hugh. McIlvanney on Boxing. 320p. 1997. pap. 19.95 (1-84018-005-6, Pub. by Mainstream Pubng) Trafalgar.
— McIlvanney on Horseracing. 288p. 1996. 34.95 (1-85158-733-0, Pub. by Mainstream Pubng); pap. 19.95 (1-85158-877-9, Pub. by Mainstream Pubng) Trafalgar.
McIlvanney, William. The Kiln. 320p. 1996. text 35.00 (0-340-65735-9) Hodder & Stought Ltd.
McIlvanney, William. The Papers of Tony Veitch. LC 82-18990. 256p. 1993. pap. 9.95 (0-15-670828-0) Harcourt.
— Shades of Grey: Glasgow, 1956-1987. (Illus.). 224p. 1993. 34.95 (1-85158-047-6, Pub. by Mainstream Pubng) Trafalgar.
— Strange Loyalties. 1993. pap. 9.95 (0-15-685644-1) Harcourt.
McIlveen, Howard, jt. auth. see Kirkland, Kevin.
McIlvene, John. Hastings Family. A Chapter in Family History. (Illus.). 137p. 1997. reprint ed. pap. 22.00 (0-8328-9038-3); reprint ed. lib. bdg. 32.00 (0-8328-9037-5) Higginson Bk Co.
McIlvenna, Ted. Meditations on the Gift of Sexuality. 77p. 1977. 12.95 (0-317-34148-0) Specific Pr.
McIlvenna, Ted, ed. The Complete Guide to Safer Sex. 2nd ed. 252p. 1999. pap. 9.95 (1-56980-135-5) Barricade Bks.
McIlvenna, Ted, et al. The Complete Guide to Safe Sex. 200p. (Orig.). 1987. pap. text 6.95 (0-930846-05-2) Specific Pr.
McIlvoy, Kevin. Hyssop. LC 98-8392. 160p. 1998. 24.95 (0-8101-5085-9, TriQuart) Northwestern U Pr.
*McIlvoy, Kevin. Hyssop, Vol. 1. 192p. 1999. pap. 12.50 (0-380-73271-8, Avon Bks) Morrow Avon.
— Little Peg: A Novel. 256p. 2000. pap. 13.00 (0-380-81476-5, Perennial) HarperTrade.
McIlvoy, Kevin. A Waltz. LC 80-26883. (Illus.). 105p. 1981. pap. 7.00 (0-89924-032-1) Lynx Hse.
McIlwain, et al. The Fifty-Plus Wellness Program. large type ed. 300p. 1991. reprint ed. 21.95 (1-56054-216-0) Thorndike Pr.
McIlwain, Bruce, et al. The Super Aspirin Cure for Arthritis. LC 99-200327. 208p. 1999. mass mkt. 5.99 (0-553-58107-4) Bantam.
McIlwain, Charles H. Constitutionalism & the Changing World: Collected Papers. LC 75-103801. (Cambridge University Press Library Editions). 320p. reprint ed. pap. 91.20 (0-608-16881-5, 2027246) Bks Demand.
— The High Court of Parliament. Mayer, J. P., ed. LC 78-67368. (European Political Thought Ser.). 1980. reprint ed. lib. bdg. 33.95 (0-405-11719-1) Ayer.
McIlwain, Harris. Osteoporosis Cure: Reverse the Crippling Effects with New Treatments. LC 97-94411. 208p. 1998. mass mkt. 5.99 (0-380-79336-9, Avon Bks) Morrow Avon.
McIlwain, Harris & Bruce, Debra. Bone Boosters: The Essential Guide to Building Strong Bones. LC 98-208440. 96p. 1998. mass mkt. 5.99 (1-57566-265-5) Kensgtn Pub Corp.
McIlwain, Harris & Bruce, Debra Fulghum. Bone Boosting Recipes. LC 99-226238. 256p. 1998. pap. 12.00 (1-57566-384-8) Kensgtn Pub Corp.
McIlwain, Harris, et al. Fifty-Plus Wellness Program. large type ed. 300p. 1992. lib. bdg. 15.95 (1-56054-975-0) Thorndike Pr.
McIlwain, Harris H. The Fibromyalgia Handbook. (Illus.). 224p. (Orig.). 1995. pap. 16.95 (0-8050-4672-0, Owl) H Holt & Co.
McIlwain, Harris H. Winning with Back Pain: How to Beat Back Pain & Take Control of Your Life. LC 93-8379. 224p. 1996. pap. 5.99 (0-471-17694-X) Wiley.
*McIlwain, Harris H. & Bruce, Debra F. The Fibromyalgia Handbook: A 7-Step Program to Halt & Even Reverse Fibromyalgia. 2nd expanded rev. ed. LC 98-39802. (Illus.). 224p. 1999. pap. 16.95 (0-8050-6115-0, Pub. by H Holt & Co) VHPS.
McIlwain, Harris H., et al. Winning with Arthritis. LC 90-28903. (Science Editions Ser.). 228p. 1991. pap. 15.95 (0-471-52847-1) Wiley.
— Winning with Arthritis. LC 90-28903. 228p. 1997. pap. 5.99 (0-471-17691-5) Wiley.
— Winning with Back Pain. LC 93-8379. 202p. 1994. pap. 12.95 (0-471-30328-3) Wiley.
— Winning with Chronic Pain: A Complete Program for Health & Well-Being. LC 94-2443. (Illus.). 222p. (C). 1994. 27.95 (0-87975-900-3); pap. 17.95 (0-87975-878-3) Prometheus Bks.
— Winning with Osteoporosis. 2nd ed. LC 93-7530. (Illus.). 160p. 1993. pap. 15.95 (0-471-30489-1) Wiley.
McIlwain, Harris H., jt. auth. see Bruce, Debra F.
McIlwain, James T. An Introduction to the Biology of Vision. (Illus.). 256p. (C). 1996. pap. text 25.95 (0-521-49890-2) Cambridge U Pr.
McIlwain, John. The DK Children's Illustrated Dictionary. LC 94-9561. (Illus.). 256p. (J). (gr. 3-6). 1994. 19.95 (1-56458-625-1) DK Pub Inc.
McIlwaine, Cathy, jt. auth. see Moser, Caroline.
McIlwaine, Cathy, jt. ed. see Chant, Sylvia H.
McIlwaine, G., jt. ed. see Dunn, P. M.
McIlwaine, H. R., ed. Journals of the House of Burgesses of Virginia, 1742-1747, 1748-1749. 427p. 1995. reprint ed. pap. text 52.00 (0-7884-0199-8) Heritage Bk.
McIlwaine, H. R. & Kennedy. Journals of the House of Burgesses of Virginia, 1770-1772. 333p. 1996. pap. 25.00 (0-7884-0494-6, H590) Heritage Bk.
McIlwaine, Henry R. Index to Obituary Notices: In the Richmond Enquirer from May 9, 1804, Through 1828, & the Richmond Whig from January 1824 through 1838. 87p. 1996. reprint ed. pap. 11.00 (0-8063-0633-5, 3570) Clearfield Co.
— The Struggle of Protestant Dissenters for Religious Toleration in Virginia. LC 78-63830. (Johns Hopkins University. Studies in the Social Sciences. Thirtieth Ser. 1912: 4). reprint ed. 11.50 (0-404-61090-0) AMS Pr.
McIlwaine, Henry R., ed. Executive Journals of the Council of Colonial Virginia: 1680-1699, 6 vols., Vol. 1. LC 26-27252. xi, 587p. 1976. 24.95 (0-88490-012-6) Library of VA.
— Executive Journals of the Council of Colonial Virginia: 1699-1705, 6 vols., Vol. 2. LC 26-27252. xi, 492p. 1976. 24.95 (0-88490-013-4) Library of VA.
— Executive Journals of the Council of Colonial Virginia: 1705-1721, 6 vols., Vol. 3. LC 26-27252. vii, 679p. 1976. 24.95 (0-88490-014-2) Library of VA.
— Executive Journals of the Council of Colonial Virginia: 1721-1739, 6 vols., Vol. 4. LC 26-27252. vii, 555p. 1978. 24.95 (0-88490-015-0) Library of VA.
— Journals of the House of Burgesses, 1752-1755, 1756-1758. (Illus.). 552p. (Orig.). 1995. pap. 66.00 (0-7884-0360-5, H589) Heritage Bk.
— Legislative Journals of the Council of Colonial Virginia. 2nd ed. LC 79-13108. xii, 1646p. 1979. reprint ed. 50.00 (0-88490-078-9) Library of VA.
— The Letters of Thomas Nelson & Benjamin Harrison. LC 27-2700. (Official Letters of the Governors of Virginia Ser: Vol. 3). xii, 510p. 1929. 19.95 (0-88490-020-7) Library of VA.
— Minutes of the Council & General Court of Colonial Virginia. 2nd ed. LC 79-13080. xviii, 668p. 1979. reprint ed. 29.95 (0-88490-077-0) Library of VA.
— Proceedings of the Committees of Safety of Cumberland & Isle of Wight Counties, Virginia, 1775-1776. 54p. 1919. text 5.00 (0-685-52452-3) Library of VA.
McIlwaine, Ia, et al, eds. Bibliography & Reading: A Festschrift in Honour of Ronald Staveley. LC 82-21489. 180p. 1983. 26.50 (0-8108-1601-6) Scarecrow.
McIlwaine, John. Maps & Mapping of Africa. LC 97-13251. 1997. 100.00 (1-873836-76-7) Bowker-Saur.
— Writings on African Archives. 200p. 1996. 75.00 (1-873836-66-X) Bowker-Saur.
McIlwaine, John, ed. Africa: A Guide to Reference Material. (Regional Reference Guides Ser.: No. 1). 592p. 1992. 135.00 (0-905450-43-4, Pub. by H Zell Pubs) Seven Hills Bk.
McIlwee, Judith S. & Robinson, J. Gregg. Women in Engineering: Gender, Power, & Workplace Culture. LC 91-2050. (SUNY Series in Science, Technology, & Society). (Illus.). 248p. (C). 1992. text 74.50 (0-7914-0869-8); pap. text 24.95 (0-7914-0870-1) State U NY Pr.
McIlwraith, Archibald K., ed. Five Elizabethan Tragedies. LC 81-6574. 399p. 1981. reprint ed. lib. bdg. 82.50 (0-313-22528-1, MCFE, Greenwood Pr) Greenwood.
McIlwraith, C. Wayne. Diagnostic & Surgical Arthroscopy in the Horse. 2nd ed. LC 89-2463. (Illus.). 227p. 1990. text 98.50 (0-8121-1186-9) Lppncott W & W.
McIlwraith, C. Wayne & Trotter, Gayle W. Joint Disease in the Horse. Valkhoff, Sandra, ed. 416p. 1996. text 132.00 (0-7216-5135-6, W B Saunders Co) Harcrt Hlth Sci Grp.
McIlwraith, C. Wayne, et al. McIlwraith & Turner's Equine Surgery: Advanced Techniques. 2nd ed. LC 98-15576. 440p. 1998. 99.00 (0-683-05770-7) Lppncott W & W.
McIlwraith, C. Wayne, jt. auth. see Turner, A. Simon.
McIlwraith, Hamish. Coping with Bereavement. 140p. 1998. pap. 10.95 (1-85168-153-1, Pub. by Onewrld Pubns) Penguin Putnam.
McIlwraith, T. F. The Bella Coola Indians, Vols. 1 & 2. 2nd ed. 1536p. 1992. text 125.00 (0-8020-2820-9); pap. text 60.00 (0-8020-7692-0) U of Toronto Pr.
McIlwraith, Thomas F. Looking for Old Ontario. LC 97-161352. (Illus.). 360p. 1997. pap. 19.95 (0-8020-7658-0); text 76.50 (0-8020-0708-2) U of Toronto Pr.
McIlwraith, W. Map of Oregon Trail: The Highway of the Pioneers to the Pacific Northwest. (J). (gr. 3-6). 1986. pap. 5.95 (0-8323-0052-7) Binford Mort.
McImoye, Leslie. Baptism. 242p. 1996. 29.95 (1-85756-280-1) Paul & Co Pubs.
McInally, Mike, ed. see Henckel, Mark.
McInally, Mike, ed. see Herman, Jeffrey & Thomas, Greg.
McIndoo, Ethel & Ham, John. Freeda Harris: Woman of Prayer. (Meet the Missionary Ser.). 64p. (J). (gr. 4-6). 1996. pap. text 5.99 (1-56309-144-5, W947121) Womans Mission Union.
McIndoo, Ethel, jt. auth. see Kizer, Kathryn.
McInelly, Phyllis A. The Warmth of a Mother's Heart. 90p. 1998. pap. 9.95 (0-7392-0007-0, PO2743) Morris Pubng.
McInerney, Claire. Find It! The Inside Story at Your Library. (Study Skills Ser.). (Illus.). 56p. (J). (gr. 4 up). 1989. lib. bdg. 15.93 (0-8225-2425-2, Lerner Publctns) Lerner Pub.
McInerney, Dan. A Traveller's History of the U. S. A. LC 99-56028. (Traveller's History Ser.). 288p. 2000. pap. 14.95 (1-56656-283-X) Interlink Pub.
McInerney, Daniel J. The Fortunate Heirs of Freedom: Abolition & Republican Thought. LC 93-37454. (Illus.). xii, 232p. 1994. text 45.00 (0-8032-3172-5) U of Nebr Pr.
*McInerney, Dennis M. Helping Kids Achieve Their Best Understanding & Using Motivation in the Classroom. (Illus.). 136p. 2000. pap. 24.95 (1-86508-202-3, Pub. by Allen & Unwin Pty) Paul & Co Pubs.
*McInerney, Francis & White, Sean. Future Wealth: Investing in the Second Great Wave of Technology Stocks. LC 99-55954. 352p. 2000. text 27.50 (0-312-25320-6, Truman Talley) St Martin.
McInerney, Francis & White, Sean. The Total Quality Corporation: How 10 Major Companies Added to Profits & Cleaned up the Environment in the 1990s. 336p. 1997. pap. 13.95 (0-452-27347-1, Truman Talley) St Martin.
*McInerney, Jay. Bacchus & Me: A Hedonist in the Wine Cellar. 224p. 2000. 24.95 (1-58574-186-8) Lyons Pr.
McInerney, Jay. Bright Lights, Big City: A Novel. LC 84-40074. (Vintage Contemporaries Ser.). 208p. 1984. pap. 10.00 (0-394-72641-3) Vin Bks.
— Brightness Falls. LC 92-50604. 1993. pap. 14.00 (0-679-74532-7) Vin Bks.
— Dressed to Kill: James Bond, the Suited Hero. (Illus.). 200p. 1996. 45.00 (2-08-013618-6, Pub. by Flammarion) Abbeville Pr.
— The Last of the Savages. 1997. pap. 12.00 (0-679-74952-7) Vin Bks.
— The Last of the Savages: A Novel. 271p. 1996. 24.00 (0-679-42845-3) Knopf.
— Model Behavior: A Novel & 7 Stories. LC 98-27859. 275p. 1998. 24.00 (0-679-42846-1) Knopf.
*McInerney, Jay. Model Behavior: A Novel & 7 Stories. 2000. pap. 11.00 (0-679-74953-5) Vin Bks.
McInerney, Jay. Ransom: A Novel. 280p. 1985. pap. 12.00 (0-394-74118-8) Vin Bks.
— Story of My Life: A Novel. (Contemporaries Ser.). 188p. 1989. pap. 12.00 (0-679-72257-2) Vin Bks.
*McInerney, Jeremy. Folds of Parnassos: Land & Ethnicity in Ancient Phokis. LC 99-14597. 368p. 2000. 50.00 (0-292-75229-6); pap. text 24.95 (0-292-75230-X) U of Tex Pr.
McInerney, Judith W. Judge Benjamin: The Superdog Rescue. (Illus.). (J). (gr. 4-6). 1987. pap. 2.75 (0-317-66178-7, Minstrel Bks) PB.
McInerney, June J. Meditations for New Members: Faithful Servants. Webber, Christopher L., ed. LC 99-37583. 96p. 1999. pap. 6.95 (0-8192-1821-9) Morehouse Pub.
McInerney, Kathleen H., jt. auth. see Courts, Patrick L.

An Asterisk (*) at the beginning of an entry indicates that the title is appearing for the first time.

McInerney, Maud B. & Salisbury, Joyce E., eds. Hildegard of Bingen: A Book of Essays. LC 98-10288. (Medieval Casebks.: Vol. 20). (Illus.). 288p. 1998. text 55.00 (*0-8153-2588-6*, H2037) Garland.

***McInerney, Maud Burnett.** I am No Woman but A Maid: The Rhetoric of Virginity from Jerome. 1999. text. write for info. (*0-312-22350-1*) St Martin.

McInerney, Merry. Burning down the House. 320p. 1995. 5.99 (*0-8125-3651-7*) Forge NYC.

— Dog People. LC 98-11955. 288p. 1998. 22.95 (*0-312-85699-7*, Pub. by Forge NYC) St Martin.

***McInerney, Merry.** Dog People. 288p. 2000. pap. text 13.95 (*0-312-87292-5*, Pub. by Forge NYC) St Martin.

***McInerney, Michael J.** Windows NT Security. LC 99-39655. (Prentice Hall Series On Microsoft Technology Ser.). 432p. 1999. pap. text 49.99 (*0-13-083990-6*) P-H.

— Windows 2000 Security. 2000. pap. 44.99 (*0-13-028124-7*) Prntice Hall Bks.

— Zero Administration Kit for Windows. LC 99-52008. (Series on Microsoft Technology). 289p. 1999. pap. text 39.99 (*0-13-084786-0*) P-H.

McInerney, Peter, jt. auth. see Maitland, Terrence.

McInerney, Peter K. HarperCollins College Outline Introduction to Philosophy. LC 91-58272. (College Outline Ser.). (Illus.). 256p. (C). 1992. pap. 15.00 (*0-06-467124-0*, Harper Ref) HarpC.

— Time & Experience. 224p. 1991. 49.95 (*0-87722-752-7*) Temple U Pr.

— Time & Experience. 296p. 1992. pap. 24.95 (*1-56639-010-9*) Temple U Pr.

McInerny, Daniel, ed. The Common Things: Essays on Thomism & Education. LC 99-18576. 290p. 2000. pap. 15.00 (*0-9669226-0-3*, Pub. by Am Maritain) Cath U Pr.

McInerny, Ralph. Aquinas Against the Averroists: On There Being Only One Intellect. LC 92-16179. (Series in the History of Philosophy). 240p. 1993. 37.95 (*1-55753-028-9*) Purdue U Pr.

— Aquinas & Analogy. LC 96-16793. 168p. (C). 1996. text 39.95 (*0-8132-0848-3*) Cath U Pr.

— Aquinas & Analogy. 1999. pap. text 14.95 (*0-8132-0932-3*) Cath U Pr.

— Aquinas on Human Action: A Theory of Practice. LC 90-27754. 244p. 1992. pap. text 19.95 (*0-8132-0761-4*) Cath U Pr.

— Art & Prudence: Studies in the Thought of Jacques Maritain. LC 88-18826. (C). 1988. pap. text 11.50 (*0-268-00620-2*) U of Notre Dame Pr.

— The Basket Case. large type ed. LC 92-18387. (Nightingale Ser.). 280p. 1992. pap. 14.95 (*0-8161-5569-0*, G K Hall Lrg Type) Mac Lib Ref.

— Boethius & Aquinas. LC 89-15705. 268p. 1990. 34.95 (*0-8132-0709-6*) Cath U Pr.

***McInerny, Ralph.** Book of Kills. 2000. 23.95 (*0-312-20346-2*) St Martin.

McInerny, Ralph. A Cardinal Offense. large type ed. LC 94-47945. (Cloak & Dagger Ser.). 694p. 1995. 22.95 (*0-7862-0402-8*) Thorndike Pr.

— Cause & Effect: An Andrew Broom Mystery. 1990. mass mkt. 3.50 (*0-373-26046-6*) Harlequin Bks.

— Desert Sinner. (WWL Mystery Ser.). 1994. per. 3.99 (*0-373-26158-6*, 1-26158-5) Harlequin Bks.

— Desert Sinner. large type ed. (Popular Ser.). 320p. 1993. reprint ed. lib. bdg. 17.95 (*1-56054-631-X*) Thorndike Pr.

— Ethica Thomistica: The Moral Philosophy of Thomas Aquinas. rev. ed. LC 97-11164. 129p. (C). 1997. pap. text 14.95 (*0-8132-0897-1*) Cath U Pr.

— A First Glance at St. Thomas Aquinas: A Handbook for Peeping Thomists. LC 89-40392. (C). 1990. pap. text 11.50 (*0-268-00975-9*) U of Notre Dame Pr.

— Frigor Mortis. 1991. reprint ed. mass mkt. 3.99 (*0-373-26080-6*) Harlequin Bks.

— Grave Undertakings: A Father Dowling Mystery. LC 99-54817. Vol. 19. 384p. 2000. text 24.95 (*0-312-20309-8*) St Martin.

***McInerny, Ralph.** Heirs & Parents: An Andrew Broom Mystery. LC 00-25473. 240p. 2000. text 23.95 (*0-312-20311-X*) St Martin.

McInerny, Ralph. A History of Western Philosophy, Vol. 3. LC 63-20526. 604p. reprint ed. pap. 187.30 (*0-608-15458-X*, 202931000003) Bks Demand.

— Irish Tenure. LC 99-16992. 256p. 1999. text 22.95 (*0-312-20345-4*) St Martin.

***McInerny, Ralph.** Irish Tenure. 272p. 2000. mass mkt. 5.99 (*0-312-97320-9*) St Martin.

— Irish Tenure: A Mystery Set at the University of Notre Dame. LC 00-37766. 2000. pap. write for info. (*0-7862-2667-6*) Thorndike Pr.

McInerny, Ralph. Judas Priest: A Father Dowling Mystery. 1994. per. 3.99 (*0-373-26156-X*, 1-26156-9) Harlequin Bks.

— Judas Priest: A Father Dowling Mystery. large type ed. LC 92-814. 331p. 1992. reprint ed. lib. bdg. 17.95 (*1-56054-376-0*) Thorndike Pr.

— Lack of the Irish: A Mystery Set at the University of Notre Dame. LC 98-21119. 224p. 1998. text 21.95 (*0-312-19294-0*) St Martin.

— Lack of the Irish: A Mystery Set at the University of Notre Dame. (Dead Letter Mysteries Ser.). 1999. mass mkt. 5.99 (*0-312-96927-9*, Minotaur) St Martin.

— Law & Ardor: An Andrew Broom Mystery. 256p. 1995. 21.00 (*0-684-80462-X*) S&S Trade.

— Let's Read Latin. 170p. (Orig.). (C). 1995. pap. text 29.95 incl. audio (*1-883357-25-X*) Dumb Ox Bks.

— The Logic of Analogy: An Interpretation of St. Thomas. 194p. 1971. pap. text 50.50 (*90-247-0104-X*, Pub. by M Nijhoff) Kluwer Academic.

— Mom & Dead: An Andrew Broom Mystery. large type ed. LC 94-6062. 302p. 1994. reprint ed. lib. bdg. 21.95 (*0-7862-0211-4*) Thorndike Pr.

— On This Rockne: A Notre Dame Mystery. LC 97-15341. 224p. 1997. text 20.95 (*0-312-17054-8*, 749186) St Martin.

— On This Rockne: A Notre Dame Mystery, Vol. 1. 320p. 1998. pap. 5.99 (*0-312-96738-1*, Pub. by Tor Bks) St Martin.

— The Question of Christian Ethics. LC 92-25511. (Michael J. McGivney Lectures of the John Paul II Institutes for Studies on Marriage & Family: Vol. 1990). 74p. 1993. 21.95 (*0-8132-0770-3*); pap. 10.95 (*0-8132-0771-1*) Cath U Pr.

— The Red Hat: A Novel. LC 97-76857. 600p. 1998. 24.95 (*0-89870-681-5*) Ignatius Pr.

— Rest in Pieces. large type ed. (Nightingale Ser.). 280p. 1991. lib. bdg. 13.95 (*0-8161-5107-5*, G K Hall Lrg Type) Mac Lib Ref.

— Rhyme & Reason: St. Thomas & Modes of Discourse. LC 81-80234. (Aquinas Lectures). 84p. (C). 1981. 15.00 (*0-87462-148-8*) Marquette.

— Saint Thomas Aquinas. LC 81-16293. 197p. (C). 1982. reprint ed. pap. text 11.50 (*0-268-01707-7*) U of Notre Dame Pr.

— Savings & Loam: An Andrew Broom Mystery. (Worldwide Library Mysteries: No. 91). 1992. mass mkt. 3.99 (*0-373-26091-1*, 1-26091-8) Harlequin Bks.

— The Search Committee. large type ed. 1991. 27.99 (*0-7089-8613-7*) Ulverscroft.

***McInerny, Ralph.** A Student's Guide to Philosophy. LC 99-66785. 1999. pap. text 5.95 (*1-882926-39-0*) ISI Books.

McInerny, Ralph. The Tears of Things. LC 96-19917. 1996. write for info. (*0-03-214746-5*) St Martin.

— What Went Wrong with Vatican II: The Catholic Crisis Explained. LC 98-29115. 176p. 1998. pap. 14.95 (*0-918477-79-4*) Sophia Inst Pr.

McInerny, Ralph, ed. Modernity & Religion. LC 93-8804. (C). 1994. text 25.50 (*0-268-01408-6*) U of Notre Dame Pr.

— New Themes in Christian Philosophy. LC 68-20439. 1968. 40.95 (*0-8290-1654-6*); pap. text 9.50 (*0-8290-1606-6*) Irvington.

McInerny, Ralph, et al. An Uncertain Legacy Vol. 1: Essays on the Pursuit of Liberty. McLean, Edward B., ed. LC 97-72119. 256p. 1997. pap. 14.95 (*1-882926-15-3*, 244) ISI Books.

McInerny, Ralph, ed. see Maritain, Jacques.

McInerny, Ralph, ed. & pref. see Wethersfield Institute Staff.

McInerny, Ralph, ed. & tr. see Aquinas, Thomas, Saint.

McInerny, Ralph, tr. & pref. see Aquinas, Thomas, Saint.

McInery, Timothy A. Private Man. 1962. 12.95 (*0-8392-1087-6*) Astor-Honor.

***McInish, Thomas H.** Capital Markets: A Global Perspective. LC 99-56767. 500p. 1999. 79.95 (*0-631-21159-4*); pap. 39.95 (*0-631-21160-8*) Blackwell Pubs.

McInish, Thomas H., jt. auth. see Kudla, Ronald J.

McInnes, Adrian. Handbook on Damages. 133p. 1992. pap. 37.00 (*0-455-21088-8*, Pub. by LawBk Co) Gaunt.

McInnes, Colin J. Hot War, Cold War: The British Army's Way in Warfare 1945-95. (Illus.). 216p. 1996. 39.95 (*1-85753-191-4*, Pub. by Brasseys) Brasseys.

McInnes, Colin J. & Rolls, Mark G., eds. Post-Cold War Security Issues in the Asia-Pacific Region. 1994. pap. 22.50 (*0-7146-4131-6*, Pub. by F Cass Pubs) Intl Spec Bk.

McInnes, Colin J. & Sheffield, Gary D., eds. Warfare in the Twentieth Century: Theory & Practice. 256p. 1988. text 55.00 (*0-04-355034-7*) Routledge.

McInnes, Colin Robert. Solar Sailing: Technology, Dynamics & Mission Applications. LC 98-43763. (Series in Space Science & Technology). xxix, 296p. 1999. 89.95 (*1-85233-102-X*) Spr-Verlag.

McInnes, D. Keith, jt. auth. see Bitran, Ricardo A.

McInnes, Edward. Woyzeck, Cuchner: Critical Monographs in English. 1993. pap. 40.00 (*0-85261-341-5*, Pub. by Univ of Glasgow) St Mut.

***McInnes, Gordon, ed.** Benefits of Valsartan. (Cardiology Ser.: Vol. 91). (Illus.). lv, 26p. 1999. 25.25 (*3-8055-6945-9*) S Karger.

McInnes, Ian. The Meritorious Service Medal to Aerial Forces. 63p. (C). 1990. pap. 24.00 (*0-902633-92-9*, Pub. by Picton) St Mut.

— The Meritorious Service Medal to Naval Forces. 63p. (C). 1987. 50.00 (*0-7855-2169-0*, Pub. by Picton) St Mut.

McInnes, Ian, ed. The Meritorious Service Medal to Naval Forces. 1990. pap. 40.00 (*0-902633-82-1*, Pub. by Picton) St Mut.

McInnes, Ian & Fraser, Mark, eds. Ashanti 1895. (Illus.). 156p. (C). 1990. 54.00 (*0-948251-12-3*, Pub. by Picton) St Mut.

McInnes, John C. Divorce Law & Practice in Scotland. 200p. 1990. boxed set 66.00 (*0-406-13210-0*, U.K., MICHIE) LEXIS Pub.

McInnes, John M., ed. Planning & Support for the Congenitally Deafblind. 644p. 1999. text 60.00 (*0-8020-4242-2*) U of Toronto Pr.

McInnes, John M. & Treffry, Jacqueline A. Deaf-Blind Infants & Children: A Development Guide. LC 82-190483. 302p. reprint ed. pap. 93.70 (*0-7837-2049-1*, 204232400004) Bks Demand.

— Deaf-Blind Infants & Children: A Developmental Guide. 1994. pap. text 17.95 (*0-8020-7787-0*) U of Toronto Pr.

***McInnes, Mary D.** Telling Histories: Installations by Ellen Rothenberg & Carrie Mae Weems. (Illus.). 56p. 2000. pap. 20.00 (*1-881450-11-2*) Boston U Art.

McInnes, Mitchell. Restitution: Developments in Unjust Enrichment. 1996. pap. 85.00 (*0-455-21430-1*, Pub. by Cavendish Pubng) Gaunt.

McInnes, Pamela M., jt. auth. see Paoletti, Lawrence C.

McInnes, Ron. Landlord-Tenant Rights in Ontario: Canadian Edition. 10th rev. ed. (Legal Ser.). 192p. 1994. pap. 9.95 (*0-88908-493-9*) Self-Counsel Pr.

McInnis, Bryant Johnson. Glory in a Snapshot: A Photographic Look at Bedford-Stuyvesant - Now & Then. Woodbury, Tina, ed. 100p. 1999. pap. write for info. (*1-889732-20-6*) Word-For-Word.

McInnis, C. Liegh. Confessions: Brainstormin' from Midnite 'Til. LC 98-91295. 110p. 1997. per. 15.00 (*0-9655775-2-X*) Psychedelic Lit.

— The Lyrics of Prince: A Literary Look at a Musical Poet, Philosopher & Storyteller. LC 96-92619. (Illus.). ix, 112p. (Orig.). 1997. per. 15.00 (*0-9655775-0-3*) Psychedelic Lit.

— Matters of Reality: Body, Mind & Soul. LC 96-9260. (Illus.). viii, 88p. (Orig.). 1997. per. 15.00 (*0-9655775-1-1*) Psychedelic Lit.

— Prose: Essays & Personal Letters. 153p. 1999. per. 15.00 (*0-9655775-5-4*) Psychedelic Lit.

— Scripts: Sketches & Tales of Urban Mississippi. LC 98-91241. 160p. 1998. per. 15.00 (*0-9655775-3-8*) Psychedelic Lit.

— Searchin' 4 Psychedelica. 97p. 1999. per. 15.00 (*0-9655775-4-6*) Psychedelic Lit.

McInnis, Carol, ed. see Allan, A. Grant.

McInnis, Cynthia. Holler If It Hurts, But Don't You Quit! 86p. 1999. pap. write for info. (*0-7392-0094-1*, PO2976) Morris Pubng.

— What Is Thy Request? Getting an Answer to Prayer. 130p. 1998. pap. 12.00 (*1-57502-749-6*, PO2083) Morris Pubng.

McInnis-Dittrich, Kathleen. Integrating Social Welfare Policy & Social Work Practice. LC 93-4781. 208p. 1993. mass mkt. 32.50 (*0-534-17430-2*) Brooks-Cole.

McInnis, Edgar, jt. auth. see Soward, Frederic H.

McInnis, J. A. Hong Kong Construction Law, 2 vols., Issue 0. 1995. ring bd. write for info. (*0-409-99783-8*, MICHIE) LEXIS Pub.

McInnis, Marina. Running Your Business with Quattro Pro for Windows. 300p. 1993. pap. 34.95 (*1-883327-42-3*) TitleWave Pr.

McInnis, Maurie D., ed. In Pursuit of Refinement: Charlestonians Abroad, 1740-1860. LC 98-58068. (Illus.). 350p. 1999. pap. 29.95 (*1-57003-315-3*) U of SC Pr.

McInnis, Michael, et al. 5x5 Singles, Vol. 2. (Illus.). 80p. (Orig.). 1997. pap. 3.95 (*0-941215-11-3*) Primal Pub.

McInnis, Nadine. The Litmus Body. 88p. 1992. pap. 12.95 (*1-55082-037-0*, Pub. by Quarry Pr) LPC InBook.

— Poetics of Desire: Essay on Dorothy Livesay. 114p. 1997. pap. 10.95 (*0-88801-181-4*, Pub. by Turnstone Pr) Genl Dist Srvs.

McInnis, Noel, ed. see Hubbard, Barbara M.

McInnis, Noel, ed. see Magdalena, Flo A.

McInnis, Raymond G. New Perspectives for Reference Service in Academic Libraries, 23. LC 77-94742. (Contributions in Librarianship & Information Science Ser.: No. 23). (Illus.). 351p. 1979. 59.95 (*0-313-20311-3*, MNP/, Greenwood Pr) Greenwood.

— Research Guide for Psychology, 1. LC 81-1377. (Reference Sources for the Social Sciences & Humanities Ser.: No. 1). (Illus.). 604p. 1982. lib. bdg. 115.00 (*0-313-21399-2*, MCR/, Greenwood Pr) Greenwood.

***McInnis, Raymond G., ed.** Discourse Synthesis: Studies in Historical & Contemporary Social Epistemology. 2001. write for info. (*0-275-97070-1*) Greenwood.

***McInnis, Thomas N.** The Christian Burial Case: An Introduction to Criminal & Judicial Procedure. 2001. write for info. (*0-275-97027-2*, Praeger Pubs); pap. write for info. (*0-275-97028-0*, Praeger Trade) Greenwood.

***McIntee, David A.** Delta Quadrant: The Unofficial Guide to Voyager. (Illus.). 288p. 2000. mass mkt. 7.95 (*0-7535-0436-7*) Virgin Pubng.

McIntee, David A. Face of the Enemy. (Doctor Who Ser.). 1998. pap. 5.95 (*0-563-40580-5*) BBC.

— Mission: Impractical. (Doctor Who Ser.). 1998. pap. 5.95 (*0-563-40592-9*) BBC.

McIntee, Jeanne D. To Comfort & to Honor: A Guide to Personalizing Rituals for the Passing of a Loved One. LC 98-19001. 128p. 1998. pap. 14.99 (*0-8066-3624-6*, 9-3624) Augsburg Fortress.

McIntire. Introduction to Psychological Testing. LC 99-29129. 448p. 1999. 63.75 (*0-07-045100-1*) McGraw.

McIntire, Alexander H., Jr. Political & Electoral Confrontation in Revolutionary Nicaragua. 65p. (C). 1985. pap. text 18.95 (*1-56000-660-9*, LA204) Transaction Pubs.

McIntire, C. T. & Perry, Marvin, eds. Toynbee: A Reappraisal. 1989. text 40.00 (*0-8020-5785-3*) U of Toronto Pr.

McIntire, Cecil L. Corpus Morphus: The Human Anatomy Board Game with 1944 Multiple Choice Quest. (Illus.). 224p. (C). 1993. rig bd. 39.95 (*0-9669824-0-1*) East Branch Pr.

McIntire, David M. The Rafter Book: A Modern Handbook for Roof Framers. LC 95-79996. (Illus.). 134p. 1995. 15.95 (*0-9647784-0-8*) Joseph Pubng.

McIntire, Deborah & Windham, Robert. Home Schooling, Vol. 3340. (Home Education Ser.). 144p. 1995. pap. 17.98 (*0-916119-84-X*) Creat Teach Pr.

McIntire, Deborah, jt. auth. see Hetzel, June.

McIntire, Dennis, jt. ed. see Cummings, David.

McIntire, Donald. The Pemaquid Loon from Temple. (Illus.). (Orig.). (J). 1988. pap. 5.99 (*0-317-92307-2*) Herit Pub Inc.

— The Pemaquid Loon from Temple. (Illus.). 24p. (Orig.). (J). (ps-4). 1988. pap. text 5.99 (*0-929537-00-9*) Herit Pub Inc.

McIntire, Donald, ed. see Chetkowski, Emily.

***McIntire, James L.** The New Eco-Order: Economic & Ecological Linkages of the World[0012]s Temperate & Boreal Forest Resources. (Illus.). 122p. 2000. reprint ed. pap. text 35.00 (*0-7881-8953-0*) DIANE Pub.

McIntire, Jamie. Santa's Christmas Surprise. LC 93-24843. (Glow-in-the-Dark Bk.). (Illus.). 24p. (J). (gr. k-3). 1996. pap. 2.95 (*0-8167-3257-4*) Troll Communs.

McIntire, John J. As I Saw It. 1977. 18.95 (*0-8369-9189-3*, 9058) Ayer.

McIntire, Larry V., jt. ed. see Rudolph, Frederick B.

***McIntire, Mac & Wheeler, Denice.** How to Create a Survivor's Journal: Preparing Your Family for Your Death or Disability. 300p. 1999. mass mkt. 29.95 (*0-9674237-0-8*) Innovative Mgm.

McIntire, Marina L., ed. Proceedings of the 9th RID National Convention, 1985: Interpreting: The Art of Cross-Cultural Mediation. 192p. (C). 1990. reprint ed. pap. 10.95 (*0-916883-05-1*) RID Pubns.

McIntire, Molly, jt. contrib. by see Mahal, Susan.

McIntire, Paul & Mester, Michael, eds. ASNT Nondestructive Testing Handbook, Vol. 4: Electromagnetic Testing. 2nd ed. (Illus.). 701p. 1986. 121.25 (*0-931403-01-4*, 129) Am Soc Nondestructive.

McIntire, Paul, jt. ed. see Bryant, Lawrence E.

McIntire, Paul, jt. ed. see Miller, Ronnie K.

McIntire, Robert C., ed. Daily Gleaner Index. 210p. 1990. disk 150.00 (*0-932265-20-0*) White Sound.

McIntire, Robert C., et al. The Bahamas Index, 1988. 400p. 1989. lib. bdg. 150.00 (*0-932265-10-3*); disk 150.00 (*0-932265-11-1*) White Sound.

McIntire, Robert C., jt. compiled by see Dodge, Steve.

McIntire, Roger. Raising Good Kids in Tough Times: 5 Crucial Habits for Great Parents. LC 99-219509. 1999. pap. 14.95 (*0-9640558-9-9*) Summit Crossrds.

McIntire, Roger W. College Keys: Getting In, Doing Well, Avoiding the 4 Big Mistakes. LC 98-122587. (YA). (gr. 11-12). 1998. pap. 11.95 (*0-9640558-7-2*) Summit Crossrds.

— Enjoy Successful Parenting: Practical Strategies for Parents of Children 2-12. 2nd rev. ed. Haavik, Eileen et al, eds. LC 96-224850. 285p. (Orig.). 1996. pap. 16.95 (*0-9640558-5-6*) Summit Crossrds.

— Teenagers & Parents: Ten Steps for a Better Relationship. 3rd rev. ed. Haavik, Eileen et al, eds. LC 96-219204. (Illus.). 264p. 1996. pap. 11.95 (*0-9640558-6-4*) Summit Crossrds.

McIntire, Ronald G. & Fessenden, John T. The Self-Directed School: Empowering the Stakeholders. LC 93-34345. 1995. 29.95 (*0-590-49267-5*, 28063m35 1994) Scholastic Inc.

McIntire-Strasburg, Janice, ed. see Twain, Mark, pseud.

***McIntire, Suzanne.** American Heritage Book of Great American Speeches for Young People. 288p. (J). 2001. pap. 14.95 (*0-471-38942-0*) Wiley.

McIntire, Tim, jt. auth. see Friedman, Robert D.

McIntire, Virginia A. Color Energy for Mind/Body/Spirit. 102p. (Orig.). 1986. reprint ed. pap. 7.50 (*0-9634894-0-2*) DeVorss.

McIntire, W. L., et al. Bending Strength of Spur & Helical Gear Teeth. (Technical Papers: Vol. P229.11). (Illus.). 20p. 1967. pap. text 30.00 (*1-55589-278-7*) AGMA.

McIntoch & Twyman, trs. The Archko Volume: Archeological Writings of the Sanhedrim & Talmuds of the Jews. 248p. 1996. pap. 16.00 (*0-7873-0598-7*) Hlth Research.

McIntosch, John. Living Abundantly Through Inner Guidance. 198p. 1998. pap. 16.95 (*1-55212-215-8*, 98-0033, Pub. by Tra3fford) Trafford Pub.

McIntosh. Aboriginal Reconciliation & the Dreaming: Warramiri Yolngu & the Quest for Equality. LC 99-461958. 148p. 1999. pap. 20.00 (*0-205-29793-5*, Longwood Div) Allyn.

McIntosh. Beacon Hill Associates: An Executive Secretary Simulation. 3rd ed. (Office Procedures Ser.). (C). 1991. 30.75 (*0-538-70394-6*) S-W Pub.

— Lifetime Aerobics. 2nd ed. 1999. pap. text 9.00 (*0-697-12653-6*) McGraw.

***McIntosh.** Peaceful Empire. 2000. 40.00 (*0-8133-3532-9*, Pub. by Westview) HarpC.

McIntosh. Real Estate Principles. 1999. pap. text, student ed. 11.25 (*0-256-12778-6*) McGraw.

— Real Estate Principles. 1999. text 11.25 (*0-256-12777-8*) McGraw.

— The Secretary: An Office Job Simulation. 3rd ed. (KM - Office Procedures Ser.). 1989. 17.75 (*0-538-60076-4*) S-W Pub.

— The Secretary: An Office Job Simulation. 3rd ed. 1989. 44.00 (*0-538-60083-7*) S-W Pub.

McIntosh, A. Towns & Cities: Competing for Survival. LC 97-202819. (Illus.). 192p. (C). (gr. 13). 1997. pap. 45.00 (*0-419-22740-7*, E & FN Spon) Routledge.

McIntosh, A., et al. Guide to a Linguistic Atlas of Late Mediaeval English. (Aberdeen University Press Bks.). 24p. 1987. pap. 6.00 (*0-08-035076-3*, Pub. by Aberdeen U Pr) Macmillan.

— A Linguistic Atlas of Late Mediaeval English, 4 vols., Set. 2400p. 1987. 670.00 (*0-08-032437-1*, Pub. by Aberdeen U Pr) Macmillan.

McIntosh, A., jt. auth. see Newman, Michael C.

McIntosh, A. V. Santa's Reindeer. (Illus.). 42p. (Orig.). (J). (ps-3). 1996. pap. 10.00 (*1-57502-360-1*, PO1165) Morris Pubng.

McIntosh, Allen A. Fitting Linear Models: An Application of Conjugate Gradient Algorithms. (Lecture Notes in Statistics Ser.: Vol. 10). (Illus.). 200p. 1982. 47.95 (*0-387-90746-7*) Spr-Verlag.

McIntosh, Ann. The Mid-Atlantic Budget Angler. LC 97-28629. (Illus.). 320p. 1998. pap. 21.95 (*0-8117-2851-X*) Stackpole.

An Asterisk (*) at the beginning of an entry indicates that the title is appearing for the first time.

***McIntosh, Anne.** Sometimes I Talk, Sometimes I Sign: Algunas Veces Hablo, Algunas Veces Uso el Lenguaje Manual. Campagna, Jeff, ed. Kidd, Dawn, tr. (Illus.). 40p. (J). (ps-3). 2000. pap. text 19.95 (*0-9679353-0-X*) Commn Conn.

McIntosh, Arthur H. & Maramorosch, Karl, eds. Arthropod Cell Culture Systems. LC 93-38285. 246p. 1994. lib. bdg. 189.00 (*0-8493-7642-4*) CRC Pr.

McIntosh, Arthur H., jt. ed. see Maramorosch, Karl.

McIntosh, Barbara-Jo. Tin Fish Gourmet: Great Seafood from Cupboard to Table. LC 98-40467. 1999. 13.95 (*1-55868-468-9*) Gr Arts Ctr Pub.

McIntosh, Bruce, jt. auth. see Kolka, James W.

McIntosh, Bruce A., jt. ed. see Halliday, Ian.

McIntosh, Burr. The Little I Saw of Cuba. 1976. lib. bdg. 59.95 (*0-8490-2174-X*) Gordon Pr.

McIntosh, C. Alison. Population Policy in Western Europe: Responses to Low Fertility in France, Sweden, & West Germany. LC 82-5840. 292p. 1983. reprint ed. pap. 90.60 (*0-8357-2616-9*, 204010300014) Bks Demand.

McIntosh, Carey. The Choice of Life: Samuel Johnson & the World of Fiction. LC 73-77160. 243p. reprint ed. pap. 75.40 (*0-8357-8073-2*, 203382200087) Bks Demand.

— The Evolution of English Prose, 1700-1800: Style, Politeness, & Print Culture. LC 97-40963. 289p. (C). 1998. 59.95 (*0-521-62424-2*) Cambridge U Pr.

McIntosh, Charles B. The Nebraska Sand Hills: The Human Landscape. LC 95-19845. (Illus.). xvi, 266p. 1996. text 70.00 (*0-8032-3184-9*) U of Nebr Pr.

McIntosh, Charles F. Brief Abstract of Lower Norfolk County & Norfolk County Wills. 223p. 1994. reprint ed. pap. 25.50 (*0-8328-4019-X*) Higginson Bk Co.

— Brief Abstract of Lower Norfolk County & Norfolk County Wills, 1637-1710 & 1710-1753, 2 vols. in 1. 566p. 1998. pap. 40.00 (*0-8063-4800-3*) Clearfield Co.

— Brief Abstracts of Norfolk County Wills, 1710-1753. 344p. 1982. reprint ed. pap. 30.00 (*0-89308-324-0*) Southern Hist Pr.

McIntosh, Christopher. Ludwig II of Bavaria. LC 98-202794. (Illus.). 240p. 1998. pap. 19.95 (*1-86064-314-0*, Pub. by I B T) St Martin.

— The Rose Cross & the Age of Reason: Eighteenth-Century Rosicrucianism in Central Europe & Its Relationship to the Enlightenment. LC 91-44752. (Brill's Studies in Intellectual History: Vol. 29). (Illus.). 200p. 1992. 81.00 (*90-04-09502-0*) Brill Academic Pubs.

— The Rosicrucians: The History, Mythology, & Rituals of an Esoteric Order. LC 97-8592. (Illus.). 188p. 1997. 22.95 (*0-87728-893-3*) Weiser.

— The Rosicrucians: The History, Mythology & Rituals of an Esoteric Order. LC 97-8592. Orig. Title: The Rosicrucians: The History, Mythology, & Rituals of an Esoteric Order. (Illus.). 192p. 1998. pap. 14.95 (*0-87728-920-4*) Weiser.

McIntosh, Clarence F., jt. auth. see Hutchinson, W. H.

McIntosh, Colin, ed. The Oxford Starter Italian Dictionary. 320p. 1999. pap. 9.95 (*0-19-860257-X*) OUP.

McIntosh, D. A. Chain of Deceit. LC 98-89501. 375p. 1998. text 25.00 (*0-7388-0237-9*); pap. text 15.00 (*0-7388-0238-7*) Xlibris Corp.

McIntosh, Daniel N. The Psychology of Religion: Theoretical Approaches. Spilka, Bernard, ed. LC 96-41128. (C). 1996. pap. text 25.00 (*0-8133-2947-7*, Pub. by Westview) HarpC.

McIntosh, Dave. High Blue Battle: The War Diary of No. 1 (401) Fighter Squadron, RCAF. (Illus.). 192p. 1990. 24.95 (*0-7737-2338-2*) Genl Dist Srvs.

— High Blue Battle: The War Diary of No. 1 (401) Fighter Squadron, RCAF. (Illus.). 192p. 1991. pap. 14.95 (*0-7737-5441-5*) Genl Dist Srvs.

— Terror in the Starboard Seat. LC 98-230947. (Illus.). 184p. 1998. pap. 17.95 (*0-7737-3089-3*) Stoddart Publ.

— Visits: On the Road to Things Past. 240p. 1990. 24.95 (*0-7737-2428-1*) Genl Dist Srvs.

— When the Work's All Done This Fall: Voices of Early Canada the Opening of the Land. (Illus.). 320p. 1989. 29.95 (*0-7737-2323-4*) Genl Dist Srvs.

— Who's Running This Country Anyhow? Ottawa Unbuttoned. 256p. 1987. 21.95 (*0-7737-2115-0*) Genl Dist Srvs.

McIntosh, David & Holmes, Majorie. Personal Injury Awards in EC Countries: An Industry Report. 199p. 1990. pap. 265.00 (*1-85044-349-1*) LLP.

McIntosh, David & Holmes, Marjorie. Civil Procedures in EC Countries. 303p. 1991. pap. 250.00 (*1-85044-435-8*) LLP.

— Personal Injury Awards in EU & EFTA Countries. 2nd ed. 456p. 1994. pap. 265.00 (*1-85044-506-0*) LLP.

McIntosh, David C. How to Build a Wooden Boat. (Illus.). 264p. 1988. 36.00 (*0-937822-10-8*) WoodenBoat Pubns.

McIntosh, David M., ed. Cleaning up the Superfund Program. (Illus.). 193p. 1999. reprint ed. pap. text 30.00 (*0-7881-8063-0*) DIANE Pub.

McIntosh, David M. & Murray, David C. Medical Malpractice Liability: An Agenda for Reform. 1994. 12.95 (*0-614-17718-9*) Hudson Instit IN.

***McIntosh, DeCourcy E. & Sandler, Irving.** The Collector as Patron in the Twentieth Century. LC 00-103091. (Illus.). 58p. 2000. pap. 25.00 (*0-615-11639-6*) Knoedler & Co.

McIntosh, DeCourcy E., ed. see Brachlianoff, Dominique.

McIntosh, Dianne & Tompkins, Iverna M. Fearless Parenting: Handle with Love. LC 96-83546. 312p. 1996. pap. 10.99 (*0-88270-691-8*) Bridge-Logos.

McIntosh, Donald. Foundations of Human Society. LC 79-84771. 1994. lib. bdg. 22.50 (*0-226-55935-1*) U Ch Pr.

— Self, Person, World: The Interplay of Conscious & Unconscious in Human Life. LC 94-47481. (Psychoanalytic Issues Ser.). 1995. 59.95 (*0-8101-1233-7*); pap. 19.95 (*0-8101-1217-5*) Northwestern U Pr.

***McIntosh, Doug.** Life's Greatest Journey. LC 00-25756. 2000. pap. 12.99 (*0-8024-6648-6*) Moody.

McIntosh, Douglas M. Love Full Circle: The Golden Rule. (Foundations of the Faith Ser.). 1999. pap. 9.99 (*0-8024-6647-8*) Moody.

McIntosh, Duncan. The Everyday Evangelist. 64p. 1984. pap. 7.00 (*0-8170-1042-4*) Judson.

McIntosh, Elaine. Internal Auditing in a Total Quality Environment. Campbell, Lee A., ed. 87p. 1992. 20.00 (*0-89413-266-0*, A7391) Inst Inter Aud.

McIntosh, Elaine N. American Food Habits in Historical Perspective. LC 95-7550. 272p. 1995. 69.50 (*0-275-94601-0*, Praeger Pubs); pap. 24.95 (*0-275-95331-9*, Praeger Pubs) Greenwood.

McIntosh, Elizabeth. Sisterhood of Spies: The Women of the OSS. 1999. mass mkt. 6.50 (*0-440-23466-2*) Dell.

McIntosh, Elizabeth P. Sisterhood of Spies: The Women of the OSS. LC 97-44242. (Illus.). 282p. 1998. 29.95 (*1-55750-598-5*) Naval Inst Pr.

McIntosh, Elspeth. The Mother's Quotation Book: A Literary Companion. (Illus.). 1997. 12.95 (*0-7090-5427-0*) Parkwest Pubns.

McIntosh-Fletcher, Donna. Teaming by Design: Real Teams for Real People. 192p. 1995. 24.95 (*0-7863-0536-3*, Irwn Prfssnl) McGraw-Hill Prof.

McIntosh, Frank S., ed. How I Got My Piece of the Rock & Vital Life Insurance Information. 1979. pap. 19.95 (*0-686-26460-6*) Ins Res Svc.

McIntosh, Gary. Arrows of Victory. Date not set. 7.99 (*1-57778-027-2*, GM-001) Albury Pub.

***McIntosh, Gary.** The Exodus Principle: A Five-Part Strategy to Free Your People for Ministry. 1999. pap. 11.99 (*0-8054-2016-9*) Broadman.

McIntosh, Gary. Get Ready for Company: How to Welcome Guests to Your Church & Develop a Follow-Up Program to Keep Them Coming Back. Spear, Cindy G., ed. 16p. 1997. pap., wbk. ed. 54.95 incl. audio (*1-57052-070-4*) Chrch Grwth VA.

McIntosh, Gary L. How to Develop a Church Policy Manual: To Insure a Consistent & Orderly Ministry. 141p. 1992. ring bd. 54.95 (*0-941005-65-8*) Chrch Grwth VA.

— How to Develop a Pastoral Compensation Plan: A Biblical Approach to Meeting the Needs of the Pastor & His Staff. Johnson, Tamara & Spear, Cindy G., eds. 100p. 1991. ring bd. 29.95 (*0-941005-43-7*) Chrch Grwth VA.

— One Size Doesn't Fit All: Bringing Out the Best in Any Size Church. LC 99-18717. (Illus.). 174p. (C). (gr. 13). 1999. pap. 11.99 (*0-8007-5699-1*) Revell.

***McIntosh, Gary L.** Staff Your Church for Growth: Building Team Ministry in the 21st Century. 208p. 2000. pap. 11.99 (*0-8010-9095-4*) Baker Bks.

McIntosh, Gary L. & Edmondson, Robert L. It Only Hurts on Monday: Why Pastors Quit & What You Can Do about It. 173p. (Orig.). 1998. pap. 9.99 (*1-889638-02-1*) ChurchSmart.

McIntosh, Gary L. & Rima, Samuel D., Sr. Overcoming the Dark Side of Leadership: The Paradox of Personal Dysfunction. LC 97-22265. 240p. 1998. pap. 12.99 (*0-8010-9047-4*) Baker Bks.

McIntosh, Gary L., jt. auth. see Martin, Glen.

***McIntosh, Gillian.** The Force of Culture: Unionist Identities in Contemporary Ireland. 248p. 2000. 65.00 (*1-85918-204-6*, Pub. by Cork Univ); pap. 25.00 (*1-85918-205-4*, Pub. by Cork Univ) Stylus Pub VA.

McIntosh, Gregory C. Antique Map Reproductions: A Directory of Publishers & Distributors of Antique Map, Atlas & Globe Facsimiles & Reproductions. LC 98-96643. 1998. pap. write for info. (*0-9667462-0-1*) Plus Ultra Pubg.

***McIntosh, Hal.** Chainsaw Carving: The Art & Craft: A Complete Guide. (Illus.). 112p. 2000. pap. 24.95 (*1-56523-128-7*, Pub. by Fox Chapel Pub) IPG Chicago.

McIntosh, Harriet. Encore Talent Agency II: A Keyboard Simulation. 3rd ed. (TA - Typing/Keyboarding Ser.). 1992. mass mkt. 10.50 (*0-538-61252-5*) S-W Pub.

McIntosh, Harriet P. Yoo Hoo: I'm over Here. (Illus.). 108p. (Orig.). 1996. pap. 9.95 (*0-614-07235-2*) Jokake Pr.

— Yoo Hoo! I'm over Here! (Illus.). 108p. (Orig.). 1996. pap. write for info. (*0-614-30154-8*) Jokake Pr.

McIntosh, Hugh. Is Christ Infallible & the Bible True? 728p. 1987. lib. bdg. 29.99 (*0-8254-5180-9*) Kregel.

McIntosh, Ian. Classical Sociological Theory: A Reader. LC 96-47035. 1997. text 50.00 (*0-8147-5573-9*); pap. text 16.50 (*0-8147-5574-7*) NYU Pr.

McIntosh, I.B. Micro Man: What Life Might Be Like If You Were Bill Gates. 128p. 1998. pap. 9.95 (*1-55152-057-5*, Pub. by Arsenal Pulp) LPC InBook.

McIntosh, J. D. Concrete & Statistics. (Illus.). 139p. 1963. 36.00 (*0-85334-038-2*) Elsevier.

***McIntosh, James.** Nimble Believing: Dickinson & the Unknown. LC 99-54534. 208p. (C). 2000. text 42.50 (*0-472-11080-2*, 11080) U of Mich Pr.

McIntosh, James, ed. see Hawthorne, Nathaniel.

McIntosh, James C. & McIntosh, Marie, trs. from FRE. The Committed Observer: Raymond Aron Interviews with Jean-Louis Missika & Dominque Wolton. LC 82-42902. 1983. 17.00 (*0-89526-624-5*) Regnery Pub.

McIntosh, James T., ed. see Davis, Jefferson.

***McIntosh, Jane.** Archeology. (Eyewitness Books). (Illus.). (J). (gr. 4-7). 2000. 19.99 (*0-7894-6605-8*) DK Pub Inc.

— Archeology. (Eyewitness Books). (J). (gr. 4-7). 2000. 15.95 (*0-7894-5864-0*) DK Pub Inc.

— Archeology. LC 94-9378. (Eyewitness Books). (J). 1994. lib. bdg. 20.99 (*0-679-96572-6*) Knopf.

— Archeology. LC 94-9378. (Eyewitness Books). (Illus.). (J). 1994. 19.00 (*0-679-86572-1*) Knopf.

McIntosh, Jane. The Practical Archaeologist: How We Know What We Know About the Past. (Illus.). 192p. 1986. 26.95 (*0-8160-1400-0*) Facts on File.

— The Practical Archaeologist: How We Know What We Know About the Past. (Illus.). 192p. 1988. pap. 15.95 (*0-8160-1814-6*) Facts on File.

— The Practical Archaeologist: How We Know What We Know About the Past. 2nd ed. LC 98-48595. 1999. 16.95 (*0-8160-3951-8*, Checkmark) Facts on File.

McIntosh, Jane. The Practical Archaeologist: How We Know What We Know About the Past. 2nd ed. LC 98-48595. (Illus.). 192p. 1999. 35.00 (*0-8160-3950-X*) Facts on File.

McIntosh, Jane B. A Pilgrimage to Senegal & the Gambia, West Africa. unabridged ed. LC 96-71572. (Illus.). 136p. (Orig.). (YA). (gr. 7-12). 1997. pap. 19.95 (*0-9655944-0-8*) Ninth Sign CA.

This is a true saga of some of the extraordinary experiences of two resolute African-American women who fulfilled their dreams of a Pilgrimage to their Motherland. The author writes that "On Saturday, July first, at one o'clock in the afternoon, Birdie & I boarded AIR AFRIQUE at JFK International Airport, New York, New York, USA. This flight would take us to Dakar, Senegal, West Africa." "As I looked around that cabin & basked in pride & glory, a voice inside me said, 'Jane, you are just about to fly on an airplane that is owned by Africa. The airline crew is African. You are at least part-African. And finally, your prayer is being answered. You are on your way to AFRICA.'" "On the large-screen TV monitor, we would chart our course & location during the entire flight. Off & on, I nodded or napped but for the most part, Birdie & I talked all the way across the Atlantic Ocean to our Motherland - AFRICA." Among their other experiences, several unfathomable incidents occurred which the author vividly depicts. With more than sixty photographs interpolated, she captivates her reader with her pervading passion to share their experiences with others. Thus emerged her literary production which she published, entitled, A PILGRIMAGE TO SENEGAL & THE GAMBIA, WEST AFRICA. To order: The Ninth Sign, Box 67 - 24470 Foothill Boulevard, Hayword, CA 94541-1061. Tel. (510) 317-7519. Fax. (510) 278-4706. *Publisher Paid Annotation.*

McIntosh, Joan. Branch & Shadow Branch. 32p. 1982. pap. 3.00 (*1-880649-11-X*) Writ Ctr Pr.

McIntosh, Joel, ed. 20 Ideas for Teaching Gifted Kids in the Middle School & High School. 132p. 1991. pap. 19.95 (*1-882664-05-1*) Prufrock Pr.

— 20 More Ideas for Teaching Gifted Kids in the Middle School & High School. 115p. 1994. pap. 19.95 (*1-882664-15-9*) Prufrock Pr.

McIntosh, Joel & Meacham, April. Creative Problem Solving in the Classroom: Teacher's Guide to Effectively Using CPS in Any Classroom. 123p. 1991. pap. 19.95 (*1-882664-00-0*) Prufrock Pr.

McIntosh, John. The Discovery of America by Christopher Columbus & the Origin of the North American Indians. (LC History-America-E). 1836. reprint ed. lib. bdg. 79.00 (*0-7812-4390-4*) Rprt Serv.

McIntosh, John. Millennium Tablets. 177p. 1996. pap. 14.95 (*0-929385-78-0*) Light Tech Pubng.

McIntosh, John, jt. auth. see Eismann, Katrin.

McIntosh, John H. History of Elbert County Georgia 1790-1935. 2nd ed. 621p. 1997. reprint ed. 35.00 (*0-9644858-9-3*) Boyd Pub Co.

McIntosh, John L., ed. Research on Suicide: A Bibliography, 2. LC 84-15706. (Bibliographies & Indexes in Psychology Ser.: No. 2). 323p. 1985. lib. bdg. 79.50 (*0-313-23992-4*, MLR/, Greenwood Pr) Greenwood.

McIntosh, John L., et al. Elder Suicide: Research, Theory, & Treatment. (Illus.). 260p. 1994. text 24.95 (*1-55798-240-6*); pap. text 19.95 (*1-55798-242-2*) Am Psychol.

McIntosh, John L., jt. compiled by see Osgood, Nancy J.

McIntosh, John S., jt. auth. see Ostrom, John H.

McIntosh, John S., jt. ed. see Kohl, Michael F.

McIntosh, John W. & McIntosh, Margaret S. The Reader's Companion, with Black Cover. 68p. 1994. ring bd. 15.00 (*0-9644092-0-8*) Creekside CO.

— The Reader's Companion, with Burgundy Cover. 68p. 1994. ring bd. 15.00 (*0-9644092-1-6*) Creekside CO.

McIntosh-Johnson, Julie. Basics of Keyboard Theory: Answer Book. 2nd rev. ed. LC TX 4 799 988. vi, 122p. 1997. teacher ed., spiral bd. 10.95 (*1-891757-11-3*, BKT-Ans) J Johnson Mus.

— Basics of Keyboard Theory: Level 1, 4th rev. ed. LC TX 3 431 937. vi, 88p. 1997. spiral bd. 8.95 (*1-891757-01-6*, BKT-1) J Johnson Mus.

— Basics of Keyboard Theory: Level 2, 4th rev. ed. LC TX 4-721-495. vi, 67p. 1997. spiral bd. 8.95 (*1-891757-02-4*, BKT-2) J Johnson Mus.

— Basics of Keyboard Theory: Level 4, 4th rev. ed. LC TX 4 721 492. vi, 91p. 1997. spiral bd. 8.95 (*1-891757-04-0*, BKT-4) J Johnson Mus.

— Basics of Keyboard Theory: Level 5, 5th rev. ed. LC TX 4 721 493. vi, 100p. 1997. spiral bd. 8.95 (*1-891757-05-9*, BKT-5) J Johnson Mus.

— Basics of Keyboard Theory: Level 6, 4th rev. ed. LC TX 4 721 498. vi, 113p. 1997. spiral bd. 9.95 (*1-891757-06-7*, BKT-6) J Johnson Mus.

— Basics of Keyboard Theory: Level 7, 3rd rev. ed. LC TX 4 721 497. vi, 132p. 1997. spiral bd. 10.45 (*1-891757-07-5*, BKT-7) J Johnson Mus.

— Basics of Keyboard Theory: Level 8, 3rd rev. ed. LC TX 4 721 496. vi, 162p. 1997. spiral bd. 11.45 (*1-891757-08-3*, BKT-8) J Johnson Mus.

— Basics of Keyboard Theory: Level 9, 3rd rev. ed. LC TX 4 721 491. vi, 180p. 1997. spiral bd. 11.95 (*1-891757-09-1*, BKT-9) J Johnson Mus.

— Basics of Keyboard Theory: Preparatory Level. 3rd rev. ed. LC TX 4 721 499. vi, 65p. 1992. spiral bd. 8.95 (*1-891757-00-8*, BKT-P) J Johnson Mus.

Mcintosh-Johnson, Julie, ed. Basics of Keyboard Theory: Level 10, LC TX 4 721 490. vi, 89p. 1997. spiral bd. 11.95 (*1-891757-10-5*, BKT-10) J Johnson Mus.

McIntosh, Jon. Hooked on Golf. (Hooked on...Sports Ser.). (Illus.). 102p. (Orig.). 1982. pap. 4.95 (*0-938864-04-1*) Ipswich Pr.

McIntosh, Laura, ed. see Gonzalez, Lorenzo.

McIntosh, Laura W., ed. Essentials of Nurse Anesthesia. LC 96-23810. (Illus.). 544p. 1996. text 49.00 (*0-07-076537-5*) McGraw-Hill HPD.

McIntosh, Lee, ed. Methods in Enzymology Vol. 297: Photosynthesis: Molecular Biology of Energy Capture. (Illus.). 395p. (C). 1998. boxed set 99.95 (*0-12-182198-6*) Acad Pr.

***McIntosh, Linda.** Are You Tired of being Tired? 2000. pap. 14.95 (*0-9577103-1-3*) Seven Hills Bk.

— How to Breathe Easily: A Natural Approach to Asthma, Sinusitis, Hay Fever & Other Respiratory Disorders. 2000. pap. 12.95 (*0-9577103-0-5*) Seven Hills Bk.

McIntosh, Malcolm, et al. Corporate Citizenship: Successful Strategies for Responsible Companies. 288p. 1998. 26.95 (*0-273-63106-3*, Pub. by F T P-H) Natl Bk Netwk.

McIntosh, Margaret E. & Draper, Roni J. Write Starts: 101 Writing Prompts for Math. Apple, Mali, ed. (Illus.). 97p. (Orig.). (YA). (gr. 6-12). 1996. pap., teacher ed. 14.95 (*0-86651-953-X*, DS21410) Seymour Pubns.

McIntosh, Margaret S., jt. auth. see McIntosh, John W.

McIntosh, Maria J. Conquest & Self-Conquest. LC 74-76928. (American Fiction Reprint Ser.). 1977. 16.95 (*0-8369-7007-1*) Ayer.

— Two Pictures. LC 72-39094. (Black Heritage Library Collection). 1977. reprint ed. 28.95 (*0-8369-9032-3*) Ayer.

McIntosh, Marie, jt. tr. see McIntosh, James C.

McIntosh, Marjorie K. Controlling Misbehavior in England, 1370-1600. LC 98-141859. (Studies in Population, Economy & Society in Past Time: No. 34). 312p. (C). 1998. text 59.95 (*0-521-62177-1*) Cambridge U Pr.

McIntosh, Mark A. Christology from Within: Spirituality & the Incarnation in Hans Urs Von Balthasar. LC 95-50918. (Studies in Spirituality & Theology: No. 3). 224p. (C). 1996. text 29.00 (*0-268-00815-9*) U of Notre Dame Pr.

***McIntosh, Mark A.** Christology from Within: Spirituality & the Incarnation in Hans Urs Von Balthasar. LC 95-50918. (Studies in Spirituality & Theology: Vol. 3). 212p. 2000. reprint ed. pap. 18.00 (*0-268-02354-9*, Pub. by U of Notre Dame Pr) Chicago Distribution Ctr.

McIntosh, Mark A. Mystical Theology: The Integrity of Spirituality & Theology. LC 97-44977. (Challenges in Contemporary Theology Ser.). 288p. 1998. 62.95 (*1-55786-906-5*); pap. 26.95 (*1-55786-907-3*) Blackwell Pubs.

***McIntosh, Mark Allen.** Mysteries of Faith. LC 99-46467. 200p. 1999. pap. 11.95 (*1-56101-175-4*) Cowley Pubns.

McIntosh, Mary. Fulfulde Syntax & Morphology. 200p. (Orig.). 1984. pap. 29.95 (*0-7103-0074-3*) Routledge.

McIntosh, Mathew. Lifetime Aerobics. 256p. (C). 1989. text. write for info. (*0-697-10562-8*) Brown & Benchmark.

McIntosh, Michael. A. H. Fox: The Finest Gun in the World. enl. rev. ed. LC 92-74003. (Illus.). 408p. 1994. 49.00 (*0-924357-24-X*, 21100-A) Countrysport Pr.

***McIntosh, Michael.** Best Guns. rev. ed. 2000. lthr. 95.00 (*0-924357-83-5*) Countrysport Pr.

McIntosh, Michael. The Gun-Review Book. LC 97-10921. (Illus.). 272p. (Orig.). 1997. pap. 15.95 (*0-89272-405-6*, Silver Quill Pr) Down East.

— More Shotguns & Shooting. LC 98-43589. (Illus.). 272p. 1998. 30.00 (*0-924357-75-4*) Countrysport Pr.

***McIntosh, Michael.** More Shotguns & Shooting. limited ed. (Illus.). 272p. 1999. write for info. (*0-924357-76-2*) Countrysport Pr.

McIntosh, Michael. Shotguns & Shooting. (Illus.). 280p. 1995. 30.00 (*0-924357-48-7*, 21150-A) Countrysport Pr.

— Traveler's Tales: The Wanderings of a Bird Hunter & Sometime Fly Fisherman. LC 97-24322. (Illus.). 312p. 1997. 22.95 (*0-89272-420-X*, Silver Quill Pr) Down East.

— Wild Things. LC 96-5226. (Illus.). 424p. 1996. 30.00 (*0-924357-57-6*, 21250-A) Countrysport Pr.

McIntosh, Michael, et al. A Breed Apart: A Tribute to the Sporting Dogs That Own Our Souls, 2 vols., Set. deluxe limited ed. Truax, Doug, ed. 1994. lthr. 175.00 (*0-924357-43-6*, 51205-B) Countrysport Pr.

— Call of the Quail: A Tribute to the Gentleman Game Bird. Smith, Steven R., ed. LC 89-60725. (Illus.). 170p. 1999. reprint ed. 35.00 (*0-924357-03-7*, 1007) Countrysport Pr.

McIntosh, Michael, ed. see Ruark, Robert C.

McIntosh, Michael, ed. see Tryon, Chuck & Tryon, Sharon.

McIntosh, N., jt. ed. see Campbell, A. G.

M

McIntosh, Ned. Little League Drills & Strategies. (Illus.). 160p. (Orig.). 1987. pap. 11.95 (*0-8092-4789-5*, 478950, Contemporary Bks) NTC Contemp Pub Co.

McIntosh, Ned. The Little League Guide to Tee Ball. LC 92-45097. 160p. 1993. pap. 6.95 (*0-8092-3791-1*, 379110, Contemporary Bks) NTC Contemp Pub Co.

McIntosh, Ned. Managing Little League Baseball. (Illus.). 192p. (Orig.). 1985. pap. 11.95 (*0-8092-5322-4*) NTC Contemp Pub Co.

***McIntosh, Ned.** Managing Little League Baseball. rev. ed. LC 00-23575. (Illus.). 208p. (Orig.). 2000. pap. 12.95 (*0-8092-2525-5*, 252550, Contemporary Bks) NTC Contemp Pub Co.

McIntosh, Neil, jt. auth. see Daniel, W. W.

McIntosh, Neil, jt. auth. see Laing, Ian A.

***McIntosh, Nina.** The Educated Heart: Professional Guidelines for Massage Therapists, Bodyworkers & Movement Teachers. (Illus.). 248p. 1999. pap. 22.95 (*0-9674122-0-X*) Decatur Bainbridge Pr.

McIntosh, Noel, et al, eds. DIU: Guide Pratique a l'Intention des Programmes de Planification Familiale. rev. ed. (FRE., Illus.). 160p. 1992. pap. text 15.00 (*0-929817-03-6*) JHPIEGO.

— DIU: Pautas para Su Uso en los Programas de Planificación Familiar. 2nd ed. (SPA., Illus.). 1996. pap. text 15.00 (*0-929817-36-2*) JHPIEGO.

— IUD Guidelines for Family Planning Service Programs: A Problem-Solving Reference Manual. 2nd ed. (Illus.). 190p. 1993. pap. text 15.00 (*0-929817-07-9*) JHPIEGO.

— Norplant: Guide Pratique a l'Intention des Programmes de Planification Familiale. 2nd rev. ed. (FRE., Illus.). 141p. 1993. pap. text 15.00 (*0-929817-05-2*) JHPIEGO.

— Norplant Implants Guidelines for Family Planning Service Programs. 2nd rev. ed. (RUS., Illus.). (Orig.). 1996. pap. 15.00 (*0-929817-02-8*) JHPIEGO.

— Norplant Implants Guidlines for Family Planning Service Programs: A Problem-Solving Reference Manual. 2nd ed. (Illus.). 1995. pap. text 15.00 (*0-929817-09-5*) JHPIEGO.

— Procedimentos DIU para Programas de Servicos de Planejamento Familiar: Un Manual de Referencia para la Solucion de Problemas. 2nd ed. (POR., Illus.). Date not set. pap. text 15.00 (*0-929817-37-0*) JHPIEGO.

McIntosh, Noel & Blumenthal, Paul. PocketGuide for Family Planning Service Providers. 2nd rev. ed. Oliveras, Elizabeth, ed. (POR., Illus.). 200p. (Orig.). 1998. pap. 15.00 (*0-929817-53-2*) JHPIEGO.

McIntosh, Noel & Blumenthal, Paul D. Guide de Poche a l'Intention des Prestataires de Services de Planification Familiale. 2nd rev. ed. Oliveras, Elizabeth, ed. Orig. Title: Guide de Poche a l'Intention des Prestatains de Planification Familiale. (FRE., Illus.). 300p. 1997. pap. 15.00 (*0-929817-49-4*) JHPIEGO.

McIntosh, Noel & Oliveras, Elizabeth. JADELLE Two-Rod Levonorgestrel Contraceptive Implant. 1997. pap. 15.00 (*0-929817-56-7*) JHPIEGO.

McIntosh, Noel & Oliveras, Elizabeth, eds. Directives de Prestations de Services pour les Programmes de Planification Familiale. Nalls, Elaine & Kleeman, Frances A., trs. from FRE. (Illus.). 96p. (Orig.). 1996. pap. text 15.00 (*0-929817-46-X*) JHPIEGO.

— PocketGuide for Family Planning Service Providers. 2nd rev. ed. (RUS., Illus.). (Orig.). 1996. pap. text 15.00 (*0-929817-48-6*) JHPIEGO.

— Service Delivery Guidelines for Family Planning Service Programs. LC 96-205961. (Illus.). 110p. 1996. pap. text 15.00 (*0-929817-10-9*) JHPIEGO.

McIntosh, Noel, jt. auth. see Blumenthal, Paul D.

McIntosh, P. D. Guide to the Soils of the Kaihiku-Hokonui Land Region. 1994. 30.00 (*0-478-04530-1*, Pub. by Manaaki Whenua) Balogh.

McIntosh, R. A., et al, eds. Wheat Rusts: An Atlas of Resistance Genes. LC 95-7869. (Illus.). 200p. (C). 1995. text 92.50 (*0-7923-3430-2*) Kluwer Academic.

McIntosh, R. A., et al. Wheat Rusts: An Atlas of Resistance Genes. (Illus.). 250p. 1995. 120.00 (*0-643-05428-6*, Pub. by CSIRO) Accents Pubns.

McIntosh, Rawle M., et al, eds. Kidney Disease: Hematologic & Vascular Problems. LC 77-7529. (Perspectives in Nephrology & Hypertension Ser.). (Illus.). 188p. reprint ed. pap. 58.30 (*0-608-10319-5*, 201519600092) Bks Demand.

McIntosh, Robert. Minimum Wage Maximum Results. 1997. pap. 12.95 (*1-887938-26-5*) Preston-Speed.

McIntosh, Robert & McIntosh, Susan, eds. The Teachings of George Albert Smith. 1996. 14.95 (*1-57008-235-9*) Bookcraft Inc.

***McIntosh, Robert K.** How Do You Know When You're Really in Love? LC 00-21325. 2000. pap. write for info. (*1-57345-647-0*) Deseret Bk.

— Minimum Wage, Maximum Results: Finding, Hiring, Training & Bringing Out the Best in Your Employees. 2nd rev. ed. 160p. 2000. pap. 20.00 (*1-893435-04-0*, Williams Custom Pub) Lakeshore Comm.

McIntosh, Robert L. Dielectric Behavior of Physically Absorbed Gases. LC 67-82258. 174p. reprint ed. pap. 54.00 (*0-608-30331-3*, 20554110002l) Bks Demand.

McIntosh, Robert P. The Forests of the Catskill Mountains. 1977. pap. 5.00 (*0-910746-07-9*, FOT01) Hope Farm.

McIntosh, Robert W., et al. Tourism: Principles, Practices & Philosophies. 7th ed. LC 94-26244. 576p. 1994. 59.95 (*0-471-01557-1*) Wiley.

— Tourism: Principles, Practices, Philosophies. 8th ed. LC 99-24944. 752p. 1999. 64.95 (*0-471-32210-5*) Wiley.

McIntosh, Robins P., jt. ed. see Barclay, William R.

McIntosh, Roderick J. The Peoples of the Middle Niger: The Island of Gold. LC 98-10817. (Peoples of Africa Ser.). (Illus.). 336p. 1998. 59.95 (*0-631-17361-7*) Blackwell Pubs.

***McIntosh, Roderick J., et al.** The Way the Wind Blows: Climate, History & Human Action. LC 99-57006. (Historical Ecology Ser.). 2000. pap. 28.00 (*0-231-11209-2*) Col U Pr.

— The Way the Wind Blows: Climate, History, & Human Action. LC 99-57006. 448p. 2000. text 65.00 (*0-231-11208-4*) Col U Pr.

McIntosh, Roderick J., jt. ed. see Schmidt, Peter R.

McIntosh, Ron. Keep the Flame Burning. LC 95-203131. 272p. 1994. pap. 12.99 (*0-89274-693-9*, HH-693) Harrison Hse.

McIntosh, Sandy. Endless Staircase. 72p. 1991. 5.75 (*0-935252-48-7*) Street Pr.

McIntosh, Sandy, jt. auth. see Galos, Jodie-Beth.

McIntosh, Sandy, ed. see Wok Talk Editors.

McIntosh, Scott A. America's Heritage: A Nation Born of God for a Divine Destiny. (Orig.). 1996. pap. 9.95 (*0-9632879-2-3*) McIntosh Pubns.

— How to Be an Angel: The Book the Devil Did Not Want Published. (Illus.). 80p. (Orig.). (YA). 1993. pap. 9.95 (*0-9632879-1-5*) McIntosh Pubns.

— Love Letters That Work: Create Some Excitement in Your Life. (Illus.). 80p. (Orig.). 1992. pap. 7.95 (*0-9632879-0-7*) McIntosh Pubns.

McIntosh, Stephen I. The Golden Mean Book & Caliper Set. (Illus.). 64p. 1997. pap. 14.99 (*0-9647645-3-9*) Now & Zen.

McIntosh, Stephen I. Triad Cards: Navigational Tools for the Dimension of Meaning. (Illus.). 130p. 1996. pap. 29.95 (*0-9647645-8-X*) Now & Zen.

McIntosh, Susan, jt. ed. see McIntosh, Robert.

***McIntosh, Susan K., ed.** Beyond Chiefdoms: Pathways to Political Complexity in Africa. LC 98-38081. (New Directions in Archaeology Ser.). (Illus.). 250p. (C). 1999. text 64.95 (*0-521-63074-6*) Cambridge U Pr.

McIntosh, Susan K., ed. Excavations at Jenne-Jeno, Hambarketolo & Kaniana (Inland Niger Delta, Mali), the 1981 Season. LC 94-35017. (Publications in Anthropology: Vol. 20). 1995. pap. 85.00 (*0-520-09785-8*, Pub. by U CA Pr) Cal Prin Full Svc.

McIntosh, Susan M., ed. Low-Fat Ways to Cook for the Holidays. LC 98-67025. (Illus.). 144p. 1998. spiral bd. 29.95 (*0-8487-2217-5*) Oxmoor Hse.

McIntosh, Terence. Urban Decline in Early Modern Germany: Schwabisch Hall & Its Region, 1650-1750. LC 96-13722. (James Sprunt Studies in History & Political Science: Vol. 62). 368p. (C). (gr. 13). 1997. lib. bdg. 37.50 (*0-8078-5063-2*) U of NC Pr.

McIntosh, Toby J. Federal Information in the Electronic Age: Policy Issues for the 1990s. LC 90-2404. 1990. 75.00 (*1-55871-170-8*, BSP 184) BNA PLUS.

McIntosh, W. E. & Shell, Harvey. Indiancraft. LC 89-3392. (Illus.). 144p. 1987. pap. 9.95 (*0-87961-171-5*) Naturegraph.

McIntosh, W. H. History of Wayne County New York. LC 75-37578. (Illus.). 1975. reprint ed. 60.00 (*0-918426-01-4*) Yankee Ped Bkshop.

McIntosh, W. Skip, jt. auth. see Shubat, Michael A.

McIntosh, Wayne V. The Appeal of Civil Law: A Political-Economic Analysis of Litigation. LC 88-29592. 240p. 1990. text 26.95 (*0-252-01628-9*) U of Ill Pr.

Mcintosh, Wayne V. & Cates, Cynthia L. Judicial Entrepreneurship: The Role of the Judge in the Marketplace of Ideas, 83. LC 97-16125. (Contributions in Legal Studies: Vol. 83). 152p. 1997. 49.95 (*0-313-30519-6*, Greenwood Pr) Greenwood.

McIntosh, William A. Guide to Effective Military Writing. 2nd ed. 256p. 1994. pap. 14.95 (*0-8117-2541-3*) Stackpole.

— Sociologies of Food & Nutrition. LC 96-31303. (Environment, Development & Public Policy Ser.). (Illus.). 290p. (C). 1996. text 54.00 (*0-306-45335-5*) Kluwer Academic.

McIntosh, William S. Location Portraiture: The Story Behind the Art. (Illus.). 223p. 1996. pap. 49.95 (*1-883403-37-5*, H 883, Silver Pixel Pr) Saunders Photo.

McIntosh-Wooten, Sara. Oprah Winfrey: Talk Show Legend. LC 98-27770. (African-American Biographies Ser.). 128p. (YA). (gr. 6 up). 1999. lib. bdg. 20.95 (*0-7660-1207-7*) Enslow Pubs.

McIntosk & Twyman, trs. The Archko Volume. LC 74-33199. 248p. 1975. 14.95 (*0-87983-067-0*, 30670K, Keats Publng) NTC Contemp Pub Co.

Mcintruff, Stephen. Look What God Made! 1999. pap. text 2.49 (*0-7847-0887-8*) Standard Pub.

McIntsoh-Johnson, Julie. Basics of Keyboard Theory: Level 3, 4th rev. ed. LC TX 4 721 494. vi, 80p. 1997. spiral bd. 8.95 (*1-891757-03-2*, BKT-3) J Johnson Mus.

McInturff, Susan L., jt. auth. see Dunne, Patrick J.

McInturff, Virginia F. A Vision for Virginia. 2nd ed. LC 95-70998. 234p. (Orig.). 1995. pap., spiral bd. 20.00 (*0-9625315-2-9*) New Faith Pub.

McIntyre. British Decolonization, 1946-1997: When, Why & How Did the British Empire Fall? LC 98-11476. 176p. 1998. text 45.00 (*0-312-21307-7*) St Martin.

— Curve of the Earth. 2000. 24.00 (*0-671-56767-5*) PB.

— Liquids for Life. 1998. 25.00 (*0-8050-5246-1*) H Holt & Co.

McIntyre, jt. auth. see Neil.

McIntyre, jt. auth. see Parker.

McIntyre, A. Contemporary Australian Collage & Its Origins. (Illus.). 224p. 1990. text 37.00 (*0-947131-31-0*) Gordon & Breach.

McIntyre, Agnes, et al. Angliller (Growing Up) large type ed. (ESK., Illus.). 8p. (J). (gr. k-3). 1999. pap. text 6.00 (*1-58084-152-X*) Lower Kuskokwim.

— Anglillra Ac'uruunam (Growing Up) large type ed. (ESK., Illus.). 8p. (J). (gr. k-3). 1999. pap. text 6.00 (*1-58084-100-7*) Lower Kuskokwim.

— Growing Up. large type ed. (Illus.). 8p. (J). (gr. k-3). 1999. pap. text 6.00 (*1-58084-099-X*) Lower Kuskokwim.

McIntyre, Albert A. The Last Grand Roundup. LC 89-90976. (Illus.). 104p. 1989. reprint ed. 12.95 (*0-9622654-0-3*) Chief Rsch.

McIntyre, Alice. Making Meaning of Whiteness: Exploring Racial Identity with White Teachers. LC 96-45473. (SUNY Series, the Social Context of Education). (Illus.). 193p. (C). 1997. text 57.50 (*0-7914-3495-8*); pap. text 18.95 (*0-7914-3496-6*) State U NY Pr.

— Role Playing: A Real Estate Training Tool. Gerth, Dawn M., ed. LC 82-83133. (Illus.). 151p. (Orig.). 1982. pap. text 16.00 (*0-913652-43-1*, BK 152) Realtors Natl.

McIntyre, Ann, jt. auth. see Harris, Rhonda.

McIntyre, Anne. The Complete Woman's Herbal: A Manual of Healing Herbs & Nutrition for Personal Well-Being & Family Care. LC 94-29291. (Reference Bks.). 1995. pap. 25.00 (*0-8050-3537-0*) H Holt & Co.

***McIntyre, Anne.** Drink to Your Health! Delicious Juices, Teas, Soups & Smoothies That Help You Look & Feel Great. LC 99-53499. (Illus.). 160p. 2000. pap. 15.00 (*0-684-86946-2*, Fireside) S&S Trade Pap.

— Flower Power: Flower Remedies for Healing Body & Soul Through Herbalism, Homeopathy, Aromatherapy & Flower Essences. (Illus.). 287p. 2000. reprint ed. pap. text 22.00 (*0-7881-9081-4*) DIANE Pub.

McIntyre, Anne. Folk Remedies for Common Ailments. (Illus.). 96p. (Orig.). 1994. pap. 12.95 (*1-55013-611-9*) Firefly Bks Ltd.

— The Good Health Garden: Growing & Using Healing Foods: Herbs, Fruits, Vegetables. LC 97-31949. (Illus.). 176p. 1998. 24.95 (*0-7621-0016-8*, Pub. by RD Assn) Penguin Putnam.

— Herbal for Mother & Child. 191p. 1992. pap. 14.95 (*1-85230-244-5*, Pub. by Element MA) Penguin Putnam.

— Herbal Medicine. (Alternative Health Ser.). (Illus.). 128p. 1993. pap. 12.95 (*0-8048-1837-1*) Tuttle Pubng.

— Herbs for Common Ailments. (Illus.). 96p. (Orig.). 1992. pap. 12.00 (*0-671-74632-4*, Fireside) S&S Trade Pap.

— The Medicinal Garden. LC 96-41112. 1995. pap. 17.95 (*0-8050-4838-3*) H Holt & Co.

***McIntyre, Anne.** A Mother's Herbal: Caring for Yourself & Your Family with Natural Remedies. 2000. pap. 24.95 (*1-86204-744-8*, Pub. by Element MA) Penguin Putnam.

McIntyre, Arnold M. Trade & Economic Development in Small Open Economies: The Case of the Caribbean Countries. LC 94-32931. 200p. 1995. 57.95 (*0-275-94745-9*, Praeger Pubs) Greenwood.

McIntyre, Barbara & Sampaio, Joao. Colloquial Portuguese: A Complete Language Course. LC 95-17041. (Colloquials Ser.). (Illus.). 322p. (gr. 13). 1995. pap. 18.99 (*0-415-12106-X*) Routledge.

McIntyre, Barbara & Sampaio, Joao. Colloquial Portuguese: A Complete Language Course. LC 95-17041. (Colloquials Ser.). (Illus.). 322p. (gr. 13). 1995. pap. 39.99 incl. audio (*0-415-12108-6*) Routledge.

McIntyre, Barbara & Sampio, Joao. Colloquial Portuguese of Brazil: Complete Course for Beginners. LC 97-8186. (Colloquials Ser.). 288p. (C). (gr. 13). 1997. pap. 27.99 incl. audio (*0-415-16138-X*) Routledge.

McIntyre, Bill. Grambling: Cradle of the Pros. Woolfolk, Doug, ed. (Illus.). 110p. 1980. 20.00 (*0-86518-015-6*) Moran Pub Corp.

McIntyre, Bryce T. Advanced Newsgathering. LC 90-38842. 304p. 1991. 69.50 (*0-275-93521-3*, C3521, Praeger Pubs); pap. 22.95 (*0-275-93522-1*, B3522, Praeger Pubs) Greenwood.

— English News Writing: A Guide for Journalists Who Use English As a Second Language. LC 97-178508. 200p. (Orig.). 1997. pap. text 22.50 (*962-201-731-2*, Pub. by Chinese Univ) U of Mich Pr.

— The English Style Guide: A Practical Writers Guide for Chinese People Who Use English As a Second Language. LC 97-177886. 172p. (Orig.). (C). 1997. pap. text 16.95 (*962-201-663-4*, Pub. by Chinese Univ) U of Mich Pr.

— Mass Media in the Asian Pacific. LC 97-20525. (Monographs on Asian Pacific Communication Ser.). 101p. 1997. 49.00 (*1-85359-397-4*, Pub. by Multilingual Matters) Taylor & Francis.

McIntyre, Catherine. Catherine McIntyre-Deliquescence. (Illus.). 100p. 1999. 49.95 (*1-890377-06-6*) Pohlmann Pr.

McIntyre, Catherine V. Writing Effective News Releases: How to Get Free Publicity for Yourself, Your Business or Your Organization. LC 91-45516. (Illus.). 144p. 1992. pap. 20.00 (*0-941599-19-1*, Pub. by Piccadilly Bks) Empire Pub Srvs.

McIntyre, Charles, jt. auth. see Knoell, Dorothy M.

McIntyre, Chris. Guide to Zambia. LC 96-31871. (Illus.). 256p. 1996. pap. text 16.95 (*0-7627-0016-5*, Pub. by Bradt Pubns) Globe Pequot.

— Namibia: The Bradt Travel Guide. LC 98-35300. (Illus.). 300p. 1998. pap. 18.95 (*1-898323-64-X*, 862132Q, Pub. by Bradt Pubns) Globe Pequot.

***McIntyre, Chris.** Zambia: The Bradt Travel Guide. 2nd ed. (Illus.). 320p. 2000. pap. 17.95 (*1-898323-99-2*, Pub. by Bradt Pubns) Globe Pequot.

McIntyre, Chris & Atkins, Simon. Guide to Namibia & Botswana. 2nd ed. (Bradt Country Guides Ser.). (Illus.). 340p. 1994. pap. 16.95 (*1-56440-541-9*, Pub. by Bradt Pubns) Globe Pequot.

McIntyre, Chris, ed. see Cunningham, Patricia M. & Hall, Dorothy P.

McIntyre, Chuck. Enrollment Simulation & Planning. (Illus.). 100p. 1999. pap. 33.00 (*0-87117-322-0*, 1434) Comm Coll Pr Am Assn Comm Coll.

***McIntyre, Cindy.** Declare Your Financial Independence! Create Wealth Through Budgeting & Investing--And Leave Your Money Problems Behind! 256p. 2000. pap. 10.95 (*1-58062-461-8*) Adams Media.

McIntyre, Cindy. Seattle, Tacoma & the Puget Sound Region. (Illus.). 128p. 1988. write for info. (*0-942381-00-9*) Sammamish Pr.

McIntyre, Cindy & Callery, Terence. The Great Eastern Mussel Cookbook. LC 95-14770. (Illus.). 128p. 1995. pap. 14.95 (*0-8397-2392-X*) Eriksson.

McIntyre, Clare. My Heart's a Suitcase & Low Level Panic. 128p. 1997. pap. 14.95 (*1-85459-246-7*, Pub. by N Hern Bks) Theatre Comm.

— The Thickness of Skin. 80p. (Orig.). 1996. pap. 13.95 (*1-85459-350-1*, Pub. by N Hern Bks) Theatre Comm.

Mcintyre, Claudia. Body Decoration: An Encyclopedia of Tradition & Culture. (Art of Living Ser.). 2001. lib. bdg. 75.00 (*0-87436-869-3*) ABC-CLIO.

***McIntyre, Connie.** Handmade Books from the Heart Kit: Tell Your Story. rev. ed. (Illus.). 18p. 1998. pap. 18.95 (*0-9677685-0-0*) C McIntyre.

McIntyre-Cooley, Thomas. A Treatise on the Constitutional Limitations Which Rest upon the Legislative Power of the States of the American Union, 1883. 5th ed. LC 98-12730. lxxxi, 886p. 1998. 120.00 (*1-886363-53-6*) Lawbk Exchange.

McIntyre, Cordelia, ed. see Drexel, Paul.

McIntyre, D. Pyrophoric Behavior & Combustion of Reactive Metals, Pub. No. 32. LC 88-61124. (MTI Publication: No. 32). (Illus.). 21p. 1988. pap. 16.00 (*0-915567-35-0*) NACE Intl.

McIntyre, D., ed. Forms of Corrosion: Recognition & Prevention. (Illus.). 146p. 1997. pap. 100.00 (*1-57590-026-2*, 37558) NACE Intl.

McIntyre, D. John & Byrd, David M. Strategies for Career-Long Teacher Education: Teacher Education Yearbook VI. (ATE Ser.). (Illus.). 264p. 1998. 65.95 (*0-8039-6673-3*); pap. 29.95 (*0-8039-6674-1*) Corwin Pr.

McIntyre, D. John & Byrd, David M., eds. Preparing Tomorrow's Teachers: The Field Experience. LC 97-11181. (Teacher Education Yearbook Ser.: Vol. 4). 309p. reprint ed. pap. 95.80 (*0-608-09125-1*, 206975700006) Bks Demand.

***McIntyre, D. John & Byrd, David M., eds.** Research on Effective Models for Teacher Education: Teacher Education Yearbook VIII. (ATE Yearbook Ser.). (Illus.). 271p. 2000. lib. bdg. 69.95 (*0-7619-7615-9*) Corwin Pr.

— Research on Effective Models for Teacher Education: Teacher Education Yearbook VIII. abr. ed. (ATE Yearbook Ser.). (Illus.). 271p. 2000. pap. 32.95 (*0-7619-7616-7*) Corwin Pr.

McIntyre, D. John & O'Hair, Mary J. The Reflective Roles of the Classroom Teacher. 353p. (C). 1995. pap. 63.95 (*0-534-17136-2*) Wadsworth Pub.

McIntyre, D. John, jt. auth. see Byrd, David M.

McIntyre, D. John, jt. ed. see Byrd, David M.

McIntyre, D. M. Prayer Life of Jesus. 5.99 (*1-85792-010-4*, Pub. by Christian Focus) Spring Arbor Dist.

McIntyre, Dale R. Experience Survey Stress Corrosion Cracking of Austenitic Stainless Steels in Water. LC TN0757.C5E87. (MTI Publication Ser.: No. 27). 36p. 1987. reprint ed. pap. 30.00 (*0-608-06690-7*, 206688700009) Bks Demand.

McIntyre, David M. Hidden Life of Prayer. 112p. 1993. pap. 6.99 (*1-55661-365-2*) Bethany Hse.

— Hidden Life of Prayer. 5.99 (*1-871676-25-8*, Pub. by Christian Focus) Spring Arbor Dist.

McIntyre, Deborah, jt. auth. see Donovan, Denis.

McIntyre, Deborah, jt. auth. see Donovan, Denis M.

McIntyre, Deni. No Place Like Lowe's: 50 Years of Retailing for the American Home. LC 96-69933. (Illus.). 160p. 1996. 40.00 (*0-9653801-0-6*) Lowes Cos.

***McIntyre, Deni & McIntyre, Will.** All over the Map: Travel Photographs & the Stories Behind Them. deluxe ed. (Illus.). 132p. 2000. write for info. (*0-9679506-0-0*) Loose Ends.

McIntyre, Donald, ed. Teacher Education Research in a New Context: Research in the Oxford Internship Scheme. LC 97-197792. 208p. 1997. pap. 29.95 (*1-85396-364-X*, Pub. by P Chapman) Taylor & Francis.

McIntyre, Donald & Gornick, F., eds. Light-Scattering from Dilute Polymer Solutions, Vol. 3. (International Science Review Ser.). (Illus.). xiv, 318p. 1964. text 307.00 (*0-677-00510-5*) Gordon & Breach.

McIntyre, Donald & Hagger, Hazel, eds. Mentors in Schools: Developing the Profession of Teaching. 192p. 1995. pap. 25.95 (*1-85346-411-2*, Pub. by David Fulton) Taylor & Francis.

McIntyre, Donald, et al. The Management of Student Teachers' Learning. 120p. 1994. pap. 19.95 (*0-7494-1034-5*, Kogan Pg Educ) Stylus Pub VA.

McIntyre, Donald, jt. auth. see Brown, Sally.

McIntyre, Donald, jt. auth. see Cooper, Paul.

McIntyre, Donald, jt. ed. see Hustler, David.

McIntyre, Donald M., ed. Law Enforcement in the Metropolis. LC 67-31465. (American Bar Foundation Publication Ser.). xvii, 219p. 1967. pap. 20.00 (*1-57588-319-8*, 304870) W S Hein.

McIntyre, Donald M., et al. Criminal Justice in the United States. rev. ed. LC 74-82708. vii, 56p. 1974. pap. 20.00 (*0-910058-65-2*, 304770) W S Hein.

McIntyre, Douglas A. & Hull, Karen S., eds. The Harvard Advocate One Hundred Twentieth Anniversary Anthology. (Illus.). 460p. 1987. 29.95 (*0-87047-029-9*) Schenkman Bks Inc.

McIntyre, Elizabeth M., jt. auth. see Rector, Brent D.

***McIntyre, Ellen, et al, eds.** Classroom Diversity: Connecting Curriculum to Students' Lives. 144p. 2001. pap. text 21.00 (*0-325-00332-7*) Heinemann.

McIntyre, Ellen & Pressley, Michael, eds. Balanced Instruction: Strategies & Skills in Whole Language. (Illus.). 328p. (C). 1996. text 43.95 (*0-926842-56-0*) CG Pubs Inc.

An Asterisk (*) at the beginning of an entry indicates that the title is appearing for the first time.

McIntyre, Ellsworth E. How to Become a Millionaire in Christian Education. (Illus.). 135p. 1997. pap. 10.00 (*0-9656853-0-6*) Nicene Pr.

McIntyre, F., ed. Lemurs of Madagascar & the Comorans: Windows Version. (World Biodiversity Database Ser.). 1997. 72.00 incl. cd-rom (*3-540-14551-6*) Spr-Verlag.

McIntyre, F. & Expert-Center for Taxonomic Identification (ETI) S, eds. Lemurs of the Madagascar & the Comorans. (World Biodiversity Database Ser.). 1997. 71.95 incl. cd-rom (*3-540-14552-4*) Spr-Verlag.

McIntyre, F. & Wilkin, L. M. Wilkin: Robert Wilkin (1766-1835) & Mary (Hyde) Wilkin, Their Parents & Descendants. (Illus.). 802p. 1995. reprint ed. pap. 115.00 (*0-8328-4948-0*); reprint ed. lib. bdg. 125.00 (*0-8328-4947-2*) Higginson Bk Co.

McIntyre, George, et al. Sustainable Tourism Development: Guide for Local Planners. LC 94-143754. (Tourism & the Environment Publication). vi, 166p. 1993. 30.00 (*92-844-0038-4*, Pub. by Wrld Tourism Org) Bernan Associates.

***McIntyre, Hal.** Securities Operations Glossary. 283p. 1998. pap. 49.95 (*0-9669178-0-4*) Summit Group.

McIntyre, Hugh C. Uranium, Nuclear Power & Canada-U. S. Energy Relations. LC 78-54112. (Canadian-American Committee Ser.). 80p. 1978. pap. 4.00 (*0-88806-035-1*) Natl Planning.

McIntyre, Ian. Dirt & Deity: Life of Robert Burns. (Illus.). 461p. 1998. pap. 15.95 (*0-00-638759-4*, Pub. by HarpC) Trafalgar.

— Dogfight: The Transatlantic Battle over Airbus. LC 92-168. 336p. 1992. 47.95 (*0-275-94278-3*, C4278, Praeger Pubs) Greenwood.

McIntyre, J. B. How to Survive in a World Out of Control. 2nd ed. LC 85-50698. (Illus.). 160p. (Orig.). 1987. pap. 14.95 (*0-9614865-0-3*) Sunburst Pub.

McIntyre, J. D., ed. see Symposium on the Chemistry & Physics of Electrocat.

McIntyre, J. E. & Daniels, P. N., eds. Textile Terms & Definitions. 10th ed. 1995. 110.00 (*1-870812-77-8*, Pub. by Textile Inst) St Mut.

McIntyre, J. E., et al. Electrostatic Charging of Textiles. (Textile Progress Ser.: Vol. 27, No. 3). 1996. pap. 36.00 (*1-870812-87-5*, Pub. by Textile Inst) St Mut.

McIntyre, J. Lewis. Giordano Bruno. 365p. 1992. reprint ed. pap. 24.95 (*1-56459-141-7*) Kessinger Pub.

McIntyre, J. Sam. The ESSO Collectibles Handbook: Memorabilia from Standard Oil of New Jersey. LC 98-84275. 184p. 1998. pap. 34.95 (*0-7643-0518-2*) Schiffer.

McIntyre, J. W., ed. see Webster, Daniel.

***McIntyre, James & Newell, Marie-Louise, eds.** Congenital & Perinatal Infections: Prevention, Diagnosis & Treatment. (Illus.). 350p. (C). 2000. pap. Price not set. (*0-521-78979-6*) Cambridge U Pr.

McIntyre, Joan. The Delicate Art of Whale Watching. LC 82-5714. (Sierra Club Guides Ser.). (Illus.). 160p. 1982. 12.50 (*0-87156-323-1*, Pub. by Sierra) Random.

McIntyre, John. Blowing Weather. 1993. reprint ed. lib. bdg. 89.00 (*0-7812-5487-6*) Rprt Serv.

McIntyre, John. Shape of Christology: Studies in the Doctrine of the Person of Christ. 2nd ed. 352p. pap. 34.95 (*0-567-08646-1*) T&T Clark Pubs.

McIntyre, John. The Shape of Pneumatology: Studies in the Doctrine of the Holy Spirit. 304p. 49.95 (*0-567-08554-6*, Pub. by T & T Clark) Bks Intl VA.

— The Shape of Soteriology. 144p. 1993. text 29.95 (*0-567-09615-7*, Pub. by T & T Clark) Bks Intl VA.

— The Shape of Soteriology. 144p. 1996. pap. 24.95 (*0-567-29290-8*, Pub. by T & T Clark) Bks Intl VA.

— Steps Going Down. 1993. reprint ed. lib. bdg. 89.00 (*0-685-62347-5*) Rprt Serv.

— Theology after the Storm: Reflections on the Upheavals in Modern Theology & Culture. Badcock, Gary, ed. & intro. by. 296p. 1997. pap. 25.00 (*0-8028-4110-4*) Eerdmans.

McIntyre, John, jt. auth. see Symes, Colin.

McIntyre, John, jt. ed. see Quisenberry, Nancy L.

McIntyre, John D., jt. auth. see Rieman, Bruce E.

McIntyre, John P. Customary Law in the "Corpus Iuris Canonici" LC 90-26653. (Distinguished Dissertations Ser.: Vol. 12). 260p. 1991. 89.95 (*0-7734-9960-1*) E Mellen.

McIntyre, John R., ed. Japan's Technical Standards: Implications for Global Trade & Competitiveness. LC 96-2212. 208p. 1997. 62.95 (*1-56720-053-2*, Quorum Bks) Greenwood.

McIntyre, John R. & Papp, Daniel S., eds. The Political Economy of International Technology Transfer. LC 85-28128. (Illus.). 280p. 1986. 72.95 (*0-89930-128-2*, MYP/, Quorum Bks) Greenwood.

McIntyre, John T. Ferment. LC 74-26117. (Labor Movement in Fiction & Non-Fiction Ser.). reprint ed. 49.50 (*0-404-58448-9*) AMS Pr.

McIntyre, John W. & Matsuki, Akitomo. Tracheal Intubation: Theory & Practice. LC 98-84426. (Illus.). 143p. 1998. pap. text 40.00 (*1-891949-03-9*, Ishiyaku EuroAmerica) Med Dent Media.

McIntyre, Joseph. E. W. Kenyon & His Message of Faith: The True Story. LC 96-71255. 1997. pap. 14.99 (*0-88419-451-5*) Creation House.

McIntyre, Judith W. The Common Loon: Spirit of Northern Lakes. LC 88-4206. (Illus.). xii, 228p. 1988. 24.95 (*0-8166-1651-5*) U of Minn Pr.

McIntyre, June. Guided Meditations with Relaxation Music. (Illus.). (J). (ps up). 1996. pap. 14.98 incl. audio compact disk (*1-889045-05-5*) J McIntyre.

— Quiet Heart Space: (Meditations & Music for Children) (Illus.). (J). (ps up). 1996. pap. 11.98 incl. audio (*1-889045-04-7*) J McIntyre.

McIntyre, Kate. The Desklamp. (Illus.). 1999. pap. 9.95 (*1-85410-596-5*, Pub. by Aurum Press Ltd) London Brdge.

***McIntyre, Keith.** Practical Drainage for Golf, Sportsturf & Horticultural. Jakobsen, Bent, ed. LC 99-53388. (Illus.). 210p. 2000. 49.95 (*1-57504-139-1*, Ann Arbor Press) Sleepng Bear.

McIntyre, Kellen K. Rio Grande Blankets: Late Nineteenth-Century Textiles in Transition. LC 92-19989. (Illus.). 88p. 1992. pap. 22.50 (*0-9633710-0-2*) Adobe Gallery.

McIntyre, Kenneth G. The Rebello Transcripts: Governor Phillip's Portugese Prelude. 257p. (C). 1984. 24.95 (*0-285-62603-5*) Intl Spec Bk.

McIntyre, Lee C., jt. ed. see Martin, Michael.

McIntyre, Lisa J. The Practical Skeptic: Core Concepts in Sociology. LC 98-19599. xiv, 313p. 1998. pap. text 24.95 (*1-55934-954-9*, 1954) Mayfield Pub.

— The Practical Skeptic Instructor's Manual. v, 205p. (C). 1998. pap. text, teacher ed. write for info. (*0-7674-0636-2*, 0636-2) Mayfield Pub.

— The Public Defender: The Practice of Law in the Shadows of Repute. LC 87-5070. (Studies in Crime & Justice). (Illus.). 1995. 24.95 (*0-226-55961-0*) U Ch Pr.

***McIntyre, Lisa J., ed.** The Practical Skeptic: Care Concepts in Sociology. LC 98-22180. xiii, 313p. 1998. pap. text 24.95 (*0-7674-0685-0*) Mayfield Pub.

McIntyre, Lisa J. & Sussman, Marvin B., eds. Families & Law. LC 94-45052. (Marriage & Family Review Ser.). (Illus.). 326p. (C). 1995. 49.95 (*1-56024-708-8*) Haworth Pr.

— Families & Law. LC 94-45052. 326p. (C). 1997. pap. 24.95 (*0-7890-0215-9*) Haworth Pr.

McIntyre, Loren. Amazonia. LC 91-6573. (Illus.). 184p. 1991. 40.00 (*0-87156-641-9*, Pub. by Sierra) Random.

McIntyre, Luther B., Jr. Help for Hurting Parents: Dealing with the Pain of Teen Pregnancy. 27p. (Orig.). 1996. pap. 3.95 (*0-9652285-0-9*, 2601) Good Life Pub.

— Help for Hurting Parents: Dealing with the Pain of Teen Pregnancy. 2nd rev. ed. 36p. (Orig.). 1997. pap. 3.95 (*0-9652285-1-7*) Good Life Pub.

— Whose Child Is This? A Biblical View of Adoption. 28p. (Orig.). (YA). (gr. 8 up). 1997. pap. 0.95 (*0-9652285-9-2*) Good Life Pub.

McIntyre, Lyle. Silver & Stone. LC 97-138002. (Illus.). 96p. 1994. 32.00 (*1-55046-114-1*, Pub. by Boston Mills) Genl Dist Srvs.

McIntyre, Margaret, compiled by. Early Childhood & Science. (Illus.). 136p. 1984. pap. text 9.95 (*0-87355-029-3*) Natl Sci Tchrs.

McIntyre, Marie. Ears to Hear: Hearts to Praise. (Greeting Book Line Ser.). (Illus.). 32p. (Orig.). 1985. pap. 1.95 (*0-89622-210-1*) Twenty-Third.

— Little Things Mean a Lot: Minute Meditations. (Greeting Book Line Ser.). (Illus.). 32p. 1982. pap. 1.95 (*0-89622-155-5*) Twenty-Third.

McIntyre, Marie G. Management Team Handbook: Five Key Strategies for Maximizing Group Performance. LC 98-8923. 1998. 34.95 (*0-7879-3973-0*) Jossey-Bass.

McIntyre, Marilyn. Super Seasonal Sampler Artic Worksheets: For R, S, L, Blends, TH, Sh, Ch. (Illus.). 170p. (J). (gr. k-5). 1995. spiral bd., wbk. ed. 27.95 (*1-58650-045-7*, BK-238) Super Duper.

McIntyre, Maureen. Solar Energy: Todays Technologies for a Sustainable Future. 1997. 20.00 (*0-89553-305-7*) Am Solar Energy.

McIntyre, Michael, et al. Peaceworld. LC 76-12410. (Illus.). 152p. (Orig.). reprint ed. pap. 47.20 (*0-7837-1955-8*, 204217200001) Bks Demand.

McIntyre, Michael J. International Income Tax Rules of the United States. 1994. ring bd., suppl. ed. write for info. (*0-614-03610-0*, MICHIE) LEXIS Pub.

— International Income Tax Rules of the United States, Vol. 1. 2nd ed. 1200p. 1999. write for info. (*0-327-00767-2*, 8124312) LEXIS Pub.

— International Income Tax Rules of the United States, Vol. 1 & 2. 2nd ed. 1200p. 1999. write for info. (*0-327-00712-5*, 8124312) LEXIS Pub.

— International Income Tax Rules of the United States, Vol. 2. 2nd ed. 1200p. 1999. write for info. (*0-327-00768-0*, 8124312) LEXIS Pub.

— International Tax Workbook. 2nd ed. xii, 352p. Date not set. spiral bd. 27.50 (*0-9651199-1-2*) M J McIntyre.

McIntyre, Michael J., ed. Internal Revenue Code: Selected International Tax Provisions. 214p. Date not set. pap., spiral bd. 13.00 (*0-9651199-2-0*) M J McIntyre.

McIntyre, Michael J., et al. Readings in Federal Taxation. 2nd ed. LC 83-16356. 625p. 1983. pap. text 24.50 (*0-88277-145-0*) Foundation Pr.

McIntyre, Michael J., jt. auth. see Arnold, Brian J.

McIntyre, Michael P., et al. Physical Geography. 5th ed. LC 90-49420. 536p. 1991. pap. 78.95 (*0-471-62017-3*) Wiley.

***McIntyre, Mike.** Class of 72 Life after Death Row. 2000. text (*0-374-12432-9*) FS&G.

McIntyre, Mike. The Kindness of Strangers: Penniless Across America. LC 97-109784. 256p. 1996. pap. 12.00 (*0-425-15455-6*) Berkley Pub.

McIntyre, Moni. Social Ethics & the Return to Cosmology: A Study of Gibson Winter. LC 92-10251. (American University Studies: Theology & Religion: Ser. VII, Vol. 131). 191p. (C). 1992. 38.95 (*0-8204-1846-3*) P Lang Pubng.

McIntyre, Moni, jt. auth. see MacKinnon, Mary H.

McIntyre, N., et al, eds. Oxford Textbook of Clinical Hepatology, 2 vols., Set. 1772p. 1992. 295.00 (*0-19-261968-3*) OUP.

McIntyre, O. Ross, ed. see Leucocyte Culture Conference Staff.

McIntyre, P. & Mercer, A. D., eds. Corrosion & Related Aspects of Materials for Potable Water Supplies. (Illus.). 285p. 1994. 160.00 (*0-901716-47-2*, Pub. by Inst Materials) Ashgate Pub Co.

— Corrosion Standards: European & International Developments. 108p. 1991. 70.00 (*0-901716-09-X*, Pub. by Inst Materials) Ashgate Pub Co.

McIntyre, P. & Mills, D. L., eds. Corrosion Standards II: National, European & International Standards, 1990-1995. (Illus.). 170p. 1996. pap. 70.00 (*1-86125-009-6*, Pub. by Inst Materials) Ashgate Pub Co.

McIntyre, Patrick. Intimacy with God. LC 92-91171. (Illus.). 128p. (Orig.). 1993. pap. 5.95 (*0-9635050-0-9*) White Harvest.

***McIntyre-Ragusa, Mary.** Eight Steps to Successful Living. 2nd rev. ed. (Illus.). 259p. 2000. pap. 16.95 (*0-9701512-0-9*) Merimac Enter.

McIntyre, Ralph L., ed. Let's Share a Devotion: A Book of Daily Meditations for Couples. 526p. 1986. pap. text 7.95 (*0-89827-032-4*) Wesleyan Pub Hse.

McIntyre, Rick. Denali National Park. 1997. pap. text 12.95 (*1-880352-48-6*) Albion Pub.

— Devali National Park: An Island in Time. (Illus.). 80p. 1989. pap. 10.95 (*0-917859-06-5*) Sunrise SBCA.

McIntyre, Rick. A Society of Wolves: National Parks & the Battle Over the Wolf. LC 93-15918. (Illus.). 128p. 1993. 14.95 (*0-89658-194-2*) Voyageur Pr.

McIntyre, Rick. A Society of Wolves: National Parks & the Battle over the Wolf. rev. ed. LC 95-40898. (Illus.). 144p. 1996. pap. 19.95 (*0-89658-325-2*) Voyageur Pr.

McIntyre, Rick, ed. War Against the Wolf: America's Campaign to Exterminate the Wolf. LC 94-28038. (Illus.). 496p. 1995. 4.95 (*0-89658-264-7*) Voyageur Pr.

McIntyre, Robert J. Bulgaria: Politics, Economics & Society. 225p. 1988. text 49.00 (*0-86187-398-X*, Pub. by P P Pubs); text 17.50 (*0-86187-399-8*, Pub. by P P Pubs) Cassell & Continuum.

McIntyre, Robert L. Electric Motor Control Fundamentals. 3rd ed. (Illus.). 448p. (C). 1974. text 90.50 (*0-07-045103-6*) McGraw.

McIntyre, Robert L. & Losee, Rex. Industrial Motor Control Fundamentals. 4th ed. 384p. 1990. text 56.18 (*0-07-045110-9*) Glencoe.

— Industrial Motor Control Fundamentals. 4th ed. 432p. 1990. teacher ed. 17.64 (*0-07-045111-7*) McGraw.

McIntyre, Ronald, jt. auth. see Smith, David W.

McIntyre, Sally. Cornelia Does Her Chores. Tuychinina, Katya, tr. (ENG & RUS.). 41p. 1997. 8.00 (*1-892067-11-0*) Patchwork Pr.

— Cornelia Does Her Chores. Raitz, Misako, tr. (ENG & JPN., Illus.). 41p. 1997. 8.00 (*1-892067-07-2*) Patchwork Pr.

— Cornelia Does Her Chores. Zhai, Ting, tr. (CHI & ENG., Illus.). 41p. 1997. 8.00 (*1-892067-01-3*) Patchwork Pr.

— Cornelia Does Her Chores (Cornelia Anoki) Oakgrove, Collins, tr. (ENG & OJI., Illus.). 41p. 1997. 8.00 (*1-892067-09-9*) Patchwork Pr.

— Cornelia Does Her Chores (Cornelia Fa Le Sue Cose) Rossetti, Germana, tr. (ENG & ITA.). 41p. 1997. 8.00 (*1-892067-06-4*) Patchwork Pr.

— Cornelia Does Her Chores (Cornelia Fait Ses Taches Domestiques) Barcenes, Greg, tr. (ENG & FRE., Illus.). 41p. (J). 1997. 8.00 (*1-892067-04-8*) Patchwork Pr.

— Cornelia Does Her Chores (Cornelia Faz Sua Tarefa) Mizutori, Ivan, tr. (ENG & POR., Illus.). 41p. 1997. 8.00 (*1-892067-10-2*) Patchwork Pr.

— Cornelia Does Her Chores (Cornelia Gengur Ao Skyldu Storfunum) Byrd, Sigfridur, tr. (ENG & ICE., Illus.). 41p. 1997. 8.00 (*1-892067-14-5*) Patchwork Pr.

— Cornelia Does Her Chores (Cornelia Gjor Sitt Husstell) Rude, Edna, tr. (ENG & NOR., Illus.). 41p. 1997. 8.00 (*1-892067-08-0*) Patchwork Pr.

— Cornelia Does Her Chores (Cornelia Gor Hendes Pligter) Clausen, Marianne F., tr. (DAN & ENG., Illus.). 41p. 1997. 8.00 (*1-892067-02-1*) Patchwork Pr.

— Cornelia Does Her Chores (Cornelia Gor Sina Hushallsysslor) O'Boyle, Monica B., tr. (ENG & SWE., Illus.). 41p. 1997. 8.00 (*1-892067-13-7*) Patchwork Pr.

— Cornelia Does Her Chores (Cornelia Hace los Quehaceres) Neff, Liz, tr. (ENG & SPA., Illus.). 41p. (J). 1997. 8.00 (*1-892067-12-9*) Patchwork Pr.

— Cornelia Does Her Chores (Cornelia Macht Ihre Arbeit) (ENG & GER.). 41p. 1997. 8.00 (*1-892067-05-6*) Patchwork Pr.

— Cornelia Does Her Chores (Cornelia Tekee Kotiaskareensa) Koutaniemi, Hannu, tr. (ENG & FIN., Illus.). 41p. 1997. 8.00 (*1-892067-03-X*) Patchwork Pr.

— Cornelia Does Her Chores (Kornelia Ben Punet e Shtepise) Qyqja, Ira, tr. (ALB & ENG., Illus.). 41p. 1997. 8.00 (*1-892067-00-5*) Patchwork Pr.

McIntyre, Sally & Goltsman, Susan M. Safety First Checklist: Audit & Inspection Program for Children's Play Areas. 2nd ed. (Illus.). 128p. 1997. pap. text 39.95 (*0-944661-19-X*) MIG Comns.

McIntyre, Stuart. A Colonial Liberalism: Lost Word of Three Victorian Visionaries. 264p. 1991. 35.00 (*0-19-554760-8*) OUP.

— Wilson Creek & the Big Bend Country, 1902-1907: An Index of the Big Bend Chief Newspaper. (Illus.). 225p. (C). 1991. 25.00 (*0-9622654-1-1*) Chief Rsch.

McIntyre, Thomas. Dreaming the Lion: Reflections on Hunting, Fishing & a Search for the Wild. LC 93-73422. (Illus.). 318p. 1993. 35.00 (*0-924357-34-7*, 61120-A) Countrysport Pr.

— Dreaming the Lion: Reflections on Hunting, Fishing & a Search for the Wild. deluxe limited ed. LC 93-73422. (Illus.). 318p. 1993. lthr. 95.00 (*0-924357-35-5*, 61120-B) Countrysport Pr.

— The Field & Stream Shooting Sports Handbook. LC 99-12871. 1999. pap. 9.95 (*1-55821-915-3*) Lyons Pr.

McIntyre, Tommy. Wolf in Sheep's Clothing: The Search for a Child Killer. LC 88-5738. (Great Lakes Bks.). 232p. 1988. 34.95 (*0-8143-1966-1*); pap. 16.95 (*0-8143-1989-0*) Wayne St U Pr.

McIntyre, Valerie J. Sheep in Wolves' Clothing: How Unseen Need Destroys Friendship & Community & What to Do about It. 2nd ed. LC 98-50492. 155p. (gr. 13). 1998. pap. 10.99 (*0-8010-5883-X*) Baker Bks.

McIntyre, Vonda N. The Crystal Star. LC 94-28939. (Star Wars Ser.). 448p. (YA). 1995. reprint ed. pap. 5.99 (*0-553-57174-5*) Bantam.

— Enterprise: The First Adventure. 1990. per. 5.99 (*0-671-73032-0*) PB.

— The Entropy Effect. (Orig.). 1986. pap. 3.50 (*0-671-62743-0*) PB.

— The Entropy Effect, No. 2. (Orig.). 1990. pap. 5.50 (*0-671-72416-9*) S&S Trade.

— The Exile Waiting. 255p. 1976. 30.00 (*0-575-02189-6*) Ultramarine Pub.

— The Moon & the Sun. LC 97-3232. 432p. 1997. 23.00 (*0-671-56765-9*, PB Hardcover) PB.

— The Moon & the Sun. 1998. mass mkt. 6.99 (*0-671-56766-7*) PB.

— The Moon & the Sun. large type ed. LC 98-28867. 1998. 30.00 (*0-7862-1591-7*) Thorndike Pr.

McIntyre, Vonda N. Star Trek: The Entropy Effect, 1. abr. ed. 1988. audio 11.00 (*0-671-66864-1*, Audioworks) S&S Trade.

McIntyre, Vonda N. Star Trek III: The Search for Spock. (Star Trek Ser.: No. 17). 1990. mass mkt. 5.50 (*0-671-73133-5*) PB.

— Star Trek II: The Wrath of Khan, No. 7. 1991. mass mkt. 5.50 (*0-671-74149-7*) PB.

— Superluminal. LC 83-8568. 298p. 1983. 25.00 (*0-89366-189-9*) Ultramarine Pub.

— Voyage Home. (Star Trek Ser.: Vol. 4). 1989. per. 5.50 (*0-671-70283-1*) PB.

McIntyre, W. A. Practical Wills Drafting. 236p. 1992. 67.00 (*0-409-89762-0*, MICHIE) LEXIS Pub.

McIntyre, W. David. Background into the Anzus Pact: Strategy & Diplomacy, 1945-55. LC 94-31762. 464p. 1995. text 75.00 (*0-312-12439-2*) St Martin.

— Background to the Anzus Pact: Policy-Making, Strategy & Diplomacy. (Illus.). 464p. (C). 1995. 39.95 (*0-908812-39-6*, Pub. by Canterbury Univ) Accents Pubns.

McIntyre, W. John. Children of Peace. (McGill-Queen's Studies in the History of Religion Ser.: No. 14). (Illus.). 280p. 1994. 60.00 (*0-7735-1195-4*, Pub. by McG-Queens Univ Pr) CUP Services.

McIntyre, Will, jt. auth. see McIntyre, Deni.

McIntyre, William. Christ's Cabinet. rev. ed. 143p. 1982. reprint ed. 4.95 (*0-86544-017-4*) Salv Army Suppl South.

McIntyre, William S., IV, et al. 101 Ways to Cut Your Business Insurance Costs Without Sacrificing Protection. 2nd ed. 199p. (C). 1996. 24.95 (*1-886813-10-8*) Intl Risk Mgt.

McIroy, M. D. UNIX RES SYS VI 10E PROGR MAN+ 2nd ed. (UNIX Programmer's Ser.: Vol. I). 702p. (C). 1990. pap. text 50.50 (*0-03-047532-5*) SCP.

— UNIX RES SYS VII 10E PPRS+ 2nd ed. (UNIX Programmer's Ser.: Vol. II). 630p. (C). 1990. pap. text 51.50 (*0-03-047529-5*) SCP.

McIrvin, Michael. The Book of Allegory. unabridged ed. (Illus.). 76p. 1998. pap. 10.00 (*1-891812-03-3*, 004-98) Cedar Hill Pubns.

— Dog. 72p. 1997. per. 10.00 (*0-944550-43-6*) Pygmy Forest Pr.

***McIrvin, Michael.** Whither American Poetry. viii, 116p. 2000. pap. 14.00 (*1-891812-26-2*, 00-026) Cedar Hill Pubns.

McIsaac, Gregory & Edwards, William R., eds. Sustainable Agriculture in the American Midwest: Lessons from Natural & Human History, Prospects for the Future. LC 93-45671. (Environment & the Human Condition Ser.). 312p. 1994. text 32.95 (*0-252-02100-2*) U of Ill Pr.

McIsaac, Joseph. Hands on C Programming. 1989. pap. 22.95 (*0-201-51816-3*) Addison-Wesley.

McIsaac, Paul, jt. ed. see Meyers, Ellen.

McIver. Great British Ghosts. 1982. pap. text. write for info. (*0-582-53043-1*, Pub. by Addison-Wesley) Longman.

McIver, Bruce. Just As Long As I'm Riding up Front: More Stories I Couldn't Tell While I Was a Pastor. LC 94-44566. 1995. pap. 10.99 (*0-8499-3597-0*) Word Pub.

McIver, Bruce & Stevenson, Ruth, eds. Teaching with Shakespeare: Critics in the Classroom. LC 92-59966. 1994. 41.50 (*0-87413-491-9*) U Delaware Pr.

McIver, Carole R., jt. auth. see Greenberg, Alan M.

McIver, Colin & Naylor, Geoffrey. Marketing Financial Services. 292p. 1981. 75.00 (*0-85297-054-4*, Pub. by Chartered Bank); pap. 39.00 (*0-85297-055-2*, Pub. by Chartered Bank) St Mut.

McIver, D. W., jt. auth. see Robbins, Marc L.

McIver, Jean & White, James P., eds. Black Alabama. 130p. 1997. pap. 12.95 (*0-916092-32-1*) Tex Ctr Writers.

McIver, Joan. 30 Irish-American Women Who Changed Our World: From Mother Jones to Grace Kelly. (Illus.). 224p. 1999. 21.95 (*1-55972-515-X*, Birch Ln Pr) Carol Pub Group.

McIver, John P. & Carmines, Edward G. Undimensional Scaling, No. 24. (Quantitative Applications in the Social Sciences Ser.: Vol. 24). (Illus.). (C). 1981. pap. 10.95 (*0-8039-1736-8*) Sage.

McIver, M. & Naylor, N., eds. Marketing Financial Services. (C). 1989. 110.00 (*0-85297-145-1*, Pub. by Chartered Bank) St Mut.

McIver, Peter B., jt. auth. see Bedessem, Anne.

***McIver, Robert K.** The Four Faces of Jesus: Four Gospel Writers, Four Unique Perspectives, Four Personal Encounters, One Complete Picture. LC 99-45762. 2000. pap. 14.99 (*0-8163-1722-4*) Pacific Pr Pub Assn.

McIver, Stuart. Glimpses of South Florida History. (Illus.). 192p. 1988. 29.95 (*0-9613236-9-8*) Florida Flair Bks.

M

— True Tales of the Everglades. (Illus.). 64p. 1989. pap. 4.95 (*0-9613236-3-9*) Florida Flair Bks.

McIver, Stuart, et al. Greater Fort Lauderdale & Broward County: The Venice of America. (Illus.). 208p. 1998. 34.95 (*0-9647106-3-3*) Copperfld Pubns.

McIver, Stuart B. Dreamers, Schemers & Scalawags. LC 93-48311. (Florida Chronicles Ser.: Vol. I). (Illus.). 264p. 1998. pap. 12.95 (*1-56164-155-3*) Pineapple Pr.

— Hemingway's Key West. LC 93-14668. (Illus.). 1993. pap. 10.95 (*1-56164-035-2*) Pineapple Pr.

— Murder in the Tropics. LC 95-30649. (Florida Chronicles Ser.: Vol. 2). (Illus.). 220p. 1995. 17.95 (*1-56164-079-4*) Pineapple Pr.

***McIver, Stuart B.** Touched by the Sun. (Florida Chronicles Ser.: Vol. 3). (Illus.). 2000. 18.95 (*1-56164-206-1*) Pineapple Pr.

McIver, Stuart B., jt. auth. see Ridings, William J., Jr.

McIver, Tom. Anti-Evolution: A Reader's Guide to Writings Before & after Darwin. LC 92-16755. 408p. 1992. reprint ed. 17.95 (*0-8018-4520-3*) Johns Hopkins.

— Anti-Evolution: An Annotated Bibliography. LC 88-42683. 400p. 1988. lib. bdg. 49.95 (*0-89950-313-6*) McFarland & Co.

***McIver, Tom.** The End of the World: An Annotated Bibliography. LC 99-15154. 398p. 1999. lib. bdg. 55.00 (*0-7864-0708-5*) McFarland & Co.

McIvor, A., jt. auth. see Duncan, R.

McIvor, A., jt. auth. see Kenefick, W.

McIvor, A. J. & Jowitt, J. A., eds. Employers & Labour in the English Textile Industry, 1850-1939. 256p. 1988. lib. bdg. 55.00 (*0-415-00354-7*) Routledge.

McIvor, Aidan. A History of the Irish Naval Service. (Illus.). 240p. 1994. boxed set 34.95 (*0-7165-2523-2*, Pub. by Irish Acad Pr) Intl Spec Bk.

***McIvor, Arthur.** A History of Work in Britain, 1880-1950. LC 00-31114. (Social History in Perspective Ser.). 2000. write for info. (*0-312-23543-7*) St Martin.

McIvor, Arthur. Organised Capital: Employers' Associations & Industrial Relations in Northern England. (Illus.). 323p. (C). 1996. text 64.95 (*0-521-55094-7*) Cambridge U Pr.

McIvor, Basil. Hope Deferred: Experiences of an Irish Unionist. LC 98-145612. 164p. 1998. pap. 25.95 (*0-85640-620-1*, Pub. by Blackstaff Pr) Dufour.

McIvor, D. E. Birding Utah. LC 97-52145. (Illus.). 400p. 1998. pap. 19.95 (*1-56044-615-3*) Falcon Pub Inc.

McIvor, Doug & Mathieson, Neil. Champagne. (Illus.). 96p. 1999. 6.99 (*0-7858-1056-0*) Bk Sales Inc.

— Port. (Pocket Guide Ser.). (Illus.). 96p. 1999. 6.99 (*0-7858-1059-5*) Bk Sales Inc.

McIvor, Eloise E. Child of the Homesteads. 1994. 21.95 (*0-943099-10-2*) M & M Pr.

McIvor, Gill. Bail Services in Scotland: The Operation & Impact of Bail Information & Accommodation Schemes. LC 96-84018. (Evaluative Studies in Social Work). 176p. 1996. 57.95 (*1-85628-626-6*, Pub. by Avebry) Ashgate Pub Co.

McIvor, Gill, ed. Working with Offenders, No. 26. LC 95-21595. 198p. 1995. pap. 27.95 (*1-85302-249-7*, Pub. by Jessica Kingsley) Taylor & Francis.

McIvor, J. S., jt. auth. see Beattie, D. R.

McIvor, Kirsten, tr. see Chugoku Newspaper Staff.

McIvor, Philip. An Ulster Wean's A to Z. 56p. (J). 1996. pap. 8.95 (*0-85640-581-7*, Pub. by Blackstaff Pr) Dufour.

Mcivor, Shirley & Mcivor, Trevor. Salute the Brave: A Pictorial Record of Queensland War Memorials. (Illus.). 340p. (Orig.). 1994. pap. 54.95 (*0-949414-54-9*, Pub. by U Sthrn Queenslnd) Accents Pubns.

McIvor, Stephanie, jt. auth. see Goodlad, Sinclair.

Mcivor, Trevor, jt. auth. see Mcivor, Shirley.

McJannet, Linda J., jt. auth. see Hattersley, Michael.

McJannet, Linda M. The Voice of Elizabethan Stage Directions: The Evolution of a Theatrical Code. LC 97-51314. (Illus.). 240p. 1999. 39.50 (*0-87413-660-1*) U of Del Sea Grant.

McJimsey, George. Harry Hopkins: Ally of the Poor & Defender of Democracy. LC 86-22764. (Illus.). 304p. 1990. 39.50 (*0-674-37287-5*) HUP.

***McJimsey, George.** The Presidency of Franklin Delano Roosevelt. LC 99-55956. (Illus.). 376p. 2000. text 34.95 (*0-7006-1012-X*) U Pr of KS.

McJoynt, Albert D., ed. & intro. see Prescott, William H.

McJunkin, Milton. The Bloody 85th: The Civil War Letters of Milton McJunkiin, a Western Pennsylvania Soldier in the Civil War. Schroeder, Patrick & Sauers, Richard, eds. (Illus.). 80p. 2000. pap. 12.95 (*1-889246-13-1*) P A Schroeder.

McKade, Kim. A True-Blue Texas Twosome (March Madness) (Intimate Moments Ser.: No. 915). 1999. per. 4.25 (*0-373-07915-X*, 1-07915-1) Harlequin Bks.

McKade, Maureen. A Dime Novel Hero. 384p. 1998. mass mkt. 5.99 (*0-380-79504-3*, Avon Bks) Morrow Avon.

***McKade, Maureen.** Mail-Order Bride. 384p. 2000. mass mkt. 5.99 (*0-380-80285-6*, Avon Bks) Morrow Avon.

McKade, Maureen. Untamed Heart. (Avon Romance Ser.). 384p. 1999. mass mkt. 5.99 (*0-380-80284-8*, Avon Bks) Morrow Avon.

— Winter Hearts. 1997. mass mkt. 5.50 (*0-380-78871-3*, Avon Bks) Morrow Avon.

McKague, Anne, jt. auth. see Smye, Marti.

McKague, Thomas R. Stormlight: Poems. LC 95-512. 64p. 1995. pap. 14.95 (*0-7734-2739-2*, Mellen Poetry Pr) E Mellen.

— The Violet Hours: Poems. LC 96-42394. 68p. 1996. pap. 14.95 (*0-7734-2689-2*, Mellen Poetry Pr) E Mellen.

McKaig, Kathleen, et al. Comprehensive Support for Families: Final Report of the Family Partnership Program. A Demonstration to Assist Families with Developmentally Disabled Children. LC 90-197879. 140p. (Orig.). 1989. pap. 15.00 (*0-88156-102-9*) Comm Serv Soc NY.

McKaig, T. Neil & Thibodeau, Jim. Bedside Assessment of Swallowing Safety: The Clinician's Software User's Guide. 44p. 1997. pap. 55.00 incl. disk (*0-7506-7004-5*, RC815) Buttrwrth-Heinemann.

McKain, David. The Common Life. LC 82-71818. 72p. 1982. pap. 3.95 (*0-914086-38-3*) Alice James Bks.

— Spirit Bodies: Poems by David McKain. LC 90-83510. (Ithaca House Poetry Ser.). 64p. (Orig.). (C). 1990. pap. 9.95 (*0-87886-133-5*) Greenfld Rev Lit.

McKain, David W. Spellbound: Growing up in God's Country. LC 88-4721. 271p. 1988. reprint ed. pap. 84.10 (*0-7837-9756-7*, 206048400005) Bks Demand.

— Spellbound: Growing up in God's Country. LC 92-37590. 272p. 1993. reprint ed. pap. 14.95 (*0-8229-5507-5*) U of Pittsburgh Pr.

McKain, James D. Index to Historic Camden Colonial & Revolutionary & Nineteenth Century. LC 94-74968. 81p. 1995. 17.50 (*0-913363-19-7*) SCMAR.

— Index to History of the Presbyterian Church in South Carolina by George Howe, D. D., \ Set. LC 95-71178. 88p. (Orig.). 1995. pap. 12.00 (*0-913363-21-9*) SCMAR.

McKain, Robert J. How to Get to the Top & Stay There. LC 80-67964. 193p. reprint ed. pap. 59.90 (*0-608-12681-0*, 202350700033) Bks Demand.

McKain, Scott & Boyle, Antonia B. Just Say Yes! A Step up to Success. LC 94-79558. 192p. 1994. text 24.95 (*0-7872-0185-5*, 41081501) Kendall-Hunt.

McKale, Donald M. Curt Prufer: German Diplomat from the Kaiser to Hitler. LC 87-4114. (Illus.). 290p. reprint ed. pap. 89.90 (*0-608-10530-9*, 207115000009) Bks Demand.

— The Swastika Outside Germany. LC 77-22304. 304p. reprint ed. pap. 94.30 (*0-8357-7043-5*, 203331600085) Bks Demand.

— War by Revolution: Germany & Great Britain in the Middle East in the Era of World War I. LC 98-13285. (Illus.). 360p. 1998. text 39.00 (*0-87338-602-7*) Kent St U Pr.

McKale, Donald M., ed. Rewriting History: The Original & Revised World War II Diaries of Curt Prufer, Nazi Diplomat. LC 88-12034. 277p. 1988. 24.00 (*0-87338-364-8*) Kent St U Pr.

Mckall, Dandi D. Don't Bug Me, Molly! Cinnamon Lake Mysteries. LC 97-9877. (Cinnamon Lake Mysteries Ser.). 80p. (J). (gr. 1-4). 1997. pap. 4.99 (*0-570-04884-2*, 56-1833) Concordia.

— The Great Meow Mystery. LC 96-45144. (Cinnamon Lake Mysteries Ser.). 80p. (J). (gr. 1-4). 1997. pap. 4.99 (*0-570-04883-4*, 56-1832) Concordia.

McKallip, Curtis. Visualizing Economics: The Art of Investing Without Statistics. (Illus.). 146p. 1991. write for info. (*1-878353-22-5*) Silent Partners.

McKallip, Jonathan, jt. auth. see Trabert, Judith A.

McKallip, Jonathan, ed. see Price, Margaret, et al.

McKalson, Peggy. The Family of Angels: A Story of Devils & Angels in an Italian Family. write for info. (*0-9657834-4-8*) Spartacus Pubns.

McKamey, Lynn. Secret of the Orient: Dwarf Rhapis Excelsa. LC 85-50589. (Illus.). 52p. (Orig.). 1983. pap. 12.00 (*0-9612130-0-0*) Rhapis Gardens.

McKamey, Stuart H. Taxonomic Catalogue of the Membracoidea (Exclusive of Leafhoppers) Second Supplement to Fascicle 1 - Membracidae of the General Catalogue of the Hemiptera. (Memoirs of the American Entomological Institute Ser.: Vol. 60). 377p. 1998. 60.00 (*1-887988-04-1*) Am Entomol Inst.

McKane, A., et al. Scale Invariance, Interfaces & Non-Equilibrium Dynamics. LC 95-17265. (NATO ASI Ser.: Ser. B, Vol. 344). (Illus.). 352p. (C). 1995. text 115.00 (*0-306-45005-4*, Kluwer Plenum) Kluwer Academic.

McKane, Elizabeth, tr. see Mandelshtam, Osip.

McKane, Helen M. The Grecian Feast: The Traditional Collection. (Illus.). 250p. 1998. 21.95 (*0-9667478-0-1*) Glenmore Farms Ltd.

McKane, Janet A. Help Wanted: All the Help You'll Ever Need for Resume & Interview Preparation. 2nd ed. 75p. (Orig.). 1995. pap. 12.00 (*0-9647084-0-X*) Exec Type.

McKane, John G. Ducks of the Mississippi Flyway. LC 79-105937. (Illus.). 1969. pap. 5.00 (*0-87839-003-0*) North Star.

McKane, John H. General Motors New Look Bus Photo Archive. (Illus.). 128p. 1999. pap. 29.95 (*1-58388-007-0*, 129099AE, Pub. by Iconografix) Motorbooks Intl.

McKane, Larry K. & Kandel, J. Microbiology: Essentials & Applications. 800p. (C). 1985. text 62.25 (*0-07-045125-7*) McGraw.

McKane, Larry K. & Kandel, Judith. Microbiology: Essentials & Applications Study Companion. 2nd ed. (C). 1995. pap., student ed. 22.19 (*0-07-035008-6*) McGraw.

McKane, Larry K. & Kandel, Judy. Microbiology: Essentials & Applications. 2nd ed. LC 94-25301. 880p. (C). 1995. 82.81 (*0-07-045154-0*) McGraw.

McKane, Larry K., jt. auth. see Brum, Gil D.

McKane, Richard, tr. see Akhmatova, Anna Andreevena.

McKane, Richard, tr. see Mandelshtam, Osip.

McKane, William. Jeremiah, Vol. 2, Chapters 26-52. Emerton, John A. et al, eds. (International Critical Commentary Ser.). 800p. 1996. 69.95 (*0-567-09732-3*, Pub. by T & T Clark) Bks Intl VA.

— Jeremiah: Chapters 1-25, Vol. 1. Cranfield, Charles E. & Emerton, John A., eds. (International Critical Commentary Ser.). 784p. 1986. 69.95 (*0-567-05042-4*, Pub. by T & T Clark) Bks Intl VA.

— Late Harvest: Reflections on the Old Testament. 1995. 39.95 (*0-567-09727-7*) Bks Intl VA.

McKane, William. Micah: Introduction & Commentary. 256p. 49.95 (*0-567-08615-1*) T&T Clark Pubs.

McKane, William. Selected Christian Hebraists. 288p. (C). 1989. text 80.00 (*0-521-35507-9*) Cambridge U Pr.

Mckanna, Clare V. Homicide, Race, & Justice in the American West, 1880-1920. LC 96-35638. 1997. 40.00 (*0-8165-1708-8*) U of Ariz Pr.

McKarns, James. Give Us This Day: Reflections for Each Day of the Liturgical Year, 3 vols., Set. Incl. Vol. 1. Year One. LC 91-7181. 145p. 1991. pap. 7.50 (*0-8189-0611-1*); Vol. 2. Year Two. LC 91-7181. 143p. 1991. pap. 7.50 (*0-8189-0612-X*); Vol. 3. Seasons & Saints. LC 91-7181. 159p. 1991. pap. 7.50 (*0-8189-0613-8*); LC 91-7181. (Orig.). 1991. 19.95 (*0-8189-0614-6*) Alba.

— Lean Against the Wind: How to Face the Future. LC 93-41498. 150p. (Orig.). 1994. pap. 5.95 (*0-8189-0690-1*) Alba.

McKasson, Stephen C. & Richards, Carol A. Speaking As an Expert: A Guide for the Identification Sciences from the Laboratory to the Courtroom. LC 97-32099. (Illus.). 228p. 1998. text 50.95 (*0-398-06840-2*); pap. text 37.95 (*0-398-06841-0*) C C Thomas.

McKaughan, Howard, ed. The Languages of the Eastern Family of the East New Guinea Highland Stock. LC 72-13131. (Anthropological Studies in the Eastern Highlands of New Guinea: No. 1). (Illus.). 848p. 1973. 40.00 (*0-295-95132-X*) U of Wash Pr.

McKaughan, Howard P. & Macaraya, Batua A. Maranao Dictionary. LC 67-13668. 878p. reprint ed. pap. 200.00 (*0-8357-9825-9*, 201611300098) Bks Demand.

McKaughan, Howard P., ed. see Benton, Richard A.

McKaughan, Howard P., ed. see Bernabe, Emma, et al.

McKaughan, Howard P., ed. see Forman, Michael L.

McKaughan, Howard P., ed. see Mirikitani, Leatrice T.

McKaughan, Howard P., ed. see Wolfenden, E. P.

McKaughan, Jeffrey D., ed. Tech Intell Vol. 2: World War II U. S. Army Technical Intelligence Reports & Summaries. (Tech Intell Ser.). (Illus.). 132p. pap. 13.95 (*0-9648793-0-1*) Darlington Prods.

McKaughan, Larry. Why Are Your Fingers Cold? LC 92-16549. (Illus.). 32p. (J). (ps-1). 1992. 14.99 (*0-8361-3604-7*) Herald Pr.

McKaughan, Paul, et al. Choosing a Future for U. S. Missions. LC 98-212808. 128p. 1998. pap. 11.95 (*1-887983-07-4*) MARC.

McKaughan, Sean, jt. auth. see Magalhaes, Antonio R.

Mckay. Grammar Strands 1. (College ESL Ser.). 182p. (J). 1996. mass mkt. 23.95 (*0-8384-4082-7*) Wadsworth Pub.

McKay. Joinery. 1974. pap. text. write for info. (*0-582-42518-2*, Pub. by Addison-Wesley) Longman.

***McKay.** Lack Brothers. 2000. pap. 17.95 (*0-593-04204-2*, Pub. by Transworld Publishers Ltd) Trafalgar.

— Mckay World Soc Sg V1. 5th ed. 1999. pap. text 17.97 (*0-395-94494-5*) HM.

— Mckay World Soc Sg V2. 5th ed. 1999. pap. text 17.97 (*0-395-94496-1*) HM.

— Mckay World Soc Va 5e. 5th ed. 1999. pap. text 35.07 (*0-395-94492-9*) HM.

— Mckay World Soc Vb. 5th ed. 1999. pap. text 35.07 (*0-395-94493-7*) HM.

— Mckay World Soc Vc. 5th ed. 1999. pap. text 35.07 (*0-395-94495-3*) HM.

— Mckay World Soc V1. 5th ed. 1999. pap. text 41.07 (*0-395-94490-2*) HM.

— Mckay World Soc V2. 5th ed. 1999. pap. text 41.07 (*0-395-94491-0*) HM.

McKay. Night Field. 1991. pap. 16.95 (*0-7710-5762-8*) McCland & Stewart.

— Reasons & Explanations: Guidelines for critical Thinking. LC 99-35782. (Philosophy). 1999. pap. 45.95 (*0-534-57411-4*) Wadsworth Pub.

— Sociology Comprehensive Exam, 5 vols. LC 94-76524. (C). Date not set. text 67.16 (*0-395-71719-1*) HM.

— Western Society Complete. 6th ed. LC 98-72226. 1998. text 56.37 (*0-395-90431-5*) HM.

— Western Society since 1400, 5 vols. (C). Date not set. pap., teacher ed., suppl. ed. 53.56 (*0-395-71725-6*) HM.

— Western Society Since 1300 6th ed. text 44.67 (*0-618-00459-9*) HM.

***McKay.** World Sociology. 5th ed. 1999. pap. text, teacher ed. 8.97 (*0-395-95399-5*) HM.

McKay & Fodors Travel Publications, Inc. Staff. Fodor's Skiing U. S. A. 30 of the Nation's Premier Ski Resorts. 1995. pap. 16.00 (*0-679-02600-2*) Fodors Travel.

McKay & Herzfeldpipkin. Grammar Strand Book 1-answer Key. (College ESL). (J). 1996. mass mkt. 6.95 (*0-8384-6975-2*) Heinle & Heinle.

***McKay & Musil.** Healing the Spirit: Stories of Recovery, Acceptance & Transformation. 200p. 2000. pap. 15.95 (*0-88347-465-4*, 661-237, Pub. by T More) BookWorld.

McKay & Pepe. Cell Reproduction/Mitosis. 1992. 76.00 (*0-697-20075-2*) McGraw.

McKay, jt. auth. see Fine Creative Media Staff.

McKay, Adam, jt. auth. see Smigel, Robert.

McKay, Alan B., et al. How to Evaluate Progressive Pharmaceutical Services. 159p. (Orig.). 1987. pap. text 31.00 (*0-930530-81-0*) Am Soc Hlth-Syst.

McKay, Alex. Tibet & the British Raj: The Frontier Cadre, 1904-1947. (SOAS London Studies on South Asia: Vol. 14). 288p. (C). 1997. text 49.00 (*0-7007-0627-5*, Pub. by Curzon Pr Ltd) UH Pr.

McKay, Alex, ed. Pilgrimage in Tibet. 260p. 1998. text 45.00 (*0-7007-0992-4*, Pub. by Curzon Pr Ltd) UH Pr.

McKay, Alex, jt. auth. see Van der Velde, Paul.

McKay, Alexander. Sexual Ideology & Schooling: Towards Democratic Sexuality Education. LC 99-37849. (C). 1999. text 54.50 (*0-7914-4523-2*); pap. text 17.95 (*0-7914-4524-0*) State U NY Pr.

McKay, Alexander G. Houses, Villas, & Palaces in the Roman World. LC 97-51608. (Illus.). 336p. 1998. reprint ed. pap. 16.95 (*0-8018-5904-2*) Johns Hopkins.

— The Two Worlds of the Poet: New Perspectives in Vergil. Wilhelm, Robert M. & Jones, Howard, eds. LC 92-30789. (Classical Studies Pedagogy: No. 19). (Illus.). 522p. reprint ed. pap. 161.90 (*0-608-10521-X*, 205443200009) Bks Demand.

— Vergil's Italy. LC 76-125595. 356p. 1970. write for info. (*0-8212-0367-3*) Little.

McKay, Alexander G., et al. Arma Virumque Vol. 1: Heroes at War; Vergil, Aeneid 10.420-509 & Aeneid 12.791-842, 887-952. (Arma Virumque Ser.: Vol. 1). (Illus.). 128p. 1998. pap. text 22.00 (*0-9662763-2-9*, 16719981) Campanian Soc.

— Arma Virumque Vol. 2: Heroes at War; Vergil, Aeneid 10.420-509 & Aeneid 12.791-842, 887-952, Vol. 2. (Illus.). 106p. 1998. pap. text 30.00 (*0-9662763-1-0*, 16719882) Campanian Soc.

McKay, Alexander G., jt. auth. see Hall, Jane H.

***McKay, Amanda.** Not Sally Marshall Again! 187p. 2000. pap. 12.95 (*0-7022-3169-X*, Pub. by Univ Queensland Pr) Intl Spec Bk.

— Sally Marshall's Not an Alien! (J). 1999. reprint ed. pap. 11.95 (*0-7022-3108-8*, Pub. by Univ Queensland Pr) Intl Spec Bk.

McKay, Ane, et al. A Mural of Leaves: Haiku, Senryu, Renku. (Illus.). 48p. (Orig.). (C). 1991. pap. text 5.00 (*0-9618009-7-6*) Vandina Pr.

McKay, B. And You Visited Me. 6.99 (*1-85792-005-8*, Pub. by Christian Focus) Spring Arbor Dist.

— Bruised but Not Broken. 6.99 (*1-85792-113-5*, Pub. by Christian Focus) Spring Arbor Dist.

— Count It All Joy. Date not set. pap. 6.99 (*1-871676-88-6*, Pub. by Christian Focus) Spring Arbor Dist.

McKay, B., jt. auth. see Allason-Jones, L.

McKay, Barry. Gay Phrase Book. 2nd ed. LC 98-144582. (Gay Studies). (Illus.). 144p. 1996. pap. 8.95 (*0-304-33775-7*) Continuum.

— Marbling Methods & Receipts from Four Centuries. 105p. 1990. 125.00 (*0-938768-21-2*, 30757) Oak Knoll.

***McKay, Barry & Isaac, Peter C.** The Human Face of the Book Trade: Print Culture & Its Creators. LC 99-30585. (Print Networks Ser.: Vol. 3). (Illus.). 228p. 1999. lib. bdg. 39.95 (*1-58456-003-7*) Oak Knoll.

McKay, Barry, jt. auth. see Isaac, Peter.

McKay, Barry, jt. auth. see Isaac, Peter C.

McKay, Barry, jt. auth. see Isaac, Peter C. G.

McKay, Bernard. Crooked River Rats: The Adventures of Pioneer Rivermen. (Illus.). 176p. 1999. pap. 16.95 (*0-88839-451-9*) Hancock House.

— Wild Trails, Wild Tales. (Illus.). 176p. (Orig.). 1996. pap. 12.95 (*0-88839-395-4*) Hancock House.

McKay, Beth, jt. auth. see Ryan, Sue.

McKay, Bev. Trash Unlimited: Linking Environmental Studies with Everyday Life. (Illus.). 64p. (Orig.). (J). (gr. 2-6). 1993. pap. text, teacher ed. 8.95 (*0-86530-276-6*, 269-8) Incentive Pubns.

McKay, Bob. How to Draw Funny People. LC 81-69658. (Illus.). 32p. (J). (gr. 2-6). 1981. lib. bdg. 17.25 (*0-89375-688-1*) Troll Communs.

— How to Draw Funny People. LC 81-69658. (Illus.). 32p. (J). (gr. 2-6). 1997. pap. 2.95 (*0-89375-408-0*) Troll Communs.

Mckay, Bob. How to Draw Funny People. 1981. 8.15 (*0-606-01057-2*, Pub. by Turtleback) Demco.

McKay, C. E. Stories of Hospital & Camp. LC 70-37312. (Black Heritage Library Collection). 1977. reprint ed. 25.95 (*0-8369-8949-X*) Ayer.

McKay, C. G. From Information to Intrigue: Studies in Secret Service: Based on the Swedish Experience, 1939-45. LC 92-35249. (Cass Series, Studies in Intelligence). 306p. 1993. 52.50 (*0-7146-3470-0*, Pub. by F Cass Pubs) Intl Spec Bk.

McKay, Carolyn, ed. see Smith, Leroy W., Jr.

McKay, Charles W. Digital Circuits: A Preparation for Microprocessors. LC 77-13058. (Illus.). 1978. 32.95 (*0-685-03835-1*) P-H.

McKay, Christine, jt. ed. see Babcock, Marguerite.

McKay, Christopher P., ed. The Case for Mars II. (Science & Technology Ser.: Vol. 62). (Illus.). 730p. 1985. pap. 20.00 (*0-87703-220-3*, Am Astronaut Soc); lib. bdg. 30.00 (*0-87703-219-X*) Univelt Inc.

McKay, Claude. Banana Bottom. (Black Classics Ser.). 1999. pap. text 10.95 (*1-874509-74-3*) X Press.

— Banana Bottom. 317p. 1971. reprint ed. 15.95 (*0-911860-03-7*) Chatham Bkseller.

— Banana Bottom. LC 73-14676. 324p. (C). 1974. reprint ed. pap. 10.00 (*0-15-610650-7*, Harvest Bks) Harcourt.

— Banjo. LC 79-17798. 336p. 1970. reprint ed. pap. 11.00 (*0-15-610675-2*, Harvest Bks) Harcourt.

— Constab Ballads. 1977. lib. bdg. 59.95 (*0-8490-1666-5*) Gordon Pr.

— The Dialect Poetry of Claude McKay, 2 vols in one. Incl. Vol. 1, Songs of Jamaica. LC 73-3801. Vol. 2, Constab Ballads. LC 73-3801. LC 73-3801. (Black Heritage Library Collection). 1977. reprint ed. 23.95 (*0-8369-8982-1*) Ayer.

— Gingertown. LC 72-37554. (Short Story Index Reprint Ser.). 1977. reprint ed. 28.95 (*0-8369-4113-6*) Ayer.

— Harlem Glory: A Fragment of Aframerican Life. 175p. 1990. pap. 12.00 (*0-88286-163-8*); lib. bdg. 24.95 (*0-88286-162-X*) C H Kerr.

— Home to Harlem. 360p. 1987. reprint ed. pap. text 15.95 (*1-55553-024-9*) NE U Pr.

— A Long Way from Home. LC 74-77507. (American Negro: His History & Literature. Series 2). 1980. reprint ed. 29.95 (*0-405-01880-0*) Ayer.

— A Long Way from Home: An Autobiography. (American Biography Ser.). 354p. 1991. reprint ed. lib. bdg. 79.00 (*0-7812-8282-9*) Rprt Serv.

An Asterisk (*) at the beginning of an entry indicates that the title is appearing for the first time.

— The Passion of Claude McKay. LC 72-95662. (Negro History Ser.). vii, 363 p. 1973. write for info. (*0-8052-3498-5*) Schocken.

— Selected Poems. LC 99-25505. (Dover Thrift Editions Ser.). 1999. pap. text 1.00 (*0-486-40876-0*) Dover.

— Selected Poems of Claude McKay. LC 70-78698. 110p. 1969. reprint ed. pap. 5.95 (*0-15-680649-5*, Harvest Bks) Harcourt.

McKay, Claudia. The Kali Connection. LC 93-42942. 190p. (Orig.). 1994. pap. 9.95 (*0-934678-54-5*) New Victoria Pubs.

— Promise of the Rose Stone. LC 86-62343. 238p. 1986. pap. 7.95 (*0-934678-09-X*) New Victoria Pubs.

— Twist of Lime: A Lynn Evans Mystery. LC 97-19531. (Lynn Evans Mystery Ser.). 166p. 1997. pap. 10.95 (*0-934678-88-X*) New Victoria Pubs.

McKay Cowing, Janet. Cowing. Genealogy of the Cowing Family. 11p. 1997. reprint ed. pap. 4.50 (*0-8328-8104-X*); reprint ed. lib. bdg. 14.50 (*0-8328-8103-1*) Higginson Bk Co.

McKay, Craig G., tr. see Lindgren, Michael.

McKay, Cynthia. The Business of Gift Baskets: A Guide for Survival, 5 vols. Doris, Carol, ed. 280p. 1998. pap. 19.95 (*0-9663083-0-1*, 0001) Sixtn Hundrd One.

McKay, D. John, ed. see Innovative Cooking Enterprises Staff.

McKay, David. Domestic Policy & Ideology: Presidents & the American State, 1964-1987. (Illus.). 240p. (C). 1989. text 59.95 (*0-521-32033-X*) Cambridge U Pr.

— Essentials of American Politics. LC 99-48143. (Essentials of Political Science Ser.). 396p. 1999. pap. 29.00 (*0-8133-6755-7*) Westview.

— Federalism & European Union: A Political Economy Perspective. 216p. 2000. 28.00 (*0-19-829677-0*) OUP.

— Rush to Union: Understanding the European Federal Bargain. (Illus.). 208p. 1996. text 55.00 (*0-19-828058-0*) OUP.

McKay, David, jt. auth. see Walker, Mark.

McKay, David, jt. ed. see Budge, Ian.

McKay, David C. The Beginner's Guide: Internet. 1995. write for info. (*1-881023-95-8*) INST Publishing.

— The Beginner's Guide: MS Access for Windows 95 Version 7.0. LC 96-158325. 1996. pap. text. write for info. (*1-881023-88-5*) INST Publishing.

— The Beginner's Guide: MS Dos 5.0-6.2 - Microsoft Windows 3.1. 1995. 29.95 (*1-881023-89-3*) INST Publishing.

— The Beginner's Guide: MS Excel 5.0. LC 96-157123. 1995. write for info. (*1-881023-83-4*) INST Publishing.

— The Beginner's Guide: MS Excel 7.0 for 95. 1995. write for info. (*1-881023-93-1*) INST Publishing.

— The Beginner's Guide: MS Office. LC 96-158304. 1995. 29.95 (*1-881023-87-7*) INST Publishing.

— The Beginner's Guide: MS Office 7.0 for 95. 1995. write for info. (*1-881023-94-X*) INST Publishing.

— The Beginner's Guide: MS Word 6.0 for Windows. LC 96-158364. 1995. write for info. (*1-881023-82-6*) INST Publishing.

— The Beginner's Guide: MS Word 7.0 for 95. 1995. write for info. (*1-881023-92-3*) INST Publishing.

— The Beginner's Guide: Quicken-QuickBook-TurboTax. 1995. write for info. (*1-881023-91-5*) INST Publishing.

— The Beginner's Guide: Windows '95. 1995. write for info. (*1-881023-90-7*) INST Publishing.

— The Beginner's Guide: Windows 95 & the Internet. 1995. write for info. (*1-881023-96-6*) INST Publishing.

— The Beginner's Guide: WordPerfect 6.1 for Windows/6.0 for DOS. LC 96-229259. 1995. write for info. (*1-881023-80-X*) INST Publishing.

McKay, David O. What E're Thou Art Act Well Thy Part: The Missionary Diaries of David O. McKay. Larson, Patricia & Larson, Stan, eds. LC 98-11619. (Illus.). 352p. 1998. text 24.95 (*0-9634732-9-8*, Blue Ribbon Books) Freethinker.

— What E're Thou Art Act Well Thy Part: The Missionary Diaries of David O. McKay. Larson, Stan & Larson, Patricia, eds. LC 98-11619. (Illus.). 352p. 1999. 149.00 (*1-890686-01-8*, Blue Ribbon Books) Freethinker.

McKay, David P. & Crawford, Richard. William Billings of Boston: Eighteenth-Century Composer. LC 74-19035. (Illus.). 314p. 1975. reprint ed. pap. 97.40 (*0-608-02501-1*, 206314500004) Bks Demand.

McKay, David W. Space Science Projects for Young Scientists. (J). 1989. pap. 6.95 (*0-531-15134-4*) Watts.

McKay, David W. & Smith, Bruce G. Space Science Projects for Young Scientists. LC 86-7745. (Projects for Young Scientists Ser.). (Illus.). 128p. (YA). (gr. 7-12). 1986. lib. bdg. 24.00 (*0-531-10244-0*) Watts.

***McKay, Dawn R.** Student's Guide to Research on the Web: The Painless Guide to Finding & Using Online Information. (Illus.). 304p. 2000. pap. text 14.95 (*0-02-863760-7*, Arco) Macmillan Gen Ref.

McKay, Deborah. Eve's Longing: The Infinite Possibilities in All Things. 139p. 1992. pap. 11.95 (*0-932511-65-1*) Fiction Coll.

McKay, Derek & Scott, H. M. The Rise of the Great Powers: The Great Powers & European States Systems, 1648-1815. (C). 1983. text. write for info. (*0-318-56830-6*) Longman.

***McKay, Don.** Another Gravity. 96p. 2001. pap. 14.95 (*0-7710-5764-4*) McCland & Stewart.

McKay, Don. Apparatus. LC 97-147668. 88p. 1997. pap. 10.95 (*0-7710-5763-6*) McCland & Stewart.

McKay, Donald C. The United States & France. LC 83-1558. 334p. (C). 1983. reprint ed. lib. bdg. 69.50 (*0-313-23885-5*, MCUW, Greenwood Pr) Greenwood.

McKay, Donald C., ed. Essays in the History of Modern Europe. LC 68-14908. (Essay Index Reprint Ser.). 1977. 21.95 (*0-8369-0652-7*) Ayer.

McKay, Eleanor, ed. Papers of John L. Lewis, 1879-1969: Guide to a Microfilm Edition. 12p. 1970. pap. write for info. (*0-89887-182-4*) Chadwyck-Healey.

McKay, Eleanor, jt. ed. see Wolff, Janet.

McKay, Elizabeth N. Franz Schubert: A Biography. (Illus.). 400p. (C). 1996. 38.00 (*0-19-816523-4*) OUP.

— Franz Schubert: A Biography. (Illus.). 378p. 1998. reprint ed. pap. text 19.95 (*0-19-816681-8*) OUP.

McKay, Erin. Weddingpages. 8th rev. ed. Werner, Tammy, ed. (Illus.). 160p. 1998. pap. 19.95 (*0-929879-03-1*) Weddingpages.

***McKay, Erin, et al.** Water Buffalo Days: Growing up in Vietnam. LC 96-35058. (Illus.). 128p. (J). (gr. 4-7). 1999. pap. 4.95 (*0-06-446211-0*) HarpC Child Bks.

McKay, Ernest A. Against Wilson & War, 1914-1917. 230p. (Orig.). (C). 1996. pap. 18.50 (*1-57524-000-9*) Krieger.

— Against Wilson & War, 1914-1917. LC 95-31584. 230p. (Orig.). (C). 1996. 26.50 (*0-89464-964-7*) Krieger.

— The Civil War & New York City. LC 90-32799. (York State Bks.). (Illus.). 392p. 1990. reprint ed. pap. 121.60 (*0-608-07619-8*, 205993400010) Bks Demand.

McKay, Everett N. Developing User Interfaces for Microsoft Windows With CDROM. LC 99-13029. (Illus.). 350p. 1999. pap. 49.99 (*0-7356-0586-6*) Microsoft.

***McKay, Everett N. & Woodring, Mike.** Debugging Windows Programs Grammers: Strategies, Tools, & Techniques for Visual C++ Programmers. 424p. 2000. pap. 44.95 (*0-201-70238-X*) Addison-Wesley.

McKay, Floyd J. An Editor for Oregon: Charles A. Sprague & the Oregon Statesman. LC 98-30120. (Illus.). 352p. 1998. 19.95 (*0-87071-439-2*) Oreg St U Pr.

McKay, Frank W. A Workable Plan for Sensible Government. 116p. (Orig.). 1984. pap. 2.95 (*0-930333-00-4*) Switz Pr.

McKay, G. An English Gaelic Key to Dwelly. 1991. pap. 7.95 (*0-8288-3343-5*, F129235) Fr & Eur.

McKay, G. A., jt. ed. see Lipin, R. B.

McKay, G. D., jt. auth. see Dinkmeyer, Don.

***McKay, Gardner.** Toyer. 496p. 1999. mass mkt. 7.50 (*0-446-60773-8*, Pub. by Warner Bks) Little.

McKay, Gardner. Toyer: A Novel. LC 97-52639. 464p. (gr. 8). 1999. 24.00 (*0-316-56118-5*) Little.

McKay, Gary & Dinkmeyer, Don. How You Feel Is up to You: The Power of Emotional Choice. LC 94-3464. 288p. 1994. pap. 13.95 (*0-915166-81-X*) Impact Pubs CA.

McKay, Gary D., jt. auth. see Dinkmeyer, Don, Sr.

McKay, Gary D., jt. auth. see Dinkmeyer, Don.

McKay, Gary D., jt. auth. see Dinkmeyer, Don C.

***McKay, Gary E.** Road Rage: "Commuter Combat in America" Hursey, Dick, ed. LC 00-131451. (Illus.). 224p. 2000. pap. 13.95 (*0-9675639-0-9*) Silvertip Bks.

McKay, George. DIY Culture. LC 98-7504. 224p. (C). 1998. 45.00 (*1-85984-878-8*) Norton.

— Diy Culture: Party & Protest in Nineties' Britain. LC 98-7504. 224p. 1998. pap. 19.00 (*1-85984-260-7*, Pub. by Verso) Norton.

***McKay, George.** Mammals. LC 99-36486. (The/Little Guides Ser.). 320p. 1999. pap. 14.95 (*1-875137-59-9*) Weldon Owen.

McKay, George. Senseless Acts of Beauty: Cultures of Resistance since the Sixties. (Illus.). 224p. (C). 1996. 60.00 (*1-85984-908-3*, Pub. by Verso) Norton.

— Senseless Acts of Beauty: Cultures of Resistence since the Sixties. (Illus.). 224p. 1996. pap. 18.00 (*1-85984-028-0*, Pub. by Verso) Norton.

McKay, George, ed. Yankee Go Home (Take Me with U) Americanization & Popular Culture. (SAP Title Ser.). 170p. 1997. pap. 20.00 (*1-85075-811-5*, Pub. by Sheffield Acad) CUP Services.

McKay, George, jt. ed. see Gould, Edwin.

McKay, George L. American Book Auction Catalogues, 1713-1943: A Union List. 560p. 1999. reprint ed. 75.00 (*1-57898-131-X*) Martino Pubng.

— Bibliography of Robert Bridges. LC 33-31729. reprint ed. 20.00 (*0-404-04132-9*) AMS Pr.

McKay, Girvan. An English-Gaelic Key to Dwelly. (C). 1989. pap. 25.00 (*0-901771-47-3*, Pub. by Gairm Pubns) St Mut.

McKay, Glynn. Mask Making. 80p. 1994. 12.98 (*0-7858-0176-6*) Bk Sales Inc.

McKay, Gordon, ed. Use of Adsorbents for the Removal of Pollutants from Wastewater. LC 95-17509. 208p. 1995. boxed set 94.95 (*0-8493-6920-7*, 6920) CRC Pr.

***McKay, H.** Birthday Wish. (Illus.). (J). 1998. mass mkt. 8.95 (*0-340-69833-0*, Pub. by Hodder & Stought Ltd) Trafalgar.

— Echo in the Chimney. (J). mass mkt. 7.95 (*0-340-72288-6*, Pub. by Hodder & Stought Ltd) Trafalgar.

— Magic in the Mirror. (Illus.). (J). mass mkt. 7.95 (*0-340-72289-4*, Pub. by Hodder & Stought Ltd) Trafalgar.

— Treasure Garden. (Illus.). mass mkt. 7.95 (*0-340-72287-8*, Pub. by Hodder & Stought Ltd) Trafalgar.

— Zoo in the Attic. (Illus.). (J). mass mkt. 7.95 (*0-340-72286-X*, Pub. by Hodder & Stought Ltd) Trafalgar.

McKay, Harvey J. St. Paul, Oregon, 1830-1890. LC 80-69228. (Illus.). 340p. 1980. 15.00 (*0-8323-0384-4*) Binford Mort.

McKay, Heather & Tom, Abigail. Teaching Adult Second Language Learners. LC 99-36775. (Handbooks for Language Teachers Ser.). 216p. (C). 1999. pap. text 20.95 (*0-521-64990-0*) Cambridge U Pr.

McKay, Heather, jt. auth. see Tom, Abigail.

McKay, Heather A. Sabbath & Synagogue Vol. 122: The Question of Sabbath in Ancient Judaism. LC 94-22552. xiii, 279p. 1994. 92.50 (*90-04-10060-1*) Brill Academic Pubs.

McKay, Heather A. & Clines, D. J. Of Prophets' Visions & the Wisdom of Sages. (JSOTS Ser.: Vol. 162). 335p. 1993. 60.00 (*1-85075-423-3*, Pub. by Sheffield Acad) CUP Services.

McKay, Henry D., jt. ed. see Shaw, Clifford R.

McKay, Hilary. The Amber Cat. LC 96-52923. 144p. (J). (gr. 4-7). 1997. 15.00 (*0-689-81360-0*) McElderry Bks.

McKay, Hilary. Dog Friday. LC 95-4446. 144p. (J). (gr. 4-7). 1995. pap. 15.00 (*0-689-80383-4*) McElderry Bks.

McKay, Hilary. Dog Friday. LC 95-4446. 144p. (J). (gr. 3-6). 1997. per. 3.99 (*0-689-81765-7*) S&S Childrens.

— Dog Friday. 1997. 9.09 (*0-606-12676-7*, Pub. by Turtleback) Demco.

***McKay, Hilary.** Dolphin Luck. LC 98-19100. 160p. (J). (gr. 4-7). 1999. per. 16.00 (*0-689-82376-2*) McElderry Bks.

McKay, Hilary. The Exiles. LC 91-38220. (Illus.). 208p. (J). (gr. 4-7). 1996. per. 3.99 (*0-689-80592-6*) Aladdin.

— The Exiles. LC 91-38220. (Illus.). 208p. (J). (gr. 4-7). 1992. 17.99 (*0-689-50555-8*) McElderry Bks.

— The Exiles. LC 91-38220. 1996. 9.09 (*0-606-09245-5*, Pub. by Turtleback) Demco.

— The Exiles at Home. LC 94-14225. (Illus.). 208p. (J). (gr. 4-8). 1997. per. 3.99 (*0-689-81403-8*) Atheneum Yung Read.

McKay, Hilary. The Exiles at Home. LC 94-14225. 208p. (J). (gr. 4-7). 1994. pap. 15.95 (*0-689-50610-4*) McElderry Bks.

McKay, Hilary. The Exiles in Love. LC 97-30237. (Illus.). 176p. (J). (gr. 4-7). 1998. per. 16.00 (*0-689-81752-5*) McElderry Bks.

— Exiles in Love. 176p. (J). 1999. per. 4.50 (*0-689-82013-5*) Aladdin.

***McKay, Hilary.** Happy & Glorious. 1999. 16.95 (*0-7540-6061-6*) Chivers N Amer.

— Pirates Ahoy! (Illus.). 32p. (J). (ps-3). 2000. 16.00 (*0-689-83114-5*) McElderry Bks.

McKay, Hilary. Where's Bear? LC 98-65819. (Illus.). 32p. (J). (ps-2). 1998. per. 15.00 (*0-689-82271-5*) S&S Trade.

McKay, Hilary & Piazza, Gail. The Amber Cat. (J). 1999. per. 3.99 (*0-689-82557-9*) Aladdin.

McKay, Ian. The Quest of the Folk: Antimodernism & Cultural Selection in Twentieth-Century Nova Scotia. (Illus.). 392p. 1994. pap. 22.95 (*0-7735-1248-9*, Pub. by McG-Queens Univ Pr) CUP Services.

— The Quest of the Folk: Antimodernism & Cultural Selection in Twentieth-Century Nova Scotia. (Illus.). 392p. 1994. 65.00 (*0-7735-1179-2*, Pub. by McG-Queens Univ Pr) CUP Services.

McKay, Ian & Leigh, Irene M., eds. Growth Factors: A Practical Approach. LC 92-27317. (Practical Approach Ser.). (Illus.). 272p. (C). 1993. pap. text 45.00 (*0-19-963359-2*); spiral bd. 95.00 (*0-19-963360-6*) OUP.

McKay, Ian A. & Brown, Kenneth D., eds. Growth Factors & Receptors: A Practical Approach. LC 98-9879. (Practical Approach Ser.: Vol. 194). (Illus.). 288p. (C). 1998. pap. text 45.00 (*0-19-963646-X*) OUP.

— Growth Factors & Receptors: A Practical Approach. LC 98-9879. (Practical Approach Ser.: Vol. 194). (Illus.). 288p. (C). 1998. text 125.00 (*0-19-963647-8*) OUP.

McKay, Irene. Beginning Interactive Grammar: Activities & Exercises. LC 92-29933. 282p. (J). 1993. mass mkt. 26.95 (*0-8384-3926-8*) Heinle & Heinle.

McKay, Irene. Intermediate Interactive Grammar: Activities & Exercises. LC 94-25621. 248p. (J). 1995. pap. 32.95 (*0-8384-5864-5*) Heinle & Heinle.

***McKay, J.** The Damned Never Die. 302p. 1999. pap. 9.95 (*0-9675722-0-7*) Bravo Pubg Grp.

McKay, J. W. Sneap '92: Proceedings of the Symposium of North Eastern Accelerator Personnel, 1992. 260p. 1995. text 78.00 (*981-02-1885-0*) World Scientific Pub.

McKay, J. W. & Hyder, H. R., eds. Northeastern Accelerator Personnel. 340p. (C). 1989. text 130.00 (*9971-5-0979-2*) World Scientific Pub.

McKay, Jack A. Schools in the Middle: Developing a Middle-Level Orientation. Herman, Jerry J. & Herman, Janice L., eds. LC 95-1463. (Road Maps to Success Ser.). (Illus.). 80p. 1995. pap. 14.95 (*0-8039-6232-0*) Corwin Pr.

McKay, James. Complete Guide to Ferrets. (Illus.). 176p. 1995. pap. 24.95 (*1-85310-433-7*, Pub. by Swan Hill Pr) Voyageur Pr.

— The Ferret & Ferreting Handbook. (Illus.). 144p. 1994. 34.95 (*1-85223-772-4*, Pub. by Crolwood) Trafalgar.

McKay, James, ed. see Guitar, Barry & Conture, Edward G.

McKay, James R., et al. The Bassoon Reed Manual: Lou Skiner's Techniques. (Published in Cooperation with the International Double Reed Society Ser.). (Illus.). 112p. 1999. pap. 29.95 (*0-253-21312-6*) Ind U Pr.

***McKay, Jenny.** The Magazines Handbook. LC 00-28186. (Media Practice Ser.). 2000. pap. write for info. (*0-415-17035-4*) Routledge.

McKay, Jim. Managing Gender: Affirmative Action & Organizational Power in Australian, Canadian, & New Zealand Sport. LC 96-53415. (SUNY Series on Sport, Culture, & Social Relations). 217p. (C). 1997. text 56.50 (*0-7914-3421-4*); pap. text 18.95 (*0-7914-3422-2*) State U NY Pr.

— The Real McKay: My Wide World of Sports. (Illus.). 336p. 1999. pap. 12.95 (*0-452-28025-7*, Plume) Dutton Plume.

McKay, Joanna. The Official Concept of the Nation in the Former GDR: Theory, Pragmatism & the Search for Legitimacy. LC 97-78097. 176p. 1998. text 55.95 (*1-85972-622-4*, Pub. by Ashgate Pub) Ashgate Pub Co.

McKay, John. Anatomy of the Ship the 24-Gun Ship Pandora. (Illus.). 128p. (C). 1992. 32.95 (*0-9615021-9-3*) Phoen Pubns.

***McKay, John.** The 100-Gun Ship Victory. (Anatomy of the Ship Ser.). (Illus.). 120p. 2000. 39.95 (*1-55750-418-0*) Naval Inst Pr.

McKay, John. The Welfare State: No Mercy for the Middle Class. LC 95-76043. 289p. 1995. 22.00 (*0-9645693-0-2*) Liberty Books.

McKay, John, ed. Finite Groups--Coming of Age. LC 85-15049. (Contemporary Mathematics Ser.: Vol. 45). 350p. 1985. pap. 42.00 (*0-8218-5047-4*, CONM/45) Am Math.

McKay, John, ed. see Locke, Robert R.

McKay, John C. A Guide to Germanic Reference Grammars: The Modern Standard Languages. LC 84-14597. (Library & Information Sources in Linguistics: Vol. 15). xviii, 239p. 1984. 55.00 (*90-272-3736-0*) J Benjamins Pubng Co.

— A Guide to Romance Reference Grammars: The Modern Standard Languages. (Library & Information Sources in Linguistics: No. 6). xviii, 126p. 1979. 39.00 (*90-272-0997-9*) J Benjamins Pubng Co.

McKay, John E. The Insiders' Guide to Civil War Sites in the Southern States. (Insiders' Guide Travel Ser.). (Illus.). 2000. pap. 19.95 (*1-57380-079-1*, The Insiders Guide) Falcon Pub Inc.

McKay, John F., jt. ed. see Miknis, Francis P.

McKay, John G., tr. see Campbell, John F.

***McKay, John P.** History of World Societies Sin. 1999. pap. text 54.96 (*0-395-95134-8*) HM.

McKay, John P. Pioneers for Profit: Foreign Entrepreneurship & Russian Industrialization, 1885-1913. LC 79-103932. 456p. 1970. lib. bdg. 36.00 (*0-226-55990-4*) U Ch Pr.

— Tramways & Trolleys: The Rise of Urban Mass Transport in Europe. LC 76-3746. 283p. reprint ed. pap. 87.80 (*0-608-02229-2*, 206013200004) Bks Demand.

— World Society, 4 vols. (C). 1996. pap., teacher ed., suppl. ed. 11.96 (*0-395-74080-0*) HM.

— World Society, 3 vols. 3rd ed. (C). 1992. pap. text, teacher ed. 3.96 (*0-395-58906-1*); pap. text, teacher ed., suppl. ed. 4.76 (*0-395-58910-X*) HM.

— World Society, 4 vols., Vol. 1. 4th ed. (C). 1996. pap. text, student ed. 21.56 (*0-395-74077-0*) HM.

— World Society, 4 vols., Vol. 2. 4th ed. (C). 1996. pap. text, student ed. 21.56 (*0-395-74078-9*) HM.

— World Sociology, 4 vols. (C). Date not set. pap., teacher ed., suppl. ed. 41.96 (*0-395-76587-0*) HM.

McKay, John P., et al. A History of Western Society, 5 vols. (C). 1994. text, teacher ed. 11.96 (*0-395-72302-7*) HM.

— A History of Western Society. 3rd ed. LC 86-81468. 1088p. (C). 1986. student ed. 8.95 (*0-685-17244-9*) HM.

— A History of Western Society, 5 vols., Vol. 1. 5th ed. 430p. (C). 1994. pap. text 43.96 (*0-395-72508-9*) HM.

— A History of Western Society, 5 vols., Vol. I. 5th ed. 600p. (C). 1994. pap. text 48.76 (*0-395-72506-2*) HM.

— A History of Western Society, 5 vols., Vol. I. 5th ed. (C). 1994. pap. text, student ed. 19.56 (*0-395-71896-1*) HM.

— A History of Western Society, 5 vols., Vol. 2. 5th ed. 370p. (C). 1994. pap. text 43.96 (*0-395-72509-7*) HM.

— A History of Western Society, 5 vols., Vol. II. 5th ed. 575p. (C). 1994. pap. text 48.76 (*0-395-72507-0*) HM.

— A History of Western Society, 5 vols., Vol. II. 5th ed. (C). 1994. pap. text, student ed. 19.56 (*0-395-71897-X*) HM.

— A History of Western Society, 5 vols., Vol. 3. 5th ed. 400p. (C). 1994. pap. text 43.96 (*0-395-72510-0*) HM.

— A History of Western Society: Since 1400, 5 vols. 5th ed. 700p. (C). 1994. pap. text 53.56 (*0-395-72511-9*) HM.

— A History of World Societies. 2nd ed. 1987. pap. 22.36 (*0-318-36898-6*) HM.

— A History of World Societies, 4 vols. 4th ed. (C). 1995. text, teacher ed. 11.96 (*0-395-74079-7*) HM.

— A History of World Societies: From Antiquity Through the Middle Ages: Rand McNally Historical Atlas of the World, 4 vols. 4th ed. 450p. (C). 1995. pap. text 41.96 (*0-395-74074-6*) HM.

— A History of World Societies Vol. 1: To 1715, 4 vols. 4th ed. LC 95-77000. 591p. (C). 1997. pap. text 49.16 (*0-395-75378-3*) HM.

— A History of World Societies Vol. C: From the French Revolution to the Present, 4 vols. 4th ed. 465p. (C). 1995. pap. text 41.96 (*0-395-74076-2*) HM.

Mckay, John P., et al. A History of World Societies Vol. B: From 1100 Through the French Revolution, 4 vols. 4th ed. 380p. (C). 1995. pap. text 41.96 (*0-395-74075-4*) HM.

McKay, John P., et al. MCKAY WORLD SOC V1 (W/ATLAS), 4 vols. 4th ed. 600p. (C). 1995. pap. text 49.16 (*0-395-74072-X*) HM.

— MCKAY WORLD SOC V2 (W/ATLAS), 4 vols. 4th ed. 675p. (C). 1995. pap. text 49.16 (*0-395-74073-8*) HM.

McKay, Joyce, et al. Drug Free Parent Booklet. (Drug Free Ser.). 1989. pap. text 14.95 (*0-88671-296-3*, 5110) Am Guidance.

McKay, Joyce L., et al. Drug Free Teachers Guide. (Drug Free Ser.). 1989. 29.95 (*0-88671-295-5*, 5101) Am Guidance.

McKay, Judith & Hirano, Nancee. The Chemotherapy & Radiation Therapy Survival Guide: Information, Suggestions, & Support to Help You Get Through Treatment. 2nd rev. ed. LC 97-69490. Orig. Title: The Chemotherapy Survival Guide. 192p. 1998. pap. 14.95 (*1-57224-070-9*) New Harbinger.

McKay, Julie. Glimpses of a Mystical Affair: Spiritual Experiences of Swami Sivananda Radha. limited ed. LC 96-19576. (Illus.). 208p. 1996. 24.95 (*0-931454-82-4*) Timeless Bks.

McKay, Julie, ed. see Radha, Sivananda.

McKay, K. L. A New Syntax of the Verb in New Testament Greek: An Aspectual Approach. LC 92-44671. (Studies in Biblical Greek: Vol. 5). 203p. (Orig.). (C). 1994. pap. text 29.95 (*0-8204-2123-5*) P Lang Pubng.

Mckay, Kathryn L. & Northwest Montana Historical Society Staff. Looking Back: A Pictorial History of the Flathead Valley, Montana. LC 97-34848. 1997. write for info. (*1-57864-019-9*) Donning Co.

M

An Asterisk (*) at the beginning of an entry indicates that the title is appearing for the first time.

M

McKay, Kenneth M. Many Glancing Colours: An Essay in Reading Tennyson, 1809-1850. 301p. 1988. text 40.00 (*0-8020-2658-3*) U of Toronto Pr.

McKay, L. R. WEESKA Electronic Communications Systems. (What Every Engineer Should Know Ser.: Vol. 25). (Illus.). 264p. 1988. text 65.00 (*0-8247-8008-6*) Dekker.

McKay, Larry. The Personal Home Inspection Guide. LC 91-14522. 96p. 1991. pap. 14.95 (*0-942963-11-3*) Distinctive Pub.

McKay, Lawrence, Jr. Caravan. LC 95-2037. (Illus.). 32p. (J). (gr. k-6). 1995. 14.95 (*1-880000-23-7*) Lee & Low Bks.

McKay, Lawrence, Jr. Journey Home. LC 97-31407. (Illus.). 32p. (YA). (gr. 1 up). 2000. 15.95 (*1-880000-65-2*) Lee & Low Bks.

*McKay, Lawrence, Jr. Journey Home. (Illus.). 32p. (YA). (gr. 1 up). 2000. pap. 6.95 (*1-58430-005-1*, Pub. by Lee & Low Bks) Publishers Group.

*McKay, Lawrence. Journey Home. (Illus.). (J). 1998. 12.40 (*0-606-18247-0*) Turtleback.

McKay, Leo, Jr. Like This. LC 95-190470. 160p. (Orig.). 1996. pap. 13.95 (*0-88784-569-X*, Pub. by Hse of Anansi Pr) Genl Dist Srvs.

McKay, Linda B. Shadow Mothers: Stories of Adoption & Reunion. (Illus.). 155p. 1998. pap. 14.95 (*0-87839-129-0*) North Star.

McKay, Lyn J., jt. auth. see Radencich, Marguerite C.

McKay, Margaret. Peacock's Progress: Aspects of Artistic Development in the Novels of Thomas Love Peacock. (Studia Anglistica Upsaliensia Ser.: No. 78). 170p. (Orig.). 1992. pap. 41.00 (*91-554-2914-9*) Coronet Bks.

*McKay, Marianne. Celine Dion. LC 99-10874. 1999. text 12.98 (*1-56799-864-X*) M Friedman Pub Grp Inc.

McKay, Mark. On Tap: A Cavalcade of Trivia & Tall Stories Celebrating 200 Years of the Australian Pub. (Illus.). 160p. 1999. pap. 14.95 (*1-86254-473-5*, Pub. by Wakefield Pr) BHB Intl.

McKay, Marlina, et al. Southern Nightmares. (Illus.). 34p. 1996. pap. 5.00 (*0-9660071-1-5*) BEAR-IN-MIND.

McKay, Mary T. & Tryillo, Lisa Rockwood. Centinela Weavers of Chimays: Unfolding Tradition. (Illus.). 96p. 1999. pap. 24.95 (*0-9668862-0-8*) Centinela Trad.

*McKay, Mathew & Rogers, Peter. The Anger Control Workbook. 160p. 2000. pap., wbk. ed. 17.95 (*1-57224-220-5*, Pub. by New Harbinger) Publishers Group.

McKay, Mathew, jt. ed. see Fanning, Patrick.

McKay, Matthew. Amor a Si Mismo. (SPA.). 1997. pap. text 9.50 (*968-403-773-2*) Selector.

McKay, Matthew & Fanning, Patrick. Being a Man: A Guide to the New Masculinity. LC 92-672206. 288p. (Orig.). 1993. pap. 12.95 (*1-879237-40-7*) New Harbinger.

— The Daily Relaxer. LC 96-71158. (Illus.). 128p. (Orig.). 1997. pap. 12.95 (*1-57224-069-5*) New Harbinger.

— Prisoners of Belief: Exposing & Changing Beliefs That Control Your Life. LC 90-63757. 160p. 1991. pap. 12.95 (*1-879237-04-0*) New Harbinger.

— Self-Esteem. 1987. mass mkt. 5.99 (*0-312-90443-6*) St Martin.

— Self Esteem. 272p. 1991. 7.98 (*1-56731-003-6*, MJF Bks) Fine Comms.

— Self-Esteem: A Proven Program of Cognitive Techniques for Assessing & Improving. 2nd ed. LC 92-62823. 288p. 1994. pap. 14.95 (*1-879237-44-X*) New Harbinger.

*McKay, Matthew & Fanning, Patrick. Self Esteem: A Proven Program of Cognitive Techniques for Assessing, Improving, & Maintaining Your Self Esteem. 3rd ed. 308p. 2000. pap. 15.95 (*1-57224-198-5*) New Harbinger.

McKay, Matthew & Fanning, Patrick. Stress Inoculation. (Relaxation Tape Ser.). 1987. audio, VHS 11.95 (*0-934986-26-6*, 7) New Harbinger.

McKay, Matthew & Paleg, Kim, eds. Focal Group Psychotherapy. LC 92-54160. 544p. 1994. text 59.95 (*1-879237-18-0*) New Harbinger.

McKay, Matthew, et al. Couple Skills: Making Your Relationship Work. LC 93-86802. 288p. 1994. pap. 14.95 (*1-879237-66-0*) New Harbinger.

— The Divorce Book: A Practical & Compassionate Guide. LC 98-68750. 304p. 1999. pap. 15.95 (*1-57224-136-5*) New Harbinger.

— How to Communicate. 272p. 1993. 7.98 (*1-56731-031-1*, MJF Bks) Fine Comms.

— Messages: The Communication Skills Book. 2nd ed. 320p. 1995. pap. 15.95 (*1-57224-022-9*) New Harbinger.

— The Self-Esteem Companion: Simple Exercises to Help you Challenge Your Inner Critic & Celebrate Your Personal Strenghts. LC 98-68753. 144p. 1999. pap. 10.95 (*1-57224-138-1*) New Harbinger.

*McKay, Matthew, et al. Taking Control of Your Moods & Your Life: A Thoughts & Feelings Workbook. 256p. 1998. 9.98 (*1-56731-302-7*, MJF Bks) Fine Comms.

McKay, Matthew, et al. Thoughts & Feelings: Taking Control of Your Moods & Your Life. 2nd rev. ed. LC 97-69491. 256p. 1998. pap. 18.95 (*1-57224-093-8*) New Harbinger.

— When Anger Hurts. 1993. 6.98 (*1-56731-028-1*, MJF Bks) Fine Comms.

— When Anger Hurts: Quieting the Storm Within. 325p. (Orig.). 1989. pap. 15.95 (*0-934986-76-2*) New Harbinger.

— When Anger Hurts Your Kids. 176p. 1997. 5.98 (*1-56731-208-X*, MJF Bks) Fine Comms.

Mckay, Matthew, et al. When Anger Hurts Your Kids: A Parent's Guide. LC 95-72228. 161p. 1996. pap. 12.95 (*1-57224-045-8*) New Harbinger.

McKay, Michael J. Torneo Catequetico 5: Juego para Aprender la Fe Catolica. Espinosa, Pedro Aguirre, tr.Tr. of Catholic Quiz 5. (SPA., Illus.). 50p. (YA). 1995. 6.95 (*1-58626-054-5*) Divinity Religious.

— Torneo Catequetico 2: Juego para Aprender la Fe Catolica. Espinosa, Pedro Aguirre, tr.Tr. of Catholic Quiz 2. (SPA., Illus.). 50p. (YA). 1995. 6.95 (*1-58626-051-0*) Divinity Religious.

— Torneo Catequetico 9: Juego para Aprender la Fe Catolica. Espinosa, Pedro Aguirre, tr.Tr. of Catholic Quiz 9. (SPA., Illus.). 50p. (YA). 1995. 6.95 (*1-58626-058-8*) Divinity Religious.

— Torneo Catequetico 8: Juego para Aprender la Fe Catolica. Espinosa, Pedro Aguirre, tr.Tr. of Catholic Quiz 8. (SPA., Illus.). 50p. (YA). 1995. 6.95 (*1-58626-057-X*) Divinity Religious.

— Torneo Catequetico 4: Juego para Aprender la Fe Catolica. Espinosa, Pedro Aguirre, tr.Tr. of Catholic Quiz 4. (SPA., Illus.). 50p. (YA). 1995. 6.95 (*1-58626-053-7*) Divinity Religious.

— Torneo Catequetico 6: Juego para Aprender la Fe Catolica. Espinosa, Pedro Aguirre, tr.Tr. of Catholic Quiz 6. (SPA., Illus.). 50p. (YA). 1995. 6.95 (*1-58626-055-3*) Divinity Religious.

— Torneo Catequetico 7: Juego para Aprender la Fe Catolica. Espinosa, Pedro Aguirre, tr.Tr. of Catholic Quiz 7. (SPA., Illus.). 50p. (YA). 1995. 6.95 (*1-58626-056-1*) Divinity Religious.

— Torneo Catequetico 3: Juego para Aprender la Fe Catolica. Espinosa, Pedro Aguirre, tr.Tr. of Catholic Quiz 3. (SPA., Illus.). 50p. (YA). 1995. 6.95 (*1-58626-052-9*) Divinity Religious.

— Torneo Catequetico 1: Juego para Aprender la Fe Catolica. Espinosa, Pedro Aguirre, tr.Tr. of Catholic Quiz 1. (SPA., Illus.). 50p. (J). (gr. 1-9). 1995. 6.95 (*1-58626-050-2*) Divinity Religious.

McKay, Michael J. & Boulton, Connie. Catholic Quiz: Confirmation - Catechism Game for Confirmation Preparation. (Illus.). 50p. (YA). (gr. 7-13). 1997. pap. 6.95 (*1-58626-010-3*) Divinity Religious.

McKay, Michael J., et al. Catholic Bible Quiz 6: Q&A about the Law, Prophets, Wisdom, Gospel & Epistles. (Illus.). 40p. 1997. spiral bd. 6.95 (*1-58626-017-0*) Divinity Religious.

— Catholic Bible Quiz 8: Q&A about the Law, Prophets, Wisdom, Gospel & Epistles. (Illus.). 40p. 1997. spiral bd. 6.95 (*1-58626-019-7*) Divinity Religious.

— Catholic Bible Quiz 5: Q&A about the Law, Prophets, Wisdom, Gospel & Epistles. (Illus.). 40p. 1997. spiral bd. 6.95 (*1-58626-016-2*) Divinity Religious.

— Catholic Bible Quiz 4: Q&A about the Law, Prophets, Wisdom, Gospel & Epistles. (Illus.). 40p. 1997. spiral bd. 6.95 (*1-58626-015-4*) Divinity Religious.

— Catholic Bible Quiz 9: Q&A about the Law, Prophets, Wisdom, Gospel & Epistles. (Illus.). 40p. 1997. spiral bd. 6.95 (*1-58626-020-0*) Divinity Religious.

— Catholic Bible Quiz 1: Q&A about the Law, Prophets, Wisdom, Gospel & Epistles. (Illus.). 40p. 1997. pap. 6.95 (*1-58626-012-X*) Divinity Religious.

— Catholic Bible Quiz 7: Q&A about the Law, Prophets, Wisdom, Gospel & Epistles. (Illus.). 40p. 1997. spiral bd. 6.95 (*1-58626-018-9*) Divinity Religious.

— Catholic Bible Quiz 3: Q&A about the Law, Prophets, Wisdom, Gospel & Epistles. (Illus.). 40p. 1997. pap. 6.95 (*1-58626-014-6*) Divinity Religious.

— Catholic Bible Quiz 2: Q&A about the Law, Prophets, Wisdom, Gospel & Epistles. (Illus.). 40p. 1997. pap. 6.95 (*1-58626-013-8*) Divinity Religious.

— Catholic Quiz 8: Catechism Game for Eighth Grade. (Illus.). (YA). (gr. 8). 1995. pap. 6.95 (*1-58626-008-1*) Divinity Religious.

— Catholic Quiz 5: Catechism Game for Fifth Grade. (Illus.). 50p. (J). (gr. 5). 1995. pap. 6.95 (*1-58626-005-7*) Divinity Religious.

— Catholic Quiz 4: Catechism Game for Fourth Grade. (Illus.). 50p. (J). (gr. 4). 1995. pap. 6.95 (*1-58626-004-9*) Divinity Religious.

— Catholic Quiz 9: Catechism Game for Ninth Grade. (Illus.). 50p. (YA). (gr. 9). 1995. spiral bd. 6.95 (*1-58626-009-X*) Divinity Religious.

— Catholic Quiz 1: Catechism Game for First Grade. (Illus.). 50p. (J). (gr. 1). 1995. pap. 6.95 (*1-58626-001-4*) Divinity Religious.

— Catholic Quiz 7: Catechism Game for Seventh Grade. (Illus.). (J). (gr. 7). 1995. pap. 6.95 (*1-58626-007-3*) Divinity Religious.

— Catholic Quiz 6: Catechism Game for Sixth Grade. (Illus.). 50p. (J). (gr. 6). 1995. pap. 6.95 (*1-58626-006-5*) Divinity Religious.

— Catholic Quiz 3: Catechism Game for Third Grade. (Illus.). 50p. (J). (gr. 3). 1995. pap. 6.95 (*1-58626-003-0*) Divinity Religious.

— Catholic Quiz 2: Catechism Game for Second Grade. (Illus.). 50p. (J). (gr. 2). 1995. pap. 6.95 (*1-58626-002-2*) Divinity Religious.

McKay, Nellie Y. Critical Essays on Toni Morrison. (Critical Essays Ser.). 216p. 1988. 49.00 (*0-8161-8884-X*, G K Hall & Co) Mac Lib Ref.

— Jean Toomer, Artist: A Study of His Literary Life & Work, 1894-1936. LC 83-21570. (Illus.). 276p. reprint ed. pap. 85.60 (*0-608-20084-0*, 207135600011) Bks Demand.

McKay, Nellie Y. & Earle, Kathryn, eds. Approaches to Teaching the Novels of Toni Morrison. LC 97-26867. (Approaches to Teaching World Literature Ser.: Vol. 59). xi, 179p. 1997. pap. 18.00 (*0-87352-742-9*, AP59P); lib. bdg. 37.50 (*0-87352-741-0*, AP59C) Modern Lang.

McKay, Nellie Y., jt. ed. see Andrews, William L.

McKay, Ogese T. Now It Can Be Told. 60p. 1991. pap. text 10.00 (*0-9629807-0-6*) Ogese T McKay.

McKay, Patricia L., et al. Microcomputers & Economic Analysis: Spreadsheet Templates for Local Government. rev. ed. (Bureau of Economic & Business Research Monographs). 182p. 1987. pap. text 15.00 (*0-930885-03-1*) Bur Econ & Bus Res.

*McKay, Patrick. A Dictionary of Ulster Place Names. (Illus.). 128p. 1999. pap. 15.95 (*0-85389-742-5*, Pub. by Inst Irish Studies) Irish Bks Media.

McKay, Quinn G. Is Lying Sometimes the Right Thing for an Honest Person to Do? How Self-Interest & the Competitive Business World Distort Our Moral Values & What We Should Do about It. (Illus.). 264p. 1997. 22.95 (*1-890009-12-1*) Exec Excell.

McKay, Ray & Putnam, Russell. Divorce Tax Practice & Planning Guide. 50p. 1996. ring bd. 165.00 (*1-886035-05-9*) Pro Tax & Business.

McKay, Raymond E., Jr., jt. auth. see Duncan, Andrew J.

McKay, Rena. Honey, I'm Home. (Romance Ser.: No. 853). 1992. per. 2.69 (*0-373-08853-1*, 5-08853-9) Silhouette.

— Romancing Cody. (Silhouette Romance Ser.). 1994. per. 2.75 (*0-373-19004-2*) Harlequin Bks.

— Romancing Cody. (Romance Ser.). 1997. per. 191.52 (*0-373-91004-5*, 5-91004-7) Silhouette.

McKay, Richard C. Donald McKay & His Famous Sailing Ships. unabridged ed. LC 95-10984. (Illus.). 480p. 1996. reprint ed. pap. text 13.95 (*0-486-28820-X*) Dover.

— South Street. LC 76-160128. (American History & Americana Ser.: No. 47). 1971. lib. bdg. 75.00 (*0-8383-1280-2*) M S G Haskell Hse.

McKay, Robert. Opportunities in Your Own Service Business. (Opportunities In . . . Ser.). (Illus.). 160p. pap. 12.95 (*0-8442-6232-3*, 297OIYOSB, VGM Career) NTC Contemp Pub Co.

— Planning Your Military Career. 160p. 1992. pap. 6.95 (*0-8442-6672-8*, NTC Business Bks) NTC Contemp Pub Co.

— Scientific Instruction in Euclid & Aristotle. 24p. 1992. 3.00 (*1-883058-28-7*, SAG&IP) Global Pubns.

— Your Own Service Business. LC 98-17652. (Opportunities in... Ser.). 160p. 1998. 14.95 (*0-8442-6465-2*, 64652); pap. 11.95 (*0-8442-6525-X*, 6525X) NTC Contemp Pub Co.

McKay, Robert B., ed. Technological Applications of Dispersions. LC 93-50099. (Surfactant Science Ser.: Vol. 52). (Illus.). 576p. 1994. text 245.00 (*0-8247-9180-0*) Dekker.

McKay, Robert F. Under the Trapeze: Being the True & Unembellished Account of the Last Original Old-Fashioned All-American Independently Owned & Operated Family Circus. 500p. 1989. 20.00 (*0-317-93517-8*) Brass Ring.

McKay, Robert J. Canadian Handbook of Flexible Benefits. 2nd ed. 608p. 1996. 175.00 (*0-471-64145-6*) Wiley.

McKay, Ronald, et al, eds. Monoclonal Antibodies to Neural Antigens. LC 81-10185. (Cold Spring Harbor Reports in the Neurosciences: No. 2). 300p. reprint ed. pap. 93.00 (*0-7837-2085-8*, 204235900004) Bks Demand.

Mckay, Ronald D. & Russell, Kenneth V., eds. Psychiatry & the Criminal Process. (Leicester Polytechnic Law School Monograph Ser.). 48p. 1986. pap. 5.00 (*0-948997-28-1*) Milltak Ltd.

McKay, S., jt. auth. see Nove, A.

McKay, Sam, ed. see York, C. Pleasants.

McKay, Sandra L. Agendas for Second Language Literacy. (Cambridge Language Education Ser.). 169p. (C). 1993. pap. text 18.95 (*0-521-44664-3*) Cambridge U Pr.

— Agendas for Second Language Literacy. (Cambridge Language Education Ser.). 169p. (C). 1993. text 49.95 (*0-521-44118-8*) Cambridge U Pr.

— Teaching English Overseas. (Illus.). 166p. 1992. pap. text 15.95 (*0-19-432814-7*) OUP.

McKay, Sandra L. & Hornberger, Nancy F., eds. Sociolinguistics & Language Teaching. (Applied Linguistics Ser.). (Illus.). 496p. (C). 1995. text 69.95 (*0-521-48205-4*) Cambridge U Pr.

— Sociolinguistics & Language Teaching. (Applied Linguistics Ser.). (Illus.). 496p. (C). 1995. pap. text 26.95 (*0-521-48434-0*) Cambridge U Pr.

*McKay, Sandra Lee & Wong, Sau-ling Cynthia. New Immigrants in the United States: Readings for Second Language Educators. LC PE1128.N384 1999. (Cambridge Language Teaching Library). (Illus.). 472p. (C). 1999. 69.95 (*0-521-66087-4*) Cambridge U Pr.

— New Immigrants in the United States: Readings for Second Language Educators. LC PE1128.N384 1999. (Cambridge Language Teaching Library). (Illus.). 472p. (C). 2000. pap. 26.95 (*0-521-66798-4*) Cambridge U Pr.

McKay, Seth S. W. Lee O'Daniel & Texas Politics, 1938-1942. LC 83-45450. reprint ed. 58.00 (*0-404-20164-4*) AMS Pr.

McKay, Sharon. Time Capsule for the 21st Century. (Illus.). 48p. (J). (gr. 1-7). 1998. pap. 19.99 (*1-58184-009-8*) Somerville Hse.

McKay, Sharon & MacLeod, David. Have a Heart! A Complete Valentine Card Kit. (Books & Stuff Ser.). (Illus.). 24p. (Orig.). (J). (ps-3). 1997. pap. 8.95 (*0-448-41609-3*, G & D) Peng Put Young Read.

*McKay, Sharon E. Pat-A-Cake Dough Book & Kit. (Illus.). 48p. (J). (ps-k). 1998. pap. 12.95 (*1-895897-62-9*) Somerville Hse.

*McKay, Sharon E. & MacLeod, David. Chalk Around the Block. (Illus.). 48p. (J). (gr. 1 up). 1998. pap. 9.95 (*0-921051-81-6*) Somerville Hse.

McKay, Sharon E. & MacLeod, David. The Halloween Book & Pumpkin Carving Kit. (Illus.). 47p. (J). (gr. 1 up). 1998. pap. 9.95 (*1-895897-05-X*) Somerville Hse.

— Have a Heart! A Complete Valentine Card Kit. (Illus.). 24p. (J). (ps-3). 1998. pap. 8.95 (*1-895897-38-6*) Somerville Hse.

*McKay, Sharon E. & MacLeod, David. The Official Kick the Can Games Book. (Illus.). 64p. (Orig.). (ps-3). 1998. pap. 13.95 (*1-895897-22-X*) Somerville Hse.

McKay, Sharon E. & Stevenson, Jane B. Make-a-Face: Face & Body Painting Kit for Kids of All Ages. (Illus.). 64p. (J). (gr. k up). 1996. spiral bd. 15.95 (*0-8362-1074-3*) Andrews & McMeel.

*McKay, Sindy. About the Rain Forest. (We Both Read Ser.). (J). 2000. pap. 3.99 (*1-891327-24-0*) Treas Bay Inc.

— About the Rain Forest. (We Both Read Ser.). (J). (gr. 1-2). 2000. 7.99 (*1-891327-23-2*) Treas Bay Inc.

McKay, Sindy. Ben & Becky Get a Pet. LC 98-60704. (We Both Read Ser.). (Illus.). 48p. (J). (gr. 1-3). 1998. 7.99 (*1-891327-06-2*) Treas Bay Inc.

— Ben & Becky Get a Pet. LC 98-60704. (We Both Read Ser.). (Illus.). 48p. (J). (gr. 1-3). 1999. pap. 3.99 (*1-891327-10-0*) Treas Bay Inc.

— Ben & Becky in the Haunted House. (We Both Read Ser.). (Illus.). 48p. (J). (gr. 1-3). 1999. 7.99 (*1-891327-14-3*); pap. 3.99 (*1-891327-18-6*) Treas Bay Inc.

— Jack & the Beanstalk. LC 97-62023. (We Both Read Ser.). (Illus.). 48p. (J). (gr. 1-2). 1998. 7.99 (*1-891327-00-3*) Treas Bay Inc.

*McKay, Sindy. June's Tune. (We Both Read). (Illus.). 48p. (J). (gr. k-1). 2000. 7.99 (*1-891327-25-9*); pap. 3.99 (*1-891327-26-7*) Treas Bay Inc.

McKay, Sindy. The New Red Bed. LC 98-61797. (We Both Read Ser.). (Illus.). 48p. (J). (gr. k-1). 1999. 7.99 (*1-891327-12-7*); pap. 3.99 (*1-891327-16-X*) Treas Bay Inc.

McKay, Stephen & Marsh, Alan. Lone Parents & Work. (DSS Research Report Ser.: No. 25). 82p. 1994. pap. 25.00 (*0-11-762148-X*, HM2148X, Pub. by Statnry Office) Bernan Associates.

*Mckay, Steven F. Social Security in Britain. LC 99-18739. 1999. text 65.00 (*0-312-22348-X*) St Martin.

McKay, Susan. Humanizing Maternity Services Through Family-Centered Care. 52p. 1982. 2.00 (*0-934024-07-3*) Intl Childbirth.

— Sophia's Story LC 98-230892. 199p. 1998. 13.95 (*0-7171-2797-4*) Gill & MacMill.

McKay, Susan, jt. auth. see Davis, Lloyd.

McKay, Thomas J. Modern Symbolic Logic. 826p. (C). 1989. text 45.00 (*0-02-379286-8*, Macmillan Coll) P-H.

*McKay, Todd. TPR Storytelling: Complete Testing Packet. (SPA.). 50p. (J). (gr. 1-9). 2000. pap. text, teacher ed. 12.00 (*1-56018-029-3*, 431) Sky Oaks Prodns.

— TPR Storytelling: Especially for Children in Elementary & Middle School. Asher, James J., ed. (SPA., Illus.). 135p. (J). (gr. 1-9). 2000. pap. text, teacher ed. 21.00 (*1-56018-032-3*, 441); pap. text, teacher ed. 21.00 (*1-56018-034-X*, 440); pap. text, teacher ed. 21.00 (*1-56018-033-1*, 442) Sky Oaks Prodns.

— TPR Storytelling: Especially for Elementary & Middle School, Vol. 1. Porrata, Samuel & Asher, James J., eds. (SPA., Illus.). 38p. (J). (gr. 1-9). 2000. pap. text 12.00 (*1-56018-023-4*, 410) Sky Oaks Prodns.

— TPR Storytelling: Especially for Elementary & Middle School, Vol. 1. Asher, James J & Porrata, Samuel, eds. (Illus.). 38p. (J). (gr. 1-9). 2000. pap. text 12.00 (*1-56018-017-X*, 400); pap. text 12.00 (*1-56018-014-5*, 420) Sky Oaks Prodns.

— TPR Storytelling: Especially for Elementary & Middle School, Vol. 2. Porrata, Samuel & Asher, James, eds. (SPA., Illus.). 38p. (J). (gr. 1-9). 2000. pap. text 12.00 (*1-56018-024-2*, 411) Sky Oaks Prodns.

— TPR Storytelling: Especially for Elementary & Middle School, Vol. 2. Asher, James J. & Porrata, Samuel, eds. (Illus.). 38p. (J). (gr. 1-9). 2000. pap. text 12.00 (*1-56018-018-8*, 401); pap. text 12.00 (*1-56018-015-3*, 421) Sky Oaks Prodns.

— TPR Storytelling: Especially for Elementary & Middle School, Vol. 3. Porrata, Samuel & Asher, James, eds. (SPA., Illus.). 38p. (J). (gr. 1-9). 2000. pap. text 12.00 (*1-56018-025-0*, 412) Sky Oaks Prodns.

— TPR Storytelling: Especially for Elementary & Middle School, Vol. 3. Asher, James J. & Porrata, Samuel, eds. (Illus.). 38p. (J). (gr. 1-9). 2000. pap. text 12.00 (*1-56018-019-6*, 402); pap. text 12.00 (*1-56018-016-1*, 422) Sky Oaks Prodns.

— TPR Storytelling: Testing Packet. (FRE.). 50p. (J). (gr. 1-9). 2000. pap. text, teacher ed. 12.00 (*1-56018-030-7*, 432); pap. text, teacher ed. 12.00 (*1-56018-031-5*, 430) Sky Oaks Prodns.

McKay, Tom & Kmetz, Deborah. Agricultural Diversity in Wisconsin. LC 87-6482. (Illus.). 93p. 1987. pap. 4.00 (*0-87020-250-2*) State Hist Soc Wis.

McKay, Valerie J., et al. Generations. (Illus.). 51p. 1998. pap. 5.95 (*0-9666849-0-7*) Valerie McKay.

McKay, Valerie M., jt. ed. see Conzen, Michael P.

McKay, W. Colin. Nagasaki Dust. 99p. 1998. pap. 5.60 (*0-87129-793-0*, N46) Dramatic Pub.

McKay, W. D. Church Government in the Writings of George Gillespie: An Ecclesiastical Republic. LC 94-21822. (Rutherford Studies in Historical Theology: Vol. 6). 372p. 1994. text 99.95 (*0-7734-1631-5*) E Mellen.

— An Ecclesiastical Republic: Church Government in the Writings of George Gillespie. (Rutherford Studies in Historical Theology). 327p. 1997. pap. text 40.00 (*0-946068-60-7*, Pub. by Rutherford Hse) OM Literature.

McKay, W. G. & Patera, J. Tables of Dimensions, Indices & Branching Rules for Representations of Simple Lie Algebras. LC 80-27663. (Lecture Notes in Pure & Applied Mathematics Ser.: Vol. 69). 331p. reprint ed. pap. 102.70 (*0-608-08960-5*, 206959500005) Bks Demand.

McKay, William B. Carpentry. 5th ed. LC 76-17606. (Building Craft Ser.). (Illus.). 233p. 1975. pap. 72.30 (*0-608-05244-2*, 206578100001) Bks Demand.

McKay, William J. Me, An Evangelist? Every Christian's Guide to Caring Evangelism. 1992. pap. text 11.95 (*0-9633831-0-8*) Stephen Minist.

— Nuts & Bolts Issues for Small Groups. rev. ed. LC 96-69489. 160p. (C). 1996. pap. 8.95 (*0-9633831-6-7*) Stephen Minist.

An Asterisk (*) at the beginning of an entry indicates that the title is appearing for the first time.

***McKay, William J. & Haugk, Kenneth C.** Stephen Ministry Training Manual, Vols. 1 & 2. Perry, R. Scott & Paap, David A., eds. (Illus.). 700p. 2000. pap. 29.95 (*0-9633831-8-3*) Stephen Minist.
— Supervision Group Facilitator's Manual. Perry, R. Scott & Paap, David A., eds. (Illus.). 200p. 2000. ring bd. 19.95 (*0-9633831-9-1*) Stephen Minist.
McKay, William J., jt. auth. see Haugk, Kenneth C.
McKay, William J., ed. see Haugk, Kenneth C.
McKaye, Bess. He Sees a Sparrow Fall. 28p. 1996. pap. 9.95 (*1-885206-45-3*, Iliad Pr) Cader Pubng.
McKaye-Ege, Arvia. The Secret Iron of the Heart. 192p. 1982. 18.00 (*0-932776-05-1*); pap. 15.00 (*0-932776-06-X*) Adonis Pr.
McKeachie, W. J., jt. ed. see Hartley, J.
McKeachie, Wilbert J. Teaching Tips: Strategies, Research & Theory for College & University Teachers. 9th ed. 444p. (C). 1994. pap. text 30.76 (*0-669-19434-4*) HM Trade Div.
McKeachie, Wilbert J. & Gibbs, Graham. Teaching Tips: Strategies, Research & Theory for College & University Teachers. 10th ed. LC 98-72060. xx, 379 p. 1998. pap. text 36.60 (*0-395-90345-9*) HM.
McKeachie, Wilbert J., jt. auth. see Eble, Kenneth E.
McKeachie, William J. & Feldman, Kenneth A. Effective Teaching in Higher Education: Research & Practice. Perry, Raymond P. & Smart, John C., eds. LC 96-19577. 464p. (C). 1997. pap. text 30.00 (*0-87586-117-2*) Agathon.
McKeachie, William J., et al. Effective Teaching in Higher Education: Research & Practice. Perry, Raymond P. & Smart, John C., eds. LC 96-19577. 464p. (C). 1997. text 64.00 (*0-87586-116-4*) Agathon.
McKeag, Douglas B. & Hough, David. Perspectives in Expencise Science & Sports Medicine Vol. 12: Volume 12: The Metabolic Basis of Performance in Sport & Exercise. Lamb, David R. & Murray, Robert, eds. (Illus.). 450p. (C). 1999. 49.00 (*1-884125-68-9*) Cooper Pubng.
***McKeag, Malcolm.** Competent Crew. (Illus.). 95p. 2000. pap. 16.95 (*1-898660-32-8*, Pub. by Fernhurst Bks) Motorbooks Intl.
McKeag, Malcolm. Cruising Crew: How to Be Welcome on Board. 96p. (C). 1990. text 59.00 (*0-906754-63-1*, Pub. by Fernhurst Bks) St Mut.
— Racing Crew. 96p. (C). 1990. text 59.00 (*0-906754-68-2*, Pub. by Fernhurst Bks) St Mut.
***McKeag, Malcolm.** Racing Crew. 1998. pap. 18.95 (*1-898660-16-6*) Fernhurst Bks.
McKeag, R. M. & Wilson, R. Studies in Operating Systems. (APIC Ser.). 1976. text 157.00 (*0-12-484350-6*) Acad Pr.
McKeagu. Intermediate Algebra. 1996. 33.50 (*0-03-018173-9*) Harcourt Coll Pubs.
— Intermediate Algebra. 3rd ed. 1998. pap. text 29.50 (*0-03-024873-6*) Harcourt Coll Pubs.
— Trigonometry. 4th ed. 1998. pap. text 29.50 (*0-03-024968-6*) Harcourt Coll Pubs.
McKeague. Algebra for College Students. 3rd ed. (Illus.). 640p. (C). 1997. text 45.00 (*0-03-019467-9*, Pub. by SCP) Harcourt.
***McKeague.** Basic Mathematics. 5th ed. (Mathematics Ser.). 2000. text 47.00 (*0-534-37892-7*) Brooks-Cole.
McKeague. Elementary Algebra. 6th ed. (C). 1999. pap. text, student ed. Price not set. (*0-03-026284-4*) Harcourt Coll Pubs.
— Elementary Algebra. 6th ed. (C). 1999. text 84.00 (*0-03-026258-5*, Pub. by Harcourt Coll Pubs) Harcourt.
— Intermediate Algebra. 5th ed. 1998. pap. text, student ed. 25.00 (*0-03-020819-X*, Pub. by Harcourt Coll Pubs) Harcourt.
— Intermediate Algebra. 6th ed. (C). 1999. text 84.00 (*0-03-026286-0*, Pub. by Harcourt Coll Pubs) Harcourt.
— Intermediate Algebra: Concepts & Graphs. 3rd ed. (Illus.). 640p. (C). 1998. text 71.50 (*0-03-019468-7*, Pub. by SCP) Harcourt.
— Intermediate Algebra: Functions & Graphs, 1E. (C). 1996. pap. text, student ed. 21.00 (*0-03-018169-0*) Harcourt Coll Pubs.
— Prealgebra. 2nd ed. (Mathematics Ser.). 1992. teacher ed. 45.00 (*0-534-14470-5*) Brooks-Cole.
— Prealgebra. 3rd ed. (Mathematics Ser.). 1995. teacher ed. 18.25 (*0-534-95274-7*) Brooks-Cole.
***McKeague.** Prealgebra. 4th ed. (Mathematics Ser.). 2000. text 47.00 (*0-534-37893-5*) Brooks-Cole.
— Solutions Manual to Accompany Algebra with Trigonometry for College Students. 4th ed. 72p. 1999. 44.50 (*0-03-020963-3*) SCP.
— Student Solutions Manual to Accompany Intermediate Algebra a Text/Workbook. 5th ed. 352p. 1999. 17.25 (*0-03-020219-1*) SCP.
McKeague. Student Solutions Manual to Accompany Trigonometry. 4th ed. 256p. (C). 1998. student ed. 8.00 (*0-03-024971-6*, Pub. by SCP) Harcourt.
— TI-83 Graphing Calculator Manual to Accompany Trigonometry. 4th ed. 104p. 1998. 12.00 (*0-03-024972-4*) SCP.
— Trigonometry. 4th ed. (C). 1998. pap. text, teacher ed. 26.75 (*0-03-024969-4*) Harcourt Coll Pubs.
Mckeague & Dykes. Basic Mathematics. 3rd ed. 1992. teacher ed. 52.00 (*0-534-14463-2*) Brooks-Cole.
McKeague, C. Patrick, jt. auth. see McKeague, Charles P.
McKeague, Charles P. Algebra with Trigonometry. 3rd ed. (C). 1993. pap. text 24.50 (*0-03-096773-2*) Harcourt Coll Pubs.
— Algebra with Trigonometry for College Students. 4th ed. LC 97-81016. 816p. (C). 1998. text 66.50 (*0-03-022314-8*, Pub. by SCP) Harcourt.
— Basic Mathematics. 2nd ed. 476p. (C). 1987. mass mkt. 34.50 (*0-534-07566-5*) Wadsworth Pub.
— Basic Mathematics. 3rd ed. 484p. (C). 1992. pap. 37.00 (*0-534-14460-8*) PWS Pubs.
— Basic Mathematics. 4th ed. 1995. mass mkt. 72.95 (*0-534-94770-0*) PWS Pubs.
— Beginning Algebra. 4th ed. LC 93-87001. (C). 1994. pap. text, wbk. ed. 74.00 (*0-03-097358-9*) Harcourt Coll Pubs.
— Beginning Algebra. 4th ed. (C). 1994. pap. text, student ed. 25.00 (*0-03-003362-4*, Pub. by Harcourt Coll Pubs) Harcourt.
— Beginning Algebra. 4th ed. (C). 1994. pap. text, teacher ed. 33.75 (*0-03-003358-6*) Harcourt Coll Pubs.
— Beginning Algebra: A Text. 4th ed. (C). 1994. pap. text, teacher ed. 40.00 (*0-03-003363-2*, Pub. by Harcourt Coll Pubs) Harcourt.
— Beginning Algebra: A Text - Workbook. 542p. (C). 1989. teacher ed., student ed. write for info. incl. VHS (*0-318-66683-9*) SCP.
— Beginning Algebra: A Text - Workbook. 3rd ed. 542p. (C). 1989. teacher ed. 5.25 (*0-15-505235-7*); pap. text, teacher ed. 20.75 (*0-15-505236-5*); disk. write for info. (*0-318-66681-2*); disk. write for info. (*0-318-66682-0*) SCP.
— Elementary Algebra. 5th ed. (C). 1994. text 76.00 (*0-03-097356-2*, Pub. by Harcourt Coll Pubs) Harcourt.
— Elementary Algebra. 5th ed. (C). 1995. pap. text, student ed. 26.50 (*0-03-009782-7*, Pub. by Harcourt Coll Pubs) Harcourt.
— Elementary Algebra: Printed Test Bank & Prepared Tests. 5th ed. (C). 1994. pap. text, suppl. ed. 49.50 (*0-03-009783-5*, Pub. by Harcourt Coll Pubs) Harcourt.
***McKeague, Charles P.** Instructor's Manual to Accompany Beginning Algebra: A Text Workbook. 5th ed. 344p. 1999. write for info. (*0-03-022683-X*, Pub. by SCP) Harcourt.
McKeague, Charles P. Intermedia Algebra: Concepts & Graphs. 3rd ed. 416p. (C). 1998. pap. text, student ed. 22.50 (*0-03-024872-8*, Pub. by SCP) Harcourt.
— Intermediate Algebra. 4th ed. LC 93-87002. (C). 1994. pap. text, wbk. ed. 74.00 (*0-03-097359-7*) Harcourt Coll Pubs.
— Intermediate Algebra. 4th ed. (C). 1994. pap. text, student ed. 24.00 (*0-03-003383-7*) Harcourt Coll Pubs.
— Intermediate Algebra. 4th ed. (C). 1994. pap. text, teacher ed. 33.75 (*0-03-003379-9*) Harcourt Coll Pubs.
— Intermediate Algebra. 4th ed. (C). 1994. pap. text, teacher ed. 40.00 (*0-03-003384-5*, Pub. by Harcourt Coll Pubs) Harcourt.
— Intermediate Algebra. 4th ed. 605p. (C). 1990. VHS. write for info. (*0-318-67022-4*); disk. write for info. (*0-318-67023-2*); disk. write for info. (*0-318-67024-0*); disk. write for info. (*0-318-67025-9*); disk. write for info. (*0-318-67026-7*); disk. write for info. (*0-318-67027-5*) SCP.
— Intermediate Algebra. 5th ed. (C). 1995. pap. text, student ed. 24.50 (*0-03-009807-6*, Pub. by Harcourt Coll Pubs) Harcourt.
— Intermediate Algebra. 5th ed. LC 94-69874. 638p. (C). 1994. text 75.00 (*0-03-097357-0*, Pub. by SCP) Harcourt.
***McKeague, Charles P.** Intermediate Algebra. 5th ed. 768p. (C). 1998. pap. text 44.00 (*0-03-022467-5*, Pub. by SCP) Harcourt.
McKeague, Charles P. Intermediate Algebra: Functions & Graphs. (C). 1995. text 71.50 (*0-03-018222-0*, Pub. by Harcourt Coll Pubs) Harcourt.
— Intermediate Algebra: Instructor's Solutions Manual. 5th ed. 280p. 1999. teacher ed. write for info. (*0-03-020822-X*, Pub. by SCP) Harcourt.
— Intermediate Algebra: Test Bank & Prepared Tests. 5th ed. (C). 1996. pap. text, suppl. ed. 33.50 (*0-03-009808-4*, Pub. by Harcourt Coll Pubs) Harcourt.
— MATH PAC W/(5.25") DISK. 3rd ed. 542p. (C). 1989. 32.00 (*0-15-555254-6*) SCP.
— Prealgebra. (Math). 462p. (C). 1987. mass mkt. 34.50 (*0-534-07596-7*) PWS Pubs.
— Prealgebra. 2nd ed. (Math). 550p. (C). 1991. mass mkt. 47.25 (*0-534-14466-7*) PWS Pubs.
— Prealgebra. 3rd ed. 1995. mass mkt. 71.95 (*0-534-94764-6*) PWS Pubs.
— Prealgebra & Basic Math: Video Workbook. 2nd ed. (Mathematics Ser.). 1992. pap., wbk. ed. 9.50 (*0-534-14455-1*) PWS Pubs.
— Printed Test Bank & Prepared Tests to Accompany Beginning Algebra: A Text-Workbook. 5th ed. 392p. (C). 1998. pap. text, wbk. ed. write for info. (*0-03-022684-8*, Pub. by SCP) Harcourt.
— Printed Test Bank & Prepared Tests to Accompany Intermediate Algebra: A Text Workbook. 5th ed. 456p. (C). 1999. pap. text, wbk. ed. write for info. (*0-03-020823-8*, Pub. by SCP) Harcourt.
***McKeague, Charles P.** Student Solutions Manual to Accompany Beginning Algebra: A Text Workbook. 5th ed. 288p. 1999. 17.00 (*0-03-022678-3*, Pub. by SCP) Harcourt.
McKeague, Charles P. Trigonometry. 3rd ed. (C). 1993. pap. text, teacher ed., suppl. ed. 246.00 (*0-03-094902-5*, Pub. by Harcourt Coll Pubs) Harcourt.
— Trigonometry. 3rd ed. (C). 1994. pap. text 40.00 (*0-03-096774-0*); pap. text, teacher ed. 28.00 (*0-03-096680-9*) Harcourt Coll Pubs.
— Trigonometry. 4th ed. LC 98-85870. 512p. (C). 1998. text 74.00 (*0-03-024783-7*, Pub. by SCP) Harcourt.
McKeague, Charles P. & Bezona. Algebra for College Students. 2nd ed. (C). 1993. pap. text, student ed. 26.50 (*0-03-096992-1*) Harcourt Coll Pubs.
McKeague, Charles P. & McKeague, C. Patrick. Electronic Companion to College Algebra. (Electronic Companion Ser.). (Illus.). 300p. (C). 1999. pap. text 34.95 (*1-58032-052-X*) Cogito Lrning.
***McKeague, Charles Patrick.** Companion to College Algebra. (Electronic Companion Ser.). 1999. text 34.95 (*1-58032-053-8*) Cogito Lrning.
McKeague, Charles R. Beginning Algebra: Text & Workbook. 5th ed. 704p. (C). 1999. pap. text, wbk. ed. 44.00 (*0-03-022464-0*, Pub. by SCP) Harcourt.
McKeague, Pat. Basic Mathematics. (Math). 608p. (C). 1981. mass mkt. 26.75 (*0-534-00905-0*) PWS Pubs.
McKeague, Patricia. Step by Step. 6th ed. 352p. 1999. per. 30.95 (*0-7872-5564-5*, 41556401) Kendall-Hunt.
McKeague, Patrick. Electronic Companion to Precalculus. Chelton, David, ed. LC 99-218224. (Electronic Companion Ser.). 300p. (C). 1998. pap. text, wbk. ed. 29.95 (*1-58032-001-5*); pap. text, wbk. ed. 29.95 incl. cd-rom (*1-888902-95-7*) Cogito Lrning.
McKean. Catholic ABC Book. 1981. 1.25 (*0-89942-202-0*, 202) Catholic Bk Pub.
— Information Masters: Secrets of the Customer Race. LC 99-13342. 300p. 1999. 29.95 (*0-471-98801-4*) Wiley.
***McKean-Casad, Lori & Whitbeck, Bill.** The Joy of Oysters: A Guide & Cookbook for Oyster Lovers in North America. (Northwest Gourmet Guides Ser.: Vol. 4). (Illus.). 256p. 2000. pap. 18.95 (*1-929258-00-3*, Pub. by Speed Graphics) Partners-West.
McKean, Charles. Banff & Buchan: An Illustrated Architectural Guide. (Illus.). 176p. (C). 1990. pap. 35.00 (*1-85158-231-2*, Pub. by Rutland Pr) St Mut.
— Creating the New Museum of Scotland. (Illus.). 160p. 1999. pap. 39.95 (*1-901663-11-6*, Pub. by Natl Mus Scotland) A Schwartz & Co.
— The District of Moray: An Illustrated Architectural Guide. (Illus.). 172p. (C). 1987. pap. 35.00 (*0-7073-0528-4*, Pub. by Rutland Pr) St Mut.
— Edinburgh: An Illustrated Architectural Guide. (Illus.). 240p. (C). 1992. pap. 45.00 (*0-9501462-4-2*, Pub. by Rutland Pr) St Mut.
— The Scottish '30s. 200p. (C). 1987. pap. 35.00 (*0-7073-0493-8*, Pub. by Rutland Pr) St Mut.
— Stirling & the Trossachs. 152p. (C). 1994. pap. 35.00 (*1-873190-21-2*, Pub. by Rutland Pr) St Mut.
McKean, Charles & Walker, David. Dundee: An Illustrated Architectural Guide. (Illus.). 184p. (C). 1993. pap. 35.00 (*1-873190-09-3*, Pub. by Rutland Pr) St Mut.
McKean, Charles, et al. Central Glasgow: An Illustrated Architectural Guide. (Illus.). 208p. (C). 1993. pap. 35.00 (*1-873190-22-0*, Pub. by Rutland Pr) St Mut.
McKean, Charles, jt. auth. see Jaques, Richard.
McKean, Dave. Cages Collection. LC 98-12318. 500p. 1998. 44.95 (*0-87816-600-9*) Kitchen Sink.
***McKean, Dave.** Cages Collection. LC 98-12318. 500p. 1998. 100.00 (*0-87816-601-7*) Kitchen Sink.
McKean, Dave. Option: Click. Haythornwaite, Clare, ed. (Illus.). 88p. 1998. 40.00 (*0-9642069-1-9*) A Spiegel Fine Arts.
McKean, Dave & Gaiman, Neil. The Collected Sandman Dustcovers, 1989-1997. LC 98-7881. (Illus.). 208p. pap. 24.95 (*0-8230-4632-X*) Watsn-Guptill.
McKean, Dave, jt. auth. see Gaiman, Neil.
McKean, Gary O. Through It All. 8p. 1994. pap. text 3.00 (*0-944561-25-X*) Chr Legal.
McKean, H. P., Jr., jt. auth. see Ito, K.
McKean, H. P., jt. ed. see Keller, J. B.
McKean, Henry & Moll, Victor. Elliptic Curves: Function Theory, Geometry, Arithmetic. (Illus.). 280p. (C). 1999. pap. 29.95 (*0-521-65817-9*) Cambridge U Pr.
McKean, Henry P., jt. auth. see Dym, Harry.
McKean, Henry P., Jr., jt. auth. see Ito, Kiyoshi.
McKean, Hugh F. Louis Comfort Tiffany. 2nd ed. Frankhanel, Heidewig, tr. (ENG & GER., Illus.). 312p. (C). 1988. 118.00 (*3-8170-2012-0*, Pub. by Knstvrlag Weingrtn) Intl Bk Import.
McKean, J. W., jt. auth. see Hettmansperger, T. P.
McKean, James. Headlong. LC 86-28200. (University of Utah Press Poetry Ser.). 78p. (Orig.). reprint ed. pap. 30.00 (*0-7837-6866-4*, 204669600003) Bks Demand.
— Tree of Heaven. LC 94-49018. (Iowa Poetry Prize Ser.) 84p. (Orig.). 1995. pap. 11.95 (*0-87745-505-8*) U of Iowa Pr.
McKean, James N. Commonsense Instrument Care: How to look after Your Violin, Viola or Cello, & Bow. 2nd rev. ed. VanClay, Mary, ed. (Illus.). 64p. 1997. pap. text 9.95 (*0-9626081-9-X*) String Letter.
Mckean, Jerome, jt. auth. see Byers, Bryan.
McKean, Jerome B., jt. auth. see Hendricks, James E.
***McKean, John.** Charles Rennie Mackintosh. rev. ed. (Illus.). 80p. 2000. pap. 9.95 (*1-84107-068-8*, Pub. by Colin Baxter Ltd) Voyageur Pr.
— Charles Rennie Mackintosh: Architect, Artist, Icon. LC 00-43418. (Illus.). 160p. 2000. 35.00 (*0-89658-519-0*) Voyageur Pr.
McKean, John. Charles Rennie MacKintosh Pocket Guide. (Illus.). 80p. 1998. pap. 9.95 (*1-900455-48-X*, Pub. by Colin Baxter Ltd) Voyageur Pr.
— Crystal Palace: London 1851 Sir Joseph Paxton. (Architecture in Detail Ser.). (Illus.). 60p. (C). 1994. pap. 29.95 (*0-7148-2925-0*, Pub. by Phaidon Press) Phaidon Pr.
***McKean, John.** Giancarlo De Carlo: Layered Places. (Illus.). 240p. 2001. 89.00 (*3-932565-12-6*) Edition A Menges.
McKean, John. Leicester Engineering Department Building: Leicester University, 1959-1963, Sirling & Gowan. (Architecture in Detail Ser.). (Illus.). 60p. (Orig.). (C). 1994. pap. 29.95 (*0-7148-3154-9*, Pub. by Phaidon Press) Phaidon Pr.
— Royal Festival Hall. (Architecture in Detail Ser.). (Illus.). 60p. 1993. pap. 29.95 (*0-7148-2773-8*, Pub. by Phaidon Press) Phaidon Pr.
McKean, Kathy, et al. Exceptions: A Handbook of Inclusion Activities for Teachers of Students at Grades 6-12 with Mild Disabilities. 2nd ed. (Illus.). 160p. 1994. pap. text, teacher ed. 19.50 (*1-57035-023-X*, 10EXCPT) Sopris.
McKean, Kay S. Our Beginning: Genesis Through the Eyes of a Woman. 152p. 1996. pap. 8.99 (*1-57782-001-0*) Discipleshp.
McKean, Kay S. & McKean, Randy, eds. The Mission (La Mision) Spanish. (Daily Power Ser.). 154p. 1995. pap. 7.99 (*1-884553-61-3*) Discipleshp.
McKean, Kay S. & Orr, Nancy. La Boda del Discipulo (The Disciple's Wedding) Planning a Wedding That Gives Glory to God. (SPA.). 72p. 1994. pap. 10.99 (*1-884553-68-0*) Discipleshp.
— The Disciple's Wedding: Planning a Wedding That Gives Glory to God. 72p. 1994. pap. 10.99 (*1-884553-21-4*) Discipleshp.
McKean, Kay S., jt. ed. see McKean, Randy.
McKean, Keith. Understanding Social Science. 384p. (C). 1995. pap. text, per. 48.95 (*0-7872-0250-9*) Kendall-Hunt.
McKean, Keith F. The Moral Measure of Literature. LC 73-2339. 137p. 1973. reprint ed. lib. bdg. 55.00 (*0-8371-6842-2*, MCMM, Greenwood Pr) Greenwood.
McKean, Kip. First Principles: Plus Revolution Through Restoration Articles I & II. 2nd ed. 1997. pap. 5.99 (*1-57782-053-3*) Discipleshp.
— Second Principles: Survey of the Old Testament. 32p. (Orig.). 1996. pap., wbk. ed. 5.50 (*1-57782-000-2*) Discipleshp.
McKean, Lise. Divine Enterprise: Gurus & the Hindu Nationalist Movement. LC 95-24600. (Illus.). 384p. 1996. pap. text 21.95 (*0-226-56010-4*); lib. bdg. 60.00 (*0-226-56009-0*) U Ch Pr.
McKean, Lori, jt. auth. see Nims, Cynthia.
McKean, M. Faith. Interplay of Realistic & Flamboyant Art Elements in the French Mysteres. LC 74-94196. (Catholic University of America. Studies in Romance Languages & Literatures: No. 60). reprint ed. 37.50 (*0-404-50360-8*) AMS Pr.
Mckean, Matthew T. Mortgage Your Way to Wealth: How Your Mortgage Lender, Realtor & Stock Broker Can Help You. 1998. pap. 21.95 (*1-890586-41-2*) Pipeline Pr.
McKean, Randy & McKean, Kay S., eds. The Mission. 154p. 1994. pap. 7.99 (*1-884553-29-X*) Discipleshp.
McKean, Randy, jt. ed. see Jones, Tom.
McKean, Randy, jt. ed. see McKean, Kay S.
McKean, Robert B. St. Petersburg Between the Revolutions: Workers & Revolutionaries, June 1907-February, 1917. LC 89-70734. (Illus.). 621p. 1990. reprint ed. pap. 192.60 (*0-608-07832-8*, 205400800010) Bks Demand.
McKean, Robert B., ed. New Perspectives on Modern Russian History: Selected Papers from the Fourth World Congress of Soviet & East European Studies, Harrogate, 1990. 300p. 1992. text 55.00 (*0-312-07594-4*) St Martin.
McKean, Robert N., ed. Issues in Defense Economics. (Universities National Bureau Conference Ser.: No. 20). 298p. 1967. 77.50 (*0-87014-490-1*) Natl Bur Econ Res.
McKean, Roland N., ed. Issues in Defense Economics. LC 67-19156. (Universities-National Bureau Conference Ser.: No. 20). 298p. reprint ed. pap. 92.40 (*0-8357-3243-6*, 205713700011) Bks Demand.
McKean, S., jt. ed. see Robinson, Dan.
Mckean, Thomas. My Evil Twin. 160p. 1998. pap. 3.99 (*0-380-79082-3*, Avon Bks) Morrow Avon.
McKean, Thomas. The Search for Sara Sanderson. 160p. (J). (gr. 3-7). 1987. pap. 2.50 (*0-380-75295-6*, Avon Bks) Morrow Avon.
— Secret of the Seven Willows. LC 91-4447. 160p. (J). 1991. pap. 12.95 (*0-671-72997-7*) S&S Trade.
— Vampire Vacation. LC 85-48073. 1986. pap. 2.50 (*0-380-89808-X*, Avon Bks) Morrow Avon.
McKean, Thomas A. Light on the Horizon: A Deeper View from Inside the Autism Puzzle. 95p. (Orig.). 1996. pap. 19.95 (*1-885477-26-0*) Fut Horizons.
— Soon Will Come the Light: A View from Inside the Autism Puzzle. Gilpin, R. Wayne, ed. (Illus.). 172p. (C). 1994. pap. 19.95 (*1-885477-11-2*) Fut Horizons.
McKean, Tom. Into the Candle Lit Room. LC 98-13070. (J). (gr. 5-9). 1999. 17.99 (*0-399-23359-8*) Putnam Pub Group.
— The Life & Songs of Iain MacNeacail. 320p. 1997. pap. 35.00 (*0-7486-6214-6*, Pub. by Polygon) Subterranean Co.
McKean, Warwick A. Equality & Discrimination under International Law. 392p. 1985. pap. 24.00 (*0-19-825519-5*) OUP.
McKeaney, Grace. Last Looks. 1984. pap. 5.25 (*0-8222-0636-6*) Dramatists Play.
McKeany, Maurine. The Absent Father & Public Policy in the Program of Aid to Dependent Children. LC 60-64080. (University of California Publications in Social Welfare: Vol. 1). 140p. reprint ed. pap. 43.40 (*0-8357-5020-5*, 202139600021) Bks Demand.
McKearney, Mick, jt. auth. see Sweetman, Chris.
McKeating, Colm. Eschatology in the Anglican Sermons of John Henry Newman. LC 92-44666. 376p. 1993. text 99.95 (*0-7734-9231-3*) E Mellen.
McKeating, Gerald. Birds of Ottawa: And Vicinity. (Illus.). 1990. pap. 9.95 (*0-919433-64-2*) Lone Pine.
— Birds of Toronto. (Illus.). 1990. pap. 9.95 (*0-919433-63-4*) Lone Pine.
McKeating, H., tr. see Simon, Marcel.
***McKeating, Henry.** Book of Jeremiah. 1998. pap. 18.00 (*0-7162-0526-2*) Epworth Pr.
— Ezekiel. (Old Testament Guides Ser.: No. 23). 128p. 1993. pap. 12.50 (*1-85075-428-4*, Pub. by Sheffield Acad) CUP Services.
McKechnie, Ann, jt. ed. see Mathews, Peter.
McKechnie, Christine. Paper Collage: Painted Pictures. 80p. 1995. pap. 19.95 (*0-85532-784-7*, 784-7, Pub. by Srch Pr) A Schwartz & Co.
***McKechnie, Gary.** Great American Motorcycle Tours. LC 99-52215. (Illus.). 384p. 2000. pap. 17.95 (*1-56261-440-1*) Avalon Travel.

M

McKechnie, Gary. Million-Dollar Frauds. Campbell, Lee A., ed. LC 99-162916. 113p. 1998. write for info. (*0-89413-402-7*) Inst Inter Aud.

McKechnie, George E., jt. ed. see Craik, Kenneth H.

McKechnie, Paul. Outsiders in the Greek Cities of the Fourth Century. 320p. 1989. 45.00 (*0-415-00340-7*) Routledge.

McKechnie, Paul & Kern, eds. Hellenica Oxyrhynchia. (Classical Texts Ser.). 1988. 59.99 (*0-85668-357-4*, Pub. by Aris & Phillips); pap. 22.00 (*0-85668-358-2*, Pub. by Aris & Phillips) David Brown.

McKechnie, Samuel. Popular Entertainments Through the Ages. LC 78-79998. (Illus.). 1972. reprint ed. 23.95 (*0-405-08768-3*) Ayer.

McKechnie, Sue. British Silhouette Artists & Their Work: 1760-1860. (Illus.). 798p. 1978. 85.00 (*0-85667-036-7*) Sothebys Pubns.

McKechnie, Therese. Dealing with Aging Relatives: Addressing the Challenges of Aging & Caregiving. (Orig.). 1999. pap. 19.95 (*0-9671175-0-X*) Prof Growth Prod.

***McKechnie, William S.** Magna Carta: A Commentary on the Great Charter of King John. LC 99-38731. 2000. write for info. (*1-58477-031-7*) Lawbk Exchange.

***McKecknie, David.** Kahoolies! 176p. 2000. pap. 12.00 (*0-9668972-0-X*) Essex Press.

McKee. Biochemistry. 2nd ed. 220p. 1998. pap., student ed. 35.00 (*0-07-290503-4*) McGraw.

— Biochemistry: An Introduction. 1996. 16.25 (*0-697-21160-6*, WCB McGr Hill) McGrw-H Hghr Educ.

— Biochemistry: An Introduction. 3rd ed. 2001. 72.00 (*0-07-231592-X*) McGraw.

Mckee. Diagnostic Cytopathology. 1996. text 175.00 (*0-7234-2449-7*) Wolfe Pubng AZ.

McKee. Essential Skin Pathology. LC 98-47945. 1999. 59.95 (*0-7234-3067-5*) Mosby Inc.

— Federal Taxation of Partnerships & Partners No. 291: 1991 Cumulative Supplement. 1991. per. 52.00 (*0-7913-0993-2*) Warren Gorham & Lamont.

— Federal Taxation of Partnerships & Partners No. 291: 1991 Cumulative Supplement, 2. 1993. 425.00 (*0-7913-1486-3*, FITP) Warren Gorham & Lamont.

— Management & Organizational Behavior. (C). 1997. text 69.50 (*0-03-003698-4*, Pub. by Harcourt Coll Pubs) Harcourt.

— Two Monsters. (J). Date not set. pap. text. write for info. (*0-05-004546-6*) Addison-Wesley.

McKee & Dickens. Public Health in Europe. 56.95 (*1-85972-634-8*) Ashgate Pub Co.

McKee & Kennedy. Correcting Common Errors in Writing. 2nd ed. 92p. (C). 1998. per. 13.95 (*0-7872-4683-2*, 41468301) Kendall-Hunt.

McKee, et al. Federal Taxation of Partners. 1992. 300.00 (*0-7913-0507-4*) Warren Gorham & Lamont.

McKee, jt. auth. see Hughes.

McKee, jt. auth. see Poirier.

McKee, jt. auth. see Tijunelis.

McKee, jt. auth. see Zanger.

McKee, jt. auth. see Zanger-Mckee.

***McKee, Alexander.** Death Raft: The Human Drama of the Medusa Shipwreck. 2000. mass mkt. 6.99 (*0-451-20044-6*, Sig) NAL.

McKee, Alexander. The Golden Wreck: The Tragedy of the 'Royal Charter' 224p. 1987. 29.95 (*0-285-62745-7*) Intl Spec Bk.

— The Queen's Corsair: Drake's Journey of Circumnavigation 1577-1580. 320p. (C). 1978. 16.95 (*0-285-62339-7*) Intl Spec Bk.

— Strike from the Sky: The Story of the Battle of Britain. LC 72-169429. (Literature & History of Aviation Ser.). 1972. reprint ed. 29.95 (*0-405-03772-4*) Ayer.

McKee, Alison. From Homeschool to College & Work: Turning Your Homeschooled Experiences into College & Job Portfolios. 2nd rev. ed. 100p. 1998. pap. 11.95 (*0-9657806-1-9*) Bittersweet Hse.

McKee-Anderson Group Staff. Things You'll Learn If You Live Long Enough So You Might As Well Know Now. 78p. (Orig.). 1989. pap. 7.95 (*0-931089-81-6*) Great Quotations.

McKee, Barry, jt. auth. see Moss, Graham.

McKee, Bill. Is Objectivity Faith? A Reconciliation of Science & Religion. 84p. (Orig.). 1995. pap. write for info. (*1-57502-036-X*) Morris Pubng.

— Is Objectivity Faith? A Reconciliation of Science & Religion. 2nd ed. LC 95-94717. 75p. (Orig.). 1998. pap. 10.00 (*1-57502-677-5*, PO0451A) Morris Pubng.

— Social Security & SSI. 65p. pap. 6.25 (*0-685-23169-0*, 41,575S) NCLS Inc.

McKee, Brian J. Historic American Covered Bridges. LC 96-26724. 160p. 1996. 43.00 (*0-7844-0189-6*) Am Soc Civil Eng.

McKee, Brian J., jt. auth. see American Society of Civil Engineers Staff.

McKee, Brian R., jt. ed. see Sheets, Payson D.

McKee, C. S., ed. see Roberts, M. W.

McKee, Charles. Ceramics Handbook: A Guide to Glaze Calculation, Materials & Processes. (Illus.). 176p. (C). 1984. pap. text 32.95 (*0-89863-072-X*) Star Pub CA.

McKee Charnas, Suzy. The Conqueror's Child. LC 99-19544. (The Holdfast Chonicles Ser.: IV). 428p. 1999. 24.95 (*0-312-85719-5*, Pub. by Tor Bks) St Martin.

***McKee Charnas, Suzy.** The Conqueror's Child. 432p. 2000. pap. 14.95 (*0-312-86946-0*, Pub. by Tor Bks) St Martin.

McKee, Christian H. The Clan Mackay Society. (Illus.). 54p. 1989. pap. 5.00 (*0-9611046-1-9*) C H McKee.

— Scottish Legends, Folklore & Superstitiion. LC 83-80904. (Illus.). 56p. (Orig.). 1983. pap. 4.75 (*0-9611046-0-0*) C H McKee.

McKee, Christopher. Edward Preble. LC 79-6044. (Navies & Men Ser.). (Illus.). 1980. reprint ed. lib. bdg. 40.95 (*0-405-13080-5*) Ayer.

— Edward Preble: A Naval Biography, 1761-1807. LC 96-2679. (Classics of Naval Literature Ser.). (Illus.). 432p. 1996. 32.95 (*1-55750-583-7*) Naval Inst Pr.

— A Gentlemanly & Honorable Profession: The Creation of the U. S. Naval Officer Corps, 1794-1815. LC 90-6232. (Illus.). 608p. 1991. 49.95 (*0-87021-283-4*) Naval Inst Pr.

— Treaty Talks in British Columbia: Negotiating a Mutually Beneficial Future. 144p. 1996. 65.00 (*0-7748-0586-2*) U of Wash Pr.

— Treaty Talks in British Columbia: Negotiating a Mutually Beneficial Future. LC 96-910499. 144p. 1997. pap. 19.95 (*0-7748-0587-0*) U of Wash Pr.

***McKee, Cynthia R.** Cash for College's Write It Right: How to Write Winning Essays for College & Scholarships. 224p. 2000. pap. 12.00 (*0-688-17108-7*, HarpRes) HarpInfo.

McKee, Cynthia R. & McKee, Philip. Cash For College, Rev. Ed. The Ultimate Guide To College Scholarships. rev. ed. LC 98-41995. 704p. 1999. pap. 19.95 (*0-688-16190-1*, Quil) HarperTrade.

McKee, Cynthia R. & McKee, Phillip C., Jr. Cash for College. LC 92-42410. 1993. pap. 16.95 (*0-688-12179-9*, Hearst) Hearst Commns.

***McKee, D.** The Hill & the Rock. 1999. pap. 9.95 (*0-86264-784-3*, Pub. by Andersen Pr) Trafalgar.

McKee, Daphne C., jt. ed. see Blumenthal, James A.

McKee, David. El Bano de Elmer (Elmer's Bath) (SPA., Illus.). 6p. (J). 1995. 5.99 (*968-16-4639-8*, Pub. by Fondo) Continental Bk.

***McKee, David.** Cebra Tiene Hippo. (Illus.). 28p. (J). (gr. k-1). 1999. pap. 6.95 (*980-257-227-6*, Pub. by Ediciones Ekare) Kane-Miller Bk.

McKee, David. El Chapuzon de Elmer (Elmer's Splash) (SPA., Illus.). 6p. (J). 1995. 5.99 (*968-16-4638-X*, Pub. by Fondo) Continental Bk.

— Elmer. (SPA.). (J). 13.95 (*84-372-6614-9*) Santillana.

— Elmer. LC 89-2285. (Illus.). 32p. (J). (ps-2). 1989. reprint ed. 14.00 (*0-688-09171-7*) Lothrop.

— Elmer. LC 89-2285. (Illus.). 32p. (J). (ps-3). 1989. reprint ed. lib. bdg. 15.93 (*0-688-09172-5*) Lothrop.

— Elmer Again. LC 91-38901. (Illus.). 32p. (J). (ps up). 1992. 15.00 (*0-688-11596-9*) Lothrop.

***McKee, David.** Elmer & the Kangaroo. LC 99-53405. (Illus.). 32p. (J). (ps-k). 2000. 14.95 (*0-688-17951-7*) Morrow Avon.

McKee, David. Elmer & the Lost Teddy Bear. LC 98-44729. 1999. 15.00 (*0-688-16912-0*) Lothrop.

— Elmer & Wilbur. LC 96-3698. (Illus.). (J). 1996. 15.00 (*0-688-14934-0*) Lothrop.

— Elmer in the Snow. LC 95-77472. (Illus.). 32p. (J). (gr. 4-7). 1995. 13.00 (*0-688-14596-5*, Wm Morrow) Morrow Avon.

— Elmer Takes Off. LC 97-19121. (Illus.). 32p. (J). (ps-1). 1998. 15.00 (*0-688-15785-8*) Lothrop.

McKee, David. Elmer's Bath. (Illus.). 10p. (J). 1995. write for info. (*0-09-950341-7*, Pub. by Hutchinson Kid) Random House.

McKee, David. Elmer's Colors. LC 94-75212. (J). 1994. pap. 4.95 (*0-688-13762-8*) Lothrop.

McKee, David. Elmers Colours. (Elmers Ser.). (Illus.). (J). 1994. 6.95 (*1-84059-055-6*) Milet Ltd.

— Elmers Colours. (Illus.). 1998. 6.95 (*1-84059-057-2*) Milet Ltd.

— Elmers Colours. (Elmers Ser.). (Illus.). (J). 1998. 6.95 (*1-84059-056-4*); 6.95 (*1-84059-058-0*); 6.95 (*1-84059-059-9*); 6.95 (*1-84059-060-2*) Milet Ltd.

McKee, David. Elmer's Day. LC 94-75215. (J). 1994. pap. 4.95 (*0-688-13759-8*) Lothrop.

***McKee, David.** Elmers Day. (Elmers Ser.). (Illus.). 1998. 6.95 (*1-84059-064-5*); 6.95 (*1-84059-066-1*); 6.95 (*1-84059-067-X*) Milet Ltd.

— Elmers Day. (Elmers Ser.). (Illus.). (J). 1998. 6.95 (*1-84059-068-8*); 6.95 (*1-84059-065-3*); 6.95 (*1-84059-062-9*) Milet Ltd.

McKee, David. Elmer's Friends. LC 94-75213.Tr. of Amigos de Elmer. (J). 1994. pap. 4.95 (*0-688-13761-X*) Lothrop.

McKee, David. Elmer's Friends. Pullin, Beatriz, tr.Tr. of Amigos de Elmer. (SPA & ENG., Illus.). 14p. (J). 1994. bds. 6.95 (*1-84059-072-6*) Milet Ltd.

— Elmers Friends. (Elmers Ser.). (Illus.). 1998. 6.95 (*1-84059-071-8*) Milet Ltd.

— Elmers Friends. (Illus.). (J). 1998. 6.95 (*1-84059-070-X*); 6.95 (*1-84059-073-4*); 6.95 (*1-84059-074-2*); 6.95 (*1-84059-075-0*); 6.95 (*1-84059-077-7*); 6.95 (*1-84059-069-6*) Milet Ltd.

— Elmer's Splash. (Illus.). 10p. (J). 1995. write for info. (*0-09-950351-4*, Pub. by Hutchinson Kid) Random House.

McKee, David. Elmer's Weather. LC 94-75214. (J). 1994. pap. 4.95 (*0-688-13760-1*) Lothrop.

***McKee, David.** Elmers Weather. (Elmers Ser.). (Illus.). 1998. 6.95 (*1-84059-081-5*) Milet Ltd.

— Elmers Weather. (Elmers Ser.). (Illus.). (J). 1998. 6.95 (*1-84059-079-3*); 6.95 (*1-84059-080-7*); 6.95 (*1-84059-082-3*); 6.95 (*1-84059-076-9*) Milet Ltd.

McKee, David. Hide-and-Seek Elmer: A Lift-the-Flap Book. (Illus.). 24p. (J). (ps-k). 1998. 11.95 (*0-688-16127-8*, Wm Morrow) Morrow Avon.

— I Can Too! Elmer Pop-up Book. LC 99-161933. (Illus.). 10p. (J). (ps up). 1997. 15.95 (*0-688-15547-2*) Lothrop.

— Minilibros - Rey Rollo. (SPA., Illus.). (J). (ps-1). boxed set 7.95 (*980-257-191-1*, Pub. by Ediciones Ekare) Kane-Miller Bk.

— The Monster & the Teddy Bear. (Illus.). 32p. (J). (ps-1). 1998. pap. 9.95 (*0-86264-762-2*, Pub. by Andersen Pr) Trafalgar.

— Not Now Bernard. (J). 1991. pap. text. write for info. (*0-05-004559-8*) Addison-Wesley.

— Otra Broma de Elmer.Tr. of Elmer Again. (SPA.). 28p. (J). (gr. 1-3). 1994. 12.99 (*968-16-4560-X*, Pub. by Fondo) Continental Bk.

— Prince Peter & the Teddy Bear. LC 96-62032. (Illus.). 32p. (J). (ps-1). 1997. 15.00 (*0-374-36123-1*) FS&G.

— Que Es Ese Ruido, Isabel? (Isabel's Noisy Tummy) (SPA.). (J). (gr. k-2). 1997. pap. 7.50 (*84-480-0102-8*) Lectorum Pubns.

— The Sad Story of Veronica Who Played the Violin. (Illus.). 32p. (J). (gr. k-4). 1991. 10.95 (*0-916291-37-5*) Kane-Miller Bk.

— Tusk Tusk. (Illus.). 32p. (J). (ps-3). 1990. reprint ed. pap. 6.95 (*0-916291-28-6*) Kane-Miller Bk.

— Zebra's Hiccups. LC 92-14453. (J). 1993. pap. 14.00 (*0-671-79440-X*) S&S Bks Yung.

McKee, David J. Tropospheric Ozone: Human Health & Agricultural Impacts. 352p. 1993. lib. bdg. 99.95 (*0-87371-475-X*, L475) Lewis Pubs.

McKee, David L. External Linkages & Growth in Small Economies. LC 93-25059. 176p. 1993. 57.95 (*0-275-94655-X*, C4655, Praeger Pubs) Greenwood.

— Growth, Development, & the Service Economy in the Third World. LC 88-14107. (Illus.). 152p. 1988. 52.95 (*0-275-92897-7*, C2897, Praeger Pubs) Greenwood.

— Schumpeter & the Political Economy of Change. LC 90-44404. 164p. 1991. 47.95 (*0-275-93679-1*, C3679, Praeger Pubs) Greenwood.

McKee, David L. Urban Environments in Emerging Economies. LC 94-7430. 192p. 1994. 55.00 (*0-275-94938-9*, Praeger Pubs) Greenwood.

McKee, David L., ed. Canadian-American Economic Relations: Conflict & Cooperation on a Continental Scale. LC 88-6610. 245p. 1988. 55.00 (*0-275-92836-5*, C2836, Praeger Pubs) Greenwood.

— Energy, the Environment, & Public Policy: Issues for the 1990s. LC 90-20000. 232p. 1991. 59.95 (*0-275-93719-4*, C3719, Praeger Pubs) Greenwood.

— Hostile Takeovers: Issues in Public & Corporate Policy. LC 89-30900. 187p. 1989. 57.95 (*0-275-93181-1*, C3181, Praeger Pubs) Greenwood.

McKee, David L. & Bennett, Richard E., eds. Structural Change in an Urban Industrial Region: The Northeastern Ohio Case. LC 86-30652. 268p. 1987. 62.95 (*0-275-92353-3*, C2353, Praeger Pubs) Greenwood.

McKee, David L. & Garner, Don E. Accounting Services, Growth, & Change in the Pacific Basin. LC 95-37480. 192p. 1996. 57.95 (*1-56720-017-6*, Quorum Bks) Greenwood.

— Accounting Services, the International Economy, & Third World Development. LC 92-16548. 176p. 1992. 57.95 (*0-275-94115-9*, C4115, Praeger Pubs) Greenwood.

McKee, David L. & Tisdell, Clement A. Developmental Issues in Small Island Economies. LC 90-31967. 216p. 1990. 57.95 (*0-275-93393-8*, C3393, Praeger Pubs) Greenwood.

McKee, David L., et al. Accounting Services & Growth in Small Economies: Evidence from the Caribbean Basin. LC 97-31516. 184p. 1998. 59.95 (*1-56720-138-5*, Quorum Bks) Greenwood.

***Mckee, David L., et al.** Accounting Services, the Islamic Middle East & the Global Economy. LC 98-30540. 200p. 1999. 65.00 (*1-56720-139-3*, Quorum Bks) Greenwood.

***McKee, David L., et al.** Offshore Financial Centers, Accounting Services & the Global Economy. LC 99-59832. 2000. write for info. (*1-56720-310-8*, Quorum Bks) Greenwood.

McKee, Dean, jt. auth. see Dimov, Ivan T.

McKee, Delber L. Chinese Exclusion vs. the Open Door Policy, 1900-1906: Clashes Over China Policy in the Roosevelt Era. LC 76-47024. (Illus.). 293p. reprint ed. pap. 90.90 (*0-608-16046-6*, 203317600084) Bks Demand.

McKee, Dierdre. My Lover & His Half-Leg. 24p. 1993. pap. 5.00 (*1-882827-03-1*) Insight to Riot.

McKee, Douglas C. Mental Mechanics: A Repair Manual for the Self. (Orig.). (C). 1997. pap. write for info. (*0-916108-14-7*) Seed Center.

McKee, E. B., jt. ed. see Davison, E. M.

McKee, E. Bates. Cascadia. (Illus.). 412p. (C). 1992. reprint ed. 105.00 (*1-878907-51-4*) TechBooks.

McKee, Edwin D. Sedimentary Structures in Dunes of the Namib Desert, South West Africa. LC 81-20155. (Geological Society of America, Special Paper: No. 188). (Illus.). 68p. reprint ed. pap. 30.00 (*0-8357-6842-2*, 203553000095) Bks Demand.

McKee, Elaine, jt. auth. see Townsend, Charles E.

McKee, Elaine M., ed. see Manley, Bob N.

McKee, Elsie Anne. Diakonia in the Classical Reformed Tradition & Today. fac. ed. LC 89-39372. 151p. (Orig.). reprint ed. pap. 46.90 (*0-7837-7963-1*, 204771900008) Bks Demand.

***McKee, Elsie Anne.** Katharina Schutz Zell, 2 Vols. Incl. Vol. 2. The Writings, a Critical Edition. LC 98-43027. (Illus.). xvi, 404p. 1999. Not sold separately (*90-04-11126-3*); Vol. 1. The Life & Thought of a Sixteenth Century Reformer. LC 98-43027. xviii, 506p. 1999. Not sold separately (*90-04-11125-5*); (Studies in Medieval & Reformation Thought: Vol. 69). (Illus.). 1999. 229.50 (*90-04-11112-3*) Brill Academic Pubs.

***McKee, Francis.** Kathy Prendergast: The End & the Beginning. 2000. pap. 29.95 (*1-85894-096-6*) Merrell Holberton.

McKee, Gerald T., jt. ed. see Schenker, Paul S.

***McKee, Gerard T. & Schenker, Paul S., eds.** Sensor Fusion & Decentralized Control in Robotic Systems II. 348p. 1999. pap. text 72.00 (*0-8194-3432-9*) SPIE.

McKee, Gerard T., jt. ed. see Schenker, Paul S.

Mckee, Gertrude & Mckee, James R. Biochemistry: An Introduction. 672p. (C). 1997. per. write for info. (*0-07-114980-5*, WCB McGr Hill) McGrw-H Hghr Educ.

McKee, Gertrude & McKee, James R. Biochemisty: An Introduction. LC 95-76544. 656p. (C). 1995. text. write for info. (*0-697-21159-2*, WCB McGr Hill) McGrw-H Hghr Educ.

McKee, Gertrude, et al. Biochemistry: Student Study Guide with Solutions Manual. 240p. (C). 1996. text, student ed. 28.12 (*0-697-21161-4*, WCB McGr Hill) McGrw-H Hghr Educ.

McKee, Glenn. Memory's Menu: Poetry. LC 99-14762. 78p. 1999. pap. text 14.95 (*0-7734-3089-X*) E Mellen.

— Picking Time. (Illus.). 26p. 1994. 5.00 (*0-9636689-1-9*) White Wave ME.

McKee, Glenn, ed. see Wixson, Jennifer.

McKee, Grace. Songs of a Happy Heart. 70p. (Orig.). 1996. pap. write for info. (*1-57502-353-9*, PO1152) Morris Pubng.

McKee, Gwen. The Little Gumbo Book: Twenty-Seven Carefully Created Recipes That Will Enable Everyone to Enjoy the Special Experience of Gumbo. LC 94-5662. (Illus.). 64p. (Orig.). 1986. 8.95 (*0-937552-17-8*) Quail Ridge.

— The Little New Orleans Cookbook: Fifty-Seven Classic Creole Recipes That Will Enable Everyone to Enjoy the Special Cuisine of New Orleans. (Illus.). 80p. (Orig.). 1991. 8.95 (*0-937552-42-9*) Quail Ridge.

— Le Petet Livre de Cuisine de la Nouvelle Orleans: French Edition of the Little New Orleans Cookbook. (FRE.). 1996. 10.95 (*0-937552-60-7*) Quail Ridge.

***McKee, Gwen & Moseley, Barbara, eds.** Best of the Best from Arizona Cookbook: Selected Recipes from Arizona's Favorite Cookbooks. (Illus.). 288p. 2000. 16.95 (*1-893062-16-3*) Quail Ridge.

— Best of the Best from California Cookbook: Selected Recipes from California's Favorite Cookbooks. 352p. 2000. pap. 16.95 (*1-893062-02-3*) Quail Ridge.

McKee, Gwen & Moseley, Barbara, eds. Best of the Best from Colorado: Selected Recipes from Colorado's Favorite Cookbooks, Vol. 25. LC 98-22431. (Illus.). 288p. 1997. spiral bd. 16.95 (*0-937552-84-4*) Quail Ridge.

— Best of the Best from Florida: Selected Recipes from Florida's Favorite Cookbooks. (Best of the Best State Cookbook Ser.). (Illus.). 288p. 1986. ring bd. 16.95 (*0-937552-16-X*) Quail Ridge.

— Best of the Best from Iowa: Selected Recipes from Iowa's Favorite Cookbooks, Vol. 26. LC 97-37161. (Illus.). 288p. 1997. spiral bd. 16.95 (*0-937552-82-8*) Quail Ridge.

— Best of the Best from Louisiana II: Selected Recipes from Louisiana's Favorite Cookbooks, Vol. 24. LC 98-17608. (Illus.). 288p. 1997. spiral bd. 16.95 (*0-937552-83-6*) Quail Ridge.

— Best of the Best from Minnesota: Selected Recipes from Minnesota's Favorite Cookbooks, Vol. 23. LC 97-23253. (Illus.). 288p. 1997. 16.95 (*0-937552-81-X*) Quail Ridge.

— Best of the Best from Texas II: Selected Recipes from Texas's Favorite Cookbooks. (Best of the Best State Cookbook Ser.). (Illus.). 352p. 1996. ring bd. 16.95 (*0-937552-62-3*) Quail Ridge.

— Best of the Best from the Great Plains: Selected Recipes from Kansas' Favorite Cookbooks, Vol. 27. LC 99-17195. (Best of the Best Ser.). (Illus.). 286p. 1999. pap. 16.95 (*0-937552-85-2*) Quail Ridge.

— Best of the Best from Wisconsin: Selected Recipes from Wisconsin's Favorite Cookbooks, Vol. 22. LC 97-16073. (Illus.). 288p. 1997. 16.95 (*0-937552-80-1*) Quail Ridge.

— "Best of the Best" State Cookbook Series: Selected Recipes from Favorite Cookbooks, 28 vols. Incl. Best of the Best from Alabama: Selected Recipes from Alabama's Favorite Cookbooks. LC 89-60781. (Illus.). 288p. 1989. ring bd. 16.95 (*0-937552-28-3*); Best of the Best from Arkansas: Selected Recipes from Arkansas' Favorite Cookbooks. LC 92-12155. (Illus.). 288p. 1992. ring bd. 16.95 (*0-937552-43-7*); Best of the Best from Georgia: Selected Recipes from Georgia's Favorite Cookbooks. LC 89-10205. (Illus.). 336p. 1989. ring bd. 16.95 (*0-937552-30-5*); Best of the Best from Illinois: Selected Recipes from Illinois' Favorite Cookbooks. (Illus.). 288p. 1995. ring bd. 16.95 (*0-937552-58-5*); Best of the Best from Indiana: Selected Recipes from Indiana's Favorite Cookbooks. (Illus.). 288p. 1995. ring bd. 14.95 (*0-937552-57-7*); Best of the Best from Kentucky: Selected Recipes from Kentucky's Favorite Cookbooks. LC 88-90826. (Illus.). 288p. 1988. pap. 16.95 (*0-937552-27-5*); Best of the Best from Louisiana: Selected Recipes from Louisiana's Favorite Cookbooks. (Illus.). 288p. 1984. ring bd. 16.95 (*0-937552-13-5*); Best of the Best from Michigan: Selected Recipes from Michigan's Favorite Cookbooks. LC 96-43779. (Illus.). 288p. 1996. ring bd. 16.95 (*0-937552-69-0*); Best of the Best from Mississippi: Selected Recipes from Mississippi's Favorite Cookbooks. rev. ed. (Illus.). 288p. 1987. pap. 16.95 (*0-937552-19-4*); Best of the Best from Missouri: Selected Recipes from Missouri's Favorite Cookbooks. LC 92-25259. (Illus.). 304p. 1992. ring bd. 16.95 (*0-937552-44-5*); Best of the Best from New England: Selected Recipes from the Favorite Cookbooks of Rhode Island, Connecticut, Massachusetts, Vermont, New Hampshire & Maine. LC 94-5578. (Illus.). 368p. 1994. ring bd. 16.95 (*0-937552-50-X*); Best of the Best from North Carolina: Selected Recipes from North Carolina's Favorite Cookbooks. LC 90-45535. (Illus.). 288p. 1990. ring bd. 16.95 (*0-937552-38-0*); Best of the Best from Ohio: Selected Recipes from Ohio's Favorite Cookbooks. LC 96-33095. (Illus.). 352p. 1996. ring bd. 16.95 (*0-937552-68-2*); Best of the Best from Oklahoma: Selected Recipes from Oklahoma's Favorite Cookbooks. LC 96-19063. (Illus.). 288p. 1996. ring bd. 16.95 (*0-937552-65-8*); Best of the Best from

An Asterisk (*) at the beginning of an entry indicates that the title is appearing for the first time.

Pennsylvania: Selected Recipes from Pennsylvania's Favorite Cookbooks. (Illus.). 320p. 1993. ring bd. 16.95 (*0-937552-47-X*); Best of the Best from South Carolina: Selected Recipes from South Carolina's Favorite Cookbooks. LC 90-42214. (Illus.). 288p. 1990. ring bd. 16.95 (*0-937552-39-9*); Best of the Best from Tennessee: Selected Recipes from Tennessee's Favorite Cookbooks. (Illus.). 288p. 1987. ring bd. 16.95 (*0-937552-20-8*); Best of the Best from Texas: Selected Recipes from Texas' Favorite Cookbooks. (Illus.). 352p. 1985. ring bd. 16.95 (*0-937552-14-3*); Best of the Best from Texas: Selected Recipes from Texas' Favorite Cookbooks. (Illus.). 352p. 1985. 18.95 (*0-937552-34-8*); Best of the Best from Virginia: Selected Recipes from Virginia's Favorite Cookbooks. LC 91-23169. (Illus.). 320p. 1991. ring bd. 14.95 (*0-937552-41-0*); 1999. 474.60 (*0-937552-64-X*) Quail Ridge.

— The Recipe Hall of Fame Cookbook: Preserving America's Food Heritage. LC 99-23538. (Illus.). 304p. (Orig.). 1999. pap. 19.95 (*1-893062-08-2*) Quail Ridge.

*__McKee, Gwen & Moseley, Barbara, eds.__ Recipe Hall of Fame Dessert Cookbook. (Best of the Best State Cookbook Ser.). 2000. 16.95 (*1-893062-19-8*) Quail Ridge.

McKee, Gwen, ed. see Fellowship Church, Baton Rouge, La, Members.

McKee, Heather, jt. auth. see Puri, Basant.

McKee, Henry S. Journeys in Understanding. LC 68-58802. (Essay Index Reprint Ser.). 1977. 18.95 (*0-8369-0122-3*) Ayer.

McKee, Jack. Builder Boards. 3rd rev. ed. LC 98-171169. Orig. Title: How to Build a Take Apart Playhouse. (Illus.). 1997. pap. 12.95 (*1-884894-52-6*) Hands On Bks.

McKee, James. His Steps My Path. 2nd large type ed. (Illus.). 144p. 1996. pap. text 16.95 (*0-9655372-0-X*) J McKee.

McKee, James B. Sociology & The Race Problem: The Failure of a Perspective. LC 92-42293. 384p. 1993. text 39.95 (*0-252-02022-7*); pap. text 19.95 (*0-252-06328-7*) U of Ill Pr.

McKee, James H. Civil War Record of the 144th Regiment NY Volunteer Infantry: Back "in War Times" (Illus.). 378p. 1994. pap. 28.00 (*0-7884-0007-X*) Heritage Bk.

McKee, James L. Lincoln: The Prairie Capital. (Illus.). 123p. 1989. reprint ed. pap. 17.95 (*0-934904-07-3*) J & L Lee.

— Lincoln, the Prairie Capital: An Illustrated History. rev. ed. (Illus.). 192p. 1984. 24.95 (*0-89781-109-7*) Am Historical Pr.

— Remember When. (Illus.). 108p. (Orig.). 1998. pap. 12.95 (*0-934904-23-5*) J & L Lee.

McKee, James L. & Zimmer, Edward F. Havelock, Nebraska. (Illus.). 96p. (Orig.). 1993. pap. 12.95 (*0-934904-33-2*) J & L Lee.

McKee, James R. Kit Carson: Man of Fact & Fiction. 1981. 27.95 (*0-405-14097-5*) Ayer.

Mckee, James R., jt. auth. see Mckee, Gertrude.

McKee, James R., jt. auth. see McKee, Gertrude.

McKee, James R., jt. auth. see McKee, Trudy.

McKee, James R., jt. auth. see Zanger, Murray.

McKee, Jasper. Physics in the Real World. (Illus.). 91p. 1999. write for info. (*0-7541-0816-3*, Pub. by Minerva Pr) Unity Dist.

*__McKee, Jeffrey Kevin.__ The Riddled Chain: Chance, Coincidence, & Chaos in Human Evolution. LC 99-45720. (Illus.). 256p. (C). 2000. 27.00 (*0-8135-2783-X*) Rutgers U Pr.

*__McKee, Jesse O.__ Ethnicity in Contemporary America: A Geographical Appraisal. 2nd ed. LC 99-88089. 400p. 2000. 45.00 (*0-7425-0034-9*) Rowman.

McKee, Jesse O., ed. Ethnicity in Contemporary America: A Geographical Appraisal. LC 84-81991. (National Council for Geographic Education, Pacesetter Ser.). (Illus.). 302p. 1985. reprint ed. pap. 93.70 (*0-7837-9724-9*, 206045500005) Bks Demand.

McKee, Jesse O., jt. ed. see Prenshaw, Peggy W.

McKee, John. A Martyr Bishop: The Life of St. Oliver Plunkett. 181p. 1975. 8.95 (*0-912414-21-9*) Lumen Christi.

Mckee, John. Photographs, 1973-1983. (Illus.). 1984. pap. 7.50 (*0-916606-06-6*) Bowdoin Coll.

McKee, John. William Allen White: Maverick on Main Street, 17. LC 74-5991. (Contributions in American Studies: No. 17). (Illus.). 264p. 1975. 55.00 (*0-8371-7533-X*, MAW/, Greenwood Pr) Greenwood.

McKee, Judy. Maximizing Customer Contact: Turning Customer Representatives into Sales Achievers. 164p. 1996. write for info. (*0-614-22081-5*) Tech Marketing.

— Sales Survival Guide. Caton, Sandra, ed. (Sales Ser.). 135p. (Orig.). 1989. pap. 12.95 (*0-685-44400-7*) Motivations Pub.

— Scriptwriting for Effective Telemarketing. Telemarketing Magazine Editorial Staff, ed. 100p. (Orig.). pap. write for info. (*0-936840-12-9*) Tech Marketing.

McKee, Judy S., ed. Play: Working Partner of Growth. LC 86-22245. 88p. 1986. pap. 11.00 (*0-87173-112-6*) ACEI.

— Play, Working Partner of Growth. LC 86-22245. (Illus.). 88p. 1986. reprint ed. pap. 30.00 (*0-608-03185-2*, 206363800007) Bks Demand.

McKee, Karen. BipQuiz. Art. LC 97-186309. 64p. (J). 1997. pap. 2.95 (*0-8069-9733-8*) Sterling.

— BipQuiz: Dinosaurs. LC 97-186314. 64p. (J). 1997. pap. 2.95 (*0-8069-9732-X*) Sterling.

— BipQuiz: Music. LC 97-186312. 64p. (J). 1997. pap. 2.95 (*0-8069-9734-6*) Sterling.

McKee, Karen A. How to Draw Airplanes. 32p. (Orig.). (J). 1990. pap. 2.95 (*0-942025-73-3*) Kidsbks.

— How to Draw Airplanes. (How to Draw Ser.). 32p. (Orig.). (J). 1991. 3.98 (*1-56156-021-9*) Kidsbks.

— How to Draw Cars. (How to Draw Ser.). 32p. (J). 1991. pap. 2.95 (*1-56156-026-X*) Kidsbks.

— How to Draw Cars. (How to Draw Ser.). 32p. (J). 1991. 3.98 (*1-56156-017-0*) Kidsbks.

— How to Draw Trucks. (How to Draw Ser.). 48p. (J). 1992. pap. 2.95 (*1-56156-145-2*) Kidsbks.

McKee, Kathryn, ed. see Schrier, Martha S.

McKee, LaVonne & Schwartz, Ted. Get Ready to Say Goodbye: A Mother's Story of Senseless Violence, Tragedy, & Triumph. 1993. 22.95 (*0-88282-079-6*) New Horizon NJ.

McKee, Linda Jones, jt. auth. see Carey, Richard.

*__McKee, Louis.__ River Architecture: Poems from Here & There. limited ed. 72p. 1999. pap. 12.00 (*0-9673401-0-1*) Cynic Pr.

McKee, Lynn. Spirit of the Turtle Woman. 352p. 1999. mass mkt. 6.99 (*0-451-40859-4*, Onyx) NAL.

McKee, Mac. Wolfer. LC 94-47095. (Novel of the West Ser.). 192p. 1995. 19.95 (*0-87131-778-8*) M Evans.

— Wolfer. large type ed. LC 97-52951. (Western Ser.). 243p. 1998. write for info. (*0-7838-8435-4*, G K Hall & Co) Mac Lib Ref.

McKee, Malcolm & Luscombe, Christopher. The Shakespeare Revue. 128p. Date not set. pap. 5.95 (*0-87129-989-5*, SD4) Dramatic Pub.

McKee, Malcolm, jt. auth. see Luscombe, Chris.

McKee, Margaret & Chisenhall, Fred. Beale Black & Blue: Life & Music on Black America's Main Street. LC 81-4995. (Illus.). 265p. 1993. pap. 16.95 (*0-8071-1886-9*) La State U Pr.

McKee, Martha. Circles. 72p. 1976. pap. 4.95 (*0-913428-26-4*) Landfall Pr.

*__McKee, Martha.__ Hugs for Teachers: Stories, Sayings, & Scriptures to Encourage & Inspire. gif. ed. LC 98-48611. (Hugs Ser.). (Illus.). 128p. 1999. 10.99 (*1-58229-007-5*) Howard Pub LA.

McKee, Martha. Single Circles. 132p. 1982. 8.95 (*0-913428-42-6*); pap. 5.95 (*0-913428-43-4*) Landfall Pr.

McKee, Martha L. Jack London in Califronia: A Guide. (Famous Footsteps Ser.). (Illus.). (Orig.). 1995. pap. 4.95 (*0-929709-12-8*) Computer Lab.

McKee, Moseley. Best of the Best from New Mexico Cookbook: Selected Recipes from New Mexico's Favorite Cookbooks. LC 99-38581. 1999. 16.95 (*0-937552-93-3*) Quail Ridge.

McKee, Nancy & Kennedy, George. Correcting Common Errors in Writing. 68p. (C). 1996. pap. text, per. 9.95 (*0-7872-1839-1*) Kendall-Hunt.

McKee, P. H., jt. auth. see Fletcher, C. D.

McKee, Pam, et al. Afternoon Teas: Recipes, History, Menus. (Between Friends Cookbook Ser.). (Illus.). 56p. (Orig.). 1995. pap. 4.99 (*1-56523-040-X*) Fox Chapel Pub.

— A Red Ribbon Christmas: Recipes & Traditions: Ideas for Entertaining. (Between Friends Cookbook Ser.). (Illus.). 60p. 1995. pap. 4.99 (*1-56523-068-X*) Fox Chapel Pub.

McKee, Pat. Orthotics in Rehabilitation: Splinting the Hand & Body. LC 97-48427. 340p. 1998. pap. text 32.95 (*0-8036-0351-7*) Davis Co.

McKee, Patricia. Heroic Commitment in Richardson, Eliot, & James. LC 85-17018. 364p. 1986. reprint ed. pap. 112.90 (*0-608-06483-1*, 206678000009) Bks Demand.

— Producing American Races: Henry James, William Faulkner, Toni Morrison. LC 98-32346. (New Americanists Ser.). 1999. write for info. (*0-8223-2329-X*) Duke.

*__McKee, Patricia.__ Producing American Races: Henry James, William Faulkner, Toni Morrison. LC 98-32346. (New Americanists Ser.). 1999. 17.95 (*0-8223-2363-X*) Duke.

McKee, Patricia. Public & Private: Gender, Class & the British Novel (1764-1878) LC 96-35350. 1997. pap. 19.95 (*0-8166-2935-8*); text 49.95 (*0-8166-2934-X*) U of Minn Pr.

McKee, Patrick & Kauppinen, Heta. The Art of Aging: A Celebration of Old Age in Western Art. (Illus.). 208p. 1986. 29.95 (*0-89885-304-4*, Kluwer Acad Hman Sci) Kluwer Academic.

McKee, Patrick, jt. auth. see McLerran, Jennifer.

McKee, Patrick A., jt. ed. see Kaufman, Christian E., Jr.

McKee, Patrick L., ed. Philosophical Foundations of Gerontology. LC 81-2922. 352p. 1982. 43.95 (*0-89885-040-1*, Kluwer Acad Hman Sci); pap. 24.95 (*0-89885-041-X*, Kluwer Acad Hman Sci) Kluwer Academic.

McKee, Patrick L. & Thiem, Jon, eds. Real Life: Ten Stories of Aging. 192p. 1994. 29.95 (*0-87081-354-4*); pap. 19.95 (*0-87081-355-2*) Univ Pr Colo.

McKee, Patrick W. & Barbe, Richard H. The Special Educator Desk Book, 1996. 350p. 1992. pap. 55.00 (*0-934753-73-3*) LRP Pubns.

McKee, Patrick W., et al. Suicide & the School: A Practical Guide to Suicide Prevention. LC 93-12083. (Crisis Intervention Ser.). (Illus.). 160p. (Orig.). 1993. pap. 24.95 (*0-934753-78-4*) LRP Pubns.

McKee, Philip, jt. auth. see McKee, Cynthia R.

McKee, Phillip C., Jr., jt. auth. see McKee, Cynthia R.

McKee, Phillip H. Pathology of the Skin. 2nd ed. 1996. 345.00 (*1-56375-588-2*) Gower-Mosby.

McKee, R., jt. auth. see Eastman, P. D.

McKee Ranger, Laurel A. High Mid-Volume Competitive Analysis. Minnella, Thomas A., ed. LC 95-75497. (Copier Productivity Ser.). 1995. write for info. (*0-9629936-3-8*) Minnella Ent.

McKee, Richard. The Clan of the Flapdragon & Other Adventures in Etymology. LC 96-45686. 224p. 1997. 24.95 (*0-8173-0881-4*) U of Ala Pr.

McKee, Robert. Story: A Guide to Screenwriting from the Film Industry's Master Teacher of Craft. unabridged ed. 1997. audio 25.00 (*0-694-51694-5*, CPN 2571) HarperAudio.

McKee, Robert. Story: Substance, Structure, Style & the Principles of Screenwriting. LC 97-24139. (Illus.). 480p. 1997. 35.00 (*0-06-039168-5*, ReganBks) HarperTrade.

McKee, Robert B., Jr., jt. auth. see Edwards, Kenneth S.

McKee, Robert D. One Fortunate Fellow. LC 95-94340. (Illus.). 150p. 1995. pap., per. 14.50 (*0-9647019-0-1*) R D McKee.

McKee, Russell, ed. Mackinac, the Gathering Place. LC 81-620009. 176p. 1981. 27.95 (*0-941912-02-7*) Mich Nat Res.

*__McKee, Sally.__ Uncommon Dominion: Venetian Crete & the Myth of Ethnic Homogeneity. LC 00-28658. (Middle Ages Ser.). 2000. write for info. (*0-8122-3562-2*) U of Pa Pr.

McKee, Sally, ed. see Laiou, Angeliki E.

McKee, Samuel. Labor in Colonial New York, 1664-1776. 193p. 1993. reprint ed. lib. bdg. 69.00 (*0-7812-5250-4*) Rprt Serv.

McKee, Sandra L. & Walters, Brenda. Life Management: Skills for Busy People. LC 96-18516. 224p. (C). 1996. pap. text 31.20 (*0-13-227539-2*) P-H.

McKee, Saundra J. American Government: The U. S. A. & West Virginia, Teacher's Manual. Buckalew, Marshall, ed. (Illus.). 353p. 1990. ring bd. 25.00 (*0-914498-12-6*) WV Hist Ed Found.

McKee, Sharon, jt. tr. see Carlile, Cynthia.

McKee, Steve. Coach. LC 93-27901. 304p. 1994. 17.95 (*0-8117-2537-5*) Stackpole.

McKee, Steven B., et al. Federal Civil Rules Handbook: 1996 Edition. 1200p. 1995. pap. write for info. (*0-314-08055-4*) West Pub.

McKee, Sue, ed. see Carrington, William G.

McKee, Suzanne P., ed. Optics, Physiology & Vision. (Vision Research Ser.: No. VR 263). 400p. 1990. 45.00 (*0-08-040692-0*, Pub. by PPI) Elsevier.

McKee, Suzi. Dear Mrs. McKee: How to Survive the Teenage Years. LC 96-95103. 110p. (Orig.). (YA). (gr. 7-12). 1996. pap. 9.97 (*0-9655399-9-7*) Indian Springs.

McKee, T. A. & McMorris, F. R. Topics in Intersection Graph Theory. LC 98-31901. (Discrete Mathematics & Application Ser.: Vol. 2). (Illus.). viii, 205p. 1999. pap. text 55.00 (*0-89871-430-3*, BKDT0002) Soc Indus-Appl Math.

McKee, Thomas E. Modern Analytical Auditing: Practical Guidance for Auditors & Accountants. LC 88-23965. 174p. 1989. 59.95 (*0-89930-354-4*; MKA/, Quorum Bks) Greenwood.

McKee, Thomas H. National Conventions & Platforms of All Political Parties, 1789-1900. LC 77-107183. 1971. reprint ed. 15.00 (*0-403-00356-3*) Scholarly.

— National Conventions & Platforms of All Political Parties, 1789-1905. 6th enl. rev. ed. LC 70-130239. 1970. reprint ed. 16.00 (*0-404-04133-7*) AMS Pr.

*__McKee, Thomas W.__ They Don't Play Me Music Anymore: How to Plan Your Future When Your World Keeps Changing. (Illus.). 120p. 1999. pap. 10.95 (*1-928685-13-7*) Advtg Point Syst.

McKee, Timothy S. No More Strangers Now: Young Voices from a New South Africa. LC 97-47293. (YA). (gr. 5 up). 1998. 19.95 (*0-7894-2524-6*) DK Pub Inc.

McKee, Trudy & McKee, James R. Biochemistry: An Introduction. 2nd ed. LC 98-4536. 1998. 82.50 (*0-07-290499-2*) McGraw.

McKee, Victoria. Working It Out: The Workaholics' Survival Book. 208p. 1995. 22.95 (*0-86051-721-7*, Robson-Parkwest) Parkwest Pubns.

McKee, W. Reid & Mason, M. E., Jr. Civil War Projectiles Vol. II: Small Arms & Field Artillery with Supplement. (Illus.). 202p. 1980. 29.95 (*0-942365-08-9*) North South Trader.

McKee, William, ed. Lectures for Bankers & Business Executives. LC 76-107724. (Essay Index Reprint Ser.). 1977. 39.95 (*0-8369-1580-1*) Ayer.

McKee, William J. Gould Farm: A Life of Sharing. (Illus.). 306p. (Orig.). 1994. pap. 11.00 (*0-9642500-2-0*) Wm J Gould.

McKee, William L. & Froeschle, Richard C. Where the Jobs Are: Identification & Analysis of Local Employment Opportunities. LC 85-10570. 175p. 1985. pap. text 12.00 (*0-88099-029-5*) W E Upjohn.

McKee, William S., et al. Federal Taxation of Partnerships & Partners. 1990. 215.00 (*0-7913-0509-0*) Warren Gorham & Lamont.

— Federal Taxation of Partnerships & Partners. 3rd ed. LC 96-61648. 1996. write for info. (*0-7913-2917-8*) Warren Gorham & Lamont.

McKee, Wilma. Heritage Celebrations: A Guide to Celebrating the History of Your Church. LC 93-73915. 100p. 1994. pap. 4.95 (*0-87303-219-5*) Faith & Life.

McKeegan, David, jt. auth. see Whitney, Norman.

McKeehan, Julie, jt. auth. see Rhodes, Neil.

McKeehan, Louis W. Yale Science: The First Hundred Years, 1701-1801. 1947. 59.50 (*0-614-00148-X*) Elliots Bks.

Mckeen, J. D. & Smith, H. R. Managing Information Systems: Strategies for Action. 374p. 1996. 70.00 (*0-471-96516-2*) Wiley.

McKeen, John, jt. auth. see Ladouceur, Norman.

McKeen, W. E., ed. Blue Mold of Tobacco. LC 88-83539. (Illus.). 288p. 1989. 47.00 (*0-89054-097-7*) Am Phytopathol Soc.

McKeen, William. The Beatles: A Bio-Bibliography. LC 89-2219. (Popular Culture Bio-Bibliographies Ser.). 191p. 1989. lib. bdg. 49.95 (*0-313-25993-3*, MBE/, Greenwood Pr) Greenwood.

— Bob Dylan: A Bio-Bibliography. LC 92-32212. (Popular Culture Bio-Bibliographies Ser.). 320p. 1993. lib. bdg. 59.95 (*0-313-27998-5*, MKY, Greenwood Pr) Greenwood.

— Hunter S. Thompson. (Twayne's United States Authors Ser.: No. 574). 144p. (C). 1991. 28.95 (*0-8057-7624-9*) Macmillan.

— Tom Wolfe. (Twayne's United States Authors Ser.). 1995. pap. 32.00 (*0-8057-4004-X*, Twyne) Mac Lib Ref.

*__McKeen, William, ed.__ Rock & Roll Is Here To Stay: An Anthology. LC 99-31759. (Illus.). 736p. 1999. text 35.00 (*0-393-04700-8*) Norton.

McKeeside, Vincent, et al. A Rising Sun: Maine Commemorates the Bicentennial of the United States Constitution. 74p. (Orig.). 1988. pap. 5.00 (*0-9621238-0-3*) Maine Commn.

McKeeve. Supernatural Power. 1990. 12.95 (*0-86694-121-5*) Omega Pubns OR.

McKeever. United States Supreme Court: A Political & Legal Analysis. LC 97-42125. 1997. 59.95 (*0-7190-4081-7*, Pub. by Manchester Univ Pr) St Martin.

— United States Supreme Court: A Political & Legal Analysis. LC 97-42125. 1997. pap. 22.50 (*0-7190-4082-5*) St Martin.

McKeever, Ann, ed. see Martel, Gloria.

McKeever, Audrey & Mickels, Kathy. Spiritual Junk Food: The Dumbing Down of Christian Youth. LC 98-83240. 256p. 1998. pap. 12.99 (*1-57921-169-0*, Pub. by WinePress Pub) BookWorld.

McKeever, Bill. Answering Mormons' Questions. 128p. 1991. pap. 7.99 (*1-55661-201-X*) Bethany Hse.

*__McKeever, Bill.__ Mormonism 101: Examining the Religion of the Latter-Day Saints. LC 99-89663. 304p. 2000. pap. 15.99 (*0-8010-1192-2*) Baker Bks.

McKeever, Bill & Johnson, E. Questions to Ask Your Mormon Friend: Effective Ways to Challenge a Mormon's Arguments Without. LC 94-16696. 192p. 1994. pap. 9.99 (*1-55661-455-1*) Bethany Hse.

McKeever, Bridget C. Hidden Addictions: A Pastoral Response to the Abuse of Legal Drugs. LC 97-37002. 96p. 1998. 29.95 (*0-7890-0266-3*, Haworth Pastrl); pap. 14.95 (*0-7890-0267-1*, Haworth Pastrl) Haworth Pr.

McKeever, Eric. Tales of the Mine Country. (Illus.). 124p. (Orig.). 1995. pap. 9.95 (*0-9643905-0-7*) E McKeever.

McKeever-Furst, Jill L. The Natural History of the Soul in Ancient Mexico. LC 95-16961. 240p. 1996. 28.50 (*0-300-06225-7*) Yale U Pr.

McKeever, George. Learn to Meditate: Journey Toward Self-Discovery. 161p. (YA). (gr. 8 up). 1998. pap. 9.95 (*1-885479-03-4*) McKeever Pubng.

McKeever, Gina W., jt. auth. see McNamara, Beth B.

*__McKeever, Gracie C.__ Dancing in the Dark. 2000. 4.50 (*1-928670-77-6*, Ennoble) Awe Struck E Bks.

McKeever, Helen C. & Greenberg, Judith E. Journal of a Revolutionary War Woman. LC 95-46727. (In Their Own Words Ser.). (Illus.). 128p. (YA). (gr. 7-11). 1996. lib. bdg. 24.00 (*0-531-11259-4*) Watts.

McKeever, Helen C., jt. auth. see Greenberg, Judith E.

McKeever, J. Ross, ed. The Community Builders Handbook (Anniversary Edition) LC 67-24963. 558p. reprint ed. pap. 173.00 (*0-608-10918-5*, 200681600060) Bks Demand.

McKeever, J. Ross, ed. see Wittausch, William K.

McKeever, James. The Future Revealed. Orig. Title: The Coming Climax of History. 320p. (C). 1982. pap. text 9.99 (*0-86694-099-5*) Omega Pubns OR.

— How to Avoid the Mark of the Beast. 24p. (C). 1990. pap. text 2.99 (*0-86694-122-3*) Omega Pubns OR.

— Is There Really Going to Be an Antichrist? 20p. (C). 1989. pap. text 2.99 (*0-86694-117-7*) Omega Pubns OR.

— Jesus for the Rest of Your Life. 20p. (C). 1989. pap. text 2.99 (*0-86694-116-9*) Omega Pubns OR.

— Only One Word. 20p. (C). 1979. pap. text 2.99 (*0-86694-001-4*) Omega Pubns OR.

— What Ever Happened to Hope? 24p. (C). 1989. pap. text 2.99 (*0-86694-115-0*) Omega Pubns OR.

— Your Key to His Kingdom. 336p. (C). 1917. text 14.99 (*0-86694-125-1*) Omega Pubns OR.

McKeever, James M. Become Like Jesus. 408p. (C). 1984. text 14.99 (*0-86694-101-0*); pap. text 9.99 (*0-86694-100-2*) Omega Pubns OR.

— Claim Your Birthright. 288p. (C). 1989. pap. text 9.99 (*0-86694-112-6*) Omega Pubns OR.

— Financial Guidance. rev. ed. 320p. (C). 1981. pap. text 9.99 (*0-931608-10-4*) Omega Pubns OR.

— How You Can Know the Will of God. 24p. (C). 1982. pap. text 2.99 (*0-86694-095-2*) Omega Pubns OR.

— It's in the Bible. 300p. (C). 1988. text 14.99 (*0-86694-109-6*); pap. text 9.99 (*0-86694-108-8*) Omega Pubns OR.

— The Knowledge of Good & Evil. 36p. (C). 1981. pap. text 2.99 (*0-86694-084-7*) Omega Pubns OR.

— The Rapture Book. 240p. (Orig.). (C). 1987. pap. text 9.99 (*0-86694-106-1*) Omega Pubns OR.

— Revelation for Laymen. 351p. (C). 1980. text 14.99 (*0-931608-08-2*); pap. text 7.95 (*0-931608-07-4*) Omega Pubns OR.

— Supernatural Power. 396p. (C). 1990. pap. text 9.99 (*0-86694-120-7*) Omega Pubns OR.

— The Victory Bible Reading Plan. 16p. (C). pap. text 1.25 (*0-86694-102-9*) Omega Pubns OR.

— Where Will You Be in 300 Years? 36p. (C). 1990. pap. text 3.99 (*0-86694-119-3*) Omega Pubns OR.

— Why Were You Created? 24p. (C). 1980. pap. text 2.99 (*0-86694-083-9*) Omega Pubns OR.

— You Can Overcome. 350p. (C). 1981. text 14.99 (*0-86694-091-X*); pap. text 9.99 (*0-86694-092-8*) Omega Pubns OR.

— Your Key to His Kingdom. 336p. (C). 1991. pap. 10.99 (*0-86694-124-X*) Omega Pubns OR.

McKeever, James M. & McKeever, Jeani. Self-Reliant Living. 420p. (C). 1994. pap. text 25.00 (*0-86694-126-6*) Omega Pubns OR.

McKeever, James M., ed. see Conus, Leon & Conus, Olga.

M

An Asterisk (*) at the beginning of an entry indicates that the title is appearing for the first time.

McKeever, James R. Apartment Development: A Strategy for Successful Decision Making. LC 74-79436. (Urban Land Institute Special Reports). 64p. reprint ed. pap. 30.00 (*0-8357-5654-8*, 202349300033) Bks Demand.

— Business Parks, Office Parks, Plazas & Centers: A Study of Development Practices & Procedures. LC 72-127217. (Urban Land Institute, Technical Bulletin Ser.: No. 65). (Illus.). 128p. reprint ed. pap. 39.70 (*0-8357-7500-3*, 201136900075) Bks Demand.

McKeever, Jeani, jt. auth. see McKeever, James M.

McKeever, Katherine. A Place for Owls: True Animal Stories. (True Animal Stories Ser.). (Illus.). 96p. (YA). (gr. 3 up). 1992. pap. 7.95 (*0-920775-24-1*, Pub. by Owl Bks) Firefly Bks Ltd.

***McKeever, Liz, ed.** ESOP Committee Guide. 136p. 2000. pap. 30.00 (*0-926902-65-2*) NCEO.

McKeever, Mairi, ed. see McKeever, S. G.

McKeever, Michael. Collecting Sports Cards. (Instant Expert Ser.). 1996. pap. 14.00 (*0-9641509-8-0*) Allian Pubng.

— Collecting Sports Memorabilia. (Instant Expert Ser.). 1996. pap. 14.00 (*0-9641509-9-9*) Allian Pubng.

— A Short History of San Diego. (Short History Ser.). (Illus.). 144p. (Orig.). 1985. pap. 12.95 (*0-938530-32-1*) Lexikos.

McKeever, Michael, jt. auth. see Green, Joel.

McKeever, Michael, jt. auth. see Kaye, Allan.

McKeever, Patrick J. Color Handbook of Skin Diseases in the Dog & Cat: A Problem-Oriented Approach to Diagnosis & Treatment. LC 99-172752. (Illus.). 288p. 1998. 59.95 (*0-8138-2983-6*) Iowa St U Pr.

McKeever, Paul E., jt. auth. see Nelson, James S.

McKeever, Robert J. Raw Judicial Power? The Supreme Court & American Society. LC 95-30875. 256p. (C). 1996. text 35.00 (*0-7190-4873-7*, Pub. by Manchester Univ Pr) St Martin.

McKeever, S. G. Paths Are Many Truth Is One: Exploring the Unity of All Religions. 2nd rev. ed. McKeever, Mairi, ed. 160p. 1998. pap. 12.95 (*1-885479-10-7*) McKeever Pubng.

— Strategy for Success: An Outline for Personal Growth. 107p. pap. 10.00 (*1-885479-00-X*) McKeever Pubng.

McKeever, S. G. & Kutt, Andrew A. America's Heroes & You. 23p. (YA). (gr. 5 up). 1995. pap. 4.95 (*1-885479-05-0*) McKeever Pubng.

McKeever, S. W. Thermoluminescence of Solids. (Cambridge Solid State Science Ser.). (Illus.). 392p. 1988. pap. text 49.95 (*0-521-36811-1*) Cambridge U Pr.

McKeever, S. W., jt. auth. see Chen, R.

McKeever, Sujantra G. Paths Are Many, Truth Is One: A Journey into the Essence of Spirituality & Religion. 150p. 1995. pap. text 9.95 (*1-885479-01-8*) McKeever Pubng.

McKeever, Susan. Ancient Rome. LC 94-24677. (DK Pockets Ser.). (Illus.). 128p. (YA). (gr. 7 up). 1995. pap. 5.95 (*1-56458-888-2*) DK Pub Inc.

— Butterflies, 2 vols. (Science Nature Guides Ser.). (Illus.). 80p. (J). (gr. 1-8). 1995. 12.95 (*1-57145-018-1*, Silver Dolph) Advantage Pubs.

— Freshwater Life. (Science Nature Guides Ser.). (Illus.). 80p. (J). (gr. 1-8). 1995. 12.95 (*1-57145-019-X*, Silver Dolph) Advantage Pubs.

McKeganey, Neil & Barnard, Marina U. AIDS, Drugs & Sexual Risk: Lives in the Balance. 160p. 1992. pap. 37.95 (*0-335-09970-X*) OpUniv Pr.

— Sex Work on the Streets: Prostitutes & Their Clients. LC 95-51048. 160p. (C). 1996. pap. 29.95 (*0-335-19400-1*) OpUniv Pr.

McKeigue, Emily, ed. see Ford, Norman.

McKeigue, Emily, ed. see Thornhill, Annette.

McKeigue, Emily, ed. see Whitney, Charlotte.

McKeith, Gillian. Dr. McKeith's 10 Steps to Perfect Health for New Mothers. 256p. 1999. pap. 16.95 (*0-87983-988-0*, Keats Publng) NTC Contemp Pub Co.

— Miracle Superfood: Wild Blue-Green Algae. (Good Health Guides Ser.). 48p. (Orig.). 1996. pap. 3.95 (*0-87983-729-2*, 37292K, Keats Publng) NTC Contemp Pub Co.

McKeithan, Daniel M. Debt to Shakespeare in Beaumont & Fletcher Plays. LC 73-128189. 240p. (C). 1970. reprint ed. 50.00 (*0-87752-070-4*) Gordian.

— Debt to Shakespeare in the Beaumont & Fletcher Plays. LC 70-126691. reprint ed. 21.50 (*0-404-04134-5*) AMS Pr.

— A Mark Twain Notebook for 1892. (Essays & Studies on American Language & Literature: Vol. 17). (Orig.). 1965. pap. 25.00 (*0-8115-0197-3*) Periodicals Srv.

— Whitman's "Song of Myself" Thirty-Four & Its Background. (Essays & Studies on American Language & Literature: Vol. 18). (Orig.). 1969. pap. 25.00 (*0-8115-0198-1*) Periodicals Srv.

McKeithen, Daniel M., ed. see Hayne, Paul H.

McKeldin, Caroline. Japanese Jive: Wacky & Wonderful Products from Japan. (Illus.). 80p. (Orig.). 1993. pap. 9.95 (*0-8348-0278-3*, Tengu Bks) Weatherhill.

— New York Smells. 1995. mass mkt. 9.99 (*0-312-95632-0*) St Martin.

McKell, Cyrus M., jt. ed. see Zeveloff, Samuel I.

McKell, Mimi, ed. see Barrell, Kay.

***McKell, William M.** Game Gourmet. LC 99-39863. 1999. write for info. (*0-9670692-0-3*) Wythe Arts Coun.

— The Game Gourmet: Recipes That Celebrate a Culinary Journey Through Mississippi. 264p. 1999. 17.95 (*1-879958-33-3*, Tradery) Wimmer Cos.

McKellar, A. R., et al, eds. Laser Spectroscopy V: Proceedings. (Optical Sciences Ser.: Vol. 30). (Illus.). 495p. 1981. 57.95 (*0-387-10914-5*) Spr-Verlag.

McKellar, Angus D. Turmoil to Triumph: The Odyssey of Captain Harris O. Machus Through Six War Devastated Countries in Search of Survival. LC 86-72281. (Illus.). 257p. 1987. 18.95 (*0-939528-00-2*) Brookside Pub.

***McKellar, Daniel P., et al.** Prognosis & Outcome Expectancy of Surgical Diseases. LC 99-27978. 465p. 1999. 85.00 (*1-57626-101-8*) Quality Med Pub.

***McKellar, Donald.** GCT & Me: Greenwood Community Theatre History. (Illus.). 300p. 1999. 35.00 (*0-87921-088-5*) Attic Pr.

McKellar, H. S. A Practical Guide to French Pronunciation. LC PC2137.. 157p. reprint ed. pap. 48.70 (*0-608-16298-1*, 202653100050) Bks Demand.

McKellar, Margaret M. Life on a Mexican Ranche. Latorre, Dolores L., ed. LC 93-42774. 1994. 38.50 (*0-934223-31-9*) Lehigh Univ Pr.

McKellar, Peter. Abnormal Psychology: Its Experience & Behavior. 352p. 1989. 49.95 (*0-415-02812-4*, A3869); pap. 14.95 (*0-415-03132-X*, A3873) Routledge.

McKellar, Robin C. Enzymes of Psychrotrophs in Raw Food. 320p. 1989. lib. bdg. 249.00 (*0-8493-6103-6*, QR121) CRC Pr.

McKellen, Ian. Acting Shakespeare. 1999. pap. write for info. (*0-14-011883-7*); pap. 18.95 (*0-670-82662-6*) Viking Penguin.

McKellips, Ann B., ed. see Youmans, J. Llewellyn.

McKellips, Roger D., ed. Northern Great Plains Rural Development Commission: Overview & Recommendation. (Illus.). 40p. (C). 1998. pap. text 20.00 (*0-7881-7464-9*) DIANE Pub.

***McKelvey.** Small Animal Anesthesia & Analgesia. 2nd ed. LC 99-25655. 1999. text 31.95 (*0-323-00273-0*) Mosby Inc.

McKelvey, et al. Hosking's Pension Schemes & Retirement Benefits. (C). 1985. 265.00 (*0-7855-4155-1*, Pub. by Witherby & Co) St Mut.

McKelvey, Blake. American Prisons: A History of Good Intentions. 2nd rev. ed. LC 75-14556. (Criminology, Law Enforcement, & Social Problems Ser.: No. 17). (Illus.). (C). 1977. 31.50 (*0-87585-704-3*) Patterson Smith.

— Rochester Institutes of Technology: A Brief History. 110p. 1984. lib. bdg. 59.95 (*0-88946-026-4*) E Mellen.

— Rochester on the Genesee: The Growth of a City. 2nd ed. LC 93-12303. (New York Classics Ser.). (Illus.). 330p. (C). 1993. pap. text 17.95 (*0-8156-2596-0*) Syracuse U Pr.

— Snow in the Cities: A History of America's Urban Response. (Illus.). 248p. (C). 1995. 50.00 (*1-878822-54-3*) Univ Rochester Pr.

McKelvey, Carole A., jt. auth. see Bascom, Barbara B.

McKelvey, Carole A., jt. auth. see Magid, Ken.

***McKelvey, Carole Conner & Boeding, Conrad J.** Children of Rage: Preventing Youth Violence after Columbine. McManus, Ed, ed. (Illus.). 350p. 2000. per. 25.00 (*0-9668302-1-0*) Human Pass Inst.

McKelvey, Charles. The African-American Movement: From Pan-Africanism to the Rainbow Coalition. LC 93-79476. 336p. (Orig.). 1994. text 38.95 (*1-882289-01-3*); pap. text 24.95 (*1-882289-00-5*) Gen Hall.

— Beyond Ethnocentrism: A Reconstruction of Marx's Concept of Science, 94. LC 90-45602. (Contributions in Sociology Ser.: No. 94). 232p. 1991. 62.95 (*0-313-27420-7*, MBD, Greenwood Pr) Greenwood.

McKelvey, David. Bobby the Mostly Silky. LC 83-73327. (Illus.). 32p. (J). (gr. 1-3). 1984. pap. 3.95 (*0-931722-27-6*) Corona Pub.

— Commander the Gander. LC 84-72455. (Illus.). 48p. (J). (gr. 4-6). 1984. pap. 3.95 (*0-931722-30-6*) Corona Pub.

— Maverick the Lucky Longhorn. (Illus.). 32p. (J). (gr. k-3). 1986. pap. 3.95 (*0-931722-47-0*); lib. bdg. 10.95 (*0-931722-48-9*) Corona Pub.

McKelvey, Dennis, tr. see Guthrie, Kari H.

***McKelvey, Diane.** Safety Handbook for Veterinary Hospital Staff. LC 99-47812. (Illus.). 130p. 1999. pap. text. write for info. (*1-58326-007-2*, AAHA Pr) Am Animal Hosp Assoc.

McKelvey, Diane & Hollingshead, K. Wayne. Small Animal Anesthesia, II. (Fundamentals Ser.: Vol. II). (Illus.). 352p. (C). (gr. 13). 1994. pap. text 33.00 (*0-8016-7961-3*, 07961) Mosby Inc.

McKelvey, Doug. Cattail, Fishscale, & Snakeskin. 45p. 1994. pap. 5.00 (*0-940895-24-2*) Cornerstone IL.

McKelvey, Douglas K. The Angel Knew Papa & the Dog. LC 95-47986. 96p. (J). (gr. 3-7). 1996. 14.95 (*0-399-23042-4*, Philomel) Peng Put Young Read.

***McKelvey, Douglas Kaine.** A Child's Christmas at St. Nicholas Circle. LC 99-36896. (Illus.). 48p. (J). 1999. 17.99 (*0-8499-5883-0*) Tommy Nelson.

McKelvey, Francis X., jt. auth. see Horonjeff, Robert.

McKelvey, G. Richard. Fisk's Homer, Willie's Catch & the Shot Heard 'Round the World: Classic Moments from Postseason Baseball, 1940-1996. LC 98-17880. (Illus.). 247p. 1998. 28.50 (*0-7864-0515-5*) McFarland & Co.

***McKelvey, G. Richard.** The MacPhails: Baseball's First Family of the Front-Office. LC 99-54849. (Illus.). 352p. 2000. 29.95 (*0-7864-0639-9*) McFarland & Co.

McKelvey, James L. George III & Lord Bute: The Leicester House Years. LC 72-96682. 161p. reprint ed. pap. 50.00 (*0-608-11985-7*, 202342300033) Bks Demand.

McKelvey, Jean T. AFL Attitudes Toward Production, 1900-1932, Vol. 2--2. LC 73-22503. (Cornell Studies in Industrial & Labor Relations: No. Vol. 2-2). 148p. 1974. lib. bdg. 49.75 (*0-8371-6375-7*, MCAP, Greenwood Pr) Greenwood.

McKelvey, Jean T., ed. The Changing Law of Fair Representation. LC 84-27831. 304p. 1985. 32.00 (*0-87546-110-7*, ILR Press); pap. text 17.95 (*0-87546-111-5*, ILR Press) Cornell U Pr.

McKelvey, Jean T., ed. see National Academy of Arbitrators, Meeting (13th, 1960, Washington, D. C.) Staff.

McKelvey, Jean T., ed. see National Academy of Arbitrators Staff.

McKelvey, John J., Jr., et al, eds. Vectors of Disease Agents: Interactions with Plants, Animals, & Men. LC 80-18676. 229p. 1980. 75.00 (*0-275-90521-7*, C0521, Praeger Pubs) Greenwood.

McKelvey, John P. Solid-State Physics for Engineering & Materials Science. LC 93-4226. 514p. (C). 1993. lib. bdg. 53.50 (*0-89464-436-X*) Krieger.

McKelvey, Kathryn. Fashion Source Book. (Illus.). 224p. (Orig.). 1996. pap. 29.95 (*0-632-03993-0*) Blackwell Sci.

— Illustrating Fashion. LC 97-8122. (Illus.). 192p. (Orig.). 1997. pap. 32.95 (*0-632-04024-6*) Blackwell Sci.

***McKelvey, KK.** Drawing for the Structural Concrete Engineer. 224p. (C). (gr. 13). 1998. pap. text 90.00 (*0-7210-0904-2*) Continuum.

McKelvey, Maureen. Evolutionary Innovation: The Business of Biotechnology. (Illus.). 334p. 1996. text 70.00 (*0-19-828996-0*) OUP.

***McKelvey, Maureen D.** Evolutionary Innovations: The Business of Biotechnology. LC 99-58420. 336p. 2000. pap. 29.95 (*0-19-829724-6*) OUP.

McKelvey, Maureen D., jt. ed. see Edquist, Charles.

***McKelvey, Peter.** Sand Forests: A Historical Perspective of the Stabilisation & Afforestation of Coastal Sands in New Zealand. LC 99-488289. (Illus.). 168p. 1999. pap. 39.95 (*0-908812-44-2*, Pub. by Canterbury Univ) Accents Pubns.

McKelvey, Peter. Steepland Forests of New Zealand: Their Conservation & Management. (Illus.). 296p. (Orig.). (C). 1995. pap. 49.95 (*0-908812-38-8*, Pub. by Canterbury Univ) Accents Pubns.

McKelvey, R., ed. Environmental & Natural Resources Mathematics. LC 85-3917. (Proceedings of Symposia in Applied Mathematics Ser.: Vol. 32). 143p. 1985. pap. 40.00 (*0-8218-0087-6*, PSAPM/32) Am Math.

McKelvey, Robert S. The Dust of Life: America's Children Abandoned in Vietnam. LC 99-22670. (Illus.). 160p. 1999. pap. text 14.95 (*0-295-97836-8*) U of Wash Pr.

McKelvey, Susan. Color for Quilters, Vol. II. (Illus.). 80p. (Orig.). 1994. 17.95 (*0-9639963-0-4*) Wallflower Designs.

— Creative Ideas for Color & Fabric. (Classic American Quilt Collection). (Illus.). 128p. 1996. text 19.95 (*0-87596-726-4*) Rodale Pr Inc.

McKelvey, Susan, jt. auth. see Cory, Pepper.

McKelvey, Susan D. Botanical Exploration of the Trans-Mississippi West, 1790-1850. LC 91-24466. (Northwest Reprints Ser.). 1200p. 1991. 99.95 (*0-87071-513-5*) Oreg St U Pr.

McKelvey, William. Outside the Box: A Book about Life. (Illus.). 110p. (Orig.). 1997. pap. 10.95 (*0-9633719-1-6*) Eclipse Pub.

McKelvey, William C. Through the Eyes & Mind of a Storyteller. LC 92-81942. (Illus.). 110p. (Orig.). 1992. pap. 10.95 (*0-9633719-0-8*) Eclipse Pub.

McKelvie, Colin. Snipe & Woodcock: Sport & Conservation. (Illus.). 224p. 1996. 37.95 (*1-85310-713-1*, Pub. by Swan Hill Pr) Voyageur Pr.

McKelvie, Roberta A. Retrieving a Living Tradition: Angelina of Montegiove. (History Ser.). 211p. 1997. pap. text 18.00 (*1-57659-131-X*) Franciscan Inst.

McKelvie, Stuart J. Vividness of Visual Imagery: Measurement, Nature, Function & Dynamics. 275p. (Orig.). (C). 1995. pap. text 30.00 (*0-913412-72-4*) Brandon Hse.

McKelvy, Charles. Baby Pictures & Other Works. unabridged ed. (Illus.). 500p. 1999. pap. 9.00 (*0-944771-25-4*) Dunery Pr.

— Clarke Barred & Other. McKelvy, Natalie, ed. 456p. 1998. pap. 8.00 (*0-944771-23-8*) Dunery Pr.

***McKelvy, Charles.** The Iceman's Path: A Ghostly Novel. unabridged ed. McKelvy, Natalie, ed. 56p. (J). (gr. 4-8). 1999. pap. 5.00 (*0-944771-26-2*) Dunery Pr.

McKelvy, Charles, ed. see McKelvy, Natalie.

McKelvy, David. Blues Harmonica Collection. 144p. 1992. per. 14.95 (*0-7935-1600-5*, 00660191) H Leonard.

McKelvy, David. Instant Harmonica: A Method for Diatonic Harmonica. (Harmonica Fun Ser.). 64p. 1989. pap. 12.95 (*0-88188-828-1*, 00850109) H Leonard.

McKelvy, David. Instant Harmonica Method. 64p. 1996. pap. 14.95 incl. audio compact disk (*0-7935-6879-X*) H Leonard.

— Instant Harmonica Pak. (Illus.). 64p. (Orig.). 1989. audio 15.95 (*0-88188-848-6*, 08720676) H Leonard.

McKelvy, James. Music for Conducting Class. 2nd ed. LC 88-82200. (Illus.). xi, 143p. 1988. pap. text 23.95 (*0-916656-26-8*, MFBK 10) Mark Foster Mus.

McKelvy, Jeffrey F., jt. ed. see Barker, Jeffery L.

McKelvy, John E., Jr Broad Reach. 223p. 1991. 20.00 (*0-9635668-0-6*) Pilot Press.

— Cruising Guide to the Nova Scotia Coast. 172p. (C). 1989. pap. 35.00 (*0-9635668-1-4*) Pilot Press.

McKelvy, John E., Jr., ed. Cruising Guide to the Nova Scotia Coast: Including Prince Edward Island, the Magdolens & Sable Island. 3rd rev. ed. (Illus.). 192p. 1999. spiral bd. 45.00 (*0-9635668-3-0*) Pilot Press.

***McKelvy, Michael.** Visual Basic 6 Desktop Applications: Exam 70-176. LC 99-61813. (MCSD Test Success Ser.). (Illus.). 448p. 1999. pap. 24.99 (*0-7821-2432-1*) Sybex.

McKelvy, Mike. Using Visual Basic 5: Special Edition. 2nd ed. LC 97-68700. 1104p. 1997. 39.99 (*0-7897-1288-1*, Pub. by Macmillan) S&S Trade.

— Using Visual Basic 4. (Illus.). 669p. 1995. 24.99 (*0-7897-0266-5*) Que.

McKelvy, Natalie. Matthew Fairlesse & Other Works. unabridged ed. 500p. 1999. pap. 9.00 (*0-944771-24-6*) Dunery Pr.

— Padma, Girl of India & Other Works. McKelvy, Charles, ed. 456p. 1998. pap. 8.00 (*0-944771-22-X*) Dunery Pr.

McKelvy, Natalie, ed. see McKelvy, Charles.

McKelway, Margaret. A World of Things to Do. Crump, Donald J., ed. (Books for World Explorers Series 8: No. 2). (Illus.). 104p. (J). 1987. lib. bdg. 12.50 (*0-87044-615-0*) Natl Geog.

McKend, H. Moving Gives Me a Stomach Ache. (Illus.). 32p. (J). (ps-8). 1988. pap. write for info. (*0-88753-178-4*) Black Moss.

McKendall, Robert R. & Stroop, William, eds. Handbook of Neurovirology. (Neurological Disease & Therapy Ser.: Vol. 27). (Illus.). 832p. 1994. text 215.00 (*0-8247-8870-2*) Dekker.

McKendree, D., ed. Barbed Wire & Rice: Poems & Songs from Japanese Prisoner-of-War Camps. (Cornell East Asia Ser.: Vol. 75). (Illus.). 212p. (Orig.). 1995. pap. 11.90 (*0-939657-75-9*, 75) Cornell East Asia Pgm.

McKendrick. Quality of Life of Lone Parents. 55.95 (*1-85972-190-7*) Ashgate Pub Co.

***McKendrick, David G., et al.** From Silicon Valley to Singapore: Location & Competitive Advantage in the Hard Disk Drive Industry. 2000. pap. 22.95 (*0-8047-4183-2*) Stanford U Pr.

McKendrick, Eddie. Sonic 3 Official Play Guide. LC 94-66340. (Illus.). 96p. 1994. pap. 12.95 (*1-55958-536-6*) Prima Pub.

McKendrick, Ewan. Force Majeure & Frustration of Contract. 2nd ed. 408p. 1995. 170.00 (*1-85044-819-1*) LLP.

— Tort. 270p. (C). 1991. 60.00 (*1-85352-799-8*, Pub. by HLT Pubns); 60.00 (*1-85352-378-X*, Pub. by HLT Pubns); pap. 60.00 (*1-85352-863-3*, Pub. by HLT Pubns) St Mut.

McKendrick, Ewan, ed. Commercial Aspects of Trusts & Fiduciary Obligations. LC 92-15521. (Illus.). 334p. 1992. text 85.00 (*0-19-825765-1*, Clarendon Pr) OUP.

McKendrick, Ewan, jt. auth. see Palmer, Norman.

McKendrick, Ewan, jt. ed. see Burrows, Andrew.

McKendrick, Ewan, jt. ed. see Palmer, Norman.

McKendrick, Jamie. The Marble Fly. 64p. 1997. pap. 11.95 (*0-19-283256-5*) OUP.

McKendrick, Melveena. Ferdinand & Isabella. LC 68-14974. (Horizon Caravel Bks.). 1544p. (YA). (gr. 7 up). 1968. lib. bdg. 15.89 (*0-06-024165-9*) HarpC Child Bks.

***McKendrick, Melveena.** Playing the King: Lope de Vega & the Limits of Conformity. LC 99-41910. (Monografias A Ser.). 256p. 2000. 75.00 (*1-85566-069-5*) Boydell & Brewer.

McKendrick, Melveena, ed. see Calderon de la Barca, Pedro.

McKendrick, S., jt. ed. see Pattie, T. S.

McKendrick, Scot. The History of Alexander the Great. LC 95-51069. (Monographs on Illuminated Manuscripts Ser.). (Illus.). 100p. 1996. 140.00 (*0-89236-371-1*, Pub. by J P Getty Trust) OUP.

McKendrick, Scot, ed. Bible Manuscripts Address Book. (Illus.). 144p. 1999. 19.95 (*0-7123-6236-3*) B23tish Library.

— Bible Manuscripts Engagement Diary 2000: Treasures of Christianity in the British Library. (Illus.). 96p. 1999. 19.95 (*0-7123-4615-5*, Pub. by B23tish Library) U of Toronto Pr.

McKendrick, Scot, jt. ed. see Brown, Michelle P.

McKendry, Maryann, jt. auth. see Double, Mary E.

McKenize, Janet. Education As a Political Issue. LC 93-3855. 314p. 1993. 72.95 (*1-85628-445-X*, Pub. by Avebry) Ashgate Pub Co.

McKenley, Yvonne. A Taste of the Caribbean. (Food Around the World Ser.). (Illus.). 48p. (J). (gr. 3-6). 1995. lib. bdg. 22.83 (*1-56847-187-4*) Raintree Steck-V.

— Taste of the Caribbean. 1995. 15.98 (*0-8172-4853-6*) Raintree Steck-V.

McKenna. Solo Speeches for under 12's. 100p. (J). (gr. 1-7). 1998. pap. 13.95 (*1-84002-013-X*, Pub. by Oberon Bks Ltd) Theatre Comm.

McKenna. Teaching Through Text. 1996. pap. 25.20 (*0-8013-1686-3*) Longman.

McKenna & O'Sullivan. Cultural Diversity in Modern Ireland. 55.95 (*1-84014-364-9*) Ashgate Pub Co.

Mckenna & University of Michigan. Conceptual Mathematics. 582p. (C). 1998. pap. text 64.00 (*0-536-01295-4*) Pearson Custom.

***McKenna & Wise.** Nursing Care of the General Pediatric Surgical Patient. 544p. 2000. 79.00 (*0-8342-1170-X*) Aspen Pub.

McKenna, jt. auth. see Brunning.

McKenna, jt. auth. see Riskin, M.

McKenna, jt. auth. see Sanders, Mick J.

McKenna & Cuneo, L.L.P. Staff, contrib. by. An Analytical Legislative History of Fdama. LC 99-168238. 518 p. 1998. 119.00 (*1-885259-56-5*) Food & Drug Law.

McKenna & Cuneo Staff. TSCA Handbook. 3rd rev. ed. LC 98-155026. 402p. 1997. pap. text 95.00 (*0-86587-566-9*, 566) Gov Insts.

McKenna & Cuneo Staff & Technology Staff. Pesticide Regulation Handbook. 513p. 1994. 110.00 (*0-471-12596-2*) Wiley.

McKenna & Cuneo Staff, et al. Pesticide Regulation Handbook. rev. ed. 1991. pap. 75.00 (*1-55840-464-3*) Exec Ent Pubns.

McKenna, A. T. Corvette. LC 98-4549. (Ultimate Cars Ser.). (J). 2000. lib. bdg. 21.35 (*1-57765-127-8*) ABDO Pub Co.

— Drag Racing. LC 97-31055. (Auto Racing Ser.). (J). 1998. lib. bdg. 14.95 (*1-56239-836-9*) ABDO Pub Co.

— Ferrari. LC 98-13021. (Ultimate Cars Ser.). (J). 1999. lib. bdg. 21.35 (*1-57765-123-5*) ABDO Pub Co.

— Formula 1 Racing. LC 97-29380. (Auto Racing Ser.). (J). 1998. pap. 14.95 (*1-56239-838-5*) ABDO Pub Co.

— Indy Racing. LC 97-46647. (Fast Tracks Ser.). (J). 1998. lib. bdg. 14.95 (*1-56239-835-0*) ABDO Pub Co.

Mckenna, A. T. Jaguar. LC 98-7297. (Ultimate Cars Ser.). 2000. lib. bdg. 21.35 (*1-57765-122-7*) ABDO Pub Co.

An Asterisk (*) at the beginning of an entry indicates that the title is appearing for the first time.

McKenna, A. T. Lamborghini. LC 98-6647. (Ultimate Cars Ser.). 2000. lib. bdg. 21.35 (*1-57765-125-1*) ABDO Pub Co.
— Mustang. LC 98-29328. (Ultimate Cars Ser.). 2000. lib. bdg. 21.35 (*1-57765-126-X*) ABDO Pub Co.
— Off Road Racing. LC 97-51445. (Fast Tracks Ser.). (J). 1998. lib. bdg. 14.95 (*1-56239-833-4*) ABDO Pub Co.
— Porsche. LC 98-29319. (Ultimate Cars Ser.). 2000. lib. bdg. 21.35 (*1-57765-124-3*) ABDO Pub Co.
— Stock Car Racing. LC 97-28477. (Auto Racing Ser.). (J). 1998. lib. bdg. 15.98 (*1-56239-837-7*) ABDO Pub Co.
— Vintage Car Racing. LC 97-38920. (Auto Racing Ser.). (J). 1998. lib. bdg. 14.98 (*1-56239-834-2*) ABDO Pub Co.
McKenna, Allen J., jt. auth. see Garwood, Thomas.
McKenna, Andrew J. Violence & Difference: Girard, Derrida, & Deconstruction. 256p. 1992. text 39.95 (*0-252-01837-0*); pap. text 15.95 (*0-252-06202-7*) U of Ill Pr.
***McKenna, Anne.** Aggressive Inline Skating. LC 98-45522. (Extreme Sports Ser.). (Illus.). 48p. (J). (gr. 4-7). 1999. 19.00 (*0-7368-0164-2*, Cpstone High Low) Capstone Pr.
— Big Air Snowboarding. LC 98-45515. (Illus.). 48p. 21.26 (*0-7368-0166-9*, Capstone Bks) Capstone Pr.
— Extreme Wakeboarding. LC 98-45517. (Illus.). 48p. 21.26 (*0-7368-0165-0*) Capstone Pr.
— Extreme Wakeboarding. 1999. 19.93 (*0-516-21782-8*) Capstone Pr.
***McKenna, Anne T.** Aggressive In-Line Skating. 1999. 19.93 (*0-516-21778-X*) Capstone Pr.
McKenna, Anne T., et al. Extreme Sports. (Illus.). 48p. 319.00 (*0-7368-0552-4*) Capstone Pr.
McKenna, Barbara. The CASE Best Book: 113 Ideas from the Nation's Award-Winning Programs. Bray, Sarah H., ed. LC 97-197515. 205p. 1997. pap. 59.00 (*0-89964-316-7*, 20156) Coun Adv & Supp Ed.
McKenna, Brian, jt. auth. see Maltby, Arthur.
McKenna, Bridget. Caught Dead. 240p. (Orig.). 1995. mass mkt. 4.99 (*0-425-14493-3*, Prime Crime) Berkley Pub.
— Dead Ahead. 208p. (Orig.). 1994. mass mkt. 4.50 (*0-425-14300-7*, Prime Crime) Berkley Pub.
McKenna, Briege. Miracles Do Happen. 1992. mass mkt. 5.99 (*0-312-92972-2*) St Martin.
— Power of the Sacraments. 32p. (Orig.). 1996. pap. 1.50 (*0-8198-5901-X*) Pauline Bks.
McKenna, Briege & Libersat, Henry. Miracles Do Happen: God Can Do the Impossible. LC 95-46595. 170p. 1987. pap. 9.99 (*0-89283-316-5*, Charis) Servant.
— Miracles Do Happen: The Best-Selling Account of One Woman's Ministry in the Church Today. 142p. 1989. pap. 22.00 (*0-86217-253-5*, Pub. by Veritas Pubns) St Mut.
Mckenna, C. J. Economics of Uncertainty. (C). 1996. text 29.50 (*0-8133-0409-1*) Westview.
McKenna, Catherine A. The Medieval Welsh Religious Lyric: Poems of the Gogynfeirdd, 1137-1282. 241p. 1991. 37.50 (*0-926689-02-9*) Ford & Bailie Pubs.
McKenna, Christine, jt. auth. see Blewett, Mary H.
McKenna, Cilla, ed. Feel It: Detached Youth Work in Action. (C). 1990. 25.00 (*0-947988-32-7*, Pub. by Wild Goose Pubns) St Mut.
McKenna, Colleen. Powerful Communication Skills: How to Communicate with Confidence. Career Press Staff, ed. LC 98-5752. 128p. 1998. pap. 10.99 (*1-56414-356-2*) Career Pr Inc.
McKenna, Colleen O. The Brightest Light. 208p. (YA). (gr. 7-9). 1992. 13.95 (*0-590-45347-5*, Scholastic Hardcover) Scholastic Inc.
— Camp Murphy. LC 92-12691. 206p. (J). (gr. 4-6). 1993. 13.95 (*0-590-45807-8*) Scholastic Inc.
— Cousins: Not Quite Sisters. 160p. (J). (gr. 4-6). 1993. pap. 2.95 (*0-590-49428-7*) Scholastic Inc.
— Cousins: Stuck in the Middle. 160p. (J). (gr. 4-6). 1993. pap. 2.95 (*0-590-49429-5*) Scholastic Inc.
— Fifth Grade: Here Comes Trouble. 144p. (J). (gr. 4-6). 1991. pap. 3.25 (*0-590-41734-7*, Apple Paperbacks) Scholastic Inc.
— Fourth Grade Is a Jinx. LC 88-23897. 176p. (J). (gr. 4-7). 1990. pap. 3.50 (*0-590-41736-3*, Apple Paperbacks) Scholastic Inc.
— Fourth Grade Is a Jinx. (J). 1989. 8.60 (*0-606-03292-4*, Pub. by Turtleback) Demco.
— Good Grief... Third Grade. LC 92-33457. 160p. (J). (gr. 2-5). 1993. 13.95 (*0-590-45123-5*) Scholastic Inc.
— Good Grief... Third Grade. LC 92-33457. 160p. (J). (gr. 4-7). 1994. pap. 2.99 (*0-590-45124-3*) Scholastic Inc.
— Merry Christmas, Miss McConnell! (J). 1990. 8.60 (*0-606-01904-9*, Pub. by Turtleback) Demco.
— Mother Murphy. 160p. (J). (gr. 4-6). 1993. pap. 2.95 (*0-590-44856-0*, Scholastic Hardcover) Scholastic Inc.
— New Friends. (Dr. Quinn, Medicine Woman Ser.: No. 1). (J). 1995. pap. 3.99 (*0-590-60372-8*) Scholastic Inc.
— Queen of the May. (Dr. Quinn, Medicine Woman Ser.: No. 02). 1996. pap. 3.99 (*0-590-60373-6*) Scholastic Inc.
— Roger Friday: Live from the Fifth Grade. LC 93-13706. 160p. (YA). (gr. 4-6). 1994. 13.95 (*0-590-46684-4*) Scholastic Inc.
— The Truth about Sixth Grade. 192p. (J). (gr. 4-6). 1992. pap. 3.50 (*0-590-44392-5*, Apple Paperbacks) Scholastic Inc.
McKenna, Colleen Oshaughnessy. Good Grief, Third Grade. LC 92-33457. 1993. 8.60 (*0-606-06417-6*, Pub. by Turtleback) Demco.
McKenna, Colleen Oshaughnessy. Valentine's Day Can Be Murder. 1997. 8.60 (*0-606-12030-0*, Pub. by Turtleback) Demco.
McKenna, Constance, ed. see Hurst, Jane.
McKenna, D. Douglas & McHenry, Jeffrey J. Positive Politics at Work. LC 93-24062. 144p. 1993. pap. 10.00 (*1-55623-879-7*, Irwn Prfssnl) McGraw-Hill Prof.
McKenna, D. L. Farewell Dublin, But Never Goodbye. 91p. (C). 1989. text 65.00 (*1-85821-011-9*, Pub. by Pentland Pr) St Mut.
McKenna, David. Love Your Work. 168p. 1990. pap. text 7.99 (*0-89693-036-X*, Victor Bks) Chariot Victor.
McKenna, David L. A Future with a History: The Wesleyan Witness of the Free Methodist Church. (Futures with a History Ser.: Vol. 1). 176p. 1995. 14.95 (*0-89367-198-3*) Light & Life Comm.
— A Future with a History: The Wesleyan Witness of the Free Methodist Church. unabridged ed. LC 95-221918. 400p. 1997. 31.95 (*0-89367-220-3*) Light & Life Comm.
— Growing Up in Christ: Realizing Our Spiritual Potential. LC 99-181064. 176p. 1998. pap. 10.99 (*0-89367-229-7*) Light & Life Comm.
— Isaiah 40-66. LC 94-180290. (Communicator's Commentary Ser.: Vol. 16B). 22.99 (*0-8499-1139-7*); pap. 14.99 (*0-8499-3563-6*) Word Pub.
— Isaiah 1-39. LC 94-180290. (Communicator's Commentary Ser.: Vol. 16A). 22.99 (*0-8499-0422-6*); pap. 14.99 (*0-8499-3562-8*) Word Pub.
— Job. (Communicator's Commentary Ser.: Vol. 12). 331p. 22.99 (*0-8499-0418-8*); pap. 14.99 (*0-8499-3551-2*) Word Pub.
— Journey Through a Bypass: The Story of an Open Heart. 93p. 1998. pap. 5.99 (*0-89367-230-0*) Light & Life Comm.
— Mark. (Communicator's Commentary Ser.: Vol. 2). 332p. 1982. 22.99 (*0-8499-0155-3*) Word Pub.
— Mark. (Mastering the Old & New Testament Ser.: Vol. 2). 1991. pap. 14.99 (*0-8499-3318-8*) Word Pub.
— What A Time to be Wesleyan! Proclaiming the Holiness Message with Passion & Purpose LC 99-18662. 152p. 1999. 14.99 (*0-8341-1769-X*) Beacon Hill.
— When Our Parents Need Us Most: Loving Care for the Aging Years. LC 93-42150. 150p. 1994. pap. 8.99 (*0-87788-902-3*, H Shaw Pubs) Waterbrook Pr.
McKenna, Dennis, jt. auth. see McKenna, Terence.
***McKenna, Diana.** One Parent Plus Kids: Leadership Manual. 128p. 1999. pap. 15.95 (*1-57921-240-9*) WinePress Pub.
McKenna, E., jt. auth. see Glendon, Ian.
McKenna, Edward, ed. The Collegeville Hymnal. 688p. 1990. text 11.95 (*0-8146-1569-4*) Liturgical Pr.
McKenna, Edward J. The Ministry of Musicians. (Ministry Ser.). 40p. (Orig.). 1981. pap. 1.95 (*0-8146-1295-4*) Liturgical Pr.
McKenna, Elizabeth P. When Work Doesn't Work Anymore: Women, Work, & Identity. 304p. 1998. pap. 12.95 (*0-385-31798-0*) Doubleday.
McKenna, Eugene & Beech, Nic. The Essence of Human Resource Management. LC 95-10434. (Essence of Management Ser.). 176p. (C). 1995. pap. text 19.95 (*0-13-076357-8*) P-H.
***McKenna, Eugene F.** Business Psychology & Organisational Behaviour: A Student's Handbook. 3rd ed. LC 99-86535. 2000. pap. write for info. (*0-86377-667-1*) Routledge.
McKenna, Eugene F. & Glendon, Ian. The Human Side of Safety. (Illus.). 304p. 1994. mass mkt. 74.95 (*0-412-40250-5*) Chapman & Hall.
McKenna, F. Raymond. Philosophical Theories of Education. LC 95-12676. 340p. (Orig.). (C). 1995. 59.50 (*0-8191-9976-1*) U Pr of Amer.
McKenna, Frank. Schooling in America. 256p. (C). 1993. per. 28.95 (*0-8403-8699-0*) Kendall-Hunt.
McKenna, Gail T. Models & Trends in Religious Education. LC 98-60277. 160p. 1998. pap. 19.95 (*0-89622-928-9*) Twenty-Third.
— Three Hundred Questions DREs Are Asking about People & Programs. 1990. pap. 8.95 (*0-8091-3185-4*) Paulist Pr.
McKenna, George. The Drama of Democracy. 3rd ed. LC 97-26801. 784p. 1997. pap. 51.56 (*0-697-32674-8*) McGraw.
— The Drama of Democracy. 3rd ed. 536p. 1998. pap., student ed. 18.75 (*0-697-32676-4*) McGraw.
— The Drama of Democracy: American Government & Politics. 2nd ed. 744p. (C). 1993. text 37.95 (*1-56134-236-X*, Dshkn McG-Hill) McGrw-H Hghr Educ.
— Guide to the Constitution: That Delicate Balance. 320p. (C). 1984. pap. 25.00 (*0-07-554649-3*) McGraw.
— Working with the Drama of Democracy. (C). 1990. per. write for info. (*0-87967-564-0*) Brown & Benchmark.
— Working with the Drama of Democracy. 2nd ed. (C). 1994. text 16.25 (*1-56134-298-X*, Dshkn McG-Hill) McGrw-H Hghr Educ.
McKenna, George & Feingold, Stanley. Taking Sides: Clashing Views on Controversial Political Issues 9Th. 10th ed. (C). 1996. text. write for info. (*0-697-35718-X*, WCB McGr Hill) McGrw-H Hghr Educ.
McKenna, George & Feingold, Stanley, eds. Taking Sides: Clashing Views on Controversial Political Issues. 9th ed. LC 94-34809. (Illus.). 416p. (C). 1995. text 13.95 (*1-56134-322-6*, Dshkn McG-Hill) McGrw-H Hghr Educ.
McKenna, George, jt. auth. see Finsterbusch, Kurt.
McKenna, George, jt. ed. see Finsterbusch, Kurt.
McKenna, George L. Art by Chance: Fortuitous Impressions. LC 89-30073. (Illus.). 96p. 1989. pap. 14.95 (*0-942614-13-5*) Nelson-Atkins.
— Prints, 1460-1995: The Collections of the Nelson-Atkins Museum of Art. LC 96-13639. (Illus.). 358p. 1997. 74.95 (*0-942614-26-7*) Nelson-Atkins.
McKenna, Gregory B. & Glotzer, Sharon C., eds. 40 Years of Entropy & the Glass Transition: Symposium Papers. (Illus.). 113p. (Orig.). (C). 1997. pap. text 40.00 (*0-7881-4509-6*) DIANE Pub.
McKenna, Gwen, ed. see Bennett, Cynthia L.
McKenna, Gwen, ed. see Haaglund, Lois F.
McKenna, Gwen, ed. see James, Will.
McKenna, Gwen, ed. see Koch, Elers.
McKenna, Gwen, ed. see Konizeski, Dick.
McKenna, Gwen, ed. see Paulson, Alan C.
McKenna, Gwen, ed. see Waitley, Douglas.
McKenna-Harmon, Kathleen M. & Harmon, Laurence C. Contemporary Apartment Marketing: Strategies & Applications. LC 92-24419. (Illus.). 236p. (Orig.). 1992. pap. text 34.95 (*0-944298-77-X*, 919) Inst Real Estate.
McKenna-Harmon, Kathleen M., jt. auth. see Harmon, Laurence C.
McKenna, Helen. Young Hickory. (J). (gr. 1-7). 1940. 6.00 (*0-87602-225-5*) Anchorage.
McKenna, Hugh. Nursing Theories & Models. (Routledge Essentials for Nurses). (Illus.). 288p. (C). 1997. 80.00 (*0-415-14222-9*); pap. 24.99 (*0-415-14223-7*) Routledge.
— Secrets of Winning at Video Poker. 32p. (Orig.). 1997. pap. 7.95 (*0-934650-18-7*) Sunnyside.
McKenna, Hugh J. Humanity. 1993. pap. 13.95 (*0-533-10563-3*) Vantage.
McKenna, Hugh P. Nursing Theories & Quality of Care. LC 94-6399. (Developments in Nursing & Health Care Ser.: Vol. 23). 272p. 1994. 72.95 (*1-85628-670-3*, Pub. by Avebry) Ashgate Pub Co.
McKenna, James. Measure for Measure: An Annotated Bibliography. Godshalk, William L., ed. (Garland Shakespeare Bibliographies Ser.). 400p. Date not set. text 60.00 (*0-8153-1500-7*) Garland.
McKenna, James & Teman, Roger, eds. ICIAM '87: Proceedings of the First International Conference on Industrial & Applied Mathematics. LC 88-61320. (Proceedings in Applied Mathematics Ser.: No. 34). xx, 380p. (C). 1988. text 63.00 (*0-89871-224-6*) Soc Indus-Appl Math.
McKenna, James A. Black Range Tales. 1991. pap. 12.00 (*0-87380-142-3*) Popular E Commerce.
— Permission Not Granted: How People Raised in Crisis-Oriented Families Carry Their Childhood Don'ts into Adulthood. LC 90-82212. (Illus.). 180p. (Orig.). 1990. pap. 10.95 (*1-878953-00-1*) Emily Pubns.
McKenna, James B., ed. see Fernandez De Figueroa, Martin.
McKenna, James J., ed. see Smith, Euclid O.
McKenna, Jamie, jt. auth. see Helfrich, Banks.
McKenna, Jill, ed. see Brice, Andrew.
McKenna, Jill, ed. see Brice, R. Andrew.
McKenna, Jill, ed. see Brice, R. Andrew & Koenen, Frank.
McKenna, Jill, ed. see Buckley, John, et al.
McKenna, Jill, ed. see Cinnamon, Gayle.
McKenna, Jill, ed. see Cohen, Ken.
McKenna, Jill, ed. see Cohen, Ken, et al.
McKenna, Jill, ed. see Corcoran, Mary & Connolly, Joe.
McKenna, Jill, ed. see Crothers, Timothy.
McKenna, Jill, ed. see Crothers, Timothy & Jones, Grant.
McKenna, Jill, ed. see Crothers, Timothy & Stanger, James.
McKenna, Jill, ed. see Flynn, John P. & Eden, Carole.
McKenna, Jill, ed. see Hartman, Shane.
McKenna, Jill, ed. see Kalwani, Sharan.
McKenna, Jill, ed. see Koenen, Frank.
McKenna, Jill, ed. see Lane, Patrick T.
McKenna, Jill, ed. see Lane, Patrick T. & Stanger, James.
McKenna, Jill, ed. see Lane, Patrick T. & Stranger, James.
McKenna, Jill, ed. see Lange, Alan.
McKenna, Jill, ed. see Lange, Alan & Lane, Susan M.
McKenna, Jill, ed. see Pease, Lisa.
McKenna, Jill, ed. see Pease, Lisa & Stranger, James.
McKenna, Jill, ed. see Pease, Lisa, et al.
McKenna, Jill, ed. see Reid, Tristan.
McKenna, Jill, ed. see Roberts, Molly.
McKenna, Jill, ed. see Roberts, Molly J.
McKenna, Jill, ed. see Roberts, Molly & Willett, Steve.
McKenna, Jill, ed. see Strack, Paul.
McKenna, Jill, ed. see Teitelbaum, Jeremy.
McKenna, Joe, ed. Joe's Magazine. 160p. 1998. pap. 45.00 (*0-9661502-0-1*, 810372) J McKenna.
McKenna, John. The Lost Village: Portrait of an Irish Village in 1925. 71p. (Orig.). 1995. reprint ed. pap. 9.95 (*1-874597-17-0*, Pub. by New Island Books) Irish Bks Media.
— Natural Alternatives to Antibiotics: Using Nature's Pharmacy to Help Fight Infections. LC 98-26253. 176p. 1999. pap. 12.95 (*0-89529-839-2*, Avery) Penguin Putnam.
McKenna, John & McKenna, Nancy. The Burning Green. 104p. (Orig.). 1996. pap. 14.00 (*0-9653517-1-8*) Wipf & Stock.
***McKenna, John & McKenna, Sally.** The Bridgestone 100 Best Places to Stay in Ireland 2000. (Illus.). 128p. 2000. pap. 14.95 (*1-874076-35-9*, Pub. by Estragon Pr Ltd) Irish Bks Media.
— 100 Best Restaurants in Ireland 2000. (Illus.). 128p. 2000. pap. 14.95 (*1-874076-34-0*, Pub. by Estragon Pr Ltd) Irish Bks Media.
McKenna, John D. & Turner, James H. Fabric Filter Baghouse I: (A Reference Text) 476p. 1993. text 85.00 (*1-882767-01-2*) ETS.
McKenna, John Emory. The Setting in Life for the Arbiter of John Philoponos, 6th Century Alexandrian Scientist. 173p. 1997. pap. 22.00 (*1-57910-090-2*) Wipf & Stock.
McKenna, John F., jt. auth. see Sikula, Andrew F.
McKenna, Jon, jt. ed. see Lindy, Julie.
McKenna, Joseph. Sign of the Stag. Ives, Edward D. & MacDougall, Pauleena M., eds. (Northeast Folklore Ser.). (Illus.). 97p. (C). 1997. pap. text. write for info. (*0-943197-24-4*) ME Folklife Ctr.
McKenna, Joseph C. Finding a Social Voice: The Church & Marxism in Africa. LC 97-8013. x, 255p. (C). 1997. 30.00 (*0-8232-1712-4*) Fordham.
— Finding a Social Voice: The Church & Marxism in Africa. LC 97-8013. (Illus.). x, 255p. (C). 1997. pap. 18.00 (*0-8232-1713-2*) Fordham.
McKenna, Judith A., ed. Structural & Other Alternatives for the Federal Courts of Appeals: Report to the U. S. Congress & the Judicial Conference of the U. S. (Illus.). 179p. (Orig.). (C). 1994. pap. text 35.00 (*0-7881-1575-8*) DIANE Pub.
McKenna, Judy, ed. see Biros, Florence W., et al.
McKenna, Judy, ed. see Perkins, Deborah L.
***McKenna, Juliet E.** The Swordsman's Oath: The Second Tale of Einarinn. 544p. 2000. mass mkt. 6.99 (*0-06-102037-0*) HarpC.
McKenna, Juliet E. The Thief's Gamble. 512p. 1999. mass mkt. 6.99 (*0-06-102036-2*) HarpC.
McKenna, K. C. Survival: A Novel of the Donner Party. 320p. (Orig.). 1994. mass mkt. 4.99 (*0-515-11405-7*, Jove) Berkley Pub.
McKenna, Katherine M. A Life of Propriety: Anne Murray Powell & Her Family, 1755-1849. 352p. 1994. 49.95 (*0-7735-1175-X*, Pub. by McG-Queens Univ Pr) CUP Services.
***McKenna, Kevin.** A Concise Guide to Canon Law: A Practical Handbook for Pastoral Ministers. 128p. 2000. pap. 10.95 (*0-87793-934-9*) Ave Maria.
McKenna, Kevin E. The Ministry of Law in the Church Today. LC 98-38658. 112p. 1999. 30.00 (*0-268-01441-8*, Pub. by U of Notre Dame Pr) Chicago Distribution Ctr.
***McKenna, Kevin E., et al, eds.** Church Finance Handbook. 368p. (C). 2000. 18.00 (*0-943616-80-8*) Canon Law Soc.
Mckenna, Kim D., jt. auth. see Sanders, Mick J.
***Mckenna, Kristine.** Strictly the High Points: A Collection of Interviews. 2000. pap. 14.95 (*1-56097-417-6*, Pub. by Fantagraph Bks) Seven Hills Bk.
Mckenna, Kristine, jt. auth. see Hopps, Walter.
McKenna, Lambert. The Social Teachings of James Connolly. 104p. 1989. pap. 22.00 (*1-85390-133-4*, Pub. by Veritas Pubns) St Mut.
McKenna, Laura, tr. see Godard, Alex.
McKenna, Laura, tr. see Hasler, Eveline.
McKenna, Laura, tr. see Holzwarth, Werner.
McKenna, Laura, tr. see Keselman, Gabiela.
McKenna, Lesley. Fantastic Book of Snowboarding. LC 97-35115. (Fantastic Book of Ser.). (Illus.). 32p. (J). (gr. 4-7). 1998. 10.95 (*0-7613-0649-8*, Copper Beech Bks) Millbrook Pr.
***McKenna, Lesley.** Fantastic Book of Snowboarding. LC 97-35115. (Fantastic Book of Ser.). (Illus.). 40p. (J). (gr. 4-7). 1998. lib. bdg. 22.40 (*0-7613-0717-6*, Copper Beech Bks) Millbrook Pr.
McKenna, Lindsay. Brave Heart. (Historical Ser.). 1993. per. 3.99 (*0-373-28771-2*, 1-28771-3) Harlequin Bks.
***McKenna, Lindsay.** Brave Heart. 2000. mass mkt. 4.50 (*0-373-82239-1*, 1-82239-4) Harlequin Bks.
McKenna, Lindsay. Captive of Fate. (Men at Work Ser.: Vol. 24). 1998. mass mkt. 4.50 (*0-373-81036-9*, 1-81036-5) Harlequin Bks.
— Commando: Morgan's Mercenaries. (Special Edition Ser.). 1993. per. 3.50 (*0-373-09830-8*, 5-09830-6) Silhouette.
***McKenna, Lindsay.** Corazon Perdido. Vol. 222. (SPA.). 2000. per. 3.50 (*0-373-35352-9*) S&S Trade.
McKenna, Lindsay. The Cougar: Cowboys of the Southwest. 1998. per. 4.25 (*0-373-24179-8*, 1-24179-3) Silhouette.
— Countdown. 1994. per. 3.50 (*0-373-09890-1*, 5-09890-0) Harlequin Bks.
— Dangerous Alliance. 1994. per. 3.50 (*0-373-09884-7*) Silhouette.
— Hangar 13. (Shadows Ser.). 1994. per. 3.50 (*0-373-27027-5*, 5-27027-7) Silhouette.
— Heart of the Eagle. (Western Lovers Ser.). 1995. per. 3.99 (*0-373-88542-3*, 1-88542-5) Harlequin Bks.
— Heart of the Hunter: Morgan's Mercenaries: The Hunters. (Special Edition Ser.: No. 1214). 1998. per. 4.25 (*0-373-24214-X*, 1-24214-8) Silhouette.
— Heart of the Wolf. (Special Edition Ser.). 1993. per. 3.50 (*0-373-09818-9*, 5-09818-1) Silhouette.
— Hunter's Pride: Morgan's Mercenaries: The Hunters. (Special Edition Ser.: No. 1274). 1999. per. 4.25 (*0-373-24274-3*, 1-24274-2) Silhouette.
— Hunter's Woman: That Special Woman! (Special Edition Ser.: Bk. 1255). 1999. per. 4.25 (*0-373-24255-7*, 1-24255-1) Silhouette.
— King of Swords. (Historical Ser.: No. 725). 1992. per. 3.99 (*0-373-28725-9*, 1-28725-9) Harlequin Bks.
***McKenna, Lindsay.** Love & Glory: A Question of Honor, No Surrender, Return of a Hero. 2000. per. 6.99 (*0-373-20173-7*, 1-20173-0) Harlequin Bks.
— A Man Alone. (Special Edition Ser.: Bk. 1357). 2000. mass mkt. 4.50 (*0-373-24357-X*, 1-24357-5) Silhouette.
— Man of Passion. (Special Edition Ser.: Bk. 1334). 2000. mass mkt. 4.50 (*0-373-24334-0*, 1-24334-4) Silhouette.
McKenna, Lindsay. Morgan's Marriage. 1996. per. 3.75 (*0-373-24005-8*, 1-24005-0) Silhouette.
— Morgan's Mercenaries: Heart of the Jaguar. 1999. pap. 5.99 (*0-373-48371-6*, 1-48371-8) Silhouette.
***McKenna, Lindsay.** Morgan's Mercenaries: Heart of the Warrior. (Silhouette Ser.). 2000. mass mkt. 5.99 (*0-373-48416-X*, 1-48416-1) Harlequin Bks.
McKenna, Lindsay. Morgan's Rescue. 1995. per. 3.75 (*0-373-23998-X*, 1-23998-7) Silhouette.
— Morgan's Son: Morgan's Mercenaries: Love & Danger. 1995. mass mkt. 3.75 (*0-373-09992-4*, 1-09992-8) Silhouette.
— Morgan's Wife. 1995. per. 3.75 (*0-373-09986-X*, 1-09986-0) Silhouette.
— No Quarter Given. (Special Ser.: No. 667). 1991. per. 3.25 (*0-373-09667-4*) Silhouette.
— Off Limits. (Special Edition Ser.: No. 733). 1992. mass mkt. 3.39 (*0-373-09733-6*, 5-09733-2) Harlequin Bks.

An Asterisk (*) at the beginning of an entry indicates that the title is appearing for the first time.

— One Man's War. (Special Edition Ser.: No. 727). 1992. mass mkt. 3.39 (*0-373-09727-1*, 5-09727-4) Harlequin Bks.

— Point of Departure: Women of Glory, That Special Woman. (Special Edition Ser.). 1993. per. 3.50 (*0-373-09853-7*, 5-09853-8) Silhouette.

— Ride the Tiger. (Special Edition Ser.: No. 721). 1992. mass mkt. 3.29 (*0-373-09721-2*, 5-09721-7) Harlequin Bks.

— The Rogue. (Special Edition Ser.). 1993. per. 3.50 (*0-373-09824-3*, 5-09824-9) Silhouette.

— Shadows & Light. (Special Edition Ser.). 1994. per. 3.50 (*0-373-09878-2*, 5-09878-5) Silhouette.

— Stallion Tamer. 1998. per. 4.25 (*0-373-24173-9*, 1-24173-6) Silhouette.

— Too near the Fire. (Men Made in America Ser.). 1995. per. 3.99 (*0-373-45185-7*, 1-45185-5) Harlequin Bks.

Mckenna, Lindsay. The Untamed Hunter: Morgan's Mercenaries: The Hunters. (Desire Ser.). 2000. per. 3.75 (*0-373-76262-3*, 1-76262-4) Silhouette.

McKenna, Lindsay. White Wolf. 1997. per. 3.99 (*0-373-24135-6*, 1-24135-5) Silhouette.

— Wild Mustang Woman. 1998. per. 4.25 (*0-373-24166-6*, 1-24166-0) Silhouette.

McKenna, Lindsay, et al. Lovers Dark & Dangerous. 1994. mass mkt. 4.99 (*0-373-48310-4*, 1-48310-6) Harlequin Bks.

McKenna, M. Olga. Micmac by Choice: Elsie Sark - An Island Legend. 194p. 1990. pap. 16.95 (*0-88780-077-7*) Formac Publ Co.

McKenna, Malcolm, et al. Classification of Mammals: Above the Species Level. LC 97-30063. 631p. 1998. 175.00 (*0-231-11012-X*) Col U Pr.

***McKenna, Malcolm C. & Bell, Susan K.** Classification of Mammals: Above the Species Level. 640p. 2000. pap. text 50.00 (*0-231-11013-8*) Col U Pr.

McKenna, Mark. The Captive Republic: A History of Republicanism in Australia 1788-1996. (Studies in Australian History). (Illus.). 348p. (C). 1997. text 64.95 (*0-521-57258-4*) Cambridge U Pr.

***McKenna, Marlene.** When Hope Never Dies: One Woman's Remarkable Recovery from Cancer; And the Natural Program That Saved Her Life. 2000. pap. text 14.00 (*1-57566-509-3*, Knsington) Kensgtn Pub Corp.

McKenna, Mary C. & Edmond, John, eds. Energy Metabolism in Brain Function & Neuroprotection Vol. 20, Nos. 4-5: Symposium, Waterville Valley, N.H., July 1997. (Developmental Neuroscience Ser.: Vol. 20, Nos. 4-5). (Illus.). 230p. 1998. pap. 49.00 (*3-8055-6691-3*) S Karger.

McKenna, Mary O. Charity Alive: Sisters of Charity of Saint Vincent de Paul, Halifax, 1950-1980. LC 97-52801. 1998. 54.00 (*0-7618-1041-2*) U Pr of Amer.

— Charity Alive: Sisters of Charity of Saint Vincent de Paul, Halifax, 1950-1980. LC 97-44729. 408p. (C). 1998. 54.00 (*0-7618-0986-4*) U Pr of Amer.

McKenna, Maureen A. Julia Thecla. (Illus.). 62p. 1986. pap. 15.00 (*0-89792-108-9*) Ill St Museum.

McKenna, Maurice, ed. Fond du Lac County: Past & Present, 2 vols., Set. (Illus.). 1114p. 1995. reprint ed. lib. bdg. 109.00 (*0-8328-5143-4*) Higginson Bk Co.

McKenna, Megan. Advent, Christmas, Epiphany: Stories & Reflections in the Sunday Readings. LC 98-7761. 256p. 1998. pap. 14.00 (*1-57075-218-4*) Orbis Bks.

— Advent, Christmas, Epiphany: The Daily Readings. LC 98-28983. 220p. 1998. pap. 12.00 (*1-57075-215-X*) Orbis Bks.

— Advent, Christmas, Epiphany: The Daily Readings - The Sunday Readings & Feast Days. 220p. 1998. boxed set 23.00 (*1-57075-220-6*) Orbis Bks.

— Angels Unawares. LC 95-25015. 176p. (Orig.). 1995. pap. 12.00 (*1-57075-030-0*) Orbis Bks.

— Blessings & Woes. LC 98-27151. (Illus.). 246p. 1999. pap. 13.00 (*1-57075-221-4*) Orbis Bks.

— Dancing with Angels: Selected Poems. LC 96-51046. 132p. 1997. pap. 13.95 (*0-8264-1044-8*) Continuum.

— Leave Her Alone. LC 99-31689. 240p. 1999. pap. 14.00 (*1-57075-265-6*) Orbis Bks.

— Lent, 2 vols. Incl. Vol. II. Lent: The Daily Readings: Reflections & Stories. LC 96-26922. 200p. (Orig.). 1996. pap. 13.00 (*1-57075-103-X*); Vol. II. The Sunday Readings Reflections & Stories. LC 96-26922. 176p. (Orig.). 1996. pap. 13.00 (*1-57075-102-1*); LC 96-45059. 1996. 23.00 (*1-57075-104-8*) Orbis Bks.

— Mary: Shadow of Grace. LC 94-46242. 176p. (Orig.). 1995. pap. 12.00 (*0-88344-996-X*) Orbis Bks.

***McKenna, Megan.** Mary, Mother of All Nations. (Illus.). 144p. 2000. pap. 20.00 (*1-57075-325-3*) Orbis Bks.

McKenna, Megan. Not Counting Women & Children: Neglected Stories from the Bible. 232p. 1994. pap. 27.00 (*0-86012-230-1*, Pub. by Srch Pr) St Mut.

McKenna, Megan. Not Counting Women & Children: Some Forgotten Stories from the Bible. LC 93-36627. 146p. (Orig.). 1994. pap. 12.00 (*0-88344-946-3*) Orbis Bks.

— Parables: The Arrows of God. LC 93-36627. 176p. (Orig.). 1994. pap. 12.00 (*0-88344-975-7*) Orbis Bks.

— Parables: The Arrows of God. 192p. (Orig.). 1994. pap. 50.00 (*0-86012-237-9*, Pub. by Srch Pr) St Mut.

— Rites of Justice: The Sacraments & Liturgy As Ethical Imperatives. LC 96-49914. 192p. (Orig.). 1997. pap. 13.00 (*1-57075-108-0*) Orbis Bks.

McKenna, Megan & Cowan, Tony. Keepers of the Story: Oral Traditions in Religion. LC 97-25239. 192p. (Orig.). 1997. pap. 13.00 (*1-57075-145-5*) Orbis Bks.

McKenna, Michael C. & Robinson, Richard D. Teaching Through Text: A Content Literacy Approach to Content Area Reading. LC 92-27870. 366p. (C). 1993. pap. text 55.00 (*0-8013-0584-5*, 79560) Longman.

— Teaching Through Text: A Content Literacy Approach to Content Area Reading. 2nd ed. LC 96-10446. 368p. (C). 1996. text 74.00 (*0-8013-1648-0*) Longman.

McKenna, Michael C., jt. ed. see Miller, John W.

McKenna, Nancy, jt. auth. see McKenna, John.

McKenna, Neil. On the Margins: Men Who Have Sex with Men in the Developing World. 112p. 1997. pap. 19.95 (*1-870670-37-X*, Pub. by Panos Bks) Paul & Co Pubs.

McKenna, P. M. Cemented Hard Carbide & Gear Making. (Technical Papers: Vol. P129.06). (Illus.). 14p. 1947. pap. text 30.00 (*1-55589-154-3*) AGMA.

McKenna, Pat. Category-Specific Names Test. 1998. pap. 295.00 (*0-86377-458-X*, Pub. by Psychol Pr) Taylor & Francis.

McKenna, Paul. A History & Bibliography of a Roycroft Printing Shop. 2nd ed. LC 81-86148. (Illus.). 200p. 1995. 35.00 (*0-939892-00-6*) Tona Graphics.

— The Hypnotic World of Paul McKenna. 224p. (Orig.). 1993. pap. 11.95 (*0-571-16802-7*) Faber & Faber.

— Paranormal World of Paul McKenna. 192p. 1997. pap. 9.95 (*0-571-19245-9*) Faber & Faber.

McKenna, Pete. Nightshift. 128p. 1996. pap. 12.95 (*1-898927-40-5*, Pub. by S T Pubng) AK Pr Dist.

— Those Fiendish Years: Interview with a Sex Fiend. (Illus.). 128p. (Orig.). 1998. pap. 26.95 (*1-898927-55-3*, Pub. by S T Pubng) AK Pr Dist.

McKenna, Peter, jt. auth. see Kirk, John M.

McKenna, Praticia, jt. ed. see Walsh, Sharon T.

McKenna, R. B., jt. auth. see Yong, C. F.

McKenna, Ralph J. The Undergraduate Reasearcher's Handbook: Creative Experimentation in Social Psychology. LC 94-32870. 300p. 1995. pap. text 44.00 (*0-205-15537-5*) Allyn.

McKenna, Regis. Big Blue. 1992. pap. write for info. (*0-201-52342-6*) Addison-Wesley.

— Real Time: Preparing for the Age of the Never Satisfied Customer. LC 97-12475. 224p. 1999. 19.95 (*0-87584-794-3*) Harvard Busn.

— Real Time: Preparing for the Age of the Never Satisfied Customer. 224p. 1999. pap. 12.95 (*0-87584-934-2*) Harvard Busn.

— Relationship Marketing: Successful Strategies for the Age of the Customer. 256p. 1993. pap. 16.00 (*0-201-62240-8*) Addison-Wesley.

McKenna, Richard. New Eyes for the Old: The Quest for Education. 1963. 2.50 (*0-87060-019-2*, OCP 7) Syracuse U Cont Ed.

— Sand Pebbles. 1962. write for info. (*0-318-66791-6*) HarpC.

McKenna, Richard. The Sand Pebbles. 608p. 1991. reprint ed. lib. bdg. 49.95 (*0-89966-857-7*) Buccaneer Bks.

— Sand Pebbles. 2000. reprint ed. pap. 21.95 (*1-55750-446-6*) Naval Inst Pr.

McKenna, Richard P., jt. auth. see Ayres, Robert U.

McKenna, Robert G., jt. ed. see Moore, Thomas M.

McKenna, Robert J., Sr. & Murphy, Gerald P., eds. Cancer Surgery. LC 93-25474. (Illus.). 829p. reprint ed. pap. 200.00 (*0-608-07182-X*, 206740700009) Bks Demand.

McKenna, Robert P., jt. auth. see Ayres, Robert U.

McKenna, Rosemary, jt. ed. see Atchity, Kenneth J.

McKenna, Sally, jt. auth. see McKenna, John.

Mckenna, Sean, ed. see Avery, Robert H.

***McKenna, Shaun.** Contemporary Scenes for Young Men. (Illus.). 86p. 2000. pap. 14.95 (*1-84002-141-1*) Theatre Comm.

— Contemporary Scenes for Young Women. 86p. 2000. pap. 14.95 (*1-84002-130-6*) Theatre Comm.

McKenna, Shaun, ed. Classics for Teenagers. 104p. 1999. pap. 13.95 (*1-84002-023-7*) Theatre Comm.

McKenna-Siddals, Mary. Millions of Snowflakes. LC 97-47733. (Illus.). (J). (ps-k). 1998. 13.00 (*0-395-71531-8*, Clarion Bks) HM.

McKenna, Stephen. Pursuit of Painting. 1997. pap. text 39.50 (*0-85331-706-2*, Pub. by Lund Humphries) Antique Collect.

— Tales of Intrigue & Revenge. LC 72-128738. (Short Story Index Reprint Ser.). 1977. 19.95 (*0-8369-3629-9*) Ayer.

McKenna, Stephen, tr. see Augustine, Saint.

McKenna, Stephen, tr. see Hilary of Poitiers.

McKenna, Steven R. Robert Henryson's Tragic Vision. LC 93-18358. (American University Studies, IV, English Language & Literature: Vol. 171). 221p. (C). 1994. text 39.95 (*0-8204-2265-7*) P Lang Pubng.

McKenna, Steven R., ed. Selected Essays on Scottish Language & Literature: A Festschrift in Honor of Allan H. MacLaine. LC 92-24194. (Illus.). 284p. 1992. text 89.95 (*0-7734-9597-5*) E Mellen.

McKenna, Tate. Legacy of Love - Captive Desire, 2 vols. in 1. 368p. 1992. pap. text, mass mkt. 4.50 (*0-8439-3326-7*) Dorchester Pub Co.

McKenna, Ted, jt. auth. see Oliverson, Ray.

McKenna, Terence. The Archaic Revival: Speculations on Psychedelic Mushrooms, the Amazon, Virtual Reality, UFOs, Evolution, Shamanism, the Rebirth of the Goddess & the End of History. LC 91-55290. (Illus.). 288p. 1992. pap. 17.00 (*0-06-250613-7*, Pub. by Harper SF) HarpC.

— Food of the Gods. 336p. 1993. pap. 16.95 (*0-553-37130-4*) Bantam.

— Synesthesia. limited ed. (Illus.). 40p. 1992. 1500.00 (*1-887123-04-0*) Granary Bks.

— True Hallucinations: Being an Account of the Author's Extraordinary Adventures in the Devil's Paradise. LC 91-58904. 256p. 1994. pap. 16.00 (*0-06-250652-8*, Pub. by Harper SF) HarpC.

McKenna, Terence, reader. History Ends in Green. 1992. 39.95 incl. audio (*1-56176-907-X*) Mystic Fire.

McKenna, Terence & McKenna, Dennis. The Invisible Landscape: Mind, Hallucinogens, & the I Ching. LC 93-5195. 256p. 1994. pap. 16.00 (*0-06-250635-8*, Pub. by Harper SF) HarpC.

McKenna, Terence & McLuhan, Marshall. Surfing on Finnegan's Wake. unabridged ed. (C). 1995. 18.95 incl. audio (*1-56176-911-8*, MYS-76911) Mystic Fire.

Mckenna, Teresa. Migrant Song: Politics & Process in Contemporary Chicano Literature. LC 96-25379. 1997. 27.50 (*0-292-76518-5*); pap. text 12.95 (*0-292-75188-5*) U of Tex Pr.

McKenna, Teresa & Ortiz, Flora I., eds. The Broken Web: The Educational Experience of Hispanic American Women. (Mujer Latina Ser.). 262p. 1989. pap. 23.95 (*0-942177-00-2*) Floricanto Pr.

McKenna, Terrence. Archaic Revival: Collected Essays & Conversations. 1991. pap. 14.95 (*0-8065-1240-7*, Citadel Pr) Carol Pub Group.

***McKenna, Terrence.** True Hallucinations & the Archaic Revival. 528p. 1998. 9.98 (*1-56731-289-6*, MJF Bks) Fine Comms.

McKenna, Theresa. The Hidden Mission Field: Caring for Single Parent Families in the 21st Century. LC 98-89461. 158p. 1999. pap. 12.95 (*1-57921-171-2*, Pub. by WinePress Pub) BookWorld.

***McKenna, Theresa.** One Parent Plus Kids: Children's Curriculum. 144p. 1999. pap. 14.95 (*1-57921-241-7*) WinePress Pub.

— One Parent Plus Kids: Parent's Workbook. Nylander, Lucy, ed. 80p. 1999. pap., wbk. ed. 11.95 (*1-57921-242-5*) WinePress Pub.

Mckenna, Thomas. Manhattan North Homicide. 1997. mass mkt. 5.99 (*0-312-96009-3*) St Martin.

McKenna, Thomas. Praying with Vincent de Paul. Koch, Carl, ed. (Companions for the Journey Ser.). (Illus.). 120p. (Orig.). 1994. pap. 8.95 (*0-88489-316-2*) St Marys.

McKenna, Thomas, et al, eds. Single Neuron Computation. (Neural Networks: Foundations to Applications Ser.). (Illus.). 644p. 1992. text 71.00 (*0-12-484815-X*) Acad Pr.

McKenna, Thomas M. Muslim Rulers & Rebels: Everyday Politics & Armed Separatism in the Southern Philippines. LC 97-49422. (Comparative Studies on Muslim Societies). 343p. 1998. 50.00 (*0-520-21015-8*, Pub. by U CA Pr); pap. 20.00 (*0-520-21016-6*, Pub. by U CA Pr) Cal Prin Full Svc.

McKenna, Tom. The Automotive Computer. Gorham, Kelly, ed. 18p. (YA). (gr. 10 up). 1990. pap., wbk. ed. 7.00 (*0-614-22215-X*, A27) Bergwall.

— Port Fuel Injection. 24p. 1988. pap., wbk. ed. 7.00 (*0-8064-0875-8*, A21) Bergwall.

McKenna, Virginia. Back to the Blue. LC 97-34229. (Born Free Wildlife Ser.). (Illus.). 40p. (J). (gr. 3-6). 1998. lib. bdg. 21.40 (*0-7613-0409-6*, Copper Beech Bks) Millbrook Pr.

McKenna, Wendy, jt. auth. see Kessler, Suzanne J.

McKenna, William, et al, eds. Apriori & World: European Contributions to Husserlian Phenomenology. (Martinus Nijhoff Philosophy: No. 2). 254p. 1981. lib. bdg. 126.50 (*90-247-2375-2*, Pub. by M Nijhoff) Kluwer Academic.

McKenna, William R. Husserl's Introduction to Phenomenology. 248p. 1982. lib. bdg. 135.00 (*90-247-2665-4*, Pub. by M Nijhoff) Kluwer Academic.

McKenna, William R. & Evans, J. Claude, eds. Derrida & Phenomenology. LC 95-20755. (Contributions to Phenomenology Ser.: Vol. 20). 224p. (C). 1995. text 110.50 (*0-7923-3730-1*) Kluwer Academic.

***McKenna/Kaesler.** Key to the Past. 2001. pap. write for info. (*0-534-52029-4*) Thomson Learn.

Mckenney. Waves of Change. 192p. 1995. 29.95 (*0-07-103600-8*) McGraw.

McKenney & Hall. Indian Tribes of North America with Biographical Sketches & Anecdotes of the Principal Chiefs, 3 vols., Set. 1974. 275.00 (*0-685-38426-8*) Scholarly.

McKenney, C. Ross & Kendall, David L. Language of the Forest. LC 96-1429. (Illus.). 158p. 1996. reprint ed. write for info. (*0-945980-55-8*) Nrth Country Pr.

McKenney, Charles E. & Long, George F., III. Federal Unfair Competition: Lanham Act s43(a) LC 89-32831. (IP Ser.). 1989. ring bd. 140.00 (*0-87632-640-8*) West Group.

Mckenney, Gerald P., ed. see Sande, Jonathan R.

McKenney, James B. Standard of Care: California Edition. Chaffee, Paul et al, eds. (Illus.). 165p. 1994. per. 19.50 (*1-885104-00-6*) Prof Pubng.

McKenney, James L., et al. Waves of Change: Business Revolution Through Information Technology. LC 94-3471. 256p. 1995. 29.95 (*0-87584-564-9*) Harvard Busn.

McKenney, Joe, jt. auth. see Hirshberg, Al.

McKenney, Kenneth. Changeling. 272p. 1985. pap. 3.50 (*0-380-89686-9*, Avon Bks) Morrow Avon.

McKenney, Mark G., et al. Understanding Surgical Disease: The Miami Manual of Surgery. LC 97-33685. 447p. 1997. 59.95 (*0-316-56001-4*, Little Brwn Med Div) Lppncott W & W.

McKenney, Ruth. Industrial Valley. (Literature of American Labor Ser.). 408p. 1992. reprint ed. pap. text 17.95 (*0-87546-183-2*, ILR Press) Cornell U Pr.

— Industrial Valley. 1993. reprint ed. lib. bdg. 89.00 (*0-7812-5389-6*) Rprt Serv.

— My Sister Eileen. 1993. reprint ed. lib. bdg. 89.00 (*0-7812-5388-8*) Rprt Serv.

McKenney, Thomas L. Memoirs, Official & Personal. LC 72-94789. (Bison Bk.: BB565). (Illus.). 368p. reprint ed. pap. 114.10 (*0-7837-6023-X*, 204583500008) Bks Demand.

— Sketches of a Tour to the Lakes: Chippeway Indians & the Treaty of Fond Du Lac. (Illus.). 1959. reprint ed. 25.00 (*0-87018-042-8*) Ross.

McKenney, Thomas L., jt. auth. see Newman, Marc.

McKenney, Tom. The Deadly Deception: Freemasonry Exposed by One of Its Top Leaders. LC 88-81728. 160p. (Orig.). 1988. pap. 9.99 (*0-910311-54-4*) Huntington Hse.

— Please Tell Me: Questions People Ask about Free Masonry - & the Answers. LC 94-75443. 224p. 1994. pap. 10.99 (*1-56384-013-8*) Huntington Hse.

McKenney, Tom C. Come & Live. LC 84-242781. (Illus.). 167p. 1981. pap. 4.95 (*0-934527-00-8*) Words Living Minis.

— Come & Live. LC 84-242781. (Illus.). 167p. 1982. 7.95 (*0-934527-01-6*) Words Living Minis.

— Holidays & Holy Days. (Illus.). 32p. (Orig.). 1987. pap. 2.50 (*0-934527-07-5*) Words Living Minis.

— Live Free. LC 84-91415. (Illus.). 317p. 1985. 12.95 (*0-934527-04-0*); pap. 8.95 (*0-934527-06-7*) Words Living Minis.

— So You're Going to Haiti? LC 88-50163. (Illus.). 56p. (Orig.). 1990. pap. 3.00 (*0-934527-08-3*) Words Living Minis.

— Trouble at the Glory Barn. LC 85-51173. (Illus.). 127p. (Orig.). 1985. pap. 6.95 (*0-934527-05-9*) Words Living Minis.

McKenney, Tom C., jt. auth. see McCormick, Joe.

McKennon, Kelly. Multipliers, Positive Functionals, Positive-Definite Functions & Fourier-Stieltjes Transforms. LC 52-42839. (Memoirs Ser.: No. 1/111). 67p. 1971. pap. 16.00 (*0-8218-1811-2*, MEMO/1/111) Am Math.

McKennon, Kelly & Robertson, Jack M. Locally Convex Spaces. LC 75-40934. (Lecture Notes in Pure & Applied Mathematics Ser.: Vol. 15). 77p. reprint ed. pap. 30.00 (*0-608-08961-3*, 206959600005) Bks Demand.

McKenny, Betsy & Schmitt, Suzanne. RIA's Complete Guide to the Federal Estate Tax Return. 624p. (Orig.). 1996. pap. text 125.00 (*0-7811-0137-9*) Res Inst Am.

McKenny, Gerald P. To Relieve the Human Condition: Bioethics, Technology, & the Body. LC 96-45998. 279p. (C). 1997. text 59.50 (*0-7914-3473-7*); pap. text 19.95 (*0-7914-3474-5*) State U NY Pr.

McKenny, Kevin. For King or Ulster: The Landed Interests, Political Ideologies & Military Campaigns of the British Settler Armies of North-West Ulster, 1620-85. (Illus.). 240p. 1997. 42.50 (*0-7165-2567-4*, Pub. by Irish Acad Pr) Intl Spec Bk.

McKenny, Margaret & Stuntz, Daniel E. The New Savory Wild Mushroom. 3rd enl. rev. ed. (Illus.). 264p. 1987. pap. 19.95 (*0-295-96480-4*) U of Wash Pr.

McKenrick, Robert, ed. Criminal Justice Ethics: Annotated Bibliography & Guide to Sources, 2. LC 90-29186. (Research & Bibliographical Guides in Criminal Justice Ser.: No. 2). 136p. 1991. lib. bdg. 47.95 (*0-313-26791-X*, SCK, Greenwood Pr) Greenwood.

McKenry. Mosby Pharmacy. 21st ed. 2000. text 56.00 (*0-323-01005-9*) Mosby Inc.

***McKenry.** Pharmacology Patient Teaching Guides. 1999. pap. text 139.00 incl. cd-rom (*0-8151-2934-3*) Mosby Inc.

McKenry, Leda. Patient Teaching Guides in Pharmacology. LC 98-45346. (Illus.). 400p. (C). 1999. text 59.95 (*0-8151-2933-5*, 31829) Mosby Inc.

McKenry, Leda M. Mosby's Pharmacology in Nursing. (Nursing Texts Ser.). 96p. (C). (gr. 13). 1998. pap. text, student ed. 14.95 (*0-8151-4516-0*, 30650) Mosby Inc.

— Mosby's Pharmacology in Nursing Package. 20th ed. 1392p. (C). (gr. 13). 1998. text 63.00 (*0-8151-4517-9*, 30651) Mosby Inc.

McKenry, Leda M. & Salerno, Evelyn. Mosby's Pharmacology in Nursing, Vol. 20. 20th ed. LC 98-220129. (Nursing Texts Ser.). (Illus.). 1200p. (C). (gr. 13). 1997. text 56.00 (*0-8151-4515-2*, 30649) Mosby Inc.

— Mosby's Pharmacology in Nursing: Includes Testbank. 20th ed. 1998. teacher ed. write for info. (*0-8151-2132-6*) Mosby Inc.

McKenry, Michael. Phytonematology Study Guide. rev. ed. (Illus.). 64p. 1985. reprint ed. pap. text 5.00 (*0-931876-51-6*, 4045) ANR Pubns CA.

McKenry, Patrick C., et al, eds. Families & Adolescents, Vol. 2 No. 1. (Vision 2010 Ser.). (Illus.). 44p. (Orig.). (C). 1995. pap. text 19.95 (*0-916174-43-3*) Natl Coun Family.

McKenry, Patrick C. & Price, Sharon J. Families & Change: Coping with Stressful Events. 336p. (C). 1994. text 55.00 (*0-8039-4925-1*) Sage.

***McKenry, Patrick C. & Price, Sharon J.** Families & Change: Coping with Stressful Events & Transitions. 2nd ed. LC 00-9215. 2000. pap. write for info. (*0-7619-1973-2*) Sage.

Mckenry, Patrick C., jt. auth. see Price, Sharon J.

McKenty, Bob. Fallout from the Nuclear Family. 63p. (Orig.). 1994. pap. text. write for info. (*1-880764-02-4*) Northwind NJ.

McKenty, Neil. The Inside Story: A Former Jesuit Priest's Story of Self-Discovery. 160p. pap. 15.95 (*1-896754-01-5*) Shoreline.

McKenzie. Engineering a Strategic Business Revolution. (Industrial Engineering Ser.). 1996. pap. 26.95 (*0-442-01930-0*, VNR) Wiley.

McKenzie & Gordon Staff. The New World Economics. 5th ed. (C). 1994. pap. text 22.50 (*0-07-045667-4*) McGraw.

McKenzie, et al. California Real Estate Principles. 6th ed. LC 98-47266. 463p. 1998. pap. 46.67 (*0-13-082661-8*) S&S Trade.

— Understanding Your Health Study Guide. 288p. 1991. pap. 14.95 (*0-8016-6654-6*) Mosby Inc.

McKenzie, jt. auth. see Baker.

McKenzie, Jim. The Five-Gallon Bucket Book: 105 Uses & Abuses for the Ultimate Recyclable. LC 98-50478. 213p. 1999. pap. 7.95 (*0-8362-8199-3*) Andrews & McMeel.

McKenzie, A., jt. auth. see Carruth, J. A.

An Asterisk (*) at the beginning of an entry indicates that the title is appearing for the first time.

McKenzie, A. B. Axial Flow Fans & Compressors: Aerodynamic Design & Performance. LC 97-1249. (Cranfield Series in Turbomachinery). (Illus.). 280p. 1997. text 105.95 (*0-291-39850-2*, Pub. by Ashgate Pub) Ashgate Pub Co.

McKenzie, A. Dean. Mystical Mirrors: Russian Icons in the Maryhill Museum of Art. (Illus.). 64p. (Orig.). 1986. pap. 14.95 (*0-9617180-0-5*) Maryhill Art.

— Russian Icons in the Santa Barbara Museum of Art. LC 82-62426. (Illus.). 54p. (Orig.). 1982. pap. 8.25 (*0-89951-049-3*) Santa Barb Mus Art.

McKenzie, Alan. How to Draw & Sell Comic Strips. (Illus.). 144p. 1998. 22.99 (*0-89134-911-1*, North Lght Bks) F & W Pubns Inc.

McKenzie, Alan T., ed. A Grin on the Interface: Word Processing for the Academic Humanist. LC 84-2032. (Technology & the Humanities Ser.: No. 1). 94p. 1984. pap. 30.00 (*0-608-05585-9*, 206604500006) Bks Demand.

Mckenzie, Alyce M. Matthew. LC 98-11626. (Interpretation Bible Studies). 112p. 1998. pap. 7.95 (*0-664-50022-6*) Geneva Press.

McKenzie, Alyce M. Preaching Proverbs: Wisdom for the Pulpit. LC 96-17775. 160p. (Orig.). 1996. pap. 17.95 (*0-664-25653-8*) Westminster John Knox.

McKenzie, Ava A. At Home in Ireland: Cooking & Entertaining with Ava Astaire McKenzie. (Illus.). 160p. 1998. pap. text 19.95 (*1-57098-204-X*) Roberts Rinehart.

*McKenzie, B. Damon Hill's Championship Year. 1999. pap. 13.95 (*0-7472-5599-7*, Pub. by Headline Bk Pub) Trafalgar.

McKenzie, B. D., jt. auth. see Wharf, Brian.

McKenzie, Barbara, ed. Fiction's Journey: 50 Stories. 559p. (C). 1978. pap. text 32.50 (*0-15-527320-5*, Pub. by Harcourt Coll Pubs) Harcourt.

McKenzie, Bert. Fringe Benefits. (Orig.). 1995. mass mkt. 5.95 (*1-56333-354-6*, Badboy) Masquerade.

McKenzie, Beryl & Day, R. H., eds. Perceptual Development in Early Infancy: Problems & Issues. (Child Psychology Ser.). 312p. 1987. text 59.95 (*0-89859-943-1*) L Erlbaum Assocs.

McKenzie-Brown, Peter, et al. The Great Oil Age: The Petroleum Industry in Canada. (Illus.). 192p. 1993. 27.95 (*1-55059-072-3*) Temeron Bks.

McKenzie, Bruce. Employment Discrimination Redress. LC 87-92036. (Illus.). 200p. (Orig.). 1988. pap. 28.00 (*0-9619802-0-6*) Starvalley Ltd Pubs.

— Medicine & the Internet: Introducing Online Resources & Terminology. 2nd ed. LC 97-219195. (Illus.). 372p. 1997. pap. text 29.50 (*0-19-262852-6*) OUP.

McKenzie, Bruce, ed. see Kreutzer, Wolfgang.

McKenzie, Bruce A. & Zachariah, Gerald. Understanding & Using Electricity. 2nd ed. 118p. 1982. 16.25 (*0-8134-2204-3*) Interstate.

McKenzie, Bruce G. The Hammermill Guide to Desktop Publishing in Business. 248p. (Orig.). 1990. pap. 24.95 (*0-9615651-1-X*) Slawson Comm.

McKenzie, C., ed. see Dickens, Charles.

McKenzie, Carole. Quotable Politicians. 208p. 1996. 14.95 (*1-85158-652-0*, Pub. by Mainstream Pubng) Trafalgar.

— Quotable Royalty. 208p. 1996. 14.95 (*1-85158-575-3*, Pub. by Mainstream Pubng) Trafalgar.

— Quotable Scots. 160p. 1996. 14.95 (*1-85158-576-1*, Pub. by Mainstream Pubng) Trafalgar.

Mckenzie, Carole. Quotable Sex, Vol. 1. 1994. mass mkt. 4.99 (*0-312-95405-0*) St Martin.

McKenzie, Carole. Quotable Vices. 208p. 1996. 14.95 (*1-85158-636-9*, Pub. by Mainstream Pubng) Trafalgar.

— Quotable Women. 208p. 1996. 14.95 (*1-85158-494-3*, Pub. by Mainstream Pubng) Trafalgar.

McKenzie, Cecile F., et al. A Parent's Guide to Houston Private Schools. 3rd ed. 200p. 1994. 14.95 (*0-9642974-0-X*) McKenzie-Kurio.

McKenzie, Charles W. Minimum Distributions from Retirement Plans. 311p. 1993. ring bd. 49.95 (*0-9638660-0-1*) Actuarial Assocs.

McKenzie, Clancy D. & Wright, Lance S. Delayed Post Traumatic Stress Disorder from Infancy: The Two Trauma Mechanism. 248p. 1996. text 31.00 (*90-5702-500-0*, Harwood Acad Pubs); pap. text 16.00 (*90-5702-501-9*, Harwood Acad Pubs) Gordon & Breach.

Mckenzie, Colin & Stutchbury, Michael, eds. Japanese Financial Markets & the Role of the Yen. 200p. pap. text 24.95 (*1-86373-240-3*, Pub. by Allen & Unwin Pty) Paul & Co Pubs.

*McKenzie, D. F. Bibliography & the Sociology of Texts. (Illus.). 140p. 1999. 49.95 (*0-521-64258-2*); pap. 17.95 (*0-521-64495-X*) Cambridge U Pr.

McKenzie, D. G. How to Make Marriage Work. (C). 1990. pap. 40.00 (*0-86439-088-2*, Pub. by Boolarong Pubns) St Mut.

— The Mango Tree Church. 84p. (C). 1990. pap. text 30.00 (*0-86439-039-4*, Pub. by Boolarong Pubns) St Mut.

McKenzie, Dan. The Infancy of Medicine: Influence of Folklore Upon Scientific Medicine. 1977. lib. bdg. 50.00 (*0-8490-2057-3*) Gordon Pr.

McKenzie, Danny L. Paks: Parents-&-Kids Science: 24 Activities for Kids & Adults to Share. 64p. (J). (gr. 1-3). 1996. 8.99 (*0-86653-865-8*, FE3865) Fearon Teacher Aids.

*McKenzie, David. The Exoneration of the Black Hand, 1917-1953. LC 98-74964. 300p. 1998. 42.00 (*0-88033-414-2*, 516, Pub. by East Eur Monographs) Col U Pr.

McKenzie Davis, Marjorie. Leap to Freedom: True Stories of Wildlife Rescue & Rehabilitation. unabridged ed. LC 98-91743. (Illus.). viii, 312p. 1998. pap. 12.95 (*0-9667286-0-2*, 98010DAV) Burley Creek Studio.

McKenzie, Dennis J. & Betts, Richard M. Essentials of Real Estate Economics. 4th ed. LC 95-31255. 470p. 1995. 43.00 (*0-13-340431-5*) P-H.

McKenzie, Dennis J., jt. auth. see Pivar, William H.

McKenzie, Donald A. Death Notices from the Canada Christian Advocate, 1858-1872. 384p. 1992. lib. bdg. 27.50 (*0-912606-35-5*) Hunterdon Hse.

— Death Notices from The Christian Guardian, 1836-1850. 368p. 1982. lib. bdg. 25.00 (*0-912606-10-X*) Hunterdon Hse.

— Death Notices from the Christian Guardian, 1851-1860. 365p. 1984. lib. bdg. 25.00 (*0-912606-25-8*) Hunterdon Hse.

— More Notices from Methodist Papers, 1830-1857. 424p. 1986. lib. bdg. 25.00 (*0-912606-29-0*) Hunterdon Hse.

— Obituaries from Ontario's Christian Guardian, 1861-1870. 405p. 1988. lib. bdg. 25.00 (*0-912606-33-9*) Hunterdon Hse.

McKenzie, Donald A., tr. see Toletana, Luisa S.

McKenzie, Donald F. The Cambridge University Press, 1696-1712: A Bibliographical Study, 2 vols., 1. LC 66-10016. (Illus.). 466p. 1966. reprint ed. pap. 144.50 (*0-8357-7982-3*, 2030610) Bks Demand.

— The Cambridge University Press, 1696-1712: A Bibliographical Study, 2 vols., 2. LC 66-10016. (Illus.). 391p. 1966. reprint ed. pap. 121.30 (*0-8357-7983-1*, 2030610) Bks Demand.

McKenzie, Douglas, jt. auth. see Opie, Brenda.

McKenzie, Douglas H., jt. ed. see Prufer, Olaf H.

*McKenzie, E. C. 14,000 Quips & Quotes: A Collection of Motivational Thoughts & Humorous One-Liners Categorized. 584p. 2000. pap. 19.95 (*1-56563-545-0*) Hendrickson MA.

McKenzie, E. C. Fourteen Thousand Quips & Quotes for Writers & Speakers. 608p. 1995. 13.99 (*0-517-42712-5*) Random Hse Value.

McKenzie, E. D. Boy at War, Men at Peace: Former Enemy Air Combatants Meet to Remember & Reconcile. Kurtenbach, K. J. & Berger, Hans G., eds. LC 97-90735. (Illus.). 313p. 1998. write for info. (*0-533-12466-2*) Vantage.

McKenzie, Earl. A Boy Named Ossie: A Jamaican Childhood. (Caribbean Writers Ser.). (Illus.). 104p. (Orig.). (C). 1991. pap. 8.95 (*0-435-98816-6*, 98816) Heinemann.

McKenzie, Edgar C., compiled by. A Catalog of British Devotional & Religious Books in German Translation from the Reformation to 1750. (Bibliographie zur Geschichte des Pietismus: Vol. 2). xxv, 514p. 1996. lib. bdg. 183.70 (*3-11-011276-0*) De Gruyter.

McKenzie, Edna B. Selected Essays on Contemporary African-American Issues. LC 98-67455. (Illus.). 54p. 1998. pap. 12.95 (*0-9667518-0-9*) McKenzie Pubns.

McKenzie, Edna C. Freedom in the Midst of a Slave Society. (YA). 1990. 12.50 (*0-87498-003-8*) Assoc Pubs DC.

McKenzie, Edward D. The Hills of Plaistow: Family Diaries Tell of Early Years in Small N. H. Town. LC 95-131508. 100p. 1994. pap. 12.50 (*0-9617909-1-1*) E D McKenzie.

— Surly Bonds of Earth. (Illus.). 160p. 1987. 20.00 (*0-9617909-0-3*) E D McKenzie.

*McKenzie, Eleanor. Chi Kung: Cultivating Personal Energy. (Illus.). 2000. pap. 14.95 (*0-600-60091-2*) P HM.

McKenzie, Eleanor. Healing Reiki: Reunite Mind, Body & Spirit with Healing Energy. LC 98-85196. (Illus.). 128p. 1998. reprint ed. pap. 16.95 (*1-56975-162-5*) Ulysses Pr.

*McKenzie, Eleanor. Pilates at Home: An Illustrated Guide to Achieving Balance, Shape & Fitness Without Equipment. (Illus.). 128p. 2000. pap. 16.95 (*1-56975-210-9*, Pub. by Ulysses Pr) Publishers Group.

McKenzie, Elizabeth, jt. ed. see Franks, James A.

McKenzie, Elizabeth, ed. see Leslie, Eliza.

McKenzie, Ellen K. A Bowl of Mischief. LC 92-24246. 144p. (J). (gr. 4-7). 1995. 14.95 (*0-8050-2090-X*, Bks Young Read) H Holt & Co.

— The Golden Bands of Eddris. LC 97 25583. (J). (gr. 4 8). 1995. 16.95 (*0-8050-4389-6*) H Holt & Co.

— The King, the Princess, & the Tinker. LC 91-31316. (Illus.). 64p. (J). (gr. 2-4). 1995. 14.95 (*0-8050-1773-9*, Redfeather BYR) H Holt & Co.

— The Perfectly Orderly House. (J). 1995. 14.95 (*0-8050-1946-4*) H Holt & Co.

— Stargone John. LC 90-34119. (Illus.). 64p. (J). (gr. 2-4). 1992. pap. 5.95 (*0-8050-2069-1*, Redfeather BYR) H Holt & Co.

— Stargone John. LC 90-34119. (Illus.). 80p. (J). (gr. 2-4). 1995. 13.95 (*0-8050-1451-9*, Redfeather BYR) H Holt & Co.

McKenzie, Ellen K. Stargone John. (Redfeather Bks.). (J). 1992. 10.15 (*0-606-02256-2*, Pub. by Turtleback) Demco.

McKenzie, Ellen K. Taash & the Jesters. LC 92-12378. 256p. (YA). (gr. 5 up). 1995. 15.95 (*0-8050-2381-X*, Bks Young Read) H Holt & Co.

— Under the Bridge. LC 94-3415. 144p. (J). (gr. 3-7). 1996. pap. 4.95 (*0-06-440629-6*, HarpTrophy) HarpC Child Bks.

McKenzie, Ellen Kindt. Under the Bridge. LC 94-3415. 1996. 9.60 (*0-606-08893-8*, Pub. by Turtleback) Demco.

Mckenzie, Evan. Privatopia: Homeowner Associations & the Rise of Residential Private Government. 1996. pap. 16.00 (*0-300-06638-4*) Yale U Pr.

McKenzie, Evan. Privatopia: Homeowner Associations & the Rise of Residential Private Government. LC 93-37340. 248p. 1994. 32.50 (*0-300-05876-4*) Yale U Pr.

McKenzie, Fred. Hickory Hill: Family Stories of Race, Religion & Romance in an East Texas Town. unabridged ed. (Illus.). 429p. 1998. 39.95 (*0-9665788-1-3*) M & M Pr TX.

McKenzie, Fred A. The American Invaders. Bruchey, Stuart & Bruchey, Eleanor, eds. LC 76-5016. (American Business Abroad Ser.). 1976. reprint ed. 24.95 (*0-405-09284-9*) Ayer.

McKenzie, Frederick A. Korea's Fight for Freedom. LC 76-111784. reprint ed. 47.50 (*0-404-04137-X*) AMS Pr.

McKenzie, Garry D. Gondwana Six: Stratigraphy, Sedimentology, & Paleontology. (Geophysical Monograph Ser.: Vol. 41). 260p. 1987. 26.00 (*0-87590-067-4*) Am Geophysical.

— Gondwana Six: Structure, Tectonics, & Geophysics. (Geophysical Monograph Ser.: Vol. 40). 338p. 1987. 33.00 (*0-87590-064-X*) Am Geophysical.

McKenzie, Garry D. & Utgard, Russell O., eds. Man & His Physical Environment: Readings in Environmental Geology. LC 79-187012. 350p. reprint ed. pap. 108.50 (*0-608-11750-1*, 201587000097) Bks Demand.

McKenzie, George. Measuring Economic Welfare: New Methods. LC 82-4422. 208p. 1983. text 74.95 (*0-521-24862-0*) Cambridge U Pr.

McKenzie, George J., tr. see Calvez, Jean Y.

McKenzie, Gordon. Organic Unity in Coleridge. LC 75-30008. reprint ed. 27.50 (*0-404-14014-9*) AMS Pr.

McKenzie, H. S. The Law of Building & Engineering Contracts & Arbitration. 4th ed. 349p. 1988. 86.00 (*0-7021-2066-9*, Pub. by Juta & Co) Gaunt.

McKenzie, Hilda. A Ray of Sunshine. 384p. 1996. pap. 10.95 (*0-7472-4917-2*, Pub. by Headline Bk Pub) Trafalgar.

— A Ray of Sunshine. large type ed. (Large Print Ser.). 560p. 1996. 27.99 (*0-7089-3636-9*) Ulverscroft.

— The Sisters. 384p. 1994. pap. 11.95 (*0-7472-4116-3*, Pub. by Headline Bk Pub) Trafalgar.

— The Sisters. large type ed. 1994. 27.99 (*0-7089-3170-7*) Ulverscroft.

McKenzie, Ian. The Squash Workshop: A Complete Game Guide. (Illus.). 272p. 1993. 39.95 (*1-85223-115-7*, Pub. by Crolwood) Trafalgar.

McKenzie, Ian K., contrib. by. The History of Criminal Investigation. LC 95-42014. (Science Discovery Ser.). 48p. (J). (gr. 6-7). 1996. lib. bdg. 24.26 (*0-8172-4558-8*) Raintree Steck-V.

McKenzie, Ian K., ed. Law, Power & Justice in England & Wales. LC 97-38546. (Law, Power & Justice in Comparative Perspective Ser.). 240p. 1998. 65.00 (*0-275-95881-7*, Praeger Pubs) Greenwood.

McKenzie, Ian M. Manual of Acute Pain Management in Children. LC 97-3034. 1997. pap. text 35.00 (*0-443-05321-9*) Church.

McKenzie, J. Ther Dictionary of the Bible. 1995. per. 19.00 (*0-684-81913-9*) S&S Trade.

McKenzie, J. J. I Will Love Unloved: A Linguistic Analysis of Woman's Biblical Importance. 386p. (Orig.). (C). 1993. pap. text 37.50 (*0-8191-9230-9*); lib. bdg. 64.50 (*0-8191-9229-5*) U Pr of Amer.

McKenzie, J. L. Bible Dictionary: Dizionario Biblico. (ITA.). 1062p. 1981. 75.00 (*0-8288-2315-4*, M7640) Fr & Eur.

McKenzie, J. L., ed. New Testament for Spiritual Reading. 25 vols. Incl. Pt. 1. Revelation of St. John. pap. 4.95 Pt. 2. Revelation of St. John. pap. 4.95 Vol. 1, Pt. 1. Gospel According to St. Matthew. pap. 4.95 Vol. 2, Pt. 1. Gospel According to St. Matthew. pap. 4.95 Vol. 3, Pt. 1. Gospel According to St. Mark. pap. 4.95 Vol. 4, Pt. 2. Gospel According to St. Mark. pap. 4.95 (*0-8245-0337-6*); Vol. 5, Pt. 1. Gospel According to St. Luke. pap. 4.95 Vol. 6, Pt. 2. Gospel According to St. Luke. pap. 4.95 Vol. 7, Pt. 1. Gospel According to St. John. pap. 4.95 Vol. 8, Pt. 2. Gospel According to St. John. 4.95 (*0-8164-1079-8*); Vol. 9, Pt. 3. Gospel According to St. John. pap. 4.95 Vol. 10. Acts of the Apostles, Pt. 1. pap. Vol. 11. Acts of the Apostles, Pt. 2. pap. 4.95 Vol. 12. Epistle to the Romans. pap. 4.95 Vol. 13. First Epistle to the Corinthians. pap. 4.95 Vol. 14. Second Epistle to the Corinthians. pap. 4.95 (*0-8245-0347-3*); Vol. 14. Second Epistle to the Corinthians. (*0-8245-0123-3*); Vol. 15. Epistle to the Galatians. pap. 4.95 Vol. 16. Epistle to the Ephesians. pap. 4.95 Vol. 17. Epistle to the Philippians, Epistle to the Colossians. pap. 4.95 (*0-8164-1088-7*); Vol. 18. First Epistle to the Thessalonians. Second Epistle to the Thessalonians. pap. 4.95 Vol. 19. First Epistle to Timothy. Second Epistle to Timothy. pap. 4.95 Vol. 20. Epistle to Titus. Epistle to Philemon. pap. 4.95 (*0-8245-0354-6*); Vol. 20. Epistle to Titus. Epistle to Philemon. (*0-8245-0129-2*); Vol. 21. Epistle to the Hebrews, Epistle to James. pap. 4.95 Vol. 22. First Epistle to Peter. Second Epistle to Peter. pap. 4.95 Vol. 23. Epistle to Jude, Three Epistles of John. pap. 4.95 123.75 (*0-8245-0135-7*) Crossroad NY.

McKenzie, J. Steven, jt. auth. see Traynor, William J.

McKenzie, James, jt. auth. see Klein, Robert.

McKenzie, James C., jt. auth. see Klein, Robert M.

McKenzie, James E. Troop Seventeen: The Making of Mounties. (Illus.). 184p. 1992. 49.95 (*1-55059-039-1*) Temeron Bks.

— War Criminals in Canada. (Illus.). 225p. (Orig.). 1995. pap. write for info. (*1-55059-109-6*) Detselig Ents.

McKenzie, James E., jt. ed. see Sperling, Gerald B.

Mckenzie, James F. Understanding Your Health. 4th ed. 288p. (C). 1994. text, student ed. 20.62 (*0-8151-5777-0*, WCB McGr Hill) McGrw-H Hghr Educ.

McKenzie, James F. & Pinger, Robert R. An Introduction to Community Health. LC 94-20883. (Health Science Ser.). 688p. (C). 1995. pap. 46.25 (*0-06-500797-2*); pap. text, teacher ed. 10.00 (*0-06-500798-0*) Jones & Bartlett.

— An Introduction to Community Health. LC 97-21863. (Health Science Ser.). 1997. pap. 52.50 (*0-7637-0584-5*) Jones & Bartlett.

McKenzie, James F. & Smeltzer, Jan L. Planning, Implementing & Evaluating Health. 2nd ed. LC 96-9109. 336p. 1996. pap. text 57.00 (*0-205-20069-9*) Allyn.

McKenzie, James F., et al. An Introduction to Community Health. 3rd ed. LC 98-41087. 697p. 1999. 53.75 (*0-7637-0872-0*) Jones & Bartlett.

*Mckenzie, Jamie. Beyond Technology: Questioning, Research & the Information Literate School. (Illus.). 184p. 2000. pap. 20.00 (*0-9674078-2-6*) FNO Pr.

— How Teachers Learn Technology Best. vi, 171p. 1999. pap. 20.00 (*0-9674078-1-8*, Pub. by FNO Pr) BookMasters.

McKenzie, Jamieson. Tools & Technologies for Securing Your Future: Administrators at Risk. 172p. 1993. 21.95 (*1-879639-27-0*) Natl Educ Serv.

McKenzie, Jamieson A. Making Change in Education: Preparing Schools for the Future. LC 86-40485. 150p. 1987. 22.95 (*0-915253-11-9*) Wilkerson Pub Co.

— Power Learning in the Classroom. Herman, Jerry J. & Herman, Janice L., eds. LC 93-10946. (Road Maps to Success Ser.). 72p. 1993. pap. 14.95 (*0-8039-6056-5*) Corwin Pr.

— Selecting, Managing & Marketing Technologies. Herman, Jerry J. & Herman, Janice L., eds. LC 93-22349. (Road Maps to Success Ser.). 72p. 1993. pap. 14.95 (*0-8039-6054-9*) Corwin Pr.

McKenzie, Jane. Paradox - The Next Strategic Dimension: Using Conflict to Re-Energize Your Business. LC 95-43633. 1996. write for info. (*0-07-709165-5*) McGraw.

McKenzie, Jim. Antiques on the Cheap: A Savvy Dealer's Tips on Buying, Restoring & Selling. LC 98-12316. (Illus.). 224p. 1998. pap. 16.95 (*1-58017-073-0*) Storey Bks.

*McKenzie, Jimmy C. Office Machines. 5th ed. LC 99-13962. (Illus.). 313p. (C). 1999. spiral bd. 51.00 (*0-13-011643-2*) P-H.

*McKenzie, John. On Time, On Target: The World War II Memoir of a Field Artillery Paratrooper in the 82d Airborne. LC 99-58260. (Illus.). 304p. 2000. 27.95 (*0-89141-714-1*) Presidio Pr.

McKenzie, John & Goldman, Robert N. The Student Edition of Minitab for Windows Manual: Release 12. LC 98-9915. 1p. 1998. cd-rom 74.00 (*0-201-39715-3*) Addison-Wesley.

— The Student Edition of Minitab for Windows Manual: Release 12. LC 98-9915. 592p. (C). 1998. pap. text 37.00 (*0-201-39711-0*) Addison-Wesley.

*McKenzie, John & Sharpe, Lesley. The Austrian Comic Tradition: A Festschrift for W. E. Yates. LC 98-191195. 304p. 1998. 95.00 (*0-7486-1086-3*, Pub. by Edinburgh U Pr) Col U Pr.

McKenzie, John A. Ecological & Evolutionary Aspects of Insecticide Resistance. (Environmental Intelligence Unit Ser.). 250p. 1996. text 79.00 (*0-12-484825-7*) Landes Bioscience.

McKenzie, John D. Uncertain Glory: Robert E. Lee at War. (Illus.). 400p. 1996. 29.95 (*0-7818-0502-3*) Hippocrene Bks.

McKenzie, John G. Nervous Disorders & Religion: A Study of Souls in the Making. LC 79-8719. 183p. 1981. reprint ed. lib. bdg. 35.00 (*0-313-22192-8*, MCND, Greenwood Pr) Greenwood.

McKenzie, John L. A Theology of the Old Testament. LC 86-9230. 336p. 1986. reprint ed. pap. text 28.50 (*0-8191-5354-0*) U Pr of Amer.

McKenzie, John L., ed. Isaiah 2. LC 68-10565. (Anchor Bible Ser.: Vol. 20). 304p. 1969. 29.00 (*0-385-05390-8*, Anchor NY) Doubleday.

McKenzie, John R., jt. ed. see Lewis, Derek.

McKenzie, John R. P., jt. ed. see Lewis, Derek.

McKenzie-Johnstone, Henry. Mission to Mexico: A Tale of British Diplomacy in the 1820s. 300p. 1992. text 59.50 (*1-85043-555-3*, Pub. by I B T) St Martin.

McKenzie, Joy. The Best in Bridalwear Design. 1998. pap. text 24.95 (*0-7134-8037-8*, Pub. by B T B) Branford.

— The Best in Swimwear Design. (Illus.). 128p. 1998. pap. text 24.95 (*0-7134-8039-4*, Pub. by B T B) Branford.

McKenzie, Judith. Pauline Jewett: A Passion for Canada. (Illus.). 232p. 32.95 (*0-7735-1822-3*) McG-Queens Univ Pr.

McKenzie, Julie & McKenzie, Thomas. Paper Plate Arts & Crafts Activities: Week-by-Week Projects Using Paper Plates. Mitchell, Judy, ed. (Illus.). 112p. (Orig.). (J). (gr. k-3). 1996. pap., teacher ed. 10.95 (*1-57310-039-0*) Teachng & Lrning Co.

McKenzie, K., ed. Antonio Pucci: Le Noie. (Elliott Monographs: Vol. 26). 1931. 35.00 (*0-527-02629-8*) Periodicals Srv.

McKenzie, K. G., ed. Shallow Tethys Two: Proceedings of the International Symposium on Shallow Tethys 2, Wagga Wagga, 15-17 September 1986. (Illus.). 587p. (C). 1987. text 168.00 (*90-6191-647-X*, Pub. by A A Balkema) Ashgate Pub Co.

McKenzie, K. G. & Jones, P. J. Ostracoda in the Earth & Life Sciences: Proceedings of the 11th International Symposium, Warrnambool, July 1991. (Illus.). 740p. (C). 1994. 168.00 (*90-5410-306-X*, Pub. by A A Balkema) Ashgate Pub Co.

McKenzie, Kate. Two Hour Mini-Quilt Projects: Over 111 Appliqued & Pieced Designs. (Illus.). 128p. 1998. pap. 14.95 (*0-8069-8705-7*) Sterling.

Mckenzie, Kate. Two-Hour Nature Crafts. LC 96-38702. (Illus.). 128p. 1997. 24.95 (*0-8069-4293-2*) Sterling.

McKenzie, Kate. Two-Hour Nature Crafts. (Illus.). 128p 1998. pap. 14.95 (*0-8069-4294-0*) Sterling.

McKenzie, Laura. Laura McKenzie's Travel Guide to Caribbean. 1996. pap. text 14.95 (*1-887161-13-9*) Boru Pubng.

— Laura McKenzie's Travel Guide to Ireland. 1996. pap. text 14.95 (*1-887161-14-7*) Boru Pubng.

— Laura McKenzie's Travel Guide to Israel. 1996. pap. text 14.95 (*1-887161-15-5*) Boru Pubng.

— Laura McKenzie's Travel Guide to London. Weems, Ann O., ed. (Laura McKenzie's Travel Guides Ser.). (Illus.). 350p. (Orig.). 1996. pap. text 14.95 (*1-887161-04-X*, Boru Bks) Boru Pubng.

M

An Asterisk (*) at the beginning of an entry indicates that the title is appearing for the first time.

— Laura McKenzie's Travel Guide to Mexico. 1996. pap. text 14.95 (*1-887161-16-3*) Boru Pubng.

— Laura McKenzie's Travel Guide to Paris. Weems, Ann O., ed. (Laura McKenzie's Travel Guides Ser.). (Illus.). 350p. (Orig.). 1996. pap. text 14.95 (*1-887161-03-1*, Boru Bks) Boru Pubng.

— Laura McKenzie's Travel Guide to Rome. Weems, Ann O., ed. (Laura McKenzie's Travel Guides Ser.). (Illus.). 350p. (Orig.). 1996. pap. text 14.95 (*1-887161-05-8*, Boru Bks) Boru Pubng.

— Laura McKenzie's Travel Guide to Spain. 1996. pap. text 14.95 (*1-887161-17-1*) Boru Pubng.

— Laura McKenzie's Travel Guide to Virginia. 1996. pap. text 14.95 (*1-887161-18-X*) Boru Pubng.

McKenzie, Leon. Adult Education & Worldview Construction. 160p. (C). 1991. lib. bdg. 22.50 (*0-89464-488-2*) Krieger.

— Pagan Resurrection Myths & the Resurrection of Jesus: A Christian Perspective. 184p. (C). 1997. 21.95 (*1-880404-13-3*, Sthrn Academic) Bkwrights.

McKenzie, Leonard. In Pictures Yosemite: The Continuing Story. LC 91-60042. 48p. (Orig.). 1991. pap. 7.95 (*0-88714-057-2*) KC Pubns.

— In Pictures Yosemite: The Continuing Story. Le Bras, Yvon, tr. (FRE., Illus.). 48p. (Orig.). 1991. pap. 8.95 (*0-88714-769-0*) KC Pubns.

— In Pictures Yosemite: The Continuing Story. Petzinger, Saori, tr. (JPN., Illus.). 48p. (Orig.). 1991. pap. 8.95 (*0-88714-770-4*) KC Pubns.

— In Pictures Yosemite: The Continuing Story. Morales, Brigitte, tr. (GER., Illus.). 48p. (Orig.). 1991. pap. 8.95 (*0-88714-768-2*) KC Pubns.

— In Pictures Yosemite: The Continuing Story. Lee, Frances Y., tr. (CHI., Illus.). 48p. (Orig.). 1992. pap. 8.95 (*0-88714-771-2*) KC Pubns.

— In Pictures Yosemite: The Continuing Story. (KOR., Illus.). 48p. (Orig.). 1993. pap. 8.95 (*0-88714-772-0*) KC Pubns.

McKenzie, Lorna. Jilted. large type ed. (Linford Romance Library). 288p. 1995. pap. 16.99 (*0-7089-7781-2*, Linford) Ulverscroft.

— Pictures in Provence. large type ed. (Linford Romance Library). 240p. 1994. pap. 16.99 (*0-7089-7513-5*, Linford) Ulverscroft.

— Storm Damage. (Rainbow Romances Ser.: No. 907). 160p. 1994. 14.95 (*0-7090-4994-3*) Parkwest Pubns.

— Storm Damage. large type ed. (Linford Romance Large Print Ser.). 240p. 1995. pap. 16.99 (*0-7089-7739-1*, Linford) Ulverscroft.

— To Sara - With Love. large type ed. (Romance Ser.). 1994. pap. 16.99 (*0-7089-7616-6*, Linford) Ulverscroft.

— Twentieth-Century Pirate. large type ed. (Linford Romance Library). 272p. 1994. pap. 16.99 (*0-7089-7545-3*, Linford) Ulverscroft.

— Vienna Masquerade. large type ed. (Linford Romance Library). 224p. 1997. pap. 16.99 (*0-7089-5038-8*) Ulverscroft.

McKenzie, M. Elizabeth, jt. auth. see Conway, Donal P.

McKenzie, Maisie. Fred McKay. 200p. (C). 1990. 90.00 (*0-86439-109-9*, Pub. by Boolarong Pubns) St Mut.

McKenzie, Margaret, jt. auth. see Connolly, Marie.

McKenzie, Marian. Choices in Your Life. (Literacy Volunteers of America Readers Ser.). 32p. (Orig.). 1988. pap. text 3.00 (*0-8428-9620-1*) Cambridge Bk.

McKenzie, Marni S. Alphabet of Bible Creatures. (Illus.). 56p. (J). (ps-8). 1993. 14.95 (*1-882630-00-9*) Mercy Pr.

— Bible Quest - God's People, God's Land - Exodus-Joshua: Student Workbook. Constance, Nellie E. & Eades, Lois, eds. 247p. (J). (gr. 7-12). 1997. pap., student ed., wbk. ed. 18.95 (*1-889015-10-5*) Explrs Bible.

— Bible Quest - Promises Fulfilled - Luke & Acts: Student Workbook. Constance, Nellie E. & Eades, Lois, eds. 235p. (J). (gr. 7-12). 1997. pap., student ed., wbk. ed. 18.95 (*1-889015-15-6*) Explrs Bible.

— Bible Quest - Words of Wisdom - Job, Psalms & Proverbs: Student Workbook. Constance, Nellie E. & Eades, Lois, eds. 266p. (YA). (gr. 7-12). 1998. pap., wbk. ed. 18.95 (*1-889015-26-1*) Explrs Bible.

— The Creed & the Christian: A Twelve-Part Study of the Apostles' Creed. unabridged ed. 56p. 1993. 24.95 incl. audio (*1-882630-01-7*); student ed. 1.95 (*1-882630-02-5*) Mercy Pr.

***McKenzie, Marni Shideler.** God's Perfect Plan: Exploring Bible Prophecy from Genesis to Revelation Study Guide, Bk. 1. 108p. 1999. pap., student ed. 12.99 (*1-889015-68-7*) Explrs Bible.

— God's Perfect Plan: Exploring Bible Prophecy from Genesis to Revelation Study Guide, Bk. 2. 122p. 1999. pap., student ed. 12.99 (*1-889015-69-5*) Explrs Bible.

— God's Perfect Plan: Exploring Bible Prophecy from Genesis to Revelation Study Guide, Bk. 3. 123p. 1999. pap., student ed. 12.99 (*1-889015-70-9*) Explrs Bible.

McKenzie, Mary. The Rule of the Strap. 144p. 34.95 (*0-9524368-8-4*, Pub. by Wildfire Club) Xclusiv Distrib.

***McKenzie, Mary A.** The Gift Children. LC 00-102821. 303p. 2000. pap. 9.95 (*0-9678882-1-2*) MBrio Bks.

McKenzie, Mary M. & Loedel, Peter H., eds. The Promise & Reality of European Security Cooperation: States, Interests & Institutions. LC 97-33705. 216p. 1998. 59.95 (*0-275-95949-X*, Praeger Pubs) Greenwood.

McKenzie, Master, ed. Butterworths Rules of Court: Criminal Court Practice - 1996. 1996. pap. write for info. (*0-406-99892-2*, BRCC1996, MICHIE) LEXIS Pub.

McKenzie, Melissa, jt. auth. see Edwards, Sally.

McKenzie, Michael. Madonna: The Early Days. deluxe ed. 96p. 1993. pap. text 19.95 (*0-9638519-3-4*) Wrldwide Televid.

***McKenzie, Michael, ed.** Donald Sultan: Visual Poetics. limited ed. (Illus.). 44p. 1998. 5000.00 (*0-9632328-5-1*) Marco Fine Arts.

McKenzie, Michael, jt. auth. see Frank, Peter.

McKenzie, Michael, jt. auth. see Worley, William.

McKenzie, Michael, ed. see Calhoun, Susan & Bradley, Jane.

***McKenzie, Michael C.** Paul Ramsey's Ethics: The Power of 'Agape' in a Postmodern World. 2000. write for info. (*0-275-96988-6*) Greenwood.

***McKenzie, Michael P.** Birds Do It, Bees Do It, So Why Can't I? Overcome the Fear of Flying. (Illus.). 220p. 2000. pap. 14.95 (*0-9700163-0-1*) Flight To Free.

***McKenzie, Michelle.** Penguin Chick. (Illus.). 12p. (J). (gr. k). 2000. bds. 5.95 (*1-878244-28-0*) Monterey Bay Aquarium.

— El Pinguino Polluelo. Bahia Translators Staff & Echibuni, Taro, trs.Tr. of Penguin Chick. (SPA., Illus.). 12p. (J). (gr. k). 2000. bds. 5.95 (*1-878244-29-9*) Monterey Bay Aquarium.

McKenzie, Mike. Arrowhead: Home of the Chiefs. Echlon, Greg, ed. LC 97-13388. 144p. 1997. 24.95 (*1-886110-11-5*); pap. 14.95 (*1-886110-12-3*) Addax Pubng.

— Oklahoma State University: History-Making Basketball. Missouri Editing Group Staff & Anderson, Kelly, eds. (Illus.). 1992. write for info. (*1-56166-049-3*) Walsworth Pub.

McKenzie-Mohr, Doug & Smith, William, Jr. Fostering Sustainable Behavior: An Introduction to Community-Based Social Marketing. (Illus.). 176p. (C). 1999. pap. 14.95 (*0-86571-406-1*, Pub. by New Soc Pubs) Consort Bk Sales.

McKenzie, Nancy F., ed. The AIDS Reader: Privacy, Poverty, Community. 1990. pap. 9.95 (*0-452-01048-9*, Mer) NAL.

McKenzie, Neil. Guests of the Nation: Manuscript Edition. 1960. pap. 13.00 (*0-8222-0488-6*) Dramatists Play.

McKenzie, Pamela, ed. see Spectra Publishing Co., Inc. Staff.

McKenzie, Paul L. How to Win at Shuffleboard. (Illus.). 40p. (Orig.). 1989. pap. 5.95 (*1-877633-03-8*) Luthers.

McKenzie, Peter. Hail Orisha! A Phenomenology of a West African Religion in the Mid-Nineteenth Century. LC 98-112696. (Studies of Religion in Africa: No. 19). ix, 578p. 1997. 147.50 (*90-04-10942-0*) Brill Academic Pubs.

McKenzie, Peter, et al, eds. Competence & Accountability in Education. 168p. 1995. text 49.95 (*1-85742-279-1*, Pub. by Arena) Ashgate Pub Co.

McKenzie, Phillip, et al. Curriculum Provision in Rural Secondary Schools. 1996. pap. 35.00 (*0-86431-195-8*, Pub. by Aust Council Educ Res) Stylus Pub VA.

McKenzie, Phillip, jt. auth. see Lokan, Jan.

McKenzie, Phillip, jt. auth. see Maclean, Rupert.

McKenzie, R. & Valeriote, M. The Structure of Decidable Locally Finite Varieties. (Progress in Mathematics Ser.: No. 79). 224p. 1989. 51.50 (*0-8176-3439-8*) Birkhauser.

McKenzie, R., jt. auth. see Hobby, D.

McKenzie, Ralph & Givant, Steven, eds. Collected Works: Tarski, 4 vols., Set. 1986. 785.50 (*0-8176-3284-0*) Birkhauser.

— Collected Works: Tarski, 4 vols., Vol. 1: 1921-1934. 1987. 230.00 (*0-8176-3280-8*) Birkhauser.

— Collected Works: Tarski, 4 vols., Vol. 2: 1935-1944. 1987. 230.00 (*0-8176-3281-6*) Birkhauser.

— Collected Works: Tarski, 4 vols., Vol. 3: 1945-1957. 1987. 230.00 (*0-8176-3282-4*) Birkhauser.

— Collected Works: Tarski, 4 vols., Vol. 4: 1958-1979. 1987. 230.00 (*0-8176-3283-2*) Birkhauser.

McKenzie, Ralph, jt. auth. see Burris, Stanley.

McKenzie, Ray, jt. ed. see Lawson, Julie.

McKenzie, Richard. Economics. 704p. (C). 1986. disk. write for info. (*0-318-60189-3*) HM.

— The Home: A Memoir of Growing Up in an Orphanage. 240p. 1997. pap. 13.00 (*0-465-03069-6*) Basic.

— The Secret Place. 4.95 (*0-913343-21-8*) Inst Psych Inc.

— Turn Left at the Black Cow: One Family's Journey from Beverly Hills to Ireland. LC 97-52321. (Illus.). 352p. 1998. 24.95 (*1-57098-205-8*) Roberts Rinehart.

McKenzie, Richard, ed. Plant Closings: Public or Private Choices? LC 84-14957. 326p. 1984. pap. 3.00 (*0-932790-42-9*) Cato Inst.

McKenzie, Richard, jt. auth. see Lee, Dwight.

McKenzie, Richard B. Bound to Be Free. (Publication Ser.: No. 255). 201p. 1982. 6.38 (*0-8179-7551-9*) Hoover Inst Pr.

— Competing Visions: The Political Conflict over America's Economic Future. LC 85-11305. 216p. 1985. 5.00 (*0-932790-51-8*); pap. 3.00 (*0-932790-52-6*) Cato Inst.

— Fugitive Industry: The Economics & Politics of Deindustrialization. LC 83-22413. (Pacific Institute on Public Policy Research Ser.). 312p. 1984. pap. 32.00 (*0-88410-951-8*, HarpBusn) HarpInfo.

— Fugitive Industry: The Economics & Politics of Deindustrialization. LC 83-22413. (Illus.). 281p. (C). 1984. 29.95 (*0-936488-66-2*); pap. 14.95 (*0-936488-67-0*) PRIPP.

— The Limits of Economic Science. 1982. lib. bdg. 73.50 (*0-89838-116-9*) Kluwer Academic.

— The Paradox of Progress: Can Americans Regain Their Confidence in a Prosperous Future? LC 96-23910. (Illus.). 256p. 1997. 27.50 (*0-19-510239-8*) OUP.

— The Political Economy of the Educational Process. (Studies in Public Choice: Vol. 2). 1979. lib. bdg. 97.50 (*0-89838-012-X*) Kluwer Academic.

— Re-Thinking Orphanages for the 21st Century. LC 98-19673. 327p. 1998. 59.95 (*0-7619-1443-9*); pap. 27.50 (*0-7619-1444-7*) Sage.

— Times Change: The Minimum Wage & the New York Times. LC 94-15800. 1994. 19.95 (*0-936488-76-X*) PRIPP.

***McKenzie, Richard B.** Trust on Trial: How the Microsoft Case is Reforming the Rules of Competition. 288p. 2000. 26.00 (*0-7382-0331-9*, Pub. by Perseus Pubng) HarpC.

McKenzie, Richard B. What Went Right in the 1980s. LC 93-7236. (Illus.). 250p. (Orig.). 1993. pap. 21.95 (*0-936488-71-9*) PRIPP.

McKenzie, Richard B. & Lee, Dwight R. Government in Retreat. 1991. pap. 10.00 (*0-943802-67-9*, 164) Natl Ctr Pol.

— Managing Through Incentives: How to Develop a More Collaborative, Productive & Profitable Organization. LC 98-14526. (Illus.). 352p. 1998. 30.00 (*0-19-511901-0*) OUP.

McKenzie, Richard B., jt. auth. see Lee, Dwight R.

McKenzie, Rita, jt. auth. see Cherry, Alan J.

McKenzie, Robert. British Political Parties: The Distribution of Power Within the Conservation & Labour Parties. (Modern Revivals in History Ser.). 694p. 1992. 72.95 (*0-7512-0067-0*, Pub. by Gregg Revivals) Ashgate Pub Co.

McKenzie, Robert & Silver, Allan. Angels in Marble: Working Class Conservatives in Urban England. LC 67-30555. (Studies in Contemporary Sociology). 307p. reprint ed. pap. 95.20 (*0-8357-5477-4*, 202405700035) Bks Demand.

Mckenzie, Robert E. Representation Before the Collection Division of the IRS. 1990. 95.00 (*0-318-41449-X*) West Group.

McKenzie, Robert E., et al. Representing the Audited Taxpayer. 1990. 69.95 (*0-685-31933-4*) West Group.

McKenzie, Robert G., jt. auth. see Houk, Carolyn S.

McKenzie, Robert T. One South or Many? Plantation Belt & Upcountry in Civil War-Era Tennessee. (Illus.). 225p. (C). 1994. text 49.95 (*0-521-46270-3*) Cambridge U Pr.

McKenzie, Robin A. The Cervical & Thoracic Spine: Mechanical Diagnosis & Therapy. (Illus.). 320p. (C). 1990. text 53.00 (*0-9597746-7-X*, Pub. by Spinal Pubns Ltd) Orthopedic Phys.

— The Lumbar Spine: Mechanical Diagnosis & Therapy. (Illus.). 164p. 1989. reprint ed. text 39.00 (*0-473-00064-4*, Pub. by Spinal Pubns Ltd) Orthopedic Phys.

— Treat Your Own Back, 7th Edition-January 1997. 7th ed. (Illus.). 80p. 1997. reprint ed. pap. text 10.00 (*0-9597746-6-1*, Pub. by Spinal Pubns Ltd) Orthopedic Phys.

— Treat Your Own Neck. 3rd ed. (Illus.). 63p. 1997. reprint ed. pap. text 10.00 (*0-473-00209-4*, Pub. by Spinal Pubns Ltd) Orthopedic Phys.

***McKenzie, Robin A. & Kubey, Craig.** 7 Steps to a Pain-Free Life: How to Rapidly Relieve Back & Neck Pain Using the McKenzie Method. (Illus.). 256p. 2000. 23.95 (*0-525-94560-1*) NAL.

McKenzie, Roderick D. Neighborhood: A Study of Local Life in the City of Columbus, Ohio. LC 71-112560. (Rise of Urban America Ser.). (Illus.). 1974. reprint ed. 19.95 (*0-405-02465-7*) Ayer.

McKenzie, Roger, et al. Daredevil: Marked for Death. LC 94-223045. (Illus.). 96p. 1990. pap. 9.95 (*0-87135-634-1*) Marvel Entrprs.

Mckenzie, Rusty. Never Far from Water. LC 98-96813. 80p. 1998. pap. write for info. (*0-9668455-0-1*) Sand Bottom.

McKenzie, Sandra. The Secrets in Your Name: Discovering the Hidden You. Caton, Patrick, ed. LC 97-71656. 168p. 1997. pap. 5.95 (*1-56245-304-1*) Great Quotations.

McKenzie, Sarah J. James. Descendants of William James. (Illus.). 93p. 1997. pap. 16.50 (*0-8328-9331-5*); lib. bdg. 26.50 (*0-8328-9330-7*) Higginson Bk Co.

McKenzie, Shawn, et al. Studies in Frank Waters Vol. 18: Afterwords. 1996. pap. 10.00 (*1-878277-13-8*) Frank Waters Soc.

McKenzie, Shirlyn B. Textbook of Hematology. LC 87-3834. (Illus.). 507p. 1988. text 48.50 (*0-8121-1096-X*) Lppncott W & W.

— Textbook of Hematology. 2nd ed. (Illus.). 768p. 1996. 56.95 (*0-683-18016-9*) Lppncott W & W.

McKenzie-Smith, I., jt. auth. see Browning, David R.

Mckenzie, Steven L. All God's Children: A Biblical Critique of Racism. LC 96-45164. 144p. (Orig.). 1997. pap. 14.95 (*0-664-25695-3*) Westminster John Knox.

***McKenzie, Steven L.** Covenant. (Understanding Biblical Themes Ser.). 2000. pap. 16.99 (*0-8272-3827-4*) Chalice Pr.

— King David: A Biography. LC 99-44315. (Illus.). 272p. 2000. 25.00 (*0-19-513273-4*) OUP.

McKenzie, Steven L. & Graham, M. Patrick, eds. Hebrew Bible Today: An Introduction to Critical Issues. LC 98-10294. 248p. 1998. pap. 24.00 (*0-664-25652-X*) Westminster John Knox.

— The History of Israel's Traditions: The Heritage of Martin Noth. LC 95-109952. (Journal for the Study of the Old Testament Supplement Ser.: Vol. 182). 326p. 1994. 85.00 (*1-85075-499-3*, Pub. by Sheffield Acad) CUP Services.

***McKenzie, Steven L. & Haynes, Stephen R., eds.** To Each Its Own Meaning: An Introduction to Biblical Criticisms & Their Application. expanded rev. ed. 304p. 1999. pap. 22.95 (*0-664-25784-4*) Westminster John Knox.

McKenzie, Steven L. & Haynes, Stephen R., eds. To Each Its Own Meaning: An Introduction to Biblical Criticisms & Their Applications. LC 92-26563. 256p. (Orig.). 1993. pap. 19.95 (*0-664-25236-2*) Westminster John Knox.

McKenzie, Steven L., jt. ed. see Graham, M. Patrick.

McKenzie, Steven L., jt. ed. see Schearing, Linda S.

McKenzie, Susan & Kunalen, S. Q & A English Legal System. 218p. 1996. pap. 22.00 (*1-85431-533-1*, Pub. by Blackstone Pr) Gaunt.

McKenzie, Thomas, jt. auth. see McKenzie, Julie.

McKenzie, V. Michael & Aveni, Anthony. Empires of Time: Calendars, Clocks, & Cultures. Wise, Gordon, ed. LC 95-14147. (Kodansha Globe Trade Paperback Ser.). 384p. 1995. pap. 16.00 (*1-56836-073-8*, Kodansha Globe) Kodansha.

McKenzie, Vashti M. Not Without a Struggle: Leadership Development for African American Women in Ministry. LC 96-26237. 160p. (Orig.). 1996. pap. 15.95 (*0-8298-1076-5*) Pilgrim OH.

McKenzie, Venetia. Creative Self-Communication. 1978. pap. 1.25 (*0-87516-254-1*) DeVorss.

***McKenzie, W. J.** History of Soe. Foot, M. R., ed. 400p. 2000. text 70.00 (*0-7146-5004-8*) F Cass Pubs.

— History of Soe. Foot, M. R., ed. Vol. 2. 400p. 2000. text 70.00 (*0-7146-5013-7*) F Cass Pubs.

McKenzie, Wendell. Genetics in Human Affairs: Course Materials & Notes. 3rd ed. 220p. (C). 1998. ring bd. 24.95 (*0-7872-5097-X*) Kendall-Hunt.

McKenzie, Wendell H. DNA Synthesis. 70p. 1994. pap. text 85.00 (*2-88124-646-X*) Gordon & Breach.

— GN 301 Genetics in Human Affairs: Course Materials & Notes. 204p. (C). 1996. ring bd. 19.95 (*0-7872-2749-8*) Kendall-Hunt.

McKenzie, Wendy. Financial Times Guide to Interpreting Company Reports & Accounts. 2nd ed. 320p. 1998. pap. 49.95 (*0-273-63099-7*, Pub. by F T P H) Trans-Atl Phila.

— Unlocking Company Reports & Accounts. 400p. 1998. pap. 57.50 (*0-273-63250-7*, Pub. by Pitman Pub) Trans-Atl Phila.

McKenzie, Wesley M., ed. see Douglas, Charles H.

McKenzie, William P., jt. ed. see Leach, James.

McKeogh, Colm. The Political Realism of Reinhold Niebuhr: A Pragmatic Approach to the Just War. LC 97-13670. 224p. 1997. text 65.00 (*0-312-17629-5*) St Martin.

McKeogh, J. P. Intellectual Property. 2nd ed. LC 94-204079. (Butterworth's Student Companion Ser.). 144p. 1994. pap. 18.00 (*0-409-30865-X*, A.T., MICHIE) LEXIS Pub.

McKeon, David, jt. auth. see Morrison, Grant.

Mckeon, Denise, jt. auth. see Samway, Katharine D.

McKeon, Denny. Kentucky Gardener's Guide: The What, Where, When, How & Why of Gardening in Kentucky. (Illus.). 2000. pap. 19.95 (*1-888608-17-X*) Cool Springs Pr.

Mckeon, Donald W., jt. auth. see Wilson, Clifford A.

McKeon, Elizabeth. Fit for a King: Elvis Presley. LC 97-43418. 240p. 1998. 7.99 (*0-517-18917-8*) Random Hse Value.

McKeon, Elizabeth & Everett, Linda. Blue Plate Special: The American Diner Cookbook. LC 96-31765. (Illus.). 272p. (Orig.). 1996. pap. 17.95 (*1-888952-01-6*) Cumberland Hse.

— Cinema under the Stars: America's Love Affair with Drive-in Movie Theaters. (Illus.). 144p. 1998. pap. 18.95 (*1-58182-002-X*) Cumberland Hse.

— The Quotable King: Hopes, Aspirations, & Memories. LC 97-6517. 192p. (Orig.). 1997. pap. 8.95 (*1-888952-44-X*) Cumberland Hse.

McKeon, Elizabeth, et al. Fit for a King: The Elvis Presley Cookbook. LC 92-25266. (Illus.). 256p. 1992. spiral bd. 14.95 (*1-55853-196-3*) Rutledge Hill Pr.

McKeon, James & Carothers, Roberta. AORA Gemstone Oracle: Cards to Explore the Crystal Realms. LC 98-85712. (Illus.). 112p. 1998. pap. 29.95 (*0-9664492-0-7*) Viktara.

McKeon, Jean. Dawn Pearl: Poems by Irene Chadwick. deluxe limited ed. 48p. 1994. 49.50 (*0-9642725-1-2*) Ietje Kooi Pr.

McKeon, Jim. Frank O'Connor: A Life. LC 99-175835. (Illus.). 192p. 1999. 35.00 (*1-84018-082-X*, Pub. by Mainstream Pubng) Trafalgar.

McKeon, John. The Serpent's Crown. 208p. 1991. 19.95 (*0-8027-1146-4*) Walker & Co.

McKeon, Joseph, ed. Managing Logistics Change Through Innovative Information Technology. 220p. 1987. pap. write for info. (*0-318-61853-2*) Leaseway Trans Corp.

McKeon, Joseph E., ed. Partnerships: A Natural Evolution in Logistics. LC 88-81504. (Logistics Resource Forum Ser.: No. 7). 126p. (Orig.). 1988. pap. text 19.95 (*0-9610146-5-2*) Leaseway Trans Corp.

Mckeon, Judith C. Gardening with Roses: Designs for Easy-Care Climbers, Ramblers & Shrubs. LC 96-36146. 1997. 30.00 (*1-56799-396-6*) M Friedman Pub Grp Inc.

McKeon, Kathryn. Mulan Saves the Day No. 18. LC 97-80399. (Disney's First Readers Ser.). (Illus.). 22p. (J). (gr. 2-4). 1998. pap. 2.95 (*0-7868-4246-6*, Pub. by Disney Pr) Time Warner.

***McKeon, Kathryn Cristaldi.** Baseball Ballerina Strikes Out. LC 98-32040. (Step into Reading Ser.: A Step 2 Book). (Illus.). 48p. (J). (gr. k-3). 2000. pap. text 3.99 (*0-679-89132-3*) Random.

McKeon, Kathryn Cristaldi. Baseball Ballerina Strikes Out. LC 98-32040. (Step into Reading Ser.: A Step 2 Book). (Illus.). 48p. (J). (gr. 1-3). 2000. lib. bdg. 11.99 (*0-679-99132-8*) Random.

***McKeon, Kathryn Cristaldi.** Baseball Ballerina Strikes Out. (Illus.). (J). 2000. 9.44 (*0-606-18483-X*) Turtleback.

McKeon, Michael. The Origins of the English Novel, 1600-1740. LC 86-18495. 544p. 1988. reprint ed. pap. text 21.95 (*0-8018-3746-4*) Johns Hopkins.

— Politics & Poetry in Restoration England: The Case of Dryden's Annus Mirabilis. LC 75-4508. (Illus.). 350p. reprint ed. pap. 108.50 (*0-7837-3867-6*, 204368900010) Bks Demand.

***McKeon, Michael, ed.** Theory of the Novel: A Historical Approach. LC 00-27120. (Illus.). 864p. 2000. 65.00 (*0-8018-6396-1*); pap. 29.95 (*0-8018-6397-X*) Johns Hopkins.

McKeon, Richard. Freedom & History & Other Essays: The Thought of Richard McKeon. McKeon, Zahava K., ed. (Illus.). 304p. 1990. pap. text 19.50 (*0-226-56029-5*) U Ch Pr.

M

An Asterisk (*) at the beginning of an entry indicates that the title is appearing for the first time.

— Freedom & History & Other Essays: The Thought of Richard McKeon. McKeon, Zahava K., ed. (Illus.). 304p. 1996. lib. bdg. 48.00 (0-226-56028-7) U Ch Pr.
— On Knowing: The Natural Sciences. McKeon, Zahava K., ed. LC 94-8953. (Illus.). 420p. 1994. pap. text 17.95 (0-226-56027-9) U Ch Pr.
— On Knowing: The Natural Sciences. McKeon, Zahava K., ed. LC 94-8953. (Illus.). 420p. 1994. lib. bdg. 65.00 (0-226-56026-0) U Ch Pr.
— The Philosophy of Spinoza: The Unity of His Thought. LC 86-28563. 345p. 1987. reprint ed. 35.00 (0-918024-47-1); reprint ed. pap. 17.50 (0-918024-48-X) Ox Bow.
— Rhetoric: Essays in Invention & Discovery. LC 86-28574. xxxiv, 220p. (C). 1987. 30.00 (0-918024-49-8) Ox Bow.
— Selected Richard McKeon, 1. McKeon, Zahava K. & Swenson, William G., eds. LC 97-10782. 528p. 1998. 50.00 (0-226-56036-8) U Ch Pr.
— Thought, Action, & Passion. LC 54-9579. (Midway Reprint Ser.). x, 305p. (C). 1993. reprint ed. pap. text 16.00 (0-226-56031-7) U Ch Pr.
McKeon, Richard, jt. ed. see Nikam, N. A.
McKeon, Richard P., ed. Introduction to Aristotle. 2nd enl. rev. ed. 812p. (C). 1974. reprint ed. lib. bdg. 23.00 (0-226-56032-5) U Ch Pr.
McKeon, Richard P., ed. see Aristotle.
McKeon, Richard P., ed. & intro. see Aristotle.
McKeon, Robert, jt. auth. see Cairns, Walter.
McKeon, Robert, tr. see Kant, Immanuel.
McKeon, Robert M., tr. see Caussade, Jean Pierre.
McKeon, Tad. Home Health Financial Management. LC 95-21945. 521p. 1995. text 93.00 (0-8342-0729-X, 20729) Aspen Pub.
McKeon, Tad, jt. auth. see Peters, Donna A.
McKeon, Zahava K. Novels & Arguments: Inventing Rhetorical Criticism. LC 82-2677. 270p. 1982. lib. bdg. 27.00 (0-226-56034-1) U Ch Pr.
McKeon, Zahava K., ed. see McKeon, Richard.
McKeone, Dermot. Measuring Your Media Profile. 250p. 1996. 78.95 (0-566-07578-4, Pub. by Gower) Ashgate Pub Co.
McKeone, Lee. Backblast. 224p. 1989. mass mkt. 3.95 (0-445-20622-5, Pub. by Warner Bks) Little.
— The Clone Crisis. 224p. (Orig.). 1992. mass mkt. 4.99 (0-446-36321-9, Pub. by Warner Bks) Little.
— Ghoster. 1988. mass mkt. 3.50 (0-445-20620-9, Pub. by Warner Bks) Little.
— Starfire Down. 1991. mass mkt. 4.95 (0-446-36137-2, Pub. by Warner Bks) Little.
McKeone, Mary. Wasting Time in School: Secondary School Chaplaincy: A Story & a Handbook. 128p. 1996. pap. 39.95 (0-85439-461-3, Pub. by St Paul Pubns) St Mut.
McKeough, Anne, et al, eds. Teaching for Transfer: Fostering Generalization in Learning. 256p. 1995. text 49.95 (0-8058-1309-8) L Erlbaum Assocs.
McKeough, Anne & Lupart, Judy L., eds. Toward the Practice of Theory-Based Instruction: Current Cognitive Theories & Their Educational Promise. 208p. (C). 1991. text 39.95 (0-8058-0773-X) L Erlbaum Assocs.
McKeough, D. Michael. The Coloring Review of Neuroscience. 2nd ed. LC 94-45666. 176p. 1995. pap. text 29.00 (0-316-56209-2, Little Brwn Med Div) Lppncott W & W.
McKeough, J. & Stewart, A. Intellectual Property in Australia. 481p. 1991. pap. 78.00 (0-409-49581-6, Austral. MICHIE) LEXIS Pub.
McKeough, J., jt. auth. see Blakeney, M. L.
McKeown. Csg (Windows) - Living with CO. 5th ed. (C). 1995. student ed. 295.00 (0-03-015367-0) Harcourt Coll Pubs.
— Field Guide to Reptiles & Amphibians in the Hawaiian Islands. 1996. 19.95 (0-9650731-1-4) Serpents Tale.
Mckeown. Working with Computers. 2nd ed. (C). 1994. pap. text, student ed. 16.75 (0-03-098206-5) Harcourt.
***McKeown, Arthur.** Titanic. (Ready-to-Read Ser.). (J). (gr. 1-3). 1998. pap. 3.99 (0-689-82476-9) Aladdin.
McKeown, Arthur & Hogan, Peter. Titanic. 48p. 1996. pap. 7.95 (1-85371-516-6, Pub. by Poolbeg Pr) Dufour.
McKeown, Barry. Ashes by Now. LC 96-10418. 330p. 1996. 18.95 (0-944957-59-5) Rivercross Pub.
McKeown, Bonni. Peaceful Patriot: The Story of Tom Bennett. 224p. 1987. pap. 8.00 (0-9621483-0-X) Peaceful Patriot Pr.
McKeown, Bruce & Thomas, Dan. Q Methodology. (Quantitative Applications in the Social Sciences Ser.: Vol. 66). 93p. (C). 1988. pap. text 10.95 (0-8039-2753-3) Sage.
McKeown, Charles & Gilliam, Terry. The Adventures of Baron Munchausen: The Screenplay. (Illus.). 256p. (Orig.). 1989. pap. 8.95 (1-55783-041-X) Applause Theatre Bk Pubs.
McKeown, Charles, jt. auth. see Gilliam, Terry.
McKeown, Ciaran. Passion of Peace. 320p. 1990. pap. 11.95 (0-85640-325-3, Pub. by Blackstaff Pr) Dufour.
McKeown, David M., et al, eds. Intergrating Photogrammetric Techniques with Scene Analysis & Machine Vision III. LC 98-122042. 27p. 1997. pap. 59.00 (0-8194-2487-0) SPIE.
McKeown, Denny. Denny McKeown's Complete Guide to Midwest Gardening. LC 84-23996. (Illus.). 408p. 1985. 24.95 (0-87833-382-7) Taylor Pub.
— The Gardening Book for Ohio: The What, Where, When, How & Why of Gardening in Ohio. LC 99-89099. (Illus.). 448p. 2000. pap. 19.95 (1-888608-39-0) Cool Springs Pr.
***McKeown, Denny.** My Kentucky Garden: A Gardener's Journal. (Illus.). 128p. 2000. spiral bd. 19.95 (1-930604-09-2) Cool Springs Pr.
— My Ohio Garden: A Gardener's Journal. (Illus.). 128p. 2000. spiral bd. 19.95 (1-930604-00-9) Cool Springs Pr.
McKeown, Ed. The Cornell Chimes: In Celebration of the Hundredth Anniversary of McGraw Tower. (Illus.). 144p. 1991. 18.95 (0-9630755-0-0) Office Acad Progs.
McKeown, Elizabeth, jt. auth. see Brown, Dorothy M.
McKeown, Elizabeth, jt. ed. see Avella, Steven M.
McKeown, J. J., et al. An Introduction to Unconstrained Optimisation. (Illus.). 132p. (C). 1990. pap. 39.00 (0-7503-0025-6); disk 270.00 (0-7503-0029-9) IOP Pub.
***McKeown, J. Leslie.** The Complete Guide to Mentoring & Coaching (TCGTMAC) Designing & Implementing a Mentoring or Coaching Program. 2nd rev. ed. (Deliver the Promise Ser.). 638p. 1999. 344.95 (0-9701760-0-7) EVNA Inc.
McKeown, James C., jt. auth. see Hopwood, Wm S.
McKeown, James M. & McKeown, Joan C. Collector's Guide to Kodak Cameras. (Illus.). 176p. (Orig.). 1981. pap. 16.95 (0-931838-02-9, CP3802, Amphoto) Watsn-Guptill.
— Price Guide to Antique & Classic Cameras, 1997-1998. 10th ed. (Illus.). 640p. 1996. pap. 69.95 (0-931838-28-2) Centennial Photo Serv.
— Price Guide to Antique & Classic Cameras 1997-1998. 10th ed. (Illus.). 640p. 1996. 79.95 (0-931838-29-0) Centennial Photo Serv.
McKeown, Jim & McKeown, Joan. McKeown's Price Guide to Antique & Classic Cameras. 11th ed. (Illus.). 672p. 1998. pap. text 69.95 (0-931838-32-0) Watsn-Guptill.
McKeown, Joan, jt. auth. see McKeown, Jim.
McKeown, Joan C. Sharing More Than a Pastor. (Illus.). 128p. (Orig.). 1993. pap. 9.95 (0-9636183-0-X) Arc Res.
McKeown, Joan C., et al. Lind's List Camera Price Guide & Master Data Catalog, 1996-1997. (Illus.). 400p. 1996. pap. 44.95 (0-931838-26-6) Centennial Photo Serv.
McKeown, Joan C., jt. auth. see McKeown, James M.
McKeown, Joan C., ed. see Wisconsin Directors of Religious Education Federat.
McKeown, Julie. Royal Doulton. (Illus.). 40p. 1998. pap. 8.50 (0-7478-0338-2, Pub. by Shire Pubns) Parkwest Pubns.
McKeown, Karen C. Hog Wild! 224p. (Orig.). 1992. mass mkt. 9.99 (0-446-39250-2, Pub. by Warner Bks) Little.
McKeown, Kate, jt. auth. see Mobley, Lou.
McKeown, Kathleen R. Text Generation: Using Discourse Strategies & Focus Constraints to Generate Natural Language Text. (Studies in Natural Language Processing). (Illus.). 256p. (C). 1992. pap. text 19.95 (0-521-43802-0) Cambridge U Pr.
McKeown, Ken. The Final Notch. large type ed. (Linford Western Library). 240p. 1996. pap. 16.99 (0-7089-7885-1) Ulverscroft.
***McKeown, Kevin.** Your Secrets Are My Business: A Security Expert Reveals How Your Trash, Telephone, License Plate, Credit Card, Computer & Even Your Mail Make You an Easy Target for Today's Information Thieves. LC 99-61754. 256p. 1999. 24.00 (1-56352-577-1) Longstreet.
***McKeown, Kevin & Stern, Dave.** Your Secrets Are My Business: A Security Expert Reveals How Your Trash, License Plate, Credit Cards, Computer & Even Your Mail Make You an Easy Target for Today's Information Thieves. 2000. reprint ed. pap. 13.00 (0-452-28204-7) Dutton Plume.
McKeown, Margaret G. & Curtis, Mary E., eds. The Nature of Vocabulary Acquisition. 208p. 1987. 39.95 (0-89859-548-7) L Erlbaum Assocs.
McKeown, Martha F. Linda's Indian Home. LC 56-8826. (Illus.). 80p. (J). (gr. 3-7). 1969. 7.95 (0-8323-0151-5) Binford Mort.
— Them Was the Days: An American Saga of the 70's. LC F 0594.M18. 298p. reprint ed. pap. 92.40 (0-7837-1641-9, 204193500024) Bks Demand.
McKeown, Mary P. & Alexander, Kern, eds. Values in Conflict: Funding Priorities for Higher Education. LC 86-20597. 360p. 1986. text 34.95 (0-88730-102-9, HarpBusn) HarpInfo.
McKeown, Neil B. Phthalocyanine Materials: Synthesis, Structure & Function. LC 97-28288. (Chemistry of Solid State Materials Ser.: Vol. 6). (Illus.). 212p. (C). 1998. text 74.95 (0-521-49623-3) Cambridge U Pr.
McKeown, Pat, jt. auth. see Gilbert, Edith.
McKeown, Patrick. Learning to Program with Visual Basic. LC 98-17343. 512p. 1998. pap. 61.95 (0-471-19814-5) Wiley.
McKeown, Patrick G. Living with Computers. 5th ed. LC 93-74844. 720p. (C). 1994. pap. text 74.00 (0-03-002069-7) Dryden Pr.
— Living with Computers. 5th ed. 200p. (C). 1995. pap. text, student ed. 29.50 (0-03-015354-9) Harcourt Coll Pubs.
— Living with Computers: Commercial Software Version. 672p. (C). 1987. teacher ed. write for info. incl. trans. (0-318-61978-4); write for info. (0-318-61977-6) Dryden Pr.
— Working with Computers. 2nd ed. LC 93-72076. 372p. (C). 1994. pap. text 44.50 (0-03-098207-3); pap. text, teacher ed. 94.00 (0-03-098205-7) Dryden Pr.
— WORKING WITH COMPUTERS, 2/E. 2nd ed. LC 93-72076. 346p. (C). 1994. pap. text 57.50 (0-03-098203-0) Dryden Pr.
McKeown, Patrick G. & Leitch, Robert A. Management Information Systems, Managing with Computers. 384p. (C). 1993. pap. text, teacher ed. 22.75 incl. trans. (0-15-500813-7) Dryden Pr.
McKeown, Patrick G. & Watson, Richard T. Metamorphosis: A Guide to the World Wide Web & Electronic Commerce, Version 2.0. 2nd ed. LC 96-49204. 192p. 1997. pap. 30.95 (0-471-18032-7) Wiley.
McKeown, Patrick G., et al. Instructor's Manual to Accompany Living with Computers Version 5.0. 5th ed. 519p. (C). 1995. pap. text, teacher ed. 36.75 (0-03-015353-0) Dryden Pr.
McKeown, Patrick G., jt. auth. see Brown, Robert D.
McKeown, R. D. & Beise, E. J., eds. Parity Violation in Electron Scattering. 244p. (C). 1990. text 66.00 (981-02-0265-2) World Scientific Pub.
McKeown, Ross. Learning Mathematics: A Program for Classroom Teachers. LC 89-19961. (Illus.). 139p. (Orig.). (C). (gr. k). 1990. pap. text 17.50 (0-435-08304-X, 08304) Heinemann.
McKeown, Sean. A Field Guide to Reptiles & Amphibians in the Hawaiian Islands. (Illus.). 1996. pap. 14.95 (0-9650731-0-6) Diamnd Head.
— The General Care & Maintenance of Day Geckos. 143p. 1993. pap. text 18.00 (1-882770-22-6) Adv Vivarium.
McKeown, Sean & Zaworski, Jim. General Care & Maintenance of Tokay Geckos. LC 96-52062. 1996. 8.50 (1-882770-38-2) Adv Vivarium.
***McKeown, Stephen A.** Mechanical Analysis of Electronic Pakaging Systems. LC 99-22027. (Mechanical Engineering Ser.). (Illus.). 376p. 1999. text 165.00 (0-8247-7033-1) Dekker.
McKeown, T. The Kids' Garden Fun Book. (Illus.). 160p. (J). 1997. spiral bd. 5.95 (1-57166-096-8) Hearts N Tummies.
McKeown, Timothy J., jt. auth. see Lynn, Leonard H.
McKerchar, M. Paper Money Bibliography. 1979. 15.00 (0-686-51600-1) S J Durst.
McKerchar, Marit, jt. auth. see Spellerberg, Ian F.
McKerchar, Marit, jt. auth. see Spellewrberg, Ian F.
McKercher, B. J. The Second Baldwin Government & the United States, 1924-1929: Attitudes & Diplomacy. (International Studies). 272p. 1984. text 69.95 (0-521-25802-2) Cambridge U Pr.
— Transition of Power: Britain's Loss of Global Preeminence to the United States, 1930-1945. LC 98-13369. 388p. (C). 1998. text 64.95 (0-521-44090-4) Cambridge U Pr.
McKercher, B. J., ed. Arms Limitation & Disarmament: Restraints on War, 1899-1939. LC 92-1193. 272p. 1992. 65.00 (0-275-94059-4, C4059, Praeger Pubs) Greenwood.
McKercher, B. J. & Hennessy, Michael A., eds. The Operational Art: Developments in the Theories of War. LC 95-52704. 232p. 1996. 65.00 (0-275-95305-X, Praeger Pubs) Greenwood.
McKercher, B. J. & Ion, A. Hamish, eds. Military Heretics: The Unorthodox in Policy & Strategy. LC 93-14116. 256p. 1993. 62.95 (0-275-94554-5, C4554, Praeger Pubs) Greenwood.
McKercher, B. J., jt. ed. see Errington, Elizabeth J.
McKercher, B. J., jt. ed. see Neilson, Keith.
***McKercher, B. J. C. & Legault, Roch, eds.** Military Planning & the Origins of the Second World War in Europe. LC 99-52826. 224p. 2000. 62.00 (0-275-96158-3, C6158, Praeger Pubs) Greenwood.
McKercher, Brian, jt. ed. see Dockrill, Michael.
McKercher, William R. Freedom & Authority. 300p. 1989. 45.99 (0-921689-31-4, Pub. by Black Rose); pap. 16.99 (0-921689-30-6, Pub. by Black Rose) Consort Bk Sales.
McKern, Bruce. Mineral Processing in ASEAN. Koomsup, Praipol, ed. 1988. pap. text 34.95 (0-04-330384-6, Pub. by Allen & Unwin Pty) Paul & Co Pubs.
— Minerals Industry of ASEAN. Koomsup, Praipol, ed. 1988. pap. text 37.95 (0-04-301284-1, Pub. by Allen & Unwin Pty) Paul & Co Pubs.
McKern, Bruce, ed. The Transnational Corporations & the Exploitation of Natural Resources. LC 93-18760. (United Nations Library on Transnational Corporations: Vol. 10). 1993. write for info. (0-415-08543-8) Routledge.
McKern, Debra & Byrne, Sherry. ALA Target Packet for Preservation Microfilming. LC 91-8677. (Illus.). (C). 1991. pap. text 25.00 (0-8389-7492-9) ALA.
McKern, W. C. Archaeology of Tonga. (BMB Ser.: No. 60). 1972. reprint ed. 25.00 (0-527-02166-0) Periodicals Srv.
— Functional Families of the Patwin. fac. ed. (University of California Publications in American Archaeology & Ethnology: Vol. 13: 7). 23p. (C). 1922. reprint ed. pap. text 2.81 (1-55567-213-2) Coyote Press.
— Patwin Houses. fac. ed. (University of California Publications in American Archaeology & Ethnology: Vol. 20: 10). (Illus.). 15p. (C). 1923. reprint ed. pap. text 1.88 (1-55567-246-9) Coyote Press.
McKernan-Cramer, Inc. Staff. Tim McKernan Barrelman. LC 95-77596. 144p. 1995. pap. text 15.95 (0-7872-1042-0) Kendall-Hunt.
McKernan, James. Curriculum Action Research: A Handbook of Methods & Resources for the Reflective Practitioner. 2nd rev. ed. LC 96-223370. 288p. 1996. pap. 35.00 (0-7494-1793-5, Kogan Pg Educ) Stylus Pub VA.
McKernan, James, jt. auth. see Keel, Sean.
***McKernan, John.** Postcard from Dublin. 32p. 1999. pap. 5.00 (1-880743-13-2, Pub. by Dead Metaphor) SPD-Small Pr Dist.
McKernan, John. Walking Along the Missouri River. LC 77-8920. (Lost Roads Poetry Ser.: No. 5). (J). 1978. pap. 4.00 (0-918786-09-6) Lost Roads.
— The Writer's Handbook. 2nd ed. 544p. (C). 1991. pap. text 32.50 (0-03-053453-4, Pub. by Harcourt Coll Pubs) Harcourt.
— Writer's Handbook. 2nd ed. (C). 1991. pap. text, teacher ed. 34.00 (0-03-054213-8) Harcourt Coll Pubs.
— The Writer's Handbook. 3rd ed. (C). 1995. pap. text. write for info. (0-15-502426-4) Harcourt Coll Pubs.
McKernan, Llewellyn. Many Waters: Poems from West Virginia. LC 93-27131. (Poetry Ser.: Vol. 7). 1993. pap. 14.95 (0-88946-568-1, Mellen Poetry Pr) E Mellen.
— This Is the Day. (Stardust Ser.). (Illus.). 24p. 1994. 4.50 (0-8378-7690-7) Gibson.
— This Is the Night. (Stardust Ser.). (Illus.). 24p. 1994. 4.50 (0-8378-7691-5) Gibson.
McKernan, Luke. Topical Budget: The Great British Newsfilm. (Illus.). 128p. 1992. 39.95 (0-253-33615-5, Pub. by British Film Inst); pap. 16.95 (0-85170-305-4, Pub. by British Film Inst) Ind U Pr.
McKernan, Luke & Terris, Olwen, eds. Walking Shadows: Shakespeare in the National Film & Television Archive. (Archive Monographs). (Illus.). 280p. 1994. pap. 21.95 (0-85170-486-7) Ind U Pr.
McKernan, Luke, jt. ed. see Herbert, Stephen.
McKernan, Maureen. The Amazing Crime & Trial of Leopold & Loeb. 380p. 1996. reprint ed. 85.00 (1-56169-215-8) Gaunt.
***McKernan, Michael.** Beryl Beaurepaire. (Illus.). 316p. 1999. 39.95 (0-7022-3110-X, Pub. by Univ Queensland Pr) Intl Spec Bk.
McKernan, Susan, ed. see Vidal, Mary T.
McKernan, Tom, ed. see Jones, Larry K.
McKernie, Grant, jt. auth. see Watson, Jack.
McKerns, Dorothy & Motchkavitz, Leslie. The Kid's Guide to Good Grammar. LC 98-20827. (Illus.). 96p. (J). (gr. 3-7). 1998. pap. 8.95 (1-56565-697-0, 06970W, Pub. by Lowell Hse Juvenile) NTC Contemp Pub Co.
McKerns, Joseph P., ed. Biographical Dictionary of American Journalism. LC 88-25098. 834p. 1989. lib. bdg. 65.00 (0-313-23818-9, MJO, Greenwood Pr) Greenwood.
McKerns, Joseph P. & Atwood, L. E. News Media & Public Policy: An Annotated Bibliography, Vol. 2. LC 83-49290. (Public Affairs & Administration Ser.: Vol. 11). 192p. 1985. text 15.00 (0-8240-9004-7) Garland.
McKerns, Kenneth W., ed. Regulation of Gene Expression by Hormones. LC 83-6310. (Biochemical Endocrinology Ser.). 278p. 1983. 85.00 (0-306-41204-7, Plenum Trade) Perseus Pubng.
— Reproductive Processes & Contraception. LC 80-20744. (Biochemical Endocrinology Ser.). 752p. 1981. 120.00 (0-306-40534-2, Plenum Trade) Perseus Pubng.
McKerns, Kenneth W. & Pantic, Vladmir, eds. Hormonally Active Brain Peptides: Stucture & Function. LC 82-9147. (Biochemical Endocrinology Ser.). 652p. 1982. 110.00 (0-306-40865-1, Plenum Trade) Perseus Pubng.
McKerns, Kenneth W., jt. ed. see Chretien, M.
McKerns, Kenneth W., ed. see International Foundation for Biochemical Endocrino.
McKerns, Kenneth W., jt. ed. see Jutisz, Marian.
***McKerracher, Archie.** Perthshire in History & Legend. 219p. 2000. pap. 19.95 (0-85976-517-2, Pub. by J Donald) Dufour.
McKerral, Helen. Gardening on a Shoestring. (Illus.). 148p. 1999. pap. 14.95 (1-86447-067-4, Pub. by Hyland Hse) Seven Hills Bk.
McKerron, Wilhelmina. The Wheel of Destiny. 1981. 30.00 (0-7223-1408-6, Pub. by A H S Ltd) St Mut.
McKerrow, Margaret, et al. The Cleverest Lawyer or Pierre Pathelin: Playscript. (Orig.). 1986. pap. 10.00 (0-88734-506-9) Players Pr.
McKerrow, Phillip. Performance Measurement of Computer Systems. (Illus.). 256p. (C). 1988. text 35.50 (0-201-17436-7) Addison-Wesley.
McKerrow, R. M., ed. see Dekker, Thomas.
McKerrow, Ronald B. Introduction to Bibliography for Literary Students. LC 94-7048. (Illus.). 400p. 1995. pap. 29.95 (1-884718-01-9) Oak Knoll.
— Printers' & Publishers' Devices in England & Scotland, 1485-1640. LC Z 1008.B545. (Bibliographical Society, Illustrated Monographs: Vol. 16). (Illus.). 309p. reprint ed. pap. 95.80 (0-608-13675-1, 205540800020) Bks Demand.
— Treatment of Shakespeare's Text by His Earlier Editors, 1709-1768. LC 79-109656. (Select Bibliographies Reprint Ser.). 1977. 15.95 (0-8369-5265-0) Ayer.
McKersie, B. D. & Brown, D. C., eds. Biotechnology & the Improvement of Forage Legumes. LC 96-48878. (Biotechnology in Agriculture Ser.: No. 17). 433p. 1997. text 140.00 (0-85199-109-2) OUP.
Mckersie, Bryan D. Stress & Stress Coping in Cultivated Plants. 260p. (C). 1994. text 186.50 (0-7923-2827-2) Kluwer Academic.
McKersie, Robert B., jt. auth. see Walton, Richard E.
McKersie, Robert B., jt. ed. see Abraham, Katherine.
McKesney, Thomas L. Indian Tribes of North America: With Biographical Sketches & Anecdotes of the Principal Chiefs, 3 vols. reprint ed. lib. bdg. 225.00 (0-7812-0302-3) Rprt Serv.
McKessock, Brenda. Mesothelioma: The Story of an Illness. LC 95-233331. 240p. 1994. pap. write for info. (1-874640-21-1, Pub. by Argyll Pubng) St Mut.
McKesson, Malcolm. Matriarchy: Freedom in Bondage. LC 96-77595. (Illus.). 208p. 1997. pap. 14.95 (0-9638129-7-1, 620221) Heck Editions.
— Matriarchy: Freedom in Bondage. deluxe limited ed. LC 96-77595. (Illus.). 208p. 1996. 34.95 (0-9638129-8-X, 620222) Heck Editions.
McKetta, ed. Encyclopedia of Chemical Processing & Design. (Illus.). 500p. 1998. text 195.00 (0-8247-2614-6) Dekker.
— Encyclopedia of Chemical Processing & Design, Vol. 61. (Illus.). 536p. 1997. text 195.00 (0-8247-2612-X) Dekker.
— Encyclopedia of Chemical Processing & Design, Vol. 62. (Illus.). 500p. 1997. text 195.00 (0-8247-2613-8) Dekker.
— Encyclopedia of Chemical Processing & Design, Vol. 64. (Illus.). 500p. 1998. text 195.00 (0-8247-2615-4) Dekker.

M

— Encyclopedia of Chemical Processing & Design, Vol. 64. (Illus.). 500p. 1998. text 195.00 (*0-8247-2615-4*) Dekker.

***McKetta, Frank. Police, Politics & Corruption. 202p. 2000. 14.00 (*0-87012-611-3*) McClain.**

A revealing story of how politics has influenced local state & federal law enforcement from the turn of the last century until very recent times. This hard cover, 201 page book covers not only some vignettes of historical political corruption in police work but some of his personal experiences in coping with the problem. Colonel McKetta offers his perspective on some approaches to lessening the corruptive influence of politics; thus positioning his book as a "primer" in the study of law enforcement in all jurisdictions. The book may be ordered from Polis Publishing, 4107 Park St., Camp Hill, PA 17011. Single copy price = $14.00 plus $3.00 shipping & handling, plus 6% Sales Tax, Total=$18.02 Checks or Money Orders accepted. ***Publisher Paid Annotation.***

McKetta, John, ed. Heat Transfer Design Methods. (Illus.). 640p. 1991. text 215.00 (*0-8247-8518-5*) Dekker.

McKetta, John J. Chemical Processing Handbook. LC 93-20256. (Illus.). 992p. 1993. text 275.00 (*0-8247-8701-3*) Dekker.

— Encyclopedia of Chemical Processes, Vol. 31. (Illus.). 512p. 1989. text 195.00 (*0-8247-2481-X*) Dekker.

— Encyclopedia of Chemical Processes, Vol. 32. (Illus.). 504p. 1989. text 195.00 (*0-8247-2482-8*) Dekker.

— Encyclopedia of Chemical Processes, Vol. 33. (Illus.). 528p. 1990. text 195.00 (*0-8247-2483-6*) Dekker.

— Encyclopedia of Chemical Processing & Design, Vol. 1. (Illus.). 496p. 1976. text 195.00 (*0-8247-2451-8*) Dekker.

— Encyclopedia of Chemical Processing & Design, Vol. 2. (Illus.). 512p. 1977. text 195.00 (*0-8247-2452-6*) Dekker.

— Encyclopedia of Chemical Processing & Design, Vol. 3. (Illus.). 512p. 1977. text 195.00 (*0-8247-2453-4*) Dekker.

— Encyclopedia of Chemical Processing & Design, Vol. 4. (Illus.). 512p. 1977. text 195.00 (*0-8247-2454-2*) Dekker.

— Encyclopedia of Chemical Processing & Design, Vol. 6. (Illus.). 504p. 1978. text 195.00 (*0-8247-2456-9*) Dekker.

— Encyclopedia of Chemical Processing & Design, Vol. 7. (Illus.). 1978. text 195.00 (*0-8247-2457-7*) Dekker.

— Encyclopedia of Chemical Processing & Design, Vol. 8. (Illus.). 526p. 1979. text 195.00 (*0-8247-2458-5*) Dekker.

— Encyclopedia of Chemical Processing & Design, Vol. 9. (Illus.). 496p. 1979. text 195.00 (*0-8247-2459-3*) Dekker.

— Encyclopedia of Chemical Processing & Design, Vol. 10. (Illus.). 464p. 1979. text 195.00 (*0-8247-2460-7*) Dekker.

— Encyclopedia of Chemical Processing & Design, Vol. 11. (Illus.). 518p. 1980. text 195.00 (*0-8247-2461-5*) Dekker.

— Encyclopedia of Chemical Processing & Design, Vol. 12. (Illus.). 408p. 1981. text 195.00 (*0-8247-2462-3*) Dekker.

— Encyclopedia of Chemical Processing & Design, Vol. 13. (Illus.). 408p. 1981. text 195.00 (*0-8247-2463-1*) Dekker.

— Encyclopedia of Chemical Processing & Design, Vol. 14. (Illus.). 504p. 1982. text 195.00 (*0-8247-2464-X*) Dekker.

— Encyclopedia of Chemical Processing & Design, Vol. 15. (Illus.). 488p. 1982. text 195.00 (*0-8247-2465-8*) Dekker.

— Encyclopedia of Chemical Processing & Design, Vol. 16. (Illus.). 456p. 1982. text 195.00 (*0-8247-2466-6*) Dekker.

— Encyclopedia of Chemical Processing & Design, Vol. 17. (Illus.). 488p. 1983. text 195.00 (*0-8247-2467-4*) Dekker.

— Encyclopedia of Chemical Processing & Design, Vol. 18. (Illus.). 512p. 1983. text 195.00 (*0-8247-2468-2*) Dekker.

— Encyclopedia of Chemical Processing & Design, Vol. 19. (Illus.). 480p. 1983. text 195.00 (*0-8247-2469-0*) Dekker.

— Encyclopedia of Chemical Processing & Design, Vol. 20. (Illus.). 520p. 1984. text 195.00 (*0-8247-2470-4*) Dekker.

— Encyclopedia of Chemical Processing & Design, Vol. 23. (Illus.). 528p. 1985. text 195.00 (*0-8247-2473-9*) Dekker.

— Encyclopedia of Chemical Processing & Design, Vol. 24. (Illus.). 520p. 1986. text 195.00 (*0-8247-2474-7*) Dekker.

— Encyclopedia of Chemical Processing & Design, Vol. 25. (Illus.). 504p. 1986. text 195.00 (*0-8247-2475-5*) Dekker.

— Encyclopedia of Chemical Processing & Design, Vol. 26. (Illus.). 520p. 1987. text 195.00 (*0-8247-2476-3*) Dekker.

— Encyclopedia of Chemical Processing & Design, Vol. 28. (Illus.). 520p. 1988. text 195.00 (*0-8247-2478-X*) Dekker.

— Encyclopedia of Chemical Processing & Design, Vol. 29. (Illus.). 528p. 1988. text 195.00 (*0-8247-2479-8*) Dekker.

— Encyclopedia of Chemical Processing & Design, Vol. 30. (Illus.). 528p. 1989. text 195.00 (*0-8247-2480-1*) Dekker.

— Encyclopedia of Chemical Processing & Design, Vol. 35. (Illus.). 520p. 1990. text 195.00 (*0-8247-2485-2*) Dekker.

— Encyclopedia of Chemical Processing & Design, Vol. 36. (Illus.). 568p. 1990. text 195.00 (*0-8247-2486-0*) Dekker.

— Encyclopedia of Chemical Processing & Design, Vol. 37. (Illus.). 520p. 1991. text 195.00 (*0-8247-2487-9*) Dekker.

— Encyclopedia of Chemical Processing & Design, Vol. 38. (Illus.). 544p. 1991. text 195.00 (*0-8247-2488-7*) Dekker.

— Encyclopedia of Chemical Processing & Design, Vol. 39. (Illus.). 528p. 1992. text 195.00 (*0-8247-2489-5*) Dekker.

— Encyclopedia of Chemical Processing & Design, Vol. 41. (Illus.). 536p. 1992. text 195.00 (*0-8247-2491-7*) Dekker.

— Encyclopedia of Chemical Processing & Design, Vol. 42. (Illus.). 528p. 1992. text 195.00 (*0-8247-2492-5*) Dekker.

— Encyclopedia of Chemical Processing & Design, Vol. 45. (Illus.). 568p. 1993. text 195.00 (*0-8247-2495-X*) Dekker.

— Encyclopedia of Chemical Processing & Design, Vol. 46. (Illus.). 552p. 1993. text 195.00 (*0-8247-2496-8*) Dekker.

— Encyclopedia of Chemical Processing & Design, Vol. 47. (Illus.). 528p. 1994. text 195.00 (*0-8247-2497-6*) Dekker.

— Encyclopedia of Chemical Processing & Design, Vol. 48. (Illus.). 496p. 1994. text 195.00 (*0-8247-2498-4*) Dekker.

— Encyclopedia of Chemical Processing & Design, Vol. 49. (Illus.). 536p. 1994. text 195.00 (*0-8247-2499-2*) Dekker.

— Encyclopedia of Chemical Processing & Design, Vol. 52. (Illus.). 544p. 1995. text 195.00 (*0-8247-2603-0*) Dekker.

— Encyclopedia of Chemical Processing & Design, Vol.5. (Illus.). 512p. 1978. text 195.00 (*0-8247-2455-0*) Dekker.

— Encyclopedia of Chemical Processing & Design: Process Control, Feedback Simulation to Process Optimization, Vol. 43. (Illus.). 552p. 1993. text 195.00 (*0-8247-2493-3*) Dekker.

— Encyclopedia of Chemical Processing & Design: Slurry Systems, Instrumentation to Solid-Liquid Separation, Vol. 51. (Illus.). 537p. 1995. text 195.00 (*0-8247-2602-2*) Dekker.

— Encyclopedia of Chemical Processing & Design: Thermoplastics to Trays, Separation, Useful Capacity, Vol. 58. (Illus.). 536p. 1996. text 195.00 (*0-8247-2609-X*) Dekker.

— Encyclopedia of Computer Processing & Design, Vol. 34. (Illus.). 420p. 1990. text 195.00 (*0-8247-2484-4*) Dekker.

McKetta, John J. Industrial Products Handbook, Vol. 1. (Illus.). 880p. 1993. text 430.00 (*0-8247-8709-9*) Dekker.

— Industrial Products Handbook, Vol. 2. (Illus.). 1760p. 1993. text 430.00 (*0-8247-8706-4*) Dekker.

McKetta, John J. Inorganic Chemicals Handbook, Vol. 1. (Illus.). 728p. 1993. text 425.00 (*0-8247-8686-6*) Dekker.

— Inorganic Chemicals Handbook, Vol. 2. (Illus.). 1456p. 1993. text 425.00 (*0-8247-8687-4*) Dekker.

McKetta, John J. Petroleum Processing Handbook. (Illus.). 792p. 1992. text 299.00 (*0-8247-8681-5*) Dekker.

McKetta, John J. Piping Design Handbook. (Illus.). 1280p. 1992. text 295.00 (*0-8247-8570-3*) Dekker.

McKetta, John J., ed. Encyclopedia of Chemical Processing & Design, Vol. 40. (Illus.). 528p. 1992. text 195.00 (*0-8247-2490-9*) Dekker.

— Encyclopedia of Chemical Processing & Design, Vol. 54. (Illus.). 528p. 1995. text 195.00 (*0-8247-2605-7*) Dekker.

— Encyclopedia of Chemical Processing & Design, Vol. 55. (Illus.). 552p. 1996. text 195.00 (*0-8247-2606-5*) Dekker.

— Encyclopedia of Chemical Processing & Design, Vol. 56. (Illus.). 528p. 1996. text 195.00 (*0-8247-2607-3*) Dekker.

— Encyclopedia of Chemical Processing & Design, Vol. 57. (Illus.). 544p. 1996. text 195.00 (*0-8247-2608-1*) Dekker.

— Encyclopedia of Chemical Processing & Design, Vol. 59. (Illus.). 528p. 1997. text 195.00 (*0-8247-2610-3*) Dekker.

— Encyclopedia of Chemical Processing & Design, Vol. 60. (Illus.). 536p. 1997. text 195.00 (*0-8247-2611-1*) Dekker.

— Encyclopedia of Chemical Processing & Design: Expanders to Finned Tubes, Vol. 21. (Illus.). 520p. 1984. text 195.00 (*0-8247-2471-2*) Dekker.

— Encyclopedia of Chemical Processing & Design: Fire Extinguishing Chemicals to Fluid Flow, Slurry Systems & Pipelines, Vol. 22. (Illus.). 440p. 1985. text 195.00 (*0-8247-2472-0*) Dekker.

— Encyclopedia of Chemical Processing & Design: Hydrogen Cyanide to Ketones Dimethyl (Acetone), Vol. 27. (Illus.). 512p. 1987. text 195.00 (*0-8247-2477-1*) Dekker.

— Encyclopedia of Chemical Processing & Design: Process Plants, Cost Estimating to Project Management, Vol. 44. (Illus.). 512p. 1993. text 195.00 (*0-8247-2494-1*) Dekker.

— Encyclopedia of Chemical Processing & Design: Settling Drums, Design of to Slag, Iron & Steel, Supply-Demand Relationships, Vol. 50. (Illus.). 520p. 1994. text 195.00 (*0-8247-2601-4*) Dekker.

— Encyclopedia of Computer Processing & Design, Vol. 53. (Illus.). 536p. 1995. text 195.00 (*0-8247-2604-9*) Dekker.

McKetta, John J., ed. Unit Operations Handbook, Vol. 1. LC 92-25562. (Illus.). 1017p. 1992. text 390.00 (*0-8247-8669-6*) Dekker.

— Unit Operations Handbook, Vol. 2. LC 92-25562. (Illus.). 1816p. 1992. text 390.00 (*0-8247-8670-X*) Dekker.

McKetta, John J., Jr., intro. Chemical Technology: An Encyclopedic Treatment, 8 vols. Incl. Vol. 7. Vegetable Food Products & Luxuries., 8 vols. (Illus.). 905p. 1975. 68.50 (*0-06-491108-X*, 06301); (Illus.). write for info. (*0-318-51000-6*) B&N Imports.

— Edible Oils & Fats & Animal Food Products, 8 vols., Vol. 8. (Illus.). 600p. 1975. 68.50 (*0-06-491109-8*, 06302) B&N Imports.

— Metals & Ores, 8 vols., Vol. 3. (Illus.). 918p. 1970. 68.50 (*0-06-491104-7*, 06297) B&N Imports.

— Natural Organic Materials & Related Synthetic Products, 8 vols., Vol. 5. (Illus.). 898p. 1972. 68.50 (*0-06-491106-3*) B&N Imports.

— Non-Metallic Ores, Silicate Industries & Solid Minerals Fuels, 8 vols., Vol. 2. 828p. 1971. 68.50 (*0-06-491103-9*) B&N Imports.

— Petroleum & Organic Chemicals, 8 vols., Vol. 4. (Illus.). 792p. 1972. 68.50 (*0-06-491105-5*) B&N Imports.

— Wood, Paper, Textiles, Plastics & Photographic Materials, 8 vols., Vol. 6. (Illus.). 686p. 1973. 68.50 (*0-06-491107-1*, 06300) B&N Imports.

McKevett, G. A. Bitter Sweets. LC 96-75281. 304p. 1996. pap. 18.95 (*1-57566-032-6*) Kensgtn Pub Corp.

— Bitter Sweets. 304p. 1997. mass mkt. 5.50 (*1-57566-169-1*, Knsington) Kensgtn Pub Corp.

McKevett, G. A. Bitter Sweets. 1997. mass mkt. 5.99 (*1-57566-693-6*, Knsington) Kensgtn Pub Corp.

— Cooked Goose, Vol. 1. 313p. 1999. mass mkt. 5.99 (*1-57566-479-8*) Kens Hse.

— Cooked Goose. LC 98-65848. (Illus.). 304p. 1998. 20.00 (*1-57566-359-7*) Kensgtn Pub Corp.

McKevett, G. A. Just Desserts. 320p. 1996. pap. 4.99 (*1-57566-037-7*) Kensgtn Pub Corp.

— Killer Calories. LC 96-79085. 304p. 1997. 18.95 (*1-57566-163-2*, Knsington) Kensgtn Pub Corp.

— Killer Calories. 320p. 1998. mass mkt. 5.99 (*1-57566-298-1*) Kensgtn Pub Corp.

***McKevett, G. A.** Killer Calories. (Savannah Reid Mystery Ser.). 2000. mass mkt. 5.99 (*1-57566-521-2*, Knsington) Kensgtn Pub Corp.

— Sugar & Spite. LC 99-63485. (Savannah Reid Mystery Ser.). 288p. 2000. 20.00 (*1-57566-493-3*) Kensgtn Pub Corp.

McKevitt, Anne. House Sensation: Spirited & Stylish Home Decorating. LC 99-24589. (Illus.). 192p. 1999. pap. 24.95 (*1-57959-034-9*) BB&T Inc.

McKevitt, Anne & Warrington, Shelley. Style on a Shoestring: Simple Ideas for Fantastic Rooms. LC 98-29372. (Illus.). 128p. 1998. pap. 19.95 (*0-912333-66-9*) BB&T Inc.

McKevitt, David & Lawton, Alan, eds. Public Sector Management: Theory, Critique & Practice. 320p. 1994. 75.00 (*0-8039-7712-3*); pap. 32.00 (*0-8039-7713-1*) Sage.

McKevitt, David & Wrigley, Len. Managing Core Public Services. LC 98-20901. 288p. (C). 1999. 69.95 (*0-631-19311-1*); pap. 39.95 (*0-631-19312-X*) Blackwell Pubs.

McKevitt, David, jt. ed. see Lawton, Alan.

McKevitt, Gerald. The University of Santa Clara: A History, 1851-1977. LC 78-65396. (Illus.). xii, 385p. 1979. 47.50 (*0-8047-1024-4*) Stanford U Pr.

McKevitt, Paul, ed. Integration of Natural Language & Vision Processing Vol. 1: Computational Models & Systems. LC 95-12. (Diverse Ser.). 309p. (C). 1995. text 110.50 (*0-7923-3379-9*) Kluwer Academic.

McKevitt, Paul, ed. Integration of Natural Language & Vision Processing Vol. 2: Intelligent Multimedia. 176p. (C). 1995. text 124.50 (*0-7923-3758-1*) Kluwer Academic.

— Integration of Natural Language & Vision Processing Vol. 3: Theory & Grounding Representations. (Diverse Ser.). 250p. (C). 1996. text 100.50 (*0-7923-3944-4*) Kluwer Academic.

— Integration of Natural Language & Vision Processing Vol. 4: Recent Advances. 228p. (C). 1996. text 97.50 (*0-7923-4114-7*) Kluwer Academic.

McKew, Howard J. Managing People in the HVAC-R Industry. Turpin, Joanna, ed. LC 94-33085. 120p. (Orig.). 1995. pap. 14.95 (*0-912524-97-9*) Busn News.

***McKewan, John.** Ultimate Horse Care. 256p. 2000. 29.95 (*1-58245-170-2*) Howell Bks.

***McKewen, Allene.** Collie. LC 99-47111. 160p. 1999. 12.95 (*1-58245-008-0*) Howell Bks.

McKewin, Robert. Behold the Man. 1988. pap. 9.95 (*0-910924-95-3*) Macalester.

McKey, D., jt. ed. see Sprent, J. I.

McKey, Jo Ann R. Accomack County, Virginia Court Order Abstracts, 1676-1678, Vol. 5. LC 98-113992. viii, 475p. 1997. pap. 13.00 (*0-7884-0733-3*, M162) Heritage Bk.

Mckey, JoAnn R. Accomack County, VA, Court Order Abstracts 1663-1666. 201p. (Orig.). 1996. pap. 21.00 (*0-7884-0448-2*, M148) Heritage Bk.

McKey, JoAnn R. Accomack County, Virginia Court Order Abstracts. 320p. 1999. pap. 28.00 (*0-7884-1092-X*, M160) Heritage.

— Accomack County, Virginia Court Order Abstracts, Vol. 4. xxiv, 195p. 1997. pap. 21.00 (*0-7884-0695-7*, M156) Heritage Bk.

— Accomack County, Virginia Court Order Abstracts Vol. 6: 1678-1682. 264p. 1998. pap. 23.50 (*0-7884-0812-7*, M163) Heritage Bk.

— Accomack County, Virginia Court Order Abstracts, 1666-1670, Vol. 2. 234p. 1998. reprint ed. pap. 21.50 (*0-7884-0568-3*, M152) Heritage Bk.

— Accomack County, Virginia Court Order Abstracts, 1671-1673, Vol. 3. (Illus.). xx, 164p. (Orig.). 1996. pap. 20.00 (*0-7884-0586-1*, M154) Heritage Bk.

— Accomack County, Virginia Court Order Abstracts, 1682-1690. 440p. 1998. pap. 35.50 (*0-7884-1038-5*, M164) Heritage Bk.

— Baptismal Records of the Dutch Reformed Churches in the City of Groningen, Netherlands 1640-1649, Vol. 1. LC 96-145920. 172p. (Orig.). 1996. pap. 28.50 (*0-7884-0439-3*, M147) Heritage Bk.

— Baptismal Records of the Dutch Reformed Churches in the City of Groningen, Netherlands 1650-1659, Vol. 2. LC 96-145920. 178p. (Orig.). 1996. pap. 29.50 (*0-7884-0440-7*, M150) Heritage Bk.

***McKey, JoAnn Riley.** Accomack County, Virginia, Court Order Abstracts, 1697-1703, Vol. 9. 208p. 1999. pap. 21.50 (*0-7884-1286-8*, M138) Heritage Bk.

— Accomack County, Virginia Court Order Abstracts, 1703-1710, No. 10. 309p. 2000. pap. 26.25 (*0-7884-1480-1*, 1480) Heritage Bk.

McKhann, Charles F. A Time to Die: The Place for Physician Assistance. LC 98-22193. 282p. 1998. 35.00 (*0-300-07631-2*) Yale U Pr.

***McKhann, Charles F.** A Time to Die: The Place for Physician Assistance. 282p. 2000. pap. 16.00 (*0-300-08698-9*) Yale U Pr.

McKibben, Alan. Hudson River Journey: An Artist's Perspective. deluxe ed. McKibben, Susan, ed. (Illus.). 84p. 1999. 49.95 (*0-9616412-6-6*, HRJOUR) Lke Champlain Pub.

McKibben, Alan A. & McKibben, Susan B. Cruising Guide to Lake Champlain: The Waterway from New York City to Montreal. 5th ed. LC 98-233875. (Illus.). 240p. 1997. pap., spiral bd. 34.95 (*0-9616412-5-8*, CGLC97) Lke Champlain Pub.

McKibben, Bill. The Age of Missing Information. 272p. 1993. pap. 13.95 (*0-452-26980-6*, Plume) Dutton Plume.

— Aperture 150: Moments of Grace: Spirit in the American Landscape. (Illus.). 80p. 1998. pap. 27.95 (*0-89381-780-5*) Aperture.

***McKibben, Bill.** The End of Nature. 2000. 26.50 (*0-8446-7129-0*) Peter Smith.

McKibben, Bill. The End of Nature. anniversary ed. 240p. 1997. pap. 14.00 (*0-385-41604-0*) Doubleday.

— Hope, Human & Wild: True Stories of Living Lightly on the Earth. LC 96-78376. 237p. (Orig.). 1997. pap. 15.00 (*1-886913-13-7*) Ruminator Bks.

— Hundred Dollar Holiday: The Case for a More Joyful Christmas. 96p. 1998. 12.00 (*0-684-85595-X*) S&S Trade.

***McKibben, Bill.** Long Distance: A Year of Living Strenuously. LC 00-55613. 2000. write for info. (*0-684-85597-6*) Simon & Schuster.

McKibben, Bill. Maybe One: A Case for Smaller Families. 256p. 1999. pap. 12.95 (*0-452-28092-3*, Plume) Dutton Plume.

— Maybe One: An Environmental & Personal Argument for Single-Child Families. LC 98-5417. 240p. 1998. 23.00 (*0-684-85281-0*) S&S Trade.

McKibben, Bill, et al. 25 Bicycle Tours in the Adirondacks: Road Adventures in the East's Largest Wilderness. LC 95-5912. (25 Bicycle Tours Ser.). (Illus.). 192p. (Orig.). 1995. pap. 13.00 (*0-88150-318-5*, Pub. by Countryman) Norton.

McKibben, Bill, jt. auth. see Rezendes, Paul.

McKibben, Carol F., jt. ed. see Goldblatt, Joe J.

McKibben, Gordon C. Cutting Edge: Gillette's Journey to Global Leadership. LC 97-25517. 496p. 1998. 35.00 (*0-87584-725-0*) Harvard Busn.

McKibben, Jorge F., tr. see Davis, Guillermo H.

McKibben, Michael T., jt. auth. see Williams, Benjamin D.

McKibben, Nancy J. The Chaos Protocol. 340p. (Orig.). 1999. pap. 19.95 (*1-893857-90-5*) Malmesbury Bks.

McKibben-Stockwell. Nuevo Lexico Griego Espanol: Greek-Spanish Lexicon of the New Testament. (SPA.). 316p. 1985. reprint ed. pap. 12.99 (*0-311-42072-9*, Edit Mundo) Casa Bautista.

McKibben, Susan, ed. see McKibben, Alan.

McKibben, Susan B., jt. auth. see McKibben, Alan A.

McKibbens, Thomas R., Jr. The Forgotten Heritage: A Lineage of Great Baptist Preaching. LC 86-705. (Orig.). 1986. pap. text 18.95 (*0-86554-186-8*, MUP-P018) Mercer Univ Pr.

McKibbens, Thomas R., Jr. & Smith, Kenneth. The Life & Work of Morgan Edwards: First Baptist Historian in the United States. Gaustad, Edwin S., ed. LC 79-5269. (Baptist Tradition Ser.). 1980. lib. bdg. 25.95 (*0-405-12438-4*) Ayer.

McKibbin, Carroll R. In Pursuit of National Interests. 2nd ed. 256p. 1994. per. 21.95 (*0-8403-8453-X*) Kendall-Hunt.

McKibbin, Elizabeth & O'Neil, Dominic. Ross: Drafting & Negotiating Commercial Leases. 4th ed. Ross, Murray J., ed. 1996. pap., suppl. ed. write for info. incl. disk (*0-406-99314-9*, RDNC4SUP, MICHIE) LEXIS Pub.

McKibbin, Frank, jt. auth. see McKibbin, Jean.

McKibbin, Jean & McKibbin, Frank. Cookbook of Foods from Bible Days. enl. rev. ed. LC 72-88527. (Illus.). 1972. reprint ed. 17.95 (*0-9601078-1-9*) Jean McKibbin.

McKibbin, L. S. Vadecum del Cuidador de Caballos. (SPA.). pap. 56.95 (*84-200-0435-9*); pap. write for info. (*0-8288-7896-X*) Fr & Eur.

An Asterisk (*) at the beginning of an entry indicates that the title is appearing for the first time.

McKibbin, Martin H., ed. What If? Exploring the Paths Not Taken in American History. (Illus.). 1995. 20.00 (*0-9641651-1-2*) Sparrowhwk Pr.
McKibbin, Nonie. The Sea in the Desert: Explorer's Guide to the Gulf of California Seaside. Thomson, Jenean et al, eds. (Illus.). 130p. (Orig.). 1989. 10.00 (*0-685-34742-7*) Golden Puffer.
McKibbin, Nonie, jt. auth. see Thomson, Donald A.
McKibbin, Ross. Classes & Cultures: England 1918-1951. LC 97-33044. 576p. (C). 1998. 45.00 (*0-19-820672-0*) OUP.
***McKibbin, Ross.** Classes & Cultures: England, 1918-1951. 580p. 2000. pap. 24.95 (*0-19-820855-3*) OUP.
— The Evolution of the Labour Party, 1910-1924. (Oxford Historical Monographs). 1984. reprint ed. pap. 16.95 (*0-19-821899-0*) OUP.
McKibbin, Stuart. Cynic's Guide to Management. 160p. 1999. 14.95 (*0-7090-6249-4*, Pub. by R Hale Ltd) Seven Hills Bk.
Mckibbin, Warwick J. Arms Reduction: Economic Implications in the Post-Cold War Era. LC 96-232396. 384p. 35.00 (*92-808-0881-8*) UN.
McKibbin, Warwick J. & Sachs, Jeffrey D. Global Linkages: Macroeconomic Interdependence & Cooperation in the World Economy. 277p. 1991. 36.95 (*0-8157-5600-3*); pap. 16.95 (*0-8157-5601-1*) Brookings.
***McKibbon, Ann K., et al.** PDQ Evidence-Based Principles & Practice. (Evidence-Based Ser.). 212p. 1999. boxed set 27.95 incl. cd-rom (*1-55009-118-2*) DEKR.
McKibbon, Hugh W. The Token Gift. (Illus.). 32p. (Orig.). (J). (gr. 1-5). 1996. pap. 6.95 (*1-55037-498-2*, Pub. by Annick); pap. 16.95 (*1-55037-499-0*, Pub. by Annick) Firefly Bks Ltd.
McKibbon, W. Stan. The Anointed One: Messiah. 215p. (Orig.). 1994. pap. write for info. (*0-9642975-0-7*) S McKibbon Min.
McKichan. Germany, 1815-1939 the Growth of Nationalism. 1994. pap. text. write for info. (*0-05-005081-8*) Addison-Wesley.
McKie. Using the Web for Social Research. 1997. 24.06 (*0-07-552851-7*) McGraw.
McKie, Angus, jt. illus. see Gibbons, Dave.
McKie, Bowlby. Gender Power & the Household. LC 99-19797. 1999. text 69.95 (*0-312-22410-9*) St Martin.
***McKie, Craig & Thompson, Keith, eds.** Transparency Masters, Vol. 3. 1999. 75.00 (*1-55077-072-1*) Thompson Educ.
McKie, David, jt. auth. see Jagtenberg, Tom.
McKie, David, tr. see Zolo, Danilo.
McKie, Douglas. Antoine Lavoisier. (Series in Science). (Illus.). 448p. 1990. reprint ed. pap. 14.95 (*0-306-80408-5*) Da Capo.
McKie, Douglas & De Heathcote, Niels. The Discovery of Specific & Latent Heats. LC 74-26274. (History, Philosophy & Sociology of Science Ser.). 1975. reprint ed. 21.95 (*0-405-06602-3*) Ayer.
McKie, Douglas, jt. auth. see Partington, James R.
McKie, James D., ed. Social Responsibility & the Business Predicament. LC 74-23967. (Studies in the Regulation of Economic Activity). 361p. 1975. 42.95 (*0-8157-5608-9*); pap. 18.95 (*0-8157-5607-0*) Brookings.
McKie, John, et al. The Allocation of Health Care Resources: An Ethical Evaluation of the "QALY" Approach. LC 97-42927. (Medico-Legal Ser.). 151p. 1998. text 76.95 (*1-85521-953-0*, Pub. by Ashgate Pub) Ashgate Pub Co.
***McKie, Robin.** Dawn of Man: The Story of Human Evolution. (Illus.). 288p. 2000. 30.00 (*0-7894-6262-1*) DK Pub Inc.
McKie, Robin, jt. auth. see Bodmer, Walter.
McKie, Robin, jt. auth. see Stringer, Christopher.
McKie, Ronald. The Emergence of Malaysia. LC 72-13868. (Illus.). 310p. 1973. reprint ed. lib. bdg. 69.50 (*0-8371-6763-9*, MCEM, Greenwood Pr) Greenwood.
McKie, Roy. The Joke Book. LC 78-62699. (Pictureback Ser.). (Illus.). (J). (ps-2). 1979. pap. 3.25 (*0-394-84077-1*, Pub. by Random Bks Yng Read); lib. bdg. 8.99 (*0-394-94077-6*, Pub. by Random Bks Yng Read) Random.
— Joke Book. (Random House Pictureback Ser.). (Illus.). (J). 1979. 8.45 (*0-606-01733-X*, Pub. by Turtleback) Demco.
— The Riddle Book. LC 77-85237. (Pictureback Ser.). (J). (ps-2). 1978. pap. 3.25 (*0-394-83732-0*, Pub. by Random Bks Yng Read) Random.
McKie, Roy & Eastman, Philip D. Snow. LC 62-15114. (Illus.). 72p. (J). (gr. 1-2). 1962. lib. bdg. 11.99 (*0-394-90027-8*) Beginner.
— Snow. LC 62-15114. (Illus.). 72p. (J). (gr. 1-2). 1962. 7.99 (*0-394-80027-3*) Beginner.
McKie, Roy, jt. auth. see Beard, Henry.
Mckie, Simon. Roll-Over Relief on Reinvestment. 140p. 1993. pap. text 48.00 (*0-406-02800-1*, UK, MICHIE) LEXIS Pub.
McKie, Stewart. The Accounting Software Handbook. 2nd ed. LC 98-25438. 225p. 1998. pap. 59.00 (*1-882419-81-2*) News Four-Hund.
— Client-Server Accounting: Reengineering Your Accounting Systems. LC 96-30767. 336p. 1997. 120.00 (*0-471-15784-8*); pap. 74.95 (*0-471-16882-3*) Wiley.
***McKie, Stewart.** Client/server Accounting: Reengineering Financial Systems, 2000 Cumulative Supplement. 144p. 2000. pap. 65.00 (*0-471-36143-7*) Wiley.
McKie, Suzanne. Legal Research: How to Find & Understand the Law. 220p. 1994. pap. 30.00 (*1-874241-50-3*, Pub. by Cavendish Pubng) Gaunt.
McKie, W. Gilmore & Lipsett, Laurence. The Contingent Worker: A Human Resources Perspective. 60p. (Orig.). 1995. 20.00 (*0-939900-68-8*) Soc Human Resc Mgmt.
McKie, William L. Scientific Hydrotherapy. 134p. 1993. reprint ed. spiral bd. 16.50 (*0-7873-0599-5*) Hlth Research.
McKiel, Mary, jt. auth. see Hemenway, Caroline G.
***McKiernan-Allen, Linda, ed.** Celebrating Covenant: A Resource for Worship. 2001. pap. 16.99 (*0-8272-0482-5*) Chalice Pr.
— Celebrating Incarnation: A Resource for Worship. LC 99-50441. 160p. 2000. pap. 16.99 (*0-8272-0478-7*) Chalice Pr.
***McKiernan-Allen, Linda & Watson, Nick.** Organizing Bodies: Policy, Institutions & Work. LC 00-26979. 2000. write for info. (*0-312-23476-7*) St Martin.
McKiernan, Dennis L. Caverns of Socrates. LC 95-9856. 432p. 1995. text 24.95 (*0-451-45455-3*, ROC) NAL.
— Caverns of Socrates. 1996. mass mkt. 6.99 (*0-451-45467-7*, ROC) NAL.
McKiernan, Dennis L. The Dragonstone. LC 96-17043. 1996. mass mkt. 24.95 (*0-451-45560-6*, ROC) NAL.
McKiernan, Dennis L. The Dragonstone. 480p. 1997. mass mkt. 6.99 (*0-451-45456-1*) NAL.
— The Eye of the Hunter. 592p. 1993. mass mkt. 6.99 (*0-451-45268-2*, ROC) NAL.
***McKiernan, Dennis L.** Into the Fire. LC 98-5247. (Hell's Crucible Ser.: Bk. 2). 480p. 1998. mass mkt. 23.95 (*0-451-45701-3*, ROC) NAL.
McKiernan, Dennis L. Into the Fire. 560p. 1999. reprint ed. mass mkt. 6.99 (*0-451-45732-3*, ROC) NAL.
— Into the Forge. LC 97-12755. 1997. mass mkt. 23.95 (*0-451-45458-8*, ROC) NAL.
— Into the Forge. (Hell's Crucible Ser.). 410p. 1998. mass mkt. 6.99 (*0-451-45700-5*, ROC) NAL.
***McKiernan, Dennis L.** Silver Wolf, Black Falcon. LC 00-24306. 496p. 2000. pap. 23.95 (*0-451-45786-2*, ROC) NAL.
McKiernan, Dennis L. Voyage of the Fox Rider. 592p. 1994. mass mkt. 6.99 (*0-451-45411-1*, ROC) NAL.
McKiernan, Dennis L., et al. Citybook 4: On the Road. Jaquays, Paul, ed. & illus. by. Dow, Tom et al, illus. 96p. 1990. pap. 11.95 (*0-940244-73-X*) Flying Buffalo.
McKiernan, Ethna. Caravan. (Orig.). (C). 1990. pap. 15.00 (*0-948268-55-7*, Pub. by Dedalus) St Mut.
— Caravan. LC 89-61292. (Illus.). 80p. (Orig.). 1989. pap. 5.95 (*0-935697-04-7*) Midwest Villages.
McKiernan, F. Mark & Launius, Roger D., eds. Missouri Folk Heroes of the Nineteenth Century. (Illus.). 1989. pap. 2.00 (*0-8309-0547-2*) Herald Pub Hse.
McKiernan, Peter. Historical Evolution of Strategic Management. (History of Management Thought Ser.). (Illus.). 820p. 1996. text 265.95 (*1-85521-797-X*, Pub. by Dartmth Pub) Ashgate Pub Co.
— Strategies of Growth: Maturity, Recovery & Internationalization. LC 91-28665. 192p. (C). 1992. pap. 21.95 (*0-415-05677-2*) Thomson Learn.
— Strategies of Growth: Maturity, Recovery & Internationalization. LC 91-28665. 192p. (C). (gr. 13 up). 1992. pap. 65.95 (*0-415-07383-9*) Thomson Learn.
McKiernan, Susan P. & King, Joann G. Building a Firm Foundation: Medina County Architecture 1811-1900. LC 95-94896. (Illus.). 160p. (Orig.). 1995. pap. 30.00 (*0-9648275-0-6*) S P McKiernan.
McKig, Jean, ed. see Silkensen, Cynthia.
McKillen, Elizabeth. Chicago Labor & the Quest for a Democratic Diplomacy, 1914-1924. 256p. 1995. text 37.50 (*0-8014-2905-6*) Cornell U Pr.
McKilligan, Neil & Savage, Ian. Bush Walks: In the Toowoomba Region. (Illus.). 77p. (Orig.). 1993. pap. 12.95 (*0-949414-67-0*, Pub. by U Sthrn Queenslnd) Accents Pubns.
McKillip, Jack. Need Analysis: Tools for the Human Services & Education. (Applied Social Research Methods Ser.: Vol. 10). 160p. 1987. text 42.00 (*0-8039-2647-2*); pap. text 18.95 (*0-8039-2648-0*) Sage.
McKillip, Jack, jt. auth. see Pitz, Gordon F.
McKillip, Patricia. Fool's Run. 1988. mass mkt. 4.95 (*0-445-20518-0*, Pub. by Warner Bks) Little.
***McKillip, Patricia.** Forgotten Beasts of Eld. (J). 1999. 13.40 (*0-613-02276-9*) Econo-Clad Bks.
McKillip, Patricia, jt. auth. see Varley, John.
McKillip, Patricia A. The Book of Atrix Wolfe. LC 94-33999. 256p. 1995. 18.95 (*0-441-00211-0*) Ace Bks.
— The Book of Atrix Wolfe. 1996. mass mkt. 5.99 (*0-441-00361-3*) Ace Bks.
— The Cygnet & the Firebird. 320p. (Orig.). 1995. mass mkt. 5.99 (*0-441-00237-4*) Ace Bks.
— The Cygnet & the Firebrand. LC 92-21149. 240p. 1993. pap. 17.95 (*0-441-12628-6*) Ace Bks.
— The Forgotten Beasts of Eld. LC 95-37915. (Magic Carpet Book Ser.). 288p. (J). (gr. 7 up). 1996. pap. 6.00 (*0-15-200869-1*) Harcourt.
— Harpist in the Wind, Vol. 3. 272p. 1985. mass mkt. 5.99 (*0-345-32440-4*) Ballantine Pub Grp.
***McKillip, Patricia A.** Riddle-Master: The Complete Trilogy. LC 99-189042. 592p. (Orig.). 1999. pap. 16.95 (*0-441-00596-9*) Ace Bks.
McKillip, Patricia A. Song for the Basilisk. LC 97-46138. 320p. 1998. pap. 22.95 (*0-441-00447-4*) Ace Bks.
***McKillip, Patricia A.** Song for the Basilisk. 1999. reprint ed. mass mkt. 6.99 (*0-441-00678-7*) Ace Bks.
— The Tower at Stony Wood. LC 99-40441. 304p. 2000. 22.95 (*0-441-00733-3*) Ace Bks.
McKillip, Patricia A. Winter Rose. LC 95-39317. 272p. 1996. pap. 19.95 (*0-441-00334 6*) Ace Bks.
— Winter Rose. 272p. 1997. mass mkt. 5.99 (*0-441-00438-5*) Ace Bks.
Mckillip, Rebecca. Art Nouveau Abstract Designs. (International Design Library). (Illus.). 48p. (Orig.). 1983. pap. 5.95 (*0-88045-023-1*) Stemmer Hse.
McKillip, Rebecca. The Celtic Design Book. 7th ed. (International Design Library). (Illus.). 48p. 1981. pap. 6.95 (*0-916144-75-5*, Naturencyclop) Stemmer Hse.
— Pennsylvania Dutch Designs. (International Design Library). (Illus.). 48p. (Orig.). 1983. pap. 5.95 (*0-88045-032-0*) Stemmer Hse.
McKillip Thrift, Kathryn, ed. see Kasseroller, Renato.
McKillop, A. Advanced Problems in Organic Reaction Mechanisms. LC 97-31811. (Tetrahedron Organic Chemistry Ser.). 1997. write for info. (*0-08-043255-7*, Pergamon Pr); write for info. (*0-08-043256-5*, Pergamon Pr) Elsevier.
— Aliphatic Chemistry, Vol. 2. 1972. 41.00 (*0-85186-512-7*) Am Chemical.
— Aliphatic Chemistry, Vol. 3. 1973. 43.00 (*0-85186-542-9*) Am Chemical.
— Aliphatic Chemistry, Vol. 4. 1974. 45.00 (*0-85186-572-0*) Am Chemical.
— Aliphatic Chemistry, Vol. 5. 1975. 61.00 (*0-85186-602-6*) Am Chemical.
McKillop, A. B. Contours of Canadian Thought. 163p. 1987. pap. 14.95 (*0-8020-6652-6*); text 30.00 (*0-8020-5740-3*) U of Toronto Pr.
— A Disciplined Intelligence: Critical Inquiry & Canadian Thought in the Victorian Era. 1979. 55.00 (*0-7735-0343-9*, Pub. by McG-Queens Univ Pr) CUP Services.
— Matters of Mind: The University in Ontario, 1791-1951. (Ontario Historical Studies). 776p. (C). 1994. text 75.00 (*0-8020-0424-5*); pap. text 35.00 (*0-8020-7216-X*) U of Toronto Pr.
McKillop, A. B., ed. see Wise, S. F.
McKillop, Alan D. The Early Masters of English Fiction. LC 79-16753. (Illus.). 233p. 1980. reprint ed. lib. bdg. 35.00 (*0-313-21291-0*, MCEE, Greenwood Pr) Greenwood.
— English Literature from Dryden to Burns. (Illus.). 1948. 76.50 (*0-89197-145-9*) Irvington.
— English Literature from Dryden to Burns. 1988. reprint ed. lib. bdg. 69.00 (*0-7812-0054-7*) Rprt Serv.
— English Literature from Dryden to Burns. reprint ed. 69.00 (*0-403-04048-5*) Somerset Pub.
McKillop, Beth. Korean Art & Design. (Illus.). 192p. 1992. pap. 34.95 (*1-85177-104-2*, Pub. by V&A Ent) Antique Collect.
McKillop, Donal. Building Societies: Structure, Performance & Change. 272p. (C). 1993. lib. bdg. 77.00 (*1-85333-880-X*, Pub. by Graham & Trotman) Kluwer Academic.
McKillop, Donald, jt. auth. see Ferguson, Charles.
McKillop, James H. & Fogelman, I., eds. Benign & Malignant Bone Disease. (Illus.). 160p. 1991. pap. text 34.00 (*0-443-04436-8*) Church.
McKillop, Sandra. Aboriginal Justice Issues. (Australian Institute Conference Proceedings Ser.: Vol. 21). 229p. 1993. pap. 35.00 (*0-642-19621-4*, Pub. by Aust Inst Criminology) Advent Bks Div.
— Preventing Youth Suicide. (Australian Institute Conference Proceedings Ser.: Vol. 13). 1992. pap. 30.00 (*0-642-17512-8*, Pub. by Aust Inst Criminology) Advent Bks Div.
McKillop, Sandra, ed. Keeping People Out of Prison. (Australian Institute Conference Proceedings Ser.: Vol. 11). 315p. 1991. pap. 30.00 (*0-642-17073-8*, Pub. by Aust Inst Criminology) Advent Bks Div.
McKillop, Sandra, et al, eds. Environmental Crime. LC 95-237478. (Australian Institute Conference Proceedings Ser.: Vol. 26). 286p. 1995. pap. 35.00 (*0-642-21348-8*, Pub. by Aust Inst Criminology) Advent Bks Div.
McKillop, Sandra & Biles, D., eds. Criminal Justice Planning & Coordination. LC 96-174369. (Australian Institute Conference Proceedings Ser.: Vol. 24). 235p. 1994. pap. 30.00 (*0-642-20269-9*, Pub. by Aust Inst Criminology) Advent Bks Div.
McKillop, Sandra & Vernon, J., eds. National Overview on Crime Prevention. (Australian Institute Conference Proceedings Ser.: Vol. 15). 310p. 1992. pap. 25.00 (*0-642-18452-6*, Pub. by Aust Inst Criminology) Advent Bks Div.
— Preventing Juvenile Crime. (Australian Institute Conference Proceedings Ser.: Vol. 9). 203p. 1991. pap. 25.00 (*0-642-16637-4*, Pub. by Aust Inst Criminology) Advent Bks Div.
McKillop, Sandra, ed. see Easteal, Patricia W.
McKim, et al. A Monograph of the Work of McKim, Mead & White, 1879-1915. LC 75-152624. 1972. 55.95 (*0-405-08770-5*, Pub. by Blom Pubns) Ayer.
McKim, David, jt. auth. see Delaney, Leslie.
McKim, Donald. Major Themes in the Reformed Tradition. 470p. 1998. pap. 37.00 (*1-57910-104-6*) Wipf & Stock.
McKim, Donald, ed. Historical Handbook of Major Biblical Interpreters. LC 98-13824. 600p. 1998. 29.99 (*0-8308-1452-3*, 1452) InterVarsity.
McKim, Donald & Wright, David F. Encyclopedia of the Reformed Faith. 384p. (C). 1992. 90.00 (*0-7855-6843-3*, Pub. by St Andrew) St Mut.
— Encyclopedia of the Reformed Faith. 384p. 1993. 85.00 (*0-7152-0660-5*) St Mut.
McKim, Donald K. The Bible in Theology & Preaching. LC 93-30549. 224p. 1994. pap. 16.95 (*0-687-44611-2*) Abingdon.
***McKim, Donald K.** The Bible in Theology & Preaching. 250p. 1999. pap. 23.00 (*1-57910-244-1*) Wipf & Stock.
Calvin's Institutes. abr. ed. 184p. 2000. pap. 16.95 (*0-664-22298-6*) Westminster John Knox.
McKim, Donald K. God Never Forgets: Faith, Hope & Alzheimer's Disease. LC 97-25541. 1997. pap. 12.00 (*0-664-25704-6*) Westminster John Knox.
***McKim, Donald K.** A Guide to Contemporary Hermeneutics: Major Trends in Biblical Interpretation. 404p. (Orig.). 1999. pap. 32.00 (*1-57910-250-6*) Wipf & Stock.
McKim, Donald K. Historical Handbook of Major Biblical Interpreters. LC 98-13824. xxiii, 643p. 1998. write for info. (*0-85111-752-X*) CE15.
— Ramism in William Perkins' Theology. (American University Studies: Theology & Religion: Ser. VII, Vol. 15). XII, 249p. (C). 1987. text 38.90 (*0-8204-0285-0*) P Lang Pubng.
***McKim, Donald K.** Readings in Calvin's Theology. 342p. (Orig.). 1998. pap. 29.00 (*1-57910-151-8*) Wipf & Stock.
McKim, Donald K. Theological Turning Points: Major Issues in Christian Thought. LC 88-45432. 240p. 1988. pap. 22.95 (*0-8042-0702-X*) Westminster John Knox.
— Westminster Dictionary of Theological Terms. 320p. 1996. 39.95 (*0-664-22089-4*); pap. 20.00 (*0-664-25511-6*) Westminster John Knox.
McKim, Donald K., ed. The Authoritative Word: Essays on the Nature of Scripture. 284p. 1998. pap. 28.00 (*1-57910-118-6*) Wipf & Stock.
— Encyclopedia of the Reformed Faith. 414p. 1992. 49.95 (*0-664-21882-2*) Westminster John Knox.
— How Karl Barth Changed My Mind. 198p. (Orig.). 1998. pap. 18.00 (*1-57910-119-4*) Wipf & Stock.
— How Karl Barth Changed My Mind. LC 86-19655. 196p. (Orig.). reprint ed. pap. 60.80 (*0-8357-4365-9*, 203719400007) Bks Demand.
— Major Themes in the Reformed Tradition. fac. ed. LC 91-36867. 467p. 1992. reprint ed. pap., per. 144.80 (*0-7837-7964-X*, 204772000008) Bks Demand.
McKim, Donald K., jt. auth. see Rogers, Jack B.
McKim, Elizabeth. Boat of the Dream: Poems. (Illus.). 108p. (Orig.). 1988. pap. 9.95 (*0-944941-01-X*) Talking Stone Pr.
— Body India. (Illus.). 56p. 1981. 12.95 (*0-938756-04-4*); pap. 6.95 (*0-938756-03-6*) Yellow Moon.
***McKim, Elizabeth & Steinbergh, Judith W.** Beyond Words, Writing Poems with Children: A Guide for Parents & Teachers. 3rd rev. ed. LC 82-70442. (Illus.). 152p. 1999. reprint ed. pap. text 19.95 (*0-944941-14-1*) Talking Stone Pr.
McKim, Elizabeth, jt. auth. see Steinbergh, Judith W.
McKim, Geoffrey. Internet Research Companion. LC 95-74875. 266p. 1996. pap. text 18.99 (*1-57576-050-9*) Que Educ & Trng.
McKim, John. Fly Tying: Adventures in Fur, Feathers & Fun. LC 82-2077. (Illus.). 158p. (Orig.). 1986. reprint ed. pap. 18.00 (*0-87842-140-8*) Mountain Pr.
McKim, LindaJo. The Presbyterian Hymnal Companion. LC 92-17830. 368p. (Orig.). 1993. pap. 25.95 (*0-664-25180-3*) Westminster John Knox.
McKim, Margaret G. The Reading of Verbal Material in Ninth Grade Algebra. LC 71-177032. (Columbia University. Teachers College. Contributions to Education Ser.: No. 850). reprint ed. 37.50 (*0-404-55850-X*) AMS Pr.
McKim, Mark G. Emil Brunner: A Bibliography. LC 96-12292. (ATLA Bibliography Ser.: No. 40). 152p. 1996. 39.00 (*0-8108-3167-8*) Scarecrow.
McKim, Mead D. Architecture of McKim Mead & White in Photographs Plans & Elevations. (Illus.). 476p. 1990. pap. 23.95 (*0-486-26556-0*) Dover.
McKim, Musa. Alone with the Moon. 1994. per. 12.00 (*0-935724-67-2*) Figures.
McKim, Priscilla, ed. Let Your Light Shine: Pioneer Women Educators of Wyoming. 2nd ed. LC 84-63062. (Illus.). 182p. 1985. write for info. (*0-930535-01-4*) Rustler Print & Pub.
McKim, Randolph. Soldier's Recollections: Leaves from the Diary of a Confederate. 1983. reprint ed. 26.95 (*0-89201-104-1*) Zenger Pub.
McKim, Randolph H. A Soldier's Recollections. 1995. 29.99 (*0-87377-172-9*) GAM Pubns.
McKim, Richard, tr. see Dragesco, Jean.
***McKim, Robert.** Religious Ambiguity & Religious Diversity. LC 99-44714. 368p. 2000. 49.95 (*0-19-512835-4*) OUP.
McKim, Robert. Thinking Visually. 1997. text 16.95 (*0-86651-423-6*) Seymour Pubns.
McKim, Robert & McMahan, Jeff, eds. The Morality of Nationalism. LC 96-21168. 384p. 1997. pap. 19.95 (*0-19-510392-0*) OUP.
McKim, Robert H. Experiences in Visual Thinking. 2nd ed. LC 80-437. (C). 1980. mass mkt. 41.95 (*0-8185-0411-0*) PWS Pubs.
McKim, Ruby S. One Hundred & One Patchwork Patterns. rev. ed. (Illus.). 124p. 1962. pap. 5.95 (*0-486-20773-0*) Dover.
McKim, Samuel J. Michigan Tax Handbook, 1998. rev. ed. 194p. 1997. pap. text 45.00 (*0-7811-0182-4*) Res Inst Am.
McKim, Samuel J., et al. Michigan Tax Handbook, 1999. rev. ed. Jenis, Richard E., ed. 216p. 1999. pap. text 35.75 (*0-7811-0195-6*) Res Inst Am.
McKim, Sandra. Whites in Skullyville County, Choctaw Nation Vol. 222: Permit Register 1889 - February 19, 1905; Choctaw. (Orig.). 1995. pap. 25.00 (*0-7884-0327-3*) Heritage Bk.
McKim-Smith, Gridley. Examining Velazquez. LC 87-31872. 162p. (C). 1988. 50.00 (*0-300-03615-9*) Yale U Pr.
McKim, Vaughn R. & Turner, Stephen, eds. Causality in Crisis? Statistical Methods & the Search for Causal Knowledge in the Social Sciences. LC 95-43072. (Studies in Science & the Humanities from the Reilly Center for Science, Technology, & Values: Ser. IV). 385p. (C). 1996. text 38.00 (*0-268-00813-2*); pap. text 22.00 (*0-268-00824-8*) U of Notre Dame Pr.
McKim, William A. Drugs & Behavior: An Introduction to Behavioral Pharmacology. 4th ed. LC 99-46144. (Illus.). 400p. (C). 1999. pap. text 54.00 (*0-13-083146-8*) P-H.
McKimens, Juanita. Aunt Birdie's Chronicles. LC 97-60734. 192p. 1997. pap. 10.00 (*1-57921-023-6*) WinePress Pub.

M

An Asterisk (*) at the beginning of an entry indicates that the title is appearing for the first time.

McKimmey, James. Cornered! large type ed. (Linford Mystery Library). 288p. 1997. pap. 16.99 (*0-7089-5157-0*) Ulverscroft.

— The Perfect Victim. large type ed. (Linford Mystery Library). 336p. 1997. pap. 16.99 (*0-7089-5102-3*, Linford) Ulverscroft.

McKinght, Bob. How to Pick Winning Horses. 1980. pap. 5.00 (*0-87980-266-9*) Wilshire.

McKinion, J. M., jt. ed. see Goodenough, J. L.

McKinlay, A. F. Thermoluminescence Dosimetry. (Medical Physics Handbook Ser.: No. 5). (Illus.). 170p. 1981. 19.00 (*0-85274-520-6*) IOP Pub.

McKinlay, Alan, jt. ed. see Melling, Joseph.

***McKinlay, Alfred.** Transport Packaging. (Illus.). 172p. (C). 1998. pap. 95.00 (*1-930268-16-5*) Packaging Prof.

***McKinlay, Archibald.** Our First Hundred Years. LC 99-41274. 1999. write for info. (*1-57864-086-5*) Donning Co.

McKinlay, Daniel B., jt. auth. see Welch, John W.

McKinlay, Deborah. Sex Secrets: A Companion's Guide. 104p. 1998. pap. 6.95 (*0-00-638357-2*, Pub. by HarpC) Trafalgar.

McKinlay, John, ed. Issues in the Political Economy of Health Care. 275p. 1984. 29.95 (*0-422-78040-5*, NO. 9330); pap. 14.95 (*0-422-78050-2*, NO. 9184) Routledge.

McKinlay, John B., jt. ed. see Hafferty, Fredric W.

McKinlay, Judith E. Gendering Wisdom the Host: Biblical Invitations to Eat & Drink. (Gender, Culture, Theory Ser.: No. 4 & 216). 280p. 1996. 80.00 (*1-85075-602-3*, Pub. by Sheffield Acad); pap. 24.50 (*1-85075-776-3*, Pub. by Sheffield Acad) CUP Services.

***McKinlay, Neil C.** The Poetry of Luis Cernuda: Order in a World of Chaos. LC 99-18395. 192p. 1999. 54.00 (*1-85566-063-6*, Pub. by Tamesis Bks Ltd) Boydell & Brewer.

Mckinlay, Robert. Third World Military Expenditure: A Political Economy Approach. 250p. 1992. 49.00 (*0-86187-721-7*, Pub. by P P Pubs) Cassell & Continuum.

McKinlay, Robert D., jt. ed. see Imbeau, Louis M.

McKinlay, Roderick G. Vegetable Crop Pests. 1992. 105.00 (*0-8493-7729-3*, SB608) CRC Pr.

McKinlay, S. L. Scottish Golf & Golfers. 203p. 1992. lib. bdg. 28.00 (*0-940889-37-4*) Classics Golf.

McKinlay, William Laird. Karluk: The Great Untold Story of Arctic Exploration. LC 77-357511. xiv, 170 p. 1976. write for info. (*0-297-77164-7*) Weidenfeld & Nicolson.

— The Last Voyage of the Karluk: The Classic Memoir of an Artic Disaster. LC 99-17672. 1999. pap. 12.95 (*0-312-20655-0*) St Martin.

Mckinley. Atlas of Histology. (C). 2001. pap. 24.00 (*0-13-796103-0*, Macmillan Coll) P-H.

McKinley. Biology: Bar Code Manual. 4th ed. 1996. pap. text. write for info. (*0-13-565714-8*) Allyn.

McKinley, jt. auth. see Valasek.

McKinley, Ann. Two Quartets: Party of Four & Melodie for Recorders. (Contemporary Consort Ser.: No. 14). i, 18p. 1991. pap. text 8.00 (*1-56571-032-0*) PRB Prods.

McKinley, Ann, ed. see Corteccia, Francesco.

McKinley, Archibald C. The Journal of Archibald C. McKinley. Humphries, Robert L., ed. LC 90-39090. 304p. 1991. 35.00 (*0-8203-1187-1*) U of Ga Pr.

Mckinley, Catherine E. & Delaney, Joyce, eds. Afrekete: A Collection of Contemporary Black Lesbian Writing. 304p. 1995. pap. 14.00 (*0-385-47355-9*, Anchor NY) Doubleday.

McKinley, Charles & Frase, Robert W. Launching Social Security: A Capture-&-Record Account, 1935-1937. LC 70-121771. 543p. reprint ed. pap. 168.40 (*0-8357-6782-5*, 203545900095) Bks Demand.

McKinley, Dale T. ANC & the Liberation Struggle: A Critical Political Biography. 175p. 1997. 54.95 (*0-7453-1282-9*, Pub. by Pluto GBR); pap. 16.95 (*0-7453-1277-2*, Pub. by Pluto GBR) Stylus Pub VA.

McKinley, Douglas. The Open Road. LC 95-60356. 320p. 1995. 22.00 (*0-9619380-1-3*) Balboa Bks.

McKinley, E. Graham. Beverly Hills, 90210: Television, Gender & Identity. LC 97-13120. (Feminist Cultural Studies, the Media, & Political Culture). (C). (gr. 13). 1997. pap. 17.50 (*0-8122-1623-7*); text 37.50 (*0-8122-3409-X*) U of Pa Pr.

McKinley, E. H. Somebody's Brother: A History of the Salvation Army Men's Social Service Department 1891-1985. LC 86-8604. (Studies in American Religion: Vol. 21). 275p. 1986. lib. bdg. 89.95 (*0-88946-665-3*) E Mellen.

McKinley, Edward H. Marching to Glory. 290p. reprint ed. pap. 8.95 (*0-86544-039-5*) Salv Army Suppl South.

McKinley, I. G. & McCombie, C., eds. Scientific Basis for Nuclear Waste Management XXI Vol. 506: Proceedings Materials Research Society Symposium. 1123p. 1998. text 95.00 (*1-55899-411-4*) Materials Res.

McKinley, James. Acts of Love. LC 87-708. 160p. 1987. 17.95 (*0-932576-47-8*); pap. 8.95 (*0-932576-67-2*) Breitenbush Bks.

— New Letters, Vol. 53, No. 3. (Illus.). 128p. 1987. pap. 4.00 (*0-317-64815-2*) New Letters MO.

— New Letters, Fall, 1986, Vol. 53, No. 1. (Illus.). 119p. 1986. pap. 4.00 (*0-317-62345-1*) New Letters MO.

— New Letters, Winter, 1986, Vol. 53, No. 2. (Illus.). 126p. 1986. pap. 4.00 (*0-317-62347-8*) New Letters MO.

McKinley, James, et al, eds. New Letters, Fall, 1987, Vol. 54, No. 1. (Illus.). 126p. 1987. write for info. (*0-318-62726-4*) New Letters MO.

McKinley, Jim. The Outdoor Cookbook. (Illus.). 210p. 1996. ring bd. 24.95 (*0-9639134-2-5*) Peak Media.

McKinley, John & Barrickman, John. Strategic Credit Risk Management. LC 93-35888. (Illus.). 120p. (Orig.). 1994. pap. text 60.00 (*0-936742-98-4*, 31176) Robt Morris Assocs.

McKinley, John E. How to Analyze Your Bank's Credit Culture. Burke, Sarah A., ed. 60p. (Orig.). 1990. pap. text 81.00 (*0-936742-75-5*, 31171) Robt Morris Assocs.

McKinley, John E., III, et al. Problem Loan Strategies. LC 84-27222. (Illus.). 168p. (Orig.). 1985. pap. text 53.00 (*0-936742-20-8*) Robt Morris Assocs.

McKinley, John E., et al. Problem Loan Strategies. rev. ed. 157p. (Orig.). 1998. pap. 53.00 (*1-57070-022-2*, 606601) Robt Morris Assocs.

***McKinley, Judy G.** A Southern Legacy: Life on a Mill Village. (Illus.). 200p. 1999. pap. 12.50 (*1-892614-24-3*) Briarwood VA.

McKinley, Kenneth F. Escudrinemos las Escrituras: La Contribucion del Antiguo Testamento al Plan de Dios para la Humanidad. (SPA.). 176p. 1997. pap. 8.99 (*0-8254-1475-X*, Edit Portavoz) Kregel.

— Hebrews: Entering the Holy of Holies. 162p. 1996. pap. 10.00 (*0-9630161-2-1*) Bible Study Min.

— Saisir le Plan - Scanning the Plan: Old Testament Survey. (FRE., Illus.). 210p. 1991. reprint ed. pap. 10.00 (*0-9630161-0-5*) Bible Study Min.

— Scanning the Plan Vol. 1: Old Testament Survey. (Illus.). 210p. 1995. reprint ed. pap. 10.00 (*0-9630161-1-3*) Bible Study Min.

McKinley, Marvin. Wheels of Farm Progress. LC 80-68925. (Illus.). 160p. 1980. pap. 15.95 (*0-916150-24-0*, HO680) Am Soc Ag Eng.

McKinley, Mary B. Words in a Corner: Studies in Montaigne's Latin Quotations. LC 80-70810. (French Forum Monographs: No. 26). 129p. (Orig.). 1981. pap. 10.95 (*0-917058-25-9*) French Forum.

McKinley, Mary B., jt. ed. see Frame, Donald M.

McKinley, Mary B., jt. ed. see Lyons, John D.

McKinley, Mary B., jt. ed. see Rubin, David L.

McKinley, Maura E. The Secret of the Eagle Feathers. LC 96-44250. (Publish-a-Book Ser.). (Illus.). 32p. (J). (gr. 1-6). 1997. lib. bdg. 22.83 (*0-8172-4436-0*) Raintree Steck-V.

McKinley, Michael. Etched in Ice: A Tribute to Hockey's Defining Moments. LC 99-172150. 1998. 24.95 (*1-55054-654-6*, Pub. by DGL) Sterling.

Mckinley, Michael. Hockey Hall of Fame Legends: The Official Book. (Illus.). 200p. 1995. pap. 24.95 (*1-57243-093-1*) Triumph Bks.

McKinley, Michael. How to Attract Birds. Burke, Ken R., ed. LC 82-63125. (Illus.). 96p. (Orig.). 1983. pap. 9.95 (*0-89721-011-5*, Ortho Bks) Meredith Bks.

— Legends: The Official Book of the Hockey Hall of Fame. (Illus.). 224p. 1996. 40.00 (*1-57243-135-0*) Triumph Bks.

— Take Care of Your Business - Or Someone Else Will. LC 97-35855. 1997. 19.95 (*1-888222-09-3*) Thinking Pubns.

Mckinley, Michael, ed. The Gulf War: Critical Perspectives. 224p. 1995. pap. 24.95 (*1-86373-606-9*) Paul & Co Pubs.

McKinley, Michael, et al. Human Anatomy Laboratory Guide & Dissection Manual. 2nd ed. 584p. (C). 1999. spiral bd. 55.00 (*0-13-010017-X*) P-H.

McKinley, Michael, jt. auth. see O'Ree, Willie.

McKinley, Michael P. Keeping Alive. 1984. pap. 6.00 (*0-9610370-7-5*) Thinking Pubns.

McKinley, Nancy L. Signs of Survival. (SOS Ser.: No. I). (Illus.). (YA). (gr. 5-12). 1996. 25.00 (*0-930599-46-2*) Thinking Pubns.

— Signs of Survival. (SOS Ser.: No. I). (Illus.). (YA). (gr. 5-12). 1997. 25.00 (*1-888222-02-6*); 25.00 (*1-888222-03-4*) Thinking Pubns.

McKinley, Nancy L. & Schwartz, Linda. Make-It-Yourself Barrier Activities. 210p. (J). (gr. k-12). 1987. pap. 37.00 (*0-930599-16-0*) Thinking Pubns.

McKinley, Nancy L., jt. auth. see Larson, Vicki L.

McKinley, Nancy L., jt. auth. see Schreiber, L. R.

McKinley, R. A. Norfolk Surnames in the Sixteenth Century. LC 70-512957. (Department of English Local History/Occasional Papers: 2). 60p. 1969. write for info. (*0-7185-2023-8*) Continuum.

McKinley, Richard. Norfolk & Suffolk Surnames in the Middle Ages. 176p. 1975. 16.00 (*0-85033-196-X*, Pub. by Leopards Head Pr) David Brown.

— The Surnames of Lancashire. 501p. 1981. 24.00 (*0-904920-05-4*, Pub. by Leopards Head Pr) David Brown.

— The Surnames of Oxfordshire. 312p. 1977. 16.00 (*0-904920-01-1*, Pub. by Leopards Head Pr) David Brown.

— The Surnames of Sussex. 483p. 1988. 34.00 (*0-904920-14-3*, Pub. by Leopards Head Pr) David Brown.

McKinley, Robert. Sculpting Dolls in Paperclay. Campbell, Barbara, ed. LC 94-66878. 76p. (Orig.). 1994. pap. text 24.95 (*0-916809-78-1*) Scott Pubns MI.

McKinley, Robert B. Bankcard Barometer 91. 200p. (Orig.). (C). 1991. pap. text 385.00 (*0-943329-72-8*) RAM Res Pub.

— Bankcard Barometer 91 No. 2: Cumulative Supplement. rev. ed. 50p. (C). 1991. pap. text 120.00 (*0-943329-73-6*) RAM Res Pub.

— Bankcard Barometer 91 No. 2: Cumulative Supplement. rev. ed. 50p. (C). 1991. pap. text 120.00 (*0-943329-74-4*) RAM Res Pub.

— Bankcard Barometer 91 No. 2: Cumulative Supplement. rev. ed. 50p. (C). 1991. pap. text 120.00 (*0-943329-75-2*) RAM Res Pub.

— Bankcard Barometer 91, No. 4 No. 4: Cumulative Supplement. rev. ed. 50p. (C). 1991. pap. text 120.00 (*0-943329-76-0*) RAM Res Pub.

— Bankcard Barometer 93. 1000p. (C). 1993. pap. text 995.00 (*0-943329-80-9*) RAM Res Pub.

— Cardsearch 91. 32p. (Orig.). (gr. 12). 1991. pap. text 25.00 (*0-943329-77-9*) RAM Res Pub.

— Cardsearch 91. rev. ed. 32p. (Orig.). 1991. pap. text 25.00 (*0-943329-78-7*) RAM Res Pub.

— Cardsearch 92. 1991. pap. text 39.95 (*0-943329-79-5*) RAM Res Pub.

— Cardsearch 93. 100p. 1993. pap. text 50.00 (*0-943329-81-7*) RAM Res Pub.

McKinley, Robert K. Dollmaking - One Artist's Approach. Nelson, Linda, ed. 166p. (Orig.). 1991. teacher ed. write for info. (*0-9628821-0-0*) McKinley Bk.

McKinley, Robert L. The Complete Neuroticist. 125p. 1969. 12.50 (*0-9609644-1-X*) Candle Bks.

— 1840 Census of Miller County, Missouri with Annotations. LC 98-100426. viii, 467p. 1997. pap. 32.00 (*0-7884-0724-4*, M157) Heritage Bk.

— The Neurotic's Handbook. 131p. (C). 1977. pap. 10.00 (*0-9609644-0-1*) Candle Bks.

— Personal Peace: Transcending Your Interpersonal Limits. 136p. 1993. pap. 11.95 (*0-934986-57-6*) New Harbinger.

Mckinley, Robin. The Blue Sword. 1987. mass mkt. 5.99 (*0-441-06880-4*) Ace Bks.

— The Blue Sword. LC 82-2895. 288p. (YA). (gr. 7-12). 1982. 16.95 (*0-688-00938-7*, Grenwillow Bks) HarpC Child Bks.

***Mckinley, Robin.** The Blue Sword. (Illus.). 288p. (J). (gr. 5 up). 2000. pap. 5.99 (*0-14-130975-X*, PuffinBks) Peng Put Young Read.

Mckinley, Robin. The Blue Sword. 1983. 11.09 (*0-606-01012-2*, Pub. by Turtleback) Demco.

— Deerskin. 320p. 1994. mass mkt. 5.99 (*0-441-00069-X*) Ace Bks.

Mckinley, Robin. Deerskin. LC 92-18460. 1993. 11.09 (*0-606-06318-8*, Pub. by Turtleback) Demco.

Mckinley, Robin. The Door in the Hedge. LC 80-21903. 224p. (J). (gr. 7 up). 1981. 15.00 (*0-688-00312-5*, Grenwillow Bks) HarpC Child Bks.

— The Hero & the Crown. 227p. (J). (gr. 4-7). 1987. mass mkt. 5.99 (*0-441-32809-1*) Ace Bks.

— The Hero & the Crown. 240p. 1998. mass mkt. 12.00 (*0-441-00499-7*) Ace Bks.

— The Hero & the Crown. (J). 1986. 34.66 incl. audio (*0-676-31297-7*) Ballantine Pub Grp.

— The Hero & the Crown. LC 84-4074. 256p. (YA). (gr. 7-12). 1984. 16.00 (*0-688-02593-5*, Grenwillow Bks) HarpC Child Bks.

***Mckinley, Robin.** The Hero & the Crown. LC 00-29092. (Illus.). 240p. (J). (gr. 5 up). 2000. pap. 5.99 (*0-14-130981-4*, PuffinBks) Peng Put Young Read.

Mckinley, Robin. The Hero & the Crown. (J). 1986. 11.09 (*0-606-03294-0*, Pub. by Turtleback) Demco.

— A Knot in the Grain & Other Stories. LC 93-17557. 208p. (J). (gr. 6 up). 1994. 14.00 (*0-688-09201-2*, Grenwillow Bks) HarpC Child Bks.

— A Knot in the Grain & Other Stories. (Trophy Bk.). 208p. (YA). (gr. 4-7). 1995. pap. 4.95 (*0-06-440604-0*, HarpTrophy) HarpC Child Bks.

— A Knot in the Grain & Other Stories. 1995. 10.05 (*0-606-08459-2*, Pub. by Turtleback) Demco.

— The Outlaws of Sherwood. 1989. mass mkt. 5.99 (*0-441-64451-1*) Ace Bks.

— The Outlaws of Sherwood. LC 88-45227. 256p. (J). (ps-3). 1988. 17.00 (*0-688-07178-3*, Grenwillow Bks) HarpC Child Bks.

— Rose Daughter. LC 96-48783. 320p. (YA). (gr. 5-9). 1997. 16.00 (*0-688-15439-5*, Grenwillow Bks) HarpC Child Bks.

***Mckinley, Robin.** Rose Daughter. 292p. 1998. reprint ed. mass mkt. 5.99 (*0-441-00583-7*) Ace Bks.

— Spindle's End. LC 99-41818. 432p. (J). (gr. 7-12). 2000. 19.99 (*0-399-23466-7*, G P Putnam) Peng Put Young Read.

Mckinley, Robin. The Stone Fey. LC 95-3915. (Illus.). 64p. (YA). 1998. 17.00 (*0-15-200017-8*) Harcourt.

Mckinley, Robin, retold by. Beauty: A Retelling of the Story of Beauty & the Beast. LC 77-25636. 256p. (YA). (gr. 5 up). 1978. 15.95 (*0-06-024149-7*) HarpC Child Bks.

— Beauty: A Retelling of the Story of Beauty & the Beast. LC 77-25636. (Trophy Bk.). 256p. (J). (gr. 7-12). 1993. pap. 4.95 (*0-06-440477-3*, HarpTrophy) HarpC Child Bks.

Mckinley, Robin, retold by. Beauty: A Retelling of the Story of Beauty & the Beast. (YA). 1993. 10.05 (*0-606-05157-0*, Pub. by Turtleback) Demco.

McKinley, Sarah, ed. & intro. see McGranaghan, Edmund.

McKinley, Steven L. Parboiled Pastor: Musings on the Joys & Pressures of Parish Ministry. LC 98-9839. 1998. pap. text 11.99 (*0-8066-3633-5*, 9-3633, Augsburg) Augsburg Fortress.

***McKinley, Tamara.** Matilda's Last Waltz. 448p. 2000. text 25.95 (*0-312-26202-7*) St Martin.

McKinley, Terry. The Distribution of Wealth in Rural China. LC 95-18471. (Socialism & Social Movements Ser.). (Illus.). 232p. (gr. 13). 1995. text 85.95 (*1-56324-614-7*, East Gate Bk); pap. text 42.95 (*1-56324-615-5*, East Gate Bk) M E Sharpe.

McKinley, Terry, jt. auth. see Griffin, Keith.

McKinley, Tony. From Paper to Web. 360p. 1997. pap. text 45.00 (*1-56830-345-9*, Pub. by Adobe Pr) Peachpit Pr.

McKinley, William J., Jr. The Cut Flower Companion. 160p. 1998. ring bd. 49.95 (*0-8134-3039-9*, 3039) Interstate.

McKinna, John. Crash Dive. 400p. 1999. mass mkt. 6.99 (*0-451-40885-3*, Onyx) NAL.

***McKinna, John.** Tiger Reef. 2000. mass mkt. 6.99 (*0-451-40919-1*, Onyx) NAL.

McKinnell, F. H., ed. Sandalwood in the Pacific Region. 43p. (Orig.). 1992. pap. 45.00 (*1-86320-086-X*) St Mut.

McKinnell, Robert G., et al. The Biological Basis of Cancer. LC 97-42369. (Illus.). 398p. (C). 1998. text 95.00 (*0-521-59298-4*); pap. text 42.95 (*0-521-59695-5*) Cambridge U Pr.

McKinney. Archery. 9th ed. 2001. pap. 13.38 (*0-07-235384-8*) McGraw.

— Current Issues in Geology: Selected Readings. 2nd ed. LC 95-151049. (Earth Science Ser.). 1995. pap. 13.00 (*0-314-06109-6*) Wadsworth Pub.

— Environmental Geology. 2002. pap. text 44.00 (*0-534-55667-1*) Brooks-Cole.

— Readings for Environmental Literacy, 1998. 2nd ed. (Biology Ser.). (C). 1997. pap. 12.95 (*0-534-54198-4*) Wadsworth Pub.

— Sew a Circle of Friends: Adorable Cloth Doll Projects. (Illus.). 128p. 1998. pap. 14.95 (*0-8069-8702-2*) Sterling.

— Walking Death Valley. pap. 11.00 (*0-06-258515-0*, Perennial) HarperTrade.

***McKinney, et al.** Current Perspectives in Geology 2000: Selected Readings. 5th ed. (Earth Science Ser.). 1999. text 18.95 (*0-534-37213-9*) Brooks-Cole.

McKinney, et al. Mediator Communication Competencies. 4th ed. 1995. pap. write for info. (*0-8087-7699-1*) Pearson Custom.

McKinney & McKinney Staff. The Texas Big Debt Survival Guide, 1988. 1988. pap. 19.95 (*0-9620366-0-9*) Marshall TX.

***McKinney, Anne.** Real Essays for College & Grad School. (Real Resumes Ser.). (Illus.). 192p. 2000. pap. 16.95 (*1-885288-20-4*, 914-012, Pub. by PREP Pubng) BookWorld.

— Real-Resumes for Career Changers: Actual Resumes & Cover Letters. (Real Resumes Ser.). (Illus.). 192p. 2000. pap. 16.95 (*1-885288-17-4*, 914-013, Pub. by PREP Pubng) BookWorld.

— Real-Resumes for Sales: Actual Job-Winning Resumes & Cover Letters. (Real Resumes Ser.). (Illus.). 192p. 2000. pap. 16.95 (*1-885288-16-6*, 914-016, Pub. by PREP Pubng) BookWorld.

— Real-Resumes for Students: Actual Resumes & Cover Letters for Students. LC 00-28560. (Real Resumes Ser.). (Illus.). 192p. 2000. pap. 16.95 (*1-885288-18-2*, 914-014, Pub. by PREP Pubng) BookWorld.

— Real-Resumes for Teachers: Actual Job-Winning Resumes & Cover Letters. (Real Resumes Ser.). (Illus.). 192p. 2000. pap. 16.95 (*1-885288-19-0*, 914-015, Pub. by PREP Pubng) BookWorld.

McKinney, Anne. Sew a Circle of Friends: Adorable Cloth Doll Projects. LC 97-7716. (Illus.). 128p. 1997. 27.95 (*0-8069-8611-5*) Sterling.

McKinney, Anne, ed. Cover Letters That Blow Doors Open: Job-Winning Cover Letters. LC 98-52224. (Anne McKinney Career Ser.). 256p. 1999. pap. 25.00 (*1-885288-13-1*, Pub. by PREP Pubng) BookWorld.

— Government Job Applications & Federal Resumes: Federal Resumes, KSAS, Forms 171 & 612, & Postal Applications. LC 98-48426. (Anne McKinney Career Ser.). (Illus.). 272p. 1999. pap. 25.00 (*1-885288-11-5*, Pub. by PREP Pubng) BookWorld.

— Letters for Special Situations: Letters to Use in the Special Situations in Life. LC 99-11353. (Anne McKinney Career Ser.). 256p. 1999. pap. 25.00 (*1-885288-09-3*, Pub. by PREP Pubng) BookWorld.

— Resumes & Cover Letters for Managers: Actual Resumes & Cover Letters Used to Obtain Management Positions. LC 98-56203. (Anne McKinney Career Ser.). 288p. 1999. pap. 25.00 (*1-885288-10-7*, Pub. by PREP Pubng) BookWorld.

— Resumes & Cover Letters That Have Worked! A Book about Changing Careers & Jobs. LC 95-19458. (Illus.). 272p. 1997. pap. 25.00 (*1-885288-04-2*, Pub. by PREP Pubng) BookWorld.

— Resumes & Cover Letters That Have Worked for Military Professionals: A Book That Translates Military Experience into Civilian Language. LC 96-33822. (Illus.). 236p. 1996. pap. 25.00 (*1-885288-06-9*, Pub. by PREP Pubng) BookWorld.

McKinney, Anne & Berteau, John T. Estate Planning in Tennessee. LC 95-39054. 272p. 1996. 24.95 (*1-56164-059-X*) Pineapple Pr.

McKinney, Antonio, jt. ed. see Fraser, George C.

McKinney, Aubrey R. Back Through the Looking Glass. LC 85-80422. (Flip Side Science Ser.). (Illus.). 177p. 1986. 24.95 (*0-914587-02-1*) Helix Pr.

— The Slender Thread. LC 84-80635. (Illus.). 384p. 1985. 24.95 (*0-914587-00-5*) Helix Pr.

McKinney, Aubrey R., ed. see Barnes, Verle.

McKinney, Aubrey R., ed. see Lotring, Alfred H.

McKinney, Aubrey R., ed. see Morris, Edwin L.

McKinney, Barbara, jt. auth. see Ross, John.

McKinney, Barbara S. A Drop Around the World. LC 97-42915. (Illus.). 36p. (J). (gr. k-7). 1998. 16.95 (*1-883220-71-8*) Dawn CA.

— A Drop Around the World. LC 97-42915. (Illus.). 32p. (YA). (gr. k up). 1998. pap. 7.95 (*1-883220-72-6*) Dawn CA.

***McKinney, Barbara S.** Pass the Energy, Please! LC 99-32181. (Sharing Nature with Children Book Ser.). (Illus.). 36p. (YA). (gr. 1 up). 2000. 16.95 (*1-58469-001-1*); pap. 7.95 (*1-58469-002-X*) Dawn CA.

***McKinney, Barbara Shaw.** Pass the Energy, Please! (Illus.). 48p. (J). (gr. 3-6). 2000. pap. text 7.95 (*1-58469-007-0*) Dawn CA.

McKinney, Beth C. & Romanski, Kate D. The English Cocker Spaniel Vol. 1: Jubilee Book of the English Cocker Spaniel Club of America, Inc., 2 vols. LC 85-82051. (Illus.). 1986. write for info. (*0-9613761-2-0*) Eng Cocker Spaniel.

— The English Cocker Spaniel Vol. 1: Jubilee Book of the English Cocker Spaniel Club of America, Inc., 2 vols., Set. LC 85-82051. (Illus.). 1987. 40.00 (*0-9613761-1-2*) Eng Cocker Spaniel.

— The English Cocker Spaniel Vol. 2: Jubilee Book of the

An Asterisk (*) at the beginning of an entry indicates that the title is appearing for the first time.

English Cocker Spaniel Club of America, Inc., 2 vols. LC 85-82051. (Illus.). 1987. write for info. (0-9613761-3-9) Eng Cocker Spaniel.
McKinney, Beth C., jt. ed. see Romanski, Kate D.
McKinney, Betty & Rieseberg, Barbara H. Beardie Basics: Beginners Guide to Bearded Collies. 3rd rev. ed. LC 97-25877. 120p. 1997. pap. 14.95 (0-931866-99-5) Alpine Pubns.
McKinney, Betty J. Sheltie Talk. 2nd ed. LC 75-45831. (Illus.). 320p. 1985. 34.95 (0-931866-17-0) Alpine Pubns.
McKinney, Betty J., ed. see Allen, Sue A.
McKinney, Betty J., ed. see Handler, Barbara S.
McKinney, Bob. Regulation of the Commodities, Futures & Options Markets. 2nd rev. ed. LC 95-25784. 1995. write for info. (0-07-172790-6) Shepards.
McKinney, Bobby J. Confederates on the Caney: An Illustrated Account of the Civil War on the Texas Gulf Coast. LC 94-79109. (Illus.). 132p. (Orig.). (C). 1994. pap. 15.00 (0-9643351-0-7) North South Trader.
Mckinney, Bruce. Hardcore Visual Basic. 2nd ed. LC 97-15486. 700p. 1997. pap. text 39.99 (1-57231-422-2) Microsoft.
McKinney, Bruce C., jt. ed. see Miller, Christine M.
***McKinney, Carol V.** Globe-Trotting in Sandals: A Field Guide to Cultural Research. 337p. 2000. pap. 32.00 (1-55671-086-0) S I L Intl.
McKinney, Carolyn. Gentle Giant of the Twenty-Sixth Division. 1994. 19.95 (0-929915-11-9) Headline Bks.
McKinney, Cherie, ed. see Lipper Analytical Services International Corporati.
McKinney, Chris. The Tattoo. Date not set. 14.95 (1-56647-248-2) Mutual Pub HI.
***McKinney, Chris.** The Tattoo. 216p. 1999. pap. 10.95 (1-56647-247-4) Mutual Pub HI.
***McKinney, David.** Can-am Cars: 1966-1974 Auto Champions. (Illus.). 112p. 1999. pap. text 19.95 (1-85532-900-X, 129047AE, Pub. by Ospry) Motorbooks Intl.
McKinney, David D., jt. auth. see McKinney, David E.
***McKinney, David E. & McKinney, David D.** Bloodlines. LC 99-97493. 2000. 19.95 (0-533-13405-6) Vantage.
McKinney, Deena. Kinfolk: Unsung Heroes. (Werewolf Ser.). (Illus.). 112p. 1999. pap. 15.00 (1-56504-308-1, 3074) White Wolf.
McKinney, Deena & Moore, Jim. Land of Eight Million Dreams. (Changeling: The Dreaming Ser.). (Illus.). 1998. pap. 18.00 (1-56504-722-2, 7308) White Wolf.
McKinney, Deena, jt. auth. see Marchinton, Buck.
McKinney, Don. Magazine Writing That Sells. 240p. 1994. 16.99 (0-89879-642-3, Wrtrs Digest Bks) F & W Pubns Inc.
McKinney, E. Doris. Motor Learning: An Experiential Guide for Teachers. 1985p. pap. 24.95 (0-932392-25-3) Mouvement Pubns.
McKinney, Elizabeth, jt. auth. see MacNair, Ray.
McKinney, Emily S., et al. Maternal-Child Nursing. Eoyang, Thomas, ed. LC 99-31878. (Illus.). 1945p. (C). 1999. text. write for info. (0-7216-8138-7, W B Saunders Co) Harcrt Hlth Sci Grp.
McKinney, F. K. & Jackson, Jeremy B. Bryozoan Evolution. (Illus.). 256p. 1987. text 55.00 (0-04-560012-0) Routledge.
McKinney, Floyd L., compiled by. Strengthening Computer Technology Programs: Examples from Developing Institutions. 120p. 1984. 10.50 (0-318-22204-3, SN49) Ctr Educ Trng Employ.
McKinney, Floyd L., et al. Increasing Job Placement Rates in Vocational Programs: Secondary & Postsecondary. 24p. 1984. 4.25 (0-318-22131-4, RD245) Ctr Educ Trng Employ.
McKinney, Francis F. Education in Violence: The Life of George H. Thomas & the History of the Army of the Cumberland. (Illus.). 530p. 1996. reprint ed. pap. 27.95 (0 9625290-5-2) Abraham Lincoln.
McKinney, Frank K. & Jackson, Jeremy B. Bryozoan Evolution. (Illus.). 252p. 1991. pap. text 18.50 (0-226-56047-3) U Ch Pr.
McKinney, Frank K. & Kriz, Jiri. Lower Devonian Fenestrata (Bryozoa) of the Prague Basin, Barrandian Area, Bohemia, Czechoslovakia. LC 86-80770. (Field Museum of Natural History, Publication 1368, Geology Ser.: Vol. 15). 96p. 1986. reprint ed. pap. 30.00 (0-608-03778-8, 206462200009) Bks Demand.
McKinney, Gage. A High & Holy Place: A Mining Camp Church at New Almaden. (Illus.). 96p. 1997. pap. write for info. (0-9657994-0-9) NAQCPA.
McKinney, George & Kritlow, William. Cross the Line. LC 97-37312. 228p. 1998. pap. 12.99 (0-7852-7246-1, J Thoma Bks) Nelson.
McKinney, Gordon B. Southern Mountain Republicans, 1865-1900: Politics & the Appalachian Community. 2nd ed. LC 97-43655. (Appalachian Echoes Ser.). 320p. (C). 1998. reprint ed. pap. text 19.00 (1-57233-009-0) U of Tenn Pr.
McKinney, Gordon B., jt. auth. see Inscoe, John C.
***McKinney, Grange B. Art Acord & the Movies: A Biography & Filmography. LC 99-71084. (Illus.). x, 164p. 2000. 39.95 (0-615-11720-1, Pub. by Wyatt Classics) Westrn Classics.**
The first comprehensive biography & filmography of the genuine cowboy & rodeo champion who ranked among the top ten silent Western film stars. Art Acord's career as a stunt man actor began in the early 1900's with the Selig Polyscope & Bison studios & continued with his popular Buck Parvin series with the Flying A Studio & with films for Fox & Universal. His self-destructive habits resulted in three failed marriages, a downgrading from major studios to the cheapest independent Western productions & ultimately to his death in Mexico at the age of forty. Some erroneous information which has appeared in print over the years is discussed & the record clarified. Both the biography & filmography are enhanced by numerous illustrations (twelve pages in full color), many appearing in print for the first time. "A meticulously researched biography & filmography,...a highly enjoyable straight forward read,...highest recommendation!" Western Clippings. "Promises to set the record straight on one of the silent era's most popular Western performers...beautifully & lavishly illustrated...Highly recommended." The Silents Majority. Also suggested as supplementary reading for film history & historiograhy classes. Visit Art Acord on the internet at http//www.mdle.com/classicfilms/guest/accord.htm. To place an order, please contact Western Classics, Post Office Box 2091, Capistrano Beach, CA 29624. Tel: 949-492-6858. Price postpaid: $39.95 (California residents add $3.10 sales tax). Payment by check or money order only. *Publisher Paid Annotation.*
McKinney, H. Lewis. Wallace & Natural Selection. LC 72-75203. (Studies in the History of Science & Medicine: No. 8). (Illus.). 116p. reprint ed. 36.00 (0-8357-9597-7, 201337300086) Bks Demand.
McKinney, H. Lewis, ed. Lamarck to Darwin: Contributions to Evolutionary Biology, 1809-1859. 124p. 1971. 10.00 (0-87291-019-9) Coronado Pr.
McKinney-Hammond, Michelle. The Genius of Temptation: What You Need to Know to Outsmart It. LC 98-5769. 1998. pap. 9.99 (1-56507-834-9) Harvest Hse.
***McKinney-Hammond, Michelle.** Get a Love Life: How to Get the Most Out of Your Relationship with God. LC 99-42962. 250p. 2000. pap. 9.99 (0-7369-0186-8) Harvest Hse.
McKinney-Hammond, Michelle. His Love Always Finds Me: God's Passionate Pursuit of His People. LC 98-53971. 364p. 1999. pap. 10.99 (0-7369-0075-6) Harvest Hse.
— The Power of Femininity: Rediscovering the Art of Being a Woman. LC 99-24433. 1999. pap. 10.99 (0-7369-0142-6) Harvest Hse.
***McKinney-Hammond, Michelle.** Prayer Guide for the Brokenhearted. LC 00-34939. 2000. write for info. (1-56955-252-5, Vine Bks) Servant.
McKinney-Hammond, Michelle. Secrets of an Irresistible Woman. LC 97-29011. 200p. 1998. pap. 9.99 (1-56507-843-8) Harvest Hse.
— What to Do until Love Finds You: Preparing Yourself for Your Perfect Mate. LC 96-41550. 250p. 1997. pap. 9.99 (1-56507-531-5) Harvest Hse.
McKinney, Hannah J. The Development of Local Public Services, 1650-1860: Lessons from Middletown, Connecticut, 166. LC 95-5269. (Contributions in Economics & Economic History Ser.: Vol. 166). 224p. 1995. 59.95 (0-313-29590-5, Greenwood Pr) Greenwood.
***Mckinney, Heather & Bradley, Clark.** Municipal Management in Poland. (Policy Papers: Vol. 4). 40p. 1999. pap. 6.50 (0-89940-575-4) LBJ Sch Pub Aff.
McKinney, Irene. Quick Fire & Slow Fire. 64p. 1989. pap. 7.95 (1-55643-046-9) North Atlantic.
— Six O'Clock Mine Report. LC 88-29084. (Pitt Poetry Ser.). 64p. 1989. pap. 10.95 (0-8229-3611-9) U of Pittsburgh Pr.
McKinney, Jack. Before the Invid Storm. (Robotech Ser.: Vol. 21). 1996. mass mkt. 5.99 (0-345-38776-7) Ballantine Pub Grp.
— Metal Fire No. 8. (Robotech Ser.: No. 8). 224p. 1987. mass mkt. 4.95 (0-345-34141-4, Del Rey) Ballantine Pub Grp.
— Robotech 3-in-1: Battlehymn; Force of Arms; Doomsday, Vols. 4-6. 512p. 1994. reprint ed. mass mkt. 5.99 (0-345-39145-4, Del Rey) Ballantine Pub Grp.
— Robotech 3-in-1: Southern Cross; Metal Fire; The Final Nightmare. 480p. 1995. mass mkt. 5.99 (0-345-39184-5, Del Rey) Ballantine Pub Grp.
— Robotech 3-in-1 Vols. 1-3: Genesis; Battle Cry; Homecoming, 3 vols., Vols. 1-3. 496p. (Orig.). 1994. mass mkt. 5.99 (0-345-38900-X, Del Rey) Ballantine Pub Grp.
— Sentinels 3-in-1: The Devil's Hand; Dark Powers; Death Dance. 1995. mass mkt. 5.99 (0-345-38901-8) Ballantine Pub Grp.
— The Zentraedi Rebellion, Vol. 19. (Robotech, Lost Generation Ser.: No. 19). 224p. (Orig.). 1994. mass mkt. 5.99 (0-345-38774-0, Del Rey Discovery) Ballantine Pub Grp.
McKinney, James. Echoes from the Past. (Orig.). 1998. pap. 10.95 (1-57532-080-0) Press-Tige Pub.
***McKinney, James C.** The Beginning Music Reader. 2nd rev. ed. (Illus.). 67p. 1999. pap. 9.95 (0-9679882-5-X, CB9006) Carol Pr.
McKinney, James C. The Diagnosis & Correction of Vocal Faults: A Manual for Teachers of Singing & for Choir Directors. (Illus.). 214p. (Orig.). 1994. pap. text, teacher ed. 29.95 incl. audio (1-56593-946-8, 1872) Singular Publishing.
— The Diagnosis & Correction of Vocal Faults: A Manual for Teachers of Singing & for Choir Directors. (Illus.). 214p. (Orig.). 1994. pap. text, teacher ed. 24.95 (1-56593-940-9, 1870) Thomson Learn.
— Lecciones Practicas Para el Canto: Practical Lessons in Singing. Herrington, Annette H., ed. Muskrat, Bruce, tr. from ENG. (SPA., Illus.). 96p. (Orig.). 1991. pap. 6.50 (0-311-32405-3) Casa Bautista.
McKinney, James L. Coming Home Empty. 122p. 1997. pap. 5.99 (0-932970-92-3) Prinit Pr.
***McKinney, Janet.** Homespun Homilies & Little Lessons: 128 Object Lessons for Bible & Sunday School Teachers. 320p. 1999. pap. 12.95 (1-58169-040-1, Evergrn Pr AL) Genesis Comm Inc.
McKinney, Jeana. Making Workshops Work. 33p. 1994. pap. text 12.00 (0-912207-29-9) NAFSA Washington.
McKinney, Jerome B. Effective Financial Management in Public & Nonprofit Agencies: A Practical & Integrative Approach. 2nd ed. LC 94-16994. 560p. 1995. text 65.00 (0-89930-925-9, Quorum Bks) Greenwood.
— Risking a Nation: U. S. Japanese Trade Failure & the Need for Political, Social, & Economic Reformation. LC 95-23283. 426p. (Orig.). (C). 1995. pap. text 34.50 (0-7618-0038-7); lib. bdg. 62.50 (0-7618-0037-9) U Pr of Amer.
McKinney, Jerome B. & Howard, Lawrence C. Public Administration: Balancing Power & Accountability. 2nd ed. LC 96-47619. 520p. 1998. 75.00 (0-275-95564-8, Praeger Pubs); pap. 29.95 (0-275-95565-6, Praeger Pubs) Greenwood.
Mckinney, John. Coast Walks 150 Adventures Along the California Coast. 1999. pap. text 14.95 (0-934161-17-8) Olympus Pr.
McKinney, John. Day Hiker's Guide to California's State Parks. (Day Hiker's Guides Ser.). 1998. pap. 14.95 (0-934161-16-X) Olympus Pr.
— Day Hiker's Guide to Southern California. (Day Hiker's Guides Ser.). 1997. pap. 14.95 (0-934161-15-1) Olympus Pr.
— Pacific Northwest. LC 97-2645. (Great Walks of North America Ser.). 1997. pap. 14.95 (0-8050-4420-5, Owl) H Holt & Co.
— A Walk along Land's End: Pioneering California's Coastal Footpath. pap. 10.00 (0-06-258607-6) HarpC.
Mckinney, John. Walking California's State Parks: Guide to over 100 Historic Parks, Preserves & Wilderness Areas. 1994. write for info. (0-318-72331-X) Harper SF.
McKinney, John, et al. Teaching about Adolescent: An Ecological Approach. LC 98-29686. (Michigan State University Series on Children, Youth, & Families: No. 5). 296p. 1998. text 70.00 (0-8153-1981-9) Garland.
McKinney, John, jt. auth. see Dirksen, Diane.
McKinney, John C. Constructive Typology & Social Theory. LC 66-25454. (Century Sociology Ser.). 1966. 30.50 (0-89197-105-X) Irvington.
McKinney, John C. & DeVyver, Frank T., eds. Aging & Social Policy. LC 66-25014. (Century Sociology Ser.). (C). 1980. reprint ed. 34.00 (0-89197-003-7); reprint ed. pap. text 15.95 (0-8290-2230-9) Irvington.
McKinney, John R. So Humble the Heart. LC 96-95326. 160p. (Orig.). 1997. pap. 12.95 (0-9656192-0-6) Humble Heart.
McKinney, Jordan. Pumpkin Painting. LC 96-15594. (Illus.). 96p. 1996. pap. 10.95 (0-8069-4858-2) Sterling.
***McKinney, Joseph A.** Created from NAFTA: The Structure, Function & Significance of the Treaty's Related Institutions. LC 99-87440. 272p. 2000. text 60.95 (0-7656-0466-3) M E Sharpe.
McKinney, Judy, et al. I Need Help Quick! Cookbook: Low-Cholesterol, Low-Fat, Low-Sodium Family Favorite Recipes. 144p. 1989. spiral bd. 11.95 (0-9624485-0-8) Health Saver.
***McKinney, Karl & McKinney, Kellie.** Relatively Loving: Family Dynamics in the Bible. (Generation Why Ser.: Vol. 4.8). 42p. (YA). (gr. 9-12). 1999. pap. 14.95 (0-87303-288-8) Faith & Life.
McKinney, Kathleen & Spencer, S., eds. Sexuality in Close Relationships. 240p. (C). 1991. text 45.00 (0-8058-0719-5) L Erlbaum Assocs.
McKinney, Kathleen & Sprecher, Susan, eds. Human Sexuality: The Societal & Interpersonal Context. LC 89-6854. 528p. 1989. pap. 49.50 (0-89391-613-7); text 125.00 (0-89391-544-0) Ablx Pub.
McKinney, Kathleen, jt. auth. see Sprecher, Susan.
McKinney, Kathleen, jt. ed. see Pryor, John B.
McKinney, Kay. Improving Math & Science Teaching: A Report on the Secretary's October 1992 Conference on Improving Math & Science Teaching & Instructional Resources. 36p. 1993. pap. 1.75 (0-16-041678-7) USGPO.
McKinney, Kellie, jt. auth. see McKinney, Karl.
McKinney, Ken, tr. see Bovon, Francois.
McKinney, Kevin. Everyday Geography: A Concise, Entertaining Review of Essential Information about the World We Live In. (Illus.). 176p. 1994. pap. write for info. (0-8092-3550-1) NTC Contemp Pub Co.
McKinney, Larry J. Equipping for Service: An Historical Account of the Bible College Movement in North America. Mondragon, Joniva M., ed. (Illus.). 254p. 1997. pap. 17.95 (1-890273-01-5) AABC.
McKinney, Laurence O. Neurotheology: Virtual Religion in the 21st Century. 172p. (Orig.). 1994. pap. 10.95 (0-945724-01-2) Am Inst Mindfulness.
McKinney, Lee & McKinney, Tag. Colorado Traveler: Gems & Minerals of Colorado - A Guide to Colorado's Native Gemstones. (American Traveler Ser.: Vol. 38). (Illus.). 48p. 1987. pap. 6.95 (1-55838-072-8) R H Pub.
McKinney, Liz. You're Not Alone: A Planning Guide for Families. 63p. (Orig.). 1990. pap. 5.00 (1-877592-17-X) GSH&MC.
McKinney, Lois, jt. ed. see Elmer, Duane H.
***McKinney, Lorrie J., et al.** Camp Jacubbi the Bubble Gummers. (Illus.). 20p. (J). (ps-6). 2000. pap. 9.95 (0-9701667-0-2) Jacubbi Enter.
McKinney, M. L. Heterochrony in Evolution: A Multidisciplinary Approach. LC 88-22573. (Topics in Geobiology Ser.: Vol. 7). (Illus.). 366p. (C). 1988. text 110.00 (0-306-42947-0, Kluwer Plenum) Kluwer Academic.
McKinney, M. L. & McNamara, K. J. Heterochrony: The Evolution of Ontogeny. (Illus.). 456p. (C). 1991. text 75.00 (0-306-43638-8, Kluwer Plenum) Kluwer Academic.
McKinney, Margaret. Footloose & Duty Free. (Illus.). 148p. (Orig.). 1985. text 9.95 (0-930982-07-X) U of Evansville Pr.
***McKinney, Maria & Gamble, Amy, eds.** Beginning Manuscript: Modern Handwriting. (Illus.). 32p. 1999. pap. 4.95 (0-88724-502-1, CD-0876) Carson-Dellos.
— Beginning Manuscript: Traditional Handwriting. (Illus.). 32p. (J). (gr. 1-3). 1999. pap. 4.95 (0-88724-503-X, CD-0877) Carson-Dellos.
— Manuscript Practice: Modern Handwriting. (Illus.). 32p. (J). (gr. 1-3). 1999. pap. 4.95 (0-88724-504-8, CD-0878) Carson-Dellos.
— Manuscript Practice: Traditional Handwriting. (Illus.). 32p. (J). (gr. 1-3). 1999. pap. 4.95 (0-88724-505-6, CD-0879) Carson-Dellos.
McKinney, Mark, jt. auth. see Hargreaves, Alec G.
McKinney, Mary Benet, see Benet McKinney, Mary.
McKinney, Mary Benet, jt. auth. see Sweetser, Thomas P.
***McKinney, Meagan.** The Cowboy Meets His Match: Matched in Montana. (Desire Ser.: Bk. 1299). 2000. per. 3.99 (0-373-76299-2, 1-76299-6) Silhouette.
McKinney, Meagan. Fair Is the Rose. large type ed. LC 93-27046. 1993. 12.95 (1-56895-031-4) Wheeler Pub.
— The Fortune Hunter. 352p. 1998. 23.00 (1-57566-262-0, Knsington) Kensgtn Pub Corp.
— The Fortune Hunter. (Zebra Bks.). 352p. 1998. pap. 6.50 (0-8217-6037-8, Zebra Kensgtn) Kensgtn Pub Corp.
— The Fortune Hunter. large type ed. LC 98-20855. 1998. 26.95 (1-57490-153-2, Beeler LP Bks) T T Beeler.
— Gentle from the Night. 352p. 1997. 21.95 (1-57566-136-5, Knsington) Kensgtn Pub Corp.
— Gentle from the Night. 352p. 1997. mass mkt. 5.99 (0-8217-5803-9, Zebra Kensgtn) Kensgtn Pub Corp.
— Gentle from the Night. large type ed. LC 98-5878. 1998. 25.95 (1-57490-136-2, Beeler LP Bks) T T Beeler.
— The Ground She Walks Upon. large type ed. LC 94-14260. 620p. 1994. lib. bdg. 24.95 (0-8161-7442-3, G K Hall Lrg Type) Mac Lib Ref.
— In The Dark. LC 98-65850. 288p. 1998. 23.00 (1-57566-371-6) Kensgtn Pub Corp.
***McKinney, Meagan.** In the Dark. large type ed. LC 99-87884. (Basic Ser.). 2000. 27.95 (0-7862-2452-5) Thorndike Pr.
— The Lawman Meets His Bride. (Intimate Moments Ser.: Bk. 1037). 2000. mass mkt. 4.50 (0-373-27107-7, 1-27107-1) Silhouette.
McKinney, Meagan. A Man to Slay a Dragon. 1996. pap. 21.95 (0-8217-5221-9) NAL.
— A Man to Slay Dragons. 416p. 1996. mass mkt. 5.99 (0-8217-5345-2, Zebra Kensgtn) Kensgtn Pub Corp.
— A Man to Slay Dragons. large type ed. LC 96-18366. 440p. 1996. lib. bdg. 23.95 (1-57490-063-3, Beeler LP Bks) T T Beeler.
***McKinney, Meagan.** The Merry Widow. 1999. 23.00 (1-57566-487-9, Knsington) Kensgtn Pub Corp.
— The Merry Widow. large type ed. 2000. 25.95 (1-56895-863-3) Wheeler Pub.
McKinney, Meagan. My Wicked Enchantress. LC 97-23464. (Five Star Romances Ser.). 408p. (Orig.). 1997. pap. 21.95 (0-7862-1206-3) Five Star.
— My Wicked Enchantress. 416p. (Orig.). 1997. pap. 5.99 (0-8217-5661-3, Zebra Kensgtn) Kensgtn Pub Corp.
— No Choice but Surrender. 384p. 1998. pap. 5.99 (0-8217-5859-4, Zebra Kensgtn) Kensgtn Pub Corp.
— No Choice but Surrender. large type ed. LC 98-39413. (Large Print Book Ser.). 1998. pap. 23.95 (1-56895-676-2) Wheeler Pub.
— One Small Secret. (Desire Ser.: No. 1222). 1999. per. 3.75 (0-373-76222-4, 1-76222-8) Silhouette.
McKinney, Meagen. In the Dark. 304p. 1999. mass mkt. 6.99 (0-8217-6341-5, Zebra Kensgtn) Kensgtn Pub Corp.
***McKinney, Megan.** Un Pequeno Secreto.Tr. of Small Secret. (SPA.). 2000. per. 3.50 (0-373-35327-8) Harlequin Bks.
McKinney, Meredith, ed. from JPN. The Tale of Saigyo: (Saigyo Monogatari) LC 97-25714. (Michigan Papers in Japanese Studies: No. 25). (Illus.). xii, 90p. 1998. pap. 11.95 (0-939512-83-1) U MI Japan.
McKinney, Meredith, tr. see Furui, Yoshikichi.
McKinney, Michael. Biodiversity Dynamics: Turnover of Populations, Taxa, & Communities. LC 98-17973. 584p. 1998. 59.95 (0-231-10414-6) Col U Pr.
— Current Issues in Geology: Selected Reading. 4th ed. LC 97-209062. (Earth Science Ser.). (C). 1997. 11.00 (0-314-20617-5) Wadsworth Pub.
***McKinney, Michael & Schoch, Robert.** Environmental Science: Systems & Solutions. 2nd ed. (Illus.). 640p. (C). 2000. pap. text 75.00 (0-7637-0918-2) JB Pubns.
McKinney, Michael & Schoch, Robert. Environmental Science Case Studies. (Earth Science Ser.). Date not set. pap. 20.00 (0-314-20397-4) Jones & Bartlett.
— ESS of Environmental Science: WWW Edition. LC 97-40642. (Earth Science Ser.). 752p. 1997. pap. 53.25 (0-7637-0613-2) Jones & Bartlett.
— Outlooks: Environmental Literacy Readings. LC 98-139749. (Earth Science Ser.). 288p. 1997. pap. 15.00 (0-7637-0658-2) Jones & Bartlett.

McKinney, Michael L. Current Issues in Geology. Westby, ed. LC 94-194121. 254p. (C). pap. text 12.25 (*0-314-03726-8*) West Pub.

— Current Issues in Geology, 1996. 3rd ed. 225p. (C). 1995. pap. 11.50 (*0-314-07568-2*) West Pub.

McKinney, Michael L. & Schoch, Robert M. Environmental Science: Systems & Solutions. (Earth Science Ser.). 650p. (C). 1996. pap. 49.50 (*0-314-06401-X*) Jones & Bartlett.

— Environmental Science: Test Bank. (Earth Science Ser.). 1996. pap. 10.00 (*0-314-20366-4*) Jones & Bartlett.

— Environmental Science Internet Activities. (Earth Science Ser.). 1996. pap. 18.75 (*0-314-09929-8*) Jones & Bartlett.

— Environmental Science Note Taking Guide. (Earth Science Ser.). 483p. 1996. pap. 20.00 (*0-314-20148-3*) Jones & Bartlett.

— Environmental Science Study Guide. (Earth Science Ser.). 173p. 1996. pap., student ed. 16.25 (*0-314-09799-6*) Jones & Bartlett.

McKinney, Michael L., jt. auth. see Parker, Sue T.

McKinney, Michael W., jt. auth. see McKinney, Wayne C.

***McKinney, Michelle.** Lost in Time. 1999. pap. write for info. (*1-58235-074-4*) Watermrk Pr.

McKinney, Mitchell S., jt. auth. see Carlin, Diana B.

McKinney, Nadine. Eyes in the Attic. LC 93-74952. 141p. (J). (gr. 3-5). 1994. pap. 7.95 (*0-943864-73-9*) Davenport.

M

McKinney, Peter & Cunningham, Bruce L. Aesthetic Facial Surgery. (Illus.). 234p. 1992. text 175.00 (*0-443-08703-2*) Church.

McKinney, Phyliss. Revelations. 20p. (Orig.). (YA). (gr. 5 up). 1992. pap. text 4.95 (*1-877860-09-3*) Eula Intl Pub.

McKinney, Richard I. Religion in Higher Education among Negroes. LC 75-38785. (Religion in America, Ser. 2). 186p. 1975. reprint ed. 20.95 (*0-405-04075-X*) Ayer.

McKinney, Richard I. & Johnson, Mordecai W. Mordecai - The Man & His Message: The Story of Mordecai Wyatt Johnson. LC 96-47507. 1997. write for info. (*0-88258-197-X*) Howard U Pr.

— Mordecai - The Man & His Message: The Story of Mordecai Wyatt Johnson. LC 96-47507. (Illus.). 354p. (C). 1997. pap. text 21.95 (*0-88258-193-7*, MCMMP) Howard U Pr.

McKinney, Richard W., ed. Creation, Christ & Culture: Studies in Honour of T. F. Torrance. 336p. 1993. 49.95 (*0-567-01019-8*, Pub. by T & T Clark) Bks Intl VA.

— Creation, Christ & Culture: Studies in Honour of T. F. Torrance. 336p. 1998. pap. 31.95 (*0-567-08558-9*, Pub. by T & T Clark) Bks Intl VA.

McKinney, Robert. Out of This World: Handbook of Ghosts, Spirits, Alien Sightings & Psychic Phenomena. (Illus.). 1985. pap. 4.95 (*0-913290-67-X*) Camaro Pub.

McKinney, Robert W., jt. ed. see Richmond, Jonathan Y.

McKinney, Rozanne M., jt. auth. see McKinney, Samuel, III.

Mckinney, Ruth A. Legal Research: A Practical Guide & Self-Instructional Workbook. LC 95-48934. (Paralegal). 264p. (C). 1996. pap. text 17.00 (*0-314-08244-1*) West Pub.

McKinney, Ruth A. Legal Research: A Practical Guide & Self-Instructional Workbook. (Miscellaneous Ser.). 79p. 1995. pap. text, teacher ed. write for info. (*0-314-09000-2*) West Pub.

***McKinney, Sally.** Adventures in Nature: New Zealand. LC 99-42001. (Illus.). 328p. 2000. pap. 18.95 (*1-56261-435-5*) Avalon Travel.

McKinney, Sally. Country Roads of Indiana. LC 92-81830. (Country Roads Ser.). (Illus.). 120p. (Orig.). 1993. pap. 9.95 (*1-56626-010-8*, Cntry Rds Pr) NTC Contemp Pub Co.

— Country Roads of Indiana: Drives, Day Trips & Weekend Excursions. 2nd ed. LC 98-30399. (Country Roads of... Ser.). (Illus.). 128p. 1999. pap. 12.95 (*1-56626-103-1*, 61031, Cntry Rds Pr) NTC Contemp Pub Co.

— Fairs & Festivals: Illinois, Indiana, & Ohio. (Travels & Vacations Ser.). (Illus.). 208p. 1996. pap. 14.95 (*1-56626-134-1*, 61341, Cntry Rds Pr) NTC Contemp Pub Co.

— Hiking Indiana. LC 98-55073. (America's Best Day Hiking Ser.). (Illus.). 200p. 1999. pap. 19.95 (*0-88011-901-2*, PMCK0901) Human Kinetics.

***McKinney, Sam.** Reach of Tide, Ring of History: A Columbia River Voyage. LC 00-9284. (Northwest Reprints Ser.). 128p. 2000. reprint ed. pap. 14.95 (*0-87071-484-8*) Oreg St U Pr.

McKinney, Samuel, III & McKinney, Rozanne M. Big Debt Survival Guide: A Practical Legal Reference for Protecting Yourself, Family, & Business from All Types of Liability Exposure in or Out of Bankruptcy. 304p. (Orig.). 1992. pap. 24.95 (*0-9620366-1-7*) Marshall TX.

McKinney, Samuel B., jt. auth. see Massey, Floyd, Jr.

McKinney, Shawn, et al. Sesquicentennial Park: The Design Competition. (Illus.). 70p. (Orig.). (C). 1987. pap. 35.00 (*0-9618107-0-X*) Cent Houst Civic.

McKinney, Tag, jt. auth. see McKinney, Lee.

McKinney, Thomas H. & Davis, Dale A. Distribution of Federal Funds for Vocational Education to Community, Technical, & Junior Colleges. LC 88-170893. (AACJC-ACCT Keeping America Working Task Force Ser.: No. 6). 70p. reprint ed. pap. 30.00 (*0-7837-2480-2*, 204263600005) Bks Demand.

McKinney, Thurman D., ed. Renal Complications of Neoplasia. 270p. 1985. 75.00 (*0-275-92031-3*, C2031, Praeger Pubs) Greenwood.

McKinney, Tim. Robert E. Lee & the Thirty Fifth Star. LC 93-84769. (Illus.). 152p. 1993. pap. 11.95 (*0-929521-75-7*) Pictorial Hist.

— Robert E. Lee at Sewell Mountain. 1990. 11.95 (*0-929521-43-9*) Pictorial Hist.

— West Virginia Civil War Almanac, Vol. 1. LC 97-69941. (Illus.). 582p. 1998. text 29.95 (*1-57510-036-3*) Pictorial Hist.

McKinney, Virginia. The Picture Plus Dictionary. (Illus.). 576p. (J). 1997. 49.00 (*1-884362-24-9*) Butte Pubns.

McKinney, W. T. Models of Mental Disorders: A New Comparative Psychiatry. LC 88-2335. (Illus.). 212p. (C). 1988. text 55.00 (*0-306-42746-X*, Kluwer Plenum) Kluwer Academic.

McKinney, W. Troy, jt. auth. see Trichter, J. Gary.

McKinney, Wayne C. & McKinney, Michael W. Archery. 7th ed. LC 92-82691. (Sports & Fitness Ser.). 234p. (C). 1993. text 10.29 (*0-697-12654-4*, WCB McGr Hill) McGrw-H Hghr Educ.

McKinney, Wayne C. & McKinney, Michael W. Archery. 8th ed. LC 95-83960. 256p. (C). 1996. text. write for info. (*0-697-27983-9*) Brown & Benchmark.

McKinney, Wayne R. & Palmer, Christopher A., eds. Gratings & Grating Monochromators for Synchrotron Radiation. LC 98-122610. 214p. 1997. 59.00 (*0-8194-2572-9*) SPIE.

— Theory & Practice of Surface-Relief Diffraction Gratings Vol. 3450: Synchrotron & Other Applications. 1998. 48.00 (*0-8194-2905-8*) SPIE.

***McKinney-Whetstone, Diane.** Blues Dancing: A Novel. 320p. 2000. pap. 13.00 (*0-688-17789-1*, Quil) HarperTrade.

— Blues Dancing: A Novel. 320p. 1999. 24.00 (*0-688-14995-2*, Wm Morrow) Morrow Avon.

McKinney-Whetstone, Diane. Tempest Rising. LC 97-40942. 288p. 1998. 24.00 (*0-688-14994-4*, Wm Morrow) Morrow Avon.

— Tempest Rising: A Novel. 288p. 1999. pap. 12.00 (*0-688-16640-7*, Quil) HarperTrade.

— Tumbling. LC 95-49146. 288p. 1996. 24.00 (*0-688-14487-X*, Wm Morrow) Morrow Avon.

— Tumbling. LC 96-51546. 1997. per. 12.00 (*0-684-83724-2*, Scribner Pap Fic) S&S Trade Pap.

McKinney, William. Radiographic Processing. 359p. 1995. spiral bd. 115.00 (*1-879575-63-9*) Acad Med Sys.

McKinnis, James A. Handcoloring Photographs. LC 93-41704. (Illus.). 144p. 1994. 24.95 (*0-8174-3972-2*, Amphoto) Watsn-Guptill.

McKinnis, Lynn. Fundamentals of Orthopedic Radiology. (Contemporary Perspectives in Rehabilitation Ser.). (Illus.). 429p. (C). 1996. text 56.00 (*0-8036-0139-5*) Davis Co.

McKinnis, Marilyn F., ed. see McGuire, Francis G.

***McKinnis, Sandra.** The Processing Program: Using Language Webs & Altered Auditory Input to Improve Comprehension, 2 vols. LC 00-21012. 2000. pap. write for info. (*1-888222-47-6*) Thinking Pubns.

McKinniss, Candace B. & Natella, Arthur A., eds. Business in Mexico: Managerial Behavior, Protocol, & Etiquette. LC 93-23222. (Illus.). 156p. 1994. 59.95 (*1-56024-406-2*) Haworth Pr.

McKinniss, Candace B. & Natella, Arthur A., eds. Business in Mexico: Managerial Behavior, Protocol, & Etiquette. LC 93-23222. 156p. 1997. pap. 19.95 (*0-7890-0129-2*) Haworth Pr.

McKinnon. Friends in Need. LC 96-61068. 192p. 1997. text 59.50 (*1-86064-138-5*, Pub. by I B T) St Martin.

Mckinnon. Information Mosaic. 300p. 1992. 29.95 (*0-07-103368-8*) McGraw.

McKinnon, Harvey. Hidden Gold: How Monthly Giving Will Build Donor Loyalty, Boost Your Organization's Income & Increase Its Financial Stability. (Illus.). 208p. 1999. pap. 39.95 (*1-56625-122-2*) Bonus Books.

***McKinnon, Al & McKinnon, Linda.** In the Trenches with Linux, Vol. I. 368p. 2000. pap. 49.95 (*1-930713-00-2*) Gearhead Pr CA.

— In the Trenches with Linux, Vol. II. 672p. 2000. pap. 69.95 (*1-930713-01-0*) Gearhead Pr CA.

McKinnon, Alan. Physical Distribution Systems. 256p. 1989. 67.50 (*0-415-00438-1*) Routledge.

McKinnon, Alastair. Falsification & Belief. (C). 1979. reprint ed. pap. text 11.00 (*0-917930-13-4*); reprint ed. lib. bdg. 27.00 (*0-917930-33-9*) Ridgeview.

McKinnon, Alastair, ed. see Kierkegaard, Soren.

McKinnon, Angus & Voss, James. Equine Reproduction. LC 91-29283. (Illus.). 1137p. 1992. text 99.50 (*0-8121-1427-2*) Lppncott W & W.

McKinnon, Angus O., jt. auth. see Rantanen, Norman W.

McKinnon-Bell, David, jt. auth. see Cawood, Ian.

McKinnon, Carolyn. Insanity Inc. LC 95-78037. (Illus.). 270p. 1996. 15.95 (*1-879418-97-5*) Audenreed Pr.

***McKinnon, Catriona & Hampsher-Monk, Iain, eds.** The Demands of Citizenship. 256p. 2000. 74.95 (*0-8264-4771-6*); pap. 27.95 (*0-8264-4772-4*) Continuum.

***McKinnon, Christine.** Character, Virtue Theories & the Vices. 300p. 1999. pap. 19.95 (*1-55111-225-6*) Broadview Pr.

***McKinnon, Colin.** Reuters Financial Glossary. 2000. pap. 39.00 (*0-273-65039-4*) F T P H.

McKinnon, Dan. Bullseye - One Reactor. 208p. (Orig.). 1987. 14.95 (*0-941437-07-8*) House Hits.

— Everything You Need to Know Before You're Hijacked. 139p. (Orig.). 1987. pap. 4.95 (*0-941437-01-9*) House Hits.

Mckinnon, Dan. The Good Life. 173p. 1973. 8.95 (*0-941437-02-7*) House Hits.

McKinnon, Dan. The Ten Second Message. LC 94-77357. 130p. 1994. pap. 9.95 (*0-941437-04-3*) House Hits.

Mckinnon, Dan. Tombstones. 106p. 1995. pap. 14.95 (*0-941437-03-5*) House Hits.

McKinnon, Dan. Words of Honor. LC 95-95330. 309p. 1996. pap. 10.00 (*0-941437-00-0*) House Hits.

McKinnon, Darryl J. Smart Things to Do Before You Divorce Him: A Woman's Guide to Planning for a Divorce. McKinnon, Sokhamony, ed. 100p. 1998. pap. 19.95 (*0-9664748-0-5*) Metropol Pubg.

McKinnon, David. War & Revolution in Leipzig, 1914-1918: Socialist Politics & Urban Evolution in a German City. LC 97-49284. 1998. write for info. (*0-7618-1019-6*) U Pr of Amer.

McKinnon, Elizabeth. Great Big Holiday Celebrations: Activities for Celebrating Major Holidays with Young Children. Bittinger, Gayle, ed. LC 91-65045. (Celebration Ser.). (Illus.). 228p. (Orig.). 1991. pap. 17.95 (*0-911019-43-X*, WPH 0704) Totline Pubns.

— Our Town: Activities for Helping Children Learn & Care about Their Community. Harrison, Brenda M. & Cubley, Kathleen, eds. LC 92-80995. (Learning & Caring About Ser.). (Illus.). 80p. (Orig.). (J). (ps). 1994. 8.95 (*0-911019-54-5*, WPH 1203) Totline Pubns.

— Preschool Theme Calendar. LC 98-61488. (Theme Calendar Ser.). (Illus.). 48p. 1999. pap. 6.95 (*1-57029-243-4*, 00191) Totline Pubns.

— Ready to Communicate: Help Your Child Develop the Skills Necessary for School Success. LC 96-60425. (Getting Ready for School Ser.). (Illus.). 96p. (Orig.). (J). (ps-k). 1997. pap. 6.95 (*1-57029-114-4*, 3204) Totline Pubns.

— Time to Learn - Colors. (Time to Learn Ser.). (Illus.). 48p. (J). (ps-k). 1998. pap. 3.95 (*1-57029-192-6*, 2810) Totline Pubns.

— Time to Learn - Drawing & Writing. LC 98-147451. (Time to Learn Ser.). (Illus.). 48p. (J). (ps-k). 1998. pap. 3.95 (*1-57029-201-9*, 2819) Totline Pubns.

— Time to Learn - Numbers. (Time to Learn Ser.). (Illus.). 48p. (J). (ps-k). 1998. pap. 3.95 (*1-57029-195-0*, 2813) Totline Pubns.

— Time to Learn - Shapes. (Time to Learn Ser.). (Illus.). 48p. (J). (ps-k). 1998. pap. 3.95 (*1-57029-197-7*, 2815) Totline Pubns.

— Time to Learn - Sorting & Matching. (Time to Learn Ser.). (Illus.). 48p. (J). (ps-k). 1998. pap. 3.95 (*1-57029-198-5*, 2816) Totline Pubns.

— Time to Learn -Letters. (Time to Learn Ser.). (Illus.). 48p. (J). (ps-k). 1998. pap. 3.95 (*1-57029-193-4*, 2811) Totline Pubns.

— Toddler Theme Calendar. LC 98-61490. (Theme Calendar Ser.). (Illus.). 48p. 1999. pap. 6.95 (*1-57029-242-6*, 00190) Totline Pubns.

McKinnon, Elizabeth, ed. More Piggyback Songs for School. LC 95-60006. (Piggyback Songs Ser.). (Illus.). 80p. (Orig.). (J). (ps-1). 1995. pap. 8.95 (*1-57029-067-9*, WPH 0211) Totline Pubns.

— Songs & Games for Threes. LC 96-61894. (Learn with Piggyback Songs Ser.). (Illus.). 48p. (Orig.). (J). (ps). 1997. pap. 3.95 (*1-57029-165-9*, 3303) Totline Pubns.

McKinnon, Elizabeth & Bittinger, Gayle, eds. Alphabet Theme-a-Saurus: The Great Big Book of Letter Recognition. LC 90-71272. (Theme-A-Saurus Ser.). (Illus.). 280p. (J). (ps-1). 1991. pap. 21.95 (*0-911019-38-3*, WPH 1004) Totline Pubns.

McKinnon, Elizabeth, jt. auth. see Bittinger, Gayle.

McKinnon, Elizabeth, ed. see Bittinger, Gayle.

McKinnon, Elizabeth, ed. see Petersen, Evelyn.

McKinnon, Elizabeth, ed. see Warren, Jean.

McKinnon, Elizabeth S. Ready to Learn Colors, Shapes & Numbers: Help Your Child Develop the Skills Necessary for School Success. LC 96-60121. (Getting Ready for School Ser.). (Illus.). 96p. (Orig.). (J). (ps-k). 1997. pap. 6.95 (*1-57029-107-1*, 3201) Totline Pubns.

— Special Day Celebrations: Seasonal Mini Celebrations to Enjoy with Young Children. Bittinger, Gayle, ed. LC 89-50765. (Celebration Ser.). (Illus.). 128p. (Orig.). (J). (ps-1). 1989. pap. 14.95 (*0-911019-24-3*, WPH 0702) Totline Pubns.

— Teaching House. Warren, Jean & Cubley, Kathleen, eds. LC 95-60511. (Learning Everywhere Ser.). (Illus.). 128p. (Orig.). 1996. pap. 6.95 (*1-57029-068-7*, 2801) Totline Pubns.

— Teaching Town. Warren, Jean & Cubley, Kathleen, eds. LC 95-60512. (Learning Everywhere Ser.). (Illus.). 128p. (Orig.). 1996. pap. 6.95 (*1-57029-069-5*, 2802) Totline Pubns.

— Teaching Trips. Warren, Jean & Cubley, Kathleen, eds. LC 95-60513. (Learning Everywhere Ser.). (Illus.). 128p. (Orig.). 1996. pap. 6.95 (*1-57029-070-9*, 2803) Totline Pubns.

McKinnon, Elizabeth S., ed. 1-2-3 Colors: Activities for Introducing Color to Young Children. LC 87-51241. (Totline 1-2-3 Ser.). (Illus.). 160p. (Orig.). (J). (ps-1). 1988. pap. 14.95 (*0-911019-17-0*, 0403) Totline Pubns.

McKinnon, Elizabeth S., jt. auth. see Warren, Jean.

McKinnon, Elizabeth S., ed. see Backer, Barbara F.

McKinnon, Elizabeth S., ed. see Miller, Susan A.

McKinnon-Evans, Stuart, tr. see Frevert, Ute.

McKinnon, Gloria. Anne's Glory Box Collection: Special Heirloom Treasures to Make. 1996. 27.95 (*1-86343-238-8*) Quilters Res.

McKinnon, Helen D. Every Woman: Adopting to Mid-Life Change. 96p. 1987. pap. 9.95 (*0-7737-5079-7*) Genl Dist Srvs.

McKinnon, James. Source Readings Vol. 2: Early Christ. rev. ed. LC 98-106574. Vol. 2. (C). 1997. pap. text 21.75 (*0-393-96695-X*) Norton.

— The Temple, the Church Fathers & Early Western Chant. LC 97-42462. (Variorum Collected Studies: Vol. 606). 350p. 1998. text 89.95 (*0-86078-688-9*, Pub. by Variorum) Ashgate Pub Co.

***McKinnon, James W.** The Advent Project: The Later Seventh-Century Creation of the Roman Mass Proper. (Illus.). 470p. 2000. 50.00 (*0-520-22198-2*, Pub. by U CA Pr) Cal Prin Full Svc.

McKinnon, K. C. Candles on Bay Street. LC 98-35729. (Illus.). 240p. 1999. 17.95 (*0-385-49128-X*) Doubleday.

***McKinnon, K. C.** Candles on Bay Street. 2000. mass mkt. write for info. (*0-449-00555-0*, GM) Fawcett.

McKinnon, K. C. Candles on Bay Street. large type ed. LC 99-19341. 1999. pap. write for info. (*1-56895-721-1*) Wheeler Pub.

— Dancing at the Harvest Moon. 1999. mass mkt. 6.99 (*0-449-00527-5*, GM) Fawcett.

— Dancing at the Harvest Moon: A Novel. LC 97-9867. (Illus.). 240p. 1997. 16.95 (*0-385-48993-5*) Doubleday.

— Dancing at the Harvest Moon: A Novel. large type ed. LC 98-14227. 1998. 25.95 (*1-56895-551-0*, Compass) Wheeler Pub.

McKinnon, Linda, jt. auth. see McKinnon, Al.

McKinnon, Lucille V. Grandma's Treasure Chest: Moral & Spiritual Values for Grandparents to share with Grandchildren. (Illus.). 124p. (Orig.). 1991. 24.95 (*0-941437-05-1*) House Hits.

Mckinnon, Mack Z. Shadowbreed. 263p. mass mkt. 4.99 (*1-55197-208-5*) Picasso Publ.

McKinnon, Matthew. The Law of Contracts. 464p. 1993. ring bd. 67.00 (*1-879581-08-6*) Lupus Pubns.

***McKinnon, Michael.** Arabia: Land, Sea, Sky. (Illus.). 224p. 1999. reprint ed. text 30.00 (*0-7881-6489-9*) DIANE Pub.

McKinnon, Michael. Arabia: Sand, Sea & Sky. (Illus.). 224p. (C). 1995. 53.00 (*0-907151-63-9*, Pub. by IMMEL Pubng) St Mut.

McKinnon, Michael, jt. auth. see Vine, Peter.

McKinnon, Patrick. Cherry Ferris Wheels. 102p. 1990. pap. 10.00 (*0-9614462-3-4*) Black Hat Pr.

***McKinnon, Pauline.** Estate Records--Keep Them Yourself. LC 98-90534. 1999. pap. 10.95 (*0-533-12842-0*) Vantage.

McKinnon, Robert S. Moose, Bruce & the Goose. 2nd rev. ed. LC 96-94057. (Illus.). 165p. (J). (gr. 4-5). 1996. pap. 12.00 (*0-9651943-0-2*) R S McKinnon.

***McKinnon, Ronald I.** Cause, Effect & Control of Accidental Loss with Accident Investigation Kit. (Illus.). 280p. (C). 2000. boxed set 129.95 (*1-56670-523-1*) Lewis Pubs.

McKinnon, Ronald I. Financial Liberalization & Economic Development: A Reassessment of Interest-Rate Policies in Asia & Latin America. 48p. 1988. pap. 9.95 (*1-55815-020-X*) ICS Pr.

— An International Standard for Monetary Stabilization. LC 83-22572. (Policy Analyses in International Economics Ser.: No. 8). 112p. (Orig.). reprint ed. pap. 34.80 (*0-8357-2825-0*, 203906100011) Bks Demand.

— Money & Capital in Economic Development. LC 72-9928. 184p. 1973. pap. 14.95 (*0-8157-5613-5*) Brookings.

— The Order of Economic Liberalization: Financial Control in the Transition to a Market Economy. 2nd ed. (Johns Hopkins Studies in Development). 224p. (C). 1993. pap. text 16.95 (*0-8018-4743-5*) Johns Hopkins.

— The Rules of the Game: International Money & Exchange Rates. LC 95-36690. (Illus.). 528p. 1996. 62.50 (*0-262-13318-0*) MIT Pr.

McKinnon, Ronald I., ed. Money & Finance in Economic Growth & Development: Essays in Honor of Edward S. Shaw: Proceedings of the Conference Held at Stanford University. LC 75-21191. (Business Economics & Finance Ser.: No. 8). 351p. reprint ed. pap. 108.90 (*0-7837-0963-3*, 204126800019) Bks Demand.

McKinnon, Ronald I., et al. Dollar & Yen: Resolving Economic Conflict Between the United States & Japan. LC 97-1584. (Illus.). 280p. 1997. 39.50 (*0-262-13335-0*) MIT Pr.

McKinnon, Sharon M. & Bruns, William J., Jr. The Information Mosaic. LC 91-46758. 288p. 1992. 27.95 (*0-87584-317-4*) Harvard Busn.

McKinnon, Sokhamony, ed. see McKinnon, Darryl J.

McKinnon, Susan. From a Shattered Sun: Hierarchy, Gender & Alliance in the Tanimbar Islands. LC 91-50325. (Illus.). 342p. 1992. pap. 19.95 (*0-299-13154-8*) U of Wis Pr.

McKinnon, Susie. Business Incubators of North America, 1998. 1998. pap. 395.00 (*1-887183-43-4*) NBIA.

McKinnon, Susie & Hayhow, Sally. The State of the Business Incubation Industry, 1998. 1998. pap. 32.00 (*1-887183-44-2*) NBIA.

McKinnon, Wayne, jt. auth. see Villeneuve, Arnold.

***McKinnon, William, compiled by.** Our Women in the War: A Series of Papers Written by Southern Ladies - South Carolina News & Courier. 401p. 1998. write for info. (*1-882194-47-0*) TN Valley Pub.

***McKinsey & Company, Inc. Staff, et al.** Valuation: Measuring & Managing the Value of Companies. 3rd ed. (Frontiers in Finance Ser.). 608p. 2000. 75.00 (*0-471-36190-9*) Wiley.

***McKinsey, C. Dennis.** Biblical Errancy: A Reference Guide. 800p. 2000. 129.95 (*1-57392-808-9*) Prometheus Bks.

McKinsey, C. Dennis. The Encyclopedia of Biblical Errancy. LC 94-40048. 553p. (C). 1995. 51.95 (*0-87975-926-7*) Prometheus Bks.

McKinsey, Elizabeth R. The Western Experiment: New England Transcendentalists in the Ohio Valley. LC 72-83467. (Essays in History & Literature Ser.). 78p. 1978. pap. 8.50 (*0-674-95040-2*) HUP.

McKinsey, Folger, jt. auth. see William, T. J.

McKinsey, James O., Jr. Managerial Accounting. Chandler, Alfred D., ed. LC 79-7551. (History of Management Thought & Practice Ser.). 1980. reprint ed. lib. bdg. 61.95 (*0-405-12335-3*) Ayer.

***McKinsey, Kristan H., et al.** Elegant Plate: Three Centuries of Precious Metals in New York, 2 vols. LC 99-55692. (Illus.). 2000. write for info. (*0-910961-11-5*) Mus City NY.

An Asterisk (*) at the beginning of an entry indicates that the title is appearing for the first time.

McKinsey, Martin, tr. & intro. see Ritsos, Yannis.

McKinstry, Asako N., jt. auth. see McKinstry, John A.

McKinstry, E. Richard, compiled by. Personal Accounts of Events, Travels, & Everyday Life in America: An Annotated Bibliography. LC 97-10832. (Winterthur Book Ser.). (Illus.). 236p. 1997. 40.00 (*0-912724-39-0*) Winterthur.

— Trade Catalogues at Winterthur: A Guide to Literature of Merchandising, 1750 to 1980. LC 93-13919. (Winterthur Bk.). 1993. reprint ed. 110.00 (*1-55655-480-X*) U Pubns Amer.

McKinstry, John A. & McKinstry, Asako N. Jinsei Annai: - 'Life's Guide' Glimpses of Japan Through a Popular Advice Column. LC 90-24303. 224p. (C). (gr. 13). 1991. 44.95 (*0-87332-762-4*, East Gate Bk) M E Sharpe.

McKinstry, John A., jt. auth. see Kerbo, Harold R.

***McKinstry, Lydia.** Experiments in Organic Chemistry. 54p. (C). 1999. pap. text 22.95 (*0-7872-6086-X*) Kendall-Hunt.

McKinstry, Pamela. Adventure Travel in Africa: An African Odyssey. 192p. (C). 1995. pap. 50.00 (*0-907151-98-1*, Pub. by IMMEL Pubng) St Mut.

— Cooking Secrets from Around the World. Marks, Judy, ed. LC 97-71562. (Illus.). 256p. 1997. pap. text 15.95 (*1-883214-15-7*) Bon Vivant Pr.

— Discovery Guide to Central Africa. 224p. (C). 1995. pap. 59.00 (*0-907151-96-5*, Pub. by IMMEL Pubng) St Mut.

— Discovery Guide to Southern Africa: Namibia, Botswana & South Africa. 256p. (C). 1994. pap. 50.00 (*0-907151-73-6*, Pub. by IMMEL Pubng) St Mut.

— Discovery Guide to the Game Parks of Southern Africa. 232p. (C). 1995. pap. 50.00 (*0-907151-97-3*, Pub. by IMMEL Pubng) St Mut.

McKinstry, Robert E. Cleft Palate Dentistry. (Illus.). 312p. 1998. 115.00 (*1-886236-07-0*) ABI Prof Pubns.

— Fundamentals of Facial Prosthetics. (Illus.). 224p. 1995. 95.00 (*1-886236-00-3*) ABI Prof Pubns.

McKinstry, Robert E., ed. Directory of Facial Prosthetic Resources: A Guide to the Literature, Products & Suppliers for the Facial Prosthetic Community. 1998. pap. 55.00 incl. disk (*1-886236-13-5*) ABI Prof Pubns.

McKinstry, Sam. Rowand Anderson. 1991. text 68.00 (*0-7486-0252-6*, Pub. by Edinburgh U Pr) Col U Pr.

McKinstry, Sam, jt. auth. see Fleming.

McKinstry, Sam, jt. auth. see Fleming, Iain.

McKinstry, Sam, jt. auth. see Stamp, Gavin.

McKinstry, Sam, jt. ed. see Stamp, Gavin.

McKinstry, Steve. A Special Gift. (Illus.). 32p. 1981. 6.95 (*0-910079-01-3*) Lucy & Co.

McKinstry, Steven R. The Attic Treasure. (Illus.). 32p. 1982. 6.95 (*0-317-62219-6*) Lucy & Co.

McKinstry, Susan J., jt. ed. see Bauer, Dale M.

McKinven, John A. The Hanlon Brothers: Their Amazing Acrobatics, Pantomimes, & Stage Spectacles. LC 97-52994. (Illus.). 133p. 1998. 39.95 (*0-916638-82-0*, D M Magic Bks) Meyerbooks.

— Stage Flying: 431 B. C. to Modern Times. LC 95-5936. 1995. 35.00 (*0-916638-81-2*, D M Magic Bks) Meyerbooks.

McKinzie, Bruce W. Objectivity, Communication, & the Foundation of Understanding. 168p. (Orig.). (C). 1994. pap. text 24.50 (*0-8191-9537-5*); lib. bdg. 47.00 (*0-8191-9536-7*) U Pr of Amer.

McKinzie, Edith. Hawaiian Genealogies, Vol. 1. Stagner, Ishmael W., ed. 128p. 1983. pap. text 23.00 (*0-939154-28-5*) Inst Polynesian.

— Hawaiian Genealogies, Vol. 2. Stagner, Ishmael W., ed. 168p. 1986. pap. text 25.00 (*0-939154-37-4*) Inst Polynesian.

McKinzie, Harry. Family Reunions: How to Plan Yours. LC 87-19615. (Reunions Ser.). 305p. (Orig.). 1994. pap. 16.95 (*0-86626-013-7*) AAIMS Pubs.

— High School Reunions: How to Plan Yours. (Reunions Ser.). 305p. (Orig.). 1994. pap. 24.95 (*0-86626-001-3*) AAIMS Pubs.

— A Message from Elvis Presley. pap. 16.95 (*0-86626-004-8*) AAIMS Pubs.

— Women in Boxing. 1994. pap. 16.95 (*0-86626-012-9*) AAIMS Pubs.

— Zthorg - God's Computer. 170p. (Orig.). pap. 24.00 (*0-86626-017-X*) AAIMS Pubs.

McKinzie, Harry & Tindimwebwa, Issy K. Names from East Africa. Campbell, Elisabeth, ed. 42p. (Orig.). (J). 1980. pap. 9.95 (*0-86626-007-2*) AAIMS Pubs.

McKinzie, Matthew G., et al. Explosive Alliance: Nuclear Weapons Simulation Research at American Universities. (Illus.). 87p. 1998. pap. 10.00 (*1-893340-15-5*) Natl Resources Defense Coun.

McKirahan, Richard. Cicero de Natura Deorum I. (Bryn Mawr Latin Commentaries Ser.). 72p. 1997. pap. 6.00 (*0-929524-89-6*) Bryn Mawr Commentaries.

McKirahan, Richard D., Jr. Philosophy Before Socrates: An Introduction with Texts & Commentary. LC 93-46837. 448p. (Orig.). (C). 1994. pap. text 16.95 (*0-87220-175-9*); lib. bdg. 39.95 (*0-87220-176-7*) Hackett Pub.

— Plato's Meno. (Greek Commentaries Ser.). 109p. (Orig.). (C). 1986. pap. text 7.00 (*0-929524-30-6*) Bryn Mawr Commentaries.

— Principles & Proofs: Aristotle's Theory of Demonstrative Science. 356p. 1992. text 52.50 (*0-691-07363-5*, Pub. by Princeton U Pr) Cal Prin Full Svc.

McKirahan, Richard D., Jr., tr. see Curd, Patricia, ed.

McKirchy, Karen. Powerful Performance Appraisals: How to Set Expectations & Work Together to Improve. LC 98-13954. Orig. Title: How to Conduct Win-Win Performance Appraisals. 128p. 1998. pap. 12.99 (*1-56414-367-8*) Career Pr Inc.

McKisack, May. The Fourteenth Century, 1307-1399. (Oxford History of England Ser.: Vol. 5). (Illus.). 620p. 1991. reprint ed. pap. 21.00 (*0-19-285250-7*) OUP.

McKisack, May. Fourteenth Century, Thirteen Seven to Thirteen Ninety-Nine. (Oxford History of England Ser.). (Illus.). 618p. 1959. text 65.00 (*0-19-821712-9*) OUP.

McKisack, May, ed. see Clarke, Maude V.

McKissack. One Family's Story. (J). 1995. 19.95 (*0-8050-1671-6*) H Holt & Co.

McKissack, Frederick. God Makes All Things New. (Illus.). 32p. (J). 1993. pap. text 5.99 (*0-8066-2653-4*, 9-2653) Augsburg Fortress.

McKissack, Frederick & McKissack, Patricia. Messey Bessey's School Desk. Rau, Dana, ed. (Rookie Readers Ser.). (Illus.). 32p. (J). 1998. pap. 4.95 (*0-516-26361-7*) Childrens.

McKissack, Frederick, jt. auth. see McKissack, Patricia.

McKissack, Frederick, jt. auth. see McKissack, Patricia C.

McKissack, Frederick L., jt. auth. see McKissack, Patricia C.

McKissack, Fredrick. Black Hoops: The History of African-Americans in Basketball. LC 98-14107. (Illus.). 176p. (YA). (gr. 5-9). 1999. 15.95 (*0-590-48712-4*) Scholastic Inc.

McKissack, Fredrick, jt. auth. see McKissack, Pat.

McKissack, Fredrick, jt. auth. see McKissack, Patricia.

McKissack, Fredrick, jt. auth. see McKissack, Patricia C.

McKissack, Fredrick, ed. see Duyff, Roberta L.

***McKissack, Fredrick L.** This Generation of Americans: A Story of the Civil Rights Movement. (Jamestown's American Portraits Ser.). (Illus.). 144p. (J). 2000. pap. 5.95 (*0-8092-0626-9*, 06269E, Jamestwn Pub) NTC Contemp Pub Co.

McKissack, Fredrick L., jt. auth. see McKissack, Patricia C.

McKissack, Pat. Goin' Someplace Special. LC 99-88258. (J). (gr. 3). 2001. 16.00 (*0-689-81885-8*) S&S Childrens.

***McKissack, Pat.** The Honest-to-Goodness Truth. LC 98-47070. (Illus.). 40p. (J). (gr. k-3). 2000. 16.00 (*0-689-82668-0*) Atheneum Yung Read.

— Miami Gets It Straight. LC 99-36116. (Road to Reading Ser.). 80p. 2000. 10.99 (*0-307-46501-2*) Gldn Bks Pub Co.

— Nettie Jo's Friends. LC 87-14080. (J). 1994. 13.19 (*0-606-06612-8*, Pub. by Turtleback) Demco.

McKissack, Pat. Run Away Home. LC 96-43673. 128p. (J). (gr. 3-7). 1997. 14.95 (*0-590-46751-4*) Scholastic Inc.

***McKissack, Pat & McKissack, Fredrick.** Ida B. Wells-Barnett: A Voice Against Violence. rev. ed. LC 00-9422. (Great African Americans Ser.). (Illus.). (J). 2001. write for info. (*0-7660-1677-3*) Enslow Pubs.

— Jesse Owens: Olympic Star. rev. ed. LC 00-9424. (Great African Americans Ser.). (Illus.). (J). 2001. write for info. (*0-7660-1681-1*) Enslow Pubs.

McKissack, Pat & McKissack, Fredrick. Messy Bessey's Holidays. LC 98-8057. (Rookie Readers Ser.). (Illus.). 32p. (J). (gr. k-3). 1999. 17.00 (*0-516-20829-2*) Childrens.

***McKissack, Pat & McKissack, Fredrick.** Paul Robeson: A Voice to Remember. rev. ed. LC 00-8294. (Great African Americans Ser.). 2000. write for info. (*0-7660-1674-9*) Enslow Pubs.

***McKissack, Pat, et al.** Miami Gets It Straight. LC 99-36116. (Road to Reading Ser.). 80p. (J). 2000. pap. 3.99 (*0-307-26501-3*, Goldn Books) Gldn Bks Pub Co.

McKissack, Patricia. The Aztec. LC 84-23142. (New True Books Ser.). (Illus.). 48p. (J). (ps-3). 1985. lib. bdg. 21.00 (*0-516-01936-8*) Childrens.

***McKissack, Patricia.** Bugs! rev. ed. LC 99-15875. (Rookie Readers Ser.). (Illus.). 32p. (J). (gr. 1-2). 2000. 17.50 (*0-516-21658-9*) Childrens.

— Bugs! rev. ed. (Rookie Readers Ser.). (Illus.). 32p. (J). (gr. 1-2). 2000. pap. 4.95 (*0-516-27046-X*) Childrens.

McKissack, Patricia. Can You Imagine? LC 96-37892. (Meet the Author Ser.). (Illus.). 32p. (J). (gr. 2-5). 1997. 14.95 (*1-878450-61-1*, 716) R Owen Pubs.

***McKissack, Patricia.** Color Me Dark: The Diary of Nellie Lee Love, the Great Migration North, Chicago, Illinois, 1919. (Dear America Ser.). (Illus.). 208p. (J). (gr. 4-8). 2000. 10.95 (*0-590-51159-9*, Dear America) Scholastic Inc.

McKissack, Patricia. The Dark-Thirty: Southern Tales of the Supernatural. LC 92-3021. (Illus.). 128p. (J). (gr. 3-7). 1996. lib. bdg. 17.99 (*0-679-91863-9*, Pub. by Knopf Bks Yng Read) Random.

— The Dark-Thirty: Southern Tales of the Supernatural. (Illus.). (J). 1996. pap. 12.00 (*0-679-88335-5*) Random.

— The Dark-Thirty: Southern Tales of the Supernatural. (Illus.). (J). 1998. pap. 4.99 (*0-679-89006-8*, Pub. by Random Bks Yng Read) Random.

McKissack, Patricia. The Dark-Thirty: Southern Tales of the Supernatural. (YA). 1992. 17.10 (*0-606-10779-7*, Pub. by Turtleback) Demco.

Mckissack, Patricia. History of Haiti. (J). 1996. 14.95 (*0-8050-3524-9*) H Holt & Co.

McKissack, Patricia. The Inca. LC 85-6712. (New True Books Ser.). (Illus.). 48p. (J). (ps-3). 1985. lib. bdg. 20.00 (*0-516-01268-1*) Childrens.

— The Inca Indians. LC 85-6712. (New True Books Ser.). (Illus.). 45p. (J). (ps-3). 1985. pap. 5.50 (*0-516-41268-X*) Childrens.

— A Long Hard Journey: The Story of the Pullman Porter. (Illus.). 158p. (YA). 1995. pap. 9.95 (*0-8027-7437-7*) Walker & Co.

— The Maya. LC 85-9927. (New True Books Ser.). (Illus.). 45p. (J). (gr. 2-3). 1985. pap. 5.50 (*0-516-41270-1*); lib. bdg. 21.00 (*0-516-01270-3*) Childrens.

— Messy Bessey. rev. ed. LC 99-22472. (Rookie Readers Ser.). 32p. (J). (gr. 1-2). 1999. 17.50 (*0-516-21650-3*) Childrens.

***McKissack, Patricia.** Messy Bessey. rev. ed. LC 99-22472. (Rookie Readers Ser.). (Illus.). 32p. (J). (gr. 1-2). 2000. pap. text 4.95 (*0-516-27003-6*) Childrens.

— Messy Bessey's Family Reunion. (Rookie Readers Ser.). (Illus.). 32p. (J). (gr. 1-2). 2000. pap. 4.95 (*0-516-26552-0*) Childrens

McKissack, Patricia. Monkey-Monkey's Trick. LC 88-3072. (Step into Reading Ser.: A Step 2 Book). (Illus.). 48p. (J). (ps-3). 1988. pap. 3.99 (*0-394-89173-2*, Pub. by Random Bks Yng Read) Random.

McKissack, Patricia. Monkey-Monkey's Trick. (Step into Reading Ser.: A Step 2 Book). (J). (gr. 1-3). 1988. 9.19 (*0-606-12428-4*, Pub. by Turtleback) Demco.

— Nzingha: Warrior Queen of Matamba, Angola, Africa, 1595. LC 00-24216. (Royal Diaries Ser.). (Illus.). 208p. (YA). (gr. 4-7). 2000. write for info. (*0-439-11210-9*) Scholastic Inc.

McKissack, Patricia. A Picture of Freedom: The Diary of Clotee, a Slave Girl, Belmont Plantation, Virginia, 1859. (Dear America Ser.). 132p. (YA). (gr. 4-9). 1997. 9.95 (*0-614-25386-1*) Scholastic Inc.

— To Establish Justice. 1900. 19.00 (*0-679-89308-3*); lib. bdg. 20.99 (*0-679-99308-8*) Knopf.

— Who Is Coming? LC 86-11805. (Rookie Readers Ser.). (Illus.). 32p. (J). (gr. k-3). 1990. pap. 4.95 (*0-516-42073-9*); lib. bdg. 17.00 (*0-516-02073-0*) Childrens.

— Who Is Who? LC 83-7361. (Rookie Readers Ser.). (Illus.). 32p. (J). (gr. k-2). 1983. pap. 4.95 (*0-516-42042-9*) Childrens.

McKissack, Patricia & Duyff, Roberta. All Our Fruits & Vegetables. unabridged ed. Hamilton, Janice, ed. LC 96-75185. (Foods I Eat, the Foods We Eat Ser.). (Illus.). 32p. (Orig.). (J). (ps). 1995. pap. write for info. (*1-888566-03-5*) Many Hands Media.

— The Foods We Eat. unabridged ed. Hamilton, Janice, ed. (Foods I Eat, the Foods We Eat Ser.). (Illus.). 16p. (Orig.). (J). (ps). 1995. pap. write for info. (*1-888566-01-9*) Many Hands Media.

— It's a Sandwich! unabridged ed. Hamilton, Janice, ed. LC 96-75184. (Foods I Eat, the Foods We Eat Ser.). (Illus.). 32p. (Orig.). (J). (ps). 1995. pap. write for info. (*1-888566-02-7*) Many Hands Media.

McKissack, Patricia & McKissack, Frederick. All Paths Lead to Bethlehem. LC 87-70472. (Illus.). 32p. (Orig.). (J). (ps-3). 1987. pap. 6.99 (*0-8066-2265-2*, 10-0220, Augsburg) Augsburg Fortress.

— A Long Hard Journey: The Story of the Pullman Porter. 144p. (J). (gr. 7-9). 1990. 17.95 (*0-8027-6884-9*); lib. bdg. 18.85 (*0-8027-6885-7*) Walker & Co.

— Messey Bessey & the Birthday Overnight. LC 98-9223. (Rookie Readers Ser.). (Illus.). (J). 1998. 17.00 (*0-516-20828-4*) Childrens.

— Red-Tail Angels: The Story of the Tuskegee Airmen of World War II. (Illus.). 144p. (YA). (gr. 5 up). 1995. 19.95 (*0-8027-8292-2*); lib. bdg. 20.85 (*0-8027-8293-0*) Walker & Co.

— Sojourner Truth: Ain't I a Woman? (Scholastic Biography Ser.). 1992. 9.09 (*0-606-06011-1*, Pub. by Turtleback) Demco.

McKissack, Patricia & McKissack, Fredrick. African-American Inventors. LC 93-42625. (Proud Heritage Ser.). (Illus.). 96p. (J). (gr. 4-6). 1994. lib. bdg. 25.90 (*1-56294-468-1*) Millbrook Pr.

— African-American Scientists. LC 93-11226. (Proud Heritage Ser.). (Illus.). 96p. (J). (gr. 4-6). 1994. lib. bdg. 25.90 (*1-56294-372-3*) Millbrook Pr.

— Big Bug Book of Counting. LC 87-61655. (Big Bug Bks.). (Illus.). 24p. (Orig.). (J). (gr. k-1). 1987. pap. text 4.95 (*0-88335-772-0*) Milliken Pub Co.

McKissack, Patricia & McKissack, Fredrick. Big Bug Book of Opposites. LC 87-61654. (Big Bug Bks.). (Illus.). 24p. (J). (gr. k-1). 1987. pap. text 4.95 (*0-88335-773-9*) Milliken Pub Co.

McKissack, Patricia & McKissack, Fredrick. Big Bug Book of Places to Go. LC 87 61652. (Big Bug Bks.). (Illus.). 24p. (Orig.). (J). (gr. k-1). 1987. pap. text 4.95 (*0-88335-775-5*) Milliken Pub Co.

— Big Bug Book of the Alphabet. LC 87-61653. (Big Bug Bks.). (Illus.). 24p. (Orig.). (J). (gr. k-1). 1987. pap. text 4.95 (*0-88335-774-7*) Milliken Pub Co.

— Big Bug Book of Things to Do. LC 87-61651. (Big Bug Bks.). (Illus.). 24p. (Orig.). (J). (gr. k-1). 1987. pap. text 4.95 (*0-88335-776-3*) Milliken Pub Co.

— Booker T. Washington: Leader & Educator. LC 92-5356. (Great African Americans Ser.). (Illus.). 32p. (J). (gr. 1-4). 1992. lib. bdg. 14.95 (*0-89490-314-4*) Enslow Pubs.

— Bugs! LC 88-22875. (Rookie Readers Ser.). (Illus.). 32p. (J). (ps-2). 1988. pap. 4.95 (*0-516-42088-7*); lib. bdg. 17.00 (*0-516-02088-9*) Childrens.

— Carter G. Woodson: The Father of Black History. LC 91-8813. (Great African Americans Ser.). (Illus.). 32p. (J). (gr. 1-4). 1991. lib. bdg. 14.95 (*0-89490-309-8*) Enslow Pubs.

— Frederick Douglass: Leader Against Slavery. LC 91-3084. (Great African Americans Ser.). (Illus.). 32p. (J). (gr. 1-4). 1991. lib. bdg. 14.95 (*0-89490-306-3*) Enslow Pubs.

— George Washington Carver: The Peanut Scientist. LC 91-8814. (Great African Americans Ser.). (Illus.). 32p. (J) (gr 1-4) 1991 lib. bdg. 14.95 (*0-89490-308-X*) Enslow Pubs.

— Great African Americans Series, 18 bks., Set. (Illus.). (J). (gr. 1-4). 1991. lib. bdg. 234.10 (*0-89490-376-4*) Enslow Pubs.

— Ida B. Wells-Barnett: A Voice Against Violence. LC 90-49848. (Great African Americans Ser.). (Illus.). 32p. (J). (gr. 1-4). 1991. lib. bdg. 14.95 (*0-89490-301-2*) Enslow Pubs.

— Insectos! Bugs! LC 88-22875. (Rookie Readers Ser.). (SPA., Illus.). 32p. (J). (ps-2). 1992. pap. 3.50 (*0-516-52088-1*) Childrens.

— Jesse Owens: Olympic Star. LC 92-3584. (Great African Americans Ser.). (Illus.). 32p. (J). (gr. 1-4). 1992. lib. bdg. 14.95 (*0-89490-312-8*) Enslow Pubs.

— Langston Hughes: Great American Poet. LC 92-2583. (Great African Americans Ser.). (Illus.). 32p. (J). (gr. 1-4). 1992. lib. bdg. 14.95 (*0-89490-315-2*) Enslow Pubs.

— Louis Armstrong: Jazz Musician. LC 91-12420. (Great African Americans Ser.). (Illus.). 32p. (J). (gr. 1-4). 1991. lib. bdg. 14.95 (*0-89490-307-1*) Enslow Pubs.

— Madam C. J. Walker: Self-Made Millionaire. LC 92-6189. (Great African Americans Ser.). (Illus.). 32p. (J). (gr. 1-4). 1992. lib. bdg. 14.95 (*0-89490-311-X*) Enslow Pubs.

— Marian Anderson: A Great Singer. LC 90-19163. (Great African Americans Ser.). (Illus.). 32p. (J). (gr. 1-4). 1991. lib. bdg. 14.95 (*0-89490-303-9*) Enslow Pubs.

— Martin Luther King, Jr. Man of Peace. LC 90-19156. (Great African Americans Ser.). (Illus.). 32p. (J). (gr. 1-4). 1991. lib. bdg. 14.95 (*0-89490-302-0*) Enslow Pubs.

— Mary Church Terrell: Leader for Equality. LC 91-3083. (Great African Americans Ser.). (Illus.). 32p. (J). (gr. 1-4). 1991. lib. bdg. 14.95 (*0-89490-305-5*) Enslow Pubs.

— Mary McLeod Bethune: A Great Teacher. LC 91-8818. (Great African Americans Ser.). (Illus.). 32p. (J). (gr. 1-4). 1991. lib. bdg. 14.95 (*0-89490-304-7*) Enslow Pubs.

— Messy Bessey. LC 87-15079. (Rookie Readers Ser.). (Illus.). (J). (ps-2). 1987. pap. 4.95 (*0-516-42083-6*) Childrens.

— Messy Bessey's Garden. LC 91-15333. (Rookie Readers Ser.). (Illus.). 32p. (J). (ps-3). 1991. pap. 4.95 (*0-516-42008-9*); lib. bdg. 17.00 (*0-516-02008-0*) Childrens.

— Messy Bessey's School Desk. LC 97-13837. (Rookie Readers Ser.). (Illus.). 32p. (J). (gr. k-2). 1998. 17.00 (*0-516-20827-6*) Childrens.

— Paul Robeson: A Voice to Remember. LC 92-2582. (Great African Americans Ser.). (Illus.). 32p. (J). (gr. 1-4). 1992. lib. bdg. 14.95 (*0-89490-310-1*) Enslow Pubs.

— Ralph J. Bunche: Peacemaker. LC 98-49849. (Great African Americans Ser.). (Illus.). 32p. (J). (gr. 1-4). 1991. lib. bdg. 14.95 (*0-89490-300-4*) Enslow Pubs.

— The Royal Kingdoms of Ghana, Mali & Songhay: Life in Medieval Africa. (Illus.). (J). (gr. 5-9). 1995. pap. 7.95 (*0-8050-4259-8*) H Holt & Co.

— Satchel Paige: The Best Arm in Baseball. LC 92-3583. (Great African Americans Ser.). (Illus.). 32p. (J). (gr. 1-4). 1992. lib. bdg. 14.95 (*0-89490-317-9*) Enslow Pubs.

— Sojourner Truth: A Voice for Freedom. LC 92-6190. (Great African Americans Ser.). (Illus.). 32p. (J). (gr. 1-4). 1992. lib. bdg. 14.95 (*0-89490-313-6*) Enslow Pubs.

— Sojourner Truth: Ain't I a Woman? 192p. (J). (gr. 4-6). 1992. 13.95 (*0-590-44690-8*, Scholastic Hardcover) Scholastic Inc.

— Los Tres Chivitos. LC 86-33450. (Start-Off Stories Ser.). (SPA., Illus.). 32p. (J). (ps-2). 1988. lib. bdg. 14.70 (*0-516-32366-0*) Childrens.

— Zora Neale Hurston: Writer & Storyteller. LC 92-2588. (Great African Americans Ser.). (Illus.). 32p. (J). (gr. 1-4). 1992. lib. bdg. 14.95 (*0-89490-316-0*) Enslow Pubs.

***McKissack, Patricia, et al.** Messy Bessey's Family Reunion. LC 99-16312. (Rookie Readers Ser.). (J). 2000. 17.50 (*0-516-20830-6*) Childrens.

McKissack, Patricia, jt. auth. see McKissack, Frederick.

McKissack, Patricia, ed. see Duyff, Roberta L.

McKissack, Patricia C. Black Diamond: The Story of the Negro Baseball Leagues. (J). 1998. pap. 5.99 (*0-590-68213-X*) Scholastic Inc.

— Black Diamond: The Story of the Negro Baseball Leagues. (J). 1994. 9.09 (*0-606-08493-2*, Pub. by Turtleback) Demco.

— Flossie & the Fox. LC 86-2024. (Illus.). 32p. (J). (ps-3). 1986. 15.99 (*0-8037-0250-7*, Dial Yng Read) Peng Put Young Read.

— Ma Dear's Aprons. LC 94-48450. (Illus.). 1997. lib. bdg. 16.99 (*0-679-95099-0*, Apple Soup Bks) Knopf Bks Yng Read.

— Ma Dear's Aprons. LC 94-48450. (Illus.). 32p. (J). (ps-2). 1997. 16.00 (*0-689-81051-2*) S&S Childrens.

***McKissack, Patricia C.** Ma Dear's Aprons. (Illus.). (J). 2000. 11.44 (*0-606-17928-3*) Turtleback.

McKissack, Patricia C. Ma Dear's Aprons. (Illus.). 32p. (J). (gr. k-3). 2000. reprint ed. per. 5.99 (*0-689-83262-1*) Aladdin.

— Messy Bessy's Holidays. (Rookie Readers Ser.). 1999. lib. bdg. 4.95 (*0-516-26476-1*) Childrens.

— A Million Fish . . . More or Less. (Illus.). 40p. (J). (gr. k-4). 1996. pap. 6.99 (*0-679-88086-0*) Random.

— A Million Fish . . . More or Less. 1996. 12.19 (*0-606-09616-7*, Pub. by Turtleback) Demco.

— Mirandy & Brother Wind. LC 87 349. (Illus.). 32p. (J). (ps-3). 1988. 17.00 (*0-394-88765-4*, Pub. by Knopf Bks Yng Read) Random.

— Mirandy & Brother Wind. LC 87-349. (Dragon Tales Ser.). (Illus.). (J). (ps-3). 1997. pap. 6.99 (*0-679-88333-9*, Pub. by Random Bks Yng Read) Random.

— Mirandy & Brother Wind. (J). 1996. 12.19 (*0-606-10877-7*, Pub. by Turtleback) Demco.

— Nettie Jo's Friends. (Dragonfly Bks.). (Illus.). 40p. (J). (ps-3). 1994. pap. 7.99 (*0-679-86573-X*, Pub. by Knopf Bks Yng Read) Random.

M

An Asterisk (*) at the beginning of an entry indicates that the title is appearing for the first time.

McKissack, Patricia C. A Picture of Freedom: The Diary of Clotee, a Slave Girl, Belmont Plantation, Virginia, 1859. LC 96-25673. (Dear America Ser.). (Illus.). 195p. (YA). (gr. 4-7). 1997. 9.95 (0-590-25988-1) Scholastic Inc.

McKissack, Patricia C. Rebels Against Slavery: American Slave Revolts. (J). (gr. 3-9). 1998. pap. text 4.50 (0-590-45736-5) Scholastic Inc.

— Rebels Against Slavery: American Slave Revolts. 176p. (YA). (gr. 5-9). 1999. pap. text 5.99 (0-590-66259-7) Scholastic Inc.

— Rebels Against Slavery: American Slave Revolts. 1998. 9.60 (0-606-13731-9, Pub. by Turtleback) Demco.

McKissack, Patricia C. & Duyff, Roberta L. So, Who's Dr. Rabbit? (Illus.). 32p. (J). (gr. 2-4). 1994. pap. text. write for info. (0-9642684-0-X) JMH Communs.

McKissack, Patricia C. & McKissack, Frederick. Messy Bessey & the Birthday Overnight. (Rookie Readers Ser.). (Illus.). 32p. (YA). (gr. k-3). 1999. pap. text 4.95 (0-516-26411-7) Childrens.

McKissack, Patricia C. & McKissack, Frederick L. Christmas in the Big House, Christmas in the Quarters. LC 92-33831. (Illus.). 80p. (J). (gr. 3-8). 1994. 17.95 (0-590-43027-0) Scholastic Inc.

— Rebels Against Slavery: American Slave Revolts. LC 94-41089. 176p. (J). (gr. 3-9). 1996. 14.95 (0-590-45735-7, Scholastic Hardcover) Scholastic Inc.

McKissack, Patricia C. & McKissack, Fredrick, Jr. Black Diamond: The Story of the Negro Baseball Leagues. LC 93-22691. (Illus.). 192p. (J). (gr. 4-6). 1994. 14.95 (0-590-45809-4) Scholastic Inc.

McKissack, Patricia C. & McKissack, Fredrick. Black Diamond: The Story of the Negro Baseball Leagues. 192p. (J). (gr. 4-7). 1996. pap. text 3.99 (0-590-45810-8) Scholastic Inc.

— Let My People Go: Bible Stories Told by a Freeman of Color. LC 97-19983. (Illus.). 144p. (YA). (gr. 3 up). 1998. 20.00 (0-689-80856-9) S&S Bks Yung.

— Messy Bessey's Closet. LC 89-34667. (Rookie Readers Ser.). (Illus.). 32p. (J). (ps-3). 1989. lib. bdg. 17.00 (0-516-02091-9) Childrens.

— Sojourner Truth: Ain't I a Woman? LC 91-45988. 192p. (YA). (gr. 4-7). 1994. pap. 3.50 (0-590-44691-6) Scholastic Inc.

McKissack, Patricia C. & McKissack, Fredrick, Jr. W. E. B. Du Bois. LC 90-37823. (Impact Biographies Ser.). (Illus.). 112p. (YA). (gr. 7-12). 1990. lib. bdg. 23.60 (0-531-10939-9) Watts.

McKissack, Patricia C. & McKissack, Fredrick L. Black Hands, White Sails: The Story of African-American Whalers. LC 99-11439. (Illus.). 152p. (J). (gr. 3-8). 1999. 15.95 (0-590-48313-7, Pub. by Scholastic Inc) Penguin Putnam.

— Young, Black & Determined: A Biography of Lorraine Hansberry. LC 97-2084. (Illus.). 156p. (YA). (gr. 5 up). 1998. pap. 18.95 (0-8234-1300-4) Holiday.

McKissic, MaryAnn. Get Out of Your Head...& into Your Life: A Weight Issues Primer. LC 95-67272. 192p. (Orig.). 1996. pap. 8.99 (0-933451-33-4) Prescott Pr.

McKissic, Rodney J. How to Play the Sports Recruiting Game & Get an Athletic Scholarship: The Handbook & Guide to Success for the African-American High School Student/Athlete. LC 97-40000. (Illus.). 158p. (YA). (gr. 10). 1998. pap. 12.95 (0-9655064-1-X) Amber Books.

McKissic, William D. & Evans, Anthony T. Beyond Roots: If Anybody Asks You Who I Am. 150p. (Orig.). 1994. pap. 7.99 (0-9625605-5-3) Renais Prodns.

McKissick Museum Staff. Baruch Collection. LC 70-120919. (C). 1993. pap. 15.95 (0-87249-959-6) U of SC Pr.

— The First Egyptians. LC 70-120919. 1993. pap. 19.95 (0-87249-952-9) U of SC Pr.

— Row upon Row: Sea Grass Baskets of the South Carolina Lowcountry. LC 70-120919. 68p. 1993. pap. 19.95 (0-87249-956-1) U of SC Pr.

McKissock, P. Color Atlas of Mammaplasty. Goin, J. M., ed. (Operative Techniques in Plastic Surgery Ser.). (Illus.). 144p. 1991. text 99.00 (0-86577-385-8) Thieme Med Pubs.

McKisson, Micki & MacRae-Campbell, Linda. Our Divided World: Poverty, Hunger, & Overpopulation. (Our Only Earth Ser.). 104p. (J). (gr. 4-12). 1990. pap. 25.00 (0-913705-52-7) Zephyr Pr AZ.

McKisson, Micki, jt. auth. see Macrae-Campbell, Linda.

McKisson, Micki, jt. auth. see MacRae-Campbell, Linda.

McKitrick, Eric L. Andrew Johnson & Reconstruction. 544p. (C). 1988. pap. text 25.95 (0-19-505707-4) OUP.

McKitrick, Eric L., jt. auth. see Elkins, Stanley M.

McKitrick, M. D. A Genealogical Record of One Branch of the Donaldson Family in America: Descendants of Moses Donaldson, Huntington, Co., Penn., 1770. (Illus.). 332p. 1993. reprint ed. pap. 54.00 (0-8328-3030-5); reprint ed. lib. bdg. 64.00 (0-8328-3029-1) Higginson Bk Co.

McKitrick, Reuben. Public Land System of Texas, 1823-1910. Bruchey, Stuart, ed. LC 78-56659. (Management of Public Lands in the U. S. Ser.). (Illus.). 1979. reprint ed. lib. bdg. 17.95 (0-405-11342-0) Ayer.

McKitterick, David. A History of Cambridge University Press Vol. 2: Scholarship & Commerce, 1698-1872. (Illus.). 544p. (C). 1998. text 125.00 (0-521-30802-X) Cambridge U Pr.

— A History of Cambridge University Press, Vol. 1: Printing & the Book Trade in Cambridge, 1534-1698. (Illus.). 524p. (C). 1992. text 125.00 (0-521-30801-1) Cambridge U Pr.

McKitterick, David, ed. The Making of the Wren Library, Trinity College, Cambridge: From the Seventeenth to the Nineteenth Century. (Illus.). 171p. (C). 1995. text 90.00 (0-521-44305-9) Cambridge U Pr.

McKitterick, David J., ed. Stanley Morison & D. B. Updike: Selected Correspondence. LC 79-87761. (Illus.). 1979. 25.00 (0-89679-001-0) Moretus Pr.

McKitterick, Rosamond. Books, Scribes & Learning in the Frankish Kingdoms, 6th-9th Centuries. LC 94-7578. (Collected Studies: No. CS 452). (Illus.). 352p. 1994. 109.95 (0-86078-406-1, Pub. by Variorum) Ashgate Pub Co.

— The Carolingians & the Written Word. (Illus.). 308p. (C). 1989. pap. text 24.95 (0-521-31565-4) Cambridge U Pr.

— Frankish Kingdom 751-987. LC 82-8944. (Illus.). 432p. (C). 1989. pap. 31.20 (0-582-49005-7, 73441) Longman.

McKitterick, Rosamond, ed. Carolingian Culture: Emulation & Innovation. LC 92-36984. (Illus.). 352p. (C). 1993. text 74.95 (0-521-40524-6); pap. text 27.95 (0-521-40586-6) Cambridge U Pr.

— The New Cambridge Medieval History Vol. 2: C. 700-c. 900. (Illus.). 1114p. (C). 1995. text 120.00 (0-521-36292-X) Cambridge U Pr.

— The Uses of Literacy in Early Medieval Europe. (Illus.). 361p. (C). 1992. pap. text 27.95 (0-521-42896-3) Cambridge U Pr.

McKitterick, Rosamond & Beadle, Richard, compiled by. Catalogue of the Pepys Library at Magdalene College, Cambridge: V.i. Medieval Manuscripts. 136p. (C). 1993. 170.00 (0-85991-341-4) Boydell & Brewer.

McKitterick, Rosamond & Quinault, Roland, eds. Edward Gibbon & Empire. 367p. (C). 1996. text 69.95 (0-521-49724-8) Cambridge U Pr.

McKitterick, Rosamund. Frankish Kings & Culture in the Early Middle Ages. (Collected Studies: Vol. CS477). 350p. 1995. 106.95 (0-86078-458-4, Pub. by Variorum) Ashgate Pub Co.

McKitterick, Thomas E. & Younger, Kenneth G., eds. Fabian International Essays. LC 75-80408. (Essay Index Reprint Ser.). 1977. 18.95 (0-8369-1057-5) Ayer.

McKittrick, David. Despatches from Belfast. rev. ed. LC 89-81776. 232p. 1990. pap. 18.95 (0-85640-427-6, Pub. by Blackstaff Pr) Dufour.

— Endgame: The Search for Peace in Northern Ireland. LC 94-234619. (Illus.). 351p. 1995. pap. 25.00 (0-85640-530-2, Pub. by Blackstaff Pr) Dufour.

— The Nervous Peace. 174p. 1996. pap. 22.95 (0-85640-575-2, Pub. by Blackstaff Pr) Dufour.

***McKittrick, David.** Through the Minefield. LC 99-488018. (Illus.). 214p. 1999. pap. 24.95 (0-85640-652-X, Pub. by Blackstaff Pr) Dufour.

McKittrick, Harold V., jt. ed. see Del Re, Robert.

McKittrick, J., et al, eds. Luminescent Materials Vol. 560: Materials Research Society Symposium Proceedings. LC 99-42465. 368p. 1999. text 73.00 (1-55899-467-X) Materials Res.

McKittrick, Michael, jt. auth. see McKittrick, Rosemary.

McKittrick, Rosemary & McKittrick, Michael. The Official Price Guide to Fine Art. 2nd ed. 896p. 1993. pap. 20.00 (0-87637-909-9) Hse Collectbls.

McKittrick, Sandra M., jt. auth. see Ayllon, Teodoro.

McKiven, Henry M., Jr. Iron & Steel: Class, Race, & Community in Birmingham, Alabama, 1875-1920. LC 94-27198. (Illus.). 290p. 1995. pap. text 18.95 (0-8078-4524-8); lib. bdg. 49.95 (0-8078-2188-8) U of NC Pr.

***McKivigan, John R.** Abolitionism & American Law. LC 99-52332. (American Abolitionist Movement Ser.). 1999. write for info. (0-8153-3109-6) Garland.

— Abolitionism & American Politics & Government. LC 99-52156. (American Abolitionist Movement Ser.). 1999. write for info. (0-8153-3107-X) Garland.

— Abolitionism & American Reform. LC 99-50015. (American Abolitionist Movement Ser.). 1999. write for info. (0-8153-3105-3) Garland.

— Abolitionism & American Religion. LC 99-52003. (American Abolitionist Movement Ser.). 1999. write for info. (0-8153-3106-1) Garland.

— Abolitionism & Issues of Race & Gender. LC 99-52641. (American Abolitionist Movement Ser.). 1999. write for info. (0-8153-3108-8) Garland.

— American Abolitionist Movement: A Collection of Scholarly Articles Illustrating Its History, 5 vols. 1999. 400.00 (0-8153-3625-X) Garland.

McKivigan, John R. The War Against Proslavery Religion: Abolitionism & the Northern Churches, 1830-1865. LC 83-45933. 328p. 1984. text 42.50 (0-8014-1589-6) Cornell U Pr.

McKivigan, John R. & Harrold, Stanley, eds. Antislavery Violence: Sectional, Racial & Cultural Conflict in Antebellum America. LC 99-6121. 336p. 1999. text 30.00 (1-57233-059-7, Pub. by U of Tenn Pr) U Ch Pr.

McKivigan, John R. & Snay, Mitchell, eds. Religion & the Antebellum Debate over Slavery. LC 98-21073. viii, 391p. 1998. pap. text 25.00 (0-8203-2076-5) U of Ga Pr.

— Religion & the Antebellum Debate over Slavery. LC 98-21073. 384p. 1998. 55.00 (0-8203-1972-4) U of Ga Pr.

McKivigan, John R., ed. see Douglass, Frederick.

McKivigan, John R., jt. ed. see Miller, Randall M.

McKivigan, John R., ed. see Redpath, James.

McKlown, Patrick & Brown, Robert D. Business Analysis with Spreadsheets Using VP Planner Plus. 464p. (Orig.). (C). 1988. pap. text 34.95 (0-8162-5543-1) Holden-Day.

McKnew, Donald, Jr., jt. auth. see Cytryn, Leon.

McKnew, Donald H., Jr., jt. auth. see Cytryn, Leon.

McKnew, Ed & Parker, Mark. Power Boat Guide: 1999 Edition. (Illus.). 1700p. 1999. pap. 79.95 (0-9622134-0-3) Amer Marine Pub.

McKnew, Ed, jt. auth. see Parker, Mark.

***McKnight.** Last Crusade. 2000. pap. 17.00 (0-8133-3385-7, Pub. by Westview) HarpC.

— Tacticas Amorosas. (SPA.). 1997. pap. text 9.98 (968-38-0398-9) Panorama Edit.

***McKnight, Susan & Thornton, Suzi.** The Mardi Gras Swamp Parade. (Illus.). 38p. (J). (gr. k-6). 2000. pap. 14.00 (1-882913-12-4) Thornton LA.

McKnight, Annie. Superstitions. 368p. 1998. mass mkt. 5.50 (0-8439-4405-6, Leisure Bks) Dorchester Pub Co.

***McKnight, Annie.** The Tombstone Rose. 368p. 2000. pap. 5.50 (0-8439-4681-4, Leisure Bks) Dorchester Pub Co.

McKnight, Bill N., ed. Biological Pollution: The Control & Impact of Invasive Exotic Species: Proceedings of a Symposium Held at the University Place Conference Center, Indiana University-Purdue University at Indianapolis on October 25 & 26, 1991. LC 93-3889. (Illus.). 270p. 1993. 30.00 (1-883362-00-8) IN Acad Sci.

McKnight, Bob. Eliminate the Losers. 1976. reprint ed. pap. 5.00 (0-87980-319-3) Wilshire.

McKnight, Brian E. Law & Order in Sung China. (Studies in Chinese History, Literature & Institutions). (Illus.). 573p. (C). 1992. text 95.00 (0-521-41121-1) Cambridge U Pr.

— Village & Bureaucracy in Southern Sung China. LC 72-159834. xii, 232p. 1983. pap. text 8.95 (0-226-56060-0) U Ch Pr.

McKnight, Brian E. & Liu, James T., trs. from CHI. The Enlightened Judgments: Ch' ing-ming Chi: The Sung Dynasty Collection. LC 99-17960. (SUNY Series in Chinese Philosophy & Culture). 640p. (C). 1999. pap. text 24.95 (0-7914-4244-6) State U NY Pr.

— The Enlightened Judgments: Ch'ing-ming Chi - The Sung Dynasty Collection. LC 99-17960. (SUNY Series in Chinese Philosophy & Culture). 640p. (C). 1999. text 73.50 (0-7914-4243-8) State U NY Pr.

McKnight, Brian E., tr. see Sung Tz'u.

McKnight, C., et al. Hypertext: A Psychological Perspective. 200p. 1993. 42.50 (0-13-441650-3) P-H.

— Hypertext in Context. (Series on Electronic Publishing: No. 4). (Illus.). 176p. (C). 1991. text 42.95 (0-521-37488-X) Cambridge U Pr.

***McKnight, C., et al.** Mathematics Education Research: A Guide for the Research Mathematician. 106p. 2000. 20.00 (0-8218-2016-8) Am Math.

McKnight, Catherine, ed. see Tillich, Paul Johannes.

McKnight, Clint. River Journal. 45p. (Orig.). 1995. pap. 3.95 (0-9651504-0-2, 11719) Dinosaur Nature.

McKnight, Clint, ed. see Hansen, Wallace.

McKnight, Darren S., jt. auth. see Dueber, Ross E.

McKnight, Darren S., jt. auth. see Johnson, Nicholas L.

McKnight, David. Australia's Spies & Their Secrets. 400p. 1994. pap. 24.95 (1-86373-661-1, Pub. by Allen & Unwin Pty) Paul & Co Pubs.

— People, Countries & the Rainbow Serpent: Systems of Classification among the Lardil of Mornington Island. LC 98-18344. (Oxford Studies in Anthropological Linguistics: No. 12). (Illus.). 280p. 1999. text 75.00 (0-19-509621-5) OUP.

McKnight, David A. Electoral System of the United States: A Critical & Historical Exposition of Its Fundamental Principles in the Constitution & the Acts & Proceedings of Congress Enforcing It. 433p. 1993. reprint ed. 52.00 (0-8377-2446-5, Rothman) W S Hein.

***McKnight, Deborah.** Indians, Indian Tribes, & State Government. 2nd ed. (Illus.). 91p. (C). 1999. pap. text 20.00 (0-7881-8549-7) DIANE Pub.

McKnight, Diane M., jt. ed. see Averett, Robert C.

McKnight, Donna, ed. see Brown, Walter L. & Jackson, Phyllis S.

McKnight, E. P. Words 'n' Action. Gaveglio, Lydia, ed. Lomax, Nancy, tr. (Illus.). 76p. (Orig.). 1997. pap. 10.00 (0-9654807-0-4) E P McKnight.

McKnight, Edgar. Jesus Christ in History & Scripture: A Poetic & Sectarian Perspective. LC 99-35521. 340p. 1999. 40.00 (0-86554-653-3) Mercer Univ Pr.

***McKnight, Edgar.** Jesus Christ in History & Scripture: A Poetic & Sectarian Perspective. LC 99-35521. 340p. 1999. pap. 20.00 (0-86554-677-0) Mercer Univ Pr.

Mcknight, Edgar V. Meaning in Texts: The Historical Shaping of a Narrative. LC 77-15238. 344p. reprint ed. pap. 106.70 (0-608-16333-3, 202688500053) Bks Demand.

McKnight, Edgar V., ed. Perspectives on Contemporary New Testament Questions: Essays in Honor of T. C. Smith. LC 92-41327. 136p. 1992. text 69.95 (0-7734-2852-6) E Mellen.

McKnight, Edgar V. & Malbon, Elizabeth S. New Literary Criticism & the New Testament. LC 94-41734. 400p. 1994. pap. 20.00 (1-56338-107-9) TPI PA.

McKnight, Edgar V. & Via, Dan O., Jr. What Is Form Criticism? 96p. (Orig.). 1997. pap. 10.00 (1-57910-055-4) Wipf & Stock.

McKnight, Edgar V., jt. ed. see Malbon, Elizabeth S.

McKnight, Floyd, tr. see Steiner, Rudolf.

McKnight, G. H., jt. ed. see Lumby, Joseph R.

McKnight, George, ed. Agent of Challenge & Defiance: The Films of Ken Loach. LC 97-5840. 240p. 1997. pap. 25.95 (0-275-96036-6, Praeger Pubs) Greenwood.

— Agent of Challenge & Defiance: The Films of Ken Loach, 64. LC 97-5840. (Contributions to the Study of Popular Culture: Vol. 64). 240p. 1997. 62.95 (0-313-30507-2, Greenwood Pr) Greenwood.

McKnight, George H. English Words & Their Background. LC 69-20052. 459p. (C). 1968. reprint ed. 75.00 (0-87752-071-2) Gordian.

— Middle English Humorous Tales in Verse. LC 78-128190. 211p. (C). 1971. reprint ed. 50.00 (0-87752-131-X) Gordian.

McKnight, George H., ed. Middle English Humorous Tales in Verse. LC 77-144435. (Belles Lettres Ser. Section II: No. 1). reprint ed. 31.50 (0-404-53611-5) AMS Pr.

McKnight, George M. St. Nicholas: His Legend & His Role in the Christmas Celebration & Other Popular Customs. 3rd unabridged ed. (Illus.). 210p. 1996. reprint ed. pap. 15.95 (0-87928-114-6) Corner Hse.

McKnight, Gerald. Woody Allen: Joking Aside LC 84-673319. (Star Book Ser.). 205p. 1983. write for info. (0-352-31281-5) BLA4.

McKnight, Harry F. Silva Mind Control Through Psychorientology. 5.95 (0-913343-40-4) Inst Psych Inc.

McKnight, Hugh. Cruising French Waterways. 3rd ed. LC 99-22891. (Cruising Guides Ser.). (Illus.). 304p. 2000. pap. text 35.00 (1-57409-087-9) Sheridan.

McKnight, Ivy. Holiday Hostess. large type ed. (Linford Romance Library). 304p. 1988. pap. 16.99 (0-7089-6473-7) Ulverscroft.

McKnight, Jean S. Law for the Layperson: An Annotated Bibliography of Self-Help Law Books. 2nd ed. LC 96-39509. xvii, 228p. 1997. pap. 47.50 (0-8377-0869-9, Rothman) W S Hein.

— The Lexis Companion: A Concise Guide to Effective Searching. LC 95-22398. 304p. (C). 1995. pap. text 19.95 (0-201-48335-1) Addison-Wesley.

— North Carolina Legal Research Guide. LC 94-46352. xiv, 124p. 1994. 38.00 (0-8377-0868-0, Rothman) W S Hein.

McKnight, Jenna. Alligator Alley. (American Romance Ser.). 1993. per. 3.50 (0-373-16512-9, 1-16512-5) Harlequin Bks.

— The Bride, the Bachelor & the Baby. 1994. per. 3.50 (0-373-16539-0, 1-16539-8) Harlequin Bks.

— The Bride, the Bachelor & the Baby. (Promo Ser.). 1999. per. 4.50 (0-373-21989-X, 1-21989-8) Harlequin Bks.

— The Cowboy Hires a Wife (1-800-HUSBAND) LC 95-22335. 251p. 1995. per. 3.50 (0-373-16605-2) Harlequin Bks.

— Cowgirl in Pearls. (American Romance Ser.). 1998. per. 3.99 (0-373-16724-5, 1-16724-6) Harlequin Bks.

— Eleven Year Match. (American Romance Ser.: No. 426). 1992. per. 3.29 (0-373-16426-2, 1-16426-8) Harlequin Bks.

— Princess in Denim. (American Romance Ser.). 1998. per. 3.99 (0-373-16719-9, 1-16719-6) Harlequin Bks.

— Three Wise Men & a Baby. 1996. per. 3.75 (0-373-16660-5, 1-16660-2) Harlequin Bks.

— Two Wedding & a Feud. (American Romance Ser.). 1996. per. 3.75 (0-373-16628-1, 1-16628-9) Harlequin Bks.

— The Wedding Knight. 1998. per. 3.50 (0-373-44055-3, 1-44055-1) Harlequin Bks.

McKnight, Jim. Straight Science? Homosexuality Evolution & Adaptation. LC 97-204891. 240p. (C). 1997. 75.00 (0-415-15772-2); pap. 24.99 (0-415-15773-0) Routledge.

McKnight, John. The Careless Society: Community & Its Counterfeits. 208p. 1996. pap. 13.50 (0-465-09126-1, Pub. by Basic) HarpC.

McKnight, John L., jt. auth. see Kretzmann, John P.

***McKnight, Joseph W. & Reppy, William A., Jr.** Texas Matrimonial Property Law. 456p. (C). 1999. ring bd. 65.00 (1-879581-70-1) Lupus Pubns.

McKnight, Juilene, ed. see Fischer, William L.

McKnight, Kathryn J. The Mystic of Tunja: The Writings of Madre Castillo, 1671-1742. LC 96-40881. (Illus.). 304p. 1997. text 45.00 (1-55849-074-4) U of Mass Pr.

McKnight, Lee W. & Bailey, Joseph P., eds. Internet Economics. LC 96-39442. (Illus.). 350p. 1997. 39.95 (0-262-13336-9) MIT Pr.

— Internet Economics. (Illus.). 544p. 1998. pap. text 20.00 (0-262-63191-1) MIT Pr.

McKnight, Linton W. Birth Flowers of the Landscape: Twelve Postcards. (Illus.). 32p. 1998. pap. 6.95 (1-891401-24-6) Commercial Publ.

— Birthflowers of the Landscape: Mystical Secrets to Year-Round Color in Your Garden. LC 97-35367. (Illus.). 128p. (Orig.). Date not set. pap. 27.95 (1-891401-09-2) Commercial Publ.

— Birthflowers of the Landscape: Mystical Secrets to Year-Round Color in Your Garden. LC 97-35367. (Illus.). 128p. (Orig.). 1998. pap. 19.95 (1-891401-10-6) Commercial Publ.

***McKnight, Linton Wright.** Birthflowers of the Landscape: Book on CD. (Illus.). 1999. cd-rom 19.95 (1-891401-07-6) Commercial Publ.

McKnight, M. F. Journey to Eternity. 2nd rev. ed. 96p. (Orig.). 1996. pap. 5.95 (1-56794-125-7, C-2447) Star Bible.

McKnight, Marianne Wilson, ed. see Petersen, Brad E.

McKnight, Marilyn & Erickson, Stephen. Mediating Divorce. (Health & Psychology Ser.). 96p. 1998. pap., wbk. ed. 19.95 (0-7879-4485-8) Jossey-Bass.

— Mediating Divorce: A Step by Step Manual, Incl. client's wkbk. & chldn's bk. (Health & Psychology Ser.). 148p. 1998. ring bd., wbk. ed. 295.00 (0-7879-4304-5) Jossey-Bass.

McKnight, Marilyn S. & Erickson, Stephen K. Mediating Divorce: Children's Book. 128p. (Orig.). 1998. pap. 9.95 (1-881111-02-4) Jossey-Bass.

McKnight, Marilyn S., jt. auth. see Erickson, Stephen K.

McKnight, Natalie. Idiots, Madmen & Other Prisoners in Dickens. LC 92-36304. 160p. 1993. text 35.00 (0-312-08596-6) St Martin.

— Suffering Mothers in Mid-Victorian Novels. LC 96-34454. 160p. 1996. text 39.95 (0-312-12295-0) St Martin.

Mcknight, Nigel. Formula 1 Technology. 130p. 1998. pap. 19.95 (1-874557-87-X, Pub. by Hazelton) Motorbooks Intl.

— Indy Car Technology. 130p. 1998. pap. 19.95 (1-874557-92-6, Pub. by Hazelton) Motorbooks Intl.

McKnight-Osborne, Juilene, ed. see Fischer, William L.

McKnight-Osborne, Juilene, ed. see Hass-Unger, Joan.

McKnight, Phillip S. The Novels of Johann Karl Wezel: Satire, Realism & Social Criticism in Late 18th Century Literature. (New York University Ottendorfer Series: Neue Folge: Vol. 14). 312p. 1981. pap. 54.00 (3-261-04797-6) P Lang Pubng.

— Understanding Christoph Hein. LC 94-18721. (Understanding Modern European & Latin American Literature Ser.). 260p. 1994. text 29.95 (1-57003-015-4) U of SC Pr.

An Asterisk (*) at the beginning of an entry indicates that the title is appearing for the first time.

McKnight, Reed. Measurement Error & Banks' Reported Earnings. LC 83-1393. (Research for Business Decisions Ser.: No. 61). 128p. 1983. reprint ed. pap. 39.70 (*0-8357-1411-X*, 207040700088) Bks Demand.
McKnight, Reginald. The Kind of Light That Shines on Texas: Stories. LC 96-9063. 208p. 1997. reprint ed. pap. 12.95 (*0-87074-414-3*) SMU Press.
— Moustapha's Eclipse. 144p. 1989. reprint ed. pap. 8.95 (*0-88001-179-3*) HarpC.
— White Boys: Stories. 224p. 1999. pap. 13.00 (*0-8050-6171-1*, Pub. by H Holt & Co) VHPS.
— White Boys: Stories. LC 97-19096. 214p. 1998. text 23.00 (*0-8050-4829-4*) St Martin.
*__McKnight, Reginald, ed.__ African American Wisdom. 2nd rev. ed. 176p. 2000. 15.95 (*1-57731-129-9*, Pub. by New Wrld Lib) Publishers Group.
McKnight, Roger. Moberg's Emigrant Novels & the Journals of Andrew Peterson. Scott, Franklyn D., ed. LC 78-15196. (Scandinavians in America Ser.). 1979. lib. bdg. 23.95 (*0-405-11649-7*) Ayer.
McKnight, Rosalind. Cosmic Journeys: My Out-of-Body Explorations with Robert A. Monroe. LC 98-73918. 320p. (Orig.). 1999. pap. 13.95 (*1-57174-123-2*) Hampton Roads Pub Co.
McKnight, Rosemary. Those Who Wait: Learning How to Wait on the Lord in an Impatient World. 140p. 1990. pap. 6.99 (*0-89225-365-7*) Gospel Advocate.
McKnight, Scot. 1 Peter. (NIV Application Commentary Ser.). 352p. 1996. 22.99 (*0-310-49290-4*) Zondervan.
— Galatians. LC 94-18276. (NIV Application Commentary Ser.). 352p. 1995. 22.99 (*0-310-48470-7*) Zondervan.
— Interpreting the Synoptic Gospels. LC 88-10502. (Guides to New Testament Exegesis Ser.). 144p. 1988. pap. 10.99 (*0-8010-6235-7*) Baker Bks.
— A New Vision of Israel: The Teachings of Jesus in National Context. LC 98-43795. (Studying the Historical Jesus Ser.). 352p. 1999. pap. 21.00 (*0-8028-4212-7*) Eerdmans.
McKnight, Scot, ed. Introducing New Testament Interpretation. LC 89-28390. (Guides to New Testament Exegesis Ser.). 200p. 1990. pap. 14.99 (*0-8010-6260-8*) Baker Bks.
McKnight Staff & Miller, Wilbur R. Power Mechanics. LC 78-53394. (Basic Industrial Arts Ser.). (Illus.). 1978. pap. 7.72 (*0-02-672870-2*) Glencoe.
— Woodworking. LC 78-53386. (Basic Industrial Arts Ser.). (Illus.). 1978. pap. 9.33 (*0-02-672800-1*) Glencoe.
McKnight, Stephen A. Eric Voegelin's Search for Order in History. exp. ed. 252p. 1988. reprint ed. pap. text 24.00 (*0-8191-6557-3*) U Pr of Amer.
— The Modern Age & the Recovery of Ancient Wisdom: A Reconsideration of Historical Consciousness, 1450-1650. (Illus.). 176p. 1991. text 29.95 (*0-8262-0781-2*) U of Mo Pr.
McKnight, Stephen A. & Price, Geoffrey L., eds. International & Interdisciplinary Perspectives on Eric Voegelin. LC 97-10987. 240p. 1997. text 39.95 (*0-8262-1105-4*) U of Mo Pr.
McKnight, Steven, ed. Genetic Flow. 1996. pap. 21.00 (*0-8243-3172-9*) Annual Reviews.
McKnight, Steven L. & Yamamoto, Keith R., eds. Transcriptional Regulation. LC 92-31461. (Monographs: Vol. 22). 1335p. 1993. 120.00 (*0-87969-410-6*); pap. 71.00 (*0-87969-425-4*) Cold Spring Harbor.
McKnight, T. S., jt. ed. see Mullins, E. J.
McKnight, Thomas. Friendly Vermin: A Survey of Feral Livestock in Australia. LC 73-62778. (University of California Publications in Social Welfare: Vol. 21). 112p. reprint ed. pap. 34.80 (*0-608-13961-0*, 202127600021) Bks Demand.
— Thomas McKnight: Windows on Paradise. (Illus.). 200p. 1997. 29.98 (*0-89660-088-2*, Artabras) Abbeville Pr.
McKnight, Thomas L. Feral Livestock in Anglo-America. LC 64-64237. (University of California Publications in Social Welfare: Vol. 16). 92p. reprint ed. pap. 30.00 (*0-608-14159-3*, 202127300022) Bks Demand.
McKnight, Thomas W. How to Win the Love You Want: Effective Techniques & Tactics For Getting the One You Love to Love. 1998. pap. text 9.99 (*1-57866-018-1*) Promntory Pr.
— Love-Tactics: Strategic Psychology to Win the One You Want. (Illus.). 76p. 1985. pap. 4.95 (*0-9615050-0-1*) Wisdom Pr.
McKnight, Thomas W. & Phillips, Robert. Love Tactics: How to Win the One You Want. unabridged ed. 1996. 16.95 incl. audio (*1-882071-62-X*) B&B Audio.
McKnight, Thomas W. & Phillips, Robert H. Love Tactics: How to Win the One You Want. LC 87-31935. 144p. pap. 7.95 (*0-89529-367-6*, Avery) Penguin Putnam.
— More Love Tactics: How to Win that Special Someone. LC 92-2729. 192p. 1993. pap. 8.95 (*0-89529-531-8*, Avery) Penguin Putnam.
McKnight, Thomas W. & Phillips, Robert H. More Love Tactics: How to Win That Special Someone. 1996. 16.95 incl. audio (*1-882071-85-9*) B&B Audio.
McKnight, Tom. Australia. LC 95-48147. (American Geographical Society Around the World Program Ser.). (Illus.). 64p. (Orig.). 1996. pap. 13.95 (*0-939923-51-3*) M & W Pub Co.
— Australia. LC 95-48147. (American Geographical Society Around the World Program Ser.). (Illus.). 64p. (Orig.). (J). 1996. 18.95 (*0-939923-52-1*) M & W Pub Co.
*__McKnight, Tom & Hess, Darrel.__ Physical Geography: A Landscape Appreciation (virtual Fieldtrip Edition) 6th ed. 604p. (C). 1999. text 78.00 incl. audio compact disk (*0-13-020263-0*) P-H.
McKnight, Tom L. Oceania: The Geography of Australia, New Zealand & the Pacific Islands. (C). 1994. text 42.00 (*0-13-123639-3*) P-H.
— Physical Geography: A Landscape Appreciation. 6th ed. LC 98-16286. 624p. (C). 1998. text 66.00 (*0-13-950445-1*) P-H.
— Regional Geography of the United States & Canada. 2nd ed. LC 96-46115. (Illus.). 512p. (C). 1997. 81.00 (*0-13-456484-7*) P-H.
McKnight-Trontz, Jennifer. Exotiquarium: Album Art from the Space Age. LC 98-41878. 1999. pap. 24.95 (*0-312-20133-8*) St Martin.
*__McKnight-Trontz, Jennifer.__ Yes You Can: Timeless Advice from Self-Help Experts. LC 99-51629. (Illus.). 96p. 2000. pap. 14.95 (*0-8118-2713-5*) Chronicle Bks.
McKnight-Trontz, Jennifer, jt. auth. see Steinweiss, Alex.
*__McKnight, W. J.__ A Pioneer History of Jefferson County, Pennsylvania & My First Recollections of Brookville, Pennsylvania, 1840-1843, When My Feet Were Bare & My Cheeks Were Brown. (Illus.). 697p. 1999. reprint ed. (*0-7884-1216-7*, M139) Heritage Bk.
McKnight, W. J. Pioneer Outline History of Northwestern Pennsylvania: Embracing the Counties of Tioga, Potter, McKean, Warren, Crawford, Venango, Forest, Clarion, Elk, Jefferson, cameron, Butler, Lawrence & Mercer; Also, a Pioneer Sketch of the Cities of Allegheny, Beaver du Bois & Towanda. (Illus.). 747p. 1997. reprint ed. lib. bdg. 76.00 (*0-8328-6380-7*) Higginson Bk Co.
*__Mcknight, Whitney.__ Dads Love Babies. LC 98-46394. (Illus.). 96p. 1999. 14.98 (*0-7651-1065-2*) Smithmark.
McKnight, William J. Jefferson County, Pennsylvania: Her Pioneers & People, 1800-1915, Vol. II: Genealogy-Biography. (Illus.). 701p. 1992. reprint ed. lib. bdg. 77.00 (*0-8328-1410-5*) Higginson Bk Co.
— A Pioneer History of Jefferson County, Pennsylvania, 1755-1844. (Illus.). 670p. 1992. reprint ed. lib. bdg. 69.50 (*0-8328-1415-6*) Higginson Bk Co.
McKnight, William M. Blue Bonnets over the Border: The 79th New York Cameron Highlanders. LC 97-46708. (Illus.). 185p. 1998. 24.95 (*1-57249-052-7*) White Mane Pub.
McKoen, Paul & Gough, Leo. The Finance Manual for Non-Financial Managers: The Power to Make Confident Financial Decisions. (Institute of Management Ser.). (Illus.). 334p. 1997. pap. 52.50 (*0-273-62559-4*, Pub. by Pitman Pub) Trans-Atl Phila.
McKoin, Florence S. Between the Rivers: A West Carroll Chronicle. 1971. 20.00 (*0-87511-082-7*) Claitors.
McKone, Harold T. Separating & Identifying Some Food & Drug Dyes by Thin-Layer Chromatography. Neidig, H. Anthony, ed. (Modular Laboratory Program in Chemistry Ser.). 7p. (C). 1994. pap. text 1.50 (*0-87540-445-6*, ANAL 445-6) Chem Educ Res.
McKoski, Martin M. & Hahn, Lynne C. Developing Sentence Sense. LC 93-36241. 192p. (C). 1997. pap. text 36.93 (*0-673-46973-5*) Addson-Wesley Educ.
— Developing Writer. 4th ed. 350p. (C). 1997. pap. text 57.00 (*0-673-46441-5*) Addson-Wesley Educ.
— Developing Writers Work. 160p. (C). 1997. pap. text 23.53 (*0-673-18399-8*) Addson-Wesley Educ.
McKotch, Robert A. & Webb, Richard, eds. Advances in P-M & Particulate Materials, 1997. (Illus.). 2000p. 1997. 900.00 (*1-878954-63-6*) Metal Powder.
McKowen. The Complete German Shorthaired Pointer. 1995. pap. 25.00 (*0-87605-155-7*) Howell Bks.
McKowen, Clark. Get Your "A" Out of College. 2nd rev. ed. Henry, Carol, ed. LC 95-83229. 328p. 1996. pap. 14.95 (*1-56052-389-1*) Crisp Pubns.
*__McKowen, Clark.__ Ligonier Sightings. (Illus.). 112p. 2000. 13.95 (*0-9665272-1-6*) Laurel Mount.
McKowen, Clark. Teaching Human Beings: The Role of Language in Education. LC 98-91640. (Illus.). 1998. text 23.95 (*0-9665272-0-8*) Laurel Mount.
*__McKowen, Ken.__ Longstreet Highroad Guide to the California Coast. LC 00-104187. (Illus.). 352p. 2000. pap. 18.95 (*1-56352-594-1*) Longstreet.
McKown, D. B. The Classical Marxist Critiques of Religion: Marx, Engels, Lenin, Kautsky. 182p. 1975. pap. text 71.50 (*90-247-1656-X*) Kluwer Academic.
McKown, David. Writing for Career Growth, Vol. 2. (IEEE Engineers Guide to Business Ser.). (Illus.). 1992. 19.95 (*0-7803-0304-0*, HL0452-3) Inst Electrical.
McKown, Delos. The Mythmaker's Magic: Behind the Illusion of "Creation Science" LC 92-34549. 180p. (C). 1993. 27.95 (*0-87975-770-1*) Prometheus Bks.
McKown, Delos B. With Faith & Fury. LC 84-43180. 444p. 1985. 29.95 (*0-87975-280-7*) Prometheus Bks.
McKown, Martha. Palm Sunday Parade. 20p. (Orig.). 1995. pap. 4.50 (*0-7880-0322-4*) CSS OH.
McKown, Ric, jt. auth. see Inches, Alison.
McKoy, Clifton. The Real McKoy. Johnson, Lois, ed. (Illus.). 136p. 1998. pap. 15.00 (*0-9662610-7-0*) Real McKoy.
*__McKoy-Hibbert, Erica.__ Mi Neva Know Sey. LC 99-97828. 167p. 2000. 12.95 (*1-930331-00-2*) Machibb.
McKoy, Lattice B. Moments of Pride, Passion, Prejudice & Spirituality. LC 97-75985. 96p. 1998. pap. 11.95 (*1-57197-103-3*) Pentland Pr.
McKoy, Thelma N. Trapped in the Lawyers' Den with Bloodsuckers. 230p. 1988. pap. 12.00 (*0-9649430-0-X*) T N McKoy.
McKray, George, jt. ed. see Roemer, Ruth.
McKrell, Judith L. Communication Problems: After a Brain Injury or Stroke. Sweetman, Richard, ed. LC 96-48516. (Illus.). 24p. (Orig.). 1996. pap. 5.95 (*0-939838-44-3*) Pritchett & Hull.
McKuen, Rod. And Autumn Came. 1969. 50.00 (*0-318-00971-4*) Cheval Bks.
— Beyond the Boardwalk. 1976. 5.95 (*0-910368-01-5*); 12.50 (*0-686-14426-0*); pap. 3.95 (*0-686-14427-9*) Cheval Bks.
— The Carols of Christmas. 1971. 3.95 (*0-394-47420-1*) Random.
— The Lovers. (Orig.). 1982. pap. 2.95 (*0-671-43615-5*) PB.
— Moment to Moment. 1972. pap. 5.95 (*0-318-00970-6*) Cheval Bks.
— The Songs of Rod McKuen. 1960. 5.95 (*0-318-00972-2*) Cheval Bks.
— Stanyan Street & Other Sorrows. 1994. lib. bdg. 25.95 (*1-56849-474-2*) Buccaneer Bks.
McKusick, James C. Coleridge's Philosophy of Language. LC 86-7731. (Yale Studies in English: No. 195). 189p. 1986. reprint ed. pap. 58.60 (*0-8357-3752-7*, 203647800003) Bks Demand.
McKusick, Marjorie. Borderland-Warfare. LC 97-178422. 308p. 1996. pap. 10.99 (*1-884369-40-5*, EBED Pubns) McDougal Pubng.
McKusick, Marshall B. The Davenport Conspiracy Revisited. LC 90-40071. (Illus.). 205p. reprint ed. pap. 63.60 (*0-608-09054-9*, 206968900005) Bks Demand.
McKusick, Marshall K., et al. The Design & Implementation of the 4.4 BSD UNIX Operating System. 608p. (C). 1996. 57.95 (*0-201-54979-4*) Addison-Wesley.
McKusick, Victor, jt. ed. see Temtamy, Samia.
McKusick, Victor A. Medical Genetics: A Self-Instruction Guide & Workbook Based on Mendelian Inheritance in Man (MIM) LC 93-31306. 128p. 1994. pap., wbk. ed. 30.00 (*0-8018-4796-6*) Johns Hopkins.
— Mendelian Inheritance in Man: A Catalog of Human Genes & Genetic Disorders. 12th ed. LC 97-26291. 1997. write for info. (*0-8018-5743-0*) Johns Hopkins.
— Mendelian Inheritance in Man: A Catalog of Human Genes & Genetic Disorders, 3 vols. 12th ed. LC 97-26291. 3972p. 1998. text 195.00 (*0-8018-5742-2*) Johns Hopkins.
— Mendelian Inheritance in Man: Catalogs of Autosomal Dominant, Autosomal Recessive, & X-Linked Phenotypes. 2nd ed. LC 68-19441. 541p. 1968. reprint ed. pap. 167.80 (*0-608-18788-7*, 2029844) Bks Demand.
— Mendelian Inheritance in Man: Catalogs of Autosomal Dominant, Autosomal Recessive, & X-Linked Phenotypes. 8th ed. LC 88-9328. 1742p. 1988. reprint ed. pap. 200.00 (*0-8357-6907-0*, 203796500009) Bks Demand.
McKusick, Victor A., ed. Medical Genetic Studies of the Amish: Selected Papers. LC 76-47386. (Illus.). 528p. 1978. 65.00 (*0-8018-1934-2*) Johns Hopkins.
McKusick, Victor A. & Osler, William. Mendelian Inheritance in Man: Catalogs of Autosomal Dominant, Autosomal Recessive, & X-Linked Phenotypes. 6th ed. LC 82-47975. 1448p. 1983. reprint ed. pap. 200.00 (*0-608-15525-X*, 2029706) Bks Demand.
McKusick, Victor A., et al. Mendelian Inheritance in Man: A Catalog of Human Genes & Genetic Disorders, 2 vols. 11th ed. 1994. text 165.00 (*0-8018-4933-0*) Johns Hopkins.
McKusick, Victor A., jt. ed. see McHugh, Paul R.
McKyes, E. Agricultural Engineering Soil Mechanics. LC 96-1405. (Developments in Agricultural Engineering Ser.: Vol. 10). 292p. 1989. 99.50 (*0-444-88080-1*) Elsevier.
McLachan, Geoffrey J. & Krishnan, Thriyambakam. The EM Algorithm & Extensions. LC 96-38417. (Wiley Probability & Mathematics Ser.). 304p. 1996. 79.95 (*0-471-12358-7*) Wiley.
McLachan, Patricia. Bebe (Baby) (SPA.). (YA). 1997. pap. 6.99 (*968-16-5440-4*, Pub. by Fondo) Continental Bk.
McLachian, Ian. U. S. A. A. F. Fighter Stories: Dramatic Accounts of American Fighter Pilots in Training & Combat Over. LC 97-61077. (Illus.). 192p. 1997. 39.95 (*1-85260-569-3*, Pub. by J H Haynes & Co) Motorbooks Intl.
McLachlan. Berlin. 2nd ed. pap. 23.95 (*962-217-657-7*) China Guides.
McLachlan, Alan. Molecular Biology of the Hepatitis B Virus. (Illus.). 312p. 1991. lib. bdg. 229.00 (*0-8493-5516-8*, QR749) CRC Pr.
*__McLachlan, Anne.__ Egypt Handbook. 3rd ed. (Footprint Handbooks Ser.). (Illus.). 2000. pap. 19.95 (*0-658-01084-0*, Passprt Bks) NTC Contemp Pub Co.
McLachlan, Anne. Morocco Handbook with Mautitania. (Illus.). 450p. 1997. 17.95 (*0-8442-4866-5*) NTC Contemp Pub Co.
Mclachlan, Anne. North African Handbook, 1994. 800p. 1994. pap. 24.95 (*0-8442-9978-2*, Passprt Bks) NTC Contemp Pub Co.
McLachlan, Anne. Tunisia Handbook with Libya. LC 96-72521. (Illus.). 480p. 1997. 18.95 (*0-8442-4867-3*) NTC Contemp Pub Co.
McLachlan, Anne & McLachlan, Keith. Egypt Handbook. 2nd ed. LC 98-65734. (Footprint Handbooks Ser.). (Illus.). 528p. 1998. 19.95 (*0-8442-4894-0*, 48940, Natl Textbk Co) NTC Contemp Pub Co.
— Egypt Handbook with Sudan. (Handbooks of the World Ser.). (Illus.). 528p. 1996. 19.95 (*0-8442-4900-9*, Passprt Bks) NTC Contemp Pub Co.
McLachlan, Anne & McLachlan, Keith, eds. Morocco & Tunisia Handbook: With Algeria, Libya & Mauritania. (Illus.). 624p. 1995. 21.95 (*0-8442-8889-6*, Passprt Bks) NTC Contemp Pub Co.
*__McLachlan, Bruce.__ Slave to Cabal. 272p. 2000. pap. 9.95 (*1-901388-55-7*, Pub. by Chimera Pubns) Firebird Dist.
McLachlan, Bryan. Shadows & Deceptions. 374p. 1999. pap. 14.95 (*1-891929-15-1*) Four Seasons.
McLachlan, Campbell & Nygh, Peter, eds. Transnational Tort Litigation: Jurisdictional Principles. 286p. 1996. text 98.00 (*0-19-825919-0*) OUP.
McLachlan, D. L. Canada-U. S. Free Trade: The Faltering Impetus for a Historic Reversal. 62p. (C). 1987. pap. text 7.95 (*0-920490-74-3*) Temeron Bks.
McLachlan, Dan, et al, eds. Crystallography in North America. LC 81-71539. 479p. 1985. reprint ed. 25.00 (*0-937140-07-4*) Polycrystal Bk Serv.
McLachlan, Dan H. & Ayres, Jak. The Fieldbook of Pacific Northwest Sea Creatures, Vol. 1. LC 79-9769. (Illus.). 208p. (C). 1979. pap. 12.95 (*0-87961-068-9*) Naturegraph.
McLachlan, Diana, ed. A Common Thread: Quilts in the Yakima Valley. (Illus.). 1985. pap. 10.00 (*1-928707-04-1*) Yakima Valley Mus.
*__McLachlan, Elizabeth P.__ With Unspeakable Persistence: Rural Teachers of the Depression Era. 224p. 1999. pap. 24.00 (*1-896300-11-1*) NeWest Pubs.
McLachlan, Elspeth M. Autonomic Ganglia. (Autonomic Nervous System Ser.). 529p. 1995. text 165.00 (*3-7186-5148-3*, Harwood Acad Pubs) Gordon & Breach.
McLachlan, G. The Planning of Health Services: Studies in 8 European Countries. (EURO Nonserial Publication Ser.). 252p. 1980. 20.00 (*92-9020-195-9*, 1340002) World Health.
McLachlan, Geoffrey. Discriminant Analysis & Statistical Pattern Recognition. LC 91-29342. (Probability & Mathematical Statistics: Applied Probability & Statistics Section Ser.: No. 1346). 544p. 1992. 129.95 (*0-471-61531-5*) Wiley.
McLachlan, Gordon. Germany. 4th ed. (Rough Guides Ser.). 1040p. 1998. pap. 23.95 (*1-85828-309-4*, Penguin Bks) Viking Penguin.
— Lithuania: The Bradt Travel Guide. 2nd ed. LC 99-14550. (Bradt Country Guides Ser.). (Illus.). 256p. 1999. pap. 17.95 (*1-898323-91-7*, Pub. by Bradt Pubns) Globe Pequot.
*__McLachlan, Gordon.__ Poland. (Illus.). 2000. pap. 19.95 (*1-84162-009-2*) Bradt Pubns.
McLachlan, Gordon, ed. Medical Education & Medical Care: A Scottish American Symposium. (Nuffield Publications). 230p. 1977. text 13.25 (*0-19-721394-4*) OUP.
McLachlan, Gordon, et al, eds. Patterns for Uncertainty? Planning for the Greater Medical Profession. 1979. pap. 14.95 (*0-19-721223-9*) OUP.
McLachlan, Gordon M. Berlin: Capital of the New Germany. (Illus.). 304p. 1994. pap. 16.95 (*0-8442-9674-0*, Passprt Bks) NTC Contemp Pub Co.
McLachlan, Ian. Eighth Air Force Bomber Stories. (Illus.). 208p. 1992. 37.95 (*1-85260-367-4*) Haynes Manuals.
McLachlan, J. L., jt. auth. see Bird, C. J.
McLachlan, James. Princetonians, 1748-1768: A Biographical Dictionary. LC 76-4063. 735p. 1976. reprint ed. pap. 200.00 (*0-608-03334-0*, 206404600008) Bks Demand.
McLachlan, James M. The Desire to Be God: Freedom & the Other in Sartre & Berdyaev. LC 91-31770. (Studies in Phenomenological Theology: Vol. 1). 215p. (C). 1992. pap. text 39.95 (*0-8204-1711-4*) P Lang Pubng.
McLachlan, John M., et al, eds. Developmental Toxicology: Mechanisms & Risk. (Banbury Reports: No. 26). (Illus.). 362p. (C). 1987. text 70.00 (*0-87969-226-X*) Cold Spring Harbor.
McLachlan, K. S. & Whittaker, W. A Bibliography of Afganistan. (C). 1983. text 50.50 (*0-906559-12-X*) Westview.
McLachlan, Keith, ed. The Boundaries of Modern Iran. LC 93-40359. (SOAS-GRC Geopolitics Ser.). 1994. text 55.00 (*0-312-12062-1*) St Martin.
McLachlan, Keith, jt. auth. see McLachlan, Anne.
McLachlan, Keith, jt. auth. see Tapper, Richard.
McLachlan, Keith, jt. ed. see Beaumont, Peter.
McLachlan, Keith, jt. ed. see McLachlan, Anne.
McLachlan, Meschach. Seizures of the Sun: First Poems. (Stewardship Ser.: No. 6). 40p. (Orig.). 1996. pap. 6.00 (*1-883197-11-2*) New Native Pr.
McLachlan, N. A., jt. ed. see Brown, A. C.
McLachlan, Sandra M., jt. auth. see Rapoport, Basil.
McLachlan, Sarah, jt. auth. see Laurita, Jaime.
McLachland, Gordon, jt. auth. see Salter, Mark.
McLachlin & Wallace. The Canadian Law of Architecture & Engineering. 512p. 1987. boxed set 115.00 (*0-409-80481-9*, MICHIE) LEXIS Pub.
McLaehlan, Ian. Final Flights: Dramatic Wartime Incidents Revealed by Archaeology. (Illus.). 256p. 1994. 34.95 (*1-85260-122-1*) J H Haynes & Co.
McLafferty, Fred W. Mass Spectral Correlations. 2nd ed. LC 81-205644. (Advances in Chemistry Ser.: No. 40). 124p. 1982. text 35.00 (*0-8412-0702-X*, Pub. by Am Chemical) OUP.
— Registry of Mass Spectral Data. 5th ed. Ep. 1989. 6000.00 incl. cd-rom (*0-471-51593-0*) Wiley.
McLafferty, Fred W., ed. Tandem Mass Spectrometry. LC 83-10528. (Wiley-Interscience Publications). 526p. reprint ed. pap. 163.10 (*0-7837-2401-2*, 204008600006) Bks Demand.
McLafferty, Fred W. & Stauffer, Douglas B. The Important Peak Index of the Registry of Mass Spectral Data, 3 vols., Set. 4080p. 1991. 825.00 (*0-471-55270-4*) Wiley.
— Wiley/NBS Registry of Mass Spectral Data. LC 87-31645. 7872p. 1989. 1099.00 (*0-471-62886-7*) Wiley.
McLafferty, Fred W. & Turecek, Frantisek. Interpretation of Mass Spectra. 4th ed. LC 92-82536. (Illus.). 400p. (C). 1993. text 34.00 (*0-935702-25-3*) Univ Sci Bks.
McLagan, Clinton R., jt. auth. see Shumaker, Gordon W.
*__McLagan, Ian.__ All the Rage: A Riotous Romp Through Rock & Roll History. LC 00-23675. (Illus.). 416p. 2000. pap. write for info. (*0-8230-7842-6*, Billboard Bks) Watsn-Guptill.
McLagan, Ian & Welch, Chris. All the Rage. (Illus.). 320p. 29.95 (*0-283-06334-3*, Pub. by S1 & J) Trafalgar.
McLagan, Patricia & Bromhead, Alison. In France: Textbook. 12.95 (*0-8219-0923-1*) EMC-Paradigm.
— In France: Workbook. 8.95 (*0-8219-0924-X*) EMC-Paradigm.
— In France: Workbook, teacher's edition. 9.95 (*0-8219-0925-8*) EMC-Paradigm.
McLagan, Patricia & Nel, Christo. The Age of Participation: New Governance for the Workplace & the World. LC 95-35766. (Illus.). 312p. 1995. 27.95 (*1-881052-56-7*) Berrett-Koehler.

M

An Asterisk (*) at the beginning of an entry indicates that the title is appearing for the first time.

— Age of Participation: New Governance for the Workplace & the World. LC 95-35766. 340p. 1997. pap. 18.95 (*1-57675-012-4*) Berrett-Koehler.

McLagan, Patricia A. Helping Others Learn: Designing Programs for Adults. 1978. 14.95 (*0-201-04617-2*) Addison-Wesley.

McLagan, Patricia A. & Krembs, Peter. On-the-Level: Performance Communication That Works. 2nd rev. ed. LC 95-18624. (Illus.). 140p. 1995. pap. 19.95 (*1-881052-76-1*) Berrett-Koehler.

McLaggan, Douglas. The Will to Survive: A Private's View As a P. O. W. LC 95-153480. (Illus.). 240p. (Orig.). 1995. pap. 17.95 (*0-86417-706-2*, Pub. by Kangaroo Pr) Seven Hills Bk.

McLaglen, John. Herne the Hunter: Billy the Kid. large type ed. (Linford Western Library). 240p. 1986. pap. 16.99 (*0-7089-6219-X*, Linford) Ulverscroft.

— Herne the Hunter: Cross-Draw. large type ed. (Linford Western Library). 272p. 1986. pap. 16.99 (*0-7089-6196-7*, Linford) Ulverscroft.

— Herne the Hunter: Death in Gold. large type ed. (Linford Western Library). 256p. 1985. pap. 16.99 (*0-7089-6190-8*) Ulverscroft.

— Herne the Hunter: Vigilante! large type ed. (Linford Western Library). 272p. 1986. pap. 16.99 (*0-7089-6203-3*, Linford) Ulverscroft.

***McLain, Bill.** Do Fish Drink Water: Puzzling And Improbable Questions And Answers. 320p. 2000. pap. 13.00 (*0-688-17908-8*) Morrow Avon.

— Do Spiders Sleep. 2000. 23.00 (*0-06-019826-5*) HarpC.

McLain, Denson K. Genetics, Diversity & the Biosphere. LC 94-72454. (Illus.). 112p. (Orig.). (C). 1995. pap. 12.99 (*1-884612-03-2*) AudioText.

— Understanding the Cell. LC 94-72550. (Illus.). 126p. (Orig.). (C). 1994. pap. 12.99 (*1-884612-01-6*) AudioText.

McLain, Denson K., ed. see Gantt, David G.

***McLain, F. Michael & Richardson, W. Mark.** Human & Divine Agency: Anglican, Catholic & Lutheran Perspectives. 296p. 1999. 54.00 (*0-7618-1470-1*); pap. 34.50 (*0-7618-1471-X*) U Pr of Amer.

McLain, Gary. The Indian Way: Learning to Communicate with Mother Earth. (Illus.). 112p. (J). (gr. 3 up). 1990. pap. 9.95 (*0-945465-73-4*) Avalon Travel.

McLain, James J. The Economic Writings of Du Pont de Nemours. LC 76-14769. 244p. 1977. 35.00 (*0-87413-114-6*) U Delaware Pr.

McLain-Kark. The Designer's AutoCAD Release 14 Tutorial. 1998. pap. 42.95 (*0-87393-821-6*) Dame Pubns.

McLain, L. ASTD Trainer's Sourcebook Series, Project Management. Roe, Richard L., ed. 250p. 1995. pap. text 39.95 (*0-07-053440-3*) McGraw.

McLain, L. Charles. My Words...Exactly. 1999. pap. write for info. (*1-58235-033-7*) Watermrk Pr.

McLain, Margaret S. Class Piano. LC 73-19659. 304p. 1974. pap. 8.95 (*0-253-31357-0*) Ind U Pr.

McLain, Michael, jt. ed. see Loades, Ann.

McLain, Patrick G., et al. Weigh to Go: Self Help Weight Loss Manual. unabridged ed. Bell, Weslea, ed. LC 98-92566. (Illus.). 200p. 1999. pap. 19.95 (*0-9663078-0-1*) Graystone Pub Co.

***McLain, Paula.** Less of Her: (Poems) (New Issues Press Poetry Ser.). 64p. 1999. 22.00 (*0-932826-81-4*, Pub. by WMU Poetry & Prose); pap. 12.00 (*0-932826-82-2*, Pub. by WMU Poetry & Prose) Partners Pubs Grp.

McLain, Rebecca J. Recommendations for a New Malian Forest Code: Observations from the Land Tenure Center's Study of Land & Tree Tenure in Mali's Fifth Region. (Research Paper Ser.: Vol. 109). (Illus.). x, 45p. (C). 1992. pap. 4.00 (*0-934519-19-6*, RP109) U of Wis Land.

— Recommendations pour un Nouveau Code Forestier Malien: Observations a Partir d'une Etude sur la Tenure des Terres et des Arbres dans la Cinquieme Region du Mali. (Research Paper Ser.: Vol. 109-F).Tr. of Recommendations for a New Malian Forest Code. (FRE., Illus.). xii, 46p. (C). 1992. pap. 4.00 (*0-934519-20-X*, RP109-F) U of Wis Land.

McLain, Rebecca J., et al. Land Tenure & Land Use in Southern Haiti: Case Studies of the Les Anglais & Grande Ravine du Sud Watersheds. (Research Paper Ser.: Vol. 95). (Illus.). xi, 252p. (C). 1988. pap. 12.00 (*0-934519-05-6*, RP95) U of Wis Land.

McLain, Timothy. Librarian's Internet Companion. Giagnocavo, Gregory & Sturm, Chris N., eds. (Illus.). 200p. (Orig.). 1995. pap. 39.95 (*0-932577-25-3*) Wentworth Worldwide.

McLain, Timothy, et al. Educator's Internet Companion: Classroom Connect's Complete Guide to Resources on the Internet. Sturm, Chris N., ed. LC 95-60749. (Illus.). 300p. (Orig.). 1995. 39.95 (*0-932577-10-5*) Wentworth Worldwide.

McLain, Timothy, jt. auth. see Giagnocavo, Gregory.

McLain, Timothy, jt. ed. see Mistry, Sanjay I.

McLain, Wayne. Resurrection Encounter: The Rufus Moseley. 1997. pap. 9.95 (*1-886158-15-0*) Macalester.

McLain, Wayne, et al. A Heavenly View: The Best of Rufus Moseley. 1993. pap. 8.95 (*0-910924-96-1*) Macalester.

McLain, William. Do Fish Drink Water: Puzzling And Improbable Questions And Answers. LC 99-15805. 320p. 1999. 22.00 (*0-688-16512-5*, Wm Morrow) Morrow Avon.

McLain, William H. New Mexico's Timber Production & Mill Residue, 1986. (Illus.). 24p. 1998. reprint ed. pap. 3.40 (*0-89904-932-X*, Ecosytems Resrch) Crumb Elbow Pub.

McLaine, Patricia. Love Is Contagious. 1961. pap. 5.25 (*0-8222-0693-5*) Dramatists Play.

***McLaine, Patricia.** The Recycling of Rosalie, Vol. 2. Read, Diana & Lanys, Bita, eds. iv, 220p. 1999. 12.95 (*0-9672510-1-X*, 102) Akasha Pubg.

— Tarot for Today: Instantaneous Insights & Effective Affirmations: A Handbook for the Apprentice. (Illus.). 2000. pap. 12.00 (*0-9672510-2-8*) Akasha Pubg.

— The Wheel of Destiny: The Tarot Reveals Your Master Plan. rev. ed. (Tarot: No. 1). (Illus.). 480p. 1999. pap. 24.95 (*0-9672510-0-1*, 101) Akasha Pubg.

McLaird, George L. The Marriage Maze: McLaird's Field Guide for the Journey. Donaldson, Doris & Fugaro, Jill, eds. LC 95-79114. (Illus.). 256p. (Orig.). 1995. pap. 17.95 (*1-887182-01-2*) AED.

McLaird, James, ed. Calamity Jane's Daughter: The Story of Maude Weir - A Story Never Before Told. LC 96-92330. (Illus.). 52p. (Orig.). 1996. pap. 11.95 (*0-9652715-0-1*, 000660821S) R Shadley.

McLamb, Jess R. Roper's North Carolina Business Resource Guide. 120p. (Orig.). 1997. pap. text 16.95 (*0-9645096-1-X*) Roper Grp.

McLamb, Jess R., ed. see Galbreath, Margaret J.

McLamb, John W., Jr. & Shiba, Wendy C. Pennsylvania Corporation Law & Practice. (National Corporation Law Ser.). 1992. ring bd. 126.00 (*0-13-110462-4*) Aspen Law.

McLamore, Jim. The Burger King: Jim McLamore & the Building of an Empire. LC 97-22285. 304p. 1997. 24.95 (*0-07-045255-5*) McGraw.

Mclanahan, David. Whole Surgery Handbook. 1999. text 23.95 (*0-525-93798-6*) Viking Penguin.

McLanahan, Kip. PowerPC Programming for Intel Programmers. 720p. 1995. pap. 49.99 (*1-56884-306-2*) IDG Bks.

McLanahan, Sara & Sandefur, Gary D. Growing up with a Single Parent: What Hurts, What Helps. LC 94-19995. (Illus.). 208p. 1994. text 19.95 (*0-674-36407-4*, MCLGRO) HUP.

— Growing up with a Single Parent: What Hurts, What Helps. (Illus.). 208p. 1996. pap. 14.00 (*0-674-36408-2*) HUP.

McLanahan, Sara S., jt. auth. see Garfinkel, Irwin.

McLanathan, Richard. Art in America: A Brief History. (Illus.). 216p. (C). 1973. pap. text 32.50 (*0-15-503466-9*, Pub. by Harcourt Coll Pubs) Harcourt.

— Peter Paul Rubens. LC 94-33330. (First Impressions Ser.). (Illus.). 92p. (J). 1995. 19.95 (*0-8109-3780-8*, Pub. by Abrams) Time Warner.

McLanathan, Richard B. Leonardo da Vinci. (First Impressions Ser.). (Illus.). 72p. (YA). (gr. 7 up). 1990. 19.95 (*0-8109-1256-2*, Pub. by Abrams) Time Warner.

— Michelangelo. LC 92-27688. (First Impressions Ser.). (Illus.). 92p. (J). 1993. 19.95 (*0-8109-3634-8*, Pub. by Abrams) Time Warner.

— Ship Models. 2nd ed. (Illus.). 48p. 1957. reprint ed. pap. 6.50 (*0-87846-220-1*) Mus Fine Arts Boston.

McLanathan, Richard B. & Brown, Gene. The Arts. (Great Contemporary Issues Ser.). 1978. 27.95 (*0-405-11153-3*) Ayer.

McLane, Bernard W., ed. The 1341 Royal Inquest in Lincolnshire. (Lincoln Record Society Ser.: No. 78). 224p. 1989. 45.00 (*0-901503-51-7*) Boydell & Brewer.

McLane, Bobbie J. Alabama Soldiers (Revolution, War of 1812 & Indian Wars) Vol. 18: Surnames Mc. 128p. (Orig.). 1996. pap. 15.00 (*0-929604-79-2*) Arkansas Ancestors.

— City of Hot Springs, Arkansas Death Records, 1896-1917. 270p. (Orig.). 1987. pap. 25.00 (*0-929604-59-8*) Arkansas Ancestors.

— Clark County, Arkansas Census, 1850. annot. ed. 53p. (Orig.). 1985. pap. 15.00 (*0-929604-37-7*) Arkansas Ancestors.

— Clark County, Arkansas Census, 1860. 104p. (Orig.). 1988. pap. 15.00 (*0-929604-44-X*) Arkansas Ancestors.

— Clark County, Arkansas Census, 1870. 408p. (Orig.). 1985. pap. 25.00 (*0-929604-61-X*) Arkansas Ancestors.

— Clark County, Arkansas Marriage Records, 1821-1879. 266p. (Orig.). 1974. pap. 22.00 (*0-929604-26-1*) Arkansas Ancestors.

— The Family of Goodin Deaton of Clark County, Arkansas, 1814-1902. (Illus.). 150p. 1997. 40.00 (*0-929604-80-6*) Arkansas Ancestors.

— Franklin County, Arkansas Census, 1860. 89p. (Orig.). 1986. pap. 12.00 (*0-929604-39-3*) Arkansas Ancestors.

— Fulton County, Arkansas Census, 1860. 61p. (Orig.). 1988. pap. 12.00 (*0-929604-40-7*) Arkansas Ancestors.

— Hempstead County, Arkansas Census with Notes Concerning 110 Families, 1850. 93p. (Orig.). 1967. pap. 15.00 (*0-929604-08-3*) Arkansas Ancestors.

— Hot Spring County, Arkansas Census, 1850, Including Marriage, Bk. A. 69p. (Orig.). 1965. pap. 12.00 (*0-929604-02-4*) Arkansas Ancestors.

— Hot Spring County, Arkansas Census, 1860. 81p. (Orig.). 1985. pap. 12.00 (*0-929604-38-5*) Arkansas Ancestors.

— Hot Spring County, Arkansas Marriage Records, 1825-1880. 155p. (Orig.). 1970. pap. 18.00 (*0-929604-21-0*) Arkansas Ancestors.

— Index to Census of Confederate Veterans - Arkansas, 1911. 280p. (Orig.). 1988. pap. 28.00 (*0-929604-57-1*) Arkansas Ancestors.

— Johnson County, Arkansas Census, 1860. 157p. (Orig.). 1988. pap. 15.00 (*0-929604-58-X*) Arkansas Ancestors.

— Lafayette County, Arkansas Census, 1860. 66p. (Orig.). 1985. pap. 12.00 (*0-929604-35-0*) Arkansas Ancestors.

— Ouachita County, Arkansas Census, 1860. annot. ed. 130p. (Orig.). 1987. pap. 18.00 (*0-929604-43-1*) Arkansas Ancestors.

— Pike County, Arkansas Census, 1860. 59p. (Orig.). 1985. pap. 12.00 (*0-929604-36-9*) Arkansas Ancestors.

McLane, Bobbie J. Saline County, Arkansas Census, 1860. 92p. (Orig.). 1986. pap. 15.00 (*0-929604-41-5*) Arkansas Ancestors.

McLane, Bobbie J., contrib. by. Alabama Soldiers (Revolution, War of 1812 & Indian Wars) Vol. 19: Surnames Ma. 101p. 1997. pap. 15.00 (*0-929604-81-4*) Arkansas Ancestors.

McLane, Bobbie J. & Allen, Desmond W. Arkansas 1850 Census Every-Name Index. 480p. 1995. 49.50 (*1-56546-063-4*) Arkansas Res.

— 1850 Census of Central Arkansas: Hot Spring, Jefferson, Montgomery, Perry, Prairie, Pulaski, Saline, Scott & Yell Counties. 119p. 1995. pap. 20.00 (*1-56546-065-0*) Arkansas Res.

— 1850 Census of Eastern Arkansas: Arkansas, Chicot, Crittenden, Desha, Greene, Mississippi, Monroe, Phillips, Poinsett & St. Francis Counties. 112p. 1995. pap. 20.00 (*1-56546-068-5*) Arkansas Res.

— 1850 Census of North Central Arkansas: Conway, Fulton, Independence, Izard, Jackson, Lawrence, Marion, Randolph, Searcy, Van Buren & White Counties. 153p. 1995. pap. 22.00 (*1-56546-067-7*) Arkansas Res.

— 1850 Census of Northwest Arkansas: Benton, Carroll, Crawford, Franklin, Johnson, Madison, Newton, Pope & Washington Counties. 170p. 1995. pap. 24.00 (*1-56546-064-2*) Arkansas Res.

— 1850 Census of Southern Arkansas: Ashley, Bradley, Clark, Dallas, Drew, Hempstead, Lafayette, Ouachita, Pike, Polk, Sevier & Union Counties. 182p. 1995. pap. 24.00 (*1-56546-066-9*) Arkansas Res.

McLane, Bobbie J. & Cline, Inez E. Garland County, Arkansas Tombstone Records Vol. 1: Eastern Area. 202p. (Orig.). 1970. pap. 18.00 (*0-929604-17-2*) Arkansas Ancestors.

— Garland County, Arkansas Tombstone Records Vol. 2: Western Area. 228p. (Orig.). 1969. pap. 18.00 (*0-929604-18-0*) Arkansas Ancestors.

— Garland County, Arkansas Tombstone Records Vol. 3: City of Hot Springs. 311p. (Orig.). 1973. pap. 28.00 (*0-929604-19-9*) Arkansas Ancestors.

— Index to Eighteen Forty Arkansas Census. 127p. (Orig.). 1967. pap. 15.00 (*0-929604-09-1*) Arkansas Ancestors.

McLane, Bobbie J. & Gandrud, Pauline J. Alabama Soldiers (Revolution, War of 1812 & Indian Wars) Vol. 1: Surnames A through Ba. 107p. (Orig.). 1975. pap. 15.00 (*0-929604-46-6*) Arkansas Ancestors.

— Alabama Soldiers (Revolution, War of 1812 & Indian Wars) Vol. 2: Surnames Be through Bond. 100p. (Orig.). 1977. pap. 15.00 (*0-929604-47-4*) Arkansas Ancestors.

— Alabama Soldiers (Revolution, War of 1812 & Indian Wars) Vol. 3: Surnames Bonner through Brynes. 152p. (Orig.). 1977. pap. 15.00 (*0-929604-48-2*) Arkansas Ancestors.

— Alabama Soldiers (Revolution, War of 1812 & Indian Wars) Vol. 4: Surnames Ca through Coker. 102p. (Orig.). 1978. pap. 15.00 (*0-929604-49-0*) Arkansas Ancestors.

— Alabama Soldiers (Revolution, War of 1812 & Indian Wars) Vol. 5: Surnames Cole through End Cs. 90p. (Orig.). 1978. pap. 15.00 (*0-929604-50-4*) Arkansas Ancestors.

— Alabama Soldiers (Revolution, War of 1812 & Indian Wars) Vol. 6: Surnames D. 128p. (Orig.). 1979. pap. 15.00 (*0-929604-51-2*) Arkansas Ancestors.

— Alabama Soldiers (Revolution, War of 1812 & Indian Wars) Vol. 7: Surnames E through Fl. 115p. (Orig.). 1983. pap. 15.00 (*0-929604-52-0*) Arkansas Ancestors.

— Alabama Soldiers (Revolution, War of 1812 & Indian Wars) Vol. 8: Surnames Forbes through Gary. 103p. (Orig.). 1983. pap. 15.00 (*0-929604-53-9*) Arkansas Ancestors.

— Alabama Soldiers (Revolution, War of 1812 & Indian Wars) Vol. 9: Surnames Gassaway through Gower. 98p. (Orig.). 1984. pap. 15.00 (*0-929604-54-7*) Arkansas Ancestors.

— Alabama Soldiers (Revolution, War of 1812 & Indian Wars) Vol. 10: Surnames Grace through Hamner. 109p. (Orig.). 1986. pap. 15.00 (*0-929604-55-5*) Arkansas Ancestors.

— Alabama Soldiers (Revolution, War of 1812 & Indian Wars) Vol. 11: Surnames Hanby through Henderson. 100p. (Orig.). 1988. pap. 15.00 (*0-929604-56-3*) Arkansas Ancestors.

— Alabama Soldiers (Revolution, War of 1812 & Indian Wars) Vol. 12: Surnames Hendon through Holland. 104p. (Orig.). 1989. pap. 15.00 (*0-929604-60-1*) Arkansas Ancestors.

— Alabama Soldiers (Revolution, War of 1812 & Indian Wars) Vol. 13: Surnames Holley through End Hs. 100p. (Orig.). 1990. pap. 15.00 (*0-929604-66-0*) Arkansas Ancestors.

— Alabama Soldiers (Revolution, War of 1812 & Indian Wars) Vol. 14: Surnames I through Jones, James. 102p. (Orig.). 1991. pap. 15.00 (*0-929604-71-7*) Arkansas Ancestors.

— Alabama Soldiers (Revolution, War of 1812 & Indian Wars) Vol. 16: Surnames Lacey Thru Lewis. 89p. (Orig.). 1995. pap. 15.00 (*0-929604-74-1*) Arkansas Ancestors.

— Alabama Soldiers (Revolution, War of 1812 & Indian Wars) Vol. 17: Surnames Lightfoot Thru Lynn. 89p. (Orig.). 1995. pap. 15.00 (*0-929604-75-X*) Arkansas Ancestors.

— Alabama Soldiers (Revolution, War of 1812 & Indian Wars) Vol.15: Surnames Jones, John Through K. 108p. (Orig.). 1992. pap. 15.00 (*0-929604-73-3*) Arkansas Ancestors.

McLane, Bobbie J. & Glazner, Capitola. Arkansas CSA Soldiers Vol. 1: Surnames A-D 1911 Census of Confederate Veterans. 160p. 1977. pap. 20.00 (*0-929604-28-8*) Arkansas Ancestors.

— Arkansas CSA Soldiers Vol. 2: Surnames E-Mc 1911 Census of Confederate Veterans. 171p. 1978. pap. 20.00 (*0-929604-29-6*) Arkansas Ancestors.

— Arkansas CSA Soldiers Vol. 3: Surnames M-Z 1911 Census of Confederate Veterans. 200p. 1979. pap. 25.00 (*0-929604-30-X*) Arkansas Ancestors.

— Hempstead County, Arkansas Census, 1860. 129p. (Orig.). 1969. pap. 15.00 (*0-929604-20-2*) Arkansas Ancestors.

— Jefferson County, Arkansas Census & Marriage, 1850, Bks. A & B. 115p. (Orig.). 1967. pap. 15.00 (*0-929604-07-5*) Arkansas Ancestors.

— Lafayette County, Arkansas Marriage Records, 1828-1907. 266p. (Orig.). 1982. pap. 25.00 (*0-929604-33-4*) Arkansas Ancestors.

— Marriage Records of Hempstead County, Arkansas, 1817-1875. 182p. (Orig.). 1969. pap. 22.00 (*0-929604-15-6*) Arkansas Ancestors.

— Missouri, an Index to the 1830 Census. 191p. (Orig.). 1966. pap. 25.00 (*0-929604-05-9*) Arkansas Ancestors.

— Mortality Schedules for Arkansas, 1850. 64p. (Orig.). 1968. pap. 15.00 (*0-929604-10-5*) Arkansas Ancestors.

— Mortality Schedules for Arkansas, 1860. 108p. (Orig.). 1969. pap. 15.00 (*0-929604-12-1*) Arkansas Ancestors.

— Mortality Schedules for Arkansas, 1870. 93p. (Orig.). 1971. pap. 15.00 (*0-929604-13-X*) Arkansas Ancestors.

— Mortality Schedules for Arkansas, 1880. 261p. (Orig.). 1975. pap. 28.00 (*0-929604-14-8*) Arkansas Ancestors.

— Pope County, Arkansas Census & Marriage, 1850, Bk. 1. 95p. (Orig.). 1966. pap. 15.00 (*0-929604-03-2*) Arkansas Ancestors.

— Pope County, Arkansas Census, 1860. 139p. (Orig.). 1967. pap. 15.00 (*0-929604-04-0*) Arkansas Ancestors.

— Pope County Arkansas Marriages, 1860-1892. 307p. (Orig.). 1972. pap. 25.00 (*0-929604-24-5*) Arkansas Ancestors.

— Sevier County, Arkansas Census, 1850 & Marriage Records Through 1852. 72p. (Orig.). 1964. pap. text 12.00 (*0-929604-00-8*) Arkansas Ancestors.

— Sevier County, Arkansas Census, 1860 & Marriage Records, Bk. 2. 145p. (Orig.). 1967. pap. 15.00 (*0-929604-06-7*) Arkansas Ancestors.

McLane, Bobbie J. & Hanks, Bill. Johnson County, Arkansas Census, 1870. 133p. (Orig.). 1989. pap. 18.00 (*0-929604-64-4*) Arkansas Ancestors.

— Logan County, Arkansas Marriage Records, the First Fifty Years. 219p. (Orig.). 1991. pap. 28.00 (*0-929604-68-7*) Arkansas Ancestors.

— Logan County Tax Book 1890: (Reconstructed 1890 Census) 118p. (Orig.). 1987. pap. 15.00 (*0-929604-42-3*) Arkansas Ancestors.

— Scott County, Arkansas Census, 1860. 147p. (Orig.). 1989. pap. 18.00 (*0-929604-62-8*) Arkansas Ancestors.

— Scott County, Arkansas Census, 1870. 221p. (Orig.). 1989. pap. 22.00 (*0-929604-63-6*) Arkansas Ancestors.

McLane, Bobbie J. & Harris, Mary S. Marriage Records of Independence County, Arkansas 1826-1877. 350p. 1970. pap. 28.00 (*0-929604-22-9*) Arkansas Ancestors.

McLane, Bobbie J. & Hubbard, Margaret. Saline County, Arkansas Marriage Records, 1836-1877. 105p. (Orig.). 1978. pap. 15.00 (*0-929604-32-6*) Arkansas Ancestors.

McLane, Bobbie J. & McConnell, Imogene. Johnson County, Arkansas Marriages, 1890-1908. 89p. (Orig.). 1990. pap. 15.00 (*0-929604-65-2*) Arkansas Ancestors.

McLane, Bobbie J. & Steele, Richard. Descendants of Hugh Jones of Orange County, VA. 239p. (Orig.). 1991. pap. 25.00 (*0-929604-77-6*) Arkansas Ancestors.

McLane, Bobbie J. & Syler, Allen B. Clark County, Arkansas - Obituaries & Death Notices, 1914-1921 Vol. 3: Southern Standard Newspaper. 117p. (Orig.). 1995. pap. 18.00 (*0-929604-78-4*) Arkansas Ancestors.

— Clark County, Arkansas Obituaries & Death Notices, 1869-1900, Vol. 1. 157p. (Orig.). 1991. pap. 20.00 (*0-929604-67-9*) Arkansas Ancestors.

— Clark County, Arkansas-Obituaries & Death Notices, 1901-1913 Vol. 2: Southern Standard Newspaper. 162p. (Orig.). 1992. pap. 22.00 (*0-929604-72-5*) Arkansas Ancestors.

McLane, Bobbie J., et al. Census Reconstruction Garland & Montgomery Counties, Arkansas, 1890. 175p. (Orig.). 1985. pap. 18.00 (*0-929604-34-2*) Arkansas Ancestors.

McLane, Bobbie J., jt. auth. see Allen, Desmond W.

McLane, Bobbie J., jt. auth. see Gandrud, Pauline J.

McLane, Bobbie Jones, see Jones McLane, Bobbie.

McLane, Carol E., jt. auth. see McLane, Charles B.

McLane, Carole, jt. auth. see McLane, Charles.

McLane, Charles & McLane, Carole. Islands of the Mid-Maine Coast Vol. III: Muscongus Bay & Monhegan Island. LC 91-67939. (Illus.). 304p. 1992. 55.00 (*0-88448-127-1*) Tilbury Hse.

— Islands of the Mid-Maine Coast Vol. III: Muscongus Bay to Monhegan. LC 91-67939. (Illus.). 304p. 1992. pap. 29.95 (*0-88448-128-X*) Tilbury Hse.

McLane, Charles B. Islands of the Mid-Maine Coast Vol. 1A: Blue Hill Bay. rev. ed. LC 83-82922. (Illus.). 160p. (Orig.). 1985. reprint ed. pap. 15.95 (*0-933858-02-7*) Tilbury Hse.

— Islands of the Mid-Maine Coast Vol. II: Mount Desert to Machias Bay. (Illus.). 406p. 1989. 45.00 (*0-933858-17-5*) Tilbury Hse.

— Islands of the Mid-Maine Coast Vol. IV: Pemaquid Point to the Kennebec. (Illus.). 288p. 1995. pap. 35.00 (*0-88448-146-8*) Tilbury Hse.

— Soviet Policy & the Chinese Communists, 1931-1946. LC 73-37861. (Select Bibliographies Reprint Ser.). 1977. reprint ed. 18.95 (*0-8369-9964-9*) Ayer.

— Soviet-Third World Relations Vol. 3: Soviet-African Relations. 190p. 1975. pap. text 46.00 (*0-903424-08-8*) Col U Pr.

McLane, Charles B. & McLane, Carol E. Islands of the Mid-Maine Coast Vol. 1: Penobscot Bay. LC 96-53524. (Illus.). 512p. 1997. pap. 35.00 (*0-88448-185-9*) Tilbury Hse.

— Islands of the Mid-Maine Coast Vol. 1: Penobscot Bay. 2nd rev. ed. LC 96-53524. (Illus.). 512p. 1997. 55.00 (*0-88448-184-0*) Tilbury Hse.

McLane, Gerard, jt. auth. see McLane, Kathryn.

McLane, Graf, Raulerson & Middleton Staff. New Hampshire Environmental Law. 2nd ed. LC 94-73602. 341p. 1994. pap. text 89.00 (*0-86587-447-6*) Gov Insts.

An Asterisk (*) at the beginning of an entry indicates that the title is appearing for the first time.

McLane, Gretel B. Kalia & the King's Horse. (Illus.). 88p. (J). (gr. 3-7). 1994. pap. 8.95 (*0-916630-70-6*) Pr Pacifica.

McLane, Helen J., jt. auth. see O'Hara, Thomas E.

McLane, Joan B. & McNamee, Gillian D. Early Literacy. (Developing Child Ser.). (Illus.). 160p. 1990. 24.95 (*0-674-22164-8*); pap. text 7.95 (*0-674-22165-6*) HUP.

McLane, John R. Indian Nationalism & the Early Congress. LC 77-72127. 417p. reprint ed. pap. 129.30 (*0-8357-8920-9*, 203339700085) Bks Demand.

McLane, John R., Jr. Judge McLane: His Life & Times. (Illus.). 512p. 1996. 35.00 (*0-914339-58-3*) P E Randall Pub.

McLane, Kathryn & McLane, Gerard. Tastefully Vegan: Creative Vegetarian Cooking. (Illus.). 302p. 1998. pap. 21.95 (*0-9664739-0-6*) Challedon Pub.

McLane, Larry L. First There Was Twogood: Pictorial History of Northern Josephine County. LC 95-188944. (Illus.). 432p. (Orig.). (J). (ps-12). 1995. 34.95 (*0-9621587-0-4*) Sexton Enter.

McLane, Louis, ed. see U. S. Treasury Department Staff.

McLane, Lucy N. In Tune with Beauty. LC 58-59534. (Illus.). xiv, 81p. 1959. 14.95 (*0-87015-083-9*) Pacific Bks.

***McLane, Maureen N.** Romanticism & the Human Sciences: Poetry, Population, & the Discourse of the Species. LC 99-87280. (Cambridge Studies in Romanticism). 324p. 2000. write for info. (*0-521-77348-2*) Cambridge U Pr.

McLane, Merrill F. The Adventure of Blueberrying: On Cape Ann Massachusetts. LC 93-74664. (Illus.). (Orig.). 1994. pap. 12.95 (*0-938813-06-4*) Carderock Pr.

— East from Granada: Hidden Andalusia & Its People. LC 88-21851. (Illus.). 184p. (Orig.). 1996. pap. 16.95 (*0-938813-07-2*) Carderock Pr.

— Proud Outcasts: The Gypsies of Spain. LC 86-70790. (Illus.). 192p. (Orig.). 1987. pap. 45.00 (*0-938813-03-X*) Carderock Pr.

McLane, Michael. Sedimentology. (Illus.). 448p. (C). 1995. text 71.95 (*0-19-507868-3*) OUP.

McLane, Mike, ed. see Nelson, Ray & Kelly, Doug.

McLane, Mike, ed. see Nelson, Ray & Mohr, Julie.

McLane, Mike, ed. see Nelson, Ray, et al.

McLane, Nanette, jt. auth. see Knapp, Shirley.

McLane, Robert M. Reminiscences, 1827-1897. LC 72-79831. (China Library). 1972. reprint ed. lib. bdg. 21.00 (*0-8420-1375-X*) Scholarly Res Inc.

McLane, S., jt. ed. see Adamek, Jiri.

McLaney, E. J. & Atrill, Peter. Introduction to Accounting. LC 98-7070. 1998. write for info. (*0-13-989716-X*) P-H.

McLaney, E. J., jt. auth. see Atrill, Peter.

McLaney, Eddie. Business Finance: Theory & Practice. 4th ed. 448p. 1997. pap. 64.50 (*0-273-62694-9*, Pub. by Pitman Pub) Trans-Atl Phila.

McLaney, Eddie, jt. auth. see Atrill, Peter.

McLaren. Australian Literature. 1990. pap. text. write for info. (*0-582-71279-3*, Pub. by Addison-Wesley) Longman.

— Business & Administrative Communication. 1993. text. write for info. (*0-256-13177-5*, Irwn McGrw-H) McGrw-H Hghr Educ.

Mclaren. Dictionary. (ZUL & ENG.). 1994. 39.95 (*0-320-03459-3*) Fr & Eur.

McLaren. E-Commerce. LC 99-206213. (Computer Applications Ser.). 1999. pap. 34.95 (*0-538-68918-8*) Thomson Learn.

— Understanding & Using the Internet. 3rd ed. (Computer Applications Ser.). 1998. pap. 34.95 (*0-538-72132-4*) S-W Pub.

McLaren, A. Douglas & Peterson, George H., eds. Soil Biochemistry, Vol. 1. LC 66-27705. 523p. reprint ed. pap. 162.20 (*0-8357-3538-9*, 202711700001) Bks Demand.

McLaren, A. Douglas, jt. ed. see Paul, Eldor A.

McLaren, Alan, jt. auth. see Indianapolis Community Hospital Staff.

McLaren, Alex C. Transmission Electron Microscopy of Minerals & Rocks. (Topics in Mineral Physics & Chemistry Ser.: No. 2). (Illus.). 399p. (C). 1991. text 95.00 (*0-521-35098-0*) Cambridge U Pr.

McLaren, Angus. History of Contraception: From Antiquity to the Present Day. 1992. pap. 27.95 (*0-631-18729-4*) Blackwell Pubs.

— A Prescription for Murder: The Victorian Serial Killings of Dr. Thomas Neill Cream. 234p. 1995. pap. 12.95 (*0-226-56068-6*) U Ch Pr.

— A Prescription for Murder: The Victorian Serial Killings of Dr. Thomas Neill Cream. LC 92-20219. (Chicago Series on Sexuality, History, & Society). (Illus.). 234p. (C). 1998. 22.50 (*0-226-56067-8*) U Ch Pr.

— Reproductive Rituals: Perceptions of Fertility in Britain from the Sixteenth Century to the Nineteenth Century. 208p. (Orig.). 1985. pap. 13.95 (*0-416-37460-3*, NO. 9340) Routledge.

— The Trials of Masculinity: Policing Sexual Boundaries, 1870-1930. LC 96-29523. (Chicago Series on Sexuality, History, & Society). 288p. 1997. 24.95 (*0-226-50067-5*) U Ch Pr.

— Trials of Masculinity: Policing Sexual Boundaries, 1870-1930. 1999. pap. text 16.00 (*0-226-50068-3*) U Ch Pr.

— Twentieth-Century Sexuality: A History. LC 98-33145. (Family, Sexuality & Social Relations in the Past Ser.). 304p. 1999. 59.95 (*0-631-20813-5*); pap. 24.92 (*0-631-20812-7*) Blackwell Pubs.

McLaren, Angus & McLaren, Arlene T. The Bedroom & the State: The Changing Practices & Politics of Contraception & Abortion in Canada, 1880-1996. 2nd ed. LC 99-179693. 208p. 1998. pap. text 19.95 (*0-19-541318-0*) OUP.

McLaren, Anne. The Chinese Femme Fatale: Stories from the Ming Period. (University of Sydney East Asian Ser.: No. 8). 176p. (C). 1994. pap. text 17.00 (*0-646-14924-5*, Pub. by Wild Peony Pty) UH Pr.

— Germ Cells & Soma: A New Look at an Old Problem. LC 81-2971. (Mrs. Hepsa Ely Silliman Memorial Lectures: No. 45). 128p. reprint ed. pap. 39.70 (*0-7837-2784-4*, 204317600006) Bks Demand.

— Political Culture in the Reign of Elizabeth I: Queen & Commonwealth, 1558-1585. LC 99-22403. (Ideas in Context Ser.: No. 56). 286p. 2000. text 54.95 (*0-521-65144-1*) Cambridge U Pr.

McLaren, Anne, jt. ed. see Finnane, Antonia.

McLaren, Anne, jt. ed. see Le Douarin, Nicole.

McLaren, Anne E. Chinese Popular Culture & Ming Chantefables. LC 98-12264. 340p. 1998. 108.00 (*90-04-10998-6*) Brill Academic Pubs.

McLaren, Arlene, jt. ed. see Gaskell, Jane.

McLaren, Arlene T., jt. auth. see McLaren, Angus.

McLaren, Arthur D. Soil Biochemistry, Vol. 4. Paul, E. A., ed. LC 66-27705. (Books in Soils & the Environment). (Illus.). 296p. 1975. reprint ed. pap. 91.80 (*0-608-07899-9*, 206788000004) Bks Demand.

McLaren, Arthur D. & Peterson, George H., eds. Soil Biochemistry, Vol. 2. LC 66-27705. (Books in Soil Science: Nos. 1 & 2). 547p. reprint ed. pap. 169.60 (*0-8357-3539-7*, 202711700002) Bks Demand.

***McLaren, Brian D.** The Church on the Other Side: Doing Ministry in the Postmodern Matrix. LC 00-39261. 2000. write for info. (*0-310-23707-6*) Zondervan.

McLaren, Brian D. Finding Faith. LC 98-48165. 1999. 17.99 (*0-310-22542-6*) HarpC.

— Reinventing Your Church. LC 97-46191. 208p. 1998. pap. 12.99 (*0-310-21654-0*) Zondervan.

McLaren, Bruce J. Black Widow: The Story of the Northrop P-61. (Illus.). 122p. 1993. pap. 16.95 (*0-934575-11-8*) Vip Pubs.

— The dBASE Management with dBASE 4 & 3 Plus. (C). 1992. pap. 16.50 (*0-06-500529-5*) Addson-Wesley Educ.

— Double Menace: P/F-82 Twin Mustang. (Illus.). 74p. 1994. pap. 16.95 (*0-934575-12-6*) Vip Pubs.

— Microcomputer Applications in Business. (C). 1997. 62.67 (*0-673-46383-4*) Addson-Wesley Educ.

McLaren, Bruce J. Working with Lotus 1-2-3. (C). 1997. 19.33 (*0-06-500530-9*) Addson-Wesley Educ.

McLaren, Bruce J. Understanding & Using Microsoft Access for Windows 95. 2nd ed. (Microcomputing Ser.). 450p. (C). 1996. mass mkt. 35.95 (*0-314-07233-0*) West Pub.

— Understanding & Using Microsoft Access 2.0. LC 94-31178. (Microcomputing Ser.). 512p. (C). 1995. mass mkt. 36.95 (*0-314-04653-4*) West Pub.

— Understanding & Using Microsoft Access 97. LC 98-115310. (Understanding & Using Ser.). 1997. pap. text 42.95 (*0-538-71966-4*) S-W Pub.

— Understanding & Using Microsoft Excel 97. (Understanding & Using Ser.). 1997. pap. 41.95 (*0-538-71986-9*) S-W Pub.

— Understanding & Using the Internet. (Microcomputing Ser.). 150p. (C). 1995. mass mkt. 15.95 (*0-314-06411-7*) West Pub.

Mclaren, Bruce J. Understanding & Using the Internet. 2nd ed. LC 96-43005. (West's Microcomputing Ser.). 150p. 1996. mass mkt. 18.95 (*0-314-20602-7*) West Pub.

McLaren, Bruce J. Understanding Internet. Date not set. pap. text, teacher ed. write for info. (*0-314-07364-7*) West Pub.

— West's Essentials of MS Access 2.0. LC 95-150067. (DF - Computer Applications Ser.). 1995. mass mkt. 9.50 (*0-314-04633-X*) West Pub.

— West's Intermediate Microsoft Access. 11th ed. LC 94-186166. (DF - Computer Applications Ser.). 1994. pap. 11.00 (*0-314-02872-2*) West Pub.

— West's Intermediate MS Access 2.0. LC 95-128545. (DF - Computer Applications Ser.). (C). 1995. mass mkt. 12.75 (*0-314-04642-9*) West Pub.

McLaren, Christie. The Last Stand. 2002. write for info. (*0-385-25760-0*) Doubleday.

McLaren, Clemence. Dance for the Land. LC 98-33761. 160p. (J). 1999. 16.00 (*0-689-82393-2*) Atheneum Yung Read.

— Inside the Walls of Troy. (YA). (gr. 7 up). Date not set. 16.00 (*0-614-19208-0*) Atheneum Yung Read.

— Inside the Walls of Troy. 208p. (YA). (gr. 7 up). 1996. 16.00 (*0-689-31820-0*) Atheneum Yung Read.

— Inside the Walls of Troy: A Novel of the Women Who Lived the Trojan War. 1998. 10.09 (*0-606-13519-7*, Pub. by Turtleback) Demco.

— Inside the Walls of Troy: A Novel of the Women Who Lived the Trojan War. 208p. (YA). (gr. 7 up). 1998. reprint ed. mass mkt. 4.99 (*0-440-22749-6*, LLL BDD) BDD Bks Young Read.

***McLaren, Clemence.** Waiting for Odysseus. LC 99-24572. (Illus.). 160p. (YA). (gr. 7). 2000. 17.00 (*0-689-82875-6*) Atheneum Yung Read.

McLaren, Darcee L., jt. ed. see Porter, Jennifer E.

McLaren, David. Lockheed T-33: A Photo Chronicle. LC 98-85940. (Illus.). 128p. (Orig.). 1999. pap. 24.95 (*0-7643-0646-4*) Schiffer.

McLaren, David R. Lockheed P-80/F-80: A Photo Chronicle. LC 95-72398. (Illus.). 184p. (YA). (gr. 10-13). 1996. pap. 24.95 (*0-88740-907-5*) Schiffer.

— Mustangs over Korea: The North American F-51 at War, 1950-1953. LC 98-87295. (Illus.). 184p. 1999. 45.00 (*0-7643-0721-5*) Schiffer.

— Republic F-84, Thunderjet, Thunderstreak & Thunderflash: A Photo Chronicle. LC 97-80165. (Illus.). 208p. 1998. pap. 29.95 (*0-7643-0444-5*) Schiffer.

McLaren, David R. & Isham, Marty J. Lockheed F-94 Starfire: A Photo Chronicle. LC 92-62387. (Illus.). 127p. (Orig.). 1993. pap. 19.95 (*0-88740-451-0*) Schiffer.

— Northrop F-89 Scorpion: A Photo Chronicle. (Illus.). 128p. 1996. pap. 24.95 (*0-7643-0065-2*) Schiffer.

McLaren, Deborah. Rethinking Tourism & Ecotravel: The Paving of Paradise & What You Can Do to Stop It. (Illus.). 190p. 1997. 48.00 (*1-56549-066-5*); pap. 21.95 (*1-56549-065-7*) Kumarian Pr.

McLaren, Diane J. Schistosoma Mansoni: The Parasite Surface in Relation to Host Immunity. LC 80-40955. (Tropical Medicine Research Studies: No. 1). (Illus.). 245p. reprint ed. pap. 76.00 (*0-8357-3527-3*, 203424700089) Bks Demand.

McLaren, Digby, jt. ed. see Mungall, Constance.

McLaren, Donald S., ed. Nutrition in the Community: A Critical Look at Nutrition. 2nd ed. LC 82-6992. (Wiley-Interscience Publications). 480p. reprint ed. pap. 148.80 (*0-7837-4517-6*, 204429600001) Bks Demand.

McLaren, Duncan, et al. Tomorrow's World: Britain's Share in a Sustainable Future. 256p. 1997. pap. 26.00 (*1-85383-511-0*, Pub. by Escan Pubns) Island Pr.

***McLaren, Glen.** Big Mobs: The Story of Australian Cattlemen. 2000. pap. 19.95 (*1-86368-247-3*, Pub. by Fremantle Arts) Intl Spec Bk.

— Life's Been Good: The Children of the Great Depression. 272p. 1999. pap. 19.95 (*1-86368-265-1*, Pub. by Fremantle Arts) Intl Spec Bk.

McLaren, Graham. Ceramics of the 1950s. (Illus.). 40p. 1997. pap. 8.50 (*0-7478-0336-6*, Pub. by Shire Pubns) Parkwest Pubns.

McLaren, I. The Sten Screen: Making & Using a Low-Cost Printing Process. 20p. (Orig.). 1983. pap. 10.00 (*1-85339-048-8*, Pub. by Intermed Tech) Stylus Pub VA.

***McLaren, Ian R.** Communication Excellence: Using NLP to Supercharge Your Business Skills. (Illus.). 220p. 2000. pap. 19.95 (*1-899836-39-X*, Pub. by Crown Hse) LPC Group.

McLaren, J. A New Concise Xhosa-English Dictionary. 193p. 1994. pap. 35.00 (*0-7859-8718-5*) Fr & Eur.

McLaren, James S. Power & Politics in Palestine: The Jews & the Governing of Their Land 100 BC-AD 70. (Journal for the Study of the New Testament, Supplement Ser.: No. 63). 248p. (C). 1991. 70.00 (*1-85075-319-9*, Pub. by Sheffield Acad) CUP Services.

***McLaren, James S.** Turbulent Times? Josephus & Scholarship on Judaea in the First Century CE. (JSP Supplement Ser.: No. 29). 312p. 1998. 85.00 (*1-85075-891-3*, Pub. by Sheffield Acad) CUP Services.

McLaren, John. New Pacific Literatures: Culture & Environment in the European Pacific. LC 92-1672. 416p. 1993. text 20.00 (*0-8153-0496-X*, H1054) Garland.

— Writing in Hope & Fear: Literature As Politics in Postwar Australia. LC 95-51531. 285p. (C). 1996. text 64.95 (*0-521-56146-9*) Cambridge U Pr.

McLaren, John, et al, eds. Law for the Elephant, Law for the Beaver: Essays in the Legal History of the North American West. 336p. 1992. pap. 19.95 (*0-88977-072-7*) Ninth Judicial CHS.

McLaren, John & Coward, Harold, eds. Religious Conscience, the State, & the Law: Historical Contexts & Contemporary Significance. LC 97-52270. (Series in Religious Studies). 288p. (C). 1998. text 65.50 (*0-7914-4001-X*); pap. text 21.95 (*0-7914-4002-8*) State U NY Pr.

***McLaren, Joseph.** African Visions: Literary Images, Political Change & Social Struggle in Contemporary Africa. Mwaria, Cheryl B. & Federici, Silvia, eds. 296p. 2000. pap. 24.95 (*0-275-97102-3*, Praeger Trade) Greenwood.

McLaren, Joseph. Langston Hughes: Folk Dramatist in the Protest Tradition, 1921-1943, 181. LC 95-48416. (Contributions in Afro-American & African Studies: Vol. 181). 248p. 1997. 49.95 (*0-313-28719-8*, Greenwood Pr) Greenwood.

McLaren, Karla. Further into the Garden: Discovering Your Chakras. LC 97-93580. (Illus.). 177p. (Orig.). 1997. pap. 9.00 (*0-9656583-1-7*) Laughing Tree Pr.

— Rebuilding the Garden: Healing the Spiritual Wounds of Childhood Sexual Assault. LC 96-95404. (Illus.). 241p. 1997. pap. 11.00 (*0-9656583-0-9*) Laughing Tree Pr.

— Your Aura & Your Chakras: The Owner's Manual. LC 98-22486. (Illus.). 288p. 1999. reprint ed. pap. 14.95 (*1-57863-047-9*) Weiser.

McLaren, Keith. Light on the Water. 160p. 1998. 35.00 (*1-55054-658-9*) DGL.

Mclaren, Keith. Light on the Water: Early Photography of Coastal British Columbia. LC 98-25896. (Illus.). 160p. 1998. 35.00 (*0-295-97748-5*) U of Wash Pr.

McLaren, Ken. Yes, with Variations. 72p. 1983. pap. 10.00 (*0-939196-00-X*) Smith.

McLaren, Linie L., compiled by. High Living: Recipes from Southern Climes. LC 72-9798. (Cookery Americana Ser.). 1973. reprint ed. pap. 13.95 (*0-405-05051-8*) Ayer.

McLaren, Lynda H., ed. see DOE Technical Information Center Staff.

McLaren, Lynn. Ebb Tide - Flood Tide: Beaufort County...Jewel of the Low Country. rev. ed. LC 91-21741. (Illus.). 120p. 1995. 36.95 (*1-881576-47-7*) Providence Hse.

McLaren, M. Stevenson & Edinburgh. LC 73-21775. (English Biography Ser.: No. 31). 1974. lib. bdg. 59.00 (*0-8383-1831-2*) M S G Haskell Hse.

McLaren, Malcolm, frwd. The Album Cover Art of Punk. (Illus.). 112p. (C). 1998. pap. 19.95 (*3-927258-61-X*) Gingko Press.

McLaren, Maria. Seven with One Blow. LC 94-32722. 24p. (J). (gr. 1-6). 1994. pap. 6.00 (*0-88734-517-4*) Players Pr.

McLaren, Mike. The Book of Crests of Scottish-American Clans. (Illus.). 273p. (Orig.). 1991. pap. 20.00 (*1-55613-401-0*) Heritage Bk.

McLaren-Owens, Iain. Articles on the Order of the Magi & Its History. 2nd ed. LC 97-77052. (Astro-Cards Reprints Ser.). (Illus.). 229p. 1997. reprint ed. pap. 22.00 (*1-885500-16-5*, AR10) Astro-Cards.

— Astro-Degree Tables: Zodiacal Data. LC 94-96299. (Astro-Degrees Ser.). 200p. 1994. pap. text 24.00 (*1-885500-00-9*, AD2) Astro-Cards.

— Spreads Set & Card Titles. LC 94-96298. (Astro-Cards System Ser.). 138p. 1994. pap. text 15.00 (*1-885500-01-7*, AC2) Astro-Cards.

McLaren-Owens, Iain, ed. see Richmond, Olney H.

McLaren-Owens, Iain, ed. & intro. see Richmond, Olney H.

McLaren-Owens, Iain, ed. & intro. see Whitehead, Willis F.

McLaren-Owens, Iain, ed. & pref. see Richmond, Olney H.

McLaren, Paul & Ladd. Soil Biochemistry, Vol. 5. (Books in Soils, Plants & the Environment: Vol. 9). (Illus.). 504p. 1981. text 210.00 (*0-8247-1131-9*) Dekker.

***McLaren, Peter.** Che Guevara, Paulo Freire & the Pedagogy of Revolution. LC 99-32890. 264p. 2000. 70.00 (*0-8476-9532-8*, Pub. by Rowman); pap. 22.95 (*0-8476-9533-6*) Rowman.

McLaren, Peter. Critical Pedagogy & Predatory Culture: Oppositional Politics in a Postmodern Era. LC 94-12153. 320p. (C). (gr. 13). 1994. 85.00 (*0-415-06424-4*, B4717) Routledge.

— Critical Pedagogy & Predatory Culture: Oppositional Politics in a Postmodern Era. LC 94-12153. 320p. (C). 1995. pap. 24.99 (*0-415-11756-9*, B4721) Routledge.

— Life in Schools. 3rd ed. 352p. (C). 1997. pap. 51.00 (*0-8013-1771-1*) Addison-Wesley.

— Life in Schools: An Introduction to Critical Pedagogy in the Foundations of Education. 2nd ed. LC 93-17627. 272p. (C). 1994. pap. text 31.95 (*0-8013-0638-8*, 78573) Longman.

Mclaren, Peter. Life in Schools: An Introduction to Critical Pedagogy in the Foundations of Education. 3rd ed. LC 97-18730. 1997. pap. write for info. (*0-8013-1772-X*) Longman.

McLaren, Peter. Revolutionary Multiculturalism. LC 97-15178. (C). 1997. pap. 27.00 (*0-8133-2571-4*, Pub. by Westview) HarpC.

— Schooling As Ritual Performance: Towards a Political Economy of Educational Symbols & Gestures. LC 99-25946. 432p. 1999. 60.00 (*0-8476-9195-0*) Rowman.

— Schooling As Ritual Performance: Towards a Political Economy of Educational Symbols & Gestures. 3rd ed. LC 99-25946. 432p. 1999. pap. 22.95 (*0-8476-9196-9*) Rowman.

McLaren, Peter & Lankshear, Colin, eds. Politics of Liberation: Paths from Freire. LC 93-825. 288p. (C). 1994. pap. 24.99 (*0-415-09127-6*, B0844) Routledge.

— Politics of Liberation: Paths from Freire. LC 93-825. 280p. (C). (gr. 13). 1994. text 62.50 (*0-415-09126-8*, B0840) Routledge.

McLaren, Peter & Leonard, Peter, eds. Paulo Freire: A Critical Encounter. LC 92-9965. 224p. (C). 1992. pap. 24.99 (*0-415-08792-9*, A9846) Routledge.

McLaren, Peter, et al. Rethinking Media Literacy: A Critical Pedagogy of Representations. LC 94-40539. (Counterpoints Ser.: Vol. 4). XVII, 260p. (C). 1995. pap. text 29.95 (*0-8204-1802-1*) P Lang Pubng.

McLaren, Peter, jt. auth. see Ovando, Carlos.

McLaren, Peter, jt. ed. see Giroux, Henry A.

McLaren, Peter, jt. ed. see Kanpol, Barry.

McLaren, Peter L. & Giarelli, James M., eds. Critical Theory & Educational Research. LC 94-11201. (SUNY Series, Teacher Empowerment & School Reform). 332p. (C). 1995. text 74.50 (*0-7914-2367-0*); pap. text 24.95 (*0-7914-2368-9*) State U NY Pr.

McLaren, Peter L., jt. ed. see Giroux, Henry A.

McLaren, Peter L., jt. ed. see Lankshear, Colin.

McLaren, Peter L., jt. ed. see Sleeter, Christine E.

McLaren, Philip. Sweet Water-Stolen Land. 1993. pap. 14.95 (*0-7022-2551-7*, Pub. by Univ Queensland Pr) Intl Spec Bk.

McLaren, R. G., jt. auth. see Cameron, K.

McLaren, Robert I. Organizational Dilemmas. LC 81-19745. (Illus.). 140p. reprint ed. pap. 43.40 (*0-8357-4601-1*, 203753400008) Bks Demand.

— The Saskatchewan Practice of Public Administration in Historical Perspective. LC 97-38813. (Canadian Studies: Vol. 19). 240p. 1997. 89.95 (*0-7734-8445-0*) E Mellen.

McLaren, Ronald. Solving Moral Problems: A Strategy for Practical Inquiry. LC 88-31730. 84p. (C). 1989. pap. text 14.95 (*0-87484-885-7*, 885) Mayfield Pub.

McLaren, Ronald, et al. Aesthetic & Ethical Values in Japanese Culture. (Occasional Papers, Institute for Education on Japan: Vol. 1, No. 4). 48p. (C). 1990. reprint ed. pap. 5.00 (*0-9619977-6-1*) Earlham Pr.

McLaren, Rory S. Troubleshooting Hydraulic Components Using Leakage Path Analysis Methods. 450p. (C). 1993. pap. text 49.95 (*0-9639619-1-8*) R McLaren FPT.

McLaren, Roy. Consensus: A Liberal Looks at His Party. 128p. 1994. pap. 5.95 (*0-88962-271-X*) Mosaic.

McLaren, S. B. & Braun, J. K., eds. GIS Applications in Mammalogy. (Illus.). 41p. (Orig.). 1993. pap. 10.00 (*1-883090-06-7*) OK Museum.

McLaren, Teri. Song of Time. (Gathering Ser.). 304p. 1996. mass mkt. 5.50 (*0-06-105622-7*, HarperPrism) HarpC.

McLaren, Tim, jt. auth. see Myers, Stephen.

McLaren, Walter W. Japanese Government Documents: Of the Meiji Era, 2 vols., Vol. 1. LC 79-65472. (Studies in Japanese History & Civilization). 249p. 1979. reprint ed. lib. bdg. 72.50 (*0-313-26912-2*, U6912) Greenwood.

— Japanese Government Documents: Of the Meiji Era, 2 vols., Vol. 2. LC 79-65472. (Studies in Japanese History & Civilization). 681p. 1979. reprint ed. lib. bdg. 89.50 (*0-313-26913-0*, U6913) Greenwood.

M

An Asterisk (*) at the beginning of an entry indicates that the title is appearing for the first time.

— Political History of Japan During the Meiji Era, 1867-1912. 379p. 1966. 35.00 (*0-7146-2018-1*, Pub. by F Cass Pubs) Intl Spec Bk.

*****McLarey, Kristina Thermaenius, et al.** When You Take a Pig to a Party. LC 99-36897. (Illus.). 32p. (J). (gr. k-4). 2000. 15.95 (*0-531-30257-1*); lib. bdg. 16.99 (*0-531-33257-8*) Orchard Bks Watts.

*****McLarey, Myra.** Water from the Well. 256p. 2000. pap. 12.00 (*0-8021-3716-4*, Grove) Grove-Atltic.

McLarey, Myra. Water from the Well. 256p. 1996. pap. 11.00 (*0-684-83097-3*) S&S Trade.

McLarin, Kim. Taming It Down. LC 99-20911. 327p. 1999. mass mkt. 13.99 (*0-446-67574-1*, Pub. by Warner Bks) Little.

— Taming It Down: A Novel. LC 97-47035. 320p. 1998. 24.00 (*0-688-15516-2*, Wm Morrow) Morrow Avon.

McLarnan, Timothy, tr. see Uspenskii, V. A.

McLarnan, Timothy, tr. see Vorobyov, N. N.

McLarney, James J. The Theism of Edgar Sheffied Brightman. LC 75-3089. reprint ed. 29.50 (*0-404-59087-X*) AMS Pr.

McLarney, William O. Freshwater Aquaculture Book: A Handbook of Small Scale Fish Culture in North America. 2nd ed. LC 98-12614. (Illus.). 602p. 1998. pap. text 45.00 (*0-88179-123-7*) Hartley & Marks.

McLarty, Barbara L., ed. A Printmaker's World: Jack McLarty (1943-1996) LC 96-95351. (Illus.). 136p. (Orig.). 1997. 70.00 (*0-9644916-2-1*); pap. 35.00 (*0-9644916-3-X*) McLartys Choice.

— World Watcher-Jack McLarty: 50 Years 1944-1994. (Illus.). 119p. 1995. 70.00 (*0-9644916-0-5*); pap. 35.00 (*0-9644916-1-3*) McLartys Choice.

McLarty, Barbara L., ed. see McLarty, Jack.

McLarty, Bruce. Journey of Faith: Walking with Jesus Through the Gospel of John. 357p. 1997. pap. 14.95 (*0-945441-25-8*) Res Pubns AR.

McLarty, Carol L., et al, eds. 1995 Florida Statistical Abstract. 29th ed. 760p. 1995. 44.95 (*0-8130-1375-5*); pap. 29.95 (*0-8130-1376-3*) U Press Fla.

McLarty, Colin. Elementary Categories, Elementary Toposes. (Oxford Logic Guides Ser.: No. 21). (Illus.). 278p. (C). 1996. pap. text 45.00 (*0-19-851473-5*) OUP.

McLarty, Donald. The Deep Blue Seize. large type ed. 384p. 1992. pap. 16.99 (*0-7089-7157-1*) Ulverscroft.

McLarty, Donald G. Essentials of Clinical Examination: A Question & Answer Guide for Students. 158p. 1991. pap. text 16.95 (*0-7020-1512-1*, Pub. by W B Saunders) Saunders.

McLarty, Jack. Michael Folden Vol. 1: The Language of Enigma. McLarty, Barbara L., ed. (Illus.). 15p. 1997. pap. 6.00 (*0-9644916-4-8*) McLartys Choice.

McLarty, John, jt. auth. see Melashenko, E. Lonnie.

McLary, Dan. Plows, Peacocks & Stars. Date not set. write for info. (*0-9659632-6-8*) Verda Publ.

McLary, Kathleen. Amish Style: Clothing, Home Furnishing, Toys, Dolls, & Quilts. LC 92-43967. 128p. (C). 1993. 39.95 (*0-253-33622-8*); pap. 24.95 (*0-253-20820-3*) Ind U Pr.

McLatchie, G. Oxford Handbook of Clinical & Operative Surgery. (Illus.). 1990. pap. 32.50 (*0-19-261710-9*) OUP.

— Skilful Karate. pap. write for info. (*0-7136-5779-0*, 91944, Pub. by A & C Blk) Midpt Trade.

McLatchie, G., et al, eds. ABC of Sports Medicine. (Illus.). 144p. (Orig.). 1995. pap. text 27.00 (*0-7279-0844-8*, Pub. by BMJ Pub) Login Brothers Bk Co.

McLatchie, G. & Leaper, David J., eds. Oxford Handbook of Operative Surgery. (Illus.). 734p. 1996. pap. 34.50 (*0-19-262097-5*) OUP.

McLatchie, G. & Lennox, C. M., eds. The Soft Tissues: Trauma & Sports Injuries. 496p. 1993. pap. text 67.50 (*0-7506-3065-5*, 71307) Buttrwrth-Heinemann.

McLatchie, G., et al. The Essentials of Sports Medicine. 2nd ed. (Illus.). 272p. (Orig.). 1993. pap. text 53.00 (*0-443-04541-0*) Church.

*****McLauchlan, Gordon.** Insight Guide to New Zealand. 1998. pap. 31.88 (*0-88729-728-5*) Langenscheidt.

McLauchlan, William P. American Legal Processes. LC 76-26579. (Viewpoints on American Politics Ser.). 233p. reprint ed. pap. 72.30 (*0-7837-3497-2*, 205783000008) Bks Demand.

— Federal Court Caseloads. LC 83-21270. 219p. 1984. 49.95 (*0-275-91226-4*, C1226, Praeger Pubs) Greenwood.

— The Indiana State Constitution: A Reference Guide, 25. LC 95-47184. (Reference Guides to the State Constitutions of the United States Ser.: No. 25). 208p. 1996. lib. bdg. 79.50 (*0-313-29208-6*, Greenwood Pr) Greenwood.

McLauchlan, William P., jt. auth. see McGillem, Clare D.

McLaughin, Robert & Sasser, Susan B. Fix Your Own LAN. 2nd ed. LC 94-21851. 89p. 1994. pap. 27.95 (*1-55828-354-4*, MIS Pr) IDG Bks.

McLaughlin. Advanced Nursing & Health Care Research. (Illus.). 393p. 1990. text 69.00 (*0-7216-3098-7*, W B Saunders Co) Harcrt Hlth Sci Grp.

— Introduction to Language Disorders. 2001. pap. 44.00 (*1-56593-116-5*) Singular Publishing.

— Powers of Their Own. 1999. 27.50 (*0-06-016781-5*) HarperTrade.

— Structural Steel Design/Fabric Drawing. (Construction & Building Trades Ser.). 1997. teacher ed. 16.95 (*0-8273-7314-7*) Delmar.

McLaughlin & Hart, eds. Cyclopedia of American Government, 3 vols., Each Volume. 1990. 24.50 (*0-8446-1142-5*) Peter Smith.

McLaughlin, Andrew M. & Maloney, William A. The European Automobile Industry: Multi-Level Governance, Policy & Politics. LC 98-31831. (Routledge Research in European Public Policy Ser.). 1999. 85.00 (*0-415-11329-6*) Routledge.

McLaughlin, A. C. Report on the Diplomatic Archives of the Department of State, 1789-1840. rev. ed. (CI Ser.). 1906. reprint ed. pap. 25.00 (*0-527-00682-3*) Periodicals Srv.

McLaughlin, Alastair, tr. see Kitaguchi, Suehiro.

McLaughlin, Andrew. Regarding Nature: Industrialism & Deep Ecology. LC 92-14076. (SUNY Series in Radical, Social & Political Theory). 280p. (C). 1993. pap. text 19.95 (*0-7914-1384-5*) State U NY Pr.

— Regarding Nature: Industrialism & Deep Ecology. LC 92-14076. (SUNY Series in Radical, Social & Political Theory). 280p. (C). 1993. text 59.50 (*0-7914-1383-7*) State U NY Pr.

McLaughlin, Andrew C. Constitutional History of the United States. 1989. reprint ed. 56.50 (*0-89197-103-3*) Irvington.

— The Courts, the Constitution & Parties. LC 70-87405. (American Scene Ser.). 312p. 1972. reprint ed. lib. bdg. 39.50 (*0-306-71549-X*) Da Capo.

— Lewis Cass. Morse, John T., Jr., ed. LC 70-128957. (American Statesmen Ser.: No. 24). reprint ed. 49.50 (*0-404-50874-X*) AMS Pr.

McLaughlin, Ann L. The Balancing Pole: A Novel. LC 91-10307. 192p. (Orig.). 1991. pap. 9.95 (*0-936784-90-3*) J Daniel.

— Lightning in July. LC 88-37410. 180p. (Orig.). 1989. pap. 9.95 (*0-936784-72-5*) J Daniel.

*****McLaughlin, Ann L.** Maiden Voyage. LC 99-21330. (Illus.). 352p. 1999. pap. 14.95 (*1-880284-38-3*) J Daniel.

McLaughlin, Ann L. Sunset at Rosalie: A Novel. LC 95-37387. 272p. (Orig.). 1996. pap. 11.95 (*1-880284-15-4*) J Daniel.

McLaughlin, Arthur J. Manual of Infection Control in Respiratory Care. 179p. 1983. spiral bd. 27.50 (*0-316-56096-0*, Little Brwn Med Div) Lppncott W & W.

McLaughlin, Barry. Second Language Acquisition in Childhood, 2 vols. 2nd ed. 280p. (C). 1987. pap. text 32.50 (*0-8058-0095-6*); pap. text 34.50 (*0-8058-0096-4*) L Erlbaum Assocs.

— Second Language Acquisition in Childhood, 2 vols., Set. 2nd ed. (C). 1987. pap. text 65.00 (*0-8058-0097-2*) L Erlbaum Assocs.

— Theories. 1995. pap. text 18.95 (*0-7131-6513-8*, Pub. by E A) St Martin.

McLaughlin, Barry, ed. Second Language Acquisition in Childhood: School-Age Children. 280p. 1984. 59.95 (*0-89859-378-6*) L Erlbaum Assocs.

— Second Language Acquisition in Childhood: School-Age Children. (Child Psychology Ser.). 304p. 1985. 59.95 (*0-89859-565-7*) L Erlbaum Assocs.

McLaughlin, Barry, jt. auth. see Weiss, Jacqueline B.

*****McLaughlin, Bob & McLaughlin, Mary.** U. S. A. Immigration & Orientation. 3rd rev. ed. LC 99-75880. x, 500p. 2000. 39.95 (*0-9657571-4-5*, Pub. by Wellesworth Pub) Brodart.

McLaughlin, Brenda, jt. auth. see Robinson, Phillip R.

McLaughlin, Brian P. & Rorty, Amelia O., eds. Perspectives on Self Deception. (Topics on Philosophy Ser.: Vol. VI). (C). 1988. pap. 22.50 (*0-520-06123-3*, Pub. by U CA Pr) Cal Prin Full Svc.

Mclaughlin, Buzz. Playwright's Process: Learning the Craft from Today's Leading Dramatists. LC 97-7977. 288p. 1997. pap. text 18.95 (*0-8230-8833-2*, Back Stage Bks) Watsn-Guptill.

McLaughlin, Catherine K. The Do's & Don'ts of Parent Involvement: How to Build a Positive School-Home Partnership. Schilling, Dianne, ed. 192p. 1993. pap. text, teacher ed. 21.95 (*1-56499-015-X*, IP9015) Innerchoice Pub.

McLaughlin, Cecil. Let Go of Your Baggage & Travel Light: A Manual for Changing Your Life. 64p. 1991. pap. 5.95 (*1-879838-00-1*) Travel Light.

McLaughlin, Charles A. Mammals of Los Angeles County, California. (Science Ser.: No. 21). (Illus.). 34p. 1959. pap. 8.00 (*0-938644-02-5*) Nat Hist Mus.

McLaughlin, Charles A. & Chiasson, Robert B. Laboratory Anatomy of the Rabbit. 3rd ed. 124p. (C). 1990. text. write for info. (*0-697-04931-0*, WCB McGr Hill) McGrw-H Hghr Educ.

McLaughlin, Charles C., ed. see Olmsted, Frederick L.

McLaughlin, Charles H., jt. auth. see Devenish, Robert J.

McLaughlin, Cheryl. Women on the Run: 7 Steps to Saving Your Health, Self & Sanity. LC 98-96753. 192p. 1999. pap. 11.95 (*0-9668497-0-1*) Gold Mine Pr.

*****McLaughlin, Chris.** Simple Techniques for Pain Relief. LC 99-26891. (Health Factfiles Ser.). 112p. 1999. pap. 12.95 (*0-7370-1605-1*) T-L Custom Pub.

McLaughlin, Chris, jt. auth. see Simmons, Michele.

McLaughlin, Christian. Glamourpuss. 256p. 1995. pap. 12.95 (*0-452-27265-3*, Plume) Dutton Plume.

— Sex Toys of the Gods. 384p. 1998. pap. 13.95 (*0-452-27519-9*, Plume) Dutton Plume.

McLaughlin, Christopher J., jt. auth. see Meyer, Roger E.

McLaughlin, Colleen, et al. Counseling & Guidance in Schools: Developing Policy & Practice. LC 96-212679. (Resource Materials for Teachers Ser.). 112p. 1996. pap. 24.95 (*1-85346-423-6*, Pub. by David Fulton) Taylor & Francis.

McLaughlin, Colleen, jt. ed. see Bovair, Keith.

McLaughlin, Corinne. How to Evaluate Psychic Guidance & Channeling. (Orig.). 1987. pap. write for info. (*0-9617783-0-X*) Sirius Pub.

McLaughlin, Corinne & Davidson, Gordon. Spiritual Politics: Changing the World from the Inside Out. LC 93-90881. 464p. (Orig.). 1994. pap. 14.00 (*0-345-36983-1*) Ballantine Pub Grp.

McLaughlin, Corrine & Davidson, Gordon. Builders of the Dawn. LC 89-29638. (Illus.). 372p. (Orig.). 1990. pap. 17.95 (*0-913990-68-X*) Book Pub Co.

McLaughlin, Craig. The Bodyworker's Muscle Reference Guide. (Illus.). 200p. 1997. spiral bd. 29.95 (*0-9655679-2-3*) BodyGuide.

McLaughlin, Curtis P. & Kaluzny, Arnold D. Continuous Quality Improvement in Health Care: Theory, Implementation & Applications. 2nd ed. LC 99-20197. 659p. 1999. 65.00 (*0-8342-1655-8*) Aspen Pub.

McLaughlin, Curtis P. & Kaluzny, Arnold D., eds. Continuous Quality Improvement in Health Care: Theory, Implementation & Applications. LC 93-48062. 467p. 1994. 63.00 (*0-8342-0536-X*, 20536) Aspen Pub.

McLaughlin, Curtis P., jt. auth. see Wilson, Marjorie P.

McLaughlin, D. W., ed. Inverse Problems: SIAM-AMS Proceedings. LC 84-392. (SIAM/AMS Proceedings Ser.: Vol. 14). 189p. 1984. text 45.00 (*0-8218-1334-X*, SIAMS/14) Am Math.

*****McLaughlin, Dan.** The Animation Primer. (Illus.). 352p. 2001. pap. 39.95 (*0-240-80451-1*, Focal) Buttrwrth-Heinemann.

McLaughlin, Dan J. El Diccionario de Tareas para los Padres. (SPA.). 1997. pap. 13.95 (*1-892565-13-7*) Damand.

*****McLaughlin, Dan J.** The Parent Educator's Ready Reference. 2nd ed. Beatty, Susan, ed. 185p. (YA). (gr. 4-12). 1999. pap. 14.95 (*0-9660937-5-5*) CHEP.

McLaughlin, Dan J. The Parent Educator's Ready Reference: A Quick Reference Guide to the Four Subject Areas for Parents & Students. Beatty, Susan, ed. 185p. 1998. pap. 14.95 (*0-9660937-3-9*) CHEP.

— Parent's Homework Dictionary. 2nd ed. 1998. pap. 15.95 (*1-892565-10-2*) Damand.

McLaughlin, Daniel. Sketch of a Trip from Omaha to Salmon River. 23p. 1976. pap. 4.95 (*0-87770-159-8*) Ye Galleon.

McLaughlin, Daniel & Tierney, William G., eds. Naming Silenced Lives: Personal Narratives & the Process of Educational Change. LC 93-20361. 224p. (C). 1993. pap. 19.99 (*0-415-90517-6*, A6581) Routledge.

McLaughlin, Dave. Take the High Ground: An Executive's Guide to Total Quality Management. LC 90-6469. (Illus.). viii, 187p. 1990. 19.95 (*0-931541-17-4*) Mancorp Pub.

McLaughlin, David. Ministering Within the Church Towards the Third Millennium Vol. 7, No. 6: Proceedings of the Sixth International Assembly of Priests' Representatives from English-Speaking Countries. (Illus.). 16p. (Orig.). 1996. pap. 3.00 (*0-9653675-2-5*) NFPC.

*****McLaughlin, David S.** Atlas of Reporductive Surgery & Assisted Reproductive Technology Procedures. 228p. 2000. 199.95 (*1-85317-710-5*, Pub. by Martin Dunitz) Blackwell Sci.

McLaughlin, Dennis, jt. ed. see Thornton, David.

*****McLaughlin, Dennis R. & McLaughlin, Lana Jo.** FoodFun Devotions for Children's Ministry. LC 99-29456. 1999. 14.99 (*0-7644-2081-X*) Group Pub.

McLaughlin, Dennis R., jt. auth. see Anthony, Michelle.

McLaughlin, Don. Heaven in the Real World: The Transforming Touch of God. LC 97-684. 224p. (Orig.). 1997. pap. 11.99 (*1-878990-54-3*) Howard Pub LA.

McLaughlin, Donal. Die Verlorene Ehre der Katharina Blum, Boll: Critical Monographs in English. 64p. 1993. pap. 32.00 (*0-85261-257-5*, Pub. by Univ of Glasgow) St Mut.

McLaughlin, Donald H. Characteristics of Small & Rural School Districts. LC 97-187871. 151p. 1997. pap. 14.00 (*0-16-049056-1*) USGPO.

McLaughlin, Doris B. Michigan Labor: A Brief History from 1818 to the Present. LC 73-633304. (Orig.). 1970. 10.00 (*0-87736-312-9*); pap. 5.00 (*0-87736-333-1*) U of Mich Inst Labor.

McLaughlin, Doris B. & Schoomaker, Anita L. The Landrum-Griffin Act & Union Democracy. LC 78-12592. 296p. reprint ed. pap. 91.80 (*0-7837-4718-7*, 205907000003) Bks Demand.

McLaughlin, E. B. Richland Co. Pioneer Directory & Scrap Book: Including the Names of 300+ Richland County Pioneers. (Illus.). 82p. 1997. reprint ed. pap. 15.00 (*0-8328-6356-4*) Higginson Bk Co.

*****McLaughlin, Ed A.** A Leavenworth Legacy: An Intriguing Story of Two Ex-Convicts from Opposite Sides of the Track. 216p. 1998. 17.00 (*0-8059-4378-1*) Dorrance.

McLaughlin, Edith M. & Curtis, T. Adrian, eds. American Cardinal Readers, Bk. 1. (Illus.). 177p. (J). (gr. 1-2). 1996. reprint ed. text 17.00 (*0-911845-36-4*) Neumann Pr.

— American Cardinal Readers, Bk. 2. (Illus.). 217p. (J). (gr. 2-3). 1996. reprint ed. text 17.00 (*0-911845-37-2*) Neumann Pr.

— American Cardinal Readers, Bk. 3. (Illus.). 249p. (J). (gr. 3-4). 1996. reprint ed. text 18.00 (*0-911845-38-0*) Neumann Pr.

— American Cardinal Readers, Bk. 4. 282p. (J). (gr. 4-5). 1996. reprint ed. text 19.00 (*0-911845-39-9*) Neumann Pr.

— American Cardinal Readers, Bk. 5. 337p. (J). (gr. 5-6). 1996. text 21.00 (*0-911845-40-2*) Neumann Pr.

— American Cardinal Readers, Bk. 6. (Illus.). 390p. (YA). (gr. 6-7). 1996. reprint ed. text 23.00 (*0-911845-41-0*) Neumann Pr.

— American Cardinal Readers: Primer. (Illus.). 98p. (J). (gr. k-1). 1997. reprint ed. text 15.00 (*0-911845-52-6*) Neumann Pr.

McLaughlin, Edward T. Studies in Medieval Life & Literature. LC 74-39101. (Essay Index Reprint Ser.). 1977. reprint ed. 18.95 (*0-8369-2701-X*) Ayer.

McLaughlin, Edward W. & Rao, Vithala R. Decision Criteria for New Product Acceptance & Success: The Role of Trade Buyers. LC 90-26408. 208p. 1991. 59.95 (*0-89930-525-3*, MDQ/, Quorum Bks) Greenwood.

McLaughlin, Eleanor, jt. auth. see Ruether, Rosemary Radford.

McLaughlin, Eugene. Community, Policing & Accountability: The Politics of Policing in Manchester in the 1980s. 208p. 1994. 61.95 (*1-85628-488-3*, Pub. by Avebry) Ashgate Pub Co.

McLaughlin, Eugene & Muncie, John, eds. Controlling Crime. 336p. (C). 1996. 79.95 (*0-7619-5000-1*); pap. 28.95 (*0-7619-5001-X*) Sage.

McLaughlin, Eugene, jt. auth. see Muncie, John.

McLaughlin, Eugene, jt. ed. see Dallos, Rudi.

McLaughlin, Evelyn G. Critical Care of the Burn Patient: A Case Study Approach. 250p. 1990. 72.00 (*0-8342-0111-9*) Aspen Pub.

McLaughlin, Frank & Gold, Mike. How to Draw Those Bodacious Bad Babes of Comics. (Illus.). 144p. 1999. pap. 19.95 (*1-58063-068-5*, Pub. by Renaissance) St Martin.

McLaughlin, G. A. A Clean Heart. 1986. pap. 2.99 (*0-88019-208-9*) Schmul Pub Co.

— Commentary on Romans. 1985. pap. 9.99 (*0-88019-167-8*) Schmul Pub Co.

McLaughlin, G. L., jt. auth. see Freedman, G.

McLaughlin, Gerald T. Letters of Credit. 500p. 1985. suppl. ed. 70.00 (*0-317-29394-X*, #H4397X) Harcourt.

*****McLaughlin, Gerald T., ed.** Loyola Law School: A Sense of Purpose & a Sense of Mission. deluxe ed. (Illus.). 134p. (C). 2000. 49.00 (*0-9679921-0-9*) Loyola Law.

McLaughlin, Gerald T. & Cohen, Neil B. Commercial Law Report. text 270.00 (*0-8205-2059-4*) Bender.

McLaughlin, Gerald T. & Freedman, George. Color Atlas of Tooth Whitening. Hacke, Gregory, ed. (Illus.). 112p. 1991. text 50.00 (*0-912791-85-3*, Ishiyaku EuroAmerica) Med Dent Media.

McLaughlin, Gerald W., et al. People, Processes, & Managing Data, No. 11. 87p. (C). 1998. pap. 15.00 (*1-882393-07-4*) Assn Instl Res.

McLaughlin, Ginger. Our Search for Yesterday. 180p. 1984. pap. 8.95 (*0-89697-154-6*) Intl Univ Pr.

McLaughlin, Gregory. Total Quality in Research & Development. (Total Quality Ser.). 272p. 1995. boxed set 54.95 (*1-884015-02-6*) St Lucie Pr.

McLaughlin, Harold J. Building Your Business Plan: A Step-by-Step Approach. LC 84-11938. (Small Business Management Ser.: No. 1-471). 297p. 1985. 32.50 (*0-471-88358-1*, Wiley-Interscience) Wiley.

Mclaughlin, Helen. Stories from Hell: A Mom's Memorable Moments. LC 98-85213. (Illus.). 87p. 1998. pap. 10.95 (*1-56167-402-8*) Am Literary Pr.

McLaughlin, Helen E. Footsteps in the Sky: An Informal Review of U. S. Airlines Inflight Service, 1920-Present. (Illus.). 352p. 1994. pap. 24.95 (*0-930161-02-5*) St of the Art Bk.

*****McLaughlin, J. Kemp.** The Mighty Eighth in WWII: A Memoir. LC 00-28305. (Illus.). 248p. 2000. 22.00 (*0-8131-2178-7*) U Pr of Ky.

McLaughlin, J. Michael & Todman, Lee D. The Insiders' Guide to Charleston, S. C. 5th rev. ed. (Insiders' Guide Travel Ser.). (Illus.). 424p. 1999. pap. 16.95 (*1-57380-088-0*, The Insiders Guide) Falcon Pub Inc.

Mclaughlin, Jack. Jefferson & Monticello: The Biography of a Builder. LC 87-23664. (Illus.). 496p. 1995. pap. 14.95 (*0-8050-1463-2*, Owl) H Holt & Co.

McLaughlin, Jack. People Piece Puzzles. (Illus.). 60p. (J). (gr. 2-8). 1973. pap. 7.95 (*0-918932-38-6*, A-1122) Activity Resources.

— To His Excellency Thomas Jefferson: Letters to a President. (Illus.). 384p. 1993. reprint ed. pap. 12.00 (*0-380-71964-9*, Avon Bks) Morrow Avon.

McLaughlin, James B., Jr., jt. auth. see Hetrick, Patrick K.

McLaughlin, Jan & Weber, Bruce. These Poems Are Not Pretty. 124p. 1992. pap. 7.95 (*0-9615619-9-8*) Palmetto.

McLaughlin, Janet, jt. auth. see Fuller, Rose.

*****McLaughlin, Janice.** Valuing Technology: Organisations Culture & Change. LC 99-17599. (Management of Technology & Innovation Ser.). 259p. 1999. pap. write for info. (*0-415-19211-0*) Routledge.

*****McLaughlin, Janice, et al.** Valuing Technology: Organisations Culture & Change. LC 99-17599. 248p. (C). 1999. text. write for info. (*0-415-19210-2*) Routledge.

McLaughlin, Janie, ed. see Cleveland Ballet Council, Cookbook Committee Staff.

*****McLaughlin, Joe-Anne.** Black Irish Blues. 36p. 2000. 25.00 (*1-892275-07-4*); pap. 10.95 (*1-892275-08-2*); text 40.00 (*1-892275-06-6*) Brooding Heron Pr.

*****McLaughlin, John.** Trusting God's Heart When You Can't Trace His Hand. LC 99-29175. 88p. 1999. pap. 7.95 (*1-57249-165-5*, Ragged Edge) White Mane Pub.

McLaughlin, John, ed. A Guide to National & State Arts Education Services. LC 87-18712. 84p. (Orig.). 1987. pap. 15.00 (*0-915400-60-X*, ACA Bks) Am for the Arts.

— Toward a New Era in Arts Education: The Interlochen Symposium. LC 88-16649. 138p. (Orig.). 1988. pap. 13.95 (*0-915400-69-3*, ACA Bks) Am for the Arts.

McLaughlin, John, jt. auth. see Mertens, Donna M.

McLaughlin, John, ed. see Allard, C. Kenneth, et al.

McLaughlin, John A., et al, eds. Evaluation Utilization. LC 85-644749. (New Directions for Evaluation Ser.: No. PE 39). 1988. pap. 22.00 (*1-55542-894-0*) Jossey-Bass.

McLaughlin, John D., jt. auth. see Dale, Peter F.

McLaughlin, John Douglas, jt. auth. see Groot, Richard.

McLaughlin, John F. & McManus, Thomas E. Competitive Uses of Regulation in the Financial Services Arena. LC 95-107122. (Illus.). 83p. (Orig.). 1994. pap. text. write for info. (*1-879716-10-0*, I-94-1) Ctr Info Policy.

McLaughlin, John M. Guidelines for Contracting with Provate Providers for Educational Services. 12p. 1995. pap. 3.50 (*0-87652-222-3*, 021-0545) Am Assn Sch Admin.

An Asterisk (*) at the beginning of an entry indicates that the title is appearing for the first time.

M

McLaughlin, W. L., ed. Trends in Radiation Dosimetry. (Illus.). 320p. 1983. pap. 28.00 (*0-08-029143-0*, Pergamon Pr) Elsevier.

McLaughlin, Walt. Elemental Surprises: Essays by Walt McLaughlin. 44p. 1995. 5.00 (*0-945251-11-4*) Great Elm.

— Wild Lilies. (Illus.). 17p. (Orig.). 1995. pap. 3.00 (*0-944048-07-2*) Timberline Missouri.

***McLaughlin, Walter H., Jr.** MicroMash MBE Review Reference: Constitutional Law/Criminal Law & Procedure/Evidence. 4th rev. ed. 487p. 1998. pap. text 75.00 (*0-15-900431-4*) Harcourt.

— MicroMash MBE Review Reference: Contracts/Real Property/Torts. 4th rev. ed. 487p. 1999. pap. text 18.95 (*0-15-900432-2*) Harcourt.

McLaughlin, Walter H. MicroMash MBE Review Reference Vol. 1: The MicroMash Way to the MBE. 3rd rev. ed. 105p. 1998. pap. text 75.00 (*0-926709-83-6*) MicroMash.

McLaughlin, Walter H., Jr. MicroMash MBE Review Reference Vol. 2: Constitutional Law/Criminal Law & Procedure/Evidence. 3rd rev. ed. 470p. 1998. pap. 75.00 (*0-926709-84-4*) MicroMash.

— MicroMash MBE Review Reference Vol. 3: Contracts/Real Property/Torts. 3rd rev. ed. 460p. 1998. pap. text 75.00 (*0-926709-85-2*) MicroMash.

McLaughlin, Wanda, ed. see Van Sickle, Lisa.

McLaughlin, Wanda J., ed. see Van Sickle, Lisa.

McLaughlin, William. At Rest in the Midwest: Poems. (Cleveland Poets Ser.: No. 28). 48p. 1980. pap. 4.50 (*0-914946-26-9*) Cleveland St Univ Poetry Ctr.

McLaughry, John, jt. auth. see Bryan, Frank.

McLaulin, J. Bryce, jt. ed. see Duffy, John C.

McLauren, Aden, jt. ed. see Majumdar, Robin.

McLaurin, Allen, jt. ed. see Majumader, Robin.

McLaurin, Ann M., jt. ed. see Pederson, William O.

McLaurin, Joe M. Richmond County Records Vols. 1-28: Journal of the Society of Richmond County Descendants. Burket, Jerri, ed. (Illus.). 665p. 1999. reprint ed. pap. 59.00 (*0-8328-9853-8*); reprint ed. lib. bdg. 69.00 (*0-8328-9852-X*) Higginson Bk Co.

McLaurin, Katie E., et al. Health System's Role in Abortion Care: The Need for a Pro-Active Approach. (Issues in Abortion Care Ser.). 34p. 1991. pap. 7.50 (*1-882220-00-5*) IPAS.

McLaurin, Katie E., ed. see Wolf, Merrill.

McLaurin, Melton, ed. You Wrote My Life: Lyrical Themes in Country Music. (Cultural Perspectives on the American Society Ser.). 180p. 1992. text 50.00 (*2-88124-548-X*); pap. text 20.00 (*2-88124-554-4*) Gordon & Breach.

McLaurin, Melton A. Celia, a Slave. LC 90-23045. 192p. 1999. mass mkt. 5.99 (*0-380-80336-4*, Avon Bks) Morrow Avon.

— Celia, a Slave. LC 90-23045. 160p. 1991. 19.95 (*0-8203-1352-1*) U of Ga Pr.

— Celia, A Slave. 192p. 1993. reprint ed. pap. 12.50 (*0-380-71935-5*, Avon Bks) Morrow Avon.

— The Knights of Labor in the South, 4. LC 77-87916. (Contributions in Labor History Ser.: No. 4). (Illus.). 232p. 1978. 55.00 (*0-313-20033-5*, MCK/, Greenwood Pr) Greenwood.

— Paternalism & Protest: Southern Mill Workers & Organized Labor, 1875-1905, 3. LC 70-111261. (Contributions in Economics & Economic History Ser.: No. 3). 265p. 1971. 59.95 (*0-8371-4662-3*, MPP&, Greenwood Pr) Greenwood.

— Separate Pasts: Growing up White in the Segregated South. 2nd ed. LC 98-15522. 192p. 1998. reprint ed. pap. 14.95 (*0-8203-2047-1*, Brown Thrasher) U of Ga Pr.

McLaurin, Melton A. & Thomason, Michael V. The Image of Progress: Alabama Photographs, 1872-1917. LC 80-11441. (Illus.). 242p. (Orig.). 1980. pap. 75.10 (*0-608-05142-X*, 206570300005) Bks Demand.

McLaurin, R. D., jt. auth. see Jureidini, Paul A.

McLaurin, Robert L., ed. Extracerebral Collections. (Advances in Neurotraumatology Ser.: Vol. 1). (Illus.). 270p. 1986. 97.00 (*0-387-81876-6*) Spr-Verlag.

McLaurin, Robert L., et al, eds. Spina Bifida: A Multidisciplinary Approach. LC 86-8184. 509p. 1986. 105.00 (*0-275-92100-X*, C2100, Praeger Pubs) Greenwood.

McLaurin, Ronald D. Middle East Foreign Policy: Issues & Processes. LC 82-13137. 325p. 1982. 45.00 (*0-275-90858-5*, C0858, Praeger Pubs) Greenwood.

McLaurin, Ronald D., ed. Military Propaganda: Psychological Warfare & Operations. LC 81-22638. 379p. 1982. 59.95 (*0-275-90859-3*, C0859, Praeger Pubs) Greenwood.

McLaurin, Thad H., jt. auth. see Holcomb, Cynthia.

McLaurin, Tim. The Acorn Plan. 1989. pap. 11.95 (*0-393-30616-X*) Norton.

— Cured by Fire. 236p. 1997. reprint ed. pap. 13.95 (*1-878086-59-6*, Pub. by Down Home NC) Blair.

— Keeper of the Moon: A Southern Boyhood. 2nd ed. 316p. 1998. reprint ed. pap. 14.95 (*1-878086-68-5*, Pub. by Down Home NC) Blair.

— Lola. LC 97-69229. 119p. 1997. 14.95 (*1-878086-62-6*, Pub. by Down Home NC) Blair.

***McLaurin, Tim.** The River Less Run: A Memoir. 280p. 2000. 23.95 (*1-878086-85-5*, Pub. by Down Home NC) Blair.

McLaurin, Tim. Woodrow's Trumpet: A Novel. LC 93-71404. 256p. 1993. reprint ed. pap. 13.95 (*1-878086-25-1*, Pub. by Down Home NC) Blair.

McLaury, Buster, et al. The Western Horse Book. LC 98-93372. (Illus.). 300p. 1999. text 60.00 (*0-922029-70-9*, Pub. by Stoecklein Pub) Gr Arts Ctr Pub.

McLaverty, Michael. Brightening Day. 278p. 1987. pap. 10.95 (*0-905169-87-5*, Pub. by Poolbeg Pr) Dufour.

— Call My Brother Back. 184p. 1979. pap. 9.95 (*0-905169-21-2*, Pub. by Poolbeg Pr) Dufour.

— The Choice. 240p. 1991. pap. 12.95 (*1-85371-110-1*, Pub. by Poolbeg Pr) Dufour.

— Collected Short Stories. 278p. 1997. pap. 14.95 (*0-905169-14-X*, Pub. by Poolbeg Pr) Dufour.

— Game Cock & Other Stories. (Illus.). 1947. 10.00 (*0-8159-5600-2*) Devin.

— In Quiet Places: Uncollected Prose, Letters & Criticism. Hillan-King, Sophia, ed. LC 89-82485. 256p. 1990. pap. 12.95 (*1-85371-040-7*, Pub. by Poolbeg Pr) Dufour.

— School for Hope. 256p. 1993. reprint ed. pap. 11.95 (*1-85371-172-1*, Pub. by Poolbeg Pr) Dufour.

— Truth in the Night. 255p. 1986. pap. 8.95 (*0-905169-72-7*, Pub. by Poolbeg Pr) Dufour.

McLaverty, Peter. The Politics of Empowerment? (Illus.). 208p. 1996. text 77.95 (*1-85521-803-8*, Pub. by Dartmth Pub) Ashgate Pub Co.

McLavin, David. Austin-Healey: Colour Classics. (Illus.). 128p. 1996. pap. 10.95 (*1-85532-647-7*, Pub. by Ospry) Stackpole.

McLaws, Galina. A Handbook of Russian Verb Morphology. LC 95-61380. (Texts Ser.). (RUS.). 60p. (Orig.). (C). 1996. pap. 12.95 (*0-941051-26-9*) Focus Pub-R Pullins.

— Integrated Russian Grammar Learning Modules I-III. LC 95-61378. (Texts Ser.). (RUS.). 81p. (C). 1996. pap. 12.95 (*0-941051-16-1*) Focus Pub-R Pullins.

— Integrated Russian Grammar Learning Modules IV-VI. LC 95-61378. (Texts Ser.). (RUS.). 96p. (C). 1996. pap. 12.95 (*0-941051-49-8*) Focus Pub-R Pullins.

— Integrated Russian Grammar Learning Modules VII-IX. LC 95-61378. (Texts Ser.). (RUS.). 96p. (C). 1996. pap. 12.95 (*0-941051-20-X*) Focus Pub-R Pullins.

— Integrated Russian Grammar Learning Modules X-XII. LC 95-61378. (Texts Ser.). (RUS.). 96p. (C). 1996. pap. 12.95 (*0-941051-36-6*) Focus Pub-R Pullins.

— An Overview of Russian Cases. LC 95-61381. (Texts Ser.). (RUS.). 96p. (Orig.). (C). 1996. pap. 12.95 (*0-941051-33-1*) Focus Pub-R Pullins.

McLay, A. L. & Toner, Peter G., eds. Subcelluar Taxonomy: An Ultrastructural Classification System with Diagnostic Applications. LC 83-10856. (Ultrastructural Pathology Publication). 86p. 1985. 78.95 (*0-89116-293-3*) Hemisp Pub.

McLay, W. D., ed. Clinical Forensic Medicine. 376p. 1991. pap. text 39.50 (*0-86187-155-3*) St Martin.

McLean. Astroelectronics. 1992. text 45.00 (*0-86187-662-8*) St Martin.

— Contemporary Geometry from an Historical Viewpoint. 512p. 1998. write for info. (*0-12-484940-7*) Acad Pr.

— Garry's First Season. 1977. pap. text. write for info. (*0-582-53688-X*, Pub. by Addison-Wesley) Longman.

— Ghost of the Glen. (Knockout Ser.). Date not set. text. write for info. (*0-582-25082-X*, Pub. by Addison-Wesley) Longman.

McLean. Medical Law. 67.95 (*1-85521-092-4*) Ashgate Pub Co.

— Medical Law & Ethics. 185.95 (*0-7546-2003-4*) Ashgate Pub Co.

— Rights. 2000. 185.95 (*0-7546-2030-1*) Ashgate Pub Co.

McLean, et al. Tumors of the Eye & Ocular Adnexa. (AFIP Atlas of Tumor Pathology Ser.: Vol. 12). (Illus.). 322p. 1995. pap. text 56.00 (*1-881041-11-5*) Am Registry Path.

McLean, jt. auth. see Marchiori.

McLean, jt. auth. see Wilson, Alan D.

***Mclean, Hellen.** Of All the Summers: A Novel. LC 99-185517. 1999. mass mkt. 14.95 (*0-88961-235-8*) Womens Pr.

McLean, A., jt. auth. see Heard, R. A.

McLean, A., jt. auth. see McPherson, N. A.

Mclean, A. C., jt. auth. see Gribble.

McLean, Adam. The Alchemical Mandala: A Survey of the Mandala in the Western Esoteric Traditions. LC 89-34803. (Hermetic Research Ser.: No. 3). (Illus.). 206p. (Orig.). 1989. pap. 17.00 (*0-933999-80-1*) Phanes Pr.

— A Commentary on the Mutus Liber. LC 90-47419. (Magnum Opus Hermetic Sourceworks Ser.: No. 11). (Illus.). 82p. (Orig.). 1991. 27.00 (*0-933999-89-5*); pap. 15.00 (*0-933999-90-9*) Phanes Pr.

— The Triple Goddess: An Exploration of the Archetypal Feminine. LC 89-34802. (Hermetic Research Ser.: No. 1). (Illus.). 125p. 1989. pap. 14.95 (*0-933999-78-X*) Phanes Pr.

— Whatever Next? (Illus.). 193p. (Orig.). 1992. pap. 9.95 (*0-948747-09-9*) Grosvenor USA.

McLean, Adam, ed. The Magical Calendar: A Synthesis of Magical Symbolism from the Seventeenth Centry Renaissance of Medieval Occultism. (Magnum Opus Hermetic Sourceworks Ser.: No. 1). (Illus.). 135p. (Orig.). 1993. pap. 18.00 (*0-933999-33-X*) Phanes Pr.

McLean, Adam C. & Gribble, Colin D. Geology for Civil Engineers. 2nd ed. (Illus.). 1985. text 49.95 (*0-04-624005-5*); pap. text 24.95 (*0-04-624006-3*) Routledge.

***McLean, Adrienne L. & Cook, David A., eds.** Headline Hollywood: A Century of Film Scandal. LC 00-39040. (Communications, Media & Culture Ser.). (Illus.). 320p. (C). 2001. text 52.00 (*0-8135-2885-2*); pap. text 22.00 (*0-8135-2886-0*) Rutgers U Pr.

McLean, Alan A. Work Stress. 1979. pap. 13.95 (*0-201-04592-3*) Addison-Wesley.

McLean, Alan c. Gary's First Season. (American Structural Readers Ser.: Stage 1). (Illus.). 16p. (Orig.). 1989. pap. text 6.31 (*0-582-79816-7*, 75066) Longman.

McLean, Alasdair W. M. Europe's Final Frontier: The Search for Security Through Space. LC 97-34374. 226p. 1997. lib. bdg. 75.00 (*1-56072-462-5*) Nova Sci Pubs.

— Western European Military Space Policy. 200p. 1992. 72.95 (*1-85521-115-7*, Pub. by Dartmth Pub) Ashgate Pub Co.

McLean, Albert F. Point Park College: The First 25 Years; An Oral History. 1985. write for info. (*0-318-60297-0*) Point Park.

Mclean, Alex, jt. auth. see Wilson, William G.

McLean, Alexander. History of Jersey City: A Record of Its Early Settlement & Corporate Progress, Sketches of Towns & Cities That Were Absorbed on the Growth of the Present Municipality...with Some Notice of the Men Who Built the City. (Illus.). 462p. 1997. reprint ed. lib. bdg. 49.50 (*0-8328-6053-0*) Higginson Bk Co.

McLean, Alexander, ed. History of McDonough County Illinois, with Biographical Sketches. (Illus.). 445p. 1998. reprint ed. lib. bdg. 48.00 (*0-8328-7084-6*) Higginson Bk Co.

McLean, Andrea & McLean, Janet. Cat Goes to Sea. (Illus.). 32p. (J). (ps-1). 1996. pap. 6.95 (*1-86373-773-1*, Pub. by Allen & Unwin Pty) IPG Chicago.

McLean, Andrew. The Chuting Gallery: A Guide to Steep Skiing in the Wasatch Mountains. (Illus.). 96p. 1998. pap. 9.95 (*0-9621935-7-7*) Thistle Pr.

***McLean, Andrew.** Josh & the Ducks. (Illus.). (J). 2000. pap. 4.95 (*1-86448-493-4*) Allen & Unwin Pty.

McLean, Andrew. Josh & the Ducks. 1999. 7.95 (*1-86448-365-2*) Allen & Unwn AT.

***McLean, Andrew & McLean, Janet.** Josh. (Illus.). 32p. (J). 2000. pap. 4.95 (*1-86448-490-X*, Pub. by Allen & Unwin Pty) IPG Chicago.

— Josh. LC 98-198223. (Little Ark Book Ser.). (Illus.). 32p. (J). (ps-3). 2000. 7.95 (*1-86448-362-8*, Pub. by Allen & Unwin Pty) IPG Chicago.

— Josh & the Monster. (Illus.). 32p. (J). 2000. 7.95 (*1-86448-364-4*, Pub. by Allen & Unwin Pty); pap. 4.95 (*1-86448-492-6*, Pub. by Allen & Unwin Pty) IPG Chicago.

— Josh & Thumper. (Illus.). 32p. (J). 2000. 7.95 (*1-86448-363-6*, Pub. by Allen & Unwin Pty); pap. 4.95 (*1-86448-491-8*, Pub. by Allen & Unwin Pty) IPG Chicago.

McLean, Andrew J. Buying & Managing Residential Real Estate. 336p. (Orig.). 1989. pap. 14.95 (*0-8092-4412-8*, 441280, Contemporary Bks) NTC Contemp Pub Co.

— Casino Player's Handbook: The Ultimate Guide to Where & How to Play in America's Casinos. (Illus.). 336p. 1997. pap. 24.95 (*0-9658499-1-0*) Scotwrite Prodns.

— How to Get a Casino Job: A Dealer, Slot Technician, Casino Host or Cashier. LC 97-91939. (Illus.). 272p. 1997. pap. 24.95 (*0-9658499-0-2*) Scotwrite Prodns.

— Investing in Real Estate. 222p. 1988. 59.95 (*0-471-60921-8*) Wiley.

— Making a Fortune Quickly in Fix-Up Properties. LC 95-22784. 368p. 1997. pap. 14.95 (*0-8092-4839-5*, 483950, Contemporary Bks) NTC Contemp Pub Co.

McLean, Andrew J. & Eldred, Gary W. Investing in Real Estate. LC 96-13042. 336p. 1996. pap. 19.95 (*0-471-15398-2*) Wiley.

McLean, Andrew M., jt. ed. see Guntner, J. Lawrence.

McLean, Anne, tr. see Bueno, Maria de Los Reyes Castillo & Castillo, Daisy.

McLean, Anne, tr. see Varsavsky, Paula.

McLean, Antonia, jt. auth. see McLean, Ruari.

McLean, Austin, ed. RadiOutlook II: New Forces Shaping the Industry. 143p. 1991. 40.00 (*0-89324-112-1*) Natl Assn Broadcasters.

McLean, B. Hudson. The Cursed Christ: Mediterranean Expulsion Rituals & Pauline Soteriology. (Journal for the Study of the New Testament, Supplement Ser.: No. 126). 263p. 1996. 75.00 (*1-85075-589-2*, Pub. by Sheffield Acad) CUP Services.

McLean, Bill. The Best Peanut Butter Sandwich in the Whole World. (Illus.). 28p. (J). (ps-2). 1990. pap. write for info. (*0-88753-207-1*) Black Moss.

McLean, Bradley H. Citations & Allusions to Jewish Scripture in Early Christian & Jewish Writings Through 180 C. E. LC 91-38309. 144p. 1992. lib. bdg. 69.95 (*0-7734-9430-8*) E Mellen.

McLean, Bradley H., ed. Origins & Method - Towards a New Understanding of Judaism & Christianity: Essays in Honour of John C. Hurd. (JSNT Supplement Ser.: Vol. 86). 409p. 1993. 85.00 (*1-85075-441-1*, Pub. by Sheffield Acad) CUP Services.

McLean, Brian J., et al, eds. New Horizons Multi Wave. LC 97-31469. (International Astronomical Union Symposia Ser.: No. 179). 508p. 1997. 182.00 (*0-7923-4802-8*); pap. 90.00 (*0-7923-4803-6*) Kluwer Academic.

McLean, Brian W. Joint Training for Night Air Warfare. LC 92-27734. 122p. 1992. pap. 7.50 (*1-58566-044-2*) Air Univ.

McLean, C. C., Jr. Carrier. History of the Carrier Family (New England) 9p. 1996. lib. bdg. 4.50 (*0-8328-6553-2*) Higginson Bk Co.

McLean, Candi. Surviving a Nuclear Powered Family. (Illus.). 119p. (Orig.). 1992. pap. 14.95 (*1-55059-045-6*) Temeron Bks.

***McLean-Carr, Carol.** Fairy Dreams. LC 99-58657. (Illus.). 32p. (J). 2000. 10.95 (*0-439-19257-9*) Scholastic Inc.

McLean-Carr, Carol A., jt. auth. see Winer, Yvonne.

McLean, Cheryl. Careers for Shutterbugs: And Other Candid Types. LC 94-3539. 160p. 1994. pap. 9.95 (*0-8442-4114-8*, 41148, VGM Career) NTC Contemp Pub Co.

— Careers for Shutterbugs & Other Candid Types. (VGM Careers for You Ser.). (Illus.). 160p. 1995. 14.95 (*0-8442-4112-1*, 41121) NTC Contemp Pub Co.

***McLean, Cheryl.** Fun with the Family in Oregon: Hundreds of Ideas for Day Trips with the Kids. 2nd ed. (Fun with the Family Ser.). (Illus.). 288p. 2000. pap. 12.95 (*0-7627-0621-X*) Globe Pequot.

McLean, Cheryl. Oregon Family Adventure Guide: Great Things to See & Do for the Entire Family. LC 95-7741. (Family Adventure Guide Ser.). (Illus.). 176p. (Orig.). 1995. pap. 9.95 (*1-56440-647-4*) Globe Pequot.

McLean, Cheryl, ed. Customer Service Letters Ready to Go. (. . . Ready to Go! Ser.). (Illus.). 160p. 1995. pap. 12.95 (*0-8442-3567-9*, NTC Business Bks) NTC Contemp Pub Co.

— Everyday Letters Ready to Go. LC 95-9355. (. . . Ready to Go! Ser.). (Illus.). 160p. 1995. pap. 12.95 (*0-8442-3568-7*, M3568-7, NTC Business Bks) NTC Contemp Pub Co.

McLean, Cheryl & Brown, Clint. Oregon's Quiet Waters: A Guide to Lakes for Canoeists & Other Paddlers. 2nd ed. (Illus.). 176p. (Orig.). 1996. pap. 14.95 (*0-943097-03-7*) Jackson Creek Pr.

McLean, Cheryl, jt. auth. see Brown, Clint.

McLean, Cheryl C. & Smiley, Linda M. Little Readers for Little Readers, Vol. I. (Illus.). 229p. (J). (gr. k-1). 1996. teacher ed., spiral bd. 50.00 (*1-929459-00-9*, Pub. by Lttle Readers) Poor Richards.

— Little Readers for Little Readers: Spanish Supplement. (ENG & SPA., Illus.). 110p. (J). (gr. k-1). 1997. teacher ed. 25.00 (*1-929459-01-7*, Pub. by Lttle Readers) Poor Richards.

— Little Readers for Little Readers, with Pointers, 2 vols., Vol. II. (Illus.). 116p. (J). (gr. k-1). 1998. teacher ed., spiral bd. 35.00 (*1-929459-02-5*, Pub. by Lttle Readers) Poor Richards.

McLean, Christopher, et al, eds. Men's Ways of Being. (New Directions in Theory & Psychology Ser.). 260p. (C). 1996. pap. 27.00 (*0-8133-2653-2*, Pub. by Westview) HarpC.

McLean, Clifton C. Singing on the Throne: And Other Tales of a Country Vet in the South. Campbell, MaryBelle, ed. (Illus.). 160p. 1993. pap., per. 18.00 (*1-879009-12-9*) Old Barn Entrprs.

— Singing on the Throne: And Other Tales of a Country Vet in the South. 2nd ed. Campbell, MaryBelle, ed. (Illus.). 160p. 1994. pap., per. 16.95 (*1-879009-16-1*) Old Barn Entrprs.

McLean, Dan, et al. Leisure Resources. LC 98-85172. (Illus.). 5p. (C). 1998. text 44.95 (*1-57167-025-4*) Sagamore Pub.

McLean, Daniel D. & Smith, S. Harold, eds. Impacting on Recreation & Park Legislation. (Illus.). 104p. (Orig.). 1990. pap. 11.50 (*0-88314-476-X*, A476X) AAHPERD.

McLean, Daniel M. Minnesota Legal Forms: Family Law. Date not set. ring bd. 95.00 (*0-327-00986-1*, 81794, MICHIE) LEXIS Pub.

McLean, Daniel W. Minnesota Legal Forms: Family Law. 240p. ring bd. 50.00 incl. disk (*0-917126-85-8*, 81795-10, MICHIE) LEXIS Pub.

— Minnesota Legal Forms: Family Law. 240p. 1994. ring bd. 69.95 incl. digital audio (*0-614-05903-8*, MICHIE); ring bd., suppl. ed. 40.00 (*0-614-03157-5*, MICHIE) LEXIS Pub.

— Minnesota Legal Forms Issue 17: Family Law. Davidson, Neil, ed. 50p. 1998. ring bd. write for info. (*0-327-00552-1*, 8179517) LEXIS Pub.

McLean, David. Timothy Pickering & the Age of the American Revolution. 1981. 60.95 (*0-405-14098-3*) Ayer.

— War, Diplomacy & Informal Empire Vol. 1: Britain, France & Latin America. 1995. text 65.00 (*1-85043-867-6*, Pub. by I B T) St Martin.

McLean, David & Preston, Antony, eds. Warship, 1997. (Illus.). 224p. 1997. 42.95 (*0-85177-722-8*) Naval Inst Pr.

McLean, David & Preston, Tony, eds. Warship, 1996. (Illus.). 256p. 1997. 42.95 (*0-85177-685-X*) Naval Inst Pr.

McLean, David, jt. ed. see Preston, Antony.

***McLean, David I., et al.** Dynamic Impact Factors for Bridges. LC 98-67633. (Synthesis of Highway Practice Ser.). 60 p. 1998. write for info. (*0-309-06819-3*) Natl Acad Pr.

***McLean, Deckle.** Essays on the First Amendment. LC 00-27617. 2000. write for info. (*0-8377-3425-8*, Rothman) W S Hein.

McLean, Deckle. Privacy & Its Invasion. LC 95-9308. 152p. 1995. 47.95 (*0-275-95335-1*, Praeger Pubs) Greenwood.

McLean, Diane, ed. see Roeder, Rick.

***McLean, Dirk.** Play Mas'! A Carnival ABC. (Illus.). 32p. (YA). (ps-3). 2000. 18.99 (*0-88776-486-X*) Tundra Bks.

McLean, Don. The Do-It-Yourself Gunpowder Cookbook. (Illus.). 80p. 1992. pap. 12.00 (*0-87364-675-4*) Paladin Pr.

— The Spy's Workshop: America's Clandestine Weapons. (Illus.). 288p. 1989. pap. 30.00 (*0-87364-512-X*) Paladin Pr.

McLean, Donald H. Recognition, Identification & Prevention of Acute Viral Infections. 389p. 1991. pap. 42.50 (*0-87527-480-3*) Green.

McLean, Donald M. & Smith, John A. Medical Microbiology Synopsis. LC 90-5597. (Illus.). 305p. 1991. pap. text 34.50 (*0-8121-1304-7*) Lppncott W & W.

McLean, Donald M. & Wong, Kathleen K. Same-Day Diagnosis of Human Virus Infections. 144p. 1984. 49.50 (*0-8493-6590-2*, QR387, CRC Reprint) Franklin.

McLean, Donald W., jt. auth. see DeRemer, Dale.

Mclean-Donaldson, Karen B. Through Students' Eyes: Combating Racism in United States Schools. LC 96-10432. 184p. 1996. 55.00 (*0-275-95478-1*, Praeger Pubs) Greenwood.

McLean, Dorothy B., ed. see McLean, John.

McLean, Duncan. Blackden. 232p. 2000. pap. 13.00 (*0-393-31975-X*) Norton.

— Bucket of Tongues. LC 99-19326. 245p. 1999. pap. 13.00 (*0-393-31897-4*) Norton.

An Asterisk (*) at the beginning of an entry indicates that the title is appearing for the first time.

— Bunker Man. LC 97-10001. 1997. 13.00 (*0-393-31616-5*); 25.00 (*0-393-04121-2*) Norton.

***McLean, Duncan.** Duncan McLean Plays: Julie Allardyce; Blackden; Rug Comes to Shuv; One Sure Thing, & I'd Rather Go Blind, Vol. 1. (Contemporary Dramatists Ser.). 304p. 2000. pap. 14.95 (*0-413-72900-1*, Methuen Drama) Methn.

McLean, Duncan. Lone Star Swing. LC 98-179517. 312p. 1998. pap. 14.00 (*0-393-31756-0*) Norton.

McLean, Duse. The Pocket Guide to Seattle: And Surrounding Areas. 5th ed. LC 96-60636. 1996. pap. text 10.95 (*0-9621935-6-9*) Thistle Pr.

McLean, Duse F. The Pocket Guide to Seattle: And Surrounding Areas. 6th rev. ed. LC 98-60791. (Illus.). 1998. pap. 10.95 (*0-9621935-8-5*) Thistle Pr.

— The Pocket Guide to Seattle, 1989: A Complete Guide to Seattle & Surrounding Areas. Hampton, Elisha, ed. (Illus.). 160p. 1996. pap. 10.95 (*0-9621935-0-X*) Thistle Pr.

McLean, Duse F., ed. see Ferguson, Robert L.

McLean, Edward B. Law & Civilization: The Legal Thought of Roscoe Pound. 342p. (C). 1992. lib. bdg. 55.00 (*0-8191-8698-8*) U Pr of Amer.

— Roman Catholicism & the Right to Work. 186p. (Orig.). (C). 1986. lib. bdg. 46.00 (*0-8191-5009-6*) U Pr of Amer.

McLean, Edward B., ed. Common Truths: New Perspectives on Natural Law. LC 00-64352. 2000. 24.95 (*1-882926-35-8*) ISI Books.

McLean, Edward B., ed. see McDonald, Forrest, et al.

McLean, Edward B., ed. see McInerny, Ralph, et al.

McLean, Edwin. Classic Music Dictionary. 1997. pap. text 8.95 (*1-56939-048-7*) FJH Music Co Inc.

McLean, Edwin, ed. see Faber, Nancy & Faber, Randall.

McLean, Edwin, ed. see Faber, Nancy, et al.

McLean, Elizabeth, ed. see Cloud, Enoch C.

***McLean, Evalyn W.** Father Struck It Rich. (Illus.). 232p. 1999. pap. 14.95 (*1-890437-26-3*) Western Reflections.

McLean, Evalyn W. Father Struck It Rich. (American Biography Ser.). 316p. 1991. reprint ed. lib. bdg. 79.00 (*0-7812-8283-7*) Rprt Serv.

McLean, Evalyn W. & Sparkes, Boyden. Father Struck It Rich. LC 75-1856. (Leisure Class in America Ser.). (Illus.). 1975. reprint ed. 26.95 (*0-405-06922-7*) Ayer.

— Father Struck It Rich. rev. ed. Benham, Jack L., ed. (Illus.). 384p. 1981. reprint ed. pap. 10.95 (*0-941026-09-4*); reprint ed. text 24.95 (*0-941026-10-8*) Bear Creek Pub.

***McLean, Evalyn Walsh & Sparkes, Boyden.** Queen of Diamonds: The Fabled Legacy of Evalyn Walsh McLean. LC 00-31939. 2000. write for info. (*1-57736-192-X*, Hillsboro Pr) Providence Hse.

Mclean, Fiona. Marketing the Museum. LC 96-22435. (Illus.). 272p. (C). 1997. 85.00 (*0-415-10392-4*); pap. 32.99 (*0-415-15293-3*) Routledge.

McLean, Francis G., et al, eds. Geotechnical Engineering Congress, 1991, Set, Vols. I & II. LC 91-17797. 1385p. 1991. pap. text 105.00 (*0-87262-806-X*) Am Soc Civil Eng.

McLean, Francis G., jt. ed. see Hansen, Kenneth D.

McLean, Francis G., jt. ed. see Ko, Hon-Yim.

McLean, Franklin C. & Urist, Marshall R. Bone: Fundamentals of the Physiology of Skeletal Tissue. 3rd rev. ed. LC 68-16703. 336p. reprint ed. pap. 104.20 (*0-8357-7339-6*, 202412100035) Bks Demand.

McLean, G. Anthony, ed. A Cry from the Hood. 140p. (Orig.). 1997. pap. write for info. (*1-889534-10-2*) Jay St Pubs.

McLean, Gary & Davison, Leslie. Electronic Keyboarding. (Illus.). 175p. (C). 1992. pap. text 39.75 (*0-939693-24-0*) Collegiate Pr.

McLean, Gary & Lyons, Art. Writing for Workplace Success. 299p. (C). 1991. pap. text 17.95 (*1-56118-228-1*) Paradigm MN.

McLean, Gary, et al. Writing: Skill Enhancement. 1994. teacher ed. 8.00 (*0-318-70383-1*); text 10.95 (*1-56118-232-X*) Paradigm MN.

— Writing for Workplace Success: Instructor's guide. 299p. (C). 1991. pap. text, teacher ed. 8.00 (*1-56118-229-X*) Paradigm MN.

McLean, Gary N. Teaching Keyboarding. rev. ed. 69p. (C). 1995. pap. text 20.00 (*1-881530-00-0*) Delta Pi Epsilon.

McLean, Gary N., et al, eds. Performance Appraisal: Perspectives on a Quality Management Approach. LC 94-70393. 218p. 1994. reprint ed. pap. 19.00 (*1-56286-004-6*) Am Soc Train & Devel.

McLean, Gary N., et al. Reading Skills Enhancement: Readings booklet, Pt. 19. 4.95 (*1-56118-207-9*) EMC-Paradigm.

McLean, George, et al, eds. Plant Virus Epidemics: Monitoring, Modeling & Predicting Outbreaks. 1986. text 146.00 (*0-12-485060-X*) Acad Pr.

Mclean, George F. Civil Society & Social Reconstruction. LC 96-20814. (Culture Heritage & Contemporary Change Series I: Vol. 16). 1996. pap. 17.50 (*1-56518-086-0*) Coun Res Values.

***McLean, George F.** Freedom, Cultural Traditions & Progress: Philosophy in Civil Society & Nation Building, Tashkent Lectures, 1999. LC 00-31601. (Cultural Heritage & Contemporary Change Ser.). 2000. write for info. (*1-56518-151-4*) Coun Res Values.

— Religion & Cooperation Between Civilizations: Islamic & Christian Cultures in a Global Horizon. LC 00-31603. (Cultural Heritage & Contemporary Change Ser.). 2000. write for info. (*1-56518-152-2*) Coun Res Values.

McLean, George F. Tradition, Harmony, & Transcendence. LC 93-4607. (Cultural Heritage & Contemporary Life Series III: Vol. 4). 1993. 45.00 (*1-56518-030-5*); pap. 17.50 (*1-56518-031-3*) Coun Res Values.

***McLean, George F.** Ways to God: Personal & Social at the Turn of the Millennia. LC 98-48111. (Cultural Heritage & Contemporary Change Ser.: Vol. 17). 460p. 1999. pap. 17.50 (*1-56518-123-9*) Coun Res Values.

McLean, George F., ed. Ethical Wisdom East &-or West. LC 78-106891. (Proceedings of the American Catholic Philosophical Association Ser.: Vol. 51). 1977. pap. 20.00 (*0-918090-11-3*) Am Cath Philo.

— The Existence of God. LC 73-161203. (Proceedings of the American Catholic Philosophical Association Ser.: Vol. 46). 1972. pap. 20.00 (*0-918090-06-7*) Am Cath Philo.

— Freedom. LC 77-153528. (Proceedings of the American Catholic Philosophical Association Ser.: Vol. 50). 1976. pap. 20.00 (*0-918090-10-5*) Am Cath Philo.

— The Human Person. LC 80-66375. (Proceedings of the American Catholic Philosophical Association Ser.: Vol. 53). 1979. pap. 20.00 (*0-918090-13-X*) Am Cath Philo.

— Immateriality. LC 79-88689. (Proceedings of the American Catholic Philosophical Association Ser.: Vol. 52). 1978. pap. 20.00 (*0-918090-12-1*) Am Cath Philo.

— Myth & Philosophy. LC 72-184483. (Proceedings of the American Catholic Philosophical Association Ser.: Vol. 45). 1971. pap. 20.00 (*0-918090-05-9*) Am Cath Philo.

— Normative Ethics & Objective Reason Vol. 1: Ethics at the Crossroads. LC 92-13187. (Cultural Heritage & Contemporary Change Series I: Vol. 7). 300p. 1997. pap. 17.50 (*1-56518-022-4*) Coun Res Values.

— Personalist Ethics & Human Subjectivity: Ethics at the Crossroads, Vol. 2. LC 92-13188. (Cultural Heritage & Contemporary Change Series I: Vol. 8). 300p. 1994. pap. 17.50 (*1-56518-024-0*) Coun Res Values.

— The Philosopher As Teacher. LC 74-166186. (Proceedings of the American Catholic Philosophical Association Ser.: Vol. 47). 1973. pap. 20.00 (*0-918090-07-5*) Am Cath Philo.

— Philosophy & Civil Law. LC 76-150281. (Proceedings of the American Catholic Philosophical Association Ser.: Vol. 49). 1975. pap. 20.00 (*0-918090-09-1*) Am Cath Philo.

— Philosophy & the Future of Man. (Proceedings of the American Catholic Philosophical Association Ser.: Vol. 42). 1968. pap. 20.00 (*0-918090-02-4*) Am Cath Philo.

— Reading Philosophy for the Twenty-First Century. LC 89-30882. (Cultural Heritage & Contemporary Life Series I. Culture & Values: Vol. 3). 336p. (Orig.). 1989. 45.00 (*0-8191-7414-9*); pap. 17.50 (*0-8191-7415-7*) Coun Res Values.

— Research on Culture & Values: The Intersection of Universities, Churches & Nations. LC 88-33914. (Cultural Heritage & Contemporary Life Series I. Culture & Values: Vol. 1). 196p. (Orig.). 1989. 45.00 (*0-8191-7352-5*); pap. 17.50 (*0-8191-7353-3*) Coun Res Values.

— Scholasticism in the Modern World. (Proceedings of the American Catholic Philosophical Association Ser.: Vol. 40). 1966. pap. 20.00 (*0-918090-00-8*) Am Cath Philo.

— Thomas & Bonaventure: A Septicentenary Commemoration. LC 75-319639. (Proceedings of the American Catholic Philosophical Association Ser.: Vol. 48). 1974. pap. 20.00 (*0-918090-08-3*) Am Cath Philo.

— Truth & the Historicity of Man. (Proceedings of the American Catholic Philosophical Association Ser.: Vol. 43). 1969. pap. 20.00 (*0-918090-03-2*) Am Cath Philo.

McLean, George F., et al, eds. Culture, Human Rights & Peace in Central America. LC 88-37136. (Cultural Heritage & Contemporary Change Series VI: Foundations of Moral Education,: Vol. 2). 220p. (Orig.). 1989. 45.00 (*0-8191-7356-8*); pap. 17.50 (*0-8191-7357-6*) Coun Res Values.

— The Place of the Person in Social Life. (Cultural Heritage & Contemporary Change Ser.: No. 6). 398p. (Orig.). 1991. 45.00 (*1-56518-013-5*, BD450.P5477) Coun Res Values.

— The Place of the Person in Social Life. (Cultural Heritage & Contemporary Change Series VI: Foundations of Moral Education,: Vol. I, No. 6). 398p. (Orig.). 1991. pap. 17.50 (*1-56518-012-7*) Coun Res Values.

McLean, George F. & Aspell, Patrick J. Ancient Western Philosophy: The Hellenic Emergence. 2nd ed. LC 97-20068. (Cultural Heritage & Contemporary Change Ser.: Vol. 8). 340p. 1997. pap. text 17.50 (*1-56518-100-X*) Coun Res Values.

McLean, George F. & Dougherty, Jude P., eds. Philosophy & Christian Theology. (Proceedings of the American Catholic Philosophical Association Ser.: Vol. 44). 1970. pap. 20.00 (*0-918090-04-0*) Am Cath Philo.

McLean, George F. & Ellrod, Frederick, eds. Philosophical Foundations for Moral Education & Character Development: Act & Agent. 2nd ed. LC 91-30829. (Cultural Heritage & Contemporary Change Series VI: Foundations of Moral Education,: Vol. I). 366p. (Orig.). 1992. 45.00 (*1-56518-001-1*, BJ1012.A26); pap. 17.50 (*1-56518-000-3*) Coun Res Values.

McLean, George F. & Kromkowski, John, eds. Relations Between Cultures. (Cultural Heritage & Contemporary Change Series I: Vol. 4). 396p. 1991. 45.00 (*1-56518-009-7*, JC330.R45); pap. 17.50 (*1-56518-008-9*) Coun Res Values.

— Urbanization & Values. (Cultural Heritage & Contemporary Change Series I: Vol. 5). 380p. 1991. 45.00 (*1-56518-011-9*, HT361.U725); pap. 17.50 (*1-56518-010-0*) Coun Res Values.

McLean, George F. & Meynell, Hugo, eds. The Nature of Metaphysical Knowledge. LC 88-164. (International Society for Metaphysics Studies in Metaphysics: Vol. IV). 180p. (Orig.). 1988. 45.00 (*0-8191-6926-9*); pap. 17.50 (*0-8191-6927-7*) Coun Res Values.

— Person & God. LC 88-161. (International Society for Metaphysics Studies in Metaphysics: Vol. III). 377p. (Orig.). 1988. 45.00 (*0-8191-6937-4*); pap. 17.50 (*0-8191-6938-2*) Coun Res Values.

— Person & Nature. LC 88-14368. (International Society for Metaphysics Studies in Metaphysics: Vol. I). 235p. (Orig.). 1988. 45.00 (*0-8191-7025-9*); pap. 17.50 (*0-8191-7026-7*) Coun Res Values.

— Person & Society. LC 88-128. (International Society for Metaphysics Studies in Metaphysics: Vol. II). 145p. (Orig.). 1988. 45.00 (*0-8191-6924-2*); pap. 17.50 (*0-8191-6925-0*) Coun Res Values.

McLean, George F. & Pegoraro, Olinto, eds. The Social Context & Values: Perspectives of the Americas. LC 88-37080. (Cultural Heritage & Contemporary Life Series I. Culture & Values). 215p. (Orig.). 1989. 45.00 (*0-8191-7354-1*); pap. 17.50 (*0-8191-7355-X*) Coun Res Values.

McLean, George F. & Voorhies, Valerie, eds. The Nature of Philosophical Inquiry. (Proceedings of the American Catholic Philosophical Association Ser.: Vol. 41). 1967. pap. 20.00 (*0-918090-01-6*) Am Cath Philo.

McLean, George F., jt. ed. see Golubovic, Zagorka.

McLean, George F., jt. ed. see Knowles, Richard T.

McLean, George F., tr. see Said, Al-Ashmawy M.

McLean, George N. The Rise & Fall of Anarchy in America. LC 72-885. (American History & Americana Ser.: No. 47). 1973. reprint ed. lib. bdg. 75.00 (*0-8383-1426-0*) M S G Haskell Hse.

McLean, Gill L. Facing Death: Conversations with a Cancer Patient. LC 93-21524. (Illus.). 224p. (Orig.). 1993. pap. text 17.95 (*0-443-04667-0*) Church.

***McLean, Glenna A.** Tadwallader: The High-Flying, Fire-Truck Riding, Pizza-Loving, Incredible, Magnificient Cat with Double Anchovies. (Illus.). 71p. 1998. pap. 5.95 (*0-9670815-0-5*) Coll Assist.

McLean, Gordon. Too Young to Die. LC 98-21950. 235p. 1998. pap. 10.99 (*1-56179-629-8*) Focus Family.

McLean, Gordon, et al. Cities of Lonesome Fear: God among the Gangs. pap. 10.99 (*0-8024-1136-3*, 115) Moody.

McLean, H. L. The Last Trump. LC 90-82592. (Illus.). 245p. (Orig.). 1990. pap. 8.95 (*0-9627225-0-2*) Epiphany Pubns.

***McLean, Harry W.** Halt, Hass & Hasa Explained: Accelerated Reliability Techniques. LC 00-38994. 2000. write for info. (*0-87389-489-8*) ASQ Qual Pr.

McLean, Hugh. Nikolai Leskov: The Man & His Art. 796p. 1977. 50.00 (*0-674-62471-8*) HUP.

McLean, Hugh, ed. In the Shade of the Giant: Essays on Tolstoy. (California Slavic Studies: No. 13). 1989. 45.00 (*0-520-06405-4*, Pub. by U CA Pr) Cal Prin Full Svc.

McLean, Hugh, et al, eds. Harvard Slavic Studies, Vol. 4: Russian Thought & Politics. LC 72-167353. (Essay Index Reprint Ser.). 1977. reprint ed. 28.95 (*0-8369-2454-1*) Ayer.

McLean, Hugh, ed. & tr. see Zoshchenko, Mikhail.

McLean, Hulda H. Tide-Drift Shells of the Monterey Bay Region. LC 92-81082. (Illus.). 72p. (Orig.). 1992. pap. 9.95 (*0-9632480-0-6*) Santa Cruz Mus Assn.

— Uncle Bert: A Biographical Portrait of Herbert Hoover. 1998. reprint ed. pap. 5.00 (*0-938469-18-5*) Hoover Lib.

McLean, Hulda Hoover, see Hoover McLean, Hulda.

McLean, Iain. Democracy & New Technology. (Illus.). 220p. 1989. text 61.95 (*0-7456-0447-1*) Blackwell Pubs.

***McLean, Iain.** The Legend of Red Clydeside. 2000. pap. 29.95 (*0-85976-516-4*, Pub. by J Donald) Dufour.

McLean, Iain, ed. The Concise Oxford Dictionary of Politics. (Oxford Paperback Reference Ser.). 570p. 1996. pap. 13.95 (*0-19-285288-4*) OUP.

McLean, Iain, et al, eds. A Mathematical Approach to Proportional Representation: Duncan Black on Lewis Carroll. 240p. (C). 1995. lib. bdg. 78.50 (*0-7923-9620-0*) Kluwer Academic.

McLean, Iain & Butler, David, eds. Fixing the Boundaries: Defining & Redefining Single-Member Electoral Districts. LC 96-19229. 302p. 1996. text 82.95 (*1-85521-778-3*, Pub. by Dartmth Pub) Ashgate Pub Co.

McLean, Iain & Urken, Arnold B., eds. Classics of Social Choice. 384p. (C). 1995. text 54.50 (*0-472-10450-0*, 10450) U of Mich Pr.

McLean, Iain S., et al, eds. The Theory of Committees & Elections & Committee Decision. 2nd rev. ed. LC 97-49380. 512p. 1998. 99.95 (*0-7923-8110-6*) Kluwer Academic.

***McLean, Ian.** TCP/IP Black Book. LC 00-24047. 2000. write for info. (*1-57610-687-X*) Coriolis Grp.

McLean, Ian. The Timex TS 2000: Your Personal Computer. (Illus.). 240p. 1984. pap. text 12.95 (*0-13-921974-9*) P-H.

— White Aborigines: Identity Politics in Australian Art. LC 97-30210. (Illus.). 228p. (C). 1998. 59.95 (*0-521-58416-7*) Cambridge U Pr.

***McLean, Ian.** Windows 2000 Security Little Black Book. LC 99-89113. (Little Black Book Ser.). (Illus.). 415p. 2000. pap. 24.99 (*1-57610-387-0*) Coriolis Grp.

McLean, Ian & Hewitt, Fiona, eds. Condorcet: Foundations of Social Choice & Political Theory. LC 93-50634. 384p. 1994. 95.00 (*1-85898-068-2*) E Elgar.

McLean, Ian, jt. auth. see Stone, Marcus.

McLean, Ian, jt. ed. see Dempster, Jack.

Mclean, Ian S. Electronic & Computer Aided Astronomy: From Eyes to Electronic Sensors. 1989. text 59.95 (*0-470-21233-0*) P-H.

McLean, Ian S., ed. Infrared Astronomy with Arrays: The Next Generation. LC 94-7722. 550p. (C). 1994. text 251.00 (*0-7923-2778-0*) Kluwer Academic.

McLean, J. A. Dimensions in Spirituality: Reflections on the Meaning of Spiritual Life & Transformation in Light of the Baha'i Faith. 336p. (Orig.). 1994. pap. 21.95 (*0-85398-376-3*) G Ronald Pub.

McLean, J. A. & Tobin, G. Animal & Human Calorimetry. (Illus.). 352p. 1988. text 100.00 (*0-521-30905-0*) Cambridge U Pr.

McLean, J. R. Two-Lane Highway Traffic Operations: Theory & Practice, Vol. 11. (Transportation Studies). xii, 408p. 1989. text 182.00 (*2-88124-725-3*) Gordon & Breach.

McLean, J. W. & Weitzel, William. Leadership - Magic, Myth, or Method? LC 91-34595. 240p. 1992. 22.95 (*0-8144-5054-7*) AMACOM.

McLean, Jack, ed. Revisioning the Sacred: Essays in Baha'i Theology. (Studies in the Babi & Baha'i Religions: Vol. 8). 1996. pap. 29.95 (*0-933770-96-0*) Kalimat.

***McLean, Jacqueline.** Teen Parenting. LC 99-37624. (Overview Ser.). (Illus.). 128p. (YA). (gr. 6-9). 2000. lib. bdg. 23.70 (*1-56006-517-6*) Lucent Bks.

— Victoria Woodhull: First Woman Presidential Candidate. LC 99-32946. (Notable Americans Ser.). (Illus.). 112p. (YA). (gr. 5 up). 1999. lib. bdg. 18.95 (*1-883846-47-1*) M Reynolds.

— Women with Wings. Anderson, Jenna, ed. (Profiles Ser.: Vol. 30). (Illus.). 160p. (YA). (gr. 5-12). 2000. lib. bdg. 18.95 (*1-881508-70-6*) Oliver Pr MN.

***McLean, James.** California Sabers; The 2nd Massachusetts Cavalry in the Civil War. LC 00-35040. (Illus.). 2000. 35.00 (*0-253-33786-0*) Ind U Pr.

McLean, James & McLean, Lee K. How Children Learn Language: A Textbook for Professionals in Early Childhood or Special Education. LC 98-50443. 224p. 1999. pap. text 48.95 (*1-56593-683-3*, 1372) Thomson Learn.

McLean, James E. Improving Education Through Action Research: A Guide for Administrators & Teachers. Herman, Jerry J. & Herman, Janice L., eds. LC 94-23860. (Road Maps to Success Ser.). (Illus.). 88p. 1995. pap. 14.95 (*0-8039-6186-3*) Corwin Pr.

McLean, James E. & Lockwood, Robert E. Why & How Should We Assess Students? The Competing Measures of Student Performance. LC 95-44371. (Roadmaps to Success Ser.). 1996. pap. 15.00 (*0-8039-6074-3*) Sage.

— Why We Assess Students - And How: The Competing Measures of Student Performance. LC 95-44371. (RTS Ser.). (Illus.). 72p. 1996. pap. 14.95 (*0-8039-6335-1*, 2444) Corwin Pr.

McLean, James H. & Gosliner, Terrence M. Taxonomic Atlas of the Benthic Fauna of the Santa Maria Basin & Western Santa Barbara Channel Vol. 9, Pt. 2: The Mollusca: The Gastropoda. Scott, Paul H. et al, eds. LC 94-68651. (Illus.). vii, 228p. (Orig.). 1996. pap. 39.00 (*0-936494-14-X*) Santa B Museum.

McLean, James H., jt. auth. see Keen, A. Myra.

McLean, James L. & McLean, Judy W., eds. Gettysburg Sources, Vol. 2. (Illus.). 187p. 1987. 23.50 (*0-935523-06-5*) Butternut & Blue.

— Gettysburg Sources, Vol. 3. (Illus.). 223p. (C). 1991. 26.50 (*0-935523-22-7*) Butternut & Blue.

McLean, Janet. Hector & Maggie. (Illus.). 32p. (J). (gr. k-3). 1993. pap. 6.95 (*0-04-442245-8*, Pub. by Allen & Unwin Pty) IPG Chicago.

***McLean, Janet, ed.** Property & the Constitution. 304p. 1999. 45.00 (*1-84113-055-9*, Pub. by Hart Pub) Intl Spec Bk.

McLean, Janet, jt. auth. see McLean, Andrea.

McLean, Janet, jt. auth. see McLean, Andrew.

McLean, Janice, ed. Directory of Fund Raising & Nonprofit Management Consultants. 390p. 1992. 50.00 (*0-930807-25-1*, 600313) Fund Raising.

***McLean, Jeanne P.** Leading from the Center: The Emerging Role of the Chief Academic Officer in Theological Schools. LC 99-17246. (Studies in Theological Education). 301p. 1999. 39.95 (*0-7885-0542-4*, 00 08 10) Duke.

***McLean, Jim.** The Complete Idiot's Guide to Improving Your Short Game. 368p. 2000. pap. 18.95 (*0-02-863889-1*, Alpha Ref) Macmillan Gen Ref.

McLean, Jim. The Eight Step Swing: A Revolutionary Golf Technique by a PGA Pro Coach. LC 93-39839. (Illus.). 160p. 1995. pap. 17.00 (*0-06-092589-2*, Harper Ref) HarpC.

***McLean, Jim.** Eight-Step Swing: Revolutionary Golf Technique by a PGA Pro. (Illus.). 2000. pap. 16.00 (*0-06-095800-6*, Quil) HarperTrade.

McLean, Jim. The Golf School: The Tuition-Free, Tee-to-Green Curriculum from Golf's Finest High-End Academy. LC 98-52979. (Illus.). 288p. 1999. 27.50 (*0-385-49287-1*) Broadway BDD.

McLean, Jim & Andrisani, John. The X-Factor Swing: And Other Secrets to Power & Distance. LC 96-43829. (Illus.). 128p. 1997. 23.00 (*0-06-270142-8*, Harper Ref) HarpC.

McLean, Jim & Dennis, Larry. The Golf Digest Book of Drills. 1990. 23.00 (*0-671-72556-4*) PB.

McLean, Jim & Pirozzolo, Fran. Putters Pocket Compa. LC 94-18734. 128p. 1994. 10.00 (*0-06-017189-8*) HarperTrade.

McLean, John. Arizona Puzzles. 64p. 1991. pap. 6.95 (*0-9631657-0-4*) AZ Puzzles.

— Notes of a Twenty-Five Years' Service in the Hudson's Bay Territory, Vol. 19. Wallace, W. S., ed. LC 68-28607. 402p. 1968. reprint ed. lib. bdg. 65.00 (*0-8371-5057-4*, MCNS, Greenwood Pr) Greenwood.

— The Science & Art of Dental Ceramics, Vol. II. (Illus.). 496p. 1980. text 160.00 (*0-931386-11-X*) Quint Pub Co.

— The Wind at My Back: Memoirs of an Irish Immigrant. McLean, Dorothy B., ed. LC 95-94525. 215p. (Orig.). 1995. pap. 15.00 (*0-9646923-0-9*) Malcolm Pubns.

McLean, John A. The Seventieth Week of Daniel 9:27 As a Literary Key for Understanding the Structure of the Apocalypse of John. LC 95-24323. (Biblical Press Ser.: Vol. 38). 332p. 1996. text 99.95 (*0-7734-2434-2*, Mellen Biblical Pr) E Mellen.

McLean, John L., ed. The Poems & Plays of Thomas Wade. LC 95-61177. xiv, 699p. 1997. 65.00 (*0-87875-463-6*) Whitston Pub.

M

***McLean, John N.** The 10 Minute Snook Book: A Quick Guide to Finding & Catching Snook on Artificial Lures. (Illus.). ix, 32p. 1999. 7.95 (*0-9670844-0-7*) McLean Multi.

McLean, John S., ed. see American Water Resources Association, Conference (23rd: 1987: Salt Lake City, UT) Staff.

McLean, John W., ed. Dental Ceramics: Proceedings of the First International Symposium on Ceramics. (Illus.). 536p. 1983. text 160.00 (*0-86715-112-9*) Quint Pub Co.

McLean, Judy W., jt. ed. see McLean, James L.

McLean, Katherine. Illustrated Bible Stories for Children. (YA). 1987. 4.98 (*0-671-07535-7*) S&S Trade.

McLean, Kathleen. Planning for People in Museum Exhibitions. (Illus.). 196p. (C). 1993. text 35.00 (*0-944040-32-2*, 67-0) AST Ctrs.

McLean, Kathleen & McNamara, John R. Academic Success in Middle School: A Guide for Parents & Students. 97p. (C). 1997. 8.00 (*1-57074-234-0*) Greyden Pr.

McLean, Kathleen, jt. ed. see Dorn, William J.

***McLean, Kathy.** The Jairus Child & the Stones of Pharaoh: An Interactive Adventure of the Initiate to the True Identity of the Great Pyramid of Giza. (Illus.). 240p. 2000. pap. 19.95 (*0-9674673-0-6*) K McLean.

McLean, Ken. Genetic Heritage. (Illus.). 240p. 1996. 80.00 (*0-9619432-1-1*) K A & C J McLean.

McLean, Lee K., jt. auth. see McLean, James.

M

McLean, Linda. JonBenet's Mother: The Tragedy & the Truth. LC 98-91774. 125p. 1998. pap. 6.99 (*0-87012-596-6*) McClain.

After three years of media frenzy with various "experts," professionals & reporters relaying topical information concerning the death of 6-year old JonBenet Ramsey, who was murdered in her Boulder, CO home Christmas Day, 1996, the family & friends of JonBenet's mother, Patsy Ramsey, are speaking out. Linda McLean, of Parkersburg, WV, a childhood friend for the past 25 years of JonBenet Ramsey's mother, Patsy Ramsey, has written her thoughts about the life of Patsy Ramsey in JONBENET'S MOTHER: THE TRAGEDY & THE TRUTH. The book chronicles the life of Patsy Ramsey, a former Miss West Virginia, from childhood through her marriage to John Ramsey & the birth of their two children, Burke & JonBenet, her struggle to beat ovarian cancer & the tragic death of her only daughter, JonBenet. Retrospectives from Patsy's two sisters, her stepchildren, a cousin & various friends from Parkersburg, Atlanta, GA & Boulder are added to express the commitment & true belief in Patsy & John Ramsey's innocence in the horrendous murder of JonBenet. This paperback biography has been featured in People magazine, LARRY KING, LEEZA, BURDEN OF PROOF, etc. & is filled with photos of the entire Ramsey family. McLean's proceeds from JONBENET'S MOTHER. THE TRAGEDY & THE TRUTH will go to the JonBenet Ramsey Memorial Fund. *Publisher Paid Annotation.*

***McLean, Linda.** Riddance. LC 00-302696. 96p. 2000. pap. 14.95 (*1-85459-465-6*) Theatre Comm.

***McLean, Lorraine A.** Dorothy Donnelly: A Life in the Theatre. LC 99-28403. (Illus.). 224p. 1999. lib. bdg. 38.50 (*0-7864-0677-1*) McFarland & Co.

McLean, M., ed. Physical & Elastic Characterisation. (Characterisation of High-Temperature Materials Ser.: No. IV). vi, 226p. 1989. text 52.50 (*0-901462-66-7*, Pub. by Inst Materials) Ashgate Pub Co.

McLean, M., jt. ed. see Hondros, E. D.

McLean, Malcolm. Devoted to the Goddess: The Life & Work of Ramprasad. LC 97-19307. (SUNY Series in Hindu Studies). 205p. (C). 1998. text 59.50 (*0-7914-3689-6*); pap. text 19.95 (*0-7914-3690-X*) State U NY Pr.

McLean, Malcolm D., ed. Papers Concerning Robertson's Colony in Texas. Incl. Introductory Volume, Robert Leftwich's Mexico Diary & Letterbook, 1822-1824. (Illus.). 611p. 1986. lib. bdg. 35.00 (*0-932408-00-1*); Vol. I, 1788-1822, The Texas Association. (Illus.). lxxi, 567p. 1980. reprint ed. lib. bdg. 30.00 (*0-932408-01-X*); Vol. II, 1823 Through September, 1826, Leftwich's Grant. (Illus.). 687p. 1975. lib. bdg. 30.00 (*0-932408-02-8*); Vol. III, October, 1826, Through April, 1830, The Nashville Colony. (Illus.). 577p. 1976. lib. bdg. 30.00 (*0-932408-03-6*); Vol. IV, May Through October 10, 1830, Tenoxtitlan, Dream Capital of Texas. (Illus.). 627p. 1977. lib. bdg. 30.00 (*0-932408-04-4*); Vol. V, October 11, 1830, Through March 5, 1831, The Upper Colony. (Illus.). 628p. 1978. lib. bdg. 30.00 (*0-932408-05-2*); Vol. VI, March 6 Through December 5, 1831, The Campaigns Against the Tawakoni, Waco, Towash & Comanche Indians. (Illus.). 632p. 1979. lib. bdg. 30.00 (*0-932408-06-0*); Vol. VII, December 6, 1831, Through October, 1833, Those Eleven-League Grants. (Illus.). 664p. 1980. lib. bdg. 30.00 (*0-932408-07-9*); Vol. VIII, November, 1833, Through September, 1834, Robertson's Colony. (Illus.). 608p. 1981. lib. bdg. 30.00 (*0-932408-08-7*); Vol. X, March 21 Through July 25, 1835, The Ranger Rendezvous. (Illus.). 600p. 1983. lib. bdg. 30.00 (*0-932408-10-9*); Vol. XI, July 26 Through October 14, 1835, Nashville-on-the-Brazos. (Illus.). 666p. 1984. lib. bdg. 30.00 (*0-932408-11-7*); Vol. XII, October 15, 1835, Through January 14, 1836, the Municipality of Milam. (Illus.). 732p. 1985. lib. bdg. 35.00 (*0-932408-12-5*); Vol. XIII, January 15 Through March 17, 1836, The Convention at Washington-on-the-Brazos. (Illus.). 792p. 1987. lib. bdg. 35.00 (*0-932408-13-3*); Vol. XIV, March 18 Through July 22, 1836, The Battle of San Jacinto & the Fall of Fort Parker. (Illus.). 620p. 1988. lib. bdg. 35.00 (*0-932408-14-1*); Vol. XV, July 23, 1836, through August 9, 1837, The Gentleman from Milam. (Illus.). 613p. 1989. 35.00 (*0-932408-15-X*); Vol. XVI, August 10, 1837, through November, 1838, The Creation of Robertson County. (Illus.). 716p. 1990. 35.00 (*0-932408-16-8*); lib. bdg. write for info. (*0-318-68008-4*) UTA Pr.

McLean, Malcolm D., ed. Papers Concerning Robertson's Colony in Texas Vol. XVIII: August 11, 1840 Through March 4, 1842: The End of an Era. 411p. 1993. 35.00 (*0-932408-18-4*) UTA Pr.

McLean, Margaret A. Barton. Roger Barton's Kinsmen: General Record of the Barton Family & a Detailed List of Roger Barton's Descendants. (Illus.). 115p. 1997. reprint ed. pap. 19.50 (*0-8328-7399-3*); reprint ed. lib. bdg. 29.50 (*0-8328-7398-5*) Higginson Bk Co.

Mclean, Margot, jt. auth. see Hillman, James.

McLean, Marianne. The People of Glengarry: Highlanders in Transition, 1745-1820. (Illus.). 312p. 1991. 65.00 (*0-7735-0814-7*, Pub. by McG-Queens Univ Pr) CUP Services.

— The People of Glengarry: Highlanders in Transition, 1745-1820. (Illus.). 312p. 1993. pap. 22.95 (*0-7735-1156-3*, Pub. by McG-Queens Univ Pr) CUP Services.

Mclean, Mary E. & Bailey, Donald B. Assessing Infants & Preschoolers with Special Needs. 2nd ed. LC 95-43484. 580p. (C). 1996. 80.00 (*0-02-379394-5*, Macmillan Coll) P-H.

McLean, Mary E., jt. ed. see Odom, Samuel L.

McLean, Mary L. & Voytek, Kenneth P. Understanding Your Economy: Using Analysis to Guide Local Strategic Planning. rev. ed. LC 92-73812. (Illus.). 245p. 1992. 52.00 (*0-918286-82-4*, Planners Press); pap. 38.95 (*0-918286-81-6*, Planners Press) Am Plan Assn.

McLean, Matthew. Locked up, Freed, Busted. LC 98-84696. 116p. 1998. pap. 8.95 (*1-56167-426-5*) Am Literary Pr.

McLean, Mervyn. An Annotated Bibliography of Oceanic Music & Dance. 2nd enl. rev. ed. LC 95-9755. (Detroit Studies in Music Bibliography: No. 74). 502p. 1995. 55.00 (*0-89990-073-9*) Harmonie Park Pr.

— Maori Music. (Illus.). 430p. 1997. 45.00 (*1-86940-144-1*, Pub. by Auckland Univ) Paul & Co Pubs.

***McLean, Mervyn.** Weavers of Song: Polynesian Music & Dance. LC 99-34404. 1999. text 42.00 incl. cd-rom (*0-8248-2271-4*) UH Pr.

McLean, Michael. Distant Serenade. LC 93-73186. (Illus.). 44p. 1993. 9.99 (*0-87579-777-6*) Deseret Bk.

— The Forgotten Carols. LC 91-30686. (Illus.). 128p. 1991. 16.95 (*0-87579-554-4*) Deseret Bk.

— Forgotten Carols: A Christmas Story & Songs. 1998. 19.95 (*1-57345-399-4*, Shadow Mount) Deseret Bk.

— The Forgotten Carols: A Christmas Story & Songs. LC 98-8353. 1998. 19.95 (*1-57345-398-6*, Shadow Mount) Deseret Bk.

— The Well-Tempered Violin. 52p. 1992. pap. text 8.95 (*0-87487-434-3*) Summy-Birchard.

McLean, Mick, ed. The Information Explosion: The New Electronic Media in Japan & Europe, 3. LC 85-12666. (Emerging Patterns of Work & Communications in an Information Age Ser.: No. 3). 130p. 1985. 49.95 (*0-313-25091-X*, MIX/) Greenwood.

— Mechatronics: Developments in Japan & Europe. LC 83-22925. 129p. 1983. 55.00 (*0-89930-087-1*, MMT/, Quorum Bks) Greenwood.

McLean, Mick & Rolland, Thomas. The INMOS Saga. LC 85-24441. 199p. 1986. 49.95 (*0-89930-165-7*, MNI/, Quorum Bks) Greenwood.

McLean, Mina G. February Holidays Handbook. LC 84-15572. (Holiday Handbooks Ser.). 96p. 1985. lib. bdg. 25.64 (*0-89565-270-6*) Childs World.

McLean, Mollie. Adventures Greek Heroes, 001. 192p. (gr. 4-7). 1972. pap. 6.95 (*0-395-13714-4*) HM.

— Adventures of the Greek Heroes. 1961. 11.05 (*0-606-10565-4*, Pub. by Turtleback) Demco.

McLean, Mollie & Wiseman, Ann S. The Adventures of Greek Heroes. 001. LC 61-10628. (Merit Ser.). (Illus.). 192p. (J). (ps-3). 1973. 18.00 (*0-395-06913-0*, Sandpiper); pap. 5.95 (*0-685-42189-9*, Sandpiper) HM.

McLean, Monica. Cinderella Bride. 1998. per. 4.25 (*0-373-07852-8*, 1-07852-6) Silhouette.

***McLean, Monica.** Just a Wedding Away. (Intimate Moments Ser.: Vol. 993). 2000. per. 4.50 (*0-373-07993-1*) Silhouette.

McLean, Oakland. The Evidence for Creation: Examining the Origin of Planet Earth. 192p. 1995. pap. 7.95 (*0-9637797-1-0*) Understand Times.

McLean, P., et al. Building Understanding (Middle) (Illus.). 80p. (J). (gr. 4-8). 1990. 9.95 (*0-918932-97-1*, A-1668) Activity Resources.

— Building Understanding (Primary) (Illus.). 64p. (J). (gr. k-4). 1990. 8.95 (*0-918932-96-3*, A-1667) Activity Resources.

McLean, Pamela D., jt. auth. see Hudson, Frederic M.

McLean, Paul D. A Triune Concept of the Brain & Behavior: Papers Presented at Queen's University, Ontario, 1969. LC 72-90742. 177p. reprint ed. pap. 54.90 (*0-608-13156-3*, 205595900041) Bks Demand.

McLean, Peggy. Mirror Explorations. (Illus.). 52p. (J). (gr. 1-5). 1993. pap. text 8.95 (*1-882293-01-0*, A-1685) Activity Resources.

McLean, Peggy & Sternberg, Betty. People Piece Primer. (Illus.). 54p. (Orig.). (J). (gr. k-3). 1975. pap. 7.95 (*0-918932-37-8*, A-1403) Activity Resources.

McLean, Peggy, et al. Let's Pattern Block It. (Illus.). 170p. (Orig.). (J). (gr. 2-8). 1973. pap. 13.95 (*0-918932-26-2*, A-1118) Activity Resources.

— Multilink Explorations. (Illus.). 48p. (J). (gr. k-4). 1986. pap. 7.95 (*0-918932-88-2*, A-5560) Activity Resources.

McLean, Peggy, jt. auth. see Jenkins, Lee.

McLean, Peggy, jt. auth. see Laycock, Mary.

McLean, Peggy, jt. auth. see Laycook, Mary.

McLean, Penny. Comunicate Con Tu Angel Guardian. 1998. pap. 9.95 (*84-8327-007-2*) E Martinez Roca.

McLean, R. Hugh. Guys & Ghouls. 32p. (Orig.). 1994. pap. 4.00 (*1-885857-08-X*) Four Wnds Pubng.

— The Sellabration of Jesus. Eldredge, A., ed. 32p. (Orig.). 1995. pap. 4.00 (*1-885857-10-1*) Four Wnds Pubng.

McLean, Raymond W. Fiddle a Little. Forbes, John, ed. (Fiddle a Little Ser.). 107p. 1983. student ed. 12.95 (*0-685-14891-2*) KET.

McLean, Richard. Zen Fables for Today: Stories Inspired by the Zen Masters. LC 97-45494. 144p. 1998. pap. 10.00 (*0-380-79561-2*, Avon Bks) Morrow Avon.

McLean, Robert A. Financial Management in Health Care Organizations. LC 96-23085. (Health Services Administration Ser.). 400p. 1997. pap. 67.95 (*0-8273-5595-5*) Delmar.

McLean, Robert A. & Anderson, Virgil L. Applied Factorial & Fractional Designs. LC 84-7015. (Statistics, Textbooks & Monographs: Vol. 55). 389p. reprint ed. pap. 120.60 (*0-7837-0271-X*, 204058000017) Bks Demand.

McLean, Robert A., jt. auth. see Anderson, Virgil L.

McLean, Roderick R., jt. auth. see Seligmann, Matthew S.

McLean, Ross, et al. Country Walks: In & Around the Niagara Escarpment. LC 97-212465. (Illus.). 176p. 1994. pap. 13.95 (*1-55046-102-8*, Pub. by Boston Mills) Genl Dist Srvs.

***McLean, Ruari.** How Typography Happens. LC 99-89050. 2000. pap. write for info. (*1-58456-019-3*) Oak Knoll.

McLean, Ruari. Jan Tschichold. LC 96-157181. (Illus.). 80p. 1996. write for info. (*0-85331-668-6*, Pub. by Lund Humphries) Antique Collect.

— Joseph Cundall, a Victorian Publisher. 96p. 1976. 28.00 (*0-900002-13-1*, Pub. by Priv Lib Assn) Oak Knoll.

— The Thames & Hudson Manual of Typography. LC 80-50803. (Illus.). 216p. 1992. pap. 16.95 (*0-500-68022-1*, Pub. by Thames Hudson) Norton.

***McLean, Ruari.** True to Type: An Autobiography of Ruari McLean. LC 99-22457. 1999. write for info. (*1-884718-96-5*) Oak Knoll.

McLean, Ruari, ed. Typographers on Type: An Illustrated Anthology. (Illus.). 180p. 1995. 27.00 (*0-393-70201-4*) Norton.

McLean, Ruari & McLean, Antonia. Benjamin Fawcett: Engraver & Colour Printer. 196p. 1988. text 113.95 (*0-85967-789-3*, Pub. by Scolar Pr) Ashgate Pub Co.

McLean, Ruari, et al. Jan Tschichold: A Life in Typography. (Illus.). 128p. 1997. pap. 19.95 (*1-56898-084-1*) Princeton Arch.

McLean, Scott, ed. see Snyder, Gary.

McLean, Sheila. Old Law, New Medicine Medical Ethics & Human Rights. 1999. pap. text 19.50 (*0-86358-402-0*) Harper SF.

— Old Law, New Medicine: Medical Ethics & Human Rights. 224p. 1999. 50.00 (*0-86358-403-9*, Pub. by Rivers Oram) NYU Pr.

Mclean, Sheila & Britton, Alison. The Case for Physician-Assisted Suicide. LC 98-212243. (Pandora Soap Box Ser.). 128p. 1997. pap. 11.95 (*0-04-440983-4*, Pub. by Rivers Oram) NYU Pr.

McLean, Sheila, jt. auth. see Pace, Nicholas A.

McLean, Sheila A. Compensation for Damage: An International Perspective. 190p. 1993. 78.95 (*1-85521-169-6*, Pub. by Dartmth Pub) Ashgate Pub Co.

— Contemporary Issues in Law, Medicine & Ethics. (Medico-Legal Ser.). (Illus.). 288p. 1995. text 89.95 (*1-85521-586-1*, Pub. by Dartmth Pub) Ashgate Pub Co.

— Death, Dying & the Law. (Medico-Legal Issues Ser.). (Illus.). 200p. 1996. text 87.95 (*1-85521-657-4*, Pub. by Dartmth Pub) Ashgate Pub Co.

— Legal Issues in Human Reproduction. (Medico-Legal Issues Ser.: Vol. 1). 1989. text 87.95 (*0-566-05393-4*, Pub. by Dartmth Pub) Ashgate Pub Co.

— Legal Issues in Human Reproduction. (Medico-Legal Issues Ser.: Vol. 1). 1990. pap. 39.95 (*1-85521-008-8*, Pub. by Dartmth Pub) Ashgate Pub Co.

— A Patient's Right to Know: Information Disclosure, the Doctor & the Law. 270p. 1989. pap. 33.95 (*1-85521-021-5*, Pub. by Dartmth Pub); text 87.95 (*1-85521-010-X*, Pub. by Dartmth Pub) Ashgate Pub Co.

McLean, Sheila A., ed. Law Reform & Human Reproduction. (Medico-Legal Issues Ser.). 200p. 1992. 81.95 (*1-85521-026-6*, Pub. by Dartmth Pub) Ashgate Pub Co.

— Law Reform & Medical Injury Litigation. (Medico-Legal Issues Ser.). (Illus.). 192p. 1995. text 81.95 (*1-85521-534-9*, Pub. by Dartmth Pub) Ashgate Pub Co.

— Legal Issues in Medicine. 234p. 1981. text 76.95 (*0-566-00428-3*) Ashgate Pub Co.

McLean, Sheila A. & Maher, Gerry. Medicine, Morals, & the Law. 113p. 1983. text 87.95 (*0-566-00533-6*) Ashgate Pub Co.

McLean, Stafford, jt. ed. see Crawley, Jacqueline N.

McLean, Susan H. Pennies for the Piper. 160p. (YA). (gr. 5 up). 1993. pap. 4.50 (*0-374-45754-9*, Sunburst Bks) FS&G.

McLean, Teresa. Seized: My Life with Epilepsy. 174p. 1996. pap. 16.95 (*1-86066-013-4*, Pub. by R Cohen Bks) Trafalgar.

McLean, Treva. The Basic Humanity Handbook: Divine Key Codes. 250p. 1999. pap. 12.95 (*1-879802-02-3*) Dancing Fish.

McLean, Trish, jt. ed. see Spaulding-Phillips, Sara.

McLean, Vianne. The Human Encounter: Teachers & Children Living Together in Preschools. 250p. 1991. 75.00 (*1-85000-724-1*, Falmer Pr); pap. 32.95 (*1-85000-725-X*, Falmer Pr) Taylor & Francis.

— The Human Encounter: Teachers & Children Living Together in the Pre-School. 224p. 1991. 50.00 (*1-85000-926-0*, Falmer Pr); pap. 22.00 (*1-85000-927-9*, Falmer Pr) Taylor & Francis.

McLean, Virginia. Pretend Passport & Currency. (Illus.). 8p. 1997. teacher ed., ring bd. 5.50 (*1-885870-03-5*) Redbird.

— Teacher's Tote to China. (Illus.). 7p. 1997. teacher ed., ring bd. 6.50 (*1-885870-00-0*) Redbird.

— Teacher's Tote to Italy. (Illus.). 7p. 1997. teacher ed., ring bd. 6.50 (*1-885870-02-7*) Redbird.

— Teacher's Tote to Kenya. (Illus.). 7p. 1997. teacher ed., ring bd. 6.50 (*1-885870-01-9*) Redbird.

McLean, Virginia O. Chasing the Moon to China. 2nd ed. LC 87-60411. (Illus.). 40p. (J). (gr. k-6). 1997. 21.95 incl. audio compact disk (*0-9606046-1-8*) Redbird.

— Pastatively Italy. LC 94-65440. (Illus.). 40p. (J). (gr. k-6). 1997. 21.95 incl. audio compact disk (*0-9606046-6-9*) Redbird.

McLean, Virginia O. & Klyce, Katherine P. Kenya, Jambo! 2nd ed. LC 88-63987. (Illus.). 36p. (J). (gr. k-6). 1997. 21.95 incl. audio compact disk (*0-9606046-4-2*) Redbird.

McLean, Will, jt. auth. see Singman, Jeffrey L.

***McLean, William.** Strongly Elliptic Systems & Boundary Integral Equations. (Illus.). 376p. (C). 2000. text 74.95 (*0-521-66332-6*); pap. text 32.95 (*0-521-66375-X*) Cambridge U Pr.

McLean, William G. & Nelson, E. W. Schaum's Outline of Engineering Mechanics. 4th ed. (Schaum's Outline Ser.). 480p. (C). 1988. pap. 14.95 (*0-07-044822-1*) McGraw.

***McLeary, Ailsa & Dingle, Tony.** Catherine: On Catherine Currie's Diary, 1873-1908. LC 98-202228. 240p. 1999. 29.95 (*0-522-84836-2*, Pub. by Melbourne Univ Pr) Paul & Co Pubs.

***McLeary, Joseph Webb, et al.** By the Numbers: Using Facts & Figures to Get Your Projects, Plans & Ideas Approved. LC 99-59434. 228p. 2000. 22.95 (*0-8144-0499-5*) AMACOM.

McLeary, Michael P., tr. see Akavia, Miriam.

McLeash, V., jt. auth. see McLeish, Kenneth.

McLeavy, Adrienne. Pet Owner's Guide to the Border Collie. (Pet Owner's Guide Ser.). (Illus.). 1996. 8.00 (*1-86054-070-8*, Pub. by Ringpr Bks) Seven Hills Bk.

***McLeay, Alison.** The Dream Maker. LC 99-48488. 413p. 1999. text 24.95 (*0-312-24423-1*) St Martin.

McLeay, Alison. Passage Home. 656p. 1991. mass mkt. 5.99 (*0-380-71532-5*, Avon Bks) Morrow Avon.

— Summer House. large type ed. LC 98-14065. (Romance Ser.). 451p. 1998. 26.95 (*0-7838-0164-5*) Thorndike Pr.

McLeay, Allison. The Summer House. LC 97-7198. 1997. text 23.95 (*0-312-15666-9*) St Martin.

McLeay, Elizabeth. The Cabinet & Political Power in New Zealand. (Readings in New Zealand Politics Ser.: No. 5). (Illus.). 266p. 1995. pap. text 42.00 (*0-19-558312-4*) OUP.

McLeay, Heather. The Knots Puzzle Book. (Illus.). (J). 1996. pap. 8.50 (*0-906212-96-0*, Pub. by Tarquin Pubns) Parkwest Pubns.

McLeay, Stuart, jt. ed. see Garrod, Neil.

McLeeland, C. & Baird, I. Low Cost CAD in Building Services. (C). 1987. 120.00 (*0-86022-114-8*, Pub. by Build Servs Info Assn) St Mut.

McLees, David, jt. auth. see Tickoo, Sham.

McLees, Mary H. A Study of the Elementary Teaching Personnel of Hunterdon, Morris, Sussex & Warren Counties, New Jersey, with Particular Reference to the State Program of Teacher Training. LC 79-177034. (Columbia University. Teachers College. Contributions to Education Ser.: No. 512). reprint ed. 37.50 (*0-404-55512-8*) AMS Pr.

***McLees, Nectaria.** A Child's Paradise of Saints. (Illus.). 52p. (J). (gr. k-5). 2000. pap. 9.49 (*0-916700-52-6*) Christ Saviour.

McLees, Nectaria, tr. see Vladimirov, Artemy.

McLeese, Don & Philbin, Marianne, eds. All We Are Saying: Popular Musicians & the Struggle for Peace. (Illus.). 1987. pap. write for info. (*0-394-75626-6*) Pantheon.

McLeester, Dick. Welcome to the Magic Theatre. 2nd ed. LC 76-29541. (Illus.). (Orig.). 1977. pap. 3.75 (*0-686-23238-0*) Health Journal.

McLeish. Seas & Oceans. (Habitats Ser.). 48p. (J). (gr. 5-6). 1996. lib. bdg. 24.26 (*0-8172-4517-0*) Raintree Steck-V.

Mcleish. Stories & Legends Bible. Date not set. pap. text. write for info. (*0-582-03406-X*, Pub. by Addison-Wesley) Longman.

McLeish, Andrew. Underwater Concreting & Repair. LC 94-36568. 148p. 1994. text 64.95 (*0-470-23403-2*) Halsted Pr.

McLeish, Barry J. Successful Marketing Strategies for Nonprofit Organizations. LC 95-1657. (Nonprofit Law, Finance, & Management Ser.). 294p. 1995. 69.95 (*0-471-10568-6*); pap. 24.95 (*0-471-10567-8*) Wiley.

McLeish, Barry L. The Donor Bond: How to Nurture Your Donors Using Strategic Marketing & Management Techniques. 173p. 1991. 27.95 (*0-930807-16-2*, 600224) Fund Raising.

McLeish, C. W., jt. auth. see Evans, G.

McLeish, D. L. & Small, C. S. The Theory & Applications of Statistical Inference Functions. (Lecture Notes in Statistics Ser.: Vol. 44). (Illus.). vi, 124p. 1988. 58.95 (*0-387-96720-6*) Spr-Verlag.

An Asterisk (*) at the beginning of an entry indicates that the title is appearing for the first time.

McLeish, D. L., jt. auth. see Small, Christopher G.

McLeish, Ewan. Europe. LC 96-30802. (Continents Ser.). 48p. (J). 1997. lib. bdg. 25.69 (*0-8172-4775-0*) Raintree Steck-V.

— Keeping Water Clean. LC 97-1257. (Protecting Our Planet Ser.). (J). 1998. 25.69 (*0-8172-4935-4*) Raintree Steck-V.

Mcleish, Ewan. South America. LC 96-41311. (Continents Ser.). 48p. (J). 1997. lib. bdg. 25.69 (*0-8172-4777-7*) Raintree Steck-V.

McLeish, Gordon, et al. A Level Law Paper, Vol. 2. (Lecture Notes Ser.). 486p. 1995. pap. 28.00 (*1-874241-75-9*, Pub. by Cavendish Pubng) Gaunt.

McLeish, I., et al. Native Orchids of Belize. (Illus.). 340p. (C). 1995. text 123.00 (*90-5410-609-3*, Pub. by A A Balkema) Ashgate Pub Co.

McLeish, John. Development of Modern Behavioural Psychology, Vol. 1. 228p. (Orig.). (C). 1981. pap. text 14.95 (*0-920490-20-4*) Temeron Bks.

McLeish, John A. Creativity in the Later Years: An Annotated Bibliography. LC 91-32398. 155p. 1992. text 10.00 (*0-8240-4645-5*, SS552) Garland.

McLeish, John L. Highlights of the Mexican Revolution. 1976. lib. bdg. 5.95 (*0-8490-1950-8*) Gordon Pr.

McLeish, Kenneth. Myth: Myths & Legends of the World Explained & Explored. 800p. 1996. 50.00 (*0-8160-3237-8*) Facts on File.

— Orpheus. 80p. 1998. pap. 12.95 (*1-84002-016-4*) Theatre Comm.

— Roman Comedy. (Inside the Ancient World Ser.). 80p. 1983. reprint ed. pap. 16.95 (*0-86292-186-4*, Pub. by Brist Class Pr) Focus Pub-R Pullins.

— Shakespeare's Characters: A Players Press Guide. 264p. 1992. 40.00 (*0-88734-608-1*) Players Pr.

McLeish, Kenneth. Sophocles: Plays Two. (Methuen World Dramatists Ser.). 227p. (C). 1990. pap. 14.95 (*0-413-62880-9*, A0459, Methuen Drama) Methn.

McLeish, Kenneth, ed. Key Ideas in Human Thought. LC 94-34096. 800p. 1995. pap. 22.95 (*1-55958-650-8*) Prima Pub.

McLeish, Kenneth & McLeash, V. Long to Reign over Us: Memories of Coronation Day & Life in the 1950s. large type ed. (Charnwood Library). (Illus.). 336p. 1993. 11.50 (*0-7089-8740-0*, Charnwood) Ulverscroft.

McLeish, Kenneth & McLeish, Valerie. Famous People. LC 90-37910. (Illus.). 96p. (J). (gr. 3-6). 1997. pap. 7.95 (*0-8167-2239-0*) Troll Communs.

— The Good Reading Guide to Murder, Crime Fiction, & Thrillers. LC 91-2027. 1991. 12.95 (*0-13-359092-5*) P-H.

— The Listener's Guide to Classical Music: An Introduction to the Great Classical Composers & their Works. 288p. 1991. 35.00 (*0-8161-7369-9*, Hall Reference) Macmillan.

— The Listener's Guide to Classical Music: An Introduction to the Great Classical Composers & their Works. 288p. 1992. 15.95 (*0-8161-7370-2*, Hall Reference) Macmillan.

— The Oxford First Companion to Composers & Their Music. (Illus.). 192p. 1982. pap. text 13.95 (*0-19-321438-5*) OUP.

— The Oxford First Companion to Instruments & Orchestras. (Illus.). 192p. 1982. pap. text 13.95 (*0-19-321435-0*) OUP.

— The Oxford First Companion to Music Round the World. (Illus.). 192p. 1982. pap. text 13.95 (*0-19-321434-2*) OUP.

— The Oxford First Companion to the Story of Music. (Illus.). 192p. 1982. pap. text 13.95 (*0-19-321437-7*) OUP.

McLeish, Kenneth & Unwin, Stephen F. A Pocket Guide to Shakespeare's Plays. 288p. (Orig.). 1999. pap. 14.00 (*0-571-19183-5*) Faber & Faber.

McLeish, Kenneth, jt. auth. see Walton, J. Michael.

McLeish, Kenneth, ed. see Buchanan, David A.

McLeish, Kenneth, ed. see McLellan, Elizabeth.

McLeish, Kenneth, ed. see Nichols, Roger & Nichols, Sarah.

McLeish, Kenneth, tr. see Aeschylus.

McLeish, Kenneth, tr. see Euripides.

McLeish, Kenneth, tr. see Feydeau, Georges.

McLeish, Kenneth, tr. see Ibsen, Henrik.

McLeish, Kenneth, tr. see Jarry, Alfred.

McLeish, Kenneth, tr. see Moliere.

McLeish, Kenneth, tr. see Sophocles.

McLeish, Kenneth, tr. see Von Horvath, Odon.

McLeish, Norman. The Nature of Religious Knowledge. 174p. 1938. 37.95 (*0-567-02193-9*, Pub. by T & T Clark) Bks Intl VA.

McLeish, Robert. Radio Production: A Manual for Broadcasters. 3rd rev. ed. LC 94-1103. 272p. 1999. pap. text 46.95 (*0-240-51366-5*, Focal) Buttrwrth-Heinemann.

***McLeish, Robert.** Radio Production: A Manual for Broadcasters. 4th ed. LC 99-23141. 336p. 2000. pap. text 49.95 (*0-240-51554-4*, Focal) Buttrwrth-Heinemann.

McLeish, Tom. Theoretical Challenges in the Dynamics of Complex Fluids: Lectures from the NATO Advanced Studies Institute Held at the Isaac Newton Institute for the Mathematical Sciences, Cambridge, U. K., March 1996. LC 97-20158. (NATO ASI Series: Series E: Applied Sciences). 1997. text 184.00 (*0-7923-4607-6*) Kluwer Academic.

McLeish, Valerie, jt. auth. see McLeish, Kenneth.

McLeish, Valerie, ed. see Buchanan, David A.

McLeish, Valerie, ed. see McLellan, Elizabeth.

McLeish, Valerie, ed. see Nichols, Roger & Nichols, Sarah.

McLellan, D. L., jt. ed. see Wilson, Barbara A.

McLellan, David. Ideology. Parkin, Frank, ed. (Concepts in the Social Sciences Ser.). 128p. (Orig.). 1995. 9.00 (*0-335-19467-2*) OpUniv Pr.

— Ideology. 2nd ed. Parkin, Frank, ed. (Concepts in the Social Sciences Ser.). 128p. (Orig.). 1995. pap. 2.00 (*0-335-19466-4*) OpUniv Pr.

— The Thought of Karl Marx. 3rd ed. 268p. 1995. pap. 26.50 (*0-333-63948-0*, Pub. by Papermac) Trans-Atl Phila.

— Unto Caesar: The Political Relevance of Christianity. LC 92-53753. (Frank M. Covey, Jr., Loyola Lectures in Political Analysis). (C). 1993. text 23.00 (*0-268-01900-2*) U of Notre Dame Pr.

McLellan, David, ed. Marxism: Essential Writings. 428p. 1988. pap. text 23.95 (*0-19-827517-X*) OUP.

McLellan, David & Sayers, Sean, eds. Socialism & Morality. 224p. 1990. pap. 14.95 (*0-312-03701-5*) St Martin.

McLellan, David, jt. ed. see Cohn-Sherbok, Daniel.

McLellan, David, ed. see Engels, Friedrich.

McLellan, David, ed. see Marx, Karl.

McLellan, David, ed. & intro. see Marx, Karl & Engels, Friedrich.

McLellan, David P. & Warrick, Bill. The Lake Shore & Michigan Southern Railway. Riehle, Ginger, ed. LC 89-20230. (Illus.). 208p. 1989. text 40.00 (*0-933449-09-7*) Transport Trails.

McLellan, David P., ed. see Marx, Karl.

McLellan, David S. Cyrus Vance. LC 85-10785. (Cooper Square American Secretaries of State & Their Diplomacy Ser.: No. 20). (Illus.). 240p. 1985. text 52.50 (*0-8476-7146-1*) Rowman.

McLellan, Dermot & Stocks, Barry. McLellan & Stocks: VAT: Input Tax Recovery. 300p. 1993. boxed set 133.00 (*0-406-01139-7*, U.K., MICHIE) LEXIS Pub.

McLellan, Dermot, jt. auth. see Scott, Howard.

***McLellan, Diana.** The Girls: Sappho Goes to Hollywood. (Illus.). 448p. 2000. 25.95 (*0-312-24647-1*) St Martin.

McLellan, Elizabeth. Minoan Crete. McLeish, Kenneth & McLeish, Valerie, eds. (Aspects of Greek Life Ser.). (Illus.). 64p. (Orig.). (gr. 7-12). 1976. pap. text 9.00 (*0-582-20671-5*, 70818) Longman.

McLellan, Evelyn. The Winter's Tale Notes. (Cliffs Notes Ser.). 72p. (Orig.). (C). 1984. pap. text 4.95 (*0-8220-0096-2*, Cliff) IDG Bks.

McLellan, Faith, jt. auth. see Jones, Anne Hudson.

McLellan, Gerald D. Massachusetts Family Law Handbook. 3rd ed. 439p. (C). 99.05 (*0-318-03672-X*) Lawyers Weekly.

McLellan, Gerald D. & Zack, Ellen, eds. Massachusetts Family Law Handbook Supplement, 1995. 1995. 39.40 (*0-318-18707-8*) Lawyers Weekly.

McLellan, Gregory. Ideology. 2nd ed. LC 95-16276. (Concepts in Social Thought Ser.). 1995. pap. 14.95 (*0-8166-2803-3*) U of Minn Pr.

McLellan, Hilary. Virtual Reality: A Selected Bibliography. Milheim, William D., ed. LC 92-8488. (Educational Technology Selected Bibliography Ser.: Vol. 6). 60p. (Orig.). 1992. pap. 24.95 (*0-87778-246-6*) Educ Tech Pubns.

McLellan, Hilary, ed. Situated Learning Perspectives. LC 95-10925. 310p. 1996. 44.95 (*0-87778-289-X*) Educ Tech Pubns.

McLellan, Hugh D. History of Gorham, Maine. LC 92-62184. (Illus.). 1088p. 1992. reprint ed. 59.50 (*0-89725-094-X*, 1418) Picton Pr.

McLellan, Janet. Many Petals of the Lotus: Five Asian Buddhist Communities in Toronto. 352p. 1999. text 60.00 (*0-8020-4421-2*); pap. text 24.95 (*0-8020-8225-4*) U of Toronto Pr.

***McLellan, Larry S. & Turco, Sharon L.** Hearts Speak. (Illus.). 60p. 2000. pap. 15.00 (*0-9702289-9-6*) L S L Pubs.

McLellan, Marjorie L. Six Generations Here: A Farm Family Remembers. LC 95-37595. (Illus.). 138p. 1997. pap. 24.95 (*0-87020-283-9*) State Hist Soc Wis.

McLellan, Mark R., jt. ed. see Day, John G.

Mclellan, Martha, ed. see Ashly, Joice.

McLellan, Robert. Hypocrite. (Orig.). 1988. pap. 10.95 (*0-7145-0280-4*) Riverrun NY.

— Linmill Stories. (Classics Ser.). 280p. 1994. pap. 11.95 (*0-86241-282-X*, Pub. by Canongate Books) Interlink Pub.

***Mclellan, Stephanie S.** Chicken Cat. (Illus.). 32p. (J). (ps-1). 2000. 14.95 (*1-55041-531-X*) Fitzhenry & W Ltd.

McLellan, Steve, jt. auth. see Hodgins, Randy.

McLellan, Tim & Karam, Fred. Pro-Engineer: Tips & Techniques. 344p. (C). 1996. pap. 59.95 (*1-56690-053-0*) Thomson Learn.

McLellan, Tom & Bragg, Alicia. Escape from Anxiety & Stress. (Encyclopedia of Psychoactive Drugs Ser.: No. 1). (Illus.). 124p. (YA). (gr. 7 up). 1988. lib. bdg. 19.95 (*0-87754-772-6*) Chelsea Hse.

McLellan, Vern. Hornet's Hoop Lines. (Illus.). 128p. 1991. write for info. (*0-926918-90-7*) Associates Pr.

***McLellan, Vern.** Thoughts That Shaped the Church. (20th Century Reference Ser.). 2000. pap. text 10.99 (*0-8423-3610-9*) Tyndale Hse.

McLellan, Vern. Wise & Wacky Wit. 160p. 1992. mass mkt. 4.99 (*0-8423-8249-6*) Tyndale Hse.

McLellan, Vernon. Happiness Is Found along the Way. Caton, Patrick, ed. 168p. 1996. pap. 5.95 (*1-56245-238-X*) Great Quotations.

— Hornets' Hoop Lines. 1991. write for info. (*0-9629189-0-3*) Associates Pr.

McLellan, Vernon, compiled by. The Complete Book of Practical Proverbs & Wacky Wit. 304p. 1996. pap. 9.99 (*0-8423-7851-0*) Tyndale Hse.

***McLellan, Vernon K.** The Complete Book of Wise Words & Quotes. LC 99-42253. 2000. pap. 9.99 (*0-8423-3671-0*) Tyndale Hse.

— Timeless Treasures. LC 00-33518. 2000. write for info. (*1-56563-542-6*) Hendrickson MA.

McLelland. Color Atlas of Avian Anatomy. 1991. text 98.00 (*0-7216-3536-9*, W B Saunders Co) Harcrt Hlth Sci Grp.

McLelland, C., jt. ed. see Wix, J.

M'Clelland, J. The Calcutta Journal of Natural History, Set: Vols. 1-5. 5645p. 1985. reprint ed. 2500.00 (*81-7089-030-6*, Pub. by Intl Bk Distr) St Mut.

McLelland, John, jt. ed. see King, A. S.

McLelland, Joseph, ed. see Vermigli, Peter M.

McLelland, Joseph C., ed. The Oxford Treatise & Disputation on the Eucharist. (Sixteenth Century Essays & Studies: Vol. 7). text 45.00 (*0-943549-89-2*) Truman St Univ.

***McLelland, Joseph C., et al, eds.** The Peter Martyr Reader. LC 99-45360. (Illus.). 256p. 1999. pap. text 30.00 (*0-943549-75-2*) Truman St Univ.

McLelland, Joseph C., ed. & tr. see Vermigli, Peter M.

McLelland, Lilith. Salem Witches' Book of Love Spells: Ancient Spells from Modern Witches. LC 98-21720. 160p. 1998. pap. 10.95 (*0-8065-2020-5*) Carol Pub Group.

— Spellcraft: A Primer for the Young Magician. LC 98-209920. (Illus.). 112p. 1998. pap. 9.95 (*1-57353-115-4*) Eschaton Prods.

Mclelland, Martha, ed. see Ashly, Joice.

McLelland, Mike. Mountain Biking Michigan: The Best Trails in the Upper Peninsula. (Illus.). 284p. 1998. pap. 14.95 (*1-882376-57-9*) Thunder Bay Pr.

***McLelland, Nicola.** Ulrich Von Zatzikhoven's Lanzelet: Narrative Style & Entertainment. LC 00-42923. (Arthurian Studies). (Illus.). 2000. write for info. (*0-85991-602-2*) Boydell & Brewer.

McLellon, Waldron M. Leather & Soul: A Civil War Odyssey. LC 93-74230. 513p. (Orig.). 1994. pap. 16.95 (*1-884489-00-1*) Butternut.

— Megabyting My Mind: 59 Plug-Ins to Add Power. LC 97-93033. (Illus.). 224p. (Orig.). Date not set. pap. 14.95 (*1-884489-01-X*) Butternut.

— One Step - Two Step: A Civil War Sequel. LC 98-93140. 334p. 1998. pap. 14.95 (*1-884489-02-8*) Butternut.

McLemee, Scott. Where the Pyramid Meets the Eye. Date not set. write for info. (*0-465-09136-9*) Basic.

— Where the Pyramid Meets the Eye. Date not set. lib. bdg. write for info. (*0-465-09140-7*) HarpC.

— Where the Pyramid Meets the Eye: Conspiracy Theory in American Culture. 1999. write for info. (*0-201-77288-4*) Addison-Wesley.

McLemee, Scott, ed. C. L. R. James & the "Negro Question" LC 96-3385. 224p. 1996. pap. 16.95 (*0-87805-823-0*); lib. bdg. 40.00 (*0-87805-807-9*) U Pr of Miss.

McLemee, Scott & Le Blanc, Paul, eds. C. L. R. James & Revolutionary Marxism: Selected Writings 1939-1949. LC 92-20631. (Revolutionary Studies). 264p. (C). 1993. pap. 18.50 (*0-391-03824-9*) Humanities.

McLemore, Anna M. No Toads Allowed! 80p. 1992. pap. 8.95 (*0-9630120-0-2*) Relational Pr.

McLemore, George. Pak: Presentational Speaking. 320p. (C). 1996. 34.95 (*0-7872-0024-7*) Kendall-Hunt.

McLemore, George, et al. Presentational Speaking & Persuasion Pak. 2nd ed. 144p. (C). 1996. 48.24 (*0-7872-2619-X*) Kendall-Hunt.

McLemore, Henry, jt. auth. see Kahn, Ely J.

McLemore, Ivy. The Texas Highschool Basketball Scrapbook. Eakin, Edwin M., ed. (Illus.). 128p. (Orig.). 1989. pap. 12.95 (*0-89015-723-5*) Sunbelt Media.

McLemore, James. Sermons for Pentecost II Based on First Lesson Texts for Cycle C: Lord, Send the Wind. LC 96-46506. (First Lesson Texts Ser.). 60p. (Orig.). 1997. pap. 8.75 (*0-7880-1039-5*) CSS OH.

McLemore, Joe, photos by. Dusk to Dawn: Charleston, SC. (Illus.). 32p. 1997. pap. 4.95 (*0-9649686-4-9*) Chrlstn Post Card.

McLemore, Joe, jt. photos by see Riggs, Bryan.

McLemore, Joy M. Quality Assurance in Diagnostic Radiology. LC 80-27154. (Illus.). 237p. reprint ed. pap. 73.50 (*0-608-18271-0*, 203300200082) Bks Demand.

McLemore, P. K. Letters to Elvis. LC 97-2742. 124p. 1997. pap. 9.95 (*0-312-16906-X*) St Martin.

McLemore, Richard A., ed. A History of Mississippi, Vol. 1. LC 72-76857. (Illus.). 781p. reprint ed. pap. 200.00 (*0-7837-1068-2*, 204159100001) Bks Demand.

— A History of Mississippi, Vol. 2. LC 72-76857. (Illus.). 743p. reprint ed. pap. 200.00 (*0-7837-1069-0*, 204159100002) Bks Demand.

McLemore, S. Dale & Romo, Harriett D. Racial & Ethnic Relations in America: Instructor's Manual & Test Bank. 5th ed. 240p. (C). 1997. text, teacher ed. write for info. (*0-205-27245-2*, T7245-8) Allyn.

McLemore, Thomas. Plan & Operation of the National Survey of Ambulatory Surgery. 128p. 1997. per. 12.00 (*0-16-061478-3*) USGPO.

McLemore, Thomas, et al. Plan & Operation of the National Survey of Ambulatory Surgery (NSAS) LC 97-36605. (Vital & Health Statistics Ser.: Series 1, No. 37). 1997. write for info. (*0-8406-0532-3*) Natl Ctr Health Stats.

McLemore, William P., ed. Teach with Discipline. LC 93-5605. 148p. (Orig.). (C). 1993. pap. text 26.00 (*0-8191-9265-1*) U Pr of Amer.

McLemorel, Thomas, jt. auth. see McCraig, Linda F.

McLenaghan, John B., et al. Currency Convertibility in the Economic Community of West African States. (Occasional Papers: No. 13). 46p. 1982. pap. 5.00 (*1-55775-059-9*) Intl Monetary.

Mclenaghan, R. G., jt. auth. see Mann, R. B.

***Mclenan, Rob, ed.** Shadowy Technicians: New Ottawa Poets. 144p. 2000. pap. 12.00 (*0-921411-71-5*) Genl Dist Srvs.

McLendon, George, et al. Surface Electron Transfer Processes. 370p. 1995. 110.00 (*0-471-18553-1*) Wiley.

McLendon, Jacquelyn Y. The Politics of Color in the Fiction of Jessie Fauset & Nella Larsen. 160p. (C). 1995. text 29.50 (*0-8139-1553-8*) U Pr of Va.

McLendon, James. Papa: Hemingway in Key West. rev. ed. LC 88-81528. (Illus.). 240p. 1990. reprint ed. 24.95 (*0-911607-08-0*) Langley Pr Inc.

— Papa: Hemingway in Key West. rev. ed. LC 88-81528. (Illus.). 240p. 1995. reprint ed. pap. 14.95 (*0-911607-07-2*) Langley Pr Inc.

McLendon, John B., Jr. African American Culture Through Sports... (Illus.). 180p. (C). Date not set. pap. text 24.00 (*1-893435-06-7*) Lakeshore Comm.

McLendon, John B., Jr., ed. see Whitted, Frederick O.

McLendon, Karen. A Challenge to Women. 22p. (Orig.). 1994. pap. 1.25 (*0-9629470-9-1*) FatherSon Pub.

***McLendon, Maureen C.** Classification Cross-Reference. 10th rev. ed. LC 99-462544. 306p. 1999. pap. 34.00 (*1-886813-47-7*) Intl Risk Mgt.

McLendon, Maureen C. IRMI's Commercial Auto Insurance Guide. LC 99-206894. 207p. (Orig.). 1998. pap. 40.00 (*1-886813-41-8*) Intl Risk Mgt.

***McLendon, Roger E., et al.** Pathology of Tumors of the Central Nervous System: A Guide to Histologic Diagnosis. (An Arnold Publication). 2000. text 179.50 (*0-340-70071-8*) E A.

McLendon, Sally. Ethnographic & Historical Sketch of the Eastern Pomo & Their Neighbors, the Southeastern Pomo. (Contributions of the University of California Archaeological Research Facility: No. 37). (Illus.). 72p. (C). 1977. reprint ed. pap. text 8.44 (*1-55567-592-1*) Coyote Press.

McLenighan, Valjean. Stop-Go, Fast-Slow. LC 81-17080. (Rookie Readers Ser.). (Illus.). 32p. (J). (ps-3). 1982. lib. bdg. 17.00 (*0-516-03617-3*) Childrens.

McLennaghan, Bonnie G., ed. Originals. 2nd rev. ed. (Illus.). 266p. 1997. reprint ed. pap. 24.95 (*0-9625396-3-5*) Lindal Cedar.

Mclennan, Alexander G. AP4 & Other Dinucleoside Polyphosphates. 368p. 1992. lib. bdg. 189.00 (*0-8493-5918-X*, QP625) CRC Pr.

McLennan, Ann, jt. auth. see Rauhauser, William.

McLennan, Bardi. Dogs & Kids: Parenting Tips. (Illus.). 240p. 1993. 18.95 (*0-87605-535-8*) Howell Bks.

***McLennan, Bardi.** Puppy Care & Training. 64p. 2000. 12.95 (*0-7938-3040-0*) TFH Pubns.

McLennan, Bardi. Puppy Care & Training: An Owner's Guide to a Happy Healthy Pet. (Owner's Guide to a Happy Healthy Pet Ser.). (Illus.). 160p. 1996. 12.95 (*0-87605-391-6*) Howell Bks.

— The Welsh Terrier Leads the Way. Luther, Luana, ed. LC 98-87267. (Pure-Bred Ser.). (Illus.). 300p. 1998. 28.50 (*0-944875-38-6*, Pub. by Doral Pub) Natl Bk Netwk.

McLennan, Bardi & Critter Press. Puppies in Your Life. LC 97-38184. 1997. write for info. (*0-87605-437-8*) Howell Bks.

***Mclennan, Bill.** Transforming Image: Painted Arts of Northwest Coast First Nations. (Illus.). 320p. 2000. 60.00 (*0-295-98024-9*) U of Wash Pr.

McLennan, D. J. A Revised Transition State Spectrum for Concerted Bimolecular B - Eliminations. 1976. pap. 15.50 (*0-08-020472-4*, Pergamon Pr) Elsevier.

McLennan, Deborah A., jt. auth. see Brooks, Daniel R.

McLennan, G. Scots Gaelic: A Brief Introduction. (ENG & GAE.). 28p. 1987. 12.95 (*0-8288-3345-1*, F132982) Fr & Eur.

McLennan, Greg. Pluralism. Parkin, Frank, ed. (Concepts in the Social Sciences Ser.). 128p. 1995. 74.00 (*0-335-19155-X*); pap. 18.95 (*0-335-19154-1*) OpUniv Pr.

McLennan, Gregory. Pluralism. (Concepts in Social Thought Ser.). 1995. pap. 14.95 (*0-8166-2815-7*); text 37.95 (*0-8166-2814-9*) U of Minn Pr.

McLennan, Hugh, et al, eds. Advances in Physiological Research. LC 81-14181. 516p. 1987. 115.00 (*0-306-42575-0*, Plenum Trade) Perseus Pubng.

McLennan, J. M., tr. see Beklemishev, V. N.

McLennan, Jim. Blue Ribbon Bow. (Illus.). 184p. pap. 19.95 (*0-921835-51-5*, Pub. by Johnson G Bk) F Amato Pubns.

McLennan, Karen J., ed. Nature's Ban: Women's Incest Literature. 384p. 1996. text 45.00 (*1-55553-252-7*); pap. text 16.95 (*1-55553-253-5*) NE U Pr.

McLennan, Kenneth, jt. ed. see Baumol, William J.

McLennan, Michael, jt. auth. see Harrison, Mark.

McLennan, Rob. Bagne, or, Criteria for Heaven. 12.00 (*1-896647-32-4*) Genl Dist Srvs.

McLennan, Rob. Growing Proteas. (Growing Ser.). (Illus.). 80p. (Orig.). 1994. pap. 13.95 (*0-86417-499-3*, Pub. by Kangaroo Pr) Seven Hills Bk.

***McLennan, Rob.** Manitoba Highway Map. 84p. 1999. pap. 10.50 (*0-921411-89-8*) Genl Dist Srvs.

— Notes on Drowning. LC 98-215213. 80p. 1998. pap. 10.50 (*0-921411-75-8*) Genl Dist Srvs.

— Poems from the Blue Horizon. 1995. pap. text 3.00 (*0-921411-34-0*) Genl Dist Srvs.

— The Richard Brautigan. 96p. 2000. pap. 10.95 (*0-88922-424-2*, Pub. by Talonbks) Genl Dist Srvs.

McLennan, Rob, ed. Written in the Skin. LC 99-180690. (Illus.). 208p. 1998. pap. 19.99 (*1-895837-37-5*) Insomniac.

McLennan, S., jt. auth. see Taylor, S.

McLennan, Scotty. Finding Your Religion: When the Faith You Grew up with Has Lost Its Meaning. LC BL624.M3977 1999. 256p. 1999. 24.00 (*0-06-065347-7*) HarpC.

***McLennan, Scotty.** Finding Your Religion: When the Faith You Grew up with Has Lost Its Meaning. LC 99-27147. 1999. write for info. (*0-06-065346-9*) Harper SF.

McLennan, W. & Australian Bureau of Statistics Staff. 1993-94 Household Expenditure Survey, Australia. LC 97-161157. 1996. write for info. (*0-642-20707-0*) Aust Inst Criminology.

M

An Asterisk (*) at the beginning of an entry indicates that the title is appearing for the first time.

McLeod. Composite Bows from Tomb of Tutankhamun. (Tutankhamuns Tomb Ser.: Vol. 3). 68p. 1970. 30.00 (*0-900416-00-9*, Pub. by Aris & Phillips) David Brown.
— Introduction to Neurology. 2nd ed. 1989. pap. 24.95 (*0-86793-017-9*) Blackwell Sci.
— Leaving Scotland. (Scottish Life, Past & Present Ser.). (Illus.). 88p. (Orig.). Date not set. pap. 6.95 (*0-948636-83-1*, 6831, Pub. by Natl Mus Scotland) A Schwartz & Co.
— Systems Analysis & Design. (C). 1994. pap. text, student ed. 33.50 (*0-03-076686-9*) Harcourt Coll Pubs.
— Writing about the World. (C). 1990. pap. text, teacher ed. 34.00 (*0-15-597755-5*) Harcourt Coll Pubs.
— Writing about the World. 2nd ed. (C). 1995. pap. text, teacher ed. 33.75 (*0-15-502173-7*) Harcourt Coll Pubs.
McLeod, ed. Conference on Pioneers & Peers, 1988. 70p. 1988. pap. 20.00 (*0-911801-37-5*, ESC-88-1) Soc Computer Sim.
McLeod, A. L., jt. auth. see Hipel, Keith W.
McLeod, A. L. Commonwealth & American Nobel Laureates in Literature: Essays in Criticism LC 98-186543. xv, 200 p. 1998. write for info. (*81-207-2007-5*) Sterling Pubs.
— Commonwealth & American Women's Discourse: Essays in Criticism. (C). 1996. write for info. (*81-207-1831-3*) Sterling Pubs.
***McLeod, A. L.** Literature of Indian Diaspora: Essays in Criticism. 2000. 42.00 (*81-207-2248-5*, Pub. by Sterling Pubs) S Asia.
McLeod, A. L., ed. Claude McKay: Centennial Studies. 200p. (C). 1992. 27.50 (*81-207-1403-2*) Apt Bks.
McLeod, A. L., ed. see Narayan, R. K.
McLeod, Alan. From a Gael with No Heartland. 96p. 1990. pap. 21.00 (*1-898218-62-5*) St Mut.
McLeod, Alex N. The Practice of Economics: Economic Systems & Decision Making in Western Societies. 368p. (C). 1992. 44.95 (*1-56000-083-X*) Transaction Pubs.
McLeod, Aminah B. African American Islam. 120p. 1996. pap. 15.95 (*0-614-21697-4*, 14) Kazi Pubns.
***McLeod, Angus.** Me, Myself, My Team: How to Become an Effective Team Player Using NLP. 300p. 2000. pap. 19.95 (*1-899836-38-1*, Pub. by Crown Hse) LPC Group.
McLeod, Barbara, jt. auth. see Yule, Peter.
***McLeod, Beatrice.** Growing Up. LC 00-9436. (Nature Undercover Ser.). (Illus.). 40p. (gr. 4-7). 2000. write for info. (*1-56711-501-2*) Blackbirch.
— Staying Alive. LC 00-9438. (Nature Undercover Ser.). 40p. 2000. write for info. (*1-56711-502-0*) Blackbirch.
***McLeod, Beth W.** Caregiving. LC 98-41472. 264p. 1999. 22.95 (*0-471-25408-8*) Wiley.
***McLeod, Beth Witrogen.** Caregiving: The Spiritual Journey of Love, Loss & Renewal. 2000. pap. text 14.95 (*0-471-39217-0*) Wiley.
McLeod, Beverly, ed. Language & Learning: Educating Linguistically Diverse Students. LC 93-11659. (SUNY Series, the Social Context of Education). 311p. (C). 1994. pap. text 23.95 (*0-7914-1892-8*) State U NY Pr.
McLeod, Bob. How to Draw Ghost Rider. (Marvel Super Heroes Ser.). 36p. (YA). (gr. 3 up). 1997. pap. 7.95 (*1-56010-204-7*, M02) W Foster Pub.
McLeod, Bob, jt. illus. see Savilik, Alex.
***McLeod, Bruce.** The Geography of Empire in English Literature, 1580-1745. LC 98-53638. (Illus.). 315p. (C). 1999. 79.95 (*0-521-66079-3*) Cambridge U Pr.
McLeod, Bruce C., et al, eds. Apheresis: Principles & Practice. LC 97-35728. 1997. text 169.00 (*1-56395-082-0*) Am Assn Blood.
McLeod-Bryan, G. Voices in the Wilderness: Twentieth-Century Prophets Speak to the New Millennium. LC 99-227066. 96p. 1999. pap. 12.95 (*0-86554-639-8*) Mercer Univ Pr.
McLeod, Charles. All Change. 222p. 1970. pap. 29.95 (*0-8464-1454-6*) Beekman Pubs.
McLeod, Chris. River of Snake. 1996. pap. 16.95 (*1-86368-168-X*, Pub. by Fremantle Arts) Intl Spec Bk.
McLeod, Christian, pseud. The Heart of the Stranger: A Story of Little Italy. LC 74-17947. (Italian American Experience Ser.). (Illus.). 240p. 1975. reprint ed. 18.95 (*0-405-06417-9*) Ayer.
McLeod, D. B. & Adams, V. M., eds. Affect & Mathematical Problem Solving. (Illus.). 280p. 1989. 63.95 (*0-387-96924-1*) Spr-Verlag.
McLeod, Daniel R., jt. ed. see Hoehn-Saric, Rudolf.
McLeod, Deanne, ed. see Dean, Becky.
McLeod, Deborah, et al. Ex Voto: Art As Invocation. 18p. 1995. pap. 3.00 incl. VHS (*1-886845-00-X*) Penin Fine Arts.
McLeod, Deborah, ed. see Pumtree, Anne.
McLeod, Dennis & King, Roger. Database System Design & Implementation. (Illus.). 400p. (C). 1987. text 35.00 (*0-13-197195-6*) P-H.
McLeod, Diane. Let Me Que You In. (Illus.). 135p. 1998. pap. 29.95 (*0-9664594-0-7*) McLeo.
McLeod, Donald C. & Miller, William A., eds. The Practice of Pharmacy: Institutional & Ambulatory Pharmaceutical Services. LC 81-51777. (Illus.). 502p. 1981. text 9.00 (*0-9606488-0-1*) H W Bks.
McLeod, Donald W. Lesbian & Gay Liberation in Canada: A Selected Annotated Chronology, 1964-75. (Illus.). 320p. 1996. pap. 30.00 (*1-55022-273-2*, Pub. by ECW) LPC InBook.
McLeod, Donald W., ed. Canadian Writers & Their Works: Cumulated Index, Fiction Series. 102p. (C). 1993. pap. text 20.00 (*1-55022-142-6*, Pub. by ECW) Genl Dist Srvs.
— Canadian Writers & Their Works: Cumulated Index, Poetry Series. 137p. (C). 1993. pap. text 20.00 (*1-55022-143-4*, Pub. by ECW) Genl Dist Srvs.
McLeod, Douglas B., jt. auth. see Lyle, Jack.
McLeod, Edythe B. The Mouse Tale: A Christmas Mouse. unabridged ed. LC 98-227232. (Illus.). 24p. (J). (gr. 1-6). 1998. pap. 9.95 (*0-9666869-0-X*) Brooks Bks.
McLeod, Eileen. Women's Experience of Feminist Therapy & Counseling. 176p. 1994. pap. 29.95 (*0-335-19221-1*) OpUniv Pr.
McLeod, Eileen, jt. auth. see Bywaters, Paul.
McLeod, Eileen, jt. ed. see Bywaters, Paul.
McLeod, Elizabeth. Dinosaurs: Fastest Fiercest Most Amazing. (J). 1994. pap. 5.95 (*1-55074-366-X*) Kids Can Pr.
***McLeod, Ellen Easton.** In Good Hands: The Women of the Canadian Handicrafts Guild. (Illus.). 361p. 1999. 39.95 (*0-88629-356-1*) McG-Queens Univ Pr.
McLeod, Emilie W. The Bear's Bicycle. (Illus.). 32p. (J). (gr. k-3). 1986. pap. 5.95 (*0-316-56206-8*, Joy St Bks) Little.
— The Bear's Bicycle. (Illus.). (J). (gr. 1-3). 1986. pap. 15.95 incl. audio (*0-87499-023-8*) Live Oak Media.
McLeod, Emilie W. The Bear's Bicycle, Set. (Illus.). (J). (gr. 1-3). 1991. reprint ed. pap. 33.95 incl. audio (*0-87499-024-6*) Live Oak Media.
McLeod, Enid, tr. see Colette, Sidonie-Gabrielle.
Mcleod-Everette, Sharon. Walk Softly with Me: Adventures of a Woman Big Game Guide in Alaska. LC 99-179107. 174p. 1998. pap. 17.00 (*0-940055-50-3*) Vanessapress.
Mcleod, Frederick G. The Image of God in the Antiochene Tradition. LC 98-21262. 278p. 1999. lib. bdg. 61.95 (*0-8132-0930-7*) Cath U Pr.
***McLeod, G.** Ho-Nikon. LC 98-68168. 192p. 1999. pap. 14.95 (*1-878044-58-3*) Mayhaven Pub.
McLeod, Gary W., jt. auth. see Hura, Myron.
McLeod, Gerald E. Texas One Day Adventures & Weekend Getaways. 1994. pap. 8.95 (*1-56943-033-0*) NTC Contemp Pub Co.
McLeod, Glenda. Virtue & Venom: Catalogs of Women from Antiquity to the Renaissance. (Women & Culture Ser.). 200p. (C). 1992. text 44.50 (*0-472-10206-0*, 10206) U of Mich Pr.
McLeod, Glenda, intro. Visitors to the City: Readers of Christine De Pizan. 225p. (Orig.). (C). 1989. pap. 20.00 (*0-941107-04-3*) MARC Pub Co.
McLeod, Glenda K., ed. The Reception of Christine De Pizan from the Fifteenth Through the Nineteenth Centuries: Visitors to the City. LC 91-44257. 184p. 1992. lib. bdg. 79.95 (*0-7734-9689-0*) E Mellen.
McLeod, Graham. Managing Information Technology Projects. 456p. 1995. pap. 40.00 (*0-7895-0176-7*) Course Tech.
McLeod, Grant, tr. see Justinian.
McLeod, Grover S. The Ghost of the Chimera. 143p. 1988. 19.95 (*0-87651-977-X*); pap. 16.95 (*0-685-46265-X*) Southern U Pr.
— Sub Duty. 581p. 1986. pap. 19.95 (*0-87651-975-3*) Southern U Pr.
— The Sultan's Gold. 138p. 1988. 19.95 (*0-87651-976-1*); pap. 16.95 (*0-685-35678-7*) Southern U Pr.
— The Trials of FAT. 260p. 1989. 19.95 (*0-87651-949-4*) Southern U Pr.
McLeod, Hew. Sikhism. LC 98-130888. 384p. 1998. pap. 14.95 (*0-14-025260-6*) Viking Penguin.
McLeod, Hugh. Piety & Poverty: Working-Class Religion in Berlin, London, & New York, 1870-1914. (Europe Past & Present Ser.). 400p. (C). 1996. text 45.00 (*0-8419-1356-0*) Holmes & Meier.
— Religion & Society in England, 1850-1914. (Social History in Perspective Ser.). 256p. 1996. pap. 19.95 (*0-312-15805-X*); text 49.95 (*0-312-15798-3*) St Martin.
— Religion & the People of Western Europe, 1789-1990. 2nd ed. LC 97-12639. (Illus.). 196p. (Orig.). 1998. pap. 16.95 (*0-19-289283-5*) OUP.
***McLeod, Hugh.** Secularisation in Western Europe, 1848-1914. LC 00-35257. (European Studies). 2000. write for info. (*0-312-23511-9*) St Martin.
McLeod, Hugh, ed. see Brown, Callum.
McLeod, Ian, jt. auth. see Eastham, Michael.
McLeod, Ian, tr. see Derrida, Jacques.
McLeod, Ian T. Law for Librarians: A Handbook for Librarians in England & Wales. LC 90-32540. 174p. Date not set. reprint ed. pap. 54.00 (*0-608-20728-4*, 207182600002) Bks Demand.
McLeod, J. K., jt. auth. see Hasler, H. G.
McLeod, Jackie O. Best of the Gift Horse Restaurant. 1993. 19.95 (*0-9634312-0-X*) Gift Horse Rest.
McLeod, Jacqueline A., jt. ed. see Hine, Darlene Clark.
McLeod, James, et al. Introductory Neurology. 3rd ed. 300p. 1995. pap. 27.95 (*0-86793-329-1*) Blackwell Sci.
McLeod, James N. & White, Bruce T. The Romance Zone: International Relationship Guide to Latin American Ladies. (Illus.). 1999. pap. 29.95 (*1-881791-05-X*, Bueno Bks) In One EAR.
McLeod, James R. Theodore Roethke: A Manuscript Checklist. LC 70-121652. (Serif Series: Bibliographies & Checklists: No. 21). 315p. reprint ed. pap. 97.70 (*0-7837-0566-2*, 204091000019) Bks Demand.
McLeod, Jenny, tr. & intro. see Schat, Peter.
***McLeod, John.** Beginning Postcolonialism. LC 99-49701. (Beginnings Ser.). 2000. write for info. (*0-7190-5209-2*, Pub. by Manchester Univ Pr) St Martin.
— Beginning Postcolonialism. LC 99-49701. 2000. text. write for info. (*0-7190-5208-4*) Manchester Univ Pr.
McLeod, John. Doing Counselling Research. 224p. 1994. 45.00 (*0-8039-7803-0*); pap. 24.95 (*0-8039-7804-9*) Sage.
— An Introduction to Counselling. 2nd ed. LC 98-9209. 352p. 1998. 95.00 (*0-335-19710-8*); pap. 29.95 (*0-335-19709-4*) OpUniv Pr.
— Narrative & Psychotherapy. LC 97-61827. 180p. 1997. 66.00 (*0-8039-7685-2*) Sage.
— Narrative & Psychotherapy. 192p. 1998. pap. 13.99 (*0-8039-7686-0*) Sage.
— Sovereignty, Power, Control: Politics in the State of Western India, 1916-1947. LC 99-11510. (Indological Library). 2p. 1999. 104.00 (*90-04-11343-6*) Brill Academic Pubs.
McLeod, John, ed. Life Sciences Simulation: Then, Now & When. 66p. 1990. pap. 32.00 (*0-911801-70-7*, EMC90-2) Soc Computer Sim.
McLeod, John & McLeod, Rita. NewGAP. 40p. (Orig.). 1990. pap. text 24.00 (*0-87879-892-7*); 22.00 (*0-87879-893-5*); 6.00 (*0-87879-894-3*) Acad Therapy.
— NewGAP, Set. 40p. (Orig.). 1990. teacher ed. 55.00 (*0-685-46301-X*) Acad Therapy.
McLeod, John, jt. auth. see House, Peter W.
McLeod, Jonathan W. Workers & Workplace Dynamics in Reconstruction-Era Atlanta: A Case Study. LC 89-963. (Afro-American Culture & Society Monographs: Vol. 10). (Illus.). 135p. 1989. pap. 15.95 (*0-934934-34-7*) CAAS Pubns.
— Workers & Workplace Dynamics in Reconstruction-Era Atlanta: A Case Study. LC 89-963. (Afro-American Culture & Society Monographs: Vol. 10). (Illus.). 138p. 1989. pap. 15.00 (*0-89215-155-2*) U Cal LA Indus Rel.
McLeod, Joseph. Rim Poems. 72p. 1990. pap. 9.95 (*0-921254-22-9*, Pub. by Penumbra Pr) U of Toronto Pr.
McLeod, Judyth A. Lavender, Sweet Lavender. (Illus.). 120p. 1994. pap. 14.95 (*0-86417-601-5*, Pub. by Kangaroo Pr) Seven Hills Bk.
***McLeod, Judyth A.** Lavender, Sweet Lavender. 2000. 16.00 (*0-7432-0065-9*) Simon & Schuster.
***Mcleod, Kate.** Beetlemania: The Story of the Car That Captured the Hearts of Millions. LC 98-49790. (Illus.). 64p. 1999. 12.98 (*0-7651-1018-0*) Smithmark.
***McLeod, Keith.** The Shore & the Shelter. 2000. pap. 17.95 (*1-86368-272-4*, Pub. by Fremantle Arts) Intl Spec Bk.
McLeod, Ken, tr. see Kongtrul, Jamgon & Erlewine, Michael.
Mcleod, Laura, compiled by. Index to Canadian Historical Review: 1971-1990. 192p. 1994. text 90.00 (*0-8020-2796-2*) U of Toronto Pr.
***McLeod, Loren.** Sea of White Impatiens. (Illus.). 2000. pap. 8.95 (*0-9676232-0-0*) Schleppie Pubg.
McLeod, Lyons. Travels in Eastern Africa, 2 vols. 1971. reprint ed. 115.00 (*0-7146-1832-2*, Pub. by F Cass Pubs) Intl Spec Bk.
McLeod, M. C., ed. see Lucian.
McLeod, M. C., ed. see Lucian, M. D.
McLeod, Malcolm & Mack, John. Ethnic Sculpture. (British Museum Ser.). (Illus.). 72p. (Orig.). 1985. pap. 14.00 (*0-674-26854-7*) HUP.
McLeod, Margaret S. G., et al. The Cathedral Libraries Catalogue. LC 84-199335. 1984. write for info. (*0-7123-4594-9*) British Lib Document.
McLeod, Marion & Manhire, Bill. Some Other Country: New Zealand's Best Short Stories. LC 96-216422. 296p. 1996. pap. 14.95 (*0-908912-28-5*) Paul & Co Pubs.
McLeod, Marion & Manhire, Bill. Some Other Country: New Zealand's Best Short Stories. 3rd ed. LC 98-126762. 1997. write for info. (*0-908912-92-7*) Bridget Williams Bks.
McLeod, Marion & Manhire, Bill, eds. New Zealand Short Story Collection. LC 98-146593. 1997. pap. 19.95 (*0-7022-3030-8*, Pub. by Univ Queensland Pr) Intl Spec Bk.
— Some Other Country: New Zealand's Best Short Stories. 256p. 1985. pap. text 14.95 (*0-86861-633-8*) Routledge.
McLeod, Marion & Wevers, Lydia. Women's Work. 240p. 1986. pap. 9.95 (*0-19-558136-9*) OUP.
McLeod, Mark S. Rationality & Theistic Belief: An Essay on Reformed Epistemology. LC 93-7544. (Cornell Studies in the Philosophy of Religion). 288p. 1993. text 42.50 (*0-8014-2863-7*) Cornell U Pr.
McLeod, Mark S., jt. ed. see Craig, William L.
McLeod, Mark W. The Vietnamese Response to French Intervention, 1862-1874. LC 90-44389. 192p. 1991. 49.95 (*0-275-93562-0*, C3562, Praeger Pubs) Greenwood.
Mcleod, Mark W., tr. see Martin, Marie A.
***Mcleod, Melvin, ed.** The Wisdom of the Dalai Lama. 2000. pap. 6.95 (*1-57062-517-4*) Random.
McLeod, Merikay. Now. 32p. (J). (ps-12). 1995. pap. 0.99 (*1-57258-060-7*) Teach Servs.
McLeod, Michel. Lonely Planet Martinique. (FRE.). 1997. 18.95 (*2-84070-072-7*) Lonely Planet.
McLeod, Neil, et al. Essential Tax Legislation. 302p. 1993. pap. 30.00 (*0-455-21185-X*, Pub. by LawBk Co) Gaunt.
— Essential Tax Legislation 1995. 4th ed. 660p. 1995. pap. 35.00 (*0-455-21311-9*, Pub. by LawBk Co) Gaunt.
McLeod, Neil S., jt. auth. see Skipper, Ann.
McLeod, Nicole J., jt. auth. see Woods, Edward G.
McLeod, Owen, jt. ed. see Pojman, Louis P.
McLeod, Penn. Til Snoring Doth Us Part. Comstock, Ariane, ed. LC 97-69857. (Illus.). 112p. 1998. pap. 8.95 (*1-889923-07-9*, Monarch Books) Monarch Westlake Village.
McLeod, Peter, et al. Introduction to Connectionist Modelling Cognitive Processes. (Illus.). 404p. 1998. text 95.00 (*0-19-852427-7*) OUP.
— Introduction to Connectionist Modelling of Cognitive Processes. (Illus.). 404p. 1998. pap. text 37.95 (*0-19-852426-9*) OUP.
McLeod, R., ed. Crisis in Editing: Texts of the English Renaissance. LC 89-17583. (Conference on Editorial Problems Ser.: No. 24). 1993. 49.50 (*0-404-63674-8*) AMS Pr.
McLeod, R. S., et al, eds. Trends in Inflammatory Bowel Disease Therapy, 1996. LC 98-172294. 320p. 1997. text 151.00 (*0-7923-8718-X*) Kluwer Academic.
McLeod, Raymond, Jr. Management Information Systems: A Study of Computer-Based Information Systems. (Illus.). 848p. (C). 1992. write for info. (*0-318-69918-4*) Macmillan.
McLeod, Raymond. Management of Information Systems. 7th ed. LC 97-13159. 655p. 1997. 93.00 (*0-13-856584-8*) P-H.
McLeod, Raymond, Jr. Systems Analysis & Design: An Organizational Approach. 804p. (C). 1994. disk 29.75 (*0-03-003028-5*) Dryden Pr.
— Systems Analysis & Design: An Organizational Approach. 498p. (C). 1994. pap. text, teacher ed. 88.25 (*0-03-076682-6*) Dryden Pr.
***McLeod, Raymond & Schell, George.** Management Information Systems. 8th ed. 688p. 2000. 89.33 (*0-13-019237-6*) P-H.
Mcleod, Reggie, et al, eds. Big River Reader: An Anthology of Stories about Upper Mississippi, from the First Four Years. (Illus.). 192p. (Orig.). 1996. pap. 15.95 (*0-9653950-1-4*) Big Riv MN.
McLeod, Rita, jt. auth. see McLeod, John.
McLeod, Robin J. & Baart, M. Louisa. Geometry & Interpolation of Curves & Surfaces. LC 97-43729. (Illus.). 416p. (C). 1998. 80.00 (*0-521-32153-0*) Cambridge U Pr.
McLeod, Robin J. & Wachspress, Eugene L., eds. Frontiers of Applied Geometry: Proceedings of a Symposium, Las Cruces, New Mexico, 1980. 128p. 1981. pap. 29.00 (*0-08-026487-5*, Pergamon Pr) Elsevier.
McLeod, Ross, jt. ed. see Garnaut, Ross.
McLeod, Russell. Feng Youlan, Jiang Qing & the "Twenty-five Poems on History" LC 83-80351. (Current Chinese Language Project Ser.: No. 21). (Illus.). 108p. 1983. pap. text 5.00 (*0-912966-59-9*) IEAS.
McLeod, Scott J. & Higgins, Kenneth F. Waterfowl & Habitat Changes after 40 Years on the Waubay Study Area. (Illus.). 40p. 1998. pap. write for info. (*0-9658936-3-4*) Dept Wildlife.
McLeod, Susan. Whither WAC? Reflections on the Silver Anniversary of Writing Across the Curriculum. Bridwell-Bowles, Lillian & Donehower, Kim, eds. (Technical Reports: Vol. 14). 11p. (Orig.). 1996. pap. 2.00 (*1-881221-22-9*) U Minn Ctr Interdis.
McLeod, Susan, et al. Writing about the World. 608p. (C). 1990. pap. text 37.00 (*0-15-597754-7*) Harcourt Coll Pubs.
— Writing about the World. 2nd ed. (Illus.). 800p. (C). 1994. pap. text 38.50 (*0-15-501314-9*, Pub. by Harcourt Coll Pubs) Harcourt.
McLeod, Susan, ed. see Pfaff, Tim.
McLeod, Susan H. Notes on the Heart: Affective Issues in the Writing Classroom. LC 96-17771. 1997. 39.95 (*0-8093-1738-9*); pap. 19.95 (*0-8093-2106-8*) S Ill U Pr.
McLeod, Susan H., ed. Strengthening Programs for Writing Across the Curriculum. LC 87-644763. (New Directions for Teaching & Learning Ser.: No. TL 36). 1988. 22.00 (*1-55542-899-1*) Jossey-Bass.
McLeod, Susan H. & Soven, Margot K., eds. Writing across the Curriculum: A Guide to Developing Programs. (Illus.). 304p. 1992. 52.00 (*0-8039-4599-X*); pap. 24.95 (*0-8039-4600-7*) Sage.
McLeod, Susan H., jt. ed. see Frederick, Bonnie.
McLeod, Thomas E. The Work of the Church Treasurer. rev. ed. LC 92-23564. 64p. 1992. pap. 11.00 (*0-8170-1189-7*) Judson.
McLeod, Thomas H., ed. Post-Secondary Education in a Technological Society: L'enseignement post-secondaire dans une societe technologique. 260p. (C). 1973. 55.00 (*0-7735-0162-2*, Pub. by McG-Queens Univ Pr) CUP Services.
McLeod, Thomas H., ed. see Nuffield Canadian Seminar Staff.
McLeod, Tom. Always Ready: The Story of the United States 147th Infantry Regiment. (Illus.). ix, 180p. (Orig.). 1996. pap. 24.95 (*0-9655987-0-5*) TMAC Pub.
McLeod, W. Self Bows & Other Archery Tackle from Tomb of Tutankhamun. (Tutankhamuns Tomb Ser.: Vol. 4). 85p. 1982. 50.00 (*0-900416-33-5*, Pub. by Aris & Phillips) David Brown.
McLeod, W. H. The Evolution of the Sikh Community: Five Essays. 1976. 36.00 (*0-19-826529-8*) OUP.
Mcleod, W. H. The Evolution of the Sikh Community: Five Essays. (Illus.). 138p. (C). 1996. pap. text 10.95 (*0-19-563737-2*) OUP.
***McLeod, W. H.** Exploring Sikhism: Aspects of Sikh Identity, Culture & Thought. 288p. 2000. text 22.00 (*0-19-564902-8*) OUP.
McLeod, W. H. Guru Nanak & the Sikh Religion. 272p. 1996. pap. text 8.95 (*0-19-563735-6*) OUP.
— Historical Dictionary of Sikhism. LC 95-15853. (Religions, Philosophies & Movements Ser.: Vol. 5). 338p. 1995. 58.00 (*0-8108-3035-3*) Scarecrow.
— The Sikhs: History, Religion, & Society. 188p. 1989. text 61.00 (*0-231-06814-X*) Col U Pr.
— The Sikhs: History, Religion, & Society. 1991. pap. text 17.50 (*0-231-06815-8*) Col U Pr.
— Way of the Sikh. (Way Ser.). 64p. (J). (gr. 4-8). 1986. pap. 10.95 (*0-7175-0731-9*) Dufour.
McLeod, W. H., ed. Sikhism. LC 84-410. (Textual Sources for the Study of Religion Ser.). 208p. 1984. 50.00 (*0-389-20479-X*, 08041) B&N Imports.
McLeod, W. H., ed. Textual Sources for the Study of Sikhism. (Textual Sources for the Study of Religion Ser.). (Illus.). x, 176p. 1990. pap. text 15.95 (*0-226-56085-6*) U Ch Pr.
McLeod, W. H., jt. ed. see Schomer, Karine.
McLeod, Wallace. The Grand Design: Selected Masonic Addresses & Papers of Wallace McLeod. LC 91-14958. 215p. 1991. 18.00 (*0-935633-10-3*) Anchor Comm.
McLeod, William A. The Boatswain's Manual. 5th ed. 332p. 1997. text 55.00 (*0-85174-644-6*) Sheridan.
McLeod, William T., ed. The Collins Paperback Thesaurus in A-to-Z Form. 632p. 1986. pap. 9.50 (*0-00-433014-5*) Shalom.

An Asterisk (*) at the beginning of an entry indicates that the title is appearing for the first time.

McLernon, Carol M. Katie - Down the Pike. 80p. (Orig.). 1997. pap. 8.00 (*1-57502-396-2*, P01236) Morris Pubng.
— Overlooking Stoneybrook. 80p. (J). (gr. 6-9). 1998. pap. 8.00 (*1-57502-864-6*, PO2356) Morris Pubng.

McLeroth, Diane. The Briard. LC 83-138458. (Illus.). 240p. 1982. 20.00 (*0-9639860-0-7*) Aubry Assocs.

McLeroy, Leigh, jt. auth. see Dyke, Larry.

McLeRoy, Sherrie S. Black Land, Red River: A Pictorial History of Grayson County, Texas. LC 93-23092. 1993. write for info. (*0-89865-868-3*) Donning Co.
— Daughter of Fortune: The Bettie Brown Story. LC 96-23324. (Women of the West Ser.). 232p. (Orig.). 1996. pap. 12.95 (*1-55622-529-6*, Rep of TX Pr) Wordware Pub.

McLeroy, Sherrie S. First in the Lone Star State: A Texas Brag Book. LC 97-36161. 1997. pap. text 14.95 (*1-55622-572-5*, Rep of TX Pr) Wordware Pub.

***McLeRoy, Sherrie S.** First in the Lone Star State II. 1999. pap. text 16.95 (*1-55622-686-1*) Wordware Pub.

McLeroy, Sherrie S. Red River Women. (Women of the West Ser.). 250p. 1996. pap. 12.95 (*1-55622-501-6*, Rep of TX Pr) Wordware Pub.
— Sports: Thematic Unit. 1997. pap. text 9.95 (*1-55734-588-0*) Tchr Create Mat.

McLeroy, Sherrie S. & McLeroy, William. More Passages: A New History of Amherst County VA. (Illus.). 189p. (Orig.). 1995. pap. 17.00 (*0-7884-0331-1*, M149) Heritage Bk.

McLeRoy, Sherrie S. & McLeRoy, William R. Strangers in Their Midst: The Free Black Population of Amherst County, Virginia. iv, 237p. (Orig.). 1993. pap. text 23.00 (*1-55613-786-9*) Heritage Bk.

McLeroy, William, jt. auth. see McLeroy, Sherrie S.

McLeRoy, William R., jt. auth. see McLeRoy, Sherrie S.

McLerran, jt. auth. see Baym, Gordon.

***McLerran, Alice.** Dragonfly. LC 00-36274. (Illus.). (J). 2000. pap. write for info. (*1-888842-15-6*) Absey & Co.

McLerran, Alice. The Ghost Dance. LC 94-34231. (Illus.). 40p. (J). (gr. 3-6). 1995. 15.95 (*0-395-63168-8*, Clarion Bks) HM.
— Hugs. (Illus.). 32p. (J). (ps-3). 1993. 4.95 (*0-590-44637-1*, Cartwheel) Scholastic Inc.
— Kisses. (Illus.). 32p. (J). (ps-3). 1993. 4.95 (*0-590-44711-4*, Cartwheel) Scholastic Inc.
— The Legacy of Roxaboxen: A Collection of Voices. 72p. 1998. 19.95 (*1-888842-08-3*) Absey & Co.
— The Mountain That Loved a Bird. (Illus.). 28p. (J). (gr. k-3). 2000. per. 5.99 (*0-689-83319-9*) Aladdin.
— The Mountain That Loved a Bird. LC 85-9391. (Illus.). 28p. (J). (ps up). 1991. 16.00 (*0-88708-000-6*, Picture Book Studio) S&S Childrens.

Mclerran, Alice. Roxaboxen. (J). (ps-3). 1991. 16.00 (*0-688-07592-4*) Lothrop.

McLerran, Alice. Roxaboxen. LC 89-8057. (J). (ps-3). 1991. lib. bdg. 15.93 (*0-688-07593-2*) Lothrop.
— Roxaboxen. (J). 1992. 11.19 (*0-606-01736-4*, Pub. by Turtleback) Demco.
— Roxaboxen. (Picture Puffin Ser.). (Illus.). 32p. (J). (ps-3). 1999. pap. 5.99 (*0-14-054475-5*) Viking Penguin.
— Roxaboxen. large type ed. (Illus.). 1993. 9.50 (*0-614-09852-1*, L-34095-00) Am Printing Hse.

McLerran, Jennifer & McKee, Patrick. Old Age in Myth & Symbol: A Cultural Dictionary. LC 91-9163. 208p. 1991. lib. bdg. 55.00 (*0-313-27845-8*, MGM, Greenwood Pr) Greenwood.

Mclerran, Jennifer, jt. auth. see Patin, Thomas.

McLerran, Jennifer, jt. ed. see Patin, Thomas.

McLeskey, Charles H., ed. Geriatric Anesthesiology. LC 96-12621. (Illus.). 703p. 1996. write for info. (*0-683-05870-3*) Lppncott W & W.

McLester, Gordon L. Oneida Indian Journey: From New York to Wisconsin, 1784-1860. 1999. write for info. (*0-299-16140-4*) U of Wis Pr.

***McLester, L. Gordon.** Oneida. (Indian Nations Ser.). (Illus.). 2000. 25.69 (*0-8172-5457-9*) Raintree Steck-V.

McLewin, Will. Linear Programming & Applications: A Course Text. (Illus.). xvi, 216p. 1990. text. write for info. (*0-904870-11-1*, Pub. by Input-Output Pub) UH Pr.

McLiam, John. The Sin of Pat Muldoon. 1957. pap. 5.25 (*0-8222-1031-2*) Dramatists Play.

McLiesh, Todd. What a Way to Go. 114p. 1998. pap. 8.95 (*0-9648608-1-3*) Verbis Pubng.

McLimore, Fred J. Strategies & Leadership: Impact on Organizational Performance. 512p. (C). 1996. pap. text, per. 54.95 (*0-7872-1784-0*, 41178401) Kendall-Hunt.

McLin, C. J., Jr. Dad, I Served: The Autobiography of C. J. McLin, Jr. LC 99-217120. (Illus.). x, 166p. 1997. pap. 16.95 (*0-9661647-0-9*) WSU Ofc Pub Rel.

McLin, Elva B. Athens State College: A Definitive History 1821-1991. 220p. 1991. 25.00 (*0-9629883-0-8*) Athens State.
— The History of Athens State College, 1821-1994. rev. ed. 220p. 1994. 25.00 (*0-614-14596-1*) Athens State.
— Madame Childs: The Lady & the Legend. 220p. 1992. 20.00 (*0-9629883-1-6*) Athens State.

McLin, Jon. Social & Economic Effects of Petroleum Development in Non-OPEC Developing Countries: Synthesis Report. xiii, 104p. (Orig.). 1986. pap. 18.00 (*92-2-105505-1*) Intl Labour Office.

McLin, Jon, jt. ed. see Huddleston, Barbara.

McLin, Jon B. Canada's Changing Defense Policy, 1957-1963: The Problems of a Middle Power in Alliance. LC 66-29907. 263p. 1967. reprint ed. pap. 81.60 (*0-608-04032-0*, 206476800011) Bks Demand.

McLin, Lena. Pulse: A History of Music. LC 77-75478. (Illus.). (YA). (gr. 6-12). 1977. pap. 10.95 (*0-8497-5600-6*, WE 3) Kjos.

McLinden, Shannon. The Me Nobody Knew: A Story of Triumph for All Girls. LC 97-35025. 112p. (J). 1997. lib. bdg. 26.95 (*0-8225-2688-3*) Lerner Pub.

McLindon, Michael P. Privatization & Capital Market Development: Strategies to Promote Economic Growth. LC 96-21320. 200p. 1996. 55.00 (*0-275-95066-2*, Praeger Pubs) Greenwood.

***McLinn, James A.** Practical Accelerated Life Testing: Practical Approaches (Tools & Techniques) Williams, Harold W., Jr., ed. & illus. by. 132p. 2000. 28.00 (*0-9701923-0-4*) Reliability Div.

***McLinn, Patricia.** At the Heart's Command. (Special Edition Ser.: Vol. 1350). 2000. mass mkt. 4.50 (*0-373-24350-2*, 1-24350-0) Harlequin Bks.

McLinn, Patricia. Grady's Wedding. (Special Edition Ser.). 1993. per. 3.39 (*0-373-09813-8*, 5-09813-2) Silhouette.

***McLinn, Patricia.** Hidden in a Heartbeat. (Special Edition Ser.: Bk. 1355). 2000. mass mkt. 4.50 (*0-373-24355-3*, 1-24355-9) Silhouette.
— Hoops. 2000. mass mkt. 4.50 (*0-373-82247-2*, 1-82247-7) Harlequin Bks.
— Lost & Found Groom. (Special Edition Ser.). 2000. mass mkt. 4.50 (*0-373-24344-8*, 1-24344-3) Silhouette.

McLinn, Patricia. The Rancher Meets His Match. 1998. per. 4.25 (*0-373-24164-X*, 1-24164-5) Silhouette.
— Rodeo Nights. (Special Edition Ser.). 1994. per. 3.50 (*0-373-09904-5*, 1-09904-3) Harlequin Bks.
— A Stranger in the Family: (The Family Way) (Special Edition Ser.). 1995. per. 3.75 (*0-373-09959-2*, 1-09959-7) Silhouette.
— A Stranger to Love. 1997. per. 3.99 (*0-373-24098-8*, 1-24098-5) Silhouette.
— Widow Woman. (Historical Ser.). 1998. per. 4.99 (*0-373-29017-9*, 1-29017-0) Harlequin Bks.

McLintock. The Voyage of the Fox. (Cloth Bound Pocket Ser.). 1998. 7.95 (*3-8290-0895-3*, 520872) Konemann.

McLintock, D. R., ed. see Bostock, J. Knight.

McLintock, David, tr. see Bernhard, Thomas.

McLintock, David, tr. see Boll, Heinrich.

McLintock, David, tr. see Meier, Christian.

McLintock, Dewar. Prototype & Dream Cars. (World of Wheels Ser.). (Illus.). (YA). (gr. 6 up). 19.95 (*0-614-21973-6*) Random.

McLintock, I. S. Bremsstrahlung from Radionuclides: Practical Guidance for Radiation Protection. 1994. pap. 150.00 (*0-948237-23-6*, Pub. by H&H Sci Cnslts) St Mut.

McLintock, I. S., jt. auth. see Connor, K. J.

McLintock, James D. Royal Cars. (Album Ser.: No. 284). (Illus.). 32p. 1989. pap. 6.25 (*0-7478-0167-3*, Pub. by Shire Pubns) Parkwest Pubns.

McLish, Rachel & Reynolds, Bill. Flex Appeal by Rachel. 1984. mass mkt. 13.99 (*0-446-38105-5*, Pub. by Warner Bks) Little.

McLish, Rachel & Vedral, Joyce L. Perfect Parts. 256p. 1987. mass mkt. 14.99 (*0-446-38534-4*, Pub. by Warner Bks) Little.

Mclleron, Geoff, et al, eds. The Complete Book of Southern African Birds. 752p. (C). 1989. 500.00 (*1-85368-019-2*, Pub. by New5 Holland) St Mut.

***Mcllwain, Harris.** Super Calcium Counter. 320p. 2000. mass mkt. 5.99 (*1-57566-565-4*) Kensgtn Pub Corp.

McLnnes, A. W., ed. Computational Mathematics. 300p. (C). 1995. text 48.00 (*981-02-0203-2*) World Scientific Pub.

Mclntyre, John R., jt. ed. see Papp, Daniel S.

McLoda. Exploring the Earth. 1996. pap. text, student ed. 30.20 (*0-13-717596-5*) P-H.

McLoda, William. Geology 102: Lab Manual. (C). 1995. pap. text 18.15 (*1-56870-123-3*) RonJon Pub.

McLogan, Russell E. Boy Soldier: Coming of Age During World War II. LC 98-60068. (Illus.). 412p. 1998. 29.95 (*0-9663444-0-5*) Terrus Pr.

McLone, David G. Pediatric Neurosurgery: Surgery of the Developing Nervous System. 4th ed. (C). 1999. text. write for info. (*0-7216-8209-X*, W B Saunders Co) Harcrt Hlth Sci Grp.

McLoone, George H. Milton's Poetry of Independence: Five Studies. LC 98-33975. (Illus.). 160p. 1999. 32.50 (*0-8387-5403-1*) Bucknell U Pr.

***McLoone, Margo.** Women Explorers of the Air. LC 99-18429. (Short Biographies Ser.). (Illus.). 48p. (YA). 1999. 19.93 (*0-7368-0310-6*, Cpstone High Low) Capstone Pr.
— Women Explorers of the Mountains. LC 99-18377. (Short Biographies Ser.). (Illus.). 48p. (YA). 1999. 19.93 (*0-7368-0311-4*, Cpstone High Low) Capstone Pr.
— Women Explorers of the Oceans. 1999. 19.93 (*0-516-21879-4*) Capstone Pr.
— Women Explorers of the Oceans: Tania Aebi, Eugenie Clark, Anne Davison, Sylvia Earle & Noami Jame. LC 99-19493. (Short Biographies Ser.). (Illus.). 48p. (YA). 1999. 19.93 (*0-7368-0312-2*, Cpstone High Low) Capstone Pr.
— Women Explorers of the World. 1999. 19.93 (*0-516-21880-8*) Capstone Pr.
— Women Explorers of the World. LC 99-19860. (Illus.). 48p. 2000. 19.93 (*0-7368-0313-0*, Cpstone High Low) Capstone Pr.

McLoone, Margo, jt. auth. see Siegel, Alice.

McLoskey, Lansing D. Twentieth Century Danish Music: An Annotated Bibliography & Research Directory, 65. LC 97-42760. (Music Reference Collection: Vol. 65). 176p. 1998. lib. bdg. 69.50 (*0-313-30293-6*, Greenwood Pr) Greenwood.

McLoskey, Mary Lou & Stack, Lydia. Voices in Literature: Gold (Advanced) Student's Journal. 1996. student ed. 7.25 (*0-8384-7028-9*) Heinle & Heinle.

McLoud, Theresa C. Thoracic Radiology - The Requisites. LC 98-18593. (Illus.). 557p. (C). (gr. 13). 1998. text 89.00 (*0-8016-6354-7*, 06354) Mosby Inc.

McLoughland, Beverly. Hippo's a Heap: And Other Animal Poems. LC 92-81074. (Illus.). 32p. (J). (ps-3). 1993. 14.95 (*1-56397-017-1*, Wordsong) Boyds Mills Pr.

McLoughlin & Magliano, James. Mathematics Appreciation. 450p. (C). 1998. per. 49.95 (*0-7872-5639-0*, 41563903) Kendall-Hunt.

Mcloughlin, Andrea. Simple Science Experiments. 1996. 7.94 (*0-606-09857-7*, Pub. by Turtleback) Demco.

McLoughlin, Barry. Building Trust: Communicating with Employees. (Communicate with Power 2000 Ser.). 150p. 2000. 20.00 (*1-886712-10-7*) McLoughlin MultiMed.
— Communicate with Power 2000 Gold Box: Communications Tools for a Changing World, 3 bks. 444p. 1999. boxed set 55.00 (*1-886712-11-5*, Pub. by McLoughlin MultiMed) Allnce Hse.
— Encountering the Media: Media Strategies & Techniques. 3rd ed. (Communicate with Power 2000 Ser.). (Illus.). 136p. 1998. spiral bd. 20.00 (*1-886712-07-7*) McLoughlin MultiMed.
— Getting Your Ideas Across: Making Effective Presentations. (Communicate with Power 2000 Ser.). 143p. 1998. reprint ed. spiral bd. 20.00 (*1-886712-08-5*) McLoughlin MultiMed.
— Overcoming Panic & Fear: Risk & Crisis Communications. (Communicate with Power 2000 Ser.). 140p. 1998. reprint ed. spiral bd. 20.00 (*1-886712-09-3*) McLoughlin MultiMed.

McLoughlin, Brendan. Developing Psychodynamic Counselling. (Developing Counselling Ser.: Vol. 5). 128p. 1995. 39.95 (*0-8039-8979-2*); pap. 19.95 (*0-8039-8980-6*) Sage.

McLoughlin Bros. Staff. Magic Mirror, an Antique Optical Toy. 81st ed. 1980. pap. 3.95 (*0-486-23847-4*) Dover.
— Pretty Village. pap. 5.95 (*0-486-23938-1*) Dover.

***McLoughlin, Cathleen T.** Shakespeare, Rabelais, & the Comical-Historical. LC 98-36829. (Currents in Comparative Romance Languages & Literatures Ser.: Vol. 80). 200p. 2000. text 46.95 (*0-8204-4098-1*) P Lang Pubng.

McLoughlin, Chris. Entree to Halkidiki: An Eat & Sleep Guide. 1995. pap. 11.95 (*1-899163-02-6*) Cimino Pub Grp.

McLoughlin, David. Adult Dyslexic: Interventions & Outcomes. 1999. pap. 39.95 (*1-86156-045-1*) Singular Publishing.

McLoughlin, David, et al. The Adult Dyslexic: Assessment, Counseling & Training. 150p. 1994. text 24.99 (*1-56593-241-2*, 0561) Thomson Learn.
— The Adult Dyslexic: Interventions & Outcomes. 150p. 1997. 39.95 (*1-56593-914-X*, 1810) Singular Publishing.

McLoughlin, Dympna. Women, Subsistence & Emigration, 1840-1870. (Women in Irish History Ser.). 192p. 2000. 49.50 (*0-7165-2563-1*, Pub. by Irish Acad Pr) Intl Spec Bk.

McLoughlin, Emmett. Letters to an Ex-Priest. 1965. 4.95 (*0-8184-0050-1*) Carol Pub Group.

McLoughlin, Ian. Creative Technological Change: The Shaping of Technology & Organisations. LC 98-28497. (Studies in the Management of Technology & Innovation). 1999. 99.99 (*0-415-17999-8*); pap. 32.99 (*0-415-18000-7*) Routledge.

McLoughlin, Ian & Clark, Jon. Technological Change at Work. 224p. 1988. 110.00 (*0-335-15417-4*) OpUniv Pr.
— Technological Change at Work. 2nd ed. LC 93-27839. 1994. pap. 40.95 (*0-335-19009-X*) OpUniv Pr.

McLoughlin, Ian & Gourlay, Stephen. Enterprise Without Unions: Industrial Relations in a Non-Union Firm. LC 94-25725. (Managing Work & Organizations Ser.). 160p. 1994. pap. 33.95 (*0-335-19030-8*) OpUniv Pr.

McLoughlin, J., ed. Environmental Pollution Control: An Introduction to Principles & Practice of Administration. (International Environmental Law & Policy Ser.). 288p. (C). 1993. lib. bdg. 117.50 (*1-85333-577-0*) Kluwer Academic.

McLoughlin, J., et al, eds. Top Tips in Urology. LC 95-11624. 117p. 1995. pap. 14.95 (*0-86542-610-4*) Blackwell Sci.

McLoughlin, J. B., jt. auth. see Diamond, Donald R.

McLoughlin, J. B., jt. auth. see Huxley, M.

McLoughlin, J. B., jt. ed. see Diamond, Donald R.

McLoughlin, J. Brian. Shaping Melbourne's Future? Town Planning, the State & Civil Society. (Illus.). 277p. (C). 1993. text 69.95 (*0-521-41334-6*) Cambridge U Pr.

McLoughlin, James A. & Lewis, Rena B. Assessing Special Students: Strategies & Procedures. 4th ed. 672p. (C). 1993. 72.00 (*0-02-379492-5*, Macmillan Coll) P-H.

***McLoughlin, James A. & Lewis, Rena B.** Assessing Students with Special Needs. 5th ed. LC 00-28143. 2000. 72.00 (*0-13-085209-0*) P-H.

McLoughlin, James A., jt. auth. see Wallace, Gerald.

McLoughlin, Jim, jt. ed. see Faulkner, Sue.

McLoughlin, John. Letters of Dr. John McLoughlin. (American Autobiography Ser.). 376p. 1995. reprint ed. lib. bdg. 89.00 (*0-7812-8587-9*) Rprt Serv.

McLoughlin, John, jt. auth. see Harris, Martin.

McLoughlin, Kate, jt. auth. see Northrop, Susan.

McLoughlin, Leslie. Colloquial Arabic of the Levant. (Colloquials Ser.). 160p. 1982. pap. 17.99 (*0-415-05107-X*, Routledge Thoemms) Routledge.
— Colloquial Arabic of the Levant. (Colloquials Ser.). 152p. 1988. pap. 14.95 (*0-7100-0668-3*, Routledge Thoemms) Routledge.

McLoughlin, Leslie. Colloquial Arabic of the Levant. (Colloquials Ser.). 1988. 14.95 incl. audio (*0-415-01854-4*, 09933) Routledge.

McLoughlin, Leslie. Colloquial Arabic of the Levant. (Colloquials Ser.). 152p. 1988. 34.99 incl. audio (*0-415-00073-4*, A2571, Routledge Thoemms) Routledge.

McLoughlin, Leslie, tr. see Algosaibi, Ghazi.

McLoughlin, Leslie J. Course in Colloquial Arabic. (ARA.). 145p. 1974. 16.95 (*0-86685-043-0*, LDL0430, Pub. by Librairie du Liban) Intl Bk Ctr.
— A Further Course in Colloquial Arabic. (ARA.). 189p. 16.95 (*0-86685-277-8*, LDL2778, Pub. by Librairie du Liban) Intl Bk Ctr.
— Ibn Saud: Founder of a Kingdom LC 93-178743. 1993. write for info. (*0-333-54938-4*) Macmillan.
— A Learner's Dictionaries of Arabic Idioms: Classical Idioms. (ARA.). 144p. 1988. pap. 13.95 (*0-86685-467-3*, LDL4673, Pub. by Librairie du Liban) Intl Bk Ctr.
— A Learner's Dictionaries of Arabic Idioms: Colloquial Idioms. (ARA.). 144p. 1988. pap. 13.95 (*0-86685-468-1*, LDL4681, Pub. by Librairie du Liban) Intl Bk Ctr.

***McLoughlin, Linda.** The Language of Magazines. LC 99-48842. (Intertext Ser.). 112p. 2000. pap. 16.99 (*0-415-21424-6*) Routledge.

McLoughlin, Marlene. Across the Aegean: An Artist's Journey from Athens to Istanbul. 132p. 1996. 18.95 (*0-8118-0862-9*) Chronicle Bks.
— Road to Rome: An Artist's Year in Italy. LC 94-27239. (Illus.). 120p. 1995. 16.95 (*0-8118-0577-8*) Chronicle Bks.

McLoughlin, Michael, ed. Great Irish Speeches of the Twentieth Century. LC 97-115913. 430p. 1996. pap. 24.95 (*1-85371-613-8*, Pub. by Poolbeg Pr) Dufour.

McLoughlin, Pat, ed. Woman's Hour Book of Short Stories 2. (Illus.). 282p. (Orig.). 1993. mass mkt. 7.99 (*0-563-36389-4*, BBC-Parkwest) Parkwest Pubns.

McLoughlin, Pat, intro. Woman's Hour Book of Short Stories. (Illus.). 256p. 1991. mass mkt. 7.99 (*0-563-20905-4*, BBC-Parkwest) Parkwest Pubns.

McLoughlin, Patrick. Commercial Leases & Insolvency. 200p. 1992. pap. 60.00 (*0-406-00640-7*, UK, MICHIE) LEXIS Pub.
— McLoughlin: Commercial Leases & Insolvency. 2nd ed. 1996. pap. write for info. (*0-406-08189-1*, MCLI02, MICHIE) LEXIS Pub.

McLoughlin, Peter F. Language Switching As an Index of Socialization in the Republic of the Sudan. LC 64-64256. (University of California Publications in Social Welfare: Vol. 1). 78p. reprint ed. pap. 30.00 (*0-608-13935-1*, 202141800021) Bks Demand.

McLoughlin, Quin. Relativistic Naturalism: A Cross-Cultural Approach to Human Science. LC 91-430. 280p. 1991. 65.00 (*0-275-93870-0*, C3870, Praeger Pubs) Greenwood.

McLoughlin, T. O. The Writings & Speeches of Edmund Burke Vol. 1: The Early Writings, 10 vols. Langford, Paul & Todd, William B., eds. 604p. 1999. text 140.00 (*0-19-822415-X*) OUP.

McLoughlin, Tom. My First Soccer Book: A Story, Coloring & Parent-Child Activity Book. (Soccer Kids Ser.). (Illus.). 16p. (J). (ps-k). 1998. pap. 4.95 (*0-9666681-8-9*) United Pubg.
— Soccer Kids: Making Soccer Fun for Four & Five Year Olds. (Illus.). 52p. 1997. pap. 11.95 (*0-9666681-9-7*) United Pubg.

McLoughlin, W. Hardbark. The Best of Hook & Bullet: If It's Out There, It's in Here. (Illus.). 176p. (Orig.). 1996. pap. 14.95 (*1-55821-316-3*, 13163) Lyons Pr.

***McLoughlin, William.** Gay in London. 1999. pap. 12.95 (*1-899858-73-3*, Pub. by Ellipsis) Norton.

McLoughlin, William & Pinnock, Jill, eds. Mary Is for Everyone. 320p. 1998. pap. 23.95 (*0-85244-429-X*, 2493, Pub. by Gra1cewing) Morehouse Pub.

McLoughlin, William G. After the Trail of Tears: The Cherokees' Struggle for Sovereignty, 1839-1880. LC 93-18532. xvi, 440p. (C). 1994. 55.00 (*0-8078-2111-X*); pap. 19.95 (*0-8078-4433-0*) U of NC Pr.
— American Evangelicals, 1800-1900: An Anthology. 1990. 16.50 (*0-8446-0793-2*) Peter Smith.
— Cherokee Renascence in the New Republic. (Illus.). 494p. 1986. pap. text 19.95 (*0-691-00627-X*, Pub. by Princeton U Pr) Cal Prin Full Svc.
— Cherokees & Missionaries, 1789-1839. LC 94-36184. 400p. 1995. pap. 18.95 (*0-8061-2723-6*) U of Okla Pr.
— New England Dissent, 1630-1833: The Baptists & the Separation of Church & State, 2 vols., Set. LC 70-131464. (Center for the Study of the History of Liberty in America Ser.). (Illus.). 1346p. 1971. 135.00 (*0-674-61175-6*) HUP.
— Revivals, Awakening, & Reform: An Essay on Religion & Social Change in America, 1607 to 1977. LC 77-27830. xvi, 256p. 1980. pap. text 12.00 (*0-226-56092-9*, P891) U Ch Pr.
— Rhode Island. 1986. pap. 12.95 (*0-393-30271-7*) Norton.
— Soul Liberty: The Baptists' Struggle in New England, 1630-1833. LC 90-43369. 357p. Date not set. reprint ed. pap. 110.70 (*0-608-20685-7*, 207179200002) Bks Demand.

McLoughlin, William G., jt. auth. see Clarke, John.

McLoughlin, William G., jt. auth. see Green, Jack P.

McLoughlin, William G., ed. see Backus, Isaac.

McLouth, Lawrence A., tr. see Zwingli, Ulrich.

McLoyd, Vonnie C. & Flanagan, Constance A., eds. Economic Stress: Effects on Family Life & Child Development. LC 85-644581. (New Directions for Child Development Ser.: No. CD 46). 1990. pap. 25.00 (*1-55542-845-2*) Jossey-Bass.

McLoyd, Vonnie C. & Steinberg, Laurence, eds. Studying Minority Adolescents: Conceptual, Methodological, & Theoretical Issues. LC 98-9400. 300p. 1998. write for info. (*0-8058-1963-0*); pap. write for info. (*0-8058-1964-9*) L Erlbaum Assocs.

McLucas, Anne D., ed. see Fechter, Charles.

McLucas, Charlotte, jt. auth. see Imus, Nola.

McLucas, John L. Space Commerce. LC 90-43957. (Frontiers of Space Ser.: No. 3). (Illus.). 234p. 1991. 36.50 (*0-674-83020-2*, MCLSPA) HUP.

McLucas, John L. & Sheffield, Charles, eds. Commercial Operations in Space 1980-2000 18th Goddard Memorial Symposium, Mar. 27-28, 1980, Washington, D.C.

M

(Science & Technology Ser.: Vol. 51). (Illus.). 214p. 1981. 30.00 (*0-87703-140-1*, Am Astronaut Soc); pap. 20.00 (*0-87703-141-X*, Am Astronaut Soc) Univelt Inc.

McLuckie, Craig W. Nigerian Civil War Literature: Seeking an "Imagined Community" LC 90-6689. (Studies in African Literature: Vol. 3). 172p. 1990. lib. bdg. 79.95 (*0-88946-727-7*) E Mellen.

***McLuckie, Craig W.** Researching McIlvanney: A Critical & Bibliographic Introduction. (Scottish Studies International: Vol. 28). 118p. (C). 1999. pap. text 26.95 (*0-8204-4313-1*) P Lang Pubng.

— Researching McIlvanney Vol. 28: A Critical & Bibliographic Introduction. 118p. 1999. 26.95 (*3-631-34535-6*) P Lang Pubng.

McLuckie, Craig W. & Colbert, Patrick J., eds. Critical Perspectives on Dennis Brutus. 269p. 1995. pap. 16.95 (*0-89410-770-4*, Three Contnts) L Rienner.

— Critical Perspectives on Dennis Brutus. 269p. 1995. 35.00 (*0-89410-769-0*, Three Contnts) L Rienner.

McLuckie, Craig W. & McPhail, Aubrey, eds. Ken Saro-Wiwa: Writer & Political Activist. LC 99-31267. 292p. 1999. lib. bdg. 59.95 (*0-89410-883-2*, Three Contnts) L Rienner.

McLuen, Dennis. Equipped to Serve: Youth Specialties' Volunteer Youth Worker Training Course. 96p. 1995. pap., teacher ed. 9.99 (*0-310-48791-9*) Zondervan.

— Equipped to Serve: Youth Specialties Volunteer Youth Worker Training Course. 96p. (J). 1995. pap. 49.99 incl. VHS (*0-310-49679-9*) Zondervan.

— Equipped to Serve Kit: Youth Specialties' Volunteer Youth Worker Training Course. 1995. pap., lab manual ed. 8.99 (*0-310-48801-X*) Zondervan.

***McLuen, Wysong.** Student Leadership Training Manual for Youth Workers: Everything You Need to Disciple Your Kids. LC 99-53469. (Youth Specialities Ser.). 2000. pap., teacher ed. 15.99 (*0-310-22797-6*) Zondervan.

McLuggage, David, jt. auth. see Higdon, Pamela L.

McLuhan. Electric Language. LC 98-3107. 192p. 1998. pap. 19.95 (*0-312-19088-3*) St Martin.

McLuhan, Elizabeth, ed. Safe Haven: The Refugee Experience of Five Families. (Illus.). 240p. 1995. pap. 28.75 (*0-919045-67-7*) U of Toronto Pr.

McLuhan, ERic. The Role of Thunder in Finnegans Wake. LC 97-169869. (Illus.). 340p. 1997. text 45.00 (*0-8020-0923-9*, PR6019) U of Toronto Pr.

McLuhan, Eric & Zingrone, Frank, eds. The Essential McLuhan. LC 96-11520. 416p. 1996. reprint ed. 18.50 (*0-465-01995-1*, Pub. by Basic) HarpC.

McLuhan, Eric, jt. auth. see McLuhan, Marshall.

***McLuhan, M.** Das Medium ist die Botschaft.Tr. of Medium is the Message. (GER., Illus.). 250p. 1998. text 16.00 (*90-5705-095-1*, Verlag Kunst) Gordon & Breach.

McLuhan, Marshall. Die Mechanische Braut Volkskultur des Industriellen Menschen. (GER., Illus.). 360p. 1996. text 33.00 (*90-5705-021-8*) Gordon & Breach.

— The Gutenberg Galaxy: The Making of Typographic Man. LC 62-4860. 294p. 1962. pap. 19.95 (*0-8020-6041-2*) U of Toronto Pr.

— Die Magischen Kanale. 540p. 1995. text 13.00 (*3-364-00308-4*) Gordon & Breach.

— Understanding Media: The Extensions of Man. 392p. 1994. pap. text 15.95 (*0-262-63159-8*) MIT Pr.

McLuhan, Marshall & Fiore, Quentin. The Medium Is the Message: An Inventory of Effects. (Illus.). 160p. 1996. reprint ed. pap. 9.95 (*1-888869-02-X*) Wired Bks.

— War & Peace in the Global Village. (Illus.). 190p. 1997. pap. 9.95 (*1-888869-07-0*) Wired Bks.

McLuhan, Marshall & McLuhan, Eric. Laws of Media: The New Science. 258p. 1988. 30.00 (*0-8020-5782-9*) U of Toronto Pr.

— Laws of Media: The New Science. 262p. 1992. pap. text 18.95 (*0-8020-7715-3*) U of Toronto Pr.

McLuhan, Marshall & Powers, Bruce R. The Global Village: Transformations in World Life & Media in the 21st Century. (Illus.). 240p. 1992. pap. text 13.95 (*0-19-507910-8*) OUP.

McLuhan, Marshall, jt. auth. see McKenna, Terence.

McLuhan, T. C. Touch the Earth. unabridged ed. (C). 1994. 10.95 incl. audio (*1-56176-910-X*, MYS-76910) Mystic Fire.

McLuhan, T. C. The Way of the Earth: Encounters with Nature in Ancient & Contemporary Thought. (Illus.). 570p. (C). 1998. pap. text 17.00 (*0-7881-5553-9*) DIANE Pub.

McLuhan, Teri. The Way of the Earth. 560p. 1994. 30.00 (*0-671-75939-6*) S&S Trade.

McLullich, Helen & Bedborough, Sheena. Scotland in the Second World War. (Scottie Bks.). (Illus.). 40p. (J). 1998. pap. 8.95 (*0-11-495814-9*, Pub. by Statnry Office) Seven Hills Bk.

McLung, James W., compiled by. Annual Report of the Librarian of Congress: For the Fiscal Year Ending September 30, 1991. 93p. 1992. 3.50 (*0-16-037931-8*) Lib Congress.

M'Clung, John A. Sketches of Western Adventure. LC 76-90184. (Mass Violence in America Ser.). 1969. reprint ed. 16.95 (*0-405-01326-4*) Ayer.

McLure, A. W. Annals of War. 840p. 1996. 14.98 (*0-7858-0706-3*) Bk Sales Inc.

McLure, Charles E., Jr. Economic Perspectives on State Taxation of Multijurisdictional Corporations. 337p. (Orig.). 1987. pap. 34.95 (*0-918255-04-X*) Tax Analysts.

— Must Corporate Income Be Taxed Twice? LC 78-27905. (Studies of Government Finance). 262p. 1979. 34.95 (*0-8157-5620-8*); pap. 14.95 (*0-8157-5619-4*) Brookings.

— Tax Policy Lessons for LDCs & Eastern Europe. 1992. pap. 9.95 (*1-55815-194-X*) ICS Pr.

McLure, Charles E., Jr. & Mieszkowski, Peter, eds. Fiscal Federalism & the Taxation of Natural Resources. LC 82-48581. 269p. reprint ed. pap. 83.40 (*0-7837-5761-1*, 204542300006) Bks Demand.

McLure, Charles E., Jr., et al. The Taxation of Income from Business & Capital in Colombia: Fiscal Reform in the Developing World. LC 89-11832. 422p. 1990. text 74.95 (*0-8223-0925-4*) Duke.

McLure, Charles E., Jr., jt. ed. see Boskin, Michael J.

M'Clure, David & Parish, Elijah. Memoirs of the Rev. Eleazar Wheelock, D. D. LC 75-38454. (Religion in America, Ser. 2). 338p. 1972. reprint ed. 24.95 (*0-405-04074-1*) Ayer.

McLure, James. The Day They Shot John Lennon. 1984. pap. 5.25 (*0-8222-0279-4*) Dramatists Play.

— Laundry & Bourbon. 1981. pap. 3.95 (*0-8222-0645-5*) Dramatists Play.

— Lone Star. 1980. pap. 3.25 (*0-8222-0685-4*) Dramatists Play.

— Max & Maxie. 1989. pap. 5.25 (*0-8222-0741-9*) Dramatists Play.

— Pvt. Wars (Full-Length) 1980. pap. 5.25 (*0-8222-0925-X*) Dramatists Play.

— Pvt. Wars (One-Act) 1980. pap. 3.25 (*0-8222-0924-1*) Dramatists Play.

— Wild Oats: A Romance of the Old West. 1985. pap. 5.25 (*0-8222-1257-9*) Dramatists Play.

McLure, John. Baba, a Louis Bakery Bread Book: The Secret Book of the Bread. Mueller, Kate & Gay, Olivia, eds. LC 93-78237. (Illus.). 132p. (Orig.). 1993. pap. 13.95 (*0-9636892-0-7*, Pub. by B A L Bakery) Chelsea Green Pub.

McLure, John R. The Ventilation of School Buildings: A Study of Present Practices & Costs in the Light of Experimental Research. LC 72-177035. (Columbia University. Teachers College. Contributions to Education Ser.: No. 157). reprint ed. 37.50 (*0-404-55157-2*) AMS Pr.

McLure, Marcia L., jt. auth. see Moynihan, James J.

McLure, Michael, jt. auth. see Wood, John C.

McLure, Patricia, jt. auth. see Newkirk, Thomas.

McLurg. Insight to Expression. 1996. pap. 26.86 (*0-07-045088-9*) McGraw.

McLuskey, Fraser, tr. see Bornkamm, Gunther.

McLuskey, Irene, tr. see Bornkamm, Gunther.

***McLuskey, Krista.** Nevada. (American States Ser.). (Illus.). 32p. (J). (gr. 3-7). 2000. write for info. (*1-930954-60-3*) Weigl Pubs.

McLuskie, Katherine. Scottish U. S. A. A Celebration of Scottish Culture in America. (Illus.). 288p. 1999. 22.50 (*1-55972-501-X*, Birch Ln Pr) Carol Pub Group.

McLuskie, Kathleen. Plays on Women: Anon, Arden of Faversham; Middleton & Dekker, The Roaring Girl; Middleton, A C. 1999. 69.95 (*0-7190-1564-2*, Pub. by Manchester Univ Pr) St Martin.

McLuskie, Kathleen E. Dekker & Heywood: Professional Dramatists. LC 93-30472. 160p. 1994. text 45.00 (*0-312-10629-7*) St Martin.

McLusky, Donald S. The Estuarine Ecosystem. 200p. 1989. 69.95 (*0-412-02091-2*, A3608, Chap & Hall NY) Chapman & Hall.

McLusky, Donald S., et al, eds. North Sea: Estuaries Interactions, Proceedings of the 18th EBSA Symposium. (Developments in Hydrobiology Ser.). (C). 1990. text 233.50 (*0-7923-0694-5*) Kluwer Academic.

McLyman, C. Transformer & Inductor Design Handbook. 2nd ed. (Electrical Engineering & Electronics Ser.: Vol. 49). (Illus.). 432p. 1988. text 85.00 (*0-8247-7828-6*) Dekker.

McLyman, William T. Designing Magnetic Components for High Frequency DC-DC Converters. 435p. 1993. 80.00 (*1-883107-00-8*) KG Magnetics.

— Magnetic Core Selection for Transformers & Inductors: A User's Guide to Practice & Specification, Vol. 102. 2nd ed. LC 97-1909. (Electrical Engineering & Electronics Ser.). (Illus.). 672p. 1997. text 99.75 (*0-8247-9841-4*) Dekker.

***McLynn.** Carl Gustav Jung. (J). 2000. pap. 22.95 (*0-552-99562-2*, Pub. by Transworld Publishers Ltd) Trafalgar.

— Robert Louis Stevenson. 24.95 (*0-7126-5893-9*, Pub. by Random) Trafalgar.

McLynn, E. J. The Jacobite Army in England, 1745: The Final Campaign. 220p. 1998. pap. 48.00 (*0-85976-488-5*, Pub. by J Donald) St Mut.

McLynn, Frank. Carl Gustav Jung. LC 97-12830. 1997. text 29.95 (*0-312-15491-7*) St Martin.

— Carl Gustav Jung. 340p. 1998. pap. 18.95 (*0-312-19445-5*) St Martin.

— Charles Edward Stuart: A Tragedy in Many Acts. 608p. 1988. text 29.95 (*0-415-00272-9*, A2597) Routledge.

— Famous Trials: Cases That Made History. LC 95-22728. (Illus.). 182p. (YA). 1995. 27.95 (*0-89577-655-3*, Pub. by RD Assn) Penguin Putnam.

— Hearts of Darkness: The European Exploration of Africa. (Illus.). 400p. 1994. pap. 14.95 (*0-7867-0084-X*) Carroll & Graf.

— The Jacobites. (Illus.). 288p. 1988. pap. text 14.95 (*0-415-00267-2*, Routledge Thoemms) Routledge.

McLynn, Neil. Ambrose of Milan: Church & Court in a Christian Capital. LC 94-2261. (Transformation of the Classical Heritage Ser.: Vol. 22). 1994. 50.00 (*0-520-08461-6*, Pub. by U CA Pr) Cal Prin Full Svc.

***McMacken, Robin.** The Dakotas: Off the Beaten Path. 3rd ed. (Off the Beaten Path Ser.). (Illus.). 192p. (Orig.). 2000. pap. 12.95 (*0-7627-0623-6*) Globe Pequot.

McMacken, Robin. The Dakotas: Off the Beaten Path: A Guide to Unique Places. 2nd ed. LC 98-15757. (Off the Beaten Path Ser.). (Illus.). 256p. 1998. pap. 12.95 (*0-7627-0171-4*) Globe Pequot.

McMackin, Dorothy J., compiled by. Newspaper Gleanings of Andrew County (MO) & Surrounding Area. LC 86-82190. 584p. 1986. 15.00 (*0-939810-05-0*) Jordan Valley.

McMackin, Frank J., et al. Mathematics of the Shop. 4th ed. LC 76-6726. 628p. (C). 1978. teacher ed. 14.00 (*0-8273-1298-9*); mass mkt. 43.00 (*0-8273-1297-0*) Delmar.

McMackin, Greg. Coaching the Defensive Backfield. LC 91-43957. (Illus.). 128p. 1992. pap. 15.00 (*0-9624779-3-1*) Harding Pr.

McMackin, Lorin. Thoughts on Freedom: Two Essays. LC 81-23297. 111p. 1982. 14.95 (*0-8093-1076-7*) S Ill U Pr.

McMahan. Mr. Brooks Goes to Bethlehem. 1994. pap. 6.95 (*1-55897-831-3*) Brentwood Music.

— Some Kind of Happenin' in Jerusalem. 1992. pap. 6.95 (*1-55897-408-3*) Brentwood Music.

Mcmahan & Funk. Here's How to Write Well. LC 98-24823. 251p. 1998. pap. text 28.00 (*0-205-27382-3*) Allyn.

McMahan, Candace, ed. Instant Group Devotions for Children's Ministry. LC 97-43837. 96p. (J). 1998. pap. 14.99 (*0-7644-2043-7*) Group Pub.

McMahan, Candace, ed. see Chapman, Chris.

McMahan, Candace, ed. see Keffer, Lois.

McMahan, Dean. Ajuna's Star. LC 90-82569. (SPA., Illus.). 24p. (J). (ps-2). 1990. pap. 4.95 (*0-9626254-3-4*) Ajuna Unlimited.

McMahan, Dean & Rose, Willi. Ajuna's Star. 1990. 8.95 incl. audio (*0-9626254-5-0*); 8.95 incl. audio (*0-9626254-6-9*) Ajuna Unlimited.

— Ajuna's Star. rev. ed. LC 90-80841. (Illus.). 24p. (J). (ps-2). 1990. reprint ed. pap. 4.95 (*0-9626254-1-8*); reprint ed. audio. write for info. (*0-9626254-2-6*) Ajuna Unlimited.

Mcmahan, Elizabeth. Literature & the Writing Process. 5th ed. LC 98-25650. 1188p. (C). 1998. pap. text 50.67 (*0-13-913211-2*) P-H.

McMahan, Elizabeth & Day, Susan. The Writer's Handbook. 2nd ed. 400p. (C). 1988. pap. 25.00 (*0-07-045432-9*) McGraw.

McMahan, Elizabeth, jt. auth. see Day, Susan X.

McMahan, Elizabeth, jt. ed. see Day, Susan.

McMahan, Ernest E. Needs: Of People & Their Communities & the Adult Educator. 55p. 1970. 3.00 (*0-88379-004-1*) A A A C E.

McMahan, Eva M. Elite Oral History Discourse: A Study of Cooperation & Coherence. LC 88-36913. (Studies in Rhetoric & Communication). 192p. (C). 1989. text 34.95 (*0-8173-0437-1*) U of Ala Pr.

McMahan, Eva M. & Rogers, Kim L., eds. Interactive Oral History Interviewing. (Communication Ser.). 184p. 1994. text 39.95 (*0-8058-0576-1*) L Erlbaum Assocs.

McMahan, Gary C. & Lawler, Edward E., 3rd. Effects of Union Status on Employee Involvement: Diffusion & Effectiveness. 29p. 1994. pap. 15.00 (*0-614-06144-X*, 2052-PP-4040) EPF.

***McMahan, Ian.** Frommer's Irreverent Guide to Manhattan. 3rd ed. (Illus.). 240p. 2000. 12.95 (*0-02-863790-9*) Macmillan.

McMahan, Ian. Get It Done! A Guide to Motivation, Determination & Achievement. 224p. (Orig.). 1996. mass mkt. 5.99 (*0-380-77970-6*, Avon Bks) Morrow Avon.

— Secrets of the Pharaohs. LC 98-26212. 231p. 1998. pap. 12.50 (*0-380-79720-8*, Avon Bks) Morrow Avon.

McMahan, Ian, jt. auth. see Murphy, Joseph.

McMahan, Jacqueline H. California Rancho Cooking. LC 83-72309. (Illus.). 248p. 1983. 14.95 (*0-9612150-0-3*) Olive Pr.

— California Rancho Cooking. (Illus.). 260p. 1998. pap. 16.95 (*1-881656-05-5*) Olive Pr.

— California Rancho Cooking. rev. ed. (Illus.). 260p. 1988. pap. 12.95 (*0-9612150-7-0*) Olive Pr.

— The Chipotle Chile Cookbook: Fire with Flavor. Hightower, Ruth, ed. (Illus.). 150p. (Orig.). 1994. pap. 14.95 (*1-881656-03-9*) Olive Pr.

— The Healthy Mexican: A Fresh Approach to Mexican Recipes. 2nd rev. ed. Hightower, Ruth, ed. (Illus.). 200p. 1994. pap. 16.95 (*1-881656-04-7*) Olive Pr.

— Mexican Breakfast Cookbook: Spicy & Sweet Morning Meals. 170p. 1992. pap. 14.95 (*1-881656-00-4*) Olive Pr.

— The Red & Green Chile Book: Southwestern & Mexican Recipes. 2nd ed. (Illus.). 210p. 1992. reprint ed. pap. 14.95 (*0-9612150-5-4*) Olive Pr.

— The Salsa Book. LC 85-63671. 160p. 1986. 12.95 (*0-9612150-2-X*); per. 9.95 (*0-9612150-3-8*) Olive Pr.

— The Salsa Book. 2nd rev. ed. (Illus.). 170p. 1989. pap. 14.95 (*0-9612150-8-9*) Olive Pr.

McMahan, Jeff. Reagan & the World: Imperial Policy in the New Cold War. 320p. 1985. pap. 12.00 (*0-85345-678-X*, Pub. by Monthly Rev) NYU Pr.

McMahan, Jeff, jt. ed. see McKim, Robert.

McMahan, Jeffery N. Somewhere in the Night: Eight Gay Tales of the Supernatural. 2nd ed. LC 97-37368. 200p. 1997. pap. 9.95 (*1-55583-432-9*) Alyson Pubns.

McMahan, Jeffrey N. Vampires Anonymous. 256p. 1991. pap. 8.95 (*1-55583-183-4*) Alyson Pubns.

McMahan, Michael K. A Breach of Faith. 196p. 1996. 22.00 (*0-9655907-0-4*) Woodland Pubns.

McMahan, Oliver. Becoming a Shepherd. 235p. 1994. pap. 11.99 (*0-87148-116-2*) Pathway Pr.

***McMahan, Oliver.** Deepening Discipleship: Contemporary Applications of Biblical Commitments. 2000. pap. 12.99 (*0-87148-274-6*) Pathway Pr.

McMahan, Oliver. Scriptural Counseling: A God-Centered Method. LC 94-69939. 269p. 1995. pap. 11.99 (*0-87148-963-5*) Pathway Pr.

McMahan, Richard H., Jr., ed. Cogeneration: Why, When & How to Assess & Implement a Project. LC 86-19795. (Series of Special Reports: No. 16). (Illus.). 367p. reprint ed. pap. 113.80 (*0-7837-0684-7*, 204101700019) Bks Demand.

McMahan, Robert. Pixel Photography. 200p. 1993. pap. 18.95 (*1-881656-01-2*) Olive Pr.

McMahan, Scott. Automating Windows with Perl. 224p. 1999. pap. 34.95 incl. cd-rom (*0-87930-589-4*, Pub. by C M P Books) Publishers Group.

McMahan, U. J., ed. Steve: Remembrances of Stephen W. Kuffler. LC 90-10383. (Illus.). 142p. (Orig.). 1990. pap. 18.95 (*0-87893-516-9*) Sinauer Assocs.

McMahen, Chris. Buddy Concrackle's Amazing Adventure. 144p. (J). (gr. 4-7). 1997. pap. 5.95 (*1-55050-101-1*, Pub. by Coteau) Genl Dist Srvs.

McMahill, Cheiron, tr. see Summerhawk, Barbara, et al, eds.

***McMahill, Kim.** On the Brink of Paradise: From Tetons to Tropics. 115p. 1999. pap. 12.95 (*0-7414-0140-1*) Buy Books.

McMahon. Bride on the Ranch. 1997. per. 3.25 (*0-373-15719-3*) Harlequin Bks.

— Development Corporation. LC 98-226044. 1998. lib. bdg. 99.00 (*90-411-0744-4*) Kluwer Law Intl.

— Nursing As Therapy. 234p. 1991. pap. 43.25 (*1-56593-012-6*, 0253) Singular Publishing.

— Origins of the Cold War. 4th ed. LC 98-72061. 1998. pap. text 14.07 (*0-395-90430-7*) HM.

— Psychology & You. Date not set. pap. text, teacher ed. 16.95 (*0-314-52495-9*) West Pub.

— Psychology & You. 1989. mass mkt., wbk. ed. 19.00 (*0-314-52496-7*) West Pub.

— Psychology & You. 2nd ed. 1994. mass mkt., teacher ed. 66.25 (*0-314-02771-8*) West Pub.

— Psychology & You. 2nd ed. (CA - Career Development Ser.). 1994. mass mkt., wbk. ed. 22.50 (*0-314-04524-4*) West Pub.

— Psychology & You. 2nd ed. (Career Development Ser.). 1996. teacher ed. 12.00 (*0-314-21636-7*) West Pub.

— Psychology & You. 3rd ed. (Career Development Ser.). 1999. pap. text, student ed., wbk. ed. 24.24 (*0-538-42663-2*) Thomson Learn.

— Psychology & You: Worksheets. 2nd ed. (Career Development Ser.). 1994. pap. 24.50 (*0-314-04662-3*) Thomson Learn.

***McMahon.** Raising the Bar, Classroom Tested Projects, Psychology & You. 3rd ed. 1999. pap. 15.75 (*0-538-42904-6*) Thomson Learn.

***McMahon & Romano.** Getting Pysched up, Classroom Test Project. 3rd ed. 1999. pap. 12.00 (*0-538-42903-8*) Thomson Learn.

— Lecture Notes for Teachers of Psychology, Psychology & You. 3rd ed. 1999. pap. 24.00 (*0-538-42901-1*) Thomson Learn.

— TAAS Performance Tasks/ Psychology & You 2e worksheet. 2nd ed. 1994. pap. 6.25 (*0-314-04647-X*) West Pub.

McMahon, jt. auth. see Arbetman.

Mcmahon, jt. auth. see Arbetman, Lee P.

McMahon, jt. auth. see Levitin.

McMahon, jt. auth. see Moore.

McMahon, jt. auth. see Norris.

McMahon, A. Michael & Morris, Stephanie A. Technology in Industrial America: Records of the Committee on Science & the Arts of the Franklin Institute, 1824-1900: A Guide. LC 77-77872. 400p. 1977. 65.00 (*0-8420-2123-X*) Scholarly Res Inc.

McMahon, Agnes, ed. Celtic Way of Life. (Illus.). 72p. 1998. pap. 9.95 (*0-86278-236-8*, Pub. by OBrien Pr) Irish Amer Bk.

McMahon, Agnes, jt. auth. see Wallace, Mike.

McMahon, Alexander R. The Karens of the Golden Chersonese. LC 77-87018. reprint ed. 42.50 (*0-404-16840-X*) AMS Pr.

McMahon, Ann P. & Brake, Kimberly A. Catalyst's Adventures in Science: Bubble Rainbows. rev. ed. LC 94-67847. (Illus.). 32p. (J). (gr. k-3). 1994. pap. 9.95 (*0-9642550-0-6*) Curiosity Unltd.

McMahon, Annette F. Petals: Change Your Perspective Change Your Life. (Illus.). 223p. (Orig.). 1987. 24.95 (*0-944005-21-7*); pap. write for info. (*0-944005-22-5*); lib. bdg. write for info. (*0-944005-23-3*) Columbia NY.

McMahon, Anthony. Damned If You Do, Damned If You Don't: Working in Child Welfare. LC 97-74453. 138p. 1998. text 55.95 (*1-85972-616-X*, Pub. by Ashgate Pub) Ashgate Pub Co.

— Taking Care of Men: Sexual Politics in the Public Mind. LC 99-25156. 288p. 1999. pap. 19.95 (*0-521-58820-0*) Cambridge U Pr.

— Taking Care of Men: Sexual Politics in the Public Mind. LC 99-25156. 288p. 1999. write for info. (*0-521-58204-0*) Cambridge U Pr.

***McMahon, April M.** Change, Chance & Optimality. (Illus.). 224p. 2000. pap. 19.95 (*0-19-824125-9*); text 60.00 (*0-19-824124-0*) OUP.

— Lexical Phonology & the History of English. (Cambridge Studies in Linguistics: No. 91). (Illus.). 300p. (C). 2000. 59.95 (*0-521-47280-6*) Cambridge U Pr.

McMahon, April M. Understanding Language Change. 373p. (C). 1994. pap. text 19.95 (*0-521-44665-1*) Cambridge U Pr.

McMahon, Barbara. Angel Bride. (Simply the Best Ser.). 1997. per. 3.25 (*0-373-03451-2*, 1-03451-1) Harlequin Bks.

— Angel Bride. large type ed. (Simply the Best Ser.). 1997. per. 3.25 (*0-373-15697-9*, 1-15697-5) Harlequin Bks.

***McMahon, Barbara.** Bachelor's Baby Promise. (Special Edition Ser.: Bk. 1351). 2000. mass mkt. 4.50 (*0-373-24351-0*, 1-24351-8) Silhouette.

McMahon, Barbara. Bluebells on the Hill. large type ed. (Magna Large Print Ser.). (Illus.). 300p. 1996. 27.99 (*0-7505-0996-1*) Ulverscroft.

— Boss Lady & the Hired Hand. 1997. per. 3.50 (*0-373-76072-8*, 1-76072-7) Silhouette.

An Asterisk (*) at the beginning of an entry indicates that the title is appearing for the first time.

— Bride of a Thousand Days. (Desire Ser.). 1996. per. 3.50 (*0-373-76017-5*, 1-76017-2) Silhouette.
— Bride on the Ranch. 1997. per. 3.25 (*0-373-03473-3*, 1-03473-5) Harlequin Bks.
— Cinderella Twin. (Desire Ser.). 1998. per. 3.75 (*0-373-76154-6*, 1-76157-3) Silhouette.
— The Cowboy & the Virgin. (Desire Ser.: No. 1215). 1999. per. 3.75 (*0-373-76215-1*, 1-76215-2) Silhouette.
— Cowboy's Bride. (Desire Ser.). 1996. per. 3.25 (*0-373-05977-9*, 1-05977-3) Silhouette.
***McMahon, Barbara.** Daddy & Daughters: Daddy Boom. 1999. per. 3.50 (*0-373-03547-0*, 1-03547-6, Harlequin); per. 3.50 (*0-373-15793-2*, 1-15793-2, Harlequin) Harlequin Bks.
McMahon, Barbara. La Dueña de Mi Corazon (The Owner of My Heart) (Deseo Ser.). (SPA.). 1998. per. 3.50 (*0-373-35230-1*, 1-35230-1) Harlequin Bks.
***McMahon, Barbara.** Georgia's Groom. (Romance Ser.: Vol. 3620). 2000. mass mkt. 3.50 (*0-373-03620-5*, 1-03620-1) Harlequin Bks.
— Georgia's Groom. large type ed. (Large Print Ser.: Vol. 466). 2000. mass mkt. 3.50 (*0-373-15866-1*, Harlequin) Harlequin Bks.
McMahon, Barbara. Island Paradise. large type ed. 1992. reprint ed. 18.95 (*0-263-13099-1*) Mac Lib Ref.
***McMahon, Barbara.** Marrying Margot. large type ed. 288p. 2000. 22.95 (*0-263-16488-8*) Thorndike Pr.
— Marrying Margot, Vol. 458. large type ed. (Large Print Ser.). 2000. mass mkt. 3.50 (*0-373-15858-0*) Harlequin Bks.
— Marrying Margot: Beaufort Brides. 2000. mass mkt. 3.50 (*0-373-03612-4*) Harlequin Bks.
— A Mother for Mollie. (Romance Ser.). 2000. mass mkt. 3.50 (*0-373-03616-7*, 1-03616-9) Harlequin Bks.
— Mother for Mollie, Vol. 462. large type ed. (Large Print Ser.: Vol. 462). 2000. mass mkt. 3.50 (*0-373-15862-9*) Harlequin Bks.
— Una Mujer Nueva: Cinderella Twin. (Deseo Ser.: No. 150).Tr. of New Woman. (SPA.). 1999. per. 3.50 (*0-373-35280-8*, 1-35280-6) Harlequin Bks.
McMahon, Barbara. The Older Man. (Desire Ser.). 1998. per. 3.75 (*0-373-76161-9*, 1-76161-8) Silhouette.
— One Stubborn Cowboy. (Desire Ser.). 1995. per. 3.25 (*0-373-05915-9*, 1-05915-3) Silhouette.
— Rent-a-Cowboy. (Romance Ser.). 1998. per. 3.50 (*0-373-03501-2*, 1-03501-3) Harlequin Bks.
— Rent-a-Cowboy. large type ed. (Back to the Ranch Ser.). 1998. per. 3.50 (*0-373-15747-9*, Harlequin) Harlequin Bks.
— Santa Cowboy. (Desire Ser.: No. 1116). 1997. per. 3.50 (*0-373-76116-3*, 1-76116-2) Harlequin Bks.
— Sheik Daddy. (Romance Ser.). 1996. per. 3.25 (*0-373-19132-9*, 1-19132-9) Silhouette.
***McMahon, Barbara.** The Sheik's Solution. (Silhouette Romance Ser.: No. 1422). 2000. per. 3.50 (*0-373-19422-6*, 1-19422-4) Harlequin Bks.
McMahon, Barbara. Un Soplo de Juventud: A Breath of Youth.Tr. of A Breath of Youth. (SPA.). 1999. per. 3.50 (*0-373-35284-0*, 1-35284-8) Harlequin Bks.
***McMahon, Barbara.** Temporary Father. large type ed. 288p. 1999. 25.99 (*0-263-16083-1*, Pub. by Mills & Boon) Ulverscroft.
McMahon, Barbara. Trial Engagement. (Larger Print Ser.). 1999. per. 3.50 (*0-373-15813-0*, 1-15813-8) Harlequin Bks.
— Trial Engagement. (Romance Ser.). 1999. per. 3.50 (*0-373-03567-5*, 1-03567-4) Harlequin Bks.
— Vamp d'Un Soir. (Rouge Passion Ser.: Vol. 501). (FRE.). 1999. mass mkt. 3.50 (*0-373-37501-8*, 1-37501-3) Harlequin Bks.
— Wanted: Perfect Wife: Bachelor Territory. (Romance Ser.: Vol. 3521). 1998. per. 3.50 (*0-373-03521-7*, 1-03521-1) Harlequin Bks.
— Wanted: Perfect Wife: Bachelor Territory. large type ed. (Larger Print Ser.: Vol. 367). 1998. per. 3.50 (*0-373-15767-3*, 1-15767-6) Harlequin Bks.
— Wanted: Wife & Mother. (Promo Ser.). 1999. per. 4.50 (*0-373-21967-9*, 1-21967-4) Harlequin Bks.
— Wanted: Wife & Mother. LC 95-13543. (Romance Ser.). 186p. 1995. per. 2.99 (*0-373-03369-9*, 1-03369-5) Harlequin Bks.
— Wanted: Wife & Mother. large type ed. (Harlequin Romance Ser.). 1995. 20.95 (*0-263-14322-8*) Mac Lib Ref.
— Wyoming Wedding. (Romance Ser.). 1996. per. 3.25 (*0-373-03428-8*, 1-03428-9) Harlequin Bks.
— Wyoming Wedding. large type ed. (Hitched Ser.). 1996. per. 3.25 (*0-373-15674-X*) Harlequin Bks.
***McMahon, Barbara.** Yours for Ninety Days. (Special Edition Ser.: No. 1282). 1999. per. 4.25 (*0-373-24282-4*, 1-24282-5) Silhouette.
McMahon, Bernard. The American Gardener's Calendar. LC 97-61547. (Illus.). 670p. (C). Date not set. reprint ed. text 45.00 (*1-882886-06-2*) T J Mem Fnd.
McMahon, Betsy M. The Days of My Life: A Journal for the Teen Years. (Illus.). 88p. (Orig.). (J). (gr. 6-9). 1987. pap. 13.95 (*0-942257-05-7*) New Chapter Pr.
McMahon, Brad & Chislovsky, Carol. Anastasia's Christmas in Paris. (Anastasia Ser.). 16p. (J). (ps-3). 1997. 6.95 (*0-694-01099-5*, HarpFestival) HarpC Child Bks.
McMahon, Brad, jt. auth. see Crosby, Greg.
McMahon, Brendan. Enemy Lines. 79p. 1996. pap. 9.95 (*3-7052-0984-1*, Pub. by Poetry Salzburg) Intl Spec Bk.
McMahon, Brian, jt. ed. see Hablutzel, Nancy.
***McMahon, Brian T.** Enabling Lives. LC 99-16192. 248p. 1999. per. 29.95 (*0-8493-0351-6*) CRC Pr.
McMahon, Brian T. & Evans, Randall W., eds. The Shortest Distance: The Pursuit of Independence for Persons with Acquired Brain Injury. LC 93-87363. 156p. (C). 1994. per. 47.95 (*1-878205-68-4*) St Lucie Pr.
McMahon, Brian T. & Shaw, Linda. Enabling Lives. 200p. 1995. lib. bdg. 29.95 (*1-57444-083-7*) St Lucie Pr.
McMahon, Brian T. & Shaw, Linda R., eds. Work Worth Doing: Advances in Brain Injury Rehabilitation. LC 91-71166. (Illus.). 432p. 1991. boxed set 57.95 (*1-878205-19-6*) St Lucie Pr.
McMahon, Bryan M. European Community Law in Ireland. 1989. boxed set 143.00 (*1-85475-000-3*, IE, MICHIE) LEXIS Pub.
McMahon, Bryan M. & Binchy, William. Irish Law of Torts. 2nd ed. 1990. boxed set 136.00 (*1-85475-155-7*, IE, MICHIE) LEXIS Pub.
McMahon, C. J., Jr. & Graham, C. D., Jr. Introduction to Engineering Materials: The Bicycle & the Walkman. LC 95-77924. 418p. (C). 1995. pap. text 39.50 (*0-9646598-0-8*) Merion Bks.
McMahon, Charles J., Jr., ed. Microplasticity, Vol. 2. LC 68-4384. (Advances in Materials Research Ser.). 439p. reprint ed. pap. 136.10 (*0-608-11667-X*, 200740200062) Bks Demand.
McMahon, Chris. Cadam: Principles, Practice & Manufacturing Management. 2nd ed. LC 98-2557. 624p. (C). 1999. pap. 100.00 (*0-201-17819-2*) Addison-Wesley.
***McMahon, Chris & Browne, Jimmie.** CAD - CAM: Principles, Practice & Manufacturing Management: Solutions Manual. 2nd rev. ed. (CAD Ser.). 1999. pap., student ed. write for info. (*0-201-34284-7*) Addison-Wesley.
McMahon, Christine A. & Harding, Joan, eds. Knowledge to Care: A Handbook for Care Assistants. LC 93-2082. 384p. 1993. pap. 19.00 (*0-632-03585-4*) Blackwell Sci.
McMahon, Christine A. & Isaacs, R. Care of the Older Person. LC 96-27717. 256p. (Orig.). 1996. pap. text 21.95 (*0-632-03985-X*) Blackwell Sci.
McMahon, Christopher. Authority & Democracy: A General Theory of Government & Management. 324p. 1994. pap. text 17.95 (*0-691-01629-1*, Pub. by Princeton U Pr) Cal Prin Full Svc.
— Authority & Democracy: A General Theory of Government & Management. LC 94-1366. (Studies in Moral, Political, & Legal Philosophy). 296p. 1994. text 45.00 (*0-691-03662-4*, Pub. by Princeton U Pr) Cal Prin Full Svc.
McMahon, Christopher, photos by. The Gardens at Filoli. LC 94-17778. (Illus.). 128p. 1994. pap. 24.95 (*1-56640-993-4*) Pomegranate Calif.
McMahon, Clara P. Education in Fifteenth-Century England, No. 35--35. LC 68-54991. (Illus.). 181p. 1969. reprint ed. lib. bdg. 55.00 (*0-8371-0586-2*, MCEC, Greenwood Pr) Greenwood.
McMahon, Colleen. Meditations for Vestry Members: Faithful Servants. Webber, Christopher L., ed. LC 98-55384. (Faithful Servants Ser.). 96p. 1999. pap. 6.95 (*0-8192-1789-1*) Morehouse Pub.
***McMahon, David.** ADO 2.1 Developer's Guide. (Application Development Ser.). 2000. pap. 49.99 (*0-07-212555-1*) Osborne-McGraw.
— Rapid Application Development with Visual C++ (Enterprise Computing Ser.). (Illus.). 2000. pap. 49.99 (*0-07-212309-5*) McGrw-H Intl.
McMahon, David. Rapid Application Development with Visual Basic 6. 448p. 1999. pap. 49.00 (*0-07-135422-0*) McGraw.
McMahon, Dierdre, tr. see Tierou, Alphonse.
***McMahon, Donna.** Dance of Knives. 2000. text 25.95 (*0-312-87431-6*) Tor Bks.
McMahon, E. J., jt. ed. see Bartnikas, R.
McMahon, Ed. For Laughin' Out Loud: My Life & Good Times. LC 98-7766. (Illus.). 355p. 1998. 23.00 (*0-446-52370-4*, Pub. by Warner Bks) Little.
McMahon, Ed & Fisher, David. For Laughing Out Loud: My Life & Good Times. (Illus.). 431p. 1999. mass mkt. 6.99 (*0-446-60742-8*, Pub. by Warner Bks) Little.
McMahon, Edward T., et al. Street Law: A Course in Practical Law. 5th ed. LC 93-44422. 1994. mass mkt. 46.50 (*0-314-02713-0*) West Pub.
McMahon, Edward T., jt. auth. see Arbetman, Lee P.
McMahon, Edwin M. Beyond the Myth of Dominance: An Alternative to a Violent Society. LC 92-38036. 288p. (Orig.). 1993. pap. 16.95 (*1-55612-563-1*) Sheed & Ward WI.
McMahon, Edwin M. & Campbell, Peter A. Addictive Religion. 24p. 1996. pap. text 2.00 (*1-55612-510-0*, LL1510) Sheed & Ward WI.
— A Bio-Spiritual Approach to Sexuality. 40p. 1996. pap. text 3.50 (*1-55612-514-3*, LL1514) Sheed & Ward WI.
— Childhood Wonder: A Doorway to the Spiritual in Focusing. 12p. 1996. pap. text 1.25 (*1-55612-507-0*, LL1507) Sheed & Ward WI.
— Focusing: Doorway to the Body-Life of Spirit. 20p. 1996. pap. text 2.00 (*1-55612-517-8*, LL1517) Sheed & Ward WI.
— Focusing & Prayer. 28p. 1996. 2.50 (*1-55612-506-2*, LL1506) Sheed & Ward WI.
— Focusing Companions. 32p. 1996. pap. text 3.00 (*1-55612-518-6*, LL1518) Sheed & Ward WI.
— Focusing Monographs, 19 cass., Set. 1996. audio 139.95 (*0-614-18806-7*, SS7500) Sheed & Ward WI.
— The Focusing Steps. 24p. 1996. pap. text 2.00 (*1-55612-502-X*, LL1502) Sheed & Ward WI.
— The Grace of Forgiving Yourself Through Focusing. 12p. 1996. pap. text 1.25 (*1-55612-509-7*, LL1509) Sheed & Ward WI.
— How Adults Can Listen to Children in a Focusing Way. 28p. 1996. pap. text 2.50 (*1-55612-516-X*, LL1516) Sheed & Ward WI.
— The Inward Connection. 16p. 1996. pap. text 1.50 (*1-55612-504-6*, LL1504) Sheed & Ward WI.
— Journeying Together in Spirit: A Conversation with Sr. Ruth McGoldrick, S. P. 20p. 1996. pap. text 2.00 (*1-55612-515-1*, LL1515) Sheed & Ward WI.
— Process Skipping: Mechanisms Which Lock in Addictive Patterns. 32p. 1996. pap. text 3.00 (*1-55612-513-5*, LL1513) Sheed & Ward WI.
— Questions Often Asked about Focusing & Spirituality. 12p. 1996. pap. text 1.25 (*1-55612-503-8*, LL1503) Sheed & Ward WI.
— Searching for God with Our Fingertips: The Body As Spiritual Guide. 12p. 1996. 1.25 (*1-55612-508-9*, LL1508) Sheed & Ward WI.
— Teaching Children to Focus: An Interview with Marianne Thompson. 20p. 1996. 2.00 (*1-55612-505-4*, LL1505) Sheed & Ward WI.
— What Is Focusing? 12p. 1996. 1.25 (*1-55612-500-3*, LL1500) Sheed & Ward WI.
— What Is Spiritual about Focusing? 12p. 1996. pap. text 1.25 (*1-55612-501-1*, LL1501) Sheed & Ward WI.
— A Woman's Prayer: Notes from a Focusing Journal. 16p. 1996. pap. text 1.50 (*1-55612-512-7*, LL1512) Sheed & Ward WI.
McMahon, Edwin M., jt. auth. see Campbell, Peter A.
McMahon-Ehalt, Teresa, tr. see Oberleitner, John L.
McMahon, Eileen. New Drug Approval in Canada. (Worldwide Pharmaceutical Regulation Ser.). (Orig.). 1995. pap. 100.00 (*1-882615-20-4*) Parexel Intl.
McMahon, Eleanor M., et al. Early Childhood Education: State Policy & Practice, an Issue Paper. LC 91-73762. 53p. 1991. reprint ed. pap. 30.00 (*0-608-05916-1*, 206625200008) Bks Demand.
McMahon, Elise N. Classics Incorporated: Cultural Studies & Seventeenth-Century French Literature. 169p. 1998. lib. bdg. 41.95 (*1-883479-21-5*) Summa Pubns.
McMahon, Ernest E. Needs - of the People & Their Communities - & the Adult Educator. 55p. 1988. 1.95 (*0-318-36408-5*, AEA1-5) A A A C E.
McMahon, Franci. Staying the Distance: A Novel. LC 93-49793. 200p. 1994. pap. 9.95 (*1-56341-046-X*); lib. bdg. 20.95 (*1-56341-047-8*) Firebrand Bks.
McMahon, Frank B. Psychology & You. 1989. mass mkt. 41.50 (*0-314-47357-2*) West Pub.
McMahon, Frank B., et al. Psychology & You. 2nd ed. LC 93-41159. 1994. mass mkt. write for info. (*0-314-02772-6*) West Pub.
McMahon, Gary, ed. Lessons in Economic Policy for Eastern Europe from Latin America. LC 95-2566. (International Political Economy Ser.). 256p. 1996. text 65.00 (*0-312-12647-6*) St Martin.
McMahon, Gary, et al. An Environmental Study of Artisanal, Small & Medium Mining in Bolivia, Chile, & Peru. LC 99-18385. (Technical Paper Ser.: No. 429). 72p. 1999. pap. 22.00 (*0-8213-4428-5*, 14428) World Bank.
McMahon, Gary, jt. ed. see Morales, Juan A.
McMahon, Gladeana, jt. ed. see Palmer, Stephen.
McMahon, Gregory. The Hittite State Cult of the Tutelary Deities. LC 91-60344. (Assyriological Studies: No. 25). xxi, 302p. 1991. pap. 30.00 (*0-918986-69-9*) Orient Inst.
McMahon, Helen. Criticism of Fiction: A Study of Trends in the Atlantic Monthly. LC 74-148278. reprint ed. 20.00 (*0-404-04144-2*) AMS Pr.
McMahon, J. Timothy. Building Managerial Effectiveness. (Work in America Institute Studies in Productivity: No. 39). 56p. 1984. pap. 39.00 (*0-317-66816-1*, Pergamon Pr) Elsevier.
— Building Managerial Effectiveness. LC 85-9352. (Studies in Productivity: Highlights of the Literature Ser.: Vol. 39). 1985. 55.00 (*0-08-029512-6*) Work in Amer.
McMahon, James. Deserts. Elliott, Charles, ed. LC 84-48674. (Audubon Society Nature Guides Ser.). (Illus.). 638p. 1985. pap. 19.95 (*0-394-73139-5*) Knopf.
— Forty-Seven Alligators. Little, Carl, ed. (Illus.). 48p. (Orig.). (J). (ps-3). 1993. pap. 6.95 (*0-932433-95-2*) Windswept Hse.
***McMahon, James A.** Law of the Common Agricultural Policy. 194p. 2000. pap. 33.50 (*0-582-30294-3*, Pub. by Pearson Educ) Gaunt.
McMahon, James M. Letting Go of Mother: Overcoming Dependence & Finding Authentic Intimacy as an Adult. LC 96-1338. 128p. 1996. pap. 8.95 (*0-8091-3662-7*) Paulist Pr.
— The Price of Wisdom: The Heroic Struggle to Become a Person. LC 95-46021. 192p. (Orig.). 1996. pap. 14.95 (*0-8245-1553-6*) Crossroad NY.
— Radical Self-Acceptance: The Spiritual Birth of the Human Person. LC 99-15981. 1999. pap. 19.95 (*0-8245-1824-1*) Crossroad NY.
McMahon, James Michael. Radical Self-Acceptance: The Spiritual Birth of the Human Person. LC 99-15981. 1999. 29.95 (*0-8245-1821-7*) Crossroad NY.
McMahon, James P. Look to Markets, Not Bureaucrats for More Recycling: Legislative Waste Control Efforts Could Prove Wasteful. (Issue Papers: No. 8-93). 5p. 1993. pap. text 8.00 (*1-57655-075-3*) Independ Inst.
— The Walking Fish. Weinberger, Jane, ed. LC 90-70520. (Illus.). 54p. (Orig.). (J). (ps-3). 1990. pap. 6.95 (*0-932433-70-7*) Windswept Hse.
McMahon, James P. & Ryan, Nancy. Buttonbush. 55p. (Orig.). (J). (gr. k-7). 1996. pap. 10.00 (*0-88734-526-3*) Players Pr.
McMahon, James R. & Hand, Janice S. Measuring the Marketplace: An Approach to Designing & Conducting a Salary Survey. (Building Blocks Ser.: Vol. 1). (Illus.). 19p. (Orig.). 1991. pap. 24.95 (*1-57963-004-9*, A0001) Am Compensation.
McMahon, Janet, jt. ed. see Curtiss, Richard H.
McMahon Jeep, Elizabeth. Children's Daily Prayer, 1998-1999. (Illus.). 352p. (J). 1998. pap. 15.00 (*1-56854-222-4*, CDP99) Liturgy Tr Pubns.
McMahon, Jim. A Leak in the Landfill: Colorado's Suppressed Report on Solid Waste Policy Finally Seeps Out. 96p. 1992. pap. text 8.00 (*1-57655-095-8*) Independ Inst.
— Resolving the Conflict Between Man & the Environment: A Model in the Philippines. (Issue Papers: No. 7-94). 7p. 1994. pap. 8.00 (*1-57655-058-3*) Independ Inst.
— Resolving the Conflict Between Man & the Environment: A Model in the Phillipines. (Issue Paper #7-94 Ser.). 7p. 1994. pap. text 8.00 (*1-57655-135-0*) Independ Inst.
McMahon, Jim & Independence Staff. Recycling & Realism: A Market Approach. (Issue Papers: No. 7-91). 12p. 1991. pap. text 8.00 (*1-57655-038-9*) Independ Inst.
McMahon, Joan, jt. auth. see Zinner, Ellen.
***McMahon, Joanne D. & Lascurain, Anna M.** Shopping for Miracles: A Guide to Psychics & Psychic Powers. 224p. 1998. pap. 16.00 (*1-56565-974-0*, 09740W, Pub. by Lowell Hse) NTC Contemp Pub Co.
McMahon, Joanne D., jt. ed. see Coly, Lisette.
McMahon, John. Almost a Lifetime. 297p. 1995. text 29.95 (*0-88982-144-5*, Pub. by Oolichan Bks) Genl Dist Srvs.
McMahon, John H., tr. see Aristotle.
McMahon, John M. Paralysin Cave: Impotence, Perception & Text in the Satyrica of Petronius. LC 97-40691. (Mnemosyne, Supplements Ser.: No. 176). (Illus.). 264p. 1998. 99.50 (*90-04-10825-4*) Brill Academic Pubs.
McMahon, John V. An Historical View of the Government of Maryland: From Its Colonization to the Present Day. LC 68-30882. (Illus.). 1968. reprint ed. 25.00 (*0-87152-046-X*) Reprint.
McMahon, Joseph. How to Select the Best Psychological Theory to Be an Effective Counselor to Your Clients. LC 88-12266. (Studies in Health & Human Services: Vol. 15). 150p. 1989. lib. bdg. 69.95 (*0-88946-004-3*) E Mellen.
McMahon, Joseph A. Education & Culture in European Community Law. (European Community Law Ser.: Vol. 8). 240p. (C). 1995. text 90.00 (*0-485-70013-1*, Pub. by Athlone Pr) Humanities.
— European Trade Policy in Agricultural Products. (C). 1988. lib. bdg. 126.50 (*90-247-3780-X*) Kluwer Academic.
McMahon, Joseph H. The Imagination of Jean Genet, 10. LC 80-16963. (Yale Romantic Studies Second Ser.: 2nd Ser., No. 10). 273p. 1980. reprint ed. lib. bdg. 35.00 (*0-313-22430-7*, MCIM, Greenwood Pr) Greenwood.
McMahon, Joseph J. Discovering the Spirit: Source of Personal Freedom. LC 93-6009. 200p. (Orig.). 1994. pap. 12.95 (*1-55612-669-7*) Sheed & Ward WI.
McMahon, June, ed. Organizing Asian Pacific Workers in Southern California. (Current Issues Ser.: No. 9). 42p. 1993. reprint ed. pap. 7.00 (*0-89215-149-8*) U Cal LA Indus Rel.
McMahon, K. Scott. Pursuit of the Shield: The U. S. Quest for Limited Ballistic Missile Defense. LC 96-52030. 408p. 1997. 62.50 (*0-7618-0686-5*); pap. 39.50 (*0-7618-0687-3*) U Pr of Amer.
McMahon, Karen, jt. auth. see Levetin, Estelle.
McMahon, Kate. A Horse of Another Colour. (Illus.). 96p. (YA). (gr. 3 up). 1999. pap. 8.95 (*1-901737-17-9*, Pub. by Anvil Books Ltd) Dufour.
McMahon, Kate & Myler, Terry. Timber Twig. LC 98-162405. 142p. 1998. pap. 9.95 (*1-901737-01-2*) Dufour.
***McMahon, Kathleen N.** Developing Non-Hierarchical Leadership on Campus: Case Studies & Best Practices in Higher Education. Outcalt, Charles L. & Faris, Shannon K., eds. LC 00-27630. (Educators' Reference Collection). 256p. 2000. lib. bdg. 65.00 (*0-313-31178-1*, Greenwood Pr) Greenwood.
McMahon, Kay. Passion's Slave. 1983. mass mkt. 3.50 (*0-685-07884-1*, Zebra Kensgtn) Kensgtn Pub Corp.
— Yankee's Lady. mass mkt. 3.95 (*0-317-43142-0*, Zebra Kensgtn) Kensgtn Pub Corp.
McMahon, Kay E., jt. auth. see Nance, Virginia L.
McMahon, Keith. Misers, Shrews & Polygamists: Sexuality & Male-Female Relations in Eighteenth-Century China. LC 94-33072. (Illus.). 384p. 1995. text 54.95 (*0-8223-1555-6*); pap. text 19.95 (*0-8223-1566-1*) Duke.
***McMahon, Kevin.** Weekend in Silverlake: A Pastoral Comedy. 256p. 2001. 25.00 (*1-85984-791-9*, Pub. by Verso) Norton.
McMahon, Kevin T. Sexuality: Theological Voices. LC 87-18201. 266p. (Orig.). 1987. pap. 14.95 (*0-935372-20-2*) NCBC.
McMahon, Linnet. The Handbook of Play Therapy. LC 91-37179. 304p. (Orig.). (C). 1992. text 99.95 (*0-415-07923-3*, A6909) Routledge.
— The Handbook of Play Therapy. LC 91-37179. (Illus.). 304p. (Orig.). (C). 1992. pap. 27.99 (*0-415-05986-0*, A6913) Routledge.
McMahon, Linnet & Ward, Adrian. Intuition Is Not Enough: Matching Learning with Practice in Therapeutic Child Care. LC 97-34706. 272p. (C). 1998. 85.00 (*0-415-15661-0*) Routledge.
— Intuition Is Not Enough: Matching Learning with Practice in Therapeutic Child Care. LC 97-34706. 272p. (C). 1998. pap. 25.99 (*0-415-15662-9*) Routledge.
McMahon, Luella E. Lovers in Midsummer. 46p. 1970. pap. 3.50 (*0-87129-148-7*, L35) Dramatic Pub.
— The People vs. Maxine Lowe. 87p. (C). 1955. pap. 5.50 (*0-87129-736-1*, P20) Dramatic Pub.
McMahon, Luella E., jt. auth. see Poe, Edgar Allan.
McMahon, Luella E., jt. auth. see Shakespeare, William.
McMahon, Lynne. Devolution of the Nude. 80p. 1993. pap. 12.95 (*0-87923-955-7*) Godine.
— Faith. LC 86-32440. (Wesleyan New Poets Ser.). 62p. 1988. pap. 12.95 (*0-8195-1135-8*, Wesleyan Univ Pr); text 25.00 (*0-8195-2133-7*, Wesleyan Univ Pr) U Pr of New Eng.

M

An Asterisk (*) at the beginning of an entry indicates that the title is appearing for the first time.

— The House of Entertaining Science. LC 99-23131. 80p. 1999. pap. 13.95 (*1-56792-106-X*) Godine.

— White Tablecloths. (International Poetry Chapbook Ser.). 11p. (Orig.). (C). 1984. pap. 4.00 (*0-936600-04-7*) Riverstone Foothills.

McMahon, M. Making of a Profession: A Century of Electrical Engineering in America. LC 83-22325. 320p. 1984. 39.95 (*0-87942-173-8*, PC01677) Inst Electrical.

McMahon, M. Catharine. Aesthetics & Art in the Astree of Honore d'Urfe. LC 78-94197. (Catholic University of America. Studies in Romance Languages & Literatures: No. 1). reprint ed. 37.50 (*0-404-50301-2*) AMS Pr.

McMahon, Maeve. Women on Guard: Discrimination & Harassment in Corrections. LC 99-226941. (Illus.). 256p. 1998. text 45.00 (*0-8020-4146-9*); pap. text 18.95 (*0-8020-7996-2*) U of Toronto Pr.

McMahon, Maeve W. The Persistent Prison? Rethinking Decarceration & Penal Reform. 320p. 1992. text 45.00 (*0-8020-2817-9*); pap. text 17.95 (*0-8020-7689-0*) U of Toronto Pr.

McMahon, Maggie. The Problem with Penpals. (Full House Michelle Ser.). (J). (gr. 2-4). 1998. pap. 3.99 (*0-671-01732-2*, Minstrel Bks) PB.

McMahon, Maria O. The General Method & the Generalist Perspective of Social Work Practice. 3rd ed. LC 95-9214. 384p. 1995. 80.00 (*0-13-063280-5*) Allyn.

— The General Method of Social Work Practice: A Generalist Perspective, Incl. Test Bank. 3rd ed. (C). 1995. teacher ed. write for info. (*0-205-18553-3*, H8553-3) Allyn.

McMahon, Marie P. The Radical Whigs, John Trenchard & Thomas Gordon: Libertarian Loyalists to the New House of Hanover. LC 89-22642. 226p. (C). 1990. lib. bdg. 41.00 (*0-8191-7627-3*) U Pr of Amer.

McMahon, Marilyn, et al. Report Writing in dBASE II. 15.95 (*0-317-06186-0*) P-H.

McMahon, Martha. Engendering Motherhood: Identity & Self-Transformation in Women's Lives. LC 95-16209. (Perspectives on Marriage & the Family Ser.). 324p. 1995. lib. bdg. 35.00 (*1-57230-002-7*) Guilford Pubns.

McMahon, Martin H., jt. auth. see Bittker, Boris I.

McMahon, Martin J., et al. Federal Income Taxation, Cases & Materials. 4th ed. LC 98-16313. (University Casebook Ser.). 1279p. 1998. text 42.75 (*1-56662-604-8*) Foundation Pr.

McMahon, Mary. Miami Job Source: Everything You Need to Know to Land the Internship Entry-Level or Middle Management Job of Your Choice in the Miami Metro Area. Psillas, Benjamin S. & Hicks, Donna C., eds. (Job Source Ser.). (Illus.). 352p. (Orig.). 1996. 15.95 (*0-9635651-6-8*) Benjamin Scott.

McMahon, Mary, et al. Baltimore Job Source: Everything You Need to Know to Land the Internship, Entry-Level, or Middle Management Job of Your Choice. Hicks, Donna C., ed. 308p. (Orig.). 1996. 15.95 (*0-9635651-4-1*) Benjamin Scott.

— Pittsburgh Job Source: Everything You Need to Know to Land the Internship, Entry-Level, or Middle Management Job of Your Choice. Hicks, Donna C., ed. 328p. (Orig.). 1996. 15.95 (*0-9635651-5-X*) Benjamin Scott.

McMahon, Mary, jt. auth. see Gage, Michael.

McMahon, Mary, jt. auth. see Psillas, Benjamin S.

***McMahon, Maureen.** Shadows in the Mist. 288p. 2000. mass mkt. 6.50 (*1-929613-36-9*, Vertigo MI) Avid MI.

McMahon, Maureen, ed. see Johnson, Cynthia & Johnson, Drew.

McMahon, Melanie M., ed. see King, Kim.

McMahon, Michael. Dead of Winter. Hunting, Constance, ed. 27p. (Orig.). 1982. pap. 3.50 (*0-913006-25-4*) Puckerbrush.

McMahon, Neil. Twice Dying: A Novel. LC 99-33341. 224p. 2000. 24.00 (*0-06-019364-6*) HarpC.

***McMahon, Neil.** Twice Dying: A Novel. 320p. 2000. mass mkt. 6.99 (*0-06-109835-3*) HarpC.

***McMahon, Paddy.** The Grand Design Vol. 1: A Simply-Stated, User-Friendly Guide to Living in the Universe. 176p. 2000. pap. 13.95 (*1-57174-154-2*) Hampton Roads Pub Co.

— The Grand Design Vol. 2: A Simply-Stated, User-Friendly Guide to Living in the Universe. 176p. 2000. pap. 13.95 (*1-57174-155-0*) Hampton Roads Pub Co.

McMahon, Patricia. Chi-Hoon: A Korean Girl. LC 92-81331. (Illus.). 48p. (J). 1998. pap. text 9.95 (*1-56397-720-6*) Boyds Mills Pr.

***McMahon, Patricia.** Dancing Wheels. LC 99-87715. (Illus.). 2000. 16.00 (*0-395-88889-1*) HM.

McMahon, Patricia. Listen for the Bus: David's Story. LC 94-73316. (Illus.). 48p. (J). (gr. k-5). 1995. 15.95 (*1-56397-368-5*) Boyds Mills Pr.

— One Belfast Boy. LC 98-28568. (Illus.). 64p. (J). (gr. 2-7). 1999. 16.00 (*0-395-68620-2*) HM.

— Six Words, Many Turtles & Three Days in Hong Kong. LC 96-44191. (Illus.). 64p. (J). (gr. 2-7). 1997. 16.00 (*0-395-68621-0*) HM.

— Summer Tunes: A Martha's Vineyard Vacation. LC 95-83980. (Illus.). 48p. (J). (gr. 2-5). 1996. 16.95 (*1-56397-572-6*) Boyds Mills Pr.

McMahon, R., et al. On Being in Charge: A Guide to Management in Primary Health Care. 2nd ed. (ENG & FRE.). vii, 472p. 1992. pap. text 30.00 (*92-4-154426-0*, 1152125) World Health.

McMahon, R. F. & Sloan, P. Essentials of Pathology for Dentistry. (Illus.). 224p. 1998. pap. write for info. (*0-443-05706-0*) Church.

McMahon, Richard. Adventuring in Hawaii: Hawaii, Maui, Molokai, Lanai, Oahu, Kauai. (Sierra Club Adventure Travel Guides Ser.). (Illus.). 368p. (Orig.). 1996. pap. 15.00 (*0-87156-428-9*, Pub. by Sierra) Random.

— Camping Hawaii: A Complete Guide. rev. ed. LC 96-36172. 1997. pap. 17.95 (*0-8248-1904-7*, Latitude Twenty) UH Pr.

***McMahon, Richard.** Camping Southern California. LC 98-49848. (Illus.). 400p. 1999. pap. 16.95 (*1-56044-711-7*) Falcon Pub Inc.

— Networking Administration for Netware Versions 4.11 & 5. 448p. 1999. pap. 46.95 (*0-538-69089-5*) Sth-Wstrn College.

McMahon, Richard. A Practical Approach to Road Traffic Law. 358p. 1993. 40.00 (*1-85431-260-X*, Pub. by Blackstone Pr) Gaunt.

McMahon, Richard & Pearson, Alan. Nursing As Therapy. 2nd ed. (Illus.). 336p. 1998. pap. 47.50 (*0-7487-3326-4*, Pub. by S Thornes Pubs) Trans-Atl Phila.

McMahon, Richard, ed. see Buckeldee, Jill.

McMahon, Richard A. Scenic Driving Hawaii. LC 97-9800. (Illus.). 152p. (Orig.). 1997. pap. 14.95 (*1-56044-556-4*) Falcon Pub Inc.

***McMahon, Richard Alan.** MCSE Windows 2000 Security Design Exam Prep. (Exam Prep Ser.). (Illus.). 800p. 2000. pap. 49.99 (*1-57610-707-8*) Coriolis Grp.

***McMahon, Robert.** Limits of Empire: The United States & Southeast Asia since World War II. LC 98-19525. 26p. 1998. pap. 17.50 (*0-231-10881-8*); lib. bdg. 45.00 (*0-231-10880-X*) Col U Pr.

McMahon, Robert. Two Poets of "Paradise Lost" LC 97-24426. 224p. 1998. text 32.50 (*0-8071-2188-6*) La State U Pr.

— Zoology Laboratory Notebook. 528p. (C). 1995. ring bd. 49.95 (*0-7872-1545-7*, 41154501) Kendall-Hunt.

McMahon, Robert J. Cold War on the Periphery: The United States, India & Pakistan. 431p. 1996. pap. 19.50 (*0-231-08227-4*) Col U Pr.

— The Cold War on the Periphery: The United States, India, & Pakistan, 1947-1965. LC 93-38724. 431p. 1994. 40.50 (*0-231-08226-6*) Col U Pr.

— Major Problems in the History of the Vietnam War. 2nd ed. LC 94-77794. (Major Problems in American History Ser.). 576p. (C). 1995. pap. text 29.16 (*0-669-35252-7*) HM Trade Div.

McMahon, Robert J., ed. Major Problems in the History of the Vietnam War: Documents & Essays. (Major Problems in American History Ser.). 635p. (C). 1990. pap. text 29.16 (*0-669-18013-0*) HM Trade Div.

McMahon, Robert J. & Peters, R. D., eds. Behavior Disorders of Adolescence: Research, Intervention, & Policy in Clinical & School Settings. LC 91-1957. (Illus.). 242p. (C). 1991. 90.00 (*0-306-43813-5*, Plenum Trade) Perseus Pubng.

McMahon, Robert J., jt. auth. see Forehand, Rex L.

McMahon, Robert J., jt. auth. see Peters, Ray D.

McMahon, Robert J., jt. ed. see Paterson, Thomas G.

McMahon, Robert J., jt. ed. see Peters, Ray D.

McMahon, Robert S. Federal Regulation of the Radio & Television Broadcast Industry in the United States: 1927-1959. Sterling, Christopher H., ed. LC 78-21727. (Dissertations in Broadcasting Ser.). 1980. lib. bdg. 30.95 (*0-405-11766-3*) Ayer.

McMahon, Robert W. Introduction to Greenhouse Production. King, Muriel N., ed. (Illus.). 321p. 1992. text, lab manual ed. 36.95 (*1-56502-002-2*, 9502M) Ohio Agri Educ.

***McMahon, Robert W.** Introduction to Greenhouse Production. 2nd ed. (Illus.). 385p. 2000. 39.95 (*1-56502-015-4*) Ohio Agri Educ.

***McMahon, Romano.** Faculty Guide: The Brain Psychology & You. 3rd ed. 1999. pap. 15.75 (*0-538-42930-5*) Thomson Learn.

— Psychological Coping Skills, Psychology & You. 3rd ed. 1999. pap. 12.00 (*0-538-42906-2*) S-W Pub.

***McMahon, Romano & Romano.** Performance Tasks & Skill Builder Worksheets, Psychology/You. 3rd ed. 1999. pap. text 15.75 (*0-538-42907-0*) Thomson Learn.

McMahon, Seamus. Memories Rekindled: Irish Folk Stories & Historical Narratives. LC 96-92004. (Illus.). 75p. pap. 4.95 (*0-9650556-0-4*) J McMahon.

McMahon, Sean. Ars Amoris: Latin for Lovers. (Illus.). 80p. 1998. 13.95 (*0-86281-665-3*, Pub. by Appletree Pr) Irish Bks Media.

— A Book of Irish Insults. LC 99-196930. 96p. 1997. pap. 11.95 (*1-85635-162-9*, Pub. by Mercier Pr) Irish Amer Bk.

— Carpe Diem: Seize the Day: A Little Book of Latin Phrases. (Illus.). 60p. 1995. 7.95 (*0-8118-0931-5*) Chronicle Bks.

— Light on Illancrone. 114p. 1990. pap. 7.95 (*1-85371-083-0*, Pub. by Poolbeg Pr) Dufour.

— A Little Book of Celtic Wisdom. (Illus.). 60p. 1995. 9.95 (*0-86281-561-4*, Pub. by Appletree Pr) Irish Bks Media.

— A Little Book of Irish Quotations. (Little Irish Book Ser.). (Illus.). 60p. 1995. 9.95 (*0-86281-480-4*, Pub. by Appletree Pr) Irish Bks Media.

— The Mercier Companion to Irish Literature. LC 98-230914. 300p. 1998. pap. 15.95 (*1-85635-216-1*, Pub. by Mercier Pr) Irish Amer Bk.

— The Poolbeg Book of Children's Verse. 240p. (J). 1987. pap. 10.95 (*1-85371-080-6*, Pub. by Poolbeg Pr) Dufour.

— The Poolbeg Book of Irish Ballads. 188p. (Orig.). 1992. pap. 9.95 (*1-85371-127-6*, Pub. by Poolbeg Pr) Dufour.

— The Poolbeg Book of Irish Placenames. 113p. (Orig.). (YA). (gr. 10-12). 1990. pap. 8.95 (*1-85371-087-3*, Pub. by Poolbeg Pr) Dufour.

— Rekindling The Faith: How The Irish Re-Christianised Europe. LC 96-151143. 128p. 1997. pap. 10.95 (*1-85635-143-2*, Pub. by Mercier Pr) Irish Amer Bk.

***McMahon, Sean.** Sam Hanna Bell: A Biography. 228p. 2000. 40.00 (*0-85640-665-1*, Pub. by Blackstaff Pr) Dufour.

McMahon, Sean. A Short History of Ireland. LC 97-202929. 224p. 1997. pap. 16.95 (*0-8023-1319-1*) Dufour.

— The Story of the Claddagh Ring. LC 97-185208. 77p. 1997. pap. 9.95 (*1-85635-189-0*, Pub. by Mercier Pr) Irish Amer Bk.

— The Three Seals. 181p. (Orig.). (J). (gr. 7-9). 1991. pap. 7.95 (*1-85371-148-9*, Pub. by Poolbeg Pr) Dufour.

McMahon, Sean, ed. A Book of Irish Quotations. 240p. 1985. 16.95 (*0-87243-127-4*) Templegate.

— Fair City: A Thousand Years of Dublin. 200p. 1989. pap. 8.95 (*1-85371-005-9*, Pub. by Poolbeg Pr) Dufour.

— My Native Land: A Celebration of Britain. 360p. 1987. pap. 12.95 (*0-905169-97-2*, Pub. by Poolbeg Pr) Dufour.

— The Poolbeg Book of Children's Verse. 240p. (J). 1987. pap. 9.95 (*0-905169-88-3*, Pub. by Poolbeg Pr) Dufour.

— Poolbeg Golden Treasury of Well Loved Poems. 208p. 1989. pap. 8.95 (*1-85371-008-3*, Pub. by Poolbeg Pr) Dufour.

— Rich & Rare. 380p. 1987. pap. 14.95 (*0-905169-86-7*, Pub. by Poolbeg Pr) Dufour.

McMahon, Sean, jt. auth. see Byrne, Art.

McMahon, Susan I. & Raphael, Taffy E., eds. The Book Club Connection: Literacy Learning & Classroom Talk. LC 96-52792. (Language & Literacy Ser.: Vol. 31). 445p. (C). 1997. text 54.00 (*0-8077-3615-5*); pap. text 21.95 (*0-8077-3614-7*) Tchrs Coll.

McMahon, Susanna. The Portable Therapist. LC 93-30957. 256p. 1994. pap. 10.95 (*0-440-50603-4*) Dell.

McMahon, Suzanne, et al, eds. A Changing World: Proceedings of the North American Serials Interest Group, Inc. LC 91-39991. (Serials Librarian Ser.: Vol. 21, Nos. 2-3). 235p. 1992. pap. text 19.95 (*1-56024-298-1*); lib. bdg. 49.95 (*1-56024-263-9*) Haworth Pr.

McMahon, T. A. & Mein, R. G. River & Reservoir Yield. 375p. 1987. text 38.00 (*0-918334-61-6*) WRP.

McMahon, T. A. & Oakland, Roger. Understand the Times: A Simplified Biblical Perspective. 171p. pap. 7.99 (*0-936728-38-8*) Word for Today.

McMahon, T. A., jt. auth. see Hunt, Dave.

McMahon, T. A., jt. auth. see Hunt, David.

McMahon, Thomas, ed. Authors & Artists for Young Adults, Vol. 20. 250p. 1997. text 82.00 (*0-7876-1136-0*, 00156240) Gale.

— Authors & Artists for Young Adults, Vol. 21. 250p. 1997. text 82.00 (*0-7876-1137-9*, 00156241) Gale.

— Authors & Artists for Young Adults, Vol. 22. 250p. 1997. text 82.00 (*0-7876-1673-7*) Gale.

McMahon, Thomas, ed. Authors & Artists for Young Adults, Vol. 25. (Illus.). 250p. (YA). (gr. 7-12). 1998. 79.00 (*0-7876-1972-8*, GML00198-111409) Visible Ink Pr.

McMahon, Thomas & Bonner, James. On Size & Life. (Scientific American Library). (Illus.). 255p. 1983. pap. text 32.95 (*0-7167-5000-7*) W H Freeman.

McMahon, Timothy, ed. Solving the Sales Manager/Sales Automation Equation. rev. ed. LC 96-83842. (Illus.). 244p. 1996. 29.95 (*0-85013-252-5*) Dartnell Corp.

McMahon, Timothy E. The McMahon Chronicles: The Story of an Irish-American Family in Rhode Island, 1870-1994. (Illus.). 115p. 1994. 35.00 (*0-9643509-9-8*) Taurus Hse Pubns.

McMahon, Tom. Big Meeting, Big Results. (Illus.). 160p. 1994. 19.95 (*0-8442-3192-4*, NTC Business Bks) NTC Contemp Pub Co.

— Big Meetings, Big Results. (Illus.). 160p. 1996. pap. text 12.95 (*0-8442-3011-1*, NTC Business Bks) NTC Contemp Pub Co.

— It Works for Us: Proven Child Care Tips from Experienced Parents Across the Country. Zion, Claire, ed. 272p. (Orig.). 1993. pap. 10.00 (*0-671-77733-5*) PB.

— Kid Tips: Proven Child-Care Tips from Experienced Parents Across the Country. (Illus.). 277p. (J). 1998. per. 14.00 (*0-671-02609-7*) S&S Trade.

— Orient: Hero Guide Dog of the Appalachian Trail. (Illus.). 32p. (J). (ps-3). 1995. 14.95 (*1-56796-006-5*) WRS Group.

— Teen Tips: A Practical Guide for Parents with Kids 11-19. 272p. (J). 1996. per. 12.00 (*0-671-89106-5*) PB.

McMahon, Trudi, jt. auth. see Klapper, John.

McMahon, Virgil E. The Artists of Washington, D. C., 1796-1996: A Directory of Painters, Sculptors & Engravers Born Before 1900. (Illus.). 300p. (Orig.). 1995. pap. 55.00 (*0-9649101-0-1*) Artists of WA.

McMahon, W. E. Hans Reichenbach's Philosophy of Grammar. (Janua Linguarum, Ser.: No. 90). 284p. 1976. text 78.50 (*90-279-3204-2*) Mouton.

***McMahon, Walter W.** Education & Development: Measuring the Social Benefits. LC 99-34156. (Illus.). 314p. 2000. text 55.00 (*0-19-829231-7*) OUP.

McMahon, William. Pine Barrens Legends, Lore & Lies. (Illus.). 149p. 1986. pap. 9.95 (*0-912608-19-6*) Mid Atlantic.

— South Jersey Towns: History & Legend. LC 78-163961. (Illus.). 384p. 1973. reprint ed. pap. 16.00 (*0-8135-0718-9*) Rutgers U Pr.

McMahon, William E. The Higher Humanism of Wallace Stevens. LC 90-22574. (Studies in American Literature: Vol. 12). 180p. 1991. lib. bdg. 79.95 (*0-88946-792-7*) E Mellen.

***McMains, H. F.** Death of Oliver Cromwell. LC 99-28854. 288p. 1999. 25.00 (*0-8131-2133-7*) U Pr of Ky.

McMains, Harvey J. & Wilcox, Lyle, eds. Alternatives for Growth: The Engineering & Economics of Natural Resources Development. LC 77-11870. 270p. reprint ed. pap. 83.70 (*0-8357-5333-6*, 205636600061) Bks Demand.

McMains, Joel M. Dog Logic: Companion Obedience-Rapport-Based Training. (Illus.). 224p. 1992. 21.95 (*0-87605-510-2*) Howell Bks.

***McMains, Joel M.** Kennels & Kenneling: A Guide for Hobbyists & Professionals. 2nd ed. (Illus.). 224p. 2000. 22.95 (*1-58245-151-6*) Howell Bks.

McMains, Joel M. Kennels & Kenneling: A Guide for Professionals & Hobbyists. LC 93-30076. (Illus.). 256p. 1994. 25.95 (*0-87605-661-3*) Howell Bks.

McMains, John R. Windows NT Backup & Recovery. LC 98-156046. (Windows NT Professional Library). (Illus.). 540p. (Orig.). 1998. pap. text 39.99 (*0-07-882363-3*) Osborne-McGraw.

McMains, June. Fast Food: Thirty Minute Gourmet Meals Without Thinking. (Illus.). 128p. (Orig.). 1988. pap. 6.95 (*0-9620721-0-9*) P Jam Pubns.

McMains, Michael J. & Mullins, Wayman C. Crisis Negotiations: Managing Critical Incidents & Hostage Situations in Law Enforcement & Corrections. LC 95-75514. (Illus.). 413p. (C). 1996. pap. 37.95 (*0-87084-595-0*) Anderson Pub Co.

***McMains, Victoria.** The Readers' Choice: 200 Book Club Favorites. LC 99-87624. 288p. 2000. pap. 14.00 (*0-688-17435-3*, Quil) HarperTrade.

McMakin, Andrea H., jt. auth. see Lundgren, Regina E.

McMakin, Jacqueline & Nary, Rhoda. The Doorways Series, Vol. 1: Encountering God in Others. LC 92-53917. 1993. 7.00 (*0-685-61102-7*) Harper SF.

McMakin, Kathy, ed. see Pullen, Martha.

McMakin, Kathy, ed. see Pullen, Martha C.

Mcmanama, Jerre, jt. auth. see Schmottlach, Neil.

McManamin, Francis G. The American Years of John Boyle O'Reilly. LC 76-6356. (Irish Americans Ser.). 1976. 29.95 (*0-405-09349-7*) Ayer.

McManamon, John M. Pierpaolo Vergerio the Elder: The Humanist as Orator. LC 96-24767. (Medieval & Renaissance Texts & Studies: Vol. 163). 240p. 1996. 26.00 (*0-86698-204-3*, MR163) MRTS.

McManamon, John M., ed. from LAT. Pierpaolo Vergerio the Elder & Saint Jerome: An Edition & Translation of "Sermones Pro Sancto Hieronymo" LC 99-19915. (Medieval & Renaissance Texts & Studies: Vol. 177). 416p. 1999. 36.00 (*0-86698-219-1*, MR177) MRTS.

McManaway, James G. Authorship of Shakespeare. LC 62-4031. (Folger Guides to the Age of Shakespeare Ser.). 1962. pap. 4.95 (*0-918016-25-8*) Folger Bks.

— Studies in Shakespeare, Bibliography, & Theatre. Hosley, Richard et al, eds. (Illus.). 417p. 1990. 50.00 (*0-918016-48-7*) Folger Bks.

McManaway, James G. & Roberts, Jeanne A. Selective Bibliography of Shakespeare: Editions, Textual Studies, Commentary. (Special Publications Ser.). 1978. 30.00 (*0-918016-02-9*); pap. 12.95 (*0-918016-03-7*) Folger Bks.

McMane, Fred. Hakeem Olajuwon. LC 96-34779. (Basketball Legends Ser.). (Illus.). 64p. (J). (gr. 3 up). 1997. lib. bdg. 15.95 (*0-7910-4385-1*) Chelsea Hse.

— Scottie Pippen. LC 95-18518. (Basketball Legends Ser.). (Illus.). 64p. (J). (gr. 3 up). 1996. lib. bdg. 15.95 (*0-7910-2498-9*) Chelsea Hse.

— Superstars of Men's Track & Field. LC 97-42869. (Male Sports Stars Ser.). (Illus.). 64p. (YA). (gr. 3 up). 1999. 15.95 (*0-7910-4591-9*) Chelsea Hse.

***McMane, Fred.** The 3,000 Hit Club. (Illus.). 256p. 2000. pap. 14.95 (*1-58261-220-X*) Sports Pub.

McManimie, Robert J. Relationships. 106p. (C). 1992. pap. text 9.95 (*0-9631253-1-1*) Devsyn.

McManis, Charles R. Unfair Trade Practices in a Nutshell. 3rd ed. (Nutshell Ser.). 471p. (C). 1993. pap. 21.00 (*0-314-01122-6*) West Pub.

McManis, Douglas R. European Impressions of the New England Coast, 1497-1620. LC 70-187026. (University of Chicago, Department of Geography, Research Paper Ser.: No. 139). 158p. 1972. reprint ed. pap. 49.00 (*0-608-02292-6*, 206293300004) Bks Demand.

***McManis, Kent.** A Guide to Hopi Katsina Dolls. (Illus.). 68p. 2000. pap. 9.95 (*1-887896-17-1*, Rio Nuevo) Treas Chest Bks.

McManis, Kent. A Guide to Zuni Fetishes & Carving Vol. II: The materials & the Carvers. (Illus.). 64p. 1998. pap. 8.95 (*1-887896-11-2*, Rio Nuevo) Treas Chest Bks.

— A Guide to Zuni Fetishes & Carvings, Vol. 1. 2nd rev. ed. (Illus.). 56p. (Orig.). 1998. pap. 8.95 (*1-887896-14-7*, Rio Nuevo) Treas Chest Bks.

McManis, Kent & Jeffries, Robert. A Guide to Navajo Weavings. LC 97-60805. (Illus.). 64p. 1997. pap. 9.95 (*1-887896-07-4*, Rio Nuevo) Treas Chest Bks.

McMann, Evelyn D. Canadian Who's Who: Index 1898-1984, Incorporating Men & Women of the Time. 528p. 1986. text 125.00 (*0-8020-4633-9*) U of Toronto Pr.

— Montreal Museum of Fine Arts, Formerly Art Association of Montreal: Spring Exhibition, 1880-1970. 418p. 1988. text 125.00 (*0-8020-2650-8*) U of Toronto Pr.

— Royal Canadian Academy of Arts: Exhibitions & Members, 1880-1979. LC 77-160467. 451p. 1997, reprint ed. pap. 75.00 (*0-8020-4139-6*) U of Toronto Pr.

McMann, Evelyn D., compiled by. Biographical Index to Artists in Canada. 240p. 1996. text 80.00 (*0-8020-2790-3*) U of Toronto Pr.

McMann, James P. Poetry in Blue: Reflections in the Eye of a Cop. LC 95-41606. 128p. (Orig.). 1995. pap. 12.95 (*0-9639290-3-8*) Good Times.

McMann, Jean. Altars & Icons: Sacred Spaces in Everyday Life. LC 97-34409. 1998. 16.95 (*0-8118-1816-0*) Chronicle Bks.

***McMann, Mary C.** Soy Protein: What You Need to Know. 48p. 2000. pap. 3.95 (*0-89529-988-7*, Avery) Penguin Putnam.

McManners, Hugh. The Backpacker's Handbook. LC 94-32042. (Illus.). 160p. 1995. 14.95 (*1-56458-852-1*) DK Pub Inc.

— The Complete Wilderness Training Book. LC 93-5686. (Illus.). 192p. 1994. 29.95 (*1-56458-488-7*) DK Pub Inc.

— The Complete Wilderness Training Book. LC 93-5686. 192p. 1998. 13.95 (*0-7894-3750-3*) DK Pub Inc.

— The Outdoor Adventure Handbook. 64p. (J). (gr. 3-7). 1996. 16.95 (*0-7894-1035-4*) DK Pub Inc.

— Top Guns. (Illus.). 224p. 1996. 29.95 (*0-563-38707-6*) BBC.

An Asterisk (*) at the beginning of an entry indicates that the title is appearing for the first time.

McManners, John. Church & Society in Eighteenth-Century France: The Clerical Establishment & Its Social Ramification, Vol. 1. (Oxford History of the Christian Church Ser.). 836p. 1998. text 155.00 (*0-19-826905-6*) OUP.
— Church & Society in Eighteenth-Century France: The Clerical Establishment & Its Social Ramification, Vol. 1. (Oxford History of the Christian Church Ser.). 836p. 1999. pap. text 49.95 (*0-19-827003-8*) OUP.
— Church & Society in Eighteenth-Century France: The Religion of the People & the Political, Vol. 2. (Oxford History of the Christian Church Ser.). 880p. 1999. pap. text 45.00 (*0-19-827004-6*) OUP.
— The Church in Eighteenth-Century France: Church, Power & Politics, Vol. 2. (Oxford History of the Christian Church Ser.). 880p. 1998. text 165.00 (*0-19-826963-3*) OUP.
— The French Revolution & the Church. LC 82-15532. 161p. (C). 1982. reprint ed. lib. bdg. 52.50 (*0-313-23074-9*, MCFR, Greenwood Pr) Greenwood.
McManners, John, ed. The Oxford History of Christianity. (Illus.). 778p. 1994. pap. text 16.95 (*0-19-285291-4*) OUP.
— The Oxford Illustrated History of Christianity. (Oxford Illustrated Histories Ser.). (Illus.). 736p. 1990. 55.00 (*0-19-822928-3*) OUP.
— The Oxford Illustrated History of Christianity. (Oxford Illustrated Histories Ser.). (Illus.). 736p. 1992. pap. 27.50 (*0-19-285259-0*) OUP.
McManness, Linda M. Lexical Categories in Spanish: The Determiner. LC 95-38845. 1995. 33.00 (*0-7618-0137-5*) U Pr of Amer.
McManness, Linda M., jt. auth. see Smith, Robert J.
McMannis, Christy, ed. see Miller, Sam.
McMannis, William J., jt. auth. see Reid, Rolland R.
McMannon, Timothy J., jt. auth. see Goodlad, John I.
McMannus, Maggie, jt. auth. see Reilly, Ed.
McManus. Classics & Feminism. LC 96-36021. 1997. 33.00 (*0-8057-9757-2*, Twayne) Mac Lib Ref.
— Jiggs is Back. 1990. pap. 12.95 (*0-913666-82-3*) Turtle Isl Foun.
— McManus Treasury, No. 2. 1995. pap. 29.96 (*0-8050-4709-3*, M&T Bks) IDG Bks.
*__McManus & Schulmeyer.__ Software Quality Assurance. 3rd ed. LC 98-36662. 784p. 1998. 62.00 (*0-13-010470-1*) P-H.
McManus, Alexander G., jt. auth. see Hunt, John E.
*__McManus, Angel.__ Y2K the Bottom Line: A Christian Approach to Preparing for January 1, 2000. 18p. 1999. pap. 5.95 (*0-9676104-2-7*) Just for You.
McManus, Ann. The Memory Jogger for Education: A Pocket Guide for Continuous Improvement in Schools. 88p. 1994. pap. 4.50 (*1-879364-24-7*) GOAL-QPC.
McManus, Anne. They Said I Was Dead: The Complete Alternative Cure for Addiction. 1993. pap. 15.50 (*1-85727-091-6*) LPC InBook.
— They Said I Was Dead: The Complete Alternative Cure for Addiction. 128p. 1994. 45.00 (*1-85727-086-X*) LPC InBook.
McManus, Barbara F., jt. auth. see Henderson, Katherine U.
McManus, Carol. Ida: Her Labor of Love. LC 98-87156. 283p. (Orig.). 1999. pap. 14.95 (*1-890437-18-2*) Western Reflections.
McManus, Catherine O. & Arnold, Krstyn E. The Lazy Cook Strikes Again: Recipes That Take 10 Minutes or Less to Prepare & Use Readily Available Ingredients. LC 98-11601. 1998. write for info. (*1-57090-087-6*) Alexander Dist.
McManus, Catherine O. & Arnold, Krystyn E. The Lazy Cook: Delicious Recipes Take 10 Minutes or Less to Prepare. Hall, Kathryn, ed. (Illus.). 208p. 1995. pap. text 12.95 (*1-57090-012-4*) Alexander Dist.
McManus, Catherine O., jt. auth. see Arnold, Krystyn E.
McManus, Donald P. & Smyth, James D. The Physiology & Biochemistry of Cestodes. (Illus.). 416p. (C). 1989 text 120.00 (*0-521-35557-5*) Cambridge U Pr.
McManus, Dorothy. Song of Sirius. Myhre, M., ed. (Illus.). 155p. (Orig.). (YA). 1990. pap. 8.00 (*0-929686-01-2*) Temple Golden Pubns.
— Touched by Love. (Illus.). 191p. (Orig.). 1994. pap. 9.95 (*0-929686-03-9*) Temple Golden Pubns.
*__McManus, Doyle.__ What's Worth Dying For? 2001. text 25.00 (*0-8050-6460-5*) H Holt & Co.
— What's Worth Dying For? 2002. pap. 14.00 (*0-8050-6461-3*) H Holt & Co.
McManus, Ed & Nicholas, Bill. We're Roasting Harry Tuesday Night: How to Plan, Write & Conduct the Business-Social Roast. 221p. 1984. 18.95 (*0-13-950163-0*, Busn) P-H.
McManus, Ed, ed. see McKelvey, Carole Conner & Boeding, Conrad J.
McManus, Edgar J. Black Bondage in the North. LC 72-12425. (Illus.). 260p. reprint ed. pap. 80.60 (*0-8357-8045-7*, 203409800087) Bks Demand.
— A History of Negro Slavery in New York. LC 66-15471. 235p. reprint ed. pap. 72.90 (*0-7837-3177-9*, 204278100006) Bks Demand.
— Law & Liberty in Early New England: Criminal Justice & Due Process, 1620-1692. LC 92-18719. 296p. 1993. 32.50 (*0-87023-824-8*) U of Mass Pr.
McManus, F., jt. auth. see Adams, M.
McManus, Fran, et al, eds. Eating Fresh from the Organic Garden State. (Illus.). 128p. 1997. pap. 14.95 (*1-883354-01-3*) Nrthest Org Farming.
McManus, Francis. Environmental Health Law in Scotland. 262p. 1989. text 82.95 (*0-566-07036-7*, Pub. by Avebry) Ashgate Pub Co.
McManus, Francis & Russell, Eleanor J. Delict. LC 97-22273. 1999. pap. text 51.95 (*0-471-96916-8*) Wiley.
McManus, Francis, tr. see Von Mises, Ludwig.
McManus, Howard R. The Battle of Cloyd's Mountain & the Virginia & Tennessee Railroad Raid. (Virginia Civil War Battles & Leaders Ser.). (Illus.). 107p. 1989. 19.95 (*0-930919-89-0*) H E Howard.
McManus, J. Re-Engineering Your Business. (Financial Times Management Briefings Ser.). 1997. pap. 89.50 (*0-273-63206-X*) F T P-H.
McManus, J. Re-Engineering Your Business: A Practical Guide. 1996. pap. 140.00 (*1-85953-002-8*, Pub. by Tech Comm) St Mut.
— The Role of the Project Manager. 1996. pap. 129.00 (*1-85953-090-7*, Pub. by Tech Comm) St Mut.
McManus, J. & Duck, R. W., eds. Geomorphology & Sedimentology of Lakes & Reservoirs. LC 92-23465. (British Geomorphological Research Group Symposia Ser.). 288p. 1993. 255.00 (*0-471-93773-8*) Wiley.
McManus, J. Donald. Toodle-oo Taxahaw: One Hundred One Tales or a Small History of the World. (Illus.). 228p. (Orig.). 1991. pap. 10.00 (*0-939710-15-3*) Meridional Pubns.
McManus, James. Going to the Sun: A Novel. 352p. 1997. pap. 13.00 (*0-06-092804-2*, Perennial) HarperTrade.
McManus, James L. Antonio Salazar Is Dead. (Illus.). 56p. (Orig.). 1980. pap. 3.00 (*0-9603794-0-1*) Syncline.
*__McManus, Jane.__ Cuba's Island of Dreams: Voices from the Isle of Pines & Youth. LC 99-43006. (Illus.). 208p. 2000. 24.95 (*0-8130-1741-6*) U Press Fla.
McManus, Jane P., jt. auth. see Marler, Don C.
*__McManus, Jeffrey P.__ Database Access with Visual Basic 6. LC 98-87577. 810p. 1999. pap. text 39.99 (*0-672-31422-3*) Sams.
McManus, Jeffrey P. How to Program Visual Basic 5.0 Control Creation Edition: Creating ActiveX. LC 98-160276. 336p. 1997. 39.99 (*1-56276-485-3*, Ziff-Davis Pr) Que.
McManus, Jim. All Generations Shall Call Me Blessed: Mary at the Millennium. LC 99-22092. 1999. pap. 14.95 (*0-8245-1787-3*) Crossroad NY.
— Hallowed Be Thy Name: A Spirituality for Today. pap. write for info. (*0-232-52129-8*) S Asia.
McManus, John. Keeping the Team in Shape. 116p. (C). 1994. pap. 30.00 (*0-85292-550-6*, Pub. by IPM Hse) St Mut.
*__McManus, John.__ Stop Breakin Down. 272p. 2000. pap. 18.00 (*0-312-26278-7*, Picador USA) St Martin.
McManus, John, jt. auth. see Botten, Neil.
McManus, John, ed. see Health Promotion Resource Center Staff.
McManus, John C. Deadly Brotherhood: The American Combat Soldier in World War II. LC 97-50358. 384p. 1998. 28.95 (*0-89141-655-2*) Presidio Pr.
*__McManus, John C.__ The Deadly Brotherhood: The American Combat Soldier in World War II. 368p. 2000. pap. 19.95 (*0-89141-721-4*) Presidio Pr.
McManus, John F. Changing Commands: The Betrayal of America's Military. LC 95-75910. 240p. (Orig.). 1995. pap. 8.95 (*1-881919-03-X*) John Birch.
— Financial Terrorism: Hijacking America under the Threat of Bankruptcy. LC 93-80358. 256p. (Orig.). 1993. pap. 8.95 (*1-881919-02-1*) John Birch.
McManus, John H. Market Driven Journalism: Let the Citizen Beware? LC 93-49517. 302p. (C). 1994. text 52.00 (*0-8039-5252-X*); pap. text 24.00 (*0-8039-5253-8*) Sage.
McManus, Judith A. Effective Business Speaking. LC 98-26231. (Basics Made Easy...Ser.). 224p. 1998. pap. 13.95 (*1-57685-146-X*) LrningExprss.
McManus, Judith A. & Osborn, Edward B. Creating an Effective Speech. (Illus.). 123p. (C). 1994. pap. text 18.95 (*0-9642994-0-2*) Annies Pr.
McManus, Kay. Land of the Five Suns. LC 97-11871. (Looking at Myths & Legends Ser.). (Illus.). 48p. 1997. 12.95 (*0-8442-4762-6*, 47626, Natl Textbk Co) NTC Contemp Pub Co.
McManus, Kevin & Institute of Popular Music Staff. Cebilbis, Jigs & Ballads: Irish Music in Liverpool LC 98-134108. (Sounds Ser.). 39 p. 1994. write for info. (*1-898806-01-2*) Univ. of Liverpool, Inst of Popular Music.
— Nashville of the North: Country Music in Liverpool. LC 98-134103. (Sounds Ser.). 37 p. 1994. write for info. (*1-898806-00-4*) Univ. of Liverpool, Inst of Popular Music.
McManus, Liz. Acts of Subversion. 236p. (Orig.). 1991. pap. 14.95 (*1-85371-124-1*, Pub. by Poolbeg Pr) Dufour.
McManus, Marianne L. Quake Stress: Preparation for the Psychological Effects of a Major Disaster. LC 88-71569. 44p. (Orig.). 1988. pap. 6.95 (*0-922248-02-8*); text 12.95 (*0-922248-08-7*); audio 7.95 (*0-922248-06-0*) Calif Psychol Pubs.
McManus, Mark, ed. 1996 Information Systems Spending Report. 200p. 1996. ring bd. 895.00 (*0-945052-31-6*) Computer Econ.
McManus, Mary G. Cheyenne: Journey to Birth. x, 141p. 1999. pap. 10.00 (*0-9664999-3-X*) Clay Mtn.
McManus, Michael. From Fate to Choice: Private Bobbies, Public Beats. 176p. 1995. 61.95 (*1-85972-099-4*, Pub. by Avebry) Ashgate Pub Co.
McManus, Michael J. Marriage Savers: A Study Guide. 96p. 1994. pap. text 4.00 (*1-885481-02-0*) Quadrus Media.
— Marriage Savers Revised Edition: Helping Your Friends & Family Stay Married. 2nd rev. ed. 320p. 1995. pap. 14.99 (*0-310-38661-6*) Zondervan.
— Political Abolitionism in Wisconsin, 1840-1861: Michael J. McManus. LC 98-12683. 288p. 1998. text 39.00 (*0-87338-601-9*) Kent St U Pr.
*__McManus, Neil.__ Portable Ventilation Systems Handbook. LC 00-42320. 2000. write for info. (*1-56032-893-2*) Taylor & Francis.
McManus, Neil. Safety & Health in Confined Spaces. LC 98-44775. 928p. 1999. 89.95 (*1-56670-326-3*) Lewis Pubs.
McManus, Niel. The Hazcom Training Program. LC 98-53508. 512p. 1999. 149.95 (*1-56670-338-7*) Lewis Pubs.
McManus, Patricia. The Babysitting Co-op Guidebook: Building a Community Support Network. (Illus.). 40p. (Orig.). (C). 1993. pap. text 15.00 (*1-56806-365-2*) DIANE Pub.
*__McManus, Patrick.__ The Deer on a Bicycle. LC 99-89160. 196p. 2000. 10.95 (*0-910055-63-7*, Pub. by East Wash Univ) U of Wash Pr.
McManus, Patrick E. A Fine & Pleasant Misery. LC 77-13452. 88p. 1995. 16.95 (*0-8050-0166-2*); pap. 7.95 (*0-8050-0032-1*, Owl) H Holt & Co.
— They Shoot Canoes, Don't They? LC 80-24131. 89p. 1995. 18.95 (*0-8050-0165-4*); pap. 7.95 (*0-8050-0030-5*, Owl) H Holt & Co.
*__McManus, Patrick F.__ The Deer on a Bicycle: Excursions into the Writing of Humor. LC 99-89160. 180p. 2000. pap. 10.95 (*0-910055-62-9*, Pub. by East Wash Univ) U of Wash Pr.
McManus, Patrick F. The Good Samaritan Strikes Again. LC 92-10633. 88p. 1995. 17.95 (*0-8050-2042-X*); pap. 7.95 (*0-8050-2922-2*) H Holt & Co.
— The Grasshopper Trap. 228p. 1995. pap. 7.95 (*0-8050-0111-5*, Owl) H Holt & Co.
— How I Got This Way. LC 94-16971. 1995. 19.95 (*0-8050-3481-1*); pap. 8.95 (*0-8050-3482-X*) H Holt & Co.
*__McManus, Patrick F.__ I Fish, Therefore I Am. 672p. 2000. 12.99 (*1-57866-097-1*) Galahad Bks.
McManus, Patrick F. Into the Twilight, Endlessly Grousing. LC 97-23502. 221p. 1998. pap. 11.00 (*0-684-84799-X*, Fireside) S&S Trade Pap.
— Into the Twilight, Endlessly Grousing. LC 97-23502. 224p. 1997. 19.50 (*0-684-84440-0*) Simon & Schuster.
McManus, Patrick F. Into the Twilight, Endlessly Grousing. abr. ed. 1997. audio 18.00 (*0-671-57724-7*) S&S Audio.
McManus, Patrick F. Kid Camping from Aaaaiii! to Zip. (Illus.). 144p. (J). (gr. 6-7). 1991. reprint ed. pap. 3.99 (*0-380-71311-X*, Avon Bks) Morrow Avon.
— The McManus Treasury I, 4 bks., Set. 1995. pap. 27.50 (*0-8050-0112-3*, Owl) H Holt & Co.
— McManus Treasury 1 & 2 Special Offer. 1993. pap. 55.00 (*0-8050-3081-6*) H Holt & Co.
— McManus Treasury II, 4 bks., Set. 1995. pap. 27.50 (*0-8050-2970-2*) H Holt & Co.
— Never Cry "Arp!" And Other Stories of the Great Outdoors. 160p. (YA). (gr. 6 up). 1995. 15.95 (*0-8050-4662-3*) H Holt & Co.
— Never Sniff a Gift Fish. LC 83-147. 88p. 1995. 17.95 (*0-8050-0527-7*); pap. 8.95 (*0-8050-0031-3*, Owl) H Holt & Co.
— The Night the Bear Ate Goombaw. 88p. 1995. 19.95 (*0-8050-1033-5*); pap. 7.95 (*0-8050-1340-7*, Owl) H Holt & Co.
— The Night the Bear Ate Goombaw. large type ed. (General Ser.). 253p. 1990. lib. bdg. 18.95 (*0-8161-4889-9*, G K Hall Lrg Type) Mac Lib Ref.
— Real Ponies Don't Go Oink! 88p. 1995. 16.95 (*0-8050-1651-1*); pap. 6.95 (*0-8050-2107-8*, Owl) H Holt & Co.
— Real Ponies Don't Go Oink! large type ed. LC 91-33249. (General Ser.). 242p. (J). 1992. 18.95 (*0-8161-5343-4*, G K Hall Lrg Type) Mac Lib Ref.
— Rubber Legs & White Tail-Hairs. LC 87-8494. 89p. 1995. 14.95 (*0-8050-0544-7*); pap. 6.95 (*0-8050-0912-4*, Owl) H Holt & Co.
McManus, Patrick F. & Creative Publishing International Staff. If Nature Calls--Hang Up! A Collection of Outdoor Humor. LC 99-38860. (Times Mirror - Outdoor Life Ser.). (Illus.). 224p. 1999. pap. 14.95 (*0-86573-106-3*) Creat Pub Intl.
McManus, Patrick F. & Gass, Patricia M. Whatchagot Stew: A Memoir of an Idaho Childhood, with Recipes & Commentaries. 288p. 1995. pap. 8.95 (*0-8050-2377-1*, Owl) H Holt & Co.
— Whatchagot Stew & the Troll's Idaho Cookbook. 89p. 1995. 16.95 (*0-8050-0922-1*) H Holt & Co.
McManus, Robert A. & O'Toole, Sean M. The Locksley Nightclub, Bar, & Restaurant Security Handbook. 320p. 1995. pap. 49.95 (*0-9647209-0-6*) Locksley Pub.
McManus, Ron & Jennings, Glen H., eds. Structured Exercises for Promoting Family & Group Strengths: A Handbook for Group Leaders, Trainers, Educators, Counselors, & Therapists. LC 95-4829. (Illus.). 303p. (C). 1996. 39.95 (*1-56024-978-1*) Haworth Pr.
— Structured Exercises for Promoting Family & Group Strengths: A Handbook for Group Leaders, Trainers, Educators, Counselors, & Therapists. LC 95-4829. 303p. (C). 1997. pap. 19.95 (*0-7890-0224-8*) Haworth Pr.
McManus, Samuel P., jt. ed. see Harris, J. Milton.
McManus, Thomas E., jt. auth. see McLaughlin, John F.
McManus, Toby, jt. auth. see Moss, Danny.
McManus, Una. Wild Irish Roses. 1998. mass mkt. 1.66 (*1-57748-336-7*) Barbour Pub.
McManus, Una & Cooper, John C. Dealing with Destructive Cults LC 84-3552. 159p. 1984. write for info. (*0-310-70281-X*) Zondervan.
McManus, Wayne W., jt. auth. see Marshall, David H.
Mcmarco, Peter. Matchbox Toys: A Collector's Guide. 1993. 17.98 (*1-55521-937-3*) Bk Sales Inc.
McMartin, Barbara. The Adirondack Park: A Wildlands Quilt. LC 98-49278. (Illus.). 196p. 1999. pap. 24.95 (*0-8156-0567-6*) Syracuse U Pr.
— Adventures in Hiking: An Introduction to Adirondack Hiking. 110p. (J). 1993. pap. 12.50 (*0-925168-25-4*) North Country.
— Caroga: An Adirondack Town Recalls Its Past. 2nd ed. LC 98-202253. Orig. Title: Caroga: The Town Recalls Its Past. (Illus.). 288p. 1998. pap. 20.00 (*1-888374-07-1*) Lake View NY.
— Discover the Adirondack High Peaks. 2nd ed. (Discover the Adirondacks Ser.: Vol. XI). (Illus.). 288p. (Orig.). 1997. pap. 13.50 (*1-888374-05-5*) Lake View NY.
— Discover the Adirondack High Peaks: Adventures Out off the Trails in the Eastern & Western High Peaks Region. 2nd ed. LC 98-162627. (Discover the Adirondacks Ser.: Vol. XI-II). (Illus.). 288p. 1998. reprint ed. pap. 13.50 (*1-888374-06-3*) Lake View NY.
— Discover the Central Adirondacks: Four-Season Adventures in the Heart of the North Woods. rev. ed. (Illus.). 168p. (Orig.). 1995. reprint ed. pap. 13.00 (*1-888374-00-4*) Lake View NY.
— Discover the Eastern Adirondacks: Four-Season Adventures near Lake George, Pharaoh Lake, & Beyond. 2nd rev. ed. (Discover the Adirondacks Ser.: Vol. 4). (Illus.). 232p. 1998. pap. 14.00 (*1-888374-09-8*) Lake View NY.
— Discover the Northern Adirondacks: Four Season Excursions from Lake Placid, Saranee Lake & Points North. 2nd rev. ed. (Discover the Adirondacks Ser.: Vol. 1X-9). (Illus.). 224p. 1998. pap. 14.00 (*1-888374-08-X*) Lake View NY.
— Discover the West Central Adirondacks: A Guide to the Western Wildernesses & the Moose River Plains. 2nd rev. ed. (Discover the Adirondacks Ser.: Vol. II). (Illus.). 296p. 1998. pap. 16.00 (*1-888374-10-1*) Lake View NY.
— 50 Hikes in the Adirondacks: Short Walks, Day Trips, & Backpacks Throughout the Park. 3rd ed. LC 97-5432. (Fifty Hikes Ser.). (Illus.). 240p. 1997. pap. 14.95 (*0-88150-399-1*, Pub. by Countryman) Norton.
— Fun on Flatwater: An Introduction to Adirondack Canoeing. LC 95-15935. (Illus.). 1995. pap. 12.50 (*0-925168-40-8*) North Country.
*__McMartin, Barbara.__ The Glove Cities: How a People & Their Craft Built Two Cities. LC 99-94082. (Illus.). 304p. 1999. 45.00 (*1-888374-13-6*) Lake View NY.
McMartin, Barbara. The Great Forest of the Adirondacks. 266p. 1994. 27.50 (*0-925168-29-7*) North Country.
— Hides, Hemlocks & Adirondack History: How the Tanning Industry Influenced the Growth of the Region. 332p. 1992. 30.00 (*0-932052-99-1*) North Country.
— To the Lake of the Skies: The Benedicts in the Adirondacks. (Illus.). 192p. 1996. pap. text 20.00 (*1-888374-02-0*) Lake View NY.
— 2020 Vision: Realizing the Recreational Potential of Adirondack Wild Forests. (Twenty Twenty Vision: Fulfilling the Promise of the Adirondack Park Ser: Vol. III). 52p. 1990. pap. 10.00 (*0-9621202-2-7*) Adirondack Council.
McMartin, Barbara & Brenning, Lee M. Adventures in Camping: A Young People's Guide to Adirondack Backpacking. LC 96-15000. (Illus.). 111p. 1996. pap. 12.50 (*0-925168-54-8*) North Country.
McMartin, Barbara, et al. 50 Hikes in the Hudson Valley: From the Catskills to the Taconics, & from the Ramapos to the Helderbergs. 2nd ed. LC 94-9722. (Fifty Hikes Ser.). (Illus.). 232p. 1994. pap. 14.95 (*0-88150-292-8*, Pub. by Countryman) Norton.
McMartin, Barbara, jt. auth. see Rosevear, Francis.
McMartin, Jim. Personality Psychology: A Student Centered Approach. 216p. 1995. text 42.00 (*0-8039-5343-7*); pap. text 19.50 (*0-8039-5344-5*) Sage.
McMaster. Using Maps & Photographs. Date not set. pap. text. write for info. (*0-582-00341-5*, Pub. by Addison-Wesley) Longman.
McMaster, Alison A. Copycat. large type ed. (Linford Romance Library). 256p. 1992. pap. 16.99 (*0-7089-7210-1*) Ulverscroft.
McMaster, Annette C., ed. see Lord, A. Roberts.
McMaster, Christopher, jt. auth. see McMaster, Marvin.
McMaster, Clara W. Sing a Happy Song: Beloved Children's Favorites. (J). 1992. 9.98 (*0-88290-451-5*, 2929) Horizon Utah.
McMaster, Darren, jt. auth. see Phillips, Todd.
McMaster, Fitz H. History of Fairfield County: From "Before the White Man Came" to 1942. (Illus.). 220p. 1997. reprint ed. lib. bdg. 29.00 (*0-8328-6921-X*) Higginson Bk Co.
McMaster, Gerald. Edward Poitras: Canada XLVI Biennale di Venezia. LC 97-186963. (ENG, FRE & ITA., Illus.). 164p. 1995. pap. 24.95 (*0-660-50753-6*, Pub. by CN Mus Civilization) U of Wash Pr.
— Reservation X: The Power of Place in Aboriginal Contemporary Art. LC 99-198835. (Illus.). 168p. 1999. pap. text 34.95 (*0-295-97775-2*) U of Wash Pr.
McMaster, H. R. Dereliction of Duty: Distrust, Deceit & the Failure of American Leadership on the Road to Vietnam. abr. ed. 1997. audio 18.00 (*0-694-51851-4*, CPN 2665) HarperAudio.
McMaster, H. R. Dereliction of Duty: Johnson, McNamara, the Joint Chiefs of Staff & the Lies that Led to Vietnam. LC 97-5152. 464p. 1997. 27.50 (*0-06-018795-6*) HarpC.
*__McMaster, H. R.__ Dereliction of Duty: Johnson, McNamara, the Joint Chiefs of Staff & the Lies That Led to Vietnam. 480p. 1998. pap. 16.00 (*0-06-092908-1*, Perennial) HarperTrade.
McMaster, H. R. A Distant Thunder. 1997. 27.50 (*0-614-27860-0*) HarpC.
McMaster, Hamilton J. The Urban Principal's Handbook. (C). 1988. 21.25 (*0-932957-28-5*) Natl School.
McMaster, James. Urban Financial Management: A Training Manual. (EDI Technical Materials Ser.). 192p. 1991. pap. 22.00 (*0-8213-1615-X*, 11615) World Bank.
McMaster, James H., ed. The ABCs of Sports Medicine. LC 80-20636. 400p. 1982. lib. bdg. 38.00 (*0-88275-890-X*) Krieger.
McMaster, James H., jt. ed. see Novak, Josef F.
McMaster, John & Stone, Frederick B. Pennsylvania & the Federal Constitution, 1787-1788, 2 vols. LC 74-87406. (American Constitutional & Legal History Ser.). 1970. reprint ed. lib. bdg. 79.50 (*0-306-71550-3*) Da Capo.

M

An Asterisk (*) at the beginning of an entry indicates that the title is appearing for the first time.

McMaster, John B. Benjamin Franklin As a Man of Letters. LC 70-125706. (American Journalists Ser.). 1978. reprint ed. 28.95 (*0-405-01687-5*) Ayer.
— With the Fathers: Studies in the History of the United States. LC 75-173113. 1972. reprint ed. 20.95 (*0-405-08771-3*, Pub. by Blom Pubns) Ayer.
McMaster, John B., ed. The American Explorer Series, 10 titles in 17 vols., Set. reprint ed. 862.50 (*0-404-54900-4*) AMS Pr.
McMaster, Juliet. Thackeray: The Major Novels. LC 76-151380. (Illus.). 246p. reprint ed. pap. 76.30 (*0-8357-8345-6*, 203401900088) Bks Demand.
— Trollope's Palliser Novels: Theme & Pattern LC 79-307755. 242p. 1978. write for info. (*0-333-23860-5*) Macmillan.
McMaster, Juliet, jt. ed. see Copeland, Edward.
McMaster, Juliet, ed. see Koppel, Gene.
McMaster, Marvin & McMaster, Christopher. GC - MS: A Practical User's Guide. LC 97-48529. 192p. 1998. 62.50 (*0-471-24826-6*, Wiley-Liss) Wiley.
McMaster, Marvin C. HPLC: A Practical User's Guide. 224p. 1994. 79.95 (*0-471-18586-8*) Wiley.
McMaster, Marvin C. HPLC, a Practical User's Guide. LC 93-42139. 1994. 55.00 (*1-56081-636-8*, Wiley-VCH) Wiley.
McMaster, Michael. Performance Management: Creating the Conditions for Results. rev. ed. LC 94-2566. 320p. (Orig.). 1993. pap. 18.95 (*1-55552-041-3*) Metamorphous Pr.
McMaster, Michael & Grinder, John. Precision: A New Approach to Communication. LC 93-28602. 304p. 1994. pap. 15.95 (*1-55552-049-9*) Grinder Delozier.
McMaster, Michael D. The Intelligence Advantage: Organizing for Complexity. 224p. 1996. pap. text 17.95 (*0-7506-9792-X*, Focal) Buttrwrth-Heinemann.
***McMaster, Michelle.** The Marriage Bargain. 320p. 2000. pap. 4.99 (*0-8439-4750-0*, Leisure Bks) Dorchester Pub Co.
McMaster, N. Balakarishnan, ed. Advances in Combinatorial Methods & Applications to Probability & Statistics. LC 97-6185. (Applied Statistics for Industry & Technology Ser.). 532p. 1997. 79.95 (*0-8176-3908-X*) Birkhauser.
McMaster, R. D. Thackeray's Cultural Frame of Reference: Allusion in The Newcomes. 208p. (C). 1991. text 65.00 (*0-7735-0838-4*, Pub. by McG-Queens Univ Pr) CUP Services.
McMaster, R. D., ed. see Dickens, Charles.
McMaster, R. E. The Art of the Trade: Mastering the Analytical & Intuitive Elements of Successful Trading. LC 98-37848. (Irwin Trader's Edge Ser.). (Illus.). 256p. 1998. 50.95 (*0-07-045542-2*) McGraw-Hill Prof.
McMaster, R. E., Jr. The Christ Within: The Church & New Age Seek Him. (Illus.). 476p. (Orig.). 1995. pap. 19.95 (*0-9647861-0-9*) A N Inc Intl.
— A Highlander's Passion: Heartfelt Poetry. (Illus.). (Orig.). 1997. pap. 14.95 (*0-9647861-1-7*) A N Inc Intl.
— No Time for Slaves. 300p. 1986. 14.95 (*0-9605316-8-8*) Reaper Pub.
— The Power of Total Perspective. 496p. 1994. 29.95 (*0-9647861-2-5*) A N Inc Intl.
— The Power of Total Perspective. 2nd ed. 523p. 1994. pap. 29.95 (*0-9643552-0-5*) A N Inc Intl.
— Wealth for All: Economics, 2 Bks., Book 2. rev. ed. 280p. 1982. 14.95 (*0-9605316-2-9*) Reaper Pub.
— Win Win Win. 1989. pap. 2.25 (*0-9605316-6-1*) Reaper Pub.
McMaster, Robert B. & Shea, K. Stuart. Generalization in Digital Cartography. Cromley, Ellen K. & Cromley, Robert G., eds. LC 92-25730. (Resource Publications for College Geography). (C). 1992. pap. 15.00 (*0-89291-209-X*) Assn Am Geographers.
McMaster, Robert C., ed. ASNT Nondestructive Testing Handbook, Second Edition: Leak Testing, Vol. 1. (Illus.). 850p. 1982. 121.25 (*0-87170-125-1*, 125) Am Soc Nondestructive.
— ASNT Nondestructive Testing Handbook, Vol. 2: Liquid Penetrant Tests. (Illus.). 616p. 1982. 121.25 (*0-87170-126-X*, 126) Am Soc Nondestructive.
McMaster, Robert C., ed. see American Society for Nondestructive Testing (ASNT).
McMaster, Shawn. The First-Timer's Guide to Magic Tricks. LC 99-73105. (Illus.). 80p. (J). (gr. 1-4). 1999. pap. 8.95 (*0-7373-0229-1*, 02291W) NTC Contemp Pub Co.
— Kidsource: Magic Tricks. LC 99-73106. (Illus.). 112p. (J). (gr. 3-7). 2000. pap. 9.95 (*0-7373-0231-3*, 02313W) NTC Contemp Pub Co.
— 60 Super Simple Magic Tricks. LC 96-390. (Sixty Super Simple Ser.). (Illus.). 80p. (J). (gr. 4-7). 1996. pap. 6.95 (*1-56565-384-X*, 03849W, Pub. by Lowell Hse Juvenile) NTC Contemp Pub Co.
— 60 Super Simple More Magic Tricks. LC 98-75616. (Illus.). 80p. (J). (gr. 2). 1999. pap. 6.95 (*0-7373-0155-4*, 01554W) NTC Contemp Pub Co.
McMaster, Steve, et al. A Guide to the Mersey Measure. LC 96-215868. (Illus.). 1996. write for info. (*0-11-752691-6*) Statnry Office.
McMaster, Susan. The Hummingbird Murders. 112p. 1992. pap. 12.95 (*1-55082-048-6*, Pub. by Quarry Pr) LPC InBook.
— Learning to Ride. (Illus.). 72p. 1994. pap. 12.95 (*1-55082-104-0*, Pub. by Quarry Pr) LPC InBook.
— Siolence: Essays on Women, Violence, & Silence. 192p. 1996. pap. text 14.95 (*1-55082-158-X*, Pub. by Quarry Pr) LPC InBook.
McMasters, Clyde V. Witnessing Throughout the Twentieth Century: First Presbyterian Church of Sapula, Oklahoma, Celebrates One Hundred Years. 256p. 1995. 16.95 (*1-881576-58-2*) Providence Hse.
McMasters, Dale. Everyday Vocabulary. (Language Arts Ser.). 24p. (gr. 4-6). 1976. student ed. 5.00 (*0-8209-0310-8*, VD-2) ESP.
McMasters, Don & Gillette, M. L. Approximating Avogadro's Number Using Glass Beads & Monomolecular Film. Stanitski, C. L., ed. (Modular Laboratory Program in Chemistry Ser.). 12p. (C). 1997. pap. text 1.50 (*0-87540-496-0*) Chem Educ Res.
***McMasters, Eric, et al.** CCNP Routing Exam Cram. LC 00-43139. 2000. write for info. (*1-57610-633-0*) Coriolis Grp.
McMasters, Jake. Blood Bounty. (White Apache Ser.: No. 7). 176p. (Orig.). 1995. pap. text, mass mkt. 3.99 (*0-8439-3790-4*) Dorchester Pub Co.
— Blood Treachery. (White Apache Ser.: No. 6). 176p. (Orig.). 1995. pap. text, mass mkt. 3.99 (*0-8439-3739-4*) Dorchester Pub Co.
— Bloodbath. (White Apache Ser.: No. 5). 176p. (Orig.). 1994. pap. text, mass mkt. 3.99 (*0-8439-3689-4*) Dorchester Pub Co.
— Desert Fury. (White Apache Ser.: No. 9). 176p. (Orig.). 1995. pap. text, mass mkt. 3.99 (*0-8439-3871-4*) Dorchester Pub Co.
— Hanged! (White Apache Ser.: No. 10). 176p. (Orig.). 1996. pap. text, mass mkt. 3.99 (*0-8439-3899-4*) Dorchester Pub Co.
— Hangman's Knot. (White Apache Ser.: No. 1). 176p. (Orig.). 1993. pap. text, mass mkt. 3.99 (*0-8439-3535-9*) Dorchester Pub Co.
— Hangman's Knot - Warpath, 2 vols. in 1. (White Apache (Double Edition) Ser.). 352p. 1997. mass mkt. 4.99 (*0-8439-4185-5*) Dorchester Pub Co.
— Quick Killer. (White Apache Ser.: No. 4). 176p. (Orig.). 1994. pap. text, mass mkt. 3.99 (*0-8439-3646-0*) Dorchester Pub Co.
— The Trackers. (White Apache Ser.: Vol. 8). 176p. (Orig.). 1995. pap. text, mass mkt. 3.99 (*0-8439-3830-7*) Dorchester Pub Co.
— Warrior Born. (White Apache Ser.: No. 3). 176p. (Orig.). 1994. pap. text, mass mkt. 3.99 (*0-8439-3613-4*) Dorchester Pub Co.
— Warrior Born & Quick Killer, 2 vols. in 1. (White Apache Ser.). 352p. 1997. reprint ed. mass mkt. 4.99 (*0-8439-4231-2*) Dorchester Pub Co.
McMasters, S. Y. A Biographical Index to the History of England. 1973. 59.95 (*0-87968-752-5*) Gordon Pr.
McMasters, William H. Originality, & Other Essays. LC 67-28759. (Essay Index Reprint Ser.). 1977. 16.95 (*0-8369-0656-X*) Ayer.
McMath, F. M. McMath: Collections for a History of the Ancient Family of McMath. (Illus.). 272p. 1992. reprint ed. pap. 43.00 (*0-8328-2324-4*); reprint ed. lib. bdg. 53.00 (*0-8328-2323-6*) Higginson Bk Co.
McMath, John M. The Now of Our Human Destiny. LC 88-71529. 1990. 12.95 (*0-8158-0453-9*) Chris Mass.
McMath, Phillip H. Arrival Point. 238p. 1991. 16.95 (*0-943099-08-0*) M & M Pr.
Mcmath, Robert. American Populism. 13p. 1992. 30.00 (*0-8090-7796-5*) Hill & Wang.
McMath, Robert. American Populism. 246p. 1990. pap. 11.00 (*0-374-52264-2*) FS&G.
— New Product Shakeout. write for info. (*0-8129-2698-6*, Times Bks) Crown Pub Group.
McMath, Robert C. Populist Vanguard: A History of the Southern Farmers' Alliance. LC 75-9751. 235p. reprint ed. pap. 72.90 (*0-7837-0294-9*, 204061500018) Bks Demand.
McMath, Robert C., Jr. William Henry Emerson: And the Scientific Discipline at Georgia Tech. 130p. 1993. write for info. (*0-9639968-9-4*) C L Emerson.
McMath, Robert C., Jr., jt. ed. see Burton, Orville V.
McMath, Robert M. & Forbes, Thomas R. What Were They Thinking? Marketing Lessons You Can Learn from Products That Flopped. 1999. pap. 13.00 (*0-8129-3203-X*, Times Bks) Crown Pub Group.
McMath, Sandy S. Africa Alone: Odyssey of an American Traveller. 2nd ed. (Illus.). 383p. 1989. reprint ed. 24.95 (*0-9622515-0-X*); reprint ed. pap. 9.95 (*0-9622515-1-8*) Columbus & Co.
— Southern Passage: Soundings Overland: Tijuana to Tierra del Fuego. (Illus.). 543p. (C). 1993. 34.95 (*0-9622515-2-6*) Columbus & Co.
McMeeken, Joan, et al. Sports Physiotherapy: Applied Science & Practice. 1995. text 149.00 (*0-443-04804-5*) Church.
McMeekin, Gail. The Power of Positive Choices. 37p. 1996. pap. 15.00 (*0-9678271-0-8*) Creative Suc.
— The 12 Secrets of Highly Creative Women: A Portable Mentor. LC 99-47814. 256p. 2000. pap. text 16.95 (*1-57324-141-5*) Conari Press.
McMeekin, Ivan. Notes for Potters in Australia. (Illus.). 310p. 1985. pap. 27.95 (*0-86840-209-5*, Pub. by New South Wales Univ Pr) Intl Spec Bk.
***McMeekin, Marie.** Yesterday, Now & Forever. 1999. pap. write for info. (*1-58235-312-3*) Watermrk Pr.
McMeel & Andrews Publishing. Doctors; Jokes, Quotes, & Anecdotes. 1999. pap. text 5.95 (*0-8362-1540-0*) Andrews & McMeel.
McMeel, Gerard. Casebook on Restitution. 558p. 1996. pap. 50.00 (*1-85431-517-X*, Pub. by Blackstone Pr) Gaunt.
McMeen, Albert, jt. auth. see Carlin, Tom.
McMeen, Albert R., III. Treasurer's & Controller's New Equipment Leasing Guide. LC 84-6994. 251p. 1984. 59.95 (*0-13-930876-8*, Busn) P-H.
***McMeen, El.** El McMeen Acoustic Guitar Treasures. 64p. 1999. pap. 11.95 (*0-7866-4353-6*, 97883) Mel Bay.
— El McMeen Acoustic Guitar/Playing Favorites. 40p. 1997. pap. 23.95 incl. audio compact disk (*0-7866-2944-4*, 95973CDP) Mel Bay.
— El McMeen Acoustic Guitar Treasures. 64p. 1999. pap. 26.95 incl. audio compact disk (*0-7866-4354-4*, 97883CDP) Mel Bay.
— El McMeen Acoustic Guitar/Playing Favorites: Intermediate Level. 40p. 1997. pap. 8.95 (*0-7866-2095-1*, 95973) Mel Bay.
McMeen, Gordon, jt. auth. see Butel, Jane.
McMelody. Rap Lyrics for My Beloved Black People. (Illus.). 56p. (Orig.). 1996. pap. 12.00 (*0-9655918-0-8*); pap. 10.00 incl. audio (*0-9655918-2-4*) Living Innov Pub.
McMenamin. Applied Microcontroller Interfacing. (C). 2000. 39.75 (*0-7668-0900-5*) Thomson Learn.
— Experiments in Electronics Devices. (Electronics Technology Ser.). (C). 1995. pap. 29.50 (*0-8273-6820-8*) Thomson Learn.
***McMenamin.** National Geographic's Ultimate Adventure Sourcebook. 384p. 2000. per. 30.00 (*0-7922-7591-8*, Pub. by Natl Geog) S&S Trade.
McMenamin, Amy L., jt. auth. see McMenamin, Mark A.
McMenamin, Ann M., jt. auth. see McMenamin, Milton J.
***McMenamin, Cindi.** Heart Hunger: Letting God Meet Your Emotional Needs. LC 99-41565. 225p. 2000. pap. 9.99 (*0-7369-0184-1*) Harvest Hse.
McMenamin, Dianna L., jt. auth. see McMenamin, Mark A.
McMenamin, Donna. Popular Arts of Mexico: 1850-1950. 240p. 1996. 59.95 (*0-7643-0026-1*) Schiffer.
McMenamin, G. R. Forensic Stylistics. 264p. 1993. 190.75 (*0-444-81544-9*) Elsevier.
McMenamin, J. Michael. Applied Electronic Devices & Analog ICS: Computerized Test Bank. (Electronics Technology Ser.). 1995. 49.95 (*0-8273-5964-0*) Delmar.
— Applied Electronic Devices & Analog Integrated Circuits. LC 94-59. (Illus.). 800p. (C). 1995. pap. 98.95 (*0-8273-5416-9*) Delmar.
— Electronic Devices: Analog ICS. (Electronics Technology Ser.). 1995. teacher ed. 16.00 (*0-8273-5417-7*) Delmar.
McMenamin, James F., ed. see Shaw, William T.
Mcmenamin, Jim. Financial Management: An Introduction. LC 98-26719. 1999. 100.00 (*0-415-18161-5*) Routledge.
McMenamin, Jim. Financial Management: An Introduction. LC 98-26719. 1999. pap. 37.99 (*0-415-18162-3*) Routledge.
McMenamin, Mark. Carthaginian Cartography: A Stylized Exergue Map. (Illus.). 26p. (Orig.). 1996. pap. text 9.95 (*0-9651136-1-2*, 101) Meanma Pr.
— The Garden of Ediacara: Discovering the First Complex Life. LC 97-38073. (Illus.). 368p. 1998. text 31.50 (*0-231-10558-4*) Col U Pr.
***McMenamin, Mark.** The Garden of Ediacara: Discovering the First Complex Life. 368p. 2000. reprint ed. pap. text 19.50 (*0-231-10559-2*) Col U Pr.
McMenamin, Mark. Thbo Tsrm Adrnm Wod Tsornm.Tr. of All about Phoenician Coinage. (Illus.). 23p. (Orig.). 1996. pap. text 9.95 (*0-9651136-0-4*, 100) Meanma Pr.
McMenamin, Mark, ed. see Vernadsky, Vladimir.
***McMenamin, Mark A.** The Carthaginians Were Here Vol. 1: Evidence for an Early Crossing of the Atlantic. (Illus.). 1999. pap. 20.00 (*0-9651136-4-7*) Meanma Pr.
McMenamin, Mark A. The Carthaginians Were Here Vol. 2: Evidence for an Early Crossing of the Atlantic. (Illus.). 131p. 1999. pap. 20.00 (*0-9651136-5-5*, 105) Meanma Pr.
— A Concise Phoenician-English English-Phoenician Dictionary. 37p. (Orig.). 1997. pap. text 15.00 (*0-9651136-2-0*, 103) Meanma Pr.
— An Introduction to Phoenician Grammar. 28p. (Orig.). 1997. pap. text 15.00 (*0-9651136-3-9*, 102) Meanma Pr.
***McMenamin, Mark A.** Phoenician Coins & Their Countermarks. (Illus.). 68p. 2000. pap. 20.00 (*0-9651136-7-1*) Meanma Pr.
— Phoenicians, Fakes & Barry Fell: Solving the Mystery of Carthaginian Coins Found in America. (Illus.). 43p. 2000. pap. 30.00 (*1-893882-01-2*) Meanma Pr.
— Rare Exonumia of the Late Twentieth Century. (Illus.). 25p. 2000. pap. 15.00 (*1-893882-00-4*) Meanma Pr.
— Sympathy for the Slide Rule: Slide Rules in Scientific Innovation & Technology Education. (Technology Quest Ser.). (Illus.). 36p. 2000. pap. 15.00 (*0-9651136-9-8*, 109) Meanma Pr.
***McMenamin, Mark A. & McMenamin, Amy L.** Make Your Own Circular Slide Rule. (Technology Quest Ser.: No. 2). (Illus.). 12p. 2000. pap. 10.00 (*0-9651136-8-X*, 108) Meanma Pr.
McMenamin, Mark A. & McMenamin, Dianna L. The Emergence of Animals: The Cambrian Breakthrough. (Illus.). 216p. 1990. pap. text 27.50 (*0-231-06647-3*) Col U Pr.
— Hypersea: Life on Land. 343p. 1996. pap. 24.00 (*0-231-07531-6*) Col U Pr.
— Hypersea: Life on the Land. LC 94-15324. (Illus.). 262p. 1994. 35.00 (*0-231-07530-8*) Col U Pr.
McMenamin, Michael. Linear Integrated Circuits: Operation & Application. (Illus.). 400p. (C). 1985. text 52.00 (*0-13-537333-6*) P-H.
McMenamin, Michael & McNamara, Walter. Milking the Public: Political Scandals of the Dairy Lobby from LBJ to Jimmy Carter. LC 80-11546. 312p. 1980. text 36.95 (*0-88229-552-7*) Burnham Inc.
McMenamin, Milton J. & McMenamin, Ann M. Designs in Drama. 188p. (C). 1991. lib. bdg. 34.50 (*0-89464-485-8*) Krieger.
McMenamin, Paul. Adventure World Sourcebook, Series I. (Illus.). 432p. 1991. pap. 24.95 (*0-685-48070-4*) Boken Commns.
***McMenamin, Richard, et al.** Cat's Got Your Tongue: A Book of Riddles. LC 98-54973. (Illus.). 144p. 1999. text 15.95 (*1-58008-066-9*) Ten Speed Pr.
McMenamin, Robert W. Clergy Malpractice. LC 86-81075. 150p. 1986. lib. bdg. 35.00 (*0-89941-483-4*, 304100) W S Hein.
McMenemin, Barbera, et al. An Investigation of Cursive vs. Printing Characteristics in Handwriting. (Illus.). (Orig.). 1982. pap. text 10.00 (*1-877772-03-8*) AHAF.
McMenemy, John. The Language of Canadian Politics: A Guide to Important Terms & Concepts. rev. ed. xx, 322p. (C). 1995. pap. 29.95 (*0-88920-230-3*) W Laurier U Pr.
McMeniman. From Inquiry to Argument. LC 98-25702. 566p. 1998. pap. text 42.00 (*0-205-20041-9*, Longwood Div) Allyn.
McMican, Ann, jt. ed. see Davey, Richard J.
McMichael, A. & Fabre, J., eds. Monoclonal Antibodies in Clinical Medicine. 1982. text 157.00 (*0-12-485580-6*) Acad Pr.
McMichael, A., jt. auth. see Browning, M.
McMichael, A. J. Planetary Overload: Global Environmental Change & the Health of the Human Species. LC 92-38292. (Illus.). 368p. (C). 1993. text 64.95 (*0-521-44138-2*) Cambridge U Pr.
— Planetary Overload: Global Environmental Change & the Health of the Human Species. (Canto Book Ser.). (Illus.). 370p. (C). 1995. pap. 13.95 (*0-521-55871-9*) Cambridge U Pr.
McMichael, A. J., et al, eds. Climate Change & Human Health: An Assessment Prepared by a Task Group on Behalf of WHO, WMO & UNEP, WHO/EHG/96.7. 314p. (Orig.). 1996. pap. 27.00 (*0-614-19510-1*, 1930091) World Health.
— Leucocyte Typing III: White Cell Differentiation Antigens. (Illus.). 1088p. 1987. 175.00 (*0-19-261552-1*) OUP.
McMichael, A. J. & Bodmer, W. F., eds. A New Look at Tumour Immunology. (Cancer Surveys Ser.: Vol. 13). (Illus.). 208p. (C). 1992. text 66.00 (*0-87969-370-3*) Cold Spring Harbor.
McMichael, Andrew J., jt. auth. see Rowland-Jones, Sarah.
McMichael, Barbara L., ed. Baby Dreams of Childless Women. LC 93-84754. (Illus.). 90p. (Orig.). 1993. pap. 5.95 (*0-9636683-0-7*) Pacific Cent.
***McMichael, Betty.** The Church Librarian's Handbook: A Complete Guide for the Library & Resource Center in Christian Education. 3rd rev. ed. LC 98-7885. 288p. 1998. pap. 17.99 (*0-8010-5772-8*) Baker Bks.
McMichael, Gary. An Ulster Voice: In Search of Common Ground in Northern Ireland. LC 98-89916. (Illus.). 288p. 1999. pap. 14.95 (*1-57098-275-9*) Roberts Rinehart.
McMichael, George. Anthology American Literature: Realism, Vol. 12. 7th ed. (C). 2000. text. write for info. (*0-13-086498-6*) P-H.
***McMichael, George.** Anthology of American Literature Vol. 2: Realism to the Present, 7th ed. LC 99-34844. Vol. 2. 2223p. (C). 1999. pap. 55.00 (*0-13-083815-2*) P-H.
McMichael, George, ed. Selected Poems of Walt Whitman: Anthology. 160p. (C). 1993. pap. text 2.20 (*0-02-379609-X*, Pub. by P-H) S&S Trade.
McMichael, George, et al. Concise Anthology of American Literature, 2 vols., Set. 4th ed. LC 97-35530. 2388p. 1997. pap. text 52.00 (*0-13-373291-6*) P-H.
McMichael, James. Each in a Place Apart. LC 93-31265. (Phoenix Poets Ser.). 70p. 1994. pap. 9.95 (*0-226-56107-0*); lib. bdg. 20.00 (*0-226-56106-2*) U Ch Pr.
— Ulysses & Justice. 198p. 1991. text 39.50 (*0-691-06547-0*, Pub. by Princeton U Pr) Cal Prin Full Svc.
— The World at Large: New & Selected Poems, 1971-1996. LC 96-15122. (Phoenix Poets Ser.). 232p. (C). 1996. pap. text 19.00 (*0-226-56105-4*); lib. bdg. 29.95 (*0-226-56104-6*) U Ch Pr.
McMichael, James F. The Spiritual Style of Management: Who Is Running This Show Anyway? 202p. (Orig.). 1997. pap. 12.00 (*0-9656668-0-8*) SFP.
McMichael, Joe & Lyons, Irish J. The Who: Concert File. (Illus.). 208p. 1997. pap. 29.95 (*0-7119-6316-9*, OP47879) Omnibus NY.
McMichael, LaVeria, jt. ed. see Rice, Ferill J.
McMichael, Leslie & Riley, Laurie. Celtic Music for Folk Harp. 76p. 1996. pap. write for info. (*0-7866-0412-3*, 95433) Mel Bay.
McMichael, Lois, compiled by. Butts County, Georgia, 1825-1976, the History Of. rev. ed. 792p. 1988. reprint ed. 37.50 (*0-89308-628-2*, BGA 85) Southern Hist Pr.
McMichael, Nancy. Snowdomes. (Illus.). 96p. 1990. 27.50 (*1-55859-036-6*) Abbeville Pr.
McMichael, Philip. Development & Social Change: A Global Perspective. LC 95-20533. (Sociology for a New Century Ser.). 1996. pap. 22.95 (*0-8039-9066-9*) Pine Forge.
— Food & Agrarian Orders in the World Economy. LC 94-17977. (Contributions in Economics & Economic History Ser.: No. 160). 304p. 1995. pap. 24.95 (*0-275-94966-4*, Greenwood Pr) Greenwood.
— Food & Agrarian Orders in the World Economy, 160. LC 94-17977. (Studies in the Political Ecomony of the World-System: No. 160). 304p. 1995. 75.00 (*0-313-29399-6*, Greenwood Pr) Greenwood.
McMichael, Philip D., ed. The Global Restructuring of Agro-Food Systems. (Food Systems & Agrarian Change Ser.). (Illus.). 320p. 1994. text 47.50 (*0-8014-2940-4*); pap. text 18.95 (*0-8014-8156-2*) Cornell U Pr.
McMichael, Ralph N., Jr., ed. Creation & Liturgy: Studies in Honor of H. Boone Porter. (Orig.). 1993. pap. text 24.95 (*1-56929-001-6*, Pastoral Press) OR Catholic.
McMichael, Tony & Fletcher, Anthony C., eds. Health at the Crossroads: Transport Policy & Urban Health. LC 96-4969. 354p. 1997. 117.95 (*0-471-96272-4*) Wiley.

An Asterisk (*) at the beginning of an entry indicates that the title is appearing for the first time.

McMichael, William H. The Mother of All Hooks: The Story of the U. S. Navy's Tailhook Scandal. LC 96-49046. 342p. 1997. text 32.95 (*1-56000-293-X*) Transaction Pubs.

McMichaels, Susan W. Journey Out of the Garden: St. Francis of Assisi & the Process of Individuation. LC 97-35893. 176p. 1998. pap. 9.95 (*0-8091-3726-7*, 3726-7) Paulist Pr.

McMickle, Marvin A. From Pulpit to Politics: Reflections on the Separation of Church & State. 180p. 1998. pap. 16.00 (*1-893435-01-6*) Lakeshore Comm.

***McMickle, Marvin A.** Preaching to the Black Middle Class: Words of Challenge, Words of Hope. LC 99-37472. 176p. 2000. pap. 16.00 (*0-8170-1328-8*) Judson.

McMilen, Marilyn M., et al. Dropout Rates in the United States (1992) (Illus.). 168p. (Orig.). (C). 1994. pap. text 35.00 (*0-7881-0892-1*) DIANE Pub.

McMillan. The Baby Zoo. 40p. (J). (gr. k-4). 1995. pap. 4.95 (*0-590-44635-5*) Scholastic Inc.

— Educational Research: Fundamentals for the Consumer. 3rd ed. LC 98-55757. 384p. (C). 1999. pap. text 65.00 (*0-321-02337-4*) Addson-Wesley Educ.

***McMillan.** Writing Papers in the Biological Sciences. 3rd ed. 2001. pap. text. write for info. (*0-312-25857-7*) St Martin.

McMillan & Gardner. Mini-Map '93: A Practical Application & Standards to Manufacturing Cell Networks. 300p. 1994. pap. 60.00 (*0-9639941-0-7*) Open I T.

McMillan, jt. auth. see Starr.

McMillan, jt. auth. see Starr, Cecie.

McMillan, A. & Scott, G. Sexually Transmitted Diseases. (Colour Aids Ser.). (Illus.). 112p. (Orig.). (C). 1991. pap. text 16.95 (*0-443-04052-4*) Church.

McMillan, A. S. & Tucker, G. M., eds. International Conference on Millimeter Wave & Far-Infrared Technology: Proceedings of the International Conference on Millimeter Wave & Far-Infrared Technology, Beijing, China, 19-23 June 1989. (International Academic Publishers Ser.). 600p. 1990. 170.00 (*0-08-037880-3*, 1105, Pub. by IAP) Elsevier.

McMillan, Alan. Electrical Installations in Hazardous Areas. 656p. 1998. text 150.00 (*0-7506-3768-4*) Buttrwrth-Heinemann.

***McMillan, Alan D.** Since the Time of the Transformers: The Ancient Heritage of the Nuu-Chah-nulth, Ditidaht & Makah. (Illus.). 264p. 2000. pap. 22.95 (*0-7748-0701-6*, Pub. by UBC Pr) U of Wash Pr.

McMillan, Alan I. Native Peoples & Cultures of Canada. 2nd rev. ed. LC 95-187910. (Illus.). 376p. 1997. pap. 19.95 (*1-55054-150-1*, Pub. by DGL) Orca Bk Pubs.

McMillan, Alex, ed. see Bee, Becky.

McMillan, Alexander, jt. ed. see Young, Hugh.

McMillan, Andrew Ian. Death in Dili. LC 93-204322. 235p. 1992. write for info. (*0-340-57849-1*, Pub. by Hodder & Stoughton Ltd) Trafalgar.

***McMillan, Ann.** Angel Trumpet: A Civil War Mystery. LC 99-34918. 224p. 1999. pap. 22.95 (*0-670-88148-1*, Viking) Viking Penguin.

McMillan, Ann. Dead March: A Civil War Mystery. 288p. 1999. pap. 5.99 (*0-14-028020-0*) Penguin Putnam.

— Dead March: A Civil War Mystery. 256p. 1998. 21.95 (*0-670-88147-3*) Viking Penguin.

McMillan, Beverly & Musick, Jack. Oceans: Life in the Deep. LC 97-8125. (Illus.). 176p. 1997. 27.98 (*1-56799-471-7*, MetroBooks) M Friedman Pub Grp Inc.

McMillan, Beverly, jt. auth. see Starr, Cecie.

McMillan, Brett, jt. auth. see McMillan, Bruce.

McMillan, Bruce. The Alphabet Symphony. (Illus.). 32p. (J). (gr. k-2). 1977. 15.00 (*0-688-80112-9*) Apple Isl Bks.

— Apples, How They Grow, 001. (Illus.). 48p. (J). (ps-3). 1979. 18.00 (*0-395-27806-6*) HM.

— A Beach for the Birds. LC 92-10920. (Illus.). 32p. (J). (gr. 2-5). 1993. 16.00 (*0-395-64050-4*) HM.

Mcmillan, Bruce. Counting Wildflowers. 1995. 10.15 (*0-606-07390-6*, Pub. by Turtleback) Demco.

McMillan, Bruce. Counting Wildflowers. LC 85-16607. (Illus.). 32p. (J). (ps up). 1995. reprint ed. mass mkt. 4.95 (*0-688-14027-0*, Wm Morrow) Morrow Avon.

— Eating Fractions. LC 90-9139. (Illus.). 32p. (J). (ps-3). 1991. 15.95 (*0-590-43770-4*, Scholastic Hardcover) Scholastic Inc.

— Eating Fractions. 32p. (J). (ps-3). 1992. 19.95 (*0-590-72732-X*) Scholastic Inc.

— Ghost Doll. rev. large type ed. (Illus.). 32p. (J). (ps-4). 1997. pap. 10.00 (*0-934313-01-6*) Apple Isl Bks.

— Gletta the Foal. LC 98-11486. (J). (ps-3). 1998. lib. bdg. 14.95 (*0-7614-5039-4*) Marshall Cavendish.

— Going on a Whale Watch. 40p. (J). (ps-3). 1993. 19.95 (*0-590-72826-1*) Scholastic Inc.

— Grandfather's Trolley. LC 95-10637. (Illus.). 32p. (J). (ps up). 1995. 15.95 (*1-56402-633-7*) Candlewick Pr.

— Growing Colors. LC 88-2767. (Illus.). 40p. (J). (ps-2). 1988. 16.00 (*0-688-07844-3*); lib. bdg. 15.93 (*0-688-07845-1*) Lothrop.

McMillan, Bruce. Growing Colors. LC 93-28804. 1994. 10.15 (*0-606-06428-1*, Pub. by Turtleback) Demco.

McMillan, Bruce. Growing Colors. LC 93-28804. (Illus.). 32p. (J). (ps-3). 1994. reprint ed. mass mkt. 4.95 (*0-688-13112-3*, Wm Morrow) Morrow Avon.

— Jelly Beans for Sale. LC 95-25864. (Illus.). 32p. (J). (ps-3). 1996. 15.95 (*0-590-86584-6*) Scholastic Inc.

— Mouse Views: What the Class Pet Saw. LC 92-25921. (Illus.). 32p. (J). (gr. k-3). 1993. lib. bdg. 16.95 (*0-8234-1008-0*) Holiday.

— Mouse Views: What the Class Pet Saw. LC 92-25921. (Illus.). 32p. (J). (ps-3). 1993. pap. 6.95 (*0-8234-1132-X*) Holiday.

Mcmillan, Bruce. Nights of the Pufflings. (Illus.). 32p. (J). 1997. pap. 4.95 (*0-395-85693-0*) HM.

McMillan, Bruce. Nights of the Pufflings. LC 94-14808. (Illus.). 32p. (J). (gr. k-5). 1995. 16.00 (*0-395-70810-9*) HM.

— Nights of the Pufflings. 1997. 10.15 (*0-606-11684-2*, Pub. by Turtleback) Demco.

— One, Two, One Pair! 32p. (J). (ps-3). 1996. pap. text 4.99 (*0-590-46082-X*) Scholastic Inc.

— One Two One Pair. (J). 1991. 10.15 (*0-606-09717-1*, Pub. by Turtleback) Demco.

— Penguins at Home: Gentoos of Antarctica. LC 92-34769. (Illus.). 40p. (J). 1993. 17.00 (*0-395-66560-4*) HM.

— Puffins Climb, Penguins Rhyme. LC 94-27225. (Illus.). 32p. (J). (ps-1). 1995. 14.00 (*0-15-200362-2*, Gulliver Bks) Harcourt.

— The Remarkable Riderless Runaway Tricycle. rev. ed. (Illus.). 48p. (J). (gr. k-4). 1985. reprint ed. pap. 10.00 (*0-934313-00-8*) Apple Isl Bks.

— Salmon for Everyone. LC 97-29679. 32p. (J). 1998. 16.00 (*0-395-84544-0*) HM.

— Samuel's Easton's Day. (J). (gr. 1-4). Date not set. pap. 5.99 (*0-614-19198-X*, Apple Paperbacks) Scholastic Inc.

— Sense Suspense. LC 93-30272. (Illus.). 40p. (J). (ps-2). 1994. 15.95 (*0-590-47904-0*) Scholastic Inc.

— Step by Step. LC 87-4195. (Illus.). 28p. (J). (ps-2). 1990. lib. bdg. 15.00 (*0-688-07234-8*) Apple Isl Bks.

— Summer Ice: Life along the Antarctic Peninsula. LC 93-38831. (Illus.). 48p. (J). (gr. 2-5). 1995. 16.00 (*0-395-66561-2*) HM.

— The Weather Sky. (Illus.). 40p. (J). (gr. 5 up). 1991. 16.95 (*0-374-38261-1*) FS&G.

— The Weather Sky. LC 90-56151. 40p. (J). (gr. 4-7). 1996. pap. 6.95 (*0-374-48266-7*) FS&G.

McMillan, Bruce. The Weather Sky. LC 90-56151. 1996. 12.15 (*0-606-10025-3*, Pub. by Turtleback) Demco.

McMillan, Bruce. Wild Flamingos. LC 97-1521. (Illus.). 32p. (J). (gr. 2-5). 1997. 15.00 (*0-395-84545-9*) HM.

McMillan, Bruce & Berenstain, Stan. My Horse of the North. LC 96-45241. (Illus.). 32p. (J). (gr. k-3). 1997. 15.95 (*0-590-97205-7*) Scholastic Inc.

McMillan, Bruce & Mallat, Kathy. The Picture That Mom Drew. LC 96-30165. (Illus.). 24p. (J). (ps-3). 1997. 14.95 (*0-8027-8617-0*); lib. bdg. 15.85 (*0-8027-8618-9*) Walker & Co.

McMillan, Bruce & McMillan, Brett. Puniddles, 001. (Illus.). 32p. (J). (gr. 2 up). 1982. pap. 6.95 (*0-395-32076-3*) HM.

McMillan, Bruce M. Fault Tolerance for Multicomputers: The Application Oriented Paradigm. (Computer Engineering & Computer Sciences Ser.). (Illus.). 200p. 1996. text 73.25 (*0-89391-884-9*) Ablx Pub.

McMillan, C. Scott, jt. auth. see Rogers, Ronald L.

McMillan, Carl H., jt. ed. see Hardt, John P.

McMillan, Catherine, ed. see Williams-Sam, Sheffra.

McMillan, Cecily. The Charleston, Savannah & Coastal Islands Book: A Complete Guide. 3rd rev. ed. LC 98-35817. (Great Destinations Ser.). (Illus.). 320p. 1998. pap. 17.95 (*1-58157-001-5*, Pub. by Berkshire Hse) Natl Bk Netwk.

McMillan, Chandler S., jt. auth. see Rogers, Ronald L.

McMillan, Charles J. The Japanese Industrial System. 3rd rev. ed. (Studies in Organization). 434p. 1996. pap. 29.95 (*3-11-015086-7*) De Gruyter.

— The Japanese Industrial System. 3rd rev. ed. LC 97-16288. (De Gruyter Studies in Organization: No. 1). xii, 434p. 1996. text 84.95 (*3-11-015087-5*) De Gruyter.

McMillan, Clare, tr. see Gehlen, Arnold.

McMillan, Claude. Mathematical Programming. LC 74-23273. (Wiley Management & Administration Ser.). 664p. (C). reprint ed. 200.00 (*0-8357-9931-X*, 201700000005) Bks Demand.

McMillan, Dana. Center Time: A Complete Guide to Learning Centers. (Illus.). 144p. (J). (ps-2). 1994. pap., teacher ed. 13.95 (*1-57310-007-2*) Teachng & Lrning Co.

— Classroom Spaces & Learning Places: How to Arrange Your Room for Maximum Learning. Mitchell, Judy, ed. (Illus.). 128p. (J). (ps-4). 1997. pap. 12.95 (*1-57310-101-X*) Teachng & Lrning Co.

***McMillan, Dana.** Farm: A Complete Theme Unit Including Learning Centers. Mitchell, Judy, ed. 32p. (J). (ps-2). 2000. pap. 5.95 (*1-57310-210-5*) Teachng & Lrning Co.

— Grocery Store: A Complete Theme Unit Including Learning Centers: PS-2. Mitchell, Judy, ed. (Illus.). 32p. (J). (ps-2). 1999. pap., teacher ed. 5.95 (*1-57310-193-1*) Teachng & Lrning Co.

— Human Body: A Complete Theme Unit Including Learning Centers: Grades PS-2. Mitchell, Judy, ed. (Illus.). 32p. 1999. pap., teacher ed. 5.95 (*1-57310-194-X*) Teachng & Lrning Co.

— Pet Store: A Complete Theme Unit Including Learning Centers. (Illus.). 32p. (J). (ps). 2000. pap. 5.95 (*1-57310-211-3*) Teachng & Lrning Co.

— Post Office: A Complete Theme Unit Including Learning Centers: Grades PS-2. Mitchell, Judy, ed. (Illus.). 32p. 1999. pap., teacher ed. 5.95 (*1-57310-195-8*) Teachng & Lrning Co.

McMillan, Dana. Time for Assessment: Evaluation Tips with Six New Learning Centers. Mitchell, Judy, ed. (Illus.). 144p. (Orig.). (J). (ps-2). 1996. pap., teacher ed. 13.95 (*1-57310-046-3*) Teachng & Lrning Co.

***McMillan, Dana.** Transportation: A Complete Theme Unit Including Learning Centers. Mitchell, Judy, ed. (Illus.). 32p. (J). (ps-2). 2000. pap. 5.95 (*1-57310-212-1*) Teachng & Lrning Co.

McMillan, Daniel. Teen Smoking: Understanding the Risk. LC 96-36323. (Issues in Focus Ser.). (Illus.). 128p. (YA). (gr. 6 up). 1998. lib. bdg. 20.95 (*0-89490-722-0*) Enslow Pubs.

McMillan, David W. Create Your Own Love Story: The Art of Lasting Relationships. LC 97-21979. 304p. 1997. 21.95 (*1-885223-60-9*); pap. 14.95 (*1-885223-66-8*) Beyond Words Pub.

McMillan, Debra B. An Ornament to the City: Historic Architecture in Downtown Fairmont. LC 96-78848. (Illus.). 304p. 1996. 34.90 (*0-929915-18-6*) Headline Bks.

McMillan, Della E. Sahel Visions: Planned Settlement & River Blindness Control in Burkina Faso. LC 94-21940. (Studies in Human Ecology). 223p. 1995. pap. text 16.95 (*0-8165-1489-5*); lib. bdg. 37.00 (*0-8165-1487-9*) U of Ariz Pr.

McMillan, Dorothy. Vile Acts. 400p. 1995. mass mkt. 4.99 (*0-8217-0100-2*, Zebra Kensgtn); mass mkt. 4.99 (*0-7860-0100-3*, Pinncle Kensgtn) Kensgtn Pub Corp.

McMillan, Dorothy, jt. auth. see Gifford, Douglas.

McMillan, Dougald & Fehsenfeld, Martha. Beckett in the Theatre: The Author As Practical Playwright & Director. LC 86-13813. (Illus.). 352p. 1989. pap. 19.95 (*0-7145-4151-6*) Riverrun NY.

McMillan, Douglas J. Approaches to Teaching Goethe's Faust. LC 86-33191. (Approaches to Teaching World Literature Ser.: No. 14). xiii, 170p. 1987. pap. 18.00 (*0-87352-502-7*, AP14P); lib. bdg. 37.50 (*0-87352-501-9*, AP14C) Modern Lang.

McMillan, Douglas J. & Fladenmuller, Kathryn S. Regular Life: Monastic, Canonical, & Mendicant Rules. LC 97-41533. (Documents of Practice Ser.). 1997. pap. 6.00 (*1-879288-95-8*) Medieval Inst.

McMillan, Duncan, jt. auth. see Lewison, Jeremy.

McMillan, E. Norman, tr. see Seleskovitch, Danica.

McMillan, Earle. The Gospel According to Mark. LC 72-86991. 1984. 12.95 (*0-915547-19-8*) Abilene Christ U.

***McMillan, Edward J.** The Audit. 385p. 2000. 15.95 (*1-930270-00-3*) Harwood.

— Budgeting & Financial Information for Chambers of Commerce. 170p. 2000. pap. 59.00 (*1-930270-03-8*) Harwood.

— Budgeting & Financial Management Handbook: For Not-for-Profit Organizations. rev. ed. LC 99-48302. (ASAE Financial Management Ser.). (Illus.). xi, 116p. 1999. pap. 46.00 (*0-88034-158-0*) Am Soc Assn Execs.

— Essential Accounting Tax & Reporting Requirements for Chambers of Commerce. 170p. 2000. pap. 59.00 (*1-930270-02-X*) Harwood.

— Model Accounting & Financial Policies & Procedures for Chambers of Commerce. 170p. 2000. pap. 59.00 (*1-930270-01-1*) Harwood.

McMillan, Edward J. Model Accounting & Financial Policies & Procedures Handbook: For Not-for-Profit Organizations. rev. ed. LC 99-32096. (ASAE Financial Management Ser.). 1999. pap. 50.00 incl. cd-rom (*0-88034-157-2*) Am Soc Assn Execs.

McMillan, Elizabeth. Living on the Water. LC 98-65890. (Illus.). 208p. 1998. 50.00 (*0-8478-2115-3*, Pub. by Rizzoli Intl) St Martin.

McMillan, Elizabeth, et al. Casa California: Spanish-Style Houses from Santa Barbara to San Clemente. LC 95-45722. (Illus.). 208p. 1996. 50.00 (*0-8478-1850-0*, Pub. by Rizzoli Intl) St Martin.

McMillan, F. R. & Tuthill, Lewis H. Concrete Primer. 4th ed. 96p. 1987. 28.25 (*0-685-72804-8*, SP-1BOW6) ACI.

McMillan, G. K. & Weiner, Stanley. How to Become an Instrument Engineer: The Making of a Prima Donna. LC 88-134784. (Illus.). 148p. 1987. pap. text 20.00 (*1-55617-007-6*, A007-6) ISA.

McMillan, G. K., jt. auth. see Weiner, S.

McMillan, Gail & Norstedt, Marilyn L., eds. New Scholarship - New Serials: Proceedings of the North American Serials Interest Group, Inc., 8th Annual Conference, June 10-13, 1993, Brown University, Providence, R.I. LC 94-6729. (Serials Librarian Ser.: Vol. 24, Nos. 3-4). (Illus.). 290p. 1994. lib. bdg. 39.95 (*1-56024-685-5*) Haworth Pr.

McMillan, George. Old Breed: A History of the First Marine Division in World War II. LC 79-16880. 1980. reprint ed. 49.95 (*0-89201-052-5*) Zenger Pub.

McMillan, George, et al. Uncommon Valor: Marine Divisions in Action. (Elite Unit Ser.: 5th). (Illus.). 272p. 1986. reprint ed. 27.95 (*0-89839-094-X*) Battery Pr.

McMillan, Gregory K. Advanced Temperature Measurement & Control. 1995. 48.00 (*1-55617-540-X*) ISA.

— Biochemical Measurement & Control. LC 87-2954. 166p. 1987. reprint ed. pap. 51.50 (*0-608-01358-7*, 206209700002) Bks Demand.

— Centrifugal & Axial Compressor Control. LC 83-216995. (Instructional Resource Package Ser.). 142p. 1983. reprint ed. pap. text, student ed. 44.10 (*0-608-01350-1*, 206209000002) Bks Demand.

— Dispersing Heat Through Conviction: The Funnier Side of Process Control. LC 99-22284. 1999. 32.00 (*1-55617-688-0*) ISA.

— PH Measurement & Control. 2nd ed. LC 84-29976. (Independent Learning Module Ser.). 304p. 1994. 60.00 (*1-55617-483-7*, A483-7) ISA.

***McMillan, Gregory K.** Pocket Guide to Good Tuning. LC 00-36958. 2000. write for info. (*1-55617-726-7*) ISA.

— Process/industrial Instruments & Controls Handbook, 5th Ed. 5th ed. LC 99-29591. 1999. 173.75 (*0-07-012582-1*) Datapro Res.

— Tuning & Control Loop Performance: A Practitioner's Guide. 3rd ed. LC 93-49410. (Illus.). 454p. reprint ed. pap. 140.80 (*0-608-20411-0*, 207166400002) Bks Demand.

McMillan, Gregory K., et al, eds. How to Become an Instrument Engineer Part 1.52: New & Improved! 52 Per Cent More Entertaining Than Original. LC 94-16752. (Illus.). 1994. 32.00 (*1-55617-520-5*) ISA.

McMillan, Ian. I Found This Shirt. 128p. 1998. pap. 12.95 (*1-85754-336-X*, Pub. by Carcanet Pr) Paul & Co Pubs.

McMillan, Ian, intro. Six: The Versewagon Poetry Manual. 128p. (C). 1988. 60.00 (*0-947612-13-0*, Pub. by Rivelin Grapheme Pr); pap. 40.00 (*0-947612-14-9*, Pub. by Rivelin Grapheme Pr) St Mut.

***McMillan, Iris P.** A Guide to Style: A Manual for Business & Professional Women. LC 00-190314. (Illus.). x, 130p. 2000. pap. 25.00 (*0-9679588-0-6*) Loganfield Inc.

McMillan, J. D., jt. auth. see Campbell, M.

McMillan, James. Classroom Assessment: Principles & Practice. LC 96-14657. 416p. 1996. pap. text 53.00 (*0-205-16587-7*) Allyn.

— Napoleon III. 200p. (C). 1995. pap. text 32.60 (*0-582-49483-4*, 78832) Longman.

McMillan, James B. James B. McMillan: Essays in Linguistics by His Friends & Colleagues. Raymond, James C. & Russell, I. Willis, eds. LC 77-7169. (Illus.). 203p. 1977. pap. 63.00 (*0-7837-8400-7*, 205921100009) Bks Demand.

McMillan, James B. & Montgomery, Michael B. Annotated Bibliography of Southern American English. LC 88-36856. 464p. (C). 1989. text 39.95 (*0-8173-0448-7*) U of Ala Pr.

McMillan, James E. A Guidebook for Electronic Court Filing LC 99-162543. 324 p. 1998. write for info. (*0-314-23340-7*) West Group.

McMillan, James E., ed. see McFarland, Ernest W.

McMillan, James F. Francaises The Social Condition of Women & the Politics on France, 1789-1914. 1998. pap. 22.95 (*1-85728-177-2*) Taylor & Francis.

— Francaises: The Social Condition of Women & the Politics of Gender in France, 1789-1914. 1998. 65.00 (*1-85728-176-4*) Taylor & Francis.

***McMillan, James F.** France & Women, 1789-1914: Gender, Society & Politics. LC 99-42213. (Illus.). 272p. 2000. pap. 27.99 (*0-415-22603-1*) Routledge.

— France & Women, 1789-1914: Gender Society & Politics. LC 99-42213. 304p. (C). 2000. text 90.00 (*0-415-22602-3*) Routledge.

McMillan, James F. Twentieth-Century France: Politics & Society in France, 1898-1991. LC 91-30407. 272p. 1992. pap. text 18.95 (*0-340-52239-9*, A6101, Pub. by E A) OUP.

McMillan, James H. Classroom Assessment: Principles & Practice for Effective Instruction. (C). 1997. pap., teacher ed. write for info. (*0-205-26351-8*, T6351-5) Allyn.

— Educational Research: Fundamentals for the Consumer. 2nd ed. LC 95-16506. (Illus.). 384p. (C). 1996. text 48.75 (*0-673-99864-9*) Addson-Wesley Educ.

— Educational Research: Fundamentals for the Consumer. 3rd ed. LC 95-16506. 384p. (C). 1997. 25.20 (*0-673-97648-3*) Addson-Wesley Educ.

— Research Education: A Conceptual Approach. 4th ed. 198p. (C). 1997. pap. text, student ed. 23.00 (*0-673-98515-6*) Addison-Wesley.

McMillan, James H. & Schumacher, Sally. Research in Education: A Conceptual Introduction. 4th ed. LC 96-18832. 704p. (C). 1997. 77.00 (*0-673-99741-3*) Longman.

McMillan, James H. & Wergin, Jon F. Understanding & Evaluating Education Research. LC 97-30618. 182p. (C). 1997. pap. text 25.00 (*0-13-193541-0*) P-H.

McMillan, James J., jt. auth. see Wason, Betty.

McMillan, Joe. Route of the Warbonnets: Santa Fe Railway in the 1970s. rev. ed. LC 77-81470. (Illus.). 176p. 1998. 39.50 (*0-934228-01-9*) McMillan Pubns.

— Wheat Lines & Super Freights. (Illus.). 1992. 64.95 (*0-934228-17-5*) McMillan Pubns.

McMillan, John. Game Theory in International Economics, Vol. 1. (Fundamentals of Pure & Applied Economics Ser.: Vol.1, pt. 1). viii, 106p. 1986. pap. text 53.00 (*3-7186-0277-6*) Gordon & Breach.

— Games, Strategies & Managers: How Managers Can Use Game Theory to Make Better Business Decisions. (Illus.). 264p. 1996. pap. 17.95 (*0-19-510803-5*) OUP.

McMillan, John & Naughton, Barry, eds. Reforming Asian Socialism: The Growth of Market Institutions. LC 96-4313. 200p. (C). 1996. text 70.00 (*0-472-10661-9*, 10661) U of Mich Pr.

McMillan, John, jt. ed. see McAfee, R. Preston.

Mcmillan, John, jt. ed. see Shepard, Alan B., Jr.

McMillan, John C., et al. Economic Growth, Political & Civil Liberties. LC 94-6152. (Occasional Papers: No. 38). 1994. pap. 9.95 (*1-55815-355-1*) ICS Pr.

McMillan, Julia A. & Oski, Frank A. Oski's Pediatrics: Principles & Practice. 3rd ed. LC 98-50639. 2446p. 1999. 150.00 (*0-7817-1618-7*) Lppncott W & W.

McMillan, Julia A., et al. Oski's Pediatrics: Principles & Practice. 3rd ed. 2848p. 150.00 (*0-7817-2012-5*) Lppncott W & W.

McMillan, Katharine K., jt. auth. see McMillan, Patricia H.

McMillan, Katherine K. & McMillan, Patricia H. House Comfortable: The Art & Science of Comfortable Living. 224p. (Orig.). 1996. pap. 13.00 (*0-399-52234-4*, Perigee Bks) Berkley Pub.

McMillan, Katherine K., jt. auth. see McMillan, Patricia H.

McMillan, Kenneth. Tales from the Yankee Dugout: A Collection of the Greatest Yankee Stories Ever Told. (Illus.). 200p. 1999. 19.95 (*1-58261-061-4*) Sprts Pubng.

***McMillan, Kenneth.** Tales from the Yankee Dugout: A Collection of the Greatest Yankee Stories Ever Told. (Illus.). 2000. pap. write for info. (*1-58261-284-6*) Sprts Pubng.

McMillan, Kenneth L. Symbolic Model Checking. LC 93-24859. 216p. (C). 1993. text 94.00 (*0-7923-9380-5*) Kluwer Academic.

M

McMillan, Kent. Hydroslide Kneeboarding: An Illustrated Guide to Learning & Mastering the Sport. Robertson, Jo, ed. LC 88-50672. (Illus.). 166p. (Orig.). (YA). 1988. pap. 12.95 (0-944406-03-3) World Pub FL.

McMillan, Lawrence G. MacMillan on Options. LC 96-27174. 592p. 1996. 69.95 (0-471-11960-1) Wiley.

***McMillan, Lawrence G.** Options As a Strategic Investment. 4p. 2001. 55.00 (0-7352-0197-8) PH Pr.

McMillan, Lawrence G. Options As a Strategic Investment. 3rd ed. LC 92-23160. 882p. (C). 1993. text 49.95 (0-13-636002-5) P-H.

McMillan, Lawrence G., jt. auth. see Gross, Leroy.

McMillan, Len D. & Wray, Marvin. First Class Male: A Christian Man's Role in Today's World. LC 94-2254. 160p. 1994. pap. 9.99 (0-8280-0786-1) Review & Herald.

— Putting up with Mr. Right. LC 96-135963. 158p. 1996. pap. 10.99 (0-8280-0967-8) Review & Herald.

McMillan, Lisa, et al. Positive Cooking: Cooking for People Living with HIV. LC 96-33390. (Illus.). 264p. 1998. pap. 12.95 (0-89529-734-5, Avery) Penguin Putnam.

McMillan, M., jt. auth. see Lowe, Nicholas.

McMillan, Malcolm C. Constitutional Development in Alabama, 1798-1901: A Study in Politics, the Negro, & Sectionalism. LC 78-2258. 1978. reprint ed. 30.00 (0-87152-258-6) Reprint.

McMillan, Malcolm C., ed. The Alabama Confederate Reader. LC 92-8817. (Library of Alabama Classics). 512p. (C). 1992. reprint ed. pap. text 24.95 (0-8173-0595-5) U of Ala Pr.

McMillan, Margaret. Education Through the Imagination: 1904 Edition. Stern, Jeffrey, ed. & intro. by. (Classics in Education Ser.). 212p. 1996. reprint ed. 75.00 (1-85506-293-3) Bks Intl VA.

McMillan, Margaret, jt. auth. see Townshend, Judith.

McMillan, Mary. Classroom Starters for Any Occasion. 144p. 1989. 10.99 (0-86653-508-X, GA1130) Good Apple.

— Lifesavers for Substitutes. (Illus.). 160p. 1992. student ed. 14.99 (0-86653-678-7, 1412) Good Apple.

— The Story of Jesus. (Color, Cut & Paste Ser.). 48p. (J). (ps-1). 1988. 7.95 (0-86653-454-7, SS1804, Shining Star Pubns) Good Apple.

McMillan, May F. The Shortest Way to the Essay: Rhetorical Strategies. LC 84-20567. xxii, 274p. (C). 1984. 19.45 (0-86554-132-9, H123) Mercer Univ Pr.

McMillan, Merna M., jt. auth. see Gentile, Lance M.

McMillan, Michael. Algorithms in Visual Basic. 1999. pap. text 54.95 (0-387-98715-0) Spr-Verlag.

— Perl from the Ground Up. (Illus.). 520p. (Orig.). 1998. pap. 34.99 (0-07-882404-4, Oracle Press) Osborne-McGraw.

— TY Programming with VB in 14 Days. LC 97-14870. 425p. 1997. 49.99 (1-57169-121-9) Sams.

McMillan, Michael, jt. auth. see Richstad, Jim.

***McMillan, Michael M.** The Administrator's Guide to Windows NT Shell Scripting. 500p. 1999. pap. 49.95 incl. cd-rom (0-12-465685-4, Pub. by Morgan Kaufmann) Harcourt.

McMillan, Michael M. Scripting Language Handbook. 800p. (C). 1999. pap. 49.95 (0-12-485680-2) Morgan Kaufmann.

McMillan, Michael M. Perl Programming for NT Blue Book, 1. 1999. pap. text 39.99 (1-57610-404-4) Coriolis Grp.

***McMillan, Mike.** Windows 2000 Script Host for System Administrators. 400p. 2000. pap. 34.99 (0-7897-2384-0) Que.

— You Can Make Big Money Writing Little Books. 3rd ed. (Illus.). 294p. 2000. pap. 29.95 (1-930385-00-5, Gypsy Girl Pr) McMillan.

McMillan, Moira. Scottish Business Law. 3rd ed. 480p. 1997. pap. 64.50 (0-273-62035-5, Pub. by Pitman Pub) Trans-Atl Phila.

McMillan, Naomi. Wish You Were Here. LC 90-85435. (Minnie 'n Me Ser.). (Illus.). 32p. (J). (gr. k-3). 1991. 5.95 (1-56282-036-2) Disney Pr.

McMillan, Norman H. Marketing Your Hospital: A Strategy for Survival LC 81-10892. ix, 117 p. 1981. write for info. (0-87258-298-1) Am Hospital.

— Marketing Your Hospital: A Strategy for Survival. LC 84-21576. ix, 117 p. 1981. 20.00 (0-939450-51-8) AHPI.

McMillan, Otis. Closing the Door: Overcoming Satanic Forces. LC 97-93146. 110p. (Orig.). 1997. pap. 6.00 (1-57502-439-X, PO1330) Morris Pubng.

McMillan, Otis T. Come, Holy Spirit, Heavenly Dove: The Holy Spirit, His Person & His Purpose. 86p. (Orig.). 1996. pap. 6.00 (1-57502-115-3) Morris Pubng.

— Right on the Money: Money, the Christian, & Financial Success. 146p. 1998. pap. 5.95 (1-57502-694-5, PO1960) Morris Pubng.

— The Tears of a Clown: Mask - What Do They Really Hide? rev. ed. 96p. 1996. pap. 6.00 (1-57502-138-2) Morris Pubng.

McMillan, P. W. Glass Ceramics. 2nd ed. 1979. text 160.00 (0-12-485660-8) Acad Pr.

McMillan, Patricia & Kennedy, James R., Jr. Library Research Guide to Sociology: Illustrated Search Strategy & Sources. LC 80-83513. (Library Research Guides Ser.: No. 5). 78p. 1981. 25.00 (0-87650-121-8) Pierian.

McMillan, Patricia H. & McMillan, Katharine K. Home Decorating for Dummies. LC 98-86179. (For Dummies Ser.). (Illus.). 384p. 1998. pap. 19.99 (0-7645-5107-8) IDG Bks.

McMillan, Patricia H. & McMillan, Katherine K. Sun Country Style. LC 99-25658. (Illus.). 144p. 1999. 39.95 (0-87905-910-9) Gibbs Smith Pub.

McMillan, Patricia H., jt. auth. see McMillan, Katherine K.

***McMillan, Patricia Hart.** Sun Country Elegant. (Illus.). 144p. 2000. 39.95 (1-58685-002-4) Gibbs Smith Pub.

McMillan, R. Bruce. Gasconade Prehistory: A Survey & Evaluation of the Archaeological Resources. Bray, Robert T., ed. (Missouri Archaeologist Ser.: Vol. 27, No. 3-4). (Illus.). 114p. (Orig.). 1965. pap. 3.00 (0-943414-45-8) MO Arch Soc.

McMillan, Richard C., et al, eds. Euthanasia & the Newborn: Conflicts Regarding Saving Lives. (Philosophy & Medicine Ser.: No. 24). 340p. 1987. lib. bdg. 117.50 (90-277-2299-4) Kluwer Academic.

McMillan, Richard C., et al. Euthanasia & the Newborn: Conflicts Regarding Saving Lives. LC 86-33835. (Philosophy & Medicine Ser.: Vol. 24). 343p. (C). 1987. pap. text 64.50 (1-55608-039-5, D Reidel) Kluwer Academic.

***McMillan, Robert.** Corporate Lunacy: How to Win (Or at Least Survive) the Corporate Game. (Illus.). 250p. 2000. 25.95 (0-9678568-0-9, Pub. by Reality Pr) ACCESS Pubs Network.

McMillan, Robin. 365 One-Minute Golf Lessons: Quick & Easy Stroke-Saving Tips. LC 94-4834. 320p. 1994. 21.95 (0-06-017087-5) HarperTrade.

— Us Against Them. 2000. 26.00 (0-06-019791-9); pap. 14.00 (0-06-095756-5) HarpC.

McMillan, Robin, ed. Golfer's Home Companion. (Illus.). 288p. 1993. 35.00 (0-671-70054-5) S&S Trade.

***McMillan, Ronald J.** Love Irony: Spacial Fashion. (Illus.). 459p. 2000. write for info. (0-7541-0915-1, Pub. by Minerva Pr) Unity Dist.

McMillan, Rosalyn. Blue Collar Blues. LC 98-19553. 352p. 1998. 23.00 (0-446-52243-0, Pub. by Warner Bks) Little.

— Blue Collar Blues. 416p. 2000. mass mkt. 7.50 (0-446-60764-9) Warner Bks.

***McMillan, Rosalyn.** The Flip Side of Sin. LC 00-27681. 352p. 2000. 24.00 (0-684-86287-5) Simon & Schuster.

McMillan, Rosalyn. Knowing. 418p. 1997. reprint ed. mass mkt. 6.50 (0-446-60376-7, Pub. by Warner Bks) Little.

— One Better. 400p. 1998. mass mkt. 7.50 (0-446-60599-9, Pub. by Warner Bks) Little.

McMillan, Sandy. How to Be a Better Communicator. (How to Be a Better...Ser.). 1997. pap. 15.95 (0-7494-2025-1) Kogan Page Ltd.

McMillan, Steve, jt. auth. see Chaisson, Eric.

McMillan, Stuart. Neither Confirm nor Deny: The Nuclear Ships Dispute Between New Zealand & the United States. LC 87-15853. 185p. 1987. 57.95 (0-275-92352-5, C2352, Praeger Pubs) Greenwood.

Mcmillan, Susan M. Foreign Direct Investment in Three Regions of the South at the End of the Twentieth Century. LC 98-35610. 208p. 1999. text 69.95 (0-312-21725-0) St Martin.

McMillan, Terry. A Day Late & a Dollar Short. 2000. 23.95 (0-670-86042-5, Viking) Viking Penguin.

— Disappearing Acts. Rosenman, Jane, ed. 384p. 1993. mass mkt. 6.99 (0-671-87200-1, Pocket Star Bks) PB.

— Disappearing Acts. LC 88-40412. 386p. 1989. 26.95 (0-670-82461-5) Viking Penguin.

— Disappearing Acts. Rosenman, Jane, ed. LC 90-36284. 400p. 1990. reprint ed. pap. 14.00 (0-671-70843-0, WSP) PB.

— Disappearing Acts, Set. abr. ed. 1993. audio 16.00 (0-453-00843-7) Penguin-HghBrdg.

— How Stella Got Her Groove Back. 1997. mass mkt. 6.99 (0-451-19200-1, Sig) NAL.

— How Stella Got Her Groove Back. 1998. mass mkt. 7.99 (0-451-19741-0, Sig) NAL.

— How Stella Got Her Groove Back. large type ed. LC 96-31677. (Large Print Bks.). 1996. 27.95 (1-56895-355-0, Compass) Wheeler Pub.

— Mama. Rosenman, Jane, ed. 260p. 1991. pap. 14.00 (0-671-74523-9, WSP) PB.

— Mama. 320p. 1994. per. 6.99 (0-671-88448-4, Pocket Star Bks) PB.

— Mama. abr. ed. 1994. 16.00 incl. audio (0-453-00865-8, Pub. by Penguin-HghBrdg) Penguin Putnam.

— Waiting to Exhale. 1995. mass mkt. 6.99 (0-671-53745-8) PB.

— Waiting to Exhale. 1996. per. 20.97 (0-671-85153-5) PB.

— Waiting to Exhale. 416p. 1992. 22.95 (0-670-83980-9, Viking) Viking Penguin.

— Waiting to Exhale. large type ed. LC 92-27196. (General Ser.). 600p. 1993. pap. 17.95 (0-8161-5618-2, G K Hall Lrg Type) Mac Lib Ref.

— Waiting to Exhale. Rosenman, Jane, ed. 416p. 1994. reprint ed. pap. 14.00 (0-671-50148-8, WSP) PB.

McMillan, Terry, ed. Breaking Ice: An Anthology of Contemporary African-American Fiction. 1990. 30.00 (0-670-82562-X) Viking Penguin.

— Breaking Ice: An Anthology of Contemporary African-American Fiction. 560p. 1990. pap. 16.95 (0-14-011697-4, Penguin Bks) Viking Penguin.

McMillan, Thomas C., jt. auth. see Collins, William J.

McMillan, Tom, jt. auth. see Lemieux, Mario.

McMillan, Tom, jt. ed. see Wood, Rodger L.

McMillan, Victoria E. Writing Papers in the Biological Sciences. 2nd ed. 192p. (C). 1996. pap. text 22.95 (0-312-11504-0) St Martin.

McMillan, W. Exercise & Fitness: HP 628 Course Study Guide. rev. ed. 249p. 1994. spiral bd. write for info. (0-933195-17-6) CA College Health Sci.

McMillan, William. Education of a Headmaster. LC 82-24372. 1986. 13.95 (0-87949-232-5) Ashley Bks.

— The Worship of the Scottish Reformed Church, 1550-1638: The Hastie Lectures in the University of Glasgow, 1930. LC 83-45585. reprint ed. 35.00 (0-404-19903-8) AMS Pr.

McMillan, William J. Let's Get America Moving Again. LC 81-85202. 101p. 1981. spiral bd. 12.95 (0-918214-08-4) F E Peters.

— Private School Management. 1977. 7.95 (0-918214-00-9, 76-51885) F E Peters.

— Private School Management. 2nd ed. LC 79-50904. 1979. 14.95 (0-918214-03-3) F E Peters.

— Private Schools: Boards & Heads. LC 80-81654. 88p. (Orig.). 1980. pap. 5.95 (0-918214-06-8) F E Peters.

— Private Schools of the Future. LC 81-66535. 117p. (C). 1981. spiral bd. 12.95 (0-918214-07-6) F E Peters.

McMillan, Zandra R. I've Got Something to Say! A Collection of Social Expression. Spenser, Pauline & Harris, Annie, eds. (Illus.). 27p. (Orig.). 1996. mass mkt. 4.95 (0-9653548-8-1) Ive Got Something.

McMillen, Conger S., ed. Sensibility in Transformation: Creative Resistance to Sentiment from the Augustans to the Romantics; Essays in Honor of Jean H. Hagstrum. LC 88-46055. (Illus.). 240p. 1990. 36.50 (0-8386-3352-8) Fairleigh Dickinson.

McMillen, Donald H. & DeGolyer, Michael E. One Culture, Many Systems: Politics in the Reunification of China. 334p. (Orig.). 1997. pap. text 26.95 (962-201-577-8, Pub. by Chinese Univ) U of Mich Pr.

McMillen, Donald H. & Si-Wai, Man, eds. The Other Hong Kong Report, 1994. (Hong Kong Ser.). 502p. 1994. pap. 49.50 (962-201-633-2, Pub. by Chinese Univ) Coronet Bks.

McMillen, Donald H., jt. ed. see MacKerras, Colin.

McMillen-Fairchild, Sally. Connections Vol. 3: Nothing Dentured, Nothing Gained - Bits of Humor & Wisdom I've Chewed on over the Years. xiv, 96p. 1998. pap., per. 8.99 (0-9665707-0-7, 101) Gami Pub Co.

McMillen, Jan, ed. Gambling Cultures: Studies in History & Interpretation. LC 95-40696. (Culture Ser.). 336p. (C). 1996. 85.00 (0-415-06820-7) Routledge.

***McMillen, John D.** Title IX Compliance & Implementation. 216p. 2000. write for info. (1-58692-014-6); write for info. (1-58692-022-7) Copyright Mgmt.

***McMillen, Kelly R., ed.** The Case for Mars VI: Making Mars an Affordable Destination. (Science & Technology Ser.: Vol. 98). 578p. 2000. 80.00 (0-87703-461-3, Am Astronaut Soc); pap. 55.00 (0-87703-462-1, Am Astronaut Soc) Univelt Inc.

McMillen, Loretta, jt. auth. see Fingado, Dorothy.

McMillen, Margot. A to Z Missouri: The Dictionary of Missouri Place Names. (Show Me Missouri Ser.). (Illus.). 224p. (Orig.). 1996. pap. 14.95 (0-9646625-4-X, MG3370) Pebble Pub.

McMillen, Margot F. Paris, Tightwad, & Peculiar: Missouri Place Names. (Missouri Heritage Readers Ser.). (Illus.). 96p. (C). 1994. pap. 8.95 (0-8262-0972-6) U of Mo Pr.

McMillen, Marilyn M. & Kaufman, Phillip. Dropout Rates in the United States (1994) 7th ed. (Illus.). 129p. (Orig.). 1997. pap. text 30.00 (0-7881-3886-3) DIANE Pub.

McMillen, Neil R. The Citizens' Council: Organized Resistance to the Second Reconstruction, 1954-64. LC 94-18858. 440p. 1994. pap. text 16.95 (0-252-06441-0) U of Ill Pr.

— Dark Journey: Black Mississippians in the Age of Jim Crow. LC 88-17123. (Illus.). 464p. 1989. pap. text 16.95 (0-252-06156-X) U of Ill Pr.

McMillen, Neil R., ed. Remaking Dixie: The Impact of World War II on the American South. LC 96-33266. 192p. 1997. text 47.50 (0-87805-927-X); pap. text 18.00 (0-87805-928-8) U Pr of Miss.

McMillen, Neil R. & Bolton, Charles C. A Synopsis of American History: Complete Edition. 8th ed. LC 97-1450. 540p. 1997. pap. text 28.25 (1-56663-160-2) I R Dee.

— A Synopsis of American History Vol. 1: Through Reconstruction. 8th ed. 243p. 1997. pap. text 22.25 (1-56663-161-0) I R Dee.

— A Synopsis of American History Vol. 2: Since the Civil War. 8th ed. 339p. 1997. pap. text 22.25 (1-56663-162-9) I R Dee.

McMillen, Pat. The Working Woman's Cookbook & Entertainment Guide. LC 83-3814. 252p. 1983. write for info. (0-672-52708-1) Macmillan.

McMillen, Persis W. Currents of Malice: Mary Towne Esty & Her Family in Salem Witchcraft. (Illus.). 650p. 1990. 35.00 (0-914339-31-1) P E Randall Pub.

McMillen, Rick. Xtreme: Air-Land-Water. 260p. 1998. 39.95 (0-88415-909-4, 5909) Gulf Pub.

***McMillen, Robert D. & Institute of Transportation Engineers Staff.** Statistical Evaluation in Traffic Safety Studies. LC 99-48624. (Illus.). 80p. 1999. pap. 38.00 (0-935403-35-3, IR-097) Inst Trans Eng.

McMillen, S. I. Nenhuma Enfermidade. Orig. Title: None of These Diseases. (POR.). 216p. 1987. pap. 8.95 (0-8297-0964-9) Vida Pubs.

— None of These Diseases: A Famous Doctor's Biblical Prescription for Healthier & Happier Living. 2nd ed. LC 63-13359. (Illus.). 160p. (YA). (gr. 10). 1993. reprint ed. mass mkt. 5.99 (0-8007-8030-2, Spire) Revell.

McMillen, S. I. & Stern, David E. None of These Diseases: The Bible's Health Secrets for the 21st Century. 3rd rev. ed. LC 99-59836. (Illus.). 288p. 2000. pap. 12.99 (0-8007-5719-X) Revell.

McMillen, Sally G. Motherhood in the Old South: Pregnancy, Childbirth, & Infant Rearing. 256p. 1997. pap. 12.95 (0-8071-2166-5) La State U Pr.

— Southern Women: Black & White in the Old South. Eisenstadt, A. S. & Franklin, John H., eds. (American History Ser.). 140p. 1992. pap. text 11.95 (0-88295-881-X) Harlan Davidson.

McMillen, Sheila, jt. ed. see Garrett, George P.

McMillen, Wheeler. Farmer. LC 66-14227. (U. S. A. Survey Ser.). (Illus.). 126p. 1966. 4.95 (0-87107-004-9) Potomac.

— Ohio Farm. LC 96-48321. 220p. 1997. pap. 18.00 (0-8142-0735-9) Ohio St U Pr.

McMillens, Marilyn M., et al. Dropout Rates in the United States (1993) (Illus.). 174p. (Orig.). (C). 1996. pap. text 30.00 (0-7881-2642-3) DIANE Pub.

McMiller, Kathryn. Being a Medical Records Clerk. 224p. (C). 1991. 43.33 (0-89303-807-5, 740504) P-H.

***McMiller, Kathryn.** Being a Medical Records Clerk. 2nd ed. LC 99-38985. (Medical Clerical Ser.). (Illus.). 208p. 1999. pap. text 43.33 (0-13-086493-5) P-H.

McMillian, Ben, ed. Hannibal: The Ultimate Warrior: The Untold Story. LC 94-93928. (Illus.). 164p. 1994. 19.95 (0-9644758-1-2) Peebco Pub.

McMillian, Elizabeth. Beach Houses: From Malibu to Laguna. LC 93-38144. (Illus.). 208p. 1994. 50.00 (0-8478-1802-0, Pub. by Rizzoli Intl) St Martin.

***McMillian, Larry.** Larry McMillan's Option Strategies Course, 3 Video Set. (Illus.). 40p. 1999. 195.00 (1-883272-32-7) Traders Lib.

McMillin, Arnold, ed. Aspects of Modern Russian & Czech Literature: Selected Papers from the Third World Congress for Soviet & East European Studies. 239p. (Orig.). 1989. pap. 22.95 (0-89357-194-6) Slavica.

***McMillin, Arnold, ed.** Reconstructing the Canon: Russian Writing in the 1980s. (Studies in Russian & European Literature: Vol. 3). 248p. 1999. text 65.00 (90-5702-593-0, Harwood Acad Pubs); pap. text 25.00 (90-5702-594-9, Harwood Acad Pubs) Gordon & Breach.

McMillin, Challace J. & Reffner, Corey, eds. Directory of College & University Coaching Education Programs. LC 98-71244. 249p. (C). 1998. pap. text 19.00 (1-885693-14-1) Fit Info Tech.

McMillin, David. Alzheimer's Disease & the Dementias: An Alternative Perspective: Based on the Readings of Edgar Cayce. LC 96-54001. (Edgar Cayce Health Ser.). 96p. 1997. pap. 12.95 (0-87604-380-5, 494) ARE Pr.

— Case Studies in Depression: Based on the Edgar Cayce Health Methods. LC 97-11151. (Edgar Cayce Health Ser.). 152p. (Orig.). 1997. pap. 14.95 (0-87604-385-6, 497) ARE Pr.

— Case Studies in Schizophrenia. LC 97-3237. (Edgar Cayce Health Ser.). 292p. (Orig.). 1997. pap. 14.95 (0-87604-382-1, 494) ARE Pr.

— Principles & Techniques of Nerve Regeneration: Alzheimer's Disease & the Dementias: Based on the Readings of Edgar Cayce. LC 97-4120. (Edgar Cayce Health Ser.). 164p. 1997. pap. 14.95 (0-87604-381-3, 496) ARE Pr.

— The Treatment of Depression: A Holistic Approach. LC 97-8533. (Edgar Cayce Health Ser.). 352p. (Orig.). 1997. pap. 16.95 (0-87604-386-4, 498) ARE Pr.

— The Treatment of Schizophrenia: A Holistic Approach Based on the Readings of Edgar Cayce. LC 97-8463. (Edgar Cayce Health Ser.). 521p. (Orig.). 1997. pap. 16.95 (0-87604-384-8, 493) ARE Pr.

***McMillin, Delorus.** Catching Hell in a Nursing Home. 2000. pap. 10.00 (0-9679662-5-6) Hardbound.

McMillin, J. Michael, ed. see Lawrence, John, Interdisciplinary Symposium on the.

McMillin, Laurence. The Schoolmaker: Sawney Webb & the Bell Buckle Story. LC 72-144336. 218p. reprint ed. pap. 67.60 (0-7837-2065-3, 204234000004) Bks Demand.

McMillin, Scott. The Elizabethan Theatre & "The Book of Sir Thomas More" LC 86-47996. 184p. 1987. text 29.95 (0-8014-2008-3) Cornell U Pr.

McMillin, Scott, ed. Restoration & Eighteenth Century Comedy. (Critical Editions Ser.). (C). 1973. pap. text 18.25 (0-393-09997-0) Norton.

McMillin, Scott, ed. Restoration & Eighteenth-Century Comedy. 2nd ed. LC 95-44942. (Critical Editions Ser.). (C). 1997. pap. text 18.25 (0-393-96334-9) Norton.

McMillin, Scott & MacLean, Sally-Beth. The Queen's Men & Their Plays. LC 97-18017. (Illus.). 272p. (C). 1998. text 59.95 (0-521-59427-8) Cambridge U Pr.

***McMillin, T. S.** Our Preposterous Use of Literature: Emerson & the Nature of Reading. LC 99-6662. 2000. 32.50 (0-252-02538-5) U of Ill Pr.

McMillion, Donna, jt. auth. see Stallings, Betty.

McMillion, Mac. Who'll Sing for Me? LC 87-91267. 122p. (Orig.). (J). 1987. pap. 6.00 (0-9619399-0-7) M McMillion Pub.

McMillion, Scott. Mark of the Grizzly: True Stories of Recent Bear Attacks & the Hard Lessons Learned. LC 98-16427. 249p. 1998. pap. 14.95 (1-56044-636-6) Falcon Pub Inc.

McMillon, Bill. The Archaeology Handbook: A Field Manual & Resource Guide. LC 91-10973. 272p. 1991. pap. 19.95 (0-471-53051-4) Wiley.

— Best Hikes with Children in San Francisco's North Bay. LC 91-45547. (Illus.). 230p. (Orig.). 1992. pap. 14.95 (0-89886-276-0) Mountaineers.

— Camping with Kids in California: The Complete Guide--Where to Go & What to Do for a Fun-Filled, Stress-Free Camping Vacation. LC 95-2141. (Travel with Kids Ser.). (Illus.). 304p. 1996. per. 15.00 (0-7615-0003-0) Prima Pub.

— Cheapskate's Guide to New York City: The Best Hotels, Shopping, Food, Sightseeing, & More. 240p. 1998. pap. 12.00 (0-8065-2050-7) Carol Pub Group.

— Country Roads of Florida. LC 93-42114. (Country Roads Ser.). (Illus.). 140p. 1994. pap. 13.95 (1-56626-039-6, Cntry Rds Pr) NTC Contemp Pub Co.

— Florida with Kids, 1998-1999. LC 97-39847. 320p. 1998. pap. 15.00 (0-7615-0474-5) Prima Pub.

— Seasonal Guide to the Natural Year: Northern California. (Illus.). 360p. 1995. pap. 15.95 (1-55591-157-9) Fulcrum Pub.

— Volunteer Vacations: Short-Term Adventures That Will Benefit You & Others. 7th rev. ed. 440p. 1999. pap. 16.95 (1-55652-363-7, Pub. by Chicago Review) IPG Chicago.

McMillon, Bill & McMillon, Kevin. Best Hikes with Children in & Around Sacramento. LC 93-2010. (Illus.). 230p. 1993. pap. 12.95 (0-89886-278-7) Mountaineers.

— Best Hikes with Children in San Francisco's South Bay. LC 92-18482. (Best Hikes with Children Ser.). (Illus.). 230p. (Orig.). 1992. pap. 12.95 (0-89886-277-9) Mountaineers.

An Asterisk (*) at the beginning of an entry indicates that the title is appearing for the first time.

McMillon, Kevin, jt. auth. see McMillon, Bill.
McMinds, Don. Mastering Osf: Motif Widgets. 2nd ed. (C). 1993. pap. text. write for info. (*0-201-59470-6*) Addison-Wesley.
McMinds, Donald L. Mastering OSF-Motif Widgets. 2nd ed. LC 92-30994. 768p. (C). 1992. pap. text 58.95 (*0-201-63335-3*) Addison-Wesley.
Mcminds, Donald L., jt. auth. see Fernandez, Charles V.
McMinn. Atlas of Human Anatomy, '95. 3rd ed. 1994. 1033.00 (*0-7234-1977-9*) Wolfe Pubng AZ.
— Concise Handbook of Human Anatomy. 192p. (C). 1998. pap. 34.95 (*0-8385-1564-9*, Apple Lange Med) McGraw.
***McMinn.** Supreme Fictions Of John Banvi. 1999. text 69.95 (*0-7190-5397-8*) St Martin.
McMinn. Supreme Fictions of John Banvi. 1999. pap. 29.95 (*0-7190-5698-5*) St Martin.
— Trato Hecho!, Vol. 2. 256p. (C). 1995. pap. text 36.33 (*0-13-459116-X*) P-H.
McMinn, Andrew, jt. auth. see Roberts, Donna.
McMinn, Bill. Une Petite Menagerie. (Orig.). 1997. pap. write for info. (*1-57553-450-9*) Watermrk Pr.
McMinn, Curtis J., ed. see Metallurgical Society of AIME Staff.
McMinn, D. G., jt. ed. see Hill, H. H.
McMinn, Derek, jt. auth. see Villar, Richard N.
McMinn, Don. Entering His Presence: Experiencing the Joy of True Worship. LC 86-70743. 257p. 1986. pap. 9.99 (*0-88270-608-X*) Bridge-Logos.
McMinn, Don, ed. see Elliff, Thomas D.
McMinn, Howard E. An Illustrated Manual of California Shrubs. 1939. 55.00 (*0-520-00847-2*, Pub. by U CA Pr) Cal Prin Full Svc.
McMinn, Howard E. & Maino, Evelyn. An Illustrated Manual of Pacific Coast Trees. 2nd ed. 1937. pap. 16.95 (*0-520-04364-2*, Pub. by U CA Pr) Cal Prin Full Svc.
McMinn, John. Trato Hecho!, Vol. 1. 1995. pap. text, wbk. ed., lab manual ed. 18.00 (*0-13-459173-9*) P-H.
— Trato Hecho!, Vol. 2. 1995. pap. text, wbk. ed., lab manual ed. 17.20 (*0-13-459140-2*) P-H.
McMinn, John, et al. Trato Hecho! Spanish for Real Life.Tr. of Contract Made!. (SPA.). 1995. text 63.67 (*0-13-327974-X*) P-H.
— Trato Hecho! Spanish for Real Life, Vol. 1&2. abr. ed.Tr. of Contract Made!. 1995. pap. text, wbk. ed., lab manual ed. 32.60 (*0-13-447012-5*) P-H.
— Trato Hecho! Vol. 1: Spanish for Real Life, Vol. 1. abr. ed. 256p. (C). 1995. pap. text 37.80 (*0-13-459108-9*) P-H.
***McMinn, John T.** Trato Hecho! Spanish for Real Life. 2nd ed. LC 99-40603. (SPA., Illus.). 494p. 1999. 61.00 (*0-13-021515-5*) P-H.
McMinn, Joseph. Jonathan Swift: A Literary Life. LC 90-42058. 210p. 1991. text 39.95 (*0-312-05275-8*) St Martin.
— Jonathan's Travels: Swift & Ireland. LC 94-3781. 1994. text 45.00 (*0-312-12354-X*) St Martin.
McMinn, Joseph, ed. Internationalism of Irish Literature & Drama. 300p. (C). 1991. text 67.50 (*0-389-20962-7*) B&N Imports.
***McMinn, Lisa G.** Growing Strong Daughters. LC 00-37891. 256p. (C). (gr. 13 up). 2000. pap. 14.99 (*0-8010-6324-8*) Baker Bks.
McMinn, M. Tratando con Deseo Incontrolado.Tr. of Dealing with Desires You Cannot Control. (SPA.). 225p. 1995. pap. write for info. (*0-614-27147-9*) Editorial Unilit.
— Tratando con Deseo Incontrolado - Dealing with Desires You Cannot Control. (SPA.). 225p. 1995. write for info. (*0-614-24405-6*) Editorial Unilit.
— Tratando con los Deseos Que Usted No Puede Controlar. (Serie Realidades - Realities Ser.).Tr. of Dealing with Desires You Cannot Control. (SPA.). 28p. pap. 1.99 (*1-56063-999-7*, 498139) Editorial Unilit.
McMinn, Mark. Cognitive Therapy. (Resources for Christian Counseling Ser.: Vol. 27). 18.99 (*0-8499-0876-0*) Word Pub.
McMinn, Mark M. Psychology, Theology, & Spirituality in Christian Counseling. LC 96-12604. (AACC Counseling Library Prof. Ser.). 327p. 1996. 24.99 (*0-8423-5252-X*) Tyndale Hse.
McMinn, Mark R. Dealing with Desires You Can't Control. 1991. pap. text 2.50 (*0-89109-318-4*) NavPress.
— The Jekyll/Hyde Syndrome: Controlling Inner Conflict Through Authentic Living. 116p. 1996. pap. 13.95 (*0-913342-79-3*) Barclay Pr.
— Making the Best of Stress: How Life's Hassles Can Form the Fruit of the Spirit. LC 95-49667. 182p. (Orig.). 1996. pap. 10.99 (*0-8308-1981-9*) InterVarsity.
McMinn, Mark R. & Foster, James D. Christians in the Crossfire: Guarding Your Mind Against Manipulation & Self-deception. LC 90-82741. 180p. 1990. pap. 9.95 (*0-913342-68-8*) Barclay Pr.
***McMinn, Merlin.** When the Dreamwalker Dances. 1998. pap. write for info. (*1-57553-913-6*) Watermrk Pr.
McMinn, R., ed. see Struns, William.
McMinn, R. M. & Hobdell, M. H. The Functional Anatomy of the Digestive System. (Illus.). 282p. 1974. pap. text 45.00 (*0-272-00123-6*) St Mut.
— Functional Anatomy of the Digestive System. 1974. pap. 16.95 (*0-8464-0434-6*) Beekman Pubs.
McMinn, R. M. H., ed. Last's Anatomy: Regional & Applied. 9th ed. LC 94-5560. (Illus.). 1994. text 66.00 (*0-443-04662-X*) Church.
McMinn, Robert M. Functional & Clinical Anatomy. 1995. 38.00 (*0-7234-0967-6*) Mosby Inc.
McMinn, Robert M., et al. A Colour Atlas of Head & Neck Anatomy. 2nd ed. LC 93-43540. (Illus.). 256p. (C). (gr. 13). 1994. reprint ed. 53.00 (*0-7234-1994-9*, Pub. by Wolfe Pub) Mosby Inc.
— The Human Skeleton. (C). (gr. 13). 1986. 41.95 (*0-8151-5795-9*, 09417) Mosby Inc.
— Picture Tests in Anatomy. (Illus.). 128p. (C). (gr. 13). 1986. 15.95 (*0-8151-5836-X*, 09146) Mosby Inc.
McMinn, Robert M., jt. auth. see Hutchings.
McMinn, Russ, ed. see Struns, William.
McMinn, Suzanne. The Billionaire & the Bassinet: Bundles of Joy. (Romance Ser.: No. 1384). 1999. mass mkt. 3.50 incl. 3.5 hd (*0-373-19384-X*, 1-19384-6) Silhouette.
— The Bride, the Trucker & the Great Escape. (Romance Ser.: No. 1274). 1998. per. 3.25 (*0-373-19274-6*, 1-19274-9) Silhouette.
— Escapade Amoureuse. (Horizon Ser.: No. 476). (FRE.). 1998. pap. 3.50 (*0-373-39476-4*, 1-39476-6) Harlequin Bks.
***McMinn, Suzanne.** Every Breath You Take, Vol. 27. (Zebra Bouquet Ser.). 1999. mass mkt. 3.99 (*0-8217-6441-1*) Kensgtn Pub Corp.
— It Only Takes a Moment, Vol. 42. (Zebra Bouquet Ser.). 2000. mass mkt. 3.99 (*0-8217-6578-7*, Zebra Kensgtn) Kensgtn Pub Corp.
McMinn, Suzanne. Make Room for Mommy. 1996. per. 3.25 (*0-373-19191-X*, 1-19191-5) Silhouette.
McMinn, Winston G. Nationalism & Federalism in Australia. 324p. 1995. pap. text 35.00 (*0-19-553667-3*) OUP.
McMlelland, David C. Psychoanalysis & Religious Mysticism. (C). 1959. pap. 4.00 (*0-87574-104-5*) Pendle Hill.
McMonagle, Barney. No Go: A Photographic Record of Free Derry. Kerr, Adrein, ed. LC 97-212807. (Illus.). 120p. 1997. pap. 21.95 (*0-946451-41-9*, Pub. by Guildhall Pr) Irish Bks Media.
McMonagle, D. Science Basic Facts. (Collins Gem Ser.). 1992. pap. 8.00 (*0-00-470304-9*) Collins.
McMonagle, Gary R. Instant Money: How to Use the Hidden Power of Your Mind to Attract Incredible Wealth. Darbey, Barbara R., ed. 197p. 1990. 19.95 (*0-9626363-0-4*) RMA Pub OH.
McMoneagle, Joe. Mind Trek: Exploring Consciousness, Time & Space Through Remote Viewing. (Illus.). 264p. 1993. pap. 12.95 (*1-878901-72-9*) Hampton Roads Pub Co.
***McMoneagle, Joseph.** Remote Viewing Secrets: A Handbook. 320p. 2000. pap. 14.95 (*1-57174-159-3*) Hampton Roads Pub Co.
McMoneagle, Joseph. The Ultimate Time Machine: A Remote Viewer's Perception of Time & Predictions for the New Millennium. LC 98-71582. 280p. 1998. pap. 12.95 (*1-57174-102-X*) Hampton Roads Pub Co.
McMonnies, Alistair & McSporran, W. S. Developing Object Oriented Data Structures Using C++ LC 94-42779. (International Software Engineering Ser.). 1995. write for info. (*0-07-707982-5*) McGraw.
***McMonus, Fran & Rickard, Wendy, eds.** Cooking Fresh from the Bay Area: The Bay Area's Best Recipes for Eating Local, Organic Produce at Its Seasonal Best. 192p. 2000. pap. 17.95 (*0-9673670-0-X*) Eating Fresh Pubns.
McMordie, W., jt. auth. see Seidl, Jennifer.
McMorland, D. E. Vendor & Purchaser. 163p. 1979. pap. 45.00 (*0-409-64522-2*, NZ, MICHIE) LEXIS Pub.
McMorland, D. E., jt. auth. see Hinde, G. E.
McMorran, Jennifer. Calgary: Ulysses Travel Guide. 2nd ed. (Ulysses Travel Guide Ser.). (Illus.). 192p. 1998. pap. 12.95 (*2-89464-168-0*) Ulysses Travel.
— The Islands of the Bahamas: Ulysses Travel Guide. (Ulysses Travel Guide Ser.). (Illus.). 288p. 1998. pap. 17.95 (*2-89464-123-0*) Ulysses Travel.
***McMorran, Jennifer.** Toronto. 2nd ed. (Ulysses Travel Guide Ser.). 1999. pap. text 13.95 (*2-89464-121-4*) Ulysses Travel.
McMorries, Edward Y. History of the First Regiment: Alabama Volunteer Infantry C.S.A. (Illus.). 142p. 1996. reprint ed. lib. bdg. 29.00 (*0-8328-5184-1*) Higginson Bk Co.
— History of the First Regiment Alabama Volunteer Infantry, C.S.A. LC 79-126243. (Select Bibliographies Reprint Ser.). 1977. reprint ed. 15.95 (*0-8369-5470-X*) Ayer.
McMorris, Bill & McMorris, Jo. Camp Cooking: A Backpacker's Pocket Guide. (Illus.). 112p. 1989. pap. 8.95 (*1-55821-023-7*) Lyons Pr.
McMorris, F. R., jt. auth. see McKee, T. A.
McMorris, Jo, jt. auth. see McMorris, Bill.
McMorris, Mark. The Black Reeds: Poems. LC 96-19306. (Contemporary Poetry Ser.). 1996. pap. 14.95 (*0-8203-1873-6*) U of Ga Pr.
— Moth-Wings: Poems. deluxe ed. (Burning Deck Poetry Chapbooks Ser.). 40p. 1996. pap. 20.00 (*1-886224-11-0*) Burning Deck.
— Palinurus Suite. 47p. (Orig.). 1992. pap. 5.00 (*0-945926-37-5*) Paradigm RI.
— Palinurus Suite. deluxe ed. (Orig.). 1992. pap. 12.00 (*0-945926-38-3*) Paradigm RI.
McMorris, Neville. The Natures of Science. LC 87-46376. 264p. 1989. 38.50 (*0-8386-3321-8*) Fairleigh Dickinson.
McMorris, Penny. The Art Quilt. LC 95-51664. (Illus.). 136p. (Orig.). 1996. pap. 24.95 (*0-8442-2649-1*, Quilt Dgst Pr) NTC Contemp Pub Co.
McMorris, Penny, intro. Nancy Crow: Work in Transition. LC 92-12986. 32p. 1992. pap. 12.95 (*0-89145-995-2*, 3331, Am Quilters Soc) Collector Bks.
McMorris, Penny & Kile, Michael M. The Art Quilt. LC 95-51664. (Illus.). 136p. (Orig.). 1986. pap. 24.95 (*0-913327-07-7*, Quilt Dgst Pr) NTC Contemp Pub Co.
McMorrow, Annalisa. Amazing Animals! Reading, Writing, & Speaking about Animals. (Super-Duper Science Ser.). (Illus.). 80p. (J). (gr. 1-3). 1998. pap. 9.95 (*1-57612-045-7*, MM2059) Monday Morning Bks.
— Bats: A Science Discovery Book. (Illus.). 48p. (J). (gr. 3-6). 1999. pap. 7.95 (*1-57612-076-7*, MM2090) Monday Morning Bks.
— Daffy-down-Dilly. (Illus.). 80p. (Orig.). (J). (ps-k). 1997. pap. 9.95 (*1-57612-009-0*, MM2037) Monday Morning Bks.
***McMorrow, Annalisa.** A Diller, a Dollar. (Illus.). (J). 1999. pap. 9.95 (*1-57612-109-7*) Monday Morning Bks.
McMorrow, Annalisa. Dinosaurs. (Illus.). 48p. (J). (gr. 1-3). 1998. pap. 7.95 (*1-57612-055-4*, MM2069) Monday Morning Bks.
***McMorrow, Annalisa.** Exciting Earth. (Illus.). (J). 1999. pap. 9.95 (*1-57612-111-9*) Monday Morning Bks.
— Leapin' Lizards & Other Reptiles. (Illus.). (J). 1999. pap. 9.95 (*1-57612-110-0*) Monday Morning Bks.
McMorrow, Annalisa. Mars. (Illus.). 48p. (J). (gr. 1-3). 1998. pap. 7.95 (*1-57612-058-9*, MM2072) Monday Morning Bks.
— Marsupials. (Illus.). (J). (gr. 1-3). 1998. pap. 7.95 (*1-57612-056-2*, MM2070) Monday Morning Bks.
***McMorrow, Annalisa.** Marvelous Money. (Illus.). (J). 1999. pap. 9.95 (*1-57612-113-5*) Monday Morning Bks.
McMorrow, Annalisa. Peculiar Plants! Readings, Writing, & Speaking about Plants. (Super-Duper Science Ser.). (Illus.). 80p. (J). (gr. 1-3). 1998. pap. 9.95 (*1-57612-044-9*, MM2058) Monday Morning Bks.
— Pussycat, Pussycat. (Illus.). 80p. (J). (ps-k). 1997. pap. 9.95 (*1-57612-008-2*, MM2036) Monday Morning Bks.
— Rain Forest: A Science Discovery Book. 48p. (J). (gr. 3-6). 1999. pap. 7.95 (*1-57612-079-1*, MM2093) Monday Morning Bks.
— Rain, Rain Go Away. (Illus.). 80p. (Orig.). (J). (ps-k). 1997. pap. 9.95 (*1-57612-010-4*, MM2038) Monday Morning Bks.
***McMorrow, Annalisa.** Snips & Snails. (Illus.). (J). 1999. pap. 9.95 (*1-57612-106-2*) Monday Morning Bks.
— Sticks & Stones. (Illus.). (J). 1999. pap. 9.95 (*1-57612-107-0*) Monday Morning Bks.
McMorrow, Annalisa. Storms. (Illus.). 48p. (J). (gr. 1-3). 1998. pap. 7.95 (*1-57612-057-0*, MM2071) Monday Morning Bks.
***McMorrow, Annalisa.** Terrific Transportation. (Illus.). (J). 1999. pap. 9.95 (*1-57612-112-7*) Monday Morning Bks.
McMorrow, Annalisa. Twinkle, Twinkle. (Super-Duper Science Ser.). (Illus.). 80p. (Orig.). (J). (ps-k). 1996. pap. 9.95 (*1-878279-87-4*, MM2016) Monday Morning Bks.
— Wacky Weather! Reading, Writing, & Speaking about Weather. (Super-Duper Science Ser.). (Illus.). 80p. (J). (gr. 1-3). 1998. pap. 9.95 (*1-57612-043-0*, MM2057) Monday Morning Bks.
— Whales. (Illus.). 48p. (J). (gr. 3-6). 1999. pap. 7.95 (*1-57612-077-5*, No. MM2091) Monday Morning Bks.
***McMorrow, Annalisa.** Wheels on the Bus. (Illus.). (J). 1999. pap. 9.95 (*1-57612-108-9*) Monday Morning Bks.
McMorrow, Annalisa, jt. auth. see Claycomb, Patty.
McMorrow, Catherine. Gold Fever! LC 95-24111. (Step into Reading Ser.: A Step 4 Book). (Illus.). (J). (ps-3). 1996. pap. 3.99 (*0-679-86432-6*) Random.
— Gold Fever! LC 95-24111. (Step into Reading Ser.: A Step 4 Book). (Illus.). (J). (ps-3). 1996. lib. bdg. 11.99 (*0-679-96432-0*) Random.
— Gold Fever! LC 95-24111. (Step into Reading Ser.: A Step 4 Book). (J). (gr. 2-4). 1996. 9.19 (*0-606-09337-0*, Pub. by Turtleback) Demco.
— The Jellybean Principal. LC 93-26537. (Step into Reading Ser.: A Step 3 Book). (Illus.). 48p. (J). (gr. 1-3). 1994. pap. 3.99 (*0-679-84743-X*, Pub. by Random Bks Yng Read) Random.
McMorrow, Catherine. The Jellybean Principal. (Step into Reading Ser.: A Step 3 Book). (J). (gr. 2-3). 1994. 9.19 (*0-606-07016-8*, Pub. by Turtleback) Demco.
McMorrow, Catherine. Quake. 2000. lib. bdg. 11.99 (*0-679-96945-4*) Random.
***McMorrow, Catherine.** Quake. 1999. pap. 3.99 (*0-679-86945-X*, Pub. by Random Bks Yng Read) Random.
McMorrow, Catherine. Stonehenge. (J). 1999. write for info. (*0-679-87499-2*) Random Bks Yng Read.
McMorrow, Debra B. & Moss, Gregory R. The TBI Annual Research Index, Vol. 1. Arokiasamy, Charles-Maria V., ed. 280p. 1990. per. 41.95 (*1-878205-39-0*) St Lucie Pr.
McMorrow, Edward J. The Educated Piano: The Structural Relationships & Specifications Essential for Fine Piano Tone. Hatfield, Phyllis, ed. (Illus.). 160p. 1989. 99.95 (*0-929738-00-4*) Light Hammer.
McMorrow, George J., tr. see Simon, Yves R.
McMorrow, Justin, et al. The Corporate University: Learning Tools for Success. Elliott, Susan, ed. (Illus.). 78p. 1998. spiral bd. 495.00 (*1-928593-02-X*) Am Prodtv Qual.
McMorrow, Martin & Fralish, Kathleen. Innovations in Head Injury Rehabilitation. 1500p. 1988. text 135.00 (*1-887515-03-8*) AHAB Press.
McMorrow, Martin J., jt. auth. see Foxx, Richard M.
McMorrow, Mary E. & Malarkey, Louise. Laboratory & Diagnostic Tests: A Pocket Guide. Eoyang, Thomas, ed. LC 97-41310. (Illus.). 480p. 1997. pap. text 19.95 (*0-7216-7303-1*, W B Saunders Co) Harcrt Hlth Sci Grp.
McMorrow, Mary E., jt. auth. see Malarkey, Louise M.
***McMorrow, Scott.** Math Start-Ups. (Illus.). (J). 1999. pap. 11.95 (*1-57612-114-3*) Monday Morning Bks.
McMorrow, Scott. Ten Minute Real World Math. (Ten-Minute Ser.). (Illus.). 96p. (Orig.). (J). (gr. 3-6). 1997. pap. 11.95 (*1-57612-021-X*, MM2041) Monday Morning Bks.
***McMorrow, Scott.** Web Start-Ups. (Illus.). (J). 1999. pap. 11.95 (*1-57612-115-1*) Monday Morning Bks.
McMorrow, Scott, jt. auth. see Suid, Murray.
McMullan, Gordon. The Politics of Unease in the Plays of John Fletcher. LC 93-28554. (Massachusetts Studies in Early Modern Culture). 352p. 1994. lib. bdg. 40.00 (*0-87023-892-2*) U of Mass Pr.
— Renaissance Configurations: Voices/Bodies/Spaces, 1580-1690 LC 97-49889. xxiii, 263p. 1998. write for info. (*0-333-67665-3*, Pub. by Macmillan) St Martin.
McMullan, Helene, jt. auth. see McMullan, Jim.
McMullan, James. High-Focus Drawing: A Revolutionary Approach to Drawing the Figure. (Illus.). 224p. 1994. 35.00 (*0-87951-536-8*, Pub. by Overlook Pr) Penguin Putnam.
— High-Focus Drawing: A Revolutionary Approach to Drawing the Figure. (Illus.). 160p. 1995. pap. 19.95 (*0-87951-604-6*, Pub. by Overlook Pr) Penguin Putnam.
McMullan, Jim & Levin, Michael. Instant Zen: A Do-It-Yourself Guide to Awareness & Discovery. 112p. 1994. spiral bd. 8.95 (*0-8048-3016-9*) Tuttle Pubng.
***McMullan, Jim & McMullan, Helene.** Happily Ever After: The Wit & Wisdom of Marriage. LC 97-45374. (Illus.). 112p. 1998. 16.95 (*1-883318-20-3*) Angel City Pr.
McMullan, Joan, tr. see Monition, Lucien, et al.
McMullan, John, jt. auth. see Gatski, Barbara.
McMullan, John, ed. see Guindon, Hubert.
McMullan, John T. Physical Techniques in Medicine, 2 vols., 1. LC 76-30281. (Illus.). reprint ed. pap. 85.30 (*0-608-15573-X*, 2029636) Bks Demand.
— Physical Techniques in Medicine, 2 vols., 2. LC 76-30281. (Illus.). reprint ed. pap. 43.70 (*0-608-15574-8*) Bks Demand.
McMullan, John T., et al. Energy Resources & Supply. LC 75-6973. (Illus.). 520p. reprint ed. pap. 161.20 (*0-608-18838-7*, 203048800069) Bks Demand.
McMullan, K. H. Class Trip to the Cave of Doom. LC 98-35524. (Dragon Slayers' Academy Ser.: No. 3). (Illus.). 96p. (J). (gr. 2-5). 1998. mass mkt. 3.99 (*0-448-41594-1*, G & D) Peng Put Young Read.
— Countdown to the Year 1000, Vol. 8. LC 99-54541. (Dragon Slayers' Academy Ser.: No. 8). (Illus.). 96p. (J). (gr. 2-5). 1999. pap. 3.99 (*0-448-42033-3*, G & D) Peng Put Young Read.
***McMullan, K. H.** Dragon Slayers' Academy Boxed Set: The New Kid at School; Revenge of the Dragon Lady. (Dragon Slayers' Academy Ser.: No. 1&2). (Illus.). (J). (gr. 2-5). 2000. boxed set 6.99 (*0-448-42289-1*, Planet Dexter) Peng Put Young Read.
— Dragon Slayers' Academy Boxed Set II: Class Trip to the Cave of Doom; A Wedding for Wiglaf? (Dragon Slayers' Academy Ser.: No. 3-4). (Illus.). (J). (gr. 2-5). 2000. boxed set 6.99 (*0-448-42290-5*, Planet Dexter) Peng Put Young Read.
McMullan, K. H. Knight for a Day. LC 99-17124. (Dragon Slayers' Academy Ser.: No. 5). (Illus.). 96p. (J). (gr. 2-5). 1999. 3.99 (*0-448-41974-2*, G & D) Peng Put Young Read.
— Knight for a Day, 1 vol., Vol. 5. LC 99-17124. (Dragon Slayers' Academy Ser.: No. 5). (Illus.). (J). (gr. 2-5). 1999. 13.89 (*0-448-42045-7*) Putnam Pub Group.
— The New Kid at School. LC 97-15520. (Dragon Slayers' Academy Ser.: No. 1). (Illus.). 92p. (J). (gr. 2-5). 1997. pap. 3.95 (*0-448-41592-5*, G & D); lib. bdg. 13.89 (*0-448-41727-8*, G & D) Peng Put Young Read.
— The New Kid at School, 1. (Dragon Slayers' Academy Ser.: No. 1). (Illus.). (J). (gr. 2-5). 1997. 9.05 (*0-606-12921-9*, Pub. by Turtleback) Demco.
— Revenge of the Dragon Lady. LC 97-31171. (Dragon Slayers' Academy Ser.: No. 2). (Illus.). 96p. (J). (gr. 2-5). 1997. 11.99 (*0-448-41593-3*, G & D); 13.89 (*0-448-41728-6*, G & D) Peng Put Young Read.
— Revenge of the Dragon Lady, 2. (Dragon Slayers' Academy Ser.). (Illus.). (J). (gr. 2-5). 1997. 9.05 (*0-606-12920-0*, Pub. by Turtleback) Demco.
— Sir Lancelot, Where Are You? LC 99-20898. (Dragon Slayers' Academy Ser.: No. 6). (Illus.). 96p. (J). (gr. 2-5). 1999. pap. text 3.99 (*0-448-41979-3*, G & D) Peng Put Young Read.
— Sir Lancelot, Where Are You?, 1 vol., Vol. 6. LC 99-20898. (Dragon Slayers' Academy Ser.: No. 6). (Illus.). (J). (gr. 2-5). 1999. 13.89 (*0-448-42046-5*) Putnam Pub Group.
— A Wedding for Wiglaf? LC 98-41532. (Dragon Slayers' Academy Ser.: No. 4). (Illus.). 96p. (J). (gr. 2-5). 1998. lib. bdg. 13.89 (*0-448-41872-X*, G & D); mass mkt. 3.99 (*0-448-41595-X*, G & D) Peng Put Young Read.
— Wheel of Misfortune, Vol. 7. LC 99-51844. (Dragon Slayers' Academy Ser.: No. 7). (Illus.). 96p. (J). (gr. 2-5). 1999. pap. 3.99 (*0-448-42031-7*, G & D) Peng Put Young Read.
McMullan, Kate. Dinosaur Hunters. LC 88-30742. (Step into Reading Ser.: A Step 4 Book). (Illus.). 48p. (J). (ps-3). 1989. pap. 3.99 (*0-394-81150-X*, Pub. by Random Bks Yng Read) Random.
— Dinosaur Hunters. (Step into Reading Ser.: A Step 4 Book). (J). (gr. 2-4). 1989. 9.19 (*0-606-04200-8*, Pub. by Turtleback) Demco.
— Fluffy Goes to School. LC 97-13843. (Hello Reader! Ser.). (Illus.). 40p. (J). (gr. 1-3). 1997. pap. 3.99 (*0-590-37213-0*) Scholastic Inc.
Mcmullan, Kate. Fluffy Meets the Dinosaurs. LC 98-28798. (Hello Reader! Ser.). (Illus.). 40p. (J). (gr. 1-3). 2000. mass mkt. 3.99 (*0-590-52310-4*) Scholastic Inc.
***McMullan, Kate.** Fluffy Meets the Dinosaurs. (Hello, Reader! Ser.). (Illus.). (J). 2000. 9.44 (*0-606-18545-3*) Turtleback.
— Fluffy Meets the Groundhog. LC 00-35812. (Hello Reader! Ser.). (Illus.). (J). 2001. write for info. (*0-439-20672-3*) Scholastic Inc.
— Fluffy Meets the Tooth Fairy. LC 99-27157. (Hello Reader! Ser.). (Illus.). (J). 2000. pap. 3.99 (*0-439-12918-4*) Scholastic Inc.
— Fluffy Saves Christmas. LC 98-24127. (Hello Reader! Ser.). (Illus.). 40p. (J). (gr. 1-3). 1999. mass mkt. 3.99 (*0-590-52308-2*, Pub. by Scholastic Inc) Penguin Putnam.

*McMullan, Kate. Fluffy Saves Christmas. (Hello, Reader! Ser.). (Illus.). (J). 2000. 9.44 (0-606-18546-1) Turtleback.

Mcmullan, Kate. Fluffy's Happy Halloween. LC 98-8379. (Hello Reader! Ser.). (Illus.). 40p. (J). (gr. 1-3). 2000. 3.99 (0-590-51222-6) Scholastic Inc.

McMullan, Kate. Fluffy's 100th Day of School. LC 98-19109. (Hello Reader! Ser.). (Illus.). 40p. (J). (gr. 1-3). 2000. 3.99 (0-590-52309-0) Scholastic Inc.

*McMullan, Kate. Fluffy's School Bus Adventure. LC 00-35782. (Hello Reader! Ser.). (Illus.). (J). 2000. pap. write for info. (0-439-20671-5) Scholastic Inc.

McMullan, Kate. Fluffy's Silly Summer. LC 97-45006. (Hello Reader! Ser.). (Illus.). 40p. (J). (gr. 1-3). 2000. 3.99 (0-590-03269-0) Scholastic Inc.

*McMullan, Kate. Fluffy's Silly Summer. (Hello, Reader! Ser.). (Illus.). (J). 2000. 9.44 (0-606-18873-8) Turtleback.

McMullan, Kate. Fluffy's Spring Break. LC 97-24001. (Hello Reader! Ser.). (Illus.). (J). 1999. 3.99 (0-590-37217-3) Scholastic Inc.

*McMullan, Kate. Fluffy's Thanksgiving. LC 97-17948. (Hello Reader! Ser.). (Illus.). 40p. (J). (gr. 1-3). 2000. pap. 3.99 (0-590-37215-7) Scholastic Inc.

McMullan, Kate. Hey, Pipsqueak! LC 95-76377. (Michael di Capua Bks.). (Illus.). 32p. (J). (ps up). 1995. 14.95 (0-06-205100-8) HarpC Child Bks.

— If You Were My Bunny. (J). 1996. pap. 4.95 (0-590-73591-8) Scholastic Inc.

— If You Were My Bunny. LC 95-9082. (Story Corner Ser.). (Illus.). 24p. (J). (ps). 1996. 6.95 (0-590-52749-5, Cartwheel) Scholastic Inc.

— If You Were My Bunny: Board Book. LC 95-9082. (Illus.). 26p. (J). (ps). 1998. reprint ed. bds. 6.99 (0-590-34126-X) Scholastic Inc.

— The Mummy's Gold. LC 95-46794. (Eek! Stories to Make You Shriek Ser.). (Illus.). 48p. (J). (gr. 1-3). 1996. pap. 3.95 (0-448-41310-8, G & D); lib. bdg. 13.99 (0-448-41345-0, G & D) Peng Put Young Read.

Mcmullan, Kate. The Mummy's Gold. (Eek! Stories to Make You Shriek Ser.). 1996. 9.15 (0-606-10884-X, Pub. by Turtleback) Demco.

McMullan, Kate. No No, Jo! LC 96-34738. (Illus.). 20p. (J). (ps-k). 1998. 9.95 (0-694-00904-0) HarpC Child Bks.

— Noel the First. LC 96-85606. (Michael di Capua Bks.). (Illus.). 32p. (J). (ps up). 1996. 14.95 (0-06-205142-3) HarpC Child Bks.

— Nutcracker Noel. LC 93-77115. (Michael di Capua Bks.). (Illus.). 32p. (J). (ps up). 1996. pap. 5.95 (0-06-205910-6, HarpTrophy) HarpC Child Bks.

— Nutcracker Noel. LC 93-77115. 1993. 11.15 (0-606-10271-X, Pub. by Turtleback) Demco.

*McMullan, Kate. Papa's Song. LC 99-34556. (Illus.). 32p. (J). (ps-3). 2000. 15.00 (0-374-35732-3) FS&G.

McMullan, Kate. The Story of Harriet Tubman. 112p. (J). 1994. pap. 3.50 (0-440-91003-X) Dell.

Mcmullan, Kate. Story of Harriet Tubman: Conductor of the Underground Railroad. 1991. 9.09 (0-606-04815-4, Pub. by Turtleback) Demco.

McMullan, Kate & Smith, Mavis. Fluffy & the Fire Fighters. LC 99-24664. (Hello Reader! Ser.). (J). 1999. pap. 10.01 (0-439-12917-6) Scholastic Inc.

*McMullan, Kate H. Fluffy's Valentine's Day. LC 97-15465. 40p. (gr. 1-3). 2000. pap. 3.99 (0-590-37216-5) Scholastic Inc.

McMullan, Kate H. Harriet Tubman No. 19: Yearling Biography. 112p. (Orig.). (J). (gr. k-6). 1990. pap. 4.50 (0-440-40400-2, Yearling) BDD Bks Young Read.

*McMullan, Patrick, photos by. Men's Show: Photography Patrick McMullan. (Illus.). 2000. 65.00 (3-908163-29-3, Pub. by Edit Stemmle) Abbeville Pr.

McMullan, R. Environmental Science in Building. 2nd ed. (Macmillan Building & Surveying Ser.). (Illus.). 283p. (C). 1990. text 80.00 (0-333-49116-5); pap. text 29.00 (0-333-49117-3) Scholium Intl.

McMullan, Randall. Dictionary of Building. 256p. 1991. 59.50 (0-87683-601-5) GP Courseware.

— Illustrated Supercalc. (Illus.). 48p. (Orig.). 1990. pap. 29.95 (0-8464-4326-0) Beekman Pubs.

— Illustrated Wordstar. (Illus.). 32p. (Orig.). 1988. pap. 32.95 (0-8464-4328-7) Beekman Pubs.

*McMullen. Morot Boating: A Motor Boat & Yachting Book. (Illus.). 92p. 2000. pap. 16.95 (0-906754-89-5, Pub. by Fernhurst Bks) Motorbooks Intl.

McMullen, Ann & Handsman, Russell G., eds. A Key into the Language of Woodsplint Baskets. LC 86-70023. (Illus.). 196p. 1987. pap. 20.00 (0-936322-04-7) Inst Amer Indian.

McMullen, Ann & Kopec, Diane, eds. An Island in Time: Three Thousand Years of Cultural Exchange on Mount Desert Island. (Robert Abbe Museum Bulletin Ser.: No. XII). 42p. 1994. reprint ed. pap. write for info. (1-885410-01-8) R Abbe Museum.

McMullen, B. Starr. Profits & the Cost of Capital to the U. S. Trunk Airline Industry under CAB Regulation. LC 92-38639. (Government & the Economy Ser.). 128p. 1993. text 10.00 (0-8153-1230-X) Garland.

McMullen, B. Starr, ed. Research in Transportation Economics, Vol. 4. 170p. 1996. 78.50 (1-55938-915-X) Jai Pr.

— Research in Transportation Economics, Vol. 5. Date not set. 78.50 (0-7623-0223-2) Jai Pr.

McMullen, B. Starr & Daughety, Andrew F., eds. Research in Transportation Economics, Vol. 3. 176p. 1994. 78.50 (0-89232-691-3) Jai Pr.

McMullen, B. Starr & Keeler, Theodore E., eds. Research in Transportation Economics, Vol. 1. 235p. 1983. 78.50 (0-89232-272-1) Jai Pr.

McMullen, B. Starr, ed. see Keeler, Theodore E.

McMullen, Bruce, jt. auth. see Morgan, Trevor.

McMullen, Charles W. Real Estate Investments: A Step-by-Step Guide. LC 80-20704. (Real Estate For Professional Practitioners Ser.). 192p. reprint ed. pap. 59.60 (0-608-14746-X, 202314300031) Bks Demand.

— Tax-Deferred Exchanges of Real Estate Investments. LC 81-3041. (Real Estate For Professional Practitioners Ser.). 100p. 1981. reprint ed. pap. 31.00 (0-7837-3456-5, 205778200008) Bks Demand.

McMullen, Clarence O. Religious Beliefs & Practices of the Sikhs in Rural Punjab. (C). 1989. 18.50 (0-945921-09-8) S Asia.

*McMullen, Conley K. Flowering Plants of the Galapagos. LC 99-31321. (Illus.). 1999. 59.95 (0-8014-3710-5); pap. 29.95 (0-8014-8621-1) Cornell U Pr.

McMullen, Curtis T. Complex Dynamics & Renormalization. LC 94-29390. (Annals of Mathematics Studies: 135). 214p. 1995. text 59.50 (0-691-02982-2, Pub. by Princeton U Pr); pap. text 24.95 (0-691-02981-4, Pub. by Princeton U Pr) Cal Prin Full Svc.

— Renormalization & 3-Manifolds Which Fiber over the Circle. LC 96-19081. (Annals of Mathematics Studies: Vol. 142). 253p. 1996. text 55.00 (0-691-01154-0, Pub. by Princeton U Pr) Cal Prin Full Svc.

McMullen, David. Atlantis: The Missing Continent. LC 77-22138. 1992. pap. 4.95 (0-8114-6850-X) Raintree Steck-V.

— Mystery in Peru: The Lines of Nazca. (Great Unsolved Mysteries Ser.). 1997. pap. 4.95 (0-8114-6861-5) Raintree Steck-V.

*McMullen, Doug, Jr. Cracking the GRE Literature. 3rd ed. 208p. 2000. pap. 18.00 (0-375-75617-5, Pub. by PRP NY) Random.

McMullen, Doug. Cracking the GRE Literature in English. 2nd ed. 1997. pap. 18.00 (0-679-78407-1) Random.

McMullen, Emerson T. William Harvey & the Use of Purpose in the Scientific Revolution: Cosmos by Chance or Universe by Design? LC 97-31966. 280p. (C). 1997. 57.00 (0-7618-0957-0); pap. 36.50 (0-7618-0958-9) U Pr of Amer.

McMullen, George. Born Many Times. LC 99-71622. (Illus.). 224p. 1999. pap. 12.95 (1-57174-131-3) Hampton Roads Pub Co.

— One White Crow. 168p. 1995. pap. 8.95 (1-57174-007-4) Hampton Roads Pub Co.

— Red Snake: A 17th Century Huron Speaks. 152p. 1993. pap. 9.95 (1-878901-58-3) Hampton Roads Pub Co.

— Running Bear: Grandson of Red Snake. LC 97-112155. 168p. (Orig.). 1996. pap. 10.95 (1-57174-037-6) Hampton Roads Pub Co.

— Two Faces: Walking in Two Worlds. LC 98-102850. 232p. (Orig.). 1997. pap. 11.95 (1-57174-071-6) Hampton Roads Pub Co.

McMullen, Glenn L., ed. The Civil War Letters of Dr. Harvey Black: A Surgeon with Stonewall. LC 95-223100. (Army of Northern Virginia Ser.: Vol. 3). 249p. 1995. 30.00 (0-935523-45-6) Butternut & Blue.

*McMullen, Haynes. American Libraries Before 1876, Vol. 6. LC 99-43164. (Beta Phi Mu Monograph). 200p. 2000. 62.50 (0-313-31277-X) Greenwood.

McMullen, I. J., jt. ed. see Kornicki, Peter F.

McMullen, James P. Cry of the Panther: Quest of a Species. LC 84-16684. (Illus.). 416p. 1984. pap. 12.95 (1-56164-118-9) Pineapple Pr.

— Idealism, Protest & the Tale of Genji: The Confucianism of Kumazawa Banzan, 1619-1691. LC 99-22790. (Oxford Oriental Monographs). 564p. 1999. text 135.00 (0-19-815251-5) OUP.

McMullen, Jeanine. My Small Country Living. (Illus.). 224p. 1985. mass mkt. 8.95 (0-446-38305-8, Pub. by Warner Bks) Little.

— Wind in the Ash Tree. (Illus.). 1989. pap. 8.95 (0-393-30627-5) Norton.

McMullen, Joan. Writing Against God: Language As Message in the Literature of Flannery O'Connor. 176p. (C). 1996. text 25.00 (0-86554-488-3, MUP/H383) Mercer Univ Pr.

McMullen, Joanne H. Writing Against God: Language As Message in the Literature of Flannery O'Connor. 1998. reprint ed. pap. text 16.00 (0-86554-620-7, P179) Mercer Univ Pr.

*McMullen, John. Advanced UNIX User's Interactive Workbook. LC 00-265893. (Illus.). 624p. 1999. pap. text, wbk. ed. 39.99 (0-13-085456-5) P-H.

McMullen, John. Breach of Employment Contracts & Wrongful Dismissal. 1995. pap. write for info. (0-406-11841-8, UK, MICHIE) LEXIS Pub.

— The Canting Crew: London's Criminal Underworld, 1550-1700. 192p. 1984. text 40.00 (0-8135-1022-8) Rutgers U Pr.

Mcmullen, John. Unix User's Interactive Workbook. LC 99-175739. 600p. 1998. pap. text, wbk. ed. 34.99 (0-13-099820-6) P-H.

McMullen, John, et al. Butterworths Employment Law Guide. 2nd ed. Osman, Christopher C., ed. 648p. 1996. pap. write for info. (0-406-01652-6, UK, MICHIE) LEXIS Pub.

McMullen, John, jt. auth. see Skinner, Todd.

McMullen, John R. Extensions of Positive-Definite Functions. LC 52-42893. (Memoirs Ser.: No. 1/117). 71p. 1972. pap. 16.00 (0-8218-1817-1, MEMO/1/117) Am Math.

McMullen, Lorraine. Ernest Thompson Seton & His Works. (Canadian Author Studies). 54p. (C). 1989. pap. text 9.95 (1-55022-051-9, Pub. by ECW) Genl Dist Srvs.

— Frances Brooke & Her Works. (Canadian Author Studies). 38p. (C). 1983. pap. text 9.95 (0-920763-38-3, Pub. by ECW) Genl Dist Srvs.

McMullen, Lorraine, ed. & intro. see Lampman Symposium, 1975, University of Ottawa Staf.

McMullen, Lynn B. The Service Load in Teacher Training Institutions of the United States. LC 73-177038. (Columbia University. Teachers College. Contributions to Education Ser.: No. 244). reprint ed. 37.50 (0-404-55244-7) AMS Pr.

McMullen, Melanie, ed. Network Remote Access & Mobile Computing: Implementing Effective Remote Access to Networks & E-Mail. (Illus.). 230p. 1994. pap. 29.95 (0-87930-334-4) Miller Freeman.

— Networks 2000: Internet, Information Super Highway Multimedia Networks, & Beyond. (Illus.). 338p. 1994. pap. 24.95 (0-87930-335-2) Miller Freeman.

*McMullen, Michael. The Baha'i: The Religious Construction of a Global Identity. LC 99-58719. 288p. 2000. text 65.00 (0-8135-2835-6); pap. text 29.00 (0-8135-2836-4) Rutgers U Pr.

McMullen, Neil. The Newly Industrializing Countries in the World Economy. (British-North American Committee Ser.). 1982. 7.00 (0-685-06045-4) Natl Planning.

McMullen, Patricia A., jt. ed. see Klein, Raymond M.

McMullen, Phillip. Grassroots of America: Index to American State Papers, Land Grants & Claims, 1789-1837. (Illus.). 520p. 1990. reprint ed. text 49.50 (0-941765-85-7) Arkansas Res.

McMullen, Richie. Enchanted Boy. 1995. per. 10.95 (0-85449-098-1, Pub. by Gay Mens Pr) LPC InBook.

— Enchanted Youth. 157p. (Orig.). 1990. pap. 12.95 (0-85449-134-1, Pub. by Gay Mens Pr) LPC InBook.

McMullen, Russell, jt. auth. see Jong, Elaine C.

McMullen, Sean. Call to the Edge. 245p. (Orig.). 1992. pap. 10.00 (1-875346-06-6, Pub. by Aphelion) Firebird Dist.

— The Centurions Empire. 416p. 1999. mass mkt. 6.99 (0-8125-6475-8, Pub. by Tor Bks) St Martin.

*McMullen, Sean. The Miocene Arrow. 2000. pap. write for info. (0-312-87547-9) St Martin.

— The Miocene Arrow. 416p. 2000. 27.95 (0-312-87054-X, Pub. by Tor Bks) St Martin.

McMullen, Sean. Mirrorsun Rising: Book Two of Greatwinter. LC 95-218557. (Greatwinter Ser.: Vol. 2). 332p. 1995. pap. 10.00 (1-875346-14-7, Pub. by Aphelion) Firebird Dist.

*McMullen, Sean. Souls in the Great Machine. 448p. 2000. pap. 15.95 (0-312-87256-9, Pub. by Tor Bks) St Martin.

McMullen, Sean. Voices in the Light Bk. 1: Greatwinter. LC 95-218558. (Greatwinter Ser.: Vol. 1). 306p. (Orig.). 1994. pap. 10.00 (1-875346-10-4, Pub. by Aphelion) Firebird Dist.

*McMullen, Thomas B., Jr. Introduction to the Theory of Constraints. LC 98-10293. (St. Lucie Press/APICS Series on Constraints Management). (Illus.). 320p. (Orig.). 1998. boxed set 39.95 (1-57444-066-7) St Lucie Pr.

McMullen, Thomas B., Jr. TOC Manufacturing Information Systems. (APICS Series on Constraints Management). 300p. 1998. 42.50 (1-57444-067-5, SL0675) St Lucie Pr.

*Mcmullen, Timothy. The Gift of a Snowflake. (Illus.). 28p. (J). (ps-3). 1998. 12.95 (0-9664050-0-5) Prspect Hill.

McMullen, W. A. Posthumous Meditations: A Dialogue in Three Acts. LC 82-916. (HPC Dialogues Ser.). 79p. (C). 1982. pap. text 3.95 (0-915145-35-9) Hackett Pub.

McMullen, William W. Soloistic English Horn Literature (1736-1984) (Juilliard Performance Guides Ser.: No. 4). (Illus.). 1994. 54.00 (0-918728-78-9) Pendragon NY.

McMullin, Cie, jt. auth. see Burwash, Lynn.

McMullin, Ernan. The Concept of Matter in Greek & Medieval Philosophy. LC 65-23511. 333p. reprint ed. pap. 103.30 (0-608-15649-3, 203190700077) Bks Demand.

— The Inference That Makes Science. LC 92-80351. (Aquinas Lectures). 1992. 15.00 (0-87462-159-3) Marquette.

McMullin, Ernan, ed. Galileo: Man of Science. (Illus.). 488p. (C). 1988. reprint ed. pap. text 14.95 (0-945726-03-1); reprint ed. lib. bdg. 50.00 (0-945726-02-3) Scholars Bookshelf.

— The Social Dimensions of Science. LC 91-50577. (Studies in Science & the Humanities from the Reilly Center for Science, Technology, & Values: Vol. III). (C). 1992. text 44.00 (0-268-01741-7) U of Notre Dame Pr.

McMullin, Ernan, jt. ed. see Cushing, James T.

McMullin, Helen L. Gifts from the Goddess: An Idaho Potatoes Cookbook. 3rd ed. (Illus.). viii, 100p. 1993. reprint ed. pap. 7.00 (1-890535-00-1) H & J Spec.

— A Potato by Any Other Name. (Illus.). 50p. 1998. pap. 3.95 (1-890535-01-X) H & J Spec.

— Potatoes, Papitas, Patatas . . . Gifts from the Goddess. (Illus.). 120p. (Orig.). 1998. pap. 11.95 (1-890535-02-8) H & J Spec.

McMullin, Neil. Buddhism & the State in Sixteenth Century Japan. LC 84-42572. 452p. reprint ed. pap. 140.20 (0-8357-3390-4, 203964700013) Bks Demand.

McMullin, Rian E. Handbook of Cognitive Therapy Techniques. (Professional Bks.). 1986. 34.95 (0-393-70035-6) Norton.

McMullin, Rian E. The New Handbook of Cognitive Therapy Techniques. LC 99-16390. 480p. 1999. 45.00 (0-393-70313-4) Norton.

McMullin, Rian E. & Casey, Bill. Talk Sense to Yourself: A Guide to Cognitive Restructuring Therapy. (Illus.). 57p. (Orig.). 1975. pap. 4.00 (0-935205-02-0) Counseling Res.

McMullin, Rian E., et al. Straight Talk to Parents: Cognitive Restructuring Training for Families. (Illus.). 63p. (Orig.). 1978. pap. 4.00 (0-935205-03-9) Counseling Res.

McMullin, Rian E., jt. auth. see Casey, Bill.

McMullin, Ross. The Light on the Hill: The Australian Labor Party, 1891-1991. (Illus.). 560p. 1991. 45.00 (0-19-554966-X) OUP.

McMullin, Stan. Thomas Chandler Haliburton & His Works. (Canadian Author Studies). 50p. (C). 1989. pap. text 9.95 (1-55022-047-0, Pub. by ECW) Genl Dist Srvs.

McMullin, Thomas A. & Walker, David. Biographical Directory of American Territorial Governors. LC 84-9095. 376p. 1984. lib. bdg. 85.00 (0-313-28101-7, MTN/, Greenwood Pr) Greenwood.

McMullins, Hilda L. Story Book Time. LC 92-45560. 64p. 1995. pap. 14.95 (0-7734-2772-4, Mellen Poetry Pr) E Mellen.

*McMullins, Hilda L. Le Turf. 72p. 1999. pap. 12.95 (0-9677145-0-8) Valee Pubns.

McMurchie, Susan. Understanding LD (Learning Differences) A Curriculum to Promote LD Awareness, Self-Esteem, & Coping Skills in Students Ages 8-13. 160p. 1994. pap. 21.95 (0-915793-75-X) Free Spirit Pub.

*McMurchy, Ian. Modern Muzzleloading for Today's Whitetails. LC 00-102689. (Illus.). 208p. 2000. 29.95 (0-87341-951-0, MODMZ) Krause Pubns.

McMurchy, Ian, jt. auth. see Hanson, Milo.

McMurdie, H. F., jt. ed. see Ondik, H. M.

McMurdie, Howard F., jt. ed. see Cook, L. P.

McMurdie, Howard F., jt. ed. see Levin, Ernest M.

*McMurdie, William F. Hey, Mac! A Combat Infantryman's Story. 208p. 2000. pap. 14.95 (1-880222-41-8) Red Apple Pub.

McMurphy, John H. Living Deliberately: Experiments in Practical Spirituality. 180p. (Orig.). 1993. pap. 13.95 (0-9635487-8-6) Amaranth Pub.

— Secrets from Great Minds. 254p. (Orig.). 1993. reprint ed. pap. 13.95 (0-9635487-9-4) Amaranth Pub.

McMurrain, T. Thomas, jt. auth. see Wilson, Gary B.

McMurran, Marshall. If It Weren't for People, Management Would Be a Science. LC 98-38649. 1998. 19.95 (0-89806-210-1) Eng Mgmt Pr.

McMurran, Mary. The Psychology of Addiction. LC 94-16356. (Contemporary Psychology Ser.). 1994. write for info. (0-7484-0187-3, Pub. by Tay Francis Ltd); pap. write for info. (0-7484-0188-1, Pub. by Tay Francis Ltd) Taylor & Francis.

McMurran, Mary & Hodge, John E., eds. The Assessment of Criminal Behaviour in Secure Settings. 200p. 1993. pap. 29.95 (1-85302-124-5) Taylor & Francis.

McMurray. Community Health Nursing. 2nd ed. 1993. pap. 29.00 (0-443-04865-7, W B Saunders Co) Harcrt Hlth Sci Grp.

McMurray, jt. auth. see Genzer.

McMurray, Becky, jt. auth. see Goodwin, Glena.

McMurray, Dean S., tr. see Boog, Horst, et al.

McMurray, Emily J. Contemporary Theatre Film & TV, Vol. 9. 450p. 1991. text 155.00 (0-8103-2072-X) Gale.

McMurray, Emily J. & Olendorf, Donna, eds. Notable Twentieth-Century Scientists, 4 vols. LC 94-5263. 2397p. 1994. 305.00 (0-8103-9181-3) Gale.

*McMurray, Enfys. Hearst's Other Castle. LC 99-204231. 95p. (Orig.). 1999. pap. 19.95 (1-85411-228-7, Pub. by Seren Bks) Dufour.

McMurray, G. R., ed. Gorda Ridge. (Illus.). 320p. 1989. 144.95 (0-387-97034-7) Spr-Verlag.

McMurray, Janice, ed. Creative Arts with Older People. LC 89-20049. (Activities, Adaptation & Aging Ser.: Vol. 14, Nos. 1-2). (Illus.). 138p. 1990. 29.95 (0-86656-929-4) Haworth Pr.

— Creative Arts with Older People. LC 89-20049. (Activities, Adaptation & Aging Ser.: Vol. 14, Nos. 1-2). 138p. 1996. pap. 14.95 (0-7890-6040-X) Haworth Pr.

McMurray, John. Organic Chemistry: Study Guide & Solutions Manual. 4th ed. (Chemistry Ser.). 1328p. 1995. student ed. 43.50 (0-534-23833-5) Brooks-Cole.

McMurray, John J. & Cleland, John G. Heart Failure in Clinical Practice. 318p. 1996. write for info. (1-85317-225-1, Pub. by Martin Dunitz) Mosby Inc.

McMurray, Madeline. Illuminations: The Healing Image. LC 88-11467. (Illus.). 86p. (Orig.). 1988. pap. 12.95 (0-914728-63-6) Wingbow Pr.

McMurray, Mark. By the Book - Galatians. (By the Book Ser.). 64p. (YA). (gr. 7 up). 1997. pap. 5.25 (0-687-12119-1) Abingdon.

McMurray, Robert G. Concepts in Fitness Programming. LC 98-31113. 320p. 1998. per. 54.95 (0-8493-8714-0) CRC Pr.

McMurray, Sara M. Quantum Mechanics. LC 93-43852. 374p. 1994. pap. 53.75 (0-685-71176-5) Addison-Wesley.

McMurray, Susan. Fundamentals of Organic Chemistry. 3rd ed. (Chemistry). 1993. mass mkt., student ed. 26.75 (0-534-21212-3) Brooks-Cole.

McMurray, William J., et al. History of the Twentieth Tennessee Regiment Volunteer Infantry, C.S.A. LC 08-19472. (Illus.). 1976. reprint ed. 200.00 (0-918450-12-8) C Elder.

McMurren, Scott. Southcentral Alaska: Including Anchorage, Matanuska-Susitna Valleys, Kenai Peninsula, & Prince William Sound. (Umbrella Guides Ser.). (Illus.). 160p. (Orig.). 1995. pap. 12.95 (0-945397-40-2, Umbrella Bks) Epicenter Pr.

McMurrer, Daniel P. & Sawhill, Isabel V. Getting Ahead: Economic & Social Mobility in America. LC 97-49260. 130p. 1998. pap. 18.95 (0-87766-674-1); lib. bdg. 49.50 (0-87766-673-3) Urban Inst.

McMurrey, David, jt. auth. see Beer, David.

McMurrian, Howard P., et al. Guide to Physicians & Other Health Care Professionals, 3 vols. Incl. Vol. 1. 1997. ring bd. 146.00 (0-7646-0304-3); Vol. 2. 1997. ring bd. 146.00 (0-7646-0305-1); Vol. 3. 1997. ring bd. 146.00 (0-7646-0306-X); 140.00 (1-56433-881-9); 140.00 (0-7646-0303-5) Prctnrs Pub Co.

— Guide to Quality Control. 1997. ring bd. 146.00 (0-7646-0115-6) Prctnrs Pub Co.

— Guide to Quality Control. 1998. ring bd. 154.00 (0-7646-0389-2) Prctnrs Pub Co.

An Asterisk (*) at the beginning of an entry indicates that the title is appearing for the first time.

McMurrin, Diane. The Splendor of His Music: The Adventures of Two Americans Living in Post-Soviet Ukraine. 192p. 1998. pap. 12.99 (*1-57921-114-3*, Pub. by WinePress Pub) BookWorld.

McMurrin, Sterling M. The Crisis of Western Culture. (Grace A. Tanner Lecture in Human Values Ser.). 15p. 1994. 7.50 (*0-910153-10-8*) E T Woolf.

— Religion, Reason, & Truth: Historical Essays in the Philosophy of Religion. LC 82-4813. 302p. reprint ed. pap. 93.70 (*0-608-17430-0*, 202985200066) Bks Demand.

— The Tanner Lectures on Human Values, Vol. 1. LC 81-641369. 268p. reprint ed. pap. 83.10 (*0-608-17429-7*, 202985100001) Bks Demand.

***McMurrin, Sterling M.** The Theological Foundations of the Mormon Religion: And the Philosophical Foundations of Mormon Theology. LC 99-41167. (Mormon Classics). 2000. pap. write for info. (*1-56085-094-9*) Signature Bks.

— Theological Foundations of the Mormon Religion: The Philosophical Foundations of Mormon Theology. LC 99-41167. (Mormon Classics: Vol. 6). 220p. 2000. reprint ed. pap. 14.95 (*1-56085-135-X*) Signature Bks.

McMurrin, Sterling M., ed. The Tanner Lectures on Human Values, Vol. VIII. 333p. (C). 1988. text 30.00 (*0-87480-302-0*) U of Utah Pr.

— The Tanner Lectures on Human Values, 1981, Vol. II. 272p. 1981. 30.00 (*0-87480-193-1*) U of Utah Pr.

— The Tanner Lectures on Human Values, 1983, Vol. IV. 300p. 1983. 30.00 (*0-87480-216-4*) U of Utah Pr.

— The Tanner Lectures on Human Values, 1984, Vol. V. 220p. 1984. 30.00 (*0-87480-234-2*) U of Utah Pr.

— The Tanner Lectures on Human Values, 1985, Vol. VI. 300p. 1985. 30.00 (*0-87480-243-1*) U of Utah Pr.

— The Tanner Lectures on Human Values, 1986, Vol. VII. 288p. 1986. 30.00 (*0-87480-259-8*) U of Utah Pr.

McMurrin, Sterling M. & Newell, L. Jackson. Matters of Conscience: Conversations with Sterling M. McMurrin on Philosophy, Education & Religion. LC 96-18068. 424p. 1996. 28.95 (*1-56085-087-6*) Signature Bks.

McMurrin, Sterling M., ed. see Ashby, Eric, et al.

McMurrin, Sterling M., ed. see Dyson, Freeman J., et al.

McMurry. Biology. 2nd ed. 1999. pap. text, student ed. 22.50 (*0-13-919408-8*) P-H.

McMurry. Fundamental General. 2nd ed. 1996. text, student ed. 33.00 (*0-13-378753-2*) Allyn.

McMurry. Fundamentals of Organic Chemistry. 4th ed. 1997. pap. 25.50 (*0-534-35216-2*) Brooks-Cole.

— Fundamentals of Organic Chemistry with InfoTrac. 4th ed. 1998. 62.25 incl. cd-rom (*0-534-36354-7*) Brooks-Cole.

— Organic Chemistry. 3rd ed. (Chemistry Ser.). 1992. pap., teacher ed. write for info. (*0-534-16223-1*) Brooks-Cole.

Mcmurry. Organic Chemistry. 4th ed. text 88.31 (*0-534-33276-5*); text 81.00 (*0-534-33255-2*) Brooks-Cole.

McMurry. Organic Chemistry. 5th ed. LC 99-16981. (Chemistry). 1999. pap. 70.00 (*0-534-36274-5*); pap. text, student ed. 42.00 (*0-534-37192-2*) Brooks-Cole.

***McMurry.** Organic Chemistry. 5th ed. LC 99-16981. 1284p. 1999. pap. 78.00 (*0-534-37366-6*) Thomson Learn.

McMurry. Organic Chemistry W/infotrac W/online Cd. 4th ed. (Chemistry). 1998. pap. 75.25 incl. cd-rom (*0-534-36355-5*) Brooks-Cole.

— Spectroscopy Workbook Organic Chemistry. 5th ed. (Chemistry). 1999. pap. text 12.00 (*0-534-37230-9*) Brooks-Cole.

Mcmurry, et al. Fundamentals of General, Organic & Biological Chemistry. 3rd ed. LC 98-32181. 849p. 1999. 95.00 (*0-13-918517-8*) P-H.

— Fundamentals of Organic & Biolgcal Chemistry. 2nd ed. LC 98-32157. 544p. 1999. pap. text 72.00 (*0-13-919390-1*) P-H.

McMurry, Dean S., tr. see Dulffer, Jost.

McMurry, Dean S., tr. see Maler, Klaus A., et al.

McMurry, Dean S., tr. see Schreiber, Gerhard, et al.

McMurry, Doug. Fresh Bread: How Jesus Draws Us to Good. LC 98-89783. (Illus.). 198p. 1999. pap. 10.00 (*1-57921-201-8*, Pub. by WinePress Pub) BookWorld.

McMurry, Doug, jt. auth. see Longfield, Bradley J.

McMurry, Douglas & Worthington, Everett L., Jr. Value Your Mate: How to Strengthen Your Marriage. LC 93-36060. (Strategic Christian Living Ser.). 128p. 1994. pap. 8.99 (*0-8010-9727-4*) Baker Bks.

McMurry, Douglas, jt. auth. see Long, Zeb Bradford.

McMurry, James. The Catskill Witch & Other Tales of the Hudson Valley. LC 74-17067. (York State Bk.). 168p. reprint ed. pap. 52.10 (*0-608-15200-5*, 202739100055) Bks Demand.

McMurry, John. Fundamentals of General Organic & Biological Chemistry. 2nd ed. 1996. text 88.00 (*0-13-342288-7*) P-H.

— Fundamentals of Organic Chemistry. LC 85-17098. (Chemistry). 600p. (C). 1986. mass mkt. 41.25 (*0-534-05280-0*) Brooks-Cole.

McMurry, John. Fundamentals of Organic Chemistry. 2nd ed. (Chemistry). 544p. (C). 1990. mass mkt. 63.25 (*0-534-12300-7*) Brooks-Cole.

— Fundamentals of Organic Chemistry. 3rd ed. LC 93-25587. (Chemistry). 536p. 1993. mass mkt. 84.95 (*0-534-21210-7*) Brooks-Cole.

McMurry, John. Fundamentals of Organic Chemistry. 4th ed. LC 97-27737. 1997. pap. 61.25 (*0-534-35215-4*) Brooks-Cole.

— Organic Chemistry. LC 83-7744. (Chemistry). 1051p. (C). 1984. mass mkt. 48.50 (*0-534-01204-3*) Brooks-Cole.

— Organic Chemistry. 2nd ed. LC 87-15835. (Chemistry). 1241p. (C). 1987. mass mkt. 60.75 (*0-534-07968-7*) Brooks-Cole.

— Organic Chemistry. 3rd ed. (Chemistry Ser.). 1992. pap., student ed. 37.00 (*0-534-16219-3*) Brooks-Cole.

— Organic Chemistry: Student Manual & Solution Manual. LC 83-7744. (Chemistry). 1051p. (C). 1984. mass mkt., student ed. 23.25 (*0-534-02675-3*) Brooks-Cole.

McMurry, John & Fay, Robert. Chemistry. 2nd ed. LC 97-29206. (Illus.). 1025p. 1997. 106.33 (*0-13-737776-2*) P-H.

McMurry, Linda O. George Washington Carver: Scientist & Symbol. (Illus.). 352p. 1982. pap. 13.95 (*0-19-503205-5*) OUP.

— Recorder of the Black Experience: A Biography of Monroe Nathan Work. LC 84-10008. (Southern Biography Ser.). (Illus.). 154p. 1985. text 27.50 (*0-8071-1171-6*) La State U Pr.

McMurry, Linda O. To Keep the Waters Troubled: The Life of Ida B. Wells. LC 98-6068. (Illus.). 416p. 1999. 35.00 (*0-19-508812-3*) OUP.

***McMurry, Linda O.** To Keep the Waters Troubled: The Life of Ida B. Wells. (Illus.). 416p. 2000. pap. 17.95 (*0-19-513927-5*) OUP.

McMurry, Mildred. Hacia Ti, Senor.Tr. of Spiritual Life Development. (SPA.). 122p. 1996. pap. text 7.99 (*0-311-12109-8*) Casa Bautista.

***McMurry, Richard M.** Atlanta 1864: Last Chance for the Confederacy. LC 99-87560. (Great Campaigns of the Civil War Ser.). (Illus.). 272p. 2000. 35.00 (*0-8032-3212-8*) U of Nebr Pr.

McMurry, Richard M. John Bell Hood & the War for Southern Independence. LC 92-12987. (Illus.). xiv, 239p. 1992. reprint ed. pap. 10.95 (*0-8032-8191-9*, Bison Books) U of Nebr Pr.

— Two Great Rebel Armies: An Essay in Confederate Military History. LC 88-14374. (Illus.). xviii, 204p. (C). 1989. 29.95 (*0-8078-1819-4*) U of NC Pr.

— Two Great Rebel Armies: An Essay in Confederate Military History. LC 88-14374. 222p. (C). 1996. pap. 18.95 (*0-8078-4569-8*) U of NC Pr.

***McMurry, Richard M.** Virginia Military Institute Alumni in the Civil War - In Bello Praesidium. (Virginia Civil War Battles & Leaders Ser.). (Illus.). 283p. 1999. 25.00 (*1-56190-111-3*) H E Howard.

McMurry, Richard M., ed. see Blue & Gray Magazine Editors.

McMurry, Robert N. The Maverick Executive. LC 73-85189. 205p. reprint ed. pap. 63.60 (*0-608-11909-1*, 202357100033) Bks Demand.

***McMurry, Sally & Adams, Annmarie, eds.** People, Power, Places: Perspectives in Vernacular Architecture, VIII. (Illus.). 328p. (C). 2000. pap. text 30.00 (*1-57233-075-9*, Pub. by U of Tenn Pr) U Ch Pr.

McMurry, Sally, jt. ed. see Adams, Annmarie.

McMurry, Sally A. Families & Farmhouses in Nineteenth Century America: Vernacular Design & Social Change. (Illus.). 288p. 1988. text 65.00 (*0-19-504475-4*) OUP.

— Families & Farmhouses in Nineteenth Century America: Vernacular Design & Social Change. LC 96-35611. (Illus.). 288p. (C). 1997. pap. text 23.00 (*0-87049-953-X*) U of Tenn Pr.

— Transforming Rural Life: Dairying Families & Agricultural Change, 1820-1885. (Revisiting Rural America Ser.). 296p. 1995. text 42.50 (*0-8018-4889-X*) Johns Hopkins.

McMurry, Sara M. Quantum Mechanic. 346p. (C). 1993. text, pap. text 70.00 incl. disk (*0-201-54439-3*) Addison-Wesley.

McMurry, Sara M. Quantum Mechanics. LC 93-43852. 1993. 26.00 (*0-685-70937-X*) Addison-Wesley.

***McMurrya, Jim.** Barbarian Science: A Humorous View from Outside the Gates of the Fortress of Formal Science. LC 99-75885. 122p. 1999. pap. 15.95 (*1-886017-24-7*) Town Sq Bks.

McMurtrey, Martin. Loose to the Wilds. 2nd ed. 162p. (YA). reprint ed. pap. 6.00 (*0-9623961-0-9*) M A McMurtrey.

— Mariachi Bishop: The Life of Patrick Flores, First Mexican-American Bishop in the U. S. LC 87-70378. (Illus.). 181p. (Orig.). 1987. pap. 6.95 (*0-931722-56-X*) Corona Pub.

McMurtrey, Martin & Cunningham, W. Patrick. Out of River's Mist: The Collected Works of Martin Mcmurtrey LC 98-84755. xiv, 313p. 1998. write for info. (*1-890549-03-7*) Alpha Pub Grp.

McMurtrey, Martin, ed. see Von Le Fort, Gertrud F.

McMurtrie, Douglas C. Check List of Kentucky Imprints, 1811-1820, with Notes in Supplement to the Check List of 1787-1810. Allen, A. H., ed. (Historical Records Survey Monographs). 1972. reprint ed. 25.00 (*0-527-01903-8*) Periodicals Srv.

— The Disabled Soldier. Phillips, William R. & Rosenberg, Janet, eds. LC 79-6921. (Physically Handicapped in Society Ser.). (Illus.). 1980. reprint ed. lib. bdg. 25.95 (*0-405-13140-2*) Ayer.

— The Evolution of National Systems of Vocational Reeducation for Disabled Soldiers & Sailors. Phillips, William R. & Rosenberg, Janet, eds. LC 79-6916. (Physically Handicapped in Society Ser.). 1980. reprint ed. lib. bdg. 31.95 (*0-405-13127-5*) Ayer.

— Historical Records Survey: Check List of the Imprints of Sag Harbor, L. I., 1791-1820, No. 12. (Historical Records Survey Monographs). 1939. pap. 25.00 (*0 527 01909 7*) Periodicals Srv.

McMurtrie, Douglas C. & Allen, A. H. American Imprints Inventory No. Five: Check List of Kentucky Imprints, 1787-1810. (Historical Records Survey Monographs). 1972. reprint ed. pap. 25.00 (*0-527-01902-X*) Periodicals Srv.

McMurtrie, Douglas C., jt. auth. see Axford, Wendy A.

McMurtrie, Douglas C., ed. see Schorbach, Karl.

McMurtrie, Mary. Scots Roses: A Botanical Album. (Illus.). 29.50 (*1-870673-26-3*, Pub. by Garden Art Pr) Antique Collect.

McMurtrie, Michael. Lost Colony: A Martian Adventure. iii, 444p. 1998. pap. 20.00 (*0-9662885-0-5*) MERC Frontiers.

McMurtrie, W. Hogin & Rikel, James E. The Coloring Review Guide to Human Anatomy. 448p. (C). 1990. text. write for info. (*0-697-03150-0*, WCB McGr Hill) McGrw-H Hghr Educ.

McMurtry. Harmony. 1994. 22.00 (*0-671-79283-0*) S&S Trade.

— Harmony. 1999. write for info. (*0-671-79284-9*) S&S Trade.

McMurtry, Jo. English Language, English Literature: The Creation of an Academic Discipline. LC 84-20534. xi, 192p. 1985. lib. bdg. 31.00 (*0-208-02060-8*, Archon Bks) Shoe String.

— Julius Caesar: A Guide to the Play. LC 98-15598. (Greenwood Guides to Shakespeare Ser.). 160p. 1998. lib. bdg. 49.95 (*0-313-30479-3*, Greenwood Pr) Greenwood.

— Shakespeare Films in the Classroom: A Descriptive Guide. LC 93-39431. (Illus.). ix, 249p. (C). 1994. lib. bdg. 39.50 (*0-208-02369-0*, Archon Bks) Shoe String.

— Understanding Shakespeare's England: A Companion for the American Reader. LC 89-32451. (Illus.). xiii, 254 p. (C). 1989. 37.50 (*0-208-02248-1*, Archon Bks) Shoe String.

— Victorian Life & Victorian Fiction: A Companion for the American Reader. LC 78-17049. (Illus.). 315p. (C). 1978. lib. bdg. 34.00 (*0-208-01744-5*, Archon Bks) Shoe String.

— Victorian Life & Victorian Fiction: A Companion for the American Reader. LC 78-17049. (Illus.). 315p. (C). 1996. pap. 27.50 (*0-208-02401-8*, Archon Bks) Shoe String.

McMurtry, John. The Cancer Stage of Capitalism. LC 98-45475. 320p. 1999. 59.95 (*0-7453-1352-3*, Pub. by Pluto GBR) Stylus Pub VA.

***McMurtry, John.** The Cancer Stage of Capitalism. 320p. 1999. pap. 19.95 (*0-7453-1347-7*, Pub. by Pluto GBR) Stylus Pub VA.

McMurtry, John. Unequal Freedoms: The Global Market As an Ethical System. LC 98-40415. 416p. 1998. pap. 24.95 (*1-56549-087-8*) Kumarian Pr.

McMurtry, John M. The Structure of Marx's World-View. LC 77-85552. 283p. reprint ed. pap. 87.80 (*0-8357-4047-1*, 203673700005) Bks Demand.

McMurtry, Ken. Beware the Snake's Venom. (Choose Your Own Nightmare Ser.: No. 2). (J). (gr. 4-8). 1995. 8.60 (*0-606-07366-3*, Pub. by Turtleback) Demco.

McMurtry, Ken. A History Mystery: The Mystery of the Roswell UFO. 96p. (Orig.). (J). 1992. pap. 3.50 (*0-380-76843-7*, Avon Bks) Morrow Avon.

— Risk Your Life Arcade. (Choose Your Own Nightmare Ser.: No. 6). (J). (gr. 4-8). 1995. 8.60 (*0-606-08506-8*, Pub. by Turtleback) Demco.

McMurtry, Larry. All My Friends Are Going to Be Strangers. LC 88-36753. 304p. 1989. pap. 11.00 (*0-671-68103-6*) S&S Trade.

***McMurtry, Larry.** All My Friends Are Going to Be Strangers. 304p. 2001. per. 12.00 (*0-684-85382-5*) S&S Trade.

McMurtry, Larry. All My Friends Are Going to Be Strangers. Grose, Bill, ed. 288p. 1992. reprint ed. mass mkt. 6.99 (*0-671-75871-3*) PB.

— Anything for Billy. Grose, Bill, ed. 416p. 1991. per. 6.99 (*0-671-74605-7*) PB.

— Anything for Billy. (J). 1989. 11.09 (*0-606-00348-7*, Pub. by Turtleback) Demco.

***McMurtry, Larry.** Boone's Lick: A Novel. 288p. 2000. 26.00 (*0-684-86886-5*) Simon & Schuster.

McMurtry, Larry. Buffalo Girls. 1995. per. 7.50 (*0-671-53615-X*) Silhouette.

— Cadillac Jack. Grose, Bill, ed. 1990. per. 6.99 (*0-671-73902-6*) PB.

— Cadillac Jack. 400p. 1987. pap. 10.00 (*0-671-63720-7*) S&S Trade.

***McMurtry, Larry.** Cadillac Jack: A Novel. 400p. 2001. per. 12.00 (*0-684-85383-3*) S&S Trade.

McMurtry, Larry. Comanche Moon. 1998. per. 7.99 (*0-671-02064-1*) PB.

— Comanche Moon. 752p. 2000. pap. 15.00 (*0-684-85755-3*) S&S Trade.

— Comanche Moon: A Novel. LC 97-29609. 752p. 1997. 28.50 (*0-684-80754-8*) S&S Trade.

— Comanche Moon: A Novel. large type ed. LC 97-52110. (Basic Ser.). 1999. pap. 30.00 (*0-7862-1392-2*) Thorndike Pr.

— Crazy Horse. LC 99-18817. 1999. 28.95 (*0-7862-1901-7*, G K Hall & Co) Mac Lib Ref.

— Crazy Horse. LC 98-26644. (Penguin Lives Ser.). 142p. 1999. 19.95 (*0-670-88234-8*) Viking Penguin.

— Dead Man's Walk. 1996. mass mkt. 6.99 (*0-671-00116-7*) PB.

— Dead Man's Walk: A Novel. LC 95-21011. 480p. 1995. 26.00 (*0-684-80753-X*) S&S Trade.

***McMurtry, Larry.** Dead Man's Walk: A Novel. (Lonesome Dove Ser.). 480p. 2000. pap. 15.00 (*0-684-85754-5*, Scribner Pap Fic) S&S Trade Pap.

McMurtry, Larry. The Desert Rose. 1976. 22.95 (*0-8488-0371-X*) Amereon Ltd.

— The Desert Rose. Grose, Bill, ed. 288p. 1990. per. 7.50 (*0-671-72763-X*) PB.

— The Desert Rose. 256p. 1987. pap. 10.00 (*0-671-63721-5*) S&S Trade.

***McMurtry, Larry.** Desert Rose: A Novel. 256p. 2001. per. 12.00 (*0-684-85384-1*) S&S Trade.

— Duane's Depressed. 528p. 1999. per. 7.99 (*0-671-02557-0*, Pocket Star Bks) PB.

McMurtry, Larry. Duane's Depressed. LC 98-45712. 432p. 1999. 26.00 (*0-684-85497-X*) S&S Trade.

— Duane's Depressed. large type ed. LC 99-26434. 1999. 29.95 (*0-7838-8631-4*, G K Hall & Co) Mac Lib Ref.

— The Evening Star. 1996. per. 6.99 (*0-671-00427-1*, PB Trade Paper) PB.

— The Evening Star. 640p. 1999. pap. 14.00 (*0-684-85751-0*) S&S Trade Pap.

— The Evening Star. large type ed. LC 92-41444. (General Ser.). 765p. 1993. pap. 18.95 (*0-8161-5649-2*, G K Hall Lrg Type) Mac Lib Ref.

— The Evening Star: A Novel. large type ed. LC 92-41444. (General Ser.). 765p. 1993. lib. bdg. 25.95 (*0-8161-5648-4*, G K Hall Lrg Type) Mac Lib Ref.

— Horseman, Pass By. 1976. 20.95 (*0-8488-0372-8*) Amereon Ltd.

***McMurtry, Larry.** Horseman, Pass By. 192p. 2001. per. 10.00 (*0-684-85385-X*) S&S Trade.

McMurtry, Larry. Horseman, Pass By. LC 93-105517. 192p. 1992. pap. 9.00 (*0-671-75499-8*, Touchstone) S&S Trade Pap.

— Horseman, Pass By. Grose, Bill, ed. 256p. 1992. reprint ed. per. 7.50 (*0-671-75384-3*) PB.

— In a Narrow Grave: Essays on Texas. 208p. 1989. pap. 9.00 (*0-671-68102-8*) S&S Trade.

— The Last Picture Show. 1976. 22.95 (*0-89190-889-7*) Amereon Ltd.

— The Last Picture Show. LC 99-24699. 1999. 30.00 (*0-7838-8632-2*) Mac Lib Ref.

— The Last Picture Show. Grose, Bill, ed. 320p. 1992. per. 6.99 (*0-671-75381-9*) PB.

— The Last Picture Show. 1999. pap. 11.00 (*0-684-00817-3*); per. 11.00 (*0-684-85386-8*) S&S Trade.

— The Last Picture Show. 224p. 1992. pap. 10.00 (*0-671-75487-4*, Touchstone) S&S Trade Pap.

— The Late Child. 480p. 1996. per. 6.99 (*0-671-56818-3*) PB.

— The Late Child. large type ed. LC 95-31811. 1995. 26.95 (*1-56895-246-5*, Compass) Wheeler Pub.

— The Late Child: A Novel. LC 95-2419. 461p. 1995. 25.00 (*0-684-80998-2*) S&S Trade.

— Leaving Cheyenne. 1976. 22.95 (*0-8488-0373-6*) Amereon Ltd.

***McMurtry, Larry.** Leaving Cheyenne. 304p. 2001. per. 12.00 (*0-684-85387-6*) S&S Trade.

McMurtry, Larry. Leaving Cheyenne. 256p. 1992. pap. 11.00 (*0-671-75490-4*, Touchstone) S&S Trade Pap.

— Leaving Cheyenne. Grose, Bill, ed. 320p. 1992. reprint ed. per. 7.50 (*0-671-75380-0*) PB.

— Lonesome Dove. 1993. pap. 6.99 (*0-671-74471-2*) PB.

— Lonesome Dove. Grose, Bill, ed. 960p. 1993. per. 7.99 (*0-671-79589-9*) PB.

— Lonesome Dove. 848p. 1985. 26.50 (*0-671-50420-7*) S&S Trade.

— Lonesome Dove. 848p. 2000. pap. 15.00 (*0-684-85752-9*) S&S Trade.

— Lonesome Dove. rev. ed. 2000. mass mkt. 7.99 (*0-671-68390-X*) PB.

— Moving On. Grose, Bill, ed. 1991. per. 7.99 (*0-671-74408-9*) PB.

— Moving On: A Novel. 800p. 1987. pap. 11.00 (*0-671-63320-1*) S&S Trade.

— Moving On: A Novel. 800p. 1999. per. 15.00 (*0-684-85388-4*) S&S Trade Pap.

— Pretty Boy Floyd. 1995. mass mkt. 6.99 (*0-671-89167-7*) PB.

***McMurtry, Larry.** Roads: Driving America's Great Highways. 208p. 2000. 24.50 (*0-684-86884-9*) S&S Trade.

McMurtry, Larry. Selected from Lonesome Dove. abr. ed. Literacy Volunteers of New York City Staff & Margolis, Seth, eds. (Writers' Voices Ser.). 64p. (Orig.). 1992. pap. text 3.95 (*0-929631-58-7*, Signal Hill) New Readers.

— Some Can Whistle. Grose, William, ed. 384p. 1990. reprint ed. per. 6.99 (*0-671-72213-1*) PB.

— Some Can Whistle: A Novel. large type ed. 399p. 1990. lib. bdg. 20.95 (*0-8161-4987-9*, G K Hall Lrg Type) Mac Lib Ref.

— Somebody's Darling. Grose, Bill, ed. 352p. 1991. per. 5.99 (*0-671-74585-9*) PB.

— Somebody's Darling: A Novel. 352p. 1987. pap. 8.00 (*0-671-63319-8*) S&S Trade.

***McMurtry, Larry.** Somebody's Darling: A Novel. 352p. 2001. per. 13.00 (*0-684-85389-2*) S&S Trade.

McMurtry, Larry. Streets of Laredo. 560p. 1995. per. 7.99 (*0-671-53746-6*) PB.

— Streets of Laredo. 560p. 2000. pap. 15.00 (*0-684-85753-7*) S&S Trade.

McMurtry, Larry. Streets of Laredo. 1993. 13.09 (*0-606-06771-X*, Pub. by Turtleback) Demco.

McMurtry, Larry. Streets of Laredo. large type ed. LC 93-47082. 795p. 1994. lib. bdg. 19.95 (*0-8161-5956-4*, G K Hall Lrg Type) Mac Lib Ref.

— Terms of Endearment. Grose, Bill, ed. 432p. 1992. per. 7.50 (*0-671-75872-1*) PB.

— Terms of Endearment. 416p. 1999. pap. 13.00 (*0-684-85390-6*) S&S Trade.

— Terms of Endearment: A Novel. 416p. 1989. pap. 11.00 (*0-671-68208-3*) S&S Trade.

— Texasville. Grose, Bill, ed. 576p. 1990. per. 7.50 (*0-671-73517-9*) PB.

— Texasville. 544p. 1999. pap. 13.00 (*0-684-85750-2*) S&S Trade.

— Texasville. large type ed. LC 99-24657. (Core Ser.). 1999. 29.95 (*0-7838-8633-0*, G K Hall Lrg Type) Mac Lib Ref.

***McMurtry, Larry.** Walter Benjamin at the Dairy Queen: Reflections at Sixty & Beyond. LC 99-19346. 208p. 1999. 20.50 (*0-684-85496-1*) S&S Trade.

— Walter Benjamin at the Dairy Queen: Reflections at Sixty & Beyond. large type ed. LC 99-47197. 1999. 28.95 (*0-7862-2264-6*) Thorndike Pr.

M

An Asterisk (*) at the beginning of an entry indicates that the title is appearing for the first time.

M

***McMurtry, Larry, ed.** Still Wild: Short Fiction of the American West - 1950 to Present. LC 99-52848. 416p. 2000. 25.50 (*0-684-86882-2*) Simon & Schuster.

McMurtry, Larry & Ossana, Diana. Pretty Boy Floyd. large type ed. LC 96-54511. 653p. 1997. 24.95 (*0-7862-1045-1*) Thorndike Pr.

— Pretty Boy Floyd: A Novel. 352p. 1994. 24.00 (*0-671-89165-0*) S&S Trade.

— Zeke & Ned. 1997. per. 7.50 (*0-671-89168-5*) PB.

— Zeke & Ned: A Novel. large type ed. LC 97-1514. (Core Ser.). 657p. 1997. lib. bdg. 28.95 (*0-7838-8094-4*, G K Hall Lrg Type) Mac Lib Ref.

— Zeke & Ned: A Novel. large type ed. LC 97-1514. 1999. pap. 26.95 (*0-7838-8095-2*, G K Hall Lrg Type) Mac Lib Ref.

McMurtry, Newell, jt. auth. see Magnani, David.

***McMurtry, R. Gerald.** Ben Hardin Helm. ix, 79p. 1999. pap. 18.00 (*0-931244-14-5*) Hardin County Historical Society.

— The Kentucky Lincolns on Mill Creek. ix, 77p. 1999. pap. 18.00 (*0-931244-12-9*) Hardin County Historical Society.

— The Lincoln Migration from Kentucky to Indiana, 1816. 46p. 1999. pap. 5.00 (*0-931244-09-9*) Hardin County Historical Society.

— A Series of Monographs Concerning the Lincolns & Hardin County, Kentucky. (Illus.). 133p. 1999. 18.00 (*0-931244-11-0*) Hardin County Historical Society.

McMurtry, R. Gerald, jt. auth. see Harkness, David J.

McMurtry, R. Gerald, jt. auth. see Neely, Mark E., Jr.

McMurtry, Richard K. John McMurtry & the American Indian: A Frontiersman in the Struggle for the Ohio Valley. LC 80-7469. (Illus.). (Orig.). 1980. pap. 14.95 (*0-936012-05-6*) Current Issues.

McMurtry, Ruth, jt. auth. see Cohen, Uriel.

McMurty, William M., ed. Selected Chansons from British Library, MS Additional 35087. Gionet, Arthur J., tr. (Recent Researches in Music of the Renaissance Ser.: Vol. RRR68). (Illus.). xliv, 59p. 1985. pap. 35.00 (*0-89579-148-X*, RRR68) A-R Eds.

McmWhorter, Kathleen T. College Reading & Study Skills. 7th ed. LC 97-2933. 512p. (C). 1997. pap. text 50.00 (*0-321-01196-1*) Addson-Wesley Educ.

McMylor, Peter, jt. ed. see Halfpenny, Peter.

McNab. Manual of Orbital Lacrimal Surgery. 4th ed. 160p. 1998. pap. text 65.00 (*0-7506-3997-0*) Buttrwrth-Heinemann.

McNab, Alex. The Tennis Doctor: The Essential Courtside Companion. (Illus.). 159p. 1999. reprint ed. text 20.00 (*0-7881-5688-8*) DIANE Pub.

McNab, Andy. Bravo Two Zero: The Harrowing True Story of a Special Forces Patrol Behind the Lines in Iraq. 432p. 1994. mass mkt. 6.99 (*0-440-21880-2*) Dell.

***McNab, Andy.** Crisis Four. 400p. 2000. 24.95 (*0-345-42807-2*) Ballantine Pub Grp.

McNab, Andy. Immediate Action. LC 96-162623. 1996. 32.95 (*0-593-03782-0*) Bantam.

— Immediate Action. 512p. 1996. mass mkt. 6.99 (*0-440-22245-1*) Dell.

— Married to the SAS. (Illus.). 290p. 1997. 25.95 (*1-85782-166-1*, Pub. by Blake Publng) Seven Hills Bk.

— Remote Control. LC 98-44167. 336p. 1999. 19.95 (*0-345-42805-6*) Ballantine Pub Grp.

***McNab, Andy.** Remote Control. 384p. 2000. mass mkt. 6.99 (*0-345-42806-4*) One Wrld.

McNab, Andy. Streeters: Rants & Raves from "This Hour Has 22 Minutes" LC 98-164792. 208p. 1998. pap. write for info. (*0-385-25717-1*) Doubleday.

McNab, Beulah. Perceptions of Phobia & Phobics: The Quest for Control. (Illus.). 253p. 1993. text 115.00 (*0-12-485960-7*) Acad Pr.

***McNab, Chris.** German Paratroopers: The History of the Fallschirmager on WWII. (Illus.). 192p. 2000. 24.95 (*0-7603-0932-9*, 130568AP, Pub. by MBI Pubg) Motorbooks Intl.

— The Illustrated History of the Vietnam War. (Illus.). 2000. 24.98 (*1-57145-266-4*, Thunder Bay) Advantage Pubs.

McNab, Claire. Body Guard. LC 94-15981. (Carol Ashton Mystery Ser.). 224p. 1994. pap. 11.95 (*1-56280-073-6*) Naiad Pr.

— Chain Letter: A Carol Ashton Mystery. LC 97-10008. 224p. (Orig.). 1997. pap. 11.95 (*1-56280-181-3*) Naiad Pr.

— Cop Out. LC 90-21907. Vol. 4. 224p. (Orig.). 1991. pap. 10.95 (*0-941483-84-3*) Naiad Pr.

McNab, Claire. Dead Certain. LC 92-18092. (Carol Ashton Mystery Ser.: No. 5). 224p. 1992. pap. 11.95 (*1-56280-027-2*) Naiad Pr.

McNab, Claire. Death Down Under. LC 88-29120. Vol. 3. 240p. 1990. pap. 11.95 (*0-941483-39-8*) Naiad Pr.

***McNab, Claire.** Death Understood: A Denise Cleever Thriller. 224p. 2000. pap. 11.95 (*1-56280-264-X*) Naiad Pr.

McNab, Claire. Double Bluff. 192p. 1995. pap. 11.95 (*1-56280-096-5*) Naiad Pr.

McNab, Claire. Fatal Reunion. LC 88-38388. Vol. 2. 224p. 1989. pap. 11.95 (*0-941483-40-1*) Naiad Pr.

McNab, Claire. Inner Circle: A Carol Ashton Mystery. 256p. 1996. pap. 11.95 (*1-56280-135-X*) Naiad Pr.

— Lessons in Murder. (Carol Ashton Mystery Ser.). 216p. 1988. pap. 11.95 (*0-941483-14-2*) Naiad Pr.

***McNab, Claire.** Murder Undercover: A Denise Cleever Thriller. LC 99-18394. 240p. 1999. pap. 11.95 (*1-56280-259-3*) Naiad Pr.

McNab, Claire. Past Due: A Detective Inspector Carol Ashton Mystery. (Carol Ashton Mystery Ser.: No. 10). 224p. 1998. pap. 11.95 (*1-56280-217-8*) Naiad Pr.

***McNab, Claire.** Set Up. LC 98-48231. (Detective Inspector Carol Ashton Mystery Ser.: No. 11). 224p. 1999. pap. 11.95 (*1-56280-255-0*) Naiad Pr.

McNab, Claire. Silent Heart. 192p. 1993. pap. 11.95 (*1-56280-036-1*) Naiad Pr.

***McNab, Claire.** Under Suspicion. (Detective Inspector Carol Ashton Mystery Ser.). 224p. 2000. pap. 11.95 (*1-56280-261-5*) Naiad Pr.

McNab, Claire. Under the Southern Cross. 224p. 1992. pap. 11.95 (*1-56280-011-6*) Naiad Pr.

McNab, Claire & Gedan, Sharon. The Loving Lesbian. LC 96-45485. 208p. (Orig.). 1997. pap. 14.95 (*1-56280-169-4*) Naiad Pr.

McNab, Colin. The Fianchetto King's Indian. LC 96-78262. (New American Batsford Chess Library). 192p. (Orig.). 1996. pap. 22.50 (*1-879479-40-0*) ICE WA.

McNab, David & Younger, James. The Planets. LC 98-89995. (Illus.). 240p. 1999. 35.00 (*0-300-08044-1*) Yale U Pr.

***McNab, David T.** Circles of Time: Aboriginal Land Rights & Resistance in Ontario. 288p. (C). 1999. pap. 29.95 (*0-88920-338-5*) Wilfrid Laurier.

— Circles of Time: Aboriginal Land Rights & Resistance in Ontario. LC 98-932488. (Illus.). 280p. 1999. text 54.95 (*0-88920-318-0*) Wilfrid Laurier.

McNab, David T., ed. Earth, Water, Air & Fire: Studies in Canadian Ethnohistory. vi, 348p. 1998. pap. 29.95 (*0-88920-297-4*) W Laurier U Pr.

McNab, Gregory, tr. see De Melo, Dias.

McNab, Helen, jt. auth. see Wynn, Anthea.

McNab, J. Strathearn, tr. see Frey, Arthur.

McNab, Nora S. The Beckoning: A Story of Love. 261p. 1990. pap. 11.95 (*0-942323-09-2*) N Amer Heritage Pr.

— Miss Merry. 210p. 1993. pap. 11.95 (*0-942323-19-X*) N Amer Heritage Pr.

— Onion Avenue. 208p. 1991. pap. 11.95 (*0-942323-14-9*) N Amer Heritage Pr.

McNab, Rosi. Teach Yourself Beginner's German, 2 cass. (ENG & GER., Illus.). 224p. 1995. pap. 8.95 (*0-8442-3778-7*, Teach Yrslf) NTC Contemp Pub Co.

— Teach Yourself Beginner's German, Set. (Teach Yourself Ser.). (GER.). 224p. 1996. pap. 17.95 incl. audio (*0-8442-3880-5*, Teach Yrslf) NTC Contemp Pub Co.

— Teach Yourself German, Beginner's. (Teach Yourself Ser.). 1992. 13.95 (*0-8288-8340-8*); 33.95 incl. audio (*0-8288-8341-6*) Fr & Eur.

McNab, Tom. Flanagan's Run. large type ed. 704p. 1983. 27.99 (*0-7089-8142-9*) Ulverscroft.

— Rings of Sand. large type ed. 432p. 1985. 27.99 (*0-7089-8247-6*) Ulverscroft.

McNab, Tom, jt. auth. see Hazeldine, Rex.

McNabb, Bill & Mabry, Steve. Teaching the Bible Creatively to Young People. 192p. 1990. pap. 10.99 (*0-310-52921-2*) Zondervan.

McNabb, David, jt. auth. see Furman, Joan.

McNabb, J. W., jt. auth. see Muvdi, Bichara B.

McNabb, Jeffrey G. Rule of Thumb Measuring System: Both English & Metric. large type ed. (Illus.). 42p. 1999. pap. text, teacher ed. 10.00 (*0-9669794-1-9*) Rule of Thumb.

***McNabb, Jeffrey G.** Rule of Thumb Measuring System: Both English & Metric. large type ed. (Illus.). (J). (gr. 4-8). 1999. pap. text 5.00 (*0-9669794-0-0*) Rule of Thumb.

***McNabb, Joe.** Ozark Hillbilly CEO: An Autobiography. LC 99-71335. 384p. 1999. pap. 39.95 (*0-9672491-3-9*) WRDSWRTH.

McNabb, Richard, jt. ed. see Enos, Theresa.

McNabb, Robert & Whitfield, Keith, eds. The Market for Training: International Perspectives on Theory, Methodology & Policy. 416p. 1994. 96.95 (*1-85628-599-5*, Pub. by Avebry) Ashgate Pub Co.

McNabb, Robert H. Thoughts on Things. 1998. pap. write for info. (*1-57553-821-0*) Watermrk Pr.

McNabb, Vincent J. Francis Thompson & Other Essays. LC 68-22117. (Essay Index Reprint Ser.). 1977. 17.95 (*0-8369-0659-4*) Ayer.

McNabb, William R. Tradition, Innovation, & Romantic Images: The Architecture of Historic Knoxville. 80p. 1991. 18.95 (*1-880174-00-6*) U TN F H McClung.

McNabney, Raymond. War Notes: From the Letters of Sgt. Raymond McNabney. Whitworth, E. Andra, ed. LC 94-71567. (Illus.). 224p. (Orig.). 1994. pap. 12.95 (*0-9640706-0-X*) Cock-a-Hoop.

McNack, Eddie C. A Study Guide for General Biology I. 156p. (C). 1989. pap. text 15.95 (*0-89641-179-6*) American Pr.

McNail, Stanley. Something Breathing. LC 87-82454. (Illus.). 58p. (Orig.). reprint ed. pap. 6.00 (*0-940945-01-0*) Embassy Hall Edns.

McNail, Stanley, ed. Sorcerer's Samplecase: Selected Poems in a Jugular Vein. (Illus.). 26p. (Orig.). (YA). (gr. 7 up). 1986. pap. 3.00 (*0-940945-00-2*) Embassy Hall Edns.

McNair, Amy. The Upright Brush: Yan Zhenqing's Calligraphy & Song Literati Politics. LC 97-39661. (Illus.). 272p. 1998. text 49.00 (*0-8248-1922-5*); pap. text 27.95 (*0-8248-2002-9*) UH Pr.

McNair, Amy, jt. auth. see McNair, Mac.

***McNair, Arnold D.** Legal Effects of War. 3rd ed. xxiii, 458p. 1999. reprint ed. 145.00 (*1-56169-470-3*) Gaunt.

McNair, Arnold D., jt. auth. see Buckland, William W.

McNair, Brian. Glasnost, Perestroika & the Soviet Media. (Communication & Society Ser.). (Illus.). 224p. (C). (gr. 13). 1991. 80.00 (*0-415-03551-1*, A5678) Routledge.

— Images of the Enemy. 288p. 1988. text 37.50 (*0-415-00645-7*); pap. text 13.95 (*0-415-00646-5*) Routledge.

— An Introduction to Political Communication. 2nd ed. LC 98-45946. (Communication & Society Ser.). 1999. 75.00 (*0-415-19921-2*); pap. 21.99 (*0-415-19922-0*) Routledge.

***McNair, Brian.** Journalism & Democracy: Evaluation of Political Public Sphere. LC 99-35507. 208p. 2000. pap. 32.99 (*0-415-21280-4*) Routledge.

— Journalism & Democracy: Evaluation of Political Public Sphere. LC 99-35507. 208p. (C). 2000. text 85.00 (*0-415-21279-0*) Routledge.

McNair, Brian. Mediated Sex: Pornography & Postmodern Culture. LC 96-543. 208p. 1996. pap. text 19.95 (*0-340-61428-5*, Pub. by E A) OUP.

— Mediated Sex: Pornography & Postmodern Culture. LC 96-543. 208p. 1996. text 55.00 (*0-340-66293-X*, Pub. by E A) Routldge.

***McNair, Brian.** News & Journalism in the U. K. A Textbook. 3rd ed. LC 98-47256. 240p. 1999. pap. write for info. (*0-415-19924-7*) Routledge.

— News & Journalism in the U. K. A Textbook. 3rd ed. LC 98-47256. 1999. write for info. (*0-415-19923-9*) Routledge.

— The Sociology of Journalism. LC 98-7067. (An Arnold Publication). (Illus.). 192p. 1998. text 65.00 (*0-340-70616-3*, Pub. by E A) OUP.

***McNair, Brian.** The Sociology of Journalism. LC 98-7067. (An Arnold Publication). (Illus.). 192p. 1998. pap. text 19.95 (*0-340-70615-5*, Pub. by E A) OUP.

***McNair, C. J. & CAM-I Cost Management Integration Team Staff.** Value Quest: Driving Profit & Performance by Integrating Strategic Management Processes. (Illus.). 400p. 2000. 35.00 (*1-890783-03-X*) CAM-I.

McNair, C. J. & Vangermeersch, Richard. Total Capacity Management: Optimizing at the Operational, Tactical & Strategic Levels. LC 98-7180. 352p. 1998. boxed set 54.95 (*1-57444-231-7*, 98328) St Lucie Pr.

McNair, Carol J. The Profit Potential: Taking High Performance to the Bottom Line. (Illus.). 224p. (C). 1994. 75.00 (*0-939246-66-X*) Wiley.

— The Profit Potential: Taking High Performance to the Bottom Line. 272p. 1995. 29.95 (*0-471-13178-4*) Wiley.

— World-Class Accounting & Finance. (APICS Ser.). 372p. 1993. 45.00 (*1-55623-550-X*, Irwn Prfssnl) McGraw-Hill Prof.

McNair, Carol J. & Leibfried, Kathleen H. Benchmarking: A Tool for Continuous Improvement. LC 93-61001. 344p. (C). 1993. pap. 18.00 (*0-939246-53-8*) Wiley.

— Benchmarking: A Tool for Continuous Improvement. abr. ed. 368p. 1995. pap. 29.95 (*0-471-13206-3*) Wiley.

McNair, Carol J. & Mosconi, William. Beyond the Bottom Line: Measuring World Class Performance. (APICS Series in Production Management). 350p. 1989. text 47.50 (*1-55623-194-6*, Irwn Prfssnl) McGraw-Hill Prof.

McNair, Chris, ed. see McNair, George R.

McNair, Clarissa. The Hole in the Edge. unabridged ed. 108p. 1997. pap. 13.95 (*0-9661087-0-1*) Hawthorne Press.

***McNair, Debra W.** Cooking on Hector's Bluff: A Personal Collection of Recipes. LC 99-91020. 248p. 1999. spiral bd. 14.95 (*0-9673665-0-X*) H Bluff.

McNair, Doug & McNair, Wallace Y. Black Organizations: A Directory. annuals 96p. 1997. pap. 125.00 (*1-887302-01-8*) Wstrn Images.

— Colorado Black Leadership Profiles Premier Edition 1989-1990: Who's Who among Colorado's Outstanding Leaders. 188p. 1989. 40.00 (*1-887302-02-6*) Wstrn Images.

— Colorado Hispanic Leadership Profiles: "Who's Who among Colorado's Outstanding Leaders" 186p. 1991. 40.00 (*0-9627600-1-3*) Wstrn Images.

— National Black Leadership Profiles: Who's Who among America's Outstanding Leaders. 153p. 1994. pap. 85.00 (*0-9627600-7-2*) Wstrn Images.

— Women Leaders of Colorado: "A Success Network of Outstanding Leaders" 78p. 1992. 40.00 (*0-9627600-2-1*) Wstrn Images.

McNair, Francis M., jt. auth. see Edmonds, Thomas P.

***McNair, Frank.** It's OK to Ask 'Em to Work: And Other Essential Maxims for Smart Managers. LC 99-50275. (Illus.). 160p. 2000. 18.95 (*0-8144-0517-7*) AMACOM.

McNair, George R. Shrub It Up: A Guide for Pacific Northwest Landscaping. McNair, Chris, ed. (Illus.). 66p. 1986. pap. 7.96 (*0-9619034-0-6*) CGM Pub Co.

McNair, Georgia T. France, 1985. Fisher, Robert C., ed. (Fisher Annotated Travel Guides Ser.). 320p. 1984. 12.95 (*0-8116-0071-8*) NAL.

McNair, Harold M. Cromatografia de Gases. Dominguez, Xorge A., tr. from SPA. (Serie de Quimica: Monografia No. 23). 90p. (C). 1981. pap. 3.50 (*0-8270-1360-4*) OAS.

McNair, Harold M. & Miller, James M. Basic Gas Chromatography. LC 97-18151. (Techniques in Analytical Chemistry Ser.). 224p. 1997. 59.95 (*0-471-17260-X*); pap. 29.95 (*0-471-17261-8*) Wiley.

McNair, Ian. Discovering the New Testament in Greek. 1996. pap. 19.99 (*0-551-02389-9*) Zondervan.

McNair, J. B. McNair, McNear & McNeir Genealogies: Second Supplement. (Illus.). 457p. 1991. reprint ed. pap. 71.00 (*0-8328-1718-X*); reprint ed. lib. bdg. 81.00 (*0-8328-1717-1*) Higginson Bk Co.

— McNair, McNear & McNeir Genealogies: Third Supplement. (Illus.). 314p. 1991. reprint ed. pap. 46.50 (*0-8328-1720-1*); reprint ed. lib. bdg. 56.50 (*0-8328-1719-8*) Higginson Bk Co.

McNair, James. Chicken. LC 86-29880. (Illus.). 96p. 1987. 19.95 (*0-87701-439-6*); pap. 11.95 (*0-87701-411-6*) Chronicle Bks.

— Cold Pasta. LC 85-363. (Illus.). 96p. 1985. pap. 11.95 (*0-87701-353-5*) Chronicle Bks.

— James McNair Cooks Southeast Asian. LC 95-12942. (Illus.). 168p. 1996. 24.95 (*0-8118-0483-6*); pap. 14.95 (*0-8118-0453-4*) Chronicle Bks.

— James McNair's Beans & Grains. (Illus.). 96p. 1997. pap. 12.95 (*0-8118-0104-7*) Chronicle Bks.

— James McNair's Cheese Cookbook. (Illus.). 96p. 1989. 19.95 (*0-87701-705-0*); pap. 11.95 (*0-87701-653-4*) Chronicle Bks.

— James McNair's Custards, Mousses & Puddings. 96p. 1993. 19.95 (*0-87701-823-5*); pap. 11.95 (*0-87701-829-4*) Chronicle Bks.

— James McNair's Fish Cookbook. (Illus.). 96p. 1991. 19.95 (*0-8118-0002-4*); pap. 11.95 (*0-87701-821-9*) Chronicle Bks.

— James McNair's Gourmet Burgers. (Illus.). 96p. 1992. 19.95 (*0-8118-0098-9*); pap. 11.95 (*0-8118-0093-8*) Chronicle Bks.

— James McNair's Grill Cookbook. (Illus.). 96p. 1990. 19.95 (*0-87701-719-0*); pap. 11.95 (*0-87701-710-7*) Chronicle Bks.

***McNair, James.** James Mcnair's New Pizza: Foolproof Techniques & Fabulous Recipes. LC 99-86781. (Illus.). 2000. pap. 19.95 (*0-8118-2364-4*) Chronicle Bks.

McNair, James. James McNair's Pasta Cookbook. (Illus.). 96p. 1990. 19.95 (*0-87701-648-8*); pap. 11.95 (*0-87701-618-6*) Chronicle Bks.

— James McNair's Pie Cookbook. LC 89-34354. (Illus.). 96p. 1989. 19.95 (*0-87701-600-3*); pap. 11.95 (*0-87701-595-3*) Chronicle Bks.

— James McNair's Potato Cookbook. LC 89-17380. (Illus.). 96p. 1989. 19.95 (*0-87701-650-X*); pap. 11.95 (*0-87701-640-2*) Chronicle Bks.

— James McNair's Rice Cookbook. (Illus.). 96p. 1988. 19.95 (*0-87701-525-2*); pap. 11.95 (*0-87701-519-8*) Chronicle Bks.

— James McNair's Salads. (Illus.). 96p. (Orig.). 1991. 19.95 (*0-87701-825-1*); pap. 11.95 (*0-87701-819-7*) Chronicle Bks.

— James McNair's Salmon Cookbook. LC 87-17382. (Illus.). 96p. 1987. 19.95 (*0-87701-478-7*); pap. 11.95 (*0-87701-453-1*) Chronicle Bks.

— James McNair's Soups. LC 90-2222. (Illus.). 96p. 1990. 19.95 (*0-87701-761-1*); pap. 11.95 (*0-87701-753-0*) Chronicle Bks.

— Pizza. LC 87-17381. (Illus.). 96p. 1987. 19.95 (*0-87701-481-7*); pap. 12.95 (*0-87701-448-5*) Chronicle Bks.

***McNair, James.** The Sutter Home Napa Valley Cookbook: New & Classic Recipes from the Wine Country. LC 99-53486. (Illus.). 160p. 2000. pap. 22.95 (*0-8118-2200-1*) Chronicle Bks.

McNair, James, photos by. James McNair's Vegetarian Pizza. LC 92-46362. (Illus.). 96p. 1993. 19.95 (*0-8118-0109-8*); pap. 12.95 (*0-8118-0100-4*) Chronicle Bks.

McNair, James & Moore, Andrew. James McNair's Cakes. LC 98-31677. (Illus.). 132p. 1999. pap. 16.95 (*0-8118-1768-7*) Chronicle Bks.

McNair, James, jt. auth. see Wolf, Rex.

McNair, James, jt. auth. see Wolfe, Rex.

McNair, James K. James McNair's Breakfasts. LC 97-39664. 1998. pap. 14.95 (*0-8118-2061-0*) Chronicle Bks.

***McNair, James K.** James McNair's Favorites. LC 99-13208. (Illus.). 616p. 1999. 29.95 (*0-8118-0115-2*) Chronicle Bks.

McNair, Jeff. The Light Team. 200p. 1998. pap. 9.95 (*1-58169-005-3*, JM101, Third Stry Window) Genesis Comm Inc.

McNair, John D. McNear: The William McNear Family, 1770-1990. 63p. 1993. reprint ed. pap. 13.00 (*0-8328-3373-8*) Higginson Bk Co.

McNair, John F. & Barlow, Thomas L. Oral Tradition from the Indus. rev. ed. Dorson, Richard M., ed. LC 77-70609. (International Folklore Ser.). (Illus.). 1977. reprint ed. lib. bdg. 17.95 (*0-405-10108-2*) Ayer.

McNair, Joseph. Multi-Cultural Awareness: Consciousness Toward a Process of Personal Transformation. 386p. (C). 1996. pap. text, per. 54.95 (*0-7872-2669-6*, 41266901) Kendall-Hunt.

***McNair, Joseph D.** Barbara Jordan: African American Politician. LC 00-26854. (Illus.). 2000. lib. bdg. write for info. (*1-56766-741-4*) Childs World.

— Leontyne Price. LC 99-44229. (YA). 2000. lib. bdg. write for info. (*1-56766-720-1*) Childs World.

***McNair, Julie.** Burning Bush: A Journey from Fear to Faith, One of Self Discovery. 2nd ed. (Illus.). 96p. 2000. 14.95 (*0-9700621-0-9*) Ritual Ves.

McNair, Kate, jt. adapted by see Garis, Roger.

McNair, Keith. Split Decision. 250p. (Orig.). 1999. pap. write for info. (*1-889732-21-4*) Word for Word.

McNair, Lord. The Law of Treaties. 800p. 1986. text 175.00 (*0-19-825152-1*) OUP.

***McNair, Mac & McNair, Amy.** Ten Principles of a Successful Marriage: Practical Lessons from the Ten Commandments. LC 99-12213. 160p. 1999. reprint ed. pap. 5.95 (*1-58182-022-4*) Cumberland Hse.

McNair, Marcia O. Kwanzaa Crafts: Gifts & Decorations for a Meaningful & Festive Celebration. LC 98-16164. (Illus.). 128p. (J). 1998. 27.95 (*0-8069-1777-6*) Sterling.

McNair, Marcia Odile. Kwanzaa Crafts: Gifts & Decorations for a Meaningful & Festive Celebration. (Illus.). 128p. (J). 1999. pap. 14.95 (*0-8069-1803-9*, Chapelle) Sterling.

***McNair, Marion.** The New America: Investment Strategies for the New Millennium. 202p. 1999. pap. 29.95 (*0-9674946-0-5*) McNair CA.

McNair, Mattie, jt. auth. see Landry, Paul.

McNair Palmer, Lisa, see Adkison, Danny M. & Palmer, Lisa McNair.

McNair, Patricia. Tossing the Pebble. LC 98-65979. 76p. 1998. pap. write for info. (*1-57502-781-X*, P02162) Morris Pubng.

McNair, Raymond F. Ascent to Greatness: The Incredible Story of America's Rise to World Super-Power. LC 75-27253. (Illus.). 550p. 1976. 14.95 (*0-685-68396-6*) Triumph Pub.

An Asterisk (*) at the beginning of an entry indicates that the title is appearing for the first time.

McNair, Sylvia. Bangkok. LC 99-10615. (Cities of the World Ser.). 64p. (YA). (gr. 4-9). 1999. 26.00 (*0-516-21195-1*) Childrens.
***McNair, Sylvia.** Bangkok. (Cities of the World Ser.). (J). 2000. pap. text 9.95 (*0-516-26531-8*) Childrens.
— Chile LC 99-12689. 2000. 32.00 (*0-516-21007-6*) Childrens.
McNair, Sylvia. Connecticut. 2nd ed. LC 98-37691. (America the Beautiful Ser.). 144p. (YA). (gr. 5-8). 1999. lib. bdg. 32.00 (*0-516-20832-2*) Childrens.
— Massachusetts. 2nd ed. LC 97-40668. (America the Beautiful Ser.). (J). 1998. 32.00 (*0-516-20635-4*) Childrens.
— Nebraska. LC 97-40704. (America the Beautiful Ser.). 144p. (YA). (gr. 5-8). 1999. 32.00 (*0-516-20689-3*) Childrens.
— New Hampshire. (America the Beautiful Ser.). 144p. (J). (gr. 5-8). 1991. lib. bdg. 28.00 (*0-516-00475-1*) Childrens.
***McNair, Sylvia.** Rhode Island LC 99-35216. (America the Beautiful Ser.). 2000. 32.00 (*0-516-21043-2*) Childrens.
McNair, Sylvia. Sweden. LC 97-26886. (Enchantment of the World Second Ser.). 144p. (YA). (gr. 5-9). 1998. 32.00 (*0-516-20607-9*) Childrens.
— Thailand. 2nd ed. LC 98-16319. (Enchantment of the World Ser.). 144 p. (J). 1998. 32.00 (*0-516-21100-5*) Childrens.
***McNair, Sylvia.** U. S. Territories. LC 00-26194. (America the Beautiful Ser.). (Illus.). (J). 2001. pap. write for info. (*0-516-21607-4*) Childrens.
McNair, Sylvia. Vermont. LC 90-21117. (America the Beautiful Ser.). (Illus.). 144p. (J). (gr. 5-8). 1991. lib. bdg. 28.00 (*0-516-00491-3*) Childrens.
McNair, Wallace Y. Black & Beautiful: A Self-Discovery Coloring Book. (Illus.). 26p. (Orig.). (J). (gr. 2 up). 1992. pap. 12.50 (*0-9627600-3-X*) Wstrn Images.
— Our African Connection: What We Brought from Home. 250p. (Orig.). (C). 1997. pap. text. write for info. (*0-9627600-5-6*) Wstrn Images.
McNair, Wallace Y., jt. auth. see McNair, Doug.
McNair, Wesley. The Dissonant Heart. (Illus.). 52p. (Orig.). 1995. pap. 12.95 (*0-913341-18-5*) Coyote Love.
***McNair, Wesley.** Mapping the Heart: Reflections on Place & Poetry. 2000. 30.00 (*1-56792-160-4*) Godine.
McNair, Wesley. Talking in the Dark. LC 98-33665. 96p. 1998. pap. 13.95 (*1-56792-094-2*) Godine.
— The Town of No & My Brother Running: Dual Volume. LC 95-35338. 176p. 1997. pap. 15.95 (*1-56792-056-X*) Godine.
— Twelve Journeys in Maine. (Illus.). 48p. 1992. 195.00 (*0-913341-16-9*); pap. 9.95 (*0-913341-15-0*) Coyote Love.
McNair, Wesley, ed. The Quotable Moose: A Contemporary Maine Reader. LC 93-38324. 269p. 1994. pap. 17.95 (*0-87451-673-0*) U Pr of New Eng.
McNair, Will L. SCR & New Technology in Electric Rig Drilling: A Safety & Efficiency Handbook. 296p. 1991. 25.00 (*0-87814-368-8*) PennWell Bks.
McNair, William & Rumley, Hilary. Pioneer Aboriginal Mission. (Illus.). 162p. (Orig.). pap. 19.95 (*0-85564-178-9*, Pub. by Univ of West Aust Pr) Intl Spec Bk.
McNairn, Alan. Behold the Hero: General Wolfe & the Arts in the Eighteenth Century. LC 99-203406. (Illus.). 328p. 1997. 44.95 (*0-7735-1539-9*, Pub. by McG-Queens Univ Pr) CUP Services.
McNairn, Colin H. Governmental & Intergovernmental Immunity in Australia & Canada. LC 78-302669. 219p. reprint ed. pap. 67.90 (*0-608-12879-1*, 202364800033) Bks Demand.
McNairn, Colin H. H., jt. auth. see Canada Staff.
McNairn, Jack & MacMullen, Jerry. Ships of the Redwood Coast. LC 45-5289. 168p. 1945. reprint ed. pap. 30.00 (*0-7837-2354-7*, 204257000005) Bks Demand.
McNairn, Peggi & Shioleno, Cindy. Quick Tech Readable, Repeatable Stories & Activities. (Illus.). 223p. (Orig.). 1994. spiral bd. 24.00 (*1-884135-08-0*) Mayer-Johnson.
McNairn, Peggi, et al. Quick Tech Magic: Music Based Stories & Activities. (Illus.). 184p. 1995. spiral bd. 29.00 (*1-884135-20-X*) Mayer-Johnson.
McNairn, William N. The Accountant's Guide to Computer-Age Accounting Manuals. (Illus.). 236p. (Orig.). 1985. student ed. 34.95 (*0-932621-00-7*) Quotamus Pr.
— The Smart Attorney's Guide to Accounting Documents for Discovery & Evidence. (Illus.). 100p. 1987. pap. text 14.95 (*0-932621-02-3*) Quotamus Pr.
McNairy, Mel. Art of Vengeance. LC 97-76807. 218p. 1998. pap. 10.95 (*0-9644007-6-6*) Filibuster Pr.
McNall, Neil A. An Agricultural History of the Genesee Valley, 1790-1860. LC 75-25260. (Illus.). 276p. 1976. reprint ed. lib. bdg. 65.00 (*0-8371-8396-0*, MCGV, Greenwood Pr) Greenwood.
McNall, Rebecca. Angel of God, What's Your Name? (Illus.). 32p. (J). (ps-2). 1996. pap. 2.95 (*0-8198-0762-1*) Pauline Bks.
McNall, Sally A. Who Is in the House? A Psychological Study of Two Centuries of Women's Fiction in America, 1795 to the Present. LC 80-26601. 153p. 1981. lib. bdg. 42.50 (*0-444-99081-X*, MWH/) Greenwood.
McNall, Sally A., jt. auth. see McNall, Scott G.
McNall, Scott G. Current Perspectives in Social Theory, Vol. 5. Agger, Ben, ed. 340p. 1985. 73.25 (*0-89232-511-9*) Jai Pr.
— The Road to Rebellion: Class Formation & Kansas Populism 1865-1900. (Illus.). xviii, 372p. 1988. lib. bdg. 60.00 (*0-226-56126-7*) U Ch Pr.
— The Road to Rebellion: Class Formation & Kansas Populism 1865-1900. (Illus.). xviii, 372p. 1999. pap. text 24.00 (*0-226-56127-5*) U Ch Pr.
McNall, Scott G., ed. Theoretical Perspectives in Sociology. 562p. 1979. pap. text 15.50 (*0-312-79633-1*) St Martin.
McNall, Scott G. & Howe, Gary N. Current Perspectives in Social Theory, Vol. 2. Agger, Ben, ed. 288p. 1981. 73.25 (*0-89232-190-3*) Jai Pr.
McNall, Scott G. & McNall, Sally A. Plains Families: Exploring Sociology Through Social History. 384p. 1983. teacher ed. write for info. (*0-318-56959-0*) St Martin.
McNall, Scott G., jt. ed. see Agger, Ben.
McNallan, Michael J., ed. see Symposium on Corrosion & Corrosive Degradation of.
McNally. Cool Places U. S. A. Backseat Books. (J). (ps-3). 1994. pap. 3.95 (*0-528-81409-5*) Rand McNally.
McNally, Bob. Bass in Depth. LC 95-94371. (Bob McNally's Complete Bks.). (Illus.). 300p. (Orig.). 1995. pap. text 16.95 (*0-9646265-0-0*) McNally Outdoor Prodns.
— Fishermen's Knots, Fishing Rigs & How to Use Them. rev. ed. LC 92-74447. (Bob McNally's Complete Bks.). (Illus.). 304p. 1995. pap. text 16.95 (*0-9646265-1-9*) McNally Outdoor Prodns.
McNally, Bruce J. Animals in Wildlife--Biology, Behavior, & Vectorisms for Disease: Index for New Information. LC 95-19213. 1995. write for info. (*0-7883-0642-1*); pap. write for info. (*0-7883-0643-X*) ABBE Pubs Assn.
McNally, Catherine, ed. see Mills, Selwyn & Weisser, Max.
McNally, Clare. Addison House. 304p. (Orig.). 1988. mass mkt. 4.50 (*0-380-75587-4*, Avon Bks) Morrow Avon.
— Blood Relations. 1997. mass mkt. 6.99 (*0-8125-5104-4*, Pub. by Tor Bks) St Martin.
— Goodnight, Sweet Angel. 1996. mass mkt. 5.99 (*0-8125-5103-6*, Pub. by Tor Bks) St Martin.
— Somebody Come & Play. 320p. 1987. pap. 4.99 (*0-8125-2164-1*, Pub. by Tor Bks) St Martin.
— Stage Fright. 256p. (Orig.). 1995. 5.99 (*0-8125-4839-6*, Pub. by Tor Bks) St Martin.
— There He Keeps Them Very Well. 368p. (Orig.). 1994. mass mkt. 4.99 (*0-8125-3525-1*) Tor Bks.
McNally, Clayton L., Jr. Micro Focus CICS Option 3.0: Developing CICS Applications on the PC. 1993. pap. 59.99 (*0-471-58406-1*, GD4604) Wiley.
McNally, Clayton L. & Molchan, Peter. Micro Focus COBOL Workbench for the Application Developer. 360p. 1993. pap. 52.00 (*0-471-58420-7*) Wiley.
McNally, Colleen, et al. Some People Think We Don't Learn Anything in This School. LC 77-71871. (Illus.). 1977. pap. 4.95 (*0-915492-03-2*) Ash Lad Pr.
McNally, David. Against the Market: Political Economy, Market Socialism & the Marxist Critique. 280p. (C). 1993. pap. 19.00 (*0-86091-606-5*, B2500, Pub. by Verso) Norton.
***McNally, David.** Bodies of Meaning: Studies on Language, Labor & Liberation. 304p. (C). 2000. text 71.50 (*0-7914-4735-9*); pap. text 23.95 (*0-7914-4736-7*) State U NY Pr.
McNally, David. The Eagle's Secret: Success Strategies for Thriving at Work & in Life. 224p. 1999. pap. 12.95 (*0-440-50845-2*, Dell Trade Pbks) Dell.
— The Eagle's Secret: Success Strategies for Thriving at Work & in Life. LC 98-11924. 224p. 1998. 22.95 (*0-385-31427-2*) Doubleday.
— Even Eagles Need a Push: Learning to Soar in a Changing World. 192p. 1994. pap. 12.95 (*0-440-50611-5*) Dell.
— Even Eagles Need a Push: Learning to Soar in a Changing World. 170p. 1990. 19.95 (*0-9626921-0-7*) Trans-Form Pr.
— Political Economy & the Rise of Capitalism: A Reinterpretation. 345p. 1989. pap. 16.95 (*0-520-07192-1*, Pub. by U CA Pr) Cal Prin Full Svc.
McNally, Deirdre, jt. compiled by see North State Cooperative Library System Advisory Bo.
McNally, Dennis. Sacred Space: An Aesthetic for the Liturgical Environment. LC 85-51230. 215p. (C). 1990. pap. 16.00 (*0-932269-45-1*); text 28.00 (*1-55605-154-9*) Wyndham Hall.
McNally, Derek, ed. Highlights of Astronomy: As Presented at the XXth General Assembly of the IAU, 1988. (C). 1989. pap. text 114.50 (*0-7923-0281-8*); lib. bdg. 261.00 (*0-7923-0280-X*) Kluwer Academic.
— Reports of Astronomy Vol. 21A: Transactions of the International Astronomical Union. (C). 1991. lib. bdg. 202.00 (*0-7923-1172-8*) Kluwer Academic.
— Transactions of the International Astronomical Union, Vol. XXB: Proceedings of the Twentieth General Assembly, Baltimore, 1988. (C). 1990. lib. bdg. 317.00 (*0-7923-0550-7*) Kluwer Academic.
— The Vanishing Universe: Adverse Environmental Impacts on Astronomy: Proceedings of the Conference Sponsored by UNESCO Held at UNESCO, Paris, June 30-July 2, 1992. LC 93-41980. (Illus.). 208p. (C). 1994. text 95.00 (*0-521-45020-9*) Cambridge U Pr.
McNally, Dorie, jt. auth. see McNally, Keith.
***McNally, Eugene J.** Protein Formulation & Delivery. LC 99-40675. (Drugs & the Pharmaceutical Sciences Ser.). (Illus.). 278p. 1999. text 150.00 (*0-8247-7883-9*) Dekker.
Mcnally, G. Soil & Rock Construction Materials. LC 98-200042. (Illus.). 416p. (C). 1998. pap. 39.99 (*0-419-21420-8*) Thomson Learn.
McNally, Hannah. Nebraska: Off the Beaten Path: A Guide to Unique Places. 2nd ed. LC 99-21462. (Off the Beaten Path Ser.). (Illus.). 225p. 1999. pap. text 12.95 (*0-7627-0459-4*) Globe Pequot.
McNally, Jeffrey A. The Adult Development of Career Army Officers. LC 91-8028. 296p. 1991. 69.50 (*0-275-93698-8*, C3698, Praeger Pubs) Greenwood.
***McNally, John.** Troublemakers. LC 00-39247. (John Simmons Short Fiction Award Ser.). 228p. 2000. pap. 15.95 (*0-87745-727-1*) U of Iowa Pr.
***McNally, John, ed.** High Infidelity: 24 Great Short Stories about Adultery by Some of Our Best Contemporary Authors. 368p. 1998. reprint ed. pap. 13.00 (*0-688-16358-0*, Quil) HarperTrade.
McNally, John, jt. auth. see Pitman, Richard.
McNally, JoLouise, jt. auth. see Borg, Quentin.
McNally, Keith & McNally, Dorie. McNally's Price Guide for Collectible Soundtrack Records. LC 94-96474. (Illus.). 240p. (Orig.). 1995. pap. 29.95 (*0-9643539-1-1*) W Pt Recs.
McNally, Kevin. Corporate Venture Capital: Bridging the Equity Gap in the Small Business Sector. LC 97-206860. (Routledge Studies in Small Business Ser.: No. 2). 240p. (C). 1997. 85.00 (*0-415-15467-7*) Routledge.
McNally, Louise. A Semantics for the English Existential Construction. rev. ed. Horn, Laurence, ed. LC 96-46189. (Outstanding Dissertations in Linguistics Ser.). 237p. 1996. text 68.00 (*0-8153-2557-6*) Garland.
McNally, Marcia, ed. see Woodbridge, Sally.
McNally, Margaret Cheney & Niles, Francis L. Norwich. LC 98-87696. (Images of America Ser.). (Illus.). 128p. 1998. pap. 16.99 (*0-7524-1270-1*) Arcadia Publng.
McNally, Mark, et al. 96 Ways You Can Save Taxes in '96: Wisconsin Edition. 128p. (Orig.). Date not set. pap. 9.95 (*0-9644913-9-7*) Loopholes Pr.
McNally, Mary. Reunion. (Illus.). 52p. 1998. pap. 9.95 (*0-9649776-3-X*) Plesnt Hill.
McNally, Mary E., jt. ed. see Bright, Frank V.
McNally, Mary M. International Wheat Subsidies: Who Really Profits? rev. ed. LC 94-23662. (Foreign Economic Policy of the United States Ser.). 176p. 1995. text 20.00 (*0-8153-2018-3*) Garland.
***McNally, Michael.** Ojibwe Singers: Hymns, Grief & a Native Culture in Motion. (Religion in America). (Illus.). 272p. 2000. text 45.00 (*0-19-513464-8*) OUP.
McNally, Michael G. & Recker, Wilfred W. Activity-Based Models of Travel Behavior: Evolution & Implementation. 300p. 2000. 65.00 (*0-08-042776-6*, Pergamon Pr) Elsevier.
McNally, Michael J. Catholic Parish Life on Florida's West Coast, 1860-1968. LC 95-71170. 503p. 1996. pap. text 16.95 (*0-9649046-0-8*) Catholic Media.
— Catholicism in South Florida, 1868-1968. LC 84-7389. 334p. (Orig.). 1984. pap. 24.95 (*0-8130-0788-7*) U Press Fla.
McNally, P., jt. auth. see Dracquer, Michael.
McNally, Patrick. Parties, Patriots & Undertakers: Parliamentary Politics in Early Hanoverian Ireland. LC 98-103973. 240p. 1997. boxed set 45.00 (*1-85182-255-0*, Pub. by Four Cts Pr) Intl Spec Bk.
McNally, Paul. Multimedia Information Resources. 216p. 1998. 69.95 (*0-7329-4092-3*, Pub. by Macmill Educ); pap. 34.95 (*0-7329-4080-X*, Pub. by Macmill Educ) Paul & Co Pubs.
McNally, Peter R., ed. GI/Liver Secrets: Questions You Will Be Asked on Rounds, in the Clinic, & on Oral Exams. LC 95-47442. (Secrets Ser.). (Illus.). 680p. (Orig.). 1996. pap. text 39.00 (*1-56053-150-9*) Hanley & Belfus.
McNally, R. T., ed. Philosophical Works of Peter Chaadaev. (C). 1991. lib. bdg. 180.50 (*0-7923-1285-6*, Pub. by M Nijhoff) Kluwer Academic.
***McNally, Raymond T. & Florescu, Radu.** In Search of Dr. Jekyll & Mr. Hyde: The True Life Story Behind the Ultimate Tale of Horror. 304p. 2000. 24.95 (*1-58063-157-6*) Renaissance.
McNally, Raymond T. & Florescu, Radu R. In Search of Dracula: The History of Dracula & Vampires. LC 94-18233. (Illus.). 318p. 1994. pap. 14.95 (*0-395-65783-0*) HM.
McNally, Raymond T., jt. auth. see Florescu, Radu.
McNally, Richard J. Panic Disorder: A Critical Analysis. LC 94-26243. 276p. 1994. lib. bdg. 38.00 (*0-89862-263-8*) Guilford Pubns.
McNally, Robert, ed. Old Ireland. LC 65-20468. 264p. reprint ed. pap. 81.90 (*0-7837-5583-X*, 204537400005) Bks Demand.
McNally, Robert A., jt. auth. see Granet, Roger.
McNally, Robert A., jt. auth. see Schoch, Robert.
McNally, Robert Aquinas, jt. auth. see Bergin, Bonnie.
McNally, Ruth & Wheale, Peter R., eds. Animal Genetic Engineering: Of Pigs, Oncomice & Men. (C). 45.00 (*0-7453-0754-X*) Pluto GBR.
McNally, Ruth, ed. see Wheale, Peter.
McNally, Ruth, jt. ed. see Wheale, Peter.
McNally Staff. Histomap of World History. 1990. pap. 6.95 (*0-528-83426-6*) Rand McNally.
McNally, Stephen. Child in Amber. LC 92-33398. 80p. 1993. pap. 9.95 (*0-87023-840-X*); lib. bdg. 20.00 (*0-87023-839-6*) U of Mass Pr.
McNally, T. M. Almost Home. LC 97-52707. 240p. 1998. 22.00 (*0-684-84469-9*) S&S Trade.
— Almost Home: A Novel. 240p. 1999. pap. 12.00 (*0-684-85445-7*, Scribner Pap Fic) S&S Trade Pap.
— Low Flying Aircraft: Stories by T. M. McNally. LC 91-14100. (Flannery O'Connor Award for Short Fiction Ser.). 176p. 1991. 19.95 (*0-8203-1378-5*) U of Ga Pr.
McNally, Terrence. And Things That Go Bump in the Night. 1969. pap. 5.25 (*0-8222-0046-5*) Dramatists Play.
— Andre's Mother & Other Short Plays. 1995. pap. 5.25 (*0-8222-1419-9*) Dramatists Play.
— Apple Pie: Three One Act Plays. 1968. pap. 5.25 (*0-8222-0061-9*) Dramatists Play.
— Bad Habits. rev. ed. 1990. pap. 5.25 (*0-8222-1435-0*) Dramatists Play.
***McNally, Terrence.** Corpus Christi. LC 99-228722. (Illus.). 1999. pap. 5.95 (*0-8222-1696-5*) Dramatists Play.
McNally, Terrence. Corpus Christi. LC 99-13624. (Illus.). 96p. 1999. pap. 12.00 (*0-8021-3635-4*, Grove) Grove-Atltic.
— Cuba Si! - Bringing It All Back Home - Last Gasps. 1970. pap. 5.25 (*0-8222-0257-3*) Dramatists Play.
— Frankie & Johnny in the Clair De Lune. 1988. pap. 5.25 (*0-8222-0420-7*) Dramatists Play.
— It's Only a Play. rev. ed. 1992. pap. 5.25 (*0-8222-0582-3*) Dramatists Play.
— Lips Together, Teeth Apart. 1992. pap. 5.25 (*0-8222-0670-6*) Dramatists Play.
— Lips Together, Teeth Apart. 112p. 1992. pap. 9.95 (*0-452-26807-9*, Plume) Dutton Plume.
— The Lisbon Traviata. 1992. pap. 5.25 (*0-8222-0673-0*) Dramatists Play.
— Love! Valour! Compassion! 1995. pap. 5.25 (*0-8222-1467-9*) Dramatists Play.
— Love! Valour! Compassion! & a Perfect Ganesh: Two Plays. (Orig.). 1997. pap. 12.95 (*0-452-27930-5*, Plume) Dutton Plume.
— Master Class. 1996. pap. 5.25 (*0-8222-1521-7*) Dramatists Play.
— Master Class. 96p. 1995. pap. 9.95 (*0-452-27615-2*, Plume) Dutton Plume.
— A Perfect Ganesh. 1994. pap. 5.25 (*0-8222-1379-6*) Dramatists Play.
— Sweet Eros & Witness: Two One-Act Plays. 1969. pap. 5.25 (*0-8222-1105-X*) Dramatists Play.
— Terrence McNally, Vol. II. (Contemporary American Playwrights Ser.). 176p. 1996. pap. 14.95 (*1-57525-061-6*) Smith & Kraus.
— Terrence McNally Vol. I: 15 Short Plays. LC 94-10070. (Contemporary Playwrights Ser.). 348p. 1994. pap. 16.95 (*1-880399-34-2*) Smith & Kraus.
— Three Plays by Terrence McNally. 256p. 1990. pap. 11.95 (*0-452-26425-1*, Plume) Dutton Plume.
— Where Has Tommy Flowers Gone? 1972. pap. 5.25 (*0-8222-1241-2*) Dramatists Play.
— Whiskey. 1973. pap. 3.25 (*0-8222-1243-9*) Dramatists Play.
McNally, Terrence, jt. auth. see Cass, Hyla.
McNally, Thomas & Storey, William G. Day by Day: The Notre Dame Prayerbook for Students. (Illus.). 208p. 1975. pap. 6.95 (*0-87793-100-3*) Ave Maria.
McNally, Thomas, jt. auth. see Storey, William G.
McNally, Tom. The Complete Book of Fly Fishing. 2nd ed. LC 97-206387. (Illus.). 368p. 1997. pap. 19.95 (*0-07-045638-0*, Ragged Mntain) McGraw-Hill Prof.
— Mostly about Dogs. (Illus.). 254p. 1972. pap. 4.95 (*0-87955-403-7*) O'Hara.
McNally, Vincent J. Reform, Revolution & Reaction: Archbishop John Thomas Troy & the Catholic Church in Ireland 1787-1817. 268p. (C). 1995. lib. bdg. 44.50 (*0-8191-9999-0*) U Pr of Amer.
McNally, William F. Bill McNally's Centrifugal Pump & Mechanical Seal Reference Manual. 800p. 1998. pap. 69.95 (*0-9670068-0-5*) McNally Inst.
— Managing Your Healthcare: A Consumer Guide to Navigating Today's Health Care Systems. 216p. 1997. pap. 19.95 (*1-886346-20-8*) Warde Pubs.
McNamara. Investigating Astronomy. 1996. 8.12 (*0-697-39586-3*) McGraw.
McNamara. Strategic Innovations: Lecturers Resource Manual. (Business Press-New Ser.). 1997. pap., teacher ed. 70.95 (*1-86152-151-0*) Thomson Learn.
McNamara, ed. Personal Financial Planning. (C). 1997. pap. text, student ed. write for info. (*0-673-99925-4*) Addison-Wesley.
McNamara, Aidan. Simple Guide to Ireland: Customs & Etiquette. 2nd ed. (Illus.). 96p. 2000. pap. text 8.95 (*1-86034-066-0*, Pub. by Global Bks) Midpt Trade.
McNamara, Andrea. Design & Practice for Printed Textiles. (Illus.). 320p. 1996. pap. text 49.95 (*0-19-553371-2*) OUP.
McNamara, B., ed. Radiation in Plasmas: Proceedings of the Topical Conference on Radiation in Plasmas, Trieste, Italy, 1983, 2 vols., 1. 1000p. 1984. write for info. (*9971-966-37-9*) World Scientific Pub.
— Twenty Years of Plasma Physics: Proceedings of the Workshop on Twenty Years of Plasma Physics (1964-1984), Trieste, Italy, September 1984. 376p. 1985. 70.00 (*9971-978-31-8*) World Scientific Pub.
McNamara, Barry & McNamara, Francine. Keys to Dealing with Bullies. LC 97-362. (Parenting Keys sER.). 176p. 1997. pap. text 6.95 (*0-7641-0163-3*) Barron.
McNamara, Barry E. Keys to Parenting a Child with a Learning Disability. LC 95-112. (Parenting Keys Ser.). 1995. pap. 6.95 (*0-8120-9033-0*) Barron.
— Learning Disabilities: Appropriate Practices for a Diverse Population. LC 97-46378. (SUNY Series, Youth Social Services, Schooling, & Public Policy). 320p. (C). 1998. text 65.50 (*0-7914-3883-X*); pap. text 21.95 (*0-7914-3884-8*) State U NY Pr.
— The Resource Room: A Guide for Special Educators. LC 88-20086. 148p. (C). 1989. pap. text 24.95 (*0-88706-984-3*) State U NY Pr.
***McNamara, Barry E. & McNamara, Francine J.** Keys to Parenting a Child with Attention Deficit Disorder: Barron's Parenting Keys. 2nd ed. 208p. 2000. pap. 7.95 (*0-7641-1291-0*) Barron.
McNamara, Barry E. & McNamara, Francine J. Keys to Parenting Children with Attention Deficit Disorders. LC 92-16966. (Parenting Keys Ser.). 208p. 1993. pap. 6.95 (*0-8120-1459-6*) Barron.
McNamara, Beth B. Baptism: The Most Precious Gift. (Illus.). 64p. (Orig.). 1996. pap. 19.95 (*0-87973-366-7*) Our Sunday Visitor.
— My Baptism Memory Book. (Illus.). 40p. (Orig.). 1996. pap. 9.95 (*0-87973-367-5*) Our Sunday Visitor.
— Welcome Letters from Your Parish. 1999. 16.95 (*0-87973-244-X*) Our Sunday Visitor.
— Welcome Letters from Your Parish: Director's Guide. 1999. write for info. (*0-87973-374-8*) Our Sunday Visitor.

M

An Asterisk (*) at the beginning of an entry indicates that the title is appearing for the first time.

McNamara, Beth B. & McKeever, Gina W. Welcoming the Little Ones: Your Guide to a Faith-Filled Parish Nursery. LC 97-69274. (Illus.). 132p. 1998. spiral bd. 19.95 (*0-87973-927-4*) Our Sunday Visitor.

McNamara, Beth B., et al. Family Moments: Monthly Ideas & Activities to Enjoy with Young Children. 24p. 1995. pap. 3.95 (*0-87973-651-8*) Our Sunday Visitor.

— Parent Letters from Your Parish, Vols. 1-7. Incl. Parent Letters from Your Parish: Letters 1-3. 1994. 9.95 (*0-87973-816-2*); 1994. 16.95 (*0-87973-818-9*) Our Sunday Visitor.

***McNamara, Beth Branigan, ed.** Christian Beginnings. (Illus.). 120p. 2000. 24.95 (*0-87973-076-5*) Our Sunday Visitor.

McNamara, Brooks. Step Right Up. LC 95-20269. (Illus.). 264p. 1995. reprint ed. pap. 16.95 (*0-87805-832-X*); reprint ed. text 40.00 (*0-87805-831-1*) U Pr of Miss.

McNamara, Brooks, ed. Plays from Contemporary American Theatre. 1988. mass mkt. 7.99 (*0-451-62753-9*) NAL.

McNamara, Brooks, et al, eds. The Drama Review: Thirty Years of Commentary on the Avant-Garde. LC 86-11316. (Theater & Dramatic Studies: No. 35). 385p. 1986. reprint ed. pap. 119.40 (*0-8357-1746-1*, 207046900095) Bks Demand.

McNamara, Brooks & Museum of the City of New York Staff. Day of Jubilee: The Great Age of Public Celebrations in New York, 1788-1909. LC 96-33237. (Illus.). 240p. (C). 1997. text 44.95 (*0-8135-2387-7*) Rutgers U Pr.

***McNamara, Chris.** Supertopo: Yosemite Big Walls. (Illus.). 160p. 2000. pap. 29.95 (*0-9672391-0-9*) Supertopo.

— Yosemite Big Wall SuperTopos. (Illus.). 220p. 2000. 29.95 (*0-9672391-1-7*) Supertopo.

McNamara, D. B., jt. ed. see Kadowitz, Philip J.

***McNamara, Daniel George.** The History of the Ninth Regiment, Massachusetts Volunteer Infantry, June, 1891-June, 1864. (Irish in the Civil War Ser.: No. 7). (Illus.). xxxviii, 558p. 2000. 29.00 (*0-8232-2055-9*); pap. 19.95 (*0-8232-2056-7*) Fordham.

McNamara, David. Classroom Pedagogy & Primary Practice. LC 93-17212. 1994. pap. write for info. (*0-415-08312-5*) Routledge.

Mcnamara, David & Harris, Robert, eds. Overseas Students in Higher Education: Issues in Teaching & Learning. (Illus.). 240p. (C). 1997. 75.00 (*0-415-13199-5*) Routledge.

McNamara, David & Harris, Robert, eds. Overseas Students in Higher Education: Issues in Teaching & Learning. (Illus.). 240p. (C). 1997. pap. 22.99 (*0-415-13200-2*) Routledge.

McNamara, Deborah, jt. auth. see Trood, Russell B.

McNamara, Deborah J., jt. auth. see Coughlan, James E.

McNamara, Deborah J., jt. ed. see Coughlan, James E.

McNamara, Dennis L. The Colonial Origins of Korean Enterprise. (Illus.). 220p. (C). 1990. text 69.95 (*0-521-38565-2*) Cambridge U Pr.

— Textiles & Industrial Transition in Japan. LC 94-43122. 288p. 1995. text 39.95 (*0-8014-3100-X*) Cornell U Pr.

***McNamara, Dennis L., ed.** Corporatism & Korean Capitalism. LC 98-31542. 168p. 1999. 75.00 (*0-415-20052-0*) Routledge.

McNamara, Derek A., et al. Introduction to the Uniform Geometrical Theory of Diffraction. fac. ed. LC 89-49004. (Illus.). 485p. 1990. reprint ed. pap. 138.30 (*0-608-00941-5*, 2061733) Bks Demand.

McNamara, Eileen. Breakdown: Sex, Suicide & the Harvard Psychiatrist. Miller, Tom, ed. 368p. 1995. pap. 6.50 (*0-671-79621-6*, Pocket Star Bks) PB.

McNamara, Elizabeth A., et al. Print & Electronic Publishing: Legal & Business Issues in Book & Magazine Publishing. LC 98-117689. (Patents, Copyrights, Trademarks, & Literary Property Course Handbook Ser.). 736 p. 1997. 39.00 (*0-87224-329-X*) PLI.

McNamara, Ellen, ed. see McNamara, Tom.

McNamara, Ellen, ed. see Nuventures Consultants, Inc. Staff.

McNamara, Ernest, et al. Australia's Defence Resources: A Compendium of Data. 3rd ed. 192p. 1986. pap. 22.00 (*0-08-029881-8*, T110, T120, T130, K122) Elsevier.

McNamara, Eugene. Keeping in Touch: New & Selected Poems. LC 98-231974. 1998. pap. 14.00 (*0-88962-673-1*) Mosaic.

— Laura As Novel, Film, & Myth. LC 92-6560. 120p. 1992. 59.95 (*0-7734-9506-1*) E Mellen.

***McNamara, Eugene.** Waterfalls. 320p. 2000. pap. 14.95 (*1-55050-162-3*, Pub. by Coteau) Genl Dist Srvs.

McNamara, Francine, jt. auth. see McNamara, Barry.

McNamara, Francine J., jt. auth. see McNamara, Barry E.

McNamara, Francis J. U. S. Counterintelligence Today. Nathan Hale Institute Staff, ed. 88p. (Orig.). 1985. 9.95 (*0-935067-06-X*) Nathan Hale Inst.

McNamara, Francis T., jt. auth. see Hill, Adrian.

***McNamara, Francis Terry.** Escape with Honor: My Last Hours in Vietnam. 1999. pap. 16.95 (*1-57488-230-9*) Brasseys.

McNamara, George. George & the Pitching Machine. LC 95-207864. (Illus.). (J). (gr. k-4). 1994. pap. 4.99 (*0-9625632-6-9*) NUVENTURES Pub.

— George & the Tricky Fish. (Illus.). (J). (ps-4). 1995. pap. 4.99 (*0-9625632-8-5*) NUVENTURES Pub.

McNamara, Helen, et al. Individual Progression. LC 74-88052. (C). 1970. pap. write for info. (*0-672-60633-X*, Bobbs) Macmillan.

McNamara, J. A., ed. Nasorespiratory Function & Craniofacial Growth. (Craniofacial Growth Ser.: Vol. 9). (Illus.). 332p. 1985. reprint ed. 59.00 (*0-929921-06-2*) UM CHGD.

McNamara, J. A., et al, eds. Developmental Aspects of Temporomandibular Joint Disorders. (Craniofacial Growth Ser.: Vol. 16). (Illus.). 298p. 1985. 59.00 (*0-929921-12-7*) UM CHGD.

— The Effect of Surgical Intervention on Craniofacial Growth. (Craniofacial Growth Ser.: Vol. 12). (Illus.). 382p. 1982. 48.00 (*0-929921-09-7*) UM CHGD.

McNamara, J. A. & Trotman, C. A., eds. Creating the Compliant Patient. (Craniofacial Growth Ser.: Vol. 33). (Illus.). 206p. 1997. 59.00 (*0-929921-29-1*) UM CHGD.

McNamara, J. A., Jr. & Trotman, Carroll-Ann, eds. Orthodontic Treatment: Management of Unfavorable Sequelae. (Craniofacial Growth Ser.: Vol. 31). (Illus.). 437p. 1996. 69.00 (*0-929921-27-5*) UM CHGD.

McNamara, J. A., jt. ed. see Carlson, D. S.

McNamara, J. A., Jr., ed. see Profit, W. R., et al.

McNamara, J. A., Jr., ed. see Samchukov, M., et al.

McNamara, J. A., Jr., ed. see Slavkin, H. C., et al.

***McNamara, J. P., et al, eds.** Modelling Nutrient Utilizatino in Farm Animals. (Cabi Publishing Ser.). 384p. 2000. text 100.00 (*0-85199-449-0*) OUP.

McNamara, J. Regis, ed. Critical Issues, Developments & Trends in Professional Psychology, Vol. 2. LC 81-15863. 321p. 1984. 59.95 (*0-275-91227-2*, C12272, Praeger Pubs) Greenwood.

McNamara, J. Regis & Appel, Margaret A., eds. Critical Issues, Developments & Trends in Professional Psychology, Vol. 3. LC 81-15863. 262p. 1986. 59.95 (*0-275-92250-2*, C22503, Praeger Pubs) Greenwood.

McNamara, J. Regis, jt. auth. see Grossman, Kandee S.

McNamara, James A. Neuromuscular & Skeletal Adaptations to Altered Orofacial Function. LC RK0280.. (Craniofacial Growth Monographs: Vol. 1). (Illus.). 194p. reprint ed. pap. 60.20 (*0-608-15983-2*, 205226400083) Bks Demand.

McNamara, James A., Jr., ed. Control Mechanisms in Craniofacial Growth: Proceedings of a Sponsored Symposium, Honoring Professor Robert E. Moyers, Held April 26th & 27th, 1974, in Ann Arbor, Michigan. LC 78-302139. (Craniofacial Growth Ser.: Monograph 3). (Illus.). 137p. 1975. pap. 42.50 (*0-608-04833-X*, 206549000004) Bks Demand.

McNamara, James A., ed. Esthetics & the Treatment of Facial Form. (Craniofacial Growth Ser.: Vol. 28). (Illus.). 216p. 1993. 55.00 (*0-929921-24-0*) UM CHGD.

McNamara, James A., Jr., et al, eds. Clinical Alteration of the Growing Face: Proceedings of a Sponsored Symposium Honoring Professor Robert E. Moyers, Held February 26 & 27, 1982, in Ann Arbor, MI. LC 83-147016. (Craniofacial Growth Monographs: No. 14). (Illus.). 339p. reprint ed. pap. 105.10 (*0-8357-7561-5*, 205232500097) Bks Demand.

McNamara, James A., Jr. & Ribbens, Katherine A., eds. Malocclusion & the Periodontium. LC RK0523.. (Craniofacial Growth Monographs: No. 15). (Illus.). 280p. reprint ed. pap. 86.80 (*0-8357-8667-6*, 205231000091) Bks Demand.

McNamara, James A., Jr., ed. see Symposium on Craniofacial Growth (2nd: 1975: Unive.

McNamara, James A., Jr., ed. see Symposium on Craniofacial Growth Staff.

McNamara, James A., jt. ed. see Trotman, Carroll-Ann.

McNamara, James F. Surveys & Experiments in Education Research. LC 94-60492. 220p. 1997. pap. text 29.95 (*1-56676-167-0*) Scarecrow.

McNamara, James F., et al. Measurement & Evaluation: Strategies for School Improvement. LC 99-22301. (School Leadership Library). 1999. 29.95 (*1-883001-78-1*) Eye On Educ.

McNamara, James F., jt. ed. see Johnston, A. P.

McNamara, Jean. A Catalog of Types of Coleoptera in the Canadian National Collection of Insects Supplement No. III. (LAT & FRE., Illus.). 65p. (Orig.). 1993. pap. 32.45 (*0-660-57939-1*, Pub. by Canadian Govt Pub) Accents Pubns.

McNamara, Jill W., jt. auth. see Westburg, Granger E.

McNamara, Jo A. A New Song: Celibate Women in the First Three Christian Centuries. LC 83-10852. (Women & History Ser.: Nos. 6 & 7). 154p. 1983. text 39.95 (*0-86656-249-4*) Haworth Pr.

— A New Song: Celibate Women in the First Three Christian Centuries. LC 85-8505. (Women & History Ser.: Nos. 6 & 7). 154p. 1985. reprint ed. pap. 11.95 (*0-918393-17-5*, Harrington Park) Haworth Pr.

— Sisters in Arms: Catholic Nuns Through Two Millennia. 768p. 1996. 35.00 (*0-674-80984-X*) HUP.

McNamara, Jo A., et al, eds. Sainted Women of the Dark Ages. LC 91-24544. 357p. 1992. text 54.95 (*0-8223-1200-X*); pap. text 19.95 (*0-8223-1216-6*) Duke.

McNamara, Jo A., tr. see Riche, Pierre.

McNamara, Jo Ann. Sisters in Arms: Catholic Nuns Through Two Millenia. 768p. 1999. pap. text 18.95 (*0-674-80985-8*) HUP.

McNamara, Joan. Adoptions & the Sexually Abused. 1990. write for info. (*0-939561-06-9*) Univ South ME.

McNamara, Joan, et al. Bruised Before Birth: Parenting Children Exposed to Parental Substance Abuse. 122p. 1995. pap. 33.00 (*1-873868-17-0*) BAAF.

McNamara, JoAnn. Gilles Aycelin: The Servant of Two Masters. LC 73-6575. 232p. reprint ed. pap. 72.00 (*0-8357-3984-8*, 203668200005) Bks Demand.

— The Ordeal of Community: Hagiography & Discipline in Merovingian Convents. Halborg, John, tr. (Translation Ser.). 103p. 1993. pap. 10.00 (*0-920669-04-2*, Pub. by Peregrina Pubng) Cistercian Pubns.

McNamara, John. Agency. 211p. 1995. 22.00 (*0-9646347-0-8*) Possiblts Pr.

— Extra: U. S. War Correspondents in Action. LC 72-10756. (Essay Index Reprint Ser.). (Illus.). 1977. reprint ed. 21.95 (*0-8369-7229-5*) Ayer.

— History in Asphalt: The Origin of Bronx Street & Place Names. 3rd ed. 1993. pap. 40.00 (*0-941980-16-2*) Bronx County.

— Local Area Networks: An Introduction to the Technology. 191p. 1996. pap. 32.95 (*1-55558-149-8*, Digital DEC) Buttrwrth-Heinemann.

— McNamara's Old Bronx. Ultan, Lloyd, ed. (Illus.). 254p. (Orig.). 1989. pap. 19.00 (*0-941980-25-1*) Bronx County.

— Present Tense & Personal Effects: A Pair of Comedies. 1986. pap. 5.25 (*0-8222-0910-1*) Dramatists Play.

McNamara, John & Twomey, Bill. Throggs Neck & Pelham Bay. LC 98-88062. (Images of America Ser.). 1998. write for info. (*0-7385-0013-5*) Arcadia Publng.

McNamara, John M., jt. auth. see Houston, Alasdair I.

McNamara, John N. Free Hand Figure Piping. rev. ed. (Illus.). 32p. 1983. pap. 8.00 (*0-932770-03-7*) McNamara Pubns.

— Lessons Learned. (Illus.). 32p. (Orig.). 1984. pap. 4.00 (*0-932770-05-3*) McNamara Pubns.

— Shaped & Cut-Out Cakes: The Easy Professional Way. (Illus.). 40p. (Orig.). (C). 1984. pap. 9.00 (*0-932770-04-5*) McNamara Pubns.

McNamara, John R. The Economics of Innovation in the Telecommunications Industry. LC 91-15932. 208p. 1991. 55.00 (*0-89930-558-X*, MEZ, Quorum Bks) Greenwood.

McNamara, John R., jt. auth. see McLean, Kathleen.

McNamara, Joseph D. The Blue Mirage. 320p. 1991. mass mkt. 5.99 (*0-449-14755-X*, GM) Fawcett.

Mcnamara, Joseph D. Code 211 Blue. 1996. mass mkt. 5.99 (*0-449-14894-7*) Fawcett.

McNamara, Joseph E. Prayer Groups. LC 94-65550. 94p. (Orig.). 1994. pap. 1.95 (*1-882972-25-2*, 3201) Queenship Pub.

McNamara, Joseph S., ed. Champions of Freedom Vol. 14: The Privatization Revolution. LC 83-641096. (Ludwig von Mises Lectures). 135p. 1989. pap. 5.00 (*0-916308-88-X*) Hillsdale Coll Pr.

— Champions of Freedom Vol. 15: The Politics of Hunger. LC 88-83508. (Ludwig von Mises Lectures). 1989. pap. 5.00 (*0-916308-86-3*) Hillsdale Coll Pr.

McNamara, K. J., ed. Evolutionary Trends. (Illus.). 368p. (Orig.). (C). 1991. pap. text 29.95 (*0-8165-1234-5*) U of Ariz Pr.

McNamara, K. J., jt. auth. see McKinney, M. L.

McNamara, Karen, jt. auth. see Lombardo, Michelle.

McNamara, Katherine. Narrow Road to the Deep North: A Journey into the Interior of Alaska. 304p. (Orig.). 1998. pap. 15.95 (*1-56279-107-9*) Mercury Hse Inc.

***McNamara, Katherine.** Narrow Road to the Deep North: A Journey Into the Interior of Alaska. (Illus.). 304p. 2001. pap. 15.95 (*1-56279-122-2*) Mercury Hse Inc.

McNamara, Kathleen R. The Currency of Ideas: Monetary Politics in the European Union. LC 97-29728. (Studies in Political Economy). (Illus.). 200p. 1998. text 29.95 (*0-8014-3432-7*) Cornell U Pr.

— Currency of Ideas: Monetary Politics in the European Union. (Cornell Studies in Political Economy). 1999. pap. text 16.95 (*0-8014-8602-5*) Cornell U Pr.

McNamara, Kelly, ed. see McNamara, Regina.

McNamara, Ken & Long, John A. The Evolution Revolution. LC 98-10109. 312p. 1998. 125.00 (*0-471-97406-4*) Wiley.

Mcnamara, Kenneth J. Evolution Revolution. LC 98-10109. 312p. 1998. pap. 39.95 (*0-471-97407-2*) Wiley.

McNamara, Kenneth J. Shapes of Time: The Evolution of Growth & Development. LC 96-29775. (Illus.). 344p. 1997. 34.95 (*0-8018-5571-3*) Johns Hopkins.

McNamara, Kenneth J., ed. Evolutionary Change & Heterochrony. 298p. 1996. 210.00 (*0-471-95837-9*) Wiley.

McNamara, Kevin. Law & Morality. 1989. pap. 25.00 (*0-86217-290-X*, Pub. by Veritas Pubns) St Mut.

— Penance. 1989. pap. 21.00 (*0-86217-216-0*, Pub. by Veritas Pubns) St Mut.

— Pluralism: Unravelling a Riddle of Our Time. 1989. 15.00 (*0-86217-265-9*, Pub. by Veritas Pubns) St Mut.

— Sacrament of Salvation. 226p. 1981. 4.95 (*0-8199-0806-1*, Frncscn Herld) Franciscan Pr.

McNamara, Kevin R. Urban Verbs: Arts & Discourses of American Cities. LC 95-42932. 1996. 39.50 (*0-8047-2645-0*) Stanford U Pr.

McNamara, Leo F. The Ionosphere: Communications, Surveillance, & Direction Finding. 248p. 1991. 74.50 (*0-89464-040-2*) Krieger.

— Radio Amateurs Guide to the Ionosphere. LC 92-32988. 176p. (Orig.). (C). 1994. pap. 39.50 (*0-89464-804-7*) Krieger.

McNamara, M. Frances. Ragbag of Legal Quotations, 1960. LC 92-74141. 334p. 1992. reprint ed. 50.00 (*0-9630106-3-8*, 307730) Lawbk Exchange.

McNamara, M. J., jt. ed. see Beattie, D. R. G.

***McNamara, Martin.** The Psalms in the Early Irish Church. (Journal for the Study of the Old Testament Supplement Ser.: No. 165). 500p. 2000. 85.00 (*1-85075-925-1*, Pub. by Sheffield Acad) CUP Services.

McNamara, Martin. Studies in Tests of Early Irish Latin Gospels (A. D. 600-1200) (C). 1990. pap. text 195.50 (*0-7923-0916-2*) Kluwer Academic.

— The Targu Neofiti 1: Genesis. (Aramaic Bible Ser.: No. 1A). 256p. (Orig.). 1992. 65.00 (*0-8146-5476-2*) Liturgical Pr.

McNamara, Martin, tr. from ARC. Targum Neofiti Vol. 5A: Deuteronomy. LC 96-22805. (Aramaic Bible (The Targums) Ser.). 200p. (Orig.). 1997. pap. text 79.95 (*0-8146-5484-3*, M Glazier) Liturgical Pr.

McNamara, Martin, tr. Targum Neofiti One - Exodus: Targum Pseudo Jonathan: Exodus. LC 94-2487. (Aramaic Bible Ser.: Vol. 2). 344p. (Orig.). 1994. 79.95 (*0-8146-5477-0*, M Glazier) Liturgical Pr.

McNamara, Martin & Clarke, Ernst. The Targum Neofiti 1 & Pseudo - Jonathan: Numbers. (Aramaic Bible Ser.: Vol. 4). 352p. (Orig.). 1995. 79.95 (*0-8146-5483-5*, M Glazier) Liturgical Pr.

McNamara, Martin, et al. The Targum of Neofiti 1 & Pseudo-Jonathan: Leviticus. (Aramaic Bible Ser.: No. 3). 264p. (Orig.). 1995. 79.95 (*0-8146-5478-9*, M Glazier) Liturgical Pr.

McNamara, Martin, jt. ed. see Herbert, Maire.

McNamara, Mary, ed. see McCarthy, Bernice.

McNamara, Mary C., et al. In a Word. (Illus.). 192p. 1998. pap., wbk. ed. 14.95 (*0-9608992-7-8*) About Learning.

McNamara, Mike. Crashproof Your BBC: Software Tips for BBC & Electron Programs. LC 84-17343. 67p. reprint ed. pap. 30.00 (*0-608-18446-2*, 203266200080) Bks Demand.

McNamara, P., et al. Appellants' Perceptions of the Planning Appeal System. (C). 1986. 45.00 (*0-7855-3830-5*, Pub. by Oxford Polytechnic) St Mut.

McNamara, Patrick. Beauty & the Priest: Finding God in the New Age. (Illus.). 250p. (Orig.). 1997. pap. 21.95 (*1-886940-01-0*) Ozark Mountn.

McNamara, Patrick. Mind & Variability. LC 98-31365. 184p. 1999. 55.00 (*0-275-96383-7*) Greenwood.

McNamara, Patrick H. Conscience First, Tradition Second: A Study of Young American Catholics. LC 90-22768. (SUNY Series in Religion, Culture, & Society). 221p. (C). 1992. text 21.50 (*0-7914-0813-2*) State U NY Pr.

McNamara, Patrick H., jt. auth. see Dowdy, Thomas E.

McNamara, Patty, et al, eds. What Research Says about Learning in Science Museums, Vol. 2. 44p. (Orig.). 1993. pap. 14.00 (*0-944040-31-4*, 68-0) AST Ctrs.

McNamara, Paul. Land Release & Development in Areas of Restraint: Restraint Policy & Development Interests. Housing in Dacorum & North Hertfordshire. (C). 1984. 35.00 (*0-7855-3843-7*, Pub. by Oxford Polytechnic) St Mut.

— Restraint Policy in Action: Housing in Dacorum & North Hertfordshire. (C). 1984. 29.00 (*0-7855-3842-9*, Pub. by Oxford Polytechnic) St Mut.

McNamara, Paul, jt. auth. see Elson, Martin.

***McNamara, Peggy.** My Tender Soul: A Story of Survival. 160p. 2000. pap. 12.95 (*1-890676-61-6*, Pub. by Beavers Pond) Bookman Bks.

McNamara, Peter. Political Economy & Statesmanship: Smith, Hamilton, & the Foundation of the Commerical Republic. LC 97-12499. 256p. 1997. lib. bdg. 35.00 (*0-87580-228-1*) N Ill U Pr.

McNamara, Peter, ed. The Noblest Minds: Fame, Honor & the American Founding. LC 99-18815. 288p. 1999. pap. 22.95 (*0-8476-8682-5*) Rowman.

— The Noblest Minds: Fame, Honor, & the American Founding. LC 99-18815. 288p. 1999. 59.00 (*0-8476-8681-7*) Rowman.

McNamara, Peter L. Loneliness of the Palm. 88p. (Orig.). 1993. pap. 8.95 (*1-879934-11-6*) St Andrews NC.

McNamara, Peter L., ed. Critics on Wallace Stevens. LC 78-173694. (Readings in Literary Criticism Ser.: No. 19). 1972. 19.95 (*0-87024-232-6*) U of Miami Pr.

***McNamara, Regina.** Lost a Job? Find a Life! Strategies for Charting a Successful Future after Losing a Job. Amorosino, Chris, ed. 70p. 1999. pap. 7.95 (*1-930311-01-X*) Kelsco.

— A Spine Is a Terrible Thing to Waste: Tips for Leading with Courage, Speed & Integrity. Amorosino, Chris, ed. 65p. 1999. pap. 7.95 (*1-930311-02-8*) Kelsco.

— Welcome to the World of Everyday Heroes: Tips for Thriving in Your First Years of Nursing Practice. McNamara, Kelly, ed. 55p. 1999. pap. 7.95 (*1-930311-03-6*) Kelsco.

McNamara, Regis & Barclay, Allan G., eds. Critical Issues, Developments, & Trends in Professional Psychology, Vol. 1. LC 81-15863. 321p. 1982. 69.50 (*0-275-90860-7*, C08601, Praeger Pubs) Greenwood.

McNamara, Richard B. Constitutional Limitations on Criminal Procedure. (Federal Publications). 419p. 1982. text 95.00 (*0-07-045674-7*) Shepards.

— Criminal Practice & Procedure, 3 vols., Vols. 1, 2 & 2A. 2nd ed. (New Hampshire Practice Ser.: Vols. 1-2A). 1530p. 1994. 210.00 (*0-88063-485-5*, MICHIE) LEXIS Pub.

McNamara, Richard B. Criminal Practice & Procedure Vols. 1, 2, & 2a. 3rd ed. (New Hampshire Practice Series). 210.00 (*0-327-12465-2*) LEXIS Pub.

McNamara, Richard B. New Hampshire Personal Injury: Tort & Insurance Practice, 1988-1993. 190p. 1993. ring bd., suppl. ed. 32.00 (*0-614-03166-4*, MICHIE) LEXIS Pub.

— New Hampshire Personal Injury: Tort & Insurance Practice, 1988-1993, Vols. 8 & 9. (New Hampshire Practice Ser.). 950p. 1988. 140.00 (*0-88063-489-8*, MICHIE) LEXIS Pub.

— New Hampshire Practice Vols. 1, 2, 2A: Criminal Practice & Procedure, 1998 Cumulative Supplement, Set. 800p. 1998. pap., suppl. ed. write for info. (*0-327-00720-6*, 8206313) LEXIS Pub.

McNamara, Richard B. Personal Injury Vols. 8-9: Tort & Insurance Practice, 2 Vols. 2nd ed. 150.00 (*0-327-12470-9*) LEXIS Pub.

McNamara, Rita. Fourteen Basic Roots & the Key to 100,000 English Words. 52p. (YA). (gr. 9-12). 1991. spiral bd. 4.95 (*0-939507-18-8*, B117) Amer Classical.

McNamara, Rita J. Energetic Bodywork: Practical Techniques. LC 98-23232. Orig. Title: Toward Balance: Psycho-Physical Integration & Vibrational Therapy. (Illus.). 208p. 1998. pap. 12.95 (*1-57863-033-9*) Weiser.

McNamara, Rob. Guitar Chords for Beginners: Easy Chords in Simplified Form, Exercises & Pop Songs. 48p. 1986. pap. 4.95 (*0-7935-5516-7*, 50394190) H Leonard.

McNamara, Robert. Bugs Bunny Buddha. (Lost City: Poetic Broadside Ser.: Vol. 1). (Illus.). 2p. 1998. pap. 2.00 (*1-892494-09-4*) Repossessed Head.

An Asterisk (*) at the beginning of an entry indicates that the title is appearing for the first time.

— Second Messengers. LC 89-32935. (Wesleyan New Poets Ser.). 64p. 1990. pap. 12.95 (0-8195-1184-6, Wesleyan Univ Pr); text 25.00 (0-8195-2182-5, Wesleyan Univ Pr) U Pr of New Eng.

McNamara, Robert, et al. Argument Without End: In Search of Answers to the Vietnam Tragedy. LC 99-11830. (Illus.). 479p. 1999. 27.50 (1-891620-22-3, Pub. by PublicAffairs NY) HarpC.

***McNamara, Robert, et al.** Argument Without End: In Search of Answers to the Vietnam Tragedy. 512p. 2000. pap. 17.00 (1-891620-87-8, Pub. by PublicAffairs NY) HarpC.

McNamara, Robert, ed. & illus. see Cecil, John, et al.

McNamara, Robert P. The Times Square Hustler: Male Prostitution in New York City. LC 94-21689. 168p. 1994. 57.95 (0-275-95003-4, Praeger Pubs); pap. 19.95 (0-275-95186-3, Praeger Pubs) Greenwood.

McNamara, Robert P., ed. Sex, Scams, & Street Life: The Sociology of New York City's Times Square. LC 95-9307. 144p. 1995. 55.00 (0-275-95002-6, Praeger Pubs); pap. 15.95 (0-275-95359-9, Praeger Pubs) Greenwood.

McNamara, Robert P. & Child Welfare League of America Staff. Beating the Odds: Crime, Poverty & Life in the Inner City. LC 99-20811. 193p. 1999. 10.95 (0-87868-765-3, CWLA Pr) Child Welfare.

McNamara, Robert P., et al. Crossing the Line: Interracial Couples in the South. LC 98-44221. 192p. 1999. pap. 19.95 (0-275-96676-3, Praeger Pubs) Greenwood.

— Crossing the Line: Interracial Couples in the South, 125. LC 98-44221. (Contributions in Sociology Ser.: Vol. 125). 192p. 1999. 59.95 (0-313-30962-0) Greenwood.

McNamara, Robert P., jt. ed. see Kenney, Dennis Jay.

McNamara, Robert P., jt. ed. see Redburn, David E.

McNamara, Robert S. In Retrospect. LC 96-218898. 1996. pap. 15.00 (0-679-76749-5) McKay.

— In Retrospect: The Tragedy & Lessons of Vietnam. 1996. pap. 15.00 (0-614-97866-1) Vin Bks.

— The McNamara Years at the World Bank: Major Policy Addresses of Robert S. NcNamara, 1968-1981. LC 81-3743. 691p. reprint ed. pap. 200.00 (0-7837-4266-5, 204395800012) Bks Demand.

— The Military Role of Nuclear Weapons: Perceptions & Misperceptions. (CISA Working Papers: No. 45). 41p. (Orig.). 1984. pap. 15.00 (0-86682-058-2) Ctr Intl Relations.

McNamara, Roderick, et al. Inland Marine Insurance, 2 vols., Set. LC 87-82150. (Orig.). (C). 1991. pap. 41.00 (0-89462-042-8, 12202/12203) IIA.

McNamara, Sheila. Traditional Chinese Medicine. LC 95-45945. 320p. 1995. pap. 14.00 (0-465-00629-9, Pub. by Basic) HarpC.

McNamara, Stephen J. Air Power's Gordian Knot: Centralized Versus Organic Control. LC 94-3790. (Illus.). 205p. 1994. pap. 13.00 (1-58566-054-X) Air Univ.

McNamara, Sylvia & Moreton, Gill. Teaching Special Needs: Strategies & Activities for Children in the Primary Classroom. 96p. 1993. pap. 25.00 (1-85346-247-0, Pub. by David Fulton) Taylor & Francis.

— Understanding Differentiation. LC 97-180578. 112p. 1996. pap. 24.95 (1-85346-457-0, Pub. by David Fulton) Taylor & Francis.

McNamara, Sylvie & Moreton, Gill. Changing Behaviour: Teaching Children with Emotional & Behavioural Difficulties in Primary & Secondary Classrooms (Resource Materials for Teachers) 96p. 1995. pap. 19.95 (1-85346-350-7, Pub. by David Fulton) Taylor & Francis.

McNamara, T. F. Measuring Second Language Performance. LC 95-26148. (Applied Linguistics & Language Ser.). 1996. pap. 35.70 (0-582-08907-7, Pub. by Addison-Wesley) Longman.

McNamara, T. F., jt. auth. see Quinn, T. J.

McNamara, Tara W. Lake Tahoe Weddings: A Destination Wedding Guide for Brides. Uzcategui-Taylor, Kristy, ed. LC 96-83130. (Illus.). 184p. (Orig.). 1996. pap. 16.95 (0-9651887-2-8) Dreamweaver Pr.

McNamara, Timothy J. Italics: Insights for Teachers & Learners Interested in Connecting with Secondary Math. (Illus.). 80p. (C). 1997. ring bd. 18.75 (0-9657801-1-2) Italics.

McNamara, Todd J., jt. auth. see Southerland, J. Alfred.

McNamara, Tom. Henry Lunt & the Ranger. 1992. pap. 5.95 (0-9625632-2-6) NUVENTURES Pub.

— Henry Lunt & the Ranger: A Novel of Espionage & High Adventure During the American Revolution. McNamara, Ellen, ed. (Illus.). 352p. 1991. 18.95 (0-9625632-3-4) NUVENTURES Pub.

— Henry Lunt & the Spymaster. (Henry Lunt Adventures Ser.: No. 2). 429p. 1994. pap. 10.95 (0-9625632-5-0) NUVENTURES Pub.

— Skull & Cross Bones. 1995. pap. 10.95 (0-9625632-7-7) NUVENTURES Pub.

McNamara, Tony. The John Wayne Principle. 1997. pap. 14.95 (0-86819-514-6, Pub. by Currency Pr) Accents Pubns.

Mcnamara, Valerie J., jt. auth. see Weber, Valerie.

McNamara, Walter, jt. auth. see McMenamin, Michael.

McNamara, William. The Catholic Church on the Northern Indiana Frontier, 1789-1844. LC 73-3567. (Catholic University of America. Studies in Romance Languages & Literatures: No. 12). reprint ed. 29.50 (0-404-57762-8) AMS Pr.

— Christian Mysticism: Psychotheology. LC 80-13139. 154p. 1981. pap. 9.50 (0-8199-0793-6, Frncscn Herld) Franciscan Pr.

McNamara, William, jt. auth. see Ernst, Tim.

Mcnamee, ed. Ethics & Sport. (Illus.). 240p. 1998. mass mkt. 32.95 (0-419-21510-7, E & FN Spon) Routledge.

McNamee, Abigail S. Children & Stress: Helping Children Cope. LC 82-16246. (Illus.). 84p. reprint ed. pap. 30.00 (0-608-09648-2, 206976400006) Bks Demand.

McNamee, Brendan. Man Who Lived in Sorcy Wood. 62p. 1987. pap. 7.95 (1-85186-026-6) Dufour.

McNamee, Catherine, tr. see Marias, Julian.

McNamee, D. Internal Audit of Purchasing. Campbell, Lee A., ed. (Practice Set Ser.). 102p. 1992. 130.00 (0-89413-280-6, A6057) Inst Inter Aud.

McNamee, Daniel, ed. TAAS Quick Review Mathematics, Grade 9. (Illus.). 112p. 1992. pap. text 14.95 (0-944459-34-X) ECS Lrn Systs.

McNamee, Daniel & Graft, Janine. TAAS Master Math, Exit Level: Teacher's Handbook for Texas Assessment of Academic Skills. Mammen, Lori, ed. (Illus.). 144p. (Orig.). 1990. pap. text 17.95 (0-944459-18-8) ECS Lrn Systs.

McNamee, Daniel, jt. auth. see Graft, Janine.

McNamee, David. Assessing Risk. Campbell, Lee A., ed. (Tool Kit Ser.). 1996. pap. 200.00 (0-89413-357-8, A6075) Inst Inter Aud.

— Business Risk Assessment. Campbell, Lee A., ed. LC 99-183463. v, 107 p. 1998. write for info. (0-89413-422-1) Inst Inter Aud.

***McNamee, David, et al.** Risk Management: Changing the Internal Auditor's Paradigm. Campbell, Lee A., ed. LC 99-181383. xiii, 218 p. 1998. write for info. (0-89413-421-3) Inst Inter Aud.

McNamee, David W. Audit Excellence: Best Practices & TQM. Campbell, Lee A., ed. (Video Ser.). 1993. pap., teacher ed. 495.00 (0-89413-303-9, A6722); pap., wbk. ed. 20.00 (0-89413-304-7, A7944) Inst Inter Aud.

— Telecommunications: Detecting & Deterring Fraud. Campbell, Lee A., ed. 1993. pap. 200.00 (0-89413-300-4, A6061) Inst Inter Aud.

McNamee, Eoin. The Language of Birds. 32p. (Orig.). 1994. pap. 9.95 (1-874597-18-9, Pub. by New Island Books) Irish Bks Media.

— The Last of Deeds. 96p. 1990. 19.95 (1-85186-053-3) Dufour.

— The Last of Deeds & Love in History. 192p. 1997. pap. 11.00 (0-312-16879-9) St Martin.

— Resurrection Man. LC 95-21825. 240p. 1996. pap. 12.00 (0-312-14716-3, Picador USA) St Martin.

McNamee, Fintan, ed. see O'Doherty, E. F.

McNamee, Fintan, ed. see Steeman, T.

McNamee, Gergory, jt. ed. see Hepworth, James R.

McNamee, Gillian D., jt. auth. see McLane, Joan B.

***McNamee, Graham.** Hate You. LC 98-8047. 128p. (YA). (gr. 7-12). 1999. 14.95 (0-385-32593-2, Delacorte Pr Bks) BDD Bks Young Read.

— Hate You. 128p. (YA). (gr. 7). 2000. mass mkt. 4.99 (0-440-22762-3, LLL BDD) BDD Bks Young Read.

— Hate You. (Illus.). (J). 2000. 10.34 (0-606-18803-7) Turtleback.

***McNamee, Gregory.** Blue Mountains Far Away: Journeys into the American Wilderness. LC 00-25899. 192p. 2000. 22.95 (1-58574-014-4) Lyons Pr.

McNamee, Gregory. A Desert Bestiary: Folklore, Literature, & Ecological Thought from the World's Dry Places. LC 96-32856. (Illus.). 192p. (Orig.). 1996. pap. 14.95 (1-55566-176-9) Johnson Bks.

— Gila: The Life & Death of an American River. LC 97-52731. 1998. pap. 14.95 (0-8263-1842-8) U of NM Pr.

— Grand Canyon Place Names. LC 97-26589. 128p. 1997. pap. 10.95 (0-89886-533-6) Mountaineers.

— Open Range & Parking Lots: Southwest Photographs. LC 99-6452. (Illus.). 104p. 1999. pap. 19.95 (0-8263-2100-3) U of NM Pr.

***McNamee, Gregory.** The Serpent's Tale: Snakes in Folklore & Literature. LC 00-20143. 168p. 2000. pap. 17.95 (0-8203-2225-3) U of Ga Pr.

McNamee, Gregory, ed. Living in Words. Interviews from the Bloomsbury Review 1981-1988. LC 88-12132. 178p. 1988. 19.95 (0-932576-62-1); pap. 8.95 (0-932576-63-X) Breitenbush Bks.

***McNamee, Gregory, ed.** The Mountain World: A Literary Journal. LC 99-46907. (Illus.). 320p. 2000. 25.00 (0-87156-898-5, Pub. by Sierra) Random.

McNamee, Gregory, ed. Named in Stone & Sky: An Arizona Anthology. LC 92-24494. 196p. (Orig.). (C). 1993. pap. 16.50 (0-8165-1348-1); lib. bdg. 34.95 (0-8165-1278-7) U of Ariz Pr.

McNamee, Gregory, ed. see Chavez, Thomas.

McNamee, Gregory, ed. see Viele, Catherine W.

McNamee, Gwen H. Bar None: 125 Years of Women Lawyers in Illinois. (Illus.). vi, 74p. 1998. pap. 15.00 (0-9663412-0-1) Chicago Bar Assn.

McNamee, Harriet, ed. see Fallen, Anne C.

McNamee, Harriet, ed. see Leahy, Christopher.

McNamee, Jennifer S., jt. auth. see Ferguson, Susan J.

McNamee, John P. Diary of a City Priest. LC 93-11924. 270p. (Orig.). 1993. pap. 14.95 (1-55612-662-X) Sheed & Ward WI.

McNamee, John P. Endurance: The Rhythm of Faith. 224p. (Orig.). 1996. pap. 14.95 (1-55612-809-6, LL1809) Sheed & Ward WI.

McNamee, John P. & McGovern, Robert. Clay Vessels & Other Poems. 80p. (Orig.). 1995. 18.95 (1-55612-812-6) Sheed & Ward WI.

***McNamee, Kevin.** National Parks of Canada. (Illus.). 224p. 1998. pap. 26.95 (1-55013-985-1, Pub. by Key Porter) Firefly Bks Ltd.

McNamee, Kevin P. The Chiropractic College Directory, 1997-98. 5th ed. (Illus.). 190p. 1997. pap. 11.95 (0-945947-04-6) KM Enterprises.

McNamee, Kevin P., et al. The Chiropractic College Directory. 6th ed. (Illus.). 236p. 1999. pap. 19.95 (0-945947-05-4) KM Enterprises.

McNamee, Lawrence, ed. Dissertations in English & American Literature: Theses Accepted by American, British & German Universities, 1865-1964. LC 68-27446. 1136p. reprint ed. pap. 200.00 (0-8357-9041-X, 201329700085) Bks Demand.

McNamee, Maurice B., ed. Essays by the Masters. LC 67-28299. (Composition & Rhetoric Ser.: No. 10). 1968. pap. 2.50 (0-672-60896-0, CR10, Bobbs) Macmillan.

McNamee, Nancy A. Don't Let the Music Die in You. pap. write for info. (0-9647604-1-X) MS Madness.

***McNamee, Patrick B.** Developing Strategies for Competitive Advantage. LC 99-32671. (Best of Long Range Planning Ser.). 285p. 1999. 75.00 (0-08-043574-2, Pergamon Pr) Elsevier.

McNamee, Patrick B. Strategic Management: A PC Based Approach. 224p. 1993. pap. text 46.95 (0-7506-0505-7) Buttrwrth-Heinemann.

— Strategic Market Planning: A Blueprint for Success. LC 97-41435. (Wiley Series in Practical Strategy). 378p. 1998. 67.50 (0-471-97932-5) Wiley.

McNamee, S. J., jt. auth. see Miller, R. K., Jr.

Mcnamee, Sheila & Gergen, Kenneth J. Relational Responsibility: Resources for Sustainable Dialogue. LC 98-25453. 1998. 48.00 (0-7619-1093-X) Sage.

McNamee, Sheila & Gergen, Kenneth J. Relational Responsibility: Resources for Sustainable Dialogue. LC 98-25453. 1998. pap. 22.95 (0-7619-1094-8) Sage.

— Therapy As Social Construction. (Inquiries in Social Construction Ser.). 224p. (C). 1992. 59.95 (0-8039-8302-6); pap. 14.99 (0-8039-8303-4) Sage.

McNamee, Stephen. And We're Off! LC 86-42963. 165p. 1987. 13.75 (0-930950-01-1); pap. 8.75 (0-930950-02-X) Nopoly Pr.

— The Devil's Disaster. LC 87-5576. 287p. 1987. 17.75 (0-930950-07-0); pap. 10.75 (0-930950-09-7) Nopoly Pr.

— A Gift of Faith. LC 87-15245. 171p. 1987. 12.75 (0-930950-10-0); pap. 8.75 (0-930950-08-9) Nopoly Pr.

— Ten Thousand Days Has Our Youth, Vol. 1. LC 86-42964. 328p. 1987. 17.75 (0-930950-03-8); pap. 10.75 (0-930950-04-6) Nopoly Pr.

McNamee, Thomas. The Grizzly Bear. LC 97-3322. (Illus.). 314p. 1997. pap. 16.95 (1-55821-610-3) Lyons Pr.

— The Return of the Wolf to Yellowstone. LC 96-39702. 352p. 1995. 27.50 (0-8050-3101-4) H Holt & Co.

— The Return of the Wolf to Yellowstone. 325p. 1998. pap. 13.95 (0-8050-5792-7, Owl) H Holt & Co.

McNamee, Tom & Cahan, Rich. The Towery Report on Lake County, IL. (Towery Report on New American Communities Ser.). (Illus.). 192p. (Orig.). 1994. pap. 9.50 (1-881096-12-2) Towery Pub.

McNamee, Tom, jt. auth. see Hayner, Don.

McNamee, Tom, jt. auth. see McGuinn, Jack.

McNamee, William L., jt. auth. see Schuler, Charles A.

***McNamer, Deirdre.** My Russian. 304p. 2000. pap. 14.00 (0-345-43951-1) Ballantine Pub Grp.

McNamer, Deirdre. My Russian. LC 99-19140. 278p. 1999. 24.00 (0-395-95637-4) HM.

McNamer, Elizabeth & Smith, Virginia. Scripture from Scratch: A Basic Bible Study Program - Participant's Manual. 130p. 1991. spiral bd. 11.95 (0-86716-146-9) St Anthony Mess Pr.

— Scripture from Scratch No. II: The World of the Bible. 96p. (Orig.). 1997. pap., student ed. 8.95 (0-86716-276-7, B2767) St Anthony Mess Pr.

McNamer, Elizabeth, jt. auth. see Smith, Virginia.

McNamer, Elizabeth M. The Education of Heloise: Methods, Content, & Purpose of Learning in the Twelfth Century. LC 91-40386. (Medieval Studies: Vol. 8). 196p. 1992. lib. bdg. 79.95 (0-7734-9657-2) E Mellen.

McNarie, Alan D. Yeshua: The Gospel of St. Thomas. 1993. 21.00 (0-916366-83-9, Pub. by Pushcart Pr) Norton.

McNarney, Betty J. The Glider Pilot Training Program, 1941-1943. (USAF Historical Studies: No. 1). 99p. 1943. pap. text 27.95 (0-89126-147-8) MA AH Pub.

McNaron, Toni. I Dwell in Possibility. LC 91-3105. (Cross-Cultural Memoir Ser.). (Illus.). 216p. 1992. 35.00 (1-55861-049-9); pap. 12.95 (1-55861-050-2) Feminist Pr.

McNaron, Toni A. Poisoned Ivy: Lesbian & Gay Academics Confronting Homophobia. LC 96-35334. 256p. (C). 1996. 54.95 (1-56639-487-2); pap. 19.95 (1-56639-488-0) Temple U Pr.

McNaron, Toni A., ed. The Sister Bond: A Feminist View of a Timeless Connection. (Athene Ser.: No. 6). (Illus.). 142p. 1985. text 35.00 (0-08-032367-7, Pergamon Pr); pap. text 14.95 (0-08-032366-9, Pergamon Pr) Elsevier.

McNaron, Toni A. & Olano, Pamela J. Multicultural Nests: Finding a Writing Voice about Literature by Women of Color. Bridwell-Bowles, Lillian & Batchelder, Susan, eds. (Technical Reports: No. 4). 28p. (Orig.). 1993. pap. 3.00 (1-881221-08-3) U Minn Ctr Interdis.

McNaron, Toni A., jt. ed. see Zimmerman, Bonnie.

McNary, Kyle. Ted "Double Duty" Radcliffe: 36 Years of Pitching & Catching in Baseball's Negro Leagues. (Illus.). 288p. (Orig.). (C). 1994. pap. 14.95 (0-9642002-0-1) K McNary.

***McNary, Robert.** Baby Doctor: Old Soul Returns to Earth. LC 99-90670. 200p. 1999. pap. 12.00 (0-9673499-0-7) Portable Schl Pr.

***McNary-Zak, Bernadette.** Letters & Asceticism in Fourth-Century Egypt. LC 99-88553. 160p. 2000. 42.50 (0-7618-1621-6) U Pr of Amer.

McNaspy, C. J. Play On! Memoirs of a Jesuit Teacher. LC 95-37834. 360p. (Orig.). (C). 1996. pap. 18.95 (0-8294-0867-3, Jesuit Way) Loyola Pr.

McNaspy, C. J., tr. see De Montoya, Antonio R.

McNatt, Kevin B., jt. auth. see Todesco, Andrew J.

McNaugher, Thomas L. Arms & Oil: U. S. Military Strategy & the Persian Gulf. LC 84-45850. 226p. 1985. 34.95 (0-8157-5624-0); pap. 14.95 (0-8157-5623-2) Brookings.

— The M-16 Controversies: Military Organizations & Weapons Acquisition. LC 83-24574. 211p. 1984. 57.95 (0-275-91741-X, C1741, Praeger Pubs) Greenwood.

— New Weapons, Old Politics: America's Military Procurement Muddle. 252p. 1989. 36.95 (0-8157-5626-7); pap. 15.95 (0-8157-5625-9) Brookings.

McNaught, A. D. & Wilkinson, A. Compendium of Chemical Terminology: The Gold Book. 2nd ed. (IUPAC Chemical Data Ser.). (Illus.). 1997. pap. text 65.00 (0-86542-684-8) Blackwell Sci.

McNaught, Allan. Race & Health Policy. 160p. 1987. lib. bdg. 45.00 (0-7099-4673-2, Pub. by C Helm) Routldge.

McNaught, Allan, ed. Managing Community Health Services. 200p. 1990. pap. 27.50 (0-412-31900-4, A5043) Chapman & Hall.

McNaught, Ann B. & Callander, Robin. Nurses' Illustrated Physiology. 4th rev. ed. (Illus.). 158p. 1989. pap. text 15.95 (0-443-02703-X) Church.

McNaught, Brian. Gay Issues in the Workplace. 1994. pap. 11.95 (0-312-11798-1) St Martin.

— Now That I'm Out What Do I Do. LC 96-53513. 240p. 1997. text 22.95 (0-312-15616-2) St Martin.

— Now That I'm Out What Do I Do. 224p. 1998. pap. 12.95 (0-312-19518-4) St Martin.

Mcnaught, Brian. On Being Gay. (Stonewall Inn Editions Ser.). 1989. pap. 10.95 (0-312-02959-4) St Martin.

McNaught, Chriss. The Beef Lover's Guide to Weight Control & Lower Cholesterol. (Illus.). 258p. 1989. spiral bd. 15.00 (0-943255-27-9) Portfolio Pub.

— What's This Green Stuff, Flo? (Flo's Cooking Ser.). (Illus.). 64p. (Orig.). 1993. pap. 6.95 (1-879894-05-X) Saratoga Pub.

McNaught, Harry. Animal Babies. LC 76-24175. (Pictureback Ser.). (Illus.). (J). (ps-1). 1977. pap. 3.25 (0-394-83570-0, Pub. by Random Bks Yng Read) Random.

— 500 Words to Grow on. LC 73-2442. (Pictureback Ser.). (Illus.). (J). (ps-1). 1973. pap. 3.25 (0-394-82668-X, Pub. by Random Bks Yng Read) Random.

— The Truck Book. LC 77-79851. (Please Read to Me Ser.). (Illus.). 34p. (J). (ps-3). 1978. pap. 3.25 (0-394-83703-7, Pub. by Random Bks Yng Read) Random.

— Trucks. (Illus.). 24p. (J). 1998. 1.99 (0-679-89185-4) Random.

McNaught, Judith. Almost Heaven. 1997. per. 3.99 (0-671-01133-2) PB.

— Almost Heaven. rev. ed. Marrow, Linda, ed. 384p. 2000. mass mkt. 7.99 (0-671-74255-8) PB.

— Double Standards. Marrow, Linda, ed. 1992. mass mkt. 7.99 (0-671-73760-0) PB.

— A Kingdom of Dreams. Marrow, Linda, ed. 464p. 1991. per. 6.99 (0-671-73761-9) PB.

— Night Whispers. LC 99-228998. 400p. 1998. 24.00 (0-671-00085-3) S&S Trade.

— Night Whispers. 1998. mass mkt. write for info. (0-671-02834-0) S&S Trade.

***McNaught, Judith.** Night Whispers. 451p. 1999. per. 7.99 (0-671-52574-3) S&S Trade.

— Night Whispers. LC 99-19122. 1999. write for info. (1-56895-647-9) Wheeler Pub.

— Night Whispers. large type ed. 2000. pap. 11.95 (1-56895-968-0) Wheeler Pub.

McNaught, Judith. Once & Always. Marrow, Linda, ed. 1990. per. 7.99 (0-671-73762-7) PB.

— Paradise. Marrow, Linda, ed. LC 91-12897. 720p. 1992. per. 7.99 (0-671-77680-0) PB.

— Perfect. large type ed. LC 93-10503. 1008p. 1993. lib. bdg. 24.95 (1-56054-731-6) Thorndike Pr.

— Perfect. large type ed. 1008p. 1994. pap. 16.95 (1-56054-876-2) Thorndike Pr.

— Perfect. Marrow, Linda, ed. 704p. 1994. reprint ed. per. 7.99 (0-671-79553-8) PB.

***McNaught, Judith.** Un Reino de Ensueno. (SPA.). 528p. 2000. pap. 9.50 (0-553-06129-1) Bantam.

McNaught, Judith. Remember When. 400p. 1996. 24.00 (0-671-52570-0, PB Hardcover) PB.

— Remember When. 418p. 1997. per. 7.99 (0-671-79555-4) PB.

— Remember When. large type ed. LC 96-49645. 1999. pap. 25.95 (0-7862-0569-5) Thorndike Pr.

— Simple Gifts. 1998. per. 12.00 (0-671-02180-X) PB.

— Something Wonderful. Marrow, Linda, ed. 432p. 1991. mass mkt. 7.99 (0-671-73763-5) PB.

— Something Wonderful. 1990. reprint ed. 20.00 (0-7278-4017-7) Severn Hse.

McNaught, Judith. Tender Triumph. rev. ed. Marrow, Linda, ed. 320p. 1991. per. 7.99 (0-671-74256-6) PB.

— Until You. 1999. 9.98 (0-671-04634-9) S&S Trade.

McNaught, Judith. Until You. large type ed. LC 94-40738. 1994. 26.95 (1-56895-160-4) Wheeler Pub.

— Until You. Marrow, Linda, ed. 448p. 1995. reprint ed. per. 7.99 (0-671-88060-8, Pocket Star Bks) PB.

***McNaught, Judith.** Water's Edge. 448p. 2000. 24.95 (0-671-52575-1, PB Hardcover) PB.

— Water's Edge. large type ed. 2000. 27.95 (1-56895-875-7) Wheeler Pub.

McNaught, Judith. Water's Edge: Export Edition. abr. ed. 2000. reprint ed. per. 14.99 (0-671-78788-8) PB.

— Whitney My Love. Marrow, Linda, ed. 1991. per. 7.99 (0-671-73764-3) PB.

— Whitney, My Love. LC 99-26631. 1999. pap. 20.00 (0-671-03685-8) PB.

— Whitney, My Love. large type ed. LC 94-17376. 1994. 25.95 (1-56895-107-8) Wheeler Pub.

***McNaught, Judith.** Whitney, My Love. 736p. 2000. reprint ed. per. 7.99 (0-671-77609-6) PB.

McNaught, Judith. Whitney, My Love, Vol. 1. 1999. 19.95 (0-671-03297-6) PB.

McNaught, Judith, et al. A Gift of Love. 464p. 1996. per. 6.99 (0-671-53661-3) PB.

M

— A Holiday of Love. Marrow, Linda & Tolley, Carolyn, eds. 384p. 1994. per. 6.99 (0-671-50252-2) PB.

McNaught, Kenneth. Conscience & History: A Memoir. (Illus.). 215p. 1999. text 30.00 (0-8020-4425-5) U of Toronto Pr.

— The Penguin History of Canada. rev. ed. 1991. pap. 16.95 (0-14-014998-8, Penguin Bks) Viking Penguin.

McNaught, L. W. Nuclear, Biological & Chemical Warfare. (Brassey's Battlefield Weapons Systems & Technology Ser.: Vol. 4). 60p. 1984. text 35.95 (0-08-028328-4, Pergamon Pr); pap. text 19.95 (0-08-028329-2, Pergamon Pr) Elsevier.

McNaught, Rosemond L., compiled by. Christmas Selections: For Readings & Recitations. LC 74-38601. (Granger Index Reprint Ser.). 1977. reprint ed. 15.95 (0-8369-6333-4) Ayer.

McNaught, Virginia E. Clark: James Clark, (Robert) Mansfield, Christopher Clark & Allied Families. 245p. 1997. pap. 37.00 (0-8328-7956-8) Higginson Bk Co.

— Clark: James Clark, (Robert) Mansfield, Christopher Clark & Allied Families. 245p. 1997. reprint ed. lib. bdg. 47.00 (0-8328-7955-X) Higginson Bk Co.

McNaughton. Boo! 32p. (C). 1999. pap. 6.00 (0-15-202110-8, Voyager Bks) Harcourt.

— Wigmore, Vol. 8. 4th ed. 1961. 145.00 (0-316-93978-1, Aspen Law & Bus) Aspen Pub.

McNaughton, Bill. Tales from a Small Tall Ship: 40 Years of Playing Boats. LC 95-83518. (Illus.). 128p. 1996. pap. 11.95 (0-9650320-0-0) Acme Pack.

McNaughton, Brian. The Throne of Bones. LC 98-102070. (Illus.). 1997. write for info. (0-9658135-0-9) Terminal Fright.

McNaughton, Colin. Boo! LC 95-30754. (Illus.). 32p. (J). 1996. 14.00 (0-15-200834-9) Harcourt.

***McNaughton, Colin.** Boo! (Illus.). (J). 1999. 11.45 (0-606-18169-5) Turtleback.

McNaughton, Colin. Captain Abdul's Pirate School. LC 93-21293. (Illus.). 40p. (J). (ps-3). 1994. 16.95 (1-56402-429-6) Candlewick Pr.

— Captain Abdul's Pirate School. LC 93-21293. (Illus.). 40p. (J). (gr. 4-7). 1996. reprint ed. pap. 7.99 (1-56402-843-7) Candlewick Pr.

***McNaughton, Colin.** Don't Step on the Crack! LC 00-24096. (Illus.). (J). 2001. write for info. (0-8037-2611-2, Dial Yng Read) Peng Put Young Read.

McNaughton, Colin. Dracula's Tomb. LC 98-70722. (Illus.). 24p. (J). (gr. k-5). 1998. 15.99 (0-7636-0495-X) Candlewick Pr.

— Guess Who's Just Moved in. Date not set. write for info. (0-679-91802-7) Random Bks Yng Read.

— Here Come the Aliens! LC 94-48912. (Illus.). 32p. (J). (ps up). 1995. 16.99 (1-56402-642-6) Candlewick Pr.

— Here Come the Aliens! LC 94-48912. (Illus.). 32p. (J). (ps-3). 1997. reprint ed. pap. 5.99 (0-7636-0295-7) Candlewick Pr.

— If Dinosaurs Were Cats & Dogs. rev. ed. LC 90-22870. (Illus.). 32p. (J). (ps-3). 1991. lib. bdg. 13.95 (0-02-765785-X, Four Winds Pr) S&S Childrens.

— Jolly Roger: And the Pirates of Captain Abdul. 2nd ed. LC 94-25703. (Illus.). 48p. (Orig.). (J). (gr. 1-5). 1995. pap. 7.99 (1-56402-512-8) Candlewick Pr.

***McNaughton, Colin.** Little Boo! (Illus.). 14p. (J). (ps-k). 2000. 5.95 (0-15-202671-1, Harcourt Child Bks) Harcourt.

— Little Suddenly! (Illus.). 14p. (J). (ps-k). 2000. 5.95 (0-15-202531-6, Harcourt Child Bks) Harcourt.

McNaughton, Colin. Making Friends with Frankenstein: A Book of Monstrous Poems & Pictures. LC 93-20027. (Illus.). 96p. (J). (ps up). 1994. 19.99 (1-56402-308-7) Candlewick Pr.

McNaughton, Colin. Making Friends with Frankenstein: A Book of Monstrous Poems & Pictures. LC 93-20027. 1996. 15.19 (0-606-10258-2, Pub. by Turtleback) Demco.

McNaughton, Colin. Making Friends with Frankenstein: A Book of Monstrous Poems & Pictures. LC 93-20027. (Illus.). 96p. (J). (gr. 1-6). 1996. reprint ed. pap. 9.99 (1-56402-962-X) Candlewick Pr.

— Oops! LC 96-44229. (Illus.). 32p. (J). (ps-3). 1997. 14.00 (0-15-201588-4, Harcourt Child Bks) Harcourt.

***McNaughton, Colin.** Oops! (Illus.). (J). (ps-3). 2000. pap. 6.00 (0-15-202458-1, Harcourt Child Bks) Harcourt.

McNaughton, Colin. Preston's Goal! LC 97-39947. (Illus.). 32p. (J). (gr. 1-3). 1998. 15.00 (0-15-201816-6) Harcourt.

***McNaughton, Colin.** Shh! (Don't Tell Mr. Wolf!) A Preston Pig Lift-the-Flap Book. (Preston Pig Story Ser.). (Illus.). 18p. (J). 2000. pap. 9.95 (0-15-202341-0, Harcourt Child Bks) Harcourt.

McNaughton, Colin. Suddenly. LC 94-12995. (Illus.). 32p. (J). (ps-3). 1995. 14.00 (0-15-200308-8) Harcourt.

— Suddenly. (Illus.). 32p. (J). 1998. pap. 6.00 (0-15-201699-6, Harcourt Child Bks) Harcourt.

— Suddenly. (ENG & SPA., Illus.). 32p. (J). (ps-2). 1997. write for info. (1-85430-532-8, Pub. by MAGI1 UK); write for info. (1-85430-530-1, Pub. by MAGI1 UK); write for info. (1-85430-531-X, Pub. by MAGI1 UK) Midpt Trade.

— There's an Awful Lot of Weirdos in Our Neighborhood. 2nd ed. LC 97-538. (Illus.). 96p. (J). (gr. 1-7). 1997. 16.99 (0-7636-0299-X) Candlewick Pr.

— Who's Been Sleeping in My Porridge? 2nd ed. LC 97-42464. (Illus.). 96p. (J). (gr. k-5). 1998. reprint ed. 16.99 (0-7636-0106-3) Candlewick Pr.

— Who's That Banging on the Ceiling? LC 91-58768. (Illus.). 32p. (J). (ps up). 1994. pap. 5.99 (1-56402-384-2) Candlewick Pr.

— Wish You Were Here (And I Wasn't) A Book of Poems & Pictures for Globe-Trotters. LC 98-51829. 64p. (YA). 2000. 16.99 (0-7636-0271-X) Candlewick Pr.

— Yum! LC 98-27980. 32p. (J). 1999. 15.00 (0-15-202064-0, Harcourt Child Bks) Harcourt.

McNaughton, David. Moral Vision: An Introduction to Ethics. 288p. 1988. pap. text 28.95 (0-631-15945-2) Blackwell Pubs.

McNaughton, Deborah. Insider's Guide to Managing Your Credit, 1 vol. 1999. mass mkt. 6.99 (0-425-16745-3) Berkley Pub.

— The Insider's Guide to Managing Your Credit: How to Establish, Maintain, Repair & Protect Your Credit. LC 97-28260. 240p. (Orig.). 1997. pap. 15.95 (0-7931-2669-X, 5680-5801) Dearborn.

McNaughton, Deborah, jt. auth. see Avanzini, John F.

McNaughton, Diana, et al. Banking Institutions in Developing Markets Vol. 1: Building Strong Management & Responding to Change, 2 vols. LC 92-27893. 184p. 1992. pap. 22.00 (0-8213-2217-6, 12217) World Bank.

— Banking Institutions in Developing Markets Vol. 2: Interpreting Financial Statements, 2 vols. LC 92-27893. 152p. 1992. pap. 22.00 (0-8213-2218-4, 12218) World Bank.

McNaughton, Duncan. Another Set / of Circumstance. LC 99-171527. 36p. 1998. pap. 60.00 (0-9666917-0-9) Hawkhaven Pr.

— Kicking the Feather. 48p. (Orig.). 1996. pap. 10.00 (1-889960-01-2) First Intensity.

— A Passage of Saint Devil. 1976. pap. 10.00 (0-88922-100-6) Genl Dist Srvs.

— The Pilot. 64p. 1991. pap. 7.00 (0-9631462-0-3) Blue Millennium.

— Valparaiso. (Poetry Ser.: No. 2). 144p. 1995. pap. text 10.00 (0-9639321-2-8) Listening Chamber.

— Valparaiso. deluxe ed. 1995. pap. 20.00 (0-9639321-3-6) Listening Chamber.

— The Wrapped Church. 32p. (Orig.). 1996. pap. 5.00 (0-9631462-1-1) Blue Millennium.

***McNaughton, Elnora.** Hold the Moon Bursting. 48p. 2000. pap. 8.00 (1-890887-11-0) Mille Grazie.

***McNaughton, Gary A. & McNaughton, Warren P.** Deployment of Mapping Systems in Distribution Cooperatives LC 99-14429. 1999. write for info. (0-917599-24-1) Natl Rural.

McNaughton, Gary A., et al. Enterprise-Wide Data Integration in Distribution Cooperative. LC 96-51766. 1996. write for info. (0-917599-20-9) Natl Rural.

McNaughton, Ian. Making Miniature Oriental Rugs & Carpets. (Illus.). 102p. 1998. pap. 12.95 (1-86108-066-2, Pub. by Guild Master) Sterling.

McNaughton, Janet. Catch Me Once, Catch Me Twice. unabridged ed. 176p. (J). (gr. 3-6). 1997. mass mkt. 5.99 (0-7736-7449-7) STDK.

— Make or Break Spring. LC 98-168564. 192p. 1999. pap. 9.95 (1-895387-93-0) Creative Bk Pub.

— To Dance at the Palais Royale. 232p. 1996. pap. 9.95 (1-895387-70-1) Creative Bk Pub.

***McNaughton, Janet.** To Dance at the Palais Royale. 220p. 1999. pap. 5.95 (0-7736-7473-X) General Publishing Co.

McNaughton, Kenneth J., jt. ed. see Chemical Engineering Magazine Editors.

***McNaughton, Marimar.** Outer Banks Architecture: An Anthology of Outposts, Lodges & Cottages. (Illus.). 130p. 2000. pap. 14.95 (0-89587-192-0) Blair.

McNaughton, Maureen. Maureen McNaughton's Potpourri. (Illus.). 54p. 1991. pap. 8.95 (0-941284-85-9) J Shaw Studio.

***McNaughton, Mildred.** Four Great Oaks. LC 99-80171. 400p. 2000. write for info. (1-893766-12-8) Aeon Pub Co.

McNaughton, Neil. Biology & Emotion. (Problems in the Behavioral Sciences Ser.). (Illus.). 256p. (C). 1989. pap. text 24.95 (0-521-31938-2) Cambridge U Pr.

McNaughton, Neil, jt. auth. see Gray, Jeffrey A.

McNaughton, Patrick R. The Mande Blacksmiths: Knowledge, Power, & Art in West Africa. LC 86-46347. (Traditional Arts of Africa Ser.). (Illus.). 270p. 1993. pap. 15.95 (0-253-20798-3) Ind U Pr.

McNaughton, Robert. Elementary Computability, Formal Languages, & Automata. LC 93-32105. (Illus.). 1993. 60.00 (0-9623885-6-4) ZB Pub Indus.

McNaughton, Rod B., jt. ed. see Green, Milford B.

McNaughton, Stuart. Being Skilled. 220p. (C). 1988. lib. bdg. 59.95 (0-416-01622-7, A2450) Routledge.

— Patterns of Emergent Literacy: Processes of Development & Transition. (Illus.). 229p. (C). 1996. pap. text 45.00 (0-19-558324-8) OUP.

***McNaughton, Virginia.** Lavender: The Grower's Guide. (Illus.). 200p. 2000. 29.95 (0-88192-478-4) Timber.

McNaughton, Warren P., jt. auth. see McNaughton, Gary A.

McNaughton, Wayne L. Business Basics: An Outline of Business Theory & Practice. (Quality Paperback Ser.: No. 317). 344p. (Orig.). 1976. pap. 13.00 (0-8226-0317-9) Littlefield.

***McNaughton, William & Ying, Li.** Reading & Writing Chinese. rev. ed. (ENG & CHI.). 368p. 1999. pap. 18.95 (0-8048-3206-4) Tuttle Pubng.

McNaughton, William, tr. see Akhmatova, Anna Andreevena.

McNay, Deborah. Precious Metals (Gold, Silver & Platinum) Industry & Trade Summary. (Illus.). 45p. (Orig.). (C). 1995. pap. text 30.00 (0-7881-2103-0) DIANE Pub.

McNay, Ian. Visions of Post-Compulsory Education. 176p. 1992. 123.00 (0-335-09779-0); pap. 39.95 (0-335-09778-2) OpUniv Pr.

***McNay, Ian & Society for Research into Higher Education Staff.** Higher Education & Its Communities. LC 00-37512. 2000. pap. write for info. (0-335-20734-0) Taylor & Francis.

McNay, Lois. Foucault & Feminism: Power, Gender & the Self. LC 92-27536. 1993. text 45.00 (1-55553-152-0) NE U Pr.

— Foucault & Feminism: Power, Gender & the Self. LC 92-27536. 1993. reprint ed. pap. text 16.95 (1-55553-153-9) NE U Pr.

***McNay, Lois.** Gender & Agency: Reconfiguring the Subject in Feminist & Social Theory. LC 99-56202. 200p. 2000. text 59.95 (0-7456-1348-9, Pub. by Polity Pr); pap. text 24.95 (0-7456-1349-7, Pub. by Polity Pr) Blackwell Pubs.

McNay, Roxi I. Close Encounters: A Journey of Spiritual Discovery & Adventure. (Illus.). 320p. (Orig.). 1991. pap. 14.95 (0-9517206-1-9) Roximillion Pubns.

McNeal. Student Active Science. LC 97-177545. (C). 1996. pap. text 47.00 (0-03-024307-6, Pub. by Harcourt Coll Pubs) Harcourt.

McNeal, Alva E. Civil Rights Compliance: An Update. 2nd ed. (Illus.). 65p. 1995. pap. text 8.50 (1-878550-18-7) Inter Dev Res Assn.

McNeal, Alva E., jt. auth. see Garza, Josephine F.

McNeal, Alvin R., jt. ed. see Protopappas, John J.

McNeal, Ann, ed. Project Impact: Disseminating Innovation in Undergraduate Education Conference Proceedings. (Illus.). 116p. (C). 1996. reprint ed. pap. text 35.00 (0-7881-3124-9) DIANE Pub.

— Project Impact - Disseminating Innovation in Undergraduate Education: Abstracts of Projects: Things That Work. 303p. 1998. reprint ed. pap. text 40.00 (0-7881-4241-0) DIANE Pub.

McNeal, Barbara. Electronic Mail among University Training Centers: A Demonstration in National Network Building. 38p. 1980. 6.00 (0-318-19194-6, R-49) Inst Future.

McNeal, Brenda. Springboards for Writing. (gr. 8-12). 1979. pap. text 15.00 (0-87879-222-8) Acad Therapy.

McNeal, C. J., ed. The Analysis of Peptides & Proteins by Mass Spectrometry. LC 88-27922. (Illus.). 234p. 1988. reprint ed. pap. 72.60 (0-608-06830-6, 206702700009) Bks Demand.

McNeal, C. J., ed. see Texas Symposium on Mass Spectrometry (3rd: 1986: T.

McNeal, Donnell. Africans: The Eyes to the Church. LC 98-70875. 220p. 2000. pap. 13.95 (1-878647-52-0) APU Pub Grp.

McNeal, E. H., jt. auth. see Thatcher, Oliver J.

McNeal, Gloria J. AACN Acute Care Procedures in the Home. 608p. spiral bd. 34.95 (0-7817-1816-3) Lppncott W & W.

McNeal, James U. Kids As Customers: A Handbook of Marketing to Children. (Illus.). 258p. 1998. text 35.00 (0-7881-5706-X) DIANE Pub.

— Kids As Customers: A Handbook of Marketing to Children. 258p. 1992. 37.00 (0-669-27627-8) Lxngtn Bks.

— The Kids Market: Myths & Realities. (Illus.). 250p. 1999. 54.95 (0-9671439-1-8) Paramount Mrkt.

McNeal, Kathleen, jt. auth. see Prater, Bayliss.

McNeal, Laura. Crooked. LC 99-19114. 346p. (gr. 7-12). 1999. lib. bdg. 18.99 (0-679-99300-2) Knopf.

McNeal, Laura & McNeal, Tom. When All the Good Holidays Are Over. LC 99-19114. 352p. (YA). (gr. 6-10). 1999. 16.95 (0-679-89300-8) Knopf.

McNeal, Laura, jt. auth. see McNeal, Tom.

McNeal, Patricia. Harder Than War: Catholic Peacemaking in Twentieth-Century America. LC 91-16814. 310p. (C). 1992. text 40.00 (0-8135-1739-7); pap. text 18.00 (0-8135-1740-0) Rutgers U Pr.

McNeal, Patricia F. The American Catholic Peace Movement, 1928-1972. (Classic Quilt Ser.). 20p. 1978. 35.95 (0-405-10840-0, 11820) Ayer.

McNeal, R. A., ed. Nicholas Biddle in Greece: The Journals & Letters of 1806. LC 92-35459. (Illus.). 240p. 1993. 40.00 (0-271-00914-4) Pa St U Pr.

McNeal, Reggie. Revolution in Leadership: Training Apostles for Tomorrow's Church. LC 98-19373. (Ministry for the Third Millennium Ser.). 160p. 1998. 16.00 (0-687-08707-4) Abingdon.

***McNeal, Reggie.** A Work of Heart: Understanding How God Shapes Spiritual Leaders. LC 99-50744. 176p. 2000. 21.00 (0-7879-4288-X) Jossey-Bass.

McNeal, Robert H. Guide to the Decisions of the Communist Party of the Soviet Union, 1917-1967. LC 75-185723. 379p. reprint ed. pap. 117.50 (0-608-14380-4, 201942900011) Bks Demand.

— Stalin: Man & Ruler. LC 88-15525. (Illus.). 400p. (C). 1990. pap. text 18.50 (0-8147-5455-4) NYU Pr.

McNeal, Stephanie Renee, ed. see Evans, Tonya Marie.

McNeal, Tom. Goodnight, Nebraska: A Novel. 336p. 1999. pap. 12.00 (0-375-70429-9) Vin Bks.

McNeal, Tom & McNeal, Laura. The Dog Who Lost His Bob. (Illus.). 32p. (J). (gr. k-4). 1996. lib. bdg. 15.95 (0-8075-1662-7) A Whitman.

McNeal, Tom, jt. auth. see McNeal, Laura.

McNeal, William W. The Life & Times of Our Family. 65p. 1993. ring bd., vinyl bd. 34.50 (0-9636747-0-6) Wrthngton Hse.

McNealy, Roderick M. Making Customer Satisfaction Happen. 208p. 1994. 29.95 (0-412-58920-6, Chap & Hall NY) Chapman & Hall.

McNease, Cathy, jt. auth. see Ni, Maoshing.

***McNee, Lisa.** Selfish Gifts: Senegalese Women's Autobiographical Discourses. LC 99-39903. (C). 2000. pap. text 18.95 (0-7914-4588-7) State U NY Pr.

— Selfish Gifts: Senegalese Women's Autobiographical Discourses. LC 99-39903. (C). 2000. text 57.50 (0-7914-4587-9) State U NY Pr.

***McNee, Mona.** C-A-T=Cat: Teach Your Child to Read with Phonics. 340p. 2000. pap. 8.95 (0-7160-2123-4, Pub. by Elliot RW Bks) Midpt Trade.

McNeece, C. Aaron & DiNitto, Diana M. Chemical Dependency: A Systems Approach. 2nd ed. LC 97-35141. 462p. 1998. pap. text 44.00 (0-205-26485-9) P-H.

McNeece, C. Aaron & Roberts, Albert R. Policy & Practice in the Justice System. LC 96-11325. (Social Work). (Illus.). 1997. pap. text 48.95 (0-8304-1417-7) Thomson Learn.

McNeece, C. Aaron, jt. auth. see Dinitto, Diana M.

McNeece, C. Aaron, jt. auth. see DiNitto, Diana M.

McNeece, C. Aaron, jt. ed. see Raffoul, Paul R.

McNeece, Lucy S. Art & Politics in Duras' India Cycle. 208p. 1996. 49.95 (0-8130-1470-0) U Press Fla.

McNeel, Cheryl B., et al. Short-Term Play Therapy for Disruptive Children. 129p. 1996. 37.95 (1-882732-51-0) Childswork.

McNeel, R. W. Beating the Stock Market. LC 63-22594. 1963. reprint ed. pap. 13.00 (0-87034-008-5) Fraser Pub Co.

McNeel, Timothy G., see Throb, Tyrone, pseud.

McNeel, William P. The Durbin Route: The Greenbrier Division of the C & O Railroad. LC 85-62875. (Illus.). 152p. 1985. pap. text 12.95 (0-933126-56-5) Pictorial Hist.

— The Greenbrier River Trail: Through the Eyes of History. LC 96-69801. (Illus.). 112p. (Orig.). 1997. pap. 9.95 (1-57510-020-7) Pictorial Hist.

McNeeley, Gene, jt. auth. see Ransom, Scott.

McNeely, Connie L. Constructing the Nation-State: International Organization & Prescriptive Action, 113. LC 95-5270. (Contributions in Sociology Ser.: Vol. 113). 208p. 1995. 57.95 (0-313-29398-8, Greenwood Pr) Greenwood.

— Public Rights, Public Rules: Constituting Citizens in the World Polity & National Policy. LC 98-35377. (States & Societies Ser.: No. 1). 424p. 1998. text 75.00 (0-8153-2126-0) Garland.

McNeely, Deldon A. Animus Aeternus: Exploring the Inner Masculine. 192p. 1995. pap. 18.00 (0-919123-50-3, Pub. by Inner City Bks) BookWorld.

— Mercury Rising: Women, Evil & the Trickster Gods. LC 96-50485. 208p. (Orig.). 1997. pap. 18.00 (0-88214-366-2) Spring Pubns.

— Touching. 128p. 1995. pap. 16.00 (0-919123-29-5, Pub. by Inner City Bks) BookWorld.

McNeely, Jeffrey A. Economics & Biological Diversity: Developing & Using Economic Incentives to Conserve Biological Resources. 256p. 1988. pap. 15.00 (2-88032-964-7, Pub. by IUCN) Island Pr.

McNeely, Jeffrey A., ed. Expanding Partnerships in Conservation. 318p. (C). 1995. pap. text 38.00 (1-55963-351-4) Island Pr.

— Protecting Nature: Regional Reviews of Protected Areas. LC 95-194741. 376p. (C). 1994. pap. text 50.00 (2-8317-0119-8, Pub. by IUCN) Island Pr.

McNeely, Jeffrey A. & Miller, Kenton R., eds. National Parks, Conservation, & Development: The Role of Protected Areas in Sustaining Society. LC 84-600007. (Illus.). 848p. 1984. pap. text 35.00 (0-87474-663-9, MCNPP) Smithsonian.

McNeely, Jeffrey A. & Sochaczewski, Paul S. Soul of the Tiger: Searching for Nature's Answers in Southeast Asia. LC 94-45557. (Illus.). 432p. 1995. pap. 13.50 (0-8248-1669-2, Kolowalu Bk) UH Pr.

McNeely, Jeffrey A., jt. auth. see Guruswamy, Lakshman D.

McNeely, Jeffrey A., jt. auth. see Munasinghe, Mohan.

McNeely, Jeffrey A., jt. auth. see World Conservation Congress Staff.

McNeely, Jerry. The Staring Match. 1957. pap. 3.25 (0-8222-1072-X) Dramatists Play.

McNeely, Kenneth. What Do We Really Know about God? LC 86-91364. 1987. 12.00 (0-87212-201-8) Libra.

McNeely, L., jt. auth. see Harrison, M.

McNeely, Richard. Judicial Jeopardy: When Business Collides with the Courts. LC 86-7945. 288p. 1986. 19.18 (0-201-05736-0) Addison-Wesley.

— Primero y Segundo de Reyes. (Comentario Biblico Portavoz Ser.). Orig. Title: First & Second Kings (Everyman's Bible Commentary). (SPA.). 160p. 1993. pap. 6.99 (0-8254-1476-8, Edit Portavoz) Kregel.

McNeely, Richard A., ed. see Dunton, Sabina M. & Fanning, Melody S.

McNeely, Richard A., ed. see Dunton, Sabina & Miller, Kathy A.

McNeely, Sarah L. Plays for the Soul. 50p. (J). (ps-12). 1997. pap. 10.00 (1-890300-03-9) NIA Pages.

McNeely, Scott & Nebeksy, Richard. Lonely Planet Czech & Slovak Republics. 2nd ed. (Illus.). 560p. 1998. pap. 19.95 (0-86442-525-2) Lonely Planet.

McNeely, Scott, et al. Europe on a Shoestring. (On a Shoestring Ser.). (Illus.). 1224p. 1999. pap. 24.95 (0-86442-648-8) Lonely Planet.

***McNeely, Scott, et al.** Europe on a Shoestring. 2nd ed. 2001. reprint ed. 24.99 (1-86450-150-2) Lonely Planet.

McNeely, Sharon L. Observing Students & Teachers Through Objective Strategies. LC 96-49745. 256p. 1997. pap. text 30.00 (0-205-26434-4) Allyn.

McNeer, May. The California Gold Rush. (Landmark Bks.). 1997. 11.09 (0-606-12902-2, Pub. by Turtleback) Demco.

Mcnees, Eleanor, ed. The Bronte Sisters: Critical Assessments, 4 vols. 2200p. (C). 1997. 535.00 (1-873403-28-3) Routledge.

McNees, Eleanor, ed. Virginia Woolf: Critical Assessments, 4 vols., Set. LC 95-108016. (Critical Assessments of Writers in English Ser.). (Illus.). 2560p. (C). (gr. 13 up). 1994. text, boxed set 535.00 (1-873403-06-2) Routledge.

M

An Asterisk (*) at the beginning of an entry indicates that the title is appearing for the first time.

McNees, Eleanor J. Eucharistic Poetry: The Search for Presence in the Writings of John Donne, Gerard Manley Hopkins, Dylan Thomas, & Geoffrey Hill. LC 90-56215. 248p. 1992. 38.50 (*0-8387-5205-5*) Bucknell U Pr.

Mcnees, Pat. Contemporary Latin American Short Stories. LC 96-96612. 1996. pap. 12.00 (*0-449-91226-4*) Fawcett.

***McNees, Pat.** Ypo: The First Fifty Years. LC 99-38806. 1999. 20.00 (*1-882203-59-3*) Orange Frazer.

***McNees, Pat, ed.** Dying: A Book of Comfort. LC 98-13933. 352p. 1998. mass mkt. 13.99 (*0-446-67400-1*, Pub. by Warner Bks) Little.

McNees, Pat & Crown Equipment Corporation Staff. By Design: The Story of Crown Equipment Corporation. LC 97-25588. 151p. 1997. 20.00 (*1-882203-15-1*) Orange Frazer.

***McNees, Wallace & Nurick Staff.** 2000 Employment Law Guide. rev. ed. Pennsylvania Chamber of Business & Industry Educational Foundation Staff, ed. 199p. 1999. pap. 99.00 (*1-929744-13-7*) Penn Chamber of Bus.

McNeese, Tim. America's Early Canals. LC 91-41353. (Americans on the Move Ser.). (Illus.). 48p. (J). (gr. 5). 1993. lib. bdg. 11.95 (*0-89686-730-7*, Crstwood Hse) Silver Burdett Pr.

— America's First Railroads. LC 91-738. (Americans on the Move Ser.). (Illus.). 48p. (J). (gr. 5). 1993. text, lib. bdg. 11.95 (*0-89686-729-3*, Crstwood Hse) Silver Burdett Pr.

— Clippers & Whaling Ships. LC 91-27187. (Americans on the Move Ser.). (Illus.). 48p. (J). (gr. 5). 1993. text, lib. bdg. 11.95 (*0-89686-735-8*, Crstwood Hse) Silver Burdett Pr.

— Conestogas & Stagecoaches. LC 91-24064. (Americans on the Move Ser.). (Illus.). 48p. (J). (gr. 5). 1993. lib. bdg. 11.95 (*0-89686-732-3*, Crstwood Hse) Silver Burdett Pr.

— The Great Wall of China. LC 92-29937. (Building History Ser.). (Illus.). (J). (gr. 4-12). 1997. lib. bdg. 22.45 (*1-56006-428-5*) Lucent Bks.

— Illustrated Myths of Native America The Southwest, Western Range, Pacific Northwest & California. (Illus.). 1999. 27.95 (*0-7137-2700-4*) Blandford Pr.

— Illustrated Myths of Native Americans. (Illus.). 160p. 1998. 24.95 (*0-7137-2666-0*, Pub. by Blandford Pr) Sterling.

— The New York Subway System. LC 96-48700. (Building History Ser.). (Illus.). (J). (gr. 4-12). 1997. lib. bdg. 22.45 (*1-56006-427-7*) Lucent Bks.

— The Panama Canal. LC 96-45623. (Building History Ser.). (Illus.). (YA). (gr. 4-12). 1997. lib. bdg. 22.45 (*1-56006-425-0*) Lucent Bks.

— The Pyramids of Giza. LC 96-45622. (Building History Ser.). (Illus.). (YA). (gr. 4-12). 1997. lib. bdg. 22.45 (*1-56006-426-9*) Lucent Bks.

— West by Steamboat. LC 91-22822. (Americans on the Move Ser.). (Illus.). 48p. (J). (gr. 5). 1993. lib. bdg. 16.95 (*0-89686-728-5*, Crstwood Hse) Silver Burdett Pr.

— Western Wagon Trains. LC 91-42076. (Americans on the Move Ser.). (Illus.). 48p. (J). (gr. 5). 1993. lib. bdg. 11.95 (*0-89686-734-X*, Crstwood Hse) Silver Burdett Pr.

McNeese, William & Klein, R. A. Statistical Methods for the Process Industries. (Quality & Reliability Ser.: Vol. 28). (Illus.). 528p. 1991. text 75.00 (*0-8247-8524-X*) Dekker.

McNeil. Curriculum. 2nd ed. LC 98-28369. 228p. 1998. pap. text 38.00 (*0-13-744384-6*) P-H.

McNeil. Curriculum Introduction. 5th ed. 480p. 1996. 86.95 (*0-471-36470-3*) Wiley.

McNeil. Curriculum Introduction: Instruction Manual. 5th ed. 1996. pap. text 25.00 (*0-471-36504-1*) Wiley.

Mcneil, jt. auth. see Wilkinson.

McNeil, Alex. Total Television: The Comprehensive Guide to Programming from 1948 to the Present. 4th ed. 1264p. (Orig.). 1996. pap. 22.95 (*0-14-024916-8*, Penguin Bks) Viking Penguin.

***McNeil, Art.** Life Is Not a Spectator Sport: Getting It on with Life Rather Than Just Getting By. vi, 256p. 2000. pap. 13.95 (*0-9681590-1-X*) FGII.

McNeil, Barbara. Biography & Genealogy Master Index, 1992. 92nd ed. 1991. 348.00 (*0-8103-4802-0*) Gale.

— Biography & Genealogy Master Index, 1993. 93rd ed. 1992. 348.00 (*0-8103-7605-9*) Gale.

— Biography & Genealogy Master Index, 1994. 94th ed. 1993. 348.00 (*0-8103-8002-1*) Gale.

McNeil, Barbara, ed. Biography & Genealogy Master Index, 1981-85, 5 vols., Set. 81st ed. 4423p. 1985. 995.00 (*0-8103-1506-8*) Gale.

— Biography & Genealogy Master Index 1984. 84th ed. 936p. 1984. 348.00 (*0-8103-1508-4*) Gale.

— Biography & Genealogy Master Index 1985. 85th ed. 664p. 1985. 348.00 (*0-8103-1507-6*) Gale.

— Biography & Genealogy Master Index, 1986. 86th ed. 650p. 1986. 348.00 (*0-8103-1511-4*) Gale.

— Biography & Genealogy Master Index, 1986-1990: Cumulation of Supplements, 3 vols., Set. 86th ed. 3600p. 1990. 995.00 (*0-8103-4803-9*) Gale.

— Biography & Genealogy Master Index, 1987. 87th ed. 823p. 1986. 348.00 (*0-8103-1513-0*) Gale.

— Biography & Genealogy Master Index, 1988. 88th ed. 1080p. 1987. 348.00 (*0-8103-1514-9*) Gale.

— Biography & Genealogy Master Index, 1989. 89th ed. 1988. 348.00 (*0-8103-2794-5*) Gale.

— Biography & Genealogy Master Index, 1991. 91st ed. 1200p. (J). 1990. 348.00 (*0-8103-4801-2*) Gale.

— Twentieth-Century Author Biographies Master Index. 539p. 1984. 39.00 (*0-8103-2096-7*) Gale.

McNeil, Barbara & Herbert, Miranda C., eds. Historical Biographical Dictionaries Master Index. LC 80-10719. (Biographical Index Ser.: No. 7). 1016p. 1980. 250.00 (*0-8103-1089-9*) Gale.

McNeil, Barbara, jt. ed. see Herbert, Miranda C.

McNeil, Barbara J. & Abrams, Herbert L. Brigham & Women's Hospital Handbook of Diagnostic Imaging. 342p. 1985. 21.00 (*0-316-56322-6*, Little Brwn Med Div) Lppncott W & W.

McNeil, Barbara J., ed. see Cravalho, Ernest G.

McNeil, Beth & Johnson, Denise, eds. Patron Behavior in Libraries: A Handbook of Positive Approaches to Negative Situations. 200p. (Orig.). 1995. pap. 28.00 (*0-8389-0662-1*, 0662-1-2045) ALA.

McNeil, Beth, ed. see Lydecker, Beatrice.

McNeil, Bill. The Dodger Encyclopedia. (Illus.). 464p. 1997. 39.95 (*1-57167-154-4*) Sports Pub.

McNeil, Brian. Christ in the Psalms. 104p. (Orig.). 1980. pap. 3.95 (*0-905092-87-2*, Pub. by Veritas Pubns) St Mut.

— God's Fidelity to Us. 160p. 1996. pap. 39.95 (*0-85439-512-1*, Pub. by St Paul Pubns) St Mut.

McNeil, Brian, ed. see Von Balthasar, Hans U.

McNeil, Brian, tr. see Fuchs, Josef.

McNeil, Brian, tr. see Klauck, Hans Josef.

McNeil, Brian, tr. see Von Balthasar, Hans U.

McNeil, Brian, tr. see Von Speyr, Adrienne.

McNeil, Bruce J. Nonqualified Deferred Compensation Plans. 210p. 1994. pap. text. write for info. (*0-314-04029-3*) West Pub.

— Nonqualified Deferred Compensation Plans. 305p. 1996. pap. text. write for info. (*0-314-20308-7*) West Pub.

— Nonqualified Deferred Compensation Plans: 1997 Edition. 328p. 1997. pap. text. write for info. (*0-314-22429-7*) West Pub.

— Nonqualified Deferred Compensation Plans, 1995 Edition. 277p. 1995. pap. text. write for info. (*0-314-07218-7*) West Pub.

— The Pension Answer Book: Nonqualified Deferred Compensation. Persons, Mark D., ed. 277p. 1991. 89.00 (*1-878375-40-7*) Panel Pubs.

McNeil, Bruce J. & Persons, Mark D. The Pension Answer Book: Nonqualified Deferred Compensation. 169p. 1990. pap. text 49.00 (*1-878375-17-2*) Panel Pubs.

***McNeil, Carla Speed.** Sin-Eater. (Finder Ser.: Vol. 1). (Illus.). 168p. 1999. pap. 15.95 (*0-9673691-0-X*) Lightspeed Pr.

McNeil, Carol, et al. Teaching Orienteering. 2nd expanded rev. ed. LC 97-17531. (Illus.). 160p. 1997. pap. text 24.00 (*0-88011-804-0*, BMCN0804) Human Kinetics.

McNeil, Caroline. Alzheimer's Disease: Unraveling the Mystery. 50p. 1996. pap. 4.00 (*0-16-048311-5*) USGPO.

McNeil, Caroline. Alzheimer's Disease: Unraveling the Mystery. (Illus.). 48p. 1997. reprint ed. pap. text 30.00 (*0-7881-3793-X*) DIANE Pub.

— Hearts & Arteries: What Scientists Are Learning about Age & the Cardiovascular System. (Illus.). 35p. 1996. reprint ed. pap. text 15.00 (*0-7881-2838-8*) DIANE Pub.

***McNeil, Caroline, et al.** Toxic & Hazardous Chemicals, Title III, & Communities: An Outreach Manual for Community Groups. 156p. 1999. reprint ed. pap. text 25.00 (*0-7881-7872-5*) DIANE Pub.

McNeil, Cheryl B., jt. auth. see Hembree-Kigin, Toni L.

McNeil, Christine. Kissing the Night. 64p. 1993. pap. 12.95 (*1-85224-220-5*, Pub. by Bloodaxe Bks) Dufour.

McNeil, Christopher, et al. The Best of Thespian Playworks Vol. I: Three Plays: God & Poker; Flambee; The Idiot & the Oddity. 111p. 1996. pap. 5.95 (*0-87129-624-1*, B78) Dramatic Pub.

McNeil, Craig. How to Ski the Blues & Blacks Without Getting Black & Blue. LC 98-74214. (Illus.). 576p. 1998. pap. 9.95 (*1-889796-08-5*) Sequoia Pub Inc.

McNeil, Dani, jt. auth. see Owen, Sandy.

McNeil, Daniel & Freiberger, Paul. Fuzzy Logic: The Revolutionary Computer Technology That Is Changing Our World. 320p. 1994. pap. 12.00 (*0-671-87535-3*, Touchstone) S&S Trade Pap.

McNeil, Daniel J. Footprints in the Heart. 149p. 1999. pap. 13.95 (*0-7414-0034-0*) Buy Books.

McNeil, David. The Grotesque Depiction of War & the Military in Eighteenth-Century English Fiction. LC 88-50584. (Illus.). 232p. 1990. 39.50 (*0-87413-369-6*) U Delaware Pr.

Mcneil, Don. Epidemiological Research Methods. 316p. 1996. 149.95 (*0-471-96195-7*); pap. 69.95 (*0-471-96196-5*) Wiley.

McNeil, Don. Moving Through Here. 1990. pap. 9.95 (*0-8065-1165-6*, Citadel Pr) Carol Pub Group.

McNeil, Donald E., jt. ed. see Childs, William M.

McNeil, Donald S., ed. Jewelers' Dictionary. 3rd ed. LC 76-26012. 268p. 1979. 39.95 (*0-931744-01-6*, CR-002) Jewlrs Circular-Keystone.

— Who's Who in the Jewelry Industry. LC 79-27501. 231p. 1980. 24.95 (*0-931744-02-4*) Jewlrs Circular-Keystone.

McNeil, E. L. Airborne Care of the Ill & Injured. (Illus.). 208p. 1982. 51.00 (*0-387-90754-8*) Spr-Verlag.

McNeil, Edna. Poems, Quotes, Mini Stories & True Life Experiences in God Power. Moore, Denise, ed. (Orig.). 1989. pap. text 24.94 (*0-9613082-3-0*, TX369163) Bootstrap.

***McNeil, Edward A.** A Span of Poetry. (Illus.). 320p. 2001. pap. write for info. (*1-57197-234-X*, Pub. by Pentland Pr) Assoc Pubs Grp.

***McNeil, Edward L.** An Interesting Way to Retire. 176p. 2001. pap. write for info. (*1-57197-241-2*, Pub. by Pentland Pr) Assoc Pubs Grp.

— Plane Reading. 224p. 2001. pap. write for info. (*1-57197-244-7*, Pub. by Pentland Pr) Assoc Pubs Grp.

— Plane Reading, Vol. II. (Illus.). 368p. 2000. write for info. (*1-57197-230-7*, Pub. by Pentland Pr) Assoc Pubs Grp.

McNeil, Florence. Miss P & Me. LC 83-48819. 128p. (J). (gr. 5-7). 1984. 11.95 (*0-06-024136-5*) HarpC Child Bks.

— Swimming Out of History: New & Selected Poems. 1991. pap. 12.95 (*0-88982-113-5*, Pub. by Oolichan Bks) Genl Dist Srvs.

McNeil, Freed H. McNeil's Mount Hood: Wyeast the Mountain Revisited. rev. ed. (Illus.). 224p. 1990. reprint ed. pap. 12.95 (*0-9614498-7-X*) Zig Zag Paper.

McNeil, Genna R. Groundwork: Charles Hamilton Houston & the Struggle for Civil Rights. LC 82-40483. (Illus.). 320p. 1983. pap. 20.95 (*0-8122-1179-0*) U of Pa Pr.

McNeil, Genna R. & Winston, Michael, eds. Historical Judgments Reconsidered: Selected Howard University Lectures in Honor of Rayford W. Logan. 270p. 1988. 24.95 (*0-88258-173-2*) Howard U Pr.

McNeil, Genna R., jt. ed. see Franklin, John H.

McNeil, George D. Tales of Pocahontas County. 1958. pap. 5.00 (*0-685-61019-5*) McClain.

McNeil, Heather. Hyena & the Moon: Stories to Tell from Kenya. (World Folklore Ser.). (Illus.). xv, 171p. 1994. lib. bdg. 23.00 (*1-56308-169-5*) Libs Unl.

McNeil, Helen, ed. Emily Dickinson. (Everyman's Poetry Ser.). 128p. 1997. 3.50 (*0-460-87895-6*, Everyman's Classic Lib) Tuttle Pubng.

McNeil, Ian, ed. An Encyclopedia of the History of Technology. (Illus.). 1088p. (C). 1990. 200.00 (*0-415-01306-2*, A3894) Routledge.

— An Encyclopedia of the History of Technology. (Illus.). 1062p. (C). 1996. pap. 60.00 (*0-415-14792-1*) Routledge.

McNeil, Ian & Day, Lance, eds. Biographical Dictionary of the History of Technology. 864p. (C). 1995. 180.00 (*0-415-06042-7*, B0378) Routledge.

McNeil, Ian, jt. ed. see Day, Lance.

McNeil, J. A. & Price, C. E. From Fundamental Fields to Nuclear Phenomena. 296p. 1991. pap. 36.00 (*981-02-0514-7*); text 93.00 (*981-02-0513-9*) World Scientific Pub.

McNeil, Jacqueline, ed. see Khanbegian, Peter.

McNeil, James. Hsing - I. LC 91-67318. 1991. 14.95 (*0-86568-155-4*, 225) Unique Pubns.

McNeil, James W. Ancient Lovemaking Secrets: The Journey Toward Immortality. LC 99-190180. 130 P. ;p. 1998. write for info. (*0-86568-169-4*) Unique Pubns.

McNeil, Jean. Costa Rica. (New Rough Guides Ser.). 1996. pap. 15.95 (*0-614-97916-1*, Penguin Bks) Viking Penguin.

— Costa Rica. 2nd ed. (Rough Guide Ser.). (Illus.). 432p. 1998. pap. text 17.95 (*1-85828-337-X*, Pub. by Rough Guides) Penguin Putnam.

— Costa Rica: The Rough Guide. 1996. write for info. (*0-614-12752-1*, Penguin Bks) Viking Penguin.

— Hunting down Home. LC 98-50078. 210p. 1999. 16.00 (*1-57131-026-6*) Milkweed Ed.

McNeil, Jean, tr. see Deleuze, Gilles & Von Sacher-Masoch, Leopold.

McNeil, Jesse J., Sr. The Preacher-Prophet in Mass Society. rev. ed. Jones, Amos, Jr., ed. LC 93-40626. 1994. text 7.95 (*0-910683-12-3*) Townsnd-Pr.

McNeil, Jim. Charleston's Navy Yard: A Picture History. (Illus.). 217p. 1985. 34.95 (*0-914432-02-8*) Coker Craft Pr.

***McNeil, John.** Art of Jazz Trumpet. 2000. pap. text 24.95 (*0-9628467-6-7*) Gerard Sarzin Pub.

McNeil, John. Spy Game. 1982. mass mkt. 2.95 (*0-686-97470-0*, Zebra Kensgtn) Kensgtn Pub Corp.

McNeil, John D. Curriculum: A Comprehensive Introduction. 5th ed. LC 95-14586. (Illus.). 480p. (C). 1996. text 72.19 (*0-673-52352-7*) Addson-Wesley Educ.

McNeil, John D. & Schave, Barbara. Issues in School Reform: A View from the Bottom-Up. LC 84-20627. (Illus.). 192p. (Orig.). 1985. pap. text 38.00 (*0-911575-50-2*) Optimization Soft.

McNeil, John D., jt. auth. see Wiles, Jon W.

McNeil, John S., et al. Military Retirement: Social, Economic & Mental Health Dilemmas. (Illus.). 156p. 1983. text 50.00 (*0-86598-078-0*) Rowman.

McNeil, John S., ed. see Health-Mental Health Conference Staff.

McNeil, Katherine, jt. auth. see Langworthy, J. Lamont.

McNeil, Kathryn K. Purchase Knob: Essays from a Mountain Notebook. LC 98-33508. (Illus.). 80p. 1999. pap. 8.00 (*1-56474-279-2*) Fithian Pr.

***McNeil, Keith & McNeil, Rusty.** Civil War Songbook: With Historical Commentary. 104p. (YA). (gr. 4 up). 1999. pap. 15.95 (*1-878360-24-8*) WEM Records.

McNeil, Keith & McNeil, Rusty. Civil War Songs: With Historical Narration. (American History Through Folksong Ser.). (Illus.). 224p. (YA). (gr. 4 up). 1989. pap. 19.95 incl. audio (*1-878360-03-5*, 507C) WEM Records.

— Colonial & Revolution Songbook: With Historical Commentary. 71p. (J). (ps-2). 1996. pap. 11.95 (*1-878360-08-6*) WEM Records.

— Colonial & Revolution Songbook & Cassette Set: With Historical Commentary. (American History Through Folksong Ser.). 71p. (YA). (gr. 4 up). 1996. pap., boxed set 29.95 incl. audio (*1-878360-17-5*) WEM Records.

— Colonial & Revolution Songbook & CD Set: With Historical Commentary. 71p. (YA). (gr. 4 up). 1996. pap., boxed set 32.95 incl. audio compact disk (*1-878360-16-7*) WEM Records.

McNeil, Keith & Reese, Terence. Bid Against the Masters: The Best of Bidding Forum. 128p. 1993. pap. 15.95 (*0-575-05450-6*, Pub. by V Gollancz) Trafalgar.

McNeil, Keith, et al. Testing Research Hypotheses Using Multiple Linear Regression. LC 75-6639. 600p. 1975. pap. text 7.95 (*0-8093-0755-3*) S Ill U Pr.

— Testing Research Hypotheses with the General Linear Model. 416p. 1996. 49.95 (*0-8093-2019-3*); pap. 24.95 (*0-8093-2020-7*) S Ill U Pr.

McNeil, Keith, jt. auth. see Wilkinson, William K.

McNeil, Keith A., jt. auth. see Newman, Isadore.

McNeil, Kent. Common Law Aboriginal Title. (Illus.). 408p. 1989. 95.00 (*0-19-825223-4*) OUP.

McNeil, Legs. Pop Culture. LC 98-17847. 208p. 2000. 24.95 (*0-671-01187-1*) S&S Trade.

McNeil, Legs & McCain, Gillian, eds. Please Kill Me: The Uncensored Oral History of Punk. LC 96-39308. (Illus.). 512p. 1997. pap. 14.95 (*0-14-026690-9*) Viking Penguin.

McNeil, Linda. Contradictions of Reform: Educational Costs of Standardized Testing. (Critical Social Thought Ser.). 256p. (C). (gr. 13). 1999. 75.00 (*0-415-92073-6*, D5476); pap. 19.99 (*0-415-92074-4*, D5480) Routledge.

— Missing a Voice: Critical Pedagogy & the Possibilities of Democratic Teaching. 1997. pap. 17.95 (*0-8133-2624-9*) Westview.

— 7 Keys to Changing: Your Life, Health & Wealth. LC 98-92010. (Illus.). 135p. 1998. pap. 12.95 (*1-891446-02-9*, Pub. by Open Mind) New Leaf Dist.

McNeil, Linda M. Contradictions of Control: School Structure & School Knowledge. (Critical Social Thought Ser.). 234p. (C). 1988. pap. 19.99 (*0-415-90075-1*) Routledge.

McNeil, Linsey. Travel in the Digital Age. (Work in the Digital Age Ser.). 1997. pap. text 19.95 (*0-906097-64-9*, Pub. by Bowerdean Pub) Capital VA.

McNeil, M. Abby Aldrich Rockefeller Folk Art Center Address Book. (Museum Gift Bks.). (Illus.). 160p. 1984. 14.95 (*0-939456-10-9*) Galison.

McNeil, Malcolm R. & Perkins, William H., eds. Clinical Management of Sensorimotor Speech Disorders. (Current Therapy of Communication Disorders Ser.). (Illus.). 352p. 1996. text 49.00 (*0-86577-527-3*) Thieme Med Pubs.

McNeil, Mark A. "Oneness Pentecostal" Movement - An Evaluation. 1993. pap. 3.00 (*1-56186-520-6*) Pilgrim Pubns.

McNeil, Mary. Earth Sciences Reference. 709p. 1991. 55.00 (*0-938905-00-7*); pap. 49.00 (*0-938905-01-5*) Flamingo Pr.

McNeil, Mary Jane. How Things Began. (Children's World Ser.). (J). (gr. 2 up). 1975. pap. 8.95 (*0-86020-199-6*, Usborne) EDC.

McNeil, Maureen, ed. National Gallery Book of Days. (Museum Gift Bks.). (Illus.). 160p. (Orig.). 1982. 10.00 (*0-939456-05-2*) Galison.

— The National Gallery of Art Heritage Address Book. (Illus.). 208p. 1982. 10.95 (*0-939456-02-8*) Galison.

McNeil, Mellicent. A Comparative Study of Entrance to Teacher-Training Institutions. LC 79-177042. (Columbia University. Teachers College. Contributions to Education Ser.: No. 443). reprint ed. 37.50 (*0-404-55443-1*) AMS Pr.

McNeil, Nellie & Egan, Martha. Rockingham County. (Images of America Ser.). 1994. pap. 14.99 (*0-7524-0005-3*) Arcadia Publng.

McNeil, Patricia W. Preparing Youth for the Information Age: A Federal Role for the 21st Century. 51p. (Orig.). 1996. pap. text 5.00 (*1-887031-55-3*) Am Youth Policy.

McNeil, Patricia W. & Kulick, Christine D. Employer's Role Is School to Work Opportunities. (Education Reform & School-to-Work Transition Ser.). 36p. 1995. pap. text, teacher ed. 12.00 (*0-614-24519-2*) Natl Inst Work.

McNeil, Robert. Tee Times the Golf Diary: Professional Edition. (Illus.). 208p. 1998. 39.95 (*0-9671342-0-X*) BOMAC Enterp.

McNeil, Robert A. & Valk, Barbara G., eds. Latin American Studies: A Basic Guide to Sources. 2nd ed. LC 89-34133. 470p. 1990. 48.00 (*0-8108-2236-9*) Scarecrow.

McNeil, Robert D. Valiant for Truth: Clarence True Wilson & Prohibition. LC 91-68406. (Illus.). 172p. (Orig.). 1992. pap. 9.95 (*0-9632048-0-7*) Rockwood UMC.

McNeil, Roosevelt, Jr. & Hobbs, Avaneda D. What Pest Control Companies Don't Want You to Know. Hobbs, Neda, ed. & illus. by. LC 97-76882. 198p. (C). 2000. pap. 19.95 (*1-878898-13-2*, Pub. by CAP Pub) ACCESS Pubs Network.

McNeil, Rusty, jt. auth. see McNeil, Keith.

McNeil, Samuel. McNeil's Travels. 57p. 1989. 14.95 (*0-87770-467-8*) Ye Galleon.

McNeil, Sarah. Ancient Romans at a Glance. LC 98-10013. (At a Glance Ser.). (Illus.). 32p. (YA). (gr. 3 up). 1997. 14.95 (*0-87226-553-6*, 65536B, P Bedrick Books) NTC Contemp Pub Co.

McNeil, Sterling. More Than a Lifetime: Far Away from Home. LC 96-92547. 240p. (Orig.). 1997. pap. 14.95 (*0-9654195-0-9*) Open Shadow.

McNeil, Sue, jt. ed. see Frost, J. David.

McNeil, Tashia "Thema". Party Ain't Over Yet! LC 97-65864. 1997. pap. 10.00 (*0-9647635-3-2*) La Caille-Nous.

McNeil, Tony D. How to Max Your PT Test & Improve Your Physical Fitness. (Illus.). 150p. (Orig.). (YA). (gr. 9 up). 1994. pap. 7.95 (*0-9644690-0-6*) TDM Pub.

Mcneil, W. K. Ozark Country. LC 95-14859. (Folklife in the South Ser.). (Illus.). 180p. 1995. pap. 16.95 (*0-87805-729-3*); text 40.00 (*0-87805-728-5*) U Pr of Miss.

McNeil, W. K. Ozark Mountain Humor. 240p. 1989. pap. 8.95 (*0-87483-086-9*) August Hse.

— Southern Mountain Folksongs: Traditional Folksongs for Worshiping, for Wooing, for Socializing, for Cradeling, for Working, & Comic Relief. (American Folklore Ser.). 240p. 1992. 24.95 (*0-87483-284-5*); pap. 12.95 (*0-87483-285-3*) August Hse.

Mcneil, W. K., ed. Appalachian Images in Folk & Popular Culture. 2nd ed. LC 94-18229. 368p. (C). 1995. pap. text 23.00 (*0-87049-866-5*) U of Tenn Pr.

McNeil, W. K. & Clements, William M., eds. An Arkansas Folklore Sourcebook. LC 92-5544. (Illus.). 288p. 1992. text 30.00 (*1-55728-254-4*) U of Ark Pr.

McNeil, W. K., ed. see Rattlehead, David.

McNeil, William, ed. see Heidegger, Martin.

M

McNeil, William C. Renegotiating International Debt: The "Young Plan" Conference of 1929. (Pew Case Studies in International Affairs). 50p. (C). 1993. pap. text 3.50 (*1-56927-208-5*) Geo U Inst Dplmcy.

***McNeil, William F.** Baseball's Other All-Stars: The Greatest Players from the Negro Leagues, the Japanese Leagues, the Mexican League & the Pre-1960 Winter Leagues in Cuba, Puerto Rico... LC 99-59170. (Illus.). 252p. 2000. pap. 29.95 (*0-7864-0784-0*) McFarland & Co.

McNeil, William F. The King of Swat: An Analysis of Baseball's Home Run Hitters from the Major, Minor, Negro & Japanese Leagues. LC 97-2179. 212p. 1997. pap. 28.50 (*0-7864-0362-4*) McFarland & Co.

— Ruth, Maris, McGwire & Sosa: Baseball's Single Season Home Run Champions. LC 99-29681. (Illus.). 252p. 1999. pap. 22.50 (*0-7864-0747-6*) McFarland & Co.

McNeil, William J., ed. Salmon Production, Management, & Allocation: Biological, Economic, & Policy Issues. LC 87-22135. (Illus.). 208p. 1988. 35.95 (*0-87071-354-X*) Oreg St U Pr.

McNeil, William J. & Himsworth, Daniel C., eds. Salmonid Ecosystems of the North Pacific. LC 80-17800. (Illus.). 348p. 1980. pap. 26.95 (*0-87071-335-3*) Oreg St U Pr.

McNeilan, Jan & McNeilan, Ray. The Pacific Northwest Gardener's Book of Lists. LC 96-52183. (Illus.). 208p. (Orig.). 1997. pap. 17.95 (*0-87833-956-6*) Taylor Pub.

McNeilan, Ray, jt. auth. see McNeilan, Jan.

McNeile, H. C. Bulldog Drummond. 1976. 20.95 (*0-8488-1151-8*) Amereon Ltd.

— Bulldog Drummond. 1999. text 7.95 (*1-902058-12-7*) Pulp Fictions.

— Bulldog Drummond Returns. 1976. reprint ed. lib. bdg. 20.95 (*0-89190-841-2*, Rivercity Pr) Amereon Ltd.

— Bulldog Drummond Strikes Back. 1976. reprint ed. lib. bdg. 24.95 (*0-89190-842-0*, Rivercity Pr) Amereon Ltd.

McNeile, Herman Cyril. Bulldog Drummond. (Gateway Mystery Ser.). 382p. 1999. pap. 14.95 (*0-89526-330-0*, Pub. by Regnery Pub) Natl Bk Netwk.

McNeill. History of Human..., Vol. 1. 5th ed. 160p. 1997. pap. text, student ed. 19.33 (*0-13-269465-4*) P-H.

— History of Human..., Vol. 2. 5th ed. 144p. 1998. pap. text, student ed. 19.33 (*0-13-269473-5*) P-H.

McNeill, Anne, jt. ed. see Sand, Michael L.

McNeill, Anthony. Chinese Lanterns from the Blue Child. 64p. 1998. pap. 12.95 (*1-900715-18-X*, Pub. by Peepal Tree Pr) Paul & Co Pubs.

McNeill, Barbara, ed. see Underwood, Paula.

McNeill, Beth & Benson, Bonnie. Teen Sexuality: Responsible Decisions. LC 95-24141. 1995. write for info. (*1-56796-126-6*) WRS Group.

McNeill, Bill. Voices of War Remembered. 392p. 1991. 27.00 (*0-385-25320-6*) Doubleday.

McNeill, Carol. Orienteering. (Skills of the Game Ser.). (Illus.). 128p. 1996. pap. 19.95 (*1-85223-990-5*, Pub. by Cro1wood) Trafalgar.

McNeill, Charles, ed. Current Controversies in Temporomandibular Disorders: Proceedings of the 10th Annual Squaw Valley Winter Seminar, Squaw Valley, California, January 23-27, 1991. LC 92-49813. (Illus.). 190p. 1992. text 62.00 (*0-86715-252-4*) Quint Pub Co.

— Science & Practice of Occlusion. LC 97-18246. (Illus.). 550p. 1997. text 148.00 (*0-86715-304-0*) Quint Pub Co.

McNeill, Charles, ed. see American Academy of Craniomandibular Disorders Staff.

McNeill, D. B., jt. auth. see Jerrard, H. G.

McNeill, Daniel. The Face. LC 98-15147. (Illus.). 384p. (gr. 8). 1998. 25.00 (*0-316-58803-2*) Little.

***McNeill, Daniel.** The Face: A Natural History. (Illus.). 384p. 2000. pap. 13.95 (*0-316-58812-1*, Back Bay) Little.

McNeill, David. Hand & Mind: What Gestures Reveal about Thought. LC 91-32575. (Illus.). 428p. 1992. 40.50 (*0-226-56132-1*) U Ch Pr.

— Hand & Mind: What Gestures Reveal about Thought. (Illus.). xii, 428p. 1995. pap. text 17.95 (*0-226-56134-8*) U Ch Pr.

***McNeill, David, ed.** Language & Gesture. (Language, Culture & Cognition Ser.: No. 2). (Illus.). 400p. (C). 2000. 64.95 (*0-521-77166-8*); pap. 24.95 (*0-521-77761-5*) Cambridge U Pr.

McNeill, Don, et al. Compassion: A Reflection on the Christian Life. LC 83-45045. (Illus.). 160p. (C). 1983. pap. 9.95 (*0-385-18957-5*, Image Bks) Doubleday.

***McNeill, Donald.** Tales from the New Barcelona: Urban Change & the European Left. LC 98-49106. 192p. 1999. 85.00 (*0-415-17062-1*) Routledge.

McNeill, Donald H., tr. see Basov, N. G., ed.

McNeill, Earldene, et al. Cultural Awareness for Young Children. rev. ed. (Illus.). 160p. 1981. pap. 14.95 (*0-317-56977-5*) CAYC Learning Tree.

McNeill, Elisabeth. A Bombay Affair. 256p. 26.00 (*0-7278-5514-X*) Severn Hse.

McNeill, Elisabeth. A Bridge in Time. 448p. 1994. pap. 8.95 (*1-85797-406-9*) Orion Pubng Grp.

— Dusty Letters. 256p. 1998. 24.00 (*0-7278-5260-4*) Severn Hse.

***McNeill, Elisabeth.** Money Troubles. 256p. 2000. 26.00 (*0-7278-5443-7*, Pub. by Severn Hse) Chivers N Amer.

— Turn Back Time. 288p. 1998. 25.00 (*0-7278-5398-8*) Severn Hse.

— Turn Back Time. large type ed. 336p. 1999. 31.99 (*0-7505-1397-7*, Pub. by Mgna Lrg Print) Ulverscroft.

McNeill, Elizabeth. Nine & a Half Weeks. 128p. 1993. reprint ed. lib. bdg. 27.95 (*1-56849-171-9*) Buccaneer Bks.

***McNeill, Ethel.** Memories in a Scrapbook: Through the Years Since 1931. 1999. pap. write for info. (*1-58235-235-6*) Watermrk Pr.

McNeill, F. M. The Silver Bough Vol. III: Festivals Halloween to Yule. 200p. 1997. 24.95 (*0-948474-04-1*) Celt Heritage Bks.

— The Silver Bough Vol. IV: Local Festivals. 200p. 1997. 24.95 (*0-948474-05-X*) Celt Heritage Bks.

Mcneill, F. Marian. The Silver Bough, 4 vols., Set. 1982. 160.00 (*0-7855-7185-X*, Pub. by Stuart Titles Ltd) St Mut.

McNeill, F. Marian. The Silver Bough Vol. I: Scottish Folklore & Folk Belief. 220p. (C). 1988. 60.00 (*0-85335-161-9*, Pub. by Stuart Titles Ltd) St Mut.

— The Silver Bough Vol. II: A Calendar of Scottish National Festivals, Candlemas to Harvest Home. 163p. (C). 1988. 40.00 (*0-7855-2387-1*, Pub. by Stuart Titles Ltd) St Mut.

— The Silver Bough Vol. III: A Calendar of Scottish National Festivals Hallowe'en to Yule. 180p. (C). 1988. 60.00 (*0-85335-162-7*, Pub. by Stuart Titles Ltd) St Mut.

— The Silver Bough Vol. IV: The Local Festivals of Scotland. 272p. (C). 1988. 60.00 (*0-85335-002-7*, Pub. by Stuart Titles Ltd) St Mut.

McNeill, F. Marina. The Scots Kitchen. 272p. 1997. pap. 40.00 (*1-873644-23-X*, Pub. by Mercat Pr Bks) St Mut.

McNeill, Frank. Passage: Over the Hill & Around the World. 162p. 1998. pap. 10.00 (*0-938711-51-2*) Tecolote Pubns.

McNeill, George E., ed. The Labor Movement: The Problem of Today: The History, Purpose & Possibilities of Labor Organizations in Europe & America. LC 66-21683. (Library of American Labor History). (Illus.). x, 639p. 1971. reprint ed. 65.00 (*0-678-00713-6*) Kelley.

McNeill, Geraldine, jt. auth. see Gillespie, Stuart.

McNeill, Ian. To Long Tan: The Second in the Official History Series of Australia's Operations in Vietnam. (Illus.). 552p. 1993. 49.00 (*1-86373-282-9*, Pub. by Allen & Unwin Pty) Paul & Co Pubs.

McNeill, J. C., III. The McNeills' SR Ranch: 100 Years in Blanco Canyon. LC 88-2204. (Centennial Series of the Association of Former Students: No. 28). (Illus.). 224p. 1988. 19.95 (*0-89096-340-1*) Tex A&M Univ Pr.

***McNeill, J. R.** Something New under the Sun: An Environmental History of the Twentieth-Century World. LC 99-54900. (Illus.). 416p. 2000. 29.95 (*0-393-04917-5*) Norton.

McNeill, John. Both Feet Firmly Planted in Midair: My Spiritual Journey. LC 98-15197. 224p. 1998. pap. 18.00 (*0-664-25808-5*) Westminster John Knox.

— The Loire Valley. (Blue Guide Ser.). (Illus.). 256p. 1995. reprint ed. pap. 15.95 (*0-393-31414-6*, Norton Paperbks) Norton.

— Normandy. (Blue Guide Ser.). (Illus.). 256p. 1993. pap. 18.95 (*0-393-30971-1*) Norton.

— TV VCR Hookups for the Electronically Impaired. LC 98-66130. (Illus.). 1998. pap. 9.95 (*1-886391-25-4*) Narwhal Pr.

McNeill, John & Williams, Bryan, eds. Containing Crime: Community Based Approaches. (Aberdeen University Press Bks.). 200p. 1991. pap. text 29.00 (*0-08-040911-3*, Pub. by Aberdeen U Pr) Macmillan.

McNeill, John, jt. auth. see Sprang, Ginny.

McNeill, John, jt. ed. see Karras, Alan L.

McNeill, John H. Experimental Models of Diabetes. LC 99-190807. 424p. 1999. boxed set 149.95 (*0-8493-1667-7*) CRC Pr.

McNeill, John H., ed. Biochemical Techniques in the Heart. LC 96-2903. (Methods in the Life Sciences-Methods in Pharmacology Ser.). 144p. 1996. spiral bd. 74.95 (*0-8493-3333-4*) CRC Pr.

— Measurement of Cardiac Function. LC 96-31525. (Methods in Pharmacology Ser.). 144p. 1996. spiral bd. 74.95 (*0-8493-3332-6*) CRC Pr.

— Measurement of Cardiovascular Function. LC 96-31524. (Methods in the Life Sciences - Methods in Pharmacology Ser.). (Illus.). 128p. 1996. spiral bd. 74.95 (*0-8493-3331-8*) CRC Pr.

McNeill, John J. The Church & the Homosexual. 4th ed. LC 94-15723. 256p. 1994. pap. 16.00 (*0-8070-7931-6*) Beacon Pr.

— Freedom, Glorious Freedom: The Spiritual Journey to the Fullness of Life for Gays, Lesbians, & Everybody Else. 256p. 1996. pap. 16.00 (*0-8070-7937-5*) Beacon Pr.

— Taking a Chance on God: Liberating Theology for Gays, Lesbians, & Their Lovers, Families & Friends - With a New Preface. 2nd ed. 288p. 1996. pap. 16.00 (*0-8070-7945-6*) Beacon Pr.

McNeill, John R. Atlantic Empires of France & Spain: Louisburg & Havana, 1700-1763. LC 85-1105. xvii, 329p. 1985. 59.95 (*0-8078-1669-8*) U of NC Pr.

McNeill, John S., jt. ed. see Lecca, Pedro J.

McNeill, John T. Books of Faith & Power. LC 75-134112. (Essay Index Reprint Ser.). 1977. 20.95 (*0-8369-1996-3*) Ayer.

— The History & Character of Calvinism. 476p. 1967. pap. text 15.95 (*0-19-500743-3*) OUP.

McNeill, John T. & Garner, Helena M. Medieval Handbooks of Penance: A Translation of the Principal Libri Poenitentiales. 476p. 1990. pap. text 20.00 (*0-231-09629-1*) Col U Pr.

McNeill, John T., ed. see Calvin, John.

McNeill, Louise. Fermi Buffalo. 104p. (Orig.). 1994. pap. 12.95 (*0-8229-5528-8*) U of Pittsburgh Pr.

— Hill Daughter: New & Selected Poems. Anderson, Maggie, ed. LC 91-8429. 168p. 1991. pap. 12.95 (*0-8229-5456-7*) U of Pittsburgh Pr.

— The Milkweed Ladies. LC 88-1334. 136p. (Orig.). 1989. pap. 10.95 (*0-8229-5406-0*) U of Pittsburgh Pr.

McNeill, M. Evelyn. Neuroanatomy Primer: Color to Learn. LC 96-46125. (Illus.). 250p. 1997. write for info. (*0-683-30067-9*) Lppncott W & W.

McNeill, Marjory. Norman MacCaig: A Study of His Life & Work. 154p. 1996. pap. 40.00 (*1-873644-46-9*, Pub. by Mercat Pr Bks) St Mut.

McNeill, Mary. The Life & Times of Mary Ann McCracken, 1770-1866: A Belfast Panorama. LC 98-114290. 328p. 1988. pap. 19.95 (*0-85640-603-1*, Pub. by Blackstaff Pr) Dufour.

— The Life & Times of Mary Ann McCracken, 1770-1866: A Belfast Panorama. 328p. 1988. reprint ed. pap. 11.95 (*0-85640-403-9*, Pub. by Blackstaff Pr) Dufour.

McNeill, Moyra. Pulled Thread Embroidery. (Illus.). 208p. 1994. reprint ed. pap. text 7.95 (*0-486-27857-3*) Dover.

McNeill, Moyra, jt. auth. see Geddes, Elisabeth.

McNeill, Patrick. Research Methods. 2nd ed. (Society Now Ser.). 160p. (C). 1990. pap. 16.99 (*0-415-04126-0*) Routledge.

McNeill, Patrick & Townley, Charles, eds. Fundamentals of Sociology. 2nd ed. 464p. (Orig.). 1986. pap. 42.50 (*0-7487-0269-5*, Pub. by S Thornes Pubs) Trans-Atl Phila.

McNeill, Patrick, jt. auth. see O'Donnell, Mike.

McNeill, Pearlie. Because You Want to Write: A Workbook for Women. 238p. 1992. pap. 17.95 (*1-85727-030-4*) LPC InBook.

— Because You Want to Write: A Workbook for Women. 238p. 1993. 49.95 (*1-85727-035-5*) LPC InBook.

McNeill, Pearlie. One of the Family: Telling the Story of a Violent Childhood & the Healing Beyond LC 90-139767. xii, 268 p. 1990. pap. write for info. (*0-7022-2301-8*, Pub. by Univ Queensland Pr) Intl Spec Bk.

McNeill, Pearlie, et al, eds. Women Talk Sex: Autobiographical Writing on Sex, Sexuality & Sexual Identity. 233p. 1992. pap. 15.50 (*1-85727-000-2*) LPC InBook.

— Women Talk Sex: Autobiographical Writing on Sex, Sexuality & Sexual Identity. 233p. 1993. 45.00 (*1-85727-010-X*) LPC InBook.

McNeill, Sarah. The Middle Ages. (Spotlights Ser.). (Illus.). 46p. (J). (gr. 4-6). 1998. 11.95 (*0-19-521394-7*) OUP.

McNeill, Shannon, jt. auth. see Keller, Debra.

McNeill, Shannon, jt. auth. see Rovetch, Lissa.

McNeill, Suzanne. Family Scrapbook Paper Pizzaz! 128p. 1997. pap. 16.99 (*1-55870-477-9*, Betrwy Bks) F & W Pubns Inc.

— Holiday Scrapbook Paper Pizzaz! 128p. 1997. pap. 16.99 (*1-55870-478-7*, Betrwy Bks) F & W Pubns Inc.

— Native American Crafts. 1997. write for info. (*0-8069-9952-7*) Sterling.

***McNeill, Suzanne, ed.** Baby Vol. 5027: 18 Acid-Free Papers for Scrapbooks & More! (Illus.). 18p. 1999. 8.45 (*1-893749-23-1*) Fiskars.

— Boys Vol. 5028: 18 Acid-Free Papers for Scrapbooks & More! (Illus.). 18p. 1999. 8.45 (*1-893749-18-5*) Fiskars.

— Child Vol. 3001: 16 Acid-Free Papers for Scrapbooks & More! (Illus.). 16p. 1999. 6.30 (*1-893749-12-6*) Fiskars.

— Childhood Vol. 3006: 16 Acid-Free Papers for Scrapbooks & More! (Illus.). 16p. 1999. 6.30 (*1-893749-14-2*) Fiskars.

— Christmas Vol. 5031: 18 Acid-Free Papers for Scrapbooks & More! (Illus.). 18p. 1999. 8.45 (*1-893749-22-3*) Fiskars.

— Family Tree Vol. 3029: 16 Acid-Free Papers for Scrapbooks & More! (Illus.). 16p. 1999. 6.30 (*1-893749-16-9*) Fiskars.

— Festive Vol. 3009: 16 Acid-Free Papers for Scrapbooks & More! (Illus.). 16p. 1999. 6.30 (*1-893749-15-0*) Fiskars.

— Girls Vol. 5029: 18 Acid-Free Papers for Scrapbooks & More! (Illus.). 18p. 1999. 8.45 (*1-893749-19-3*) Fiskars.

— Love Vol. 3034: 16 Acid-Free Papers for Scrapbooks & More! (Illus.). 16p. 1999. 6.30 (*1-893749-17-7*) Fiskars.

— Party Vol. 5026: 18 Acid-Free Papers for Scrapbooks & More! (Illus.). 18p. 1999. 8.45 (*1-893749-21-5*) Fiskars.

— Petals Vol. 5034: 18 Acid-Free Papers for Scrapbooks & More! (Illus.). 18p. 1999. 8.45 (*1-893749-20-7*) Fiskars.

— School Time Vol. 3005: 16 Acid-Free Papers for Scrapbooks & More! (Illus.). 16p. 1999. 6.30 (*1-893749-13-4*) Fiskars.

McNeill, Suzanne & Stiles, Lani. Family Memories: Capturing the Best Memories with Photos, Albums & Journals. LC 96-85256. (Illus.). 128p. (Orig.). 1996. pap. 21.99 (*1-57421-005-X*) Design Orgnls.

McNeill, T. E. Castles in Ireland: Feudal Power in a Gaelic World. LC 96-46689. (Illus.). 280p. (C). 1997. 60.00 (*0-415-16537-7*) Routledge.

McNeill, T. W., jt. auth. see Andersson, Gunnar B.

***McNeill, Tom.** Castles in Ireland: Feudal Power in a Gaelic World. (Illus.). 2000. pap. 20.95 (*0-415-22853-0*) Routledge.

McNeill, Walter G., jt. auth. see Green, Edward F.

McNeill, William. Compassion. 1993. pap. write for info. (*0-385-42682-8*) Doubleday.

***McNeill, William.** First Time Resume. 128p. 2000. pap. 7.95 (*1-58062-292-5*) Adams Media.

McNeill, William. The Glance of the Eye: Heidegger, Aristotle & the Ends of Theory. LC 98-48871. (SUNY Series, Contemporary Continental Philosophy). 374p. (C). 1999. pap. text 19.95 (*0-7914-4228-4*) State U NY Pr.

— The Glance of the Eye: Heidegger, Aristotle & the Ends of Theory. LC 98-48871. (SUNY Series in Contemporary Continental Philosophy). 371p. (C). 1999. text 59.50 (*0-7914-4227-6*) State U NY Pr.

— A History of the Human Community Vol. 1: Prehistory to 1500. 5th ed. (Illus.). 384p. (C). 1996. pap. text 57.00 (*0-13-266289-2*) P-H.

— A History of the Human Community Vol. 2: 1500 to Present. 5th ed. (Illus.). 368p. (C). 1996. pap. text 57.00 (*0-13-266297-3*) P-H.

— A History of the Human Community Combined. 5th ed. LC 96-19658. 715p. (C). 1996. 74.00 (*0-13-262510-5*) P-H.

McNeill, William & Feldman, Karen S., eds. Continental Philosophy: An Anthology. (Philosophy Anthologies Ser.). 656p. 1998. pap. 34.95 (*1-55786-561-2*) Blackwell Pubs.

— Continental Philosophy: An Anthology. 656p. 1998. 78.95 (*1-55786-700-3*) Blackwell Pubs.

McNeill, William, tr. see Haar, Michel.

McNeill, William, tr. see Heidegger, Martin.

McNeill, William H. The Age of Gunpowder Empires, 1450-1800. Adas, Michael, ed. LC 89-84997. (Essays on Global & Comparative History Ser.). 49p. 1989. pap. 6.00 (*0-87229-043-3*) Am Hist Assn.

— La Civilizacion de Occidente: Manual de Historia. 6th ed. 586p. (C). 1995. pap. 11.25 (*0-8477-0833-0*) U of PR Pr.

— Europe's Steppe Frontier, 1500-1800. LC 64-22248. (Midway Reprint Ser.). 256p. reprint ed. pap. 79.40 (*0-608-09476-5*, 205427600005) Bks Demand.

— Historia del Mundo. Millares Vazquez, Manuel et al, trs. from ENG. (Illus.). 523p. 1969. reprint ed. 6.50 (*0-8477-0834-9*) U of PR Pr.

— History of Western Civilization: A Handbook. 6th ed. LC 85-24545. (Illus.). xviii, 704p. 1986. pap. text 22.00 (*0-226-56160-7*); lib. bdg. 48.00 (*0-226-56159-3*) U Ch Pr.

— The Human Condition & Other Essays. 168p. 1993. text 35.00 (*0-691-08648-6*, Pub. by Princeton U Pr) Cal Prin Full Svc.

— Hutchins' University: A Memoir of the University of Chicago, 1929-1950. LC 91-9322. (Centennial Publication Ser.). (Illus.). 204p. 1991. lib. bdg. 35.00 (*0-226-56170-4*) U Ch Pr.

— Keeping Together in Time: Dance & Drill in Human History. LC 95-8794. (Illus.). 293p. (C). 1995. 22.00 (*0-674-50229-9*) HUP.

— Keeping Together in Time: Dance & Drill in Human History. (Illus.). 216p. 1997. reprint ed. pap. 14.95 (*0-674-50230-2*) HUP.

— The Metamorphosis of Greece since World War II. LC 77-26105. (Illus.). 272p. 1996. 15.95 (*0-226-56156-9*) U Ch Pr.

— The Metamorphosis of Greece since World War II. LC 77-26105. 272p. reprint ed. pap. 84.40 (*0-608-09023-9*, 206965800005) Bks Demand.

— Mythistory & Other Essays. LC 85-8584. x, 226p. 1995. 23.95 (*0-226-56135-6*) U Ch Pr.

— Plagues & People. LC 76-2798. (Illus.). 368p. 1977. pap. 14.95 (*0-385-12122-9*, Anchor NY) Doubleday.

— Plagues & People. 1992. 25.50 (*0-8446-6492-8*) Peter Smith.

— Polyethnicity & National Unity in World History. 1986. pap. 10.95 (*0-8020-6643-7*) U of Toronto Pr.

— Polyethnicity & National Unity in World History. LC 88-128714. (Donald G. Creighton Lectures: No. 1985). 97p. reprint ed. pap. 30.10 (*0-7837-1791-1*, 204199200001) Bks Demand.

— The Pursuit of Power: Technology, Armed Force & Society since A. D. 1000. LC 81-24095. (Illus.). x, 416p. 1984. pap. text 16.00 (*0-226-56158-5*) U Ch Pr.

— The Rise of the West: A History of the Human Community. 860p. 1991. pap. 24.00 (*0-226-56141-0*) U Ch Pr.

— The Rise of the West: A History of the Human Community. LC 63-13067. 1997. pap. 14.95 (*0-226-56144-5*, P385) U Ch Pr.

— Venice: The Hinge of Europe, 1081-1797. LC 73-84192. xviii, 334p. 1993. pap. text 18.95 (*0-226-56149-6*) U Ch Pr.

— A World History. 4th ed. (Illus.). 656p. (C). 1998. pap. text 37.95 (*0-19-511616-X*) OUP.

M

An Asterisk (*) at the beginning of an entry indicates that the title is appearing for the first time.

McNeill, William H. & Adams, Ruth S., eds. Human Migration: Patterns & Policies. LC 77-23685. 460p. reprint ed. pap. 142.60 (*0-608-13203-9*, 205604700044) Bks Demand.

McNeill, William H. & Waldman, Marilyn R., eds. The Islamic World. LC 83-18246. xviii, 486p. 1984. pap. text 17.95 (*0-226-56155-0*) U Ch Pr.

McNeill, William H., ed. see Acton, John E.

McNeill, William H., ed. see Callender, Ann B.

McNeill, William H., ed. see Heath, Roy E.

McNeill, William H., ed. see Krukones, James H.

McNeill, William H., ed. see Shkolnik, Esther S.

***McNeilley, Michael.** Situational Reality. Dancing Bear Staff, ed. (Illus.). 80p. 1999. 12.95 (*0-9659307-0-X*) Dream Horse Pr.

McNeillie, Andrew. The Essays of Virginia Woolf Vol. I: 1904-1912. 1987. 19.95 (*0-318-42591-2*, Harvest Bks) Harcourt.

***McNeillie, Andrew.** Pigeons of the World: The Magna Illustrated Guide. (Illus.). 160p. 1999. reprint ed. text 20.00 (*0-7881-6574-7*) DIANE Pub.

McNeillie, Andrew, ed. The Essays of Virginia Woolf Vol. II: 1912-1918. Vol. II. 384p. 1990. pap. 14.95 (*0-15-629055-3*, Harvest Bks) Harcourt.

— The Essays of Virginia Woolf Vol. III: 1919-1924. 544p. 1989. 22.95 (*0-15-129057-1*) Harcourt.

McNeillie, Andrew, intro. The Essays of Virginia Woolf Vol. II: 1912-1918. 448p. 1988. 22.95 (*0-15-129056-3*) Harcourt.

McNeillie, Andrew, ed. see Woolf, Virginia.

McNeilly, Mark R. Sun Tzu & the Art of Business: Six Strategic Principles for Managers. LC 96-26080. (Illus.). 272p. 1996. 25.00 (*0-19-509996-6*) OUP.

***McNeilly, Mark R.** Sun Tzu & the Art of Business: Six Strategic Principles for Managers. (Illus.). 272p. 2000. pap. 13.95 (*0-19-513789-2*) OUP.

McNeilly, Rob & Brown, Jenny. Healing with Words. 108p. (Orig.). 1994. pap. 14.95 (*0-85572-246-0*) Seven Hills Bk.

***McNeilly, Robert B.** Healing the Whole Person: A Solution-Focused Approach to Using Empowering Language, Emotions & Actions in Therapy. LC 99-52758. 192p. 2000. text 45.00 (*0-471-38274-4*) Wiley.

McNeilly, Steven. How to Read Weather Statements & Charts. LC 93-31899. (Illus.). 181p. 1993. reprint ed. pap. 56.20 (*0-608-07690-2*, 206778000010) Bks Demand.

McNeils, E. B. & Saylgh, S. Solar Electricity for Development. (C). 1989. 130.00 (*0-7855-4211-6*, Pub. by Interntl Solar Energy Soc) St Mut.

McNeilus, James. The Three Legged Chair. 476p. 1988. reprint ed. 16.75 (*0-9620256-0-7*) J McNeilus.

McNeily, Curtlan R., jt. auth. see Moriarty, John P.

McNeir, Clive L. Multilingual Dictionary of Local Government & Business. 2nd ed. 704p. 1997. 130.00 (*0-304-32949-5*) Continuum.

McNeir, Leo. Cassell Multilingual Dictionary of Local Government & Business. (ENG, FRE & GER.). 288p. 1993. text 110.00 (*0-304-32715-8*) Continuum.

McNeir, Waldo F. Merchant of Venice Notes. (Cliffs Notes Ser.). 72p. 1961. pap. 4.95 (*0-8220-0052-0*, Cliff) IDG Bks.

— Studies in English Renaissance Literature. (Essay Index Reprint Ser.). 1977. reprint ed. 22.95 (*0-518-10153-3*) Ayer.

McNeir, Waldo F. & Levy, Leo B., eds. Studies in American Literature. (Essay Index Reprint Ser.). 1977. reprint ed. 17.95 (*0-518-10152-5*) Ayer.

McNeish, Cameron. The Best Hillwalking in Scotland. (Illus.). 1998. pap. 17.95 (*1-897784-73-2*, Pub. by N Wilson Pubng) Interlink Pub.

— The Corbett Almanac. (Illus.). 160p. 1996. 13.95 (*1-897784-14-7*, Pub. by N Wilson Pubng) Interlink Pub.

— The Munro Almanac. rev. ed. (Illus.). 144p. 1996. 14.95 (*1-897784-39-2*, Pub. by N Wilson Pubng) Interlink Pub.

— The Munros: Scotland's Highest Mountains. (Illus.). 228p. 1997. 45.00 (*1-900455-13-7*, Pub. by Colin Baxter Ltd) Voyageur Pr.

— The Trossachs. (Twenty-Five Walks Ser.). (Illus.). vii, 102p. 1994. pap. 18.00 (*0-11-495166-7*, Pub. by Statnry Office) Seven Hills Bk.

McNeish, James. The Mask of Sanity: The Bain Murders. LC 98-140451. (Illus.). 1997. 24.95 (*0-908990-46-4*) David Ling Pub.

McNeley, James K. Holy Wind in Navajo Philosophy. LC 80-27435. 115p. 1981. pap. 15.95 (*0-8165-0724-4*) U of Ariz Pr.

McNelis, B. & Morton, J. Solar Energy for Developing Countries . . . Power for Villages (C44) 83p. (C). 1986. 95.00 (*0-7855-3804-6*, Pub. by Interntl Solar Energy Soc) St Mut.

McNelis, B. & Morton, J., eds. Solar Energy for Developing Countries . . . Power for the Villages. (C). 1986. 110.00 (*0-7855-4202-7*, Pub. by Interntl Solar Energy Soc) St Mut.

McNelley, T. R., et al. Proceedings of ReX'96: The Third International Conference on Recrystallization & Related Phenomena. (Illus.). 720p. 1997. text 125.00 (*0-9645943-6-6*, ReX'96) MIAS.

McNelley, Terry R., ed. see Minerals, Metals & Materials Society Staff.

***McNellis, Grace.** Home on the Vandevert Ranch. 140p. 1999. pap. 14.95 (*1-880222-40-X*) Red Apple Pub.

McNellis, Jerry & Nettles, Jack. Compression Planning. (Illus.). (Orig.). 1990. write for info. (*0-318-66540-9*) Braintrain.

— Exploding the Meeting Myth: Compression Planning... a Proven System for Better, Faster, Sharper Solutions. 240p. 1992. pap. 24.95 (*0-9625078-4-9*) Braintrain.

McNelly, Jeff. Play Ball: All I Ever Learned I Forgot by the Third Inning. 1999. pap. text 9.95 (*1-57243-328-0*) Triumph Bks.

***McNelly, Theodore.** The Origins of Japan's Democratic Constitution. LC 99-87956. 240p. 2000. 52.00 (*0-7618-1636-4*); pap. 29.50 (*0-7618-1637-2*) U Pr of Amer.

McNelly, Theodore. Politics & Government in Japan. 3rd ed. (Illus.). 284p. (Orig.). 1985. reprint ed. pap. text 18.50 (*0-8191-4359-6*) U Pr of Amer.

McNemar, Pat. Oregon Coast Visitors Guide. 110p. (Orig.). 1997. pap. 8.95 (*1-57502-478-0*, P01432) Morris Pubng.

McNemee, Andrew J. "Brother Mack" the Frontier Preacher. 153p. 1980. 14.95 (*0-87770-236-5*) Ye Galleon.

Mcnergney, Robert, jt. auth. see Keller, Clayton.

McNergney, Robert F., et al, eds. Educating for Democracy: Case-Method Teaching & Learning. LC 98-39825. 216p. 1999. pap. 24.50 (*0-8058-2483-9*) L Erlbaum Assocs.

McNergney, Robert F. & Herbert, Joanne M. Foundations of Education: The Challenge of Professional Practice. 2nd ed. LC 97-15153. 588p. 1997. 76.00 (*0-205-27009-3*) P-H.

— Foundations of Education: The Challenge of Professional Practice: Examination Copy. 2nd ed. 608p. (C). 1997. text. write for info. (*0-205-27666-0*, T7666-5) Allyn.

McNergney, Robert F., jt. auth. see Kent, Todd W.

McNerney. Sports Injuries of the Lower Extremity. 1996. text. write for info. (*0-7216-3746-9*, W B Saunders Co) Harcrt Hlth Sci Grp.

McNerney, Colleen & Davis, Norah D. Education for Sustainability: An Agenda for Action. 86p. (Orig.). (C). 1997. pap. text 25.00 (*0-7881-3961-4*) DIANE Pub.

McNerney, Gerald. Enter the Third Level. rev. ed. Orig. Title: Terrorism & Fear. 256p. 1994. reprint ed. pap. 10.95 (*0-9642956-0-1*) Contemporary Pr.

— Terrorism & Fear: Enter the Third Level. LC 93-86071. 210p. (Orig.). 1994. pap. 10.95 (*0-9637293-5-7*) Storm Pub.

McNerney, Joan. Noah's Daughters. (Kestrel Ser.: No. 10). 24p. (Orig.). 1984. pap. 3.00 (*0-914974-42-4*) Holmgangers.

McNerney, Kathleen. Tirant Lo Blanc Revisited: A Critical Study. LC 83-62143. (Medieval & Renaissance Monograph: Vol. 4). 139p. reprint ed. pap. 43.10 (*0-608-18710-0*, 202702500053) Bks Demand.

McNerney, Kathleen, ed. On Our Own Behalf: Women's Tales from Catalonia. LC 87-12465. (European Women Writers Ser.). viii, 234p. 1988. text 45.00 (*0-8032-3122-9*) U of Nebr Pr.

— Voices & Visions: The Words & Works of Merce Rodoreda. LC 98-30642. 280p. 1999. 45.00 (*1-57591-018-7*) Susquehanna U Pr.

McNerney, Kathleen & Enriques De Salamanca, Cristina, eds. Double Minorities of Spain: A Bio-Bibliographic Guide to Women Writers of the Catalan, Galician, & Basque Countries. LC 94-27639. 432p. 1994. lib. bdg. 50.00 (*0-87352-397-0*, D312C) Modern Lang.

McNerney, Kathleen & Vosburg, Nancy, eds. The Garden Across the Border: Merce Rodoreda's Fiction. LC 93-44028. (C). 1994. 42.50 (*0-945636-63-6*) Susquehanna U Pr.

McNerney, Kathleen, jt. auth. see Oliver, Maria-Antaonia.

McNerney, Kathleen, jt. ed. see Galerstein, Carolyn L.

McNerney, Kathryn. American Oak Furniture. (Illus.). 176p. 1994. pap. 9.95 (*0-89145-250-8*, 1457) Collector Bks.

— American Oak Furniture, Bk. II. 2nd ed. 1996. pap. 12.95 (*0-89145-557-4*, 3716) Collector Bks.

— Antique Iron. (Illus.). 224p. 1996. pap. 9.95 (*0-89145-238-9*, 1880) Collector Bks.

— Antique Tools: Our American Heritage. (Illus.). 153p. 1996. pap. 9.95 (*0-89145-125-0*, 1868) Collector Bks.

— Blue & White Stoneware. (Illus.). 160p. 1996. pap. 9.95 (*0-89145-179-X*, 1312) Collector Bks.

— Kitchen Antiques, 1750-1940. 1995. pap. 14.95 (*0-89145-447-0*, 2216) Collector Bks.

— Primitives: Our American Heritage, Second Series, Vol. 2. 2nd ed. (Illus.). 160p. 1996. pap. 14.95 (*0-89145-331-8*, 1759) Collector Bks.

— Victorian Furniture: Our American Heritage. (Illus.). 252p. 1981. pap. 9.95 (*0-89145-164-1*, 1885) Collector Bks.

— Victorian Furniture: Our American Heritage. 2nd ed. 1994. pap. 9.95 (*0-89145-598-1*, 3829) Collector Bks.

McNerney, Michael J. & Meyer, Herb. Early Pioneer Gravestones of Pope County, Illinois. LC 94-72149. (Illus.). 22p. (Orig.). 1994. pap. 9.95 (*0-913415-07-3*) Am Kestrel Pr.

***McNerney, Michael T.** Airport Facilities: Innovations for the Next Century. LC 98-7392. 616p. 1998. 79.00 (*0-7844-0351-1*) Am Soc Civil Eng.

McNerney, Rebecca A. The Changing Structure of the Electric Power Industry: An Update. (Illus.). 182p. 1998. pap. text 30.00 (*0-7881-7363-4*) DIANE Pub.

McNerney, Therese, jt. auth. see Lewis, Carole.

McNerney, Therese, jt. auth. see Lewis, Carole B.

McNerney, Therese, ed. see Lewis, Carole B.

McNett, Ian. Charting a Course: A Guide to the Excellence Movement in Education. 55p. (C). 1984. pap. 8.95 (*0-931989-06-X*) Coun Basic Educ.

McNett, Ian, ed. Early Alert: The Impact of Federal Education Cutbacks on the States. 64p. (Orig.). 1983. pap. 6.95 (*0-937846-99-6*) Inst Educ Lead.

— Let's Not Reinvent the Wheel: Profiles of School-Business Collaboration. 72p. (Orig.). 1983. pap. 6.95 (*0-937846-97-X*) Inst Educ Lead.

McNetty, Jeffrey A., et al. Conserving the World's Biological Diversity. 200p. (Orig.). 1990. pap. 14.95 (*0-915825-42-2*, MCCWP, Pub. by IUCN) World Resources Inst.

Mcnevin, David, jt. auth. see O'Connor, Gerry.

McNew, Delbert A., jt. auth. see Seacrest, Betty R.

***McNew, Rusty, et al.** Emergency Department Compliance Manual. 3rd ed. LC 99-56982. (AHLCC Compliance Ser.). (Illus.). 450p. 2000. pap. 100.00 (*0-8342-1771-6*) Aspen Pub.

McNey, Martha, text. Leslie's Story: A Book about a Girl with Mental Retardation. LC 95-35621. (Illus.). (J). 1996. lib. bdg. 21.27 (*0-8225-2576-3*, Lerner Publctns) Lerner Pub.

McNichol, Andrea & Nelson, Jeffrey A. Handwriting Analysis. LC 97-168687. (Illus.). 368p. (Orig.). 1994. pap. 18.95 (*0-8092-3566-8*, 356680, Contemporary Bks) NTC Contemp Pub Co.

McNichol, Janet, jt. auth. see Cole, Pat.

McNichol, Stella. The Early Twentieth Century British Novel: A Modern Introduction. 224p. 1992. pap. 16.95 (*0-7131-6540-5*, A5372, Pub. by E A) Routldge.

McNicholas, Dick. Amusement Machines: Your Route to Success. 48p. (Orig.). 1981. pap. 6.95 (*0-943592-00-3*, TX 773-174) Publishers Pr.

McNicholas, Shelagh. Goat in the Garden. (Animal Ark Ser.: No. 4). (J). (gr. 4-7). 1997. pap. text 3.99 (*0-590-18752-X*) Scholastic Inc.

***McNicholas, Shelagh.** Puppies in the Pantry. (Animal Ark Ser.: No. 3). (J). (gr. 3-5). 1998. 9.09 (*0-606-13131-0*, Pub. by Turtleback) Demco.

McNicholas, T. A., jt. ed. see Tinker, Jack.

McNicholl, Geoffrey & Cain, Mead, eds. Rural Development & Population: Institutions & Policy - A Supplement to Population & Development Review, Vol. 15, 1989. (Population & Development Review Supplements Ser.: No. 1). 376p. 1991. text 35.00 (*0-19-506847-5*); pap. text 15.00 (*0-19-506849-1*) OUP.

***McNichols, Ann.** Falling from Grace. (YA). (gr. 5-8). 2000. 16.95 (*0-8027-8750-9*) Walker & Co.

McNichols, Charles W. IBM-PC Statistics: BASIC Programs & Applications. 1984. write for info. (*0-318-57662-7*) P-H.

McNichols, Donald. Portrait of a Quaker: A Biography of Levi T. Pennington. LC 80-66654. (Illus.). 180p. 1980. 12.50 (*0-913342-24-6*) Barclay Pr.

— Seattle Pacific University: A Growing Vision. LC 89-10574. (Illus.). 288p. 1989. pap. text 19.95 (*0-9602642-3-X*); lib. bdg. 19.95 (*0-9602642-2-1*) Seattle Pac Univ.

***McNickie, D'Arcy.** They Came Here First: The Epic of the American Indian. (LC History-America-E). 325p. 1999. reprint ed. lib. bdg. 89.00 (*0-7812-4263-0*) Rprt Serv.

McNickle. Hawk Is Hungry. LC 92-8623. (Sun Tracks Ser.: Vol. 22). 180p. (Orig.). 1992. pap. 16.95 (*0-8165-1331-7*) U of Ariz Pr.

— Wind from an Enemy Sky. LC 87-17575. 268p. 1988. reprint ed. pap. 12.95 (*0-8263-1100-8*) U of NM Pr.

McNickle, Chris. To Be Mayor of New York: Ethnic Politics in the City. Jackson, Kenneth T., ed. LC 92-32583. (Columbia History of Urban Life Ser.). (Illus.). 300p. (C). 1993. 44.00 (*0-231-07636-3*) Col U Pr.

McNickle, D'Arcy. The Hawk Is Hungry & Other Stories. Hans, Birgit, ed. LC 92-8623. (Sun Tracks Ser.: Vol. 22). 180p. (Orig.). 1992. lib. bdg. 33.95 (*0-8165-1326-0*) U of Ariz Pr.

— Runner in the Sun. LC 87-5986. (Zia Bks.). (Illus.). 260p. (J). 1987. reprint ed. pap. 13.95 (*0-8263-0974-7*) U of NM Pr.

— The Surrounded. LC 77-91886. (Zia Bks.). 305p. 1978. pap. 12.95 (*0-8263-0469-9*) U of NM Pr.

McNicol, jt. auth. see Jones, Alan.

McNicol, Allan J. Jesus' Directions for the Future Vol. 9: A Source & Reaction History of the Use of Eschatological Traditions in Paul & in the Synoptic Accounts of Jesus' Last Eschatological Discourse. 180p. 1996. text 35.00 (*0-86554-497-2*, MUP/H390) Mercer Univ Pr.

McNicol, Allan J., et al, eds. Beyond the Q Impasse: Luke's Use of Matthew. LC 96-36858. 352p. 1996. pap. 25.00 (*1-56338-184-2*) TPI PA.

McNicol, Donald. Radio's Conquest of Space: The Experimental Rise in Radio Communication. LC 74-4689. (Telecommunications Ser.). (Illus.). 388p. 1974. reprint ed. 31.95 (*0-405-06052-1*) Ayer.

McNicol, Jane. Your Child's Food Allergies: Detecting & Treating Hyperactivity, Congestion, Irritability & Other Symptoms Caused by Common Food Allergies. LC 91-34661. 176p. 1992. pap. 9.95 (*0-471-55801-X*) Wiley.

McNicol, S. B. & Mortimer, D. Evidence. (Butterworths Tutorial Ser.). 352p. 1996. pap. write for info. (*0-409-30778-5*, MICHIE) LEXIS Pub.

McNicol, Suzanne B. The Law of Privilege. 562p. 1992. 120.00 (*0-455-21149-3*, Pub. by LawBk Co) Gaunt.

McNicoll, A. W. Hellenistic Fortifications from the Aegean to the Euphrates. (Oxford Monographs on Classical Archaeology). (Illus.). 256p. 1997. text 125.00 (*0-19-813228-X*) OUP.

McNicoll, Andre, jt. auth. see Croes, Martin.

McNicoll, Geoffrey, jt. auth. see Hicks, George L.

McNicoll, R. E., ed. see Miami University, Hispanic American Institute Staf.

***McNicoll, Sylvia.** Bringing up Beauty. (Illus.). 204p. (J). (gr. 4-7). 2000. pap. 5.95 (*0-7736-7479-9*, Stoddart Kids) Stoddart Publ.

— Grave Secrets. large type ed. (Illus.). 228p. (J). (gr. 3-7). 1999. pap. 8.95 (*0-7737-6015-6*) Genl Dist Srvs.

McNie, Maggie. Champagne. (Illus.). 272p. 1999. text 30.00 (*0-571-17468-X*) Faber & Faber.

***McNie, Maggie.** Champagne. (Illus.). 208p. 2000. pap. 15.00 (*0-571-17469-8*) Faber & Faber.

McNiece, Gerald. Shelley & the Revolutionary Idea. LC 75-88808. 317p. reprint ed. pap. 98.30 (*0-8357-9178-5*, 201160100078) Bks Demand.

McNiece, Ray. The Bone-Orchard Conga. 2nd rev. ed. (Illus.). 70p. 1994. pap. 6.95 (*1-883731-08-9*) Poetry Alive.

— The Road That Carried Me Here. (Working Lives Ser.). 112p. 1998. pap. 9.95 (*0-933087-51-9*) Bottom Dog Pr.

McNiece, Ray. The Road That Carried Me Here, Vol. 1. abr. ed. 1997. 9.95 incl. audio (*0-933087-56-X*) Bottom Dog Pr.

McNiel, N. A. & Magill, C. W. Genetics. 2nd ed. (Illus.). 225p. 1977. pap. text 14.95 (*0-89641-004-8*) American Pr.

McNiff, B., jt. auth. see Errichello, Robert L.

McNiff, Jean. Action Research Principles & Practice. 194p. (C). 1995. pap. 20.99 (*0-415-09096-2*) Routledge.

— Teaching As Learning: An Action Research Approach. LC 92-32095. 144p. (C). 1993. pap. 20.99 (*0-415-08390-7*, B0179) Routledge.

Mcniff, Jean. You & Your Action Research Project. LC 96-222720. 168p. (C). 1996. pap. 20.99 (*0-415-14475-2*) Routledge.

McNiff, Jean & Collins, Una, eds. Rethinking Pastoral Care. LC 98-35448. 14p. (C). (gr. 13). 1999. 75.00 (*0-415-19441-5*, D6298); pap. 22.99 (*0-415-19442-3*, D6302) Routledge.

McNiff, Kathy, jt. auth. see Pitt, Esmond.

McNiff, Philip J., ed. Switzerland: A View from Boston. 1984. pap. 10.00 (*0-89073-077-6*, 299) Boston Public Lib.

— Twelve Mayors of Boston, 1900-1970. (Illus.). 1970. 2.00 (*0-89073-033-4*, 137) Boston Public Lib.

McNiff, Shaun. Art As Medicine: Creating a Therapy of the Imagination. LC 92-50117. (Illus.). 224p. (Orig.). 1992. pap. 18.00 (*0-87773-658-8*, Pub. by Shambhala Pubns) Random.

— The Arts & Psychotherapy. (Illus.). 260p. 1981. pap. 26.95 (*0-398-06277-3*); text 39.95 (*0-398-04112-1*) C C Thomas.

— Depth Psychology of Art. (Illus.). 258p. 1989. pap. 35.95 (*0-398-06278-1*) C C Thomas.

— Depth Psychology of Art. (Illus.). 258p. (C). 1989. text 51.95 (*0-398-05535-1*) C C Thomas.

— Educating the Creative Arts Therapist: A Profile of the Profession. 296p. 1986. pap. 36.95 (*0-398-06279-X*) C C Thomas.

— Educating the Creative Arts Therapist: A Profile of the Profession. 296p. (C). 1986. text 49.95 (*0-398-05172-0*) C C Thomas.

— Fundamentals of Art Therapy. (Illus.). 262p. 1988. pap. 35.95 (*0-398-06280-3*) C C Thomas.

— Fundamentals of Art Therapy. (Illus.). 262p. (C). 1988. text 51.95 (*0-398-05388-X*) C C Thomas.

— Trust the Process. LC 97-40182. 1998. pap. 14.95 (*1-57062-357-0*, Pub. by Shambhala Pubns) Random.

McNiff, Timothy J., et al. Opening a New Catholic School: A Series of Case Studies. Kealey, Robert J., ed. LC 97-216084. 69p. 1997. pap. 10.00 (*1-55833-189-1*) Natl Cath Educ.

McNiff, Veronica, jt. auth. see Niles, Bo.

McNiff, William J. Heaven on Earth: A Planned Mormon Society. LC 72-8632. reprint ed. 29.50 (*0-404-11007-X*) AMS Pr.

McNiffe, Liam. A History of the Garda Siochana. LC 97-146284. (Illus.). 288p. 1997. 29.95 (*0-86327-581-8*, Pub. by Wolfhound Press) Irish Amer Bk.

McNight, C. The Underachieving Curriculum: Assessing U. S. School Mathematics from an International Perspective. Travers, Kenneth J., ed. 140p. 1987. pap. text 8.00 (*0-87563-298-X*) Stipes.

Mcnight, Kent. Mushrooms: Flashguides. (Illus.). 12p. 1996. pap. 7.95 (*0-395-82999-2*) HM.

***McNinch, Barbara L.** Rottweiler. LC 99-31347. (Training Your Pet Ser.). (Illus.). 176p. 1999. pap. 11.95 (*0-7641-0849-2*) Barron.

McNinch, Marjorie G. Bridges, Vol. 1. (Illus.). xiii, 105p. 1995. 24.95 (*0-9657328-6-X*, 106) Cedar Tree Bks.

— Festivals, Vol. 1. (Illus.). xvii, 122p. 1996. 24.95 (*0-9657328-7-8*, 107) Cedar Tree Bks.

— The Silver Screen, Vol. 1. LC 98-207285. (Illus.). x, 118p. 1997. 24.95 (*0-9657328-8-6*, 108) Cedar Tree Bks.

McNish, Jacquie. The Big Score: Robert Friedland, Inco, & The Voisey's Bay Hustle. LC 99-173910. 368p. 1998. 27.95 (*0-385-25758-9*) Bantam.

— The Big Score: Robert Friedland, Inco, & The Voisey's Bay Hustle. 368p. 1999. pap. 15.95 (*0-385-25906-9*) Bantam.

McNish, Susan, jt. ed. see Hanson, Jim.

McNitt. Richard Wetherill, Anasazi: Anasazi. rev. ed. LC 65-29102. (Illus.). 380p. 1974. reprint ed. pap. 16.95 (*0-8263-0329-3*) U of NM Pr.

McNitt, Lawrence L. The Handbook of APL for the IBM PC. (Illus.). 350p. 1988. text 34.95 (*0-89433-268-6*, NO. 8227) Petrocelli.

— Invitation to APL for the IBM Personal Computer. (Illus.). 250p. 1988. pap. text 24.95 (*0-89433-267-8*, NO. 8221) Petrocelli.

— Invitation to "C" Programming Language. (Illus.). 300p. 1987. 29.95 (*0-89433-280-5*, NO. 8143); pap. text 24.95 (*0-89433-300-3*) Petrocelli.

— Invitaton to Turbo Pascal. (Illus.). 280p. 1988. pap. 24.95 (*0-89433-282-1*, NO. 8231) Petrocelli.

McNitt, Robert W. Sailing at the U. S. Naval Academy: An Illustrated History. LC 96-13061. (Illus.). 224p. 1996. 41.95 (*1-55750-573-X*) Naval Inst Pr.

McNitt, Virgil B., ed. A Tale of Two Conventions: An Account of the Republican & Democratic National Conventions of June, 1912. LC 73-19136. (Politics & People Ser.). (Illus.). 336p. 1974. reprint ed. 25.95 (*0-405-05860-8*) Ayer.

McNiven, Daniel A. The Kilted Ladies from Hell. large type ed. 176p. (Orig.). 1996. pap. 12.95 (*0-9654680-2-X*) Pilgrimage Pr.

McNiven, Helen & McNiven, Peter. Making Masks. (First Arts & Crafts Ser.). (Illus.). 32p. (J). (gr. 1-6). 1994. lib. bdg. 21.40 (*1-56847-212-9*) Raintree Steck-V.

M

— Models. LC 94-22442. (First Arts & Crafts Ser.). (Illus.). 32p. (J). (gr. 1-6). 1994. 21.40 (*1-56847-214-5*) Raintree Steck-V.

— Puppets. (First Arts & Crafts Ser.). (Illus.). 32p. (J). 1994. lib. bdg. 21.40 (*1-56847-215-3*) Raintree Steck-V.

— Toys & Games. (First Arts & Crafts Ser.). (Illus.). 32p. (J). (gr. 1-6). 1994. lib. bdg. 21.40 (*1-56847-213-7*) Raintree Steck-V.

McNiven-Hine, Ellen. A Critical Study of Condillac's Traite des Systemes. (Archives Internationales d'Histoire des Idees (International Archives of the History of Ideas) Ser.: No. 93). 1979. lib. bdg. 171.00 (*90-247-2120-2*) Kluwer Academic.

McNiven, Ian J., et al, eds. Constructions of Colonialism: Perspectives on Eliza Fraser's Shipwreck. LC 97-51839. (Illus.). 192p. 1998. 75.00 (*0-7185-0139-X*, Pub. by Leicester U Pr); pap. 24.95 (*0-7185-0171-3*, Pub. by Leicester U Pr) Cassell & Continuum.

***McNiven, J. D. & Plumstead, J. E., contrib. by.** Comparative Perspectives on Regional Development. LC 99-212441. 77 p. 1998. write for info. (*0-662-27441-5*, Pub. by Can7 Govern Pub) Intl Spec Bk.

McNiven, Peter, jt. auth. see McNiven, Helen.

McNorgan, David. Preparing the Environment for Worship. (Preparing for Liturgy Ser.). 48p. 1997. pap. 3.95 (*0-8146-2443-X*) Liturgical Pr.

McNulty, Diane, jt. auth. see Coe, Linda.

McNulty, Edward N. Let's Go to the Movies for Young Adults: Alternative Studies for Christian Growth. Patton, Vincent, ed. LC 98-52040. 16p. 2000. 5.95 (*1-57895-028-7*) Curriculm Presbytrn KY.

— Let's Go to the Movies for Younger & Older Youth: Alternative Studies for Christian Growth. Patton, Vincent, ed. LC 98-52001. 16p. (YA). (gr. 7-12). 1999. 5.95 (*1-57895-029-5*) Curriculm Presbytrn KY.

***McNulty, Edward N.** Let's Go to the Movies: Alternative Studies for Christian Growth. LC 00-36117. 2000. write for info. (*1-57895-031-7*) Bridge Resources.

McNulty, Elizabeth. Boston: Then & Now. LC 99-29319. (Then & Now Ser.: Vol. 2). 144p. 1999. 17.98 (*1-57145-177-3*, Thunder Bay) Advantage Pubs.

***McNulty, Elizabeth.** Chicago Then & Now. LC 00-33792. (Illus.). 2000. write for info. (*1-57145-278-8*, Thunder Bay) Advantage Pubs.

— St. Louis Then & Now. LC 00-36450. (Then & Now Ser.). (Illus.). 144p. 2000. 17.98 (*1-57145-243-5*, Thunder Bay) Advantage Pubs.

McNulty, Elizabeth, ed. see Collins, James.

McNulty, Elizabeth W. Planted in Love: The Enneagram-Reasoning & Conversion. 142p. 1996. pap. 39.95 (*0-85439-502-4*, Pub. by St Paul Pubns) St Mut.

McNulty, Faith. The Burning Bed. 288p. 1981. pap. 3.95 (*0-05-024747-6*) Bantam.

— The Burning Bed: The True Story of an Abused Wife. 320p. 1989. mass mkt. 4.50 (*0-380-70771-3*, Avon Bks) Morrow Avon.

— Dancing with Manatees. LC 93-7593. (Hello Reader! Ser.: Level 4). (Illus.). 40p. (J). (ps-3). 1994. pap. 3.99 (*0-590-46401-9*) Scholastic Inc.

Mcnulty, Faith. Dancing with Manatees. (Hello, Reader! Ser.). 1994. 9.19 (*0-606-06305-6*, Pub. by Turtleback) Demco.

McNulty, Faith. The Elephant Who Couldn't Forget. LC 79-2741. (I Can Read Bks.). (Illus.). 64p. (J). (ps-3). 1980. 11.95 (*0-06-024145-4*); lib. bdg. 14.89 (*0-06-024146-2*) HarpC Child Bks.

— Endangered Animals. LC 95-13236. (Hello Reader! Ser.: Level 3). (Illus.). 32p. (J). (gr. k-3). 1996. pap. 3.50 (*0-590-22859-5*, Cartwheel) Scholastic Inc.

Mcnulty, Faith. Endangered Animals. (Hello, Reader! Ser.). 1996. 8.70 (*0-606-09240-4*, Pub. by Turtleback) Demco.

McNulty, Faith. How to Dig a Hole in the Other Side of the Earth. (Illus.). (J). (gr. 2-4). 1991. 24.95 incl. audio (*0-87499-234-6*) Live Oak Media.

— How to Dig a Hole to the Other Side of the World. LC 78-22479. (Trophy Picture Bk.). (Illus.). 32p. (J). (ps-3). 1990. pap. 5.95 (*0-06-443218-1*, HarpTrophy) HarpC Child Bks.

— How to Dig a Hole to the Other Side of the World. (Illus.). (J). (gr. 2-4). pap. 15.95 incl. audio (*0-87499-233-8*) Live Oak Media.

— How to Dig a Hole to the Other Side of the World. (J). 1979. 10.15 (*0-606-03827-2*, Pub. by Turtleback) Demco.

— How to Dig a Hole to the Other Side of the World, 4 bks., Set. (Illus.). (J). (gr. 2-4). pap. 33.95 incl. audio (*0-87499-235-4*) Live Oak Media.

McNulty, Faith. How Whales Walked Into the Sea. (Illus.). write for info. (*0-439-06016-8*) Scholastic Inc.

McNulty, Faith. How Whales Walked Into the Sea. LC 98-38211. (Illus.). (J). 1999. pap. write for info. (*0-590-89831-0*) Scholastic Inc.

— How Whales Walked Into the Sea. LC 98-38211. (Illus.). 32p. (J). (gr. 2-5). 1999. 16.95 (*0-590-89830-2*) Scholastic Inc.

— Hurricane. LC 79-2672. (Illus.). 64p. (J). (gr. 3-5). 1983. 11.95 (*0-06-024142-X*) HarpC Child Bks.

— The Lady & the Spider. LC 85-5427. (Illus.). 48p. (J). (gr. 1-4). 1986. 15.00 (*0-06-024191-8*) HarpC Child Bks.

— The Lady & the Spider. LC 85-5427. (Trophy Picture Bk.). (Illus.). 48p. (J). (ps-3). 1987. pap. 5.95 (*0-06-443152-5*, HarpTrophy) HarpC Child Bks.

McNulty, Faith. Lady & the Spider. (J). 1987. 11.15 (*0-606-03598-2*, Pub. by Turtleback) Demco.

McNulty, Faith. Listening to Whales Sing. LC 94-40993. (Hello Reader! Ser.: Level 4). (Illus.). 32p. (J). (ps-3). 1996. pap. 3.99 (*0-590-47871-0*, Cartwheel) Scholastic Inc.

— Listening to Whales Sing. (Hello, Reader! Ser.). 1996. 9.19 (*0-606-09558-6*, Pub. by Turtleback) Demco.

— The Orphan. 40p. (J). 1992. 11.95 (*0-590-43838-7*, Scholastic Hardcover) Scholastic Inc.

— Peeping in the Shell: A Whooping Crane Is Hatched. LC 85-45837. (Illus.). 64p. (J). (gr. 3-7). 1986. 11.95 (*0-06-024134-9*) HarpC Child Bks.

***McNulty, Faith.** Red Wolves. LC 99-41359. (Hello Reader! Ser.). (Illus.). (J). 2000. pap. write for info. (*0-439-08751-1*) Scholastic Inc.

McNulty, Faith. The Silly Story of a Flea & His Dog. LC 98-44088. (Hello Reader! Ser.). (Illus.). (J). 1999. write for info. (*0-590-22860-9*) Scholastic Inc.

— A Snake in the House. LC 92-27939. (Illus.). 32p. (J). (ps-3). 1994. 14.95 (*0-590-44758-0*) Scholastic Inc.

— When I Lived with Bats. LC 98-6548. (Hello Readers! Ser.). (Illus.). 48p. (J). (gr. 2-4). 1998. 3.99 (*0-590-04980-1*) Scholastic Inc.

McNulty, Faith & Durrell, Julie. If Dogs Ruled the World. LC 99-24785. (Hello Reader! Ser.). 1999. pap. write for info. (*0-439-08752-X*) Scholastic Inc.

McNulty, Faith & Shiffman, Lena. Le Chant Des Baleines. (Hello Reader! (Je Peux Lire!) Ser.). (FRE., Illus.). 40p. (J). mass mkt. 5.99 (*0-590-16027-3*) Scholastic Inc.

McNulty, Ian, ed. X-Ray Microfocusing Vol. 3449: Applications & Techniques. LC 99-211184. 1998. 59.00 (*0-8194-2904-X*) SPIE.

McNulty, J. Bard. The Narrative Art of the Bayeux Tapestry Master. LC 86-47841. (Studies in the Middle Ages: No. 13). 47.50 (*0-404-61443-4*) AMS Pr.

McNulty, J. Bard, ed. The Correspondence of Thomas Cole & Daniel Wadsworth. (Illus.). 96p. (Orig.). 1983. pap. 14.75 (*0-940748-88-6*) Conn Hist Soc.

McNulty, J. Bard, jt. ed. see Bickford, Christopher P.

McNulty, J. G. Interventional Radiology of the Gallbladder: Percutaneous Cholecystostomy. (Illus.). xiii, 65p. 1990. pap. 64.00 (*0-387-52905-5*) Spr-Verlag.

— Minimally Invasive Therapy of the Liver & Biliary System. LC 93-42224. (Illus.). 205p. 1994. 115.00 (*0-86577-514-1*) Thieme Med Pubs.

McNulty, J. G., ed. see International Conference on Flow Measurement Staff.

McNulty, James F. Words of Power. LC 83-2514. 226p. (Orig.). 1983. pap. 8.95 (*0-8189-0442-9*) Alba.

McNulty, Jean, jt. auth. see Lorimer, Rowland.

McNulty, John K. Federal Estate & Gift Taxation in a Nutshell. 5th ed. (Nutshell Ser.). 486p. (C). 1994. pap. 22.95 (*0-314-04247-4*) West Pub.

— Federal Income Taxation of Individuals in a Nutshell. 4th ed. (Nutshell Ser.). 503p. 1992. reprint ed. pap. text 17.00 (*0-314-42967-0*) West Pub.

— Federal Income Taxation of Individuals in a Nutshell. 5th ed. LC 95-32870. (Nutshell Ser.). 520p. (C). 1995. pap. 21.95 (*0-314-06580-6*) West Pub.

— Federal Income Taxation of S Corporations. (University Textbook Ser.). 216p. 1991. pap. text 14.50 (*0-88277-972-9*) Foundation Pr.

McNulty, K. K., Sr. Is It I? rev. ed. (One of the Answers Ser.). (Illus.). 280p. 1989. 21.95 (*0-935025-03-0*) Data & Res Tech.

— Is It I? The Witness of Monsignor Charles Owen Rice. (One of the Answers Ser.). (Illus.). 247p. (Orig.). (C). 1989. pap. text 19.95 (*0-935025-01-4*) Data & Res Tech.

— Proper-T-Care: How to Win at Real Estate! (One of the Answers Ser.). (Illus.). 320p. 1989. 19.95 (*0-935025-02-2*) Data & Res Tech.

***Mcnulty, Karsten D.** Romanian Folk Art. LC 99-72107. (Illus.). 2000. pap. text 19.95 (*0-9670899-0-5*) Aid to Artisans.

McNulty, Leon J. A King's Love Story: A Book of Inspirational Poems. 24p. 1999. pap. 7.00 (*0-8059-4775-2*) Dorrance.

McNulty, Lyndi S. Wallace-Homestead Price Guide to Plastic Collectibles: Updated Prices. (Illus.). 208p. 1992. pap. 19.95 (*0-87069-652-1*, Wllce-Homestd) Krause Pubns.

McNulty, M. S. & McFerran, J. B., eds. Recent Advances in Virus Diagnosis. (Current Topics in Veterinary Medicine & Animal Science Ser.). 1984. text 141.50 (*0-89838-674-8*) Kluwer Academic.

McNulty, M. S., jt. ed. see McFerran, J. B.

McNulty, Marjorie G. Glastonbury - From Settlement to Suburb: A History of the 300-Year-Old Town. 4th rev. ed. (Illus.). 185p. 1995. 14.00 (*0-9610676-0-8*) Hist Soc Glastonbury.

McNulty, Maureen, jt. auth. see Johansen, Robert.

McNulty, Paul J. The Origins & Development of Labor Economics. 1984. reprint ed. pap. text 12.95 (*0-262-63097-4*) MIT Pr.

McNulty, Robert, ed. see Booth, Kathy.

McNulty, Robert H., et al. The State of the American Community: Empowerment for Local Action. Page, Clint, ed. LC 95-152659. (Illus.). 156p. 1994. pap. 19.95 (*0-941182-19-3*) Partners Livable.

McNulty, T., jt. ed. see Byars, E. A.

McNulty, Tim. As a Heron Unsettles a Quiet Pool: Nine Poems for Mary. 16p. 1988. 5.00 (*1-882623-05-3*) Exiled-Am Pr.

***McNulty, Tim.** In Blue Mountain Dusk. 96p. 1999. pap. 12.95 (*0-9651413-8-1*) Pleasure Boat.

McNulty, Tim. Last Year's Poverty. 1987. 25.00 (*0-918116-41-4*) Brooding Heron Pr.

— Olympic National Park: A Natural History. 272p. 1999. pap. 16.95 (*1-57061-168-8*) Sasquatch Bks.

— Washington's Mount Rainier National Park: A Centennial Celebration. LC 98-20931. (Illus.). 144p. 1998. 35.00 (*0-89886-582-4*) Mountaineers.

— Washington's Wild Rivers: The Unfinished Work. LC 89-13562. (Illus.). 144p. 1990. 14.95 (*0-89886-170-5*) Mountaineers.

McNulty, Tim, et al. Washington's Mount Rainier National Park. LC 98-20931. 144p. 2000. pap. 18.95 (*0-89886-621-9*) Mountaineers.

***McNulty, Tom, ed.** Accessible Libraries on Campus: A Practical Guide for the Creation of Disability-Friendly Libraries. LC 99-34534. 193p. 1999. pap. 22.00 (*0-8389-8035-X*) Assn Coll & Res Libs.

McNulty, Tom & Suvino, Dawn M. Access to Information: Materials, Technologies, & Services for Print-Impaired Readers. (LITA Monographs: No. 2). 161p. 1993. pap. 7.00 (*0-8389-7641-7*) ALA.

McNurlin. Information & Statistics. 4th ed. 1998. text 116.25 (*0-13-923294-X*) P-H.

McNurlin, Barbara, jt. auth. see Stockwell, Shelley L.

McNurlin, Barbara C., jt. auth. see Sprague, Ralph H.

McNurney, John M., jt. ed. see Dowden, Lisa G.

McNutt, et al. System Administrator Tools. (Illus.). (Orig.). 1995. pap. 59.95 (*1-56592-118-6*) Thomson Learn.

McNutt, Charles H. Early Puebloan Occupations of Tesuque By-Pass & in the Upper Rio Grande Valley. LC 79-631330. (University of Michigan, Museum of Anthropology, Anthropological Papers: No. 40). (Illus.). 158p. reprint ed. pap. 49.00 (*0-8357-8601-3*, 203499700091) Bks Demand.

McNutt, Charles H., ed. The Archaic Period in the Mid-South: Proceedings of the 1989 Mid-South Archaeological Conference. LC 91-620836. (Mississippi Department of Archives & History Archaeological Reports: No. 24). (Illus.). 95p. 1991. 9.00 (*0-938896-60-1*) Mississippi Archives.

— Prehistory of the Central Mississippi Valley. LC 95-21893. (Illus.). 344p. (Orig.). (C). 1996. pap. text 34.95 (*0-8173-0807-5*) U of Ala Pr.

McNutt, James A., Jr. Exploring the West Indies. (Nautilus Explorer Ser.). 112p. 1993. pap. 19.00 (*1-884104-01-0*) Hydrodyne Marine.

— Quest for Shipwrecks: Era of New Shipwreck Discovery, 2 vols., Set, Vols. 1 & 2. 2nd ed. (Nautilus Explorer Ser.). (Illus.). 248p. 1997. pap. 22.00 (*1-884104-00-2*, QSII) Hydrodyne Marine.

McNutt, James S., Jr. Business & Careers in Marine Sciences. 332p. 1993. pap. text 24.00 (*1-884104-02-9*) Hydrodyne Marine.

McNutt, Jean-Isabel. Echoes of Eden: Being a Commonplace Book about Animals, Lovers, Food, Eccentrics, Artists, & Me. LC 93-3386. 143p. 1993. 15.00 (*0-374-14637-3*) FS&G.

McNutt, Jim. A Single Journey: Biblical Sketches for Life on Your Own. LC 98-49327. 265p. 1999. pap. 12.99 (*1-56955-053-0*) Servant.

McNutt, Jim, ed. see Whipple, Melvin.

McNutt, John. Counting Money. 1992. 149.00 (*1-56304-032-8*) J Stanfield.

McNutt, John & Boggs, Lesley P. Running Wild: Dispelling the Myths of the African Wild Dog. LC 97-168346. (Illus.). 150p. 1996. 45.00 (*1-56098-717-0*) Smithsonian.

McNutt, John G., jt. ed. see Hoff, Marie D.

McNutt, L. Summer Point. LC 97-165858. 157p. 1999. pap. text 16.95 (*1-896951-01-5*) Cormor Bks.

McNutt, Nan. The Bentwood Box. 5th ed. (Northwest Coast Indian Art Ser.). (Illus.). 36p. (Orig.). (J). (gr. 3-8). 1994. pap. text 9.95 (*0-9614534-7-8*) N McNutt Assocs.

— The Bentwood Box: A Northwest Coast Indian Art Activity Book. (Illus.). 36p. (J). (gr. 4-7). 1997. reprint ed. pap. 10.95 (*1-57061-116-5*) Sasquatch Bks.

— The Button Blanket. 4th ed. (Northwest Coast Indian Art Ser.). (Illus.). 44p. (J). (ps-3). 1994. pap. 9.95 (*0-9614534-3-5*) N McNutt Assocs.

— The Button Blanket: A Northwest Coast Indian Art Activity Book. LC 97-16045. (Illus.). 44p. (gr. 1-5). 1997. reprint ed. pap. 10.95 (*1-57061-118-1*) Sasquatch Bks.

— The Cedar Plank Mask. (Illus.). 34p. (J). (gr. 3-6). 1991. pap. 9.95 (*0-9614534-2-7*) N McNutt Assocs.

— The Cedar Plank Mask: A Northwest Coast Indian Art Activity Book. LC 97-16047. (Illus.). 36p. (J). (gr. 4-7). 1997. reprint ed. pap. 10.95 (*1-57061-117-3*) Sasquatch Bks.

— The Spindle Whorl: A Northwest Coast Indian Art Activity Book. (Illus.). 44p. (Orig.). (J). 1997. pap. 10.95 (*1-57061-115-7*) Sasquatch Bks.

McNutt, Patrick. The Economics of Public Choice: Contemporary Issues in the Political Economy of Governing. LC 96-14166. (Illus.). 272p. (C). 1996. 95.00 (*1-85278-514-4*) E Elgar.

— The Economics of Public Choice: Contemporary Issues in the Political Economy of Governing. LC 96-14166. 272p. 1997. pap. 30.00 (*1-85898-522-6*) E Elgar.

McNutt, Patty L. Horse & Handler Safety: A Safety Guide for All Equistrians. (Illus.). 64p. 1998. pap. 7.00 (*1-890050-24-5*) Carlisle Press.

McNutt, Paula M. The Forging of Israel: Iron Technology, Symbolism & Tradition in Ancient Society. (Journal for the Study of the Old Testament Supplement Ser.: 108). 307p. 1990. 85.00 (*1-85075-263-X*, Pub. by Sheffield Acad) CUP Services.

— Reconstructing the Society of Ancient Israel. LC 98-31938. (Library of Ancient Israel). 288p. 1999. 27.00 (*0-664-22132-7*) Westminster John Knox.

McNutt, Paula M., ed. see Lind, Michael.

McNutt, Paula M., ed. see Weeks, John M.

McNutt, Randy. Ghosts: Ohio's Haunted Landscapes, Lost Arts & Forgotten Places. LC 96-68627. 261p. 1996. pap. 19.95 (*1-882203-14-3*) Orange Frazer.

— Ghosts: Ohio's Haunted Landscapes, Lost Arts, Forgotten Places. LC 96-68627. (Illus.). 261p. 1996. text 24.95 (*1-882203-05-4*) Orange Frazer.

***McNutt, Randy.** Too Hot to Handle: An Illustrated Encyclopedia of American Recording Studies of the 20th Century. LC 00-132431. (Illus.). 192p. 2000. pap. 30.00 (*0-940152-09-6*) Hamilton Hobby.

McNutt, Randy. We Wanna Boogie: An Illustrated History of the American Rockabilly Movement. 2nd ed. (Illus.). 288p. 1989. pap. 25.00 (*0-940152-05-3*) Hamilton Hobby.

McNutt, Randy, compiled by. No Left Turns, a Handbook for Conservatives: Based on the Writings of John M. Ashbrook. LC 85-80376. (Illus.). 128p. 1986. pap. 15.00 (*0-940152-03-7*) Hamilton Hobby.

McNutt, Randy, jt. auth. see Kennedy, Rick.

***McNutt, Stacey.** Churches & Cathedrals, 1. 1998. pap. text 10.95 (*1-57717-031-8*) Todtri Prods.

McNutt, Timothy E., Sr. Alley Alligator's Awesome Smile. (Illus.). (J). (ps). 1994. pap. text 3.95 (*0-9642475-0-X*) T E McNutt.

McNutt, Todd A. Other People's Secrets: A Techno-Expose' on the Legal Invasion of Privacy by Computers. 2nd ed. 60p. (YA). (gr. 11 up). 1999. pap. 9.95 (*1-885037-06-6*) SEEBIC Pubng.

McNutty, Faith. How to Dig a Hole to the Other Side of the World. (Illus.). (J). (gr. 1-3). 1979. 7.66 (*0-06-024147-0*, 630859) HarpC.

McOle, Christopher. Death of a Tyrant, 6. 100p. 1997. 25.00 (*0-7278-5210-8*) Severn Hse.

McOmber, Howard J., II. With Love As Our Weapon. Holt, Pamela, ed. (Illus.). 104p. (Orig.). (C). 1990. pap. 9.95 (*0-9626734-0-4*) Plowshare Prodns.

McOmber, Rachel & Kassing, Perry. McOmber Adult Book 5 - Ben (Short e) (Illus.). 78p. 1994. pap. 10.00 (*1-56861-008-4*) Swift Lrn Res.

— McOmber Adult Book 4 - Muff (Short u) (Illus.). 78p. 1994. pap. 10.00 (*1-56861-007-6*) Swift Lrn Res.

— McOmber Adult Book 1 - Max (Short a) (Illus.). 78p. 1994. pap. 10.00 (*1-56861-004-1*) Swift Lrn Res.

— McOmber Adult Book 6 - Ben & Peggy (Review) (Illus.). 78p. 1994. pap. 10.00 (*1-56861-009-2*) Swift Lrn Res.

— McOmber Adult Book 3 - Rob (Short o) (Illus.). 78p. 1994. pap. 10.00 (*1-56861-006-8*) Swift Lrn Res.

— McOmber Adult Book 2 - Kim (Short i) (Illus.). 78p. 1994. pap. 10.00 (*1-56861-005-X*) Swift Lrn Res.

McOmber, Rachel B., ed. Bags... Bags (Animals) rev. ed. (Illus.). (J). write for info. (*0-944991-97-1*) Swift Lrn Res.

— Bags... Bags (Holidays) rev. ed. (Illus.). (J). write for info. (*0-944991-98-X*) Swift Lrn Res.

— McOmber Phonics Storybooks. rev. ed. (Illus.). (J). write for info. (*0-944991-72-6*) Swift Lrn Res.

— McOmber Phonics Storybooks: A Box. rev. ed. (Illus.). (J). write for info. (*0-944991-13-0*) Swift Lrn Res.

— McOmber Phonics Storybooks: A Game for Champions. rev. ed. (Illus.). (J). write for info. (*0-944991-68-8*) Swift Lrn Res.

— McOmber Phonics Storybooks: A Hum-Bug. rev. ed. (Illus.). (J). write for info. (*0-944991-20-3*) Swift Lrn Res.

— McOmber Phonics Storybooks: A Nifty Ball of String. rev. ed. (Illus.). (J). write for info. (*0-944991-50-5*) Swift Lrn Res.

— McOmber Phonics Storybooks: A Night to Celebrate. rev. ed. (Illus.). (J). write for info. (*0-944991-71-8*) Swift Lrn Res.

— McOmber Phonics Storybooks: A Package from Hong Kong. rev. ed. (Illus.). (J). write for info. (*0-944991-61-0*) Swift Lrn Res.

— McOmber Phonics Storybooks: A Red Hen. rev. ed. (Illus.). (J). write for info. (*0-944991-25-4*) Swift Lrn Res.

— McOmber Phonics Storybooks: A Trip to China. rev. ed. (Illus.). (J). write for info. (*0-944991-70-X*) Swift Lrn Res.

— McOmber Phonics Storybooks: At the Fair. rev. ed. (Illus.). (J). write for info. (*0-944991-60-2*) Swift Lrn Res.

— McOmber Phonics Storybooks: Ben Has a Pet. rev. ed. (Illus.). (J). write for info. (*0-944991-26-2*) Swift Lrn Res.

— McOmber Phonics Storybooks: Ben in Bed. rev. ed. (Illus.). (J). write for info. (*0-944991-29-7*) Swift Lrn Res.

— McOmber Phonics Storybooks: Ben Will Get Well. rev. ed. (Illus.). (J). write for info. (*0-944991-30-0*) Swift Lrn Res.

— McOmber Phonics Storybooks: Boe E. Toad. rev. ed. (Illus.). (J). write for info. (*0-944991-54-8*) Swift Lrn Res.

— McOmber Phonics Storybooks: Boyer's Toy Store. rev. ed. (Illus.). (J). write for info. (*0-944991-69-6*) Swift Lrn Res.

— McOmber Phonics Storybooks: Bug. rev. ed. (Illus.). (J). write for info. (*0-944991-19-X*) Swift Lrn Res.

— McOmber Phonics Storybooks: Chatsworth. rev. ed. (Illus.). (J). write for info. (*0-944991-74-2*) Swift Lrn Res.

— McOmber Phonics Storybooks: Choose Which One - 1. rev. ed. (Illus.). (J). write for info. (*0-944991-67-X*) Swift Lrn Res.

— McOmber Phonics Storybooks: Everyone Knows a Pitcher. rev. ed. (Illus.). (J). write for info. (*0-944991-79-3*) Swift Lrn Res.

— McOmber Phonics Storybooks: Fizz in the Pit. rev. ed. (Illus.). (J). write for info. (*0-944991-12-2*) Swift Lrn Res.

— McOmber Phonics Storybooks: Fizz Mix. rev. ed. (Illus.). (J). write for info. (*0-944991-11-4*) Swift Lrn Res.

— McOmber Phonics Storybooks: Fizz Mud. rev. ed. (Illus.). (J). write for info. (*0-944991-21-1*) Swift Lrn Res.

— McOmber Phonics Storybooks: Hello Again. rev. ed. (Illus.). (J). write for info. (*0-944991-84-X*) Swift Lrn Res.

— McOmber Phonics Storybooks: Hen Pox. rev. ed. (Illus.). (J). write for info. (*0-944991-28-9*) Swift Lrn Res.

M

An Asterisk (*) at the beginning of an entry indicates that the title is appearing for the first time.

— McOmber Phonics Storybooks: Humps & Lumps. rev. ed. (Illus.). (J). write for info. (*0-944991-62-9*) Swift Lrn Res.

— McOmber Phonics Storybooks: In the Dell. rev. ed. (Illus.). (J). write for info. (*0-944991-32-7*) Swift Lrn Res.

— McOmber Phonics Storybooks: Jud & Nell. rev. ed. (Illus.). (J). write for info. (*0-944991-33-5*) Swift Lrn Res.

— McOmber Phonics Storybooks: Kim. rev. ed. (Illus.). (J). write for info. (*0-944991-07-6*) Swift Lrn Res.

— McOmber Phonics Storybooks: Max. rev. ed. (Illus.). (J). write for info. (*0-944991-01-7*) Swift Lrn Res.

— McOmber Phonics Storybooks: Max Is Six. rev. ed. (Illus.). (J). write for info. (*0-944991-43-2*) Swift Lrn Res.

— McOmber Phonics Storybooks: Max Ran. rev. ed. (Illus.). (J). write for info. (*0-944991-02-5*) Swift Lrn Res.

— McOmber Phonics Storybooks: Max the Grand. rev. ed. (Illus.). (J). write for info. (*0-944991-57-2*) Swift Lrn Res.

— McOmber Phonics Storybooks: Me & the Bee. rev. ed. (Illus.). (J). write for info. (*0-944991-46-7*) Swift Lrn Res.

— McOmber Phonics Storybooks: Miss Vie. rev. ed. (Illus.). (J). write for info. (*0-944991-48-3*) Swift Lrn Res.

— McOmber Phonics Storybooks: Mom & Dad Hop-Jig. rev. ed. (Illus.). (J). write for info. (*0-944991-16-5*) Swift Lrn Res.

— McOmber Phonics Storybooks: Number Fun. rev. ed. (Illus.). (J). write for info. (*0-944991-58-0*) Swift Lrn Res.

— McOmber Phonics Storybooks: On TV. rev. ed. (Illus.). (J). write for info. (*0-944991-17-3*) Swift Lrn Res.

— McOmber Phonics Storybooks: Pete's Bike Ride. rev. ed. (Illus.). (J). write for info. (*0-944991-40-8*) Swift Lrn Res.

— McOmber Phonics Storybooks: Razz. rev. ed. (Illus.). (J). write for info. (*0-944991-06-8*) Swift Lrn Res.

— McOmber Phonics Storybooks: Razz Visits Raz in Israel. rev. ed. (Illus.). (J). write for info. (*0-944991-75-0*) Swift Lrn Res.

— McOmber Phonics Storybooks: Robin Hood's Cook. rev. ed. (Illus.). (J). write for info. (*0-944991-64-5*) Swift Lrn Res.

— McOmber Phonics Storybooks: Snores & More. rev. ed. (Illus.). (J). write for info. (*0-944991-59-9*) Swift Lrn Res.

— McOmber Phonics Storybooks: Tale of the Green Glob. rev. ed. (Illus.). (J). write for info. (*0-944991-65-3*) Swift Lrn Res.

— McOmber Phonics Storybooks: Teacher's Manual. rev. ed. (Illus.). teacher ed. write for info. (*0-944991-00-9*) Swift Lrn Res.

— McOmber Phonics Storybooks: Ten in the Hut. rev. ed. (Illus.). (J). write for info. (*0-944991-27-0*) Swift Lrn Res.

— McOmber Phonics Storybooks: The Bag. rev. ed. (Illus.). (J). write for info. (*0-944991-03-3*) Swift Lrn Res.

— McOmber Phonics Storybooks: The Big Deal. rev. ed. (Illus.). (J). write for info. (*0-944991-47-5*) Swift Lrn Res.

— McOmber Phonics Storybooks: The Big Hole. rev. ed. (Illus.). (J). write for info. (*0-944991-38-6*) Swift Lrn Res.

— McOmber Phonics Storybooks: The Bon-Bon Box. rev. ed. (Illus.). (J). write for info. (*0-944991-14-9*) Swift Lrn Res.

— McOmber Phonics Storybooks: The Box Mix. rev. ed. (Illus.). (J). write for info. (*0-944991-15-7*) Swift Lrn Res.

— McOmber Phonics Storybooks: The Cake. rev. ed. (Illus.). (J). write for info. (*0-944991-44-0*) Swift Lrn Res.

— McOmber Phonics Storybooks: The Confection Connection. rev. ed. (Illus.). (J). write for info. (*0-944991-73-4*) Swift Lrn Res.

— McOmber Phonics Storybooks: The Cove of Gloom. rev. ed. (Illus.). (J). write for info. (*0-944991-83-1*) Swift Lrn Res.

— McOmber Phonics Storybooks: The Fumes. rev. ed. (Illus.). (J). write for info. (*0-944991-39-4*) Swift Lrn Res.

— McOmber Phonics Storybooks: The Gal Pals. rev. ed. (Illus.). (J). write for info. (*0-944991-42-4*) Swift Lrn Res.

— McOmber Phonics Storybooks: The Haircut. rev. ed. (Illus.). (J). write for info. (*0-944991-53-X*) Swift Lrn Res.

— McOmber Phonics Storybooks: The Hum-Bug Hop. rev. ed. (Illus.). (J). write for info. (*0-944991-31-9*) Swift Lrn Res.

— McOmber Phonics Storybooks: The Invisible Crocodiles. rev. ed. (Illus.). (J). write for info. (*0-944991-80-7*) Swift Lrn Res.

— McOmber Phonics Storybooks: The Kit. rev. ed. (Illus.). (J). write for info. (*0-944991-08-4*) Swift Lrn Res.

— McOmber Phonics Storybooks: The Land of Morning. rev. ed. (Illus.). (J). write for info. (*0-944991-82-3*) Swift Lrn Res.

— McOmber Phonics Storybooks: The Lemonade Sale. rev. ed. (Illus.). (J). write for info. (*0-944991-41-6*) Swift Lrn Res.

— McOmber Phonics Storybooks: The Magic "E" rev. ed. (Illus.). (J). write for info. (*0-944991-37-8*) Swift Lrn Res.

— McOmber Phonics Storybooks: The Map. rev. ed. (Illus.). (J). write for info. (*0-944991-05-X*) Swift Lrn Res.

— McOmber Phonics Storybooks: The Neat Trick. rev. ed. (Illus.). (J). write for info. (*0-944991-55-6*) Swift Lrn Res.

— McOmber Phonics Storybooks: The Pit Kit. rev. ed. (Illus.). (J). write for info. (*0-944991-09-2*) Swift Lrn Res.

— McOmber Phonics Storybooks: The Prime Time Trick. rev. ed. (Illus.). (J). write for info. (*0-944991-56-4*) Swift Lrn Res.

— McOmber Phonics Storybooks: The Prize. rev. ed. (Illus.). (J). write for info. (*0-944991-49-1*) Swift Lrn Res.

— McOmber Phonics Storybooks: The Quiz Is (1) rev. ed. (Illus.). (J). write for info. (*0-944991-34-3*) Swift Lrn Res.

— McOmber Phonics Storybooks: The Quiz Is (2) rev. ed. (Illus.). (J). write for info. (*0-944991-35-1*) Swift Lrn Res.

— McOmber Phonics Storybooks: The Rope. rev. ed. (Illus.). (J). write for info. (*0-944991-45-9*) Swift Lrn Res.

— McOmber Phonics Storybooks: The Sub. rev. ed. (Illus.). (J). write for info. (*0-944991-22-X*) Swift Lrn Res.

— McOmber Phonics Storybooks: The Tan Cab. rev. ed. (Illus.). (J). write for info. (*0-944991-04-1*) Swift Lrn Res.

— McOmber Phonics Storybooks: The Time Box. rev. ed. (Illus.). (J). write for info. (*0-944991-52-1*) Swift Lrn Res.

— McOmber Phonics Storybooks: The Tin Lid. rev. ed. (Illus.). (J). write for info. (*0-944991-10-6*) Swift Lrn Res.

— McOmber Phonics Storybooks: The Tub. rev. ed. (Illus.). (J). write for info. (*0-944991-24-6*) Swift Lrn Res.

— McOmber Phonics Storybooks: The TV Box. rev. ed. (Illus.). (J). write for info. (*0-944991-18-1*) Swift Lrn Res.

— McOmber Phonics Storybooks: The Video Show. rev. ed. (Illus.). (J). write for info. (*0-944991-63-7*) Swift Lrn Res.

— McOmber Phonics Storybooks: The Wizz Kid. rev. ed. (Illus.). (J). write for info. (*0-944991-23-8*) Swift Lrn Res.

— McOmber Phonics Storybooks: Tid Bits. rev. ed. (Illus.). (J). write for info. (*0-944991-36-X*) Swift Lrn Res.

— McOmber Phonics Storybooks: Under the Rainbow. rev. ed. (Illus.). (J). write for info. (*0-944991-81-5*) Swift Lrn Res.

— McOmber Phonics Storybooks: Yellow Crocodile. rev. ed. (Illus.). (J). write for info. (*0-944991-76-9*) Swift Lrn Res.

— McOmber Phonics Storybooks: You Can Make It. rev. ed. (Illus.). (J). write for info. (*0-944991-51-3*) Swift Lrn Res.

— McOmber Phonics Storybooks Vol. 1: Writing Book. rev. ed. (Illus.). (J). write for info. (*0-944991-93-9*) Swift Lrn Res.

— McOmber Phonics Storybooks Vol. 2: Writing Book. rev. ed. (Illus.). (J). write for info. (*0-944991-94-7*) Swift Lrn Res.

— String Art Vol. 1: For All Seasons. rev. ed. (Illus.). (J). write for info. (*0-944991-95-5*) Swift Lrn Res.

— String Art Vol. 2: For All Seasons. rev. ed. (Illus.). (J). write for info. (*0-944991-96-3*) Swift Lrn Res.

M'Conechy, James, ed. Papers Illustrative of the Political Condition of the Highlands of Scotland. LC 75-175587. (Maitland Club, Glasgow. Publications: No. 64). reprint ed. 32.50 (*0-404-53071-0*) AMS Pr.

McOntyre, A. M. Australian Contemporary Drawings. 162p. (C). 1990. 120.00 (*0-86439-037-8*, Pub. by Boolarong Pubns) St Mut.

McOscar, Diane L., ed. see Gross, Andrew C., et al.

McOwan. The Day the Mountain Moved. 1996. pap. text 9.00 (*0-7152-0688-5*, Pub. by St Andrew) St Mut.

— Light on Dumyat. 1996. pap. text 9.00 (*0-7152-0697-4*, Pub. by St Andrew) St Mut.

— Robert Burns for Beginners. 1996. pap. text 11.98 (*0-7152-0715-6*, Pub. by St Andrew) St Mut.

McOwan, Rennie. Light on Dumyat. 152p. (C). 1992. pap. 32.00 (*0-7855-7006-3*, Pub. by St Andrew) St Mut.

— Light on Dumyat. 152p. 1993. pap. 22.00 (*0-7152-0544-7*, Pub. by St Andrew) St Mut.

— Magic Mountains. (Illus.). 160p. 1996. 29.95 (*1-85158-707-1*, Pub. by Mainstream Pubng) Trafalgar.

— Walks in the Trossachs & Rob Roy Country. 184p. (C). 1991. pap. text 39.00 (*86-15-30563-3*, Pub. by St Andrew) St Mut.

— Walks in the Trossachs & Rob Roy Country. 192p. (C). 1992. pap. 35.00 (*0-685-66160-1*, Pub. by St Andrew) St Mut.

— Walks in the Trossachs & Rob Roy Country. 192p. 1993. pap. 35.00 (*0-7152-0563-3*, Pub. by St Andrew) St Mut.

— The White Stag Adventure. 160p. (C). 1992. pap. 32.00 (*0-7855-6833-6*, Pub. by St Andrew) St Mut.

— The White Stag Adventure. 160p. 1993. pap. 30.00 (*0-7152-0665-6*, Pub. by St Andrew) St Mut.

McOwan, Rennie, jt. auth. see Gray, Affleck.

McOwen, Robert C. Partial Differential Equations: Theory & Applications. LC 95-21357. 420p. 1995. 85.33 (*0-13-121880-8*) P-H.

MCP Staff. Eight Friends in All. (Little Book Practice Reader). 1996. write for info. (*0-8136-1471-6*) Modern Curr.

— Kangaroo in the Kitchen. (Little Book Practice Reader). 1998. write for info. (*0 8136 0741 8*) Modern Curr.

MCP Staff. Ten Minute Guide to Office for Windows 95 Bundle. 1997. pap. text 12.99 (*0-7897-0667-9*) Que.

— Webster's New World Dictionary: School Edition. (Illus.). 23.50 (*0-8136-1995-5*, J619955) Good Apple.

— The Word Book. (J). (gr. 1). 1986. 9.00 (*0-8136-1976-9*) Modern Curr.

McParland, Stephen, jt. auth. see Blair, John.

McParland, Stephen J. It's Party Time: A Musical Appreciation of the Beach Party Film Genre. (Illus.). 204p. (Orig.). 1992. pap. 25.00 (*0-9601880-2-9*) J Blair.

McParlin, Audrey. Flight. 25p. 1997. 10.00 (*0-533-12327-5*) Vantage.

McParr, Nigel. Dark Sisters. 1998. mass mkt. 6.95 (*1-56333-698-7*) Masquerade.

— The Transformation of Emily. (Orig.). 1997. mass mkt. 6.50 (*1-56333-519-0*) Masquerade.

McPartlan, Paul. The Eucharist Makes the Church: Henri de Lubac & John Zizioulas in Dialogue. 368p. 1996. pap. 33.95 (*0-567-29263-0*, Pub. by T & T Clark) Bks Intl VA.

— One in 2000? Towards Catholic-Orthodox Unity. 192p. 1996. pap. 39.95 (*0-85439-439-7*, Pub. by St Paul Pubns) St Mut.

— Sacrament of Salvation: An Introduction to Eucharistic Ecclesiology. 144p. pap. 24.95 (*0-567-29299-1*, Pub. by T & T Clark) Bks Intl VA.

McPartland. Take It Easy. 2nd ed. LC 99-56986. 240p. (C). 2000. pap. text 33.27 (*0-13-660812-4*, Macmillan Coll) P-H.

McPartland, jt. auth. see ABC Staff.

McPartland, Brian J. & McPartland, Joseph F. Handbook of Practical Electrical Design. 3rd ed. LC 98-30222. 723p. 1999. 64.95 (*0-07-046642-4*) McGraw.

McPartland, Brian J., jt. auth. see McPartland, Joseph F.

McPartland-Fairman, Pamela. Stars & Stripes: Facts & Folklore about the U. S. A. LC 98-152581. vi, 106 p. 1998. write for info. (*0-07-115799-9*) McGraw.

— Stars & Stripes: Stories about the U.S.A., Yesterday & Today. LC 98-152581. 112p. 1998. pap. 17.81 (*0-07-045993-2*) McGraw.

McPartland, J. F. McGraw-Hill's National Electrical Code Handbook: Based on the 1996 National Electrical Code. 22nd ed. (Illus.). 1264p. 1996. 65.00 (*0-07-045992-4*) McGraw.

McPartland, J. F., et al. McGraw-Hill's Handbook of Electrical Construction Calculations. LC 93-3994. (Illus.). 368p. 1993. 54.50 (*0-07-045682-8*) McGraw.

McPartland, Joe, ed. Ulster Reciter: Ballads, Poems & Recitations for Every Occasion. 90p. 1984. pap. 7.95 (*0-685-25949-8*, Pub. by Blackstaff Pr) Dufour.

— Ulster Reciter: Ballads, Poems & Recitations for Every Occasion. 90p. 1984. pap. 10.95 (*0-85640-321-0*) Dufour.

McPartland, John. Danger for Breakfast. large type ed. (Linford Mystery Library). 288p. 1992. pap. 16.99 (*0-7089-7304-3*) Ulverscroft.

— The Face of Evil. large type ed. (Linford Mystery Library). 1991. pap. 16.99 (*0-7089-7076-1*) Ulverscroft.

— Love Me Now. large type ed. (Linford Mystery Library). 400p. 1994. pap. 16.99 (*0-7089-7475-9*, Linford) Ulverscroft.

McPartland, John M. & Zigler, Mitch. Counterstrain Technique. rev. ed. LC 98-93924. (Illus.). 66p. 1998. pap. 33.00 (*1-893553-02-7*) AMRITA Pr.

***McPartland, Joseph F.** McGraw-Hill's National Electrical Code Handbook. 1300p. 1999. 115.00 (*0-07-134598-1*) McGraw.

McPartland, Joseph F. & McGraw-Hill Book Company Staff. McGraw-Hill's Handbook of Electrical Construction Calculations. 2nd ed. LC 97-29144. 464p. 1998. 59.95 (*0-07-046641-6*) McGraw.

McPartland, Joseph F. & McPartland, Brian J. McGraw-Hill's National Electrical Code Handbook. 23rd ed. (Illus.). 1360p. 1998. 92.95 (*0-07-047234-3*) McGraw-Hill Prof.

— 1998 Yearbook Supplement to McGraw-Hill's National Electrical Code Handbook. (Illus.). 176p. 1998. 29.95 (*0-07-046604-1*) McGraw-Hill Prof.

McPartland, Joseph F. & Novak, William J. Electrical Design Details. LC 82-94. 240p. 1983. reprint ed. 21.50 (*0-89874-412-1*) Krieger.

McPartland, Joseph F., jt. auth. see McPartland, Brian J.

***McPartland, M., et al.** Hemp Diseases & Pests: Management with an Emphasis on Biological Control. (CABI Publishing Ser.). 208p. 2000. text 90.00 (*0-85199-454-7*) C A B Intl.

McPartland, Marian. The Artistry of Marian McPartland. 1995. pap. 14.95 (*0-89898-415-7*, TPF0135) Wrner Bros.

McPartland, Martha R. History of East Greenwich, R.I., 1677-1960, with Related Genealogy. (Illus.). 300p. 1996. lib. bdg. 39.50 (*0-8328-5219-8*) Higginson Bk Co.

McPartland, Pamela. Take It Easy: American Idioms & Two Word Verbs for Students of English As a Foreign Language. (English As a Second Language Ser.). 176p. (C). 1981. pap. text 25.40 (*0-13-882902-0*) P-H.

McPartland, Pamela. Take It Easy American Idioms. (English As a Second Language Ser.). 176p. (C). 1981. 17.50 incl. audio (*0-13-882910-1*) P-H.

McPartland, Pamela. What's Up? 192p. (C). 1989. pap. text 23.00 (*0-13-955766-0*) P-H.

McPartland, Pamela, et al. Connect with English: Home Viewer's Guide: Chinese/English Edition. 112p. 1998. pap. 16.88 (*0-07-292774-7*) McGraw.

— Connect with English: Home Viewer's Guide: English Edition. 120p. 1998. pap. 16.88 (*0-07-292772-0*) McGraw.

— Connect with English: Home Viewer's Guide: Korean/English Edition. 112p. 1998. pap. 16.88 (*0-07-292775-5*) McGraw.

— Connect with English: Home Viewer's Guide: Spanish/English Edition. 112p. 1998. pap. 16.88 (*0-07-292773-9*) McGraw.

— Connect with English: Home Viewer's Guide: Thai/English Edition. 112p. 1998. pap. 16.88 (*0-07-292776-3*) McGraw.

McPartland, Patricia A. Promoting Health in the Workplace. xiv, 266p. (C). 1991. text 58.00 (*3-7186-0528-7*) Gordon & Breach.

McPartland, Scott. Edwin Land: Photographic Pioneer. LC 93-22077. (Masters of Invention Ser.). 48p. (J). (gr. 4-8). 1993. lib. bdg. 21.60 (*0-86592-150-4*) Rourke Enter.

— Gertrude Elion: Master Chemist. LC 93-22315. (Masters of Invention Ser.). 48p. (J). (gr. 4-8). 1993. lib. bdg. 21.27 (*0-86592-130-X*) Rourke Enter.

— Gordon Gould: Laser Man. LC 93-2819. (Masters of Invention Ser.). 48p. (J). (gr. 4-8). 1993. lib. bdg. 21.27 (*0-86592-079-6*) Rourke Enter.

McPeak-Bailey, Bobbi. Chicken Pox Christmas. (Illus.). 64p. (Orig.). (J). (gr. k-4). 1994. pap. 8.95 (*0-9625005-2-6*) Wee Pr.

— The Christmas Tree That Cried. 2nd ed. (Illus.). 40p. 1995. reprint ed. pap. text 6.95 (*0-9625005-3-4*) Wee Pr.

— Emma's Happy Birthday Piano. (Illus.). 36p. (J). (gr. k-4). 1991. pap. 5.95 (*0-9625005-1-8*) Wee Pr.

— Sweet Dreams: A Garden Lullaby. (Illus.). 48p. (Orig.). (J). (gr. k-3). 1995. pap. 8.95 (*0-9625005-4-2*) Wee Pr.

McPeak, Ron H. Amphibians & Reptiles of Baja California. LC 99-51722. 104p. 1999. pap. 20.95 (*0-930118-28-6*, 8M) Sea Chall.

McPeak, Ronald H. Amber Forest: Beauty & Biology of California's Submarine Forests. (Illus.). 144p. 39.95 (*0-922769-01-X*) Aqua Quest.

McPeak, Ronald H., et al. The Amber Forest: Beauty & Biology of California's Submarine Forests. LC 88-51680. (Illus.). 144p. (Orig.). 1988. pap. 29.95 (*0-922769-00-1*) Aqua Quest.

— The Amber Forest: Beauty & Biology of California's Submarine Forests. Brunton, Jolee & Loyst, Ken, eds. LC 88-51680. (Illus.). 160p. (Orig.). 1988. 39.95 (*0-685-23081-3*) Watersport Pub.

McPeake, Francis. Pocket Tin Whistle Tutor. (Appletree Pocket Guides Ser.). 72p. 1983. pap. 7.95 (*0-86281-112-0*, Pub. by Appletree Pr) Irish Bks Media.

McPeake, Robert. EC Competition Law in Practice. LC 98-167710. (Inns of Court School of Law Ser.). 229p. 1998. pap. 48.00 (*1-85431-718-0*, 15593, Pub. by Blackstone Pr) Gaunt.

— EC Competition Law in Practice. 2nd ed. 227p. 1999. pap. 50.00 (*1-85431-902-7*, Pub. by Blackstone Pr) Gaunt.

***McPeake, Robert.** EC Competition Law in Practice. 3rd ed. (Inns of Court School of Law Ser.). 241p. 2000. pap. 46.00 (*1-84174-005-5*, Pub. by Blackstone Pr) Gaunt.

McPeck, Philip, ed. see Johnston, Barbara.

McPeek, George, jt. auth. see Masterson, Steve.

McPeek, George, jt. auth. see McGraw, Gerald.

McPeek, James A., jt. auth. see Baldwin, Robert.

McPhail. Big Brown Bear. 20p. (J). 2000. 10.95 (*0-15-202345-3*) Harcourt.

— Harvey Been's Christmas. (J). (ps-3). 2000. write for info. (*0-689-82198-0*) S&S Trade.

— Introduction to Santhali. 1983. 19.95 (*0-8288-8468-4*) Fr & Eur.

— Santa's Scholar. (Illus.). (J). 1997. pap. 5.95 (*0-316-58846-6*) Little.

McPhail, Aubrey, jt. ed. see McLuckie, Craig W.

McPhail, Beverly, jt. auth. see Stout, Karen D.

McPhail, Bob. The Tijuana Handbook & Souvenir Guide. 48p. 1996. reprint ed. pap. text 3.00 (*0-9646406-0-0*) CF Pub CA.

McPhail, Brenda M., ed. NAFTA Now! The Changing Political Economy of North America. 145p. (C). 1995. pap. 19.50 (*0-8191-9702-5*); lib. bdg. 48.00 (*0-8191-9701-7*) U Pr of Amer.

McPhail, Clark. Myth of the Madding Crowd. (Social Institutions & Social Change Ser.). 295p. (Orig.). 1991. pap. text 27.95 (*0-202-30375-6*) Aldine de Gruyter.

— The Myth of the Madding Crowd. (Social Institutions & Social Change Ser.). 295p. 1991. lib. bdg. 51.95 (*0-202-30424-8*) Aldine de Gruyter.

McPhail, David. The Bear's Toothache. (Illus.). 32p. (J). (gr. k-3). 1988. pap. 5.95 (*0-316-56325-0*, Joy St Bks) Little.

— The Bear's Toothache. (J). 1988. 11.15 (*0-606-12180-3*, Pub. by Turtleback) Demco.

— The Bear's Toothache. unabridged ed. (Illus.). (J). (gr. k-2). 1986. reprint ed. 24.95 incl. audio (*0-87499-081-5*); reprint ed. pap. 15.95 incl. audio (*0-87499-080-7*) Live Oak Media.

— The Bear's Toothache, 4 bks., Set. unabridged ed. (Illus.). (J). (gr. k-2). 1986. reprint ed. pap. 33.95 incl. audio (*0-87499-082-3*) Live Oak Media.

— Big Brown Bear. LC 98-15568. (Green Light Readers Ser.). (Illus.). 20p. (J). 1999. pap. 3.95 (*0-15-201999-5*, Gulliver Bks) Harcourt.

***McPhail, David.** A Bug, a Bear & a Boy. (Hello, Reader! Ser.). (J). (ps-1). 1998. 8.70 (*0-606-13231-7*, Pub. by Turtleback) Demco.

McPhail, David. A Bug, a Bear & a Boy Go to School. LC 98-32127. (Hello Reader! Ser.: Level 1). (Illus.). 32p. (J). (gr. k-2). 1999. pap. 3.99 (*0-439-07783-4*, Pub. by Scholastic Inc) Penguin Putnam.

— Can Do Pigs. 32p. 1999. pap. 5.99 (*0-14-056256-7*, PuffinBks) Peng Put Young Read.

— David McPhail's Animals A to Z. (J). (ps-1). 1989. pap. 2.50 (*0-590-40347-8*) Scholastic Inc.

— The Day the Dog Said, "Cock-a-Doodle Doo!" LC 95-30063. (Hello Reader! Ser.: Level 2). (Illus.). (J). (gr. 2). 1997. 3.50 (*0-590-73887-9*) Scholastic Inc.

McPhail, David. The Day the Dog Said, "Cock-a-Doodle Doo!" (Hello, Reader! Ser.). 1997. 8.70 (*0-606-11241-3*, Pub. by Turtleback) Demco.

— El Dia Que El Perro Dijo, "Quiquiriqui!" The Day the Dog Said "Cock-A-Doodle-Doo", 1 vol. (SPA., Illus.). 32p. (gr. k-2). 1999. pap. text 3.99 (*0-439-07164-X*) Scholastic Inc.

McPhail, David. Drawing Lessons from a Bear. LC 98-54966. (Illus.). 32p. (J). (ps-3). 2000. 14.95 (*0-316-56345-5*) Little.

— Ed & Me. LC 86-3175. (Illus.). 32p. (J). (ps-3). 1996. pap. 5.00 (*0-15-201269-9*) Harcourt.

M

An Asterisk (*) at the beginning of an entry indicates that the title is appearing for the first time.

— Edward & the Pirates. LC 95-38451. (Santa's Book of Names Ser.). (Illus.). 32p. (J). (gr. k-3). 1997. 15.95 (*0-316-56344-7*) Little.

— Edward & the Pirates. (J). (ps-3). 1997. 15.95 (*0-316-58845-8*) Little.

— Edward in the Forest of Long Ago 2002. write for info. (*0-316-56391-9*) Little.

— Emma's Pet. (Illus.). (J). (ps-2). pap. 15.95 incl. audio (*0-87499-106-4*) Live Oak Media.

— Emma's Pet. 1999. pap. 18.99 (*0-14-055290-1*) NAL.

— Emma's Pet, Set. (Illus.). (J). (ps-2). pap., teacher ed. 31.95 incl. audio (*0-87499-108-0*) Live Oak Media.

— Farm Morning. LC 84-19167. (Illus.). 32p. (J). (ps-3). 1985. 15.95 (*0-15-227299-2*, Harcourt Child Bks) Harcourt.

— Farm Morning. D'Andrade, Diane, ed. LC 84-19167. (Illus.). 32p. (J). (ps-3). 1991. pap. 7.00 (*0-15-227300-X*, Harcourt Child Bks) Harcourt.

— First Flight. (Illus.). 32p. (J). (ps-3). 1991. reprint ed. pap. 5.95 (*0-316-56332-3*, Joy St Bks) Little.

— Fix-It. (Illus.). (J). (gr. k-3). 1988. pap. 15.95 incl. audio (*0-87499-083-1*) Live Oak Media.

— Fix-It, 4 bks., Set. (Illus.). (J). (gr. k-3). 1988. pap., student ed. 31.95 incl. audio (*0-87499-085-8*) Live Oak Media.

— Fix It All. (Illus.). (J). (ps). 1992. pap. 4.99 (*0-14-054752-5*, PuffinBks) Peng Put Young Read.

M

*__McPhail, David.__ A Girl, a Goat & a Goose. (Hello Reader! Ser.). (Illus.). 32p. (J). (ps-1). 2000. pap. 3.99 (*0-439-09978-1*) Scholastic Inc.

McPhail, David. Goldilocks & the Three Bears. LC 93-43992. (David McPhail's Favorite Tales Ser.). (Illus.). 32p. (J). (ps-k). 1995. bds. 4.95 (*0-590-48117-7*) Scholastic Inc.

— Great Race, Level 2. (Hello, Reader! Ser.). (J). 1997. 8.70 (*0-606-12957-X*, Pub. by Turtleback) Demco.

— In Flight with David McPhail. LC 95-40132. (Creative Sparks Ser.). (Illus.). 41p. (Orig.). (J). 1996. 15.95 (*0-435-08132-2*, 08132) Heinemann.

— Little Red Riding Hood. LC 93-43990. (David McPhail's Favorite Tales Ser.). (Illus.). 32p. (J). (ps-k). 1995. bds. 4.95 (*0-590-48116-9*) Scholastic Inc.

— Lost! (Illus.). 32p. (J). (gr. k-3). 1993. pap. 5.95 (*0-316-56336-6*, Joy St Bks) Little.

— Lost, Vol. 1. (Illus.). (J). (ps-3). 1990. 14.95 (*0-316-56329-3*, Joy St Bks) Little.

— Mole Music. LC 98-21318. (Illus.). 40p. (J). (gr. k-5). 1999. 15.95 (*0-8050-2819-6*) H Holt & Co.

— The Party. 1990. 14.95 (*0-316-88860-5*) Little.

— The Party. (J). (ps-4). 1990. 14.95 (*0-316-56330-7*, Joy St Bks) Little.

— Pig Pig Gets a Job. LC 89-25606. (Pig Pig Ser.). (Illus.). 24p. (J). (ps-3). 1990. 14.99 (*0-525-44619-2*, Dutton Child) Peng Put Young Read.

— Pig Pig Grows Up. (Pig Pig Ser.). (J). (ps-3). 1992. pap. 5.99 (*0-14-054779-7*) NAL.

— Pig Pig Grows Up. unabridged ed. (Pig Pig Ser.). (Illus.). (J). (ps-3). 1985. pap. 15.95 incl. audio (*0-941078-94-9*) Live Oak Media.

— Pig Pig Grows Up, 4 bks., Set. unabridged ed. (Pig Pig Ser.). (Illus.). (J). (ps-3). 1985. pap., teacher ed. 31.95 incl. audio (*0-941078-95-7*) Live Oak Media.

— Pigs Ahoy! LC 95-17753. (Illus.). 32p. (J). (ps-2). 1995. 14.99 (*0-525-45334-2*, Dutton Child) Peng Put Young Read.

— Pigs Ahoy. 32p. (J). (gr. 3-7). 1998. pap. 5.99 (*0-14-055819-5*) Viking Penguin.

*__McPhail, David.__ The Puddle. (Illus.). 32p. (J). (ps-k). 2000. pap. 4.95 (*0-374-46030-2*) FS&G.

McPhail, David. Santa's Book of Names. LC 92-37279. (Illus.). 32p. (J). (ps-3). 1993. 14.95 (*0-316-56335-8*, Joy St Bks) Little.

— Santa's Book of Names. (Illus.). 32p. (J). (gr. k-3). 1997. reprint ed. pap. 5.95 (*0-316-11534-7*) Little.

— Sisters. LC 84-3775. (Illus.). 32p. (J). (ps-3). 1984. 14.00 (*0-15-275319-2*, Harcourt Child Bks) Harcourt.

— Sisters. LC 84-3775. (Illus.). 32p. (J). (ps-3). 1990. pap. 5.00 (*0-15-275320-6*, Voyager Bks) Harcourt.

*__McPhail, David.__ Teddy Bear. 2001. text 16.95 (*0-8050-6414-1*) St Martin.

McPhail, David. Those Can-Do Pigs. LC 96-14689. (Illus.). 32p. (J). (ps-4). 1996. 14.99 (*0-525-45495-0*, Dutton Child) Peng Put Young Read.

— Tinker & Tom & the Star Baby. LC 96-45439. (Illus.). 32p. (J). (gr. k-3). 1998. 14.95 (*0-316-56349-8*) Little.

*__McPhail, David.__ Tinker & Tom & the Star Baby. 32p. (J). (ps-3). 2000. pap. 5.95 (*0-316-56389-7*) Little.

McPhail, David. Train. (J). (ps-3). 1990. write for info. (*0-318-66965-X*, Joy St Bks) Little.

— Where Can an Elephant Hide? 1979. write for info. (*0-385-12941-6*) Doubleday.

McPhail, David, jt. auth. see Austin, Margot.

*__McPhail, David M.__ Big Pig & Little Pig. LC 00-9725. (Green Light Readers Ser.). (Illus.). (J). 2001. write for info. (*0-15-216510-X*) Harcourt.

McPhail, David M. A Bug, a Bear & a Boy. LC 97-26877. (Hello Reader! Ser.). (Illus.). 32p. (J). 1998. 3.50 (*0-590-14904-0*) Scholastic Inc.

— Cerdos a Montones, Cerdos a Granel! Orig. Title: Pigs Aplenty, Pigs Galore!. 1996. 10.19 (*0-606-10386-4*, Pub. by Turtleback) Demco.

— The Day the Sheep Showed Up. LC 97-27355. (Hello Reader! Ser.). (J). 1998. 3.50 (*0-590-84910-7*) Scholastic Inc.

*__McPhail, David M.__ The Day the Sheep Showed Up. (Hello, Reader! Ser.). (J). 1998. 9.44 (*0-606-13318-6*) Turtleback.

McPhail, David M. Ed & Me. LC 86-3175. 1996. 10.20 (*0-606-09227-7*, Pub. by Turtleback) Demco.

Mcphail, David M. First Flight. 1987. 10.15 (*0-606-04918-5*, Pub. by Turtleback) Demco.

*__McPhail, David M.__ Girl, a Goat & a Goose. (Hello, Reader! Ser.). (Illus.). (J). 2000. 9.44 (*0-606-18875-4*) Turtleback.

McPhail, David M. The Glerp. LC 94-20298. (Illus.). 32p. (J). 1994. pap. 5.95 (*0-382-24670-5*); lib. bdg. 15.95 (*0-382-24668-3*) Silver Burdett Pr.

— The Great Race. LC 97-2244. (Hello Reader! Ser.). (Illus.). (J). (gr. k-2). 1997. 3.50 (*0-590-84909-3*) Scholastic Inc.

— In the Summer I Go Fishing. pap. 5.00 (*0-201-04612-1*) Addison-Wesley.

— Lost. (J). 1990. 11.15 (*0-606-05916-4*, Pub. by Turtleback) Demco.

— Pigs Ahoy! 1998. 11.19 (*0-606-13705-X*, Pub. by Turtleback) Demco.

— Pigs Aplenty, Pigs Galore! (Illus.). 32p. (J). 1996. pap. 5.99 (*0-14-055313-4*) NAL.

— Pigs Aplenty, Pigs Galore! LC 92-27986. (Illus.). (J). (ps-2). 1993. 15.99 (*0-525-45079-3*, Dutton Child) Peng Put Young Read.

— Pigs Aplenty, Pigs Galore! (J). 1996. 11.19 (*0-606-10904-8*, Pub. by Turtleback) Demco.

— The Puddle. LC 97-10872. 32p. (J). (ps-k). 1998. 15.00 (*0-374-36148-7*) FS&G.

— Santa' Book of Names. 1997. 11.15 (*0-606-13758-0*, Pub. by Turtleback) Demco.

— Sisters. 1984. 10.20 (*0-606-04538-4*, Pub. by Turtleback) Demco.

*__McPhail, David M.__ Sled: And Other Fox & Rabbit Stories. (First Flight Bks.). (Illus.). 32p. (J). 1999. lib. bdg. 9.95 (*1-55041-515-8*) Fitzhenry & W Ltd.

McPhail, David M. Yesterday I Lost a Sneaker (And Found the Great Goob Sick) LC 94-22862. (Illus.). (J). 1995. 13.95 (*0-382-24906-2*); pap. text 5.95 (*0-382-24907-0*); lib. bdg. 15.95 (*0-382-24905-4*) Silver Burdett Pr.

*__McPhail, David M. & O'Connor, John.__ The Sled: Fox & Rabbit Stories. (First Flight Bks.). (Illus.). 32p. (J). (ps). 1999. pap. 3.95 (*1-55041-517-4*) Fitzhenry & W Ltd.

McPhail, David M., jt. auth. see MacDonald, Steven.

McPhail, Doug, jt. auth. see Fletcher, David C.

*__McPhail, Helen.__ Long Silence: Civilian Life under the German Occupation of Northern. 256p. 2000. text 59.50 (*1-86064-479-1*) St Martin.

— On the Trail of the Poets of the Great War: Edmund Blunden. (Battleground Europe Ser.). 1999. pap. text. write for info. (*0-85052-678-7*) Pen & Sword Bks Ltd.

McPhail, Helen & Guest, Philip. Wilfred Owen. 1999. pap. 16.95 (*0-85052-614-0*, Pub. by Leo Cooper) Combined Pub.

McPhail, Helen, tr. see Becker, Annette.

McPhail, Helen, tr. see French Ramblers Association Staff.

McPhail, Helen, tr. see Gimpel, Jean.

McPhail, Helen, tr. see Laidi, Zaki, ed.

McPhail, Helen, tr. see Noiriel, Gerard.

McPhail, Helen, tr. see Prost, Antoine.

McPhail, Ian. How to Avoid California Probate & Estate Taxes: Preserving Your Estate for Your Heirs. 200p. (Orig.). 1992. pap. 16.95 (*1-55958-178-6*) Prima Pub.

— Planning Your Will with Your Family in Mind: How Your Estate Planning Decisions Will Affect the Ones You Love. LC 93-17734. 320p. 1993. pap. 14.95 (*1-55958-364-9*) Prima Pub.

McPhail, Inger C. Deer. LC 98-74369. (Illus.). 64p. 1998. pap. 10.00 (*0-935132-26-0*) C H Fairfax.

Mcphail, Jannetta, jt. auth. see Kerr, Janet Ross.

McPhail, Kathryn & Davy, Aidan. Integrating Social Concerns into Private Sector Decisionmaking: A Review of Corporate Practices in the Mining, Oil, & Gas Sectors. LC 98-9991. (Discussion Paper Ser.: No. 384). 120p. 1998. pap. 22.00 (*0-8213-4188-X*, 14188) World Bank.

McPhail, Mac. Emma's Pet. (J). (ps). 1993. pap. 4.99 (*0-14-054749-5*, Dutton Child) Peng Put Young Read.

McPhail, Mark L. The Rhetoric of Racism. LC 93-8188. 170p. (C). 1994. lib. bdg. 41.00 (*0-8191-9180-9*) U Pr of Amer.

— Zen in the Art of Rhetoric: An Inquiry into Coherence. LC 95-15882. (SUNY Series in Speech Communication). 220p. (C). 1995. text 57.50 (*0-7914-2803-6*); pap. text 18.95 (*0-7914-2804-4*) State U NY Pr.

McPhail, Thomas L. Electronic Colonialism. rev. ed. (Library of Social Research: Vol. 126). 256p. (Orig.). 1987. pap. text 26.00 (*0-8039-2731-2*) Sage.

— Electronic Colonialism. 2nd rev. ed. (Library of Social Research: Vol. 126). 256p. (Orig.). 1987. text 59.95 (*0-8039-2730-4*) Sage.

— Electronic Colonialism: The Future of International Broadcasting & Communication. 2nd rev. ed. LC 86-6635. (Sage Library of Social Research: No. 126). 311p. reprint ed. pap. 96.50 (*0-8357-4777-8*, 203771400009) Bks Demand.

McPhail, Virginia, ed. see James, Earl.

*__McPhail, Weldon.__ Drug Control: Information on High Intensity Drug Trafficking Areas Program. (Illus.). 51p. 1999. pap. text 20.00 (*0-7881-8278-1*) DIANE Pub.

— Drug Control: INS & Customs Can Do More to Prevent Drug-Related Employee Corruption. (Illus.). 64p. (C). 1999. pap. text 20.00 (*0-7881-8423-7*) DIANE Pub.

McPhail, Weldon. Drug Control: Observations on Elements of the Federal Drug Control Strategy. (Illus.). 68p. 1999. reprint ed. pap. text 20.00 (*0-7881-7729-X*) DIANE Pub.

McPharlin, Linda H. Privacy Rights of Employees. Hagelstein, Marie, ed. 62p. 1994. pap. text 20.00 (*0-88124-754-5*, BU-32600) Cont Ed Bar-CA.

McPharlin, Michalene, jt. auth. see Rumwell, Claudia.

McPharlin, Michalene, jt. auth. see Rumwell, Claudia B.

McPharlin, Michalene, jt. ed. see Rumwell, Claudia B.

McPharlin, Michalene, jt. ed. see Rumwell, Claudia.

McPharlin, Paul. A Repertory of Marionette Plays. LC 97-26982. (Studies in Puppetry: No. 2). 382p. 1997. text 39.95 (*0-7734-8575-9*) E Mellen.

McPhatter, Thomas H. Caught in the Middle: A Dichotomy of an African American Man (They Called Him Troublemaker) (Illus.). xii, 452p. (Orig.). (C). 1993. write for info. (*0-9634658-0-5*); pap. 24.95 (*0-9634658-1-3*) Audacity Pubns.

McPhaul, John. What Is Child Support? No. 3: 25 Definitions Your Children Want to Know About. McPhaul, Lisa, ed. 25p. (YA). (gr. 4-9). Date not set. pap. text. write for info. (*0-9655777-0-8*) Small Grp Cnslt.

McPhaul, Lisa, ed. see McPhaul, John.

McPhedran, Pete. Microsoft Exchange Server Survival Guide. LC 96-67960. 840p. 1996. 49.99 (*0-672-30890-8*) Sams.

McPhedran, R. C., jt. auth. see Melrose, Donald B.

McPhee. Pathophysiology of Disease: An Introduction to Clinical Medicine. 3rd ed. (Illus.). 662p. (C). 1999. pap. 39.95 (*0-8385-8160-9*, Apple Lange Med) McGraw.

McPhee, Allan. Economic Revolution in British West Africa. 322p. 1971. reprint ed. 45.00 (*0-7146-2766-6*, Pub. by F Cass Pubs) Intl Spec Bk.

*__McPhee, Andrew T.__ AIDS. LC 99-45288. 2000. 24.00 (*0-531-11779-0*) Watts.

— Sleep & Dreams. LC 00-28971. 2001. write for info. (*0-531-11735-9*) Watts.

McPhee, Arthur G. Friendship Evangelism: The Caring Way to Share Your Faith. 1979. pap. 6.70 (*0-310-37311-5*, 11262P) Zondervan.

McPhee, Carol A. Staying Under. LC 97-43626. 224p. 1998. 22.95 (*1-57601-056-2*) McPhee.

McPhee, Charles. Stop Sleeping Through Your Dreams: A Guide to Awakening Consciousness During Dream Sleep. LC 95-22519. 304p. 1995. pap. 12.95 (*0-8050-2515-4*) H Holt & Co.

McPhee, Colin. The Balinese Wajang Koelit & Its Music. LC 77-86983. 56p. reprint ed. 32.50 (*0-404-16765-9*) AMS Pr.

*__McPhee, Colin.__ A House in Bali. 213p. 2000. pap. 19.95 (*962-593-629-7*, Pub. by Periplus) Tuttle Pubng.

McPhee, Colin. A House in Bali. LC 77-86965. (Illus.). reprint ed. 32.50 (*0-404-16766-7*) AMS Pr.

McPhee, Ian, jt. auth. see Buttrey, T. V.

McPhee, James. Blood Quest. (Survival Two Thousand Ser.: No. 1). 1991. mass mkt. 3.50 (*0-373-63201-0*) Harlequin Bks.

— Frozen Fire. (Survival Two Thousand Ser.: No. 03). 1991. per. 3.50 (*0-373-63203-7*) Harlequin Bks.

— Renegade War. (Survival Two Thousand Ser.: No. 2). 1991. per. 3.50 (*0-373-63202-9*) Harlequin Bks.

McPhee, Jenny, tr. see Maurensig, Paolo.

McPhee, John. Annals of the Former World. LC 97-39660. (Illus.). 696p. 1998. text 35.00 (*0-374-10520-0*) FS&G.

— Annals of the Former World, 2 vols. (Illus.). 696p. 2000. pap. 17.00 (*0-374-51873-4*) FS&G.

— Annals of the Former World, 2 bks. limited ed. 1983. text 75.00 (*0-374-10519-7*) FS&G.

— Assembling California. 1993. text 21.00 (*0-374-10645-2*) FS&G.

— Assembling California. 224p. 1994. pap. 13.00 (*0-374-52393-2*) FS&G.

— Basin & Range. (Illus.). 216p. (C). 1981. text 23.00 (*0-374-10914-1*) FS&G.

— Basin & Range. LC 80-28679. (Illus.). 216p. (C). 1982. pap. 10.00 (*0-374-51690-1*) FS&G.

— Coming into the Country. 1982. mass mkt. 4.95 (*0-553-25527-4*) Bantam.

— Coming into the Country. LC 77-12249. 438p. 1977. 22.95 (*0-374-12645-3*) FS&G.

— Coming into the Country. 272p. 1991. pap. 15.00 (*0-374-52287-1*) FS&G.

— The Control of Nature. 272p. 1990. pap. 12.00 (*0-374-52259-6*) FS&G.

*__McPhee, John.__ The Control of Nature. large type ed. LC 99-42399. (Core Ser.). 1999. 26.95 (*0-7838-8774-4*, G K Hall & Co) Mac Lib Ref.

McPhee, John. The Crofter & the Laird. LC 77-113774. (Illus.). 160p. 1970. 18.95 (*0-374-13192-9*) FS&G.

— The Crofter & the Laird. LC 77-113774. (Illus.). 160p. 1992. pap. 12.00 (*0-374-51465-8*) FS&G.

— The Curve of Binding Energy. 224p. 1974. 19.95 (*0-374-13373-5*) FS&G.

— The Curve of Binding Energy. 236p. 1994. pap. 11.00 (*0-374-51598-0*) FS&G.

— The Deltoid Pumpkin Seed. 192p. 1973. 18.95 (*0-374-13781-1*) FS&G.

— The Deltoid Pumpkin Seed. 186p. 1992. pap. 11.00 (*0-374-51635-9*) FS&G.

— Encounters with the Archdruid. 256p. 1971. 25.00 (*0-374-14822-8*) FS&G.

— Encounters with the Archdruid. 256p. 1977. pap. 13.00 (*0-374-51431-3*) FS&G.

— Giving Good Weight. (Illus.). 261p. 1979. text 19.95 (*0-374-16306-5*) FS&G.

— Giving Good Weight. (Illus.). 264p. 1994. pap. 14.00 (*0-374-51600-6*) FS&G.

— The Headmaster: Frank L. Boyden of Deerfield. 149p. 1966. text 16.95 (*0-374-16860-1*) FS&G.

— The Headmaster: Frank L. Boyden of Deerfield. 148p. 1992. pap. 10.00 (*0-374-51496-8*) FS&G.

— Heirs of General Practice. 120p. 1986. pap. 8.00 (*0-374-51974-9*) FS&G.

— Heirs of General Practice. 1994. 20.00 (*0-8446-6733-1*) Peter Smith.

— In Suspect Terrain. LC 82-21031. (Illus.). 210p. 1983. text 23.50 (*0-374-17650-7*) FS&G.

— In Suspect Terrain. LC 82-21031. (Illus.). 210p. 1984. pap. 14.00 (*0-374-51794-0*) FS&G.

— Irons in the Fire. LC 96-32358. 216p. 1997. text 22.00 (*0-374-17726-0*) FS&G.

— Irons in the Fire. 224p. 1998. pap. text 12.00 (*0-374-52545-5*, Noonday) FS&G.

*__McPhee, John.__ Irons in the Fire. 1999. 24.50 (*0-8446-6988-1*) Peter Smith.

McPhee, John. The John McPhee Reader. Howarth, William L., ed. 385p. 1976. text 25.00 (*0-374-17992-1*) FS&G.

— The John McPhee Reader. Howarth, William L., ed. 385p. 1982. pap. 15.00 (*0-374-51719-3*) FS&G.

— Levels of the Game. 160p. 1969. text 18.95 (*0-374-18568-9*) FS&G.

— Levels of the Game. 152p. 1979. pap. 9.00 (*0-374-51526-3*) FS&G.

— Looking for a Ship. 242p. 1990. 18.95 (*0-374-19077-1*) FS&G.

— Looking for a Ship. 248p. 1991. pap. 12.00 (*0-374-52319-3*) FS&G.

— Oranges. LC 66-20125. 149p. 1967. 20.00 (*0-374-22688-1*) FS&G.

— Oranges. LC 66-20125. 152p. 1975. pap. 10.00 (*0-374-51297-3*) FS&G.

— Pieces of the Frame. 320p. 1975. 19.95 (*0-374-23281-4*) FS&G.

— Pieces of the Frame. LC 75-4960. 320p. 1979. pap. 13.00 (*0-374-51498-4*) FS&G.

— The Pine Barrens. LC 67-22439. (Illus.). 157p. 1978. 27.50 (*0-374-23360-8*); pap. 11.00 (*0-374-51442-9*) FS&G.

— La Place de la Concorde Suisse. LC 83-27466. 152p. 1984. pap. 12.00 (*0-374-51932-3*) FS&G.

— The Ransom of Russian Art. LC 94-14723. 1994. 20.00 (*0-374-24682-3*) FS&G.

— The Ransom of Russian Art. (Illus.). 192p. 1996. pap. 12.00 (*0-374-52450-5*) FS&G.

— Rising from the Plains. 224p. 1986. 23.00 (*0-374-25082-0*) FS&G.

— Rising from the Plains. 224p. 1987. pap. 11.00 (*0-374-52065-8*) FS&G.

— A Roomful of Hovings & Other Profiles. LC 68-23746. 250p. 1969. 19.95 (*0-374-25208-4*) FS&G.

— A Roomful of Hovings & Other Profiles. LC 68-23746. 256p. 1979. pap. 11.00 (*0-374-51501-8*) FS&G.

— The Second John McPhee Reader. Strachan, Patricia, ed. & selected by by. LC 95-33519. 416p. 1996. pap. 14.00 (*0-374-52463-7*) FS&G.

— Sense of Where You Are. rev. ed. 1999. 25.00 (*0-374-26099-0*) FS&G.

— A Sense of Where You Are: A Profile of William Warren Bradley. (Illus.). 172p. 1978. pap. 12.00 (*0-374-51485-2*) FS&G.

— A Sense of Where You Are: A Profile of William Warren Bradley. 2nd ed. (Illus.). 206p. 1978. 19.95 (*0-374-26093-1*) FS&G.

— A Sense of Where You Are: Bill Bradley at Princeton. rev. ed. 1999. pap. text 12.00 (*0-374-52689-3*) FS&G.

— The Survival of the Bark Canoe. LC 75-26558. (Illus.). 146p. 1975. 18.95 (*0-374-27207-7*) FS&G.

— The Survival of the Bark Canoe. (Illus.). 132p. 1982. pap. 10.00 (*0-374-51693-6*) FS&G.

— Table of Contents. 293p. 1985. 19.95 (*0-374-27241-7*) FS&G.

— Table of Contents. 294p. 1986. pap. 14.00 (*0-374-52008-9*) FS&G.

McPhee, John, jt. auth. see Rowell, Galen A.

McPhee, John, ed. see Una Publicacion Pastoral Redentorista Staff.

McPhee, John, ed. see Van Valkenburgh, A. Richard.

McPhee, Jonathan & Burakoff, Suzanne. The Nutcracker: Story & Music. (Boston Ballet Presents Ser.: Vol. 1). (Illus.). 32p. (Orig.). (J). (gr. k-6). 1996. pap. 12.95 (*0-9640792-1-6*) Hare & Hatter.

McPhee, Kevin. Reflections by Kevin. 42p. (Orig.). 1996. pap. 14.95 (*0-9653332-0-5*) Olive or Twist.

McPhee, Laura, jt. auth. see Beahan, Virginia.

McPhee, Mark S., et al. Key References in Gastroenterology: An Annotated Guide. LC 82-14661. (Key References in Internal Medicine Ser.). 127p. reprint ed. pap. 39.40 (*0-7837-2563-9*, 204272200006) Bks Demand.

McPhee, Marnie. Western Oregon: Portrait of the Land & Its People. LC 87-19341. (Oregon Geographic Ser.: No. 2). (Illus.). 104p. (Orig.). 1987. pap. 6.95 (*0-938314-34-3*) Am Wrld Geog.

McPhee, Martha. Bright Angel Time. LC 98-15053. 256p. 1999. pap. 12.00 (*0-15-600586-7*, Harvest Bks) Harcourt.

*__McPhee, Martha.__ Girls: Ordinary Girls & Their Extraorinary Pursuits. 192p. 2000. 30.00 (*0-375-50167-3*) Random.

McPhee, Norma H., et al. Sensitivity & Awareness: A Guide for Developing Understanding among Children. 3rd rev. ed. LC 97-42840. (Illus.). 96p. 1998. pap. text 14.95 (*0-944727-34-4*, Turtle Books) Jason & Nordic Pubs.

McPhee, Penelope O., jt. auth. see Schulke, Flip.

McPhee, Peter. Carnival: A Scream in High Park Reader. 216p. pap. 18.99 (*1-895837-38-3*) Insomniac.

— The Politics of Rural Life: Political Mobilization in the French Countryside 1846-1852. (Illus.). 320p. 1992. text 75.00 (*0-19-820225-3*) OUP.

— Revolution & Environment in Southern France: Peasants, Lords & Murder in the Corbieres, 1780-1830. LC 98-51333. (Illus.). 288p. 1999. text 75.00 (*0-19-820717-4*) OUP.

McPhee, Robert D. & Tompkins, Phillip K., eds. Organizational Communication: Traditional Themes & New Directions. LC 85-14488. (Sage Annual Reviews of Communications Research Ser.: No. 13). 296p. 1985. reprint ed. pap. 91.80 (*0-608-01189-4*, 205948700001) Bks Demand.

McPhee, Shamus, compiled by. Our Destiny: A Treasury of Travellers Verse. 128p. 1998. pap. 24.00 (*1-898218-82-X*) St Mut.

An Asterisk (*) at the beginning of an entry indicates that the title is appearing for the first time.

McPhee, Stephen J. & Ganong. Pathophysiology of Disease: An Introduction to Clinical Medicine. 2nd ed. 624p. (C). 1997. pap. text 36.95 (*0-8385-7678-8*, A-7678-4, Apple Lange Med) McGraw.

***McPhee, Stephen J., et al.** CMDT 2000 on CD-Rom: Current Medical Diagnosis & Treatment. 2nd ed. 2000. cd-rom 99.95 (*0-8385-1559-2*) McGraw.

McPhee, William N. & Glaser, William A., eds. Public Opinion & Congressional Elections. LC 80-29534. (Illus.). 326p. 1981. reprint ed. lib. bdg. 65.00 (*0-313-22779-9*, MCOP, Greenwood Pr) Greenwood.

McPheeters, Annie L. Library Service in Black & White: Some Personal Recollections, 1921-1980. LC 88-1979. (Illus.). 184p. 1988. 27.50 (*0-8108-2104-4*) Scarecrow.

McPheeters, D. W. Camilo Jose Cela. LC 74-75876. (Twayne's World Authors Ser.). 1969. lib. bdg. 20.95 (*0-8057-2204-1*) Irvington.

— Estudios Humanisticos Sobre La "Celestina" 110p. 1984. 20.00 (*0-916379-09-4*) Scripta.

McPheeters, D. W., ed. Guia de Nuevos Temas De Literatura Espanola. 415p. 1972. pap. 9.00 (*0-87535-118-2*) Hispanic Soc.

McPheeters, Kenneth L., jt. auth. see Dorsey, R. Stephen.

McPhelimy, Lynn. In the Checklist of Life: A Working Book to Help You Live & Leave Life. 2nd rev. ed. McPhelimy, Martin, ed. (Illus.). 140p. 1997. pap. 19.95 (*0-9657843-5-5*) AAIP.

McPhelimy, Martin, ed. see McPhelimy, Lynn.

McPheron, Bruce A. & Steck, Gary A., eds. Fruit Fly Pests: A World Assessment of Their Biology & Management. (Illus.). 608p. 1996. boxed set 139.95 (*1-57444-014-4*) St Lucie Pr.

McPheron, Bruce A., jt. auth. see Chung Kim.

McPheron, William. Bibliography of Contemporary American Fiction, 1945-1988: An Annotated Checklist. 190p. 1989. lib. bdg. 42.95 (*0-313-27702-8*) Greenwood.

— Bibliography of Contemporary American Poetry, 1945-1985. 72p. 1986. lib. bdg. 42.95 (*0-313-27703-6*) Greenwood.

— Edward Dorn. LC 87-73498. (Western Writers Ser.: No. 85). (Illus.). 53p. (Orig.). 1988. pap. 4.95 (*0-88430-084-6*) Boise St U W Writ Ser.

— Gilbert Sorrentino: A Descriptive Bibliography. LC 90-3674. (Bibliography Ser.: No. 2). (Illus.). 240p. 1991. 49.95 (*0-916583-67-8*) Dalkey Arch.

McPheron, William & Sheppard, Jocelyn. Bibliography of Contemporary American Fiction, 1945-1988: An Annotated Checklist. LC 88-13522. (Literary Bibliographies Ser.). 190 p. 1989. 39.50 (*0-88736-167-6*) Mecklermedia.

McPherran, Mark L. The Religion of Socrates. LC 95-45059. 1996. 35.00 (*0-271-01581-0*) Pa St U Pr.

— The Religion of Socrates. 366p. 1999. pap. 19.95 (*0-271-01829-1*) Pa St U Pr.

McPherren, Charlotte. Love & Fortune. LC 94-147303. 368p. (Orig.). 1994. pap. text, mass mkt. 4.50 (*0-8439-3560-X*) Dorchester Pub Co.

McPherron, Alan & Srejovic, Dragoslav, eds. Divostin & the Neolithic of Central Serbia. LC 87-83523. (Ethnology Monographs: No. 10). (Illus.). xiv, 492p. 1988. ring bd., boxed set 56.00 (*0-945428-00-6*) Ethnology Monographs.

***McPherron, Shannon P. & Roth, Barbara J.** Virtual Dig: A Simulated Archaeological Excavation of a Middle Paleolithic Site in France. LC 99-17296. 160p. 1999. pap. text 29.95 incl. audio compact disk (*0-7674-0245-6*) Mayfield Pub.

McPherson. How to Break the Poverty Syndrome. 1995. pap. 8.00 (*0-927936-61-5*); pap. text 8.00 (*0-927936-48-8*) Vincom Pubng Co.

***McPherson.** Introduction to Neuroscience for Occupational Therapy. 2001. pap. 44.00 (*0 7693 0035 9*) Thomson Learn.

McPherson. Plain English Please. 5th ed. 1987. teacher ed. 18.12 (*0-07-555049-0*) McGraw.

— Tietz Clinical Guide to Lab Tests. 4th ed. (C). 1999. pap. text. write for info. (*0-7216-7975-7*, W B Saunders Co) Harcrt Hlth Sci Grp.

McPherson, jt. auth. see Spearman, Charles E.

McPherson, Alan. Fifty Nature Walks in Southern Illinois. (Illus.). 300p. 1993. pap. text 13.95 (*0-9627422-3-6*) Cache River Pr.

— Indian Names in Indiana. 1993. pap. 12.50 (*0-9636978-0-3*) A McPherson.

— Nature Walks in Northern Indiana. Strickholm, Alfred, ed. LC 97-105665. (Illus.). 496p. (Orig.). 1996. pap. 15.95 (*0-9628469-1-0*) Hoosier Chap-Sierra Club.

— Nature Walks in Orange County. (Illus.). 200p. (Orig.). 1990. pap. 9.95 (*0-939919-09-5*) Bear Flag Bks.

— Nature Walks in Southern Indiana. Strickholm, Alfred, ed. (Illus.). 416p. (Orig.). 1991. pap. 15.95 (*0-9628469-0-2*) Hoosier Chap-Sierra Club.

— One Hundred Nature Walks in the Missouri Ozarks. (Illus.). 352p. (Orig.). 1997. pap. 17.95 (*1-889899-00-3*) Cache River Pr.

McPherson, Alan & Clark, Sue A. Wild Food Plants of Indiana & Adjacent States. 2nd ed. (Illus.). 215p. 1994. reprint ed. pap. 12.50 (*0-9636978-1-1*) A McPherson.

McPherson, Alan J. Hoosier: Illustrated Origins of Indiana's Sobriquet. (Illus.). 35p. (Orig.). 1996. pap. 5.95 (*0-9636978-2-X*) A McPherson.

McPherson, Alexander. Crystallization of Biological Macromolecules. LC 98-26897. (Illus.). ix, 586 p. (C). 1999. text 97.00 (*0-87969-527-7*) Cold Spring Harbor.

— The History of Faulkner Co., Arkansas 1873-1927. Sperry, Phillip A. & Goss, Joe R., eds. (Illus.). 133p. 1993. reprint ed. 24.95 (*1-56869-010-X*); reprint ed. pap. 17.95 (*1-56869-011-8*) Oldbuck Pr.

— History of the Greenbrier Baptist Association. Sperry, Phillip A., ed. (Illus.). 93p. 1994. reprint ed. 22.95 (*1-56869-008-8*); reprint ed. pap. 14.95 (*1-56869-009-6*) Oldbuck Pr.

— Preparation & Analysis of Protein Crystals. LC 88-32577. 384p. (C). 1989. reprint ed. lib. bdg. 59.00 (*0-89464-355-X*) Krieger.

McPherson, Andrew & Raab, Charles. The Making of Scottish Educational Policy: Government & Secondary Schooling Since 1945. 352p. 1988. 60.00 (*0-85224-515-7*, Pub. by Edinburgh U Pr) Col U Pr.

McPherson, Andrew, jt. auth. see Gow, Lesley.

McPherson, Ann, ed. Women's Problems in General Practice. 3rd ed. LC 92-48910. (Oxford General Practice Ser.: No. 22). 512p. 1993. pap. 39.50 (*0-19-262065-7*) OUP.

McPherson, Ann & Waller, Deborah, eds. Women's Health. 4th ed. LC 97-790. (Oxford General Practice Ser.). (Illus.). 664p. 1997. pap. text 62.50 (*0-19-262750-3*) OUP.

McPherson, Ann, jt. auth. see Austoker, Joan.

McPherson, B. H. The Supreme Court of Queensland: History, Jurisdiction, Procedure. 464p. 1989. boxed set 120.00 (*0-409-49444-5*, Austral, MICHIE) LEXIS Pub.

McPherson, Barry, jt. ed. see Marshall, Victor.

McPherson, Barry D., et al. The Social Significance of Sport: An Introduction to the Sociology of Sport. LC 89-1975. (Illus.). 352p. (C). 1989. text 36.00 (*0-87322-235-0*, BMCPO235) Human Kinetics.

McPherson, Barry D., ed. see Olympic Scientific Congress (1984: Eugene, OR) Sta.

McPherson, Betty. A Mayflower Adventure. (Pocket Tales Ser.: Bk. 1). (Illus.). 32p. (J). (ps-1). 1985. 6.00 (*0-918823-00-5*) Boyce-Pubns.

— A Picnic at Bull Run. (Pocket Tales Ser.: Bk. 3). (Illus.). 40p. (J). (ps-1). 1991. 6.00 (*0-918823-05-6*) Boyce-Pubns.

— The Small Patriot. (Pocket Tales Ser.: Bk. 2). (Illus.). 32p. (J). (ps-1). 1987. 6.00 (*0-918823-01-3*) Boyce-Pubns.

McPherson, Brian. Get It in Writing: A Musicians Guide to Music Law. 352p. 1999. per. 29.95 (*0-7935-6699-1*, 00330239) H Leonard.

McPherson, Bruce & Klein, James. Measure by Measure: A History of New England Conservatory from 1867. (Illus.). 152p. 1995. text 45.00 (*0-9648857-0-0*) New Eng Conser.

McPherson, Bruce R., ed. see DeGrazia, Emilio, et al.

McPherson, C. W. Grace at This Time: Praying the Daily Office. LC 99-34670. 176p. 1999. pap. 16.95 (*0-8192-1784-0*, 5977) Morehouse Pub.

McPherson, Carole, jt. auth. see Post, Jory.

***McPherson, Catriona.** Existence & Truth in Discourse. (Publications of the Philological Society). 250p. 2000. pap. 29.95 (*0-631-22165-4*) Blackwell Pubs.

McPherson, Charles W., jt. ed. see Van Hoosier, G. L., Jr.

McPherson, Christopher. Everything but the Truth. 144p. (Orig.). 1997. pap. 12.95 (*1-55152-035-4*, Pub. by Arsenal Pulp) LPC InBook.

McPherson Co, History Book Committee. Families-Fiction-Facts, McPherson Co. 784p. text 40.00 (*0-9615586-8-7*) Loup Valley.

***McPherson, Conor.** Dublin Carol. 2000. pap. 11.95 (*1-55936-185-9*) Theatre Comm.

McPherson, Conor. I Went Down. 160p. Date not set. pap. 20.95 (*1-85459-393-5*) Theatre Comm.

McPherson, Conor. This Lime Tree Bower. pap. 5.25 (*0-8222-1707-4*) Dramatists Play.

— The Weir. pap. 5.95 (*0-8222-1706-6*) Dramatists Play.

McPherson, Conor. The Weir & Other Plays. LC 99-18988. 240p. 1999. pap. 15.95 (*1-55936-167-0*, Pub. by Theatre Comm) Consort Bk Sales.

McPherson, C.W. Understanding Faith: An Exploration of Christian Theology. LC 98-39096. 176p. 1998. pap. 18.95 (*0-8192-1767-0*) Morehouse Pub.

McPherson, D. Jayne. Afterbeats. Mycue, Edward, ed. (Took Modern Poetry in English Ser.: No. 20). (Illus.). 28p. (Orig.). 1991. pap. 3.00 (*1-879457-19-9*) Norton Coker Pr.

McPherson, Dave & Watson, Derek. A Tale of Two Cities: The Dave McPherson Story. (Illus.). 192p. 1997. 34.95 (*1-85158-879-5*, Pub. by Mainstream Pubng) Trafalgar.

McPherson, David. Shakespeare, Jonson, & the Myth of Venice. LC 89-40722. (Illus.). 160p. 1991. 33.50 (*0-87413-397-1*) U Delaware Pr.

McPherson, David L. Late Potentials of the Auditory System. LC 95-34210. (Evoked Potentials Ser.). 170p. 1995. 39.95 (*1-56593-163-7*, 0473) Thomson Learn.

***McPherson, Debbie.** Ol' Bug Eye Fly. 60p. (J). (gr. 1-4). 2000. pap. 8.99 (*1-57532-268-4*) Press-Tige Pub.

***McPherson, Dell.** My Stepping Stones to Prayer: Prayer Channel. 236p. 1999. pap. 13.00 (*0-7392-0468-8*, PO3784) Morris Pubng.

McPherson, E. & Ashton, D. L. Metric Engineering Drawing Examples. LC TA0175.M3. (Illus.). 69p. (Orig.). reprint ed. pap. 30.00 (*0-608-18149-8*, 203283700081) Bks Demand.

McPherson, E. W. Holcombe. The Holcombes: Nation Builders. (Illus.). 1346p. 1991. reprint ed. pap. 142.50 (*0-8328-1990-5*); reprint ed. lib. bdg. 152.50 (*0-8328-1989-1*) Higginson Bk Co.

McPherson, Ed. The Year 2000: Will Your Information Systems Survive? 650p. 1997. 39.99 (*0-7897-0993-7*) Que.

McPherson, Edward. Handbook of Politics, 12 vols. in 4. LC 72-146558. (Law, Politics & History Ser.). 1973. reprint ed. lib. bdg. 225.00 (*0-306-70030-1*) Da Capo.

— The Political History of the U. S. A. During the Period of Reconstruction. Hyman, Harold & Trefousse, Hans, eds. LC 77-127288. (Studies in American History & Government). 648p. 1973. reprint ed. lib. bdg. 85.00 (*0-306-71206-7*) Da Capo.

— Political History of the United States of America During the Great Rebellion. LC 73-127287. (American Constitutional & Legal History Ser.). 1972. reprint ed. lib. bdg. 75.00 (*0-306-71207-5*) Da Capo.

McPherson, Edwin M. Plant Location Selection Techniques. LC 95-22727. (Illus.). 260p. 1996. 129.00 (*0-8155-1378-X*) Noyes.

***McPherson, Elizabeth.** Exercises for the Microbiology Laboratory. 200p. (C). 1999. spiral bd. 33.95 (*0-7872-6229-3*, 41622901) Kendall-Hunt.

McPherson, Elizabeth & Cowan, Gregory. Plain English Please. 5th ed. 480p. (C). 1986. pap. 43.75 (*0-07-554227-7*) McGraw.

McPherson, Emma S. Reveries of Raleigh. 286p. 1987. 75.00 (*0-942179-02-1*); pap. 35.00 (*0-685-19192-3*) Shelby Hse.

***McPherson, Fiona.** The Memory Key: Unlock the Secrets to Remembering. LC 00-23336. 224p. 2000. pap. 12.99 (*1-56414-470-4*) Career Pr Inc.

***McPherson, Frank.** How to Do Everything with Your Pocket PC & Handheld PC. (Illus.). 512p. 2000. pap. 24.99 (*0-07-212420-2*) McGraw.

McPherson, Gene. When I Am Dictator of the U. S. A. A Plan to Save America. LC 94-185065. 231p. 1994. pap. 9.95 (*0-9640797-0-4*) Mt Adams Media.

McPherson, George & Laramore, Robert D. An Introduction to Electrical Machines & Transformers. 2nd ed. 216p. 1989. pap. text, teacher-ed. 20.75 (*0-471-51929-4*) Wiley.

— An Introduction to Electrical Machines & Transformers. 2nd ed. LC 89-33699. 592p. 1990. text 105.95 (*0-471-63529-4*) Wiley.

McPherson, Geri, jt. auth. see McPherson, John.

McPherson, Geri, ed. see McPherson, John.

McPherson, Gertrude H. Small Town Teacher. LC 71-188349. 259p. 1972. reprint ed. pap. 80.30 (*0-7837-4170-7*, 205901900012) Bks Demand.

McPherson, Gladys R. Harding. Ancestry of Addie Clark Harding, Daughter of Abner Clark Harding, Jr., & Maud McCain. (Illus.). 165p. 1997. reprint ed. pap. 25.00 (*0-8328-8969-5*); reprint ed. lib. bdg. 35.00 (*0-8328-8969-5*) Higginson Bk Co.

McPherson, Guy R. Ecology & Management of North American Savannas. LC 97-4813. 1997. 35.00 (*0-8165-1624-3*) U of Ariz Pr.

McPherson, Harry. A Political Education: A Washington Memoir. LC 94-32805. (Illus.). 520p. 1995. pap. 19.95 (*0-292-75181-8*) U of Tex Pr.

McPherson, Heather. Barbecue! Great Ideas for Backyard Get-Togethers. LC 98-22523. 1998. write for info. (*0-8092-2773-8*) NTC Contemp Pub Co.

McPherson, Heather J. Good Eating's Entertain with Ease. LC 97-24286. 1997. write for info. (*0-8092-2924-2*) NTC Contemp Pub Co.

McPherson, Hugo. Hawthorne As Myth-Maker: A Study in Imagination. LC 76-430856. (University of Toronto, Department of English Studies & Texts: No. 16). 274p. reprint ed. pap. 85.00 (*0-608-16821-1*, 202640900049) Bks Demand.

McPherson, J. B. Holy Bible. 276p. 1992. pap. 14.95 (*0-9633589-7-9*) Splendor Pub.

McPherson, J. C., jt. auth. see Eckert, W. J.

McPherson, J. E. The Pentatomoidea (Hemiptera) of Northeastern North America With Emphasis on the Fauna of Illinois. LC 81-9167. (Illus.). 253p. 1982. 31.95 (*0-8093-1040-6*) S Ill U Pr.

***McPherson, J. E. & McPherson, R. M.** Stink Bugs of Economic Importance in America North of Mexico. LC 00-31279. (Illus.). 2000. write for info. (*0-8493-0071-1*) CRC Pr.

McPherson, J. G. Fun with Electronics. (Pocket Scientist Ser.). 64p. (J). (gr. 3-6). 1983. lib. bdg. 12.95 (*0-88110-160-5*) EDC.

McPherson, James A. Crabcakes: A Memoir. 288p. 1999. pap. 13.00 (*0-684-84796-5*, Touchstone) S&S Trade Pap.

— Crabcakes: A Memoir. LC 97-36412. 288p. 1998. 22.50 (*0-684-83465-0*) Simon & Schuster.

— Elbow Room: Stories. (Black History Titles Ser.). 1986. mass mkt. 5.99 (*0-449-21357-9*, Crest) Fawcett.

— A Region Not Home: Reflections from Exile. LC 99-56063. 320p. 2000. 24.00 (*0-684-83464-2*) S&S Trade.

McPherson, James M. The Abolitionist Legacy: From Reconstruction to the NAACP. LC 75-22101. 452p. 1976. pap. text 16.95 (*0-691-10039-X*, Pub. by Princeton U Pr) Cal Prin Full Svc.

— The Abolitionist Legacy: From Reconstruction to the NAACP. LC 75-22101. 450p. reprint ed. pap. 139.50 (*0-7837-3876-5*, 204371800010) Bks Demand.

— Abraham Lincoln & the Second American Revolution. (Illus.). 192p. 1992. pap. 12.95 (*0-19-507606-0*) OUP.

— Battle Chronicles of the Civil War: Biographies & Index, Vol. 6. 1990. 28.00 (*0-02-897276-7*) Mac Lib Ref.

— Battle Chronicles of the Civil War 1861, Vol. 1. 1991. 28.00 (*0-02-897271-6*) Mac Lib Ref.

— Battle Chronicles of the Civil War 1862, Vol. 2. 1990. 28.00 (*0-02-897272-4*) Mac Lib Ref.

— Battle Chronicles of the Civil War 1863, Vol. 3. 1990. 28.00 (*0-02-897273-2*) Mac Lib Ref.

— Battle Chronicles of the Civil War 1864, Vol. 4. 1990. 28.00 (*0-02-897274-0*) Mac Lib Ref.

— Battle Chronicles of the Civil War 1865, Vol. 5. 1990. 28.00 (*0-02-897275-9*) Mac Lib Ref.

— The Battle Cry of Freedom: The Era of the Civil War. 928p. 1989. pap. 18.00 (*0-345-35942-9*) Ballantine Pub Grp.

— Battle Cry of Freedom: The Era of the Civil War. (Oxford History of United States: Vol. 6). (Illus.). 928p. (C). 1988. 45.00 (*0-19-503863-0*) OUP.

— Civil War & Reconstruction, Vol. 1. 2000. pap. text 29.95 (*0-312-11632-2*) St Martin.

— Drawn with the Sword: Reflections on the American Civil War. 272p. 1997. reprint ed. pap. 14.95 (*0-19-511796-4*) OUP.

— For Cause & Comrades: Why Men Fought in the Civil War. 256p. 1998. reprint ed. pap. 13.95 (*0-19-512499-5*) OUP.

— For Cause & Comrades: Why Men Fought the Civil War. LC 96-24760. 256p. 1997. 25.00 (*0-19-509023-3*) OUP.

— Is Blood Thicker Than Water? Crises of Nationalism in the Modern World. LC 99-11781. 112p. 1999. pap. 11.00 (*0-375-70428-0*) Vin Bks.

— Marching Toward Freedom: Blacks in the Civil War, 1861-1865. (Library of American History). (Illus.). 160p. (YA). (gr. 7-12). 1991. 19.95 (*0-8160-2337-9*) Facts on File.

— Marching Toward Freedom: Blacks in the Civil War, 1861-1865. (Library of American History). (Illus.). 160p. 1994. reprint ed. pap. 8.95 (*0-8160-3092-8*) Facts on File.

— Ordeal by Fire. 2nd ed. LC 92-23635. 208p. (C). 1993. 38.44 (*0-07-045837-5*) McGraw.

— Ordeal by Fire. 3rd ed. 2000. 49.00 (*0-07-231736-1*) McGraw.

— Ordeal by Fire, Vol. 2. 2nd ed. LC 92-23635. (C). 1993. 38.44 (*0-07-045838-3*) McGraw.

— Ordeal by Fire: Civil War, Vol. 2. 3rd ed. 480p. 2000. pap. 38.44 (*0-07-232065-6*) McGraw.

— Ordeal by Fire: Coming of War, Vol. 1. 3rd ed. 224p. 2000. pap. 38.44 (*0-07-232064-8*) McGraw.

— Ordeal by Fire: The Civil War & Reconstruction. 2nd ed. LC 81-11832. 800p. (C). 1991. 62.50 (*0-07-045842-1*) McGraw.

***McPherson, James M.** To the Best of My Ability: The American Presidents. LC 00-21569. (Illus.). 480p. (J). 2000. 29.95 (*0-7894-5073-9*) DK Pub Inc.

McPherson, James M. What They Fought for, 1861-1865. LC 94-38423. 112p. 1995. pap. 10.95 (*0-385-47634-5*, Anchor NY) Doubleday.

— What They Fought for, 1861-1865. LC 93-36934. (Walter Lynwood Fleming Lectures in Southern History). 96p. (C). 1994. 16.95 (*0-8071-1904-0*) La State U Pr.

McPherson, James M., ed. The Atlas of the Civil War. LC 94-16962. (Illus.). 224p. 1994. per. 40.00 (*0-02-579050-1*) Macmillan.

— We Cannot Escape History: Lincoln & the Last Best Hope of Earth. LC 95-2279. 184p. 1995. 27.95 (*0-252-02190-8*) U of Ill Pr.

McPherson, James M., intro. 1863: Turning Point of the Civil War. LC 98-27656. (Illus.). 320p. (gr. 11). 1999. 34.95 (*0-7370-0028-7*) T-L Custom Pub.

***McPherson, James M., et al, readers.** American Heritage's Great Minds of American History. abr. ed. 1999. audio 36.00 (*0-671-04384-6*) S&S New Media.

McPherson, James M., text. Gettysburg: The Paintings of Mort Kunstler. LC 98-14832. (Illus.). 128p. 1998. 24.95 (*1-55853-617-5*) Rutledge Hill Pr.

McPherson, James M. & Cooper, William J., Jr., eds. Writing the Civil War: The Quest to Understand. LC 98-19681. 352p. 1998. 29.95 (*1-57003-259-9*) U of SC Pr.

***McPherson, James M. & Cooper, William J., Jr., eds.** Writing the Civil War: The Quest to Understand. 352p. 2000. pap. 16.95 (*1-57003-389-7*) U of SC Pr.

McPherson, James M. & Katz, William L., eds. Anti-Slavery Crusade in America, 70 vols., Set. 1970. 1102.00 (*0-405-00600-4*) Ayer.

McPherson, James M. & McPherson, Patricia R., eds. Lamson of the Gettysburg: The Civil War Letters of Lieutenant Roswell H. Lamson, U. S. Navy. LC 97-11129. (Illus.). 272p. 1997. 25.00 (*0-19-511698-4*) OUP.

— Lamson of the Gettysburg: The Civil War Letters of Lieutenant Roswell H. Lamson, U. S. Navy. (Illus.). 272p. 1999. pap. 15.95 (*0-19-513093-6*) OUP.

***McPherson, James M. & Pohanka, Brian C.** Writing & Fighting the Civil War: Soldier Correspondence to the New York Sunday Mercury, Vol. 1. Styple, William B., ed. (Writing & Fighting Ser.: Vol. 1). (Illus.). 380p. 2000. 27.00 (*1-883926-13-0*) Belle Grv Pub.

McPherson, James M., et al. The Union, the Confederacy, & the Atlantic Rim. LC 94-32424. (Illus.). 181p. 1995. 29.95 (*1-55753-060-2*) Purdue U Pr.

McPherson, James M., et al. The Union, the Confederacy, & the Atlantic Rim. May, Robert E., ed. LC 94-32424. (Illus.). 181p. 1995. pap. 16.95 (*1-55753-061-0*) Purdue U Pr.

McPherson, James M., jt. auth. see Grant, Ulysses S.

McPherson, James M., ed. see McGuire, Bill & Wheeler, Leslie.

McPherson, James M., ed. see Sharpe Reference Staff.

McPherson, James M., tr. see Turnbull, Michael.

McPherson, Jan. In the Cold, Cold Dawn. LC 92-31918. (Voyages Ser.). (J). 1993. 4.25 (*0-383-03578-3*) SRA McGraw.

McPherson, John. Build Your Own Router Tables. (Illus.). 160p. 1997. pap. 21.99 (*1-55870-459-0*, Betrwy Bks) F & W Pubns Inc.

— Close to Home. (Illus.). 128p. 1994. pap. 6.95 (*0-8362-1750-0*) Andrews & McMeel.

— Close to Home Postcard Book. (Illus.). 1995. pap. text 8.95 (*0-8362-0649-5*) Andrews & McMeel.

— Close to Home Revisited: A Close to Home Treasury. (Illus.). 224p. 1995. pap. 12.95 (*0-8362-0427-1*) Andrews & McMeel.

***McPherson, John.** Close to Home Survival Guide. 144p. 1999. pap. 9.95 (*0-7407-0011-1*) Andrews & McMeel.

— Close to Home Survival Guide. (Close to Home Collection). 1999. pap. 9.99 (*0-310-23403-4*) Zondervan.

— Close to Home Uncut. (Close to Home Collection). 144p. 2000. pap. 9.95 (*0-7407-0613-6*) Andrews & McMeel.

M

M

McPherson, John. Close to Home Unplugged. (Close to Home Anthology Ser.: No. 2). 224p. 1997. pap. 12.95 (*0-310-22219-2*) Zondervan.
— Close to Home Unplugged: The Second Close to Home Anthology. LC 97-71640. (Illus.). 224p. 1997. pap. 12.95 (*0-8362-3658-0*) Andrews & McMeel.
— Get Well Book. LC 97-74516. (Main Street Editions Ser.). 1998. 6.95 (*0-8362-5257-8*) Andrews & McMeel.
— Home: The Final Frontier. (Close to Home Collection). (Illus.). 128p. (Orig.). 1996. pap. 7.95 (*0-8362-1030-1*) Andrews & McMeel.
— The Honeymoon Is Over. LC 96-84108. (Close to Home Collection). (Illus.). 128p. 1996. pap. 7.95 (*0-8362-2134-6*) Andrews & McMeel.
— Honeymoon Is Over. 1996. pap. 7.95 (*0-310-21399-1*) Zondervan.
***McPherson, John.** "How-to" Build This Log Cabin for $3,000. (Illus.). 140p. 1999. pap. 24.95 (*0-89745-980-6*) Sunflower U Pr.
McPherson, John. McPherson Goes to Church. (Illus.). 128p. 1994. pap. 8.99 (*0-310-48181-3*) Zondervan.
— McPherson's Marriage Album. 112p. 1991. pap. 7.99 (*0-310-53901-3*) Zondervan.
McPherson, John. Primitive Wilderness Living & Survival Skills: Naked into the Wilderness. McPherson, Geri, ed. (Illus.). 408p. 1993. reprint ed. pap. 24.95 (*0-9678777-7-6*) Prairie Wolf.
McPherson, John. The Silence of the Lamberts: A Close to Home Collection. LC 96-79242. (Illus.). 128p. (Orig.). 1997. pap. 7.95 (*0-8362-2698-4*) Andrews & McMeel.
— The Silence of the Lamberts: A Close to Home Collection. 128p. (Orig.). 1997. pap. 7.95 (*0-310-21912-4*) Zondervan.
— Striking Close to Home. 1998. pap. 8.99 (*0-310-22789-5*) Zondervan.
— Striking Close to Home: A Close to Home Collection. LC 98-85350. (Close to Home Collection). (Illus.). 144p. 1998. pap. 8.95 (*0-8362-6824-5*) Andrews & McMeel.
McPherson, John. Advent Church Resource Manual. (Nineteen Ninety-Seven Seasonal Advent Celebration Ser.). 176p. 1997. 49.00 (*1-57849-075-8*) Mainstay Church.
McPherson, John. What to Do When You Don't Know What to Do: Church Leader's Manual. (Nineteen Ninety-Six 50-Day Spiritual Adventure Ser.). 320p. 1995. ring bd. 50.00 (*1-879050-87-0*) Chapel of Air.
McPherson, John & McPherson, Geri. Primitive Wilderness Living & Survival Skills. (Illus.). 408p. 1993. pap. 24.95 (*0-89745-997-0*) Sunflower U Pr.
McPherson, John & McPherson, Geri. Primitive Wilderness Living & Survival Skills 2: Applied & Advanced. (Illus.). 296p. 1996. pap. 24.95 (*0-89745-984-9*) Sunflower U Pr.
McPherson, John, jt. illus. see Robertson, Andy.
McPherson, John H. History of Liberia. LC 78-63806. (Johns Hopkins University. Studies in the Social Sciences. Thirtieth Ser. 1912: No. 9). reprint ed. 29.50 (*0-404-61069-2*) AMS Pr.
McPherson, Joseph M. Primitive Beliefs in the North-East of Scotland. Dorson, Richard M., ed. LC 77-70605. (International Folklore Ser.). 1977. reprint ed. lib. bdg. 26.95 (*0-405-10109-0*) Ayer.
McPherson, Joseph W. The Moulids of Egypt: Egyptian Saints-Days. LC 77-87654. reprint ed. 28.50 (*0-404-16408-0*) AMS Pr.
McPherson, Joyce. The Ocean of Truth: The Story of Sir Isaac Newton. (Illus.). 144p. (Orig.). (J). (gr. 5-12). 1997. pap. 7.95 (*1-882514-50-5*) Greenleaf TN.
— A Piece of the Mountain: The Story of Blaise Pascal. 128p. (YA). (gr. 5-12). 1995. pap. 7.95 (*1-882514-17-3*) Greenleaf TN.
McPherson, Joyce B. The River of Grace: The Story of John Calvin. (Illus.). 140p. (YA). (gr. 5-12). 1999. pap. 7.95 (*1-882514-54-8*) Greenleaf TN.
McPherson, Kate, jt. ed. see Kinsley, Carol W.
McPherson, Katharyn R. Problem Solving Strategies: Parent-Teacher Guide to Improving Your Child's Test Scores. 52p. Date not set. pap. text, spiral bd. 12.95 (*0-9647611-1-4*) McPhrsn Prob.
— Problem Solving Strategies: Parent/Teacher Guide to Improving Your Child's Test Scores in Math, Writing, Reading (Grades 1 - College) 53p. (J). (gr. 1-13). 1996. pap. text 15.95 (*0-9647611-0-6*) McPhrsn Prob.
— Problem Solving Strategies (Adaptable for Grades 1 - 12) Improve Test Scores in Math, Writing, Reading. 2nd ed. 40p. (Orig.). (J). (gr. 1-12). 1992. pap. 9.95 (*0-9647611-8-1*) McPhrsn Prob.
McPherson, Kathryn, et al. Gendered Pasts: Historical Essays on Femininity & Masculinity in Canada. (Canadian Social History Ser.). (Illus.). 302p. (C). 1999. pap. text 19.95 (*0-19-541449-7*) OUP.
McPherson, Kathryn Read, jt. ed. see Brown, Amy Benson.
McPherson, Kathy. Second Nature, Vol. 1. 70p. 1998. pap. 10.50 (*1-56770-427-1*) S Scheewe Pubns.
***McPherson, Kathy.** Second Nature II. (Illus.). 70p. 1999. pap. 10.50 (*1-56770-463-8*) S Scheewe Pubns.
McPherson, Kenneth. Indian Ocean: A History of People. (Essaus in World History Ser.). (C). 1996. text 32.50 (*0-8133-1242-6*); pap. text 10.95 (*0-8133-1243-4*) Westview.
— The Indian Ocean: A History of People & the Sea. (Oxford India Paperbacks Ser.). (Illus.). 338p. 1998. reprint ed. pap. text 14.95 (*0-19-564243-0*) OUP.
— The Indian Ocean: A History of Peoples & the Sea. (Illus.). 328p. (C). 1994. text 28.00 (*0-19-563374-1*) OUP.
McPherson, Klim, jt. auth. see Shetty, Prakash S.
McPherson Library - Reference Division - Universit. Creative Canada: A Biographical Dictionary of Twentieth-Century Creative & Performing Artists, 2 vols., 2. LC 73-80898. 1972. text 35.00 (*0-8020-3285-0*) U of Toronto Pr.
McPherson, Linda. Modern Collectible Tins: Identification & Values. LC 98-153333. 1998. pap. text 19.95 (*1-57432-054-8*, 5051) Collector Bks.
McPherson, M., jt. auth. see Feldman, Ron.
McPherson, M. B. Prospects for Metropolitan Water Management. 240p. 1970. pap. 3.00 (*0-87262-026-3*) Am Soc Civil Eng.
McPherson, M. J., et al, eds. PCR: A Practical Approach. (Practical Approach Ser.). (Illus.). 274p. 1991. pap. text 55.00 (*0-19-963196-4*) OUP.
— PCR 2: A Practical Approach. LC 96-176054. (The Practical Approach Ser.: No. 150). (Illus.). 3360p. 1995. text 95.00 (*0-19-963425-4*); pap. text 55.00 (*0-19-963424-6*) OUP.
***McPherson, M. J. & Moller, S.** PCR. Beynon, R. J. & Howe, C. D., eds. (Basics Ser.). 120p. 2000. pap. text (*0-387-91600-8*) Spr-Verlag.
***McPherson, M. L.** Accurizing the Factory Rifle. (Illus.). 335p. 1999. pap. 44.95 (*0-9670948-3-6*) Precision Shootg.
McPherson, M. L. Metallic Cartridge Reloading. 3rd ed. LC 81-70996. (Illus.). 352p. 1996. pap. 21.95 (*0-87349-180-7*, MCR3, DBI Bks) Krause Pubns.
McPherson, M. L., jt. auth. see Fackler, Kurt D.
McPherson, M. L., ed. see Barnes, Frank C.
McPherson, Malcolm. Executive Guide to Speech-Driven Computer Systems. Ennals, Richard et al, eds. LC 95-34080. (Executive Guides Ser.). (Illus.). 128p. 1995. 31.95 (*3-540-19911-X*) Spr-Verlag.
McPherson, Malcolm F. & Radelet, Steven C., eds. Economic Recovery in the Gambia: Insights for Adjustment in Sub-Saharan Africa. LC 95-36778. (Studies in International Development). 336p. 1996. pap. 30.00 (*0-674-22975-4*) HUP.
McPherson, Marion W., jt. auth. see Popplestone, John.
McPherson, Marion W., jt. auth. see Popplestone, John A.
McPherson, Marlys. Psychopathic Personality Commitment Law: A Study of Its Implementation in Minnesota. (Illus.). 48p. 1997. reprint ed. pap. text 25.00 (*0-7881-4707-2*) DIANE Pub.
McPherson, Mary. Telling Tales Out of School. LC 97-166581. 180 p. 1996. write for info. (*0-86417-807-7*) Seven Hills Bk.
McPherson, Michael. Singing with the Owls. 58p. 1983. pap. 5.95 (*0-932136-05-2*) Petronium HI.
***McPherson, Michael S.** The Student Aid Game: Meeting Need & Rewarding Talent in American Higher Education. 176p. 1999. pap. 14.95 (*0-691-00536-2*, Pub. by Princeton U Pr) Cal Prin Full Svc.
McPherson, Michael S., et al, eds. Paying the Piper: Productivity, Incentives, & Financing in U. S. Higher Education. (Economics of Education Ser.). 344p. (C). 1994. text 70.00 (*0-472-10404-7*, 10404) U of Mich Pr.
McPherson, Michael S. & Schapiro, Morton O. Keeping College Affordable: Government & Educational Opportunity. 262p. 1991. 36.95 (*0-8157-5642-9*); pap. 16.95 (*0-8157-5641-0*) Brookings.
— The Student Aid Game: Meeting Need & Rewarding Talent in American Higher Education. LC 97-14999. 152p. 1998. text 29.95 (*0-691-05783-4*, Pub. by Princeton U Pr) Cal Prin Full Svc.
McPherson, Michael S., jt. auth. see Hausman, Daniel M.
McPherson, Michael S., ed. see Pechman, Joseph.
McPherson, Michael S., jt. ed. see Pechman, Joseph A.
McPherson, Michelle. Meditations of a Bulldog. (Illus.). 250p. (Orig.). 1995. pap. 13.95 (*1-883893-26-7*) WinePress Pub.
***McPherson, Miles.** Bad to the Bone: Fifteen Cool Bible Heroes Who Lived Radical Lives for God. LC 99-6529. 192p. 1999. pap. text 8.99 (*0-7642-2280-5*) Bethany Hse.
— Parenting the Wild Child. 192p. 2000. pap. 11.99 (*0-7642-2370-4*) Bethany Hse.
McPherson, Miles. The Power of Believing in Your Child: Unleash Your Power as a Parent to Help Your Kids Be All They Can Be. 28p. 1998. pap. 10.99 (*0-7642-2078-0*) Bethany Hse.
— 21 Jump-Start Devotional. 128p. 1998. pap. 6.99 (*0-7642-2146-9*) Bethany Hse.
McPherson, Miles & Rice, Wayne. One Kid at a Time: Mentoring As a Model for Youth Ministry. Southern, Randy, ed. (YA). (gr. 6-12). 1997. pap., teacher ed. 8.99 (*0-7814-5205-8*, 29728) Cook.
McPherson, Murray B. Regional Earth Science Information in Local Water Management. 185p. 1975. pap. 5.00 (*0-87262-151-0*) Am Soc Civil Eng.
McPherson, N. A. & McLean, A. Continuous Casting: Non-Metallic Inclusions in Continuously Cast Steel, Vol. VII. LC 95-79148. 324p. 1995. 70.00 (*1-886362-04-1*) Iron & Steel.
— Continuous Casting Vol. VI: Tunidsh to Mold Transfer Operations, Vol. VI. LC 83-81654. 234p. 1992. 70.00 (*0-932897-72-X*) Iron & Steel.
— Continuous Casting Vol. 8: Transverse Cracking in Continuously Cast Products. 272p. 1997. 70.00 (*1-886362-20-3*, P-PC98/097) Iron & Steel.
McPherson, Natalie. Machines & Economic Growth: The Implications for Growth Theory, 156. LC 93-44509. (Contributions in Economics & Economic History Ser.). 280p. 1994. 59.95 (*0-313-29255-8*, Greenwood Pr) Greenwood.
McPherson, Nina, tr. see Huong, Duong Thu.
McPherson, Nina, tr. see Thu-Huong, Duong.
McPherson, Nina, tr. see Vu, Tran.
McPherson, Patricia R., jt. ed. see McPherson, James M.
McPherson, R. M., jt. auth. see McPherson, J. E.
***McPherson, Rett.** A Comedy of Heirs: A Torie O'Shea Mystery. 224p. 2000. mass mkt. 5.99 (*0-312-97133-8*, Minotaur) St Martin.
McPherson, Richard A., jt. auth. see Sacher, Ronald A.
McPherson, Robert E., jt. auth. see King, Christopher T.
McPherson, Robert S. The Northern Navajo Frontier, 1860-1900: Expansion Through Adversity. LC 88-8593. (Illus.). 143p. 1988. reprint ed. pap. 44.40 (*0-608-04131-9*, 206486400011) Bks Demand.
— Sacred Land, Sacred View: Navajo Perceptions of the Four Corners Region. LC 91-33322. (Monographs in Western History: No. 19). (Illus.). 152p. 1992. pap. 8.95 (*1-56085-008-6*, C Redd Ctr Wstrn Studies) Signature Bks.
***McPherson, Robert S., ed.** The Journey of Navajo Oshley: An Autobiography & Life History. (Illus.). 272p. 2000. 39.95 (*0-87421-290-1*); pap. 19.95 (*0-87421-291-X*) Utah St U Pr.
***McPherson, Roosevelt.** Let Not Your Heart Be Troubled: Living with God in the Worst of Times & the Best of Times. LC 98-74731. 85p. 1999. pap. 12.00 (*1-878647-59-8*) APU Pub Grp.
McPherson, Ryan. The Color of Money: Campaign Contributions & Race. (Illus.). 167p. (C). 1999. pap. text 30.00 (*0-7881-7750-8*) DIANE Pub.
McPherson, Sandra. Edge Effect: Trails & Portrayals. LC 95-33661. (Wesleyan Poetry Ser.). 95p. 1996. pap. 12.95 (*0-8195-2226-0*, Wesleyan Univ Pr) U Pr of New Eng.
— Edge Effect: Trails & Portrayals. LC 95-33661. (Wesleyan Poetry Ser.). (Illus.). 95p. 1996. text 25.00 (*0-8195-2225-2*, Wesleyan Univ Pr) U Pr of New Eng.
— Elegies for the Hot Season. LC 81-5455. (American Poetry Ser.: Vol. 23). 71p. 1982. reprint ed. pap. 5.95 (*0-912946-92-X*, Ecco Press) HarperTrade.
— Floralia. (Poetry Ser.). (Illus.). 24p. (Orig.). 1985. pap. 9.95 (*0-317-39884-9*) Seluzicki Fine Bks.
— Floralia. deluxe ed. (Poetry Ser.). (Illus.). 24p. (Orig.). 1985. 50.00 (*0-317-39885-7*) Seluzicki Fine Bks.
— The God of Indeterminacy: Poems. LC 92-14714. (Illus.). 104p. (C). 1993. 11.95 (*0-252-06271-X*) U of Ill Pr.
— Patron Happiness. LC 82-11490. (American Poetry Ser.). 70p. 1984. pap. 6.50 (*0-88001-022-3*) HarpC.
— The Spaces Between Birds: Mother - Daughter Poems, 1967-1995. LC 95-39746. (Wesleyan Poetry Ser.). 75p. 1996. pap. 12.95 (*0-8195-2228-7*, Wesleyan Univ Pr) U Pr of New Eng.
— Streamers. LC 88-4253. 1989. pap. 7.95 (*0-88001-214-5*) HarpC.
— The Year of Our Birth. LC 77-85295. (American Poetry Ser.: No. 15). 1978. pap. 6.95 (*0-912946-49-0*, Ecco Press) HarperTrade.
McPherson, Sara, ed. see Trombello, Joseph.
McPherson, Scott. Marvin's Room. 1992. pap. 5.25 (*0-8222-1312-5*) Dramatists Play.
Mcpherson, Scott. Marvin's Room. 128p. 1996. reprint ed. pap. 9.95 (*0-452-27819-8*, Plume) Dutton Plume.
McPherson, Sigrid R. The Refiner's Fire: Memoirs of a German Girlhood. 208p. 1995. pap. 20.00 (*0-919123-54-6*, Pub. by Inner City Bks) BookWorld.
McPherson, Stehpanie S. Ordinary Genius: The Story of Albert Einstein. (Illus.). 96p. (J). 1997. pap. text 6.95 (*1-57505-067-6*, Carolrhoda) Lerner Pub.
McPherson, Stephanie. Martha Washington: First Lady. LC 97-23478. (Historical American Biographies Ser.). (Illus.). 128p. (YA). (gr. 6 up). 1998. lib. bdg. 20.95 (*0-7660-1017-1*) Enslow Pubs.
McPherson, Stephanie S. I Speak for the Women: A Story about Lucy Stone. LC 92-13786. (Creative Minds Ser.). (Illus.). (J). 1993. lib. bdg. 19.95 (*0-87614-740-6*, Carolrhoda) Lerner Pub.
— Ordinary Genius: The Story of Albert Einstein. LC 93-1408. (Trailblazers Ser.). 96p. (J). (gr. 3-7). 1995. lib. bdg. 22.60 (*0-87614-788-0*, Carolrhoda) Lerner Pub.
— Peace & Bread: The Story of Jane Addams. LC 93-6736. (J). (gr. 4-7). 1993. lib. bdg. 22.60 (*0-87614-792-9*, Carolrhoda) Lerner Pub.
— Rooftop Astronomer: A Story about Maria Mitchell. (Illus.). 32p. (J). (gr. 3-6). 1990. lib. bdg. 14.95 (*0-87614-410-5*, Carolrhoda) Lerner Pub.
***McPherson, Stephanie S.** Sisters Against Slavery: A Story about Sarah & Angelina Grimkbe. LC 98-46741. (Creative Minds Biography Ser.). 64p. (J). (gr. 3-6). 1999. 21.27 (*1-57505-361-6*, Carolrhoda) Lerner Pub.
McPherson, Stephanie S. TV's Forgotten Hero: The Story of Philo Farnsworth. LC 95-26383. (J). 1996. lib. bdg. 16.95 (*1-57505-017-X*, Carolrhoda) Lerner Pub.
— Workers' Detective: A Story about Aliee Hamilton. (Illus.). (J). (gr. 3-6). 1992. lib. bdg. 14.95 (*0-87614-699-X*, Carolrhoda) Lerner Pub.
***McPherson, Stephanie Sammartino.** Lau vs. Nichols: Bilingual Education in Public Schools. (Landmark Supreme Court Cases Ser.). (Illus.). 104p. (YA). (gr. 6 up). 2000. lib. bdg. 20.95 (*0-7660-1472-X*) Enslow Pubs.
McPherson, Thomas. The Dodge Story. LC 92-26168. (Crestline Ser.). (Illus.). 320p. 1976. 44.95 (*0-87938-697-5*, Crestline Pub) MBI Pubg.
McPherson, Tim, contrib. by. Prescriptions from God's Word. 28p. 1997. 1.35 (*0-89827-185-1*) Wesleyan Pub Hse.
McPherson, Tom, jt. auth. see McCall, Walt.
McPherson, William. The Stephen Lawrence Inquiry: Appendices. rev. ed. (Command Papers (All) Ser.: No. 4262-II). 350p. 1999. pap. 55.00 (*0-10-142624-0*, HM26240, Pub. by Statnry Office) Balogh.
McPherson, William H. Public Employee Relations in West Germany. LC 77-634396. (Comparative Studies in Public Employment Labor Relations Ser.). 1971. 10.95 (*0-87736-009-X*); pap. 5.95 (*0-87736-010-3*) U of Mich Inst Labor.
McPherson, Woodrow W., ed. Economic Development of Tropical Agriculture: Theory, Policy, Strategy, & Organization. LC 68-24368. (Illus.). 344p. reprint ed. pap. 106.70 (*0-7837-5102-8*, 204480100004) Bks Demand.
McPherson, Yaffa. Yaffa, God's Prickly Pear. LC 92-97176. 208p. (Orig.). 1992. pap. 10.95 (*0-9634792-0-2*) Intimate Awe.
McPhetres, Sam. The Practical User's Guide to the Trust Territory Archives. (Educational Ser.: No. 14). 45p. 1992. pap. 7.50 (*1-878453-12-2*) Univ Guam MAR Ctr.
McPhilemy, Sean. The Committee: Political Assassination in Northern Ireland. (Illus.). 418p. 1998. 24.95 (*1-57098-211-2*) Roberts Rinehart.
McPhillimy, Bill. Controlling Your Class: A Teacher's Guide to Managing Classroom Behaviour. LC 96-25546. 1996. pap. text 34.95 (*0-471-96568-5*) Wiley.
McPhillips. The New Formalism. 1998. 22.95 (*0-8057-4614-5*, Twyne) Mac Lib Ref.
McPhillips, Martin. The Constitutional Convention. LC 85-40169. (Turning Points in American History Ser.). (Illus.). 64p. (J). (gr. 5 up). 1985. lib. bdg. 14.95 (*0-382-06827-0*) Silver Burdett Pr.
McPhillips, Scott. Superman Doesn't Live Here Anymore: Drugs Are a Lie, Jesus Is the Truth. LC 98-65353. (Illus.). 66p. 1998. pap. 9.95 (*0-9662205-7-9*) Mac on the Attack.
McPhillips, Shirley, jt. auth. see Flynn, Nick.
McPhun, Delwyn. East Africa Pilot. (Illus.). (C). 1998. pap. 125.00 (*0-85288-251-3*, Pub. by Laurie Norie & Wilson Ltd) St Mut.
McPoil, Thomas G. Physical Therapy of the Foot & Ankle. 2nd ed. Hunt, Gary C., ed. LC 95-7870. (Clinics in Physical Therapy Ser.). 1995. pap. text 49.00 (*0-443-08925-6*) Church.
Mcpoil, Thomas G., ed. see Malone.
McPolin, James. John. enl. rev. ed. LC 79-64670. (New Testament Message Ser.: Vol. 6). 273p. 1979. pap. 14.95 (*0-8146-5129-1*) Liturgical Pr.
McPolin, M. John. enl. rev. ed. LC 79-64670. 1989. pap. 30.00 (*0-86217-013-3*, Pub. by Veritas Pubns) St Mut.
McPolin, Paul, et al. Rights of the Accused. LC 00-24992. (Crime, Justice, & Punishment Ser.). (Illus.). (YA). (gr. 7-12). 1999. lib. bdg. 19.95 (*0-7910-4303-7*) Chelsea Hse.
McProud, C. G., ed. Audio Anthology Vol. 1: When Audio Was Young. LC 87-62118. (Illus.). 124p. 1987. pap. text 16.95 (*0-8338-0195-3*) Audio Amateur.
— Audio Anthology Vol. 2: When Audio Was Young. (Illus.). 124p. 1989. pap. text 16.95 (*0-8338-0197-X*) Audio Amateur.
— Audio Anthology Vol. 3: When Audio Was Young. LC 90-80999. (Illus.). 124p. 1990. pap. text 16.95 (*0-9624191-1-7*) Audio Amateur.
— Audio Anthology Vol. 4: When Audio Was Young. LC 91-72106. (Illus.). 144p. 1991. pap. text 16.95 (*0-9624191-9-2*) Audio Amateur.
McQ, Joe. The Steps We Took. (Illus.). 180p. (Orig.). 1990. pap. 11.95 (*0-87483-151-2*) August Hse.
McQain, Jeff, jt. auth. see Malless, Stan.
McQquade. Reading Images Viewing Texts. 2000. pap. text 38.95 (*0-312-18016-0*) St Martin.
McQuade. Cases in Financial Accounting & Reporting. 1992. 28.75 (*0-07-045656-9*) McGraw.
— Cc Writers Presence. 2nd ed. 1997. pap. text 1.85 (*0-312-14493-8*) St Martin.
***McQuade.** The Harper American Literature. 3rd ed. 352p. 1999. 18.00 (*0-321-02739-6*) Addson-Wesley Educ.
McQuade. Principles of Scientific Man, Vol. 1. 2000. pap. text. write for info. (*0-312-11595-4*) St Martin.
Mcquade. The Schirmer Biographical Dictionary of Dance. 1998. 95.00 (*0-02-860306-0*, Schirmer Books) Mac Lib Ref.
McQuade. The Schirmer Biographical Dictionary of Dance. Date not set. 95.00 (*0-02-864511-1*, Schirmer Books) Mac Lib Ref.
***Mcquade.** Supplementioneers - Harper American Literature. 3rd ed. 1998. 65.33 (*0-201-58772-6*) Addison-Wesley.
***Mcquade & Atwan.** Writers Presence. 3rd ed. 2000. pap. text 35.95 (*0-312-19767-5*) St Martin.
Mcquade, Atwan. Traditions of Essay, Vol. 1. 2000. pap. text. write for info. (*0-312-02016-3*) St Martin.
McQuade, Donald, ed. The Harper American Literature. 3rd ed. LC 98-36994. 3000p. (C). 1998. pap. 56.00 (*0-321-01269-0*) Addson-Wesley Educ.
McQuade, Donald & Atwan, Robert. HarperCollins' American Literature, 2 vols., Vol. 1. 2nd ed. 2500p. (C). 1997. pap. 67.00 (*0-06-500964-9*) Addson-Wesley Educ.
— Resources for Teaching "The Writer's Presence" 2nd ed. 272p. 1997. pap. text 13.33 (*0-312-14488-1*) St Martin.
— Thinking in Writing. 4th ed. LC 97-25635. 584p. 1997. pap. 31.88 (*0-07-045983-5*) McGraw.
McQuade, Donald & Atwan, Robert, eds. Popular Writing in America: The Interaction of Style & Audience. 5th ed. (Illus.). 96p. 1993. pap. text (*0-19-508283-4*) OUP.
McQuade, Donald, ed. see Emerson, Ralph Waldo.
McQuade, Donald A., ed. The Territory of Language: Linguistics, Stylistics, & the Teaching of Composition. LC 85-2080. 376p. (Orig.). (C). 1986. text 31.95 (*0-8093-1217-4*); pap. text 21.95 (*0-8093-1215-8*) S Ill U Pr.
McQuade, Finlay & Champagne, David W. How to Make a Better School. LC 94-2066. 256p. (C). 1994. 52.00 (*0-205-14120-X*) Allyn.
***McQuade, J. Stanley.** Reading Medical Records: The McQuade System. Davila-Lizardi, Luis A., ed. (Illus.). iv, 333p. (C). 1999. pap. 49.95 (*0-941787-00-1*) Davila Assocs.

An Asterisk (*) at the beginning of an entry indicates that the title is appearing for the first time.

McQuade, Jacqueline. At Preschool with Teddy Bear. Goyette, Cecile, ed. LC 98-30114. (Illus.). 26p. (J). (ps). 1999. pap. 5.99 (0-8037-2394-6, Dial Yng Read) Peng Put Young Read.
— At the Petting Zoo with Teddy Bear. Goyette, Cecile, ed. LC 98-30113. (Illus.). 26p. (J). (ps). 1999. pap. 5.99 (0-8037-2395-4, Dial Yng Read) Peng Put Young Read.
— Christmas with Teddy Bear. LC 95-53761. (Illus.). 32p. (J). (ps-2). 1996. 13.99 (0-8037-2075-0, Dial Yng Read) Peng Put Young Read.
McQuade, Joe. Baptized in Dirty Water. LC 95-62288. 208p. (Orig.). 1995. pap. 12.00 (0-9623712-8-9) Tafford Pub.
McQuade, Joseph M., jt. auth. see Glick, Robert R.
McQuade, Lawerence C. East-West Trade: Managing Encounter & Accommodation. 194p. 1977. pap. 5.95 (0-317-33692-4) Atl Coun US.
McQuade, Margaret C. & Castro, Jaime C. Talavera Poblana: Four Centuries of a Mexican Ceramic Tradition. (ENG & SPA., Illus.). 112p. 1999. 30.00 (1-879128-19-5) Americas Soc.
***McQuade, Molly.** Barbarism. LC 99-71364. 71p. 2000. pap. 13.95 (1-884800-27-0, Pub. by Four Way Bks) SPD-Small Pr Dist.
McQuade, Molly. Stealing Glimpses: Of Poetry, Poets & Things in Between. LC 98-26855. 288p. 1999. 24.00 (1-889330-25-6, Pub. by Sarabande Bks); pap. 14.95 (1-889330-26-4, Pub. by Sarabande Bks) Consort Bk Sales.
— An Unsentimental Education: Writers & Chicago. LC 94-43441. 270p. 1995. 18.95 (0-226-56210-7) U Ch Pr.
***McQuade, Molly, ed.** By Herself: Women Reclaim Poetry. LC 99-67240. 430p. 2000. pap. 16.00 (1-55597-297-7, Pub. by Graywolf) SPD-Small Pr Dist.
McQuade, Pam, jt. auth. see Sortor, Toni.
McQuade, Pamela, jt. auth. see Sortor, Toni.
McQuade, Ralph J. Cases in Financial Accounting & Reporting. LC 92-20563. 256p. (C). 1993. pap. 40.94 (0-07-045655-0) McGraw.
McQuade, Stanley. Medical Information Systems for Lawyers, 2 vols. 2nd ed. LC 93-73676. 1993. ring bd. 225.00 (0-685-59889-6) West Group.
McQuade, Susan. Great-Grandpa. LC 92-27235. (Voyages Ser.). (Illus.). (J). 1993. 3.75 (0-383-03622-4) SRA McGraw.
McQuaid, C. D., jt. ed. see Mill, Peter J.
McQuaid, Donald. Grimsby. unabridged ed. (Grimsby Ser.). (Illus.). 44p. 1998. 17.95 (0-9671196-0-X, McJA-ESFA) McJA ESFA.
McQuaid, E. Patrick & Stahl, Barbara J. How to Get into an Ivy League School. write for info. (0-318-59705-5) S&S Trade.
McQuaid, Elwood. Come Walk with Me. LC 89-82580. 1990. pap. 8.95 (0-915540-47-9) Frnds Israel.
***McQuaid, Elwood.** Hay Esperanza. (SPA.). 150p. 2000. write for info. (0-915540-64-9) Frnds Israel.
McQuaid, Elwood. It Is No Dream. LC 78-51766. 1978. pap. 8.95 (0-915540-21-5) Frnds Israel.
— Not to the Strong. LC 91-71438. 1991. pap. 8.95 (0-915540-45-2) Frnds Israel.
— The Outpouring. LC 85-29866. 1990. pap. 8.95 (0-915540-49-5) Frnds Israel.
***McQuaid, Elwood.** II Peter: Standing Fast in the Last Days. 200p. (C). 2000. pap. write for info. (0-915540-65-7) Frnds Israel.
McQuaid, Elwood. There Is Hope. 1996. pap. 8.95 (0-915540-11-8) Frnds Israel.
— The Zion Connection: Destroying the Myths - Forging an Alliance. LC 95-43853. 1996. pap. 9.95 (0-915540-40-1) Frnds Israel.
— Zvi. LC 78-56149. 202p. 1978. pap. 8.95 (0-915540-23-1) Frnds Israel.
***McQuaid, Elwood.** Zvi. (SPA.). 210p. 2000. pap. write for info. (0-915540-62-2) Frnds Israel.
McQuaid, Elwood. ZVI & the Next Generation. LC 88-80875. 1988. pap. 8.95 (0-915540-43-6) Frnds Israel.
***McQuaid, Elwood.** Zvi y la Generacion Signviente. (SPA.). 160p. 2000. pap. write for info. (0-915540-63-0) Frnds Israel.
McQuaid, Kim. Uneasy Partners: Big Business in American Politics, 1945-1990. LC 93-17520. (American Moment Ser.). 272p. (C). 1993. text 38.95 (0-8018-4651-X); pap. text 14.95 (0-8018-4652-8) Johns Hopkins.
McQuaid, Kim, jt. auth. see Berkowitz, Edward D.
McQuaid, Linda, et al. Children's Nursing. LC 96-25830. 1996. text 49.00 (0-443-05087-2) Church.
McQuaid, Matilda. Lilly Reich: Designer. LC 95-81466. (Illus.). 64p. (Orig.). 1996. pap. text 18.95 (0-8109-6159-8, Pub. by Abrams) Time Warner.
— Lilly Reich: Designer. (Illus.). 64p. (Orig.). 1996. pap. 16.95 (0-87070-144-4, 0-8109-6159-8, Pub. by Mus of Modern Art) Abrams.
— Santiago Calatrava: Structure & Expression. (Illus.). 40p. 1993. pap. 9.95 (0-685-65844-9) Abrams.
McQuaid, Matilda, jt. auth. see McCarty, Cara.
McQuaid, Matilda, jt. ed. see Berkeley, Ellen P.
McQuaid, Robert W. The Craft of Writing Technical Manuals. LC 82-91154. (Illus.). 54p. 1983. 15.00 (0-912259-00-0) R W McQuaid.
— The Craft of Writing Technical Manuals. 2nd ed. LC 82-91154. (Handbook Edition Ser.). (Illus.). 107p. (C). 1990. student ed. 20.00 (0-912259-01-9) R W McQuaid.
McQuaid, Ronald, jt. auth. see Glancey, Keith.
McQuaid, Ronald, jt. ed. see Breheny, Michael.
McQuaid, Sarah. The Irish Dadgad Guitar. 96p. pap. 9.95 (0-946005-74-5, OS 00108, Pub. by Ossian) Music Sales.
— The Irish Dadgad Guitar. 1996. pap. text 17.95 (0-946005-93-1, Pub. by Ossian) Dufour.
McQuaig, Becky, jt. auth. see McQuaig, Charles.
McQuaig, Charles & McQuaig, Becky. It Happens All the Time. LC 98-39131. 144p. 1998. pap. 7.99 (1-56722-223-4) Word Aflame.
McQuaig, Douglas J. The Accounting Cycle. (C). 1995. pap. text 24.36 (0-395-77936-7) HM.
— College Accounting, 5 vols. (C). 1992. pap., teacher ed. 7.56 (0-395-63856-9) HM.
— College Accounting, 5 vols. (C). 1993. pap., teacher ed., suppl. ed. 3.96 (0-395-63858-5) HM.
— College Accounting, 5 vols. (C). 1993. pap., teacher ed. 7.56 (0-395-63857-7) HM.
— College Accounting, 5 vols. (C). 1993. pap., suppl. ed. 5.96 (0-395-65547-1) HM.
— College Accounting, 5 vols. (C). 1994. pap., teacher ed. 3.96 (0-395-63861-5) HM.
— College Accounting. (C). 1995. pap. 57.96 (0-395-77937-5) HM.
— College Accounting. 4th ed. 1989. teacher ed. write for info. (0-318-63321-3) HM.
— College Accounting Fundamentals. LC 76-15788. (Illus.). (C). 1977. 5.25 (0-685-02285-4); text 21.50 (0-395-18986-1) HM.
— College Accounting Fundamentals, 2 vols. 2nd ed. (C). 1981. text 21.95 (0-395-29409-6); text 18.95 (0-395-29410-X) HM.
McQuaig, Douglas J. College Accounting Fundamentals, 3 vols. 3rd ed. (C). 1984. text 41.16 (0-395-35679-2) HM.
McQuaig, Douglas J. College Accounting Video Guide, 5 vols. (C). 1993. pap. 5.96 (0-395-65548-X) HM.
— College Accounting 1-29: Exams, 4 vols. (C). Date not set. text 50.36 (0-395-49433-8) HM.
— CW Hale Medical Practice Set. 2nd ed. 12.95 (0-685-42419-7) HM.
— Phoenix Mountn Bikes II. (C). 1995. pap. write for info. (0-395-77034-3) HM.
McQuaig, Douglas J. & Bille, Patricia A. College Accounting: Chpts. 1-13, 6 vols. 6th ed. 544p. (C). 1996. text 53.96 (0-395-79700-4); text, teacher ed. 11.96 (0-395-80991-6) HM.
— College Accounting: Chpts. 1-13, 6 vols. 6th annot. ed. (C). 1996. text, teacher ed. 55.16 (0-395-82905-4) HM.
— College Accounting: Chpts. 1-26, 6 vols. 6th ed. 512p. (C). 1996. text 43.16 (0-395-79701-2) HM.
— College Accounting: Chpts. 1-8, 6 vols. 6th ed. 352p. (C). 1996. text 43.16 (0-395-79702-0) HM.
— College Accounting: Chpts. 14-26, 6 vols. (C). 1996. text, teacher ed. 11.96 (0-395-80992-4) HM.
— College Accounting: Chpts. 14-26, 6 vols. 6th annot. ed. (C). 1996. text, teacher ed. 69.96 (0-395-82904-6) HM.
McQuaig, Douglas J., jt. auth. see Bille, Patricia A.
McQuaig, Jack H. Your Business, Your Son & You. 192p. 1979. 10.00 (0-686-62444-0) B Klein Pubns.
McQuail, Denis. Audience Analysis. LC 97-4855. 200p. 1997. text 44.00 (0-7619-1001-8); pap. text 18.95 (0-7619-1002-6) Sage.
— Communication Models for the Study of Mass Communications. LC 75-11683. (A.O.M.S. Social Processes Ser.). (Illus.). 240p. 1975. pap. text 14.95 (0-582-29578-5) Longman.
— Mass Communication Theory: An Introduction. 3rd ed. 448p. 1994. 65.00 (0-8039-7784-0); pap. 27.50 (0-8039-7785-9) Sage.
— Media Performance: Mass Communication & the Public Interest. 352p. (C). 1992. text 65.00 (0-8039-8294-1); pap. text 21.95 (0-8039-8295-X) Sage.
— Towards a Sociology of Mass Communications. 1969. pap. text. write for info. (0-686-66487-6, 97480) Macmillan.
***McQuail, Denis & Graber, Doris, eds.** The Politics of News: The News of Politics. LC 98-2661. 200p. (C). 1998. 39.95 (1-56802-413-4) Congr Quarterly.
McQuail, Denis & Windahl, Sven. Communication Models for the Study of Mass Communication. 2nd ed. LC 92-28665. (C). 1994. pap. text 36.00 (0-582-03650-X, 79758) Longman.
McQuail, Denis, jt. ed. see Graber, Doris.
McQuail, Lisa. Treasures of Two Nations: Thai Royal Gifts to the United States of America. (Illus.). 1997. 49.95 (1-891739-01-8); pap. 37.50 (1-891739-02-6) Smithsonian Asian.
McQuail, Lisa, jt. auth. see Government Public Relations Office of the Prime Minister.
McQuain, Jeff, jt. auth. see Malless, Stan.
McQuain, Jeffery. Never Enough Words: How Americans Invented Expressions As Ingenious, Ornery & Colorful As Themselves. LC 99-12356. 1999. 24.95 (0-679-45804-2) Random Ref & Info.
McQuain, Jeffrey. Power Language: Getting the Most Out of Your Words. LC 95-48830. 224p. 1996. pap. 13.00 (0-395-71255-6) HM.
McQuain, Jeffrey & Malless, Stanley. Coined by Shakespeare: Words & Meanings First Penned by the Bard. LC 97-48561. (Illus.). 1998. 14.95 (0-87779-353-0) Merriam-Webster Inc.
McQuain, Jeffrey, jt. ed. see Manser, Martin H.
McQuany, Joe. Big Book Study Guide. 145p. 1986. pap. text 8.95 (1-883094-00-3) Kelly Fnd.
— Recovery Dynamics: Client Guide Book. 104p. 1989. pap. text 15.00 (1-883094-02-X) Kelly Fnd.
— Recovery Dynamics: Counselors Manual. 400p. 1989. text 60.00 (1-883094-01-1) Kelly Fnd.
— Recovery Dynamics: Individual Evaluation Packet. 96p. 1989. pap. text 14.00 (1-883094-03-8) Kelly Fnd.
McQuarie, Donald. Marx: Sociology-Social Change-Capitalism. 15.95 (0-7043-3221-3, Pub. by Quartet); pap. 6.95 (0-686-82876-3, Pub. by Quartet) Charles River Bks.
Mcquarie, Donald & Denisoff, R. Serge, eds. Readings in Contemporary Sociological Theory: From Modernity to Post-Modernity. LC 94-3991. 440p. 1994. pap. text 45.00 (0-13-104266-1) P-H.
McQuarie, Donald, jt. ed. see McGuire, Patrick.
McQuarrie, Allan D. & Tsai, Chih-Ling. Regression & Time Series Model Selection. LC 98-190995. 455p. 1998. 38.00 (981-02-3242-X) World Scientific Pub.
McQuarrie, Carole, jt. auth. see Cox, Heather.
McQuarrie, Donald & Simon, John. Molecular Thermodynamics. LC 98-48543. (Illus.). xiii, 656p. (C). 1999. text 78.00 (1-891389-05-X) Univ Sci Bks.
McQuarrie, Donald A. CTB-MAC General Chemistry. (C). 1992. 40.00 (0-7167-2266-6) W H Freeman.
— General Chemistry. 2nd ed. (C). 1986. pap. text. write for info. (0-7167-1913-4) W H Freeman.
— General Chemistry. 3rd ed. (C). 1991. pap. text 34.40 (0-7167-2169-4) W H Freeman.
— General Chemistry Package. (C). 1991. pap. text 80.00 (0-7167-2305-0) W H Freeman.
— Quantum Chemistry. LC 82-51234. (Physical Chemistry Ser.). (Illus.). 517p. (C). 1983. text 61.50 (0-935702-13-X) Univ Sci Bks.
— Quantum Chemistry Solutions Manual. (Physical Chemistry Ser.). 241p. (C). 1985. student ed. 22.00 (0-935702-16-4) Univ Sci Bks.
***McQuarrie, Donald A.** Statistical Mechanics. LC 00-21962. (Illus.). 640p. 2000. reprint ed. text 85.00 (1-891389-15-7) Univ Sci Bks.
McQuarrie, Donald A. Statistical Thermodynamics. 343p. (C). 1985. pap. text 48.00 (0-935702-18-0) Univ Sci Bks.
— Test Book Chemistry. (C). 1991. 13.60 (0-7167-2222-4) W H Freeman.
McQuarrie, Donald A. & Simon, John D. Physical Chemistry: A Molecular Approach. LC 97-142. (Illus.). 1200p. 1997. text 92.00 (0-935702-99-7) Univ Sci Bks.
McQuarrie, Donald G. Reoperative General Surgery. 2nd ed. Humphrey, Edward N., ed. LC 96-46310. (Illus.). 960p. (C). (gr. 13). 1996. text 180.00 (0-8151-7028-9, 27465) Mosby Inc.
McQuarrie, Edward F. Customer Visits: Building a Better Market Focus. 2nd ed. LC 97-45475. 241p. 1998. write for info. (0-7619-0883-8); pap. write for info. (0-7619-0884-6) Sage.
— Customer Visits: Tools to Build Market Focus. (Illus.). 176p. (C). 1993. text 49.95 (0-8039-4669-4); pap. text 22.95 (0-8039-4670-8) Sage.
— The Market Research Toolbox: A Concise Guide for Beginners. (Illus.). 184p. 1996. 46.00 (0-8039-5856-0); pap. 19.50 (0-8039-5857-9) Sage.
McQuarrie, John. Cowboyin' II: A Legend Lives On. LC 97-900725. (Illus.). 176p. 1997. 39.95 (0-9699761-4-3) Mountain Pr.
— Til We Meet Again. LC 92-238213. 1992. 34.95 (0-07-551301-3, Pub. by McG-H Ryerson) Howell Pr VA.
Mcquarrie, Ralph. Star Wars ArtBox: The Art of Ralph Mcquarrie. (Star Wars Ser.). 1996. 18.95 (0-8118-1320-7) Chronicle Bks.
McQuarrie, Ralph. The Illustrated Star Wars Universe. 208p. 1997. reprint ed. pap. 18.95 (0-553-37484-2) Bantam.
McQuarrie, Rock. General Chemistry. 3rd ed. LC 90-3706. (Illus.). 1184p. (C). 1991. 56.00 (0-7167-2187-2) W H Freeman.
— General Chemistry. 3rd ed. LC 90-3706. (Illus.). 1184p. (C). 1991. teacher ed. 13.60 (0-7167-2185-6); trans. 160.00 (0-7167-2186-4) W H Freeman.
McQuater, Ruth, jt. auth. see Dale, Barrie.
McQuattie, Shiela, jt. auth. see Dale, Catherine.
McQuay, Chris. Behold, Thy Handmaid. 208p. (Orig.). (C). 1992. pap. 7.95 (0-9619761-1-X) Chris Life Ctr.
McQuay, Henry & Moore, Andrew. An Evidence-Based Resource for Pain Relief. (Illus.). 272p. 1998. pap. text 65.00 (0-19-263048-2) OUP.
McQuay, Mike, jt. auth. see Kube-McDowell, Michael P.
McQueary, Carl R. & Paulisen, May N. Ma's in the Kitchen: You'll Know When It's Done. (Illus.). 216p. 1994. 16.95 (0-89015-953-X) Sunbelt Media.
McQueary, Carl R. & Paulissen, May N. Miriam: The Southern Belle Who Became the First Woman Governor Of Texas. Eakin, Ed, ed. LC 94-4455. 400p. 1995. 27.95 (0-89015-971-8) Sunbelt Media.
***McQueen.** Television: A Media. 288p. 1998. text 55.00 (0-340-71976-1, Pub. by E A) OUP.
McQueen, Alex S. History of Charlton County. LC 78-12909. (Illus.). 305p. 1988. reprint ed. 25.00 (0-87152-286-1) Reprint.
***McQueen, Alex S.** History of Charlton County (GA) With Genealogical Sketches. 1932p. 2000. 34.50 (0-7404-0035-5) Higginson Bk Co.
McQueen, Alex S. History of Charlton County, Georgia. (Illus.). 269p. 1993. reprint ed. lib. bdg. 32.50 (0-8328-2933-1) Higginson Bk Co.
McQueen, Bob, jt. auth. see McQueen, Judy.
McQueen, C. Richard & Crestol, Jack. Federal Tax Aspects of Bankruptcy. LC 84-11. (Tax & Estate Planning Ser.). 776p. 1984. 110.00 (0-685-42684-X) Shepards.
McQueen, C. Richard & Williams, Jack F. Tax Aspects of Bankruptcy Law & Practice. 3rd ed. LC 97-65756. 1997. write for info. (0-8366-9002-8) West Group.
McQueen, Charlene A. In Vitro Toxicology. 450p. 1989. lib. bdg. 88.00 (0-936923-23-7, RA1199) CRC Pr.
***McQueen, Cilla.** Markings: Poems & Drawings. (Illus.). 64p. 2000. pap. 24.95 (1-877133-92-2, Pub. by Univ Otago Pr) Intl Spec Bk.
***McQueen, Clyde.** Black Churches in Texas: A Guide to Historic Congregations. LC 99-45373. 288p. 2000. 39.95 (0-89096-902-7) Tex A&M Univ Pr.
— Black Churches in Texas: A Guide to Historic Congregations. LC 99-45373. Vol. 85. (Illus.). 288p. 2000. pap. 24.95 (0-89096-941-8) Tex A&M Univ Pr.
McQueen, Cyrus B. Field Guide to the Peat Mosses of Boreal North America. LC 89-40615. (Illus.). 154p. 1990. pap. 25.00 (0-87451-522-X) U Pr of New Eng.
McQueen, David. Television: A Media Student's Guide. LC 98-14852. (An Arnold Publication). (Illus.). 288p. 1999. pap. text 18.95 (0-340-70604-X) OUP.
McQueen, David V., jt. ed. see Martin, Claudia J.
McQueen, H. J., et al. Hot Workability & TMP of Ferrous & Non-Ferrous Alloys. 1996. 115.00 (0-919086-66-7) CIM.
McQueen, H. J., ed. see Metallurgical Society of AIME Staff.
Mcqueen, Ian L. Japan: A Budget Travel Guide. 1997. pap. text 20.00 (4-7700-2047-3, Pub. by Kodansha Intl) Kodansha.
McQueen, John & McQueen, Winifred, eds. Walter Bower's Scotichronicon, Bks. III & IV. (Scotichronicon Ser.). 400p. 1989. text 70.00 (0-08-036410-1, Pub. by Aberdeen U Pr) Macmillan.
McQueen, Judy, ed. IOLS, '92: Proceedings of the 7th Integrated Online Library Systems Meeting, May 6-7, 1992. 200p. 1992. pap. 30.00 (0-938734-62-8) Info Today Inc.
McQueen, Judy & McQueen, Bob. Intelligent Transportation Systems Architectures. LC 99-10826. 443p. 1998. 95.00 (0-89006-525-X, C8525) Artech Hse.
McQueen, Judy, jt. auth. see Basch, N. Bernard.
McQueen, Kelly & Fassler, David. Let's Talk Trash: The Kids' Book about Recycling. LC 90-21400. (Illus.). 168p. (J). (ps-6). 1991. pap. 14.95 (0-914525-19-0); 18.95 (0-914525-20-4) Waterfront Bks.
McQueen, Kelly, jt. auth. see Fassler, David.
McQueen, Kevin. Getting a Mortgage Loan. Askerooth, Gary & Fisher, Kathryn, eds. (Realizing the American Dream Ser.). (Illus.). 37p. (Orig.). 1995. pap., teacher ed. 3.00 (1-884356-07-9); pap., teacher ed., wbk. ed. 5.00 (1-884356-12-5) Neighborhd Reinvest.
— Shopping for a Home. Askerooth, Gary & Fisher, Kathryn, eds. (Realizing the American Dream Ser.). (Illus.). 39p. (Orig.). 1995. pap., teacher ed. 5.00 (1-884356-11-7); pap., wbk. ed. 3.00 (1-884356-06-0) Neighborhd Reinvest.
McQueen, Larry R. Joel & the Spirit: The Cry of a Prophetic Hemeneutic. (JPT Supplement Ser.: No. 8). 125p. 1995. pap. 13.95 (1-85075-736-4, Pub. by Sheffield Acad) CUP Services.
McQueen, Lucinda. Baby Farm Animals. (Illus.). 24p. (J). (ps). 1988. 2.95 (0-448-09251-4, G & D) Peng Put Young Read.
— La Gallinita Roja.Tr. of Little Hen. (SPA.). 32p. (J). (ps-2). 1989. 19.95 (0-590-71879-7) Scholastic Inc.
— La Gallinita Roja.Tr. of Little Hen. (SPA.). 32p. (J). (ps-2). 1991. pap. 3.95 (0-590-44927-3) Scholastic Inc.
— Little Bunny's Easter Surprise, 1 vol. 1999. 3.50 (0-590-65029-7) Scholastic Inc.
— Little Chick's Easter Surprise. 1999. pap. 3.50 (0-590-64985-X) Scholastic Inc.
— Little Duck's Easter Surprise, 1 vol. 1999. 3.50 (0-590-68130-3) Scholastic Inc.
— Little Lamb's Easter Surprise, 1 vol. 1999. 3.50 (0-590-41968-4) Scholastic Inc.
— The Little Red Hen. (FRE., Illus.). (Orig.). (J). pap. 6.99 (0-590-71720-0); pap. 13.99 incl. audio (0-590-73915-8) Scholastic Inc.
— Pet the Baby Farm Animals: Their Fur Feels Real! LC 93-84532. (Illus.). 16p. (J). (ps-2). 1994. 8.95 (0-590-47687-4, Cartwheel) Scholastic Inc.
— Santa's Christmas Surprise. (Sparkling Christmas Tree Bks.). (Illus.). 10p. (J). (ps). 1994. bds. 4.95 (0-590-48041-3, Cartwheel) Scholastic Inc.
— Snowman's Christmas Surprise. (Sparkling Christmas Tree Bks.). (Illus.). 10p. (J). (ps-1). 1994. bds. 4.95 (0-590-48042-1, Cartwheel) Scholastic Inc.
McQueen, Lucinda. The Little Red Hen. (Easy-to-Read Folktales Ser.). 32p. (Orig.). (J). (ps-3). 1985. pap. 2.99 (0-590-41145-4) Scholastic Inc.
— The Little Red Hen. Big bk. (Easy-to-Read Folktales Ser.). 32p. (Orig.). (J). (ps-3). 1985. 19.95 (0-590-71718-9) Scholastic Inc.
McQueen, Lucinda, jt. auth. see Alistir, K. A.
McQueen, Lucinda, ed. see Wolcott, Patty.
McQueen, Marcia, jt. auth. see Faughn, Jackie.
McQueen, Margaret, jt. auth. see Jupiter, Jesse.
***McQueen, Mary.** Tidings of Joy: Scriptures for the Church Seasons - Advent 1999. 48p. 1999. pap. 3.95 (0-687-07499-1) Abingdon.
McQueen, Mary P. The Farmers Market Cookbook. 142p. Date not set. 18.95 (0-8488-2368-0) Amereon Ltd.
McQueen, Matthew, et al. ACP-EU Trade & Aid Cooperation. 169p. 1997. pap. 11.95 (0-85092-538-X, Pub. by Comm Sec) Stylus Pub VA.
McQueen, Matthew J., et al, eds. Advances in Critical Care Testing: The IFCC-AVL Award 1996. LC 97-12403. (Illus.). 180p. 1997. pap. 63.00 (3-540-62590-9) Spr-Verlag.
***McQueen, Mike, et al.** Blue Horizons: Images from a Golden Age of Travel. (Illus.). 144p. 1999. pap. 27.50 (0-9521908-5-0, Pub. by Peak Pubg Ltd) Trans-Atl Phila.
McQueen, Priscilla L. Around the World in Twenty Legends. (Basic Readers Ser.). 1970. teacher ed. 3.25 (0-685-36208-6); student ed. 2.30 (0-685-36209-4) McQueen.
— Carousel of Stories. (Basic Readers Ser.). 1970. 10.98 (0-917186-13-3); student ed. 7.53 (0-917186-14-1) McQueen.
— Getting Ready for Reading, Writing & Arithmetic. (Illus.). teacher ed. 3.42 (0-685-16724-0) McQueen.
— How Many. (Illus.). (J). (gr. k). 1968. pap. 2.54 (0-685-16725-9) McQueen.

M

An Asterisk (*) at the beginning of an entry indicates that the title is appearing for the first time.

— Imagine That. (Basic Readers Ser.). 1970. teacher ed. 3.25 (*0-685-36210-8*); teacher ed. 2.30 (*0-685-36211-6*) McQueen.
— Our Own Country. (Basic Readers Ser.). 1970. teacher ed. 3.25 (*0-685-36212-4*); student ed. 2.30 (*0-685-36213-2*) McQueen.
— We Can Read: Story Pack - 54 Little Stories. (J). 1973. pap. 18.66 (*0-685-47089-X*) McQueen.
— What Kind. (Illus.). (J). (gr. k). 1968. pap. 2.07 (*0-685-16726-7*) McQueen.
— Which One? (Illus.). (J). (gr. k). 1968. pap. 6.15 (*0-685-16727-5*) McQueen.
McQueen, R. A. & Knussen, Christina. Research Methods in Psychology: A Practical Introduction. LC 98-31834. 1999. write for info. (*0-13-899238-X*) P-H.
McQueen, Rod. The Eatons: The Rise & Fall of Canada's Royal Family. LC 98-226571. (Illus.). 368p. 1998. 26.95 (*0-7737-3120-2*) Stoddart Publ.
— Last Best Hope: How to Start & Grow Your Own Business. 288p. 1996. 29.99 (*0-7710-5630-3*) McCland & Stewart.
McQueen, Rod. Last Best Hope: How to Start & Grow Your Own Business. 312p. 1997. pap. text 16.95 (*0-7710-5634-6*) McCland & Stewart.
McQueen, Rod. Who Killed Confederation Life? The Inside Story. (Illus.). 320p. 1997. 26.95 (*0-7710-5631-1*) McCland & Stewart.
— Who Killed Confederation Life? The Inside Story. (Illus.). 320p. 1997. pap. text 19.99 (*0-7710-5638-9*) McCland & Stewart.
McQueen, Shawna, jt. auth. see Eisenhauer, Jack.
McQueen, Steffani S. Dr. Mom's Low-Fat, No-Fat Fix It Fast Cookbook. 180p. 1994. pap. 11.95 (*0-9643854-0-6*) Sterling Texas.
***McQueen-Teasley, Regenia.** Regina McQueen - Born to Search. LC 00-90448. 2000. pap. 7.95 (*0-533-13501-X*) Vantage.
McQueen, Tom. Near-Life Experiences: Discovering New Powers for Personal Growth. LC 97-93191. 126p. 1997. 19.95 (*0-9656679-3-6*) J E M Pub.
— Passing the FAA Written Exam: Commercial. 1991. pap. 9.95 (*0-8306-3579-3*) McGraw-Hill Prof.
McQueen, William A., intro. A Selection of Emblems. LC 92-22032. (Augustan Reprints Ser.: No. 155-156). 1972. reprint ed. 21.50 (*0-404-70155-8*, PR1209) AMS Pr.
McQueen-Williams, Morvyth & Apisson, Barbara. A Diet for One Hundred Healthy Happy Years: Health Secrets from the Caucasus. Ober, Norman, ed. LC 76-30710. 1977. 9.95 (*0-685-03832-7*) P-H.
McQueen, Winifred, jt. ed. see McQueen, John.
McQueeney, Robert M. & Vacon, Bob. Unpardonable Sins: A Father's Fight for Justice. LC 91-68140. 1992. 21.95 (*0-88282-068-0*) New Horizon NJ.
McQuere, Gordon D. Russian Theoretical Thought in Music. LC 83-9097. (Russian Music Studies: No. 10). (Illus.). 404p. reprint ed. pap. 125.30 (*0-8357-1457-8*, 207051000097) Bks Demand.
McQuerry, Cleta. You Had to Be There. 90p. (Orig.). 1996. pap. 9.95 (*1-57502-131-5*) Morris Pubng.
McQuerry, James P., jt. ed. see Culp, Robert D.
***McQuerry, Maureen & Tetyana, Tetyana.** Nuclear Legacy: Students of Two Atomic Cities. LC 99-58585. 328p. 2000. boxed set 22.50 (*1-57477-087-X*) Battelle.
McQuigg, Jackson. History of Steel Wheels: Trains at the North Carolina Transportation Museum. LC 96-69322. (Illus.). 95p. 1996. pap. write for info. (*0-9642749-0-6*) NC Transptn Hist.
— Tampa Union Station. (Images of America Ser.). (Illus.). 128p. 1998. pap. 16.99 (*0-7524-0461-X*) Arcadia Publng.
McQuilken, Kim. The Road to Athletic Scholarship: What Every Student-Athlete, Parent & Coach Needs to Know. LC 96-19530. 210p. (C). 1996. text 37.50 (*0-8147-5530-5*); pap. text 13.50 (*0-8147-5546-1*) NYU Pr.
McQuilkin. Runner's Outdoor Sports Photography. (Illus.). 1982. 9.95 (*0-02-499580-0*, Macmillan Coll) P-H.
McQuilkin, Eleanor A. Every Sky. LC 98-92503. 69p. 1998. pap. 13.00 (*0-9662783-0-5*) Antrim Hse.
— Mornings. 80p. (Orig.). 1986. 13.95 (*0-9608824-2-1*); pap. 8.95 (*0-9608824-3-X*) Stereopticon Pr.
McQuilkin, Frank. Forgottenville, the Town that Arrested Santa Claus. unabridged ed. (Forgottenville Ser.). (Illus.). 48p. (J). (ps-7). 1982. 18.95 incl. audio (*0-941316-00-9*) TSM Books.
McQuilkin, J. Robertson. A Promise Kept. LC 98-16753. 1998. 14.99 (*0-8423-5099-3*) Tyndale Hse.
— Understanding & Applying the Bible. pap. 14.99 (*0-8024-9091-3*, 309) Moody.
McQuilkin, J. Robertson, compiled by. Free & Fulfilled: Victorious Living in the 21st Century. LC 96-50234. 352p. 1997. 24.99 (*0-7852-7556-8*) Nelson.
McQuilkin, Rennie. North Northeast: New England Poems. LC 85-13343. (Illus.). 96p. (Orig.). 1985. pap. 12.00 (*0-87233-081-8*) Bauhan.
McQuilkin, Robert. Comfort Below Freezing. LC 79-28741. (Illus.). 176p. (Orig.). 1980. pap. 5.95 (*0-89037-184-9*) Anderson World.
— How to Cut Photo Costs. rev. ed. Campbell, Susan, ed. LC 85-117511. (Illus.). 206p. 1985. 14.95 (*0-911445-02-1*) Page Prods.
— Runner's World Outdoor Sports Photography Book. 200p. 1982. pap. 9.95 (*0-89037-243-8*) Anderson World.
McQuilkin, Robert C. Our Lord's Parables. 1980. pap. 5.95 (*0-310-41541-1*) Zondervan.
***McQuilkin, Robertson.** The Great Omission: A Biblical Basis for World Evangelism. 103p. 1999. pap. 6.99 (*1-884543-23-5*) O M Lit.
— Life in the Spirit. LC 99-47243. 256p. 2000. pap. 12.99 (*0-8054-2079-7*) Broadman.
McQuilkin, Robertson J. An Introduction to Biblical Ethics. rev. ed. LC 94-42397. 560p. 1995. pap. 19.99 (*0-8423-1731-7*) Tyndale Hse.
McQuillan, Alan D. & McQuillan, M. K. Titanium. LC 56-4724. (Metallurgy of the Rarer Metals Ser.: No. 4). 486p. reprint ed. pap. 150.70 (*0-608-15056-8*, 202575900046) Bks Demand.
McQuillan, Alan G. & Preston, Ashley L., eds. Globally & Locally: Seeking a Middle Path to Sustainable Development. LC 98-15317. 484p. (C). 1998. 49.00 (*0-7618-1126-5*) U Pr of Amer.
***McQuillan, Alice.** They Call Them Grifters: The True Story of Sante & Kenneth Kimes. 2000. mass mkt. 6.99 (*0-451-40907-8*, Onyx) NAL.
Mcquillan, Claudia. Chips & Dips: 60 Terrific Recipes. LC 96-28038. 1997. 14.95 (*0-8118-1271-5*) Chronicle Bks.
McQuillan, D. Aidan. Prevailing over Time: Ethnic Adjustment on the Kansas Prairies, 1875-1925. LC 89-28957. xx, 292p. 1990. text 50.00 (*0-8032-3143-1*) U of Nebr Pr.
McQuillan, Dan. Ireland Guide. 2nd ed. 432p. 1998. pap. 17.95 (*1-883323-83-5*) Open Rd Pub.
***McQuillan, Dan.** Scotland Guide. 2000. 17.95 (*1-892975-33-5*) Open Rd Pub.
McQuillan, Deirdre. The Aran Sweater. (Little Irish Bookshelf Ser.). (Illus.). 60p. 1993. 9.95 (*0-86281-391-3*, Pub. by Appletree Pr) Irish Bks Media.
— The Dublin Style Guide: An Insider's Guide to Shopping for Style in Dublin. (Illus.). 172p. 1998. pap. 10.95 (*1-86059-015-2*, Pub. by Town Hse) Roberts Rinehart.
McQuillan, Jeff. The Literacy Crisis: False Claims, Real Solutions. LC 98-17263. 115p. 1998. pap. 16.00 (*0-325-00063-8*) Heinemann.
McQuillan, Jeff, jt. auth. see Krashen, Stephen.
McQuillan, John, ed. ATM Year 97 - Conference Proceedings: Asynchronous Transfer Mode. (Illus.). ring bd. 595.00 (*0-614-28396-5*) Tech Trans Inst.
McQuillan, Karin. Deadly Safari. (Boston Mysteries Ser.). 272p. 1991. mass mkt. 4.99 (*0-345-37057-0*) Ballantine Pub Grp.
— Deadly Safari. large type ed. 1994. 27.99 (*0-7089-3189-8*) Ulverscroft.
— Elephants' Graveyard. (Boston Mysteries Ser.). 272p. 1994. mass mkt. 4.99 (*0-345-38862-3*) Ballantine Pub Grp.
***McQuillan, Kevin.** Culture, Religion, & Demographic Behaviour: Catholics & Lutherans in Alsace, 1750-1870. 1999. text 60.00 (*0-7735-1860-6*) McG-Queens Univ Pr.
***McQuillan, Lawrence J.** The Case Against the International Monetary Fund. LC 99-46269. (Essays in Public Policy Ser.: No. 98). 29p. 1999. pap. 5.00 (*0-8179-4332-3*) Hoover Inst Pr.
McQuillan, Lawrence J. & Montgomery, Peter C., eds. The International Monetary Fund--Financial Medic to the World? A Primer on Mission, Operations & Public Policy. LC 99-11874. (Publication Ser.: Vol. 456). 245p. 1999. pap. 19.95 (*0-8179-9642-7*) Hoover Inst Pr.
McQuillan, M. K., jt. auth. see McQuillan, Alan D.
***McQuillan, Martin.** The Narrative Reader. LC 00-32308. 2000. pap. write for info. (*0-415-20533-6*) Routledge.
— Post-Theory: New Directions in Criticism. 224p. 2000. pap. 28.00 (*0-7486-1065-0*, Pub. by Edinburgh U Pr) Col U Pr.
***McQuillan, Martin & Byrne, Eleanor J.** Deconstructing Disney. LC 99-34635. 176p. 2000. 59.95 (*0-7453-1456-2*, Pub. by Pluto GBR); pap. 18.95 (*0-7453-1451-1*, Pub. by Pluto GBR) Stylus Pub VA.
McQuillan, Melissa. Van Gogh. (Illus.). 1989. pap. 14.95 (*0-500-20232-X*, Pub. by Thames Hudson) Norton.
McQuillan, Patrick J. Educational Opportunity in an Urban American High School: A Cultural Analysis. LC 96-52324. 243p. (C). 1997. text 57.50 (*0-7914-3499-0*); pap. text 18.95 (*0-7914-3500-8*) State U NY Pr.
McQuillan, Patrick J., jt. auth. see Muncey, Donna E.
McQuillan, Robert & Ardus, D. A. Exploring the Geology of Shelf Seas. LC QE0039.M25. (Illus.). 246p. reprint ed. pap. 76.30 (*0-608-18789-5*, 203014000068) Bks Demand.
***McQuillan, S.** Summus Pontifex Ecclesiae, 380-1534. 2000. pap. 18.00 (*0-7388-2211-6*) Xlibris Corp.
McQuillan, Susan & Saltzman, Edward. Complete Idiot's Guide to Losing Weight. LC 97-80967. 336p. 1997. 17.95 (*0-02-862113-1*) Macmillan Gen Ref.
McQuillan, Susan, jt. auth. see Ricketts, David.
McQuillan, Thomas, tr. see Norberg-Schulz, Christian.
McQuillen, Connie, ed. Robert Burton, Philosophaster. (Medieval & Renaissance Texts & Studies: Vol. 103). 240p. 1993. 25.00 (*0-86698-123-3*, MR103) MRTS.
McQuillen, Connie, tr. A Comedy Called Susenbrotus. LC 97-4586. 231p. (C). 1997. text 39.50 (*0-472-10756-9*, 10756) U of Mich Pr.
McQuillen, Connie, tr. see Schleiner, Louise.
McQuillen, Kevin & Prince, Anne. DOS-VSE Assembler Language. rev. ed. LC 85-63465. 492p. 1986. pap. 45.00 (*0-911625-31-3*) M Murach & Assoc.
— MVS Assembler Language. rev. ed. LC 86-63830. 528p. 1987. pap. 45.00 (*0-911625-34-8*) M Murach & Assoc.
McQuillen-Martensen, Kathy. Exercises in Positioning. LC 95-17703. 1996. pap. text 39.95 (*0-7216-4981-5*, W B Saunders Co) Harcrt Hlth Sci Grp.
— Exercises in Radiographic Critique: Text & Exercises Package. (Illus.). 465p. 1996. text 84.00 (*0-7216-6179-3*, W B Saunders Co) Harcrt Hlth Sci Grp.
— Radiograhic Critique. (Illus.). 320p. 1996. text 52.50 (*0-7216-4978-5*, W B Saunders Co) Harcrt Hlth Sci Grp.
— Radiographic Critique. (Illus.). 438p. 1996. teacher ed. write for info. (*0-7216-4979-3*, W B Saunders Co) Harcrt Hlth Sci Grp.
McQuillen, Michael J. Eriez Magnetics: From Pioneer to World Leader. LC 91-75933. 120p. 1991. 15.00 (*0-9630652-0-3*) Eriez Mfg.
McQuillin, F. J., ed. Homogeneous Hydrogenation in Organic Chemistry. LC 75-37874. (Homogeneous Catalysis in Organic & Inorganic Chemistry: No. 1). vi, 146p. 1975. text 94.00 (*90-277-0646-8*) Kluwer Academic.
McQuillis, Nellie R. Buying Hyacinths. LC 99-158760. (Illus.). 1998. 9.95 (*0-944128-19-X*) SW PA Geneal Servs.
McQuinn, Caitlin, jt. auth. see McQuinn, Conn.
McQuinn, Conn. Chess for Kids, Incl. chessboard & chess pieces. (Illus.). 32p. (J). (gr. 3-7). 1998. pap. 8.95 (*0-8167-4464-5*) Troll Communs.
— Fun with Electronics. (Illus.). 72p. (J). 1994. pap. 19.95 (*0-8362-4231-9*) Andrews & McMeel.
***McQuinn, Conn.** Glitter Bead Buddies. 8p. (J). (gr. 2-9). 1999. pap. 5.95 (*0-8167-4947-7*) Troll Communs.
— Kidbiz: Everything You Need to Start Your Own Business. LC 97-49142. (Illus.). 96p. (J). (gr. 3 up). 1999. pap. 10.99 (*0-14-038811-7*, PuffinBks) Peng Put Young Read.
McQuinn, Conn. Would You Rather? 150 Wild & Wacky Choices. (Illus.). 96p. (J). (gr. 3-7). 1998. pap. 4.95 (*0-8167-4807-1*) Troll Communs.
McQuinn, Conn & McQuinn, Caitlin. Bead Buddies. (Illus.). 8p. (J). (gr. 2-9). 1998. 5.95 (*0-8167-4716-4*) Troll Communs.
McQuinn, Conn, jt. auth. see Colombo, Luann.
McQuinn, Conn, jt. auth. see Columbo, Luann.
McQuinn, Donald E. Warrior. (Military Science Fiction Promotion Ser.). 672p. 1991. mass mkt. 5.99 (*0-345-37348-0*, Del Rey) Ballantine Pub Grp.
— Witch. (Orig.). 1995. mass mkt. 6.99 (*0-345-39737-1*, Del Rey) Ballantine Pub Grp.
— With Full Honors. 1997. mass mkt. 5.99 (*0-345-40045-3*, Del Rey) Ballantine Pub Grp.
McQuire, Scott. Visions of Modernity: Representation, Memory, Time, & Space in the Age of the Cinema. 264p. 1997. 75.00 (*0-7619-5300-0*); pap. 32.00 (*0-7619-5301-9*) Sage.
McQuiston. Solution Manual to Accompany Heating, Ventilating & Air Conditioning. 216p. 1994. pap. text 16.95 (*0-471-30900-1*) Wiley.
McQuiston, Chris M. & Webb, Adele A. Foundations of Nursing Theory: Contributions of 12 Key Theorists. 650p. 1995. text 69.95 (*0-8039-7136-2*); pap. text 32.00 (*0-8039-7137-0*) Sage.
McQuiston, Debra, jt. auth. see McQuiston, Don.
McQuiston, Don & McQuiston, Debra. Dolls & Toys of Native America: A Journey Through Childhood. LC 94-34678. (Illus.). 120p. 1995. pap. 19.95 (*0-8118-0570-0*) Chronicle Bks.
— Visions of the North: Native Arts of the Northwest Coast. LC 96-163546. (Illus.). 120p. 1995. pap. 19.95 (*0-8118-0859-9*) Chronicle Bks.
***McQuiston, Don, et al.** Visions of the North: Native Art of the Northwest Coast. (Illus.). 120p. 2000. reprint ed. pap. text 20.00 (*0-7881-9130-6*) DIANE Pub.
McQuiston, F. W., Jr. Gold: The Saga of the Empire Mine, 1850-1956. Steinfeld, Charles, ed. (Illus.). 96p. (Orig.). 1986. pap. 9.95 (*0-931892-07-4*) B Dolphin Pub.
McQuiston, F. W. & Shoemaker, Robert S. Gold & Silver Cyanidation Plant Practice, Vol. 1. fac. ed. LC 75-309162. (Illus.). 245p. 1975. reprint ed. pap. 76.00 (*0-7837-7862-7*, 204762100001) Bks Demand.
— Gold & Silver Cyanidation Plant Practice, Vol. 2. fac. ed. LC 75-309162. (Illus.). 323p. 1981. reprint ed. pap. 100.20 (*0-7837-7863-5*, 204762100002) Bks Demand.
McQuiston, F. W. & Shoemaker, Roberts. Primary Crushing Plant Design. LC 77-94869. (Illus.). 297p. reprint ed. pap. 92.10 (*0-608-18319-9*, 203159100075) Bks Demand.
McQuiston, Faye C. & Parker, Jerald D. Heating, Ventilating, & Air Conditioning. 3rd ed. LC 87-34604. 200p. 1988. pap. text 7.50 (*0-471-61224-3*) Wiley.
— Heating, Ventilation & Air Conditioning Analysis & Design. 4th ed. 768p. 1993. text 100.95 (*0-471-58107-0*) Wiley.
***McQuiston, Faye C., et al.** Heating, Ventilating, & Air Conditioning: Analysis & Design. 5th ed. LC 99-58908. 656p. 2000. 102.95 incl. cd-rom (*0-471-35098-2*) Wiley.
McQuiston, John, 2nd. Always We Begin Again: The Benedictine Way of Living. LC 95-52770. 96p. (Orig.). 1996. pap. 7.95 (*0-8192-1648-8*) Morehouse Pub.
McQuiston, L. B. McQuiston-McCuiston-McQuesten Families, 1620-1937. 750p. 1991. reprint ed. lib. bdg. 119.00 (*0-8328-1929-8*) Higginson Bk Co.
McQuiston, Liz. Graphic Agitation: Social & Political Graphics since The Sixties. (Illus.). 240p. 1995. pap. 35.00 (*0-7148-3458-0*, Pub. by Phaidon Press) Phaidon Pr.
— Graphic Agitation: Social & Political Graphics since the Sixties. (Illus.). 240p. (C). 1993. reprint ed. text 55.00 (*0-7148-2878-5*, Pub. by Phaidon Press) Phaidon Pr.
— Suffragettes to She-Devils. (Illus.). 240p. 1997. 59.95 (*0-7148-3619-2*, Pub. by Phaidon Press) Phaidon Pr.
McQuiston, Mary G., jt. auth. see Jones, David P.
McQuiston, Susan, jt. auth. see Garrison, William T.
McQuitty, Louis L. Pattern-Analytical Clustering: Theory, Method, Research & Configural Findings. LC 87-13346. (Illus.). 816p. 1987. lib. bdg. 102.00 (*0-8191-6449-6*) U Pr of Amer.
McQuoid-Mason, D. J., et al. Consumer Law. (Human Rights for All Ser.: Bk. 3). 108p. 1988. pap., student ed. write for info. (*0-7021-2469-9*, Pub. by Juta & Co) Gaunt.
— Consumer Law. (Human Rights for All Ser.: Bk. 3). 91p. 1991. pap., teacher ed. write for info. (*0-7021-2470-2*, Pub. by Juta & Co) Gaunt.
— Criminal Law & Juvenile Justice. (Human Rights for All Ser.: Bk. 2). 79p. 1987. pap., teacher ed. write for info. (*0-7021-2466-4*, Pub. by Juta & Co); pap., student ed. write for info. (*0-7021-2465-6*, Pub. by Juta & Co) Gaunt.
— Family Law. (Human Rights for All Ser.: Bk. 4). 82p. 1990. pap., teacher ed. write for info. (*0-7021-2411-7*, Pub. by Juta & Co); pap., student ed. write for info. (*0-7021-2410-9*, Pub. by Juta & Co) Gaunt.
— Street Law - Allemansreg, Bk. 1: Introduction to South African Law & the Legal System. (Human Rights for All Ser.). 70p. 1987. pap., student ed. write for info. (*0-7021-2461-3*, Pub. by Juta & Co) Gaunt.
— Street Law - Allemansreg, Bk. 1: Introduction to South African Law & the Legal System. (Human Rights for All Ser.). 93p. 1990. pap., teacher ed. write for info. (*0-7021-2462-1*, Pub. by Juta & Co) Gaunt.
McQuoid-Mason, David. Consumer Law in South Africa. LC 98-126563. xlxvi, 386p. 1997. pap. 52.00 (*0-7021-3856-8*, Pub. by Juta & Co) Gaunt.
McQuone, Shelly, jt. auth. see Eisele, David W.
McQuown, Judith. Incorporate Yourself. (Illus.). 304p. 1999. 27.50 (*0-7679-0223-8*) Broadway BDD.
***McQuown, Judith H.** Inc. Yourself: How to Profit by Setting up Your Own Corporation. 9th ed. 304p. 2000. pap. 15.00 (*0-7679-0225-4*) Broadway BDD.
McQuown, N. A., jt. ed. see Wauchope, Robert.
McQuown, Norman A. Spoken Turkish, Bk. 1, Units 1-12. LC 74-152747. (Spoken Language Ser.). 378p. (gr. 9-12). 1971. pap. 20.00 (*0-87950-240-1*) Spoken Lang Serv.
— Spoken Turkish, Bk. 2, Units 13-30. LC 74-152747. (Spoken Language Ser.). 378p. (gr. 9-12). 1971. pap. 20.00 (*0-87950-241-X*) Spoken Lang Serv.
McQuown, Norman A. & Kaylan, Sadi. Spoken Turkish. LC 74-152747. (Spoken Language Ser.). 378p. (gr. 9-12). 1971. audio 75.00 (*0-87950-245-2*) Spoken Lang Serv.
McQuown, Norman A. & Kaylan, Sadi. Spoken Turkish, Bk. 1. LC 74-152747. (Spoken Language Ser.). 378p. (gr. 9-12). 1971. pap. 95.00 incl. audio (*0-87950-246-0*) Spoken Lang Serv.
McQuown, Richard C., jt. auth. see Henning, Harry L.
McQustra, Christopher. Love in the Economy: Social Doctrine of the Church for the Individual in the Economy. 220p. (C). 1996. pap. 39.95 (*0-85439-324-2*, Pub. by St Paul Pubns) St Mut.
McRae. The Elvis Mystery. 1992. pap. text. write for info. (*0-17-556083-8*) Addison-Wesley.
— Who Was Nancy? 1992. pap. text. write for info. (*0-17-556000-5*) Addison-Wesley.
Mcrae. The World in 2020. 1995. 24.95 (*0-07-103616-4*) McGraw.
McRae, Andrew. God Speed the Plough: The Representation of Agrarian England, 1500-1660. (Past & Present Publications). (Illus.). 351p. (C). 1996. text 69.95 (*0-521-45379-8*) Cambridge U Pr.
McRae, Barbara & Leverette, Rebekah. Macon County NC in the 1850 Census: A Snapshot in Time. 183p. 1997. pap. 22.00 (*0-9638930-3-3*) Teresita Pr.
McRae, Barbara S. Franklin's Ancient Mound: Myth & History of Old Nikwasi, Franklin, N.C. (Illus.). 56p. (Orig.). 1993. pap. 6.95 (*0-9638930-0-9*) Teresita Pr.
— Records of Macon County, NC, 1849-1858: Deed Books F, G, H & I. 136p. Date not set. pap. 25.00 (*0-9638930-4-1*) Teresita Pr.
McRae, Barbara S., ed. Atahita Journal: A Collection of Prose & Poetry from the Southern Mountains. 78p. (Orig.). 1994. pap. 8.00 (*0-9638930-1-7*) Teresita Pr.
***McRae, Barbara Sears.** Records of Old Macon County, North Carolina, 1829-1850. 212p. 2000. reprint ed. pap. 25.00 (*0-8063-1302-1*, Pub. by Clearfield Co) ACCESS Pubs Network.
McRae, Barry. The Jazz Cataclysm. LC 84-1827. (Roots of Jazz Ser.). 198p. 1985. reprint ed. lib. bdg. 25.00 (*0-306-76240-4*) Da Capo.
— The Jazz Handbook. (Monograph Ser.). 272p. 1990. 30.00 (*0-8161-9096-8*, Hall Reference); 18.95 (*0-8161-1828-0*, Hall Reference) Macmillan.
McRae, Bill. Lonely Planet Seattle. (Illus.). 222p. 1998. pap. 14.95 (*0-86442-537-6*) Lonely Planet.
McRae, Bill & Jewell, Judy. Lonely Planet Pacific Northwest: U. S. A. Guide. (Illus.). 896p. 1995. pap. 19.95 (*0-86442-240-7*) Lonely Planet.
McRae, Bill, et al. Frommer's Canada. 10th ed. (Frommer's Travel Guides Ser.). 816p. 1998. pap. 19.95 (*0-02-862051-8*, Frommer) Macmillan Gen Ref.
— Lonely Planet Pacific Northwest: Travel Survival Kit. 2nd ed. (Lonely Planet Travel Guides Ser.). (Illus.). 912p. 1999. pap. text 24.95 (*0-86442-534-1*) Lonely Planet.
McRae, Bobbi A. Colors from Nature: Growing, Collecting, & Using Natural Dyes. Steege, Gwen, ed. LC 92-53808. (Illus.). 168p. 1993. 26.95 (*0-88266-806-4*, Storey Pub); pap. 17.95 (*0-88266-799-8*, Storey Pub) Storey Bks.
— The Frugal Gardener - More Than 200 Ways to Save Resources (& Money) by Recycling in Your Garden. (Illus.). 96p. (Orig.). 1992. pap. 8.95 (*0-944577-04-0*) Limestone.
— Nature's Dyepot: A Resource Guide for Spinners, Weavers & Dyers. (Illus.). 65p. (Orig.). 1991. pap. 8.95 (*0-944577-02-4*) Limestone.
— The New Fiberworks Sourcebook: Being an Essential Mail-Order Guide to Supplies & Services for the Fiber Arts. LC 93-12584. (Illus.). 320p. (Orig.). 1993. pap. 15.95 (*0-944577-06-7*) Limestone.
McRae Books Agency Staff, jt. auth. see Ross, Stewart.
McRae, Brad. Negotiating & Influencing Skills: The Art of Creating & Claiming Value. LC 97-21051. 176p. 1997. 42.00 (*0-7619-1184-7*) Sage.
— Negotiating & Influencing Skills: The Art of Creating & Claiming Value. LC 97-21051. xii, 195 p. 1998. pap. 19.95 (*0-7619-1185-5*) Sage.

An Asterisk (*) at the beginning of an entry indicates that the title is appearing for the first time.

McRae, Bradley C. Practical Time Management: How to Get More Things Done in Less Time. 2nd ed. (Business Ser.). 144p. 1992. pap. 7.95 (*0-88908-281-2*) Self-Counsel Pr.

McRae, David. Developing the VCE. 95p. 1992. pap. 45.00 (*0-7300-1388-X*, ECT436, Pub. by Deakin Univ) St Mut.

McRae, David & Frenkel, Dean. The Essential Meditation Guide. (Illus.). 64p. (Orig.). 1995. pap. 8.95 (*0-85572-253-3*, Pub. by Hill Content Pubng) Seven Hills Bk.

McRae, Donald. Dark Trade: Lost in Boxing. (Illus.). 304p. 1998. pap. 19.95 (*1-85158-999-6*, Pub. by Mainstream Pubng) Trafalgar.

McRae, Donald, jt. ed. see Kaplan, William.

McRae, Donald M. & Steger, Debra P., eds. Understanding the Free Trade Agreement. 254p. 1989. pap. text 23.95 (*0-88645-079-9*, Pub. by Inst Res Pub) Ashgate Pub Co.

McRae, Floyd W., Jr., ed. see Dickey, Thomas S. & George, Peter C.

McRae, Gail C. Borzois. (Illus.). 192p. 1989. 9.95 (*0-86622-676-1*, KW-167) TFH Pubns.

McRae, Glen, et al. An Ounce of Prevention: Waste Reduction Strategies for Health Care Facilities. (Illus.). 222p. (Orig.). 1993. pap. 50.00 (*0-87258-637-5*, 057007) Am Hospital.

McRae, Hamish. Japan's Role in the Emerging Global Securities Markets. (Occasional Paper Ser.: No. 17). 30p. 1985. pap. 7.00 (*1-56708-016-2*) Grp of Thirty.

— The World in 2020: Power, Culture & Prosperity. LC 94-24545. 320p. 1995. 24.95 (*0-87584-604-1*) Harvard Busn.

— The World in 2020: Power, Culture & Prosperity. 320p. 1996. pap. 14.95 (*0-87584-738-2*) Harvard Busn.

McRae, Heather, et al. Indigenous Legal Issues: Commentary & Materials. 2nd ed. LC 97-153750. 540p. 1997. pap. 68.00 (*0-455-21468-9*, Pub. by LawBk Co) Gaunt.

McRae, I. I. The Geodetic World Map. 126p. 1988. 16.00 (*0-86690-349-6*, M2822-014) Am Fed Astrologers.

McRae, James. MTA - A Word Game Mystery about the 3C's: Conspiracy, Corruption & Control. 333p. Date not set. pap. text 15.00 (*0-9651347-2-5*) J McRae.

— "We Are Not Beggars" - a Private Sector: Economic Revitalization Plan for the Black Inner City. 2nd ed. LC 96-144912. 57p. (Orig.). 1996. pap. text 10.00 (*0-9651347-1-7*) J McRae.

— Youngmaster - The Mistakes We Make As Youth, & the Regrets Such Cause Us, As Adults. 544p. Date not set. pap. text 15.00 (*0-9651347-0-9*) J McRae.

McRae, James J., jt. auth. see Coffey, William J.

McRae, James J., ed. see Ali, Ansara.

McRae, Jenna. Brick Paths & Clay Pots Vol. 3: Gardens of a Lifetime. (Rose Cottage Papers Ser.: Vol. 3). (Illus.). 80p. (Orig.). 1998. pap. 12.00 (*1-887106-15-4*) McRae Banker.

— Renderings. (Rose Cottage Papers). (Illus.). 34p. (Orig.). 1995. pap. 7.00 (*1-887106-00-6*) McRae Banker.

McRae, John. Blood of the Lion. 240p. 1994. 16.98 (*0-88290-509-0*, 1981) Horizon Utah.

— Fire in the Snow. LC 93-27311. 239p. 1993. pap. 10.95 (*0-87579-752-0*) Deseret Bk.

— The Language of Poetry. LC 97-17316. (Intertext Ser.). 168p. (C). 1998. pap. 16.99 (*0-415-16928-3*) Routledge.

McRae, John & Boardman, Roy. Reading Between the Lines, 2 cass. 120p. 1984. pap. 31.95 incl. audio (*0-521-25992-4*); pap. text 15.95 (*0-521-27790-6*); pap. text 14.95 (*0-521-27789-2*) Cambridge U Pr.

McRae, John & Vethamani, Malachi E. Now Read On: A Multicultural Anthology of Literature in English. LC 98-38478. 1999. 65.00 (*0-415-18216-6*); pap. 21.99 (*0-415-18217-4*) Routledge.

McRae, John, jt. auth. see Carter, Ronald.

McRae, John, tr. see Numata Center for Buddhist Translation & Research.

McRae, John M. Elderly in the Environment: Northern Europe. LC 76-352614. 121p. (Orig.). reprint ed. pap. 37.60 (*0-7837-4912-0*, 204457700004) Bks Demand.

McRae, John M., ed. see Southern Conference on Gerontology Staff.

McRae, John R., tr. see Sengaku, Mayeda & Inada, Kenneth K., eds.

McRae, Kenneth D. Conflict & Compromise in Multilingual Societies: Belgium. Vol. 2. xiv, 387p. (C). 1986. pap. 19.95 (*0-88920-195-1*) W Laurier U Pr.

— Conflict & Compromise in Multilingual Societies: Belgium, Vol. 2. 3rd ed. xiv, 387p. (C). 1986. text 45.00 (*0-88920-163-3*) W Laurier U Pr.

— Conflict & Compromise in Multilingual Societies Vol. 1: Switzerland. 2nd ed. xxii, 274p. 1998. reprint ed. 44.95 (*0-88920-313-X*) W Laurier U Pr.

— Conflict & Compromise in Multilingual Societies Vol. 3: Finland. 447p. 1997. 55.00 (*0-88920-283-4*) W Laurier U Pr.

McRae, L. E., jt. auth. see Holtz, M. H.

McRae, Lee. Handbook of Renaissance Society & Its Songs: Western Europe & England, 1400-1600 & the Place of Music in the Renaissance. rev. ed. (YA). (gr. 7-12). 1999. pap. write for info. (*0-9626075-4-1*) L McRae.

— Handbook of the Renaissance: Europe: 1400-1600. 3rd ed. (Illus.). 56p. 1995. reprint ed. pap. 12.00 (*0-9626075-2-5*) L McRae.

McRae, Linda & Kelliher. African Ethnonyms: Index to Art Producing Peoples of Africa. LC 96-19439. 378p. 1996. 95.00 (*0-7838-1532-8*, G K Hall & Co) Mac Lib Ref.

McRae, Linda & White, Lynda S. Artmarc Sourcebook: Cataloging Art, Architecture, & Their Surrogate Images. LC 97-39441. 287p. 1998. 75.00 (*0-8389-0723-7*) ALA.

***McRae, Melinda.** Miss Chadwick's Companion. (Signet Regency Romance Ser.). 2000. mass mkt. 4.99 (*0-451-19857-3*, Sig) NAL.

Mcrae, Melinda. Temporary Duke. (Signet Regency Romance Ser.). 224p. 1998. mass mkt. 4.99 (*0-451-19577-9*, Sig) NAL.

McRae, Melinda. The Unrepentant Rake. 224p. 1999. mass mkt. 4.99 (*0-451-19779-8*, Sig) NAL.

McRae, Michael J. Continental Drifter: Dispatches from the Uttermost Parts of the Earth. (Illus.). 224p. 1993. 21.95 (*1-55821-243-4*) Burford Bks.

McRae, Murray, et al. New Works: Visiting Hours; House;The Prairie Church of Buster Galloway;Wetland Roy; LC 88-107476. 548p. (Orig.). 1997. pap. 18.95 (*0-88754-451-7*) Theatre Comm.

McRae, Norman. Greater Detroit: The First City of the Midwest. Parks, Lori, ed. LC 99-73081. (Illus.). 350p. 2000. 49.95 (*1-886483-31-0*, Pub. by Heritge Media) Sunbelt Pubns.

McRae, Ocee. Romance in the Oil Fields of Texas. 182p. 1990. 6.95 (*0-917724-01-X*, 962) Lunan-Ferguson.

McRae, Patricia B., tr. see Mandel, Richard D.

McRae, R., et al. Key Topics in Otolaryngology. 368p. (Orig.). 1995. pap. 57.50 (*1-872748-68-6*, Pub. by Bios Sci) Coronet Bks.

McRae, Renee. Truth in Rhyme: By Renee McRae. 2nd rev. ed. ix, 55p. 1996. spiral bd. 12.95 (*0-9670542-0-6*) McRae Ents.

McRae, Robert. The Problem of the Unity of the Sciences: Bacon to Kant. LC 62-2304. 160p. reprint ed. pap. 49.60 (*0-8357-8905-5*, 201431800095) Bks Demand.

McRae, Robert F. Leibniz: Perception, Apperception, & Thought. LC 76-6084. 158p. reprint ed. pap. 49.00 (*0-8357-3647-4*, 203637400003) Bks Demand.

McRae, Robert Grant. Philosophy & the Absolute: The Modes of Hegel's Speculation. 1985. lib. bdg. 118.00 (*90-247-3151-8*) Kluwer Academic.

McRae, Ronald. Clinical Orthopedic Examination. 4th ed. LC 97-10029. 1997. pap. text 36.95 (*0-443-05602-1*) Church.

— Clinical Orthopedic Examination. 4th ed. LC 97-10029. 1998. write for info. (*0-443-05812-1*) Church.

McRae, Ronald K. Practical Fracture Treatment. 3rd ed. LC 93-7651. 384p. 1994. pap. text 60.00 (*0-443-04809-6*) Church.

McRae, Ronald K. & Kinninmonth, A. W. Orthopaedics & Trauma: An Illustrated Colour Text. LC 96-39211. (Illus.). 152p. 1997. pap. text 34.95 (*0-443-05135-6*) Church.

McRae, Shirley W. Angel at the Door: Southern Folksongs for Voices & Orff Instruments. 36p. 1981. pap. 6.50 (*0-918812-16-X*) MMB Music.

— Chatter with the Angels: Folk Songs from the American Black Tradition for Voices & Orff Instruments. 44p. 1980. pap. 8.95 (*0-918812-09-7*, SE 0239) MMB Music.

McRae, Stuart G. Practical Pedology. 300p. 1988. text 52.95 (*0-470-21062-1*) P-H.

McRae, Susan. Cross-Class Families: A Study of Wives' Occupational Superiority. 224p. 1986. 59.00 (*0-19-827264-2*) OUP.

McRae, Susan, ed. Changing Britain: Families & Households in the 1990s. LC 99-24527. 512p. 2000. text 72.00 (*0-19-829636-3*) OUP.

McRae, T. W. Managing Your Finances. LC 97-12805. 1997. 17.99 (*1-86152-049-2*, Pub. by ITBP) Thomson Learn.

McRae, Thomas W. Computers & Accounting. LC 75-6793. 179p. reprint ed. pap. 55.50 (*0-8357-2590-1*, 205237000013) Bks Demand.

— Statistical Sampling for Audit & Control. LC 73-19329. (Wiley-Interscience Publications). 299p. reprint ed. pap. 92.70 (*0-7837-4518-4*, 204429700001) Bks Demand.

McRae, Thomas W., jt. auth. see Fothergill, Kenneth R.

McRae, W. A., jt. auth. see Chambers, W. A.

McRae, W. C. Road Trip U. S. A. Getaways: Seattle - Northwest Driving Adventures Beyond the Metro Area. (Illus.). 60p. 2000. pap. 9.95 (*1-56691-156-7*, Roadtrip) Avalon Travel.

McRae, W. C. & Jewell, Judy. Moon Handbooks: Montana: Including Glacier National Park. 4th rev. ed. Vol. 4. (Illus.). 490p. 1999. pap. 17.95 (*1-56691-142-7*, Moon Handbks) Avalon Travel.

McRae, W. C., jt. auth. see Weir, Bill.

McRae, Wallace. Cowboy Curmudgeon: And Other Poems. (Illus.). 144p. (Orig.). 1992. pap. 12.95 (*0-87905-463-8*) Gibbs Smith Pub.

McRae, William J. Preparing for Your Marriage. 211p. (Orig.). 1980. pap. 10.99 (*0-310-42761-4*, 9366P) Zondervan.

McRaild, Donald M. Culture, Conflict & Migration: The Irish in Victorian Cumbria. 256p. 1998. 44.95 (*0-85323-652-6*, Pub. by Liverpool Univ Pr); pap. 19.95 (*0-85323-662-3*, Pub. by Liverpool Univ Pr) Intl Spec Bk.

McRandle, James H. The Antique Drums of War. LC 93-41325. (Military History Ser.: No. 33). (Illus.). 232p. 1994. 39.50 (*0-89096-591-9*); pap. 18.95 (*0-89096-611-7*) Tex A&M Univ Pr.

McRann, Penelope Kister, ed. see Morrison, Marvin L.

McRaven, Charles. Building & Restoring the Hewn Log House. LC 93-39370. (Illus.). 176p. 1994. pap. 21.99 (*1-55870-325-X*, Betrwy Bks) F & W Pubns Inc.

— Building with Stone. LC 88-62875. (Illus.). 192p. 1989. reprint ed. pap. 17.95 (*0-88266-550-2*, Garden Way Pub) Storey Bks.

— Building with Stone. LC 88-62875. (Illus.). 192p. 1991. reprint ed. 24.95 (*0-88266-569-3*, Garden Way Pub) Storey Bks.

— Stonework: Techniques & Projects. McHale, Elizabeth, ed. LC 97-28290. (Illus.). 192p. 1997. pap. 18.95 (*0-88266-976-1*, Storey Pub) Storey Bks.

McRaven, William H. Spec Ops: Case Studies in Special Operations Warfare: Theory & Practice. (Illus.). 402p. 1998. text 28.00 (*0-7881-5620-9*) DIANE Pub.

— Spec Ops: Case Studies in Special Operations Warfare, Theory & Practice. LC 94-46452. (Illus.). 432p. 1996. pap. 19.95 (*0-89141-600-5*) Presidio Pr.

McRay, John. Archaeology & the New Testament. LC 91-11663. 432p. (Orig.). 1990. 39.99 (*0-8010-6267-5*) Baker Bks.

McRay, Ron. Through the Water, Through the Fire. 64p. 1992. per. 3.95 (*0-9631167-0-3*) R McRay.

McReady, William, jt. ed. see Cafferty, Pastora.

McRedmond, Louis. Modern Irish Lives: A Dictionary of Twentieth-Century Biography. LC 96-30676. 400p. 1996. text 35.00 (*0-312-16478-5*) St Martin.

— Thrown among Strangers: John Henry Newman in Ireland. 223p. (Orig.). 1990. pap. 16.95 (*1-85390-180-6*, Pub. by Veritas Pubns) St Mut.

***McRedmond, Louis, ed.** Modern Irish Lives: Dictionary of 20th-Century Biography. LC 99-193915. xix, 328 p. 1998. write for info. (*0-7171-2786-9*, Pub. by Gill & MacMill) St Mut.

McRee, Duncan E. Practical Protein Crystallography. (Illus.). 386p. 1993. text 73.00 (*0-12-486050-8*) Acad Pr.

— Practical Protein Crystallography. 2nd ed. 500p. 1999. 75.00 (*0-12-486052-4*) Acad Pr.

***McRee, Livia.** Instant Fabric: Quilted Projects from Your Home Computer. (Illus.). 96p. 2000. pap. 24.95 (*1-56477-338-8*) Martingale & Co.

McRee, Nancy J., jt. auth. see Ringwald, Barbara.

McReynolds. The Chalice & the Blade. 464p. 1998. reprint ed. mass mkt. 6.50 (*0-553-57430-2*, Fanfare) Bantam.

McReynolds, Anne & Packer, Jo. The Power to Bring Them Back. pap. 11.98 (*1-55517-318-7*) CFI Dist.

McReynolds, B.S. The 007 Dossier. LC 99-177401. 1999. 23.95 (*0-9667203-7-7*) BS Bk Pubg.

— Presidential Blips: Dips, Flips, Lip, Pips, Quips, Rips, Slips, Tips & Zips. LC 98-231375. 1998. pap. 19.95 (*0-9667203-6-9*) BS Bk Pubg.

McReynolds, Edwin C. Oklahoma: History of the Sooner State. rev. ed. LC 54-10052. (Illus.). 477p. 1962. 24.95 (*0-8061-0302-7*) U of Okla Pr.

— Seminoles. LC 57-11198. (Civilization of the American Indian Ser.: No. 47). (Illus.). 1975. reprint ed. pap. 16.95 (*0-8061-1255-7*) U of Okla Pr.

McReynolds, Edwin C., et al. Oklahoma: The Story of Its Past & Present. LC 61-17309. (Illus.). 500p. 1961. 22.95 (*0-8061-0509-7*) U of Okla Pr.

McReynolds, Elaine, jt. auth. see McReynolds, Ray.

McReynolds, George E., jt. auth. see Tupper, Eleanor.

***McReynolds, Glenna.** Dream Stone. 464p. 2000. reprint ed. mass mkt. 6.50 (*0-553-57431-0*) Bantam.

McReynolds, Janet. Something Supernatural. 103p. 1986. pap. 3.95 (*0-88144-038-8*) Christian Pub.

McReynolds, Katherine. Susanna Wesley. (Women of Faith Ser.). 16p. 1998. mass mkt. 4.99 (*0-7642-2003-9*, 202003) Bethany Hse.

McReynolds, Kathy. Catherine Marshall. LC 99-6443. (Women of Faith Ser.). 160p. 1999. pap. text 4.99 (*0-7642-2167-1*) Bethany Hse.

McReynolds, Kathy & Luter, Boyd. Women As Christ's Disciples. LC 96-32480. 208p. (gr. 11). 1997. pap. 11.99 (*0-8010-5711-6*) Baker Bks.

McReynolds, Louise. The News under Russia's Old Regime: The Development of a Mass-Circulation Press. LC 91-13671. 327p. 1991. reprint ed. pap. 101.40 (*0-608-04577-2*, 206534600003) Bks Demand.

McReynolds, Louise, jt. ed. see Von Geldern, James.

McReynolds, Louise, ed. & tr. see Nagrodskaia, E.

McReynolds, Louise, ed. & tr. see Nagrodskaia, Evdokia.

McReynolds, Patricia J. Almost Americans: A Quest for Dignity. LC 97-37227. (Red Crane Literature Ser.). (Illus.). 264p. (Orig.). 1997. pap. 16.95 (*1-878610-64-3*) Red Crane Bks.

McReynolds, Paul. Lightner Witmer: His Life & Times. LC 97-17508. 353p. 1997. 24.95 (*1-55798-444-1*) Am Psychol.

McReynolds, Paul, ed. Advances in Psychological Assessment, Vol. 3. LC 73-21077. (Jossey-Bass Behavioral Science Ser.). 572p. reprint ed. pap. 177.40 (*0-8357-5181-3*, 202108800003) Bks Demand.

— Advances in Psychological Assessment, 3 vols., Vol. 4. LC 78-647160. (Jossey-Bass Social & Behavioral Science Ser.). (Illus.). 611p. 1977. reprint ed. pap. 189.50 (*0-8357-4714-X*, 202108800004) Bks Demand.

— Advances in Psychological Assessment, 3 vols., Vol. 5. LC 78-647160. (Jossey-Bass Social & Behavioral Science Ser.). (Illus.). 582p. 1981. reprint ed. pap. 180.50 (*0-8357-4715-8*, 202108800005) Bks Demand.

— Advances in Psychological Assessment, 3 vols., Vol. 6. LC 78-647160. (Jossey-Bass Social & Behavioral Science Ser.). (Illus.). 399p. 1984. reprint ed. pap. 123.70 (*0-8357-4716-6*, 202108800006) Bks Demand.

McReynolds, Paul, et al. Advances in Psychological Assessment, Vol. 7. LC 78-647160. (Illus.). 330p. (C). 1990. 65.00 (*0-306-43399-0*, Plenum Trade) Perseus Pubng.

McReynolds, Paul, jt. auth. see Rosen, J. C.

McReynolds, Paul, ed. see Hutcheson, Francis, et al.

***McReynolds, Paul R., ed.** Greek-English New Testament: Word Study. 3rd ed. LC 98-56040. 5624p. 1999. 34.99 (*0-8423-8290-9*) Tyndale Hse.

McReynolds, Peter. Process Control Charting with Quattro Pro for Windows. 250p. 1993. pap. 39.95 (*1-883327-41-5*) TitleWave Pr.

McReynolds, Ray. Home Plumbing: A Step-by-Step Guide. 2nd ed. (How-to Ser.). (Illus.). 56p. (Orig.). 1995. pap. 4.95 (*1-55180-017-9*) Self-Counsel Pr.

— Room Finishing: A Step-by-Step Guide. (How-to Ser.). 48p. (Orig.). 1991. pap. 4.95 (*0-88908-957-4*) Self-Counsel Pr.

— Step by Step Guide Book on Home Plumbing. (Illus.). 56p. 1975. pap. text. write for info. (*0-9619201-1-4*) S by S Guide.

— Step by Step Guide Book on Home Wiring. (Illus.). 48p. 1982. pap. text. write for info. (*0-9619201-0-6*) S by S Guide.

— Step by Step Guide Book on Sprinkling Systems. (Illus.). 38p. (Orig.). (C). 1974. pap. text. write for info. (*0-9619201-2-2*) S by S Guide.

— Step by Step Guide Books on Home Wiring Diagrams. (Illus.). 48p. 1982. pap. text. write for info. (*0-9619201-4-9*) S by S Guide.

McReynolds, Ray & McReynolds, Elaine. Basic Home Wiring Diagrams: A Step-by-Step Guide. (How-to Ser.). (Illus.). 48p. (Orig.). (C). 1989. pap. 2.95 (*0-88908-869-1*) Self-Counsel Pr.

McReynolds, Roger & Reading, Ben. Darktown: The Apocalyptic Cycle. (Illus.). 136p. 1998. pap. 18.95 (*1-890305-17-0*) Gold Rush.

McReynolds, Ronald W. Telling of Bees: And Other Poems. (Illus.). 96p. 1998. pap. 10.00 (*0-910479-05-4*) Mid-America Pr.

M'Crie, Thomas. The Reformation History in Spain. 272p. 1997. reprint ed. pap. 13.95 (*0-923309-58-6*) Hartland Pubns.

M'Crindle, John. The Invasion of India by Alexander the Great. LC 74-155621. reprint ed. 45.00 (*0-404-04119-1*) AMS Pr.

McRobb, Max. Specification Writing & Management. (Quality & Reliability Ser.: Vol. 20). (Illus.). 240p. 1989. text 99.75 (*0-8247-8082-5*) Dekker.

McRobb, William L. McCrave: A Mental Operations Manual for the Seemingly Hopeless. unabridged ed. LC 97-95129. (Illus.). xx, 178p. 1998. spiral bd. 21.95 (*0-9662533-0-2*, ALK1.101) McCrave.

McRobbie. The Fourth Caution. (Clipper Fiction Ser.). 1991. pap. text. write for info. (*0-582-87536-6*, Pub. by Addison-Wesley) Longman.

— Head over Heels. 1990. pap. text. write for info. (*0-582-86892-0*) Longman.

— Outworld. (Clipper Fiction Ser.). 1994. pap. text. write for info. (*0-582-80266-0*, Pub. by Addison-Wesley) Longman.

— Punch Lines. 1987. pap. text. write for info. (*0-582-66799-2*, Pub. by Addison-Wesley) Longman.

— Timelock. (Clipper Fiction Ser.). 1993. pap. text. write for info. (*0-582-91190-7*, Pub. by Addison-Wesley) Longman.

McRobbie, Angela. British Fashion Design: Rag Trade or Image Industry? LC 98-2983. (Illus.). 224p. (C). 1998. pap. 19.99 (*0-415-05781-7*) Routledge.

— Fashion Style Image. LC 98-2983. (Illus.). 224p. (C). 1998. 75.00 (*0-415-05780-9*) Routledge.

— In Culture Society: Art Fashion & Popular Music. LC 99-14223. 1999. pap. 20.99 (*0-415-13750-0*) Routledge.

***McRobbie, Angela.** In the Culture Society: Art, Fashion & Popular Music. LC 99-14223. 208p. (C). 1999. text 65.00 (*0-415-13749-7*) Routledge.

McRobbie, Angela. Postmodernism & Popular Culture. LC 93-41812. (Illus.). 232p. (C). 1994. pap. 20.99 (*0-415-07713-3*, B4295) Routledge.

McRobbie, Angela, ed. Back to Reality: Social Experience & Cultural Studies. LC 95-39216. (Illus.). 224p. 1997. text 74.95 (*0-7190-4454-5*); text 24.95 (*0-7190-4455-3*, Pub. by Manchester Univ Pr) St Martin.

McRobbie, James. What the Bible Teaches. pap. 8.99 (*0-88019-122-8*) Schmul Pub Co.

McRobbie, Kenneth. Karl Polanyi in Vienna. 256p. 1999. pap. 34.99 (*1-55164-142-9*) Consort Bk Sales.

McRobbie, Kenneth, ed. Humanity, Society & Commitment: On Karl Polanyi, Vol. 4. 178p. 1995. 48.99 (*1-895431-85-9*, Pub. by Black Rose); pap. 19.99 (*1-895431-84-0*, Pub. by Black Rose) Consort Bk Sales.

McRobbie, Kenneth & Polanyi-Levitt, Kari, eds. Karl Polanyi in Vienna: The Contemporary Significance of the Great Transformation. 256p. 1999. 53.99 (*1-55164-143-7*) Consort Bk Sales.

McRobbie, M. A. & Slaney, J. K., eds. Automated Deduction - CADE-13: Proceedings of the International Conference on Automated Deduction, 13th, New Brunswick, NJ, July 30 - August 3, 1996, Vol. 110. LC 96-29057. (Lecture Notes in Artificial Intelligence). 764p. 1996. 113.00 (*3-540-61511-3*) Spr-Verlag.

McRobbie-Utasi, Zita. Quantity in the Skolt (Lappish) Saami Language: An Acoustic Analysis. LC 99-70017. (Uralic & Altaic Ser.: Vol. 165). 255p. 1999. 35.00 (*0-933070-45-4*) Ind U Res Inst.

McRobert, Iain. Windows Black Pentecostalism in Britain: Origins, Functions & Theology. 352p. 1993. pap. 40.00 (*0-86153-154-X*, Pub. by St Andrew) St Mut.

McRobert, Stuart. Beyond Brawn: The Encyclopedia on How to Build Muscle & Might. LC 98-853. (Illus.). 496p. 1999. pap. 24.95 (*9963-616-06-2*, Pub. by CS Pubng Ltd) CS Pubng.

— Beyond Brawn: The Insider's Encyclopedia on How to Build Muscle & Might. LC 98-853. (Illus.). 496p. 1999. 34.95 (*9963-616-07-0*, Pub. by CS Pubng Ltd) CS Pubng.

— Brawn: Bodybuilding for the Drug-Free & Genetically Typical. 2nd ed. 232p. 1999. pap. 19.95 (*9963-616-08-9*, Pub. by CS Pubng Ltd) ACCESS Pubs Network.

— The Insider's Tell-All Handbook on Weight-Training Technique: The Illustrated Step-by-Step Guide to Perfecting Your Exercise Form for Injury-Free Maximum Gains. LC 96-231205. (Illus.). 216p. (Orig.). (YA). 1996. 39.95 (*9963-616-03-8*, Pub. by CS Pubng Ltd); pap. 29.95 (*9963-616-04-6*, Pub. by CS Pubng Ltd) CS Pubng.

— The Insider's Tell-All Handbook on Weight-Training Technique: The Illustrated Step-by-Step Guide to Perfecting Your Exercise Form for Injury-Free Maximum Gains. (Illus.). 216p. (Orig.). 1999. pap. 24.95 (*9963-616-09-7*, Pub. by CS Pubng Ltd) ACCESS Pubs Network.

M

— The Muscle & Might Training Tracker: The Week-by-Week Journal for Charting Training Success. 136p. 1998. spiral bd. 19.95 (*9963-616-05-4*) CS Pubng Ltd.

McRoberts, Greg. Good Dirt. (Illus.). 1998. pap. 14.95 (*0-9665953-0-0*) Perpetual Motion.

McRoberts, Greg & Deppe, Darla. Sun Spots - The Adventurous Travelers Guide to Sun Valley, Idaho. (Illus.). 116p. 1999. pap. 10.95 (*0-9665953-1-9*) Perpetual Motion.

***McRoberts, Kenneth.** Catalonia. 224p. 2000. pap. 22.00 (*0-19-541481-0*) OUP.

McRoberts, Kenneth, ed. Beyond Quebec: Taking Stock of Canada. 448p. 1995. pap. 24.95 (*0-7735-1314-0*, Pub. by McG-Queens Univ Pr) CUP Services.

— Beyond Quebec: Taking Stock of Canada. 448p. 1995. 65.00 (*0-7735-1301-9*, Pub. by McG-Queens Univ Pr) CUP Services.

— Misconceiving Canada: The Struggle for National Unity. LC 97-183213. 288p. (Orig.). 1997. pap. text 35.00 (*0-19-541233-8*) OUP.

McRoberts, Kenneth & Monahan, Patrick J., eds. The Charlottetown Accord: The Referendum, & the Future of Canada. LC 93-94681. 361p. 1993. text 55.00 (*0-8020-2989-2*) U of Toronto Pr.

McRoberts, Kerry D. New Age or Old Lie? LC 89-12831. 138p. 1989. pap. 7.95 (*0-943575-30-3*) Hendrickson MA.

McRoberts, Robert. Lip Service. LC 76-55803. 59p. 1976. 3.50 (*0-87886-078-9*, Greenfld Rev Pr) Greenfld Rev Lit.

McRoberts Ward, Ruth. Appreciation: What Every Woman Still Needs. 144p. (YA). (gr. 10). 1989. pap. 7.99 (*0-8010-9697-9*) Baker Bks.

— Blending Temperaments: Improving Relationships - Yours & Others. 256p. (YA). (gr. 10). 1988. pap. 9.99 (*0-8010-9687-1*) Baker Bks.

McRobie, Alan, jt. auth. see Jackson, Keith.

McRobie, Alan, jt. auth. see Jackson, William K.

McRovie, Louise, ed. see Klein, John.

McRoy, C. Peter & Helfferich, Carla, eds. Seagrass Ecosystems: A Scientific Perspective. LC 76-9466. (Marine Science Ser.: No. 4). 328p. reprint ed. pap. 101.70 (*0-608-15917-4*, 203086800071) Bks Demand.

McRoy, Ruth G. Special Needs Adoptions: Practice Issues. LC 98-30946. (Illus.). 288p. 1998. 58.00 (*0-8153-2776-5*, SS1151) Garland.

McRoy, Ruth G. & Zurcher, Louis A., Jr. Transracial & Inracial Adoptees: The Adolescent Years. 168p. 1983. pap. 21.95 (*0-398-06282-X*); text 34.95 (*0-398-04840-1*) C C Thomas.

McRoy, Ruth G., et al. Emotional Disturbance in Adopted Adolescents: Origins & Development. LC 87-1053. 226p. 1988. 62.95 (*0-275-92913-2*, C2913, Praeger Pubs) Greenwood.

— Openness in Adoption: New Practices, New Issues. LC 88-2471. 171p. 1988. 55.00 (*0-275-92933-7*, C2933, Praeger Pubs) Greenwood.

McRoy, Ruth G., jt. auth. see Altstein, Howard.

McRoy, Ruth G., jt. auth. see Grotevant, Harold D.

McRoy, Susan, jt. ed. see Ali, Syed.

McRoy, Susan, jt. ed. see Haller, Susan.

McRue, Robert. The Queer Renaissance: Contemporary American Literature & the Reinvention of Lesbian & Gay Identities. LC 96-51220. 1997. text 50.00 (*0-8147-5554-2*) NYU Pr.

McRuer, Duane, et al. Aircraft Dynamics & Automatic Control. LC 73-134350. (Illus.). 809p. (Orig.). 1974. pap. text 55.00 (*0-691-02440-5*, Pub. by Princeton U Pr) Cal Prin Full Svc.

McRuer, Robert. The Queer Renaissance: Contemporary American Literature & the Reinvention of Lesbian & Gay Identities. LC 96-51220. 1997. pap. text 19.00 (*0-8147-5555-0*) NYU Pr.

***MCSE Majors Staff.** MCSE Windows Network Server 4 for Dummies. 2nd ed. (For Dummies Ser.). 504p. 1999. pap. 29.99 incl. cd-rom (*0-7645-0611-0*) IDG Bks.

McSean, Tony. Library Association Directory of Suppliers & Services, 1994-95. 2nd ed. LC 94-55995. (Illus.). 113p. 1994. reprint ed. pap. 35.10 (*0-608-07778-X*, 206786600010) Bks Demand.

McSean, Tony, ed. Health Information: New Possibilities. LC 95-21647. 281p. (C). 1995. text 114.50 (*0-7923-3584-8*) Kluwer Academic.

McSeveney, Angela. Coming Out with It. 1993. 12.95 (*0-7486-6137-9*, Pub. by Polygon) Subterranean Co.

McShane. Esther. 1996. pap. 9.99 (*0-946351-48-1*) Loizeaux.

McShane & Williams, eds. Victims of Crime & the Victimization Process. LC 96-39140. (Criminal Justice Ser.: Vol. 6). 392p. 1997. text 85.00 (*0-8153-2513-4*) Garland.

McShane, A. Joshua. 1996. pap. 11.99 (*0-946351-40-6*, Pub. by John Ritchie) Loizeaux.

— Lessons for Leaders. 1996. 21.99 (*0-946351-23-6*, Pub. by John Ritchie) Loizeaux.

McShane, B., jt. auth. see Murphy, J.

McShane, Barbara, tr. see Rodgers, Mary.

McShane, Clay. The Automobile: A Chronology of Its Antecedents, Development & Impact. LC 97-12771. 272p. 1997. lib. bdg. 69.50 (*0-313-30308-8*, Greenwood Pr) Greenwood.

— Down the Asphalt Path: The Automobile & the American City. 288p. 1995. pap. 19.50 (*0-231-08391-2*) Col U Pr.

McShane, Clay, ed. The Automobile: A Chronology of Its Antecedents, Development, & Impact. 1997. lib. bdg. 65.00 (*1-57958-021-1*) Fitzroy Dearborn.

McShane, E. J. Order - Preserving Maps & Integration Processes. (Annals of Mathematics Studies: No. 31). 1974. reprint ed. 25.00 (*0-527-02747-2*) Periodicals Srv.

— A Riemann-Type Integral That Includes Lebesgue-Stieltjes, Bochner & Stochastic Integrals. LC 52-42839. (Memoirs Ser.: No. 1/88). 54p. 1983. reprint ed. pap. 17.00 (*0-8218-1288-2*, MEMO/1/88) Am Math.

McShane, Frank, ed. Mid Twentieth Century Novelists: Ford Maddox Ford. (Critical Heritage Ser.). 288p. (C). 1997. 125.00 (*0-415-15921-0*) Routledge.

McShane, Frank, ed. see Chandler, Raymond.

McShane, Ivan & Westburg, Martial R. The First Selected Poems of Ivan McShane. Westburg, John E., ed. (Illus.). 80p. 1965. 10.00 (*0-87423-001-2*) Westburg.

McShane, John, jt. auth. see Dockrell, Julie.

McShane, Joseph M. Sufficiently Radical: Catholicism, Progressivism, & the Bishops' Program of 1919. LC 86-9735. 319p. 1986. reprint ed. pap. 98.90 (*0-7837-9117-8*, 204991800004) Bks Demand.

McShane, Kim, ed. see Knox, Gary A.

McShane, Larry. Cops under Fire. 224p. 1998. 24.95 (*0-89526-357-2*, Pub. by Regnery Pub) Natl Bk Netwk.

McShane, Marilyn & Williams, eds. The American Court System. LC 96-39145. (Criminal Justice Ser.: Vol. 5). 424p. 1997. text 81.00 (*0-8153-2512-6*) Garland.

— Criminological Theory. LC 96-39144. (Criminal Justice Ser.: Vol. 3). 424p. 1997. text 81.00 (*0-8153-2509-6*) Garland.

— The Philosophy & Practice of Corrections. LC 96-45337. (Criminal Justice Ser.: Vol. 4). 392p. 1997. text 76.00 (*0-8153-2510-X*) Garland.

McShane, Marilyn & Williams, Franklin P., eds. Drug Use & Drug Policy. LC 96-37307. (Criminal Justice Series Ser.: Vol. 2). 464p. 1997. text 85.00 (*0-8153-2511-8*) Garland.

Mcshane, Marilyn D. Altered States of Mind: Critical Observations of the Drug War. Kraska, Peter B. & Williams, Frank P., eds. LC 93-7387. 288p. 1993. text 52.00 (*0-8153-0898-1*) Garland.

McShane, Marilyn D. & Krause, Wesley. Community Corrections. LC 92-24. (Illus.). 507p. (C). 1992. pap. text 71.00 (*0-02-379765-7*, Macmillan Coll) P-H.

McShane, Marilyn D. & Williams, Frank P., III. Encyclopedia of American Prisons. LC 95-41593. (Reference Library of the Humanities: Vol. 1748). (Illus.). 560p. 1996. text 100.00 (*0-8153-1350-0*, H1748) Garland.

— The Management of Correctional Institutions. LC 92-27791. (Current Issues in Criminal Justice Ser.: Vol. 5). 352p. 1993. text 64.00 (*0-8153-1082-X*, SS869) Garland.

McShane, Marilyn D. & Williams, Frank P., 3rd, eds. Law Enforcement Operations & Management. LC 96-39143. (Criminal Justice Ser.: Vol. 1). 440p. 1997. text 81.00 (*0-8153-2508-8*) Garland.

McShane, Marilyn D., jt. auth. see Williams, Frank P., III.

McShane, Marilyn D., ed. see Carroll, Leo.

McShane, Marilyn D., ed. see Palmer, Ted.

McShane, Marilyn D., ed. see Roebuck, Julian B. & Murty, Komanduri S.

McShane, Mark. The Hostage Game. (Orig.). 1979. mass mkt. 2.25 (*0-89083-458-X*, Zebra Kensgtn) Kensgtn Pub Corp.

— Seance on a Wet Afternoon. 17.95 (*0-89190-628-2*) Amereon Ltd.

— Seance on a Wet Afternoon. 189p. 1990. mass mkt. 3.95 (*0-88184-615-5*) Carroll & Graf.

McShane, Paul A. That They Might Live. 217p. 1997. pap. 14.95 (*1-57901-025-3*) Intl Promotions.

McShane, Philip. The Shaping of the Foundations: Being at Home in the Transcendental Method. 24.00 (*0-8191-0209-1*) U Pr of Amer.

McShane, Philip J., ed. see Lonergan, Bernard.

McShane, Roger. Exploring Applesoft. 170p. 1983. pap. 18.95 (*0-13-295916-X*) P-H.

McShane, Roger B. The Foreign Policy of the Attalids of Pergamun. LC 63-7251. (Illinois Studies in the Social Sciences: Vol.53). 253p. reprint ed. pap. 78.50 (*0-608-11742-0*, 201503800098) Bks Demand.

McShane, Rudolph, jt. tr. see Cutler, Ann.

McShane, Stephen G., ed. see Chicago, South Shore & South Bend Railroad Staff, et al.

***McShane, Steven Lattimore & Von Glinow, Mary A. Young.** Organizational Behavior LC 99-37328. 2000. write for info. (*0-256-22896-5*, Irwn McGrw-H) McGrw-H Hghr Educ.

McShane, Susan P. Outcomes & Measures in Family Literacy Programs. Hayes, Andrew E., ed. 73p. (Orig.). 1996. pap. text 15.00 (*1-884458-01-7*) Natl Ctr Fmly Lit.

McShane, Terry. Working Well...? How to Correct the Unhealthy Workplace: The Ergonomic Approach. 2nd rev. ed. (Illus.). 128p. (Orig.). 1996. pap. 16.95 (*0-9636940-1-4*) T&M Assocs.

McShane, Thomas O., jt. auth. see Adams, Jonathan S.

McSharry, Patra. Good Sports: Fair Play & Foul. (Icarus World Issues Ser.). (Illus.). (YA). (gr. 7-12). 1992. pap. 8.95 (*0-8239-1379-1*); lib. bdg. 16.95 (*0-8239-1378-3*) Rosen Group.

McSharry, Patra & Rosen, Roger, eds. Apartheid: Calibrations of Color. (Icarus World Issues Ser.: Vol. 2). (Illus.). 176p. (YA). (gr. 7-12). 1991. lib. bdg. 16.95 (*0-8239-1330-9*) Rosen Group.

— Apartheid: Calibrations of Color. (Icarus World Issues Ser.: Vol. 2). (Illus.). 176p. (YA). (gr. 7-12). 1991. pap. 8.95 (*0-8239-1331-7*) Rosen Group.

— Coca Cola Culture: Icons of Pop. (Icarus World Issues Ser.). (Illus.). (YA). (gr. 7-12). 1993. pap. 8.95 (*0-8239-1594-8*); lib. bdg. 16.95 (*0-8239-1593-X*) Rosen Group.

— On Heroes & the Heroic: In Search of Good Deeds. (Icarus World Issues Ser.). (Illus.). (YA). (gr. 7-12). 1993. pap. 8.95 (*0-8239-1385-6*); lib. bdg. 16.95 (*0-8239-1384-8*) Rosen Group.

— The People of This Place: Natural & Unnatural Habitats. (Icarus World Issues Ser.). (Illus.). (YA). (gr. 7-12). 1993. pap. 8.95 (*0-8239-1382-1*); lib. bdg. 16.95 (*0-8239-1381-3*) Rosen Group.

— Urbanities: Visions of the Metropolis. (Icarus World Issues Ser.). (Illus.). (YA). (gr. 7-12). 1993. pap. 8.95 (*0-8239-1388-0*); lib. bdg. 16.95 (*0-8239-1387-2*) Rosen Group.

McSharry, Patra, ed. see Epshtein, Yaacov.

McSharry, Patra, ed. see Gindin, Irina.

McSharry, Patra, ed. see Kilov, Haim, et al.

McSharry, Patra, ed. see Kokoshvili, Simon, et al.

McSharry, Patra, ed. see Litvin, Valentin.

McSharry, Patra, ed. see Rosen, Roger.

McSharry, Patra, jt. ed. see Rosen, Roger.

McShea, Robert J. Morality & Human Nature: A New Route to Ethical Theory. 240p. 1990. 49.95 (*0-87722-735-7*) Temple U Pr.

— The Political Philosophy of Spinoza. LC 73-89037. 835p. reprint ed. pap. 200.00 (*0-608-08662-2*, 206918500003) Bks Demand.

McShea, Susanna H. Hometown Heroes. (Hometown Heroes Ser.). 320p. 1992. mass mkt. 4.99 (*0-380-71675-5*, Avon Bks) Morrow Avon.

— Ladybug, Ladybug. (Hometown Heroes Mystery Ser.). 352p. 1995. reprint ed. mass mkt. 5.50 (*0-380-71981-9*, Avon Bks) Morrow Avon.

— The Pumpkin-Shell Wife. (Hometown Heroes Ser.). 352p. 1993. mass mkt. 4.99 (*0-380-71980-0*, Avon Bks) Morrow Avon.

McShea, William J., et al, eds. The Science of Overabundance: Deer Ecology & Population Management. LC 97-3327. (Illus.). 432p. 1997. text 39.95 (*1-56098-681-6*) Smithsonian.

McSheehy, William R. Skid Row: An Institutional Analysis. 160p. 1975. pap. 11.95 (*0-87073-181-5*) Schenkman Bks Inc.

***McSheffrey, Gerald.** Planning Derry: Planning & Politics in Northern Ireland. 368p. 1999. 72.95 (*0-86356-714-2*, Pub. by Liverpool Univ Pr); pap. 45.95 (*0-85323-724-7*, Pub. by Liverpool Univ Pr); pap. 45.95 (*0-86356-724-X*, Pub. by Liverpool Univ Pr) Intl Spec Bk.

McSheffrey, Shannon. Gender & Heresy: Women & Men in Lollard Communities, 1420-1530. (Middle Ages Ser.). (Illus.). 264p. 1995. text 39.95 (*0-8122-3310-7*); pap. text 18.95 (*0-8122-1549-4*) U of Pa Pr.

McSheffrey, Shannon, tr. Love & Marriage in Late Medieval London. LC 94-47339. (Documents of Practice Ser.). 1995. pap. 6.00 (*1-879288-53-2*) Medieval Inst.

McSherry, Frank, et al, eds. Eastern Ghosts. LC 90-44724. (American Ghost Ser.). 208p. (Orig.). 1990. pap. 9.95 (*1-55853-091-6*) Rutledge Hill Pr.

— New England Ghosts. LC 90-43189. (American Ghost Ser.). 214p. (Orig.). 1990. pap. 9.95 (*1-55853-090-8*) Rutledge Hill Pr.

McSherry, Frank D., Jr., et al, eds. Dixie Ghosts. LC 88-1991. (American Ghost Ser.). 1988. pap. 9.95 (*0-934395-73-X*) Rutledge Hill Pr.

McSherry, Frank D., et al, eds. Ghosts of the Heartland: Haunting, Spine Chilling Stories from the American Midwest. LC 90-30532. 224p. (Orig.). 1990. pap. 9.95 (*1-55853-068-1*) Rutledge Hill Pr.

McSherry, Frank D., Jr., et al, eds. Great American Ghost Stories. 512p. 1998. pap. 14.95 (*1-55853-581-0*) Rutledge Hill Pr.

— Great American Ghost Stories, Vol. II. 272p. 1993. mass mkt. 4.99 (*0-425-13623-X*) Berkley Pub.

— Western Ghosts. LC 90-8072. (American Ghost Ser.). 224p. (Orig.). 1990. pap. 9.95 (*1-55853-069-X*) Rutledge Hill Pr.

McSherry, Frank D., Jr., jt. ed. see Waugh, Charles G.

McSherry, J. Patrice. Incomplete Transition: Military Power & Democracy in Argentina. LC 96-48927. 408p. 1997. text 49.95 (*0-312-16252-9*) St Martin.

McSherry, James. History of Maryland. James, Bartlett B., ed. LC 68-30881. (Illus.). 1968. reprint ed. 20.00 (*0-87152-047-8*) Reprint.

McSherry, Richard M. The National Medals of the United States. LC 72-14409. (Maryland Historical Society. Fund-Publications: No. 25). reprint ed. write for info. (*0-404-57625-7*) AMS Pr.

McShine, Kynaston. The Museum as Muse: Artists Reflect. LC 98-68644. (Illus.). 296p. 1999. 49.50 (*0-8109-6197-0*, Pub. by Abrams) Time Warner.

***McShine, Kynaston.** The Museum as Muse: Artists Reflect. LC 98-68644. 296p. 1999. 50.00 (*0-87070-091-X*, Pub. by Mus of Modern Art) Abrams.

— Museum as Muse: Artists Reflect. LC 98-68644. 296p. 1999. pap. 29.95 (*0-87070-092-8*) Mus of Modern Art.

McShine, Kynaston, ed. Joseph Cornell. (Illus.). 296p. 1990. 65.00 (*3-7913-1063-1*, Pub. by Prestel) te Neues.

McShine, Kynaston, jt. ed. see D'Harnoncourt, Anne.

McShulskis, Jacquelyn & Taylor, Scott Warren, eds. The Boskage Standard Desk Reference of U.S. Customs & International Trade Terms & Procedures. 3rd ed. (ACT - Automated Customs Training Ser.). 295p. Price not set. incl. VHS (*1-893495-02-7*, PN 3307, Boskage Commerce) Boskage Pr.

McShulskis, Jacquelyn, ed. see Stetson, Robert.

McShulskis, Jacquelyn, ed. see Taylor, Scott W.

McShulskis, Jacquelyn, ed. see Taylor, Scott Warren.

Mcsloy, Peter. For Jazz. 1995. 23.75 (*0-936156-01-5*); pap. text 12.00 (*0-936156-02-3*) Hit & Run Pr.

McSmith, Alexander. Children of Wax. 2nd ed. 1999. pap. text 11.95 (*1-56656-314-3*) Interlink Pub.

McSmith, Andy. Faces of Labour. LC 97-40793. 1997. pap. 16.00 (*1-85984-093-0*) Norton.

— Faces of Labour: The Inside Story. 1996. 25.00 (*1-85984-968-7*, Pub. by Verso) Norton.

McSorley, Edward. Our Own Kind. LC 76-6357. (Irish Americans Ser.). 1976. reprint ed. 26.95 (*0-405-09350-0*) Ayer.

McSorley, Joseph. Be of Good Heart: Sustaining Christian Hope in Our Difficult Days. abr. ed. LC 98-55717. Orig. Title: Be of Good Heart: A Plea for Christian Optimism. 144p. 1999. pap. 12.95 (*0-918477-91-3*) Sophia Inst Pr.

— Isaac Hecker & His Friends. 314p. 1972. pap. 1.45 (*0-8091-1605-7*) Paulist Pr.

McSorley, Joseph F. A Portable Guide to Federal Conspiracy Law. LC 96-31821. 1996. pap. 64.95 (*1-57073-368-6*) Amer Bar Assn.

McSorley, Richard. It's a Sin to Build a Nuclear Weapon: The Collected Works on War & Christian Peacemaking. 348p. (Orig.). 1991. 22.95 (*1-879175-07-X*); pap. 16.95 (*1-879175-06-1*) Fortkamp.

— Kill? for Peace. 2nd rev. ed. LC 70-135455. 140p. (C). 1982. reprint ed. pap. 3.75 (*0-912239-06-9*) Ctr Peace Studies.

— Peace Eyes. LC 77-9240. 219p. 1978. pap. 3.75 (*0-912239-03-4*) Ctr Peace Studies.

McSorley, Richard T. My Path to Peace & Justice. 350p. (Orig.). 1996. pap. 17.00 (*1-879175-19-3*) Fortkamp.

McSpadden. Wireless Power Transmission. write for info. (*0-471-15417-2*) Wiley.

McSpadden, Anna B. McSpadden. "Way Back When . . ." Happenings We Remember & Genealogies (Descendants of Samuel McSpadden of Tenn. & Related Families) (Illus.). 160p. 1998. reprint ed. pap. 14.00 (*0-8328-9683-7*); reprint ed. lib. bdg. 24.00 (*0-8328-9682-9*) Higginson Bk Co.

***McSpadden, J. Walker.** Robin Hood. LC 99-52851. 2000. pap. 2.50 (*0-486-41021-8*) Dover.

— Stories from Great Operas. 20.00 (*0-8196-2006-8*) Biblo.

— The Story of Robin Hood & His Merry Outlaws. abr. ed. Marshall, Michael J., ed. (Core Classics Ser.: Vol. 7). (Illus.). 224p. (J). (gr. 4-6). 2000. pap. 7.95 (*1-890517-16-X*) Core Knowledge.

McSpadden, Joseph W. Famous Sculptors of America. LC 68-57331. (Essay Index Reprint Ser.). 1977. 27.95 (*0-8369-0086-3*) Ayer.

McSpadden, Joseph W., ed. Famous Dogs in Fiction, Vol. 1. rev. ed. LC 72-4373. (Short Story Index Reprint Ser.). 1977. reprint ed. 25.95 (*0-8369-4184-5*) Ayer.

— Famous Ghost Stories. LC 70-152949. (Short Story Index Reprint Ser.). 1977. reprint ed. 18.95 (*0-8369-3808-9*) Ayer.

— Famous Psychic & Ghost Stories, 2 Vols. LC 73-77. (Short Story Index Reprint Ser.). 1977. reprint ed. 44.95 (*0-8369-4248-5*) Ayer.

McSpadden, Larry, jt. auth. see Littell, Robert S.

McSpadden, Lynn. Four & Twenty: Songs for the Mountain Dulcimer. (Illus.). 44p. 1977. pap. 11.95 (*0-8256-2635-8*, AM41229) Music Sales.

McSparran, Frances, ed. Octovian: Medieval Studies. (OS 289 Ser.). (Illus.). 244p. 1986. 29.95 (*0-19-722291-9*) OUP.

McSparren, Carolyn. Fathers & Sons. (Superromance Ser.: No. 829). 1999. mass mkt. 4.25 (*0-373-70829-7*, 1-70829-6) Harlequin Bks.

— If Wishes Were Horses. (Superromance Ser.: No. 772). 1998. per. 3.99 (*0-373-70772-X*) Harlequin Bks.

— Mr. Miracle: By the Year 2000: Celebrate! 1999. per. 4.25 (*0-373-70852-1*, 1-70852-8) Harlequin Bks.

— The Only Child. 1997. per. 3.99 (*0-373-70725-8*, 1-70725-6) Silhouette.

— Ride a Painted Pony. 1998. per. 4.25 (*0-373-70804-1*) Harlequin Bks.

***McSparren, Carolyn.** The Wrong Wife. (Superromance Ser.: Bk. 921). 2000. per. 4.50 (*0-373-70921-8*, 1-70921-1) Harlequin Bks.

McSpiritt, Marian, jt. auth. see McLaughlin, Mercedes.

McSporran, W. S., jt. auth. see McMonnies, Alistair.

McSquare, Eddy. Led Zeppelin: Good Times, Bad Times. (Illus.). 64p. 1991. pap. 12.95 (*0-8256-1312-4*, BO10138) Music Sales.

McStay, Kyran P. The Efficiency of New Issue Markets. rev. ed. LC 92-34079. (Financial Sector of the American Economy Ser.). 144p. 1992. text 15.00 (*0-8153-0966-X*) Garland.

***McSwain.** Basic EMT: Comprehensive Prehospital Care Curriculum. 2nd ed. 2000. text. write for info. (*0-323-01116-0*) Mosby Inc.

McSwain, Harold W. A Relational Aesthetic. LC 93-22887. (New Studies in Aesthetics: Vol. 18). XXIV, 307p. (C). 1994. text 58.95 (*0-8204-2185-5*) P Lang Pubng.

McSwain, Kate. Art-Istry for Children: Color. 212p. (Orig.). 1992. pap. 32.95 (*1-878347-39-X*) NL Assocs.

McSwain, Larry C. & Treadwell, Williams C., Jr. Conflict Ministry in the Church. 143p. 1997. 5.95 (*1-57847-012-9*) Genl Conf Svnth-day.

McSwain, Mary E. & Morihara, Bonnie V. VIA-U. S. A.'s Living & Working in America, Vol. I. Higuchi, Yuko & Ikeda, Kazuko, trs. (ENG & JPN., Illus.). ix, 178p. (Orig.). (C). 1988. VHS 200.00 (*0-685-21729-9*) VIA Pr.

— VIA-U. S. A.'s Living & Working in America, Vol. II. (Illus.). 150p. (Orig.). (C). 1989. VHS 250.00 (*0-685-21730-2*) VIA Pr.

— VIA-U. S. A.'s Living & Working in America, Vol. III. (Illus.). (Orig.). (C). 1989. VHS 250.00 (*0-685-21728-0*) VIA Pr.

McSwain, Mary J. Florida Gardening by the Sea. LC 97-19009. (Illus.). 336p. 1997. 24.95 (*0-8130-1529-4*) U Press Fla.

McSwain, Norman E. The Basic EMT. 896p. (gr. 13). 1996. pap. text, teacher ed. 49.95 (*0-8151-4579-9*) Mosby Inc.

— The Basic EMT. 1p. (gr. 13). 1996. text, wbk. ed. 45.95 (*0-8151-4580-2*, 30571) Mosby Inc.

— The Basic EMT: Comprehensive Pre-Hospital Patient Care. (Illus.). 864p. (C). (gr. 13). 1996. pap. text 37.95 (*0-8151-4647-7*, 29889) Mosby Inc.

McSwain, Norman E. & Ware, Drue N. Atlas of Emergency Trauma Surgical Procedures. LC 90-4546. (Illus.). 184p. 1994. 98.50 (*0-89640-179-0*) Igaku-Shoin.

McSwain, Norman E., et al. The Basic EMT: Comprehensive Prehospital Patient Care. 1996. text, wbk. ed. write for info. (*0-8151-5979-X*) Mosby Inc.

— The Basic EMT: Comprehensive Prehospital Patient Care Text. 1996. text, wbk. ed. write for info. (*0-8151-4581-0*) Mosby Inc.

McSwain, Norman E., Jr., et al. The Basic EMT Prehospital Patient Care. LC 96-8004. (Illus.). 928p. (C). (gr. 13). 1996. text 39.95 (*0-8151-5961-7*, 25287) Mosby Inc.

McSwain, Norman E., et al. EMT & Paramedic Quick Reference. (Illus.). 336p. (C). 1994. pap. text. write for info. (*1-884225-02-0*) Communs Skills.

McSwain, Ross. Another Look Out Yonder, Vol. 2. 190p. write for info. (*0-943639-15-8*) Anchor Pub Co.

— Texas Sheep & Goat Raisers Association History. (Illus.). 288p. 1996. 42.75 (*0-943639-27-1*) Anchor Pub Co.

***McSwane, David Z., et al.** Essentials of Food Safety. 2nd ed. LC 99-53961. 464p. (C). 1999. pap. text 44.00 (*0-13-017371-1*) P-H.

— Essentials of Food Safety & Sanitation & Pti Test Voucher. 2nd ed. 1999. pap. text 67.00 (*0-13-088828-1*, Prentice Hall) P-H.

McSwane, David Z., jt. auth. see Rue, Nancy.

McSween, H. Y., Jr., et al. An Introduction to the Petrographic Microscope: A Programmed Text. (Illus.). iii, 53p. (C). 1982. student ed. 5.00 (*0-910249-04-0*) U of Tenn Geo.

Mcsween, Harry Y. Fanfare for Earth. LC 96-23898. 272p. 1997. text 23.95 (*0-312-14601-9*) St Martin.

McSween, Harry Y., Jr. Meteorites & Their Parent Planets. LC 98-26494. (Illus.). 254p. (C). 1999. pap. text 29.95 (*0-521-58751-4*) Cambridge U Pr.

— Meteorites & Their Parent Planets. 2nd ed. LC 98-26494. (Illus.). 304p. (C). 1999. text 74.95 (*0-521-58303-9*) Cambridge U Pr.

McSween, Harry Y. Stardust to Planets: A Geological Tour of the Universe. LC 95-17153. 1995. pap. 14.95 (*0-312-13188-7*, St Martin Griffin) St Martin.

McSween, Terry E. A Values Based Approach. (Illus.). 304p. 1995. text 54.95 (*0-442-01945-9*, VNR) Wiley.

McSween, Terry E. The Values-Based Safety Process: Improving You Safety Culture with a Behavioral Approach. (Industrial Health & Safety Ser.). 320p. 1995. 64.95 (*0-471-28672-9*, VNR) Wiley.

McSweeney. Moral Issues Internat Affairs. LC 97-40513. 265p. 1998. text 65.00 (*0-312-21128-7*) St Martin.

***McSweeney, Bill.** Security, Identity & Interests: A Sociology of International Relations. LC 99-11332. (Cambridge Studies in International Relations: No. 69). 300p. (C). 1999. 54.95 (*0-521-66177-3*); pap. 19.95 (*0-521-66630-9*) Cambridge U Pr.

McSweeney, Cherie, jt. auth. see Wawrychuk, Carol.

McSweeney, Jeanne & Leocha, Charles. Getting to Know Kids in Your Life: Activities, Questions & Ways to Get to Know Kids Better. 160p. (Orig.). 1995. pap. 6.95 (*0-915009-27-7*) World Leis Corp.

— Getting to Know You: Three Hundred Sixty-Five Questions & Activities to Enhance Relationships. rev. ed. 160p. 1994. pap. 6.95 (*0-915009-30-7*) World Leis Corp.

McSweeney, John. Street Karate: A Complete Course in Self-Defense. LC 98-209086. (Illus.). 96p. 1998. pap. 12.00 (*0-87364-966-4*) Paladin Pr.

McSweeney, John, jt. auth. see Cascio, Pat.

McSweeney, Kerry. Four Contemporary Novelists: Angus Wilson, Brian Moore, John Fowles, V. S. Naipaul. 232p. 1983. 44.95 (*0-7735-0399-4*, Pub. by McG-Queens Univ Pr) CUP Services.

— Invisible Man: Race & Identity. (Masterwork Studies: No. 17). 168p. 1988. 23.95 (*0-8057-7977-9*) Macmillan.

— The Language of the Senses: Sensory-Perceptual Dynamics in Wordsworth, Coleridge, Thoreau, Whitman, & Dickinson. 218p. 1998. text 60.00 (*0-7735-1740-5*, Pub. by McG-Queens Univ Pr) CUP Services.

— Middlemarch. (Unwin Critical Library). 176p. 1984. text 39.95 (*0-04-800031-0*); pap. text 19.95 (*0-04-800032-9*) Routledge.

— Moby Dick: Ishmael's Mighty Book. (Twayne's Masterwork Studies: No. 3). 120p. (C). 1986. 23.95 (*0-8057-7954-X*, Twyne); pap. 13.95 (*0-8057-8002-5*, Twyne) Mac Lib Ref.

— Supreme Attachments: Studies in Victorian Love Poetry. LC 98-12823. (Nineteenth Century Ser.). 192p. 1998. text 69.95 (*1-84014-202-2*, PR595.L7M38, Pub. by Ashgate Pub) Ashgate Pub Co.

— Tennyson & Swinburne As Romantic Naturalists. 240p. 1981. text 30.00 (*0-8020-2381-9*) U of Toronto Pr.

McSweeney, Kerry, ed. see Carlyle, Thomas.

McSweeney, Mary A., jt. auth. see Savage, Warren J.

McSweeney, Phil & Alexander, Don. Managing Volunteers Effectively. LC 96-84014. 176p. 1996. 55.95 (*1-85742-294-5*, Pub. by Arena); pap. 33.95 (*1-85742-293-7*, Pub. by Arena) Ashgate Pub Co.

McSweeney, Terry. Great Gift & the Wish-Fulfilling Gem. LC 86-19767. (Jataka Tales Ser.). 32p. (J). (gr. k-5). 1987. pap. 7.95 (*0-89800-143-9*); lib. bdg. 16.95 (*0-89800-157-9*) Dharma Pub.

McSweeney, Thomas J. & Raha, Stephanie, eds. Better to Light One Candle: The Christophers' Three Minutes a Day Millennial Edition. LC 99-12654. (Three Minutes a Day Ser.). 376p. 1999. 20.00 (*0-8264-1163-0*); pap. 14.95 (*0-8264-1162-2*) Continuum.

McSweeney, William. Moral Issues in International Affairs: Problems of European Integration LC 97-40513. viii, 265 p. 1998. 5.25 hd. write for info. (*0-333-69848-7*) Macmillan.

McSweeny & Grant Staff. Chronic Obstructive Pulmonary Disease: A Behavioral Perspective. (Lung Biology in Health & Disease Ser.: Vol. 36). (Illus.). 336p. 1988. text 175.00 (*0-8247-7693-3*) Dekker.

McSweeny, Mary A., jt. auth. see Savage, Warren J.

McSwigan, Marie. Snow Treasure. (Illus.). 156p. (J). (gr. 3-7). 1988. pap. 3.50 (*0-590-42537-4*) Scholastic Inc.

— Snow Treasure. (J). 1942. 9.09 (*0-606-01076-9*, Pub. by Turtleback) Demco.

McSwiggan, Kevin. Silhouettes. (Album Ser.: No. 335). (Illus.). 32p. 1997. pap. 6.25 (*0-7478-0359-5*, Pub. by Shire Pubns) Parkwest Pubns.

McSwiney, S. Start a Craft: Greeting Cards. 48p. 1996. 8.98 (*0-7858-0611-3*) Bk Sales Inc.

McSwite, O. C. Legitimacy in Public Administration: A Discourse Analysis. LC 96-51270. (Advances in Public Administration Ser.: Vol. 4). 288p. 1997. 49.95 (*0-7619-0273-2*); pap. 21.50 (*0-7619-0274-0*) Sage.

McTaggart, Bonnie, jt. auth. see Bryant, Jill.

McTaggart-Cowan, Ian, jt. ed. see Geist, Valerius.

McTaggart, Debra, jt. auth. see McTaggart, Stephen.

McTaggart, Douglas. Bigwin Inn. Hudson, Noel, ed. (Illus.). 144p. 35.00 (*1-55046-035-8*, Pub. by Boston Mills) Genl Dist Srvs.

— Economics in Action. (C). 1993. text. write for info. (*0-201-53953-5*) Addison-Wesley.

McTaggart Ellis, John & Keeling, S. V. Philosophical Studies. LC 99-56430. (Key Texts Ser.). Date not set. pap. text. write for info. (*1-890318-66-3*) St Augustines Pr.

McTaggart, J. E. Philosophical Studies. Keeling, S. V., ed. & intro. by. Rochelle, Gerald, intro. (Key Texts Ser.). 300p. 1996. pap. 22.00 (*1-85506-479-0*) Bks Intl VA.

McTaggart, J. M. Some Dogmas of Religion. (Key Texts Ser.). 299p. 1997. reprint ed. pap. 24.00 (*1-85506-519-3*) Thoemmes Pr.

McTaggart, James M., et al. The Value Imperative: Managing for Superior Shareholder Returns. 288p. 1994. 40.00 (*0-02-920670-7*) Free Pr.

McTaggart, John M. The Nature of Existence, 2 vols., Set. 1968. 69.00 (*0-403-00129-3*) Scholarly.

— Philosophical Studies. Keeling, S. V., ed. LC 67-22104. (Essay Index Reprint Ser.). 1977. 20.95 (*0-8369-0660-8*) Ayer.

— Studies in Hegelian Cosmology. 2nd ed. 1986. reprint ed. pap. 27.95 (*0-935005-60-9*); reprint ed. lib. bdg. 44.95 (*0-935005-59-5*) Lincoln-Rembrandt.

McTaggart, Lynne. What Doctors Don't Tell You: The Truth about the Dangers of Modern Medicine. LC 98-92431. 400p. 1998. pap. 12.50 (*0-380-79607-4*, Avon Bks) Morrow Avon.

— What Doctors Don't Tell You: The Truth about the Dangers of Modern Medicine. 416p. 1999. mass mkt. 6.99 (*0-380-80761-0*, Avon Bks) Morrow Avon.

McTaggart, M. Horse & His Schooling. (Illus.). 98p. 1984. reprint ed. pap. text 15.00 (*0-87556-385-6*) Saifer.

McTaggart, Robin. Action Research: A Short Modern History. 134p. (C). 1995. pap. 55.00 (*0-7300-1217-4*, EED402, Pub. by Deakin Univ) St Mut.

— Getting Started in Arts Education Research: Monograph, No. 1. 1991. pap. 29.00 (*0-646-06270-0*, Pub. by Deakin Univ) St Mut.

McTaggart, Robin, ed. Participatory Action Research: International Contexts & Consequences. LC 96-52807. (SUNY Series, Teacher Preparation & Development). (Illus.). 283p. (C). 1997. pap. text 19.95 (*0-7914-3534-2*) State U NY Pr.

— Participatory Action Research: International Contexts & Consequences. LC 96-52807. (SUNY Series, Teacher Preparation & Development). (Illus.). 283p. (C). 1997. text 59.50 (*0-7914-3533-4*) State U NY Pr.

McTaggart, Robin, jt. auth. see Kemmis, Stephen.

McTaggart, Stephen & McTaggart, Debra. ABC Talking Book Adventures. (Talking Book Adventures Ser.). (Illus.). 12p. (J). (ps up). text 16.95 (*0-9627001-2-6*) Futech Educ Prods.

— Bookee Presents 1, 2, 3 Count with Me. (Talking Book Adventures Ser.). (Illus.). 14p. (J). (ps up). text 16.95 (*0-9627001-3-4*) Futech Educ Prods.

— Bookee's Sounds Around. (Talking Book Adventures Ser.). (Illus.). 12p. (J). (ps up). text 16.95 (*0-9627001-0-X*) Futech Educ Prods.

McTaggart, T. The Big Box. (C). 1989. pap. 60.00 (*0-907526-27-6*, Pub. by Alloway Pub) St Mut.

— Pioneers of Heavy Haulage. (C). 1988. pap. 60.00 (*0-907526-17-9*, Pub. by Alloway Pub) St Mut.

McTaggart, Timothy, ed. Jardin Musical, Contenant Plusieurs Belles Fleurs de Chansons a Quatre Parties, Le Tiers Livre, Antwerp, c.1556. LC 92-23321. (Sixteenth-Century Chanson Ser.: Vol. 2). (Illus.). 216p. 1992. text 83.00 (*0-8240-3101-6*) Garland.

— Jardin Musiqual, Contenant Plusieurs Belles Fleurs De Chansons . . . Le Premier Livre (Antwerp, c. 1556) And Jardin Musical Contenant Plusieurs Belles Fleurs De Chansons Spirituelles a Quatre Parties..Livre Second (Antwerp, c. 1556) LC 92-23321. (Sixteenth Century Chanson Ser.: Vol. 1). 272p. 1992. text 94.00 (*0-8240-3100-8*) Garland.

McTaggart, Timothy, ed. see Susato, Tielman, et al.

McTaggart, W. Donald. Industrial Development in West Malaysia, 1968. 65p. 1972. pap. 6.00 (*0-939252-00-7*) ASU Ctr Asian.

***McTaggart, William R.** Butternut Moon, 1. 112p. (J). (gr. 2-7). 2000. 13.95 (*0-9669285-4-7*) Gramma Bks.

McTaggart, William R. Companion Reader, 3 vols. Incl. Ten More Christmas Stories: Plus Two Christmas Classics: Yes, Virginia There Is a Santa Claus & Twas the Night Before Christmas. (Illus.). 144p. (J). (gr. k-5). 1999. 16.00 (*0-9669285-0-4*); (Illus.). (J). (ps-6). 1999. 53.00 (*0-9669285-2-0*) Gramma Bks.

— A Companion Reader of Ten Christmas Stories. LC 98-85079. (Illus.). 104p. (J). (ps-7). 1998. 16.00 (*1-890394-20-3*, Sage Creek) Rhodes & Easton.

***McTaggart, William R.** A Companion Reader of Ten Christmas Stories, Vol. 1. (Companion Reader Ser.). (Illus.). 127p. (J). (gr. k-5). 1999. 16.00 (*0-9669285-3-9*) Gramma Bks.

McTaggart, William R. A Treasury of Ten Summertime Children's Stories. (Companion Reader Ser.). (Illus.). 128p. (J). (gr. k-5). 1999. 16.00 (*0-9669285-1-2*) Gramma Bks.

Mctaggert, Douglas. Economics in Action. (C). 1993. text. write for info. (*0-201-53952-7*) Addison-Wesley.

McTaggert, J. M. A Commentary on Hegel's Logic. (C). 1986. reprint ed. pap. 28.95 (*0-935005-50-1*) Lincoln-Rembrandt.

McTaggert, Lynne. Field. 25.00 (*0-06-019300-X*); pap. 14.00 (*0-06-093117-5*) HarpC.

McTaggert, T. The Iron Men of the Road. (C). 1988. pap. 68.00 (*0-907526-41-1*, Pub. by Alloway Pub) St Mut.

McTague, Brendan. Windows NT Technical Support. 1998. pap. 29.99 (*1-56205-927-0*) New Riders Pub.

McTague, Richard H., jt. auth. see Rogers, Shawn B.

McTaugue, I. Jams, Jellies, & Preserves. 1983. pap. 2.95 (*0-88266-206-6*, Storey Pub) Storey Bks.

McTavish. Social Research Workbook. (C). 1999. pap. 20.00 (*0-321-04786-9*) Addson-Wesley Educ.

McTavish, ed. Social Research: Achieved Design. LC 98-39829. 448p. (C). 1999. text 66.00 (*0-321-01375-1*) Allyn.

— Social Research: Achived Design-Topics in Research Methods & Exercises. (C). 1999. write for info. (*0-321-40385-1*) Addison-Wesley.

McTavish, Donald G., jt. auth. see Loether, Herman J.

McTavish, Hugh. Ending War in Our Lifetime: A Concrete, Realistic Plan. LC 94-169328. 320p. (Orig.). 1993. 24.95 (*0-9636865-0-X*); pap. 17.95 (*0-9636865-1-8*) West Fork Pr.

McTavish, John. Tomorrow We Go to Bethlehem. 1986. pap. 5.25 (*0-687-42330-9*) Abingdon.

McTavish, John B., ed. see Barth, Karl.

McTavish, Ronald, ed. Linking Marketing & Technology Strategies: December 3-5, 1989. LC 90-162. 49p. 1990. reprint ed. pap. 30.00 (*0-608-04083-5*, 206481500011) Bks Demand.

McTeague, Frank. Shared Reading in the Middle & High School Years: In the Middle & High School Years. LC 92-39116. 93p. (C). (gr. 5). 1992. pap. text 16.50 (*0-435-08735-5*, 08735) Heinemann.

McTeague, James H. Before Stanislavsky: American Professional Acting Schools & Acting Theory, 1875-1925. LC 93-26669. 1993. 41.50 (*0-8108-2657-7*) Scarecrow.

— Playwrights & Acting: Acting Methodologies of Brecht, Ionesco, Pinter & Shepard, 59. LC 94-17979. (Contributions in Drama & Theatre Studies). 216p. 1994. 55.00 (*0-313-28975-1*, Greenwood Pr) Greenwood.

McTear, M. & Creaney, N., eds. AI & Cognitive Science, 1990: Proceedings of the Third Irish Conference on Artificial Intelligence & Cognitive Science 20-22 September 1990, Ulster. (Workshops in Computing Ser.). xv, 392p. 1991. pap. 59.00 (*0-387-19653-6*) Spr-Verlag.

Mctear, Michael, ed. Understanding Cognitive Science. 1988. text 57.95 (*0-470-21175-X*) P-H.

McTear, Michael & Anderson, Terry. Understanding Knowledge Engineering. (Information Technology Ser.). 1990. text 61.95 (*0-470-21646-8*) P-H.

McTear, Michael F. & Conti-Ramsden, Gina, eds. Pragmatic Disability in Children: Studies in Disorders of Communication. (Illus.). 246p. (C). 1991. pap. 45.00 (*1-879105-56-X*, 0237) Thomson Learn.

McTee, Charly, ed. see Brothers, Al & Ray, Murphy E., Jr.

McTee, Cindy. A Music Calligrapher's Handbook: Tools, Materials, & Techniques. 44p. (Orig.). 1987. pap. 3.95 (*0-918812-55-0*, SB 0006) MMB Music.

***McTeer, Maureen A.** Tough Choices: Living & Dying in the 21st Century. xii, 212p. 1999. pap. 19.95 (*1-55221-040-5*, Pub. by Irwin Law) Gaunt.

McTernan. Gods Final Warning. LC 99-173796. 160p. 1998. pap. 12.95 (*1-57558-027-6*) Hearthstone OK.

McTernan, William F. & Kaplan, Edward, eds. Risk Assessment for Groundwater Pollution Control. LC 90-20924. 376p. 1990. pap. text 6.00 (*0-87262-784-5*) Am Soc Civil Eng.

McThenia, Andrew W., jt. auth. see Epstein, David J.

***Mctiernan, Anne.** Breast Cancer Optimal Health & Exercise Plan. 2000. text 24.95 (*0-312-25312-5*) St Martin.

McTighe, James. Roadside History of Colorado. rev. ed. LC 89-84757. (Illus.). 400p. (Orig.). 1989. pap. 13.95 (*1-55566-054-1*) Johnson Bks.

McTighe, Jan, jt. auth. see Wiggins, Grant.

McTighe, Jay & Ferrara, Steven. Assessing Learning in the Classroom. LC 98-28469. (Student Assessment Ser.). 1998. 7.95 (*0-8106-2070-7*) NEA.

***McTighe, Jay & Wiggins, Grant.** The Understanding by Design Handbook. (Illus.). 287p. 1999. spiral bd. write for info. (*0-87120-340-5*) ASCD.

McTighe, Jay, jt. auth. see Arter, Judith A.

McTighe, Michael J. A Measure of Success: Protestants & Public Culture in Antebellum Cleveland. LC 93-26789. 283p. (C). 1994. text 74.50 (*0-7914-1825-1*); pap. text 24.95 (*0-7914-1826-X*) State U NY Pr.

McTighe, Sheila. Nicolas Poussin's Landscape Allegories. (Illus.). 226p. (C). 1996. text 74.95 (*0-521-48214-3*) Cambridge U Pr.

McTigue, Bernard, intro. Nature Illustrated: An Address Book. (Illus.). 144p. 1990. 17.95 (*0-8109-1389-5*, Pub. by Abrams) Time Warner.

McTigue, G. Gaynor. Life's Little Frustration Book. 1994. mass mkt. 6.99 (*0-312-95215-5*) St Martin.

Mctigue, G. Gaynor. More Life's Little Frustration Book. 1997. mass mkt. 6.99 (*0-312-96098-0*) St Martin.

McTigue, G. Gaynor. You Know You're Middle-Aged When . . . LC 95-110354. 96p. 1994. mass mkt. 4.50 (*0-7860-0066-X*, Pinncle Kensgtn) Kensgtn Pub Corp.

McTigue, Geraldine, ed. see Washington, Booker T.

McTigue, James. A Survival Manual for Consumers: Get Mad Then Get Even. (Self Confidence - Self Competence Ser.). 200p. (Orig.). 1987. pap. 11.95 (*0-932123-03-1*) Stone Trail Pr.

McTigue, Nancy E. National Assessment of Particle Removal by Filtration. LC 98-8140. 1998. write for info. (*0-89867-964-8*) Am Water Wks Assn.

McTigue, William R., Jr., jt. auth. see Phifer, Russell W.

McTurk, Rory, tr. see Hallberg, Peter.

McTwigan, Michael. Ron Nagle: A Survey Exhibition. LC 93-79949. 84p. 1993. pap. 25.00 (*0-9638030-0-X*) Mills Art Gal.

McTyeire, Holland N., et al. Duties of Masters to Servants. LC 79-154084. (Black Heritage Library Collection). 1977. 18.95 (*0-8369-8795-0*) Ayer.

McTyre, Joe, jt. auth. see Glover, James Bolan, V.

McTyre, Ruthann B., compiled by. Library Resources for Singers, Coaches & Accompanists: An Annotated Bibliography, 1970-1997, 71. LC 98-23959. (Music Reference Collection: Vol. 71). 176p. 1998. lib. bdg. 65.00 (*0-313-30266-9*, Greenwood Pr) Greenwood.

Mcullen, John. Quick Clips: 120 Tips to Improve Your Technique, Performance & Equipment. 1997. pap. 7.95 (*1-887216-08-1*) Elk Mtn Pr.

McVan, Alice J. Antonio Machado. (Illus.). 1959. 10.00 (*0-87535-095-X*) Hispanic Soc.

McVarish, Emily, tr. see Lichtenstein, Jacqueline.

McVaugh, Julia A., ed. see Swalin, Benjamin.

McVaugh, Machael, ed. see Maimonides, Moses.

McVaugh, Michael, jt. ed. see Sylla, Edith.

McVaugh, Michael R. & Ogden, Margaret, eds. Guigonis de Caulhiaco: Inventarium sive Chirurgia Magna, Vol. 2: Commentary. (Studies in Ancient Medicine: No. 14.2). vi, 438p. 1997. 170.50 (*90-04-10784-3*) Brill Academic Pubs.

McVaugh, Michael R. & Siraisi, Nancy G. Renaissance Medical Learning: Evolution of Tradition. (Osiris Ser.: Vol. 6). 244p. 1994. lib. bdg. 39.00 (*0-934235-18-X*) U Ch Pr.

— Renaissance Medical Learning: Evolution of Tradition. (Osiris Ser.: Vol. 6). 244p. 1994. pap. text 25.00 (*0-934235-17-1*) U Ch Pr.

McVaugh, Michael R., jt. auth. see Mauskopf, Seymour H.

McVaugh, Michael R., ed. see De Caulhiaco, Guigonis.

***McVaugh, Rogers.** Botanical Results of the Sesse & Mocino Expedition (1787-1803) A Guide to Relevent Scientific Names of Plants, Vol. VII. 626p. 2000. 55.00 (*0-913196-68-1*) Hunt Inst Botanical.

McVaugh, Rogers. Edward Palmer, Plant Explorer of the American West. LC 56-11234. (Illus.). 1977. reprint ed. 15.00 (*0-913728-26-8*) Theophrastus.

Mcvay. The Esenin Imaginists & the Peasant Poets. 1998. 50.00 (*0-8161-9078-X*, G K Hall Lrg Type) Mac Lib Ref.

McVay, Barry L. Compliance with the Defense Priorities & Allocations System: It's the Law! (Panoptic Federal Contracting Ser.). 28p. (Orig.). 1998. pap. 19.95 (*0-912481-15-3*) Panoptic Ent.

— Facilities Capital Cost of Money. (Panoptic Federal Contracting Ser.). 21p. (Orig.). 1997. pap. 19.95 (*0-912481-19-6*) Panoptic Ent.

— The Federal Procurement Process. 37p. (Orig.). 1998. pap. 19.95 (*0-912481-22-6*) Panoptic Ent.

— Federal Profit Policy. 27p. (Orig.). 1997. pap. 19.95 (*0-912481-11-0*) Panoptic Ent.

— Getting Started in Federal Contracting: A Guide Through the Federal Procurement Maze. 4th rev. ed. LC 96-68905. (Panoptic Federal Contracting Ser.). 396p. 1996. pap. 39.95 (*0-912481-24-2*) Panoptic Ent.

— The History of Federal Procurement. 2nd rev. ed. (Panoptic Federal Contracting Ser.). 21p. 1998. pap. 19.95 (*0-912481-23-4*) Panoptic Ent.

— The Panoptic Federal Protest Package: How to Challenge Improprieties & Errors in the Procurement Process. (Federal Contracting Ser.). 138p. 1997. ring bd. 39.95 (*0-912481-17-X*) Panoptic Ent.

— The Panoptic Federal Supply & Service Code Book. (Panoptic Federal Contracting Ser.). 124p. (Orig.). 1997. pap. 24.95 (*0-912481-20-X*) Panoptic Ent.

— Proposals That Win Federal Contracts: How to Plan, Price, Write & Negotiate to Get Your Fair Share of Government Business. LC 88-62678. (Federal Contracting Ser.). 334p. (Orig.). 1989. pap. 24.95 (*0-912481-08-0*) Panoptic Ent.

— Providing Foreign Products to the Federal Government. 3rd rev. ed. (Panoptic Federal Contracting Ser.). 35p. 1998. pap. 29.95 (*0-912481-14-5*) Panoptic Ent.

***McVay, Barry L.** Small Business Set-Asides & Preference Programs. (Federal Contracting Ser.). 54p. 1999. pap. 29.95 (*0-912481-25-0*) Panoptic Ent.

McVay, Freda, et al. Lubbock: City of Land & Sky. LC 94-21463. (Urban Tapestry Ser.). (Illus.). 256p. 1994. 39.50 (*1-881096-09-2*) Towery Pub.

McVay, Gwyn. Brother Ikon. limited ed. (Orig.). 1996. pap. write for info. (*0-9651608-0-7*) Inkstone Pr.

— This Natural History. 35p. 1997. pap. 5.00 (*1-877603-45-7*) Pecan Grove.

***McVay, Marguerita.** How to Be a Successful Distance Student: Learning on the Internet. 180p. (C). 1998. pap. text 25.00 (*0-536-01711-5*) Pearson Custom.

M

An Asterisk (*) at the beginning of an entry indicates that the title is appearing for the first time.

McVea, Harry. Financial Conglomerates & the Chinese Wall: Regulating Conflicts of Interest. LC 92-47415. (Illus.). 302p. 1993. text 58.00 (*0-19-825713-9*, Clarendon Pr) OUP.

McVea, Harry & Cumper, Peter. Learning Exam Skills. 122p. 1996. pap. 22.00 (*1-85431-451-3*, Pub. by Blackstone Pr) Gaunt.

McVea, Mildred L. Sugar Petite. (Illus.). 184p. 1989. pap. 9.95 (*0-8071-1622-X*) La State U Pr.

McVeagh, Diana. New Grove Twentieth Century English Masters. pap. write for info. (*0-393-31595-9*) Norton.

McVeagh, Diana, et al. The New Grove Twentieth Century English Masters: Elgar, Delius, Vaughan, Tippett, Holst, Williams, Walton & Britten. 1986. pap. 16.95 (*0-393-30351-9*) Norton.

McVeagh, J. P. Land Valuation Law. 7th ed. 1979. boxed set 58.00 (*0-409-64584-2*, NZ, MICHIE) LEXIS Pub.

McVeagh, John. All Before Them: 1660-1780, Vol. 1. LC 88-7489. (English Literature & the Wider World Ser.). (Illus.). 320p. (C). 1990. text 55.00 (*0-948660-08-2*, Pub. by Ashfield Pr) Humanities.

— Irish Travel Writing: A Bibliography. 176p. 1997. 55.00 (*0-86327-503-6*, Pub. by Wolfhound Press) Irish Amer Bk.

McVeagh, John, ed. Richard Pococke's Irish Tours. (Illus.). 240p. 1995. 39.50 (*0-7165-2539-9*, Pub. by Irish Acad Pr) Intl Spec Bk.

McVeagh, John, jt. ed. see Hadfield, Andrew.

McVeigh, Alice. Ghost Music. 376p. 1998. 27.00 (*1-85797-693-2*, Pub. by Orion Pubng Grp); pap. 10.95 (*0-7528-0920-2*, Pub. by Orion Pubng Grp) Trafalgar.

McVeigh, Amy. Mackinac Connection: The Insider's Guide to Mackinac Island. 3rd rev. ed. LC 92-23695. (Illus.). 152p. 1998. pap. 12.95 (*0-9623213-3-8*) Mackinac Pub.

McVeigh, Amy, jt. auth. see Jolliffe, Susan D.

McVeigh, Brian J. Life in a Japanese Women's College: Learning to Be Ladylike. LC 96-19652. (Nissan Institute/Routledge Japanese Studies Ser.). 288p. (C). 1997. 90.00 (*0-415-14456-6*) Routledge.

— Nature of the Japanese State: Rationality & Rituality. LC 98-34179. (Nissan Institute/Routledge Japanese Studies Ser.). 280p. (C). 1998. 85.00 (*0-415-17106-7*) Routledge.

— Spirits, Selves & Subjectivity in a Japanese New Religion: The Cultural Psychology of Belief in Shukyo Mahikari. LC 97-39718. (Studies in Asian Thought & Religion Ser.: Vol. 21). 272p. 1997. 89.95 (*0-7734-8430-2*) E Mellen.

*__McVeigh, Brian J.__ Wearing Ideology: State, Schooling & Self-Presentation in Japan. (Dress, Body, Culture Ser.). (Illus.). 224p. 2000. 65.00 (*1-85973-485-5*, Pub. by Berg Pubs); pap. 19.50 (*1-85973-490-1*, Pub. by Berg Pubs) NYU Pr.

McVeigh, C. A. A Dictionary of the High Court Rules. 216p. 1989. pap. 63.00 (*0-409-78793-0*, NZ, MICHIE) LEXIS Pub.

McVeigh, J. C., jt. ed. see Sayigh, A. A.

McVeigh, Jane & Ellis, Mary Lynn. With a Poet's Eye: Children Translate the World. LC 97-30220. (J). 1997. pap. text 25.00 (*0-435-07242-0*) Heinemann.

McVeigh, Jane T. Rose Virginie Pelletier: The Woman & Her Legacy. LC 96-53027. 232p. 1997. text 39.50 (*0-7618-0690-3*) U Pr of Amer.

*__McVeigh, Jim.__ Executed: Tom Williams & the IRA. (Illus.). 120p. 1999. pap. 13.95 (*1-900960-05-2*, Pub. by Beyond the Pale) Irish Bks Media.

— Garvaghy: A Community under Siege. (Illus.). 120p. 1999. pap. 17.95 (*1-900960-06-0*, Pub. by Beyond the Pale) Irish Bks Media.

McVeigh, Joseph, jt. ed. see Trommler, Frank.

McVeigh, Kate. The Favor Factor. pap. 5.99 (*0-89274-967-9*) Harrison Hse.

*__McVeigh, Kate.__ Get Over It: Overcoming the Enemy's Strategy of Offense. 1999. pap. 5.99 (*1-57794-172-1*) Harrison Hse.

McVeigh, Mark, jt. auth. see Canizares, Susan.

McVeigh, Robbie, jt. ed. see Levin, Ronit.

McVeigh, Ruth, jt. auth. see Turner, Trudy.

McVeigh, Ruth M. & Turner, Trudy. Fogswamp. (Illus.). 255p. 1977. pap. 11.95 (*0-88839-104-8*) Hancock House.

McVeigh, Shaun & Wheeler, Sally. Law, Health & Medical Regulation. (Contemporary Legal Issues Ser.). 250p. 1993. 81.95 (*1-85521-283-8*, Pub. by Dartmth Pub) Ashgate Pub Co.

McVeigh, Simon W. Concert Life in London from Mozart to Hadyn. LC 92-565. (Illus.). 322p. (C). 1993. text 69.95 (*0-521-41353-2*) Cambridge U Pr.

McVeigh, Terrence A., tr. from LAT. Wyclif on Simony. LC 92-9844. ix, 179p. 1992. 27.00 (*0-8232-1349-8*) Fordham.

McVeity. The Fifty Dollar Fall. (Clipper Fiction Ser.). 1991. pap. text. write for info. (*0-582-87517-X*, Pub. by Addison-Wesley) Longman.

— Where R the Billabongs? (Clipper Fiction Ser.). 1994. pap. text. write for info. (*0-582-80270-9*, Pub. by Addison-Wesley) Longman.

McVeity, Jen. On Different Shores. LC 98-4481. 167p. (YA). (gr. 5 up). 1998. lib. bdg. 17.99 (*0-531-33115-6*) Orchard Bks Watts.

— On Different Shores. LC 98-4481. (Illus.). 167p. (YA). (gr. 5-9). 1998. 16.95 (*0-531-30115-X*) Orchard Bks Watts.

— You Choose. 1998. pap. 5.95 (*0-207-19188-3*) HarpC.

McVety, et al. The Menu & the Cycle of Cost Control. 288p. (C). 1997. per. 66.95 (*0-7872-4215-2*, 41421501) Kendall-Hunt.

McVety, Paul J. Fundamentals of Menu Planning. 232p. 1989. pap. 46.95 (*0-442-26492-5*, VNR) Wiley.

McVety, Paul J. & Ware, Bradley J. Fundamentals of Menu Planning. 240p. 1989. pap. 49.95 (*0-471-28945-0*, VNR) Wiley.

McVey & Associates Staff. Job Interviews. (Follet Coping Skills Ser.). 64p. 1988. pap. text. write for info. (*0-8428-2329-8*) Cambridge Bk.

— Using Transportation. (Follet Coping Skills Ser.). 64p. 1988. pap. text 5.50 (*0-8428-2330-1*) Cambridge Bk.

McVey, James P. Handbook of Mariculture: Finfish Aquaculture, Vol. II. LC 90-2451. 1991. lib. bdg. 152.00 (*0-8493-0219-6*, SH138, CRC Reprint) Franklin.

McVey, James P., ed. Handbook of Mariculture: Crustacean Aquaculture, Vol. I. 456p. 1983. 212.95 (*0-8493-0220-X*, SH138) CRC Pr.

*__McVey, Janice M.__ Hope over Struggle. LC 00-90924. 2000. pap. 7.95 (*0-533-13541-9*) Vantage.

McVey, Kathleen, ed. see St. Ephrem the Syrian.

McVey, Kathleen E., intro. Ephrem the Syrian. (Classics of Western Spirituality Ser.). 1989. pap. 24.95 (*0-8091-3093-9*) Paulist Pr.

McVey, Kelly, ed. Proceedings of the 1997 Sensors & Electron Devices Symposium. (Illus.). 425p. (Orig.). 1997. pap. write for info. (*0-9603590-8-7*) ERI MI.

*__McVey, Mary.__ Streetwise Spanish Dictionary/Thesaurus: The User-Friendly Guide to Spanish Slang & Idioms. (Streetwise Ser.). (SPA & ENG.). 320p. 2000. pap. 21.19 (*0-8442-2551-7*) NTC Contemp Pub Co.

McVey, Mary A. Bridge Basics: An Introduction to the Game. 2nd ed. 120p. 1982. pap. 5.50 (*0-910475-01-6*) KET.

— Play Bridge! 1983. pap. 6.50 (*0-910475-22-9*) KET.

McVey, Mary A. & Lehtcmaa, Linda R. Play More Bridge. (Bridge Ser.). 228p. 1985. pap. text 7.00 (*0-910475-32-6*) KET.

McVey, Michael, jt. illus. see Mancini, Mark.

McVey, Philip M. Terrorism & Local Law Enforcement: A Multidimensional Challenge for the Twenty-First Century. LC 97-7427. (Illus.). 188p. 1997. text 53.95 (*0-398-06774-0*); pap. text 39.95 (*0-398-06775-9*) C C Thomas.

McVey, R. Steve, jt. auth. see Capozzoli, Thomas K.

McVey, Rick, adapted by see Henry, O.

*__McVey, Ruth.__ Money & Power in Provincial Thailand. LC 99-34360. 288p. 2000. pap. text 21.95 (*0-8248-2273-0*) UH Pr.

McVey, Ruth. The Soviet View of the Indonesian Revolution, No. 7. (Modern Indonesia Project Ser.: Vol. 7). 90p. 1957. reprint ed. 2.50 (*0-87763-018-6*) Cornell SE Asia.

*__McVey, Ruth, ed.__ Money & Power in Provincial Thailand. LC 99-34360. 288p. 2000. 55.00 (*0-8248-2272-2*) UH Pr.

McVey, Ruth T., ed. Southeast Asian Capitalists. (Studies on Southeast Asia: No. 9). 220p. (Orig.). (C). 1992. pap. text 16.00 (*0-87727-708-7*) Cornell SE Asia.

McVey, Ruth T. & Suddard, Adrienne, eds. Southeast Asian Transitions: Approaches Through Social History. LC 78-4171. (Yale Southeast Asia Studies: No. 8). 252p. reprint ed. pap. 78.20 (*0-7837-2989-8*, 204319400006) Bks Demand.

McVey, Ruth T., jt. auth. see Anderson, Benedict R.

McVey, Ruth T., jt. ed. see Benda, Harry J.

McVey, Ruth T., jt. ed. see Lev, Daniel S.

McVey, Sharel. Excel Version 5 for Windows: The Original Step-by-Step Approach Corporate Edition. 1994. 29.99 (*1-56529-730-X*) Que.

McVey, Steve. Grace Rules: Living in the Kingdom of God Where . . . LC 98-12643. 220p. 1998. pap. 8.99 (*1-56507-897-7*) Harvest Hse.

— Grace Walk. LC 94-47485. (Orig.). 1995. pap. 8.99 (*1-56507-321-5*) Harvest Hse.

McVicar, Andrew, jt. auth. see Clancy, John.

McVicar, Clyde, ed. see Fotiades, John M.

McVicar, George, jt. ed. see Davie, Cedric T.

McVicar, Jekka. Good Enough to Eat: Growing & Cooking Edible Flowers. (Illus.). 160p. 1998. 29.95 (*1-85626-227-8*, Pub. by Cathie Kyle) Trafalgar.

— Herbs for the Home. 256p. 1999. pap. write for info. (*0-14-025678-4*) Viking Penguin.

McVicar, Murray, jt. auth. see Midwinter, Arthur F.

McVicar, Wes. Clown Act Omnibus: Everything You Need to Know about Clowning Plus over 200 Clown Stunts. LC 87-42958. (Illus.). 192p. (YA). (gr. 9 up). 1986. reprint ed. pap. 14.95 (*0-916260-41-0*, B118) Meriwether Pub.

McVicar, Will. The Sons of God: Teachings From "A Course in Miracles" LC 97-94089. 195p. (Orig.). 1998. pap. 12.95 (*0-9658888-1-9*, 1013) Love Pub.

McVickar, John. Outlines of Political Economy. LC 64-22240. (Reprints of Economic Classics Ser.). vi, 242p. 1965. reprint ed. 45.00 (*0-678-00118-9*) Kelley.

*__McVicker, Carrie.__ Children & the HIV/AIDS Crisis: Youth Who Are Infected & Affected. Barnitz, Laura A., ed. 38p. 1999. pap. 6.00 (*0-9663709-6-1*) Youth Advocate.

McVicker, Dee. Easy Recycling Handbook: What to Recycle & How to Buy Recycled...Without All the Garbage. LC 93-79984. (Illus.). 128p. (Orig.). 1994. pap. 8.95 (*0-9638428-5-4*) Grassroots Bks.

McVicker, Donald, et al. Testimony of Images: Pre-Columbian Art. LC 92-85435. (Illus.). 200p. (Orig.). (C). 1992. pap. 25.00 (*0-940784-15-7*) Miami Univ Art.

McVicker, Galina. Citizen, Turn Back! A Russian-American Odyssey. LC 93-24256. (Illus.). 128p. (Orig.). 1993. 16.95 (*1-56474-076-5*); pap. 8.95 (*1-56474-070-6*) Fithian Pr.

McVicker, Jeanette, ed. see Woolf, Virginia, et al.

McVicker, Marilyn G. Sauna Detoxification Therapy: A Guide for the Chemically Sensitive. LC 96-51802. (Illus.). 175p. 1997. pap. 29.95 (*0-7864-0359-4*) McFarland & Co.

McVicker, Mary L. The Writings of J. Frank Dobie: A Bibliography. LC 68-23421. 1968. 13.95 (*0-685-85505-8*) Mus Great Plains.

— The Writings of J. Frank Dobie: A Bibliography. deluxe limited ed. LC 68-23421. 1968. boxed set 25.00 (*0-685-85504-X*) Mus Great Plains.

McVie, J. G., et al, eds. Clinical & Experimental Pathology of Lung Cancer. (Developments in Oncology Ser.). 1985. text 160.00 (*0-89838-764-7*) Kluwer Academic.

McVie, J. Gordon, et al, eds. Autologous Bone Marrow Transplantation & Solid Tumors. LC 84-13380. (Monograph Series of the European Organization for Research on Treatment of Cancer: No. 14). (Illus.). 208p. 1984. reprint ed. pap. 64.50 (*0-7837-9561-0*, 206031000005) Bks Demand.

McVinney, L. Donald. Chemical Dependency Treatment: Innovative Group Approaches. LC 97-37554. 125p. 1997. 39.95 (*0-7890-0354-6*) Haworth Pr.

McVinney, L. Donald, ed. Picasso Linoleum Cuts: The Mr. & Mrs. Charles Kramer Collection in the Metropolitan Museum of Art. 1985. 60.00 (*0-394-54692-X*) Random.

McVittie, Donald R. Describing Nonstandard Gears: An Alternative to the Rack Shift Coefficient. (Nineteen Eighty-Six Fall Technical Meeting Ser.: Vol. 86FTM1). (Illus.). 23p. 1986. pap., pap. text 30.00 incl. audio compact disk (*1-55589-465-8*, 86-FTM1) AGMA.

McVittie, Donald R. & Errichello, Robert L. Application of Miner's Rule to Industrial Gear Drives. (Nineteen Eighty-Eight Fall Technical Meeting Ser.: Vol. 88FTM9). (Illus.). 22p. 1988. pap. text 30.00 (*1-55589-514-X*) AGMA.

McVitty, Walter. Getting It Together: Organizing the Reading-Writing Classroom. LC 90-26355. (Orig.). 1991. write for info. (*0-435-08585-9*) Heinemann.

McVitty, Walter, ed. Children & Learning. (Illus.). 120p. (Orig.). (C). 1985. pap. text 16.50 (*0-909955-53-0*, 00586) Heinemann.

— Getting It Together: Organizing the Reading-Writing Classroom. (Illus.). 122p. (Orig.). (C). 1987. pap. text 21.00 (*0-909955-63-8*, 00590) Heinemann.

McVoy, Cullen. Finding Ro-Hun: Awakening Through Spiritual Therapy. (Illus.). 80p. (Orig.). 1996. mass mkt. 5.00 (*0-9640545-0-7*) Pooka Pubns.

McVoy, L. C. Louisiana in the Short Story. LC 73-130264. (American History & Americana Ser.: No. 47). 1970. reprint ed. lib. bdg. 75.00 (*0-8383-1171-7*) M S G Haskell Hse.

McWade, Mickie. Getting up, Getting over, Getting On: A Twelve Step Guide to Divorce Recovery. 1999. pap. 14.95 (*1-891400-13-4*) Champion Pr.

McWade, Patricia. Financing Graduate School: How to Get Money for Your Master's or PhD. 2nd rev. ed. LC 96-31265. 220p. (Orig.). 1996. pap. 16.95 (*1-56079-638-3*) Petersons.

McWaid, Helen & Machac, Kathy. Home Stuff: Teach Away with Toss Aways. (Home-School-Education Ser.). (Illus.). 159p. 1982. pap. text 9.95 (*0-9611480-0-4*) Custom Curriculum.

McWalter, Ronald S., jt. auth. see Hayes, Peter C.

McWalter, Tony, jt. ed. see Ross, George M.

McWalters, Edward, et al. Heroes of the Faith. 54p. 1994. pap. 5.95 (*1-57326-022-3*) Core Ministries.

McWane, John W., jt. auth. see Smith, Malcolm K.

McWard, Larry J., jt. auth. see Zimmerman, Fred W.

McWaters, J. F., jt. auth. see Milacic, V. R.

McWaters, J. Glenn. Deep Water Exercise for Health & Fitness. LC 87-35861. (Illus.). 192p. (Orig.). 1988. 16.95 (*0-913581-07-0*); pap. 10.95 (*0-913581-08-9*) Publitec.

McWaters, Marcus M. & Lin, You-Feng. Intermediate Algebra. LC 84-80462. 517p. (C). 1985. text 65.56 (*0-669-05123-3*) HM Trade Div.

McWatters, Alicia. A Guide to a Naturally Healthy Bird. rev. ed. LC 97-69046. 80p. 2000. pap. 9.95 (*1-884820-21-2*) SAFE GOODS.

McWay, Dana C. Legal Aspects of Health Information Management. LC 96-8394. (Nursing Education Ser.). 300p. (C). 1996. mass mkt. 49.95 (*0-8273-5576-9*) Delmar.

McWayne, W. Robynne. Radical Reality: How Consciousness Transforms Itself into the Material Stuff of the Universe: The Physics of Reality Has Wildly Liberating Everyday Applications. (Illus.). 230p. 1998. pap. 14.95 (*1-891969-26-9*) RealityWrks.

McWeeny, R. & Sutcliffe, B. J., eds. Methods of Molecular Quantum Mechanics. 2nd ed. (Theoretical Chemistry Ser.). 573p. 1989. text 198.00 (*0-12-486551-8*) Acad Pr.

McWeeny, Roy, et al, eds. Quantum Systems in Chemistry & Physics: Trends in Methods & Applications. LC 98-136403. (Topics in Molecular Organization & Engineering Ser.: No. 16). 300p. 1997. 137.00 (*0-7923-4699-8*) Kluwer Academic.

McWeeny, Roy, ed. see Coulson, Charles A.

McWethy, Patricia J., ed. Basic Biological Concepts: What Should the World's Children Know? LC 94-211589. 1994. 3.00 (*0-941212-14-9*) Natl Assn Bio Tchrs.

McWhan, D. B., ed. Crystal Structure at High Pressure. (Transactions of the American Crystallographic Association Ser.: Vol. 5). 162p. 1969. pap. 25.00 (*0-686-60376-1*) Polycrystal Bk Serv.

McWhiney, Grady. Braxton Bragg & Confederate Defeat, Vol. I. LC 91-3554. 440p. 1991. 29.95 (*0-8173-0545-9*) U of Ala Pr.

— Cracker Culture: Celtic Ways in the Old South. LC 86-16052. (Illus.). 336p. 1989. pap. 22.95 (*0-8173-0458-4*) U of Ala Pr.

McWhiney, Grady, et al, eds. Fear God & Walk Humbly: The Agricultural Journal of James Mallory, 1843-1877. LC 96-6268. (Illus.). 600p. 1997. text 49.95 (*0-8173-0832-6*) U of Ala Pr.

McWhiney, Grady & Jamieson, Perry D. Attack & Die: Civil War Military Tactics & the Southern Heritage. LC 81-902. (Illus.). 232p. 1984. pap. text 15.95 (*0-8173-0229-8*) U of Ala Pr.

McWhinney, Edward. Conflict & Compromise: International Law & World Order in a Revolutionary Age. LC 80-29045. 152p. (C). 1981. 32.00 (*0-8419-0694-7*); pap. 18.00 (*0-8419-0696-3*) Holmes & Meier.

— Constitution-Making: Principles, Process, Practices. 240p. 1981. 30.00 (*0-8020-5553-2*) U of Toronto Pr.

*__McWhinney, Edward.__ From Gatt to the WTO: The Multilateral Trading System. 200p. 2000. 79.50 (*90-411-1253-7*) Kluwer Law Intl.

McWhinney, Edward. The International Court of Justice & the Western Tradition of Internationl Law. LC 87-10985. (Legal Aspects of International Organizations Ser.: No. 7). 1987. lib. bdg. 99.00 (*90-247-3524-6*) Kluwer Academic.

— Judge Manfred Lachs & Judicial Law-Making: Opinions on the International Court of Justice, 1967-1993. (Judges Ser.: Vol. 2). 1995. lib. bdg. 143.00 (*90-411-0125-X*) Kluwer Academic.

— Quebec & the Constitution, 1960 to 1978. LC 79-316335. 186p. reprint ed. pap. 57.70 (*0-8357-4159-1*, 203693300007) Bks Demand.

*__McWhinney, Edward.__ The United Nations & a New World Order for A New Millennium - Self-Determination, State Succession & Humanitarian. 120p. 2000. pap. 45.00 (*90-411-1371-1*) Kluwer Law Intl.

McWhinney, Edward. United Nations Law Making: Cultural & Ideological Relativism & International Law for an Era of Transition. 310p. (C). 1984. 34.50 (*0-8419-0948-2*); pap. 24.50 (*0-8419-1008-1*) Holmes & Meier.

McWhinney, Edward, ed. Law, Foreign Policy & the East-West Detente. LC 65-899. 131p. reprint ed. pap. 40.70 (*0-608-30687-8*, 201432100089) Bks Demand.

McWhinney, Edward J. The International Law of Detente. 260p. 1978. lib. bdg. 87.00 (*90-286-0338-7*) Kluwer Academic.

— Judge Shigeru Oda & the Progressive Development of International Law: Opinions, Declarations, Separate Opinions, Dissents, on the International Court of Justice, 1976-1992. LC 93-884. (Judges Ser.). 1993. lib. bdg. 189.50 (*0-7923-2257-6*) Kluwer Academic.

— Judicial Settlement of International Disputes: Jurisdiction Justiciability & Judicial Law-Making of the Contemporary International Court. (C). 1991. lib. bdg. 93.00 (*0-7923-0991-X*) Kluwer Academic.

— Supreme Courts & Judicial Law-Making: Constitutional Tribunals & Constitutional Review. 1986. lib. bdg. 136.50 (*90-247-3203-4*) Kluwer Academic.

— The World Court & the Contemporary International Law-Making Process. 227p. 1979. lib. bdg. 80.00 (*90-286-0908-3*) Kluwer Academic.

McWhinney, Edward J., ed. From Coexistence to Cooperation: International Law & Organization in the Post-Cold War Era. 312p. (C). 1991. lib. bdg. 121.50 (*0-7923-1401-8*) Kluwer Academic.

McWhinney, Edward J., et al, eds. Federalism in the Making: Contemporary Canadian & German Constitutionalism, National & Transnational. LC 92-31199. 1992. lib. bdg. 90.50 (*0-7923-1975-3*) Kluwer Academic.

McWhinney, Edward J., jt. auth. see Singh, Nagendra K.

McWhinney, Ian R. A Textbook of Family Medicine. 2nd ed. (Illus.). 464p. 1997. text 60.00 (*0-19-511517-1*); pap. text 39.50 (*0-19-511518-X*) OUP.

McWhinney, Will. Creating Paths of Change: Managing Issues & Resolving Problems in Organizations. 2nd ed. LC 97-4640. 1997. pap. 21.95 (*0-7619-1007-7*) Sage.

— Paths of Change: Stragetic Choices for Organizations & Society. (Illus.). 280p. 1992. 52.00 (*0-8039-3930-2*); pap. 24.00 (*0-8039-3931-0*) Sage.

— Paths of Change: Strategic Choices for Organizations & Society. LC 97-4628. 1997. pap. 24.00 (*0-7619-1017-4*) Sage.

McWhir, Anne, ed. see Shelley, Mary Wollstonecraft.

McWhirter, Benedict, jt. auth. see McWhirter, J.

McWhirter, Darien A. The End of Affirmative Action: Where Do We Go from Here? 224p. 1996. 19.95 (*1-55972-339-4*, Birch Ln Pr) Carol Pub Group.

— Equal Protection. LC 94-37866. (Exploring the Constitution Ser.). 216p. 1994. 29.95 (*0-89774-855-7*) Oryx Pr.

— Freedom of Speech, Press, & Assembly. LC 94-4842. (Exploring the Constitution Ser.). 208p. 1994. 29.95 (*0-89774-853-0*) Oryx Pr.

— The Legal 100: A Ranking of the Individuals Who Have Most Influenced the Law. LC 97-17536. (Illus.). 416p. 1997. 27.50 (*0-8065-1860-X*, Citadel Pr) Carol Pub Group.

— Search Seizure & Privacy. LC 94-27882. (Exploring the Constitution Ser.). 192p. 1994. 29.95 (*0-89774-854-9*) Oryx Pr.

— The Separation of Church & State. LC 93-40703. (Exploring the Constitution Ser.). 208p. 1994. 29.95 (*0-89774-852-2*) Oryx Pr.

— Sharing Ownership: The Business Manager's Guide to ESOP's & Other Ownership Incentive Plans. LC 92-46584. 288p. 1993. 34.95 (*0-471-57733-2*) Wiley.

McWhirter, Darien A. & Bible, Jon D. Privacy As a Constitutional Right: Sex, Drugs, & the Right to Life. LC 91-47986. 224p. 1992. 55.00 (*0-89930-638-1*, MWV, Quorum Bks) Greenwood.

McWhirter, Darien A., jt. auth. see Bible, Jon D.

McWhirter, David. Millennial Harbinger - Index. LC 81-65031. (Millennial Harbinger Ser.). 776p. (C). 1981. 19.99 (*0-89900-228-5*) College Pr Pub.

McWhirter, David, ed. Henry James's New York Edition: The Construction of Authorship. (Illus.). 352p. 1998. pap. 19.95 (*0-8047-3518-2*) Stanford U Pr.

An Asterisk (*) at the beginning of an entry indicates that the title is appearing for the first time.

McWhirter, David & Rowe, John C., eds. Henry James's New York Edition: The Construction of Authorship. LC 95-1325. (Illus.). xxvi, 333p. 1995. 49.50 (*0-8047-2564-0*) Stanford U Pr.

McWhirter, David P. & Mattison, Andrew M. The Male Couple: How Relationships Develop. xv, 341 p. 1985. 18.95 (*0-13-547661-5*, Busn) P-H.

McWhirter, Ellen H. Counseling for Empowerment. LC 94-3945. 270p. 1994. pap. text 39.95 (*1-55620-135-4*, 72517) Am Coun Assn.

McWhirter, George. A Staircase for All Souls. 128p. 1993. pap. text 10.95 (*0-88982-120-8*, Pub. by Oolichan Bks) Genl Dist Srvs.

McWhirter, George, ed. see Pacheco, Jose E.

McWhirter, J. & McWhirter, Benedict. At-Risk Youth: A Comprehensive Response. 2nd ed. LC 97-21569. (Counseling Ser.). 384p. 1997. mass mkt. 57.95 (*0-534-34580-8*) Brooks-Cole.

McWhirter, J. G. Mathematics in Signal Processing III. (Institute of Mathematics & Its Applications Conference Series, New Ser.: No. 49). (Illus.). 460p. 1994. text 110.00 (*0-19-853480-9*) OUP.

McWhirter, J. G., ed. Mathematics in Signal Processing, No. II. (Institute of Mathematics & Its Applications Conference Series, New Ser.: New Series 26). (Illus.). 840p. 1990. 175.00 (*0-19-853641-0*) OUP.

McWhirter, J. G. & Proudler, I. K., eds. Mathematics in Signal Processing IV. (Institute of Mathematics & Its Applications Conference Ser.: No. 67). (Illus.). 352p. 1999. text 175.00 (*0-19-850202-8*) OUP.

McWhirter, J. R., ed. Use of High Purity Oxygen in the Activated Sludge Process, 2 vols., Vol. 1. (Uniscience Ser.). 296p. 1978. 89.00 (*0-8493-5101-4*, TD756, CRC Reprint) Franklin.

— Use of High Purity Oxygen in the Activated Sludge Process, 2 vols., Vol. 2. (Uniscience Ser.). 292p. 1978. 89.00 (*0-8493-5102-2*, CRC Reprint) Franklin.

McWhirter, Jeffries, et al. At-Risk Youth: A Comprehensive Response. LC 92-26966. 353p. 1992. mass mkt. 26.50 (*0-534-19842-2*) Brooks-Cole.

Mcwhirter, Kore L. & O'Toole, Donna R. Aarvy Aardvark Finds Hope: A Read-Aloud Story for People of All Ages. (Illus.). 80p. (Orig.). (J). (ps up). 1989. teacher ed. 6.95 (*1-878321-26-9*, Compassion Pr); pap. 11.95 (*1-878321-25-0*, Compassion Pr) Compassion Bks.

McWhirter, Louis. Astrology & Stock Market Forecasting. Weingarten, Henry, ed. 1977. reprint ed. 49.00 (*0-88231-034-8*) ASI Pubs Inc.

McWhirter, Norris. Book of Millennium Records. 1999. text 24.95 (*1-85227-805-6*) Virgin Pr.

— Guinness Book of World Records, 1987. 1987. pap. 4.95 (*0-685-57360-5*) Bantam.

Mcwhirter, Norris. The Guinness Book of World Records 1997. 800p. 1997. mass mkt. 6.99 (*0-553-54284-2*) Bantam.

McWhirter, Norris. Guinness Book 1995. 1994. mass mkt. 8.99 (*0-553-54190-0*) Bantam.

— Guinness Book 1995. 1995. mass mkt. 8.99 (*0-553-85069-5*) Bantam.

— Guinness Book 1996. 1995. mass mkt. 8.99 (*0-553-54227-3*) Bantam.

— Guinness...1987. 1987. pap. 4.95 (*0-685-52275-X*) Bantam.

McWhite. Down Rae's Creek. 2nd rev. ed. (Illus.). 112p. 1994. reprint ed. per. 10.00 (*0-9662195-0-3*) M C White.

McWhorter. Efficient & Flexible Reading. 5th ed. LC 98-19302. 456p. (C). 1998. pap. text 48.00 (*0-321-01244-5*) Addson-Wesley Educ.

— Guide to College Reading. 5th ed. LC 99-25373. 535p. 1999. pap. text 48.00 (*0-321-03793-6*) Addson-Wesley Educ.

— Study & Critical Thinking Skills in College. 4th ed. 448p. (C). 1999. pap. text. write for info. (*0-321-03795-2*) Addson-Wesley Educ.

McWhorter. Successful College Writing. pap. text. write for info. (*0-312-24364-2*); pap. text. write for info. (*0-312-24366-9*) St Martin.

McWhorter. Successful College Writing. 1999. pap. text 44.95 (*0-312-15276-0*) St Martin.

***McWhorter.** Successful College Writing: Shorter Edition. 1999. pap. text 39.95 (*0-312-24534-3*) St Martin.

McWhorter. The Writer's Compass. (C). 1994. pap. text 37.96 (*0-395-66701-1*) HM.

— Writers Express. (C). 1992. pap. 37.16 (*0-395-59895-8*) HM.

— The Writer's Express, 2 vols. 2nd ed. LC 96-76930. (C). 1996. pap. text 37.16 (*0-395-78292-9*) HM.

— Writer's Handbook. LC 97-162051. (C). Date not set. pap. 22.76 (*0-395-72820-7*); pap. text 22.76 (*0-395-72819-3*) HM.

McWhorter, ed. College Reading Study Skill Writer. 1997. cd-rom 132.00 (*0-673-55017-6*) P-H.

McWhorter, ed. I'm Academic Reading. 2nd ed. 176p. 1997. text 11.00 (*0-673-54362-5*) P-H.

McWhorter & Harden, O. Elizabeth. Maria Edgeworth's Art of Prose Fiction. 258p. 1971. text 35.40 (*3-10-800307-0*) Mouton.

McWhorter, jt. auth. see Needles, Belverd E., Jr.

McWhorter, Abner. An Introduction to Business for African-American Youth. Adams, Debra, ed. (Illus.). 162p. (Orig.). (YA). (gr. 6-12). 1995. pap. 10.95 (*0-9645840-1-8*) Xpression Pub.

McWhorter, C. G. & Gebhardt, M. R., eds. Methods of Applying Herbicides. 358p. 1988. text 35.00 (*0-911733-08-6*) Weed Sci Soc.

McWhorter, David B. & Sunada, Daniel K. Ground Water Hydrology & Hydraulics. LC 77-74259. 1981. reprint ed. 45.00 (*0-918334-18-7*) WRP.

McWhorter, Don & McWhorter, Jane. Living Together in Knowledge: What Husbands & Wives Can Learn about Marriage from Each Other. 172p. 1988. pap. text 5.95 (*0-929540-00-X*) Pub Designs.

McWhorter, Eugene W. The Club & the Town: The Rotary Club & the City of Longview, Texas, Year by Year from 1920-1995. LC 95-75960. (Illus.). 112p. 1995. 25.00 (*0-9646100-9-4*) Longview Rotary Endow Fund.

— Traditions of the Land: The History of Gregg County, Texas. LC 89-80785. (Illus.). 128p. (C). 1989. 29.95 (*0-9623844-0-2*) Gregg Cty Hist Found.

McWhorter, Frankie. Cowboy Fiddler in Bob Wills' Band. LC 96-50451. (Illus.). 168p. 1997. reprint ed. pap. 16.95 (*1-57441-025-3*) UNTX Pr.

McWhorter, George T. Burroughs Dictionary: An Alphabetical List of Proper Names, Word, Phrases & Concepts Contained in the Published Works of Edgar Rice Burroughs. LC 87-14266. (Illus.). 462p. 1987. lib. bdg. 65.00 (*0-8191-6512-3*) U Pr of Amer.

***McWhorter, Jame.** Friendship - Handle with Care. 1999. pap. 7.99 (*0-89225-383-5*) Gospel Advocate.

McWhorter, Jane. Caterpillars or Butterflies. (Illus.). 1977. pap. 7.15 (*0-89137-410-8*) Quality Pubns.

— Let This Cup Pass. (Illus.). 1979. pap. 7.15 (*0-89137-414-0*) Quality Pubns.

— Meet My Friend David. 1982. 7.15 (*0-89137-420-5*) Quality Pubns.

— Now I Can Fly! 1985. pap. 7.15 (*0-89137-437-X*) Quality Pubns.

— She Hath Done What She Could. 1973. 7.15 (*0-89137-405-1*) Quality Pubns.

McWhorter, Jane, jt. auth. see McWhorter, Don.

***McWhorter, John.** Losing the Race: Self-Sabotage in Black America. 288p. 2000. 24.00 (*0-684-83669-6*) Free Pr.

McWhorter, John. Spreading the Word: Language & Dialect in America. LC 99-42846. 2000. pap. text. write for info. (*0-325-00198-7*) Heinemann.

— Towards a New Model of Creole Genesis. (Studies in Ethnolinguistics: Vol. 3). XIII, 199p. (C). 1997. text 44.95 (*0-8204-3312-8*) P Lang Pubng.

— The Word on the Street: Fact & Fable about American English. LC 98-28441. (Illus.). 302p. (C). 1998. 27.95 (*0-306-45994-9*, Plenum Trade) Perseus Pubng.

***McWhorter, John H.** The Missing Spanish Creoles. LC 99-41957. 283p. 2000. 45.00 (*0-520-21999-6*, Pub. by U CA Pr) Cal Prin Full Svc.

McWhorter, John H., ed. see Society for Pidgin & Creole Linguistics Staff.

McWhorter, Kathleen. The Writer's Express: A Paragraph & Essay Text with Readings, 2 vols. 2nd ed. (C). 1997. text, teacher ed. 11.96 (*0-395-84069-4*) HM.

— The Writer's Selections: Shaping Our Lives. 288p. (C). 1996. pap. text 27.56 (*0-395-72821-5*) HM.

***McWhorter, Kathleen T.** College Reading & Study Skills. 8th ed. LC 00-29641. 2001. write for info. (*0-321-04957-8*) Longman.

McWhorter, Kathleen T. Efficient & Flexible Reading. 5th ed. 128p. 1998. 12.00 (*0-321-02672-1*) Addson-Wesley Educ.

— Guide to College Reading. LC 96-2358. (C). 1996. write for info. (*0-673-52491-4*) Addson-Wesley Educ.

— Guide to College Reading. 2nd ed. (C). 1989. 28.20 (*0-673-39665-7*) Addson-Wesley Educ.

— The Writer's Compass. 2nd ed. LC 98-72062. 1998. pap. text 30.57 (*0-395-87410-6*) HM.

— The Writer's Compass: A Sentence & Paragraph Text with Readings. annot. ed. (C). 1994. text, teacher ed. 39.16 (*0-395-72141-5*) HM.

— The Writer's Compass: A Sentence & Paragraph Text with Readings. 2nd ed. LC 98-72062. xiv, 514p. 1999. write for info. (*0-395-88544-2*) HM.

McWhorter, Kathleen T., ed. Academic Reading. 3rd ed. LC 97-11027. 450p. (C). 1997. pap. text 50.00 (*0-321-01222-4*) Addson-Wesley Educ.

McWhorter, LaDelle. Bodies & Pleasures. LC 98-49787. 1999. 18.95 (*0-253-21325-8*) Ind U Pr.

— Heidegger & the Earth: Essays in Environmental Philosophy. 98p. (C). 1992. 25.00 (*0-943549-08-6*) Truman St Univ.

***McWhorter, Larry.** Cowboy Poetry Contemporary Verse by Larry McWhorter. Coggin, Janice, ed. (Illus.). 192p. 2000. 19.95 (*0-9662091-3-3*) Cowboy Miner.

***McWhorter, Lucille Vigil. The Border Settlers of Northwestern Virginia. 6th ed. 538p. 2000. reprint ed. 16.95 (*0-87012-609-1*) McClain.**

In the contest for land Jesse Hughes bore a part far beyond that of the average settler. He was one of those woodsmen in whom was concentrated the hardihood, the daring, the fierce & uncontrollable spirit of our barbarous ancestors in the fens & on the swamp shores of Northwestern Europe. It was a war, danger, adventure. On the trail of the wild Indian his soul hardened to iron & Jesse's nature grew more savage than that of the man he hunted. He was grim, cruel, relentless & bloodthirsty. But he was the product of the age in which he lived. (One of the Big Four) (Sixth Printing. *Publisher Paid Annotation.*

McWhorter, Lucullus V. The Border Settlers of Northwestern Virginia, from 1768 to 1795: Embracing the Life of Jesse Hughes & Other Noted Scouts of the Great Woods of the Trans-Allegheny. (Illus.). 520p. 2000. reprint ed. pap. 16.95 (*0-8063-0600-9*, 3630, Pub. by Clearfield Co) ACCESS Pubs Network.

In the contest for land Jesse Hughes bore a part far beyond that of the average settler. He was one of those woodsmen in whom was concentrated the hardihood, the daring, the fierce & uncontrollable spirit of our barbarous ancestors in the fens & on the swamp shores of Northwestern Europe. It was war, danger adventure. On the trail of the wild Indian his soul hardened to iron & Jesse's nature grew more savage that of the man he hunted.He was grim, cruel, relentless & bloodthirsty. Be he was the product of the age he which he lived. (One of the Big Four.) Sixth Printing, 2000. *Publisher Paid Annotation.*

— Hear Me, My Chiefs: Nez Perce Legend & History. LC 52-5209. (Illus.). 640p. 1984. reprint ed. 27.95 (*0-87004-316-1*); reprint ed. pap. 19.95 (*0-87004-310-2*) Caxton.

— Tragedy of the Wahk-Shum: The Death of Andrew J. Bolon, Yakima Indian Agent As Told by Sue-el-lil, Eyewitness; Also, The Suicide of Gen. Geo. A. Custer As Told by Owl Child, Eyewitness. Hines, Donald M., ed. LC 94-79277. (Illus.). 105p. 1995. pap. text 10.95 (*0-9629539-4-6*) Great Eagle Pub.

— Yellow Wolf: His Own Story. LC 85-16659. (Illus.). 324p. 1984. reprint ed. pap. 16.95 (*0-87004-315-3*) Caxton.

McWhorter, Margaret L. Autumn Leaves. LC 81-51943. (Illus.). 60p. (Orig.). 1981. pap. 5.95 (*0-9604342-1-6*) Ransom Hill.

— Poems That Tell Me Who I Am. LC 80-51481. (Illus.). 57p. 1978. reprint ed. pap. 5.95 (*0-9604342-0-8*) Ransom Hill.

— Tea Cup Tales. 2nd rev. ed. Andrecht, Summer, ed. 112p. 1997. pap. 9.95 (*0-941903-23-0*) Ransom Hill.

McWhorter, Minnie S. McWhorter History of the Henry McWhorter Family of N. J. & W. Va. (Illus.). 248p. 1995. reprint ed. pap. 39.00 (*0-8328-4804-2*); reprint ed. lib. bdg. 49.00 (*0-8328-4803-4*) Higginson Bk Co.

McWhorter, Mitzi, jt. ed. see Randle, Michael C.

McWhorter, Patricia J. Cry of Our Native Soul: Our Instinct for Creation-Centered Spirituality. LC 97-30295. 104p. 1998. pap. 12.95 (*1-56825-067-3*, 067-3) Rainbow Books.

McWhorter, Paul J., jt. ed. see Varadan, Vijay K.

McWhorter, R. Clayton, jt. auth. see Hardy, Owen B.

***McWhorter Sember, Brette.** Tenants' Rights in New York. (Legal Survival Guides Ser.). 224p. 2000. pap. 14.95 (*1-57248-122-6*, Sphinx Pubng) Sourcebks.

McWhorter Sember, Brette & Warda, Mark. How to Form a Corporation in New York. LC 99-33980. (Legal Survival Guides Ser.). 224p. 1999. pap. 19.95 (*1-57248-105-6*, Sphinx Pubng) Sourcebks.

McWiliams, Judith. Deception. 352p. 1999. mass mkt. 4.99 (*0-8217-6099-8*) Kensgtn Pub Corp.

***McWilliam, Augustus.** English Potpourri: English Help at Your Fingertips. LC 99-90208. 212p. 1999. pap. text 14.95 (*0-9670034-0-7*) L A M Pub.

***McWilliam, Candia.** Shorts II: The Macallan/Scotland on Sunday Short Story Collection. LC 00-303244. 256p. 2000. pap. 12.95 (*0-7486-6268-5*, Pub. by Edinburgh U Pr) Col U Pr.

McWilliam, Emma, jt. auth. see Phillips, Rena.

McWilliam, Erica. In Broken Images: Feminist Tales for a Different Teacher Education. 208p. (C). 1995. text 40.00 (*0-8077-3387-3*); pap. text 19.95 (*0-8077-3386-5*) Tchrs Coll.

***McWilliam, Erica.** Pedagogical Pleasures. LC 99-19789. (Eruptions Ser.: Vol. 1). 216p. (C). 1999. pap. text 29.95 (*0-8204-3800-6*) P Lang Pubng.

McWilliam, Erica & Taylor, Peter, eds. Pedagogy, Technology & the Body. LC 96-848. (Counterpoints Ser.: Vol. 29). VIII, 217p. (C). 1996. pap. text 29.95 (*0-8204-3089-7*) P Lang Pubng.

McWilliam, G. H., tr. & intro. see Boccaccio, Giovanni.

McWilliam, J. Book of Freezing. 1977. reprint ed. 20.00 (*0-85941-010-2*) St Mut.

McWilliam, Joanne, ed. see Barnes, Timothy D., et al.

McWilliam, N., jt. ed. see Winser, Shane.

McWilliam, Neil. Dreams of Happiness: Social Art & the French Left, 1830-1850. LC 92-38222. (Illus.). 424p. 1993. text 59.50 (*0-691-03155-X*, Pub. by Princeton U Pr) Cal Prin Full Svc.

— Monumental Intolerance: Jean Baffier, A Nationalist Sculptor in Fin-de-Siaecle France. LC 99-17642. 2000. write for info. (*0-271-01965-4*) Pa St U Pr.

McWilliam, Neil, ed. A Bibliography of Salon Criticism from the July Monarchy to the Second Republic, 1831-1851, Vol. 2. (Studies in the History of Art). 320p. (C). 1991. text 16.95 (*0-521-40091-0*) Cambridge U Pr.

— A Bibliography of Salon Criticism in Paris from the Ancien Regime to the Restoration, 1699-1827, Vol. 1. (Studies in the History of Art). 283p. (C). 1991. text 16.95 (*0-521-34634-7*) Cambridge U Pr.

***McWilliam, P.** Lives in Progress: Case Stories in Early Intervention. LC 99-31077. 1999. pap. text 32.00 (*1-55766-365-3*) P H Brookes.

McWilliam, P. J., et al. Practical Strategies for Family-Centered Early Intervention. (Early Childhood Intervention Ser.). (Illus.). 212p. (Orig.). 1996. pap. 39.95 (*1-879105-94-2*, 0355) Thomson Learn.

McWilliam, R. A. Rethinking Pull-Out Services in Early Intervention: A Professional Resource. 384p. 1996. pap. text 43.95 (*1-55766-242-8*, 2428) P H Brookes.

McWilliam, Rohan. Popular Politics in Nineteenth-Century England. LC 97-49376. (Historical Connections Ser.). 144p. (C). 1998. 60.00 (*0-415-18675-7*) Routledge.

— Popular Politics in Nineteenth-Century England. LC 97-49376. (Historical Connections Ser.). 144p. (C). 1998. pap. 17.99 (*0-415-10841-1*) Routledge.

McWilliams. Sewing & Serging Techniques for Blouses & Shirts. (Illus.). 96p. 1998. pap. 12.95 (*0-8069-8695-6*) Sterling.

McWilliams, et al. Cleft Palate Speech. 2nd ed. (Illus.). 400p. (C). 1989. text 65.95 (*1-55664-238-5*) Mosby Inc.

***McWilliams, A. L.** Eye of the Cat. LC 00-28847. 2000. write for info. (*0-7862-2495-9*) Five Star.

McWilliams, Bernard, ed. Nuestro Libro de Oracion Familiar. (SPA., Illus.). 405p. 1967. 29.95 (*0-915741-28-8*) C D Stampley Ent.

McWilliams, Bernard F., tr. see Dussel, Enrique D.

McWilliams, Bernard F., tr. see Paoli, Arturo.

***McWilliams, Bill.** Return to Glory: The Untold Story of Honor, Dishonor & Triumph at the United States Military Academy, 1950-53. LC 00-132973. (Illus.). 600p. 2000. write for info. (*1-890306-22-3*) Warwick Hse.

McWilliams, Brendan. Weather Eye. (Illus.). 160p. (Orig.). 1994. pap. 11.95 (*1-874675-38-4*, Pub. by Lilliput Pr) Irish Bks Media.

***McWilliams, Calvin, III.** Visions. 2000. pap. write for info. (*1-58235-387-5*) Watermrk Pr.

McWilliams, Carey. Ambrose Bierce, a Biography. (BCL1-PS American Literature Ser.). 358p. 1992. reprint ed. lib. bdg. 89.00 (*0-7812-6677-7*) Rprt Serv.

— California, the Great Exception. LC 98-42930. 385p. 1999. pap. 14.95 (*0-520-21893-0*, Pub. by U CA Pr) Cal Prin Full Svc.

***McWilliams, Carey.** Factories in the Field: The Story of Migratory Farm Labor in California. LC 99-45099. 345p. 2000. 14.95 (*0-520-22413-2*, Pub. by U CA Pr) Cal Prin Full Svc.

McWilliams, Carey. Ill Fares the Land: Migrants & Migratory Labor in the United States. Cortes, Carlos E., ed. LC 76-1255. (Chicano Heritage Ser.). 1977. reprint ed. 35.95 (*0-405-09514-7*) Ayer.

— A Mask for Privilege: Anti-Semitism in America. LC 78-26197. 299p. 1979. reprint ed. lib. bdg. 65.00 (*0-313-20880-8*, MCMP, Greenwood Pr) Greenwood.

— A Mask for Privilege: Anti-Semitism in America. 2nd ed. LC 99-12370. 299p. 1999. pap. write for info. (*0-7658-0612-6*) Transaction Pubs.

— North from Mexico: The Spanish-Speaking People of the United States. Meier, Matt S., ed. LC 89-38043. 372p. 1990. pap. 19.95 (*0-275-93224-9*, B3224, Greenwood Pr) Greenwood.

— North from Mexico: The Spanish-Speaking People of the United States, 140. Meier, Matt S., ed. LC 89-17031. 376p. 1990. 65.00 (*0-313-26631-X*, MNX/, Greenwood Pr) Greenwood.

— Southern California: An Island on the Land. LC 73-77787. 415p. 1973. pap. 16.95 (*0-87905-007-1*) Gibbs Smith Pub.

— Southern California Country: An Island on the Land. LC 76-111847. (Essay Index Reprint Ser.). 1977. 29.95 (*0-8369-1674-3*) Ayer.

McWilliams, Catherine, jt. auth. see Maxwell, Marion.

McWilliams, Courtney. The Beatles: Yesterday & Tomorrow. LC 96-9850. 209p. (gr. 10). 1997. pap. 29.95 (*0-7643-0135-7*) Schiffer.

— Beatles Collectibles: "With a Little Help from My Friends" LC 98-85864. 176p. 1998. pap. 29.95 (*0-7643-0657-X*) Schiffer.

— The Beatles, Yesterday & Tomorrow: A Collector's Guide to Beatles Memorabilia. 2nd rev. ed. (Illus.). 209p. 1999. pap. 29.95 (*0-7643-0852-1*) Schiffer.

McWilliams, D., jt. auth. see Congdon, Tim.

McWilliams, Dean. John Gardner. (Twayne's United States Authors Ser.). 152p. 1990. 21.95 (*0-8057-7602-8*, TUSAS 561, Twyne) Mac Lib Ref.

McWilliams, Dean, jt. auth. see Chesnutt, Charles Waddell.

McWilliams, Dee-Dee. Yesterday's Lifestyle-Today's Survival: The Life of a Real Ozark Mountain Hillbilly. (Illus.). 80p. (Orig.). 1983. pap. 7.95 (*0-943962-01-3*) Viewpoint Pr.

McWilliams, Donald B., jt. auth. see Pinney, William E.

McWilliams, Esther. The Beauty of the Big Horns. LC 98-22671. 1998. write for info. (*0-89802-699-7*) Beautiful Am.

McWilliams, Gerald M. & Brauning, Daniel W. The Birds of Pennsylvania. LC 99-38164. (Illus.). 668p. 2000. 39.95 (*0-8014-3643-5*) Cornell U Pr.

McWilliams, J., jt. ed. see Herring, J.

McWilliams, James. Mark Twain in the "St. Louis Post-Dispatch", 1874-1891. abr. ed. LC 95-61176. viii, 291p. 1997. 39.00 (*0-87875-469-5*) Whitston Pub.

McWilliams, Jane Wilson & Patterson, Carol Cushard. Bay Ridge on the Chesapeake: An Illustrated History. LC 86-72096. (Illus.). 205p. 1986. 29.95 (*0-9617617-0-9*) Brighton Editions.

McWilliams, Jimmie. Corn Pone: Half-Baked, Half-Fried Staple Corn Bread Patties. (Illus.). 216p. (Orig.). 1992. pap. 19.95 (*0-9633194-1-8*) D R Virtue Pr.

McWilliams, Joan H. Creating Parenting Plans That Work. 32p. 1999. pap. 12.45 (*1-883726-37-9*) Bradford Pub.

McWilliams, John. Last of the Mohicans: Civil Savagery & Savage Civility. LC 94-14564. (Twayne's Masterwork Studies: No. 143). (Illus.). 128p. 1994. 29.00 (*0-8057-8389-X*, Twyne) Mac Lib Ref.

McWilliams, John, photos by. Land of the Deepest Shade. (Illus.). 108p. 1989. 53.00 (*0-89381-392-3*) Aperture.

McWilliams, John, ed. & intro. see Cooper, James Fenimore.

***McWilliams, John C.** The 1960s Cultural Revolution. LC 99-58963. (Greenwood Press Guides to Historic Events of the Twentieth Century Ser.). 2000. write for info. (0-313-29913-7, Greenwood Pr) Greenwood.

McWilliams, John C. The Protectors: Harry J. Anslinger & the Federal Bureau of Narcotics, 1930-1962. LC 88-40328. 256p. 1990. 40.00 (0-87413-352-1) U Delaware Pr.

McWilliams, John P., Jr. The American Epic: Transformations of a Genre 1770-1860. (Cambridge Studies in American Literature & Culture: No. 36). 294p. (C). 1990. text 59.95 (0-521-37322-0) Cambridge U Pr.

McWilliams, John P., Jr., jt. ed. see Dekker, George.

McWilliams, Joyce. Roses Are Dead: Divorce Means Never Having to Say I Love You. (Illus.). 110p. (Orig.). 1991. pap. 6.95 (0-9630605-0-3) PrimRose CA.

McWilliams, Judith. Another Man's Baby. 1997. per. 3.50 (0-373-76095-7, 1-76095-8) Silhouette.

— Anything's Possible! (Desire Ser.). 1995. mass mkt. 3.25 (0-373-05911-6, 1-05911-2) Silhouette.

— Betrayed: Northpoint. (Historical Ser.). 1994. per. 3.99 (0-373-28849-2, 1-28849-7) Harlequin Bks.

— The Boss, the Beauty & the Bargain. (Desire Ser.: No. 1122). 1998. per. 3.50 (0-373-76122-8, 1-76122-0) Silhouette.

— Une Etrangere a Athenes. (Rouge Passion Ser.: Vol. 468). (FRE.). 1998. mass mkt. 3.50 (0-373-37468-2, 1-37468-5) Harlequin Bks.

— Honorable Intentions, Bk. 32. (Born in the U. S. A. Ser.). 1997. mass mkt. 4.50 (0-373-47182-3, 1-47182-0) Harlequin Bks.

— In Good Faith. (Men Made in America Ser.). 1995. per. 3.59 (0-373-45182-2, 1-45182-2) Harlequin Bks.

— Instant Husband. (Desire Ser.). 1996. per. 3.50 (0-373-76001-9, 1-76001-6) Silhouette.

— The Man from Atlantis: Spellbound. 1995. per. 3.25 (0-373-05954-X) Harlequin Bks.

— Matrimonio a Ciegas: Instant Husband. 1997. per. 3.50 (0-373-35178-X, 1-35178-2) Harlequin Bks.

— Not My Baby! (Temptation Ser.). 1993. per. 2.99 (0-373-25540-3, 1-25540-5) Harlequin Bks.

— Practice Husband. (Desire Ser.). 1997. per. 3.50 (0-373-76062-0, 1-76062-8) Silhouette.

— The Sheik's Secret. (Desire Ser.: Bk. 1228). 1999. per. 3.75 (0-373-76228-3, 1-76228-5) Silhouette.

— Suspicion. (Historical Ser.). 1994. per. 3.99 (0-373-28815-8, 1-28815-8) Harlequin Bks.

McWilliams, K. Richard, jt. auth. see El-Najjar, Mahmoud Y.

McWilliams, Lois R., ed. So Blow Ye Winds: A Diary of Oscar Rice. (Illus.). 85p. (Orig.). 1990. pap. 9.95 (0-9625505-1-5) SOS Pubns NJ.

McWilliams, Lorraine, ed. see Edgar, Elaine.

McWilliams, Margaret. Experimental Foods. 4th ed. (Illus.). 356p. 1994. pap., lab manual ed. 20.95 (0-916434-13-3) Plycon Pr.

— Food Fundamentals. 7th ed. LC 98-151941. (Illus.). 620p. 1998. pap. text 43.95 (0-916434-39-7) Plycon Pr.

Mcwilliams, Margaret. Foods: Experimental Perspectives. 3rd ed. LC 96-18910. 607p. (C). 1996. 84.00 (0-13-520990-0) P-H.

***McWilliams, Margaret.** Foods: Experimental Perspectives. 4th ed. LC 00-21914. (Illus.). 544p. 2000. 73.33 (0-13-021282-2) P-H.

McWilliams, Margaret. Fundamentals of Meal Management. 3rd ed. (Illus.). 368p. (C). 1997. pap. text 34.95 (0-916434-31-1) Plycon Pr.

— Illustrated Guide to Food Preparation. 8th ed. (C). 1998. pap. text 20.95 (0-916434-12-5) Plycon Pr.

McWilliams, Martha, jt. auth. see Saecker Schneider, Julie.

***McWilliams, Nancy.** Psychoanalytic Case Formulation. LC 98-56044. 240p. 1999. 36.00 (1-57230-462-6) Guilford Pubns.

McWilliams, Nancy. Psychoanalytic Diagnosis: Understanding Personality Structure in the Clinical Process. LC 94-8549. 398p. 1994. lib. bdg. 44.00 (0-89862-199-2) Guilford Pubns.

McWilliams, Patrick, ed. see Day, Angelique.

McWilliams, Patrick, jt. ed. see Day, Angelique.

McWilliams, Peter. Ain't Nobody's Business If You Do: The Absurdity of Consensual Crimes in a Free Society. 818p. 1993. 11.47 (0-931580-53-6) Prelude Press.

— Ain't Nobody's Business If You Do: The Absurdity of Consensual Crimes in Our Free Country. LC 97-162195. 1995. pap. 5.95 (0-931580-58-7) Prelude Press.

***McWilliams, Peter.** Come Love with Me & Be My Life: The Collected Romantic Poetry of Peter McWilliams. LC 98-198821. 1998. write for info. (0-931580-99-4) Prelude Press.

McWilliams, Peter. Come Love with Me & Be My Life: The Complete Romantic Poetry of Peter McWilliams. 250p. 1991. pap. 12.95 (0-931580-03-X) Prelude Press.

— Come Love with Me & Be My Life: The Complete Romantic Poetry of Peter McWilliams, 2 audiotapes, Set. 250p. 1991. audio 12.95 (0-931580-74-9) Prelude Press.

— Do It. 1997. 12.95 (0-931580-63-3) Prelude Press.

— I Marry You Because. 192p. 1993. pap. 5.95 (0-931580-85-4) Prelude Press.

— Its Okay to Be Gay. 1995. pap. text 9.95 (0-931580-62-5) Prelude Press.

— Life 101. 1997. 12.95 (0-931580-64-1) Prelude Press.

— Life 101 Quote Book. 1997. pap. text 7.95 (0-931580-67-6) Prelude Press.

— Life 102: What to Do When Your Guru Sues You. 423p. 1994. 19.95 (0-931580-34-X) Prelude Press.

— Life One-0-One: Everything We Wish We Had Learned about Life in School But Didn't. unabridged rev. ed. (Life 101 Ser.). 400p. 1994. pap. 22.95 incl. audio (0-931580-78-1) Prelude Press.

— Love 101: To Love Oneself Is the Beginning of a Lifelong Romance. (Life 101 Ser.). 432p. (Orig.). 1995. pap. 11.95 (0-931580-70-6) Prelude Press.

— Love 101: To Love Oneself Is the Beginning of a Lifelong Romance. (Orig.). 1997. pap. text 5.95 (0-931580-72-2) Prelude Press.

— Peter McWilliams' Personal Electronics Book, 1988. 1989. pap. 10.95 (0-318-32500-4) P-H.

— The Portable Do It! rev. ed. 1995. pap. text 5.95 (0-931580-42-0) Prelude Press.

— The Portable Life 101. rev. ed. 1995. pap. text 5.95 (0-931580-41-2) Prelude Press.

— Portraits: A Book of Photographs by Peter McWilliams. (Illus.). 252p. 1992. 34.95 (0-931580-77-3) Prelude Press.

— Question of Compassion. 1998. 14.95 (0-931580-76-5) Prelude Press.

— That Book about Drugs. 384p. 1994. pap. 5.95 (0-931580-60-9) Prelude Press.

***McWilliams, Peter.** Wealth 101: Getting What You Want, Enjoying What You've Got. 1999. mass mkt. 6.95 (0-931580-18-8) Prelude Press.

McWilliams, Peter. What Jesus & the Bible Really Said about Drugs, Sex, Gays, Gambling, Prostitution, Alternative Healing, Assisted Suicide, & Other Consensual "Sins" 1994. pap. 5.95 (0-931580-59-5) Prelude Press.

— Word Processor Book. 2000. 14.95 (0-698-11200-8) Putnam Pub Group.

— You Can't Afford the Luxury of a Negative Thought. 1997. 12.95 (0-931580-57-9) Prelude Press.

— You Can't Afford the Luxury of a Negative Thought: A Book for People with Any Life-Threatening Illness - Including Life. rev. ed. 622p. 1995. pap. 5.95 (0-931580-24-2) Prelude Press.

McWilliams, Peter & Bloomfield, Harold. Hypericum & Depression. 1997. pap. text 7.95 (0-931580-36-6) Prelude Press.

McWilliams, Peter, jt. auth. see Bloomfield, Harold H.

McWilliams, Peter, jt. auth. see John-Roger.

McWilliams, Richebourg. Iberville's Gulf Journals. 208p. 1991. pap. text 19.95 (0-8173-0539-4) U of Ala Pr.

McWilliams, Roger, ed. Radio-Frequency Power in Plasmas. LC 89-45805. (AIP Conference Proceedings Ser.: No. 190). 520p. 1989. lib. bdg. 70.00 (0-88318-397-8) Am Inst Physics.

McWilliams, Stephen K. The Watering of the Lawn. 1998. pap. write for info. (1-57553-845-8) Watermrk Pr.

McWilliams, Susan B., jt. ed. see Stephenson, Thomas L.

McWilliams, Tennant S. Hannis Taylor: The New Southerner As an American. LC 77-17124. 176p. 1978. reprint ed. pap. 54.60 (0-608-01676-4, 206233200002) Bks Demand.

McWilliams, Thomas P. How to Use Sequential Statistical Methods, Vol. 13. 49p. 1989. pap. 22.00 (0-87389-049-3, T3513) ASQ Qual Pr.

McWilliams Tullberg, Rita. Women at Cambridge. LC 98-30190. (Illus.). 256p. (C). 1998. pap. text 22.95 (0-521-64464-X) Cambridge U Pr.

McWilliams, Warren. Christ & Narcissus: Prayer in a Self-Centered World. LC 91-36400. 160p. (Orig.). 1992. pap. 11.99 (0-8361-3569-5) Herald Pr.

***McWilliams, Warren.** Dear Chris: Letters on the Life of Faith. LC 98-31369. 198p. 1999. pap. text 16.95 (0-918954-70-3) Baylor Univ Pr.

McWilliams, Wayne C. & Piotrowski, Harry. The World since 1945: A History of International Relations. 4th ed. LC 97-17880. 632p. 1997. 59.95 (1-55587-788-5) L Rienner.

— The World since 1945: A History of International Relations. 4th ed. LC 97-17880. 632p. 1997. pap. 23.50 (1-55587-621-8) L Rienner.

***McWilliams, Wayne C. & Piotrowski, Harry.** The World Since 1945: A History of International Relations. 5th ed. 600p. (C). 2001. pap. write for info. (1-55587-899-7) L Rienner.

***McWilliams, Wilson C.** Beyond the Politics of Disappointment? American Elections, 1980-1998. 2nd ed. LC 99-6789. (Illus.). 184p. (C). 1999. pap. text 21.95 (1-889119-18-0, Chatham House Pub) Seven Bridges.

McWilliams, Wilson C. & Gibbons, Michael T., eds. The Federalists, the Antifederalists & the American Political Tradition, 287. LC 91-25724. (Contributions in Political Science Ser.: No. 287). 144p. 1992. 47.95 (0-313-27724-9, GFI, Greenwood Pr) Greenwood.

***McWilliams, Wilson C., et al.** Friends & Citizens: Essays in Honor of Wilson Carey McWilliams. LC 00-25893. 2000. write for info. (0-8476-9746-0) Rowman.

McWilliams, Wilson C., jt. ed. see Best, Judith A.

McWilliams, Wilson C., ed. see Lowi, Theodore J. & Romance, Joseph.

McWilliams, Peter. Do It! Let's Get Off Our Buts. rev. ed. (Life 101 Ser.). 509p. 1994. pap. 5.95 (0-931580-79-X) Prelude Press.

McWorkman, Lee G. From Two to Seventy-Two. (Illus.). 284p. (Orig.). 1989. pap. 9.95 (0-9624492-0-2) McWorkman.

— Oilfield.Doc. (Illus.). 184p. 1988. 9.95 (0-933512-40-6) McWorkman.

Mda, Zakes. When People Play People: Development Communications Through Theatre. LC 93-18987. 288p. (C). 1993. text 65.00 (1-85649-199-4, Pub. by Zed Books) St Martin.

MDC Sdn. Bhd, ed. Hong Kong Management Cases for Supervisors. (Chinese University Press Staff). (Illus.). (C). pap. text. write for info. (962-201-743-6, Pub. by Chinese Univ) U of Mich Pr.

Mddox, Gregory H., ed. & tr. see Mnyampala, Mathias E.

MDRT Annuity Task Force Staff. The MDRT Annuity Sales Manual. 2nd rev. ed. 220p. 1998. ring bd. 225.00 (1-891042-00-9) Million Dollar.

M'Duffee, John. Oregon Crisis. 30p. 1999. reprint ed. pap. 5.95 (0-87770-063-X) Ye Galleon.

Mea, Giuseppe. Italian-Portuguese Dictionary. (ITA & POR.). 2256p. 95.00 (0-8288-9427-2) Fr & Eur.

— Portuguese - Italian Dictionary. (ITA & POR.). 2256p. 95.00 (0-8288-9426-4) Fr & Eur.

Meaburn, J. Detection & Spectrometry of Faint Light. (Astrophysics & Space Science Library: No. 56). 1976. lib. bdg. 123.50 (90-277-0678-6) Kluwer Academic.

— Detection & Spectrometry of Faint Light. (Astrophysics & Space Science Library: No. 56). 1980. pap. text 81.00 (90-277-1198-4) Kluwer Academic.

Meacci, Ferdinando, ed. Italian Economists of the 20th Century. LC 97-39370. 320p. 1998. 90.00 (1-85278-886-0) E Elgar.

Meacham, Brian J., jt. auth. see Custer, Richard L. P.

Meacham, Alfred B. Wi-Ne-Ma the Woman-Chief & Her People. LC 76-43773. reprint ed. 27.50 (0-404-15628-2) AMS Pr.

Meacham, Andrew. Selling Serenity: Life among the Recovery Stars. LC 97-44281. 418p. (Orig.). 1999. pap. 15.00 (0-89777-708-5, Upton Bks) SIRS Mandarin.

Meacham, April, jt. auth. see McIntosh, Joel.

Meacham, Beth, ed. Terry's Universe. 288p. 1989. pap. 3.95 (0-8125-4592-3, Pub. by Tor Bks) St Martin.

Meacham, Carla M. Haliotis Ornaments of the Windmiller Culture, Central California. (Illus.). iv, 233p. 1979. reprint ed. pap. text 25.00 (1-55567-028-8) Coyote Press.

Meacham, Charles M. History of Christian County, Kentucky. (Illus.). 695p. 1993. reprint ed. lib. bdg. write for info. (0-8328-2927-7) Higginson Bk Co.

Meacham, Cory J. How the Tiger Lost Its Stripes. LC 96-39845. 288p. (C). 1997. 24.00 (0-15-100279-7) Harcourt.

Meacham, Daniel. The Magic of Self-Confidence. 1985. pap. 5.95 (0-671-54193-5, Fireside) S&S Trade Pap.

Meacham, Esther A. & Sarbaugh, Mabel M., eds. Professional Development. 113p. (Orig.). (C). 1979. pap. text 9.00 (0-89894-022-2) Advocate Pub Group.

Meacham Gould, Virginia, ed. Chained to the Rock of Adversity: To Be Free, Black & Female in the Old South. LC 98-14341. (Southern Voices from the Past Ser.). 168p. 1998. 35.00 (0-8203-1996-1); pap. 17.50 (0-8203-2083-8) U of Ga Pr.

Meacham, J. A. & Kuhn, Deanna, eds. On the Development of Developmental Psychology. (Contributions to Human Development Ser.: Vol. 8). (Illus.). xii, 160p. 1982. pap. 42.75 (3-8055-3568-6) S Karger.

***Meacham, John A.** Honey, He Shrunk My Head! And Other Tall Huntin' & Fishin' Tales. LC 00-190461. v, 187p. 2000. pap. 14.95 (0-9679594-0-3) Lordnose.

Meacham, John A., ed. Family & Individual Development. (Contributions to Human Development Ser.: Vol. 14). (Illus.). x, 114p. 1985. 63.50 (3-8055-4037-X) S Karger.

— Interpersonal Relations: Family, Peers, Friends. (Contributions to Human Development Ser.: Vol. 18). (Illus.). x, 134p. 1987. 78.50 (3-8055-4515-0) S Karger.

***Meacham, Jon.** Voices in Our Blood: America's Best on the Civil Rights Movement. LC 00-41474. 2001. write for info. (0-679-46296-1) Random.

Meacham, Kenneth S. MRI Study Guide for Technologists. LC 95-10164. (Illus.). 224p. 1995. 32.95 (0-387-94489-3) Spr-Verlag.

***Meacham, Leonida & Meacham, Ralph.** Bankruptcy Basics. 2nd ed. 67p. (C). 1999. pap. text 20.00 (0-7881-8543-8) DIANE Pub.

***Meacham, Maggie.** Turning Seventeen, No. 6. 2001. pap. write for info. (0-06-447242-6, HarpTrophy) HarpC Child Bks.

Meacham, Margaret. Call Me Cathy. Clancy, Lisa, ed. (Real Life Ser.). 160p. (Orig.). (YA). (gr. 6 up). 1995. mass mkt. 3.50 (0-671-87272-9) PB.

— Oyster Moon. LC 96-15057. (Illus.). 112p. (J). (gr. 4-8). 1996. pap. 9.95 (0-87033-459-X, Tidewtr Pubs) Cornell Maritime.

— The Secret of Heron Creek. LC 90-50373. (Illus.). 136p. (Orig.). (J). (gr. 5-8). 1991. pap. 7.95 (0-87033-414-X, Tidewtr Pubs) Cornell Maritime.

Meacham, Mary, jt. auth. see Carroll, Frances L.

Meacham, Mary, jt. ed. see Carroll, Frances L.

Meacham, Ralph, jt. auth. see Meacham, Leonida.

Meacham, Standish. Lord Bishop: The Life of Samuel Wilberforce, 1805-1873. LC 70-102669. (Illus.). 338p. 1970. 29.00 (0-674-53913-3) HUP.

— Regaining Paradise: Englishness & the Early Garden City Movement. LC 98-44370. (Illus.). 272p. 1999. 35.00 (0-300-07572-3) Yale U Pr.

— Toynbee Hall & Social Reform, 1880-1914: The Search for Community. LC 86-28269. (Illus.). 233p. reprint ed. pap. 72.30 (0-7837-4536-2, 208026300004) Bks Demand.

Meacham, Standish, ed. see Bulwer Lytton, Edward.

Meacham, Standish, ed. & intro. see Bulwer Lytton, Edward.

***Meacham, William C.** Lest We Forget: The Kingsmen, 101st Aviation Battalion 1968. 1999. mass mkt. 6.99 (0-8041-1917-1) Ivy Books.

Meachem, Mary, jt. auth. see Lenz, Millicent.

Meachen, Dana. A Box Can Be Many Things. (Rookie Readers Ser.). (J). (ps-2). 1997. pap. 4.95 (0-516-26153-3) Childrens.

Meachen, George N. A Short History of Tuberculosis. LC 75-23738. reprint ed. 31.50 (0-404-13295-2) AMS Pr.

Meachen-Rau, Dana. Panama. LC 98-2812. (Geography Ser.). (J). 1999. 32.00 (0-516-21189-7) Childrens.

Meacher. Diffusing Power: The Key to Socialist Revival. (C). pap. 16.95 (0-7453-0693-4, Pub. by Pluto GBR) Stylus Pub VA.

Meacher, Michael & Beckett, Margaret. Making the Poor Poorer: The Welfare State after the Fowler Reviews. 1986. 40.00 (0-85124-425-4); pap. 40.00 (0-85124-435-1) St Mut.

Meachum, Virginia. Jane Goodall: Protector of Chimpanzees. LC 97-2881. (People to Know Ser.). (Illus.). 104p. (YA). (gr. 6 up). 1997. lib. bdg. 20.95 (0-89490-827-8) Enslow Pubs.

— Martha Stewart: Successful Businesswoman. LC 97-43578. (People to Know Ser.). 112p. (YA). (gr. 6 up). 1998. lib. bdg. 20.95 (0-89490-984-3) Enslow Pubs.

***Meachum, Virginia.** Rosie O'Donnell: Talk Show Host & Comedian. LC 99-26875. (People to Know Ser.). (Illus.). 112p. (gr. 6 up). 2000. lib. bdg. 20.95 (0-7660-1148-8) Enslow Pubs.

Meachum, Virginia. Steven Spielberg: Hollywood Filmmaker. LC 95-39022. (People to Know Ser.). 112p. (YA). (gr. 6 up). 1996. lib. bdg. 20.95 (0-89490-697-6) Enslow Pubs.

***Meacock, Heather.** An Anthropological Approach to Theology: A Study of John Hick's Theology of Religious Pluralism, Towards Ethical Criteria for a Global Theology of Religions. LC 00-29887. 2000. write for info. (0-7618-1690-9) U Pr of Amer.

Mead. Brown's Signal Reminder. (C). 1987. 30.00 (0-85174-127-4) St Mut.

***Mead.** Common Conditions. LC 98-40970. (C). 1999. 16.95 (0-443-06021-5) Church.

Mead. Crossing Starlight Bridge. (J). 1998. pap. 3.95 (0-87628-343-1) Ctr Appl Res.

— Experience of Finland Bh. 24.95 (1-85065-165-5) C Hurst.

— How Spiders Got Eight Legs. LC 97-17705. 24p. (J). (gr. 1-2). 1998. 19.97 (0-8172-5163-4) Raintree Steck-V.

— Passive Vibration Control. LC 98-48784. 554p. 1999. 270.00 (0-471-94203-0) Wiley.

Mead, jt. auth. see Tolley.

Mead, Alice. Adem's Cross. 144p. (YA). (gr. 5 up). 1998. mass mkt. 3.99 (0-440-22735-6, LLL BDD) BDD Bks Young Read.

— Adem's Cross. LC 96-1414. 160p. (YA). (gr. 7-12). 1996. 15.00 (0-374-30057-7) FS&G.

— Adem's Cross. 1998. 9.09 (0-606-13110-8, Pub. by Turtleback) Demco.

— Billy & Emma. LC 98-49760. (Illus.). 32p. (J). (ps-3). 2000. 16.00 (0-374-30705-9) FS&G.

— Crossing the Starlight Bridge. LC 93-40978. 128p. (J). 1995. per. 3.95 (0-689-80105-X) Aladdin.

— Crossing the Starlight Bridge. 128p. (J). (gr. 4-6). 1994. lib. bdg. 15.00 (0-02-765950-X, Bradbury S&S) S&S Childrens.

— Crossing the Starlight Bridge. 1995. 9.05 (0-606-07403-1, Pub. by Turtleback) Demco.

— Journey to Kosova. 204p. 1995. pap. 8.00 (1-888034-00-9) Loose Cannon.

— Junebug. (J). 1996. pap. 4.99 (0-440-91275-X) BDD Bks Young Read.

— Junebug. 112p. (J). (gr. 3-7). 1997. pap. 4.50 (0-440-41245-5, YB BDD) BDD Bks Young Read.

— Junebug. LC 95-5421. 112p. (J). (gr. 4-7). 1995. 14.00 (0-374-33964-3) FS&G.

— Junebug. (J). 1997. 9.09 (0-606-11528-5, Pub. by Turtleback) Demco.

***Mead, Alice.** Junebug & the Reverend. (Illus.). 192p. (J). 2000. pap. 4.50 (0-440-41571-3, YB BDD) BDD Bks Young Read.

Mead, Alice. Junebug & the Reverend. LC 97-48893. 192p. (J). (gr. 4-7). 1998. 16.00 (0-374-33965-1) FS&G.

***Mead, Alice.** Junebug & the Reverend. (Illus.). (J). 2000. 9.85 (0-606-18785-5) Turtleback.

— Soldier Mom. LC 98-55434. 160p. (J). (gr. 3-7). 1999. 16.00 (0-374-37124-5) FS&G.

Mead, Alice. Walking the Edge. 192p. (J). (gr. 6-8). 1995. lib. bdg. 14.95 (0-8075-8649-8) A Whitman.

Mead, Alice & Neptume, Arnold, eds. Giants of the Dawnland: Ancient Wabanaki Tales. 76p. (YA). Date not set. pap. 8.00 (1-888034-01-7) Loose Cannon.

Mead, Andrew. An Introduction to the Music of Milton Babbit. LC 92-37178. (Illus.). 264p. (C). 1993. text 35.00 (0-691-03314-5, Pub. by Princeton U Pr) Cal Prin Full Svc.

***Mead, Arden W.** Hand Me My Harp: Some Sermons on Selected Psalms. 134p. 2000. pap. 11.99 (1-889387-18-5) Crtve Commns MO.

Mead Art Museum Staff. Collegial Collectors: American Art from the Class of 1967. (Illus.). 12p. (Orig.). 1992. pap. 5.00 (0-914337-15-7) Mead Art Mus.

Mead, B. A. Apollonius of Tyana, the Philosopher-Reformer of the First Century A.D. 159p. 1996. pap. 14.00 (0-7873-0600-2) Hlth Research.

— The Gospels & the Gospel. 215p. 1996. reprint ed. spiral bd. 16.50 (0-7873-0602-9) Hlth Research.

— Plotinus: The Theosophy of the Greeks. 48p. 1996. reprint ed. spiral bd. 9.00 (0-7873-0601-0) Hlth Research.

Mead, C. & Tolley, Emelie. Cooking with Herbs. 1995. 24.00 (0-517-88380-5) Random.

Mead, Carl D. Yankee Eloquence in the Middle West: The Ohio Lyceum, 1850-1870. LC 77-5130. 1977. reprint ed. lib. bdg. 65.00 (0-8371-9323-0, MEYE, Greenwood Pr) Greenwood.

Mead, Carver. Analog VLSI. (C). 1989. text. write for info. (0-201-50371-9) Addison-Wesley.

— Analog VLSI & Neural Systems. (Computation & Neural Systems Ser.). (Illus.). 384p. (C). 1989. text 56.95 (0-201-05992-4) Addison-Wesley.

Mead, Carver & Ismail, Mohammed I., eds. Analog VLSI Implementation of Neural Systems. (C). 1989. text 100.50 (0-7923-9040-7) Kluwer Academic.

*Mead, Carver A. Collective Electrodynamics: Quantum Foundations of Electromagnetism. LC 00-28180. 157p. (C). 2000. 22.95 (0-262-13378-4) MIT Pr.

Mead, Charles. The Gingerbread Man. LC 95-7140. (HandClaps & FingerSnaps Ser.: Bk. 1). (Illus.). 32p. (J). (ps up). 1995. 17.95 incl. audio (0-918812-84-4) MMB Music.

Mead, Charles, jt. auth. see Rychner, Lorenz M.

Mead, Charles R. Application for Employment: A Campaign Document. (Orig.). 1988. pap. 9.50 (0-317-91373-5) Mead Comm.

Mead, Cheryl. The Matt Dillon Scrap Book. (Illus.). 96p. 1984. pap. 7.95 (0-312-52301-7) St Martin.

Mead, Chris. Owls. (Illus.). 128p. text 19.95 (0-905483-59-6, Pub. by Whittet Bks) Diamond Farm Bk.

— Robins. (Illus.). 128p. text 19.95 (0-905483-36-7, Pub. by Whittet Bks) Diamond Farm Bk.

Mead, Chris & Tolley, Emelie. Gardening with Herbs. LC 94-23825. (J). 1995. 45.00 (0-517-58332-1) C Potter.

Mead, Chris, jt. auth. see Hodgkinson, Loraine.

Mead, Chris, jt. auth. see Tolley, Emelie.

Mead, Chris, jt. auth. see Tolley, Emilie.

Mead, Chris, Inc. Staff. Herbal Pantry. 1992. 20.00 (0-517-58331-3) C Potter.

Mead, Christine, compiled by. Disaster Work, Journeys of Discovery: Creative Learning from Disasters. 1990. pap. 40.00 (1-899942-07-6, Pub. by Natl Inst Soc Work) St Mut.

Mead, Christopher. Architecture of Bart Prince: The Pragmatics of Place. LC 98-31921. (Illus.). 176p. 1999. text 60.00 (0-393-73032-8) Norton.

— Charles Garnier's Paris Opera: Architectural Empathy & the Renaissance of French Classicism. (Illus.). 352p. 1991. 75.00 (0-262-13275-3) MIT Pr.

— Space for the Continuous Present in the Residential Architecture of Bart Prince. (Illus.). 49p. (Orig.). 1989. pap. 9.95 (0-944282-03-2) UNM Art Mus.

*Mead, Christopher. Victor Baltard Making Modern Paris. 1999. 60.00 (0-226-51678-4) U Ch Pr.

Mead, Christopher C. Houses by Bart Prince: An American Architecture for the Continuous Present. LC 90-49352. (Illus.). 125p. 1991. reprint ed. pap. 38.80 (0-608-04124-6, 206485700011) Bks Demand.

Mead, Clifford S. Thomas Pynchon: A Bibliography of Primary & Secondary Materials. LC 88-30415. (Illus.). 176p. 1989. 39.95 (0-916583-37-6) Dalkey Arch.

Mead, Clifford S. & Wallace, Janet, eds. The Pauling Catalogue: Ava Helen & Linus Pauling Papers at Oregon State University. (Illus.). 305p. 1991. 35.00 (0-9629082-0-7) Kerr Lib.

Mead, D. Eugene. Effective Supervision: A Task-Oriented Model for the Mental Health Professions. LC 90-2257. 200p. 1990. text 27.95 (0-87630-600-8) Brunner-Mazel.

Mead, D. J., jt. ed. see Richards, E. J.

Mead, Dana G. & Hayes, Thomas C. High Standards, Hard Choices: A CEO's Journey of Courage, Risk & Change. LC 99-33866. 231p. (C). 1999. 29.95 (0-471-29613-9) Wiley.

*Mead, Daniel M. History of Greenwich, Fairfield Co. (CT) With Many Important Statistics. 318p. 2000. 37.00 (0-7404-0029-0) Higginson Bk Co.

Mead, Daniel M. A History of the Town of Greenwich, Fairfield County, CT. 318p. 1993. reprint ed. lib. bdg. 35.00 (0-8328-3200-6) Higginson Bk Co.

Mead, Daniel R. Encyclopedia of Slot Machines. (Illus.). 400p. 2002. write for info. (0-934422-17-6) Mead Pub Corp.

Mead, Daniel R. Handbook of Slot Machine Reel Strips. 296p. 1983. 17.95 (0-934422-11-7, BKS-100117) Mead Pub Corp.

Mead, Daniel R. Loose Change Red Book Price Guide for Trade Stimulators & Counter Games: A Price Guide to Relative Current Value - 1997-1998 (Approved Through 2003) 3rd ed. LC 96-94664. 110p. 1996. per. 17.95 (0-934422-48-6, BKS-100486) Mead Pub Corp.

Mead, Daniel R., ed. Loose Change Blue Book for Slot Machines: A Price Guide to Relative Current Value 1997-1998 (Approved Through 2003) 4th rev. ed. LC 96-94665. 368p. 1997. per. 39.95 (0-934422-52-4, BKS-100324) Mead Pub Corp.

Mead, Daniel R., jt. auth. see Geddes, Robert N.

Mead, Daniel R., jt. auth. see Mead, Deborah L.

Mead, Daniel R., jt. auth. see Saul, David L.

Mead, Daniel R., ed. see Schulte, Richard F.

Mead, Daniel R., ed. & illus. see Geddes, Robert N.

Mead, Daniel R., ed. & illus. see Meyer, Joseph.

Mead, Daniel R., ed. & illus. see Vinson, Barney.

Mead Data Central, Inc. Staff, contrib. by. Proceedings of the Conference on Teaching Legal & Factual Research in Private Law Libraries: Westfields International Conference Center, Chantilly, Virginia, April 26-29, 1990. LC 91-17748. ix, 210p. 1991. 32.50 (0-8377-0911-3, Rothman) W S Hein.

*Mead, Dave. Beyond the Asphalt: A Quick & Easy Survival Guide. 45p. 1999. pap. 7.95 (1-929374-01-1) Fire Mt Pr.

— Beyond the Asphalt: A Quick & Easy Survival Guide, Including Survival Kit. 45p. 1999. pap. 16.95 (1-929374-00-3) Fire Mt Pr.

*Mead, David. 100 Guitar Tips You Should Have Been Told: Including Hints from 20 of the World's Greatest Guitarists. (Illus.). 200p. 2000. pap. 20.00 (1-86074-295-5) Sanctuary Pub.

Mead, David. Ten Minute Guitar Workout. 1999. pap. 25.95 (1-86074-239-4) Sanctuary Pubng.

Mead, Deborah L. & Mead, Daniel R. Owner's Pictorial Guide for the Care & Understanding of the Pace Bell Slot Machine. LC 82-73747. (Owner's Pictorial Guide Ser.). (Illus.). 142p. 1983. pap. 29.95 (0-934422-03-6, 100285) Mead Pub Corp.

*Mead, Don, et al. Disappearing Peasantries? Land & Labour in Latin America, Asia & Africa. (Illus.). 352p. 2000. pap. 29.95 (1-85339-477-7, Pub. by Intermed Tech) Stylus Pub VA.

Mead, Donald C. Direct Broadcast Satellite Communications: An MPEG Enabled Service. LC 98-56157. 320p. (C). 1999. 65.00 (0-201-69582-0) Addison-Wesley.

Mead, Donald C., jt. auth. see Liedholm, Carl.

Mead, Douglas S. Literary Comparison in Jacobean Prose. (English Literature Ser.: No. 33). 1970. reprint ed. pap. 24.95 (0-8383-0054-5) M S G Haskell Hse.

Mead, Edna. The Bronx Triangle: A Portrait of Norwood. Hermalyn, Gary D. & Ultan, Lloyd, eds. (Illus.). 141p. 1982. 12.00 (0-941980-09-X) Bronx County.

Mead, Elwood. Irrigation Institutions: A Discussion of the Economic & Legal Questions Created by the Growth of Irrigated Agriculture in the West. LC 72-2856. (Use & Abuse of America's Natural Resources Ser.). 406p. 1972. reprint ed. 28.95 (0-405-04520-4) Ayer.

Mead, Frank S. Handbook of Denominations. 9th rev. ed. LC 90-32830. 336p. 1990. 13.95 (0-687-16572-5) Abingdon.

— The Handbook of Denominations in the United States. 10th ed. 320p. 1995. 15.95 (0-687-01478-6) Abingdon.

*Mead, Frank S. Saints & Sinners in the Bible: Lively Portraits of the Fascinating Men & Women of the Old & New Testaments. 250p. 1999. reprint ed. text 25.00 (0-7881-6801-0) DIANE Pub.

Mead, Frank S. Ten Decisive Battles of Christianity. LC 72-117823. (Essay Index Reprint Ser.). 1977. 18.95 (0-8369-1812-6) Ayer.

*Mead, Frank S., ed. 12,000 Inspirational Quotations: A Treasury of Spiritual Insights & Practical Wisdom. LC 00-103124. (Webster's New Explorer Ser.). Orig. Title: Encyclopedia of Religious Quotations. 544p. 2000. 10.98 (1-892859-17-3) Federal St Pr.

Mead, G. C., jt. ed. see Richardson, R. I.

Mead, G. M. Current Issues in Cancer. (Illus.). 147p. 1992. pap. text 8.00 (0-7279-0775-1, Pub. by BMJ Pub) Login Brothers Bk Co.

Mead, G. R. Apollonius of Tyana. 196p. 1980. pap. 15.00 (0-89005-350-2) Ares.

— Apollonius of Tyana. 170p. 1992. reprint ed. pap. 13.95 (1-56459-131-X) Kessinger Pub.

— The Chaldaean Oracles, Set, Vols. 1 & 2. 190p. 1992. reprint ed. pap. 18.00 (1-56459-250-2) Kessinger Pub.

— Concerning H. P. Blavatsky. 50p. 1992. reprint ed. pap. 9.00 (1-56459-252-9) Kessinger Pub.

— Did Jesus Live One Hundred B. C.? 440p. 1993. spiral bd. 27.50 (0-7873-0603-7) Hlth Research.

— Did Jesus Live One Hundred B. C.? 440p. 1992. reprint ed. pap. 26.95 (1-56459-130-1) Kessinger Pub.

— Did Jesus Live One Hundred Years B. C. An Inquiry into the Talmud Jesus Stories, the Toldoth, Jeschu, a Study of Christian Origins. 1991. lib. bdg. 79.95 (0-8490-4304-2) Gordon Pr.

— The Divine Pymander of Hermes Trismegistus. 1990. pap. 5.95 (1-55818-152-0) Holmes Pub.

— The Doctrine of the Subtle Body in Western Tradition. 164p. 1996. reprint ed. spiral bd. 12.00 (0-7873-0607-X) Hlth Research.

— The Doctrine of the Subtle Body in Western Tradition. 109p. 1993. reprint ed. pap. 11.95 (1-56459-312-6) Kessinger Pub.

— Five Years of Theosophy: Mystical, Philosophical, Theosophical, Historical & Scientific Essay. LC 75-36850. (Occult Ser.). 1976. reprint ed. 33.95 (0-405-07966-4) Ayer.

— Fragments of a Faith Forgotten. 633p. 1992. reprint ed. pap. 29.95 (0-922802-22-X) Kessinger Pub.

— Fragments of a Faith Forgotten. 2nd ed. 633p. 1997. reprint ed. pap. 34.50 (0-7873-0605-3) Hlth Research.

— Fragments of a Faith Forgotten: Gnostics & Christian Origins. 1991. lib. bdg. 79.95 (0-8490-4285-2) Gordon Pr.

— The Gnostic Crucifixion. 1994. reprint ed. pap. 6.95 (1-55818-176-8) Holmes Pub.

— The Gnostic Crucifixion. 83p. 1992. reprint ed. pap. 5.95 (1-56459-129-8) Kessinger Pub.

— Gnostic John the Baptizer: Selections from the Mandaean John-Book Together with Studies on John & Christian Origins, the Slavonic Josephus' Account of John & Jesus, & John & the Fourth Gospel Proem. 137p. 1993. reprint ed. pap. 14.95 (1-56459-375-4) Kessinger Pub.

— The Gospels & the Gospel. 215p. 1992. reprint ed. pap. 15.95 (0-922802-78-5) Kessinger Pub.

— The Hymn of Jesus. 76p. 1992. reprint ed. pap. 9.95 (1-56459-158-1) Kessinger Pub.

— The Hymn of the Robe of Glory. 99p. 1993. reprint ed. pap. 14.95 (1-56459-360-6) Kessinger Pub.

— The Hymns of Hermes. LC 91-27216. 70p. (Orig.). 1991. pap. 7.00 (0-933999-17-8) Phanes Pr.

— The Hymns of Hermes. (Orig.). 1991. reprint ed. pap. 6.95 (1-55818-144-X) Holmes Pub.

— A Mithraic Ritual. 1994. pap. 6.95 (1-55818-288-8) Holmes Pub.

— Mithriac Ritual. 77p. (Orig.). 1992. reprint ed. pap. 9.95 (1-56459-117-4) Kessinger Pub.

— Mysteries of Mithra. 90p. 1992. reprint ed. pap. 5.95 (1-56459-249-9) Kessinger Pub.

— Mysteries of Mithras. 1993. reprint ed. pap. 6.95 (1-55818-209-8) Holmes Pub.

— Orpheus. 208p. 1996. reprint ed. pap. 19.95 (1-56459-611-7) Kessinger Pub.

— Orphic Pantheon. 1984. pap. 8.95 (0-916411-18-4) Holmes Pub.

— Pistis Sophia. 325p. 1992. reprint ed. pap. 24.95 (0-922802-87-4) Kessinger Pub.

— Pistis Sophia: A Gnostic Gospel. 1991. lib. bdg. 88.75 (0-8490-5036-7) Gordon Pr.

— Pistis Sophia: A Gnostic Gospel. 394p. 1996. reprint ed. spiral bd. 34.50 (0-7873-1104-9) Hlth Research.

— Pistis Sophia: A Gnostic Gospel. 3rd ed. LC 83-83170. 408p. 1984. reprint ed. lib. bdg. 28.50 (0-89345-041-3, Spir Sci Lib) Garber Comm.

— Plotinus. 1983. reprint ed. pap. 8.95 (0-916411-01-X) Holmes Pub.

— Plotinus: The Theosophy of the Greeks (1895) 51p. 1996. reprint ed. pap. 7.95 (1-56459-743-1) Kessinger Pub.

— Quests Old & New. 338p. 1992. reprint ed. pap. 29.95 (0-922802-79-3) Kessinger Pub.

— Simon Magus. 1978. reprint ed. pap. 10.00 (0-89005-258-1) Ares.

— Simon Magus: An Essay on the Founder of Simonianism Based on the Ancient Sources with a Re-Evaluation of His Philosophy & Teachings. Holmes, J. D., ed. 1991. pap. 9.95 (1-55818-177-6) Holmes Pub.

— Simon Magus: An Essay on the Founder of Simonianism Based on the Ancient Sources with a Re-Evaluation of His Philosophy & Teachings. 91p. 1994. reprint ed. pap. 7.95 (1-56459-439-4) Kessinger Pub.

— Some Mystical Adventures. 303p. 1993. reprint ed. pap. 19.95 (1-56459-359-2) Kessinger Pub.

— Thrice Greatest Hermes, 3 vols. 1986. reprint ed. pap. 70.00 (0-7873-0604-5) Hlth Research.

— Thrice Greatest Hermes: Studies in Hellenistic Theosophy & Gnosis Being a Translation of the Extant Sermons & Fragments of the Trismegistic Literature with Prolegomena, Commentaries, & Notes. 864p. 1992. reprint ed. pap. 39.95 (1-56459-186-7) Kessinger Pub.

— The Upanishads, 2 vols. 237p. 1992. reprint ed. pap. 14.95 (0-922802-77-7) Kessinger Pub.

— The Virgin of the World: or Apple of the Eye of the World. 1990. reprint ed. pap. text 8.95 (1-55818-129-6) Holmes Pub.

— The Vision of Aridaeus. 74p. 1996. reprint ed. pap. 12.95 (1-56459-614-1) Kessinger Pub.

— The Wedding Song of Wisdom. 107p. 1992. reprint ed. pap. 5.95 (1-56459-155-7) Kessinger Pub.

— The Wedding Song of Wisdom: Gnosticism & the Rite of Scared Marriage. 1999. reprint ed. pap. 7.95 (1-55818-383-3, Alexandrian) Holmes Pub.

— The World Mystery. 200p. 1992. reprint ed. pap. 14.95 (0-922802-91-2) Kessinger Pub.

— The World Mystery. 2nd ed. 200p. 1996. reprint ed. spiral bd. 15.50 (0-7873-0606-1) Hlth Research.

Mead, G. R., ed. Select Works of Plotinus. Taylor, Thomas, tr. 421p. 1994. reprint ed. pap. 37.00 (1-56459-429-7) Kessinger Pub.

Mead, G. R., ed. & intro. see Blavatsky, Helena P.

Mead, G. R. S. The Dream of Raven: A Mystery (1895) 220p. 1998. reprint ed. pap. 19.95 (0-7661-0150-9) Kessinger Pub.

*Mead, G. R. S. Gnosis of the Mind (1906) 70p. 1999. reprint ed. pap. 9.95 (0-7661-0751-5) Kessinger Pub.

*Mead, Gary. The Doughboys: America & the First World War. 2000. 37.95 (1-58567-061-8, Pub. by Overlook Pr) Penguin Putnam.

Mead, Gary. South Africa. (Illus.). 336p. 1997. pap. 17.95 (0-8442-4851-7, 48517, Passprt Bks) NTC Contemp Pub Co.

Mead, Gary. South Africa. 2nd ed. pap. 23.95 (962-217-620-8) China Guides.

Mead, George C., jt. auth. see Miller, Herbert E.

Mead, George F., Jr., et al, eds. Introductory Algebra. 2nd ed. LC 92-18690. 396p. 1992. 34.50 (0-931541-41-7) Mancorp Pub.

Mead, George Herbert. George Herbert Mead on Social Psychology. Strauss, Anselm L., ed. LC 64-23419. 384p. 1964. pap. text 17.95 (0-226-51665-2, P170) U Ch Pr.

— The Individual & the Social Self: Unpublished Work of George Herbert Mead. Miller, David L., ed. LC 82-4885. (Chicago Original Paperback Ser.). 232p. (C). 1992. lib. bdg. 26.00 (0-226-51673-3) U Ch Pr.

— The Individual & the Social Self: Unpublished Work of George Herbert Mead. Miller, David L., ed. LC 82-4885. (Chicago Original Paperback Ser.). 232p. (C). 1995. pap. text 16.00 (0-226-51674-1) U Ch Pr.

— The Individual & the Social Self: Unpublished Work of George Herbert Mead. Miller, David L., ed. LC 82-4885. 238p. reprint ed. pap. 73.80 (0-608-09479-X, 205427900005) Bks Demand.

— Mind, Self, & Society: From the Standpoint of a Social Behaviorist. Morris, Charles W., ed. 448p. 1967. pap. text 15.95 (0-226-51668-7) U Ch Pr.

— The Philosophy of the Present. Murphy, Arthur E., ed. LC 80-16334. 240p. 1996. pap. text 8.95 (0-226-51670-9, P909) U Ch Pr.

*Mead, George Herbert. Play, School & Society, Ser. 11. Deegan, Mary Jo, ed. LC 97-20825. (American University Studies: Vol. 71). (Illus.). CXII, 157p. 1999. text 50.00 (0-8204-3823-5) P Lang Pubng.

Mead, George Herbert. Selected Writings, George Herbert Mead. Reck, Andrew J., ed. LC 80-27048. lxxii, 488p. (C). 1998. pap. text 12.95 (0-226-51671-7) U Ch Pr.

— The Social Self. (Reprint Series in Sociology). (C). 1993. reprint ed. pap. text 1.00 (0-8290-2918-4, S-187) Irvington.

Mead, George R. The Hymn of Jesus: Echoes from the Ghosts. 78p. 1973. reprint ed. pap. 2.95 (0-8356-0432-2, Quest) Theos Pub Hse.

Mead, Gretchen, jt. auth. see Chioffi, Nancy.

Mead, Hayden. Concise Guide for the Next Century: The Concise Guide to On-Line & E-Mail Terms. LC 97-117478. (Orig.). 1997. mass mkt. 5.99 (0-425-15692-3) Berkley Pub.

— Concise Guides for the Next Century: Instant Styles for Writers. LC 97-114958. 144p. (Orig.). 1997. mass mkt. 5.99 (0-425-15546-3) Berkley Pub.

— Concise Guides for the Next Century: The Concise Guide to Legal Terms. LC 97-146385. 192p. 1997. mass mkt. 5.99 (0-425-15712-1) Berkley Pub.

— Essentials of Grammar. 1996. mass mkt. 5.99 (0-425-15446-7) Berkley Pub.

— Spelling Made Simple. 1996. mass mkt. 5.99 (0-425-15524-2) Berkley Pub.

Mead, Hayden & Clark, Andy, compiled by. Concise Guides for the Next Century: The On-Line Research Handbook. 224p. 1997. mass mkt. 5.99 (0-425-15667-2) Berkley Pub.

Mead, Helen. Wyving & Thryving: The Making of the English Gementwoman 1550-1750. (C). 1988. 45.00 (0-9515798-3-5, Pub. by H Copeman) St Mut.

Mead, Hunter. Types & Problems of Philosophy. 3rd ed. LC 59-6277. 1959. text 37.95 (0-03-006240-3) Irvington.

Mead, Irene K., tr. see DeBry-Pexton, Patricia.

Mead, J. F., et al. Lipids: Chemistry, Biochemistry & Nutrition. LC 85-19304. (Illus.). 494p. (C). 1986. text 130.00 (0-306-41990-4, Kluwer Plenum) Kluwer Academic.

Mead, James, et al. Investigating Child Abuse. (Illus.). 145p. (C). 1987. reprint ed. ring bd. 100.00 (0-939925-18-4) R C Law & Co.

— Investigating Child Abuse. 2nd ed. (Illus.). 145p. 1987. reprint ed. pap. 25.00 (0-939925-17-6) R C Law & Co.

Mead, Jane. The Lord & the General Din of the World. LC 95-23868. 96p. 1996. pap. 12.95 (0-9641151-1-5) Sarabande Bks.

Mead, Jane, ed. Many & More: A Celebration of Love in Later Life. LC 94-5303. 246p. 1994. 20.00 (0-943221-21-8) Timken Pubs.

Mead, Jane & Sherline, Reid, eds. Acts of Faith: Stories. 180p. 1995. pap. 18.95 (0-943221-25-0) Timken Pubs.

Mead, Jere. Handbook of Physiology: Section 3, The Respiratory System, Vol. III, Pts. 1 & 2: Mechanics of Breathing. Macklem, Peter T., ed. (American Physiological Society Book). (Illus.). 834p. 1988. text 245.00 (0-19-520669-X) OUP.

Mead, Jeremiah P. Fables by Phaedrus. (LAT.). 105p. (YA). Date not set. spiral bd. 13.00 (0-939507-54-4, B725) Amer Classical.

Mead, Jim L., jt. ed. see Steadman, David W.

Mead, Joan T., jt. auth. see Gilliland, Joan F.

Mead, John. Selenium. Andrick, Frank, ed. (Illus.). 52p. 1998. pap. 5.00 (1-892453-00-2) AMP Pr.

Mead, John, ed. see Andrick, Frank.

Mead, John S. Haynes Peugeot 504 (Diesel) Owners Workshop Manual, No. 663: '74-'83. 16.95 (1-85010-376-3) Haynes Manuals.

— Haynes VW Vanagon (Air-Cooled) Owners Workshop Manual, 1980-1983. 17.95 (1-85010-029-2) Haynes Manuals.

Mead, John S. & Hawse, Mara L., eds. Proceedings Coal, Energy & Environment. (Illus.). 632p. 1994. lib. bdg. write for info. (1-885189-02-8) Coal Res Ctr.

Mead, Julie F., jt. auth. see Underwood, Julie K.

Mead, Juliette. Intimate Strangers. LC 96-7659. 320p. 1996. 22.00 (0-671-53794-6) S&S Trade.

— Intimate Strangers. 1997. per. 6.99 (0-671-53795-4) S&S Trade.

Mead, Kate C. A History of Women in Medicine from the Earliest Times to the Beginning of the 19th Century. LC 75-23739. (Illus.). reprint ed. 72.50 (0-404-13296-0) AMS Pr.

Mead, Katherine. Gail Devers: A Runner's Dream. 1998. pap. 4.95 (0-8172-7975-X) Raintree Steck-V.

— How Spiders Got Eight Legs. 1998. pap. 4.95 (0-8172-7979-2) Raintree Steck-V.

Mead, Katherine, retold by. Why the Leopard has Spots. 1998. pap. 4.95 (0-8172-7980-6) Raintree Steck-V.

Mead, Katherine H., ed. The Preston Morton Collection of American Art. LC 81-52029. (Illus.). 272p. (Orig.). 1981. pap. 12.00 (0-89951-043-4) Santa Barb Mus Art.

Mead, Kenneth E. Highway Contracting: Disadvantaged Business Program Meets Contract Goal, But Refinements Are Needed. (Illus.). 67p. (Orig.). (C). 1994. pap. text 25.00 (0-7881-1328-3) DIANE Pub.

Mead, Kenneth M. Information Superhighway: Issues Affecting Development. (Illus.). 76p. (Orig.). (C). 1994. pap. text 30.00 (0-7881-1421-2) DIANE Pub.

— Railroad Safety: Continued Emphasis Needed for an Effective Track Safety Inspection Program. (Illus.). 60p. (Orig.). (C). 1994. pap. text 20.00 (0-7881-1466-2) DIANE Pub.

Mead, Larry, jt. auth. see Jason-Lloyd, Leonard.

Mead, Lawrence M. Beyond Entitlement: The Social Obligations of Citizenship. 336p. (C). 1985. 35.00 (0-02-920890-4) Free Pr.

— The New Politics of Poverty: The Nonworking Poor in America. LC 91-55458. 368p. 1993. pap. 16.00 (0-465-05069-7, Pub. by Basic) HarpC.

Mead, Lawrence M., ed. The New Paternalism: Supervisory Approaches to Poverty. LC 97-33742. 355p. 1997. 42.95 (0-8157-5650-X); pap. 18.95 (0-8157-5651-8) Brookings.

Mead, Lawrence M., et al. From Welfare to Work: Lessons from America. (IEA Health & Welfare Unit Choice in Welfare Ser.: No. 39). 154p. 1997. pap. 22.50 (0-255-36399-0, Pub. by Inst Economic Affairs) Coronet Bks.

*Mead, Leon & Acret, James. Construction Industry Guide to Mechanics Liens for CA, NV, AZ 2000 Edition. 250p. 2000. pap. text 65.00 (1-55701-328-4) BNI Pubns.

*Mead, Linda. The ABCs of Making Teddy Bears. (Illus.). 156p. 2000. pap. 27.95 (1-56477-332-9) Martingale & Co.

Mead, Loren B. Critical Moment of Ministry: A Change of Pastors. LC 86-72582. 78p. (Orig.). 1986. pap. 8.95 (1-56699-017-3, AL94) Alban Inst.

M

An Asterisk (*) at the beginning of an entry indicates that the title is appearing for the first time.

— Financial Meltdown in the Mainline? (Money, Faith, & Lifestyle Ser.). 1998. pap. 13.95 (*1-56699-197-8*, AL188) Alban Inst.

— Financial Meltdown in the Mainline? LC 97-78127. 144 p. 1998. write for info. (*1-56688-197-8*) Bur For At-Risk.

— Five Challenges for the Once & Future Church. LC 96-85718. (Once & Future Church Ser.). 112p. 1996. pap. 12.25 (*1-56699-175-7*, AL177) Alban Inst.

— More Than Numbers: The Ways Churches Grow. LC 92-75724. 1993. pap. 11.25 (*1-56699-109-9*, AL141) Alban Inst.

— The Once & Future Church: Reinventing the Congregation for a New Mission Frontier. LC 91-72968. (Once & Future Church Ser.). 100p. (Orig.). 1992. pap. 10.95 (*1-56699-050-5*, AL129) Alban Inst.

— Transforming Congregations for the Future. LC 93-74587. (Once & Future Church Ser.). 154p. 1994. pap. 12.95 (*1-56699-126-9*, AL152) Alban Inst.

Mead, Loren B., et al. The Experience of Judicatory Leadership: Research with Episcopal Bishops & Their Spouses. pap. 9.75 (*1-56699-070-X*) Alban Inst.

Mead, Lucia A. Swords & Ploughshares: Or, the Supplanting of the System of War by the System of Law. LC 71-143431. (Peace Movement in America Ser.). xiv, 249p. 1972. reprint ed. lib. bdg. 32.95 (*0-89198-079-2*) Ozer.

***Mead, Lucy.** Fathers Are Special. LC 99-43265. 2000. 5.99 (*0-517-20956-X*) Random Hse Value.

— Friends Are Special. LC 00-37664. (Illus.). (J). 2001. pap. write for info. (*0-517-16312-8*) Bell T.

— Graduates Are Special. LC 00-37666. 2001. pap. write for info. (*0-517-16263-6*) Bell T.

— Grandparents Are Special: A Tribute to Those Who Love, Encourage & Inspire. LC 00-21802. 64p. 2000. 5.99 (*0-517-16265-2*) Random Hse Value.

— Lovers Are Special. 2000. 5.99 (*0-517-16183-4*) Crown Pub Group.

— Mothers Are Special. LC 99-43266. 2000. 5.99 (*0-517-20955-1*) Random Hse Value.

***Mead, Margaret.** And Keep Your Powder Dry: An Anthropologist Looks at America. LC E169.1.M5 1999. (Margaret Mead Ser.: Vol. 2). 256p. 2000. 69.95 (*1-57181-217-2*); pap. 17.50 (*1-57181-218-0*) Berghahn Bks.

Mead, Margaret. And Keep Your Powder Dry: An Anthropologist Looks at America. LC 77-156694. (Essay Index Reprint Ser.). 1977. reprint ed. 20.95 (*0-8369-2416-9*) Ayer.

— Blackberry Winter. 1990. 25.25 (*0-8446-6290-9*) Peter Smith.

— Changing Culture of an Indian Tribe. LC 72-84468. (Columbia University. Contributions to Anthropology Ser.: No. 15). reprint ed. 32.50 (*0-404-50565-1*) AMS Pr.

— Continuities in Cultural Evolution. LC 99-17824. 488p. 1999. pap. 29.95 (*0-7658-0604-5*) Transaction Pubs.

— Inquiry into the Question of Cultural Stability in Polynesia. LC 70-82354. (Columbia Univ. Contributions to Anthropology Ser.: Vol. 9). reprint ed. 27.50 (*0-404-50559-7*) AMS Pr.

***Mead, Margaret.** Kinship in the Admiralty Islands. 380p. 2001. 29.95 (*0-7658-0764-5*) Transaction Pubs.

Mead, Margaret. Kinship in the Admiralty Islands. LC 91-41796. 175p. 1992. reprint ed. lib. bdg. 29.50 (*0-86527-403-7*) Fertig.

***Mead, Margaret.** Letters from the Field 1925-75. 2000. pap. 13.00 (*0-06-095804-9*) HarpC.

Mead, Margaret. Male & Female: A Study of the Sexes in a Changing World. 1996. pap. 12.00 (*0-688-14676-7*, Quil) HarperTrade.

— Male & Female: The Classic Study of the Sexes. Date not set. pap. 12.00 (*0-614-97758-4*, Harvest Bks) Harcourt.

***Mead, Margaret.** New Lives for Old. 2000. pap. 16.00 (*0-06-095806-5*) HarpC.

Mead, Margaret. Paper Coming Age in Samo. annuals 1971. pap. 13.00 (*0-688-30974-7*, Quil) HarperTrade.

— Paper Sex & Temperment. 335p. 1971. pap. 12.95 (*0-688-06016-1*, Quil) HarperTrade.

— Soviet Attitudes Toward Authority: An Interdisciplinary Approach to Problems of Soviet Character. LC 78-10846. 148p. 1979. reprint ed. lib. bdg. 55.00 (*0-313-21081-0*, MESO, Greenwood Pr) Greenwood.

— To Grandmother with Love: A Special Tribute. (Illus.). 96p. 1992. 15.00 (*0-8362-8001-6*) Andrews & McMeel.

Mead, Margaret, ed. Cultural Patterns & Technical Change. LC 85-14839. 348p. 1985. reprint ed. lib. bdg. 55.50 (*0-313-24839-7*, MEPA, Greenwood Pr) Greenwood.

Mead, Margaret & Byers, Paul. The Small Conference. 1968. text 21.55 (*90-279-6049-6*) Mouton.

Mead, Margaret & Lutkehaus, Nancy. Blackberry Winter: My Earlier Years. Turner, Philip, ed. (Globe Trade Paperback Ser.). (Illus.). 336p. 1995. pap. 15.00 (*1-56836-069-X*, Kodansha Globe) Kodansha.

Mead, Margaret & Metraux, Rhoda, eds. The Study of Culture at a Distance. LC GN345.S88 1999. (Margaret Mead Ser.: Vol. 1). 512p. 2000. 69.95 (*1-57181-215-6*); pap. 19.50 (*1-57181-216-4*) Berghahn Bks.

Mead, Margaret & Wolfenstein, Martha, eds. Childhood in Contemporary Cultures. LC 55-10248. 1994. pap. text 6.50 (*0-226-51507-9*, P124) U Ch Pr.

***Mead, Margaret, et al.** Russian Culture. (Study of Contemporary Western Culture: Vol. 3). 320p. 2000. 69.95 (*1-57181-230-X*); pap. 19.95 (*1-57181-234-2*) Berghahn Bks.

Mead, Margaret, jt. auth. see Bateson, Gregory.

Mead, Margaret, ed. see Benedict, Ruth.

Mead, Marian. Four Studies in Wordsworth. LC 65-15890. (Studies in Wordsworth: No. 29). 1969. reprint ed. lib. bdg. 75.00 (*0-8383-0596-2*) M S G Haskell Hse.

Mead, Marica S. The Virginia County Supervisors' Manual. 5th rev. ed. 360p. 1988. 25.00 (*0-318-04157-X*) U VA Ctr Pub Serv.

Mead, Mary A. Michigan Tax Handbook. 328p. 1988. pap. 17.00 (*0-13-580457-4*) P-H.

— Michigan Tax Handbook. 1987th ed. 1986. pap. 17.00 (*0-13-579913-9*) P-H.

— Michigan Tax Handbook, 1985. write for info. (*0-318-58206-6*) P-H.

Mead, Mary A., jt. auth. see George, Peter.

Mead, Matthew. The Administration of Things. 64p. 1970. 21.00 (*0-900977-24-8*, Pub. by Anvil Press); pap. 13.95 (*0-900977-26-4*, Pub. by Anvil Press) Dufour.

— The Almost Christian Discovered. Kistler, Don, ed. 166p. 1989. 16.95 (*1-877611-72-7*) Soli Deo Gloria.

— The Midday Muse. 64p. 1979. pap. 14.95 (*0-85646-050-8*, Pub. by Anvil Press) Dufour.

— A Name in Heaven. 132p. 1995. reprint ed. 18.95 (*1-57358-030-9*) Soli Deo Gloria.

— The Sermons of Matthew Mead. 435p. 1991. reprint ed. 21.95 (*1-877611-29-8*) Soli Deo Gloria.

Mead, Matthew, tr. see Bobrowski, Johannes.

Mead, Melissa. Shadowcaster Clue Book: Illuminations. (Illus.). 80p. (Orig.). 1993. pap. 14.95 (*0-929373-15-4*) Origin Syst.

— ULTIMA VIII Clue Book: Pentology. (Illus.). 96p. (Orig.). 1994. pap. 14.95 (*0-929373-18-9*) Origin Syst.

— Wings of Glory Playtesters' Guide. (Illus.). 64p. (Orig.). pap. 9.95 (*0-929373-20-0*) Origin Syst.

Mead, Michael. Aids to General Practice. 2nd ed. (Illus.). 170p. 1991. pap. text 22.00 (*0-443-04589-5*) Church.

— Aids to General Practice. 3rd ed. LC 94-43949. 1995. pap. text 27.95 (*0-443-05277-8*) Church.

— Tutorials in General Practice. 3rd ed. LC 98-48319. 1999. write for info. (*0-443-06197-1*) Church.

Mead, Michael & Patterson, Henry. Tutorials in General Practice. 2nd ed. (Illus.). 206p. 1992. pap. text 37.95 (*0-443-04332-9*) Church.

Mead, Michael, jt. auth. see Cracknell, Ian D.

Mead, Murray. The Secrets to Staying Happily Married. (Illus.). 60p. (Orig.). 1994. pap. text 19.95 (*0-9642629-9-1*) Murray Pubng.

Mead, P. J. Census of India, 1911 Bombay, 2 vols., Set. 923p. (C). 1987. 135.00 (*0-8364-2166-3*, Pub. by Usha) S Asia.

Mead, Petr. Orde Wingate & the Historians. (C). 1989. 50.00 (*0-86303-318-0*, Pub. by Merlin Bks) St Mut.

Mead, Philip. Kenneth Slessor: Critical Readings. LC 97-187351. (Illus.). 320p. 1997. pap. 29.95 (*0-7022-2687-4*, Pub. by Univ Queensland Pr) Intl Spec Bk.

Mead, Philip, ed. European Business Law: A Review for Corporate Legal Advisers. viii, 210p. 1991. text 237.00 (*2-88316-005-8*) Gordon & Breach.

Mead, Philip, jt. ed. see Tranter, John.

***Mead, Philip B., et al.** Protocols for Infectious Diseases in Obstetrics & Gynecology. 2nd ed. LC 99-30332. (Protocols in Obstetrics & Gynecology Ser.). (Illus.). 605p. 1999. pap. 49.95 (*0-632-04324-5*) Blackwell Sci.

Mead, R. J. The Exchanged Life - Walking on the Water in the Storms of Life. 171p. 1997. pap. 10.00 (*0-9662438-0-3*) Free Indeed.

— Jesus Took Me to the Cross with Him. (Illus.). 14p. (J). (gr. 6-8). 1998. pap. 1.95 (*0-9662438-1-1*) Free Indeed.

Mead, Ralph. The Solo Sex Joke Book: Jokes, Cartoons, & Limericks about the World's Most Popular Sex Act. (Illus.). 110p. 1999. pap. 9.95 (*1-887650-17-2*) Factor Pr.

***Mead, Richard.** Cases & Projects in International Management: Cross-Cultural Dimentions. 192p. 2000. 64.95 (*0-631-21832-7*) Blackwell Pubs.

Mead, Richard. A Discourse on the Plague. 9th enl. rev. ed. LC 75-23742. reprint ed. 45.00 (*0-404-13297-9*) AMS Pr.

— International Management. 1998. write for info. (*0-631-21032-6*) Blackwell Pubs.

— International Management: Cross Cultural Dimensions. 488p. 1994. pap. 44.95 (*0-631-18369-8*) Blackwell Pubs.

— International Management: Cross-Cultural Dimensions. 2nd ed. LC 97-38758. 528p. 1998. pap. 47.95 (*0-631-20003-7*) Blackwell Pubs.

— International Management: Cross-Cultural Dimensions. 2nd ed. LC 97-38758. 528p. 1998. 78.95 (*0-631-20935-2*) Blackwell Pubs.

— Malaysia's National Language Policy & the Legal System. LC 87-50360. (Monographs: No. 30). ix, 118p. 1988. pap. 13.00 (*0-938692-30-5*) Yale U SE Asia.

— The Medical Works of Richard Mead. LC 75-23740. reprint ed. 94.50 (*0-404-13550-1*) AMS Pr.

***Mead, Richard, ed.** Cases & Projects in International Management. 192p. 1999. pap. text 34.95 (*1-55786-849-2*) Blackwell Pubs.

Mead, Rita. Henry Cowell's New Music, 1925-1936: The Society, the Music Editions, & the Recordings. Buelow, George, ed. LC 81-1510. (Studies in Musicology: No. 40). (Illus.). 636p. 1981. reprint ed. pap. 197.20 (*0-8357-1170-6*, 207002400063) Bks Demand.

Mead, Rita H. Doctoral Dissertations in American Music: A Classified Bibliography. LC 74-18893. (I.S.A.M. Monographs: No. 3). 155p. (Orig.). 1974. pap. 10.00 (*0-914678-02-7*) Inst Am Music.

Mead, Robert G., ed. Foreign Languages: Key Links in the Chain of Learning. (Reports of the Northeast Conference on the Teaching of Foreign Languages). 169p. 1983. pap. 10.95 (*0-915432-83-8*) NE Conf Teach Foreign.

Mead, Robert G., Jr., ed. Language Teaching: Broader Contexts. 104p. 1966. pap. 10.95 (*0-915432-66-8*) NE Conf Teach Foreign.

Mead, Robin. Haunted Hotels: A Guide to American & Canadian Inns & Their Ghosts. LC 95-25168. 224p. (Orig.). 1995. pap. 9.95 (*1-55853-369-9*) Rutledge Hill Pr.

Mead, Roger. The Design of Experiments: Statistical Principles for Practical Applications. (Illus.). 634p. (C). 1990. pap. text 52.95 (*0-521-28762-6*) Cambridge U Pr.

Mead, Rowland. Andalucia Handbook. LC 97-188735. (Illus.). write for info. (*0-900751-94-0*) Footprint Handbooks Ltd.

Mead, Rowland. Andalucia Handbook. LC 97-188735. (Illus.). 336p. 1997. 17.95 (*0-8442-4868-1*) NTC Contemp Pub Co.

— Andalucia Handbook. 2nd ed. (Footprint Handbook Ser.). 368p. 1999. pap. 17.95 (*0-8442-2125-2*, 21252) NTC Contemp Pub Co.

***Mead, Rowland.** Globetrotter Travel Guide to Costa Rica. (Globetrotter Travel Guides Ser.). (Illus.). 128p. 1999. pap. 10.95 (*1-85368-896-7*, Pub. by New5 Holland) Globe Pequot.

— Walking England's Cathedral Cities. (Walking Ser.). (Illus.). 192p. 2000. pap. 14.95 (*0-658-00366-6*, 003666) NTC Contemp Pub Co.

Mead, Ruth, jt. auth. see Sabais, Heinz W.

Mead, Ruth, tr. see Bienek, Horst.

Mead, Ruth, tr. see Bobrowski, Johannes.

Mead, Samuel. The FamilyPC Guide to Cool PC Projects. LC 96-208017. (Illus.). 320p. (J). 1996. pap. 24.45 (*0-7868-8207-7*, Pub. by Hyperion) Time Warner.

Mead, Sidney. The Lively Experiment Continued: Essays in Honor of Sidney E. Mead. Brauer, Jerald C., ed. LC 87-2752. 288p. 1987. pap. 18.95 (*0-86554-290-2*, P049) Mercer Univ Pr.

Mead, Sidney E. History & Identity. LC 78-26543. (American Academy of Religion. Studies in Religion: No. 19). 71p. reprint ed. pap. 30.00 (*0-7837-5477-9*, 204524200005) Bks Demand.

— Love & Learning. Doyle, Mary L., ed. 1978. pap. 5.00 (*0-914914-12-X*); lib. bdg. 12.95 (*0-914914-13-8*) New Horizons.

Mead, Sidney M. Landmarks, Bridges & Visions: Aspects of Maori Culture: Essays LC 97-161634. 266 p. 1997. write for info. (*0-86473-317-8*) Lubrecht & Cramer.

Mead, Spencer P. Abstract of Church Records of the Town of Stamford, County of Fairfield, from the Earliest Records to 1850. 499p. 1997. reprint ed. lib. bdg. 51.50 (*0-8328-5687-8*) Higginson Bk Co.

— Abstract of Probate Records at Fairfield, County of Fairfield, 1648-1750. (Illus.). 363p. 1997. reprint ed. lib. bdg. 37.50 (*0-8328-5644-4*) Higginson Bk Co.

— Abstract of Probate Records for the District of Stamford, County of Fairfield, 1729-1848, 2 vols. 928p. 1997. reprint ed. lib. bdg. 104.00 (*0-8328-5688-6*) Higginson Bk Co.

— History & Genealogy of the Mead Family of Fairfield County, Connecticut, Eastern New York, Western Vermont, & Western Pennsylvania from 1180-1900. (Illus.). 480p. 1989. reprint ed. pap. 72.00 (*0-8328-0865-2*); reprint ed. lib. bdg. 80.00 (*0-8328-0864-4*) Higginson Bk Co.

— Ye Historie of Ye Town of Greenwich, Co. of Fairfield & State of Conn., with Genealogical Notes on (Many) Families. (Illus.). 768p. 1995. reprint ed. lib. bdg. 77.50 (*0-8328-4605-8*) Higginson Bk Co.

— Ye Historie of Ye Town of Greenwich, Connecticut. LC 92-60184. (Illus.). 862p. 1992. reprint ed. 49.50 (*0-89725-079-6*, 1348) Picton Pr.

Mead, Stephen. Grandpa, Tell Me More! A Colorful Portrait of a Country Lad. VanStratt, Teresa & Urbaniak, Christine, eds. (Illus.). 124p. (J). (gr. 3-12). 1995. 15.00 (*0-9644211-0-0*) T VanStratt.

— You Can Win! Blackjack Made Easy. (Illus.). 44p. 1999. pap. 9.95 (*0-8059-4674-8*) Dorrance.

***Mead, Sue.** Monster Trucks & Tractors. LC 98-8216. (Race Car Legends Ser.). (Illus.). 64p. (YA). (gr. 3 up). 1999. lib. bdg. 16.95 (*0-7910-5021-1*) Chelsea Hse.

— Off-Road Racing. (Race Car Legends Ser.). (Illus.). 2000. 16.95 (*0-7910-5851-4*) Chelsea Hse.

— Off-Road Racing. (Race Car Legends Ser.). (Illus.). 2001. pap. 5.95 (*0-7910-5852-2*) Chelsea Hse.

Mead, Syd. Kronolog: Syd Mead's Kronovid, Kronoteko, & Kronovecta. (Illus.). 471p. 1991. 500.00 (*0-929463-07-2*) Oblagon.

— Kronoteko: Art of Syd Mead. (Illus.). 143p. 1991. 149.95 (*0-929463-05-6*) Oblagon.

— Kronovecta: Concept Designs of Syd Mead. (Illus.). 328p. 1991. pap. 149.95 (*0-929463-06-4*) Oblagon.

— Oblagon Vol. 2: Concepts of Syd Mead. 2nd ed. Ichikawa, Mieko, tr. (ENG & JPN., Illus.). 168p. 1996. reprint ed. per. 50.00 (*4-06-201520-0*) Oblagon.

Mead, Sydney J. Sentinel II. (Sentinelkodansha Ser.). (JPN., Illus.). 116p. 1987. per. 49.50 (*4-06-202322-9*) Oblagon.

— Studio Image "RGB" Set: Red, Green, Blue Studio Image Books, 3vols. Incl. Studio Image 1. (Illus.). (Orig.). 1988. pap. 17.00 (*0-929463-00-5*); Studio Image 3. Servick, Roger, ed. (Illus.). 36p. 1994. pap. 21.00 (*0-929463-02-1*); Studio Image 2. (Illus.). (Orig.). 1989. pap. 19.00 (*0-929463-01-3*); (Illus.). 108p. 1994. Set pap. 57.00 (*0-929463-03-X*) Oblagon.

Mead, Tray C. & Price, Robert C. Mesa: In the Shadow of the Superstitions. 144p. 1988. 29.95 (*0-89781-254-9*, 5274) Am Historical Pr.

Mead, Virginia H., jt. auth. see Cutietta, Robert A.

Mead, W. L., ed. Advances in Mass Spectrometry: Proceedings of a Conference Held in Paris, September, 1964, Vol. 3. LC QC0454.I61. 1098p. reprint ed. pap. 200.00 (*0-8357-5171-6*, 202399300003) Bks Demand.

Mead, Walter J., et al. Offshore Lands: Oil & Gas Leasing & Conservation on the Outer Continental Shelf. LC 85-63548. (Illus.). 172p. (Orig.). (C). 1985. 29.95 (*0-936488-10-7*); pap. 10.95 (*0-936488-01-8*) PRIPP.

Mead, Walter J., jt. auth. see Yousuf Hasan Mohammad.

Mead, Walter R. The Low-Wage Challenge to Global Growth: The Labor Cost-Productivity Imbalance in Newly Industrialized Countries. 48p. 1990. 12.00 (*0-944826-21-0*) Economic Policy Inst.

Mead, William B. & Dickson, Paul. Baseball: The Presidents' Game. LC 96-49052. (Illus.). 230p. 1997. pap. 16.95 (*0-8027-7515-2*) Walker & Co.

Mead, William B., jt. auth. see Strassels, Paul N.

Mead, William E. The Grand Tour in the Eighteenth Century. LC 72-83604. (Illus.). 1972. reprint ed. 30.95 (*0-405-08784-5*) Ayer.

Mead, William E., ed. Squyr of Lowe Degre: A Middle English Metrical Romance Edited in All Extant Forms, with Introduction, Notes & Glossary. LC 76-178506. reprint ed. 27.50 (*0-404-56676-6*) AMS Pr.

Meadbra, Michael. Learn Windows 98 in a Weekend. LC 97-69602. (Computer Bks.). 225p. 1998. per. 19.99 (*0-7615-1296-9*) Prima Pub.

Meade. Basic Circuits Manual. (Electronics Technology Ser.). 1990. pap., lab manual ed. 26.00 (*0-8273-2995-4*) Delmar.

— Foundations of Electron. (Electronics Technology Ser.). 1994. 72.95 (*0-8273-6402-4*) Delmar.

— Foundations of Electronics. (Electronics Technology Ser.). 1990. pap. 50.95 (*0-8273-2993-8*) Delmar.

— Foundations of Electronics. 2nd ed. (Electronic Technology Ser.). 1994. pap. 69.95 (*0-8273-6463-6*, VNR) Wiley.

— Foundations of Electronics. 3rd ed. (Electronics Technology Ser.). (C). 1998. pap., lab manual ed. 26.50 (*0-7668-0430-5*) Delmar.

***Meade.** Foundations of Electronics: Instructor's Guide. 400p. 1999. teacher ed. 32.95 (*0-7668-0429-1*) Delmar.

Meade. Foundations of Electronics - CTB. 2nd ed. (Electronics Technology Ser.). 1994. 59.95 (*0-8273-6462-8*) Delmar.

***Meade.** Partners in Movement. (C). 1999. pap. text 49.00 (*0-12-785026-0*) Acad Pr.

Meade. Thrombosis. 1995. text 105.00 (*0-443-05154-2*, W B Saunders Co) Harcrt Hlth Sci Grp.

— Transistor Circuit Development wth Math CAD. (Electrical Trades Ser.). (C). 1994. pap. 29.50 (*0-8273-9100-5*) Delmar.

Meade & Heiserman. Foundations of Electronics: Circuits & Devices. 3rd ed. LC 98-41641. 1168p. (C). 1998. text 107.95 (*0-7668-0427-5*) Delmar.

Meade, jt. auth. see Delmar.

Meade, Bishop. Old Churches, Ministers, & Families of Virginia, 2 vols., Set. (Illus.). 1067p. (Orig.). 1993. reprint ed. pap. text 58.00 (*1-55613-691-9*) Heritage Bk.

Meade, C. Wade. Egyptology & Rome: A Handbook for Students of Egyptian Archaeology in Rome. 97p. (Orig.). 1987. pap. text 16.95 (*0-936638-02-8*) Palatine Pubns.

— Ruins of Rome: A Guide to the Classical Antiquities. LC 80-81128. (Illus.). 1980. 21.95 (*0-936638-00-1*); pap. 16.95 (*0-936638-01-X*) Palatine Pubns.

Meade, Catherine M. My Nature Is Fire: Saint Catherine of Siena. LC 91-9224. 1991. pap. 12.50 (*0-8189-0615-4*) Alba.

Meade, Dorothy C. Heart Bags & Hand Shakes: The Story of the Cook Collection. LC 94-66130. (Illus.). xii, 60p. (Orig.). (YA). (gr. 7-12). 1994. pap. 10.95 (*0-9628075-4-0*) Natl Woodlands Pub.

***Meade, Douglas & Bourkoff, Etan.** Maple V for Engineers. 1999. teacher ed. write for info. (*0-8053-6446-3*) Benjamin-Cummings.

Meade, Douglas & Bourkoff, Etan. Maple V for Engineers: Toolkit. 128p. 1997. pap. 23.33 (*0-8053-6445-5*) Benjamin-Cummings.

Meade, Erica H. Tell It by Heart: Women & the Healing Power of Story. 281p. 1995. 38.95 (*0-8126-9301-9*); pap. 17.95 (*0-8126-9302-7*) Open Court.

Meade, Everard. The Dragonfly. 174p. 1987. 14.95 (*0-933905-00-9*) Claycomb Pr.

— The Dragonfly. 1992. pap. 7.95 (*0-933905-20-3*) Claycomb Pr.

Meade, F. H., et al. Religions of the World. rev. ed. (Illus.). (C). 1988. 90.00 (*0-7157-2355-3*) St Mut.

Meade, George. The Life & Letters of George Gordon Meade, Major-General United States Army. Meade, George G., ed. (Army of the Potomac Ser.). (Illus.). 965p. (C). 1994. text 100.00 (*0-935523-38-3*) Butternut & Blue.

Meade, George G., ed. see Meade, George.

Meade, Glenn. Brandenburg. 1998. mass mkt. 6.99 (*0-312-96525-7*, Pub. by Tor Bks) St Martin.

— Brandenburg: A Novel. LC 96-54630. 1997. text 24.95 (*0-312-15483-6*) St Martin.

— The Sands of Sakkara. LC 99-12725. 436p. 1999. 25.95 (*0-312-20201-6*, Thomas Dunne) St Martin.

***Meade, Glenn.** The Sands of Sakkara. 544p. 1999. pap. 6.99 (*0-312-97108-7*) St Martin.

Meade, Glenn. Snow Wolf. 1997. mass mkt. 6.99 (*0-312-96211-8*) St Martin.

Meade, Holly. John Willy & Freddy McGee. LC 97-50362. (Illus.). 32p. (J). (ps-3). 1998. 15.95 (*0-7614-5033-5*) Marshall Cavendish.

Meade, J. E. Agathotopia: The Economics of Partnership. (David Hume Papers: No. 16). 150p. 1989. pap. text 14.00 (*0-08-037967-2*, Pub. by Aberdeen U Pr) Macmillan.

— Full-Employment Regained? (Cambridge Department of Applied Economics Occasional Papers: No. 61). 114p. (C). 1995. pap. text 14.95 (*0-521-55697-X*) Cambridge U Pr.

— Full-Employment Regained? (Cambridge Department of Applied Economics Occasional Papers: No. 61). 114p. (C). 1996. text 49.95 (*0-521-55327-X*) Cambridge U Pr.

— Liberty, Equality, & Efficiency: Apologia Pro Agathotopia Mea. LC 92-34923. (C). 1993. text 65.00 (*0-8147-5491-0*) NYU Pr.

Meade, James E. The Intelligent Radical's Guide to Economic Policy: The Mixed Economy. 1975. pap. text 10.95 (*0-04-330257-2*) Routledge.

— The Just Economy. (Principles of Political Economy Ser.: Vol. 4). 1977. reprint ed. pap. text 21.95 (*0-04-330279-3*) Routledge.

— A Neo-Classical Theory of Economic Growth. LC 83-1748. 185p. (C). 1983. reprint ed. lib. bdg. 49.75 (*0-313-23965-7*, MENE, Greenwood Pr) Greenwood.

— Principles of Political Economy Vol. 3: Just Economy. LC 65-26549. 247p. (C). 1976. text 29.50 (*0-87395-205-7*) State U NY Pr.

Meade, James E., et al. Economic & Social Structure of Mauritius. 246p. 1968. reprint ed. 32.00 (*0-7146-1233-2*, Pub. by F Cass Pubs) Intl Spec Bk.

Meade, James G. Power Excel for Windows 95. 1995. pap. 29.95 (*1-55828-440-0*, MIS Pr) IDG Bks.

***Meade, James G.** Robohelp 7 for Dummies. (For Dummies Ser.). 408p. 1999. pap. 24.99 incl. cd-rom (*0-7645-0560-2*) IDG Bks.

Meade, Jeff. Home Sweet Office: The Ultimate Out-of-Office Experience: Working Your Company Job from Home. LC 93-8563. 208p. (Orig.). 1993. pap. 12.95 (*1-56079-240-X*) Petersons.

Meade, Jim. Wannabe Guide to Marketing. (Illus.). 100p. 2001. pap. 9.95 (*1-57143-056-3*) RDR Bks.

Meade, Jim, jt. auth. see Hirao, Joey.

Meade, L. T. Stories from the Diary of a Doctor. LC 75-32767. (Literature of Mystery & Detection Ser.). (Illus.). 1976. reprint ed. 31.95 (*0-405-07886-2*) Ayer.

***Meade, L. T. & Eustace, Robert.** The Detections of Miss Cusack. (Doyleana & Other Victorian Literature Ser.). 1998. 22.00 (*1-55246-064-9*) Battered Silicon.

Meade, M. L. Senales & Sistemas, Modelos & Comportamientos. (SPA.). (C). 1993. pap. text 12.33 (*0-201-60138-9*) Addison-Wesley.

Meade, Marion. Buster Keaton: Cut to the Chase. LC 97-17745. (Illus.). 464p. 1997. reprint ed. pap. 16.95 (*0-306-80802-1*) Da Capo.

— Dorothy Parker: What Fresh Hell Is This? (Illus.). 480p. 1989. pap. 17.95 (*0-14-011616-8*, Penguin Bks) Viking Penguin.

— Eleanor of Aquitaine. 1991. pap. 16.95 (*0-14-015338-1*, Penguin Bks) Viking Penguin.

— Stealing Heaven. LC 79-1182. (Hera Ser.). 415p. 1994. pap. 15.00 (*1-56947-011-1*) Soho Press.

— The Unruly Life of Woody Allen: A Biography. LC 99-45482. (Illus.). 384p. 2000. 26.00 (*0-684-83374-3*) Scribner.

Meade, Melinda, et al. Human Health in the Balance. (Active Learning Modules on the Human Dimensions of Global Change Ser.). (Illus.). 193p. (C). 1997. pap., teacher ed. 20.00 (*0-89291-249-9*); pap., student ed., wbk. ed. 8.75 (*0-89291-250-2*) Assn Am Geographers.

***Meade, Melinda S. & Earickson, Robert J.** Medical Geography. 2nd ed. 480p. 2000. lib. bdg. 49.95 (*1-57230-558-4*) Guilford Pubns.

Meade, Michael J. Men & the Water of Life: Initiation & the Tempering of Men. LC 92-56405. 464p. 1994. reprint ed. pap. 17.00 (*0-06-250726-5*, Pub. by Harper SF) HarpC.

Meade, Patricia S. Healthcare Advertising & Marketing: A Practical Approach to Effective Communications. LC 98-31110. (Illus.). 225p. 1998. 55.00 (*0-07-041236-7*) McGraw.

Meade, Robert D. Judah P. Benjamin: Confederate Statesman. LC 74-29506. (Modern Jewish Experience Ser.). (Illus.). 1975. reprint ed. 38.95 (*0-405-06733-X*) Ayer.

Meade, Russell L. Computer Test Bank for Foundations of Electronics. 1991. 69.95 (*0-8273-4588-7*) Delmar.

— Foundations of Electronics. 345p. 1994. teacher ed. 26.00 (*0-8273-6466-0*) Delmar.

— Foundations of Electronics. 2nd ed. LC 93-38058. (C). 1994. pap. 90.95 (*0-8273-5971-3*) Delmar.

— Foundations of Electronics. 3rd ed. LC 98-41278. (C). 1998. pap. 93.95 (*0-7668-0424-0*) Delmar.

— Foundations of Electronics: Circuits & Devices. LC 93-38059. 1137p. (C). 1994. mass mkt. 102.95 (*0-8273-5970-5*) Delmar.

— Foundations of Electronics: PC Lab Sampler. 1991. pap., teacher ed. 33.43 (*0-8273-4822-3*) Delmar.

— Foundations of Electronics & Circuits & Devices: Lab Manual. 2nd ed. 401p. (C). 1994. pap. text 40.95 (*0-8273-6467-9*) Delmar.

— Foundations of Electronics Instructors Guide. 1991. pap. 21.00 (*0-8273-2994-6*) Delmar.

Meade, Russell L. & Wilson, Edward A. Foundations of Electronics: Flashcards. 186p. 1994. 20.50 (*0-8273-6461-X*) Delmar.

***Meade, Scottee.** Boston Terrier: An Owner's Guide to a Happy Healthy Pet. LC 00-38475. (Guide to a Happy Healthy Pet Ser.). (Illus.). 160p. 2000. 12.95 (*1-58245-159-1*) Howell Bks.

Meade, Shepherd. How to Succeed in Business Without Really Trying. 1995. reprint ed. lib. bdg. 24.95 (*1-56849-596-X*) Buccaneer Bks.

***Meade, Starr.** Training Hearts, Teaching Minds: Family Devotions Based on the Shorter Catechism. LC 00-37511. (Illus.). 2000. pap. 14.99 (*0-87552-392-7*) P & R Pubng.

Meade, T. W., ed. Anticoagulants & Myocardial Infarction: A Reappraisal. LC 84-5053. (Wiley-Medical Publication). (Illus.). 284p. reprint ed. pap. 88.10 (*0-8357-4620-8*, 203755200008) Bks Demand.

Meade, Teresa & Walker, Mark, eds. Science, Medicine & Cultural Imperialism. LC 90-45331. 190p. 1991. text 45.00 (*0-312-04779-7*) St Martin.

Meade, Teresa A. Civilizing Rio: Reform & Resistance in a Brazilian City, 1889-1930. LC 96-6452. 1997. 48.50 (*0-271-01607-8*); pap. 19.95 (*0-271-01608-6*) Pa St U Pr.

Meade, Tina, jt. auth. see Johnson, James.

Meade, Tom. Essential Fly Fishing: An All-Color Guide. LC 94-18502. (Illus.). 160p. 1994. pap. 15.95 (*1-55821-334-1*) Lyons Pr.

Meade, Vicki L., ed. see Albrant, Daniel H. & Harteker, Linda R.

Meade, Walter F. In the Catskill Mountains: A Personal Approach to Nature. LC 91-12887. (Illus.). 127p. 1991. 15.00 (*0-935796-20-7*) Purple Mnt Pr.

Meade, William. Old Churches, Ministers & Families of Virginia, 2 vols. (Illus.). 985p. 1997. reprint ed. lib. bdg. 99.00 (*0-8328-7178-8*) Higginson Bk Co.

— Old Churches, Ministers, & Families of Virginia: Digested Index & Genealogical Guide, 2 vols. 1100p. 1995. reprint ed. 70.00 (*0-8063-0238-0*) Genealog Pub.

Meaden, G. & Chi, T. Do. Geographical Information Systems - Applications to Marine Fisheries. (Fisheries Technical Papers: No. 356). 362p. 1996. pap. 46.00 (*92-5-103829-5*, F38295, Pub. by FAO) Bernan Associates.

***Meaden, Terence.** Secrets of the Avebury Stones: Britain's Greatest Megalithic Temple. (Illus.). 150p. 2000. pap. 20.00 (*1-58394-009-X*) Frog Ltd CA.

Meaden, Terence. Stonehenge: The Secret of the Solstice. (Illus.). 176p. (Orig.). 1997. pap. 16.95 (*0-285-63364-3*, Pub. by Souvenir Pr Ltd) IPG Chicago.

Meader, Greg & Michaels, John H. Golf Games. (Illus.). 1999. 7.95 (*0-9671638-0-3*) J Michaels.

Meader, J. W. The Merrimack River: Its Source & Its Tributaries. 320p. 1998. reprint ed. pap. 24.50 (*0-7884-0900-X*, M105) Heritage Bk.

Meader, James L. Normal School Education in Connecticut. LC 74-177065. (Columbia University. Teachers College. Contributions to Education Ser.: No. 307). reprint ed. 37.50 (*0-404-55307-9*) AMS Pr.

Meader, John T. Dell Turner: The Stories of His Life. Ives, Edward D., ed. (Northeast Folklore Ser.: Vol. XXVII). (Illus.). 150p. (Orig.). 1988. pap. 10.00 (*0-943197-19-8*) ME Folklife Ctr.

Meader, Jonathan. In Praise of Women. LC 97-26260. 144p. 1997. pap. 24.95 (*0-89087-842-0*) Celestial Arts.

— Wordless Travel Book. (Illus.). 18p. (Orig.). 1995. pap. 4.95 (*0-89815-809-5*) Ten Speed Pr.

Meader, Martin, jt. auth. see Giles, David.

Meader, Robert F. Illustrated Guide to Shaker Furniture. (Illus.). 146p. 1972. pap. 10.95 (*0-486-22819-3*) Dover.

***Meader, Vera.** Cold War Story. 2000. pap. text 14.95 (*1-889534-32-3*) Jay St Pubs.

Meaders, Daniel E., compiled by. Eighteenth-Century White Slaves: Fugitive Notices, Pennsylvania, 1729-1760, Vol. 1. LC 93-8973. (Documentary Reference Collections). 608p. 1993. lib. bdg. 115.00 (*0-313-27987-X*, Greenwood Pr) Greenwood.

Meaders, Daniel E., ed. Advertisements for Runaway Slaves in Virginia, 1801-1820. LC 97-1500. (Studies in African American History & Culture). 418p. 1997. text 87.00 (*0-8153-2737-4*) Garland.

Meadhra, Michael. The ABCs of Online Banking with Quicken. 368p. 1996. pap. text 19.99 (*0-7821-1901-8*) Sybex.

***Meadhra, Michael.** Kde for Linux. (For Dummies Ser.). 384p. 2000. pap. 24.99 incl. cd-rom (*0-7645-0658-7*) IDG Bks.

Meadhra, Michael. Smartsuite X for Dummies. 432p. 1998. pap. 19.99 (*0-7645-0353-7*) IDG Bks.

***Meadhra, Michael.** Staroffice for Linux for Dummies. 432p. 1999. pap. 19.99 (*0-7645-0576-9*) IDG Bks.

Meadhra, Ruairi O. Modeling of the Kinetics of Suspension Crystallizers: A New Model for Secondary Nucleation. (Illus.). 199p. (Orig.). 1995. pap. 59.50 (*90-407-1190-9*, Pub. by Delft U Pr) Coronet Bks.

Meadley, Walter. Picking Your Kids Dog. Adams, Milton, ed. (Illus.). 160p. 1997. pap. 12.95 (*1-890676-08-X*) Beavers Pond.

Meadmore, Clement. The Modern Chair: Classic Designs by Thonet, Breuer, Le Corbusier, Eames & Others. LC 97-19699. (Illus.). 192p. 1997. pap. 13.95 (*0-486-29807-8*) Dover.

Meadmore, Daphne, jt. auth. see Symes, Colin.

Meador, Betty D. Uncursing the Dark: Treasures from the Underworld. LC 92-23029. 192p. (Orig.). 1992. pap. 15.95 (*0-933029-65-9*) Chiron Pubns.

***Meador, Betty De Shong.** Inanna, Lady of Largest Heart: Poems of the Sumerian High Priestess Enheduana. LC 00-36407. (Illus.). 256p. 2001. 40.00 (*0-292-75241-5*) U of Tex Pr.

— Inanna, Lady of Largest Heart: Poems of the Sumerian High Priestess Enheduanna. LC 00-36407. (Illus.). 256p. 2001. pap. 22.95 (*0-292-75242-3*) U of Tex Pr.

Meador, C., tr. see Andreyev, Leonid.

Meador, Celine W. Dream Big, by Durn! (Illus.). 64p. (Orig.). 1996. pap. 10.95 (*1-889299-01-4*, ARC3014) ARC Pubns.

— Just Wait 'til We're Diamond. (Illus.). 32p. (J). (ps-6). 1993. 14.95 (*1-889299-00-6*, BK386) ARC Pubns.

***Meador, Clifton K.** A Little Book of Doctors' Rule No. II: A Compilation. LC 99-63780. 80p. (C). 1999. pap. text 9.95 (*1-56053-365-X*, Pub. by Hanley & Belfus) Mosby Inc.

Meador, Clifton K. A Little Book of Doctors' Rules. 128p. (Orig.). 1992. pap. text 9.95 (*1-56053-061-8*) Hanley & Belfus.

Meador, Clifton K. Memory Lapse: An Artist's Book. (Illus.). 192p. 55.00 (*0-932526-83-7*) Nexus Pr.

Meador, Clifton K., jt. auth. see Wadlington, William.

Meador, Clifton K., jt. ed. see Hammerschmidt, Rosalie.

Meador, D. J. His Father's House. LC 93-37982. 384p. 1994. text 25.00 (*1-56554-032-8*) Pelican.

Meador, Dale. Along Dusty Roads. Patten, G. Z., ed. 200p. (Orig.). 1996. pap. 9.95 (*0-9652124-0-8*) Tres Bien.

Meador, Daniel. Appellate Courts: 1994 Edition. 1193p. 1994. text 60.00 (*1-55834-192-7*, 12315-10, MICHIE) LEXIS Pub.

Meador, Daniel J. Habeas Corpus & Magna Carta: Dualism of Power & Liberty. LC 65-28634. (Magna Carta Essays Ser.). 94p. reprint ed. pap. 30.00 (*0-8357-9801-1*, 201003600071) Bks Demand.

— Unforgotten. LC 98-6070. 400p. 1999. 25.00 (*1-56554-349-1*) Pelican.

Meador, Daniel J., ed. The Korean War in Retrospect: Lessons for the Future. 216p. (C). 1998. 36.00 (*0-7618-1073-0*) U Pr of Amer.

Meador, Daniel J. & Bernstein, Jordana S. Appellate Courts in the United States. 151p. 1994. pap. 14.50 (*0-314-03748-9*) West Pub.

Meador, Daniel J. & Kempin, Frederick G. American Courts. 113p. (C). 1991. reprint ed. pap. 14.50 (*0-314-86717-1*) West Pub.

Meador, Daniel John & Kempin Jr., Frederick G. HISTORIAL INTRO TO ANGLO-AMERICAN LAW IN A NUTSHELL 3E. 3rd ed. (Paralegal). 323p. (C). 1990. reprint ed. pap. text 15.50 (*0-314-74708-7*) West Pub.

Meador, Karen. It's in the Bag: Creative Thinking for School & Home. (Illus.). 64p. 1999. pap. 10.95 (*1-880505-48-7*, CLC0232) Pieces of Lrning.

Meador, Karen S. Creative Thinking & Problem Solving for Young Learners. LC 97-33633. (Gifted Treasury Ser.). (Illus.). 150p. 1997. pap. 21.50 (*1-56308-529-1*) Libs Unl.

Meador, Kristen A., jt. ed. see Phillips, Scarlett L.

Meador, Mary, ed. see Workman, Joe.

Meador, Nancy, jt. auth. see Harman, Betty.

Meador, Nancy, jt. ed. see Harman, Betty.

***Meador, Prentice A.** Great Story. 2000. pap. 9.99 (*0-89098-147-7*) Twent Cent Christ.

***Meador, Prentice A., Jr.** More Than We Imagined: Parables of the Kingdom of God. LC 00-105861. 150p. 2000. pap. 9.95 (*0-89112-446-2*, Hill Crest Pubg) Abilene Christ U.

***Meador, Prentice A.** Promises to Keep: The Calling, Character & Cost of Commitment. 1998. pap. 11.99 (*0-89098-199-X*) Twent Cent Christ.

— Walk with Me: Hear My Voice, Watch My Actions, Follow My Steps, Come... 1998. pap. 9.99 (*0-89098-153-1*) Twent Cent Christ.

Meador, Roy. Guidelines for Preparing Proposals. 2nd ed. LC 91-24732. (Illus.). 224p. 1991. boxed set 54.95 (*0-87371-588-8*, L588) Lewis Pubs.

Meadors, Edward P. Jesus the Messianic Herald of Salvation. 388p. 1997. pap. 19.95 (*1-56563-268-0*) Hendrickson MA.

Meadors, Gary. New Testament Essays. 1991. 17.50 (*0-88469-231-0*) BMH Bks.

Meadow. Lecture Notes on Paediatrics. 5th ed. 1986. 17.95 (*0-8016-3372-9*) Mosby Inc.

***Meadow & Auger, Giselle.** The Insiders' Guide to Maine's Southern Coast. 2nd ed. (Insiders' Guide Travel Ser.). 1999. pap. 14.95 (*1-57380-115-1*, The Insiders Guide) Falcon Pub Inc.

Meadow, Anthony. System 7 Revealed. 400p. (C). 1991. pap. text 22.95 (*0-201-55040-7*) Addison-Wesley.

Meadow, Anthony & Feiler, Jesse. Essential OpenDoc: Cross-Platform Development for OS/2, Macintosh & Windows Programmers. 304p. (C). 1996. pap., pap. text 24.95 incl. cd-rom (*0-201-47958-3*) Addison-Wesley.

Meadow, Barry. Blackjack Autumn: A True Tale of Life, Death & Splitting 10's in Winnemucca. LC 99-457867. 255p. 1999. 27.95 (*0-945322-03-8*) TR Pub.

— Money Secrets at the Racetrack. LC 87-51583. 148p. (Orig.). 1990. pap. 24.95 (*0-945322-02-X*) TR Pub.

— Success at the Harness Races. 1976. reprint ed. pap. 7.00 (*0-87980-320-7*) Wilshire.

Meadow, Charles T. Ink into Bits: A Web of Converging Media. LC 98-16854. (Illus.). 304p. 1998. 45.00 (*0-8108-3507-X*); pap. 24.50 (*0-8108-3508-8*) Scarecrow.

— Text Information Retrieval Systems. (Library & Information Science Ser.). (Illus.). 302p. 1992. text 55.00 (*0-12-487410-X*) Acad Pr.

***Meadow, Charles T.** Text Information Retrieval Systems. 2nd ed. 450p. 1999. 64.96 (*0-12-487405-3*) Acad Pr.

Meadow, H. Lee, ed. see Academy of Marketing Science Staff.

Meadow, Mary J. Gentling the Heart: Buddhist Loving-Kindness Practice for Christians. 160p. (Orig.). 1994. pap. 13.95 (*0-8245-1434-3*) Crossroad NY.

— Through a Glass Darkly: A Spiritual Psychology of Faith. LC 95-13753. 144p. 1995. pap. 14.95 (*0-8245-1510-2*) Crossroad NY.

Meadow Orlans, Kathryn P. & Wallace, Ruth A., eds. Gender & the Academic Experience: Berkeley Women Sociologists. LC 93-27763. (Illus.). x, 268p. (C). 1994. pap. text 20.00 (*0-8032-8606-6*) U of Nebr Pr.

***Meadow-Orlans, Kathryn P., et al.** The Deaf Child in the Family & at School: Essays in Honor of Kathryn P. Meadow-Orlans LC 99-34490. 1999. write for info. (*0-8058-3221-1*) L Erlbaum Assocs.

Meadow-Orlans, Kathryn P., jt. ed. see Moores, Donald F.

Meadow, Pauline M., jt. ed. see Bull, Alan T.

Meadow, Phyllis W., jt. auth. see Spotnitz, Hyman.

Meadow, Richard H. & Zeder, Melinda A., eds. Approaches to Faunal Analysis in the Middle East. LC 78-50908. (Peabody Museum Bulletins Ser.: No. 2). (Illus.). 186p. 1978. pap. 12.00 (*0-87365-951-1*) Peabody Harvard.

Meadow, Robert G. & Jackson-Beeck, Marilyn. The Presidential Debates: Media, Electoral & Policy Perspective. Bishop, George F. et al, eds. LC 78-70323. 324p. 1978. 69.50 (*0-275-90285-4*, C0285, Praeger Pubs) Greenwood.

Meadow, Rosalyn M. Women's Conflicts about Eating & Sexuality: The Relationship Between Food & Sex. LC 91-19205. 1992. pap. 10.95 (*0-918393-98-1*, Harrington Park) Haworth Pr.

Meadow, Rosalyn M. & Weiss, Lillie. Women's Conflicts about Eating & Sexuality: The Relationship Between Food & Sex. LC 91-4120. 212p. 1992. lib. bdg. 39.95 (*1-56024-131-4*) Haworth Pr.

Meadow, Roy, ed. ABC of Child Abuse. 3rd ed. 100p. 1997. pap. text 29.00 (*0-7279-1106-6*, Pub. by BMJ Pub) Login Brothers Bk Co.

Meadowbrook. Feed Me, I'm Yours. 1986. spiral bd. 8.00 (*0-671-62278-1*) S&S Trade.

Meadowbrook Creations Staff. Our Baby's First Year: A Baby Record Calendar. 30p. 1983. pap. 10.00 (*0-88166-003-5*) Meadowbrook.

Meadowcourt, Richard & Dunster, Charles. Milton's Paradise Regained: Two Eighteenth-Century Critiques, 2 vols. in 1. LC 76-161937. 344p. 1971. reprint ed. 50.00 (*0-8201-1087-6*) Schol Facsimiles.

Meadowcraft, James, jt. ed. see Lafferty, William M.

Meadowcraft, Stan, jt. auth. see Hardy, Ron.

Meadowcroft, Barry, jt. auth. see Starr, Fred.

Meadowcroft, Cedric. The Homeowner's Guide to the Law. 152p. 1987. 95.00 (*1-85190-023-3*, Pub. by Fourmat Pub) St Mut.

Meadowcroft, D. B., jt. ed. see Grabke, H. J.

Meadowcroft, Enid L. By Wagon & Flatboat. LC 38-32408. (Illus.). (J). (gr. 5 up). 1944. 13.95 (*0-690-16502-1*) HarpC Child Bks.

Meadowcroft, James. Conceptualizing the State: Innovation & Dispute in British Political Thought, 1880-1914. LC 96-113990. (Oxford Historical Monographs). 258p. 1995. text 59.00 (*0-19-820601-1*) OUP.

Meadowcroft, James, ed. The Liberal Political Tradition: Contemporary Reappraisals. LC 95-19663. 208p. 1996. 85.00 (*1-85898-083-6*) E Elgar.

Meadowcroft, James, jt. auth. see Lafferty, William M.

Meadowcroft, James, ed. see Hobhouse, Leonard T.

Meadowcroft, James, jt. ed. see Kenny, Michael.

Meadowcroft, James, jt. ed. see Laffernty, William M.

Meadowcroft, P., tr. see Reinken, Gunter.

Meadowcroft, Pamela & Trout, Barbara A., eds. Troubled Youth in Treatment Homes: A Handbook of Therapeutic Foster Care. (Trilogy Ser.: Bk. 2). 1990. pap. 11.50 (*0-87868-354-2*) Child Welfare.

Meadowcroft, Sam, jt. auth. see Brown, Dave.

Meadowcroft, T. J. Aramaic Daniel & Greek Daniel: A Literary Comparison. (JSOT Supplement Ser.: No. 198). 336p. 1995. 85.00 (*1-85075-551-5*, Pub. by Sheffield Acad) CUP Services.

***Meadows.** Communications Engineering. 2000. pap. 34.95 (*0-7506-4645-4*) Buttrwrth-Heinemann.

Meadows. Measurement of Geometric Tolerances in Manufacturing. LC 98-17836. (Illus.). 496p. 1998. text 175.00 (*0-8247-0163-1*) Dekker.

Meadows, A. J. Stellar Evolution. 2nd ed. 1978. text 87.00 (*0-08-021668-4*, Pub. by Pergamon Repr) Franklin.

Meadows, A. J. & Meadows, Charles T. Communicating Research. LC 97-23432. (Library & Information Science Ser.). (Illus.). 264p. 1997. text 59.95 (*0-12-487415-0*) Morgan Kaufmann.

Meadows, Adela. Quimper Pottery: A Guide to Origins, Styles, & Values. LC 97-31915. 1998. 49.95 (*0-7643-0421-6*) Schiffer.

Meadows, Anne. Digging up Butch & Sundance. rev. ed. LC 96-11934. (Illus.). xii, 406p. 1996. pap. 19.95 (*0-8032-8225-7*, Bison Books) U of Nebr Pr.

Meadows, Anne, ed. see National Research Council, Panel on Child Care Pol.

Meadows, Anthony. System 7 Revealed. (JPN.). (C). 1992. pap. text. write for info. (*0-201-55675-8*) Addison-Wesley.

***Meadows, B. J. & Saltzman, Marilyn.** Building School Communities: Strategies for Leaders. LC 99-87758. (Illus.). 184p. 2000. pap. 19.95 (*1-55591-981-2*) Fulcrum Pub.

Meadows, C. Julia. Natural Bodycare: Creating Aromatherapy Cosmetics for Health & Beauty. LC 98-7385. (Illus.). 128p. 1998. 24.95 (*0-8069-4245-2*) Sterling.

***Meadows, Carl.** How to Organize Group Travel for Fun & Profit: Make Money, Travel Free, Make New Friends, Live the Good Life! (Illus.). xvi, 352p. 2000. pap. 29.95 (*0-9670380-0-6*) E T C Pub Inc.

Meadows, Carolyn J., ed. see Meadows, Iris C.

Meadows, Carolyn Jean, jt. auth. see Culver Meadows, Iris.

Meadows, Cecil A. The Victorian Ironmonger. (Album Ser.: No. 32). (Illus.). 32p. 1989. pap. 5.25 (*0-85263-704-7*, Pub. by Shire Pubns) Parkwest Pubns.

Meadows, Charles T., jt. auth. see Meadows, A. J.

Meadows, Daniel. Set Pieces: Being about Film Stills, Mostly. (Illus.). 116p. (C). 1993. 52.95 (*0-85170-389-5*, Pub. by British Film Inst); pap. 22.95 (*0-85170-390-9*, Pub. by British Film Inst) Ind U Pr.

Meadows, David. Creative Sermon Designs: Adding Zest to Preaching. 1996. 11.95 (*1-55673-972-9*, Fairway Pr) CSS OH.

Meadows, Denis. Five Remarkable Englishmen. (Illus.). 1961. 10.00 (*0-8159-5506-5*) Devin.

— A Saint & a Half. 220p. 1963. 10.00 (*0-8159-6803-5*) Devin.

— A Short History of the Catholic Church. 246p. 1959. 14.95 (*0-8159-6813-2*) Devin.

M

Meadows, Donella H. The Global Citizen. LC 90-20899. 297p. 1991. pap. 17.95 (*1-55963-058-2*); text 30.00 (*1-55963-059-0*) Island Pr.

Meadows, Donella H., et al. Beyond the Limits. 300p. 1992. 19.95 (*0-614-02997-X*) Amer Forum.

— Beyond the Limits: Confronting Global Collapse, Envisioning a Sustainable Future. (Illus.). 320p. 1992. 19.95 (*0-930031-55-5*) Chelsea Green Pub.

— Beyond the Limits: Confronting Global Collapse, Envisioning a Sustainable Future. (Illus.). 320p. 1993. reprint ed. pap. 16.95 (*0-930031-62-8*) Chelsea Green Pub.

— Groping in the Dark: The First Decade of Global Modelling. fac. ed. LC 81-14713. (Illus.). 339p. 1994. pap. 105.10 (*0-7837-7660-8*, 204741300007) Bks Demand.

Meadows, Eddie S. Jazz Research & Performance Materials: A Select Annotated Bibliography. rev. ed. LC 95-20905. (Library of Music Ethnology: No. 4), 854p. 1995. text 100.00 (*0-8153-0373-4*, ML128) Garland.

— Theses & Dissertations on Black American Music. LC 80-128580. (Front Music Publications: No. 1). ii, 19p. (Orig.). 1980. pap. 5.00 (*0-934082-01-4*) Theodore Front.

Meadows, Eddie S., jt. auth. see Djedje, Jacqueline C.

Meadows, Edward S. U. S. Military Holsters & Pistol Cartridge Boxes. (Illus.). 432p. 1987. 45.00 (*0-9618191-0-3*) Ordnance Pubns.

Meadows, F. L. & Ames, J. M. Reed, Descendants of Reade or Reed: William Reade & Mabel (Kendall), His Wife; Supply Reed & Susannah (Byam), His Wife; John Reed & Rebecca (Bearce), His Wife. 285p. 1993. reprint ed. pap. 44.00 (*0-8328-3240-5*); reprint ed. lib. bdg. 54.00 (*0-8328-3239-1*) Higginson Bk Co.

Meadows, Ferguson B., Jr., et al. Using Guidance Skills in the Classroom. (Illus.). 314p. 1982. pap. 38.95 (*0-398-06283-8*) C C Thomas.

— Using Guidance Skills in the Classroom. (Illus.). 314p. (C). 1982. 51.95 (*0-398-04597-6*) C C Thomas.

Meadows, Graham. Animals Are Not Like Us Series, 4 bks. Incl. Cats. LC 98-18764. (Illus.). 24p. (J). (ps up). 1998. lib. bdg. 19.93 (*0-8368-2251-X*); Dogs. LC 98-18763. (Illus.). 24p. (J). (ps up). 1998. lib. bdg. 19.93 (*0-8368-2252-8*); Horses. LC 98-18761. (Illus.). 24p. (J). (ps up). 1998. lib. bdg. 19.93 (*0-8368-2253-6*); Pigs. LC 98-18762. (Illus.). 24p. (J). (ps up). 1998. lib. bdg. 19.93 (*0-8368-2254-4*); (Illus.). (YA). (ps up). 1998. Set lib. bdg. 79.73 (*0-8368-2250-1*) Gareth Stevens Inc.

Meadows, Iris C. Jenny of the Ozark Mountains: Growing up in Rural South Missouri in the 1920's & '30's. Meadows, Carolyn J., ed. LC 89-84927. (Illus.). 219p. (Orig.). 1989. pap. 5.95 (*0-9624710-0-3*) Culver-Meadows.

— Jenny of the Ozark Mountains: Growing up in Rural South Missouri in the '20s & '30s. 2nd ed. Meadows, Carolyn J., ed. LC 93-91477. (Illus.). 203p. 1993. 5.95 (*0-9624710-1-1*) Culver-Meadows.

Meadows, Iris C., jt. auth. see Hatch, Aileen M.

Meadows, Jack. The Great Scientists. (Illus.). 256p. 1987. 45.00 (*0-19-520620-7*) OUP.

— The Great Scientists. (Illus.). 256p. 1989. pap. 25.00 (*0-19-520815-3*) OUP.

— Innovation in Information: Twenty Years of the British Library Research & Development Department. LC 94-9975. (British Library Research). 175p. 1994. 40.00 (*1-85739-100-4*) Bowker-Saur.

— Project Elvyn: An Experiment in Electronic Journal Delivery. LC 94-185519. (British Library Research). 200p. 1995. 60.00 (*1-85739-161-6*) Bowker-Saur.

Meadows, Jack, ed. Information Technology & the Individual. 1992. text 57.50 (*0-86187-877-9*, Pub. by P P Pubs) Cassell & Continuum.

Meadows, Jack, jt. ed. see Rowland, Fytton.

Meadows, James D. Case Studies in Orthopaedic Physical Therapy. LC 98-49161. 264p. 1999. pap. 42.00 (*0-07-041235-9*) McGraw.

Meadows, James D. Geometric Dimensioning & Tolerancing: Applications & Techniques for Use in Design, Manufacturing, & Inspection. LC 95-12153. (Mechanical Engineering Ser.: Vol. 96). (Illus.). 624p. 1995. text 69.75 (*0-8247-9309-9*) Dekker.

Meadows, James D. Geometric Dimensioning & Tolerancing: Workbook & Answerbook. (Mechanical Engineering Ser.). (Illus.). 240p. 1997. text, wbk. ed. 29.95 (*0-8247-0076-7*) Dekker.

***Meadows, James D.** Jesse Jackson. LC 00-27575. (Illus.). (J). 2000. write for info. (*1-56766-742-2*) Childs World.

Meadows, Janice. The Antarctic. LC 95-125241. (World Bibliographical Ser.). 412p. 1994. lib. bdg. 87.50 (*1-85109-121-1*) ABC-CLIO.

Meadows, John, jt. auth. see Leask, Marilyn.

***Meadows, Julia.** Natural Bodycare: Recipes for Health & Beauty. (Illus.). 128p. 1999. pap. 14.95 (*0-8069-2487-X*) Sterling.

Meadows, Kenneth. Beaver. LC 97-42267. (Little Earth Medicine Library). 64p. 1998. 8.95 (*0-7894-2885-7*) DK Pub Inc.

***Meadows, Kenneth.** The Book of Rune Wisdom: How to Create & Read Your Own Runes. 2000. pap. 12.95 (*1-86204-392-2*) Element MA.

Meadows, Kenneth. Brown Bear. LC 97-42267. (Little Earth Medicine Library). 64p. 1998. 8.95 (*0-7894-2877-6*) DK Pub Inc.

— Crow. LC 97-42267. (Little Earth Medicine Library). 64p. 1998. 8.95 (*0-7894-2878-4*) DK Pub Inc.

— Deer. LC 97-42267. (Little Earth Medicine Library). 64p. 1998. 8.95 (*0-7894-2886-5*) DK Pub Inc.

— Earth Medicine: Revealing Hidden Teachings of the Native American Medicine Wheel. 1996. pap. 16.95 (*1-85230-668-8*, Pub. by Element MA) Penguin Putnam.

— Falcon. LC 97-42267. (Little Earth Medicine Library). 64p. 1998. 8.95 (*0-7894-2884-9*) DK Pub Inc.

— Goose. LC 97-42267. (Little Earth Medicine Library). 64p. 1998. 8.95 (*0-7894-2881-4*) DK Pub Inc.

— Medicine Way: How to Live the Teachings of the Native American Medicine Wheel: A Shamanic Path to Self-Mastery. 256p. 1997. pap. 17.95 (*1-86204-022-2*, Pub. by Element MA) Penguin Putnam.

— Otter. LC 97-42267. (Little Earth Medicine Library). 64p. 1998. 8.95 (*0-7894-2882-2*) DK Pub Inc.

— Owl. LC 97-42267. (Little Earth Medicine Library). 64p. 1998. 8.95 (*0-7894-2880-6*) DK Pub Inc.

— Rune Power: The Secret Knowledge of the Wise Ones. 208p. 1996. pap. 15.95 (*1-85230-706-4*, Pub. by Element MA) Penguin Putnam.

— Salmon. LC 97-42267. (Little Earth Medicine Library). 64p. 1998. 8.95 (*0-7894-2876-8*) DK Pub Inc.

— The Shamanic Experience: A Practical Guide to Shamanism for the New Millennium. (Illus.). 256p. 1993. pap. 15.95 (*1-85230-226-7*, Pub. by Element MA) Penguin Putnam.

— Snake. LC 97-42267. (Little Earth Medicine Library). 64p. 1998. 8.95 (*0-7894-2879-2*) DK Pub Inc.

— Where Eagles Fly: A Shamanic Way to Inner Wisdom. 1995. pap. 16.95 (*1-85230-620-3*, Pub. by Element MA) Penguin Putnam.

— Where Eagles Fly: A Shamanic Way to Personal Fulfillment. 272p. 1998. pap. 15.95 (*1-86204-284-5*, Pub. by Element MA) Penguin Putnam.

— Wolf. LC 97-42267. (Little Earth Medicine Library). 64p. 1998. 8.95 (*0-7894-2883-0*) DK Pub Inc.

— Woodpecker. (Little Earth Medicine Library). 64p. 1998. 8.95 (*0-7894-2875-X*) DK Pub Inc.

***Meadows, Lee E.** Above Suspicion. (Lincoln Keller Mystery Ser.). 432p. 2000. 24.95 (*1-882792-93-9*) Proctor Pubns.

Meadows, Lee E. Silent Conspiracy: A Lincoln Keller Mystery. LC 96-72290. 270p. 1997. 24.95 (*1-882792-38-6*) Proctor Pubns.

Meadows, Leon R. A Study of the Teaching of English Composition in Teachers Colleges of the United States, with a Suggested Course of Procedure. LC 78-177066. (Columbia University. Teachers College. Contributions to Education Ser.: No. 311). reprint ed. 37.50 (*0-404-55311-7*) AMS Pr.

Meadows, Matthew. Pablo Picasso. (Art for Young People Ser.). (Illus.). 32p. (J). 1996. 14.95 (*0-8069-6160-0*) Sterling.

***Meadows, Michael E.** Voices in the Wilderness: Indigenous Australians & the News Media, 59. (Contributions to the Study of Mass Media & Communications Ser.: Vol. 59). 224p. 2000. 64.00 (*0-313-31566-3*, Greenwood Pr) Greenwood.

Meadows, Michael E. & Sala, Maria, eds. Soil Erosion & Land Degradation in Regions of Mediterranean. (Zeitschrift fuer Geomorphologie - Annals of Geomorphology Ser.: Supplementband 107). (Illus.). vi, 93p. 1996. pap. 37.00 (*3-443-21107-0*, Pub. by Gebruder Borntraeger) Balogh.

***Meadows, Mike.** GPS for VFR: A Practical GPS Guide for VFR Pilots. (Illus.). 2000. 19.95 (*0-615-11108-4*) M Meadows.

Meadows, N., et al, eds. Petroleum Geology of the Irish Sea & Adjacent Areas. (Geological Society Special Publication Ser.: No. 124). (Illus.). 408p. 1997. 125.00 (*1-897799-84-5*, Pub. by Geol Soc Pub Hse) AAPG.

Meadows, Patrick A. Francis Ponge & the Nature of Things: From Ancient Atomism to a Modern Poetics. LC 97-6998. 176p. 1997. 32.50 (*0-8387-5360-4*) Bucknell U Pr.

Meadows, Peter, ed. The Indus River: Biodiversity, Resources, Humankind. (Illus.). 500p. 1999. text 54.00 (*0-19-577905-3*) OUP.

Meadows, Robert J. Understanding Violence & Victims. LC 97-40881. 220p. 1998. pap. 46.00 (*0-13-452129-3*) P-H.

***Meadows, Robert J.** What Price for Blood: Murder & Justice in Saudi Arabia. LC 99-66905. 224p. 2000. 21.95 (*1-885003-31-5*, Pub. by R D Reed Pubs) Midpt Trade.

Meadows, Rose. The Christmas Rebellion. large type ed. 1995. 27.99 (*0-7089-3435-8*) Ulverscroft.

— The Crinoline Empress. large type ed. (Large Print Ser.). 304p. 1996. 27.99 (*0-7089-3574-5*) Ulverscroft.

— Pretty Maids All in a Row. large type ed. (Linford Romance Library). 368p. 1997. pap. 16.99 (*0-7089-7985-8*, Linford) Ulverscroft.

— Remember the Valiant. large type ed. (Large Print Ser.). 304p. 1996. 27.99 (*0-7089-3654-7*) Ulverscroft.

— Slander Most Savage. large type ed. (Large Print Ser.). 320p. 1997. 27.99 (*0-7089-3688-1*) Ulverscroft.

Meadows, Roy W., ed. see Hatch, Aileen M. & Meadows, Iris C.

Meadows, Sandy, jt. auth. see Blair, George.

Meadows, Sara. The Child As Thinker: The Development & Acquisition of Cognition in Childhood. LC 92-40457. 480p. (C). 1993. pap. 27.99 (*0-415-01143-4*, B0777) Routledge.

— Parenting Behaviour & Children's Cognitive Development. (Essays in Developmental Psychology Ser.). 160p. 1996. pap. 19.95 (*0-86377-403-2*) Psychol Pr.

***Meadows, Shane & Fraser, Paul.** A Room for Romeo Brass. (Illus.). 196p. 2000. pap. 14.95 (*1-901680-45-2*, Pub. by ScreenPr Bks) Midpt Trade.

Meadows, Susan, tr. from ITA. Where Muses Dwell. LC 96-71418. (Illus.). 192p. 1997. 55.00 (*0-8478-2027-0*, Pub. by Rizzoli Intl) St Martin.

Meadows, Taylor. The Confessions of a Thug. LC 98-909886. 1988. reprint ed. 17.50 (*81-206-0330-3*, Pub. by Asian Educ Servs) S Asia.

— Tippoo Sultan: A Tale of Mysore War. 460p. 1986. reprint ed. 22.00 (*0-8364-1734-8*, Pub. by Usha) S Asia.

Meadows, William C. Kiowa, Apache & Comanche Military Societies. LC 98-49958. 576p. 1999. 65.00 (*0-292-75212-1*) U of Tex Pr.

Meads, Geoff. Oceans Without Continents. LC 97-9200. 1997. write for info. (*1-85775-270-8*, Radcliffe Med Pr) Scovill Paterson.

— The Unsupported Middle: Future Developments in a Primary Care-LED NHS. LC 97-5138. 1997. write for info. (*1-85775-109-4*, Radcliffe Med Pr) Scovill Paterson.

Meads, Geoff, ed. Future Options for General Practice: Primary Care Development. 1995. write for info. (*1-85775-079-9*, Radcliffe Med Pr) Scovill Paterson.

Meads, Kat. Born Southern & Restless. LC 96-25366. (Emerging Writers in Creative Nonfiction Ser.). 220p. 1996. 24.95 (*0-8207-0275-7*); pap. text 16.95 (*0-8207-0276-5*) Duquesne.

Meads, M. J. The Weta Book. (Illus.). 36p. 1990. pap. 12.50 (*0-477-02585-4*) Balogh.

Meads, Roger F., ed. see Griffin, Julie.

***Meads, Sue & Brown, Faye.** ICD-10 Coding Fundamentals. 2nd ed. LC 99-19557. (Illus.). 240p. 1999. pap. 34.95 (*1-57066-134-0*) Practice Mgmt Info.

Meads, Sue & Brown, Faye. ICD-10 Coding Fundamentals: A Comprehensive Coding Guide for Healthcare Professionals. LC 97-20325. (Illus.). 250p. 1997. text 44.95 (*1-57066-115-4*, ME081) Practice Mgmt Info.

Meadwell, Kenneth W. L' Avalee des Avales, l'Hiver De Force et les Enfantomes De Rejean Ducharme: Une Fiction Mot a Mot et Sa Litterarite. LC 90-20062. (Canadian Studies: Vol. 11). (FRE.). 284p. 1990. lib. bdg. 89.95 (*0-88946-382-4*) E Mellen.

Meager. Gene Therapy Technologies & Regulations: From Laboratory to Clinic. LC 99-15301. 438p. 1999. 150.00 (*0-471-96709-2*) Wiley.

Meager, Tony. The Molecular Biology of Cytokines. LC 97-44184. (Molecular Medical Science Ser.). 422p. 1998. 159.95 (*0-471-98272-5*) Wiley.

Meagher. Crime & Justice in America. (C). 1996. pap. text 49.00 (*0-15-501290-8*) Harcourt Coll Pubs.

— Criminal Justice in America. (C). 1996. pap. text, teacher ed. 6.00 (*0-15-501508-7*) Harcourt.

— Critical Reading Handbook. (C). 1996. pap. text, teacher ed. 28.00 (*0-15-503060-4*) Harcourt Coll Pubs.

Meagher, et al. Doctors & Hospitals: Legal Duties. 464p. 1991. boxed set 81.00 (*0-409-89767-1*, MICHIE) LEXIS Pub.

— History of Tioga County. (Illus.). 1186p. 1989. reprint ed. lib. bdg. 109.00 (*0-8328-0577-7*) Higginson Bk Co.

Meagher, Christine A. Satellite Regulatory Compendium. LC 85-206066. 1985. 197.00 (*0-934960-26-7*) Phillips Business.

***Meagher, David K.** As It Is Said: A Selected, Annotated Bibliography in Death & Dying. 2nd rev. ed. 104p. 1999. reprint ed. spiral bd. 16.00i (*0-930194-58-6*) Ctr Thanatology.

***Meagher, Denise.** Wings for Honey. (Illus.). 32p. (J). 2000. 22.95 (*1-57532-205-6*) Press-Tige Pub.

Meagher, Don. Handbook for Critical Reading. LC 96-75655. 240p. (C). 1996. pap. text 19.50 (*0-15-503057-4*, Pub. by Harcourt Coll Pubs) Harcourt.

Meagher, Ellen, jt. auth. see Kahn, Renee.

Meagher, F. Robert. Law & Social Change: Indo-American Reflection. (C). 1988. 110.00 (*0-7855-3672-8*) St Mut.

Meagher, Jack & Boughton, Pat. Sportsmassage: A Complete Program for Increasing Performance in Fifteen Popular Exercises. rev. ed. (Illus.). 224p. 1990. pap. 16.95 (*0-88268-096-X*) Station Hill Pr.

Meagher, James L. How Christ Said the First Mass or the Lord's Last Supper. LC 82-74246. 438p. 1985. reprint ed. pap. 18.50 (*0-89555-207-8*) TAN Bks Pubs.

Meagher, John C. Clumsy Construction in Mark's Gospel: A Critique of Form & Redaktionsgeschichte. LC 79-66373. (Toronto Studies in Theology: Vol. 3). 178p. 1979. lib. bdg. 79.95 (*0-88946-876-1*) E Mellen.

— Shakespeare's Shakespeare: How the Plays Were Made. LC 74-78439. 240p. 1997. 34.50 (*0-8264-1007-3*) Continuum.

***Meagher, John C.** Shakespeare's Shakespeare: How the Plays Were Made. 240p. 1999. pap. 19.95 (*0-8264-1202-5*) Continuum.

Meagher, Judy, jt. auth. see Novelli, Joan.

Meagher, Justice. Equity: Doctrines & Remedies. 1992. boxed set 162.00 (*0-614-05470-2*, Austral, MICHIE) LEXIS Pub.

— Equity: Doctrines & Remedies. 3rd ed. 1992. pap. 119.00 (*0-409-30187-6*, Austral, MICHIE) LEXIS Pub.

Meagher, Linda D. & Devine, Thomas G. Handbook of College Teaching. LC 91-14532. 300p. (C). 1993. text 35.00 (*0-89341-637-1*, Longwood Academic); pap. text 18.50 (*0-89341-638-X*, Longwood Academic) Hollowbrook.

— The Reading Connection: Reading Skills & College Success. 1997. teacher ed. 11.18 (*0-256-23156-7*, Irwn McGrw-H) McGrw-H Hghr Educ.

Meagher, Linda D., jt. auth. see Devine, Thomas.

Meagher, Linda D., jt. auth. see Devine, Thomas G.

Meagher, Mark, et al. Frommer's Ireland from $50 a Day. 17th ed. 592p. 1998. 18.95 (*0-02-862046-1*, Pub. by Macmillan) S&S Trade.

Meagher, Mary. Yellowstone & the Biology of Time Photographs Across a Century. 1999. pap. text 32.95 (*0-8061-3006-7*) U of Okla Pr.

Meagher, Mary & Houston, Doug. Yellowstone & the Biology of Time: Photographs Across a Century. LC 97-40591. (Illus.). 304p. 1998. 80.00 (*0-8061-2996-4*) U of Okla Pr.

Meagher, Mary E. Vignettes Unveiled: Memos from the Twentieth Century. 1997. pap. write for info. (*1-57553-436-3*) Watermrk Pr.

Meagher, Paul K., jt. auth. see Vann, Gerald.

Meagher, R. P. & Gummow, Justice. Jacobs' Law of Trusts in Australia. 5th ed. 1986. 116.00 (*0-409-49076-8*, AT, MICHIE); pap. 94.00 (*0-409-49079-2*, AT, MICHIE) LEXIS Pub.

Meagher, R. P. & Gummow, W. M. Jacobs' Law of Trusts in Australia. 6th ed. LC 97-179672. 1008p. 1996. write for info. (*0-409-30537-5*, MICHIE) LEXIS Pub.

Meagher, R. P., et al. Equity Doctrines & Remedies. 3rd ed. 1992. pap. text 119.00 (*0-614-05551-2*, Austral, MICHIE); boxed set 162.00 (*0-409-30186-8*, Austral, MICHIE) LEXIS Pub.

***Meagher, Robert.** Frommer's Ireland 2001. (Illus.). 2000. pap. 19.99 (*0-7645-6135-9*) IDG Bks.

Meagher, Robert. Survey of Document Imaging Systems in Local Government. 82p. 1997. pap. 42.00 (*0-933887-73-6*, A4505) ARMA Intl.

Meagher, Robert E. Helen. LC 85-16480. (Illus.). 144p. 1986. pap. text 14.95 (*0-87023-506-0*) U of Mass Pr.

— Helen: Myth, Legend & the Culture of Misogyny. 224p. 1995. 29.50 (*0-8264-0850-8*) Continuum.

Meagher, Robert E., tr. from GEC. Euripides Iphigenia at Aulis & Iphigenia in Taurus. 176p. 1993. 16.00 (*0-86516-266-2*) Bolchazy-Carducci.

Meagher, Robert E., ed. see Augustine, Saint.

Meagher, Robert E., tr. see Aeschylus.

Meagher, Robert E., tr. see Euripides.

Meagher, Robert E., tr. & comment see Euripides.

Meagher, Robert E., tr. & intro. see Euripides.

Meagher, Robert F. Law & Social Change Indo-American Reflections. (C). 1988. 100.00 (*0-89771-287-0*) St Mut.

***Meagher, Timothy J.** Inventing Irish America: Generation, Class, & Ethnic Identity in a New England City, 1880-1928. LC 00-30255. (Irish in America Ser.). 472p. 2000. pap. 22.00 (*0-268-03154-1*); lib. bdg. 50.00 (*0-268-03153-3*) U of Notre Dame Pr.

Meagher, Timothy J., ed. From Paddy to Studs: Irish American Communities in the Turn of the Century Era, 1880-1920, 13. LC 85-27304. (Contributions in Ethnic Studies: No. 13). 216p. 1986. 57.95 (*0-313-24670-X*, MPD/, Greenwood Pr) Greenwood.

Meagher, Timothy J., jt. ed. see Bayor, Ronald H.

Meah, M. N., ed. see Tice, P. A., et al.

Meahdra, Michael, jt. auth. see Weingarten, Jan.

***Meahl, Elizabeth.** Snack Art: Creative Kids. (Illus.). 160p. 1999. pap., teacher ed. 14.95 (*1-57690-318-4*, TCM2318) Tchr Create Mat.

Meaker, Gerald H. The Revolutionary Left in Spain, 1914-1923. LC 73-80622. xii, 564p. 1974. 62.50 (*0-8047-0845-2*) Stanford U Pr.

— The Revolutionary Left in Spain, 1914-1923. LC 73-80622. 576p. 1974. reprint ed. pap. 30.00 (*0-608-00525-8*, 206140400007) Bks Demand.

Meakin, Annette M. Ribbon of Iron. LC 70-115540. (Russia Observed, Series I). 1970. reprint ed. 20.95 (*0-405-03050-9*) Ayer.

— Russia: Travels & Studies. LC 72-115565. (Russia Observed Ser.). (Illus.). 1971. reprint ed. 35.95 (*0-405-03086-X*) Ayer.

Meakin, B. The Land of the Moors. 490p. 1986. 350.00 (*1-85077-100-6*, Pub. by Darf Pubs Ltd) St Mut.

***Meakin, David, ed.** Vian: L'Ecume des Jours. 80p. 1999. pap. 35.00 (*0-85261-528-0*, Pub. by U of Glasgow) St Mut.

Meakin, David, ed. & intro. see Robbe-Grillet, Alain.

Meakin, H. L. John Donne's Articulations of the Feminine. LC 98-26941. (Oxford English Monographs). 288p. 1999. text 65.00 (*0-19-818455-7*) OUP.

Meakin, J. D., jt. ed. see Coutts, T. J.

Meakin, J. O., jt. ed. see Coutts, J.

Meakin, Paul. Fractals, Scaling & Growth Far from Equilibrium. LC 96-44263. (Nonlinear Science Ser.: Vol. 5). (Illus.). 688p. (C). 1998. text 125.00 (*0-521-45253-8*) Cambridge U Pr.

Meakin, Paul, et al, eds. Fractal Aspects of Materials. (MRS Symposium Proceedings Ser.: Vol. 367). 534p. 1995. 89.00 (*1-55899-268-5*, 367) Materials Res.

Meakin, W. The New Industrial Revolution. Wilkins, Mira, ed. LC 76-29998. (European Business Ser.). 1977. reprint ed. lib. bdg. 25.95 (*0-405-09756-5*) Ayer.

Meakins, G. D. Functional Groups: Characteristics & Interconversions. (Oxford Chemistry Primers Ser.: No. 35). (Illus.). 98p. (C). 1996. pap. text 12.95 (*0-19-855867-8*) OUP.

Meakins, Jonathan L., ed. Surgical Infections: Diagnosis & Treatment. LC 93-29195. (Illus.). 500p. (C). 1993. text 89.00 (*0-89454-016-5*) Sci Am Medicine.

Mealand, David L., jt. auth. see Guting, Eberhard W.

Meale, Carol M., ed. Readings in Medieval English Romance. LC 93-47652. 246p. (C). 1994. 60.00 (*0-85991-404-6*, DS Brewer) Boydell & Brewer.

— Women & Literature in Britain, 1150-1500. 2nd ed. (Illus.). 233p. 1997. pap. text 19.95 (*0-521-57620-2*) Cambridge U Pr.

Mealer, Cathy, ed. see Lansing, David.

Mealer, Tamara. My World in French. (My World in...Coloring Book Ser.). (FRE., Illus.). 96p. (J). 1994. pap. 4.95 (*0-8442-1393-4*, 13934, Natl Textbk Co) NTC Contemp Pub Co.

— My World in German Coloring Book. LC 97-43146. (My World in...Coloring Book Ser.). (GER., Illus.). 96p. (J). 1994. pap. 4.95 (*0-8442-2169-4*, 21694, Natl Textbk Co) NTC Contemp Pub Co.

— My World in Italian Coloring Book. (ITA., Illus.). 96p. (J). (ps-3). 1994. pap. 4.95 (*0-8442-8067-4*, 80674, Natl Textbk Co) NTC Contemp Pub Co.

— My World in Spanish Coloring Book. (SPA., Illus.). 96p. (J). 1994. pap. 4.95 (*0-8442-7552-2*, 75522, Natl Textbk Co) NTC Contemp Pub Co.

An Asterisk (*) at the beginning of an entry indicates that the title is appearing for the first time.

Mealey, Andrew N. Future Sight: Biblical Prophecy of the End Times Focused on Major Events & Entities. (Illus.). 224p. (Orig.). 1997. pap. 14.95 (*0-9656384-4-8*) NorRem Pub.

— Last Exodus: Every Race, People, & Tribe Inherit God's Promised Land. (Illus.). 224p. (Orig.). 1997. pap. 14.95 (*0-9656384-6-4*) NorRem Pub.

Mealey, Catherine E. Best of Wyoming. xvi, 203p. 1990. pap. 12.95 (*0-9627054-0-3*) Meadowlark Wy.

***Mealey, Linda R.** Sex Differences: Development & Evolutionary Strategies. LC 99-62784. 458p. 1999. 69.95 (*0-12-487460-6*) Acad Pr.

Mealiea, Laird W. Skills for Managers in Organizations. LC 94-1347. (C). 1994. text 21.50 (*0-256-15948-3*, Irwn McGrw-H) McGrw-H Hghr Educ.

Mealiea, Laird W. & Latham, Gary P. Skills for Managerial Success: Theory, Experience, & Practice. LC 95-12121. 544p. (C). 1995. text 41.50 (*0-256-12454-X*, Irwn McGrw-H) McGrw-H Hghr Educ.

Mealing, Ronald W. On Vol. 1: A Book of Poetry. deluxe limited large type ed. LC 96-984788. 314p. 1996. 49.95 (*0-9654293-3-4*) R Mealing Ent.

— On Vol. 1: A Book of Poetry. limited large type ed. LC 96-984788. 314p. 1996. 34.95 (*0-9654293-0-X*) R Mealing Ent.

Mealing, S. R., ed. The Jesuit Relations & Allied Documents: A Selection. 169p. reprint ed. pap. text 10.95 (*0-88629-037-6*, Pub. by McG-Queens Univ Pr) CUP Services.

Mealing, Stuart. The Art & Science of Computer Animation. (Illus.). 308p. (Orig.). 1992. text 39.95 (*1-871516-16-1*, Pub. by Intellect) Cromland.

— Mac3D: Three Dimensional Modeling & Rendering on the Macintosh. (Illus.). 246p. (Orig.). 1994. pap. text 34.95 (*1-871516-46-3*, Pub. by Intellect) Cromland.

Mealing, Stuart, et al. Principles of Modelling & Rendering with 3D Studio. LC 98-4539. 1998. 69.00 (*90-265-1523-5*) Swets.

Mealing, Stuart, jt. ed. see Dudley, Esther.

Meals, Hank, jt. auth. see Lamela, Susan.

Meals, Jim. The Price of Sparrows. Date not set. pap. 15.95 (*0-934468-50-8*) Gaslight.

Meals, Robert W. All Flesh Is Vulnerable. 1986. write for info. (*0-935087-15-X*) Wright Pub Co.

Meals, Roy A. Hand Surgery Review. 4th ed. 153p. 1995. pap. text 28.95 (*0-942219-82-1*) Quality Med Pub.

— 100 Orthopaedic Conditions Every Doctor Should Understand. (Illus.). 328p. 1992. pap. 36.00 (*0-942219-37-6*) Quality Med Pub.

Meals, Roy A. & Lesavoy, Malcolm A. Hand Surgery Review. 2nd ed. LC 85-3677. 364p. pap. 112.90 (*0-8357-7860-6*, 203627700002) Bks Demand.

Mealy, Doug. Put Yourself on the Fast Track: A Guide for Supervisors & Managers Who Want to Get Promoted. LC 84-28648. (Illus.). 104p. 1986. pap. 12.95 (*0-88280-110-4*) ETC Pubns.

Mealy, J. Webb. After the Thousand Years: Resurrection & Judgment in Revelation 20. (JSNT Supplement Ser.: No. 70). 273p. (C). 1992. 75.00 (*1-85075-363-6*, Pub. by Sheffield Acad) CUP Services.

Mealy, Norman & Rock, Judith. Music, Dance & Religion: The Performing Arts in Worship. (Illus.). 192p. 1985. 15.95 (*0-13-607219-4*); pap. 8.95 (*0-13-607201-1*) P-H.

Mealy, Virginia T. Newbery Books. 2nd ed. (Illus.). 128p. 1991. pap. 12.95 (*1-879287-02-1*, BL012) Pieces of Lrning.

Meana, Janet, jt. auth. see Mcgrath, Gerald.

Meaney. Childhood Stress. 2000. pap. text. write for info. (*0-7167-3663-2*) St Martin.

Meaney, Carron, jt. ed. see Bekoff, Marc A.

Meaney, Clare, et al. A Home for Lady Liberty. Ellington, Darcy, ed. (Illus.). 26p. 1995. 15.95 (*1-880352-40-0*) Albion Pub.

Meaney, Constance S. Stability & the Industrial Elite in China & the Soviet Union. LC 87-83158. (China Research Monographs: No. 34). ix, 158p. 1988. pap. 15.00 (*0-912966-98-X*) IEAS.

Meaney, F. J., jt. auth. see Davis, M.

Meaney, Gerardine. Sex & Nation: Women in Irish Culture & Politics. (C). 1989. 60.00 (*1-85594-015-9*) St Mut.

Meaney, Helen E. My True Feelings. 1998. pap. write for info. (*1-57553-763-X*) Watermrk Pr.

Meaney, James A. How to Buy a Franchise: An Experienced Franchise Lawyer Shows How to Find, Evaluate & Negotiate for the Right Franchise. rev. ed. LC 98-30264. (New Entrepreneur Ser.). 218p. 1999. pap. 14.95 (*0-87576-217-4*) Pilot Bks.

Meaney, John W. O'Malley of Notre Dame. LC 90-50968. (Orig.). 1991. pap. text 13.00 (*0-268-01505-8*) U of Notre Dame Pr.

Meaney, Mark E. Capital As Organic Unity: The Role of Hegel's "Science of Logic" in Marx's "Grundrisse" 264p. 1998. 55.00 (*0-391-04053-7*) Humanities.

Meaney, Terence. Working Windows: A Guide to the Repair & Restoration of Wood Windows. LC 98-10244. (Illus.). 128p. 1998. pap. 14.95 (*1-55821-707-X*) Lyons Pr.

Meanley, Brooke. Birdlife at Chincoteague: And the Virginia Barrier Islands. LC 79-27187. (Illus.). 128p. 1981. pap. 7.95 (*0-87033-257-0*, Tidewtr Pubs) Cornell Maritime.

— Birds & Marshes of the Chesapeake Bay Country. LC 75-17558. (Illus.). 172p. 1975. pap. 8.95 (*0-87033-207-4*, Tidewtr Pubs) Cornell Maritime.

— Blackwater. LC 78-35. 160p. 1978. reprint ed. pap. 49.60 (*0-608-02465-1*, 206310900004) Bks Demand.

— The Great Dismal Swamp. (Illus.). 39p. 1973. 1.50 (*0-318-20251-4*) Audubon Naturalist.

Meanley, John A., ed. Maritime Services Directory, 1995. 960p. 1995. pap. 89.00 (*0-9623031-2-7*) Aegis Pubns.

— Maritime Services Directory, 1999. 1999. pap. 95.00 (*0-9623031-7-8*) Aegis Pubns.

Meanor, Patrick. Bruce Chatwin. LC 97-10211. 1997. 32.00 (*0-8057-4568-8*, Twyne) Mac Lib Ref.

— John Cheever Revisited. LC 94-11347. (Twayne's United States Authors Ser.: No. 647). 232p. 1994. 32.00 (*0-8057-3999-8*, Twyne) Mac Lib Ref.

***Means & Henson.** Communication for the Workplace. (C). 1999. pap. 15.50 (*0-538-72355-6*); pap., student ed. 25.50 (*0-538-72356-4*) Thomson Learn.

Means, jt. auth. see Henson.

Means, Alexander. Diary for 1861. (American Autobiography Ser.). 46p. 1995. reprint ed. lib. bdg. 69.00 (*0-7812-8588-7*) Rprt Serv.

Means, Anthony R. Calcium Regulation of Cellular Function, No. 30. (Advances in Second Messenger & Phosphoprotein Research Ser.: Vol. 30). (Illus.). 404p. 1994. text 110.00 (*0-7817-0233-X*) Lppncott W & W.

Means, Anthony R. & O'Malley, Bert W. Hormone Action Pt. G: Calmodulin & Calcium-Binding Proteins. (Methods in Enzymology Ser.: Vol. 102). 1983. text 188.00 (*0-12-182002-5*) Acad Pr.

Means, Anthony R., jt. ed. see Conn, P. Michael.

Means, Barbara. Technology & Education Reform. 196p. 1997. pap. 14.00 (*0-16-048882-6*) USGPO.

Means, Barbara, ed. Technology & Education Reform: The Reality Behind the Promise. LC 93-45336. (Education Ser.). 256p. 1994. text 32.95 (*1-55542-625-5*) Jossey-Bass.

Means, Barbara, et al, eds. Teaching Advanced Skills to At-Risk Students: Views from Research & Practice. 2nd ed. LC 91-21683. (Education-Higher Education Ser.). 317p. 1991. text 36.45 (*1-55542-393-0*) Jossey-Bass.

Means, Barbara & Olson, Kerry. Technology & Education Reform: Studies of Education Reform. (Illus.). 180p. 1998. pap. text 25.00 (*0-7881-2632-6*) DIANE Pub.

Means, Barbara, jt. auth. see Cole, Michael.

Means, Beth & Lindner, Lindy. Teaching Writing in Middle School: Tips, Tricks, & Techniques. LC 97-39412. (Illus.). 160p. 1998. pap. 23.00 (*1-56308-562-3*) Libs Unl.

Means Coleman, Robin R. African American Viewers & the Black Situation Comedy: Situating Racial Humor. LC 98-35902. (Studies in African American History & Culture). xvii, 349 p. 1998. 70.00 (*0-8153-3125-8*) Garland.

***Means Coleman, Robin R.** African American Viewers & the Black Situation Comedy: Situating Racial Humor. LC 99-53437. (Studies in African American History & Culture). 2000. 20.00 (*0-8153-3781-7*) Garland.

***Means, David.** Assorted Fire Events: Stories. 256p. 2000. 22.00 (*1-893956-05-9*, Pub. by Context Bks) Publishers Group.

Means, Dennis R. E. A. Bartlett's Nantasket Beach: A Pictorial Introduction to Hull, Massachusetts During the 1890s. (Illus.). 80p. (Orig.). 1995. pap. 19.95 (*0-943361-01-X*) Means Library.

Means, Eldred K. Black Fortune. LC 72-4739. (Black Heritage Library Collection). 1977. reprint ed. 27.95 (*0-8369-9110-9*) Ayer.

— E. K. Means: Negro Stories. 1977. 20.95 (*0-8369-9190-7*, 9059) Ayer.

— Further E. K. Means. LC 72-4648. (Black Heritage Library Collection). (Illus.). 1977. reprint ed. 31.95 (*0-8369-9111-7*) Ayer.

— More E. K. Means. LC 72-4738. (Black Heritage Library Collection). (Illus.). 1977. reprint ed. 32.95 (*0-8369-9112-5*) Ayer.

Means, Elizabeth R. The Dream Spoilers: A Quadriplegic's Nightmare. LC 97-123443. (Orig.). 1996. pap. 12.95 (*0-9652561-0-3*) Pelican Pr CA.

***Means, Elizabeth R.** The Youngest Hobos: A Story of Survival. 150p. (YA). (gr. 4-12). 2000. pap. write for info. (*0-9652561-2-X*) Pelican Pr CA.

Means, Evan. Hiking Tennessee Trails: Hikes along the Appalachian Trail, Natchez Trace, Cumberland Trail, John Muir Trail, Over Mountain Victory Trail. 5th ed. Brown, Robert, ed. (Illus.). 160p. 1998. pap. 12.95 (*0-7627-0225-7*) Globe Pequot.

Means, Florence C. The Moved-Outers. LC 92-13706. 156p. (J). 1993. pap. 6.95 (*0-8027-7386-9*) Walker & Co.

Means, Florence G. But What, My Dear, Do You Know about Hotels? And Other Stories about Old Times in Colorado. Mason, Lorna C., ed. (Illus.). 144p. (Orig.). 1992. pap. 8.95 (*0-944720-02-1*) Greenridge Pr.

Means, Gardiner C. A Monetary Theory of Employment. Samuels, Warren J. & Lee, Frederic S., eds. LC 94-26135. (Studies in Institutional Economics Ser.). 292p. (C). (gr. 13). 1994. text 81.95 (*1-56324-477-2*) M E Sharpe.

— A Monetary Theory of Employment. Samuels, Warren J. & Lee, Frederic S., eds. LC 94-26135. (Studies in Institutional Economics). 292p. (gr. 13). 1994. pap. text 40.95 (*1-56324-478-0*) M E Sharpe.

— Pricing Power & the Public Interest: A Study Based on Steel. LC 75-39260. (Getting & Spending: The Consumer's Dilemma Ser.). (Illus.). 1976. reprint ed. 31.95 (*0-405-08033-6*) Ayer.

Means, Gardiner C., jt. auth. see Berle, Adolf A.

Means, Gardiner C., jt. auth. see Berle, Adolf A., Jr.

Means, Gay G. The Guy Mannering Letters of Henry Watkins Allen: A Journey Through the South in 1853. 1985. 10.00 (*0-940981-25-3*) Univ LA Lafayette.

Means, Gordon P. Malaysian Politics: The Second Generation. (South-East Asian Social Science Monographs). (Illus.). 388p. 1991. 65.00 (*0-19-588983-5*) OUP.

***Means, Grady & Schneider, David.** MetaCapitalism: The E-Business Revolution & the Design of 21st Century Companies & markets. 160p. 2000. 24.95 (*0-471-39335-5*) Wiley.

Means, Howard. Colin Powell. 352p. 1993. mass mkt. 5.99 (*0-345-38381-8*) Ballantine Pub Grp.

— C.s.a.--confederate States of America: A Novel. LC 98-27461. 352p. 1998. 24.00 (*0-688-16187-1*, Wm Morrow) Morrow Avon.

***Means, J. Jeffrey & Nelson, Mary Ann.** Trauma & Evil: Healing the Wounded Soul. 2000. pap. 20.00 (*0-8006-3270-2*, Fortress Pr) Augsburg Fortress.

Means, Jeffery L. & Hinchee, Robert E., eds. Emerging Technology for Bioremediation of Metals 2(4) LC 94-2906. 160p. 1994. lib. bdg. 85.00 (*1-56670-085-X*, L1085) Lewis Pubs.

***Means, Jeffrey L. & Hinchee, Robert E., eds.** Wetlands & Remediation: An International Conference, Salt Lake City, Utah, November 16-17, 1999. LC 99-57261. (Illus.). 450p. 2000. 79.95 (*1-57477-089-6*) Battelle.

Means, Jeffrey L., et al. The Application of Solidification-Stabilization to Waste Materials. 368p. 1994. lib. bdg. 85.00 (*1-56670-080-9*, L1080) Lewis Pubs.

— Remedial Options for Metals-Contaminated Sites. LC 95-14984. 240p. 1995. lib. bdg. 85.00 (*1-56670-180-5*, L1180) Lewis Pubs.

Means, Jeffrey L., jt. auth. see Smith, Lawrence.

Means, Jim. A Lesser People: America's Real Problem. 104p. (Orig.). 1997. pap. 9.95 (*1-880710-03-X*) Monterey Pacific.

Means, John. Maryland's Catoctin Mountain Parks: An Interpretive Guide to Catoctin Mountain Park & Cunningham Falls State Park. (Illus.). 174p. (Orig.). 1995. pap. text 14.95 (*0-939923-38-6*) M & W Pub Co.

Means, Laurel, ed. Medieval Lunar Astrology: A Collection of Representative Middle English Texts. LC 93-22743. 372p. 1993. text 99.95 (*0-7734-9299-2*) E Mellen.

Means, Louis S. The Quality of Mercy. LC 97-101664. 320p. (Orig.). 1996. pap. write for info. (*0-9652561-1-1*) Pelican Pr CA.

Means, Marie H. A Tentative Standardization of a Hard Opposites Test. (Psychological Monographs General & Applied: Vol. 30). 1974. reprint ed. pap. 36.00 (*0-8115-1429-3*) Periodicals Srv.

***Means, Marsha.** Living with Your Husband's Secret Wars. LC 99-41564. 224p. 1999. pap. 10.99 (*0-8007-5710-6*) Revell.

Means, Michael H. The Consolatio Genre in Medieval English Literature. LC 73-178985. (University of Florida Humanities Monographs: No. 36). 114p. reprint ed. pap. 35.40 (*0-7837-4966-X*, 204463200004) Bks Demand.

Means, Patrick A. Men's Secret Wars. LC 96-16252. (Illus.). 256p. (gr. 10). 1996. 15.99 (*0-8007-1721-X*) Revell.

***Means, Patrick A.** Men's Secret Wars. 288p. 1999. pap. 10.99 (*0-8007-5717-3*) Revell.

Means, Philip A. Ancient Civilization of the Andes. LC 64-8175. 586p. 1964. reprint ed. 80.00 (*0-87752-072-0*) Gordian.

— Biblioteca Andina, Pt. One: The Chroniclers, or, the Writers of the Sixteenth & Seventeenth Centuries Who Treated of the Pre-Hispanic History & Culture of the Andean Countries. (Connecticut Academy of Arts & Sciences Ser., Trans.: Vol. 29). 1928. pap. 100.00 (*0-685-22806-1*) Elliots Bks.

— Fall of the Inca Empire & the Spanish Rule in Peru, 1530-1780. LC 64-8176. (Illus.). 351p. 1964. reprint ed. 80.00 (*0-87752-073-9*) Gordian.

— History of the Spanish Conquest of Yucatan & of the Itzas. (HU PMP Ser.). (Illus.). 1917. 30.00 (*0-527-01210-6*) Periodicals Srv.

— Spanish Main: Focus of Envy, 1492-1700. LC 65-24994. (Illus.). 278p. 1965. reprint ed. 75.00 (*0-87752-074-7*) Gordian.

— A Study of Andean Social Institutions. (Connecticut Academy of Arts & Sciences Ser., Trans.: Vol. 27). 1925. pap. 69.50 (*0-685-22815-0*) Elliots Bks.

— A Survey of Ancient Peruvian Art. (Connecticut Academy of Arts & Sciences Ser., Trans.: Vol. 21). 1917. pap. 75.00 (*0-685-44363-9*) Elliots Bks.

Means, R. S., Co. Engineering Staff, jt. ed. see Reynolds, Donald E.

Means, R. S., Co., Inc. Staff. ADA Compliance Pricing Guide: Costs for the Seventy-Five Most Needed ADA Compliance Projects. Greene, Mary & Waier, Philip, eds. LC 95-113602. (Illus.). 300p. 1994. pap. 72.95 (*0-87629-351-8*, 67310) R S Means.

— Means Estimating Handbook. (Illus.). 900p. 1990. 99.95 (*0-87629-177-9*, 67276) R S Means.

Means, R. S., Staff. How to Estimate with Metric Units. 190p. 1993. pap. 49.95 (*0-87629-317-8*, 67304) R S Means.

— Illustrated Construction Dictionary Condensed. (Illus.). 500p. 1991. pap. 59.95 (*0-87629-219-8*, 67282) R S Means.

— Means Electrical Estimating Methods. 2nd ed. 1995. boxed set 64.95 (*0-87629-358-5*, 67230A) R S Means.

— Means Forms for Building Construction Professionals. 2nd ed. 325p. 1986. ring bd. 94.95 (*0-911950-87-7*, 67231) R S Means.

— Means Forms for Contractors. 1991. ring bd. 79.95 (*0-87629-214-7*, 67288) R S Means.

— Means Mechanical Estimating Methods. 2nd ed. 1992. 64.95 (*0-87629-213-9*, 67294) R S Means.

— Means Unit Price Estimating Methods. 2nd ed. 432p. 1993. pap. 59.95 (*0-87629-315-1*, 67303) R S Means.

Means, Robert C. Underdevelopment & the Development of Law: Corporations & Corporation Law in Nineteenth Century Colombia. LC 79-23936. (Studies in Legal History). 350p. reprint ed. pap. 108.50 (*0-8357-3894-9*, 203662600004) Bks Demand.

Means, Robin, jt. ed. see Malpass, Peter.

Means, R.S. Staff, jt. auth. see Langdon, Davis & Everest Staff.

Means, Russell & Wolf, Marvin J. Where White Men Fear to Tread. 4th ed. (Illus.). 592p. 1996. pap. 17.95 (*0-312-14761-9*) St Martin.

Means, Spencer, jt. auth. see Weiner, Alan R.

Means, Sterling. Ethiopia: The Missing Link in African History. pap. 6.95 (*0-686-00436-1*) Hakims Pubs.

***Means, Sterling M.** Ethiopia & the Missing Link in African History. 250p. 1999. pap. 9.95 (*1-930097-05-0*) Lushena Bks.

Means, Sterling M. Ethiopia & the Missing Link in African History. (Illus.). 161p. 1998. reprint ed. pap. 40.00 (*1-58073-013-2*) BCP Bks.

Means, Thomas L., jt. auth. see Henson, Carol.

Means, W. D. Stress & Strain: Basic Concepts of Continuum Mechanics for Geologists. (Illus.). 336p. (C). 1991. 49.95 (*0-387-07556-9*) Spr-Verlag.

Meany, Janet & Pfaff, Paula. Rag Rug Handbook. (Illus.). 128p. 1996. reprint ed. pap. 19.95 (*1-883010-28-4*) Interweave.

Meany, Janet & Pfaff, Paula. Rag Rug Handbook. 3rd ed. 1992. pap. 19.95 (*0-932394-21-3*) Dos Tejedoras.

Meany, Terence. Working Windows: Repair & Restoration of Wood Windows. unabridged ed. (Illus.). vii, 104p. 1997. pap. 9.95 (*0-9659344-0-3*) Meany Pr.

***Meany, Terry.** Complete Idiot's Guide to Electrical Repair. (Complete Idiot's Guides Ser.). 2000. pap. text 16.95 (*0-02-863896-4*, Alpha Ref) Macmillan Gen Ref.

— The Complete Idiot's Guide to Plumbing. (Complete Idiot's Guide Ser.). 360p. 2000. pap. 16.95 (*0-02-863893-X*, Alpha Ref) Macmillan Gen Ref.

Meaor, Maureen. Pots & People: That Have Shaped the Heritage of Medieval & Later England. LC 97-186379. (Illus.). 80p. 1998. pap. 13.95 (*1-85444-080-2*, 0801, Pub. by Ashmolean Mus) A Schwartz & Co.

Meara, Anne. After-Play. 1996. pap. 5.25 (*0-8222-0459-2*) Dramatists Play.

***Meara, R. J. & Koller, W. C., eds.** Parkinson's Disease & Parkinson's Syndrome in the Elderly. (Illus.). 280p. (C). 2000. text. write for info. (*0-521-62884-9*) Cambridge U Pr.

Meard, Jack. The Complete Idiot's Guide to Buying or Leasing a Car. LC 96-84589. 239p. 1996. 14.95 (*0-02-861274-4*) Macmillan Gen Ref.

Meares, Ainslie. Ainslie Meares Compendium: Dialogue on Meditation, from the Quiet Place & a Kind of Believing. 156p. (Orig.). 1994. pap. 12.95 (*0-85572-195-2*, Pub. by Hill Content Pubng) Seven Hills Bk.

— The Introvert. 150p. (Orig.). 1994. pap. 10.95 (*0-85572-076-X*) Seven Hills Bk.

— Thoughts. 62p. (Orig.). 1994. pap. 7.95 (*0-85572-116-2*, Pub. by Hill Content Pubng) Seven Hills Bk.

— A Way of Doctoring. 180p. (Orig.). 1994. pap. 12.95 (*0-85572-150-2*, Pub. by Hill Content Pubng) Seven Hills Bk.

— The Wealth Within. 170p. 1994. pap. 13.95 (*0-85572-086-7*, Pub. by Hill Content Pubng) Seven Hills Bk.

Meares, Alison, jt. auth. see Loudiyi, Dounia.

Meares, Bernard, tr. see Mandelshtam, Osip.

***Meares, Carol A. & Sargent, John F., Jr.** The Digital Work Force: Building Infotech Skills at the Speed of Innovation. (Illus.). 122p. (C). 2000. pap. text 30.00 (*0-7881-8801-1*) DIANE Pub.

Meares, Charlotte E., jt. auth. see Caron, George R.

Meares, Claude F., ed. Perspectives in Bioconjugate Chemistry. LC 93-15385. (Illus.). 210p. 1993. pap. text 38.00 (*0-8412-2672-5*, Pub. by Am Chemical) OUP.

Meares, Don. The Church's Ultimate Goal: Corporate Destiny in the Local Church. LC 97-205921. 160p. 1995. pap. 8.99 (*1-880089-26-2*, Pub. by Albury Pub) Appalach Bk Dist.

Meares, Jannie L. Dynamic Drama in the Church: How to Develop a Local Church Drama Ministry. Spear, Cindy G., ed. 1997. ring bd. 109.95 incl. VHS (*1-57052-060-7*) Chrch Grwth VA.

Meares, John. The Memorial of John Meares. 97p. 1985. reprint ed. 14.95 (*0-87770-341-8*) Ye Galleon.

Meares, L. G. & Hymowitz, C. E. Simulating with Spice. Marks, S. N. & Robson, J. T., eds. (Spice Ser.). (Illus.). 283p. (Orig.). 1988. pap. 15.00 (*0-923345-00-0*) INTUSOFT.

— Spice Applications Handbook, Vol. 2. 2nd ed. (Illus.). 200p. (Orig.). (C). 1990. pap. 49.95 (*0-923345-01-9*) INTUSOFT.

***Meares, Russell.** Intimacy & Alienation: Memory, Trauma & Personal Being. LC 99-36239. 2000. write for info. (*0-415-22030-0*) Routledge.

***Meares, Tracey L. & Kahan, Dan M.** Urgent Times: Policing & Rights in Inner-City Communities. LC 99-23658. 80p. 1999. pap. 12.00 (*0-8070-0605-X*) Beacon Pr.

Mearin, M. L. & Mulder, Chris J., eds. Coeliac Disease: Forty Years Gluten-Free. (Developments in Gastroenterology Ser.). (C). 1991. text 146.50 (*0-7923-1160-4*) Kluwer Academic.

Mearing, Judith S. Working for Children. LC 78-1148. (Jossey-Bass Social & Behavioral Science Ser.). 368p. reprint ed. pap. 114.10 (*0-608-30131-0*, 202173100022) Bks Demand.

Mearns, Barbara & Mearns, Richard. Biographies for Birdwatchers: The Lives of Those Commemorated in Western Palearctic Bird Names. (Books about Birds). 490p. 1988. text 53.00 (*0-12-487422-3*) Acad Pr.

— The Bird Collectors. (Poyser Books about Birds). (Illus.). 608p. 1997. text 49.95 (*0-12-487440-1*) Morgan Kaufmann.

***Mearns, Dan.** Seattle Slew. LC 00-104789. (Thoroughbred Legends Ser.: Vol. 5). (Illus.). 144p. 2000. 24.95 (*1-58150-047-5*, Pub. by Blood-Horse) IPG Chicago.

Mearns, Dan, jt. ed. see Paulick, Raymond S.

Mearns, Dave. Person-Centered Counselling Training. LC 98-121483. 240p. 1997. 59.95 (*0-7619-5290-X*); pap. 24.50 (*0-7619-5291-8*) Sage.

M

An Asterisk (*) at the beginning of an entry indicates that the title is appearing for the first time.

Mearns, Dave & Dryden, Windy, eds. Experiences of Counselling in Action. (Counselling in Action Ser.). 160p. (C). 1989. text 49.95 (*0-8039-8192-9*); pap. text 21.50 (*0-8039-8193-7*) Sage.

Mearns, Dave & Thorne, Brian. Developing Person-Centered Counselling. 192p. 1994. 39.95 (*0-8039-8981-4*); pap. 18.95 (*0-8039-8982-2*) Sage.

— Person Centered Counselling in Action. (Counselling in Action Ser.). 160p. (C). 1988. text 49.95 (*0-8039-8049-3*); pap. text 21.50 (*0-8039-8050-7*) Sage.

Mearns, David J. Shiva's Other Children: Religion & Social Identity Amongst Overseas Indians. 299p. 1995. 45.00 (*0-8039-9249-1*) Sage.

Mearns, David J., jt. ed. see Gray, John N.

Mearns, Edgar A. Mammals of the Mexican Boundary of the United States Pt. 1: Catalogue of the Species of Mammals Occurring in That Region, Families Didelphildae to Muridae. LC 73-18787. (Natural Sciences in America Ser.). 576p. 1974. reprint ed. 44.95 (*0-405-05777-6*) Ayer.

Mearns, James. Early Latin Hymnaries. 127p. reprint ed. lib. bdg. 31.07 (*0-685-13869-0*, 05102527) G Olms Pubs.

— Early Latin Hymnaries. xx, 107p. 1970. reprint ed. write for info. (*0-318-71173-7*) G Olms Pubs.

Mearns, Richard, jt. auth. see Mearns, Barbara.

Mearns, Robin, jt. auth. see Leach, Melissa.

Mears, Arthur I. Colorado Avalanche Area Studies & Guidelines for Avalanche-Hazard Planning. (Special Publications: No. 7). (Illus.). 124p. (Orig.). 1979. pap. 8.00 (*1-884216-36-6*) Colo Geol Survey.

— Snow-Avalanche Hazard Analysis for Land-Use Planning & Engineering. (Bulletin Ser.: No. 49). (Illus.). 55p. (Orig.). 1992. pap. 12.00 (*1-884216-10-2*) Colo Geol Survey.

Mears, Catherine & Chowdhury, Sue. Health Care for Refugees & Displaced People. (Practical Health Guide Ser.: Vol. 9). (Illus.). 64p. (C). 1994. pap. 9.95 (*0-85598-225-X*, Pub. by Oxfam Pub) Stylus Pub VA.

Mears, Catherine & Young, Helen. Acceptability & Use of Cereal-Based Foods in Refugee Camps: Case Studies from Nepal, Ethiopia & Tanzania. (Oxfam Working Papers Ser.). 160p. 1998. pap. 18.95 (*0-85598-402-3*, Pub. by Oxfam Pub) Stylus Pub VA.

Mears, Eileen. What's Cooking "Down Home" (Illus.). 494p. (Orig.). 1994. spiral bd. 16.50 (*0-9641341-0-1*) E Mears.

Mears, Eileen, ed. A Treasury of Farm Women's Humor. 300p. 1994. pap. 12.95 (*0-942936-25-6*) Lincoln-Herndon Pr.

Mears, Eliot G. Resident Orientals on the American Pacific Coast. Daniels, Roger, ed. LC 78-54827. (Asian Experience in North America Ser.). 1979. reprint ed. lib. bdg. 40.95 (*0-405-11284-X*) Ayer.

Mears, F. Gary. Psychotropic Drugs: Understanding Adverse Reactions. 352p. 1999. 42.00 (*0-393-70284-7*) Norton.

Mears, Gillian, ed. Ride a Cock Horse. 164p. (C). 1990. 30.00 (*0-947087-12-5*, Pub. by Pascoe Pub) St Mut.

Mears, Helen. Year of the Wild Boar. LC 73-7457. 346p. 1973. reprint ed. lib. bdg. 65.00 (*0-8371-6936-4*, MEWB, Greenwood Pr) Greenwood.

Mears, Henrietta C. De Que Trata la Biblia.Tr. of What the Bible Is All About. (SPA.). 36p. 1986. 14.99 (*1-56063-164-3*, 498490) Editorial Unilit.

— De Que Trata la Biblia: Jovenes Exploradores.Tr. of What the Bible Is All About: Young Explorers. (SPA.). 365p. 1986. pap. 12.99 (*1-56063-325-5*, 498491) Editorial Unilit.

— Lo Que Nos Dice la Biblica.Tr. of What the Bible Is All About. (SPA.). 624p. 1980. 14.99 (*0-8297-0485-X*) Vida Pubs.

***Mears, Henrietta C.** What the Bible Is All about. LC 99-14830. 447p. 1999. 19.99 (*0-8307-2431-1*) Gospel Lght.

Mears, Henrietta C. What the Bible Is All About. rev. ed. 585p. 1987. pap. 12.99 (*0-8423-7902-9*) Tyndale Hse.

— What the Bible Is All About: NIV Edition. LC 98-17735. 720p. 1998. 15.99 (*0-8307-1830-3*, Regal Bks) Gospel Lght.

— What the Bible Is All About - NIV Edition. LC 98-17735. 720p. 1998. pap. 10.99 (*0-8307-1897-4*, Regal Bks) Gospel Lght.

Mears, Henrietta C., jt. auth. see Blankenbaker, Frances.

***Mears, Isabella.** Tao Teh King. LC 99-80176. 128p. 2000. write for info. (*1-893766-15-2*) Aeon Pub Co.

Mears, Isabella, tr. The Tao Teh King. 1983. pap. 9.95 (*0-7229-0300-6*) Theos Pub Hse.

Mears, James A., compiled by. Plant Taxonomic Literature Microfiche Collection: Bibliographic Guide. 177p. 1989. write for info. (*0-85964-217-8*) Chadwyck-Healey.

— Types & Special Collections (Flowering Plants & Ferns) of the Herbarium of the Academy of Natural Sciences of Philadelphia: Indices to the Microfiche. 274p. 1984. write for info. (*0-930466-87-X*) Chadwyck-Healey.

— United States National Arbaretum Vascular Plaant Type & Cultivar Collection. 78p. 1985. write for info. (*0-930466-94-2*) Chadwyck-Healey.

Mears, Jane, jt. auth. see Watson, Elizabeth A.

Mears, Jo. Endometriosis: A Natural Approach. (Natural Approach Ser.). (Illus.). 184p. (Orig.). 1997. pap. 9.95 (*1-56975-088-2*) Ulysses Pr.

Mears, Patrick E. Bankruptcy Law & Practice in Michigan. LC 87-80722. 552p. 1987. ring bd. 110.00 (*0-685-22684-0*, 87-007) U MI Law CLE.

— Bankruptcy Law & Practice in Michigan. LC 87-80722. 552p. 1992. suppl. ed. 60.00 (*0-685-22685-9*, 92-028) U MI Law CLE.

Mears, Peter. Healthcare Teams: Building Continuous Quality Improvement. (Illus.). 200p. 1994. student ed., per. 36.95 (*1-884015-41-7*) St Lucie Pr.

— Healthcare Teams: Building Continuous Quality Improvement Facilitator's Guide. (Illus.). 120p. 1994. teacher ed., per. 57.95 (*1-884015-43-3*) St Lucie Pr.

— Organization Teams: Building Continuous Quality Improvement Facilitator's Guide. (Illus.). 120p. 1994. teacher ed., per. 57.95 (*1-884015-44-1*) St Lucie Pr.

— Quality Improvement: Tools & Techniques. LC 94-34752. 1995. text 49.95 incl. disk (*0-07-041229-4*) McGraw.

— Quality Improvement Tools & Techniques. LC 94-34752. 326p. 1994. 32.95 (*0-07-041219-7*) McGraw.

— Quality Improvement Tools & Techniques. LC 94-34752. 1995. disk 19.95 (*0-07-852726-0*) McGraw.

— Team Building Instructor's Manual: A Structured Learning Approach. (Illus.). 120p. (C). 1994. spiral bd. 57.95 (*1-884015-14-X*) St Lucie Pr.

Mears, Peter & Voehl, Frank. The Executive Guide to Implementing Quality Systems. 232p. 1995. per. 49.95 (*1-884015-53-0*) St Lucie Pr.

— Team Building: A Structured Learning Approach. (Illus.). 192p. (C). 1994. per. 31.95 (*1-884015-15-8*) St Lucie Pr.

Mears, Peter M. The Keyboard Instructor for the Apple IIe. 158p. 1987. pap. text 35.50 (*0-314-58913-9*) West Pub.

— The Keyboard Instructor for the IBM PC. 174p. 1987. pap. text 35.50 (*0-314-58914-7*) West Pub.

— Teach Yourself Apple BASIC. 192p. 1983. spiral bd. write for info. (*0-318-57868-9*) Addison-Wesley.

Mears, R. Ray Mears' World of Survival. 128p. 1997. 26.95 (*0-00-472083-0*, Pub. by HarpC) Trafalgar.

Mears, Raymond. A Look at Life: A Collection of Poems. 72p. 1999. pap. 8.00 (*1-891774-13-1*, Path Pubng in Christ) Path Pubng.

— The Outdoor Survival Handbook: A Guide to the Resources & Material Available in the Wild & How to Use Them for Food, Shelter, Warmth, & Navigation. LC 93-9683. (Illus.). 240p. (Orig.). 1993. pap. 14.95 (*0-312-09359-4*) St Martin.

***Mears, Raymond & Bliss, Ronald.** Big Orange Memories: Ray Mears & the Tennessee Basketball Program. (Illus.). 224p. 2000. 24.95 (*1-58382-052-3*) Sports Pub.

Mears, Richard C. Ebb of the River. LC 86-19545. 208p. 1986. pap. 8.95 (*0-88191-044-9*) Freundlich.

Mears, Rona R., jt. auth. see Fagan, Wayne I.

Mears, Rona R., jt. ed. see Gitlin, Richard A.

Mears, Susan Fielder. Your Living Legacy. LC 98-13270. 176p. 1998. pap. 19.95 (*0-8092-2905-6*, 290560, Contemporary Bks) NTC Contemp Pub Co.

Mears, T. Lambert, tr. The Institutes of Gaius & Justinian: The Twelve Tables, & the CXVIIIth & CXVIIth Novels. LC 93-79703. 686p. 1994. reprint ed. 145.00 (*1-56169-061-9*) Gaunt.

Mears, Walter R., jt. auth. see Chancellor, John.

Mears, William H., jt. auth. see Clapp, Alfred C.

Mearsheimer, John J. Conventional Deterrence. LC 83-5317. (Cornell Studies in Security Affairs). 296p. (C). 1983. 42.50 (*0-8014-1569-1*); pap. text 16.95 (*0-8014-9346-3*) Cornell U Pr.

— Liddell Hart & the Weight of History. LC 88-47748. (Cornell Studies in Security Affairs). 264p. 1988. text 37.50 (*0-8014-2089-X*) Cornell U Pr.

***Measday, Ellen & Knight, Lisa F.** Speak Out! Authentic Communication Activities For The Intermediate & Advanced Esl Student. 176p. (C). 1998. per. (*0-7872-4843-6*) Kendall-Hunt.

Measday, Ellen & Knight, Lisa F. Speak Out! Authentic Communication Activities for the Intermediate & Advanced ESL Student. 160p. (C). 1994. per. 17.95 (*0-8403-9536-1*) Kendall-Hunt.

Measday, Stephen. The News on Aliens. LC 97-188212. 163p. (YA). 1997. pap. 12.95 (*0-7022-2887-7*, Pub. by Univ Queensland Pr) Intl Spec Bk.

— The News They Didn't Use. (YA). 1995. pap. 12.95 (*0-7022-2711-0*, Pub. by Univ Queensland Pr) Intl Spec Bk.

Mease, Gary, ed. see Mushala, Paul S.

Mease, Gladys P. & Hartzel, Gwendolyn P. Nyce: The Abraham & Leanna (Godshall) Nyce Family: Their Ancestors & Descendants. (Illus.). 109p. 1995. reprint ed. pap. 19.50 (*0-8328-4932-4*); reprint ed. lib. bdg. 29.50 (*0-8328-4931-6*) Higginson Bk Co.

Mease, James. Picture of Philadelphia. LC 75-112561. (Rise of Urban America Ser.). (Illus.). 1970. reprint ed. 23.95 (*0-405-02466-5*) Ayer.

Measell, James. New Martinsville Glass, 1900-1944. (Illus.). 240p. 1994. pap. 34.95 (*0-915410-85-0*) Antique Pubns.

Measell, James, ed. Fenton Glass: The 1980s Decade. (Illus.). 176p. 1996. 44.95 (*1-57080-020-0*); pap. 34.95 (*1-57080-019-7*) Antique Pubns.

— Imperial Glass Encyclopedia Vol. 2: Cape Cod - L. (Illus.). 272p. 1997. 44.95 (*1-57080-022-7*); pap. 34.95 (*1-57080-021-9*) Antique Pubns.

***Measell, James, ed.** Imperial Glass Encyclopedia Vol. III: M-Z. (Illus.). 272p. 1999. 44.95 (*1-57080-066-9*); pap. 34.95 (*1-57080-065-0*) Antique Pubns.

Measell, James & Roetteis, W. C. The L. G. Wright Glass Company. LC 98-104831. (Illus.). 1997. 44.95 (*1-57080-031-6*); pap. 34.95 (*1-57080-030-8*) Antique Pubns.

Measell, James & Smith, Don E. Findlay Glass. (Illus.). 148p. 1986. pap. 19.95 (*0-915410-25-7*) Antique Pubns.

Measell, James & Wiggins, Berry. Great American Glass: Glass of the Roaring 20's - Depression Era. LC 98-199763. (Illus.). 208p. 1998. pap. write for info. (*1-57080-050-2*) Antique Pubns.

— Great American Glass No. 1: Glass of the Roaring 20's/Depression Era. (Illus.). 208p. 1998. pap. 34.95 (*1-57080-049-9*) Antique Pubns.

***Measell, James & Wiggins, Berry.** Great American Glass of the Roaring 20s & Depression Era, Bk. 2. (Illus.). 208p. 2000. 44.95 (*1-57080-064-2*); pap. 34.95 (*1-57080-063-4*) Antique Pubns.

Measell, James, et al. Dugan Diamond: The Story of Indiana, Pennsylvania Glass. (Illus.). 212p. 1993. pap. 34.95 (*0-915410-91-5*) Antique Pubns.

Measell, James, ed. see McGee, Marie.

Measell, James, ed. see National Imperial Glass Collector's Society Staff.

Measell, James S. Teaching the Introductory Public Relations Course: Communication Perspective. Lewis, Warren W., ed. LC 90-14056. (Illus.). 85p. (C). 1990. pap. 9.50 (*0-927516-20-9*) ERIC-REC.

***Measham, Anthony R. & Chatterjee, Meera.** Wasting Away: The Crisis of Malnutrition in India. LC 99-28089. (Directions in Development Ser.). 88p. 1999. pap. 22.00 (*0-8213-4435-8*, 14435) World Bank.

Measham, Anthony R. & Heaver, Richard A. India's Family Welfare Program: Moving to a Reproductive & Child Health Approach. LC 95-52404. 72p. 1996. pap. 22.00 (*0-8213-3448-4*, 13448) World Bank.

***Measham, Terence.** Christian Dior: The Magic of Fashion. (Illus.). 64p. 2000. pap. 24.95 (*1-86317-048-0*) Museum Applied Arts.

— Ken Done: The Art of Design. (Illus.). 120p. 2000. pap. 32.95 (*1-86317-049-9*) Museum Applied Arts.

— Treasures of the Powerhouse Museum. (Illus.). 192p. 2000. pap. 50.00 (*1-86317-047-2*) Museum Applied Arts.

Measher, R., jt. auth. see Bowman, J.

Measom, George. The Illustrated Guide to the Great Western Railway 1852. 64p. 1987. 30.00 (*0-905392-47-7*) St Mut.

Measor, Lynda & Sikes, Patricia J. Gender & Schools. 192p. 1992. pap. text 25.00 (*0-304-32397-7*, Tycooly Pub) Weidner & Sons.

Meastro, Betsy. Snow Day. 32p. (J). (ps-3). 1992. pap. 4.95 (*0-590-46083-8*) Scholastic Inc.

Meastro, Betsy C. & DelVecchio, Ellen. Big City Port. (Illus.). 32p. (J). (gr. k-3). 1984. pap. 4.95 (*0-590-41577-8*) Scholastic Inc.

***Measurement Comparison Committee.** Guide for Inter-Laboratory Comparsions: RP 15. unabridged ed. (Illus.). 48p. 1999. 15.00 (*1-58464-025-1*) Natl Conf Stds Labs.

Measurements Group, Inc. Technical Staff. Strain Gage Based Transducers: Their Design & Construction. (Illus.). 74p. (Orig.). (C). 1988. pap. 10.00 (*0-9619057-0-0*) Measure Grp.

***Measures.** Structural Monitoring with Fiber Optic Technology. 720p. 2000. 115.00 (*0-12-487430-4*) Acad Pr.

Measures, Raymond M., ed. Laser Remote Chemical Analysis. LC 87-13380. (Chemical Analysis Ser.). 560p. 1988. 215.00 (*0-471-81640-X*) Wiley.

***Meat Loaf.** To Hell & Back. 2000. pap. 16.00 (*0-06-098876-2*) HarpC.

Meat Loaf, et al. To Hell & Back: An Autobiography. LC 99-48892. (Illus.). 304p. 1999. 24.95 (*0-06-039293-2*, ReganBks) HarperTrade.

Meath-Lang, Bonnie, jt. auth. see Lang, Harry G.

Meats, Stephen. Looking for the Pale Eagle. 62p. (Orig.). 1993. pap. 8.00 (*0-939391-18-X*) B Woodley Pr.

Meaus. Basic Medical Terminology Instructors Guide. 3rd ed. 1987. 11.10 (*0-02-685470-8*) Macmillan.

***Mebane, Felicia E.** Medicare Politics: Exploring the Media Coverage, Political Information & Political Participation. LC 00-42232. (Health Care Policy in the United States Ser.). 2000. write for info. (*0-8153-3717-5*) Garland.

Mebane, John C. The April of Her Age: The Buried Treasure of Robert Louis Stevenson & Princess Victoria Kaiulani. LC 94-233516. (Illus.). 248p. (Orig.). 1994. pap. 14.95 (*0-9641844-1-9*) Windward HI.

Mebane, John S. Renaissance Magic & the Return of the Golden Age: The Occult Tradition & Marlowe, Jonson & Shakespeare. LC 88-22068. (Illus.). xviii, 317p. 1989. reprint ed. pap. text 20.00 (*0-8032-8179-X*, Bison Books) U of Nebr Pr.

Mebane, Mary E. Mary. LC 98-49044. (Chapel Hill Book Ser.). 242p. (C). 1999. pap. 16.95 (*0-8078-4821-2*) U of NC Pr.

— Mary, Wayfarer. LC 98-46858. (Chapel Hill Book Ser.). 230p. 1999. pap. 17.95 (*0-8078-4822-0*) U of NC Pr.

***Mebane, Robert C.** Adventures with Science Series. (Illus.). (J). 1998. 44.75 (*0-7660-1324-3*) Enslow Pubs.

Mebane, Robert C. & Rybolt, Thomas R. Adventures with Atoms & Molecules Bk. I: Chemistry Experiments For Young People. (Adventures with Science Ser.). (Illus.). 82p. (J). (gr. 4-9). 1998. pap. 10.95 (*0-7660-1224-7*) Enslow Pubs.

— Adventures with Atoms & Molecules Bk. II: Chemistry Experiments For Young People. (Adventures with Science Ser.). (Illus.). 96p. (J). (gr. 4-9). 1998. pap. 10.95 (*0-7660-1225-5*) Enslow Pubs.

— Adventures with Atoms & Molecules Bk. III: Chemistry Experiments for Young People. (Adventures with Science Ser.). (Illus.). 96p. (J). (gr. 4-9). 1998. pap. 10.95 (*0-7660-1226-3*) Enslow Pubs.

— Adventures with Atoms & Molecules Bk. IV: Chemistry Experiments for Young People. (Adventures with Science Ser.). (Illus.). 96p. (J). (gr. 4-9). 1998. pap. 10.95 (*0-7660-1227-1*) Enslow Pubs.

— Adventures with Atoms & Molecules Bk. V: Chemistry Experiments for Young People. LC 85-10177. (Adventures with Science Ser.). (Illus.). 96p. (J). (gr. 4-9). 1995. lib. bdg. 10.95 (*0-89490-606-2*) Enslow Pubs.

— Adventures with Atoms & Molecules Bk. V: Chemistry Experiments for Young People. (Adventures with Science Ser.). (Illus.). 96p. (J). (gr. 4-9). 1998. pap. 10.95 (*0-7660-1228-X*) Enslow Pubs.

— Air & Other Gases. (Everyday Material Science Experiments Ser.). (Illus.). 64p. (J). (gr. 5-8). 1995. lib. bdg. 18.90 (*0-8050-2839-0*) TFC Bks NY.

— Metals. (Everyday Material Science Experiments Ser.). (Illus.). 64p. (J). (gr. 5-8). 1995. lib. bdg. 18.90 (*0-8050-2842-0*) TFC Bks NY.

— Plastics & Polymers. (Everyday Material Science Experiments Ser.). (Illus.). 64p. (J). (gr. 5-8). 1995. lib. bdg. 18.90 (*0-8050-2843-9*) TFC Bks NY.

— Salts & Solids. (Everyday Material Science Experiments Ser.). (Illus.). 64p. (J). (gr. 5-8). 1995. lib. bdg. 18.90 (*0-8050-2841-2*) TFC Bks NY.

— Water & Other Liquids. (Everyday Material Science Experiments Ser.). (Illus.). 64p. (J). (gr. 5-8). 1995. lib. bdg. 18.90 (*0-8050-2840-4*) TFC Bks NY.

Mebane, Robert C., jt. auth. see Rybolt, Thomas R.

Mebane, Rodney M., jt. auth. see Calderon-Young, Estelita.

Mebane, Walter R. Political Analysis: The Methodology Section of the American Political Science, Vol. 7. annuals (Political Analysis Ser.). 218p. 1999. text 49.50 (*0-472-11074-8*, 11074) U of Mich Pr.

Meberg, Marilyn. Choosing the Amusing Finding Humor & Joy Beneath the Rubble of Life, 1. LC 99-17564. 1999. pap. text 10.99 (*0-8499-3744-2*) Word Pub.

— I'd Rather Be Laughing. LC 97-52653. 208p. 1998. pap. 12.99 (*0-8499-3989-5*) Word Pub.

***Meberg, Marilyn, contrib. by.** I'd Rather Be Laughing. 1998. pap. 10.99 incl. audio (*0-8499-6283-8*) Word Pub.

Meberg, Marilyn, et al. Overjoyed: 60 Devotions. LC 98-11682. 208p. 1999. 14.99 (*0-310-22653-8*) Zondervan.

Mebrate, Assefa, jt. auth. see Kalb, Jon E.

Mebs, Gudrun, jt. auth. see Shier, W. Thomas.

Mebust, Larry E. Gray Whales, a Bird's-Eye View: A Fieldguide for Boat Skippers & Whalewatchers. 37p. 1992. pap. 7.95 (*0-9635485-0-6*) Offshore Pub.

Mebust, Leanne & Gismoruli, Regina. Little Witch. LC 97-216261. (Illus.). (J). 1997. write for info. (*0-7853-2360-0*) Pubns Intl Ltd.

Mecartea, Bruce. Quest for a Tomorrow. 407p. (Orig.). 1995. pap. 6.95 (*0-9646744-0-8*) Dawn Pub CA.

MECC Staff. Africa Trail. 1995. 39.02 (*0-7929-0909-7*) MECC.

Mecca, Andrew M., ed. Prevention Action Plan for Alcohol-Related Problems. (Illus.). 90p. (Orig.). (C). 1994. pap. text 30.00 (*0-7881-1430-1*) DIANE Pub.

— Prevention 2000 - A Public-Private Partnership. (Illus.). 126p. 1994. reprint ed. pap. text 30.00 (*0-7881-1429-8*) DIANE Pub.

Mecca, Andrew M., et al. Toward a State of Esteem: The Final Report of the California Task Force to Promote Self-Esteem & Personal & Social Responsibility. (Illus.). 160p. 1990. pap. 8.00 (*0-8011-0846-2*) Calif Education.

Mecca, C. Michael Jackson American Master. (Illus.). 272p. 1996. 54.95 (*0-9655174-0-3*) CAM Publng CA.

Mecca, C., et al. Michael Jackson American Master. 2nd rev. ed. (Illus.). 280p. 1997. 54.95 (*0-9655174-1-1*) CAM Publng CA.

Mecca, Judy T. Plays That Teach: Plays, Activities, & Songs with a Message. Keeling, Jan, ed. (Illus.). 96p. (Orig.). (J). (gr. 3-6). 1992. pap. text 10.95 (*0-86530-153-0*, 195-2) Incentive Pubns.

— Real-Life Drama for Real, Live Students: A Collection of Monologues, Duet Acting Scenes, & a Full-Length Play. Keeling, Jan, ed. LC 97-150548. (Illus.). 112p. (J). (gr. 5-8). 1997. pap. text 10.95 (*0-86530-352-5*, 195-3) Incentive Pubns.

— Special Plays for Special Days: 30 Minute Holiday & Seasonal Plays. (Illus.). 96p. (Orig.). (J). (gr. k-6). 1991. pap. text 10.95 (*0-86530-203-0*, IP 194-4) Incentive Pubns.

— What a World: A Musical for You & Your Friends to Perform (6 Scripts & Production Guide) Weiss, Andrea, ed. LC 97-43029. (Theater Kits Ser.). (Illus.). (J). (gr. 3-7). 1998. pap., boxed set 9.95 (*1-56247-616-5*, Amer Girl Library) Pleasant Co.

Mecca, July Truesdell. Multicultural Plays: A Many-Splendored Tapestry Honoring Our Global Community. (Illus.). 128p. (J). (gr. 1-7). 1999. pap. 12.95 (*0-86530-411-4*, IP 411-4) Incentive Pubns.

Mecca, Stephen J. & Robertshaw, Joseph E. Home Energy Management: Principles & Practices. (Illus.). 160p. 1981. 12.95 (*0-89433-146-9*) Petrocelli.

Mecca, Stephen J., jt. auth. see Robertshaw, Joseph E.

***Mecca, Tommi Avicolli, et al, eds.** Hey Paesan! Writing by Lesbians & Gay Men of Italian Descent. 320p. 1999. pap. 12.95 (*0-9675586-0-3*) Three Guineas.

Mecca, Tommi Avicolli, et al. Fuori: Essays by Italian/American Lesbians & Gays. Tamburri, Anthony Julian, ed. (VIA Folios Ser.: No. 6). 111p. 1995. pap. 10.00 (*1-884419-05-4*) Bordighera.

Meccariello, Bryan. Plastic Cup Collectibles. LC 97-80679. 128p. 1998. pap. 14.95 (*0-7643-0473-9*) Schiffer.

Mech, Doris. Joy with Honey. LC 94-47239. 1995. pap. 13.95 (*0-312-11836-8*) St Martin.

Mech, Edmund V., ed. Independent-Living Services for At-Risk Adolescents. 138p. 1988. pap. 14.95 (*0-87868-359-3*) Child Welfare.

Mech, Edmund V. & Rycraft, Joan R., eds. Preparing Foster Youths for Adult Living: Proceedings of an Invitational Research Conference. LC 95-185119. 1995. pap. text 7.50 (*0-87868-593-6*) Child Welfare.

Mech, L. David. The Arctic Wolf - Updated 10th Anniversary Edition: Ten Years with the Pack. 2nd rev. ed. LC 97-885. (Illus.). 144p. 1997. reprint ed. 9.95 (*0-89658-353-8*) Voyageur Pr.

— Handbook of Animal Radio-Tracking. LC 83-6733. (Illus.). 120p. (C). 1983. pap. 11.95 (*0-8166-1221-8*) U of Minn Pr.

— The Way of the Wolf. LC 91-14415. (Illus.). 120p. 1991. 29.95 (*0-89658-163-2*) Voyageur Pr.

— The Way of the Wolf. LC 91-14415. (Illus.). 120p. 1995. pap. text 19.95 (*0-89658-179-9*) Voyageur Pr.

An Asterisk (*) at the beginning of an entry indicates that the title is appearing for the first time.

— The Wolf: The Ecology & Behavior of an Endangered Species. LC 80-27364. (Illus.). 385p. (C). 1981. reprint ed. pap. 18.95 (*0-8166-1026-6*) U of Minn Pr.

— The Wolves of Denali. LC 97-34687. 1998. 29.95 (*0-8166-2958-7*) U of Minn Pr.

***Mech, L. David, ed.** The Wolves of Minnesota: Howl in the Heartland. LC 00-36467. (Illus.). 128p. 2000. 24.95 (*0-89658-464-X*) Voyageur Pr.

Mech, L. David, photos by. Wolves of the High Arctic: An International Wolf Center Book. LC 92-21714. (Illus.). 128p. 1995. pap. text 9.95 (*0-89658-222-1*) Voyageur Pr.

***Mech, Susan Delaney.** Rx for Quilters: Stitcher-Friendly Advice for Every Body. LC 99-6696. (Illus.). 112p. 2000. pap. 14.95 incl. audio (*1-57120-092-4*, 10209) C & T Pub.

Mech, Terrence F. & McCabe, Gerard B., eds. Leadership & Academic Librarians. LC 97-53106. (Greenwood Library Management Collection). 288p. 1998. lib. bdg. 65.00 (*0-313-30271-5*, Greenwood Pr) Greenwood.

Mech, Terrence F., jt. ed. see Farmer, D. W.

Mecham, Tisha. Bio-Kinetic Testing for Health: How to Take the Guesswork Out of Healing. Adams, Stacey, ed. (Bio-Kinetic Testing Ser.: Vol. 1). (Illus.). 288p. 1998. pap. 24.97 (*0-9666409-0-X*) Alliance Press.

***Mecham, Evan.** Wrongful Impeachment. 356p. 1999. 20.00 (*1-929360-00-2*) Prime News Pr.

Mecham, John L. Church & State in Latin America: A History of Politico Ecclesiastical Relations. rev. ed. LC 66-15511. 477p. reprint ed. pap. 147.90 (*0-7837-0315-5*, 204063700018) Bks Demand.

Mecham, L. Ralph, ed. Long Range Plan for the Federal Courts. 205p. (C). 1998. pap. text 35.00 (*0-7881-7159-3*) DIANE Pub.

Mecham, Leonidas R. National Wiretap Report (1996) (Illus.). 193p. (Orig.). (C). 1997. pap. text 40.00 (*0-7881-4527-4*) DIANE Pub.

Mecham, Leonidas R., ed. National Wiretap Report, 1997. (Illus.). 207p. (C). 1998. pap. text 35.00 (*0-7881-7318-9*) DIANE Pub.

Mecham, Leonidas Ralph. Judicial Business of the United States Courts: 1997 Report of the Director. 388p. 1998. per. 31.00 (*0-16-042731-2*) USGPO.

***Mecham, Leonidas Ralph.** Judicial Business of the United States Courts, 1999 Report of the Director. 396p. 2000. per. 36.00 (*0-16-059068-X*) USGPO.

Mecham, Merlin J. Cerebral Palsy. 2nd ed. Halpern, Harvey, ed. LC 86-3271. (PRO-ED Studies in Communicative Disorders). (Illus.). 180p. (Orig.). 1996. pap. text 26.00 (*0-89079-627-0*, 7318) PRO-ED.

Mecham, Robert, ed. see Arri.

Mecham, Robert P. & Schwartz, Stephen M., eds. The Vascular Smooth Muscle Cell: Molecular & Biological Responses to the Extracellular Matrix. (Biology of the Extracellular Matrix Ser.). (Illus.). 410p. 1995. text 100.00 (*0-12-632310-0*) Acad Pr.

Mecham, Robert P., jt. ed. see Cheresh, David A.

Mecham, Robert P., jt. ed. see Roberts, David D.

Mechan, D., jt. auth. see Dalgleish, G.

Mechan, D. J., jt. auth. see Hubbard, L.

Mechan, Derek J., jt. auth. see Hubbard, D. J.

Mechan, Derek J., jt. auth. see Hubbard, Judy L.

***Mechan, Norma Lu & Druesedow, Jean.** Collection by Design: 150 Years of Costume from the Silverman/Rodgers Collection of the Kent State University Museum. (Illus.). 32p. 1999. pap. 10.95 (*0-89672-421-2*) Tex Tech Univ Pr.

Mechanic. Mental Health & Social Policy. 4th ed. LC 97-32789. 289p. 1998. pap. 60.00 (*0-205-26993-1*) P-H.

Mechanic, David. Inescapable Decisions: The Imperatives of Health Reform. LC 93-13425. 256p. (C). 1993. text 39.95 (*1-56000-121-6*) Transaction Pubs.

— Painful Choices: Research & Essays on Health Care. 320p. 1989. 39.95 (*0-88738-258-4*) Transaction Pubs.

— Students under Stress: A Study in the Social Psychology of Adaptation. LC 77-91058. 267p. reprint ed. pap. 82.80 (*0-608-09917-1*, 206925500003) Bks Demand.

— Symptoms, Illness Behavior, & Help-seeking. LC 82-25012. (Series in Psychosocial Epidemiology). 1982. write for info. (*0-8135-1005-8*) Rutgers U Pr.

— Symptoms, Illness Behavior, & Help-seeking. LC 82-3856. (Monographs In Psychosocial Epidemiology). 157 p. 1982. write for info. (*0-88202-134-6*, N Watson) Watson Pub Intl.

Mechanic, David, ed. Improving Mental Health Services: What the Social Sciences Can Tell Us. LC 87-646993. (New Directions for Mental Health Services Ser.: No. MHS 36). 1987. pap. 25.00 (*1-55542-944-0*) Jossey-Bass.

Mechanic, David, jt. ed. see Aiken, Linda H.

Mechanic, Janevive J. The Logic of Decision Making: An Introduction to Critical Thinking. (American University Studies: Philosophy: Ser. V, Vol. 39). X, 205p. 1988. text 35.50 (*0-8204-0484-5*) P Lang Pubng.

Mechanical Failures Prevention Group, Meeting (35t. Time-Dependent Failure Mechanisms & Assessment Methodologies: Proceedings of the 35th Meeting of the Mechanical Failures Prevention Group, National Bureau of Standards, Gaithersburg, MD, April 20-22, 1982. Early, James G. et al, eds. LC 82-19892. 331p. reprint ed. pap. 94.40 (*0-608-15715-5*, 2031643) Bks Demand.

Mechanisms of Vasodilatation Symposium Staff. Mechanisms of Vasodilation Symposium, Abstracts. Vanhoutte, P. M., ed. (Journal: Blood Vessels: Vol. 17, No. 3). 56p. 1980. pap. 32.25 (*3-8055-1252-X*) S Karger.

Mechem, Floyd R. Elements of the Law of Partnership. LC 12-36583. (Business Enterprises Reprint Ser.). xxxviii,277p. 1982. reprint ed. text 44.00 (*0-89941-180-0*, 302300) W S Hein.

Mechem, Floyd R., jt. auth. see Atkinson.

Mechem, K. The Shepherd & His Love: Instrument Parts-Piccolo, Viola, Piano. 8p. 1993. pap. 5.95 (*0-7935-2695-7*) H Leonard.

— Songs of the Slave: Vocal Score. 64p. 1994. pap. 7.95 (*0-7935-3859-9*, 50482274) H Leonard.

— Tartuffe Libretto. 52p. 1994. pap. 5.95 (*0-7935-3476-3*) H Leonard.

Mechem, Kirke, ed. see Owen, Jennie S.

Mecherle, G. Stephen, ed. Free-Space Laser Communication Technologies IX, Vol. 2990. 320p. 1997. 69.00 (*0-8194-2401-3*) SPIE.

— Free-Space Laser Communication Technologies X, Vol. 3266. 252p. 1998. 59.00 (*0-8194-2705-5*) SPIE.

***Mecherle, G. Stephen, ed.** Free-Space Laser Communication Technologies XI. 370p. 1999. pap. text 84.00 (*0-8194-3085-4*) SPIE.

Mecherle, G. Stephen, jt. ed. see Christopher, Paul.

Mechery, F. A. & Tikekar, Maneesha, eds. Indian Socialism: Past & Present. xii, 231p. 1985. 16.00 (*0-685-67627-7*, Pub. by Himalaya Pub) Nataraj Bks.

Mechie, Stewart. The Church & Scottish Social Development, 1780-1870, 1957. LC 75-3740. 181p. 1975. reprint ed. lib. bdg. 55.00 (*0-8371-8060-0*, MECS, Greenwood Pr) Greenwood.

Mechikoff, Robert A. & Estes, Steven. History & Philosophy of Sport & Physical Education: From the Ancient Greeks to the Present. 416p. (C). 1992. text. write for info. (*0-697-12159-3*) Brown & Benchmark.

— A History & Philosophy of Sport & Physical Educations from Ancient Civilizations to the Modern World. 2nd ed. LC 97-60303. 416p. (C). 1997. text. write for info. (*0-697-25883-1*, WCB McGr Hill) McGrw-H Hghr Educ.

Mechikoff, Robert A., jt. auth. see Estes, Steven G.

Mechino. Break the Weight Loss Barrier. (C). 1998. 19.95 (*0-13-080553-X*, Macmillan Coll) P-H.

Mechler. Programmierung Neuronaler Netze. (GER.). (C). 1991. text. write for info. (*0-201-55942-0*) Addison-Wesley.

Mechler, Gary. Constellations of the Northern Skies. LC 94-34032. (National Audubon Society Pocket Guides Ser.). 1995. pap. 9.00 (*0-679-77998-1*) Knopf.

***Mechler, Gary.** Night Sky. LC 98-51876. (National Audubon Society First Field Guides Ser.). (Illus.). 160p. (YA). (gr. 3-7). 1999. 17.95 (*0-590-64085-2*, Pub. by Scholastic Inc); vinyl bd. 11.95 (*0-590-64086-0*, Pub. by Scholastic Inc) Penguin Putnam.

Mechler, Gary, et al. The Sun & the Moon. LC 94-42421. 1995. pap. 7.99 (*0-679-76056-3*) Knopf.

Mechling, Allen R. History of the Old Kittanning Cemetery, 1811-1960. 113p. 1995. per. 14.95 (*1-55856-202-8*, 251) Closson Pr.

Mechling, Allen R. & Mechling, Marla K. Patients with Communicable Diseases in the Borough of Kittanning, PA 1907-1955. 136p. 1995. per. 6.00 (*1-55856-210-9*, 106) Closson Pr.

Mechling, Jay. Church, State, & Public Policy: The New Shape of the Church - State Debate. LC 79-17711. (AEI Symposia Ser.: No. 79F). (Illus.). 136p. reprint ed. pap. 42.20 (*0-8357-4449-3*, 203728600008) Bks Demand.

Mechling, Jay, et al, eds. Children's Folklore: A Sourcebook. LC 95-5152. (Illus.). 392p. 1995. text 66.00 (*0-8240-5418-0*, SS647) Garland.

Mechling, Jay, jt. ed. see Gillespie, Angus K.

Mechling, Marla K., jt. auth. see Mechling, Allen R.

***Mechmann, Edward T.** God, Society & the Human Person: Catholic Social Teaching As Presented in the Catechism of the Catholic Church. 96p. (YA). 2000. pap. 9.95 (*0-8189-0886-6*, Saint Pauls) Alba.

Mechner, Vicki, ed. Healing Journeys: The Power of Rubenfeld Synergy. LC 98-67158. xii, 355p. 1998. pap. 14.95 (*0-9664261-3-4*) OmniQuest Pr.

Mechnikov, et al. Founders of Modern Medicine. Berger, D., tr. LC 78-142669. (Essay Index Reprint Ser.). 1977. 23.95 (*0-8369-2111-9*) Ayer.

Mecholsky, J. J. & Powell, S. R., Jr., eds. Fractography of Ceramic & Metal Failures - STP 827. LC 83-71813. 272p. 1984. text 42.00 (*0-8031-0215-1*, STP827) ASTM.

Mechoso, Carlos, jt. ed. see Clymer, Mark.

Mechoulam, Raphael. Cannabinoids As Therapeutic Agents. 200p. 1986. 115.00 (*0-8493-5772-1*, RM666, CRC Reprint) Franklin.

Mechtel. Flucht Ins Fremde Paradies: C Level. text 8.95 (*0-8219-0870-7*) EMC-Paradigm.

Mechthild of Magdeburg. Mechthild of Magdeburg: The Flowing Light of the Godhead. Tobin, Frank, tr. from GEH. & intro. by. LC 97-44826. (Classics of Western Spirituality Ser.: No. 91). 560p. 1998. 34.95 (*0-8091-0495-4*) Paulist Pr.

***Mechthild of Magdeburg.** Meditations from Mechthild of Magdeburg. Carrigan, Henry L., Jr., ed. LC 99-11222. (Living Library). Orig. Title: Selections from the Flowing Light of the Godhead. 126p. 1999. pap. 11.95 (*1-55725-217-3*, 930-020, Pub. by Paraclete MA) BookWorld.

Mechtild of Hackeborn. Booke of Gostlye Grace of Mechtild of Hackeborn. Halligan, Theresa A., ed. pap. text 13.14 (*0-88844-046-4*) Brill Academic Pubs.

***Mechtingen, Von.** Eliska. 1998. pap. text 8.95 (*1-897809-46-8*) Silver Moon.

Mechtly, E. H. The International System of Units. 1977. pap. 2.80 (*0-87563-139-8*) Stipes.

***Mechworks Software Inc., Inc.** Solving Mechanics of Materials Problems with Matlab. LC 99-10487. 175p. (C). 1999. pap. text 27.67 (*0-13-021537-6*) P-H.

Mecimore, Charles D., jt. auth. see Hildreth, W. Bartley.

Mecimore, Charles D., jt. auth. see King, Betty A.

Meck, Charles R. Fishing Small Streams with a Fly Rod. LC 91-3400. (Illus.). 224p. 1991. pap. 15.00 (*0-88150-202-2*, Pub. by Countryman) Norton.

— Patterns, Hatches, Tactics, & Trout. LC 95-12008. (Illus.). 350p. 1995. 24.95 (*1-55629-050-0*) Vivid Pub.

— Trout Streams & Hatches of Pennsylvania: A Complete Fly-Fishing Guide to 140 Rivers & Streams. 3rd rev. ed. (Trout Streams Ser.). (Illus.). 384p. 1999. pap. 21.95 (*0-88150-453-X*, Pub. by Countryman) Norton.

Meck, Charles R. & Rohmer, John J. Arizona Trout Streams & Their Hatches: Fly-Fishing in the High Deserts of Arizona & Western New Mexico. LC 98-29660. (Trout Streams Ser.). (Illus.). 256p. 1998. pap. 17.95 (*0-88150-423-8*, Pub. by Countryman) Norton.

Meck, Charles R., et al. Mid-Atlantic Trout Streams & Their Hatches: Overlooked Angling in Pennsylvania, New York, & New Jersey. LC 97-10386. (Trout Streams Ser.). (Illus.). 192p. (Orig.). 1997. pap. 17.00 (*0-88150-397-5*, Pub. by Countryman) Norton.

Meck, Charles R., jt. auth. see Hoover, Greg.

Meck, Stuart & Pearlman, Kenneth. Ohio Planning & Zoning Law. 730p. (Orig.). 1997. pap. 55.00 (*0-8322-0674-1*) Banks-Baldwin.

Meck, Stuart, jt. auth. see Klein, William.

Mecke, Gunter. Hair, or, the Ligurinus Shock: On a Narcissistic Crisis in Puberty & Its Recurrence in the Man of Fifty. LC 74-82753. 1975. 10.00 (*0-87212-044-9*) Libra.

Meckel, Adrienne M., jt. auth. see Duke, Daniel L.

Meckel, Christoph. Snow Creatures & Other Stories. Bedwell, Carol, tr. from GER. LC 90-37811. (Studies in German Language & Literature: Vol. 3). (Illus.). 104p. 1991. lib. bdg. 59.95 (*0-88946-581-9*) E Mellen.

— Zund & Other Stories. Bedwell, Carol, tr. from GER. LC 90-37947. (Studies in German Language & Literature: Vol. 2). (Illus.). 120p. 1991. lib. bdg. 59.95 (*0-88946-580-0*) E Mellen.

Meckel, Daniel J., ed. see Hall, James A.

Meckel, Daniel J., ed. see Moore, Robert L.

Meckel, Mary V. A Sociological Analysis of the California Taxi-Dancer: The Hidden Halls. LC 94-38355. (Women's Studies: Vol. 8). 168p. 1995. text 79.95 (*0-7734-9039-6*) E Mellen.

Meckel, Richard A. Save the Babies: American Public Health Reform & the Prevention of Infant Mortality, 1850-1929. LC 89-15389. (Henry E. Sigerist Series in the History of Medicine). (Illus.). 360p. 1990. text 55.00 (*0-8018-3879-7*) Johns Hopkins.

— Save the Babies: American Public Health Reform & the Prevention of Infant Mortality, 1850-1929. LC 98-26843. (Ann Arbor Paperbacks Ser.). 336p. 1998. pap. text 19.95 (*0-472-08556-5*, 08556) U of Mich Pr.

***Meckelnborg, Christina & Schneider, Bernd.** Opusculum Fabularum: Die Fabelsammlung Der Berliner Handschrift Theol. Lat. Fol. 142. 208p. 1999. 68.00 (*90-04-11333-9*) Brill Academic Pubs.

Meckenstock, Guenter, ed. Schleiermacher's Bibliothek: Bearbeitung des Faksimilierten Rauchschen Auktionskatalogs & der Hauptbuecher des Verlages G. Reimer. (Schleiermacher-Archiv Ser.: Bd 10). (GER.). vii, 349p. (C). 1993. lib. bdg. 152.35 (*3-11-013619-8*) De Gruyter.

Meckenstock, Guenter, jt. ed. see Ringleben, Joachim.

Meckenstock, Guenter, ed. see Schleiermacher, Friedrich Daniel Ernst.

Meckenstock, Gunter. Wirtschaftsethik. 415p. 1997. text 52.00 (*3-11-015559-1*); pap. text 32.00 (*3-11-015558-3*) De Gruyter.

Meckert, U. Russian for Restaurant & Hotels: Russisch fuer das Gaststaetten-und Hotelwesen. 3rd ed. (GER & RUS.). 184p. 1982. 29.95 (*0-8288-1476-7*, M15241) Fr & Eur.

Meckes, Richard L., jt. auth. see Brette, Michael N.

Meckier, Jerome. Hidden Rivalries in Victorian Fiction: Dickens, Realism, & Revaluation. LC 87-6177. 320p. 1987. 38.00 (*0-8131-1622-8*) U Pr of Ky.

Meckier, Jerome, ed. Critical Essays on Aldous Huxley. LC 95-12209. (Critical Essays on British Literature Ser.). 1995. 49.00 (*0-8161-8873-4*, G K Hall & Co) Mac Lib Ref.

Meckier, Jerome, jt. ed. see Clubbe, John.

Mecklenbrauker, W. & Hlawatsch, F., eds. The Wigner Distribution: Theory & Applications in Signal Processing. LC 97-27475. 480p. 1997. 225.00 (*0-444-88856-X*) Elsevier.

Mecklenburg, Frank, tr. see Bloch, Ernst.

Mecklenburg, Frank, tr. see Degenhart, Bernhard & Schmitt, Annegrit.

Mecklenburg, R. E., et al. Tobacco Effects in the Mouth. (Illus.). 28p. (Orig.). (C). 1995. pap. text 25.00 (*0-7881-2182-0*) DIANE Pub.

Mecklenburg, Virginia. Edward Hopper: Watercolors. LC 99-6287. 192p. 1999. text 39.95 (*0-393-04849-7*) Norton.

Mecklenburg, Virginia M. Modern American Realism: The Sara Roby Foundation Collection. 2nd ed. LC 08-474691. (Illus.). 148p. (Orig.). 1998. pap. 21.95 (*0-87474-691-4*) Smithsonian.

— The Patricia & Phillip Frost Collection: American Abstraction, 1930-45. LC 89-43055. (Illus.). 200p. (C). 1989. pap. 29.95 (*0-87474-717-1*) Smithsonian.

Mecklenburg, Virginia M. & Ausfeld, Margaret L. Advancing American Art: Politics & Aesthetics in the U. S. State Department Exhibition, 1946-48. LC 83-19301. (Illus.). 120p. 1984. pap. 12.00 (*0-89280-021-6*) Montgomery Mus.

Mecklenburg, Virginia M., et al. Edward Hopper: The Watercolors. LC 99-6287. 1999. write for info. (*0-937311-58-8*) Natl Mus Amer Art.

Mecklenburger, James A. & Hostrop, Richard W., eds. Education Vouchers: From Theory to Alum Rock. LC 72-8872. 410p. 1972. pap. 23.95 (*0-88280-002-7*) ETC Pubns.

Mecklenburgh, J. C. Plant Layout: A Guide to the Layout of Process Plant & Sites. LC 74-181804. 160p. reprint ed. pap. 49.60 (*0-608-13147-4*, 202523400043) Bks Demand.

Mecklenburgh, J. C. & Hartland, S. The Theory of Backmixing: The Design of Continuous Flow Chemical Plant with Backmixing. LC 74-32190. 529p. reprint ed. pap. 164.00 (*0-608-14928-4*, 202597700048) Bks Demand.

Meckler, Alan M. Micropublishing: A History of Scholarly Micropublishing in America, 1938-1980, 40. LC 81-6955. (Contributions in Librarianship & Information Science Ser.: No. 40). (Illus.). 179p. 1982. 55.00 (*0-313-23096-X*, MMP/) Greenwood.

Meckler, Alan M., jt. ed. see O'Sullivan, John.

Meckler, Jack M. & Treasury Management Association Staff. The Corporate Guide to Payments Systems Risk: Assessing & Controlling Payments Risk. (Illus.). 186p. (C). 1995. 60.00 (*1-55738-885-7*) Treasry Mgmt.

Meckler, Milton. Improving Indoor Air Quality. 284p. (C). 1996. 79.00 (*0-13-231820-2*) P-H.

— Improving Indoor Air Quality Through Design, Operation, & Maintenance. LC 95-49207. 1996. 74.00 (*0-88173-208-7*) Fairmont Pr.

— Innovative Energy Design for the '90s. (Illus.). 403p. 64.00 (*0-88173-123-4*, 0263) Fairmont Pr.

Meckler, Milton, ed. Indoor Air Quality - Design Guidebook. 283p. 1991. 74.00 (*0-88173-088-2*) Fairmont Pr.

— Retrofitting of Buildings for Energy Conservation. LC 94-4801. 489p. 1994. 75.00 (*0-88173-183-8*) Fairmont Pr.

Meckler, R. Wippo, jt. auth. see Koren, Leonard.

Meckley, David. Field Experiences 328, 428 & 450. (C). pap. text. write for info. (*0-7872-6742-2*) Kendall-Hunt.

— Field Experiences 451 & 468. (C). pap. text. write for info. (*0-7872-6745-7*) Kendall-Hunt.

Meckley, Ilene L. Sharing & Caring--The Key to Taking Your Business up, up, & Away! (Illus.). viii, 185p. 1998. pap. 15.00 (*1-892464-00-4*) Meckley Pubng Co.

Meckley, Stephanie R., et al. Just Like Mom. (Illus.). 24p. (J). (gr. k-2). 1998. pap. 3.00 (*1-892464-03-9*) Meckley Pubng Co.

Mecklin, John M. Democracy & Race Friction. LC 70-124244. (Select Bibliographies Reprint Ser.). 1977. reprint ed. 20.95 (*0-8369-5432-7*) Ayer.

— Democracy & Race Friction: A Study in Social Ethics. LC 78-172717. reprint ed. 24.50 (*0-404-00090-8*) AMS Pr.

Meckna, Michael. Twentieth-Century Brass Soloists: Bio-Critical Source Books on Musical Performance. LC 93-23943. 344p. 1994. lib. bdg. 85.00 (*0-313-26468-6*, MTC/, Greenwood Pr) Greenwood.

— Virgil Thomson: A Bio-Bibliography, 4. LC 86-14229. (Bio-Bibliographies in Music Ser.: No. 4). 217p. 1986. lib. bdg. 55.00 (*0-313-25010-3*, MVN/, Greenwood Pr) Greenwood.

Meckna, Michael, ed. The Collected Works of Alfred B. Sedgwick. LC 94-707. (Nineteenth-Century American Musical Theater Ser.: No. 7). 488p. 1994. reprint ed. text 149.00 (*0-8153-1369-1*) Garland.

Meconis, Charles A. & Makeeev, Boris N. U. S. - Russian Naval Cooperation. LC 95-30655. 192p. 1995. 59.95 (*0-275-95387-4*, Praeger Pubs) Greenwood.

***Meconis, Charles A. & Wallace, Michael D.** East Asian Naval Weapons Acquisitions in the 1990s: Causes, Consequences, & Responses. LC 99-26749. 248p. 2000. write for info. (*0-275-96251-2*, Praeger Pubs) Greenwood.

Med-Facts, Inc. Staff. Injury & Illness Prevention Program. rev. ed. 122p. 1992. 199.95 (*1-884006-26-4*) Med-Facts.

— OSHA's Bloodborne Pathogen Procedures Made Cost Effective: FED-OSHA Mandated Exposure Control for Occupational Exposure Control to Bloodborne Pathogens. rev. ed. 118p. 1993. student ed. 495.00 (*1-884006-25-6*) Med-Facts.

Meda, L., jt. auth. see Cerofolini, G. F.

Medalia, Leon S., Jr. My First Ninety Years. 300p. 1974. 12.00 (*0-685-41734-4*) Fountainhead.

Medalia, Nahum Z. & Larsen, Otto N. Diffusion & Belief in a Collective Delusion: The Seattle Windshield Pitting Epidemic. (Reprint Series in Social Sciences). (C). 1993. reprint ed. pap. text 5.00 (*0-8290-2718-1*, S-602) Irvington.

Medalie, David. Encounters: An Anthology of South African Short Stories. LC 98-137327. 272p. 1998. pap. 49.95 (*1-86814-325-2*, U Pr W Africa) Intl Scholars.

Medard, Louis A. Accidental Explosions, Vol. 1: Physical & Chemical Properties. (Applied Science Ser.). 1989. text 74.95 (*0-470-21530-5*) P-H.

— Accidental Explosions, Vol. 2: Types of Explosive Substances. (Applied Science Ser.). 1989. text 74.95 (*0-470-21532-1*) P-H.

— Gas Encyclopedia. 1150p. 1976. 481.00 (*0-444-41492-4*) Elsevier.

Medaris, Gene. Ted McRoberts: North Country Marshal. 224p. 1987. pap. 19.95 (*0-937708-06-2*) Great Northwest.

Medaris, L. G., Jr., ed. Early Proterozoic Geology of the Great Lakes Region. LC 83-11509. (Geological Society of America Ser.: Vol. 160). (Illus.). 148p. 1983. reprint ed. pap. 45.90 (*0-608-07711-9*, 206779900010) Bks Demand.

Medawar. Murder on the Boundary. 1999. text. write for info. (*0-312-20938-X*) St Martin.

Medawar, J. S., jt. auth. see Medawar, Peter Brian.

***Medawar, Mardi.** Fort Larned Incident. 2000. text 23.95 (*0-312-20878-2*) St Martin.

Medawar, Mardi Oakley. Death at Rainy Mountain. 288p. 1998. mass mkt. 5.99 (*0-425-16141-2*, Prime Crime) Berkley Pub.

An Asterisk (*) at the beginning of an entry indicates that the title is appearing for the first time.

— Murder at Medicine Lodge. LC 98-37611. 272p. 1999. text 23.95 (*0-312-19925-2*) St Martin.
— People of the Whistling Waters. 442p. 1993. 19.95 (*1-879915-05-7*) Affil Writers America.
Medawar, Peter Brian. Advice to a Young Scientist. 128p. 1981. reprint ed. pap. 14.00 (*0-465-00092-4*, Pub. by Basic) HarpC.
— Consejo a un Joven Cientifico. (Breviarios Ser.). (SPA.). pap. 6.99 (*968-16-1317-1*, Pub. by Fondo) Continental Bk.
— Induction & Intuition in Scientific Thought. LC 69-17272. (Memoirs Ser.: Vol. 75). 1980. pap. 10.00 (*0-87169-075-6*, M075-MEP) Am Philos.
— Memoir of a Thinking Radish. large type ed. 16p. 1989. reprint ed. 19.95 (*1-85089-301-2*, Pub. by ISIS Lrg Prnt) Transaction Pubs.
Medawar, Peter Brian & Medawar, J. S. Aristotle to Zoos: A Philosophical Dictionary of Biology. LC 84-16529. (Illus.). 319p. 1983. pap. text 13.00 (*0-674-04537-8*) HUP.
— Aristotle to Zoos: A Philosophical Dictionary of Biology. (Illus.). 319p. 1983. 37.50 (*0-674-04535-1*) HUP.
Medbery, James D., jt. ed. see Culp, Robert D.
Medbh, Maighread. The Making of a Pagan. 66p. (Orig.). 1990. pap. 11.95 (*0-85640-455-1*, Pub. by Blackstaff Pr) Dufour.
***Medbh, Maighread.** Tenant. LC 99-490279. 96p. 2000. pap. 13.95 (*1-897648-52-9*, Pub. by Salmon Poetry) Dufour.
Medcalf, Bill. Adventure in Writing: How to Write Adventure Stories & Books - And Get Them Published. (Illus.). 115p. 1997. pap. 8.95 (*0-9620226-1-6*) Wildwood TX.
— Retrieve: A New, Gentle Approach to Retriever Training. (Illus.). 200p. 1990. 15.95 (*0-9620226-0-8*) Wildwood TX.
Medcalf, Donald, jt. auth. see Russell, Ronald.
Medcalf, Gordon, ed. see Eveleigh, Mark.
Medcalf, Gordon, ed. see Riches, Sue & Riches, Victoria.
Medcalf, John. A Parish at War: Letters from Nicaragua. 110p. 1989. pap. 7.95 (*0-87243-182-7*) Templegate.
Medcalf, Linda J. Law & Identity: Lawyers, Native Americans & Legal Practice. LC 78-588. (Sage Library of Social Research: Vol. 62). 148p. reprint ed. pap. 45.90 (*0-608-31009-3*, 202193100026) Bks Demand.
Medcalf, Linda J., jt. auth. see Dolbeare, Kenneth M.
***Medcalf, Peter.** War in the Shadows: Bougainville 1944-45. rev. ed. (Illus.). 170p. 2000. pap. 19.95 (*0-7022-3144-4*, Pub. by Univ Queensland Pr) Intl Spec Bk.
Medcalf, Stephen, ed. The Later Middle Ages. LC 81-6509. (Context of English Literature Ser.). 300p. 1981. pap. 21.50 (*0-8419-0726-9*) Holmes & Meier.
— Poems for All Purposes: Selected Poems of G. K. Chesterton. (Illus.). 208p. 1994. 19.95 (*0-7126-5881-5*, Pub. by Pimlico) Trafalgar.
***Medcom.** Age Specific Video. 1998. 198.67 (*0-8359-5404-8*) P-H.
— Infection Control Video. 2nd ed. 1998. 155.00 (*0-8359-5402-1*) P-H.
Medcraft, Rosalie & Gee, Valda. The Sausage Tree. 200p. 1995. pap. 16.95 (*0-7022-2783-8*, Pub. by Univ Queensland Pr) Intl Spec Bk.
Meddaugh, et al. Cost Accounting for Managerial Planning, Decision Making & Control. 4th ed. LC 91-73135. 744p. 1992. pap., student ed. 23.95 (*0-87393-137-8*) Dame Pubns.
Meddaugh, Susan. Beast Pa, 001. LC 80-24851. 32p. (J). (ps-3). 1985. pap. 6.95 (*0-395-38366-8*) HM.
***Meddaugh, Susan.** The Best Place. LC 98-50184. (Illus.). 32p. (J). (ps-3). 1999. 15.00 (*0-395-97994-3*, W Lorraine) HM.
Meddaugh, Susan. Cinderella's Rat. LC 97-2156. (Illus.). 32p. (J). (ps-3). 1997. 15.00 (*0-395-86833-5*) HM.
— Hog-Eye. LC 95-3951. (Illus.). 32p. (J). (ps-3). 1998. pap. 5.95 (*0-395-93746-9*) HM.
***Meddaugh, Susan.** Martha & Skits. LC 00-23988. (Illus.). (J). 2000. 15.00 (*0-618-05776-5*) HM.
Meddaugh, Susan. Martha Blah Blah. (Illus.). 32p. (J). 1996. 14.95 (*0-395-79755-1*) HM.
— Martha Blah Blah. LC 95-53275. (Illus.). 32p. (J). (ps-3). 1998. pap. 5.95 (*0-395-90118-9*) HM.
— Martha Calling. LC 93-50611. 1994. 10.15 (*0-606-10259-0*, Pub. by Turtleback) Demco.
— Martha Speaks. LC 91-48455. (Illus.). 32p. (J). (ps-3). 1992. 15.00 (*0-395-63313-3*) HM.
— Martha Speaks. LC 91-48455. (Illus.). 32p. (J). (ps-3). 1995. pap. 5.95 (*0-395-72952-1*, Sandpiper) HM.
— Martha Speaks. (J). 1995. 10.85 (*0-606-07844-4*, Pub. by Turtleback) Demco.
— Martha Walks the Dog. LC 97-47172. 32p. (J). (gr. k-3). 1998. 15.00 (*0-395-90494-3*) HM.
— Tree of Birds. (Illus.). 32p. (J). (gr. k-3). 1990. 16.00 (*0-395-53147-0*) HM.
— Tree of Birds. 32p. (J). (ps-3). 1994. pap. 5.95 (*0-395-68978-3*) HM.
— The Witches' Supermarket. (Illus.). 32p. (J). (gr. k-3). 1991. 13.95 (*0-395-57034-4*, Sandpiper) HM.
— The Witches' Supermarket. (Illus.). 32p. (J). 1994. pap. 4.95 (*0-395-70092-2*) HM.
— The Witches' Supermarket. (J). 1991. 10.15 (*0-606-08394-4*, Pub. by Turtleback) Demco.
Meddaugh, Susan. Hog-Eye. LC 95-3951. 32p. (J). (gr. k-3). 1995. 14.95 (*0-395-74276-5*) HM.
— Martha Calling. 32p. (J). 1994. 14.95 (*0-395-69825-1*) HM.
— Martha Calling. LC 93-50611. 32p. (J). (ps-3). 1996. pap. 5.95 (*0-395-82741-8*) HM.
— Martha Habla (Martha Speaks) Date not set. 14.95 (*1-880507-32-3*) Lectorum Pubns.
— Two Ways to Count to Ten: A Liberian Folktale. LC 86-33513. 32p. (J). (ps-2). 1995. 14.95 (*0-8050-0407-6*, Bks Young Read) H Holt & Co.
Meddeb, Abdelwahab, intro. Vital: Three Contemporary African Artists. LC 97-122809. (Illus.). 48p. (C). 1996. pap. 20.00 (*1-85437-170-3*, Pub. by Tate Gallery) U of Wash Pr.
Meddemmen, John, tr. see Segre, Cesare.
Meddick, Jim. Primary Crullers: A Robotman Book. LC 97-71633. (Illus.). 128 p. (Orig.). 1997. pap. 9.95 (*0-8362-3662-9*) Andrews & McMeel.
Meddin, Sheryl & Frisch, Bennett. Stressed Is Just Desserts Spelled Backwards: A Collection of Great American Desserts. LC 96-79804. (Illus.). 144p. 1997. 16.95 (*1-56352-378-7*) Longstreet.
Medding, Peter Y. The Founding of Israeli Democracy, 1948-1967. 264p. 1990. text 65.00 (*0-19-505648-5*) OUP.
— Mapai in Israel: Political Organisation & Government in a New Society. LC 75-184900. 338p. reprint ed. pap. 96.40 (*0-608-16859-9*, 2027240) Bks Demand.
Medding, Peter Y., ed. Israel: State & Society, 1948-1988. (Studies in Contemporary Jewry: Vol. V). 448p. 1989. 29.95 (*0-685-27143-9*) OUP.
— Studies in Contemporary Jewry Vol. V: Israel: State & Society, 1948-1988. 448p. 1989. text 55.00 (*0-19-505827-5*) OUP.
— Studies in Contemporary Jewry Vol. XIV: Coping with Life & Death: Jewish Families in the Twentieth Century. LC 98-31030. 376p. 1999. text 55.00 (*0-19-512820-6*) OUP.
— Studies in Contemporary Jewry, Values, Interests & Identity Vol. 11: Jews & Politics in a Changing World, Vol. 11. (Illus.). 384p. (C). 1996. text 55.00 (*0-19-510331-9*) OUP.
Meddock, Sally. Super Soups, Vol. 14. Winquist, Jeannine, ed. 64p. (Orig.). 1986. pap., per. 3.95 (*0-942320-23-9*) Am Cooking.
Medearis. African-American Arts Series. 1997. 50.94 (*0-8050-5616-5*) H Holt & Co.
Medearis, Angela S. The Adventures of Sugar & Junior. LC 94-42368. (Illus.). 32p. (J). (gr. k-3). 1995. lib. bdg. 15.95 (*0-8234-1182-6*) Holiday.
— The African-American Kitchen: Cooking from Our Heritage. 272p. 1997. pap. 14.95 (*0-452-27638-1*, Plume) Dutton Plume.
— Annie's Gifts. LC 92-71998. (Feeling Good Ser.). (Illus.). 32p. (J). (gr. 1-4). 1994. 14.95 (*0-940975-30-0*); pap. 6.95 (*0-940975-31-9*) Just Us Bks.
— Annie's Gifts. 1994. 12.15 (*0-606-08690-0*, Pub. by Turtleback) Demco.
— Art. LC 97-8073. (J). 1997. lib. bdg. 16.98 (*0-8050-4483-3*) H Holt & Co.
— Best Friends in the Snow. LC 98-24329. (My First Hello Reader Ser.). (Illus.). (J). 1999. 4.99 (*0-590-52284-1*) Scholastic Inc.
— Bye-Bye, Babies! LC 94-41791. (Illus.). 14p. (J). (ps). 1995. bds. 4.95 (*1-56402-258-7*) Candlewick Pr.
— Cooking. LC 97-8071. (African-American Arts Ser.). 80p. (YA). (gr. 5 up). 1997. 20.40 (*0-8050-4484-1*) TFC Bks NY.
— Dancing with the Indians. LC 90-28666. (Illus.). 32p. (J). (gr. k-3). 1991. lib. bdg. 16.95 (*0-8234-0893-0*) Holiday.
— Dancing with the Indians. (Illus.). (J). (ps-4). 2000. 24.95 incl. audio (*0-87499-333-4*); pap. 15.95 incl. audio (*0-87499-332-6*) Live Oak Media.
— Dancing with the Indians. (Illus.). (J). (ps-3). 1991. reprint ed. pap. 6.95 (*0-8234-1023-4*) Holiday.
— Dancing with the Indians, 4 bks., Set. unabridged ed. (Illus.). (J). (gr. k-3). 2000. pap., teacher ed. 37.95 incl. audio (*0-87499-334-2*) Live Oak Media.
— Dare to Dream: Coretta Scott King & the Civil Rights Movement. LC 93-33573. (Rainbow Biography Ser.). (Illus.). 64p. (J). (gr. 3-6). 1994. 13.99 (*0-525-67426-8*, Dutton Child) Peng Put Young Read.
— Eat, Babies, Eat! LC 94-41790. (Illus.). 14p. (J). (ps). 1995. bds. 4.95 (*1-56402-257-9*) Candlewick Pr.
— The Ghost of Sifty-Sifty Sam. LC 96-37489. (Illus.). 32p. (J). (gr. k-4). 1997. 15.95 (*0-590-48290-4*); pap. write for info. (*0-590-48291-2*) Scholastic Inc.
— Haunts: Five Hair-Raising Tales. LC 96-17336. (Illus.). 48p. (J). (gr. 4-6). 1996. lib. bdg. 15.95 (*0-8234-1280-6*) Holiday.
— Here Comes the Snow. LC 95-17364. (Hello Reader! Ser.: Level 1). (Illus.). 32p. (J). (ps-1). 1996. pap. 3.50 (*0-590-26266-1*, Cartwheel) Scholastic Inc.
— Holidays & Celebrations. (J). 1997. lib. bdg. 16.98 (*0-8050-4487-6*) H Holt & Co.
— Jugamos Bajo la Lluvia - We Play on a Rainy Day. Noda, Yolanda, tr. (SPA., Illus.). 32p. (J). (ps-3). 1996. pap. 3.50 (*0-590-73881-X*) Scholastic Inc.
— Literature & Drama. (J). 1997. lib. bdg. 16.98 (*0-8050-4488-4*) H Holt & Co.
— Nannie. LC 95-10360. (Illus.). (J). 1997. 16.00 (*0-689-31858-8*) Atheneum Yung Read.
— 100th Day of School. LC 95-13214. (Hello Reader! Ser.: Level 2). (Illus.). 30p. (J). (gr. k-2). 1996. pap. 2.95 (*0-590-25944-X*, Cartwheel) Scholastic Inc.
— Politics & Civil Rights. (J). 1997. lib. bdg. 16.98 (*0-8050-4486-8*) H Holt & Co.
— Poppa's Itchy Christmas. LC 96-40170. (Illus.). (J). (gr. k-3). 1998. 15.95 (*0-8234-1298-9*) Holiday.
— Poppa's New Pants. LC 94-20489. (Illus.). 32p. (J). (ps-3). 1995. lib. bdg. 15.95 (*0-8234-1155-9*) Holiday.
— Princess of the Press: The Story of Ida B. Wells-Barnett. LC 97-8520. (Rainbow Biography Ser.). (Illus.). 48p. (J). (gr. 2-5). 1997. 14.99 (*0-525-67493-4*, Dutton Child) Peng Put Young Read.
— Religion. (J). 1995. lib. bdg. 16.98 (*0-8050-4485-X*) H Holt & Co.
— Rum-a-Tum-Tum. LC 94-9929. (Illus.). 32p. (J). (gr. k-3). 1997. lib. bdg. 16.95 (*0-8234-1143-5*) Holiday.
— Seeds Grow! LC 98-23888. (Hello Reader! Ser.). (Illus.). 32p. (J). (ps-1). 2000. mass mkt. 3.99 (*0-590-37974-7*) Scholastic Inc.
— The Singing Man: Adapted from a West African Folktale. LC 93-4219. (Illus.). 32p. (J). (gr. k-3). 1994. lib. bdg. 16.95 (*0-8234-1103-6*) Holiday.
— Skin Deep Vol. 1: And Other Teenage Reflections. rev. ed. (Illus.). 48p. (YA). (gr. 10 up). 1997. reprint ed. pap. 10.00 incl. VHS (*0-9660873-0-5*) Diva Prodns.
— Spray-Paint Mystery. (Illus.). 102p. (J). (gr. 5-7). 1996. pap. 2.99 (*0-590-48474-5*) Scholastic Inc.
— Too Much Talk. LC 95-16184. (Illus.). 32p. (J). (ps-3). 1995. 15.95 (*1-56402-323-0*) Candlewick Pr.
Medearis, Angela S. Too Much Talk. (J). 1997. 11.19 (*0-606-13855-2*, Pub. by Turtleback) Demco.
Medearis, Angela S. Too Much Talk. LC 95-16184. (Illus.). 32p. (J). (ps-3). 1997. reprint ed. pap. 5.99 (*0-7636-0398-8*) Candlewick Pr.
— Treemonisha. (Illus.). 40p. (J). (gr. k-4). 1995. 15.95 (*0-8050-1748-8*) H Holt & Co.
— We Eat Dinner in the Bathtub. LC 95-26300. (Hello Reader! Ser.: Level 1). (Illus.). 32p. (J). (gr. k-2). 1996. 3.99 (*0-590-73886-0*) Scholastic Inc.
— We Play on a Rainy Day. (Hello Reader! Ser.). (Illus.). 32p. (J). (ps-1). 1996. pap. 3.50 (*0-590-26265-3*, Cartwheel) Scholastic Inc.
— What Did I Do to Deserve a Sister Like You? LC 95-26358. (J). 1997. 14.00 (*0-689-31935-5*) Atheneum Yung Read.
Medearis, Angela Shelf. Dance. (African-American Arts Ser.). 1997. 20.40 (*0-8050-4481-7*) TFC Bks NY.
Medearis, Angela Shelf. Dare to Dream: Coretta Scott King & the Civil Rights Movement. (Rainbow Biography Ser.). (Illus.). 60p. (gr. 3-7). 1999. pap. 4.99 (*0-14-130202-X*, PuffinBks) Peng Put Young Read.
Medearis, Angela Shelf. Here Comes the Snow. (Hello, Reader! Ser.). 1996. 8.70 (*0-606-09407-5*, Pub. by Turtleback) Demco.
— A Kwanzaa Celebration: Festive Recipes & Homemade Gifts from an African-American Kitchen. 194p. 1999. reprint ed. text 18.00 (*0-7881-6803-7*) DIANE Pub.
— 100th Day of School. (J). 1996. 8.70 (*0-606-08467-3*, Pub. by Turtleback) Demco.
Medearis, Angela Shelf. Seven Days of Kwanzaa: How to Celebrate Them. 128p. (J). (gr. 4-7). 1994. pap. 3.50 (*0-590-46360-8*) Scholastic Inc.
Medearis, Angela Shelf. Seven Days of Kwanzaa: How to Celebrate Them. 1994. 8.60 (*0-606-06728-0*, Pub. by Turtleback) Demco.
— Seven Spools of Thread: A Kwanzaa Story. LC 00-8101. (Illus.). 40p. (J). (gr. 2-7). 2000. lib. bdg. 15.95 (*0-8075-7315-9*) A Whitman.
Medearis, Angela Shelf. The Zebra-Riding Cowboy: A Folk Song from the Old West. LC 91-27941. (Illus.). 89p. (J). (ps-2). 1995. 14.95 (*0-8050-1712-7*, Bks Young Read) H Holt & Co.
— The Zebra-Riding Cowboy: A Folk Song from the Old West. (J). 1997. pap. text 5.95 (*0-8050-5302-6*) H Holt & Co.
— The Zebra-Riding Cowboy: A Folk Song from the Old West. (J). 1997. 11.15 (*0-606-12135-8*, Pub. by Turtleback) Demco.
Medearis, Angela Shelf, jt. auth. see Medearis, Michael.
Medearis, Kenneth G. Report on an Investigation of the Feasibility of Establishing a National Civil Engineering Software Center to the American Society of Civil Engineers for the Research Council on Computer Practices. LC 79-302366. 128p. reprint ed. pap. 39.70 (*0-608-12130-4*, 202382200034) Bks Demand.
***Medearis, Michael & Medearis, Angela Shelf.** Daisy & the Doll. (Family Heritage Ser.). (Illus.). 32p. (J). (gr. 1-5). 2000. 14.95 (*0-916718-15-8*, Pub. by VT Folklife Ctr) IPG Chicago.
Medearis, Angela S. Ideas for Entertaining from the African-American Kitchen: Recipes & Traditions for Holidays Throughout the Year. (Illus.). 320p. 1998. pap. 14.95 (*0-452-27537-7*, Plume) Dutton Plume.
Medeiros, Arthur C. & Loope, Lloyd L. Rare Plants & Animals of Haleakala National Park. (Illus.). 58p. (Orig.). 1995. pap. text 7.95 (*0-940295-13-X*) HI Natural Hist.
Medeiros, Benjamin A. Surplus Values Revisited. 1993. 14.95 (*0-533-10394-0*) Vantage.
Medeiros, Denis M. & Wildman, Robert E. Advanced Human Nutrition. (Modern Nutrition Ser.). 608p. 1999. boxed set 79.95 (*0-8493-8566-0*) CRC Pr.
***Medeiros, Flavio Henrique & Almada, Carlos.** Brazilian Rhythms for Solo Guitar. 56p. 1999. pap. write for info. incl. audio compact disk (*0-7866-4700-0*, 98226BCD) Mel Bay.
Medeiros, Mark D., jt. auth. see Zingg, Paul J.
Medeiros-Neto, Geraldo A., jt. ed. see Gaitan, Eduardo.
Medeiros, Phyllis P. The Seeds & the Soil: The Planting of the Freewill Baptist Church in Hollis, Buxton & Gorham, Maine, 1780-1820. LC 97-44450. 96p. (C). 1997. text 21.50 (*0-7618-0983-X*) U Pr of Amer.
Medeiros, Selene De, see De Medeiros, Selene.
Medeiros, Teresa. Breath of Magic. 400p. (Orig.). 1996. mass mkt. 5.99 (*0-553-56334-3*) Bantam.
***Medeiros, Teresa.** The Bride & the Beast. LC 00-23707. 384p. 2000. 15.95 (*0-553-80125-2*, Spectra) Bantam.
Medeiros, Teresa. Charming the Prince. 352p. 1999. mass mkt. 5.99 (*0-553-57502-3*) Bantam.
— Fairest of Them All. 400p. 1995. mass mkt. 5.99 (*0-553-56333-5*) Bantam.
— Fairest of Them All. LC 96-86157. (Five Star Romances Ser.). 1996. lib. bdg. 23.95 (*0-7862-0864-3*) Five Star.
— Heather & Velvet. 400p. 1992. mass mkt. 5.99 (*0-553-29407-5*) Bantam.
— Lady of Conquest. 400p. 1998. mass mkt. 5.99 (*0-553-58114-7*) Bantam.
— Nobody's Darling. 400p. 1998. mass mkt. 5.99 (*0-553-57501-5*) Bantam.
— Nobody's Darling. large type ed. LC 98-39411. (Large Print Bks.). 1998. pap. 22.95 (*1-56895-675-4*) Wheeler Pub.
— Once an Angel. 432p. 1993. mass mkt. 5.99 (*0-553-29409-1*) Bantam.
— Shadows & Lace. 368p. 1996. mass mkt. 5.99 (*0-553-57623-2*, Fanfare) Bantam.
— Thief of Hearts. 432p. 1994. mass mkt. 5.99 (*0-553-56332-7*) Bantam.
— Thief of Hearts. large type ed. LC 94-40173. 623p. 1995. lib. bdg. 20.95 (*0-7862-0372-2*) Thorndike Pr.
— Touch of Enchantment. 352p. 1997. mass mkt. 5.99 (*0-553-57500-7*, Fanfare) Bantam.
— Touch of Enchantment. LC 98-47829. (Large Print Bks.). 1998. 22.95 (*1-56895-590-1*) Wheeler Pub.
— A Whisper of Roses. 416p. 1993. mass mkt. 5.99 (*0-553-29408-3*) Bantam.
— A Whisper of Roses. large type ed. LC 93-33801. 609p. 1994. lib. bdg. 21.95 (*0-7862-0070-7*) Thorndike Pr.
Medel-Anonuevo, Carolyn. Women Reading the World: Policies & Practices of Literacy in Asia. 134p. 1996. pap. 20.00 (*92-820-1069-4*, U6940, Pub. by UNESCO) Bernan Associates.
Medem, R. Argali. deluxe limited ed. (Illus.). 304p. 1994. boxed set 150.00 (*1-57157-027-6*); boxed set 150.00 (*84-604-9495-0*) Safari Pr.
Medema, K. Gorgles. Vreeman, J., ed. (Orig.). (J). 1985. pap. 3.95 (*0-918789-05-2*) FreeMan Prods.
— Rennis the Nam. Vreeman, J., ed. (Illus.). 16p. (Orig.). (J). 1985. pap. 3.95 (*0-918789-04-4*) FreeMan Prods.
Medema, Steven G. Coasean Economics: Law & Economics & the New Institutional Economics. LC 97-37029. (Recent Economic Thought Ser.). 288p. 1997. lib. bdg. 104.50 (*0-7923-8034-7*) Kluwer Academic.
Medema, Steven G., ed. The Legacy of Ronald Coase in Economic Analysis, 2 vols., Set. LC 94-32261. (Intellectual Legacies in Modern Economics Ser.). 1088p. 1995. 400.00 (*1-85898-010-0*) E Elgar.
Medema, Steven G. & Samuels, Warren J., eds. Foundations of Research in Economics: How do Economists do Economics? LC 96-13005. (Advances in Economic Methodology Ser.). (Illus.). 320p. (C). 1996. text 95.00 (*1-85898-163-8*) E Elgar.
— Foundations of Research in Economics: How Do Economists Do Economics? LC 96-13005. (Advances in Economic Methodology Ser.). 320p. (Orig.). (C). 1998. pap. 30.00 (*1-85898-771-7*) E Elgar.
Medema, Steven G., jt. auth. see Mercuro, Nicholas.
Medema, Steven G., jt. auth. see Samuels, Warren J.
Medenbach de Rooy, J. M. van, see Van der Maesen, L. J.
Medenbach, O. & Wilk, H. The Magic of Minerals. White, J. S., tr. from GER. (Illus.). 204p. 1989. 95.95 (*0-387-15730-1*) Spr-Verlag.
Meder, Heinz. Karibische Geschichten: Dominikanische Republik von und fur "Insider" (GER., Illus.). 216p. 1993. pap. 14.00 (*1-886254-00-1*) Edic Nue Mun.
— Tales of a Caribbean Isle: The Dominican Republic by & for an Insider. (Illus.). 197p. 1994. pap. 14.00 (*1-886254-06-0*) Edic Nue Mun.
Meder, J. & Handbuck, Ein. Durer-Katalog. LC 75-87642. (Graphic Art Ser.: Vol. 12). (Illus.). 358p. 1971. reprint ed. lib. bdg. 85.00 (*0-306-71788-3*) Da Capo.
Meder, Joseph. The Mastery of Drawing, 2 vols., Set. Ames, Winslow, tr. from GER. LC 76-22300. (Illus.). 720p. lib. bdg. 115.00 (*0-913870-16-1*) Abaris Bks.
Meder, Marylouise D., ed. Library School Review, Vol. 16. 1976. pap. 2.00 (*0-941044-00-9*) Sch Lib Sci.
— Library School Review, Vol. 18. 1979. pap. 2.00 (*0-686-26897-0*) Emporia State.
— Library School Review, Vol. 18. 1979. pap. 2.00 (*0-941044-02-5*) Sch Lib Sci.
— Library School Review, Vol. 19. 1980. pap. 2.00 (*0-941044-03-3*) Sch Lib Sci.
Medford, Connie, jt. auth. see Medford, Robert.
Medford, Connie, jt. auth. see Medford, Robert J.
Medford, Constanza R., jt. auth. see Medford, Robert J.
Medford, Edna Greene, jt. ed. see Greenburg, Martin H.
***Medford, Lorrie.** Why Can't I Lose Weight? 304p. 1999. pap. 17.95 (*0-9676419-0-X*) L D N Pubng.
Medford, Robert & Medford, Connie. The Families of Haywood & Jackson Counties, North Carolina: Based on the 1850 Census Records. LC 95-107271. 144p. 1994. pap. 23.00 (*1-56664-070-9*) WorldComm.
— The Families of Haywood County: Based on the 1860 Census Records. 136p. 1995. pap. text 23.00 (*1-56664-071-7*) WorldComm.
— The Families of Haywood County 1880 Census Records. (Families of Haywood County Ser.: Vol. 4). 234p. 1995. pap. text 23.00 (*1-56664-085-7*) WorldComm.
— The Families of Haywood County 1870 Census Records. (Families of Haywood County Ser.: Vol. 3). 190p. 1995. pap. 23.00 (*1-56664-079-2*) WorldComm.
— The Families of Haywood County 1910 Census, 6 vols., Vol. 6. LC 98-199093. (Families of Haywood County Ser.). 506p. 1998. pap. 28.00 (*1-56664-131-4*) WorldComm.
— The Families of Haywood County, 1900 Census. (Families of Haywood County Ser.: Vol. 5). 380p. 1996. pap. 26.00 (*1-56664-089-X*) WorldComm.
***Medford, Robert, et al.** Kinslands & Related Lines. 360p. 2000. 67.00 (*0-7404-0074-6*); pap. 55.00 (*0-7404-0075-4*) Higginson Bk Co.
— Suttons & Related Lines: Some Descendants of John Sutton of Attleborough, England. 965p. 2000. 125.00 (*0-7404-0958-1*); pap. 115.00 (*0-7404-0959-X*) Higginson Bk Co.

M

–MDR Domestic 2000, 2 vols. rev. ed. (Illus.). 3500p. 2000. 325.00 (*1-56363-348-5*) Med Econ.
The only single-source listing of every medical supplier licensed to sell products in the U.S. - with over 1,000 new companies added this year. Fast access to the facts on over 12,000 companies & more than 65,000 products. The 2000 edition contains more ISO 9000 Series Registration & CE-marked device data as well as e-mail & WWW addresses than ever before. Two fully cross-referenced volumes: Volume I - Product Directory: every medical device & supply & diagnostic available in the U.S. Unique 5-character FDA code identifying the medical specialty & the device name; Full company name, address & telephone number for every manufacturer of the product. Prices & product specifications (when available) to help compare products from different suppliers. Volume II - Supplier Profiles: complete background on each company including number of employees, ownership, method of distribution, sales volume, revenue & net income. Handy indexes include Keyword Index, Trade Name Index, Supplier Geographical Index & OEM (Original Equipment Manufacturer) Index. 3,200 pages. Available: January 2000. (Special combo package of WinMDR & MDR print edition also available. ISBN: 1-56363-351-5, $499.00. Call for details.) *Publisher Paid Annotation.*

–MDR International, 2000. rev. ed. (Illus.). 1100p. 2000. 275.00 (*1-56363-349-3*, PDR) Med Econ.
For those interested in medical supplies & companies outside the U.S., this invaluable resource covers more than 7,000 suppliers & 25,000 products from over 70 countries including Canada. Organized in the same easy format as the U.S. edition, the MDR International Edition saves valuable research time. Detailed supplier profile directory includes manufacturer's address & telephone numbers, contracts, financial data, number of employees, method of distribution, a complete list of products available & more. Also includes Trade Name Index & Supplier Geography Index, all cross-referenced, making it easy to quickly find the right companies & products. 1,100 pages. Available: January 2000. *Publisher Paid Annotation.*

–PDR Companion Guide 2000. 54th rev. ed. (Illus.). 2000p. 2000. 59.95 (*1-56363-340-X*, PDR) Med Econ.
Cross-referenced to the 2000 editions of the PDR, PDR for Opthalmology & PDR for Nonprescription Drugs & Dietary Supplements, this unique, time-saving, all-in-one clinical reference assures safe & appropriate drug selection with nine critical checkpoints: Interactions Index, Food Interactions Cross-Reference, Side Effects Index, Indications Index, Contraindications Index, Off-Label Treatment Guide, Cost of Therapy Guide, International Drug Guide, Generic Availability Table, New for 2000, an Imprint Identification Guide which enables readers to quickly identify thousands of drugs by imprint alone. (i.e. strength, color, form, shape, etc.) *Publisher Paid Annotation.*

–PDR for Nonprescription Drugs & Dietary Supplements. 21st rev. ed. (Illus.). 500p. 2000. 49.95 (*1-56363-341-8*, PDR) Med Econ.
The 2000 PDR for Nonprescription Drugs & Dietary Supplements provides critical information on those ingredients that move from prescription to nonprescription status as well as new over-the-counter drugs that are introduced every year. The 2000 edition contains: a section on dietary supplements including nutritionals, herbals, & functional foods; full detailed descriptions of the most commonly used nonprescription drugs & products; color photos of hundreds of OTC drugs for quick ID - cross referenced to the detailed descriptions; four separate indices for quick ID (by category, product name, manufacturer & active ingredient), comprehensive coverage of ingredients, indications, drug interactions, dosage, administration & more. And a Companion Drug Index to common diseases & frequently encountered side effects. *Publisher Paid Annotation.*

–PDR for Ophthalmology 2000. 28th rev. ed. (Illus.). 250p. 1999. 54.95 (*1-56363-339-6*, PDR) Med Econ.
Exclusive product information on the care & treatment of the eye. This indispensable guide is the definitive directory of drug & product data relating uniquely to the practice of Ophthalmology & Optometry. 230 pages. Available: November 1999 *Publisher Paid Annotation.*

–PDR Nurses Drug Handbook, 2000. 6th ed. (C). 1999. pap. 29.95 (*0-7668-1086-0*) Thomson Learn.
Lightweight & portable, the PDR Nurse's Handbook puts essential drug data at your fingertips & offers crystal-clear explanations of the information the practicing nurse needs to do their job effectively. Published in cooperation with Delmar Publishers, the 2000 edition is easier & quicker to use than ever. Arranged in a handy A-Z format, the Handbook provides complete, alphabetically arranged descriptions of each drug, including contents, dosage, side effects, overdose symptoms & treatments. Free internet updates. Instructions included with the book. Detailed listings for the most widely prescribed retail drugs, commonly administered hospital medications, & numerous drugs used in long-term & home health care. Available: August 1999. Also available in CD-ROM format. Call for details. *Publisher Paid Annotation.*

–PDR Supplements, 2000: Combined Supplements A & B. 54th rev. ed. (Illus.). 300p. 2000. 29.95 (*1-56363-344-2*, PDR) Med Econ.
PDR Supplements provide every important update between annual editions of the PDR. And they fit neatly inside the front cover of the PDR where they are always available for ready reference. *Publisher Paid Annotation.*

–PDR 2000: Bookstore Version. 54th rev. ed. (Illus.). 3000p. 1999. 82.95 (*1-56363-335-3*, PDR) Med Econ.
Completely revised & updated, the 2000 PDR provides FDA-approved drug information on more than 4,000 prescription drugs, over 2,100 full-color, actual-size photos of medicines for instant identification, & important data on over 250 drug manufacturers. New medicines, new drug interaction data, the most recent side effects findings, & certain drugs now removed from the market make it absolutely critical that medical professionals keep up-to-date with the very latest prescription drug information. The 2000 PDR contains: the newest drugs--which drugs are indicated for the diagnosed condition; how different drugs interact; latest findings on side effects caused by the prescribed drug; recommended dosages; clinical pharmacology; pediatric use; contraindications; FDA use-in-pregnancy ratings; & more. Hundreds of new drugs added including: Avandia, Celebrex, Vioxx, Enbrel, Pletal, Agenerase, & many more. New larger trim allows dramatically improved readability. 3,000 pages. Available: November 1999 *Publisher Paid Annotation.*

–2000 HMO PPO Directory. (Illus.). 340p. 1999. 215.00 (*1-56363-352-3*, PDR) Med Econ.
The 2000 HMO/PPO Directory is an invaluable resource which provides detailed information on over 600 HMO's & more than 1,000 PPO's with listings organized alphabetically by state & city - including name, address, phone number & key decision makers by title & name, plus e-mail addresses whenever available. 100
verified by our Data Verification Group, the book also contains difficult to find details such as: current member enrollments, number of affiliated physicians & affiliated hospitals, average claim compensation categories for both physicians & hospitals; year founded; employer references; federal qualifications; profit or non-profit status; type of HMO/PPO (staff, IPA, group, network) Six cross referenced indexes that include listings alphabetically by organization, by personnel, & by the number of members enrolled. 340 pages, Available: November 1999. (Special combo package of WinHMO/PPO on CD-ROM & print edition also available. ISBN: 1-56363-354-X. $499.00. Call for details.) *Publisher Paid Annotation.*

–Red Book 2000. 104th rev. ed. (Illus.). 800p. 2000. pap. 61.95 (*1-56363-357-4*, PDR) Med Econ.
Celebrating 104 years of service, Red Book remains the pharmacy's most reliable source for accurate product information & prices on prescription drugs, OTC items & reimbursable medical supplies. With valuable clinical & pharmaceutical reference information, Red Book is the essential resource healthcare professionals reach for every day. The new 2000 Red Book contains extensive updates & additions & provides the latest pricing & product information on over 100,000 Rx & OTC items but also includes the broad spectrum of healthcare information in one volume, to cope with pharmacy's changing role in the medical, pharmaceutical & retail marketplace. Sections include: Nationally recognized Average Wholesale Prices (AWPs), Direct Prices, & Federal Upper Limit prices for prescription drugs; Suggested Retail prices for OTC products; NDC numbers for all FDA-approved drugs; Complete package information including dosage form, route of administration, strength & size, "Orange Book" codes-FDA's Approved Drug Products with Therapeutic Equivalent Evaluations; Vitamin Comparison Table: Amounts of vitamins & minerals in over 50 popular multivitamin products; Common Laboratory Values: Answers to the most common patient questions about urine sugar level, cholesterol, book pressure & more; Guide to Leading Alternative Medicines; Pharmacy Buying Groups-Group Purchasing Organizations in the pharmaceutical marketplace; NCPDP Billing Standards; Controlled Substance Inventory Sheet. Full color photos. *Publisher Paid Annotation.*

— 2000 Physicians' Desk Reference. 54th rev. ed. (Illus.). 3000p. 1999. 82.95 (*1-56363-330-2*, PDR) Med Econ.

Medical Economics Staff, ed. Veterinary Pharmaceutical & Biologicals: The Veterinanan's PDR. 11th rev. ed. 1300p. 1998. 79.95 (*0-935078-73-8*) Veterinary Med.
"The Veterinarian's PDR" - the most complete source of veterinary products available. An easy-to-use source of prescribing information on more than 4,300 veterinary products, including those approved by FDA, USDA & EPA. Organized by brand & generic name for instant accessibility, it covers therapeutic indications, dosage & administration, precautions, adverse reactions & more. Plus, a brand & generic name index for quick cross-referencing between veterinary & human drugs. 1,300 pages. Published biennially in cooperation with Veterinary Medicine Publishing Co. Available: December 1998. *Publisher Paid Annotation.*

***Medical Economics Staff & Williams & Wilkins Staff.** PDR Medical Dictionary. 2nd rev. ed. 2100p. 2000. 49.95 (*1-56363-338-8*, PDR) Med Econ.

Medical Education Board. Preparation for the United States Medical Licensing Examinations, Step 1, Bk. F. (USMLE Ser.). (Illus.). 150p. (C). 1997. 18.00 (*1-884083-08-0*) Maval Pub.

Medical Education Board, jt. auth. see Waintrub, Mauricio L.

Medical Education Board Staff, jt. auth. see Waintrub, Mauricio L.

Medical Education Board Staff, jt. auth. see Waintrub, Mauricio W.

Medical Follow Up Agency Staff, jt. auth. see Institute of Medicine Staff.

Medical Library Association Staff. Directory of the Medical Library Association, 1989-1990. 151p. 1989. pap. 43.75 (*0-912176-27-X*) Med Lib Assn.

— Directory of the Medical Library Association, 1990-1991. 168p. 1990. pap. 43.75 (*0-912176-31-8*) Med Lib Assn.

— Directory of the Medical Library Association, 1991-1992. 175p. 1991. pap. 95.00 (*0-912176-32-6*) Med Lib Assn.

— Directory of the Medical Library Association, 1993-1994. 200p. 1993. pap. 150.00 (*0-912176-35-0*) Med Lib Assn.

— Salary Survey, 1992. 39p. 1992. pap. 52.00 (*0-912176-33-4*) Med Lib Assn.

Medical Library Association Staff, jt. auth. see Johnson, Mary E.

Medical Library Association Staff, jt. auth. see Shedlock, James.

Medical Library Staff. Directory of the Medical Library Association 1994-1995. 224p. 1996. pap. 150.00 (*0-912176-36-9*) Med Lib Assn.

Medical Management Institute Staff. The Medical Office Policy Manual. LC 95-39519. (Illus.). 199p. (Orig.). 1996. pap. text 44.95 (*0-07-600796-0*, ME109) Practice Mgmt Info.

***Medical Officers of Schools Association Staff.** The Handbook of School Health. 18th rev. ed. 334p. 1999. pap. 39.95 (*1-85856-081-0*, Trentham Bks) Stylus Pub VA.

Medical Records Staff. Healthcare Information Management. 1994. text 70.00 (*0-7602-0047-5*, Irwn Prfssnl) McGraw-Hill Prof.

Medical Review Staff. Behavioral Science, 1996: Digging up the Bones, Vol. 5. (Medical Review Ser.). (Illus.). 86p. 1997. pap. 18.95 (*0-07-038218-2*) McGraw-Hill HPD.

— Pharmacology, 1995: Digging up the Bones, Vol. 1. (Medical Review Ser.). (Illus.). 99p. 1997. pap. 18.95 (*0-07-038214-X*) McGraw-Hill HPD.

— Psychiatry, 1995: Digging up the Bones, Vol. 6. (Medical Review Ser.). (Illus.). 108p. 1997. pap. 18.95 (*0-07-038219-0*) McGraw-Hill HPD.

Medical Support Systems Staff, ed. Complications of Laparoscopy & Flexible Endoscopy: Postgraduate Course of the Annual Meeting of the Society of American Gastrointenstinal Endoscopic Surgeons (SAGES) 1994. 1994. 170.00 (*0-387-14219-3*) Spr-Verlag.

Medical Tribune, Inc. Staff. Medicine: The Year in Review, 1992. 320p. 1992. 49.95 (*0-931861-81-0*) Med Tribune.

Medical View Staff. Stedman's English-Japanese-English Medical Dictionary. 2nd ed. 1973p. 1984. 250.00 (*0-8288-1850-9*) Fr & Eur.

Medici, Angelo, ed. see Warren, Bert.

Medici, Geraldine A. Drug Dosages & Solutions. 2nd ed. 373p. (C). 1988. pap. text 28.95 (*0-8385-1775-7*, A1775-4) Appleton & Lange.

Medici, Marina. Good Magic. 256p. 1989. pap. 20.00 (*0-671-76316-4*) Simon & Schuster.

— Love Magic. LC 93-3847. 256p. 1994. pap. 16.00 (*0-671-79684-4*, Fireside) S&S Trade Pap.

Medici, Mario, jt. ed. see Conati, Marcello.

Medicine, Beatrice, jt. auth. see Albers, Patricia.

Medicine Eagle, Brooke. Buffalo Woman Comes Singing: The Spirit Song of a Rainbow Medicine Woman. 480p. (Orig.). 1991. pap. 12.50 (*0-345-36143-1*) Ballantine Pub Grp.

Medicine Grizzlybear Lake. Native Healer. 1993. pap. 5.50 (*0-685-66342-6*, Harp PBks) HarpC.

Medicine Hawk & Grey Cat. American Indian Ceremonies: A Practical Workbook & Study Guide to the Medicine Path. (Illus.). 144p. 1992. reprint ed. 15.00 (*0-938294-72-5*) Inner Light.

Medicine, Story. Children of the Morning Light: Wampanoag Tales As Told by Manitonquat. LC 92-32328. (Illus.). 80p. (J). (gr. 1 up). 1994. mass mkt. 16.95 (*0-02-765905-4*) Macmillan.

***Medicines Control Agency Staff.** Rules & Guidance for Pharmaceutical Manufacturers & Distributors, 1997. LC 98-147000. viii, 234p. 1999. 40.00 (*0-11-321995-4*, Pub. by Statnry Office) Balogh.

Medicins Sans Frontieres Staff. World in Crisis: Politics of Survival at the End of the Twentieth Century. LC 97-148635. (Illus.). 248p. (C). 1996. pap. 20.99 (*0-415-15378-6*) Routledge.

***Medicode, Inc. Staff.** Clinical Documentation Compliance Handbook. (Illus.). 1999. pap. write for info. (*1-56337-347-5*) Medicode Inc.

— 1999 Physician ICD-9-CM, Compact Edition: International Classification of Diseases. 9th rev. ed. (Illus.). vi, 1478p. (C). 1999. pap. write for info. (*1-56337-284-3*) Thomson Learn.

— 1999 Procedural Coding Crosswalk. ii, 329p. (C). 1999. pap. write for info. (*1-56337-288-6*) Thomson Learn.

***Medicode, Med-Index Division Staff.** Coders' Desk Reference: Everything a Coder Needs to Know. (Illus.). 908p. (C). 1999. pap. 80.00 (*1-56337-324-6*) Medicode Inc.

— Compact Physician ICD9-CM, 1999-2000, Vol. 1-2. (C). 1999. pap. 48.00 (*1-56337-313-0*) Thomson Learn.

— Deluxe Physician ICD-9-CM, 1999-2000, Vols. 1-2. (C). 1999. pap. 56.00 (*1-56337-314-9*) Thomson Learn.

— Drug Guide 2000. (C). 1999. 72.00 (*1-56337-307-6*) Thomson Learn.

— Medicare Billing Guide 2000. (C). 2000. 80.00 (*1-56337-328-9*) Thomson Learn.

— Modifiers Made Easy 2000. (C). 1999. 64.00 (*1-56337-346-7*) Thomson Learn.

Medicode, Med-Index Division Staff. Physician ICD 9 CM: 1999 Edition. (C). 1999. pap. 69.95 (*1-56337-283-5*) Thomson Learn.

***Medicode, Med-Index Division Staff.** Procedural Coding Crosswalk, 2000. (C). 1999. 80.00 (*1-56337-309-2*) Thomson Learn.

— 2000 Surgical Cross Coder. (Illus.). vii, 882p. (C). 2000. pap. 114.00 (*1-56337-326-2*) Medicode Inc.

Medicode Staff. 1998 Icd-10 Made Easy. (Illus.). iv, 213p. (C). 1999. pap. 63.95 (*1-56337-237-1*) Thomson Learn.

— 1999 Physician ICD-9-CM: International Classification of Diseases, Clinical Modification. 9th ed. iii, 774p. (C). 1998. pap. write for info. (*1-56337-285-1*) Thomson Learn.

Medicus, F. Johann Gottlieb Fichte: Thirteen Vorlesungen, Gehalten An der Universitat Halle. 240p. reprint ed. write for info. (*0-318-71928-2*) G Olms Pubs.

Medicus, Fritz. On Being Human: The Life of Truth & Its Realization. LC 72-178170. 324p. 1973. 9.75 (*0-8044-5673-9*) Green.

Medicus, Heinrich A., jt. auth. see Bitter, Francis.

Medicus Staff & Hubbard, L. Ron. All about Radiation. 1989. 30.00 (*0-88404-446-7*) Bridge Pubns Inc.

Mediero, Manuel M. A Love Too Beautiful. Halsey, Martha T., ed. Cazorla, Hazel, tr. from SPA. LC 94-61737. (Contemporary Spanish Plays Ser.: Vol. 8).Tr. of Juana del Amor Hermoso. (Illus.). 80p. (Orig.). 1995. pap. 6.00 (*0-9631212-7-8*) Estreno.

Medieros, Wendy A. Marbling Techniques: How to Create Traditional & Contemporary Designs on Paper & Fabric. LC 94-19095. (Illus.). 144p. 1994. pap. 24.95 (*0-8230-3005-9*) Watsn-Guptill.

Medieval Hebrew Masters Staff. Hiddushe Haramah We-Shitot Kadmonim Al Massekheth Gittin, 2 vols., Set. (HEB.). 779p. (C). 1989. 32.00 (*1-881255-02-6*) OFEQ Inst.

— Hiddushe Haramah We-Shitot Kadmonim Al Massekheth Gittin, Vol. I. (HEB.). 347p. (C). 1989. 16.00 (*1-881255-00-X*) OFEQ Inst.

M

An Asterisk (*) at the beginning of an entry indicates that the title is appearing for the first time.

— Hiddushe Haramah We-Shitot Kadmonim Al Massekheth Gittin, Vol. II. (HEB.). 432p. (C). 1989. 16.00 (1-881255-01-8) OFEQ Inst.

— Sifra on Leviticus: Vayiqra Dibura DeHobah, Vol. 3. (HEB.). 550p. (C). 1992. 24.00 (1-881255-10-7) OFEQ Inst.

— Sifra on Leviticus Vol. I: Baraita de-R. Ishmael (The 13 Hermeneutic Rules of R. Ishmael) LC 91-60934. (HEB.). 142p. (C). 1991. 14.00 (1-881255-09-3) OFEQ Inst.

Medieval Institute Publication Staff, ed. Studies in Iconography: Journal - Annual - Volumes 15 & Beyond, 20 vols. 1994. pap. 35.00 (1-58044-003-7) Medieval Inst.

Medigovich, William, jt. auth. see Fisher, Lyle.

Medill, Robert. Klondike Diary. (American Autobiography Ser.). 188p. 1995. reprint ed. lib. bdg. 69.00 (0-7812-8589-5) Rprt Serv.

Medin. Cognitive Psychology. 2nd ed. (C). 1997. pap. text 33.50 (0-15-504006-5, Pub. by Harcourt Coll Pubs) Harcourt.

— Cognitive Psychology. 3rd ed. (C). 1999. text. write for info. (0-15-508057-1) Harcourt Coll Pubs.

Medin, Dean E. Small Mammal Responses to Diameter-Cut Logging in an Idaho Douglas-Fir Forest. 10p. 1997. reprint ed. pap. 1.50 (0-89904-694-0, Wildlife Resrch Grp) Crumb Elbow Pub.

Medin, Donald L., ed. The Psychology of Learning & Motivation, Vol. 37. (Illus.). 350p. 1997. text 79.95 (0-12-543337-9) Morgan Kaufmann.

Medin, Doug L., et al, eds. Psychology of Learning & Motivation- Advances in Research & Theory: Categorization by Human & Machines, Vol. 29. (Illus.). 552p. 1993. text 99.95 (0-12-543329-8) Acad Pr.

***Medin, Douglas L.** Psychology of Learning & Motivation, Vol. 39. Vol. 39. 276p. 1999. 79.95 (0-12-543339-5) Acad Pr.

Medin, Douglas L., ed. The Psychology of Learning & Motivation, Vol. 31. (Illus.). 366p. 1994. text 99.95 (0-12-543331-X) Acad Pr.

— The Psychology of Learning & Motivation, Vol. 33. (Illus.). 296p. 1995. text 85.00 (0-12-543333-6) Acad Pr.

— The Psychology of Learning & Motivation, Vol. 35. (Illus.). 337p. 1996. text 69.95 (0-12-543335-2) Acad Pr.

— Psychology of Learning & Motivation, Vol. 38. (Illus.). 306p. (C). 1998. boxed set 89.95 (0-12-543338-7) Acad Pr.

— The Psychology of Learning & Motivation Vol. 28: Advances in Research & Theory. (Illus.). 296p. 1992. text 99.95 (0-12-543328-X) Acad Pr.

Medin, Douglas L., et al, eds. The Psychology of Learning & Motivation Vol. 32: Decision Making from a Cognitive Perspective. (Illus.). 426p. 1995. text 99.95 (0-12-543332-8) Acad Pr.

— The Psychology of Learning & Motivation Vol. 34: Causal Learning. (Illus.). 442p. 1996. text 74.95 (0-12-543334-4) Acad Pr.

Medin, Douglas L. & Atran, Scott, eds. Folkbiology. LC 98-50861. (Illus.). 470p. 1999. 65.00 (0-262-13349-0, Bradford Bks); pap. 32.50 (0-262-63192-X, Bradford Bks) MIT Pr.

Medin, Douglas L. & Ross, Brian H. Cognitive Psychology. 2nd ed. LC 96-78285. 626p. (C). 1996. text 74.00 (0-15-502843-X, Pub. by Harcourt Coll Pubs) Harcourt.

Medin, Douglas L., jt. auth. see Smith, Edward E.

Medin, Tzvi. Cuba: The Shaping of Revolutionary Consciousness. LC 89-39433. 192p. 1990. lib. bdg. 40.00 (1-55587-187-9) L Rienner.

— Ortega y Gasset en la Cultura Hispanoamerican (Ortega y Gasset in Hispanomarican Culture) (SPA.). 318p. 1994. pap. 14.99 (968-16-4251-1, Pub. by Fondo) Continental Bk.

Medina. Designing Esl Lessons. Date not set. pap. text. write for info. (0-312-19138-3) St Martin.

***Medina.** Inspiration for a New Beginning. 1999. 8.95 (0-7459-4258-X, Pub. by Lion Pubng) Trafalgar.

Medina, Alvin L. The Santa Rita Experimental Range: History & Annotated Bibliography (1903-1988) (Illus.). 67p. (Orig.). 1997. pap. text 30.00 (0-7881-3753-0) DIANE Pub.

Medina, Amelia C. A Comparative Analysis of Evaluation Theory & Practice for the Instructional Component of Bilingual Programs. Cordasco, Francesco, ed. LC 77-90549. (Bilingual-Bicultural Education in the U. S. Ser.). 1978. lib. bdg. 33.95 (0-405-11089-8) Ayer.

Medina, Andres. Recuentos y Figuraciones: Ensayos de Antropologia Mexicana. (SPA.). 288p. 1996. pap. 23.00 (968-36-5633-1, UN49, Pub. by Instit de Invest) UPLAAP.

Medina, Andres, et al, eds. Origen y Formacion del Estado en Mesoamerica. 198p. 1986. pap. 9.14 (968-837-959-X, UN029) UPLAAP.

Medina, Angel. Diccionario de Musica Sevilla 1818. (SPA.). 107p. 1991. write for info. (0-7859-6225-5, 8474682924) Fr & Eur.

Medina, Antonio T. Asian Economic Tigers--A Philippine Comparison. 104p. 1996. lib. bdg. 32.00 (0-7618-0251-7) U Pr of Amer.

Medina, Augusto G., jt. ed. see Singh, R. Paul.

Medina, Barbara F. Structured System Analysis: A New Technique. xiv, 82p. 1981. text 160.00 (0-677-05570-6) Gordon & Breach.

***Medina, C. C.** A Little Love. LC 99-51757. 368p. 2000. 18.95 (0-446-52448-4, Pub. by Warner Bks) Little.

Medina, Cecila. The Legal Status of Indians in Brazil. 10.00 (0-944253-64-4) Inst Dev Indian Law.

Medina, Cecilia. The Legal Status of Indians in Bolivia. 10.00 (0-944253-63-6) Inst Dev Indian Law.

— The Legal Status of Indians in Chile. 10.00 (0-944253-65-2) Inst Dev Indian Law.

— The Legal Status of Indians in Columbia. 10.00 (0-944253-66-0) Inst Dev Indian Law.

— The Legal Status of Indians in Guatemala. 15.00 (0-944253-67-9) Inst Dev Indian Law.

— The Legal Status of Indians in Paraguay. 10.00 (0-944253-68-7) Inst Dev Indian Law.

Medina County Historical Society Staff, ed. History of Medina County, Ohio. 419p. 1993. reprint ed. lib. bdg. 43.50 (0-8328-2833-5) Higginson Bk Co.

Medina, Cuauhtemoc & Mellado, Justo Pastor. Monica Castillo: Yo Es un Otro. (ENG & SPA., Illus.). 72p. 1998. pap. 20.00 (1-889195-23-5) Smart Art Pr.

Medina, Cuauhtemoc, jt. auth. see Florez, Fernando Castro.

***Medina, Cynthia.** Nuevos Destinos: Spanish in Review. 112p. (C). 1999. pap. 20.63 (0-07-233815-6) McGrw-H Hghr Educ.

Medina, D., et al. Cellular & Molecular Biology of Mammary Cancer. LC 87-25756. (Illus.). 528p. (C). 1988. text 139.50 (0-306-42761-3, Kluwer Plenum) Kluwer Academic.

Medina, Dante. La Dama de la Gardenia (The Maiden of the Gardenia) (SPA.). 260p. pap. 8.99 (968-16-3870-0, Pub. by Fondo) Continental Bk.

Medina, David. Elohim's Nursery. 158p. 1984. 40.00 (0-7212-0626-3, Pub. by Regency Pr GBR) St Mut.

Medina, Dena, jt. auth. see Medina, Rudy A.

Medina, Dennis, ed. We Like Ike: The Eisenhower Presidency & 1950s America. LC 90-70503. (Illus.). 114p. (Orig.). 1990. pap. 5.00 (0-939324-42-3) Wichita Art Mus.

Medina, E., et al, eds. Biodiversity & Savanna Ecosystem Processes: A Global Perspective. (Ecological Studies: Vol.121). 236p. 1996. 89.00 (0-387-57949-4) Spr-Verlag.

Medina, Eduardo, ed. see Kaur, Bibi Inderjit.

Medina, Enrique. Las Tumbas: The Tombs. LC 92-23401. (Library of World Literature in Translation: Vol. 4). 334p. 1992. text 20.00 (0-8240-7436-X) Garland.

Medina, Ernesto, et al, eds. Biodiversity & Savanna Ecosystem Processes: A Global Perspective. (Ecological Studies: Vol. 121). 1995. write for info. (3-540-57949-4) Spr-Verlag.

Medina, Francis X. & Marra, Dorothy B. Ciao, Francesco. 224p. 1995. 19.95 (0-9645371-0-9) F X Medina.

Medina, Francisco. Sismicidad y Volcanismo en Mexico. (Ciencia para Todos Ser.). (SPA.). 126p. pap. 6.99 (968-16-5174-X, Pub. by Fondo) Continental Bk.

Medina-Gaud, Silverio, jt. auth. see Maldonado-Capriles, Jenaro.

Medina, Grover J., tr. see Bernard, David K.

Medina, Harold R. Corrected Opinion of Harold R. Medina, United States Circuit Judge in United States of America, Plaintiff, v. Henry S. Morgan, Harold Stanley et al... LC 75-2647. (Wall Street & the Security Market Ser.). 1975. reprint ed. 35.95 (0-405-06972-3) Ayer.

Medina, Jane. My Name Is Jorge: On Both Sides of the River. LC 99-60227. (SPA., Illus.). 48p. (YA). (gr. 2-5). 1999. 14.95 (1-56397-811-3) Boyds Mills Pr.

***Medina, Jane.** My Name Is Jorge: On Both Sides of the River. (SPA., Illus.). 48p. (YA). (gr. 4-7). 1999. 7.95 (1-56397-842-3, Wordsong) Boyds Mills Pr.

Medina, John. Depression: How It Happens, How It's Healed. LC 97-69493. (Illus.). 125p. (Orig.). 1998. pap. 14.95 (1-57224-100-4) New Harbinger.

***Medina, John.** The Genetic Inferno: Inside the Seven Deadly Sins. LC 99-86430. (Illus.). 368p. 2000. 24.95 (0-521-64064-4) Cambridge U Pr.

Medina, John J. The Clock of Ages: Why We Age--How We Age--Winding Back the Clock. (Illus.). 344p. (C). 1996. text 29.95 (0-521-46244-4) Cambridge U Pr.

— The Clock of Ages: Why We Age--How We Age--Winding Back the Clock. (Illus.). 352p. 1997. pap. 15.95 (0-521-59456-1) Cambridge U Pr.

— What You Need to Know about Alzheimer's. LC 98-67410. (Illus.). 165p. 1999. pap. 15.95 (1-57224-127-6) New Harbinger.

Medina, Jose, tr. see Lafont, Cristina.

Medina, Joyce. Cezanne & Modernism: The Poetics of Painting. LC 94-31716. (SUNY Series, The Margins of Literature). (Illus.). 250p. (C). 1995. text 59.50 (0-7914-2231-3); pap. text 19.95 (0-7914-2232-1) State U NY Pr.

Medina, Juvenal. Fenomenos Geodinamicos. 88p. 1991. pap. 17.00 (1-85339-026-7, Pub. by Intermed Tech) Stylus Pub VA.

Medina, Juvenal R. Los Desastres Si Avisan. 171p. pap. 19.00 (1-85339-036-4, Pub. by Intermed Tech) Stylus Pub VA.

Medina, Luis. Hacia el Nuevo Estado (Toward a New State) Mexico, 1920-1993. 2nd ed. (SPA.). 362p. 1995. pap. 12.99 (968-16-4703-3, Pub. by Fondo) Continental Bk.

Medina Machine Tools Co. Staff. Automated Manufacturing-Lathe. (Illus.). 120p. (J). (gr. 7-8). 1997. text 99.95 (1-58100-017-0) Beckley Cardy.

— Automated Manufacturing-Mill. (Illus.). 120p. 1997. text 99.95 (1-58100-016-2) Beckley Cardy.

Medina, Manuel, ed. see IFIP TC6-WG6.5 International Working Conference St.

Medina, Maria D. De, see Bernstein, David E. & De Medina, Maria D., eds.

Medina, Marjorie B., jt. ed. see Moats, William A.

Medina, Mit. Mobilization for Evangelism. pap. 4.95 (1-884213-00-6) Vision Christ.

Medina, Pablo. Arching into the Afterlife. LC 90-24943. 96p. 1991. pap. 9.00 (0-927534-12-6) Biling Rev-Pr.

— The Floating Island. LC 99-42661. 104p. 1999. pap. 14.00 (1-893996-01-8, Pub. by White Pine) Consort Bk Sales.

***Medina, Pablo.** The Return of Felix Nogara: A Novel. 272p. 2000. 25.95 (0-89255-251-4) Persea Bks.

Medina, Pat. Paralegal Discovery: Procedures & Forms, 1. 2nd ed. 704p. 1994. boxed set 89.00 (0-471-31076-X) Wiley.

***Medina, Pat.** Paralegal Discovery: Procedures & Forms. 3rd ed. 984p. 1999. boxed set 110.00 (0-7355-1101-2) Panel Pubs.

Medina, Pol, Jr. The Best of Pugad Baboy. (Tagalog Ser.). (Illus.). 78p. (Orig.). 1991. pap. 7.50 (971-10-0440-2, Pub. by New Day Pub) Cellar.

— Pugad Baboy Three. (TAG., Illus.). 80p. (Orig.). 1992. pap. text 7.50 (971-10-0518-2, Pub. by New Day Pub) Cellar.

Medina-Quiroga, Cecilia. The Battle of Human Rights. (C). 1988. lib. bdg. 131.00 (90-247-3687-0) Kluwer Academic.

Medina, Rick. Humaliens: Lexicon's Mission. 150p. (J). (gr. 4-7). 1999. pap. 4.99 (1-892587-00-9) Dualstar.

— Humaliens Vol. 2: The Clone Formula. 150p. (gr. 4-7). 1999. pap. 4.99 (1-892587-01-7) Dualstar.

— Humaliens Vol. 3: World Wide Web Attack. 150p. (gr. 4-7). 1999. pap. 4.99 (1-892587-02-5) Dualstar.

— Humaliens Vol. 4: Robots Everywhere. 150p. (J). (gr. 4-7). 1999. pap. 4.99 (1-892587-03-3) Dualstar.

— Humaliens Vol. 5: Milky Way vs. Andromeda, Special Edition. 200p. (gr. 4-7). 1999. pap. 5.99 (1-892587-04-1) Dualstar.

***Medina, Robert C.** Caramba! Southwest Spoken Spanish Composition. LC 99-94666. (Illus.). 80p. 1999. pap. write for info. (0-933196-06-7) Bilingue Pubns.

Medina, Robert C., ed. see Maze, Carol M.

Medina, Roberto. Fabian No Se Muere. LC 78-7307. (SPA.). (Orig.). 1978. pap. text 4.95 (0-933196-01-6) Bilingue Pubns.

Medina, Ruben. Amor de Lejos: Fools' Love. (Illus.). (J). 1986. 12.35 (0-606-17953-4) Turtleback.

Medina, Rudy A. Electrical Fires & Their Causes. 99p. 1996. pap. text 15.00 (0-9649477-0-6) Medina Ent.

***Medina, Rudy A. & Medina, Dena.** The Coming of Ecaot. 140p. 2000. 18.00 (0-9649477-1-4) Medina Ent.

Medina, Standish F., Jr. Things Magic. LC 97-91073. (Illus.). 128p. 1998. write for info. (0-9660954-9-9, 500) S F Medina.

***Medina, Tony.** Memories of Eating. LC 99-48825. 1999. write for info. (0-9654738-3-X) Lng Shot Prods.

Medina, Tony. No Noose Is Good Noose. 180p. 1996. pap. 12.00 (0-86316-109-X) Writers & Readers.

— Sermons from the Smell of a Carcass Condemned to Begging. LC 98-26932. 1998. write for info. (0-9654738-2-1) Lng Shot Prods.

Medina, Tony, jt. ed. see Anderson, S. E.

Medina, Tony, ed. see Simmons, Sharrif.

Medina, Vincente. Social Contract Theories. 188p. (C). 1990. lib. bdg. 48.50 (0-8476-7624-2) Rowman.

Medina, William A. Changing Bureaucracies. (Public Administration & Public Policy Ser.: Vol. 11). (Illus.). 160p. 1982. text 85.00 (0-8247-1672-8) Dekker.

Medine, Allen & Anderson, Michael, Jr., eds. Environmental Engineering. LC 83-71587. 989p. 1983. pap. 11.00 (0-87262-369-6) Am Soc Civil Eng.

Medine, Peter E. Thomas Wilson. (Twayne's English Authors Ser.: No. 431). 216p. 1986. 32.00 (0-8057-6929-3) Macmillan.

Medine, Peter E. & Wittreich, Joseph, eds. Soundings of Things Done: Essays in Early Modern Literature in Honor of S. K. Heninger Jr. LC 96-1363. (Illus.). 344p. 1997. 48.50 (0-87413-606-7) U Delaware Pr.

Medinets, Dave. PHP3: Programming Browser-Based Applications. 448p. 1999. pap. 39.99 (0-07-135342-9) McGraw.

Medinets, David. Perl 5 by Example. LC 96-69960. 696p. 1996. 39.99 (0-7897-0866-3) Que.

— UNIX Shell Programming Tools. LC 99-18756. 568p. 1999. pap. 39.99 (0-07-913790-3) McGraw.

Meding, Dorothee Von, see Von Meding, Dorothee.

Meding, Wichmann Von, see Von Meding, Wichmann.

Medinger, Ann, jt. ed. see Spagnolo, Samuel V.

Medinger, Daniel, ed. see Kenney, Jeremiah.

Medinger, Patti, ed. A Taste of Catholicism II: A New Generation. 215p. 1997. pap. 15.00 (1-885938-10-1) Cathdrl Fndtn Pr.

Medinnus, Gene R., ed. Readings in the Psychology of Parent-Child Relations. LC 67-12565. 384p. reprint ed. 119.10 (0-8357-9973-5, 205514600008) Bks Demand.

Medinnus, Gene R., jt. auth. see Johnson, Ronald C.

Medio, Alfredo. Chaotic Dynamics: Theory & Applications to Economics. (Illus.). 344p. (C). 1995. pap. 20.95 (0-521-48461-8) Cambridge U Pr.

Medio, Alfredo & Gallo, Giampaolo. Chaotic Dynamics: Theory & Applications to Economics. (Illus.). 250p. (C). 1993. pap. 56.95 (0-521-42107-1) Cambridge U Pr.

***Medioni, Gerard, et al.** A Computational Framework for Segmentation & Grouping. LC 00-23205. 2000. write for info. (0-444-50353-6) Elsevier.

Mediresky, J. Laszlo. A Time to Love & a Time to Kill. Muzoleski, Pamela, ed. (Orig.). 1997. pap. 11.95 (1-57532-039-8) Press-Tige Pub.

Medish, Vadim. The Soviet Union. 4th rev. ed. 432p. (C). 1990. pap. text 46.67 (0-13-818196-9) P-H.

Medish, Vadim, ed. see Zyuganov, Gennady A.

MediSphere Health Partner Staff. Managed Care Contract Reference Guide. 65p. 1998. pap. 30.50 (1-56829-091-8) Med Group Mgmt.

Mediterraneo Staff. Basic Illustrated Spanish-English Dictionary: Diccionario Basico Ilustrado Espanol-Ingles, 4 vols., Set. (ENG & SPA.). 1200p. 1982. 395.00 (0-8288-2321-9, S2567) Fr & Eur.

Mediterreneo Staff. Diccionario Basico Ilustrado Espanol-Ingles-Euskera, 4 vols., Set. (ENG & SPA.). 1200p. 1982. 395.00 (0-7859-3370-0, M29970) Fr & Eur.

— Diccionario Basico Illustrado Espanol Ingles Gallego, 4 vols. (ENG & SPA.). 1200p. 1982. 395.00 (0-7859-3445-6) Fr & Eur.

Meditz, Sandra W. Spain: A Country Study. 2nd ed. Solsten, Eric & Keefe, Eugene K., eds. LC 90-6127. (Area Handbook Ser.). (Illus.). 444p. 1991. boxed set 25.00 (0-16-028550-X, 008-020-1235-1) USGPO.

Meditz, Sandra W. Zaire: A Country Study. 452p. 1994. boxed set 25.00 (0-16-061167-9) USGPO.

Medlam, Sarah. The Bettine, Lady Abingdon Collection: The Bequest of Mrs. T. R. P. Hole: a Handbook. LC 97-170976. (Illus.). 104p. 1996. 50.00 (1-85177-179-4, Pub. by V&A Ent) Antique Collect.

***Medland, K.** Blind Fear. 1999. pap. 11.00 (0-7472-5659-4, Pub. by Headline Bk Pub) Trafalgar.

Medland, Mary. Plays: A Study Guide. Friedland, J. & Kessler, R., eds. (Novel-Ties Ser.). 1990. pap. text, student ed. 15.95 (0-88122-863-X) Lrn Links.

— The Red Badge of Courage: A Study Guide. (Novel-Ties Ser.). (YA). (gr. 9-12). 1990. pap. text 15.95 (0-88122-414-6) Lrn Links.

— Where the Lilies Bloom: A Study Guide. Friedland, Joyce & Kessler, Rikki, eds. (Novel-Ties Ser.). 30p. (J). (gr. 6-8). 1990. pap. text 15.95 (0-88122-399-9) Lrn Links.

Medland, Maurice. Point of Honor. 304p. 1997. 21.95 (1-57566-193-4, Knsington) Kensgtn Pub Corp.

— Point of Honor. 384p. 1998. pap. 5.99 (0-7860-0489-4, Pinncle Kensgtn) Kensgtn Pub Corp.

Medland, Michael B. Happier Families: Raising Responsible, Self-Managed Children. 185p. (Orig.). 1992. pap. 11.95 (0-9633009-6-2) Barcroft Pub.

— Self-Management Strategies: Theory, Curriculum & Teaching Procedures. LC 90-31211. 312p. 1990. 65.00 (0-275-93519-1, C3519, Praeger Pubs) Greenwood.

Medland, William J. The Cuban Missile Crisis of Nineteen Sixty-Two: Needless or Necessary? LC 87-36025. 175p. 1988. 52.95 (0-275-92844-6, C2844, Praeger Pubs) Greenwood.

***Medlen, Virginia Shaw.** Intellectual Property Protection: What Engineers & Other Inventors Need to Know. 3rd ed. LC 99-47208. 104p. 2000. 26.95 (1-888577-46-0, IPP3) Prof Pubns CA.

Medler, John T. Insects of Nigeria. (Memoir Ser.: No. 30). 919p. 1980. 75.00 (1-56665-028-3) Assoc Pubs FL.

— New Guinea Flatidae (Homoptera) Species Collected on Economic & Other Plants, with Descriptions of New Species. (Bishop Museum Bulletin in Entomology Ser.: Vol. 2). (Illus.). 79p. (C). 1989. pap. 21.00 (0-930897-38-2) Bishop Mus.

Medley. New High School Spanish, Level 1. (Secondary Spanish Ser.). (C). 2001. mass mkt., teacher ed. 14.00 (0-8384-7743-7) Heinle & Heinle.

— New High School Spanish, Level 2. (Secondary Spanish Ser.). 2002. mass mkt. 15.95 (0-8384-7907-3) Heinle & Heinle.

— New High School Spanish, Level 3. (Secondary Spanish Ser.). 2001. text 15.95 (0-8384-7899-9); text, teacher ed. 15.95 (0-8384-7908-1) Heinle & Heinle.

— New High School Spanish Level 1. (Secondary Spanish Ser.). 2001. pap. text 25.00 (0-8384-7752-6) Heinle & Heinle.

— New High School Spanish Level 3. 2001. pap. text, wbk. ed. 15.00 (0-8384-7996-0) Heinle & Heinle.

— New Spanish, Level 1. (Secondary Spanish Ser.). 2001. pap. text, wbk. ed. 15.95 (0-8384-7898-0) Heinle & Heinle.

— Spanish, Level 1. (Secondary Spanish Ser.). 2001. text 62.95 (0-8384-7889-1) Heinle & Heinle.

— Spanish, Level 2. (Global ESL/ELT Ser.). 2002. pap. text, wbk. ed. 15.95 (0-8384-7890-5) Heinle & Heinle.

— Spanish, Level 13. (Secondary Spanish Ser.). 2001. text, wbk. ed. 15.95 (0-8384-7882-4) Heinle & Heinle.

— Spanish Program, Level 1. (Secondary Spanish Ser.). 2001. text 49.95 (0-8384-7880-8) Heinle & Heinle.

Medley, Anthony. Complete Idiot's Guide to Bridge. 384p. 1997. 16.95 (0-02-861735-5) Macmillan Gen Ref.

Medley, Bill & Medley, Pat. Serenade in D Major. (Alfred Signature Ser.). 4p. 1994. pap. 2.50 (0-7390-0778-5, 12885) Alfred Pub.

Medley, Frank. A Proposito! 1992. mass mkt. 15.95 (0-8384-2399-X) Heinle & Heinle.

— Sin Duda. 1992. mass mkt. 16.95 (0-8384-2378-7) Heinle & Heinle.

Medley, G., jt. ed. see Isham, V.

Medley, Geoffrey R. National Engineering Conference, 1996: The Darwin Summit - Engineering Tomorrow Today. (National Conference Proceedings Ser.: Vol. 96/03). (Illus.). 510p. 1996. pap. 96.00 (0-85825-647-9, Pub. by Inst Engrs Aust-EA Bks) Accents Pubns.

Medley, H. Anthony. Sweaty Palms: The Neglected Art of Being Interviewed. rev. ed. (Illus.). 254p. 1992. reprint ed. pap. 8.95 (0-89815-403-0) Ten Speed Pr.

Medley, J. Inside the Rainbow. 1997. pap. 10.95 (0-943383-09-9) FirstHand Ltd.

Medley, James. Huck & Billy. (Orig.). 1994. mass mkt. 4.95 (1-56333-245-0, Badboy) Masquerade.

— The Revolutionary & Other Stories. (Orig.). 1996. mass mkt. 5.95 (1-56333-417-8, Badboy) Masquerade.

Medley, Joseph E., jt. auth. see Wiegersma, Nancy.

Medley, Linda. Castle Waiting: The Curse of Brambly Hedge. 2nd rev. ed. (Illus.). 96p. (Orig.). 1999. pap. 9.00 (0-9651852-1-4) Olio.

***Medley, Linda.** Castle Waiting: The Lucky Road. (Illus.). 184p. 2000. pap. 16.95 (1-888963-07-7) Cartoon Bks.

Medley, Margaret. The Chinese Potter: A Practical History of Chinese Ceramics. (Illus.). 288p. (Orig.). Date not set. pap. 22.95 (0-7148-2593-X, Pub. by Phaidon Press) Phaidon Pr.

Medley, Mary L. A History of Anson County, North Carolina, 1750-1976. (Illus.). 417p. 1997. reprint ed. pap. 35.00 (0-8063-4755-4, 9238) Clearfield Co.

M

M

Medley, Max W., jt. auth. see Allen, James L.

Medley, Michael J., jt. auth. see Akansu, Ali N.

Medley, Pat, jt. auth. see Medley, Bill.

Medley, Steven P. The Complete Guidebook to Yosemite National Park. 3rd rev. ed. LC 94-10712. (Illus.). 112p. 1994. pap. 9.95 (0-939666-85-5) Yosemite Assn.

— Map & Guide to Tuolumne Meadows. (Illus.). 1994. pap. 2.50 (0-939666-72-3) Yosemite Assn.

— Map & Guide to Wawona & Mariposa Grove. Reineck & Reineck Staff, tr. (Illus.). 1991. pap. 2.95 (0-939666-29-4) Yosemite Assn.

— Der Vollstaendige Fuehrer des Yosemite National Parkes - Complete Guidebook to Yosemite National Park. (GER., Illus.). 112p. 1993. pap. 10.95 (0-939666-64-2) Yosemite Assn.

Medley, Steven P., jt. ed. see Bates, Craig D.

Medley, Steven P., ed. see Bunnell, Lafayette H.

Medley, Steven P., ed. see Ross, Michael E.

Medley, Tom. Hot Rod History Bk. 2, Bk. 2. (Illus.). 200p. 1994. pap. 22.95 (1-884089-08-9) CarTech.

— Hot Rod History, Bk. 1: The Beginnings. (Illus.). 202p. 1994. pap. 22.95 (1-884089-05-4) CarTech.

Medley, Wes. Original Arizona Cookin' Mohanna, Tim, ed. (Illus.). 1992. pap. write for info. (0-9633651-1-8) Orig Western.

— Original Cowboy Cookbook. (Illus.). 106p. pap. text 12.95 (0-9633651-0-X) Orig Western.

Medlicott, Joan Avna. Belonging: A Caribbean Love Story. 2nd ed. LC 96-61403. (Illus.). 222p. 1996. reprint ed. pap. 13.95 (0-9657695-0-X) Picara Point.

***Medlicott, Joan Avna.** Ladies of Covington Send Their Love. LC 99-89922. 352p. 2000. text 24.95 (0-312-25329-X) St Martin.

Medlicott, Joan Avna. Virgin Islands Tales of Olden Days. LC 97-67332. 96 p. 1997. write for info. (0-9657695-1-8) Picara Point.

***Medlicott, Mary.** Tales from Africa. LC 99-88383. (Illus.). 96p. (J). 2000. pap. 11.95 (0-7534-5290-1, Kingfisher) LKC.

Medlicott, Mary, ed. The River That Went to the Sky: Twelve Tales of African Stories Tellers. LC 94-44607. (Illus.). 96p. (J). (gr. 1 up). 1995. 17.95 (1-85697-608-4, Kingfisher) LKC.

Medlicott, William N. Congress of Berlin & After. 442p. 1963. 49.50 (0-7146-1501-3, Pub. by F Cass Pubs) Intl Spec Bk.

Medlik, S. The Business of Hotels. 3rd ed. 206p. 1995. pap. 32.95 (0-7506-2080-3) Buttrwrth-Heinemann.

***Medlik, S.** Business of Hotels. 4th ed. 2000. pap. 29.95 (0-7506-4115-0) Buttrwrth-Heinemann.

Medlik, S. Dictionary of Travel, Tourism & Hospitality. 2nd ed. LC 97-108241. 360p. 1996. pap. 31.95 (0-7506-2864-2) Buttrwrth-Heinemann.

— Managing Tourism. LC 91-140078. (Illus.). 358p. 1991. reprint ed. pap. 111.00 (0-608-07965-0, 206793700012) Bks Demand.

***Medlik, S.** Tourism & Hospitality in the 21st Century. 320p. 2000. 66.95 (0-7506-4676-4) Buttrwrth-Heinemann.

— Understanding Tourism. 256p. 1997. pap. 24.95 (0-7506-3654-8) Buttrwrth-Heinemann.

***Medlik, S.** Understanding Tourism. 1999. pap. 24.95 (0-7506-4352-8, Digital DEC) Buttrwrth-Heinemann.

Medlik, S., ed. Managing Tourism. LC 95-195718. (Illus.). 358p. 1991. reprint ed. pap. 111.00 (0-608-08866-8, 206950500004) Bks Demand.

Medlin, D. M. The Verbal Art of Jean Francois Regnard, Vol. 1. 156p. 1966. pap. 7.00 (0-912788-00-3) Tulane Romance Lang.

Medlin, Dorothy, jt. ed. see Merrick, Jeffrey W.

Medlin, Eugene & Doane, Colin. The French Modele Nineteen Thirty-Five Pistols: Thirty Twos with a French Accent. LC 90-82574. (Illus.). 288p. 1990. 40.00 (0-9627605-0-1) BFH.

Medlin, Julie J. Michigan Lichens. LC 96-83208. (Bulletin Ser.: No. 60). (Illus.). 100p. (Orig.). 1996. pap. 12.00 (0-87737-039-7) Cranbrook.

Medlin, L. & Priddle, J. Polar Marine Diatoms. (Illus.). 214p. 1990. 45.00 (0-85665-140-0, Pub. by Brit Antarctic Surv) Balogh.

Medlin, Virgil D., ed. The Russian Revolution. LC 79-4332. (European Problem Studies). 218p. 1979. reprint ed. pap. 11.50 (0-88275-907-X) Krieger.

Medlin, Virgil D., ed. see Nabokov, Vladimir.

Medlin, William K. Fire Mountain: A Nation's Heritage in Jeopardy. LC 95-31587. 1996. pap. 14.95 (0-86534-228-8) Sunstone Pr.

Medlock, Ronald D. & Laffrey, David C., eds. Structural Materials Technology III Vol. 3400: An NDT Conference. 544p. 1998. 107.00 (0-8194-2849-3) SPIE.

Medlock, Scott. Extra Innings: Baseball Poems. LC 92-13013. 48p. (J). (gr. 3-7). 1993. 16.00 (0-15-226833-2) Harcourt.

— Opening Days: Sports Poems. LC 94-43364. 48p. (J). (gr. 3-7). 1996. 16.00 (0-15-200270-7) Harcourt.

Medlycott, James. 100 Years of the Wimbledon Tennis Championships. LC 78-309650. 4-93p. 1977. write for info. (0-600-38768-2, Pub. by Hamlyn Publishing Group Ltd) Sterling.

Medlycott, Mervyn, jt. auth. see Gibson, J. S. W.

Mednick. Elements of Verilog Style. (C). 1999. 40.00 (0-13-780420-2, Pub. by P-H) S&S Trade.

Mednick, Birgitte R., jt. auth. see Baker, Robert L.

Mednick, Christina S. San Cristobal: Voices & Visions of the Galisteo Basin. LC 96-22539. 1996. pap. 35.00 (0-89013-294-1) Museum NM Pr.

Mednick, Fred. Rebel Without a Car: Surviving & Appreciating Your Child's Teen Years. 224p. (Orig.). 1996. pap. 12.95 (1-57749-014-2) Fairview Press.

Mednick, Murray. The Coyote Cycle: Seven Plays by Murray Mednick. (Illus.). 175p. (Orig.). 1993. pap. 15.95 (0-9630126-1-4) Padua Hills Play.

— Switchback: or Lost Child in the Terror Zone. LC 97-43811. (Classics Ser.: No. 140). 60p. (Orig.). 1997. pap. 9.95 (1-55713-309-3) Sun & Moon CA.

Mednick, Murray, et al, eds. Best of the West: An Anthology of Plays from the 1989 & 1990 Padua Hills Playwrights Festivals. 2nd ed. 320p. (Orig.). 1994. pap. 14.95 (0-9630126-2-2) Padua Hills Play.

Mednick, Murray & Barsha, Tony. The Hawk: An Improvisational Play. LC 68-29295. (Illus.). 113p. 1968. 14.95 (0-910278-37-7) Boulevard.

Mednick, Sarnoff A., et al, eds. Developmental Neuropathology of Schizophrenia. (NATO ASI Ser.: Vol. 217). (Illus.). 256p. (C). 1992. text 114.00 (0-306-44081-4, Kluwer Plenum) Kluwer Academic.

— Handbook of Longitudinal Research Vol. 1: Birth & Childhood Cohorts, 2 vols. LC 83-24723. 740p. 1981. 125.00 (0-275-90681-7, C06811, Praeger Pubs) Greenwood.

— Handbook of Longitudinal Research Vol. 2: Teenage & Adult Cohorts, 2 vols. LC 83-24723. 608p. 1984. 105.00 (0-275-91228-0, C12282, Praeger Pubs) Greenwood.

Mednick, Sarnoff A. & Hollister, J. Meggin, eds. Neural Development & Schizophrenia: Theory & Research, No. 275. LC 95-3584. (NATO ASI Ser.: Ser. A, Vol. 275). (Illus.). 272p. (C). 1995. text 89.50 (0-306-44996-X) Plenum.

Mednick, Sarnoff A., et al. Psychology: Explorations in Behavior & Experience. LC 74-22239. 606p. reprint ed. pap. 187.90 (0-7837-3457-3, 205778300008) Bks Demand.

Mednick, Sarnoff A., jt. auth. see Van Dusen, Katherine Teilmann.

Mednick, Sarnoff A., jt. ed. see Goodwin, Donald W.

Mednick, Sarnoff A., jt. ed. see Moffitt, Terrie E.

Mednicki, Bernard & Wachsberger, Ken. Never Be Afraid: A Jew in the Maquis. LC 96-95134. 212p. 1997. pap. 16.00 (1-879461-04-8) Azenphony Pr.

Mednikova, E. M. English-Russian Dictionary of Verbal Collocations. 636p. (C). 1986. 115.00 (0-7855-6673-2, Pub. by Collets); 110.00 (0-7855-5358-4, Pub. by Collets) St Mut.

— English-Russian Dictionary of Verbal Collocations. 668p. (C). 1990. 75.00 (0-89771-825-9, Pub. by Collets) St Mut.

Mednikova, E. M., ed. English-Russian Dictionary of Verbal Collocations. 2nd rev. ed. 672p. (C). 1990. 21.95 (0-8285-5165-0) Firebird NY.

Mednikova, E. M. & Apresjan, Yuri D., eds. New English-Russian Dictionary, 3 vols., Set. 4th rev. ed. 2496p. (C). 1993. 120.00 (0-8285-5001-8) Firebird NY.

Mednikova, E. M. & Gal'Perin, L., eds. English-Russian Dictionary, 2 vols., Set. 2110p. (C). 1987. 295.00 (0-7855-6853-0, Pub. by Collets) St Mut.

Mednis, E. Cadogan Chess: Most Game Grandmaster. 1999. text 19.95 (1-85744-534-1) Cadgn Bks.

Mednis, Edmar. Advanced Endgame Strategies. 129p. (Orig.). 1996. pap. 10.95 (0-945470-59-2) Chess Ent.

— From the Middlegame into the Endgame. (Chess Ser.). (Illus.). 185p. 1987. pap. 19.90 (0-08-032038-4, Pergamon Pr) Elsevier.

— From the Middlegame into the Endgame. 220p. 1994. pap. 17.95 (1-85744-060-9) S&S Trade.

— From the Opening into the Endgame. (Chess Ser.). (Illus.). 176p. 1983. 25.90 (0-08-026917-6, Pergamon Pr); pap. 15.90 (0-08-026916-8, Pergamon Pr) Elsevier.

— Gewinne das Endspiel! (Praxis Schach Ser.: Bd. 7). (GER.). 240p. 1992. write for info. (3-283-00251-7) G Olms Pubs.

— How Karpov Wins. 2nd enl. rev. ed. (Illus.). 400p. 1994. reprint ed. pap. text 11.95 (0-486-27881-6) Dover.

— How to Be a Complete Tournament Player. (Chess Library). 160p. 1991. pap. 15.95 (0-08-037795-5, Pub. by CHES) Macmillan.

— How to Beat Bobby Fischer. LC 97-29737. (Illus.). 320p. 1998. pap. 9.95 (0-486-29844-2) Dover.

— How to Defeat a Superior Opponent. Darin, Dodd M., ed. (Illus.). 336p. 1989. pap. 16.95 (0-945806-00-0) Summit CA.

— How to Defeat a Superior Opponent. (Illus.). 312p. 1995. pap. 14.95 (0-945806-01-9) Summit CA.

— How to Play Good Opening Moves. 1986. pap. 13.00 (0-679-14109-X) McKay.

— The King in the Endgame. 104p. 1997. pap. 8.95 (0-945470-65-7) Chess Ent.

— The King in the Opening. (Illus.). 100p. 1998. pap. 8.95 (0-945470-72-X) Chess Ent.

— Practical Knight Endings. 188p. (Orig.). 1993. pap. 12.95 (0-945470-35-5) Chess Ent.

— Practical Opening Tips. 144p. 1997. pap. text 19.95 (1-85744-186-9, Pub. by Cadgn Bks) Macmillan.

— Practical Rook Endings. (Illus.). 71p. (Orig.). 1982. pap. 6.00 (0-931462-16-9) Chess Ent.

— Questions & Answers on Practical Endgame Play. 135p. (Orig.). 1987. pap. 7.95 (0-931462-69-X) Chess Ent.

— Rate Your Endgame. rev. ed. 1997. pap. 19.95 (1-85744-174-5) Macmillan.

— Spiele Gute Eroffnungszuge! (Praxis Schach Ser.: Bd. 6). (GER.). 120p. 1992. write for info. (3-283-00250-9) G Olms Pubs.

— Strategic Chess: Mastering the Closed Game. LC 99-12951. 256p. 1999. pap. text 9.95 (0-486-40617-2) Dover.

— Strategic Chess: Mastering the Closed Game. 236p. 1993. pap. 14.95 (0-945806-11-6) Summit CA.

— Strategic Themes in the Opening & Beyond. 124p. (Orig.). 1990. pap. 8.95 (0-931462-94-0) Chess Ent.

Mednis, Edmar & Crouch, Colin. Rate Your Endgame. (Chess Library). 200p. 1991. pap. 19.95 (0-08-037803-X, Pub. by CHES) Macmillan.

— Rate Your Endgame. 244p. 1992. pap. 19.95 (1-85744-020-X, Pub. by Cadgn Bks) Macmillan.

Mednis, Edmar, jt. auth. see Wall, Bill.

Medoff, Mark. Big Mary. 1989. pap. 5.25 (0-8222-0117-8) Dramatists Play.

— Children of a Lesser God. 1980. pap. 5.25 (0-8222-0203-4) Dramatists Play.

— Dreams of Long Lasting. 560p. 1993. mass mkt. 5.99 (0-446-36460-6, Pub. by Warner Bks) Little.

— Four Short Plays by Mark Medoff. 1974. pap. 5.25 (0-8222-0744-3) Dramatists Play.

— The Hands of Its Enemy. 1987. pap. 5.25 (0-8222-0494-0) Dramatists Play.

— The Heart Outright. 1990. pap. 5.25 (0-8222-0506-8) Dramatists Play.

— The Homage That Follows. 1995. pap. 5.25 (0-8222-1469-5) Dramatists Play.

— The Kramer. 1976. pap. 5.25 (0-8222-0620-X) Dramatists Play.

— Kringle's Window. 1994. pap. 5.25 (0-8222-1356-7) Dramatists Play.

— The Majestic Kid. 1986. pap. 5.25 (0-8222-0717-6) Dramatists Play.

— Stefanie Hero. LC 95-150061. 1994. pap. 5.25 (0-8222-1370-2) Dramatists Play.

— Stumps. 1995. pap. 5.25 (0-8222-1434-2) Dramatists Play.

— The Wager. 1975. pap. 5.25 (0-8222-1214-5) Dramatists Play.

— When You Comin' Back, Red Ryder? 1974. pap. 5.25 (0-8222-1240-4) Dramatists Play.

Medoff, Mark & Johnson, Carleene. The Odyssey of Jeremy Jack. 1973. pap. 5.25 (0-8222-0835-0) Dramatists Play.

Medoff, Mark & Marks, Ross. Showdown on Rio Road. 1998. pap. 5.25 (0-8222-1620-5) Dramatists Play.

Medoff, Mark & Treon, Phil. Crunch Time. 1998. pap. 5.25 (0-8222-1621-3) Dramatists Play.

Medoff, Norman J. Creating TV Projects. LC 95-194730. (Illus.). 244p. 1994. pap. 32.95 (0-86729-334-9, Focal) Buttrwrth-Heinemann.

Medoff, Norman J. & Tanquary, Tom. Portable Video: ENG & EFP. 3rd ed. LC 97-20550. (Illus.). 304p. 1997. pap. 39.95 (0-240-80285-3, Focal) Buttrwrth-Heinemann.

— Portable Video: ENG & EFP. (Professional Librarian Ser.). (Illus.). 191p. (C). 1988. 50.00 (0-86729-147-8, Hall Reference); pap., student ed. 27.95 (0-86729-148-6, Hall Reference) Macmillan.

Medoff, Norman J., jt. auth. see Kaye, Barbara K.

Medoff, Peter & Sklar, Holly. Streets of Hope: The Fall & Rise of an Urban Neighborhood. LC 94-4613. 337p. (C). 1994. pap. 18.00 (0-89608-482-5); lib. bdg. 40.00 (0-89608-483-3) South End Pr.

***Medoff, Rafael.** Militant Zionism in America: The Rise & Impact of the Jabotinsky Movement in the U. S., 1926-1948. 2000. 39.95 (0-8173-1071-1) U of Ala Pr.

Medoff, Rafael. Zionism & the Arabs: An American Jewish Dilemma, 1898-1948. LC 96-47482. 200p. 1997. 55.00 (0-275-95824-8, Praeger Pubs) Greenwood.

***Medoff, Rafael & Waxman, Chaim I.** Historical Dictionary of Zionism. 382p. 2000. 60.00 (0-8108-3773-0) Scarecrow.

Medova, Marie-Laure. Ballet for Beginners.Tr. of Danse Classique. (Illus.). 112p. (J). 1997. pap. 12.95 (0-8069-3877-3) Sterling.

Medovar, B. I., et al, eds. Electroslag Technology. (Material Research & Engineering Ser.). (Illus.). xxii, 270p. 1991. 119.95 (0-387-97333-8) Spr-Verlag.

Medovar, B. I., et al. Arc-Slag Remelting Steel & Alloys. 160p. 1995. pap. 74.00 (1-898326-21-5, Pub. by CISP) Balogh.

— Welding & Surfacing Reviews: Special Electrometallurgy (A Review), Vol. 1, No. 5. Paton, B. E., ed. (Soviet Technology Reviews Ser.: Vol. 1, Pt. 5). iv, 68p. 1989. pap. text 75.00 (3-7186-4976-4) Gordon & Breach.

***Medoza, Staci & Bourne, David.** Guide For Life: Palm Reading. 64p. 2000. pap. 6.95 (1-84215-068-5) Anness Pub.

Medrano. Hispanic Poetry. 1999. pap. text 10.60 (0-201-57548-5) Addison-Wesley.

Medrano, Fidel A. Historia de los Hospitales Coloniales de Hispanoamerica: Historia de los Hospitales Coloniales de Ecuador y Bolivia, Vol. X. Camps, Janett, ed. (Illus.). 321p. (C). Date not set. text 50.00 (0-9641506-4-6) Edit Interamerica.

— Historia de los Hospitales Coloniales de Hispanoamerica: Historia de los Hospitales Coloniales de Venezuela, Vol. IX. Garcia, Lucia, ed. (Illus.). (C). 1994. text 50.00 (0-9641506-1-1) Edit Interamerica.

Medrano, G. & Lieb, K., eds. Reactor Physics for Developing Countries & Nuclear Spectroscopy Research: Proceedings of the Conference on Reactor Physics for Developing Countries & Nuclear Spectroscopy Research. 770p. 1986. text 144.00 (9971-5-0203-8) World Scientific Pub.

Medrano, Mignon. Todo lo Dieron por Cuba: A Shocking Testimony by 30 Women Political Prisoners. 220p. 1995. pap. text 25.00 (1-884619-04-5) Endowment CAS.

Medrek, Joseph S. New Creations. unabridged ed. 52p. 1998. pap. 3.98 (1-58339-175-4, E11) Triangle Press.

Medrich, Alice. Alice Medrich's Cookies & Brownies. LC 99-11794. (Illus.). 160p. 1999. 23.95 (0-446-52382-8, Pub. by Warner Bks) Little.

— Chocolate & the Art of Low-Fat Desserts. (Illus.). 192p. 1994. 35.00 (0-446-51666-X, Pub. by Warner Bks) Little.

— Cocolat: Extraordinary Chocolate Desserts. (Illus.). 192p. 1990. 35.00 (0-446-51419-5, Pub. by Warner Bks) Little.

Medrich, Elliott. Preparation for Work. 22p. 1997. pap. 4.00 (0-16-048970-9) USGPO.

Medrich, Elliott A., et al. The Serious Business of Growing Up: A Study of Children's Lives Outside School. LC 81-7630. 419p. reprint ed. pap. 129.90 (0-7837-4754-3, 204450100003) Bks Demand.

Medsger, Betty. Winds of Change: Challenges Confronting Journalism Education. 185p. (Orig.). 1996. pap. write for info. (0-9655091-0-9) Freedm Forum.

***Medsger, Oliver Perry.** Edible Wild Plants: The Classic Guide to the Flavor & Lore of the North American Outdoors. (Illus.). 2001. pap. 16.95 (0-07-136443-9) McGraw.

Medsker, Karen L. Conditions of Learning: Training Applications. 1995. pap. text, teacher ed. write for info. (0-15-503086-8) Harcourt Coll Pubs.

Medsker, Karen L., jt. auth. see Gagne, Robert M.

***Medsker, L. R. & Jain, L. C.** Recurrent Neural Networks: Design & Applications. LC 99-49146. (International Series on Computational Intelligence). 392p. 1999. write for info. (0-8493-7181-3) CRC Pr.

Medsker, Larry, ed. Frontiers in Soft Computing & Decision Systems: Papers from the 1997 Fall Symposium. (Technical Reports: No. FS-97-04). (Illus.). 1998. spiral bd. 25.00 (1-57735-079-0) AAAI Pr.

Medsker, Larry R. Hybrid Intelligent Systems. LC 95-17214. 312p. (C). 1995. text 118.50 (0-7923-9588-3) Kluwer Academic.

— Hybrid Neural Network & Expert Systems. LC 93-38572. 256p. (C). 1993. text 131.50 (0-7923-9423-2) Kluwer Academic.

Medtner, Nikolai. Complete Book of Piano Sonatas. Date not set. 14.95 (0-486-29979-1) Dover.

— Complete Piano Sonatas: Series I. 1998. 13.95 (0-486-29978-3) Dover.

Meduna, ed. Theory of Computation. (C). 1998. text. write for info. (0-321-01065-5) Addson-Wesley Educ.

Meduna, Alexander. Automata & Languages: Theory & Applications. LC 98-52375. 560p. 1999. 149.00 (1-85233-074-0, Pub. by Spr-Verlag) Spr-Verlag.

Meduna, Ladislas J. Oneirophrenia: The Confusional State. LC 50-6278. (Illus.). 112p. reprint ed. pap. 34.80 (0-608-30242-2, 201502300096) Bks Demand.

Meduna, Veronika, jt. auth. see Tan, Choon.

Medunitsyn, N. V., et al. Mediators of the Immune Response. xiv, 326p. 1987. text 216.00 (3-7186-0310-1) Gordon & Breach.

Meduno, Michael. Technical Diving. 288p. 1993. pap. 29.95 (0-8016-7478-6) Mosby Inc.

Meduri, P. J. The Crib & the Cross: A Students Guide Through the Life of Christ. 162p. (Orig.). (YA). (gr. 6 up). 1994. pap. 8.95 (1-887002-18-9) Cross Trng.

Medve, Mary L., jt. auth. see Medve, Richard J.

Medve, Richard J. & Medve, Mary L. Edible Wild Plants of Pennsylvania & Neighboring States. LC 89-22830. (Illus.). 256p. 1990. pap. 18.95 (0-271-00697-8); lib. bdg. 35.00 (0-271-00690-0) Pa St U Pr.

Medve, William J., jt. auth. see Peto, Gloria J.

Medvec, Emily, ed. see Adams, Ansel.

Medveczky, P. G., et al, eds. Herpesviruses & Immunity. (Infectious Agents & Pathogenesis Ser.). (Illus.). 340p. (C). 1998. text 115.00 (0-306-45890-X, Kluwer Plenum) Kluwer Academic.

Medved, Diane. The Case Against Divorce. 272p. 1990. mass mkt. 5.99 (0-8041-0633-9) Ivy Books.

Medved, Diane, jt. auth. see Medved, Michael.

Medved, Diane, jt. auth. see Quayle, Dan.

Medved, M. Fundamentals of Dynamical Systems & Bifurcation Theory. (Illus.). 308p. 1992. 137.00 (0-7503-0150-3) IOP Pub.

Medved, Maureen. The Tracey Fragments. LC 98-199190. 156p. 1999. pap. 14.95 (0-88784-624-6) Genl Dist Srvs.

Medved, Michael. Hollywood vs. America: Popular Culture & the War Against Traditional Values. LC 92-52604. 416p. 1993. reprint ed. pap. 14.00 (0-06-092435-7, Perennial) HarperTrade.

— Riding High. 1999. pap. 23.95 (0-525-93617-3) NAL.

Medved, Michael & Medved, Diane. Saving Childhood: How to Protect Your Children from the National Assault on Innocence. LC 98-11850. 336p. 1998. 24.00 (0-06-017372-6) HarpC.

— Saving Childhood: How to Protect Your Children from the National Assault on Innocence. 336p. 1999. pap. 13.00 (0-06-093224-4) HarpC.

Medved, Robert. Excel for Windows 95 Now! (Now! Ser.). (Illus.). 208p. 1998. spiral bd. 19.95 (0-8442-2920-2) NTC Contemp Pub Co.

— Windows '95 NOW! A Simple Guide to Learning Windows '95 Quickly & Easily! LC 95-60747. (Illus.). 240p. (Orig.). 1996. pap. 19.99 (0-9643450-3-X) Easel Pubng.

— Windows 3.1 Now! (Now! Ser.). (Illus.). 208p. 1998. spiral bd. 19.95 (0-8442-2922-9) NTC Contemp Pub Co.

— Windows 3.1 NOW! A Simple Guide to Learning Windows Quickly & Easily! 2nd ed. Murray, Katharine, ed. LC 95-60174. (Illus.). 216p. 1995. pap. 17.99 (0-9643450-0-5) Easel Pubng.

— Windows 95 Now! (Now! Ser.). 208p. 1998. spiral bd. 19.95 (0-8442-2919-9) NTC Contemp Pub Co.

— Word NOW! (for Windows '95) A Simple Guide to Learning Word Quickly & Easily. (Illus.). 224p. (Orig.). 1996. pap. 19.99 (0-9643450-4-8) Easel Pubng.

— WordPerfect 6.1 for Windows Now! (Now! Ser.). 208p. 1998. spiral bd. 19.95 (0-8442-2923-7) NTC Contemp Pub Co.

Medved, Robert & Ames, Jennifer. Excel NOW! (for Windows '95) A Simple Guide to Learning Excel Quickly & Easily! LC 95-60748. (Illus.). 240p. (Orig.). 1996. pap. 19.99 (0-9643450-2-1) Easel Pubng.

— Word 6 NOW! (for Windows 3.1) A Simple Guide to Learning Word Quickly & Easily. LC 95-60569. (Illus.). 208p. (Orig.). 1995. pap. 18.99 (0-9643450-1-3) Easel Pubng.

An Asterisk (*) at the beginning of an entry indicates that the title is appearing for the first time.

— Word 6 for Windows Now! (... Now! Ser.). 208p. 1998. spiral bd. 19.95 (*0-8442-2921-0*) NTC Contemp Pub Co.

Medved, Robert, jt. auth. see Temple, Scott.

Medved, Vladimir. Measurement of Locomotion. 208p. 1999. 95.00 (*0-8493-7675-0*) CRC Pr.

Medvedev, Anthony. The Young Elder: From Ambrose of Milkova. 70p. 1974. pap. 3.00 (*0-317-30442-9*) Holy Trinity.

Medvedev, E. S. & Osherov, V. I. Radiationless Transitions in Polyatomic Molecules. LC 94-19897. (Series in Chemical Physics: Vol. 57).Tr. of Teoriia Bezylzluchatelnykh Perekhodov v Mnogoatomnykh Moleculakh. 1994. 141.95 (*3-387-57769-6*) Spr-Verlag.

Medvedev, F. A. Scenes from the History of Real Functions. (Science Networks Historical Studies: Vol. 7). 268p. 1992. 156.00 (*0-8176-2572-0*) Birkhauser.

Medvedev, G. S. Keys to the Insects of the European Part of the U. S. S. R., Vol. IV, Pt. II. (C). 1989. 75.00 (*81-7087-047-X*) S Asia.

— Keys to the Insects of the European Part of the U. S. S. R. Vol. 4, Pt. VI: Megaloptera, Raphidioptera, Neuroptera, Mecoptera & Trichoptera. (Illus.). 314p. 1998. 95.00 (*1-57808-006-1*) Science Pubs.

Medvedev, G. S., ed. Keys to the Insects of the Eastern Part of the U. S. S. R. Lepidoptera, Vol. IV, Pt. III. (Keys to the Insects of the Eastern Part of the USSR Ser.). 650p. (C). 1996. text 175.00 (*1-886106-25-8*) Science Pubs.

— Keys to the Insects of the European Part of the U. S. S. R. Vol. 4: Lepidoptera, Pt. 2. (Illus.). x, 1092p. 1990. 209.50 (*90-04-08926-8*) Brill Academic Pubs.

Medvedev, G. V., ed. Keys to the Insects of the European Part of the U. S. S. R. Pt. 4, Braconidae: Hymenoptera, Vol. III. Kothekar, V. S. & Sharma, S. K., trs. from RUS. 900p. 1995. text 147.50 (*1-886106-23-1*) Science Pubs.

— Keys to the Insects of the European Part of the U. S. S. R. Pt. 5, Braconidae: Hymenoptera, Vol. III. Kothekar, V. S., tr. from RUS. 490p. 1995. text 95.00 (*1-886106-24-X*) Science Pubs.

Medvedev, N. Ya, jt. auth. see Kopytov, V. M.

Medvedev, O. S. Cardiology Reviews Vol. 3, Pt. 1: The Role of Endogenous Epinephrine in the Development of Experimental Hypertension, Vol. 3. (Soviet Medical Reviews Ser.: Section A). 128p. 1991. pap. text 184.00 (*3-7186-5234-X*, Harwood Acad Pubs) Gordon & Breach.

Medvedev, Pavel N. Formalizm i Formalisty. (GER.). 208p. 1973. reprint ed. write for info. (*3-487-04618-0*) G Olms Pubs.

— Formal'nyi Metod v Literaturovedenii. (Documenta Semiotica: Serie 2). (GER.). 247p. 1974. reprint ed. write for info. (*3-487-05290-3*) G Olms Pubs.

Medvedev, Pavel N. & Bakhtin, Mikhail M. The Formal Method in Literary Scholarship: A Critical Introduction to Sociological Poetics. LC 77-15529. (Goucher College Ser.). 218p. reprint ed. pap. 67.60 (*0-608-13995-5*, 202222600025) Bks Demand.

Medvedev, Pavel N., jt. auth. see Bakhtin, Mikhail M.

Medvedev, Roy. In Search of Common Sense. Date not set. 60.00 (*0-393-01578-5*) Norton.

***Medvedev, Roy.** Post-Soviet Russia: A Journey Through the Yeltsin Era. Shriver, George, tr. (RUS.). 640p. 2000. text 37.50 (*0-231-10606-8*) Col U Pr.

Medvedev, Roy. Problems in the Literary Biography of Mikhail Sholokhov. Briggs, A. D., tr. LC 76-14032. 235p. reprint ed. pap. 67.00 (*0-608-12059-6*, 2024491) Bks Demand.

Medvedev, Roy A. Let History Judge: The Origins & Consequences of Stalinism. enl. rev. ed. Shriver, George, ed. & tr. by. 891p. 1989. text 87.50 (*0-231-06350-4*) Col U Pr.

— Let History Judge: The Origins & Consequences of Stalinism. rev. ed. 1990. pap. text 29.00 (*0-231-06351-2*) Col U Pr.

— On Soviet Dissent: Interviews with Piero Ostellino. Packer, William A., tr. from ITA. LC 79-27877. 158p. 1980. text 44.00 (*0-231-04812-2*) Col U Pr.

— On Soviet Dissent: Interviews with Piero Ostellino. Packer, William A., tr. from ITA. LC 79-27877. 158p. 1985. pap. text 17.50 (*0-231-04813-0*) Col U Pr.

— Political Essays. (European Socialist Thought Ser.: No. 8). 151p. 1976. 33.50 (*0-85124-151-4*, Pub. by Spkesman) Coronet Bks.

Medvedev, Roy A., ed. The Samizdat Register 1. (C). 1977. 15.25 (*0-393-05652-X*) Norton.

Medvedev, Roy A. & Medvedev, Zhores A. Khrushchev: The Years in Power. 1978. reprint ed. pap. 10.95 (*0-393-00879-7*) Norton.

Medvedev, Roy A., et al. Khrushchev: The Years in Power. LC 76-19104. 197p. 1976. text 49.50 (*0-231-03939-5*) Col U Pr.

***Medvedev, Roy Aleksandrovich.** Post-Soviet Russia: A Journey Through the Yeltsin Era. LC 00-40443. (Illus.). 2000. write for info. (*0-231-10607-6*) Col U Pr.

Medvedev, S. V. Physiology & General Biology Reviews Vol. 5, Pt. 3: A New Ideology of Studies of the Neurophysiological Correlates to Mental Activity, Vol. 5. (Soviet Scientific Reviews Ser.: Section F). 50p. 1991. text 52.00 (*3-7186-5177-7*, Harwood Acad Pubs) Gordon & Breach.

Medvedev, V. A., jt. ed. see Glushko, V. P.

Medvedev, Zhores A. The Legacy of Chernobyl. (Illus.). 376p. 1992. pap. 10.95 (*0-393-30814-6*) Norton.

— National Frontiers & International Scientific Cooperation. (Medvedev Papers: Vol. 1). 296p. (Orig.). 1975. pap. 28.50 (*0-85124-127-1*, Pub. by Spkesman) Coronet Bks.

— Protein Biosynthesis & Problems of Heredity Development & Aging. LC 67-71423. 606p. reprint ed. pap. 187.90 (*0-608-13803-7*, 202070200018) Bks Demand.

— The Rise & Fall of T. D. Lysenko. Lawrence, Lucy G., ed. Lerner, I. Michael, tr. LC 79-77519. 304p. reprint ed. pap. 94.30 (*0-608-12295-5*, 202377000034) Bks Demand.

Medvedev, Zhores A., jt. auth. see Medvedev, Roy A.

Medvedeva, Natallia. Mama, Ia Zhulika Liubliu. (RUS.). 170p. (Orig.). 1988. pap. 15.00 (*0-89830-114-9*) Russica Pubs.

Medvedkov, Yuri, ed. Amelioration of the Human Environment: IGU Congress, Moscow, 1976, Proceedings, Pt. 1. 1977. pap. 23.00 (*0-08-021322-7*, Pergamon Pr) Elsevier.

— Regional Systems: IGU Congress, Moscow, 1976, Proceedings, Pt. 2. 1977. pap. 23.00 (*0-08-021323-5*, Pergamon Pr) Elsevier.

— Urbanization: IGU Congress, Moscow, Proceedings, Pt. 3. 1977. pap. 23.00 (*0-08-021324-3*, Pergamon Pr) Elsevier.

***Medvedow, Jill & McElreavy, Tim.** Home: Photographs by Shellburne Thurber. Donnelly, Nora, ed. (Illus.). 40p. 2000. pap. 25.00 (*0-910663-56-4*, Pub. by ICA Inc) Dist Art Pubs.

Medvedow, Jill & Phillpot, Clive. What Are You Waiting For? LC 84-7777. (Illus.). 32p. 1984. pap. 6.00 (*0-941104-11-7*) Real Comet.

Medvedow, Jill, jt. auth. see Morgan, Jessica.

Medvedow, Jill S., et al. Bamboo Echoes: A New Work by Mona Higuchi Dedicated to the Comfort Women. (Illus.). 26p. 1996. pap. 10.00 (*0-9648475-2-3*) I S Gardner Mus.

Medvei, V. C. The History of Clinical Endocrinology. (History of Medicine Ser.). (Illus.). 451p. 1993. 128.00 (*1-85070-427-9*) Prthnon Pub.

— A History of Endocrinology. (Illus.). 900p. 1982. text 286.50 (*0-85200-245-9*) Kluwer Academic.

Medvene, Arnold, intro. Storms & Rainbows: The Many Faces of Death. 200p. (Orig.). 1992. pap. 9.95 (*0-9630598-0-7*) Lilith Pr.

Medvene, Mark. Foilrigami. (Illus.). (J). (gr. 4-7). 1968. 10.95 (*0-685-06619-3*) Astor-Honor.

Medvic, Emily F., jt. auth. see Fisher, Bobbi.

Medwadowski, Stefan J., jt. ed. see Popov, Egor P.

Medwadowski, Stefan J., ed. see Syymposium on Concrete Thin shells (1970: New York.

Medwall, Henry. Nature One & Two. LC 71-133709. (Tudor Facsimile Texts. Old English Plays Ser.: No. 17). reprint ed. 59.50 (*0-404-53317-5*) AMS Pr.

— The Plays of Henry Medwall. Nelson, Alan H., ed. (Tudor Interludes Ser.: No. II). 245p. 1980. 75.00 (*0-85991-054-7*) Boydell & Brewer.

Medwar, Mardi O. Witch of the Palo Duro, 1 vol. 1999. mass mkt. 5.99 (*0-425-16735-6*) Berkley Pub.

Medway, Frederic & Cafferty, Thomas, eds. School Psychology: A Social Psychological Perspective. 496p. 1991. text 89.95 (*0-8058-0536-2*) L Erlbaum Assocs.

***Medway, Gareth J.** Lure of the Sinister: The Unnatural History of Satanism. LC 99-49577. 2000. 29.95 (*0-8147-5645-X*) NYU Pr.

Medway, Peter. Finding a Language: Autonomy & Learning in School. (Chameleon Education Ser.). 148p. (Orig.). 1981. pap. 4.95 (*0-906495-41-5*) Writers & Readers.

Medway, Peter, ed. Shifting Relations: Science, Technology & Technoscience. 110p. 1995. pap. 40.00 (*0-7300-1606-4*, ESC810, Pub. by Deakin Univ) St Mut.

Medway, Peter, jt. auth. see Torbe, Mike.

Medway, Peter, jt. ed. see Freedman, Aviva.

Medwed, Mameve. Host Family. LC 99-29473. 304p. 2000. 23.95 (*0-446-52166-3*, Pub. by Warner Bks) Little.

***Medwed, Mameve.** Host Family. 320p. 2001. pap. write for info. (*0-446-67661-6*) Warner Bks.

Medwed, Mameve. Mail. 320p. 1998. reprint ed. mass mkt. 11.99 (*0-446-67375-7*, Pub. by Warner Bks) Little.

Medwell, Jane, jt. auth. see Wray, David.

Medwell, Jane, jt. ed. see Wray, David.

***Medwick, Cathleen.** Teresa of Avila: The Progress of a Soul. LC 99-18921. (Illus.). 304p. 1999. 26.00 (*0-394-54794-2*) Knopf.

— Teresa of Avila: The Progress of a Soul. 2001. reprint ed. pap. 12.95 (*0-385-50129-3*) Doubleday.

Medwid, Daria, jt. auth. see Weston, Denise C.

***Medwid, Linda M.** The Makers of Classical Archaeology: A Reference Work. LC 99-462362. 320p. 2000. 99.95 (*1-57392-826-7*, Humanity Bks) Prometheus Bks.

Medwin, Herman & Clay, Clarence S. Fundamentals of Acoustical Oceanography. LC 97-35785. (Applications of Modern Acoustics Ser.). (Illus.). 712p. 1997. text 75.00 (*0-12-487570-X*) Morgan Kaufmann.

***Medwin, Thomas.** Lady Singleton. LC 99-85755. 2000. write for info. (*0-8201-1529-0*) Schol Facsimiles.

Medwin, Thomas. The Life of Percy Bysshe Shelley. 1988. reprint ed. lib. bdg. 59.00 (*0-7812-0194-2*) Rprt Serv.

— Life of Percy Bysshe Shelley. 1971. reprint ed. 59.00 (*0-403-01100-0*) Scholarly.

Medyckyi & Scott. Human Factors in Geographic Information Systems. 1993. 79.95 (*1-85293-262-7*, Belhaven) Halsted Pr.

Medzhitova, E. D. & Trofimov, A. A., eds. Chuvash Folk Art. (CHV & RUS., Illus.). 246p. 1981. 250.00 (*0-7855-1579-8*) St Mut.

Medzini, Meron. French Policy in Japan During the Closing Years of the Tokugawa Regime. (East Asian Monographs: No. 41). 257p. 1971. pap. 11.00 (*0-674-32230-4*) HUP.

Medzirasky, Joseph. Caveman Hunters. 125p. (Orig.). 1998. pap. 10.95 (*1-57532-077-0*) Press-Tige Pub.

Mee, Bob. Boxing: The Hall of Fame. (Illus.). 352p. 1997. 29.98 (*0-7858-0778-0*) Bk Sales Inc.

Mee, Bob, jt. auth. see Bunce, Steve.

Mee, C. D. Magnetic Recording Technology. 2nd ed. LC 95-44642. 704p. 1996. 65.00 (*0-07-041276-6*) McGraw.

Mee, C. Denis & Daniel, Eric D. Magnetic Recording Handbook. 2nd ed. LC 96-19057. (Illus.). 624p. 1996. 89.50 (*0-07-041275-8*) McGraw.

Mee, C. Dennis. The Physics of Magnetic Recording. (North-Holland Personal Library). xviii, 270p. 1986. reprint ed. pap. 56.75 (*0-444-87043-1*, North Holland) Elsevier.

Mee, Charles L. History Plays. LC 97-28922. (PAJ Bks.). 352p. 1998. text 45.00 (*0-8018-5805-4*); pap. text 16.95 (*0-8018-5792-9*) Johns Hopkins.

— Meeting at Potsdam. 1995. pap. text 14.95 (*1-879957-50-7*, Franklin Sq Pr) Harpers Mag Found.

— A Nearly Normal Life: A Memoir. LC 98-25245. 240p. (gr. 8). 1999. 24.00 (*0-316-55852-4*, Back Bay) Little.

— A Nearly Normal Life: A Memoir. 240p. 2000. pap. 12.95 (*0-316-55836-2*, Back Bay) Little.

***Mee, Charles L.** A Nearly Normal Life: A Memoir. large type ed. LC 00-20110. (Americana Series). 2000. 27.95 (*0-7862-2488-6*) Thorndike Pr.

Mee, Charles L., Jr. Playing God: Seven Fateful Moments When Great Men Met to Change the World. 269p. 1999. reprint ed. text 23.00 (*0-7881-6343-4*) DIANE Pub.

Mee, Christopher & Forbes, Hamish, eds. A Rough & Rocky Place: The Landscape & Settlement History of the Methana Peninsula, Greece. (Illus.). 370p. 1997. 69.95 (*0-85323-741-7*, Pub. by Liverpool Univ Pr) Intl Spec Bk.

Mee, Christopher & Steel, Louise. Corpus of Cypriote Antiquities: The Cypriote Collections in the University of Liverpool & the Williamson Art Gallery & Museum. (Studies in Mediterranean Archaeology: Vol. XX:17). (Illus.). 70p. 1998. pap. 67.50 (*91-7081-182-2*, Pub. by P Astroms) Coronet Bks.

Mee, Christopher, jt. auth. see Cavanagh, William.

Mee, Cynthia S. 2,000 Voices: Young Adolescents' Perceptions & Curriculum Implications. LC 97-5315. 1997. pap. write for info. (*1-56090-116-0*) Natl Middle Schl.

Mee, Graham. Miners, Adult Education & Community Service, 1920-1984. (C). 1985. 65.00 (*1-85041-006-2*, Pub. by Univ Nottingham) St Mut.

Mee, Graham & Wiltshire, Harold. Structure & Performance in Adult Education. LC 77-7051. 1978. pap. text 9.50 (*0-582-48944-X*) Longman.

Mee, Graham, jt. auth. see Wallis, J.

Mee, John. Date Tech: Dating Technology for Men. unabridged ed. (Illus.). 240p. 1999. pap. 12.95 (*1-892654-16-4*) Bayshore Ent.

— The Property Rights of Unmarried Cohabitees. 388p. 1999. 54.00 (*1-901362-76-0*, Pub. by Hart Pub) Northwestern U Pr.

Mee, John M. Direct Mass Spectrometry of Body Metabolites: Quantitative Methodology & Clinical Applications. (Illus.). ix, 135p. 1984. pap. 15.00 (*0-318-04438-2*) Brandon-Lane-Pr.

Mee-kau, Nyaw & Si-ming, Li, eds. The Other Hong Kong Report, 1996. (Illus.). 537p. (Orig.). 1997. pap. text 34.50 (*962-201-715-0*, Pub. by Chinese Univ) U of Mich Pr.

Mee Kim, Eun, see Kim, Eun Mee, ed.

***Mee, Laurence D. & Topping, Graham, eds.** Black Sea Pollution Assessment. (Black Sea Environmental Ser.: Vol. 10). 380p. 1999. 25.00 (*92-1-129506-8*) UN.

Mee-Lee, David, et al. Patient Placement Criteria for the Treatment of Substance-Related Disorders: ASAM PPC-2. 2nd ed. Wilford, Bonnie B., ed. LC 97-108914. 170p. 1996. 100.00 (*1-880425-03-3*) Am Soc Addict Med.

Mee, Michelle. The Sky Is Blue with Clouds Like Fishbones. (Storybridge Ser.). 64p. (J). (gr. 1-4). 1995. pap. 9.95 (*0-7022-2707-2*, Pub. by Univ Queensland Pr) Intl Spec Bk.

Mee, Susie. The Undertaker's Daughter. LC 92-71921. 80p. 1992. pap. 9.00 (*1-881523-01-2*) Junction CA.

Mee, Susie, ed. Downhome: An Anthology of Southern Women Writers. LC 95-18978. 480p. (YA). 1995. pap. 17.00 (*0-15-600121-7*) Harcourt.

Meece. Gender & Education Achievement. (Educational Psychology Ser.: Vol. 28, No. 4). 1993. 20.00 (*0-8058-9985-5*) L Erlbaum Assocs.

Meece, Alan E. Horoscope for the New Millennium. LC 96-35825. (Illus.). 432p. 1999. 19.95 (*1-56718-461-8*) Llewellyn Pubns.

***Meece, Allen.** The Abel Mutiny. LC 00-191003. 2000. 25.00 (*0-7388-2189-6*); pap. 18.00 (*0-7388-2190-X*) Xlibris Corp.

Meece, Allen, et al. Once upon an Island: A Collection of New Key West Authors. LC 97-68162. 150p. 1997. pap. 9.95 (*1-57502-515-9*, PO1529) Morris Pubng.

Meece, Judith L. Child & Adolescent Development for Educators. LC 96-39264. 400p. (C). 1997. pap. 37.19 (*0-07-041297-9*) McGraw.

Meece, Judith L., jt. ed. see Schunk, Dale H.

Meech-Pekarik, Julia. The Hogen & Heiji Battle Screens in the Metropolitan Museum of Art. Ruzicka, Molly B., ed. (Illus.). 1984. pap. 12.00 (*0-916235-00-9*) Jacksonville Art.

— The World of the Meiji Print: Impressions of a New Civilization. (Illus.). 299p. 1986. 60.00 (*0-8348-0209-0*) Weatherhill.

Meech-Pekarik, Julia, jt. auth. see Pal, Pratapaditya.

Meech, Sanford B. Design in Chaucer's Troilus. LC 76-88981. 529p. 1969. reprint ed. lib. bdg. 38.50 (*0-8371-2118-3*, MECT, Greenwood Pr) Greenwood.

Meech, Susan B. A Supplement to the Descendants of Peter Spicer Containing Additions & Corrections. (Illus.). 269p. reprint ed. pap. 42.00 (*0-8328-1653-1*); reprint ed. lib. bdg. 52.00 (*0-8328-1652-3*) Higginson Bk Co.

Meechan, John. Pain & Anxiety Control for the Conscious Dental Patient. (Illus.). 396p. 1998. text (*0-19-262849-6*) OUP.

Meechan, John G., et al. Pain & Anxiety Control for the Conscious Dental Patient. LC 97-34665. (Illus.). 396p. 1998. pap. text 69.50 (*0-19-262848-8*) OUP.

Meeck, Julia. Rain & Snow: The Umbrella in Japanese Art. (Illus.). 143p. 1993. pap. text 32.00 (*0-913304-36-0*) Japan Soc.

Meed, Douglas V. Bloody Border: Riots, Battles & Adventures along the Turbulent U. S.-Mexican Borderlands. (Great West & Indian Ser.: Vol. 58). (Illus.). 1992. 26.95 (*0-87026-081-2*) Westernlore.

***Meed, Douglas V.** Texas Ranger: Johnny Klevenhagen. (Illus.). 275p. 2000. pap. 18.95 (*1-55622-793-0*, Rep of TX Pr) Wordware Pub.

Meed, Douglas V. Texas Wanderlust: The Adventures of Dutch Wurzbach. LC 96-27122. (Centennial Series of the Association of Former Students: No. 65). (Illus.). 192p. 1996. 29.95 (*0-89096-726-1*); pap. 12.95 (*0-89096-734-2*) Tex A&M Univ Pr.

— They Never Surrendered: Bronco Apaches of the Sierra Madres, 1890-1935. (Great West & Indian Ser.: Vol. 59). (Illus.). 1994. 26.95 (*0-87026-086-3*) Westernlore.

Meed, Steven, tr. see Meed, Vladka.

Meed, Vladka. On Both Sides of the Wall. Meed, Steven, tr. LC 78-71300. (Illus.). 304p. 1979. pap. 13.95 (*0-89604-013-5*, Holocaust Library) US Holocaust.

Meeden, G., jt. auth. see Ghosh, M.

Meeder, J. P. Numerical Simulation of Chemical Reactions in Point-Source Plumes. (Illus.). 117p. 1998. pap. 39.50 (*90-407-1639-0*, Pub. by Delft U Pr) Coronet Bks.

Meedith Press Staff. Step-by-Step Decorative Painting. LC 96-78040. (Do-It-Yourself Ser.). (Illus.). 96p. 1997. pap. 12.95 (*0-696-20678-1*) Meredith Bks.

Meedk, Stephen. Autobiography of a Mountain Man. (American Autobiography Ser.). 17p. 1995. reprint ed. lib. bdg. 69.00 (*0-7812-8590-9*) Rprt Serv.

***Meeds, Bridget.** Tuning the Beam: Synchrotron Poems. (Illus.). 48p. 2000. pap. 15.00 (*0-9702498-0-2*) B Meeds.

Meegan, C. A., et al, eds. Gamma-Ray Bursts: 4th Huntsville Symposium, 2 pts. LC 97-70902. (AIP Conference Proceedings Ser.: Vol. 428). (Illus.). 966p. 1998. 245.00 (*1-56396-766-9*) Am Inst Physics.

Meegan, Richard, jt. ed. see Massey, Doreen.

Meegan, William J. The Conquest of Genesis: A Study in Universal Creation Mathematics. LC 98-7595. 200p. 1998. text 79.95 (*0-7734-8987-8*) E Mellen.

Meegoda, Jay N., et al, eds. Dredging & Management of Dredged Materials: Proceedings of 3 Sessions Held in Conjunction with Geo-Logan. LC 97-19528. (Geotechnical Special Publications). 208p. 1997. 25.00 (*0-7844-0254-X*) Am Soc Civil Eng.

Meegoda, Jay N., et al. Engineered Contaminated Soils & Interaction of Soil Geomembranes: Proceedings of Sessions Sponsored by the Soil Properties Committee of the ASCE Geotechnical Engineering Division in Conjunction with the ASCE National Convention in Washington, D. C., November 10-14, 1996. LC 96-44711. (Geotechnical Special Publications). 144p. 1996. 25.00 (*0-7844-0213-2*) Am Soc Civil Eng.

Meegoda, Namunu J. Engineering Properties of Contaminated Soils. (C). 2001. write for info. (*0-13-337387-8*, Macmillan Coll) P-H.

Meehan. Life & Letters of G. Stratton-Porter. 1976. 24.95 (*0-8488-0833-9*) Amereon Ltd.

Meehan, Aidan. The Book of Kells Painting Book. LC 99-70863. (Illus.). 64p. 1999. pap. 9.95 (*0-500-28146-7*, Pub. by Thames Hudson) Norton.

— Celtic Alphabets. LC 97-60249. (Illus.). 96p. (Orig.). 1998. pap. 15.95 (*0-500-27980-2*, Pub. by Thames Hudson) Norton.

— Celtic Borders. LC 98-60189. (Illus.). 96p. 1999. pap. 15.95 (*0-500-28067-3*, Pub. by Thames Hudson) Norton.

— Celtic Design: A Beginner's Manual. LC 90-71434. (Illus.). 160p. (Orig.). 1991. pap. 15.95 (*0-500-27629-3*, Pub. by Thames Hudson) Norton.

— Celtic Design: Animal Patterns. LC 91-67307. (Illus.). 160p. 1992. pap. 15.95 (*0-500-27662-5*, Pub. by Thames Hudson) Norton.

— Celtic Design: Illuminated Letters. LC 92-80339. (Illus.). 160p. 1992. pap. 15.95 (*0-500-27685-4*, Pub. by Thames Hudson) Norton.

— Celtic Design: Knotwork. LC 90-71465. (Illus.). 160p. (Orig.). 1991. pap. 15.95 (*0-500-27630-7*, Pub. by Thames Hudson) Norton.

— Celtic Design: Maze Patterns. LC 93-61000. (Illus.). 160p. 1994. pap. 15.95 (*0-500-27747-8*, Pub. by Thames Hudson) Norton.

— Celtic Design: Spirals. LC 92-62132. (Illus.). 160p. 1993. pap. 15.95 (*0-500-27705-2*, Pub. by Thames Hudson) Norton.

— Celtic Design: The Dragon & the Griffin. LC 94-60346. (Illus.). 160p. (Orig.). 1995. pap. 15.95 (*0-500-27792-3*, Pub. by Thames Hudson) Norton.

— Celtic Design: The Tree of Life. LC 94-61399. (Illus.). 160p. (Orig.). 1995. pap. 15.95 (*0-500-27827-X*, Pub. by Thames Hudson) Norton.

— Celtic Patterns: For Painting & Crafts. LC 96-61459. (Illus.). 64p. (Orig.). 1997. pap. 9.95 (*0-500-27938-1*, Pub. by Thames Hudson) Norton.

***Meehan, Aidan.** The Lindisfarne Painting Book. LC 99-65175. (Illus.). 64p. 2000. pap. 9.95 (*0-500-28184-X*, Pub. by Thames Hudson) Norton.

***Meehan, Alacoque.** Brunch with an Irish Flavour. (Illus.). 128p. 1998. pap. 15.95 (*1-899047-53-0*, Pub. by A A Farmar) Irish Bks Media.

Meehan, Anita M. & Astor-Stetson, Eileen. Adolescent Psychology, '98/'99. 2nd ed. (Annual Ser.). (Illus.). 240p. 1998. pap. text 12.25 (*0-697-39128-0*, Dshkn McG-Hill) McGrw-H Hghr Educ.

— Adolescent Psychology 97/98. annuals (Annual Ser.). (Illus.). 256p. (C). 1996. text 12.25 (*0-697-35417-2*, Dshkn McG-Hill) McGrw-H Hghr Educ.

M

M

***Meehan, Anthony.** Computer Consulting in the United States: An Internation Guide, 2000. 1999. pap. text 39.95 (*1-894450-00-0*) Medias & Co.

Meehan, Anthony & Jagpal, Amardeep, eds. Canadian Directory of Search Firms 1999: The Complete Guide to Canada's Recruitment Industry. 4th ed. 336p. 1999. pap. 44.95 (*0-9681447-6-4*) MED.

— Who's Hiring 2000: 5000 Canadian Employers Indexed by Occupation. annuals 4th ed. 532p. 1999. pap. 29.95 (*0-9681447-7-2*) MED.

Meehan, Anthony, jt. ed. see Yerema, Richard.

Meehan, Bernard. The Book of Durrow: An Illustrated Introduction. LC 95-74900. (Illus.). 96p. 1995. 19.95 (*1-57098-053-5*) Roberts Rinehart.

— The Book of Kells. 2nd rev. ed. LC 94-60268. (Illus.). 96p. 1995. pap. 19.95 (*0-500-27790-7*, Pub. by Thames Hudson) Norton.

Meehan, Bill. Collector's Guide to Lu-ray Pastels: Ts&T Premier Potters of America. (Illus.). 160p. 1994. pap. 18.95 (*0-89145-608-2*, 3876) Collector Bks.

***Meehan, Bob.** Beyond the Yellow Brick Road: Our Children & Drugs. rev. ed. xi, 210p. 2000. pap. 20.00 (*0-9702327-0-5*) Meek Pubng.

Meehan, Brian. Plain Song. 24p. 1982. pap. 10.00 (*0-936576-07-3*) Symposium Pr.

***Meehan, Bridget.** Praying with Visionary Women. LC 99-35188. 200p. 1999. pap. 12.95 (*1-58051-063-9*) Sheed & Ward WI.

Meehan, Bridget M. Delighting in the Feminine Divine. LC 93-44593. (Illus.). 132p. (Orig.). 1994. pap. 9.95 (*1-55612-658-1*) Sheed & Ward WI.

— Exploring the Feminine Face of God: A Prayerful Journey. LC 91-60016. (Illus.). 120p. (Orig.). 1991. pap. 8.95 (*1-55612-454-6*, LL1454) Sheed & Ward WI.

— God Delights in You: A Four-Week Prayer Journal. LC 94-60352. (Orig.). 1994. pap. 7.95 (*0-89622-603-4*) Twenty-Third.

— The Healing Power of Prayer. rev. ed. LC 95-45412. 160p. (Orig.). 1996. pap. 9.95 (*0-89243-866-5*) Liguori Pubns.

— Prayers, Activities, Celebrations (& More) for Catholic Families. LC 94-61850. 80p. (Orig.). 1995. pap. 7.95 (*0-89622-641-7*) Twenty-Third.

— Praying with Women of the Bible. LC 98-3176. 176p. 1998. pap. 12.95 (*0-7648-0231-3*, Liguori Triumph) Liguori Pubns.

— Your Prayerful Journal for Lent. LC 93-79677. 180p. (Orig.). 1994. spiral bd. 13.95 (*0-89243-534-8*) Liguori Pubns.

Meehan, Bridget M. & Oliver, Regina M. Heart Talks with Mother God. 48p. (Orig.). 1995. 14.95 (*0-8146-2069-8*) Liturgical Pr.

— Praying with a Passionate Heart. LC 98-35989. 128p. 1999. pap. 12.95 (*0-7648-0212-7*) Liguori Pubns.

— A Promise of Presence: Weekly Reflections & Daily Prayer Activities. LC 99-62047. 232p. 1999. pap. 9.95 (*0-87946-200-0*, 283) ACTA Pubns.

Meehan, Bridget M., jt. auth. see Beben, Mary.

Meehan, Christine, ed. see Healy, Gene.

Meehan, Christopher H. Blood on the Bridge. 1998. pap. 14.95 (*1-882376-59-5*) Thunder Bay Pr.

— Murder on the Grand. 1997. pap. 14.95 (*1-882376-49-8*) Thunder Bay Pr.

Meehan, Denis, tr. see Gregory of Nazianzus, St.

Meehan, Eileen. Home Buying & Selling for the Clueless: Everything a Beginner Needs to Know. LC 98-29045. (Illus.). 224p. 1998. pap. 10.95 (*0-8065-2022-1*, Citadel Pr) Carol Pub Group.

Meehan, Elizabeth. Citizenship & the European Community. (Illus.). 224p. 1993. 45.00 (*0-8039-8428-6*); pap. 19.95 (*0-8039-8429-4*) Sage.

***Meehan, Elizabeth.** Twentieth-Century American Writers. LC 99-50796. (History Makers Ser.). 144p. (YA). (gr. 4-12). 2000. 18.96 (*1-56006-671-7*) Lucent Bks.

Meehan, Elizabeth & Sevenhuijsen, Selma, eds. Equality Politics & Gender. (Modern Politics Ser.: Vol. 29). 224p. (C). 1991. text 55.00 (*0-8039-8482-0*); pap. text 19.95 (*0-8039-8483-9*) Sage.

Meehan, Elizabeth M. Women's Rights at Work: Campaigns & Policy in Britain & the United States. LC 84-1597. 253p. 1985. text 35.00 (*0-312-88793-0*) St Martin.

Meehan, Elizabeth M., jt. ed. see Kahn, Peggy.

Meehan, Elizabeth M., jt. ed. see Larres, Klaus.

Meehan, Eugene J. Assessing Governmental Performance: An Analytical Framework, 310. LC 92-25740. (Contributions in Political Science Ser.: No. 310). 216p. 1992. 55.00 (*0-313-28720-1*, GM8720, Greenwood Pr) Greenwood.

— Cognitive Education & Testing: A Methodological Approach, 47. LC 91-3. (Contributions to the Study of Education Ser.: No. 47). 224p. 1991. 55.00 (*0-313-27889-X*, MGN, Greenwood Pr) Greenwood.

— Economics & Policymaking: The Tragic Illusion, 47. LC 81-20331. (Contributions in Economics & Economic History Ser.: No. 47). (Illus.). 194p. 1982. 52.95 (*0-313-23313-6*, MEE/, Greenwood Pr) Greenwood.

— Ethics for Policymaking: A Methodological Analysis, 257. LC 89-25763. (Contributions in Political Science Ser.: No. 257). 248p. 1990. 62.95 (*0-313-27342-1*, MEW/, Greenwood Pr) Greenwood.

— The Quality of Federal Policymaking: Programmed Failure in Public Housing. LC 78-27663. 256p. reprint ed. pap. 79.40 (*0-7837-3200-7*, AU0042800007) Bks Demand.

— Reasoned Argument in Social Science, 53. LC 80-1198. (Linking Research to Policy Ser.). (Illus.). 218p. 1981. 57.95 (*0-313-22481-1*, MRE/, Greenwood Pr) Greenwood.

— Social Inquiry: Needs, Possibilities, Limits. LC 93-39678. 224p. (Orig.). (C). 1994. pap. text 29.95 (*1-56643-006-2*, Chatham House Pub) Seven Bridges.

— The Thinking Game: A Guide to Effective Study. LC 88-4335. (Chatham House Studies in Political Thinking). (Illus.). 256p. (C). 1988. pap. text 22.95 (*0-934540-64-0*, Chatham House Pub) Seven Bridges.

Meehan, Francis J. Contrast in Shakespeare's Historical Plays. LC 72-8981. (Studies in Shakespeare: No. 24). 1973. reprint ed. lib. bdg. 59.00 (*0-8383-1681-6*) M S G Haskell Hse.

Meehan, Francis X. A Contemporary Social Spirituality. LC 82-2253. 143p. (Orig.). reprint ed. pap. 44.40 (*0-608-20203-7*, 207146200012) Bks Demand.

Meehan, J. F., et al. Managua, Nicaragua Earthquake of December 23, 1972. 214p. 1973. pap. 12.00 (*0-318-16321-7*, EP-12) Earthquake Eng.

Meehan, J. Johanna, ed. Feminists Read Habermas: Gendering the Subject of Discourse. LC 94-20585. (Thinking Gender Ser.). 256p. (C). (gr. 13). 1995. pap. 18.99 (*0-415-90714-4*, A9798) Routledge.

Meehan, J. P. The Lady of the Limberlost: A Biography. 24.95 (*0-8488-0094-X*) Amereon Ltd.

Meehan, James, jt. auth. see Bruyn, Severyn T.

Meehan, James R., jt. auth. see Polisky, Mildred K.

Meehan, James W., Jr., jt. ed. see Larner, Robert J.

Meehan, Jeannette P. Freckles Comes Home. reprint ed. lib. bdg. 24.95 (*0-89190-931-1*, Rivercity Pr) Amereon Ltd.

***Meehan, Jim.** Hearts Have Reasons. 96p. 2000. pap. 7.95 (*0-88347-451-4*, Pub. by T More) BookWorld.

— Reasons Have Hearts Too. 96p. 2000. pap. 7.95 (*0-88347-452-2*, Pub. by T More) BookWorld.

Meehan, Joe, jt. ed. see Hinterobermaier, Chris.

Meehan, Joseph. Manual SLRs. LC 95-151239. (Magic Lantern Guides Ser.). (Illus.). 176p. (Orig.). (C). 1998. pap. 19.95 (*1-883403-10-3*, H 153, Silver Pixel Pr) Saunders Photo.

— Panoramic Photography. LC 95-49226. (Illus.). 144p. 1996. pap. 27.50 (*0-8174-5347-4*, Amphoto) Watsn-Guptill.

***Meehan, Joseph.** Pentax ZX-M/K 1000. LC 99-26593. (Magic Lantern Guides Ser.). 176p. 1999. 19.95 (*1-883403-55-3*, Silver Pixel Pr) Saunders Photo.

Meehan, Joseph. The Photographer's Guide to Using Filters. (Illus.). 144p. 1992. pap. 22.50 (*0-8174-5449-7*, Amphoto) Watsn-Guptill.

— The Photographer's Guide to Using Filters. rev. ed. LC 98-11624. 144p. 1998. pap. 24.95 (*0-8174-5452-7*) Watsn-Guptill.

Meehan, Kerry F. & Nowicki, Joseph J. The Collaborative Social Studies Classroom: A Resource for Teachers. LC 95-13741. 208p. (C). 1995. pap. text 33.00 (*0-205-17391-8*) Allyn.

Meehan, Kerry F., jt. auth. see Nowicki, Joseph J.

Meehan, Les, jt. auth. see Meehan, Patricia.

Meehan, Maria, jt. auth. see O'Regan, Donal.

Meehan, Maude. Washing the Stones: Selected Poems, 1975-1995. LC 95-29997. 240p. (Orig.). 1996. pap. 13.00 (*0-918949-85-8*) M Meehan.

Meehan, Michael. Liberty & Poetics in Eighteenth Century England. LC 85-22404. 1985. 37.50 (*0-7099-4623-6*, Pub. by C Helm) Routldge.

Meehan, Norma L. Art Deco Paper Doll Wardrobe 1920-1939. (Illus.). 1994. pap. text 4.95 (*0-87588-422-9*, 4734) Hobby Hse.

— Fashions of the 40s & 50s: Paper Doll Wardrobe. (Illus.). 24p. Date not set. pap. text 5.95 (*0-87588-465-2*, 5198) Hobby Hse.

— Heroine of the Limberlost: A Paper Doll Biography of Gene Stratton-Porter. (Illus.). 32p. 1998. pap. 9.95 (*0-89672-396-8*) Tex Tech Univ Pr.

— Nana's Trunk Paperdolls. (Illus.). 24p. 1995. pap. text 4.95 (*0-87588-438-5*) Hobby Hse.

Meehan, Patricia. Blooms & Bouquets: Quick & Easy Projects for the Modern Home. (Patricia Meehan's Stencil Classics Ser.). (Illus.). 32p. 1999. pap. 12.95 (*1-85585-666-2*, Pub. by Collins & Br) Sterling.

— Magic & Moonlight: Quick & Easy Projects for the Modern Home. (Patricia Meehan's Stencil Classics Ser.). (Illus.). 32p. 1999. pap. 12.95 (*1-85585-667-0*, Pub. by Collins & Br) Sterling.

— Stencil Source Book: Over Two Hundred Designs to Make Stencils for All Around the Home. (Illus.). 144p. 1994. 22.95 (*0-89134-586-8*, North Lght Bks) F & W Pubns Inc.

— Stencil Source Book 2, Vol. 2. (Illus.). 144p. 1995. 22.99 (*0-89134-695-3*, North Lght Bks) F & W Pubns Inc.

Meehan, Patricia & Meehan, Les. The Creative Stencil Source Book: 200 Inspiring & Original Designs. (Illus.). 1999. 24.95 (*1-85585-609-3*, Pub. by Collins & Br) Trafalgar.

***Meehan, Patricia & Meehan, Les.** The Creative Stencil Source Book: 200 Inspiring & Original Motifs. (Illus.). 144p. 2000. pap. 17.95 (*1-85585-658-1*, Pub. by Collins & Br) Sterling.

Meehan, Patrick J. Frank Lloyd Wright: A Research Guide to Archival Sources. LC 81-47447. 681p. 1983. text 160.00 (*0-8240-9342-9*) Garland.

— Frank Lloyd Wright Remembered. (Illus.). 256p. 1995. 29.95 (*0-471-14383-9*) Wiley.

Meehan, Patrick J., ed. see Wright, Frank Lloyd.

Meehan, Paul. Saucer Movies: A UFOlogical History of the Cinema. LC 98-29743. 376p. 1998. 55.00 (*0-8108-3573-8*) Scarecrow.

Meehan, Paula. The Man Who Was Marked by Winter. 66p. 1994. pap. 12.00 (*0-910055-14-9*) East Wash Univ.

— The Man Who Was Marked by Winter. 66p. 1994. reprint ed. 21.00 (*0-910055-13-0*) East Wash Univ.

— Pillow Talk. LC 94-217445. 74p. 1994. pap. 13.95 (*1-85235-133-0*) Dufour.

Meehan, Richard L. The Atom & the Fault: Experts, Earthquakes, & Nuclear Power. 184p. 1984. reprint ed. 23.00 (*0-262-13199-4*) MIT Pr.

— Getting Sued & Other Tales of the Engineering Life. 254p. 1983. reprint ed. pap. text 13.95 (*0-262-63089-3*) MIT Pr.

Meehan, Robert H. & Lemesis, G. Victor. Determining Compensation Costs: An Approach to Estimating & Analyzing Expense. (Building Blocks Ser.: Vol. 3). (Illus.). 24p. (Orig.). 1992. pap. 24.95 (*1-57963-006-5*, A0003) Am Compensation.

Meehan, Roberta M. Fundamentals of Anatomy & Physiology. 3rd ed. 1995. pap. text, lab manual ed. 48.00 (*0-13-340910-4*) P-H.

— Laboratory Manual for Fundamentals of Anatomy & Physiology. 4th ed. 751p. (C). 1997. pap. text, lab manual ed. 33.33 (*0-13-751850-1*) P-H.

Meehan, Rosario, tr. see Ancell, Carolyn D.

Meehan, Rosario, tr. see Deitering-Ancell, Carolyn.

Meehan, Rosario, tr. see Fanning, Regine.

Meehan, Sheila, jt. ed. see Dowdall, Mike.

Meehan, Suzi, ed. see Moreno, Richard.

Meehan, Thomas C., tr. see Sorrentino, Fernando.

***Meehan, Tim.** Suit Yourself: A Practical Guide to Men's Attire. McGhee, Stephen, ed. (Illus.). 101p. 1999. pap. 16.95 (*0-9670738-0-4*) J T Meehan Pubg.

Meehan, Tom. When the Sacred Marriage Ends. LC 95-94377. 271p. (Orig.). 1995. pap. 14.40 (*0-9646166-0-2*) Dollar Spec Pubns.

Meehan, Tony. Goodbye Maigida. 176p. (C). 1989. text 45.00 (*1-872795-18-8*, Pub. by Pentland Pr) St Mut.

Meehan, Trudy, ed. see Davis, Lynn.

Meehan, Valerie C. Experiments for Medical Chemistry. 128p. (C). 1995. 13.95 (*0-8403-9219-2*) Kendall-Hunt.

Meehan, Virginia M. Christopher Marlowe Poet & Playwright Studies in Poetical Method. LC 74-79321. (De Proprietatibus Litterarum, Ser. Practica: No. 81). 100p. 1974. pap. text 52.35 (*90-279-3382-0*) Mouton.

Meehan, W. R., ed. Influences of Forest & Rangeland Management on Salmonid Fishes & Their Habitat. LC 91-55216. (Special Publication Ser.: No. 19). 751p. (C). 1991. text 81.00 (*0-913235-68-7*, 510.15C) Am Fisheries Soc.

Meehan-Waters, Brenda. Holy Women of Russia: The Lives of Five Orthodox Women Offer Spiritual Guidance for Today. LC 96-31010. 1996. pap. 9.95 (*0-88141-157-4*) St Vladimirs.

Meehl, Joanne H. The Recovering Catholic: Personal Journeys of Women Who Left the Church. LC 94-22774. 288p. 1995. 25.95 (*0-87975-927-5*) Prometheus Bks.

Meehl, Paul E. Clinical Versus Statistical Prediction: A Theoretical Analysis & a Review of the Evidence. LC 54-11774. 159p. reprint ed. pap. 49.30 (*0-608-14126-7*, 205589000039) Bks Demand.

— Clinical vs. Statistical Prediction: A Theoretical Analysis & a Review of the Evidence. LC 96-5094. 1996. reprint ed. 40.00 (*1-56821-831-1*) Aronson.

— Psychodiagnosis: Selected Papers. LC 72-95440. (Illus.). 383p. 1973. reprint ed. pap. 118.80 (*0-608-00838-9*, 206162900010) Bks Demand.

— Select Philosophical Methodical Papers. 512p. (C). 1991. text 44.95 (*0-8166-1855-0*) U of Minn Pr.

Meehl, Paul E., jt. auth. see Waller, Niels G.

Meek, A. J., photos by. The Gardens of Louisiana: Places of Work & Wonder. LC 96-53547. (Illus.). 272p. 1997. 49.95 (*0-8071-2107-X*) La State U Pr.

Meek, A. J., jt. auth. see Gassan, Arnold.

Meek, Anne. Communicating with the Public: A Guide for School Leaders. LC 99-6199. 144p. 1999. pap. 22.95 (*0-87120-343-X*, 199052) ASCD.

Meek, Anne, ed. Designing Places for Learning. LC 95-4409. 1995. pap. 25.95 (*0-87120-248-4*, 195082) ASCD.

Meek, Basil, ed. Twentieth Century History of Sandusky County, Ohio. (Illus.). 934p. 1993. reprint ed. lib. bdg. 95.00 (*0-8328-3448-3*) Higginson Bk Co.

Meek, Bill. Moonpenny. 145p. pap. 11.95 (*0-946005-30-3*, OS 10181, Pub. by Ossian) Music Sales.

Meek, C. & Simms, K., eds. The Fragility of Her Sex? Medieval Irish Women in Their European Context. 208p. 1996. 45.00 (*1-85182-172-4*, Pub. by Four Cts Pr); pap. 25.00 (*1-85182-206-2*, Pub. by Four Cts Pr) Intl Spec Bk.

Meek, Caroline. The Butter Business: How a Butter Tub Cover Is Related to the Mill, the Cooper, & the Farmer. (Illus.). 112p. (Orig.). 1995. pap. 6.50 (*1-879444-03-8*) Hanford Mills Museum.

Meek, Carroll L., ed. Post-Traumatic Stress Disorder: Assessment, Differential Diagnosis, & Forensic Evaluation. LC 89-43413. 264p. 1990. 30.95 (*0-943158-35-4*, PTSDBP) Pro Resource.

Meek, Charles J. Conducting Made Easy for Directors of Amateur Musical Organizations. LC 88-18356. (Illus.). 150p. 1988. 26.00 (*0-8108-2167-2*); pap. 18.00 (*0-8108-2179-6*) Scarecrow.

Meek, Charles K. Colonial Law: A Bibliography with Special Reference to Native African Systems of Law & Land Tenure. LC 78-14383. 58p. 1979. lib. bdg. 55.00 (*0-313-21011-X*, MECL, Greenwood Pr) Greenwood.

— Land Law & Custom in the Colonies. 2nd ed. 337p. 1968. reprint ed. 45.00 (*0-7146-1698-2*, Pub. by F Cass Pubs) Intl Spec Bk.

— Law & Authority in a Nigerian Tribe. LC 76-44756. reprint ed. 37.50 (*0-404-15951-6*) AMS Pr.

— Northern Tribes of Nigeria: Ethnographical Account of the Northern Provinces of Nigeria Together with a Report of the 1921 Decennial Census, 2 vols. (Illus.). 1971. reprint ed. 145.00 (*0-7146-2686-4*, Pub. by F Cass Pubs) Intl Spec Bk.

— Tribal Studies in Northern Nigeria, 2 vols. LC 74-15066. reprint ed. 155.00 (*0-404-12107-1*) AMS Pr.

Meek, Charles S. Beyond the Crash: The Real World of Investing. (Illus.). 200p. 1988. 19.95 (*0-938619-41-1*) Live Oak TX.

— Money Matters: Financial Planning & Investment Ideas for the Non Finance Professional. 1991. text 24.95 (*1-55738-136-4*, Irwn Prfssnl) McGraw-Hill Prof.

Meek, Christine E. The Commune of Lucca Under Pisan Rule, 1342-1369. LC 78-70245. 1980. 20.00 (*0-910956-69-3*, SAM6); pap. 12.00 (*0-910956-80-4*) Medieval Acad.

Meek, Christine E., ed. Women in Late Medieval & Early Modern Europe. 208p. 2000. pap. 29.95 (*1-85182-424-3*, Pub. by Four Cts Pr); boxed set 55.00 (*1-85182-423-5*, Pub. by Four Cts Pr) Intl Spec Bk.

Meek, Christopher B. & Woodworth, Werner P. Creating Labor-Management Partnerships. (Illus.). 240p. (C). 1994. pap. 40.00 (*0-201-58823-4*) Addison-Wesley.

Meek, Cindy. Catalog of Nonsmoking Hotel Rooms: A Consumer Service. rev. ed. 146p. (Orig.). 1986. pap. 43.50 (*0-938619-24-1*) Live Oak TX.

Meek, D. Caran an T-Saoghail. 1998. pap. 21.95 (*1-874744-67-X*, Pub. by Birlinn Ltd) Dufour.

Meek, Devon W., jt. ed. see Alyea, Elmer C.

Meek, Doris & MacCarthy, Mike. Norska: A Viking Woman's Journey. 260p. (Orig.). 1995. pap. 14.50 (*1-885516-01-0*) SD Writs Mnthly.

Meek, Ed. Flying: Poems. LC 92-15308. 64p. 1992. pap. 14.95 (*0-7734-0040-0*) E Mellen.

Meek, Esther L., jt. auth. see MacNair, Donald J.

Meek, Forrest B. Michigan's Heartland. (Illus.). 449p. 1979. lib. bdg. 24.95 (*0-9602472-0-3*) Edgewood.

— Michigan's Timber Battleground. 2nd rev. ed. (Illus.). 483p. 1991. reprint ed. lib. bdg. 34.95 (*0-9602472-1-1*) Edgewood.

Meek, Frank. Haynes Kawasaki 250, 350 & 400 (3-cyl) Models '72-'79, No. M134. 1979. 23.95 (*0-85696-134-5*) Haynes Manuals.

— Haynes Triumph Trident & BSA Rocket 3 Owners Workshop Manual, No. 136: '69-'75. 1979. 23.95 (*0-85696-136-1*) Haynes Manuals.

Meek, Gary E., et al. Business Statistics. 800p. 1986. write for info. (*0-685-17397-6*) P-H.

Meek, Gary K., ed. Country Studies in International Accounting: Americas & the Far East. LC 96-2504. (Library of International Accounting: Vol. 3). 512p. 1996. 205.00 (*1-85898-225-1*) E Elgar.

Meek, Geoffrey A. Practical Electron Microscopy for Biologists. 2nd ed. LC 75-4955. 550p. reprint ed. pap. 170.50 (*0-608-17744-X*, 205224200069) Bks Demand.

Meek, George W. Enjoy Your Own Funeral: And Live a Happy Forever. LC 99-27092. (Illus.). 320p. 1999. pap. 16.95 (*1-880090-85-6*) Galde Pr.

Meek, Harold A. Guarino Guarini. LC 87-24636. 256p. (C). 1988. 70.00 (*0-300-03989-1*) Yale U Pr.

— Guarino Guarini & His Architecture. 256p. (C). 1990. reprint ed. pap. 30.00 (*0-300-04748-7*) Yale U Pr.

— Horn & Conductor: Reminiscences of a Practitioner. Mann, Alfred, ed. LC 96-44230. 120p. 1997. pap. 19.95 (*1-878822-83-7*) Univ Rochester Pr.

— The Synagogue: The Complete History of the Art & Architecture of the Synagogue. (Illus.). 240p. (C). 1995. text 59.95 (*0-7148-2932-3*, Pub. by Phaidon Press) Phaidon Pr.

Meek, J. L. Computer Methods in Structural Analysis. (Illus.). 520p. (C). 1991. pap. 60.00 (*0-419-15440-X*, E & FN Spon) Routledge.

Meek, J. L., jt. auth. see Gupta, Kajal K.

Meek, J. M. & Craggs, J. D. Electrical Breakdown of Gases. LC 77-2784. 888p. reprint ed. 200.00 (*0-8357-9879-8*, 201947200012) Bks Demand.

Meek, James. Drivetime. 288p. (Orig.). 1996. pap. 15.95 (*0-7486-6205-7*, Pub. by Polygon) Subterranean Co.

— Last Orders: And Other Stories. 184p. (Orig.). 1992. pap. 14.95 (*0-7486-6127-1*, Pub. by Polygon) Subterranean Co.

— McFarlane Boils the Sea. 1989. 18.00 (*0-7486-6006-2*, Pub. by Polygon) Subterranean Co.

Meek, James A. Did Jesus Say That? (Discover Life Ser.). 30p. pap. 5.35 (*1-56212-244-4*) CRC Pubns.

— DL Spiritual Fitness Study Guide. 14p. 1991. pap., student ed. 3.25 (*1-56212-166-9*) CRC Pubns.

— Jesus - His Powerful Life: Leader Guide. (Discover Life Ser.). 54p. 1996. pap. 5.35 (*1-56212-138-3*) CRC Pubns.

— Jesus His Triumph over Death: Leader Guide. (Discover Life Ser.). 43p. pap. 0.95 (*1-56212-209-6*) CRC Pubns.

— Jesus His Triumph over Death: Student Guide. (Discover Life Ser.). 14p. pap., student ed. 3.25 (*1-56212-210-X*) CRC Pubns.

— A New Kind of Life: Study Guide. (Discover Life Ser.). 18p. 1990. pap., student ed. 3.25 (*1-56212-229-0*) CRC Pubns.

Meek, James A. Steps to Success. (Discover Life Ser.). 1994. pap. 5.75 (*1-56212-091-3*) CRC Pubns.

Meek, Jay. Drawing on the Walls. LC 79-51607. (Poetry Ser.). 1980. pap. 11.95 (*0-915604-32-9*) Carnegie-Mellon.

— Drawing on the Walls. LC 79-51607. (Poetry Ser.). 1980. 20.95 (*0-915604-31-0*) Carnegie-Mellon.

— Earthly Purposes. 1984. pap. 11.95 (*0-915604-95-7*) Carnegie-Mellon.

— Earthly Purposes. 1984. 20.95 (*0-915604-94-9*) Carnegie-Mellon.

— Good Lives. 34p. 1996. 3.50 (*0-941127-20-6*) Dacotah Terr Pr.

— Headlands: New & Selected Poems. LC 96-83424. 120p. 1997. 20.95 (*0-88748-234-1*); pap. 11.95 (*0-88748-235-X*) Carnegie-Mellon.

— Stations. LC 88-70525. 80p. 1989. pap. 11.95 (*0-88748-081-0*) Carnegie-Mellon.

— Windows. LC 93-73472. (Poetry Ser.). 80p. (Orig.). 1994. pap. 11.95 (*0-88748-171-X*) Carnegie-Mellon.

An Asterisk (*) at the beginning of an entry indicates that the title is appearing for the first time.

M

An Asterisk (*) at the beginning of an entry indicates that the title is appearing for the first time.

— The Writings of St. Paul. (Critical Editions Ser.). 454p. (C). 1972. pap. 14.75 (*0-393-09979-2*) Norton.

Meeks, Wayne A., ed. The HarperCollins Study Bible: New Revised Standard Version (with the Apocryphal/ Deuterocanonical Books) LC 92-56127. 2368p. 1993. 42.00 (*0-06-065580-1*, Pub. by Harper SF) HarpC.

Meeks, Wayne A., ed. see Cohen, Shaye J. D.

Meeldijk, Victor. The Component Identifier & Source Book, No. 2. 2nd ed. LC 99-185020. (Illus.). 416p. 1999. pap. 34.95 (*0-7906-1159-7*) Prompt Publns.

Meeldijk, Victor. Electronic Components: Selection & Application Guidelines. LC 93-44638. (Illus.). 864p. 1997. pap. 135.00 (*0-471-18972-3*) Wiley.

Meeldijk, Victor. Electronic Components: Selection & Application Guidelines 1995 Update Supplement. 128p. 1996. pap. 65.00 (*0-471-13301-9*) Wiley.

Meelis, Evert, jt. auth. see Haccou, Patsy.

Meellone, Michael A. & Planty, Earl. Planty's Encyclopedia of Cacheted F. D. C.'s, Vol. 10. (Illus.). 1978. pap. 9.95 (*0-317-16574-7*) FDC Pub.

Meelu, O. P. & Singh-Yadvinder. Green Manuring for Soil Productivity Improvement. (World Soil Resources Reports: No. 76). 133p. 1994. pap. 16.00 (*92-5-103515-6*, F35156, Pub. by FAO) Bernan Associates.

Meem, J. L. Two Group Reactor Theory. xiv, 417p. 1964. text 389.00 (*0-677-00520-2*) Gordon & Breach.

Meema, K. M., jt. auth. see Hutchinson, Thomas C.

Meema, K. M., jt. ed. see Hutchinson, Thomas C.

Meena, James C. The Very Best of X: Lifestyles in Christ Meditations on Orthodox Christian Living. 118p. (Orig.). 1995. pap. 8.95 (*0-9634940-5-8*) York Pub.

Meenaghan, Thomas M. & Gibbons, W. Eugene. Generalist Practice Skills in Larger Systems: Knowledge & Skill Concepts. 188p. (C). 2000. pap. text 22.95 (*0-925065-31-5*) Lyceum IL.

Meenaghan, Thomas M. & Kilty, Keith. Policy Analysis & Research Technology: Political & Ethical Considerations. LC 93-30524. 248p. 1994. pap. text 28.95 (*0-925065-46-3*) Lyceum IL.

Meenaghan, Thomas M., et al. Macro-Level Practice in the Human Services: An Introduction to Planning, Administration & Evaluation. (Illus.). 288p. (C). 1982. 29.95 (*0-02-920850-5*) Free Pr.

Meenai, S. A. The Islamic Development Bank: A Case Study of Islamic Co-Operation. 200p. 1989. 69.50 (*0-7103-0329-7*) Routledge.

— Money & Banking Pakistan. 3rd ed. 318p. 1985. pap. text 21.95 (*0-19-577327-6*) OUP.

Meenakshi. Hindi-English Dictionary. 2nd ed. 802p. 1984. 49.95 (*0-8288-1743-X*) Fr & Eur.

Meenan, Daniel F., tr. see Iparraguirre, Ignacio.

Meengs, Karen L. & Eby, Deborah R. The Holistic & Metaphysical Resource Book for Maryland, Virginia & Washington D. C., 1997-1998. (Illus.). x, 362p. 1997. 19.95 (*0-9661147-0-1*) Over Cliff.

Meer, Ameena. Bombay Talkie. 1999. pap. 11.99 (*1-85242-707-8*) Serpents Tail.

Meer, Antonia Van der, see Katzenbach, John & Van der Meer, Antonia.

Meer, Antonia Van Der, see Van Der Meer, Antonia.

Meer, Claudia G. Customer Education. LC 84-6938. 168p. 1985. lib. bdg. 41.95 (*0-8304-1049-X*) Burnham Inc.

Meer, Claudia G., et al. Sex Role Stereotyping in Occupational Choices: A Career Counseling Manual. 62p. 1982. 6.00 (*0-941312-01-1*) Inst Mgmt & Labor.

Meer, Cor Van der, see Rees, Roy & Van der Meer, Cor.

Meer, H. G. Van der, see Van der Meer, H. G.

Meer, H. V. Van der, see Van der Meer, H. V.

Meer, J. C. Van Der, see Van Der Meer, J. C.

Meer, J. M. Van der, see Van der Meer, J. M., ed.

Meer, J. W. Van Der, see Van Der Meer, J. W., ed.

Meer, Jeff. Drugs & Sports. (Encyclopedia of Psychoactive Drugs Ser.: No. 2). (Illus.). 128p. (YA). (gr. 7 up). 1987. lib. bdg. 19.95 (*1-55546-226-X*) Chelsea Hse.

— Drugs & Sports. (Encyclopedia of Psychoactive Drugs Ser.: No. 2). (Illus.). 128p. (YA). (gr. 7 up). 1988. pap. 8.95 (*0-7910-0794-4*) Chelsea Hse.

— Drugs & Sports. (Encyclopedia of Psychoactive Drugs - Compact Paperback Library). (Illus.). 32p. (YA). (gr. 5 up). 1991. pap. 4.49 (*1-55546-996-5*) Chelsea Hse.

Meer, Jitse M. Van Der, see Van Der Meer, Jitse M., ed.

Meer, Mary F. Wooing the Meadowlark: A Collection of Haiku. LC 98-107388. (Illus.). 24p. 1997. pap. text 6.00 (*1-887381-08-2*) Vandina Pr.

Meer, Mary Ter, see Galeana, Jamie G. & Ter Meer, Mary.

Meer, N. C. Van Setten van der, see Van Setten van der Meer, N. C.

Meer, Patrick Van der, see Van der Meer, Patrick.

Meer, Shamim, ed. Women, Land, & Authority: Perspectives from South Africa. 160p. 1997. pap. 15.95 (*0-85598-375-2*, Pub. by Oxfam Pub) Stylus Pub VA.

Meera, Mother. Answers. (Illus.). 112p. (Orig.). 1991. pap. text 9.95 (*0-9622973-3-X*) Meeramma Pubns.

Meerbaum, Samuel, ed. Myocardial Perfusion, Reperfusion, Coronary Venous Retroperfusion. 160p. 1990. 102.00 (*0-387-91362-9*) Spr-Verlag.

Meerbaum, Samuel & Melzer, Richard, eds. Myocardial Contrast Two Dimensional Echocardiography. (Developments in Cardiovascular Medicine Ser.). (C). 1989. text 182.50 (*0-7923-0205-2*) Kluwer Academic.

Meerbote, Ralf & Hudson, H., eds. Kant's Aesthetics. (North American Kant Society Studies in Philosophy: Vol. 1). viii, 146p. (Orig.). 1991. pap. text 18.00 (*0-924922-06-0*); lib. bdg. 36.00 (*0-924922-56-7*) Ridgeview.

Meerhaeghe, M. A. Van, see Van Meerhaeghe, M. A.

Meerloo, Joost A. Patterns of Panic. LC 50-5823. 120p. reprint ed. pap. 37.20 (*0-608-11209-7*, 201044500070) Bks Demand.

— The Two Faces of Man: Two Studies on the Sense of Time & on Ambivalence. LC 54-12141. (Illus.). 251p. reprint ed. pap. 77.90 (*0-608-11153-8*, 201070300070) Bks Demand.

Meerman, Michael V. The Complete Credit & Collection Letters Kit. 140p. 1994. pap. 37.50 (*0-934914-90-7*) NACM.

Meermann, Rolf, jt. auth. see Vandereycken, Walter.

Meeropol, Michael. Surrender: How the Clinton Administration Completed the Reagan Revolution. LC 98-25387. (Illus.). 400p. 1998. 32.50 (*0-472-10952-9*, 10952) U of Mich Pr.

***Meeropol, Michael.** Surrender: How the Clinton Administration Completed the Reagan Revolution. (Illus.). 400p. (C). 2000. pap. 19.95 (*0-472-08676-6*, 08676) U of Mich Pr.

Meeropol, Michael, ed. The Rosenberg Letters: A Complete Edition of the Prison Correspondence of Julius & Ethel Rosenberg. LC 93-40860. 792p. 1994. text 35.00 (*0-8240-5948-4*, H1184) Garland.

Meeropol, Michael, jt. auth. see Meeropol, Robert.

Meeropol, Robert & Meeropol, Michael. We Are Your Sons: The Legacy of Ethel & Julius Rosenberg. 2nd ed. LC 85-30892. (Illus.). 508p. 1986. text 34.95 (*0-252-01263-1*) U of Ill Pr.

Meerow, A. W. Flora of Ecuador No. 202: Amaryllidaceae. (Opera Botanica Series B). 53p. 1990. pap. 34.00 (*87-88702-46-4*, Pub. by Coun Nordic Pubs) Balogh.

Meerow, Alan W., jt. auth. see Broschat, Timothy K.

Meers, Mark. Bringing Home the Sushi: An American Businessman & His Family Take on '90s Japan. LC 95-73159. 1996. 21.95 (*1-887472-05-3*) Sunstar Pubng.

Meers, Peter, et al. Hospital Infection Control for Nurses. LC 92-49510. 1992. 41.50 (*1-56593-060-6*, 0366) Singular Publishing.

Meers, Peter, jt. auth. see Sedgwick, J.

Meers, Trevor. 101 Best Web Sites for Kids. 160p. 1999. mass mkt. 5.99 (*0-7853-3931-0*) Pubns Intl Ltd.

Meerschaer. Mathematical Modeling. 2nd ed. LC 98-19869. 351p. (C). 1998. text 59.95 (*0-12-487652-8*) Acad Pr.

Meerschaert, Mark M. Mathematical Modeling. (Illus.). 287p. 1993. text 53.00 (*0-12-487650-1*) Acad Pr.

Meerschaut, A., ed. Incommensurate Sandwiched Layered Compounds. 436p. 1992. text 175.00 (*0-87849-643-2*, Pub. by Trans T Pub) Enfield Pubs NH.

Meerschwam. Break Financial Boundaries. 300p. 1991. 37.50 (*0-07-103305-X*) McGraw.

***Meersman, H., et al, eds.** World Transport Research. 2714p. 1999. 485.00 (*0-08-043590-4*) Elsevier.

***Meersman, R. A., et al.** Database Semantics: Semantic Issues in Multimedia Systems: IFIP TC2/WG2.6 8th Working Conference on Database Semantics (DS-8), New Zealand, January 4-8, 1999 LC 99-188348. xi, 456 p. 1999. pap. write for info. (*0-7923-8405-9*) Kluwer Academic.

Meersman, R. A., jt. ed. see Steel, T. B., Jr.

Meerson, Felix Z. Adaptive Protection of the Heart: Protecting Against Stress & Ischemic Damage. (Illus.). 320p. 1990. lib. bdg. 139.00 (*0-8493-5150-2*, QP114) CRC Pr.

— The Failing Heart: Adaptation & Deadaptation. Katz, Arnold M., ed. Bobrov, Nicholas & Levant, Leonid, trs. from RUS. LC 83-2974. (Illus.). 341p. 1983. reprint ed. pap. 105.80 (*0-608-00611-4*, 206119800007) Bks Demand.

***Meerson, Michael Aksionou.** The Trinity of Love in Modern Russian Theology: The Love Paradigm & the Retricual of Western Medieval Love Mysticism in Modern Russian Trinitarian Thought. 255p. 1998. pap. 15.95 (*0-8199-0987-4*) Franciscan Pr.

Meerson, Olga. Dostoevsky's Taboos. 232p. 1998. 55.00 (*3-931828-48-4*, Pub. by Dresden Univ Pr) Paul & Co Pubs.

— "Svobodnaia Veshch" Poetika Neostraneniia u Andreia Platonova. (RUS., Illus.). 136p. (C). 1997. pap. text 14.00 (*1-57201-038-X*) Berkeley Slavic.

Meerstadt, P. W. & Batty, Daphne. Model Business Plan. 1995. pap. 30.00 (*1-873868-29-4*) BAAF.

Meerstadt, P. W. & Gyll, Catherine. Manual of Neonatal Emergency X-Ray Interpretation. (Illus.). 301p. 1995. pap. text 33.95 (*0-7020-1567-9*, Pub. by W B Saunders) Saunders.

Meertens, Donny, jt. auth. see Sanchez, Gonzalo.

Meerwarth, Rudolf, et al. Die Einwirkung des Krieges Auf Bevolkerungsbewegung, Einkommen Und Lebenshaltung in Deutschland. (Wirtschafts-Und Sozialgeschichte des Weltkrieges (Osterreichische Und Ungarische Serie)). (GER.). 1932. 150.00 (*0-317-27461-9*) Elliots Bks.

Mees, A. I. Dynamics of Feedback Systems. LC 80-40501. (Illus.). 224p. reprint ed. pap. 69.50 (*0-8357-6651-9*, 203532000094) Bks Demand.

***Mees, Alistair, ed.** Nonlinear Dynamics & Statistics. (Illus.). 493p. 2000. 89.95 (*0-8176-4163-7*) Birkhauser.

***Mees, Alistair I., et al.** Progress in Optimization: Contributions from Australasia. 354p. 2000. 149.00 (*0-7923-6286-1*) Kluwer Academic.

Mees, Arthur. Choirs & Choral Music. LC 69-13995. 250p. 1970. reprint ed. lib. bdg. 45.00 (*0-8371-1967-7*, MECM, Greenwood Pr) Greenwood.

— Choirs & Choral Music. LC 68-25296. (Studies in Music: No. 42). 1969. reprint ed. lib. bdg. 75.00 (*0-8383-0308-0*) M S G Haskell Hse.

Mees, Burke. Notes of a Seaplane Instructor: An Instructional Guide to Seaplane Flying. LC 97-39177. (Focus Series Book). (Illus.). 1998. pap. 19.95 (*1-56027-310-0*, ASA-NSI) ASA Inc.

Mees-Christeller, Eva. The Practice of Artistic Therapy. Vunderink, Margreet, tr. from DUT. (Illus.). 78p. (Orig.). 1985. pap. 8.00 (*0-936132-77-9*) Merc Pr NY.

Mees, G. F. Geographical Variation in Birds of Java. (Publications of the Nuttall Ornithological Club: No. 26). (Illus.). 119p. 1996. 25.00 (*1-877973-38-6*, 26) Nuttall Ornith.

Mees, Inger, jt. auth. see Collins, Beverley.

Mees, Inger, jt. auth. see Collins, Beverly.

Mees, L. F. Blessed by Illness. 248p. (Orig.). 1983. reprint ed. pap. 10.95 (*0-88010-054-0*) Anthroposophic.

***Mees, Paul.** A Very Public Solution: Getting Around in the Dispersed City. 331p. 2000. pap. 29.95 (*0-522-84867-2*, Pub. by Melbourne Univ Pr) Paul & Co Pubs.

Mees, Philip, tr. see Lievegoed, Bernard.

Mees, Rudolf. Money for a Better World. 64p. 1991. pap. 10.95 (*1-869890-26-4*, Pub. by Hawthorn Press) Anthroposophic.

***Meese.** Teaching & Learning with Mild Disabilities: Integrating Reseach & Practice. 2nd ed. (Education Ser.). 2000. 68.95 (*0-534-57852-7*) Wadsworth Pub.

***Meese, Edwin.** Familiar Exposition of the Constitution of the United States: Joseph Story, Supreme Court Justice. 2000. 29.95 (*0-89526-284-3*, Gateway Editions) Regnery Pub.

Meese, Edwin, III. With Reagan: The Inside Story. LC 92-4222. (Illus.). 350p. 1992. 24.95 (*0-89526-522-2*) Regnery Pub.

Meese, Edwin, 3rd & Moffit, Robert E., eds. Making America Safer: What Citizens & Their State & Local Officials Can Do to Combat Crime. 206p. 1997. pap. 19.95 (*0-89195-069-9*) Heritage Found.

Meese, Elizabeth A. Crossing the Double-Cross: The Practice of Feminist Criticism. LC 85-20920. xiii, 180p. 1986. 34.95 (*0-8078-1683-3*); pap. 17.95 (*0-8078-4149-8*) U of NC Pr.

— Ex-Tensions: Re-Figuring Feminist Criticism. 224p. 1990. text 27.50 (*0-252-01682-3*); pap. text 11.95 (*0-252-06105-5*) U of Ill Pr.

— Sem, Erotics: Theorizing Lesbian: Writing. (Cutting Edge: Lesbian Life & Literature Ser.). 304p. (C). 1992. text 45.00 (*0-8147-5469-4*); pap. text 16.00 (*0-8147-5470-8*) NYU Pr.

Meese, Elizabeth A. & Parker, Alice A., eds. The Difference Within: Feminism & Critical Theory. LC 88-7916. (Critical Theory Ser.: Vol. 8). xi, 219p. (C). 1989. 65.00 (*1-55619-042-5*) J Benjamins Pubng Co.

Meese, Elizabeth A., jt. ed. see Parker, Alice A.

Meese, Michael J. Amred Forces Guide to Personal Financial Planning. 4th ed. LC 97-37606. 400p. 1998. pap. 19.95 (*0-8117-2664-9*) Stackpole.

Meese, R. Gregory, ed. see Technical Association of the Pulp & Paper Industry.

Meese, Richard, jt. ed. see Al-Nauimi, Najeeb.

Meese, Ruth. Strategies for Teaching Students with Emotional & Behavioral Disorders. LC 95-42261. (Special Education Ser.). 480p. 1996. pap. 72.95 (*0-534-24288-X*) Brooks-Cole.

Meese, Ruth L. Teaching Learners with Mild Disabilities: Integrating Research & Practice. LC 93-28274. 474p. 1993. 43.75 (*0-534-21102-X*) Brooks-Cole.

Meeske. Copywriting For The Electronic Media: A Practical Guide. 4th ed. (Radio/TV/Film). 2001. 37.00 (*0-534-52660-8*) Wadsworth Pub.

Meeske, Harrison F. The Hudson Valley Dutch & Their Houses. LC 98-44141. 414p. 1999. pap. 29.00 (*0-916346-64-1*) Purple Mnt Pr.

Meeske, Milan D. Copywriting for the Electronic Media. 3rd ed. LC 97-13202. (Radio/TV/Film Ser.). (C). 1997. 60.95 (*0-534-50754-9*) Wadsworth Pub.

Meeske, Milan D. & Norris, R. C. Copywriting for the Electronic Media: A Practical Guide. 367p. (C). 1986. pap. write for info. (*0-534-06636-4*) Wadsworth Pub.

Meeson, Nigel. Admiralty Jurisdiction & Practice. (Lloyds Shipping Law Library). 544p. 1993. 170.00 (*1-85044-368-8*) LLP.

— Ship & Aircraft Mortgages. 217p. 1988. 110.00 (*1-85044-104-9*) LLP.

Meesook, Kanita, et al. IMF Economic Reviews No. 2: Marshall Islands & the Federated States of Micronesia, 1995. 1995. pap. 15.00 (*0-614-11640-6*) Intl Monetary.

Meessen, Karl M. Extraterritorial Jurisdiction in Theory & Practice. LC 96-20674. 1996. 195.00 (*90-411-0899-8*) Kluwer Law Intl.

Meessen, Karl M., ed. International Law of Export Control: Jurisdictional Issues. 208p. (C). 1992. lib. bdg. 109.00 (*1-85333-483-9*, Pub. by Graham & Trotman) Kluwer Academic.

Meester, Conrad De, see De Meester, Conrad.

***Meester, G.** Plants & Politics. 255p. 1999. pap. 67.00 (*90-74134-72-6*) Wageningen Pers.

Meester, Geert T. & Pinciroli, Francesco, eds. Databases for Cardiology. (Developments in Cardiovascular Medicine Ser.). (C). 1991. text 306.50 (*0-7923-0886-7*) Kluwer Academic.

Meester, Geert T., jt. ed. see Serruys, Patrick W.

Meester, J. & Setzer, H. W., eds. The Mammals of Africa: An Identification Manual. LC 70-169904. 505p. reprint ed. pap. 156.60 (*0-608-17752-0*, 205649600069) Bks Demand.

Meester, Ronald & Roy, Rahul. Continuum Percolation. (Cambridge Tracts in Mathematics Ser.: Vol. 119). (Illus.). 248p. (C). 1996. text 54.95 (*0-521-47504-X*) Cambridge U Pr.

Meeta, Madhu. Diseases of Ornamental Plants in India. (C). 1994. 42.50 (*81-7035-129-4*, Pub. by Daya Pub Hse) S Asia.

Meeter, Daniel J. Bless the Lord, O My Soul: The New-York Liturgy of the Dutch Reformed Church, 1767. LC 98-23171. (Drew University Studies in Liturgy: No. 6). 376p. 1998. 65.00 (*0-8108-3518-5*) Scarecrow.

— Meeting Each Other in Church Doctrine, Liturgy, & Government: The Bicentennial of the Celebration of the Constitution of the Reformed Church in America. LC 93-5093. (Historical Series of the Reformed Church in America: No. 24). 240p. (Orig.). 1993. pap. text 13.00 (*0-8028-0717-8*) Eerdmans.

Meeter, Glenn. Letters to Barbara. LC 81-15235. 274p. reprint ed. pap. 85.00 (*0-608-14505-X*, 202533600043) Bks Demand.

Meeter, Glenn, jt. ed. see Detweiler, Robert.

Meeter, H. Henry. The Basic Ideas of Calvinism. 6th ed. LC 90-33204. 224p. 1990. pap. 12.99 (*0-8010-6269-1*) Baker Bks.

Meeter, Merle, ed. The Armor of Light. 208p. (Orig.). (C). 1979. pap. 6.95 (*0-932914-01-2*) Dordt Coll Pr.

Meeth, Louis R. Quality Education for Less Money. LC 73-18502. (Jossey-Bass Higher Education Ser.). 224p. reprint ed. pap. 69.50 (*0-608-14791-5*, 202566300045) Bks Demand.

Meeth, Louis R., jt. ed. see Hodgkinson, Harold L.

Meetham, A. R., et al. Atmospheric Pollution: Its History, Origins & Prevention. 4th ed. (Illus.). 288p. 1981. 113.00 (*0-08-024003-8*, Pub. by Pergamon Repr) Franklin.

Meetham, G. W., jt. auth. see Van de Voorde, Marcel H.

Meeting on Animal Models in Human Reproduction Sta. Animal Models in Human Reproduction. Sergio, Mario & Martini, Luciano, eds. LC 79-5314. (Illus.). 500p. reprint ed. pap. 155.00 (*0-608-00609-2*, 206119600007) Bks Demand.

Meeting on Critical Evaluation of Cardiac Rehabili. Critical Evaluation of Cardiac Rehabilitation, Tel-Aviv, Nov.-Dec. 1975: Proceedings of the Meeting on Critical Evaluation of Cardiac Rehabilitation, Tel-Aviv, Nov.-Dec. 1975. Kellermann, J. J., ed. (Bibliotheca Cardiologica Ser.: No. 36). (Illus.). 1977. 54.00 (*3-8055-2373-4*) S Karger.

Meeting on Physical Techniques in Cardiological Im. Physical Techniques in Cardiological Imaging: Proceedings of the Meeting on Physical Techniques in Cardiological Imaging Held at the Medical & Biological Sciences Building, University of Southampton, 8-9 July 1982. fac. ed. Short, M. D. et al, eds. LC 83-20768. (Illus.). 221p. 1983. reprint ed. pap. 68.60 (*0-7837-8014-1*, 204777000008) Bks Demand.

***Meetsos, Achilleas & Mossialos, Elias.** Contemporary Greece & Europe. LC 00-42039. (Illus.). 2000. write for info. (*1-84014-728-8*, Pub. by Ashgate Pub) Ashgate Pub Co.

Meetze, Walter. Ages - Poetic Stories & Poems. LC 97-91328. 1998. pap. 8.95 (*0-533-12642-8*) Vantage.

Meeus, Jean H. Astronomical Algorithms. 1991. 24.95 (*0-943396-35-2*) Willmann-Bell.

— Astronomical Algorithms 2nd ed. LC 98-55091. 1998. write for info. (*0-943396-63-8*) Willmann-Bell.

— Astronomical Formulae for Calculators. 4th ed. 1988. pap. 14.95 (*0-943396-22-0*) Willmann-Bell.

— Astronomical Tables of the Sun, Moon & Planets. 2nd ed. LC 95-3657. 1995. 24.95 (*0-943396-45-X*) Willmann-Bell.

— Elements of Solar Eclipses, 1951-2200. 1989. pap. 19.95 (*0-943396-21-2*) Willmann-Bell.

— Mathematical Astronomy Morsels. LC 97-22651. 1997. 24.95 (*0-943396-51-4*) Willmann-Bell.

— Transits. 1990. pap. 14.95 (*0-943396-26-3*) Willmann-Bell.

Meeus, Jean H., jt. auth. see Grosjean, C.

Meeus, Wim, et al, eds. Adolescence, Careers, & Cultures. LC 92-45751. (Prevention & Intervention in Childhood & Adolescence Ser.: No. 13). x, 428p. (C). 1993. lib. bdg. 127.15 (*3-11-013679-1*) De Gruyter.

Meeusen, Wim, ed. Economic Policy in the European Union: Current Perspectives. LC 99-17605. 272p. 1999. 90.00 (*1-84064-036-7*) E Elgar.

Meeuwissen, Tony. Remarkable Animals: 1,000 Amazing Amalgamations. LC 97-13686. (Illus.). 24p. (J). (gr. k-4). 1998. pap. 15.95 (*0-531-30066-8*) Orchard Bks Watts.

Meeuwsen, Teery. Near to the Heart of God: God's Words of Encouragement for Women. LC 97-35181. Orig. Title: He Touched Me. 256p. 1998. pap. 17.99 (*0-7852-7060-4*, J Thoma Bks) Nelson.

Meeuwsen, Terry. Just Between Friends. LC 98-53698. 128p. 1999. 12.99 (*0-7852-7496-0*) Nelson.

Meeuwsen, Terry, compiled by. Christmas Memories: From Our Hearts to Yours. 128p. 1996. 12.99 (*0-7852-7253-4*) Nelson.

Meezan, William & Shireman, Joan F., eds. Care & Commitment: Foster Parent Adoption Decisions. LC 85-2730. 247p. (C). 1985. text 64.50 (*0-88706-103-6*); pap. text 21.95 (*0-88706-104-4*) State U NY Pr.

Meezan, William, jt. auth. see McCroskey, Jacquelyn.

Meffe, Gary K. & Carroll, C. Ronald. Principles of Conservation Biology. 2nd ed. LC 97-8018. (Illus.). 673p. (C). 1997. text 69.95 (*0-87893-521-5*) Sinauer Assocs.

Meffert, John W., jt. auth. see Jacoby, Mary Moore.

Meffert, Lisa, jt. auth. see Wells, Dan.

Meg Publications Staff, ed. see Bankston, Julie A.

Mega Books Staff. Learning Adventures in Math. (Learning Adventures Ser.). (Illus.). 80p. (J). (gr. 1-2). 1998. 6.95 (*0-684-84427-3*) S&S Trade.

— Power Play Science: Grades 1-2. 80p. (gr. 1-2). 1998. 6.95 (*0-684-84426-5*) S&S Trade.

Mega, Voula & Sweeney, Margaret. Enterprise & the Environment Highlights of Research & Case Study in Ireland. 80p. 1996. pap. 15.00 (*92-827-6035-9*, SY93-96-928-ENC, Pub. by Comm Europ Commun) Bernan Associates.

Megahead, S., et al. Rechargeable Lithium & Lithium Ion (RCT) Batteries. (Proceedings Ser.: Vol. 94-28). 510p. 1995. 70.00 (*1-56677-087-4*) Electrochem Soc.

M

An Asterisk (*) at the beginning of an entry indicates that the title is appearing for the first time.

M

— Francis Thompson: The Poet of Earth in Heaven. (BCL1-PR English Literature Ser.). 288p. 1992. reprint ed. lib. bdg. 79.00 (0-685-54939-9) Rprt Serv.
— Three Sitwells: A Biographical & Critical Study. LC 79-145174. 1971. reprint ed. 29.00 (0-403-01102-7) Scholarly.
— Walter De La Mare: A Biography & Critical Study. 1988. reprint ed. lib. bdg. 69.00 (0-7812-0050-4) Rprt Serv.
— Walter De La Mare: A Biography & Critical Study. LC 72-145175. 305p. 1972. reprint ed. 39.00 (0-403-01103-5) Scholarly.
Megson, G. M. An Introduction to Systolic Algorithm Design. (Illus.). 360p. 1992. 79.00 (0-19-853813-8) OUP.
Megson, G. M., jt. auth. see Aleksandrov, V. N.
Megson, T. H. Aircraft: Structures for Engineering Students. 2nd ed. LC 89-70453. 569p. 1990. pap. text 79.95 (0-470-21653-0) Halsted Pr.
— Structural & Stress Analysis. 641p. 1996. pap. text 49.95 (0-470-23563-2) Halsted Pr.
Megson, T.U.G. Aircraft Structures for Engineering Students. 3rd ed. 590p. 1999. pap. 79.95 (0-470-34937-9) Halsted Pr.
***Meguid, Ibrahim Abedel.** Other Place. 316p. 1999. 29.50 (977-424-456-7, Pub. by Am Univ Cairo Pr) Col U Pr.
Meguid, S. A., ed. Micromechanical Modelling & Damage Characteriztion of Advanced Materials Vol. 199-55: Micromechanical Modelling & Damage Characterization of Advanced Materials. LC 95-76451. (1995 Joint ASME Applied Mechanics Summer Meeting Ser.). 120p. 1995. 80.00 (0-7918-1313-4, H00945) ASME.
***Megura, Jim.** Bottles - Official Price Guide. 13th ed. Vol. 13. (Illus.). 2000. pap. 17.00 (0-676-60184-7) Ballantine Pub Grp.
Megura, Jim. The Official Price Guide to Bottles. 12th ed. (Illus.). 480p. 1998. pap. 17.00 (0-676-60009-3) Random.
Megurd, K. & Katayama, T., eds. Seismic Risk Management for Countries of the Asia Pacific Region: Proceedings of the WSSI Workshop. (Illus.). 192p. (Orig.). (C). 1995. pap. text 40.00 (0-7881-2588-5) DIANE Pub.
Megyery, Kathy & Sader, Frank. Facilitating Foreign Participation in Privatization. (Foreign Investment Advisory Service Occasional Paper Ser.: No. 8). 50p. 1997. pap. 22.00 (0-8213-3824-2, 13824) World Bank.
Megyesy, Eugene F. Pressure Vessel Handbook. 10th ed. 490p. 1995. 118.00 (0-914458-18-3) Pressure Vessel.
***Megyesy, Eugene F.** Pressure Vessel Handbook. 11th ed. LC 98-91427. (Illus.). 1998. write for info. (0-914458-19-1) Pressure Vessel.
Mehafdi, Messaoud, jt. auth. see Emmanuel, Clive R.
Mehaffey, J. R., ed. Mathematical Modeling of Fire, Vol. STP 983. 140p. 1988. pap. 26.00 (0-8031-0992-X, STP983) ASTM.
Mehaffey, Karen R. Victorian American Women, 1840-1880: An Annotated Bibliography. LC 91-22206. 192p. 1991. text 15.00 (0-8240-7142-5) Garland.
— Women & the American Civil War: A Handbook. (History-Reference Ser.). 350p. Date not set. text 52.00 (0-8153-2133-3) Garland.
Mehaffey, Robert H. You Can Win Your Florida Election: A Step-by-Step Guide. 239p. 1992. 29.95 (0-9634145-0-X) R H Mehaffey & Assocs.
Mehaffy, Bob & Mehaffy, Carolyn. Cruising Guide to the Hawaiian Islands. (Illus.). 312p. 1998. pap. 29.95 (0-939837-26-9) Paradise Cay Pubns.
Mehaffy, Bob, jt. auth. see Mehaffy, Carolyn.
Mehaffy, Carolyn & Mehaffy, Bob. Cruising Guide to San Francisco Bay. 2nd rev. ed. (Illus.). 250p. 1999. pap. 29.95 (0-939837-31-5) Paradise Cay Pubns.
— Destination Mexico. LC 95-67194. 1995. 19.95 (0-9634635-4-3) Caractacus.
Mehaffy, Carolyn & Mehaffy, Bob. Destination Mexico: Planning a Cruise to Mexico. (Illus.). 186p. 1995. pap. 15.95 (0-939837-41-2, Pub. by Paradise Cay Pubns) R Hale & Co.
Mehaffy, Carolyn, jt. auth. see Mehaffy, Bob.
Mehaffy, George L., jt. auth. see Lanman, Barry A.
Mehaffy, Irene, jt. auth. see Mehaffy, Robert E.
Mehaffy, Robert E. & Mehaffy, Irene. Writing on the Job. 2nd ed. Orig. Title: Writing for the Real World. 380p. (C). 1993. pap. text 23.95 (0-917962-29-X) T H Peek.
Mehale, Alilali G. Deep Water Training & Aerobics: A New Approach to a Total Physical Fitness. Davis, Denise et al, eds. (Illus.). 80p. (Orig.). (C). 1994. pap. text 9.00 (0-9642960-6-3) Scientific Sports.
Mehale, George A. Personal Guide for Physical Fitness. (Illus.). 63p. 1998. pap. 14.99 (0-9642960-5-5) Scientific Sports.
Mehan, Hugh. Learning Lessons: Social Organization in the Classroom. LC 78-24298. (Illus.). 247p. reprint ed. pap. 76.60 (0-8357-8205-0, 203393700087) Bks Demand.
Mehan, Hugh, et al. Constructing School Success: The Consequences of Untracking Low Achieving Students. (Illus.). 254p. (C). 1996. pap. text 17.95 (0-521-56826-9) Cambridge U Pr.
— Constructing School Success: The Consequences of Untracking Low Achieving Students. (Illus.). 254p. (C). 1996. text 54.95 (0-521-56076-4) Cambridge U Pr.
— Handicapping the Handicapped: Decision Making in Students' Educational Careers. LC 85-22084. (Illus.). xvi, 193p. 1986. 35.00 (0-8047-1304-9) Stanford U Pr.
Mehan, Richard J. & Dierker, Robert H. Missouri Causes of Action: Torts. 400p. 1993. spiral bd. 95.00 (1-56257-326-8, MICHIE) LEXIS Pub.
Mehan, Richard J., jt. auth. see Dierker, Robert H.
Mehan, Vivek K., jt. auth. see Meier, Bernhard.
Meharg, Amy, jt. ed. see Griffin, Linda.
Mehary, Hagos. The Strained U. S. - Ethiopian Relations. 175p. (Orig.). 1989. pap. 41.00 (91-22-01321-0) Coronet Bks.
***Mehat, Narindar & Wardell, Margaret.** When Love Prevails: A Sikh Woman Finds Christ. 135p. 1998. reprint ed. mass mkt. 9.99 (1-85078-288-1, Pub. by O M Pubng) OM Literature.
Mehay, Stephen L., jt. auth. see Shoup, Donald C.
Mehay, Stephen L., jt. ed. see Eitelberg, Mark J.
Mehden, Fred R. Von der, see Von der Mehden, Fred R.
Mehdi, Charef. Tea in the Harem. Emery, Ed, tr. from FRE. 160p. (Orig.). 1991. 13.99 (1-85242-151-7) Serpents Tail.
Mehdi, Majed, ed. see Dahesh.
Mehdi, Mohammad T. Islam & Intolerance, a Reply to Salman Rushdie. 1990. 7.95 (0-685-66741-3, 14) Tahrike Tarsile Quran.
— Kennedy & Sirhan, Why. LC 68-57262. (Illus.). (Orig.). pap. 10.00 (0-911026-04-5, KSW) New World Press NY.
— Nation of Lions . . . Chained. LC 62-17245. 1963. pap. 15.00 (0-911026-05-3) New World Press NY.
— Peace in Palestine. LC 75-43266. 1976. pap. 10.00 (0-911026-08-8) New World Press NY.
— Terrorism: Why America Is the Target! LC 87-62974. 128p. 1988. pap. 10.00 (0-911119-10-8) New World Press NY.
Mehdi, Mohammad T., ed. Palestine & the Bible. LC 71-114557. 1971. pap. 5.00 (0-911026-06-1) New World Press NY.
Mehdi, Rubya. The Islamization of the Law in Pakistan. (Scandinavian Institute of Asian Studies: No. 60). 340p. (C). 1993. pap. 55.00 (0-7007-0236-9, Pub. by Curzon Pr Ltd) Paul & Co Pubs.
Mehedinti, S. What Is Transylvania? 124p. 1986. write for info. (0-937019-02-X); pap. 15.00 (0-937019-03-8) Romanian Hist.
Mehegan, J. J. O'Higgins of Chile. 1976. lib. bdg. 59.95 (0-8490-2366-1) Gordon Pr.
Mehegan, John. Improvising Jazz Piano. (Illus.). 104p. 1985. audio 9.95 (0-318-70317-3, AM72844) Music Sales.
— Improvising Jazz Piano. (It's Easy to Play Ser.). (Illus.). 104p. 1985. pap. 14.95 (0-8256-2256-5, AM32483) Music Sales.
— Jazz Rhythm & the Improvised Line. LC 58-13525. (Jazz Improvisation Ser.: Vol. 2). 1962. pap. 22.95 (0-8230-2572-1) Music Sales.
— Swing & Early Progressive Piano Styles. LC 58-13525. (Jazz Improvisation Ser.). 1964. pap. 22.95 (0-8230-2573-X) Music Sales.
— Swing & Early Progressive Piano Styles. LC 58-13525. (Jazz Improvisation Ser.: Vol. 4). 1965. pap. 22.95 (0-8230-2574-8) Music Sales.
— Tonal & Rhythmic Principles. LC 58-13525. 208p. 1959. pap. 22.95 (0-8230-2559-4) Music Sales.
Mehendale, H. M. Mechanisms of Lung Injury. 90p. 1989. text 84.00 (2-88124-410-6) Gordon & Breach.
Mehendiratta, Pradeep. University Administration in India & the U. S. A. 1985. 28.50 (0-8364-1308-3, Pub. by Oxford IBH) S Asia.
Mehetra, S. S. Molecular Basis of Cytoplasmic Male Sterility in Crop Plants. 196p. 1995. pap. 79.00 (81-7089-208-2, Pub. by Intl Bk Distr) St Mut.
Mehetre, M. G. Energy Crisis in India. 1990. 40.00 (81-85076-89-8, Pub. by Chugh Pubns) S Asia.
Meheut, M. Animal Studies: 550 Illustrations of Mammals, Birds, Fish & Insects. (Illus.). 112p. 1999. pap. 9.95 (0-486-40266-5) Dover.
Mehew, Ernest, jt. ed. see Booth, Bradford A.
Mehew, Ernest, jt. ed. see Booth, Bradford E.
Mehew, Ernest, ed. see Stevenson, Robert Louis.
Mehew, Karen, jt. auth. see Mehew, Randall.
Mehew, Randall & Mehew, Karen. The Best Manners Book Ever. (Virtue & Values Ser.). (Illus.). 68p. (J). 1990. pap. text 5.95 (0-929985-55-9) Jackman Pubng.
— Gospel Basic Busy Book, Vol. I. (Illus.). 100p. (J). 1989. reprint ed. pap. text 6.95 (0-910613-13-3) Millenial Press.
— Gospel Basic Busy Book, Vol. II. (Illus.). 100p. (J). 1990. pap. text 6.95 (0-910613-08-7) Millenial Press.
Mehew, Randall K. A Most Convincing Witness. (Personal Enrichment Ser.). 41p. (Orig.). 1991. pap. write for info. (0-929985-63-X) Jackman Pubng.
— Organizing Families & Reunions. (Personal Enrichment Ser.). 125p. (Orig.). 1991. pap. write for info. (0-929985-76-1) Jackman Pubng.
— Our Family History. (Personal Enrichment Ser.). 27p. (Orig.). 1991. write for info. (0-929985-74-5) Jackman Pubng.
— Personal Life History. (Personal Enrichment Ser.). 32p. (Orig.). 1991. pap. write for info. (0-929985-73-7) Jackman Pubng.
— Seeds of Faith. (Personal Enrichment Ser.). 132p. (Orig.). 1991. pap. write for info. (0-929985-75-3) Jackman Pubng.
Mehigan, Simon. Confidential Information. 1995. write for info. (0-406-03493-1, MCI, MICHIE) LEXIS Pub.
***Mehigan, Tim, ed.** Heinrich von Kleist und die Aufklarung. (GER.). 258p. 2000. 65.00 (1-57113-047-0, Pub. by Camden Hse) Boydell & Brewer.
Mehihan, Thomas J. John C. Menihan Lithographs & Watercolors. Menihan, John C., Enterprises Staff, ed. (Illus.). 36p. (Orig.). pap. text 20.00 (0-9639675-0-9) J C Menihan.
Mehl, Dieter. Shakespeare's Tragedies: An Introduction. 298p. 1987. pap. text 19.95 (0-521-31690-1) Cambridge U Pr.
Mehl, Dieter, ed. see Lawrence, D. H.
Mehl, Duane. The High Road. 208p. (Orig.). 1988. pap. 9.95 (1-56838-097-6) Hazelden.
Mehl, James V., ed. In Laudem Caroli: Renaissance & Reformation Studies for Charles G. Nauert, Jr. LC 98-3775. (Sixteenth Century Essays & Studies: No. 49). 242p. 1998. 40.00 (0-940474-53-0) Truman St Univ.
Mehl, Lewis E. Healing Ceremonies: Bridging Native American Medicine & Spirituality with the Modern World Frontiers & Consciousness. 250p. write for info. (0-8290-5205-4) Irvington.
Mehl, Lewis E. & Peterson, Gayle. Art of Healing. 350p. text. write for info. (0-8290-1804-2); audio. write for info. (0-318-61266-6) Irvington.
Mehl, Lewis E. & Peterson, Gayle H. Mind Body Medicine Vol. 1: The Stages of Healing. (Frontiers of Consciousness Ser.). (Illus.). 250p. write for info. (0-8290-2468-9) Irvington.
— Mind Body Medicine Vol. 2: The Language of Healing. (Frontiers of Consciousness Ser.). 250p. write for info. (0-8290-2469-7) Irvington.
Mehl-Madrona, Lewis. Coyote Medicine: Lessons from Native American Healing. LC 96-32714. 1997. 23.50 (0-684-80271-6, Scribner Pap Fic) S&S Trade Pap.
— Coyote Medicine: Lessons from Native American Healing. 304p. 1998. per. 13.00 (0-684-83997-0, Fireside) S&S Trade Pap.
Mehl, Roger. Condition of the Christian Philosopher. Kushner, Eva, tr. 221p. 1963. 9.00 (0-227-67654-8) Attic Pr.
Mehl, Ron. Clay Story. (J). Date not set. pap. 6.99 (1-57673-321-1) Multnomah Pubs.
— The Cure for a Troubled Heart: Meditations on Psalm 37. LC 96-43245. 140p. 1996. 12.99 (1-57673-017-4, Multnomah Bks) Multnomah Pubs.
— Dios Tambien Trabaja de Noche.Tr. of God Works the Night Shift. (SPA.). 224p. 1997. pap. text 12.50 (0-311-46149-2) Casa Bautista.
— God Works the Night Shift: Acts of Love Your Father Performs Even While You Sleep. Libby, Larry R., ed. 289p. 1995. pap. 12.99 (0-88070-718-6) Multnomah Pubs.
***Mehl, Ron.** Just in Case I Can't Be There: A Dad's Counsel to a Son or Daughter Leaving Home. LC 98-50572. 160p. 1999. 14.99 (1-57673-542-7) Multnomah Pubs.
— Love Found a Way: Stories of Christmas. LC 99-33692. 160p. 1999. 12.95 (1-57856-276-7) Waterbrook Pr.
Mehl, Ron. Meeting God at a Deadend: Discovering Heaven's Best When Life Closes In. 240p. 1998. pap. 12.99 (1-57673-339-4) Multnomah Pubs.
— Surprise Endings: Ten Good Things about Bad Things. 232p. 1993. pap. 9.99 (0-88070-828-X, Multnomah Bks) Multnomah Pubs.
— Ten(der) Commandments. LC 98-23085. 224p. 1998. 18.99 (1-57673-304-1) Multnomah Pubs.
***Mehl, Ron.** What God Whispers in the Dark. 2000. 16.99 (1-57673-706-3) Multnomah Pubs.
Mehlberg, Henry. Time, Causality & the Quantum Theory, 2 vols. Benecerraf, Paul, tr. from FRE. Incl. Vol. 1. Essay on the Causal Theory of Time. 322p. 1980. lib. bdg. 104.50 (90-277-0721-9, D Reidel); Vol. 1. Essay on the Causal Theory of Time. 322p. 1980. pap. text 62.50 (90-277-1074-0, D Reidel); (Boston Studies in the Philosophy of Science: No. 19). 1980. write for info. (0-318-53991-8) Kluwer Academic.
— Time in a Quantized Universe, Vol. 2. Benecerraf, Paul, tr. (Boston Studies in the Philosophy of Science). 296p. 1980. pap. text 62.50 (90-277-1076-7, D Reidel); lib. bdg. 88.00 (90-277-1075-9, D Reidel) Kluwer Academic.
Mehlem, Ulrich. Zweisprachigkeit Marokkanischer Kinder in Deutschland: Untersuchungen Zu Sprachgebrauch, Spracheinstellungen und Sprachkompetenzen Marokkanischer Kinder in Deutsch, Marokkanischem Arabisch und Berber (Masirisch) in Dortmund. (Europaische Hochschulschriften Ser.: Series 21, Band 196). (GER.). 334p. 1998. pap. 51.95 (3-631-32488-X) P Lang Pubng.
Mehler, Howard S. Lactic Acid Metabolism: A Monograph on Carbohydrate Metabolism in the Blood & Brain of the Suckling Rat. LC 88-90631. (Illus.). 115p. (C). 1988. 69.95 (0-9621181-0-9) Mehler Pub.
Mehler, Irving M., jt. auth. see Faulk, Martha.
Mehler, Jacques A. & Dupoux, Emmanuel. What Infants Know: The New Cognitive Science of Early Development. Southgate, Patsy, tr. LC 93-10147. 240p. 1994. pap. 25.95 (1-55786-370-9) Blackwell Pubs.
Mehler, Jacques A. & Franck, Susana, eds. Cognition on Cognition. LC 95-32771. (Special Issues of Cognition Ser.). (Illus.). 500p. 1995. pap. text 45.00 (0-262-63167-9, Bradford Bks) MIT Pr.
Mehler, Jacques A. & Noizet, Georges, eds. Textes pour une Psycholinguistique. Noizet, Yvonne, tr. (Textes de Sciences Sociales Ser.: No. 10). 1974. pap. 41.55 (90-279-7285-0) Mouton.
Mehler, Jacques A., jt. ed. see Pinker, Steven.
Mehler, Kelly. The Table Saw Book. (Illus.). 192p. 1993. pap. 27.95 (1-56158-011-2, 70155) Taunton.
Mehler, Mark, jt. auth. see Crispin, Gerry.
Mehler, Philip S. Eating Disorders: A Guide to Medical Care & Complications. LC 99-27939. 200p. 1999. pap. 18.95 (0-8018-6277-9) Johns Hopkins.
***Mehler, Philip S. & Andersen, Arnold E., eds.** Eating Disorders: A Guide to Medical Care & Complications. LC 99-27939. (Illus.). 200p. 1999. 38.00 (0-8018-6276-0) Johns Hopkins.
***Mehler, Robert E.** How the Circulatory System Works. Sompayrac, Lauren M., ed. LC 00-39753. (How It Works Ser.). (Illus.). 111p. (C). 2000. pap. 19.95 (0-86542-548-5) Blackwell Sci.
Mehlhausen, Joachim. Vestigia Verbi: Aufsatze zur Geschichte der Evangelischen Theeologie. 520p. 1998. 168.00 (3-11-015053-0) De Gruyter.
Mehlhorn, H., ed. Parasitology in Focus. (Illus.). 1040p. 1988. 288.00 (0-387-17838-4) Spr-Verlag.
Mehlhorn, K., et al, eds. VLSI Algorithms & Architecture. (Lecture Notes in Computer Science Ser.: Vol. 227). viii, 328p. 1986. 39.00 (0-387-16766-8) Spr-Verlag.
Mehlhorn, Kurt. Data Structures & Algorithms One: Sorting & Searching. (EATCS Monographs on Theoretical Computer Science). (Illus.). xiv, 336p. 1987. 50.00 (0-387-13302-X) Spr-Verlag.
Mehlhorn, Kurt, jt. auth. see Naher, S.
Mehlich. Technical Writing for Success. 1997. mass mkt. 27.95 (0-538-68296-5) S-W Pub.
Mehlich, S. Blackline Masters, Technical Writing for Success. (EC - HS Communication/English Ser.). 1995. 35.00 (0-538-63674-2) S-W Pub.
Mehlich, S. & Smith-Worthington, D. Technical Writing for Success: A School-to-Work Approach. (EC - HS Communiction/English Ser.). 448p. 1997. text 27.95 (0-538-63673-4) S-W Pub.
Mehling, Betty, jt. auth. see Pendleton, Bonnie.
Mehling, Franz N. Knaurs Lexicon Von A-Z. (GER.). 1119p. 1996. 75.00 (0-320-00109-1) Fr & Eur.
— Knaurs Lexikon Von A-Z. (GER.). 1088p. 1991. 65.00 (0-7859-6929-2) Fr & Eur.
Mehling, Gunther. Naturstein-Lexikon: Fur Handwerk und Industrie. 4th ed. (GER.). 668p. 1993. 135.00 (0-7859-8458-5, 3766710540) Fr & Eur.
Mehling, M. B. Cowdrey - Cowdrey - Cowdray Genealogy: William Cowdery of Lynn, Mass., 1630, & His Descendants. (Illus.). 451p. 1989. reprint ed. pap. 69.50 (0-8328-0431-2); reprint ed. lib. bdg. 79.50 (0-8328-0430-4) Higginson Bk Co.
Mehlinger, Howard D. School Reform in the Information Age. LC 95-92373. (Illus.). 165p. (Orig.). 1995. pap. 14.95 (0-9645857-0-7) IN Univ Excell.
Mehlinger, Howard D. & Davis, O. J., Jr., eds. The Social Studies. LC 80-83744. (National Society for the Study of Education Publication Ser.: No. 80, Pt II). 290p. (C). 1981. lib. bdg. 16.00 (0-226-60131-5) U Ch Pr.
Mehlinger, Howard D., et al. Global Studies for American Schools. LC 79-13014. (Developments in Classroom Instruction Ser.). 88p. reprint ed. pap. 30.00 (0-608-15073-8, 202592300047) Bks Demand.
Mehlman, Ira, jt. auth. see Garling, Scipio.
Mehlman, Ira H., jt. auth. see Fox, Robert W.
Mehlman, Israel. Genozot Sefarim: Bibliographical Essays. 1979. 12.95 (0-405-12617-4) Ayer.
Mehlman, Jeffrey. Cataract: A Study in Diderot. LC 76-65332. 121p. reprint ed. pap. 37.60 (0-7837-0217-5, 204052500017) Bks Demand.
***Mehlman, Jeffrey.** Emigre New York: French Intellectuals in Wartime Manhattan, 1940-1944. LC 99-44901. 2000. 38.00 (0-8018-6286-8) Johns Hopkins.
Mehlman, Jeffrey. Genealogies of the Text Literature, Psychoanalysis & Politics in Modern France. (Cambridge Studies in French: No. 54). 274p. (C). 1995. text 64.95 (0-521-47213-X) Cambridge U Pr.
— Legacies of Anti-Semitism in France. LC 83-3685. 155p. reprint ed. pap. 48.10 (0-7837-2934-0, 205752000006) Bks Demand.
— Walter Benjamin for Children: An Essay on His Radio Years. LC 92-28496. 126p. (C). 1993. 19.95 (0-226-51865-5) U Ch Pr.
Mehlman, Jeffrey, tr. see Foucault, Michel & Blanchot, Maurice.
Mehlman, Jeffrey, tr. see Hollier, Denis.
Mehlman, Jeffrey, tr. see Laplanche, Jean.
Mehlman, Jeffrey, tr. see Sartre, Jean-Paul.
Mehlman, Jeffrey, tr. see Vidal-Naquet, Pierre.
Mehlman, Maxwell J. & Botkin, Jeffrey R. Access to the Genome: The Challenge to Equality. LC 97-37974. 160p. 1998. 39.95 (0-87840-677-8); pap. 14.95 (0-87840-678-6) Georgetown U Pr.
Mehlman, Maxwell J. & Youngner, Stuart J., eds. Delivering High Technology Home Care: Issues for Decisionmakers. LC 91-4741. 256p. 1991. 33.95 (0-8261-7610-0) Springer Pub.
Mehlman, Maxwell J., jt. auth. see Murray, Thomas H.
Mehlman, Maxwell J., jt. ed. see Grubb, Andrew.
Mehlman, Myron A. Identification & Control of Environmental & Occupational Diseases Pt. 1: Asbestos & Cancers. (Advances in Modern Environmental Toxicology Ser.: Vol. 22). (Illus.). 518p. 1994. 135.00 (0-911131-50-7) Specialist Journals.
— Identification & Control of Environmental & Occupational Diseases Pt. 2: Hazards & Risks of Chemicals in Oil Refining Industry. (Advances in Modern Environmental Toxicology Ser.). (Illus.). 700p. 1994. 135.00 (0-911131-51-5) Specialist Journals.
Mehlman, Myron A., ed. Benchmarks: Alternative Methods in Toxicology. LC 88-63539. 219p. 1989. 50.00 (0-911131-19-1) Specialist Journals.
— Environmental & Occupational Cancer: Scientific Update. LC 89-6864. 348p. 1990. 65.00 (0-911131-17-5) Specialist Journals.
— Health Hazards & Risks from Exposure to Complex Mixtures & Air Toxic Chemicals. (Advances in Modern Environmental Toxicology Ser.: Vol. 19). (Illus.). 241p. 1991. 65.00 (0-911131-24-8) Specialist Journals.
— Safety Evaluation: Toxicology, Methods, Concepts & Risk Assessment. LC 87-609437. (Toxicology & Industrial Health Ser.: Vol. 10). (Illus.). 278p. 1987. 65.00 (0-911131-13-2) Specialist Journals.
Mehlman, Myron A., et al, eds. Assessment of Reproductive & Tetragenic Hazards. LC 82-62165. (Advances in Modern Environmental Toxicology Ser.: Vol. 3). (Illus.). 1983. reprint ed. text 58.00 (0-911131-03-5) Specialist Journals.
— Occupational Health Hazards of Solvents. rev. ed. LC 86-61325. (Advances in Modern Environmental Toxicology Ser.: Vol. 2). (Illus.). 259p. 1986. text 60.00 (0-911131-02-7) Specialist Journals.
— Phosgene Induced Edema: Diagnosis & Therapeutic

M

An Asterisk (*) at the beginning of an entry indicates that the title is appearing for the first time.

Mehrotra, R. C. & Arora, R. K. Education, Science & Human Values: Essays in Honor of Professor D. S. Kothari. LC 94-902557. 1994. write for info. (*81-224-0614-9*, Pub. by Wiley Estrn) Franklin.

Mehrotra, Raja R. Nehru, Man among Men. 1990. 21.50 (*81-7099-196-X*, Pub. by Mittal Pubs Dist) S Asia.

— Sociolinguistics in Hindi Contexts. (Contributions to the Sociology of Language Ser.: No. 38). xii, 153p. 1985. 73.10 (*0-89925-139-0*) Mouton.

Mehrotra, Raja R., ed. Book of Indian Names. (C). 1994. 22.00 (*81-7167-149-7*, Pub. by Rupa) S Asia.

Mehrotra, Raja Ram. Indian English: Text & Interpretation. LC 97-50618. (Varieties of English Around the World General Ser.: No. T7). x, 148p. 1998. lib. bdg. 45.00 (*1-55619-720-9*) J Benjamins Pubng Co.

Mehrotra, Ram C. & Singh, Anirudh. Organometallic Chemistry: A Unified Approach. LC 87-29632. 634p. 1991. text 105.00 (*0-470-21019-2*) Halsted Pr.

Mehrotra, S. R. History of the Indian National Congress Vol. 1: 1885-1918. (C). 1995. 48.00 (*0-7069-8071-9*, Pub. by Vikas) S Asia.

— Towards India's Freedom & Partition. 322p. 1979. 24.95 (*0-7069-0712-4*) Asia Bk Corp.

Mehrotra, Santosh & Jolly, Richard, eds. Development with a Human Face: Experiences in Social Achievement & Economic Growth. LC 97-26762. (Illus.). 508p. 1998. text 90.00 (*0-19-829076-4*) OUP.

***Mehrotra, Santosh & Jolly, Richard, eds.** Development with a Human Face: Experiences in Social Achievement & Economic Growth. (Illus.). 512p. 2000. pap. 35.00 (*0-19-829657-6*) OUP.

Mehrotra, Santosh K. India & the Soviet Union: Trade & Technology Transfer. (Cambridge Russian, Soviet & Post-Soviet Studies: No. 73). (Illus.). 258p. (C). 1991. text 69.95 (*0-521-36202-4*) Cambridge U Pr.

Mehrtens, Cristina, tr. see De Jesus, Carolina M.

Mehrtens, John M. Living Snakes of the World in Color. LC 87-9932. (Illus.). 480p. 1987. 65.00 (*0-8069-6460-X*) Sterling.

— Turtles. (Illus.). 80p. 1984. pap. text 6.95 (*0-86622-512-9*, PB-129) TFH Pubns.

Mehrtens, Patricia A. One Hundred Years Ago in Burrillville (RI) Selected Stories from the Local Newspapers. viii, 231p. (Orig.). 1993. pap. 21.00 (*1-55613-716-8*) Heritage Bk.

Mehrtens, Patricia Zifchock. Burrillville. (Images of America Ser.). 128p. 1996. pap. 16.99 (*0-7524-0259-5*) Arcadia Publng.

Mehrtens, Susan, jt. auth. see Maynard, Herman B., Jr.

Mehrtens, Susan E. Dreaming to Wake to Life: One Example of the Archetypal "Hero's Journey" LC 96-70642. (Illus.). xiv, 220p. (Orig.). 1996. 29.95 (*1-889919-01-2*); pap. 18.95 (*1-889919-02-0*) Potlatch Group Inc.

— The New Business Landscape: Taking Your Business into the Twenty-First Century. LC 96-92996. 137p. (Orig.). 1997. pap. 15.95 (*1-889919-03-9*) Potlatch Group Inc.

— Revisioning Science: Essays Toward a New Knowledge Base for Our Culture. LC 96-70641. (Illus.). 304, xxiip. (Orig.). 1997. pap. 24.95 (*1-889919-00-4*) Potlatch Group Inc.

Mehrtens, Susan E., jt. auth. see Nahser, F. Byron.

Mehrtens, Susan E., jt. auth. see Pehrson, John B.

***Mehta.** Caste, Clan & Ethnicity: A Study of Mehtas in Rajasthan. 1999. 34.00 (*81-7033-543-4*, Pub. by Rawat Pubns) S Asia.

Mehta. Chemistry 101 Quickprint. (C). 1998. pap. text 25.00 (*0-536-01593-7*) Pearson Custom.

— Concrete Microstructure. 2nd ed. (Orig.). 1996. pap. 57.81 (*0-07-041344-4*) McGraw.

— An Introduction to Quality Control for the Apparel Industry. LC 92-19333. (Quality & Reliability Ser.: Vol. 36). (Illus.). 296p. 1992. text 62.50 (*0-8247-8679-3*) Dekker.

— Liberalism & Empire. LC 98-40812. 1999. pap. text 17.00 (*0-226-51882-5*); lib. bdg. 45.00 (*0-226-51881-7*) U Ch Pr.

Mehta & Johnson, et al. Architectural Acoustics. LC 98-22448. 446p. (C). 1998. 81.00 (*0-13-793795-4*) P-H.

Mehta, Anita J., ed. Estuarine Cohesive Sediment Dynamics. (Lecture Notes on Coastal & Estuarine Studies: Vol. 14). vi, 473p. 1986. pap. 65.00 (*0-387-96296-4*) Spr-Verlag.

— Granular Matter: An Interdisciplinary Approach. (Illus.). 300p. 1993. write for info. (*3-540-94065-0*) Spr-Verlag.

— Granular Matter: An Interdisciplinary Approach. LC 93-1503. (Illus.). 296p. 1993. 98.95 (*0-387-94065-0*) Spr-Verlag.

Mehta, Arun B., ed. Common Musculoskeletal Problems. LC 96-20354. (Illus.). 400p. (Orig.). 1996. pap. text 33.95 (*1-56053-173-8*) Hanley & Belfus.

Mehta, Arun C. & National Institute of Educational Planning and Administration (India) Staff. Education for All in India: Enrolment Projections. LC 98-915998. xvii, 249 p. 1998. write for info. (*81-259-0625-8*) Vikas.

Mehta, Ashish J., ed. Nearshore & Estuarine Cohesive Sediment Transport. (Coastal & Estuarine Studies: Vol. 42). 1993. 54.00 (*0-87590-256-1*) Am Geophysical.

Mehta, Asoka. Perception of Asian Personality. 264p. 1978. 16.95 (*0-940500-63-9*) Asia Bk Corp.

Mehta, Atul, jt. ed. see Wang, Ko-Pen.

Mehta, Atul B. Self-Assessment Color Review of Clinical Haematology. 1995. pap. text 28.00 (*0-316-56557-1*, Little Brwn Med Div) Lppncott W & W.

Mehta, Atul B., jt. auth. see Hoffbrand, A. Victor.

Mehta, B. C. Agrarian Relations & Rural Exploitation. 268p. (C). 1987. 31.50 (*81-7024-163-4*, Pub. by Ashish Pub Hse) S Asia.

— Fertility Behaviour of Tribals in Rajasthan. 211p. 1994. pap. 125.00 (*81-85880-41-7*, Pub. by Print Hse) St Mut.

— Rural Poverty in India. 1993. 23.00 (*81-7022-432-2*, Pub. by Concept) S Asia.

Mehta, Brenda. Corps Infirme, Corps Infame: La Femme Dans le Roman Balzacien. LC 92-81520. (FRE.). 128p. 1992. lib. bdg. 29.95 (*0-917786-86-6*) Summa Pubns.

Mehta, Chetan S. Environmental Protection & the Law. (C). 1991. 28.00 (*81-7024-381-5*, Pub. by Ashish Pub Hse) S Asia.

Mehta, Cyrus R. & Patel, Nitin R. Proc-StatXact for SAS Users. (Illus.). 509p. 1997. pap. 95.00 (*1-889592-00-5*) Cytel Software.

Mehta, D. Paul & Thumann, Albert. Handbook of Energy Engineering. 2nd ed. LC 89-34318. 429p. 1989. text 67.00 (*0-88173-096-3*, 0287) Fairmont Pr.

Mehta, D. Paul, jt. auth. see Thumann, Albert.

Mehta, D. S. Handbook of Disabled in India. 392p. (C). 1983. 24.95 (*0-685-08979-7*, Pub. by Allied Pubs) Asia Bk Corp.

— Mass Communication & Journalism in India. (C). 1992. pap. 14.00 (*81-7023-353-4*, Pub. by Allied Pubs) S Asia.

— Mass Communication & Journalism in India. 313p. 1979. 20.95 (*0-318-37284-3*) Asia Bk Corp.

***Mehta, Deepa.** Speaking of Eating for a Healthy Life: For Calorie-Conscious People. 1998. pap. 8.00 (*81-207-1983-2*, Pub. by Sterling Pubs) S Asia.

Mehta, Deepak. Work, Biography, Ritual: A Muslim Community in North India. LC 96-912041. (Illus.). 296p. 1997. 26.00 (*0-19-564021-7*) OUP.

Mehta, Dina. Brides Are Not for Burning: A Play in Two Acts. (C). 1993. pap. 9.00 (*81-7167-114-4*, Pub. by Rupa) S Asia.

— The Other Woman & Other Stories. 121p. 1981. 16.95 (*0-685-21572-5*) Asia Bk Corp.

Mehta, Dinesh. Atlas of Endoscopic Sinonasal Surgery. (Illus.). 118p. 1992. text 95.00 (*0-8121-1471-X*) Lppncott W & W.

Mehta, Dinesh, jt. auth. see Mehta, Meera.

Mehta, Dinshh. Mahatma Gandhi the Beloved Patient. (Illus.). 180p. (Orig.). 1996. pap. 22.00 (*0-934676-85-2*) Greenlf Bks.

Mehta, G., jt. auth. see Bridges, D.

Mehta, G. S. Socio-Economic Aspects of Migration. (C). 1991. 20.00 (*81-7100-362-1*, Pub. by Deep & Deep Pubns) S Asia.

Mehta, Ghanshyam, jt. auth. see Bridges, Douglas.

Mehta, Gita. Karma Cola Marketing Mystic Earth. 1991. pap. 12.00 (*0-449-90604-3*) Fawcett.

— Raj. 1991. pap. 12.50 (*0-449-90566-7*) Fawcett.

— A River Sutra. 1994. pap. 12.00 (*0-679-75247-1*) Vin Bks.

— Snakes & Ladders: Glimpses of Modern India. 320p. 1998. pap. 11.95 (*0-385-49169-7*, Anchor NY) Doubleday.

Mehta, Gurleena & Narang, Harish. Apartheid in Fiction. 1990. 33.00 (*81-7169-052-1*, Commonwealth) S Asia.

Mehta, H. S., ed. Fatigue & Fracture, 1. LC 96-85013. 416p. 1996. pap. text 130.00 (*0-7918-1770-9*, TS283) ASME Pr.

— Fatigue, Environmental Factors, & New Materials: Proceedings, ASME/JSME Joint Pressure Vessels & Piping Conference (1998, San Diego, CA) LC 98-73178. 377p. 1998. pap. 130.00 (*0-7918-1870-5*) ASME.

— Fracture Mechanics - Applications & New Materials. (PVP Ser.: Vol. 260). 224p. 1993. 50.00 (*0-7918-0987-0*, H00819) ASME.

— Fracture Mechanics Applications: Proceedings of the Pressure Vessels & Piping Conference, Minneapolis, MN, 1994. LC 94-71666. (PVP Ser.: Vol. 287). 165p. 1994. pap. 50.00 (*0-7918-1360-6*) ASME.

Mehta, H. S., et al, eds. Fatigue & Fracture Mechanics in Pressure Vessels & Piping. (Proceedings of the 1995 ASME/JSME Pressure Vessels & Piping Conference Ser.: PVP-Vol. 304). 596p. 1995. 150.00 (*0-7918-1335-5*, H00967) ASME.

— Fatigue & Fracture, 1997: Proceedings ASME Pressure Vessels & Piping Conference (1997, Orlando, FL) LC 97-73337. (PVP Ser.: Vol. 350). 503p. 1997. pap. 160.00 (*0-7918-1567-6*) ASME Pr.

Mehta, Haroobhai & Patel, H., eds. Dynamics of Reservation Policy. 315p. 1986. 31.00 (*0-8364-1818-2*, Pub. by Minerva) S Asia.

Mehta, Ila A. Vasant Chhalke (Gujerati) large type ed. (Charnwood Large Print Ser.). 1990. 27.99 (*0-7089-2269-4*, Charnwood) Ulverscroft.

Mehta, J. B. Presidential System: A Better Alternative. (Illus.). 79p. 1979. 7.95 (*0-318-36606-1*) Asia Bk Corp.

Mehta, J. K. Gandhian Thought: An Analytical Study. 1985. 26.00 (*0-8364-1388-1*, Pub. by Ashish Pub Hse) S Asia.

— Gandhian Thought: An Analytical Study. 243p. 1985. 37.95 (*0-318-36649-5*) Asia Bk Corp.

Mehta, J. L. India & the West: The Problem of Understanding - Selected Essays of J.L. Mehta. (Studies in World Religions: No. 4). 268p. (C). 1985. pap. 14.75 (*0-89130-827-X*, 03 00 04) Harvard U Wrld Relig.

Mehta, Jagat S. Third World Militarization: A Challenge to Third World Diplomacy. LC 85-50860. (Tom Slick World Peace Ser.). 295p. 1985. pap. 8.00 (*0-89940-006-X*) LBJ Sch Pub Aff.

Mehta, Jashwant B. Electoral Reforms. (C). 1990. 40.00 (*0-89771-243-9*) St Mut.

— Quest for a Better Democratic Alternative. LC 94-904208. (C). 1995. 18.00 (*0-7069-8491-9*, Pub. by Vikas) S Asia.

***Mehta, K., ed.** Human CD38 & Related Molecules. (Chemical Immunology Ser.: Vol. 75). (Illus.). xii, 282p. 1999. 238.25 (*3-8055-6923-8*) S Karger.

Mehta, Kalyani, ed. Untapped Resources: Women in Aging Societies Across Asia. LC 97-945802. 168p. 1997. pap. 25.00 (*981-210-106-3*, Pub. by Times Academic) Intl Spec Bk.

Mehta, Kishor C., et al, eds. Guide to the Use of the Wind Load Provisions of ASCE 7-88. LC 91-38210. 99p. 1991. pap. text 22.00 (*0-87262-852-3*) Am Soc Civil Eng.

Mehta, Kishor C. & Marshall, Richard D. Guide to the Use of the Wind Provisions of ASCE 7-95. LC 97-45835. 112p. 1997. pap. text 30.00 (*0-7844-0302-3*, 40302-3) Am Soc Civil Eng.

Mehta, M. K. & Schmidt, J. J. Applied Nuclear Theory & Nuclear Model Calculations for Nuclear Technology Application. 936p. (C). 1989. text 138.00 (*9971-5-0897-4*) World Scientific Pub.

— Computation & Analysis of Nuclear Data: Relevant to Nuclear Energy & Safety. 1000p. 1993. text 178.00 (*981-02-1224-0*) World Scientific Pub.

Mehta, Madan. Fundamentals of Building Construction. 700p. (C). 2001. 60.00 (*0-13-367533-5*, Macmillan Coll) P-H.

— The Principles of Building Construction. LC 96-33105. 362p. 1996. 49.60 (*0-13-205881-2*) P-H.

Mehta, Madan L. Random Matrices. 2nd enl. rev. ed. 562p. 1990. text 111.00 (*0-12-488051-7*) Acad Pr.

Mehta, Makrand, jt. auth. see Tripathi, Dwijendra.

Mehta, Markand, ed. Regional Roots of Indian Nationalism: Gunarat, Maharashtra & Rajasthan. (C). 1990. 42.00 (*0-8364-2485-9*, Pub. by Criterion) S Asia.

Mehta, Mayur & Vieira, Gary. Small Business Computer Systems. 2nd ed. 144p. 1993. ring bd. 13.95 (*0-8403-7908-0*) Kendall-Hunt.

Mehta, Meera & Mehta, Dinesh. Metropolitan Housing Market: A Study of Ahmedabad. 192p. (C). 1990. text 25.00 (*0-8039-9596-2*) Sage.

Mehta, Mira. How to Use Yoga: A Step-by-Step Guide to the Lyengar Method of Yoga for Relaxation, Health & Well-Being. Collins, Elaine, ed. LC 97-76653. (Illus.). 96p. 1998. pap. 14.95 (*0-9627138-6-4*) Rodmell Pr.

— Yoga. 1990. pap. 23.00 (*0-679-72287-4*) Knopf.

Mehta, N. K., tr. see Meschyan, S. R.

Mehta, N. K., tr. see Petrukhin, V. P.

Mehta, N. K., tr. see Shvets, V. B.

Mehta, N. K., tr. see Ter-Martirosyan, Z. G.

Mehta, N. K., tr. see Tseitlin, A. I. & Kusainov, A. A.

***Mehta, Narendra.** Indian Head Massage. (Illus.). 160p. 1999. 27.00 (*0-7225-3791-3*) Thorsons PA.

— Indian Head Massage: Discover the Power of Touch. 2000. 18.95 (*0-7225-3940-1*) Thorsons PA.

Mehta, P. C. & Vyas, N. N. Changing Land Relations in Tribal India. (C). 1994. 17.50 (*81-7033-234-6*, Pub. by Rawat Pubns) S Asia.

Mehta, P. C., jt. auth. see Rampal, V. V.

Mehta, P. D. Buddhahood. 200p. 1993. pap. 15.95 (*1-85230-055-8*, Pub. by Element MA) Penguin Putnam.

— Heart of Religion. 1993. pap. 22.50 (*1-85230-014-0*, HERELP, Pub. by Element MA) Penguin Putnam.

— Holistic Consciousness. 1989. pap. 13.95 (*1-85230-108-2*, Pub. by Element MA) Penguin Putnam.

***Mehta, P. I. & Verma, Neena.** Human Rights under the Indian Constitution: The Philosophy & Judicial Gerrymandering. LC 99-931180. 1999. 30.00 (*81-7629-126-9*, Pub. by Deep & Deep Pubns) S Asia.

Mehta, P. Kumar. Concrete: Structure, Properties, & Materials. (Illus.). 416p. (C). 1986. text 43.95 (*0-685-10931-3*) P-H.

Mehta, P. Kumar, ed. Cement Standards: Evolution & Trends - STP 663. 119p. 1986. pap. 20.00 (*0-8031-0298-4*, STP663) ASTM.

Mehta, P. Kumar & Malhotra, V. M. Pozzolanic & Cementitious Materials. (Advances in Concrete Technology Ser). 136p. 1996. text 39.00 (*2-88449-235-6*) Gordon & Breach.

Mehta, Parkash. Operations Research in Agriculture. 1986. 32.50 (*0-8364-1551-5*, Pub. by Ashish Pub Hse) S Asia.

Mehta, Parkash & Kumari, Anjala. Poverty & Farm Size in India. 1990. 17.00 (*81-7099-199-4*, Pub. by Mittal Pubs Dist) S Asia.

Mehta, Praful. ISO 9000 Audit Questionnaire & Registration Guidelines. LC 94-26830. (Briefing Ser.). 44p. 1994. 15.00 (*0-87389-299-2*, MB102) ASQ Qual Pr.

Mehta, Prayag. Bureaucracy, Organisational Behaviour, & Development. 188p. (C). 1989. text 24.00 (*0-8039-9614-4*) Sage.

— A Psychological Strategy for Alternative Human Development: India's Performance since Independence. LC 98-7051. 256p. 1998. 35.00 (*0-7619-9257-X*) Sage.

Mehta, Priti. World of Rice. 1991. 45.00 (*1-869828-06-2*, Pub. by Moonstone Bks) St Mut.

Mehta, R. J. Divorced Hindu Women. 173p. 1975. 12.95 (*0-7069-0385-4*) Asia Bk Corp.

Mehta, Rama. Inside the Haveli. pap. 17.95 (*0-7043-4394-0*, Pub. by Womens Press) Trafalgar.

Mehta, Rama. Sociolegal Status of Women in India. 192p. 1987. 24.00 (*0-8364-2080-2*, Pub. by Mittal Pubs Dist) S Asia.

Mehta, Rohit. Call of the Upanishads. (C). 1996. 18.00 (*81-208-0747-2*, Pub. by Motilal Bnarsidass) S Asia.

— The Creative Silence. 1986. 9.95 (*81-7059-017-5*, 7224, Quest) Theos Pub Hse.

— Dialogue with Death: Shri Aurobindo's Savitri, a Mystical Approach. (C). 1994. reprint ed. 18.50 (*81-208-1222-0*, Pub. by Motilal Bnarsidass); reprint ed. pap. 12.50 (*81-208-1223-9*, Pub. by Motilal Bnarsidass) S Asia.

— From Mind to Super Supermind: Commentary on the Bhagvad Gita. (C). 1995. reprint ed. 15.00 (*81-208-0964-5*, Pub. by Motilal Bnarsidass) S Asia.

— The Fullness of the Void: The Yoga of Theosophy, the Transcendental Wisdom. (C). 1982. 15.00 (*0-8364-2506-5*, Pub. by Motilal Bnarsidass) S Asia.

— J. Krishnamurti & the Nameless Experience. (C). 1989. reprint ed. 22.50 (*81-208-0589-5*, Pub. by Motilal Bnarsidass); reprint ed. pap. 14.50 (*81-208-0590-9*, Pub. by Motilal Bnarsidass) S Asia.

— The Journey with Death. (C). 1987. reprint ed. 9.50 (*81-208-0295-0*, Pub. by Motilal Bnarsidass) S Asia.

— Science of Meditation. (C). 1991. reprint ed. 12.50 (*81-208-0297-7*, Pub. by Motilal Bnarsidass) S Asia.

— Science of Meditation. (C). 1995. reprint ed. pap. 9.00 (*81-208-0298-5*, Pub. by Motilal Bnarsidass) S Asia.

— The Secret of Self-Transformation: A Synthesis of Tantra & Yoga. (C). 1987. pap. text 10.00 (*81-208-0402-3*, Pub. by Motilal Bnarsidass) S Asia.

— The Secret of Self-Transformation: A Synthesis of Tantra & Yoga. (C). 1997. 18.00 (*81-208-0381-7*, Pub. by Motilal Bnarsidass) S Asia.

— Seek Out the Way. 1990. pap. 3.95 (*81-7059-146-5*, 7201, Quest) Theos Pub Hse.

— Yoga: The Art of Integration. 1990. 22.95 (*81-7059-129-5*, 7513, Quest) Theos Pub Hse.

Mehta, Rohit, ed. Dialogue with Death: Shri Aurobindo's Savitri, A Mystical Approach. (C). 1983. reprint ed. 17.50 (*0-8364-2507-3*, Pub. by Motilal Bnarsidass) S Asia.

Mehta, Rohit & Mehta, Shridevi. J. Krishnamurti & Sant Kabir: A Study in Depth. 1990. 21.00 (*81-208-0667-0*, Pub. by Motilal Bnarsidass) S Asia.

Mehta, Rustam J. Masterpieces of Indian Textiles. (Illus.). 132p. 1979. 42.95 (*0-318-36266-X*) Asia Bk Corp.

Mehta, S. M. Indian Constitutional Law. rev. ed. (C). 1990. 188.00 (*0-89771-202-1*) St Mut.

Mehta, S. R. Society & Health: A Sociological Perspective. 1992. 18.50 (*0-7069-6394-6*, Pub. by Vikas) S Asia.

Mehta, S. R., ed. Poverty, Population & Sustainable Development: Essays in Honour of Professor Victor S. D'Souza. LC 97-904553. (Illus.). xii, 430p. 1997. 43.00 (*81-7033-407-1*, Pub. by Rawat Pubns) Nataraj Bks.

Mehta, Samir, et al. Step-Up: A High-Yield Systems Based Review for the USMLE Step 1 Exam. 250p. 22.95 (*0-683-30755-X*) Lppncott W & W.

Mehta, Satish C. Development Planning in an African Economy Vol. I: The Experience of Nigeria: 1950-1980. 1990. 36.00 (*81-85163-14-6*, Pub. by Kalinga) S Asia.

— Development Planning in an African Economy Vol. 1: The Experience of Nigeria: 1950-1980. (Illus.). vii, 244p. 1990. 22.00 (*0-685-63300-4*, Pub. by Kalinga) Nataraj Bks.

— Development Planning in an African Economy, 1950-1980 Vol. 1: The Experience of Nigeria. (Illus.). vii, 244p. 1990. 22.00 (*0-685-62647-4*, Pub. by Kalinga) Nataraj Bks.

Mehta, Shekhar, et al. Controlling Pollution: Incentives & Regulations. LC 96-46554. 132p. 1997. 21.95 (*0-8039-9348-X*) Sage.

Mehta, Shirin. The Peasantry & Nationalism. 16.00 (*0-8364-1222-2*, Pub. by Manohar) S Asia.

Mehta, Shridevi, jt. auth. see Mehta, Rohit.

Mehta, Swarnjit. Migration: A Spatial Perspective. (C). 1990. 19.00 (*81-7033-096-3*, Pub. by Rawat Pubns) S Asia.

Mehta, T. A Handbook of Forest Utilization. 208p. 1981. 100.00 (*0-7855-3111-4*, Pub. by Intl Bk Distr) St Mut.

Mehta, T. A Handbook of Forest Utilization. 208p. (C). 1981. text 160.00 (*0-89771-585-3*, Pub. by Intl Bk Distr) St Mut.

Mehta, Uday S. The Anxiety of Freedom: Imagination & Individuality in Locke's Political Thought. LC 92-8147. 199p. reprint ed. pap. 61.70 (*0-608-20922-8*, 207202100003) Bks Demand.

Mehta, Usha. Gandhi's Contribution to the Emancipation of Women. (C). 1991. 14.00 (*81-7154-536-X*, Pub. by Popular Prakashan) S Asia.

Mehta, Usha, et al. Women & Men Voters: The 1977-80 Experiment. 120p. 1981. 120.00 (*0-7855-1836-3*, Pub. by Archives Pubs) St Mut.

Mehta, V. Attitudes of Educated Women Towards Social Issues. 126p. 1979. 15.95 (*0-318-37044-1*) Asia Bk Corp.

Mehta, V. R. Foundations of Indian Political Thought: An Interpretation (from Manu to the Present Day) 1996. 14.00 (*81-7304-157-1*, Pub. by Manohar) S Asia.

— Ideology Modernisation & Politics in India. (C). 1988. reprint ed. 24.00 (*0-317-90977-0*, Pub. by Manohar) S Asia.

Mehta, Ved. Mahatma Gandhi & His Apostles. LC 92-83709. 288p. (C). 1993. reprint ed. pap. 17.00 (*0-300-05539-0*) Yale U Pr.

— Portrait of India. LC 92-83817. 544p. (C). 1993. reprint ed. pap. 20.00 (*0-300-05538-2*) Yale U Pr.

— Rajiv Gandhi & Rama's Kingdom. LC 94-15420. (Illus.). 224p. 1994. 25.00 (*0-300-06038-6*) Yale U Pr.

— Rajiv Gandhi & Rama's Kingdom. (Illus.). 208p. 1996. pap. 15.00 (*0-300-06858-1*) Yale U Pr.

— Remembering Mr. Shawn's New Yorker: The Invisible Art of Editin. 416p. 1999. pap. 16.95 (*0-87951-707-7*, Pub. by Overlook Pr) Penguin Putnam.

— Remembering Mr. Shawn's New Yorker: The Invisible Art of Editing. LC 98-10022. 368p. 1998. 27.95 (*0-87951-876-6*, Pub. by Overlook Pr) Penguin Putnam.

— Sound-Shadows of the New World. LC 85-5045. 1987. pap. 8.95 (*0-393-30437-X*) Norton.

— A Ved Mehta Reader: The Craft of the Essay. LC 97-39079. 416p. 1998. 40.00 (*0-300-07189-2*); pap. 18.00 (*0-300-07561-8*) Yale U Pr.

— Vedi. (Illus.). 272p. 1987. reprint ed. pap. 7.95 (*0-393-30417-5*) Norton.

Mehta, Vera, jt. ed. see Constable, Robert.

Mehta, Vinod. The Sanjay Story. 192p. 1978. 9.95 (*0-318-37220-7*) Asia Bk Corp.

Mehta, Vyfen L., tr. see Rasp, Richard A.

Mehtabdin, Khalid R. Comparative Management: Business Styles in Japan & the United States. LC 86-16395. (Mellen Studies in Business: Vol. 1). 140p. 1986. pap. 69.95 (*0-88946-153-8*) E Mellen.

An Asterisk (*) at the beginning of an entry indicates that the title is appearing for the first time.

— Reaganomics: Successes & Failures. LC 86-21674. 1986. pap. 59.95 (*0-88946-204-6*) E Mellen.

Mehtar, Shaheen. Hospital Infection Control: Setting Up a Cost-Effective Resources. LC 92-49489. (Illus.). 208p. (C). 1992. 45.00 (*0-19-262266-8*); 29.50 (*0-19-262033-9*) OUP.

Mehul, Etienne N. Melidore et Phrosine: Drame Lyrique. Bartlet, Elizabeth, ed. LC 85-75346. (French Opera in the 17th & 18th Centuries Ser.: No. 4,vol. LXXIII). (Illus.). 300p. 1990. lib. bdg. 82.00 (*0-918728-81-9*) Pendragon NY.

Mehul, Etienne-Nicolas. Etienne-Nicolas Mehul: Symphony No. 1 in G Minor. Charlton, David, ed. (Recent Researches in Music of the 19th & Early 20th Centuries Ser.: Vol. RRN6). (Illus.). xviii, 106p. 1985. pap. 40.00 (*0-89579-174-9*) A-R Eds.

Mehuron, Kate, jt. auth. see Percesepe, Gary J.

Mehuron, Tamar A., ed. Points of Light: New Approaches to Ending Welfare Dependency. 154p. (C). 1991. pap. 12.95 (*0-89633-152-0*); lib. bdg. 38.50 (*0-89633-151-2*) Ethics & Public Policy.

Mei, C., ed. see American Society of Mechanical Engineers Staff.

Mei, C. C. The Applied Dynamics of Ocean Surface Waves. (Advanced Series in Ocean Engineering: Vol. 1). 764p. 1994. text 76.00 (*9971-5-0773-0*, E-B752); pap. text 38.00 (*9971-5-0789-7*) World Scientific Pub.

Mei Cherng & Wang Bor. Mei Cherng's Seven Stimuli & Wang Bor's Pavilion of King Terng. Mair, Victor H., tr. from CHI. LC 87-23959. (Illus.). 154p. 1987. lib. bdg. 89.95 (*0-88946-020-5*) E Mellen.

Mei, Chiang C. Mathematical Analysis in Engineering: How to Use the Basic Tools. (Illus.). 478p. (C). 1995. text 85.00 (*0-521-46053-0*) Cambridge U Pr.

— Mathematical Analysis in Engineering: How to Use the Basic Tools. (Illus.). 478p. 1997. pap. text 37.95 (*0-521-58798-0*) Cambridge U Pr.

Mei, Elizabeth. Elizabeth: A True Story. LC 96-94273. 300p. 1996. 13.00 (*0-9648277-0-0*) Mei Pubng.

Mei, Fu P. Fu Pei Mei's Chinese Cookbook. 1995. 23.95 (*4-07-974788-8*) Shufu No.

Mei, Huang. Transforming the Cinderella Dream: From Frances Burney to Charlotte Bronte. 200p. 1990. 35.00 (*0-8135-1522-X*) Rutgers U Pr.

Mei Hui Huang, jt. tr. see Smith, Larry.

Mei, J. P., jt. auth. see Malkiel, Burton Gordon.

Mei, Jacqueline T. The Yacht Chef's Guide to Freelancing. LC 95-68752. 80p. (Orig.). 1995. pap. text 15.00 (*0-9646837-0-9*) Clouseau Pubns.

Mei, Jian-Ping. New Methods for the Arbitrage Pricing Theory & the Present Value Model. 100p. 1994. text 30.00 (*981-02-1839-7*) World Scientific Pub.

Mei Ling Rein, et al, eds. Abortion: An Eternal Social & Moral Issue. 10th rev. ed. (Information Plus Reference Ser.). (Illus.). 176p. 1998. pap. text 26.95 (*1-57302-060-5*) Info Plus TX.

— Capital Punishment: Cruel & Unusual? 11th rev. ed. (Information Plus Reference Ser.). (Illus.). 116p. 1998. pap. text 25.95 (*1-57302-061-3*) Info Plus TX.

Mei, Sui-Sheng & Truesdell, Keith A., eds. High-Power Lasers: Solid State, Gas Excimer & Other Advanced Lasers II. LC 98-227271. (Proceedings of SPIE Ser.: Vol. 3549). 272p. 1998. 80.00 (*0-8194-3010-2*) SPIE.

— High-Power Lasers Vol. 2889: Solid State, Gas, Excimer & Other Advanced Lasers. 524p. 1996. 102.00 (*0-8194-2290-8*) SPIE.

Mei, Sui-Sheng, et al. Proceedings, ICLOE'92: 1992 International Conference on Lasers & Optoelectronics, 16-18 October, 1992, Beijing, China. LC 93-83315. (Spie Proceedings Ser.). xvii, 830 p. 1993. write for info. (*0-8194-1225-2*) Routledge.

Mei, V., jt. ed. see Den Braven, K. R.

Mei, V., jt. ed. see Herold, K. E.

Mei Xia, et al. The Re-Emerging Securities Market in China. LC 92-9824. 200p. 1992. 52.95 (*0-89930-755-8*, GEF, Quorum Bks) Greenwood.

Mei, Yuan. I Don't Bow to Buddhas: Selected Poems of Yuan Mei. Seaton, J. P., tr. LC 96-51284. 124p. 1997. pap. text 14.00 (*1-55659-120-9*) Copper Canyon.

***Mei, Zhen.** Numerical Bifurcation Analysis for Reaction-Diffusion Equations. LC 00-41043. (Series in Computational Mathematics: Vol. 28). xiv, 414p. 2000. 84.00 (*3-540-67296-6*) Spr-Verlag.

Mei, Zu-yan, ed. Mechanical Design & Manufacturing of Hydraulic Machinery. (Hydraulic Machinery Bks.). 574p. 1991. 119.95 (*1-85628-820-X*, Pub. by Avebury Technical) Ashgate Pub Co.

***Meibach, Howard.** Hollywood Literary Sales Directory Vol. 3: July, 1998 - January, 1999. 3rd ed. 70p. 1999. pap. 15.95 (*0-9666188-2-3*) In Good Co.

— Spec Screenplay Sales Directory, 1991-1999, Vol. 3. 3rd rev. deluxe ed. 1999. pap. 59.95 (*0-9666188-1-5*) In Good Co.

***Meibach, Howard, ed.** Hollywood Literary Sales Directory Vol. 4: January 1999 - July 1999. 4th rev. ed. 73p. 1999. pap. 15.95 (*0-9666188-3-1*) In Good Co.

Meibach, Howard, ed. Hollywood Literary Sales Directory, January, 1998-July, 1998, Vol. 2. 2nd rev. ed. 63p. 1998. pap. 15.95 (*0-9666188-0-7*) In Good Co.

Meibar, Basheer. Political Culture, Foreign Policy & Conflict: The Palestine Area Conflict System, 63. LC 81-427. (Contributions in Political Science Ser.: No. 63). (Illus.). 312p. 1982. 59.95 (*0-313-22941-4*, MEP/, Greenwood Pr) Greenwood.

Meibetaner, Iris, jt. auth. see Klein, Josef.

***MeiBner, Bjorn.** Das Verstehen fordern: Bericht vom wissenschaftlichen Ehrenkolloquium aus AnlaB des 65. Geburtstages von Eva Maria Krech. 1999. 26.95 (*3-631-33142-8*) P Lang Pubng.

Meibom, Marcus. Antiquae Musicae Auctores Septem, 2 vols. fac. ed. (Monuments of Music & Music Literature in Facsimile Ser., Series II: Vol. 51). (Illus.). 1977. lib. bdg. 125.00 (*0-8450-2251-2*) Broude.

Meiburg, Peter. Saxonische Taktonik und Schollenkinematik Am Ostrand des Rheinischen Massivs. (Geotektonische Forschungen Ser.: Vol. 62). (GER.). 267p. 1982. 114.00 (*3-510-50028-8*, Pub. by E Schweizerbartsche) Balogh.

Meichenbaum, D. & Jaremko, M. Stress Reduction & Prevention. (Illus.). 512p. (C). 1983. 52.50 (*0-306-41066-4*, Plenum Trade) Perseus Pubng.

Meichenbaum, D. & Turk, D. C. Facilitating Treatment Adherence: A Practitioner's Guidebook. LC 87-15397. (Illus.). 310p. (C). 1987. 44.50 (*0-306-42638-2*, Plenum Trade) Perseus Pubng.

Meichenbaum, Donald & Biemiller, Andrew. Nurturing Independent Learners: Helping Students Take Charge of Their Learning. LC 97-50477. 256p. 1997. pap. text 24.95 (*1-57129-047-8*) Brookline Bks.

Meiczinger, John. How to Draw Indian Arts & Crafts. LC 88-50807. (How to Draw Ser.). (Illus.). 32p. (J). (gr. 2-6). 1989. lib. bdg. 17.25 (*0-8167-1537-8*) Troll Communs.

— How to Draw Indian Arts & Crafts. LC 88-50807. (How to Draw Ser.). (Illus.). 32p. (J). (gr. 2-6). 1996. pap. 2.95 (*0-8167-1515-7*) Troll Communs.

— How to Draw Indian Arts & Crafts. (J). 1989. 7.70 (*0-606-02357-7*, Pub. by Turtleback) Demco.

***Meiczinger, John.** HT Draw Indian Arts & Crafts. (Illus.). 1999. pap. text 9.90 (*0-7857-6351-1*) Econo-Clad Bks.

Meid, Volker, jt. auth. see Yingling.

Meid, Wolfgang, jt. auth. see Krahe, Hans.

Meidan & Lewis. Readings in Financial Services Marketing. 1998. pap. 21.99 (*1-86152-453-6*) Thomson Learn.

Meidan, Arthur. Insurance Marketing. 158p. 1984. pap. 100.00 (*0-907721-16-8*, Pub. by Graham Burn Prods) St Mut.

Meidan, Arthur, ed. Insurance Marketing. (C). 1984. 75.00 (*0-7855-4129-2*, Pub. by Witherby & Co) St Mut.

Meiden, Walter, jt. auth. see Carlut, Charles.

Meiden, Walter, jt. auth. see Euwe, Max.

Meiden, Walter, jt. auth. see Iglesias, Mario.

***MEIDINGER, WERNER.** Naturally Healthy with Evening Primrose Oil. 96p. 1999. pap. text 11.95 (*0-8069-2035-1*) Sterling.

Meidl, James H., jt. auth. see Kenley.

Meidleman, Saul L., jt. ed. see Laskin, Allen I.

Meienberg, Otmar. Saccadic Eye Movements in Neurological & Ophthalmological Diagnosis. (Neurology Ser.: Vol. 29). (Illus.). xii, 115p. 1988. 94.95 (*0-387-18547-X*) Spr-Verlag.

Meienberger, Norbert. The Emergence of Constitutional Government in China, 1905-1908: The Concept Sanctioned by the Empress Dowager Tz'u-Hsi. (Schweizer Asiatische Studien-Monographien: Vol. 1). 115p. 1980. 22.00 (*3-261-04620-1*) P Lang Pubng.

Meier. Black Experience: Transformation of Activism. LC 72-94820. 203p. 1970. pap. 19.95 (*0-87855-558-7*) Transaction Pubs.

— Elements of Counseling. 4th ed. (Counseling Ser.). 2000. pap. 19.95 (*0-534-36640-6*) Brooks-Cole.

— Politics & the Bureaucracy. 4th ed. (C). 1999. text 28.00 (*0-15-505523-2*, Pub. by Harcourt Coll Pubs) Harcourt.

— Statistical Methods in Analytical Chemistry. 2nd ed. LC 99-25291. 464p. 2000. 94.95 (*0-471-29363-6*) Wiley.

— Teachings of Carl Schmitts. LC 98-23580. 179p. 1998. 26.00 (*0-226-51890-6*) U Ch Pr.

***Meier.** What Works. 2000. 60.00 (*0-8133-9781-2*, Pub. by Westview); pap. 23.00 (*0-8133-9782-0*, Pub. by Westview) HarpC.

Meier & Davis. Dealing with Managed Care: A Primer for Students. (Counseling Ser.). (C). 2000. pap. text 17.00 (*0-534-54974-8*) Wadsworth Pub.

Meier, et al. Regulation & Consumer Protection: Politics, Bureaucracy & Economics. 3rd ed. LC 97-67113. 1997. pap. 48.95 (*0-87393-640-X*) Dame Pubns.

— The Shaman from Elko. Hill, Gareth, ed. & frwd. by. 272p. (C). 1978. pap. 17.00 (*0-932630-00-6*) C G Jung Frisco.

Meier, jt. ed. see Newport, Slobin.

Meier, Ann, ed. see Hirzy, Ellen C.

Meier-Arendt, W. Die Hinkelstein-Gruppe. Der Uebergang vom Frueh-zum Mittelneolithikum in Suedwestdeutschland: Text-Vol. & Vol. with Plates. (Roemisch-Germanische Forschungen Ser.: Vol. 35). (Illus.). x, 237p. (C). 1975. 200.00 (*3-11-004758-6*) De Gruyter.

Meier, Arnold R., et al. A Curriculum for Citizenship: A Total School Approach to Citizenship Education. LC 52-13495. 425p. reprint ed. pap. 131.80 (*0-7837-3673-8*, 204354700009) Bks Demand.

Meier, August. Negro Thought in America, 1880-1915: Racial Ideologies in the Age of Booker T. Washington. LC 63-14008. 352p. 1963. text 44.50 (*0-472-64230-8*, 64230); pap. text 22.95 (*0-472-06118-6*, 06118, Ann Arbor Bks) U of Mich Pr.

— A White Scholar & the Black Community, 1945-1965: Essays & Reflections. LC 92-3205. 248p. 1992. 40.00 (*0-87023-809-4*); pap. 17.95 (*0-87023-810-8*) U of Mass Pr.

Meier, August, et al, eds. Black Protest in the Sixties: Essays from the New York Times Magazine, 1990. 2nd ed. LC 90-13071. 396p. 1991. text 34.95 (*1-55876-031-8*); pap. text 14.95 (*1-55876-032-6*) Wiener Pubs Inc.

Meier, August & Rudwick, Elliott. Black Detroit & the Rise of the UAW. (Illus.). 302p. 1981. pap. text 13.95 (*0-19-502895-3*) OUP.

— Black History & the Historical Profession, 1915-1980. LC 85-16817. (Blacks in the New World Ser.). 400p. 1986. pap. text 16.95 (*0-252-01274-7*) U of Ill Pr.

— Core: A Study in the Civil Rights Movement, 1942-1968. LC 72-92294. 580p. 1975. reprint ed. pap. text 15.95 (*0-252-00567-8*) U of Ill Pr.

— From Plantation to Ghetto. 3rd ed. (American Century Ser.). (Illus.). 406p. 1976. pap. 13.00 (*0-8090-0122-5*) Hill & Wang.

Meier, August, jt. auth. see Litwack, Leon.

Meier, August, jt. ed. see Franklin, John H.

Meier, August, jt. ed. see Litwack, Leon F.

***Meier, Barbara.** Women & Migration: Anthropological Perspectives. 2000. text 59.95 (*0-312-23239-X*) St Martin.

Meier, Barbara, jt. auth. see Strauch, Inge.

Meier, Bernadette, ed. see Fejer, Paul H.

Meier, Bernhard. The Modes of Renaissance Vocal Polyphony. Beebe, Ellen S., tr. (Illus.). 1988. lib. bdg. 50.00 (*0-8450-7025-8*) Broude.

Meier, Bernhard & Mehan, Vivek K. Atlas of Coronary Balloon Angioplasty. LC 94-30841. (Fundamental & Clinical Cardiology Ser.: Vol. 23). (Illus.). 272p. reprint ed. pap. 84.40 (*0-608-08962-1*, 206959700005) Bks Demand.

Meier, Bill. Autorental Europe: A Guide to Choosing & Driving a Rental Car in Europe. 192p. 1993. pap. text 12.95 (*0-9634749-0-1*) Lansing Pubns.

Meier-Brugger, Michael. Griechische Sprachwissenschaft, Vol. 1. (Sammlung Goschen Ser.: No. 2241). (GER.). (C). 1992. pap. 22.95 (*3-11-012550-1*, 54-92) De Gruyter.

— Griechische Sprachwissenschaft, Vol. 2. (Sammlung Goschen Ser.: No. 2242). (GER.). (C). 1992. pap. 20.65 (*3-11-013526-4*) De Gruyter.

***Meier-Brugger, Michael.** Indogermanische Sprachwissenschaft: Unter Mitarbeit von Matthias Fritz und Manfred Mayrhofer. (De Gruyter Studienbuch Ser.). 310p. 2000. 30.00 (*3-11-014478-6*) Mouton.

Meier, C. A. Healing Dream & Ritual. 213p. 1995. pap. 17.95 (*3-85630-510-6*) Continuum.

— Personality: The Individuation Process in the Light of C. G. Jung's Typology. LC 76-15650. 214p. 1997. pap. 16.95 (*3-85630-549-1*) Continuum.

Meier, Carl A. The Psychology of C. G. Jung. Rolfe, Eugene, tr. LC 85-13996. (Unconscious in Its Empirical Manifestations Ser.: Vol. I). (Illus.). 236p. (C). 1985. 35.00 (*0-938434-10-1*); pap. 16.95 (*0-938434-68-3*) Sigo Pr.

— The Psychology of C. G. Jung: The Meaning & Significance of Dreams, Vol. II. 163p. 1987. 40.00 (*0-938434-11-X*); pap. 16.95 (*0-938434-69-1*) Sigo Pr.

— The Psychology of C. G Jung, Vol. III: Consciousness, Vol. III. Roscoe, David, tr. from GER. (Illus.). 128p. (C). 1989. 40.00 (*0-938434-12-8*); pap. 16.95 (*0-938434-70-5*) Sigo Pr.

***Meier, Carla.** Blue Is for Advent: Colors & Seasons of the Church Year. (Illus.). 13p. (J). (ps). 2000. write for info. (*0-9661326-2-9*) Metrop NY Mission.

Meier, Cheryl. I Know Just How You Feel. LC 93-44820. 1994. 7.99 (*0-8407-4399-8*) Nelson.

Meier, Christian. Athens: A Portrait of the City in Its Golden Age. Kimber, Robert & Kimber, Rita, trs. LC 98-14091. 800p. 1998. 37.50 (*0-8050-4840-5*) H Holt & Co.

— Caesar: A Biography. McLintock, David, tr. from GER. (Illus.). 592p. 1996. 30.00 (*0-465-00894-1*, Pub. by Basic) HarpC.

— Caesar: A Biography. (Illus.). 528p. 1997. pap. 17.00 (*0-465-00895-X*, Pub. by Basic) HarpC.

— The Greek Discovery of Politics. McLintock, David, tr. 352p. 1990. 46.50 (*0-674-36232-2*) HUP.

— The Political Art of Greek Tragedy. 250p. (C). 1993. text 37.50 (*0-8018-4727-3*) Johns Hopkins.

Meier, Cominicus M. Die Rechtswirkungen der Klosterlichen Profeb: Eine Rechtsgeschichtliche Untersuchung der Monastischen Profeb und Ihrer Rechtswirkungen Unter Berucksichtigung des Staatskirchenrechts. (Europaische Hochschulschriften Ser.: Reihe 23, Bd. 486). (GER.). 550p. 1993. 77.95 (*3-631-46188-7*) P Lang Pubng.

Meier, D. J. Molecular Basis of Transitions & Relaxations, Vol. 4. (Midland Macromolecular Monographs). xii, 430p. 1978. text 428.00 (*0-677-11240-8*) Gordon & Breach.

Meier, D. J., ed. Block Copolymers: Science & Technology. (MMI Press Symposium Ser.: Vol. 3). x, 200p. 1983. text 280.00 (*3-7186-0144-3*) Gordon & Breach.

Meier, Daniel. Learning in Small Moments: Life in an Urban Classroom. (Practitioners Inquiry Ser.: Vol. 3). 176p. (C). 1997. text 44.00 (*0-8077-3627-9*); pap. text 18.95 (*0-8077-3626-0*) Tchrs Coll.

***Meier, Daniel.** Scribble Scrabble, Learning to Read & Write: Success with Diverse Teachers, Children & Families. LC 99-48786. 168p. 2000. pap. 19.95 (*0-8077-3882-4*) Tchrs Coll.

***Meier, Daniel R.** Scribble Scrabble--Teaching Children to Become Successful Readers & Writers. LC 99-48786. 168p. 2000. write for info. (*0-8077-3883-2*) Tchrs Coll.

***Meier, Dave.** Accelerated Learning Handbook: A Creative Guide to Designing & Delivering Faster, More Effective Training Programs. (Illus.). 350p. 2000. 29.95 (*0-07-135547-2*) McGraw.

Meier, Deborah. Becoming a Teacher. (DeGarmo Lectures: No. 16). 1991. 10.00 (*0-685-51004-2*) Soc Profs Ed.

***Meier, Deborah.** Is Standardized Testing Good for Education? LC 99-89137. 104p. 2000. pap. 12.00 (*0-8070-0441-3*) Beacon Pr.

Meier, Deborah. The Power of Their Ideas: Lessons for America from a Small School in Harlem. 208p. 1996. pap. 13.00 (*0-8070-3111-9*) Beacon Pr.

Meier, Ernst. Deutsche Volksmarchen Aus Schwaben. (GER.). xii, 325p. 1977. reprint ed. write for info. (*3-487-04098-0*) G Olms Pubs.

Meier, Ernst Von, see Von Meier, Ernst.

Meier-Evert, K. & Okawa, M. Sleep-Wake Disorders: Proceedings of a Japanese-German International Symposium Held in Erfurt, Germany, October 9-10, 1996. LC 97-42703. (Illus.). 199p. 1998. 95.00 (*0-306-45771-7*, Kluwer Plenum) Kluwer Academic.

Meier, G. E. Francisco Goya. (GER.). 70p. 1982. 60.00 (*0-7855-1504-6*) St Mut.

Meier, G. E. & Schnerr, G. H., eds. Control of Flow Instabilities & Unsteady Flows, Vol. VII. (CISM International Centre for Mechanical Sciences Ser.: Vol. 369). (Illus.). 325p. 1996. pap. 87.00 (*3-211-82807-9*) Spr-Verlag.

Meier, G. E. & Thompson, P. A. Adiabatic Waves in Liquid-Vapor Systems. (International Union of Theoretical & Applied Mechanics Symposia Ser.). (Illus.). 456p. 1990. 96.00 (*0-387-50203-3*) Spr-Verlag.

Meier, Gary & Meier, Gloria. Brewed in the Pacific Northwest: A History of Beer Making in Oregon & Washington. LC 91-23402. (Western Writers Ser.: No. 3). 216p. (Orig.). 1991. 25.95 (*0-940242-54-0*) Fjord Pr.

— Naughty Ladies of the Old Northwest. (Illus.). 144p. 1990. pap. 12.95 (*0-89288-180-1*) Maverick.

— Oregon Outlaws. LC 97-165187. (Illus.). 254p. (Orig.). 1996. pap. 17.95 (*1-886609-05-5*) Tamarack Bks.

Meier, Georg F. Anfangsgruende Aller Schoenen Wissenschaften. (Documenta Linguistica Ser.: Bd. 3, Reihe V). (GER.). cxc, 1830p. 1976. reprint ed. write for info. (*3-487-06072-8*) G Olms Pubs.

— Beurtheilung der Gottschedischen Dichtkunst. (GER.). viii, 362p. 1975. reprint ed. write for info. (*3-487-05512-0*) G Olms Pubs.

Meier, Georg F., jt. ed. see Lange, Samuel G.

Meier, Gerald M. Data Disk, 4th ed. 4th ed. 1996. pap. text 246.00 (*0-15-505455-4*) Harcourt Coll Pubs.

— Emerging from Poverty: The Economics that Really Matters. 268p. 1985. pap. text 21.95 (*0-19-503714-6*) OUP.

— Financing Asian Development: Performance & Prospects. LC 86-23328. (Asian Agenda Reports: No. 6). (Illus.). 88p. (Orig.). (C). 1987. pap. text 10.50 (*0-8191-5682-5*) U Pr of Amer.

— Financing Asian Development: Performance & Prospects. LC 86-23328. (Asian Agenda Reports: No. 6). (Illus.). 88p. (Orig.). (C). 1987. lib. bdg. 25.50 (*0-8191-5681-7*) U of PR Pr.

— The International Environment of Business: Competition & Governance in the Global Economy. LC 97-29841. (Illus.). 480p. (C). 1998. pap. text 44.95 (*0-19-511641-0*) OUP.

— Politics & Policy Making in Developing Countries. 369p. 1991. 34.95 (*1-55815-095-1*); pap. 19.95 (*1-55815-079-X*); 6.95 (*1-55815-135-4*) ICS Pr.

***Meier, Gerald M. & Rauch, James E.** Leading Issues in Economic Development. 7th ed. LC 99-59308. (Illus.). 600p. (C). 2000. pap. text 49.95 (*0-19-511589-9*) OUP.

Meier, Gerald M. & Steel, William F., eds. Industrial Adjustment in Sub-Saharan Africa. (EDI Series in Economic Development). (Illus.). 312p. 1989. text 35.00 (*0-19-520784-X*) OUP.

Meier, Gerald M., jt. ed. see Stiglitz, Joseph E.

Meier, Gisela. Minorities. LC 91-11651. (Women Today Ser.). 64p. (J). (gr. 5-7). 1991. lib. bdg. 17.95 (*0-86593-124-0*); lib. bdg. 17.27 (*0-685-59203-0*) Rourke Corp.

Meier, Gladys H. & Martindale, Robert R. Hall. History of the Hall Family & Allied Lines. (Illus.). 185p. 1997. reprint ed. pap. 28.00 (*0-8328-8910-5*); reprint ed. lib. bdg. 38.00 (*0-8328-8909-1*) Higginson Bk Co.

Meier, Gloria, jt. auth. see Meier, Gary.

Meier-Graefe, Julius. Degas. (Fine Art Ser.). (Illus.). 128p. 1988. reprint ed. pap. 4.50 (*0-486-25702-9*) Dover.

— Dostoevsky, the Man & His Work. LC 71-7153. (Studies in European Literature: No. 56). 406p. 1972. reprint ed. lib. bdg. 75.00 (*0-8383-1390-6*) M S G Haskell Hse.

— Modern Art, Being a Contribution to a New System of Aesthetics, 2 vols. LC 68-9239. (Contemporary Art Ser.). (Illus.). 1968. reprint ed. 96.95 (*0-405-00719-1*) Ayer.

— Modern Art, Being a Contribution to a New System of Aesthetics, 2 vols., Vol. 1. LC 68-9239. (Contemporary Art Ser.). (Illus.). 1968. reprint ed. 48.95 (*0-405-00826-0*) Ayer.

— Modern Art, Being a Contribution to a New System of Aesthetics, 2 vols., Vol. 2. LC 68-9239. (Contemporary Art Ser.). (Illus.). 1968. reprint ed. 48.95 (*0-405-00827-9*) Ayer.

— Vincent Van Gogh: A Biographical Study. Holroyd-Reece, John, tr. LC 76-109788. 239p. 1970. reprint ed. lib. bdg. 35.00 (*0-8371-4278-4*, MEVG, Greenwood Pr) Greenwood.

— Vincent Van Gogh: A Biography. 160p. 1987. reprint ed. pap. 5.95 (*0-486-25253-1*) Dover.

Meier, Gretl S. Job Sharing: A New Pattern for Quality of Work & Life. LC 79-4145. 187p. 1979. pap. 8.00 (*0-911558-59-4*) W E Upjohn.

— Worker Learning & Worktime Flexibility: A Policy Discussion Paper. LC 83-1348. 64p. (Orig.). 1983. pap. text 4.00 (*0-88099-007-4*) W E Upjohn.

Meier, H. & Marthinsen, J. Switzerland: A Guide to the Capital & Money Markets. 1996. 170.00 (*1-85564-373-1*, Pub. by Euromoney) Am Educ Systs.

Meier, Hans W. Library of Specifications Sections, 4 vols., Set. LC 82-10149. 1983. ring bd. 250.00 (*0-686-84600-1*, Busn) P-H.

— Library of Specifications Sections, 4 vols., Set. 2nd ed. 1568p. 1988. ring bd. 295.00 (*0-13-535352-1*, Busn) P-H.

— Understanding & Using Today's Construction Contract Documents. rev. ed. (Illus.). 123p. 1996. pap. 19.95 (*1-889892-05-X*) Builders Bk Inc.

M

Meier, Heinrich. Carl Schmitt & Leo Strauss: The Hidden Dialogue; Including Strauss's Notes on Schmitt's Concept of the Political & Three Letters from Strauss to Schmitt. Lomax, J. Harvey, tr. LC 95-8803. 156p. 1995. 19.95 (*0-226-51889-2*) U Ch Pr.

Meier, Heinz K. Friendship under Stress: U. S.-Swiss Relations, 1900-1950. 423p. 1970. 45.00 (*3-261-00611-0*) P Lang Pubng.

— Switzerland. LC 91-121289. (World Bibliographical Ser.). 430p. 1990. lib. bdg. 98.00 (*1-85109-107-6*) ABC-CLIO.

Meier, Helmt M. E. Enciclopedia Agropecuaria Sistematica: Plantas Cultivos y Cosechas, Ganderia, Tecnologia Agropecuaria y Forestal, 3 vols., Set. (SPA.). 1492p. 1978. 125.00 (*0-8288-5208-1*, S50556) Fr & Eur.

Meier, Henri B. The Swiss Equity Market. LC 85-12195. (Illus.). 210p. 1986. 49.95 (*0-89930-147-9*, MEQ/, Quorum Bks) Greenwood.

Meier, Joe, jt. auth. see Sellier, Charles E., Jr.

Meier, Joe, jt. auth. see Sellier, Charles E.

Meier, Joe, jt. auth. see Sellier, Charles E., Jr.

Meier, Joel F. Backpacking. 2nd rev. ed. LC 91-68424. (Illus.). 150p. 1993. pap. 14.30 (*0-915611-53-8*, L1538) AAHPERD.

Meier, Joel F. & Mitchell, Viola. Camp Counseling: Leadership & Programming for the Organized Camp. 7th ed. 544p. (C). 1992. text. write for info. (*0-697-10967-4*) Brown & Benchmark.

Meier, John & Rishel, Thomas. Writing in the Teaching & Learning of Mathematics. LC 98-86032. (MAA Notes). 115p. 1998. pap. text 18.95 (*0-88385-158-X*) Math Assn.

Meier, John P. Marginal Jew - Rethinking the Historical Jesus Vol. 1: Roots of the Problem & the Person, Vol. 1. 496p. 1991. 39.95 (*0-385-26425-9*) Doubleday.

— Marginal Jew - Rethinking the Historical Jesus Vol. 2: Mentor, Message & Miracles, Vol. 2. 1136p. 1994. 37.50 (*0-385-46992-6*) Doubleday.

Meier, Judith A. Advertisements & Notices of Interest from Norristown Vol. II: 1822-1827. 187p. 1989. per. 19.95 (*1-55856-031-9*, 171) Closson Pr.

— Advertisements & Notices of Interest from Norristown, Pennsylvania Newspapers, Vol. 3. 199p. 1990. per. 19.95 (*1-55856-057-2*, 172) Closson Pr.

— Advertisements & Notices of Interest from Norristown, Pennsylvania Newspapers, Vol. 6: 1844-1848. 324p. 1992. per. 22.95 (*1-55856-108-0*, 175) Closson Pr.

— Advertisements & Notices of Interest from Norristown, Pennsylvania Newspapers, 1799-1821. 1988. pap. text 19.95 (*0-933227-89-2*, 170) Closson Pr.

— Runaway Women Elopements & Other Miscreant Deeds As Advertised in the Pennsylvania Gazette, 1728-1789. 113p. 1993. per. 10.95 (*1-55856-119-6*, 369) Closson Pr.

Meier, Judy. Making Beautiful Wax Dolls. LC 89-61679. (Orig.). 1989. pap. text 15.95 (*0-916809-32-3*) Scott Pubns MI.

Meier, Juergen, ed. Menschenbilder - Philosophie Im Krankenhaus. (GER.). vi, 121p. 1994. write for info. (*3-487-09884-9*) G Olms Pubs.

Meier, Jurg & White, Julian, eds. Handbook of Clinical Toxicology of Animal Venoms & Poisons. 768p. 1995. boxed set 139.95 (*0-8493-4489-1*, 4489) CRC Pr.

***Meier, Kenneth J.** Applied Statistics for Public Administration. 1998. pap., teacher ed. 30.00 (*0-15-505456-2*) Harcourt.

Meier, Kenneth J. Applied Statistics for Public Administration. 3rd ed. (C). 1991. pap. text 35.25 (*0-534-19591-1*) Harcourt.

— The Political Economy of Regulation: The Case of Insurance. LC 87-33769. (SUNY Series in Public Administration). (Illus.). 230p. (C). 1988. pap. text 24.95 (*0-88706-732-8*) State U NY Pr.

— The Political Economy of Regulation: The Case of Insurance. LC 87-33769. (SUNY Series in Public Administration). (Illus.). 230p. (C). 1988. text 74.50 (*0-88706-731-X*) State U NY Pr.

Meier, Kenneth J. The Politics of Sin: Drugs, Alcohol & Public Policy. LC 93-14454. (Bureaucracies, Public Administration & Public Policy Ser.). (Illus.). 279p. (C). (gr. 13). 1994. pap. text 32.95 (*1-56324-299-0*) M E Sharpe.

Meier, Kenneth J. The Politics of Sin: Drugs, Alcohol & Public Policy. LC 93-14454. (Bureaucracies, Public Administration & Public Policy Ser.). (Illus.). 279p. (C). (gr. 13). 1994. text 76.95 (*1-56324-298-2*) M E Sharpe.

Meier, Kenneth J. & Brudney, Jeffrey L. Applied Statistics for Public Administration. 4th ed. LC 96-76827. 512p. (C). 1996. pap. text 65.00 (*0-03-019378-8*, Pub. by Harcourt Coll Pubs) Harcourt.

Meier, Kenneth J. & Stewart, Joseph, Jr. The Politics of Hispanic Education: Un Paso Pa'lante y Dos Pa'tras. LC 90-33101. (SUNY Series, United States Hispanic Studies). 275p. (C). 1991. text 64.50 (*0-7914-0507-9*); pap. text 21.95 (*0-7914-0508-7*) State U NY Pr.

Meier, Kenneth J., et al. Race, Class & Education: The Politics of Second Generation Discrimination. LC 89-40262. 240p. (Orig.). (C). 1990. pap. text 15.95 (*0-299-12214-X*) U of Wis Pr.

Meier, Kenneth J., jt. auth. see McFarlane, Deborah R.

Meier, Kenneth J., jt. auth. see Smith, Kevin B.

Meier, Klaus V., jt. auth. see Morgan, William J.

Meier, Kurt. Die Theologischen Fakultaeten Im Dritten Reich. (GER.). vi, 500p. (C). 1996. text 80.00 (*3-11-015226-6*); pap. text 50.40 (*3-11-013761-5*) De Gruyter.

Meier, Leslie. Back to School Murder: A Lucy Stone Mystery. 256p. 1997. 18.95 (*1-57566-216-7*, Knsington) Kensgtn Pub Corp.

— Back to School Murder: A Lucy Stone Mystery. 272p. 1998. pap. 5.99 (*1-57566-330-9*) Kensgtn Pub Corp.

***Meier, Leslie.** Christmas Cookie Murder, Vol. 1. 256p. 1999. 20.00 (*1-57566-476-3*) Kens Hse.

— Christmas Cookie Murder. (Lucy Stone Mysteries Ser.). (Illus.). (J). 2000. mass mkt. 5.99 (*1-57566-691-X*) Kensgtn Pub Corp.

Meier, Leslie. Mail-Order Murder. 1999. pap. 5.95 (*0-14-015832-4*, Viking) Viking Penguin.

— Mistletoe Murder. (Lucy Stone Mystery Ser.). Orig. Title: Mail-order Murder. 224p. 1998. mass mkt. 5.99 (*1-57566-370-8*, Knsington) Kensgtn Pub Corp.

— Tippy Toe Murder. 256p. 1996. mass mkt. 4.99 (*1-57566-099-7*, Knsington) Kensgtn Pub Corp.

— Tippy Toe Murder. 256p. 1999. mass mkt. 5.99 (*1-57566-392-9*) Kensgtn Pub Corp.

— Trick or Treat Murder. 256p. 1997. mass mkt. 5.99 (*1-57566-219-1*, Knsington) Kensgtn Pub Corp.

***Meier, Leslie.** Turkey Day Murder. (Lucy Stone Mysteries Ser.). (Illus.). (J). 2000. 20.00 (*1-57566-605-7*) Kensgtn Pub Corp.

— Valentine Murder. 256p. 1999. 20.00 (*1-57566-390-2*) Kensgtn Pub Corp.

***Meier, Leslie.** Valentine Murder. (Lucy Stone Mystery Ser.). 2000. mass mkt. 5.99 (*1-57566-499-2*) Kensgtn Pub Corp.

Meier, Levi. Ancient Secrets: Using the Stories of the Bible to Improve Our Everyday Lives. LC 99-42864. 288p. 1999. pap. 16.95 (*1-58023-064-4*) Jewish Lights.

— Jacob. 132p. (C). 1994. pap. text 19.95 (*0-8191-9668-1*); lib. bdg. 42.00 (*0-8191-9667-3*) U Pr of Amer.

— Jewish Values in Health & Medicine. 220p. (Orig.). (C). 1991. pap. text 26.50 (*0-8191-8174-9*); lib. bdg. 49.50 (*0-8191-8173-0*) U Pr of Amer.

— Jewish Values in Jungian Psychology. 198p. (Orig.). (C). 1991. pap. text 22.50 (*0-8191-8324-5*); lib. bdg. 48.50 (*0-8191-8323-7*) U Pr of Amer.

— Moses - The Prince, the Prophet: His Life, Legend & Message for Our Lives. LC 98-35473. 224p. 1998. 23.95 (*1-58023-013-X*) Jewish Lights.

— Moses - The Prince, the Prophet: His Life, Legend & Message for Our Lives. 224p. 1999. pap. 16.95 (*1-58023-069-5*) Jewish Lights.

Meier, Levi, ed. Jewish Values in Bioethics. 195p. 1986. 35.95 (*0-89885-299-4*, Kluwer Acad Hman Sci) Kluwer Academic.

Meier, M. Matthew. 1989. pap. 30.00 (*0-7855-6987-1*, Pub. by Veritas Pubns) St Mut.

Meier, Manfred, et al, eds. Neuropsychological Rehabilitation. LC 87-154. 468p. 1987. lib. bdg. 57.95 (*0-89862-702-8*) Guilford Pubns.

***Meier, Marcie.** Activities Using the State of the World Atlas. 6th ed. Bongiorno, Linda & Motgomery, Mark, eds. (Illus.). 150p. 2000. pap. 25.00 (*0-943804-08-6*) U of Denver Teach.

Meier, Marcie. A Fitting Bar Mitzvah. (Illus.). (YA). 1996. pap. text 12.95 (*965-229-127-7*, Pub. by Gefen Pub Hse) Gefen Bks.

Meier, Matt S. Mexican American Biographies: A Historical Dictionary, 1836-1987. LC 87-12025. 279p. 1988. lib. bdg. 55.00 (*0-313-24521-5*, MMX/, Greenwood Pr) Greenwood.

Meier, Matt S., compiled by. Bibliography of Mexican American History. LC 83-18585. 500p. 1984. lib. bdg. 75.00 (*0-313-23776-X*, MBI/, Greenwood Pr) Greenwood.

Meier, Matt S. & Ribera, Feliciano. Mexican Americans, American Mexicans: From Conquistadors to Chicanos. rev. ed. LC 93-3385. (American Century Ser.). 288p. 1994. pap. 13.00 (*0-8090-1559-5*) Hill & Wang.

Meier, Matt S. & Rivera, Feliciano, eds. Dictionary of Mexican American History. LC 80-24750. (Illus.). 498p. 1981. lib. bdg. 65.00 (*0-313-21203-1*, NMD/, Greenwood Pr) Greenwood.

Meier, Matt S., et al. Notable Latino Americans: A Biographical Dictionary. LC 96-27392. 448p. (J). (gr. 7). 1997. 65.00 (*0-313-29105-5*) Greenwood.

Meier, Matt S., ed. see McWilliams, Carey.

Meier, Michael. A Quick Reference Guide to Using Early Recollections in Treating Personality Disorders. LC 87-92202. (Orig.). (C). 1988. pap. text. write for info. (*0-945628-00-5*) Diagnostic Solns.

Meier-Mitchell. Camp Counseling. 8th ed. 2000. 37.00 (*0-697-25884-X*, WCB McGr Hill) McGrw-H Hghr Educ.

Meier, Moritz H. & Schomann, Georg F. Der Attische Process. Vlastos, Gregory, ed. LC 78-19370. (Morals & Law in Ancient Greece Ser.). (GER & GRE.). 1979. reprint ed. lib. bdg. 61.95 (*0-405-11561-X*) Ayer.

Meier, Nancy. Operating Room Policy & Procedures. 1993. 145.00 (*1-879575-35-3*) Acad Med Sys.

***Meier, Nicholas & Adams, R. J.** Plain English for Cops. LC 99-66963. 152p. 1999. pap. 15.00 (*0-89089-846-4*) Carolina Acad Pr.

Meier, Nicholas, jt. auth. see Close, Daryl.

Meier, Norman C., ed. Studies in the Psychology of Art, Vol. 2. (Psychological Monographs General & Applied: Vol. 48). 1974. reprint ed. 55.00 (*0-8115-1447-1*) Periodicals Srv.

— Studies in the Psychology of Art, Vol. 3. LC 73-2977. (Classics in Psychology Ser.). 1976. reprint ed. 15.95 (*0-405-05149-2*) Ayer.

Meier-Oeser, Stephan. Die Spur des Zeichens: Das Zeichen und Seine Funktion in der Philosophie des Mittelalters und der Fruhen Neuzeit. xix, 483p. 1997. 169.00 (*3-11-015526-5*) De Gruyter.

Meier, Paul. Consejos a los Padres de Ninos Preescolar. (Serie Enfoque a la Familia - Focus on the Family Ser.).Tr. of Advice to Parents of Preschoolers. (SPA.). 21p. 1994. pap. 1.99 (*1-56063-334-4*, 497427) Editorial Unilit.

— Don't Let Jerks Get the Best of You. 256p. 1995. pap. 11.99 (*0-7852-8019-7*) Nelson.

— Happiness Is a Choice for Teens. LC 96-41864. (J). 1997. pap. 12.99 (*0-7852-7574-6*) Nelson.

— Que los Odiosos No Acaben Contigo!Tr. of Don't Let the Jerks Get the Best of You. (SPA.). 1997. 10.99 (*0-88113-412-0*, B001-4120) Caribe Betania.

— El Tercer Milenio.Tr. of Third Millenium. (SPA.). 313p. 1995. 11.99 (*0-88113-307-8*, B001-3078) Caribe Betania.

— The Third Millennium. LC 93-18464. 320p. 1993. pap. 12.99 (*0-8407-7571-7*) Nelson.

— Tu Puedes Evitar el Divorcio. (Serie Tu Puedes - You Can Ser.).Tr. of You Can Avoid Divorce. (SPA.). 24p. pap. 1.79 (*1-56063-156-2*, 490490) Editorial Unilit.

Meier, Paul & Ratcliff, Donald. Raising Your Child: From Birth to Twelve. 3rd abr. ed. 160p. (C). (gr. 13). 1999. mass mkt. 5.99 (*0-8007-8663-7*, Spire) Revell.

Meier, Paul & Wise, Robert. Beyond the Millennium. LC 97-36564. 300p. 1998. pap. 12.99 (*0-7852-7196-1*) Nelson.

— The Secret Code: A Novel. LC 98-38983. 324p. 1999. pap. 12.99 (*0-7852-7090-6*) Nelson.

Meier, Paul & Wise, Robert L. The Fourth Millennium. 324p. 1996. pap. 12.99 (*0-7852-8149-5*) Nelson.

Meier, Paul, et al. Introduction to Psychology & Counseling: Christian Perspectives & Applications. 2nd ed. LC 91-9525. (Illus.). 368p. 1991. 34.99 (*0-8010-6275-6*) Baker Bks.

— WWJD? The Question That Will Change Your Life: A Devotional. LC 98-21709. 192p. 1998. 12.99 (*0-7852-7521-5*) Nelson.

Meier, Paul, jt. auth. see Meier, Richard.

Meier, Paul, jt. auth. see Minirth, Frank B.

Meier, Paul D. Mega Millennium Series: Third, Fourth & Beyond. 1998. 15.99 (*0-7852-6971-1*) Nelson.

Meier, Paul D., et al. Christian Childrearing & Personality Development. 2nd ed. LC 93-23808. 256p. (YA). (gr. 10). 1996. pap. 10.99 (*0-8010-5611-X*) Baker Bks.

Meier, Paul D., jt. auth. see Minirth, Frank B.

Meier, Peg. Bring Warm Clothes: Letters & Photos from Minnesota's Past. LC 81-11236. (Illus.). 340p. (Orig.). 1981. pap. 19.95 (*0-932272-06-1*) Neighbors Pub.

— Coffee Made Her Insane: And Other Nuggets from Old Minnesota Newspapers. (Illus.). 314p. 1988. pap. 14.95 (*0-933387-01-6*) Neighbors Pub.

— The Last of the Tearoom Ladies: And Other Minnesota Tales. (Illus.). 240p. (Orig.). 1990. pap. 9.95 (*0-933387-02-4*) Neighbors Pub.

— Too Hot, Went to Lake: Seasonal Photos from Minnesota's Past. (Illus.). (Orig.). 1993. pap. 24.95 (*0-933387-03-2*) Neighbors Pub.

Meier, Peg & Wood, Dave. The Pie Lady of Winthrop: And Other Minnesota Tales. (Illus.). 244p. (Orig.). 1985. pap. 8.95 (*0-933387-00-8*) Neighbors Pub.

Meier, Peter & Munasinghe, Mohan. Incorporating Environmental Concerns into Power Sector Decision-Making: A Case Study of Sri Lanka. LC 93-45458. (Environment Papers: No. 6). 176p. 1994. pap. 22.00 (*0-8213-2746-1*, 12746) World Bank.

Meier, Peter, jt. auth. see Hobbs, B. F.

Meier, Peter, jt. auth. see Munasinghe, Mohan.

Meier, Peter C. & Zund, Richard E. Statistical Methods in Analytical Chemistry. LC 92-27288. (Chemical Analysis Ser.: Vol. 123). 344p. 1993. 89.95 incl. disk (*0-471-58454-1*) Wiley.

***Meier, Philipp.** Autonomie und Souveranitat Oder das Scheitern der Sprache: Hegel Im Denken Von Georges Bataille. (Europaische Hochschulschriften Serie: Bd. 574). 180p. 1999. 30.95 (*3-906761-59-2*, Pub. by P Lang) P Lang Pubng.

Meier, R. H., III, jt. ed. see Atkins, D. J.

Meier, Regula A. Liechtenstein. LC 94-160591. (World Bibliographical Ser.). 146p. 1993. lib. bdg. 63.00 (*1-85109-201-3*) ABC-CLIO.

Meier, Richard. Ackerberg House & Addition. LC 96-5627. (Illus.). 72p. 1996. pap. 19.95 (*1-885254-27-X*, Pub. by Monacelli Pr) Penguin Putnam.

— Building the Getty. LC 97-29326. (Illus.). 204p. 1997. 35.00 (*0-375-40043-5*) Knopf.

— Building the Getty. LC 99-20219. 224p. 1999. pap. 24.95 (*0-520-21730-6*, Pub. by U CA Pr) Cal Prin Full Svc.

— Dante O. Benini: Intuition & Precision/intuizione E Rigore. 1999. pap. text 25.00 (*88-7838-059-8*) L'Arca IT.

— Richard Meier, Architect. Koshalek, Richard & Hutt, Dana, eds. LC 99-35830. (Illus.). 336p. 1999. text 60.00 (*1-58093-044-1*, Pub. by Monacelli Pr) Penguin Putnam.

— Richard Meier, Architect, Vol. 2. LC 90-48765. (Illus.). 432p. 1991. 65.00 (*0-8478-1320-7*, Pub. by Rizzoli Intl) St Martin.

— Richard Meier, Architect, Vol. 2. abr. ed. LC 90-48765. (Illus.). 432p. 1991. pap. 49.50 (*0-8478-1321-5*, Pub. by Rizzoli Intl) St Martin.

— Richard Meier's Barcelona. LC 97-28060. 1997. pap. 25.00 (*1-885254-56-3*, Pub. by Monacelli Pr) Penguin Putnam.

***Meier, Richard & Allen, Stan.** Richard Meier, Architect. LC 99-35830. 1999. 45.00 (*1-58093-061-1*, Pub. by Monacelli Pr) Penguin Putnam.

Meier, Richard & Meier, Paul. 7 Secrets for a Happy Family. alternate ed. 128p. (gr. 12). 1997. mass mkt. 4.99 (*0-8007-8642-4*, Family Foundati, Spire) Revell.

Meier, Richard & Partners Staff & Brawne, Michael. The Getty Center: Los Angeles, 1997. LC 99-170850. (Illus.). 120p. 1998. pap. 29.95 (*0-7148-3799-7*) Phaidon Pr.

Meier, Richard L. Urban Futures Observed: In the Asian Third World. LC 79-28624. (Policy Studies on International Development). 256p. 1980. 78.00 (*0-08-025954-5*, Pergamon Pr) Elsevier.

Meier, Rick, jt. auth. see Simms, Phil.

Meier, Robert F., ed. Major Forms of Crime. (Criminal Justice System Annuals Ser.: Vol. 21). 320p. (Orig.). (C). 1984. pap. text 26.00 (*0-8039-2095-4*) Sage.

— Major Forms of Crime. LC 84-15953. (Sage Criminal Justice System Annuals Ser.: Vol. 21). 247p. (Orig.). 1984. reprint ed. pap. 76.60 (*0-608-02790-1*, 206385700007) Bks Demand.

— Theoretical Methods in Criminology. LC 84-27716. 247p. reprint ed. pap. 76.60 (*0-8357-4831-6*, 203776800009) Bks Demand.

***Meier, Robert F., et al, eds.** The Process & Structure of Crime. (Criminal Events & Crime Analysis Advances in Criminological Theory Ser.: Vol. 9). 317p. 2000. 44.95 (*0-7658-0004-7*) Transaction Pubs.

Meier, Robert F. & Geis, Gilbert. Victimless Crime? Prostitution, Drugs, Homosexuality, Abortion. LC 96-37333. 210p. (Orig.). (C). 1997. pap. text. write for info. (*0-935732-46-2*) Roxbury Pub Co.

Meier, Robert F., jt. auth. see Clinard, Marshall B.

Meier, Robert F., jt. auth. see Miethe, Terance D.

Meier, Robert J., et al, eds. Evolutionary Models & Studies in Human Diversity. (World Anthropology Ser.). xiv, 376p. 1978. 58.50 (*90-279-7640-6*) Mouton.

Meier, Rudolf, jt. auth. see Wheeler, Quentin.

Meier-Ruge, W., ed. CNS Aging & Its Neuropharmacology: Experimental & Clinical Aspects. (Interdisciplinary Topics in Gerontology Ser.: Vol. 15). (Illus.). 1979. pap. 76.75 (*3-8055-2980-5*) S Karger.

— Die Dementielle Hirnerkrankung im Alter. (Geriatrie fuer die Taegliche Praxis Ser.: Vol. 3). viii, 216p. 1993. pap. 28.00 (*3-8055-4509-6*) S Karger.

— Dementing Brain Disease in Old Age. (Teaching & Training in Geriatric Medicine Ser.: Vol. 3). viii, 216p. 1993. pap. 31.50 (*3-8055-4478-2*) S Karger.

— The Elderly Patient in General Practice. (Teaching & Training in Geriatric Medicine Ser.: Vol. 1). viii, 256p. 1988. pap. 31.50 (*3-8055-4476-6*) S Karger.

— Le Malade Age en Pratique Medicale. (Geriatrie en Pratique Quotidienne Ser.: Vol. 1). viii, 256p. 1990. pap. 31.50 (*3-8055-5292-0*) S Karger.

— Patologie Vascolari Cerebrali Dell'Anziano. (Insegnamento E Formazione in Medicina Geriatrica Ser.: Vol. 2). viii, 188p. 1991. pap. 24.50 (*3-8055-5365-X*) S Karger.

— I Paziente Anziano Nella Pratica Medica. viii, 256p. 1990. pap. 31.50 (*3-8055-5286-6*) S Karger.

— Vascular Brain Disease in Old Age. (Teaching & Training in Geriatric Medicine Ser.: Vol. 2). viii, 188p. 1989. pap. 24.50 (*3-8055-4477-4*) S Karger.

— Vaskulaere Hirnerkrankung im Alter. (Geriatrie fuer die Taegliche Praxis Ser.: Vol. 2). viii, 188p. 1989. pap. 21.00 (*3-8055-4508-8*) S Karger.

Meier-Ruge, W., ed. see Workshop on Advances in Experimental Pharmacology.

Meier, Samuel A. Speaking of Speaking: Marking Direct Discourse in the Hebrew Bible. LC 92-16149. (Supplements to Vetus Testamentum Ser.: Vol. 46). xvi, 386p. 1992. 139.50 (*90-04-09602-7*) Brill Academic Pubs.

Meier, Scott T. The Elements of Counseling. LC 88-18754. 85p. (C). 1988. pap. 9.00 (*0-534-09900-9*) Brooks-Cole.

Meier, Scott T., jt. auth. see Davis, Susan.

Meier, Shirley. Shadow's Daughter. 1991. per. 4.99 (*0-671-72096-1*) Baen Bks.

Meier, Shirley, et al. Shadow's Son. 1991. per. 4.99 (*0-671-72091-0*) Baen Bks.

Meier, Shirley, jt. auth. see Stirling, S. M.

***Meier, Susan.** The Baby Bequest: (Brewster Baby Boom) (Silhouette Romance Ser.: No. 1420). 2000. per. 3.50 (*0-373-19420-X*, 1-19420-8) Harlequin Bks.

— Bringing up Babies. (Romance Ser.: Vol. 142). 2000. mass mkt. 3.50 (*0-373-19427-7*) Silhouette.

Meier, Susan. Guess What? We're Married! Texas Family Ties. (Silhouette Romance Ser.: No. 1338). 1998. per. 3.50 (*0-373-19338-6*, 1-19338-2) Silhouette.

***Meier, Susan.** His Expectant Neighbor. (Silhouette Romance Ser.: Vol. 1468). 2000. mass mkt. 3.50 (*0-373-19468-4*, 1-19468-7) Harlequin Bks.

— Hunter's Vow. 2001. mass mkt. 3.50 (*0-373-19487-0*, 1-19487-7) Silhouette.

Meier, Susan. Husband from 9 to 5 (Loving the Boss) (Silhouette Romance Ser.: No. 1354). 1999. per. 3.50 (*0-373-19354-8*, 1-19354-9) Harlequin Bks.

— In Care of the Sheriff. 1998. per. 3.50 (*0-373-19283-5*, 1-19283-0) Silhouette.

— Merry Christmas, Daddy. 1996. per. 3.25 (*0-373-19192-8*, 1-19192-3) Silhouette.

***Meier, Susan.** Oh, Babies! (Romance Ser.: Vol. 144). 2000. per. 3.50 (*0-373-19433-1*) Silhouette.

Meier, Susan. The Rancher & the Heiress: Texas Family Ties. (Romance Ser.: No. 1374). 1999. per. 3.50 (*0-373-19374-2*, 1-19374-7, Harlequin) Harlequin Bks.

— Stand-In Mom. (Romance Ser.). 1994. per. 2.75 (*0-373-19022-0*, 1-19022-2) Harlequin Bks.

— Temporarily Hers. 1995. per. 2.99 (*0-373-19109-X*, 1-19109-7) Silhouette.

— Wife in Training. (Romance Ser.). 1996. per. 3.25 (*0-373-19184-7*, 1-19184-0) Silhouette.

Meier, T. & Fahrenholz, F., eds. A Laboratory Guide to Biotin-Labeling in Biomolecule Analysis. LC 96-11381. 1996. write for info. (*0-8176-5206-X*) Birkhauser.

— A Laboratory Guide to Biotin-Labeling in Biomolecule Analysis. LC 96-11381. 240p. 1996. 89.50 (*3-7643-5206-X*) Birkhauser.

Meier, Thomas J. Ed Tangen, the Pictureman: A Photographic History of the Boulder Region, Early Twentieth Century. (Illus.). 384p. (Orig.). 1994. pap. 29.95 (*0-9641297-1-X*) Boulder Creek.

Meier, Traci, jt. auth. see Pitti, Mary J.

Meier, Urs & Betti, Raimondo, eds. Recent Advances in Bridge Engineering: Advanced Rehabilitation, Durable Materials, Non Destructive Evaluation & Management. LC 97-40518. 408p. 1997. 30.00 (*0-9659573-0-6*) Col Univ Dept.

An Asterisk (*) at the beginning of an entry indicates that the title is appearing for the first time.

Meier, Viktor. Yugoslavia: History of Its Demise. LC 98-32356. 1999. pap. 25.00 (*0-415-18596-3*) Routledge.
— Yugoslavia: History of Its Demise. LC 98-32356. 1999. text 85.00 (*0-415-18595-5*) Routledge.
Meier, W. M. & Uytterhoeven, J. B., eds. Molecular Sieves: The 3rd International Conference Co-Sponsored by the Eidgenossische Technische Hochschule & the Swiss Chemical Society at Zurich, Switzerland, Sept. 3-7, 1973. LC 73-83768. (Advances in Chemistry Ser.: Vol. 121). 648p. 1973. reprint ed. pap. 200.00 (*0-608-03899-7*, 206434600008) Bks Demand.
Meier, Winfried. Flora & Vegetation des Avila-Nationalparks (Venezuela/Kuestenkordillere) Unter Besonderer Beruecksichtigung der Nebelwaldstufe. (Dissertationes Botanicae Ser.). (GER., Illus.). 486p. 1998. pap. 78.00 (*3-443-64208-X*) Balogh.
Meierhoefer, Barbara. Mandatory Minimum Penalties in the Federal Criminal Justice System. (Illus.). 244p. 1997. reprint ed. pap. text 45.00 (*0-7881-4677-7*) DIANE Pub.
Meierhofer, Maynard C. A Simple Way to Solve the Health Care Crisis: Both the Health Care & the Cost of Health Care. 1995. 12.95 (*0-533-11353-9*) Vantage.
Meierotto, Brigid, jt. auth. see Bukowiecki, Angeline.
Meiers, David D. From Mott to May-Port. unabridged ed. (Illus.). v, 144p. (Orig.). 1997. pap. 12.95 (*0-9657945-0-4*) JEM Sales.
Meiers, Marion, jt. auth. see McGregor, Robert.
Meiers, Michael. Was Jonestown a CIA Experiment? A Review of the Evidence. LC 88-30698. (Studies in American Religion: Vol. 35). (Illus.). 575p. 1988. 119.95 (*0-88946-013-2*) E Mellen.
Meifang, Zhang, et al. Threads of Light: Chinese Embroidery from Suzhou & the Photography of Robert Glenn Ketchum. LC 98-31905. (UCLA Fowler Museum of Cultural History Textile Ser.: Vol. 3). (Illus.). 170p. 1999. 70.00 (*0-930741-70-6*); pap. 39.00 (*0-930741-71-4*) UCLA Fowler Mus.
Meiggs, Russell. The Athenian Empire. (Illus.). 648p. 1979. reprint ed. pap. text 45.00 (*0-19-814843-7*) OUP.
— Roman Ostia. 2nd ed. (Illus.). 684p. 1985. text 89.00 (*0-19-814810-0*) OUP.
— Trees & Timber in the Ancient Mediterranean World. (Illus.). 572p. 1983. text 125.00 (*0-19-814840-2*) OUP.
Meiggs, Russell & Lewis, David M., eds. A Selection of Greek Historical Inscriptions to the End of the Fifth Century B.C. 2nd rev. ed. 338p. 1989. pap. text 35.00 (*0-19-814487-3*) OUP.
Meigham, Michael. How to Design & Deliver Induction Training Programmes. 2nd ed. 128p. 1995. pap. 25.00 (*0-7494-1667-X*, Kogan Pg Educ) Stylus Pub VA.
Meighan, C. E. & Squier, R. J. Papers on California Archaeology, Nos. 19-20. (Reports of the University of California Archaeological Survey: No. 19). (Illus.). 58p. 1953. pap. 6.88 (*1-55567-340-6*) Coyote Press.
Meighan, Clement W. Archaeology & Anthropological Ethics. 19p. 1986. pap. text 1.95 (*0-937523-00-3*) Wormwood Pr.
— Archaeology for Money. LC 86-24607. (Illus.). 151p. (Orig.). (C). 1986. pap. text 10.95 (*0-937523-01-1*) Wormwood Pr.
Meighan, Clement W. & Baumhoff, Martin A. Papers on California Archaeology, Nos. 32-33. fac. ed. (Reports of the University of California Archaeological Survey: No. 30). 103p. 1955. reprint ed. pap. 11.56 (*1-55567-348-1*) Coyote Press.
Meighan, Clement W. & Gonsalves, W. C. Papers on California Archaeology, Nos. 30-31. fac. ed. (Reports of the University of California Archaeological Survey: No. 29). (Illus.). 56p. 1955. reprint ed. pap. 6.88 (*1-55567-347-3*) Coyote Press.
Meighan, Clement W. & Riddell, Francis A. The Maru Cult of the Pomo Indians: A California Ghost Dance Survival. 134p. 1972. 12.50 (*0-916561-51-8*) Southwest Mus.
Meighan, Clement W., jt. auth. see Sanger, Kay K.
Meighan, Roland. The Next Learning System: And Why Home-Schoolers Are Trailblazers. 1997. pap. 13.95 (*1-900219-04-2*, Pub. by Educ Heretics) Intl Spec Bk.
Meighan, Thomas. An Investigation of the Self-Concept of Blind & Visually Handicapped Adolescents. LC 79-155921. 49p. reprint ed. pap. 30.00 (*0-608-16875-0*, 202735100055) Bks Demand.
Meighen, Arthur. The Greatest Englishman of History. LC 76-51374. (Studies in Shakespeare: No. 24). 1977. lib. bdg. 49.00 (*0-8383-2136-4*) M S G Haskell Hse.
Meighen, Mary, jt. auth. see Pratt, Marjorie.
Meigret. Traite Touchant . . . L'Escrite Francoise. Cameron, ed. (Exeter French Texts Ser.: Vol. 33). (FRE.). 121p. Date not set. pap. text 19.95 (*0-85989-039-2*, Pub. by Univ Exeter Pr) Northwestern U Pr.
Meigs. Accounting. 11th ed. (Ready Notes Ser.: Vol. 1). 1998. pap. 16.25 (*0-07-303907-1*) McGraw.
— Accounting. 11th ed. (Ready Notes Ser.: Vol. 2). 144p. 1998. pap. 16.25 (*0-07-303908-X*) McGraw.
— Accounting, Vol. 1. 11th ed. 1998. pap., student ed. 25.31 (*0-07-303909-8*) McGraw.
— Financial Accounting Te! 1998. 64.50 (*0-07-233833-4*) McGraw.
— Financial Accounting U. S. General Ledger. 9th ed. 1998. 16.25 (*0-07-847704-2*) McGraw.
— Student Accounting. 11th ed. 1999. text 12.00 (*0-07-236878-0*) McGraw.
Meigs, A. James. Free Reserves & the Money Supply. LC 62-17136. (Economic Research Studies). 1992. lib. bdg. 10.00 (*0-226-51901-5*) U Ch Pr.
Meigs, A. James & Goodman, John C. Federal Deposit Insurance Corp. A Case for Radical Reform. 1990. pap. 10.00 (*0-943802-58-X*, 155) Natl Ctr Pol.
Meigs, A. James, jt. auth. see Goodman, John C.
Meigs, Alexander J. Free Reserves & the Money Supply. LC 62-17136. (University of Chicago Economics Research Center Studies in Economics). (Illus.). 134p. reprint ed. pap. 41.60 (*0-608-09020-4*, 206965500005) Bks Demand.
Meigs, Anna S. Food, Sex & Pollution: A New Guinea Religion. 196p. (C). 1988. pap. text 16.00 (*0-8135-1306-5*) Rutgers U Pr.
Meigs, Cornelia. Invincible Louisa: The Story of the Author of Little Women. 256p. (J). (gr. 3-7). 1995. pap. 5.95 (*0-316-56594-6*) Little.
— Invincible Louisa: The Story of the Author of Little Women. LC 68-21174. 1968. 11.05 (*0-606-09471-7*, Pub. by Turtleback) Demco.
— Invisible Louisa. 256p. (J). (gr. 4-6). 1988. pap. 3.50 (*0-590-44818-8*) Scholastic Inc.
— Swift Rivers. (Newbery Honor Roll Ser.). (YA). 1994. 12.05 (*0-606-06792-2*, Pub. by Turtleback) Demco.
— Swift Rivers. LC 94-2339. (Newberry Honor Roll Ser.). (Illus.). 288p. (J). (gr. 4-7). 1994. reprint ed. pap. 6.95 (*0-8027-7419-9*) Walker & Co.
Meigs, Frances B. My Grandfather, Thornton W. Burgess: An Intimate Portrait. LC 98-17258. (Illus.). 192p. 1998. 21.95 (*1-889833-05-3*, Commonwealth Eds) Memoirs Unltd.
Meigs, Jonathan. Corbin. The Corbins of Virginia: Genealogical Record of the Descendants of Henry Corbin, Who Settled in Virginia in 1654. 49p. 1997. reprint ed. pap. 11.00 (*0-8328-8050-7*); reprint ed. lib. bdg. 21.00 (*0-8328-8049-3*) Higginson Bk Co.
Meigs, Mark. Optimism at Armageddon: Voices of American Participants in World War I. 280p. (C). 1997. text 45.00 (*0-8147-5548-8*) NYU Pr.
Meigs, Mary. The Box Closet. 224p. 1987. pap. 14.95 (*0-88922-253-3*, Pub. by Talonbks) Genl Dist Srvs.
— In the Company of Strangers. LC 93-128414. (Illus.). 176p. 1991. pap. 13.95 (*0-88922-294-0*, Pub. by Talonbks) Genl Dist Srvs.
— Lily Briscoe: A Self-Portrait. 264p. 1981. pap. 16.95 (*0-88922-195-2*, Pub. by Talonbks) Genl Dist Srvs.
— The Medusa Head. LC 83-91368. 160p. 1983. pap. 12.95 (*0-88922-210-X*, Pub. by Talonbks) Genl Dist Srvs.
— The Time Being. LC 98-135103. 176p. 1997. pap. 12.95 (*0-88922-374-2*, Pub. by Talonbks) Genl Dist Srvs.
Meigs, Mary A., jt. auth. see Meigs, Robert F.
Meigs, Montgomery C. Slide Rules & Submarines: American Scientists & Subsurface Warfare in World War 2. LC 90-5793. (Illus.). 295p. 1990. per. 12.00 (*0-16-018591-2*, 008-020-01193-2) USGPO.
Meigs, Robert F. Accounting: The Basis for Business Decisions. 9th ed. 1993. pap. text. write for info. (*0-07-043071-3*); pap. text. write for info. (*0-07-043072-1*) McGraw.
— Accounting--The Basis for Business Decisions. 11th ed. LC 98-39391. 1136p. 1998. 89.69 (*0-07-289709-0*) McGraw.
— Financial Accounting. 8th rev. ed. LC 94-21842. (C). 1994. text 68.74 (*0-07-043344-5*) McGraw.
— Financial Accounting. 9th ed. LC 97-24229. 896p. (C). 1997. 87.81 (*0-07-043436-0*) McGraw.
— Financial Accounting. 10th ed. 2000. 68.74 (*0-07-231637-3*) McGraw.
Meigs, Robert F. & Meigs, Mary A. Accounting: The Basis for Business Decisions. 10th ed. (C). 1995. pap., student ed. 25.31 (*0-07-043202-3*) McGraw.
Meigs, Robert F. & Meigs, Walter B. Financial Accounting. 8th ed. (C). 1995. pap. text, student ed. 22.50 (*0-07-043350-X*) McGraw.
— Financial Accounting/Accounting Worksheets. 8th ed. (C). 1994. text 23.00 (*0-07-043343-7*) McGraw.
Meigs, Robert F., et al. Accounting: The Basis for Business Decisions. 10th ed. LC 95-41255. (C). 1995. text 68.75 (*0-07-043360-7*) McGraw.
— Accounting: The Basis for Business Decisions, Chs. 1-15, Worksheets A. 10th ed. LC 95-41255. (C). 1995. pap. text 23.44 (*0-07-043203-1*) McGraw.
— Accounting: The Basis for Business Decisions, Chs. 14-26, Worksheets A. 10th ed. (C). 1995. pap. text 23.44 (*0-07-043204-X*) McGraw.
***Meigs, Robert F., et al.** Accounting: The Basis for Business Decisions, Ch. 1-14, Vol. 1. 332p. (C). 1998. pap. 23.44 (*0-07-303910-1*) McGrw-H Hghr Educ.
— Accounting: The Basis for Business Decisions, Ch. 15-24 Working Papers, Vol. 2. 224p. (C). 1998. pap. 23.44 (*0-07-303911-X*) McGrw-H Hghr Educ.
Meigs, Robert F., et al. Accounting: The Basis for Business Decisions, Student Interactive Templates (Excel) (C). 1996. pap. text 25.00 (*0-07-840794-X*) McGraw.
Meigs, Robert F., jt. auth. see Meigs, Walter B.
Meigs, Walter B. & Meigs, Robert F. Accounting: The Basis for Business Decisions. (Illus.). 1136p. (C). 1983. disk 12.50 (*0-07-041617-6*); Apple II 12.50 (*0-07-041616-8*) McGraw.
Meigs, Walter B., jt. auth. see Meigs, Robert F.
Meigs, William M. Growth of the Consitution in the Federal Convention of 1787: An Effort to Trace the Origin & Development of Each Separate Clause from Its First Suggestion in That Body to the Form Finally Approved Containing Also a Facsimile of a Heretofore Unpublished Manuscript of the First Draft of the Instrument Made for Use in the Committee of Detail. 374p. 1987. reprint ed. 45.00 (*0-8377-2436-8*, Rothman) W S Hein.
— Relation of the Judiciary to the Constitution. LC 73-124896. (American Constitutional & Legal History Ser). 1971. reprint ed. lib. bdg. 35.00 (*0-306-71988-6*) Da Capo.
Meihy, Jose C., ed. see De Jesus, Carolina M.
Meij, Lestse, et al. Haute Couture & Pret-A-Porter: Mode 1750-2000, 1. LC 99-183012. (Illus.). 128p. 1999. pap. text 30.00 (*90-400-9290-7*) Waandrs.
Meij, A. W., jt. ed. see Luijten, Ger.
Meij, Dick Van der, see Van der Meij, Dick.
Meij, H. Van der, see Van der Meij, H.
Meij, J. L. Depreciation & Replacement Policy. (Accounting Ser.). 248p. 1986. text 15.00 (*0-8240-7884-5*) Garland.
Meijard, E., jt. auth. see Rijksen, H. D.
Meijboom, Alfred P. & Prins, Corien, eds. The Law of Information Technology in Europe, 1992: A Comparison with the U. S. A. (Computer - Law Ser.: Vol. 9). 1991. pap. 67.00 (*90-6544-554-4*) Kluwer Law Intl.
Meijboom, B. R. Planning in Decentralized Firms. (Lecture Notes in Economics & Mathematical Systems Ser.: Vol. 289). x, 168p. 1987. 33.90 (*0-387-17795-7*) Spr-Verlag.
Meijboom, Erik J. Textbook of Fetal Cardiology. 300p. 1997. text. write for info. (*0-7817-0295-X*) Lppncott W & W.
Meijboom, Hajo U. A History & Critique of the Origin of the Marcan Hypothesis, 1835-1866: A Contemporary Report Rediscovered. Kiwiet, John J., ed. & tr. by. (New Gospel Studies: No. 8). 190p. 1992. text 25.00 (*0-86554-407-7*, MUP/H330) Mercer Univ Pr.
Meijden, R. Van der, see Van der Meijden, R.
Meijer, ed. New Perspectives in Special Educational Needs. 176p. (C). 1996. pap. 24.99 (*0-415-08337-0*) Routledge.
Meijer, Anton & Peeters, Paul. Computer Network Architectures. LC 82-22165. (Electrical Engineering, Telecommunications, & Signal Processing Ser.). 396p. (C). 1982. pap. text 56.95 (*0-7167-8075-5*, Computer Sci Pr) W H Freeman.
Meijer, D. J., ed. Natural Phenomena: Their Meaning, Depiction & Description in the Ancienct Near East. 316p. pap. 53.25 (*0-444-85759-1*, North Holland) Elsevier.
Meijer, Erik, jt. ed. see Jeuring, Johan.
Meijer, G. C., ed. see Van Herwaarden, A. W.
Meijer, Gerrit, ed. New Perspectives on Austrian Economics. LC 94-32065. 272p. (C). (gr. 13). 1995. 90.00 (*0-415-12283-X*, C0482) Routledge.
Meijer, Jan M. Knowledge & Revolution: The Russian Colony in Zuerich (1870-1873); A Contribution to the Study of Russian Populism. 1955. pap. 79.50 (*0-317-07649-3*) Elliots Bks.
Meijer, Jan M., ed. Dutch Contributions to the Eighth International Congress of Slavists, Zagerb, Ljubljana, September 3-9, 1978. iv, 425p. 1979. pap. 82.00 (*90-272-2010-7*) J Benjamins Pubng Co.
Meijer, Jan M., ed. see Dostoyevsky, Fyodor.
Meijer, L., et al. Progress in Cell Cycle Research, Vol. 3. 326p. 1998. 95.00 (*0-306-45810-1*, Kluwer Plenum) Kluwer Academic.
Meijer, Laurent, et al, eds. Progress in Cell Cycle Research, Vol. 2. 292p. (C). 1997. text 95.00 (*0-306-45507-2*, Kluwer Plenum) Kluwer Academic.
Meijer, Laurent & Guidet, Silvana, eds. Progress in Cell Cycle Research, Vol. 1. (Illus.). 384p. 1996. 95.00 (*0-306-45280-4*, Kluwer Plenum) Kluwer Academic.
***Meijer, Laurent, et al.** Progress in Cell Cycle Research. 256p. 2000. 120.00 (*0-306-46305-9*, Kluwer Plenum) Kluwer Academic.
Meijer, Maaike, ed. The Defiant Muse: Dutch & Flemish Feminist Poems from the Middle Ages to the Present. LC 97-34847. (Defiant Muse Ser.). 240p. 1998. pap. 17.95 (*1-55861-152-5*); lib. bdg. 42.00 (*1-55861-151-7*) Feminist Pr.
Meijer, Marinus J. Introduction to Modern Criminal Law in China. LC 76-29206. (Studies in Chinese Government & Law). 214p. 1976. reprint ed. lib. bdg. 62.50 (*0-313-26964-5*, U6964, Greenwood Pr) Greenwood.
Meijer, P. A. Plotinus on the Good or the 1 (Enneads) Vol. 9: An Analytical Commentary. (Amsterdam Classical Monographs (ACM): Vol. I). 397p. 1992. pap. 80.00 (*90-5063-082-0*, Pub. by Gieben) J Benjamins Pubng Co.
Meijer, P. A., jt. ed. see Bos, E. P.
Meijer, P. H., ed. Group Theory & Solid State Physics, Vol. 7. (International Science Review Ser.). x, 294p. 1964. text 306.00 (*0-677-00530-X*) Gordon & Breach.
— Quantum Statistical Mechanics, Vol. 7. (Documents on Modern Physics Ser.). x, 172p. (Orig.). 1966. text 235.00 (*0-677-01310-8*) Gordon & Breach.
Meijer, Reinder P. Literature of the Low Countries: A Short History of Dutch Literature in the Netherlands & Belgium. 1978. pap. 12.95 (*0-89197-825-9*); text 42.50 (*0-8057-3431-7*) Irvington.
Meijer, Rob R., ed. Person-Fit Reserach: Theory & Applications. 109p. 1995. pap. write for info. (*0-8058-9929-4*) L Erlbaum Assocs.
Meijer, Roel. Cosmopolitanism Identity & Authenticity in the Middle East. 250p. 1998. 75.00 (*0-7007-1059-0*, Pub. by Curzon Pr Ltd); pap. 29.95 (*0-7007-1056-6*, Pub. by Curzon Pr Ltd) Paul & Co Pubs.
Meijere, A. de, ed. Small Ring Compounds in Organic Synthesis V. (Topics in Current Chemistry Ser.: Vol. 178). (Illus.). x, 182p. 1996. 139.00 (*3-540-60495-2*) Spr-Verlag.
Meijere, Armin De, see De Meijere, Armin, ed.
Meijering, E. P. Athanasius Teil I: Die Dritte Rede Gegen die Arianer: Kapitel 1-25 Einleitung, Ubersetzung, Kommentar, (GER.). 276p. 1996. pap. 57.00 (*90-5063-187-8*, Pub. by Gieben) J Benjamins Pubng Co.
— Athanasius Teil II: Die Dritte Rede Gegen die Arianer: Kapitel 26-58. Ubersetzung und Kommentar. (GER.). 318p. 1997. pap. 65.00 (*90-5063-367-6*, Pub. by Gieben) J Benjamins Pubng Co.
— Athanasius de Incarnatione Verbi. (GER.). 431p. (C). 1989. pap. 97.00 (*90-5063-023-5*, Pub. by Gieben) J Benjamins Pubng Co.
— Augustine: De Fide et Symbolo: Introduction, Translation, Commentary. 197p. (C). 1987. pap. 40.00 (*90-70265-78-8*, Pub. by Gieben) J Benjamins Pubng Co.
— Die Hellenisierung des Christentums im Urteil Adolf von Harnacks: Proceedings of the Colloquium, Amsterdam, the Netherlands, 15-18 October 1990. (Verhandelingen der Koninklijke Nederlandse Akademie van Wetenschappen, Afd. Letterkunde, Nieuwe Reeks Ser.: No. 128). (ENG & GER.). 150p. 1985. 50.00 (*0-444-85623-4*) Elsevier.
— F. C. Baur Als Patristiker: Die Bedeutung Seiner Geschichtsplilosophie und Quellenforschung. (GER.). 193p. (C). 1986. pap. 40.00 (*90-70265-68-0*, Pub. by Gieben) J Benjamins Pubng Co.
— Der Ganze un der Wahre Luther. 46p. pap. 11.00 (*0-444-85582-3*) Elsevier.
— Die Geschichte der Christlichen Theologie im Urteil J. L. Von Mosheims. 460p. 1995. pap. 80.00 (*90-5063-437-0*, Pub. by Gieben) J Benjamins Pubng Co.
— Von Den Kirchenvatern Zu Karl Barth: Das Altkirchliche Dogma in der "Kerchlichen Dogmatik" (GER.). 513p. 1993. pap. 80.00 (*90-5063-126-6*, Pub. by Gieben) J Benjamins Pubng Co.
Meijering, Roos. Literary & Rhetorical Theories in Greek Scholia. xi, 327p. (C). 1987. 52.00 (*90-6980-011-X*, Pub. by Egbert Forsten) Hod1der & Stoughton.
Meijerink, Sander V. Conflict & Cooperation on the Scheldt River Basin: A Case Study of Decision Making on International Scheldt Issues Between 1967 & 1997. LC 99-18795. (Environment & Policy Ser.). 1999. write for info. (*0-7923-5650-0*) Kluwer Academic.
Meijers, Daniel. Ascetic Hasidism in Jerusalem: The Guardian-of-the-Faithful Community of Mea Shearim. LC 91-41067. (Studies in Judaism in Modern Times: Vol. 10). viii, 144p. 1992. 71.00 (*90-04-09562-4*) Brill Academic Pubs.
Meijler, A. P. Automation in Anesthesia: A Relief? (Illus.). 210p. 1987. 66.95 (*0-387-18204-7*) Spr-Verlag.
Meijler, F. L. & Burchell, H. B., eds. Professor Dirk Durrer: 35 Years of Cardiology in Amsterdam. 648p. 1986. text 135.00 (*0-444-85656-0*); pap. text. write for info. (*0-444-85654-4*) Elsevier.
Meijn, Robert. Mahakam. LC 98-85360. 192p. 1999. pap. 11.95 (*1-56315-193-6*, Pub. by SterlingHse) Natl Bk Netwk.
***Meikle.** Marx. LC 99-55612. 540p. 2000. 166.95 (*1-84014-707-5*) Ashgate Pub Co.
Meikle, Barry, ed. Ontario Legal Directory, 1999. annuals (Toronto Legal Directory Ser.). 1000p. 1999. 48.00 (*0-8020-4929-X*); write for info. (*0-8020-4930-3*) U of Toronto Pr.
Meikle, A. Wayne, ed. Hormone Replacement Therapy. LC 99-13398. (Contemporary Endocrinology Ser.: Vol. 13). (Illus.). 439p. 1999. 125.00 (*0-89603-601-4*) Humana.
Meikle, Barry H. Bastards I Have Sailed With. LC 98-169155. 173 p. 1997. write for info. (*0-473-04912-0*) The Bradbury Hse.
Meikle, Betty A., jt. auth. see Ireton, Donna S.
Meikle, Betty A. Forsaken: Official Strategy Guide. 1998. pap. 19.99 (*1-57840-995-0*) Acclaim Bks.
— Forsaken 64: Official Strategy Guide. 1998. pap. text 12.99 (*1-57840-997-7*) Acclaim Bks.
— Shadowman PC Strategy Guide. 1999. pap. 19.99 (*1-57840-992-6*) Acclaim Bks.
***Meikle, Betty A.** WWF: Warzone. (Illus.). 1998. pap. 12.99 (*1-57840-990-X*) Acclaim Bks.
Meikle, Denis. A History of Horrors: The Rise & Fall of the House of Hammer. (Scarecrow Filmmakers Ser.: No. 51). 472p. 1996. 55.00 (*0-8108-2959-2*) Scarecrow.
Meikle, Jeffrey. Design in the Contemporary World: A Paper Prepared from the Proceedings of the Stanford Design Forum 1988. 100p. (Orig.). 1989. write for info. (*0-318-65097-5*) Pentagram Design.
Meikle, Jeffrey L. American Plastic: A Cultural History. LC 95-15187. (Illus.). 500p. (C). 1995. text 49.95 (*0-8135-2234-X*) Rutgers U Pr.
***Meikle, Jeffrey L.** Twentieth Century Limited: Industrial Design in America, 1925-1939. (Illus.). 249p. 2000. reprint ed. pap. text 25.00 (*0-7881-6291-8*) DIANE Pub.
Meikle, Lyndel, ed. Very Close to Trouble: The Johnny Grant Memoir. (Illus.). 240p. 1996. 35.00 (*0-87422-140-4*); pap. 17.95 (*0-87422-139-0*) Wash St U Pr.
Meikle, R. D. Flora of Cyprus, Vol. 1. (Illus.). 832p. 1977. 40.00 (*0-9504876-3-5*, Pub. by Royal Botnic Grdns) Balogh.
— Flora of Cyprus: Pinaceae to Theligonaceae, Vol. 2. (Illus.). 1136p. 1985. 60.00 (*0-9504876-4-3*, Pub. by Royal Botnic Grdns) Balogh.
Meikle, Scott. Aristotle's Economic Thought. 224p. 1997. reprint ed. pap. text 21.00 (*0-19-815225-6*) OUP.
Meikle, W. Eric, et al, eds. Contemporary Issues in Human Evolution. (Memoirs of the California Academy of Sciences Ser.: Vol. 21). (Illus.). 204p. (Orig.). 1996. pap. 35.00 (*0-940228-45-9*) Calif Acad Sci.
Meikle, W. Eric & Parker, Sue T. Naming Our Ancestors: An Anthology of Hominid Taxonomy. (Illus.). 254p. (C). 1994. pap. text 15.95 (*0-88133-799-4*) Waveland Pr.
Meiklejohn, Alexander. Education Between Two Worlds. LC 71 167385. (Essay Index Reprint Ser.). 1977. reprint ed. 22.95 (*0-8369-2565-3*) Ayer.
— The Experimental College. LC 75-165724. (American Education, Ser, No. 2). 1977. reprint ed. 33.95 (*0-405-03712-0*) Ayer.
***Meiklejohn, Alexander.** Free Speech & Its Relation to Self-Government, 1948. LC 99-87204. 2000. write for info. (*1-58477-087-2*) Lawbk Exchange.
Meiklejohn, Alexander. Freedom & the College. LC 75-99641. (Essay Index Reprint Ser.). 1977. 21.95 (*0-8369-1990-4*) Ayer.

M

— Liberal College. LC 79-89203. (American Education: Its Men, Institutions, & Ideas. Series 1). 1975. reprint ed. 18.95 (*0-405-01441-4*) Ayer.
— What Does America Mean? 272p. (C). 1972. reprint ed. pap. 3.00 (*0-393-00658-1*) Norton.
Meiklejohn, Donald. Freedom & the Public: Public & Private Morality in America. LC 65-23650. 175p. reprint ed. pap. 54.30 (*0-608-15207-2*, 202740100055) Bks Demand.
Meiklejohn, J. M., tr. see Kant, Immanuel.
***Meiklejohn, Susan Turner.** Wages, Race, Skills & Space: Lessons from Employers in Detroit's Auto Industry. LC 99-51638. (Garland Reference Library of Social Science). 2000. write for info. (*0-8153-2844-3*) Garland.
Meiksins, Peter F. Engineering Labour: Technical Workers in Comparative Perspective. (C). 1996. 65.00 (*1-85984-994-6*) Routledge.
— Engineering Labour: Technical Workers in Comparative Perspective. (C). 1996. pap. 20.00 (*1-85984-135-X*, Pub. by Verso) Norton.
Meiksins-Wood, Ellen. Pristine Culture of Capitalism: Historical Essay on Old Regimes & Modern States. 200p. (C). 1991. pap. 18.00 (*0-86091-572-7*, Pub. by Verso) Norton.
Meikson, Z. H. & Thackray, Philip C. Electronic Design with Off-the-Shelf Integrated Circuits. 220p. 1980. 27.95 (*0-13-250282-8*, Parker Publishing Co) P-H.
Meil, Joanne. New World Plants & Their Uses: A Guide to Selected Literature & Genetic Resources 1980-1993. (Illus.). 39p. (Orig.). (C). 1995. pap. text 20.00 (*0-7881-1613-4*) DIANE Pub.
Meilach, Dona Z. The Best Bagels Are Made at Home. (Illus.). 176p. (Orig.). 1995. pap. 8.95 (*1-55867-131-5*, Nitty Gritty Ckbks) Bristol Pub Ent CA.
— The Best 50 Bruschettas. LC 99-213384. (Best 50 Ser.). 80p. 1999. pap. 4.95 (*1-55867-220-6*) Bristol Pub Ent CA.
— The Best 50 Homemade Liqueurs. LC 96-173656. (Best 50 Ser.). 80p. (Orig.). 1996. pap. 4.95 (*1-55867-141-2*) Bristol Pub Ent CA.
— Contemporary Stone Sculpture. LC 71-108070. (Illus.). 224p. 1987. pap. 24.95 (*0-88740-089-2*) Schiffer.
— Decorative & Sculptural Ironwork: Tools, Techniques, Inspiration. 2nd ed. LC 98-53076. 312p. 1999. write for info. (*0-7643-0790-8*) Schiffer.
— Gourmet Gifts. LC 98-125197. (Illus.). 176p. (Orig.). 1997. pap. 8.95 (*1-55867-176-5*, Nitty Gritty Ckbks) Bristol Pub Ent CA.
— Making Your Own Biscotti & Dunking Cookies. LC 96-226673. 1996. 14.00 (*0-517-70495-1*) Random.
— Marinades: Make Ordinary Foods Extraordinary. (Illus.). 176p. 1995. pap. 8.95 (*1-55867-119-6*, Nitty Gritty Ckbks) Bristol Pub Ent CA.
— Wraps & Roll-Ups. LC 99-191146. (Illus.). 176p. 1998. pap. 8.95 (*1-55867-209-5*) Bristol Pub Ent CA.
Meilach, Dona Z. & Mandel, Elias. Doctor Talks to Five to Eight Year Olds. (Illus.). 1988. pap. 5.50 (*0-318-37509-5*) Budlong.
Meilach, Dona Z., et al. Let's Learn Bible. LC 98-164997. 1991. 7.95 (*0-88125-399-5*) Ktav.
Meilach, Dona Z., jt. auth. see Birch, William G.
Meilach, Dona Z., jt. auth. see Davis, M. Edward.
Meilach, Michael D. There Shall Be One Christ: A Collection of Essays on Teilhard de Chardin. (Spirit & Life Ser.). x, 85p. 1968. pap. 2.50 (*1-57659-095-X*) Franciscan Inst.
Meilaender, Gilbert. The Taste for the Other: The Social & Ethical Thought of C. S. Lewis. 256p. 1998. pap. text 16.00 (*0-8028-4492-8*) Eerdmans.
***Meilaender, Gilbert.** Things That Count. 2000. 24.95 (*1-882926-36-6*) ISI Books.
Meilaender, Gilbert C. Bioethics: A Primer for Christians. LC 96-22967. 131p. 1996. pap. 10.00 (*0-8028-4234-8*) Eerdmans.
— Body, Soul, & Bioethics. LC 95-17486. 144p. (C). 1998. reprint ed. pap. text 15.00 (*0-268-02153-8*) U of Notre Dame Pr.
— Faith & Faithfulness: Basic Themes in Christian Ethics. LC 90-50966. (C). 1991. text 26.50 (*0-268-00982-1*) U of Notre Dame Pr.
— Faith & Faithfulness: Basic Themes in Christian Ethics. LC 90-50966. (C). 1992. pap. text 14.00 (*0-268-00983-X*) U of Notre Dame Pr.
— Friendship: A Study in Theological Ethics. LC 81-50459. (Revisions: A Series of Books on Ethics). 128p. 1985. pap. text 9.50 (*0-268-00969-4*) U of Notre Dame Pr.
— The Limits of Love: Some Theological Explorations. LC 87-42548. 156p. 1992. 30.00 (*0-271-00611-0*); pap. text 12.95 (*0-271-00862-8*); pap. text 12.95 (*0-271-00790-7*) Pa St U Pr.
Meilaender, Gilbert C., Jr. The Theory & Practice of Virtue. LC 83-40598. 208p. (C). 1984. pap. text 13.00 (*0-268-01853-7*) U of Notre Dame Pr.
Meilaender, Gilbert C., ed. Working: Its Meaning & Its Limits. (Ethics of Everyday Life Ser.). 272p. 2000. 25.00 (*0-268-01961-4*, Pub. by U of Notre Dame Pr); pap. 15.00 (*0-268-01962-2*, Pub. by U of Notre Dame Pr) Chicago Distribution Ctr.
Meilan, Chen, pref. Six Contemporary Chinese Women Writers. 374p. 1995. 8.95 (*7-5071-3175-0*, Pub. by Panda Bks) China Bks.
Meiland, Jack W. & Krausz, Michael, eds. Relativism: Cognitive & Moral. LC 81-19834. 272p. 1982. pap. 18.00 (*0-268-01612-7*) U of Notre Dame Pr.
Meile, B. Verhaltensauffaellige Schueler. (Sozialmedizinische und Paedagogische Jugendkunde Ser.: Band 16). xii, 84p. 1982. pap. 20.00 (*3-8055-3552-X*) S Karger.
Meile, Frank, ed. see Fraley, John.
Meilgaard, Morten C., et al. Sensory Evaluation Techniques. 2nd ed. rev. ed. 376p. 1991. boxed set 136.95 (*0-8493-4280-5*, TA418) CRC Pr.
— Sensory Evaluation Techniques. 3rd ed. LC 99-19553. 416p. 1999. boxed set 129.95 (*0-8493-0276-5*) CRC Pr.
Meilgaard, Morten C., jt. auth. see Carr.
Meilhac, Henri & Halevy, Ludovic. The Brazilian. Shapiro, Norman R., tr. from FRE. (Farce Ser.: Vol. 3). 56p. 1987. pap. 6.95 (*0-936839-59-7*) Applause Theatre Bk Pubs.
Meili, Neil. Buffalo Chips. 28p. (Orig.). 1996. pap. 7.00 (*1-890636-01-0*) New Tex Pr.
— Cowboys, Poets & Pilots. 48p. (Orig.). 1995. pap. 7.00 (*1-890636-03-7*) New Tex Pr.
— Prairie Boy on the Trail. 48p. (Orig.). 1997. pap. 7.00 (*1-890636-02-9*) New Tex Pr.
— Prairie Boy's Springtime. 24p. (Orig.). 1994. pap. 5.00 (*1-890636-00-2*) New Tex Pr.
Meilikhov, Evgenii Z., jt. auth. see Lazarev, Sergey D.
Meilikhov, Evgenii Z., jt. ed. see Grigoriev, Igor S.
Meilin, Zhu & Yusheng, Zhang. Internal Combustion Engines: Proceedings of the International Conference Wuhan, China, 22-24 October, 1997. (Illus.). xvi, 778p. 1997. 196.00 (*7-80003-394-5*) World Scientific Pub.
Meiling, Phillip S. The Paths of Heaven: The Evolution of Airpower Theory. LC 97-24531. (Illus.). 680p. 1997. pap. 39.00 (*1-58566-027-2*) Air Univ.
Meilinger, Phillip S. American Airpower Biography: A Survey of the Field. rev. ed. (Illus.). 65p. 1997. pap. 5.00 (*1-58566-011-6*) Air Univ.
Meilinger, Phillip S. Hoyt S. Vandenberg: The Life of a General. LC 88-45097. (Illus.). 294p. 1989. 11.95 (*0-253-32862-4*) Ind U Pr.
Meilland, Alain. Meilland: A Life in Roses. Keating, Richard C. & Keating, Louis Clark, trs. LC 83-14996. (Illus.). 176p. 1984. 26.95 (*0-8093-1111-9*) S Ill U Pr.
Meillassoux, Claude. The Anthropology of Slavery: The Womb of Iron & Gold. Dasnois, Alide, tr. 422p. 1991. pap. text 21.95 (*0-226-51912-0*); lib. bdg. 57.50 (*0-226-51911-2*) U Ch Pr.
— Urbanization of an African Community. LC 84-45538. (American Ethnological Society Monographs: No. 45). 1988. reprint ed. 30.00 (*0-404-62943-1*) AMS Pr.
Meillassoux, Claude, ed. Maidens, Meal & Money. Edholm, Felicity, tr. from FRE. LC 79-52834. (Themes in the Social Sciences Ser.). 200p. 1981. pap. text 24.95 (*0-521-29708-7*) Cambridge U Pr.
Meillet, A. Comparative Method in Historical Linguistics. Ford, G. B., Jr., tr. 1967. pap. 29.95 (*0-685-00758-8*) Adlers Foreign Bks.
Meillet, A., jt. auth. see Ernout, A.
Meillet, Antoine. Altarmenisches Elementarbuch. LC 80-24325. (Anatolian & Caucasian Studies). 228p. 1981. reprint ed. 50.00 (*0-88206-043-0*) Caravan Bks.
Meillet, Antoine & Buck, George C. Introduction a l'Etude Comparative des Langues Indo-Europeennes. LC 64-64958. (Alabama Linguistic & Philological Ser.: No. 3). (FRE.). 536p. 1964. pap. 166.20 (*0-7837-8394-9*, 205920500009) Bks Demand.
Meilleur, Brien A., et al. Hala & Wauke in Hawaii. (Bulletin in Anthropology Ser.: Vol. 7). (Illus.). 64p. (C). 1997. pap. 14.95 (*0-930897-96-X*) Bishop Mus.
Meilman, Patricia. Titian & the Altarpiece in Renaissance Venice. LC 98-51718. (Illus.). 288p. (C). 2000. 75.00 (*0-521-64095-4*) Cambridge U Pr.
Meilman, Philip, jt. auth. see Grayson, Paul.
Meilman, Philip W., jt. auth. see Grayson, Paul A.
Meilstrup, Jon W., ed. Imaging Atlas of the Normal Gallbladder & Its Variants. LC 93-44006. 160p. 1994. lib. bdg. 139.00 (*0-8493-4788-2*) CRC Pr.
Meima, Karla L., jt. auth. see Grant, Christin N.
Mein, Annemieke. Art of Annemieke Mein. 160p. 1997. pap. 50.00 (*0-85532-775-8*, Pub. by Srch Pr) A Schwartz & Co.
Mein, Annemmieke. The Art of Annemieke Mein: Wildlife Artist in Textiles. (Illus.). 160p. 1995. 50.00 (*1-879504-03-0*, 403-0, Pub. by Srch Pr) A Schwartz & Co.
Mein, Carolyn L. Different Bodies, Different Diets: Men's Edition. (Twenty-Five Body Type System Ser.). (Illus.). 546p. 1999. 29.95 (*0-9661381-1-2*) Visionware.
— Different Bodies, Different Diets: Women's Edition. (Twenty-Five Body Type System Ser.). (Illus.). 550p. 1999. 29.95 (*0-9661381-0-4*) Visionware.
***Mein, Carolyn L.** Releasing Emotional Patterns with Essential Oils. 2nd ed. 170p. 2000. pap. 11.95 (*0-9661381-4-7*, Pub. by Visionware) ACCESS Pubs Network.
Mein, Eric A. Keys to Health. 1995. mass mkt. 4.99 (*0-312-95616-9*, Pub. by Tor Bks) St Martin.
Mein, Eric A., ed. see Hunt, Anne E.
Mein, Margaret & Stockwell, Arthur H., eds. Winston Churchill & Christian Fellowship. 1996. pap. 35.00 (*0-7223-2694-2*, Pub. by A H S Ltd) St Mut.
Mein, R. G., jt. auth. see McMahon, T. A.
Meinander, Henrik, et al, eds. The Nordic World: Sports in Society. LC 97-43918. (Sport in the Global Society Ser.). 200p. (C). 1998. text 52.50 (*0-7146-4825-6*, Pub. by F Cass Pubs); pap. text 22.50 (*0-7146-4391-2*, Pub. by F Cass Pubs) Intl Spec Bk.
Meinardi, H., et al. Quantitative Assessment in Epilepsy Care. LC 93-26823. (NATO ASI Series A, Life Sciences: Series A, Vol. 255). (Illus.). 222p. (C). 1993. text 85.00 (*0-306-44620-0*) Plenum.
Meinardus, Gunter & Nurnberger, Gunter. Delay Equations, Approximation, & Application. (International Series of Numerical Mathematics: No. 74). 356p. 1985. 124.00 (*0-8176-1733-7*) Birkhauser.
Meinardus, Gunter, jt. ed. see Collatz, Lothar.
Meinardus, Otto F. The Holy Family in Egypt: In the Steps of the Tradition. 1987. pap. 12.50 (*977-424-129-0*, Pub. by Am Univ Cairo Pr) Col U Pr.
— Monks & Monasteries of the Egyptian Deserts. rev. ed. 200p. 1989. pap. 20.00 (*977-424-188-6*, Pub. by Am Univ Cairo Pr) Col U Pr.
— St. John of Patmos & the Seven Churches of Asia Minor. (Illus.). 150p. 1974. reprint ed. pap. 12.00 (*960-7269-15-2*, Pub. by Lycabettus Pr) Bosphorus Bks.
— St. John of Patmos & the Seven Churches of the Apocalypse. LC 78-51245. (In the Footsteps of the Saints Ser.). (Illus.). 160p. 1979. 17.50 (*0-89241-070-1*); pap. 6.95 (*0-89241-043-4*) Caratzas.
— St. Paul in Ephesus & the Cities of Galatia & Cyprus. LC 78-51246. (In the Footsteps of the Saints Ser.). (Illus.). 160p. 1979. 17.50 (*0-89241-071-X*); pap. 6.95 (*0-89241-044-2*) Caratzas.
— St. Paul in Greece. LC 78-51244. (In the Footsteps of the Saints Ser.). 160p. 1979. 17.50 (*0-89241-072-8*); pap. 6.95 (*0-89241-045-0*) Caratzas.
— St. Paul in Greece. 6th ed. (Illus.). 127p. 1972. reprint ed. pap. 12.00 (*960-7269-17-9*, Pub. by Lycabettus Pr) Bosphorus Bks.
— St. Paul's Last Journey. LC 78-51247. (In the Footsteps of the Saints Ser.). (Illus.). 160p. 1979. 17.50 (*0-89241-073-6*); pap. 6.95 (*0-89241-046-9*) Caratzas.
— Two Thousand Years of Coptic Christianity. LC 99-895732. 368p. 1999. 24.50 (*977-424-511-3*, Pub. by Am Univ Cairo Pr) Col U Pr.
Meinbach, Anita M. & Rothlein, Liz C. Legacies: Using Children's Literature in the Classroom. LC 94-34987. (C). 1995. pap. text, teacher ed. 18.00 (*0-673-55344-2*) Addson-Wesley Educ.
Meinbach, Anita M., jt. auth. see Rothlein, Liz C.
***Meinbach, Anita Meyer, et al.** The Complete Guide to Thematic Units: Creating the Integrated Curriculum. 2nd rev. ed. 356p. 2000. pap. text, teacher ed. 44.95 (*1-929024-10-X*, 417) CG Pubs Inc.
Meinck, Fritz & Mohle, Helmut. Elsevier's Dictionary of Water & Sewage Engineering in German, English, French & Italian: Woerterbuch fur das Wasserfach und Abwasserfach. 4th ed. (ENG, FRE, GER & ITA.). 661p. 1993. 395.00 (*0-8288-0961-5*, M 7889) Fr & Eur.
Meinck, Fritz & Mohle, K. Dictionary of Water & Sewage Engineering. 2nd rev. ed. (ENG, FRE, GER & ITA.). 738p. 1980. 274.75 (*0-444-99811-X*) Elsevier.
Meincke, Mike. Complete Guide to Stationary Gas Engines. (Illus.). 192p. 1996. pap. 29.95 (*0-7603-0121-2*) MBI Pubg.
Meinders, LaDonna K. Leaves in the Wind. LC 89-81374. (Illus.). 152p. (J). 1989. 15.95 (*0-934188-31-9*) Evans Pubns.
Meinders, Miriam, jt. auth. see Enns, Aiden S.
Meindert, Jong De. Wheel on the School. 1972. 10.05 (*0-606-05081-7*, Pub. by Turtleback) Demco.
Meinderts, Koos & Fienieg, Annette. The Rat of Few Words. Van Deventer, Eric, tr. from DUT. LC 97-23383. (Illus.). 25p. (J). 1998. 10.95 (*1-57379-072-9*, K1002) High-Scope.
Meindertsma, J. D. Income Diversity & Farming Systems: Modelling of Farming Households in Lombok, Indonesia LC 99-176506. xvi, 239 p. 1997. write for info. (*90-6832-115-3*, Pub. by Royal Tropical) Eiron.
Meindl, Dieter. American Fiction & the Metaphysics of the Grotesque. 264p. (C). 1996. 39.95 (*0-8262-1079-1*) U of Mo Pr.
Meindl, James D. Micropower Circuits. LC 68-28502. (Illus.). 258p. reprint ed. pap. 80.00 (*0-608-09956-2*, 201017800068) Bks Demand.
Meindl, James D., ed. Brief Lessons in High Technology. (Portable Stnaford Bks.). 249p. 1991. pap. 12.95 (*0-916318-41-9*) Stanford Alumni Assn.
Meindl, James R., et al, eds. Cognition Within & Between Organizations. LC 96-4525. (Organizational Science Ser.). 528p. 1996. 69.95 (*0-7619-0113-2*) Sage.
Meindl, Karl & Schroeder, Walter. Brandenburg D.1. LC 98-220800. (Great War Aircraft in Profile Ser.). (Illus.). 64p. 1997. pap. 24.95 (*1-891268-01-5*) Flying Machines.
Meine, Curt. Aldo Leopold: His Life & Work. LC 87-40367. (Illus.). 654p. 1991. reprint ed. pap. 27.95 (*0-299-11494-5*) U of Wis Pr.
***Meine, Curt.** Humans & Other Catastrophes: Perspectives on Extinction. (Illus.). 32p. 1999. pap. write for info. (*1-930465-07-6*) Ctr Biodiv & Conserv.
Meine, Curt. Wallace Stegner & the Continental Vision: Essays on Literature, History, & Landscape. LC 97-14838. 240p. 1997. write for info. (*1-55963-537-1*) Island Pr.
Meine, Curt & Biodiversity Support Program Staff. Bulgaria's Biological Diversity: Conservation Status & Needs Assessment LC 99-168938. 1998. write for info. (*1-887531-21-1*) Biodivers Supp Prog.
Meine, Curt D., ed. see Leopold, Aldo.
Meine, Franklin J. Tall Tales of the Southwest. 1988. reprint ed. lib. bdg. 49.00 (*0-7812-0188-8*) Rprt Serv.
— Tall Tales of the Southwest. LC 78-166809. (Illus.). 1971. reprint ed. 79.00 (*0-403-01424-7*) Scholarly.
Meineck, Peter, ed. & tr. see Sophocles.
Meineck, Peter, tr. see Aristophanes.
Meineck, Peter, tr. & notes see Aeschylus.
Meineck, Peter, tr. & notes see Aristophanes.
Meinecke, Fred K., tr. see Landgraf, Anne K.
Meinecke, Friedrich. Machiavellism. Scott, Douglas, tr. LC 97-16855. 480p. 1997. pap. text 27.95 (*1-56000-970-5*) Transaction Pubs.
— The Warfare of a Nation. 1977. 59.95 (*0-8490-2807-8*) Gordon Pr.
Meinecke, Michael. Patterns of Stylistic Changes in Islamic Architecture: Local Traditions Versus Migrating Artists. LC 95-5508. (Hagop Kevorkian Series on Near Eastern Art & Civilization). 180p. (C). 1996. text 75.00 (*0-8147-5492-9*) NYU Pr.
Meineke, A. Ethnikon: A Geographical Lexicon on Ancient Cities, Peoples, Tribes & Toponyms. (GRE.). vi, 817p. (C). 1992. pap. text 40.00 (*0-89005-411-8*) Ares.
Meineke, August. Analecta Alexandrina. vii, 440p. 1964. reprint ed. write for info. (*0-318-70975-9*) G Olms Pubs.
— Poetarum Comicorum Graecorum Fragmenta. x, 807p. 1989. reprint ed. write for info. (*3-487-09213-1*) G Olms Pubs.
Meineke, Stefan. Friedrich Meinecke: Persoenlichkeit und Politisches Denken Bis Zum Ende des Ersten Weltkrieges. (Veroeffentlichungen der Historischen Kommission zu Berlin Ser.: Bd. 90). (GER.). xii, 384p. (C). 1995. lib. bdg. 143.10 (*3-11-013979-0*) De Gruyter.
Meinel, Aden B. & Meinel, Marjorie P. Applied Solar Energy. 400p. (C). 1976. text 38.25 (*0-201-04719-5*) Addison-Wesley.
Meinel, Aden B., et al. Catalog of Emission Lines in Astrophysical Objects. 2nd ed. LC QB0465.M38. 169p. reprint ed. pap. 52.40 (*0-608-12781-7*, 202348000032) Bks Demand.
Meinel, C. Modified Branching Programs & Their Computational Power. (Lecture Notes in Computer Science Ser.: Vol. 370). vi, 132p. 1989. 27.00 (*0-387-51340-X*) Spr-Verlag.
Meinel, Carolyn. The Happy Hacker: A Guide to (Mostly) Harmless Computer Hacking. 2nd rev. ed. (Illus.). 400p. 1998. pap. 34.95 (*0-929408-25-X*) Amer Eagle Pubns Inc.
Meinel, Christopher & Theobald, Thorsten. Algorithms & Data Structures in VLSI Design: OBDD - Foundations & Applications. LC 98-26197. (Illus.). 270p. 1998. pap. 49.95 (*3-540-64486-5*) Spr-Verlag.
Meinel, Hans. A Course in Scientific German. 248p. 1972. 32.75 (*3-19-001103-6*) Adlers Foreign Bks.
Meinel, Marjorie P., jt. auth. see Meinel, Aden B.
Meinel, Wulf. Frontiers of European Broadcasting Legislation. (European Media Monograph). 96p. 1996. pap. text 12.95 (*0-85170-413-1*) Ind U Pr.
Meiner, Sue. Nursing Documentation: Legal Focus Across Practice Settings. LC 99-10239. 17p. 1999. 65.00 (*0-7619-1071-9*) Sage.
***Meiner, Sue.** Nursing Documentation: Legal Focus Across Practice Settings. LC 99-10239. 1999. pap. write for info. (*0-7619-1072-7*) Sage.
Meiner, Sue E., jt. ed. see Luggen, Ann Schmidt.
Meiners. The Legal Environment of Business. 5th ed. (LA - Business Law Ser.). 1994. pap. write for info. (*0-314-03378-5*) West Pub.
— Managing in the Legal Environment. 3rd ed. (SWC-Business Law). (C). 1995. mass mkt., student ed. 20.95 (*0-314-06326-9*) S-W Pub.
— Study Guide Legal Environment Of Business 5. 5th ed. (SWC-Business Law). 1994. mass mkt., student ed. 17.50 (*0-314-03588-5*) West Pub.
Meiners & Ringleb. Legal Environment of Busines. 6th ed. (LA - Business Law Ser.). (C). 1996. mass mkt., student ed. 18.25 (*0-314-20770-8*) S-W Pub.
Meiners, Phyllis A. National Directory of Foundation Grants for Native Americans. LC 97-65768. (Multicultural Grant Guides: Vol. 4). (Illus.). 224p. (Orig.). 1998. pap. 99.95 (*0-9633694-8-2*) CRC EagleRock.
Meiners, Phyllis A. & Sanford, Greg A. National Directory of Church Philanthropy. (Illus.). 400p. pap. write for info. (*0-9633694-4-X*) CRC Pub CO.
Meiners, Phyllis A. & Tun-Atz, Hilary H. Corporate & Foundation Fundraising Manual for Native Americans. 3rd rev. ed. LC 96-83771. (Multicultural Grant Guides: No. 2). (Illus.). 290p. 1996. spiral bd., wbk. ed. 129.95 (*0-9633694-6-6*) CRC EagleRock.
Meiners, Phyllis A., jt. auth. see Tun-Atz, Hilary H.
Meiners, Phyllis A., ed. see Bailey, Susan D.
Meiners, Phyllis A., ed. see Sanford, Greg A.
Meiners, R. K. Journeying Back to the World: Poems. LC 74-30339. (Breakthrough Bks.). 88p. 1975. text 18.95 (*0-8262-0173-3*) U of Mo Pr.
— Last Alternatives: Allen Tate. LC 72-4614. (American Literature Ser.: No. 49). 1972. reprint ed. lib. bdg. 75.00 (*0-8383-1594-1*) M S G Haskell Hse.
***Meiners, Roger & Morriss, Andrew, eds.** The Common Law & the Environment: Rethinking the Statutory Basis for Modern Environmental Law. LC 99-45508. (Political Economy Forum Ser.). 376p. 2000. pap. 24.95 (*0-8476-9709-6*); text 70.00 (*0-8476-9708-8*) Rowman.
***Meiners, Roger E.** The Legal Environment of Business. 7th ed. LC 99-23199. 1999. pap. 99.95 (*0-324-00423-0*) Thomson Learn.
Meiners, Roger E. & Amacher, Ryan C., eds. Federal Support of Higher Education. LC 89-10189. 360p. (C). 1989. pap. text 15.95 (*0-943852-78-1*) Prof World Peace.
Meiners, Roger E. & Yandle, Bruce, eds. The Economic Consequences of Liability Rules: In Defense of Common Law Liability. LC 91-185. 256p. 1991. 65.00 (*0-89930-649-7*, MQS/, Quorum Bks) Greenwood.
— Regulation & the Reagan Era. LC 89-7594. (Independent Studies in Political Economy). 304p. (C). 1989. 49.95 (*0-8419-1174-6*) Independent Inst.
— Regulation & the Reagan Era: Politics, Bureaucracy & the Public Interest. 304p. 1989. lib. bdg. 45.95 (*0-945999-71-2*, 6068) Independent Inst.
— Regulation & the Reagan Era: Politics, Bureaucracy & the Public Interest. (Illus.). 304p. 1989. pap. text 19.95 (*0-945999-70-4*, 6065) Independent Inst.
— Taking the Environment Seriously. (Political Economy Forum Ser.). 288p. (C). 1993. text 64.00 (*0-8476-7873-3*) Rowman.
— Taking the Environment Seriously. 288p. 1995. pap. 24.95 (*0-8476-8054-1*) Rowman.
Meiners, Roger E., et al. The Legal Environment of Business. 5th ed. Fenton, ed. LC 93-33086. (SWC-Business Law). 825p. (C). 1993. mass mkt. 58.00 (*0-314-02690-8*) West Pub.

— The Legal Environment of Business. 6th ed. LC 96-26926. 880p. 1996. mass mkt. 84.95 (*0-314-09953-0*) West Pub.

Meiners, Roger E., jt. auth. see Clarkson, Kenneth W.

Meiners, Roger E., jt. ed. see Hill, Peter J.

Meiners, Roger E., jt. ed. see Stroup, Richard L.

***Meiners, Willem.** Those Who Win Are Those Who Think They Can. 182p. 2000. pap. write for info. (*1-893162-27-3*) Erica Hse.

Meinert, Curtis L. Clinical Trials: Design, Conduct & Analysis. (Monographs in Epidemiology & Biostatistics: No. 8). (Illus.). 512p. (C). 1986. text 89.50 (*0-19-503568-2*) OUP.

–Clinical Trials Dictionary: Terminology & Usage Recommendations. LC 95-94294. 480p. Date not set. text 95.00 (*0-9646424-0-9*) C L Meinert.
"Dr. Meinert has produced in this dictionary a treasure for those of you who aim to write about clinical trials with precision & brevity. It goes well beyond the general dictionaries of medicine in representing detail & great accuracy the large & complex vocabulary needed to describe clearly the methods & results of clinical trials. It also provides a thorough index to the entries of its main section that facilitates the findings of terms associated with particular concepts & practical steps in trials. But perhaps its most extraordinary & admirable section is that on usage. Here Dr. Meinert gives us a deeply perceptive & strongly illuminating discourse on nuances in the rhetoric of scientific speech & writing as seen by him through his long & fruitful engagement with designing, running, reporting, & interpreting clinical trials. For these reasons this new dictionary is going to be a classic at birth. It merits an audience far wider than just authors reporting clinical trials. That audience should include authors' editors, journal editors & their manuscript editor, indexers of clinical trials papers, meta-analysts, teachers of clinical epidemiology, & anyone else who reads reports of trials & assesses their scientific strength & clinical value. I believe it will get that wide audience."--Edward J. Huth, Editor Emeritus, ANNALS OF INTERNAL MEDICINE. Order from: Center for Clinical Trials, 615 North Wolfe Street, Room 5010, Baltimore, MD 21205. (410) 955-8197, FAX (410) 955-0932. *Publisher Paid Annotation.*

Meinert, Roland, et al, eds. Postmodernism, Religion & the Future of Social Work. LC 98-16142. (Social Thought Monograph Ser.: Vol. 18, No. 3). 92p. 1998. 29.95 (*0-7890-0516-6*, Haworth Pastrl) Haworth Pr.

***Meinert, Roland, et al, eds.** Social Work: Seeking Relevancy in the Twenty-First Century. LC 99-45999. (Illus.). 221p. 1999. lib. bdg. 39.95 (*0-7890-0644-8*) Haworth Pr.

— Social Work: Seeking Relevancy in the Twenty-First Century. LC 99-45999. (Illus.). 152p. 2000. pap. text 24.95 (*0-7890-1050-X*) Haworth Pr.

Meinert, Roland G., et al. Issues in Social Work: A Critical Analysis. LC 93-32125. 208p. 1994. 57.95 (*0-86569-209-2*, Auburn Hse) Greenwood.

Meinesz, Alexandre. Killer Algae: The True Tale of a Biological Invasion. Simberloff, Daniel, tr. from FRE. LC 99-32502. (Illus.). 352p. 1999. 25.00 (*0-226-51922-8*) U Ch Pr.

***Meinhardt, D. & Volker, S.** Beyond the Borders: Crossover in Creative Culture. (Illus.). 240p. 2000. pap. 46.00 (*3-540-65589-1*) Spr-Verlag.

Meinhardt, F. Untersuchungen Zur Genetik Des Fortpflanzungsverhaltens und der Fruchtkoerper- und Antibiotikabbildung Des Basidiomyceten Agrocybe Aegerita. (Bibliotheca Mycologica Ser.: No. 75). (GER., Illus.). 128p. 1981. pap. text 32.00 (*3-7682-1275-0*) Lubrecht & Cramer.

Meinhardt, H. Algorithmic Beauty of Sea Shells. (Illus.). 204p. 1995. 49.95 incl. disk (*0-387-57842-0*) Spr-Verlag.

— The Algorithmic Beauty of Sea Shells. (Illus.). 204p. 1995. 49.95 incl. disk (*3-540-57842-0*) Spr-Verlag.

— Models of Biological Pattern Formation. 1982. text 125.00 (*0-12-488620-5*) Acad Pr.

Meinhardt, Hans. The Algorithmic Beauty of Sea Shells. 2nd enl. ed. LC 98-2590. (Virtual Laboratory Ser.). (Illus.). xiii, 236p. 1998. 54.95 incl. disk (*3-540-63919-5*) Spr-Verlag.

Meinhardt, Peter & Davis, Nigel. Company Law in Great Britain. 196p. 1982. text 78.95 (*0-566-02389-X*, Pub. by Dartmth Pub) Ashgate Pub Co.

Meinho, Ulrike & Richardson, Kay, eds. Text, Discourse & Context: Representations of Poverty in Britain. LC 93-50744. (Real Language Ser.). 1994. write for info. (*0-582-10214-6*, Pub. by Addison-Wesley) Longman.

— Text, Discourse & Context: Representations of Poverty in Britain (Real Language Series) LC 93-50744. (Real Language Ser.). 1993. pap. text 24.10 (*0-582-10213-8*) Addison-Wesley.

Meinhof, Carl. Die Dichtung der Afrikaner. (B. E. Ser.: No. 43). (GER.). 1911. 30.00 (*0-8115-2994-0*) Periodicals Srv.

— Introduction to the Study of African Languages. Werner, A., tr. LC 75-172719. reprint ed. 34.00 (*0-404-07955-5*) AMS Pr.

Meinhof, Carl, et al, eds. Deutsche Kolonialsprachen Vol. 1: Die Sprache der Herero in Deutsch-Sudwest-Afrika, 1937, 5 vols. (B. E. Ser.: No. 177). 1937. 25.00 (*0-8115-3087-6*) Periodicals Srv.

— Deutsche Kolonialsprachen Vol. 3: Die Sprache der Haussa in Zentalafrika, 5 vols. (B. E. Ser.: No. 177). 1972. 25.00 (*0-8115-3088-4*) Periodicals Srv.

— Deutsche Kolonialsprachen Vol. 5: Die Sprache der Jaund in Kamerun, 5 vols. (B. E. Ser.: No. 177). 1972. 25.00 (*0-8115-3089-2*) Periodicals Srv.

***Meinhof, Ulrike.** Intertextuality & the Media. (Illus.). 176p. 2000. pap. 19.95 (*0-7190-4713-7*, Pub. by Manchester Univ Pr); text 59.95 (*0-7190-4712-9*, Pub. by Manchester Univ Pr) St Martin.

Meinhof, Ulrike, jt. auth. see Richardson, Kay.

Meinhold. Child Psychology: Development & Behavior Analysis. 304p. (C). 1993. pap. text 42.95 (*0-8403-8253-7*) Kendall-Hunt.

Meinhold, C. B. Radiation Safety Concerns for Pregnant or Breast Feeding Patients: Positions of the NCRP & the ICRP. 22p. 1997. pap. 4.00 (*0-16-062804-0*) USGPO.

Meinhold, Charles B., intro. Advising the Public about Radiation Emergencies: A Document for Public Comment. LC 94-37114. (NCRP Commentaries Ser.: No. 10). (Illus.). 29p. (Orig.). 1994. pap. text 20.00 (*0-929600-38-X*) NCRP Pubns.

— Considerations Regarding the Unintended Radiation Exposure of the Embryo, Fetus or Nursing Child. LC 94-18566. (Commentary Ser.: No. 9). 21p. (Orig.). 1994. pap. text 20.00 (*0-929600-36-3*) NCRP Pubns.

— Dose Control at Nuclear Power Plants. LC 94-40857. (Report Ser.: No. 120). 138p. (Orig.). 1994. pap. text 30.00 (*0-929600-39-8*) NCRP Pubns.

— An Introduction to Efficacy in Diagnostic Radiology & Nuclear Medicine (Justification of Medical Radiation Exposure) LC 95-24596. (NCRP Commentaries Ser.: No. 13). 29p. 1995. pap. text 20.00 (*0-929600-45-2*) NCRP Pubns.

— Limitation of Exposure to Ionizing Radiation. LC 93-7142. (Report Ser.: No. 116). 70p. (Orig.). 1993. pap. text 35.00 (*0-929600-30-4*) NCRP Pubns.

— Maintaining Radiation Protection Records. LC 92-49562. (Report Ser.: No. 114). 86p. (Orig.). 1992. pap. text 30.00 (*0-929600-27-4*) NCRP Pubns.

— Misadministration of Radioactive Material in Medicine - Scientific Background. LC 91-35005. (Commentary Ser.: No. 7). 49p. 1991. pap. text 25.00 (*0-929600-22-3*) NCRP Pubns.

— A Practical Guide to the Determination of Human Exposure to Radio Frequency Fields. LC 93-45910. (Report Ser.: No. 119). 233p. (Orig.). 1993. pap. 40.00 (*0-929600-35-5*) NCRP Pubns.

— Principles & Application of Collective Dose in Radiation Protection. LC 95-26030. (NCRP Reports: No. 121). 106p. (Orig.). 1995. pap. 25.00 (*0-929600-46-0*) NCRP Pubns.

— Radiation Exposure & High Altitude Flight. LC 95-21369. (NCRP Commentaries Ser.: No. 12). 25p. (Orig.). 1995. pap. 20.00 (*0-929600-44-4*) NCRP Pubns.

— Radiation Protection in the Mineral Extraction Industry. LC 93-33554. (Report Ser.: No. 118). 1993. pap. text 30.00 (*0-929600-33-9*) NCRP Pubns.

— Research Needs for Radiation Protection. LC 93-34922. (Report Ser.: No. 117). 1993. pap. text 30.00 (*0-929600-32-0*) NCRP Pubns.

— Risk Estimates for Radiation Protection. LC 93-44242. (Report Ser.: No. 115). 148p. (Orig.). 1993. pap. text 35.00 (*0-929600-34-7*) NCRP Pubns.

— Sources & Magnitude of Occupational & Public Exposures from Nuclear Medicine Procedures: Recommendations of the National Council on Radiation Protection & Measurements. LC 96-690. (NCRP Reports: Vol. 124). 77p. (Orig.). 1996. pap. 25.00 (*0-929600-51-7*) NCRP Pubns.

— Uncertainty in NCRP Screening Models Relating to Atmosphere Transport, Deposition & Uptake by Humans. LC 92-36388. (Commentary Ser.: No. 8). (Illus.). 56p. 1993. pap. text 30.00 (*0-929600-28-2*) NCRP Pubns.

Meinhold, Charles B., pref. Dose Limits for Individuals Who Receive Exposure from Radionuclide Therapy Patients. LC 95-3556. (NCRP Commentaries Ser.: No. 11). 21p. (Orig.). 1995. pap. text 20.00 (*0-929600-42-8*) NCRP Pubns.

Meinhold, Margit. Sri Lanka Phrasebook. 80p. (Orig.). 1987. pap. 2.95 (*0-908086-94-6*) Lonely Planet.

Meinholz, Norman M. & Kuehn, Steven R. The Deadman Slough Site (47 Pr-46) LC 96-4808. (Archaeology Research Ser.: No. 4). 1996. write for info. (*0-87020-282-0*) State Hist Soc Wis.

Meinholz, Norman M., et al. The Statz Site: A Late Woodland Community & Archaic Lithic Workshop in Dane County, Wisconsin. LC 97-24197. (Archaeology Research Ser.). 1997. pap. write for info. (*0-87020-280-4*) State Hist Soc Wis.

Meinick, Ralph. The Life & Work of Ludwig Lewisohn Vol. II: This Dark & Desperate Age. 1998. 39.95 (*0-8143-2765-6*, Great Lks Bks) Wayne St U Pr.

Meinig, Donald W. The Great Columbia Plain: A Historical Geography, 1805-1910. LC 95-35777. (Weyerhaeuser Environmental Classics Ser.). (Illus.). 598p. (C). 1995. pap. 19.95 (*0-295-97485-0*) U of Wash Pr.

— Imperial Texas: An Interpretive Essay in Cultural Geography. 145p. 1969. pap. 11.95 (*0-292-73807-2*) U of Tex Pr.

— On the Margins of the Good Earth. 246p. (C). 1989. pap. text 40.00 (*0-89771-022-3*, Pub. by Bob Mossel) St Mut.

— The Shaping of America: A Geographical Prespective on 500 Years of History, Vol. 2: Continental. LC 85-17962. Vol. 2. 1995. pap. 25.00 (*0-300-06290-7*) Yale U Pr.

— The Shaping of America Vol. 1: A Geographical Perspective on 500 Years of History. LC 85-17962. Vol. 1. 512p. (C). 1988. reprint ed. pap. 25.00 (*0-300-03882-8*) Yale U Pr.

— The Shaping of America Vol. 2: A Geological Perspective on 500 Years of American History: Continental America, 1800-1867. LC 85-17962. Vol. 2. (Illus.). 656p. (C). 1993. 55.00 (*0-300-05658-3*) Yale U Pr.

— The Shaping of America Vol. 3: A Geographical Perspective on 500 Years of History: Transcontinental America, 1850-1950. LC 85-17962. Vol. 3. (Illus.). 480p. 1998. 50.00 (*0-300-07592-8*) Yale U Pr.

***Meinig, Donald W.** The Shaping of America Vol. 3: A Geographical Perspective on 500 Years of History: Transcontinental America, 1850-1950. Vol. 3. (Illus.). 480p. 2000. pap. 25.00 (*0-300-08290-8*) Yale U Pr.

Meinig, Donald W. Southwest: Three Peoples in Geographical Change, 1600-1970. (Historical Geography of North America Ser.). (Illus.). 164p. (Orig.). (C). 1971. text 22.95 (*0-19-501289-5*) OUP.

Meinig, Donald W., ed. The Interpretation of Ordinary Landscapes. (Illus.). 266p. 1979. pap. text 26.95 (*0-19-502536-9*) OUP.

Meinig, George E. New Trition: How to Achieve Optimum Health. (Illus.). 326p. (Orig.). 1988. pap. write for info. (*0-945196-08-3*) Bion Pub.

— Root Canal Cover-Up. 2nd ed. Koonce, Charlene & Lovendale, Mark, eds. LC 93-72133. (Illus.). 257p. 1994. pap. 19.95 (*0-945196-14-8*) Bion Pub.

— Root Canal Cover-Up. 5th ed. Lovendale, Mark & Koonce, Charlene, eds. LC 93-72133. (Illus.). 230p. 1993. reprint ed. pap. 19.95 (*0-945196-19-9*) Bion Pub.

Meinikov, O. English-Russian Astronomical Dictionary. (ENG & RUS.). 504p. 1980. 75.00 (*0-569-06519-4*) St Mut.

— English-Russian Dictionary of Astronomy. (ENG & RUS.). 504p. 1980. write for info. (*0-8288-0772-8*) Fr & Eur.

Meininger, Anne-Marie, ed. see Balzac, Honore de.

***Meininger, Irmgard.** Chittor: Historical View & a Guide. (Illus.). 80p. 2000. pap. 19.50 (*81-246-0150-X*, Pub. by D K Printwrld) Nataraj Bks.

— City Palace of Udaipur: Historical View & a Guide. (Illus.). 96p. 2000. pap. 24.00 (*81-246-0149-6*, Pub. by D K Printwrld) Nataraj Bks.

— The Kingdom of Mewar: Great Struggles & Glory of the World's Ruling Dynasty. (Illus.). xii, 208p. 2000. 115.00 (*81-246-0144-5*, Pub. by D K Printwrld) Nataraj Bks.

Meininger, Peter L., jt. ed. see Goodman, Steven M.

Meininger, Richard C., ed. Effects of Aggregates & Mineral Fillers on Asphalt Mixture Performance. LC 92-31159. (Special Technical Publication Ser.: Vol. 1147). (Illus.). 360p. 1992. text 58.00 (*0-8031-1468-0*, STP1147) ASTM.

Meininger, Thomas A. The Formation of Nationalist Bulgarian Intelligentsia, 1835-1878. (Modern European History Ser.). 552p. 1988. text 20.00 (*0-8240-8028-9*) Garland.

Meininghaus. Five Centuries of Scent & Elegant Flacons. 1998. 75.00 (*3-925369-82-1*) Arnoldsche Art Pubs.

Meinke, Karl, ed. Many-Sorted Logic & Its Applications. LC 93-138982. (Wiley Professional Computing Ser.). (Illus.). 415p. 1993. reprint ed. pap. 128.70 (*0-608-05263-9*, 206580100001) Bks Demand.

Meinke, Karl, jt. auth. see Moller, Bernard.

Meinke, Peter. Howard Nemerov. LC 68-64753. (University of Minnesota Pamphlets on American Writers Ser.: No. 70). 48p. (Orig.). reprint ed. pap. 30.00 (*0-7837-2873-5*, 205758200006) Bks Demand.

— Liquid Paper: New & Selected Poems. LC 91-50108. (Poetry Ser.). 120p. (C). 1991. pap. 12.95 (*0-8229-5455-9*); text 29.95 (*0-8229-3681-X*) U of Pittsburgh Pr.

— The Night Train & the Golden Bird. LC 76-43966. (Pitt Poetry Ser.). 79p. reprint ed. pap. 30.00 (*0-608-16768-1*, 202631600049) Bks Demand.

— Night Watch on the Chesapeake. LC 86-25040. (Poetry Ser.). 96p. 1987. pap. 10.95 (*0-8229-5390-0*) U of Pittsburgh Pr.

— The Piano Tuner. LC 85-28864. (Flannery O'Connor Award for Short Fiction Ser.). 168p. 1994. pap. 12.95 (*0-8203-1645-8*) U of Ga Pr.

— Scars. (Poetry Ser.). 76p. (Orig.). 1996. pap. 10.95 (*0-8229-5592-X*) U of Pittsburgh Pr.

— Scars. (Poetry Ser.). 76p. (Orig.). (C). 1996. text 24.95 (*0-8229-3935-5*) U of Pittsburgh Pr.

— The Shape of Poetry. LC 99-13050. 10p. 1999. pap. 13.95 (*0-87116-186-9*) Writer.

***Meinke, Peter.** Zinc Fingers: Poems from A to Z. 96p. 2000. pap. 12.95 (*0-8229-5724-8*) U of Pittsburgh Pr.

Meinkoff. Treasure Island. 1995. 24.95 (*0-8057-8804-2*, Twyne) Mac Lib Ref.

Meinkohn, D. & Haken, H., eds. Dissipative Structures in Transport Processes & Combustion: Interdisciplinary Seminar, Bielefeld, 17-21 July, 1989. (Synergetics Ser.: Vol. 48). (Illus.). 256p. 1990. 71.00 (*0-387-52751-6*) Spr-Verlag.

Meinkoth, Michael C. The Sister Creeks Site Mounds: Middle Woodland Mortuary Practices in the Illinois River Valley. LC 95-44995. (Transportation Archaeological Research Reports: Vol. 2). (Illus.). 148p. (C). 1995. pap. 8.00 (*0-9644881-1-6*) ITARP.

Meinkoth, Norman A., jt. auth. see Audubon Society Staff.

Meins, Elizabeth. Security of Attachment & the Social Development of Cognition. LC 98-106166. (Essays in Develomental Psychology Ser.). 192p. 1997. 44.95 (*0-86377-468-7*, Pub. by Psychol Pr) Taylor & Francis.

***Meinster, Barry.** Getting Started: Microsoft Windows NT Four Point O. 1998. pap. 12.00 (*0-538-72189-8*) Thomson Learn.

Meinster, Barry. MCSE Six Pack. (Certification Study Guides Ser.). 600p. 1999. 49.99 incl. cd-rom (*0-7645-3274-X*) IDG Bks.

— South-Western's Microsoft Windows NT 4.O Certification. LC 97-29230. 1998. 46.95 (*0-538-71938-9*) S-W Pub.

***Meinster, Barry, et al.** Networking Essentials, MS Windows Nt 4.0. LC 98-29340. (Computer Applications Ser.). 1998. pap. 46.95 (*0-538-68477-1*) Thomson Learn.

— South-Western Networking Essentials. 1998. pap. 12.00 (*0-538-68479-8*) Thomson Learn.

Meintel, Deirdre. Race, Culture & Portuguese Colonialism in Cabo Verde. (Foreign & Comparative Studies Program, African Ser.: No. 41). (Orig.). 1984. pap. text 12.50 (*0-915984-66-0*) Syracuse U Foreign Comp.

Meintjes, Ria & Athey, Jackie. The Bride's Choice. LC 79-52243. (Continental's Creative Cake Ser.). (Illus.). 64p. (Orig.). 1979. pap. 7.95 (*0-916096-22-X*) Books Bakers.

Meintosh, Ron. Quest for Revival: Experiencing Great Revivals of the Past Empowering You for God's Move Today! LC 99-180282. 325p. 1997. 19.99 (*1-57794-053-9*, HH2-053-9) Harrison Hse.

Meints, Graydon M. Along the Tracks: A Directory of Named Places on Michigan Railroads. LC 87-405797. 1987. pap. 15.00 (*0-916699-12-9*) CMU Clarke Hist Lib.

— Michigan Railroads & Railroad Companies. LC 92-32966. (C). 1993. 35.00 (*0-87013-318-7*) Mich St U Pr.

Meinwald, Jerrold, ed. see National Academy of Sciences Staff.

M

Meinz, Daniel W., jt. auth. see Young, Jeffrey F.

Meinz, David L. Eating by the Book: What the Bible Says about Food, Fat, Fitness, & Faith. LC 97-78373. (Illus.). 301p. 1999. pap. 21.95 (*0-9644253-5-1*) Gilbert Pr VA.

Meinzen-Dick, Ruth S. Groundwater Markets in Pakistan: Participation & Productivity, Vol. 105. LC 96-50382. (Research Reports). 1996. write for info. (*0-89629-108-1*) Intl Food Policy.

Meinzen-Dick, Ruth S. & Svendsen, Mark, eds. Future Directions for Indian Irrigation. 475p. 1991. 33.00 (*0-89629-316-5*); teacher ed. 24.00 (*0-87006-988-8*); student ed. 8.40 (*0-87006-987-X*) Intl Food Policy.

Meinzen-Dick, Ruth S., jt. ed. see Burns, Bryan Randolph.

Meinzer, Oscar E. Plants As Indicators of Ground Water. (Illus.). 100p. 1997. reprint ed. pap. 49.95 (*0-9641628-7-3*) Karo Hollow.

Meinzer, Wyman. Coyote. LC 95-31162. 1995. 37.50 (*0-89672-352-6*); pap. 19.95 (*0-89672-353-4*) Tex Tech Univ Pr.

— Coyote: The Postcards. 1996. pap. text 9.95 (*0-89672-366-6*) Tex Tech Univ Pr.

— The Roadrunner. LC 92-33693. (Illus.). 128p. 1993. 37.50 (*0-89672-243-0*); pap. 19.95 (*0-89672-244-9*) Tex Tech Univ Pr.

— Texas Sky. LC 97-45309. (Illus.). 132p. 1998. 29.95 (*0-292-75218-0*) U of Tex Pr.

Meir Ai-Nai-Yim. Polychrome Historical Haggadah. (Illus.). 1974. 40.00 (*0-686-10317-3*) J Freedman Liturgy.

Meir, Avinoam. As Nomadism Ends: The Israeli Bedouin of the Negev. LC 96-11295. 272p. (C). 1996. pap. 69.00 (*0-8133-8959-3*, Pub. by Westview) HarpC.

— As Nomadism Ends: The Israeli Bedouin of the Negev. 272p. 1998. pap. 19.00 (*0-8133-3556-6*, Pub. by Westview) HarpC.

Meir, Avinoan, jt. ed. see Stern, Eliahu.

Meir, Colin. The Ballads & Songs of W. B. Yeats: The Anglo-Irish Heritage in Subject & Style. LC 75-322711. viii, 141p. 1974. write for info. (*0-333-15839-3*) Macmillan.

***Meir, Eli.** EcoBeaker 2.0. (Illus.). 416p. (C). 1999. 24.00 (*0-9671306-0-3*) BeakerWare.

Meir Friedman, Lawrence. The Horizontal Society. LC 98-31594. 336p. 1999. 29.95 (*0-300-07545-6*) Yale U Pr.

Meir, Goldo & Syrkin, Marie. Golda Meir Speaks Out. LC 74-164426. 251 p. 1973. write for info. (*0-297-99558-8*) Trafalgar.

Meir, Samuel Ben, see Ben Meir, Samuel.

Meir, Yehyda Ben. Civil-Military Relations in Israel. LC 94-33142. 288p. 1995. 34.50 (*0-231-09684-4*) Col U Pr.

Meire, Hylton B. & Farrant, Pat. Basic Ultrasound. LC 94-40651. 234p. 1995. pap. 78.50 (*0-471-91691-9*) Wiley.

Meireavn, Teoppil M. & Vijayalakshmi, M. The Story of a Seaside Village. LC 98-915276. 171p. 1998. write for info. (*81-250-1544-2*) Orient Longman Ltd.

Meireis, Torsten. Theologiestudium im Kontext. 320p. 1997. text 124.00 (*3-11-015737-3*) De Gruyter.

Meirelles, Janet. Diabetes Is Not a Piece of Cake: Prescribed for Family, Friends & Co-workers of Folks with Diabetes. LC 94-75824. (Illus.). 1994. pap. 15.95 (*1-884929-75-3*) Lincoln Pubng.

— Diabetes Is Not a Piece of Cake: Prescribed for Family, Friends & Coworkers of Folks with Diabetes. 3rd ed. LC 97-73536. 1997. pap. 15.95 (*1-884929-77-X*) Lincoln Pubng.

— Diabetes is Not a Piece of Cake Cookbook. 128p. (Orig.). 1995. pap. 11.75 (*1-884929-82-6*) Lincoln Pubng.

— Love Can Be Sweet Even with Diabetes. 1999. pap. 18.95 (*1-58040-012-4*) Am Diabetes.

Meireran, Sigmund, tr. see Sanne, Karl U.

Meiri, Baruch & Elagar, Rachamin. Chalom Ben Soragim. (HEB.). 168p. 1998. 19.95 (*965-229-192-7*, Pub. by Gefen Pub Hse) Gefen Bks.

Meiring, Bernard J. Educational Aspects of the Legislation of the Councils of Baltimore, 1829-1884. 1978. 28.95 (*0-405-10844-3*, 11821) Ayer.

Meiring, P. De V., ed. Textbook of Geriatric Medicine. (Illus.). 433p. (C). 1990. pap. text 65.25 (*0-7021-2387-0*, Pub. by Juta & Co) Intl Spec Bk.

Meiring, Steven P., et al. A Core Curriculum: Making Mathematics Count for Everyone. Hirsch, Christian R., ed. LC 92-6996. (Curriculum & Evaluation Standards for School Mathematics Addenda Ser.). (Illus.). 150p. 1992. pap. 19.95 (0-87353-328-3) NCTM.

Meirleir, K., jt. ed. see Osteaux, M.

Meirmanov, Anvarbek M., et al. Evolution Equations & Lagrangian Coordinates. LC 96-54303. (De Gruyter Studies in Mathematics Ser.: Vol. 24). xiii, 311p. (C). 1997. text 148.95 (3-11-014875-7) De Gruyter.

Meirovitch. Elements Vibration Analysis. 2nd ed. 1986. student ed. 28.75 (0-07-041343-6) McGraw.

— Fundamentals of Vibrations. 704p. 2000. 95.63 (0-07-041345-2) McGraw.

Meirovitch, Leonard. Analytical Methods in Vibrations. 576p. (C). 1967. text 65.20 (0-02-380140-9, Macmillan Coll) P-H.

— Computational Methods in Structural Dynamics. 1980. text 112.50 (90-286-0580-0) Kluwer Academic.

— Dynamics & Control of Structures. LC 89-22710. 448p. 1990. 150.00 (0-471-62858-1) Wiley.

— Elements of Vibration Analysis. 2nd ed. 560p. (C). 1986. 99.38 (0-07-041342-8) McGraw.

— Introduction to Dynamics & Control. LC 84-20938. 140p. 1985. pap. text, teacher ed. 15.00 (0-471-82282-5) Wiley.

— Introduction To Dynamics & Control. LC 84-20938. 416p. 1985. text 103.95 (0-471-87074-9) Wiley.

— Methods of Analytical Dynamics. 485p. (C). 1970. 111.25 (0-07-041455-6) McGraw.

— Principles & Techniques of Vibrations. 694p. (C). 1996. 105.00 (0-02-380141-7, Macmillan Coll) P-H.

Meirovitz, Marco & Dods, Stuart. Muscles of the Mind Program: Verbal Thinking. 1992. pap. 14.99 (0-89824-193-6) Trillium Pr.

Meirovitz, Marco & Jacobs, Paul. Muscles of the Mind Program. 1992. pap. 14.99 (0-89824-186-3) Trillium Pr.

— Muscles of the Mind Program: Brain Muscle Builders. 1992. pap. 14.99 (0-89824-185-5) Trillium Pr.

— Muscles of the Mind Program: Visual Thinking. 1992. pap. 14.99 (0-89824-184-7) Trillium Pr.

Meirovitz, Marco, et al. Thinkability. 1995. teacher ed. write for info. (1-57004-012-5); wbk. ed. write for info. (1-57004-028-1) Lrning NJ.

— Thinkability, Addtional Game Kits. 1995. 149.00 (1-57004-018-4) Lrning NJ.

— Thinkability, Set. 1995. teacher ed., student ed. 239.00 (1-57004-027-3); student ed., wbk. ed. 119.50 (1-57004-017-6) Lrning NJ.

— Thinkability: A Practical Program to Improve Thinking Skills Using Games. 1995. teacher ed. 89.00 (0-570-04012-4) L Erlbaum Assocs.

— Thinkability: A Practical Program to Improve Thinking Skills Using Games, 10 wkbks., Set. 1995. student ed. 119.50 (0-570-04017-5); 149.00 (0-570-04018-3) L Erlbaum Assocs.

— Thinkability: A Practical Program to Improve Thinking Skills Using Games, Set, incl. 10 wkbks. & 5 game kits. 1995. teacher ed. 239.00 (0-570-04027-2) L Erlbaum Assocs.

Meirowitz, Claire, jt. ed. see Kershen, Harry.

Meis, Jeanne M. & Enzinger, Franz M. Atlas of Soft Tissue Tumors. (C). 1993. VHS, disk 500.00 (1-56815-019-9) Mosby Inc.

Meis-Kindblom, Jeanne M. & Enzinger, Franz M. Color Atlas of Soft Tissue Tumors. LC 95-9592. (Illus.). 320p. (C). (gr. 13). 1995. text 129.00 (0-8151-5895-5, 24079) Mosby Inc.

Meis, M. Indian Women & Patriarchy. 113p. 1979. 23.95 (0-318-37057-3) Asia Bk Corp.

Meis, Morgan. Angelus Novus. 144p. 1993. pap. write for info. (1-887128-02-6) Soft Skull Pr.

Meis, Reinhard. Pocket Watches. LC 86-63367. (Illus.). 316p. 1987. 79.95 (0-88740-084-1) Schiffer.

Meis, Ron. Understanding Bats: Discovering the Secret Lives of These Gentle Mammals. 32p. (Orig.). 1996. pap. 3.95 (1-880241-12-9) Bird Watchers.

Meis, Ron & Williams, Kim. Understanding Bats: Discovering the Secret Lives of These Gentle Mammals. Thompson, William H., III et al, eds. (Illus.). 32p. (Orig.). 1996. pap. write for info. (0-614-30206-4) Bird Watchers.

Meisami, Esmail, ed. Handbook of Human Growth & Developmental Biology, Vol. 2, Pt. A. 368p. 1989. boxed set 260.00 (0-8493-3184-6, QP187) CRC Pr.

— Handbook of Human Growth & Developmental Biology, Vol. 2, Pt. B. 376p. 1990. lib. bdg. 249.00 (0-8493-3185-4, RJ131) CRC Pr.

— Handbook of Human Growth & Developmental Biology, Vol. III, Pt. A. 256p. 1990. lib. bdg. 159.00 (0-8493-3186-2, RJ131) CRC Pr.

— Handbook of Human Growth & Developmental Biology, Vol. 3, Pt. B. 240p. 1990. boxed set 170.00 (0-8493-3187-0, RJ131) CRC Pr.

Meisami, Esmail & Timiras, Paola S., eds. Handbook of Human Growth & Development, Vol. I: Neural, Sensory, Motor & Integrative Development, 3 pts., Pt. C: Factors Influencing Brain Development. 192p. 1988. lib. bdg. 140.00 (0-8493-3183-8, RJ131) CRC Pr.

— Handbook of Human Growth & Development, Vol. I: Neural, Sensory, Motor & Integrative Development, 3 pts., Pt. B: Sensory, Motor & Integrative Development. 240p. 1988. lib. bdg. 200.00 (0-8493-3182-X, RJ131) CRC Pr.

— Handbook of Human Growth & Development, Vol. I: Neural, Sensory, Motor & Integrative Development, 3 Pts., Vol. 1. 216p. 1988. boxed set 199.00 (0-8493-3181-1, RJ131) CRC Pr.

Meisami, Esmail, ed. see International Symposium on Developmental Neurobiology Staff.

Meisami, Julie S. Medieval Persian Court Poetry. LC 87-1743. (Illus.). 360p. 1987. reprint ed. pap. 111.60 (0-608-06482-3, 206677900009) Bks Demand.

***Meisami, Julie S.** Persian Historiography. 288p. 1999. 72.00 (0-7486-0743-9, Pub. by Edinburgh U Pr); pap. 31.00 (0-7486-1276-9, Pub. by Edinburgh U Pr) Col U Pr.

Meisami, Julie S., ed. from PER. The Sea of Precious Virtues: A Medieval Islamic Mirror for Princes. LC 88-27858. 468p. 1990. 39.95 (0-87480-313-6) U of Utah Pr.

Meisami, Julie S., tr. The Sea of Precious Virtues. 330p. 1996. 39.95 (0-614-21339-8, 1451) Kazi Pubns.

Meisami, Julie S., jt. ed. see Starkey, Paul.

Meisami, Julie S., ed. & tr. see Nizami, Ganjaui.

Meisburger, W. F. History of Papa Frog. LC 93-74950. (Illus.). 24p. (J). (ps-3). 1994. pap. 4.95 (0-943864-72-0) Davenport.

Meisch, Lynn A., ed. Traditional Textiles of the Andes: Life & Cloth in the Highlands. LC 97-60320. (Illus.). 157p. (Orig.). 1997. pap. 24.95 (0-500-27985-3, Pub. by Thames Hudson) Norton.

Meisch, M. V., jt. auth. see Lancaser, J. L.

Meise, Jutta. Lessings Anglophilie. (Europaische Aufklarung in Literatur und Sprache Ser.: No. 10). XI, 238p. 1997. 51.95 (3-631-31301-2) P Lang Pubng.

Meise, Reinhold & Vogt, Dietmar. Introduction to Functional Analysis. Ramanujan, M. S. et al, trs. LC 97-12597. (Oxford Graduate Texts in Mathematics Ser.). 448p. 1997. text 90.00 (0-19-851485-9) OUP.

Meisei Co., Ltd. Editors. Hotel Facilities. (New Concept in Architecture & Design Ser.). (Illus.). 224p. 1997. 85.00 (4-938812-28-2, Pub. by Puroto Gyarak) Bks Nippan.

— Religious Facilities. LC 98-100434. (New Concept in Architecture & Design Ser.). (Illus.). 224p. 1997. 85.00 (4-938812-27-4, Pub. by Puroto Gyarak) Bks Nippan.

— Transportation Facilities. Watanabe, Hiroshi, tr. from JPN. LC 98-100430. (New Concept in Architecture & Design Ser.). (Illus.). 224p. 1997. 85.00 (4-938812-26-6, Pub. by Puroto Gyarak) Bks Nippan.

Meisei Publications Editorial Staff. Bar & Nightclub Graphics. (Illus.). 224p. 1996. 89.95 (4-938812-40-1, Pub. by Meisei Co Ltd) Bks Nippan.

— Cakes & Sweets Graphics: New Concepts in Architecture & Design. (Illus.). 224p. 1996. 89.95 (4-938812-20-7, Pub. by Meisei Co Ltd) Bks Nippan.

— Educational Facilities. (New Concept in Architecture & Design Ser.). (Illus.). 224p. 1994. 85.00 (4-87246-293-9, Pub. by Tenpo Syst Study) Bks Nippan.

Meisei Publications Editorial Staff. Laboratories & Research Facilities. (New Concept in Architecture & Design Ser.). (Illus.). 320p. 1997. 85.00 (4-938812-25-8, Pub. by Puroto Gyarak) Bks Nippan.

— Libraries. (New Concept in Architecture & Design Ser.). (Illus.). 224p. 1996. 85.00 (4-938812-21-5, Pub. by Puroto Gyarak) Bks Nippan.

Meisei Publications Editorial Staff. Medical Facilities. (New Concept in Architecture & Design Ser.). (Illus.). 224p. 1994. 85.00 (4-87246-294-7, Pub. by Tenpo Syst Study) Bks Nippan.

— New Hotel Architecture. (Illus.). 400p. 1993. 115.00 (4-87246-282-3, Pub. by Meisei Co Ltd) Bks Nippan.

Meisei Publications Editorial Staff. Theaters & Halls. LC 96-152250. (New Concept in Architecture & Design Ser.). 1996. 85.00 (4-938812-09-6, Pub. by Puroto Gyarak) Bks Nippan.

Meisel, Alan, et al. X-Ray Spectra & Chemical Binding. (Chemical Physics Ser.: Vol. 37). (Illus.). 465p. 1989. 157.95 (0-387-13325-9) Spr-Verlag.

Meisel, Allen D., et al. Atlas of Osteoarthritis. LC 83-253444. 208p. reprint ed. pap. 64.50 (0-7837-2727-5, 204310700006) Bks Demand.

***Meisel, Anthony.** To a Most Dangerous Sea: Adventure, Exploration, & Survival on Savage Waters. 320p. 2000. 39.98 (1-57912-113-6) Blck Dog & Leventhal.

Meisel, Anthony, ed. see Mails, Thomas E.

Meisel, Anthony C. & Del Mastro, M. L., trs. The Rule of St. Benedict. LC 74-33611. 128p. 1975. pap. 6.95 (0-385-00948-8, Image Bks) Doubleday.

Meisel, Barry. Losing the Edge: The Rise & Fall of Stanley Cup Champion New York Rangers. (Illus.). 256p. 1995. 23.00 (0-684-81519-2) S&S Trade.

Meisel, C. Julius, ed. Mainstreaming Handicapped Children: Outcomes, Controversies, & New Directions. 312p. (C). 1986. text 59.95 (0-89859-582-1) L Erlbaum Assocs.

Meisel, D., jt. ed. see Kamat, Prashant V.

Meisel, Dan, jt. auth. see Kamat, Prashant V.

Meisel, Frank, jt. auth. see Harvey, Brian.

Meisel, J. M., ed. Two First Languages - Early Grammatical Development in Bilingual Children. (Studies on Language Acquisition: No. 10). iv, 318p. 1990. pap. 83.10 (3-11-013133-1) Mouton.

Meisel, Jacqueline D. South Africa at the Crossroads. LC 94-8350. (Headliners Ser.). (Illus.). 64p. (J). (gr. 5-8). 1994. lib. bdg. 23.40 (1-56294-511-4) Millbrook Pr.

Meisel, James H. The Genesis of George Sorel: An Account of His Formative Period Followed by a Study of His Influence. LC 82-11860. 320p. 1982. reprint ed. lib. bdg. 69.50 (0-313-23658-5, MEGS, Greenwood Pr) Greenwood.

Meisel, James H., pref. The Myth of the Ruling Class: Gaetano Mosca & the "Elite" LC 80-13080. 432p. 1980. reprint ed. lib. bdg. 65.00 (0-313-22346-7, MEMR, Greenwood Pr) Greenwood.

Meisel, Janet. Barons of the Welsh Frontier: The Corbet, Pantulf, & Fitz Warin Families, 1066-1272. LC 80-10273. 251p. reprint ed. pap. 77.90 (0-7837-6886-9, 204671600003) Bks Demand.

Meisel, Jurgen M., ed. The Acquisition of Verb Placement: Functional Categories & V2 Phenomena in Language Acquisition. LC 92-23956. (Studies in Theoretical Psycholinguistics: Vol. 16). 464p. (C). 1992. text 212.00 (0-7923-1906-0) Kluwer Academic.

— Bilingual First Language Acquisition: French & German Grammatical Development. LC 94-23215. (Language Acquisition & Language Disorders (LALD) Ser.: No. 7). vi, 282p. 1994. lib. bdg. 70.00 (1-55619-242-8) J Benjamins Pubng Co.

— Bilingual First Language Acquisition: French & German Grammatical Development. LC 94-23215. (Language Acquisition & Language Disorders (LALD) Ser.: No. 7). vi, 282p. 1994. pap. 29.95 (1-55619-243-6) J Benjamins Pubng Co.

Meisel, Jurgen M., jt. ed. see Pam, Martin D.

Meisel, Louis & Cooper, Joseph. Political Parties: Development & Decay. LC 76-46782. (Sage Electoral Studies Yearbook: Vol. 4). 344p. reprint ed. pap. 106.70 (0-608-31006-9, 202192700026) Bks Demand.

Meisel, Louis K., selected by. Photorealism since 1980. LC 92-21997. (Illus.). 368p. 1993. 95.00 (0-8109-3720-4, Pub. by Abrams) Time Warner.

Meisel, Louis K., jt. auth. see Martignette, Charles G.

Meisel, Louis K., jt. auth. see Martinette, Charles G.

Meisel, Martin. Shaw & the Nineteenth Century Theatre. LC 75-25495. (Illus.). 477p. 1976. reprint ed. lib. bdg. 87.50 (0-8371-8416-9, MESN, Greenwood Pr) Greenwood.

Meisel, Max. Bibliography of American Natural History, 3 vols. 1100p. 1994. reprint ed. 195.00 (1-57898-029-1) Martino Pubng.

Meisel, Paul. Making Lawn Ornaments in Wood: Complete Building Techniques & Patterns. 130p. (Orig.). 1998. pap. 14.95 (1-56523-104-X) Fox Chapel Pub.

— Pencil Play Word Games for Girls. (gr. 9-12). 1999. pap. text 1.95 (1-56247-730-7) Pleasant Co.

— Zaras Hats. 1999. 14.99 (0-525-45465-9) NAL.

Meisel, Paul, jt. auth. see Berger, Melvin.

Meisel, Paul, jt. auth. see Elliott, David.

Meisel, Paul, jt. auth. see Spielman, Patrick.

Meisel, Perry. The Absent Father: Virginia Woolf & Walter Pater. LC 79-19289. 1980. 45.00 (0-300-02401-0) Yale U Pr.

— The Cowboy & the Dandy: Crossing over in Romanticism & Rock & Roll. LC 97-23789. (Illus.). 166p. 1998. 24.95 (0-19-511817-0) OUP.

— Thomas Hardy: The Return of the Repressed; a Study of the Major Fiction. LC 77-182211. (Yale College Ser.: No. 12). 189p. reprint ed. pap. 58.60 (0-8357-8349-9, 203382400087) Bks Demand.

Meisel, Steven, jt. ed. see Forray, Jean.

Meisel, Susan L., ed. see Vanhyning, Memory L.

***Meisel, Susan Pear & Harris, Ellen.** The Hamptons: Life Behind the Hedges. LC 99-462336. (Illus.). 172p. 2000. 39.95 (0-8109-3431-0, Pub. by Abrams) Time Warner.

Meisel, Tony. Cruising under Sail & Power. 272p. 1990. text 35.00 (0-02-583935-7) Macmillan.

Meisel-Valdez, Catherine S., jt. auth. see Scott, Joseph R., Jr.

Meisel, Wayne & Wolf, Maura, eds. Light One Candle: Quotes for Hope & Action. (Gift Editions Ser.). (Illus.). 64p. 1991. 7.99 (0-88088-357-X) Peter Pauper.

Meiselas, Susan & Whitley, A. Kurdistan: In the Shadow of History. LC 96-53931. (Illus.). 408p. 1997. 100.00 (0-679-42389-3) Random.

Meiselas, Susan, ed. see Dorfman, Ariel & de la Parra, Marco Antonio.

Meiselman, David & Shapiro, Eli. The Measurement of Corporate Sources & Uses of Funds. (Technical Papers: No. 18). 301p. 1964. reprint ed. 78.30 (0-87014-424-3) Natl Bur Econ Res.

Meiselman, David I. Welfare Reform & the Carter Public Service Employment Program: A Critique. LC 77-95219. 1978. pap. 2.50 (0-916770-05-2) Law & Econ U Miami.

Meiselman, David J. Attorney Malpractice Law & Procedure. LC 79-89562. 1980. 135.00 (0-685-59903-5) West Group.

Meiselman, David M., ed. Varieties of Monetary Experience. LC 70-116027. (Economic Research Studies). 1993. lib. bdg. 30.00 (0-226-51930-9) U Ch Pr.

***Meiselman, Herbert.** Dimensions of the Meal. LC 99-44079. 368p. 2000. 129.00 (0-8342-1641-8, 16418) Aspen Pub.

Meiselman, Karin C. Incest: A Psychological Study of Causes & Effects with Treatment Recommendations. LC 78-62557. 382p. reprint ed. pap. 108.90 (0-7837-6513-4, 2045625) Bks Demand.

Meiselman, Moshe. Jewish Woman in Jewish Law. (Library of Jewish Law & Ethics: Vol. 6). pap. 16.95 (0-87068-329-2) Ktav.

Meiselman, Shulamit S. The Soloveitchik Heritage: A Daughter's Memoir. LC 95-17674. 1995. 25.00 (0-88125-525-4) Ktav.

Meisels, Alexander. Cytopathology of the Uterine Cervix. 1991. sl. 200.00 (0-89189-341-5) Am Soc Clinical.

Meisels, Alexander & Morin, Carol. Cytopathology of the Uterus. 2nd ed. LC 96-41995. (ASCP Theory & Practice of Cytopathology Ser.). 1996. 116.00 (0-89189-383-0) Am Soc Clinical.

Meisels, Murray, jt. auth. see Shapiro, E. R.

Meisels, Murray, jt. ed. see Lane, Robert C.

Meisels, Samuel J. Developmental Screening in Early Childhood: A Guide. 3rd ed. LC 89-61119. 58p. pap. text 4.50 (0-935989-27-7, NAEYC#121) Natl Assn Child Ed.

Meisels, Samuel J. & Atkins-Burnett, Sally. Developmental Screening in Early Childhood: A Guide. LC 94-68837. 60p. 1994. pap. text 5.00 (0-912674-63-6, NAEYC121) Natl Assn Child Ed.

Meisels, Samuel J. & Atkins-Burnett, Sally. Developmental Screening in Early Childhood: A Guide. 4th ed. LC 94-68837. 60p. (C). 1994. pap. 6.00 (0-935989-64-1) Natl Assn Child Ed.

Meisels, Samuel J. & Fenichel, Emily, eds. New Visions for the Developmental Assessment of Infants & Young Children. 408p. (Orig.). 1996. pap. 35.00 (0-943657-35-0) ZERO TO THREE.

Meisels, Samuel J. & Shonkoff, Jack P., eds. Handbook of Early Childhood Intervention. (Illus.). 784p. (C). 1990. pap. text 36.95 (0-521-38777-9) Cambridge U Pr.

Meisels, Samuel J. & Wiske, Martha S. Early Screening Inventory. (C). 1983. 43.95 (0-8077-6080-3) Tchrs Coll.

Meisels, Samuel J., et al. Screening & Assessment: Guidelines for Identifying Young Disabled & Developmentally Vulnerable Children & Their Families. 68p. (Orig.). 1989. reprint ed. pap. 8.00 (0-943657-15-6, 07) ZERO TO THREE.

***Meisels, Samuel J., et al.** Winning Ways to Learn: Ages 3, 4, & 5. LC 00-102856. (Parenting Guide Ser.). (Illus.). 184p. 2000. pap. 15.95 (0-9666397-6-6) Goddard Pr.

— Winning Ways to Learn: Ages 6, 7, & 8. LC 00-102858. (Parenting Guide Ser.). (Illus.). 184p. 2000. pap. 15.95 (0-9666397-7-4) Goddard Pr.

Meisels, Samuel J., jt. ed. see Shonkoff, Jack P.

Meisenberg, Gerhard & Simmons, William H. Principles of Medical Biochemistry. LC 98-2505. (Illus.). 768p. (C). (gr. 13). 1998. pap. text 38.95 (0-8151-4410-5, 30897) Mosby Inc.

Meisenheimer, Adel. Song Crafters Tool Kit: The Basics, Special Gospel Music Edition, Vol. I. 1987. 39.95 incl. audio (0-944582-00-1) Song Crafters.

Meisenheimer, Adel, ed. Song Crafters Tool Kit: The Basics, Vol. I. 1987. 39.95 incl. audio (0-944582-02-8) Song Crafters.

Meisenheimer, Adel, ed. see Boitos, Myra E.

Meisenheimer, Bernadette, ed. see Meisenheimer, Jim.

Meisenheimer, Claire G. Improving Quality: A Guide to Effective Programs. 2nd ed. LC 97-5136. 400p. 1997. 65.00 (0-8342-0910-1) Aspen Pub.

— Quality Assurance for Home Health Care. 288p. 1989. 77.00 (0-8342-0026-0, 20026) Aspen Pub.

Meisenheimer, Jim. 50 More Ways to Sell Smarter. 144p. (Orig.). 1996. pap. 19.95 (0-9637479-1-6) Helbern Grp.

— Forty-Seven Ways to Sell Smarter. LC 93-78918. 144p. 1993. pap. 19.95 (0-9637479-0-8) Helbern Grp.

— How to Double Your Sales Without Quadrupling Your Effort. Meisenheimer, Bernadette, ed. 125p. 1999. pap. 19.95 (0-9637479-2-4) Helbern Grp.

Meisenheimer, Klaus & Roser, Hermann-Josef, eds. Hot Spots in Extragalactic Radio Sources. (Lecture Notes in Physics Ser.: Vol. 327). xii, 301p. 1989. 48.00 (0-387-50993-3) Spr-Verlag.

Meisenheimer, Klaus, jt. auth. see Roser, Hermann-Josef.

Meisenheimer, Lucky J. Lucky's Collectors Guide to 20th Century Yo-Yos: History & Values. LC 99-612740. (Illus.). 240p. 1998. write for info. (0-9667612-1-9); pap. 29.95 (0-9667612-0-0) Lucky Js Swim & Surf.

Meisenheimer, Sharon. Color Days. (J). (gr. k-3). 1988. pap. 8.99 (0-8224-1641-7) Fearon Teacher Aids.

— Special Ways with Ordinary Days. (J). (gr. k-3). 1988. pap. 12.99 (0-8224-6347-4) Fearon Teacher Aids.

Meisenhelder, Susan E. Hitting a Straight Lick with a Crooked Stick: Race & Gender in The Work of Zora Neale Hurston. LC 98-58023. 264p. 1999. 34.95 (0-8173-0965-9) U of Ala Pr.

Meiser & Laider, Keith J. Physical Chemistry. LC 96-1823. (Illus.). xvi, 919p. 1982. text 49.50 (0-8053-5682-7) Benjamin-Cummings.

Meiser & Laidler, Keith J. Physical Chemistry: A Solution Manual. (C). 1982. pap. text, teacher ed. 16.25 (0-8053-5683-5) Benjamin-Cummings.

Meiser, Frances, et al. The Brain Train. (Illus.). 32p. 1998. pap. 4.95 (1-884820-31-X) SAFE GOODS.

Meiser, John H., jt. auth. see Laidler, Keith J.

Meiser, Joy. Bed & Breakfast Guide to Rhode Island, 1990-1992. 6th ed. (Illus.). 110p. 1990. pap. 4.95 (0-685-31413-8) Bed Brkfst RI.

Meiser, Kenneth. Tenant-Landlord. (Illus.). 90p. 1989. pap. 35.00 (0-685-14672-3) NJ Inst CLE.

Meiser, Louis K. Photorealism. (Illus.). 448p. 1989. pap. 39.98 (0-8109-8092-4, Pub. by Abrams) Time Warner.

Meiser, Mary, jt. auth. see Maxwell, Rhoda J.

Meiser, Mary J. Good Writing! 2nd ed. LC 97-32641. 538p. (C). 1998. pap. text 42.00 (0-205-27334-3) Allyn.

Meisiek, Cornelius H. Evangelisches Theologiestudium Im Dritten Reich. (Europaische Hochschulschriften Ser.: Reihe 23, Bd. 481). (GER., Illus.). 422p. 1993. 59.80 (3-631-45566-6) P Lang Pubng.

Meisinger, Amy L. First Words: A Little Husker Book. (Illus.). 16p. (J). 1998. pap. 6.99 (0-9665572-0-4) U Lead.

Meisinger, Hubert. Liebesgebot und Altruismusforschung: Ein Exegetischer Beitrag Zum Dialog Zwischen Theologie und Naturwissenschaft. (Novum Testamentum et Orbis Antiquus Ser.: Vol. 33). (GER.). 336p. 1996. text 68.75 (3-7278-1093-9, Pub. by Presses Univ Fribourg) Eisenbrauns.

Meisinger, J. J., et al, eds. Nitrification Inhibitors: Potentials & Limitations. (ASA Special Publications: No. 38). (Illus.). 129p. 1980. pap. 5.25 (0-89118-063-X) Am Soc Agron.

Meisinger, Richard J., Jr. College & University Budgeting: An Introduction for Faculty & Academic Administrators. 2nd ed. LC 94-20513. 1994. 60.00 (0-915164-94-9) NACUBO.

Meisl, Josef. Haskalah: Geschichte der Aufklarungsbewegung unter den Juden in Russland. Katz, Steven, ed. LC 79-7147. (Jewish Philosophy, Mysticism & History of Ideas Ser.). 1980. reprint ed. lib. bdg. 23.95 (0-405-12277-2) Ayer.

An Asterisk (*) at the beginning of an entry indicates that the title is appearing for the first time.

Meisler, Alan. Flower Children: Thirty Original Victorian Postcards from the World-Class Meisler Collection. (Original Victorian Postcard Book Series from the World-Class Meisler Collection). (Illus.). 34p. (Orig.). 1994. pap. 8.95 (*1-886584-01-X*) Sentimental Times.

— Vegetable People: Thirty Original Victorian Postcards from the World-Class Meisler Collection. (Original Victorian Postcard Book Series from the World-Class Meisler Collection). (Illus.). 34p. (Orig.). 1994. pap. 8.95 (*1-886584-00-1*) Sentimental Times.

Meisler, Andy. Resist or Serve: Official Guide to The X-Files Volume 4. LC 99-181152. Vol. 4. (Illus.). 288p. 1999. pap. 16.00 (*0-06-107309-1*, HarperPrism) HarpC.

— X-Files The End & the Beginning: Episode Guide Volume 5, Vol. 5. Vol. 5. (Illus.). 304p. 2000. pap. 16.95 (*0-06-107595-7*, HarpEntertain) Morrow Avon.

Meisler, Andy & Rey, Michael. What Not to Name Your Baby. (Illus.). 64p. (Orig.). 1996. pap. 5.95 (*0-89815-814-1*) Ten Speed Pr.

Meisler, Jules. Effective Psychotherapy for Patient & Therapist. LC 91-2881. 208p. 1991. 55.00 (*0-275-93985-5*, C3985, Praeger Pubs) Greenwood.

Meisler, Meryl & Popper, Evelyn. Bulletin Board Displays. Pliakas, Stephanie, ed. (Thinking Skills Library). (Illus.). 108p. (Orig.). (J). (gr. 2-5). 1997. pap., teacher ed. 9.95 (*1-56784-707-2*) Newbridge Educ.

Meisler, Stanley. United Nations: The First Fifty Years. 416p. 1997. reprint ed. pap. 15.00 (*0-87113-656-2*, Atlntc Mnthly) Grove-Atltic.

Meislich, Herbert. Organic Chemistry. 1999. pap. text 8.95 (*0-07-052718-0*) McGraw-Hill Pubng.

Meislich, Herbert, et al. Schaum Three Thousand Solved Problems in Organic Chemistry. LC 92-23614. (Schaum's Solved Problems Ser.). 704p. (C). 1994. pap. 27.95 (*0-07-056424-8*) McGraw.

— Schaum's Outline of Organic Chemistry. 2nd ed. (Schaum's Outline Ser.). 512p. (C). 1991. pap. 14.95 (*0-07-041458-0*) McGraw.

Meislin, Marcia C. Internal Consultant: A Fifty-Minute Book. LC 96-86717. 95p. 1997. pap. text 10.95 (*1-56052-417-0*) Crisp Pubns.

Meisner, James, Jr. & Ruth, Amy. American Revolutionaries & Founders of the Nation. LC 98-30351. (Collective Biographies Ser.). (Illus.). 112p. (YA). (gr. 6 up). 1999. lib. bdg. 20.95 (*0-7660-1115-1*) Enslow Pubs.

Meisner, Jane S., jt. auth. see Davis, Judy M.

Meisner, Maurice. The Deng Xiaoping Era: An Inquiry into the Fate of Chinese Socialism, 1978-1994. LC 95-49995. 500p. 1996. 30.00 (*0-8090-7815-5*) Hill & Wang.

— Mao's China & After. enl. rev. ed. 1986. pap. 18.95 (*0-02-920880-7*) Free Pr.

— Mao's China & After. 3rd rev. ed. 1998. 16.00 (*0-02-920882-3*) Free Pr.

— Mao's China & After: A Hisrory of the People's Republic. 3rd ed. LC 98-31734. 608p. 1999. 19.95 (*0-684-85635-2*) S&S Trade.

— Marxism, Maoism & Utopianism: Eight Essays. 276p. 1982. 17.95 (*0-299-08420-5*) U of Wis Pr.

Meisner, Maurice, jt. ed. see Dirlik, Arif.

Meisner, Sanford & Longwell, Dennis. Sanford Meisner on Acting. LC 86-46187. 1987. pap. 13.00 (*0-394-75059-4*) Vin Bks.

Meisner, Ulf-G, ed. Effective Field Theories of the Standard Model: Proceedings of the Workshop, Dobogoko, Hungary, 22-26 August 1991. LC 92-9939. 500p. 1992. text 95.00 (*981-02-1001-9*) World Scientific Pub.

Meisonnier, Etienne. Dictionnaire des Medicaments Veterinaires et des Parapharmacies Animales. 6th ed. (FRE.). 1328p. 1992. pap. 110.00 (*0-7859-8659-6*, 286326091x) Fr & Eur.

Meiss, J. D., jt. auth. see Mackay, R. S.

Meiss, Kathleen A. Work, Welfare & Social Work Practice: A Study of Theoretical & Practice Relationships with Applications from Occupational Social Work. (Stockholm Studies in Social Work: No. 6). 253p. (Orig.). 1991. pap. 52.50 (*91-22-01411-X*) Coronet Bks.

Meiss, Millard. French Painting in the Time of Jean, Duke of Berry: The Limbourgs & Their Contemporaries, 2 vols. LC 73-90120. (Illus.). 1975. boxed set 110.00 (*0-8076-0734-7*) Braziller.

— Giotto & Assisi. LC 60-9443. (Walter W. S. Cook Alumni Lectures). 80p. reprint ed. pap. 30.00 (*0-608-30034-9*, 205084100061) Bks Demand.

— Les Tres Riches Heures of Jean, Duke of Berry. LC 73-90120. (Illus.). 290p. 1969. boxed set 100.00 (*0-8076-0512-3*) Braziller.

— Les Tres Riches Heures of Jean, Duke of Berry. LC 73-90120. (Illus.). 290p. 1989. pap. 24.95 (*0-8076-1220-0*) Braziller.

Meiss, Millard & Longdon, Jean. Les Tres Riches Heures: The Medieval Seasons. 1969. 50.00 (*0-8076-1226-X*, Pub. by Braziller) Norton.

Meiss, Millard & Longnon, Jean. Les Tres Riches Heures: The Medieval Seasons. 1995. 10.95 (*0-8076-1399-1*) Braziller.

Meiss, Millard & Thomas, Marcel. The Rohan Master: A Book of Hours. LC 73-77880. (Illus.). 248p. 1994. 65.00 (*0-8076-1358-4*, Pub. by Braziller) Norton.

Meiss, Millard & Thomas, Marcel, intros. The Rohan Master. LC 73-77880. (Illus.). 247p. 1973. boxed set 100.00 (*0-8076-0690-1*) Braziller.

Meiss, Millard, jt. auth. see Tintori, Leonetto.

Meiss, Millard, jt. intro. see Kirsch, Edith W.

***Meiss, Rich & Arch, Dave.** Warming up the Crowd! 57 Pre-Session Training Activities. LC 99-42893. 144p. 1999. pap. 24.95 (*0-7879-5141-2*, Pfffr & Co) Jossey-Bass.

Meiss, Von, see Von Meiss.

Meissel, Chris. Young Children Rap to Learn about Famous African-Americans. Keeling, Jan, ed. (Illus.). 80p. (Orig.). (J). (ps). 1993. pap. text 9.95 (*0-86530-265-0*, 265-0) Incentive Pubns.

Meisser, Meryl & Popper, Evelyn. Mapping Skills. Pliakas, Stephanie, ed. (Thinking Skills Library). (Illus.). 110p. (Orig.). (J). (gr. 2-5). 1997. pap., teacher ed. 9.95 (*1-56784-711-0*) Newbridge Educ.

Meissner. Florida Law Enforcement Manual, 2 vols., Set. 1988. pap. 24.00 (*0-614-05821-X*, MICHIE) LEXIS Pub.

Meissner, Bill. Hitting into the Wind: Stories. LC 96-51732. 224p. 1997. reprint ed. pap. 12.95 (*0-87074-416-X*) SMU Press.

Meissner, Bill & Driscoll, Jack. Twin Sons of Different Mirrors: Poems in Dialogue. LC 89-3106. (Illus.). 64p. (Orig.). 1989. pap. 6.95 (*0-915943-35-2*) Milkweed Ed.

Meissner, Boris. The Communist Party of the Soviet Union. Reshetar, John S., Jr., ed. Holling, Fred, tr. LC 75-27684. (Foreign Policy Research Institute Ser.: No. 4). 276p. 1976. reprint ed. lib. bdg. 65.00 (*0-8371-8461-4*, MECP) Greenwood.

Meissner, C. Latin Phrase Book. 347p. (C). 1992. pap. text 25.95 (*0-7156-1470-3*, Pub. by G Duckworth) Focus Pub-R Pullins.

— Latin Phrase Book. Auden, H. W., tr. from GER. 338p. 1989. reprint ed. pap. text 15.95 (*0-89341-567-7*, Longwood Academic) Hollowbrook.

Meissner, Collin. Henry James & the Language of Experience. LC 98-39565. 248p. (C). 1999. 59.95 (*0-521-62398-7*) Cambridge U Pr.

Meissner, Frank. Seeds of Change: Stories of IDB Innovation in Latin America. 132p. (Orig.). (C). 1991. pap. text 12.50 (*0-940602-39-3*) IADB.

— Technology Transfer in the Developing World: The Case of the Chile Foundation. LC 87-36127. 177p. 1988. 49.95 (*0-275-92926-4*, C2926, Praeger Pubs) Greenwood.

Meissner, Franz-Joseph. Langenscheidts Woerterbuch der Ungangssprache Franzoesisch. (FRE & GER.). 245p. 1992. 39.95 (*0-7859-8389-9*, 3468201583) Fr & Eur.

Meissner, Gerd. SAP: Inside the Secret Software Power. 238p. 2000. 24.95 (*0-07-134785-2*) McGraw.

***Meissner, Gunter & Folsom, Randall.** Outperform the Dow: Using Options, Futures & Portfolio Strategies to Beat the Market. (Trading Advantage Ser.). 224p. 2000. 39.95 (*0-471-39311-8*) Wiley.

Meissner, H. G. Strategic International Marketing. (Illus.). 260p. 1990. 71.95 (*0-387-52254-9*) Spr-Verlag.

Meissner, Henriette M. Rehtorik und Theologie: Der Dialog Gregors von Nyssa "De Anima et Resurrectione" (Patrologia Ser.: Bd. 1). (GER.). XV, 474p. 1992. 55.80 (*3-631-44032-4*) P Lang Pubng.

Meissner, Larry, jt. ed. see Patrick, Hugh T.

Meissner, Loren P. Essential Fortran 90 & 95: Common Subset Edition. LC 97-60215. 490p. (Orig.). (C). 1997. pap. 40.00 (*0-9640135-3-3*) Unicomp.

Meissner, Loren P. FORTRAN 90. 492p. (C). 1995. pap. 67.95 (*0-534-93372-6*) PWS Pubs.

Meissner, Loren P. & Organick, Elliot I. FORTRAN 77: Featuring Structured Programming. 3rd ed. LC 78-74689. 500p. (C). 1980. pap. text 34.69 (*0-201-05499-X*) Addison-Wesley.

Meissner, M. & Pohl, R. O., eds. Phonon Scattering in Condensed Matter VII: Proceedings of the Seventh International Conference. (Solid-State Sciences Ser.: Vol. 112). 1993. 119.95 (*0-387-56395-4*); write for info. (*3-540-56395-4*) Spr-Verlag.

Meissner, Paul A. Florida Law Enforcement Manual. rev. ed. 592p. (C). 1996. pap. text 49.00 (*0-9645280-0-2*) P A Meissner.

Meissner, R., et al, eds. Continental Lithosphere: Deep Seismic Reflections. (Geodynamics Ser.: Vol. 22). 452p. 1991. 55.00 (*0-87590-522 6*, GD0225226) Am Geophysical.

Meissner, R. & Bortfeld, R. K., eds. DEKORP-Atlas. (Illus.). 390p. 1990. 118.95 (*0-387-52512-2*) Spr-Verlag.

***Meissner, Renate.** Die Sudjemenitischen Juden: Versuch einer Rekonstruktion Ihrer Traditionellen Kultur Vor Dem Exodus. (Europaische Hochschulschriften Ser.). 197p. 1999. 37.95 (*3-631-34775-8*) P Lang Pubng.

Meissner, Rolf. The Continental Crust: A Geophysical Approach. (International Geophysics Ser.). 1986. pap. text 75.00 (*0-12-488951-4*) Acad Pr.

Meissner, W. W. Freud & Psychoanalysis. (Gethsemani Studies in Psychological & Religious Anthropology). 310p. 2000. 40.00 (*0-268-02854-0*, Pub. by U of Notre Dame Pr); pap. 20.00 (*0-268-02855-9*, Pub. by U of Notre Dame Pr) Chicago Distribution Ctr.

— To the Greater Glory: A Psychological Study of Ignatian Spirituality. LC 98-25328. (Studies in Theology). 1998. write for info. (*0-87462-640-4*) Marquette.

— Vincent's Religion: The Search for Meaning. LC 96-23183. (Reshaping of Psychoanalysis Ser.: Vol. 8). (Illus.). XIII, 279p. (C). 1997. 52.95 (*0-8204-3390-X*) P Lang Pubng.

Meissner, Werner. Philosophy & Politics in China: The Controversy over Dialectical Materialism in the 1930's. LC 89-51664. 230p. 1990. 42.50 (*0-8047-1772-9*) Stanford U Pr.

Meissner, William W. The Assault on Authority: Dialogue or Dilemma? LC 70-152878. 320p. reprint ed. pap. 99.20 (*0-8357-8807-5*, 203346500086) Bks Demand.

***Meissner, William W.** The Cultic Origins of Christianity: The Dynamics of Religious Development. LC 99-54673. 296p. 2000. pap. 27.95 (*0-8146-5076-7*, M Glazier) Liturgical Pr.

Meissner, William W. Ignatius of Loyola: The Psychology of a Saint. LC 92-1270. 529p. 1994. pap. 20.00 (*0-300-06079-3*) Yale U Pr.

— Internalization in Psychoanalysis, No. 50. LC 80-13867. (Psychological Issues Monographs: No. 50). ix, 279p. 1980. 42.50 (*0-8236-2726-8*, BN02713) Intl Univs Pr.

— Life & Faith: Psychological Perspectives on Religious Experience. fac. ed. LC 85-8026. 328p. 1987. reprint ed. pap. 101.70 (*0-7837-7782-5*, 204753700007) Bks Demand.

— Psychoanalysis & Religious Experience. LC 83-51296. 254p. 1986. pap. 18.00 (*0-300-03751-1*, Y-599) Yale U Pr.

— Psychotherapy & the Paranoid Process. LC 85-15614. 432p. 1994. 60.00 (*0-87668-752-4*) Aronson.

— The Therapeutic Alliance. LC 96-13037. 100p. 1996. 42.00 (*0-300-06684-8*) Yale U Pr.

— Thy Kingdom Come: Psychoanalytic Perspectives on the Messiah & the Millennium. 256p. (Orig.). 1995. pap. 29.95 (*1-55612-750-2*) Sheed & Ward WI.

— Treatment of Patients in the Borderline Spectrum. LC 88-10526. 648p. 1995. pap. 60.00 (*1-56821-495-2*) Aronson.

— What Is Effective in Psychoanalytic Therapy? The Move from Interpretation to Relation. LC 90-14509. 216p. 1991. 40.00 (*0-87668-572-6*) Aronson.

Meissonnier, Juste A. Oeuvre de Juste Aurele Meissonnier: The Complete Suite of Engravings of His Designs. LC 69-16909. (Illus.). 1978. reprint ed. 54.95 (*0-405-08785-3*, Pub. by Blom Pubns) Ayer.

***Meistad, Tore.** Martin Luther & John Wesley on the Sermon on the Mount. LC 98-45129. (Pietist & Wesleyan Studies: No. 10). (Illus.). 352p. 1999. 55.00 (*0-8108-3567-3*) Scarecrow.

Meistas, E. G., jt. ed. see Solheim, S. E.

Meister. Archaeology in the Classroom. 112p. 1995. pap., per. 10.50 (*0-7872-1875-8*) Kendall-Hunt.

Meister, ed. Daretis Phrygii. (LAT.). 1991. reprint ed. 26.95 (*3-8154-1960-3*, T1960, Pub. by B G Teubner) U of Mich Pr.

Meister & AIA Staff. Excavations in Israel. 144p. 1995. pap. text, per. 30.00 (*0-7872-0486-2*) Kendall-Hunt.

Meister, et al. Archaeology on Film. 2nd ed. LC 94-73389. 128p. 1994. pap., per. 13.50 (*0-8403-9016-5*) Kendall-Hunt.

Meister, Albert. Participation, Associations, Development & Change. Ross, Jack L., tr. from FRE. (Illus.). 286p. 1984. 39.95 (*0-87855-423-8*) Transaction Pubs.

Meister, Alton. Advances in Enzymology & Related Areas of Molecular Biology, Vol. 67. 528p. 1993. 239.95 (*0-471-58279-4*) Wiley.

— Advances in Enzymology & Related Areas of Molecular Biology, Vol. 71. 11th ed. LC 41-9213. 288p. 1995. 210.00 (*0-471-12701-9*) Wiley.

Meister, Alton, ed. Advances in Enzymology: And Related Areas of Molecular Biology, 6 vols., Vol. 63. 551p. 1990. 239.95 (*0-471-50984-1*) Wiley.

— Advances in Enzymology: And Related Areas of Molecular Biology, 6 vols., Vol. 64. 494p. 1991. 239.95 (*0-471-50949-3*) Wiley.

— Advances in Enzymology: And Related Areas of Molecular Biology, 6 vols., Vol. 65. 448p. 1992. 239.95 (*0-471-52760-2*) Wiley.

— Advances in Enzymology: And Related Areas of Molecular Biology, Vol. 61, 6 vols., Vol. 61. 557p. 1988. 239.95 (*0-471-81830-5*) Wiley.

— Advances in Enzymology: And Related Areas of Molecular Biology, Vol. 62, 6 vols., Vol. 62. 455p. 1989. 225.00 (*0-471-61770-9*) Wiley.

— Advances in Enzymology & Related Areas of Molecular Biology. 633p. 1995. pap. text 59.00 (*0-471-12648-9*) Wiley.

— Advances in Enzymology & Related Areas of Molecular Biology, Vol. 66. 344p. 1993. 239.95 (*0-471-55769-2*) Wiley.

— Advances in Enzymology & Related Areas of Molecular Biology, Vol. 68. 237p. 1994. 239.95 (*0-471-31071-9*) Wiley.

— Advances in Enzymology & Related Areas of Molecular Biology, Vol. 69. 316p. 1994. 239.95 (*0-471-01767-1*) Wiley.

Meister, Alton, ed. Advances in Enzymology & Related Areas of Molecular Biology, Vol. 60, 6 vols., Vol. 60. 417p. 1987. 239.95 (*0-471-81282-X*) Wiley.

Meister, Alton, ed. Advances in Enzymology & Related Areas of Molecular Biology, Vol. 70, Vol. 70. LC 41-9213. 344p. 1995. 210.00 (*0-471-04097-5*) Wiley.

Meister, Anton D., et al. Quadratic Programming Models Applied to Agricultural Policies. LC 77-25931. (Illus.). 120p. 1978. reprint ed. pap. 37.20 (*0-608-00023-X*, 206078900006) Bks Demand.

Meister, Barbara. Art Song: The Marriage of Music & Poetry. LC 91-12788. 300p. (C). 1992. text 35.00 (*0-89341-635-5*, Longwood Academic) Hollowbrook.

— Nineteenth-Century French Song: Faur, Chausson, Duparc, & Debussy. LC 98-145953. 416p. 1998. 24.95 (*0-253-21175-1*) Ind U Pr.

— Nineteenth-Century French Song: Faure, Chausson, Duparc & Debussy. LC 79-2171. 416p. 1980. 39.95 (*0-253-34075-6*) Ind U Pr.

Meister, Cari. Amazon River. LC 98-8662. (Rivers & Lakes Ser.). (J). 2002. lib. bdg. 19.92 (*1-57765-101-4*) ABDO Pub Co.

— Blizzards. LC 98-11989. (Nature's Fury Ser.). (Illus.). 32p. (J). 1999. lib. bdg. 19.93 (*1-57765-085-9*, ABDO & Dghtrs) ABDO Pub Co.

***Meister, Cari.** Busy, Busy City Street. LC 99-42058. (Illus.). 32p. (J). (ps-3). 2000. 15.99 (*0-670-88944-X*, Viking Child) Peng Put Young Read.

Meister, Cari. Canada. LC 98-10139. (Going Places Ser.). (Illus.). 24p. (J). 2000. lib. bdg. 18.60 (*1-57765-028-X*, Checkerboard Library) ABDO Pub Co.

— Catch That Cat. LC 98-53056. (J). 2000. 15.00 (*0-516-21689-9*) Childrens Pict.

***Meister, Cari.** Catch That Cat! (Rookie Readers Ser.). (J). 2000. pap. text 4.95 (*0-516-26541-5*) Childrens.

Meister, Cari. Disney World. LC 98-9768. (Going Places Ser.). (Illus.). 24p. (J). 2000. lib. bdg. 18.60 (*1-57765-025-5*, Checkerboard Library) ABDO Pub Co.

— Earthquakes. LC 98-19467. (Nature's Fury Ser.). (Illus.). 32p. (J). (gr. 4-6). 1999. lib. bdg. 19.93 (*1-57765-083-2*, ABDO & Dghtrs) ABDO Pub Co.

— Floods. LC 98-6648. (Nature's Fury Ser.). (Illus.). 32p. (J). 1998. lib. bdg. 19.93 (*1-57765-082-4*, ABDO & Dghtrs) ABDO Pub Co.

— Grand Canyon. LC 98-4809. (Going Places Ser.). (Illus.). 24p. (J). 2000. lib. bdg. 18.60 (*1-57765-024-7*, Checkerboard Library) ABDO Pub Co.

— Great Bear Lake. LC 98-4149. (Lakes Ser.). (J). 2000. lib. bdg. 19.92 (*1-57765-108-1*) ABDO Pub Co.

— Hurricanes. LC 98-13130. (Nature's Fury Ser.). (Illus.). 32p. (J). (gr. 4-6). 1999. lib. bdg. 19.93 (*1-57765-080-8*, ABDO & Dghtrs) ABDO Pub Co.

— Mexico. LC 98-10131. (Going Places Ser.). (Illus.). 24p. (J). 2000. lib. bdg. 18.60 (*1-57765-029-8*, Checkerboard Library) ABDO Pub Co.

— The Nile. LC 98-29324. (Rivers & Lakes Ser.). (J). 2002. lib. bdg. 19.92 (*1-57765-098-0*) ABDO Pub Co.

— The Ocean. LC 98-11751. (Going Places Ser.). (Illus.). 24p. (J). 2000. lib. bdg. 18.60 (*1-57765-027-1*, Checkerboard Library) ABDO Pub Co.

***Meister, Cari.** Tiny Goes Camping. LC 00-8185. (Illus.). (J). 2000. pap. write for info. (*0-14-056741-0*, PuffinBks) Peng Put Young Read.

— Tiny Goes to the Library. LC 98-51134. (Illus.). 32p. (J). (ps-2). 2000. 13.89 (*0-670-88556-8*, Viking Child) Peng Put Young Read.

— Tiny Goes to the Library. LC 98-51134. (Easy-to-Read Ser.). (Illus.). (J). 2000. pap. 3.99 (*0-14-130488-X*, PuffinBks) Peng Put Young Read.

Meister, Cari. Tiny's Bath. LC 98-3844. (Illus.). 32p. (J). (ps-2). 1999. 13.89 (*0-670-87962-2*); pap. 3.99 (*0-14-130267-4*, Viking) Viking Penguin.

— Volcanoes. LC 98-15730. (Nature's Fury Ser.). (Illus.). 32p. (J). 1999. lib. bdg. 19.93 (*1-57765-084-0*, ABDO & Dghtrs) ABDO Pub Co.

— When Tiny Was Tiny. LC 98-47827. (J). 1999. pap. 3.99 (*0-14-130419-7*) Viking Penguin.

— The Yangtze. LC 98-20923. (Rivers Ser.). (J). 2002. lib. bdg. 19.92 (*1-57765-103-0*) ABDO Pub Co.

— Yellowstone National Park. LC 98-10605. (Going Places Ser.). (Illus.). 24p. (J). 2000. lib. bdg. 18.60 (*1-57765-026-3*, Checkerboard Library) ABDO Pub Co.

Meister, Cari & Brooks, David. Catch That Cat. LC 98-53056. (Rookie Readers Ser.). 24p. (J). (gr. k-1). 1999. 15.00 (*0-516-21614-7*) Childrens.

***Meister, Cari & Davis, Rich.** Tiny the Snow Dog. LC 99-88385. (Easy-to-Read Ser.). (J). 2001. pap. write for info. (*0-14-056708-9*) Viking Penguin.

Meister, Carl. Lake Victoria. LC 98-7298. (Lakes Ser.). 2002. lib. bdg. 19.92 (*1-57765-105-7*) ABDO Pub Co.

— Tornadoes. LC 98-12064. (Nature's Fury Ser.). (Illus.). 32p. (J). 1999. lib. bdg. 19.93 (*1-57765-081-6*, ABDO & Dghtrs) ABDO Pub Co.

Meister, Cary W. Historical Demography of the Pima & Maricopa Indians, 1846-1974, 2 vols. (Studies in Historical Demography). 775p. 1990. reprint ed. text 50.00 (*0-8240-3364-7*) Garland.

Meister, Charles W. Religion: Bane or Blessing? LC 99-61058. 384p. 1999. pap. 16.95 (*1-56184-141-2*) New Falcon Pubns.

Meister, D. Psychology of System Design. (Advances in Human Factors/Ergonomics Ser.: Vol. 17). 548p. 1991. 201.25 (*0-444-88378-9*) Elsevier.

Meister, David. Conceptual Aspects of Human Factors. LC 88-32055. (Illus.). 278p. reprint ed. pap. 86.20 (*0-608-08798-X*, 206943700004) Bks Demand.

— The History & Characteristics of Human Factors - Ergonomics. LC 98-49609. 400p. 1999. pap. 36.00 (*0-8058-2769-2*) L Erlbaum Assocs.

— The History & Characteristics of Human Factors-Ergonomics. LC 98-49609. 300p. 1999. 79.95 (*0-8058-2768-4*) L Erlbaum Assocs.

— Human Factors Testing & Evaluation. (Advances in Human Factors-Ergonomics Ser.: No. 5). 424p. 1986. 204.50 (*0-444-42701-5*) Elsevier.

Meister, David, jt. auth. see Bedny, Gregory.

Meister, Denise, jt. auth. see Nolan, James L., Jr.

Meister, Erhard, et al, eds. Modern Mathematical Methods in Diffraction Theory & Its Applications in Engineering: Proceedings of the Sommerfeld '96 Workshop, Freudenstadt, 30 September-4 October 1996. LC 97-22715. (Methoden und Verfahren der Mathematischen Physik Ser.: Bd. 42). (GER., Illus.). vi, 308p. 1997. pap. 57.95 (*3-631-30878-7*) P Lang Pubng.

— Modern Mathematical Methods in Diffraction Theory & Its Applications in Engineering: Proceedings of the Sommerfeld '96 Workshop, Freudenstadt, 30 September-4 October 1996. LC 97-22715. (Methoden und Verfahren der Mathematischen Physik Ser.: Bd. 42). (Illus.). VI, 308p. 1997. pap. 57.95 (*0-8204-3230-X*) P Lang Pubng.

Meister, Ernst. Room Without Walls: Selected Poems. Gugelberger, George M., ed. Orig. Title: Wandloser Raum. 64p. 1981. pap. 4.00 (*0-88031-057-X*) Invisible-Red Hill.

Meister, Gail. Help for New Teachers: Developmental Practices That Work. 97p. 1990. pap. 21.95 (*1-56602-036-0*) Research Better.

Meister, Gail, jt. auth. see Austin, Susan.

Meister, Gerd. Es Grunte die Tanne, Es Wuchs das Erz. (GER.). 220p. 1991. write for info. (*3-487-09317-0*) G Olms Pubs.

M

M

Meister, H. The Purification Problem for Constrained Games with Incomplete Information. (Lecture Notes in Economics & Mathematical Systems Ser.: Vol. 295). 140p. 1987. 23.95 (*0-387-18429-5*) Spr-Verlag.

Meister, J. J. Polymer Modification: Principles, Techniques, & Applications. (Plastics Engineering Ser.). (Illus.). Date not set. text. write for info. (*0-8247-0078-3*) Dekker.

Meister, Jeanne. 1998 Survey of Corporate University Future Directions. unabridged ed. Eisenstat, Adam & Roberts, Stephanie, eds. (Illus.). 100p. 1998. pap. 895.00 (*0-9656453-1-2*) Corp Univ Xchange.

Meister, Jeanne C. Corporate Quality Universities: Lessons Learned from Programs That Produce Results. LC 93-1268. 276p. 1993. text 42.50 (*1-55623-790-1*, Irwn Prfssnl) McGraw-Hill Prof.

— Corporate Universities: Lessons in Building A World-Class Work-Force. 2nd rev. ed. LC 97-32842. 1998. text 40.00 (*0-7863-0787-0*, Irwn Prfssnl) McGraw-Hill Prof.

— 1997 Survey of Corporate University Future Directions. unabridged ed. Roberts, Stephanie, ed. (Illus.). 100p. 1997. pap. 895.00 (*0-9656453-0-4*) Corp Univ Xchange.

Meister, John, ed. see Law, William.

Meister, Maureen, ed. H. H. Richardson: The Architect, His Peers & Their Era. LC 99-26903. (Illus.). 155p. 1999. 20.00 (*0-262-13356-3*) MIT Pr.

Meister, Michael, ed. Blessed Ambiguity: Brothers in the Church. LC 93-74489. (Christian Brothers Seminar, 1993 Ser.). 263p. (Orig.). 1994. pap. 10.00 (*1-884904-00-9*) Christian Brothers.

Meister, Michael F., ed. The Declaration: Text & Contexts. (Christian Brothers Seminar, 1994 Ser.). 337p. (Orig.). 1995. pap. text 8.00 (*1-884904-05-X*) Christian Brothers.

Meister, Michael F., ed. Charism & Identity: Who Do We Say We Are? (Christian Brothers Seminar, 1995 Ser.). 129p. (Orig.). 1996. pap. 12.00 (*1-884904-06-8*) Christian Brothers.

Meister, Michael W., ed. Cooking for the Gods: The Art of Home Ritual in Bengal. (Illus.). 96p. (Orig.). 1996. pap. 29.95 (*0-8122-1589-3*) U of Pa Pr.

Meister, Michael W., et al, eds. Encyclopaedia of Indian Temple Architecture: North India: Foundations of North Indian Style, c. 250 B. C.-A. D. 1100, Vol. 2, Pt. 1. LC 82-50173. (Illus.). 440p. 1988. reprint ed. pap. 136.40 (*0-608-07149-8*, 206737500002) Bks Demand.

— Encyclopaedia of Indian Temple Architecture: North India: Foundations of North Indian Style, c. 250 B. C.-A. D. 1100, Vol. 2, Pt. 1, Plates. LC 82-50173. (Illus.). 388p. 1988. reprint ed. pap. 120.30 (*0-608-07150-1*, 206737500003) Bks Demand.

Meister, Michael W., pref. Making Things in South Asia: The Role of Artist & Craftsman. (Proceedings of the South Asia Seminar Ser.: No. 4). (Illus.). 216p. (Orig.). 1988. pap. 10.00 (*0-936115-03-3*) U Penn South Asia.

Meister, Michael W., ed. see Coomaraswamy, Amanda K.

Meister, Michael W., ed. see Coomaraswamy, Ananda K.

Meister, Michael W., ed. see Ghosh, Pika.

Meister, Peter, ed. Arthurian Literature & Christianity: Notes from the Twentieth Century. LC 99-11198. (Reference Library of the Humanities). (Illus.). 224p. 1999. reprint ed. 50.00 (*0-8153-3262-9*, H2134) Garland.

Meister, Peter W. & Reber, Horst. European Porcelain of the 18th Century. LC 81-66539. (Illus.). 320p. 1983. text 105.00 (*0-8014-1443-1*) Cornell U Pr.

Meister, Robert, tr. see Fuchs, Peter.

Meister, Susan B., jt. ed. see Nightingale, Elena O.

Meister, T. Jeff, jt. auth. see Eckersley, John S.

Meister, Teddy. Pardon Me, but Your References Are Showing! 32 Proven & Fun Activities to Build Reference Skills for Grades 4-8. 2nd ed. LC 96-4320. 48p. 1996. pap. 12.95 (*0-917846-80-X*, Alleyside) Highsmith Pr.

Meister, U. Usha Meister's Vegetarian Kitchen: Low-Fat Epicurean Delights. 1997. pap. text. write for info. (*0-9681142-0-2*) U Meister.

***Meister, Wil L.** Hearts of Childhood. LC 99-96807. (J). (ps-k). 2000. pap. 9.95 (*0-533-13350-5*) Vantage.

Meisterfeld, C. W. Jelly Bean vs. Dr. Jekyll & Mr. Hyde: Written for the Safety of Our Children & the Welfare of Our Dogs. LC 89-91639. (Illus.). 176p. 1989. 24.95 (*0-9601292-5-1*) M R K.

— Psychological Dog Training: Behavior Conditioning with Respect & Trust. (Illus.). 232p. (Orig.). (YA). (gr. 6 up). 1991. pap. 18.00 (*0-9601292-6-X*) M R K.

— Tails' of a Dog Psychoanalyst. LC 78-58492. (Illus.). 1978. 19.95 (*0-9601292-2-7*) M R K.

Meisterfeld, C. W. & Pecci, Ernest F. Crazy Dogs-Crazy People: Looking at Behavior in Our Society. Blakely, Kristine & Steinmueller, Heidi, eds. LC 92-81548. (Illus.). 272p. 1993. 26.95 (*0-9601292-7-8*) M R K.

Meisterhans, Konrad. Grammatik Der Attischen Inschriften. xiv, 288p. 1971. reprint ed. write for info. (*3-487-04079-4*) G Olms Pubs.

***Meistorfeld, C. W.** Dog Whisper: Intuitive Communication. LC 99-75795. (Illus.). 224p. 1999. 21.95 (*0-9601292-8-6*) M R K.

Meiswand. Colour Comedies: International Architects' & Designers' Workshop. 1993. 39.95 (*3-926048-90-5*, Pub. by Nieswand-Verlag) Dist Art Pubs.

Meital, Yoram. Egypt's Struggle for Peace: Continuity & Change, 1967-1971. LC 97-29622. 256p. 1997. 49.95 (*0-8130-1533-2*) U Press Fla.

Meitam, Carol, ed. see Birnholz, Mary B., et al.

Meites, Joseph, ed. Neuroendocrinology of Aging. LC 83-10937. 400p. 1983. 85.00 (*0-306-41310-8*, Plenum Trade) Perseus Pubng.

Meites, Louis. Polarographic Techniques. 2nd ed. LC 65-19735. (Illus.). 770p. reprint ed. pap. 200.00 (*0-608-18196-X*, 205659800078) Bks Demand.

Meites, Louis, et al, eds. Handbook Series in Inorganic Electrochemistry, Vol. VIII. 552p. 1988. lib. bdg. 160.00 (*0-8493-0369-9*, QD557) CRC Pr.

— Handbook Series in Inorganic Electrochemistry: (Mn-Np), Vol. IV. 536p. 1984. lib. bdg. 112.00 (*0-8493-0364-8*, QD557, CRC Reprint) Franklin.

— Handbook Series in Inorganic Electrochemistry: (O-Pd), Vol. V. 552p. 1985. lib. bdg. 110.00 (*0-8493-0365-6*, QD557, CRC Reprint) Franklin.

Meites, Louis & Zuman, Petr. Handbook of Organic Electrochemistry, Vol. 5. 472p. 1982. 259.00 (*0-8493-7225-9*, QD272, CRC Reprint) Franklin.

— Handbook Series in Inorganic Electrochemistry, 6 vols., Set. LC 80-17900. 1742.00 (*0-8493-0360-5*, CRC Reprint) Franklin.

— Handbook Series in Inorganic Electrochemistry, Vol. VI. 552p. 1983. lib. bdg. 302.00 (*0-8493-7226-7*, QD272, CRC Reprint) Franklin.

— Handbook Series in Organic Electrochemistry, Vol. 3. LC 77-24273. 1978. 372.00 (*0-8493-7223-2*, CRC Reprint) Franklin.

Meites, Louis & Zuman, Petr, eds. Handbook Series in Inorganic Electrochemistry: (Eu-Mg), Vol. III. 488p. 1983. lib. bdg. 111.00 (*0-8493-0363-X*, QD557, CRC Reprint) Franklin.

Meites, Louis, et al. Handbook of Inorganic Electrochemistry, Vol. VI: PM-SC. (CRC Handbook Series in Inorganic Electrochemistry). 544p. 1986. 300.00 (*0-8493-0366-4*, QD557, CRC Reprint) Franklin.

— Handbook of Inorganic Electrochemistry, Vol. VII: SC-TM. (CRC Handbook Series in Inorganic Electrochemistry). 512p. 1986. 284.00 (*0-8493-0367-2*, CRC Reprint) Franklin.

— Handbook Series in Inorganic Electrochemistry: (Ag-Co), Vol. I. 512p. 1980. 283.00 (*0-8493-0361-3*, QD557, CRC Reprint) Franklin.

— Handbook Series in Inorganic Electrochemistry: (Cr-Er), Vol. II. Zuman, Petr, ed. 560p. 1981. 303.00 (*0-8493-0362-1*, QD557, CRC Reprint) Franklin.

Meites, Samuel, jt. ed. see Faulkner, Willard R.

Meitin, Alberta. Teaching Basic Ceramics. LC 90-63281. 54p. 1990. pap. text 4.95 (*0-916809-45-5*) Scott Pubns MI.

Meitler. Texas Instrument's Graphic Calculator College Mathematics. 1997. pap. text 21.33 (*0-13-749517-X*) P-H.

Meitler, Carolyn L. College Algebra with Trigonometry: Graphing Calculator Enhancement. 5th ed. 1993. pap. text. write for info. (*0-07-041368-1*) McGraw.

— Graphing Calculator. 5th ed. (Mathematics Ser.). 1992. pap., suppl. ed. 19.75 (*0-534-16745-4*) PWS Pubs.

— Graphing Calculator Enhancement for Elementary Algebra: TI-81, Casio FX-7700G, & TI-85 Graphing Calculators. LC 92-39470. 96p. (C). 1993. pap. 14.38 (*0-07-041369-X*) McGraw.

— Graphing Calculator Enhancement for Intermediate Algebra: TI-81, Casio FX-7700G, & TI-85 Graphing Calculators. LC 92-35331. 96p. (C). 1993. pap. 15.63 (*0-07-041370-3*) McGraw.

— A Guide to TI Graphing Calculators. LC 94-32478. (C). 1994. pap. text 21.25 (*0-07-041371-1*) McGraw.

— Precalculus: Functions & Graphs, Calculator Enhancement for Precalculus. 3rd ed. 1993. pap. text. write for info. (*0-07-041367-3*) McGraw.

Meitler Consultants, Inc. Staff, tr. New Catholic Schools 1985 to 1995. LC 97-204552. (Illus.). 120p. 1997. pap. 16.00 (*1-55833-187-5*) Natl Cath Educ.

Meitlis, Jakob. Das Ma'asse-Buch. Entstehung und Quellengeschichte. (GER.). xiv, 152p. 1987. reprint ed. write for info. (*3-487-07833-3*) G Olms Pubs.

Meitner, Lise, jt. auth. see Rife, Patricia.

Meitus, Irv J., jt. auth. see Weinberg.

Meitzler, Charles & Isham, R. General Physics 118. (C). 1996. pap. text 18.51 (*1-56870-235-3*) RonJon Pub.

Meitzler, Leland K., ed. United States County Courthouse Address Book. 63p. 1988. pap. 3.95 (*0-945433-03-4*) Herit Quest.

Meitzner, Laura S. & Price, Martin L. Amaranth to Zai Holes: Ideas for Growing Food under Difficult Conditions. (Illus.). 416p. (Orig.). 1996. pap. 29.95 (*0-9653360-0-X*) ECHO Inc.

***Meiwes-Broer, Karl-Heinz.** Metal Clusters at Surfaces: Structure, Quantum Properties, Physical Chemistry. LC 99-56372. (Cluster Physics Ser.). (Illus.). 300p. (C). 2000. 79.95 (*3-540-66562-5*) Spr-Verlag.

Meixel, Steven A., jt. auth. see Franko, John P.

Meixner. A Practice Set for Intermediate 1: Acme Box Company. 1997. pap. 19.95 (*0-87393-733-3*) Dame Pubns.

Meixner, Barbara. Suzuki Harp Ensemble Music. 29p. 1994. pap. text 5.95 (*0-87487-753-9*) Summy-Birchard.

— Suzuki Piano Ensemble Music: 2 Pianos, 4 Hands, Vol. 1. 25p. 1995. pap. text 6.95 (*0-87487-750-4*) Summy-Birchard.

— Suzuki Piano Ensemble Music: 2 Pianos, 4 Hands, Vol. 2. 32p. 1995. pap. text 6.95 (*0-87487-751-2*) Summy-Birchard.

— Suzuki Piano Ensemble Music Vol. 1: 1 Piano, 4 Hands. 22p. 1995. pap. text 6.95 (*0-87487-749-0*) Summy-Birchard.

— Suzuki Piano Ensemble Music Vols. 3-4: 2 Pianos, 4 Hands. 30p. 1995. pap. text 6.95 (*0-87487-752-0*) Summy-Birchard.

Meixner, Elizabeth, jt. auth. see Cummings, Gerald R.

Meixner, Laura L. French Realist Painting & the Critique of American Society, 1865-1900. (Illus.). 336p. (C). 1995. text 110.00 (*0-521-46103-0*) Cambridge U Pr.

Meixner, Uwe. Axiomatic Formal Ontology. LC 97-214694. (Synthese Library: No. 264). 404p. 1997. text 160.50 (*0-7923-4717-X*) Kluwer Academic.

Meizel, Janet E. Spanish for Medical Personnel. 1993. per. 26.95 (*1-56930-001-1*) Skidmore Roth Pub.

Meizhen, Cheng, jt. compiled by see Dejin, Li.

Meizlish, Saul, ed. A Child's Passover Haggadah. (Illus.). 76p. (J). (gr. 1-6). 1987. 9.95 (*0-915361-70-1*) Lambda Pubs.

Meizner, Israel & Bar-Ziv, Jacob. In Utero Diagnosis of Skeletal Disorders: An Atlas of Prenatal Sonographic & Postnatal Radiologic Correlation. LC 92-48449. 304p. 1993. lib. bdg. 179.00 (*0-8493-5130-8*, R6629) CRC Pr.

***Meja, Volker & Stehr, Nico, eds.** The Sociology of Knowledge, 2 vols. LC 99-47651. (International Library of Critical Writings in Sociology). 1286p. 1999. 465.00 (*1-85898-588-9*) E Elgar.

Meja, Volker, jt. auth. see Kettler, David.

Meja, Volker, jt. ed. see Stehr, Nico.

Mejdal, S., tr. see Koplowitz, George B., ed.

Mejdal, S., tr. see Koplowitz, George B. & Warren, Alan, eds.

Mejia, jt. auth. see Gomez.

Mejia, A. & Pizurki, H. Physician & Nurse Migration Analysis & Policy Implications. 476p. 1979. 64.00 (*92-4-156059-2*) World Health.

Mejia, A., jt. auth. see Abbatt, F.

Mejia, Arthur, jt. ed. see Thompson, J. A.

Mejia, Aurelio. Diccionario Enciclopedico Tecnico Actualizado. (SPA.). 748p. 1996. 24.95 (*958-95655-2-2*, Pub. by Divulgacion Tecnica) ISCA.

— Guia Practica para Manejar el Computador. (SPA.). 460p. 1999. 21.95 (*958-95655-6-5*, Pub. by Divulgacion Tecnica) ISCA.

— Guia Practica para Manejar StarOffice. (SPA.). 336p. 2000. 21.95 (*958-95655-7-3*, Pub. by Divulgacion Tecnica) ISCA.

— Hipnosis Regresiones a Vidas Pasadas. (SPA.). 230p. 1997. 19.95 (*958-95655-5-7*, Pub. by Divulgacion Tecnica) ISCA.

— Vidas Antes de la Vida: Guia Practica para Hacer Regresiones. (SPA.). 300p. 1997. 19.95 (*958-95655-8-1*, Pub. by Divulgacion Tecnica) ISCA.

Mejia Caldwell, Frances, jt. auth. see Taylor, Nicole.

Mejia, Carlos R. Trampas de Luz. (Ciencia para Todos Ser.). (SPA.). pap. 6.99 (*968-16-2544-7*, Pub. by Fondo) Continental Bk.

Mejia, Elizabeth, ed. Comalcalco. 335p. 1992. pap. 12.00 (*968-29-4504-6*, IN045) UPLAAP.

Mejia, Elizabeth A. & O'Connor, Frederick. Five Star Films: An Intermediate Listening/Speaking Text. LC 93-44648. 176p. (C). 1994. pap. text 27.73 (*0-13-035536-4*) P-H.

Mejia, Elizabeth A., et al. American Picture Show: A Cultural Reader. 240p. (C). 1991. pap. text 31.93 (*0-13-029687-2*) P-H.

— Very Teachable Films. 224p. (C). 1994. pap. 20.80 (*0-13-106824-5*) P-H.

Mejia, Joan, jt. auth. see Genkos, Mary.

Mejia, Manuel J., jt. auth. see Landau, Rubin.

Mejia-Niconchuk, Marta, tr. see Long, Caroline B.

Mejia-Niconchuk, Marta, tr. see Long, Caroline C.

Mejia, Paul S. Genetic Technology: Index of New Information & Research Guide with Bibliography. 160p. 1997. 47.50 (*0-7883-1530-7*); pap. 44.50 (*0-7883-1531-5*) ABBE Pubs Assn.

Mejia Prieto, Jorge. Albures y Refranes de Mexico. (Panorama Ser.). (SPA.). 157p. 1997. pap. 10.50 (*968-38-0132-3*) Panorama Edit.

Mejias, jt. auth. see Bacon, Susan.

Mejias, Alicia, tr. see Moore, Ryamond S. & Moore, Dorothy N.

Mejias, Antonio. Refrigeration License Examinations. LC 93-6800. 304p. 1993. per. 25.00 (*0-671-86705-9*, Arc) IDG Bks.

***Mejias, Antonio, ed. Isla Brava, Epica Del Indio Taino, 1. (SPA.). 100p. (Orig.). (YA). 2000. pap. 10.00 (*0-9661557-3-4*) Infante Pubns Inc.**

Isla Brava Epica del Indio Taino de Boriquen: description: Isla Brava is an historical story of the Taino Indians of Boriquen, known today as Puerto Rico. The story covers the origins of the Taino Indians before Christopher Columbus, proceeded by the domination of the Spanish & concludes with the extermination for the collector of Puerto Rican history. Isla Brava es una obra en verso, basada en la cultura del indio Taino. Esta historia esta llena de romance y mitololgia Taina. Los personajes se presentan como un drama teatral. La obra se desarrolla desde antes del descubrimiento por Cristobal Colon, hasta despues de la dominacion Espanola y el exterminacion total de la cultura Taina. Es una obra de conciencia. Se recomienda como una representacion de la Literatura Poetica. *Publisher Paid Annotation.*

Mejias, Antonio I., jt. auth. see Perez, Jose A.

Mejias-Bikandi, Errapel, jt. auth. see Farrell, Patrick.

Mejias, Ignacio Sanchez, see Sanchez Mejias, Ignacio.

Mejinas, Antonio I., jt. auth. see Perez, Jose A.

Mejstrik, Michael, et al. The Privatization Process in East-Central Europe: Evolutionary Process of Czech Privatizations. LC 96-24590. (International Series in Economics & Econometrics). 352p. (C). 1996. lib. bdg. 151.50 (*0-7923-4096-5*) Kluwer Academic.

Meju, Max A. Geophysical Data Analysis: Understanding Inverse Problem Theory & Practice. LC 94-41168. (Course Notes Ser.: Vol. 6). 1994. pap. 30.00 (*1-56080-027-5*, 256A) Soc Expl Geophys.

Mekas, Jonas. I Had Nowhere to Go. (Illus.). 480p. (Orig.). 1991. pap. 14.95 (*0-9628181-0-0*) Black Thistle Pr.

— Zefiro Torna or Scenes from the Life of George Maciunas (Fluxus) (Illus.). 28p. (Orig.). 1997. pap. 10.00 (*1-889873-00-4*, Arthse Bks) Arthouse.

Mekeel, Arthur. The Quakers & the American Revolution. 432p. 1999. pap. 41.00 (*1-85072-176-9*, Pub. by W Sessions) St Mut.

Mekeirle, Joseph O. Multinational Corporations: The ECISM Guide to Information Sources. LC 78-62333. 480p. 1978. 125.00 (*0-275-90307-9*, C0307, Praeger Pubs) Greenwood.

Mekemson, Mary J. A Critical, Modern-Spelling Edition of James Shirley's The Opportunity. LC 91-13770. (Renaissance Imagination Ser.). 368p. 1991. text 20.00 (*0-8153-0455-2*) Garland.

Meketa, Charles & Meketa, Jacqueline D. One Blanket & Ten Days Rations. Dodson, Carolyn & Jackson, Earl, eds. LC 79-67811. (Illus.). 112p. (Orig.). 1980. pap. 5.00 (*0-911408-54-1*) SW Pks Mnmts.

Meketa, Jacqueline D. From Martyrs to Murderers: The Old Southwest's Saints, Sinners, & Scalawags. LC 93-60808. (Illus.). 224p. (Orig.). 1993. 18.95 (*1-881325-09-1*); pap. 12.95 (*1-881325-08-3*) Yucca Tree Pr.

Meketa, Jacqueline D., jt. auth. see Meketa, Charles.

Meketa, Jacqueline D., ed. see Chacon, Rafael.

Meketa, Ray. Luther Rector Hare. 1976. 25.95 (*0-8488-1097-X*) Amereon Ltd.

***Mekgwe-Magocha, Pinkie.** Sunshine at Midnight. 1999. pap. write for info. (*1-57553-980-2*) Watermrk Pr.

Mekjavic, jt. auth. see Banister.

Mekler, D. L. Sefer Hazichronos: Memoirs of Rabbi Joseph I. Schneersohn. 3rd ed. LC 85-23288. (YID.). 1988. reprint ed. write for info. (*0-8266-5420-7*) Kehot Pubn Soc.

— Sefer Hazichronos: Memoirs of Rabbi Joseph I. Schneersohn, Vol. 1. 3rd ed. LC 85-23288. (YID.). 1988. reprint ed. 15.00 (*0-8266-5418-5*) Kehot Pubn Soc.

— Sefer Hazichronos: Memoirs of Rabbi Joseph I. Schneersohn, Vol. 2. 3rd ed. LC 85-23288. (YID.). 1988. reprint ed. 15.00 (*0-8266-5419-3*) Kehot Pubn Soc.

Mekler, Eva. Sunrise Shows Late: A Novel. LC 96-43464. 288p. 1997. 21.95 (*1-882593-17-0*) Bridge Wrks.

Mekler, Eva, jt. auth. see Schulman, Michael.

Mekler, Eva, jt. ed. see Schulman, Michael.

Mekler, S., ed. Academicorum Philosophorum Index Herculanensis. (GER.). xxxvi, 135p. 1958. write for info. (*3-296-10100-4*) G Olms Pubs.

Mekula, Janice. Frozen Sunshine. LC 80-81596. (Illus.). 64p. 1980. 10.00 (*0-8187-0038-6*) Harlo Press.

Mekz, Andrew K. Knicks Grit: Words of Wisdom from the Brash, Bold, Big Hearted 1994 New York Knicks. Broussard, Anne E., ed. 52p. (Orig.). 1994. pap. 6.95 (*0-9640033-4-1*) Wit Press.

— Rangers' Wit: Reflections, Retorts & Reminiscences from the Stanley Cup Champs. Broussard, Anne E., ed. (Orig.). 1994. pap. 6.95 (*0-9640033-6-8*) Wit Press.

— Rockets Wit: Words of Wisdom from the Captivating, Charismatic, Clutch NBA Champs. Broussard, Anne E., ed. (Orig.). 1994. pap. 5.95 (*0-9640033-5-X*) Wit Press.

Mel, B. New Wine: Spiritual Roots/12 Step Miracle. 1991. pap. 12.95 (*0-89486-772-5*) Hazelden.

Mel Bay Publications Incorporated Staff. Classic Rags of Scott Joplin. 124p. 1996. spiral bd. 22.95 incl. audio compact disk (*0-7866-2563-5*) Mel Bay.

***Mel Bay Publications Incorporated Staff, ed.** Art of Fingerstyle Guitar: Intermediate Level. 112p. 1998. spiral bd. 19.95 incl. audio compact disk (*0-7866-3459-6*) Mel Bay.

— What Child Is This? 7p. 1998. pap. 1.40 (*0-7866-4027-8*) Mel Bay.

***Mel Bay Staff.** Classic Guitar Method, Vol. I. 48p. 1998. pap. write for info. incl. audio compact disk (*0-7866-4474-5*, 93207BCD) Mel Bay.

Mel Bay Staff. Classic Melodies Encyclopedia. 288p. 1998. pap. 24.95 (*0-7866-4087-1*) Mel Bay.

***Mel Bay Staff.** 50 New Anthems for Mixed Voices. 272p. 2000. pap. 19.95 (*0-7866-5672-7*) Mel Bay.

— Fun with the Ukulele. 40p. 1998. pap. 19.95 incl. audio compact disk (*0-7866-4653-5*, 93270CDP) Mel Bay.

Mel Bay Staff. Plectrum Banjo Melody Chord Playing System. 112p. 1979. spiral bd. 11.95 (*1-56222-332-1*, 93628) Mel Bay.

— Songs of the Jewish People/Piano-Vocal: Intermediate. 120p. 1996. pap. 14.95 (*0-7866-1417-X*) Mel Bay.

***Mel Bay Staff.** 2000 Fingerpicking Book/3-CD Set. 408p. 2000. pap. 39.95 incl. audio compact disk (*0-7866-5290-X*, 98370BCD) Mel Bay.

***Mel Bay Staff, compiled by.** 2000 Blues Guitar. 232p. 2000. 29.95 incl. audio compact disk (*0-7866-4724-8*, 98424BCD) Mel Bay.

— 2000 Hammered Dulcimer. 72p. 2000. pap. 24.95 incl. audio compact disk (*0-7866-5295-0*, 98375BCD) Mel Bay.

***Mel Bay Staff & Bay, William.** Fun with the Guitar. 40p. 1998. pap. 19.95 incl. audio compact disk (*0-7866-4659-4*, 93262CDP) Mel Bay.

— Fun with the Mandolin. 40p. 1998. pap. 19.95 incl. audio compact disk (*0-7866-4657-8*, 93258CDP) Mel Bay.

***Mel Bay Staff, et al.** Fun with the Banjo. 40p. 1998. pap. 19.95 incl. audio compact disk (*0-7866-4655-1*, 93268CDP) Mel Bay.

Mel Bay Staff, jt. auth. see Silverman, Jerry.

Mel, Jeanne, ed. see Marrs, Samuel.

Mel Pepper & Janet Adams. Neonatal Care Policy & Procedure Guideline Manual. 260p. 1997. spiral bd. 110.00 (*1-879575-85-X*) Acad Med Sys.

An Asterisk (*) at the beginning of an entry indicates that the title is appearing for the first time.

Mel, Peter. Christopher Columbus: Two Civilizations Come Together. (Illus.). 192p. (Orig.). 1992. pap. 14.92 (*1-882234-03-0*) Heritage CA.

Mela, Pomponius & Berry, Paul. Geography de Situ Orbis A. D. 43. LC 98-100838. (Studies in Classics). vii, 159 p. 1997. write for info. (*0-7734-8558-9*) E Mellen.

Mela, Pomponius, jt. auth. see Romer, F. E.

Melack, John M., ed. Saline Lakes. (Developments in Hydrobiology Ser.). (C). 1988. text 299.00 (*90-6193-648-9*) Kluwer Academic.

Melady, John. Korea: Canada's Forgotten War. (Illus.). 219p. 1988. pap. 4.95 (*0-7715-9278-7*) Genl Dist Srvs.

Melady, Margaret B. The Rhetoric of Pope John Paul II. LC 98-44672. 272p. 1999. 65.00 (*0-275-96298-9*, Praeger Pubs) Greenwood.

Melady, Margaret B., jt. auth. see Melady, Thomas P.

Melady, Thomas P. The Ambassador's Story: The United States & the Vatican in World Affairs. LC 93-87230. 224p. 1994. 19.95 (*0-87973-702-6*, 702) Our Sunday Visitor.

— Burundi: The Tragic Years. LC 73-89357. (Illus.). 128p. reprint ed. pap. 39.70 (*0-8357-8822-9*, 203347000086) Bks Demand.

Melady, Thomas P. & Melady, Margaret B. Uganda: The Asian Exiles. LC 76-10321. 96p. reprint ed. pap. 30.00 (*0-8357-7062-1*, 203355000086) Bks Demand.

Melakopides, Costas. Pragmatic Idealism: Canadian Foreign Policy, 1945-1995. 248p. 1998. text 39.95 (*0-7735-1722-7*, Pub. by McG-Queens Univ Pr) CUP Services.

Melam, Lawrence E., jt. auth. see Brown, Steven R.

Melamed, Barbara G., jt. auth. see Schneiderman, Neil.

Melamed, Daniel R. J. S. Bach & the German Motet. (Illus.). 245p. (C). 1995. text 59.95 (*0-521-41864-X*) Cambridge U Pr.

Melamed, Daniel R., ed. Bach Studies, No. 2. (Illus.). 252p. (C). 1996. text 64.95 (*0-521-47067-6*) Cambridge U Pr.

Melamed, Daniel R. & Marissen, Michael. An Introduction to Bach Studies. LC 97-40406. 208p. (C). 1998. text 45.00 (*0-19-512231-3*) OUP.

Melamed, Evelyn B., jt. auth. see Minkoff, Harvey.

Melamed, Frances. Janova: Portrait of a Jewish Lithuanian Village in Revolutionary & Communist Russia 1914-1920. LC 75-38045. (Illus.). 229p. 1976. 22.50 (*0-917294-01-7*) Janova Pr.

***Melamed, I. Dan.** Empirical Methods for Exploiting Parallel Texts. (Illus.). 198p. 2001. 32.95 (*0-262-13380-6*) MIT Pr.

Melamed, Leo. Leo Melamed on the Markets: Twenty Years of Financial History As Seen by the Man Who Revolutionized the Markets. LC 95-22150. 304p. 1992. 29.95 (*0-471-57524-0*) Wiley.

Melamed, Leo, ed. The Merits of Flexible Exchange Rates: An Anthology. 450p. (Orig.). (C). 1988. pap. text 35.00 (*0-913969-15-X*); lib. bdg. 68.50 (*0-913969-14-1*) Univ Pub Assocs.

Melamed, Leo & Tamarkin, Bob. Leo Melamed: Escape to the Futures. LC 96-15316. 480p. 1996. 27.95 (*0-471-11215-1*) Wiley.

Melamed, Myron R., et al, eds. Flow Cytometry & Sorting. 2nd ed. LC 89-13091. 836p. 1990. 215.00 (*0-471-56235-1*) Wiley.

Melamed, V. Z., et al. Coal Cutting by Winning Machines. Sarve, S. D., tr. from RUS. (Russian Translation Ser.: No. 74). (Illus.). 288p. (C). 1990. text 116.00 (*90-6191-909-6*, Pub. by A A Balkema) Ashgate Pub Co.

Melamid, Alexander, jt. auth. see Komar, Vitaly.

Melammed, Renee L. Heretics or Daughters of Israel? The Crypto-Jewish Women of Castile. LC 97-50630. 264p. 1999. text 45.00 (*0-19-509580-4*) OUP.

Melamu, Moteane. Children of the Twilight. 165p. 1998. 29.95 (*0-86543-678-9*); pap. 12.95 (*0-86543-679-7*) Africa World.

— Living & Partly Living. 146p. 1999. pap. 12.95 (*0-86543-677-0*) Africa World.

Melanchthon, Paul. Messages of Understanding & the Missing Answers. LC 96-94392. 201p. 1997. pap. 12.00 (*0-9662948-0-7*, M-1) Melanchthon Hse.

Melanchthon, Philip. The Augsburg Confession. Jacobs, Henry E., ed. Krauth, Charles P., tr. from LAT. Orig. Title: Confessio Augustana. 38p. 1997. reprint ed. pap. 2.50 (*1-891469-08-8*) Repristination.

— The Confessyon of the Fayth of the Germaynes in the Councell, 2 pts., Set. LC 76-57351. (English Experience Ser.: No. 771). 1977. reprint ed. lib. bdg. 45.00 (*90-221-0771-X*) Walter J Johnson.

— The Epistle of P. Melancton Made unto Kynge Henry the Eyght, for the Revokynge of the Six Artycles. Wesel, J. C., tr. from LAT. LC 72-216. (English Experience Ser.: No. 336). 32p. 1971. reprint ed. 45.00 (*90-221-0336-6*) Walter J Johnson.

— Epistolae, Judicia, Consilia, Testimonia Aliorumque Ad Eum Epistolae Quae in Corpore Reformatorum Desiderantur. (GER.). x, 614p. 1975. reprint ed. write for info. incl. 3.5 hd (*3-487-05726-3*) G Olms Pubs.

— The Justification of Man by Faith Only. Lease, Nicholas, tr. LC 79-84123. (English Experience Ser.: No. 942). 204p. 1979. reprint ed. lib. bdg. 35.00 (*90-221-0942-9*) Walter J Johnson.

— The Life & Arts of Martin Luther. Orig. Title: Hymns of the Reformation. 46p. 1997. pap. 3.00 (*1-891469-10-X*) Repristination.

— The Loci Communes of Philip Melanchthon. Hill, Charles L., tr. LC 83-45649. reprint ed. 32.50 (*0-404-19858-9*) AMS Pr.

— Paul's Letter to the Colossians. Parker, D. C., tr. & intro. by. (Historic Texts & Interpreters Ser.: Vol. 7). 126p. 1989. 30.00 (*1-85075-210-9*, Pub. by Sheffield Acad) CUP Services.

— Philip Melanchthon: Orations on Philosophy & Education. Kusukawa, Sachiko, ed. Salazar, Christine F., tr. LC 98-8077. (Texts in the History of Philosophy Ser.). 320p. (C). 1999. text 59.95 (*0-521-58350-0*); pap. text 22.95 (*0-521-58677-1*) Cambridge U Pr.

— A Very Godly Defense, Defending the Marriage of Priests. Beuchame, L., tr. LC 76-25643. (English Experience Ser.: No. 199). 1969. reprint ed. 20.00 (*90-221-0199-1*) Walter J Johnson.

Melanchthon, Philip, jt. auth. see Chytraeus, David.

Melancon, Michael S. The Socialist Revolutionaries & the Russian Anti-War Movement, 1914-1917. LC 90-39908. 380p. reprint ed. pap. 117.80 (*0-608-09856-6*, 206982100006) Bks Demand.

Melancon, Richard, jt. auth. see Mayer, Morris F.

***Melancon, Robert M.** The Secrets of Executive Search: Professional Strategies for Managing Your Personal Job Search. 200p. 2000. pap. 29.95 (*0-9675140-0-2*) Melancon Co.

Meland, Bernard E. Essays in Constructive Theology: A Process Perspective. LeFevre, Perry D., ed. & intro. by. LC 87-82148. 329p. 1988. text 31.95 (*0-913552-38-0*); pap. text 18.95 (*0-913552-39-9*) Exploration Pr.

— Fallible Forms & Symbols: Discourses on Method in a Theology of Culture. LC 76-7868. 226p. reprint ed. pap. 70.10 (*0-608-16921-8*, 202695700053) Bks Demand.

— Future of Empirical Theology. Braver, J. C., ed. LC 78-83980. (Essays in Divinity Ser.: Vol. 7). 398p. 1997. lib. bdg. 24.00 (*0-226-51955-4*) U Ch Pr.

— Reawakening of Christian Faith. LC 72-142670. (Essay Index Reprint Ser.). 1977. reprint ed. 18.95 (*0-8369-2663-3*) Ayer.

***Melander, Erik.** Anarchy Within: The Security Dilemma Between Ethnic Groups in Emerging Anarchy. (Illus.). 254p. 1999. 62.50 (*91-506-1329-4*, Pub. by Uppsala Universitet) Coronet Bks.

Melander, Goran. Refugees in Somalia. (Research Report Ser.: No. 56). 48p. 1980. write for info. (*91-7106-169-X*, Pub. by Nordic Africa) Transaction Pubs.

Melander, Goran, ed. Modern Issues in European Law: Nordic Perspectives. LC 97-19435. 233p. 1997. 93.00 (*90-411-0423-2*) Kluwer Academic.

Melander, Goran, et al, eds. The Raoul Wallenberg Compilation of Human Rights Instruments, Vol. 1 RAWA. LC 95-45769. 1997. 198.00 (*0-7923-3646-1*) Kluwer Law Intl.

Melander, Goran & Nobel, Peter, eds. African Refugees & the Law. (Seminar Proceedings Ser.: No. 11). 98p. 1978. write for info. (*91-7106-129-0*, Pub. by Nordic Africa) Transaction Pubs.

— International Legal Instruments on Refugees in Africa (Instruments Legaux Internationaux sur les Refuges en Afrique) 413p. 1979. write for info. (*91-7106-154-1*, Pub. by Nordic Africa) Transaction Pubs.

Melander, John M. & Lauersdorf, Lynn R., eds. Masonry: Design & Construction, Problems & Repair. LC 93-1147. (STP Ser.: Vol. 1180). (Illus.). 430p. 1993. 47.00 (*0-8031-1492-3*, STP1180) ASTM.

Melander, Lars & Saunders, William H., Jr. Reaction Rates of Isotopic Molecules. LC 85-23200. 348p. 1986. reprint ed. 49.50 (*0-89874-940-9*) Krieger.

Melander, Leigh. The Lyra System of Relaxation No. 1: Star Songs, Star Path, Star Dance, Star Thoughts. Ferrandino, Rita, ed. 1998. 39.95 (*1-58425-004-6*) Lyra Enterprises.

— Star Path: A Guide to Building Relaxation into Your Life. Ferrandino, Rita, ed. (Lyra System of Relaxation Ser.: #1). 54p. 1998. 10.95 (*1-58425-001-1*) Lyra Enterprises.

— Star Path & Star Thoughts Bundle: A Constellation of Creative Wellness. Ferrandino, Rita, ed. (Lyra System of Relaxation Ser.). 1998. 14.95 (*1-58425-005-4*) Lyra Enterprises.

— Star Songs & Star Path Bundle No. 1: A Constellation of Creative Wellness. Ferrandino, Rita, ed. (Lyra System of Relaxation Ser.). 1998. 19.95 (*1-58425-006-2*) Lyra Enterprises.

— Star Thoughts: A Playbook of Relaxation Activities. Ferrandino, Rita, ed. (Lyra System of Relaxation Ser.: #1). 32p. 1998. pap. 5.00 (*1-58425-003-8*) Lyra Enterprises.

Melander, Rochelle & Eppley, Harold. Dancing in the Aisle: Spiritual Lessons We've Learned from Children. LC 99-30817. 144p. 1999. pap. 15.95 (*0-8298-1352-7*) Pilgrim OH.

— Growing Together: Spiritual Exercises for Church Committees. LC 98-18985. 112p. 1998. pap. 9.99 (*0-8066-3716-1*, 9-3716) Augsburg Fortress.

Melander, Sheila & Bucher, Linda. Pocket Companion for Critical Care Nursing. Carter, Robin, ed. LC 98-43361. 475p. 1999. pap. text 23.95 (*0-7216-6919-0*, W B Saunders Co) Harcrt Hlth Sci Grp.

Melander, Sheila, jt. auth. see Bucher, Linda.

Melander, Sheila D. Review of Critical Care Nursing: Case Studies & Applications. Cullen, Barbara N., ed. (Illus.). 426p. 1996. pap. text 32.00 (*0-7216-5537-8*, W B Saunders Co) Harcrt Hlth Sci Grp.

Melandri, B. A., et al. Bioelectrochemistry 4: Nerve Muscle Function - Bioelectrochemistry, Mechanisms, Bioenergetics, & Control. (NATO ASI Ser.: 267). (Illus.). 386p. (C). 1994. text 125.00 (*0-306-44813-0*, Kluwer Plenum) Kluwer Academic.

***Melaney, William D.** After Ontology: Literary Theory & Modernist Poetics. (C). 2001. pap. text 18.95 (*0-7914-4958-0*) State U NY Pr.

— After Ontology: Literary Theory & Modernist Poetics. (C). 2001. text 57.50 (*0-7914-4957-2*) State U NY Pr.

Melanie, M., jt. auth. see Cooper.

Melanos, Jack. Rapunzel & the Witch. (J). 1950. 5.00 (*0-87602-186-0*) Anchorage.

— Sinbad & the Evil Genii. (J). (gr. k up). 1986. pap. 6.00 (*0-87602-251-4*) Anchorage.

Melanson. Time It. 2nd ed. (C). 1992. pap. text. write for info. (*0-7730-5210-0*) Addison-Wes.

Melanson, Leo. Winning Secrets of a Master Sports Bettor - Football. 32p. (Orig.). 1997. pap. 7.95 (*0-934650-19-5*) Sunnyside.

Melanson, Mia S. Effective Telephone Communication Skills. Bultema, Patrick et al, eds. (Illus.). 31p. (Orig.). pap. write for info. (*1-57125-023-9*) Help Desk Inst.

Melanson, Philip H. The Murkin Conspiracy: An Investigation into the Assassination of Dr. Martin Luther King, Jr. LC 88-15262. 219p. 1989. 39.95 (*0-275-93029-7*, C3029, Praeger Pubs) Greenwood.

Melanson, Richard A. American Foreign Policy since the Vietnam War: The Search for Consensus from Nixon to Clinton. 2nd ed. LC 95-32053. 334p. (C). (gr. 13). 1996. pap. text 32.95 (*1-56324-522-1*) M E Sharpe.

— American Foreign Policy Since the Vietnam War: The Search for Consensus from Nixon to Clinton. 2nd ed. LC 95-32053. 334p. (gr. 13). 1996. text 79.95 (*1-56324-521-3*) M E Sharpe.

— American Foreign Policy since the Vietnam War: The Search for Consensus from Nixon to Clinton. 3rd ed. LC 99-43618. 352p. 1999. text 69.95 (*0-7656-0272-5*); pap. text 25.95 (*0-7656-0273-3*) M E Sharpe.

— Writing History & Making Policy, Vol. VI: The Cold War, Vietnam, & Revisionism, Vol. VI. LC 83-10362. (Exxon Education Foundation Series on Rhetoric & Political Discourse). 260p. (C). 1983. pap. text 21.00 (*0-8191-3353-1*); lib. bdg. 50.50 (*0-8191-3352-3*) U Pr of Amer.

Melanson, Richard A., ed. Neither Cold War nor Detente? Soviet-American Relations in the 1980's. fac. ed. LC 81-16299. 253p. 1982. reprint ed. pap. 78.50 (*0-7837-7984-4*, 204774000008) Bks Demand.

Melanson, Richard A. & Mayer, David, eds. Reevaluating Eisenhower: American Foreign Policy in the Fifties. LC 86-4363. (Illus.). 288p. 1987. text 29.95 (*0-252-01340-9*); pap. text 15.95 (*0-252-06067-9*) U of Ill Pr.

Melanson, Richard A. & Thompson, Kenneth W., eds. Foreign Policy & Domestic Consensus, Vol. II. LC 85-15655. (Credibility of Institutions, Policies & Leadership Ser.). 212p. (Orig.). 1985. lib. bdg. 46.00 (*0-8191-4865-2*) U Pr of Amer.

***Melanson, Yvette D. & Safran, Claire.** Looking for Lost Bird: A Jewish Woman Discovers Her Navajo Roots. 240p. 2000. pap. 12.00 (*0-380-79553-1*, Avon Bks) Morrow Avon.

Melanson, Yvette D. & Safran, Claire. Looking for Lost Bird: A Jewish Woman's Discovery of Her Navajo Roots. LC 98-42110. 240p. 1999. 22.00 (*0-380-97601-3*, Avon Bks) Morrow Avon.

Melara, Julio A. Do You Have the Time for Success? 115p. 1994. pap. 12.00 (*0-9642430-0-8*) Time For Action.

— It Only Takes Everything You've Got! Lessons for a Life of Success. large type ed. 148p. 1998. 17.00 (*0-9642430-1-6*) Time For Action.

Melaragno. Preliminary Design of Modern Bridges for Architects & Engineers. LC 98-25608. (Illus.). 552p. 1998. text 195.00 (*0-8247-0184-4*) Dekker.

Melaragno, M. Severe Storm Engineering for Structural Design. 450p. 1995. pap. text 50.00 (*2-88449-126-0*) Gordon & Breach.

— Severe Storm Engineering for Structural Design. 450p. 1996. text 59.00 (*2-88449-150-3*) Gordon & Breach.

Melaragno, Michele. The French Interpreter. 150p. 1996. pap. text 11.95 (*1-889421-00-6*) Minerva Archit.

— The German Interpreter. 150p. 1996. pap. text 11.95 (*1-889421-01-4*) Minerva Archit.

— The Italian Interpreter. 150p. 1996. pap. text 11.95 (*1-889421-02-2*) Minerva Archit.

— The Japanese Interpreter. 150p. 1996. pap. text 11.95 (*1-889421-03-0*) Minerva Archit.

— The Russian Interpreter. 150p. 1996. pap. text 11.95 (*1-889421-04-9*) Minerva Archit.

— The Spanish Interpreter. 150p. 1996. pap. text 11.95 (*1-889421-05-7*) Minerva Archit.

Melaragno, Michele G. Introduction to Shell Structures: The Art & Science of Vaulting. LC 90-41113. (Illus.). 352p. (C). (gr. 13). 1991. text 84.95 (*0-442-23725-1*) Chapman & Hall.

— Quantification in Science. (Illus.). 336p. (C). (gr. 13). 1991. ring bd. 83.95 (*0-442-00641-1*, Chap & Hall CRC) CRC Pr.

Melaragno, Ralph J. Tutoring with Students: A Handbook for Establishing Tutorial Programs in Schools. LC 75-40045. 172p. 1976. pap. 34.95 (*0-87778-090-0*) Educ Tech Pubns.

Melaren, James T. South Carolina Family Court Handbook. 619p. (Orig.). 1996. pap. 50.00 (*0-943856-67-1*) SC Bar CLE.

Melaro, Constance. Bitter Harvest: The Odyssey of a Teacher. 1965. 12.95 (*0-8392-1148-1*) Astor-Honor.

Melas, E. M. The Islands of Karpathos, Saros & Kasos in the Neolithic & Bronze Age. (Studies in Mediterranean Archaeology: Vol. LXVIII). (Illus.). 337p. (Orig.). 1985. pap. 165.00 (*91-86098-23-3*, Pub. by P Astroms) Coronet Bks.

Melas-Kyriazi, Lisa. Motif & Meaning. LC 87-71912. (Illus.). 30p. (Orig.). 1987. pap. 4.00 (*0-934358-18-4*) Fuller Mus Art.

Melas, Viatcheslav B., jt. auth. see Ermakov, Sergei M.

Melashenko, E. Lonnie & Crosby, Timothy E. In the Presence of Angels: A Collection of Inspiring, True Angel Stories. LC 95-6966. 1995. pap. 10.99 (*0-8163-1261-3*) Pacific Pr Pub Assn.

Melashenko, E. Lonnie & Crosby, Timothy E. The Television Time Bomb. Holt, B. Russell, ed. 64p. 1993. pap. 0.47 (*0-8163-1168-4*) Pacific Pr Pub Assn.

***Melashenko, E. Lonnie & Jones, Brian.** Angels among Us Magabook: A Collection of Inspiring True Angel Stories. Holt, B. Russell, ed. (Illus.). 95p. 2000. pap. 5.99 (*0-8163-1792-5*) Pacific Pr Pub Assn.

***Melashenko, E. Lonnie & Jones, Brian D.** Walking with Angels: More True Stories from the Author of "In the Presence of Angels" Lale, Tim, ed. LC 99-59068. 189p. 2000. pap. 12.99 (*0-8163-1785-2*) Pacific Pr Pub Assn.

Melashenko, E. Lonnie & McLarty, John. An Insider's Guide to the Kingdom: The Beatitudes as a Map to Joy & Freedom. LC 95-13760. 1995. 2.29 (*0-8163-1269-9*) Pacific Pr Pub Assn.

— Stand at the Cross & Be Changed. LC 96-48568. 1997. pap. 8.99 (*0-8163-1384-9*) Pacific Pr Pub Assn.

Melashenko, E. Lonnie & Smith, David B. More Than Amazing Grace. Holt, B. Russell. ed. 48p. 1995. pap. 1.49 (*0-8163-1268-0*) Pacific Pr Pub Assn.

— Popcorn, the Peraly Gates, & Other Kernels of Truth. LC 96-13827. 1996. pap. 1.97 (*0-8163-1347-4*) Pacific Pr Pub Assn.

— A Suitcase Full of Faith. 64p. 1995. pap. 1.99 (*0-8163-1309-1*) Pacific Pr Pub Assn.

***Melashenko, Lonnie.** Rock-Solid Living in a Run-Amok World. 1999. pap. 14.99 (*0-8280-1341-1*) Review & Herald.

Melashenko, Lonnie, jt. auth. see Crosby, Timothy.

Melasuo, Tuomo. National Movements & World Peace. 189p. 1990. text 72.95 (*1-85628-079-9*, Pub. by Avebry) Ashgate Pub Co.

Melaville, Atelia I. & Blank, Martin J. Together We Can: A Guide for Crafting a Profamily System of Education & Human Services. Asayesh, Gelareh, ed. 1995. lib. bdg. 251.95 (*0-8490-6685-9*) Gordon Pr.

Melaville, Atelia I. & Blank, Martin J. Together We Can: A Guide to Crafting a Profamily System of Education & Human Services. Asayesh, Gelareh, ed. 169p. 1993. pap. 12.00 (*0-16-041721-X*) USGPO.

Melaville, Atelia I., et al. Together We Can: A Guide for Crafting a Profamily System of Education & Human Services. Thompson, Bruce A., ed. 158p. (C). 1993. pap. text 25.00 (*0-7881-0098-X*) DIANE Pub.

Melazzo, Lucio, jt. ed. see Herzfeld, Michael.

Melba, Nellie. Melodies & Memories. LC 73-107821. (Select Bibliographies Reprint Ser.). 1977. 26.95 (*0-8369-5192-1*) Ayer.

— Melodies & Memories. LC 71-126694. reprint ed. 34.00 (*0-404-04287-2*) AMS Pr.

— Melodies & Memories. 339p. 1990. reprint ed. lib. bdg. 79.00 (*0-7812-9103-8*, 10103) Rprt Serv.

***Melbaa, Gadaa.** Oromia: An Introduction to the History of the Oromo People. rev. ed. LC 99-33590. 150p. 1999. pap. 12.00 (*1-886513-18-X*) Kirk Hse Pubs.

Melber, G., ed. see Brownell, David.

Melber, Henning, et al. Namibia & External Resources: The Case of Swedish Development Assistance. LC 95-129814. (Research Reports: Vol. 96). 122p. 1994. pap. text 16.95 (*91-7106-351-X*) Transaction Pubs.

Melbin, Murray. Night As Frontier: Colonizing the World after Dark. 1987. text 29.95 (*0-02-920940-4*) Free Pr.

Melbon, Gary B. & Denstbier, Richard A., eds. Nebraska Symposium on Motivation, 1985: The Law as a Behavioral Instrument. LC 53-11655. (Nebraska Symposium on Motivation Ser.: Vol. 33). xxvii, 291p. 1986. text 45.00 (*0-8032-3100-8*) U of Nebr Pr.

Melbourne Art Directors Club Staff. 15th M. A. D. C. Annual, 1. 15th ed. (Illus.). 1999. 29.95 (*1-56970-541-0*) Bks Nippan.

— Melbourne Art Director's Annual, 1996. (Illus.). 200p. 1997. pap. 29.95 (*1-56970-549-6*) Bks Nippan.

Melbourne, Bertram L. Alpha Through Omega: A User Friendly Guide to New Testament Greek. LC 96-31410. (ENG & GRE.). 250p. 1996. pap. text 19.50 (*0-7618-0457-9*) U Pr of Amer.

— Slow to Understand: The Disciples in Synoptic Perspective. LC 88-22771. 224p. (Orig.). (C). 1988. lib. bdg. 41.50 (*0-8191-7154-9*) U Pr of Amer.

Melbourne, David. Politically Correct Bible Stories. 1995. 12.95 (*1-888121-11-4*) ST Publ.

Melbourne, David & Adams, Helen. Your Dreams & Your Stars. LC 98-181735. (Illus.). 192p. 1998. 12.95 (*0-7137-2689-X*, Pub. by Blandford Pr) Sterling.

Melbourne, David & Hearne, Keith. Dream Interpretation: The Secret. 192p. 1998. 12.95 (*0-7137-2670-9*, Pub. by Blandford Pr) Sterling.

Melbourne, David F. Dream Oracle: A Unique Guide to Interpreting Message-Bearing Dreams. LC 00-551009. (Illus.). 176p. 1999. pap. text 9.95 (*1-85368-976-9*) New5 Holland.

***Melbourne, David F. & Heaine, Keith.** The Meaning of Your Dreams: An Interactive Guide. 224p. 2000. pap. 12.95 (*0-7137-2778-0*, Pub. by Blandford Pr) Sterling.

Melbourne, Roy M. Conflict & Crisis: A Foreign Service Story. rev. ed. LC 97-6262. 298p. 1997. 39.50 (*0-7618-0729-2*) U Pr of Amer.

Melby, Alan K. & Warner, Terry. The Possibility of Language: A Discussion of the Nature of Language, with Implications for Human & Machine Translation. LC 95-45373. (Benjamins Translation Library Ser.: Vol. 14). xxvi, 276p. 1995. 49.00 (*1-55619-695-4*) J Benjamins Pubng Co.

Melby, Alan K., jt. ed. see Makkai, Adam.

Melby, Barbara M., jt. auth. see Halvey, John H.

Melby, Christopher L. & Hyner, Gerald C. Exercise & Physical Fitness: A Personalized Approach. 116p. 1988. pap. text 16.95 (*0-912855-83-5*) E Bowers Pub.

Melby, Christopher L., jt. auth. see Hyner, Gerald C.

Melby, Craig A. & Utzman, Jane. Leasing Smart. LC 96-36097. 100p. (Orig.). 1997. pap. text 14.95 (*0-945456-43-3*) PT Pubns.

Melby, Edward C., Jr., ed. see Charles River International Symposium on Laborator.

Melby, Eric D. Oil & the International System: The Case of France, 1918-1969. Bruchey, Stuart, ed. LC 80-2816. (Dissertations in European Economic History Ser.). (Illus.). 1981. lib. bdg. 42.95 (*0-405-14000-2*) Ayer.

Melby, Ernest O. The Education of Free Men, 1955. LC 77-1248. (Horace Mann Lectures). 75p. 1977. lib. bdg. 49.50 (*0-8371-9501-2*, MEEF, Greenwood Pr) Greenwood.

Melby, Ernest O. & Puner, Morton, eds. Freedom & Public Education. LC 72-14106. (Essay Index Reprint Ser.). 1977. reprint ed. 18.95 (*0-518-10019-7*) Ayer.

Melby, J. S. Biblical Baptism. 20p. 1977. pap. 0.95 (*1-58572-014-3*) Ambasdor Pubns.

Melby, John F. The Mandate of Heaven: A Record of Civil War, China, 1945-49. LC 68-9736. (Illus.). 327p. reprint ed. pap. 101.40 (*0-608-11792-7*, 201436300090) Bks Demand.

Melby, John F. & Straka, W. W., eds. Constantine Nabokov: Letters of a Russian Diplomat to an American Friend, 1906-1922. LC 88-11770. (Slavic Studies: Vol. 1). 430p. 1988. lib. bdg. 109.95 (*0-88946-014-0*) E Mellen.

Melby, Pete. Simplified Irrigation Design. 2nd ed. 1995. pap. 36.95 (*0-442-01822-3*, VNR) Wiley.

Melby, Pete. Simplified Irrigation Design: Professional Designer & Installer Version. 2nd ed. (Landscape Architecture Ser.). 240p. 1995. pap. 49.95 (*0-471-28622-2*, VNR) Wiley.

Melcer, Donald. Self Development Through Meditative Practice. 1983. pap. 4.50 (*0-916786-70-6*, Saint George Pubns) R Steiner Col.

M

Melcher. Health Assessment. Date not set. text. write for info. (*0-7216-1913-4*, W B Saunders Co) Harcrt Hlth Sci Grp.

Melcher, Alyssa S. Peekaboo Bunny: Friend in the Snow. (Illus.). 24p. (J). (ps-k). 1995. 6.95 (*0-590-50318-9*, Cartwheel) Scholastic Inc.

Melcher, Harold & Melcher, Joan. The Way to Greece. LC 84-18400. (Illus.). 113p. (Orig.). 1984. pap. 8.95 (*0-87233-077-X*) Bauhan.

***Melcher, Inc. Staff, creator.** Clean & Serene: Meditations for the Bath. (Soapdish Editions Ser.). 2000. 7.95 (*0-8118-2973-1*) Chronicle Bks.

— Hot & Steamy: Erotic Baths for Two. (Soapdish Editions Ser.). 2000. 7.95 (*0-8118-2969-3*) Chronicle Bks.

— Makin' Waves: Fun with Kids in the Tub. (Soapdish Editions Ser.). 2000. 7.95 (*0-8118-2971-5*) Chronicle Bks.

— Rub-a-Dub-Dub: Baby in the Tub. (Soapdish Editions Ser.). 2000. 7.95 (*0-8118-2970-7*) Chronicle Bks.

— Soothing Soaks: Relaxation for the Bath. (Soapdish Editions Ser.). 2000. 7.95 (*0-8118-2972-3*) Chronicle Bks.

— Splish Splash: Recipes for the Bath. (Soapdish Editions Ser.). 2000. 7.95 (*0-8118-2968-5*) Chronicle Bks.

Melcher, James R., jt. auth. see Woodson, Herbert H.

Melcher, Joan, jt. auth. see Melcher, Harold.

Melcher, Marguerite F. Shaker Adventure. 319p. 1986. pap. 4.95 (*0-937942-08-1*) Shaker Mus.

Melcher, Mary. Mommy, Who Does God Love? (J). (ps-k). 1997. 10.95 (*0-689-81036-9*) S&S Childrens.

Melcher, Michael. Parallel to the Shore. (Illus.). 19p. (Orig.). 1992. pap. 5.00 (*0-926935-68-2*) Runaway Spoon.

Melcher, Nancy, ed. International Home Cooking: The United Nations International School Fiftieth Anniversary Cookbook. anniversary ed. LC 98-104761. (Illus.). xviii, 332p. 1997. pap. 20.00 (*0-9658603-1-0*) UN Intl Schl.

Melcher, Robert A., et al. Music for Study. 3rd ed. 256p. 1988. pap. write for info. (*0-318-62256-4*) P-H.

Melcher, Ryan, jt. auth. see Patterson, Jeff.

***Melcher, Suzanne.** Introduction to Writing Goals & Objectives: A Manual for Recreation Therapy Students & Entry-Level Professionals. x, 60p. 1999. pap. text, wbk. ed. 14.95 (*1-892132-10-9*, WGO112) Venture Pub PA.

Melcher, Trini, jt. auth. see Iqbal, Zafar.

Melcher, Willard F. & Warch. Music for Study. 3rd ed. 256p. 1988. 70.00 (*0-13-607474-X*) P-H.

Melchers. Structural Reliability: Analysis & Prediction. (Engineering Science Ser.). 1987. text 94.95 (*0-470-20873-2*) P-H.

***Melchers.** Structural Reliability Analysis. 2nd ed. LC 98-53106. 456p. 1999. 170.00 (*0-471-98324-1*) Wiley.

— Structural Reliability Analysis. 2nd ed. LC 98-53106. 456p. (C). 1999. pap. 70.00 (*0-471-98771-9*) Wiley.

Melchers, F., et al, eds. Lymphocyte Hybridomas: Second Workshop. (Illus.). 1979. 34.95 (*0-387-09670-1*) Spr-Verlag.

— Mechanisms of B Cell Neoplasia 1998 15th Workshop: Proceedings of the Workshop Held at the Basel Institute for Immunology 4th - 6th October 1998, No. 246. (Current Topics in Microbiology & Immunology Ser.). (Illus.). xxvix, 415p. 1999. 250.00 (*3-540-65759-2*) Spr-Verlag.

— Progress in Immunology, Vol. VII. (Illus.). 1408p. 1989. 207.00 (*0-387-51053-2*) Spr-Verlag.

Melchers, F. & Potter, M., eds. Mechanisms in B-Cell Neoplasia. (Current Topics in Microbiology & Immunology Ser.: Vol. 132). (Illus.). 390p. 1986. 106.00 (*0-387-17048-0*) Spr-Verlag.

Melchers, F., jt. ed. see Potter, M.

Melchers, Gunnel & Johannesson, Nils-Lennart, eds. Nonstandard Varieties of Language. (Stockholm Studies in English: No. 84). 220p. 1994. pap. 46.50 (*91-22-01635-X*) Coronet Bks.

Melchers, Gunnel & Warren, Beatrice, eds. Studies in Anglistics: Lexicology, Grammar, & Language Contact. (Stockholm Studies in English: No. 85). 316p. 1995. 52.50 (*91-22-01672-4*) Coronet Bks.

***Melchers, R. E. & Stewart, M. G., eds.** Applications of Statistics & Probability - Civil Engineering Reliability & Risk Analysis: Proceedings of the ICASP-8 Conference, Sydney, NSW, Australia, 12-15 December 1999, 2 vols. (Illus.). 1250p. (C). 1999. text 185.00 (*90-5809-086-8*, Pub. by A A Balkema) Ashgate Pub Co.

Melchers, R. E. & Stewart, M. G., eds. Probabalistic Risk & Hazard Assessment. 253p. 1993. 123.00 (*90-5410-349-3*, Pub. by A A Balkema) Ashgate Pub Co.

— Proceedings of the Conference, New Castle, NSW, Australia, 1-2 June 1995. 220p. 1995. 85.00 (*90-5410-555-0*, Pub. by A A Balkema) Ashgate Pub Co.

Melchers, R. E., jt. ed. see Stewart, M. G.

***Melchers, Rose S.** Of Fifty Summers. LC 99-74745. (Illus.). 136p. 1999. pap. 12.95 (*0-9673493-1-1*) Les Cheneaux Hist.

***Melchert, Charles F.** Biblical Wisdom & Educational Ministry: Biblical Wisdom & Educational Ministry. LC 98-9684. 336p. 1998. pap. 28.00 (*1-56338-139-7*) TPI PA.

— Voyeur. LC 99-37287. 192p. 1999. 35.00 (*0-06-019522-3*) HarpC.

Melchert, Christopher. The Formation of the Sunni Schools of Law, 9th-10th Centuries C. E. LC 97-40209. (Studies in Islamic Law & Society: No. 4). xxviii, 244p. 1997. 82.00 (*90-04-10952-8*) Brill Academic Pubs.

Melchert, Norman. The Great Conversation: A Historical Introduction to Philosophy. 3rd ed. LC 98-4462. xiii,720p. 1998. text 55.95 (*0-7674-0012-7*) Mayfield Pub.

— The Great Conversation: Pre-Socrates Through Deseartes. 3rd ed. LC 98-4464. 400p. 1998. pap. text 37.95 (*0-7674-0468-8*) Mayfield Pub.

— The Great Conversation Vol. 2: Deseartes Through Heidegger. 3rd ed. LC 98-4464. xii,419p. 1998. pap. text 37.95 (*0-7674-0469-6*) Mayfield Pub.

— Who's to Say: A Dialogue on Relativism. LC 94-21086. 96p. (C). 1994. pap. text 5.95 (*0-87220-271-2*); lib. bdg. 24.95 (*0-87220-272-0*) Hackett Pub.

Melchert, Paul A. & Roebke, John. A Will Is Not Enough: A Helpful Guide for Your Family. (Illus.). 24p. (Orig.). 1993. write for info. (*0-9638509-0-3*) Waconia Pubng.

Melchert, Wanda R. Machine Sewn Rag Baskets. 2nd rev. ed. LC 95-136447. (Illus.). 64p. (Orig.). 1994. pap. 11.95 (*0-9641199-0-0*) Desert Cntry.

Melchin, Kenneth R. Living with Other People: Directions in Christian Ethics from Bernard Lonergan. 120p. 1998. pap. 17.95 (*0-8146-5940-3*) Liturgical Pr.

Melchinger, Glenn. Japanese Written Word: A Unique Reader. 1998. pap. text 22.00 (*4-7700-2126-7*, Pub. by Kodansha Intl) Kodansha.

Melchiode, Gerald & Sloan, Bill. Beyond Viagra: A Common-Sense Guide to Building a Healthy Sexual Relationship for Men & Women. LC 98-43122. 256p. 1999. pap. 14.95 (*0-8050-6060-X*, Pub. by H Holt & Co) VHPS.

Melchionda, N., et al, eds. Recent Advances in Obesity & Diabetes Research. LC 83-19133. (Serono Symposia Publications from Raven Press: No. 8). (Illus.). 442p. 1984. reprint ed. pap. 137.10 (*0-7837-9530-0*, 206027900005) Bks Demand.

Melchior, Bernhard. Re-Visioning the Self Away from Home Vol. 340: Autobiographical & Cross-Cultural Dimensions in the Works of Paule Marshall. (European Univeristy Studies: Series 14). 358p. (C). 1998. pap. text 51.95 (*0-8204-3523-6*) P Lang Pubng.

***Melchior-Bonnet, Sabine.** The Mirror: A History. Jewett, Katharine, tr. from FRE. 2001. 27.50 (*0-415-92447-2*) Routledge.

Melchior, Daniel C. & Bassett, R. L., eds. Chemical Modeling of Aqueous Systems II. LC 89-28446. (ACS Symposium Ser.: No. 416). (Illus.). 576p. 1990. reprint ed. pap. 178.60 (*0-608-03972-1*, 205256400012) Bks Demand.

Melchior, H., ed. Bildgebende Systeme in der Urologie. (Beitraege zur Urologie Ser.: Vol. 4). (GER., Illus.). xiv, 386p. 1986. 188.75 (*3-8055-4335-2*) S Karger.

Melchior, Paul, ed. IUGG Union Lectures. (Special Publications). 1992. 15.00 (*0-87590-461-0*) Am Geophysical.

— Seismic Activity in Western Europe: With Particular Consideration to the Liege Earthquake of November 8, 1983. 1984. text 206.50 (*90-277-1889-X*) Kluwer Academic.

Melchior, Paul, jt. auth. see Chapralis, Jim C.

Melchior, Paul, ed. see International Astronomical Union Staff.

Melchior, William T. Insuring Public School Property. LC 75-177068. (Columbia University. Teachers College. Contributions to Education Ser.: No. 168). reprint ed. 37.50 (*0-404-55168-8*) AMS Pr.

***Melchiore, Susan.** Caesar Rodney. (Colonial Leaders Ser.). 2000. 18.95 (*0-7910-5968-5*) Chelsea Hse.

— Caesar Rodney. (Colonial Leaders Ser.). (Illus.). 2000. pap. 8.95 (*0-7910-6125-6*) Chelsea Hse.

Melchiori, Giorgio. Shakespeare's Dramatic Meditations: An Experiment in Criticism. (C). 1976. 34.00 (*0-19-812073-7*) OUP.

— Shakespeare's Garter Plays: Edward Third to Merry Wives of Windsor. LC 93-48123. (C). 1994. 29.50 (*0-87413-518-4*) U Delaware Pr.

— The Tightrope Walkers: A Greenwood Archival Edition. LC 73-14036. 277p. 1974. reprint ed. lib. bdg. 65.00 (*0-8371-7141-5*, METW, Greenwood Pr) Greenwood.

— The Whole Mystery of Art: Pattern into Poetry in the Work of W. B. Yeats. LC 72-12553. (Illus.). 306p. 1978. lib. bdg. 35.00 (*0-8371-6719-1*, MEMA, Greenwood Pr) Greenwood.

Melchiori, Giorgio, jt. ed. see Marrapodi, Michele.

Melchiori, Giorgio, ed. see Shakespeare, William.

Melchiorri, Claudio & Tornamb, Antonio E. Modelling & Control of Mechanisms & Robots: Bertinoro, Italy, 22-26 July 1996. LC 96-21727. 304p. 1996. write for info. (*981-02-2724-8*) World Scientific Pub.

Melchiorri, F., jt. ed. see Signore, M.

***Melchizedek, Drunvalo.** Ancient Secret of the Flower of Life. (Illus.). 228p. 1999. pap. 25.00 (*1-891824-17-1*) Light Tech Pubng.

— Ancient Secret of the Flower of Life. (Flower of Life Ser.: No. 2). (Illus.). 2000. pap. 25.00 (*1-891824-21-X*, Pub. by Light Tech Pubng) New Leaf Dist.

Melchoir, Daniel C. & Bassett, R. L., eds. Chemical Modeling of Aqueous Systems II. LC 89-28446. (ACS Symposium Ser.: No. 416). (Illus.). 538p. 1989. 94.95 (*0-8412-1729-7*) Am Chemical.

Melchoir, P. The Tides of the Planet Earth. 2nd ed. LC 82-16567. (Illus.). 648p. 1983. 284.00 (*0-08-026248-1*, Pub. by Pergamon Repr) Franklin.

Melchor, Lisa P. Italian-American Artists, 1945-1968: A Limited Survey, Works on Paper. (Illus.). 48p. (Orig.). 1994. pap. text 7.50 (*1-885998-01-5*) Hunter College.

Mel'cuk, Igor A. Dependency Syntax: Theory & Practice. LC 86-14542. (SUNY Series in Linguistics). 428p. (C). 1987. pap. text 21.50 (*0-88706-451-5*) State U NY Pr.

— Dependency Syntax: Theory & Practice. LC 86-14542. (SUNY Series in Linguistics). 428p. (C). 1988. text 21.50 (*0-88706-450-7*) State U NY Pr.

Mel'cuk, Igor A., jt. auth. see Gladkij, Aleksej V.

Mel'cuk, Igor K. & Pertsov, Nikolaj V. Surface Syntax of English: A Formal Model within the Meaning-Text Framework. Stern, Lev, tr. LC 86-6884. (Linguistic & Literary Studies in Eastern Europe: No. 13). xv, 526p. 1986. 190.00 (*90-272-1515-4*) J Benjamins Pubng Co.

Melczer, William. The Pilgrim's Guide to Santiago de Compostela. LC 93-18623. (Historical Travel Ser.). (Illus.). 368p. (Orig.). 1993. pap. 20.00 (*0-934977-25-9*) Italica Pr.

***Meldal-Johnsen, Trevor.** Always. 2nd rev. ed. 320p. 1999. 24.95 (*0-9673285-0-0*) Bamboo Grove Pubs.

Meldau, Fred J. The Prophets Still Speak: Messiah in Both Testaments. 1988. 8.95 (*0-915540-42-8*) Frnds Israel.

Meldehout, M. & Seneor, R. Mathematical Physics: Eighth International Congress. 892p. 1987. pap. 43.00 (*9971-5-0209-7*); text 148.00 (*9971-5-0208-9*) World Scientific Pub.

Melden, A. I. Essays Moral Philosophy. LC 58-10483. 288p. 1966. pap. 8.00 (*0-295-74049-3*, WP20) U of Wash Pr.

— Ethical Theories: A Book of Readings with Revisions. 2nd ed. (C). 1967. text 45.80 (*0-13-290122-6*) P-H.

Melder, Keith. City of Magnificent Intentions: A History of Washington, District of Columbia. 2nd rev. ed. Stuart, Melinda Y., ed. (Illus.). 688p. 1997. text 45.00 (*0-913137-01-4*) Intac.

— Hail to the Candidate: Presidential Campaigns from Banners to Broadcasts. LC 91-5179. (Illus.). 224p. 1992. pap. 24.95 (*1-56098-178-4*) Smithsonian.

Meldgaard, Helle & Aagaard, Johannes, eds. Religious Movements in Europe. (Renner Ser.: Vol. 3). 192p. 1997. pap. 26.95 (*87-7288-548-3*, Pub. by Aarhus Univ Pr) David Brown.

Meldin, Madeleine. The Tender Bud: A Physician's Journey Through Breast Cancer. LC 92-49967. 232p. 1993. 29.95 (*0-88163-157-4*) Analytic Pr.

Meldman & Schadewald. Practical Guide to U. S. Taxation of International Transactions. LC 96-158623. 384p. 1996. 89.00 (*0-8080-0090-X*, 26595BLS01) CCH INC.

Meldman, Louis W. Mystical Sex: Love, Ecstasy & the Mystical Experience. LC 96-42203. 208p. 1997. pap. 14.95 (*1-85230-957-1*, Pub. by Element MA) Penguin Putnam.

Meldman, Robert & Sideman, Richard. Federal Taxation: Practice & Procedure. 5th ed. LC 98-173128. 600p. (C). 1998. text 89.00 (*0-8080-0257-0*) CCH INC.

Meldman, Robert E. & Schadewald, Michael S. A Practical Guide to U. S. Taxation of International Transactions. LC 98-117568. 400p. 1998. 125.00 (*90-411-0622-7*) Kluwer Law Intl.

— A Practical Guide to U. S. Taxation of International Transactions. 2nd ed. LC 98-117568. 400p. 1996. 95.00 (*0-8080-0171-X*) CCH INC.

***Meldman, Robert E. & Schadewald, Michael S.** A Practical Guide to U. S. Taxation of International Transactions. 3rd ed. 496p. (C). 2000. text 99.00 (*0-8080-0491-3*) CCH INC.

Meldman, Robert E. & Sideman, Richard J. Federal Taxation Practice & Procedure Problem Supplement. Norris, Lawrence M., ed. 64p. (C). 1998. pap. text, suppl. ed. 40.00 (*0-8080-0265-1*) CCH INC.

Meldman, Robert E., jt. auth. see Petrie.

Meldolesi, Luca. Discovering the Possible: The Surprising World of Albert O. Hirschman. LC 94-42834. (C). 1995. text 34.95 (*0-268-00877-9*) U of Notre Dame Pr.

Meldrum, Barbara H. Sophus K. Winther. LC 82-74094. (Western Writers Ser.: No. 60). (Illus.). 52p. (Orig.). 1983. pap. 4.95 (*0-88430-034-X*) Boise St U W Writ Ser.

Meldrum, Barbara H., ed. Old West - New West: Centennial Essays. LC 92-29828. 352p. (C). 1993. pap. 29.95 (*0-89301-163-0*); lib. bdg. 36.00 (*0-89301-166-5*) U of Idaho Pr.

Meldrum, Barbara H., ed. Under the Sun: Myth & Realism in Western American Literature. LC 85-50609. (Illus.). viii, 230p. 1985. 45.00 (*0-87875-303-6*) Whitston Pub.

Meldrum, Brian S., ed. Excitatory Amino Acid Antagonists. (Frontiers in Pharmacology & Therapeutics Ser.). (Illus.). 368p. 1991. 125.00 (*0-632-02737-1*) Blackwell Sci.

Meldrum, Brian S., et al, eds. Anatomy of Epileptogenesis. (Current Problems in Epilepsy Ser.: Vol. 6). 187p. 1988. 69.95 (*0-86196-155-2*, Pub. by J Libbey Med) Bks Intl VA.

— Excitatory Amino Acids. LC 91-18568. (Fidia Research Foundation Symposium Ser.: No. 5). (Illus.). 816p. 1991. reprint ed. pap. 200.00 (*0-608-05807-6*, 205977200007) Bks Demand.

Meldrum, Brian S. & Porter, Roger J. New Anticonvulsant Drugs. (Current Problems in Epilepsy Ser.: Vol. 4). (Illus.). 350p. 1986. 82.95 (*0-86196-063-7*, Pub. by J Libbey Med) Bks Intl VA.

Meldrum, D. H. Fighting Fire with Foam: Basics of Effective Systems. 1979. 3.50 (*0-686-25956-4*, TR 79-2) Society Fire Protect.

Meldrum, David R., jt. auth. see Wisot, Arthur L.

Meldrum, David S., ed. see Galt, John.

Meldrum, Douglas G. The Night Two Thousand Men Came to Dinner: And Other Appetizing Anecdotes. (Illus.). 160p. 1994. 16.95 (*0-02-583960-8*, Scribners Ref) Mac Lib Ref.

Meldrum, Helen. Interpersonal Communication in Pharmaceutical Care. LC 93-31220. 154p. 1994. pap. 14.95 (*1-56024-867-X*); lib. bdg. 49.95 (*1-56024-866-1*) Haworth Pr.

Meldrum, J. P. D. Wreath Products. 1995. 120.00 (*0-582-02693-8*, Pub. by Addison-Wesley) Longman.

***Meldrum, Timothy.** Domestic Service & Gender, 1660-1750. LC 00-21674. (Women & Men in History Ser.). 2000. write for info. (*0-582-31208-6*) Addison-Wesley.

Mele, Alfred R. Autonomous Agents: From Self-Control to Autonomy. 288p. 1995. text 60.00 (*0-19-509454-9*) OUP.

***Mele, Alfred R.** Self-Deception Unmasked. LC 00-32626. (Monographs in Philosophy). 160p. 2000. 15.95 (*0-691-05745-1*) Princeton U Pr.

— Self-Deception Unmasked. 160p. 2001. 49.50 (*0-691-05744-3*) Princeton U Pr.

Mele, Alfred R. Springs of Action: Understanding Intentional Behavior. 288p. 1992. text 65.00 (*0-19-507114-X*) OUP.

Mele, Alfred R., ed. The Philosophy of Action. LC 96-8682. (Oxford Readings in Philosophy). 320p. (C). 1997. text 71.00 (*0-19-875174-5*); pap. text 21.95 (*0-19-875175-3*) OUP.

Mele, Alfred R., jt. ed. see Heil, John.

Mele, Antonio, jt. auth. see Fornari, Fabio.

Mele, Audre. Polluting for Pleasure. LC 92-43498. 224p. 1993. 22.95 (*0-393-03510-7*) Norton.

***Mele, Christopher.** Selling the Lower East Side: Culture, Real Estate, & Resistance in New York City. LC 99-57397. 408p. 2000. pap. 19.95 (*0-8166-3182-4*) U of Minn Pr.

***Mele, Frank.** Small in the Eye of A River. 1999. 30.00 (*1-55821-963-3*) Lyons Pr.

Mele, Jim. The Calculation of Two. 68p. 1982. pap. 3.95 (*0-916696-21-9*) Cross Country.

— An Oracle of Love. 24p. 1976. pap. 1.00 (*0-916696-01-4*) Cross Country.

— The Sunday Habit. 1978. pap. 3.00 (*0-916696-07-3*) Cross Country.

Mele, Joan F., tr. see Baudelaire, Charles.

Mele, M., jt. ed. see Creazza, G.

Mele, Michael. A Gift for the Contessa. LC 96-42181. (Illus.). 40p. (J). 1997. 15.95 (*1-56554-216-9*) Pelican.

Mele, Michael, ed. see Tise, Larry E.

Mele, P. E. Ceylon. (Illus.). 90p. lib. bdg. 9.95 (*0-8288-3932-8*) Fr & Eur.

Mele, Pietro F. Tibet. (Illus.). 92p. 1988. 14.95 (*0-937938-63-7*) Snow Lion Pubns.

Melear, Lawrence. Educator's Guide to Drug Prevention. (Illus.). 165p. 1990. teacher ed. 48.00 (*0-945207-00-X*) Melear.

Melebea, jt. auth. see Calisto.

Meleca, Robert J., jt. auth. see Dworkin, James P.

Melegari, Vezic, et al. Travels Back in Time. (Illus.). 40p. (YA). 1997. 1.99 (*0-517-18454-0*) Random Hse Value.

Melehy, Hassan. Writing Cogito: Montaigne, Descartes, & the Institution of the Modern Subject. LC 97-679. (SUNY Series, The Margins of Literature). 210p. (C). 1997. text 59.50 (*0-7914-3571-7*); pap. text 19.95 (*0-7914-3572-5*) State U NY Pr.

Melehy, Hassan, tr. see Dosse, Francois.

Melehy, Hassan, tr. see Ranciere, Jacques.

Meleis, Afaf I. Theoretical Nursing: Development & Progress. 3rd ed. LC 96-36612. 688p. 1997. text 39.95 (*0-397-55259-9*) Lppncott W & W.

***Meleis, Afaf Ibrahim, et al.** Immigrant Women & Their Health: An Olive Paper. (Monographs). 59p. (C). 1998. pap. text 20.00 (*0-9656391-6-9*, 1057) Sigma Theta Tau.

Meleisea, Penelope Schoeffel. Sociocultural Issues & Economic Development in the Pacific Islands. LC 98-947641. (Studies). 17 p. 1996. write for info. (*971-561-081-1*) Paul & Co Pubs.

Melek, Jacob E. Poems of the Holocaust. (Illus.). 276p. (Orig.). 1996. pap. 24.00 (*0-614-95918-7*) J Melek.

Melek, Jacques. California Apartment Ownership: Orange County, 16 vols., Set. (Orig.). 1983. write for info. (*0-318-56682-6*) J Melek.

— California Apartment Ownership: San Bernandino County, Set. (Orig.). 1983. pap. 48.00 (*0-942330-18-8*) J Melek.

— California Apartment Ownership: San Bernandino County, Vol 1. (Orig.). 1983. pap. 480.00 (*0-942330-19-6*) J Melek.

— California Commercial Industrial Directories, 60 Vols., No. 32. (Plumas Ser.). 200p. (Orig.). 1982. pap. write for info. (*0-942330-53-6*) J Melek.

— California Commercial Industrial Directories, No. 33. (Riverside Ser.). 200p. (Orig.). 1983. 96.00 (*0-686-35962-3*); pap. write for info. (*0-942330-54-4*) J Melek.

— California Commercial Industrial Directories: Alamedia, No. 1. 200p. (Orig.). 1983. 96.00 (*0-942330-22-6*) J Melek.

— California Commercial Industrial Directories: Alamedia, Set. 200p. (Orig.). 1983. pap. 48.00 (*0-686-35979-8*) J Melek.

— California Commercial Industrial Directories: Alpine, No. 2. 150p. (Orig.). 1983. 96.00 (*0-942330-23-4*) J Melek.

An Asterisk (*) at the beginning of an entry indicates that the title is appearing for the first time.

— California Commercial Industrial Directories: Amador, No. 3. 200p. (Orig.). 1983. 96.00 (*0-942330-24-2*) J Melek.

— California Commercial Industrial Directories: Butte, Vol 4. 200p. (Orig.). 1983. 96.00 (*0-942330-25-0*) J Melek.

— California Commercial Industrial Directories: Calaveras, Vol. 5. 150p. (Orig.). 1983. 96.00 (*0-942330-27-7*) J Melek.

— California Commercial Industrial Directories: Central Sierra Counties, Vol. 7. 200p. (Orig.). 1983. 96.00 (*0-686-35977-1*) J Melek.

— California Commercial Industrial Directories: Contra Costa, Vol. 6. 200p. (Orig.). 1983. 96.00 (*0-942330-28-5*) J Melek.

— California Commercial Industrial Directories: Del Norte, Vol. 8. 200p. (Orig.). 1983. 96.00 (*0-942330-29-3*) J Melek.

— California Commercial Industrial Directories: El Dorado, Vol. 9. 150p. (Orig.). 1983. 96.00 (*0-942330-30-7*) J Melek.

— California Commercial Industrial Directories: Fresno, No. 10. 200p. (Orig.). 1982. pap. write for info. (*0-942330-31-5*) J Melek.

— California Commercial Industrial Directories: Fresno, Set. 200p. (Orig.). 1982. pap. 48.00 (*0-685-05927-8*) J Melek.

— California Commercial Industrial Directories: Glenn, No. 11. 200p. (Orig.). 1983. 96.00 (*0-942330-32-3*) J Melek.

— California Commercial Industrial Directories: Humboldt, No. 12. 200p. (Orig.). 1983. 96.00 (*0-942330-33-1*) J Melek.

— California Commercial Industrial Directories: Imperial, No. 13. 200p. (Orig.). 1983. 96.00 (*0-942330-34-X*) J Melek.

— California Commercial Industrial Directories: Inyo, No. 14. 200p. (Orig.). 1983. 96.00 (*0-942330-35-8*) J Melek.

— California Commercial Industrial Directories: Kern, No. 15. 200p. (Orig.). 1983. 96.00 (*0-942330-36-6*) J Melek.

— California Commercial Industrial Directories: Kings, No. 16. 200p. (Orig.). 1983. 96.00 (*0-942330-37-4*) J Melek.

— California Commercial Industrial Directories: Lake, No. 17. 200p. (Orig.). 1983. 96.00 (*0-942330-38-2*) J Melek.

— California Commercial Industrial Directories: Lassen, No. 18. 200p. (Orig.). 1983. pap. 96.00 (*0-685-05926-X*) J Melek.

— California Commercial Industrial Directories: Los Angeles, No. 19. 200p. (Orig.). 1983. pap. write for info. (*0-942330-40-4*) J Melek.

— California Commercial Industrial Directories: Madera, No. 20. 200p. (Orig.). 1983. 96.00 (*0-942330-41-2*) J Melek.

— California Commercial Industrial Directories: Marin, No. 21. 200p. (Orig.). 1983. 96.00 (*0-686-98669-5*); pap. write for info. (*0-942330-42-0*) J Melek.

— California Commercial Industrial Directories: Mariposa, No. 22. 200p. (Orig.). 1983. pap. write for info. (*0-942330-43-9*) J Melek.

— California Commercial Industrial Directories: Mendocino, No. 23. 200p. (Orig.). 1983. pap. write for info. (*0-318-56681-8*) J Melek.

— California Commercial Industrial Directories: Merced, No. 24. 200p. (Orig.). 1983. pap. write for info. (*0-318-56680-X*) J Melek.

— California Commercial Industrial Directories: Modoc, No. 25. 200p. (Orig.). 1983. pap. write for info. (*0-942330-46-3*) J Melek.

— California Commercial Industrial Directories: Mono, No. 26. 200p. (Orig.). 1983. pap. write for info. (*0-942330-47-1*) J Melek.

— California Commercial Industrial Directories: Monterey, No. 27. 200p. (Orig.). 1983. pap. write for info. (*0-942330-48-X*) J Melek.

California Commercial Industrial Directories: Napa, No 28. 200p. (Orig.). 1983. 96.00 (*0-685-05925-1*) J Melek.

— California Commercial Industrial Directories: Nevada, No. 29. 150p. 1983. pap. write for info. (*0-942330-50-1*) J Melek.

— California Commercial Industrial Directories: Northern Sierra Counties, No. 59. 200p. (Orig.). 1983. 96.00 (*0-942330-80-3*) J Melek.

— California Commercial Industrial Directories: Northern State Counties, No. 58. 200p. (Orig.). 1983. 96.00 (*0-686-98787-X*); pap. write for info. (*0-942330-79-X*) J Melek.

— California Commercial Industrial Directories: Orange, No. 30. 200p. (Orig.). 1983. 96.00 (*0-942330-51-X*) J Melek.

— California Commercial Industrial Directories: Placer, No. 31. 150p. (Orig.). 1983. pap. write for info. (*0-942330-52-8*) J Melek.

— California Commercial Industrial Directories: San Benito, No. 35. 200p. 1983. pap. write for info. (*0-942330-56-0*) J Melek.

— California Commercial Industrial Directories: San Bernardino, No. 36. 200p. (Orig.). 1983. pap. write for info. (*0-942330-57-9*) J Melek.

— California Commercial Industrial Directories: San Diego, No. 37. 200p. 1983. pap. write for info. (*0-942330-58-7*) J Melek.

— California Commercial Industrial Directories: San Francisco, No. 38. 200p. (Orig.). 1983. pap. write for info. (*0-942330-59-5*) J Melek.

— California Commercial Industrial Directories: San Joaquin, Vol. 39. 200p. (Orig.). 1983. 96.00 (*0-942330-60-9*) J Melek.

— California Commercial Industrial Directories: San Luis Obispo, No. 40. 200p. (Orig.). 1983. pap. 96.00 (*0-942330-61-7*) J Melek.

— California Commercial Industrial Directories: San Mateo, No. 41. 200p. (Orig.). 1983. 96.00 (*0-942330-62-5*) J Melek.

— California Commercial Industrial Directories: Sanislaus, No. 50. 200p. (Orig.). 1983. 96.00 (*0-942330-71-4*) J Melek.

— California Commercial Industrial Directories: Santa Barbara, No. 42. 200p. (Orig.). 1983. pap. 96.00 (*0-942330-63-3*) J Melek.

— California Commercial Industrial Directories: Santa Clara, No. 43. 200p. (Orig.). 1983. 96.00 (*0-942330-64-1*) J Melek.

— California Commercial Industrial Directories: Santa Cruz, No. 44. 200p. (Orig.). 1983. 96.00 (*0-942330-65-X*) J Melek.

— California Commercial Industrial Directories: Shasta, No. 45. 200p. (Orig.). 1983. 96.00 (*0-942330-66-8*) J Melek.

— California Commercial Industrial Directories: Sierra, No. 46. 150p. 1982. 96.00 (*0-942330-67-6*) J Melek.

— California Commercial Industrial Directories: Siskiyou, No. 47. 200p. 1983. 96.00 (*0-942330-68-4*) J Melek.

— California Commercial Industrial Directories: Solano, No. 48. 200p. (Orig.). 1983. pap. 96.00 (*0-942330-69-2*) J Melek.

— California Commercial Industrial Directories: Sonoma, No. 49. 200p. (Orig.). 1983. 96.00 (*0-942330-70-6*) J Melek.

— California Commercial Industrial Directories: Tehama, No. 51. 200p. (Orig.). 1983. 96.00 (*0-942330-72-2*) J Melek.

— California Commercial Industrial Directories: Trinity, No. 52. 200p. 1983. 96.00 (*0-942330-73-0*) J Melek.

— California Commercial Industrial Directories: Tulane, No. 53. 150p. (Orig.). 1983. 96.00 (*0-942330-74-9*) J Melek.

— California Commercial Industrial Directories: Tuolumne, No. 54. 200p. (Orig.). 1983. 96.00 (*0-942330-75-7*) J Melek.

— California Commercial Industrial Directories: Ventura, No. 55. 200p. (Orig.). 1983. 96.00 (*0-942330-76-5*) J Melek.

— California Commercial Industrial Directories: Yuba, No. 54. 200p. (Orig.). 1983. 96.00 (*0-942330-78-1*) J Melek.

— Cancer: Acute & Chronic Deleterious Effects of the Present Conventional Medical Therapy to Cancer Patients. 600p. (Orig.). 1984. pap. text 19.95 (*0-942330-04-8*, Sunbright Bks) J Melek.

— Cancer: Affinity & Pool of Iron from the Red Blood Cells by the Highly Acidic Chromosomal Nucleic Acid of Cancer Cell As the Source of Energy of Cancer Cell & Loss of Weight by Cancer Patient. 400p. (Orig.). 1984. pap. text 8.95 (*0-942330-07-2*, Sunbright Bks) J Melek.

— Cancer: All the Hazards & Risks You Cannot Afford to Take & the Preventive Natural, Universal Approaches to Prevention of This Dreadful Disease. (Illus.). 600p. (Orig.). 1984. pap. 19.95 (*0-685-09129-5*, Sunbright Bks) J Melek.

— Cancer: Allergic Induced Immune Response Effect on Cancer Cells. 600p. (Orig.). pap. text 24.95 (*0-685-09130-9*, Sunbright Bks) J Melek.

— Cancer: An Iotragenic Environmental Disease-the Cause & Effect. 600p. (Orig.). 1984. pap. text 24.95 (*0-685-09132-5*, Sunbright Bks) J Melek.

— Cancer: Calcification Effect of Cancer Cell Membrane with Calcium Hydroxide Solution in Cure & Control of Cancer. (Illus.). 300p. (Orig.). 1984. pap. text 24.95 (*0-685-09136-8*, Sunbright Bks) J Melek.

— Cancer: Constant, Continuous Titration of Calcium Bicarbonate Solution Effect of Calcification Shell on the Membrane of Cancer Cells. 500p. (Orig.). 1984. pap. text 24.50 (*0-685-09137-6*, Sunbright Bks) J Melek.

— Cancer: Egg-Shell Formation on Cancer Cell. (Illus.). 500p. (Orig.). 1984. pap. text 19.95 (*0-942330-05-6*, Sunbright Bks) J Melek.

— Cancer: Iron Supplement & Increase Iron Rich Food. (Illus.). 250p. (Orig.). 1984. pap. text 8.95 (*0-685-09145-7*, Sunbright Bks) J Melek.

— Cancer-Anaphylactic: The Jacques Melek Cytokinetic Induced Respond Immune Response & Molecular Theory Effect on Cancer Cells. 600p. (Orig.). 1984. pap. 24.95 (*0-942330-03-X*, Sunbright Bks) J Melek.

— Cancer-Biological Theory of Jacques Melek: Concepts of the Mechanism & Production of the First Cancer Cell. 250p. (Orig.). 1984. pap. text 9.50 (*0-685-09134-1*, Sunbright Bks) J Melek.

— Cancer Oxidation. 300p. (Orig.). 1984. pap. text 8.95 (*0-685-09146-5*, Sunbright Bks) J Melek.

— The Court Fox. 500p. 1983. pap. 24.95 (*0-942330-49-8*, Sunrise Pubns) J Melek.

— Lyrics of Love Vol. 1: Songs & Poems. 120p. 1981. write for info. (*0-318-56567-6*, Sunrise Pubns); pap. 6.00 (*0-686-96966-9*, Sunrise Pubns) J Melek.

— Risks & Hazards You Cannot Afford. (Illus.). (Orig.). 1984. pap. 8.95 (*0-685-08399-3*, Sunrise Pubns) J Melek.

— U. S. Tax Law Dictionary. (Tax Law Dictionary Ser.). (Illus.). 638p. (Orig.). 1996. pap. 24.95 (*0-942330-00-5*) J Melek.

Melek, Jacques, jt. auth. see American Medical Association.

Meleka, Fikri M. Dimensions of the Cancer Problem. xii, 144p. 1983. pap. 42.75 (*3-8055-3622-4*) S Karger.

Melekhin, V. N., jt. auth. see Kapitza, S. P.

***Melekhina, Alisa.** The Frog Princess: A Russian Fairy Tale. (Illus.). 25p. (J). (gr. 1-3). 2000. pap. 5.95 (*0-533-13238-X*) Vantage.

MeleMcCarthy. Textbook of Language Assessment. 2000. 27.00 (*1-56593-177-7*) Thomson Learn.

Melendez, A. Gabriel. So All Is Not Lost: The Poetics of Print in Nuevomexicano Communities, 1834-1958. LC 97-4583. (Paso por Aqui Ser.). 281p. 1997. 50.00 (*0-8263-1776-6*); pap. 24.95 (*0-8263-1806-1*) U of NM Pr.

Melendez, Andres A., ed. Libro de Concordia. (SPA.). 1989. 19.95 (*0-570-09902-1*, 16-1009) Concordia.

Melendez, Carlos, jt. auth. see Oquli, Ramon.

Melendez-Carrucini, G. & Melendez-Lugo, Ruben H. Ingreso Tributable: Inclusiones & Doctrinas. (SPA., Illus.). 742p. 1990. text 75.00 (*1-878186-00-0*) Inst Cont PR.

Melendez, Concha. Antologia y Cartas de Sus Amigos. (SPA.). 368p. 1995. pap. 16.95 (*0-8477-0236-7*) U of PR Pr.

Melendez De Stone, Bunny, tr. see Smith, John L.

Melendez, E., et al. Hispanics in the Labor Force: Issues & Policies. (Environment, Development, & Public Policy: Public Policy & Social Services Ser.). (Illus.). 328p. (C). 1991. 65.00 (*0-306-43799-6*, Plenum Trade) Perseus Pubng.

Melendez, Edgardo. El Movimiento Anexionista en Puerto Rico. 1993. pap. 16.95 (*0-8477-0186-7*) U of PR Pr.

***Melendez, Edgardo.** Puerto Rican Government & Politics: A Comprehensive Bibliography. LC 00-24784. 350p. 2000. lib. bdg. 75.00 (*1-55587-894-0*) L Rienner.

Melendez, Edgardo. Puerto Rico's Statehood Movement, 220. LC 88-10249. (Contributions in Political Science Ser.: No. 220). 212p. 1988. 52.95 (*0-313-26131-8*, MPH/, Greenwood Pr) Greenwood.

Melendez, Edgardo, jt. ed. see Melendez, Edwin.

Melendez, Edwin & Melendez, Edgardo, eds. Colonial Dilemma: Critical Perspectives on Contemporary Puerto Rico. 350p. 1993. 40.00 (*0-89608-442-6*); pap. 16.00 (*0-89608-441-8*) South End Pr.

Melendez, Edwin & Uriarte, Miren, eds. Latino Poverty & Economic Development in Massachusetts. LC 93-34381. 212p. (Orig.). 1994. pap. 14.95 (*0-87023-894-9*) U of Mass Pr.

Melendez, Esteban N. Plantas Venenosas de Puerto Rico. (SPA.). 290p. 1990. pap. 12.75 (*0-8477-2341-0*) U of PR Pr.

Mele'ndez, Gloria S., tr. see Nervo, Amado.

Melendez, Guillermo. Seeds of Promise: The Prophetic Church in Central America. 1990. pap. 6.95 (*0-377-00204-6*) Friendship Pr.

Melendez-Lugo, Ruben H., jt. auth. see Melendez-Carrucini, G.

Melendez, Robles De, see De Melendez, Robles.

Melendez, Sarah E., jt. auth. see Ambert, Alba N.

Melendez Valdes, Juan. Poesias. Real Ramos, Cesar, ed. (Nueva Austral Ser.: Vol. 217). (SPA.). 1991. pap. text 24.95 (*84-239-7217-8*) Elliots Bks.

— Poesias Ineditas de Juan Melendez Valdes. Rodriguez Monino, Antonio, ed. (SPA.). 259p. 1968. 100.00 (*0-614-00218-4*) Elliots Bks.

Melendez, Winifred. The Universities of Puerto Rico: A Historical, Sociological & Cultural Study Including a Directory of Puerto Rico Scholars. 1979. lib. bdg. 250.00 (*0-8490-1247-3*) Gordon Pr.

Melendo, R. P., jt. auth. see Gallego, J. F.

Melendres, C. A., ed. Synchrotron Techniques in Interfacial Electrochemistry: Proceedings of the NATO Advanced Research Workshop, Funchal, Madeira, Portugal, December 14-18, 1992. (NATO Advanced Science Institutes C: Mathematical & Physical Sciences Ser.). 500p. (C). 1994. text 298.50 (*0-7923-2844-2*) Kluwer Academic.

Melendres, C. A., jt. ed. see Gutierrez, C.

Melendy, H. Brett. Hawaii, America's Sugar Territory 1898-1959. LC 99-26436. (Studies in American History: Vol. 25). 360p. 1999. text 99.95 (*0-7734-7998-8*) E Mellen.

— Walter Francis Dillingham, 1875-1963: Hawaiian Entrepreneur & Statesman. LC 96-3699. (Studies in American History: Vol. 10). (Illus.). 356p. 1996. 99.95 (*0-7734-8793-X*) E Mellen.

Melenski, Aaron, ed. see Arpante, Barbara A.

Melentiev, A. & Rudenko, Y. N. Energy Reviews: Scientific & Engineering Problems of Energy Systems Reliability, 3. (Soviet Technology Reviews Ser.: Vol. 3). xvi, 350p. (C). 1987. reprint ed. text 500.00 (*3-7186-0281-4*) Gordon & Breach.

Melentiev, L. A., ed. Energy Reviews: Nuclear Power Systems. (Soviet Technology Reviews Ser.: Vol. 1). x, 344p. 1982. text 572.00 (*3-7186-0071-4*) Gordon & Breach.

— Energy Reviews Vol. 6, Pt. 4: Optimization of Development of Heat & Water Supply Systems, Vol. 6. (Soviet Technology Reviews Ser.). 166p. 1994. pap. text 92.00 (*3-7186-5539-X*) Gordon & Breach.

— Unified Gas Supply System of the U. S. S. R. (Soviet Technology Reviews Ser.: Vol. 2). xii, 316p. 1985. text 503.00 (*3-7186-0152-4*) Gordon & Breach.

***Melerski, Edmund S.** Design Analysis of Beams, Cicular Plates & Cylindrical Tanks on Elastic Foundations. (Illus.). 306p. 2000. 39.00 (*90-5809-304-2*, Pub. by A A Balkema) Ashgate Pub Co.

— Design Analysis of Beams, Cicular Plates & Cylindrical Tanks on Elastic Foundations: With IBM Compatible Software. (Illus.). 306p. 2000. 85.00 incl. cd-rom (*90-5809-303-4*, Pub. by A A Balkema) Ashgate Pub Co.

Melese-D'Hospital, G., jt. auth. see Howe, J. P.

Melese, Gilbert & Katz, Robert. Thermal & Flow Design of Helium-Cooled Reactors. 432p. 1985. 65.00 (*0-89448-027-8*, 300019) Am Nuclear Soc.

Meleshko, V. V. & Konstantinov, M. Yu. Vortex Dynamics & Chaotic Phenomena. 300p. 1997. text 61.00 (*981-02-0871-5*) World Scientific Pub.

***Melet, Ed.** Sustainable Architecture. LC 99-514573. 1999. pap. 47.50 (*90-5662-118-1*) NAi Uitgevers.

Melet, Ed. Sustainable Architecture: The Pursuit of a More Contrast-rich Environment. (Illus.). 208p. 1999. pap. 47.50 (*90-5662-089-4*, Pub. by NAi Uitgevers) Dist Art Pubs.

Meletinsky, Eleazar M. The Poetics of Myth. Segal, Robert A., ed. Lanoue, Guy & Sadetsky, Alexandre, trs. LC 97-24453. (Theorists of Myth Ser.: Vol. 9). 520p. 1998. text 85.00 (*0-8153-2134-1*) Garland.

Meletis, Chris & Fitzgerald, Susan M. Better Sex Naturally: A Consumer's Guide to Herbs & Other Natural Supplements That Can Jump Start Your Sex Life. LC 99-87987. 224p. 2000. pap. 14.00 (*0-06-273688-4*) HarpC.

***Meletis, Chris D. & Jacobs, Thad.** Interactions Between Drugs & Natural Medicines: What the Physician & Pharmacist Must Know about Vitamins, Minerals, Foods & Herbs. LC 99-75715. 368p. 1999. 35.00 (*1-888483-10-5*) Eclectic Med.

Meletis, Efstathios I., jt. ed. see Sagues, Alberto A.

***Meleton, Marcus P., Jr.** Liberal Man: Final Mission. (Illus.). 168p. 2000. pap. 14.95 (*0-9635826-5-8*) Sharkbait Pr.

Meleton, Marcus P., Jr. Nice Guys Don't Get Laid. rev. ed. LC 93-83581. 112p. 1993. pap. 7.95 (*0-9635826-0-7*) Sharkbait Pr.

Meleton, Marucs P. Hunting for Lawyers: A Modest Proposal. LC 95-92039. 128p. (Orig.). 1995. pap. 9.95 (*0-9635826-2-3*) Sharkbait Pr.

Meleze-Modrzejewski, Joseph. Statut Personnel et Liens de Famille dans les Droits de l'Antiquite. (Collected Studies: Vol. 411). 320p. 1993. 109.95 (*0-86078-376-6*, Pub. by Variorum) Ashgate Pub Co.

Melfa, Frank A. Bodybuilding a Realistic Approach: How You Can Have a Great Body. 2nd ed. LC 97-95132. (Illus.). 437p. (Orig.). 1998. pap. 16.95 (*0-9641640-7-8*) Power Writings.

Melfe, Thomas A., jt. auth. see Train, John.

Melfi, Charles V. MC68 HC11 Laboratory Manual: Software & Hardware Interfacing. LC 98-6997. (C). 2000. pap. 22.50 (*0-7668-0482-8*) Delmar.

Melfi, Leonard. The Little Venice Makes a Good Drink: or The Family That Stays Together... LC 96-37912. 80p. Date not set. pap. 6.95 (*1-55783-258-7*) Applause Theatre Bk Pubs.

Melfi, Mary. A Bride in Three Acts, Vol. 1. 96p. pap. 5.00 (*0-919349-33-1*) Guernica Editions.

— Infertility Rites. 182p. 1991. pap. 13.00 (*0-920717-51-9*) SPD-Small Pr Dist.

— Office Politics. (Essential Poets Ser.: Vol. 88). 96p. 1999. pap. 10.00 (*1-55071-085-0*) Guernica Editions.

— A Queen Is Holding a Mummified Cat, Vol. 1. 88p. pap. 5.00 (*0-919349-09-9*) Guernica Editions.

— Sex Therapy: A Black Comedy. LC 95-75022. (Drama Ser.: No. 13). 120p. (C). 1996. pap. 10.00 (*1-55071-035-4*) Guernica Editions.

— Stages: Selected Poems. LC 98-72849. (Essential Poets Ser.: Vol. 77). 180p. 1998. pap. 13.00 (*1-55071-050-8*) Guernica Editions.

Melfi, Mary, ed. Painting Moments: Art, AIDS & Nick Palazzo. LC 97-72805. 150p. 1998. pap. 18.00 (*1-55071-067-2*) Guernica Editions.

Melfi, Rudy C. Permar's Oral Embryology & Microscopic Anatomy: A Textbook for Students in Dental Hygiene. 9th ed. LC 93-5248. (Illus.). 278p. 1994. 34.00 (*0-8121-1659-3*) Lppncott W & W.

Melford, Michael, photos by. Big Sky Country: The Best of Montana, North Dakota, Wyoming & Idaho. LC 96-16309. (Illus.). 176p. 1996. 50.00 (*0-8478-1964-7*, Pub. by Rizzoli Intl) St Martin.

Melford, Michael, jt. auth. see Ferguson, Gary.

Melford, S. J. & Anysas, J. A. Identifying a Liquid Using Physical Properties. Neidig, H. Anthony, ed. (Modular Laboratory Program in Chemistry Ser.). 11p. (C). 1994. pap. text 1.50 (*0-87540-440-5*, PROP 440-5) Chem Educ Res.

Melger, Boyd A., see Re'lem, Dyob, pseud.

Melger, Boyd A., jt. auth. see Re'lem, Dyob, pseud.

Melger, Boyd A., pseud. High Bloodpressures, Infarction, Diagrams. LC 88-92898. (Illus.). 63p. (Orig.). 1988. pap. write for info. (*0-9622463-0-1*) B Melger.

— Lantana Malangii: Kembang Tembelehan Boyhood Impressions. (Illus.). 107p. (Orig.). 1991. pap. write for info. (*0-9622463-5-2*) B Melger.

— Lantana Malangii: Kembang Tembelehan Jeugd Impressies. (DUT., Illus.). 90p. (Orig.). 1991. pap. write for info. (*0-9622463-4-4*) B Melger.

Melges, Buddy & Mason, Charles. Sailing Smart: Winning Techniques, Tactics & Strategies. LC 82-15557. (Illus.). 208p. 1995. pap. 9.95 (*0-8050-0351-7*, Owl) H Holt & Co.

Melhado, Evan M. Jacob Berzelius: The Emergence of His Chemical System. LC 81-7593. 360p. 1981. reprint ed. 45.00 (*0-299-08970-3*) U of Wis Pr.

Melhado, Evan M. & Frangsmyr, Tore, eds. Enlightenment Science in the Romantic Era: The Chemistry of Berzelius & Its Cultural Setting. (Illus.). 260p. (C). 1992. text 59.95 (*0-521-41775-9*) Cambridge U Pr.

Melham, Lynnea. If You Cook for Children: A Healthy Approach. 57p. 1997. pap. 9.99 (*0-9659195-0-1*) Wellness Object.

Melham, T. F., jt. ed. see Gordon, M. J.

Melham, Thomas F. Higher Order Logic & Hardware Verification. (Tracts in Theoretical Computer Science Ser.: No. 31). (Illus.). 179p. (C). 1993. text 47.95 (*0-521-41718-X*) Cambridge U Pr.

Melham, Thomas F. & Camilleri, Juanito, eds. Higher Order Logic Theorum Proving & Its Application: Proceedings of the Seventh International Workshop, Valletta, Malta, September 19-22, 1994. LC 94-35140. (Lecture Notes in Computer Science Ser.: Vol. 859). 1994. 65.95 (*3-540-58450-1*) Spr-Verlag.

— Higher Order Logic Theorum Proving & Its Application: Proceedings of the Seventh International Workshop, Valletta, Malta, September 19-22, 1994, 859. LC 94-35140. (Lecture Notes in Computer Science Ser.). 1994. 62.00 (*0-387-58450-1*) Spr-Verlag.

Melheim, Rich. The Christmiss Guest. (Illus.). (J). (gr. k-4). 1995. 16.95 (*0-9635106-7-3*) Creat Outlet.

M

— 101 Ways to Get Your Adult Children to Move Out: (And Make Them Think it Was Their Idea) LC 95-32761. 64p. 1996. pap. 6.95 (*0-385-48006-7*, Main St Bks) Doubleday.

— One Hundred One Ways to Get Your Adult Children to Move Out (& Make Them Think It Was Their Idea) (Illus.). 76p. (Orig.). 1994. pap. 9.95 (*0-9635106-6-5*) Creat Outlet.

Melheim, Richard A. Lust. 336p. 1994. 19.95 (*0-9635106-3-0*) Creat Outlet.

— Unfinished Business: Saddam Hussein, George Bush, & an American Arab in Military Intelligence Who Knew Too Much. 240p. 1992. 20.00 (*0-9635106-0-6*) Creat Outlet.

Melhem, D. H. Blight. LC 94-13017. (Illus.). 160p. 1995. 21.95 (*0-7145-4274-1*) Riverrun NY.

— Country: An Organic Poem. LC 97-24177. 1998. 25.00 (*0-89304-222-6*); pap. 15.00 (*0-89304-223-4*) Cross-Cultrl NY.

— Heroism in the New Black Poetry: Introductions & Interviews. LC 89-22756. (Illus.). 288p. 1990. pap. 18.00 (*0-8131-0807-1*) U Pr of Ky.

— Notes on Ninety Fourth Street. 66p. 1972. write for info. (*0-318-64125-9*) Poets Pr.

— Reaching Exercises: The IWWG Workshop Book. LC 81-67876. 1981. reprint ed. 10.95 (*0-935468-04-8*) Dovetail.

— Rest in Love. 2nd ed. 109p. 1995. reprint ed. pap. 9.95 (*0-913057-22-3*) Confront Mag Pr.

Melhem, G. Advanced Consequence Modelling. (Chemical Engineering Ser.). 1991. text. write for info. (*0-442-00755-8*, VNR) Wiley.

Melhem, G. A., ed. see Design Institute for Emergency Releif Systems User.

Melhnish, Clare. Odile Decq Benoit Cornette. LC 97-112985. (Illus.). 160p. 1996. 49.95 (*0-7148-3343-6*, Pub. by Phaidon Press) Phaidon Pr.

Melhoramentos. Dicionario Practico da Lingua Portuguesa. (POR.). 1044p. 1987. 95.00 (*0-7859-9314-2*) Fr & Eur.

Melhoramentos, ed. Minidicionario da Lingua Portuguesa. (POR.). 568p. 1992. 24.95 (*0-7859-9313-4*) Fr & Eur.

Melhorn, W. N. & Kempton, J. P., eds. Geology & Hydrogeology of the Teays-Mahomet Bedrock Valley System. (Special Papers: No. 258). (Illus.). 136p. 1991. pap. 18.00 (*0-8137-2258-6*) Geol Soc.

Melhuish, Charles, ed. Road Safety in Asia & the Pacific: Report of the Escap/ADB Seminar-cum-Workshop. 89p. (C). 1998. pap. text 30.00 (*0-7881-7398-7*) DIANE Pub.

***Melhuish, Clare.** Modern House 2. (Illus.). 2000. 59.95 (*0-7148-3987-6*) Phaidon Pr.

Melhuish, Clare. Odile Decq Benoit Cornette. (Illus.). 160p. 1998. pap. 29.95 (*0-7148-3771-7*, Pub. by Phaidon Press) Phaidon Pr.

— The Pallas Guide to Modern London No. 1: The City & East End. (Illus.). 464p. (Orig.). 1995. pap. 23.95 (*1-873429-10-X*, Pub. by Pallas Athene) Cimino Pub Grp.

Melhuish, Martin. Celtic Tide: Traditional Music in a New Age. (Illus.). 304p. 1998. pap. 15.95 (*1-55082-205-5*, QP00793, Pub. by Quarry Pr) LPC InBook.

— Oh What a Feeling: A Vital History of Canadian Music. (Illus.). 208p. 1996. pap. 24.95 (*1-55082-177-6*, Pub. by Quarry Pr) LPC InBook.

— Oh What a Feeling: A Vital History of Canadian Music. LC 97-193174. (Illus.). 208p. 1996. 19.95 (*1-55082-164-4*, Pub. by Quarry Pr) LPC InBook.

Melhuish, Martin, jt. auth. see Hall, Mark.

Melhuus, Marit & Anne, Kristi. Machos, Mistresses & Madonnas: Contesting the Power of Latin American Gender Imagery. LC 96-48949. (C). 1996. pap. 20.00 (*1-85984-160-0*, Pub. by Verso) Norton.

Meli, Domenico B. Equivalence & Priority: Newton versus Leibniz - Including Leibniz's Unpublished Manuscripts on the Principia. (Illus.). 328p. 1997. reprint ed. pap. text 46.95 (*0-19-850143-9*) OUP.

Meli, Francis. South Africa Belongs to Us: A History of the ANC. LC 88-39946. (Illus.). 290p. 1989. pap. 15.95 (*0-253-28591-7*) Ind U Pr.

Meli, Franco. A Cheyenne. LC 99-19389. (Day with Ser.). 48p. (J). (gr. 5-7). 1999. 22.60 (*0-8225-1920-8*, Runestone Pr) Lerner Pub.

Meli, Giovanni. Don Chisciotti & Sanciu Panza. Sbrocchi, Leonard G., ed. (Biblioteca di Quaderni d'Italianistica Ser.: Vol. 2). (Illus.). 324p. (Orig.). 1986. pap. 20.00 (*0-317-04132-0*, Pub. by Can Soc Ital Stu) Speedimpex.

— Moral Fables. Sbrocchi, Leonard G., ed. Cipolla, Gaetano, tr. from ENG. & intro. by. (Biblioteca di Quaderni d'Italianistica Ser.: Vol. 6). (Illus.). 146p. (Orig.). 1988. pap. 20.00 (*0-9691979-5-0*, Pub. by Can Soc Ital Stu) Speedimpex.

— Moral Fables & Other Poems Vol. III: A Bilingual Anthology (Sicillian - English) Cipolla, Gaetano, ed. & tr. by. from ENG. LC 94-47001. (Pueti D'arba Sicula - Poets of ARBA Sicula: Vol. 3). (ITA., Illus.). 216p. (Orig.). 1995. pap. 16.00 (*1-881901-07-6*) LEGAS.

Melia. Electrodynamics. 1996. pap. text 22.00 (*0-226-51958-9*); lib. bdg. 50.00 (*0-226-51957-0*) U Ch Pr.

Melia, Daniel F., jt. ed. see Matonis, A. T.

Melia, Kath M., et al. Ethical Issues in Caring. 200p. 1988. text 63.95 (*0-566-05266-0*, Pub. by Avebry) Ashgate Pub Co.

Melia, Margot, jt. ed. see Bosworth, Richard.

Melia, Paul, ed. David Hockney. LC 94-42848. (Critical Introductions to Art Ser.). 1995. text 79.95 (*0-7190-4404-9*) Manchester Univ Pr.

— David Hockney. LC 94-42848. (Critical Introductions to Art Ser.). (Illus.). 288p. 1995. text 19.95 (*0-7190-4405-7*, Pub. by Manchester Univ Pr) St Martin.

***Melia, Paul & Luckhardt, Ulrich.** David Hockney. (Illus.). 200p. 2000. pap. 29.95 (*3-7913-2413-6*) Prestel.

Melia, Paul & Luckhardt, Ulrich. David Hockney Paintings. (Illus.). 200p. 1994. 55.00 (*3-7913-1381-9*, Pub. by Prestel) te Neues.

Melia, Paul & Woods, Alan. Peter Greenaway. 160p. 1999. text 79.95 (*0-7190-5623-3*) Manchester Univ Pr.

— Peter Greenaway: Artworks, 63-98. 160p. 1999. pap. 24.95 (*0-7190-5624-1*, Pub. by Manchester Univ Pr) St Martin.

Melia, Pius. The Origin, Persecutions, & Doctrines of the Waldenses from Documents: Many Now for the First Time Collected & Edited. LC 77-84716. reprint ed. 37.50 (*0-404-16122-7*) AMS Pr.

Melia, Richard P. Vocational Rehabilitation: Its Relationship to Vocational Education. 16p. 1986. 2.75 (*0-318-22246-9*, OC 120) Ctr Educ Trng Employ.

Melia, Trevor & Ryder, Nova. Lucifer State: A Novel Approach to Rhetoric. 2nd ed. (Illus.). 208p. (C). 1994. per. 16.95 (*0-8403-6847-X*, 40305701) Kendall-Hunt.

Melia, Trevor, jt. auth. see Thames, Richard.

Melia, Trevor, jt. ed. see Simons, Herbert W.

***Melian, Jose Cardenes.** 60-second Spanish Grammer Workout: 140 Speed Tests to Boost Your Fluency. (60 Second Ser.). 144p. 2000. pap. 9.06 (*0-658-00429-8*, 004298) NTC Contemp Pub Co.

— 60-Second Spanish Vocabulary Workout: 140 Speed Tests to Boost Your Fluency. (60 Second Ser.). 144p. 2000. pap. 9.06 (*0-658-00427-1*, 004271) NTC Contemp Pub Co.

Melica, F., ed. AIDS & Reproduction. (Illus.). xii, 196p. 1992. 147.00 (*3-8055-5481-8*) S Karger.

Melich, Anna, jt. auth. see Reif, Karlheinz.

Melich, Tanya. No Place for a Woman: Misogyny in the Republican Party. 1996. 23.95 (*0-614-15509-6*) Bantam.

Melichar, Emanuel O. State Individual Income Taxes. LC 94-76234. xxii, 424p. 1994. reprint ed. 55.00 (*0-89941-885-6*, 308490) W S Hein.

Melichar, G., et al, eds. Invasives und Nichtinvasives Monitoring von Atmung, Beatmung, Kreislauf, und Stoffwechsel. (Beitraege zur Intensiv und Notfallmedizin Ser.: Vol. 4). (Illus.). viii, 260p. 1986. 65.25 (*3-8055-4267-4*) S Karger.

***Melicher.** Financial Analysis Tools Worksheet. 10th ed. 1999. 57.25 (*0-324-04180-2*) Thomson Learn.

***Melicher, Norton.** Finance: An Introduction to Institutions, Investment & Management. 10th ed. LC 99-29145. (SWC-Finance Ser.). 677p. 1999. pap. 91.95 (*0-324-00430-3*) Sth-Wstrn College.

Melicher, Ronald W. Finance: Introduction to Institutes, Investment & Management. 9th ed. LC 96-8686. (Finance Ser.). 1996. mass mkt. 75.95 (*0-538-83993-7*) S-W Pub.

Melicher, Ronald W., jt. auth. see Welshans, Merle T.

Melick, Andrew. Euros 04. 1996. 16.95 (*3-86187-073-8*) B Gmunder.

Melick, Cletus. The Silent War. (J). (gr. 3-8). 1997. pap. 2.50 (*1-57514-295-3*, 3076) Encore Perform Pub.

Melick, Harry C. The Manor of Fordham & Its Founder. LC 50-11879. (Illus.). 234p. reprint ed. pap. 72.60 (*0-7837-5584-8*, 204537600005) Bks Demand.

***Melick, Jeffrey C.** Massachusetts Basic Practice Manual: Preparing & Trying Your First Civil Case. (Massachusetts Basic Practice Ser.). 150p. 1999. pap. write for info. (*1-57589-175-1*) Mass CLE.

Melick, Richard R., Jr. Philippians, Colossians, Philemon. (New American Commentary Ser.: Vol. 32). 416p. 1991. 27.99 (*0-8054-0132-6*) Broadman.

Meligari, Linda E., ed. see Wayne, Bill.

***Melikan, Rose.** John Scott, Lord Eldon, 1751-1838: The Duty of Loyalty. LC 98-42867. (Studies in English Legal History). 356p. (C). 1999. write for info. (*0-521-62395-2*) Cambridge U Pr.

Melikian, Abraham, tr. from FRE. Shirak Songbook Charles Aznavour (Ser Serdi Djampov) (ARM.). 128p. 1980. pap. 10.00 (*1-58253-024-6*) Shirak.

Melikian, Anahid. Byron & the East. 1977. 19.95 (*0-8156-6049-9*, Pub. by Am U Beirut) Syracuse U Pr.

— Byron & the East. LC PR4392.N4M44. 124p. 1977. reprint ed. pap. 38.50 (*0-608-07620-1*, 205993500010) Bks Demand.

Melikian, Anahid, ed. see Smith, Byron P.

Melikov, Edward, et al. Soviet Defense Decision-Making: An Integrated View, Vol. II. (Illus.). 331p. (Orig.). 1989. pap. text 125.00 (*1-55831-100-9*) Delphic Associates.

Melikyan, A. A. Generalized Characteristics of First Order PDEs: Applications in Optimal Control & Differential Games. LC 98-4739. 350p. 1998. 79.95 (*0-8176-3984-5*) Birkhauser.

Melilli, Albert S., ed. Handbook of Comparative World Steel Standards: Sekai Tekko Zairyo Kikaku Hikaku Taisho Soran: U. S. A., United Kingdom, West Germany, France, U. S. S. R., Japan, Canada, Australia, International. LC 96-9914. (Data Ser.: Vol. 67). 552p. 1996. pap. text 250.00 (*0-8031-1825-2*, DS67) ASTM.

Melilli, Albert S. & Nisbett, Edward G., eds. Residual & Unspecified Elements in Steel. LC 89-32224. (Special Technical Publication Ser.: No. STP 1042). (Illus.). 320p. 1989. text 64.00 (*0-8031-1259-9*, STP1042) ASTM.

Melilli, Albert S., ed. see American Society for Testing & Materials Staff.

Melilli, Albert S., jt. ed. see Behal.

Melilli, Albert S., jt. ed. see Nisbett, Edward G.

Melillo, David G., jt. auth. see Heys, Richard.

Melillo, Jerry M., jt. ed. see Galloway, James N.

Melillo, Joseph V. Market the Arts. 1995. pap. text 26.00 (*1-884345-04-2*) ARTS Action.

Melillo, Marcie. The Ultimate Barbie Doll Book. LC 96-76686. 256p. 1996. 39.95 (*0-87341-397-0*) Krause Pubns.

Melin, Anders, jt. ed. see Hormander, Lars.

***Melin, Charlotte, ed.** German Poetry in Transition, 1945-1990--Bilingual Edition. LC 99-24866. (GER & ENG.). 405p. 1999. text 50.00 (*0-87451-914-4*) U Pr of New Eng.

Melin, Charlotte, jt. auth. see Zorach, Cecile.

***Melin, Mark.** Computer Inselligence: Transform Your Bottom Line with Interactive Marketing Magic. 306p. 2000. 24.95 (*1-886284-57-1*, Pub. by Chandler Hse) Natl Bk Netwk.

Melin, Nancy J., ed. The Serials Collection: Organization & Administration. LC 82-81133. (Current Issues in Serials Management Ser.: No. 1). 168p. 1982. 30.00 (*0-87650-140-4*) Pierian.

Melin, Nancy J. & Lisanti, Suzana. Essential Guide to the Library IBM PC. Incl. Vol. 1. Hardware: Set-Up & Expansion. LC 85-10535. 1985. (*0-88736-033-5*); Vol. 2. Operating System: PC-DOS. LC 85-10535. 1985. (*0-88736-034-3*); Vol. 3. Library Application Software. LC 85-10535. 1985. (*0-88736-035-1*); Vol. 4. Data Communications: Going Online. LC 85-10535. 1986. (*0-88736-036-X*); Vol. 5. Buying & Installing Generic Software for Library Use. LC 85-10535. 1986. (*0-88736-037-8*); LC 85-10535. 34.95 (*0-317-38262-4*) Mecklermedia.

***Melina, Livio & Catholic Church Staff.** Sharing in Christ's Virtues: For a Renewal of Moral Theology in Light of Veritatis Splendor. LC 99-87318. 2001. write for info. (*0-8132-0989-7*) Cath U Pr.

Melina, Lois R. Adoption: An Annotated Bibliography. LC 86-31964. (Reference Books on Family Issues: Vol. 10). 314p. 1987. text 51.00 (*0-8240-8942-1*, SS374) Garland.

— Making Sense of Adoption: A Parent's Guide. LC 89-45106. 288p. (Orig.). 1989. pap. 13.00 (*0-06-096319-0*, PL 6319, Perennial) HarperTrade.

— Raising Adopted Children. LC 85-45648. 288p. 1986. pap. 12.50 (*0-06-096039-6*, Perennial) HarperTrade.

— Raising Adopted Children, Revised Edition: A Manual for Adoptive Parents. rev. ed. LC 98-11880. 384p. (gr. 10). 1998. pap. 13.00 (*0-06-095717-4*) HarpC.

Melina, Lois R. & Roszia, Sharon K. Open Adoption Experience: Complete Guide for Adoptive & Birth Families - From Making the Decision Throug. LC 92-56254. 416p. 1993. pap. 15.00 (*0-06-096957-1*, Perennial) HarperTrade.

Melina, Vesanto & Forest, Joseph. Cooking Vegetarian: Healthy, Delicious & Easy Vegetarian Cuisine. LC 99-162240. 224p. 1998. pap. 18.95 (*1-56561-172-1*) Wiley.

***Melina, Vesanto & Forest, Joseph.** Cooking Vegetarian: Healthy, Delicious, & Easy Vegetarian Cuisine. 248p. 1998. pap. 18.95 (*0-471-34673-X*) Wiley.

Melina, Vesanto, et al. Becoming Vegetarian: The Complete Guide to Adopting a Healthy Vegetarian Diet. LC 95-30573. 262p. (Orig.). 1995. pap. 15.95 (*1-57067-013-7*) Book Pub Co.

Melindez, Mariselle. Raza, Ginero E Hibridez en el Lazarillo de Ciegos Caminantes. No. 264. 160p. 1999. pap. 27.50 (*0-8078-9268-8*) U of NC Pr.

Melinkov, V. N., jt. ed. see De Sabbata, Venzo.

Melino, Gerry. Biochemistry of Neuroectodermal Tumors. 129p. 1994. pap. text 180.00 (*3-7186-5500-4*, Harwood Acad Pubs) Gordon & Breach.

— Biochemistry of Neuroectodermal Tumors, Pt. I. 130p. 1994. pap. text 182.00 (*3-7186-5491-1*, Harwood Acad Pubs) Gordon & Breach.

Melino, Gerry, et al, eds. Biochemistry of Neuroectodermal Tumors. (Clinical Chemistry & Enzymology Communications Ser.). iv, 178p. 1990. pap. text 293.00 (*3-7186-5019-3*) Gordon & Breach.

Melinosky, Theodore F. The K1BV DX Awards Directory: Worldwide Listing of over 2600 Different Amateur Awards from 122 Countries. 255p. 1998. pap. 22.00 (*0-9662503-0-3*) KOneBV DX Awards.

Melion, Walter S. Shaping the Netherlandish Canon: Karel Van Mander's Schilder-Boeck. LC 91-2806. (Illus.). 385p. 1992. 52.00 (*0-226-51959-7*) U Ch Pr.

Melion, Walter S., jt. ed. see Barnes, Susan J.

Meliopoulos, A. P. Sakis. Power System Grounding & Transients: An Introduction. (Electrical Engineering & Electronics Ser.: Vol. 50). (Illus.). 472p. 1988. text 185.00 (*0-8247-7908-8*) Dekker.

Melious, Jean O. Land Banking Revisited: Massachusetts Breaks the Mold. (Land Policy Roundtable Ser.: No. 107). 51p. (Orig.). 1986. pap. text 5.25 (*1-55844-107-7*) Lincoln Inst Land.

Melipoulos, A. P. Power System Modeling, Analysis & Control. (Electrical Engineering & Electronics Ser.). (Illus.). Date not set. text. write for info. (*0-8247-9734-5*) Dekker.

Melis, Ildiko, jt. ed. see Gonzalez, Roseann Dvenas.

***Melis-Spielkamp, Bianca.** Pragmatische Schriftlichkeit in Englischen Arthurischen Romanzen. 357p. 1999. 52.00 (*3-631-34400-7*) P Lang Pubng.

***Melischek, Gabriele & Seethaler, Josef.** Die Wiener Tageszeitungen: Eine Dokumentation BD. 5: 1945-1955 Mit einem Uberblick Uber die Osterreichische Tagespresse der Zweiten Republik Bis 1998. (Illus.). 284p. 1999. 45.95 (*3-631-33036-7*) P Lang Pubng.

Melish, Joanne P. Disowning Slavery: Gradual Emancipation & "Race" in New England, 1780-1860. LC 97-46669. 1998. pap. write for info. (*0-8014-8437-5*) Cornell U Pr.

— Disowning Slavery: Gradual Emancipation & "Race" in New England, 1780-1860. LC 97-46669. (Illus.). 320p. 1998. text 35.00 (*0-8014-3413-0*) Cornell U Pr.

Melish, John H. Surveys for Travellers, Emigrants & Others. LC 75-22829. (America in Two Centuries Ser.). 1976. 33.95 (*0-405-07701-7*) Ayer.

Melish, William B., ed. The History of the Imperial Council Ancient Arabic Order Nobles of the Mystic Shrine for North America 1872 to 1921 (1921) 282p. 1998. reprint ed. pap. 19.95 (*0-7661-0256-4*) Kessinger Pub.

Melissa, Ma P., ed. see Osho.

Melissen. Innovation Diplomatic Practice. LC 98-17571. 1999. text 69.95 (*0-312-21592-4*) St Martin.

Melissinos. Ten Minute Addresses. 1994. pap. 4.00 (*0-88053-356-0*, S411) Macoy Pub.

Melissinos, et al. Experiments in Modern Physics. 2nd ed. 650p. 1997. write for info. (*0-12-489851-3*) Acad Pr.

Melissinos, A., jt. auth. see Jones, C.

Melissinos, Adrian C. Experiments in Modern Physics. 1966. text 70.00 (*0-12-489850-5*) Acad Pr.

— Principles of Modern Technology. (Illus.). 350p. (C). 1990. pap. text 39.95 (*0-521-38965-8*) Cambridge U Pr.

— Principles of Modern Technology. (Illus.). 351p. (C). 1990. text 95.00 (*0-521-35249-5*) Cambridge U Pr.

Melissinos, Adrian C., jt. auth. see Das, Ashok.

Melito of Sardis. On Pascha & Fragments. Hall, Stuart G., ed. (Oxford Early Christian Texts Ser.). 1979. text 49.95 (*0-19-826811-4*) OUP.

Melitz, Leo L. The Opera Goers' Complete Guide. Salinger, Richard, tr. LC 80-2293. reprint ed. 54.50 (*0-404-18859-1*) AMS Pr.

Melius, Ken, ed. see Kersten, John.

Melius, Kenneth W., ed. see Melius, Michael M.

Melius, Michael M. Cloud Peak Primitive Area: Trail Guide, History & Photo Odyssey. Melius, Kenneth W., ed. LC 93-60487. (Illus.). 120p. (Orig.). 1995. pap. 15.00 (*0-937603-12-0*) Melius Pub.

— Plants & Animals Rare in South Dakota: A Field Guide. LC 87-50402. (Illus.). 120p. (Orig.). 1987. pap. 3.00 (*0-937603-05-8*) Melius Pub.

— True. 112p. 1991. per. 8.00 (*0-614-24797-7*) Tesseract SD.

— True. 112p. 1991. 15.00 (*0-614-24796-9*) Tesseract SD.

— True: Notes from Journeys in South Dakota. LC 91-52925. (Illus.). 130p. 1991. 15.00 (*0-937603-11-2*, Tensleep Pubns); pap. 8.00 (*0-937603-10-4*, Tensleep Pubns) Melius Pub.

— Under Wing & Sky: Birds of the Badlands & Black Hills. (Illus.). 88p. 1995. per. 12.00 (*0-912410-13-2*) Tesseract SD.

Melius, Paul, jt. auth. see Friedman, Michael E.

Meliveo, Elena. Mastering Spanish Business Vocabulary. LC 96-78917. 1997. pap. text 11.95 (*0-8120-9826-9*) Barron.

Meliza, Raymond W. How to Find a Job (12 Simple Techniques) (Illus.). 16p. 1994. pap. 3.00 (*1-884241-30-1*, AO401) Energeia Pub.

— Teaching Adults Improvement Skills in the Workplace. (Illus.). 24p. 1996. pap. 3.50 (*1-884241-38-7*, SPSO319) Energeia Pub.

— Time Management for High School Students. (Illus.). 8p. (YA). 1995. pap. 2.50 (*0-9626591-9-3*, AO402) Energeia Pub.

— Time Management Techniques. (Illus.). 8p. (Orig.). 1997. pap. 2.50 (*0-9626591-3-4*, SPS0341) Energeia Pub.

Melka, Kevin W. Supernumerary. Stahl, Patricia, ed. (Illus.). 48p. 1998. pap. 5.00 (*1-892519-11-9*, AAE-2001) Archangel Ent.

Melka, Steven E., jt. auth. see Schend, Steven.

Melke, Sabine. Cichlids from Lake Malawi & Tanganyika, Success with. (Illus.). 192p. 1993. 29.95 (*0-86622-489-0*, TT030) TFH Pubns.

Melker, Alexander I., ed. International Workshop on New Approaches to High-Tech Materials Vol. 3345: Nondestructive Testing & Computer Simulations in Materials Science & Engineering. 328p. 1998. 69.00 (*0-8194-2792-6*) SPIE.

***Melker, Alexander I., ed.** Nondestructive Testing & Computer Simulations in Science & Engineering. 488p. 1999. pap. text 92.00 (*0-8194-3161-3*) SPIE.

Melkers, Julia, jt. ed. see Bozeman, Barry.

Melki, Samir A., jt. auth. see Azar, Dimitri T.

Melkman, R., ed. The Construction of Objectivity: A New Look at the First Months of Life. (Contributions to Human Development Ser.: Vol. 19). (Illus.). xiv, 130p. 1988. 86.25 (*3-8055-4746-3*) S Karger.

Melko, Matthew. The Nature of Civilizations. LC 69-15527. (Extending Horizons Ser.). (Illus.). 224p. (C). 1969. 4.95 (*0-87558-044-0*) Porter Sargent.

— Peace in Our Time. 217p. 1990. 24.95 (*1-55778-055-2*) Prof World Peace.

— A Professor's Work. LC 98-29101. (Illus.). 268p. 1998. 54.00 (*0-7618-1216-4*); pap. 36.50 (*0-7618-1217-2*) U Pr of Amer.

Melko, Matthew & Scott, Leighton R., eds. The Boundaries of Civilizations in Space & Time. LC 87-10718. (Illus.). 480p. (Orig.). (C). 1987. text 68.50 (*0-8191-6492-5*); pap. text 37.00 (*0-8191-6493-3*) U Pr of Amer.

Melko, Matthew, jt. auth. see Cargan, Leonard.

Melkonian, Carole, tr. see Hanh, Thich Nhat.

Melkonian, Haigazoun, tr. see Koushagian, Torkom.

Melkonian, Markar. Richard Rorty's Politics: Liberalism at the End of the American Century. LC 99-37145. 250p. 2000. 64.95 (*1-57392-724-4*, Humanity Bks) Prometheus Bks.

***Melkonian, Markar.** Richard Rorty's Politics: Liberalism at the End of the American Century. LC 99-37145. 250p. 2000. pap. 19.95 (*1-57392-725-2*, Humanity Bks) Prometheus Bks.

Melkonian, Martin, jt. ed. see Silver, Marc L.

Melkonian, Michael, et al, eds. The Cytoskeleton of Flagellate & Ciliate Protists. (Illus.). v, 167p. 1992. 182.95 (*0-387-82294-1*) Spr-Verlag.

Melkonian, Michael & Dring, Matthew J., eds. Algal Cell Motility. (Current Phycology Ser.). 192p. (gr. 13). 1991. text 54.95 (*0-412-02431-4*, A4037, Chap & Hall NY) Chapman & Hall.

Melkonian, Michael, ed. see Geider, Richard J. & Osborne, Bruce A.

An Asterisk (*) at the beginning of an entry indicates that the title is appearing for the first time.

Melkote, R. Srinivas. Communication for Development in the Third World: Theory & Practice from 1950's to 1990's. 252p. (C). 1991. text 29.95 (*0-8039-9683-7*); pap. text 14.95 (*0-8039-9684-5*) Sage.

Melkote, Srinivas R., et al, eds. International Satellite Broadcasting in South Asia: Political, Economic & Cultural Implications. LC 98-26805. 352p. 1998. 62.00 (*0-7618-1201-6*); pap. 39.00 (*0-7618-1202-4*) U Pr of Amer.

Melkov, G. A., jt. auth. see Gurevich, A. G.

Mell, Donald C., ed. Pope, Swift, & Women Writers. LC 96-16288. 256p. 1996. 39.50 (*0-87413-590-7*) U Delaware Pr.

Mell, Donald C., Jr., et al, eds. Contemporary Studies of Swift's Poetry. LC 79-21610. (Illus.). 240p. 1980. 35.00 (*0-87413-173-1*, 173) U Delaware Pr.

— Man, God, & Nature in the Enlightenment. LC 87-51123. (Medieval Studies : No. 2). 247p. 1988. 39.95 (*0-937191-03-5*); pap. 14.95 (*0-937191-13-2*) Mich St U Pr.

Mell, George. Writing Antiques. (Album Ser.: No. 54). (Illus.). 32p. 1988. pap. 4.75 (*0-85263-519-2*, Pub. by Shire Pubns) Parkwest Pubns.

Mell, P. H. The Life of Patrick Hughes Mell. 1995. 17.99 (*0-87377-167-2*) GAM Pubns.

— A Southern Baptist Looks at Predestination. 1992. pap. 10.99 (*0-87377-961-4*) GAM Pubns.

Mell, Ulrich. Neue Schoepfung: Eine Traditionsgeschichtliche und Exegetische Studie zu einem soteriologischen Grundsatz Paulinischer Theologie. (Beiheft zur Zeitschrift fuer die Neuetestamentliche Wissenschaft Ser.: No. 56). (GER.). xv, 436p. (C). 1989. lib. bdg. 119.25 (*3-11-011831-9*) De Gruyter.

Mella, Cesar T. A Priest to the World & Other Prose Works. 77p. (Orig.). 1984. pap. 7.50 (*971-10-0180-2*, Pub. by New Day Pub) Cellar.

Mella, Dorothee L. Candle Power: A Game of Light. 48p. 1992. pap. 4.95 (*0-9636345-0-X*) Domel.

— Functional Color A to Z: Energy Power of Colors. 56p. 1994. pap. 4.95 (*0-9636345-2-6*) Domel.

— The Language of Color. (Illus.). 128p. (Orig.). 1988. mass mkt. 11.99 (*0-446-38781-9*, Pub. by Warner Bks) Little.

— Stone Power. 1988. mass mkt. 13.99 (*0-446-38696-0*, Pub. by Warner Bks) Little.

Mella, Dorothee L. & Lusson, Michelle. GEM Pharmacy: Nature's Mineral Supports. 56p. 1992. pap. 4.95 (*0-9636345-1-8*) Domel.

Mella, Leanne & Stainback, Charles A. Along the Frontier: Hamilton, Nauman, Torres, Viola. (Illus.). 96p. 1996. write for info. (*0-933642-23-7*) Intl Ctr Photo.

Mella, Piero. Diccionario Enciclopedico De Contabilidad. (SPA.). 1989. 39.95 (*0-7859-6504-1*) Fr & Eur.

Mellaart, James & Murray, Ann. Beycesultan Vol. III, Pt. II: Late Bronze Age & Phrygian Pottery & Middle & Late Bronze Age Small Objects. (Occasional Publications of the British Institute of Archaeology at Ankara: No. 12). (Illus.). 150p. 1995. 55.00 (*1-898249-06-7*, Pub. by Brit Inst Arch) David Brown.

Mellado De Hunter, Elena. Anglicimos Profesionales De Puerto Rico. LC 80-17935. (Coleccion Mente y Palabra). (SPA.). 204p. 1981. 6.00 (*0-8477-0578-1*); pap. 5.20 (*0-8477-0579-X*) U of PR Pr.

Mellado de Hunter, Elena. El Estoicismo de Angel Ganivet. (UPREX, Estudios Literarios Ser.: No. 10). 193p. (C). 1972. pap. 1.50 (*0-8477-0010-0*) U of PR Pr.

***Mellado, Jim.** How to Change Your Church: Without Killing It. (Illus.). 220p. 2000. 21.99 (*0-8499-1660-7*) Word Pub.

Mellado, Joaquin & Aldana, Maria J., eds. Eulogius von Cordoba-Concordantia in Eulogium Cordubensem. (Alpha-Omega, Reihe B Ser.: Bd. VI). (GER.). viii, 645p. 1993. write for info. (*3-487-09657-9*) G Olms Pubs.

Mellado, Justo P. Prospect & Perspective: Recent Art from Chile. Adams, Beverly, ed. & intro. by. (Illus.). 48p. 1997. pap. write for info. (*1-883502-09-8*) San Ant Mus Art.

Mellado, Justo Pastor, jt. auth. see Medina, Cuauhtemoc.

Mellado, Ramon. Puerto Rico y Occidente. 6th ed. (UPREX, Ensayo Ser.: No. 31). 189p. (C). 1973. pap. 1.50 (*0-8477-0031-3*) U of PR Pr.

Mellah, Fawzi. Elissa. 188p. 1993. 19.95 (*0-7043-2704-X*, Pub. by Quartet) Interlink Pub.

Mellan, I. Industrial Plasticizers. LC 62-8734. 1963. 139.00 (*0-08-010144-5*, Pub. by Pergamon Repr) Franklin.

Mellan, Olivia. Money Harmony. 246p. 1995. pap. 9.95 (*0-8027-7456-3*) Walker & Co.

— Money Harmony: Resolving Money Conflicts in Your Life & Relationships. LC 93-37876. 256p. 1994. 19.95 (*0-8027-1285-1*) Walker & Co.

— Overcoming Overspending: A Winning Plan for Spenders & Their Partners. 216p. 1997. reprint ed. pap. 12.95 (*0-8027-7495-4*) Walker & Co.

Mellan, Olivia & Christie, Sherry. Overcoming Overspending: A Winning Plan for Spenders & Their Spouse. 216p. 1995. 20.95 (*0-8027-1309-2*) Walker & Co.

Mellanby, K. Scabies. 87p. 1972. 20.00 (*0-7855-0673-X*) St Mut.

Melland, Frank H. In Witchbound Africa. (Illus.). 316p. 1967. reprint ed. 45.00 (*0-7146-1044-5*, Pub. by F Cass Pubs) Intl Spec Bk.

Mellander, Deane, jt. auth. see Carstens, Harold H.

Mellander, Erik & Jansson, Leif. Conrad: A Maximum Likelihood Program for Estimation of Non-Linear Simultaneous Equations Models. 94p. 1987. pap. 55.00 (*91-7204-283-4*, Pub. by Industriens) Coronet Bks.

Mellander, Klas. The Power of Learning: Fostering Employee Growth. LC 92-47432. 225p. 1993. 27.50 (*1-55623-893-2*, Irwn Prfssnl) McGraw-Hill Prof.

Mellar, Harvey, et al, eds. Learning with Artificial Worlds: Computer Based Modelling in the Curriculum. LC 94-11536. 218p. 1994. 85.00 (*0-7507-0312-1*, Falmer Pr); pap. 29.95 (*0-7507-0313-X*, Falmer Pr) Taylor & Francis.

Mellard, Evelyn. In the Circles of Time. (Illus.). 120p. 1975. 15.00 (*0-685-58282-5*) A Jones.

Mellard, James M. Doing Tropology: Analysis of Narrative Discourse. LC 86-11370. 192p. 1987. text 24.95 (*0-252-01356-5*) U of Ill Pr.

— The Exploded Form: The Modernist Novel in America. LC 79-25993. 224p. 1980. text 24.95 (*0-252-00801-4*) U of Ill Pr.

— Using Lacan, Reading Fiction. 264p. 1991. text 36.50 (*0-252-01786-2*); pap. text 14.95 (*0-252-06173-X*) U of Ill Pr.

Mellard, Rudolph. Along the Way with Horses & Me. (Illus.). 165p. 1975. 15.00 (*0-685-58281-7*) A Jones.

— Stagecoach 22-San Antonio-El Paso Line. (Illus.). 1977. 15.00 (*0-685-87381-1*) A Jones.

— The Track of the Albatross. (Illus.). 1974. 15.00 (*0-685-50194-9*) A Jones.

Mellard, trevor. Automotive Electronic Systems. 1988. 27.00 (*0-434-91257-3*) CRC Pr.

Mellars, Paul. The Neanderthal Legacy: An Archaeological Perspective from Western Europe. LC 95-4300. 480p. 1995. text 75.00 (*0-691-03493-1*, Pub. by Princeton U Pr) Cal Prin Full Svc.

Mellars, Paul, ed. The Emergence of Modern Humans: An Archaeological Perspective. 576p. 1991. text 72.50 (*0-8014-2614-6*) Cornell U Pr.

— Excavations on Oronsay: Prehistoric Ecology on a Small Island. (Illus.). 200p. 1987. 50.00 (*0-85224-544-0*, Pub. by Edinburgh U Pr) Col U Pr.

Mellars, Paul & Dark, Petra, eds. Star Carr in Context: New Archaeological & Palaeoecological Investigations at the Early Mesolithic Site of Star Carr, North Yorkshire. (Monographs Ser.): (Illus.). xiv, 250p. 1999. 70.00 (*0-9519420-4-2*, Pub. by McDonald Inst) David Brown.

Mellars, Paul & Gibson, Kathleen, eds. Modelling the Early Human Mind. (Monographs Ser.). (Illus.). x, 229p. 1996. 50.00 (*0-9519420-1-8*, Pub. by McDonald Inst) David Brown.

Mellars, Paul & Stringer, Christopher, eds. The Human Revolution: Behavioural & Biological Perspectives on the Origins of Modern Humans. (Illus.). 690p. 1989. text 69.50 (*0-691-08539-0*, Pub. by Princeton U Pr) Cal Prin Full Svc.

Mellars, Paul, jt. ed. see Dibble, Harold L.

Mellberg, James R. & Ripa, Louis W. Fluoride in Preventive Dentistry. (Illus.). 1288p. 1983. text 84.00 (*0-86715-102-1*) Quint Pub Co.

Mellberg, William F. Famous Airliners: From Biplane to Jetliner the Story of Travel by Air. 2nd ed. (Illus.). 196p. (Orig.). 1999. pap. 24.95 (*1-882663-13-6*) Plymouth VT.

— Famous Airliners: Seventy Years of Aviation & Transport Progress. (Illus.). 180p. (Orig.). 1994. pap. text 14.95 (*1-882663-02-0*) Plymouth VT.

— Moon Missions: Mankind's First Voyages to Another World. LC 98-114035. (Illus.). 198p. (Orig.). 1997. pap. 19.95 (*1-882663-12-8*) Plymouth VT.

Melle, A. G. Van, see Gerritsen, W. P. & Van Melle, A. G., eds.

Melle, Julie. My 911 Book for Help. LC 92-71606. (Illus.). 16p. (J). (ps-6). 1992. pap. text 9.99 (*1-881402-00-2*) CA Storybook.

— My 911 Book & Tape for Help. 2nd rev. ed. Hagan, Maureen, ed. Work for Hire, tr. & illus. by. Hutnick, Liz, illus. LC 97-69634. (ENG & SPA.). 36p. (J). (gr. k-5). 1997. per. 15.99 (*1-881402-01-0*) CA Storybook.

Melle, P. J. Van, see Van Melle, P. J.

Melle, Ullrich, ed. see Husserl, Edmund.

Melle, William J. Van, see Van Melle, William J.

Mellema, Gregory. Beyond the Call of Duty: Supererogation, Obligation, & Offence. LC 90-45680. (SUNY Series in Ethical Theory). 226p. (C). 1991. pap. text 21.95 (*0-7914-0738-1*) State U NY Pr.

— The Bottom Line: Making Christian Choices in the Marketplace. LC 94-22303. (Issues in Christian Living Ser.). 1994. pap. 7.75 (*1-56212-064-6*) CRC Pubns.

— Individuals, Groups, & Shared Moral Responsibility. (American University Studies: Philosophy: Ser. V, Vol. 61). 224p. (C). 1988. text 33.50 (*0-8204-0855-7*) P Lang Pubng.

Mellen, Barbara. She Walks in Beauty: Jennifer, a Celebration of Life. (Illus.). 80p. (Orig.). 1993. pap. 10.00 (*0-9636524-0-0*) B Mellen.

Mellen, Diana L. Yesterday: The Hampton, McCracken, Longwith, Mabry, & Wells Families. (Illus.). vi, 324p. (Orig.). 1991. pap. 26.00 (*1-55613-505-X*) Heritage Bk.

Mellen, Frank. If Only I Could Whistle Loudly. LC 96-76389. (Illus.). 44p. (J). (ps-6). 1996. 15.95 (*1-880851-23-7*) Greene Bark Pr.

Mellen, George W. Argument on the Unconstitutionality of Slavery, Embracing an Abstract of the Proceedings of the National & State Conventions on This Subject. LC 70-172720. reprint ed. 34.50 (*0-404-00089-4*) AMS Pr.

Mellen, Joan. Bobby Knight: His Own Man. 384p. 1989. mass mkt. 5.99 (*0-380-70809-4*, Avon Bks) Morrow Avon.

— Filmguide to The Battle of Algiers. LC 73-75787. (Indiana University Press Filmguide Ser.: No. 8). 92p. reprint ed. pap. 30.00 (*0-8357-9210-2*, 201762900007) Bks Demand.

***Mellen, Joan.** Gabriel Garcia Marquez. (Literary Masters Ser.: Vol. 5). (Illus.). 176p. 2000. 49.95 (*0-7876-3970-2*) Gale.

Mellen, Joan. Kay Boyle: Author of Herself. LC 94-654. 1994. text 35.00 (*0-374-18098-9*) FS&G.

***Mellen, Joan.** Magic Realism. (Literary Topics Ser.: Vol. 5). (Illus.). 179p. 2000. 49.95 (*0-7876-3972-9*) Gale.

— One Hundred Years of Solitude. Gale Group Publishing Staff, ed. (Literary Masterpieces Ser.: Vol. 5). (Illus.). 210p. 2000. 49.95 (*0-7876-3971-0*) Gale.

Mellen, Philip. Gerhart Hauptmann: Religious Syncretism & Eastern Religions. (American University Studies: Germanic Languages & Literature: Ser. I, Vol. 24). XI, 328p. (Orig.). 1983. pap. text 30.55 (*0-8204-0060-2*) P Lang Pubng.

Mellen, Rachael. The Handy Book to English Genealogy. 3rd ed. (Illus.). 228p. (Orig.). 1990. pap. 15.00 (*1-55613-359-6*) Heritage Bk.

Mellen, Stephanie. A Bear in the Chair: Beginning Reader. LC 94-75065. (Illus.). 50p. (J). (gr. k-2). 1994. pap. 6.95 (*0-9637414-1-1*) Meltec.

— The Crystal Rabbit. LC 93-91632. (Illus.). 52p. 1993. pap. 7.95 (*0-9637414-0-3*) Meltec.

— God Doesn't Leave the Toilet Seat Up--Why Would She? LC 95-94943. (Illus.). 64p. 1997. pap. 8.95 (*0-9637414-3-8*) Meltec.

— The Golden Angel. LC 94-79576. (Illus.). 64p. 1995. pap. 7.95 (*0-9637414-2-X*) Meltec.

Mellen, Stephanie, jt. auth. see Polakiewicz, David M.

Mellencamp, John. Mellencamp. LC 98-27556. (Illus.). 160p. 1998. 40.00 (*0-06-055372-3*, Perennial) HarperTrade.

— Mellencamp: Paintings & Reflections. LC 98-27556. (Illus.). 160p. 1998. pap. 25.00 (*0-06-095295-4*, Perennial) HarperTrade.

Mellencamp, Patricia. A Fine Romance...Five Ages of Film Feminism. LC 95-33540. (Culture & the Moving Image Ser.). 288p. (C). 1996. 69.95 (*1-56639-400-7*) Temple U Pr.

— A Fine Romance...Five Ages of Film Feminism. LC 95-33540. (Culture & the Moving Image Ser.). (Illus.). 288p. (C). 1996. pap. text 22.95 (*1-56639-401-5*) Temple U Pr.

— High Anxiety: Catastrophe, Scandal, Age, & Comedy. LC 91-46255. (Arts & Politics of the Everyday Ser.). (Illus.). 448p. 1992. 42.00 (*0-253-33744-5*); pap. 19.95 (*0-253-20735-5*, MB-735) Ind U Pr.

— Indiscretions: Avant-Garde Film, Video, & Feminism. LC 89-45804. (Theories of Contemporary Culture Ser.). 254p. 1990. 32.00 (*0-253-33743-7*) Ind U Pr.

Mellencamp, Patricia, ed. Logics of Television: Essays in Cultural Criticism. LC 89-46004. (Theories of Contemporary Culture Ser.). 318p. 1990. pap. 15.95 (*0-253-20582-4*, MB-582) Ind U Pr.

Mellencamp, Patricia & Rosen, Philip T., eds. Cinema Histories, Cinema Practices. LC 83-22457. 150p. (C). 1984. pap. 19.95 (*0-313-27003-1*, P7003) Greenwood.

— Cinema Histories, Cinema Practices, 4. LC 83-22457. 150p. (C). 1984. lib. bdg. 45.00 (*0-313-27037-6*, U7037) Greenwood.

Mellencamp, Patricia, jt. ed. see Heath, Stephen.

Mellenthin, F. W. Von, see Von Mellenthin, F. W.

Mellenthin, Horst. Das Proportionsproblem in der Architekturanschauung: Frankreich, 18. (Studien Zur Kunstgeschichte Ser.: Vol. 90). (GER.). 347p. 1995. write for info. (*3-487-09958-6*) G Olms Pubs.

Mellentin, Kath. Bible Pops No. 1: Moses in the Bulrushes. (Illus.). 6p. (J). (ps-2). 1996. 5.99 (*0-689-80922-0*) S&S Childrens.

— Bible Pops No. 2: Joshua & the Battles of Jericho. (Illus.). 6p. (J). (ps-2). 1996. pap. 5.99 (*0-689-80923-9*) S&S Childrens.

— Bible Pops No. 3: David & Goliath. (Illus.). 6p. (J). (ps-2). 1996. 5.99 (*0-689-80924-7*) S&S Childrens.

— Bible Pops No. 4: Joseph & the King of Egypt. (Illus.). 6p. (J). (ps-2). 1996. 5.99 (*0-689-80925-5*) S&S Childrens.

— Book - Plus Project, Bk. 1. (Illus.). 24p. (J). (ps-2). 1997. 9.99 (*0-689-80903-4*) S&S Bks Yung.

— Let's Build an Airport. LC 98-25776. (J). (gr. 1-5). 1998. 14.95 (*1-84089-026-6*) Zero to Ten.

— Wheels on the Bus. (Illus.). 16p. (J). (ps). 1998. 13.99 (*1-884628-37-0*, Flyng Frog) Allied Pub MD.

Mellentin, Kath & Wood, Tim. Dear Tooth Fairy. (Illus.). (J). (ps-2). 1997. 9.99 (*0-614-29101-1*) Litle Simon.

— Farm Babies Pack, 4 bks. (Farm Babies Ser.). (Illus.). 40p. (J). 1997. bds. 13.99 (*1-884628-61-3*, Flyng Frog) Allied Pub MD.

— Learn with Teddy Colors. (Illus.). 12p. (J). 1997. 11.99 (*1-884628-56-7*, Flyng Frog) Allied Pub MD.

— Learn with Teddy Numbers. (Illus.). 12p. (J). 1997. 11.99 (*1-884628-55-9*, Flyng Frog) Allied Pub MD.

— Little Piggy. (Farm Babies Ser.). (Illus.). 10p. (J). 1997. bds. 3.50 (*1-884628-60-5*, Flyng Frog) Allied Pub MD.

— Little Pony. (Farm Babies Ser.). (Illus.). 10p. (J). 1997. bds. 3.50 (*1-884628-57-5*, Flyng Frog) Allied Pub MD.

— Miss Polly Had a Dolly. (Illus.). 20p. (J). 1997. 14.95 (*0-7641-7057-0*) Barron.

— A New Suit for Santa. (Illus.). 12p. (J). 1997. 6.95 (*0-7641-5059-6*) Barron.

— Pet Corner, 6 bks. (Illus.). 8p. (J). (ps-k). 1998. 9.95 (*0-7641-7210-7*) Barron.

— Thank You God for All My Friends. (Thank You God Ser.). (Illus.). 24p. (J). (ps). 1997. 6.99 (*1-884628-07-9*, Flyng Frog) Allied Pub MD.

— Thank You God for the Wonderful World. (Thank You God Ser.). (Illus.). 24p. (J). (ps). 1997. 6.99 (*1-884628-32-X*, Flyng Frog) Allied Pub MD.

Mellentin, Kath & Woods, Tim. Little Calf. (Farm Babies Ser.). (Illus.). 10p. (J). 1997. bds. 3.50 (*1-884628-58-3*, Flyng Frog) Allied Pub MD.

— Little Lamb. (Farm Babies Ser.). (Illus.). 10p. (J). 1997. bds. 3.50 (*1-884628-59-1*, Flyng Frog) Allied Pub MD.

Mellentin, Kath, et al. Animal Hospital, 6 bks. (Animal Hospital Ser.). (Illus.). 6p. (J). 1997. 9.95 (*0-7641-7085-6*) Barron.

Mellentin, Kath, jt. auth. see Wood, Tim.

Mellentin, Kath, jt. auth. see Wood, Tom.

Meller. European Cities. 84.00 (*0-471-96598-7*) Wiley.

***Meller, Bronwyn, et al.** Reading Fictions: Applying Literacy Theory to Short Stories. (NCTE Chalkface Ser.). 100p. 2000. pap. write for info. (*0-8141-3869-1*, 38691) NCTE.

Meller, Eric. Rabbit Who Overcame Fear: A Jataka Tale. LC 90-48400. (Jataka Tales Ser.). 32p. (Orig.). (J). (gr. k-4). 1991. 16.95 (*0-89800-212-5*) Dharma Pub.

— Rabbit Who Overcame Fear: A Jataka Tale. LC 90-48400. (Jataka Tales Ser.). 32p. (Orig.). (J). (ps up). 1991. pap. 7.95 (*0-89800-211-7*) Dharma Pub.

Meller, Eriv. The Value of Friends. LC 86-24164. (Jataka Tales Ser.). 32p. (Orig.). (J). (ps-3). 1986. pap. 7.95 (*0-89800-140-4*) Dharma Pub.

Meller, Helen. Patrick Geddes: Social Evolutionist & City Planner. LC 93-4323. (Geography, Environment & Planning Ser.). (Illus.). 384p. (C). 1994. pap. 27.99 (*0-415-10393-2*) Routledge.

— Towns, Plans & Society in Modern Britain. LC 97-493. (New Studies in Economic & Social History: Vol. 31). 150p. (C). 1997. text 44.95 (*0-521-57227-4*); pap. text 12.95 (*0-521-57644-X*) Cambridge U Pr.

Meller, Hugh. London Cemeteries: An Illustrated Guide & Gazetteer. 3rd ed. (Illus.). 368p. 1994. pap. 43.95 (*0-85967-997-7*, Pub. by Scolar Pr) Ashgate Pub Co.

Meller, Michael N., ed. International Patent Litigation: A Country-by-Country Analysis (1993-99), vol. 1. 1999. ring bd., suppl. ed. 325.00 (*1-57018-013-X*, 1097-PR8) BNA Books.

— International Patent Litigation: A Country-by-Country Analysis, 1998 Supplement. 142p. 1998. suppl. ed. 195.00 (*1-57018-096-2*, 1096-PR8) BNA Books.

— International Patent Litigation: A Country-by-Country Analysis, 1999 Supplement. 176p. 1997. ring bd. 195.00 (*1-57018-047-4*, 1047-PR7) BNA Books.

***Meller, Michael N., ed.** International Patent Litigation: A Country-by-Country Analysis, 1999 Supplement. 280p. 1999. pap. 195.00 (*1-57018-141-1*, 1141-PR9) BNA Books.

Meller, Norman. Constitutionalism in Micronesia. (Illus.). 406p. (C). 1986. pap. 24.00 (*0-939154-39-0*) Inst Polynesian.

***Meller, Patricio.** The Unidad Popular & the Pinochet Dictatorship: A Political Analysis. LC 00-33294. 2000. write for info. (*0-312-23771-5*) St Martin.

Meller, Patricio, jt. ed. see Blomstrom, Magnus.

Meller, Patricio, jt. ed. see Engel, Eduardo.

Meller, Susan & Elffers, Joost. Textile Designs: Two Hundred Years of European & American Patterns for Printed Fabrics. (Illus.). 464p. 1991. 85.00 (*0-8109-3853-7*, Pub. by Abrams) Time Warner.

Meller, Susan, jt. auth. see Elffers, Joost.

Meller, Walter C. A Knight's Life in the Days of Chivalry. LC 78-63506. (Illus.). 328p. reprint ed. 38.50 (*0-404-17155-9*) AMS Pr.

***Mellerio, Andre & Harrison, Sharon.** Redon's Etchings & Lithographs: A Catalogue Raisonne. (FRE & ENG., Illus.). 416p. 2000. 175.00 (*1-55660-309-6*) A Wofsy Fine Arts.

Mellerio, Louis. Lexique de Ronsard. lxxv, 250p. 1974. reprint ed. write for info. (*3-487-05248-2*) G Olms Pubs.

Mellerowicz, H. Der Kreislauf des Jugendlichen bei Arbeit und Sport. 2nd ed. (Illus.). viii, 60p. 1980. pap. 14.00 (*3-8055-1140-X*) S Karger.

Mellerowicz, H., jt. ed. see Loellgen, H.

Mellers, Barbara A. & Baron, Jonathan, eds. Psychological Perspectives on Justice: Theory & Applications. LC 92-27263. (Series on Judgment & Decision Making). (Illus.). 360p. (C). 1993. text 59.95 (*0-521-43199-9*) Cambridge U Pr.

Mellers, Wilfrid. Between Old Worlds & New: Occasional Writings on Music. Paynter, John, ed. & intro. by. LC 97-49644. 328p. 1998. 45.00 (*0-8386-3798-1*) Fairleigh Dickinson.

— Caliban Reborn: Renewal in Twentieth-Century Music. LC 79-14238. (Music Reprint Ser.). 1979. reprint ed. lib. bdg. 29.50 (*0-306-79569-8*) Da Capo.

— Francis Poulenc. (Oxford Studies of Composers). (Illus.). 208p. 1995. reprint ed. pap. text 21.00 (*0-19-816338-X*) OUP.

— Percy Grainger. (Oxford Studies of Composers). (Illus.). 176p. 1992. pap. text 28.00 (*0-19-816270-7*) OUP.

Mellersh, H. E. Chronology of Ancient World, 10,000 B.C. to A.D. 799. LC 94-30474. 1995. 85.00 (*0-13-326422-X*) S&S Trade.

— Chronology of World History. 516p. 1995. lib. bdg. 49.50 (*0-87436-866-9*) ABC-CLIO.

Mellersh, H. E., et al. Chronology of World History, 4 vols. 1995. 350.00 (*0-13-326430-0*) Mac Lib Ref.

Mellert, Robert. Seven Ethical Theories. 172p. 1995. pap. text 18.95 (*0-7872-0567-2*) Kendall-Hunt.

Melles, B. Production Control in Construction: Different Approaches to Control, Use of Information & Automated Data Processing. 334p. 1997. pap. 57.50 (*90-6275-937-8*, Pub. by Delft U Pr) Coronet Bks.

Mellett, Catherine. Saturday Afternoon in My Kitchen. (Poetry New York Pamphlet Ser.). 20p. 1998. pap. 5.00 (*0-923389-30-X*) Meet Eyes Bind.

Mellett, Dorothy W. Gravestone Art in Rockland County, New York. LC 90-85609. (Illus.). 160p. (Orig.). 1991. pap. 22.50 (*0-9630484-0-6*) Hudson Valley.

Mellett, Howard J., et al. Financial Management in the NHS: A Manager's Handbook. LC 93-34382. 1993. 64.95 (*0-412-47320-8*, Chap & Hall NY) Chapman & Hall.

Mellett, Howard J., jt. auth. see Edwards, Dick.

Mellett, Howard J., jt. auth. see Edwards, J. R.

M

Mellett, J. S. Paleobiology of North American Hyaenodon (Mammalia Creodonta) Szalay, F. S., ed. (Contributions to Vertebrate Evolution Ser.: Vol. 1). 1976. 65.25 (*3-8055-2379-3*) S Karger.

Mellett, Jennifer N. Texas Limitations Manual, 1987-1993. 650p. 1993. suppl. ed. 85.00 (*0-685-17764-5*, MICHIE) LEXIS Pub.

— Texas Probate Code Manual. 1200p. 1994. ring bd. 175.00 (*0-614-05979-8*, MICHIE) LEXIS Pub.

— Texas Probate Code Manual, 1984-1993, 2 vols. 1040p. 1993. suppl. ed. 49.00 (*0-685-46136-X*, MICHIE) LEXIS Pub.

Mellett, Jennifer N., suppl. Texas Personal Injury Law, 1981-1992, 2 vols. 2nd ed. 1994. ring bd., suppl. ed. 65.00 (*0-685-74466-3*, MICHIE) LEXIS Pub.

— Texas Personal Injury Law, 1981-1992, 2 vols., Set. 2nd ed. 1024p. ring bd. 170.00 (*0-409-25621-8*, MICHIE) LEXIS Pub.

Mellett, Jennifer Nosler, jt. auth. see Steves, Sterling W.

Mellett, M., jt. ed. see Edwards, E.

***Mellett, Peter.** Expert Guide Series, 4 bks. 32p. 1999. 96.88 (*1-57572-878-8*) Heinemann Lib.

— Fantastic Facts: Trees. 64p. (J). 2000. pap. 6.95 (*1-84215-094-4*) Anness Pub.

Mellett, Peter. Flight: A Fascinating Fact File & Learn-It-Yourself Project Book. (Learn about Ser.). (Illus.). 64p. (J). (gr. 3-7). 1997. 7.95 (*1-85967-311-2*, Lorenz Bks) Anness Pub.

***Mellett, Peter.** Flying the Atlantic. LC 98-44517. (Expert Guide Ser.). (Illus.). 32p. 1999. lib. bdg. 24.22 (*1-57572-687-4*) Heinemann Lib.

Mellett, Peter. Launching a Satellite. LC 98-52725. (Expert Guide Ser.). 32p. 1999. write for info. (*1-57572-781-1*) Heinemann Lib.

— Solving a Crime. LC 98-52717. (Expert Guide Ser.). 32p. 1999. write for info. (*1-57572-782-X*) Heinemann Lib.

Mellett, Peter & James, John. Filming a Blockbuster. LC 98-44448. (Expert Guide Ser.). (Illus.). 32p. 1999. lib. bdg. 24.22 (*1-57572-686-6*) Heinemann Lib.

Mellett, Peter G. Mididictionary of Science. LC 92-40594. (C). 1993. write for info. (*0-19-211680-0*) OUP.

Mellett, Peter G., ed. Learning & Psychosomatic Approach to the Nature & Treatment of Illness: 18th Annual Conference of the Society for Psychosomatic Research. 1977. pap. 53.00 (*0-08-020881-9*, Pergamon Pr) Elsevier.

Mellett, Peter G., jt. ed. see Christie, Margaret J.

Mellette, Charles. Obedience: The Key to God's Divine Favor. 96p. (Orig.). 1996. pap. 9.99 (*1-889389-05-6*) End-Time Wave.

Mellette, Robert S. Children of the Trees: A Guidebook for the Journey Through Your Emotional Forest. large type ed. Date not set. pap. 14.95 (*1-892873-05-2*) Ginger Pubns.

Melleuish, Gregory. Cultural Liberalism in Australia: A Study in Intellectual & Cultural History. 234p. (C). 1995. text 64.95 (*0-521-47444-2*) Cambridge U Pr.

— The Packaging of Australia: Politics & Culture Wars. LC 98-198373. 143p. 1997. pap. 24.95 (*0-86840-584-1*, Pub. by New South Wales Univ Pr) Intl Spec Bk.

***Melley, Timothy.** Empire of Conspiracy: The Culture of Paranoia in Postwar America. LC 99-41667. 264p. 1999. pap. text. write for info. (*0-8014-8606-8*) Cornell U Pr.

Mellgren. New Horizons in English. 1980. text 63.07 (*0-201-60403-5*) Addison-Wesley.

Mellgren. New Horizons in English. 2nd ed. 1983. pap. text 20.08 (*0-201-04589-3*) S&S Trade.

Mellgren, L. Yes! English for Children. 1978. 78.87 (*0-201-04958-9*); text 78.87 (*0-201-04960-0*) S&S Trade.

Mellgren, L., ed. Intracellular Calcium Dependent Proteolipis. 304p. 1990. lib. bdg. 210.00 (*0-8493-6570-8*, QP609) CRC Pr.

***Mellgren, Mary.** FTCE French. (C). 2000. per. 10.00 (*1-58197-086-2*) XAM.

— PRAXIS II French. (Praxis Ser.). (C). 2000. per. 10.00 (*1-58197-059-5*) XAM.

Melli, P. & Brebbia, Carlos A., eds. Supercomputing in Engineering Structures. LC 88-63525. 305p. 1989. 72.00 (*0-945824-07-6*) Computational Mech MA.

Melli, Roberto, jt. auth. see Sciubba, E.

Mellibovsky, Matilde. Circle of Love over Death: The Story of the Mothers of the Plaza de Mayo. Proser, Matthew & Proser, Maria A., trs. from SPA. LC 96-24501.Tr. of Circulo de Amor Sobre la Muerte. 250p. (Orig.). 1996. pap. 14.95 (*1-880684-38-1*) Curbstone.

Mellichamp, Joseph M. Ministering in the Secular University: A Guide for Christian Professors & Staff. LC 97-26127. 1997. write for info. (*0-929510-09-7*) Lewis & Stanley.

Mellichamp, Larry, jt. auth. see Loewer, Peter H.

Mellichamp, Leslie. We Thought at Least the Roof Would Fall. LC 87-2231. (Illus.). 140p. (Orig.). 1987. pap. 5.95 (*0-936015-07-1*) Pocahontas Pr.

Mellick, Andrew D., Jr. The Story of an Old Farm: or Life in New Jersey in the 18th Century: With a Genealogical Appendix. 742p. 1991. reprint ed. lib. bdg. 75.00 (*0-8328-2248-5*) Higginson Bk Co.

Mellick, J. S., ed. see Kingsley, Henry.

Mellick, Jill. The Natural Artistry of Dreams: Creative Ways to Bring the Wisdom of Dreams to Waking Life. (Illus.). 256p. 1996. pap. 14.95 (*1-57324-019-2*) Conari Press.

Mellick, Jill & Shutes, Jeanne. The Worlds of P'otsunu: Geronima Cruz Montoya of San Juan Pueblo. LC 95-4412. (Illus.). 252p. 1996. 24.95 (*0-8263-1643-3*) U of NM Pr.

Mellick, Jill, jt. auth. see Woodman, Marion.

Mellier, Y., et al, eds. Gravitational Lensing: Proceedings of a Workshop Held in Toulouse, France, September 13-15, 1989. (Lecture Notes in Physics Ser.: Vol. 360). xv, 315p. 1990. 52.95 (*0-387-52648-X*) Spr-Verlag.

Melligun, Ron. Cooke County - It's History, Economics & Culture. (C). 1998. text 14.67 (*1-56870-293-0*) RonJon Pub.

Mellin, Barbara. Paint by Numbers. 16p. 1996. pap. 20.00 (*0-201-48999-6*) Addison-Wesley.

Mellin, Bob. Railbike: Cycling on Abandoned Railroads. LC 95-94676. (Illus.). 144p. (Orig.). 1996. pap. 16.95 (*0-935902-29-5*) Balboa Pub.

— Waterhole: How to Dig Your Own Well. LC 91-72454. (Illus.). 75p. 1992. pap. 12.00 (*0-935902-21-X*) Balboa Pub.

Mellin, Bob, ed. & photos by see Mellin, Joe.

Mellin, Jeanne. The Complete Morgan Horse. 5th ed. (Illus.). 372p. 1995. reprint ed. 24.00 (*0-9652884-0-4*) Am Morgan Horse.

— Illustrated Horseback Riding for Beginners. 1970. pap. 5.00 (*0-87980-196-4*) Wilshire.

Mellin, Joe. Starting Young: Getting a Jump on Getting Ahead in Business. Mellin, Bob, ed. & photos by by. LC 98-92644. (Illus.). 112p. (J). (gr. 4-12). 1999. pap. 12.00 (*0-935902-33-3*) Balboa Pub.

Mellin, Laurel. The Solution: No More Dieting! No More Drugs! No More Weight Problems! unabridged ed. 1997. audio 18.00 (*0-694-51791-7*, Caedmon) HarperAudio.

Mellin, Laurel. The Solution: 6 Winning Ways to Permanent Weight Loss. (Illus.). 416p. 1998. pap. 13.00 (*0-06-098724-3*, ReganBks) HarperTrade.

Mellin, Laurel M. Shapedown: Just for Kids!, Level 1, Ages 6-8. 5th ed. LC 88-70316. (Illus.). 155p. 1995. pap. 18.95 (*0-935902-19-8*) Balboa Pub.

— Shapedown: Just for Kids!, Level 2, Ages 9-10. 5th ed. LC 88-70316. (Illus.). 140p. 1995. pap. 18.95 (*0-935902-20-1*) Balboa Pub.

— Shapedown: Just for Kids!, Level 3, Ages 11-12. 5th ed. LC 88-70316. (Illus.). 202p. 1995. pap. 18.95 (*0-935902-23-6*) Balboa Pub.

— Shapedown: Just for Teens! 5th ed. LC 86-71125. (Illus.). 284p. 1995. pap. 18.95 (*0-935902-27-9*) Balboa Pub.

— Shapedown: Parent's Guide to Supporting Your Child. 5th ed. LC 88-70316. (Illus.). 244p. 1995. pap. 18.95 (*0-935902-18-X*) Balboa Pub.

— Shapedown: Parent's Guide to Supporting Your Teen. 5th ed. LC 86-71125. (Illus.). 284p. 1995. pap. 18.95 (*0-935902-28-7*) Balboa Pub.

— Shapedown Instructor's Guide. 5th ed. LC 86-71125. (Illus.). 394p. 1987. teacher ed., ring bd. 49.95 (*0-935902-08-2*) Balboa Pub.

— YES: Shapedown Youth Evaluation Scale. 2nd rev. ed. LC 86-71116. (Illus.). 269p. 1986. write for info. (*0-935902-10-4*) Balboa Pub.

Mellin, Marc, tr. see Casarjian, Robin.

Mellin, Maribeth. Costa Rica. (Traveler's Companion Ser.). 1998. pap. text 22.95 (*0-7627-0242-7*) Globe Pequot.

— Traveler's Companion Mexico. (Traveler's Companion Ser.). 356p. 1998. pap. text 23.95 (*0-7627-0254-0*) Globe Pequot.

Mellin, Maribeth, ed. San Diego Best Places. 8th ed. (Illus.). 363p. 1999. pap. 18.95 (*1-57061-197-1*) Sasquatch Bks.

Mellin, Maribeth, jt. auth. see Yogerst, Joe.

Mellin, Maribeth, jt. auth. see Yogurst, Joe.

Mellin-Olsen, Stieg. The Politics of Mathematics Education. (Mathematics Education Library: Vol. 4). 264p. 1987. lib. bdg. 155.50 (*90-277-2350-8*, D Reidel) Kluwer Academic.

Melling. My First Spanish Words. (My First ...Words to See Ser.). (SPA., Illus.). 48p. 1999. 11.95 (*0-8442-2399-9*, 23999, Passprt Bks) NTC Contemp Pub Co.

Melling, jt. auth. see French.

Melling, D. J. Understanding Plato. (Illus.). 192p. 1987. pap. 15.95 (*0-19-289116-2*) OUP.

Melling, D. J., jt. ed. see Barry.

***Melling, David.** Over the Moon! Best-Loved Nursery Rhymes. (Illus.). 24p. (J). (ps-3). 2000. 14.99 (*0-525-46498-0*, Dutton Child) Peng Put Young Read.

Melling, David, et al, eds. The Blackwell Dictionary of Eastern Christianity. LC 98-33150. (Illus.). 576p. 1999. 74.95 (*0-631-18966-1*) Blackwell Pubs.

Melling, David. My First French Words. LC 98-46154. (My First ...Words to See Ser.). (FRE.). 48p. 1999. 11.95 (*0-8442-2406-5*, 24065, Passprt Bks) NTC Contemp Pub Co.

Melling, David, jt. auth. see Morris, Neil.

***Melling, E. H.** Guide for the Young Composer. 281p. 2000. reprint ed. lib. bdg. 59.00 (*0-7812-9318-9*) Rprt Serv.

Melling, J. K. Discovering London's Guilds & Liveries. 1989. pap. 35.00 (*0-85263-971-6*, Pub. by Shire Pubns) St Mut.

Melling, John K. Discovering London Guilds & Liveries. 5th rev. ed. (Handbook Ser.: No. 180). (Illus.). 112p. 1995. pap. 9.50 (*0-7478-0299-8*, Pub. by Shire Pubns) Parkwest Pubns.

— Murder Done to Death: Parody & Pastiche in Detective Fiction. LC 95-15442. 296p. 1996. 46.00 (*0-8108-3034-5*) Scarecrow.

Melling, John K., jt. auth. see Brecknock, John L.

Melling, Joseph. Insanity, Institutions & Society, 1800-1914. (Studies in the Social History of Medicine Ser.). 1999. write for info. (*0-415-18441-X*) Routledge.

Melling, Joseph & McKinlay, Alan, eds. Management, Labour & Industrial Politics in Modern Europe: The Quest for Productivity Growth during the Twentieth Century. LC 95-49464. (Illus.). 208p. 1996. 80.00 (*1-85898-016-X*) E Elgar.

Melling, Maggie, jt. auth. see Fritchie, Rennie.

Melling, Phil. Man of Amman: The Life of Dai Davies. LC 94-239037. 135p. 1994. pap. 24.00 (*1-85902-083-6*, Pub. by Gomer Pr) St Mut.

— Mann of Amman: The Life of Dai Davies. 135p. 1994. pap. 23.95 (*0-8464-4667-7*) Beekman Pubs.

Melling, Phil & Roper, Jon. America, France & Vietnam: Cultural History & Ideas of Conflict. 250p. 1991. 77.95 (*1-85628-072-1*, Pub. by Avebry) Ashgate Pub Co.

Melling, Phil & Roper, Jon, eds. Americanisation & the Transformation of World Cultures: Melting Pot or Cultural Chernobyl? LC 96-13411. 280p. 1996. text 89.95 (*0-7734-8811-1*) E Mellen.

Melling, Philip H. Vietnam in American Literature: The Puritan Heritage. (Twayne's Literature & Society Ser.: No. 1). 256p. 1990. text 20.95 (*0-8057-8850-6*) Macmillan.

***Melling, Phillip.** Fundamentalism in America: Millennialism, Identity & Militant Religion. 223p. 1999. 35.00 (*1-57958-261-3*) Fitzroy Dearborn.

Mellinger, George B., ed. Environmental & Waste Management Issues in the Ceramic Industry. LC 93-47662. (Ceramic Transactions Ser.: Vol. 39). 463p. 1994. 74.00 (*0-944904-71-8*, CT039) Am Ceramic.

— Nuclear Waste Management, No. III. (Ceramic Transactions Ser.: Vol. 9). (Illus.). 595p. 1990. 10.00 (*0-944904-24-6*, CT009) Am Ceramic.

Mellinger, J., ed. Animal Nutrition & Transport Processes, No. 1: Nutrition in Wild & Domestic Animals. (Comparative Physiology Ser.: Vol. 5). viii, 288p. 1990. 221.75 (*3-8055-5157-6*) S Karger.

Mellinger, Maria. Saying Hello to an Unpublished Maria. 96p. 1998. pap. 12.00 (*0-944920-29-2*) Bellowing Ark Pr.

— The Year of Weddings. 2000. 45.00 (*0-06-019298-4*) HarpC.

Mellinger, Martha. Little Ones Praise. 1981. pap. 4.35 (*0-87813-518-9*) Christian Light.

Mellings, Joan. It's Fun to Go to School. LC 85-45771. (Illus.). 32p. (J). (gr. k-2). 1986. 6.95 (*0-694-00125-2*) HarpC Child Bks.

Mellink, Machteld J. Ancient Anatolia: Aspects of Change & Cultural Development: Essays in Honor of Machteld J. Mellink. Canby, Jeanny V. et al, eds. LC 86-40059. (Wisconsin Studies in Classics). (Illus.). 139p. 1986. reprint ed. pap. 43.10 (*0-608-07476-4*, 206769800009) Bks Demand.

— A Hittite Cemetery at Gordion. LC 58-1735. (University of Pennsylvania, University Museum, Anthropological Publications). 130p. reprint ed. pap. 40.30 (*0-608-14326-X*, 205201200026) Bks Demand.

— Kizilbel: An Archaic Painted Tomb Chamber in Northern Lycia. LC 97-45359. (Archaeological Monographs). 1998. 45.00 (*0-924171-53-7*) U Museum Pubns.

Mellink, Machteld J., ed. Troy & the Trojan War: A Symposium Held at Bryn Mawr College, October 1984. (Bryn Mawr Archaeological Monographs). (Illus.). xii, 101p. (Orig.). (C). 1986. pap. text 10.00 (*0-929524-59-4*) Bryn Mawr Commentaries.

Mellinkoff, David. The Conscience of a Lawyer. 304p. (C). 1973. reprint ed. 25.50 (*0-314-28402-8*) West Pub.

— Dictionary of American Legal Usage. 708p. (C). 1992. reprint ed. pap. 41.00 (*0-314-00068-2*); reprint ed. pap. 25.00 (*0-314-01060-2*) West Pub.

— The Language of the Law. 544p. 1963. pap. text 34.00 (*0-316-56627-6*, Aspen Law & Bus) Aspen Pub.

— Legal Writing-Sense & Nonsense: Sense & Nonsense. 242p. (C). 1981. reprint ed. pap. text 19.00 (*0-314-63275-1*) West Pub.

Mellinkoff, Ruth. The Devil at Isenheim: Reflections of Popular Belief in Grunewald's Altarpiece. (Discovery Ser.: No. 1). 100p. 1988. 55.00 (*0-520-06204-3*, Pub. by U CA Pr) Cal Prin Full Svc.

— The Horned Moses in Medieval Art & Thought. (Illus.). 322p. 1997. pap. 35.00 (*1-57910-088-0*) Wipf & Stock.

— The Mark of Cain. LC 80-18589. (Quantum Bks.: No. 20). 128p. 1981. 45.00 (*0-520-03969-6*, Pub. by U CA Pr) Cal Prin Full Svc.

— Outcasts: Signs of Otherness in Northern European Art of the Late Middle Ages, 2 vols., Vol. Set. (California Studies in the History of Art: No. 32). 1994. 225.00 (*0-520-07815-2*, Pub. by U CA Pr) Cal Prin Full Svc.

Mellion, Morris B. Sports Medicine Secrets. 2nd rev. ed. LC 98-43414. (Secrets Ser.). (Illus.). 500p. 1998. pap. text 39.00 (*1-56053-308-0*) Hanley & Belfus.

Mellion, Morris B., ed. Office Sports Medicine. 2nd ed. (Illus.). 400p. 1999. 54.00 (*1-56053-120-7*) Hanley & Belfus.

Mellion, Morris B., et al, eds. The Team Physician's Handbook. 2nd rev. ed. LC 96-45304. (Illus.). 680p. 1996. pap. text 64.95 (*1-56053-174-6*) Hanley & Belfus.

Mellis, Charles J. Committed Communities: Fresh Streams for World Missions. LC 76-53548. 138p. 1981. reprint ed. pap. 6.95 (*0-87808-426-6*, WCL426-6) William Carey Lib.

Mellis, Craig, jt. auth. see Van Asperen, Peter.

Mellis, James & Thomaneck, J. K., eds. Politics, Government & Society in the German Democratic Republic: Basic Documents. 373p. 1989. 19.50 (*0-85496-247-6*) Berg Pubs.

Mellis, Louis & Scinto, David. Gangster No. 1. (Oberon Bks.). 60p. 1997. pap. 12.95 (*1-870259-56-4*) Theatre Comm.

Mellish, C. S. Computer Interpretation of Natural Language Descriptions. LC 85-14660. (Artificial Intelligence Ser.). 182p. 1985. text 31.95 (*0-470-20219-X*) P-H.

Mellish, C. S., jt. auth. see Clocksin, W. F.

Mellish, Chris, jt. ed. see Hallam, John.

Mellish, J. M. Evaluation of Clinical Nursing. 72p. 1987. pap. text 25.00 (*0-409-10256-3*) Buttrwrth-Heinemann.

— Introduction to Ethos of Nursing. 1989. pap. text 32.50 (*0-409-10007-2*) Buttrwrth-Heinemann.

Mellish, J. M., jt. auth. see Brink.

Mellish, Joseph, tr. see Schiller, Friedrich.

Melliss, C. L. Tradable & Non-Tradable Prices in the U. K. & EC: Measurement & Explanation. LC HF1414.. (Bank of England, Economics Division, Working Paper Ser.: Vol. 15). (Illus.). 92p. 1993. reprint ed. pap. 30.00 (*0-608-07532-9*, 206774800009) Bks Demand.

Melliss, C. L. & Cornelius, M. New Currencies in the Former Soviet Union: A Recipe for Hyperinflation or the Path to Price Stability. LC HG1076.1. (Bank of England, Economics Division. Working Paper Ser.: No. 26). 99p. reprint ed. pap. 30.70 (*0-608-20164-2*, 207142800011) Bks Demand.

Mellitt, B., et al, eds. Computers in Railways IV Vol. 2: Railway Operations. LC 94-72459. (COMPRAIL Ser.: Vol. 4). 1994. 218.00 (*1-56252-283-3*, 3595) Computational Mech MA.

Mellitzer, Jurgen, jt. auth. see Brunner, Doris.

Mellizo, Carlos. Una Cuestion de Tiempo: Relatos. LC 90-86071. (Coleccion Hispanica - Narrativa: No. 1). (SPA.). 93p. (Orig.). 1991. pap. 9.95 (*0-89729-591-9*) Ediciones.

— Historia de Sonia y Otras Historias. LC 87-70083. 104p. 1987. pap. 10.00 (*0-916950-74-3*) Biling Rev-Pr.

Mellke, Hans, jt. contrib. by see Muller, Christian.

Mello, Anthony De, see De Mello, Anthony.

Mello, D', see D'Mello.

Mello, Henry J., ed. The Art of Prevention: Arts Serving Youths at Risk in Human Service & Correctional Setting. 58p. 1998. reprint ed. pap. text 20.00 (*0-7881-4049-3*) DIANE Pub.

Mello, J. M., jt. auth. see Hastings, N. A.

Mello, Luiz S. Homen De, see Homen De Mello, Luiz S., ed.

Mello, M. Chaves de. Portuguese - English, English - Portuguese Legal Dictionary: Diccionario Juridico. 3rd ed. (ENG & POR.). 515p. 1987. pap. 95.00 (*0-8288-0401-X*, F51280) Fr & Eur.

Mello, Michael. The United States of America vs. Theodore John Kaczynski: Ethics, Power, & the Invention of the Unabomber. 368p. Date not set. 24.95 (*1-893956-01-6*) Context Bks.

Mello, Michael A. Dead Wrong: A Death Row Lawyer Speaks Out Against Capital Punishment. LC 97-6427. 420p. 1997. 29.95 (*0-299-15340-1*) U of Wis Pr.

Mello, Nancy K., ed. Advances in Substance Abuse, Vol. 4. 300p. (Orig.). 1991. 88.00 (*1-85302-080-X*) Taylor & Francis.

Mello, Nancy K. & Mendelson, Jack H., eds. Medical Diagnosis & Treatment of Alcoholism. (Illus.). 656p. 1992. text 65.00 (*0-07-041491-2*) McGraw-Hill HPD.

Mello, Nancy K., jt. ed. see Mendelson, Jack H.

Mello, P., ed. see Associazione Italiana per l'intelligenza Artificiale Staff.

Mello, P., jt. ed. see Lamma, E.

***Mello, Raphael.** Janet, Librarian. 160p. 2000. mass mkt. 7.95 (*1-56201-155-3*, Pub. by Blue Moon Bks) Publishers Group.

Mello, Tara B. The Pit Crew. LC 98-19266. (Race Car Legends Ser.). (Illus.). 64p. (YA). (gr. 3 up). 1999. lib. bdg. 16.95 (*0-7910-5022-X*) Chelsea Hse.

— Rusty Wallace. LC 98-25713. (Race Car Legends Ser.). (Illus.). 64p. (YA). (gr. 3 up). 1999. lib. bdg. 16.95 (*0-7910-5023-8*) Chelsea Hse.

Mello, Tara Baukus. George Washington. LC 99-23987. 1999. 16.95 (*0-7910-5352-0*) Chelsea Hse.

— George Washington. (Revolutionary War Leaders Ser.). (Illus.). 80p. (gr. 3 up). 1999. pap. 8.95 (*0-7910-5695-3*) Chelsea Hse.

— John Smith. LC 99-24004. (Illus.). 80p. (gr. 3 up). 1999. 15.95 (*0-7910-5345-8*) Chelsea Hse.

— John Smith. (Colonial Leaders Ser.). (Illus.). 80p. (J). (gr. 3 up). 1999. pap. 8.95 (*0-7910-5688-0*) Chelsea Hse.

— Mark Martin. LC 99-15640. (Illus.). 64p. 1999. 16.95 (*0-7910-5411-X*) Chelsea Hse.

— Mark Martin. (Race Car Legends Ser.). (Illus.). 64p. (gr. 4-7). 1999. pap. 7.95 (*0-7910-5677-5*) Chelsea Hse.

***Mello, Tara Baukus.** Need for Speed. (Race Car Legends Ser.). (Illus.). (J). 2000. 16.95 (*0-7910-6015-2*) Chelsea Hse.

— Rusty Wallace. (Race Car Legends Ser.). (Illus.). 64p. (gr. 4-7). 1999. pap. text 8.95 (*0-7910-5757-7*) Chelsea Hse.

Mello, Tara Baukus. Stunt Driving. LC 99-15641. (Illus.). 64p. (gr. 4-7). 1999. 16.95 (*0-7910-5415-2*); pap. 7.95 (*0-7910-5681-3*) Chelsea Hse.

***Mello, Tara Baukus.** Tony Stewart. LC 00-30519. (Race Car Legends Ser.). (Illus.). (J). 2000. pap. write for info. (*0-7910-5842-5*) Chelsea Hse.

— Tony Stewart. (Race Car Legends Ser.). 2000. 16.95 (*0-7910-5841-7*) Chelsea Hse.

Mello, Walmor C. De, see De Mello, Walmor C., ed.

Melloch, Mike & Reed, Mark A. Compound Semiconductors 1997: Proceedings of the IEEE Twenty-Fourth International Symposium on Compound Semiconductors Held in San Diego, California, 8-11 September 1997. LC 98-4287. (Institute of Physics Publishing Conference Ser.). 666p. 1998. 245.00 (*0-7503-0556-8*) IOP Pub.

Mellody, Peggy, jt. auth. see Noyes, Diane D.

Mellody, Peggy, jt. auth. see Zimmerman, Linda.

Mellody, Pia. Breaking Free: A Recovery Handbook for Facing Codependence" LC 88-45702. 448p. 1989. pap. 18.00 (*0-06-250590-4*, Perennial) HarperTrade.

Mellody, Pia, et al. Facing Codependence: Mellody,&Pia. abr. ed. 1990. audio 11.00 (*1-55994-286-X*, CPN 1871) HarperAudio.

Mellody, Pia, et al. Facing Codependence: What It Is, Where It Comes from, How It Sabotages Our Lives. LC 88-45662. (Illus.). 256p. 1989. pap. 15.00 (*0-06-250589-0*, Pub. by Harper SF) HarpC.

— Facing Love Addiction: Giving Yourself the Power to Change the Way You Love. LC 91-55289. 256p. 1992. pap. 15.00 (*0-06-250604-8*, Pub. by Harper SF) HarpC.

An Asterisk (*) at the beginning of an entry indicates that the title is appearing for the first time.

Mellon, Andrew W. Taxation: The People's Business. LC 73-2521. (Big Business; Economic Power in a Free Society Ser.). 1973. reprint ed. 19.95 (*0-405-05101-8*) Ayer.

Mellon, Charles D. Everything You Need to Know to Understand & Live with Depression. (Illus.). 112p. 1996. pap. 11.85 (*0-9653362-2-0*) Genetics Heritage.

— The Genetic Basis of Abnormal Human Behavior. LC 96-77828. (Illus.). 260p. 1997. pap. 19.95 (*0-9653362-4-7*) Genetics Heritage.

— Hereditary Madness: The Evolution of Psychiatric Genetic Thought. LC 96-77792. 172p. (C). 1996. 24.95 (*0-9653362-5-5*) Genetics Heritage.

Mellon, Charles D., ed. see Chetverikov, S. S.

Mellon, Charles D., ed. see Lucas, Prosper.

***Mellon, Charles David.** The Individual & Liberty: 91 Things That You Can Do to Protect Your Freedom. LC 99-96475. 100p. 1999. pap. 10.00 (*0-9653362-7-1*) Genetics Heritage.

Mellon, Charles E. How to Invest Your Way to Wealth, Vol. 2. 2nd ed. LC 97-91587. (Illus.). 155p. 1999. pap. 29.95 (*0-9656479-0-0*, 96-9901, Sierra Pubns) Gupur Ent.

Mellon, Constance A. Naturalistic Inquiry for Library Science: Methods & Applications for Reseach, Evaluation & Teaching, 64. LC 89-27276. (Contributions in Librarianship & Information Science Ser.: No. 64). 218p. 1990. 59.95 (*0-313-25653-5*, MNC/) Greenwood.

***Mellon, F., et al.** Mass Spectrometry of Natural Substances in Food. 312p. 2000. 129.00 (*0-85404-571-6*, Pub. by Royal Soc Chem) Spr-Verlag.

Mellon, Francis X. Limited Liability Companies. rev. ed. 138p. 1996. pap. text 65.00 (*0-7811-0146-8*) Res Inst Am.

— State Tax Treatment of LLCs. 52p. (Orig.). Date not set. pap. text 25.95 (*0-7811-0113-1*) Res Inst Am.

Mellon, Fred & Sanstrom, Brittmarie, eds. Stable Isotopes in Human Nutrition Studies. (Food Science & Technology International Ser.). (Illus.). 172p. 1996. text 56.00 (*0-12-490540-4*) Acad Pr.

Mellon Institute Staff. Influence of Solute Elements & Thermoelastic Martensites on the Strength & Super-Elasticity of Copper-Based Alloys. 64p. 1967. 9.60 (*0-317-34530-3*, 86) Intl Copper.

Mellon, J. K. & Thorpe, A. C. Synopses in Urology. LC 97-42814. 155p. 1998. write for info. (*0-632-05072-1*) Blackwell Sci.

Mellon, James. African Hunter. (Illus.). 522p. 1996. 125.00 (*1-57157-051-9*); pap. text 75.00 (*1-57157-050-0*) Safari Pr.

Mellon, James, ed. Bullwhip Days Slave Reme. (Illus.). 480p. 1990. pap. 14.00 (*0-380-70884-1*, Avon Bks) Morrow Avon.

Mellon, John C. Finding Jesus in Sobriety: A Millennial Translation of the Gospel of Mark. LC 99-164670. 136p. 1999. pap. 12.00 (*0-9666431-2-7*) Markos Bks.

— Mark As Recovery Story: Alcoholism & the Rhetoric of Gospel Mystery. LC 94-24082. 296p. 1995. 26.95 (*0-252-02165-7*) U of Ill Pr.

Mellon, Linda F., tr. see Lucas, Prosper.

Mellon, Margaret, jt. auth. see Rissler, Jane.

Mellon, Nancy. The Art of Storytelling. 192p. 1998. pap. text 16.95 (*1-86204-346-9*, Pub. by Element MA) Penguin Putnam.

— Storytelling & the Art of Imagination. 1992. pap. 13.95 (*1-85230-339-5*, Pub. by Element MA) Penguin Putnam.

Mellon, R. H. Larimer, McMasters & Allied Families. (Illus.). 196p. 1990. reprint ed. pap. 31.00 (*0-8328-1483-0*); reprint ed. lib. bdg. 39.00 (*0-8328-1482-2*) Higginson Bk Co.

Mellon, Steve & Baker, Don. Evansville - Then & Now. Baumann, J. Bruce, ed. (Illus.). 112p. 1995. text 29.95 (*1-884850-06-5*) Scripps Howard.

Mellon, Steve & Noyes, Charlene. Sacramento: Then & Now. Baumann, J. Bruce, ed. (Illus.). 128p. 29.95 (*1-884850-04-9*) Scripps Howard.

Mellon, Susan, jt. auth. see Crawford, Tad.

Mellon, Thomas. Thomas Mellon & His Times. (Illus.). 560p. (C). 1996. pap. 22.95 (*0-8229-5572-5*) U of Pittsburgh Pr.

— Thomas Mellon & His Times. 2nd rev. ed. (Illus.). 560p. (C). 1996. text 35.00 (*0-8229-3777-8*) U of Pittsburgh Pr.

Mellone, Michael. Photo Encyclopedia of Cacheted First Day Covers, 1901-1939, Vol. 1. (Illus.). 110p. 1994. pap. 17.97 (*0-89794-051-2*) FDC Pub.

— Photo Encyclopedia of Cacheted First Day Covers, 1901-1939, Vol. 2. (Illus.). 110p. 1994. pap. 17.97 (*0-89794-052-0*) FDC Pub.

— Photo Encyclopedia of Cacheted First Day Covers, 1901-1939, Vol. 3. (Illus.). 110p. 1995. pap. 17.97 (*0-89794-053-9*) FDC Pub.

— Photo Encyclopedia of Cacheted First Day Covers, 1901-1939, Vol. 4. (Illus.). 110p. 1995. pap. 17.97 (*0-89794-054-7*) FDC Pub.

— Photo Encyclopedia of Cacheted First Day Covers, 1901-1939, Vol. 5. (Illus.). 110p. 1996. pap. 17.97 (*0-89794-055-5*) FDC Pub.

— Photo Encyclopedia of Cacheted First Day Covers, 1901-1939, Vol. 6. (Illus.). 110p. (C). 1996. pap. 17.97 (*0-89794-056-3*) FDC Pub.

— Photo Encyclopedia of Cacheted First Day Covers, 1901-1939, Vol. 7. (Illus.). 110p. 1997. pap. 17.97 (*0-89794-057-1*) FDC Pub.

— Photo Encyclopedia of Cacheted First Day Covers, 1901-1939, Vol. 8. (Illus.). 110p. 1997. pap. 17.97 (*0-89794-058-X*) FDC Pub.

— Photo Encyclopedia of Cacheted First Day Covers, 1901-1939, Vol. 9. (Illus.). 110p. 1999. pap. 17.97 (*0-89794-059-8*) FDC Pub.

— Photo Encyclopedia of Cacheted First Day Covers, 1901-1939, Vol. 10. (Illus.). 110p. 1999. pap. 17.97 (*0-89794-060-1*) FDC Pub.

— Photo Encyclopedia of Cacheted First Day Covers, 1901-1939, Vol. 11. (Illus.). 110p. 2000. pap. 17.97 (*0-89794-061-X*) FDC Pub.

— Photo Encyclopedia of Cacheted First Day Covers, 1901-1939, Vol. 12. (Illus.). 110p. 2000. pap. 17.97 (*0-89794-062-8*) FDC Pub.

Mellone, Michael & Planty, Earl. Planty's Encyclopedia of Cacheted F. D. C.'s, Vol. 6. (Illus.). 1978. pap. 9.95 (*0-89794-014-8*) FDC Pub.

Mellone, Michael A. The Cachet Identifier of U. S. Cacheted First Day Covers. (Illus.). 1977. pap. 6.95 (*0-89794-004-0*) FDC Pub.

— Mellone's Specialized Cachet Catalogue of First Day Covers of the 1940's, 2 vols. 2nd ed. (Illus.). 1979. pap. 8.95 (*0-89794-019-9*) FDC Pub.

— Mellon's Specialized Cachet Catalog of First Day Covers of the 1950's, 2 vols. 1984. pap. 8.95 (*0-685-73681-4*); pap. 8.95 (*0-685-73682-2*) FDC Pub.

— Scott 95 U. S. First Day Cover Catalogue & Checklist. 1994. pap. 6.95 (*0-89487-199-4*) Scott Pub Co.

Mellone, Michael A. & Planty, Earl. Planty's Encyclopedia of Cacheted F. D. C.'s, 10 vols. (Illus.). 1979. pap. 99.98 (*0-89794-008-3*) FDC Pub.

— Planty's Encyclopedia of Cacheted F. D. C.'s, Vol. 3. (Illus.). 1978. pap. 8.95 (*0-89794-011-3*) FDC Pub.

— Planty's Encyclopedia of Cacheted F. D. C.'s, Vol. 4. (Illus.). 1978. pap. 9.95 (*0-89794-012-1*) FDC Pub.

— Planty's Encyclopedia of Cacheted F. D. C.'s, Vol. 5. (Illus.). 1978. pap. 9.95 (*0-89794-013-X*) FDC Pub.

— Planty's Encyclopedia of Cacheted F. D. C.'s, Vol. 7. (Illus.). 1979. pap. 9.95 (*0-89794-015-6*) FDC Pub.

— Planty's Encyclopedia of Cacheted F. D. C.'s, Vol. 8. (Illus.). 1979. pap. 9.95 (*0-89794-016-4*) FDC Pub.

— Planty's Encyclopedia of Cacheted F. D. C.'s, Vol. 9. (Illus.). 1978. pap. 9.95 (*0-317-16573-9*) FDC Pub.

— Planty's Encyclopedia of Cacheted F. D. C.'s, 1923-1928, Vol. 1. (Illus.). 1977. pap. 9.95 (*0-89794-009-1*) FDC Pub.

— Planty's Encyclopedia of Cacheted F. D. C.'s, 1928-1929, Vol. 2. (Illus.). 1977. pap. 9.95 (*0-89794-010-5*) FDC Pub.

Mellone, Michael A., ed. see Newton, Barry.

Mellone, Michael A., ed. see Roessler, A. C.

Mellone, Sydney H. Western Christian Thought in the Middle Ages. 1977. lib. bdg. 250.00 (*0-8490-2816-7*) Gordon Pr.

Melloni, B. John. Illustrated Dictionary of Medicine: Diccionario de Medicina Ilustrado. (SPA., Illus.). 650p. 1982. 75.00 (*0-8288-1868-1*, S29945) Fr & Eur.

Melloni, B. John & Dox, Ida G. Melloni's Illustrated Dictionary of Medical Abbreviations. LC 98-11886. (Illus.). 492p. 1998. pap. 26.95 (*1-85070-708-1*) Prthnon Pub.

Melloni, B. John, et al. Melloni's Illustrated Dictionary of the Musculoskeletal System. LC 98-2796. (Illus.). 314p. 1998. pap. 29.95 (*1-85070-667-0*) Prthnon Pub.

Melloni, B. John, jt. auth. see Dox, Ida G.

Melloni, J. L., jt. auth. see Dox, I. G.

Melloni, June L., et al. Melloni's Illustrated Review of Human Anatomy: By Structures-Arteries, Bones, Muscles, Nerves, Veins. LC 88-722. (Illus.). 278p. 1988. reprint ed. pap. 86.20 (*0-608-04701-5*, 206542200004) Bks Demand.

— Melloni's Student Atlas of Human Anatomy. LC 96-53894. 286p. 1997. pap. 34.95 (*1-85070-770-7*) Prthnon Pub.

Mellonie, Bryan & Ingpen, Robert R. Lifetimes: The Beautiful Way to Explain Death to Children. 40p. 1983. pap. 11.95 (*0-553-34402-1*) Bantam.

Mellonig, James, jt. ed. see Nevins, Myron.

Mellonig, James T., ed. see Fiorellini, Joseph P.

***Mellor.** Logbook for Cruising under Sail. 96p. 2000. pap. 14.95 (*1-898660-35-2*, Pub. by Fernhurst Bks) Motorbooks Intl.

Mellor, A. M. Design of Modern Turbine Combustors. (Combustion Ser.). 557p. 1990. text 276.00 (*0-12-490055-0*) Acad Pr.

Mellor, Alec. Strange Masonic Stories. (Illus.). xii, 184p. 1985. pap. 11.95 (*0-88053-082-0*, M-313) Macoy Pub.

Mellor, Alfred, et al. Mellor Meigs & Howe: A Monograph of the Work of Mellor Meigs & Howe. LC 90-47377. (American Architectural Classics Ser.). (Illus.). 228p. 1992. reprint ed. 85.00 (*1-878650-01-7*) Archit CT.

Mellor, Allec. Dictionnaire de la Franc-Maconnerie et des Francs-Macons. (FRE.). 324p. 1989. reprint ed. pap. 49.95 (*0-7859-4834-1*) Fr & Eur.

***Mellor, Anne.** Mothers of the Nation: Women's Political Writing in England, 1780-1830. LC 99-47328. (Illus.). 208p. 2000. 39.95 (*0-253-33713-5*) Ind U Pr.

Mellor, Anne K. English Romantic Irony. LC 80-10687. 228p. (C). 1980. 30.50 (*0-674-25690-5*) HUP.

— Mary Shelley: Her Life, Her Fiction, Her Monsters. (Illus.). 350p. 1988. 35.00 (*0-415-02591-5*) Routledge.

— Mary Shelley: Her Life, Her Fiction, Her Monsters. (Illus.). 350p. (C). 1989. pap. 23.99 (*0-415-90147-2*) Routledge.

— Romanticism & Gender. LC 92-22902. 288p. (C). 1992. pap. 24.99 (*0-415-90664-4*, A7604) Routledge.

Mellor, Anne K. & Matlak, Richard E. British Literature, 1780-1830. (C). 1995. text 62.50 (*0-15-500260-0*, Pub. by Harcourt Coll Pubs) Harcourt.

Mellor, Anne K., ed. see Shelley, Mary Wollstonecraft.

Mellor, Anne Kostelanetz, jt. ed. see Novak, Maximillian E.

Mellor, Barbara, jt. ed. see Douglas-Cooper, Helen.

Mellor, Bernard. Lugard in Hong Kong: Empires, Education & a Governor at Work, 1907-1912. (Illus.). 232p. 1992. 68.50 (*962-209-316-7*, Pub. by HK Univ Pr) Coronet Bks.

— The University of Hong Kong: An Informal History, 2 vols. (Illus.). 428p. 1980. 87.50 (*962-209-023-0*, Pub. by HK Univ Pr) Coronet Bks.

Mellor, Bernard, jt. auth. see Blunden, Edmund C.

***Mellor, Bronwyn.** Reading Hamlet. LC 99-46417. (Chalkface Ser.). (Illus.). 112p. 1999. pap. 12.95 (*0-8141-3870-5*, 38705) NCTE.

***Mellor, Bronwyn, et al.** Reading Stories: Activities & Texts for Critical Readings. (Chalkface Ser.). 115p. 2000. pap. write for info. (*0-8141-3911-6*, 39116) NCTE.

Mellor, Bronwyn, jt. auth. see Martino, Wayne.

Mellor, Constance. Natural Remedies for Common Ailments. 134p. 1980. 17.95 (*0-8464-1073-7*) Beekman Pubs.

Mellor, D. H. The Facts of Causation. LC 95-5708. 256p. (C). (gr. 13). 1995. 60.00 (*0-415-09779-7*, B3181) Routledge.

— The Facts of Causation. (International Library of Philosophy). 264p. (C). (gr. 13). 1999. pap. 27.99 (*0-415-19756-2*, D6134) Routledge.

— The Matter of Chance. LC 70-152629. 203p. reprint ed. pap. 57.90 (*0-608-13305-1*, 2025592) Bks Demand.

— Real Time II. LC 98-14910. 160p. (C). 1998. 65.00 (*0-415-09780-0*); pap. 22.99 (*0-415-09781-9*) Routledge.

Mellor, D. H. & Oliver, Alex, eds. Properties. LC 97-164761. (Oxford Readings in Philosophy). 288p. 1997. text 60.00 (*0-19-875177-X*); pap. text 19.95 (*0-19-875176-1*) OUP.

Mellor, David. Gramophone Good Classical CD Guide: 1997 Edition. 10th rev. ed. 1340p. 1996. pap. 25.95 incl. audio compact disk (*0-902470-78-7*, GG19970, Pub. by Gramophone) Music Sales.

— How to Become a Record Producer. (Illus.). 128p. 1997. pap. 15.95 (*1-870775-48-1*, XC8026, Pub. by PC Pubg) Cimino Pub Grp.

— How to Set up a Home Recording Studio. 2nd ed. 144p. 1995. pap. 15.95 (*1-870775-43-0*) Cimino Pub Grp.

— How to Set up Home Recording. 1991. pap. text 30.00 (*1-870075-30-7*, Pub. by Quiller Pr) St Mut.

— A Paradise Lost: The Neo-Romantic Imagination In. (Illus.). 144p. (C). 1987. reprint ed. pap. 45.00 (*0-85331-532-9*, Pub. by Lund Humphries) Antique Collect.

— Recording Techniques: For Small Studios. (Illus.). 160p. 1996. pap. 15.95 (*1-870775-29-5*, Pub. by PC Pubg) Cimino Pub Grp.

— The '60s Art Scene in London. (Illus.). 240p. (C). 1993. pap. 35.00 (*0-7148-2910-2*, Pub. by Phaidon Press) Phaidon Pr.

***Mellor, David.** A Sound Person's Guide to Video. (Illus.). 272p. 2000. pap. 39.95 (*0-240-51595-1*, Focal) Buttrwrth-Heinemann.

Mellor, David A. Arthur Tress: Requiem for a Paperweight. Glenn, Constance W., ed. & intro. by. (Illus.). 16p. (Orig.). 1994. pap. 10.00 (*0-936270-33-0*) CA St U LB Art.

— David Hiscock. (Illus.). 1996. 65.00 (*0-9518371-9-2*, Pub. by Cheatle Zelda) Dist Art Pubs.

Mellor, David A. & Bucklow, Christopher. Under the Sun. 1996. 35.00 (*1-881997-01-4*) Fraenkel Gal.

Mellor, David A. & Gervereau, Laurent, eds. The '60s: Britain & France, 1962-1973 the Utopian Years. (Illus.). 288p. 1997. 65.00 (*0-85667-467-2*, Pub. by P Wilson) Antique Collect.

Mellor, David Allan. David Levinthal: Dark Light--Photographs 1984-1994. (Illus.). 48p. 1995. pap. 17.50 (*0-907879-43-8*) Dist Art Pubs.

Mellor, David H. Matters of Metaphysics. (Illus.). 315p. (C). 1991. text 54.95 (*0-521-41117-3*) Cambridge U Pr.

Mellor, David H., ed. Ways of Communicating: The Darwin College Lectures, 1989. (Illus.). 171p. (C). 1991. 39.95 (*0-521-37074-4*) Cambridge U Pr.

***Mellor, Don.** American Rock. 2000. pap. 21.00 (*0-88150-428-9*, Pub. by Countryman) Norton.

Mellor, Don. Climbing in the Adirondacks: A Guide to Rock & Ice Routes in Adirondack Park. (Illus.). 240p. (Orig.). 1986. suppl. ed. 4.50 (*0-9615992-1-9*); pap. 15.95 (*0-685-11832-0*) Lake Placid Climb.

— Climbing in the Adirondacks: A Guide to Rock & Ice Routes in the Adirondack Park. 3rd ed. LC 89-59. 480p. 1996. pap. 24.95 (*0-935272-79-8*) ADK Mtn Club.

— Rock Climbing: A Trailside Guide. LC 96-52821. (Trailside Series Guide). (Illus.). 192p. 1997. pap. 18.95 (*0-393-31653-X*, Norton Paperbks) Norton.

Mellor, Eloise. Youth Open the Door. 1969. 5.00 (*0-87516-710-1*); pap. 3.00 (*0-87516-114-6*) DeVorss.

Mellor, George L. Introduction to Physical Oceanography. (Illus.). 273p. 1996. reprint ed. pap. 55.00 (*1-56396-210-1*) Spr-Verlag.

Mellor, Grant. Flying Tinsel. (Illus.). 136p. (J). (gr. 5-8). 1993. pap. text 12.95 (*0-938587-33-1*) Cuisenaire.

Mellor, J. E. Falconry Notes by Mellor. 1972. 15.00 (*0-914802-07-0*) Falcon Head Pr.

Mellor, Joanna, jt. auth. see Rzetelny, Harriet.

Mellor, John. The Art of Pilotage. (Illus.). 192p. 1990. 27.50 (*0 924486 04 X*) Sheridan.

— Boat Handling under Power. (Illus.). 190p. 1993. pap. 16.50 (*0-924486-43-0*) Sheridan.

***Mellor, John.** Cruising: A Skipper's Guide. (Illus.). 96p. 2000. pap. 16.95 (*1-898660-66-2*, 130047AE) Fernhurst Bks.

Mellor, John. Cruising Skipper. 96p. (C). 1990. text 59.00 (*0-906754-71-2*, Pub. by Fernhurst Bks) St Mut.

— Handling Troubles Afloat: What to Do When It All Goes Wrong. (Illus.). 208p. 1996. pap. 19.95 (*1-57409-009-7*) Sheridan.

— Log Book for Cruising under Sail. 96p. (C). 1990. text 59.00 (*0-906754-62-3*, Pub. by Fernhurst Bks) St Mut.

— The Sailing Cruiser Manual. (Illus.). 196p. 1989. 26.50 (*0-911378-87-1*) Sheridan.

— A Small Boat Guide to the Rules of the Road: The Collision Regulations Simplified. (Illus.). 64p. (C). 1998. pap. 12.95 (*0-906754-54-2*, 128337AE, Pub. by Fernhurst Bks) St Mut.

Mellor, John W. Economics of Agricultural Development. LC 66-19491. (Illus.). 418p. 1970. pap. text 19.95 (*0-8014-9102-9*) Cornell U Pr.

Mellor, John W., ed. Agriculture on the Road to Industrialization. (International Food Policy Research Institute Ser.). 488p. 1995. text 57.50 (*0-8018-5012-6*) Johns Hopkins.

Mellor, John W., et al, eds. Accelerating Food Production in Sub-Saharan Africa. LC 86-10684. 437p. 1987. reprint ed. pap. 135.50 (*0-608-03670-6*, 206449600009) Bks Demand.

Mellor, John W. & Ahmed, Raisuddin, eds. Agricultural Price Policy for Developing Countries. LC 87-26862. 352p. 1988. text 35.00 (*0-8018-3586-0*) Johns Hopkins.

Mellor, John W. & Desai, Gunvant M., eds. Agricultural Change & Rural Poverty: Variations on a Theme by Dharm Narain. LC 85-50. 256p. 1985. 28.50 (*0-8018-3275-6*) Johns Hopkins.

Mellor, John W., jt. auth. see Desai, Bhupat M.

Mellor, M. Joanna, ed. Special Aging Populations & Systems Linkages. LC 96-7980. (Journal of Gerontological Social Work: Vol. 25, Nos. 1/2). 155p. 1996. 39.95 (*1-56024-831-9*) Haworth Pr.

Mellor, M. Joanna, et al, eds. Geriatric Social Work Education. LC 92-1702. (Journal of Gerontological Social Work Ser.: Vol. 18. Nos. 3-4). (Illus.). 218p. 1992. 39.95 (*1-56024-297-3*) Haworth Pr.

Mellor, M. Joanna & Solomon, Renee, eds. Geriatric Social Work Education. LC 92-1702. (Journal of Gerontological Social Work: Vol. 18. Nos. 3-4). 218p. 1996. reprint ed. pap. 19.95 (*0-7890-0053-9*) Haworth Pr.

Mellor, M. Joanna, jt. ed. see Getzel, George S.

Mellor, Mary. Feminism & Ecology. LC 97-34294. 232p. 1997. text 50.00 (*0-8147-5600-X*); pap. text 18.50 (*0-8147-5601-8*) NYU Pr.

Mellor, Mike. The American West, 1840-1895. LC 98-207525. (History Program Ser.). (Illus.). 112p. (C). 1998. pap. 13.95 (*0-521-58633-X*) Cambridge U Pr.

Mellor, P. B., jt. auth. see Johnson, W.

Mellor, P. S. African Horse Sickness. LC 98-216667. (Archives of Virology Ser.). 342p. 1998. (*3-211-83132-0*) Spr-Verlag.

***Mellor, P. S., et al, eds.** African Horse Sickness. LC 98-216667. (Illus.). 280p. 1998. 179.00 (*3-211-83133-9*) Spr-Verlag.

Mellor, Philip A. & Shilling, Chris. Re-Forming the Body: Religion, Community, & Modernity. Featherstone, Mike, ed. LC 97-65104. (Theory, Culture & Society Ser.). 256p. 1997. 75.00 (*0-8039-7722-0*); pap. 26.95 (*0-8039-7723-9*) Sage.

Mellor, Ronald. The Historians of Ancient Rome. LC 97-21974. 531p. 1997. pap. 25.99 (*0-415-91268-7*) Routledge.

— The Historians of Ancient Rome. LC 97-21974. 531p. (C). 1997. 80.00 (*0-415-91267-9*) Routledge.

— The Roman Historians. LC 98-27442. 1999. 70.00 (*0-415-11773-9*); pap. 21.99 (*0-415-11774-7*) Routledge.

— Tacitus. 200p. (C). (gr. 13). 1994. pap. 20.99 (*0-415-91002-1*, B4411) Routledge.

Mellor, Ronald, ed. Tacitus: The Classical Heritage. LC 95-6076. (Classical Heritage Ser.: Vol. 6). 304p. 1995. text 64.00 (*0-8153-0933-3*) Garland.

***Mellor, Ronald, et al, eds.** Text & Tradition: Studies in Greek History & Historiography in Honor of Mortimer Chambers. LC 99-28852. 1999. pap. 19.95 (*0-941690-92-X*) Regina Bks.

***Mellor, Ronald & Tritle, Lawrence A., eds.** Text & Tradition: Studies in Greek History & Historiography in Honor of Mortimer Chambers. 1999. 39.95 (*0-941690-91-1*) Regina Bks.

Mellor, Stephen, jt. auth. see Therriault, Daniel.

Mellor, Stephen J. Structured Development for Real-Time Systems Vol. 1: Introduction & Tools, Vol. 1. 1986. pap. text 37.60 (*0-13-854787-4*) P-H.

Mellor, Stephen J. & Shalaer, Sally. Object Life Cycles: Modeling the World in States. LC 91-13591. (Yourdon Press Computing Ser.). 251p. 1991. pap. 61.00 (*0-13-629940-7*, Yourdon) P-H.

Mellor, Stephen J. & Shlaer, Sally. Object Oriented Systems Analysis: Modeling the World in Data. (Yourdon Press Computing Ser.). (Illus.). 144p. (C). 1988. pap. 58.00 (*0-13-629023-X*) P-H.

Mellor, Stephen J., jt. auth. see Ward, Paul T.

Mellor, Stuart, jt. auth. see Read, Michael D.

Mellor, Suzanne. Literacy & Competencies. 1996. pap. 35.00 (*0-86431-185-0*, Pub. by Aust Council Educ Res) Stylus Pub VA.

Mellor, Suzanne. Literacy & the Competencies: Teachers' Perspectives. 1966. 100.00 (*0-86431-216-4*, Pub. by Aust Council Educ Res) St Mut.

Mellor, Tony, jt. auth. see Ellis, Steve.

***Mellor, Zoe.** Double Knits: Pairs of Patterns for Babies & Toddlers. (Illus.). 2000. 19.95 (*1-57076-167-1*, Trafalgar Sq Pub) Trafalgar.

Mellor, Zoe. Head to Toe Knits. LC 97-81252. (Illus.). 80p. 1998. 22.95 (*1-57076-116-7*, Trafalgar Sq Pub) Trafalgar.

Mellors, Alan, jt. auth. see McGowan, John C.

Mellors, Anthony, ed. see Crane, Stephen.

M

Mellott, Douglas W., Jr. New Product Planning Management of the Marketing-R & D Interface: An Annotated Bibliography. LC 76-57928. (American Marketing Association Bibliography Ser.: No. 26). 51p. reprint ed. pap. 30.00 (*0-608-11938-5*, 202335300032) Bks Demand.

Mellott, Jack. West Virginia University. (Illus.). 112p. 1987. 37.50 (*0-916509-13-3*) Harmony Hse Pub.

Mellott, Jack, photos by. Northwestern University. (First Edition Ser.). (Illus.). 112p. 1988. 39.00 (*0-916509-46-X*) Harmony Hse Pub.

Mellott, Richard, jt. auth. see Woodso, Yoko.

Mellow, James. Things As They Are. 1999. 29.95 (*0-670-86685-7*) Viking Penguin.

— Things As They Are: Walker Evans Biography. 1996. write for info. (*0-201-62465-6*) Addison-Wesley.

Mellow, James R. Hemingway: A Life Without Consequences. (Illus.). 720p. 1993. pap. 22.00 (*0-201-62620-9*) Addison-Wesley.

— Nathaniel Hawthorne in His Time. LC 98-2623. 684p. 1998. reprint ed. pap. 19.95 (*0-8018-5900-X*) Johns Hopkins.

— Walker Evans. LC 99-35406. (Illus.). 654p. 1999. 40.00 (*0-465-09077-X*, Pub. by Basic) HarpC.

Mellowe, Chalcey & Spiezio, Elmer. The Loot Players. 170p. 1998. pap. 16.95 (*1-57502-717-8*) Morris Pubng.

Mellowe, Clancey. The Loot Players. 208p. 1998. pap. 19.95 (*1-57502-608-2*, PO1745) Morris Pubng.

Mellowe, Clancey & Spiezio, Elmer A. A Symphony of Love. 168p. 1994. 16.95 (*1-57087-059-4*) Prof Pr NC.

Mellown, Elgin W., compiled by. A Descriptive Catalogue of the Bibliographies of Twentieth Century British Poets, Novelists & Dramatists. 2nd enl. rev. ed. LC 79-193301. xvi, 414p. 1978. 45.00 (*0-87875-137-8*) Whitston Pub.

Mellown, Elgin W., jt. compiled by see Hoy, Peter C.

Mellown, Robert. The University of Alabama: A Guide to the Campus. LC 87-26205. (Illus.). 128p. 1988. pap. 9.95 (*0-8173-0395-2*) U of Ala Pr.

Mellows, Anthony R. Taxation for Executors & Trustees. 7th ed. 1993. pap. 101.00 (*0-406-62401-1*, U.K., MICHIE) LEXIS Pub.

Mellows, Clayton R. Absenteeism, Work Loss & Illness Behavior: Medical Analysis Index with Reference Bibliography. LC 85-47855. 150p. 1987. pap. 34.50 (*0-88164-385-8*) ABBE Pubs Assn.

— Sex Counseling - Guidelines, Assessment & Treatment: Index of Modern Authors & Subjects with Guide for Rapid Research. LC 90-56284. 160p. 1991. 47.50 (*1-55914-350-9*); pap. 44.50 (*1-55914-351-7*) ABBE Pubs Assn.

— Workman's Compensation: Index of Modern Information. LC 88-47986. 150p. 1989. 47.50 (*1-55914-064-X*); pap. 44.50 (*1-55914-065-8*) ABBE Pubs Assn.

Mellows, F. Russellism - The Latest Blasphemy: Millions-Now-Living-Will-Never-Die-Ism. 23p. 1988. reprint ed. pap. 1.95 (*1-883858-50-X*) Witness CA.

Mellows, Joan. A Different World. large type ed. 1989. 27.99 (*0-7089-2077-2*) Ulverscroft.

— The Marriage Trap. large type ed. 455p. 1989. 27.99 (*0-7089-1935-9*) Ulverscroft.

Mellows, Mary. A Lamp for Orchid. 126p. 1986. pap. 22.00 (*0-7223-1987-8*, Pub. by A H S Ltd) St Mut.

***Mellows, Meinert.** Testen Und Auswahlen Von Nichtlinearen Zeitreihenmodellen Mit Dem Bootstrap-Verfahren. (Illus.). 144p. 1999. 31.95 (*3-631-34614-X*) P Lang Pubng.

Melloy, Kevin & Schmidt, Ken. Street Fighter Alpha 3: Official Fighting Guide, 1. (Illus.). 143p. 1999. pap. 11.99 (*1-56686-886-6*) Brady Pub.

Melloy, Kristine J., et al. Developing Social Competence in Children & Youth with Challenging Behaviors. 48p. 1997. pap. text 11.40 (*0-86586-307-5*) Coun Exc Child.

Melloy, Kristine J., jt. auth. see Zirpoli, Thomas J.

Mellquist, Peter E., jt. auth. see Hewlett-Packard Company Staff.

Mellstrom. Protective Gloves for Occupational Use. 336p. 1994. boxed set 141.95 (*0-8493-7359-X*, RL244) CRC Pr.

Melluish, T. W., jt. auth. see Kinchin Smith, F.

Melluish, T. W., jt. auth. see Kinchin-Smithma, F.

Melly, Brian W. Comparison of Several Computer Hydraulics Programs for the IBM PC & Compatibles. 1987. 7.50 (*0-318-23463-7*, TR87-1) Society Fire Protect.

***Melly, Christopher.** General Agreement on Trade in Services: Examination of South American Trading Partners' Schedules of Commitments. (Illus.). 300p. (C). 1999. reprint ed. pap. text 40.00 (*0-7881-7899-7*) DIANE Pub.

Melly, George. Towards Laughter: Paintings by Maggi Hambling. (Illus.). 64p. (C). 1993. pap. 27.50 (*0-85331-647-3*, Pub. by Lund Humphries) Antique Collect.

Melly, George, jt. contrib. by see Gooding, Mel.

Melly, Peter J., jt. auth. see Ringenbach, Paul T.

Melman, Billie, ed. Borderlines: Genders & Identities in War & Peace 1870-1930. LC 97-12078. 432p. (C). 1998. 75.00 (*0-415-91113-3*); pap. 22.99 (*0-415-91114-1*) Routledge.

***Melman, Ilona.** Holistic Healing. (Pocket Healing Bks.). (Illus.). 72p. 2000. pap. 4.95 (*965-494-100-7*) Astrolog Pub.

Melman, Yossi. The Master Terrorist: The True Story Behind Abu-Nidal. Himmelstein, Shmuel, tr. LC 86-10820. 216p. 1986. 16.95 (*0-915361-52-3*) Lambda Pubs.

— The Master Terrorist: The True Story Behind Abu-Nidal. 296p. 1987. pap. 3.95 (*0-380-70428-5*, Avon Bks) Morrow Avon.

— The New Israelis: An Intimate View of a Changing People. 320p. 1992. 19.95 (*1-55972-129-4*, Birch Ln Pr) Carol Pub Group.

Melman, Yossi & Raviv, Dan. Behind the Uprising: Israelis, Jordanians, & Palestinians, 238. LC 89-7486. (Contributions in Political Science Ser.: No. 238). 255p. 1989. 59.95 (*0-313-26787-1*, MBU/, Greenwood Pr) Greenwood.

— Friends in Deed: Inside the U. S.-Israel Alliance. LC 93-42416. (Illus.). 560p. (J). 1995. pap. 14.45 (*0-7868-8090-2*, Pub. by Hyperion) Time Warner.

Melmans & Valenza, Samuel W., Jr. Creation of Nothing: Supplement to the U. S. Patents #4616,556 & #3601,077. 1989. write for info. (*0-936918-12-8*) Intergalactic NJ.

Melmed, Jolyne S. Interpreting the Parcellation of Peruvian Agricultural Producer Cooperatives. (Research Paper Ser.: Vol. 96). (Illus.). 39p. (C). 1988. pap. 4.00 (*0-934519-06-4*, RP96) U of Wis Land.

Melmed, Laura Krauss. Capital ABC. 1924. write for info. (*0-688-17561-9*) Lothrop.

Melmed, Laura Krauss. First Song Ever Sung. (J). 1995. 11.19 (*0-606-07519-4*, Pub. by Turtleback) Demco.

— I Love You As Much... LC 92-27677. (Illus.). 24p. (J). (ps-k). 1993. 16.00 (*0-688-11718-X*); lib. bdg. 15.93 (*0-688-11719-8*) Lothrop.

***Melmed, Laura Krauss.** I Love You As Much. 2000. write for info. (*0-688-17728-X*, Wm Morrow) Morrow Avon.

— I Love You As Much... Board Book. LC 98-122396. (Illus.). 19p. (J). (ps up). 1998. bds. 6.95 (*0-688-15978-8*, Wm Morrow) Morrow Avon.

Melmed, Laura Krauss. Jumbo's Lullaby. LC 98-48138. 24p. (J). 1999. 16.00 (*0-688-16550-8*) Morrow Avon.

***Melmed, Laura Krauss.** Jumbo's Lullaby. LC 98-48138. 24p. (J). 1999. 15.89 (*0-688-16996-1*) Morrow Avon.

Melmed, Laura Krauss. Little Oh. LC 95-25427. (Illus.). (J). (ps-3). 1997. lib. bdg. 15.93 (*0-688-14209-5*) Lothrop.

— Little Oh. LC 95-25427. (Illus.). (J). (ps up). 1997. 16.00 (*0-688-14208-7*) Lothrop.

— The Marvelous Market on Mermaid. LC 93-32621. (Illus.). 24p. (J). (ps-1). 1996. 15.00 (*0-688-13053-4*) Lothrop.

— Moishe's Miracle: A Hanukkah Story. LC 99-27640. 32p. (J). 2000. 15.95 (*0-688-14682-1*, Wm Morrow); lib. bdg. 15.89 (*0-688-14683-X*, Wm Morrow) Morrow Avon.

— Prince Nautilus. LC 93-37432. (Illus.). (J). 1994. 16.00 (*0-688-04566-9*) Lothrop.

— The Rainbabies. LC 91-16877. (Illus.). 32p. (J). (gr. 1 up). 1992. 16.00 (*0-688-10755-9*); lib. bdg. 15.93 (*0-688-10756-7*) Lothrop.

— This First Thanksgiving Day. LC 96-14215. 24p. (J). (ps-3). 2000. 15.95 (*0-688-14554-X*); lib. bdg. 15.89 (*0-688-14555-8*) Morrow Avon.

***Melmed, Laura Krauss.** UPC I Love You as Much. 2000. pap. 6.95 (*0-688-16806-X*) HarpC.

Melmed, Raun D., jt. auth. see Nicholls, Christopher J.

Melmed-Sanjak, Jolyne, et al, eds. Recovery or Relapse in the Global Economy: Comparative Perspectives on Restructuring in Central America. LC 93-17117. 256p. 1993. 62.95 (*0-275-94605-3*, C4605, Praeger Pubs) Greenwood.

Melmed, Shlomo. Oncogenesis & Molecular Biology of Pituitary Tumors. (Frontiers of Hormone Research Ser.: Vol. 20). (Illus.). vi, 198p. 1996. 198.25 (*3-8055-6254-3*) S Karger.

— The Pituitary. (Illus.). 752p. 1990. 59.95 (*0-86542-126-9*) Blackwell Sci.

Melmed, Shlomo, ed. Molecular & Clinical Advances in Pituitary Disorders - 11993: Proceedings of the 3rd International Pituitary Congress. 400p. 1993. pap. 30.00 (*0-9637943-0-2*) Endocrine Res.

Melmed, Shlomo, jt. ed. see Conn, P. Michael.

Melmon, Kenneth L., et al, eds. Clinical Pharmacology. 3rd ed. 1991. 79.51 (*0-08-040305-0*, Pub. by PPI); pap. 42.51 (*0-08-040644-0*, Pub. by PPI) McGraw.

Melmon, Kenneth L., et al. Melmon & Morrelli's Clinical Pharmacology: Basic Principles in Therapeutics. 3rd ed. (Illus.). 1141p. 1992. pap. text 65.00 (*0-07-105385-9*) McGraw-Hill HPD.

***Melmon, Kenneth L., et al.** Melmon & Morrelli's the Essentials Clinical Pharmacology: Principles & Practical Applications of Therapeutics. 4th ed. (Illus.). 1200p. 1999. pap. text 64.00 (*0-07-105406-5*) McGraw-Hill HPD.

Melmoth, Sebastian. Degas. 1993. 5.98 (*1-55521-826-1*) Bk Sales Inc.

— Egon Schiele. 1994. 5.98 (*0-7858-0208-8*) Bk Sales Inc.

— Klimt. 1994. 5.98 (*0-7858-0211-8*) Bk Sales Inc.

Melnechuk, Theodore, jt. ed. see Baxter, Claude F.

Melner, Samuel. Great Fishing Tackle Catalogs of the Golden Age. 344p. 1998. pap. text 18.95 (*1-55821-902-1*) Lyons Pr.

Melnick, Ana, jt. auth. see Lomnitz, Larissa.

Melnick, Ana, jt. auth. see Lomnitz, Larissa Adler.

Melnick, Arnold. Professionally Speaking: Public Speaking for Health Professionals. LC 98-22026. (Illus.). 113p. 1998. 39.95 (*0-7890-0600-6*); pap. 19.95 (*0-7890-0601-4*) Haworth Pr.

Melnick, Arthur. Representation of the World: A Naturalized Semantics. (Revisioning Philosophy Ser.: Vol. 26). XI, 355p. (C). 1997. text 57.95 (*0-8204-3350-0*) P Lang Pubng.

— Space, Time, & Thought in Kant. 576p. (C). 1989. lib. bdg. 207.50 (*0-7923-0135-8*, Pub. by Kluwer Academic) Kluwer Academic.

***Melnick, Daniel & Rouse, Beatrice A.** Portrait of Health in the United States: Major Statistical Trends & Guide to Resources. 500p. 2000. pap. 89.00 (*0-89059-189-X*) Bernan Pr.

Melnick, Daniel C. Fullness of Dissonance: Modern Fiction & the Aesthetics of Music. LC 93-8332. 1994. 32.50 (*0-8386-3525-3*) Fairleigh Dickinson.

***Melnick, Edward L., et al.** Creating Value in Financial Services. LC 99-47411. 1999. write for info. (*0-7923-8572-1*) Kluwer Academic.

Melnick, Gregory. Icon Painter's Notebook: An Anthology of Source Materials (The Bolshakov Edition) 260p. 1994. per. 22.95 (*1-879038-19-6*) Oakwood Pubns.

— An Iconographer's Sketchbook Vol. II: The Tyulin Collection. (Illus.). 250p. 1997. per. 19.95 (*1-879038-22-6*) Oakwood Pubns.

— Iconographer's Sketchbook, the Postnikov Collection Vol. 1: Ancient Icon Figures. (Postnikov Collection). 250p. 1997. per. 19.95 (*1-879038-10-2*) Oakwood Pubns.

Melnick, Hugh D. & Intrator, Nancy. The Pregnancy Prescription: The Success-Oriented Approach to Overcoming Infertility. LC 97-94304. (Illus.). 184p. (Orig.). 1998. pap. 17.95 (*0-9660419-0-9*, JO) Josara Pub.

Melnick, Jeffrey, jt. ed. see Rubin, Rachel.

***Melnick, Jeffrey P.** Black-Jewish Relations on Trial: Leo Frank & Jim Conley in the New South. 160p. 2000. pap. 18.00 (*1-57806-287-X*); lib. bdg. 45.00 (*1-57806-286-1*) U Pr of Miss.

Melnick, Jeffrey P. A Right to Sing the Blues: African Americans, Jews, & American Popular Song. LC 98-33877. 277p. 1999. 27.95 (*0-674-76976-7*) HUP.

Melnick, Joseph L., ed. Enteric Viruses in Water. (Monographs in Virology: Vol. 15). (Illus.). x, 238p. 1984. 142.75 (*3-8055-3803-0*) S Karger.

— Progress in Medical Virology, Vol. 12. 1970. 75.00 (*3-8055-0409-8*) S Karger.

— Progress in Medical Virology, Vol. 13. 1971. 95.75 (*3-8055-1181-7*) S Karger.

— Progress in Medical Virology, Vol. 14. 1972. 82.75 (*3-8055-1291-0*) S Karger.

— Progress in Medical Virology, Vol. 16. (Illus.). 1973. 85.25 (*3-8055-1601-0*) S Karger.

— Progress in Medical Virology, Vol. 17. 400p. 1974. 85.25 (*3-8055-1642-8*) S Karger.

— Progress in Medical Virology, Vol. 20. (Illus.). 400p. 1975. 86.25 (*3-8055-2161-8*) S Karger.

— Progress in Medical Virology, Vol. 22. 250p. 1976. 103.50 (*3-8055-2315-7*) S Karger.

— Progress in Medical Virology, Vol. 23. (Illus.). 1977. 95.75 (*3-8055-2423-4*) S Karger.

— Progress in Medical Virology, Vol. 24. (Illus.). 1978. 94.00 (*3-8055-2810-8*) S Karger.

— Progress in Medical Virology, Vol. 25. (Illus.). 1979. 77.50 (*3-8055-2978-3*) S Karger.

— Progress in Medical Virology, Vol. 26. (Illus.). viii, 240p. 1980. 129.75 (*3-8055-0702-X*) S Karger.

— Progress in Medical Virology, Vol. 28. (Illus.). x, 234p. 1982. 128.75 (*3-8055-2983-X*) S Karger.

— Progress in Medical Virology, Vol. 29. (Illus.). x, 246p. 1984. 128.75 (*3-8055-3618-6*) S Karger.

— Progress in Medical Virology, Vol. 31. (Illus.). x, 234p. 1984. 142.75 (*3-8055-3909-6*) S Karger.

— Progress in Medical Virology, Vol. 33. (Illus.). viii, 182p. 1986. 129.75 (*3-8055-4155-4*) S Karger.

— Progress in Medical Virology, Vol. 34. (Illus.). x, 206p. 1987. 150.50 (*3-8055-4468-5*) S Karger.

— Progress in Medical Virology, Vol. 35. (Illus.). viii, 220p. 1988. 173.25 (*3-8055-4711-0*) S Karger.

— Progress in Medical Virology, Vol. 36. (Illus.). viii, 210p. 1989. 164.50 (*3-8055-4834-6*) S Karger.

— Progress in Medical Virology, Vol. 37. (Illus.). x, 250p. 1990. 197.50 (*3-8055-5077-4*) S Karger.

— Progress in Medical Virology, Vol. 39. (Illus.). x, 270p. 1992. 231.50 (*3-8055-5428-1*) S Karger.

— Progress in Medical Virology, Vol. 40. (Illus.). viii, 224p. 1993. 230.50 (*3-8055-5600-4*) S Karger.

— Viruses, Oncogenes & Cancer. (Progress in Medical Virology Ser.: Vol. 32). (Illus.). viii, 224p. 1985. 146.25 (*3-8055-3976-2*) S Karger.

Melnick, Joseph L., et al, eds. Viral Hepatitis in China: Problems & Control Strategies. (Monographs in Virology: Vol. 19). (Illus.). xii, 160p. 1991. 155.75 (*3-8055-5364-1*) S Karger.

Melnick, Joseph L. & Hummeler, K., eds. Progress in Medical Virology, Vol. 30. (Illus.). viii, 212p. 1984. 135.00 (*3-8055-3851-0*) S Karger.

Melnick, Joseph L. & Khan, N. C., eds. Human Immunodeficiency Virus: Innovative Techniques for Isolation & Identification of HIV & for Monitoring of AIDS Patients. (Monographs in Virology: Vol. 18). viii, 130p. 1990. 116.75 (*3-8055-5182-7*) S Karger.

Melnick, Joseph L. & Maupas, P., eds. Hepatitis B Virus & Primary Liver Cancer. (Progress in Medical Virology Ser.: Vol. 27). (Illus.). viii, 212p. 1981. 108.75 (*3-8055-1784-X*) S Karger.

Melnick, Joseph L., ed. see Becker, I.

Melnick, Joseph L., ed. see Hotchin, J.

Melnick, Joseph L., ed. see International Congress for Virology Staff.

Melnick, Joseph L., ed. see Lonberg-Holm, K. & Philipson, L.

Melnick, Joseph L., jt. ed. see Ras, V. Shalapati.

Melnick, Joseph L., ed. see Tinsley, T. W. & Harrap, K. A.

Melnick, Michael, et al, eds. Clinical Dysmorphology of Oral-Facial Structures. LC 81-19816. 543p. reprint ed. pap. 168.40 (*0-8357-7871-1*, 203628800002) Bks Demand.

Melnick, Michael & Jorgenson, Ronald, eds. Developmental Aspects of Craniofacial Dysmorphology. LC 79-2487. (Alan R. Liss Ser.: Vol. 15, No. 8). 1979. 19.00 (*0-685-42252-6*) March of Dimes.

Melnick, Michael S., et al. Managing Back Pain. (Orig.). 1989. pap. text 4.00 (*0-9616461-6-0*) Saunders Grp.

Melnick, Michael S., jt. auth. see Saunders, H. Duane.

Melnick, Mimi. Manhole Covers. (Illus.). 272p. 1994. 45.00 (*0-262-13302-4*) MIT Pr.

— Manhole Covers. (Illus.). 274p. 1996. pap. text 22.50 (*0-262-63174-1*) MIT Pr.

Melnick, R. Shep. Between the Lines: Interpreting Welfare Rights. 344p. (C). 1994. 42.95 (*0-8157-5664-X*); pap. 18.95 (*0-8157-5663-1*) Brookings.

— Regulation & the Courts: The Case of the Clean Air Act. LC 83-7694. 404p. 1983. 36.95 (*0-8157-5662-3*); pap. 16.95 (*0-8157-5661-5*) Brookings.

Melnick, Ralph. The Life & Work of Ludwig Lewisohn Vol. 1: "A Touch of Wildness" LC 97-36411. (Illus.). 752p. 1998. 39.95 (*0-8143-2692-7*) Wayne St U Pr.

— The Stolen Legacy of Anne Frank: Meyer Levin, Lillian Hellman, & the Staging of the Diary. LC 96-46853. (Illus.). 268p. 1997. 30.00 (*0-300-06907-3*) Yale U Pr.

Melnick, Robert, jt. auth. see Alanen, Arnold R.

Melnick, S. L., et al. A Guide for Epidemiological Studies of Oral Manifestations of HIV Infection. (ENG, FRE & SPA.). ix, 27p. 1993. pap. text 9.00 (*92-4-154453-8*, 1150399) World Health.

***Melnick, Sharon M. & Bassuk, Ellen L.** Identifying & Responding to Violence Among Poor & Homeless Women. (Illus.). 42p. 1999. pap. text. write for info. (*0-9672165-1-6*) Bettr Homes Fund.

Melnick, Shep, jt. ed. see Keller, Morton.

***Melnick, Steven A.** Quality Control of Home Schooling in Pennsylvania. Shoop, Diane E., ed. 32p. 1999. pap. 20.00 (*1-58036-137-4*) Penn State Data Ctr.

Melnick, Vijaya L. & Dubler, Nancy N., eds. Alzheimer's Dementia: Dilemmas in Clinical Research. LC 85-11740. (Contemporary Issues in Biomedicine, Ethics, & Society Ser.). 312p. 1985. 69.50 (*0-89603-067-9*) Humana.

Melnicoe, William B. & Mennig, Jan. Elements of Police Supervision. 2nd ed. 336p. (C). 1978. text 57.00 (*0-02-476000-5*, Macmillan Coll) P-H.

Melnik, Arie, jt. auth. see Allen, Bruce T.

Melnik, Jan. How to Start a Home-Based Resume Service. 2nd rev. ed. LC 98-16496. (How to Start a Home-Based Business Ser.). (Illus.). 288p. 1997. pap. 17.95 (*0-7627-0068-8*) Globe Pequot.

— How to Start a Home-Based Secretarial Services Business. 3rd ed. LC 99-41011. (How to Start a Home-Based Business Ser.). (Illus.). 336p. 1999. pap. text 17.95 (*0-7627-0515-9*) Globe Pequot.

***Melnik, Milan, et al.** Crystallographic & Structural Analysis of Iron Carbonyls. 176p. 2000. lib. bdg. 89.00 (*1-56072-827-2*) Nova Sci Pubs.

Melnik, Peg, jt. auth. see Fish, Tim.

Melnikoff, Pamela. Plots & Players. LC 96-3777. (Illus.). (J). (gr. 3 up). 1996. pap. 9.95 (*0-8276-0576-5*) JPS Phila.

— The Star & the Sword. LC 94-5813. (Illus.). 140p. (J). (gr. 3 up). 1994. pap. 8.95 (*0-8276-0528-5*) JPS Phila.

Melnikoff, Tatyana, ed. & intro. see Kesey, Ken, et al.

***Mel'nikov, A. V.** Financial Markets: Stochastic Analysis & the Pricing of Derivative Securities. LC 99-17735. (Translations of Mathematical Monographs: Vol. 184). xiv, 133p. 1999. 49.00 (*0-8218-1082-0*) Am Math.

Melnikov, G. P. Systemology & Linguistic Aspects of Cybernetics. (Studies in Cybernetics: Vol. 16). xvi, 440p. 1988. text 527.00 (*2-88124-665-6*) Gordon & Breach.

Melnikov, I. A. The Sea Ice Ecosystem. 221p. 1997. text 49.00 (*2-919875-04-3*) Gordon & Breach.

Melnikov, Mya & Smirnov, V. A. Handbook of Photochemistry of Organic Radicals: Absorption & Emission Properties, Mechanisms, Aging. LC 96-34050. 1996. write for info. (*1-56700-071-1*) Begell Hse.

Melnikov, O., et al. Exercises in Graph Theory. LC 97-46594. (Texts in the Mathematical Sciences Ser.). 354p. 1998. lib. bdg. 149.00 (*0-7923-4906-7*) Kluwer Academic.

Melnikov, V. M. & Koshelev, V. A. Large Space Structures Formed by Centrifugal Forces. (Earth Space Institute Book Ser.: Vol. 4). 164p. 1998. text 39.00 (*90-5699-112-4*, ECU55, Harwood Acad Pubs) Gordon & Breach.

Melnikov, Yuri A. Green's Functions in Applied Mechanics. 288p. 1995. 130.00 (*1-85312-387-0*) Computational Mech MA.

Melnikov, Yuri A. Green's Functions Method in Applied Mechanics. LC 95-68892. (Topics in Engineering Ser.: Vol. 27). 288p. 1995. 130.00 (*1-56252-311-2*, 3870) Computational Mech MA.

— Influence Functions & Matrices. LC 98-45743. (Mechanical Engineering Ser.: No. 119). (Illus.). 488p. 1998. text 185.00 (*0-8247-1941-7*) Dekker.

Melnikova, A. M., jt. auth. see Givargizov, E. I.

Melnikova-Levigne, Sonia, jt. auth. see Soltes, Ori Z.

Melnychuk, Taras. From Behind Prison Bars. LC 82-50025. (Ukrainian Ser.). 83p. 1982. pap. 3.25 (*0-914834-48-7*) Smoloskyp.

Melnyczuk, Askold, ed. Agni: Issue Focuses on State Control & the Arts. 322p. (C). 1990. write for info. (*0-318-66933-1*) New Cambrdge.

— Agni: The Used World. 312p. (Orig.). (C). 1989. pap. write for info. (*0-318-66934-X*) New Cambrdge.

Melnyczuk, Askold, ed. see Aizenberg, Susan, et al.

Melnyczuk, Askold, ed. see Barber, Jennifer, et al.

Melnyczuk, Askold, ed. see Ellis, Thomas S., et al.

Melnyk. Apple, Computer Masters. (DF - Computer Applications Ser.). 1992. pap. write for info. (*0-314-00527-7*) S-W Pub.

Melnyk. Clarisworks 4.0: Computer Skill resource Guide. 2nd ed. (Computer Applications). 1997. pap. 28.25 (*0-314-13011-X*) West Pub.

— Microsoft Works 4.0 for Mac: Computer Skill Resource Guide. 2nd ed. (Computer Applications). 1997. pap. 28.25 (*0-314-13009-8*) West Pub.

— Microsoft Office for Windows: Skills Resource Guide. 2nd ed. (Computer Applications). 1998. pap. 28.25 (*0-314-13005-5*) West Pub.

An Asterisk (*) at the beginning of an entry indicates that the title is appearing for the first time.

— Microsoft Works 3.0 Windows 3.0: Computer Skills Resource Guide. 2nd ed. (Computer Applications). 1997. pap. 28.25 (*0-314-13007-1*) West Pub.

Melnyk. Operational Management. 1996. teacher ed. 49.06 (*0-256-23010-2*) McGraw.

Melnyk & Hardman. Computers: Tools for Today, Apple. (DF - Computer Applications Ser.). 1992. 46.50 (*0-314-91176-6*) West Pub.

— Integrator, Computer Literacy System. (DC - Introduction to Computing Ser.). (C). 1993. mass mkt. 28.25 (*0-314-00526-9*) West Pub.

Melnyk, Doug. Naked Croquet. 1997. pap. 7.95 (*0-88801-122-9*, Pub. by Turnstone Pr) Genl Dist Srvs.

Melnyk, Eugenie. My Darling Elia. LC 99-13110. 278p. 1999. text 23.95 (*0-312-20565-1*) St Martin.

Melnyk, George. Beyond Alienation: Political Essays on the West. 122p. (Orig.). 1993. pap. text 13.95 (*1-55059-060-X*) Temeron Bks.

— The Search for Community: From Utopia to a Cooperative Society. 170p. 1985. 45.99 (*0-920057-53-5*, Pub. by Black Rose); pap. 16.99 (*0-920057-52-7*, Pub. by Black Rose) Consort Bk Sales.

Melnyk, George, jt. ed. see Quarter, Jack.

Melnyk, Julie, ed. Women's Theology in Nineteenth-Century Britain: Transfiguring the Faith of Their Fathers. LC 97-34074. (Literature & Society in Victorian Britain Ser.: Vol. 3). 264p. 1997. text 60.00 (*0-8153-2793-5*, H2055) Garland.

Melnyk, Steven. Operations Management: Study Guide. 192p. (C). 1996. text 26.25 (*0-256-23009-9*, Irwn McGrw-H) McGrw-H Hghr Educ.

Melnyk, Steven & Narasimhan, Ram. Computer Integrated Manufacturing: A Source Book. 344p. 1990. 49.95 (*1-55822-051-8*) Am Prod & Inventory.

Melnyk, Steven A. & Carter, Phillip L. Production Activity Control: A Practical Guide. (APICS Series in Production Management). 200p. 1987. text 47.50 (*0-87094-970-5*, Irwn Prfssnl) McGraw-Hill Prof.

— Shop Floor Control Principles & Practices & Case Studies. LC 87-72180. 535p. 1987. pap. text 60.00 (*0-935406-95-6*) Am Prod & Inventory.

Melnyk, Steven A. & Denzler, David. Operations Management: A Value Driven Approach. 962p. (C). 1996. text 73.75 (*0-256-12381-0*, Irwn McGrw-H) McGrw-H Hghr Educ.

Melnyk, Steven A., et al. Shop Floor Control. LC 85-70568. 1985. text 47.50 (*0-87094-628-5*, Irwn Prfssnl) McGraw-Hill Prof.

Melo, Carlos A. De, see De Melo, Carlos A.

Melo, Dias De, see De Melo, Dias.

Melo, Esperanca, jt. auth. see Lewis, Amanda.

Melo, Gloria. A Minha Mao Esquerda: Poemas. unabridged ed. Peregrinacao Publications Staff, ed. (Poetry/ Poesia Ser.: No. 5). (POR.). 96p. 1998. boxed set 12.00 (*1-889358-14-2*, 10) Peregrinacao.

Melo, Ireneia, jt. auth. see Telleria, M. Teresa.

Melo, L. F., et al, eds. Biofilms - Science & Technology. LC 92-34848. (NATO Advanced Study Institutes Series E, Applied Sciences: Vol. 223). 1992. text 363.00 (*0-7923-2022-0*) Kluwer Academic.

— Fouling Science & Technology. (C). 1988. text 380.00 (*90-247-3729-X*) Kluwer Academic.

Melo-Mart In, Inmaculada De Staff. Making Babies: Biomedical Technologies, Reproductive Ethics, & Public Policy. LC 98-20219. 1998. write for info. (*0-7923-5116-9*) Kluwer Academic.

Melo Neto, Joao Cabral De, see Cabral De Melo Neto, Joao.

***Melo, Patricia.** In Praise of Lies. Landers, Clifford E., tr. 192p. 1999. 13.95 (*1-58234-058-7*) Bloomsbury Pubg.

Melo, Patricia. The Killer: A Psychological Thriller. Landers, Clifford, tr. LC 97-22948. 192p. 1997. text 23.00 (*0-88001-574-8*) HarpC.

— The Killer: A Psychological Thriller. Landers, Clifford E., tr. 217p. 1999. reprint ed. pap. 14.00 (*0-88001-608-6*) HarpC.

Melo, Welington De, see De Melo, Welington.

Meloan. The International Global Market. 3rd ed. 2000. 45.25 (*0-07-231473-7*) McGraw.

Meloan, jt. auth. see James.

Meloan, Becky, jt. auth. see Bryant, Kim.

Meloan, C. E., ed. Pesticides Laboratory Training Manual. (Illus.). xviii, 484p. 1996. pap. 79.00 (*0-935584-60-9*) AOAC Intl.

***Meloan, Clifton E.** Chemical Separations: Principles, Techniques & Experiments. LC 99-36208. 752p. 1999. 99.95 (*0-471-35197-0*) Wiley.

Meloan, Clifton E. Instrumental Analysis Using Spectroscopy. LC 68-20179. (Medical Technology Ser.: No. 1). 178p. reprint ed. pap. 55.20 (*0-608-10187-7*, 205034900063) Bks Demand.

Meloan, Clifton E., jt. auth. see Pomeranz, Y.

Meloan, Taylor W. & Graham, John L. International & Global Marketing: Concepts & Cases. 2nd ed. LC 97-5424. (C). 1997. text. write for info. (*0-256-21894-3*, Irwn Prfssnl) McGraw-Hill Prof.

Meloan, Taylor W. & Graham, John L., eds. International & Global Marketing: Concepts & Cases. LC 94-17867. (Series in Marketing). 640p. (C). 1994. text 48.95 (*0 256 15723-5*, Irwn McGrw-H) McGrw-H Hghr Educ.

Melocarro, Lynne, ed. see Johnson, Samuel & Knight, Ellis C.

Meloche, Joseph. Introductory CD-ROM Searching: The Key to Effective Ondisc Searching. LC 92-44616. (Illus.). 205p. 1994. lib. bdg. 49.95 (*1-56024-412-7*) Haworth Pr.

Meloche, Renee, jt. auth. see DeTellis, Jeanne.

Melodia, Thomas V., jt. auth. see Malinowski, Stanley B.

Melody. Love Is in the Earth - Kaleidoscopic Pictorial Supplement Z. Augustine, Leodeciae, ed. (Illus.). 384p. 1998. pap. 18.95 (*0-9628190-5-0*) Earth-Love Pub Hse.

***Melody.** Teaching America About Sex. 1999. pap. text 18.50 (*0-8147-5619-0*) NYU Pr.

Melody, A. Love Is in the Earth - A Kaleidoscope of Crystals Update: The Reference Book Describing the Metaphysical Properties of the Mineral Kingdom. Jackson, R. R., ed. LC 94-61710. (Illus.). 728p. (Orig.). 1995. pap. 18.95 (*0-9628190-3-4*) Earth-Love Pub Hse.

Melody, A. Love Is in the Earth - Kaleidoscopic Pictorial: Supplement A. LC 96-86276. (Illus.). 384p. (Orig.). 1996. pap. 18.95 (*0-9628190-7-7*) Earth-Love Pub Hse.

Melody, A. Love Is in the Earth - Laying-on-of-Stones: The Journey Continues. Jackson, R. R. & Augustine, L., eds. LC 91-771320. (Illus.). 273p. (Orig.). 1992. pap. 12.95 (*0-9628190-1-8*) Earth-Love Pub Hse.

— Love Is in the Earth - Mineralogical Pictorial: Treasures of the Earth. Jackson, Bob, ed. LC 93-73772. (Illus.). 416p. (Orig.). 1994. pap. 27.95 (*0-9628190-2-6*) Earth-Love Pub Hse.

Melody Beattie. The Language of Letting Go: 365 Daily Reflections from Melody Beattie. 366p. 1999. 9.95 (*1-56838-325-8*) Hazelden.

Melody, David, tr. see Bak, Samuel.

Melody, Laura, jt. auth. see Killingsworth, Paul S.

Melody, M. E. & Peterson, Linda M. Teaching America about Sex: Marriage Guides & Sex Manuals from the Late Victorians to Dr. Ruth. LC 99-6300. 287p. 1999. 28.95 (*0-8147-5532-1*) NYU Pr.

Melody, William H. Children's Television: The Economics of Exploitation. LC 73-80079. 176p. reprint ed. pap. 54.60 (*0-8357-8069-4*, 203382500087) Bks Demand.

Melodyev, Martin. Shliuz. LC 98-48569. (RUS.). 88p. 1998. pap. write for info. (*1-55779-116-3*) Hermitage Pubs.

Meloe, Torleif. United States Control of Petroleum Imports: A Study of the Federal Government's Role in the Management of Domestic Oil Supplies. Bruchey, Stuart, ed. LC 78-22701. (Energy in the American Economy Ser.). (Illus.). 1979. lib. bdg. 28.95 (*0-405-12003-6*) Ayer.

Meloen, Jos, jt. auth. see Farnen, Russell F.

Melograno, Vincent J. Designing the Physical Education Curriculum. 3rd ed. LC 95-20773. (Illus.). 288p. (C). 1995. text 35.00 (*0-87322-525-2*, BMEL0525) Human Kinetics.

— Professional & Student Portfolios for Physical Education. LC 97-45626. (Illus.). 208p. 1998. pap. text 22.00 (*0-88011-809-1*, BMEL0809) Human Kinetics.

Melograno, Vincent J. & Klinzing, James E. An Orientation to Total Fitness. 5th ed. 240p. 1993. per. 19.95 (*0-8403-6745-7*) Kendall-Hunt.

Melohn, Tom. The New Partnership: A Straight-Talking Guide to Bringing Out the Best in People at Work. 265p. 1996. pap. 14.95 (*0-471-14738-9*) Wiley.

Melon & Laguerre, Enrique A. El Jibaro de Puerto Rico. 1968. 14.95 (*0-87751-007-5*) E Torres & Sons.

Melon, jt. auth. see Rosa-Nieves.

Melon Diaz, Esther. La Narrativa De Marta Brunet. (UPREX, Literarios Ser.: No. 41). 272p. (C). 1975. pap. 1.50 (*0-8477-0041-0*) U of PR Pr.

Melon, Ester & Laguerre, Enrique A. The Jibaro in Puerto Rico: Symbol & Figure. (Puerto Rico Ser.). 1979. 59.95 (*0-8490-2951-1*) Gordon Pr.

Melonakos, C. M. Tracting Made Easy. 48p. 1987. pap. 3.95 (*0-9616024-1-4*) Paramount Bks.

Melonakos, Christine. Turn Your Little Ones into Book of Mormon Whiz Kids. LC 90-85979. 167p. (Orig.). 1991. pap. 15.98 (*0-88290-407-8*) Horizon Utah.

Melonakos, Kathleen. Saunders Pocket Reference for Nurses. 2nd ed. LC 94-20443. (Illus.). 733p. 1994. pap. text 24.00 (*0-7216-4459-7*, W B Saunders Co) Harcrt Hlth Sci Grp.

Melone, Albert P. Creating Parliamentary Government: The Transition to Democracy in Bulgaria. LC 98-16298. (Parliaments & Legislatures Ser.). (Illus.). 350p. 1998. text 50.00 (*0-8142-0769-3*, MELCRE); pap. text 21.95 (*0-8142-0770-7*, MELCRX) Ohio St U Pr.

— Researching Constitution Law. 224p. (C). 1997. pap. text 44.00 (*0-673-52086-2*) Addson-Wesley Educ.

***Melone, Albert P.** Researching Constitutional Law. 2nd ed. 243p. 2000. pap. 17.95 (*1-57766-140-0*) Waveland Pr.

Melone, Albert P. & Mace, George. Judicial Review & American Democracy. LC 88-634. 303p. 1988. reprint ed. pap. 94.00 (*0-608-00146-5*, 206092700006) Bks Demand.

Melone, Albert P., et al. North Dakota Lawyers: Mapping the Socio-Political Dimensions. LC 75-4047. (Publisher's Social Science Report: No. 1). (Illus.). 54p. 1975. pap. 1.75 (*0-911042-20-2*) NDSU Inst Reg.

Melone, Joseph J. Collectively Bargained Multi-Employer Pension Plans. (C). 1963. 11.50 (*0-256-00654-7*, Irwn McGrw-H) McGrw-H Hghr Educ.

Melone, Mark. The Mystery Believed, Pt. 1. LC 96-77418. (Light for Life Ser.). 112p. (Orig.). 1995. pap. text 10.00 (*1-887158-07-3*) God With Us.

— The Mystery Celebrated. LC 96-77418. (Light for Life Ser.: Pt. 2). 108p. (Orig.). 1996. pap. 10.00 (*1-887158-09-X*) God With Us.

Melone, Mary A. & Parik, Carol. Low Fat Great Tasting Kids' Snacks: Healthy & Delicious Recipes. (Cooking Books for Children: Vol. 5). (Illus.). 96p. (J). (gr. 3-8). 1996. lib. bdg. 18.95 (*1-56674-177-7*, HTS Bks) Forest Hse.

Meloney, Jim. Distributed COM Application Development Using Visual Basic 6.0. LC 99-24599. (Illus.). 720p. 1999. pap. text 49.99 incl. audio compact disk (*0-13-021343-8*) P-H.

Meloni, Alberto C., ed. see Kavasch, E. Barrie.

Meloni, C., et al. Say the Right Thing! 1982. pap. text 15.76 (*0-201-10205-6*) Addison-Wesley.

Meloni, Francesco. Severini's Graphic Work. limited ed. (ITA., Illus.). 218p. 1982. 275.00 (*1-55660-001-1*) A Wofsy Fine Arts.

Meloni, Franco, jt. auth. see Fiorentini, Vincenzo.

***Meloni, Julie.** PHP Essentials. 400p. 2000. pap. 39.99 (*0-7615-2729-X*, Prima Tech) Prima Pub.

Melonio, Francoise. Tocqueville & the French. Raps, Beth G., tr. from FRE. LC 97-33328.Tr. of Tocqueville & les Francais. 352p. 1998. text 37.50 (*0-8139-1778-6*) U Pr of Va.

Melore, Philip M. Your Personal PLC Tutor - A Guide to Understanding PLCs. (Illus.). 96p. 1998. spiral bd. 29.95 (*0-9664859-0-4*) P Melore.

Melosh, Barbara. Engendering Culture: Manhood & Womanhood in New Deal Public Art & Theater. LC 90-9948. (New Directions in American Art Ser.). (Illus.). 312p. (C). 1991. pap. text 27.95 (*0-87474-721-X*) Smithsonian.

— Engendering Culture: Manhood & Womanhood in New Deal Public Art & Theater. LC 90-9948. (New Directions in American Art Ser.). (Illus.). 312p. (C). 1991. text 65.00 (*0-87474-720-1*) Smithsonian.

— Physician's Hand. (C). 1982. pap. text 22.95 (*0-87722-290-8*) Temple U Pr.

Melosh, Barbara, ed. Gender & American History since 1890. LC 92-20212. (Rewriting Histories Ser.). (Illus.). 320p. (C). 1993. pap. 24.99 (*0-415-07676-5*, A7389) Routledge.

Melosh, H. J. Impact Cratering: A Geologic Process. (Monographs on Geology & Geophysics: No. 11). (Illus.). 256p. (C). 1996. pap. text 45.00 (*0-19-510463-3*) OUP.

Melosh, H. J., ed. Origins of Planets & Life. LC 98-110021. 354p. 1997. pap. 15.00 (*0-8243-2098-0*) Annual Reviews.

Melosh, Robert J. Structural Engineering Analysis by Finite Elements. 384p. 1990. boxed set 53.00 (*0-13-855701-2*) P-H.

Melosi, Martin V. Coping with Abundances. (C). 1985. pap. text 23.74 (*0-07-554666-3*) McGraw.

***Melosi, Martin V.** Sanitary City: Urban Infrastructure in America from Colonial Times to the Present. LC 99-29417. (Creating the North American Landscape Ser.). 608p. 1999. 59.95 (*0-8018-6152-7*) Johns Hopkins.

Melosi, Martin V. Thomas A. Edison & the Modernization of America. 221p. (C). 1997. pap. 19.00 (*0-673-39625-8*) Addson-Wesley Educ.

Melosi, Martin V., ed. Urban Public Policy: Historical Modes & Methods. LC 93-15358. (Issues in Policy History Se.: No. 3). 206p. 1993. pap. 16.95 (*0-271-01093-2*) Pa St U Pr.

Melosi, Martin V. & Scarpino, Philip, eds. Public History & the Environment. 2000. write for info. (*1-57524-071-8*) Krieger.

Melossi, Dario, ed. The Sociology of Punishment. LC 97-30505. (International Library of Criminology, Criminal Justice & Penology). (Illus.). 524p. 1997. text 193.95 (*1-85521-799-6*, Pub. by Ashgate Pub) Ashgate Pub Co.

Melot, Michel. Chateaux of the Loire. (Evergreen Ser.). 1997. 29.99 (*3-8228-8256-9*) Taschen Amer.

— The Impressionist Print. Beamish, Caroline, tr. from FRE. LC 95-50606. (Illus.). 296p. 1996. 70.00 (*0-300-06792-5*) Yale U Pr.

Melott, Ronald K. Is Energy Conservation Firesafe? 1978. 2.50 (*0-686-12081-7*, TR 78-8) Society Fire Protect.

Melouk, H. A. & Shokes, F. M., eds. Peanut Health Management. LC 95-76524. (Health Management Ser.). (Illus.). 137p. (Orig.). 1995. pap. 55.00 (*0-89054-203-1*) Am Phytopathol Soc.

Meloun, Milan, et al. Chemometrics For Analyhtical Chemistry Vol. 1: PC-Aided Statistical Data Analysis. 500p. (C). 1992. 75.00 (*0-13-126376-5*) P-H.

Meloy, Betty T. Idaho Museum Guide. (Illus.). 72p. (Orig.). 1989. pap. 5.95 (*0-9623630-0-6*) B T Meloy.

Meloy, Ellen. The Last Cheater's Waltz: Beauty & Violence in the Desert Southwest. LC 98-30325. 229p. 1999. 23.00 (*0-8050-4065-X*) H Holt & Co.

— Raven's Exile. 1995. write for info. (*0-8050-2497-2*) H Holt & Co.

— Raven's Exile: A Season on the Green River. (Illus.). 272p. 1995. pap. 12.95 (*0-8050-3807-8*, Owl) H Holt & Co.

Meloy, Glenn R., ed. Innovative Powerhouse Design: Proceedings of a Session Sponsored by the Energy Division. 42p. 1985. 3.00 (*0-87262-505-2*) Am Soc Civil Eng.

Meloy, J. Reid. The Psychopathic Mind: Origins, Dynamics, & Treatment. LC 88-3454. 496p. 1988. 60.00 (*0-87668-922-5*) Aronson.

— Violent Attachments. LC 92-10469. 392p. 1997. pap. 50.00 (*0-7657-0061-1*) Aronson.

Meloy, J. Reid, ed. The Psychology of Stalking. LC 98-84369. (Illus.). xvii, 327p. (C). 1998. text 59.95 (*0-12-490560-9*) Acad Pr.

Meloy, J. Reid, et al, eds. Contemporary Rorschach Interpretation: A Casebook. LC 96-49872. (Personlity & Clinical Psychology Ser.). 450p. 1997. 49.50 (*0-8058-1920-7*) L Erlbaum Assocs.

Meloy, J. Reid, et al. Clinical Guidelines for Involuntary Outpatient Treatment. Smith, Harold H., Jr., ed. LC 89-43652. (Practitioner's Resource Ser.). 78p. (Orig.). 1990. pap. 16.45 (*0-943158-45-1*, CGIBP) Pro Resource.

Meloy, J. Reid, jt. auth. see Gacono, Carl B.

Meloy, Judith. Writing the Qualitative Dissertation: Understanding by Doing. 128p. 1994. text 29.95 (*0-8058-1416-7*) L Erlbaum Assocs.

— Writing the Qualitative Dissertation: Understanding by Doing. 128p. 1994. pap. 14.95 (*0-8058-1417-5*) L Erlbaum Assocs.

Melrose, jt. auth. see Brown.

Melrose, A. R. The Pooh Dictionary: The Complete Guide to the Words of Pooh & All the Animals in the Forest. LC 95-6033. (Illus.). 252p. (J). (gr. 4 up). 1995. 18.99 (*0-525-45395-4*, Dutton Child) Peng Put Young Read.

Melrose Abbey Staff. Chronica De Mailros. Stephenson, Joseph, ed. LC 73-172721. (Bannatyne Club, Edinburgh. Publications: No. 49). reprint ed. 37.50 (*0-404-52759-0*) AMS Pr.

— Liber Sancte Marie de Melros, 2 vols. Innes, Cosmo N., ed. LC 77-172722. (Bannatyne Club, Edinburgh, Publications: No. 56). reprint ed. 115.00 (*0-404-52910-0*) AMS Pr.

Melrose, Andres, jt. auth. see Brown, Brian.

Melrose, Andrew. Sink or Swim. (Storykeepers Juvenile Ser.: Bk. 5). (Illus.). 64p. (J). (gr. 2-5). 1997. pap. 3.99 (*0-310-20341-4*) Zondervan.

— Sink or Swim. (Storykeepers Easy Reader Ser.: Bk. 5). (J). (ps-3). 1997. pap. 3.99 (*0-310-20343-0*) Zondervan.

— Starlight Escape. (Storykeepers Juvenile Ser.: Bk. 6). (Illus.). 64p. (J). (gr. 2-5). 1997. pap. 3.99 (*0-310-20337-6*) Zondervan.

Melrose, Andrew & Brown, Brian. Story Keepers Raging Waters. (Storykeepers Ser.: Vol. 2). (J). 1995. 14.99 incl. VHS (*0-310-20579-4*) Zondervan.

Melrose, Andrew, jt. adapted by see Brown, Brian.

Melrose, Andrew, jt. auth. see Brown, Brian.

Melrose, D. B. Instabilities in Space & Laboratory Plasmas. (Illus.). 288p. 1986. text 80.00 (*0-521-30541-1*) Cambridge U Pr.

— Plasma Astrophysics: Nonthermal Processes in Diffuse Magnetized Plasm: Astrophysical Applications, 2 vols., Vol. 2. 714p. 1980. text 600.00 (*0-677-03490-3*) Gordon & Breach.

— Plasma Astrophysics Vol. 1: Nonthermal Processes in Diffuse Magnetized Plasmas: The Emission, Absorption & Transfer of Waves in Plasmas. x, 270p. 1980. text 335.00 (*0-677-02340-5*) Gordon & Breach.

Melrose, Dianna. Bitter Pills: Medicines & the Third World Poor. (Illus.). 277p. (C). 1982. pap. 18.50 (*0-85598-065-6*, Pub. by Oxfam Pub) Stylus Pub VA.

— Nicaragua: The Threat of a Good Example? 80p. (C). 1985. pap. text 30.00 (*0-85598-070-2*, Pub. by Oxfam Pubns) St Mut.

Melrose, Donald B. & McPhedran, R. C. Electromagnetic Processes in Dispersive Media. (Illus.). 431p. (C). 1991. text 115.00 (*0-521-41025-8*) Cambridge U Pr.

Melrose, Georgiana. A Strange Occupation. 128p. 1989. 30.00 (*0-7223-2200-3*, Pub. by A H S Ltd) St Mut.

Melrose, Jennifer. To a Good Home Only. 230p. 1987. 70.00 (*1-85200-009-0*, Pub. by United Writers Pubns) St Mut.

Melrose, John & Melrose, Krisan K. BUCOMCO: A Business Communication Simulation. 2nd ed. LC 93-38289. 1993. write for info. (*1-56118-530-2*) Paradigm MN.

Melrose, Ken. Making the Grass Greener on Your Side: A CEO's Journey to Leading by Serving. LC 95-34423. (Illus.). 250p. 1995. 24.95 (*1-881052-21-4*) Berrett-Koehler.

Melrose, Krisan K., jt. auth. see Melrose, John.

Melrose, Margaret, jt. auth. see Dean, Hartley.

Melrose Press Staff. International Who's Who in Music: Popular Music, Vol. 2. 2nd ed. 1998. 175.00 (*0-948875-97-6*) Taylor & Francis.

Melrose, Richard. The Atiyah-Patodi-Singer Index Theorem. LC 93-1405. (Research Notes in Mathematics Ser.). (Illus.). 392p. (C). 1993. text 66.00 (*1-56881-002-4*) AK Peters.

Melrose, Richard B. Geometric Scattering Theory. (Stanford Lectures: No. 1). (Illus.). 130p. (C). 1995. text 54.95 (*0-521-49673-X*); pap. text 16.95 (*0-521-49810-4*) Cambridge U Pr.

Melrose, Robin. The Communicative Syllabus: A Systematic Functional Approach to Language Teaching. 224p. 1992. text 59.00 (*0-86187-137-5*, Pub. by P P Pubs) Cassell & Continuum.

— Communicative Syllabus: A Systemic-Functional Approach to Language. 1995. pap. 22.95 (*1-85567-341-X*) St Martin.

Melrose, Susan. A Semiotics of the Dramatic Text. LC 93-17914. (New Directions in Theatre Ser.). 1994. text 45.00 (*0-312-10086-8*) St Martin.

Mels, Reinhard, jt. auth. see Lane, Gerd R.

Melsa, James L. & Sage, Andrew P. An Introduction to Probability & Stochastic Processes. (Illus.). 448p. 1973. pap. text 54.00 (*0-13-034850-3*) P-H.

Melsa, James L., jt. auth. see Gibson, Jerry D.

Melsen, Birte, ed. Current Controversies in Orthodontics. (Illus.). 314p. 1991. text 99.00 (*0-86715-174-9*) Quint Pub Co.

Melson, et al. Maternal-Infant Care Planning. 3rd ed. LC 98-36726. 368p. 1998. 34.95 (*0-87434-951-6*) Springhouse Corp.

Melson, Brenda K. Runaway Adolescents: A Family Systems Perspective. rev. ed. LC 95-25280. (Children of Poverty Ser.). 132p. 1995. text 46.00 (*0-8153-2334-4*) Garland.

Melson, Charles D. Condition Red: Marine Defense Battalions in World War II. (Illus.). 33p. (Orig.). 1996. pap. text 20.00 (*0-7881-3529-5*) DIANE Pub.

— U. S. Marine in Vietnam, 1965-1974. (Illus.). 64p. 1996. pap. 12.95 (*1-85532-542-X*, Pub. by Ospry) Stackpole.

— Up the Slot: Marines in the Central Solomons. (Illus.). 37p. 1996. pap. text 25.00 (*0-7881-3522-8*) DIANE Pub.

— Vietnam Marines, 1965-73. (Elite Ser.: No. 43). (Illus.). 64p. pap. 12.95 (*1-85532-251-X*, 9458, Pub. by Ospry) Stackpole.

— The War That Would Not End: U. S. Marines in Vietnam - 1971-73. LC 97-42531. Orig. Title: U. S. Marines in Vietnam: The War That Would Not End. 378p. 1999. pap. 19.95 (*1-55571-420-X*, Hellgate Pr) PSI Resch.

M

An Asterisk (*) at the beginning of an entry indicates that the title is appearing for the first time.

M

Melson, Chuck & Applegate, Rex. The Close Combat Files of Colonel Rex Applegate. LC 99-186257. (Illus.). 208p. 1998. 39.95 (*0-87364-998-2*) Paladin Pr.

***Melson, Dave.** In Search of Druid Gold. (Illus.). 122p. 2000. pap. write for info. (*0-7541-0507-5*, Pub. by Minerva Pr) Unity Dist.

Melson, Gail F., jt. ed. see Fogel, Alan.

Melson, Gordon A. & Figgis, Brian N., eds. Transition Metal Chemistry, Vol. 9. fac. ed. LC 65-27431. 320p. 1985. pap. 99.20 (*0-7837-8638-7*, 202712700009) Bks Demand.

— Transition Metal Chemistry, 1982, Vol. 8. LC 65-27431. (Illus.). 478p. 1982. reprint ed. pap. 148.20 (*0-7837-0915-3*, 204122000008) Bks Demand.

Melson, James. The Golden Boy. LC 91-36061. 230p. 1992. pap. 14.95 (*1-56023-015-0*, Harrington Park); lib. bdg. 54.95 (*1-56024-243-4*, Harrington Park) Haworth Pr.

Melson, Kathryn A. Practice Problems for Dosage Calculations. 1991. pap., teacher ed. 11.00 (*0-8273-4401-5*) Delmar.

Melson, Kathryn A. & Jaffe, Maries S. Pediatric & Post Partum Home Health Nursing: Assessment & Care Planning. (Illus.). 496p. (C). (gr. 13). 1996. spiral bd. 29.95 (*0-8151-4876-3*, 25760) Mosby Inc.

***Melson, Robert.** False Papers: Deception & Survival in the Holocaust. 232p. 2000. 26.95 (*0-252-02594-6*) U of Ill Pr.

Melson, Robert. Revolution & Genocide: On the Origins of the Armenian Genocide & the Holocaust. LC 91-47944. 386p. 1992. 32.50 (*0-226-51990-2*) U Ch Pr.

— Revolution & Genocide: On the Origins of the Armenian Genocide & the Holocaust. (Illus.). 364p. 1996. reprint ed. pap. text 16.95 (*0-226-51991-0*) U Ch Pr.

Melson, Tom. Using Maps & Globes. De Weese, Bob, ed. (People & Places Ser.). (Illus.). 31p. (J). (gr. 4-6). Date not set. pap., wbk. ed. 3.50 (*1-58610-130-7*) Learn Horizon.

Melson, William G., jt. auth. see Mason, Brian H.

Meltabarger, P. J. Baaz. (Illus.). 94p. (J). (gr. 4-7). 1996. 16.50 (*1-56763-188-6*) Ozark Pub.

— The Ballad of Padre Island, Vol. 1. Samuelson, Arnold & Samuelson, Billie, eds. (Illus.). 28p. (Orig.). (J). (gr. 1-5). 1987. pap. text 3.95 (*0-923133-00-3*) JM Pub.

— The Karankawa Indians, Pt. 2. Samuelson, Arnold & Samuelson, Billie, eds. (Ballad of Padre Island Ser.). (Illus.). 28p. (Orig.). (J). (gr. 1-5). 1988. pap. text 3.95 (*0-923133-01-1*) JM Pub.

— Livingston: The Pedigreed Pooch of Padre Island. Samuelson, Arnold & Samuelson, Billie, eds. (Illus.). 150p. (YA). (gr. 7-10). 1988. 19.95 (*0-923133-02-X*) JM Pub.

— Prince Leapinhigh. 26p. (J). (ps). 1996. 12.95 (*1-56763-173-8*); pap. text 3.95 (*1-56763-172-X*) Ozark Pub.

— Princess Tappintoe. 21p. (J). (ps). 1996. 12.95 (*1-56763-175-4*); pap. text 3.95 (*1-56763-174-6*) Ozark Pub.

Melter, Robert A., et al, eds. Vision Geometry VII, Vol. 3454. 1998. 80.00 (*0-8194-2909-0*) SPIE.

— Vision Geometry V, Vol. 2826. 352p. 1996. 66.00 (*0-8194-2214-2*) SPIE.

— Vision Geometry VI, Vol. 3168. 402p. 1997. 80.00 (*0-8194-2590-7*) SPIE.

Meltesen, Clarence R. After the Battle...Ranger Evasion & Escape. (Illus.). 255p. 1997. pap. text 15.00 (*0-9627005-1-7*) C R Meltesen.

— Roads to Liberation from Oflag 64. 2nd ed. LC 90-91707. (Illus.). 535p. 1990. 20.00 (*0-9627005-0-9*) C R Meltesen.

Meltesen, Clarence R. & Garris, Herbert L. The Men of Oflag 64: August 1943-January 1945. LC 97-216462. 146p. 1997. pap. 20.00 (*0-9627005-2-5*) C R Meltesen.

Melton, A. C. The Mycota: A Comprehensive Treatise on Fungi As Experimental Systems for Basic & Applied Research, Vol. 2. Esser, Karl & Lemke, P. A., eds. 648p. 1995. 299.95 (*0-387-58003-4*) Spr-Verlag.

Melton, A. C., ed. Mathematical Foundations of Programming Semantics. (Lecture Notes in Computer Science Ser.: Vol. 239). vi, 395p. 1986. 42.00 (*0-387-16816-8*) Spr-Verlag.

***Melton, A. E.** Nitrox Mixing Handbook Vol. 1: U. S. Standard - Imperial. (Illus.). 304p. (C). 1999. 50.00 (*0-915539-05-5*, M-6116) IANTD.

— Nitrox Mixing Handbook Vol. 2: Metric. (Illus.). 192p. (C). 1999. 50.00 (*0-915539-06-3*, M-6117) IANTD.

Melton, Alan. Caring Beyond Words: The Power of Christian Symbols to Heal the Soul. LC 95-10837. 96p. 1997. pap. 11.00 (*1-57312-012-X*) Smyth & Helwys.

Melton, Arthur W. Problems of Installation in Museums of Art. Robinson, Edward S., ed. & intro. by. 276p. (C). 1996. reprint ed. pap. text 30.00 (*0-931201-25-X*) Am Assn Mus.

Melton, Arthur W., et al. Measuring Museum Based Learning: Experimental Studies of the Education of Children in a Museum of Science. (Illus.). 106p. 1996. reprint ed. pap. 13.50 (*0-931201-33-0*) Am Assn Mus.

Melton, Austin. Software Measurement: Understanding Software Engineering. 1995. mass mkt. 47.50 (*0-412-55180-2*) Chapman & Hall.

Melton, Buckner F., Jr. The First Impeachment: The Constitution's Framers & the Case of Senator William Blount. LC 98-9236. 400p. 1998. 40.00 (*0-86554-597-9*, H449) Mercer Univ Pr.

***Melton, Carol K.W.** Between War & Peace: Woodrow Wilson & the American Expeditionary Force in Siberia, 1918-1921. 2001. 39.95 (*0-86554-692-4*, H512) Mercer Univ Pr.

Melton, Carroll. 1999: The Crash of America. 300p. 1997. 22.95 (*0-943015-30-8*) Power Press.

Melton, Charles E. Ancient Diamond Time Capsules: Secrets of Life & the World. (Illus.). 167p. 1985. 9.95 (*0-9614901-0-1*); pap. 5.95 (*0-9614901-2-8*) Melton-Giardini Bk.

— Principles of Mass Spectrometry & Negative Ions. LC 72-134445. 327p. reprint ed. pap. 101.40 (*0-608-17004-6*, 202711100054) Bks Demand.

Melton, Dana D. & Ledbetter, Frances M. Hooked on Games. (Illus.). 150p. (Orig.). (J). (gr. k-6). 1989. pap. 9.95 (*0-685-29409-9*) Hooked Games.

Melton, David. A Boy Called Hopeless. LC 86-27557. (Illus.). 231p. (J). (gr. 4-8). 1986. reprint ed. lib. bdg. 14.95 (*0-933849-32-X*) Landmark Edns.

— A Boy Called Hopeless. LC 86-27557. (Illus.). 232p. (J). (gr. 4 up). 1986. reprint ed. pap. 5.95 (*0-933849-07-9*) Landmark Edns.

— How to Capture Live Authors & Bring Them to Your Schools. LC 85-81416. 1986. pap. 16.95 (*0-933849-03-6*) Landmark Edns.

— The One & Only Autobiography of Ralph Miller: The Dog Who Knew He Was a Boy. LC 86-27551. (Illus.). 104p. (J). (gr. 2-6). 1986. reprint ed. pap. 5.95 (*0-933849-05-2*); reprint ed. lib. bdg. 14.95 (*0-933849-30-3*) Landmark Edns.

— The One & Only Second Autobiography of Ralph Miller: The Dog Who Knew He Was a Boy. LC 86-27556. (Illus.). 128p. (J). (gr. 2-6). 1986. reprint ed. pap. 5.95 (*0-933849-06-0*); reprint ed. lib. bdg. 14.95 (*0-933849-31-1*) Landmark Edns.

— Todd. (Gentle Revolution Ser.). (Illus.). 266p. 1985. 12.95 (*0-936676-52-3*) Inst Achieve Human Pot.

— Written & Illustrated By . . . LC 85-50637. 1985. pap. 16.95 (*0-933849-00-1*) Landmark Edns.

— You Can Improve Your Students' Writing Skills Immediately! A Revolutionary, No-Nonsense, Two-Brain Approach for Teaching Your Students How To Write Better & Enjoy It More. LC 97-19445. (Illus.). 96p. (Orig.). 1997. pap. text, teacher ed. 16.95 (*0-933849-67-2*) Landmark Edns.

Melton, David, compiled by. Images of Greatness: A Celebration of Life. LC 87-26300. (Illus.). 64p. (J). (gr. 4 up). 1987. 16.95 (*0-933849-11-7*) Landmark Edns.

Melton, David, jt. auth. see Teachers of the School District of Independence, M.

Melton, Dennis W. Bubba on Business: Common Sense from Common People about Work, Leadership & Results. 110p. 1998. pap. 12.95 (*1-890777-03-X*) Select Pr.

Melton, Douglas A., ed. Antisense RNA & DNA. LC 88-205987. (Current Communications in Molecular Biology Ser.). 161p. reprint ed. pap. 50.00 (*0-7837-6439-1*, 204643900012) Bks Demand.

Melton, E. J. History of Cooper County, Missouri: An Account from Early Times to the Present. (Illus.). 584p. 1997. reprint ed. lib. bdg. 59.00 (*0-8328-7132-X*) Higginson Bk Co.

Melton, Gary B. Child Advocacy: Psychological Issues & Interventions. LC 83-2255. 242p. 1983. 45.00 (*0-306-41156-3*, Plenum Trade) Perseus Pubng.

Melton, Gary B., ed. Adolescent Abortion: Psychological & Legal Issues, Report of the Interdivisional Committee on Adolescent Abortion, American Psychological Association. LC 85-31812. (Children & the Law Ser.). 160p. 1986. reprint ed. pap. 49.60 (*0-608-02039-7*, 206269200003) Bks Demand.

— Legal Reforms Affecting Child & Youth Services. LC 82-6204. (Child & Youth Services Ser.: Vol. 5, Nos. 1 & 2). 150p. 1983. text 49.95 (*0-86656-105-6*); pap. text 19.95 (*0-86656-216-8*) Haworth Pr.

— Nebraska Symposium on Motivation, 1994: The Individual, the Family & Social Good: Personal Fulfillment in Times of Change. LC 53-11655. (Nebraska Symposium on Motivation Ser.: No. 42). 200p. Date not set. 45.00 (*0-8032-3185-7*) U of Nebr Pr.

— Nebraska Symposium on Motivation, 1994: The Individual, the Family & Social Good: Personal Fulfillment in Times of Change. LC 53-11655. (Nebraska Symposium on Motivation Ser.: No. 42). 200p. (C). 1995. pap. text 25.00 (*0-8032-8221-4*) U of Nebr Pr.

— Neighbors Helping Neighbors: A New National Strategy for the Protection of Children. 196p. (Orig.). (YA). (gr. 12 up). 1994. pap. text 40.00 (*0-7881-0859-X*) DIANE Pub.

— Reforming the Law: Impact of Child Development Research. LC 87-31. (Law & Behavior Ser.). 307p. 1987. lib. bdg. 42.00 (*0-89862-278-6*) Guilford Pubns.

Melton, Gary B., et al, eds. Children's Competence to Consent. LC 82-18631. (Critical Issues in Social Justice Ser.). (Illus.). 286p. (C). 1983. 71.00 (*0-306-41069-9*, Plenum Trade) Perseus Pubng.

Melton, Gary B. & Barry, Frank D., eds. Protecting Children from Abuse & Neglect: Foundations for a New National Strategy. LC 94-18298. 451p. 1994. lib. bdg. 50.00 (*0-89862-265-4*, 2265) Guilford Pubns.

Melton, Gary B. & Dienstbier, Richard A., eds. Nebraska Symposium on Motivation, 1985: The Law as a Behavioral Instrument. LC 53-11655. (Nebraska Symposium on Motivation Ser.: Vol. 33). xxvii, 291p. 1986. pap. text 25.00 (*0-8032-8132-3*) U of Nebr Pr.

Melton, Gary B., et al. Community Mental Health Centers & the Courts: An Evaluation of Community-Based Forensic Services. LC 84-25751. 177p. 1985. reprint ed. pap. 54.90 (*0-608-01844-9*, 206249400003) Bks Demand.

— No Place to Go: The Civil Commitment of Minors. LC 97-28085. (Children & the Law Ser.). vii, 228p. 1998. text 45.00 (*0-8032-3095-8*) U of Nebr Pr.

— Psychological Evaluations for the Courts: A Handbook for Mental Health Professionals & Lawyers. 2nd ed. LC 97-10163. (Law & Behavior Ser.). 794p. 1997. lib. bdg. 75.00 (*1-57230-236-4*, 0236) Guilford Pubns.

Melton, Gary B., jt. ed. see Childs, Alan W.

Melton, George E. Darlan: Myth & Reality. LC 97-32541. 264p. 1998. 59.95 (*0-275-95973-2*, Praeger Pubs) Greenwood.

Melton, H. Keith. The Ultimate Spy Book. LC 95-44054. 176p. 1996. 29.95 (*0-7894-0443-5*) DK Pub Inc.

Melton, Henry. Clean Slate Word Processing for the TRS-80. 1983. write for info. (*0-318-57972-3*) Macmillan.

Melton, Hollis, ed. see Clark, VeVe A., et al.

Melton, Holly. A Day at Moss Lake. (Illus.). 24p. (J). (gr. k-2). write for info. (*1-58605-010-9*) Knowledge Kids.

— The Day Leap Are Olives. (Illus.). 24p. (J). (gr. k-2). write for info. (*1-58605-011-7*) Knowledge Kids.

— Tad's Good Night. (Illus.). 24p. (J). (gr. k-2). write for info. (*1-58605-009-5*) Knowledge Kids.

Melton, Howard E. Melton Art Reference Library, 2 vols., Set, Vols. 1 & 2. 390p. 1993. spiral bd., ring bd. 195.00 (*0-9640163-0-3*) Melton Art Ref.

***Melton, J. Gordon.** American Religions: An Illustrated History. 2000. lib. bdg. 99.00 (*1-57607-222-3*) ABC-CLIO.

Melton, J. Gordon. Biographical Dictionary of American Cult & Sect Leaders. LC 83-48226. (Library of Social Sciences). 354p. 1986. text 60.00 (*0-8240-9037-3*, SS212) Garland.

***Melton, J. Gordon.** The Church of Scientology. LC 99-86785. (Studies in Contemporary Religions). 2000. pap. write for info. (*1-56085-139-2*) Signature Bks.

Melton, J. Gordon. The Cult Controversy: A Guide to Sources. (Religious Information Systems Ser.: Vol. 6). 300p. 1992. 45.00 (*0-8153-0860-4*, H1601) Garland.

— Encyclopedia of American Religions. 6th ed. 1243p. 1998. 205.00 (*0-8103-8417-5*) Gale.

— Encyclopedia of American Religions Vol. II: Religious Creeds. 2nd ed. 505p. 1993. 150.00 (*0-8103-5491-8*) Gale.

***Melton, J. Gordon.** Encyclopedia of World Religions, 4 Vols. 2002. lib. bdg. 375.00 (*1-57607-223-1*) ABC-CLIO.

Melton, J. Gordon. Encyclopedic Handbook of Cults in America. rev. ed. LC 92-11540. (Religious Information Systems Ser.: Vol. 7). 424p. 1992. pap. text 24.95 (*0-8153-1140-0*) Garland.

— Encyclopedic Handbook of Cults in America. 2nd rev. ed. LC 92-11540. (Religious Information Systems Ser.: Vol. 7). 424p. 1992. text 72.00 (*0-8153-0502-8*, H#SS797) Garland.

— Finding Enlightenment: Ramtha's School of Ancient Wisdom. LC 97-21810. (Illus.). 232p. 1997. 19.95 (*1-885223-61-7*) Beyond Words Pub.

— National Directory of Churches, Synagogues, & Other Houses of Worship, 4 Vols. Krol, John, ed. 2400p. 1993. 315.00 (*0-8103-8989-4*, 101773) Gale.

— National Directory of Churches, Synagogues, & Other 1 Houses of Worship, Vol. 1: Northeastern States. Krol, John, ed. 600p. 1993. 89.00 (*0-8103-8990-8*, 101774) Gale.

— National Directory of Churches, Synagogues, & Other 1 Houses of Worship, Vol. 2: Midwestern States, Vol. 2. Krol, John, ed. 600p. 1993. 89.00 (*0-8103-8991-6*, 101775) Gale.

— National Directory of Churches, Synagogues, & Other 1 Houses of Worship, Vol. 3: Southern States, Vol. 3. Krol, John, ed. 600p. 1993. 89.00 (*0-8103-8992-4*, 101776) Gale.

— National Directory of Churches, Synagogues, & Other 1 Houses of Worship, Vol. 4: Western States, Vol. 4. Krol, John, ed. 600p. 1993. 89.00 (*0-8103-8993-2*, 101777) Gale.

— New Age Almanac. 1990. pap. 16.95 (*0-8103-9402-2*) Visible Ink Pr.

— Religious Bodies in the United States: A Directory. LC 91-41564. (Religious Information Systems Ser.: Vol. 1). 340p. 1992. text 20.00 (*0-8153-0806-X*, H#1568) Garland.

— Religious Leaders of America: A Biographical Guide to Founders & Leaders of Religious Bodies, Churches & Spiritual Groups in North America. 2nd ed. 700p. 1998. 99.00 (*0-8103-8878-2*, 008162) Gale.

***Melton, J. Gordon.** The Vampire Book: Encyclopedia of the Undead. 2nd ed. LC 99-161873. (Illus.). 919p. 1998. pap. 19.95 (*1-57859-071-X*) Visible Ink Pr.

Melton, J. Gordon. The Vampire Book: The Encyclopedia of the Undead. (Illus.). 792p. 1994. 16.95 (*0-8103-2295-1*) Visible Ink Pr.

— The Vampire Gallery: A Who's Who of the Undead. LC 99-160747. (Illus.). 500p. 1998. text 19.95 (*1-57859-053-1*) Visible Ink Pr.

— Videohound's Vampire Film Guide. LC 97-4010. (Illus.). 335p. 1997. 17.95 (*1-57859-002-7*, 00156897) Visible Ink Pr.

Melton, J. Gordon, ed. Cults & New Religions: Sources for the Study of Nonconventional Religious Groups in Nineteenth & Twentieth-Century America, 22 vols., Set. 1992. 2420.00 (*0-8153-0000-X*) Garland.

— Encyclopedia of American Religions Vol. 1: Religious Creeds. 838p. 1987. 150.00 (*0-8103-2132-7*) Gale.

— The Unification Church, Vol. II. (Cults & New Religions Ser.: Vol. 16). 600p. 1990. reprint ed. text 40.00 (*0-8240-4490-8*) Garland.

Melton, J. Gordon & Koszegi, Michael A. Religious Information Sources: A Worldwide Guide. LC 91-47697. (Religious Information Systems Ser.: Vol. 2). 581p. 1992. text 20.00 (*0-8153-0859-0*, H#1593) Garland.

Melton, J. Gordon & Poggi, Isotta. Magic, Witchcraft, & Paganism in America: A Bibliography. 2nd ed. LC 91-45867. (Religious Information Systems Ser.: Vol. 3). 422p. 1992. text 30.00 (*0-8153-0499-4*, SS#723) Garland.

Melton, J. Gordon & Shepard, Leslie A. Encyclopedia of Occultism & Parapsychology, 2 vols. 4th ed. 1511p. 1996. 315.00 (*0-8103-5487-X*) Gale.

Melton, J. Gordon, jt. auth. see Johnson, J.

Melton, J. Gordon, jt. auth. see Pruter, Karl.

Melton, J. Gordon, jt. auth. see Ward, Gary L.

Melton, J. Gordon, jt. ed. see Koszegi, Michael A.

Melton, J. Gordon, jt. ed. see Lewis, James R.

Melton, Jack W., Jr. & Pawl, Lawrence E. Melton & Pawl's Guide to Civil War Artillery Projectiles. 96p. 1996. pap., per. 9.95 (*0-614-30270-6*) Kennesaw Mtn.

— Melton & Pawl's Guide to Civil War Artillery Projectiles. LC 94-80240. (Illus.). 96p. 1996. 19.95 (*0-9635861-1-4*) Kennesaw Mtn.

Melton, James & Keenan, Matthew. The Socially Responsive Portfolio: Balancing Politics & Profits in Institutional Money Management. 275p. 1993. text 45.00 (*1-55738-501-7*, Irwn Prfssnl) McGraw-Hill Prof.

Melton, James E. Vital Enthusiasm. LC 82-81903. 232p. 1983. 12.95 (*0-9604752-1-4*) Global Pubns CA.

— Your Right to Fly. LC 80-82961. (Illus.). 218p. 1979. pap. 8.95 (*0-9604752-0-6*) Global Pubns CA.

Melton, James V. Absolutism & the Eighteenth-Century Origins of Compulsory Schooling in Prussia & Austria. (Illus.). 288p. 1988. text 74.95 (*0-521-34668-1*) Cambridge U Pr.

Melton, James V., jt. ed. see Lehmann, Hartmut.

Melton, James V., tr. see Brunner, Otto.

***Melton, Jerry L.** Habas Bks. 1 & 2: The Pineville Incident & The Missouri Irregulars. LC 98-94015. 1999. pap. 16.95 (*0-533-12946-X*) Vantage.

— The Sandestos. LC 99-94015. 2000. pap. 16.95 (*0-533-13138-3*) Vantage.

Melton, Jim. Understanding the New SQL/PSM: A Complete Guide. 2nd ed. LC 97-50141. 343p. (Orig.). 1998. pap. text 34.95 (*1-55860-461-8*) Morgan Kaufmann.

Melton, Jim & Eisenberg, Andrew. Understanding the New SQLJ: A Complete Guide. Gray, Jim, ed. (Data Management Systems Ser.). 512p. 2000. pap. 44.95 incl. cd-rom (*1-55860-562-2*, Pub. by Morgan Kaufmann) Harcourt.

Melton, Jim & Simon, Alan. Understanding the New SQL: A Complete Guide. 2nd ed. 300p. 1999. pap. text 39.95 (*1-55860-456-1*, Pub. by Morgan Kaufmann) Harcourt.

Melton, Jim & Simon, Alan R. Understanding the New SQL: A Complete Guide. 536p. (C). 1998. pap. text 46.95 (*1-55860-245-3*) Morgan Kaufmann.

Melton, John. Astrolagaster: or The Figvre-Caster. LC 92-550. (Augustan Reprints Ser.: No. 174X). 1975. reprint ed. 14.50 (*0-404-70173-6*, BF1681) AMS Pr.

Melton, John G., ed. see Bromley, David G. & Cutchin, Diane G.

***Melton, Joy T.** Safe Sanctuaries: Reducing the Risk of Child Abuse in the Church. LC 97-66519. 80p. 1998. pap. 15.95 (*0-88177-220-8*, DR220) Discipleship Res.

Melton, Judith M. The Face of Exile: Autobiographical Journeys. LC 98-24440. 232p. 1998. text 29.95 (*0-87745-649-6*) U of Iowa Pr.

Melton, L. Joseph, III, jt. ed. see Riggs, B. Lawrence.

Melton, L. R. An Introductory Guide to Information Sources in Physics. fac. ed. LC 79-313118. (Illus.). 48p. 1978. reprint ed. pap. 30.00 (*0-7837-8011-7*, 204776700008) Bks Demand.

Melton, Les, ed. see Evans, Lori & Velasquez, Barb.

Melton, Lisa & Ladizinsky, Eric. 50 Nifty Science Experiments. (50 Nifty Ser.). (Illus.). 64p. (J). (ps-3). 1992. pap. 5.95 (*0-929923-92-8*, 00928W, Pub. by Lowell Hse) NTC Contemp Pub Co.

Melton, Lisa T. The Man Who Climbed the Mountain. 360p. 1989. 25.00 (*0-9623449-0-7*) M Okada Assn.

Melton, Lisa T., et al. 50 Nifty Super Science Experiments. LC 97-14823. (Fifty Nifty Super Ser.). (Illus.). 80p. (J). 1997. pap. 6.95 (*1-56565-726-8*, 07268W, Pub. by Lowell Hse Juvenile) NTC Contemp Pub Co.

Melton, Louisa & Pickett, Winston. Using Multiple Intelligences in Middle School Reading. Walling, Donovan R., ed. LC 97-65149. (Fastback Ser.: Vol. 411). 41p. 1997. pap. 3.00 (*0-87367-611-4*) Phi Delta Kappa.

***Melton, Louisa, et al.** Improving K-8 Reading Using Multiple Intelligences. (Fastback Ser.: No. 448). 33p. 1999. pap. 3.00 (*0-87367-648-3*, FB# 448) Phi Delta Kappa.

Melton, Luke. Introduction to Statistics for Process Studies. 2nd ed. (C). 1992. pap. text 10.74 (*0-07-041449-1*) McGraw.

Melton, Mary. Lost with All Hands: A Family Forever Changed. LC 98-88764. (Illus.). 254p. 1998. pap. 14.95 (*0-89725-364-7*, 1903, Penobscot Pr) Picton Pr.

Melton, Melanie. Observing for the Fun of It: Backyard Astronomy for the Whole Family. Spohn, Terry, ed. LC 96-153916. (Illus.). 104p. (Orig.). 1996. per. 14.95 (*0-913135-26-7*, 18545) Kalmbach.

— Will Black Holes Devour the Universe? And 100 Other Questions & Answers about Astronomy. 1994. pap. 14.95 (*0-913135-20-8*, 18541) Kalmbach.

Melton, Michael R. The Complete Guide to Whiplash. LC 98-96767. (Illus.). 108p. 1998. pap. text 29.95 (*0-9668091-0-6*) Body-Mind.

Melton, Paul. Going Global with Equities: Profit from the World's Equity Bargains. (Illus.). 256p. 1996. 50.00 (*0-273-61973-X*) F T P-H.

Melton, R. G. & Knox, R. J., eds. Enzyme-Prodrug Strategies for Cancer Therapy. LC 98-37682. (Illus.). 255p. (C). 1999. text 125.00 (*0-306-45895-0*, Kluwer Plenum) Kluwer Academic.

Melton, Reginald F. Instructional Models for Course Design & Development. LC 81-5538. (Illus.). 198p. 1982. 39.95 (*0-87778-178-8*) Educ Tech Pubns.

An Asterisk (*) at the beginning of an entry indicates that the title is appearing for the first time.

Melton, Robert G., et al, eds. AAS/AIAA Spaceflight Mechanics Meeting, Feb. 22-24, 1993, Pasadena, CA. LC 57-43769. (Advances in the Astronautical Sciences Ser.: Vol. 82). (Illus.). 1454p. 1993. 240.00 (*0-87703-368-4*, Am Astronaut Soc) Univelt Inc.

Melton, Robert G. & Society of Automotive Engineers Staff. Space Station Technology. LC 96-69315. viii, 527p. 1996. write for info. (*1-56091-746-6*) Soc Auto Engineers.

***Melton, Rollan D.** Sonny's Story: A Journalist's Memoir. (Illus.). x, 224p. 1999. 24.95 (*1-56475-376-X*) U NV Oral Hist.

Melton, Terry W., jt. ed. see Eckhardt, Robert B.

Melton, Timothy. For Black Men Who Have Considered Living... 48p. 1991. 4.95 (*1-877610-05-4*) Sea Island.

Melton, Victoria, ed. see Williams, Stephen J. & Sanchez, Julianne P.

Melton, W. F. The Rhetoric of John Donne's Verse. 1972. 59.95 (*0-8490-0953-7*) Gordon Pr.

Melton, William. Even Lovers Drown. LC 99-62038. 365p. 1999. 25.00 (*0-7388-0390-1*); pap. 15.00 (*0-7388-0391-X*) Xlibris Corp.

Meltser, David, jt. auth. see Levin, Vladimir.

Meltsner, Arnold J. Rules for Rulers: The Politics of Advice. 208p. 1990. 27.95 (*0-87722-685-7*) Temple U Pr.

Meltsner, Arnold J., ed. Politics & the Oval Office: Towards a Presidential Governance. 332p. 1981. 39.95 (*0-87855-428-9*); pap. 24.95 (*0-685-07094-8*) Transaction Pubs.

Meltsner, Arnold J., et al. Political Feasibility of Reform in School Financing: The Case of California. LC 72-92461. (Special Studies in U. S. Economic, Social & Political Issues). 1973. 39.50 (*0-685-70526-9*) Irvington.

Meltsner, Michael, jt. auth. see Schrag, Philip G.

Meltsner, Susan. Body & Soul. 235p. 1996. 7.98 (*1-56731-114-8*, MJF Bks) Fine Comms.

Meltsner, Susan, jt. auth. see Paster, Zorba.

Meltsner, Susan, ed. see Earle, Ralph H.

Meltz, Barbara. Put Yourself in Their Shoes: Understanding How Your Child Sees the World. LC 98-38609. 432p. 1999. pap. 12.95 (*0-440-50823-1*, Dell Trade Pbks) Dell.

Meltz, Eva S. & Osgood, Rae G. And the Winds Blew Cold: Stalinist Russia as Experienced by an American Emigrant. LC 99-53822. (Illus.). 506p. 2000. pap. 22.95 (*0-939923-76-9*) M & W Pub Co.

***Meltz, Eva Stolar & Osgood, Rae Gunter.** And the Winds Blew Cold: Stalinist Russia As Experienced by an American Emigrant. LC 99-53822. (Illus.). 504p. 2000. 32.95 (*0-939923-85-8*, Pub. by M & W Pub Co) Midpt Trade.

Meltz, Noah M. Industrial Relations Theory: Its Nature, Scope, & Pedagogy. Adams, Roy J., ed. LC 93-9898. (Institute of Management & Labor Relations Ser.: No. 4). (Illus.). 408p. 1993. 47.50 (*0-8108-2678-X*) Scarecrow.

Meltz, Noah M., et al. Sharing the Work: An Analysis of the Issues in Worksharing & Jobsharing. LC 81-188245. 98p. reprint ed. pap. 30.40 (*0-608-14638-2*, 205582600038) Bks Demand.

Meltz, Robert & Merriam, Dwight. The Takings Issue: Constitutional Limits on Land Use Control & Environmental Regulation. LC 98-34885. 525p. 1998. text 60.00 (*1-55963-380-8*) Island Pr.

Meltzer. Politics of Plagiarism. 300p. (C). 1990. pap. text 14.95 (*0-226-51968-6*); lib. bdg. 34.95 (*0-226-51967-8*) U Ch Pr.

***Meltzer.** U. S. History 2000. (Illus.). 604p. 2000. pap. 6.95 (*0-375-75550-0*) Random.

Meltzer & Shapiro. Judicial Code & Rules of Procedure in the Federal Courts. rev. ed. 1998. pap., student ed. write for info. (*1-56662-630-7*) Foundation Pr.

Meltzer, Albert. Anarchism: Arguments for & Against. 1999. pap. text 11.95 (*1-873176-57-0*) AK Pr Dist.

— I Couldn't Paint Golden Angels: Sixty Years of Common Place Life & Anarchist Agitation. (Illus.). 400p. (Orig.). 1996. pap. 19.95 (*1-873176-93-7*, AK Pr San Fran) AK Pr Dist.

Meltzer, Albert, ed. A New World in Our Hearts: The Faces of Spanish Anarchism. 1979. pap. 4.50 (*0-932366-00-7*) Black Thorn Bks.

***Meltzer, Allan H.** History Federal Reserve, Vol. 1. 1998. 60.00 (*0-226-51999-6*); pap. text 25.00 (*0-226-52000-5*) U Ch Pr.

— History Federal Reserve, Vol. 2. 1998. 60.00 (*0-226-52001-3*); pap. text 25.00 (*0-226-52002-1*) U Ch Pr.

Meltzer, Allan H. Keynes's Monetary Theory: A Different Interpretation. (Illus.). 352p. (C). 1989. text 74.95 (*0-521-30615-9*) Cambridge U Pr.

— Money, Credit & Policy. (Economists of the Twentieth Century Ser.). 448p. 1995. 100.00 (*1-85898-208-1*) E Elgar.

***Meltzer, Allan H.** Report of the International Financial Institution Advisory Commission, March 2000. 192p. 2000. per. 18.00 (*0-16-050325-6*) USGPO.

Meltzer, Allan H. U. S. Leadership & Postwar Progress. LC 93-24884. (Occasional Papers: No. 42). 1993. pap. 9.95 (*1-55815-254-7*) ICS Pr.

Meltzer, Allan H., jt. auth. see Brunner, Karl.

Meltzer, Allan H., jt. auth. see Ott, David J.

Meltzer, Annabelle H., jt. auth. see Rothwell, Kenneth S.

***Meltzer, Barnet.** Food Swings: Make the Life-Changing Connection Between the Foods You Eat & Your Emotional Health & Well-Being. LC 99-44602. (Illus.). 256p. 1999. pap. 14.95 (*1-56924-682-3*, Pub. by Marlowe & Co) Publishers Group.

Meltzer, Barnet. The Ten Rules of High Performance Living. LC 97-51867. 256p. 1997. pap. 14.95 (*1-57071-208-5*) Sourcebks.

Meltzer, Bernard, jt. auth. see Findler, N. V.

Meltzer, Bernard D. Supplement Labor '88. 1988. pap. 12.95 (*0-316-56649-7*, Aspen Law & Bus) Aspen Pub.

Meltzer, Bernard D. & Henderson, Stanley D. Labor Law: Cases, Materials & Problems. 3rd ed. LC 84-81751. (C). 1985. 52.00 (*0-316-56647-0*, Aspen Law & Bus) Aspen Pub.

— Statutory Supplement to Labor Law: Cases, Materials & Problems. LC 84-81751. (C). 1985. pap. 11.95 (*0-316-56648-9*, Aspen Law & Bus) Aspen Pub.

Meltzer, Bernard N., et al. Symbolic Interactionism: Genesis, Varieties & Criticisms. (Monographs in Social Theory). 1977. reprint ed. pap. 13.95 (*0-7100-8056-5*, Routledge Thoemms) Routledge.

Meltzer, Brad. Dead Even. LC 98-5935. 368p. 1998. 25.00 (*0-688-15090-X*, Wm Morrow) Morrow Avon.

***Meltzer, Brad.** Dead Even. 529p. 1999. mass mkt. 7.50 (*0-446-60733-9*, Pub. by Warner Bks) Little.

— Dead Even: Burton,&Kate, Set. abr. ed. 1998. audio 25.00 (*0-694-51991-X*, Pub. by HarperAudio) Lndmrk Audiobks.

— The First Counsel. 496p. 2001. 25.95 (*0-446-52728-9*) Warner Bks.

Meltzer, Brad. The Tenth Justice. LC 96-44815. 400p. 1997. 23.00 (*0-688-15089-6*, Wm Morrow) Morrow Avon.

— The Tenth Justice. 496p. 1998. mass mkt. 7.99 (*0-446-60624-3*, Pub. by Warner Bks) Little.

— The Tenth Justice. large type ed. LC 97-43879. (Large Print Bks.). 1998. 26.95 (*1-56895-518-9*) Wheeler Pub.

Meltzer, Brad. The Tenth Justice: Gibson,&Thomas. abr. ed. 1997. audio 18.00 (*0-694-51807-7*, CPN 2645, Pub. by HarperAudio) Lndmrk Audiobks.

Meltzer, C. Rips. Billy's Blues. LC 97-21537. 176p. 1998. 24.00 (*1-57962-005-1*) Permanent Pr.

Meltzer, Daniel J. & Shapiro, David L. Federal Courts & the Federal System, 1993 Supplement. 3rd ed. (University Casebks.). 216p. 1993. pap. text. write for info. (*1-56662-102-X*) Foundation Pr.

— The Judicial Code & Rules of Procedure in the Federal Courts, Student's Edition. rev. ed. 744p. 1996. pap. text. write for info. (*1-56662-384-7*) Foundation Pr.

— The Judicial Code & Rules of Procedure in the Federal Courts, 1994. rev. ed. 738p. 1994. pap. text 18.95 (*1-56662-177-1*) Foundation Pr.

Meltzer, Daniel J. & Shapiro, David L., eds. The Judicial Code & Rules of Procedure in the Federal Courts: 1995 Edition. rev. ed. 750p. 1995. pap. text, student ed. 19.95 (*1-56662-286-7*) Foundation Pr.

Meltzer, David. The Agency Trilogy. LC 95-204274. (Orig.). 1994. pap. 12.95 (*1-56333-216-7*, R Kasak Bks) Masquerade.

— Arrows: Selected Poetry, 1957-1992. LC 94-26540. 180p. (C). 1994. 25.00 (*0-87685-939-2*) Black Sparrow.

— Arrows: Selected Poetry, 1957-1992. LC 94-26540. 180p. (C). 1994. pap. 13.00 (*0-87685-938-4*) Black Sparrow.

— The Art - The Veil. (Illus.). 64p. 1982. pap. 10.00 (*0-87924-040-7*) Membrane Pr.

— Blue Rags. 1974. 5.00 (*0-685-48375-4*); pap. 1.50 (*0-685-48377-0*) Oyez.

— Blue Rags. deluxe ed. 1974. 15.00 (*0-685-48376-2*) Oyez.

— The Eyes, the Blood. (Orig.). 1973. pap. 3.00 (*0-914726-13-7*) Mudra.

— Harps. 1974. 5.00 (*0-685-56671-4*); pap. 2.00 (*0-685-56672-2*) Oyez.

— Journal of the Birth. 1967. pap. 0.50 (*0-685-04670-2*) Oyez.

— The Name: Selected Poetry 1973-1983. LC 84-454. 160p. 1984. pap. 8.50 (*0-87685-491-9*) Black Sparrow.

***Meltzer, David.** No Eyes: Lester Young. LC 00-36101. (Illus.). 200p. 2000. pap. 30.00 (*1-57423-130-8*) Black Sparrow.

— No Eyes: Lester Young. LC 00-36101. (Illus.). 200p. 2000. pap. 16.00 (*1-57423-129-4*) Black Sparrow.

— No Eyes: Lester Young. aut. ed. (Illus.). 200p. 2000. 40.00 (*1-57423-131-6*) Black Sparrow.

Meltzer, David. Orf. 1993. reprint ed. mass mkt. 6.95 (*1-56333-110-1*) Masquerade.

— Six. LC 76-40038. (Illus.). 130p. (Orig.). 1976. pap. 4.00 (*0-87685-270-3*) Black Sparrow.

— Two-Way Mirror. 1977. 6.95 (*0-685-80005-9*); 2.95 (*0-685-80006-7*) Oyez.

— Under. (Orig.). 1995. mass mkt. 6.95 (*1-56333-290-6*, Rhinoceros) Masquerade.

Meltzer, David, ed. The Secret Garden: An Anthology in the Kabbalah. LC 98-7237. 240p. (Orig.). 1998. pap. 16.95 (*1-886449-53-8*, P9538) Barrytown Ltd.

— Tree: Five, the Snake, the Apple. (Illus.). 200p. (Orig.). 1975. pap. 15.00 (*0-686-10822-1*) Tree Bks.

— Tree: Four, Raa. (Illus.). (Orig.). 1974. pap. 15.00 (*0-686-17262-0*) Tree Bks.

— Tree: Six, Messiah. (Illus.). (Orig.). 1978. pap. 10.00 (*0-686-31720-3*) Tree Bks.

— Tree: Three, Shekinah. (Illus.). (Orig.). 1973. pap. 15.00 (*0-686-27969-7*) Tree Bks.

— Tree: Two, Yetzirah. (Illus.). (Orig.). 1972. pap. 15.00 (*0-686-27968-9*) Tree Bks.

— Writing Jazz. LC 99-30298. (Illus.). 208p. (Orig.). 1999. pap. 16.95 (*1-56279-096-X*, Pub. by Mercury Hse Inc) Consort Bk Sales.

Meltzer, David J. Search for the First Americans. LC 93-29453. (Exploring the Ancient World Ser.). (Illus.). 176p. 1996. text 24.95 (*0 89599 035 0*) Smithsonian.

Meltzer, David J., et al, eds. American Archaeology Past & Future: A Celebration of the Society for American Archaeology, 1935-1985. LC 85-600308. (Illus.). 480p. (C). 1986. pap. text 19.95 (*0-87474-693-0*, MEAAP) Smithsonian.

Meltzer, David J. & Dunnell, Robert C., eds. The Archaeology of William Henry Holmes. LC 91-27847. (Illus.). 736p. (Orig.). (C). 1992. pap. text 34.95 (*1-56098-152-0*) Smithsonian.

Meltzer, David J., jt. auth. see Dillehay, Thomas D.

Meltzer, David J., ed. see Squier, Ephraim G. & Davis, Edwin H.

***Meltzer, Eleanor, ed.** Official Insignia of Native American Tribes: Study Pursuant to P. L. 105-330. (Illus.). 47p. 2000. pap. write for info. (*0-9668180-3-2*) Work Grp Intell Rghts.

Meltzer, Ellen, ed. The New Book of American Rankings. rev. ed. 272p. 1997. 50.00 (*0-8160-2878-8*) Facts on File.

Meltzer, Ellen, jt. auth. see Aronson, Marc.

Meltzer, Eric, jt. ed. see Hulbert, Mark J.

Meltzer, Francoise. Hot Property: The Stakes & Claims of Literary Originality. LC 93-6275. 184p. (C). 1994. 27.50 (*0-226-51975-9*) U Ch Pr.

— Hot Property: The Stakes & Claims of Literary Originality. LC 93-6275. (C). 1997. pap. text 18.95 (*0-226-51976-7*) U Ch Pr.

***Meltzer, Francoise.** Joan of Arc. 1998. pap. text 16.95 (*0-226-51982-1*); lib. bdg. 45.00 (*0-226-51981-3*) U Ch Pr.

Meltzer, Francoise. Salome & the Dance of Writing: Portraits of Mimesis in Literature. LC 86-24983. (Illus.). xii, 240p. (C). 1987. 29.95 (*0-226-51971-6*) U Ch Pr.

— Salome & the Dance of Writing: Portraits of Mimesis in Literature. LC 86-24893. xii, 238p. 1989. reprint ed. pap. text 16.95 (*0-226-51972-4*) U Ch Pr.

— The Trial(s) of Psychoanalysis. 296p. 1988. pap. text 17.00 (*0-226-51970-8*); lib. bdg. 34.00 (*0-226-51969-4*) U Ch Pr.

Meltzer, Francoise, tr. see Poulet, Georges.

Meltzer, Francoise, tr. & intro. see Poulet, Georges.

Meltzer, Herbert Y., ed. Novel Antipsychotic Drugs. LC 92-3453. (Illus.). 284p. 1992. reprint ed. pap. 88.10 (*0-608-05808-4*, 205977300007) Bks Demand.

Meltzer, Herbert Y., et al, eds. Psychopharmacology: The Third Generation of Progress in Association with the American College of Neuropsychopharmacology. LC 85-43136. 1824p. 1987. reprint ed. pap. 200.00 (*0-608-03430-4*, 206413100008) Bks Demand.

Meltzer, Howard. Economic Activity & Social Functioning of Adults with Psychiatric Disorders Report 3: OPCS Surveys of Psychiatric Morbidity in Great Britain. xviii, 168p. 1996. 34.00 (*0-11-691653-2*, Pub. by Statnry Office) Balogh.

— Economic Activity & Social Functioning of Residents with Psychiatric Disorders Report 6: OPCS Surveys of Psychiatric Morbidity in Great Britain. xxvi, 58p. 1996. 30.00 (*0-11-691663-X*, Pub. by Statnry Office) Balogh.

— Physical Complaints, Service Use & Social Functioning of Residents with Psychiatric Disorders Report 5: OPCS Surveys of Psychiatric Morbidity in Great Britain. xviii, 55p. 1996. 30.00 (*0-11-691662-1*, Pub. by Statnry Office) Balogh.

— Physical Complaints, Service Use & Treatment of Adults with Psychiatric Disorders Report 2: OPCS Surveys of Psychiatric Morbidity in Great Britain. xvi, 81p. 1996. 24.00 (*0-11-691651-6*, Pub. by Statnry Office) Balogh.

— The Prevalence of Psychiatric Morbidity among Adults Living in Institutions Report 4: OPCS Surveys of Psychiatric Morbidity in Great Britain. x, 101p. 1995. 32.00 (*0-11-691661-3*, Pub. by Statnry Office) Balogh.

Meltzer, Howard. The Prevalence of Psychiatric Morbidity among Adults Living in Private Households Report 1: OPCS Surveys of Psychiatric Morbidity in Great Britain. xii, 174p. 1995. 35.00 (*0-11-691627-3*, HM16273, Pub. by Statnry Office) Balogh.

Meltzer, Jack. Metropolis to Metroplex: The Social & Spatial Planning of Cities. LC 83-49195. 215p. reprint ed. pap. 66.70 (*0-608-08797-1*, 206943600004) Bks Demand.

Meltzer, James D., jt. auth. see Shands, Harley C.

Meltzer, Judith, et al, eds. Policy Options in Long-Term Care. LC 81-10445. (C). 1995. lib. bdg. 34.00 (*0-226-51973-2*) U Ch Pr.

— Policy Options in Long-Term Care. LC 81-10445. (C). 1995. pap. text 15.00 (*0-226-51974-0*) U Ch Pr.

— Policy Options in Long-Term Care. LC 81-10445. (Illus.). 254p. reprint ed. pap. 78.80 (*0-608-09021-2*, 206965600005) Bks Demand.

Meltzer-Kleinhenz, Sydnie. More for Me. (Hello Reader! Level 1 Ser.). (J). 1997. 8.70 (*0-606-12994-4*, Pub. by Turtleback) Demco.

Meltzer, Lisa. Bruce Coville's Book of Monsters II: More Tales to Give You the Creeps. 1996. 9.09 (*0-606-09109-2*, Pub. by Turtleback) Demco.

— One-Two-Three Look at Me. (Baby Shaped Board Bks.). (Illus.). 28p. (J). (ps). 1990. 2.95 (*0-02-689486-6*) Checkerboard.

Meltzer, Lynn J., ed. Strategy Assessment & Instruction for Students with Learning Disabilities: From Theory to Practice. LC 91-48272. 424p. 1993. text 41.00 (*0-89079-540-1*, 5194) PRO-ED.

Meltzer, Lynn J., et al. Strategies for Success: Classroom Teaching Techniques for Students with Learning Problems. rev. ed. LC 95-18217. (Illus.). 183p. (C). 1996. pap. text 29.00 (*0-89079-673-4*, 7313) PRO-ED.

Meltzer, M., et al. Metal-Bearing Waste Streams: Minimizing, Recycling & Treatment. 406p. 1990. 89.00 (*0-8155-1260-0*) Noyes.

Meltzer, Marilyn & Palau, Susan M. Acquiring Critical Thinking Skills. (Illus.). 1996. pap., teacher ed. write for info. (*0-7216-4226-8*, W B Saunders Co) Harcrt Hlth Sci Grp.

— Acquiring Critical Thinking Skills. 1996. pap. text 26.95 (*0-7216-6151-3*, W B Saunders Co) Harcrt Hlth Sci Grp.

— Learning Strategies in Nursing: Reading, Study, & Test-Taking. 2nd ed. Eoyang, Thomas, ed. LC 96-20650. (Illus.). 400p. 1997. pap. text 26.00 (*0-7216-6342-7*, W B Saunders Co) Harcrt Hlth Sci Grp.

Meltzer, Mark, et al, eds. 1996 Officer Compensation Report: The Executive Compensation Survey for Small to Medium-Sized Businesses. annuals 208p. 1995. pap. 395.00 (*1-56706-114-1*) Panel Pubs.

Meltzer, Mark, jt. auth. see Goldsmith, Howard B.

Meltzer, Mark, jt. auth. see Howard, Clark.

Meltzer, Milton. The American Promise: Voices of a Changing Nation, 1945-Present. (Illus.). 192p. (YA). (gr. 7 up). 1990. 15.95 (*0-553-07020-7*, Starfire BDD) BDD Bks Young Read.

Meltzer, Milton. American Revolutionaries: A History in Their Own Words, 1750-1800. 1987. 12.05 (*0-606-05117-1*, Pub. by Turtleback) Demco.

Meltzer, Milton. The American Revolutionaries: A History in Their Own Words 1750-1800. LC 86-47846. (Trophy Bk.). (Illus.). 224p. (J). (gr. 7 up). 1993. pap. 6.95 (*0-06-446145-9*, HarpTrophy) HarpC Child Bks.

— Andrew Jackson: And His America. (Milton Meltzer Biographies Ser.). (Illus.). 144p. (YA). (gr. 7-12). 1993. lib. bdg. 28.00 (*0-531-11157-1*) Watts.

— The Bill of Rights: How We Got It & What It Means. LC 90-1537. 180p. (YA). (gr. 7 up). 1990. 15.00 (*0-690-04805-X*) HarpC Child Bks.

Meltzer, Milton. The Black Americans: A History in Their Own Words, 1619-1983. rev. ed. LC 83-46160. (Trophy Nonfiction Bk.). (Illus.). 320p. (YA). (gr. 7 up). 1987. pap. 10.95 (*0-06-446055-X*, HarpTrophy) HarpC Child Bks.

M

— Bread & Roses: The Struggle of American Labor, 1865-1915. Scott, John Anthony, ed. (Illus.). 176p. (YA). 1999. 22.95 (*0-7351-0216-3*) Replica Bks.

Meltzer, Milton. Brother, Can You Spare a Dime: The Great Depression of 1929-1933. (Library of American History). (Illus.). 144p. (YA). 1990. 19.95 (*0-8160-2372-7*) Facts on File.

***Meltzer, Milton.** Carl Sandburg: A Biography. LC 98-46373. 144p. (YA). (gr. 7 up). 1999. lib. bdg. 29.90 (*0-7613-1364-8*) TFC Bks NY.

— Civil Rights Landmark. LC 99-89550. 2000. pap. write for info. (*0-375-80414-5*) Random.

Meltzer, Milton. Columbus & the World Around Him. LC 89-24764. (Biography Ser.). 160p. (YA). (gr. 9-12). 1990. lib. bdg. 28.00 (*0-531-10899-6*) Watts.

— Crime in America. LC 90-5698. 176p. (YA). (gr. 7 up). 1990. 12.95 (*0-688-08513-X*, Wm Morrow) Morrow Avon.

***Meltzer, Milton.** Dorothea Lange: A Photographer's Life. LC 99-26674. 416p. 1999. pap. text 24.95 (*0-8156-0622-2*) Syracuse U Pr.

— Driven from the Land: The Story of the Dust Bowl. LC 98-47501. (Great Journeys Ser.). 111p. (J). (gr. 5-9). 2000. lib. bdg. 31.36 (*0-7614-0968-8*, Benchmark NY) Marshall Cavendish.

Meltzer, Milton. Food: How We Hunt & Gather It, How We Grow & Eat It. LC 98-5097. (Illus.). 96p. (YA). (gr. 5 up). 1999. 23.90 (*0-7613-0354-5*, Copper Beech Bks) Millbrook Pr.

— A History of Jewish Life from Eastern Europe to America. LC 95-16065. 352p. 1996. 40.00 (*1-56821-433-2*) Aronson.

— Hold Your Horses! A Feedbag Full of Fact & Fable. LC 95-2983. (Illus.). 144p. (J). (gr. 3-7). 1995. lib. bdg. 15.89 (*0-06-024478-X*) HarpC Child Bks.

— The Landscape of Memory. 1999. pap. 4.99 (*0-14-031985-9*) Viking Penguin.

— Langston Hughes: A Biography. LC 68-21952. (YA). (gr. 7 up). 1968. 14.95 (*0-690-48525-5*) HarpC Child Bks.

— Langston Hughes: An Illustrated Edition. LC 97-1403. (Illus.). 240p. (YA). (gr. 5 up). 1997. pap. 16.95 (*0-7613-0327-8*); lib. bdg. 39.40 (*0-7613-0205-0*) Millbrook Pr.

— The Many Lives of Andrew Carnegie. LC 96-40144. (Meltzer Biographies Ser.). 160p. (YA). (gr. 7 up). 1997. lib. bdg. 28.00 (*0-531-11427-9*) Watts.

— The Many Lives of Andrew Carnegie. LC 96-40144. (Milton Meltzer Biographies Ser.). (J). 1997. write for info. (*0-531-11388-4*) Watts.

— Mark Twain: A Writer's Life. LC 85-5108. (Illus.). 128p. (YA). (gr. 9-12). 1985. lib. bdg. 28.00 (*0-531-10072-3*) Watts.

— Mary McCleod Bethune. (Women of Our Time Ser.). (Illus.). (J). (gr. 2-6). 1988. pap. 3.50 (*0-317-69647-5*, PuffinBks) Peng Put Young Read.

— Mary McLeod Bethune: Voice of Black Hope. (Women of Our Time Ser.). (J). 1988. 10.19 (*0-606-03613-X*, Pub. by Turtleback) Demco.

— Mary McLeod Bethune: Voice of Black Hope. (Women of Our Time Ser.). (Illus.). 64p. (J). (gr. 2-6). 1988. reprint ed. pap. 4.99 (*0-14-032219-1*, PuffinBks) Peng Put Young Read.

— Never to Forget: The Jews of the Holocaust. LC 75-25409. (YA). (gr. 7 up). 1976. lib. bdg. 15.89 (*0-06-024175-6*) HarpC Child Bks.

— Never to Forget: The Jews of the Holocaust. LC 75-25409. (Trophy Nonfiction Bk.). (Illus.). 240p. (YA). (gr. 7-12). 1991. pap. 7.95 (*0-06-446118-1*, HarpTrophy) HarpC Child Bks.

— Never to Forget: The Jews of the Holocaust. 1991. 12.05 (*0-606-01103-X*, Pub. by Turtleback) Demco.

— Rescue: The Story of How Gentiles Saved Jews in the Holocaust. LC 87-47816. (Illus.). 224p. (YA). (gr. 7 up). 1988. 16.00 (*0-06-024209-4*); lib. bdg. 16.89 (*0-06-024210-8*) HarpC Child Bks.

— Rescue: The Story of How Gentiles Saved Jews in the Holocaust. LC 87-47816. (Trophy Nonfiction Bk.). (Illus.). 176p. (J). (gr. 12 up). 1991. pap. 7.95 (*0-06-446117-3*, HarpTrophy) HarpC Child Bks.

Meltzer, Milton. Rescue, the Story of How Gentiles Saved Jews in the Holocaust. 1991. 12.05 (*0-606-12498-5*, Pub. by Turtleback) Demco.

Meltzer, Milton. Slavery: A World History. (Illus.). 616p. 1993. reprint ed. pap. 22.50 (*0-306-80536-7*) Da Capo.

— The Teaching of Non-Fiction in Elementary & Secondary Classrooms: Essays by Milton Meltzer. Saul, Wendy, ed. (Language & Literacy Ser.). 216p. (C). 1994. text 40.00 (*0-8077-3378-4*); pap. text 18.95 (*0-8077-3377-6*) Tchrs Coll.

— Ten Queens: Portraits of Women of Power. LC 97-36428. (Illus.). 144p. (YA). (gr. 7). 1998. 24.99 (*0-525-45643-0*, Dutton Child) Peng Put Young Read.

— The Terrorists. LC 82-48858. (Illus.). 192p. (YA). (gr. 7 up). 1983. 12.95 (*0-06-024193-4*) HarpC Child Bks.

— Theodore Roosevelt & His America. LC 94-17369. (Illus.). 160p. (YA). (gr. 9-12). 1994. lib. bdg. 28.00 (*0-531-11192-X*) Watts.

***Meltzer, Milton.** There Comes a Time. LC 99-89550. 192p. (J). 2001. 16.95 (*0-375-80407-2*); lib. bdg. 18.99 (*0-375-90407-7*) Random Bks Yng Read.

— They Came in Chains: The Story of the Slave Ships. LC 98-47456. (Great Journeys Ser.). 96p. (YA). (gr. 5-9). 2000. lib. bdg. 31.36 (*0-7614-0967-X*) Marshall Cavendish.

Meltzer, Milton. Thomas Jefferson: The Revolutionary Aristocrat. LC 91-15943. (Non-Fiction Ser.). (Illus.). 160p. (YA). (gr. 9-12). 1991. lib. bdg. 28.00 (*0-531-11069-9*) Watts.

— Tom Paine: Voice of Revolution. LC 96-11956. (Milton Meltzer Biographies Ser.). 192p. (J). 1996. lib. bdg. 28.00 (*0-531-11291-8*) Watts.

— Tongue of Flame: The Story of Lydia Maria Child. LC 65-15228. 224p. (J). (gr. 5 up). 1991. lib. bdg. 13.89 (*0-690-04903-X*) HarpC Child Bks.

— Underground Man. LC 90-36277. 224p. (J). (gr. 3-7). 1990. pap. 4.95 (*0-15-292846-4*, Gulliver Bks) Harcourt.

— Underground Man. LC 90-36277. (Great Episodes Ser.). 224p. (J). (gr. 3-7). 1990. 14.95 (*0-15-200617-6*, Gulliver Bks) Harcourt.

Meltzer, Milton. Underground Man. 1990. 10.05 (*0-606-04836-7*, Pub. by Turtleback) Demco.

Meltzer, Milton. Weapons & Warfare: From the Stone Age to the Space Age. LC 95-48464. (Illus.). 96p. (J). (gr. 3-7). 1996. 16.95 (*0-06-024875-0*) HarpC Child Bks.

— Weapons & Warfare: From the Stone Age to the Space Age. LC 95-48464. (Illus.). 96p. (J). (gr. 4-7). 1996. lib. bdg. 16.89 (*0-06-024876-9*) HarpC Child Bks.

— Who Cares? Millions Do-- LC 94-4082. (J). 1994. lib. bdg. 16.85 (*0-8027-8325-2*) Walker & Co.

— Who Cares? Millions Do-- LC 94-4082. (Illus.). 144p. (J). 1994. 15.95 (*0-8027-8324-4*) Walker & Co.

***Meltzer, Milton.** Who Cares? Millions Do... A Book about Altruism. (Illus.). 164p. (YA). (gr. 6-8). 2000. reprint ed. text 17.00 (*0-7881-9056-3*) DIANE Pub.

Meltzer, Milton. Witches & Witch Hunts. LC 97-36999. (Illus.). 1999. write for info. (*0-590-48630-6*) Scholastic Inc.

— Witches & Witch-Hunts: A History of Persecution. LC 97-36999. 128p. (J). (gr. 3-9). 1999. 16.95 (*0-590-48517-2*, Pub. by Scholastic Inc) Penguin Putnam.

Meltzer, Milton, compiled by. The Mexican-American War. 39.00 (*1-56696-091-6*) Jackdaw.

— Reconstruction. 39.00 (*1-56696-051-7*) Jackdaw.

Meltzer, Milton, ed. Frederick Douglass: In His Own Words. LC 94-14524. (Illus.). 240p. (YA). (gr. 7 up). 1995. 22.00 (*0-15-229492-9*, Gulliver Bks) Harcourt.

— Voices from the Civil War: A Documentary History of the Great American Conflict. large type ed. 1995. 61.50 (*0-614-09614-6*, L-81913-00) Am Printing Hse.

Meltzer, Milton, jt. auth. see Hughes, Langston.

Meltzer, Morton F. Information, the Ultimate Management Resource: How to Find, Use, & Manage It. LC 81-66222. 223p. reprint ed. pap. 69.20 (*0-608-13415-5*, 205574900036) Bks Demand.

Meltzer, Otto & Kahrstedt, Ulrich. Geschichte der Karthager, 3 vols., Set. LC 75-7330. (Roman History Ser.). (GER.). 1975. reprint ed. 150.95 (*0-405-07105-1*) Ayer.

— Geschichte der Karthager, 3 vols., Vol. 1. LC 75-7330. (Roman History Ser.). (GER.). 1975. reprint ed. 50.95 (*0-405-07106-X*) Ayer.

— Geschichte der Karthager, 3 vols., Vol. 2. LC 75-7330. (Roman History Ser.). (GER.). 1975. reprint ed. 51.95 (*0-405-07107-8*) Ayer.

— Geschichte der Karthager, 3 vols., Vol. 3. LC 75-7330. (Roman History Ser.). (GER.). 1975. reprint ed. 51.95 (*0-405-07108-6*) Ayer.

Meltzer, Peter D., et al. Passport to New York Restaurants. 12th rev. ed. Orig. Title: Passport to New York the 400 Restaurants That Matter Most. (Illus.). 212p. 1998. pap. 10.95 (*0-937413-12-7*) Passport NYC.

Meltzer, Richard. The Aesthetics of Rock. (Illus.). 360p. 1987. pap. 11.95 (*0-306-80287-2*) Da Capo.

— Gulcher: Post-Rock Cultural Pluralism in America (1649-1993) 1990. pap. 9.95 (*0-8065-1197-4*, Citadel Pr) Carol Pub Group.

— Holes: A Book Not Entirely about Golf. 48p. 1999. 4.00 (*1-892061-02-3*) Future Tense.

***Meltzer, Richard.** A Whore Just Like the Rest: The Music Writing of Richard Meltzer. LC 99-58212. 608p. 2000. pap. text 17.00 (*0-306-80953-2*) Da Capo.

Meltzer, Richard S., et al, eds. Echocardiography in Coronary Artery Disease. (Developments in Cardiovascular Medicine Ser.). (C). 1988. text 179.50 (*0-89838-979-8*) Kluwer Academic.

Meltzer, Richard S., jt. auth. see Roelandt, Jos R.

Meltzer, Robert. Biomedical & Clinical Instrumentation: Fast Tracking from Concept Through Production in a Regulated Environment. 274p. 1993. 135.00 (*0-935184-50-3*) Interpharm.

Meltzer, Sol. Herb Gardening in Texas. 3rd ed. 208p. (Orig.). 1997. pap. 16.95 (*0-88415-329-0*, 5329) Gulf Pub.

Meltzer, Stanton L., et al. Guide to Divorce Engagements, 2 vols., Set. 1995. ring bd. 150.00 (*1-56433-689-1*) Prctnrs Pub Co.

— Guide to Divorce Engagements, Vol. 1. 1995. ring bd. write for info. (*1-56433-690-5*) Prctnrs Pub Co.

— Guide to Divorce Engagements, Vol. 2. 1995. ring bd. write for info. (*1-56433-691-3*) Prctnrs Pub Co.

— Guide to Divorce Engagements, Vol. 2. 1996. ring bd. write for info. (*0-7646-0022-2*) Prctnrs Pub Co.

Meltzer, Stephen, ed. PCR in Bioanalysis. LC 97-37496. (Methods in Molecular Biology Ser.: Vol. 92). (Illus.). xi, 281p. 1998. 69.50 (*0-89603-361-9*) Humana.

Meltzer, Stephen J., ed. PCR in Bioanalysis. (Methods in Molecular Biology Ser.: Vol. 92). (Illus.). 292p. 1998. 89.50 (*0-89603-497-6*) Humana.

Meltzer, Steve. Photographing Your Craftwork: A Hands-On Guide for Craftspeople. 2nd ed. 136p. (Orig.). 1993. reprint ed. pap. 12.95 (*0-934026-81-5*) Interweave.

Meltzer, Theodore H. Filtration in the Pharmaceutical Industry. (Advances in Parenteral Science Ser.: Vol. 3). (Illus.). 1120p. 1986. text 295.00 (*0-8247-7519-8*) Dekker.

— High-Purity Water Preparation: For the Semiconductor, Pharmaceutical, & Power Industries. 2nd ed. LC 92-85421. 833p. 1997. 125.00 (*0-927188-02-3*) Tall Oaks Pub.

— Pharmaceutical Water Systems. 865p. 1996. 145.00 (*0-927188-06-6*) Tall Oaks Pub.

Meltzer, Theodore H. & Jornitz, Maik W. Filtration in the Biopharmaceutical Industry. 2nd ed. LC 97-43494. (Illus.). 952p. 1998. text 225.00 (*0-8247-9896-1*) Dekker.

Meltzer, Tom. Cracking the CLEP 1999. (Princeton Review Ser.). 440p. 1998. pap. 20.00 (*0-375-75212-9*) Villard Books.

***Meltzer, Tom & Foglino, Paul.** Cracking the Clep. 4th ed. 448p. 2000. pap. 20.00 (*0-375-76151-9*, Pub. by PRP NY) Random.

Meltzoff, Andrew N., jt. auth. see Gopnik, Alison.

Meltzoff, Julian. Critical Thinking about Research: Psychology & Related Fields. LC 97-30477. 300p. 1997. pap. 24.95 (*1-55798-455-7*, 431-8640) Am Psychol.

Meltzoff, Sarah K. & Lipuma, Edward S. A Japanese Fishing Joint Venture: Worker Experience & National Development in the Solomon Islands. (ICLARM Technical Reports: No. 12). (Illus.). 63p. (Orig.). 1983. pap. text 11.00 (*0-89955-386-9*, Pub. by ICLARM) Intl Spec Bk.

Melucci. Nomads of the Present. 1992. pap. write for info. (*0-09-172872-X*, Pub. by Random) Random House.

Melucci, Alberto. Challenging Codes: Collective Action in the Information Age. (Cambridge Cultural Social Studies). 454p. (C). 1996. text 64.95 (*0-521-57051-4*); pap. text 25.95 (*0-521-57843-4*) Cambridge U Pr.

— The Playing Self: Person & Meaning in the Planetary Society. (Cultural Social Studies). 184p. (C). 1996. text 54.95 (*0-521-56401-8*); pap. text 16.95 (*0-521-56482-4*) Cambridge U Pr.

Melugin, Roy F. Formation of Isaiah 40-55. (Beiheft zur Zeitschrift fuer die Alttestamentliche Wissenschaft Ser.: No. 141). (C). 1976. text 83.85 (*3-11-005820-0*) De Gruyter.

Melugin, Roy F. & Sweeney, Marvin A., eds. New Visions of Isaiah. (JSOT Supplement Ser.: No. 214). 344p. 1996. 90.75 (*1-85075-584-1*, Pub. by Sheffield Acad) CUP Services.

Melum, Mara M. Total Quality Outcomes Management: A Guide to Integrating Outcomes Measurement & TQM to Improve Health. 333p. 1995. pap. write for info. (*1-879364-48-4*) GOAL-QPC.

Melum, Mara M. & Collett, Casey. Breakthrough Leadership: Achieving Organizational Alignment Through Hoshin Planning. LC 94-48029. 344p. 1995. 69.00 (*1-55648-133-0*) AHPI.

Melum, Mara M. & Sinioris, Marie K. Total Quality Management: The Health Care Pioneers. LC 92-11056. 404p. 1992. pap. 69.00 (*1-55648-089-X*, 169410) AHPI.

Melusky. American Political System. LC 99-29137. 400p. 1999. pap. 31.88 (*0-697-39592-8*) McGraw.

Melusky, Joseph A. The Constitution: Our Written Legacy. LC 89-18963. 338p. (Orig.). 1991. 29.50 (*0-89464-334-7*); pap. 23.50 (*0-89464-550-1*) Krieger.

Melusky, Joseph A. & Ridgway, Whitman H. The Bill of Rights: Our Written Legacy. 268p. (C). 1993. pap. 19.50 (*0-89464-827-6*); text 28.50 (*0-89464-533-1*) Krieger.

Melvern, Linda. Last Resort. 1992. write for info. (*0-679-41218-2*) McKay.

***Melvern, Linda.** A People Betrayed: The Role of the West in Rwanda. 288p. 2000. pap. 19.95 (*1-85649-831-X*, Pub. by Zed Books) St Martin.

— A People Betrayed: The Role of the West in Rwanda. 2000. text 69.95 (*1-85649-830-1*, Pub. by Zed Books) St Martin.

Melvile, Hermann. Typee: A Peep at Polynesian Life. 1976. 26.95 (*0-8488-0581-X*) Amereon Ltd.

Melville, A. D., tr. see Ovid.

Melville, A. D., tr. see Statius.

Melville, Alan. Finanical Accounting. 393p. (Orig.). 1997. pap. 47.50 (*0-7121-1428-9*, Pub. by Pitman Pub) Trans-Atl Phila.

— Taxation. 550p. 1998. pap. 120.00 (*0-85297-475-2*, Pub. by Chartered Bank) St Mut.

— Taxation: British Finance Act, 1998. 640p. 1998. pap. 62.50 (*0-273-63870-X*, Pub. by Pitman Pub) Trans-Atl Phila.

Melville, Ann. A Clean Break. large type ed. 386p. 1995. pap. 18.99 (*1-85389-558-X*, Dales) Ulverscroft.

Melville, Annabelle M. Elizabeth Bayley Seton. 1976. 25.00 (*0-684-14735-1*, Scribners Ref) Mac Lib Ref.

***Melville, Anne.** The Eyes of the World. large type ed. 576p. 1999. 31.99 (*0-7505-1366-7*, Pub. by Mgna Lrg Print) Ulverscroft.

Melville, Anne. Just What I Wanted. 224p. 25.00 (*0-7278-5232-9*) Severn Hse.

Melville, Annette. Resource Strategies in the 90s Vol. 16: Trends in ARL University Libraries. (Occasional Papers). 40p. 1994. pap. 25.00 (*0-918006-72-4*) ARL.

Melville, Annette & Simon, Scott, eds. Redefining Film Preservation: A National Plan: Recommendations of the Librarian of Congress in Consultation with the National Film Preservation Board. LC 94-29345. 1994. write for info. (*0-8444-0819-0*) Lib Congress.

Melville, Anthony, tr. see Jarry, Alfred.

Melville, Anthony, tr. see Satie, Erik.

***Melville, Beth & Namovicz-Peat, Susan, eds.** Health Care Report Cards, 1998-99. 4th rev. ed. 158p. 1998. pap. 93.00 (*0-929156-41-2*) Atlantic Info Services Inc.

***Melville, Bruce W. & Coleman, Stephen E.** Bridge Scour. LC 99-71116. 575p. 1999. pap. 78.00 (*1-887201-18-1*) WRP.

Melville, Charles, ed. History & Literature in Iran. (Pembroke Persian Papers). 224p. 1993. text 65.00 (*1-85043-652-5*) I B T.

— Safavid Persia: The History & Politics of an Islamic Society. LC 96-60443. 256p. 1996. pap. 19.95 (*1-86064-086-9*) St Martin.

Melville, Charles & Smith, eds. Christians & Moors in Spain, 711-1501: Arabic Sources, No. 3. (Hispanic Classics Ser.). 1992. 59.95 (*0-85668-449-X*, Pub. by Aris & Phillips); pap. 25.00 (*0-85668-450-3*, Pub. by Aris & Phillips) David Brown.

Melville, Chuck. Felicia: Melari's Wish. (Illus.). 184p. (Orig.). 1995. pap. 14.95 (*1-883847-09-5*) MU Press.

Melville, Chuck, ed. see Hill, Cathy.

***Melville, D. A.** Canadians & the Victoria Cross: Men of Valor: They Fight for You. (Illus.). 64p. 1999. pap. write for info. (*1-55125-045-4*) Vanwell Publ.

Melville, Douglas, ed. see Ames, Joseph B.

Melville, Douglas, ed. see Anderson, Olof W.

Melville, Douglas, ed. see Arnold, Edwin L.

Melville, Douglas, ed. see Atkins, Frank.

Melville, Douglas, ed. see Bennet, Robert A.

Melville, Douglas, ed. see Bennett, Gertrude B.

Melville, Douglas, ed. see Blackwood, Algernon.

Melville, Douglas, ed. see Bramah, Ernest.

Melville, Douglas, ed. see Bruce, Muriel.

Melville, Douglas, ed. see Burton, Alice E.

Melville, Douglas, ed. see Chambers, Robert W.

Melville, Douglas, ed. see Channing, Mark.

Melville, Douglas, ed. see Chester, George R.

Melville, Douglas, ed. see Clock, Herbert & Boetzel, Eric.

Melville, Douglas, ed. see Coblentz, Stanton A.

Melville, Douglas, ed. see Constantine, Murray.

Melville, Douglas, ed. see Cook, William W.

Melville, Douglas, ed. see Cowan, Frank.

Melville, Douglas, ed. see De Comeau, Alexander.

Melville, Douglas, ed. see Dunn, Allan J.

Melville, Douglas, ed. see Eddison, Eric R.

Melville, Douglas, ed. see Fleckenstein, Alfred C.

Melville, Douglas, ed. see Fyne, Neal.

Melville, Douglas, ed. see Gillmore, Inez H.

Melville, Douglas, ed. see Gompertz, Martin L.

Melville, Douglas, ed. see Green, Fitzhugh.

Melville, Douglas, ed. see Gregory, Jackson.

Melville, Douglas, ed. see Griffith, George.

Melville, Douglas, ed. see Guthrie, Thomas A.

Melville, Douglas, ed. see Haggard, H. Rider.

Melville, Douglas, ed. see Haldane, Charlotte.

Melville, Douglas, ed. see Harris, Burland.

Melville, Douglas, ed. see Hartmann, Franz.

Melville, Douglas, ed. see Hodder, William R.

Melville, Douglas, ed. see Kingsmill, Hugh, pseud.

Melville, Douglas, ed. see Knowles, Vernon.

Melville, Douglas, ed. see Kummer, Frederic A.

Melville, Douglas, ed. see Large, E. C.

Melville, Douglas, ed. see Le Queux, William T.

Melville, Douglas, ed. see Leroux, Gaston.

Melville, Douglas, ed. see Lindsay, David.

Melville, Douglas, ed. see Linklater, Eric.

Melville, Douglas, ed. see London, Jack.

Melville, Douglas, ed. see Marshall, Sidney J.

Melville, Douglas, ed. see McHugh, Vincent.

Melville, Douglas, ed. see Merritt, Abraham.

Melville, Douglas, ed. see Morris, Kenneth.

Melville, Douglas, ed. see Murray, G. G.

Melville, Douglas, ed. see Owen, Frank F.

Melville, Douglas, ed. see Potter, Margaret H.

Melville, Douglas, jt. ed. see Reginald, R.

Melville, Douglas, ed. see Rolfe, Frederick W., et al.

Melville, Douglas, ed. see Rosynyaine, J. H.

Melville, Douglas, ed. see Savile, Frank.

Melville, Douglas, ed. see Scott, G. Firth.

Melville, Douglas, ed. see Sheldon-Williams, Miles.

Melville, Douglas, ed. see Sinclair, Upton.

Melville, Douglas, ed. see Todd, Ruthven.

Melville, Douglas, ed. see Vivian, Charles E.

Melville, Douglas, ed. see Wells, H. G.

Melville, Elinor G. A Plague of Sheep: Environmental Consequences of the Conquest of Mexico. LC 96-5374. (Studies in Environment & History). (Illus.). 219p. (C). 1994. text 69.95 (*0-521-42061-X*) Cambridge U Pr.

— A Plague of Sheep: Environmental Consequences of the Conquest of Mexico. (Illus.). 219p. 1997. pap. text 17.95 (*0-521-57448-X*) Cambridge U Pr.

Melville, H. Ancestry of John Whitney, Who Emigrated from London in 1635, & Settled in Watertown, Mass., the First of the Name in America & the One from Whom a Great Majority of the Whitneys in the U. S. Are Descended. (Illus.). 313p. 1989. reprint ed. pap. 38.50 (*0-8328-1263-3*); reprint ed. lib. bdg. 48.50 (*0-8328-1262-5*) Higginson Bk Co.

Melville, Henry. Veritas: Revelation of Mysteries Biblical, Historical, & Social, by Means of the Mediann & Persian Laws. 160p. 1993. reprint ed. pap. 17.95 (*1-56459-396-7*) Kessinger Pub.

Melville, Herman. Apple Tree Table: And Other Sketches. (BCL1-PS American Literature Ser.). 329p. 1992. reprint ed. lib. bdg. 89.00 (*0-7812-6793-5*) Rprt Serv.

— Apple-Tree Table & Other Sketches. LC 70-88907. 329p. 1969. reprint ed. lib. bdg. 35.00 (*0-8371-2245-7*, MEAT, Greenwood Pr) Greenwood.

— The Apple-Tree Table & Other Sketches. (Notable American Authors Ser.). 1999. reprint ed. lib. bdg. 125.00 (*0-7812-4554-0*) Rprt Serv.

— Bartleby & Benito Cereno. 112p. 1990. pap. 1.00 (*0-486-26473-4*) Dover.

— Bartleby & Benito Cereno. 1998. lib. bdg. write for info. (*1-56723-076-8*) Yestermorrow.

— Battle-Pieces & Aspects of the War. LC 60-5042. 1979. reprint ed. lib. bdg. 50.00 (*0-8201-1252-6*) Schol Facsimiles.

— Battle-Pieces & Aspects of the War: Civil War Poems. LC 95-20053. 282p. 1995. reprint ed. pap. 13.95 (*0-306-80655-X*) Da Capo.

— Battle-Pieces & Aspects of the War (Poems) (Notable American Authors Ser.). 1999. reprint ed. lib. bdg. 125.00 (*0-7812-4550-8*) Rprt Serv.

— Billy Budd. 1998. pap. text 14.95 (*1-55701-236-9*) BNI Pubns.

— Billy Budd. Stern, Milton, ed. LC 73-8967. (Library of Literature: No. 43). 244p. 1975. pap. 7.95 (*0-672-61040-X*, Bobbs) Macmillan.

— Billy Budd. write for info. (*0-318-54489-X*) NAL.

— Billy Budd. 1990. per. 3.99 (*0-671-73144-0*, PB Trade Paper) PB.

— Billy Budd. (Now Age Illustrated V Ser.). (Illus.). 64p. (J). (gr. 4-12). 1979. student ed. 1.25 (*0-88301-409-2*); pap. text 2.95 (*0-88301-385-1*) Pendulum Pr.

— Billy Budd. 1992. pap. 2.50 (*0-8125-0426-7*, Pub. by Tor Bks) St Martin.

Melville, Herman. Billy Budd. large type ed. 1997. pap. 19.95 (*1-55701-218-0*) BNI Pubns.

Melville, Herman. Billy Budd. (Notable American Authors Ser.). 1999. reprint ed. lib. bdg. 125.00 (*0-7812-4556-7*) Rprt Serv.

— Billy Budd: Sailor. 120p. 1999. per. 5.99 (*0-671-02833-2*) S&S Trade.

— Billy Budd & Other Stories. 416p. 1993. pap. 4.95 (*0-460-87205-2*, Everyman's Classic Lib) Tuttle Pubng.

— Billy Budd & Other Tales. LC 97-62337. (Signet Classics Ser.). 496p. 1998. mass mkt. 4.95 (*0-451-52687-2*, Sig Classics) NAL.

Melville, Herman. Billy Budd & Other Tales. (Signet Classics). 1948. 9.05 (*0-606-02340-2*, Pub. by Turtleback) Demco.

— Billy Budd & Other Tales. (Illus.). (J). 1992. 8.34 (*0-606-18635-2*) Turtleback.

Melville, Herman. Billy Budd & the Encatadas. (Airmont Classics Ser.). (YA). (gr. 9 up). 1965. mass mkt. 2.50 (*0-8049-0116-3*) Airmont.

— Billy Budd & Typee. (Barron's Book Notes Ser.). (Orig.). (C). 1984. pap. 2.50 (*0-8120-3404-X*) Barron.

— Billy Budd, Foretopman. Date not set. lib. bdg. 17.95 (*0-89190-891-9*, Am Repr) Amereon Ltd.

— Billy Budd Readalong. 64p. 1994. pap. 14.95 incl. audio (*0-7854-0790-1*, 40543) Am Guidance.

— Billy Budd, Sailor. Hayford, Harrison & Sealts, Merton M., Jr., eds. LC 62-17135. 228p. 1962. pap. 9.95 (*0-226-32132-0*, P99) U Ch Pr.

— Billy Budd, Sailor. large type ed. LC 97-9266. (Perennial Ser.). 24.95p. 1997. lib. bdg. 24.95 (*0-7838-8195-9*, G K Hall Lrg Type) Mac Lib Ref.

— Billy Budd, Sailor & Other Stories. (Bantam Classics Ser.). 288p. (gr. 7-12). 1982. mass mkt. 4.95 (*0-553-21274-5*) Bantam.

— Billy Budd, Sailor & Other Stories. Beaver, Harold, ed. Incl. Bell Tower. 1968. Benito Cereno. 1968. Cock-a-Doodle-Doo. 1968. Daniel Orme. 1968. Encantadas. 1968. John Marr. 1968. (English Library). 466p. 1968. Set pap. 2.50 (*0-14-043029-6*) Viking Penguin.

— Billy Budd, Sailor & Selected Tales. Milder, Robert, ed. & intro. by. LC 97-8211. (The World's Classics Ser.). 464p. 1997. pap. 7.95 (*0-19-283303-0*) OUP.

— Billy Budd, Sailor & Selected Tales. Milder, Robert, ed. LC 97-8211. (Oxford World's Classics Ser.). (Illus.). 464p. 2001. pap. 7.95 (*0-19-283903-9*) OUP.

— Clarel. Hayford, Harrison et al, eds. LC 90-60361. (Northwestern-Newberry Edition of the Writings of Herman Melville: Vol. 12). 893p. 1991. 89.95 (*0-8101-0906-9*); pap. text 29.95 (*0-8101-0907-7*) Northwestern U Pr.

— Clarel: A Poem & a Pilgrimage to the Holy Land. (Notable American Authors Ser.). 1999. reprint ed. lib. bdg. 125.00 (*0-7812-4555-9*) Rprt Serv.

— Collected Poems. (BCL1-PS American Literature Ser.). 548p. 1993. reprint ed. lib. bdg. 99.00 (*0-7812-6987-3*) Rprt Serv.

— Collected Poems (except Clarel) annot. ed. Vincent, Howard P., ed. (Complete Works of Herman Melville Ser.). reprint ed. spiral bd. 69.50 (*0-87532-007-4*) Hendricks House.

— Complete Short Fiction. LC 98-102392. 478p. 1997. 20.00 (*0-375-40068-0*) Everymns Lib.

— The Confidence Man. 26.95 (*0-89190-890-0*) Amereon Ltd.
— The Confidence Man. LC 71-141591. (Critical Editions Ser.). 376p. (C). 1971. pap. text 12.50 (*0-393-09968-7*) Norton.
— The Confidence Man. LC 95-9643. (Literary Classics Ser.). 296p. 1995. pap. 8.95 (*1-57392-038-X*) Prometheus Bks.
— The Confidence-Man. Hayford, Harrison et al, eds. (Northwestern-Newberry Edition of the Writings of Herman Melville: Vol. 10). 518p. 1984. 59.95 (*0-8101-0324-9*); pap. text 19.95 (*0-8101-0325-7*) Northwestern U Pr.
— The Confidence-Man. Matterson, Stephen, ed. & intro. by. 400p. 1991. pap. 10.95 (*0-14-044547-1*, Penguin Classics) Viking Penguin.
— The Confidence Man. annot. ed. Foster, Elizabeth S., ed. (Complete Works of Herman Melville Ser.). 1979. 29.95 (*0-87532-009-0*) Hendricks House.
— The Confidence-Man. 260p. 1990. reprint ed. lib. bdg. 21.95 (*0-89966-714-7*) Buccaneer Bks.
— The Confidence-Man: His Masquerade. Franklin, H. Bruce, ed. LC 66-30445. 1967. pap. 6.95 (*0-672-60986-X*, LL13, Bobbs) Macmillan.
— The Confidence-Man: His Masquerade. (Oxford World Classics Ser.). 416p. 1999. pap. 9.95 (*0-19-283762-1*) OUP.
— The Confidence-Man His Masquerade: An Authoritative Text, Backgrounds & Sources, Reviews, Criticism & an Annotated Bibliography. LC 71-141591. (Norton Critical Editions Ser.). (Illus.). xvii, 376p. (J). 1971. write for info. (*0-393-04345-2*) Norton.
— Correspondence. Horth, Lynn, ed. (Northwestern-Newberry Edition of the Writings of Herman Melville: Vol. 14). (Illus.). 924p. 1993. 99.95 (*0-8101-0981-6*); pap. text 29.95 (*0-8101-0995-6*) Northwestern U Pr.
— Encantadas: or Enchanted Isles. (BCL1-PS American Literature Ser.). 118p. 1993. reprint ed. lib. bdg. 69.00 (*0-7812-6988-1*) Rprt Serv.
— Family Correspondence of Herman Melville. Paltsits, Victor H., ed. (American Literature Ser.: No. 49). 1976. lib. bdg. 75.00 (*0-8383-2111-9*) M S G Haskell Hse.
— Great Short Works Melv. 512p. 1970. pap. 8.00 (*0-06-083094-8*) HarpC.
— Herman Melville: Authentic Anecdotes of Old Zack. Starosciak, Kenneth, ed. & intro. by. 1973. reprint ed. pap. 5.00 (*0-686-02647-0*) K Starosciak.
— Herman Melville: Selected Poems. limited ed. Vendler, Helen H., ed. (Illus.). 156p. 1995. text 700.00 (*0-910457-31-X*) Arion Pr.
— Israel Potter. Reagar, Daniel, ed. (Masterworks of Literature Ser.). 1999. pap. 12.95 (*0-8084-0476-8*) NCUP.
— Israel Potter. Hayford, Harrison et al, eds. LC 82-81178. (Northwestern-Newberry Edition of the Writings of Herman Melville: Vol. 8). 401p. 1982. 59.95 (*0-8101-0552-7*); pap. text 19.95 (*0-8101-0553-5*) Northwestern U Pr.
— Israel Potter: His Fifty Years of Exile. LC 90-56158. (Illus.). 497p. 1991. reprint ed. pap. 19.95 (*0-8232-1323-4*) Fordham.
— Israel Potter: His Fifty Years of Exile. (BCL1-PS American Literature Ser.). 301p. 1992. reprint ed. lib. bdg. 89.00 (*0-7812-6794-3*) Rprt Serv.
— Israel Potter: His Fifty Years of Exile. rev. ed. LC 90-56158. (Illus.). 497p. 1991. 60.00 (*0-8232-1322-6*) Fordham.
— Israel Potter: His Fifty Years of Exiles. (Notable American Authors Ser.). 1999. reprint ed. lib. bdg. 125.00 (*0-7812-3998-2*) Rprt Serv.
— John Marr & Other Sailers (Poems) (Notable American Authors Ser.). 1999. reprint ed. lib. bdg. 125.00 (*0-7812-4552-4*) Rprt Serv.
— Journal of a Visit to Europe & the Levant, 1856-57, No. 35--35. Horsford, Howard, ed. LC 75-27655. (Princeton Studies in English Ser.: No.35). (Illus.). 299p. 1976. reprint ed. lib. bdg. 35.00 (*0-8371-8448-7*, MEJV, Greenwood Pr) Greenwood.
— Journals. Horsford, Howard & Horth, Lynn, eds. (Northwestern-Newberry Edition of the Writings of Herman Melville: Vol. 15). (Illus.). 683p. 1989. 89.95 (*0-8101-0822-4*); pap. text 29.95 (*0-8101-0823-2*) Northwestern U Pr.
— Mardi. (FRE.). 1983. pap. 20.95 (*0-7859-4190-8*) Fr & Eur.
— Mardi. Hillway, Tyrus, ed. (Masterworks of Literature Ser.). 1973. 25.95 (*0-8084-0016-9*); pap. 18.95 (*0-8084-0017-7*) NCUP.
— Mardi. Hayford, Harrison et al, eds. LC 67-21602. (Northwestern-Newberry Edition of the Writings of Herman Melville: Vol. 3). 1970. 79.95 (*0-8101-0015-0*); pap. text 29.95 (*0-8101-0014-2*) Northwestern U Pr.
— Mardi. annot. ed. Wright, Nathalia, ed. (Complete Works of Herman Melville Ser.). 1990. 29.95 (*0-87532-015-5*) Hendricks House.
— Mardi: And a Voyage Thither. LC 98-29409. (Northwestern-Newberry Edition of the Writings of Herman Melville). 704p. 1998. pap. 17.95 (*0-8101-1690-1*) Northwestern U Pr.
— Mardi: And a Voyage Thither. 2 vols., Set. (BCL1-PS American Literature Ser.). 1992. reprint ed. lib. bdg. 150.00 (*0-7812-6795-1*) Rprt Serv.
— Moby Dick. Date not set. lib. bdg. 49.95 (*0-8488-0183-0*) Amereon Ltd.
— Moby Dick. (Cyber Classics Ser.). 486p. 1997. pap. text 14.95 (*1-55701-195-8*) BNI Pubns.
— Moby Dick. Walcutt, Charles C., ed. & intro. by. 608p. (YA). (gr. 7-12). 1981. mass mkt. 4.95 (*0-553-21311-3*, Bantam Classics) Bantam.
— Moby Dick. 61p. (YA). (gr. 7 up). 1998. pap. 5.50 (*0-87129-782-5*, M68) Dramatic Pub.

Melville, Herman. Moby Dick, 001. Kazin, Alfred, ed. LC 56-14087. (YA). (gr. 9 up). 1956. pap. 13.96 (*0-395-05108-8*, RivEd) HM.
Melville, Herman. Moby Dick. Carlson, Donna, ed. (Illustrated Classics Ser.). (Illus.). 128p. (J). 1992. pap. 2.95 (*1-56156-093-6*) Kidsbks.
— Moby Dick. (Cloth Bound Pocket Series). 240p. 1998. 7.95 (*3-89508-088-8*) Konemann.
***Melville, Herman.** Moby Dick. (Classics Ser.). 2000. pap. 11.95 (*0-679-78327-X*) Modern Lib NY.
Melville, Herman. Moby Dick. (C). 1967. pap. text 16.00 (*0-393-09670-X*) Norton.
— Moby Dick. LC 97-11062. (Oxford Illustrated Classics Ser.). (Illus.). 104p. (J). (gr. 4 up). 1997. 25.00 (*0-19-274156-X*) OUP.
— Moby Dick. Tanner, Tony, ed. & intro. by. (Oxford World's Classics Ser.). 656p. 1998. pap. 6.95 (*0-19-283385-5*) OUP.
***Melville, Herman.** Moby Dick. (Oxford World's Classics Hardcovers Ser.). 640p. 2000. 18.00 (*0-19-210041-6*) OUP.
Melville, Herman. Moby Dick. Shapiro, Irwin, ed. LC 73-75458. (Now Age Illustrated Ser.). (Illus.). 64p. (J). (gr. 5-10). 1973. pap. 2.95 (*0-88301-099-2*) Pendulum Pr.
***Melville, Herman.** Moby Dick. (SPA.). 1998. pap. 15.95 (*84-08-02226-1*) Planeta.
Melville, Herman. Moby Dick. Vogel, Malvina, ed. (Great Illustrated Classics Ser.: Vol. 16). (Illus.). 240p. (J). (gr. 3-6). 1990. 9.95 (*0-86611-967-1*) Playmore Inc.
— Moby Dick. (American Collection Short Classics). (J). (gr. 4-7). 1993. pap. 4.95 (*0-8114-6834-8*) Raintree Steck-V.
— Moby Dick. LC 00-502456. (Illus.). 600p. 1999. per. 5.99 (*0-671-02835-9*) S&S Trade.
— Moby Dick. 640p. 1998. mass mkt. 5.99 (*0-8125-4156-1*, Pub. by Tor Bks) St Martin.
— Moby Dick. LC 87-16788. (Illus.). 48p. (J). (gr. 3-6). 1996. pap. 4.95 (*0-8167-1208-5*) Troll Communs.
— Moby Dick. (Classics Library). 608p. pap. 3.95 (*1-85326-008-8*, 0088WW, Pub. by Wrdsworth Edits) NTC Contemp Pub Co.
— Moby-Dick. (J). (gr. 8). 1996. mass mkt. 3.99 (*0-8125-4307-6*, Pub. by Tor Bks) St Martin.
Melville, Herman. Moby-Dick. 1955. 10.05 (*0-606-01084-X*, Pub. by Turtleback) Demco.
Melville, Herman. Moby-Dick. Lee, A. Robert, ed. 512p. 1993. pap. 3.95 (*0-460-87307-5*, Everyman's Classic Lib) Tuttle Pubng.
— Moby Dick. LC 96-27942. (Illus.). 32p. (J). (gr. k-3). 1997. 16.00 (*0-374-34997-5*) FS&G.
Melville, Herman. Moby Dick. abr. ed. 1991. audio 17.00 (*1-55994-394-7*, DCN 2077) HarperAudio.
Melville, Herman. Moby-Dick. abr. ed. 1996. pap. 23.95 incl. audio (*0-14-086172-6*, Png AudioBks) Viking Penguin.
Melville, Herman. Moby Dick. large type ed. 1997. pap. 21.95 (*1-55701-219-9*) BNI Pubns.
Melville, Herman. Moby Dick. 687p. 1983. reprint ed. lib. bdg. 35.95 (*0-89966-478-4*) Buccaneer Bks.
— Moby Dick. rev. ed. LC 98-6469. 555p. 1998. mass mkt. 4.95 (*0-451-52699-6*, Sig Classics) NAL.
— Moby Dick. rev. ed. Dixson, Robert J., ed. (American Classics Ser.: Bk. 2). (gr. 9 up). 1987. audio 65.00 (*0-13-024662-X*, 58219) Prentice ESL.
— Moby Dick. unabridged ed. (Classics Ser.). (YA). (gr. 11 up). 1964. mass mkt. 3.95 (*0-8049-0033-7*, CL-33) Airmont.
***Melville, Herman.** Moby-Dick. 2nd ed. (Critical Editions Ser.). 1999. pap. 11.50 (*0-393-97283-6*) Norton.
Melville, Herman. Moby Dick. 2nd ed. (Illustrated Classic Book Ser.). (Illus.). 61p. (J). (gr. 3 up). 1998. reprint ed. pap. text 4.95 (*1-56767-235-3*) Educ Insights.
— Moby Dick, Tome I. (FRE.). 1980. pap. 11.95 (*0-7859-4134-7*) Fr & Eur.
— Moby Dick, Tome II. 1980. pap. 11.95 (*0-7859-4135-5*) Fr & Eur.
***Melville, Herman.** Moby Dick: Heston,&Charlton, Set. abr. ed. 95p. 1998. audio 18.00 (*0-694-52018-7*, Caedmon) HarperAudio.
Melville, Herman. Moby Dick: Or the Whale. LC 92-50222. (Illus.). 864p. 1992. 21.00 (*0-679-60010-8*) Modern Lib NY.
— Moby Dick: Or the Whale. Parker, Hershel & Tanselle, G. Thomas, eds. (Northwestern-Newberry Edition of the Writings of Herman Melville: Vol. 6). 1043p. (C). 1988. 99.95 (*0-8101-0268-4*); pap. text 29.95 (*0-8101-0269-2*) Northwestern U Pr.
— Moby Dick: Or the Whale. annot. ed. Vincent, Howard P. & Mansfield, Luther S., eds. (Complete Works of Herman Melville Ser.). 909p. 1962. 29.95 (*0-87532-001-5*) Hendricks House.
— Moby Dick: Or the Whale. LC 81-40320. (Illus.). 600p. 1981. reprint ed. 55.00 (*0-520-04354-5*, Pub. by U CA Pr); reprint ed. 395.00 (*0-520-04549-1*, Pub. by U CA Pr); reprint ed. pap. 24.95 (*0-520-04548-3*, Pub. by U CA Pr) Cal Prin Full Svc.
— Moby Dick: Or the Whale. rev. ed. LC 92-19289. (Illus.). 624p. 1993. pap. 16.99 (*0-14-039084-7*, Penguin Classics) Viking Penguin.
— Moby Dick: Or the White Whale. (Oxford Illustrated Classics Ser.). (Illus.). 104p. 1998. reprint ed. pap. 12.95 (*0-19-278153-7*) OUP.
— Moby Dick: Original Lithographs by Leonard Baskin. (Illus.). 20p. 1970. boxed set 1200.00 (*1-55660-295-2*) A Wofsy Fine Arts.
— Moby Dick Readalong. (Illustrated Classics Collection 1). 64p. 1994. pap. 14.95 incl. audio (*0-7854-0709-X*, 40351) Am Guidance.
— Monarch Moby Dick. 1976. 3.95 (*0-671-00623-1*, Arco) Macmillan Gen Ref.
— Omoo. 1976. 23.95 (*0-8488-1098-8*) Amereon Ltd.

***Melville, Herman.** Omoo. LC 99-43708. 320p. 2000. text 8.95 (*0-486-40873-6*) Dover.
Melville, Herman. Omoo. Hayford, Harrison et al, eds. LC 67-11991. (Northwestern-Newberry Edition of the Writings of Herman Melville: Vol. 2). 380p. 1968. 59.95 (*0-8101-0162-9*); pap. text 19.95 (*0-8101-0160-2*) Northwestern U Pr.
— Omoo. (BCL1-PS American Literature Ser.). 299p. 1992. reprint ed. lib. bdg. 79.00 (*0-7812-6796-X*) Rprt Serv.
— Omoo: A Narrative of Adventures in the South Seas. LC 99-41391. 336p. 1999. pap. 16.95 (*0-8101-1765-7*) Northwestern U Pr.
Melville, Herman. Omoo: Adventures in the South Seas. (Pacific Basin Bks.). 220p. (Orig.). 1985. pap. 14.95 (*0-7103-0133-2*) Routledge.
Melville, Herman. The Piazza Tales. 21.95 (*0-89190-877-3*) Amereon Ltd.
— The Piazza Tales. LC 95-53225. 1996. 14.50 (*0-679-60198-8*) Modern Lib NY.
— Piazza Tales. Reagan, Daniel, ed. (Masterworks of Literature Ser.). 1994. 14.95 (*0-8084-0443-1*) NCUP.
— Piazza Tales. (BCL1-PS American Literature Ser.). 250p. 1993. reprint ed. lib. bdg. 79.00 (*0-7812-6989-X*) Rprt Serv.
— The Piazza Tales & Other Prose Pieces, 1839-60. Parker, Hershel & Tanselle, G. Thomas, eds. (Northwestern-Newberry Edition of the Writings of Herman Melville: Vol. 9). (Illus.). 847p. (C). 1987. 89.95 (*0-8101-0550-0*); pap. text 29.95 (*0-8101-0551-9*) Northwestern U Pr.
— Pierre. (Twelve-Point Ser.). 1999. lib. bdg. 24.00 (*1-58287-113-2*) North Bks.
— Pierre. Hayford, Harrison et al, eds. (Northwestern-Newberry Edition of the Writings of Herman Melville: Vol. 7). 435p. 1972. 59.95 (*0-8101-0266-8*); pap. text 19.95 (*0-8101-0267-6*) Northwestern U Pr.
— Pierre. 435p. 1995. pap. 14.95 (*0-8101-1412-7*) Northwestern U Pr.
— Pierre: Or the Ambiguities. Spengemann, William C., ed. LC 95-32700. (Penguin Classics Ser.). 400p. 1996. pap. 12.95 (*0-14-043484-4*, Penguin Bks) Viking Penguin.
— Pierre: Or the Ambiguities. annot. ed. Murray, Henry A., ed. (Complete Works of Herman Melville Ser.). 608p. 1962. 29.95 (*0-87532-003-1*) Hendricks House.
— Pierre, Israel Potter, the Confidence-Man, Tales & Billy Budd. Hayford, Harrison, ed. LC 84-11259. 1478p. 1985. 40.00 (*0-940450-24-0*, Pub. by Library of America) Penguin Putnam.
— Pierre, or the Ambiguities: Kraken Edition, The. Parker, Hershel, ed. (Illus.). 560p. 1995. 16.00 (*0-06-118009-2*) HarperTrade.
— Redburn. Hayford, Harrison et al, eds. (Northwestern-Newberry Edition of the Writings of Herman Melville: Vol. 4). 384p. 1972. 69.95 (*0-8101-0013-4*); pap. text 19.95 (*0-8101-0016-9*) Northwestern U Pr.
— Redburn. Beaver, Harold, ed. (English Library). 448p. 1977. pap. 14.95 (*0-14-043105-5*, Penguin Classics) Viking Penguin.
— Redburn. (BCL1-PS American Literature Ser.). 346p. 1993. reprint ed. lib. bdg. 89.00 (*0-7812-6990-3*) Rprt Serv.
— Redburn: His First Voyage. 1998. lib. bdg. write for info. (*1-56723-077-6*) Yestermorrow.
— Redburn: ou Sa Premiere Croisiere. (FRE.). 1980. pap. 13.95 (*0-7859-4142-8*) Fr & Eur.
— Redburn, White-Jacket, Moby-Dick. Tanselle, G. Thomas, ed. LC 82-18677. 1436p. 1983. 35.00 (*0-940450-09-7*, Pub. by Library of America) Penguin Putnam.
— Selected Poems of Herman Melville. 3rd ed. Cohen, Hennig, ed. LC 91-55378. xviii, 259p. 1991. reprint ed. pap. 17.00 (*0-8232-1336-6*) Fordham.
— Selected Tales & Poems. 29.95 (*0-89190-681-9*) Amereon Ltd.
— Shorter Novels of Herman Melville. (Black & Gold Library). 1978. pap. 12.95 (*0-87140-122-3*, Pub. by Liveright) Norton.
— Three Short Novels: Bartleby, Benito Cereno, Billy Budd. large type ed. 381p. 1997. reprint ed. lib. bdg. 24.00 (*0-939495-20-1*) North Bks.
— Timoleon. 1972. 35.00 (*0-8490-1215-5*) Gordon Pr.
— Timoleon & Other Poems. (Notable American Authors Ser.). 1999. reprint ed. lib. bdg. 125.00 (*0-7812-4553-2*) Rprt Serv.
— Typee. (Classics Illustrated Ser.). (Illus.). 1997. pap. text 4.99 (*1-57840-061-9*, Pub. by Acclaim Bks) Penguin Putnam.
— Typee. (FRE.). 1984. pap. 17.95 (*0-7859-4199-1*) Fr & Eur.
— Typee. (Twelve-Point Ser.). 360p. 1999. lib. bdg. 24.00 (*1-58287-097-7*) North Bks.
— Typee. Hayford, Harrison et al, eds. LC 67-11990. (Northwestern-Newberry Edition of the Writings of Herman Melville: Vol. 1). (Illus.). 374p. (C). 1968. 59.95 (*0-8101-0161-0*); pap. text 19.95 (*0-8101-0159-9*) Northwestern U Pr.
— Typee. Blair, Ruth, ed. (The World's Classics Ser.). (Illus.). 386p. 1996. pap. 8.95 (*0-19-282307-8*) OUP.
— Typee. 293p. 1993. pap. 3.95 (*0-460-87276-1*, Everyman's Classic Lib) Tuttle Pubng.
— Typee. 210p. pap. 4.00 (*1-85326-230-7*, Pub. by Wrdsworth Edits) NTC Contemp Pub Co.
***Melville, Herman.** Typee. large type ed. 465p. 1999. lib. bdg. 24.00 (*0-939495-73-2*) North Bks.
— Typee: A Peep at Polynesian Life. LC 95-32699. 320p. 1996. pap. 12.95 (*0-14-043488-7*, Penguin Bks) Viking Penguin.
Melville, Herman. Typee: A Peep at Polynesian Life. (Notable American Authors Ser.). 1999. reprint ed. lib. bdg. 125.00 (*0-7812-3991-5*) Rprt Serv.
— Typee: Four Months Residence in the Marquesas Islands. (Pacific Basin Bks.). 300p. (Orig.). 1985. pap. 14.95 (*0-7103-0132-4*) Routledge.

— Typee, Omoo, Mardi. Tanselle, G. Thomas, ed. LC 81-18600. 1333p. 1982. 40.00 (*0-940450-00-3*, Pub. by Library of America) Penguin Putnam.
— Whale: The Anti-Moby Dick Edition. Darling, Tom, ed. 300p. (Orig.). 1996. pap. 12.00 (*1-889543-02-0*) Beachchair Pr.
— White-Jacket. Hayford, Harrison et al, eds. LC 67-21603. (Northwestern-Newberry Edition of the Writings of Herman Melville: Vol. 5). 499p. 1970. 59.95 (*0-8101-0257-9*); pap. 19.95 (*0-8101-0258-7*) Northwestern U Pr.
— White-Jacket. LC 88-2650. (Classics of Naval Literature Ser.). 736p. 1988. reprint ed. 32.95 (*0-87021-788-7*) Naval Inst Pr.
***Melville, Herman.** White-Jacket: or The World in a Man of War. 2000. pap. 16.95 (*0-8101-1828-9*) Northwestern U Pr.
— The World in a Man-of-War. (Oxford World's Classics Ser.). 496p. 2000. pap. 8.95 (*0-19-283801-6*) OUP.
Melville, Herman & Hayford, Harrison. The Piazza Tales. LC 96-34027. 187p. 1996. 14.95 (*0-8101-1467-4*) Northwestern U Pr.
***Melville, Herman & Robillard, Douglas.** The Poems of Herman Melville. rev. ed. LC PS2382.R63 2000. 2000. pap. 29.00 (*0-87338-660-4*) Kent St U Pr.
Melville, Herman & Stern, Milton R. Billy Budd, Sailor: An Inside Narrative. LC 73-8967. (Library of Literature: Vol. 43). ix, 184 p. 1975. write for info. (*0-672-51466-4*, Bobbs) Macmillan.
Melville, Herman, et al. Four Great American Classics. 752p. 1992. mass mkt. 7.50 (*0-553-21362-8*, Bantam Classics) Bantam.
Melville, Herman, et al. Israel Potter: His Fifty Years of Exile. LC 97-29546. (Writings of Herman Melville Ser.). 240p. 1997. pap. 14.95 (*0-8101-1591-3*) Northwestern U Pr.
Melville, Herman, et al. Moby Dick. (Classics Illustrated Ser.). (Illus.). 52p. (YA). pap. 4.95 (*1-57209-003-0*) Classics Int Ent.
Melville, Herman, jt. auth. see Center for Learning Network Staff.
Melville, Herman, jt. auth. see Schatt, Stanley.
Melville, Herman, jt. auth. see Wegener, Larry E.
***Melville, Ian.** Marketing in Japan. (Illus.). 256p. 2000. pap. text 39.95 (*0-7506-4145-2*) Buttrwrth-Heinemann.
Melville, James. The Body Wore Brocade: A Superintendent Otani Mystery. 224p. 1992. text 20.00 (*0-684-19413-9*, Scribners Ref) Mac Lib Ref.
— The Body Wore Brocade: A Superintendent Otani Mystery. large type ed. (Ulverscroft). 304p. 1994. 27.99 (*0-7089-3064-6*) Ulverscroft.
— The Chrysanthemum Chain. large type ed. 370p. 1982. 27.99 (*0-7089-0758-X*) Ulverscroft.
— Diary of Mr. James Melville, 1556-1601. LC 70-172723. (Bannatyne Club, Edinburgh. Publications: No. 34). reprint ed. 32.50 (*0-404-52740-X*) AMS Pr.
— Memoirs of His Own Life. LC 74-172724. (Maitland Club, Glasgow. Publications: No. 21). reprint ed. 64.50 (*0-404-52718-3*) AMS Pr.
— The Ninth Netsuke. large type ed. 320p. 1986. 27.99 (*0-7089-1404-7*) Ulverscroft.
— The Reluctant Spy. 224p. 1995. 20.00 (*0-7278-4773-2*) Severn Hse.
— Sayonara, Sweet Amaryllis. large type ed. 304p. 1986. 27.99 (*0-7089-1433-0*) Ulverscroft.
— A Tarnished Phoenix. large type ed. (Adventure Suspense Ser.). 432p. 1992. 27.99 (*0-7089-2666-5*) Ulverscroft.
***Melville, Jennie.** Dead Again: A Charmian Daniels Mystery. LC 00-32052. 2000. write for info. (*0-7838-9099-0*, G K Hall & Co) Mac Lib Ref.
Melville, Jennie. Dead Set: A Charmian Daniels Mystery. LC 95-269. (WWL Mystery Ser.). 252p. 1995. per. 3.99 (*0-373-26174-8*, 1-26174-2) Harlequin Bks.
— Footsteps in the Blood. large type ed. LC 94-2047. 322p. 1994. lib. bdg. 18.95 (*0-7862-0189-4*) Thorndike Pr.
— The Morbid Kitchen. large type ed. LC 95-53281. 1996. pap. 21.95 (*0-7862-0642-X*) Thorndike Pr.
— Murder Has a Pretty Face. large type ed. (Magna Large Print Ser.). 407p. 1996. 27.99 (*0-7505-1047-1*, Pub. by Mgna Lrg Print) Ulverscroft.
— Murder Has a Pretty Face. 1991. reprint ed. per. 3.99 (*0-373-26079-2*) Harlequin Bks.
— Whoever Has the Heart. large type ed. LC 94-7116. 330p. 1994. lib. bdg. 17.95 (*0-7862-0207-6*) Thorndike Pr.
— Windsor Red. 1990. mass mkt. 3.50 (*0-373-26051-2*) Harlequin Bks.
Melville, John. Crystal Gazing & the Wonders of Clairvoyance: Embracing Practical Instructions in the Art, History, & Philosophy of This Ancient Science (1910) 98p. 1996. reprint ed. pap. 14.95 (*1-56459-750-4*) Kessinger Pub.
— Crystal-Gazing & the World of Clairvoyance. 87p. 1996. reprint ed. spiral bd. 12.00 (*0-7873-1269-X*) Hlth Research.
Melville-Jones, J. A Dictionary of Ancient Greek Coins. (Illus.). 253p. (Orig.). 1990. lib. bdg. 75.00 (*0-900652-81-0*) S J Durst.
Melville-Jones, John. A Dictionary of Ancient Roman Coins. (Illus.). 329p. 1990. lib. bdg. 65.00 (*1-85264-026-X*) S J Durst.
Melville, K. F., ed. Guide to Coal Contracts, 1991. 731p. 1991. pap. 237.00 (*0-935453-40-7*) Pasha Pubns.
Melville, Keith. Marriage & Family Today. 3rd ed. 492p. (C). 1983. text. write for info. (*0-318-57008-4*) Random.
— Pocketbook Pressures: Who Benefits from Economic Growth? LC 96-154973. (National Issues Forums Ser.). 28p. 1995. write for info. (*0-7872-1637-2*) Kendall-Hunt.
Melville, Keith, jt. auth. see Bird, Gloria.
Melville, Keith, jt. auth. see Doble, John.

M

Melville, Kirsty & Chester, Jonathan. Splash! A Penguin Counting Book. LC 97-8047. (Illus.). 24p. (J). (ps-1). 1997. 12.95 (*1-883672-56-2*) Tricycle Pr.

Melville, Lawrence. The Fair Land of Gowrie. 1987. 70.00 (*0-900323-20-5*, Pub. by W Culross & Son Ltd) St Mut.

Melville, Leslie W. Forms & Agreements on Intellectual Property & International Licensing, 3 vols., Set. 3rd ed. LC 78-17576. 1979. ring bd. 375.00 (*0-685-00782-0*) West Group.

Melville, Lewis, ed. Trial of the Duchess of Kingston. (Notable British Trials Ser.). x, 328p. 1995. reprint ed. 102.00 (*1-56169-126-7*) Gaunt.

Melville, Margarita B., ed. Mexicanas at Work in the United States. (Mexican American Studies: No. V). (Illus.). (Orig.). (C). 1988. pap. text 11.95 (*0-939709-04-X*) Univ Houston Mex Amer.

Melville, Mary H. The Temporary Worker in the Nuclear Power Industry: An Equity Analysis. LC 81-65590. (CENTED Monographs: No. 1). (Illus.). 70p. 1981. pap. text 5.00 (*0-939436-00-0*) Ctr Tech Environ.

Melville, Michael L. The Story of the Lovat Scouts. 118p. 1981. 100.00 (*0-7152-0474-2*) St Mut.

Melville, Pauline. The Migration of Ghosts. LC 98-215800. 209p. 1998. write for info. (*0-7475-3675-9*) AMACOM.

— The Migration of Ghosts. 224p. 1999. 23.95 (*1-58234-020-X*) Bloomsbury Pubg.

***Melville, Pauline.** The Migration of Ghosts. 2000. pap. 13.95 (*1-58234-074-9*) Bloomsbury Pubg.

Melville, Pauline. The Ventriloquist's Tale. 368p. 1998. 23.95 (*1-58234-009-9*) Bloomsbury Pubg.

***Melville, Pauline.** The Ventriloquist's Tale. 1999. pap. 13.95 (*1-58234-026-9*) Bloomsbury Pubg.

Melville, Ronald, tr. see Lucretius.

Melville, S. & Goddard, W. Research Methodology: An Introduction for Science & Engineering Students. 175p. 1996. pap. 23.60 (*0-7021-3562-3*, Pub. by Juta & Co) Intl Spec Bk.

Melville, Sally. Sally Melville Styles: Knitting Techniques & 26 Patterns for Using Leftover Yarns. Rowley, Elaine, ed. LC 98-90712. (Illus.). 128p. 1998. 28.95 (*0-9646391-4-9*) XRX Inc.

***Melville, Sarah C.** The Role of Naziq/Zakutu in Sargonid Politics. (State Archives of Assyria Studies: Vol. IX). xiv, 139p. 1999. pap. text 29.50 (*951-45-9040-6*, Pub. by Neo-Assyrian Text) Eisenbrauns.

Melville-Singleton, Pamela, ed. & intro. see Trollope, Frances M.

Melville, Stephen. Seams: Art as a Philosophical Context. Gilbert-Rolfe, Jeremy, ed. & intro. by. 160p. 1996. pap. 18.95 (*90-5701-021-6*, 610381, Pub. by G & B) Dist Art Pubs.

— Seams: Art as a Philosophical Context. Gilbert-Rolfe, Jeremy, ed. & intro. by. (Critical Voices in Art, Theory, & Culture Ser.: Vol. 2). (Illus.). 160p. 1996. 35.00 (*90-5701-031-3*, 610382, Pub. by G & B) Dist Art Pubs.

Melville, Stephen, contrib. by. Hirsch Perlman. (Illus.). 32p. 1988. pap. 10.00 (*0-941548-16-3*) Ren Soc U Chi.

Melville, Stephen & Readings, Bill, eds. Vision & Textuality. LC 94-39995. (Illus.). 288p. 1995. text 54.95 (*0-8223-1630-7*); pap. text 18.95 (*0-8223-1644-7*) Duke.

Melville, Stephen W. Philosophy Beside Itself: On Deconstruction & Modernism. LC 85-14025. (Theory & History of Literature Ser.: No. 27). (Illus.). 219p. (Orig.). 1986. reprint ed. pap. 67.90 (*0-608-00839-7*, 206163000010) Bks Demand.

Melville, Sue. Crafts for All Abilities. 64p. 1997. pap. 16.95 (*0-85532-822-3*, 8223, Pub. by Srch Pr) A Schwartz & Co.

Melville, Tom. Cricket for Americans: Playing & Understanding the Game. LC 92-7488. 214p. 1993. 25.95 (*0-87972-606-7*) Bowling Green Univ Popular Press.

— The Tented Field: A History of Cricket in America. LC 98-4030. 280p. 1998. 48.95 (*0-87972-769-1*); pap. 19.95 (*0-87972-770-5*) Bowling Green Univ Popular Press.

Melville-Walmsley. Elementary Health & PE. 208p. (C). 1998. per. 35.95 (*0-7872-5071-6*, 41507101) Kendall-Hunt.

Melville, William L. Leven & Melville Papers. LC 78-172725. (Bannatyne Club, Edinburgh. Publications: No. 77). reprint ed. 67.50 (*0-404-52798-1*) AMS Pr.

Melvin. Architectural Life of Frs. York. pap. write for info. (*0-471-48960-3*) Wiley.

Melvin, ed. I'm International Money & Finiancial. 4th ed. 1997. text 11.00 (*0-673-55554-2*) S&S Trade.

Melvin, jt. auth. see Plant.

Melvin, Billy A. Free Will Baptist Minister's Manual. 1974. ring bd. 10.95 (*0-89265-024-9*) Randall Hse.

Melvin, Billy A., jt. auth. see O'Donnell, J. D.

***Melvin, Brian.** Tao of Drumming: A Philosophical & Rhythmic Study for All Instruments. 60p. 1999. pap. text 25.00 (*0-9677922-0-7*) B Melvin.

Melvin, Bruce L. Rural Youth on Relief. LC 74-37899. (Select Bibliographies Reprint Ser.). 1977. reprint ed. 20.95 (*0-8369-6737-2*) Ayer.

— Rural Youth on Relief. LC 78-165686. (Research Monographs: Vol. 11). 1971. reprint ed. lib. bdg. 19.50 (*0-306-70343-2*) Da Capo.

Melvin, Bruce L. & Smith, Elna N. Youth in Agricultural Villages. LC 79-165603. (Research Monographs: Vol. 21). 1971. reprint ed. lib. bdg. 19.50 (*0-306-70353-X*) Da Capo.

Melvin, Bruce L., jt. auth. see Smith, E. N.

Melvin, Don, jt. auth. see Kunerth, Jeff.

Melvin, Eric. Plan - Predict - Prevent: How to Reinvest in Public Buildings. (Special Reports: No. 62). 83p. (Orig.). 1992. pap. text 50.00 (*0-917084-11-X*) Am Public Works.

Melvin, Frances. The Boughs of Innocence. large type ed. 356p. 1983. 27.99 (*0-7089-1005-X*) Ulverscroft.

— Camberwell Beauty. large type ed. 352p. 1984. 27.99 (*0-7089-1105-6*) Ulverscroft.

Melvin, Frank E. Napoleon's Navigation System. LC 79-135721. reprint ed. 47.50 (*0-404-04288-0*) AMS Pr.

Melvin, Gail. Yahweh, Yahshua & You LC 98-91512. xiv, 327 p. 1998. write for info. (*0-9665602-0-5*) Jubilee Pubns.

Melvin, George F., jt. auth. see Albert, Dave.

Melvin, George F., jt. auth. see Plant, Jeremy F.

Melvin, J. L., ed. Evaporites, Petroleum & Mineral Resources. (Developments in Sedimentology Ser.: No. 50). 556p. 1991. 168.75 (*0-444-88680-X*) Elsevier.

Melvin, J. L., jt. ed. see Chino, N.

Melvin, James R. The Effects of Energy Price Changes on Commodity Prices, Interprovincial Trade & Employment. LC 76-27870. (Ontario Economic Council Research Studies: No. 3). (Illus.). 112p. reprint ed. pap. 34.80 (*0-8357-3999-6*, 203669900005) Bks Demand.

— Interregional Effects of Canadian Tariffs & Transportation Policy. (Ontario Economic Council Research Studies). 151p. 1987. pap. text 12.95 (*0-8020-6630-5*) U of Toronto Pr.

— Trade in Services: A Theoretical Analysis. 195p. 1989. pap. text 29.95 (*0-88645-090-X*, Pub. by Inst Res Pub) Ashgate Pub Co.

Melvin, Jeanne. Fibromyalgia Syndrome - Getting Healthy. (Illus.). 60p. (Orig.). 1996. pap. text 6.00 (*1-56900-041-7*, 1144) Am Occup Therapy.

***Melvin, Jeanne & Gall, Victoria, eds.** Adult Rheumatic Diseases. (Rheumatologic Rehabilitation Ser.: Vol. 2). (Illus.). 2000. pap. write for info. (*1-56900-139-1*) Am Occup Therapy.

Melvin, Jeanne & Gall, Victoria, eds. Surgical Rehabilitation. (Rheumatologic Rehabilitation Ser.: Vol. 5). (Illus.). 1999. pap. 52.00 (*1-56900-114-6*, 1205) Am Occup Therapy.

Melvin, Jeanne & Wright, Virginia, eds. Pediatric Rheumatic Diseases. (Rheumatologic Rehabilitation Ser.: Vol. 3). (Illus.). Date not set. pap. write for info. (*1-56900-087-5*) Am Occup Therapy.

***Melvin, Jeanne & Wright, Virginia, eds.** Pediatric Rheumatic Diseases. (Rheumatologic Rehabilitation Ser.: Vol. 3). (Illus.). 2000. pap. write for info. (*1-56900-140-5*) Am Occup Therapy.

Melvin, Jeanne L. Scleroderma: Caring for Your Hands & Face. (Illus.). 28p. 1994. pap. text 6.00 (*1-56900-006-9*) Am Occup Therapy.

Melvin, Jeanne L. & Jensen, Gail, eds. Rheumatologic Rehabilitation Vol. I: Assessment & Mangement. LC 98-204415. (Illus.). 450p. 1997. text 50.00 (*1-56900-086-7*, 1201) Am Occup Therapy.

***Melvin, Jeremy.** The Architecture of London. (Illus.). 320p. 2001. 42.00 (*3-932565-08-8*) Edition A Menges.

— Young British Architects. LC 99-86884. (Illus.). 128p. 2000. pap. 49.95 (*3-7643-6153-0*) Birkhauser.

Melvin, John, jt. ed. see Nahum, Alan.

Melvin, John W., jt. auth. see Nahum, Alan M.

Melvin, Michael, jt. auth. see Boyes, William.

Melvin, Michael, jt. auth. see Boyes, William J.

Melvin, Michael H. International Money & Finance. 4th ed. LC 94-17773. 304p. (C). 1997. pap. text 74.00 (*0-673-99207-1*) Addson-Wesley Educ.

— International Money & Finance. 5th ed. LC 96-16002. (C). 1997. text 68.44 (*0-673-98375-7*) Addson-Wesley Educ.

— International Money & Finance. 6th ed. LC 99-12765. 269p. (C). 1999. 75.00 (*0-321-05051-7*) Addson-Wesley Educ.

Melvin, Michael H., jt. auth. see Husted, Steven L.

Melvin, Neil. Russians Beyond Russia: The Politics of National Identity. LC 96-124124. 176p. 1996. pap. 15.95 (*1-85567-233-2*) Bks Intl VA.

***Melvin, Neil J.** Uzbekistan Vol. 7: Transition to Authoritarianism on the Silk Road. 150p. 2000. 33.00 (*90-5823-029-5*, Harwood Acad Pubs); pap. 19.95 (*90-5823-030-9*, Harwood Acad Pubs) Gordon & Breach.

Melvin, Particia M., ed. American Community Organizations: A Historical Dictionary. LC 86-9961. 252p. 1986. lib. bdg. 59.95 (*0-313-24053-1*, MLV/, Greenwood Pr) Greenwood.

Melvin, Patricia M. The Organic City: Urban Definition & Community Organization, 1880-1920. LC 87-13322. 240p. 1987. 29.95 (*0-8131-1585-X*) U Pr of Ky.

Melvin, Patricia M., jt. auth. see Miller, Zane L.

Melvin, Robert. Profiles in Flowers: The Story of San Diego County Floriculture. Ecke, Paul, Jr., ed. 168p. 1989. write for info. (*0-9623551-0-0*) P Ecke Ranch Pr.

Melvin, Sean. The Entrepreneur's Handbook for Business Law: The Business Owner's Answer Book to Most Common Legal Questions. LC 97-71169. 256p. 1997. 15.95 (*0-02-861751-7*) Macmillan.

Melvin, Sean P. Settle Your Tax Debt: How to Save Thousands Using the IRS Offer-in-Compromise Program. LC 98-8158. 192p. 1998. pap. 19.95 (*0-7931-2836-5*, 56807101) Dearborn.

***Melvin, Sean P.** The Y2K Business & Legal Survival Guide: Surviving Litigation - Managing the Crisis - Dealing with Liability & Insurance. LC 99-38229. 208p. 1999. pap. 19.95 (*0-7931-3486-2*) Dearborn.

Melvin, Sean P., jt. auth. see Nicholas, Ted.

Melvin, Shelley. Not Just Cheesecake! A Yogurt Cheese Cookbook. 2nd rev. ed. LC 97-6928. 224p. 1997. pap. 16.95 (*0-937404-45-4*) Triad Pub FL.

Melvin, William H. First Day of Forever & One Hundred Additional Poems. 110p. 1989. pap., per. 7.95 (*0-89697-308-5*) Intl Univ Pr.

Melvoin, Richard I. New England Outpost: War & Society in Colonial Frontier Deerfield. 368p. 1992. pap. 14.95 (*0-393-30808-1*) Norton.

Melvold, Robert W., et al. Sorbents for Liquid Hazardous Substance Cleanup & Control. LC 87-31550. (Pollution Technology Review Ser.: No. 150). (Illus.). 154p. 1988. 36.00 (*0-8155-1159-0*) Noyes.

Melwani, Mona. Indian Cooking Overseas: Traditional Cuisine Survives. (C). 1995. pap. write for info. (*81-207-1613-2*) Sterling Pubs.

Melyan, Gary. The Pocket I-Ching. LC 88-50327. (Illus.). 182p. 1988. reprint ed. pap. 8.95 (*0-8048-1566-6*) Tuttle Pubng.

Melyan, Gary G. The Pocket I-Ching. 1999. 5.99 (*0-7858-1122-2*) Bk Sales Inc.

Melyan, Wesley R. & Bonetti, Lee. Rolling Thunder: July 1965-December, 1966. 149p. 1993. reprint ed. pap. 18.50 (*0-923135-70-7*) Dalley Bk Service.

Melynk, Steven A. & Narasimhan, Ram. Computer Integrated Manufacturing: Guidelines & Applications from Industrial Leaders. (APICS Series in Production Management). 378p. 1991. 50.00 (*1-55623-538-0*, Irwn Prfssnl) McGraw-Hill Prof.

Melzack, Ronald, ed. Pain Measurement & Assessment. fac. ed. LC 82-40296. (Illus.). 311p. pap. 96.50 (*0-7837-7506-7*, 204700000005) Bks Demand.

Melzack, Ronald & Wall, P. Challenge of Pain. 1996. pap. 17.95 (*0-14-025670-9*, Pub. by Pnguin Bks Ltd) Trafalgar.

Melzack, Ronald, jt. ed. see Turk, Dennis C.

Melzack, Ronald, jt. ed. see Wall, Patrick D.

***Melzak, Sheila.** Children in Exile: Therapeutic Work in the Community & the Clinic with Child Survivors of Political Violence & War. LC 99-41645. 300p. 1999. 29.95 (*1-85302-585-2*) Jessica Kingsley.

Melzak, Z. Alex. Companion to Concrete Mathematics Vol. 1: Mathematical Techniques & Various Applications. LC 72-14171. (Wiley Series in Pure & Applied Mathematics). 284p. reprint ed. pap. 88.10 (*0-608-30895-1*, 202249200027) Bks Demand.

— Companion to Concrete Mathematics Vol. 2: Mathematical Ideas, Modelling & Applications. LC 72-14171. (Wiley Series in Pure & Applied Mathematics). 432p. reprint ed. pap. 134.00 (*0-608-30894-3*, 205516500002) Bks Demand.

Melzer, Annabelle H. Latest Rage the Big Drum: Dada & Surrealist Performance. LC 80-22656. (Studies in the Fine Arts: The Avant-Garde: No. 7). (Illus.). 290p. reprint ed. pap. 89.90 (*0-8357-1639-2*, 207023100065) Bks Demand.

Melzer, Arthur M. The Natural Goodness of Man: On the System of Rousseau's Thought. 368p. 1998. pap. text 22.50 (*0-226-51979-1*) U Ch Pr.

— The Natural Goodness of Man: On the System of Rousseau's Thought. LC 89-20587. 328p. reprint ed. pap. 101.70 (*0-608-09480-3*, 205428000005) Bks Demand.

— The Natural Goodness of Man: The Study of Behavior Without a Goal. 368p. 1996. lib. bdg. 61.50 (*0-226-51978-3*) U Ch Pr.

Melzer, Arthur M., et al, eds. History & the Idea of Progress. 272p. 1995. text 39.95 (*0-8014-2986-2*); pap. text 15.95 (*0-8014-8182-1*) Cornell U Pr.

— Technology in the Western Political Tradition. 352p. 1993. text 45.00 (*0-8014-2724-X*); pap. text 17.95 (*0-8014-8006-X*) Cornell U Pr.

Melzer, Arthur M., ed. see Simon, John, et al.

Melzer, Arthur M., ed. see Symposium on Science, Reason, & Modern Democracy S.

Melzer, Emmanuel. No Way Out: The Politics of Polish Jewry, 1935-1939. LC 96-30841. (Monographs of the Hebrew Union College: Vol. 19). Orig. Title: Ma'avak Medini Be-Malkodet. (HEB.). 248p. (C). 1997. 39.95 (*0-87820-418-0*) Hebrew Union Coll Pr.

Melzer, James E. & Moffitt, Kirk. Head-Mounted Displays: Designing for the User. LC 96-49041. (Optical & Electro-Optical Engineering Ser.). (Illus.). 352p. 1996. 65.00 (*0-07-041819-5*) McGraw.

Melzer, John T. Fourteen Days to Field Spanish. 60p. 1985. pap. 7.95 (*0-317-01524-9*, Pub. by Univ Ed) Taylor & Francis.

— Oilfield Spanish Thousands of Words & Terms in Spanish & English from Company Man to Roughneck from Toolpusher to Roustabout: A Vocabulary of Walk-Around Rio-Spanish from Spud to Tank Battery from Reserve Pit to Crom Block. Special Section on Pumps. Ricci, Doris R., tr. LC TN865.M45.Tr. of Castellano para el Campo Petrolifero. (ENG & SPA., Illus.). 324p. 1997. pap. 56.95 (*0-9664440-0-0*) Oakbowery Bks.

Melzer, Marilyn. Learning Strategies for Allied Health Students. LC 95-901. (Illus.). 368p. 1995. pap. text 26.95 (*0-7216-5603-X*, W B Saunders Co) Harcrt Hlth Sci Grp.

Melzer, Milton, ed. Lincoln: In His Own Words. LC 92-17431. (Illus.). 224p. (J). (gr. 3-7). 1993. 22.95 (*0-15-245437-3*) Harcourt.

— Lincoln, in His Own Words. limited ed. LC 92-17431. (Illus.). 240p. (J). 1993. 150.00 (*0-15-245438-1*) Harcourt.

***Melzer, Richard.** Breakdown, How the Secret of the Atomic Bomb Was Stolen: An Expose. LC 99-52053. (Illus.). 160p. 2000. pap. 16.95 (*0-86534-304-7*) Sunstone Pr.

— Coming of Age in the Great Depression: The Civilian Conservation Corps in New Mexico. 2000. 25.00 (*1-881325-41-5*) Yucca Tree Pr.

Melzer, Richard. Ernie Pyle in the American Southwest: A Focused Biography. LC 95-40232. (Illus.). 176p. (Orig.). 1996. pap. 18.95 (*0-86534-243-1*) Sunstone Pr.

— Madrid Revisited: Life & Labor in a New Mexican Mining Camp in the Great Depression. 2nd ed. (Illus.). 64p. 1997. reprint ed. pap. 9.95 (*1-58096-000-6*) Ancient City Pr.

Melzer, Richard, jt. ed. see Meerbaum, Samuel.

***Melzer, Sara E. & Norberg, Kathryn.** From Royal to Republican Body: Incorporating the Political in Seventeenth & Eighteenth Century France. LC 97-22678. 286p. 1998. 50.00 (*0-520-20806-4*, Pub. by U CA Pr); pap. 18.00 (*0-520-20807-2*, Pub. by U CA Pr) Cal Prin Full Svc.

Melzer, Sondra. The Rhetoric of Rage: Women in Dorothy Parker. LC 95-36389. (Writing about Women Ser.: Vol. 22). XI, 190p. (C). 1997. text 44.95 (*0-8204-3038-2*) P Lang Pubng.

Melzer, Werner. Beekeeping: An Owner's Manual. 1989. pap. 6.95 (*0-8120-4089-9*) Barron.

***Melzi, Gaetano.** Dizionario di Opere Anonime e Pseudonime di Scrittori Italiani, 3 vols. 1666p. 1999. reprint ed. 195.00 (*1-57898-161-1*) Martino Pubng.

Melzi, R. C. Langenscheidt Italian Standard Dictionary, Thumb-Indexed. 1990. 20.95 (*0-88729-060-4*) Langenscheidt.

Melzi, Robert C. Bantam New College Italian/English Dictionary. (ENG & ITA.). 736p. 1984. mass mkt. 5.99 (*0-553-27947-5*) Bantam.

— The New International Webster's Italian & English Dictionary. Orig. Title: The Bantam New College Italian & English Dictionary. xiii, 719p. 1998. reprint ed. 24.95 (*1-888777-46-X*) Trident Pr Intl.

Melzian, H. I., jt. auth. see Westermann, Diedrich.

Member Inns of the Wisconsin Bed & Breakfast Association Staff. Mornings Inn Style: A Cookbook & Travel Guide from the Wisconsin Bed & Breakfast Assn. LC 98-86310. (Illus.). 176p. 1999. pap. 15.95 (*0-942495-83-7*) Palmer Pubns Inc.

***Members & Friends of Mercersburg Historical Society Staff.** The Tuscarora Reader. (Illus.). 300p. (J). (gr. 3-4). 2000. 25.00 (*0-9702361-0-7*) Mercersburg Hist Soc.

***Members & Friends of the California's Sesquicentennial Wagon Train.** California's Sesquicentennial Wagon Train: A Celebration of the Use of Animal Motive Power in the Settling & Commerce of California. (Illus.). viii, 178p. 1999. pap. 15.00 (*0-9675855-0-3*) CA Sesquicen.

Members of Assistance League of St. Louis. Fare to Remember: A Sampling of St. Louis Cuisine. LC 98-73283. 290p. 1998. 19.95 (*0-9666305-0-5*, Pub. by Asst League St Louis) Wimmer Bks.

***Members of Bell LabsTechnical Staff.** Handbook of CDMA System Design, Engineering & Optimization. Kim, Kyoung-Jin, ed. LC 99-55012. 274p. 1999. 80.00 incl. cd-rom (*0-13-017572-2*) P-H.

Members of ESRC Inner Cities Research Programme St & Hausner, Victor A., eds. Urban Economic Change: Five City Studies. (ESRC Inner Cities Research Programme Ser.: No. 2). (Illus.). 280p. 1988. text 69.00 (*0-19-823280-2*) OUP.

Members of Freshfields' Construction & Engineering. Management Contracting Law & Practice. 165p. 1994. pap. 50.00 (*1-874241-18-X*, Pub. by Cavendish Pubng) Gaunt.

Members of Haiku Society of America. From a Kind Neighbor: Haiku Society of America 1997 Members' Anthology. Stevenson, John, ed. 96p. 1997. pap. 9.00 (*0-9631467-5-0*) Haiku Soc.

Members of JSC, jt. auth. see Friends & Family of JSC Members.

Members of Moosewood College Staff. Low-Fat Favorites: Flavorful Recipes for Healthful Meals. LC 96-49430. (Moosewood Collective Ser.). 1996. 35.00 (*0-517-70210-X*) Crown.

Members of Poetry Workshop Staff. Festival of Poetry Bk. 1: Anthology of Poems by Members of Margaret Tyler's Scottsdale Library Poetry Workshop. 64p. (Orig.). 1989. pap. 2.50 (*0-9622775-0-9*) Tyler-Balstrode.

Members of Sublette County Artists' Guild. Seed-Ke-Dee Revisited: Land of Blue Granite & Silver Sage. LC 98-60583. (Illus.). 480p. 1998. text 39.95 (*1-57579-127-7*) Pine Hill Pr.

Members of TFCE Staff. Texas Temptations. 350p. 1993. 12.00 (*0-9637300-0-2*) TX Assn Fmly.

***Members of the Blue Bird Circle.** Gathered Again: A Collection of Recipes. (Illus.). 304p. 1998. 18.00 (*0-9617897-1-9*) Blue Bird Cir.

Members of the Department of Otolaryngology Staff, et al. Management of Voice Disorders. (Illus.). 256p. (C). 1994. pap. 55.00 (*1-56593-311-7*, 0464) Thomson Learn.

Members of the Emiliano Zapata Liberation Movement. Zapatistas! Documents of the New Mexican Revolution. 360p. Date not set. 12.00 (*1-57027-014-7*) Autonomedia.

Members of the Faculty of Theology of the Universi. Navarre Bible: Acts of the Apostles. (Navarre Bible Ser.). (ENG & LAT.). 272p. pap. 14.95 (*1-85182-044-2*, Pub. by Four Cts Pr) Intl Spec Bk.

— Navarre Bible: St. John. (LAT & ENG.). 247p. 1989. pap. 14.95 (*1-85182-094-9*) Scepter Pubs.

— Navarre Bible: St. Luke. (Navarre Bible Ser.). (ENG & LAT.). pap. 14.95 (*1-85182-040-X*, Pub. by Four Cts Pr) Intl Spec Bk.

— St. Mark. (Navarre Bible Ser.). pap. 14.95 (*1-85182-092-2*, Pub. by Four Cts Pr) Intl Spec Bk.

— Thessalonians & Pastoral: Thessalonians & Pastoral Epistles. (Navarre Bible Ser.). 183p. 1992. pap. 14.95 (*1-85182-077-9*, Pub. by Four Cts Pr) Intl Spec Bk.

Members of the Faculty of Theology of the Universi & Casciaro, Jose M. Navarre Bible: Captivity Epistles. Adams, Michael, tr. from SPA. (ENG & LAT., Illus.). 207p. 1991. pap. 14.95 (*1-85182-079-5*) Scepter Pubs.

— Navarre Bible: Catholic Epistles. Adams, Michael, tr. from SPA. (ENG & LAT., Illus.). 240p. 1991. pap. 14.95 (*1-85182-087-6*) Scepter Pubs.

— Navarre Bible: Corinthians. Adams, Michael, tr. from SPA. (ENG & LAT., Illus.). 250p. 1990. pap. 14.95 (*1-85182-065-5*) Scepter Pubs.

An Asterisk (*) at the beginning of an entry indicates that the title is appearing for the first time.

— Navarre Bible: Hebrews. Adams, Michael, tr. from SPA. (ENG & LAT., Illus.). 198p. 1990. pap. 14.95 (*1-85182-069-8*) Scepter Pubs.
— Navarre Bible: Revelation. Adams, Michael, tr. from SPA. (ENG & LAT., Illus.). 192p. 1992. pap. 14.95 (*1-85182-089-2*) Scepter Pubs.
Members of the International Food, Wine & Travel W. Windows to the World: Inside Look at Food, Wine & Travel. KaSaker, Ray & Jackson, D. K., eds. (Illus.). 254p. 1989. 7.98 (*0-9621891-1-1*) D & A Pub CA.
***Members of the Scientific Committee of the XIVth EAU Congress, ed.** European Association of Urology (EAU) XIVth Congress, Stockholm, April 1999: Abstracts, Vol. 1 & 2. (European Urology Ser.: Vol. 35, Suppl. 2). xiv, 192p. 1999. pap. 45.25 (*3-8055-6850-9*) S Karger.
***Members of the Scientific Committee of the XVth EAU Congress, ed.** European Association of Urology: XVth Congress, Brussels, April 2000: Abstracts. (European Urology Ser.: Vol. 37, Suppl. 2). (Illus.). xvi, 176p. 2000. pap. 45.25 (*3-8055-7068-6*) S Karger.
Members of the Society Staff. Proceedings: Papers from the 6th Regional Meeting. 588p. 1970. pap. 7.00 (*0-914203-01-0*) Chicago Ling.
Members of the U.S. Congress. Profiles in Character. 288p. 1996. 19.99 (*0-7852-7356-5*) Nelson.
Members of the Washington State, jt. auth. see Hoague, Eleanore.
Members of the 455th Bomb Squadron Association. Marauder Squadron Albums - A Trilogy from the 455th Bombardment Squadron: Includes Marauder Memoirs - History of the 455th Bombardment Squadron in WW II - World War II Combat Drawings & Memoirs of Benedict I. Goldsmith - Prisoners of War . . . Missing in Action & the Squadron Beyond, 3 vols. Mulrenin, Paul E., ed. LC 97-70441. (Illus.). 1230p. (C). 1997. pap. 75.00 (*0-9619535-2-7*) Four Fifty Fifth.
Members of Women's American ORT Staff. ORT Cooks Around the World. (Illus.). 229p. (Orig.). 1994. pap. 12.95 (*0-9652450-0-4*) Wom Am ORT.
Membery, York. Keanu Reeves. LC 97-16041. (Superstars of Film Ser.). (Illus.). 48p. (YA). (gr. 5 up). 1999. lib. bdg. 15.95 (*0-7910-4646-X*) Chelsea Hse.
— Pierce Brosnan: The Biography. (Illus.). 224p. 1997. mass mkt. 7.95 (*0-7535-0158-9*, Pub. by Virgin Bks) London Brdge.
— Ralph Fiennes: The Biography. (Illus.). 224p. 1998. pap. 16.95 (*0-233-99290-1*, Pub. by Chameleon) Trafalgar.
Membrane Processes for Industry Symposium Staff. Proceedings of the Membrane Processes for Industry Symposium, May 19-20, 1986. Feazel, Charles E. & Lacey, Robert E., eds. LC 66-30620. (Illus.). 268p. 1966. pap. 5.00 (*0-940824-00-0*) S Res Inst.
***Membre, Michele.** Mission to the Lord Sophy of Persia (1539-1542) Translated with Introduction & Notes. 2nd ed. Morton, A. H., ed. 144p. (C). 1999. pap. 32.00 (*0-906094-43-7*, Pub. by Gibb Memorial Trust) David Brown.
Membrives, Eva P., ed. see Aleman, Manuel M.
Memdovic, Olga, et al, eds. Globalization of Labour Markets: Challenges, Adjustment & Policy Response in the European Union & Less Developed Countries. LC 97-33607. 360p. 1997. 151.50 (*0-7923-9986-2*) Kluwer Academic.
Meme-Fun Dai, tr. see Graham, Billy.
Memering, W. Dean. Prentice Hall Guide to Research Writing. 2nd ed. 384p. (C). 1989. pap. text 20.60 (*0-13-774480-3*) P-H.
Memering, W. Dean, jt. auth. see Howell, James F.
Memering, W. Dean, jt. auth. see O'Hare, Frank.
Memling, Claude. Little Cottontail. (Little Golden Storybks.). (Illus.). (J). 1998. 3.99 (*0-307-16158-7*, 16158, Goldn Books) Gldn Bks Pub Co.
***Memmel, Norbert & Kohler, Anette.** Classic Dolomite Climbs. (Illus.). 232p. 2000. pap. 29.95 (*0-89886-693-6*) Mountaineers.
Memmer, Wayne. Tiger: A True Champion. LC 91-62540. 56p. 1993. 6.95 (*0-944957-32-3*) Rivercross Pub.
Memmi, Albert. Agar. (FRE.). 1984. pap. 10.95 (*0-7859-4210-6*) Fr & Eur.
— The Colonizer & the Colonized. rev. ed. LC 90-24035. 208p. 1991. pap. 15.50 (*0-8070-0301-8*) Beacon Pr.
— Desert Ou la Vie et les Aventures de Joubair Ouali El-Mammi. (Folio Ser.: No. 2034). (FRE.). 1989. pap. 10.95 (*2-07-038122-6*) Schoenhof.
— Jews & Arabs. Levieux, Eleanor, tr. from FRE. LC 75-10697. 224p. 1975. 9.95 (*0-87955-327-8*); pap. 7.95 (*0-87955-328-6*) O'Hara.
— The Pillar of Salt: A Novel. LC 91-16952. 352p. 1992. reprint ed. pap. 16.00 (*0-8070-8327-5*) Beacon Pr.
***Memmi, Albert.** Racism. Martinot, Steve, tr. from FRE. LC 99-47227. 176p. 1999. pap. 15.95 (*0-8166-3165-4*, Pub. by U of Minn Pr); lib. bdg. 39.95 (*0-8166-3164-6*, Pub. by U of Minn Pr) Chicago Distribution Ctr.
Memmi, Albert. Scorpion. (Folio Ser.: No. 1715). (FRE.). 270p. 1986. pap. 10.95 (*2-07-037715-6*) Schoenhof.
— The Scorpion. 2nd ed. LC 79-114950. 242p. 1975. reprint ed. 9.95 (*0-87955-908-X*); reprint ed. pap. 7.95 (*0-87955-906-3*) O'Hara.
— Statue de Sel. (Folio Ser.: No. 206). (FRE.). 377p. 1984. pap. 9.95 (*2-07-036206-X*) Schoenhof.
Memmler, Ruth L. The Human Body in Health & Disease. 8th ed. LC 95-17706. 480p. 1995. pap. text 30.95 (*0-397-55175-4*) Lppncott W & W.
— Structure & Function of the Human Body. 6th ed. LC 95-38675. 368p. 1995. text 34.00 (*0-397-55173-8*); pap. text, student ed. 16.95 (*0-397-55190-8*) Lppncott W & W.
Memmler, Ruth L., et al. The Human Body in Health & Disease. 8th ed. LC 95-17706. (Illus.). 480p. 1995. text 36.00 (*0-397-55174-6*) Lppncott W & W.
— Structure & Function of the Human Body. 6th ed. LC 95-38675. (Illus.). 368p. 1996. pap. 29.95 (*0-397-55172-X*) Lppncott W & W.
Memmott, David. House on Fire. 68p. 1992. pap. 9.00 (*1-877655-06-6*) Wordcraft Oregon.
— The Larger Earth: Descending Notes of a Grounded Astronaut. (Illus.). 104p. (Orig.). 1996. pap. 9.95 (*1-882633-18-0*) Permeable.
***Memmott, David.** Shadow Bones: Stories. (Wordcraft Speculative Writers Ser.: No. 19). 116p. 1999. pap. 10.00 (*1-877655-28-7*) Wordcraft Oregon.
Memmott, David, ed. see Beasley, Conger, Jr.
Memmott, David, ed. see Evenson, Brian.
Memmott, David, ed. see Kennedy, Thomas E.
Memmott, David, ed. see Olsen, Lance.
Memmott, Harry. An Artist's Guide to Firing Pottery. (VCP Ser.). 127p. 1995. pap. 65.00 (*0-909184-28-3*, Pub. by Deakin Univ) St Mut.
— An Artist's Guide to the Use of Ceramic Oxides. 114p. 1995. pap. 54.00 (*0-8495-8006-4*, Pub. by Deakin Univ) St Mut.
Memo, Rosemary & Haney, Shirley. Communication, Compromise & Commitment. 88p. (YA). (gr. 7-12). 1994. pap. 6.95 (*1-57515-045-X*) PPI Pubng.
Memon, Ali N. The Islamic Nation: Status & Future of Muslims in the New World Order. LC 95-6017. 261p. 1995. pap. 15.00 (*0-9627854-7-4*) Writers Inc.
— Pakistan: Islamic Nation in Crisis. LC 97-18601. 1996. pap. 16.95 (*0-915957-66-3*) amana pubns.
***Memon, Amina.** Handbook of the Psychology of Interviewing. LC 98-41438. 380p. 1999. 82.95 (*0-471-97443-9*) Wiley.
***Memon, Amina, et al.** Psychology & Law: Truthfulness, Accuracy & Credibility. (C). 1998. pap., student ed. 56.56 (*0-07-709316-X*) McGrw-H Hghr Educ.
***Memon, Mohammad Siddique G.** Sukkur: Then & Now. (Illus.). 225p. 1999. text 11.95 (*0-19-579069-3*) OUP.
Memon, Mohammad U., jt. auth. see Husain, Initzar.
Memon, Muhammad U., ed. Colour of Nothingness: Modern Urdu Short Stories. LC 98-930522. 230p. 1999. 21.95 (*0-19-577897-9*) OUP.
Memon, Muhammad U., ed. The Tale of the Old Fisherman: Contemporary Urdu Short Stories. 197p. 1991. 25.00 (*0-89410-681-3*, Three Contnts); pap. 11.95 (*0-89410-682-1*, Three Contnts) L Rienner.
Memon, Muhammad U., tr. see Hussein, Abdullah.
Memon, Muhammad Umar. An Epic Unwritten. LC 98-906488. xviii, 369 p. 1998. write for info. (*0-14-027227-5*) Penguin Books.
Memon, Muhammad Umar, ed. see Mastur, Khadija.
Memon, Muhammad Umar, ed. see Qasimi, Ahmad Nadeem.
Memon, P. Ali. Keeping New Zealand Green. 1996. 39.95 (*0-908569-70-X*, Pub. by Univ Otago Pr) Intl Spec Bk.
Memon, Siddique G. Tomb of the Kalhora Chiefs at Hyderabad. (Illus.). 86p. 1995. 55.00 (*0-19-577502-3*) OUP.
Memorial Hospital Junior Auxiliary Easton Maryland. A Cook's Tour of the Eastern Shore. 2nd ed. LC 59-15724. (Illus.). 386p. 1959. spiral bd. 15.95 (*0-87033-001-2*, Tidewtr Pubs) Cornell Maritime.
Memorial Sloan-Kettering Cancer Center. International Alumni Directory, 1986-1988. Wood, Denise D., ed. 1986. 50.00 (*0-911315-01-2*) Memorial Sloan-Kettering.
Memory, J. D., jt. auth. see Stejskal, E. O.
Memory, John M. Some Relationships: Everything I Know about Intimate, Sometimes Intimate & Supposed-to-Be Intimate Relationships. LC 97-92568. (Illus.). 150p. 1997. pap. 7.95 (*0-9659703-0-2*) Madison Pub.
***Memory, John M. & Aragon, Randall.** Patrol Officer Problem Solving & Solutions. 450p. 2000. pap. write for info. (*0-89089-857-X*) Carolina Acad Pr.
Memory Trade: A Prehistory of Cyberculture. Memory Trade: A Prehistory of Cyberculture. (Illus.). 132p. 1998. pap. text 15.00 (*90-5704-181-2*, Pub. by Harvey Miller) Gordon & Breach.
Memphis Herb Society Staff. Today's Herbal Kitchen: How to Cook & Design with Herbs Through the Seasons. Boker, Carol, ed. LC 95-61099. (Illus.). 256p. 1996. 19.95 (*1-879958-28-7*, Tradery) Wimmer Cos.
Memrino, Marcia L. & Russell, Paul A., eds. Paxton, Massachusetts Births, Marriages & Deaths, 1748-1850. xx, 138p. (Orig.). 1996. pap. 22.00 (*0-7884-0564-0*, R877) Heritage Bk.
Men, Alexander. About Christ & the Church. Vinogradov, Alexis, tr. 112p. 1996. pap. 6.95 (*1-879038-29-3*) Oakwood Pubns.
— Awake to Life! Sermons from the Paschal (Easter) Cycle. 96p. 1996. 4.45 (*1-879038-26-9*) Oakwood Pubns.
— Christianity for the Twenty-First Century: The Prophetic Writings of Alexander Men. Shukman, Ann & Roberts, Elizabeth, eds. 224p. 1996. pap. 19.95 (*0-8264-0894-X*) Continuum.
— Son of Man: The Story of Christ & Christianity. Brown, Samuel, tr. from RUS. 256p. 1998. pap. 11.95 (*1-879038-28-5*) Oakwood Pubns.
Men, Hunbatz. Secrets of Mayan Science - Religion. LC 89-6637. (Illus.). 156p. (Orig.). 1989. pap. 12.00 (*0-939680-63-7*) Bear & Co.
Men of the Middle Tennessee WWII Fighter Pilots As. Missions Remembered: Recollections of the World War II Air War. LC 97-48517. (Illus.). 220p. 1998. 22.95 (*0-07-001649-6*) McGraw.
Mena, Alicia, tr. see Rumble, Patricia B.
Mena, Andres I. Perez y, see Perez y Mena, Andres I.
Mena, Andres I. Perez y, see Stevens-Arroyo, Anthony M. & Perez y Mena, Andres I., eds.
Mena, Cesar A. Historia de la Medicina en Cuba Vol. III: 1898-1902. (SPA.). Date not set. pap. write for info. (*0-89729-686-9*) Ediciones.
— Historia de la Medicina en Cuba II: Ejercicios y Ensenanza de las Ciencias Medicas en la Epoca Colonial. LC 91-76473. (Coleccion Cuba y sus Jueces). (SPA., Illus.). 380p. (Orig.). 1993. pap. 39.00 (*0-89729-646-X*) Ediciones.
— Historia de la Odontologia en Cuba: Cuba Comunista y en el Exilio 1959-1983, Vol. IV. LC 81-652235. (Coleccion Cuba y sus Jueces). (SPA., Illus.). 752p. (Orig.). 1984. pap. 33.00 (*0-89729-344-4*) Ediciones.
— Historia de la Odontologia en Cuba: Vol. 1, Periodo Colonial(1492-1898), Vol. I. LC 81-65235. (Coleccion Cuba y sus Jueces). (SPA., Illus.). 394p. (Orig.). 1981. pap. 29.00 (*0-89729-293-6*) Ediciones.
— Historia de la Odontologia en Cuba: Vol. 2, Intervencion Norteamericana, 1899-1902, 1906-1909, 3 vols. LC 81-65235. (Coleccion Cuba y sus Jueces). (SPA., Illus.). 293p. (Orig.). 1982. pap. 29.00 (*0-89729-310-X*) Ediciones.
— Historia de la Odontologia en Cuba: Vol. 3, Periodo Repubicano 1940-1958, 3 vols. LC 81-65235. (Coleccion Cuba y sus Jueces). (SPA., Illus.). 293p. (Orig.). 1982. pap. 29.00 (*0-89729-311-8*) Ediciones.
— Santa Apolonia (Patrona Dental) LC 86-80092. (SPA., Illus.). 79p. (Orig.). 1985. pap. 10.00 (*0-89729-388-6*) Ediciones.
Mena, Cesar A. & Cobelo, Armando F. Historia de la Medicina en Cuba, Vol. 1: Hospitales y Centros Beneficos en Cuba Colonial. LC 91-76473. (Coleccion Cuba y sus Jueces). (SPA., Illus.). 717p. (Orig.). 1992. pap. 49.00 (*0-89729-624-9*) Ediciones.
Mena, Fernando de, tr. see Lopez, Estrada F., ed.
Mena, Hector R. Index to Costa Rican Philatelic Literature, Pt. II. vi, 59p. 1993. 5.00 (*0-9645247-1-6*) SCRC.
Mena, Hector R., ed. Costa Rica Postal Catalogue. 2nd ed. (Illus.). 248p. 1997. pap. 30.00 (*0-9645247-4-0*, SOCORICO) SCRC.
Mena, Jesus. Data Mining Your Website. LC 99-22694. 400p. 1999. pap. 39.95 (*1-55558-222-2*, Digital DEC) Buttrwrth-Heinemann.
Mena, Juan De, see De Mena, Juan.
Mena, Maria C. The Collected Stories of Maria Cristina Mena. Doherty, Amy, ed. LC 97-22160. (Recovering the U. S. - Hispanic Literary Heritage Ser.). 208p. 1997. pap. 12.95 (*1-55885-211-5*) Arte Publico.
Mena, Patricio V. A Revision of the Genus Arcytophyllum Rubiaceae: Hedyotideae. LC 90-6284. (Memoirs Ser.: No. 60). (Illus.). 28p. 1990. pap. 7.25 (*0-89327-355-4*) NY Botanical.
Mena, Patricio V., jt. auth. see Balslev, H.
Mena, Paul. Tenement Landscapes. LC 96-203625. 20p. (Orig.). 1995. pap. 3.00 (*1-888431-02-4*) ASGP.
Menache, Alberto. Understanding Motion Capture for Character Animation & Video Games. 350p. 1999. pap. text 54.95 (*0-12-490630-3*) Morgan Kaufmann.
Menache, Sophia. Clement V. LC 97-27894. (Cambridge Studies in Medieval Life & Thought: No. 36). 375p. (C). 1998. text 69.95 (*0-521-59219-4*) Cambridge U Pr.
Menache, Sophia, ed. Communication in the Jewish Diaspora: The Pre-Modern World. (Brill's Series in Jewish Studies: Vol. 16). 1996. 140.50 (*90-04-10189-6*) Brill Academic Pubs.
Menachem, Kollel, contrib. by. Kovets Divrei Torah. Vol. 18. (HEB.). 294p. 1992. pap. 5.00 (*0-8266-6025-8*) Kehot Pubn Soc.
— Kovets Divrei Torah, Vol. 19. (HEB., Illus.). 144p. 1993. pap. 8.00 (*0-8266-6026-6*) Kehot Pubn Soc.
Menage, Ronald H. The Practical Book of Greenhouse Gardening. 168p. 1983. 7.95 (*0-312-63461-7*) St Martin.
Menagh, Melanie, jt. auth. see Gallagher, Dawn.
Menaghan, Elizabeth G., jt. auth. see Parcel, Toby L.
***Menaghan, John.** All the Money in the World. LC 99-460528. 96p. 2000. pap. 13.95 (*1-897648-45-6*, Pub. by Salmon Poetry) Dufour.
Menahem, Samuel E. When Therapy Isn't Enough: The Healing Power of Prayer & Psychology. Elliott, Ryan & Hauser, Joe, eds. 250p. (Orig.). 1995. pap. 14.95 (*0-9615140-4-3*) Relaxed Bks.
Menai, M. N., jt. tr. see Zakir, Mohammed.
Menair, Peter, et al. Down from the Shimmering Sky: Masks of the Northwest Coast. LC 98-15997. (Illus.). 192p. 1998. pap. text 30.00 (*0-295-97709-4*) U of Wash Pr.
Menaker, Austin H., jt. auth. see Kutz, Kenneth J.
Menaker, Daniel. The Treatment. LC 97-49475. 288p. 1998. 23.00 (*0-679-42206-4*) Knopf.
— The Treatment. 272p. 1999. pap. 14.00 (*0-671-03263-1*, WSP) PB.
Menaker, Donald. Family Trees. limited ed. Lott, Clarinda H., ed. (Illus.). 1983. 2.00 (*0-932616-12-7*) Brick Hse Bks.
— The Nearest Living Horizon. 64p. (Orig.). 1997. pap. 10.00 (*0-932616-58-5*) Brick Hse Bks.
Menaker, Esther. The Freedom to Inquire: Self Psychological Perspectives on Women's Issues, Masochism, & the Therapeutic Relationship. LC 94-49182. 360p. 1995. 50.00 (*1-56821-475-8*) Aronson.
— Masochism & the Emergent Ego. LC 96-10226. (Master Works). 1996. reprint ed. pap. 50.00 (*1-56821-837-0*) Aronson.
— Misplaced Loyalties. LC 94-24042. 1995. pap. 21.95 (*1-56000-816-4*) Transaction Pubs.
Menaker, Esther & Menaker, William. Ego in Evolution. (Psychoanalysis: Examined & Re-Examined Ser.). 280p. 1984. reprint ed. lib. bdg. 32.50 (*0-306-76236-6*) Da Capo.
Menaker, Michael, ed. Extraretinal Photoreception in Circadian Rhythms & Related Phenoma: Proceedings of a Symposium, Vancouver. 1976. pap. 26.00 (*0-08-020965-3*, Pergamon Pr) Elsevier.
Menaker, William, jt. auth. see Menaker, Esther.
Menal, Pere. Collected Works of Pere Menal. 1996. 69.00 (*3-7643-5147-0*) Birkhauser.
Menamin, Margaret. Sonnets for a Second Summer. 60p. 1996. 15.95 (*1-882935-23-3*) Westphalia.
Menan, Janet W. Faces of Deception. LC 97-91440. 1998. pap. 14.95 (*0-533-12681-9*) Vantage.
Menand. Future of Academic Freedom. 1998. pap. 15.00 (*0-226-52005-6*) U Ch Pr.
***Menand, Louis.** Metaphysical Club. 2000. text (*0-374-19963-9*) FS&G.
Menand, Louis. Pragmatism: A Reader. LC 97-9328. 1997. pap. 16.00 (*0-679-77544-7*) Random.
Menand, Louis, ed. The Future of Academic Freedom. 256p. 1996. 24.95 (*0-226-52004-8*) U Ch Pr.
Menander. Four Plays: The Hero - Epitrepontes - Periceiromene - Samia. Capps, Edward, ed. & intro. by. (College Classical Ser.). (GRE.). (C). 1981. text 32.50 (*0-89241-364-6*); pap. text 16.00 (*0-89241-113-9*) Caratzas.
— Menander: The Bad-Tempered Man. Ireland, Stanley, ed. & tr. by. from GRE. (Classical Texts Ser.). 192p. 1995. pap. 22.00 (*0-85668-611-5*, Pub. by Aris & Phillips); text 59.99 (*0-85668-610-7*, Pub. by Aris & Phillips) David Brown.
— Menander, the Principal Fragments. Allinson, Frank G., tr. LC 70-109789. 539p. 1970. reprint ed. lib. bdg. 75.00 (*0-8371-4279-2*, MEFR, Greenwood Pr) Greenwood.
— Plays & Fragments: Menander. Miller, Norma, tr. & intro. by. 272p. 1988. pap. 12.95 (*0-14-044501-3*, Penguin Classics) Viking Penguin.
— Rhetor. Wilson, N. G. & Russell, Donald A., eds. 1981. 115.00 (*0-19-814013-4*) OUP.
— Das Schiedsgericht. Von Wilamowitz-Moellendorff, Ulrich, ed. viii, 219p. 1974. write for info. (*3-296-14600-8*) G Olms Pubs.
Menander, et al. Menander. LC 98-9966. (Greek Drama Ser.). 296p. 1998. 40.00 (*0-8122-3444-8*); pap. 17.95 (*0-8122-1652-0*) U of Pa Pr.
Menapace, John, photos by. Letter in a Klein Bottle. LC 84-80980. (Illus.). 1984. 30.00 (*0-912330-56-2*) Jargon Soc.
Menarchik, Douglas. Powerlift - Getting to Desert Storm: Strategic Transportation & Strategy in the New World Order. LC 93-2857. 216p. 1993. 55.00 (*0-275-94642-8*, C4642, Praeger Pubs) Greenwood.
Menard. The Santa Venera Pottery. (Illus.). (C). text. write for info. (*0-472-10900-6*) U of Mich Pr.
Menard, Christine. More Bright & Bold Bulletin Boards. (Illus.). 64p. 1995. pap. 12.95 (*0-917846-61-3*, 34009, Alleyside) Highsmith Pr.
Menard, Claude, ed. Transaction Cost Economics: Recent Developments. LC 96-26476. 192p. 1997. 75.00 (*1-85898-483-1*) E Elgar.
Menard, David W. Before Centuries: USAFE Fighters, 1948-1959. (Illus.). 144p. 1998. 34.95 (*1-57427-079-6*) Howell Pr VA.
— F-100 Super Sabre. (Colors & Markings Ser.: Vol. 14). (Illus.). 1990. pap. 12.95 (*0-8306-8538-3*) McGraw-Hill Prof.
— North American F-86 SabreJet Day Fighters. (Warbird Tech Ser.: Vol. 3). (Illus.). 100p. (Orig.). 1996. pap. 16.95 (*0-933424-66-3*) Specialty Pr.
— USAF Plus Fifteen: A Photo History, 1947-1962. LC 92-63123. (Illus.). 144p. (Orig.). 1993. pap. 24.95 (*0-88740-483-9*) Schiffer.
Menard, Eusebe. At All Times, in Every Age. 122p. 1977. pap. 2.95 (*0-8199-0663-8*, Frncscn Herld) Franciscan Pr.
Menard, Henry W. The Ocean of Truth: A Personal History of Global Tectonics. LC 85-43300. (Princeton Series in Geology & Paleontology). (Illus.). 368p. 1986. reprint ed. pap. 114.10 (*0-608-06472-6*, 206676900009) Bks Demand.
— Science: Growth & Change. LC 77-156138. (Illus.). 229p. reprint ed. pap. 71.00 (*0-7837-4171-5*, 205902000012) Bks Demand.
Menard, Kevin. Dynamic Mechanical Analysis: An Introduction, Technique & Applications. LC 98-53025. 14p. 1999. lib. bdg. 69.95 (*0-8493-8688-8*) CRC Pr.
Menard, Louis. Dictionary of Accounting & of Financial Management. (ENG & FRE.). 994p. 1994. 156.60 (*0-7859-8886-6*) Fr & Eur.
— French/English - English/French Dictionary of Accounting Terms. 2nd ed. (ENG & FRE.). 650p. 1994. 175.00 (*0-7859-8752-5*) Fr & Eur.
***Menard, Mark M.** Mountain Biking Chico. LC 98-49085. (Illus.). 160p. 1999. pap. 10.95 (*1-56044-804-0*) Falcon Pub Inc.
Menard, Mathilde. Dictionnaire des Termes Economiques. (FRE.). 94p. 1990. pap. 15.95 (*0-7859-7890-9*, 2501014154) Fr & Eur.
Menard, Orville D. Political Bossism in Mid-America: Tom Dennison's Omaha, 1900-1933. LC 88-33697. (Illus.). 360p. (C). 1989. lib. bdg. 50.00 (*0-8191-7342-8*) U Pr of Amer.
Menard, Russell R., jt. auth. see McCusker, John J.
Menard, Scott. Applied Logistic Regression Analysis, No. 106. (Quantitative Applications in the Social Science Ser.: Vol. 108). 96p. (C). 1995. pap. 10.95 (*0-8039-5757-2*) Sage.
— Longitudinal Research, No. 76. (Quantitative Applications in the Social Sciences Ser.: Vol. 76). (Illus.). 96p. 1991. pap. 10.95 (*0-8039-3753-9*) Sage.
Menard, Shirley W., ed. The Clinical Nurse Specialist: Perspectives on Practice. 1989. pap. text 33.50 (*0-8273-4311-6*) Delmar.
Menard, Valene. Oscar de la Hoya: Champion Boxer. LC 97-43509. (Real-Life Reader Biographies Ser.). (Illus.). 32p. (J). (gr. 3-8). 1998. lib. bdg. 15.95 (*1-883845-58-0*) M Lane Pubs.
Menard, Valerie. Cristina Saralegui. LC 97-43427. (Real-Life Reader Biographies Ser.). (Illus.). 32p. (J). (gr. 3-8). 1998. lib. bdg. 15.95 (*1-883845-60-2*) M Lane Pubs.

M

An Asterisk (*) at the beginning of an entry indicates that the title is appearing for the first time.

*Menard, Valerie. Jennifer Lopez. (Real-Life Reader Biography Ser.). (Illus.). 32p. (J). (gr. 3-8). 2000. lib. bdg. 15.95 (1-58415-025-4) M Lane Pubs.
— The Latino Holiday Book: From Cinco de Mayo to Dia de los Muertos - The Celebrations & Traditions of Hispanic-Americans. 240p. 2000. pap. 15.95 (1-56924-646-7) Marlowe & Co.
— Ricky Martin. (Real Life Reader Biography Ser.). (Illus.). 32p. (J). (gr. 3-8). 1999. lib. bdg. 15.95 (1-58415-059-9) M Lane Pubs.
Menard, Valerie. Salma Hayek. LC 99-29471. (Real-Life Reader Biography Ser.). (Illus.). 32p. (J). (gr. 3-8). 1999. lib. bdg. 15.95 (1-58415-018-1) M Lane Pubs.
— Trent Dimas: Gold Medal Olympic Gymnast. LC 97-21984. (Real Life Reader Biographies Ser.). (Illus.). 32p. (J). (gr. 3-8). 1997. lib. bdg. 15.95 (1-883845-50-5) M Lane Pubs.
*Menard, Valerie. Winona Ryder. (Real-Life Reader Biography Ser.). (Illus.). 32p. (J). (gr. 3-8). 2000. lib. bdg. 15.95 (1-58415-039-4) M Lane Pubs.
Menardon, M. Encyclopedie de l'Automobile: Le Moteur a Explosion: Encyclopedia of the Automobile; the Internal Combustion Engine. (FRE.). 240p. 1980. pap. 95.00 (0-8288-4696-0, M14350) Fr & Eur.
Menaria, Rajendra. Environmental Conservation & Planning. 1989. 22.50 (81-7024-259-2, Pub. by Ashish Pub Hse) S Asia.
Menarini, Piero, ed. see Garcia Lorca, Federico.
Menasce, Daniel A. Capacity Planning: A Practical Approach. 1993. 44.00 incl. disk (0-685-70954-X) P-H.
*Menasce, Daniel A. Capacity Planning for Web Performance: Metrics, Methods & Benchmarks. LC 98-3499. 336p. (C). 1998. pap. 58.00 (0-13-693822-1, Prentice Hall) P-H.
Menasche, Ann E. Leaving the Life. 1997. pap. 17.99 (0-906500-53-2, Pub. by Onlywomen Pr) LPC InBook.
*Menasche, Emile. What's a Sampler? A Basic Guide to the World of Digital Sampling. rev. ed. 48p. 2000. pap. 5.95 (0-634-01342-4) H Leonard.
— What's a Sequencer? A Basic Guide to Their Features & Use. rev. ed. 64p. 2000. pap. 5.95 (0-634-01345-9) H Leonard.
— What's a Synthesizer? rev. ed. 64p. 2000. pap. 5.95 (0-634-01344-0) H Leonard.
— What's MIDI? Making Musical Instruments Work Together. rev. ed. 64p. 2000. pap. 5.95 (0-634-01343-2) H Leonard.
Menasche, Lionel. Writing a Research Paper. rev. ed. 160p. 1997. pap. text 16.95 (0-472-08369-4, 08369) U of Mich Pr.
Menasche, Lionel, jt. auth. see Furey, Patricia R.
Menase, Lev. Art Treasures of Slovenia. 208p. 1981. 131.00 (0-7855-1507-0) St Mut.
Menashe, Samuel. Collected Poems. 220p. 1986. pap. 14.95 (0-915032-43-0) Natl Poet Foun.
*Menashe, Samuel. The Niche Narrows: New & Selected Poems. 2000. 37.95 (1-58498-013-3); pap. 16.95 (1-58498-012-5) Talisman Hse.
Menashri, David. Education & the Making of Modern Iran. LC 91-55567. 376p. 1992. text 52.50 (0-8014-2612-X) Cornell U Pr.
— Iran: A Decade of War & Revolution. LC 90-4787. 424p. 1990. 49.95 (0-8419-0949-0); pap. 24.95 (0-8419-0950-4) Holmes & Meier.
— Revolution at a Crossroads: Iran's Domestic Politics & Regional Ambitions. LC 96-43152. (Policy Papers: No. 43). 92p. 1997. pap. 8.00 (0-944029-68-X) Wash Inst NEP.
Menashri, David, ed. Central Asia Meets the Middle East. LC 97-19801. 256p. (C). 1998. text 52.50 (0-7146-4600-8, Pub. by F Cass Pubs); pap. text 24.50 (0-7146-4129-4, Pub. by F Cass Pubs) Intl Spec Bk.
Menaster, Albert J. West's California Criminal Defense. LC 95-46982. 500p. (C). 1995. ring bd. 39.00 (0-314-08726-5) West Pub.
Menat, E. Dictionnaire de la Pratique Dietetique. (FRE.). 1998. 75.00 (0-320-00164-4) Fr & Eur.
MENC Committee on Performance Standards. Performance Standards for Music: Strategies & Benchmarks for Assessing Progress Toward the National Standards, Grades PreK-12. 136p. 1996. pap. 20.00 (1-56545-099-X, 1633) MENC.
Mence, Neil, jt. auth. see Boyd, Norah.
Mench, J. A., jt. ed. see Moberg, G.
Mench, Joy A. & Krulisch, Lee, eds. Canine Research Environment. LC 89-62910. 82p. 1990. pap. 20.00 (0-685-59680-X) Scientists Ctr.
Menchaca, Angelita V., ed. see Vrattos, Stephen.
Menchaca, Frank. Al. LC 97-95018. 50p. 1999. pap. 6.95 (0-9628159-2-6) Front Rm.
— Nicolo G - And the Days of November. LC 90-84969. 56p. (Orig.). 1990. pap. 4.95 (0-9628159-0-X) Front Rm.
Menchaca, Martha. The Mexican Outsiders: A Community History of Marginalization & Discrimination in California. LC 94-46190. (Illus.). 272p. (C). 1995. 40.00 (0-292-75173-7); pap. 18.95 (0-292-75174-5) U of Tex Pr.
Menchaca Rocha, Arturo. El Discreto Encanto de las Particulas. (Ciencia para Todos Ser.). (SPA.). pap. 6.99 (968-16-2949-3, Pub. by Fondo) Continental Bk.
*Menchene, Ron. Propaganda Postcards of World War II. (Illus.). 160p. 2000. pap. 21.95 (1-58221-024-1, Antique Trader) Krause Pubns.
Mencher. Basic Media Writing. 5th ed. 1995. teacher ed. 18.75 (0-697-27003-3, WCB McGr Hill) McGrw-H Hghr Educ.
*Mencher. Basic Media Writing. 6th ed. LC 98-17590. 528p. 1998. pap. 40.00 (0-697-35368-0) McGrw-H Hghr Educ.
Mencher. News Reporting & Writing. 7th ed. 1997. 16.25 (0-697-28902-8, WCB McGr Hill) McGrw-H Hghr Educ.
— News Reporting & Writing. 8th ed. LC 99-25513. 1999. 38.50 (0-07-230011-6); pap. 25.31 (0-07-230012-4) McGraw.
Mencher, Elaine, jt. ed. see Robinson, Ian.
Mencher, George T., et al. Audiology & Auditory Dysfunction. LC 96-26053. (Illus.). 288p. (C). 1996. 58.00 (0-205-16101-4) Allyn.
Mencher, George T., jt. ed. see Gerber, Sanford E.
Mencher, Georges T., ed. see Nova Scotia Conference on Early Identification of.
Mencher, Joan, jt. ed. see Brink, Judy.
Mencher, Joan P., et al. Anthropology: CUNY: Rethinking the Disciplines, Vol. 8A. LC 98-226509. (Women in the Curriculum Ser.). 54p. 1997. pap. 10.00 (1-885303-09-2) Towson St Univ.
Mencher, Melvin. Basic Media Writing. 5th ed. 480p. (C). 1995. text 22.50 (0-697-27002-5) Brown & Benchmark.
— Basic Media Writing. 5th ed. 480p. (C). 1995. text. write for info. (0-697-27001-7) Brown & Benchmark.
— News Reporting & Writing LC 77-81895. 437 p. 1977. write for info. (0-697-04308-8, WCB McGr Hill) McGrw-H Hghr Educ.
— News Reporting & Writing. 7th ed. LC 95-83695. 736p. (C). 1996. text 46.75 (0-697-28901-X) Brown & Benchmark.
— News Reporting & Writing. 7th ed. 288p. (C). 1997. text, wbk. ed. 22.50 (0-697-28903-6) Brown & Benchmark.
— News Reporting & Writing. 7th ed. 736p. (C). 1997. per. write for info. (0-07-114585-0) McGraw.
— Reporter's Checklist & Notebook. 160p. (C). 1995. text. write for info. (0-697-29404-8) Brown & Benchmark.
Menchik, Mark D. Individual Equilibrium-Seeking Behavior: A Definition & a Test. (Discussion Papers: No. 33). 1969. pap. 10.00 (1-55869-056-5) Regional Sci Res Inst.
— Residential Environmental Preferences & Choice: Some Preliminary Empirical Results Relevant to Urban Form. (Discussion Papers: No. 46). 1971. pap. 10.00 (1-55869-108-1) Regional Sci Res Inst.
Menchik, Paul L. Household & Family Economics. LC 96-36207. (Recent Economic Thought Ser.). 272p. (C). 1996. lib. bdg. 109.00 (0-7923-9654-5) Kluwer Academic.
Menchin, Robert. 101 Classic Jewish Jokes: Jewish Humor from Groucho Marx to Jerry Seinfeld. LC 97-36233. (Illus.). 96p. 1997. pap. 9.95 (0-914457-88-8) Mustang Pub.
Menchin, Robert S. The Mature Market: A Gold Mine of Ideas for Tapping the 50 Plus Market. 265p. 1991. per. 24.95 (1-55738-236-0, Irwn Prfssnl) McGraw-Hill Prof.
Menchine, Ron. A Picture Postcard History of U. S. Baseball. LC 92-16270. (Illus.). 124p. 1992. pap. 14.95 (0-930256-21-2, Vestal Pr) Madison Bks UPA.
— Tuff Stuff's Baseball Postcard Collection: A Comprehensive Reference & Price Guide. (Illus.). 208p. 1999. pap. 24.95 (0-930625-53-6, Antique Trader) Krause Pubns.
Menchini, Paul, ed. see Bhasker, J.
Menchk, Karl-Wolfgang, ed. see Kebschull, Dietrich, et al.
Menchu, Rigoberta. Crossing Borders: An Autobiography. LC 98-30118. 242p. 1998. 25.00 (1-85984-893-1, Pub. by Verso) Norton.
*Menchu, Rigoberta. Crossing Borders: An Autobiography. 1999. pap. 18.00 (1-85984-201-1, Pub. by Verso) Norton.
Menchu, Rigoberta. I, Rigoberta Menchu: An Indian Woman in Guatemala. Burgos-Debray, Elizabeth, ed. Wright, Ann, tr. from SPA. 252p. (C). 1987. pap. 18.00 (0-86091-788-6, A0663, Pub. by Verso) Norton.
— Rigoberta: La Nieta de Los Mayas. LC 98-171338. (SPA.). 1998. 11.95 (84-03-59526-3) Santillana.
Mencia, Mario. The Fertile Prison: Fidel Castro in Batista's Jails. (Illus.). 250p. 1994. pap. 15.95 (1-875284-08-7) Ocean Pr NJ.
Mencik, Jaroslav. Mechanics of Components with Treated or Coated Surfaces, Vol. 42. LC 95-31283. (Solid Mechanics & Its Applications Ser.). 384p. (C). 1996. text 191.50 (0-7923-3700-X) Kluwer Academic.
Mencik van Zebinsky, A. A. European Union External Competence & External Relations in Air Transport. LC 95-34225. 1996. lib. bdg. 66.00 (90-411-0111-X) Kluwer Academic.
Mencius. Mencius. Hinton, David, tr. from CHI. LC 98-30083. 304p. 1999. pap. 13.00 (1-887178-62-7, Pub. by Counterpt DC) HarpC.
— Mencius. Hinton, David, tr. from CHI. 320p. 1999. reprint ed. pap. text 14.00 (1-58243-020-9, Pub. by Counterpt DC) HarpC.
— Mencius, Vols. 1 & 2. Lau, D. C., tr. from CHI. (Chinese Classics Ser.: Vol. 2). 206p. (C). 1997. 34.50 (962-201-313-9, Pub. by Chinese Univ) U of Mich Pr.
Menck, Herman & Smart, Charles, eds. Central Cancer Registries: Design, Management, & Use. LC 94-1853. 312p. 1994. text 55.00 (3-7186-0579-1) Gordon & Breach.
— Central Cancer Registries: Design, Management & Use. 312p. 1994. pap. text 25.00 (3-7186-0587-2) Gordon & Breach.
*Menckel, Ewa & Westerholm, Peter. Evaluation in Occupational Health Practice. LC 99-29660. 235p. 1999. text 72.00 (0-7506-4303-X) Buttrwrth-Heinemann.
Mencken. Sociology. 1998. student ed. 17.74 (0-07-233315-4) McGraw.
Mencken, August. The Railroad Passenger Car: An Illustrated History of the First Hundred Years, with Accounts by Contemporary Passengers. LC 57-13290. 223p. reprint ed. pap. 69.20 (0-608-11720-X, 200291500016) Bks Demand.
*Mencken, August. The Railroad Passenger Car: An Illustrated History of the First 100 Years with Accounts by Contemporary Passengers. LC 00-30931. (Illus.). 226p. 2000. 27.95 (0-8018-6541-7) Johns Hopkins.
Mencken, H. L. The American Language. 1977. 22.95 (0-07-544766-5) McGraw.
— The American Language, 3 vols. 4th ed. Incl. Vol. 1. American Language. 1936. 55.00 (0-394-40075-5); Vol. 2. American Language No. 1. 1945. 50.00 (0-394-40076-3); Vol. 3. American Language No. 1. 1948. 50.00 (0-394-40077-1); write for info. (0-318-54003-7) Knopf.
— Book of Burlesques. 1971. reprint ed. 49.00 (0-403-00666-X) Scholarly.
— A Book of Prefaces. (BCL1-PS American Literature Ser.). 283p. 1992. reprint ed. lib. bdg. 79.00 (0-7812-6612-2) Rprt Serv.
— A Carnival of Buncombe: Writings on Politics. Moos, Malcolm C., ed. LC 83-24163. 416p. 1993. pap. 12.95 (0-226-51977-5) U Ch Pr.
— The Editor, the Bluenose, & the Prostitute: H. L. Mencken's History of the "Hatrack" Censorship Case. Bode, Carl, ed. (Illus.). 175p. 1988. 65.00 (0-911797-40-8) Roberts Rinehart.
— The Editor, the Bluenose, & the Prostitute: H. L. Mencken's History of the "Hatrack" Censorship Case. limited ed. Bode, Carl, ed. (Illus.). 175p. 1988. 29.95 (0-911797-48-3) Roberts Rinehart.
— Friedrich Nietzsche. LC 92-34210. 280p. (C). 1993. pap. 24.95 (1-56000-649-8) Transaction Pubs.
— George Bernard Shaw: His Plays. LC 75-30843. (George Bernard Shaw Ser.: No. 92). 1975. lib. bdg. 75.00 (0-8383-2073-2) M S G Haskell Hse.
— The H. L. Mencken Baby Book: Comprising the Contents of H.L. Mencken's What You Ought to Know About Your Baby. (Illus.). 224p. 1990. text 21.00 (0-932883-22-2) Hanley & Belfus.
— H. L. Mencken on Music: A Selection of His Writings on Music Together with an Account of H. L. Mencken's Musical Life. 222p. 1990. reprint ed. lib. bdg. 69.00 (0-7812-9177-1) Rprt Serv.
Mencken, H. L. Happy Days, 1880-1892. (Maryland Paperback Bookshelf Ser.). 330p. (C). 1996. reprint ed. pap. 15.95 (0-8018-5338-9) Johns Hopkins.
— Heathen Days, 1890-1936. (Maryland Paperback Bookshelf Ser.). 320p. 1996. reprint ed. pap. 15.95 (0-8018-5339-7) Johns Hopkins.
Mencken, H. L. In Defense of Women. large type ed. LC 99-34546. 125p. 1999. 27.95 (1-56000-481-9) Transaction Pubs.
— A Mencken Chrestomathy. 1982. pap. 19.00 (0-394-75209-0) Pantheon.
— Minority Report: H. L. Mencken's Notebooks. LC 97-4116. (Maryland Paperback Bookshelf Ser.). 296p. 1997. reprint ed. pap. 15.95 (0-8018-5658-2) Johns Hopkins.
— My Life As Author & Editor. Yardley, Jonathan, ed. & intro. by. 1993. 30.00 (0-679-41315-4) Knopf.
Mencken, H. L. Newspaper Days, 1899-1906. LC 95-52240. (Maryland Paperback Bookshelf Ser.). 336p. 1996. reprint ed. pap. 15.95 (0-8018-5340-0) Johns Hopkins.
Mencken, H. L. On Politics: A Carnival of Buncombe. Moos, Malcolm, ed. LC 96-10531. (Maryland Paperback Bookshelf Ser.). 377p. 1996. reprint ed. pap. 15.95 (0-8018-5342-7) Johns Hopkins.
— Prejudices: A Selection. Farrell, James T., ed. & intro. by. LC 95-42524. (Maryland Paperback Bookshelf Ser.). 280p. (C). 1996. reprint ed. pap. 15.95 (0-8018-5341-9) Johns Hopkins.
— Prejudices: First Series. 285p. 1998. reprint ed. 25.00 (0-936128-89-5) De Young Pr.
— A Second Mencken Chrestomathy. Teachout, Terry, ed. LC 94-12087. 1995. 30.00 (0-679-42829-1) Knopf.
— Thirty-Five Years of Newspaper Work: A Memoir. Hobson, Fred et al, eds. LC 94-2077. 1994. 34.95 (0-8018-4791-5) Johns Hopkins.
— Thirty-Five Years of Newspaper Work: A Memoir. Hobson, Fred et al, eds. (Maryland Paperback Bookshelf Ser.). (Illus.). 416p. (C). 1996. reprint ed. pap. 16.95 (0-8018-5380-X) Johns Hopkins.
— Treatise on the Gods. 400p. 1998. reprint ed. 35.00 (0-936128-92-5) De Young Pr.
— Treatise on the Gods. 2nd ed. LC 96-51594. (Maryland Paperback Bookshelf Ser.). 375p. 1997. reprint ed. pap. 15.95 (0-8018-5654-X) Johns Hopkins.
— Vintage Mencken. 1976. 22.95 (0-8488-0465-1) Amereon Ltd.
— The Vintage Mencken. LC 89-40542. 1990. pap. 12.00 (0-679-72895-3) Vin Bks.
Mencken, H. L., ed. New Dictionary of Quotations on Historical Principles from Ancient & Modern Sources. 1942. 75.00 (0-394-40079-8) Knopf.
Mencken, H. L. & Goodman, Philip. Do You Remember? The Whimsical Letters of H. L. Mencken & Philip Goodman. Sanders, Jack, ed. LC 96-29348. (Illus.). 208p. 1996. 24.95 (0-938420-54-2) MD Hist.
— Do You Remember? The Whimsical Letters of H. L. Mencken & Philip Goodman. limited ed. Sanders, Jack, ed. LC 96-29348. (Illus.). 208p. 1996. boxed set 75.00 (0-938420-57-7) MD Hist.
Mencken, H. L., jt. auth. see La Monte, Robert R.
Mencken, H. L., jt. auth. see Nathan, George J.
Mencken, H. L., jt. ed. see Nathan, George J.
Mencken, H. L., tr. see Nietzsche, Friedrich Wilhelm.
Menconi, Al. Dear Mr. Gothard: A Common Sense Response to Criticisms of Today's Christian Music. 2nd ed. Hart, Dave, ed. 66p. 1995. reprint ed. pap. 4.95 (0-942925-07-6) New Song Pub.
Menconi, Stephen J., jt. auth. see Bronson, Gary J.
Menconi, Stephen J., ed. see Bronson, Gary J. & Silver, Howard I.
Mencotti, jt. auth. see Stark.
Menczel, J., et al, eds. Osteoporosis: Proceedings of an International Symposium Held at the Jerusalem Osteoporosis Center in June, 1981. LC 81-19822. (Illus.). 452p. reprint ed. pap. 140.20 (0-608-15575-6, 202963700062) Bks Demand.
Menczer, Bela. Tensions of Order & Freedom: Catholic Political Thought, 1789-1848. LC 93-21080. 210p. (C). 1993. text 34.95 (1-56000-133-X) Transaction Pubs.
Menczer, Leonard F., jt. ed. see Wolfe, Richard J.
Mendaes France, Michel, jt. auth. see Tenenbaum, Gerald.
Mendall, Howard L. & Aldous, Clarence M. The Ecology & Management of the American Woodcock. (Illus.). 201p. 1984. reprint ed. 17.95 (0-936075-02-3) Gunnerman Pr.
Mende, Barbara. How to Get a Job Through Want Ads. pap. 12.95 (0-931790-96-4) Brick Hse Pub.
Mende Conny, Beth. Why Worry? (Charming Petites Ser.). (Illus.). 80p. 1999. 4.95 (0-88088-386-3) Peter Pauper.
Mende, Emilie. Pictorial Family Tree of Brass Instruments in Europe Since the Early Middle Ages. (ENG, FRE & GER., Illus.). 1978. 20.00 (2-88039-003-6) Brass Pr.
Mende, Matthias. Baldung (Hans) The Graphic Work. (GER., Illus.). 336p. 1978. 125.00 (1-55660-168-9) A Wofsy Fine Arts.
Mende, W., jt. auth. see Peschel, M.
Mendel, Alfred O. Personality in Handwriting: A Step-by-Step Guide to Unlocking Hidden Talents & Desires In... 1990. pap. 14.95 (0-87877-153-0) Newcastle Pub.
Mendel, Arthur. Vision & Violence. 328p. (C). 1992. text 39.50 (0-472-10275-3, 10275) U of Mich Pr.
Mendel, Arthur, jt. auth. see Howard, John T., Jr.
Mendel, Arthur, tr. see Bekker, Paul.
Mendel, Arthur, tr. see Einstein, Alfred.
Mendel, Arthur P. Michael Bakunin: Roots of Apocalypse. LC 81-5168. 517p. 1981. 65.00 (0-275-91699-5, C1699, Praeger Pubs) Greenwood.
*Mendel, Arthur P. Vision & Violence. 352p. 1999. pap. 24.95 (0-472-08636-7, 08636) U of Mich Pr.
Mendel, Carol. San Diego on Foot. 9th rev. ed. (Illus.). 96p. 1994. pap. 6.95 (0-935179-20-8) Carol Mendel.
Mendel, Donald J. The Oahe Sub-District: A Case Study in Water Resources Administration. 1963. 1.00 (1-55614-074-6) U of SD Gov Res Bur.
Mendel, G. Versuche Ueber Pflanzenhybriden. 1966. reprint ed. pap. 12.00 (3-7682-0013-2) Lubrecht & Cramer.
Mendel, Gregor Johann. Experiments in Plant-Hybridisation. LC 67-9611. 48p. 1965. pap. 10.50 (0-674-27800-3) HUP.
Mendel, J. M. Maximum-Likelihood Deconvolution. (Illus.). xiv, 227p. 1989. 89.95 (0-387-97208-0) Spr-Verlag.
Mendel, Jerry. A Prelude to Neural Networks: Adaptive & Learning Systems. 1993. text 41.25 (0-685-70703-2) P-H.
Mendel, Jerry M. Discrete Techniques of Parameter Estimation: The Equation Error Formulation. (Control & Systems Theory Ser.: Vol. 1). (Illus.). 408p. 1973. text 185.00 (0-8247-1455-5) Dekker.
— Lessons in Estimation Theory. 2nd ed. LC 94-15781. (Signal Processing Ser.). 592p. 1995. 90.00 (0-13-120981-7) P-H.
Mendel, Kathleen L. Ancestral Shadows: The Native American Spirit. LC 94-60585. (Illus.). 30p. (Orig.). (C). 1994. pap. 5.20 (1-878142-17-8) Telstar MI.
— Ancient Hearts Whisper: Egyptian Love Poetry. Brethauer, Candy K., ed. & pref. by. LC 92-97166. 36p. (Orig.). (C). 1992. pap. 7.10 (1-878142-28-3) Telstar MI.
— Ankh - Eternal Light: Eternal Light. LC 94-60587. (Illus.). 40p. (Orig.). (C). 1994. pap. 7.10 (1-878142-38-0) Telstar MI.
— Calliope Garden. Brethauer, Candy K., ed. LC 91-77829. 40p. (Orig.). (C). 1992. pap. 6.10 (1-878142-25-9) Telstar MI.
— Coyote Solitude: A Wilderness Meditation. Brethauer, Candy K., ed. LC 92-71827. 20p. (Orig.). (YA). 1993. pap. 5.20 (1-878142-32-1) Telstar MI.
— Gateways. Brethauer, Candy K., ed. LC 91-77549. 46p. (Orig.). (C). 1992. pap. 6.10 (1-878142-27-5) Telstar MI.
— Into a Silhouette. LC 90-70182. 52p. 1990. pap. 6.10 (0-9624384-5-6) Telstar MI.
— Journey into Physical-Spiritual Self. 40p. (Orig.). 1995. pap., student ed. 10.15 (1-878142-39-9) Telstar MI.
— Silent Stones Sacred Light: Sacred Light. LC 94-60584. (Illus.). 40p. (Orig.). (C). 1994. pap. 7.10 (1-878142-37-2) Telstar MI.
— Whispering Clay. Brethauer, Candy K., ed. LC 92-71598. (Illus.). 30p. (Orig.). (J). 1992. pap. 7.20 (1-878142-29-1) Telstar MI.
Mendel, Kathleen L., ed. Lions, Lizards & Ladybugs. LC 89-51485. (Illus.). 80p. (J). (gr. k-6). 1989. pap. 9.95 (0-9624384-2-1) Telstar MI.
— Sentinel. LC 90-70012. (Illus.). 146p. (Orig.). 1990. pap. 12.95 (0-9624384-4-8) Telstar MI.
Mendel, Kathleen L., ed. see Quinn, Dawn & Malachowski, Cindy.
*Mendel, Kathleen Lee. Greeting the Moon. 27p. 2000. pap. 7.10 (1-878142-62-3) Telstar MI.
— Silent Mind Peaceful Heart. 30p. 2000. mass mkt. 6.20 (1-878142-63-1) Telstar MI.
Mendel, Lisa L. & Danhauer, Jeffrey L. Audiologic Evaluation & Management & Speech Perception Assessment. LC 96-29149. 290p. 1996. pap. 57.95 (1-56593-692-2, 1366) Thomson Learn.
Mendel, Lisa L., et al. Singular's Pocket Dictionary of Audiology. LC 98-55561. 14p. 1999. pap. 45.00 (0-7693-0042-1) Thomson Learn.
Mendel, Lisa Lucks, et al. Singular's Illustrated Dictionary of Audiology. LC 98-52949. (Illus.). 14p. 1999. pap. 59.95 (1-56593-950-6, 1876) Thomson Learn.

An Asterisk (*) at the beginning of an entry indicates that the title is appearing for the first time.

Mendel, Matthew P. The Male Survivor: The Impact of Sexual Abuse. 264p. 1994. 46.00 (*0-8039-5441-7*); pap. 21.00 (*0-8039-5442-5*) Sage.

Mendel, Max, et al. Engineering Probabilistic Design & Maintenance for Flood Protection. Cooke, Roger, ed. LC 96-52465. (Diverse Ser.). 228p. (C). 1997. text 120.50 (*0-7923-4399-9*) Kluwer Academic.

Mendel, Menachem. Cheshbon Hanefesh. (ENG & HEB.). 1995. 17.95 (*0-87306-681-2*) Feldheim.

— Cheshbon Hanefesh. (ENG & HEB.). 1996. 9.95 (*0-87306-774-6*) Feldheim.

Mendel, Menachem. Derech Mitzvasecha. (HEB.). 601p. 20.00 (*0-8266-5590-4*) Kehot Pubn Soc.

Mendel, Nissan. Dertseil Mir ah Maaseh, Vol. 3. LC 88-12796.Tr. of Storyteller. (YID., Illus.). 318p. (J). (gr. 4-8). 1999. 12.00 (*0-8266-0388-2*, Merkos LInyonei Chinuch) Kehot Pubn Soc.

Mendel-Reyes, Meta. Reclaiming Democracy: The Sixties in Politics & Memory. (Illus.). 244p. (C). 1996. pap. 17.99 (*0-415-91820-0*) Routledge.

— Reclaiming Democracy: The 60s in Politics & Memory. 208p. 1996. pap. 15.95 (*0-415-91135-4*) Routledge.

Mendel, Richard A. The American School-to-Career Movement: A Background Paper for Policymakers & Foundations Officers. 24p. 1995. pap. text. write for info. (*1-887031-53-7*) Am Youth Policy.

— Prevention or Pork? A Hard Headed Look at Youth-Oriented Anti-Crime Programs. 33p. 1995. pap. text. write for info. (*1-887031-50-2*) Am Youth Policy.

Mendel, Roberta. And My Hand Ran Away with My Brain Like the Cow Jumped over the Moon. (Serendipity Ser.). 33p. (Orig.). 1995. pap. 10.00 (*0-936424-17-6*, 011) Pin Prick.

— At Random: A Book of Wisdom: Epigrams, Witticisms, & Interesting Definitions. (Books for Browsers Ser.). 24p. 1995. reprint ed. pap. 10.00 (*0-936424-03-6*, 005) Pin Prick.

— The Book of Poetic Forms. (Chameleon Ser.). 71p. 1997. pap. 10.00 (*0-936424-20-6*, 016) Pin Prick.

— Deft & Daffy Definitions (& Then Some) for 'Tweens & Adults. aut. ed. (Meanderthal Ser.). (Illus.). 39p. 1997. pap. 10.00 (*0-936424-24-9*, 018) Pin Prick.

— Epigrams to Live & Die By. (Sketchbook Ser.). (Illus.). 36p. 1995. reprint ed. pap. 10.00 (*0-936424-08-7*, 007) Pin Prick.

— The Eye ("I") Hodge Podge Theology Anthology. 42p. 1999. pap. 10.00 (*0-936424-21-4*) Pin Prick.

— The First Book of Whimsy: Bits of Almost-Haiku & Other Things. 2nd rev. ed. (Books for Browsers Ser.). (Illus.). 24p. (Orig.). 1996. pap. 10.00 (*0-936424-19-2*, 001) Pin Prick.

— Jewish Poems. (Holocaust Ser.). 48p. 1994. reprint ed. pap. text 10.00 (*0-936424-09-5*, 009) Pin Prick.

— Kabbalah (The Journey) A Longpoem. aut. ed. (Enigma Ser.). 72p. 1999. pap. 28.00 (*0-936424-27-3*, 019) Pin Prick.

— Landscapes (of Time, Mind, Heart, Place, Space, Things, Beings & of Souls) (Sketchbook Ser.). 54p. (Orig.). 1995. pap. 10.00 (*0-936424-18-4*, 013) Pin Prick.

— Life Is... aut. ed. (Enigma Ser.). (Illus.). 33p. 1997. pap. 10.00 (*0-936424-23-0*, 017) Pin Prick.

***Mendel, Roberta.** One * Liners. aut. ed. (Jots & Gists Ser.). 42p. 1999. pap. 10.00 (*0-936424-26-5*, 021) Pin Prick.

Mendel, Roberta. Patterns: Poems of Form & Substance - An Exercise in Experimentation or Obfuscation, a Work in Progress. (Chameleon Ser.). 1997. pap. 10.00 (*0-936424-22-2*, 014) Pin Prick.

— Philosophical Mutterings about Things of Some Importance. (Sketchbook Ser.). (Illus.). 24p. 1980. reprint ed. pap. 10.00 (*0-936424-05-2*, 004) Pin Prick.

— The Pin Prick Press Annual Index of Serial & Chapbook Publications, 1980. 28p. (Orig.). 1981. pap. 3.00 (*0-936424-07-9*, 008) Pin Prick.

— Puzzle Poems: Poems of Form & Substance - An Exercise in Experimentation, a Work in Progress. (Chameleon Ser.). 1997. pap. 10.00 (*0-936424-16-8*, 015) Pin Prick.

— The Second Book of Whimsey: Word Paintings, Political Grotesqueries, & Other Things. (Books for Browsers Ser.). (Illus.). 24p. 1994. reprint ed. pap. 10.00 (*0-936424-01-X*, 002) Pin Prick.

— A Survival Manual for the Independent Woman Traveler. limited aut. ed. LC 82-80695. 128p. (Orig.). 1982. pap. 14.00 (*0-936424-06-0*) Pin Prick.

— The Third Book of Whimsey: Poignant Fragments, Serpentine Thoughts, & Other Things. (Books for Browsers Ser.). 24p. 1996. reprint ed. pap. 10.00 (*0-936424-02-8*, 003) Pin Prick.

— War Poems: A War Poem Folio. (Death Song Ser.). 21p. (Orig.). 1996. pap. 10.00 (*0-936424-10-9*, 012) Pin Prick.

— Women's Prisms. (Xantippe Ser.). 24p. 1994. reprint ed. pap. 10.00 (*0-936424-04-4*, 006) Pin Prick.

— Writing for Me. (Scribbler Ser.). 7p. (Orig.). 1984. pap. 5.00 (*0-936424-11-7*) Pin Prick.

— Writing for Me. rev. ed. (Scribbler Ser.). 7p. (Orig.). 1994. pap. 5.00 (*0-936424-15-X*, 010) Pin Prick.

Mendel, S., tr. see Hauff, Wilhelm.

Mendel, Stephanie. March, Before Spring. 32p. 1999. reprint ed. pap. 13.00 (*0-9668431-1-8*, Pub. by O & W Pub) SPD-Small Pr Dist.

Mendel, Werner M., et al. Schizophrenia: The Experience & Its Treatment. LC 76-20083. (Jossey-Bass Behavioral Science Ser.). 192p. reprint ed. pap. 59.60 (*0-8357-4995-9*, 203792800009) Bks Demand.

Mendel, William W. & Bradford, David G. Interagency Cooperation: A Regional Model for Overseas Operations. 99p. (C). 1996. reprint ed. pap. text 30.00 (*0-7881-3676-3*) DIANE Pub.

Mendeleyev, William, jt. auth. see Nasibova, Aida.

Mendelker, Scott. From Elsewhere: The Subculture of Those Who Claim to Be of Non Earthly Origins; Being E.T. in America. 272p. 1995. 18.95 (*1-55972-304-1*, Birch Ln Pr) Carol Pub Group.

Mendell, Adrienne. How Men Think: The Seven Essential Rules for Making It. 1996. pap. 11.00 (*0-614-12580-4*, Columbine) Fawcett.

— How Men Think: The Seven Essential Rules for Making It in a Man's World. 256p. 1996. pap. 11.00 (*0-449-90978-6*, Columbine) Fawcett.

Mendell, Dale, ed. Body & Self: An Exploration of Early Female Development. LC 94-32618. 276p. 1995. pap. text 50.00 (*1-56821-396-4*) Aronson.

Mendell, Edward. Wildlife Odyssey: A Photographer's Travelogue. (Illus.). 144p. 1990. pap. 55.00 (*0-9515863-0-0*) Neal-Schuman.

Mendell, Elizabeth L. Romanesque Sculpture in Saintonge. (Illus.). 1940. 150.00 (*0-685-89780-X*) Elliots Bks.

Mendell, J. Handbook of Peripheral Neuropathies. (Neurological Disease & Therapy Ser.). Date not set. write for info. (*0-8247-8827-3*) Dekker.

MENDELL, JANET. My Kitchen in Spain. 25.00 (*0-06-019526-6*) HarpC.

Mendell, Jay S. & Pessolano, F. John, eds. Nonextrapolative Methods in Business Forecasting: Scenarios, Vision, & Issues Management. LC 84-18093. (Illus.). 222p. 1985. 65.00 (*0-89930-066-9*, MHF/, Quorum Bks) Greenwood.

***Mendell, Jerry R., et al.** Diagnosis & Management of Peripheral Nerve Disorders. (Contemporary Neurology Ser.). (Illus.). 768p. 2000. text 165.00 (*0-19-513301-3*) OUP.

Mendell, Lorne M., jt. ed. see Binder, Marc D.

Mendell, Marguerite & Nielsen, Klas, eds. Europe: Central & East. (Critical Perspectives on Historic Issues Ser.: Vol. 6). 300p. 1995. 48.99 (*1-895431-91-3*, Pub. by Black Rose); pap. 19.99 (*1-895431-90-5*, Pub. by Black Rose) Consort Bk Sales.

Mendell, Marguerite, jt. ed. see Cangiani, Michele.

Mendell, Marguerite, jt. ed. see Leys, Colin T.

***Mendell, Pierre.** At First Sight. (Illus.). 240p. 2000. 65.00 (*3-907044-49-5*, Pub. by Lars Muller) Princeton Arch.

Mendell, Ronald L. How to Conduct Business Investigations & Competitive Intelligence Gathering. (Orig.). 1997. pap. text 35.00 (*0-918487-13-7*) Thomas Investigative.

***Mendell, Ronald L.** How to Do Financial Asset Investigations: A Practical Guide for Private Investigators, Collections Personnel, & Asset Recovery Specialists. 2nd ed. LC 94-769. (Illus.). 208p. (C). 2000. text 38.95 (*0-398-07044-X*) C C Thomas.

— How to Do Financial Asset Investigations: A Practical Guide for Private Investigators, Collections Personnel & Asset Recovery Specialists. 2nd ed. LC 99-54997. 208p. 2000. 27.95 (*0-398-07045-8*) C C Thomas.

Mendell, Ronald L. Investigating Computer Crime: A Primer for Security Managers. LC 98-20736. (Illus.). 198p. 1998. 44.95 (*0-398-06890-9*); pap. 30.95 (*0-398-06891-7*) C C Thomas.

Mendell, W. W., ed. Lunar Bases & Space Activities of the Twenty-First Century. LC 86-50. (Illus.). 865p. (C). 1986. 20.00 (*0-942862-02-3*) Lunar & Planet Inst.

Mendeloff, Albert & Dunn, James P. Digestive Diseases. LC 71-158432. (Vital & Health Statistics Monographs, American Public Health Association). (Illus.). 190p. 1971. 31.00 (*0-674-20580-4*) HUP.

Mendeloff, John. The Dilemma of Toxic Substance Regulation: How Overregulation Causes Underregulation. (Regulation of Economic Activity Ser.: No. 17). 450p. 1988. 42.00 (*0-262-13230-3*) MIT Pr.

Mendelowitsch, A. Clinical Aspects of Microdialysis. LC 96-18565. (Acta Neurochirugica - Supplementum Ser.). 75p. 1996. 89.00 (*3-211-82834-6*) Spr-Verlag.

Mendelowitz, Daniel M. Children Are Artists: An Introduction to Children's Art for Teachers & Parents. 2nd rev. ed. (Illus.). xiv, 158p. (C). 1963. 27.50 (*0-8047-0450-3*) Stanford U Pr.

— Drawing. LC 80-50905. (Illus.). xvi, 464p. 1980. reprint ed. 47.50 (*0-8047-1089-9*) Stanford U Pr.

— A History of American Art. 2nd ed. LC 71-111303. (C). 1973. pap. text 71.00 (*0-03-089475-1*, Pub. by Harcourt Coll Pubs) Harcourt.

Mendelowitz, Daniel M. & Wakeham, Duane A. A Guide to Drawing. 5th ed. 336p. (C). 1993. pap. text 64.00 (*0-03-055487-X*, Pub. by SCP) Harcourt.

***Mendels, Doron.** Identity, Religion & Historiography: Studies in Hellenistic History. (JSP Supplement Ser.: No. 24). 480p. 1998. 85.00 (*1-85075-682-1*, Pub. by Sheffield Acad) CUP Services.

Mendels, Doron. Land of Israel As a Political Concept in Hasmonean Literature: Recourse to History in Second Century B.C. Claims to the Holy Land. 200p. 1987. text 63.50 (*3-16-145147-3*, Pub. by JCB Mohr) Coronet Bks.

— The Media Revolution of Early Christianity: An Essay on Eusebius's "Ecclesiastical History" 269p. 1999. pap. 24.00 (*0-8028-4610-6*) Eerdmans.

— The Rise & Fall of Jewish Nationalism. LC 97-13245. 462p. 1997. pap. 35.00 (*0-8028-4329-8*) Eerdmans.

Mendels, Franklin F. Industrialization & Population Pressure in Eighteenth-Century Flanders. Bruchey, Stuart, ed. LC 80-2817. (Dissertations in European Economic History Ser.). (Illus.). 1981. lib. bdg. 35.95 (*0-405-14001-0*) Ayer.

Mendels, J., ed. Psychobiology of Affective Disorders. (Illus.). viii, 220p. 1981. pap. 34.00 (*3-8055-1400-X*) S Karger.

Mendels, Ora. A Taste for Treason. 1990. 17.95 (*1-55972-047-6*, Birch Ln Pr) Carol Pub Group.

Mendelsohn, jt. auth. see Baker.

Mendelsohn, Berk, et al. The Molecular Basis of Cancer. 2nd ed. 700p. 1999. text. write for info. (*0-7216-7291-4*, W B Saunders Co) Harcrt Hlth Sci Grp.

***Mendelsohn, Bob.** Who Ever Heard of a Jewish Missionary? A Jew for Jesus Tells His Story. Perlman, Susan, ed. (Illus.). 56p. 1999. pap. 3.00 (*1-881022-43-9*, BK072) Purple Pomegranate.

Mendelsohn, Charles J., jt. auth. see Friedman, William F.

Mendelsohn, Daniel. Cavafy. 1999. pap. write for info. (*0-375-70089-7*) Vin Bks.

Mendelsohn, Daniel. The Elusive Embrace: Desire & the Riddle of Identity. 208p. 1999. 24.00 (*0-375-40095-8*) Knopf.

***Mendelsohn, Daniel.** The Elusive Embrace: Desire & the Riddle of Identity. 224p. 2000. pap. 12.00 (*0-375-70697-6*) Vin Bks.

Mendelsohn, David. Expanding Our Vision: Insights for Language Teachers. (Illus.). 10p. 1999. pap. 21.95 (*0-19-541398-9*) OUP.

Mendelsohn, Elliot. Introduction to Mathematical Logic. 3rd ed. LC 86-11084. (Mathematics Ser.). 341p. (C). 1987. boxed set 53.50 (*0-534-06624-0*) Chapman & Hall.

Mendelsohn, Erich. Amerika: Bilderbuch Tines Architekten. LC 76-40319. (Architecture & Decorative Art Ser.). (GER.). 1977. reprint ed. lib. bdg. 55.00 (*0-306-70830-2*) Da Capo.

— Mendelsohn's Amerika: 82 Photographs. LC 93-2259. 96p. 1993. reprint ed. pap. 11.95 (*0-486-27591-4*) Dover.

Mendelsohn, Erich, jt. auth. see Zevi, Bruno.

Mendelsohn, Everett. Heat & Life: The Development of the Theory of Animal Heat. LC 64-16067. 222p. reprint ed. pap. 68.90 (*0-7837-5937-1*, 204573600007) Bks Demand.

Mendelsohn, Everett, jt. auth. see Boutwell, Jeffrey.

Mendelsohn, Everett, jt. auth. see Fortun, Michael.

Mendelsohn, Everett I., et al, eds. Human Aspects of Biomedical Innovation. LC 74-160027. (Studies in Technology & Society). (Illus.). 246p. 1971. 45.50 (*0-674-41331-8*) HUP.

— The Social Production of Scientific Knowledge. (Sociology of the Sciences Yearbook Ser.: Vol. 1). 1977. pap. text 64.50 (*90-277-0776-6*); lib. bdg. 88.00 (*90-277-0775-8*) Kluwer Academic.

Mendelsohn, Everett I. & Nowotny, Helga, eds. Science Between Utopia & Dystopia, 1984. (Sociology of the Sciences Yearbook Ser.: No. 8). 310p. 1984. pap. text 73.50 (*90-277-1721-4*); lib. bdg. 122.50 (*90-277-1719-2*) Kluwer Academic.

Mendelsohn, Everett I. & Segal, Howard P. Technology, Pessimism, & Postmodernism. LC 93-23651. (Sociology of the Sciences Yearbook Ser.). 224p. (C). 1994. lib. bdg. 152.50 (*0-7923-2630-X*, Pub. by Kluwer Academic) Kluwer Academic.

Mendelsohn, Everett I., jt. ed. see Grene, Marjorie.

Mendelsohn, Everett I., ed. see Maasen, Sabine.

Mendelsohn, Ezra. Essential Papers on Jews & the Left. LC 97-3723. 1997. text 75.00 (*0-8147-5570-4*) NYU Pr.

— Essential Papers on Jews & the Left. LC 97-3723. 1997. pap. text 27.50 (*0-8147-5571-2*) NYU Pr.

— The Jews of East Central Europe Between the World Wars. LC 81-48676. (Illus.). 320p. 1983. 39.95 (*0-253-33160-9*) Ind U Pr.

— The Jews of East Central Europe Between the World Wars. LC 81-48676. (Illus.). 320p. 1987. pap. 15.95 (*0-253-20418-6*, MB-418) Ind U Pr.

— On Modern Jewish Politics. (Studies in Jewish History). (Illus.). 184p. 1993. text 60.00 (*0-19-503864-9*); pap. text 19.95 (*0-19-508319-9*) OUP.

— Zionism in Poland: The Formative Years, 1915-1926. LC 81-10301. 387p. 1981. reprint ed. pap. 120.00 (*0-7837-3324-0*, 205772900007) Bks Demand.

Mendelsohn, Ezra, ed. Studies in Contemporary Jewry: Literary Strategies: Jewish Texts & Contexts, Vol. XII. 400p. 1997. text 60.00 (*0-19-511203-2*) OUP.

— Studies in Contemporary Jewry Vol. III: Jews & Other Ethnic Groups in a Multi-Ethnic World. (Illus.). 360p. 1987. text 55.00 (*0-19-504896-2*) OUP.

— Studies in Contemporary Jewry Vol. IX: Modern Jews & Their Musical Agendas. (Illus.). 400p. 1994. text 65.00 (*0-19-508617-1*) OUP.

***Mendelsohn, Ezra, ed.** Studies in Contemporary Jewry Vol. XV: People of the City: Jews & the Urban. LC 99-25988. (Illus.). 288p. 2000. text 45.00 (*0-19-513468-0*) OUP.

Mendelsohn, Ezra & Cohen, Richard I., eds. Studies in Contemporary Jewry: Art & Its Uses: The Visual Image & Modern Jewish Society, Vol. 6. (Illus.). 432p. 1990. text 65.00 (*0-19-506188-8*) OUP.

Mendelsohn, Ezra & Shatz, Marshall S., eds. Imperial Russia, Seventeen Hundred to Nineteen Seventeen: State, Society, Opposition Essays in Honor of Marc Raeff. 331p. 1989. text 38.00 (*0-87580-143-9*) N Ill U Pr.

Mendelsohn, Harold. Mass Entertainment. 1966. pap. 14.95 (*0-8084-0218-8*) NCUP.

Mendelsohn, Harvey, tr. see Szondi, Peter.

Mendelsohn, Henry N. An Author's Guide to Social Work Journals. 3rd ed. LC 90-20573. 284p. 1992. 29.95 (*0-87101-219-7*) Natl Assn Soc Wkrs.

Mendelsohn, Isaac. Slavery in the Ancient Near East: A Comparative Study of Slavery in Babylonia, Assyria, Syria & Palestine, from the Middle of the Third Millennium to the End of the First Millenium. LC 78-6962. 162p. 1978. reprint ed. lib. bdg. 45.00 (*0-313-20499-3*, MESA) Greenwood.

Mendelsohn, Jack. Being Liberal in an Illiberal Age: Why I Am a Unitarian Universalist. 1995. pap. 14.00 (*1-55896-332-4*, Skinner Hse Bks) Unitarian Univ.

— Channing: The Reluctant Radical. LC 79-17863. (Illus.). 308p. 1980. reprint ed. lib. bdg. 65.00 (*0-313-22101-4*, MECH, Greenwood Pr) Greenwood.

Mendelsohn, Jane. I Was Amelia Earhart. 1997. pap. 10.00 (*0-679-77636-2*) Random.

— I Was Amelia Earhart: A Novel. large type ed. LC 96-27420. 1996. 24.95 (*0-7862-0858-9*) Thorndike Pr.

— I Was Amelia Earhart: A Novel. large type ed. LC 96-27420. 1999. 22.95 (*0-7862-0859-7*) Thorndike Pr.

***Mendelsohn, Jane.** Innocence. 208p. 2000. 21.95 (*1-57322-164-3*, Riverhead Books) Putnam Pub Group.

Mendelsohn, John, ed. Covert War, 18 vols. 6150p. 1989. 1065.00 (*0-8153-0021-2*) Garland.

Mendelsohn, John, et al. The Molecular Basis of Cancer. (Illus.). 640p. 1994. text 149.00 (*0-7216-6483-0*, W B Saunders Co) Harcrt Hlth Sci Grp.

Mendelsohn, Joyce. Touring the Flatiron: Walks in Four Historic Neighborhoods. 146p. 1998. pap. 12.00 (*0-9647061-2-1*, Pub. by NY Landmarks) City & Co.

Mendelsohn, L., ed. see Lenin, Vladimir Il'ich.

Mendelsohn, Lotte. Healthy Mexican Regional Cookery: A Culinary Travelogue. (Regional Cooking Ser.: No. 2). (Illus.). 288p. 1995. pap. 17.95 (*1-883280-06-0*) Font & Ctr Pr.

Mendelsohn, Lotte & Lazzaro, Bea. Italian Regional Cookery: A Culinary Travelogue. LC 93-25341. (Illus.). 360p. 1993. reprint ed. pap. 15.95 (*1-883280-00-1*) Font & Ctr Pr.

Mendelsohn, M. S. Commercial Banks & the Restructuring of Cross-Border Debt. (Report Ser.). 36p. 1983. pap. 10.00 (*1-56708-061-8*) Grp of Thirty.

Mendelsohn, M. Stefan. The Debt of Nations: A Twentieth Century Fund Paper. (International Debt Ser.). 67p. (Orig.). (C). 1984. pap. 7.00 (*0-87078-158-8*) Century Foundation.

Mendelsohn, Mac, jt. auth. see A & T Staff.

Mendelsohn, Mac, jt. auth. see Harper, J.

Mendelsohn, Martin. The Guide to Franchising. 3rd ed. LC 78-40961. 1982. text 28.00 (*0-08-025845-X*, Pergamon Pr) Elsevier.

— The Guide to Franchising. 5th ed. 352p. 1993. pap. text 45.00 (*0-304-32814-6*) Continuum.

— The Guide to Franchising. 6th ed. 352p. 1999. pap. 32.95 (*0-304-70483-0*) Continuum.

Mendelsohn, Martin, ed. Franchising in Europe. 432p. 1993. pap. text 35.00 (*0-304-32812-X*) Continuum.

***Mendelsohn, Martin & Brennan, Michael, eds.** The International Encyclopaedia of Franchising. 1998. ring bd. 135.00 (*90-411-0779-7*) Kluwer Law Intl.

Mendelsohn, Michael. Braunwald's Heart Disease: Review & Assessment. 3rd ed. (Illus.). 300p. 1997. pap. text 52.00 (*0-7216-6631-0*, W B Saunders Co) Harcrt Hlth Sci Grp.

Mendelsohn, Mortimer, ed. Genes, Cancer & Radiation Protection. LC 92-49792. (Annual Meeting Proceedings Ser.: No. 13). 350p. (Orig.). 1992. pap. text 40.00 (*0-929600-24-X*) NCRP Pubns.

Mendelsohn, Mortimer L., et al. Biomarkers: Medical & Workplace Applications. LC 98-3882. 500p. (C). 1998. text 69.95 (*0-309-06422-8*) Natl Acad Pr.

Mendelsohn, Oliver & Vicziany, Marika. The Untouchables: Subordination, Poverty & the State in Modern India. LC 97-27947. (Contemporary South Asia Ser.: No. 4). 308p. (C). 1998. text 64.95 (*0-521-55362-8*); pap. text 22.95 (*0-521-55671-6*) Cambridge U Pr.

Mendelsohn, Patrick, jt. ed. see Lewis, Robert.

Mendelsohn, R. M. The Synthesis of Self Vol. 1: The I of Consciousness: Development from Birth to Maturity, 4 vols. LC 87-25798. (Illus.). 370p. (C). 1987. text 70.00 (*0-306-42711-7*, Kluwer Plenum) Kluwer Academic.

— The Synthesis of Self Vol. 2: It All Depends on How You Look at It: The Development of Pathology in the Cohesive Disorders, 4 vols. LC 87-25798. (Illus.). 272p. (C). 1987. text 70.00 (*0-306-42712-5*, Kluwer Plenum) Kluwer Academic.

— The Synthesis of Self Vol. 3: Believing Is Seeing: The Pathology of Development in the Noncohesive Disorders, 4 vols. LC 87-25798. (Illus.). 392p. (C). 1987. text 70.00 (*0-306-42713-3*, Kluwer Plenum) Kluwer Academic.

— The Synthesis of Self Vol. 4: The Principles That Guide the Ideal Therapist, 4 vols. LC 87-25798. (Illus.). 266p. (C). 1987. text 70.00 (*0-306-42714-1*, Kluwer Plenum) Kluwer Academic.

Mendelsohn, Richard. Sammy Marks: "The Uncrowned King of the Transvaal" LC 90-28333. (Illus.). 320p. 1991. pap. 19.95 (*0-8214-0999-9*) Ohio U Pr.

Mendelsohn, Richard L. & Schwartz, Lewis M. Basic Logic. 320p. (C). 1986. pap. text 36.80 (*0-13-062548-5*) P-H.

Mendelsohn, Richard L., jt. auth. see Fitting, Melvin.

***Mendelsohn, Robert.** The Greening of Global Warming. 37p. 1999. pap. 9.95 (*0-8447-7132-5*, Pub. by Am Enterprise) Pub Resources Inc.

Mendelsohn, Robert & Neumann, James E., eds. The Impact of Climate Change on the United States Economy. LC 97-35704. (Illus.). 344p. (C). 1999. text 59.95 (*0-521-62198-4*) Cambridge U Pr.

Mendelsohn, Robert & Shaw, Daigee, eds. The Economics of Pollution Control in the Asia Pacific. LC 96-5865. (New Horizons in Environmental Economics Ser.). (Illus.). 384p. (C). 1996. text 95.00 (*1-85898-307-X*) E Elgar.

Mendelsohn, Robert S. Confessions of a Medical Heretic. 208p. 1990. reprint ed. pap. 16.95 (*0-8092-4131-5*, 413150, Contemporary Bks) NTC Contemp Pub Co.

— How to Raise a Healthy Child in Spite of Your Doctor. 304p. 1987. mass mkt. 5.99 (*0-345-34276-3*) Ballantine Pub Grp.

Mendelsohn, Roy M. How Can Talking Help? An Introduction to the Technique of Analytic Therapy. LC 91-35243. 328p. 1992. 50.00 (*0-87668-503-3*) Aronson.

M

An Asterisk (*) at the beginning of an entry indicates that the title is appearing for the first time.

— Leaps: Facing Risks in Offering a Constructive Therapeutic Response When Unusual Measures Are Necessary. LC 90-22584. 320p. 1992. 55.00 (*0-87668-566-1*) Aronson.

— The Manifest Dream & Its Use in Therapy. LC 93-30140. 300p. 1990. 50.00 (*0-87668-766-4*) Aronson.

Mendelsohn, Samuel. The Criminal Jurisprudence of the Jews. (Studies in Jewish Jurisprudence: Vol. 6). 280p. (C). 1991. 25.00 (*0-87203-122-5*) Hermon.

Mendelsohn, Stephany, ed. Poetry. 1979. 4.95 (*1-55708-175-1*, MCR263) McDonald Pub Co.

Mendelsohn, Steven B. Tax Options & Strategies for People with Disabilities. 2nd rev. ed. 313p. 1996. pap. 29.95 (*0-939957-85-X*) Demos Medical.

Mendelson. Intro To Mathematical Logic. 2nd ed. (Math). 1979. 32.75 (*0-534-25307-5*) Brooks-Cole.

— Women's Imaging. (Illus.). 760p. (C). (gr. 13). 2000. text 160.00 (*0-8151-8468-9*, 28891) Mosby Inc.

Mendelson, Abby. Pittsburgh: A Place in Time. LC 98-32214. 180p. 1999. pap. 15.95 (*1-887969-08-X*) Cathedral PA.

— Pittsburgh Steelers. 1996. 36.95 (*0-87833-957-4*) Taylor Pub.

— Pittsburgh Steelers. limited ed. 1996. 75.00 (*0-87833-134-4*) Taylor Pub.

Mendelson, Alexander. Plasticity: Theory & Application. LC 68-12718. (Macmillan Series in Applied Mechanics). 367p. reprint ed. pap. 113.80 (*0-608-11610-6*, 200354000034) Bks Demand.

M

— Plasticity: Theory & Application. LC 82-21231. 368p. (C). 1983. reprint ed. lib. bdg. 43.50 (*0-89874-582-9*) Krieger.

Mendelson, Anne. Stand Facing the Stove: The Story of the Woman Who Gave America the Joy of Cooking. (Illus.). 474p. 1995. 29.95 (*0-8050-2904-4*) H Holt & Co.

Mendelson, Anne, ed. see Martinez, Zarela.

Mendelson, Bert. Introduction to Topology. 3rd ed. 224p. 1990. pap. 7.95 (*0-486-66352-3*) Dover.

***Mendelson, Carole R., ed.** Endocrinology of the Lung: Development & Surfactant Synthesis. LC 99-52787. (Contemporary Endocrinology Ser.). 346p. 2000. 149.50 (*0-89603-676-6*) Humana.

Mendelson, Cheryl. Home Comforts: The Art & Science of Keeping House. LC 99-37555. 896p. 1999. 34.50 (*0-684-81465-X*) Scribner.

Mendelson, Danuta. The Interfaces of Medicine & Law: The Liability of Negligently Caused Psychiatric Injury (Nervous Shock) LC 98-18563. 319p. 1998. text 68.95 (*1-85521-924-7*, K925.M46, Pub. by Ashgate Pub) Ashgate Pub Co.

Mendelson, E. Introduction to Mathematical Logic. 4th ed. 440p. 1997. ring bd. 74.95 (*0-412-80830-7*) Chapman & Hall.

Mendelson, E., tr. see Kushner, B.

Mendelson, E., tr. see Sanin, Nikolai A.

Mendelson, E. Michael. Sangha & State in Burma: A Study of Monastic Sectarianism & Leadership. Ferguson, John P., ed. LC 75-13398. (Illus.). 416p. 1975. 55.00 (*0-8014-0875-X*) Cornell U Pr.

***Mendelson, Edward.** Early Auden. 448p. 2000. pap. 15.00 (*0-374-52695-8*) FS&G.

Mendelson, Edward. Early Auden. 448p. 1983. 19.50 (*0-674-21986-4*) HUP.

Mendelson, Edward. Later Auden. LC 98-27384. 608p. 1999. text 30.00 (*0-374-18408-9*) FS&G.

***Mendelson, Edward.** Later Auden. 608p. 2000. pap. 16.00 (*0-374-52699-0*) FS&G.

Mendelson, Edward, ed. Selected Poems of W. H. Auden. 240p. 1990. pap. 13.00 (*0-679-72483-4*) Vin Bks.

Mendelson, Edward, ed. see Auden, W. H.

Mendelson, Edward, ed. see Auden, W. H. & Isherwood, Christopher.

Mendelson, Edward, ed. see Auden, W. H. & Kallman, Chester.

Mendelson, Edward, jt. ed. see Seidel, Michael.

Mendelson, Elliot. Introduction to Mathematical Logic. 3rd ed. (C). (gr. 13). 1987. text 61.95 (*0-412-06971-7*, Chap & Hall CRC) CRC Pr.

— Schaum Boolean Algebra & Switching Circuits. (Schaum's Outline Ser.). 224p. (C). 1970. pap. 14.95 (*0-07-041460-2*) McGraw.

— Schaum's Outline to Beginning Calculus. 2nd ed. LC 96-39852. (Illus.). 400p. (C). 1996. pap. 15.95 (*0-07-041733-4*) McGraw.

Mendelson, Elliot, jt. auth. see Ayres, Frank, Jr.

Mendelson, George. Psychiatric Aspects of Personal Injury Claims. (Illus.). 296p. 1988. pap. 40.95 (*0-398-06286-2*) C C Thomas.

— Psychiatric Aspects of Personal Injury Claims. (Illus.). 296p. (C). 1988. text 58.95 (*0-398-05411-8*) C C Thomas.

Mendelson, Haim & Ziegler, Johannes. Survival of the Smartest: Managing Information for Rapid Action & World-Class Performance. LC 98-41566. 255p. 1999. 29.95 (*0-471-29560-4*) Wiley.

Mendelson, Jack H., ed. Experimentally Induced Chronic Intoxication & Withdrawal in Alcoholics. (Journal of Studies on Alcohol: Suppl. No. 2). 1964. 5.00 (*0-911290-00-1*) Rutgers Ctr Alcohol.

Mendelson, Jack H. & Mello, Nancy K., eds. Encyclopedia of Psychoactive Drugs: Series 2, 18 vols. (Illus.). 3328p. (YA). (gr. 7 up). 1989. lib. bdg. 359.10 (*1-55546-202-2*) Chelsea Hse.

Mendelson, Jack H., jt. ed. see Mello, Nancy K.

Mendelson, Lee, et al. Red Riding Hood. write for info. (*0-318-58236-8*) P-H.

Mendelson, Littler, jt. auth. see Susser, Peter.

***Mendelson, Lynn.** Chicken! Chicken! Chicken! rev. ed. 160p. 2000. pap. 14.95 (*1-55285-015-3*) Carlton Bks Ltd.

Mendelson, Morton J. Becoming a Brother: A Child Learns about Life, Family & Self. (Illus.). 272p. 1993. pap. text 11.00 (*0-262-63146-6*, Bradford Bks) MIT Pr.

Mendelson, Paul. 100 Tips for Better Bridge: The Macallan the Malt. 128p. 1995. pap. 19.95 (*0-09-180767-0*, Pub. by Random) Trafalgar.

— The Right Way to Play Bridge. (Illus.). 192p. 2001. pap. 8.95 (*0-7160-2028-9*, Pub. by Elliot RW Bks) Midpt Trade.

Mendelson, Phyllis C., jt. ed. see Hall, Sharon K.

Mendelson, Robert. Family Divided: A Divorced Father's Struggle with the Child Custody Industry. LC 97-14239. 547p. 1997. 27.95 (*1-57392-151-3*) Prometheus Bks.

Mendelson, Sara & Crawford, Patricia. Women in Early Modern England 1550-1720. LC 97-33337. (Illus.). 480p. 1998. 35.00 (*0-19-820124-9*) OUP.

— Women in Early Modern England 1550-1720. (Illus.). 510p. 2000. pap. 19.95 (*0-19-820812-X*) OUP.

Mendelson, Sara Heller, ed. see Newcastle, Margaret C.

***Mendelson, Sarah E.** Changing Course: Ideas, Politics & the Soviet Withdrawl from Afghanistan. LC 97-18082. (Princeton Studies in International History & Politics). 168p. 1998. text 35.00 (*0-691-01677-1*, Pub. by Princeton U Pr) Cal Prin Full Svc.

Mendelson, Steve. The Emperor's New Clothes. LC 91-42606. 32p. (J). (gr. k-3). 1992. 7.50 (*1-55670-232-9*) Stewart Tabori & Chang.

***Mendelson, Susan.** The Lazy Gourmet. (Illus.). 224p. 2000. pap. 16.95 (*1-55110-966-2*) Whitecap Bks.

Mendelson, W. B. Human Sleep: Research & Clinical Care. LC 87-7372. (Illus.). 456p. (C). 1987. text 80.00 (*0-306-42627-7*, Kluwer Plenum) Kluwer Academic.

Mendelson, Wallace. Judicial Review & Party Politics. (Reprint Series in Social Sciences). (C). 1993. reprint ed. pap. text 1.00 (*0-8290-2759-9*, PS-201) Irvington.

— Justices Black & Frankfurter: Conflict in the Court. 2nd ed. LC 61-5781. 165p. reprint ed. pap. 51.20 (*0-608-13409-0*, 202410000035) Bks Demand.

— Supreme Court Statecraft: The Rule of Law & Men. LC 85-2489. 362p. 1985. reprint ed. pap. 112.30 (*0-608-00181-3*, 206096300006) Bks Demand.

Mendelssohn-Bartholdy, C., ed. see Mendelssohn, Felix.

Mendelssohn-Bartholdy, Karl. Geschichte Griechenlands von der Eroberung Konstantinopels durch die Turken im Jahre 1453 bis auf Unsere Tage, 2 vols. (GER.). write for info. (*0-318-70437-4*); write for info. (*0-318-70438-2*) G Olms Pubs.

— Geschichte Griechenlands von der Eroberung Konstantinopels durch die Turken im Jahre 1453 bis auf Unsere Tage, 2 vols., Set. (GER.). write for info. (*0-318-70436-6*) G Olms Pubs.

Mendelssohn-Bartholdy, Paul, ed. see Mendelssohn, Felix.

Mendelssohn, Cecille, jt. auth. see Mendelssohn, Felix.

Mendelssohn, Fanny, jt. auth. see Mendelssohn, Felix.

Mendelssohn, Felix. Chamber Works for Piano & Strings. 384p. 1989. pap. 19.95 (*0-486-26117-4*) Dover.

— Complete Chamber Music for Strings. Rietz, Julius, ed. 283p. 1978. reprint ed. pap. 13.95 (*0-486-23679-X*) Dover.

— Complete Works for Piano & Orchestra in Full Score. 208p. 1996. pap. 12.95 (*0-486-29032-8*) Dover.

— Complete Works for Pianoforte Solo, 2 vols., 1. 416p. 1975. pap. 11.95 (*0-486-23136-4*) Dover.

— Complete Works for Pianoforte Solo, 2 vols., 2. 2nd ed. 416p. 1975. pap. 11.95 (*0-486-23137-2*) Dover.

— Concerto in E Minor Opus 64: Violin & Piano. 32p. 1986. pap. 7.95 (*0-7935-4859-4*) H Leonard.

— Elijah: An Oratorio for Piano & Vocal Score. 198p. 1986. per. 8.95 (*0-7935-4559-5*, 50323790) H Leonard.

— Elijah in Full Score. 352p. 1995. pap. 16.95 (*0-486-28504-9*) Dover.

***Mendelssohn, Felix.** Felix Mendelssohn - Concerto for Two Pianos & Orchestra in E Major (1823) Original Version of the First Movement. fac. ed. Lindeman, Stephan D., ed. (Recent Researches in the Music of the 19th & Early 20th Centuries Ser.: Vol. N28). (Illus.). xiv, 117p. 1999. pap. 55.00 (*0-89579-439-X*) A-R Eds.

Mendelssohn, Felix. Goethe & Mendelssohn. LC 70-122622. (Studies in German Literature: No. 13). 1970. reprint ed. lib. bdg. 75.00 (*0-8383-0902-X*) M S G Haskell Hse.

— How Lovely Are the Messengers from St. Paul. 8p. 1986. pap. 1.25 (*0-7935-5499-3*, 50294260) H Leonard.

— Hymn of Praise: Vocal Score Three Solo Voices & Piano. 112p. 1986. per. 6.95 (*0-7935-4709-1*, 50323970) H Leonard.

— Letters from Italy & Switzerland. Wallace, Lady, tr. LC 70-114866. (Select Bibliographies Reprint Ser.). 1977. 26.95 (*0-8369-5271-5*) Ayer.

— Letters of Felix Mendelssohn-Bartholdy from 1833-1847. Mendelssohn-Bartholdy, Paul & Mendelssohn-Bartholdy, C., eds. LC 73-114867. (Select Bibliographies Reprint Ser.). 1977. 29.95 (*0-8369-5272-3*) Ayer.

— Letters of Felix Mendelssohn to Ignaz & Charlotte Moscheles. Moscheles, Felix, ed. & tr. by. LC 77-107822. (Select Bibliographies Reprint Ser.). 1977. 29.95 (*0-8369-5217-0*) Ayer.

— Letters of Felix Mendelssohn to Ignaz & Charlotte Moscheles. Moscheles, Felix, ed. LC 76-173116. (Illus.). 1972. reprint ed. 30.95 (*0-405-08786-1*, Pub. by Blom Pubns) Ayer.

— Lift Thine Eyes to the Mountains: From Elijah a Capella. 4p. 1986. pap. 0.95 (*0-7935-5485-3*, 50292660) H Leonard.

— Major Orchestral Works in Full Score. 406p. 1975. pap. 18.95 (*0-486-23184-4*) Dover.

***Mendelssohn, Felix.** Mendelssohn Masterpieces for Solo Piano: 25 Works. 2000. pap. 9.95 (*0-486-41161-3*) Dover.

Mendelssohn, Felix. The Music Composed for Shakespeare's A Midsummer Night's Dream. 1976. lib. bdg. 59.95 (*0-8490-2307-6*) Gordon Pr.

— Songs Without Words for Piano. 152p. 1986. per. 8.95 (*0-7935-2596-9*) H Leonard.

— Symphony No. 5 ("Reformation") in Full Score. 96p. 1994. pap. 9.95 (*0-486-27875-1*) Dover.

***Mendelssohn, Felix.** Symphony Number 4 in A Major OP 90. 1998. 2.95 (*0-486-29953-8*, 741739Q) Dover.

— Violin Concerto in E Minor, Op. 64. unabridged ed. 64p. 1999. pap. 3.50 (*0-486-40639-3*) Dover.

Mendelssohn, Felix. The Watching over Israel from Elijah. 8p. 1986. pap. 1.25 (*0-7935-5479-9*, 50293760) H Leonard.

Mendelssohn, Felix & Mendelssohn, Cecille. The Mendelssohns on Honeymoon: The 1837 Diary of Felix & Cecille Mendelssohn Bartholdy, Together with Letters to Their Families. Jones, Peter W., ed. LC 97-5419. (Illus.). 256p. 1997. text 65.00 (*0-19-816597-8*) OUP.

Mendelssohn, Felix & Mendelssohn, Fanny. Mendelssohn/Twenty-Four Songs: Medium Voice. Paton, John G., ed. 96p. (C). 1992. pap. 9.95 (*0-88284-523-3*, 3388) Alfred Pub.

— Mendelssohn/Twenty-Four Songs, Medium Voice. Paton, John G., ed. 96p. (C). 1992. pap. 9.95 (*0-88284-499-7*, 3387) Alfred Pub.

Mendelssohn, Felix & Viereck, eds. Appiani Vol. II: Bella Civilia. (GRE.). 1986. reprint ed. 85.00 (*3-322-00272-1*, T1054, Pub. by B G Teubner) U of Mich Pr.

Mendelssohn, Moses. Jerusalem: Or on Religious Power & Judaism. Arkush, Allan, tr. LC 83-40015. (Illus.). 262p. 1983. pap. 19.95 (*0-87451-264-6*) U Pr of New Eng.

— Love Letters to His Bride. Regan, Frauke, tr. from GER. (Illus.). 120p. 1991. 21.95 (*0-941062-55-4*) Begos & Rosenberg.

— Phaedon: or The Death of Socrates. LC 73-2219. (Jewish People; History, Religion, Literature Ser.). 1973. reprint ed. 24.95 (*0-405-05282-0*) Ayer.

Mendelssohn, Peter De, see De Mendelssohn, Peter.

Mendelssohn, Sidney. The Jews of Asia: Especially in the Sixteenth & Seventeenth Centuries. LC 77-87612. (Illus.). 256p. reprint ed. 37.50 (*0-404-16436-6*) AMS Pr.

— Judaic or Semitic Legends & Customs Amongst South African Natives. 1976. lib. bdg. 59.95 (*0-8490-2111-1*) Gordon Pr.

— South African Bibliography, 2 vols. 2147p. 1993. reprint ed. 175.00 (*1-57898-030-5*) Martino Pubng.

***Mendelzon, A., ed.** 8th World Wide Web Conference. 716p. 1999. 71.00 (*0-444-50266-1*) Elsevier.

Mendenhall. A Brief Course in Business Statistics. (Business Statistics Ser.). 1994. pap., student ed. 17.95 (*0-534-25293-1*) Wadsworth Pub.

— A Course in Business. 4th ed. (Business Statistics Ser.). 1995. pap., teacher ed. 28.00 (*0-534-26510-3*) PWS Pubs.

— A Course in Business Statistics. (Business Statistics Ser.). 1984. teacher ed. 7.25 (*0-87150-789-7*) PWS Pubs.

— A Course in Business Statistics. 4th ed. (Business Statistics Ser.). 1995. pap., student ed. 18.95 (*0-534-26509-X*) Wadsworth Pub.

— Math Statistics with Applications. 3rd ed. (Statistics Ser.). 1986. teacher ed. 3.00 (*0-87150-942-3*) PWS Pubs.

— Mathematical Statistics with Applications. (Statistics Ser.). 1973. 25.00 (*0-87872-047-2*) PWS Pubs.

— Minitab Handbook A Course In Bus Stat 2e. 2nd ed. (Business Statistics). 1988. 13.50 (*0-534-91522-1*) Brooks-Cole.

— Statistics for Management & Economics. (Business Statistics Ser.). 1971. 15.75 (*0-87872-005-7*) PWS Pubs.

— Statistics for Management & Economics. 3rd ed. (Business Statistics Ser.). Date not set. teacher ed. 6.75 (*0-87150-680-7*) PWS Pubs.

— Statistics for Management & Economics. 7th ed. (Business Statistics Ser.). 1993. pap., student ed. 18.95 (*0-534-93301-7*) Wadsworth Pub.

— Statistics for Managmen & Economics. 2nd ed. (Business Statistics Ser.). 1974. 17.50 (*0-87872-058-8*) PWS Pubs.

— Understanding Statistics. 3rd ed. (Statistics Ser.). 1980. teacher ed. 7.50 (*0-87150-685-8*) PWS Pubs.

Mendenhall & Beaver. Statistics for Management & Economics. 6th ed. 1989. teacher ed. 13.50 (*0-534-91661-9*) Thomson Learn.

— Statistics for Management & Economics. 7th ed. (Business Statistics Ser.). 1993. pap., student ed. 26.95 (*0-534-93304-1*) Wadsworth Pub.

— Statistics for Manangement & Economics. 4th ed. (Business Statistics Ser.). 1982. student ed. 9.00 (*0-87150-425-1*) PWS Pubs.

Mendenhall & Scheaffer. Elementary Survey Sampling. 3rd ed. (Statistics Ser.). 1986. teacher ed. 4.50 (*0-87150-948-2*) PWS Pubs.

Mendenhall & Sincich, Terry. Simon & Schuster a Second Course in Statistics. 5th ed. 1996. pap. text, student ed. 29.33 (*0-13-456468-5*) P-H.

Mendenhall, jt. auth. see Boudreau.

Mendenhall, jt. auth. see Ott.

Mendenhall, jt. auth. see Schaeffer.

Mendenhall, jt. auth. see Scheaffer.

Mendenhall, jt. auth. see Wackerly.

Mendenhall, Bethany, ed. see Morehouse, Brian.

Mendenhall, Charles. The Air Racer. rev. ed. (Illus.). 192p. 1994. pap. 19.95 (*0-933424-01-9*) Specialty Pr.

Mendenhall, Charles A. The Gee Bees Racers: A Legacy of Speed. (Illus.). 179p. 1994. pap. 19.95 (*0-933424-05-1*) Specialty Pr.

***Mendenhall, Corwin.** Sea Stories. (Illus.). 368p. 2000. pap. 19.00 (*0-8059-4804-X*) Dorrance.

Mendenhall, Corwin. Submarine Diary: The Silent Stalking of Japan. LC 90-40440. (Bluejacket Paperback Ser.). (Illus.). 308p. 1995. pap. 15.95 (*1-55750-582-9*) Naval Inst Pr.

Mendenhall, Deb, jt. auth. see Joseph, Leisha.

***Mendenhall, George E.** The Bible in Popular Context. 240p. 2000. pap. 20.00 (*1-56338-321-7*) TPI PA.

Mendenhall, George E. The Syllabic Inscriptions from Byblos. 194p. 1986. text 40.00 (*0-8156-6077-4*, Pub. by Am U Beirut) Syracuse U Pr.

Mendenhall, Harlan. Fall of the House of Gacy. (Illus.). 267p. (Orig.). 1996. pap. 12.95 (*1-887827-01-3*) New Authors Pubns.

Mendenhall, Harlan H., jt. auth. see Lockwood, Brocton.

Mendenhall, John. American Trademarks, 1930-1950, Vol. 2. (Illus.). 160p. 1983. reprint ed. pap. text 22.50 (*0-88108-112-4*) Art Dir.

— Character Trademarks. (Illus.). 144p. (Orig.). 1990. pap. 16.95 (*0-87701-752-2*) Chronicle Bks.

— Early Modernism: Swiss & Austrian Trademarks 1920-1950. LC 96-40895. (Illus.). 132p. 1997. pap. 16.95 (*0-8118-1283-9*) Chronicle Bks.

— French Trademarks: The Art Deco Era. (Illus.). 144p. (Orig.). 1991. pap. 16.95 (*0-87701-853-7*) Chronicle Bks.

— High Tech Trademarks. LC 85-61876. 160p. 1985. 19.95 (*0-88108-024-1*) Art Dir.

— High Tech Trademarks, No. 2. LC 85-61876. 160p. 1988. 27.50 (*0-88108-058-6*) Art Dir.

— Nederland Trademarks, 1900-1950. LC 94-79354. (Illus.). (Orig.). 1995. pap. text 17.95 (*0-88108-150-7*) Art Dir.

— Penmanship & Fine Lettering: A Resource for Designers. LC 97-73401. (Illus.). 112p. 1997. pap. 11.95 (*0-88108-202-3*) Art Dir.

— Scan This Book, Vol. 3. LC 97-74890. (Illus.). 128p. 1998. pap. 16.95 (*0-88108-205-8*) Art Dir.

Mendenhall, John, ed. American Trade Marks, 1930-1950, Vol. 1. LC 83-7316. (Illus.). 160p. 1991. reprint ed. pap. text 22.50 (*0-88108-095-0*) Art Dir.

— American Trademarks, 1930-1950, Vol. 3. LC 86-81966. 160p. 1991. text 24.95 (*0-88108-080-2*) Art Dir.

— Scan This Book. LC 91-77465. (Illus.). 120p. 1991. pap. text 15.95 (*0-88108-099-3*) Art Dir.

— Scan This Book, Vol. 2. (Illus.). 1991. pap. text 15.95 (*0-88108-193-0*) Art Dir.

Mendenhall, Kitty. Parade. 70p. (Orig.). 1997. pap. 9.95 (*1-884754-29-5*) Potpourri Pubns.

Mendenhall, M., ed. Tactical Missile Aerodynamics: Prediction Methodology. (PAAS Ser.: Vol. 142). 700p. 1992. 79.95 (*1-56347-016-0*, V-142) AIAA.

Mendenhall, Mark & Oddou, Gary, eds. Readings & Cases in International Human Resources Management. 2nd ed. LC 94-37700. (C). 1995. mass mkt. 37.95 (*0-538-84737-9*) S-W Pub.

Mendenhall, Mark, jt. ed. see Oddou, Gary.

***Mendenhall, Mark A.** Readings & Cases in International Human Resource Managment. 3rd ed. LC 99-27527. 523p. (Orig.). 1999. pap. 50.95 (*0-324-00634-9*) Thomson Learn.

Mendenhall, Mark E., ed. see Stahl, Gunter K.

Mendenhall, Michael J., ed. The Constitution of the United States of America. (Orig.). 1999. pap. 3.00 (*0-9623713-9-4*) Sept Svntnth Pubg.

Since 1989 relied on by schools from elementary level through graduate school, by professionals & laypersons from every walk of life who demand accuracy & reliability. Derived directly from the original documents & meticulously researched, this edition of the Constitution has become the most sought after copy in America & throughout the world. Contains the long forgotten preamble to the Bill of Rights as a special bonus. Printed in handy 4x6 pocket size for ease of use. This edition contains the Declaration of Independence. "It is with great pleasure that I recommend the Definitive Edition of The Constitution of the United States...I have used it in classes ranging from high school history & government to upper division college political science & have found it to have no equal for easy & clear application of the basic principles of our system of government." -Henry M. Littlefield, Ph.D., Faculty Member, Golden Gate University. Place your order by mail, phone, fax or e-mail: september17thgyaloo.com. September 17th Publishing 1015 Cass St., Suite 10, Monterey, CA 93940. Phone: 831-373-1787, Fax: 831-375-9307.
Publisher Paid Annotation.

Mendenhall, Ruth D., jt. auth. see Prater, Yvonne.

Mendenhall, Thomas, jt. auth. see Howard, James.

Mendenhall, Thomas C. The Harvard-Yale Boat Race, 1852-1924: And the Coming of Sport to the American College. (Illus.). 386p. 1993. 49.95 (*0-913372-64-1*) Mystic Seaport.

Mendenhall, W. C. Three Hundred Twenty Desert Watering Places in Southeastern California & Southwestern Nevada. 104p. 1982. 14.95 (*0-913814-62-8*) Nevada Pubns.

Mendenhall, Wackerly-Sheaffer. Math Statistics with Applications. 4th ed. (Adaptable Courseware-Hardside Ser.). 26.00 (*0-534-32052-5*) Brooks-Cole.

Mendenhall, William. Beginning Statistics: A to Z. 525p. (C). 1993. pap. 64.95 (*0-534-19122-3*) Wadsworth Pub.

— Introduction to Probability & Statistics. 5th ed. (Statistics Ser.). 1979. mass mkt. 21.75 (*0-87150-377-8*) PWS Pubs.

An Asterisk (*) at the beginning of an entry indicates that the title is appearing for the first time.

— Introduction to Probability & Statistics. 6th ed. 800p. 1983. mass mkt. 28.25 (*0-87150-365-4*, 4760) PWS Pubs.

— Introduction to Probability & Statistics. 7th ed. (C). 1987. mass mkt. 39.75 (*0-87150-046-9*, 36G0150) PWS Pubs.

— Introduction to Probability & Statistics. 9th ed. (Statistics Ser.). 1994. pap. 49.00 (*0-534-20887-8*) Brooks-Cole.

***Mendenhall, William.** Introduction to Probability & Statistics. 10th ed. (Statistics Ser). 1998. pap. 13.50 (*0-534-36208-7*) Brooks-Cole.

Mendenhall, William & Beaver. Introduction to Probability & Statistics. 6th ed. (Statistics Ser.). Date not set. teacher ed. 7.50 (*0-87150-403-0*) PWS Pubs.

Mendenhall, William & Beaver. Introduction to Probability & Statistics. 6th ed. (Statistics Ser.). 1983. student ed. 9.50 (*0-87150-381-6*) PWS Pubs.

— Introduction to Probability & Statistics. 9th ed. (Statistics Ser.). 1994. pap., student ed. 26.95 (*0-534-20888-6*) Wadsworth Pub.

Mendenhall, William & Beaver. Introduction to Probability & Statistics. 10th ed. LC 98-15311. (Statistics Ser.). 1998. pap. 86.95 (*0-534-35778-4*) Brooks-Cole.

— Introduction to Probability & Statistics. 10th ed. (Statistics Ser.). 1998. pap., student ed. write for info. (*0-534-36170-6*) PWS Pubs.

***Mendenhall, William & Beaver.** Introduction to Probability & Statistics. 10th ed. 1998. pap. 20.50 (*0-534-36172-2*) Thomson Learn.

Mendenhall, William & Beaver, Robert J. A Brief Course in Business Statistics. LC 94-17706. 654p. 1994. pap., text, mass mkt. 67.95 incl. 3.5 hd (*0-534-25290-7*) Wadsworth Pub.

Mendenhall, William & Beaver, Robert J. A Course In Business: Statistics. 2nd ed. (Business Statistics Ser.). 832p. (C). 1988. mass mkt. 41.50 (*0-534-91488-8*) PWS Pubs.

Mendenhall, William & Beaver, Robert J. A Course in Business Statistics. 3rd ed. 800p. 1992. text 51.75 (*0-534-92989-3*) Wadsworth Pub.

— A Course in Business Statistics. 3rd ed. 800p. 1992. pap., teacher ed. 12.50 (*0-534-92996-6*) Wadsworth Pub.

— Introduction to Probability & Statistics. 8th ed. 848p. (C). 1991. text 55.95 (*0-534-92409-3*); teacher ed. 14.95 (*0-534-92548-0*); student ed. 20.95 (*0-534-92551-0*) Wadsworth Pub.

— Introduction to Probability & Statistics. 9th ed. 704p. 1994. pap. 63.00 (*0-534-20886-X*) Wadsworth Pub.

Mendenhall, William & Ott, Lyman. Understanding Statistics. 3rd ed. LC 79-20914. (C). 1980. pap. 23.00 (*0-87150-421-9*) PWS Pubs.

Mendenhall, William & Ott, R. Lyman. Understanding Statistics. 6th ed. 598p. 1994. pap. 70.95 (*0-534-20922-X*) Wadsworth Pub.

Mendenhall, William & Reinmuth, James E. Statistics for Management & Economics. 4th ed. (C). 1982. pap. 27.25 (*0-87150-411-1*) PWS Pubs.

— Statistics for Management & Economics. 5th ed. (C). 1986. pap. 37.25 (*0-87150-972-5*, 36G8340) PWS Pubs.

— Statistics for Management & Economics. 5th ed. (C). 1986. pap. 15.00 (*0-87150-974-1*, 36G8345) PWS Pubs.

Mendenhall, William & Scheaffer, Richard L. Mathematical Statistics with Applications. 2nd ed. (C). 1981. pap. 28.25 (*0-87150-410-3*) PWS Pubs.

Mendenhall, William & Sincich, Terry. A Second Course in Statistics. 5th ed. 766p. (C). 1996. 105.00 (*0-13-396821-9*) P-H.

— Statistics for Engineering & the Sciences. 4th ed. LC 94-41303. 1008p. 1995. 105.00 (*0-02-380581-1*, Macmillan Coll) P-H.

Mendenhall, William & Wackerly, Dennis D. Mathematical Statistics with Applications. 5th ed. (Statistics Ser.). 1996. pap., student ed. 17.95 (*0-534-20918-1*) Wadsworth Pub.

***Mendenhall, William, et al.** A Brief Course in Business Statistics. 2nd ed. LC 00-30850. (Illus.). 2000. write for info. (*0-534-38130-8*) Course Tech.

Mendenhall, William, et al. A Course in Business Statistics. 4th ed. (C). 1995. text, mass mkt. 97.95 incl. 3.5 hd (*0-534-26508-1*) Wadsworth Pub.

Mendenhall, William, et al. Mathematical Statistics W/ Applications. 4th ed. (Statistics Ser.). 752p. (C). 1989. pap. 60.75 (*0-534-92026-8*) PWS Pubs.

Mendenhall, William, et al. Statistics For Management & Economics. 6th ed. Payne, Michael, ed. (Business Statistics Ser.). 992p. (C). 1989. pap. 49.25 (*0-534-91658-9*) Wadsworth Pub.

— Statistics for Management & Economics. 7th ed. LC 92-30933. 1062p. 1993. pap. 73.95 (*0-534-93299-1*) Wadsworth Pub.

— Statistics for Psychology. LC 77-23194. (C). 1973. pap. 14.00 (*0-87872-045-6*) PWS Pubs.

Mendenhall, William, jt. auth. see Beaver, Robert J.

Mendenhall, William, jt. auth. see Ott.

Mendenhall, William, jt. auth. see Ott, R. Lyman.

Mender, Mona. Extraordinary Women in Support of Music. LC 96-40068. 272p. 1997. 48.00 (*0-8108-3278-X*) Scarecrow.

— Music Manuscript Preparation: A Concise Guide. LC 90-8373. (Illus.). 222p. 1991. 34.50 (*0-8108-2294-6*) Scarecrow.

Mendershausen, Horst. Changes in Income Distribution During the Great Depression. LC 75-19726. (National Bureau of Economic Research Ser.). (Illus.). 1975. reprint ed. 20.95 (*0-405-07604-5*) Ayer.

— Changes in Income Distribution During the Great Depression. (Studies in Income & Wealth: No. 7). 191p. 1946. reprint ed. 49.70 (*0-87014-162-7*) Natl Bur Econ Res.

— Coping with the Oil Crisis: French & German Experiences. LC 75-35485. 127p. reprint ed. pap. 39.40 (*0-7837-3048-9*, 202380700034) Bks Demand.

— German Economics. LC 73-21101. (Contributions in Economic Analysis Ser.: No. 8). (Illus.). 130p. 1974. reprint ed. lib. bdg. 65.00 (*0-8371-6000-6*, MEGE, Greenwood Pr) Greenwood.

Mendes, A. J. Economic Integration & Growth in Europe. 160p. 1986. 49.95 (*0-7099-4664-3*, Pub. by C Helm) Routldge.

Mendes, Anthony. Inspiring Commitment: How to Win Employee Loyalty in Chaotic Times. 125p. 1995. pap. 19.95 (*0-7863-0422-7*, Irwn Prfssnl) McGraw-Hill Prof.

Mendes, Bob. Vengeance: Prelude to Saddam's War. Smittenaar, H. S., tr. from DUT. 303p. 1996. pap. 9.95 (*1-881164-71-3*) Intercont VA.

Mendes, Chico & Gross, Tony. Fight for the Forest: Chico Mendes in His Own Words. rev. ed. (Latin America Bureau Ser.). (Illus.). 128p. (C). 1992. pap. text 12.00 (*0-85345-866-9*, Pub. by Lat Am Bur) Monthly Rev.

Mendes, Clelia. City with Sea. 1998. 10.95 (*0-533-12521-9*) Vantage.

Mendes de Leon, Pablo M., jt. ed. see Masson-Zwaan, Tanja L.

***Mendes, Errol P., et al, eds.** Democratic Policing & Accountability: Global Perspectives. 248p. 1999. text 69.95 (*0-7546-1173-6*, Pub. by Ashgate Pub) Ashgate Pub Co.

Mendes-Flohr, Paul R. Divided Passions: Jewish Intellectuals & the Experience of Modernity. LC 89-22557. 450p. 1991. 44.95 (*0-8143-2030-9*) Wayne St U Pr.

— From Mysticism to Dialogue: Martin Buber's Transformation of German Social Thought. LC 88-20689. 194p. 1989. 32.95 (*0-8143-2028-7*); pap. 16.95 (*0-8143-2029-5*) Wayne St U Pr.

— German Jews: A Dual Identity. LC 98-32151. 149p. 1999. 18.50 (*0-300-07623-1*) Yale U Pr.

Mendes-Flohr, Paul R., ed. Ecstatic Confessions: The Heart of Mysticism. Cameron, Esther, tr. LC 96-31865. (Martin Buber Library). 160p. 1996. reprint ed. pap. 16.95 (*0-8156-0422-X*, BUECP) Syracuse U Pr.

— Gershom Scholem: The Man & His Work. LC 93-47893. (SUNY Series in Judaica: Hermeneutics, Mysticism, & Religion). 127p. (C). 1994. text 44.50 (*0-7914-2125-2*); pap. text 14.95 (*0-7914-2126-0*) State U NY Pr.

Mendes-Flohr, Paul R., jt. auth. see Cohen, Arthur A.

Mendes-Flohr, Paul R., jt. auth. see Rotenstreich, Nathan.

Mendes-Flohr, Paul R., jt. ed. see Glatzer, Nahum N.

Mendes-Flohr, Paul R., jt. ed. see Reinharz, Jehuda.

Mendes-Flohr, Paul R., ed. & comment see Buber, Martin.

Mendes, Guy. Another Page, Bk. 1. (Another Page TV Ser.). 118p. 1988. student ed. 6.95 (*0-910475-46-6*) KET.

— Another Page, Bk. 2. (Another Page TV Ser.). 167p. 1988. student ed. 6.95 (*0-910475-47-4*) KET.

— Another Page, Bk. 3. (Another Page TV Ser.). 124p. 1988. student ed. 6.95 (*0-910475-48-2*) KET.

— Another Page, Bk. 4. (Another Page TV Ser.). 142p. 1988. student ed. 6.95 (*0-910475-49-0*) KET.

— Another Page, Bk. 5. (Another Page TV Ser.). 132p. 1988. student ed. 6.95 (*0-910475-50-4*) KET.

— Light at Hand: Photographs, 1970-85. LC 85-81724. (Illus.). 64p. 1986. 22.50 (*0-917788-30-3*) Gnomon Pr.

Mendes, H. Pereira. Looking Ahead: Twentieth Century Happenings. LC 79-154451. (Utopian Literature Ser.). 1976. reprint ed. 29.95 (*0-405-03533-0*) Ayer.

Mendes, Joel, jt. ed. see Rosen, Howard.

***Mendes-Llewellyn, Cristina, contrib. by.** Talk Portuguese, Set. LC 99-23206. (Talk...Language Ser.). (POR.). 128p. 1999. pap. 18.95 incl. audio (*0-8442-2328-X*, 2328X, Passprt Bks) NTC Contemp Pub Co.

Mendes, Manuel & Silva, J. M. Theoretical & Experimental Modal Analysis. LC 96-38057. (Mechanical Engineering Research Studies). 1997. write for info. (*0-86380-208-7*) Wiley.

Mendes, Peter. Clandestine Erotic Fiction in English, 1800-1930: A Bibliographic Study. 497p. 1993. 156.95 (*0-85967-919-5*, Pub. by Scolar Pr) Ashgate Pub Co.

Mendes, R. V., jt. auth. see Garrido, M. S.

Mendes, Reva. Words for the Quiet Moments. 35p. 1973. reprint ed. pap. 3.50 (*0-87516-185-5*) DeVorss.

Mendes, Richard. Prose & Cons. 128p. 1993. pap. 8.95 (*1-880365-41-3*) Prof Pr NC.

Mendes, Sam, jt. auth. see Ball, Alan.

Mendes, V. D. The Victoria & Albert Museum's Textile Collection Vol. 2: British Textiles from 1900 to 1937. (Illus.). 1992. pap. 36.00 (*1-85177-114-X*, Pub. by V&A Ent) Antique Collect.

***Mendes, Valerie.** Dressed in Black. 144p. 2000. 45.00 (*0-8109-6689-1*, Pub. by Abrams) Time Warner.

Mendes, Valerie & De La Haye, Amy. 20th Century Fashion. LC 98-61433. (World of Art Ser.). (Illus.). 280p. 1999. pap. 16.95 (*0-500-20321-0*, Pub. by Thames Hudson) Norton.

Mendes, Valerie, jt. auth. see Wilcox, Claire.

Mendes, Valerie, jt. auth. see Wilcox, Claire.

Mendez. Evidence-California Code & Federal Rules-Problem Approach. 2nd ed. LC 99-462588. (Paralegal Ser.). (C). 1999. pap. 32.25 (*0-314-23896-4*) West Pub.

— Habla Espanol. 5th ed. (C). 1993. pap. text, student ed. 77.50 (*0-15-500012-8*) Harcourt.

— Habla Espanol: Manual De Ejercicios Y Laboratorio. 5th ed. (C). 1993. pap. text, wbk. ed., lab manual ed. 40.50 (*0-03-075903-X*) Harcourt Coll Pubs.

— Habla Espanol: Testing Progress. 5th ed. (C). 1993. pap. text, teacher ed., suppl. ed. 10.00 (*0-03-075907-2*, Pub. by Harcourt Coll Pubs) Harcourt.

— Habla Espanol Essentials. 5th ed. (SPA.). (C). 1993. student ed. 74.00 incl. audio (*0-15-500654-1*) Harcourt.

Mendez. Hablemos Espanol. 6th ed. (SPA.). 1997. pap., student ed. 82.00 incl. cd-rom (*0-03-023606-1*) Harcourt Coll Pubs.

Mendez, Jr. El Que Sigue. LC 94-61480. (Coleccion Humor: No. 1). (SPA., Illus.). 86p. (Orig.). 1994. pap. 9.95 (*0-89729-659-1*) Ediciones.

— Textos. (C). 1996. pap. text 33.50 (*0-15-504481-8*) Harcourt Coll Pubs.

***Mendez- Ramirez, Hugo.** Neruda's Ekphrastic Experience: Mural Art & "Canto General" LC 98-47708. (Illus.). 248p. 1999. 43.50 (*0-8387-5398-1*) Bucknell U Pr.

***Mendez- Trelles, Ignacio.** Dictionary of Gastronomy & Hotel Management. (ENG & SPA.). 288p. 1999. pap. 69.95 (*0-320-01781-8*) Fr & Eur.

Mendez, A. Diccionario Tecnico de la Industria del Petroleo y Derivados. (ENG, FRE & SPA.). 588p. 1980. 95.00 (*0-8288-0715-9*, S37582) Fr & Eur.

Mendez, A., jt. ed. see Fernandez, E.

Mendez, Adriana. Cubans in America. LC 93-14339. (In America Ser.). (Illus.). 72p. (J). (gr. 5 up). 1994. pap. 5.95 (*0-8225-1039-1*, Lerner Publctns); lib. bdg. 19.93 (*0-8225-1953-4*, Lerner Publctns) Lerner Pub.

Mendez, Amalia Cardos de, see Cardos de Mendez, Amalia.

***Mendez, Ana.** Shaking the Heavens. 2000. pap. 10.99 (*0-8307-2496-6*, Renew) Gospel Lght.

Mendez, Ana T. Merced De, see Merced de Mendez, Ana T.

***Mendez, Antonio J.** Master of Disguise: My Secret Life in the CIA. (Illus.). 2000. pap. 14.00 (*0-06-095791-3*) HarpC.

***Mendez, Antonio J. & McConnell, Malcolm.** The Master of Disguise: My Secret Life in the CIA. LC 99-23066. (Illus.). 368p. 1999. 25.00 (*0-688-16302-5*, Wm Morrow) Morrow Avon.

Mendez, Carlos M. Critica al Poder Politico. LC 81-67847. (SPA., Illus.). 269p. (Orig.). 1981. pap. 14.95 (*0-89729-298-7*) Ediciones.

— El Manifiesto Democrata. LC 82-71115. (Coleccion Cuba y sus Jueces). (SPA.). 40p. (Orig.). 1982. pap. 2.00 (*0-89729-313-4*) Ediciones.

Mendez, Carmen, jt. auth. see Rizzo, Ann-Marie.

Mendez, Clark R. Onetti y la Fidelidad a las Reglas del Juego. (SPA.). 188p. (Orig.). (C). 1992. text 46.00 (*0-8191-8889-1*); pap. text 26.50 (*0-8191-8890-5*) U Pr of Amer.

Mendez, Connie. Metafisica 4 en 1.Tr. of Metaphysics Four in One. 1997. pap. text 14.98 (*980-6114-26-4*) Bienes.

Mendez, Connie. Metafisica 4 en 1.Tr. of Metaphysics Four in One. (SPA.). 1997. pap. text 14.98 (*980-6329-00-7*) Bienes.

Mendez, Connie. Que Es la Metafisica. 1997. pap. text 7.98 (*980-6114-34-5*) Bienestar.

Mendez, Connie. Te Regalo Lo Que Se Te Antoje. (SPA.). 1997. pap. text 5.50 (*980-6114-06-X*) Bienes.

Mendez, E. E. & Von Klitzing, K., eds. Physics & Applications of Quantum Wells & Superlattices. (NATO ASI Series B, Physics: Vol. 170). (Illus.). 442p. 1988. 125.00 (*0-306-42823-7*, Plenum Trade) Perseus Pubng.

Mendez, Eugenio F. Cronicas De Puerto Rico: Desde la Conquista Hasta Nuestros Dias, 1493-1955. 2nd ed. (C). reprint ed. pap. 8.00 (*0-8477-0811-X*) U of PR Pr.

— Identity & Culture. (Puerto Rico Ser.). 1979. lib. bdg. 59.95 (*0-8490-2943-0*) Gordon Pr.

Mendez, Eugenio Fernandez, see Fernandez Mendez, Eugenio, ed.

Mendez-Faith, Kienzle. Habla Espanol? 4th ed. Price, Julia, ed. (SPA., Illus.). 614p. (C). 1989. write for info. (*0-03-026229-1*) Harcourt Coll Pubs.

— Habla Espanol? 4th ed. Price, Julia, ed. (SPA., Illus.). 614p. (C). 1990. teacher ed. 35.00 (*0-685-22795-2*); audio. write for info. (*0-03-026658-0*) Harcourt Coll Pubs.

— Habla Espanol? 4th annot. ed. Price, Julia, ed. (SPA., Illus.). 614p. (C). 1990. teacher ed. write for info. (*0-03-013918-X*) Harcourt Coll Pubs.

Mendez-Faith, Teresa. Contextos: Literarios Hispanoamericanos. 228p. (C). 1986. pap. text 28.75 (*0-03-063844-5*) Harcourt Coll Pubs.

— HABLAEMOS 6E. 6th ed. 848p. (C). 1997. text 67.50 (*0-03-020439-9*) Harcourt Coll Pubs.

— Panoramas Literarios: Hispanoamerica. (SPA.). 416p. (C). 1997. pap. text 35.56 (*0-669-21805-7*) HM Trade Div.

Mendez-Faith, Teresa & Gill, Mary M. Habla Espanol? Essentials. 4th ed. (ENG & SPA.). 440p. (C). 1991. write for info. (*0-318-69168-X*) Harcourt Coll Pubs.

— Habla Espanol? The Essentials. 5th ed. LC 93-36981. (C). 1993. text 73.00 (*0-15-500650-9*) Harcourt Coll Pubs.

— Viewer's Manual: Videomundo. 4th ed. (ENG & SPA.). 440p. (C). 1989. pap. text, student ed. 30.50 (*0-03-020732-0*) Harcourt Coll Pubs.

Mendez-Faith, Teresa, et al. Habla Espanol? 5th ed. (Illus.). 600p. (C). 1993. text 77.50 (*0-03-074997-2*, Pub. by Harcourt Coll Pubs) Harcourt.

— Habla Espanol? An Introductory Course. 5th ed. (Illus.). 600p. (C). 1993. teacher ed. write for info. (*0-03-075908-0*) Harcourt Coll Pubs.

Mendez-Faith, Teresa, jt. auth. see Kienzle, Beverly M.

Mendez, Jose L. Como Leer a Garcia Marquez: Una Interpretacion Sociologica. LC 89-5381. 224p. (Orig.). 1992. pap. text 12.50 (*0-8477-3640-7*) U of PR Pr.

— Introduccion a la Sociologia de la Literatura. LC 80-25694. (Coleccion Mente y Palabra). 143p. 1982. 5.50 (*0-8477-0580-3*); pap. 5.00 (*0-8477-0581-1*) U of PR Pr.

Mendez, Juan. HCO Spanish Grammar. LC 90-56014. (College Outline Ser.). 336p. 1991. pap. 15.00 (*0-06-467129-1*, Harper Ref) HarpC.

***Mendez, Juan E., et al, eds.** The (Un)Rule of Law & the Underprivileged in Latin America. LC 98-31846. (From the Helen Kellogg Institute for International Studies). 368p. 1999. 48.00 (*0-268-04301-9*); pap. 28.00 (*0-268-04302-7*) U of Notre Dame Pr.

Mendez Luengo, Ernesto. Llanto Por un Lobo Muerto. (Nueva Austral Ser.: Vol. 49). (SPA.). 1991. pap. text 24.95 (*84-239-1849-1*) Elliots Bks.

Mendez, Luis F. Julian del Casal: Estudio Comparativo de Prosa y Poesia. LC 78-70499. 1979. pap. 10.00 (*0-89729-213-8*) Ediciones.

Mendez, M. Albert, jt. auth. see Russell, Lee.

Mendez, Miguel. The Cristobal Colon Project: A Transnational Negotiation Simulation. (Pew Case Studies in International Affairs). 50p. (C). 1996. text 3.50 (*1-56927-217-4*) Geo U Inst Dplmcy.

— The Dream of Santa Maria de las Piedras. Foster, David W., tr. from SPA. LC 89-61106. 194p. 1989. 25.00 (*0-916950-98-0*); pap. 15.00 (*0-916950-99-9*) Biling Rev-Pr.

— Entre Letras y Ladrillos. (SPA.). 112p. (Orig.). 1996. pap. 11.00 (*0-927534-58-4*) Biling Rev-Pr.

— From Labor to Letters: A Novel Autobiography. Foster, David W., tr. from SPA. LC 97-3271. 128p. 1997. 20.00 (*0-927534-70-3*); pap. 11.00 (*0-927534-66-5*) Biling Rev-Pr.

— Peregrinos de Aztlan. LC 90-27640. (Clasicos Chicanos - Chicano Classics Ser.: No. 6). 192p. 1991. pap. 15.00 (*0-927534-14-2*) Biling Rev-Pr.

— Pilgrims in Aztlan. Foster, David W., tr. LC 92-23636. 184p. 1992. 25.00 (*0-927534-22-3*); pap. 15.00 (*0-927534-23-1*) Biling Rev-Pr.

Mendez, Miguel A. The California Code & the Federal Rules: A Problem Approach. LC 95-20151. (American Casebook Ser.). 564p. (C). 1995. pap. text 37.00 (*0-314-06686-1*) West Pub.

— Evidence: The California Code & the Federal Rules a Problem Approach Answers to Questions. (American Casebook Ser.). 83p. 1995. pap. 9.50 (*0-314-06913-5*) West Pub.

Mendez, Phil. The Black Snowman. (Illus.). 48p. (J). (gr. 2-5). 1989. 15.95 (*0-590-40552-7*) Scholastic Inc.

— The Black Snowman. LC 87-4774. (Illus.). 48p. (J). (gr. 4-7). 1991. pap. 5.99 (*0-590-44873-0*, Blue Ribbon Bks) Scholastic Inc.

— The Black Snowman. 1989. 11.19 (*0-606-00318-5*, Pub. by Turtleback) Demco.

Mendez, Prudewcio. Paraguay, the Democratic Revolution: Why the Colorados. (C). 1993. pap. text 2.00 (*0-9625497-0-3*) P Mendez.

Mendez, Ramon T. Costumbre Nacionales, 1809-1883. (SPA., Illus.). 1978. lib. bdg. 35.00 (*0-8288-3941-7*) Fr & Eur.

Mendez, Raul H., ed. Visualization in Supercomputing. (Illus.). 224p. 1990. 54.95 (*0-387-97149-1*) Spr-Verlag.

Mendez, Raul H. & Orszag, S. A. Japanese Supercomputing. (Lecture Notes in Engineering Ser.: Vol. 36). (Illus.). 150p. 1988. 62.95 (*0-387-96765-6*) Spr-Verlag.

Mendez, Ruben P. International Public Finance: Global Relations in a New Perspective. (Illus.). 368p. (C). 1992. pap. text 36.95 (*0-19-507195-6*) OUP.

Mendez, Salvador P., et al. Arqueologia del Norte de Michoacan: Investigacion de Salvamento en una Carretera. (SPA., Illus.). 104p. 1996. pap. 11.00 (*968-29-9488-8*, IN96, Pub. by Dir Gen Pubicaiones) UPLAAP.

Mendez, V. & Nestor, J. Sediment Transport in Irrigation Canals. (IHE Thesis Ser.: No. 15). (Illus.). 286p. (C). 1998. pap. text 48.00 (*90-5410-413-9*, Pub. by A A Balkema) Ashgate Pub Co.

Mendez Ventura, Sylvia. Chief Justice Cesar Bengzon: A Filipino in the World Court. LC 96-946568. ix, 202 p. 1996. write for info. (*971-27-0576-5*) Anvil Pub Inc.

Mendez-Villarrubia, Jose M., jt. auth. see Labruzza, Anthony L.

Mendez y Mercado, Leticia I. Identidad, III Coloquio Paul Kirchhoff: Analisis y Teoria, Simbolismo, Sociedades Complejas, Nacionalismo y Etnicidad. (SPA.). 290p. 1996. pap. 18.50 (*968-36-4848-7*, UN052, Pub. by Instit de Invest) UPLAAP.

Mendgen, K. & Lesemann, D. E., eds. Electron Microscopy of Plant Pathogens. (Illus.). 352p. 1990. 159.00 (*0-387-52777-X*) Spr-Verlag.

Mendhall. Statistics for Management & Economics. 5th ed. (Business Statistics Ser.). 1986. student ed. 4.50 (*0-87150-976-8*) PWS Pubs.

Mendheim, Beverly. Ritchie Valens, the First Latino Rocker. LC 87-71700. 176p. 1987. pap. 15.00 (*0-916950-79-4*) Biling Rev-Pr.

***Mendicino, L. & Simpson, L., eds.** Environmental Issues in the Electronics & Semiconductor Industries: Proceedings of the Second International Symposium. LC 99-64654. 246p. 1999. 52.00 (*1-56677-230-3*, PV 99-8) Electrochem Soc.

Mendieta, Ana, jt. auth. see Blocker, Jane.

Mendieta, Eduardo, ed. Karl-Otto Apel - Selected Essays Vol. 1: Towards a Transcendental Semiotics. LC 93-12057. 192p. (C). 1994. text 60.00 (*0-391-03807-9*) Humanities.

Mendieta, Eduardo, jt. auth. see Dussel, Enrique D.

Mendieta, Eduardo, jt. ed. see Batstone, David.

Mendieta, Eduardo, ed. & intro. see Apel, Karl-Otto.

Mendieta, Eduardo, ed. & tr. see Dussel, Enrique.

Mendieta, Eva. El Prestamo en el Espanol de los Estados Unidos. (Studies in Ethnolinguistics: Vol. 1). (SPA.). 192p. (C). 1999. text 44.95 (*0-8204-4036-1*, 40361) P Lang Pubng.

Mendieta, Fray Geronimo de, see Geronimo de Mendieta, Fray.

Mendietta, Eduardo, jt. auth. see Alcoff, Eduardo.

Mendiguren, Xabier. Por Que no Canta el Petirro. pap. text 5.95 (*84-246-5407-2*) Lectorum Pubns.

Mendillo, M., jt. auth. see Haerendel, G.

Mendillo, M., jt. ed. see Brenning, N.

M

Mendiluce, J. Maria. Pura Vida. LC 99-168490. (Autores Espanoles E Iberoamericanos Ser.). 1999. 22.95 (*84-08-02848-0*) Planeta.

Mendina, G. T. Ethics & Electronic Information in the Twenty-First Century. 1998. 34.95 (*1-55753-138-2*) Purdue U Pr.

***Mendini, Allesandro.** Alessi. 152p. 1998. pap. 44.95 (*0-471-97857-4*) Wiley.

Mendini, Allessandro & Niesewand, Nonie, eds. Alessi: The Design Factory. (Illus.). 144p. 1997. pap. 38.00 (*1-85490-356-X*) Academy Ed UK.

Mendiola, Marina P. De, see De Mendiola, Marina P., ed.

Mendiola, Marina Perez de, see Perez de Mendiola, Marina.

Mendiones, Ruchira C., jt. auth. see Jones, Robert B.

Mendiones, Ruchira C., jt. ed. see Anderson, Benedict R.

Mendis, Garrett C. The Early History of Ceylon. (Illus.). 120p. 1986. reprint ed. 14.00 (*0-8364-1743-7*, Pub. by Manohar Bk Srv) S Asia.

— The Early History of Ceylon & Its Relations with India & Other Foreign Countries. LC 70-179224. (Illus.). 103p. reprint ed. 29.50 (*0-404-54851-2*) AMS Pr.

Mendis, N. K., ed. The Questions of King Milinda: Abr't of Milindapanha. 208p. 1993. 12.00 (*955-24-0067-8*, Pub. by Buddhist Pub Soc) Vipassana Res Pubns.

Mendis, Patrick. Human Environment & Spatial Relationships in Agricultural Production: The Case Study of Sri Lanka & Other Tea Producing Countries. LC 91-43603. (American University Studies: Economics: Ser. XVI, Vol. 8). (Illus.). XXIV, 256p. (C). 1992. text 48.95 (*0-8204-1735-1*) P Lang Pubng.

***Mendita.** Global Ethics. 94th ed. 2002. pap. text. write for info. (*0-534-52065-0*) Thomson Learn.

Menditto, Joseph & Kirsch, Debbie. Genetic Engineering, DNA & Cloning: A Bibliography in the Future of Genetics. LC 82-50417. xiv, 783p. 1983. 65.00 (*0-87875-241-2*) Whitston Pub.

Mendizabal. Diccionario de Informatica/Dictionary of Computing, English-Spanish/Spanish-English. 2nd ed. (ENG & SPA.). 760p. 1993. 150.00 (*0-7859-9264-2*) Fr & Eur.

— Oxford English & Spanish Computer Dictionary: Diccionario Oxford de Informatica. 2nd ed. (ENG & SPA.). 450p. 1986. 125.00 (*0-8288-0256-4*, S8231) Fr & Eur.

Mendizabal, Juan C., jt. auth. see Erro-Orthmann, Nora.

Mendizabal, Juan Cruz, see Guerra Garrido, Raul & Cruz Mendizabal, Juan.

Mendizabal, Max. Refranero Popular Mexicano. (SPA.). 1997. pap. text 7.98 (*968-403-985-9*) Selector.

Mendl, James W., jt. auth. see Machann, Clinton.

Mendl, James W., Jr., jt. ed. see Machann, Clinton.

Mendl, Wolf. Japan's Asia Policy: Regional Security & Global Interests. 256p. (C). 1997. pap. 27.99 (*0-415-16466-4*) Routledge.

— The Study of War As a Contribution to Peace. LC 82-83955. (Orig.). (C). 1983. pap. 4.00 (*0-87574-247-5*) Pendle Hill.

Mendle, Michael. Dangerous Positions: Mixed Government, the Estates of the Realm & the Making of the Answer to the XIX Propositions. LC 83-4798. 269p. pap. 83.40 (*0-7837-8395-7*, 205920600009) Bks Demand.

— Henry Parker & the English Civil War: The Political Thought of the Public's 'Privado' (Cambridge Studies in Early Modern British History). 227p. (C). 1995. text 64.95 (*0-521-48227-5*) Cambridge U Pr.

***Mendler, Allen N.** Discipline with Dignity for Challenging Youth. 1999. pap. 24.95 (*1-879639-65-3*) Natl Educ Serv.

Mendler, Allen N. What Do I Do When...? How to Achieve Discipline with Dignity in the Classroom. LC 98-160767. 184p. (Orig.). 1992. pap. 21.95 (*1-879639-21-1*) Natl Educ Serv.

Mendler, Allen N., jt. auth. see Curwin, Richard L.

Mendler, Edward C. Massachusetts Conveyancers' Handbook. 3rd ed. LC 83-83043. 1984. 115.00 (*0-318-01918-3*) West Group.

— Massachusetts Conveyancers' Handbook. 3rd ed. LC 83-83043. 1993. suppl. ed. 54.00 (*0-317-03246-1*) West Group.

***Mendler, Sandra.** The HOK Guidebook to Sustainable Design. 256p. 2000. text 69.95 (*0-471-37906-9*) Wiley.

Mendlesohn, Esther. Teaching Primary Math with Music: Grades K-3. LC 93-716697. 1997. pap. 11.95 (*0-86651-512-7*) Seymour Pubns.

Mendleson, Eliot. Schaum's Three Thousand Solved Problems in Calculus. rev. ed. 1988. pap. 24.95 (*0-07-041523-4*) McGraw.

Mendlewicz, J. & Racagni, Giorgio, eds. Target Receptors for Anxiolytics & Hypnotics: From Molecular Pharmacology to Therapeutics. (International Academy for Biomedical & Drug Research Ser.: Vol. 3). (Illus.). vi, 162p. 1992. 152.25 (*3-8055-5602-0*) S Karger.

Mendlewicz, Julien. New Trends in Suicide Prevention. Wilmotte, J., ed. (Bibliotheca Psychiatrica Ser.: No. 162). (Illus.). vi, 106p. 1982. pap. 41.75 (*3-8055-3430-2*) S Karger.

Mendlewicz, Julien, ed. Genetics & Psychopharmacology. (Modern Problems of Pharmacopsychiatry Ser.: Vol. 10). viii, 132p. 1975. 50.50 (*3-8055-2117-0*) S Karger.

— Psychoneuroendocrinology & Abnormal Behavior. (Advances in Biological Psychiatry Ser.: Vol. 5). (Illus.). vi, 130p. 1980. pap. 50.50 (*3-8055-0599-X*) S Karger.

Mendlewicz, Julien, et al, eds. Depressive Illness. (Advances in Biological Psychiatry Ser.: Vol. 7). (Illus.). viii, 244p. 1981. pap. 64.50 (*3-8055-2482-X*) S Karger.

— New Therapeutic Indications of Antidepressants: Workshop, Bruges, March 1996. LC 97-4322. (International Academy for Biomedical & Drug Research Ser.: Vol. 12, 1997). (Illus.). vi, 138p. 1997. 139.25 (*3-8055-6436-8*) S Karger.

Mendlewicz, Julien & Hippius, H., eds. Genetic Research in Psychiatry: C.I.N.P. President's Workshop, 2nd, Munchner Genetikgesprache, September 12-15, 1991. (Illus.). 280p. 1992. 118.00 (*0-387-54827-0*) Spr-Verlag.

Mendlewicz, Julien & Van Praag, H. M., eds. Childhood Psychopharmacology: Current Concepts. (Advances in Biological Psychiatry Ser.: Vol. 2). (Illus.). 1978. pap. 34.00 (*3-8055-2901-5*) S Karger.

Mendlewicz, Julien & Van Praag, Herman M., eds. Management of Depressions with Monoamine Precursors. (Advances in Biological Psychiatry Ser.: Vol. 10). (Illus.). vi, 202p. 1983. pap. 108.75 (*3-8055-3645-3*) S Karger.

Mendlewicz, Julien, jt. auth. see Racagni, Giorgio.

Mendlewicz, Julien, jt. auth. see Van Praag, Herman M.

Mendlewicz, Julien, ed. see Alcoholism Symposium Staff.

Mendlovitz, Saul H. The Struggle for a Just World Order: An Agenda of Inquiry & Praxis for the 1980's. 23p. 1982. pap. 12.95 (*0-911646-26-4*) Transaction Pubs.

Mendlovitz, Saul H. & Weston, Burns H., eds. Preferred Futures for the United Nations. LC 95-31316. 528p. 1996. 75.00 (*1-57105-008-6*) Transnatl Pubs.

Mendlovitz, Saul H., jt. frwd. see Weiss, Peter.

Mendlowitz, Benjamin. The Book of Wooden Boats, Vol. 2. 49.95 (*0-393-04899-3*) Norton.

Mendlowitz, Benjamin. Guide to Wooden Boats; Sail. (Illus.). 160p. 1996. 19.95 (*0-393-04045-3*) Norton.

— Guide to Wooden Power Boats. LC 98-29152. (Illus.). 160p. 1998. 22.50 (*0-393-04660-5*) Norton.

— Wood, Water, & Light. 1992. 50.00 (*0-393-03327-9*) Norton.

Mendlowitz, Benjamin, photos by. The Book of Wooden Boats. LC 92-10533. (Illus.). 192p. 1992. 55.00 (*0-393-03417-8*) Norton.

— Wood, Water, & Light: A Celebration of Classic Wooden Boats. (Illus.). 1989. 100.00 (*0-393-03332-5*) Norton.

Mendlowitz, Edward. The Biggest Mistakes Taxpayers Make & How to Avoid Them. 220p. 1984. 14.95 (*0-13-077074-4*); pap. 6.95 (*0-13-077066-3*) P-H.

Mendlowitz, Edward & Weitsen, Peter A. New Business Kit & Tax Compliance Guide. rev. ed. (Illus.). 165p. 1998. pap. 29.95 (*0-9656711-0-0*) Pract Programs.

Mendocino Coast Geneal Soc. Staff. Birth, Deaths & Marriages on California's Mendocino Coast, 1930-1939, Vol. 4. 363p. 1998. pap. 42.00 (*0-7884-0937-9*, M167) Heritage Bk.

Mendocino Coast Genealogical Soc. Staff. Births, Deaths & Marriages on California's Mendocino Coast, Vol. 2, 1910-1919. LC 96-112610. vi, 317p. (Orig.). 1997. pap. 46.00 (*0-7884-0609-4*, M155) Heritage Bk.

***Mendocino Coast Genealogical Society Staff.** Births, Deaths & Marriages on California's Mendocino Coast Vol. 7: Items from the Fort Bragg Advocate-News, 1960-1969. 449p. 2000. pap. 42.50 (*0-7884-1436-4*, 1436) Heritage Bk.

Mendocino Coast Genealogical Society Staff. Births, Deaths & Marriages on California's Mendocino Coast, 1920-1929, Vol. 3. LC 96-112610. 280p. 1998. pap. 29.50 (*0-7884-0822-4*, M165) Heritage Bk.

— Births, Deaths, & Marriages on California's Mendocino Coast, 1940-1949: Items from the Fort Bragg Advocate & News. 500p. 1999. 69.00 (*0-7884-1101-2*, M168) Heritage Bk.

***Mendocino Coast Genealogical Society Staff.** Births, Deaths & Marriages on California's Mendocino Coast, 1950-1959 Vol. 6: Items from the Fort Bragg Advocate-News. 434p. 1999. pap. 61.00 (*0-7884-1289-2*, M158) Heritage Bk.

Mendocino Coast Genealogical Society Staff, ed. Births, Deaths & Marriages on California's Mendocino Coast Vol. 1: 1889-1902. 330p. (Orig.). 1995. pap. 44.00 (*0-7884-0350-8*) Heritage Bk.

Mendola. Human Thought. 1997. pap. text 93.50 (*0-7923-4402-2*) Kluwer Academic.

Mendola, Joseph. Human Thought. LC 96-53319. (Philosophical Studies). 1997. lib. bdg. 190.00 (*0-7923-4401-4*) Kluwer Academic.

Mendola, Leonard R., jt. auth. see Crowl, Thomas K.

Mendola, Rich. I Am. (Bible Studies). 1986. pap. 2.95 (*0-317-04071-5*); pap., teacher ed. 3.95 (*0-317-04072-3*) Intl Students Inc.

Mendola, Sharon. Design Workbook. 96p. (C). 1995. spiral bd. 17.95 (*0-7872-0617-2*) Kendall-Hunt.

Mendon, Laurie. Rocky Mountain National Park Trail Guide & Journal. LC 94-66661. 225p. 1994. pap. 12.95 (*0-9641329-6-6*) Pinnacle Ventures.

Mendonca, Claire, jt. auth. see Botta, Kathleen.

Mendonca, Maisa L., jt. ed. see Benjamin, Medea.

Mendonca, Manuel, jt. auth. see Kanungo, Rabindra N.

Mendonca, Manuel, jt. ed. see Kanungo, Rabindra N.

***Mendonca, Stephen.** Instant Advantage.com: Winning Strategies for the Online Economy. 272p. 2000. pap. 39.99 (*0-13-017908-6*) P-H.

Mendonqa, Augustine. Rotal Anthology: An Annotated Index of Rotal Decisions from 1971-1988. 771p. 1992. 45.00 (*0-943616-59-X*) Canon Law Soc.

Mendonsa, Arthur A. Helping Children Become Successful Adults: A Planning Manual for Communities. LC 97-50392. (Illus.). 102p. 1998. pap. 14.95 (*0-89854-191-3*) U of GA Inst Govt.

Mendonsa, Gilda. Best of Goan Cooking. (Illus.). 106p. (Orig.). 1997. pap. 8.95 (*0-7818-0584-8*) Hippocrene Bks.

***Mendonsa, Gilda.** Best of Goan Cooking. (Orig.). 1998. reprint ed. pap. 12.00 (*81-7476-028-8*, Pub. by UBS Pubs) S Asia.

Mendonsa, Ray. Linux Administrator's Guide. 800p. 2000. pap. 49.99 (*0-7615-2157-7*) Prima Pub.

Mendoza. Glosas y Decimas de Mexico. (SPA.). pap. 11.99 (*968-16-0384-2*, Pub. by Fondo) Continental Bk.

Mendoza. Trato Personal. (C). 1997. text 4.66 (*0-673-19223-7*) Addison-Wesley.

Mendoza, Al C. The Art of Western Floral Design: A Study of Design Principles & Elements. Mendoza, Michelle L., ed. (Illus.). 70p. 1997. write for info. (*0-9656165-0-9*) Am Intl Acad.

Mendoza, Andres De, see De Almansa, Andres & De Mendoza, Andres.

Mendoza, Antonio Cuesta, see Cuesta Mendoza, Antonio.

Mendoza, Antonio Hurtado De, see Hurtado de Mendoza, Antonio.

Mendoza, Carlos. Earth Refugees of the Aquarian Age. 130p. (Orig.). 1982. pap. text 4.95 (*0-686-38949-2*) C Mendoza.

— Rendezvous. LC 92-90877. 250p. (Orig.). 1992. pap. 10.00 (*0-9608420-1-2*) C Mendoza.

Mendoza, Celia, tr. see Edge, Findley B.

Mendoza, Daniel. The Memoirs of the Life of Daniel Mendoza. Magriel, Paul, ed. LC 74-29507. (Modern Jewish Experience Ser.). (Illus.). 1975. reprint ed. 20.95 (*0-405-06734-8*) Ayer.

Mendoza, David, jt. auth. see Naylor, Kim.

Mendoza, E. Feliciano. Juana de Ibarbourou: Oficio de Poesia. LC 80-20020. (Coleccion Mente y Palabra). (SPA., Illus.). xi, 370p. 1981. 8.00 (*0-8477-0572-2*); pap. 7.20 (*0-8477-0573-0*) U of PR Pr.

Mendoza, Eduardo. The City of Marvels. Molloy, Bernard, tr. 432p. 1988. 19.95 (*0-15-118040-7*) Harcourt.

— La Verdad Sobre el Caso Savolta. 17th ed. (SPA.). 432p. 1992. pap. 17.95 (*0-7859-0578-2*, S29407) Fr & Eur.

— The Year of the Flood. 118p. 1997. pap. text 10.00 (*1-86046-045-3*) Harvill Press.

***Mendoza, Everett.** Radical & Evangelical: Portrait of a Filipino Christian. LC 00-39616. 2000. pap. write for info. (*0-9679101-2-9*) Intl Academic Pubs.

Mendoza-Fernandez, J. J. Quick-to-Solve Brainteasers. LC 98-34888.Tr. of Quick to Solve Brain Teasers. (SPA., Illus.). 96p. 1998. 6.95 (*0-8069-6151-1*) Sterling.

Mendoza, George. Fishing the Morning Lonely. (Illus.). 1974. 7.95 (*0-88395-029-4*) Freshet Pr.

— Hunter I Might Have Been. (Illus.). (J). (gr. 3-5). 1968. 10.95 (*0-8392-3064-8*) Astor-Honor.

— Norman Rockwell Illustrated Cookbook. 1989. 17.95 (*0-685-33408-2*) Random Hse Value.

— Norman Rockwell's Scrapbook for a Young Boy. deluxe ed. (Illus.). (J). 1979. 17.95 (*0-89659-026-7*) Abbeville Pr.

— Piece of String. (Illus.). 1965. 10.95 (*0-8392-1160-0*) Astor-Honor.

Mendoza, Guillermo R., jt. auth. see Sander, Nancy J.

Mendoza, Guillermo R., ed. see Sander, Nancy.

Mendoza, Jonathan. Blood Strategies & Secrets. Date not set. pap. 19.99 incl. cd-rom (*0-7821-1793-7*) Sybex.

— Quake II: The Reckoning: Official Strategies & Secrets. 1998. pap. 14.99 (*0-7821-2300-7*) Sybex.

— Sybex Unofficial Unreal Strategy. 240p. 1998. 19.99 (*0-7821-2127-6*) Sybex.

Mendoza, Jose, jt. auth. see Cembranos, Pilar.

Mendoza, Kenneth. Talking Books: Ethnopoetics, Translation, Text. LC 93-23760. (ENGL Ser.). xii, 102p. 1993. 39.95 (*1-879751-78-X*) Camden Hse.

Mendoza, Kenneth, ed. see Timm, Eitel.

***Mendoza, Lisa.** Hi, It's Me, Your Dog! (Illus.). 176p. 2000. pap. 14.95 (*1-884956-16-5*) Quill Driver.

Mendoza, Lydia. Lydia Mendoza: A Family Autobiography. LC 92-45111. 400p. 1993. pap. 17.95 (*1-55885-066-X*); text 32.95 (*1-55885-065-1*) Arte Publico.

Mendoza, Manuel G., jt. auth. see Napoli, Vincent.

Mendoza, Marcela, tr. see Roberts, Phil.

***Mendoza, Maria Luisa.** Fuimos es Mucha Gente. 2000. pap. 15.95 (*968-19-0512-1*) Aguilar.

Mendoza, Meyra S. & Rosegrant, Mark W. Pricing Behavior in Philippine Corn Markets: Implications for Market Efficiency. LC 95-8312. (International Food Policy Research Institute Research Report Ser.: Vol. 101). 1995. write for info. (*0-89629-104-9*) Intl Food Policy.

Mendoza, Michelle L., ed. see Mendoza, Al C.

Mendoza, Miguel Rodrigez. Trade Rules in the Making: Challenges in Regional & Multilateral Negotiations. LC 99-6279. 546p. 1999. pap. text 22.95 (*0-8157-5679-8*) Brookings.

Mendoza, Miguel Rodrigez & Kip, Michael. Hemispheres. LC 99-18942. 64p. 1999. pap. text 14.95 (*0-7734-3109-8*) E Mellen.

Mendoza, Parick M., et al. Four Great Rivers to Cross: Cheyenne History, Culture & Traditions. LC 97-30742. (Illus.). 131p. 1998. lib. bdg. 20.00 (*1-56308-471-6*) Teacher Ideas Pr.

Mendoza, Patrick. Song of Sorrow: Massacre at Sand Creek. LC 93-93930. 43p. 1993. teacher ed. 2.75 (*0-9636362-1-9*); pap. 10.95 (*0-9636362-0-0*) Willow Wind.

Mendoza, Patrick M. Extraordinary People in Extraordinary Times. LC 99-14238. (Illus.). x, 142p. 1999. pap., teacher ed. 18.00 (*1-56308-611-5*) Libs Unl.

Mendoza, Plinio A., et al. Guide to the Perfect Latin American Idiot. Ames, Michaela, tr. LC 99-55248. 256p. 2000. 24.95 (*1-56833-134-7*, Pub. by Madison Bks UPA) Natl Bk Netwk.

***Mendoza, Plinio Apuleyo.** Aquellos Tiempos Con Gabo. (SPA.). 2000. pap. 14.95 (*0-553-06112-7*) Bantam.

Mendoza, Plinio Apuleyo. Los Fabricantes de Miseria.Tr. of Manufactures of Poverty. 317p. 1998. pap. 14.95 (*0-553-06094-5*) Bantam.

Mendoza, Plinio Apuleyo. Manual Del Perfecto Idiota Latinamericano. (SPA.). 336p. 1997. mass mkt. 9.99 (*0-553-06060-0*) Bantam.

Mendoza, Rachel. Recomendaciones para la Poda del Arboles. (SPA.). 15p. 1996. pap. text 7.00 (*1-881956-17-2*) Int Soc Arboricult.

Mendoza, Ramon G. The Acentric Labyrinth. 1995. pap. 26.95 (*1-85230-640-8*, Pub. by Element MA) Penguin Putnam.

— Outside Humanity: A Study of Kafka's Fiction. 310p. (Orig.). (C). 1986. pap. text 26.00 (*0-8191-5516-0*) U Pr of Amer.

Mendoza, Richard H., jt. ed. see Martinez, Joe L., Jr.

Mendoza, Ruben. Loteria: And Other Stories. LC 97-40636. 128p. 1998. pap. 12.95 (*0-312-18129-9*) St Martin.

Mendoza, Ruben, contrib. by. Donde Tu Eres Mi Sol. unabridged ed.Tr. of Where Are You My Sun. (SPA.). 166p. 1995. pap. 14.95 (*0-9659827-9-3*) J L Seco.

Mendoza, Sally P., jt. ed. see Barchas, Patricia R.

Mendoza, Sally P., jt. ed. see Mason, William A.

***Mendoza, Sylvia.** Salsa Serenade/Serenata. 2000. mass mkt. 5.99 (*0-7860-1096-7*, Encanto) Kensgtn Pub Corp.

Mendoza, Tony. Cuba: Going Back. LC 98-51938. 155p. 1999. pap. 22.95 (*0-292-75233-4*) U of Tex Pr.

***Mendoza, Tony.** Cuba: Going Back. LC 98-51938. 156p. 1999. 50.00 (*0-292-75232-6*) U of Tex Pr.

— Ernie: A Photographer's Memoir. LC 00-24089. (Illus.). (Orig.). 2001. write for info. (*0-8118-2963-4*) Chronicle Bks.

Mendoza, Vicente. El Corrido Mexicano (The Mexican Folk Song) (SPA.). 468p. 1954. pap. 11.99 (*968-16-0982-4*, Pub. by Fondo) Continental Bk.

Mendoza, Vicente T. Canciones Mexicanas.Tr. of Mexican Folksongs. 126p. 1948. 3.00 (*0-318-14245-7*) Hispanic Inst.

Mendoza, Vincent L. Son of Two Bloods. LC 95-50326. (North American Indian Prose Award Ser.). (Illus.). 200p. 1999. pap. 12.00 (*0-8032-8257-5*, Bison Books) U of Nebr Pr.

***Mendoza, Zoila S.** Shaping Society Through Dance. 2000. lib. bdg. 50.00 (*0-226-52010-2*) U Ch Pr.

— Shaping Society Through Dance: Mestizo Ritual Performance in the Peruvian Andes LC 99-40310. (Studies in Ethnomusicology). (Illus.). 264p. 1999. pap. text 29.00 (*0-226-52009-9*) U Ch Pr.

Mendras, H. & Mihailescu, I. Theories & Methods in Rural Community Studies. LC 82-16508. (Vienna Centre Ser.: No. 9). 304p. 1982. 139.00 (*0-08-025813-1*, Pub. by Pergamon Repr) Franklin.

Mendras, Henri. Social Change in Modern France: Towards a Cultural Anthropology of the Fifth Republic. 256p. (C). 1991. 49.95 (*0-521-39108-3*); pap. text 18.95 (*0-521-39998-X*) Cambridge U Pr.

Mendrick, Michael. New York State Trivia. LC 97-34333. 192p. 1997. pap. 6.95 (*1-55853-534-9*) Rutledge Hill Pr.

Mendrinos, Roxanne B. Using Educational Technology with At-Risk Students: A Guide for Library Media Specialists & Teachers. LC 96-51139. (Greenwood Professional Guides in School Librarianship). (Illus.). 240p. 1997. 39.95 (*0-313-29369-4*, Greenwood Pr) Greenwood.

Mendrinou, Maria M., jt. auth. see Lavdas, Kostas A.

Menduina, Claudio Sanchez-Albornoz Y, see Sanchez-Albornoz y Menduina, Claudio.

Mendum, J. P. & Bennett, D. M., prods. Revelations of Antichrist: Christ & Christianity. 432p. pap. 8.00 (*0-944379-33-8*) CPA Bk Pub.

Mendus, Susan. The Politics of Toleration: Tolerance & Intolerance in Modern Life. LC 99-32392. 170p. 2000. 16.95 (*0-8223-2498-9*) Duke.

Mendus, Susan & Edwards, David, eds. On Toleration. 152p. 1988. text 49.95 (*0-19-827529-3*) OUP.

Mendus, Susan & Rendall, Jane. Sexuality & Subordination: Interdisciplinary Studies of Gender in the Nineteenth Century. 256p. 1989. 49.50 (*0-415-01368-2*) Routledge.

Mendus, Susan, jt. ed. see Bell, J. M.

Mendus, Susan, jt. ed. see Horton, John.

Mendy, Peter K., jt. auth. see Lobban, Richard A., Jr.

Mendyk, Dennis, ed. Living in the Reader's World, 4 bks., Bk. 1. (Adult Reading Ser.: Levels 2-6). (Illus.). 160p. 1988. pap. text 6.30 (*0-8428-9514-0*) Cambridge Bk.

— Living in the Reader's World, 4 bks., Bk. 2. (Adult Reading Ser.: Levels 2-6). (Illus.). 160p. 1988. pap. text 6.00 (*0-8428-9515-9*) Cambridge Bk.

— Living in the Reader's World, 4 bks., Bk. 4. (Adult Reading Ser.: Levels 2-6). (Illus.). 160p. 1988. pap. text 6.00 (*0-8428-9517-5*) Cambridge Bk.

Mendyk, Dennis, ed. see Cyzyk, Janet L.

Mendyk, Stanley A. Speculum Britanniae: Regional Study, Antiquarianism, & Science in Britain to 1700. (Illus.). 432p. 1989. text 45.00 (*0-8020-5744-6*) U of Toronto Pr.

Menear, Pauline & Hawkins, Terry. Stage Management & Theater Administration. rev. ed. (Theater Manuals Ser.). (Illus.). 128p. 1995. reprint ed. pap. 14.95 (*0-7148-2516-6*, Pub. by Phaidon Press) Phaidon Pr.

Menebroker, Ann, et al, eds. Landing Signals: An Anthology of Sacramento Poets. (Illus.). 256p. (Orig.). 1986. pap. 10.00 (*0-914485-09-1*); audio 10.00 (*0-914485-11-3*) Trill Pr.

Menedez, Josefa, et al. Words of Love. LC 84-51596. 95p. (Orig.). 1994. reprint ed. pap. 6.00 (*0-89555-244-2*) TAN Bks Pubs.

Meneely, A. Howard. War Department, 1861. LC 72-127434. (Columbia University. Studies in the Social Sciences: No. 300). 1970. reprint ed. 27.50 (*0-404-51300-X*) AMS Pr.

Meneely, Janie. Santa & the Skipjack. (Illus.). 32p. (J). (gr. k-6). 1991. write for info. (*0-9618461-1-9*) BaySailor Bks.

Meneely, Jerome A. Proverbs to Live By: Wisdom from Ages Past. 128p. 1998. pap. 6.98 (*0-88290-639-9*, 1094) Horizon Utah.

— Words to Live By: 110 Modern Mottos. 128p. 1998. 6.98 (*0-88290-630-5*, 1093) Horizon Utah.

Menefee, Angelo K. With the Help of Love I Can Do Anything. (Illus.). (J). (gr. 1-4). 1996. 7.95 (*0-533-11694-5*) Vantage.

An Asterisk (*) at the beginning of an entry indicates that the title is appearing for the first time.

Menefee, Campbell A. Historical & Descriptive Sketchbook of Napa, Sonoma, Lake, & Mendocino. 268p. 1994. 29.95 (*1-885852-00-2*) J D Stevenson.

Menefee, Christine, jt. ed. see Mountaingrove, Jean.

***Menefee-Libey, David.** The Triumph of Campaign-Centered Politics. LC 99-6066. (Illus.). 256p. (C). 1999. pap. text 24.95 (*1-889119-19-9*, Chatham House Pub) Seven Bridges.

Menefee, Sarah. The Blood about the Heart. LC 91-58997. 75p. (Orig.). 1993. pap. 10.95 (*0-915306-53-0*) Curbstone.

Menefee, Sarah. I'm Not Thousandfurs. LC 85-48297. 62p. (Orig.). 1986. pap. 8.00 (*0-915306-59-X*) Curbstone.

Menefee, Selden C. Vocational Training & Employment of Youth. LC 70-166953. (Research Monographs: Vol. 25). 1971. reprint ed. lib. bdg. 22.50 (*0-306-70357-2*) Da Capo.

Meneghini, Giuseppe. Algae Italianae e Dalmatiche illustrata. (Illus.). 1970. 55.00 (*90-6123-094-2*) Lubrecht & Cramer.

Meneghini, Robert & Kozu, Toshiaka. Spaceborne Weather Radar. (Radar Library). 208p. 1990. text 10.00 (*0-89006-382-6*) Artech Hse.

Meneguzzi, Maurice, et al, eds. Small-Scale Structures in Three-Dimensional Hydrodynamic & Magnetohydrodynamic Turbulence: Proceedings of a Workshop, Held at Nice, France 10-13 January 1995. LC 95-44629. (Lecture Notes in Physics Ser.: Vol. 462). (Illus.). 420p. 1995. 101.95 (*3-540-60486-3*) Spr-Verlag.

Meneguzzo, Marco & Vettese, Angela. Meisterschule. (Illus.). 48p. 1998. pap. 16.95 (*88-8158-169-8*, Pub. by Charta) Dist Art Pubs.

Meneilly, Robert. Pray As You Go: On Living Your Faith in the Nineties. 160p. 1996. 19.95 (*0-8362-2170-2*) Andrews & McMeel.

Menelaus, Malcolm B. The Orthopaedic Management of Spina Bifida Cystica. 2nd ed. LC 79-40044. (Current Problems in Orthopaedics Ser.). 227p. reprint ed. pap. 70.40 (*0-8357-3375-0*, 203962100013) Bks Demand.

Menelaus, Malcolm B., ed. The Management of Limb Inequality. (Current Problems in Orthopaedics Ser.). (Illus.). 236p. 1991. text 145.00 (*0-443-04298-5*) Church.

Meneley, Anne. Tournaments of Value: Sociability & Hierarchy in a Yemeni Town. (Anthropological Horizons Ser.). (Illus.). 248p. 1996. text 45.00 (*0-8020-0883-6*); pap. text 18.95 (*0-8020-7868-0*) U of Toronto Pr.

Menell. Environmental Law. LC 94-75303. 1280p. 1994. 60.00 (*0-316-55157-0*, Aspen Law & Bus) Aspen Pub.

Menell, A. & Bazin, Michael J. Mathematics for the Biological Sciences. 200p. 1988. text 41.95 (*0-470-21167-9*) P-H.

Menell, Jeff. Howard Stern: Big Mouth. 192p. 1993. mass mkt. 4.99 (*1-55817-796-5*, Pinncle Kensgtn) Kensgtn Pub Corp.

Menell, Peter S., jt. auth. see Dwyer, John P.

Menell, Zoe, ed. see Musgrave, Beatrice.

Menell, Zoe, jt. ed. see Musgrave, Beatrice.

Menen, Audrey. The Ramayana: As Told by Audrey Menen. LC 72-598. 276p. 1972. reprint ed. lib. bdg. 49.50 (*0-8371-6181-9*, VARA, Greenwood Pr) Greenwood.

Menendaz, Marilu, ed. Cuba: The Elusive Island. (Illus.). 143p. 1998. text 27.00 (*0-7881-5596-2*) DIANE Pub.

Menendez, Al & Menendez, Shirley. Maryland Trivia. LC 92-6746. 192p. (Orig.). 1992. pap. 6.95 (*1-55853-164-5*) Rutledge Hill Pr.

Menendez, Al & Menendez, Shirley, compiled by. New Jersey Trivia. LC 93-12564. 192p. (Orig.). 1993. pap. 6.95 (*1-55853-223-4*) Rutledge Hill Pr.

Menendez, Al, jt. auth. see Doerr, Edd.

Menendez, Albert J. Christmas in the White House. LC 83-3629. (Illus.). 128p. 1983. 16.95 (*0-664-21392-8*) Westminster John Knox.

— Church & State in Canada. LC 96-3037. 140p. 1996. 24.95 (*1-57392-079-7*) Prometheus Bks.

— The December Dilemma: Christmas in American Public Life. 104p. (Orig.). 1988. pap. 6.95 (*0-9617164-1-X*) AURF.

— December Wars: Religious Symbols & Ceremonies in the Public Square. LC 93-5591. 170p. 1993. 23.95 (*0-87975-857-0*) Prometheus Bks.

— Evangelicals at the Ballot Box. LC 96-22931. (Illus.). 340p. 1996. 25.95 (*1-57392-093-2*) Prometheus Bks.

— The Perot Voters & the Future of American Politics. LC 96-3754. (Illus.). 277p. 1996. 25.95 (*1-57392-044-4*) Prometheus Bks.

— Visions of Reality: What Fundamentalist Schools Teach. LC 92-33260. 158p. (Orig.). (C). 1993. pap. 16.95 (*0-87975-802-3*) Prometheus Bks.

***Menendez, Albert J. & Menendez, Shirley C.** Christmas Songs Made in America. LC 99-46610. (Illus.). 160p. 1999. 12.95 (*1-58182-046-1*, Cumberland Hearthside) Cumberland Hse.

Menendez, Albert J., jt. auth. see Doerr, Edd.

Menendez, Anthony L., jt. auth. see Bullock, Lyndal M.

Menendez, Antonio V. Power & Television in Latin America: The Dominican Case. LC 92-383. 208p. 1992. 55.00 (*0-275-94275-9*, C4275, Praeger Pubs) Greenwood.

***Menendez-Aponte, Emily.** When Mom & Dad Divorce: A Kid's Resource. LC 99-76078. (Illus.). 32p. (J). (ps-6). 1999. pap. 5.95 (*0-87029-333-8*) Abbey.

Menendez, Aurelio. Access to Basic Infrastructure by the Urban Poor. (Economic Development Institute Policy Seminar Report Ser.: No. 28). 96p. 1991. pap. 22.00 (*0-8213-1815-2*, 11815) World Bank.

— Estimating Capital & Operating Costs in Urban Transportation Planning. LC 92-9806. 200p. 1993. 52.95 (*0-275-94219-8*, C4219, Praeger Pubs) Greenwood.

Menendez-Botet, Celia J. & St Germain, Jean M., eds. Hazardous Waste: Facts & Fallacies. 64p. 1990. 20.00 (*0-915274-55-8*) Am Assn Clinical Chem.

Menendez, Elvira. Pablo y su Elefante. 2nd ed. (Punto Infantil Ser.).Tr. of Paul & his Elephant. (SPA.). 1991. 10.60 (*0-606-05529-0*) Turtleback.

Menendez, Emilio. Lecciones de Derecho de Familia. LC 76-961. (SPA.). 393p. (Orig.). (C). 1981. 9.60 (*0-8477-3018-2*); pap. 7.50 (*0-8477-3007-7*) U of PR Pr.

— Lecciones de Teoria General del Derecho. LC 79-16559. (SPA.). 262p. 1980. pap. text 7.20 (*0-8477-3017-4*) U of PR Pr.

Menendez, Enrique C. Only the Wind. Armas, Jose, ed. Hernandez, Frances, tr. from SPA. (Illus.). 182p. 1980. 9.00 (*0-918358-05-1*); pap. 7.00 (*0-686-64685-1*) Pajarito Pubns.

Menendez, J. Alberb, ed. The Catholic Novel: An Annotated Bibliography. LC 88-1718. 344p. 1988. text 20.00 (*0-8240-8534-5*) Garland.

Menendez, Josefa. A Call to Souls. 25p. 1998. pap. 1.00 (*0-89555-614-6*, 1537) TAN Bks Pubs.

— Christ's Appeal for Love. Keppel, L., tr. from SPA. 1993. reprint ed. pap. 7.00 (*0-89555-013-X*) TAN Bks Pubs.

— I Wait for You: Jesus' Lament Over Man's Indifference (Excerpts from the Way of Divine Love) 32p. (Orig.). 1994. pap. 0.75 (*0-89555-285-X*) TAN Bks Pubs.

— The Way of Divine Love. LC 79-112493. 504p. 1993. reprint ed. pap. 18.50 (*0-89555-030-X*); reprint ed. pap. 8.50 (*0-89555-276-0*) TAN Bks Pubs.

Menendez, Ken. Taming the Lawyers. LC 96-75087. 305p. 1996. pap. 19.95 (*1-56343-133-5*) Silver Lake.

***Menendez, Kenneth.** Taming the Lawyers: What to Expect in a Lawsuit & How to Make Sure Your Attorney Gets Results. 2nd ed. 310p. 2000. pap. 17.95 (*1-56343-175-0*, Pub. by Silver Lake) Natl Bk Netwk.

Menendez Pidal, Ramon. Antologia de Prosistas Espanoles, No. 110. (SPA.). 261p. 1978. 10.95 (*0-8288-8556-7*, S2322) Fr & Eur.

— La Crisis del Siglo XVII. Vargas, V. F. et al, eds. (Historia de Espana Ser.: Vol. 24). (SPA.). 796p. 1992. 195.00 (*0-7859-0561-8*, 842394994X) Fr & Eur.

— La Espana de los Reyes Catolicos: La Edificacion del Estado y la Politica Exterior. Fernandez, L. S. & Alvarez, M. F., eds. (Historia de Espana Ser.: Vol. 19). (SPA.). 810p. 1992. 195.00 (*0-7859-0559-6*, 842394820X) Fr & Eur.

— Espana Primitiva: Prerromana. Almagro, M. et al, eds. (Historia de Espana Ser.: Vol. 3). (SPA.). 1992. 195.00 (*0-7859-0557-X*, 842394803X) Fr & Eur.

— Los Espanoles en la Historia. (Nueva Austral Ser.: Vol. 182). (SPA.). 1991. pap. text 24.95 (*84-239-1982-X*) Elliots Bks.

— Estudios Literarios, No. 28. (SPA.). 212p. 1968. write for info. (*0-318-69890-0*) Fr & Eur.

— Flor Nueva de Romances Viejos. (Nueva Austral Ser.: Vol. 202). (SPA.). 1991. pap. text 12.95 (*84-239-7202-X*) Elliots Bks.

— Historia de Espana, 37 vols. (SPA.). 1992. write for info. (*0-7859-0510-3*, 8423948005) Fr & Eur.

— Historia de Espana Vol. 1: Espana Primitiva: La Prehistoria. Pacheco, F. H. et al, eds. (SPA.). 1000p. 1992. 195.00 (*0-7859-0511-1*, 8423948013) Fr & Eur.

— Historia de Espana Vol. 2: Espana Primitiva: La Protohistoria. Almagro, M. & Bellido, A. G., eds. (SPA.). 720p. 1992. 195.00 (*0-7859-0512-X*, 8423948021) Fr & Eur.

— Historia de Espana Vol. 4: Espana Romana: La Conquista y la Explotacion Economia. rev. ed. Duque, Angel M. & Martinez, J. M., eds. (SPA.). 762p. 1992. 195.00 (*0-7859-0533-2*, 8423949834) Fr & Eur.

— Historia de Espana Vol. 5: Espana Romana: La Sociedad, el Derecho y la Cultura. rev. ed. Manjarres, J. M. et al, eds. (SPA.). 764p. 1992. 195.00 (*0-7859-0534-0*, 8423949842) Fr & Eur.

Historia de Espana Vol. 6: Espana Visigoda: Las Invasiones, las Sociedades, la Iglesia. Diaz, M. C. et al, eds. (SPA.). 596p. 1992. 195.00 (*0-7859-0540-5*, 8423949958) Fr & Eur.

— Historia de Espana Vol. 8: Espana Musulmana (711-1031): La Conquista, el Emirato, el Califato. Levi-Provencal, E., ed. (SPA.). 568p. 1992. 195.00 (*0-7859-0513-8*, 8423948064) Fr & Eur.

— Historia de Espana Vol. 9: Espana Musulmana (711-1031): Instituciones y Vida Social y Intelectual. Levi-Provencal, E., ed. (SPA.). 862p. 1992. 195.00 (*0-7859-0514-6*, 8423948072) Fr & Eur.

— Historia de Espana Vol. 11: La Espana Cristiana de los Siglos VII al XI: Vol. 1 (722-1037) Sanchez-Albornoz, Claudio, ed. (SPA.). 886p. 1992. 195.00 (*0-7859-0531-6*, 8423949818) Fr & Eur.

— Historia de Espana Vol. 14: Expansion Peninsular y Mediterranea (1212-1350): La Corona de Castilla. Fontes, J. T. et al, eds. (SPA.). 660p. 1992. 195.00 (*0-7859-0517-0*, 8423948153) Fr & Eur.

— Historia de Espana Vol. 15: Expansion Peninsular y Mediterranea (1212-1350): El Reino de Navarra, la Corona de Aragon, Portugal. Lacarra, J. M. et al, eds. (SPA.). 660p. 1992. 195.00 (*0-7859-0520-0*, 8423948242) Fr & Eur.

— Historia de Espana Vol. 16: La Crisis de la Reconquista (1350-1410) Fernandez, L. S. & Campistol, J. R., eds. (SPA.). 862p. 1992. 195.00 (*0-7859-0518-9*, 8423948161) Fr & Eur.

— Historia de Espana Vol. 18: La Espana de los Reyes Catolicos: La Bases del Reinado, la Guerra de Sucesion, la Guerra de Granada. Fernandez, L. S. & Carriazo, J., eds. (SPA.). 1046p. 1992. 195.00 (*0-7859-0519-7*, 8423948196) Fr & Eur.

— Historia de Espana Vol. 20: El Siglo XVI. Alvarez, M. F., ed. (SPA.). 778p. 1992. 195.00 (*0-7859-0521-9*, 8423948277) Fr & Eur.

— Historia de Espana Vol. 21: La Espana de Carlos V: El Hombre, la Politica Espanola y la Politica Europea. Alvarez, M. F., ed. (SPA.). 1072p. 1992. 195.00 (*0-7859-0522-7*, 8423948285) Fr & Eur.

— Historia de Espana Vol. 22: Felipe II: El Hombre y la Politica, Vol I 1556-1568. Fernandez, L. S. & Fernandez de Retana, eds. (SPA.). 868p. 1992. 195.00 (*0-7859-0523-5*, 8423948307) Fr & Eur.

— Historia de Espana Vol. 23: Felipe II: El Hombre y la Politica, Vol. II 1569-1598. Fernandez, L. S. & Fernandez de Retana, eds. (SPA.). 920p. 1992. 195.00 (*0-7859-0524-3*, 8423948315) Fr & Eur.

— Historia de Espana Vol. 25: La Espana de Felipe III. Bustamente, C. P., ed. (SPA.). 660p. 1992. 195.00 (*0-7859-0525-1*, 8423948323) Fr & Eur.

— Historia de Espana Vol. 26: La Espana de Felipe IV. Tomas y Valiente, F. et al, eds. (SPA.). 880p. 1992. 195.00 (*0-7859-0526-X*, 8423948331) Fr & Eur.

— Historia de Espana Vol. 27: El Siglo del Quijote (1580-1680): Vol. I, Religion, Filosofia, Ciencia. Martin, M. A. et al, eds. (SPA.). 913p. 1992. 195.00 (*0-7859-0536-7*, 8423949907) Fr & Eur.

— Historia de Espana Vol. 28: El Siglo de Quijote (1580-1680): Vol. II, las Letras, las Artes. (SPA.). 879p. 1992. 195.00 (*0-7859-0537-5*, 8423949915) Fr & Eur.

— Historia de Espana Vol. 29: La Epoca de los Primeros Borbones: La Nueva Monarquia (1700-1759) Sanchez, F. C. et al, eds. (SPA.). 778p. 1992. 195.00 (*0-7859-0527-8*, 8423948374) Fr & Eur.

— Historia de Espana Vol. 31: La Epoca de la Ilustracion: El Estado y la Cultura (1759-1808) Recio, L. M. et al, eds. (SPA.). 1088p. 1992. 195.00 (*0-7859-0529-4*, 8423948390) Fr & Eur.

— Historia de Espana Vol. 32: La Epoca de la Ilustracion: Las Indias y la Politica Exterior. Rikles, C. D. et al, eds. (SPA.). 904p. 1992. 195.00 (*0-7859-0530-8*, 8423949796) Fr & Eur.

— Historia de Espana Vol. 34: La Era Isabelina y el Sexenio Democratico (1834-1874) Villarroya, Joaquin T. et al, eds. (SPA.). 1208p. 1992. 195.00 (*0-7859-0532-4*, 8423949826) Fr & Eur.

— Historia de Espana Vol. 35: La Epoca del Romanticismo (1808-1874): Origenes, Religion, Filosofia, Ciencia. Juretschke, H. et al, eds. (SPA.). 786p. 1992. 195.00 (*0-7859-0538-3*, 8423949923) Fr & Eur.

— Historia de Espana Vol. 37: La Comienzos del Siglo XX: La Problacion, la Economia, la Sociedad (1898-1931) Delgado, J. L. et al, eds. (SPA.). 782p. 1992. 195.00 (*0-7859-0535-9*, 8423949850) Fr & Eur.

— La Lengua Castellana en el Siglo XVII. (Nueva Austral Ser.: Vol. 208). (SPA.). 1991. pap. text 24.95 (*84-239-7208-9*) Elliots Bks.

— Poesia Juglaresca & Juglares. Origenes de las Literaturas Romanicas. (Nueva Austral Ser.: No. 159). (SPA.). 1991. pap. text 39.95 (*84-239-1959-5*) Elliots Bks.

— Los Trastamaras de Castilla y Aragon en el Siglo XV. Fernandez, L. S. et al, eds. (Historia de Espana Ser.: Vol. 17). (SPA.). 1026p. 1992. 195.00 (*0-7859-0558-8*, 842394817X) Fr & Eur.

— Visigoda: La Monarquia, la Cultura, las Artes. Prendes, J. M., ed. (Historia de Espana Ser.: Vol. 7). (SPA.). 510p. 1992. 195.00 (*0-7859-0545-6*, 9423949966) Fr & Eur.

Menendez Pidal, Ramon & Riquer, Martin D., intros. Cantar de Mio Cid: Texto Antiguo De Ramon Menendez Pidal Version Moderna De Alfonso Reyes. (Nueva Austral Ser.: No. 20). (SPA.). 1991. pap. text 24.95 (*84-239-1820-3*) Elliots Bks.

Menendez Pidal, Ramon & Stiffoni, Giovanni. Historia de Espana Vol. 30: La Epoca de los Primeros Borbones: La Cultura Espanola entre el Barroco y la Illustracion (1680-1759) (SPA.). 557p. 1992. 195.00 (*0-7859-0528-6*, 8423948382) Fr & Eur.

Menendez Pidal, Ramon, et al. Historia de Espana Vol. 2, No. 26: El Siglo del Quijote (1580-1680): Las Letras, las Artes. 879p. 1992. 189.50 (*84-239-4991-5*) Elliots Bks.

Menendez, Ramon & Musca, Tom. Stand & Deliver. 112p. 1997. pap. 5.50 (*0-87129-740-X*, SB3) Dramatic Pub.

Menendez, Ricardo. La Seguridad Siempre Llama dos Veces . . . Y los Orichas Tambien. LC 96-86651. (Coleccion Caniqui). (SPA.). 320p. 1997. pap. 18.00 (*0-89729-817-9*) Ediciones.

Menendez, Shirley, jt. auth. see Menendez, Al.

Menendez, Shirley, jt. compiled by see Menendez, Al.

Menendez, Shirley C., jt. auth. see Menendez, Albert J.

Meneray, Wilbur E. & Favrot, Anne, eds. The Favrot Family Papers Vol. Iv: A Documentary Chronicle of Early Louisiana. Hampshire, Carole & Smith, Snn, trs. from FRE. write for info. (*0-87409-005-9*) Tulane Univ.

Menes, Orlando R. Borderlands with Angels. 32p. (Orig.). (C). 1994. pap. 5.00 (*0-9637849-5-1*) Bacchae Pr.

Meneses, Carole. The Personal Recorder: How to Be Positively Absolutely Organized. 3rd rev. ed. (Illus.). 168p. (YA). 1996. ring bd. 30.00 (*0-9653644-4-5*) Potto Publng.

Meneses, Eloise H., jt. auth. see Hiebert, Paul G.

Meneses, Mary De, see Pinnell, Norma N. & De Meneses, Mary.

Menestrier, Claude-Francois. Traite des tournois, joustes, carrousels et autres spectacles publics. LC 76-43926. (Music & Theatre in France in the 17th & 18th Centuries Ser.). reprint ed. 84.50 (*0-404-60174-X*) AMS Pr.

Menet, J. M., jt. auth. see Thiebaut, D.

Menetra, Louis. Journal of My Life. Roche, Daniel, ed. Goldhammer, Arthur, tr. from FRE. 400p. 1986. text 57.50 (*0-231-06128-5*) Col U Pr.

— Journal of My Life: The Autobiography of Jacques-Louis Menetra. Goldhammer, Arthur, tr. from FRE. 400p. 1989. pap. text 21.00 (*0-231-06129-3*) Col U Pr.

Menetrier, Pierre, jt. auth. see Wenk, Jay.

Meney, Kathy A. & Pate, John S., eds. Australian Rushes: Biological Identifications & Conservation of Restionacae & Allied Families. (Illus.). 496p. 1999. 95.00 (*1-876268-01-8*, Pub. by Univ of West Aust Pr) Intl Spec Bk.

Menez, Ernani G., jt. auth. see Phillips, Ronald C.

Menez, Herminia. Explorations in Philippine Folklore. LC 96-946518. 174p. 1997. pap. text 17.00 (*971-550-211-3*, Pub. by Ateneo de Manila Univ Pr) UH Pr.

Menez, Herminia Q. Folklore Communication Among Filipinos in California. Dorson, Richard M., ed. LC 80-733, (Folklore of the World Ser.). 1981. lib. bdg. 26.95 (*0-405-13320-0*) Ayer.

Menezes, Alfred J. Elliptic Curve Public Key Cryptosystems. LC 93-10961. (International Series in Engineering & Computer Science, VLSI, Computer Architecture, & Digital Screen Processing: Vol. 234). 144p. (C). 1993. text 120.00 (*0-7923-9368-6*) Kluwer Academic.

Menezes, Alfred J., jt. auth. see Vanstone, Scott A.

Menezes, Alfred J., ed. see Gao, XuHong & Mullin, Ronald C.

***Menezes, Allan.** The Complete Guide to the Pilates Method. (Illus.). 224p. 2000. pap. 19.95 (*0-89793-285-4*, Pub. by Hunter Hse) Publishers Group.

Menezes, Arnold H. & Sonntag, Volker K., eds. Principles of Spinal Surgery, 2 vols. LC 95-30569. 1520p. 1995. text 295.00 (*0-07-912043-1*) McGraw-Hill HPD.

Menezes, Mary N., ed. Amerindians in Guyana, 1803-1873: A Documentary History. 314p. 1979. 55.00 (*0-7146-3054-3*, Pub. by F Cass Pubs) Intl Spec Bk.

Meng. Business Opportunities in India. (C). 1997. 17.95 (*0-13-732975-X*, Macmillan Coll) P-H.

— Business Opportunities in Sichuan Province, China. (C). 1997. 17.95 (*0-13-732967-9*, Macmillan Coll) P-H.

— Business Opportunities in the Yangtze River Delta, China. (C). 1997. 17.95 (*0-13-732983-0*, Macmillan Coll) P-H.

Meng, An-Kuo, jt. auth. see Suffet, I. H.

Meng, Brita, jt. auth. see Somogyi, Stephan.

Meng, C. I., et al, eds. Auroral Physics. (Illus.). 484p. (C). 1991. text 150.00 (*0-521-38049-9*) Cambridge U Pr.

***Meng, Cheng-Shun & Birch, Cyril.** Mistress & Maid: Jiaohongji. LC 00-34583. (Translations from the Asian Classics). 2000. pap. 17.50 (*0-231-12169-5*) Col U Pr.

Meng-chia, Yao, ed. see Echo Books Staff & Chen, Lydia.

Meng, Frank P. I Don't Believe This World: Why I Am an Iconoclast. 220p. (Orig.). 1988. pap. 10.00 (*0-9619707-0-7*) Venice Pr.

Meng, Low A. & Liang, Foo S. Issues & Development in Auditing. LC 95-35311. 1995. write for info. (*0-201-88901-3*) Addison-Wesley.

Meng, Low A. & Liang, Tan W. Entrepreneurs, Entrepreneurship, & Enterprising Culture. LC 95-44345. 1995. write for info. (*0-201-88912-9*) Addison-Wesley.

Meng, Paul, et al. Standard Operating Procedures for Investigators. LC 97-41919. 210p. 1998. pap. 72.95 (*0-471-96936-2*) Wiley.

Meng, R. Business Opportunities in the Phillipines. (C). 1997. 17.95 (*0-13-733016-2*, Macmillan Coll) P-H.

Meng, S. M. Tsungli Yamen: Its Organization & Functions. LC 62-53393. (East Asian Monographs: No. 13). 151p. 1962. pap. 11.00 (*0-674-91095-8*) HUP.

***Meng, Tan Teck, et al.** U.S.-Asean Relations: Implications for Business. 351p. 1998. pap. text 29.99 (*0-13-789868-1*, Prentice Hall) P-H.

Meng, Teresa H. Synchronization Design for Digital Systems. (C). 1990. text 103.50 (*0-7923-9128-4*) Kluwer Academic.

Meng, Teresa H. & Malik, Sharad, eds. Asynchronous Circuit Design for VLSI Signal Processing. LC 93-33160. 184p. (C). 1994. text 162.50 (*0-7923-9397-X*) Kluwer Academic.

Meng, U. C. & Pinar, M. Radiative Transfer - II Vol. II: Proceedings of the Second International Symposium on Radiation Transfer, Kusadasi, Turkey, July 1997. LC 98-24472. 632p. 1998. 55.00 (*1-56700-116-5*) Begell Hse.

Meng, Weiyi, jt. auth. see Yu, Clement.

***Meng, Xin.** Labour Market Reform in China. LC 99-29696. (Trade & Development Ser.). (Illus.). 229p. (C). 2000. 74.95 (*0-521-77126-9*) Cambridge U Pr.

Meng, Zhaoqian, ed. Metrology for Quality Control in Production (IAP) Proceedings of the IMEKO TC 14 International Symposium on Metrology for Quality Control in Production, Beijing, China, 9-12 May 1989, No. 2. (International Academic Publishers Ser.). 382p. 1989. 110.00 (*0-08-037515-4*, Pergamon Pr) Elsevier.

Menga, Tan Y. Formal Specification Techniques for Engineering Modular C Programs. (International Series in Software Engineering: Vol. 1). 232p. (C). 1995. text 120.50 (*0-7923-9653-7*) Kluwer Academic.

***Mengal, Paul.** Statistique Descriptive Appliquee aux Sciences Humaines. 5th ed. 111p. 1999. 25.95 (*3-906759-35-0*) P Lang Pubng.

— Statistique Descriptive Appliquee aux Sciences Humaines. 6th ed. (FRE.). viii, 109p. 1999. 25.95 (*3-906763-62-5*, Pub. by P Lang Pubng) P Lang Pubng.

***Mengali, U. & D'Andrea, A. N.** Synchronization Techniques for Digital Receivers. LC 97-41674. (Applications of Communications Theory Ser.). (Illus.). 534p. (C). 1998. 125.00 (*0-306-45725-3*, Plenum Trade) Perseus Pubng.

Mengarini, Gregory. Selish or Flat-Head Grammar. LC 10-30201. (Library of American Linguistics: No. 2). reprint ed. 42.75 (*0-404-50982-7*) AMS Pr.

Menge, H. Grossworterbuch German/Altgriechisch/German. 29th ed. (GER & GRE.). 762p. 1997. 175.00 (*0-320-01032-5*) Fr & Eur.

Menge, Hermann. Langenscheidt German & Ancient Greek Pocket Dictionary: Langenscheidt Taschenwoerterbuch Altgriechisch. (GER & GRE.). 1027p. 1986. 49.95 (*0-8288-0510-5*, F19902) Fr & Eur.

M

An Asterisk (*) at the beginning of an entry indicates that the title is appearing for the first time.

— Langenscheidt Pocket Latin Dictionary: Langenscheidt Taschenwoerterbuch Lateinisch. 35th ed. (GER & LAT.). 1036p. 1983. 45.00 (0-8288-1028-1, F58022) Fr & Eur.

Menge, Hermann & Guthling, O. Langenscheidt Grosswoerterbuch Altgriechisch-Deutsch: Ancient Greek & German. 24th ed. (GER & GRE.). 762p. 1981. 135.00 (0-8288-0509-1, F 19904) Fr & Eur.

— Langenscheidt Large German-Latin Dictionary: Langenscheidt Grosswoerterbuch Deutsch-Latein. 13th ed. (GER & LAT.). 740p. 1982. 95.00 (0-8288-1026-5, F58000) Fr & Eur.

— Langenscheidt Large Latin-German Dictionary: Langenscheidt Grosswoerterbuch Lateinisch-Deutsch. 21st ed. (GER & LAT.). 813p. 1981. 95.00 (0-8288-1027-3, F57990) Fr & Eur.

Menge, R. & Preuss, S. Lexicon Caesarianum. (GER.). 1972. 175.00 (0-8288-6405-5, M-7284) Fr & Eur.

Menge, Walter O. & Fischer, Carl H. The Mathematics of Life Insurance. 2nd ed. LC 65-12855. (C). 1965. text 12.95 (0-914004-00-X) Ulrich.

Mengech, Annalee N., et al, eds. Integrated Pest Management in the Tropics: Current Status & Future Prospects. LC 95-20219. 186p. 1996. 170.00 (0-471-96076-4) Wiley.

Mengel & Schwiebert. Ambulatory Medicine. 3rd ed. (Illus.). 750p. 1999. spiral bd. 33.95 (0-8385-0387-X) Appleton & Lange.

Mengel, Dana. Bells of Christmas. 1.25 (0-687-50362-0) Abingdon.

— Blessed Be the Name. 1.25 (0-687-02777-2) Abingdon.

— Christ Was Born Today. 1.25 (0-687-50332-9) Abingdon.

— Come, Christian Sing. 1.00 (0-687-50123-7) Abingdon.

— Come, Follow Me. 1.25 (0-687-07145-3) Abingdon.

— From the Rising of the Sun. 1.25 (0-687-07115-1) Abingdon.

— Hail That Ever-Happy Dawn. 1.25 (0-687-50143-1) Abingdon.

— Have Your Own Way, Lord. 1.50 (0-687-02712-8) Abingdon.

— Rejoice, Rejoice This Happy Morn. 1.10 (0-687-50321-3) Abingdon.

— Song of the Wise Men. 1.75 (0-687-50163-6) Abingdon.

Mengel, Dora. Song of Victory. 1.25 (0-687-06168-7) Abingdon.

Mengel, Elias F., Jr., ed. Poems on Affairs of State: Augustan Satirical Verse, 1660-1714, Vol. 2. 575p. 1965. 150.00 (0-300-00766-3) Elliots Bks.

Mengel, Ewald. On First Looking into Arden's Goethe: Adaptations & Translations of German Plays for the Modern English Stage. (GERM Ser.). x, 198p. 1994. 60.00 (1-879751-84-4) Camden Hse.

Mengel, Gail Epstein. The Homework Organizer: Assignment Notebook & Guide. 2nd ed. 96p. (YA). (gr. 6-12). 1991. 9.95 (0-9631705-0-3) Get Organized.

Mengel, J. Dansk-Italiensk Ordborg: Danish-Italian Dictionary. (DAN & ITA.). 660p. 1979. 39.95 (0-8288-4724-X, M1292) Fr & Eur.

Mengel, K. & Pilbeam, D. J., eds. Nitrogen Metabolism in Plants. (Proceedings of the Phytochemical Society of Europe Ser.: No. 33). (Illus.). 304p. 1992. 95.00 (0-19-857752-4) OUP.

Mengel, Mark B., ed. Principles of Clinical Practice: An Introductory Textbook. (Illus.). 432p. (C). 1991. text 45.00 (0-306-43847-X, Kluwer Plenum) Kluwer Academic.

Mengel, Mark B. & Fields, Scott A., eds. Introduction to Clinical Skills: A Patient-Centered Textbook. LC 96-39432. (Illus.). 519p. (C). 1997. text 59.50 (0-306-45350-9, Kluwer Plenum) Kluwer Academic.

Mengel, Mark B. & Holleman, Warren L., eds. Fundamentals of Clinical Practice: A Textbook on the Patient, Doctor & Society. LC 96-46673. (Illus.). 517p. (C). 1996. text 71.00 (0-306-45348-7, Kluwer Plenum) Kluwer Academic.

Mengel, Mark B. & Schwiebert, L. Peter, eds. Clinical Manual of Ambulatory Medicine: The Primary Care of Families. 2nd ed. 647p. (C). 1996. pap. text 44.95 (0-8385-1466-9, A1466-0, Apple Lange Med) McGraw.

Mengel, Robert M. Birds of Kentucky. American Ornithologists' Union Staff, ed. 581p. 1965. 25.00 (0-943610-03-6) Am Ornithologists.

Mengel, Robert M., ed. Papers in Vertebrate Paleontology Honoring Robert Warren Wilson. LC 84-71697. (Special Publications: No. 9). (Illus.). 192p. (Orig.). 1984. pap. 25.00 (0-935868-09-7) Carnegie Mus.

Mengel, Robert M., jt. auth. see Jenkinson, Marion A.

Mengel, Robert M., jt. auth. see Tordoff, Harrison B.

Mengel, Robert M., ed. see Daly, Eleanor.

Mengel, Swetlana. Wege Der Herausbildung Der Wortbildungsnorm Im Ostslawischen Des 11.-17. Jahrhunderts. (Berliner Slawistische Arbeiten Ser.: No. 2). (Illus.). 343p. 1997. 57.95 (3-631-31348-9) P Lang Pubng.

Mengel, Wolfgang, jt. ed. see Fonkalsrud, Eric W.

Mengelkoch, Louise, jt. compiled by see Nerburn, Kent.

Menger, Anton. The Right to the Whole Produce of Labour: The Origin & Development of the Theory of Labour's Claim to the Whole Product of Industry. LC 68-54737. (Reprints of Economic Classics Ser.). cxviii, 271p. 1970. reprint ed. lib. bdg. 45.00 (0-678-00714-4) Kelley.

Menger, Carl. Investigations into the Method of the Social Sciences. 234p. 1996. pap. 14.95 (0-910884-30-7) Libertarian Press.

— Principles of Economics. 328p. 1994. pap. 17.95 (0-910884-27-7) Libertarian Press.

***Menger, Connie.** The Carpenter Returns. (Illus.). 184p. 1999. 15.00 (0-9670428-2-8) Min Universal Wisdom.

Menger, Connie, jt. auth. see Menger, Howard.

Menger, F. M. & Mandell, L. Electronic Interpretation of Organic Chemistry: A Problems-Oriented Text. LC 79-21718. 224p. 1980. pap. text 39.50 (0-306-40391-9, Plenum Trade) Perseus Pubng.

Menger, Fredric M. Problems in Organic Reaction Mechanisms. LC 68-28060. (Appleton-century-crofts Chemistry Ser.). vii, 121p. 1969. write for info. (0-390-62638-4) McGraw.

— Problems in Organic Reaction Mechanisms. LC 68-28060. (Appleton-Century-Crofts Series in Chemistry). 128p. reprint ed. pap. 39.70 (0-608-12431-1, 205569100030) Bks Demand.

***Menger, Howard & Menger, Connie.** The High Bridge Incident. large type ed. (Illus.). 145p. 1999. pap. 24.95 (0-9670428-3-6) Min Universal Wisdom.

— Threads of Light to You. large type ed. 146p. 1999. pap. 24.95 (0-9670428-4-4) Min Universal Wisdom.

Menger, Karl. Kurventheorie. 2nd rev. ed. LC 63-11314. 1968. 18.95 (0-8284-0172-1) Chelsea Pub.

— Morality, Decisions, & Social Organization Toward a Logic of Ethics. Mulder, Henk L., ed. Van Der Schalie, E., tr. from GER. LC 74-81941. (Vienna Circle Collection: No. 6). 124p. 1974. pap. text 73.50 (90-277-0319-1, D Reidel); lib. bdg. 78.00 (90-277-0318-3, D Reidel) Kluwer Academic.

— Reminiscences of the Vienna Circle & the Mathematical Colloquium. Golland, Louise, ed. LC 94-5014. (Vienna Circle Collection: Vol. 20). 272p. (C). 1994. pap. text 28.00 (0-7923-2873-6) Kluwer Academic.

— Reminiscences of the Vienna Circle & the Mathematical Colloquium. Golland, Louise, ed. LC 94-5014. (Vienna Circle Collection: Vol. 20). 272p. (C). 1994. lib. bdg. 127.50 (0-7923-2711-X, Pub. by Kluwer Academic) Kluwer Academic.

— Selected Papers in Logic & Foundations, Didactics, & Economics. (Vienna Circle Collection: No. 10). 354p. 1979. pap. text 91.00 (90-277-0321-3, D Reidel); lib. bdg. 146.00 (90-277-0320-5, D Reidel) Kluwer Academic.

Menger, Michael D., jt. ed. see Messmer, K.

Menger, Pierre-Michel, jt. auth. see Ginsburgh, Victor.

Mengerink, William C. Hand in Hand: Funding Strategies for Human Service Agencies. 92nd ed. 115p. 1992. 40.00 (0-930807-37-5, 600317) Fund Raising.

Mengersen, Ernest, jt. auth. see Philip, Hugh.

Mengert, et al. Institution of Education. 1992. 22.55 (0-536-58222-X) Pearson Custom.

Mengert, Jim, jt. auth. see Linver, Sandy.

Menges. How to Make Injection Molds. 1987. 74.95 (0-02-947570-8) Free Pr.

Menges, A., ed. see Werner, F.

Menges, Constantiine C., ed. Russia & the New Independent States: The Political & Economic Transitions. 300p. (C). 1994. pap. text 27.50 (0-8191-9551-0) U Pr of Amer.

Menges, Constantine C., ed. Partnerships for Peace, Democracy & Prosperity. LC 97-17069. 270p. (C). 1997. pap. 29.50 (0-7618-0796-9) U Pr of Amer.

— Transitions from Communism in Russia & Eastern Europe: Analysis & Perspectives. LC 93-6192. 320p. 1993. 62.50 (0-8191-9296-1); pap. 28.50 (0-8191-9297-X) U Pr of Amer.

***Menges, Constantine C., ed.** The Marshall Plan from Those Who Made It Succeed. 424p. 2000. pap. 39.50 (0-7618-1658-5) U Pr of Amer.

Menges, Georg, et al, eds. Experts Systems in Production Engineering. (Lecture Notes in Engineering Ser.: Vol. 29). iv, 239p. 1987. 47.95 (0-387-17927-5) Spr-Verlag.

Menges, Georg & Mohren, Paul. How to Make Injection Molds. 2nd ed. 540p. 1993. 129.50 (1-56990-062-0) Hanser-Gardner.

Menges, Georg, jt. auth. see Osswald, Tim A.

Menges, George. Concise Encyclopedia of Polymer Science & Engineering. Mark, Herman F. et al, eds. LC 89-70674. 1376p. 1990. 270.00 (0-471-51253-2) Wiley.

Menges, Gunter, ed. Information, Inference & Decision. LC 73-91432. (Theory & Decision Library: No. 1). 1974. pap. text 65.50 (90-277-0423-6); lib. bdg. 88.00 (90-277-0422-8) Kluwer Academic.

Menges, Karl, et al, eds. Herder Yearbook, Vol. 1. (GERM Ser.). x, 152p. 1992. 50.00 (1-879751-22-4) Camden Hse.

Menges, Karl, ed. see Herder, Johann G.

Menges, Matthew C. The Concept of Univocity Regarding to the Predication of God & Creature According to William Ockham. (Philosophy Ser.). xi, 196p. 1952. pap. 8.00 (1-57659-098-4) Franciscan Inst.

Menges, Patricia A., ed. see August, B. Alan.

Menges, Patricia A., ed. see Levin, David S.

Menges, Patricia A., ed. see Nance, Kimi.

Menges, Patricia A., ed. see Pinnacle Communications Staff.

Menges, Patricia A., ed. see Young, Natalie B.

Menges, Phil. Beyond Revolution: The Guide to Complete Political & Social Reform. 260p. (Orig.). 1994. pap. 14.95 (0-9643663-0-4) Outside NY.

Menges, Robert. Faculty in New Jobs. LC 98-40284. 1999. text 24.95 (0-7879-3878-5) Jossey-Bass.

Menges, Robert J. & Svinicki, Marilla D., eds. College Teaching: From Theory to Practice. LC 85-644763. (New Directions for Teaching & Learning Ser.: No. TL 45). 1991. pap. 22.00 (1-55542-799-5) Jossey-Bass.

Menges, Robert J. & Weimer, Maryellen G., eds. Teaching on Solid Ground: Using Scholarship to Improve Practice. (Higher & Adult Education Ser.). 422p. 1995. text 36.95 (0-7879-0133-4) Jossey-Bass.

Menges, Robert J., jt. auth. see Brinko, Kathleen.

***Menges, Tracey.** Mid-Atlantic Region. (Annual Directory of American & Canadian Bed & Breakfasts Ser.: Vol. II). 255p. 2000. pap. 9.95 (1-57748-772-9) Barbour Pub.

— The Midwest. (Annual Directory of American & Canadian Bed & Breakfasts Ser.: Vol. IV). (Illus.). 179p. 2000. pap. 9.95 (1-57748-774-5) Barbour Pub.

— New England. (Annual Directory of American & Canadian Bed & Breakfasts Ser.: Vol. I). (Illus.). 293p. 2000. pap. 9.95 (1-57748-771-0) Barbour Pub.

Menges, Tracey. 1999 Annual Directory of Western Bed & Breakfasts. 1998. pap. 12.95 (1-55853-681-7) Rutledge Hill Pr.

— 1999 Annual Directory of Midwestern Bed & Breakfasts. 1998. pap. 9.95 (1-55853-682-5) Rutledge Hill Pr.

— 1999 Annual Directory of Southern Bed & Breakfasts. 1998. pap. 9.95 (1-55853-683-3) Rutledge Hill Pr.

— 1999 Annual Directory of Mid-Atlantic Bed & Breakfasts. 1998. pap. 9.95 (1-55853-684-1) Rutledge Hill Pr.

— 1999 Annual Directory of New England Bed & Breakfasts. 1998. pap. 9.95 (1-55853-685-X) Rutledge Hill Pr.

***Menges, Tracey.** The South. (Annual Directory of American & Canadian Bed & Breakfasts Ser.: Vol. III). (Illus.). 273p. 2000. pap. 9.95 (1-57748-773-7) Barbour Pub.

— The West. (Annual Directory of American & Canadian Bed & Breakfasts Ser.: Vol. V). (Illus.). 431p. 2000. pap. 12.95 (1-57748-775-3) Barbour Pub.

***Menges, Tracey, ed.** The Annual Directory of American & Canadian Bed & Breakfasts, 2000 Edition: New England. (Illus.). 320p. 1999. pap. 9.95 (1-55853-775-9) Rutledge Hill Pr.

Mengesha, Astair G. Women's Work: A Crosscultural Comparison of Roles in Cameroon & India. (Illus.). 128p. 1998. pap. 13.00 (0-9642068-9-7) Nyala Pubng.

***Mengham, Rod.** Introduction to Contemporary Fiction: International Writing in English Since, 1970. LC 98-46821. 1999. 59.95 (0-7456-1956-8) Blackwell Pubs.

Mengham, Rod. An Introduction to Contemporary Fiction: International Writing in English Since 1970. 288p. pap. 24.95 (0-7456-1957-6) Polity Pr.

Mengham, Rod, ed. see Forster, E. M.

Menghi, A. Nuovo Dizionario di Terminologia Giuridica: New Dictionary of Legal Terms. (ITA.). 1979. pap. 49.95 (0-8288-4830-0, M9654) Fr & Eur.

Menghi, Umberto. Mamma's Kitchen: The Flavors of Tuscany. (Illus.). 180p. 1998. pap. 29.95 (1-55054-506-X, Pub. by DGL) Orca Bk Pubs.

Menghini, Luverna, jt. auth. see Einolf, David M.

Mengin, Robert. No Laurels for De Gaulle. Allen, Jay, tr. from FRE. LC 78-179734. (Biography Index Reprint Ser.). 1977. reprint ed. 24.95 (0-8369-8102-2) Ayer.

Mengisteab, Kidane. Ethiopia: Failure of Land Reform & Agricultural Crisis, 137. LC 90-32335. (Contributions in Afro-American & African Studies: No. 137). 240p. 1990. 62.95 (0-313-27423-1, MFJ, Greenwood Pr) Greenwood.

— Globalization & Autocentricity in Africa's Development in the 21st Century. LC 96-48230. 1996. write for info. (0-86543-558-8); pap. write for info. (0-86543-559-6) Africa World.

Mengisteab, Kidane & Daddieh, Cyril, eds. State Building & Democratization in Africa: Faith, Hope & Realities. LC 98-21642. 312p. 1999. 65.00 (0-275-96353-5, Praeger Pubs) Greenwood.

Mengisteab, Kidane & Logan, Ikubolajeh, eds. Beyond Economic Liberalization in Africa: Structural Adjustment & the Alternatives. LC 95-13680. (Illus.). 320p. (C). 1995. text 25.00 (1-85649-294-X, Pub. by Zed Books) St Martin.

Mengle, Kathy. Tools for Healing: Working Toward Harmony & Balance. LC 84-72359. (Illus.). 172p. (Orig.). 1985. pap. 10.95 (0-87516-548-6) DeVorss.

***Mengozzi, Paolo.** European Community Law: From the Treaty of Rome to the Treaty of Amsterdam. 2nd ed. Del Duca, Patrick, tr. 320p. 1999. text 150.00 (90-411-1240-5) Kluwer Law Intl.

Mengual, Ana, tr. see Junyent, Sebastian.

Menguc, M. Pinar, ed. Radiative Heat Transfer: Proceedings of the First International Symposia on Radiative Heat Transfer. 400p. 1996. 127.50 (1-56700-060-6) Begell Hse.

— Radiative Transfer-I: Proceedings of the First International Symposium on Radiation Transfer, Kusadasi, Turkey, August 13-18, 1995. LC 96-17763. 1996. write for info. (1-56700-068-1) Begell Hse.

***Menha, Francha Roffe.** School Violence: Deadly Lessons. LC 99-43566. (Teen Issues Ser.). (Illus.). 64p. (YA). (gr. 6 up). 2000. lib. bdg. 17.95 (0-7660-1358-8) Enslow Pubs.

Menhart, David, jt. auth. see Dalessandro, James.

Menhart, John & Lynn, Donald. Welding Management: Techniques for Welding Leadership. Nickel, Amy J., ed. LC 97-175036. (Illus.). 115p. (Orig.). 1997. pap. 50.00 (1-881113-10-8) Croydon Grp.

Menhart, W. H., et al. Atlas of Cancer Incidence in the Former German Democratic Republic, 1978-1982. (IARC Scientific Publications: No. 106). (Illus.). 384p. 1993. pap. 95.00 (92-832-2106-0) OUP.

Menhennet, Alan. Grimmelshausen the Storyteller: A Study of the "Simplician" Novels. LC 96-52520. (GERM Ser.). (GER.). 220p. 1997. 50.00 (1-57113-102-7) Camden Hse.

— Romantic Movement. (Literary History of Germany Ser.: Vol. 6). 276p. 1981. 58.50 (0-389-20104-9, N6878) B&N Imports.

Menhennet, Alan, tr. see Hasek, Jaroslav.

Menhennet, David & Palmer, John. Parliament in Perspective. LC 67-73291. 1967. 18.95 (0-8023-1125-3) Dufour.

Menhinick, Edward F. The Freshwater Fishes of North Carolina. (Illus.). vi, 227p. (C). 1991. 34.70 (0-9628949-0-7) NC Wildlife.

Menhinick, G. Grampian Cookbook. 89p. 1984. pap. 6.00 (0-08-032420-7, Pergamon Pr) Elsevier.

Menhinick, Gladys. The Grampian Cookbook. 100p. 1989. pap. 40.00 (1-873644-22-1, Pub. by Mercat Pr Bks) St Mut.

Menhinick, Oliver N., ed. Plant Propagation: Insight, Fundamentals & Techniques. 72p. 1990. pap. 25.00 (0-948251-74-3, Pub. by Picton) St Mut.

Menichelli, Edward & Crocetta, Lionel. You Shall Not Kill, Vol. 6. (Reflections on the Commandments Ser.). 63p. 1995. pap. 2.95 (0-8198-8803-6) Pauline Bks.

Menick, jt. auth. see Burget.

Menick, Jim. Lingo. 336p. 1992. pap. 10.95 (0-88184-812-3) Carroll & Graf.

Menick, Stephen. The Muffin Child. LC 97-51817. 208p. (J). (gr. 5-9). 1998. 17.99 (0-399-23303-2, Philomel) Peng Put Young Read.

Menicucci, David F. Catholic Home & School Association Guidebook. 108p. (Orig.). 1990. pap. 6.00 (1-55833-058-5) Natl Cath Educ.

Menicucci, Wayne. The Rookie Card Collector. (Illus.). 42p. (Orig.). 1987. pap. 4.95 (0-942755-57-X) Diamond M Bks.

Menides. Elizabeth Bishop. 2000. 24.95 (0-8057-1632-7) Mac Lib Ref.

***Menides, Laura J. & Dorenkamp, Angela, eds.** In Worcester, Massachusetts: Essays on Elizabeth Bishop from the 1997 Elizabeth Bishop Conference at WPI. LC 98-46159. (WPI Studies: Vol. 18). (Illus.). ix, 361p. (C). 1999. pap. text 36.00 (0-8204-4149-X) P Lang Pubng.

Menier, Juan A. Cuba Por Dentro: El Minint. LC 93-74509. (Coleccion Cuba y sus Jueces). (SPA.). 173p. (Orig.). 1994. pap. 18.00 (0-89729-718-0) Ediciones.

Menigoz, Robin S., et al. Affordable Landscaping. LC 94-67708. 96p. (Orig.). 1995. pap. 9.95 (0-89721-274-6, UPC05431, Ortho Bks) Meredith Bks.

Menigoz, Robin S., jt. auth. see Lutsko, Ron.

Menihan, Cydney A. OB/GYN Ultrasound Triage & Evaluation for Advanced Practice Nurses. LC 97-24741. 224p. 1997. spiral bd. 37.00 (0-397-55383-8) Lppncott W & W.

Menihan, John C., Enterprises Staff, ed. see Mehihan, Thomas J.

Menik, Jaroslav. Strength & Fracture of Glass & Ceramics. (Glass & Science Technology Ser.: Vol. 12). 358p. 1992. 153.75 (0-444-98685-5) Elsevier.

Menikoff, Barry. Psychiatric Home Care. 288p. (C). 1999. text 59.95 (0-12-490940-X) Acad Pr.

Menikoff, Barry, ed. & intro. see Stevenson, Robert Louis.

***Meninger, William & Francis.** The Committed Life: An Adaptation of the Introduction to the Devout Life by St. Francis de Sales. LC 00-31403. 2000. write for info. (0-8264-1285-8) Continuum.

Meninger, William A. Bringing the Imitation of Christ into the Twenty-First Century. LC 92-36883. 144p. 1998. pap. 11.95 (0-8264-1101-0) Continuum.

— The Loving Search for God: Contemplative Prayer & "The Cloud of Unknowing" LC 82-40274. 142p. (C). 1995. pap. 11.95 (0-8264-0851-6) Continuum.

— The Process of Forgiveness. 156p. 1997. pap. 12.95 (0-8264-1008-1) Continuum.

— The Temple of the Lord: And Other Stories. LC 97-23225. 96p. 1997. pap. 11.95 (0-8264-1062-6) Continuum.

— Ten-Twelve Monastery Road. (Illus.). 120p. (Orig.). 1989. pap. 8.95 (0-932506-73-9) St Bedes Pubns.

Menini, Claudia, jt. ed. see Facchini, Alberto.

Menino, Holly. Forward Motion: Horses, Humans & the Competitive Enterprise. LC 96-17487. 208p. 1996. 23.00 (0-86547-493-1) N Point Pr.

— Forward Motion: World-Class Riders & the Horses Who Carry Them. LC 98-28429. 208p. 1999. pap. 14.95 (1-55821-692-8) Lyons Pr.

Meniru, Godwin I., et al, eds. A Handbook of Intrauterine Insemination. (Illus.). 260p. (C). 1997. pap. text 44.95 (0-521-58676-3) Cambridge U Pr.

Menissier, F., jt. auth. see King, J. W.

Menitove, Jay E., ed. Standards for Blood Banks & Transfusion Services. 17th rev. ed. 86p. 1996. pap. text 75.00 (1-56395-086-3, PC97-ST9617) Am Assn Blood.

— Standards for Hematopoietic Progenitor Cells. 36p. 1996. pap. text 30.00 (1-56395-071-5, PC97-935720) Am Assn Blood.

***Menjivar, Cecilia.** Fragmented Ties: Salvadoran Immigrant Networks in America. 326p. 2000. pap. 19.95 (0-520-22211-3, Pub. by U CA Pr) Cal Prin Full Svc.

***Menjmvar, Cecilia.** Fragmented Ties: Salvadoran Immigrant Networks in America. 326p. 2000. 48.00 (0-520-22210-5, Pub. by U CA Pr) Cal Prin Full Svc.

Menjot, Denis, jt. auth. see Pinol, Jean-Luc.

Menjou, Adolphe. It Took Nine Tailors. (American Autobiography Ser.). 238p. 1995. reprint ed. lib. bdg. 79.00 (0-7812-8591-7) Rprt Serv.

Menk, James. Lillian's Fish. LC 97-12331. (Illus.). 176p. (J). (gr. 3-4). 1997. 14.95 (1-56145-158-4) Peachtree Pubs.

Menk, Martha, tr. see Sweetkind, Irene S., ed.

Menk, Patricia H. To Live in Time: The Sesquicentennial History of Mary Baldwin College. 500p. 1992. 40.00 (0-9633486-0-4) M Baldwin Coll.

Menkart, Deborah & Sunshine, Catherine A., eds. Puerto Rico: Classroom Resources for Secondary Schools. LC 90-62779. (Caribbean Connections Ser.). (Illus.). 106p. (Orig.). 1990. pap. 12.00 (1-878554-04-2) Netwrk of Educ.

Menkart, Deborah, jt. ed. see Sunshine, Catherine A.

Menkart, Deborah, jt. ed. see Sunshine, Catherine H.

Menke, Anne M., tr. see Kristeva, Julia.

Menke, Arnold S., ed. The Semiaquatic & Aquatic Hemiptera of California: Heteroptera: Hemiptera. LC 77-91755. (Bulletin of the California Insect Survey Ser.: Vol. 21). 178p. reprint ed. pap. 55.20 (0-608-14568-8, 202493500040) Bks Demand.

An Asterisk (*) at the beginning of an entry indicates that the title is appearing for the first time.

M

An Asterisk (*) at the beginning of an entry indicates that the title is appearing for the first time.

Mennonite Board of Congregational Ministries Staff. Congregational Discipling: A Threefold Vision for Worship, Community & Mission. LC 97-12503. 1997. 8.99 (*0-8361-9450-0*) Herald Pr.

Mennonite Board of Congregational Ministries Staff, jt. auth. see Ministerial Leadership Services of the General Con.

Mennonite Central Committee Kenya. More Treasured Mennonite Recipes II: Food, Fun & Fellowship from the Mennonite Relief Sales. (Illus.). 224p. 1995. pap. 12.95 (*1-56523-028-0*) Fox Chapel Pub.

Mennonite Church Staff. Mennonite Confession of Faith. LC 63-22593. 32p. (Orig.). 1963. pap. 1.99 (*0-8361-1314-4*) Herald Pr.

Mennonite Church Staff, jt. auth. see General Boards of the General Conference.

Mennonite Relief Sale Volunteers Staff. Treasured Mennonite Recipes: Favorite Recipes from Mennonite Relief Sale Volunteers. 200p. 1993. pap. 11.95 (*1-56523-025-6*) Fox Chapel Pub.

Meno, Joe. Tender As Hellfire. LC 98-37687. 256p. 1999. text 22.95 (*0-312-20051-X*) St Martin.

Menocal, Maria R. A First Rate Place. 2000. write for info. (*0-316-56688-8*) Little.

— Shards of Love: Exile & the Origins of the Lyric. LC 93-26530. 312p. 1993. text 54.95 (*0-8223-1405-3*); pap. text 18.95 (*0-8223-1419-3*) Duke.

— Writing in Dante's Cult of Truth: From Borges to Boccaccio. LC 90-45998. 232p. 1991. text 49.95 (*0-8223-1104-6*); pap. text 17.95 (*0-8223-1117-8*) Duke.

***Menocal, Maria Rosa, et al, eds.** The Literature of Al-Andalus. (The Cambridge History of Arabic Literature). (Illus.). 600p. (C). 2000. Price not set. (*0-521-47159-1*) Cambridge U Pr.

Menocal, Narcisco G., ed. & intro. see Wright, John L.

Menocal, Narcisco G. Architecture As Nature: The Transcendentalist Idea of Louis Sullivan. LC 80-5118. (Illus.). 253p. reprint ed. pap. 78.50 (*0-608-20453-6*, 207170600002) Bks Demand.

Menocal, Narcisco G., ed. Wright Studies Vol. 1: Taliesin 1911-1914. (Illus.). 160p. (C). 1991. pap. 21.95 (*0-8093-1625-0*) S Ill U Pr.

— Wright Studies Vol. 1: Taliesin 1911-1914. (Illus.). 160p. (C). 1992. 41.95 (*0-8093-1624-2*) S Ill U Pr.

***Menocal, Narciso G., ed.** Wright Studies Vol. 2: Fallingwater & Pittsburgh. (Illus.). 144p. 2000. pap. 24.95 (*0-8093-1957-8*) S Ill U Pr.

— Wright Studies Vol. 2: Fallingwater & Pittsburgh. Vol. 2. (Illus.). 144p. 2000. 44.95 (*0-8093-1956-X*) S Ill U Pr.

Menocal, Richard De, see De Menocal, Richard.

Menolascino, F. J., jt. auth. see McGee, J. J.

Menolascino, Frank J. & Egger, Michael L. Medical Dimensions of Mental Retardation. LC 76-16503. 501p. 1978. reprint ed. pap. 155.40 (*0-608-01842-2*, 206249200003) Bks Demand.

Menolascino, Frank J. & Stark, Jack A., eds. Handbook of Mental Illness in the Mentally Retarded. LC 84-13263. (Illus.). 472p. (C). 1984. 114.00 (*0-306-41648-4*, Plenum Trade) Perseus Pubng.

Menon, A. G. A Systematic Monograph of the Tongue Soles of the Genus Cynoglossus Hamilton-Buchanan (Pisces, Cynoglossidae) LC 76-608109. (Smithsonian Contributions to Zoology Ser.: No. 238). 135p. reprint ed. pap. 41.90 (*0-608-13713-8*, 205528600013) Bks Demand.

***Menon, Anand.** France, Nato & the Limits of Independence, 1981-97: The Politics of Ambivalence. LC 99-43337. 2000. text 65.00 (*0-312-22931-3*) St Martin.

Menon, Anand & Howorth, Jolyon, eds. European Union & National Defense Policy. LC 98-118502. (State & the European Union Ser.). 200p. (C). 1997. 85.00 (*0-415-16484-2*); pap. 27.99 (*0-415-16485-0*) Routledge.

Menon, Anand, jt. ed. see Forder, James.

***Menon, Anil & Sharma, Arun, eds.** AMA Winter Educators' Conference, 1999 Vol. 10: Marketing Theory & Applications. 276p. 1999. pap. 50.00 (*0-87757-275-5*) Am Mktg.

Menon, Aric K., jt. ed. see Bhatia, C. S.

Menon, Bhashkar P. Bridges Across the South: Technical Cooperation among Developing Countries. (Policy Studies). 1980. text 56.00 (*0-08-024645-1*, Pergamon Pr); pap. text 18.00 (*0-08-024646-X*, Pergamon Pr) Elsevier.

Menon, Elizabeth K. The Complete Mayeux: Use & Abuse of a French Icon. LC 97-52736. (Illus.). XXXIV, 436p. (C). 1998. pap. text 60.95 (*0-8204-3427-2*) P Lang Pubng.

Menon, Elizabeth K., jt. auth. see Weisberg, Gabriel P.

***Menon, Geeta.** Sociological Explorations: Introductory Sociology on the Internet. 56p. (C). 1999. pap. text 20.95 (*0-7872-6437-7*, 41643701) Kendall-Hunt.

Menon, Goutham M., jt. ed. see Coe, Jo Ann R.

Menon, Jayant. Exchange Rates & Prices: The Case of Australian Manufactured Imports. (Lecture Notes in Economics & Mathematical Systems Ser.: Vol. 433). (Illus.). 313p. 1996. pap. text 71.00 (*3-540-60801-X*) Spr-Verlag.

Menon, K. P. A Dictionary of Kathakali. (Illus.). 80p. 1979. 14.95 (*0-318-36308-9*) Asia Bk Corp.

— Memories & Musings. 361p. 1979. 14.95 (*0-318-36594-4*) Asia Bk Corp.

Menon, K. R. Maritime Strategy & Continental Wars. LC 97-28051. (Naval Policy & History Ser.: No. 3). 232p. (C). 1998. 47.50 (*0-7146-4793-4*, Pub. by F Cass Pubs); pap. 22.50 (*0-7146-4348-3*, Pub. by F Cass Pubs) Intl Spec Bk.

Menon, K. S. Style Book: For Journalists & Writers. 132p. 1990. text 18.95 (*81-220-0183-1*, Pub. by Konark Pubs Pvt Ltd) Advent Bks Div.

Menon, Krish. Sams Teach Yourself CGI Programming in a Week. 3rd ed. 387p. 1998. pap. 29.99 (*1-57521-381-8*) Sams.

Menon, M. G. Human Genome Research: Emerging Ethical, Legal, Social & Economic Issues. LC 99-933299. xviii, 252p. 1999. write for info. (*81-7023-862-5*) Allied Pubs.

Menon, N. C. Mother of Battles: Saddam's Folly. (Illus.). 181p. 1992. text 25.00 (*81-220-0254-4*, Pub. by Konark Pubs Pvt Ltd) Advent Bks Div.

***Menon, Nirup M.** The Impact of Information Technology: Evidence from the Healthcare Industry. rev. ed. (Studies in Industrial Productivity). 121p. 1999. 40.00 (*0-8153-3447-8*) Garland.

Menon, Nivedita. Gender & Politics in India. LC 99-939171. (Themes in Politics Ser.). (Illus.). 552p. 2000. text 35.00 (*0-19-564641-X*) OUP.

Menon, P. G., jt. auth. see Paal, E.

Menon, P. K. The Law of Recognition in International Law: Basic Principles. LC 94-33966. 1994. write for info. (*0-7734-9109-0*) E Mellen.

— The Law of Treaties Between States & International Organizations. LC 92-22554. 264p. 1992. text 89.95 (*0-7734-9590-8*) E Mellen.

— The Succession of States in Respect to Treaties, State Property, Archives, & Debts. LC 90-22575. (Studies in World Peace: Vol. 6). 265p. 1991. lib. bdg. 89.95 (*0-88946-263-1*) E Mellen.

— The United Nations Efforts to Control Arms in Outer Space: A Brief History with Key Documents. LC 87-24727. (Studies in World Peace: Vol. 1). 212p. 1989. lib. bdg. 89.95 (*0-88946-587-8*) E Mellen.

Menon, P. K., jt. ed. see Kodilinye, Gilbert.

Menon, P. Shungoonny. History of Travancore: From the Earliest Time. LC 98-904960. xv, 523 p. 1998. write for info. (*81-206-0169-6*) Asian Educ Servs.

Menon, R. G. & International Fertilizer Development Center Staff. Compaction of Phosphate Rocks with Soluble Phosphates: An Alternative Technology to Partial Acidulation of Phosphate Rocks with Low Reactivity: IFDC Experience. LC 96-46811. (Technical Bulletin Ser.: No. T-44). 23p. 1996. pap. 30.00 (*0-88090-114-4*) Intl Fertilizer.

Menon, Raghava. The Hindustan Times Presents: The World of Amjad Ali Khan. (C). 1996. 48.00 (*81-85273-81-2*, Pub. by UBS Pubs Dist) S Asia.

***Menon, Rajan.** A Nuclear Strategy for India. LC 00-38744. 2000. pap. write for info. (*0-7619-9450-5*) Sage.

— Soviet Power & the Third World. 261p. 1986. 18.00 (*0-300-03500-4*) Yale U Pr.

Menon, Rajan. Soviet Power & the Third World. LC 85-40988. 272p. (C). 1989. reprint ed. pap. 19.00 (*0-300-04489-5*) Yale U Pr.

Menon, Rajan & Nelson, Daniel N., eds. Limits to Soviet Power. 230p. 1997. reprint ed. pap. text 15.00 (*0-7881-5021-9*) DIANE Pub.

Menon, Rajan, jt. auth. see Ebel, Robert E.

Menon, Raman V. K., tr. see Michaud, J., ed.

Menon, Ramarkrishnan. Writing to Learn Mathematics: Student Journals & Student Constructed Questions. 1993. pap. 45.00 (*0-7300-2059-2*, Pub. by Deakin Univ) St Mut.

Menon, Ritu & Bhasin, Kamla. Borders & Boundaries: How Women Experienced the Partition of India. LC 98-17638. 276p. (C). 1998. pap. 20.00 (*0-8135-2552-7*) Rutgers U Pr.

— Borders & Boundaries: Women in India's Partition. LC 98-902564. 1998. 24.00 (*81-86706-00-3*, Pub. by Kali for Women) S Asia.

— Borders & Boundaries: Women in India's Partition. LC 98-17638. 276p. (C). 1998. 50.00 (*0-8135-2551-9*) Rutgers U Pr.

Menon, S. V. Renormalization Group Theory of Critical Phenomena. (IPA Monographs in Physics). 1995. write for info. (*81-224-0701-3*, Pub. by Wiley Estrn) Franklin.

Menon, Sangeetha, jt. auth. see Williams, George M.

Menon, Sathis. PBS C Workbook. 288p. (C). 1993. pap. 41.88 (*0-07-041576-5*) McGraw.

Menon, T. K. A Primer of Malayalam Literature. (C). 1990. text 15.00 (*81-206-0603-5*, Pub. by Asian Educ Servs) S Asia.

Menon, T. K., ed. see Padmanabha, K. P.

Menon, T. V. The Thousand Names of the Divine Mother: Sri Lalita Sahasranama with Commentary. Kev, K. V., ed. Namboodiri, M. N., tr. 468p. 1996. 18.95 (*1-879410-67-2*) M A Ctr.

Menon, V. P. Transfer of Power in India. 1997. reprint ed. pap. 28.00 (*81-250-0884-5*) Orient Longman Ltd.

Menon, Vapal P. The Story of the Integration of the Indian States. LC 72-4282. (World Affairs Ser.: National & International Viewpoints). (Illus.). 542p. 1972. reprint ed. 36.95 (*0-405-04575-1*) Ayer.

***Menon, Vivek.** On the Brink: Travels in the Wilds of India. LC 99-936253. (Illus.). 1999. write for info. (*0-14-027826-5*) Penguin Books.

Menorah Park Center for the Aging Residents Staff & Myers, R. H., Tenants. Cameo Recollections: From Generation to Generation. 100p. 1991. pap. text 5.00 (*0-9631040-0-4*) Menorah Pk Ctr Age.

Menos, Dennis. Arms over Diplomacy: Reflections on the Persian Gulf War. LC 91-44450. 192p. 1992. 49.95 (*0-275-94160-4*, C4160, Praeger Pubs) Greenwood.

— The Superpowers & Nuclear Arms Control: Rhetoric & Reality. LC 89-36700. 200p. 1990. 52.95 (*0-275-93458-6*, C3458, Praeger Pubs) Greenwood.

— A Test of Allegiance. vii, 252p. 1997. pap. 15.00 (*0-9660404-0-6*) Vergina Pr.

Menotti, Gian-Carlo. Amahl & the Night Visitors. LC 84-27196. (Illus.). 64p. (J). (ps up). 1986. 21.00 (*0-688-05426-9*, Wm Morrow); lib. bdg. 19.88 (*0-688-05427-7*, Wm Morrow) Morrow Avon.

— Amahl & the Night Visitors: Chorus Parts Opera in One Act. 16p. 1986. pap. 4.00 (*0-7935-5359-8*, 50337800) H Leonard.

— Amahl & the Night Visitors: Easy Piano. 40p. 1993. pap. 7.95 (*0-7935-2778-3*) H Leonard.

— Concerto: For Violin-Piano-Orchestra. 1987. pap. 24.00 (*0-7935-2016-9*, 50287850) H Leonard.

— Concerto for Violin & Orchestra: Full Score. 96p. 1992. per. 35.00 (*0-7935-2056-8*, 50480208) H Leonard.

— The Consul: Vocal Score. 304p. 1986. pap. 35.00 (*0-7935-1136-4*, 50337690) H Leonard.

— Intro March & Shepherds Dance Concert Band. 1991. pap. 50.00 (*0-7935-0488-0*) H Leonard.

— Medium: The Vocal Score Tragedy in Two Acts. (ENG & FRE.). 128p. 1986. pap. 25.00 (*0-7935-1546-7*, 50337670) H Leonard.

— Suite for Two Cellos & Piano. 44p. 1986. pap. 18.00 (*0-7935-4068-2*, 50291680) H Leonard.

— Telephone, the Or l'Amour a 'Trois Vocal Score. (ENG & FRE.). 56p. 1986. pap. 11.95 (*0-7935-5370-9*, 50337660) H Leonard.

Menotti, Giulia. Lourdes: English Edition. Orling, Merry, tr. 64p. pap. text 9.95 (*88-7009-025-6*, Pub. by Bonechi) Eiron.

***Menrad, Klaus.** Communicating Genetic Engineering in the Agro-Food Sector to the Public. 82p. (C). 2000. reprint ed. pap. text 25.00 (*0-7881-8986-7*) DIANE Pub.

***Menrad, Klaus, et al.** Future Impacts of Biotechnology on Agriculture, Food Production & Food Processing: A Delphi Survey. Fraunhofer Institute for Systems & Innovation Rese, ed. LC 99-45438. (Technology, Innovation & Policy Ser.: Vol. 10). (Illus.). xx, 406p. 1999. pap. 89.00 (*3-7908-1215-3*) Spr-Verlag.

Men's Fitness Staff & Tomkiw, Beth. Total Sex: Men's Fitness Magazine's Complete Guide to Everything Men Need to Know & Want to Know about Sex. LC 98-31338. (Illus.). 320p. (Orig.). 1999. pap. 21.00 (*0-06-273629-9*) HarpC.

Men's Garden Clubs of America Staff. A to Z Hints for the Vegetable Gardener: From the 10,000 Members of the Men's Garden Clubs of America. LC 75-39519. (Illus.). 128p. 1983. reprint ed. pap. 7.95 (*0-88266-106-X*, Garden Way Pub) Storey Bks.

Mens, H. L. Van, see Gordon, D. H. & Van Mens, H. L.

***Men's Health Book Editors, ed.** The Complete Book of Men's Health: The Definitive, Illustrated Guide to Healthy Living, Exercise, & Sex. (Illus.). 288p. 2000. pap. 19.95 (*1-57954-298-0*) Rodale Pr Inc.

Men's Health Books Editors. Command Respect: Cultivate the Qualities That Inspire & Impress Others. Garfinkel, Perry & Kaufman, Brian P., eds. 176p. 1998. pap. 14.95 (*0-614-31249-3*) Rodale Pr Inc.

— The Complete Book of Men's Health: The Definitive, Illustrated Guide to Healthy Living, Exercise, & Sex. LC 98-8658. (Illus.). 288p. 1998. text 31.95 (*0-87596-528-8*) Rodale Pr Inc.

— The Doctor's Book of Home Remedies for Men: From Heart Disease & Headaches to Flabby Abs & Road Rage, over 2,000 Simple Solutions. LC 98-46311. 1999. text 29.95 (*0-87596-529-6*) Rodale Pr Inc.

***Men's Health Books Editors.** The Men's Health Hard Body Plan: The Ultimate 12-Week Plan for Burning Fat & Building Muscle. Keller, Larry, ed. (Illus.). 384p. 2000. pap. 19.95 (*1-57954-229-8*) Rodale Pr Inc.

— The Men's Health Longevity Program. 2001. pap. 18.95 (*1-57954-366-9*) Rodale Pr Inc.

Men's Health Books Editors, et al. Healing Power: Natural Methods for Achiving Whole-Body Health. LC 98-48717. (Men's Health Life Improvement Guides Ser.: Vol. 14). 1999. pap. 14.95 (*0-87596-506-7*) Rodale Pr Inc.

— Maximum Style: Look Sharp & Feel Confident in Every Situation. LC 97-3799. (Men's Health Life Improvement Guides Ser.). (Illus.). 176p. 1997. 14.95 (*0-87596-379-X*) Rodale Pr Inc.

Men's Health Books Editors, ed. see Raskin, Doma.

Mens Health Books Staff. Doctors Book of Home Remedies for Men. 2000. 89.85 (*1-57954-108-9*) Rodale Pr Inc.

Men's Health Books Staff, et al. Age Erasers for Men: Hundreds of Fast & Easy Ways to Beat the Years. (Illus.). 500p. 1994. text 27.95 (*0-87596-213-0*) Rodale Pr Inc.

— Powerfully Fit: Dozens of Ways to Boost Strength, Increase Endurance, & Chisel Your Body. LC 95-25484. (Men's Health Life Improvement Guides Ser.). (Illus.). 176p. (Orig.). 1996. pap. 14.95 (*0-87596-279-3*) Rodale Pr Inc.

Men's Health Books Staff, ed. see Bauman, Alisa & Kaufman, Brian.

Men's Health Books Staff, ed. see Caine, K. Winston & Garfinkel, Perry.

Men's Health Magazine Editors. Men's Health - a Guide to Staying Young. 320p. 1995. reprint ed. 7.98 (*1-56731-069-9*, MJF Bks) Fine Comms.

Mens Health Magazine Editors, MEN HLTH MAG. Mens Health Day Log98. 1997. spiral bd. 14.95 (*0-87596-431-1*, Pub. by Rodale Pr Inc) St Martin.

***Men's Journal Staff.** The Great Life: A Man's Guide to Sports, Skills, Fitness & Serious Fun. Evans, Sid, ed. (Illus.). 384p. 2000. pap. 19.00 (*0-14-029626-3*) Penguin Putnam.

Mensa, Dean L. High Resolution Radar Cross-Section Imaging. fac. ed. LC 90-1140. (Artech House Radar Library). (Illus.). 283p. 1991. reprint ed. pap. 87.80 (*0-608-00938-5*, 206173000011) Bks Demand.

Mensa Publications Staff. IQ Workout. 1998. pap. text 7.99 (*0-7858-0959-7*) Bk Sales Inc.

MENSA Publications Staff. MENSA Presents Number Puzzles for Math Geniuses. 1993. pap. 13.00 (*0-8129-2214-X*, Times Bks) Crown Pub Group.

— MENSA Presents Word Puzzles for Language Geniuses. 1993. pap. 13.00 (*0-8129-2213-1*, Times Bks) Crown Pub Group.

Mensa Publications Staff. Mind Obstacle Course. 1998. pap. text 7.99 (*0-7858-0955-4*) Bk Sales Inc.

— Word Shapes. 1998. pap. text 7.99 (*0-7858-0958-9*) Bk Sales Inc.

Mensah, Barbara, jt. auth. see Goodman, Andrew.

Mensah, Nsorowa. L. I. F. E. Life Is War. LC 97-90397. 53p. 1998. pap. 8.95 (*0-533-12381-X*) Vantage.

Mensah, Patrick, tr. see Derrida, Jacques.

Mensah, Thomas A., contrib. by. Ocean Governance: Strategies & Approaches for the 21st Century. LC 96-46528. (Proceedings of the Annual Conference of the Law of the Sea Institute Ser.: No. P28). 1996. 58.00 (*0-911189-31-9*) Law Sea Inst.

— Ocean Governance for Hawaii. (Law of the Sea Institute Ser.: Vol. 3). 1995. pap. 15.00 (*0-911189-29-7*) Law Sea Inst.

Mensah, Thomas A., ed. Ocean Governance: Strategies & Approaches for the 21st Century. (Proceedings of the Law of the Sea Institute's Annual Conference Ser.: Vol. 28). 700p. 1996. write for info. (*0-614-23966-4*) Law Sea Inst.

***Mensch, Barbar S.** Uncharted Passage: Girls' Adolescence in the Developing World. LC 98-40824. 31p. 1998. pap. 15.00 (*0-87834-093-9*) Population Coun.

Mensch, Barbara. The Last Waterfront: The People of South Street. LC 84-18779. (Illus.). 188p. 1985. 20.00 (*0-88191-012-0*) Freundlich.

Mensch, Elizabeth & Freeman, Alan. The Politics of Virtue: Is Abortion Debatable? LC 92-41302. 279p. 1993. text 49.95 (*0-8223-1331-6*); pap. text 17.95 (*0-8223-1349-9*) Duke.

Mensch, Elizabeth & Freeman, Alan, eds. Property Law, 2 vols., 1. LC 92-33815. (International Library of Essays in Law & Legal Theory: Vol. 14). (C). 1993. lib. bdg. 125.00 (*0-8147-5488-0*) NYU Pr.

— Property Law, 2 vols., 2. LC 92-33815. (International Library of Essays in Law & Legal Theory: Vol. 14). (C). 1993. lib. bdg. 125.00 (*0-8147-5489-9*) NYU Pr.

— Property Law, 2 vols., Set. LC 92-33815. (International Library of Essays in Law & Legal Theory: Vol. 14). (C). 1993. lib. bdg. 250.00 (*0-8147-5475-9*) NYU Pr.

Mensch, Hermann, jt. auth. see Normann, H.

Mensch, James R. After Modernity: Husserlian Reflections on a Philosophical Tradition. LC 95-33584. (Illus.). 319p. (C). 1996. text 65.50 (*0-7914-2985-7*); pap. text 21.95 (*0-7914-2986-5*) State U NY Pr.

— The Gospel According to St. John: Philosophical Perspectives. LC 91-38847. (American University Studies: Philosophy: Ser. V, Vol. 121). 219p. (C). 1992. text 40.95 (*0-8204-1583-9*) P Lang Pubng.

— Intersubjectivity & Transcendental Idealism. LC 87-18047. (SUNY Series in Contemporary Continental Philosophy). 430p. (C). 1988. pap. text 21.95 (*0-88706-752-2*) State U NY Pr.

— Knowing & Being: A Postmodern Reversal. LC 97-18014. (Illus.). 232p. 1996. 50.00 (*0-271-01554-3*); pap. 18.95 (*0-271-01555-1*) Pa St U Pr.

Menschell, Mindy. J My Name Is Jess: Big Book. large type ed. (Little Books & Big Bks.). (Illus.). 8p. (J). (ps-1). 1998. pap. text 19.89 (*0-8215-0871-7*) Sadlier.

Mensching, Glenn E., Jr. & Mensching, Teresa B., eds. Coping with Information Illiteracy: Bibliographic Instruction for the Information Age. (Library Orientation Ser.: No. 20). 202p. 1990. pap. 35.00 (*0-87650-267-2*) Pierian.

***Mensching, Guido.** Infinitive Constructions with Specified Subjects: A Syntactic Analysis of the Romance Languages. LC 99-38156. (Oxford Studies in Comparative Syntax). 336p. 2000. pap. 29.95 (*0-19-513304-8*); text 60.00 (*0-19-513303-X*) OUP.

Mensching, Herausgegeben V. & Rottgen, Karl-Heinz. Studien Zu Romanischen Fachtexten Aus Mittelalter und Fruher Neuzeit. (Romanistische Texte und Studien: Bd. 6). (GER.). 1995. write for info. (*3-487-09944-6*) G Olms Pubs.

Mensching, Teresa B., ed. Reaching & Teaching Diverse Library User Groups. (Library Orientation Ser.: No. 19). 169p. 1989. pap. 35.00 (*0-87650-258-3*) Pierian.

Mensching, Teresa B. & Stanger, Keith J., eds. Bibliographic Instruction & Computer Database Searching. (Library Orientation Ser.: No. 17). 173p. 1988. pap. 35.00 (*0-87650-251-6*) Pierian.

Mensching, Teresa B., jt. ed. see Bunge, Mary B.

Mensching, Teresa B., jt. ed. see Mensching, Glenn E., Jr.

Mensching, Wilhelm. Conscience. LC 61-16821. (Orig.). 1961. pap. 4.00 (*0-87574-117-7*) Pendle Hill.

Mense, Siegfried & Simons, David. Muscle Pain: Understanding Its Nature, Diagnosis & Treatment. 304p. 65.00 (*0-683-05928-9*) Lppncott W & W.

Menser, Gery P. Hallucinogenic & Poisonous Mushroom Field Guide. 2nd ed. (Illus.). 146p. (Orig.). 1996. pap. 14.95 (*0-914171-89-5*) Ronin Pub.

Mensh, Elaine & Mensh, Harry. Black, White, & "Huckleberry Finn" Re-Imagining the American Dream. LC 99-6204. 1999. 29.95 (*0-8173-0995-0*) U of Ala Pr.

— The IQ Mythology: Class, Race, & Inequality. 160p. (C). 1991. 19.95 (*0-8093-1666-8*) S Ill U Pr.

Mensh, Harry, jt. auth. see Mensh, Elaine.

Mensh, Stephanie, jt. auth. see Berger, Paul.

Mensh, Stephanie, jt. auth. see Berger, Paul E.

***Mensha Ridge Press Staff.** Unofficial Guide to Bed & Breakfasts in the Southeast. (Unofficial Guides Ser.). (Illus.). 400p. 2000. pap. 16.99 (*0-7645-6222-3*) IDG Bks.

***Mensha Ridge Press Staff, ed.** Unofficial Guide to Disneyland 2001. (Illus.). 304p. 2000. pap. 13.99 (*0-02-863726-7*) Macmillan Gen Ref.

An Asterisk (*) at the beginning of an entry indicates that the title is appearing for the first time.

— Unofficial Guide to Walt Disney World 2001. (Illus.). 768p. 2000. pap. 16.99 (0-02-863727-5) Macmillan Gen Ref.

Mensier, Paul. Dictionnaire des Huiles Vegetales. (FRE.). 771p. 1957. pap. 165.00 (0-7859-7964-6, 2720504211) Fr & Eur.

Mensing, Katia Von, see Von Mensing, Katia.

Mensing, Margo, jt. auth. see Ziek, Bhakti.

Mensing, Steve. Gold in the Black Hills. (Orig.). 1993. 13.00 (0-86025-203-5, Pub. by I Henry Pubns) Empire Pub Srvs.

— Hell Riders. large type ed. (Linford Western Library). 272p. (Orig.). 1985. pap. 16.99 (0-7089-6083-9) Ulverscroft.

Menski, Werner. Coping with 1997: Gems 2. 1995. pap. 18.00 (0-948080-99-X, Trentham Bks) Stylus Pub VA.

***Menskifi, M. B.** Quantum Measurements & Decoherence: Models & Phenomenology. LC 00-28408. (Fundamental Theories of Physics Ser.). 2000. write for info. (0-7923-6227-6) Kluwer Academic.

Mensky, M. B. Continuous Quantum Measurements & Path Integrals. (Illus.). 188p. 1993. 126.00 (0-7503-0228-3) IOP Pub.

Men'Sov, D. E. Limits of Indeterminacy in Measure of T-Means of Subseries of a Trigonometric Series. LC 81-14992. (Steklov Institute of Mathematics Ser.: No. 149). 56p. 1981. pap. 34.00 (0-8218-3043-0, STEKLO/149) Am Math.

Ment, Merriam. First Start in Spanish Activity. 1994. pap. 7.95 (0-8442-7532-8) NTC Contemp Pub Co.

Menta, Ed. The Magic World Behind the Curtain: Andrei Serban in the American Theatre. 2nd ed. LC 94-22375. (Artists & Issues in the Theatre Ser.: Vol. 5). (Illus.). XIV, 208p. (C). 1997. reprint ed. pap. 22.95 (0-8204-3728-X) P Lang Pubng.

Mentasi, Rosa B. Venetian Glass, 1890-1990. (Illus.). 208p. 1992. 95.00 (88-7743-119-9, Pub. by Arsenale Editrice) Antique Collect.

Mente, B. Etiquette Guide to Japan. 154p. 1995. pap. text 5.95 (4-900737-04-6, Pub. by Yen Bks) Tuttle Pubng.

Mente, Boye De, see De Mente, Boye.

Mentel. Short Cuts B2. 1997. 13.13 (0-07-041890-X) McGraw.

— Short Cuts B3. 1997. 13.13 (0-07-042020-3) McGraw.

Mentel, James R. Short Cuts: An Interactive English Course, Vol. 1. 196p. (C). 1996. pap. 14.06 (0-07-041886-1) McGraw.

— Short Cuts: An Interactive English Course, Vol. 2. (C). 1996. pap. text 13.13 (0-07-041891-8) McGraw.

— Short Cuts: An Interactive English Course, Vol. 2. LC 96-77577. 192p. (C). 1996. pap. 14.06 (0-07-041887-X) McGraw.

Mentel, James R., jt. auth. see Hartmann, Pamela.

Mentel, Jim, jt. auth. see Hartmann, Pamela.

Menten. Victorian Parlor. 1998. pap. 3.95 (0-486-23115-1) Dover.

Menten, T. Little Animals Stained Glass Book. 1991. text 1.00 (0-486-25733-9) Dover.

Menten, T. Little Halloween Stained Glass. (J). 1991. pap. 1.00 (0-486-25736-3) Dover.

Menten, Ted. Easy-to-Duplicate Menu Designs: 60 Copyright-Free Forms. (Quick Copy Ser.). (Illus.). 48p. 1986. pap. 5.95 (0-486-25173-X) Dover.

— Easy-to-Duplicate Sales Designs: 58 Copyright-Free Forms. (Quick Copy Ser.). (Illus.). 48p. 1986. pap. text 4.95 (0-486-25192-6) Dover.

— Ready-to-Use Art Deco Borders on Layout Grids. (Clip Art Ser.). (Illus.). 64p. 1988. text 5.95 (0-486-25732-0) Dover.

— Ready-to-Use Art Deco Small Frames & Borders. (Clip Art Ser.). (Illus.). 64p. 1987. pap. text 5.95 (0-486-25343-0) Dover.

— Ready-to-Use Christmas & New Year's Mortised Cuts. (Clip Art Ser.). (Illus.). 64p. 1987. pap. 4.95 (0-486-25443-7) Dover.

— Ready-to-Use Decorative Corners. (Clip Art Ser.). (Illus.). 64p. 1987. pap. 5.95 (0-486-25303-1) Dover.

— Ready-to-Use Santa Claus Illustrations. (Clip Art Ser.). (Illus.). 64p. 1986. pap. 4.95 (0-486-25155-1) Dover.

— Ready-to-Use Starbursts. (Clip Art Ser.). (Illus.). 64p. 1986. pap. 5.95 (0-486-25050-4) Dover.

— Ready-to-Use Victorian Borders. (Clip Art Ser.). (Illus.). 64p. 1986. pap. 5.95 (0-486-25190-X) Dover.

Menten, Theodore. After Goodbye: How to Begin Again after the Death of Someone You Love. LC 93-85506. 128p. 1994. 12.95 (1-56138-295-7) Running Pr.

— Art Deco Cut & Use Stencils, Vol. 181. (J). 1977. pap. 5.95 (0-486-23551-3) Dover.

— Art Nouveau Decorative Ironwork: One Hundred & Fifty Photographic Illustrations. (Illus.). 128p. 1981. pap. 9.95 (0-486-23986-1) Dover.

— Baby Bears, Bunnies & Other Little Critters. 81st ed. 1985. pap. 3.95 (0-486-24782-1) Dover.

Menten, Theodore. Baby Teddy Bear Sticker Paper Doll. (Illus.). (J). 1991. pap. 1.00 (0-486-26839-X) Dover.

Menten, Theodore. Clown Masks Punch Out Stencils. 81st ed. (Toy Bks.). (Illus.). 16p. 1984. pap. 3.95 (0-486-24633-7) Dover.

— Cut & Use Stencil Bunny Rabbit. 81st ed. (J). 1985. pap. 6.95 (0-486-24909-3) Dover.

— Decorative Labels for Home Canning. 1975. pap. 4.95 (0-486-23219-0) Dover.

— Easy to Duplicate News Designs. 1986. pap. 5.95 (0-486-25216-7) Dover.

— Favorite Storybook Characters. 81st ed. 1987. pap. 5.95 (0-486-25448-8) Dover.

— Folk Art Cut & Use Stencils. (J). 1985. pap. 5.95 (0-486-24838-0) Dover.

— Gentle Closings: How to Say Goodbye to Someone You Love. LC 91-52787. 160p. 1992. 12.95 (1-56138-004-0) Running Pr.

— Illuminated Alphabet. (Illus.). 48p. 1971. pap. 4.95 (0-486-22745-6) Dover.

— Make Your Own Teddy Bear Calendar Coloring Book, Vol. 181. (Illus.). (J). 1991. pap. 2.50 (0-486-26911-6) Dover.

— Ready-to-Use Art Deco Borders. 81st ed. 64p. (Orig.). 1985. pap. 5.95 (0-486-24967-0) Dover.

— Ready-to-Use Art Nouveau Borders. (Illus.). 64p. (Orig.). 1983. pap. 5.95 (0-486-24431-8) Dover.

— Ready-to-Use Art Nouveau Small Frames & Borders. 81st ed. 64p. (Orig.). 1985. pap. 5.95 (0-486-24975-1) Dover.

— Ready-to-Use Banners. (Clip Art Ser.). (Illus.). 1979. pap. 5.95 (0-486-23899-7) Dover.

— Ready-to-Use Teddy Bear Illustrations. 81st ed. 64p. (Orig.). 1985. pap. 5.95 (0-486-24943-3) Dover.

— Ships & Boats Punch Out Stencils. (J). 1986. pap. 3.95 (0-486-25049-0) Dover.

— Teddy Bear-Cut & Use Stencils. (J). 1983. pap. 5.95 (0-486-24595-0) Dover.

— Teddy Bear Punch Out Stencils. 81st ed. (J). 1985. pap. 3.95 (0-486-24832-1) Dover.

— Teddy Bear Sticker Paper Doll. 80th ed. (Illus.). (J). (gr. k-3). 1990. pap. 1.00 (0-486-26235-9) Dover.

— Teddy Bear Stickers & Seals. 1985. 3.95 (0-486-24928-X) Dover.

— Victorian Fashion Paper Dolls from Harper's Bazaar, 1867-1898. (Illus.). (J). 1977. pap. 4.95 (0-486-23453-3) Dover.

Menten, Theodore. Wizard of Oz: Postcard Book. (Illus.). 1986. pap. 4.95 (0-486-25033-4) Dover.

Menten, Theodore, ed. Advertising Art in the Art Deco Style. LC 74-27703. (Pictorial Archive Ser.). (Illus.). 175p. 1975. pap. 11.95 (0-486-23164-X) Dover.

— The Art Deco Style in Household Objects, Architecture, Sculpture, Graphics, Jewelry. (Illus.). 183p. (Orig.). 1972. pap. 11.95 (0-486-22824-X) Dover.

— Chinese Cut Paper Designs. LC 75-22240. (Pictorial Archive Ser.). (Illus.). 97p. (Orig.). 1975. pap. 6.95 (0-486-23198-4) Dover.

— Japanese Border Designs. LC 75-13124. (Pictorial Archive Ser.). Orig. Title: Kodal Moshiki Zuko. (Illus.). 96p. 1975. reprint ed. pap. 5.95 (0-486-23180-1) Dover.

— Ready-to-Use Arrows. (Clip Art Ser.). (Illus.). 1979. pap. 4.95 (0-486-23783-4) Dover.

— Ready-to-Use Borders. (Clip Art Ser.). (Illus.). 1979. pap. 4.95 (0-486-23782-6) Dover.

— Ready-to-Use Headlines. (Clip Art Ser.). 1979. pap. 4.95 (0-486-23454-1) Dover.

Menten, Theodore, ed. see Clusius, Carolus.

Menten, Theodore, ed. see Munting, Abraham.

Menter, Ian. Work & Identity in the Primary School: A Post-Fordist Analysis. LC 96-19874. 160p. 1996. 88.95 (0-335-19724-8) OpUniv Pr.

Menter, Ian, et al. Work & Identity in the Primary School: A Post-Fordist Analysis. LC 96-19874. 160p. 1996. pap. 30.95 (0-335-19723-X) OpUniv Pr.

Menteshashvili, Avtandil. Trouble in the Caucasus. (Illus.). 107p. (C). 1994. lib. bdg. 65.00 (1-56072-177-4) Nova Sci Pubs.

Menteshashvili, Z. R., jt. ed. see Garsevanishvili, V. R.

Mentgen, Janet & Bulbrook, Mary Jo. Healing Touch: Level I Notebook. 100p. 1994. pap. text 12.00 (1-889293-01-6) NC Ctr Healing.

— Healing Touch: Level I Notebook. 100p. 2000. pap. text 15.00 (1-889293-08-3) NC Ctr Healing.

— Healing Touch: Level II Notebook. 206p. 1995. pap. text 20.00 (1-889293-02-4) NC Ctr Healing.

— Healing Touch: Level II Notebook. 175p. 2000. pap. text 20.00 (1-889293-07-5) NC Ctr Healing.

Mentha, Jean-Pierre, tr. see Hyvrard, Jeanne.

Mentienne, A. La Decouverte de la Photographie en 1839. Bunnell, Peter C. & Sobieszek, Robert A., eds. LC 76-23037. (Sources of Modern Photography Ser.). (FRE.). 1979. reprint ed. lib. bdg. 15.95 (0-405-09600-3) Ayer.

Menting, Peter. The Last Crusade: A Novel. LC 92-3346. 148p. (Orig.). 1993. pap. 14.95 (0-86534-158-3) Sunstone Pr.

Mention, Philippe & Ramio, Christian. Cartridges of the Gras System. LC 88-82737. (Illus.). 147p. 1988. 37.95 (0-939683-02-4) Armory Pubns.

Mentis, Mandia, jt. ed. see Skuy, Mervyn.

Mentkowski, Marcia. Learning That Lasts: Integrating Learning, Development & Performance in College & Beyond. LC 99-50759. 576p. 2000. 38.95 (0-7879-4482-3) Jossey-Bass.

Mentley, Kaye W., jt. auth. see Ludwig, Sally A.

Menton, Jane. The Grove a Florida Home Through Seven Generations. LC 98-61133. (Illus.). 160p. 1998. write for info. (1-889574-06-1) Sentry Press.

Menton, Jane A. The Grove: The History of a Florida Home & the Family That Loved It Through Seven Generations. (Illus.). 140p. 1998. write for info. (1-889574-05-8) Sentry Press.

Menton, Linda K., jt. auth. see Tamura, Eileen H.

Menton, Seymour. El Cuento Hispanoamericano: Antologia Critico-Historica. 3rd ed. (Coleccion Popular Ser.). (SPA.). 1994. pap. 15.99 (968-16-0016-9) Fondo.

— Latin America's New Historical Novel. LC 93-787. (Texas Pan American Ser.). 240p. (C). 1993. text 30.00 (0-292-75157-5) U of Tex Pr.

— Prose Fiction of the Cuban Revolution. LC 75-5993. (Latin American Monographs: No. 37). 364p. reprint ed. pap. 112.90 (0-8357-7713-8, 203607000002) Bks Demand.

Menton, Seymour & Herrera-Sobek, Maria, eds. Saga de Mexico. LC 91-33663. 348p. 1991. pap. 22.00 (0-927534-11-8) Biling Rev-Pr.

Menton, Seymour, jt. ed. see Martins, Wilson.

Menton, Seymour, tr. see Cepeda Samudio, Alvaro.

Mentor Circle of Poets Staff. One Score & Two Years of Uncommon Fanfare: Anthology of Award-Winning Poems from the Annual Poetry Contests Sponsored by the North American Mentor Magazine, 1964-1985. LC 85-52334. (Illus.). xii, 244p. 1986. pap. 10.00 (0-87423-040-3) Westburg.

Mentor Editorial Staff, jt. auth. see Schubi Editorial Staff.

Mentre, Mireille. The Illuminated Manuscripts of Medieval Spain. LC 96-60236. (Illus.). 304p. 1997. 75.00 (0-500-01732-8, Pub. by Thames Hudson) Norton.

Mentre, Paul. The Fund, Commercial Banks & Member Countries. (Occasional Papers: No. 26). 39p. 1984. pap. 5.00 (1-55775-067-X) Intl Monetary.

Ments, Morry Van, see Van Ments, Morry.

Mentschikoff, Soia & Stotzky, Irwin R. The Theory & Craft of American Law. LC 80-70678. 1981. write for info. (0-8205-0211-1, 382) Bender.

Mentzas, Ioannis, jt. auth. see Machida, Soho.

***Mentze, Mark J.** Pass the EXCET on Your First Try: Study Manual for the Texas EXCET Exam: Professional Development. LC 99-63369. (Illus.). 85p. 1999. pap. 28.95 (0-9671860-0-5) Express Design.

Mentzel, Sven-Morten. Real Exchange Rate Movements: An Econometric Investigation into Causes of Fluctuations in Some Dollar Real Exchange Rates. LC 97-51873. (Contributions to Economics Ser.). (Illus.). x, 109p. 1998. pap. 56.00 (3-7908-1081-9) Spr-Verlag.

Mentzer, John T. & Bienstock, Carol C. Sales Forecasting Management: Understanding the Techniques, Systems, & Management of the Sales Forecasting Process. LC 97-33746. 274p. 1998. 67.00 incl. audio compact disk (0-7619-0823-4); pap. write for info. (0-7619-0822-6) Sage.

Mentzer, M. Electro-Optic Technology & Applications. (Optical Engineering Ser.). Date not set. write for info. (0-8247-9933-X) Dekker.

Mentzer, Mark A. Principles of Optical Circuit Engineering. (Optical Engineering Ser.: Vol. 26). (Illus.). 328p. 1990. text 155.00 (0-8247-8202-X) Dekker.

Mentzer, Mark A. & Ziegler, David C. Living with Epilepsy. LC 81-71463. (Illus.). 144p. (Orig.). 1981. pap. 7.95 (0-9607240-0-1) Bubba Pr.

Mentzer, Mike. Mike Mentzer's High Intensity Training Program: Secrets to Building Muscles in Minutes. 40p. 1997. 39.95 incl. audio (1-889462-02-0) Advanced Research Pr.

Mentzer, Raymond A., Jr. Blood & Belief: Family Survival & Confessional Identity among the Provincial Huguenot Nobility. LC 93-25955. 280p. 1994. 38.95 (1-55753-041-6) Purdue U Pr.

Mentzer, Raymond A., ed. Sin & the Calvinists: Morals Control & the Consistory in the Reformed Tradition. LC 94-25541. (Sixteenth Century Essays & Studies: Vol. 32). 206p. 1995. 40.00 (0-940474-34-4, SCJP) Truman St Univ.

Mentzer, Richard C. The Core Package. Longdom, Danny G., ed. LC 79-23416. (Instructional Design Library). 124p. 1980. 27.95 (0-87778-141-9) Educ Tech Pubns.

Mentzer, Robert M. Adenosine, Cardioprotection, & Its Clinical Application. LC 97-14689. (Developments in Cardiovascular Medicine Ser.). 256p. 1997. text 55.00 (0-7923-9954-4) Kluwer Academic.

Mentzer, William C. & Wagner, Gail M., eds. The Hereditary Hemolytic Anemias. fac. ed. LC 88-23751. (Illus.). 488p. 1989. reprint ed. pap. 151.30 (0-7837-7889-9, 204764500007) Bks Demand.

Mentzos, John, jt. ed. see Katz, Judith.

Menu, Bernadette. Ramses II, Greatest of the Pharaohs. LC 98-43843. (Discoveries Ser.). 1999. 12.95 (0-8109-2870-1, Pub. by Abrams) Time Warner.

Menu, J., jt. auth. see Parkhouse, J.

Menuez, Doug & Kounalakis, Markos. Defying Gravity: The Making of Newton. Livingston, Julie, ed. (Illus.). 192p. 1993. 29.95 (0-941831-94-9) Beyond Words Pub.

Menuge, Angus J. Christ & Culture in Dialogue: Constructive Themes & Practical Applications. LC 99-13295. 336p. 1999. pap. 19.95 (0-570-04273-9) Concordia.

***Menuge, Noel James.** Medieval Women & the Law. LC 00-28941. 192p. 2000. 75.00 (0-85115-775-0) Boydell & Brewer.

Menuhin, Yehudi. Unfinished Journey: Twenty Years Later. (Illus.). 544p. 1999. pap. 19.00 (0-88064-229-7) Fromm Intl Pub.

— Unfinished Journey: Twenty Years Later. expanded ed. LC 97-9122. (Illus.). 552p. 1997. 35.00 (0-88064-179-7) Fromm Intl Pub.

— Violin. (Illus.). 304p. 1996. 50.00 (2-08-013623-2, Pub. by Flammarion) Abbeville Pr.

Menuhin, Yehudi, et al. Violin & Viola. (Illus.). 1976. write for info. (0-318-54251-X); pap. 9.95 (0-685-03273-6) Macmillan.

Menunqua. Medicine Bear. 72p. 1997. pap. 10.95 (1-882376-50-1) Thunder Bay Pr.

Menut, Albert D., tr. Nicole Oresme: Highlights from His French Commentary on Aristotle's Politics. 237p. 1979. 25.00 (0-87291-132-2) Coronado Pr.

Menut, Albert D., ed. & tr. see Oresme, Nicole.

Menville, Douglas A. A Historical & Critical Survey of the Science Fiction Film. LC 74-16509. (Science Fiction Ser.). 177p. 1977. 16.95 (0-405-06330-X) Ayer.

— The Work of Ross Rocklynne: An Annotated Bibliography & Guide. Clarke, Boden, ed. LC 88-34360. (Bibliographies of Modern Authors Ser.: No. 17). 70p. (C). 1989. pap. 13.00 (0-8095-1511-3) Millefleurs.

Menville, Douglas A. & Reginald, R. Things to Come: An Illustrated History of the Science Fiction Film. LC 83-8789. 212p. 1983. reprint ed. lib. bdg. 33.00 (0-89370-019-3) Millefleurs.

Menville, Douglas A., jt. auth. see Wakefield, H. Russell.

Menville, Douglas A., ed. see Ainsworth, William H.

Menville, Douglas A., ed. see Arlen, Michael J.

Menville, Douglas A., ed. see Balzac, Honore de.

Menville, Douglas A., ed. see Benson, Edward F.

Menville, Douglas A., ed. see Blackwood, Algernon.

Menville, Douglas A., ed. see Boothby, Guy.

Menville, Douglas A., ed. see Burrage, Alfred McLelland.

Menville, Douglas A., ed. see Campbell, Praed.

Menville, Douglas A., ed. see Carew, Henry.

Menville, Douglas A., ed. see Carnegie, James.

Menville, Douglas A., ed. see Coppard, Alfred E.

Menville, Douglas A., ed. see Crawford, Francis M.

Menville, Douglas A., ed. see Dalton.

Menville, Douglas A., ed. see De La Mare, Walter J.

Menville, Douglas A., ed. see Doughty, Francis W.

Menville, Douglas A., ed. see Erckmann, Emile & Erckmann, Alexandre.

Menville, Douglas A., ed. see Ewers, Hanns H.

Menville, Douglas A., ed. see Fielding, Henry.

Menville, Douglas A., ed. see Gautier, Theophile.

Menville, Douglas A., ed. see Griffith, George.

Menville, Douglas A., ed. see Hadley, George.

Menville, Douglas A., ed. see Haggard, H. Rider.

Menville, Douglas A., ed. see Harvey, William F.

Menville, Douglas A., ed. see Hecht, Ben.

Menville, Douglas A., ed. see Heron-Allen, Edward.

Menville, Douglas A., ed. see Holmes, Oliver W.

Menville, Douglas A., ed. see Housman, Clemence.

Menville, Douglas A., ed. see Ingram, Elanor M.

Menville, Douglas A., ed. see James, Montague R.

Menville, Douglas A., ed. see Keller, David H.

Menville, Douglas A., ed. see Machen, Arthur.

Menville, Douglas A., ed. see MacKay, Mary.

Menville, Douglas A., ed. see Marrat, Florence.

Menville, Douglas A., ed. see Moresby, Lily & Beck, Adams.

Menville, Douglas A., ed. see Odell, Eric.

Menville, Douglas A., ed. see O'Donnell, Elliot.

Menville, Douglas A., ed. see Paget, Violet.

Menville, Douglas A., ed. see Paine, Albert B.

Menville, Douglas A., ed. see Phillpotts, Eden.

Menville, Douglas A., ed. see Powys, John Cowper.

Menville, Douglas A., jt. ed. see Reginald, R.

Menville, Douglas A., ed. see Reynolds, George W.

Menville, Douglas A., ed. see Sicard, Clara.

Menville, Douglas A., ed. see Stewart, Mary L.

Menville, Douglas A., ed. see Viereck, George S.

Menville, Douglas A., ed. see Vivan, Charles E.

Menville, Douglas A., ed. see Ward, Arthur Henry Sarsfield.

Menville, Douglas A., ed. see Whiting, Sydney.

Meny, Yves & Knapp, Andrew. Government & Politics in Western Europe: Britain, France, Italy, Germany. 3rd ed. LC 98-2539. (Illus.). 508p. 1998. text 75.00 (0-19-878222-5); pap. text 24.95 (0-19-878221-7) OUP.

Meny, Yves & Wright, Vincent, eds. The Politics of Steel: Western Europe & the Steel Industry in the Crisis Years (1974-1984) (European University Institute, Series C (Political & Social Science): No. 7). x, 812p. 1986. lib. bdg. 242.35 (3-11-010517-9) De Gruyter.

Meny, Yves, et al. Adjusting to Europe: The Impact of the European Union on National Institutions & Policies. LC 96-19654. (European Public Policy Ser.). (Illus.). 200p. (C). 1996. pap. 25.99 (0-415-14409-4) Routledge.

Meny, Yves, jt. auth. see DellaPorta, Donatella.

Meny, Yves, jt. auth. see Duhamel, Olivier.

Menyuk, Curtis R., jt. ed. see Willner, Alan E.

Menyuk, Paula. The Development of Speech. LC 74-173981. (Studies in Communicative Disorders). 1972. pap. text 2.15 (0-672-61276-3, Bobbs) Macmillan.

— Language & Maturation. 1981. pap. text 12.00 (0-262-63075-3) MIT Pr.

— Reading & Linguistic Development. Chall, Jeanne S., ed. LC 99-11226. (From Reading Research to Practice Ser.: Vol. 4). 64p. 1999. pap. 9.95 (1-57129-071-0) Brookline Bks.

— Sentences Children Use. 1969. 10.00 (0-262-13045-9) MIT Pr.

— Sentences Children Use. (Press Research Monographs: No. 52). 176p. 1972. pap. text 12.00 (0-262-63043-5) MIT Pr.

Menyuk, Paula, et al. Early Language Development in Full-Time & Premature Infants. 256p. 1995. 59.95 (0-8058-1772-7); pap. 32.50 (0-8058-1773-5) L Erlbaum Assocs.

Menz, A. The Fishery Potential & Productivity of the Pelagic Zone of Lake Malawi, Niassa. 1995. pap. 25.00 (0-902500-57-0, Pub. by Nat Res Inst) St Mut.

Menz, Deb. Color in Spinning. LC 97-43428. (Illus.). 240p. 1998. 39.95 (1-883010-37-3) Interweave.

Menz, Fredric C. & Stevens, Sarah A., eds. Economic Opportunities in Freer U. S. Trade with Canada. LC 90-34663. 203p. (C). 1991. pap. text 21.95 (0-7914-0531-1) State U NY Pr.

Menz, Fredric C., jt. auth. see Mutti.

Menz, Kenneth M. Rainfed Rice Production in the Philippines: A Combined Agronomic-Economic Study. 90p. 1989. pap. 90.00 (0-949511-73-0, Pub. by ACIAR) St Mut.

— Rice Production in Sri Lanka: A Combined Agronomic-Economic Study in the Intermediate & Dry Zones. 1990. pap. 63.00 (1-86320-022-3, Pub. by ACIAR) St Mut.

— Weed Control Economics. Tisdell, Clement A. et al, eds. (Applied Botany & Crop Science Ser.). 177p. 1987. text 83.00 (0-12-068278-8) Acad Pr.

Menz, Kenneth M., et al, eds. Economics of Fishery Management in the Pacific Islands Region. 169p. 1989. pap. 117.00 (0-949511-95-1, Pub. by ACIAR) St Mut.

Menz, Kenneth M., jt. auth. see Fleming, E. M.

M

An Asterisk (*) at the beginning of an entry indicates that the title is appearing for the first time.

M

Menz, Kenneth M., jt. ed. see Ryland, G. J.

Menz, Robert L. A Memoir of a Pastoral Counseling Practice. LC 97-10894. 95p. 1997. 29.95 (0-7890-0268-X, Haworth Pastrl); pap. 14.95 (0-7890-0269-8, Haworth Pastrl) Haworth Pr.

Menz, W., jt. auth. see Fukuda, T.

Menza, Claudia. Cage of Wild Cries. 1991. pap. 12.95 (0-88962-445-3) Mosaic.

Menze, Clemens. Bildung und Bildungswesen. (Hildesheimer Beitrage Zu Den Erziehungs und Sozial Wissenschaften Ser.: Bd. 13). (GER.). 236p. 1980. 25.00 (3-487-07008-1) G Olms Pubs.

Menze, Dietmar W. Baryons: Proceedings of the 8th International Conference on the Structure of Baryons Bonn, Germa. 880p. 1999. 128.00 (981-02-3865-7) World Scientific Pub.

Menze, Ernest A., ed. & tr. see Herder, Johann G.

Menze, Ernest A., tr. see Kinder, Herman & Hilgemann, Werner.

Menze, Scott A., jt. auth. see Davis, Jeffrey G.

Menzefricke, Ulrich. Statistics for Managers. 682p. 1994. text 97.95 (0-534-23538-7) Wadsworth Pub.

Menzel. Fingerprint Detection with Lasers. 2nd ed. LC 99-18798. (Illus.). 312p. 1999. text 85.00 (0-8247-1974-3) Dekker.

Menzel, Randolf, jt. auth. see Frederici, Angela D.

Menzel, Adolf. Hellenika. Vlastos, Gregory, ed. LC 78-19372. (Morals & Law in Ancient Greece Ser.). (GER & GRE.). 1979. reprint ed. lib. bdg. 17.95 (0-405-11562-8) Ayer.

Menzel, Adolph F. Von, see Von Menzel, Adolph F.

Menzel, Barbara J. Would You Rather? LC 81-6810. (Illus.). 32p. (J). (ps-3). 1982. 16.95 (0-89885-076-2, Kluwer Acad Hman Sci) Kluwer Academic.

Menzel, David W., ed. Ocean Processes: U. S. Southeast Continental Shelf: A Summary of Research Conducted in the South Atlantic Bight under the Auspices of the U. S. Department of Energy from 1977 to 1991. LC 93-13553. 112p. 1993. pap. 27.00 (0-87079-598-8, DE93010744); fiche 12.50 (0-87079-599-6, DE93010744) DOE.

Menzel, Donald C., ed. The American County: Frontiers of Knowledge. (Illus.). 272p. 1996. pap. text 29.95 (0-8173-0803-2) U of Ala Pr.

Menzel, Donald C., jt. ed. see Bowman, James S.

Menzel, Donald H. Fundamental Formulas of Physics, 2 vols., Vol. 1. 2nd ed. (Illus.). 1960. pap. text 11.95 (0-486-60595-7) Dover.

— Fundamental Formulas of Physics, 2 vols., Vol. 2. 2nd ed. (Illus.). 1960. pap. text 11.95 (0-486-60596-5) Dover.

— Mathematical Physics. 412p. 1961. pap. text 11.95 (0-486-60056-4) Dover.

Menzel, Donald H., ed. Radio Noise Spectrum. LC 60-7997. (Illus.). 191p. 1960. 30.50 (0-674-74675-9) HUP.

Menzel, Donald H., ed. see Martin, Martha E.

Menzel, E. Roland. Fingerprint Detection with Lasers. 120p. 1980. text 70.00 (0-8247-6974-0) Dekker.

— An Introduction to Lasers, Forensic Lights & Fluorescent Fingerprint Detection. LC 91-76835. (Illus.). 55p. (Orig.). (C). 1991. pap. 14.95 (0-9622305-6-1, 8-5043) Lightning Powder.

— Laser Spectroscopy: Techniques & Applications. LC 94-5323. (Practical Spectroscopy Ser.: 18). (Illus.). 320p. 1994. text 165.00 (0-8247-9265-3) Dekker.

Menzel, George. Portrait of a Flying Lady. LC 94-60145. (Illus.). 248p. 1994. 29.95 (1-56311-136-5) Turner Pub KY.

Menzel, Nancy N. Workers' Comp Management from A to Z: A "How To" Guide with Forms. 2nd ed. 224p. 1998. spiral bd. 80.00 (1-883595-01-0, 23025, OEM Pr) OEM Health.

Menzel, Paul T. Strong Medicine: The Ethical Rationing of Health Care. 256p. (C). 1990. text 37.95 (0-19-505710-4) OUP.

Menzel, Peter. Material World: A Global Family Portrait. LC 94-8588. (Illus.). 255p. 1994. 35.00 (0-87156-437-8, Pub. by Sierra) Random.

Menzel, Peter & D'Aluisio, Faith. Man Eating Bugs. 1998. text 24.95 (1-58008-051-0) Ten Speed Pr.

— Man Eating Bugs. LC 98-4411. (Illus.). 192p. 1998. pap. 19.95 (1-58008-022-7) Ten Speed Pr.

***Menzel, Peter & D'Aluisio, Faith.** Robo Sapiens: Evolution of a New Species. (Illus.). 240p. (C). 2000. 29.95 (0-262-13382-2, Material Wrld Bks) MIT Pr.

Menzel, Peter & Sierra Club Staff. Material World: A Global Family Portrait. LC 94-8588. (Illus.). 256p. 1995. pap. 25.00 (0-87156-430-0, Pub. by Sierra) Random.

Menzel, Peter, jt. auth. see D'Aluisio, Faith.

Menzel, Peter, jt. auth. see Ramos-Elorduy, Julieta.

***Menzel, Ralf.** Photonics: Using Laser Light as a Tool. LC 00-38820. (Advanced Texts in Physics Ser.). (Illus.). 2000. pap. write for info. (3-540-67074-2) Spr-Verlag.

Menzel, Scott, jt. auth. see Fraser, Bryna S.

Menzel, Scott, jt. auth. see Hubbard, Susan.

Menzel, Scott, jt. auth. see Rogers, Anne M.

Menzel, Sewall H. Bullets versus Ballots: Political Violence & Revolutionary War in El Salvador, 1979-1991. LC 94-772. (University of Miami North-South Center Ser.). 120p. (C). 1994. pap. 14.95 (1-56000-689-7, Pub. by U Miami N-S Ctr) L Rienner.

— Cocaine Quagmire: Implementing the U. S. Anti-Drug Policy in the North Andes-Colombia. LC 97-9257. 232p. 1997. 32.50 (0-7618-0751-9) U Pr of Amer.

— Fire in the Andes: U. S. Foreign Policy & Cocaine Politics in Bolivia & Peru. LC 96-3424. 300p. 1996. lib. bdg. 44.00 (0-7618-0507-9) U Pr of Amer.

— Fire in the Andes: U. S. Foreign Policy & Cocaine Politics in Bolivia & Peru. 300p. (C). 1997. pap. text 27.50 (0-7618-1001-3) U Pr of Amer.

Menzel, Suzanne. A201 Lab Manual: Exercises in C. (C). 1993. student ed. 14.00 (1-881592-28-6) Hayden-McNeil.

Menzel Symposium on High Pressure Steam Curing Sta. Menzel Symposium on High Pressure Steam Curing. Kuenning, W. H., ed. LC 77-186848. (ACI Publication: No. SP-32). (Illus.). 296p. reprint ed. pap. 91.80 (0-7837-5216-4, 204494700005) Bks Demand.

Menzel, Theophil, tr. see Andrae, Tor.

Menzel, Winston. Cytoskeleton of the Algae. 480p. 1992. lib. bdg. 219.00 (0-8493-6679-8, QK565) CRC Pr.

— Estuarine & Marine Bivalve Mollusk Culture. (Illus.). 432p. 1991. lib. bdg. 259.00 (0-8493-4936-2, SH370) CRC Pr.

Menzer, Joe. Carolina Panthers: The First Season of the Most Successful Expansion Team in NFL History. 256p. 1996. 22.95 (0-02-861396-1, Pub. by Macmillan) S&S Trade.

— Four Corners: How UNC, N. C. State, Duke, & Wake Forest Made North Carolina the Crossroads of the Basketball Universe. LC 98-47550. (Illus.). 304p. 1999. 25.00 (0-684-84674-8) Simon & Schuster.

Menzer, Joe & Graeff, Burt. CAVS: From Fitch to Fratello. LC 94-68644. (Illus.). 250p. 1994. 23.95 (1-57167-006-8) Sports Pub.

Menzer, Michael. Fond du Lac: A Gift of the Glacier County. 200p. 1991. lib. bdg. 29.95 (0-9631213-0-8) Fond Du Lac CHS.

Menzer, Robert E., jt. ed. see Ragsdale, Nancy N.

***Menzhausen, J.** Kulturlandschaft Sachsen. (GER., Illus.). 304p. 1998. text 43.00 (90-5705-059-5, Verlag Kunst) Gordon & Breach.

Menzi, Donald W. & Padeh, Zwe. The Tree of Life, The Palace of Adam Kadmon Vol. I: Chayyim Vital's Introduction to the Kabbalah of Isaac Luria. 1998. 50.00 (0-7657-6011-8) Aronson.

Menzies. The Development of Early Christian Pneumatology: With Special Reference to Luke-Acts. (JSNT Supplement Ser.: No. 54). 370p. (C). 1991. 70.00 (1-85075-306-7, Pub. by Sheffield Acad) CUP Services.

***Menzies.** Modern & Past Glacial Environments. 352p. 2000. pap. text 59.95 (0-7506-4226-2) Buttrwrth-Heinemann.

Menzies, Donald, jt. auth. see Dunn, David C.

Menzies, Edna. Storytime. (Illus.). 128p. (J). (gr. 1-3). 1993. pap. 5.95 (1-879224-15-1) Mailbox.

Menzies, Heather. By the Labour of Their Hands: The Story of Ontario Cheddar Cheese. LC 95-118701. (Illus.). 240p. 1994. pap. 19.95 (1-55082-102-1, Pub. by Quarry Pr) LPC InBook.

Menzies, J. & Rose, J., eds. Drumlin Symposium: Proceedings of the Drumlin Symposium-First International Conference on Geomorphology, Manchester, 16-18 September 1985. 362p. 1987. text 136.00 (90-6191-792-1, Pub. by A A Balkema) Ashgate Pub Co.

Menzies, John. Modern Glacial Environments: Processes, Dynamics & Sediments. (Glacial Environments Ser.: Vol. 1). (Illus.). 392p. 1995. pap. text 85.95 (0-7506-2351-9) Buttrwrth-Heinemann.

Menzies, John, ed. Past Glacial Environments: Sediments, Forms & Techniques. LC 95-34315. (Glacier Environments Ser.: Vol. 2). (Illus.). 605p. 1996. pap. text 85.95 (0-7506-2352-7, Prgamon Press) Buttrwrth-Heinemann.

Menzies, Nicholas K. Forest & Land Management in China since the Seventeenth Century. (Studies on the Chinese Economy). 200p. 1994. text 79.95 (0-312-10254-2) St Martin.

Menzies, Nicholas K., jt. auth. see Daniels, Christian.

Menzies, Robert. The Riches of His Grace. 175p. 1956. 9.50 (0-227-67583-5) Attic Pr.

Menzies, Robert G. Central Power in the Australian Commonwealth: An Examination of the Growth of Commonwealth Power in the Australian Federation. LC 67-28061. (Virginia Legal Studies). 208p. reprint ed. pap. 64.50 (0-8357-8061-9, 203397300087) Bks Demand.

Menzies, Robert J. Survival of the Sanest: Order & Disorder in a Pretrial Psychiatric Clinic. 310p. 1989. pap. 18.95 (0-8020-6737-9); text 40.00 (0-8020-5827-2) U of Toronto Pr.

Menzies, Robert J., et al. Abyssal Environment & Ecology of the World Oceans. LC 72-8780. 488p. 1979. 42.50 (0-471-59440-7) Krieger.

Menzies, Robert P. Empowered for Witness: The Spirit in Luke-Acts. (Journal of Pentecostal Theology Supplement Ser.: No. 6). 290p. 1994. pap. 21.95 (1-85075-721-6, Pub. by Sheffield Acad) CUP Services.

Menzies, Robert P., jt. auth. see Menzies, William W.

Menzies, Robert P., jt. ed. see Ma, Wonsuk.

Menzies, S. W., et al. Atlas of the Surface Microscopy of Pigmented Skin Tumors. (Illus.). 208p. 1996. text 74.00 (0-07-470206-8) McGraw-Hill HPD.

Menzies, W. Doctrinas Biblicas Pentecostal.Tr. of Bible Doctrine & Pentecostal. (SPA.). 270p. 1996. pap. 11.99 (0-8297-1853-2) Vida Pubs.

Menzies, William M., jt. auth. see Horton, Stanley M.

Menzies, William W. Anointed to Serve: The Story of the Assemblies of God. LC 79-146707. (Illus.). 436p. 1971. 15.95 (0-88243-465-9, 02-0465) Gospel Pub.

— Understanding the Times of Christ. LC 91-70704. 117p. 1991. reprint ed. pap. 2.95 (0-88243-622-8, 02-0622) Gospel Pub.

Menzies, William W. & Horton, Stanley H. Bible Doctrines: A Pentecostal Perspective. enl. rev. ed. LC 92-43219. 304p. 1993. 20.95 (0-88243-318-0) Gospel Pub.

***Menzies, William W. & Menzies, Robert P.** Power to Serve: A Theology of Pentecost. LC 00-28975. 2000. write for info. (0-310-23507-3) Zondervan.

Menzies, Yve. Living in Italy: The Essential Guide for Property Purchasers & Residents. 5th ed. (Illus.). 224p. 1999. pap. 16.95 (0-7090-6311-3) Seven Hills Bk.

Menzinsky, George & Blomberg, Erik. Sweden: Lion Type Stamps 1862-1872 & Ring Type Stamps 1872-1892. Koplowitz, George B. et al, eds. Ahman, Sven, tr. from SWE. (Illus.). 123p. (Orig.). 1985. pap. text 17.50 (0-936493-05-4) Scand Philatelic.

Menzinsky, George, et al. Sweden Skilling Banco Stamps, 1855-1858 & Black Local Stamp & 1862 Provisional of Local Stamp Type. Stone, Lauson et al, eds. Ahman, Sven, tr. (Illus.). 91p. 1985. pap. text 17.50 (0-936493-06-2) Scand Philatelic.

Menzione, A. & Scribano, A. Calorimetry in High Energy Physics: Proceedings. 696p. 1994. text 124.00 (981-02-1672-6) World Scientific Pub.

Meo, D. De, see Bovo, F.

Meo, Leila. Lebanon, Improbable Nation: A Study in Political Development. LC 75-46621. 246p. 1976. reprint ed. lib. bdg. 65.00 (0-8371-8727-3, MELE, Greenwood Pr) Greenwood.

— U. S. Strategy in the Gulf. (Monographs: No. 14). 130p. (Orig.). 1981. pap. 6.00 (0-937694-50-9) Assn Arab-Amer U Grads.

Meo, Leila, et al. The Arab Boycott of Israel. (Other Works: No. 2). 35p. (Orig.). 1976. pap. text 2.00 (0-937694-12-6) Assn Arab-Amer U Grads.

Meo, Mel, jt. auth. see Groshowski, Nita.

Meola, Patricia E. Summit. LC 98-86342. (Images of America Ser.). 1998. write for info. (0-7524-1349-X) Arcadia Publng.

Meopham, Brian. Commercial Guide to F. I. D. I. C. Conditions of Contract. (Waterlow Practitioner's Library). 352p. 1986. 69.00 (0-08-039234-2, K130, Pergamon Pr) Elsevier.

— Commercial Guide to GC-Works-1 Conditions of Contract. (Waterlow Practitioner's Library). 336p. 1985. 59.00 (0-08-039233-4, Pergamon Pr) Elsevier.

— Commercial Guide to I. C. E. Conditions Contract. (Waterlow Practitioner's Library). 336p. 1985. 59.00 (0-08-039232-6, Pergamon Pr) Elsevier.

Mep, Alan D. & Ulrich, Heidi. Partners for Prosperity: The Group of Seven & the European Community. 53p. (Orig.). (C). 1994. pap. text 25.00 (0-7881-0687-2) DIANE Pub.

Mepham, Ben, ed. Food Ethics. LC 96-2493. (Professional Ethics Ser.). 192p. (C). 1996. 70.00 (0-415-12451-4); pap. 22.99 (0-415-12452-2) Routledge.

Mepham, John. Virginia Woolf: A Literary Life. LC 91-9081. (Literary Lives Ser.). 240p. 1991. text 29.95 (0-312-06204-4) St Martin.

Mepham, Lydie, jt. intro. see Elliott, David.

Mepham, M. J. Accounting in Eighteenth Century Scotland. (Foundations of Accounting Ser.: No. 11). 666p. 1988. text 15.00 (0-8240-6117-9) Garland.

Mepham, Michael S. Computation in Language Text Analysis. LC 75-305923. 242p. reprint ed. pap. 75.10 (0-608-12044-8, 202459100038) Bks Demand.

Mepham, T. B. Physiology of Lactation. 224p. 1991. 255.00 (0-471-93246-9, Wiley-Liss) Wiley.

Mepham, T. B., et al, eds. Issues in Agricultural Bioethics. 413p. 1999. 200.00 (1-897676-23-9, Pub. by Nottingham Univ Pr) St Mut.

Mepham, Virginia, jt. auth. see Molloy, William.

Meppelink, F. Jean. Putting Faith to Work: Lessons of Help & Hope for Women. 118p. 1992. ring bd. 15.00 (0-9657979-3-7) Growing Life.

Meppelink, Jean. Angels in Heaven & Earth. 50p. 1998. pap. 5.00 (0-9657979-4-5) Growing Life.

— Finding God in the Tangles of Life: Lesson from Ruth. 131p. (Orig.). 1994. pap. 6.95 (0-9657979-2-9) Growing Life.

— Peace in the Parsonage: A Handbook for Pastors' Wives. 78p. (Orig.). 1992. pap. 5.95 (0-9657979-0-2) Growing Life.

— Places of Victory: Lessons from Psalm 23. 135p. (Orig.). 1993. pap. 6.95 (0-9657979-1-0) Growing Life.

Mepton, Nancy. Moon Power Starguide, 1999. (Moon Power Ser.: Vol. 5). 314p. 1999. pap. 19.95 (0-9667312-0-4) Startheme Pubns.

Mera, H. P. Spanish-American Blanketry: Its Relationship to Aboriginal Weaving in the Southwest. LC 87-12715. (Illus.). 81p. (Orig.). 1987. pap. 15.95 (0-933452-22-5) Schol Am Res.

Mera, Harry P. Pueblo Designs: One Hundred Seventy-Six Illustrations of the Rain Bird. (Illus.). 113p. 1970. reprint ed. pap. 8.95 (0-486-22073-7) Dover.

— Pueblo Indian Embroidery. LC 94-34722. (Illus.). 80p. 1995. pap. text 6.95 (0-486-28418-2) Dover.

— Reconnaissance & Excavation in Southeastern New Mexico. LC 39-14217. (AAA Memoirs: No. 51). 1938. 25.00 (0-527-00550-9) Periodicals Srv.

— Style Trends in Pueblo Pottery in the Rio Grande & Little Colorado Cultural Areas from the Sixteenth to the Nineteenth Century. LC 76-43776. (Laboratory of Anthropology, Memoirs: Vol. 3). reprint ed. write for info. (0-404-15630-4) AMS Pr.

***Mera, Koichi & Renaud, Bertrand, eds.** Asia's Financial Crisis & the Role of Real Estate. (Illus.). 296p. 2000. 72.95 (0-7656-0641-0) M E Sharpe.

Mera, S. Understanding Disease: Pathology & Prevention. 856p. 1997. pap. (0-7487-3178-4) S Thornes Pubs.

Mera, S. Understanding Disease: Pathology & Prevention. (Illus.). 600p. (C). 1997. pap. text 55.00 (1-56593-428-8, 1095) Singular Publishing.

Merabti, Madjid, et al, eds. Performance Engineering of Computer & Telecommunications Systems: Proceedings of the UKPEW '95, Liverpool John Moores University, 5-6 September 1995. LC 95-53986. ix, 381p. 1996. pap. 69.95 (3-540-76008-3) Spr-Verlag.

***Merad, Ali.** Christian Hermit in an Islamic World: A Muslim's View of Charles de Foucauld. Herzov, Zoe, tr. from FRE. LC 99-47039. 144p. 2000. pap. 12.95 (0-8091-3903-0) Paulist Pr.

Meral, Jean. Paris in American Literature. LC 88-33910. 296p. reprint ed. pap. 91.80 (0-608-08616-9, 206913900003) Bks Demand.

Meran, Patti. Pet Sitting for Profit. 2nd ed. LC 97-27615. 224p. 1997. 17.95 (0-87605-596-X) Howell Bks.

Merandonk, M. Basic Gurkhali Dictionary. 1991. 45.00 (0-7855-0266-1, Pub. by Ratna Pustak Bhandar) St Mut.

Merani, Alberto L. Dictionary of Child Psychiatry & Psychology: Diccionario de Psicologia y Psiquiatria Infantil. (SPA.). 176p. 1983. 28.50 (0-8288-2221-2, S39839) Fr & Eur.

— Dictionary of Psychology: Diccionario de Psicologia. 5th ed. (ENG & SPA.). 280p. 1985. write for info. (0-7859-4968-2) Fr & Eur.

***Merante, Marla.** Scenes of the Ausable River Velley: Twenty Tear-Out Post Cards. 20p. 1999. pap. 10.00 (0-9672668-0-7) Ausable Pr.

Meranto, Philip J. Politics of Federal Aid to Education in 1965: A Study in Political Innovation. LC 67-16846. (Orig.). 1967. pap. 16.95 (0-8156-2107-8) Syracuse U Pr.

Meranze, Michael. Laboratories of Virtue: Punishment, Revolution, & Authority in Philadelphia, 1760-1835. LC 95-45117. (Published for the Institute of Early American History & Culture Ser.). 384p. (C). 1996. text 19.95 (0-8078-2277-9) U of NC Pr.

Merari, Ariel, ed. On Terrorism & Combating Terrorism. LC 84-22037. 188p. 1985. pap. 19.95 (0-313-27061-9, P7061); lib. bdg. 49.95 (0-313-27047-3, U7047) Greenwood.

Meras, Phyllis. Exploring Rhode Island: A Visitor's Guide to the Ocean State. 82p. 1984. pap. 4.95 (0-685-10922-4) Providence Journ.

— The Mermaids of Chenonceaux: And 828 Other Stories. 352p. 1982. 16.95 (0-312-92525-5) St Martin.

Meras, Phyllis & Gannon, Tom. Rhode Island: An Explorer's Guide. 2nd ed. LC 97-24575. (Explorer's Guide Ser.). (Illus.). 296p. (Orig.). 1998. pap. 16.00 (0-88150-391-6, Pub. by Countryman) Norton.

— Rhode Island: An Explorer's Guide. 3rd ed. LC 99-28861. (Explorer's Guide Ser.). (Illus.). 324p. (Orig.). 2000. pap. 17.00 (0-88150-465-3, Pub. by Countryman) Penguin Books.

Merashi, Mehdi, jt. auth. see Marashi, Mehdi.

Meraviglia-Crivelli, Graf. Wappen des Boemischen Adels. (CZE & GER.). 316p. 1990. reprint ed. 152.00 (0-317-03842-7) Szwede Slavic.

Meraw, Ken, ed. see Ahoy, Christopher K. & King, Frederick W.

Meray, Tibor, jt. auth. see Aczel.

Meray, Tibor, jt. auth. see Aczel, Tamas.

Merayo, F. Garcia, see Garcia Merayo, F.

***Merback, Mitchell B.** Thief, The Cross, & The Wheel: Pain & The Spectacle Of Punishment in Medieval & Renaissance Europe. 1999. 42.00 (0-226-52015-3) U Ch Pr.

Merbler, John, jt. auth. see Braaten, Sheldon.

Merbreier, Carter & Riley, Linda C. Television: What's Behind What You See. LC 95-13605. (Illus.). 40p. (J). (gr. 4-7). 1995. 16.00 (0-374-37388-4) FS&G.

Merbs, Charles F., jt. ed. see Miller, R.

Merbury, Charles. A Briefe Discourse of Royall Monarchie, Wherunto Is Added a Collection of Italian Proverbes, Etc. LC 70-38209. (English Experience Ser.: No. 474). 94p. 1972. reprint ed. 20.00 (90-221-0474-5) Walter J Johnson.

Mercadante, Frank. Growing Teen Disciples: Strategies for Really Effective Youth Ministry. LC 98-226455. 304p. 1998. pap. 21.95 (0-87793-652-8) Ave Maria.

Mercadante, Linda A. Victims & Sinners: Spiritual Roots of Addiction & Recovery. LC 96-18498. 256p. (Orig.). 1996. pap. 22.95 (0-664-25508-6) Westminster John Knox.

Mercadel, Walter F. Stutsbear & the Bionic Busboy: My Secret Diary So Stay Out Unless You Are My Friend This Means You. LC 93-78988. (Orig.). 1994. pap. 8.95 (0-9634332-1-0) Lithodendron.

Mercado, Carmen. Teach & Learn Across Culture. Fetterman, David M., ed. (Studies in Education & Culture). 250p. Date not set. text 37.50 (0-8153-0914-7) Garland.

Mercado, Carol. A Voice from the Grave. (Orig.). 1996. mass mkt. 5.99 (0-425-15511-0) Berkley Pub.

Mercado, James. Why? Boddah You? A Collection of Cartoons & Illustrations. (Illus.). 120p. (Orig.). 1996. pap. 9.95 (0-913611-07-7) W E C Plant.

Mercado, Juan C. Building a Nation: The Case of Echeverria. 252p. (C). 1995. lib. bdg. 39.00 (0-7618-0114-6) U Pr of Amer.

Mercado, Julio. Del Camino. (SPA.). 120p. 1923. 1.00 (0-318-14254-6) Hispanic Inst.

Mercado, Leonardo N. The Filipino Mind. LC 94-28262. (Cultural Heritage & Contemporary Change Series III: Vol. 8). 1994. 45.00 (1-56518-063-1); pap. 17.50 (1-56518-064-X) Coun Res Values.

Mercado, Leticia I. Mendez y, see Mendez y Mercado, Leticia I.

Mercado, Mario R. The Evolution of Mozart's Pianistic Style. LC 91-8696. (Illus.). 272p. (C). 1992. 36.95 (0-8093-1690-0) S Ill U Pr.

Mercado, Mary Margaret. Splat! LC 99-22473. (Rookie Readers Ser.). 24p. (J). (gr. k-1). 1999. 15.00 (0-516-21615-5) Childrens.

Mercado, Monina A., ed. People Power: An Oral & Photographic History of the Philippines Revolution of 1986. (Illus.). 320p. (Orig.). 1987. pap. 19.95 (0-86316-131-6) Writers & Readers.

An Asterisk (*) at the beginning of an entry indicates that the title is appearing for the first time.

Mercado, Nestor J. God Bless America: A Discussion of Family Values. 122p. Date not set. pap. text 12.95 (*0-9649504-0-5*) Mercado Info.

Mercado, O. A. An Atlas of Foot Surgery Vol. II: Rear Foot Surgery. (Illus.). 75.00 (*0-940542-04-8*) Carolando.

— An Atlas of Podiatric Surgery: Forefoot Surgery, Vol. 1. (Illus.). 290p. 1980. 75.00 (*0-940542-03-X*) Carolando.

— Mercado Atlas of Foot Anatomy. Orig. Title: An Atlas of Podiatric Anatomy. (Illus.). 1995. spiral bd. 50.00 (*0-940542-05-6*) Carolando.

Mercado, P., jt. auth. see Miranda, J.

Mercado, Sergio R. Baile de Mascaras (Masquerade Ball) 304p. 1995. pap. 14.95 (*0-679-76334-1*) Vin Bks.

***Mercado, Tununa.** In a State of Memory. Kahn, Peter, tr. 2001. pap. 15.00 (*0-8032-8269-9*, Bison Books); text 45.00 (*0-8032-3157-1*) U of Nebr Pr.

Mercado, Walter. Mas Alla del Horizonte. abr. ed. (SPA.). 272p. 1997. audio 12.98 (*1-57042-526-4*, Pub. by Warner Bks) Little.

— Mas Alla del Horizonte: Visiones del Nuevo Milenio. 1997. 20.00 (*0-446-52077-2*) Warner Bks.

— Mas Alla del Horizonte: Visiones del Nuevo Milenio. 304p. 1997. mass mkt. 9.99 (*0-446-67353-6*, Pub. by Warner Bks) Little.

Mercandante, Saverio. Elena Da Feltre. (Italian Opera Ser., 1810-1840: Vol. 20). 250p. 1985. text 30.00 (*0-8240-6569-7*) Garland.

Mercat Press Staff. The Handbook to Edinburgh. 251p. (C). 1987. pap. 40.00 (*0-901824-88-7*, Pub. by Mercat Pr Bks) St Mut.

— Handbook to Edinburgh. LC 99-172076. (Illus.). 270p. 1998. pap. 40.00 (*1-873644-73-6*, Pub. by Mercat Pr Bks) St Mut.

Mercatante, Anthony S. The Facts on File Encyclopedia of World Mythology & Legend. (Illus.). 832p. 1988. 95.00 (*0-8160-1049-8*) Facts on File.

— Who's Who in Egyptian Mythology. 2nd ed. Bianchi, Robert S., ed. 256p. 1995. 34.50 (*0-8108-2967-3*) Scarecrow.

— Zoo of the Gods: The World of Animals in Myth & Legend. LC 98-36093. (Illus.). 208p. 1999. reprint ed. pap. 15.95 (*1-56975-160-9*) Ulysses Pr.

Mercati, Cynthia. The American Car. (Illus.). 80p. 1997. pap. 5.00 (*0-87440-049-X*) Bakers Plays.

— Snapshots. 1996. pap. 5.00 (*0-87440-029-5*) Bakers Plays.

— Strength of Our Spirit. 39p. 1998. pap. 3.25 (*0-87440-068-6*) Bakers Plays.

Mercati, Cynthia. To See the Stars. 80p. Date not set. pap. 5.60 (*0-87129-997-6*, TC7) Dramatic Pub.

— A Trip Through Time. (Cover-To-Cover Bks.). 64p. 2000. 10.60 (*0-7807-9510-5*, Covercraft); 5.60 (*0-7891-5190-1*) Perfection Learn.

Mercati, Cynthia, adapted by. Girls to the Rescue. 80p. Date not set. pap. 5.00 (*0-87440-033-3*) Bakers Plays.

Mercati, Maria. The Handbook of Chinese Massage: Tuina Techniques to Awaken Body & Mind. LC 97-17132. (Illus.). 144p. 1997. pap. 19.95 (*0-89281-745-3*) Inner Tradit.

— Thai Massage Manual: Natural Therapy for Flexibility, Relaxation & Energy Balance. LC 98-43572. (Illus.). 144p. 1998. pap. 17.95 (*0-8069-1755-5*) Sterling.

***Mercati, Maria.** Tui Na Massage for a Healthier & Brighter Child. 2000. pap. 16.95 (*1-56649-161-4*) Welcome Rain.

Mercator, Gerardos. Atlas (of the World) cd-rom 50.00 (*1-891788-26-4*, 26-4) Octavo Corp.

Merced de Mendez, Ana T. Luceros de Amor. (Illus.). 100p. 1990. write for info. (*0-9627442-0-4*) A T Merced de Mendez.

Merced De Mendez, Ana T. Tales from the Island: Puerto Rican Stories. LC 94-77801. (Illus.). 60p. (J). (gr. 6-10). 1995. 20.00 (*0-9627442-1-2*); wbk. ed. 12.95 (*0-9627442-2-0*) A T Merced de Mendez.

Merced, Stoka A., jt. auth. see Brenner, R.

Mercede, Frank J. Fault Calculations for Industrial - Commercial Power Systems. Griffith, M. Shan & Huening, Walter C., eds. 636p. 1993. student ed., wbk. ed. 399.00 (*0-7803-0350-4*, HL4598) Inst Electrical.

Mercedes, Ana. Ana Mercedes Hoyos. (Illus.). 24p. 1993. 10.00 (*0-9626731-3-7*) Yoshii Gallery.

Mercedes, Sari. Portraits in Pen. (Illus.). 100p. 1995. pap. 10.00 (*0-9647225-0-X*) Sari.

— Sketchbook Travels. Justice, L. A., ed. (Illus.). (Orig.). Date not set. pap. 20.00 (*0-9647225-1-8*) Sari.

Mercedes, Sari. Sketchbook Travels. 200p. (Orig.). 1999. pap. write for info. (*0-614-29376-6*) Sari.

***Mercedes, Sister.** The Art of Sister Mercedes: Paintings & Drawings. LC 00-130952. (Illus.). 110p. 2000. 40.00 (*1-886060-11-8*) Galerija.

Mercenier, Jean & Srinivasan, T. N., eds. Applied General Equilibrium & Economic Development. 376p. 1994. text 80.00 (*0-472-10382-2*, 10382) U of Mich Pr.

Mercer. Child & Adolescent Development. (Psychology Ser.). 2001. pap. 61.95 (*0-534-34986-2*) Brooks-Cole.

— Infant Development with InfoTrac. (Psychology Ser.). 1998. 46.50 (*0-534-36356-3*) Brooks-Cole.

***Mercer.** Your Divorce Advisor. 2001. pap. write for info. (*0-684-87068-1*, Fireside) S&S Trade Pap.

***Mercer & Kotabe, Masaaki.** Marketing Management. 2nd ed. 2000. pap. text 18.75 (*0-324-04171-3*) Thomson Learn.

Mercer, jt. auth. see Reid.

Mercer, A. D. Progress in the Understanding & Prevention of Corrosion: 10th European Corrosion Congress. Costa, J. M., ed. 960p. 1993. 160.00 (*0-901716-36-7*, Pub. by Inst Materials) Ashgate Pub Co.

Mercer, A. D., jt. auth. see Lewis, J. R.

Mercer, A. D., jt. ed. see McIntyre, P.

Mercer, A. S. Banditti of the Plains. LC 54-5940. (Western Frontier Library: No. 2). (Illus.). 1975. pap. 11.95 (*0-8061-1315-4*) U of Okla Pr.

— Big Horn County, Wyoming: The Gem of the Rockies. 116p. 1986. reprint ed. pap. 10.00 (*0-8466-0156-7*, S-156, Shorey Pubns) Shoreys Bkstore.

Mercer, Alan D., et al. Operational Distribution Research. 196p. 1978. pap. 31.00 (*0-85066-168-4*) Taylor & Francis.

Mercer, Alex. Disease, Mortality & Population in Transition. 1991. text 69.00 (*0-7185-1344-4*) St Martin.

Mercer, Ann R. Teaching Students with Learning Problems. 5th ed. LC 97-15652. 645p. (C). 1997. pap. text 64.00 (*0-13-490228-9*) P-H.

Mercer, Basil W., jt. auth. see Dawson, Gaynor W.

Mercer, Bill. Lena Taku Waste (These Good Things) Selections from the Elizabeth Cole Butler Collection of Native American Art. LC 98-180312. (Illus.). 127p. 1997. pap. 20.00 (*1-883124-05-0*) Portland Art Mus.

Mercer, Blaine & Covey, Herbert C. Theoretical Frameworks in the Sociology of Education. 139p. 1980. pap. 11.95 (*0-87073-855-0*) Schenkman Bks Inc.

Mercer, Blaine & Hey, Steven. People in Schools. LC 80-13278. 382p. 1981. 39.95 (*0-87073-856-9*) Schenkman Bks Inc.

Mercer, Calvin R. Norman Perrin's Interpretation of the New Testament. Mabee, Charles, ed. LC 84-27335. (Studies in American Biblical Hermeneutics: No. 2). 192p. 1986. 24.95 (*0-86554-219-8*, MUP-H197) Mercer Univ Pr.

***Mercer, Carolyn Ayres.** Continuous Improvement in the Mathematics Classroom. LC 99-57218. 2000. write for info. (*0-87389-432-4*) ASQ Qual Pr.

Mercer, Cavalie. Journal of the Waterloo Campaign. 416p. 1995. reprint ed. pap. 15.95 (*0-306-80651-7*) Da Capo.

***Mercer, Christia.** Leibniz's Metaphysics: Its Origins & Development. 448p. (C). 1999. 64.95 (*0-521-40301-4*) Cambridge U Pr.

Mercer, Dave, jt. auth. see Klander, Lars.

Mercer, David. Managing the External Environment: A Strategic Perspective. 312p. (C). 1992. text 60.00 (*0-8039-8628-9*); pap. text 24.00 (*0-8039-8629-7*) Sage.

— Marketing. 2nd ed. (Illus.). 576p. (C). 1996. pap. 38.95 (*0-631-19638-2*) Blackwell Pubs.

— Marketing: The Encyclopedic Dictionary. LC 98-26085. 576p. 1998. 69.95 (*0-631-19107-0*); pap. 39.95 (*0-631-21126-8*) Blackwell Pubs.

***Mercer, David.** Marketing Strategy: The Challenge of the External Environment. LC 97-62267. viii, 325p. 1998. pap. write for info. (*0-7619-5876-2*) Sage.

Mercer, David. Mercer: Plays Two. 370p. 1995. pap. 15.95 (*0-413-65200-9*, A0708, Methuen Drama) Methn.

— Microsoft Access 2000 Exam Cram. (Exam Cram / Coriolis' Certification Insi Ser.). 1999. pap. text 26.99 (*1-57610-511-3*) Coriolis Grp.

— Microsoft Access 97. 10th ed. LC 98-29401. (Exam Cram Ser.). 300p. (C). 1998. mass mkt. 26.99 (*1-57610-223-8*) Coriolis Grp.

Mercer, David. New Marketing Practice: Rules for Success in a Changing World. 304p. 1997. pap. 19.95 (*0-14-024078-0*, Pub. by Pnguin Bks Ltd) Trafalgar.

Mercer, David. No Limits to Love. 69p. (C). 1988. pap. 8.95 (*0-413-48260-X*, A0191) Heinemann.

— A Question of Balance: Natural Resources Conflict Issues in Australia. 2nd ed. LC 95-139052. 350p. 1995. pap. 39.00 (*1-86287-163-9*, Pub. by Federation Pr) Gaunt.

***Mercer, David.** A Question of Balance: Natural Resources Conflict Issues in Australia. 3rd ed. 366p. 2000. pap. 39.95 (*1-86287-342-9*, Pub. by Federation Pr) Gaunt.

Mercer, David & Laing, Stuart. Mercer: Plays One. LC 90-27136. (Methuen World Dramatists Ser.). 362p. (Orig.). (C). 1990. pap. 14.95 (*0-413-63450-7*, A0462, Methuen Drama) Methn.

Mercer, David, jt. auth. see Mason, Tom.

Mercer, Deborah B., jt. auth. see Burkhart, Joyce L.

***Mercer, Delinda E.** Individual Drug Counseling Approach to Treat Cocaine Addiction: The Collaborative Cocaine Treatment Study Model. LC 99-489402. 91p. 1999. pap. 8.75 (*0-16-050144-X*) USGPO.

***Mercer, Delinda E. & Woody, George E.** Individual Drug Counseling Approach to Cocaine Addiction: The Collaborative Cocaine Treatment Study Model. 83p. 2000. pap. text 25.00 (*0-7881-8850-X*) DIANE Pub.

Mercer, Donald W., jt. auth. see Herberman, Ronald B.

Mercer, Dorothy L. Injury: Learning to Live Again. LC 94-1058. 192p. 1994. pap. 9.95 (*0-934793-54-9*) Pathfinder CA.

Mercer, E. Ian, jt. tr. see Scott, Thomas A.

Mercer, Edward, et al. Experiments in General Chemistry. 1994. per. 20.00 (*0-88252-168-3*) Paladin Hse.

Mercer, Gina. Janet Frame: Subversive Fictions. 304p. 1996. pap. 29.95 (*0-908569-82-3*, Pub. by Univ Otago Pr) Intl Spec Bk.

Mercer, Ginger, jt. auth. see Bach, Bob.

***Mercer, Graham.** Globetrotter Travel Parks of Australia. (Illus.). 1999. 14.95 (*1-85974-110-X*) New5 Holland.

— Globetrotter Travel Parks of Kenya. (Illus.). 1999. 14.95 (*1-85974-123-1*) New5 Holland.

— Globetrotter Travel Parks of South Africa. (Illus.). 1999. 14.95 (*1-85974-135-5*) New5 Holland.

— Globetrotter Travel Parks of Sydney. (Illus.). 1999. 14.95 (*1-85974-138-X*) New5 Holland.

— Globetrotter Travel Parks of Tanzania. (Illus.). 1999. 14.95 (*1-85974-141-X*) New5 Holland.

Mercer, Gwen & Mercer, Maxine. Legitimate Sisters. 84p. 1994. pap. 7.00 (*0-969112-0-5*) RghtBrain.

Mercer, Gwen & Newton, Violette. Art Songs. 91p. 1995. pap. 10.00 (*0-9649112-1-3*) RghtBrain.

Mercer, Helen. Constructing a Competitive Order: The Hidden History of British Anti-Trust Policies. (Illus.). 286p. (C). 1995. text 64.95 (*0-521-41292-7*) Cambridge U Pr.

Mercer, Helen, et al, eds. Labour Government & Private Industry: The Experience of the 1945-51 Governments. 240p. 1993. 68.00 (*0-7486-0339-5*, Pub. by Edinburgh U Pr) Col U Pr.

***Mercer, Henry C.** Ancient Carpenter's Tools: Illustrated & Explained, Together with the Implements of the Lumber. LC 99-86242. (Illus.). 2000. pap. 19.95 (*0-486-40958-9*) Dover.

Mercer, Henry C. Dating of Old Houses. (Illus.). 28p. 1976. reprint ed. pap. 2.00 (*0-910302-03-0*) Bucks Co Hist.

***Mercer, Hugh.** Recalling Education. 2000. 19.95 (*1-882926-55-2*) ISI Books.

Mercer, I. F. Crystals. (Illus.). 60p. 1990. pap. 15.00 (*0-11-310013-2*, Pub. by Statnry Office) Sterling.

Mercer, Ian. Crystals. (British Museum of Natural History Ser.). (Illus.). 60p. 1990. pap. text 9.95 (*0-674-17914-5*) HUP.

Mercer, Ian, jt. auth. see Van Rose, Susanna.

Mercer, J. Edward. Nature Mysticism (1913) 273p. 1996. reprint ed. pap. 24.95 (*1-56459-583-8*) Kessinger Pub.

Mercer, J. F. B., jt. ed. see Leone, A.

Mercer, James L. Public Management in Lean Years: Operating in a Cutback Management Environment. LC 92-15782. 288p. 1992. 62.95 (*0-89930-357-9*, MEB, Quorum Bks) Greenwood.

— Strategic Planning for Public Managers. LC 90-47590. 240p. 1991. 59.95 (*0-89930-355-2*, MSZ/, Quorum Bks) Greenwood.

Mercer, James L. & Philips, Ronald J. Public Technology: Key to Improved Government Productivity. LC 80-69693. 287p. reprint ed. pap. 89.00 (*0-608-12907-0*, 202353800033) Bks Demand.

Mercer, James L., et al. Managing Urban Government Services: Strategies, Tools, & Techniques for the Eighties. LC 81-66228. 256p. reprint ed. pap. 79.40 (*0-608-12155-X*, 202391200034) Bks Demand.

Mercer, James W. DNAPL Site Evaluation. LC 93-18972. 384p. 1993. lib. bdg. 85.00 (*0-87371-977-8*, LS977) Lewis Pubs.

Mercer, Jean. To Everything There Is a Season: Development in the Context of the Lifespan. 584p. (Orig.). (C). 1991. lib. bdg. 71.00 (*0-8191-8391-1*) U Pr of Amer.

Mercer, Jeremy. The Champagne Gang: Living High on Crime. (Illus.). 224p. (Orig.). 1997. pap. 14.95 (*1-895629-97-7*) Warwick Publ.

***Mercer, Jerry L.** Living Deeply Our New Life in Christ: A Wesleyan Spirituality for Today. LC 98-88822. 120p. 2000. pap. 16.95 (*0-88177-275-5*, DR275) Discipleship Res.

Mercer, Jerry L. & Wesley, John. Being Christian: A United Methodist Vision for the Christian Life. LC 93-72074. 104p. 1993. pap. 10.95 (*0-88177-125-2*, DR125) Discipleship Res.

Mercer, Jerry L., jt. auth. see Stobbe, Brenda.

Mercer, John. Infant Development. LC 96-52400. (Psychology Ser.). 519p. 1997. pap. 43.75 (*0-534-33977-8*) Brooks-Cole.

— The Informational Film. LC 80-54273. (Illus.). 200p. (C). 1981. pap. text 6.80 (*0-87563-197-5*) Stipes.

— An Introduction to Cinematography. (Illus.). (C). 1979. spiral bd. 12.80 (*0-87563-168-1*) Stipes.

Mercer, John E. Alchemy, Its Science & Romance. LC 79-8617. (Illus.). reprint ed. 27.50 (*0-404-18481-2*) AMS Pr.

***Mercer, John W., ed.** Anyone, Anywhere, Anytime: Learning Technologies at @Minnesota.US@Superhighway. 49p. (C). 1999. reprint ed. pap. text 15.00 (*0-7881-8216-1*) DIANE Pub.

Mercer, Jonathan. Reputation & International Politics. (Studies in Security Affairs). 264p. 1996. text 37.50 (*0-8014-3055-0*) Cornell U Pr.

Mercer, Joyce A. Behind the Mask of Adolescent Satanism. LC 91-72991. (Illus.). 160p. 1991. pap. 9.95 (*0-925190-22-5*) Fairview Press.

***Mercer, Judy.** Blind Spot. 480p. 2000. 23.95 (*0-671-03424-3*, PB Hardcover) PB.

Mercer, Judy. Double Take. LC 97-8777. 1997. 22.00 (*0-671-55707-6*) PB.

— Fast Forward. Date not set. pap. 3.99 (*0-671-02431-0*, Pocket Books) PB.

— Fast Forward. Chernoff, Dona, ed. 352p. 1995. 22.00 (*0-671-89960-0*) PB.

— Fast Forward. 1997. mass mkt. 6.50 (*0-614-27768-X*); per. 6.50 (*0-671-89961-9*) PB.

— Split Image. LC 99-166545. 340p. 1998. 23.00 (*0-671-55602-9*, PB Hardcover) PB.

— Split Image. 1999. per. 6.99 (*0-671-55603-7*) PB.

***Mercer, Judy.** Split Image. large type ed. LC 99-46164. 1999. 25.95 (*1-56895-780-7*, Compass) Wheeler Pub.

Mercer, Julia E. Bermuda Settlers of the 17th Century: Genealogical Notes from Bermuda. LC 82-81220. 276p. 1992. reprint ed. 14.00 (*0-8063-0987-3*) Genealog Pub.

Mercer, June. The Clearing Mist. large type ed. 320p. 1987. 27.99 (*0-7089-1668-6*) Ulverscroft.

— Death-Line. large type ed. 304p. 1987. 27.99 (*0-7089-1614-7*) Ulverscroft.

Mercer, K. Lynne, jt. auth. see Cross, Patricia C.

Mercer, Kobena. Welcome to the Jungle: New Positions in Black Cultural Studies. LC 93-48150. 288p. (C). (gr. 13). 1994. pap. 49.95 (*0-415-90635-0*) Routledge.

— Welcome to the Jungle: New Positions in Black Cultural Studies. LC 93-48150. 288p. (C). (gr. 13). 1994. 80.00 (*0-415-90634-2*) Routledge.

Mercer, Lance, jt. photos by see Peterson, Charles.

***Mercer, Lee.** Hiking Wyoming's Teton & Washakie Wilderness. (Hiking Guides Ser.). (Illus.). 130p. 2000. pap. 16.95 (*1-56044-887-3*) Falcon Pub Inc.

Mercer, Lloyd J. E. H. Harriman: Master Railroader. Perkins, Edwin, ed. (Twayne's Evolution of American Business Ser.: No. 3). 1985. 33.00 (*0-8057-9802-1*, 605, Twyne) Mac Lib Ref.

Mercer, Lloyd J., et al. California City & County User Charges: Change & Efficiency since Proposition 13. LC 84-10828. (Illus.). 114p. reprint ed. pap. 35.40 (*0-608-20126-X*, 207139800011) Bks Demand.

Mercer, M. Ray, jt. auth. see Butler, Kenneth M.

Mercer, Malcolm V. Schooling the Poorer Child: Elementary Education in Sheffield, 1560-1902. (Illus.). 328p. 1996. pap. 19.95 (*1-85075-534-5*, Pub. by Sheffield Acad) CUP Services.

Mercer, Mary E. The Art of Becoming Human. LC 96-47874. 146p. 1997. 19.95 (*1-57392-120-3*) Prometheus Bks.

Mercer, Maxine, jt. auth. see Mercer, Gwen.

Mercer, Mayer. Frog Where Are You. (J). 1994. pap. 4.99 (*0-14-054632-4*, Dial Yng Read) Peng Put Young Read.

***Mercer, Michael.** Absolutely Fabulous Organizational Change. LC 99-76325. 250p. 2000. 24.95 (*0-938901-21-4*, Pub. by Castlegate Pubs) Midpt Trade.

Mercer, Michael. Goodnight Disgrace. 120p. 1986. pap. 11.95 (*0-88922-238-X*, Pub. by Talonbks) Genl Dist Srvs.

Mercer, Michael W. Hire the Best...& Avoid the Rest. 176p. 1993. 19.95 (*0-8144-0207-0*) AMACOM.

— Turning Your Human Resources Department into a Profit Center. LC 88-48024. 265p. 1989. 59.95 (*0-8144-5841-6*) AMACOM.

Mercer, Michael W. & Troiani, Maryann V. Spontaneous Optimism: Proven Strategies for Health, Prosperity & Happiness. LC 97-75101. 272p. 1998. pap. 14.95 (*0-938901-09-5*) Castlegate Pubs.

Mercer, Michael W., jt. auth. see Troiani, Maryann V.

Mercer, Mick. Gothic Rock: All You Ever Wanted to Know... (Orig.). 1993. pap. 19.98 (*0-614-13015-8*) Cleopatra.

— Hex Files: The Goth Bible. LC 96-50280. (Illus.). 240p. (Orig.). 1997. pap. 23.95 (*0-87951-783-2*, Pub. by Overlook Pr) Penguin Putnam.

Mercer, Morris A., Jr. To All My Friends. (Illus.). 64p. (Orig.). 1986. pap. write for info. (*0-9617362-0-8*) M A Mercer.

Mercer, Neil. The Guided Construction of Knowledge: Talk Amongst Teachers & Learners. 160p. 1995. 48.00 (*1-85359-263-3*, Pub. by Multilingual Matters); pap. 15.95 (*1-85359-262-5*, Pub. by Multilingual Matters) Taylor & Francis.

***Mercer, Neil.** Words & Minds: How We Use Language to Think Together & Get Things Done. LC 00-22280. 2000. pap. write for info. (*0-415-22476-4*) Routledge.

Mercer, Neil, jt. auth. see Edwards, Derek.

Mercer, Neil, ed. see Swann, Joan.

Mercer, Nelda, et al. The M-Fit Grocery Shopping Guide: Your Guide to Healthier Choices. 4th rev. ed. LC 96-177886. 397p. 1995. pap. 18.95 (*0-9649656-0-7*) U MI Med Ctr.

Mercer, Nelda, jt. auth. see Burt, Lizzie.

Mercer, Nick, jt. auth. see Gaukroger, Stephen.

Mercer, Patrick J. Give Them a Volley & Charge! The Battle of Inkermann, 1854. 224p. 1997. write for info. (*1-86227-025-2*, Pub. by Spellmnt Pubs) St Mut.

Mercer, Patrick J. Inkerman, 1854. (Campaign Ser.: No. 51). (Illus.). 96p. 1998. pap. 16.95 (*1-85532-618-3*, Pub. by Ospry) Stackpole.

Mercer, Peter. "Hamlet" & the Acting of Revenge. LC 86-82701. 277p. (C). 1987. text 33.95 (*0-87745-171-0*) U of Iowa Pr.

***Mercer, Peter.** Not by Strength by Guile. (Illus.). 16p. 2000. 26.00 (*1-85782-368-0*) Blake Publng.

Mercer, Philip. The Life of the Gallant Pelham. (Illus.). 189p. 1995. reprint ed. 25.00 (*1-56837-316-3*) Broadfoot.

Mercer, R., et al, eds. Advances in Artificial Intelligence: 12th Biennial Conference of the Canadian Society for Computational Studies of Intelligence, AI, '98, Vancouver, BC, Canada, June 18-20, 1998. LC 98-22153. (Lecture Notes in Computer Science Ser.: Vol. 1418). xii, 467p. 1998. pap. 69.00 (*3-540-64575-6*) Spr-Verlag.

Mercer, R. & Hill, P. H. Archaeological Field Survey in N. Scotland Vol. III: 1982-83. 278p. 1985. pap. 24.00 (*0-614-21828-4*) David Brown.

Mercer, R. B. Industrial Control Wiring Guide. 2nd ed. (Newnes Practitioner Ser.). (Illus.). 128p. 2000. spiral bd. 33.00 (*0-7506-3140-6*, Newnes) Buttrwrth-Heinemann.

Mercer, R. J. Causewayed Enclosures. (Archaeology Ser.: No. 61). (Illus.). 72p. 1989. pap. 10.50 (*0-7478-0064-2*, Pub. by Shire Pubns) Parkwest Pubns.

Mercer, Ramona T. Becoming a Mother: Research on Maternal Role Identity from Rubin to the Present. LC 95-2601. (Focus on Women Ser.: Vol. 18). (Illus.). 408p. 1995. 58.95 (*0-8261-8970-9*) Springer Pub.

Mercer, Ramona T., et al. Transitions in a Woman's Life: Major Life Events in Developmental Context. (Focus on Women Ser.). 224p. 1989. 32.95 (*0-8261-6560-5*) Springer Pub.

Mercer, Richard, jt. auth. see Hungerford, Thomas W.

Mercer, Rick. Computing Fundamentals with C++ 2nd ed. LC 98-18880. 814p. 1998. pap. 49.95 (*1-887902-36-8*) Franklin Beedle.

— Operating in the Dark: The Accountability Crisis in Canada's Health Care System. 336p. 1998. 24.95 (*0-385-25719-8*) Doubleday.

— Programming with C++ Using, Modifying & Implementing Object Classes. LC 99-27204. 1998. pap. 49.95 (*1-887902-39-2*) Franklin Beedle.

— Streeters. 1999. mass mkt. 5.99 (*0-7704-2837-1*) Bantam.

Mercer, Robert, jt. auth. see Martine, Roberta.

M

Mercer, Robert A. Sculpture in Verse. (Illus.). 54p. (Orig.). 1996. pap. 12.95 (*0-9655433-0-7*) Merwood Pr.

Mercer, Roger. Archaeological Field Survey in N. Scotland Vol. I: 1976-79, Vol. I. 155p. 1980. pap. text 15.00 (*0-614-21821-7*) David Brown.

— Archaeological Field Survey in N. Scotland Vol. II: 1980. 170p. 1981. pap. 12.00 (*0-614-21824-1*) David Brown.

— Excavation of a Neolithic Enclosure at Helman Tor, Lanlivery, Cornwall, 1986: Interim Report. 18p. 1986. pap. 6.00 (*0-614-21839-X*) David Brown.

Mercer, Roger, ed. Farming Practices in Prehistoric Britain. 245p. 1984. 68.00 (*0-85224-501-7*, Pub. by Edinburgh U Pr) Col U Pr.

Mercer, Rosemary, tr. from JPN. Deep Words: Miura Baien's System of Natural Philosophy. LC 90-21719. (Philosophy of History & Culture Ser.: No. 4). (Illus.). x, 216p. 1991. 86.00 (*90-04-09351-6*) Brill Academic Pubs.

Mercer, Russell. The True Israel of God. LC 97-70782. 112p. (Orig.). 1997. pap. 7.95 (*1-883928-21-4*) Longwood.

Mercer, Samuel A. Assyrian Grammar. LC 22-17308. (Columbia University. Oriental Studies: No. 29). reprint ed. 27.50 (*0-404-50519-8*) AMS Pr.

— Egyptian Hieroglyphic Grammar: With Vocabularies, Exercises, Chrestomathy. viii, 184p. 1980. 15.00 (*0-89005-203-4*) Ares.

— Ethiopic Liturgy. LC 76-141034. reprint ed. 47.50 (*0-404-04308-9*) AMS Pr.

— Handbook of Egyptian Hieroglyphs: A Study of the Ancient Language. 1998. pap. text 16.95 (*0-7818-0625-9*) Hippocrene Bks.

— Sumero - Babylonian Sign List. LC 18-16548. (Columbia University. Oriental Studies: No. 14). reprint ed. 34.50 (*0-404-50504-X*) AMS Pr.

Mercer, Samuel A. & Hallock, Frank H., eds. The Tell El-Amarna Tablets, 2 vols., Set. LC 78-72764. (Ancient Mesopotamian Texts & Studies). (Illus.). 942p. 1983. reprint ed. 145.00 (*0-404-18216-X*) AMS Pr.

Mercer, Sherry L., jt. auth. see Wattenbarger, James L.

Mercer, Steve, ed. see Miller, Randy, et al.

***Mercer, Susan O.** Women as They Age. 2nd ed. Garner, J. Dianne, ed. LC 00-39713. 274p. 2000. pap. text 24.95 (*0-7890-1126-3*); lib. bdg. 69.95 (*0-7890-1125-5*) Haworth Pr.

Mercer, Susan O., ed. Women As They Age: Challenge, Opportunity & Triumph. LC 88-34803. (Journal of Women & Aging: Vol. 1, Nos. 1-3). (Illus.). 415p. 1989. text 59.95 (*0-86656-805-0*); pap. text 22.95 (*0-86656-873-5*) Haworth Pr.

Mercer, Susan O., et al. Geriatric Case Practice in the Nursing Home. (Geriatric Case Practice Training Ser.: Vol. 1). (Illus.). 280p. 1991. 46.00 (*0-8039-2916-1*); pap. 22.95 (*0-8039-2917-X*) Sage.

***Mercer-Taylor, Peter.** The Life of Mendelssohn. LC 99-58441. (Musical Lives Ser.). (Illus.). 200p. (C). 2000. text 49.95 (*0-521-63025-8*); pap. text 17.95 (*0-521-63972-7*) Cambridge U Pr.

Mercer, Tony. Chronometer Makers of the World. (Illus.). 291p. 1991. 75.00 (*0-7198-0240-7*, Pub. by NAG Press) Antique Collect.

Mercer, Viola. Memories. 76p. 1998. pap. 9.95 (*1-885206-59-3*) Cader Pubng.

Mercer, William W., jt. ed. see Keeling, David A.

Mercer, Z. Christopher. Quantifying Marketability Discounts: Developing & Supporting Marketability Discounts in the Appraisal of Closely Held Business Interests. 525p. 1997. 115.00 (*0-9658358-0-4*) Peabody Pub LP.

Merceron, Jacques. Le Message & sa Fiction: La Communication par Messager dans la Litterature Francaise Des XII, Vol. 128. (FRE.). 416p. 1998. pap. 45.00 (*0-520-09822-6*, Pub. by U CA Pr) Cal Prin Full Svc.

Mercersburg Woman's Club Staff. Old Mercersburg (Historical & Genealogical Sketches) (Illus.). 215p. 1997. reprint ed. lib. bdg. 29.50 (*0-8328-6429-3*) Higginson Bk Co.

Merch. Grover's Tubby. LC 96-158624. (J). 1996. 4.99 (*0-679-87864-5*) Random.

***Mercham, John.** The Photographs of Frederick C. Marcham. LC 00-31497. 112p. 2000. 29.95 (*0-942690-45-1*) DeWitt Hist.

Merchan, M. A., et al. The Mammalian Cochlear Nuclei: Organization & Function. (NATO ASI Ser.: Vol. 239). (Illus.). 532p. (C). 1993. text 145.00 (*0-306-44406-2*, Kluwer Plenum) Kluwer Academic.

Merchand, H. Latinoamerica en Dos Mil Conciertos. (SPA.). 122p. 1974. 5.00 (*0-8288-7063-2*) Fr & Eur.

Merchant. Rewarding Results. 272p. 1989. 35.00 (*0-07-103258-4*) McGraw.

— Three Marriage Plays: The Wise-Woman of Hogsdon/The English Traveller/The Captives. (Illus.). 304p. 1996. text 74.95 (*0-7190-2221-5*, Pub. by Manchester Univ Pr) St Martin.

Merchant, Alexander N. From Barter to Slavery: The Economic Relations of Portuguese & Indians in the Settlement of Brazil, 1500-1580. LC 78-64184. (Johns Hopkins University. Studies in the Social Sciences. Thirtieth Ser. 1912: 1). reprint ed. 27.50 (*0-404-61292-X*) AMS Pr.

Merchant, B., jt. ed. see Gershwin, M. Eric.

Merchant, Carolyn. The Death of Nature: Women, Ecology, & the Scientific Revolution. LC 89-24516. 384p. 1990. pap. 16.00 (*0-06-250595-5*, Pub. by Harper SF) HarpC.

— Earthcare: Women & the Environment. 288p. (gr. 13). 1995. pap. 18.99 (*0-415-90888-4*, B3092) Routledge.

— Ecological Revolutions: Nature, Gender, & Science in New England. LC 89-30945. (H. Eugene & Lillian Youngs Lehman Ser.). (Illus.). xviii, 380p. (C). 1989. 55.00 (*0-8078-1858-5*); pap. 18.95 (*0-8078-4254-0*) U of NC Pr.

— Radical Ecology: The Search for a Livable World. LC 92-12542. (Reactionary Thought/Radical Movements Ser.). (Illus.). 224p. (gr. 13). 1992. pap. 18.99 (*0-415-90650-4*, A7618) Routledge.

Merchant, Carolyn, ed. Green vs. Gold: Sources in California's Environmental History. LC 98-3346. (Illus.). 416p. 1998. text 45.00 (*1-55963-579-7*); pap. text 25.00 (*1-55963-580-0*) Island Pr.

— Major Problems in American Environmental History: Documents & Essays. (Major Problems in American History Ser.). 544p. (C). 1993. pap. text 29.16 (*0-669-24993-9*) HM Trade Div.

Merchant, Carolyn & Gottleib, Roger, eds. Ecology. LC 94-3090. (Key Concepts in Critical Theory Ser.). 320p. (C). 1994. pap. 17.50 (*0-391-03795-1*) Humanities.

Merchant, Christina S., jt. auth. see Constantino, Cathy A.

Merchant, Darlene A. Treating Abused Adolescents: A Program for Providing Individual & Group Therapy. 1990. pap. text 14.95 (*1-55691-017-7*, 177) Learning Pubns.

Merchant, Dean. The Lore of the Fried Clam & a History of the Soft-Shell Clam Industry. (Illus.). 160p. 2000. pap. 19.95 (*0-914339-79-6*, Pub. by P E Randall Pub) U Pr of New Eng.

Merchant, Ella, jt. auth. see Jones, Alice I.

Merchant, Guy. Coordinating Primary Language & Literacy: The Subject Leader's Handbook. 1998. pap. 26.95 (*1-85396-370-4*) B&N Imports.

***Merchant, Guy.** Picture Books for the Literacy Hour: Activities for Primary Teachers. (Illus.). 1999. pap. 27.95 (*1-85346-627-1*) David Fulton.

Merchant, H. D., ed. Creep & Stress Relaxation in Miniature Structure & Components. LC 97-70340. (Illus.). 299p. 1997. 104.00 (*0-87339-373-2*, 3732) Minerals Metals.

Merchant, H. D., ed. see Metallurgical Society of AIME Staff.

Merchant, Harish D. Problems in Material Science. x, 476p. 1972. text 489.00 (*0-677-13450-9*) Gordon & Breach.

Merchant, Harish D., ed. Defect Structure, Morphology & Properties: Symposium on Defect Structure, Morphology & Properties of Deposits (1994: Rosemont, IL) (Illus.). 432p. 1995. 20.00 (*0-87339-290-6*, 2906) Minerals Metals.

Merchant, Harish D., ed. see AIME, Metallurgical Society Staff.

Merchant, Harish D., ed. see Metallurgical Society of AIME Staff.

Merchant, Harish D., ed. see Minerals, Metals & Materials Society Staff.

Merchant, Ismail. Ismail Merchant's Paris: Filming & Feasting in France LC 99-11027. 144p. 1999. 39.95 (*0-8109-4162-7*, Pub. by Abrams) Time Warner.

— Ismail Merchant's Passionate Meals: The New Indian Cuisine for Fearless Cooks & Adventurous Eaters. LC 93-37147. (Illus.). 288p. (J). 1994. 27.00 (*0-7868-6015-4*, Pub. by Hyperion) Time Warner.

— The Proprietor: The Screenplay & Story Behind the Film. LC 96-31367. (Illus.). 224p. 1996. 24.95 (*1-55704-306-X*, Pub. by Newmarket) Norton.

Merchant, Kalpana M. Pharmacological Regulation of Gene Expression in the CNS: Towards An Understanding of Basal Ganglial Functions. LC 96-18410. (Pharmacology & Toxicology: Basic & Clinical Aspects Ser.). 224p. 1996. boxed set 139.95 (*0-8493-8550-4*) CRC Pr.

Merchant, Kenneth A. Fraudulent & Questionable Financial Reporting: A Corporate Perspective. LC 87-80813. 88p. 1987. 20.00 (*0-910586-64-0*, 072-87) Finan Exec.

— Modern Management Control Systems. LC 97-15527. 848p. 1997. 105.00 (*0-13-554155-7*) P-H.

Merchant, Linda K., jt. ed. see Dupuis, Mary M.

Merchant, M. N. Quranic Laws. 1991. pap. 10.50 (*0-933511-30-2*) Kazi Pubns.

Merchant, Michael. Exploring Electricity: Techniques & Troubleshooting. LC 95-30312. 576p. 1995. 66.00 (*0-02-380555-2*, Macmillan Coll) P-H.

— Exploring Electronics: Techniques & Troubleshooting. LC 97-23979. 620p. 1997. text 60.00 (*0-02-380571-4*) Macmillan.

Merchant, Moelwyn. A Bundle of Papyrus. 124p. 1998. pap. 20.95 (*0-8464-4770-3*) Beekman Pubs.

— A Bundle of Papyrus. 124p. (C). 1989. pap. 30.00 (*0-86383-544-9*, Pub. by Gomer Pr) St Mut.

— Fire from the Heights. (Princeton Theological Monographs: No. 27). 126p. (Orig.). 1991. pap. 8.00 (*1-55635-011-2*) Pickwick.

— Fragments of a Life. 367p. 1990. 47.95 (*0-8464-4668-5*) Beekman Pubs.

— Inherit the Land. 203p. 1991. pap. 19.95 (*0-8464-4796-7*) Beekman Pubs.

— Inherit the Land. 203p. (C). 1991. pap. 21.00 (*0-86383-817-0*, Pub. by Gomer Pr) St Mut.

— Jeshua, Nazareth to Jerusalem. LC 91-7927. (Princeton Theological Monographs: No. 26). xviii, 426p. (Orig.). 1991. pap. 15.00 (*1-55635-010-4*) Pickwick.

— Seeking Perfection. 131p. 1996. pap. 20.95 (*0-8464-4626-X*); pap. 20.85 (*0-8464-4797-5*) Beekman Pubs.

Merchant, Moelwyn, ed. Breaking the Code. (C). 1975. 30.00 (*0-85088-327-X*, Pub. by Gomer Pr) St Mut.

— Fragments of a Life. 367p. (C). 1990. 63.00 (*0-86383-647-X*, Pub. by Gomer Pr) St Mut.

Merchant, Muhammad V. Book of Quranic Laws. 204p. 1996. pap. 10.50 (*0-614-21048-8*, 1536) Kazi Pubns.

Merchant, Pat. Proceeding Without Anecdotal Details of Imagery. (Orig.). 1992. pap. 16.00 (*0-913412-62-7*) Brandon Hse.

Merchant, Paul, ed. Wendell Berry. LC 91-73134. (American Authors Ser.). 250p. 1991. pap. 15.00 (*0-917652-88-6*) Confluence Pr.

Merchant, Paul, ed. see Berry, Wendell.

Merchant, Ronald. Basic Business Math & Electronic Calculators. 384p. (C). 1995. pap. text 36.95 (*0-89863-189-0*) Star Pub CA.

— Basic Business Math & Electronic Calculators. 384p. (C). 1997. pap. text 36.95 (*0-89863-190-4*) Star Pub CA.

— Basic Business Math & Electronic Calculators. 4th ed. 306p. 1989. pap. text 29.95 (*0-89863-130-0*) Star Pub CA.

— Business Math with Electronic Accuracy. 320p. (C). 1987. pap. text 29.95 (*0-89863-107-6*) Star Pub CA.

— Calculator Proficiency. 144p. 1989. pap. text 18.95 (*0-89863-123-8*) Star Pub CA.

Merchant, Vicki, jt. ed. see Adkins, Lisa.

Merchant, W. D. Home on the Hill: A Bombay Girlhood. (Illus.). 133p. 1992. pap. text 10.50 (*0-89410-713-5*, Three Contnts) L Rienner.

Merchant, W. Moelwyn. Creed & Drama: An Essay in Religious Drama. LC 66-23222. 127p. reprint ed. pap. 39.40 (*0-608-17188-3*, 202786700056) Bks Demand.

Merchant, W. Moelwyn, ed. see Shakespeare, William.

Merchiers. Credit Insurance. 1993. pap. text 28.00 (*90-6544-765-2*) Kluwer Academic.

Merchuk, J. C., jt. auth. see Asenjo, Juan A.

***Mercia, Leonard.** Storey's Guide to Raising Poultry: Breeds, Care, Health. 352p. 2000. pap. 18.95 (*1-58017-263-6*) Storey Bks.

— Storey's Guide to Raising Turkeys: Breeds, Care, Health. 208p. 2000. pap. 18.95 (*1-58017-261-X*) Storey Bks.

Mercia, Leonard S. Raising Poultry the Modern Way. 1983. pap. 8.95 (*0-88266-058-6*) Storey Bks.

— Raising Poultry the Modern Way. rev. ed. Foster, Kimberly, ed. LC 89-45738. (Illus.). 240p. 1990. pap. 12.95 (*0-88266-577-4*) Storey Bks.

— Raising Your Own Turkeys. LC 81-6353. (Illus.). 144p. (Orig.). 1983. pap. 12.95 (*0-88266-253-8*, Garden Way Pub) Storey Bks.

Mercie, Christine. The Sons of God. 158p. 1954. pap. 7.95 (*0-87516-059-X*) DeVorss.

Mercie, Susan. Substances & Safety: Drugs & the New Workplace. rev. ed. 1999. pap. 0.50 (*0-89230-201-1*) Do It Now.

Mercier, Andre, jt. ed. see Svilar, Maja.

Mercier, Andree, jt. auth. see Lister, Brenda J.

Mercier, B. An Introduction to the Numerical Analysis of Spectral Methods. (Lecture Notes in Physics Ser.: Vol. 318). v, 154p. 1989. 34.95 (*0-387-51106-7*) Spr-Verlag.

— Lectures on Topics in Finite Element Solution of Elliptic Problems. (Tata Institute Lectures on Mathematics). (Illus.). 191p. 1980. 31.95 (*0-387-09543-8*) Spr-Verlag.

Mercier, Cathryn M. & Bloom, Susan P. Presenting Avi. LC 96-53878. (Twayne's United States Young Adult Authors Ser.). 206p. (gr. 6 up). 1997. 24.95 (*0-8057-4569-6*, Twyne) Mac Lib Ref.

Mercier, Cathryn M., jt. auth. see Bloom, Susan P.

Mercier, Charles. Terence: Brothers (Adelphoe) (Focus Classical Library). 120p. 1998. pap. 6.95 (*0-941051-72-2*) Focus Pub-R Pullins.

Mercier, Charles & Rieber, Robert W. Criminal Responsibility. (Historical Foundations of Forensic Psychiatry & Psychology Ser.). 256p. 1980. reprint ed. lib. bdg. 27.50 (*0-306-76064-9*) Da Capo.

Mercier, Claude. Petrochemical Industry & the Possibilities of Its Establishment Developing Countries. (Illus.). 202p. (C). 1966. 155.00 (*2-7108-0058-6*, Pub. by Edits Technip) Enfield Pubs NH.

Mercier, Denis. Mass Media Issues. 5th ed. 512p. (C). 1995. pap. text, per. 35.95 (*0-7872-0507-9*) Kendall-Hunt.

— Mass Media Issues. 6th ed. 500p. 1997. 36.95 (*0-7872-4436-8*) Kendall-Hunt.

Mercier, Francois. Recollections of the Youkon. Yarborough, Linda F., ed. (Alaska Historical Commission Studies in History: No. 188). (Illus.). 1986p. (Orig.). 1986. pap. 10.00 (*0-943712-19-X*) Alaska Hist.

Mercier, Francoise. QuickCheck French. LC 97-31024. (Barron's Quickcheck Language Ser.). (ENG & FRE.). 160p. 1998. pap. 8.95 (*0-7641-0308-3*) Barron.

Mercier, Geselle, tr. from ENG. Botero in Chicago. (SPA., Illus.). 64p. (Orig.). 1994. pap. 20.00 (*0-938903-17-9*) Cty of Chicago.

Mercier, Jacques. Art That Heals: The Image As Medicine in Ethiopia. LC 96-80093. (Illus.). 128p. 1997. 49.95 (*3-7913-1606-0*, Pub. by Prestel) te Neues.

— Petit Dictionnaire Franco-Belge, Belgo-Francais: Mots et Expressions Usuels. (FRE.). 286p. 1990. 49.95 (*0-7859-8175-6*, 2871760098) Fr & Eur.

Mercier, Jean. Downstream & Upstream Ecologists: The People, Organizations & Ideas Behind the Movement. LC 97-3628. 240p. 1997. 59.95 (*0-275-95927-9*, Praeger Pubs) Greenwood.

— Lexique Anglais-Francais du Compteur D'electricite: Principes et Pieces Composantes. (ENG & FRE.). 42p. 1973. pap. 9.95 (*0-8288-6312-1*, M-6407) Fr & Eur.

— Lexique Anglais-Francais du Programmateur De Cuisiniere: Fonctionnement et Pieces Composantes. (ENG & FRE.). 29p. 1973. pap. 9.95 (*0-8288-6313-X*, M-6406) Fr & Eur.

Mercier, Jean & Belanger, Francine. Vocabulary of Metal Working: Vocabulaire du Travail des Metaux en Fauilles, Barres, Tubes et Profils. (ENG & FRE.). 99p. 1984. pap. 9.95 (*0-8288-1916-5*, M4663) Fr & Eur.

Mercier, Joyce & Garasky, Steven, eds. Family Policy, Vol. 25.1. 109p. 1997. pap. 15.00 (*0-944285-49-X*) Pol Studies.

***Mercier, Joyce M., et al, eds.** Redefining Family Policy: Implications for the 21st Century. LC 00-38317. 336p. 2000. 54.95 (*0-8138-2590-3*) Iowa St U Pr.

Mercier, Judith D., jt. auth. see Mercier, Peter J.

Mercier, Laurie, contrib. by. Margaret Hurley: An Oral History. (Illus.). xii, 211p. (Orig.). 1995. pap. write for info. (*1-889320-01-3*) WA St Oral Hist.

Mercier, Laurie & Buckendorf, Madeline. Using Oral History in Community History Projects. (Pamphlet Ser.: Vol. 4). (Orig.). 1992. pap. text 8.00 (*0-614-32270-7*) Oral Hist.

Mercier, Lonnie R. Practical Orthopedics. 4th ed. LC 95-12842. (Illus.). 528p. (C). (gr. 13). 1995. pap. text 74.95 (*0-8151-5903-X*, 24430) Mosby Inc.

Mercier, Lonnie R. Practical Orthopedics. 5th ed. (Illus.). 560p. Date not set. pap. text. write for info. (*0-323-00827-5*) Mosby Inc.

Mercier, Louis-Sebastien. Du Theatre. xvi, 372p. 1973. reprint ed. write for info. (*3-487-04908-2*) G Olms Pubs.

— Memoirs of the Year 2500. LC 77-6804. 360p. 1977. 35.00 (*0-8398-2380-0*) Ultramarine Pub.

— Memoirs of the Year 2500. Hooper, W., tr. from FRE. LC 68-56258. xi, 360p. 1973. reprint ed. 49.50 (*0-678-00915-5*) Kelley.

— Le Nouveau Paris, 6 pts. in 3. xxxviii, 1486p. reprint ed. write for info. (*0-318-71379-9*) G Olms Pubs.

— Oeuvres Dramatiques, 2 vols. in 1. 726p. 1984. reprint ed. write for info. (*3-487-07477-X*) G Olms Pubs.

***Mercier, Louis-Sebastien.** Panorama of Paris: Selections from Tableau de Paris. Popkin, Jeremy D., ed. LC 98-51840. 235p. 1999. 50.00 (*0-271-01930-1*) Pa St U Pr.

Mercier, Louis-Sebastien. Panorama of Paris: Selections from Tableau de Paris. Popkin, Jeremy D., ed. 322p. 1999. pap. 17.00 (*0-271-01931-X*) Pa St U Pr.

Mercier, Louis-Sebastien & Popkin, Jeremy D. In Search of Peace & Prosperity: New German Settlements in Eighteenth-Century Europe & America. LC 98-51840. 1999. 21.50 (*0-271-01929-8*) Pa St U Pr.

Mercier, M., ed. Criteria (Dose Effect Relationships) for Organichlorine Pesticides: Report of a Working Group of Experts Prepared for the Commission of the European Communities. 400p. 1981. pap. 184.00 (*0-08-023441-0*, Pub. by Pergamon Repr) Franklin.

Mercier, Mary. Johnny No-Trump. 1968. pap. 5.25 (*0-8222-0598-X*) Dramatists Play.

Mercier, Michele. Crimes Without Punishment: Humanitarian Action in Former Yugoslavia. LC 95-36109. 224p. 1995. 54.95 (*0-7453-1080-X*, Pub. by Pluto GBR); pap. 19.95 (*0-7453-1081-8*, Pub. by Pluto GBR) Stylus Pub VA.

***Mercier, Peter J. & Mercier, Judith D.** Battle Cries on the Home Front: Violence in the Military Family. LC 99-50281. 238p. 2000. pap. 29.95 (*0-398-07035-0*) C C Thomas.

Mercier, Pierre, jt. auth. see Barral, Jean-Pierre.

Mercier, Pierre-Yves, ed. Knopf Guide to Amsterdam. (Illus.). 1993. pap. 25.00 (*0-679-74914-4*) Random.

Mercier, R., ed. see Cesaire, Aime.

Mercier, R., ed. see Dadie, Bernard B.

Mercier, Richard. The Songs of Hans Pfitzner: A Guide & Study, 64. LC 97-41922. (Music Reference Collection: Vol. 64). 232p. 1998. lib. bdg. 69.50 (*0-313-30533-1*, Greenwood Pr) Greenwood.

Mercier, Ron. Dance the River Whale. LC 98-94935. 256p. 1999. pap. 13.95 (*0-9668527-0-2*) Deerbridge Bks.

Mercier, Sheryl, jt. auth. see Hoover, Evalyn.

Mercier, Sheryl A., jt. auth. see Ostlund, Karen L.

***Mercier, Susan K. & Elskoe-Long, Susan.** Exploring Words: Developmental Word Sorts Allowing Students to Discover Common Features about Words. (Illus.). 191p. 1999. teacher ed. 32.95 (*0-9675954-0-1*) SueMer.

Mercier, Vivian. Modern Irish Literature: Sources & Founders. Dillon, Eilis, ed. LC 93-24542. 398p. (C). 1994. text 48.00 (*0-19-812074-5*, Clarendon Pr) OUP.

Mercik, Agnes. Applique Innovations. (Illus.). 128p. 1998. pap. 14.95 (*0-8069-8707-3*) Sterling.

— Applique Innovations: New Techniques for Beautiful Clothing. LC 97-12796. (Illus.). 127p. 1997. 27.95 (*0-8069-0355-4*) Sterling.

Mercilliott, Frederick. Arson in the First Degree. 196p. (Orig.). 1995. pap. 12.99 (*0-936285-24-9*) U New Haven Pr.

Merck & Co., Inc. Staff. El Manual Merck de Diagnostico y Terapeutica. 9th ed. Berkow, Robert, ed. (SPA.). 3122p. 1994. 150.00 (*0-7859-9597-8*) Fr & Eur.

— The Merck Manual of Medical Information: Home Edition. Berkow, Robert et al, eds. LC 96-80494. (Illus.). 1509p. 1997. 29.95 (*0-911910-87-5*) Merck.

Merck, Bobbie J. Delay Is Not Denial. 83p. (Orig.). (C). 1994. pap. 5.95 (*0-929263-08-1*) Great Love Church Intl.

— Hope. 123p. (Orig.). (C). 1992. pap. text 6.95 (*0-929263-05-7*) Great Love Church Intl.

— Power of the Secret Place. 78p. (Orig.). 1990. pap. 5.95 (*0-929263-03-0*) Great Love Church Intl.

— Spoiling Python's Schemes. 217p. (Orig.). (C). 1991. pap. 8.95 (*0-929263-02-2*) Great Love Church Intl.

Merck, David W. Maintaining Dating Purity. LC 96-42567. 1996. 3.75 (*1-889520-01-2*) Truth for Eternity.

Merck, Dohme, jt. auth. see Merck, Sharp.

Merck, E. M., jt. auth. see Merck, Timothy.

Merck Editors. The Merck Veterinary Manual. 8th rev. ed. 1998. 32.00 (*0-911910-29-8*) Merck.

Merck Editors, ed. Merck Manual: Portugese Language Edition. (POR.). Date not set. 150.00 (*0-7859-9662-1*) Fr & Eur.

— Merck Manual: Russian Language Edition. (RUS.). Date not set. 195.00 (*0-7859-9663-X*) Fr & Eur.

— Merck Manual: Turkish Language Edition. (TUR.). Date not set. 150.00 (*0-7859-9664-8*) Fr & Eur.

Merck, Mandy. After Diana: Irreverent Elegies. LC 98-30116. 160p. 1998. pap. 16.00 (*1-85984-265-8*, Pub. by Verso) Norton.

Merck, Mandy. In Your Face: 9 Sexual Studies. pap. 17.95 (*0-8147-5639-5*); text 55.00 (*0-8147-5638-7*) NYU Pr.

An Asterisk (*) at the beginning of an entry indicates that the title is appearing for the first time.

Merck, Mandy, ed. Pervisions: Deviant Readings by Mandy Merck. (Illus.). 224p. (C). (gr. 13). 1993. pap. 17.99 (*0-415-90792-6*, B0639) Routledge.

— The Sexual Subject: Screen Reader in Sexuality. LC 91-40140. 352p. (C). 1992. pap. 22.99 (*0-415-07467-3*, A7174) Routledge.

— The Sexual Subject: Screen Reader in Sexuality. LC 91-40140. (Illus.). 352p. (C). (gr. 13). 1992. 80.00 (*0-415-07466-5*, A7170) Routledge.

Merck, Mandy, et al. Coming Out of Feminism? LC 98-4889. 224p. 1998. 62.95 (*1-55786-701-1*); pap. 29.95 (*1-55786-702-X*) Blackwell Pubs.

Merck, Robert M. Deck the Halls... Treasures of Christmas Past. (Illus.). 96p. 1992. 27.50 (*1-55859-267-9*) Abbeville Pr.

Merck, Russell. How to Succeed in Activity-Based Selling: Creating the Self-Motivation Needed for Peak Sales Performance. LC 96-76375. (Illus.). 224p. (Orig.). 1996. pap. 19.95 (*0-9652524-0-X*) Gld Star Pub.

Merck, Sharp & Dohme. The Merck Manual for Veterinarians: El Manual Merck de Veterinaria. 2nd ed. (SPA.). 1386p. 1981. 75.00 (*0-8288-2389-8*, S39845) Fr & Eur.

Merck, Sharp & Merck, Dohme. Merck Manual: El Manual Merck. 7th ed. (SPA.). 1986. 75.00 (*0-8288-1869-X*, S37592) Fr & Eur.

Merck, Timothy & Merck, E. M. Christmas Ornament Legends Vol. 1: The Genuine Collection of Stories, Traditions, & Folklore from the Old World. (Illus.). 80p. 1995. 12.95 (*0-9648534-0-X*) Old Wrld Christmas.

Merck, Wilson. Review of Imagery Uses in Twentieth Century Literature. (Orig.). 1990. pap. 9.90 (*0-913412-15-5*) Brandon Hse.

Merckel, Curt. Die Ingenieurtechnik Im Alterthum. xix, 658p. 1969. reprint ed. write for info. (*0-318-70783-7*) G Olms Pubs.

Mercker, Mary R. Northumberland Dreaming: A Past Life Remembered. LC 98-72214. 424p. 1998. pap. text 14.95 (*1-57174-086-4*) Hampton Roads Pub Co.

Mercogliano, Chris. Making It up As We Go Along: The Story of the (Albany) Free School. LC 97-51792. 1998. pap. 21.00 (*0-325-00043-3*, Pub. by Boynton Cook Pubs) Heinemann.

Mercogliano, Chris, jt. auth. see Gatto, John T.

Mercredi, Morningstar. Fort Chipewyan Homecoming: A Journey to Native Canada. LC 96-15786. (Illus.). (J). 1996. pap. 6.95 (*0-8225-9731-4*, Lerner Publctns); lib. bdg. 21.27 (*0-8225-2659-X*, Lerner Publctns) Lerner Pub.

Mercugliano, Marianne, et al. The Clinician's Practical Guide to Attention-Deficit Hyperactivity Disorder. LC 98-35194. 1998. 39.95 (*1-55766-358-0*) P H Brookes.

Mercuri, Carmela. Beauty & the Beast: Story with Music. (Illus.). 24p. (Orig.). (YA). (gr. 8-12). 1976. pap. 4.95 (*0-935474-24-2*) Carousel Pubns Ltd.

— The Best of Vaudeville 3. (Dear Teacher, I've Always Wanted to Play the Piano Ser.). (Illus.). 32p. (Orig.). 1982. pap. 5.95 (*0-935474-05-6*, CAR1122) Carousel Pubns Ltd.

— Christmas Songs 1, No. 1. (Dear Teacher, I've Always Wanted to Play the Piano Ser.). (Illus.). 32p. (Orig.). 1982. pap. 5.95 (*0-935474-04-8*, CAR1111) Carousel Pubns Ltd.

— Classical Themes, Level 1. (Dear Teacher, I've Always Wanted to Play the Piano Ser.: No. 4). (Illus.). 32p. (Orig.). 1982. pap. 5.95 (*0-935474-06-4*) Carousel Pubns Ltd.

— Classical Themes: Level Two, Themes 5. (Dear Teacher, I've Always Wanted to Play the Piano Ser.). (Illus.). 32p. (Orig.). 1982. pap. 5.95 (*0-935474-07-2*, CAR1134) Carousel Pubns Ltd.

— Music Theory in Practice, Bk. 1. 32p. 1984. pap. 5.95 (*0-935474-01-3*) Carousel Pubns Ltd.

— My First Theory Book: Note Names for Coloring. (Illus.). 32p. (Orig.). (J). (gr. 1-6). 1987. pap. text 5.95 (*0-935474-20-X*) Carousel Pubns Ltd.

— Popular Folks Songs 1. (Dear Teacher, I've Always Wanted to Play the Piano Ser.). (Illus.). 32p. (Orig.). 1982. pap. 5.95 (*0-935474-02-1*, CAR1100) Carousel Pubns Ltd.

— The Recorder Book: The Beginners Recorder Book. (Illus.). (Orig.). 1993. pap. 5.95 (*0-935474-23-4*) Carousel Pubns Ltd.

— Toot-in-Time Band: Introducing Children to the World of Music. (Illus.). (Orig.). (J). (gr. 1-6). 1993. pap. 16.95 (*0-935474-21-8*) Carousel Pubns Ltd.

Mercuri, Carmela, ed. Modes in All Keys for Piano. (Orig.). 1993. pap. 6.95 (*0-935474-22-6*) Carousel Pubns Ltd.

Mercuri, Carmela & Smith, Robin A. World in Tune - An Integrative Approach to World Music, Musical Instrument Included: Music of the Ancient World. (Illus.). 142p. 1997. pap., teacher ed. 300.00 (*0-935474-27-7*) Carousel Pubns Ltd.

Mercuri, Carmela, ed. see Mozart, Wolfgang Amadeus.

Mercuri, Michele, et al, eds. Non-Invasive Imaging of Atherosclerosis. LC 97-37849. (Developments in Cardiovascular Medicine Ser.: No. 199). 245p. 1997. text 159.50 (*0-7923-8036-3*) Kluwer Academic.

Mercurialis-Hieronymus. De Arte Gymnastica, Libre Sex. Tanis, Norman E., ed. (Northridge Facsimile Ser.: Pt. X). 1978. pap. 5.00 (*0-937048-09-7*) Santa Susana.

Mercurian, Barbara J., ed. Genocide & Human Rights: Lessons from the Armenian Experience. LC 93-19321. xi, 436p. 1993. pap. 25.00 (*0-935411-11-9*) Natl Assn Arm.

*__Mercurio, Carl & Sigel, Efrem.__ Online Pharmacy Rush: Gold Mine or Fool's Gold? 135p. 1999. pap. 11.95 (*0-9662321-3-5*) Corp Res Grp.

Mercurio, Gian & Peschel, Max. Mesa Verde: Fuerher Durch Den Nationalpark. Glosser, Margie, tr. (Illus.). (Orig.). 1991. pap. 4.95 (*0-9627377-0-4*) Lonewolf Pub.

Mercurio, Gian & Peschel, Maxymilian L. The Guide to Trading Posts & Pueblos. (Illus.). 72p. (Orig.). 1994. pap. 8.95 (*0-9627377-2-0*) Lonewolf Pub.

— Mesa Verde: A Complete Guide. (Illus.). 50p. (Orig.). 1992. pap. 4.95 (*0-9627377-1-2*) Lonewolf Pub.

Mercurio, Helen C. The Miracle Santa's Beard. Mercurio, Mary M., ed. (Illus.). 29p. (J). 1985. 12.00 (*0-9616079-0-4*) Tiffany Pub.

Mercurio, Louis. Instant Travel Art Vol. 1: Cruises. 48p. 1982. pap. 20.95 (*0-916032-17-5*) Delmar.

Mercurio, Mary M., ed. see Mercurio, Helen C.

Mercurio, Robert, tr. see Zoja, Luigi.

Mercurius, Kether, jt. auth. see Caballion, Invicta.

Mercuro, Nicholas, ed. Ecology, Law & Economics: The Simple Analytics of Natural Resource & Environmental Economics. 2nd ed. LC 97-27625. 244p. (C). 1997. 52.00 (*0-7618-0863-9*); pap. 34.50 (*0-7618-0864-7*) U Pr of Amer.

— Family Law & Gender Bias: Comparative Perspectives. (International Review of Comparative Public Policy Ser.: Vol. 4). 256p. 1993. 78.50 (*1-55938-400-X*) Jai Pr.

— Taking Property & Just Compensation: Lew & Economics Perspectives of the Takings Issue. (Recent Economic Thought Ser.). 240p. (C). 1992. lib. bdg. 116.50 (*0-7923-9233-7*) Kluwer Academic.

Mercuro, Nicholas & Medema, Steven G. Economics & the Law: From Posner to Post-Modernism. LC 96-46300. 256p. 1997. text 29.95 (*0-691-01174-5*, Pub. by Princeton U Pr) Cal Prin Full Svc.

Mercuro, Nicholas & Ryan, Timothy. Law, Economics & Public Policy. Breit, William & Elzinga, Kenneth G., eds. LC 84-4406. (Political Economy & Public Policy Ser.: Vol. 3). 184p. 1984. 78.50 (*0-89232-396-5*) Jai Pr.

Mercuro, Nicholas, et al. Ecology, Law & Economics: The Simple Analytics of Natural Resource & Environment Economics. LC 94-17739. (Illus.). 212p. (Orig.). (C). 1994. reprint ed. pap. text 32.50 (*0-8191-9594-4*); reprint ed. lib. bdg. 49.50 (*0-8191-9593-6*) U Pr of Amer.

Mercuro, Nicholas, jt. ed. see Leonhard, Alan T.

Mercury, Catherine J. Think of Wind. Stranges, Dawn M., ed. (Illus.). 28p. (Orig.). (J). 1996. pap. 14.95 (*0-9654447-1-6*) One Big Pr.

Mercury, Catherine J., jt. auth. see Stranges, Dawn M.

*__Mercury, Maureen.__ Pagan Fleshworks: The Alchemy of Body Modification. LC 00-35700. 2000. pap. 19.95 (*0-89281-809-3*) Inner Tradit.

Mercy, Deborah. Frostbite & Other Cold Injuries. 2nd ed. (Fisheries Safety & Survival Ser.: No. 7). 19p. 1990. reprint ed. pap., student ed. 4.00 (*1-56612-008-X*) AK Sea Grant CP.

Merdeka Thien-Ly Huong Do. Caodaiism an Introduction: Cao Dai Indigenous Vietnamese Religion. LC 94-74876. 106p. 1994. pap. text. write for info. (*0-9644543-0-0*) Cao Dai Temple.

Merdinger, J. E. Rome & the African Church in the Time of Augustine. LC 96-20999. 288p. 1997. 42.00 (*0-300-04017-2*) Yale U Pr.

*__Merdlowitz, Edward.__ IRA Distributions What You Should Know Before You Have to Take Distributions from Your IRA Accounts. 40p. 2000. pap. 29.95 (*0-9656711-1-9*) Pract Programs.

Mere, Gallogo, tr. see Woodbury, Michael A., ed.

Mereday, Emma W. On the Outside. 80p. (Orig.). 1995. pap. 25.00 (*0-9647131-0-1*) Emmae.

Mereday, Meta J. Reaching Out Just a Little Farther. rev. ed. (Illus.). 64p. 1995. pap. 15.00 (*0-9647131-9-5*) Emmae.

Meredig, John, tr. see Makaev, E. A.

Meredith. The Calling. 124p. 1995. pap. 5.99 (*1-886820-03-1*) Meredith WA.

— Essentials of Project Management. pap. text. write for info. (*0-471-37162-9*) Wiley.

— Note Book of an Unknown Writer. 143p. 1995. pap. text 4.99 (*1-886820-02-3*) Meredith WA.

— Poetry of Meredith. 55p. 1995. pap. 2.99 (*1-886820-01-5*) Meredith WA.

*__Meredith.__ Project Management: A Managerial Approach. 4th ed. 640p. 1999. text 98.95 (*0-471-29829-8*) Wiley.

Meredith. Strange Valentine. 168p. 1995. pap. 5.99 (*1-886820-00-7*) Meredith WA.

— Xplore IBM Bk/Disk. 288p. 1993. pap. text 37.33 (*0-13-014226-3*) P-H.

Meredith & Turban. Quantitative Business Analysis. 1999. 45.00 (*0-324-01600-X*) Sth-Wstrn College.

Meredith, jt. auth. see Radrobe.

Meredith, Albert. Charles Haddon Spurgeon's Lectures to My Students. LC 98-21294. (Shepherd's Notes Ser.). 1999. 5.95 (*0-8054-9196-1*) Broadman.

Meredith, Anthony. The Cappadocians. LC 95-15076. 129p. (Orig.). 1995. pap. 11.95 (*0-88141-112-4*) St Vladimirs.

— The Cappadocians LC 94-134861. (Outstanding Christian Thinkers Ser.). xiii, 129p. 1995. write for info. (*0-225-66707-X*, Pub. by G Chapman) Bks Intl VA.

Meredith, Anthony & Gregory. Gregory of Nyssa. LC 98-24529. (Early Church Fathers Ser.). 1999. 85.00 (*0-415-11839-5*); pap. 25.99 (*0-415-11840-9*) Routledge.

Meredith, Barbara, jt. auth. see Lewis, Jane.

Meredith, Barbara, jt. auth. see Lewis, Jane E.

*__Meredith Books Staff.__ All about Backyard Structures. (Illus.). 96p. 2000. pap. 11.95 (*0-89721-447-1*, Ortho Bks) Meredith Bks.

— All about Carpentry Basics. (Illus.). 96p. 2000. pap. 11.95 (*0-89721-436-6*, Ortho Bks) Meredith Bks.

— All about Deck & Patio Upgrades. (All about Basics Ser.). (Illus.). 96p. 2000. pap. 11.95 (*0-89721-441-2*, Ortho Bks) Meredith Bks.

— All about Decks. (All about Basics Ser.). (Illus.). 96p. 2000. pap. 11.95 (*0-89721-442-0*, Ortho Bks) Meredith Bks.

— All about Landscape Construction Basics. (All about Basics Ser.). (Illus.). 96p. 2000. pap. 11.95 (*0-89721-437-4*, Ortho Bks) Meredith Bks.

— All about Masonry Basics. (All about Basics Ser.). (Illus.). 96p. 2000. pap. 11.95 (*0-89721-438-2*, Ortho Bks) Meredith Bks.

— All about Patios. (Illus.). 96p. 2000. pap. 11.95 (*0-89721-443-9*, Ortho Bks) Meredith Bks.

— All about Plumbing Basics. (All about Basics Ser.). (Illus.). 96p. 2000. pap. 11.95 (*0-89721-439-0*, Ortho Bks) Meredith Bks.

— All about Wiring Basics. (All about Basics Ser.). (Illus.). 96p. 2000. pap. 11.95 (*0-89721-440-4*, Ortho Bks) Meredith Bks.

Meredith Books Staff. Kraft Halloween. LC 98-68024. (Illus.). 96p. 1999. 12.95 (*0-696-20901-2*) Meredith Bks.

— Kraft No Oven Summer Sensations: Easy Tips from the Kraft Creative Kitchens. 96p. 1998. 12.95 (*0-696-20840-7*) Meredith Bks.

Meredith, Bronwen. Is Your Cat Too Fat? (Illus.). 128p. 1999. 18.95 (*1-56649-040-5*); pap. 12.95 (*1-56649-039-1*) Welcome Rain.

Meredith, Carol. Contemporary Interiors. (Room by Room Ser.). (Illus.). 160p. 1998. 35.00 (*1-56496-427-2*, Pub. by Rockport Pubs) F & W Pubns Inc.

— Country Interiors. (Room by Room Ser.). (Illus.). 160p. 1998. 35.00 (*1-56496-425-6*, Pub. by Rockport Pubs) F & W Pubns Inc.

— Eclectic Style: New with Old in Interior Design. (Illus.). 160p. 1998. 34.99 (*1-56496-413-2*) Rockport Pubs.

— Jamie Anderson Wouldn't. (Illus.). 24p. (J). (ps-2). 1998. lib. bdg. 15.95 (*1-55037-457-5*, Pub. by Annick) Firefly Bks Ltd.

*__Meredith, Carol.__ Jamie Anderson Wouldn't. (Illus.). 24p. (J). (ps-2). 1998. pap. 5.95 (*1-55037-456-7*, Pub. by Annick) Firefly Bks Ltd.

— Room by Room: Contemporary Interiors. 2000. pap. 20.00 (*1-56496-696-8*) Rockport Pubs.

— Room by Room: Country Interiors. 2000. pap. 20.00 (*1-56496-700-X*) Rockport Pubs.

Meredith, Carol, jt. auth. see Prosser, Alex.

Meredith, Christopher. Griffri. 256p. 1995. 30.00 (*1-85411-059-4*) Dufour.

— Shifts. 180p. 1997. pap. 17.95 (*1-85411-199-X*, Pub. by Seren Bks) Dufour.

— Snaring Heaven. 80p. 1990. pap. 13.95 (*1-85411-026-8*, Pub. by Seren Bks) Dufour.

Meredith, Christopher, jt. ed. see Huzzard, Ron.

Meredith Custom Publishing Staff. Kraft Holiday Homecoming (MCP) 87 Festive Recipes. 96p. 1997. 12.95 (*0-696-20763-X*) Meredith Bks.

Meredith, D., compiled by. Tabula Imperii Romani: Map of the Roman Empire, Coptos. (Illus.). 1958. pap. 5.00 (*0-85431-253-6*, Pub. by Soc Antiquaries) David Brown.

*__Meredith, D. R.__ By Hook or By Book. 272p. 2000. mass mkt. 5.99 (*0-425-17465-4*, Prime Crime) Berkley Pub.

Meredith, D. R. The Homefront Murders. (Southwest Mysteries Ser.). 1995. mass mkt. 4.99 (*0-345-38050-9*) Ballantine Pub Grp.

— Murder by Reference. 272p. 1991. mass mkt. 4.99 (*0-345-36861-4*) Ballantine Pub Grp.

— Murder by Sacrilege. 1993. mass mkt. 4.99 (*0-345-37693-5*) Ballantine Pub Grp.

*__Meredith, D. R.__ Murder in Volume. 2000. mass mkt. 5.99 (*0-425-17309-7*, Prime Crime) Berkley Pub.

Meredith, Dale D., et al. Design & Planning of Engineering Systems. (Civil Engineering & Engineering Mechanics Ser.). (Illus.). 384p. 1973. 34.95 (*0-685-03823-8*) P-H.

*__Meredith, David & Dyster, Barrie.__ Australia in the Global Economy: Continuity & Change. LC 99-37270. (Illus.). 400p. 2000. 64.95 (*0-521-63127-0*); pap. 24.95 (*0-521-63730-9*) Cambridge U Pr.

Meredith, David & Dyster, Barrie. Australia in the International Economy in the Twentieth Century. (Illus.). 378p. (C). 1990. pap. text 29.95 (*0-521-33689-9*) Cambridge U Pr.

Meredith, David, jt. auth. see Havinden, Michael.

Meredith, Dawn, jt. auth. see Koonin, Steven E.

*__Meredith, Don.__ Two...Becoming One: Applying God's Best for Your Marriage. 1999. pap., wbk. ed. 14.99 (*0-8024-3446-0*) Moody.

— Two...Becoming One: Discovering God's Best for Your Marriage. 1999. pap. 12.99 (*0-8024-3445-2*) Moody.

— Where the Tigers Were: Travels Through Literary Landscapes. 160p. 2001. 21.95 (*1-57003-380-3*) U of SC Pr.

Meredith, Don & Meredith, Sally. Becoming One. 2nd rev. ed. (Illus.). 282p. 1997. pap. 11.95 (*0-9657965-0-7*) Christian Family.

Meredith, Doris R. The Sheriff & the Branding Iron Murders. 160p. 1986. pap. 2.95 (*0-380-70050-6*, Avon Bks) Morrow Avon.

— The Sheriff & the Branding Iron Murders. 159p. 1985. 14.95 (*0-8027-4050-2*) Walker & Co.

— The Sheriff & the Folsom Man Murders. 208p. 1987. pap. 2.95 (*0-380-70364-5*, Avon Bks) Morrow Avon.

— The Sheriff & the Folsom Man Murders. 192p. 1987. 16.95 (*0-8027-5663-8*) Walker & Co.

— The Sheriff & the Folsom Man Murders. large type ed. LC 99-13451. (Paperback Ser.). 268p. 1999. pap. 23.95 (*0-7838-8582-2*) Thorndike Pr.

Meredith, Elaine C. A Lifetime of Poetry. (Illus.). 221p. (Orig.). 1986. pap. 25.00 (*0-9614058-1-3*) Southco.

Meredith, Elandra K., jt. ed. see Clagett, Alice B.

Meredith, Ellen. Listening In: Dialogues with the Wiser Self. LC 93-77564. 304p. (Orig.). 1993. pap. 14.95 (*0-9636073-5-9*) Horse Mtn Pr.

Meredith, Fred. Tempting Fortune: The Way Business Really Works. Piper, David, ed. 144p. 1996. pap. 14.95 (*0-88962-571-9*) Mosaic.

Meredith, Gary. Small Business Management in Australia. 2nd ed. 352p. 1982. 18.50 (*0-07-451006-1*) McGraw.

Meredith, George. The Adventures of Harry Richmond. Hergenban, L. T., ed. & intro. by. LC 78-88088. 651p. 1970. reprint ed. pap. 200.00 (*0-608-01841-4*, 206249100003) Bks Demand.

— Diana of the Crossways. reprint ed. lib. bdg. 79.00 (*0-7812-0098-9*) Rprt Serv.

— Diana of the Crossways. LC 70-145177. 1971. reprint ed. 89.00 (*0-403-01105-1*) Scholarly.

— The Egoist. Adams, Robert M., ed. LC 77-25313. (Critical Editions Ser.). 561p. (C). 1979. pap. text 16.75 (*0-393-09171-6*) Norton.

— George Meredith (1828-1909) Selected Poems. Hanley, Keith, ed. 1983. pap. 8.50 (*0-85635-416-3*) Carcanet Pr.

— George Meredith's Essay "On Comedy" & Other "New Quarterly Magazine" Publications: A Critical Edition. Ives, Maura C., ed. LC 97-41276. 368p. 1998. 49.50 (*0-8387-5349-3*) Bucknell U Pr.

— Letters of George Meredith, 2 vols., Set. (BCL1-PR English Literature Ser.). 1992. reprint ed. lib. bdg. 150.00 (*0-7812-7594-6*) Rprt Serv.

— The Ordeal of Richard Feverel: A History of a Father & Son. LC 99-461805. 524p. 1999. pap. 11.95 (*0-14-043483-6*, PuffinBks) Peng Put Young Read.

— The Poems of George Meredith. Bartlett, Phyllis B., ed. LC 73-77142. 1978. 175.00 (*0-300-01283-7*) Yale U Pr.

— Selected Poems. Hough, Graham G., ed. LC 79-2564. 95p. 1980. reprint ed. lib. bdg. 42.50 (*0-313-22034-4*, MESP, Greenwood Pr) Greenwood.

— Short Stories. rev. ed. LC 73-144162. (Short Story Index Reprint Ser.). 1977. reprint ed. 20.95 (*0-8369-3777-5*) Ayer.

— The Tragic Comedians: A Study in a Well-Known Story. (Revised Edition) LC 74-29508. (Modern Jewish Experience Ser.). 1975. reprint ed. 17.95 (*0-405-06735-6*) Ayer.

— Works, 29 vols., Set. (BCL1-PR English Literature Ser.). 1992. reprint ed. lib. bdg. 2610.00 (*0-7812-7593-8*) Rprt Serv.

*__Meredith, George.__ Works of George Meredith, 29 vols. Incl. Beauchamp's Career. 355p. 1999. reprint ed. lib. bdg. 90.00 (*1-58201-199-0*); Farina & The Case of General Ople & Lady Camper. 206p. 1999. reprint ed. lib. bdg. 90.00 (*1-58201-213-X*); Poems. 233p. 1999. reprint ed. lib. bdg. 90.00 (*1-58201-214-8*); Shaving of Shagpat: An Arabian Entertainment. 315p. 1999. reprint ed. lib. bdg. 90.00 (*1-58201-210-5*); Tale of Chloe & The House on the Beach. 204p. 1999. reprint ed. lib. bdg. 90.00 (*1-58201-212-1*); Tragic Comedians: A Study in a Well-Known Story. 211p. 1999. reprint ed. lib. bdg. 90.00 (*1-58201-211-3*); Pt. 1. Adventures of Harry Richmond. 378p. 1999. reprint ed. lib. bdg. 90.00 (*1-58201-196-6*); Pt. 1. Amazing Marriage. 278p. 1999. reprint ed. lib. bdg. 90.00 (*1-58201-208-3*); Pt. 1. Diana of the Crossways: A Novel. 282p. 1999. reprint ed. lib. bdg. 90.00 (*1-58201-202-4*); Pt. 1. Egoist: A Comedy in Narrative. 351p. 1999. reprint ed. lib. bdg. 90.00 (*1-58201-200-8*); Pt. 1. Evan Harrington. 316p. 1999. reprint ed. lib. bdg. 90.00 (*1-58201-188-5*); Pt. 1. Lord Ormont & His Aminta: A Novel. 201p. 1999. reprint ed. lib. bdg. 90.00 (*1-58201-206-7*); Pt. 1. One of Our Conquerors. 270p. 1999. reprint ed. lib. bdg. 90.00 (*1-58201-204-0*); Pt. 1. Ordeal of Richard Feverel: A History of a Father & Son. 308p. 1999. reprint ed. lib. bdg. 90.00 (*1-58201-186-9*); Pt. 1. Rhoda Fleming: A Story. 273p. 1999. reprint ed. lib. bdg. 90.00 (*1-58201-194-X*); Pt. 1. Sandra Belloni. 327p. 1999. reprint ed. lib. bdg. 90.00 (*1-58201-190-7*); Pt. 1. Vittoria. 350p. 1999. reprint ed. lib. bdg. 90.00 (*1-58201-192-3*); Pt. 2. Adventures of Harry Richmond. 382p. 1999. reprint ed. lib. bdg. 90.00 (*1-58201-197-4*); Pt. 2. Amazing Marriage. 290p. 1999. reprint ed. lib. bdg. 90.00 (*1-58201-209-1*); Pt. 2. Diana of the Crossways: A Novel. 279p. 1999. reprint ed. lib. bdg. 90.00 (*1-58201-203-2*); Pt. 2. Egoist: A Comedy in Narrative. 353p. 1999. reprint ed. lib. bdg. 90.00 (*1-58201-201-6*); Pt. 2. Evan Harrington. 320p. 1999. reprint ed. lib. bdg. 90.00 (*1-58201-189-3*); Pt. 2. Lord Ormont & His Aminta: A Novel. 194p. 1999. reprint ed. lib. bdg. 90.00 (*1-58201-207-5*); Pt. 2. One of Our Conquerors. 316p. 1999. reprint ed. lib. bdg. 90.00 (*1-58201-205-9*); Pt. 2. Ordeal of Richard Feverel: A History of a Father & Son. 303p. 1999. reprint ed. lib. bdg. 90.00 (*1-58201-187-7*); Pt. 2. Rhoda Fleming: A Story. 278p. 1999. reprint ed. lib. bdg. 90.00 (*1-58201-195-8*); Pt. 2. Sandra Belloni. 340p. 1999. reprint ed. lib. bdg. 90.00 (*1-58201-191-5*); Pt. 2. Vittoria. 342p. 1999. reprint ed. lib. bdg. 90.00 (*1-58201-193-1*); 1999. reprint ed. Set lib. bdg. 2610.00 (*1-58201-185-0*) Classic Bks.

Meredith, Gertrude E. The Descendants of Hugh Amory, 1605-1805, British & American. (Illus.). 373p. 1988. reprint ed. pap. 58.50 (*0-8328-0217-4*); reprint ed. lib. bdg. 68.50 (*0-8328-0216-6*) Higginson Bk Co.

Meredith, Gina, jt. auth. see Hartwig, Laurie.

Meredith, Gloria E. & Arbuthnott, Gordon W., eds. Morphological Investigations of Single Neurons in Vitro. LC 93-10269. (IBRO Handbook Series: Methods in the Neurosciences: No. 16). 210p. 1993. pap. 230.00 (*0-471-93928-5*) Wiley.

Meredith, H. O., jt. ed. see Dickinson, G. Lowes.

Meredith, H. V. Physical Growth of White Children. (SRCD M Ser.: Vol. 1, No. 2). 1936. pap. 25.00 (*0-527-01487-7*) Periodicals Srv.

Meredith, Henry. Account of the Gold Coast of Africa. (Illus.). 264p. 1967. 35.00 (*0-7146-1039-9*, Pub. by F Cass Pubs) Intl Spec Bk.

Meredith, Henry, ed. see Scarlatti, Alessandro.

Meredith, Howard & Williams, John. Bacone Indian University. 163p. 1980. 10.00 (*0-86546-006-X*) Indian U Pr OK.

An Asterisk (*) at the beginning of an entry indicates that the title is appearing for the first time.

M

Meredith, Howard L. Dancing on Common Ground: Tribal Cultures & Alliances on the Southern Plains. LC 94-23557. (Illus.). x, 222p. 1995. 29.95 (0-7006-0694-7) U Pr of KS.
— Modern American Indian Tribal Government & Politics: An Interdisciplinary Study. 169p. 1993. pap. 16.95 (0-912586-76-1) Dine College Pr.
Meredith, Howard L. & Milan, Virginia E. A Cherokee Vision of Eloh' Proctor, Wesley, tr. (CHR & ENG.). 37p. 1981. pap. 8.00 (0-940392-04-6) Indian U Pr OK.
Meredith, Howard L. & Sobral, Virginia M., eds. A Cherokee Vision of Eloh' Proctor, Wesley, tr. (CHR & ENG., Illus.). 40p. 1997. pap. text 15.00 (0-9660164-0-8) Noksi Pr.
Meredith, Howard L., jt. auth. see Newkumet, Vynola B.
Meredith, Isabel. A Girl among the Anarchists. LC 92-12212. xiv, 302p. (C). 1992. pap. 9.95 (0-8032-8190-0, Bison Books) U of Nebr Pr.
Meredith, J. C., tr. see Kant, Immanuel.
Meredith, J. L. Meredith's Second Book of Bible Lists. LC 83-3807. 192p. (Orig.). 1983. pap. 7.99 (0-87123-319-3) Bethany Hse.
Meredith, Jack & Shafer, Scott. Operations Management: A Process-Based Approach with Spreadsheets. LC 97-46370. 860p. 1998. text 80.95 (0-471-16545-X) Wiley.
Meredith, Jack R. The Management of Operations. 3rd ed. 148p. 1987. pap. 34.95 (0-471-85582-0) Wiley.
— The Management of Operations. 4th ed. LC 91-33361. 800p. (C). 1992. text 86.95 (0-471-50909-4) Wiley.
— The Management of Operations. 4th ed. 1992. pap. text 25.00 (0-471-54352-7) Wiley.
***Meredith, Jack R.** Operations Management for MBAs. LC 98-40650. (Illus.). 380p. 1998. pap. 46.95 (0-471-29828-X) Wiley.
Meredith, Jack R. & Mantel, Samuel J. Project Management: A Managerial Approach. 3rd ed. (Series in Production-Operations Management). 784p. 1995. text 95.95 (0-471-01626-8) Wiley.
Meredith, Jack R. & Shafer, Scott. Fundamentals of Management Science. 6th ed. 80p. (C). 1994. per. write for info. (0-256-11868-X, Irwn McGrw-H) McGrw-H Hghr Educ.
Meredith, Jack R., jt. auth. see Turban, Efraim.
Meredith, James E., jt. auth. see Chinousky, Paul S.
***Meredith, James H.** Understanding the Literature of World War II: A Student Casebook to Issues, Sources & Historical Documents. LC 98-44591. 272p. 1999. 39.95 (0-313-30417-3) Greenwood.
Meredith, Jane. Around & about the Custom House. (Illus.). 96p. 1997. pap. 15.00 (1-85182-308-5, Pub. by Four Cts Pr) Intl Spec Bk.
Meredith, Jill, jt. auth. see Kiefer, Carol Solomon.
Meredith, Jill, jt. ed. see Bruzelius, Caroline.
Meredith, Joel L. Meredith's Big Book of Bible Lists. 1998. pap. text 9.99 (0-88486-197-X, Inspirational Pr) Arrowood Pr.
— Meredith's Book of Bible Lists. LC 80-14486. 288p. (Orig.). 1980. pap. 9.99 (0-87123-023-2, 210023) Bethany Hse.
Meredith, John. The Omdurman Diaries, 1898: Eye-Witness Accounts of the Legendary Campaign. 1998. 39.95 (0-85052-607-8, Pub. by Leo Cooper) Trans-Atl Phila.
Meredith, Joseph. Hunter's Moon: Poems from Boyhood to Manhood. LC 92-41085. 122p. 1993. 18.95 (1-877770-83-3); pap. 12.50 (1-877770-84-1); audio 12.95 (1-877770-85-X) Time Being Bks.
Meredith, Joseph C. The CAI Author-Instructor: An Introduction & Guide to the Preparation of Computer-Assisted Instruction Materials. LC 70-125876. 144p. 1971. 29.95 (0-87778-014-5) Educ Tech Pubns.
— A Handful of Emeralds: On Patrol with the "Hanna" in the Postwar Pacific. LC 97-8510. (Illus.). 240p. 1997. 32.95 (1-55750-590-X) Naval Inst Pr.
Meredith, Kenneth T. Depression Kid. (Illus.). 172p. 1999. pap. 10.00 (1-928590-03-9) Golden Stone CO.
— You Are with Me: A Personal Story of God's Sustaining Grace. LC 96-122368. 80p. 1995. pap. 6.99 (0-8341-1551-4) Beacon Hill.
***Meredith, Laurence.** BMW: Classic Cars of the 60s & 70s. (Illus.). 200p. 2000. 34.95 (1-86126-250-7, 129779AE, Pub. by Crolwood) Motorbooks Intl.
Meredith, Laurence. Essential Mercedes-Benz SL: 190SL & Pagoda Models, the Cars & Their Story 1955-71. (Essential Ser.). (Illus.). 80p. 1997. pap. 15.95 (1-870979-89-3, Bay View Bks) MBI Pubg.
— Essential Volkswagen Karmann-Ghia: The Cars & Their Story 1955-74. (Essential Ser.). (Illus.). 80p. 1994. pap. 15.95 (1-870979-52-4, Bay View Bks) MBI Pubg.
— Original Porsche 356: The Restoration Guide to All Coupe, Cabriolet, Roadster & Speedster Models 1950-65. (Illus.). 112p. 1995. pap. 34.95 (1-870979-58-3, Bay View Bks) MBI Pubg.
— Original VW Beetle, Updated ed. The Guide to European Models 1945-1978. rev. ed. LC 99-40953. (Illus.). 144p. 1999. 36.95 (1-901432-27-0) MBI Pubg.
— The Original VW Bus: The Restorers Guide to All Bus, Panel Van & Pick up Models 1950-79. (Original Ser.). (Illus.). 128p. 1997. 35.95 (1-870979-84-2, Bay View Bks) MBI Pubg.
***Meredith, Laurence.** Porsche 911. (Illus.). 160p. 2000. 24.95 (0-7509-2281-8) Sutton Publng.
— Porsche 911 Model by Model. (Illus.). 160p. 2000. 44.95 (1-86126-346-5, 130699AE, Pub. by Crolwood) Motorbooks Intl.
Meredith, Laurence. VW Beetle. 1999. pap. text 19.95 (0-7509-2133-1) Sutton Pub Ltd.
— VW Beetle: Model by Model. (Illus.). 160p. 1999. 44.95 (1-86126-273-6, Pub. by Crolwood) Motorbooks Intl.
— VW Bus. 1999. pap. text 21.95 (0-7509-2201-X) Sutton Pubg.
— VW Bus Custom Handbook. (Illus.). 205p. 1994. pap. text 19.95 (1-870979-47-8, Bay View Bks) MBI Pubg.
***Meredith, Laurence.** VW Golf. (Illus.). 160p. 2000. pap. 19.95 (0-7509-2314-8) Sutton Publng.
Meredith, Laurence. VW Transporter - The Complete Story. (Illus.). 200p. 1998. 35.95 (1-86126-159-4, Pub. by Crolwood) Motorbooks Intl.
Meredith, Lawrence. Life Before Death: A Religion of the Body. 1999. 28.95 (0-89334-292-0, Humanics Pub) Humanics Ltd.
Meredith, Lynne. How to Cook a Vulture: The End of the IRS's Immaculate Deception. (Illus.). 224p. 1998. pap. text 49.95 (0-9645192-7-5) Prsprty Pub.
— Vultures in Eagle's Clothing: Breaking Free from Ignorance Related Surgery (IRS) (Illus.). 223p. 1994. reprint ed. pap. text 39.95 (0-9645192-6-7) Prsprty Pub.
Meredith, M. European Initiatives in Public Procurement. (European Community Law Ser.). 63p. 1990. pap. text 134.00 (2-88316-004-X) Gordon & Breach.
***Meredith, Marilyn.** The Astral Gift. deluxe ed. 271p. 1998. pap. 6.99 (1-891940-00-7) Gold Eagle Pr.
Meredith, Marilyn. Cooking for a Big Family & Large Groups. (Illus.). 112p. 1990. pap. 7.95 (0-929935-05-5) Countrywomans Pr.
***Meredith, Marilyn.** Deadly Omen. (Tempe Crabtree Mystery Ser.). 255p. 1999. pap. 7.95 (1-891940-03-1) Gold Eagle Pr.
Meredith, Marilyn. The Demon Fire. 197p. 1984. 6.95 (0-89697-132-5) Intl Univ Pr.
— When the Cook Camps Out. (Illus.). 112p. (Orig.). 1990. pap. 7.95 (0-929935-03-9) Countrywomans Pr.
Meredith, Mark, ed. Trading with Uncertainty: Foreign Investment Trends in the Soviet Union. viii, 87p. 1991. text 293.00 (2-88316-007-4) Gordon & Breach.
Meredith, Martin. Coming to Terms: South Africa's Search for Truth. LC 99-40362. (Illus.). 400p. 2000. 27.50 (1-891620-33-9, Pub. by PublicAffairs NY) HarpC.
— In the Name of Apartheid: South Africa in the Postwar Era. LC 88-45044. 320p. 1988. 25.00 (0-06-430163-X) HarperTrade.
— Nelson Mandela: A Biography. LC 97-49351. (Illus.). 596p. 1998. text 29.95 (0-312-18132-9) St Martin.
— Nelson Mandela: A Biography. 608p. 1999. pap. 17.95 (0-312-19992-9) St Martin.
Meredith, Mary, ed. see Demou, Doris B.
Meredith, Michael J., ed. Animal Breeding & Infertility. (Illus.). 508p. 1996. 125.00 (0-632-04038-6) Blackwell Sci.
Meredith-Owens. Mesair Ussuara: Tezkere of Asik Celebi. (Gibb Memorial New Ser.: Vol. 24). 1971. 72.00 (0-7189-0200-9, Pub. by Aris & Phillips) David Brown.
Meredith, P. Instruments of Communication. 1966. 284.00 (0-08-010663-3, Pub. by Pergamon Repr) Franklin.
Meredith, P. L. Space Law - A Case Study for the Practitioner: Implementing a Telecommunications Satellite Business Concept. 408p. (C). 1992. lib. bdg. 168.00 (0-7923-1786-6) Kluwer Academic.
Meredith, Pamela & Horan, Nancy Mathes. Adult Primary Care. LC 99-26387. (Illus.). 750p. 1999. text 65.00 (0-7216-6037-1, W B Saunders Co) Harcrt Hlth Sci Grp.
Meredith, Paul, jt. auth. see Landin, Leslie.
Meredith, Peter. The Mary Play: From the N. Town Manuscript. (Exeter Medieval English Texts & Studies Ser.). 196p. 1997. pap. 19.95 (0-85989-547-5, Pub. by Univ Exeter Pr) Northwestern U Pr.
— The Passion Play. 1990. text. write for info. (0-582-49079-0, Pub. by Addison-Wesley) Longman.
Meredith, Peter & Tailby, John, eds. The Staging of Religious Drama in Europe in the Middle Ages: Texts & Documents in English Translation. 2nd ed. Sleeman, Margaret et al, trs. (Early Drama, Art & Music Monograph: No. 4). 1990. reprint ed. boxed set 24.95 (0-918720-23-0) Medieval Inst.
Meredith, Philip & Beattie, Alan. Sex Education: Political Issues in Britain & Europe. 250p. (C). 1989. lib. bdg. 49.95 (0-415-00604-X) Routledge.
Meredith Press Staff. Step-by-Step Exterior Painting. LC 96-78039. (Do-It-Yourself Ser.). (Illus.). 96p. 1997. pap. 12.95 (0-696-20677-3) Meredith Bks.
— Step-by-Step Interior Painting. LC 96-78038. (Do-It-Yourself Ser.). (Illus.). 96p. 1997. pap. 12.95 (0-696-20676-5) Meredith Bks.
— Step-by-Step Stenciling. LC 96-78043. (Do-It-Yourself Ser.). (Illus.). 96p. 1997. pap. 12.95 (0-696-20679-X) Meredith Bks.
***Meredith Press Staff, contrib. by.** Simply Handmade: 365 Projects for Every Occasion. (Illus.). 216p. 2000. 29.95 (0-696-21037-1, Better Homes) Meredith Bks.
Meredith, R. The Structures & Properties of Fibres. 85p. 1975. 70.00 (0-7855-7227-9) St Mut.
Meredith, R. & Hearle, John W., eds. Physical Methods of Investigating Textiles. LC 59-13795. (Illus.). 441p. reprint ed. pap. 136.80 (0-608-11497-9, 201195500080) Bks Demand.
Meredith, R. Alan, jt. auth. see Anderson, C. Dixon.
Meredith, R. J. Engineers' Handbook of Industrial Microwave Heating. (Power Ser.: No. 25). 377p. 1998. 119.00 (0-85296-916-3, PO025) INSPEC Inc.
— Power System Commissioning & Maintenance Practice. (Power Ser.: No. 24). 520p. 1998. 139.00 (0-85296-909-0, PO024) INSPEC Inc.
Meredith, R. J., jt. auth. see Metaxas, A. C.
Meredith, Rebecca, jt. auth. see Doty, Betty.
***Meredith, Richard K.** My Bold Decision to Walk with Christ. (Illus.). 32p. 1999. pap. write for info. (0-9674471-0-0, 555) Harv Evangel Min.
Meredith, Robert, ed. The Environmentalist's Bookshelf. 272p. 1993. 45.00 (0-8161-7359-1, Hall Reference) Macmillan.
Meredith, Robert C. Anthology for Young Writers. 252p. 1975. pap. 18.33 (0-8442-5604-8) NTC Contemp Pub Co.
Meredith, Robert C. & Fitzgerald, John D. Structuring Your Novel: From Basic Idea to Finished Manuscript. LC 70-170126. 240p. 1993. reprint ed. pap. 13.00 (0-06-273170-X, Harper Ref) HarpC.
Meredith, Roy. Mr. Lincoln's Camera Man: Mathew B. Brady. LC 73-92262. (Illus.). 368p. 1946. reprint ed. pap. 18.95 (0-486-23021-X) North South Trader.
Meredith, Ruby F., jt. ed. see O'Kunewick, James P.
Meredith, Russell, jt. auth. see Howard, Michaela.
Meredith, S., jt. auth. see Gee, Robyn.
Meredith, Sally, jt. auth. see Meredith, Don.
Meredith, Scott. Writing to Sell. 4th ed. LC 95-41413. 240p. 1996. 17.99 (0-89879-750-0, Wrtrs Digest Bks) F & W Pubns Inc.
Meredith, Scott, ed. Bar One: Roundup of Best Western Stories. LC 79-75782. (Short Story Index Reprint Ser.). 1977. 20.95 (0-8369-3032-0) Ayer.
— Bar Six: Roundup of Best Western Stories. LC 79-75782. (Short Story Index Reprint Ser.). 1977. 20.95 (0-8369-3056-8) Ayer.
— Bar Three: Roundup of Best Western Stories. LC 79-75782. (Short Story Index Reprint Ser.). 1977. 20.95 (0-8369-3055-X) Ayer.
— Bar Two: Roundup of Best Western Stories. LC 79-75782. (Short Story Index Reprint Ser.). 1977. 20.95 (0-8369-3033-9) Ayer.
Meredith, Scott, ed. see Meredith, Sue.
Meredith, Scott, jt. ed. see Wodehouse, P. G.
Meredith, Sheena. Natural Way: Eczema: A Comprehensive Guide to Gentle, Safe & Effective Treatment. (Natural Way Ser.). 128p. 1994. pap. 5.95 (1-85230-493-6, Pub. by Element MA) Penguin Putnam.
Meredith, Sue. Bar Five: A Roundup of Best Western Stories. Meredith, Scott, ed. LC 79-75782. (Short Story Index Reprint Ser.). 1977. 20.95 (0-8369-3007-X) Ayer.
— Why Are People Different? (Starting Point Science Ser.). (Illus.). 24p. (J). (gr. 1-4). 1993. pap. 3.95 (0-7460-1014-1, Usborne) EDC.
— Why Are People Different? (Starting Point Science Ser.). (Illus.). 24p. (J). (gr. 1-5). 1993. lib. bdg. 12.95 (0-88110-642-9, Usborne) EDC.
— World Religions. (Illus.). 64p. (J). (gr. 4-7). 1996. lib. bdg. 17.95 (0-88110-830-8, Usborne) EDC.
Meredith, Sue, jt. auth. see Gee, R.
Meredith, Sue, jt. auth. see Mosely, F.
Meredith, Sue, jt. auth. see Tahta, S.
Meredith, Susan. Alaska's Search for a Killer: A Seafaring Medical Adventure 1946-1948. (Illus.). xv, 273p. 1998. pap. 21.95 (0-9659849-1-5) Alaska Pub Hlth.
***Meredith, Susan.** Starting Computers. (Usborne Computer Guides Ser.). (Illus.). (gr. k-3). 2000. 17.95 (1-58086-264-0) EDC.
Meredith, Susan. World Religions. rev. ed. (Illus.). 64p. (J). (gr. 5-9). 2000. pap. 9.95 (0-7460-1750-2, Pub. by Usbrne Pbng UK) EDC.
Meredith, Susan, ed. Growing Up. (Facts of Life Ser.). (Illus.). 48p. (YA). (gr. 5 up). 1999. lib. bdg. 15.95 (1-58086-184-9, Usborne) EDC.
— Growing Up: Revised Edition. (Facts of Life Ser.). (Illus.). 48p. (YA). (gr. 5 up). 1999. pap. 7.95 (0-7460-3142-4, Usborne) EDC.
— Hacerse Mayor/Growing Up. (Facts of Life Ser.). (Illus.). 48p. (YA). (gr. 5 up). 1999. pap. 7.95 (0-7460-3423-7, Usborne) EDC.
— Hamsters. (First Pets Ser.). (Illus.). 32p. (J). (ps-3). 1999. 4.95 (0-7460-2979-9, Usborne); lib. bdg. 12.95 (1-58086-167-9, Usborne) EDC.
***Meredith, Susan, ed.** Starting Computers. (Computer Guides Ser.). (Illus.). 48p. (gr. k-3). 2000. pap. 9.95 (0-7460-3464-4, Pub. by Usbrne Pbng UK) EDC.
Meredith, Suzanne, jt. auth. see Velluto, Sharon.
Meredith, Sydney. Fitness Unfolding: How to Begin & Maintain a Quality, Healthy Lifestyle. Tips, Guidelines, & Resources. 233p. (Orig.). 1991. pap. 13.95 (0-911107-01-0) Markbks.
Meredith, T. J., et al. Antidotes for Poisoning by Cyanide. LC 93-32558. (IPCS-CEC Evaluation of Antidotes Ser.: No. 2). 203p. (C). 1994. text 57.95 (0-521-45458-1) Cambridge U Pr.
— Antidotes for Poisoning by Paracetamol. (IPCS-CES Evaluation of Antidotes Ser.: No. 3). (Illus.). 109p. (C). 1995. text 54.95 (0-521-49576-8) Cambridge U Pr.
— Naloxone, Flumazenil & Dantrolene As Antidotes. LC 93-32098. (IPCS-CEC Evaluation of Antidotes Ser.: No. 1). 114p. (C). 1994. text 47.95 (0-521-45459-X) Cambridge U Pr.
Meredith, Thomas K. Lust for Innocence Vol. 1: A Guide to Recognizing Pedophilia. unabridged ed. (Illus.). xi, 91p. 1997. pap. 19.95 (0-9661056-0-5) World Patriot.
***Meredith, Thomas K.** Thomas's New Nicotine Chewing Gum Home Recipe. 26p. 1999. pap. 9.99 (0-9661056-1-3) World Patriot.
Meredith, Travis. Atlas of Vitreo-Retinal Surgery. LC 98-22343. (Illus.). 256p. (C). (gr. 13). 1998. text 175.00 (0-8151-2834-7, 30963) Mosby Inc.
Meredith, William. Effort at Speech: New & Selected Poems. LC 97-9679. 256p. 1997. 39.95 (0-8101-5070-0); pap. 17.95 (0-8101-5071-9) Northwestern U Pr.
— Love Letter from an Impossible Land. LC 70-144748. (Yale Series of Younger Poets: No. 42). reprint ed. 18.00 (0-404-53842-8) AMS Pr.
— Poems Are Hard to Read. 258p. 1990. pap. 13.95 (0-472-06427-4, 06427, Ann Arbor Bks) U of Mich Pr.
Meredith, William, ed. Poets of Bulgaria. Levertov, Denise et al, trs. from BUL. 150p. 1985. 25.00 (0-87775-189-7); pap. 15.00 (0-87775-190-0) Unicorn Pr.
Meredith, William, ed. Poets of Bulgaria. 92p. 1988. reprint ed. pap. 16.95 (0-948259-39-6, Pub. by Forest Bks) Dufour.
Meredith, William, jt. ed. see Harteis, Richard.
Meredith, Willis C., jt. auth. see Margeton, Stephen G.
***Merehurst.** International School of Sugarcraft: Book One: Beginners. 1999. pap. text 19.95 (1-85391-748-6) Merehurst Ltd.
— International School of Sugarcraft: Book Two: Advanced. 1999. pap. text 19.95 (1-85391-753-2) Merehurst Ltd.
Merehurst. International School of Sugarcraft: Sugar Flowers. 1999. 24.95 (1-897730-80-2) Premier Eds.
— Merehurst Cake Book. 1992. 24.95 (1-85391-263-8) Sterling.
Merehurst Ltd. Staff. Salt Dough Projects. 1999. pap. text 16.95 (1-85391-582-3) Merehurst Ltd.
Merehurst Ltd. Staff, et al. Art & Craft of Paper, 1. (Illus.). 144p. 1995. 19.95 (1-85391-437-1) Merehurst Ltd.
Merejkowski, Demitri. The Death of the Gods. Trench, Herbert, tr. from RUS. & intro. by. LC 82-82473. 464p. 1987. reprint ed. pap. 15.95 (0-8334-0021-5, Spir Lit Lib) Garber Comm.
Merejkowski, Dimitri. Dostoievsky. LC 73-21712. (Studies in Dostoyevsky: No. 86). (C). 1974. lib. bdg. 75.00 (0-8383-1816-9) M S G Haskell Hse.
Merejkowski, Dmitri. The Death of the Gods. 464p. 1997. reprint ed. pap. 15.50 (0-7661-0114-2) Kessinger Pub.
Merek, Jack. Blackbird. 368p. 1992. mass mkt. 5.99 (0-446-36192-5, Pub. by Warner Bks) Little.
— Target Stealth. LC 88-40095. 352p. 1990. mass mkt. 4.95 (0-446-34843-0, Pub. by Warner Bks) Little.
Merel, Henri. Germinal: Une Documentation Integrale. 326p. 1993. 60.00 (0-85261-248-6, Pub. by Univ of Glasgow) St Mut.
Merello, Barbara S., tr. see Amado, Jorge.
Merelman, Richard M. Making Something of Ourselves: On Culture & Politics in the United States. LC 83-5959. 200p. (C). 1984. pap. 12.95 (0-520-04915-2, Pub. by U CA Pr) Cal Prin Full Svc.
— Partial Visions: Culture & Politics in Britain, Canada, & the United States. LC 91-9089. 300p. (Orig.). (C). 1991. pap. 14.95 (0-299-12994-2); lib. bdg. 32.95 (0-299-12990-X) U of Wis Pr.
— Representing Black Culture: Race & Cultural Politics in the United States. 288p. (C). 1995. pap. 19.99 (0-415-91075-7, B4660) Routledge.
Merena, Marjorie. My Christmas Diary: A Journal for the Holiday Season Through the Years. 240p. 1998. 16.00 (0-380-97753-2, Avon Bks) Morrow Avon.
Merenbach, Dennis G. & Stephen, Anthony. How to Be an Expert Witness: Credibility in Oral Testimony. (Illus.). 64p. (Orig.). 1993. pap. 8.95 (1-56474-048-X) Fithian Pr.
Merenbloom, Elliot Y. The Team Process: A Handbook for Teachers. 3rd enl. ed. 168p. (C). 1991. pap. text 18.00 (1-56090-054-7) Natl Middle Schl.
Mereness, Newton D. Maryland As a Proprietary Province. xx, 530p. 1997. pap. 35.00 (0-7884-0667-1, M161) Heritage Bk.
Mereness, Newton D., jt. auth. see Alsop, George.
Mereness, Newton D., jt. auth. see Leland, G. Waldo.
Merenga, Hirzo. Electronic Structure Calculations on Cerium-Containing Crystals: Towards a Better Understanding of Scintillation in Ionic Crystals. 181p. (Orig.). 1997. pap. 44.50 (90-407-1427-4, Pub. by Delft U Pr) Coronet Bks.
Merenstein, Gerald B. Handbook of Pediatrics. 18th rev. ed. 1029p. (C). 1996. pap. text 31.95 (0-8385-3625-5, A3625-9, Apple Lange Med) McGraw.
***Merenstein & Kaplan Staff.** Handbook of Pediatrics. 19th ed. 1999. 31.95 (0-8385-3568-2) McGraw.
Merenstein, Gerald B. Handbook of Neonatal Intensive Care. 4th ed. LC 97-20146. (Illus.). 792p. (C). (gr. 13). 1997. pap. text 45.95 (0-8151-3696-X, 31038) Mosby Inc.
Meres, Clare La, see La Meres, Clare.
Meres, Francis. Palladis Tamia. LC 39-10093. 192p. 1978. reprint ed. 50.00 (0-8201-1188-0) Schol Facsimiles.
***Meres, Jonathan.** The Big Bad Rumor. LC 99-89323. (Illus.). 40p. (J). (gr. k-1). 2000. 15.95 (0-531-30292-X) Orchard Bks Watts.
Meres, Jonathan. Somewhere Out There. (Illus.). 32p. (J). (gr. 1-4). 1998. 19.95 (0-09-176638-9, Pub. by Hutchnson) Trafalgar.
Meresh-Hemery, Kathleen. The Brightest Star. LC 97-45809. (Illus.). (J). 1998. 6.95 (1-56123-102-9) Centering Corp.
Meret, Dimas P. Oraculo del Dilogun. (SPA.). 881p. 1997. 175.00 (0-9661781-1-4) Edit Osha.
— Tratado de Ozain. (SPA., Illus.). 130p. 1996. 49.95 (0-9661781-0-6) Edit Osha.
Mereu, Lunella, ed. Boundaries of Morphology & Syntax. LC 99-15509. (Current Issues in Linguistic Theory Ser.: Vol. 180). viii, 314p. 1999. 79.00 (1-55619-957-0) J Benjamins Pubng Co.
Mereweather-Thompson, Cornelius. Christian Approaches to Dialogue with Other Faith Communities. LC 94-47432. 148p. 1995. text 69.95 (0-7734-8979-7) E Mellen.
Merewether, Charles, jt. auth. see Cameron, Dan.
Merewether, F. H. A Tour Through the Famine Districts of India. 1986. reprint ed. 34.00 (0-8364-1615-5, Pub. by Usha) S Asia.
Merezhkovsky, Dmitri S. Malen'Kaya Tereza. LC 84-22518. 208p. 1989. pap. 9.50 (0-938920-43-X) Hermitage Pubs.
— Tolstoi As Man & Artist. LC 69-13996. 310p. 1970. reprint ed. lib. bdg. 65.00 (0-8371-4098-6, METO, Greenwood Pr) Greenwood.
Merezhkovsky, Dmitri S., jt. auth. see Allen, Paul M.

Merezkovskij, Dmitrij S. Polnoe Sobranie Socinenij, 24 bde. in 6 banden. (GER.). xii, 6043p. 1973. reprint ed. write for info. (*3-487-04808-6*) G Olms Pubs.

Merfeld. Siddur Haverim Kol Yisrael. write for info. (*0-88125-680-3*) Ktav.

MERG Policy Group. Making Democracy Work: A Framework for Macroeconomic Policy in South Africa. 348p. 1994. pap. 18.95 (*1-86808-183-4*) OUP.

Mergal, Angel M., jt. ed. see Williams, George H.

Mergal, Margaret Z. Communication for Business. 238p. 1974. pap. 2.50 (*0-8477-2610-X*) U of PR Pr.

— Speech Improvement: Tapescripts for Business English Three-Zero-One. 2nd ed. 112p. 1979. pap. 3.50 (*0-8477-2611-8*) U of PR Pr.

Mergal, Margaret Z., ed. see Flechas, Genaro.

Mergault, Jean. Apollo Larousse French-English, English-French Dictionary: Dictionnaire Larousse Apollo Francais-Anglais-Francais. (ENG & FRE.). 1028p. 1993. 23.95 (*0-7859-4734-5*) Fr & Eur.

— New Larousse Adonis French-English-French. 532p. 1987. pap. 11.95 (*0-7859-4735-3*) Fr & Eur.

— Nouveau Dictionnaire Larousse: Mars French - English, English - French. (ENG & FRE.). 478p. 1989. 49.95 (*0-7859-7651-5*, 2034016211) Fr & Eur.

Mergen, Bernard. Play & Playthings: A Reference Guide. LC 82-6139. (American Popular Culture Ser.). (Illus.). 281p. 1982. lib. bdg. 65.00 (*0-313-22136-7*, MGT/, Greenwood Pr) Greenwood.

— Recreational Vehicles & Travel: A Resource Guide. LC 84-28974. (American Popular Culture Ser.). 221p. 1985. lib. bdg. 65.00 (*0-313-23672-0*, MER/, Greenwood Pr) Greenwood.

— Snow in America. LC 97-12247. (Illus.). 336p. 1997. 24.95 (*1-56098-780-4*) Smithsonian.

— Snow in America. (Illus.). 322p. 1999. pap. 15.95 (*1-56098-381-7*) Smithsonian.

Mergen, Bernard, ed. Cultural Dimensions of Play, Games, & Sport. LC 86-10563. (Association for the Anthropological Study of Play Ser.: No. 10). 223p. 1986. reprint ed. pap. 69.20 (*0-608-07117-X*, 206734300009) Bks Demand.

Mergener, Robert J. College Algebra: A Functions Approach. 5th ed. 480p. 1995. per. 52.95 (*0-8403-7764-9*) Kendall-Hunt.

— Trigonometry: A Functions Approach. 304p. 1989. per. 37.95 (*0-8403-5308-1*) Kendall-Hunt.

Mergenhagen, Paula. Targeting Transitions: Marketing to Consumers During Life Changes. LC 93-73829. 253p. (Orig.). 1994. 39.95 (*0-936889-29-2*); pap. 29.95 (*0-936889-30-6*) American Demo.

Mergenhagen, Stephan E. & Rosan, Burton, eds. Molecular Basis of Oral Microbial Adhesion. LC 84-20504. 242p. reprint ed. pap. 75.10 (*0-7837-4041-7*, 204387100011) Bks Demand.

Mergenthaler, Volker. Medusa Meets Holofernes: Poetologische, Semiologische und Intertextuelle Diskursivierung von Enthauptung. LC 97-206185. (GER., Illus.). 153p. 1997. 28.95 (*3-906757-47-1*, Pub. by P Lang) P Lang Pubng.

Merger, Robert P., et al. Intellectual Property in the New Technological Age. 1300p. 1997. teacher ed. write for info. (*1-56706-531-7*, 65317) Panel Pubs.

Merges, Robert. Patent Law & Policy Statutes, Rules & Treaties: 1997 Edition. 301p. 1997. pap. 12.00 (*1-55834-458-6*, 12306-11, MICHIE) LEXIS Pub.

Merges, Robert P. Patent Law & Policy: Cases & Materials. 2nd ed. LC 96-79718. (Illus.). 1368p. 1997. text 58.00 (*1-55834-445-4*, 12305-11, MICHIE) LEXIS Pub.

***Merges, Robert P., et al.** Intellectual Property in the New Technological Age. 2nd ed. LC 99-89259. 2000. boxed set 63.00 (*0-7355-1226-4*) Panel Pubs.

— Intellectual Property in the New Technological Age: 1999-2000 Case & Statutory Supplement. rev. ed. 380p. 1999. pap. write for info. (*0-7355-0041-X*, 0041X) Panel Pubs.

Merges, Thomas. Patent Law & Policy Cases & Materials: 1992 Edition. 1034p. 1992. text. write for info. (*0-87473-986-1*, 12305-10, MICHIE) LEXIS Pub.

Merghan, Clement W. The Coville Rock Shelter, Inyo County, California. fac. ed. Olson, Ronald L. et al, eds. (University of California Publications: No. 12:5). (Illus.). 58p. (C). 1953. reprint ed. pap. 6.88 (*1-55567-130-6*) Coyote Press.

Mergins, Catherine G., jt. auth. see Alissi, Albert S.

Mergler, Wayne, ed. The Last New Land: Stories of Alaska, Past & Present. LC 96-30733. (Illus.). 816p. 1996. 34.95 (*0-88240-481-4*, Alaska NW Bks); pap. 22.95 (*0-88240-483-0*, Alaska NW Bks) Gr Arts Ctr Pub.

Mergner, T. & Hlavacka, F., eds. Multisensory Control of Posture: Proceedings of an International Symposium on Sensory Interaction in Posture & Movement Control Held in Smolenice, Slovakia, September 9-11, 1994, As a Satellite Symposium to the European Neuroscience Association Meeting of 1994. LC 95-30547. (Illus.). 370p. 1995. 95.00 (*0-306-45101-8*, Kluwer Plenum) Kluwer Academic.

Mergner, W. J. Cell Death. 1990. 110.00 (*0-938607-39-1*) Field & Wood Inc Medical.

Mergo, Patricia. Imaging of the Chest: A Teaching File. 340p. text 89.00 (*0-683-30473-9*) Lppncott W & W.

Merguerian, Barbara, ed. see Topalian, Naomi G.

Merguerian, Barbara J. & Jafferian, Doris D., eds. Armenian Women in a Changing World: Papers Presented at the First International Conference of the Armenian International Women's Association. 280p. 1995. pap. 20.00 (*0-9648787-0-4*) AIWA.

Merguet, Hugo. Handlexikon Zu Cicero. pap. write for info. (*0-318-70790-X*) G Olms Pubs.

— Handlexikon Zu Cicero. 816p. 1962. reprint ed. write for info. (*0-318-72050-7*) G Olms Pubs.

— Handlexikon Zu Cicero. (Olms Paperbacks Ser.: Bd. 7.2). (GER.). vi, 816p. 1997. reprint ed. write for info. (*3-487-00839-4*) G Olms Pubs.

— Lexikon Zu Den Philosophischen Schriften Ciceros, 3 vols., Set. 1971. reprint ed. write for info. (*0-318-72052-3*) G Olms Pubs.

— Lexikon Zu Den Philosophischen Schriften Cicero's: Mit Angabe Saemtlicher Stellen, 3 vols., Set. (GER & LAT.). 1987. reprint ed. lib. bdg. 575.00 (*3-487-00052-0*) G Olms Pubs.

— Lexikon Zu Den Reden des Cicero, 4 vols., Set. (Lexikon Zu den Schriften Cicero's Ser.: Teil 1). 3513p. 1973. write for info. (*3-487-05028-5*) G Olms Pubs.

— Lexikon Zu Den Reden des Cicero, 4 vols., Set. 1962. reprint ed. write for info. (*0-318-72051-5*) G Olms Pubs.

— Lexikon Zu Den Schriften Casars, 2 vols., Set. iv, 1142p. 1963. reprint ed. write for info. (*0-318-71175-3*); reprint ed. write for info. (*0-318-72049-3*) G Olms Pubs.

— Lexikon Zu Den Schriften Casars. Entwicklung. pap. write for info. (*0-318-70798-5*) G Olms Pubs.

— Lexikon Zu Vergilius. 786p. 1969. reprint ed. write for info. (*0-318-72053-1*) G Olms Pubs.

— Lexikon Zu Vergilius Mit Angabe Samtlicher Stellen. pap. write for info. (*0-318-70800-0*) G Olms Pubs.

— Lexikon Zu Vergilius Mit Angabe Samtlicher Stellen. 786p. 1969. reprint ed. write for info. (*0-318-71176-1*); reprint ed. pap. write for info. (*0-318-70519-2*); reprint ed. pap. write for info. (*0-318-71177-X*) G Olms Pubs.

Merguet, Hugo, ed. Lexikon Zu Den Philosophischen Schriften Cicero's, 3 vols. (Lexikon Zu den Schriften Cicero's Ser.: Pt. 2). 2715p. 1987. reprint ed. 700.00 (*3-487-00051-2*) G Olms Pubs.

Merh, Kusum Pradeep. Yama: The Glorious Lord of the Other World. (Illus.). xvi, 302p. (C). 1996. 26.00 (*81-246-0066-X*, Pub. by D K Printwrld) Nataraj Bks.

***Merhari, L., et al, eds.** Materials Issues & Modeling for Device Nanofabrication Vol. 584: Materials Research Society Symposium Proceedings. (Materials Research Society Symposium Proceedings Ser.). 2000. text 93.00 (*1-55899-492-0*) Materials Res.

Merhav, S. Aerospace Sensors Systems & Applications. (Illus.). 480p. 1996. 79.95 (*0-387-94605-5*) Spr-Verlag.

Merholz, Jorg K., jt. auth. see van der Mei, Sicco Henk.

Meriam. Engineering Mechanics: Dynamics, 2. 4th ed. 160p. 1997. pap., student ed. 36.95 (*0-471-19099-3*) Wiley.

— Statistics & Dynamics 4th ed. 1999. pap. 105.00 (*0-471-38122-5*) Wiley.

Meriam, J. L. & Kraige, L. G. Engineering Mechanics, SI Version: Statics, Vol. 1. 4th ed. 123p. 1997. pap., student ed. 36.95 (*0-471-19075-6*) Wiley.

Meriam, J. L. & Kraige, L. Glenn. Engineering Mechanics. 4th ed. LC 96-22505. 544p. 1996. text 103.95 (*0-471-59764-3*) Wiley.

— Engineering Mechanics Vol. 2: Dynamics. 4th ed. LC 96-22505. 752p. 1997. text 103.95 (*0-471-59767-8*) Wiley.

Meriam, James L. Statics. 2nd ed. LC 71-136719. (Illus.). 394p. reprint ed. pap. 122.20 (*0-608-30336-4*, 201928800011) Bks Demand.

Meriam, Junius L. Normal School Education & Efficiency in Teaching. LC 77-177071. (Columbia University. Teachers College. Contributions to Education Ser.: No. 1). reprint ed. 37.50 (*0-404-55001-0*) AMS Pr.

Meriam, Lewis, jt. auth. see Bachman, George W.

Merian, Ernest, ed. Carcinogenic & Mutagenic Metal Compounds, Vol. 14. (Current Topics in Environmental & Toxicology Ser.). xvi, 638p. 1991. text 303.00 (*2-88124-781-4*) Gordon & Breach.

— Metals & Their Compounds in the Environment: Occurrence, Analysis, Biological Relevance. LC 90-12615. 1439p. 1990. 294.00 (*3-527-26521-X*, Wiley-VCH) Wiley.

Merian, Ernest, et al. Carcinogenic & Mutagenic Metal Compounds 2, Vol. 11. xiv, 544p. 1988. text 203.00 (*2-88124-663-X*) Gordon & Breach.

Merian, Maria S. Flowers, Butterflies & Insects: All One Hundred Fifty-Four Engravings. (Illus.). 160p. pap. 10.95 (*0-486-26636-2*) Dover.

— Maria Sibylla Merian: Artist & Naturalist. Wettengl, Kurt, ed. (Illus.). 256p. 1998. text 65.00 (*3-7757-0723-9*, 810812, Pub. by Gerd Hatje) Dist Art Pubs.

Merian, Maria S. The Wondrous Transformation of Caterpillars: Fifty Engravings Selected from Erucarum Ortus (1718) LC 78-317912. 33 p. 1978. write for info. (*0-85967-407-X*) Ashgate Pub Co.

***Merian, Maria S., pref.** Maria Sibylla Merian - Neues Blumenbuck: (New Book of Flowers) (Illus.). 80p. 1999. 125.00 (*3-7913-2060-2*) te Neues.

Merian, Maria Sibylla, see Sibylla Merian, Maria.

Merian, Matthaus. 1,300 Real & Fanciful . . . LC 98-16166. 144p. 1998. pap. 11.95 (*0-486-40237-1*) Dover.

Merians, Linda E., ed. The Secret Malady: Venereal Disease in Eighteenth-Century Britain & France. LC 96-20580. 280p. 1997. pap. 18.00 (*0-8131-0888-8*) U Pr of Ky.

— The Secret Malady: Venereal Disease in Eighteenth-Century Britain & France. LC 96-20580. (Illus.). 280p. 1997. text 42.50 (*0-8131-1989-8*) U Pr of Ky.

Merical, Nancy. Just for Kids: A Year of Program Resources. 1999. pap. 6.99 (*0-8341-9945-9*) Lillenas.

Merick, Amy, et al. In Our Own Hands: The History of Student Housing Cooperatives at the University of Michigan. Goldstein, Margaret, ed. LC 94-75279. 128p. 1994. 20.00 (*0-9639935-1-8*) Inter-Cooperative.

Mericle, Charice. So Many Strange Things. 2001. write for info. (*0-316-60000-8*) Little.

Mericle, Suzanne. Trippin with Mabel & Margaret. LC 98-84873. 1998. mass mkt., per. 14.95 (*1-889131-28-8*) CasAnanda.

***Mericsko, Robert J., ed.** Advances in Computer-Assisted Recognition. 276p. 1999. pap. text 72.00 (*0-8194-3054-4*) SPIE.

Merida, Carlos. Modern Mexican Artists: Critical Notes. LC 68-22931. (Essay Index Reprint Ser.). 1977. 23.95 (*0-8369-0701-9*) Ayer.

Merida, Rolando. The Succession. (Illus.). 64p. (C). 1997. pap. 15.00 (*1-886458-16-2*) Avenue Servs.

Merideth, Lee W. Civil War Times: 30 Year Comprehensive Index, April 1959 - February 1989. LC 90-62096. 228p. (Orig.). 1990. pap. 29.95 (*0-9626237-0-9*) Hist Indexes.

— Guide to Civil War Periodicals, Vol. II. 528p. 1997. 39.95 (*0-9626237-3-3*) Hist Indexes.

***Merideth, Lee W.** 1912 Facts about Titanic. (Illus.). iv, 224p. 1999. pap. 12.95 (*0-9626237-4-1*) Hist Indexes.

Merideth, Lee W. 1912 Facts about Titanic. ("Facts About" History Ser.: Vol. 1). (Illus.). 224p. 1999. pap. 11.95 (*1-882810-33-3*) Savas Pub.

Merideth, Lee W., ed. Guide to Civil War Periodicals, 1991, Vol. I. LC 91-77550. 368p. (Orig.). 1991. 37.00 (*0-9626237-2-5*); pap. 32.00 (*0-9626237-1-7*) Hist Indexes.

Merideth, Robert. The Politics of the Universe: Edward Beecher, Abolition, & Orthodoxy. LC 68-21869. 286p. reprint ed. pap. 88.70 (*0-608-06263-4*, 206659200008) Bks Demand.

Meridian Creative Group Staff. CBL Explorations in Algebra for the TI-82 & TI-83: Calculator - Based Laboratory. 100p. (Orig.). (C). 1996. 19.95 (*0-9639121-8-6*) Meridian Creative.

— CBL Explorations in Calculus for the TI-85: Calculator-Based Laboratory. 101p. 1995. 19.95 (*0-9639121-2-7*) Meridian Creative.

— CBL Explorations in Chemistry for the TI-82 & TI-83: Calculator - Based Laboratory. 100p. (Orig.). (C). 1996. 19.95 (*0-9639121-9-4*) Meridian Creative.

— CBL Explorations in Precalculus for the TI-82: Calculator-Based Laboratory. 1995. 19.95 (*0-9639121-3-5*) Meridian Creative.

— CBL Explorations in Precalculus for the TI-85: Calculator-Based Laboratory. 101p. 1995. 19.95 (*0-9639121-4-3*) Meridian Creative.

Meridian Publishing Staff. My Heart, Christ's Home. 1995. pap. text 14.95 (*1-56570-058-9*) Meridian MI.

— Tyranny of the Urgent. 1995. pap. text 14.95 (*1-56570-063-5*) Meridian MI.

***Meridian Securities Markets Staff.** Handbook of World Stock Indices. 3rd ed. (Illus.). 445p. 1999. pap. 125.00 (*1-891518-11-9*) Meridian Securities.

— Ranking of World Stock Markets. 3rd ed. (Illus.). 196p. 1999. pap. 95.00 (*1-891518-12-7*) Meridian Securities.

***Meridian Securities Markets Staff, ed. World Stock Exchange Fact Book: Historical Securities Data for the International Investor. (Illus.). 695p. 2000. 325.00 (*1-891518-13-5*) Meridian Securities.**

The Fact Book is a comprehensive annual reference publication covering over 45 international stock exchanges. With regulatory information & up to 25 years of historical data collected directly from the exchanges, it provides an exceptional single-source reference on international stock markets. Stock Exchange & Government Regulations - Listing & disclosure requirements, investor protection codes, rules of mergers & acquisitions, restrictions on foreign investment, taxation & repatriation regulations. Stock Market Statistics - Market capitalization, trading value & volume, domestic & foreign breakdown, P E & P BV ratios & dividend yield, stock ownership & trading profiles, number of listed companies & market capitalization broken down by sector. All figures in local currency & in US$ adjusted for inflation. Stock index Data - Monthly high, low, close & average data on the official exchange indices & other prominent Indices (Dow Jones, S&P, FTSE, Nikkei, Hang Seng, etc.). Index calculation methodology & constituent stocks arranged by industry. Also see Ranking of World Stock Markets. Handbook of World Stock Indices & Handbook of North American Stock Exchanges. Contact: Meridian Securities Markets, 16928 Bar Harbor Bend, Round Rock, TX 78681. Phone: 512-238-0162. Fax: 512-238-6067. e-mail: info@meridiansecurities.com. Web Address: www.meridiansecurities.com. *Publisher Paid Annotation.*

Meridian Securities Markets Staff, ed. World Stock Exchange Fact Book: Historical Securities Data for the International Investor. annuals 5th unabridged ed. (Illus.). 680p. 1999. pap. 325.00 (*1-891518-09-7*) Meridian Securities.

Meridien, Anne. Simple Thoughts on Finding Love & Marriage. LC 97-26203. 96p. 1997. pap. 7.00 (*1-56170-428-8*) Hay House.

***Meridith, Shelley.** Hide n' Seek at Home with Josh B'Gosh. 10p. (J). 1998. 6.99 (*1-929174-10-1*) Oshkosh BGosh.

Meridith, Susan & Gee, Robyn. Facts of Life. rev. ed. (Illus.). 96p. (J). (gr. 5 up). 1998. pap. 12.95 (*0-7460-3143-2*, Usborne) EDC.

— Facts of Life. rev. ed. (Illus.). 96p. (YA). (gr. 5 up). 1998. lib. bdg. 20.95 (*0-88110-974-6*, Usborne) EDC.

Merieux, Ch, ed. see International Symposium on Requirements for Poultry Viruses Vaccines Staff.

Merieux, Regine, jt. auth. see Berger, Dominique.

Merigan, Thomas C., Jr., et al, eds. Textbook of AIDS Medicine. 2nd ed. LC 97-42697. 1063p. 1998. 155.00 (*0-683-30216-7*) Lppncott W & W.

Merila, Edith. Liability Insurance: The Purchaser's Guide. 36p. 1986. 5.00 (*0-932622-08-9*) Ctr Public Rep.

***Merilees, Bill.** Gardening for Wildlife: A Guide for Nature Lovers. rev. ed. (Illus.). 192p. 2000. pap. 14.95 (*1-55110-954-9*) Whitecap Bks.

Merilees, William J. Attracting Backyard Wildlife: A Guide for Nature Lovers. LC 89-5516. (Illus.). 176p. (Orig.). 1990. pap. 4.95 (*0-89658-130-6*) Voyageur Pr.

Merilees, William J., jt. auth. see Lyons, Chess.

Merill, Elmer D. Index Rafinesquianus: The Plant Names Published by C. S. Rafinesque with Reductions, & a Consideration of His Methods, Objectives & Attainments. Cohen, I. Bernard, ed. LC 79-7984. 1980. reprint ed. lib. bdg. 28.95 (*0-405-12566-6*) Ayer.

Merillat, Herbert C. Guadalcanal Remembered. 1990. pap. 3.95 (*0-380-76102-5*, Avon Bks) Morrow Avon.

— Land & the Constitution in India. LC 79-127362. (Studies of the South Asian). 337p. reprint ed. 104.50 (*0-8357-9066-5*, 201538900093) Bks Demand.

Merillat, Herbert L. Island: A History of the First Marine Division on Guadalcanal, August 7 - December 9, Nineteen Forty-Two. LC 79-18779. 1981. reprint ed. 25.00 (*0-89201-067-3*) Zenger Pub.

Merillon, J. M., jt. ed. see Ramawat, K. G.

Merillou, Catherine, jt. auth. see Vicars, Robert E.

Merimee. Carmen. pap. text 4.25 (*0-88436-906-4*) EMC-Paradigm.

Merimee. Colomba. (FRE.). (C). 1964. pap. 9.95 (*0-8442-1967-3*, VF1967-3) NTC Contemp Pub Co.

Merimee, Prosper. Les Ames du Purgatoire. (FRE.). 192p. 1973. 10.95 (*0-7859-0078-0*, M2466) Fr & Eur.

— Carmen. Gibson, Dick, tr. (ENG & FRE.). 98p. 1997. pap. text 19.50 (*1-58085-002-2*) Interlingua VA.

— Carmen. Loyd, Mary, tr. from FRE. 37p. 1997. pap. 14.95 (*0-9666591-1-2*) Seconda Donna.

— Carmen & Other Stories. Jotcham, Nicholas, tr. & intro. by. (Oxford World's Classics Ser.). 400p. 1999. pap. 11.95 (*0-19-283722-2*) OUP.

— Carmen et Autres Nouvelles. (FRE., Illus.). 1965. write for info. (*0-318-63444-9*) Fr & Eur.

— Carmen et Autres Nouvelles. unabridged ed. (FRE.). pap. 7.95 (*2-87714-146-2*, Pub. by Bookking Intl) Distribks Inc.

— Carmen et Treize Autres Nouvelles. (Folio Ser.: No. 560). (FRE., Illus.). 1965. pap. 9.95 (*2-07-036560-3*) Schoenhof.

— Carmen, Les Ames du Purgatoire. (FRE.). 1983. pap. 10.95 (*0-7859-2969-X*, 2080702637) Fr & Eur.

— Le Carrosse du Saint-Sacrement. (FRE.). 256p. 1989. 18.95 (*0-7859-1574-5*, 2903638225) Fr & Eur.

— Chronique du Regne de Charles Neuf. Josserand, Pierre, ed. (FRE.). 1979. pap. 4.95 (*0-7859-1446-3*, 2211054609) Fr & Eur.

— Colomba. (Coll. GF). (FRE.). 247p. 1992. pap. 11.95 (*0-7859-4765-5*) Fr & Eur.

— Colomba et Autre Nouvelles. (FRE.). 1973. pap. 10.95 (*0-7859-3064-7*) Fr & Eur.

— Colomba et Autres Nouvelles. unabridged ed. (FRE.). pap. 7.95 (*2-87714-143-8*, Pub. by Bookking Intl) Distribks Inc.

— The Conspirators. Vaughn, Paul, tr. (Absolute Classics Ser.). 128p. 1997. pap. 12.95 (*1-899791-10-8*) Theatre Comm.

— Correspondance, 17 tomes. Parturier, ed. Incl. Tome XVII. Supplement, Additions et Corrections, Index et Tables. (FRE.). 538p. 1962. pap. 50.00: 1832-1835. (FRE.). 1972. pap. 50.00 (*0-7859-1522-2*, 2708926012); 1836-1840. (FRE.). 658p. 1964. pap. 50.00 (*0-7859-1523-0*, 2708926020); 1844-1846. (FRE.). 584p. 1943. pap. 45.00 (*0-7859-1524-9*, 2708926047); 1847-1849. (FRE.). 567p. 1945. pap. 45.00 (*0-7859-1525-7*, 2708926055); 1850-1852. (FRE.). 492p. 1946. pap. 40.00 (*0-7859-1526-5*, 2708926063); 1853-1855. (FRE.). 560p. 1947. pap. 45.00 (*0-7859-1527-3*, 2708926071); 1856-1858. (FRE.). 1964. pap. 50.00 (*0-7859-1611-3*, 270892608X); 1859-1860. (FRE.). 574p. 1955. pap. 45.00 (*0-7859-1528-1*, 2708926098); 1860-1861. (FRE.). 450p. 1961. pap. 35.00 (*0-7859-1529-X*, 2708926101); 1862-1863. (FRE.). 596p. 1962. pap. 45.00 (*0-7859-1612-1*); 1864-1865. (FRE.). 640p. 1964. pap. 52.00 (*0-7859-1530-3*, 2708926128); 1866-1867. (FRE.). 650p. 1958. pap. 55.00 (*0-7859-1531-1*, 2708926136); 1868-1869. (FRE.). 712p. 1960. pap. 60.00 (*0-7859-1532-X*, 2708926144); 1870. (FRE.). 256p. 1960. pap. 25.00 (*0-7859-1533-8*, 2708926152); Supplement. (FRE.). 468p. 1961. pap. 35.00 (*0-7859-1534-6*, 2708926160); (FRE.). 1964. pap. write for info. (*0-318-51970-4*) Fr & Eur.

— Etudes Sur les Arts du Moyen-Age. (FRE., Illus.). 282p. 1967. pap. 10.95 (*0-7859-1391-2*, 2080101692) Fr & Eur.

— Lettres a Fanny Lagden. 12.50 (*0-686-54756-X*) Fr & Eur.

— Lokis. 164p. 19.95 (*0-686-54757-8*) Fr & Eur.

— Notes d'Un Voyage en Corse, 1840. (FRE.). 110p. 1989. pap. 19.95 (*0-7859-1559-1*, 2876600358) Fr & Eur.

— Nouvelles Completes: Carmen et 10 Autres Nouvelles, 2 vols. Josserand, Pierre, ed. 1974. pap. 12.95 (*0-7859-2880-4*) Fr & Eur.

— Nouvelles Completes Vol. 1: Colomba et 10 Autres Nouvelles. (FRE.). 1976. pap. 12.95 (*0-7859-3387-5*) Fr & Eur.

— Romans et Nouvelles, 2 tomes. Parturier, ed. (Coll. Prestige). 69.90 (*0-685-34944-6*) Fr & Eur.

— Romans et Nouvelles: Charles IX; Mateo Falcone; Vision

M

de Charles IX; Enlevement de la Redoute; Tamango; Federico. Parturier, ed. (FRE.). 318p. 1969. pap. 29.95 (*0-7859-4875-9*, F68021) Fr & Eur.

— Tamango: Mateo Falcone et Autres Nouvelles. (FRE.). 1983. pap. 10.95 (*0-7859-2983-5*) Fr & Eur.

— Theatre: Romans et Nouvelles. (FRE.). 1979. lib. bdg. 110.00 (*0-8288-3566-7*, F68014) Fr & Eur.

— Theatre: Romans et Nouvelles. rev. ed. 54.95 (*0-686-56540-1*) Fr & Eur.

— Theatre de Clara Gazul. (FRE.). 1968. 7.95 (*0-7859-0028-4*, F68310) Fr & Eur.

— La Venus d'Ille: Les Ames du Purgatoire. (FRE., Illus.). 135p. 1991. pap. 8.95 (*0-7859-4691-8*) Fr & Eur.

— La Venus d'Ille et Autres Nouvelles: Dossier de Lectures. (FRE.). 1982. pap. 10.95 (*0-7859-2980-0*) Fr & Eur.

Merimee, Prosper & Auzas, Pierre M. Notes de Voyage. (FRE.). 785p. 1989. 89.95 (*0-7859-1560-5*, 2876600366) Fr & Eur.

Merimee, Prosper & Connes, Georges. Etudes Anglo-Americaines. (FRE.). 369p. 1930. pap. 79.95 (*0-7859-5382-5*) Fr & Eur.

Merimee, Prosper & Jourda, Pierre. Colomba. (Folio Ser.: No. 819). (FRE.). 188p. 1947. 10.95 (*2-07-036819-X*) Schoenhof.

— Colomba - Mateo Falcone. (FRE.). 188p. 1989. reprint ed. pap. 10.95 (*0-7859-3227-5*, 2266030728) Fr & Eur.

— La Jacquerie. (Horizons et Visages Ser.). 462p. 1931. pap. 79.95 (*0-7859-5384-1*) Fr & Eur.

Merimee, Prosper & Levaillant, Maurice. Mosaique. (FRE.). 530p. 1933. pap. 105.00 (*0-7859-0026-8*, F68008) Fr & Eur.

Merimee, Prosper & Mandel, Oscar. Two Romantic Plays: The Spaniards in Denmark by Prosper Merimee & the Rebels of Nantucket by Oscar Mandel. unabridged ed. LC 96-68760. (Illus.). 175p. (Orig.). 1996. pap. 15.95 (*0-914502-11-5*) Spectrum Prods.

Merimee, Prosper & Mongault, Henri. Etudes de Litterature Russe: Gogol, Tourguenev..., Vol. 2. (FRE.). 608p. 1932. pap. 79.95 (*0-7859-5383-3*) Fr & Eur.

Merimee, Prosper & Trahard, Pierre. Lettre a Francisque Michel, 1848-1870. (FRE.). 238p. 1930. pap. 79.95 (*0-7859-5385-X*) Fr & Eur.

Merin, Saul. Inherited Eye Diseases: Diagnosis & Clinical Management. (Illus.). 528p. 1991. text 250.00 (*0-8247-7410-8*) Dekker.

Merin, Saul, ed. see Jersualem Conference on Impaired Vision In childho.

Merin, Yehuda, jt. ed. see Porter, Jack N.

Merinar, John R., Jr. Before You Say, "You're Fired" 54p. 1996. spiral bd. 47.00 (*0-925773-27-1*) M Lee Smith.

Merinero, Antonio. Marketing y Ventas en la Oficina de Farmacia. (SPA.). 304p. 1997. pap. 29.00 (*84-7978-316-8*, Pub. by Ediciones Diaz) IBD Ltd.

Mering, T. A., jt. auth. see Adrianov, O. S.

Meringer, Rudolf & Mayer, Carl. Versprechen und Verlesen: Eine Psychologisch-Linguistische Studie. (Classics in Psycholinguistics Ser.: No. 2). xl, xiv 207p. 1978. 65.00 (*90-272-0973-1*) J Benjamins Pubng Co.

Meringolo, Denise D., jt. auth. see Mayo, Edith P.

Meringolo, Vince, ed. see Technical Association of the Pulp & Paper Industry.

Merini, Alda. A Rage of Love. Verdicchio, Pasquale, tr. from ITA. LC 93-81344. (Prose Ser.: No. 30). 80p. 1995. pap. 10.00 (*1-55071-013-3*) Guernica Editions.

Merini, Rafika. Two Major Francophone Women Writers: Assia Djebar & Leila Sebbar. LC 94-30420. (Francophone Cultures & Literatures Ser.: Vol. 5). 159p. 1995. 43.95 (*0-8204-2635-0*) P Lang Pubng.

Merino. Atlas of Breast Pathology. 1999. text. write for info. (*0-7216-6116-5*, W B Saunders Co) Harcrt Hlth Sci Grp.

— Diccionario de Dudas del Ingles. 4th ed. (ENG & SPA.). 1990. write for info. (*0-7859-3701-3*, 8428318123) Fr & Eur.

Merino, Barbara D. Business Income & Price Levels: The Accounting, Legal, & Political Views. Brief, Richard P., ed. LC 80-1460. (Dimensions of Accounting Theory & Practice Ser.). 1980. lib. bdg. 31.95 (*0-405-13482-7*) Ayer.

Merino, Barbara Dubis, jt. auth. see Previts, Gary John.

Merino, Barbara J., et al, eds. Language & Culture in Learning: Teaching Spanish to Native Speakers of Spanish. LC 93-26831. 290p. 1994. 89.95 (*0-7507-0230-3*, Falmer Pr); pap. 27.95 (*0-7507-0231-1*, Falmer Pr) Taylor & Francis.

Merino, Beatriz L., jt. ed. see Garcia, Angel.

Merino-Bustamante, Jose. Auxiliary Dictionary of the Translator Spanish-English. 2nd ed. 240p. 1991. pap. 39.95 (*0-7859-5041-9*) Fr & Eur.

— Vocabulario Ingles-Espanol, Espanol-Ingles. 8th ed. (ENG & SPA.). 192p. 1990. pap. write for info. (*0-7859-5082-6*) Fr & Eur.

Merino Carrion, Beatriz L., jt. compiled by see Garcia Cook, Angel.

Merino Carrion, Beatriz L., jt. ed. see Garcia Cook, Angel.

Merino, Donald N., jt. auth. see Lang, Hans J.

Merino, Elias M., ed. DX Centers: Donors in AlGaAs & Related Compounds. (Defect & Diffusion Forum Ser.: Vol. 108). (Illus.). 186p. (C). 1994. text 120.00 (*3-908450-03-9*, Pub. by Trans T Pub) Enfield Pubs NH.

***Merino, Erica.** Life, Italian Style: Quotes & Quips from Notable Italian Americans. LC 99-33500. 176p. 1999. pap. 12.00 (*0-380-79696-1*, Avon Bks) Morrow Avon.

Merino, Hugo Z., jt. auth. see Petras, James F.

Merino, J. English-Spanish Dictionary of Word Usage. (ENG & SPA.). 1990. pap. 28.00 (*0-7859-8959-5*) Fr & Eur.

— English-Spanish Dictionary of Word Usage. (ENG & SPA.). 304p. 1990. pap. 29.50 (*84-283-1812-3*, Pub. by Paraninfo) IBD Ltd.

— Spanish-English - English-Spanish Thematic Dictionary. (ENG & SPA.). 597p. 1977. pap. 23.75 (*84-283-1765-8*) IBD Ltd.

Merino, Jose M. La Edad de la Aventura (The Age of Adventure) 1997. 29.95 (*84-372-2195-1*) Santillana.

— The Gold of Dreams. 224p. (YA). 1994. pap. 4.95 (*0-374-42584-1*) FS&G.

— La Orilla Oscura (The Dark Edge of the Water) 352p. 1995. pap. 16.95 (*0-679-76348-1*) Vin Bks.

Merino, Jose Maria. Beyond the Ancient Cities. Lane, Helen, tr. from SPA. LC 93-35482.Tr. of Tierra del Tiempo Perdido. 208p. (J). 1994. 16.00 (*0-374-34307-1*) FS&G.

Merino, Jose Maria, see Maria Merino, Jose, adapted by.

Merino-Morais, Jane. Difference et Repetition dans les Contes de la Fontaine. LC 82-24846. (University of Florida Monographs: Vol. 52). (FRE.). 152p. 1983. reprint ed. pap. 47.20 (*0-608-04484-9*, 206522900001) Bks Demand.

Merino, Orlando, jt. auth. see Helton, J. William.

Merinoff, Linda, see Bundy, Peg, pseud.

Merion, Anne & Yun-Kan, Shio. China: The Land & Its People. rev. ed. LC 85-72107. (Countries Ser.). (Illus.). 48p. (J). (gr. 5 up). 1991. lib. bdg. 14.95 (*0-382-24242-4*) Silver Burdett Pr.

Merion-Jones, Gwyn & Jones, Michael, eds. Manorial Domestic Buildings in England & Northern France. (Society of Antiquaries Occasional Papers: No. 15). (Illus.). 223p. 1994. pap. 35.00 (*0-85431-263-3*, Pub. by Soc Antiquaries) David Brown.

***Merish, Lori.** Sentimental Materialism: Gender, Commodity Culture & Nineteenth-Century American Literature. LC 99-50027. (New Americanists Ser.). 2000. pap. 64.95 (*0-8223-2480-6*); pap. 21.95 (*0-8223-2516-0*) Duke.

Merisotis, Jamie P., ed. The Changing Dimensions of Student Aid. LC 85-644752. (New Directions for Adult & Continuing Education Ser.: No. HE 74). 1991. pap. 22.00 (*1-55542-790-1*) Jossey-Bass.

Merisotis, Jamie P., jt. auth. see Hauptman, Arthur M.

Merisotis, Jamie P., jt. auth. see Lee, John B.

Merit. Merit Student Encyclopedia 1991, Vol. 13. 1991. 45.00 (*0-02-943743-1*) Mac Lib Ref.

— Merit Students Encyclopedia 1991, Vol. 11. 1991. 45.00 (*0-02-943741-5*) Mac Lib Ref.

Merit, Don. Excellence in Customer Service Within the Graphic Arts Industry: A Nuts & Bolts Approach to Quality Customer Service Within the Printing Trade. 32p. (Orig.). (C). 1991. pap. 9.95 (*0-933600-06-2*) Graph Arts Pub.

***Merit, Don.** Printing Estimating Primer. (Illus.). 120p. (C). 2000. pap. text 25.00 (*0-88362-313-7*) GATFPress.

Merit Group Staff, ed. see Raffery, Jeanne.

Meritt, Benjamin D. The Athenian Calendar in the Fifth Century. 1977. 44.95 (*0-8369-5012-7*) Ayer.

— Inscriptions from the Athenian Agora. (Excavations of the Athenian Agora Picture Bks.: No. 10). (Illus.). 32p. 1966. pap. 3.00 (*0-87661-610-4*) Am Sch Athens.

Meritt, Benjamin D. & Traill, John S. Inscriptions, the Athenian Councillors. LC 54-5697. (Athenian Agora Ser.: Vol. 15). (Illus.). xii, 486p. 1974. 55.00 (*0-87661-215-X*) Am Sch Athens.

Meritt, Benjamin D., et al. The Athenian Tribute Lists, Vol. 3. LC 75-10396. xx, 366p. 1968. reprint ed. 35.00 (*0-87661-913-8*) Am Sch Athens.

Meritt, Lucy S. History of the American School of Classical Studies at Athens, 1939-1980. LC 83-22495. (Illus.). xv, 411p. 1984. 15.00 (*0-87661-942-1*) Am Sch Athens.

***Meritt, Lucy Shoe & Edlund-Berry, Ingrid E. M.** Etruscan & Republican Roman Mouldings. 2nd ed. LC 99-55340. 1999. write for info. (*0-924171-77-4*) U Museum Pubns.

Meritts. Environmental Geography & Atmosphere. 1998. 60.30 (*0-7167-3494-X*) W H Freeman.

Merivale. Checkpoints with Readings: Developing College English Skills. 3rd ed. 352p. 2000. pap. 39.95 (*0-201-61411-1*) Addison-Wesley.

Merivale, Herman. Lectures on Colonization & Colonies Delivered Before the University of Oxford in 1839, 1840, & 1841. 2nd ed. LC 67-25954. (Reprints of Economic Classics Ser.). xix, 685p. 1967. reprint ed. 57.50 (*0-678-00273-8*) Kelley.

Merivale, Patricia. Pan, the Goat-God: His Myth in Modern Times. LC 69-12729. (Harvard Studies in Comparative Literature: No. 30). 319p. reprint ed. pap. 98.90 (*0-608-17496-3*, 202999600067) Bks Demand.

Merivale, Patricia, ed. Detecting Texts: The Metaphysical Detective Story from Poe to Postmodernism. LC 98-27815. 304p. 1998. 45.00 (*0-8122-3469-3*); pap. 19.95 (*0-8122-1676-8*) U of Pa Pr.

Merivale, Phillipa. Healing with Color: The Experience of Aura-Soma. LC 98-16942. 1998. pap. 12.95 (*1-86204-185-7*, Pub. by Element MA) Penguin Putnam.

Meriweather, Mary B. Illustrated Bulletin Boards. (Illus.). 58p. (Orig.). 1992. pap. 6.95 (*1-56794-031-5*, C2280) Star Bible.

Meriwether, Colyer. History of Higher Education in South Carolina, with a Sketch of the Free School System. LC 75-187369. (Illus.). 283p. 1972. reprint ed. 25.00 (*0-87152-097-4*) Reprint.

Meriwether, David. My Life in the Mountains & on the Plains: The Newly Discovered Autobiography. Griffen, Robert A., ed. LC 65-11240. (American Exploration & Travel Ser.: 46). 324p. reprint ed. pap. 100.50 (*0-608-12408-7*, 205213200039) Bks Demand.

Meriwether, Doug. Mister, I Am the Band! Buddy Rich - His Life & Travels. LC 97-42489. 464p. 1998. per. 49.95 (*0-7935-8243-1*, HL00330320) H Leonard.

Meriwether, Elizabeth A. Recollections of 92 Years, 1824-1916. LC 94-23586. (Illus.). 256p. 1994. pap. 14.95 (*0-939009-84-6*, EPM) Howell Pr VA.

Meriwether, J. W., ed. Atmospheric Sciences in Antartica. 298p. 1989. 22.00 (*0-87590-685-0*) Am Geophysical.

Meriwether, Louise. Daddy Was a Number Runner. LC 86-9019. 240p. 1986. pap. 10.95 (*0-935312-57-9*) Feminist Pr.

— Fragments of the Ark. Rosenman, Jane, ed. 352p. 1995. pap. 10.00 (*0-671-79948-7*, WSP) PB.

***Meriwether, Louise.** Shadow Dancing. 320p. 2000. mass mkt. 12.95 (*0-345-42595-2*) Ballantine Pub Grp.

Meriwether, Margaret. The Kin Who Count. 304p. 1999. 45.00 (*0-292-75223-7*) U of Tex Pr.

Meriwether, Margaret L., ed. see Tucker, Judith.

Meriwether, Margaret Lee. The Kin Who Count: Family & Society in Ottoman Aleppo, 1770-1840. (Illus.). 278p. 1999. pap. 22.00 (*0-292-75224-5*) U of Tex Pr.

Meriwether, Nell. Strategies for Writing Successful Essays. LC 97-18518. 352p. 1997. pap. 16.95 (*0-8442-5992-6*) NTC Contemp Pub Co.

***Meriwether, Nell W.** Successful Research Papers in 12 Easy Steps. 2000. pap. 14.95 (*0-658-01214-2*) NTC Contemp Pub Co.

— 12 Easy Steps to Successful Research Papers. LC 96-858. (Illus.). 176p. (C). 1996. pap. 7.95 (*0-8442-5891-1*, 58911) NTC Contemp Pub Co.

Meriwether, Robert L. The Expansion of South Carolina, 1729-1765. LC 73-16348. (Perspectives in American History Ser.: No. 17). (Illus.). viii, 294p. 1974. reprint ed. lib. bdg. 39.50 (*0-87991-345-2*) Porcupine Pr.

Merk, Ann & Meek, Jim. Clouds. LC 94-13324. (Weather Report Discovery Library). 24p. (J). (gr. k-4). 1994. lib. bdg. 10.95 (*0-86593-389-8*) Rourke Corp.

— Storms. LC 94-13321. (Weather Report Discovery Library). 24p. (J). (gr. k-4). 1994. lib. bdg. 10.95 (*0-86593-386-3*) Rourke Corp.

Merk, Ann & Merk, Jim. Rain, Snow & Ice. LC 94-13325. (Weather Report Discovery Library). 24p. (J). (gr. k-4). 1994. lib. bdg. 10.95 (*0-86593-390-1*) Rourke Corp.

— Studying Weather. LC 94-13320. (Weather Report Discovery Library). 24p. (J). (gr. k-4). 1994. lib. bdg. 10.95 (*0-86593-385-5*) Rourke Corp.

— Weather & Us. LC 94-13322. (Weather Report Discovery Library). 24p. (J). (gr. k-4). 1994. lib. bdg. 10.95 (*0-86593-387-1*) Rourke Corp.

— Weather Signs. LC 94-13323. (Weather Report Discovery Library). 24p. (J). (gr. k-4). 1994. lib. bdg. 10.95 (*0-86593-388-X*) Rourke Corp.

Merk, David, jt. ed. see Lewis, John F.

Merk, Frederick. Economic History of Wisconsin During the Civil War Decade. 2nd ed. LC 72-180453. (Illus.). 414p. 1971. reprint ed. 27.50 (*0-87020-117-4*) State Hist Soc Wis.

— Manifest Destiny & Mission in American History. 304p. (Orig.). (C). 1995. pap. text 16.50 (*0-674-54805-1*) HUP.

— Manifest Destiny & Mission in American History. (Orig.). 1966. pap. text 8.95 (*0-07-553693-5*) McGraw.

— The Oregon Question: Essays in Anglo-American Diplomacy & Politics. LC 67-14345. 443p. reprint ed. pap. 137.40 (*0-7837-2300-8*, 205738800004) Bks Demand.

Merk, Frederick & Merk, Lois B. Fruits of Propaganda in the Tyler Administration. LC 79-135547. (Illus.). 269p. 1971. 23.95 (*0-674-32676-8*) HUP.

— Manifest Destiny & Mission in American History: A Reinterpretation. LC 82-25146. 265p. (C). 1983. reprint ed. lib. bdg. 41.50 (*0-313-23844-8*, MERM, Greenwood Pr) Greenwood.

Merk, Frederick, ed. see Simpson, George.

Merk, H. F., ed. Porphyria. (Skin Pharmacology & Applied Skin Physiology Ser.: Vol. 11, No. 6). (Illus.). 98p. 1999. pap. 34.00 (*3-8055-6908-4*) S Karger.

Merk, H. F. & Jackson, E. M., eds. International Symposium on Cosmetic Efficacy: 3rd Symposium, Cologne, May, 1998. (Skin Pharmacology & Applied Skin Physiology Ser.: Vol. 12, No. 3). (Illus.). 62p. 1999. pap. 25.25 (*3-8055-6929-7*) S Karger.

Merk, Jim, jt. auth. see Merk, Ann.

Merk, Lois B., jt. auth. see Merk, Frederick.

Merk, Otto & Wolter, Michael, eds. Im Zeichen des Kreuzes: Aufsatze von Erich Dinkler. (Beiheft zur Zeitschrift fuer die Neuetestamentliche Wissenschaft Ser.: No. 61). (GER.). x, 578p. (C). 1992. lib. bdg. 167.70 (*3-11-013017-3*) De Gruyter.

Merke, F. History & Iconography of Endemic Goitre & Cretinism. 330p. 1984. 68.00 (*3-456-81189-6*) Hogrefe & Huber Pubs.

Merkel. Hotel Builders. text. write for info. (*0-471-48961-1*) Wiley.

Merkel-Holguin, Lisa A. Children Who Lose Their Parents to HIV/AIDS: Agency Guidelines for Adoptive & Kinship Placement. LC 96-122141. 1996. pap. 9.95 (*0-87868-631-2*) Child Welfare.

Merkel-Holguin, Lisa A., jt. ed. see Smith, Eve P.

***Merkel, Inge & Latimer, Renate.** Odysseus & Penelope: An Ordinary Marriage. unabridged ed. LC 95-53237. (Studies in Austrian Literature, Culture, & Thought Ser.).Tr. of Eine ganz gewohnliche Ehe. 391p. 2000. pap. 29.50 (*1-57241-075-2*) Ariadne CA.

Merkel, Ingrid, jt. ed. see Debus, Allen G.

Merkel, J. Die Vegetation in Gebiet des Messtischblattes 6434 Hersbruck. (Dissertationes Botanicae Ser.: No. 51). (GER., Illus.). 176p. 1980. pap. text 40.00 (*3-7682-1235-1*) Lubrecht & Cramer.

Merkel, Jayne S. In Its Place: The Architecture of Carl Strauss & Ray Roush. (Illus.). 60p. 1985. pap. 15.95 (*0-917562-36-4*) Contemp Arts.

— Michael Graves & Riverbend: A Summer Pavillion for the Cincinnati Symphony Orchestra. (Illus.). 1987. 15.95 (*0-917562-33-X*) Contemp Arts.

Merkel, Jeanne S. Nine Boats & Nine Kids: A True Chronicle. LC 84-19422. (Illus.). 162p. (Orig.). 1984. 14.95 (*0-931447-01-1*); pap. 9.95 (*0-931447-00-3*) Ledge Bks.

Merkel, Judi K., ed. Indiana State Fair Cookbook: Hoosier Heritage Edition. 246p. 1993. spiral bd. 17.95 (*0-89730-230-3*, State Fair Bks) R J Berg.

Merkel, Keith W. & Hoffman, Robert S. Proceedings of the California Eelgrass Symposium, Chula Vista, CA, May 27 & 28, 1988. 78p. 1990. pap. 17.50 (*0-931950-02-3*) Sweetwater River Pr.

*** Merkel, Klaus.** The Reading of Time in the Text of Nature. (Illus.). 96p. 2000. 45.00 (*3-907044-40-1*) Lars Muller.

Merkel, Margaret. Sunshine at the End of Life. Zagury, Carolyn S., ed. LC 97-60583. 108p. 1997. pap. 12.95 (*1-880254-43-3*) Vista.

Merkel, Richard H. Well Log Formation Evaluation. LC TN0860.A32. (AAPG Continuing Education Course Note Ser.: Vol. 14). 92p. 1979. reprint ed. pap. 30.00 (*0-608-02773-1*, 206383900007) Bks Demand.

Merkel, Robert A., jt. auth. see Boggs, Donald L.

Merkel, Robert S. Textile Product Serviceability: By Specification. 400p. (C). 1991. text 55.51 (*0-02-380565-X*, Macmillan Coll) P-H.

Merkel, Robyn A. Art Talk: Year 'Round Art Activities for S, R, L & Blends. (Illus.). 220p. (J). (gr. 1-6). 1997. spiral bd., wbk. ed. 26.95 (*1-58650-060-0*, BK-257) Super Duper.

Merkel, Susan L. Certifiably Bulimic. LC 91-14993. 136p. 1991. pap. 12.95 (*0-942963-15-6*) Distinctive Pub.

Merkel, Udo. Racism & Xenophobia in European Football. pap. text 17.95 (*3-89124-343-X*) Meyer & Meyer.

Merkelio, R., ed. see Ovid.

Merken. Oht Physical Science W/Mod Appl 5e. 5th ed. (C). 1993. teacher ed. 246.00 (*0-03-096041-X*, Pub. by Harcourt Coll Pubs) Harcourt.

— Physical Science. 4th ed. (C). 1989. pap. text, teacher ed. 28.00 (*0-03-023322-4*) Harcourt Coll Pubs.

Merken, ed. Organic Chemistry. (C). 1986. text, teacher ed. write for info. (*0-321-40544-7*) Addison-Wesley Educ.

Merken, jt. auth. see Smith.

Merken, Kathleen, tr. see Makabe, Tomoko.

Merken, Melvin. Physical Science with Modular Applications. 5th ed. (C). 1993. pap. text 66.50 (*0-03-096010-X*, Pub. by Harcourt Coll Pubs) Harcourt.

Merker, Gloria S. The Hellenistic Sculpture of Rhodes. (Studies in Mediterranean Archaeology: Vol. XL). (Illus.). 64p. (Orig.). 1973. pap. 22.50 (*91-85058-58-0*) P Astroms.

***Merker, Gloria S.** The Sanctuary of Demeter & Kore: Terracotta Figurines of the Classical, Hellenistic & Roman Periods. LC 99-87774. (Corinth Ser.). (Illus.). 400p. 2000. text 100.00 (*0-87661-184-6*, Pub. by Am Sch Athens) U Museum Pubns.

Merker, Hannah. Listening: Ways of Hearing in a Silent World. LC 99-46960. 224p. 1999. reprint ed. pap. 12.95 (*0-87074-448-8*, Pub. by SMU Press) Tex A&M Univ Pr.

Merker, Kyle. The Fitness Guide: Where to Work Out When You're on the Road. LC 96-94075. (Illus.). 208p. (Orig.). 1997. pap. 14.95 (*0-9650685-7-9*) Incline Press Publishing.

Merker, Milton, jt. ed. see Shen, Benjamin S.

Merkert, Jorn, jt. ed. see Smith, David.

Merkes-Frei, Christa & Tietze, Ulrike, eds. Trommle Mein Herz fur das Leben: Schone-Liederbuch. (GER.). 92p. 1996. spiral bd. 10.00 (*0-942017-31-5*, 310-6456SL); spiral bd. write for info. incl. audio (*0-942017-32-3*) Amer Assn Teach German.

Merkhofer, Miley W. Decision Science & Social Risk Management. (C). 1986. text 147.00 (*90-277-2275-7*) Kluwer Academic.

Merkhoher, Miley W., jt. auth. see Covello, Vincent T.

***Merki.** Give Your Students the Latest Facts about AIDS: HIV/AIDS (Teen Health) annot. ed. 1999. teacher ed. 10.81 (*0-02-652585-2*) Glencoe.

— Glencoe Health: Teacher's Wraparound Edition. 1999. teacher ed. 56.23 (*0-02-651563-6*) Glencoe.

— HIV/AIDS & Society (Glencoe Health) annot. ed. 1999. teacher ed. 9.39 (*0-02-651589-X*) Glencoe.

— Teen Health: Course 1: Teacher's Wraparound Edition. 1999. teacher ed. 38.91 (*0-02-651838-4*) Glencoe.

— Teen Health: Course 2: Teacher's Wraparound Edition. 1999. teacher ed. 47.57 (*0-02-653129-1*) Glencoe.

Merki. Teen Health: Course 3: Teacher's Wraparound Edition. 1999. teacher ed. 52.99 (*0-02-653206-9*) Glencoe.

Merki, Don, jt. auth. see Merki, Mark.

Merki, Mark & Merki, Don. Jumping Through the Hoops: A Survival Guide to Graduate School. (From the Trenches Survival Guides Ser.: No. 1). (Illus.). 128p. (Orig.). 1995. pap. 9.95 (*0-945872-10-0*) Great Activities Pub Co.

Merki, Mary B. Glencoe Health: A Guide to Wellness. 1986. 43.94 (*0-02-652380-9*) Glencoe.

Merkies, A. H. Selection of Models by Forecasting Intervals. Van Holten-De Wolff, M., tr. LC 73-83565. 1973. lib. bdg. 115.00 (*90-277-0342-6*) Kluwer Academic.

Merkies, A. H., jt. auth. see Van Daal, Jan.

Merkin, Daphne. The Discovery of Sex. 2004. 25.00 (*0-517-70625-3*) Random Hse Value.

— Dreaming of Hitler. LC 98-15052. 384p. 1999. pap. 13.00 (*0-15-600611-1*, Harvest Bks) Harcourt.

— Enchantment. 304p. 1986. 16.95 (*0-15-128791-0*) Harcourt.

Merkin, David R. Introduction to the Theory of Stability. Smirnov, Andrei L. & Afagh, Fred, trs. from RUS. LC 96-15277. (Texts in Applied Mathematics Ser.: Vol. 24). 319p. 1996. 49.95 (*0-387-94761-2*) Spr-Verlag.

An Asterisk (*) at the beginning of an entry indicates that the title is appearing for the first time.

M

An Asterisk (*) at the beginning of an entry indicates that the title is appearing for the first time.

Merlin-Walch, Olivier & Amoros Rica, Narciso. Dictionnaire Juridique, Diccionario Juridico: French - Spanish, Spanish - French. 3rd ed. (FRE & SPA.). 933p. 1993. 195.00 (*0-7859-1078-6*, S36030) Fr & Eur.

Merlin-Walch, Olivier & Rica, Amoros. Diccionario Juridico Frances-Espanol-Frances. (FRE & SPA.). 800p. 1986. 175.00 (*0-8288-0407-9*, S 36030) Fr & Eur.

***Merling, Andrew, et al.** The Wedding: A Family's Coming Out Story. Wythe, Douglas, ed. LC 99-59512. 288p. 2000. 23.00 (*0-380-97691-9*, Avon Bks) Morrow Avon.

Merling, David, Sr. The Book of Joshua: Its Theme & Role in Archaeological Discussions. (Seminary Doctoral Dissertation Ser.: No. 23). 353p. 1997. pap. 19.99 (*1-883925-17-7*) Andrews Univ Pr.

Merling, David, ed. To Understand the Scriptures: Essays in Honor of William H. Shea. LC 97-75234. (Illus.). xxx, 330p. 1997. pap. 15.00 (*0-9642060-2-1*) Inst of Archaeol.

Merling, David & Geraty, Lawrence T., eds. Hesban after 25 Years. LC 94-77622. (Illus.). xxix, 379p. (Orig.). 1994. pap. 15.00 (*0-9642060-0-5*) Inst of Archaeol.

Merlini, L., et al, eds. Current Concepts in Childhood Spinal Muscular Atrophy. (Illus.). 227p. 1989. 120.00 (*0-387-82131-7*) Spr-Verlag.

Merlini, Marco P., ed. Surgery of the Arteria Profunda Femuralis. LC 94-12558. 1994. 132.00 (*0-387-58067-0*) Spr-Verlag.

***Merlino, Jennifer A.** Reflection in Time. 10p. 1998. 6.95 (*1-885206-67-4*) Cader Pubng.

Merlino, Kim. Science: Insects & Spiders. (Illus.). 32p. (J). (gr. 2-3). 1997. pap. 2.25 (*0-88743-292-1*, 02160) Sch Zone Pub Co.

Merlio, Gilbert & Pelletier, Nicole, eds. Bordeaux au Temps de Holdrelin. (Contacts, Serie II: Vol. 20). (FRE., Illus.). vi, 360p. 1997. 43.95 (*3-906754-70-7*, Pub. by P Lang) P Lang Pubng.

Merlis, Bob & Seay, David. Heart & Soul: A Celebration of Black Music Style in America 1930-1975. LC 97-3186. (Illus.). 160p. 1997. 40.00 (*1-55670-538-7*) Stewart Tabori & Chang.

Merlis, Brian. Brooklyn - the Centennial Edition. (Illus.). 128p. (Orig.). 1997. per. 19.95 (*1-878741-33-0*) Israelowitz Pub.

— Brooklyn - The Way It Was. 250p. 1995. 39.95 (*1-878741-21-7*); pap. 24.95 (*1-878741-20-9*) Israelowitz Pub.

— Brooklyn's Gold Coast. LC 97-75158. 1997. pap. text 19.95 (*1-878741-49-7*) Israelowitz Pub.

— Brooklyn's Gold Coast: The Sheepshead Bay Communities. LC 97-75158. 160qp. 1997. 24.95 (*1-878741-48-9*) Israelowitz Pub.

***Merlis, Brian.** Brooklyn's Park Slope: A Photographic Retrospective. 165p. 1999. 29.95 (*1-878741-47-0*) Israelowitz Pub.

Merlis, Brian & Israelowitz, Oscar. Welcome Back to Brooklyn. 172p. 1993. 19.95 (*1-878741-14-4*) Israelowitz Pub.

Merlis, Mark. American Studies. 288p. 1996. reprint ed. pap. 10.95 (*0-14-025090-5*) Viking Penguin.

— An Arrow's Flight. LC 97-53088. 384p. 1998. text 24.95 (*0-312-18675-4*) St Martin.

— An Arrow's Flight. 376p. 1999. pap. 13.95 (*0-312-24288-3*) St Martin.

Merlo, Alida V. Women, Law & Social Control. 283p. (C). 1994. pap. text 38.00 (*0-02-380567-6*, Macmillan Coll) P-H.

***Merlo, Alida V. & Benekos, Peter J.** What's Wrong with the Criminal Justice System: Ideology, Politics & the Media. LC 99-41038. 207p. 1999. pap. 28.95 (*0-87084-933-6*) Anderson Pub Co.

Merlo, Alida V., jt. ed. see Benekos, Peter J.

Merlo, Catherine M. Legacy of a Shared Vision: The History of Calcot. 192p. 1995. lib. bdg. 32.00 (*0-9645117-0-3*) Calcot.

***Merlo, Claudio.** The History of Art: Masterpieces of the World. LC 99-48577. (Illus.). 128p. (J). 2000. 29.95 (*0-87226-531-5*, 65315B, P Bedrick Books) NTC Contemp Pub Co.

Merlo, Claudio. Three Masters of the Renaissance: Leonardo, Michelangelo, Raphael. Rosenberg, Marion Lignana, tr. from ITA. LC 98-76194. (Bravo Ser.). (Illus.). 120p. (YA). (gr. 6 up). 1999. 8.95 (*0-7641-0946-4*) Barron.

Merlo, Juan C. Y Equipo. Diccionario Enciclopedico: El Ateneo. 3rd ed. (SPA.). 995.00 (*0-7859-0709-2*, S-33045) Fr & Eur.

Merlo, Paola & Slap. Parsing with Principles & Classes of Information. LC 96-206051. (Studies in Linguistics & Philosophy). 246p. (C). 1996. text 93.50 (*0-7923-4103-1*) Kluwer Academic.

Merlo, Thecia. Those Who Listen Hear His Voice: An Awareness Journal. 256p. spiral bd. 9.50 (*0-8198-7378-0*) Pauline Bks.

Merlo, Vicente A. Diccionario de Historia Eclesiastica de Espana, Vol. 3. 2nd ed. (SPA.). 128p. 1990. pap. 15.95 (*0-7859-5157-1*) Fr & Eur.

— Diccionario de Historia Eclesiastica de Espana, Vol. 4. 4th ed. (SPA.). 224p. 1990. pap. 14.95 (*0-7859-5158-X*, S19856) Fr & Eur.

Merlone, Mark S. Inspirational Spiritual Healing Through Poetry. 88p. 1998. pap. 10.95 (*1-892896-97-4*) Buy Books.

Merlonghi, Ferdinando. Oggi in Italia, 5 vols. (C). 1993. text 63.96 (*0-395-66859-X*) HM.

— Oggi in Italia, 5 vols. (C). 1993. pap., wbk. ed. 33.96 (*0-395-68534-6*) HM.

Merlonghi, Ferdinando, et al. Oggi in Italia: A First Course in Italian. 2nd ed. LC 81-85378. 1982. reel tape 270.00 (*0-685-42421-9*) HM.

— Oggi in Italia: A First Course in Italian, 5 vols. 5th ed. (ITA.). (C). 1994. text, teacher ed., wbk. ed. 7.56 (*0-395-68535-4*) HM.

— Oggi in Italia: A First Course in Italian, 5 vols. 5th annot. ed. (ITA.). (C). 1993. text, teacher ed. 65.16 (*0-395-66860-3*) HM.

— Racconti di Oggi. 176p. (C). 1991. pap. text. write for info. (*0-395-55423-3*) HM Soft Schl Col Div.

Merlonghi, Ferdinando, jt. auth. see Merlonghi, Franca C.

Merlonghi, Franca, et al. Oggi in Italia: A First Course in Italian. 6th ed. (ITA.). 608p. (C). 1997. text 63.96 (*0-395-85900-X*) HM.

— Oggi in Italia: A First Course in Italian. 6th ed. (ITA.). (C). 1998. pap. text, wbk. ed. 34.76 (*0-395-87970-1*) HM.

— Oggi in Italia: A First Course in Italian. 6th annot. ed. (ITA.). (C). 1998. teacher ed. 65.16 (*0-395-85901-8*) HM.

Merlonghi, Franca C. & Merlonghi, Ferdinando. Andiamo Avanti! Lingua e Cultura. 352p. (C). 1992. pap. text 40.60 (*0-13-031451-X*) P-H.

Merlonghi, Franca C., et al. Andiamo Avanti: Attualita e Racconti. 200p. (C). 1991. pap. text 24.40 (*0-13-036542-4*) P-H.

Merlonghi, Franca C., jt. auth. see Valencia, Pablo.

Merloyd, Lawrence, ed. see Greenspan, Stanley L.

Merluzzi, Thomas V., et al, eds. Cognitive Assessment. LC 80-24870. (Guilford Clinical Psychology & Psychotherapy Ser.). (Illus.). 548p. reprint ed. pap. 169.90 (*0-7837-0689-8*, 204102200019) Bks Demand.

Merluzzi, Thomas V., ed. see Glass, Carol R. & Genest, Myles.

Merluzzi, Vincent J. & Adams, Julian, eds. The Search for Anti-Inflammatory Drugs: Case Histories from Concept to Clinic. LC 95-1583. (Illus.). 314p. 1995. 87.50 (*0-8176-3685-4*) Birkhauser.

Merluzzi, Vincent J., jt. ed. see Adams, Julian.

Merlyn, Vaughan, et al. Development & Effectiveness: Strategies for IS Organizational Transition. (Ernst & Young Information Management Ser.). 390p. 1994. 45.00 (*0-471-58954-3*) Wiley.

Mermall, Thomas. The Rhetoric of Humanism: Spanish Culture after Ortega y Gasset. LC 76-45293. 1976. pap. 12.00 (*0-916950-16-6*); lib. bdg. 20.00 (*0-916950-02-6*) Biling Rev-Pr.

Mermann, Alan C. Some Chose to Stay: Faith & Ethics in a Time of Plague. LC 96-52123. (Society/Religion/Religion/Society Ser.). 1997. pap. 17.50 (*0-391-04029-4*); text 55.00 (*0-391-04028-6*) Humanities.

***Mermann, Alan C.** Some Chose to Stay: Faith & Ethics in a Time of Plague. 1999. pap. 59.95 (*1-57392-624-8*) Prometheus Bks.

Mermann, Alan C. To Do No Harm: Learning to Care for the Seriously Ill. 128p. 1998. 45.00 (*0-391-04084-7*); pap. 15.00 (*0-391-04085-5*) Humanities.

— To Do No Harm: Learning to Care for the Seriously Ill. LC 99-10115. 128p. 1999. 39.95 (*1-57392-667-1*, Humanity Bks) Prometheus Bks.

***Mermann, Alan C.** To Do No Harm: Learning to Care for the Seriously Ill. LC 99-10115. 128p. 1999. pap. 14.95 (*1-57392-666-3*, Humanity Bks) Prometheus Bks.

Mermel, Anita & Simons, Judy. Women & World Development: An Education & Action Guide for Making Global Connections in Your Community. OEF International Staff, ed. LC 89-7220. 92p. (Orig.). 1991. pap., student ed. 16.00 (*0-912917-21-0*) UNIFEM.

***Mermelstein, Jeff.** Sidewalk. 2000. 45.00 (*1-899235-62-0*) Dewi Lewis.

Mermelstein, Mel. By Bread Alone: The Story of A-4685. LC 78-1206. (Illus.). 290p. 1981. pap. 10.00 (*0-686-86305-4*) M Mermelstein.

— By Bread Alone: The Story of A-4685. 2nd ed. LC 78-1206. (Illus.). 290p. 1981. 15.00 (*0-9606534-0-6*, 7901) M Mermelstein.

Mermelstein, Shoshana & Shapiro, Chava. Arts & Crafts Around the Jewish Calendar, Vol. 1. 1997. pap. 4.95 (*0-914131-00-1*, A470) Torah Umesorah.

— Arts & Crafts Around the Jewish Calendar, Vol. 2. 1997. pap. 4.95 (*0-914131-01-X*, A471) Torah Umesorah.

Mermet, Jean M., jt. auth. see Jerraya, Ahmed A.

Mermet, Jean P., ed. Fundamentals & Standards in Hardware Description Languages: Proceedings of the NATO Advanced Study Institute, In Ciocco, Barga, Italy, April 16-26, 1993. LC 93-20899. (NATO Advanced Science Institutes Series C: Mathematical & Physical Sciences). 480p. (C). 1993. text 254.00 (*0-7923-2513-3*) Kluwer Academic.

— VHDL for Simulation, Synthesis, & Formal Proofs of Hardware. LC 92-16266. (International Series in Engineering & Computer Science, VLSI, Computer Architecture, & Digital Screen Processing: Vol. 183). 316p. (C). 1992. text 155.00 (*0-7923-9253-1*) Kluwer Academic.

Mermet, Jean P., jt. ed. see Nebel, Wolfgang.

Mermet, Michel, jt. ed. see Henry, Jean-Pierre.

***Mermier, Guy R.** France: Past & Present. LC 99-51813. (Studies in Modern European History: Vol. 37). 312p. (C). 2000. pap. text 29.95 (*0-8204-4455-3*) P Lang Pubng.

Mermier, Guy R., ed. Contemporary Readings of Medieval Literature. LC 81-50963. (Michigan Romance Studies: Vol. 8). 226p. 1989. pap. 15.00 (*0-939730-07-3*) Mich Romance.

Mermier, Guy R., ed. Courtly Romance: A Collection of Essays. LC 84-60235. (Medieval & Renaissance Monograph Ser.: Vol. 6). 320p. reprint ed. pap. 99.20 (*0-608-15899-2*, 203082600071) Bks Demand.

— Synopsis, 1991-92, Vol. 3. 124p. 1993. text 49.95 (*0-7734-9237-2*) E Mellen.

Mermier, Guy R., tr. Le Jeu d'Adam le Bocu d'Arras - The Play of Adam the Hunchback from Arras. LC 93-50731. 76p. 1994. 49.95 (*0-7734-9142-2*) E Mellen.

— A Medieval Book of Beasts: Pierre de Beauvais' Bestiary Followed by a Diplomatic Transcription of the Malines (Mechelen) Manuscript of Pierre de Beauvais, Short Version, & with in Appendix, an English Translation of the Cambrai Bestiary. LC 91-37833. (Illus.). 364p. 1991. lib. bdg. 99.95 (*0-7734-9629-7*) E Mellen.

— The Romance of Jehan de Paris (Le Romant de Jehan de Paris) LC 92-45566. (Studies in French Literature: Vol. 15). 120p. 1993. text 59.95 (*0-7734-9225-9*) E Mellen.

Mermier, Guy R. & Boilly-Widmer, Yvette. Explication de Texte: Theorie et Pratique. LC 93-18841. 206p. 1993. pap. 29.95 (*0-7734-9261-5*) E Mellen.

Mermier, Guy R. & DuBruck, Edelgard E., eds. Fifteenth Century Studies, Vol. 1. LC 78-5176. 327p. 1978. reprint ed. pap. 101.40 (*0-8357-0312-6*, 201986100001) Bks Demand.

— Fifteenth Century Studies, Vol. 2. LC 79-640105. 252p. 1979. reprint ed. pap. 78.20 (*0-8357-0392-4*, 201986100002) Bks Demand.

— Fifteenth Century Studies, Vol. 3. LC 79-640105. 252p. 1980. reprint ed. pap. 78.20 (*0-8357-0505-6*, 201986100003) Bks Demand.

Mermier, Guy R. & Vaquero, Mercedes, eds. Synopsis. (Medieval & Renaissance Monograph). (Orig.). 1988. pap. 5.00 (*0-941107-02-7*) MARC Pub Co.

Mermier, Guy R., jt. ed. see DuBruck, Edelgard E.

Mermier, Guy R., ed. see Fifteenth-Century Studies Staff.

Mermier, Guy R., tr. see De La Halle, Adam.

Mermier, Martha B. Coping with Severe Mental Illness: Families Speak Out. LC 93-20490. (Studies in Health & Human Services: Vol. 23). 212p. 1993. text 89.95 (*0-7734-9285-2*) E Mellen.

Mermilliod, J. C., jt. ed. see Milone, E. F.

Mermilliod, Jean-Claude & Mermilliod, Monique. Catalog of Mean UBV Data on Stars. 1994. 159.95 (*0-387-94355-2*); write for info. (*3-540-94355-2*) Spr-Verlag.

Mermilliod, Monique, jt. auth. see Mermilliod, Jean-Claude.

Mermin, Dorothy. Elizabeth Barrett Browning: The Origins of a New Poetry. LC 88-28680. (Women in Culture & Society Ser.). 328p. 1989. pap. text 18.95 (*0-226-52039-0*) U Ch Pr.

— Godiva's Ride: Women of Letters in England, 1830-1880. LC 92-45186. 204p. (C). 1993. pap. 6.50 (*0-253-20824-6*) Ind U Pr.

Mermin, Jonathan. Debating War & Peace: Media Coverage of U. S. Intervention in the Post-Vietnam Era. LC 98-43564. 168p. 1999. 16.95 (*0-691-00534-6*, Pub. by Princeton U Pr) Cal Prin Full Svc.

***Mermin, Jonathan.** Debating War & Peace: Media Coverage of U. S. Intervention in the Post-Vietnam Era. LC 98-43564. 168p. 1999. 45.00 (*0-691-00533-8*, Pub. by Princeton U Pr) Cal Prin Full Svc.

Mermin, Jonathan, jt. auth. see Granich, Reuben.

Mermin, N. David. Boojums All the Way Through: Communicating Science in a Prosaic Age. (Illus.). 330p. (C). 1990. pap. 21.95 (*0-521-38880-5*) Cambridge U Pr.

— Boojums All the Way Through: Communicating Science in a Prosaic Age. (Illus.). 330p. (C). 1990. text 59.95 (*0-521-38231-9*) Cambridge U Pr.

— Space & Time in Special Relativity. (Illus.). 240p. (C). 1989. reprint ed. pap. text 21.95 (*0-88133-420-0*) Waveland Pr.

Mermin, N. David, jt. auth. see Ashcroft, Neil W.

Mermin, Rob. Circus Smirkus: A True Story of High Adventure & Low Comedy. LC 97-215520. (Illus.). v, 96p. (J). 1997. pap. 14.95 (*0-9658076-0-6*, Circus Smirkus) Circus Barn.

Mermin, Samuel. Jurisprudence & Statecraft: The Wisconsin Development Authority & Its Implications. LC 63-15054. 264p. reprint ed. pap. 81.90 (*0-608-14666-8*, 202114100021) Bks Demand.

— Law & the Legal System: An Introduction. 2nd ed. LC 81-83102. 496p. (C). 1982. pap. 25.00 (*0-316-56731-0*) Little.

Mermut, A., jt. ed. see Ahmad, N.

Mermut, Ahmed R., ed. Layer Charge Characteristics of 2:1: Silicate Clay Minerals. (CMS Workshop Lectures: Vol. 6). (Illus.). 144p. (C). 1994. pap. text 17.00 (*1-881208-07-9*) Clay Minerals.

Mermut, Ahmed R., jt. ed. see Miedema, Rienk.

***Merna & Dubey Staff.** Financial Engineering in the Procurement of Projects. Asia Law & Practice Staff, ed. 150p. 1999. pap. text 170.00 (*962-936-047-0*, Pub. by Asia Law & Practice) Am Educ Systs.

Merna & Owen Staff. Understanding the Private Finance Initiative: The New Dynamics of Project Finance. 168p. 1998. pap. 170.00 (*962-360-031-3*, Pub. by Asia Law & Practice) Am Educ Systs.

Merna, Tony, jt. auth. see Nijru, Cyrus.

Mernagh, Dawn & Cartwright, Jennifer. Health & Beauty Therapy: A Practical Approach for NVQ Level 3. 312p. (Orig.). 1995. pap. 39.50 (*0-7487-1817-6*, Pub. by S Thornes Pubs) Trans-Atl Phila.

Mernagh-Ward, Dawn & Cartwright, Jennifer. Good Practice in Salon Management, Level 3. (Illus.). 180p. (Orig.). 1997. pap. 42.50 (*0-7487-2887-2*, Pub. by S Thornes Pubs) Trans-Atl Phila.

Mernissi, Fatima. Beyond the Veil: Male-Female Dynamics in Modern Muslim Society. rev. ed. LC 86-46034. 224p. 1987. 35.00 (*0-253-31162-4*); pap. 12.95 (*0-253-20423-2*, MB-423) Ind U Pr.

— Doing Daily Battle: Interviews with Moroccan Women. Lakeland, Jo, tr. LC 88-34211. 224p. (C). 1989. text 35.00 (*0-8135-1417-7*) Rutgers U Pr.

— Dreams of Trespass: Tales of a Harem Girlhood. LC 93-39523. (Illus.). 1994. 23.00 (*0-201-62649-7*) Addison-Wesley.

— Dreams of Trespass: Tales of a Harem Girlhood. 256p. 1995. pap. 13.00 (*0-201-48937-6*) Addison-Wesley.

— The Forgotten Queens of Islam. 238p. 1997. pap. 16.95 (*0-8166-2439-9*) U of Minn Pr.

— Islam & Democracy: Fear of the Modern World. Lakeland, Mary J., tr. 300p. 1992. 24.95 (*0-201-60883-9*) Addison-Wesley.

— Islam & Democracy: Fear of the Modern World. (Illus.). 208p. 1993. pap. 14.00 (*0-201-62483-4*) Addison-Wesley.

— The Veil & the Male Elite: A Feminist Interpretation of Women's Rights in Islam. (Illus.). 240p. 1992. pap. 16.00 (*0-201-63221-7*) Addison-Wesley.

— Women & Islam: An Historical & Theological Enquiry. (C). 1991. 22.50 (*81-85107-71-8*, Pub. by Kali for Women) S Asia.

— Women's Rebellion & Islamic Memory. Agar, Emily, tr. 224p. (C). 1996. text 55.00 (*1-85649-397-0*, Pub. by Zed Books); text 19.95 (*1-85649-398-9*, Pub. by Zed Books) St Martin.

***Mernit, Billy.** Writing the Romantic Comedy: How to Craft a Screenplay That Will Sell. 288p. 2000. 24.00 (*0-06-019568-1*, HarpRes) HarpInfo.

Mernit, Susan. Everything You Need to Know about Changing Schools. (Need to Know Library). (Illus.). 64p. (YA). (gr. 7-12). 1992. lib. bdg. 17.95 (*0-8239-1326-0*) Rosen Group.

***Mernit, William.** That's How Much I Love You. (Illus.). 95p. 2000. pap. 8.95 (*0-9676061-0-1*) Tallfellow.

Mernitz, Scott. Mediation of Environmental Disputes: A Sourcebook. LC 80-7503. 202p. 1980. 57.95 (*0-275-90523-3*, C0523, Praeger Pubs) Greenwood.

Mero, Everett B., ed. American Playgrounds. LC 78-143063. 1982. 24.95 (*0-8434-0433-7*, Pub. by McGrath NH) Ayer.

Mero, L. Ways of Thinking: The Limits of Rational Thought & Artificial Intelligence. 260p. (C). 1990. text 61.00 (*981-02-0266-0*); pap. text 30.00 (*981-02-0267-9*) World Scientific Pub.

Mero, Laszlo. Moral Calculations: Game Theory, Logic, & Human Frailty. LC 98-17443. 300p. 1998. 27.00 (*0-387-98419-4*) Spr-Verlag.

***Mero, Rena & Hill, Joe B.** Undefeated: The Rena Mero Story. deluxe ed. Hill, Chip, ed. (Illus.). 200p. 2000. 29.95 (*1-890262-09-9*) Total Power Pubg.

Merod, Jim. Jazz As a Cultural Archives. 1995. pap. text 12.00 (*0-8223-6431-X*) Duke.

— The Political Responsibility of the Critic. LC 86-47977. 288p. 1987. 39.95 (*0-8014-1976-X*); pap. 16.95 (*0-8014-9555-5*) Cornell U Pr.

— The Political Responsibility of the Critic. LC 86-47977. (Cornell Paperbacks Ser.). 283p. reprint ed. pap. 87.80 (*0-608-20923-6*, 207202200003) Bks Demand.

Meroff, D. Huellas en el Mar.Tr. of Footsteps in the Sea. 7.99 (*0-7899-0144-7*, 497275) Editorial Unilit.

Meroff, Deborah. Captain, My Captain. LC 97-40841. 1997. pap. 12.90 (*0-921100-79-5*) Inhtce Pubns.

— Captain, My Captain. 208p. 1985. pap. 4.70 (*0-310-41551-9*, 9158P) Zondervan.

— Coronation of Glory: The Story of Lady Jane Grey. LC 97-40840. 1998. pap. 12.90 (*0-921100-78-7*) Inhtce Pubns.

— Touch of the Master. 1999. pap. 9.99 (*1-884543-10-3*) O M Lit.

Merola, Carmela, tr. see Braghin, Andrea & Caruana, Edmund.

Merola, Tony. Floribbean Flavors: A Reflection of Florida's New Cuisine. LC 96-86522. (Illus.). 132p. 1996. 19.95 (*0-9654211-0-4*) Brooks Tropic.

***Merolla, Carol.** Quiet Reflections: A Careful Thinking of Poetry. 1999. pap. write for info. (*1-58235-335-2*) Watermrk Pr.

Merolle, Vincenzo, ed. The Correspondence of Adam Ferguson, 2 vols. (Pickering Masters Ser.). 608p. 1996. 195.00 (*1-85196-140-2*, Pub. by Pickering & Chatto) Ashgate Pub Co.

Meron, Theodor. Bloody Constraint: Chivalry in Shakespeare. LC 98-14533. 256p. 1998. 29.95 (*0-19-512383-2*) OUP.

— Henry's Wars & Shakespeare's Laws: Perspectives on the Law of War in the Later Middle Ages. 248p. 1994. text 49.95 (*0-19-825811-9*) OUP.

— Human Rights in Internal Strife: Their International Protection. 185p. (C). 1987. text 120.00 (*0-949009-04-0*, Pub. by Grotius Pubns Ltd) St Mut.

— War Crimes Law Comes of Age: Essays. 346p. 1999. text 65.00 (*0-19-826856-4*) OUP.

Meron, Tyrus. The Edge of Darkness. LC 90-82184. (C). 1991. 19.95 (*1-56062-037-4*) CIS Comm.

Meronek, Theodora, jt. auth. see Cheney, Georgeann.

Meroney, Howard. Poems Made & Remade. 1966. pap. 10.00 (*0-685-62615-6*) Atlantis Edns.

Meroney, John W. Word Processing Applications in Practice. (DF - Computer Applications Ser.). 1983. mass mkt. 16.00 (*0-538-23750-3*) S-W Pub.

— Word Processing Applications in Practice. 2nd ed. (DF - Computer Applications Ser.). 1988. mass mkt. 18.95 (*0-538-23830-5*) S-W Pub.

— Word Processing Applications in Practice. 3rd ed. (DF - Computer Applications Ser.). 1995. 83.95 (*0-538-62757-3*); mass mkt. 20.95 (*0-538-62529-5*) S-W Pub.

Meroney, Robert N. & Bienkiewicz, Bogusz. Computational Wind Engineering 2: Proceedings of the 2nd International Symposium on Computational Wind Engineering (CWE 96), Fort Collins, Colorado, August 4-8, 1996. LC 97-46797. 950p. 1997. 324.00 (*0-444-82878-8*) Elsevier.

Meroni, M., et al, eds. Glomerulonephritis in the Elderly. (Contributions to Nephrology Ser.: Vol. 105). (Illus.). viii, 184p. 1993. 49.75 (*3-8055-5752-3*) S Karger.

An Asterisk (*) at the beginning of an entry indicates that the title is appearing for the first time.

— Hereditary Nephritis. (Contributions to Nephrology Ser.: Vol. 80). (Illus.). x, 168p. 1990. 29.75 (*3-8055-5172-X*) S Karger.

Meroni, Rudolf, jt. ed. see Campbell, Dennis.

Merot, Alain. French Painting in the Seventeenth Century. LC 95-60931. 324p. 1995. 70.00 (*0-300-06550-7*) Yale U Pr.

Merot, Alain. Nicolas Poussin. (Illus.). 336p. 1990. 125.00 (*1-55859-120-6*) Abbeville Pr.

Merquior, Jose G. Liberalism Old & New. Roth, Michael, ed. (Studies in Intellectual & Cultural History: No. 1). 208p. 1991. pap. 14.95 (*0-8057-8627-9*, Twyne); text 24.95 (*0-8057-8602-3*, Twyne) Mac Lib Ref.

Merrell, Barbara. Sign of Death. (YA). (gr. 7 up). 1981. mass mkt. 2.50 (*0-89083-781-3*, Zebra Kensgtn) Kensgtn Pub Corp.

Merrell, Betty & Tunnel, Priscilla. Stories That Won't Go Away. Hansen, Susan, ed. (Illus.). 205p. 1995. pap. text 8.95 (*1-56309-112-7*, N954118, New Hope) Womans Mission Union.

Merrell, Bruce, ed. see Muir, John.

Merrell, David J. The Adaptive Seascape: The Mechanism of Evolution. LC 93-29841. 1994. 34.95 (*0-8166-2348-1*) U of Minn Pr.

***Merrell, Floyd.** Change Through Signs of Body, Mind & Language. 140p. (C). 2000. pap. 10.95 (*1-57766-136-2*) Waveland Pr.

Merrell, Floyd. Pararealities: The Nature of Our Fictions & How We Know Them. (Purdue University Monographs in Romance Languages: No. 12). xii, 170p. 1983. 44.00 (*90-272-1722-X*) J Benjamins Pubng Co.

— Peirce, Signs & Meaning. (Toronto Studies in Semiotics). (Illus.). 408p. 1997. pap. text 24.95 (*0-8020-7982-2*) U of Toronto Pr.

— Peirce, Signs & Meaning. LC B945.P44M465 1997. (Illus.). 384p. 1997. text 65.00 (*0-8020-4135-3*, B840) U of Toronto Pr.

— Semiosis in the Postmodern Age. LC 94-21557. (Illus.). 360p. 1995. 49.95 (*1-55753-055-6*) Purdue U Pr.

— Semiotic Foundations: Steps Toward An Epistemology of Written Texts. LC 81-48631. (Illus.). 191p. 1982. pap. 59.30 (*0-7837-3718-1*, 205789600009) Bks Demand.

— A Semiotic Theory of Texts. (Approaches to Semiotics Ser.: No. 70). x, 234p. 1985. 93.85 (*0-89925-035-1*) Mouton.

— Sign, Textuality, World. LC 91-26984. (Advances in Semiotics Ser.). (Illus.). 283p. 1992. pap. 87.80 (*0-608-05034-2*, 205969500004) Bks Demand.

— Signs Becoming Signs: Our Perfusive, Pervasive Universe. LC 90-49160. (Illus.). 263p. 1991. pap. 81.60 (*0-608-05049-0*, 205971000004) Bks Demand.

— Signs Grow: Semiosis & Life Processes. LC 96-209097. (Toronto Studies in Semiotics). 356p. 1996. text 65.00 (*0-8020-0778-3*) U of Toronto Pr.

— Signs Grow: Semiosis & Life Processes. (Toronto Studies in Semiotics). 400p. 1996. pap. text 24.95 (*0-8020-7142-2*) U of Toronto Pr.

— Simplicity & Complexity: Pondering Literature, Science, & Painting. LC 97-40774. (Studies in Literature & Science). 384p. (C). 1998. text 49.50 (*0-472-10860-3*, 10860) U of Mich Pr.

***Merrell, Floyd.** Sobre las Culturas y Civilizaciones Latinoamericanas. LC 99-49112. (SPA.). 432p. 1999. pap. 39.50 (*0-7618-1541-4*) U Pr of Amer.

Merrell, Floyd. Unthinking Thinking: Jorge Luis Borges, Mathematics, & the New Physics. LC 90-20128. (Illus.). 320p. 1991. 39.95 (*1-55753-011-4*) Purdue U Pr.

Merrell, Floyd, jt. ed. see Anderson, Myrdene.

Merrell, Gerald, ed. Maryland Business Almanac. rev. ed. (Illus.). 500p. 1996. pap. write for info. (*0-9649819-2-0*) Baltimore Sun.

Merrell, James H. The Indians' New World: Catawbas & Their Neighbors from European Contact Through the Era of Removal. (C). 1991. pap. text 14.75 (*0-393-96017-X*) Norton.

— The Indians' New World: Catawbas & Their Neighbors from European Contact Through the Era of Removal. LC 88-22658. (Illus.). xviii, 382p. (C). 1989. 49.95 (*0-8078-1832-1*) U of NC Pr.

— Into the American Woods: Negotiators on the Pennsylvania Frontier. (Illus.). 464p. 2000. pap. 14.95 (*0-393-31976-8*) Norton.

Merrell, James H., jt. ed. see Mancall, Peter C.

Merrell, James Hart, jt. ed. see Mancall, Peter C.

Merrell, Joann. Simple Machines. (Hands-On Minds-On Science Ser.). (Illus.). 1994. pap., teacher ed. 11.95 (*1-55734-644-5*) Tchr Create Mat.

***Merrell, Ken.** The Landlord. Anderson, Stevens, ed. 460p. 2000. pap. 7.99 (*0-9678510-1-7*) Kay Dee.

Merrell, Kenneth W. Behavioral, Social, & Emotional Assessment of Children & Adolescents. LC 98-8363. 340p. 1998. 55.00 (*0-8058-2886-9*) L Erlbaum Assocs.

— Preschool & Kindergarten Behavior Scales. LC 94-12893. 60p. 1994. 19.95 (*0-88422-152-0*) Clinical Psych.

Merrell, Kenneth W. & Gimpel, Gretchen A. Special Skills of Children & Adolescents: Conceptualization, Assessment, Treatment. LC 97-11805. 250p. 1997. 55.00 (*0-8058-2655-6*); pap. write for info. (*0-8058-2656-4*) L Erlbaum Assocs.

Merrell, Patricia. Art & Craft of Applique, Bk. 1: Sew Quick, Sew Easy. 24p. 1990. pap. 9.95 (*1-883504-01-5*) Sew-Art Int.

— Art & Craft of Applique, Bk. 2: Those Crazy Birds & Other Designs. 2nd ed. 32p. 1990. reprint ed. pap. 9.95 (*1-883504-02-3*) Sew-Art Int.

— Creative Fabric Embellishment. 60p. pap. 12.95 (*1-883504-12-0*) Sew-Art Int.

— Renaissance Thread Methods & Ideas. 24p. 1994. pap. 6.95 (*1-883504-00-7*) Sew-Art Int.

Merrell, Patrick. Double-Cross Mazes. (Amazing Mazes Ser.). (Illus.). 32p. (J). (gr. 3-7). 1998. pap. 3.95 (*0-8167-4820-9*) Troll Communs.

— Mastermind Mazes. (Illus.). 32p. (J). (gr. 3-7). 1997. pap. 3.95 (*0-8167-4399-1*) Troll Communs.

— Maze Mania. (Illus.). 64p. (Orig.). (J). (gr. 3-7). 1996. pap. 3.95 (*0-8167-4111-5*) Troll Communs.

***Merrell, Patrick.** Mazes on Mars: An Astronishing Assortment of Astronomical Mazes. 1999. pap. 3.95 (*0-8167-5945-6*) Troll Communs.

Merrell, Patrick. Monster Mazes. (Illus.). 32p. 1997. pap. text 3.95 (*0-8167-4400-9*) Troll Communs.

— Pipsqueak! Maze School, 1. (Read with Me Paperback Ser.). (Illus.). 32p. (ps-1). 1999. pap. text 3.25 (*0-590-03712-9*) Scholastic Inc.

— Pipsqueaks! Maze Party. 1999. pap. text 3.25 (*0-590-03713-7*) Scholastic Inc.

— Puzzled Penguins. LC 99-175238. (Illus.). 32p. (J). (ps-1). 1998. pap. 3.50 (*0-8167-4937-X*) Troll Communs.

— Rhymes with Bug. LC 98-212548. (Beginner Phonics Ser.). (J). 1998. write for info. (*0-7853-3153-0*) Pubns Intl Ltd.

— Rhymes with Cat. LC 98-212424. (Beginner Phonics Ser.). (J). 1998. write for info. (*0-7853-3154-9*) Pubns Intl Ltd.

— Rhymes with Cub. LC 98-212540. (Beginner Phonics Ser.). (J). 1998. write for info. (*0-7853-3155-7*) Pubns Intl Ltd.

— Rhymes with Dog. LC 98-212556. (Beginner Phonics Ser.). (J). 1998. write for info. (*0-7853-3156-5*) Pubns Intl Ltd.

Merrell, Patrick. I Can Read! LC 98-235002. (J). 1997. write for info. (*0-7853-2453-4*) Pubns Intl Ltd.

Merrell, Patrick, et al. Shapes & Colors. LC 98-208286. 1998. write for info. (*0-7853-2706-1*) Pubns Intl Ltd.

Merrell, Ronald C. & Olson, Robert M., III, eds. Laparoscopic Surgery: A Colloquium. LC 98-15837. (Illus.). 328p. 1998. 99.00 (*0-387-98396-1*) Spr-Verlag.

Merrell, Susan S. Accidental Bond: The Power of Sibling Relationships. 1997. pap. 12.00 (*0-449-91119-5*) Fawcett.

***Merrell, Susan S.** A Member of the Family: A Novel. LC 99-34923. 368p. 2000. 25.00 (*0-06-019280-1*, Pub. by Harper SF) HarpC.

Merrell, Todd. Party Fabulous: 12 Parties to Change the World. LC 96-215956. (Illus.). 224p. 1996. pap. text 14.00 (*0-425-15530-7*) Berkley Pub.

Merrell, V. Dallas. Huddling: The Informal Way to Management Success. LC 78-31941. 224p. reprint ed. pap. 69.50 (*0-608-30690-8*, 202262100028) Bks Demand.

Merrell, William. Insurance Claims Investigation & Agency Practice: How to Make $100,000 per Year Conducting Insurance Claims Investigations. 201p. 1998. pap. 35.00 (*1-891247-16-6*) Thomas Investigative.

Merrell-Wolff, Franklin. Franklin Merrell-Wolff's Experience & Philosophy: A Personal Record of Transformation & a Discussion of Transcendental Consciousness: Containing His Philosophy of Consciousness Without an Object & His Pathways Through to Space. LC 93-30880. 445p. (C). 1994. reprint ed. pap. text 21.95 (*0-7914-1964-9*) State U NY Pr.

— Franklin Merrell-Wolff's Experience & Philosophy: A Personal Record of Transformation & a Discussion of Transcendental Consciousness: Containing His Philosophy of Consciousness Without an Object & His Pathways Through to Space. LC 93-30880. 445p. (C). 1994. reprint ed. text 64.50 (*0-7914-1963-0*) State U NY Pr.

— Transformations in Consciousness: The Metaphysics & Epistemology. LC 95-13896. 326p. (C). 1995. text 59.50 (*0-7914-2675-0*); pap. text 19.95 (*0-7914-2676-9*) State U NY Pr.

Merrens, Matthew R. & Brannigan, Gary G. Experiences in Personality: Research, Assessment & Change. LC 97-15015. 240p. 1997. pap. 30.95 (*0-471-13937-8*) Wiley.

Merrens, Matthew R. & Brannigan, Gary G., eds. The Developmental Psychologists: Research Adventures Across the Life Span. (McGraw-Hill Series in Developmental Psychology). 310p. (C). 1995. pap. 23.75 (*0-07-007259-0*) McGraw.

Merrens, Matthew R., jt. auth. see Shaffer, Lary.

Merrens, Matthew R., jt. ed. see Brannigan, Gary G.

Merrett, Alicia. Make Your Own Teddy Bear Book & Kit: Everything You Need to Create Your Very Own Bear. LC 94-67766. (Illus.). 48p. 1995. pap. 9.95 (*1-56138-541-7*) Running Pr.

Merrett, Alicia, et al. The Complete Book of Teddy Bear Making Techniques: A Step-by-Step Visual Directory with an Inspirational Gallery of Original Bears. LC 98-65181. (Encyclopedia of Art Ser.). (Illus.). 176p. 1998. 24.95 (*0-7624-0349-7*) Running Pr.

Merrett, Christopher. A Culture of Censorship: Secrecy & Intellectual Repression in South Africa. LC 94-32888. 1995. text 18.95 (*0-86554-455-7*, MUP-P117) Mercer Univ Pr.

— State Censorship & the Academic Process in South Africa. (Occasional Papers: No. 192). 1991. pap. 5.00 (*0-685-56565-3*) U of Ill Grad Sch.

Merrett, Christopher D. Free Trade: Neither Free Nor about Trade. LC 95-79354. 320p. 1995. 52.99 (*1-55164-045-7*, Pub. by Black Rose); pap. 23.99 (*1-55164-044-9*, Pub. by Black Rose) Consort Bk Sales.

***Merrett, Christopher D. & Walzer, Norman, eds.** A Cooperative Approach to Local Economic Development. LC 00-32814. 2000. write for info. (*1-56720-395-7*, Quorum Bks) Greenwood.

***Merrett, David.** Business Institutions & Behavior in Australia. LC 99-87143. 150p. 2000. pap. 22.50 (*0-7146-8055-9*) F Cass Pubs.

— Business Institutions & Behaviour in Australia. LC 99-87143. 150p. 1999. 45.00 (*0-7146-4994-5*) F Cass Pubs.

Merrett, Frank. Encouragement Works Best: Positive Approaches to Classroom Management. 144p. 1993. pap. 25.00 (*1-85346-254-3*, Pub. by David Fulton) Taylor & Francis.

— Improving Reading: A Teacher's Guide to Peer-Tutoring. 112p. 1994. pap. 19.95 (*1-85346-326-4*, Pub. by David Fulton) Taylor & Francis.

Merrett, John. Famous Voyages in Small Boats. (Illus.). 1957. 26.95 (*0-87599-073-8*) S G Phillips.

Merrett, Nigel R. & Haedrich, R. L. Deep-Sea Demersal Fish & Fisheries. 296p. 1997. write for info. (*0-412-39410-3*) Kluwer Academic.

Merrett, P., ed. see Platnick, Norman I.

Merrett, Patricia & Butcher, Ronald, eds. The Hunting Journal of Robert Briggs Struthers 1852-56 in the Zulu Kingdom & the Tsonga Regions. 216p. 1991. pap. 24.95 (*0-86980-788-9*, Pub. by Univ Natal Pr) Intl Spec Bk.

Merrett, Stephen. Introduction to the Economics of Water Resources: An International Perspective. (Illus.). 256p. 1997. 67.50 (*0-8476-8710-4*); pap. 26.95 (*0-8476-8711-2*) Rowman.

— Introduction to the Economics of Water Resources: An International Perspective. LC 97-199057. 211p. 1997. 79.95 (*1-85728-636-7*) Taylor & Francis.

Merrett, Stephen. Introduction to the Economics of Water Resources: An International Perspective. LC 97-199057. 1997. pap. 29.95 (*1-85728-637-5*) UCL Pr Ltd.

Merrett, T. G., jt. ed. see Said El Shami, A.

Merri, ed. see Hasbin, Almost A.

Merriam. An A B C of Boats. (J). 1998. pap. 13.00 (*0-689-81028-8*) S&S Childrens.

— 12 Ways Get 11. (J). 1998. pap. 5.99 (*0-87628-369-5*) Ctr Appl Res.

Merriam, Alan P. African Music on LP: An Annotated Discography. LC 72-111629. 214p. reprint ed. pap. 66.40 (*0-8357-5238-0*, 201027200068) Bks Demand.

— An African World: The Basongye Village of Lupupa Ngye. LC 74-377. (Illus.). 370p. 1974. reprint ed. pap. 114.70 (*0-7837-9661-7*, 205929400005) Bks Demand.

— Anthropology of Music. 358p. 1964. pap. 19.95 (*0-8101-0607-8*) Northwestern U Pr.

— Congo, Background of Conflict. LC 61-11381. (Northwestern University African Studies Ser.: No. 6). (Illus.). 386p. reprint ed. pap. 119.70 (*0-8357-9451-2*, 201671400004) Bks Demand.

— Ethnomusicology of the Flathead Indians. LC 68-100257. (Viking Fund Publications in Anthropology: No. 44). 435p. reprint ed. pap. 134.90 (*0-608-10708-5*, 200639800059) Bks Demand.

***Merriam, Allen H.** People of the Millennium. LC 99-94964. 2000. pap. 12.95 (*0-533-13244-4*) Vantage.

Merriam, C. Hart. Ethnogeographic & Ethnosynonymic Data from Northern California Tribes. (Research Facility Miscellaneous Publications). 157p. (C). 1976. reprint ed. pap. 16.88 (*1-55567-599-9*) Coyote Press.

— Ethnographic Notes on California Indian Tribes. fac. ed. Heizer, R. F., ed. (Reports of the University of California Archaeological Survey: No. 68:I). (Illus.). 186p. 1966. reprint ed. pap. 20.00 (*1-55567-382-1*) Coyote Press.

— Ethnographic Notes on California Indian Tribes No. II: Northern & Southern California Indian Tribes. fac. ed. Heizer, R. F., ed. (Reports of the University of California Archaeological Survey: No. 68:II). 96p. 1967. reprint ed. pap. 10.94 (*1-55567-383-X*) Coyote Press.

— Ethnographic Notes on California Indian Tribes No. III: Ethnological Notes on Central California Indian Tribes. fac. ed. Heizer, R. F., ed. (Reports of the University of California Archaeological Survey: No. 68:III). 200p. 1967. reprint ed. pap. 21.25 (*1-55567-384-8*) Coyote Press.

— Village Names in Twelve California Mission Records. fac. ed. Heizer, Robert, ed. (Reports of the University of California Archaeological Survey: No. 74). 182p. 1968. reprint ed. pap. 19.38 (*1-55567-390-2*) Coyote Press.

Merriam, C. Hart, ed. The Dawn of the World: Myths & Tales of the Miwok Indians of California. LC 92-42566. x, 273p. 1993. pap. 9.95 (*0-8032-8193-5*, Bison Books) U of Nebr Pr.

Merriam, C. Hart, ed. The Dawn of the World: Myths & Weird Tales Told by the Mewan Indians of California. fac. ed. (Illus.). 273p. (C). 1910. reprint ed. pap. text 30.00 (*1-55567-660-X*) Coyote Press.

Merriam, C. Hart, ed. see Woiche, Istet.

Merriam, Caroline R. & Borrus, Kathy. The North American Markets Directory for Artisans. (ENG & SPA.). 250p. (Orig.). 1997. pap. 25.00 (*0-9625480-2-2*) Crafts Ctr.

Merriam, Charles E. American Political Ideas. LC 70-97887. reprint ed. 20.00 (*0-404-04310-0*) AMS Pr.

— Chicago: A More Intimate View of Urban Politics. LC 71-112579. (Rise of Urban America Ser.). 1976. reprint ed. 24.95 (*0-405-02467-3*) Ayer.

— Four American Party Leaders. (History - United States Ser.). 104p. 1992. reprint ed. lib. bdg. 69.00 (*0-7812-6191-0*) Rprt Serv.

— Four American Party Leaders: Henry Ward Beecher Foundation Lectures, Amherst College. LC 67-23247. (Essay Index Reprint Ser.). 1977. 14.95 (*0-8369-0702-7*) Ayer.

— History of the Theory of Sovereignty since Rousseau. LC 76-76667. (Columbia University. Studies in the Social Sciences: No. 33). reprint ed. 34.50 (*0-404-51033-7*) AMS Pr.

— History of the Theory of Sovereignty since Rousseau. 1900. LC 98-32385. 1999. 65.00 (*1-886363-76-5*) Lawbk Exchange.

— New Aspects of Politics. 3rd ed. LC 77-114809. 1994. lib. bdg. 20.00 (*0-226-52061-7*) U Ch Pr.

— New Aspects of Politics. 3rd enl. ed. LC 77-114809. 1993. pap. text 2.95 (*0-226-52062-5*, P374) U Ch Pr.

— The Role of Politics in Social Change. LC 83-1490. 149p. 1983. reprint ed. lib. bdg. 55.00 (*0-313-23852-9*, MERO, Greenwood Pr) Greenwood.

Merriam, Clinton H. The Classification & Distribution of the Pit River Indian Tribes of California. LC 76-43779. (Smithsonian Miscellaneous Collections: Vol. 78, No. 3). reprint ed. write for info. (*0-404-15633-9*) AMS Pr.

— The Mammals of the Adirondack Region, Northwestern New York: Introductory Chapter Treating of the Location & Boundaries of the Region, Its Geological History, Topography, Climate, General Features, Botany & Faunal Position. LC 73-17832. (Natural Sciences of America Ser.). 320p. 1974. reprint ed. 23.95 (*0-405-05750-4*) Ayer.

Merriam, Clinton H., ed. An-Nik-a-Del: The History of the Universe as Told by the Modes-Se Indians of California. LC 76-43777. reprint ed. write for info. (*0-404-15632-0*) AMS Pr.

Merriam, D. F., jt. auth. see Forster, A.

Merriam, D. F., jt. auth. see Harff, J.

Merriam, Daniel B. The Art of Daniel Merriam: The Impetus of Dreams. Beebee, Yale, ed. (Illus.). 128p. 1997. 39.95 (*0-9658347-0-0*) Monarch Edits.

Merriam, Daniel F., ed. Capture, Management & Display of Geological Data: With Special Emphasis on Energy & Mineral Resources. LC 76-56893. 1977. pap. 50.00 (*0-08-021422-3*, Pergamon Pr) Elsevier.

— Computer Assisted Instruction in Geology: Proceedings of the 4th Geochautauqua, Syracuse University, 1975. 1976. pap. 50.00 (*0-08-021040-6*, Pergamon Pr) Elsevier.

— Computer Software for the Geosciences: Proceedings of the Geochautauqua, 5th, 1976. LC 77-30468. 1977. pap. 50.00 (*0-08-022090-8*, Pergamon Pr) Elsevier.

Merriam, Daniel F., ed. Current Trends in Geomathematics. (Computer Applications in the Earth Sciences Ser.). (Illus.). 334p. 1988. 75.00 (*0-306-43087-8*, Plenum Trade) Perseus Pubng.

Merriam, Daniel F., ed. Management, Analysis & Display of Geoscience Data: Proceedings of the First Annual Conference, Golden, CO, January 27-29, 1982. 60p. 1983. pap. 57.00 (*0-08-030248-3*, Pergamon Pr) Elsevier.

— Quantitative Stratigraphic Correlation: Proceedings of the 6th Geochautauqua, Syracuse University, October 1977. (Illus.). 112p. 1979. pap. 50.00 (*0-08-023979-X*, Pergamon Pr) Elsevier.

— Recent Advances in Geomathematics: An International Symposium. 245p. 1978. 387.25 (*0-08-022095-9*, Pergamon Pr) Elsevier.

Merriam, Daniel F. & Kurzl, Hans, eds. Use of Microcomputers in Geology. LC 92-29735. (Computer Applications in the Earth Sciences Ser.). (Illus.). 302p. (C). 1992. 132.00 (*0-306-44310-4*, Plenum Trade) Perseus Pubng.

Merriam, Daniel F., jt. ed. see Gaal, G.

Merriam, Daniel F., jt. ed. see Hanley, J. T.

***Merriam, Dena.** Gift of Imagination. 1999. 27.95 (*1-56833-150-9*) Madison Bks UPA.

Merriam, Dena. Trinity: A Church, a Parish, a People. LC 96-14804. (Illus.). 152p. 1996. 45.00 (*0-7892-0249-2*, Cross Riv Pr) Abbeville Pr.

Merriam, Dena & Munro, Eleanor. Carole A. Feuerman: Sculptor. LC 98-50690. (Illus.). 160p. 1999. 45.00 (*1-55595-177-5*) Hudson Hills.

Merriam, Dwight, jt. auth. see Meltz, Robert.

Merriam, Eve. Bam, Bam, Bam. LC 94-20300. (Illus.). 88p. (J). 1995. 14.95 (*0-8050-3527-3*) H Holt & Co.

— Bam Bam Bam. (Illus.). 32p. (J). 1998. pap. 5.95 (*0-8050-5796-X*) H Holt & Co.

— Bam Bam Bam. 1998. 11.15 (*0-606-13179-5*, Pub. by Turtleback) Demco.

— Blackberry Ink. Cohn, Amy, ed. LC 84-16633. (Illus.). 40p. (J). (ps up). 1994. reprint ed. mass mkt. 5.95 (*0-688-13080-1*, Wm Morrow) Morrow Avon.

— Blackberry Ink: Poems. LC 84-16633. 1994. 10.15 (*0-606-06236-X*, Pub. by Turtleback) Demco.

— A Conversation Against Death. 25p. 2000. 5.95 (*0-930194-24-1*) Ctr Thanatology.

— Daddies At Work. (Illus.). 32p. (J). (ps-2). 1996. 3.25 (*0-689-80998-0*) Aladdin.

— Embracing the Dark: Poetry. Whitman, Ruth, ed. LC 94-75911. 80p. (Orig.). 1994. pap. 13.00 (*1-882329-04-X*) Garden St Pr.

***Merriam, Eve.** Emma Lazarus Rediscovered. 2nd ed. Orig. Title: Emma Lazarus: Woman with a Torch. 184p. 1999. 14.95 (*0-930395-29-8*) Biblio NY.

Merriam, Eve. Emma Lazarus Rediscovered. 2nd expanded ed. Schappes, Morris U., ed. & intro. by. Orig. Title: Emma Lazarus: Woman with a Torch. (Illus.). 184p. 1999. reprint ed. pap. 10.95 (*0-930395-28-X*) Biblio NY.

Merriam, Eve. Halloween A B C. 1995. 11.19 (*0-606-07605-0*, Pub. by Turtleback) Demco.

Merriam, Eve. Halloween ABC. LC 86-23772. (Illus.). 32p. (J). 1995. mass mkt. 5.99 (*0-689-80198-X*) Aladdin.

— Higgle, Wiggle. LC 92-29795. (Illus.). 40p. 1997. mass mkt. 4.95 (*0-688-14547-7*, Wm Morrow) Morrow Avon.

— Higgle Wiggle: Happy Rhymes. LC 92-29795. (Illus.). 40p. (J). (ps up). 1994. 15.00 (*0-688-11948-4*, Wm Morrow) Morrow Avon.

Merriam, Eve. Higgle Wiggle: Happy Rhymes. 1997. 10.15 (*0-606-11459-9*, Pub. by Turtleback) Demco.

Merriam, Eve. The Hole Story. (Illus.). 40p. (J). (ps-2). 1995. 16.00 (*0-671-88353-4*) S&S Bks Yung.

— The Inner City Mother Goose. 3rd ed. LC 95-22553. (Illus.). 80p. (YA). (gr. 7 up). 1996. 16.00 (*0-689-80677-9*) S&S Bks Yung.

M

— Mommies at Work. (Illus.). 32p. (J). (ps-2). 1996. 3.25 (*0-689-80999-9*) Aladdin.
— The Singing Green: New & Selected Poems for All Seasons. LC 91-31205. (Illus.). 112p. (J). (gr. 4-7). 1992. 14.00 (*0-688-11025-8*, Wm Morrow) Morrow Avon.
— Ten Rosy Roses. LC 98-27473. (Illus.). 32p. (J). (ps-1). 1999. 14.95 (*0-06-027887-0*) HarpC Child Bks.
— Ten Rosy Roses. LC 98-27473. (Illus.). 32p. (J). (ps-2). 1999. lib. bdg. 14.89 (*0-06-027888-9*) HarpC Child Bks.
— Thinking of You. (Illus.). 40p. 1991. lib. bdg. 7.95 (*0-8378-0372-1*) Gibson.
— Train Leaves the Station. (Illus.). (J). (gr. 3). 1995. pap. 5.95 (*0-8050-3547-8*) H Holt & Co.
— Train Leaves the Station. LC 91-28009. (Illus.). 32p. (J). (ps). 1995. 14.95 (*0-8050-1934-0*, B Martin BYR) H Holt & Co.
— Twelve Ways to Get to Eleven. LC 92-25810. (Illus.). 40p. (J). (ps-1). 1993. mass mkt. 15.00 (*0-671-75544-7*) S&S Bks Yung.
— Twelve Ways to Get to Eleven. (J). (ps-1). 1996. mass mkt. 5.99 (*0-689-80892-5*) S&S Bks Yung.
— What in the World. LC 96-42346. (Illus.). 20p. (J). (ps-3). 1998. 9.95 (*0-694-01036-7*) HarpC Child Bks.
— Where Is Everybody? LC 88-19800. (Illus.). (J). (ps-1). 1989. pap. 14.95 (*0-671-64964-7*) S&S Bks Yung.
***Merriam, Eve.** The Wise Woman & Her Secret. LC 90-42406. (Illus.). 40p. (J). (ps-3). 1999. pap. 5.99 (*0-689-82381-9*) Aladdin.
Merriam, Eve. The Wise Woman & Her Secret. LC 90-42406. (Illus.). 40p. (J). (ps-3). 1991. pap. 16.00 (*0-671-72603-X*) S&S Bks Yung.
— You Be Good & I'll Be Night: Jump-on-the-Bed Poems. LC 87-24859. 40p. (J). 1996. mass mkt. 4.95 (*0-688-13984-1*, Wm Morrow) Morrow Avon.
Merriam, Eve. You Be Good & I'll Be Night: Jump-on-the-Bed Poems. (J). 1994. 10.15 (*0-606-08910-1*, Pub. by Turtleback) Demco.
Merriam, Eve, ed. Growing up Female in America: Ten Lives. LC 86-47761. (Illus.). 308p. 1987. reprint ed. pap. 16.50 (*0-8070-7009-2*) Beacon Pr.
Merriam, Eve, retold by. That Noodlehead Epaminondas. (Illus.). (J). 1992. reprint ed. pap. 8.95 (*0-89966-962-X*) Buccaneer Bks.
Merriam, Eve & Greenberg, Melanie. On My Street. LC 98-74004. (Growing Tree Ser.). (Illus.). 24p. (YA). (ps up). 2000. 9.95 (*0-694-01258-0*, HarpFestival) HarpC Child Bks.
Merriam, George S. Life & Times of Samuel Bowles, 2 vols., Set. LC 76-108512. 1970. reprint ed. 49.00 (*0-403-00220-6*) Scholarly.
— Negro & the Nation. LC 75-95441. (Studies in Black History & Culture: No. 54). 1970. reprint ed. lib. bdg. 75.00 (*0-8383-0994-1*) M S G Haskell Hse.
Merriam, George S., ed. see Bowles, Samuel.
Merriam, Harold G., ed. see Linderman, Frank B.
Merriam, Joan. Little Girl Lost. 1998. mass mkt. 5.99 (*0-7860-0487-8*, Pinncle Kensgtn) Kensgtn Pub Corp.
Merriam, Kendall. Medvedb's Journal. 32p. 1991. pap. 5.00 (*0-942396-64-2*) Blackberry ME.
***Merriam, Ray.** Pearl Harbor Casualties: Military & Civilian Plus Casualties & Survivors of the U. S. S. Arizona. (World War II Monograph Ser.: Vol. 39). (Illus.). 70p. 1999. pap. 10.50 (*1-57638-155-2*, 39-S) Merriam Pr.
***Merriam, Ray, ed.** Battle of the Bulge. (World War II Journal Ser.: Vol. 3). (Illus.). 100p. 1999. pap. 14.95 (*1-57638-165-X*, J3-S) Merriam Pr.
— Gebirgsjaeger: Germany's Mountain Troops. (World War II Arsenal Ser.: Vol. 3). (Illus.). 60p. 1999. pap. 9.95 (*1-57638-163-3*, A3-S) Merriam Pr.
— Pearl Harbor: "This Is No Drill!" (World War II Journal Ser.: Vol. 2). (Illus.). 96p. 1999. pap. 12.50 (*1-57638-154-4*, J2-S) Merriam Pr.
— The Russo-German Conflict. (World War II Journal Ser.: Vol. 4). (Illus.). 100p. 1999. pap. 14.95 (*1-57638-166-8*, J4-S) Merriam Pr.
— U. S. Army. (World War II Arsenal Ser.: Vol. 2). (Illus.). 100p. 1999. pap. 14.95 (*1-57638-169-2*, A2-S) Merriam Pr.
— U. S. Warplanes. (World War II Arsenal Ser.: Vol. 1). (Illus.). 100p. 1999. pap. 14.95 (*1-57638-167-6*, A1-S) Merriam Pr.
— Waffen-SS. (World War II Arsenal Ser.: Vol. 7). (Illus.). 90p. 1999. pap. 14.95 (*1-57638-168-4*, A7-S) Merriam Pr.
— War in the Philippines. (World War II Journal Ser.: Vol. 5). (Illus.). 98p. 1999. pap. 14.95 (*1-57638-164-1*, J5-S) Merriam Pr.
— World War II Anthology. (World War II Journal Ser.: Vol. 1). (Illus.). 100p. 1999. pap. 16.95 (*1-57638-153-6*, J1-S) Merriam Pr.
Merriam, Robert L. ABC of Revolution. (Illus.). 52p. (Orig.). 1976. pap. 1.75 (*0-686-32502-8*) R L Merriam.
— Abigail Challenges the Telephone Company. (Illus.). 8p. (Orig.). (J). (ps-6). 1972. pap. 1.50 (*0-686-32483-8*) R L Merriam.
— The Ancient Art of Skating. (Illus.). 25p. 1957. pap. 1.50 (*0-686-33162-1*) R L Merriam.
— Curious Emily. (Illus.). 29p. 1980. pap. 2.00 (*0-686-32487-0*) R L Merriam.
— The Darling Twins. (Illus.). 25p. (Orig.). 1976. pap. 2.00 (*0-686-32493-5*) R L Merriam.
— The Energy Crisis. (Illus.). 7p. (Orig.). 1974. pap. 2.00 (*0-686-32494-3*) R L Merriam.
— Eunice Williams. (Illus.). 32p. (Orig.). 1984. 35.00 (*0-918507-58-8*) R L Merriam.
— Helen Childs Boyden. (Illus.). 32p. 1989. 35.00 (*0-317-99671-1*) R L Merriam.
— J. Hamilton Rose. (Illus.). 29p. (Orig.). 1979. pap. 2.00 (*0-686-32488-9*) R L Merriam.
— John Carson. (Illus.). 23p. (Orig.). 1977. pap. 2.00 (*0-686-37766-4*) R L Merriam.
Merriam, Robert L. Lucy Terry Prince. (Illus.). 32p. 1983. 35.00 (*0-686-40220-0*) R L Merriam.
Merriam, Robert L. Maple Sugar. (Illus.). 32p. (Orig.). 1982. 35.00 (*0-685-05823-9*); pap. 2.50 (*0-686-35762-0*) R L Merriam.
— Moses Washington. (Illus.). 31p. 1978. pap. 2.00 (*0-686-32489-7*) R L Merriam.
— Pleasant Beth. (Illus.). 24p. (Orig.). 1975. pap. 2.00 (*0-686-32490-0*) R L Merriam.
— Santa Claus' Snack. (Illus.). 14p. (J). (ps-6). 1970. pap. 2.00 (*0-686-32491-9*) R L Merriam.
— Six Vignettes. (Illus.). 38p. 1981. 2.00 (*0-686-32492-7*) R L Merriam.
— The Stories of the Ants. (Illus.). 19p. (Orig.). 1981. pap. 2.00 (*0-686-32495-1*) R L Merriam.
Merriam, Sharan B. Adult Development: Implications for Adult Education. 39p. 1984. 4.75 (*0-318-22018-0*, IN282) Ctr Educ Trng Employ.
— Case Study Research in Education: A Qualitative Approach. LC 88-42795. (Illus.). 248p. reprint ed. pap. 76.90 (*0-7837-6523-1*, 204563500007) Bks Demand.
— Qualitative Research & Case Study Applications in Education. LC 97-7167. (Joint Publication of the Jossey-Bass Education Series & the Jossey-Bass Higher & Adult Education Ser.). 1997. 21.95 (*0-7879-1009-0*) Jossey-Bass.
— Themes of Adulthood Through Literature. 432p. 1983. pap. text 21.95 (*0-8077-2731-8*) Tchrs Coll.
Merriam, Sharan B., ed. Selected Writings on Philosophy & Adult Education. 2nd ed. LC 95-24355. 332p. (C). 1995. pap. 29.50 (*0-89464-887-X*) Krieger.
— An Update on Adult Learning Theory. LC 85-644750. (New Directions for Adult & Continuing Education Ser.: No. ACE57). 116p. (Orig.). 1993. pap. 22.00 (*1-55542-684-0*) Jossey-Bass.
Merriam, Sharan B. & Baumgartner, Lisa, eds. Adult Learning & Development: Multicultural Stories. LC 99-21494. (C). 1999. write for info. (*1-57524-104-8*); pap. 28.50 (*1-57524-097-1*) Krieger.
Merriam, Sharan B. & Brockett, Ralph G. Profession & Practice of Adult Education: An Introduction. LC 96-22517. (Higher & Adult Education Ser.). 334p. 1996. 32.95 (*0-7879-0290-X*) Jossey-Bass.
Merriam, Sharan B. & Caffarella, Rosemary S. Learning in Adulthood. 2nd ed. LC 98-25498. (Education Ser.). 480p. 1998. 34.95 (*0-7879-1043-0*) Jossey-Bass.
Merriam, Sharan B. & Clark, M. Carolyn. Lifelines: Patterns of Work, Love, & Learning in Adulthood. LC 91-10280. (Social & Behavioral Science Ser.). 280p. 1991. 34.95 (*1-55542-364-7*) Jossey-Bass.
Merriam, Sharan B. & Cunningham, Phyllis M., eds. The Handbook of Adult & Continuing Education. LC 89-45601. (Higher Education Ser.). 750p. 1989. 60.00 (*1-55542-161-X*) Jossey-Bass.
Merriam, Sharan B. & Simpson, Edwin L. A Guide to Research for Educators & Trainers of Adults. 2nd ed. 250p. (C). 1994. lib. bdg. 29.50 (*0-89464-849-7*) Krieger.
***Merriam, Sharan B. & Simpson, Edwin L.** A Guide to Research for Educators & Trainers of Adults. 2nd rev. ed. LC 99-56257. 254p. 2000. text 32.50 (*1-57524-142-0*) Krieger.
Merriam, Sharon B., ed. The Research-to-Practice Dilemma. 13p. 1987. 3.00 (*0-318-23414-9*, OC123) Ctr Educ Trng Employ.
Merriam, Sharon B., jt. auth. see Elias, John L.
Merriam, Thornton W. The Relations Between Scholastic Achievement in a School of Social Work & Six Factors in Students Background. LC 70-177072. (Columbia University. Teachers College. Contributions to Education Ser.: No. 616). reprint ed. 37.50 (*0-404-55616-7*) AMS Pr.
Merriam-Webster Editors. Addenda Section 1993: A Supplement to Webster's Third New International Dictionary. unabridged ed. 1993. pap. 5.00 (*0-87779-100-7*) Merriam-Webster Inc.
— Merriam-Webster Concise School & Office Thesaurus. 1991. 15.05 (*0-606-05462-6*, Pub. by Turtleback) Demco.
— The Merriam-Webster Dictionary. rev. ed. LC 95-5824. 896p. (C). 1994. mass mkt. 5.99 (*0-87779-911-3*) Merriam-Webster Inc.
— The Merriam-Webster Dictionary of Quotations. 512p. 1995. mass mkt. 4.99 (*0-87779-904-0*) Merriam-Webster Inc.
— Merriam-Webster Dictionary of Quotations. 1992. 10.09 (*0-606-05463-4*, Pub. by Turtleback) Demco.
— The Merriam-Webster New Book of Word Histories. 544p. 1995. pap. 9.95 (*0-87779-603-3*) Merriam-Webster Inc.
— The Merriam-Webster Thesaurus. 672p. 1995. mass mkt. 4.99 (*0-87779-902-4*) Merriam-Webster Inc.
— Merriam-Webster's Biographical Dictionary. rev. ed. LC 94-43025. 1184p. 1995. 27.95 (*0-87779-743-9*) Merriam-Webster Inc.
— Merriam-Webster's Collegiate Dictionary. 10th deluxe ed. LC 98-13387. (Illus.). 1998. im. lthr. 45.00 (*0-87779-714-5*) Merriam-Webster Inc.
— Merriam-Webster's Collegiate Dictionary. 10th deluxe large type ed. LC 93-20206. (Illus.). 1600p. 1993. im. lthr. 34.95 (*0-87779-711-0*) Merriam-Webster Inc.
— Merriam Webster's Collegiate Dictionary. 10th rev. ed. Mish, Frederick C., ed. LC 93-20206. (Illus.). 1600p. 1995. text 19.95 (*0-87779-707-2*) Merriam-Webster Inc.
— Merriam Webster's Collegiate Dictionary. 10th rev. ed. FCM Staff, ed. LC 93-20206. (Illus.). 1600p. 1997. im. lthr. 27.95 (*0-87779-710-2*) Merriam-Webster Inc.
Merriam-Webster Editors. Merriam Webster's Collegiate Dictionary. 10th rev. ed. Mish, Frederick C., ed. LC 96-42529. (Illus.). 1600p. 1997. kivar 22.95 (*0-87779-708-0*) Merriam-Webster Inc.
Merriam-Webster Editors. Merriam Webster's Collegiate Dictionary: Thumb-Indexed. 10th rev. ed. FCM Staff, ed. LC 93-20206. (Illus.). 1600p. (C). 1998. 24.95 (*0-87779-709-9*) Merriam-Webster Inc.
— Merriam-Webster's Collegiate Dictionary Tenth Edition & Electronic Edition. 10th ed. 1600p. 1996. 39.95 incl. cd-rom (*0-87779-713-7*) Merriam-Webster Inc.
— Merriam-Webster's Concise Dictionary. large type ed. LC 97-50501. 1998. pap. 19.95 (*0-87779-624-6*) Merriam-Webster Inc.
— Merriam-Webster's Concise Handbook for Writers. 2nd ed. LC 97-40797. 1998. pap. 9.95 (*0-87779-625-4*) Merriam-Webster Inc.
— Merriam-Webster's Crossword Puzzle Dictionary. 2nd ed. 784p. 1997. mass mkt. 5.99 (*0-87779-919-9*) Merriam-Webster Inc.
— Merriam-Webster's Crossword Puzzle Dictionary. 2nd rev. ed. LC 96-24796. 784p. 1996. 18.95 (*0-87779-121-X*) Merriam-Webster Inc.
***Merriam-Webster Editors.** Merriam-Webster's Crossword Quest, Vol. 2. 80p. 1999. pap. 8.95 (*0-87779-654-8*) Merriam-Webster Inc.
Merriam-Webster Editors. Merriam-Webster's Deluxe Dictionary. 10th ed. LC 98-18666. 1998. write for info. (*0-7621-0300-0*) RD Assn.
— Merriam-Webster's Dictionary of Law. 656p. 1996. pap. 15.95 (*0-87779-604-1*) Merriam-Webster Inc.
— Merriam-Webster's Dictionary of Synonyms. 944p. 1994. 21.95 (*0-87779-341-7*) Merriam-Webster Inc.
***Merriam-Webster Editors.** Merriam-Webster's Encyclopedia of World Religions: An A-Z Guide to the World's Religions. Doniger, Wendy, ed. LC 99-33147. (Illus.). 1200p. 1999. 49.95 (*0-87779-044-2*) Merriam-Webster Inc.
Merriam-Webster Editors. Merriam-Webster's Everyday Language Reference Set: Dictionary, Thesaurus, Vocabulary Builder. 1994. pap., boxed set 16.99 (*0-87779-970-9*) Merriam-Webster Inc.

–Merriam-Webster's French-English Dictionary. (FRE.). 864p. 2000. pap. 5.99 (*0-87779-917-2*) Merriam-Webster Inc.
A bilingual, bidirectional guide to French & North American English, with extensive coverage of Canadian French. Over 80,000 words & phrases. Designed for all skill levels. Abundant examples. Durable hardcover format. *Publisher Paid Annotation.*

— Merriam-Webster's Guide to Punctuation & Style. 352p. 1995. mass mkt. 4.99 (*0-87779-912-1*) Merriam-Webster Inc.
— Merriam-Webster's Legal Secretaries Handbook. 2nd rev. ed. 512p. 1996. 19.95 (*0-87779-134-1*) Merriam-Webster Inc.
— Merriam-Webster's Manual for Writers & Editors. LC 97-40798. 448p. 1998. pap. 17.95 (*0-87779-622-X*) Merriam-Webster Inc.
— Merriam-Webster's Medical Dictionary. 771p. 1995. mass mkt. 6.99 (*0-87779-914-8*) Merriam-Webster Inc.
— Merriam-Webster's Medical Office Handbook. 2nd rev. ed. 544p. 1996. 19.95 (*0-87779-235-6*) Merriam-Webster Inc.
— Merriam-Webster's Notebook Dictionary. 96p. 1996. pap., student ed. 3.95 (*0-87779-650-5*) Merriam-Webster Inc.
— Merriam-Webster's Notebook Guide to Punctuation. LC 96-199726. 64p. 1996. pap., student ed. 3.95 (*0-87779-651-3*) Merriam-Webster Inc.
— Merriam-Webster's Pocket Biographical Dictionary. 384p. 1996. pap. 3.95 (*0-87779-507-X*) Merriam-Webster Inc.
— Merriam-Webster's Pocket Dictionary. LC 95-4773. 416p. 1995. pap. 3.95 (*0-87779-500-2*) Merriam-Webster Inc.
— Merriam-Webster's Pocket Geographical Dictionary. LC 96-13760. 368p. 1996. pap. 3.95 (*0-87779-506-1*) Merriam-Webster Inc.
— Merriam-Webster's Pocket Guide to English Usage. LC 97-27858. 400p. 1998. pap. 3.95 (*0-87779-514-2*) Merriam-Webster Inc.
— Merriam-Webster's Pocket Guide to Punctuation. 320p. 1995. pap. 3.95 (*0-87779-502-9*) Merriam-Webster Inc.
— Merriam-Webster's Pocket Guide to Synonyms. 368p. 1995. pap. 3.95 (*0-87779-501-0*) Merriam-Webster Inc.
— Merriam-Webster's Premium Gift Set: Merriam-Webster's Collegiate Dictionary & Collegiate Thesaurus. 10th deluxe ed. 1993. boxed set, im. lthr. 49.95 (*0-87779-712-9*) Merriam-Webster Inc.
— Merriam-Webster's Reader's Handbook: A Complete Guide to Literary Terms. LC 97-26659. 608p. 1997. pap. 14.95 (*0-87779-620-3*) Merriam-Webster Inc.
— Merriam-Webster's Rhyming Dictionary. 369p. 1995. mass mkt. 4.99 (*0-87779-913-X*) Merriam-Webster Inc.
— Merriam-Webster's School Thesaurus. LC 88-26859. 704p. (YA). (gr. 9-12). 1995. 15.95 (*0-87779-178-3*) Merriam-Webster Inc.
— Merriam-Webster's Secretarial Handbook. 3rd ed. LC 96-10632. 608p. 1993. 17.95 (*0-87779-236-4*) Merriam-Webster Inc.
— The Official Scrabble Players Dictionary. large type ed. LC 97-43212. 1998. pap. 29.95 (*0-87779-623-8*) Merriam-Webster Inc.
— The Official Scrabble Players Dictionary. 3rd ed. LC 95-20437. 704p. 1995. 19.95 (*0-87779-220-8*) Merriam-Webster Inc.
— The Official Scrabble Players Dictionary. 3rd ed. 672p. 1996. pap. 6.50 (*0-87779-915-6*) Merriam-Webster Inc.
— Webster's Compact Rhyming Dictionary. LC 86-33165. 400p. 1995. 6.50 (*0-87779-185-6*) Merriam-Webster Inc.
Merriam-Webster Editors. Webster's Middle School Dictionary 1996. 1997. 20.40 (*0-03-096483-0*) Harcourt Coll Pubs.
***Merriam Webster Editors.** Webster's New Explorer Dictionary & Thesaurus. LC 99-62651. (Webster's New Explorer Ser.). (Illus.). 1456p. 1999. 19.98 (*1-892859-06-8*) Federal St Pr.
***Merriam-Webster Editors.** Webster's New Explorer Medical Dictionary. LC 99-62652. (Webster's New Explorer Ser.). Orig. Title: Merriam Webster's Medical Dictionary. 800p. 1999. 8.98 (*1-892859-07-6*) Federal St Pr.
— Webster's New Explorer Spanish-English Dictionary. LC 99-62653. (Webster's New Explorer Ser.). Orig. Title: Merriam-Webster's Spanish English Dictionary. (SPA., Illus.). 800p. 1999. 8.98 (*1-892859-08-4*) Federal St Pr.
Merriam-Webster Editors. Webster's II New Riverside Children's Dictionary. (J). 1984. 18.10 (*0-606-02686-X*, Pub. by Turtleback) Demco.
— Webster's Synonyms, Antonyms & Homonyms. 252p. 1994. 6.99 (*0-517-06366-2*) Random Hse Value.
Merriam-Webster Editors, ed. The Merriam-Webster & Garfield Dictionary. LC 99-25351. 816p. 1999. pap. 12.95 (*0-87779-626-2*) Merriam-Webster Inc.
— Merriam-Webster Dictionary. 1994. 11.34 (*0-606-07859-2*) Turtleback.
— Merriam-Webster Dictionary. 1995. 17.30 (*0-606-07860-6*) Turtleback.
— The Merriam-Webster Dictionary of Synonyms & Antonyms. 448p. 1995. mass mkt. 4.99 (*0-87779-906-7*) Merriam-Webster Inc.
***Merriam-Webster Editors, ed.** Merriam-Webster's Collegiate Reference Set with CD-ROM. 1999. boxed set 49.95 incl. cd-rom (*0-87779-715-3*) Merriam-Webster Inc.
Merriam-Webster Editors, ed. Merriam-Webster's Collegiate Thesaurus. deluxe ed. LC 93-3177. 894p. 1993. im. lthr. 21.95 (*0-87779-170-8*) Merriam-Webster Inc.
— Merriam-Webster's Crossword Quest, Vol. 3. 80p. 1999. pap. 8.95 (*0-87779-655-6*) Merriam-Webster Inc.
— Merriam-Webster's Crossword Quest, Vol. 4. 1999. pap. 8.95 (*0-87779-656-4*) Merriam-Webster Inc.
***Merriam-Webster Editors, ed.** Merriam-Webster's Crossword Quest, Vol. 5. 88p. 2000. pap. 8.95 (*0-87779-657-2*) Merriam-Webster Inc.
— Merriam-Webster's Crossword Quest, Vol. 6. 88p. 2000. pap. 8.95 (*0-87779-658-0*) Merriam-Webster Inc.
Merriam-Webster Editors, ed. Merriam-Webster's Dictionary of Basic English. LC 94-49524. (Illus.). 736p. 1995. pap. 9.95 (*0-87779-605-X*) Merriam-Webster Inc.
— Merriam-Webster's Dictionary of Basic English. 1995. 15.30 (*0-606-07861-4*) Turtleback.
— Merriam-Webster's Elementary Dictionary. LC 93-41502. (Illus.). 608p. (J). (gr. 2-6). 1994. 15.95 (*0-87779-575-4*) Merriam-Webster Inc.
— Merriam-Webster's English & Spanish Reference Set. (SPA & ENG.). 1999. pap., boxed set 16.99 (*0-87779-976-8*) Merriam-Webster Inc.
— Merriam Webster's Geographical Dictionary. 3rd rev. ed. LC 96-52365. (Illus.). 1392p. 1997. 29.95 (*0-87779-546-0*) Merriam-Webster Inc.
— Merriam-Webster's Guide to Business Correspondence. 2nd ed. 402p. 1996. reprint ed. 17.95 incl. cd-rom (*0-87779-231-3*) Merriam-Webster Inc.
— Merriam-Webster's Intermediate Dictionary. LC 98-4995. (Illus.). 960p. (YA). (gr. 6-9). 1994. 15.95 (*0-87779-479-0*) Merriam-Webster Inc.
— Merriam Webster's Medical Desk Dictionary. rev. ed. LC 96-15564. 928p. 1993. 25.95 (*0-87779-125-2*) Merriam-Webster Inc.
— Merriam-Webster's Medical Desk Dictionary with CD-ROM. (Illus.). 1998. 49.95 incl. cd-rom (*0-87779-027-2*) Merriam-Webster Inc.
— Merriam-Webster's Notebook Atlas. (Illus.). 68p. 1996. pap., student ed. 3.95 (*0-87779-652-1*) Merriam-Webster Inc.
— Merriam-Webster's Pocket Atlas. (Illus.). 272p. 1998. pap. 6.95 (*0-87779-515-0*) Merriam-Webster Inc.
— Merriam-Webster's School Dictionary. LC 98-12888. (Illus.). 1184p. (YA). (gr. 9-12). 1994. 15.95 (*0-87779-380-8*) Merriam-Webster Inc.
— Merriam-Webster's Spanish-English Dictionary. LC 98-5887. (ENG & SPA.). 848p. 1998. 19.95 (*0-87779-165-1*); pap. 5.99 (*0-87779-916-4*) Merriam-Webster Inc.
— Webster's Basic English Dictionary. LC 83-13709. (Illus.). 608p. 1995. 14.95 (*0-87779-150-3*) Merriam-Webster Inc.
— Webster's Compact Dictionary. LC 87-21956. 432p. 1995. 6.50 (*0-87779-488-X*) Merriam-Webster Inc.
— Webster's Instant Word Guide. LC 79-20748. 384p. 1995. 6.50 (*0-87779-273-9*) Merriam-Webster Inc.
— Webster's Medical Speller. 2nd ed. LC 87-26947. 400p. 1995. 6.50 (*0-87779-137-6*) Merriam-Webster Inc.
***Merriam-Webster Editors, ed.** Webster's New Explorer Crossword Challenge, No. 1. 160p. 2000. pap. 5.98 (*1-892859-18-1*) Federal St Pr.
— Webster's New Explorer Crossword Challenge, No. 2. 160p. 2000. pap. 5.98 (*1-892859-19-X*) Federal St Pr.
— Webster's New Explorer Large Print Dictionary. large type ed. LC 00-103125. (Webster's New Explorer Ser.). 768p. 2000. 12.98 (*1-892859-16-5*) Federal St Pr.
Merriam-Webster Editors, ed. Webster's Third New International Dictionary. rev. unabridged ed. LC 93-10630. (Illus.). 2783p. 1961. 119.00 (*0-87779-201-1*) Merriam-Webster Inc.

M

Merriam-Webster Editors, jt. auth. see Kenkyusha Ltd. Staff.
Merriam-Webster Editors, jt. ed. see Encyclopedia Britannica Staff.
Merriam-Webster Editors, ed. see Kenkyusha Ltd. Staff.
Merriam-Webster Staff. Discover Works for Windows 95 Version 4, With Disk. Date not set. disk 24.95 (*1-86398-176-4*) Wbstr & Assocs.
— Merriam-Webster Children's Illustrated Dictionary. LC 99-43274. (Illus.). 912p. (J). 2000. 17.95 (*0-7894-5238-3*, D K Ink) DK Pub Inc.
Merriam-Webster Staff. The Merriam-Webster Dictionary, Home & Office Edition. LC 97-39927. (Illus.). 720p. 1998. pap. 11.95 (*0-87779-606-8*) Merriam-Webster Inc.
— The Merriam-Webster Thesaurus, Home & Office Edition. LC 95-19061. 704p. 1996. pap. 9.95 (*0-87779-607-6*) Merriam-Webster Inc.
— Merriam-Webster's Collegiate Thesaurus. LC 93-3177. 894p. 1995. 17.95 (*0-87779-169-4*) Merriam-Webster Inc.
— Merriam-Webster's Dictionary of English Usage. rev. ed. LC 93-19289. Orig. Title: Webster's Dictionary of English Usage. 992p. 1993. 24.95 (*0-87779-132-5*) Merriam-Webster Inc.
***Merriam-Webster Staff.** Merriam-Webster's French-English Dictionary. (FRE & ENG.). 2000. 19.95 (*0-87779-166-X*) Merriam-Webster Inc.

***Merriam-Webster Staff, ed. Merriam-Webster's Elementary Dictionary. (Illus.). 640p. (J). (gr. 2-6). 2000. pap. 11.95 (0-87779-630-0) Merriam-Webster Inc.**
Copyright 2000! A new, revised trade paperback version of our popular hardcover at a great price! A first real dictionary for children ages 7-11. Delivers over 32,000 entries, hundreds of illustrations & special sections including U.S. presidents. *Publisher Paid Annotation.*

Merrians, Deborah. I Can Read about Earthquakes & Volcanoes. LC 95-5944. (Illus.). 48p. (J). (gr. k-3). 1996. pap. 4.95 (*0-8167-3649-9*) Troll Communs.
— I Can Read About Earthquakes & Volcanoes. LC 74-24966. (Illus.). (J). (gr. 2-4). 1997. pap. 2.95 (*0-89375-067-0*) Troll Communs.
— I Can Read About Insects. LC 76-54493. (Illus.). (J). (gr. 2-5). 1997. pap. 2.95 (*0-89375-040-9*) Troll Communs.
— I Can Read About Spiders. LC 76-54576. (Illus.). (J). (gr. 2-5). 1977. pap. 2.95 (*0-89375-043-3*) Troll Communs.
— I Can Read about Spiders. LC 96-225987. 1997. pap. 4.95 (*0-8167-4204-9*) Troll Communs.
Merrick. How to Manage Your Multi-Age Classroom. 1996. pap. text, wbk. ed. 24.95 (*1-55734-468-X*) Tchr Create Mat.
— Reconceiving Black Adolescent Pregnancy. 110p. 2000. 65.00 (*0-8133-6816-2*, Pub. by Westview) HarpC.
Merrick, A., tr. see Sor, Ferdinand.
Merrick, Barbara L. & Williams, Alicia C., eds. Middleborough, Massachusetts, Vital Records, Vol. 1. 487p. 1986. text 35.00 (*0-942445-00-7*) MA Soc Mayflower Descendants.
— Middleborough, Massachusetts, Vital Records, Vol. 2. 360p. 1990. text 35.00 (*0-942445-01-5*) MA Soc Mayflower Descendants.
***Merrick, Catherine.** Fabric Quantity Handbook: For Soft Furnishings. 1999. 17.50 (*0-9516841-7-5*) Merk & Day.
— Professional Patterns for Tie-Backs. 1999. pap. 25.00 (*0-9516841-3-2*) Merk & Day.
— Swag & Tail Design & Pattern Book, 1. (Illus.). 104p. 1999. 75.00 (*0-9516841-1-6*) Merk & Day.
***Merrick, Catherine.** Swag & Tail Design & Pattern Book. (Illus.). 104p. 1999. 75.00 (*0-9516841-8-3*) Merk & Day.
Merrick, Catherine & Day, Rebecca. Encyclopaedia of Curtains: Complete Curtain Maker. (Illus.). 240p. 1998. 50.00 (*0-9516841-4-0*, Pub. by Merrick & Day) Randall Intl.
Merrick, Charles I. & Titchenal, Kay H. Change Master: Principles for Mastering Change. 210p. 1995. pap. 12.95 (*0-9647018-0-4*) Candlewick Sq.
Merrick, Daniel B. & Polk, David P., eds. Chalice Hymnal. 832p. 1995. 15.99 (*0-8272-8029-7*) Chalice Pr.
Merrick, Dave. Social Work & Child Abuse. LC 96-2573. (State of Welfare Ser.). 240p. (C). 1996. pap. 24.99 (*0-415-13068-9*) Routledge.
Merrick, David & Marshall, Richard, eds. Energy Vol. 1: Present & Future Options. LC 80-41416. (Illus.). 354p. reprint ed. pap. 109.80 (*0-608-17672-9*, 203038900001) Bks Demand.
Merrick, Elliot. Northern Nurse. (Illus.). 336p. 1994. reprint ed. pap. 14.00 (*0-88150-299-5*, Pub. by Countryman) Norton.
Merrick, Elliott. Green Mountain Farm. LC 99-38142. 212p. 1999. pap. 14.95 (*0-88150-435-1*, Pub. by Countryman) Norton.
— The Long Crossing & Other Labrador Stories. LC 91-32226. (Illus.). 158p. (Orig.). (C). 1992. pap. 13.95 (*0-89101-074-2*) U Maine Pr.
— True North. LC 88-38068. 375p. 1989. reprint ed. pap. 116.30 (*0-608-02783-9*, 206385000007) Bks Demand.
Merrick, G. B. Genealogy of the Merrick-Merick-Myrick Family of Massachusetts, 1636-1902. (Illus.). 502p. 1989. reprint ed. pap. 75.00 (*0-8328-0869-5*); reprint ed. lib. bdg. 83.00 (*0-8328-0867-9*) Higginson Bk Co.
Merrick, Gordon. Forth into Light. 256p. 1996. reprint ed. pap. 11.95 (*1-55583-292-X*) Alyson Pubns.
***Merrick, Gordon.** Great Urge Downward. 438p. 2000. pap. 14.95 (*1-55583-296-2*) Alyson Pubns.
Merrick, Gordon. An Idol for Others. LC 98-11230. 400p. 1998. pap. 14.95 (*1-55583-295-4*) Alyson Pubns.
— The Lord Won't Mind. 256p. 1996. reprint ed. pap. 11.95 (*1-55583-290-3*) Alyson Pubns.
— Now Let's Talk about Music. LC 97-7282. 256p. 1997. reprint ed. pap. 12.95 (*1-55583-293-8*) Alyson Pubns.
— One for the Gods, Vol. 2. 312p. 1996. reprint ed. pap. text 11.95 (*1-55583-291-1*) Alyson Pubns.
— Perfect Freedom. LC 99-11461. 464p. 1999. reprint ed. pap. 14.95 (*1-55583-297-0*, Pub. by Alyson Pubns) Consort Bk Sales.
— The Quirk. LC 98-20555. 400p. 1998. reprint ed. pap. 12.95 (*1-55583-294-6*, Alyson Bks) Alyson Pubns.
— The Strumpet Wind. 256p. 1992. reprint ed. lib. bdg. 18.95 (*0-89966-892-5*) Buccaneer Bks.
Merrick, Gordon & Hulse, Charles. The Good Life. LC 97-35633. 350p. (Orig.). 1997. pap. 14.95 (*1-55583-298-9*) Alyson Pubns.
***Merrick, Helen H. & Williams, Tess, eds.** Women of Other Worlds: Excursions Through Science Fiction & Feminism. 472p. 1999. pap. 29.95 (*1-876268-32-8*, Pub. by Univ of West Aust Pr) Intl Spec Bk.
Merrick, Janna, jt. auth. see Blank, Robert H.
Merrick, Janna, jt. ed. see Blank, Robert H.
Merrick, Janna C. & Blank, Robert H., eds. The Politics of Pregnancy: Policy Dilemmas in the Maternal-Fetal Relationship. LC 93-5723. (Women & Politics Ser.: Vol. 13, Nos. 3 & 4). (Illus.). 245p. 1994. pap. 14.95 (*1-56023-047-9*, Harrington Park); lib. bdg. 49.95 (*1-56024-478-X*) Haworth Pr.
Merrick, Janna C., jt. auth. see Blank, Robert H.
Merrick, Jeffrey, intro. Early Modern European History: Selected Course Outlines & Reading Lists from Leading American Colleges & Universities. 3rd enl. ed. LC 88-17406. (History Syllabi Ser.). 300p. (C). 1988. pap. 16.95 (*0-910129-93-2*) Wiener Pubs Inc.
***Merrick, Jeffrey & Ragan, Bryant T., eds.** Homosexuality in Early Modern France: A Documentary Collection. LC 99-87275. 272p. (C). 2000. pap. text 35.00 (*0-19-510257-6*) OUP.
Merrick, Jeffrey & Ragan, Bryant T., Jr., eds. Homosexuality in Modern France. (Studies in the History of Sexuality). 264p. 1996. pap. 19.95 (*0-19-509304-6*); text 55.00 (*0-19-509303-8*) OUP.
Merrick, Jeffrey W. & Medlin, Dorothy, eds. Andre Morellet (1727-1819) in the Republic of Letters & the French Revolution. LC 94-12273. (Eighteenth Century French Intellectual History Ser.: Vol. 2). X, 252p. (C). 1995. text 57.95 (*0-8204-2494-3*) P Lang Pubng.
Merrick, Jonathan. Sams Teach Yourself PL/SQL in 21 Days. LC 97-66672. (Teach Yourself Ser.). 346p. 1997. 39.99 (*0-672-31123-2*) Sams.
Merrick, Kenneth A. German Aircraft Interiors, 1935-1945. Hitchcock, Thomas H., ed. LC 94-75879. (German Aircraft Interiors Ser.: Vol. 1). (Illus.). 256p. 1997. 54.95 (*0-914144-41-3*) Monogram Aviation.
Merrick, Kenneth A. German Aircraft Markings, 1939-1945 LC 78-308383. 176p. 1977. write for info. (*0-7110-0739-X*, Pub. by Ian Allan) Motorbooks Intl.
— Luftwaffe Colors. LC 74-14272. 1975. write for info. (*0-668-03652-4*, Arco) Macmillan Gen Ref.
Merrick, M. V. Essentials of Nuclear Medicine. 2nd ed. LC 97-34666. (Illus.). v, 334p. 1997. pap. 89.00 (*3-540-76205-1*) Spr-Verlag.
Merrick, Minerva. Light of the Ages Recently Written by Ancient Immortals & the Death Blow to Poverty. 304p. 1998. reprint ed. pap. 24.95 (*0-7661-0639-X*) Kessinger Pub.
Merrick, Patrick. Avalanches. LC 97-11260. (Forces of Nature Ser.). (Illus.). 32p. (J). (gr. 2-6). 1997. lib. bdg. 22.79 (*1-56766-414-8*) Childs World.
— Bears. LC 98-38135. (Illus.). 32p. (J). 1999. lib. bdg. 22.79 (*1-56766-585-3*) Childs World.
— Biting Flies. LC 98-45791. (J). 1999. lib. bdg. write for info. (*1-56766-631-0*) Childs World.
— Blizzards. LC 97 28751. (Forces of Nature Ser.). (Illus.). 32p. (J). (gr. 2-6). 1998. lib. bdg. 22.79 (*1-56766-469-5*) Childs World.
— Cardinals. LC 98-38134. (Illus.). 32p. (J). 1999. lib. bdg. 22.79 (*1-56766-592-6*) Childs World.
— Caterpillars. LC 96-46956. (Nature Books Ser.). 32p. (J). (gr. 2-6). 1997. lib. bdg. 22.79 (*1-56766-380-X*) Childs World.
— Dragonflies. LC 96-47042. (Nature Books Ser.). (Illus.). 32p. (J). (gr. 2-6). 1997. lib. bdg. 22.79 (*1-56766-381-8*) Childs World.
— Droughts. LC 97-28750. (Forces of Nature Ser.). (Illus.). 32p. (J). (gr. 2-6). 1998. lib. bdg. 22.79 (*1-56766-470-9*) Childs World.
— Eagles. LC 98-27795. (Illus.). 32p. (J). 1999. lib. bdg. 22.79 (*1-56766-588-8*) Childs World.
— Earthworms. LC 97-28747. (Illus.). 32p. (J). 1998. lib. bdg. 22.79 (*1-56766-501-2*) Childs World.
— Easter Bunnies. LC 98-33380. (Holiday Symbols Ser.). (Illus.). 32p. (J). (gr. 2-3). 1999. lib. bdg. 15.95 (*1-56766-639-6*) Childs World.
— Forest Fires. LC 97-3064. (Forces of Nature Ser.). (Illus.). 32p. (J). (gr. 2-6). 1997. lib. bdg. 22.79 (*1-56766-415-6*) Childs World.
— Fourth of July Fireworks. LC 98-51661. (Holiday Symbols Ser.). (Illus.). 32p. (J). (gr. 2-3). 1999. lib. bdg. 15.95 (*1 56766 640 X*) Childs World.
***Merrick, Patrick.** Honduras LC 99-38770. 2000. lib. bdg. write for info. (*1-56766-736-8*) Childs World.
Merrick, Patrick. Leeches. LC 98-44320. (Illus.). 32p. (J). 1999. lib. bdg. write for info. (*1-56766-633-7*) Childs World.
***Merrick, Patrick.** Lice. LC 98-45209. (Illus.). 32p. (J). 1999. lib. bdg. write for info. (*1-56766-634-5*) Childs World.
Merrick, Patrick. Loons. LC 98-38203. (Illus.). 32p. (J). 1999. lib. bdg. 22.79 (*1-56766-595-0*) Childs World.
***Merrick, Patrick.** Morocco. LC 99-40504. (J). 2000. lib. bdg. write for info. (*1-56766-737-6*) Childs World.
Merrick, Patrick. Raccoons. LC 97-27835. (Illus.). 32p. (J). 1998. lib. bdg. 22.79 (*1-56766-504-7*) Childs World.
— Snow Leopards. LC 97-28748. (Nature Books Ser.). (Illus.). 32p. (J). (gr. 2-6). 1998. lib. bdg. 22.79 (*1-56766-474-1*) Childs World.
***Merrick, Patrick.** Thanksgiving Turkeys. LC 98-50659. (Illus.). 32p. 1999. lib. bdg. 22.79 (*1-56766-642-6*) Childs World.
Merrick, Patrick. Ticks. LC 96-47082. (Nature Books Ser.). (Illus.). 32p. (J). (gr. 2-6). 1997. lib. bdg. 22.79 (*1-56766-384-2*) Childs World.
— Toads. LC 97-27838. (Illus.). 32p. (J). 1998. lib. bdg. 22.79 (*1-56766-502-0*) Childs World.
— Vampire Bats. LC 98-37312. (Illus.). 32p. 1999. lib. bdg. write for info. (*1-56766-636-1*) Childs World.
— Walkingsticks. LC 96-46957. (Nature Books Ser.). (Illus.). 32p. (J). (gr. 2-6). 1997. lib. bdg. 22.79 (*1-56766-383-4*) Childs World.
Merrick, R. Valve Selection & Specification. 1990. text 69.95 (*0-442-31870-7*) Chapman & Hall.
Merrick, Robert G. Stand Alone, Inventor! And Make Money with Your New Product Ideas! (Illus.). 310p. (Orig.). 1997. pap. 19.95 (*0-9643832-0-9*) Lee Pubng.
Merrick, Sam. F. Slade Dale - The Life of His Choice. (Illus.). 173p. 1998. pap. 19.95 (*0-941965-11-2*) Ocean Cnty Hist.
Merrick, Sandra. Early Childhood Units for Holidays. (Illus.). 112p. (Orig.). (J). (ps-1). 1992. student ed. 11.95 (*1-55734-019-6*) Tchr Create Mat.
— Early Childhood Units for Math. (Whole Language Units Ser.). (Illus.). 144p. 1993. student ed. 12.95 (*1-55734-200-8*) Tchr Create Mat.
— Early Childhood Units for Nursery Rhymes. Goldfluss, Karen J., ed. (Illus.). 112p. (Orig.). 1992. student ed. 10.95 (*1-55734-020-X*) Tchr Create Mat.
Merrick, Thomas W. & Graham, Douglas H. Population & Economic Development in Brazil, 1800 to the Present. LC 78-20523. 408p. 1979. reprint ed. pap. 126.50 (*0-608-03671-4*, 206449700009) Bks Demand.
Merrick, William C., ed. see Cornesky, Robert, et al.
Merrick, William G. Tan Vat. LC 93-83571. 124p. (Orig.). 1992. pap. 8.50 (*0-9635951-0-5*) Piedmont Coll.
Merricks, John & Walker, Ian. High Performance Racing: A Winning Approach from the 1996 Olympic Medallists. (Illus.). 1999. pap. 18.95 (*1-898660-30-1*) Fernhurst Bks.
Merricks, Linda. The World Made New: Frederick Soddy, Science, Politics, & Environment. (Illus.). 246p. (C). 1996. text 115.00 (*0-19-855934-8*) OUP.
Merricks, Paul, jt. ed. see Jones, Peter.
***Merridale, Catherine.** Night of Stone. 2001. 29.95 (*0-670-89474-5*, Viking) Viking Penguin.
Merridale, Catherine & Ward, Chris, eds. Perestroika: The Historical Perspective. 256p. 1995. text 19.95 (*0-340-55789-3*, A6288, Pub. by E A) St Martin.
***Merriden, Trevor.** Cold Calling: Business the Nokia Way. (Business Way Ser.). 2000. 21.95 (*1-84112-104-5*) Capstone Pub NH.
Merrienboer, Jeroen J. Van, see Van Merrienboer, Jeroen J.
***Merrier, Patricia.** Basics of Business Communication. 2nd ed. (Communication-English Ser.). (C). 2000. 38.95 (*0-538-72295-9*) S-W Pub.
Merrifield, et al. Labor Relation Law: Cases & Materials, 1993 Cumulative Supplement. 1994. write for info. (*1-55834-116-1*, 13122-10, MICHIE) LEXIS Pub.
— Labor Relation Law: Cases & Materials, 1997 Cumulative Supplement. 136p. 1997. pap. text 11.00 (*1-55834-262-1*, 13122-13, MICHIE) LEXIS Pub.
— Labor Relations Law: 92 Cumulative Supplement. 8th ed. 107p. 1992. write for info. (*0-87473-668-4*, 13121-10, MICHIE) LEXIS Pub.
Merrifield, Andy & Swyngedouw, E. The Urbanization of Injustice. LC 96-47841. 1997. text 50.00 (*0-8147-5575-5*); pap. text 17.50 (*0-8147-5576-3*) NYU Pr.
Merrifield, Bruce. Bruce Merrifield: Life During a Golden Age of Peptide Chemistry: The Concept & Development of Solid-Phase Synthesis. LC 92-42159. (Profiles, Pathways, & Dreams Ser.). (Illus.). 297p. 1993. text 36.00 (*0-8412-1842-0*, Pub. by Am Chemical) OUP.
Merrifield, Calvin & Merrifield, Rebecca. Call Me Ret Man & Have a Ball: Comic Book. 1979. write for info. (*0-917476-13-1*) A Ellis Institute.
Merrifield, D. Bruce. Strategic Analysis, Selection, & Management of R & D Projects. LC 77-14599. (AMA Management Briefing Ser.). 54p. reprint ed. pap. 30.00 (*0-608-14415-0*, 205169900002) Bks Demand.
Merrifield, Doris F. Deutsche Wirtschaftssprache fur Amerikaner. 2nd ed. LC 88-31549. 282p. 1989. 50.95 (*0-471-61374-6*) Wiley.
— Deutsche Wirtschaftssprache Fur Amerikaner. 3rd ed. 336p. 1994. pap. 49.95 (*0-471-30947-8*) Wiley.
— Deutsche Wirtschaftssprache Fur Amerikaner. 3rd ed. (GER.). 1995. pap. text 20.95 (*0-471-00883-4*) Wiley.
— Praktische Anleitung Zur Interpretation Von Dichtung. LC 81-40127. 246p. (Orig.). 1982. pap. text 21.50 (*0-8191-2054-5*) U Pr of Amer.
Merrifield, Doris F., jt. auth. see Haas, Werner.
Merrifield, Ed A. The Urbanization of Injustice. (C). 1996. pap. write for info. (*0-85315-842-8*, Pub. by Lawrence & Wishart) NYU Pr.
Merrifield, Edward. Luke Swetland's Captivity & Rescue from the Indians: An Early Settler of the Wyoming Valley & a Soldier of the American Revolution. LC 98-88847. (Pennsylvania History & Legends Ser.). (Illus.). 66p. 1998. reprint ed. pap. 8.95 (*1-889037-15-X*) Wennawoods.
Merrifield, Fred, ed. Modern Religious Verse & Prose: An Anthology. LC 79-51964. (Granger Poetry Library). 1980. reprint ed. 35.00 (*0-89609-186-4*) Roth Pub Inc.
Merrifield, Gladys. Twentieth Reunion & Other Poems. limited ed. LC 84-70671. (Living Poets' Library: No. 31). 1984. 5.00 (*0-934218-31-5*) Dragons Teeth.
— Windows on Manhattan. (Living Poets' Library). 1986. pap. 5.00 (*0-934218-33-1*) Dragons Teeth.
Merrifield, Heyoehkah. Magical Art. LC 87-401423. (Illus.). (Orig.). (C). 1986. pap. 12.95 (*0-945122-00-4*) Rain Bird Pubs.
Merrifield, Heyoka. Sacred Art Sacred Earth: Transformative Art - Birthing a New Myth. (Illus.). 144p. (Orig.). (YA). 1994. pap. 19.95 (*0-945122-01-2*) Rain Bird Pubs.
Merrifield, Jeff. Damanhur: The Community They Tried to Brand a Cult. (Illus.). 1999. pap. 16.00 (*0-7225-3700-X*) Thorsons PA.
Merrifield, Juanita. The Little Purple Cow of Murphysboro. 18p. (Orig.). (J). (ps-6). 1995. pap. 6.00 (*0-9656822-0-X*) Purple Cow.
Merrifield, Juliet. Life at the Margins: Literacy, Language, & Technology in Everyday Life. LC 97-30137. (Language & Literacy Ser.). 1997. 49.00 (*0-8077-3665-1*) Tchrs Coll.
Merrifield, Juliet, et al. Life at the Margins: Literacy, Language, & Technology in Everyday Life. LC 97-30137. 256p. 1997. pap. 22.95 (*0-8077-3664-3*) Tchrs Coll.
Merrifield, Kathy. A Christian Cline: Observations about Life & God. 250p. (Orig.). 1992. pap. write for info. (*0-9630692-1-7*) Selaginella.
— The Oregon Gull Identification Workbook. 38p. 1991. pap. 9.95 (*0-9630692-0-9*) Selaginella.
Merrifield, Leroy S., et al. Labor Relations Law: Cases & Materials. 9th ed. LC 94-75594. (Contemporary Legal Education Ser.). xxii, 1040 p. 1994. write for info. (*1-55834-138-2*) LEXIS Pub.
Merrifield, Margaret. Come Sit by Me. (Illus.). 32p. (J). reprint ed. pap. 5.95 (*0-88961-141-6*, Pub. by Womens Pr) LPC InBook.
— Come Sit by Me. 2nd ed. LC 98-226144. (Illus.). 30p. (J). (ps-2). 1998. reprint ed. pap. 5.50 (*0-7737-5958-1*) STDK.
Merrifield, Margaret. Morning Light: An Educational Storybook for Children & Caregivers about AIDS & Saying Goodbye. unabridged ed. (Illus.). 30p. (J). (ps-2). 1996. pap. 6.99 (*0-7737-5704-X*) STDK.
***Merrifield, Mary.** Medieval & Renaissance Treatises on the Arts of Painting. LC 98-48799. 918p. 1999. pap. text 34.95 (*0-486-40440-4*) Dover.
Merrifield, Michael. Colorado Gonzo Rides Vol. 1: A Mountain Biker's Guide to Colorado's Best Single Track Trails. LC 91-71647. 192p. 1991. pap. 12.95 (*0-9628867-0-X*) Blue Clover.
Merrifield, Michael, jt. auth. see Binney, James.
Merrifield, Ralph. The Archaeology of Ritual & Magic. (Illus.). 224p. (C). 1988. 25.00 (*0-941533-25-5*, NAB); pap. 15.95 (*0-941533-26-3*, NAB) I R Dee.
Merrifield, Ralph, jt. auth. see Hall, Jenny.
Merrifield, Rebecca, jt. auth. see Merrifield, Calvin.
Merrifield, Richard E., jt. auth. see Simmons, Howard.
Merrifield, Scott. North Sulawesi Language Survey. LC 95-68478. (Publications in Sociolinguistics: No. 1). 336p. (Orig.). 1997. pap. 28.00 (*1-55671-000-3*) S I L Intl.
Merrifield, William, et al, eds. Laboratory Manual for Morphology & Syntax. rev. ed. 291p. 1987. pap. text 18.75 (*0-88312-785-7*) S I L Intl.
Merrifield, William R. Proto Otomanguean Kinship. LC 80-50558. (International Museum of Cultures Publications: No. 11). 400p. (Orig.). 1981. pap. 12.50 (*0-88312-161-1*) S I L Intl.
Merrifield, William R., ed. Five Amazonian Studies on Worldview & Cultural Change. LC 85-80411. (International Museum of Cultures Publications: No. 19). (Illus.). 96p. (Orig.). 1985. pap. 11.00 (*0-88312-174-3*) S I L Intl.
— South American Kinship: Eight Kinship Systems from Brazil & Colombia. LC 85-80410. (International Museum of Cultures Publications: No. 18). (Illus.). 132p. (Orig.). 1985. pap. 12.00 (*0-88312-173-5*) S I L Intl.
Merrifield, William R., et al, eds. Gods, Heroes, Kinsmen: Ethnographic Studies from Irian Jaya, Indonesia. LC 83-80231. (International Museum of Cultures Publications: No. 17). 300p. (Orig.). 1983. pap. 16.00 (*0-88312-112-3*) S I L Intl.
***Merrigan, Kathleen A., ed.** Pesticide Data Program: Annual Summary, Calendar Year 1998. (Illus.). 160p. 2000. pap. text 25.00 (*0-7567-0033-7*) DIANE Pub.
Merrigan, Michael W., jt. auth. see Amrhein, James E.
Merrigan, Terrence. Clear Heads & Holy Hearts: The Religious & Theological Ideal of John Henry Newman. (Louvain Theological & Pastoral Monographs). 272p. (Orig.). 1992. pap. 25.00 (*0-8028-0567-1*) Eerdmans.
Merrihew, Raymond. In the Valley Below. 1998. pap. write for info. (*1-57553-976-4*) Watermrk Pr.
Merriiam, Robert L. A Christmas Legend. (Illus.). 9p. (Orig.). 1970. pap. 1.50 (*0-686-32485-4*) R L Merriam.
Merril. Sensing Semiosis: Toward the Possibility of Complementary Culture Logics. LC 97-48752. 286p. 1998. text 55.00 (*0-312-17693-7*) St Martin.
Merril, William L. A Calculator Tutorial. (Illus.). 1994. pap. text 8.95 (*0-914534-11-4*) Stokes.
Merrilees, Cynthia & Haack, Pamela. Write on Target: Practical Advice from Real Teachers. (Illus.). 63p. 1992. reprint ed. pap. 8.95 (*0-9627389-2-1*, Crystal Spgs) Soc Dev Educ.
Merrill. Ethical Foundations for Journalists. (C). 1996. pap. text. write for info. (*0-15-501795-0*) Harcourt Coll Pubs.

M

An Asterisk (*) at the beginning of an entry indicates that the title is appearing for the first time.

— Journalism Ethics. 257p. 1996. pap. text 28.95 (*0-312-13899-7*) St Martin.
— Magnetic Field of the Earth. (C). 1998. pap. text 54.95 (*0-12-491246-X*) Acad Pr.
Merrill. Muddy Boots: Ethical in the Construction Field. 33.00 (*0-534-55169-6*) Thomson Learn.
Merrill. Raymond Chandler. (Critical Essays Ser.). Date not set. 48.00 (*0-7838-8462-1*) Mac Lib Ref.
— Systems Physiology. 1998. lab manual ed. 8.74 (*0-07-228974-0*) McGraw.
Merrill, jt. auth. see Hutt.
Merrill, Iv, ed. see Haviland, John B. & Hart, Roger.
Merrill, A. Marion & Sprague, Grace E. Contemporary Verse. LC 72-8281. (Granger Index Reprint Ser.). 1977. reprint ed. 45.95 (*0-8369-6392-X*) Ayer.
Merrill, A. Roger, jt. auth. see Covey, Stephen R.
Merrill, Andrea & Jacobson, Judy. Montana Almanac. LC 97-13198. (Illus.). 500p. (Orig.). 1997. pap. 18.95 (*1-56044-493-2*) Falcon Pub Inc.
Merrill, Arch. Shadows on the Wall. LC 87-24477. (Arch Merrill's New York Ser.: Vol. 11). (Illus.). 168p. 1987. reprint ed. pap. 12.95 (*1-55787-000-4*, NY36045, Empire State Bks) Hrt of the Lakes.
— Stagecoach Towns. (Arch Merrill's New York Ser.: Vol. 6). 208p. 1991. reprint ed. pap. 12.95 (*1-55787-002-0*, 76040, Empire State Bks) Hrt of the Lakes.
— The Underground & Other Upstate Tales: Freedom's Road. (Illus.). 182p. 1996. reprint ed. pap. 12.95 (*0-932771-50-5*) Creek.
— Upstate Echos. (Arch Merrill's New York Ser.: Vol. 9). (Illus.). 168p. 1992. reprint ed. pap. 12.95 (*1-55787-003-9*, 76043, Empire State Bks) Hrt of the Lakes.
Merrill, Arthur A. Battle of White Plains. (Illus.). (YA). (gr. 7 up). 1976. pap. 3.00 (*0-911894-27-6*) Analysis.
— Behavior of Prices on Wall Street. 2nd rev. ed. (Illus.). 147p. 1984. 35.00 (*0-911894-49-7*) Analysis.
— Chess Openings Simplified. 1974. pap. 3.75 (*0-911894-24-1*) Analysis.
— Circumpolar Constellations. (Illus.). 1962. pap. 3.00 (*0-911894-37-3*) Analysis.
— Filtered Waves, Basic Theory. LC 77-77420. (Illus.). 1977. 15.00 (*0-911894-36-5*) Analysis.
— Fitting Linear & Curvilinear Regression Lines with a Pocket Calculator. 1978. pap. 3.00 (*0-911894-40-3*) Analysis.
— Log Scale Construction. 29p. 1966. pap. 4.00 (*0-911894-31-4*) Analysis.
— Merrill MW Waves. (Illus.). 1979. 20.00 (*0-911894-44-6*) Analysis.
— Remembering Names: Improvement Is Easy. (Illus.). 57p. 1985. 9.75 (*0-911894-50-0*) Analysis.
— Revolutionary War: An Outline & Calendar. (Illus.). (YA). (gr. 7 up). 1976. pap. 2.00 (*0-911894-35-7*) Analysis.
Merrill, Arthur L. United Theological Seminary of the Twin Cities: An Ecumenical Venture. LC 92-41819. (Illus.). 340p. 1993. text 99.95 (*0-7734-9201-1*) E Mellen.
Merrill, Arthur L. & Overholt, Thomas W., eds. Scripture in History & Theology: Essays in Honor of J. Coert Rylaarsdam. LC 77-12106. (Pittsburgh Theological Monographs: No. 17). 1977. pap. 10.00 (*0-915138-32-8*) Pickwick.
Merrill, Barbara. Gender, Change & Identity: Mature Women Studies in Universities. LC 99-72663. 254p. 1999. text 65.95 (*1-84014-993-0*, Pub. by Ashgate Pub) Ashgate Pub Co.
— Learn about Teaching from Children: An Outstanding Guide for All early Childhood Educators. 5th ed. LC 83-73668. (Illus.). 53p. 1984. 5.00 (*0-9613271-1-1*) RAEYC.
Merrill, Bob, jt. auth. see Styne, Julie.
Merrill, Bob, jt. auth. see Trapani, Iza.
Merrill, Bonnie. Fun with the Family in Maine: Hundreds of Ideas for Day Trips with the Kids. 2nd ed. LC 99-48434. (Illus.). 288p. 2000. pap. text 12.95 (*0-7627-0536-1*) Globe Pequot.
Merrill, Boynton, Jr. A Bestiary. LC 75-3549. (Illus.). 72p. 1976. 15.00 (*0-8131-1329-6*) U Pr of Ky.
Merrill, Byron. Elijah: Yesterday, Today & Tomorrow. LC 97-73197. 1997. 13.95 (*1-57008-331-2*) Bookcraft Inc.
Merrill, C. S. O'Keeffe: Days in a Life. 140p. (Orig.). 1995. pap. 12.00 (*0-9631909-8-9*) La Alameda Pr.
***Merrill, Cade.** The Dark Room. (Blair Witch Files Ser.). 176p. (J). (gr. 8-12). 2000. mass mkt. 4.99 (*0-553-49363-9*) BDD Bks Young Read.
— The Witch's Daughter. (Blair Witch Files Ser.). 176p. (J). (gr. 8-12). 2000. mass mkt. 4.99 (*0-553-49362-0*) BDD Bks Young Read.
Merrill, Caroline E., jt. auth. see Merrill, John V.
Merrill Carriere, Fanie, compiled by. Merrill Genealogy. (Illus.). 66p. 1995. pap. 8.95 (*0-937242-17-9*) Scandia Pubs.
Merrill, Charles. Emily's Year. 1992. pap. 7.95 (*0-917320-34-4*) Mho & Mho.
— The Great Ukrainian Partisan Movement & Other Tales of the Eisenhower Years. LC 83-11758. 245p. (Orig.). 1983. pap. 10.95 (*0-87233-071-0*) Bauhan.
Merrill, Charles S., jt. ed. see Cernyak-Spatz, Susan E.
Merrill, Chris, ed. see Adler, Lucile.
Merrill, Christopher. The Grass of Another Country: A Journey Through the World of Soccer. LC 93-4022. 160p. 1995. 20.00 (*0-8050-2771-8*); pap. 12.95 (*0-8050-3591-5*) H Holt & Co.
— The Old Bridge: The Third Balkan War & the Age of the Refugee. LC 95-20061. 100p. 1995. pap. 6.95 (*1-57131-208-0*) Milkweed Ed.
— Only Nails Remain. 1995. 20.00 (*0-8050-3049-2*) H Holt & Co.
— Only the Nails Remain: Scenes from the Balkan Wars. LC 99-16783. 416p. 1999. 27.95 (*0-8476-9820-3*, Pub. by Rowman) Natl Bk Netwk.
— Watch Fire. LC 95-124640. 192p. (Orig.). 1994. pap. 14.00 (*1-877727-43-1*) White Pine.
Merrill, Christopher & Bradbury, Ellen, eds. From the Faraway Nearby: Georgia O'Keeffe As Icon. LC 97-33004. (Illus.). 293p. 1998. pap. 19.95 (*0-8263-1834-7*) U of NM Pr.
Merrill, Christopher, ed. see Salamun, Tomaz.
Merrill, Christopher, ed. & intro. see Hay, John.
Merrill, Christopher, tr. see Debeljak, Ales.
Merrill, Claire. A Seed Is a Promise. 32p. (J). (gr. 1-4). 1990. pap. 2.50 (*0-590-43454-3*) Scholastic Inc.
— A Seed Is a Promise. (J). 1973. 7.70 (*0-606-04536-8*, Pub. by Turtleback) Demco.
Merrill, D. Liderazgo con Amor: Funcion Hombre Hogar. (Serie Enfoque a la Familia - Focus on the Family Ser.).Tr. of Loving Leader: The Man's Role at Home. (SPA.). 1.99 (*1-56063-559-2*, 497443) Editorial Unilit.
Merrill, Daniel D. Augustus De Morgan & the Logic of Relations. (New Synthese Historical Library). 272p. 1990. lib. bdg. 191.50 (*0-7923-0758-5*, Pub. by Kluwer Academic) Kluwer Academic.
Merrill, Daniel D., jt. auth. see Grimm, Robert H.
Merrill, Daniel D., ed. see Oberlin Colloquium in Philosophy Staff.
Merrill, David, jt. auth. see Hayden, Keavin.
Merrill, David, ed. see Gips, Kathleen.
Merrill, David W. Life Is a Test & You Will Pass. (Illus.). 40p. 1995. pap. 9.95 (*1-879418-96-7*) Audenreed Pr.
Merrill, Dean. Another Chance: How God Overrides Our Big Mistakes. 160p. (Orig.). 1981. pap. 6.95 (*0-310-35331-9*, 11325P) Zondervan.
— The God Who Won't Let Go: Divine Grace in the Face of Guilt, Tragedy & Failure. LC 97-41433. 160p. 1998. pap. 10.99 (*0-310-21848-9*) Zondervan.
— Sinners in the Hands of an Angry Church: Finding a Better Way to Influence Our Culture. LC 97-23181. 183p. 1997. pap. 12.99 (*0-310-21308-8*) Zondervan.
Merrill, Dean, jt. auth. see Cymbala, Jim.
Merrill, Deborah M. Caring for Elderly Parents: Juggling Work, Family & Caregiving in Middle & Working Class Families. LC 96-45347. 248p. 1997. 55.00 (*0-86569-269-6*, Auburn Hse) Greenwood.
Merrill, Dennis. Bread & the Ballot: The United States & India's Economic Development, 1947-1963. LC 90-50012. (Illus.). xvi, 282p. (C). 1990. 55.00 (*0-8078-1920-4*) U of NC Pr.
Merrill, Dennis J., jt. auth. see Paterson, Thomas G.
Merrill, Durwood. You're Out & You're Ugly Too: Confessions of an Umpire With an Attitude. Dent, Jim, ed. 328p. 1999. mass mkt. 6.50 (*0-312-96900-7*) St Martin.
Merrill, Durwood & Dent, Jim. You're Out & You're Ugly Too: Confessions of an Umpire with an Attitude. LC 97-36577. xvi, 270p. 1998. text 22.95 (*0-312-18237-6*) St Martin.
Merrill, E. D. A Bibliography of Eastern Asiatic Botany. 1999. reprint ed. 85.00 (*1-57898-130-1*) Martino Pubng.
— A Commentary on Loureiro's "Flora Cochinchinensis" 1935. pap. 15.00 (*0-934454-24-8*) Lubrecht & Cramer.
— A Flora of Manila. 1968. reprint ed. 96.00 (*3-7682-0548-7*) Lubrecht & Cramer.
— Polynesian Botanical Bibliography, 1773-1935. (BMB Ser.: No. 144). 1937. 30.00 (*0-527-02252-7*) Periodicals Srv.
Merrill, E. D. & Walker, E. H. A Bibliography of Eastern Asiatic Botany: Supplement 1. 1960. 45.00 (*0-934454-11-6*) Lubrecht & Cramer.
Merrill, Edward M. Lottery. 336p. mass mkt. 4.99 (*1-55197-105-4*) Picasso Publ.
Merrill, Elmer D. Plantae Elmerianae Borneenses. LC 29-219. (University of California Publications in Social Welfare: Vol. 15). 320p. reprint ed. pap. 99.20 (*0-608-18022-X*, 201475100096) Bks Demand.
Merrill, Elmer T., ed. see Catullus, Gaius Valerius.
Merrill, Emily Y., jt. auth. see Merrill, Yvonne Y.
Merrill, Eugene H. Deuteronomy. LC 94-12543. (New American Commentary Ser.: Vol. 4). 480p. 1994. 27.99 (*0-8054-0104-0*) Broadman.
— An Historical Survey of the Old Testament. 2nd ed. LC 91-31821. 352p. 1991. pap. 19.99 (*0-8010-6283-7*) Baker Bks.
— Kingdom of Priests: A History of Old Testament Israel. LC 87-30853. 546p. 1997. pap. 24.99 (*0-8010-2103-0*) Baker Bks.
Merrill, Frances & Merrill, Mason. Nudism Comes to America. LC 72-9773. reprint ed. 45.00 (*0-404-57476-9*) AMS Pr.
Merrill, Francis, tr. see Guerin, Daniel.
Merrill, Frederic, ed. see Kloppenberg, Lisa.
Merrill, Frederick T. Japan & the Opium Menace. Grob, Gerald N., ed. LC 80-1264. (Addiction in America Ser.). 1981. reprint ed. lib. bdg. 18.95 (*0-405-13607-2*) Ayer.
Merrill, Fredric R. The Oregon Rules of Civil Procedure in the Courts. 194p. (Orig.). 1988. pap. text 18.50 (*0-317-92497-4*) Oregon Law Inst.
Merrill, Gary & Pathak, Dhiraj, eds. Knowledge Sharing Across Biological & Medical Knowledge-Based Systems: Papers from the AAAI Workshop. (Technical Reports: Vol. WS-98-04). (Illus.). 50p. 1998. spiral bd. 25.00 (*1-57735-057-X*) AAAI Pr.
Merrill, George. Studies in Comparative Jurisprudence & the Conflict of Laws. LC 33-33040. (Historical Reprints in Jurisprudence & Classical Legal Literature Ser.). xii, 247p. 1984. reprint ed. lib. bdg. 48.00 (*0-89941-340-4*, 303440) W S Hein.
— Studies in Comparative Jurisprudence & the Conflict of Laws. xii, 247p. 1985. reprint ed. lib. bdg. 30.00 (*0-8377-0850-8*, Rothman) W S Hein.
Merrill, George P. First One Hundred Years of American Geology. (Illus.). 773p. 1969. reprint ed. lib. bdg. 20.00 (*0-02-849180-7*) Lubrecht & Cramer.
— The Geology & Natural History of Lower California. 48p. 1975. reprint ed. pap. 10.00 (*0-8466-0158-3*, S-158, Shorey Pubns) Shoreys Bkstore.
Merrill, George P. & Albritton, Claude C., eds. Contributions to a History of American State Geological & Natural History Surveys. LC 77-6529. (History of Geology Ser.). (Illus.). 1978. reprint ed. lib. bdg. 54.95 (*0-405-10450-2*) Ayer.
Merrill, George R., photos by. Reflections: Psychological & Spiritual Images of the Heart. (Illus.). 1990. pap. 6.95 (*0-8091-3127-7*) Paulist Pr.
Merrill, Georgia D. History of Androscoggin County. (Illus.). 893p. 1989. reprint ed. lib. bdg. 94.00 (*0-8328-0561-0*) Higginson Bk Co.
— History of Carroll County, New Hampshire. LC 73-181351. (Illus.). 1103p. 1991. reprint ed. 59.50 (*0-912274-13-1*, 1308) Picton Pr.
Merrill, Georgia D., ed. Allegany County & Its People: A Centennial Memorial History of Allegany County, Also, Histories of the Towns of the County. (Illus.). 951p. 1995. reprint ed. lib. bdg. 95.00 (*0-8328-4707-0*) Higginson Bk Co.
— History of Carroll County, New Hampshire. (Illus.). 987p. 1993. reprint ed. lib. bdg. 99.50 (*0-8328-3170-0*) Higginson Bk Co.
Merrill, Georgia Drew. Carroll County, NH, History & Index. 1103p. 1991. 68.00 (*0-89725-337-X*) Picton Pr.
Merrill, Ginette B., ed. see Howells, Elinor M.
Merrill, Henry A. Alexander Gifford, or, Vi'let's Boy: A Story of Negro Life. LC 72-1821. (Black Heritage Library Collection). 1977. reprint ed. 31.95 (*0-8369-9036-6*) Ayer.
Merrill, Horace S. Bourbon Democracy of the Middle West, 1865-1896. LC 53-8592. (Americana Library Ser.: No. 2). (Illus.). 1969. reprint ed. pap. 10.00 (*0-295-95032-3*, ALP2) U of Wash Pr.
— William Freeman Vilas: Doctrinaire Democrat. (Illus.). 324p. 1991. reprint ed. 24.95 (*0-87020-269-3*) State Hist Soc Wis.
Merrill, Hugh. Esky: The Early Years at Esquire. LC 94-39575. (Illus.). 220p. (C). 1995. 27.95 (*0-8135-2165-3*) Rutgers U Pr.
***Merrill, Hugh.** Red Hot Typewriter: The Life of John D. MacDonald. 272p. 2000. text 24.95 (*0-312-20905-3*) St Martin.
Merrill, Irving R., ed. Bound for Idaho: The 1864 Trail Journal of Julius Merrill. LC 87-38315. (Illus.). 236p. 1989. reprint ed. pap. 13.95 (*0-89301-124-X*) U of Idaho Pr.
Merrill, J. E., ed. The Role of Microglial Cells & Astrocytes in Pathology. (Journal Ser.: Vol. 16, No. 3-4, 1994). (Illus.). 124p. 1994. pap. 50.50 (*3-8055-6086-9*) S Karger.
Merrill, J. L., ed. History of Acworth, New Hampshire: With the Proceedings of the Centennial Anniversary, Genealogical Records & Register of Farms. (Illus.). 306p. 1988. reprint ed. lib. bdg. 36.00 (*0-8328-0039-2*, NH0037) Higginson Bk Co.
Merrill, J. W. Yellow Spring & Huron: A Local History Containing Sketches of All the People, Institutions & Events, from the Earliest Settlement to Date of Publication. (Illus.). 433p. 1997. reprint ed. lib. bdg. 46.50 (*0-8328-6712-8*) Higginson Bk Co.
Merrill, James. Another Language of Flowers. LC 98-41304. 64p. 1998. 25.00 (*0-8076-1448-3*) Braziller.
— The Changing Light at Sandover: A Poem. 1993. pap. 22.00 (*0-679-74736-2*) Knopf.
— The Changing Light at Sandover: Including the whole of the Book of Ephraim, Mirabell's Books of Number, Scripts for the pageant, & A New Coda, The Higher Keys. LC 81-70062. (Illus.). 512p. 1983. 25.00 (*0-689-11282-3*) Atheneum Yung Read.
— The Diblos Notebook. LC 65-12401. (C). 1975. pap. 2.95 (*0-689-70519-0*, 209) Atheneum Yung Read.
— The Diblos Notebook. LC 94-9180. 160p. 1994. reprint ed. pap. 9.95 (*1-56478-064-3*) Dalkey Arch.
— A Different Person: A Memoir. LC 92-37974. 1993. 25.00 (*0-679-42317-6*) Knopf.
— The Inner Room: Poems. LC 88-45265. 112p. 1988. pap. 15.00 (*0-679-72049-9*) Knopf.
— Santorini: Stopping the Leak. (Metacom Limited Edition Ser.: No. 8). 24p. 1982. 37.50 (*0-911381-07-4*) Metacom Pr.
— A Scattering of Salts: Poems. 1995. 20.00 (*0-679-44158-1*) Knopf.
— A Scattering of Salts: Poems. 1996. pap. 14.00 (*0-679-76590-5*) Knopf.
— Selected Poems, 1946-1985. 1993. pap. 20.00 (*0-679-74731-1*) Knopf.
— Self-Portrait in Tyvek Windbreaker. 32p. 1995. pap. 10.95 (*1-873790-79-1*) Dufour.
***Merrill, James & Garney, John.** Voice of the Poet: James Merrill. 1999. pap. 15.95 incl. audio (*0-375-40667-0*) Random AudioBks.
***Merrill, James Ingram, et al.** The Collected Poems of James Merrill. LC 00-40542. 2001. write for info. (*0-375-70941-X*) Knopf.
Merrill, James M. Battle Flags South: Story of the Civil War Navies on Western Waters. LC 71-86652. 334p. 1975. 32.50 (*0-8386-7448-8*) Fairleigh Dickinson.
Merrill, Jan. The Push Cart War. (J). 1996. pap. 5.99 (*0-440-91157-5*) BDD Bks Young Read.
Merrill, Jane. Monday Through Friday: Day Care Alternatives. fac. ed. LC 82-3364. 236p. 1982. reprint ed. pap. 73.20 (*0-7837-8260-8*, 204903800009) Bks Demand.
***Merrill, Jane P. & Sunderland.** Boarding the Ark Today: Featuring Hundreds of Tasty Recipes for the 21st Century. (Illus.). 1999. pap. 14.95 (*0-9621168-4-X*, 30001102) Sunrise Pubs.
Merrill, Jane P. & Sunderland, Karen M. Set for Life: Eat More - Weigh Less - Feel Terrific! 2nd rev. ed. (Illus.). 326p. 1995. pap. 19.95 (*0-9621168-3-1*, 3000427) Sunrise Pubs.
Merrill, Jean. The Girl Who Loved Caterpillars. (Illus.). 32p. (J). (gr. k up). 1997. pap. 5.99 (*0-698-11393-4*, PapStar) Peng Put Young Read.
— The Girl Who Loved Caterpillars. (J). 1997. 11.15 (*0-606-11390-8*, Pub. by Turtleback) Demco.
— The Girl Who Loved Caterpillars: A Twelfth-Century Tale from Japan. LC 91-29054. (Illus.). 32p. (J). (ps up). 1992. 15.95 (*0-399-21871-8*, Philomel) Peng Put Young Read.
— The Pushcart War. 224p. (J). 1978. pap. 4.99 (*0-440-47147-8*, YB BDD) BDD Bks Young Read.
— Pushcart War. (J). 1964. 10.09 (*0-606-01278-8*, Pub. by Turtleback) Demco.
— The Toothpaste Millionaire, 001. LC 73-22055. (Illus.). 96p. (J). (gr. 2-5). 1974. 16.00 (*0-395-18511-4*) HM.
— The Toothpaste Millionaire. 96p. (J). (gr. 4-7). 1993. pap. 5.95 (*0-395-66954-5*) HM.
— The Toothpaste Millionaire. (Illus.). 96p. (J). (gr. 2-5). 1999. pap. 4.95 (*0-395-96063-0*) HM.
— The Toothpaste Millionaire. (J). 1993. 10.05 (*0-606-12545-0*, Pub. by Turtleback) Demco.
***Merrill, Jean.** The Toothpaste Millionaire, Set. unabridged ed. (J). (gr. 5). 1998. 33.20 incl. audio Recorded Bks.
Merrill, Jeffrey C., ed. Mental Health Services in the United States & England: Struggling for Change: Collected Papers Prepared for the Joint United States-England Conference on Mental Health Services Princeton, New Jersey, February 25-28, 1990. LC 91-61190. (Illus.). 160p. (Orig.). 1991. pap. write for info. (*0-942054-03-2*) R W Johnson Found.
Merrill, Jo L. Texas Family Law Trial Guide, 1 vol. 750p. 75.00 (*0-8205-1767-4*) Juris Pubng.
Merrill, Joan. Camcorder Video: Shooting & Editing Techniques. 320p. (C). 1992. pap. text 28.95 (*0-13-110925-1*) P-H.
Merrill, John. D. P. R. Korea: Politics, Economics & Society. (Marxist Regimes Ser.). 220p. 1987. 47.50 (*0-86187-424-2*); pap. 17.50 (*0-86187-425-0*) St Martin.
— Korea: The Peninsular Origins of the War. LC 85-40990. (Illus.). 240p. 1989. 36.50 (*0-87413-300-9*) U Delaware Pr.
Merrill, John C. The Dialectic in Journalism: Toward a Responsible Use of Press Freedom. LC 88-7851. 259p. 1993. pap. text 15.95 (*0-8071-1889-3*) La State U Pr.
— The Imperative of Freedom. 246p. (C). 1990. reprint ed. pap. text 27.25 (*0-932088-44-9*) Freedom Hse.
— The Imperative of Freedom. 2nd ed. 246p. (C). 1990. reprint ed. lib. bdg. 42.00 (*0-932088-45-7*) Freedom Hse.
***Merrill, John C.** Legacy of Wisdom: Great Thinkers & Journalism. LC 99-462344. 200p. 2000. pap. 24.95 (*0-8138-2040-5*) Iowa St U Pr.
Merrill, John C. The Princely Press: Machiavelli on American Journalism. LC 98-10555. 160p. (C). 1998. 52.00 (*0-7618-1035-8*); pap. 29.50 (*0-7618-1036-6*) U Pr of Amer.
Merrill, John C., et al. Modern Mass Media. 2nd ed. 476p. (C). 1997. 75.00 (*0-673-99025-7*) Addson-Wesley Educ.
***Merrill, John C., et al.** Twilight of Press Freedom: The Rise of People's Journalism. 200p. 2000. write for info. (*0-8058-3663-2*); pap. write for info. (*0-8058-3664-0*) L Erlbaum Assocs.
Merrill, John C., jt. auth. see Dennis, Everette E.
Merrill, John F. Outperforming the Market: Everyone's Guide to High-Profit, Low-Risk Investing. LC 98-13950. (Illus.). 280p. 1998. 27.95 (*0-07-041979-5*) McGraw.
Merrill, John N. Arkwright of Cromford. 36p. 1987. 25.00 (*0-907496-35-0*, Pub. by JNM Pubns) St Mut.
— Canal Walks, Vol. 1: Derbyshire & Nottinghamshire. 1986. 25.00 (*0-907496-30-X*, Pub. by JNM Pubns) St Mut.
— Circular Walks in Western Peakland. 48p. 1986. 25.00 (*0-907496-44-X*, Pub. by JNM Pubns) St Mut.
— Customs of the Peak District & Derbyshire. 48p. 1987. 25.00 (*0-907496-34-2*, Pub. by JNM Pubns) St Mut.
— Derbyshire Inns - An A to Z Guide. 120p. 1987. 30.00 (*0-907496-71-7*, Pub. by JNM Pubns) St Mut.
— Derbyshire Punishment. 60p. 1987. 35.00 (*0-907496-33-4*, Pub. by JNM Pubns) St Mut.
— Halls & Castles of the Peak District & Derbyshire. 96p. 1987. 35.00 (*0-907496-72-5*, Pub. by JNM Pubns) St Mut.
— Hike to Be Fit...Strolling with John. 32p. 1987. 45.00 (*0-907496-51-2*, Pub. by JNM Pubns) St Mut.
— The John Merrill Walk Record Book. 72p. 1987. 40.00 (*0-907496-47-4*, Pub. by JNM Pubns) St Mut.
— John Merrill's Dark Peak Challenge - 24 Miles. 32p. 1987. 29.00 (*0-907496-66-0*, Pub. by JNM Pubns) St Mut.
— John Merrill's Lakeland Challenge Walk - 18 Miles. 32p. 1987. 29.00 (*0-907496-50-4*, Pub. by JNM Pubns) St Mut.
— John Merrill's Staffordshire Moorland Challenge Walk - 22 Miles. 32p. 1987. 45.00 (*0-907496-67-9*, Pub. by JNM Pubns) St Mut.
— John Merrill's Yorkshire Dales Challenge Walk - 23 Miles. 32p. 1987. 55.00 (*0-907496-28-8*, Pub. by JNM Pubns) St Mut.
— Long Circular Walks in the Peak District. 64p. 1986. 25.00 (*0-907496-42-3*, Pub. by JNM Pubns) St Mut.
— Lost Industries of Derbyshire. 120p. 1987. 35.00 (*0-907496-32-6*, Pub. by JNM Pubns) St Mut.
— North Yorkshire Moors Challenge Walk - 24 Miles. 32p. 1986. 29.00 (*0-907496-36-9*, Pub. by JNM Pubns) St Mut.

An Asterisk (*) at the beginning of an entry indicates that the title is appearing for the first time.

— The Peak District . . . Something to Remember Her By. (Illus.). 96p. (C). 1989. 50.00 (0-907496-53-9, Pub. by JNM Pubns) St Mut.
— Peak District Challenge Walk - 25 Miles. 32p. 1987. 29.00 (0-907496-43-1, Pub. by JNM Pubns) St Mut.
— Peak District End to End Walks - 23 & 24 Miles. 52p. 1987. 29.00 (0-907496-39-3, Pub. by JNM Pubns) St Mut.
— The River's Way. 36p. 1986. 45.00 (0-907496-41-5, Pub. by JNM Pubns) St Mut.
— Touring the Peak District & Derbyshire by Car. 60p. 1989. 50.00 (0-907496-22-9, Pub. by JNM Pubns) St Mut.
— Turn Right at Death Valley. 1986. 50.00 (0-907496-26-1, Pub. by JNM Pubns) St Mut.
— Turn Right at Land's End. 208p. (C). 1989. 45.00 (0-907496-74-1, Pub. by JNM Pubns) St Mut.
— Winster - A Visitor's Guide. 20p. 1987. 60.00 (0-907496-21-0, Pub. by JNM Pubns) St Mut.
— With Mustard on My Back. 76p. (Orig.). 1985. pap. 30.00 (0-907496-27-X) St Mut.
Merrill, John R. Using Computers in Physics. LC 80-5681. 271p. 1980. pap. text 23.00 (0-8191-1134-1) U Pr of Amer.
Merrill, John V. & Merrill, Caroline E. Sketches of Historic Bennington. (Illus.). 99p. 1997. reprint ed. pap. 18.50 (0-8328-6500-1); reprint ed. lib. bdg. 28.50 (0-8328-6499-4) Higginson Bk Co.
Merrill, Joseph. Cases in Cost Accounting. 128p. (C). 1994. spiral bd. 19.95 (0-8403-9445-4) Kendall-Hunt.
— History of Amesbury, Massachusetts: Including the First Seventeen Years of Salisbury, to the Separation in 1654; & Merrimac, from Its Incorporation in 1876. (Illus.). 451p. 1989. reprint ed. lib. bdg. 45.00 (0-8328-0800-8, MA0002) Higginson Bk Co.
Merrill, K., ed. see Wergeland, Agnes M.
Merrill, Kathleen & Rinder, Lawrence. Sophie Calle: Proofs. LC 93-39485. 1993. pap. 4.95 (0-944722-16-4) Hood Mus Art.
Merrill, Kathryn L., jt. auth. see Christian, Kristy L.
Merrill, Kathy C. Tailgating Without a Hitch: Tailgate Cooking Made Fun. LC 96-70134. 100p. (Orig.). 1996. pap. 12.95 (1-882792-32-7) Proctor Pubns.
Merrill Library, Special Collections Dept. Staff. Name Index to the Library of Congress Collection of Mormon Diaries. LC 75-636249. (Western Text Society Ser.: Vol. 1, No. 2). 395p. reprint ed. pap. 122.50 (0-8357-6231-9, 203460600090) Bks Demand.
Merrill, Linda. An Ideal Country: Paintings by Dwight William Tryon in the Freer Gallery of Art. LC 90-35669. (Illus.). 200p. 1990. pap. 30.00 (0-87451-539-4) U Pr of New Eng.
— The Peacock Room: A Cultural Biography. LC 98-21534. (Illus.). 408p. 1998. 65.00 (0-300-07611-8) Yale U Pr.
Merrill, Linda, ed. With Kindest Regards: The Correspondence of Charles Lang Freer & James McNeill Whistler, 1890-1903. LC 94-48202. (Illus.). 224p. 1995. text 25.95 (1-56098-532-1) Smithsonian.
Merrill, Linda & Ridley, Sarah. The Princess & the Peacocks: Or, the Story of the Room. LC 92-72019. (Illus.). 32p. (J). (gr. k-4). 1993. lib. bdg. 14.89 (1-56282-328-0, Pub. by Hyprn Child) Little.
— The Princess & the Peacocks: or The Story of the Room. LC 92-72019. (Illus.). 32p. (J). (gr. k-4). 1993. 14.95 (1-56282-327-2, Pub. by Hyprn Child) Little.
Merrill, Lisa. When Romeo Was a Woman. LC 98-41314. (Triangulations Ser.). (Illus.). 328p. 1999. text 37.50 (0-472-10799-2, 10799) U of Mich Pr.
***Merrill, Lisa.** When Romeo Was a Woman: Charlotte Cushman & Her Circle of Female Spectators. (Triangulations Ser.). (Illus.). 352p. (C). 2000. pap. 19.95 (0-472-08749-5, 08749) U of Mich Pr.
Merrill, Lisa, jt. auth. see Borisoff, Deborah.
Merrill, Lisa, jt. ed. see Longmire, Linda.
Merrill, Lois J., jt. ed. see Forbes, Malcolm H.
Merrill Lynch Staff. Merril Lynch Guide to Retirement. 1999. pap. 15.95 (0-14-017329-3) Viking Penguin.
— Merrill Lynch GT Financial Plan. 1985. pap. 17.95 (0-671-25460-X) S&S Trade.
Merrill, M. A., jt. auth. see Terman, Lewis M.
Merrill, M. David. Instructional Design Theory. Twitchell, David G., ed. LC 93-45441. 450p. 1994. 59.95 (0-87778-275-X) Educ Tech Pubns.
Merrill, M. David, et al. Teaching Concepts: An Instructional Design Guide. 2nd ed. LC 92-15348. (Illus.). 232p. 1992. 37.95 (0-87778-247-4) Educ Tech Pubns.
— Ticcit. Langdon, Danny G., ed. LC 79-24448. (Instructional Design Library). 144p. 1980. 27.95 (0-87778-160-5) Educ Tech Pubns.
Merrill, Madeline O. & Merrill, Richard. Dolls & Toys at the Essex Institute. LC 76-40405. (E.I. Museum Booklet Ser.). 1976. 5.95 (0-88389-066-6, PEMP190, Essx Institute) Peabody Essex Mus.
Merrill, Margery B. Jessie's Tree: Orlando Remembered. LC 95-41638. (Illus.). 120p. (Orig.). 1996. pap. 16.95 (1-877633-29-1) Luthers.
Merrill, Marlene D. Yellowstone & the Great West: Journals, Letters, & Images from the 1871 Hayden Expedition. LC 99-12068. (Illus.). 1999. 29.95 (0-8032-3148-2) U of Nebr Pr.
Merrill, Marlene D., jt. ed. see Lasser, Carol.
***Merrill, Martha.** Reference Services & Media. LC 99-30029. 130p. 1999. 49.95 (0-7890-0695-2) Haworth Pr.
Merrill, Martha, jt. auth. see McCain, Mary M.
Merrill, Mary L., et al. A Light unto My Path. (Illus.). 185p. 1981. reprint ed. 10.00 (0-686-33180-X) Pathway Pubns.
Merrill, Mary P. Financial Planning in the Bank. Johns, Rebecca B., ed. (Illus.). 380p. 1990. text 55.00 (0-89982-364-5) Am Bankers.
Merrill, Mason, jt. auth. see Merrill, Frances.
Merrill, Milton R. Reed Smoot: Apostle in Politics. LC 89-22621. (Western Experience Ser.). 447p. 1990. reprint ed. pap. 138.60 (0-7837-9254-9, 204999400004) Bks Demand.
Merrill, Nan C. Meditations & Mandalas: Simple Songs for the Spiritual Life. LC 73-163479. (Illus.). 208p. 1999. 19.95 (0-8264-1151-7) Continuum.
Merrill, Nan C. Psalms for Praying: An Invitation to Wholeness. LC 66-21737. 312p. 1997. pap. 16.95 (0-8264-1045-6) Continuum.
***Merrill, Nan C.** Psalms for Praying: An Invitation to Wholeness. 320p. 2000. 22.95 (0-8264-1286-6) Continuum.
Merrill, Nancy O. A Concise History of Glass Represented in the Chrysler Museum Glass Collection. LC 89-63529. (Illus.). 227p. 1989. pap. 35.00 (0-940744-58-9) Chrysler Museum.
— Contemporary Glass: Virginia & North Carolina Artists. (Illus.). 12p. 1979. pap. 1.00 (0-940744-23-6) Chrysler Museum.
Merrill-Oldham, Jan. Conservation & Preservation of Library Materials. LC 82-1875. 65p. 1982. pap. text 3.50 (0-917590-07-4) Univ Conn Lib.
— Preservation Planning Program Resource Guides: Managing a Library Binding Program. 159p. 1993. pap. 15.00 (0-918006-68-6) ARL.
Merrill-Oldham, Jan, et al. Preservation Program Models: A Study Project & Report. 54p. 1991. pap. 45.00 (0-918006-20-1) ARL.
Merrill, Orin S. Mysterious Scott: The Monte Cristo of Death Valley. LC 72-93067. (Illus.). 216p. 1972. reprint ed. pap. 8.50 (0-912494-10-7) Commun Print.
Merrill, Paul F., et al. Computers in Education. 3rd ed. LC 95-22603. 384p. 1995. pap. text 59.00 (0-205-18517-7) Allyn.
— Computers in Education. 3rd ed. (C). 1995. pap., teacher ed. write for info. (0-205-18519-3, H8519-4) Allyn.
Merrill, Peter. Do It Right the Second Time: Benchmarking Best Practices in the Quality Change Process. LC 97-783. (Illus.). 265p. 1997. 27.00 (1-56327-175-3) Productivity Inc.
Merrill, Peter C. German-American Artists in Early Milwaukee: A Biographical Dictionary. 165p. 1997. 22.50 (0-924119-01-2) German-Am Cult Soc.
***Merrill, Peter C.** German-American Urban Culture: Writers & Theaters in Early Milwaukee. (Illus.). 2000. pap. 19.95 (0-924119-03-9) German-Am Cult Soc.
Merrill, Peter C. German Immigrant Artists in America: A Biographical Dictionary. LC 96-39017. 352p. 1996. 49.00 (0-8108-3266-6) Scarecrow.
Merrill, Peter R. Taxation of Financial Services under a Consumption Tax. LC 97-161344. (AEI Studies in Tax Reform). 50p. (Orig.). 1997. pap. 9.95 (0-8447-7072-8, AEI Pr) Am Enterprise.
Merrill, Peter T., jt. auth. see Birnbaum, Henrik.
***Merrill, Philip & Aiono, Uluaipou-o-Malo.** Baltimore. (Images of America Ser.). (Illus.). 128p. 1999. pap. 18.99 (0-7385-0132-8) Arcadia Publng.
Merrill, R. B. Proceedings of the 6th Lunar Science Conference. 1975. 1655.00 (0-08-020566-6, Pub. by Pergamon Repr) Franklin.
Merrill, R. Dale. The Church Business Meeting. LC 68-28075. 1968. pap. 9.00 (0-8170-0409-2) Judson.
Merrill, Richard. Calls from the Granite State: Stories. LC 96-42280. 128p. 1997. 17.95 (1-880284-22-7) J Daniel.
Merrill, Richard, jt. auth. see Merrill, Madeline O.
Merrill, Richard, jt. auth. see Ortiz, Joe.
Merrill, Richard A., jt. auth. see Hutt, Peter B.
Merrill, Richard A., ed. see Hutt, Peter B.
Merrill, Robert. Critical Essays on Kurt Vonnegut. (Critical Essays on American Literature Ser.). 248p. 1989. 48.00 (0-8161-8893-9, G K Hall & Co) Mac Lib Ref.
— Norman Mailer. rev. ed. (Twayne's United States Authors Ser.). 160p. 1992. 32.00 (0-8057-3967-X, Twyne) Mac Lib Ref.
Merrill, Robert, ed. Ethics-Aesthetics. (Post Modern Positions Ser.: Vol. 1). 195p. 1988. pap. text 11.95 (0-944624-01-4) Maisonneuve Pr.
— Ethics-Aesthetics: Post-Modern Positions. LC B155.E74. 195p. 1988. lib. bdg. 22.96 (0-944624-00-6) Maisonneuve Pr.
Merrill, Robert K., ed. Source & Migration Processes & Evaluation Techniques. (Treatise of Petroleum Geology, Handbook of Petroleum Geology Ser.). (Illus.). 213p. 1991. 10.00 (0-89181-600-3, 436) AAPG.
Merrill, Ronald E. The Ideas of Ayn Rand. LC 91-11283. 203p. (C). 1991. 34.95 (0-8126-9157-1); pap. 17.95 (0-8126-9158-X) Open Court.
Merrill, Ronald E. & Sedgwick, Henry D. The New Venture Handbook: Everything You Need to Know to Start & Run Your Own Business. LC 86-47818. 366p. reprint ed. pap. 113.50 (0-7837-4237-1, 204392600012) Bks Demand.
Merrill, Russell G. The Vitamin, Mineral & Herb Guide: A Quick Overview of the Benefits of Vitamins, Minerals & Herbs. Mills, Kathy & Prelozni, Sue, eds. (Illus.). 130p. 1998. pap. 9.95 (0-9661633-0-3) ARM Pubns.
Merrill, Ruth E. Plants Used in Basketry by the California Indians. fac. ed. (University of California Publications in American Archaeology & Ethnology: Vol. 20: 13). 30p. (C). 1923. reprint ed. pap. text 3.44 (1-55567-249-3) Coyote Press.
— Plants Used in Basketry by the California Indians. (Illus.). 1980. reprint ed. pap. 6.95 (0-686-77544-9) Acoma Bks.
Merrill, Samuel. Making Multicandidate Elections More Democratic. LC 87-25856. (Illus.). 150p. 1988. reprint ed. pap. 46.50 (0-608-06487-4, 206678400009) Bks Demand.
— Newspaper Libel: A Handbook for the Press. (Handbook for the Press Ser.). 304p. 1995. reprint ed. 45.00 (0-8377-2476-7, Rothman) W S Hein.
Merrill, Samuel, III & Grofman, Bernard. A Unified Theory of Voting: Directional & Proximity Spatial Models. (Illus.). 240p. 1999. 54.95 (0-521-66222-2); pap. 19.95 (0-521-66549-3) Cambridge U Pr.
Merrill, Sandra D. Donald's Story. LC 96-90046. (Illus.). 260p. 1996. per. 14.95 (0-9649541-4-1) Tebidine.
Merrill, Sarah A., et al. Abeunt Studia in Mores: A Festschrift for Helga Doblin on Philosophies of Education, & Personal Learning in the Humanities & Moral Sciences. XXVII, 364p. (C). 1990. text 38.00 (0-8204-1224-4) P Lang Pubng.
Merrill, Sarah B. Defining Personhood: Toward the Ethics of Quality in Clinical Care. LC 99-173197. (Value Inquiry Book Ser.). x, 222 p. 1998. write for info. (90-420-0571-8) Editions Rodopi.
Merrill, Selah. Ancient Jerusalem. Davis, Moshe, ed. LC 77-70724. (America & the Holy Land Ser.). (Illus.). 1977. reprint ed. lib. bdg. 44.95 (0-405-10267-4) Ayer.
— East of the Jordan. 256p. 1986. 350.00 (1-85077-089-1, Pub. by Darf Pubs Ltd) St Mut.
Merrill, Stephen. The Doctrine of Salvation. 80p. 1980. 3.85 (0-7399-0220-2, 2220) Rod & Staff.
— The Doctrine of Salvation. 128p. 1993. pap. 4.50 (0-7399-0221-0, 2221) Rod & Staff.
Merrill, Stuart. Pastels in Prose. 1975. 250.00 (0-87968-310-4) Gordon Pr.
— Une Voix dans la Foule. 1972. 250.00 (0-8490-1267-8) Gordon Pr.
— The White Tomb: Selected Writings. 1999. 34.95 (1-883689-86-4) Talisman Hse.
Merrill, Susan C., ed. Occupational Therapy Across Cultural Boundaries: Theory, Practice & Professional Development. LC 91-36744. (Occupational Therapy in Health Care Ser.). 116p. 1992. lib. bdg. 39.95 (1-56024-223-X) Haworth Pr.
Merrill, Susan C., intro. Occupational Therapy & Psychosocial Dysfunction. LC 92-30263. (Occupational Therapy in Health Care Ser.: Vol. 8, Nos. 2 & 3). (Illus.). 247p. 1993. pap. text 19.95 (1-56024-331-7); lib. bdg. 39.95 (1-56024-330-9) Haworth Pr.
Merrill, Thomas F. The Poetry of Charles Olson: A Primer. LC 81-40341. 224p. 1982. 32.50 (0-87413-196-0) U Delaware Pr.
— William Perkins 1558-1602, English Puritanist--His Pioneer Works on Casuistry: Discourse on Conscience & the Whole Treatise of Cases of Conscience. xx, 242p. 1966. text 67.50 (90-6004-115-1, Pub. by B De Graaf) Coronet Bks.
Merrill, Tim. Guyana & Belize: Country Studies. 452p. 1993. boxed set 28.00 (0-16-061156-3) USGPO.
Merrill, Tim L. Guyana & Belize Country Studies: Area Handbook. 2nd ed. LC 93-10956. (Department of the Army, Area Handbook Ser.). 1993. 22.00 (0-8444-0778-X) Lib Congress.
Merrill, Tim L. Honduras: A Country Study. 348p. 1995. boxed set 22.00 (0-16-061176-8) USGPO.
— Mexico: A Country Study. 464p. 1997. boxed set 29.00 (0-16-061205-5) USGPO.
Merrill, Tim L., ed. Guyana & Belize: Country Studies. 2nd ed. (Illus.). 408p. (Orig.). (C). 1995. text 50.00 (0-7881-0992-8) DIANE Pub.
***Merrill, Tim L., ed.** Nicaragua: A Country Study. 3rd ed. (Illus.). 300p. 1999. reprint ed. text 50.00 (0-7881-8115-7) DIANE Pub.
Merrill, Tim L. & Miro, Ramon, eds. Mexico: A Country Study. LC 97-13481. (Area Handbook Ser.). 414p. 1997. 25.00 (0-8444-0855-7, F1208, Pub. by Lib Congress) Bernan Associates.
Merrill, Tim L., jt. auth. see Metz, Helen C.
Merrill, Tim L., ed. see Federal Research Division Staff.
Merrill, Timothy. Learning to Fall: A Guide for the Spiritually Clumsy. LC 97-50224. 144p. 1998. pap. 12.99 (0-8272-2126-6) Chalice Pr.
— You Might Be a UCCer If . . . LC 97-44938. 68p. 1998. pap. 5.00 (0-8272-4408-8) Chalice Pr.
Merrill, Timothy F., et al, contrib. by. SourceBook of Weddings. 257p. 1998. text 43.00 (0-930921-12-7, WED) Comm Res OH.
Merrill, Toni. Activities for the Aged & Infirm: A Handbook for the Untrained Worker. (Illus.). 392p. 1979. 61.95 (0-398-01294-6); pap. 45.95 (0-398-06287-0) C C Thomas.
Merrill, W. K. Vacationing with Saddle & Packhorse. 1976. 8.95 (0-668-03486-6, ARCO) Macmillan.
Merrill, Walter M. Against Wind & Tide: A Biography of William Lloyd Garrison. LC 63-10871. (Illus.). 415p. 1963. reprint ed. pap. 128.70 (0-7837-1718-0, 205724700024) Bks Demand.
Merrill, Walter M., ed. see Garrison, William L.
Merrill, William. Code for Classifiers: Principles Governing the Consistent Placing of Books in a System of Classification. 2nd ed. LC Z 0696.M57. 189p. reprint ed. pap. 58.60 (0-608-12426-5, 202425900036) Bks Demand.
Merrill, William L. An Investigation of Ethnographic & Archaeological Specimens of Mescalbeans (Sophora secundiflora) in American Museums. (Technical Reports Ser.: No. 6). (Illus.). 1977. pap. 2.00 (0-932206-15-8) U Mich Mus Anthro.
— Raramuri Souls: Knowledge & Social Process in Northern Mexico. LC 87-62623. (Series in Ethnographic Inquiry). (Illus.). 248p. 1995. pap. text 15.95 (1-56098-653-0) Smithsonian.
Merrill, William L., ed. see Haviland, John B. & Hart, Roger.
Merrill, William M., ed. Beyond Fantasy. 215p. 16.95 (0-9618391-0-4) Inland Pub.
Merrill, Yvonne D. The Social Construction of Western Women's Rhetoric Before 1750. LC 95-46894. (Women's Studies: Vol. 9). 284p. 1996. 89.95 (0-7734-8851-0) E Mellen.
***Merrill, Yvonne Y.** Hands-On Africa: Art Activities for All Ages. (Illus.). 70p. 2000. pap. 20.00 (0-9643177-7-X, Pub. by K-ITS) Publishers Group.
— Hands-On Alaska. (Illus.). 20.00 (0-9643177-0-2) Todd Commns.
Merrill, Yvonne Y. Hands-On Alaska: Art Activities for All Ages. (Illus.). 81p. (J). (gr. k). pap. 20.00 (0-9643177-3-7) K-ITS.
***Merrill, Yvonne Y.** Hands-On Asia: Art Activities for All Ages. (Illus.). 87p. (J). (gr. 5 up). 1999. pap. 20.00 (0-9643177-5-3, Pub. by K-ITS) Publishers Group.
Merrill, Yvonne Y. Hands-On Celebrations: Art Activities for All Ages. (Illus.). 81p. (J). (gr. k). pap. 20.00 (0-9643177-4-5) K-ITS.
— Hands-On Latin America: Art Activities for All Ages. (Illus.). 85p. (J). (gr. 3-7). 1998. pap. text 20.00 (0-9643177-1-0) K-ITS.
— Hands-On Rocky Mountains: Art Activities about Anasazi, American Indians, Settlers, & Trappers. (Illus.). 88p. 1997. pap. text 16.95 (0-9643177-2-9) K-ITS.
Merrill, Yvonne Y. & Merrill, Emily Y. Hands-On Pioneers: Art Activities for All Ages. LC 95-70453. (Illus.). 88p. (Orig.). 1995. pap. 19.95 (1-57345-085-5, Shadow Mount) Deseret Bk.
Merrillees, R. S. Trade & Transcendence in the Bronze Age Levant. (Studies in Mediterranean Archaeology: Vol. XXXIX). (Illus.). 81p. (Orig.). 1974. pap. 36.50 (91-85058-61-0, Pub. by P Astroms) Coronet Bks.
Merrills, J. & Fisher, J. Pharmacy Law & Practice. 384p. 1995. pap. 39.95 (0-632-03232-4, Pub. by Blckwll Scitfc UK) Blackwell Sci.
Merrills, J. G. The Development of International Law by the European Court of Human Rights. 2nd ed. (Melland Schill Monographs in International Law). 272p. 1995. text 32.50 (0-7190-4560-6, Pub. by Manchester Univ Pr) St Martin.
— International Dispute Settlement. enl. ed. 310p. (C). 1991. pap. 85.00 (0-949009-94-6, Pub. by Grotius Pubns Ltd) St Mut.
— International Dispute Settlement. 3rd ed. LC 98-20492. 320p. (C). 1999. text 90.00 (0-521-63003-7); pap. text 39.95 (0-521-63993-X) Cambridge U Pr.
Merrills, J. G. & Fitzmaurice, Gerald, eds. Judge Sir Gerald Fitzmaurice & the Discipline of International Law: Opinions on the International Court of Justice, 1961-1973. LC 97-47052. (Judges Ser.). 356p. 1998. 123.00 (90-411-0538-7) Kluwer Law Intl.
Merrills, J. G., jt. auth. see Robertson, A. H.
Merrills, Jonathan & Fisher, Jonathan. Pharmacy Law & Practice. 2nd ed. LC 97-25805. 1997. pap. 55.00 (0-632-04809-3) Blackwell Sci.
Merrill's Marauders Association. Merrill's Marauders. LC 87-71198. (Illus.). 112p. 1987. 34.95 (0-938021-14-1) Turner Pub KY.
Merrim, Stephanie. Early Modern Women's Writing & Sor Juana Ines de la Cruz. LC 99-6029. 432p. (C). 1999. 47.95 (0-8265-1330-1) Vanderbilt U Pr.
— Early Modern Women's Writing & Sor Juana Ines de la Cruz. LC 99-6029. 432p. 1999. pap. 21.95 (0-8265-1338-7) Vanderbilt U Pr.
— Feminist Perspectives on Sor Juana Ines de La Cruz. 1999. pap. 19.95 (0-8143-2216-6) Wayne St U Pr.
— Logos & the Word. LC 83-47648. (Utah Studies in Literature & Linguistics: Vol. 23). 106p. 1983. pap. 13.70 (0-8204-0003-3) P Lang Pubng.
Merrimack Historical Committee. Merrimack. (Images of America Ser.). 128p. 1996. pap. 16.99 (0-7524-0279-X) Arcadia Publng.
Merriman, Brian. The Midnight Court. 72p. 1990. pap. 14.95 (0-86278-205-8) Dufour.
— Midnight Court. 1987. pap. 16.95 (0-85342-658-9) Dufour.
— The Midnight Court: Cuirt an Mhean-Oiche. 3rd ed. LC 96-111122. 1990. pap. 7.95 (0-85342-244-3) Dufour.
The Midnight Court & the Adventures of a Luckless Fellow. Ussher, Percy A., tr. from GAE. LC 75-28825. (Illus.). 80p. reprint ed. 24.50 (0-404-13817-9) AMS Pr.
Merriman, Brigid O. Searching for Christ: The Spirituality of Dorothy Day. LC 93-23827. (Studies in American Catholicism: Vol. 13). (C). 1994. text 34.50 (0-268-01750-6) U of Notre Dame Pr.
Merriman, Chad. The Avengers. 1998. 17.50 (0-7540-8015-3, Gunsmoke) Chivers N Amer.
***Merriman, Chad.** Mighty Big River. 1999. 19.00 (0-7540-8071-4, Gunsmoke) Chivers N Amer.
Merriman, D., jt. ed. see Davis, J. D.
Merriman, D., jt. ed. see Sears, M.
Merriman, David. The Control of Municipal Budgets: Toward the Effective Design of Tax & Expenditure Limitations. LC 87-2495. 180p. 1987. 55.00 (0-89930-217-3, MTM/, Quorum Bks) Greenwood.
Merriman, Henry S. Young Mistley. Van Thal, Herbert, ed. 1966. 12.95 (0-685-09212-7); pap. 8.95 (0-304-93090-3) Dufour.
Merriman, John. History of Modern Europe. 1997. pap. 32.00 (0-393-98338-2) Norton.
Merriman, John. History of Modern European Vol. 2: Study Guide. 1996. pap., student ed. write for info. (0-393-97017-5) Norton.
Merriman, John, ed. Consciousness & Class Experience in 19th Century Europe. LC 79-16032. 261p. (C). 1979. 39.95 (0-8419-0444-8) Holmes & Meier.
— French Cities in the Nineteenth Century: Class, Power, & Urbanization. LC 81-2520. 256p. 1982. 37.95 (0-8419-0464-2) Holmes & Meier.
Merriman, John M. The History of Modern Europe. (Illus.). 1200p. (C). 1996. pap. text 62.50 (0-393-96885-5) Norton.
— The History of Modern Europe: Test Item File. (C). 1996. pap. text, teacher ed. write for info. (0-393-96887-1) Norton.

M

— The History of Modern Europe Vol. 1: From the Renaissance to the Age of Napoleon. Vol. 1. (Illus.). 650p. (C). 1996. pap. text 37.50 (*0-393-96888-X*, Norton Paperbks) Norton.

— The History of Modern Europe Vol. 1: Study Guide. (C). 1996. pap., student ed. write for info. (*0-393-96886-3*) Norton.

— The History of Modern Europe Vol. 2: From the French Revolution to the Present. Vol. 2. (Illus.). 650p. (C). 1996. pap. text 39.00 (*0-393-96928-2*, Norton Paperbks) Norton.

Merriman, John M., jt. auth. see Van Loon, Hendrik W.

Merriman, Linda M. & Tollafield, David R., eds. Assessment of the Lower Limb. LC 94-44955. 1995. text 56.00 (*0-443-05030-9*) Church.

Merriman, Linda M., jt. auth. see Tollafield, David R.

Merriman, Margarita. A New Look at Sixteenth-Century Counterpoint. LC 81-40924. (Illus.). 230p. (Orig.). 1982. lib. bdg. 56.00 (*0-8191-2391-9*) U Pr of Amer.

Merriman, Marion & Lerude, Warren. American Commander in Spain: Robert Hale Merriman & the Abraham Lincoln Brigade. LC 86-1360. (Wilbur S. Shepperson Series in History & Humanities: No. 21). (Illus.). 272p. 1986. 29.95 (*0-87417-106-7*) U of Nev Pr.

Merriman, Michael W., ed. The Baptismal Mystery & the Catechumenate. 168p. 1990. 19.95 (*0-89869-182-6*) Church Pub Inc.

Merriman, Nick. Beyond the Glass Case: The Past, the Heritage & the Public. 200p. 1992. text 59.00 (*0-7185-1349-5*) St Martin.

***Merriman, Nick.** Early Humans. (Eyewitness Books). (Illus.). (J). (gr. 4-7). 2000. 19.99 (*0-7894-6559-0*) DK Pub Inc.

— Early Humans. (Eyewitness Books). (J). (gr. 4-7). 2000. 15.95 (*0-7894-5806-3*) DK Pub Inc.

Merriman, Nick. Making Early Histories in Museums. LC 98-37092. (Making Histories in Museums Ser.). 1999. 89.50 (*0-7185-0110-1*, Pub. by Leicester U Pr) Cassell & Continuum.

Merriman, Nick, tr. see Bourdieu, Pierre & Darbel, Alain.

Merriman, P. A. & Browitt, C. W., eds. Natural Disasters: Protecting Vulnerable Communities. 600p. 1993. 134.00 (*0-7844-1936-1*) Am Soc Civil Eng.

— Natural Disasters: Protecting Vulnerable Communities: Proceedings of the Conference Held in London, October 13-15, 1993. 600p. 1993. 134.00 (*0-7277-1936-X*) Am Soc Civil Eng.

Merriman, Paul A. & Buck, Richard. Beating the Market with the Enhanced Index Funds. 2000. 24.95 (*0-9672379-0-4*) P A Merriman.

Merriman, Rachel. The Tale of Tobias. LC 95-4812. 32p. (J). (ps-3). 1996. 15.99 (*1-56402-692-2*) Candlewick Pr.

Merriman, Raymond A. Basic Principles of Geocosmic Signatures Related to Financial Market Timing. 63p. 1995. per. 15.95 (*0-930706-22-6*) Seek-It Pubns.

— Evolutionary Astrology: The Journey of the Soul Through States of Consciousness. 255p. 1991. per. 25.00 (*0-930706-18-8*) Seek-It Pubns.

— Merriman on Market Cycles: The Basics. 64p. 1994. per. 25.00 (*0-930706-20-X*) Seek-It Pubns.

— The New Solar Return Book of Prediction. rev. ed. 160p. 1998. pap., per. 15.95 (*0-930706-34-X*) Seek-It Pubns.

— The Sun, the Moon & the Silver Market: Secrets of a Silver Trader. 112p. 1992. per. 75.00 (*0-930706-19-6*) Seek-It Pubns.

Merriman, Raymond A. & Woodsmall, John. F. A. R. Manual: The Financial Astrological Research Program for Market Timing. 60p. 1994. per. 10.00 (*0-930706-21-8*) Seek-It Pubns.

Merriman, Rebecca. Simply Free. Gill, Vicki, ed. 96p. 1998. pap. 6.95 (*1-891825-00-3*) Ridgetop Pubg.

Merriman, Roger B. Life & Letters of Thomas Cromwell, 2 vols. Incl. Vol. 1. Life, Letters of 1535. 1902. Vol. 2. Letters from 1536, Notes, Index. 1902. 1969. 85.00 (*0-19-822305-6*) OUP.

Merriman, Scott A., jt. auth. see Trinkle, Dennis A.

Merriman, William E. & Bowman, Laura L. The Mutual Exclusivity Bias in Children's Word Learning. (Monographs of the Society for Research in Child Development: No. 220). 138p. 1990. pap. text 15.00 (*0-226-52066-8*) U Ch Pr.

Merriman, William E., jt. ed. see Tomasello, Michael.

Merriman, Woodene, ed. see Clark, Jayne & Wingenbach, Gerry.

***Merrin, Jeredith.** Bat Ode. LC 00-27727. (Phoenix Poets Ser.). 2000. pap. 12.00 (*0-226-52058-7*); lib. bdg. 26.00 (*0-226-52057-9*) U Ch Pr.

Merrin, Jeredith. An Enabling Humility: Marianne Moore, Elizabeth Bishop, & the Uses of Tradition. LC 89-70037. 184p. (C). 1990. text 35.00 (*0-8135-1547-5*); pap. text 19.00 (*0-8135-1623-4*) Rutgers U Pr.

— Shift. 96p. 1996. pap. 9.95 (*0-226-52064-1*) U Ch Pr.

— Shift. LC 95-39347. (Phoenix Poets Ser.). 96p. 1996. lib. bdg. 20.00 (*0-226-52063-3*) U Ch Pr.

Merrin, John. Fly Fishing. (Trailside Series Guide). (Illus.). 192p. 1996. pap. 17.95 (*0-393-31476-6*, Norton Paperbks) Norton.

Merrin, Leona M. Standing Ovations . . . Devi Dja: Woman of Java. Baum, Mary, ed. (Illus.). 417p. (Orig.). 1990. pap. 8.95 (*0-9624120-0-7*) Lee & Lee Pub.

Merriner, James L. Mr. Chairman: Power in Dan Rostenkowski's America. LC 98-54247. 320p. 1999. 29.95 (*0-8093-2280-5*) S Ill U Pr.

Merriner, James L. & Senter, Thomas P. Against Long Odds: Citizens Who Challenge Congressional Incumbents. LC 99-15394. 216p. 1999. 35.00 (*0-275-96642-9*) Greenwood.

Merringer, John, tr. see Colletti, Lucio.

Merrins, Matther R., jt. ed. see Brannigan, Gary G.

Merrion, Daid R. Diesel Engine Design for the Nineties: Fortieth Buckendale Lecture: SAE International Congress & Exposition 1994. LC 93-87523. (Special Publications). 160p. 1994. pap. 15.00 (*1-56091-463-7*, SP-1011) Soc Auto Engineers.

Merrion, Margaret, ed. What Works: Instructional Strategies for Music Education. (Illus.). 144p. 1989. pap. 18.25 (*0-940796-61-9*, 1501) MENC.

Merrion, Margaret & Rubin, Janet E. Creative Approaches to Elementary Curriculum. LC 96-45749. 1996. pap. text 25.00 (*0-435-08698-7*) Heinemann.

Merrion, Margaret, jt. auth. see Rubin, Janet.

Merrion, Margaret, jt. auth. see Rubin, Janet E.

Merris, Russell. Combinatorics. LC 95-20724. (Prindle, Weber, & Schmidt Series In Advanced Mathematics). 1995. mass mkt. 105.95 (*0-534-95154-6*) PWS Pubs.

***Merris, Russell.** Graph Theory. 256p. 2000. 79.95 (*0-471-38925-0*) Wiley.

Merris, Russell. Multilinear Algebra, Vol. 8. (Algebra, Logic & Applications Ser.). 340p. 1997. text 59.00 (*90-5699-078-0*) Gordon & Breach.

Merris, William E. & Griswold, David H. A Composition Handbook. 3rd ed. 278p. (YA). (gr. 7-10). 1985. reprint ed. pap. text 14.67 (*1-877653-50-0*) Wayside Pub.

Merrison, Tim. Books. Stefoff, Rebecca, ed. LC 90-13868. (Media Story Ser.). (Illus.). 32p. (J). (gr. 4-8). 1991. lib. bdg. 17.26 (*0-944483-96-8*) Garrett Ed Corp.

— Field Athletics. LC 90-27451. (Olympic Sports Ser.). (Illus.). 48p. (J). (gr. 6). 1991. lib. bdg. 13.95 (*0-89686-665-3*, Crstwood Hse) Silver Burdett Pr.

— Movies. Stefoff, Rebecca, ed. LC 90-3964. (Media Story Ser.). (Illus.). 32p. (J). (gr. 4-8). 1991. lib. bdg. 17.26 (*0-944483-94-1*) Garrett Ed Corp.

Merriss, William E. & Griswold, David H. A Composition Handbook. 3rd ed. 1985. pap. text 8.50 (*0-88334-084-4*) Longman.

— A Composition Handbook. 3rd ed. (J). 1985. teacher ed. 10.84 (*0-8013-0074-6*, 75738); pap. text 17.28 (*0-88334-186-7*, 76152) Longman.

Merrit, A. Dwellers in the Mirage. 1993. reprint ed. lib. bdg. 18.95 (*0-89968-407-6*, Lghtyr Pr) Buccaneer Bks.

— The Moon Pool. 1993. reprint ed. lib. bdg. 18.95 (*0-89968-408-4*, Lghtyr Pr) Buccaneer Bks.

Merrit, Chris. Crossing the Border: The Canada-United States Boundary. (Borderlands Monographs: No. 5). 19-55p. (C). 1991. pap. text 5.00 (*0-614-04707-2*) Canadian-Amer Ctr.

Merrit, Ella A., jt. ed. see Chenery, William L.

***Merrit Frederick's Publishing Staff.** Merrit's Civil Engineers Platinum Edition: The Premier Reference Collection. 1. 2800p. 1999. pap. text 225.00 (*0-07-135536-7*) McGraw.

Merrit, J. I. The Best of Field & Stream. 320p. 1996. per. 14.00 (*0-684-81831-0*, Fireside) S&S Trade Pap.

***Merrit, Natacha.** Natacha Merrit: Digital Diaries. 2000. 29.99 (*3-8228-6398-X*) Taschen Amer.

Merrit, Paul H., jt. ed. see Steiner, Todd D.

Merrit, Robert G., Jr., jt. auth. see Cheatham, Robert W.

Merrit, Walter. History for the League for Industrial Rights. LC 76-120852. (Civil Liberties in American History Ser.). 1970. reprint ed. lib. bdg. 22.50 (*0-306-71961-4*) Da Capo.

Merrithew, Cathy. The Shetland Sheepdog: An Owner's Guide to a Happy, Healthy Pet. (Owner's Guide to a Happy, Healthy Pet Ser.). (Illus.). 160p. 1995. 12.95 (*0-87605-385-1*) Howell Bks.

Merritt. Doppler Color Imaging. 2nd ed. 1999. text. write for info. (*0-443-07511-5*, W B Saunders Co) Harcrt Hlth Sci Grp.

Merritt & McEwen. Mass Spectronomy, Pt. A. (Practical Spectroscopy Ser.: Vol. 3). (Illus.). 304p. 1979. text 180.00 (*0-8247-6749-7*) Dekker.

Merritt, A. Creep, Shadow, Creep! 1991. reprint ed. lib. bdg. 21.95 (*1-56849-033-X*) Buccaneer Bks.

— Dwellers in the Mirage. 288p. 1991. pap. 5.95 (*0-02-022872-4*) Macmillan.

***Merritt, A.** The Moon Pool. (Bison Frontiers of Imagination Ser.). 254p. 2001. pap. 10.95 (*0-8032-8268-0*, Bison Books) U of Nebr Pr.

Merritt, Abraham. The Face in the Abyss. (Illus.). 1991. 30.00 (*0-937986-01-1*); 60.00 (*0-937986-00-3*) D M Grant.

— The Face in the Abyss. 288p. 1992. pap. 9.00 (*0-02-022873-2*) Macmillan.

— The Fox Woman & Other Stories. Reginald, R. & Melville, Douglas, eds. LC 77-84256. (Lost Race & Adult Fantasy Ser.). 1978. reprint ed. lib. bdg. 19.95 (*0-405-11000-6*) Ayer.

— The Metal Monster. (Orig.). 1991. reprint ed. lib. bdg. 21.95 (*1-56849-081-X*) Buccaneer Bks.

— The Moon Pool. 448p. 1993. pap. 4.95 (*0-88184-891-3*) Carroll & Graf.

Merritt, Abraham & Bok, Hannes. The Fox Woman & the Blue Pagoda & the Black Wheel, 2 vols. LC 75-46293. (Supernatural & Occult Fiction Ser.). 1976. reprint ed. lib. bdg. 23.95 (*0-405-08153-7*) Ayer.

Merritt, Alicia. Book of Dollmaking. 1998. 19.99 (*0-7858-0887-6*) Bk Sales Inc.

— Bunny Kit. LC 96-164413. (Illus.). 48p. 1995. 19.95 (*0-312-13447-9*) St Martin.

Merritt, Andrew. Jesus Destroyed the Works of the Devil. Temperance Publishing House Staff, ed. (Illus.). 20p. (Orig.). 1993. pap. 2.95 (*0-9637640-0-4*) A & V Pub.

— The Marriage Enrichment Handbook: Godly Principles for a Successful Marriage. Temperance Publishing House Staff, ed. (Illus.). 197p. (Orig.). 1993. pap. 9.95 (*0-9637640-1-2*) A & V Pub.

— My Faith Is Taking Me Someplace. LC 97-65689. 1997. pap. 11.99 (*0-88419-458-2*) Creation House.

Merritt, Anna J. & Merritt, Richard L., compiled by. Politics, Economics, & Society in the Two Germanies, 1945-75: A Bibliography of English-Language Works. LC 77-26853. 288p. 1978. text 29.95 (*0-252-00684-4*) U of Ill Pr.

Merritt, Anna J. & Merritt, Richard L., eds. Public Opinion in Occupied Germany: The OMGUS Surveys, 1945. LC 74-94397. (Illus.). 350p. reprint ed. pap. 108.50 (*0-608-30423-9*, 202022300016) Bks Demand.

Merritt, Anna J., jt. ed. see Merritt, Richard L.

Merritt, Arthur T. Sixteenth-Century Polyphony: A Basis for the Study of Counterpoint. LC 39-25128. (Illus.). 233p. 1939. reprint ed. pap. 72.30 (*0-7837-6086-8*, 205913200007) Bks Demand.

Merritt, Ashleigh C., jt. auth. see Helmreich, Robert L.

Merritt, Bruce. The Patmos Conspiracy. LC 90-80821. 287p. 1990. pap. 9.95 (*0-916035-38-7*) Evangel Indiana.

Merritt, C. Guide to Defamation Law. 204p. 1995. pap. write for info. (*0-409-31033-6*, MICHIE) LEXIS Pub.

Merritt, Cathlee M. & Bernhard, Keith. Getting Started with the ClarisWorks Database. 64p. Date not set. pap. text 14.95 (*0-9620807-7-2*) AppleWorks.

Merritt, Cathleen & Bernhard, Keith, eds. Getting Started with AppleWorks Spread Sheet. 128p. Date not set. pap. text 19.95 (*0-9620807-8-0*) Natl AppleWrks.

Merritt, Cathleen, jt. auth. see Bernhard, Keith.

Merritt, Cathleen, jt. ed. see Williams, Warren.

Merritt, Charles, Jr. & McEwen, Charles N., eds. Mass Spectrometry. LC 78-24085. (Practical Spectroscopy Ser.: No. 3). (Illus.). 415p. reprint ed. pap. 128.70 (*0-7837-0670-7*, 204100500002) Bks Demand.

Merritt, Christopher R., ed. Doppler Color Imaging, Vol. 27. (Clinics in Diagnostic Ultrasound Ser.: Vol. 27). (Illus.). 282p. 1992. text 149.95 (*0-443-08763-6*) Church.

Merritt Company Staff. California Insurance Code & Ethics Supplement. LC 98-118302. 1992. write for info. (*1-56343-057-6*) Silver Lake.

— OSHA Construction Manual. 1995. ring bd. 397.00 (*1-56343-069-X*) Silver Lake.

— OSHA Reference Manual. 1995. ring bd. 397.00 (*0-930868-03-X*) Silver Lake.

— Risk Management Manual. LC 98-120377. 1995. ring bd. 397.00 (*0-930868-02-1*) Silver Lake.

— Spanish Glossary of Insurance Terms. 2nd ed. 209p. 1994. pap. 9.95 (*0-930868-83-8*) Silver Lake.

***Merritt, Constance.** A Protocol for Touch. Cairns, Scott, ed. LC 99-54652. (Vassar Miller Prize in Poetry Ser.: Vol. 7). 86p. 1999. pap. 12.95 (*1-57441-083-0*, Pub. by UNTX Pr) Tex A&M Univ Pr.

Merritt, D. Building Expert Systems in Prolog. (Compass International Ser.). (Illus.). xv, 358p. 1989. 79.95 (*0-387-97016-9*) Spr-Verlag.

— Building Expert Systems Prolog. 1989. 248.00 (*0-387-97015-0*) Spr-Verlag.

— Merritt. rev. ed. 204p. 1991. reprint ed. pap. 33.50 (*0-8328-2077-6*); reprint ed. lib. bdg. 43.50 (*0-8328-2076-8*) Higginson Bk Co.

Merritt, David H., ed. Aesthetics in the Constructed Environment: Proceedings of the 24th Annual Water Resources Planning & Management Conference. LC 97-71305. 840p. 1997. 68.00 (*0-7844-0228-0*) Am Soc Civil Eng.

Merritt, Davis. Telling the News Is Not Enough: An Editor's Challenge to Journalism. LC 95-3294. (Communication Ser.). 144p. 1995. pap. 17.50 (*0-8058-1983-5*); text 36.00 (*0-8058-1982-7*) L Erlbaum Assocs.

Merritt, Davis B. Public Journalism & Public Life. 2nd ed. LC 97-15069. 216p. 1997. text. write for info. (*0-8058-2707-2*); pap. text. write for info. (*0-8058-2708-0*) L Erlbaum Assocs.

Merritt, Dennis. Reflection. LC 92-71914. (Illus.). 114p. (Orig.). 1993. pap. 9.95 (*1-881674-00-2*) Amziod.

Merritt, Dodie, et al. Primary Education Thinking Skills. (Illus.). 208p. (Orig.). 1997. pap., teacher ed. 18.95 (*1-880505-24-X*, CLC0199) Pieces of Lrning.

Merritt, Donna D. & Culatta, Barbara. Collaborative Language Intervention in the Classroom. LC 97-29146. (School-Age Children Ser.). 300p. 1997. pap. 49.95 (*1-56593-619-1*, 1287) Thomson Learn.

***Merritt, Douglas.** Coxe & Connected Families. fac. ed. 49p. 1999. reprint ed. pap. 10.00 (*0-8328-9926-7*) Higginson Bk Co.

— Coxe & Connected Families. 49p. 1999. reprint ed. 20.00 (*0-8328-9925-9*) Higginson Bk Co.

Merritt, Douglas. Graphic Design for Television. LC 93-17390. (Illus.). 160p. 1993. pap. 56.95 (*0-240-51326-6*, Focal) Buttrwrth-Heinemann.

Merritt Editors. How to Insure Your Car: A Step by Step Guide to Buying the Coverage You Need at Prices You Can Afford. LC 95-79504. (How to Insure Ser.). 265p. 1996. pap. 12.95 (*1-56343-117-3*) Silver Lake.

— How to Insure Your Income: A Step by Step Guide to Buying the Coverage You Need at Prices You Can Afford. LC 97-75913. (How to Insure Ser.). 274p. (Orig.). 1996. pap. 12.95 (*1-56343-148-3*) Silver Lake.

Merritt Editors, ed. How to Insure Your Home. (How to Insure Ser.). 240p. 1996. pap. 12.95 (*1-56343-132-7*) Silver Lake.

Merritt Editors & Silver Lake Editors. How to Insure Your Possessions: A Step by Step Guide to Buying the Coverage You Need at Prices You Can Afford. (How to Insure Ser.). 240p. 1999. pap. 12.95 (*1-56343-156-4*) Silver Lake.

Merritt Editors & Wilson, Reg. How to Insure Your Life. (How to Insure Ser.). 240p. 1996. pap. 12.95 (*1-56343-135-1*) Silver Lake.

Merritt, Emma F. Lady of Summer. 400p. (Orig.). 1995. mass mkt. 5.50 (*0-380-77984-6*, Avon Bks) Morrow Avon.

— Lady of Winter. 384p. (Orig.). 1996. mass mkt. 5.99 (*0-380-77985-4*, Avon Bks) Morrow Avon.

— Lord of Fire. 400p. (Orig.). 1994. mass mkt. 4.50 (*0-380-77288-4*, Avon Bks) Morrow Avon.

— Lord of Thunder. 432p. (Orig.). 1994. mass mkt. 4.99 (*0-380-77290-6*, Avon Bks) Morrow Avon.

— Night Lace. 320p. 1996. mass mkt. 5.50 (*0-8217-5251-0*, Zebra Kensgtn) Kensgtn Pub Corp.

Merritt, Evelyn B. & Hall, Sharlot M. Arizona's First Capital. (Old Capitol Booklets Ser.: Vol. 3). (Illus.). 15p. 1973. pap. 2.00 (*0-927579-16-2*, 6075-13-66) Sharlot Hall Mus Pr.

***Merritt, Frederick S.** Building Design & Construction Handbook. 6th ed. (Illus.). 2000. 115.00 (*0-07-041999-X*) McGraw.

Merritt, Frederick S., et al, eds. Standard Handbook for Civil Engineers. 4th ed. LC 95-11425. (Illus.). 1600p. 1995. 150.00 (*0-07-041597-8*) McGraw.

Merritt, Greg. Celluloid Mavericks: A History of American Independent Filmmaking. LC 99-43696. (Illus.). 464p. 1999. pap. 18.95 (*1-56025-232-4*, Thunders Mouth) Avalon NY.

— Film Production: The Complete Uncensored Guide to Filmmaking. LC 97-25549. (Illus.). 350p. (Orig.). 1997. pap. 24.95 (*0-943728-99-1*) Lone Eagle Pub.

Merritt, H. Wayne. In Word & Deed: Understanding Moral Integrity in Paul. LC 92-42844. (Emory Studies in Early Christianity: Vol. 1). XI, 190p. (C). 1993. text 41.95 (*0-8204-1103-5*) P Lang Pubng.

Merritt, Hardy L., ed. see Boykin, Milton L.

Merritt, Helen. Modern Japanese Woodblock Prints: The Early Years. LC 89-27923. (Illus.). 344p. 1990. text 48.00 (*0-8248-1200-X*) UH Pr.

Merritt, Helen & Yamada, Nanako. Guide to Modern Japanese Woodblock Prints, 1900-1975. LC 91-40576. (Illus.). 384p. 1995. reprint ed. pap. text 55.00 (*0-8248-1732-X*) UH Pr.

***Merritt, Helen & Yamada, Nanako.** Woodblock Kuchi-e Prints: Reflections of Meiji Culture. LC 99-32145. 2000. 45.00 (*0-8248-2073-8*) UH Pr.

Merritt, Herbert E. Hydraulic Control Systems. 368p. 1991. 160.00 (*0-471-59617-5*, Wiley-Interscience) Wiley.

Merritt, Hiram H. & Yahr, Melvin D., eds. H. Houston Merritt: Memorial Volume. fac. ed. LC 82-23106. (Illus.). 231p. pap. 71.70 (*0-7837-7199-1*, 204710000005) Bks Demand.

Merritt, Howard S. To Walk with Nature: The Drawings of Thomas Cole. LC 81-84873. (Illus.). 64p. (Orig.). 1981. pap. 5.00 (*0-943651-11-5*) Hudson Riv.

Merritt, J. F., ed. The Political World of Thomas Wentworth, Earl of Strafford, 1621-1641. 307p. (C). 1996. text 64.95 (*0-521-56041-1*) Cambridge U Pr.

Merritt, Jackie. Accidental Bride. (Desire Ser.). 1995. mass mkt. 3.25 (*0-373-05914-0*, 1-05914-6) Silhouette.

— Amores Rebeldes - Rebel Love. (Silhouette Deseo - Silhouette Desire Ser.: Vol. 139).Tr. of Rebel Love. (ENG & SPA.). 1996. per. 3.50 (*0-373-35139-9*) Harlequin Bks.

— Assignment: Marriage. (Desire Ser.). 1996. per. 3.50 (*0-373-05980-9*, 1-05980-7) Silhouette.

— Big Sky Billionaire: The World's Most Eligible Bechelors. 1998. per. 4.50 (*0-373-65022-1*, 1-65022-5, Mira Bks) Harlequin Bks.

***Merritt, Jackie.** Black Creek Ranch. 2000. mass mkt. 4.50 (*0-373-82248-0*, 1-82248-5) Harlequin Bks.

Merritt, Jackie. For the Love of Sam. 1998. per. 4.25 (*0-373-24180-1*, 1-24180-1) Silhouette.

— Hesitant Husband. (Desire Ser.). 1995. per. 3.25 (*0-373-05935-3*, 1-05935-1) Silhouette.

***Merritt, Jackie.** Hired Bride. 256p. 2000. pap. 4.50 (*0-373-65041-8*, 1-65041-5, Harlequin) Harlequin Bks.

— The Kincaid Bride. Vol. 1321. 2000. mass mkt. 4.50 (*0-373-24321-9*) Harlequin Bks.

Merritt, Jackie. The Lady & the Lumberjack. (Desire Ser.: No. 683). 1991. per. 2.79 (*0-373-05683-4*) Harlequin Bks.

— Letter to a Lonesome Cowboy: Montana Mavericks: Return to Whitehorn. (Special Edition Ser.: No. 1154). 1998. per. 4.25 (*0-373-24154-2*, 1-24154-6) Silhouette.

— A Man & a Million. 1995. per. 3.75 (*0-373-09988-6*, 1-09988-6) Silhouette.

— Mi Mujer Ideal. (Deseo Ser.: No. 217).Tr. of My Ideal Woman. (SPA.). 1997. per. 3.50 (*0-373-35217-4*, 1-35217-8) Harlequin Bks.

— Mision: Matrimonio. (SPA.). 1996. per. 3.50 (*0-373-35161-5*, 1-35161-8) Harlequin Bks.

— Montana Christmas. 1996. per. 3.50 (*0-373-76039-6*, 1-76039-6) Silhouette.

— Montana Fever. (Desire Ser.: No. 1014). 1996. per. 3.50 (*0-373-76014-0*, 1-76014-9) Silhouette.

— Montana Lovers. 1996. per. 3.99 (*0-373-24065-1*, 1-24065-4) Silhouette.

— A Montana Man. (Desire Ser.). 1998. per. 3.75 (*0-373-76159-7*, 1-76159-2) Silhouette.

— Montana Passion. (Special Edition Ser.). 1996. per. 3.99 (*0-373-24051-1*, 1-24051-4) Silhouette.

— Montana Sky. (Desire Ser.). 1993. per. 2.99 (*0-373-05790-3*, 5-05790-6) Silhouette.

— Mystery Lady. (Desire Ser.). 1994. per. 2.99 (*0-373-05849-7*, 5-05849-0) Silhouette.

— Nevada Drifter. (Desire Ser.). 1994. per. 2.99 (*0-373-05866-7*, 1-05866-8) Silhouette.

— The Rancher Takes a Wife. (Montana Mavericks Ser.). 1994. per. 3.99 (*0-373-50169-2*, 1-50169-1) Harlequin Bks.

— Rebel Love. 1995. per. 3.25 (*0-373-05965-5*, 1-05965-8) Silhouette.

— The Secret Daughter: Christmas Arch/The Benning Legacy. (Special Edition Ser.: No. 1218). 1998. per. 4.25 (*0-373-24218-2*, 1-24218-9) Silhouette.

An Asterisk (*) at the beginning of an entry indicates that the title is appearing for the first time.

— Una Sonrisa Irresistible: (An Irresistible Smile) (Deseo Ser.: No. 131).Tr. of Irresistible Smile. (SPA.). 1998. per. 3.50 (*0-373-35261-1*, 1-35261-6) Harlequin Bks.
— Tennessee Waltz. (Desire Ser.). 1993. per. 2.89 (*0-373-05774-1*, 5-05774-0) Silhouette.
***Merritt, Jackie.** Tough to Tame: Man of the Month. (Desire Ser.: Bk. 1297). 2000. per. 3.99 (*0-373-76297-6*, 1-76297-0) Silhouette.
Merritt, Jackie. The Widow & the Rodeo Man. (Montana Mavericks Ser.). 1994. per. 3.99 (*0-373-50166-8*, 1-50166-7) Silhouette.
***Merritt, Jackie.** A Willing Wife, No. 4. (Fortunes of Texas Ser.). 1999. per. 4.50 (*0-373-65033-7*) Silhouette.
Merritt, Jackie. Wind River Ranch. (Desire Ser.: No. 1085). 1997. per. 3.50 (*0-373-76085-X*, 1-76085-9) Silhouette.
— Wrangler's Lady. (Desire Ser.). 1994. per. 2.99 (*0-373-05841-1*, 5-05841-7) Silhouette.
— Wyoming Territory. (Historical Ser.: No. 714). 1992. per. 3.99 (*0-373-28714-3*, 1-28714-3) Harlequin Bks.
***Merritt, James.** Friends, Foes & Fools: Wisdom from Proverbs for Fathers. (Illus.). 1999. pap. 10.99 (*0-8054-2081-9*) Broadman.
— Trout Dreams: A Gallery of Fly-Fishing Profiles. LC 00-35843. (Illus.). 240p. 2000. 24.95 (*1-58667-011-5*, Pub. by Derrydale Pr) Natl Bk Netwk.
Merritt, Jeffrey. Practical ISDN. 1997. pap. text 24.95 (*1-55828-520-2*, MIS Pr) IDG Bks.
Merritt, Jim. Passing the Torch: Preserving Indiana's Heritage. 1997. pap. 20.00 (*1-57860-008-1*) Guild Pr IN.
Merritt, John. The Making of the Australian Workers Union, 1886-1911. (Illus.), 340p. 1986. 38.00 (*0-19-554667-9*) OUP.
Merritt, John, jt. ed. see Curthoys, Ann.
Merritt, John E., ed. see World Congress on Reading Staff.
Merritt, Jon. Empowering Children: A Parent's Guide to Building-in Success & Self-Esteem. 161p. 1990. pap. 8.95 (*1-880360-01-2*) Parent Res.
— A Parent's Primer: Seven Short Lessons in Child-Raising. 100p. 1991. pap. 8.95 (*0-685-50035-7*) Parent Res.
Merritt, Jon, jt. auth. see Bloch, Douglas.
Merritt, Joseph F. Guide to the Mammals of Pennsylvania. LC 87-40157. (Illus.). 448p. 1987. pap. 19.95 (*0-8229-5393-5*) U of Pittsburgh Pr.
Merritt, Joseph F., ed. Winter Ecology of Small Mammals. LC 84-72213. (Special Publications: No. 10). (Illus.). 390p. 1984. 47.50 (*0-935868-10-0*) Carnegie Mus.
Merritt, Judy. Mountain Rising: A Novel. LC 95-33615. 250p. (Orig.). 1996. pap. write for info. (*1-887786-09-0*) Sky & Sage Bks.
Merritt, Justine. Journey: Poems of a Peacemaker. LC 93-10737. 192p. 1993. 22.00 (*0-932727-68-9*) Hope Pub Hse.
Merritt, King, jt. auth. see Crawley, Sharon J.
Merritt, LeRoy C., et al. Reviews in Library Book Selection. LC 58-62836. (Wayne State University Studies: Humanities: No. 3). 205p. reprint ed. pap. 63.60 (*0-7837-3821-8*, 204364100010) Bks Demand.
Merritt, Lyn. 3D Modeling from Photos: Build 3D Models Fast Using Desktop Photogrammetry. LC 97-90875. (Illus.). 363p. (Orig.). 1997. pap. 59.00 (*0-9659471-0-6*) ThreeD Construct.
Merritt, Margaret. Drawing Plants, Trees & Flowers. (Understand How to Draw Ser.: No. 3). (Illus.). 32p. pap. 4.95 (*0-85532-571-2*, 571-2, Pub. by Srch Pr) A Schwartz & Co.
Merritt, Marion. Riding Sidesaddle on the Seesaw. 1997. pap. 12.95 (*0-916897-30-3*) Andrew Mtn Pr.
— Uphill Both Ways. LC 85-13349. (Illus.). 100p. 1985. pap. 6.95 (*0-916897-05-2*) Andrew Mtn Pr.
Merritt, Mark W. Employment Guide for the Military, Intelligence & Special Operations Communities. 1997. 30.00 (*0-938609-10-6*) Graduate Group.
Merritt, Martha R. Nosmo King. LC 96-83022. (Illus.). 35p. (YA). (gr. 3-12). 1996. pap. 6.95 (*0-9650661-0-X*) Beekman Hill Pub.
Merritt, Michael L., ed. see ERDA Techinal Information Center Staff.
Merritt, Michael L., ed. see ERDA Technical Information Center Staff.
Merritt, Nancy. Teen & Young Adult Suicide. rev. ed. 2000. pap. 0.50 (*0-89230-237-2*) Do It Now.
Merritt, Nancy-Jo. Understanding Immigration Law: How to Enter, Work & Live in the United States. 96p. 1992. pap. 9.95 (*0-9630356-2-2*) Makai.
Merritt, Onera. An American Child. (American Autobiography Ser.). 192p. 1995. reprint ed. lib. bdg. 69.00 (*0-7812-8592-5*) Rprt Serv.
Merritt, Patty & Wells, Rosie. Rosie Wells Enterprises' Official Price Guide for Precious Moments Applause Dolls. 88p. (Orig.). 1995. pap. 9.95 (*1-886812-04-7*) R Wells.
Merritt Publishing Staff. Glossary of Insurance Terms. 1996. pap. 14.95 (*1-56343-154-8*) Silver Lake.
Merritt Publishing Staff & Silver Lake Editors. Get Your Claim Paid: Making Sure the Insurance You've Bought Works When You Suffer a Loss. 340p. 2000. pap. 19.95 (*1-56343-168-8*) Silver Lake.
Merritt, R., et al. Atlas of the Dragonflies of Britain & Ireland. LC 96-164120. (Illus.). 169p. 1996. pap. 35.00 (*0-11-701561-X*, HM1561X, Pub. by Statnry Office) Balogh.
Merritt, Ray, jt. ed. see Barth, Miles.
Merritt, Raymond W. & Ennico, Clifford R., eds. Corporate Counseling, Vols. 1 & 2. 1323p. 1988. 90.00 (*0-942954-20-3*) NYS Bar.
— New York Securities Law: Practice & Policy. 244p. 1990. pap. 32.00 (*0-614-26659-9*, 4165) NYS Bar.
— Transfer of Wealth. 165p. 1993. pap. 32.00 (*0-614-26658-0*, 4230) NYS Bar.
Merritt, Raymond W., ed. see Abramowitz, Elkan & Williamson, Allan P.
Merritt, Raymond W., ed. see Douglass, Catherine J. & Lieberman, Ellen.
Merritt, Raymond W., ed. see Manno, Christopher E. & Gartner, Steven J.
Merritt, Raymond W., ed. see New York State Bar Association Staff.
Merritt, Richard. Aquatic Insects of North America. 1995. 73.95 (*0-7872-3241-6*) Kendall-Hunt.
Merritt, Richard & Cummins, Kenneth. Aquatic Insects of North America. 880p. (C). 1995. pap. text, per. 78.95 (*0-7872-1761-1*) Kendall-Hunt.
Merritt, Richard F., jt. auth. see Miller, Susann C.
Merritt, Richard L. Foreign Policy Analysis. 176p. 1985. reprint ed. lib. bdg. 39.50 (*0-8191-5145-9*) U Pr of Amer.
Merritt, Richard L., ed. Foreign Policy. (C). 1974. pap. 15.00 (*0-918592-09-7*) Pol Studies.
— Foreign Policy Analysis. 176p. 1975. boxed set 34.95 (*0-669-00251-8*) Transaction Pubs.
— Foreign Policy Analysis. LC 75-27808. (Policy Studies Organization Ser.: No. 9). (Illus.). 175p. reprint ed. pap. 54.30 (*0-8357-8880-6*, 203358100086) Bks Demand.
Merritt, Richard L. & Hanson, Elizabeth C. Science, Politics, & International Conferences: A Functional Analysis of the Moscow Political Science Congress. LC 88-18322. (GSIS Monograph in World Affairs). 1989. lib. bdg. 20.00 (*1-55587-134-8*) L Rienner.
Merritt, Richard L. & Merritt, Anna J., eds. Innovation in the Public Sector. LC 84-17839. (Advances in Political Science Ser.: No. 4). 312p. 1985. reprint ed. pap. 96.80 (*0-608-01153-3*, 205945300001) Bks Demand.
— Living with the Wall: West Berlin, 1961-1985. LC 85-10234. (Duke Press Policy Studies). (Illus.). xiv, 242p. 1985. 37.00 (*0-8223-0657-3*) Duke.
Merritt, Richard L. & Pyszka, Gloria L. Students Political Scientists Handbook. 192p. 1975. pap. 13.95 (*0-87073-251-X*) Schenkman Bks Inc.
Merritt, Richard L., et al. Democracy Imposed: U. S. Occupation Policy & the German Public, 1945-1949. LC 95-4263. 1995. 50.00 (*0-300-06037-8*) Yale U Pr.
— International Event-Data Developments. 248p. 1993. text 47.50 (*0-472-10427-6*, 10427) U of Mich Pr.
Merritt, Richard L., jt. compiled by see Merritt, Anna J.
Merritt, Richard L., jt. ed. see Merritt, Anna J.
Merritt, Richard W., jt. ed. see Kim, Ke Chung.
Merritt, Robert. Early Music & the Aesthetics of Ezra Pound: Hush of Older Song. LC 93-32242. 176p. 1993. 79.95 (*0-7734-9371-9*) E Mellen.
— To the Death. 320p. 1990. mass mkt. 4.50 (*0-380-70904-X*, Avon Bks) Morrow Avon.
Merritt, Robert C. Extractive Metallurgy of Uranium. LC 71-157076. (Illus.). 576p. 1979. reprint ed. 12.00 (*0-918062-10-1*) Colo Sch Mines.
Merritt, Robert E. The Merritt's Tradition. large type ed. (Illus.). 200p. 1995. 45.00 (*0-9652821-0-4*) R Merritt.
Merritt, Robert E. & Corey, Arthur. Christian Science & Liberty. LC 70-132847. 1970. pap. 8.95 (*0-87516-060-3*) DeVorss.
***Merritt, Robert E., et al.** California Subdivision Map Act Practice: March 2000 Update. LC 87-70121. 200p. 2000. 53.00 (*0-7626-0415-8*, RE-32354) Cont Ed Bar-CA.
Merritt, Robert E., et al. Understanding Development Regulations. 248p. (Orig.). 1994. pap. 26.00 (*0-923956-19-0*) Solano Pr.
Merritt, Robert E., jt. auth. see Curtin, Daniel J., Jr.
Merritt, Robert E., ed. see Sutter, John A.
Merritt, Russell & Kaufman, J. B. Walt in Wonderland: The Silent Films of Walt Disney. 176p. (C). 1994. 39.95 (*0-8018-4907-1*) Johns Hopkins.
***Merritt, Russell & Kaufman, J. B.** Walt in Wonderland: The Silent Films of Walt Disney. (Illus.). 2000. pap. text 19.95 (*0-8018-6429-1*) Johns Hopkins.
Merritt, Stephanie. Mind, Music & Imagery: Unlocking the Treasures of Your Mind. LC 95-43811. 256p. (Orig.). 1996. pap. 13.95 (*0-944031-62-5*) Aslan Pub.
***Merritt, Steve.** All about Self-Directed IRA Investing. 2000. pap. 12.95 (*1-887063-09-9*) Halyard Pr.
Merritt, Steve. All about the New IRA: How to Cash in on the New Tax Law Changes. 128p. 1998. pap. 12.95 (*1-887063-07-2*) Halyard Pr.
Merritt, Steve. How to Build Wealth with Your 401(K) Everything You Need to Know to Become More Than a Millionaire. 2nd ed. LC 97-197254. 1997. pap. text 19.95 (*1-887063-04-8*) Halyard Pr.
Merritt, Steve. How to Build Wealth with Your 401(K) Everything You Need to Know to Become More Than a Millionaire Over the Course of Your Working Lifetime. 224p. 1996. pap. text 19.00 (*1-887063-00-5*) Halyard Pr.
— Investor's Resource Guide: Hard-to-Find Information at Your Fingertips. 160p. 1998. pap. 12.95 (*1-887063-06-4*) Halyard Pr.
***Merritt, Steve.** What to Do with Your Retirement Account When You Leave the Company. 2000. pap. 15.95 (*1-887063-08-0*) Halyard Pr.
Merritt, Susan, jt. auth. see Davis, Jack.
Merritt, Susan E. Her Story II: Women from Canada's Past. (Illus.). vii, 184p. (YA). 1998. pap. write for info. (*1-55125-022-5*) Vanwell Publ.
***Merritt, Susan E.** Her Story II: Women from Canada's Past. (Illus.). 192p. (YA). 1999. pap. write for info. (*1-55125-037-3*) Vanwell Publ.
— Sleep Little Centipede, Sleep. (Illus.). 58p. (J). 1999. pap. write for info. (*1-55125-021-7*) Vanwell Publ.
— The Stone Orchard. 168p. (J). 1999. pap. write for info. (*1-55125-030-6*) Vanwell Publ.
Merritt, Susan E. Women from Canada's Past. (Her Story Ser.). (Illus.). 172p. (YA). (gr. 5 up). 1993. pap. 12.95 (*1-55125-000-4*) ACCESS Pubs Network.
***Merritt, Susan E. & Cienik, Andy.** When Pigs Go Bad. (Illus.). 58p. (J). 1999. pap. write for info. (*1-55125-027-6*) Vanwell Publ.
Merritt, Susan H. Pinter in Play: Critical Strategies & the Plays of Harold Pinter. LC 90-31163. 367p. (C). 1995. text 49.95 (*0-8223-1040-6*) Duke.
— Pinter in Play: Critical Strategies & the Plays of Harold Pinter. LC 90-31163. 376p. 1995. pap. text 17.95 (*0-8223-1674-9*) Duke.
Merritt, Susan M. & Stix, Allen. Migrating from Pascal to C++ LC 96-11796. (Undergraduate Texts in Computer Science Ser.). 565p. 1996. 54.95 (*0-387-94730-2*) Spr-Verlag.
Merritt, Sydney. Guided Meditations for Teens: Living Through the Church Year. LC 97-33508. 216p. (Orig.). (YA). (gr. 9-12). 1997. pap. 19.95 (*0-89390-402-3*) Resource Pubns.
Merritt, Sydney A. Guided Meditations for Adult Catechumens. LC 98-52094. 1999. 19.95 (*0-89390-452-X*) Resource Pubns.
— Guided Meditations for Children: 40 Scripts & Activities Based on Sunday Lectionary. LC 94-48152. 184p. (J). (gr. 1-4). 1995. pap. 19.95 (*0-89390-336-1*) Resource Pubns.
Merritt, T. Allen, jt. auth. see Miller, Herbert C.
Merritt, Tillman, ed. see Gabrieli, Andrea.
***Merritt, Timothy.** The Christian's Manual: A Treatise of Christian Perfection with Directions to Obtaining. 80p. 1998. pap. 5.99 (*0-88019-382-4*) Schmul Pub Co.
Merritt, Valerie J. California Probate Workflow Manual: March 1994 Update. Tom, Janette, ed. LC 79-53359. 184p. 1994. 42.00 (*0-88124-719-7*, ES-31564) Cont Ed Bar-CA.
— California Probate Workflow Manual Vols. 1 & 2: March 1993 Update. rev. ed. Tom, Janette, ed. LC 79-53359. 268p. 1993. ring bd. 40.00 (*0-88124-600-X*, ES-31563) Cont Ed Bar-CA.
— California Probate Workflow Manual Vols. 1 & 2: October 1991 Update. rev. ed. Dworin, Christopher D., ed. LC 79-53359. 275p. 1991. ring bd. 45.00 (*0-88124-437-6*, ES-31562) Cont Ed Bar-CA.
Merritt, W. W., Sr. A History of Montgomery County, Iowa from the Earliest Days to 1906. (Illus.). 343p. 1994. reprint ed. lib. bdg. 35.00 (*0-8328-3818-7*) Higginson Bk Co.
Merritt, W. W. A History of the County of Montgomery (Iowa) (Illus.). 344p. 1993. reprint ed. lib. bdg. 39.50 (*0-8328-3445-9*) Higginson Bk Co.
Merritt, Wesley. Three Indian Campaigns. 24p. reprint ed. pap. 10.00 (*0-8466-4037-6*, I37) Shoreys Bkstore.
Merritts. Enviroment Geology & Earth Matters. 1998. 59.00 (*0-7167-3304-8*) W H Freeman.
— Environmental Geology. 1997. write for info. (*0-7167-3213-0*); 48.00 (*0-7167-3214-9*) W H Freeman.
— Environmental Geology. 1998. teacher ed. 24.00 (*0-7167-2762-5*); pap. 24.00 (*0-7167-3240-8*) W H Freeman.
***Merritts & Dewet, Andrew.** Whole Earth: Earth System Science & Global Change. 2001. pap. text. write for info. (*0-7167-3740-X*) W H Freeman.
Merriweather, Curtis A. How to Put on the Whole Armor of God. 38p. (Orig.). 1995. pap. 7.00 (*0-9623431-3-7*) Faith Christ Ch.
— How to Take Charge of Your Future. 56p. (Orig.). (C). 1994. pap. 5.95 (*0-9623431-6-1*) Faith Christ Ch.
— Life Is Your Choice. 18p. (Orig.). (C). 1989. pap. 1.00 (*0-9623431-0-2*) Faith Christ Ch.
— Taking the Shield of Faith. 45p. (Orig.). 1994. pap. 3.95 (*0-9623431-5-3*) Faith Christ Ch.
— Why Satan Wants to Steal God's Word from You. 29p. (Orig.). 1993. pap. 2.95 (*0-9623431-4-5*) Faith Christ Ch.
Merrix, Robert P. & Ranson, Nicholas, eds. Ideological Approaches to Shakespeare: The Practice of Theory. LC 92-29122. 312p. 1992. text 99.95 (*0-88946-079-5*) E Mellen.
Merron, Keith. Riding the Wave: Designing Your Organization's Architecture for Enduring Success. 448p. 1994. 34.95 (*0-442-01803-7*, VNR) Wiley.
Merron, Keith. Riding the Wave: Designing Your Organization's Architecture for Enduring Success. (Industrial Engineering Ser.). 448p. 1994. 34.95 (*0-471-28617-6*, VNR) Wiley.
Merrow, Bill, jt. auth. see Gamble, Jesse.
Merrow, O. E. Merrow: Henry Merrow of Reading, Massachusetts & His Descendants named Marrow, Marrow & Merry. (Illus.). 659p. 1991. reprint ed. pap. 98.00 (*0-8328-1934-4*); reprint ed. lib. bdg. 108.00 (*0-8328-1933-6*) Higginson Bk Co.
Merrullo, Victor D. Arboriculture & the Law. (C). 1992. text 45.00 (*1-881956-01-6*) Int Soc Arboricult.
Merry. 300 Best Aviation Web Sites. LC 99-29312. 340p. 1999. pap. 24.95 (*0-07-134835-2*) McGraw.
Merry, Barbara. The Splicing Handbook. (Illus.). 112p. 1988. pap. text 10.95 (*0-87742-952-9*) Intl Marine.
***Merry, Barbara.** Splicing Handbook: Techniques for Modern & Traditional Ropes. 2nd ed. LC 99-57607. 150p. 2000. pap. 13.95 (*0-07-135438-7*) McGraw.
Merry, Barbara & Darwin, John. The Splicing Handbook: Techniques for Modern & Traditional Ropes. 112p. 1988. pap. 10.95 (*0-07-156371-7*) McGraw.
Merry, Barbara L. Menippean Elements in Paul Scarron's Roman Comique. LC 91-16266. (American University Studies: Romance Languages & Literature: Ser. II, Vol. 172). 132p. (C). 1992. text 35.95 (*0-8204-1578-2*) P Lang Pubng.
Merry, Bruce, tr. see D'Aragona, Tullia.
Merry, Eleanor C. Goethe's Approach to Colour. 45p. 1996. reprint ed. spiral bd. 10.00 (*0-7873-0608-8*) Hlth Research.
Merry, Eleanor C., tr. from NOR. The Dream Song of Olaf Asteson. 2nd ed. 48p. 1988. pap. 12.95 (*0-85440-706-5*, Pub. by R Steiner Pr) Anthroposophic.
Merry, Henry J. The Constitutional System: The Group Character of the Elected Institutions. LC 86-15162. 225p. 1986. 55.00 (*0-275-92185-9*, C2185, Praeger Pubs) Greenwood.
— Five-Branch Government: The Full Measure of Constitutional Checks & Balances. LC 79-22499. 286p. reprint ed. pap. 88.70 (*0-608-30983-4*, 202277500029) Bks Demand.
Merry, John A. 200 Best Aviation Web Sites: And 100 More Worth Bookmarking. LC 98-10909. 240p. 1998. pap. 19.95 (*0-07-001646-1*) McGraw.
Merry, John F., ed. History of Delaware County & Its People, 2 vols., Set. (Illus.). 901p. 1995. reprint ed. lib. bdg. 95.00 (*0-8328-4671-6*) Higginson Bk Co.
Merry, Karen, jt. ed. see Feeney, Mary.
Merry, Malcolm. Hong Kong Tenancy Law: An Introduction to the Law of Landlord & Tenant. 2nd ed. 430p. 1989. boxed set 138.00 (*0-409-99576-2*, MICHIE) LEXIS Pub.
— Hong Kong Tenancy Law: An Introduction to the Law of Landlord & Tenant. 2nd rev. ed. xxii, 430p. 1989. pap. write for info. (*0-409-99580-0*, MICHIE) LEXIS Pub.
Merry, Roger. Successful Child, Successful Teachering. LC 97-17212. (Enriching the Primary Curriculum - Child, Teacher, Context Ser.). 160p. 1997. pap. 23.95 (*0-335-19742-6*); pap. 79.00 (*0-335-19743-4*) OpUniv Pr.
Merry, Sally E. Getting Justice & Getting Even: Legal Consciousness among Working-Class Americans. (Language & Legal Discourse Ser.). (Illus.). 238p. 1990. pap. text 24.00 (*0-226-52069-2*) U Ch Pr.
— Getting Justice & Getting Even: Legal Consciousness among Working-Class Americans. (Language & Legal Discourse Ser.). (Illus.). 238p. 1997. lib. bdg. 48.00 (*0-226-52068-4*) U Ch Pr.
— Urban Danger: Life in a Neighborhood of Strangers. 278p. 1986. pap. 18.95 (*0-87722-425-0*) Temple U Pr.
Merry, Sally E. & Milner, Neal, eds. The Possibility of Popular Justice: A Case Study of Community Mediation in the United States. LC 93-23588. (Law, Meaning, & Violence Ser.). 504p. (Orig.). (C). 1993. text 64.50 (*0-472-10426-8*, 10426) U of Mich Pr.
— The Possibility of Popular Justice: A Case Study of Community Mediation in the United States. LC 93-24588. 504p. (Orig.). (C). 1995. pap. text 25.95 (*0-472-08344-9*, 08344) U of Mich Pr.
***Merry, Sally Engle.** Colonizing Hawaii: The Cultural Power of Law. LC 99-30345. (Illus.). 364p. 2000. 59.50 (*0-691-00931-7*, Pub. by Princeton U Pr) Cal Prin Full Svc.
— Colonizing Hawaii: The Cultural Power of Law. LC 99-30345. 364p. 2000. pap. 18.95 (*0-691-00932-5*, Pub. by Princeton U Pr) Cal Prin Full Svc.
Merry, T. Invitation to Person Centered Psychology. 166p. 1994. 49.95 (*1-56593-510-1*, 1178) Singular Publishing.
Merry, Uri. Coping with Uncertainty: Insights from the New Sciences of Chaos, Self-Organization. LC 94-16996. 224p. 1995. 59.95 (*0-275-94910-9*, Praeger Pubs) Greenwood.
— Coping with Uncertainty: Insights from the New Sciences of Chaos, Self-Organization & Complexity. LC 94-16996. 224p. 1995. pap. 19.95 (*0-275-95152-9*) Greenwood.
Merry, Uri & Brown, George. The Neurotic Behavior of Organizations. (Gestalt Institute of Cleveland Press Book Ser.). 300p. 1987. pap. 24.95 (*0-88163-250-3*) Analytic Pr.
Merry, Uri, jt. auth. see Levy, Amir.
Merry, Wayne. Official Wilderness First-Aid Guide. (Illus.). 416p. 1994. pap. 14.95 (*0-7710-8253-3*) McCland & Stewart.
— Official Wilderness First-Aid Guide. 390p. 1997. pap. 14.95 (*0-7710-8250-9*) McCland & Stewart.
Merryfield, Merry M. International Trade & Manpower Development: Policy Changes & Economic Realities in Nigeria. (Graduate Student Term Papers Co-Winner). 1983. pap. text 2.00 (*0-941934-44-6*) Indiana Africa.
— Making Connections Between Multicultural & Global Education Teacher Educators & Teacher Education. 1996. 25.00 (*0-89333-134-1*) AACTE.
Merryfield, Merry M., ed. Lessons from Africa. (Illus.). 99p. 1989. pap. text 12.00 (*0-941339-07-6*) Ind U SSDC.
Merryfield, Merry M. & Remy, Richard C., eds. Teaching about International Conflict & Peace. LC 94-13643. (SUNY Series, Theory, Research, & Practice in Social Education). 374p. (C). 1995. pap. text 21.95 (*0-7914-2374-3*) State U NY Pr.
— Teaching about International Conflict & Peace. LC 94-13643. (SUNY Series, Theory, Research, & Practice in Social Education). 374p. (C). 1995. text 64.50 (*0-7914-2373-5*) State U NY Pr.
Merryfield, Merry M., et al. Preparing Teachers to Teach Global Perspectives: A Handbook for Teacher Educators. LC 97-4905. (Illus.). 288p. 1996. 69.95 (*0-8039-6518-4*); pap. 32.95 (*0-8039-6519-2*) Corwin Pr.
Merrylees, Peter. Effective Use of Health Care Information: A Review of Recent Research. LC 97-228546. (British Library Research). 262 p. 1997. write for info. (*1-85739-230-2*) Bowker-Saur.
Merryman, et al. Civil Law Tradition: Europe, Latin America, East Asia: Cases & Materials, 1994 Edition. 1994. text 62.00 (*1-55834-180-3*, 12310-10, MICHIE) LEXIS Pub.
Merryman, Gregory K. Regulation of Corporate Political Activity. 3rd ed. (Corporate Practice Series Portfolio: No. 16). 1988. 92.00 (*0-87179-998-7*) BNA.

M

An Asterisk (*) at the beginning of an entry indicates that the title is appearing for the first time.

Merryman, J. H. The United States Life-Saving Service, 1880. Jones, William R., ed. LC 97-34121. (Illus.). 1997. pap. 6.95 (*0-89646-071-1*) Vistabooks.

Merryman, John H. The Civil Law Tradition: An Introduction to the Legal Systems of Western Europe & Latin America. 2nd ed. LC 84-50153. 184p. 1985. 29.50 (*0-8047-1247-6*); pap. 11.95 (*0-8047-1248-4*) Stanford U Pr.

— The Loneliness of the Comparative Lawyer & Other Essays in Foreign & Comparative Law. LC 99-27523. 1999. 168.00 (*90-411-1215-4*) Kluwer Law Intl.

Merryman, John H. & Clark, David S. Comparative Law: Western European & Latin American Legal Systems. 2nd ed. (Contemporary Legal Education Ser.). 1993. 25.00 (*0-685-48590-0*, MICHIE) LEXIS Pub.

Merryman, John H. & Elsen, Albert E. Law, Ethics, & the Visual Arts. 3rd ed. LC 98-21891. 1998. 270.00 (*90-411-0697-9*) Kluwer Law Intl.

— Law, Ethics, & the Visual Arts, 2 vols., Set. 2nd ed. LC 79-65005. (Illus.). 960p. 1987. text 109.95 (*0-8122-8052-0*) U of Pa Pr.

Merryman, Louis M. Fragrance of a New Dawn. 1991. pap. 4.95 (*1-55673-287-2*, 9120) CSS OH.

— Halloween Alternatives. 128p. 1996. pap. write for info. (*1-883893-51-8*) WinePress Pub.

Merryman, Marjorie. The Music Theory Handbook. LC 96-76368. 272p. (C). 1996. pap. text 18.00 (*0-15-502662-3*, Pub. by Harcourt Coll Pubs) Harcourt.

Merryman, Molly. Clipped Wings: The Rise & Fall of the Women Airforce Service Pilots (WASPs) LC 97-21217. 1997. text 30.00 (*0-8147-5567-4*) NYU Pr.

Merryman-Waterman, Bev B. Channels of Mercy. (Illus.). 64p. (Orig.). 1996. pap. 9.95 (*0-9653232-0-X*) Leslie-J Pr.

Merryweather, F. Somner. Bibliomania in the Middle Ages. 1977. lib. bdg. 59.95 (*0-8490-1503-0*) Gordon Pr.

— Bibliomania in the Middle Ages. rev. ed. Copinger, H. B., ed. LC 72-83748. 288p. 1972. reprint ed. 24.95 (*0-405-08787-X*, Pub. by Blom Pubns) Ayer.

Merryweather, James. York Music, 1304-1896. 1999. pap. 21.00 (*1-85072-034-7*, Pub. by W Sessions) St Mut.

Merryweather, Marilyn W. The Only Home They Ever Knew: Summit County & the Children's Home. (Illus.). 112p. 1991. text. write for info. (*0-9621895-5-3*) Summit Cty Hist Soc.

Mers, Gilbert. Working the Waterfront: The Ups & Downs of a Rebel Longshoreman. LC 88-2168. (Illus.). 308p. 1988. 19.95 (*0-292-76022-1*) U of Tex Pr.

Mers, Joyce La, see La Mers, Joyce.

Mersand, Joseph E. American Drama, 1930-1940: Essays on Playwrights & Plays. LC 75-157968. (Essay Index Reprint Ser.). 1977. reprint ed. 18.95 (*0-8369-2245-X*) Ayer.

— Traditions in American Literature. (BCL1-PS American Literature Ser.). 247p. 1993. reprint ed. lib. bdg. 79.00 (*0-7812-6566-5*) Rprt Serv.

Mersand, Joseph E., ed. Three Comedies of American Family Life. Incl. Three Comedies of American Family Life. 320p. 1988. pap. 5.50 (*0-671-66430-1*); 320p. 1981. Set pap. 3.95 (*0-671-42886-1*, WSP) PB.

Mersand, Joseph E., et al. Spelling the Easy Way. 3rd ed. 352p. 1996. pap. 12.95 (*0-8120-9143-4*) Barron.

Merse, Anna Szinyel. The Hungarian National Gallery. 160p. 1999. 25.00 (*963-13-3929-7*, Pub. by Corvina Bks) St Mut.

Merser, Cheryl. The Garden Design Book. Garden Design Staff, ed. 304p. 1997. 55.00 (*0-06-039207-X*, ReganBks) HarperTrade.

Merser, Russell M., jt. auth. see Dudgeon, Dan E.

Mersereau, John, Jr. Russian Romantic Fiction. 270p. 1983. pap. 13.95 (*0-88233-740-8*) Ardis Pubs.

Mersereau, Larry. Shoestring Marketing: Marketing 101 for Small Business, Indispensable Marketing Tools... 1996. pap. text 14.95 (*1-882180-57-7*) Griffin CA.

Mersereau, Russell M. & Smith, Mark J. Digital Filtering: A Computer Laboratory Textbook. 240p. (C). 1993. pap. 52.95 (*0-471-51694-5*) Wiley.

Mersereau, Russell M., jt. auth. see Smith, Mark J.

Mersereau, Shirley W., jt. auth. see Coerper, Lois H.

Merseth, ed. Case Studies in Teacher Education. (C). 1998. text. write for info. (*0-321-01150-3*) Addison-Wesley Educ.

Merseth, Katherine K. Caes in Educational Administration. LC 96-16823. 320p. (C). 1997. pap. text 36.93 (*0-673-99003-6*) Addson-Wesley Educ.

Mersey, Charles C. Chief Ministers of England, Nine Hundred Twenty to Seventeen Twenty. LC 67-30222. (Essay Index Reprint Ser.). 1977. 26.95 (*0-8369-0703-5*) Ayer.

— Chief Ministers of England, Nine Hundred Twenty to Seventeen Twenty. LC 67-30222. (Essay Index Reprint Ser.). reprint ed. lib. bdg. 26.00 (*0-8290-0845-4*) Irvington.

— Prime Ministers of Britain. LC 74-86772. (Essay Index Reprint Ser.). 1977. 36.95 (*0-8369-1422-8*) Ayer.

Mersey, Clive B. Viceroys & Governors-General of India, 1757-1947. LC 70-160925. (Biography Index Reprint Ser.). 1977. reprint ed. 21.95 (*0-8369-8088-3*) Ayer.

Mershart, Ronald V., compiled by. Pioneers of Superior, Wisconsin. (Orig.). 1996. pap. 24.95 (*0-915709-24-4*) Pk Geneal Bk.

Mershart, Ronald V., ed. They Remembered Superior. (Illus.). 56p. 1998. pap. 7.95 (*0-9664281-0-2*) Douglas Cty Hist.

Mershchikova, I., tr. see Naumova, T. N.

Mershon Center Staff. Economics & National Security. 1989. pap. text. write for info. (*0-201-26289-4*) Addison-Wesley.

Mershon, Jerry L. Juvenile Justice, the Adjudicatory Process. LC 82-154236. (Juvenile Justice Textbook Ser.: No. 501). 73p. 1982. 7.50 (*0-318-00253-1*) Natl Juv & Family Ct Judges.

Mershon, Sherie & Schlossman, Steven L. Foxholes & Color Lines: Desegregating the U. S. Armed Forces. LC 97-27031. (Rand Bks.). (Illus.). 408p. 1998. 34.95 (*0-8018-5690-6*) Johns Hopkins.

Merskey, Harold, ed. The Analysis of Hysteria. 2nd ed. 504p. 1996. text 52.50 (*0-88048-647-3*) Am Psychiatric.

Merskey, Harold, jt. auth. see Vaery, Henning.

Merskey, Harold, ed. see International Assn. for the Study of Pain, Task Fo.

Merskey, Peter B. The Grim Reapers: Fighting Squadron 10 in WW II. (Illus.). 131p. 1986. pap. 11.95 (*0-912173-09-2*) Champlin Museum.

Mersky, Peter. F-8 Crusader Fighter Units of the Vietnam War. (Illus.). 96p. 1998. pap. 16.95 (*1-85532-724-4*, Pub. by Ospry) Motorbooks Intl.

— RF-8 Crusader Units over Cuba & Vietnam. (Combat Aircraft Ser.: No. 12). (Illus.). 96p. 1999. pap. 17.95 (*1-85532-782-1*, Pub. by Ospry) Motorbooks Intl.

Mersky, Peter B. Israeli Fighter Aces. (Illus.). 144p. 1997. 24.95 (*1-883809-15-0*) Specialty Pr.

— Time of the Aces: Marine Pilots in the Solomons, 1942-1944. (Illus.). 41p. 1996. reprint ed. pap. text 20.00 (*0-7881-3521-X*) DIANE Pub.

Mersky, Ray M., jt. auth. see Jacobstein, J. Myron.

***Mersky, Roy M.** A Documentary History of the Legal Aspects of Abortion in the United States. LC 99-52896. (A Documentary History of the Legal Aspects of Abortion in the United States: No. 4). xi, 413p. 1999. 95.00 (*0-8377-0871-0*, 323270) W S Hein.

— Documentary History of the Legal Aspects of Abortion in the United States: Griswold V. Connecticut. No. 5. 2000. write for info. (*0-8377-0872-9*) W S Hein.

Mersky, Roy M. Louis Dembitz Brandeis, 1856-1941: A Bibliography. (Yale Law Library Publications: No. 15). ii, 44p. 1987. reprint ed. pap. 15.00 (*0-8377-2437-6*, Rothman) W S Hein.

Mersky, Roy M., et al, eds. Index to Periodical Articles Related to Law, 1979-1998. (Retrospective Cumulative Issues Ser.: No. 4). 1999. pap. 900.00 (*0-87802-055-1*) Glanville.

Mersky, Roy M. & Dunn, Donald J., eds. Index to Periodical Articles Related to Law: Five-Year Cumulative Index: 1989-1993. 1994. 130.00 (*0-87802-068-3*) Glanville.

— Index to Periodical Articles Related to Law: Five-Year Cumulative Index: 1994-1998. 470p. 1999. 130.00 (*0-87802-069-1*) Glanville.

Mersky, Roy M. & Hartman, Gary. Landmark Legal Cases in American History. (Library in a Book Ser.). 320p. 1998. 50.00 (*0-8160-2452-9*) Facts on File.

Mersky, Roy M. & Hartman, Gary R., compiled by. Documentary History of the Legal Aspects of Abortion in the United States: Roe vs. Wade, 3 vols., Set. LC 93-1977. No. 2. 1993. 175.00 (*0-8377-0866-4*, Rothman) W S Hein.

— Documentary History of the Legal Aspects of Abortion in the United States: Webster vs. Reproductive Health Services, 8 vols. No. 1. 1990. 525.00 (*0-8377-0863-X*, Rothman) W S Hein.

Mersky, Roy M. & Jacobstein, J. Myron, eds. Index to Periodical Articles Related to Law, Thirty Year Cumulation, Vols. 1-30: 1958-1988, 4 vols., Set. 1989. 400.00 (*0-87802-063-2*) Glanville.

— Supreme Court of the United States Hearings & Reports On Successful & Unsuccessful Nominations of Supreme Court Justices By The Senate Judiciary Committee: 1916-1990 & 1983 Supplement, 11 vols. LC 75-13630. (Illus.). 1977. fiche 205.00 (*1-57588-269-8*, 301031) W S Hein.

— Supreme Court of the United States Hearings & Reports on Successful & Unsuccessful Nominations of Supreme Court Justices by the Senate Judiciary Committee: 1916-1994 & 1983 Supplement, 10 vols. in 38. LC 75-13630. (Illus.). 1977. lib. bdg. 3495.00 (*0-930342-48-8*, 301030) W S Hein.

Mersky, Roy M. & Leiter, Richard A., compiled by. Spirit of Law Librarianship: A Reader. LC 91-19305. ix, 264p. 1991. 37.50 (*0-8377-0865-6*, Rothman) W S Hein.

Mersky, Roy M. & Young, Suzanne F., compiled by. Documentary History of the Legal Aspects of Abortion in the United States: Planned Parenthood vs. Casey, 6 vols. LC 95-22961. No. 3. 1996. 325.00 (*0-8377-0867-2*, Rothman) W S Hein.

Mersky, Roy M., jt. auth. see Blaustein, Albert P.

Mersky, Roy M., jt. auth. see Jacobstein, J. Myron.

Mersky, Roy M., jt. auth. see Middleton, Kent.

Mersky, Roy M., ed. see Carson, Hampton L.

Mersky, Roy M., ed. see Cogswell, Robert E.

Mersky, Roy M., ed. see DeHart, William C.

Mersky, Roy M., ed. see Field, Moses.

Mersky, Roy M., ed. see Foulkes, William D.

Mersky, Roy M., ed. see Gasaway, Laura N., et al.

Mersky, Roy M., ed. see Goodenow, J. M.

Mersky, Roy M., ed. see Kennedy, John P.

Mersky, Roy M., ed. see Maine, Henry S.

Mersky, Roy M., ed. see Parker, Edward G.

Mersky, Roy M., ed. see Pollock, Frederick.

Mersky, Roy M., ed. see Pulling, Alexander.

Mersky, Roy M., ed. see Thorpe, William G.

Mersky, Roy M., ed. see Tiedeman, Christopher G.

Mersman, Hans, ed. see Mozart, Wolfgang Amadeus.

Mersmann, A. Crystallization Technology Handbook. (Illus.). 704p. 1994. text 215.00 (*0-8247-9233-5*) Dekker.

Mersmann, A. B. & Schroll, S. E., eds. Fundamentals of Adsorption. LC 90-84745. 1007p. 1991. 50.00 (*0-8169-0540-1*) Am Inst Chem Eng.

Mersmann, Alfons B. & Scholl, Stephan E. Fundamentals of Adsorption. LC 90-84745. 500p. 1991. 50.00 (*0-939204-43-6*) Eng Found.

Mersmann, H., jt. auth. see Stanton, H.

***Merson, et al.** Introduction to International Health. 2000. 65.00 (*0-8342-1228-5*) Aspen Pub.

Merson, A. Britain Fascism & the Popular Front. (C). 1985. pap. 19.50 (*0-85315-642-5*, Pub. by Lawrence & Wishart) NYU Pr.

— Communist Resistance in Nazi Germany. (C). 1985. pap. 22.50 (*0-85315-602-6*, Pub. by Lawrence & Wishart) NYU Pr.

***Merson, Jay.** Private Tuition. 1999. pap. 9.99 (*1-897809-58-1*) Silver Moon.

Merson, Stephen & Baldwin, David. Psychiatric Emergencies, No. 11. (Oxford Handbooks in Emergency Medicine Ser.: Vol. 11). 134p. 1995. text 69.50 (*0-19-262478-4*); pap. text 35.00 (*0-19-262477-6*) OUP.

Merte, H. J., ed. Genesis of Glaucoma. (Documenta Ophthalmologica Proceedings Ser.: No. 16). 1978. text 171.00 (*90-6193-156-8*) Kluwer Academic.

— Societas Ergophthalmologica Internationalis: 5th Symposium, Bordeux 1974. 6th Symposium, Hamburg 1976. 7th Symposium, Nagoya 1978. (Problems of Industrial Medicine in Ophthalmology Ser.: Vol. 5-7). (Illus.). xx, 760p. 1982. pap. 216.75 (*3-8055-3003-X*) S Karger.

Mertel, Kenneth D. Year of the Horse: Vietnam-1st Air Cavalry in the Highlands, 1965-1967. LC 96-69810. (Illus.). 384p. 1997. 35.00 (*0-7643-0138-1*) Schiffer.

Mertelsmann, R., ed. Lymphohaematopoietic Growth Factors in Cancer Therapy II. LC 92-49430. 1993. 123.00 (*0-387-55953-1*) Spr-Verlag.

Mertelsmann, R. & Veronesi, U., eds. Lymphohaematopoietic Growth Factors in Cancer Therapy. (EOS Monographs). (Illus.). vii, 90p. 1990. 62.95 (*0-387-53086-X*) Spr-Verlag.

Mertelsmann, R., jt. auth. see Gillis, S.

Mertelsmann, R., jt. auth. see Levitt.

Mertelsmann, R., jt. ed. see Bartsch, Hans H.

Mertelsmann, R., jt. ed. see Hiddemann, W.

Mertelsmann, Roland & Herrmann, Friedhelm, eds. Hematopoietic Growth Factors in Clinical Applications. 2nd expanded rev. ed. LC 94-22881. (Illus.). 424p. 1994. text 180.00 (*0-8247-9268-8*) Dekker.

Merten, Cyndie, jt. auth. see Apple, Daniel K.

Merten, Otto-Wilhelm, et al, eds. New Developments & New Applications in Animal Cell Technology. LC 98-2862. 1998. text 345.00 (*0-7923-5016-2*) Kluwer Academic.

Mertens. We the People. 2nd ed. 1999. pap. text, student ed. 12.00 (*0-393-97321-2*) Norton.

Mertens, Charles De, see De Mertens, Charles.

Mertens, Donna M. Research Methods in Education & Psychology: Integrating Diversity with Quantitative & Qualitative Approaches. LC 97-4890. 444p. 1997. 49.00 (*0-8039-5827-7*); pap. 23.00 (*0-8039-5828-5*) Sage.

Mertens, Donna M., ed. Creative Ideas for Teaching Evaluation. (C). 1989. lib. bdg. 140.50 (*0-7923-9021-0*) Kluwer Academic.

Mertens, Donna M. & McLaughlin, John. Research Methods in Special Education. (Applied Social Research Methods Ser.: Vol. 37). 168p. 1994. 42.00 (*0-8039-4808-5*); pap. 18.95 (*0-8039-4809-3*) Sage.

Mertens, Eberhard. Die Groben Deutschen Filme: Ausgewählte Kinoprogramme 1930-1945. (GER., Illus.). 290p. 1995. write for info. (*3-487-08367-1*) G Olms Pubs.

Mertens, Eberhard, ed. Die Groben Deutschen Unterhaltungsfilme 1930-1940. (Filmprogramme Ser.). (GER., Illus.). 160p. 1979. write for info. (*3-487-08202-0*) G Olms Pubs.

— Die Groben Preubenfilme: Produktion 1921-1932. (Filmprogramme Ser.: Vol. 5). (GER., Illus.). 130p. 1981. write for info. (*3-487-08229-2*) G Olms Pubs.

— Die Groben Preubenfilme: Produktion 1932-1945. (Filmprogramme Ser.: Vol. 6). (GER., Illus.). 130p. 1981. write for info. (*3-487-08230-6*) G Olms Pubs.

— Hans Albers in Seinen Groben Erfolgsfilmen. (Filmprogramme Ser.: Vol. 4). (GER., Illus.). 160p. 1979. write for info. (*3-487-08205-5*) G Olms Pubs.

— Die Schonsten Hollywoodfilme. (Filmprogramme Ser.: Vol. 7). (GER., Illus.). 130p. 1982. write for info. (*3-487-08240-3*) G Olms Pubs.

Mertens, F. G., jt. auth. see Spatschek, K. H.

Mertens, Fredrik, ed. see Mitelman, Felix.

Mertens, G. Cell Surface-Associated Heparan Sulfate Proteoglycans: Binding Properties & Subcellular Expression. No. 93. 106p. (Orig.). 1994. pap. 42.50 (*90-6186-637-5*, Pub. by Leuven Univ) Coronet Bks.

Mertens, Herman-Emiel. Not the Cross, but the Crucified. (Louvain Theological & Pastoral Monographs). 1993. pap. text 25.00 (*0-8028-0571-X*) Eerdmans.

Mertens, Jean-Francois, ed. Game-Theoretic Methods in General Equilibrium Analysis: Proceedings of the NATO Advanced Study Institute on Long Island, NY, U. S. A., July 1-12, 1991. (NATO ASI Series D: Behavioural & Social Sciences). 272p. (C). 1994. lib. bdg. 166.50 (*0-7923-3011-0*) Kluwer Academic.

Mertens, John. The Fall of America. LC 98-139835. v, 408p. 1998. pap. 18.00 (*1-891211-05-6*) Gazelle Books.

— The Other Half of the Truth about the Holocaust & Other Things. LC 99-164312. iv, 29p. 1997. pap. 12.00 (*1-891211-02-1*) Gazelle Books.

Mertens, Lothar. Davidstern unter Hammer und Zirkel. (Haskala Ser.: Bd. 18). 492p. 1997. write for info. (*3-487-10332-X*) G Olms Pubs.

Mertens, Nicholas. A General Introduction to Western Philosophy. LC 97-35186. 237p. 1998. lib. bdg. 55.00 (*1-56072-492-7*) Nova Sci Pubs.

Mertens, R. P., jt. auth. see Van OverStraeten, R. J.

Mertens, Randy. Purr Diem: A Daily Calendar of Cats. (Illus.). 366p. 1994. spiral bd. 7.50 (*1-882835-26-3*) STA-Kris.

Mertens, Robert G. The Theory of the Time-Energy Relationship: A Scientific Treatise. rev. ed. Weber, Diana, ed. LC 95-81487. (Illus.). 350p. 1995. pap. 13.20 (*1-889398-01-2*); lib. bdg. 26.53 (*1-889398-00-4*) Gamma Publng.

— The Theory of the Time-Energy Relationship: A Scientific Treatise. 2nd ed. Weber, Diana, ed. LC 96-77368. (Illus.). 350p. 1996. pap. 16.50 (*1-889398-03-9*); lib. bdg. 29.50 (*1-889398-02-0*) Gamma Publng.

Mertens, Thomas R. & Hammersmith, Robert L. Genetics: Laboratory Investigations. 11th ed. LC 97-315. 275p. 1997. pap. text 52.00 (*0-13-575986-2*) P-H.

Mertens, William J., jt. auth. see Crump, David.

Mertens, Wim. American Minimal Music. (Illus.). 128p. reprint ed. pap. 12.50 (*0-912483-15-6*) Pro-Am Music.

Mertes, Jack, ed. see Versace, Dick.

Mertes, James D., jt. auth. see Kaiser, Ronald A.

Mertes, John E., jt. auth. see Wright, John S.

Mertes, Michael, et al, eds. In Search of Germany. LC 95-45854. 319p. 1996. pap. text 24.95 (*1-56000-880-6*) Transaction Pubs.

Mertig, Angela G., jt. ed. see Dunlap, Riley E.

Mertin, Josef. Early Music: Approaches to Performance Practice. Levarie, Siegmund, tr. from GER. (Music Ser.).Tr. of Alte Musik: Wege zur Auffuhrungspraxis. 300p. 1986. lib. bdg. 29.50 (*0-306-76286-2*) Da Capo.

Mertin, Roger. Roger Mertin, Records 1976-1978. Desmarais, ed. LC 78-17219. 46p. 1978. pap. 3.95 (*0-932026-02-8*) Columbia College Chi.

***Mertins.** Signal Analysis. LC 98-49131. 330p. 1999. 100.00 (*0-471-98626-7*) Wiley.

Mertins, J. W., jt. auth. see Coppel, H. C.

***Mertins, K. & Jochem, R.** Quality-Oriented Design of Business Processes LC 99-29500. 1999. write for info. (*0-7923-8484-9*) Kluwer Academic.

***Mertins, K., et al.** Global Protection Management: IFIP WG5.7 International Conference on Advances in Production Management Systems, September 6-10, 1999, Berlin, Germany. LC 99-27700. 1999. write for info. (*0-7923-8605-1*) Kluwer Academic.

Mertins, Lisa. Ginkgo & Moon. LC 94-40960. (Illus.). 32p. (J). (ps-3). 1996. 14.95 (*0-395-73576-9*) HM.

Mertlich, Robert. Goldfish: A Complete Introduction. 128p. 1988. pap. 8.95 (*0-86622-350-9*, CO-019S) TFH Pubns.

Mertner, Edgar, jt. auth. see Camden, William.

Merton. Silver Burdett Countries: China. 1989. 15.96 (*0-382-09253-8*) Silver Burdett Pr.

Merton, Andrew, compiled by. In Your Own Voice: A Writer's Reader. LC 94-9460. 512p. (C). 1997. pap. text 45.00 (*0-06-501763-3*) Addson-Wesley Educ.

Merton, Don & Butler, David E. The Black Robin: Saving the World's Most Endangered Bird. (Illus.). 308p. 1993. pap. text 49.95 (*0-19-558260-8*) OUP.

Merton, Marshall. A Complete Introduction to Rabbits. (Illus.). 128p. 1987. pap. 5.95 (*0-86622-281-2*, CO022S) TFH Pubns.

Merton, Reginald. Magicians, Seers, & Mystics: Apollonius of Tyana; The Unknown Master of the Albigeneses; Christian Rosenkreutz & the Rosicrucians; Mystery of the Templars; Nicholas Flamen & the Philosophers Stone; Saint-German the Immortal; Madame Blavatsky & the Theosophists. Magre, Maurice, tr. 287p. 1994. reprint ed. pap. 19.95 (*1-56459-432-7*) Kessinger Pub.

Merton, Robert. Social Research & the Practicing Professions. 1982. pap. 19.75 (*0-685-05493-4*); text 30.00 (*0-89011-569-9*) Abt Bks.

Merton, Robert C. Continuous-Time Finance. (Macroeconomics & Finance Ser.). (C). 1992. pap. 37.95 (*0-631-18508-9*) Blackwell Pubs.

Merton, Robert K. The Focused Interview: A Manual of Problems & Procedures. 2nd ed. 1990. pap. 15.95 (*0-02-920986-2*) Free Pr.

— Mass Persuasion: The Social Psychology of a War Bond Drive. LC 77-136076. 210p. 1971. reprint ed. lib. bdg. 49.75 (*0-8371-5226-7*, MEMP, Greenwood Pr) Greenwood.

— On Social Structure & Science. Sztompka, Piotr, ed. 400p. 1996. pap. text 19.95 (*0-226-52071-4*) U Ch Pr.

— On Social Structure & Science. Sztompka, Piotr, ed. 400p. 1996. lib. bdg. 55.00 (*0-226-52070-6*) U Ch Pr.

— On the Shoulders of Giants: A Shandean Postscript. LC 65-12859. (Illus.). 302p. 1985. 14.95 (*0-15-169962-3*) Harcourt.

— On the Shoulders of Giants: The Post-Italianate Edition. LC 92-43871. (Illus.). xxxii, 348p. (C). 1993. pap. text 18.00 (*0-226-52086-2*) U Ch Pr.

— On Theoretical Sociology: Five Essays, Old & New. 1967. pap. 16.95 (*0-02-921150-6*) Free Pr.

— Puritanism, Pietism, & Science. (Reprint Series in Social Sciences). (C). 1993. reprint ed. pap. text 2.30 (*0-8290-2664-9*, S-192) Irvington.

— The Role-Set: Problems in Sociological Theory. (Reprint Series in Sociology). (C). 1993. reprint ed. pap. text 5.00 (*0-8290-3696-2*, S-193) Irvington.

— Science, Technology & Society in Seventeenth Century England. LC 79-82308. 1970. 40.00 (*0-86527-178-X*) Fertig.

— Social Research & the Practicing Professions. 300p. 1984. reprint ed. lib. bdg. 59.00 (*0-8191-4111-9*) U Pr of Amer.

— Social Structure & Anomie. (Reprint Series in Social Sciences). (C). 1993. reprint ed. pap. text 5.00 (*0-8290-3491-9*, S-194) Irvington.

— Social Theory & Social Structure. LC 68-28789. 1968. 35.00 (*0-02-921130-1*) Free Pr.

— Sociological Ambivalence & Other Essays. LC 76-1033. (Illus.). 1976. pap. 19.95 (*0-02-921120-4*) Free Pr.

— The Sociology of Science: An Episodic Memoir. LC 79-9962. (Arcturus Books Paperbacks). 164p. 1979. pap. 7.95 (*0-8093-0925-4*) S Ill U Pr.
— The Sociology of Science: Theoretical & Empirical Investigations. Storer, Norman W., ed. LC 72-97623. 640p. 1979. pap. text 29.00 (*0-226-52092-7*, P846) U Ch Pr.
— Varieties of Political Expression in Sociology. LC 72-81104. 239p. reprint ed. pap. 74.10 (*0-608-16606-5*, 202678200052) Bks Demand.
Merton, Robert K., ed. Authority & the Individual. LC 73-14144. (Perspectives in Social Inquiry Ser.). 386p. 1974. reprint ed. 23.95 (*0-405-05491-2*) Ayer.
— Factors Determining Human Behavior. LC 73-14153. (Perspectives in Social Inquiry Ser.). 186p. 1974. reprint ed. 12.95 (*0-405-05500-5*) Ayer.
— Studies in Social Psychology in World War 2, 3 vols. LC 73-14180. (Perspectives in Social Inquiry Ser.). 1662p. 1974. reprint ed. 106.95 (*0-405-05523-4*) Ayer.
Merton, Robert K., et al, eds. Qualitative & Quantitative Social Research: Papers in Honor of Paul F. Lazarsfeld. LC 78-24752. 1979. 29.95 (*0-02-920930-7*) Free Pr.
— Student-Physician: Introductory Studies in the Sociology of Medical Education. LC 57-12526. (Commonwealth Fund Publications Ser). (Illus.). 372p. reprint ed. 115.40 (*0-8357-9179-3*, 201102300072) Bks Demand.
Merton, Robert K. & Lazarsfeld, Paul F., eds. Continuities in Social Research: Studies in the Scope & Method of the American Soldier. LC 73-14168. (Perspectives in Social Inquiry Ser.). 260p. 1978. reprint ed. 18.95 (*0-405-05514-5*) Ayer.
Merton, Robert K. & Nisbet, Robert A., eds. Contemporary Social Problems. 4th ed. 782p. (C). 1976. write for info. (*0-318-52965-3*) Harcourt Coll Pubs.
Merton, Robert K. & Riley, Matilda W., eds. Sociological Traditions from Generation to Generation: Glimpses of the American Experience. LC 79-26693. (Modern Sociology Ser.). (Illus.). 184p. (C). 1980. pap. 39.50 (*0-89391-061-9*); text 73.25 (*0-89391-034-1*) Ablx Pub.
Merton, Robert K. & Sills, David L., eds. Social Science Quotations. 437p. 1992. 25.00 (*0-02-897397-6*) Macmillan.
Merton, Robert K., et al. The Work of Robert K. Merton & Contemporary Sociology. LC 97-16720. 357p. 1997. text 44.95 (*1-56000-318-9*) Transaction Pubs.
Merton, Robert K., jt. auth. see Fischer, Claude S.
Merton, Robert K., jt. auth. see Janowitz, Morris.
Merton, Robert K., jt. auth. see Sills, David L.
Merton, Robert K., ed. see Allison, Paul D.
Merton, Robert K., ed. see Angell, Robert C.
Merton, Robert K., ed. see Bales, Robert F.
Merton, Robert K., ed. see Barber, Bernard.
Merton, Robert K., ed. see Beaver, Donald D.
Merton, Robert K., ed. see Becker, Howard S.
Merton, Robert K., ed. see Birnbaum, Norman.
Merton, Robert K., ed. see Bittner, Egon.
Merton, Robert K., ed. see Bredemeier, Harry C.
Merton, Robert K., ed. see Breed, Warren.
Merton, Robert K., ed. see Caplovitz, David.
Merton, Robert K., ed. see Clark, Burton R.
Merton, Robert K., ed. see Cohen, Steven M.
Merton, Robert K., ed. see Cole, Stephen.
Merton, Robert K., ed. see Costner, Herbert L.
Merton, Robert K., ed. see Davis, Arthur K.
Merton, Robert K., ed. see Davis, Kingsley.
Merton, Robert K., ed. see Davison, W. Phillips.
Merton, Robert K., ed. see Devereux, Edward C., Jr.
Merton, Robert K., ed. see Duncan, Otis D.
Merton, Robert K., ed. see Elder, Glen H., Jr.
Merton, Robert K., ed. see Elkana, Yahuda, et al.
Merton, Robert K., ed. see Etzioni, Amitai.
Merton, Robert K., ed. see Fleck, Ludwig.
Merton, Robert K., ed. see Friedman, Nathalie S.
Merton, Robert K., ed. see Ginsberg, Ralph B.
Merton, Robert K., ed. see Goode, Erich.
Merton, Robert K., ed. see Goss, Mary E.
Merton, Robert K., ed. see Hammond, Phillip E.
Merton, Robert K., ed. see Hill, Robert B.
Merton, Robert K., ed. see Hyman, Herbert H.
Merton, Robert K., ed. see Keller, Suzanne I.
Merton, Robert K., ed. see Keyfitz, Nathan.
Merton, Robert K., ed. see Kohn, Melvin L.
Merton, Robert K., ed. see Levine, Donald N.
Merton, Robert K., ed. see March, James G.
Merton, Robert K., ed. see Marsh, Robert M.
Merton, Robert K., ed. see Moore, Wilbert E.
Merton, Robert K., ed. see Mullins, Nicholas C.
Merton, Robert K., ed. see Nettler, Gwynn.
Merton, Robert K., ed. see Nisbet, Robert A.
Merton, Robert K., ed. see O'Gorman, Hubert J.
Merton, Robert K., ed. see Reskin, Barbara F.
Merton, Robert K., ed. see Rosenberg, Morris.
Merton, Robert K., ed. see Rossi, Alice S.
Merton, Robert K., ed. see Ryder, Norman B.
Merton, Robert K., ed. see Schuessler, Karl F.
Merton, Robert K., ed. see Short, James F., Jr.
Merton, Robert K., ed. see Sills, David L.
Merton, Robert K., ed. see Simmons, Roberta G.
Merton, Robert K., ed. see Skolnick, Jerome H.
Merton, Robert K., ed. see Storer, Norman W.
Merton, Robert K., ed. see Stouffer, Samuel A.
Merton, Robert K., ed. see Strodtback, Fred L.
Merton, Robert K., ed. see Swanson, Guy E.
Merton, Robert K., ed. see Thielens, Wagner P., Jr.
Merton, Robert K., ed. see Trow, Martin A.
Merton, Robert K., ed. see Vidich, Arthur J.
Merton, Robert K., ed. see White, Harrison C.
Merton, Robert K., ed. see Wright, Charles R.
Merton, Robert K., ed. see Wrong, Dennis H.
Merton, Robert K., ed. see Yinger, J. Milton.
Merton, Robert K., jt. ed. see Zuckerman, Harriet.
Merton, Robert K. . On the Shoulders of Giants: A Shandean Postscript. LC 65-12859. (Illus.). 290p. 1967. pap. 4.95 (*0-15-668781-X*, Harvest Bks) Harcourt.
Merton, Stephen. Mark Rutherford: (William Hale White) 189p. 1967. 49.50 (*0-685-63213-X*) Elliots Bks.
Merton, Thomas. The Ascent to Truth. LC 80-26736. 356p. 1981. pap. 12.00 (*0-15-608682-4*, Harvest Bks) Harcourt.
— The Ascent to Truth. 252p. 1994. pap. 30.00 (*0-86012-024-4*, Pub. by Srch Pr) St Mut.
— The Asian Journal of Thomas Merton. Stone, Naomi B. et al, eds. LC 71-103370. (Illus.). 448p. 1975. pap. 15.95 (*0-8112-0570-3*, NDP394, Pub. by New Directions) Norton.
— Basic Principles of Monastic Spirituality. LC 96-60151. (Illus.). 128p. 1996. pap. 10.95 (*0-87243-222-X*) Templegate.
— Bread in the Wilderness. 180p. 1986. pap. 9.95 (*0-8146-0406-4*) Liturgical Pr.
— Bread in the Wilderness. LC 97-509. (Illus.). 160p. 1997. reprint ed. pap. 12.95 (*0-8112-1348-X*, NDP840, Pub. by New Directions) Norton.
— Cables to the Ace. 100p. 1986. 12.50 (*0-87775-192-7*) Unicorn Pr.
— The Climate of Monastic Prayer. (Cistercian Studies: No. 1). 154p. 1969. pap. 12.95 (*0-87907-801-4*) Cistercian Pubns.
— The Collected Poems of Thomas Merton. LC 77-9902. 1088p. 1980. pap. 29.95 (*0-8112-0769-2*, NDP504, Pub. by New Directions) Norton.
— Conjectures of a Guilty Bystander. LC 66-24311. 368p. 1968. pap. 13.00 (*0-385-01018-4*, Image Bks) Doubleday.
— Conjectures of a Guilty Bystander. 358p. 1994. pap. 33.00 (*0-86012-242-5*, Pub. by Srch Pr) St Mut.
— Contemplation in a World of Action: Restored & Corrected Edition. LC 98-46482. (Gethsemani Studies in Psychological & Religious Antropology: No. 1). 280p. 1999. pap. 14.00 (*0-268-00834-5*) U of Notre Dame Pr.
— Contemplative Prayer. 128p. 1971. reprint ed. pap. 8.95 (*0-385-09219-9*, Image Bks) Doubleday.
— Courage for Truth. 336p. 1994. pap. 15.95 (*0-15-600004-0*) Harcourt.
— The Courage for Truth: Letters to Writers. Bochen, Christine M., ed. LC 92-37078. 1993. 25.00 (*0-374-13055-8*) FS&G.
— Dancing in the Water of Life: Seeking Peace in the Hermitage: 1963-1965. LC 96-48223. (Journals of Thomas Merton: Vol. 5). 384p. 1998. pap. 15.00 (*0-06-065483-X*, Pub. by Harper SF) HarpC.
— Disputed Questions. LC 79-14717. 310p. (C). 1985. pap. 11.00 (*0-15-626105-7*, Harvest Bks) Harcourt.
— Eighteen Poems. deluxe limited ed. 1986. 200.00 (*0-8112-1012-X*, Pub. by New Directions) Norton.
— Entering the Silence: Becoming a Monk & Writer: 1941-1952. Montaldo, Jonathan, ed. LC 95-30457. (Journals of Thomas Merton: Vol. 2). 528p. 1997. pap. 16.00 (*0-06-065477-5*, Pub. by Harper SF) HarpC.
— Faith & Violence: Christian Teaching & Christian Practice. 1968. pap. 14.00 (*0-268-00094-8*) U of Notre Dame Pr.
— The Geography of Lograire: Long Poem. LC 78-88727. 1969. pap. 7.95 (*0-8112-0098-1*, NDP283, Pub. by New Directions) Norton.
— Honorable Reader: Reflections on My Work. 184p. 1991. reprint ed. pap. 9.95 (*0-8245-1125-5*, Crsrd) Crossroad NY.
***Merton, Thomas.** The Intimate Merton. LC 99-33239. 2001. 15.00 (*0-06-251629-9*) Harper SF.
Merton, Thomas. Intimate Merton: His Life from His Journals. Hart, Patrick & Monaldo, Jonathan, eds. LC 99-33239. (Illus.). 400p. 1999. 28.00 (*0-06-251620-5*) HarpC.
— Introductions East & West. 175p. 1992. 17.95 (*0-88962-129-2*); pap. 9.95 (*0-88962-130-6*) Mosaic.
— The Last of the Fathers: Saint Bernard of Clairvaux & the Encyclical Letter, Doctor Mellifluus. LC 81-4105. 128p. 1981. pap. 8.00 (*0-15-649438-8*, Harvest Bks) Harcourt.
— Life & Holiness. 128p. 1969. pap. 8.95 (*0-385-06277-X*, D183, Image Bks) Doubleday.
— Life & Holiness. 160p. 1995. pap. 6.00 (*0-385-48048-2*, Image Bks) Doubleday.
— The Literary Essays of Thomas Merton. Hart, Patrick, ed. LC 84-2056. Vol. 587. 549p. 1985. pap. 18.95 (*0-8112-0931-8*, NDP587, Pub. by New Directions) Norton.
— The Living Bread. 124p. 1994. pap. 45.00 (*0-86012-025-2*, Pub. by Srch Pr) St Mut.
— Love & Living. Stone, Naomi B. & Hart, Patrick, eds. LC 79-14717. 240p. (C). 1985. pap. 11.00 (*0-15-653895-4*, Harvest Bks) Harcourt.
— Mornings with Thomas Merton: 120 Daily Readings. LC 97-45998. 1998. 15.99 (*1-56955-009-3*) Servant.
— My Argument with the Gestapo: A Macaronic Journal. LC 69-20082. 256p. 1975. pap. 10.95 (*0-8112-0586-X*, NDP403, Pub. by New Directions) Norton.
— Mystics & Zen Masters. 320p. 1999. pap. 14.00 (*0-374-52001-1*) FS&G.
— The New Man. 256p. 1999. pap. 13.00 (*0-374-51444-5*) FS&G.
— The New Man. 184p. 1994. pap. 21.00 (*0-7855-2734-6*, Pub. by Srch Pr) St Mut.
— New Seeds of Contemplation. rev. ed. LC 61-17869. 297p. 1974. pap. 10.95 (*0-8112-0099-X*, NDP337, Pub. by New Directions) Norton.
— No Man Is an Island. 256p. 1994. pap. 21.00 (*0-86012-004-X*, Pub. by Srch Pr) St Mut.
— No Man Is an Island. large type ed. 384p. 1986. pap. 15.95 (*0-8027-2527-9*) Walker & Co.
— No Man Is an Island. LC 78-7108. 288p. 1978. reprint ed. pap. 9.00 (*0-15-665962-X*, Harvest Bks) Harcourt.
— Opening the Bible. 96p. 1970. pap. 6.95 (*0-8146-0408-0*) Liturgical Pr.
— The Other Side of the Mountain: The End of the Journey: 1967-1968. Hart, Patrick, ed. LC 98-12655. (Journals of Thomas Merton: Vol. 7). 368p. 1998. 30.00 (*0-06-065486-4*, Pub. by Harper SF) HarpC.
— The Other Side of the Mountain: The End of the Journey, 1967-1968, Vol. 7, 1967-1968. Hart, Patrick, ed. LC 98-12655. (Journals of Thomas Merton: Vol. 7). (Illus.). 368p. 1999. pap. 15.00 (*0-06-065487-2*, Pub. by Harper SF) HarpC.
— Passion for Peace: The Social Essays. Shannon, William H., ed. & intro. by. 360p. 1995. 29.95 (*0-8245-1494-7*) Crossroad NY.
— Passion for Peace: The Social Essays. Shannon, William H., ed. & intro. by. 348p. 1997. pap. 17.95 (*0-8245-1657-5*, Herdr & Herdr) Crossroad NY.
— Praying the Psalms. 48p. 1956. pap. 3.95 (*0-8146-0548-6*) Liturgical Pr.
— Raids on the Unspeakable. LC 66-17823. 1966. pap. 10.95 (*0-8112-0101-5*, NDP213, Pub. by New Directions) Norton.
— Raids on the Unspeakable. 142p. 1994. pap. 30.00 (*0-86012-046-5*, Pub. by Srch Pr) St Mut.
— The Road to Joy: Letters to New & Old Friends. Daggy, Robert E., ed. 672p. 1989. 27.95 (*0-374-25123-1*) FS&G.
— Run to the Mountain: The Story of a Vocation: 1939-1941. Hart, Patrick, ed. LC 94-43414. (Journals of Thomas Merton: Vol. 1). 512p. 1996. pap. 16.00 (*0-06-065475-9*, Pub. by Harper SF) HarpC.
— A Search for Solitude: Pursuing the Monk's True Life: 1952-1960. Cunningham, Lawrence S., ed. LC 95-46821. (Journals of Thomas Merton: Vol. 3). 432p. 1997. pap. 17.00 (*0-06-065479-1*, Pub. by Harper SF) HarpC.
— Selected Poems. enl. ed. LC 67-23488. 1967. pap. 9.95 (*0-8112-0100-7*, NDP85, Pub. by New Directions) Norton.
— The Seven Storey Mountain. 300p. 1991. reprint ed. lib. bdg. 22.95 (*0-89966-864-X*) Buccaneer Bks.
— The Seven Storey Mountain. 50th anniversary ed. 496p. (C). 1998. 35.00 (*0-15-100413-7*) Harcourt.
— The Seven Storey Mountain: An Autobiography of Faith. 50th ed. 496p. 1999. pap. 15.00 (*0-15-601086-0*, Harvest Bks) Harcourt.
— The Sign of Jonas. LC 79-10283. 382p. 1979. pap. 12.00 (*0-15-682529-5*, Harvest Bks) Harcourt.
— The Silent Life. 192p. 1999. pap. 12.00 (*0-374-51281-7*) FS&G.
— Spiritual Direction & Meditation. 108p. 1960. pap. 5.95 (*0-8146-0412-9*) Liturgical Pr.
— The Springs of Contemplation: A Retreat at the Abbey of Gethsemani. Richardson, Jane M., ed. LC 96-47761. 208p. 1997. reprint ed. pap. 9.95 (*0-87793-598-X*) Ave Maria.
— Thomas Merton. (Modern Spirituality Ser.). 96p. 1990. pap. 4.95 (*0-87243-174-6*) Templegate.
— Thomas Merton: Introductions East & West. 144p. 1994. 17.95 (*0-88962-136-5*) Mosaic.
— Thomas Merton in Alaska: Prelude to the Asian Journal. LC 87-24028. (Illus.). 224p. 1989. 9.95 (*0-8112-1048-0*, Pub. by New Directions) Norton.
— A Thomas Merton Reader. rev. ed. McDonnell, Thomas P., ed. LC 74-29. 528p. 1974. pap. 13.95 (*0-385-03292-7*, Image Bks) Doubleday.
— Thoughts in Solitude. 128p. 1998. 17.00 (*0-374-27649-8*) FS&G.
— Thoughts in Solitude. 114p. 1994. pap. 30.00 (*0-86012-017-1*, Pub. by Srch Pr) St Mut.
— Thoughts in Solitude. LC 92-50736. 168p. 1993. reprint ed. pap. 6.00 (*0-87773-920-X*, Pub. by Shambhala Pubns) Random.
— Thoughts on the East. LC 95-5377. (New Directions Bibelot Ser.). 96p. (Orig.). 1995. pap. 6.00 (*0-8112-1293-9*, NDP802, Pub. by New Directions) Norton.
— A Vow of Conversation. 256p. 1988. 17.95 (*0-374-28535-7*) FS&G.
— The Waters of Siloe. LC 79-10372. (Illus.). 416p. 1979. pap. 14.00 (*0-15-694954-7*, Harvest Bks) Harcourt.
— The Way of Chuang Tzu. LC 65-27556. (Illus.). 1969. reprint ed. pap. 8.95 (*0-8112-0103-1*, NDP276, Pub. by New Directions) Norton.
— The Way of Chuang Tzu: A Personal & Spiritual Interpretation of the Classic Philosopher of Taoism. 160p. 1994. pap. 21.00 (*0-86012-239-5*, Pub. by Srch Pr) St Mut.
— Ways of the Christian Mystics. LC 94-8330. (Pocket Classics Ser.). 200p. 1994. pap. 6.00 (*1-57062-030-X*, Pub. by Shambhala Pubns) Random.
— What Is Contemplation? (Illus.). 80p. 1981. pap. 9.95 (*0-87243-103-7*) Templegate.
— The Wisdom of the Desert. 128p. 1996. pap. 35.00 (*0-86012-276-X*, Pub. by Srch Pr) St Mut.
— The Wisdom of the Desert: Sayings from the Desert Fathers. LC 59-15021. 1970. pap. 7.95 (*0-8112-0102-3*, NDP295, Pub. by New Directions) Norton.
— Witness to Freedom: The Letters in Times of Crisis. Shannon, William H., ed. & selected by by. LC 95-22488. (Harvest Bks.). 368p. 1995. reprint ed. pap. 16.00 (*0-15-600274-4*, Harvest Bks) Harcourt.
— Zen & the Birds of Appetite. LC 68-25546. 1968. pap. 9.95 (*0-8112-0104-X*, NDP261, Pub. by New Directions) Norton.
— Zen & the Birds of Appetite. LC 93-16313. (Pocket Classics Ser.). 304p. 1993. reprint ed. pap. 6.00 (*0-87773-936-6*, Pub. by Shambhala Pubns) Random.
Merton, Thomas, ed. Monks Pond: Thomas Merton's Little Magazine. LC 89-8918. (Illus.). 368p. 1989. 40.00 (*0-8131-1694-5*) U Pr of Ky.
Merton, Thomas & Bochen, Christine M. Learning to Love: Exploring Solitude & Freedom, 1966-1967. LC 97-19840. (Journals of Thomas Merton: Vol. 6). 416p. 1998. pap. 15.00 (*0-06-065485-6*, Pub. by Harper SF) HarpC.
Merton, Thomas & Daggy, Robert E. Dancing In The Water Of Life Volume 5: 1963-1965: Seeking Peace in the Hermitage. LC 96-48223. (Journals of Thomas Merton: Vol. 5). 384p. 1997. 30.00 (*0-06-065482-1*, Pub. by Harper SF) HarpC.
Merton, Thomas & Kramer, Victor A. Turning Toward the World: The Pivotal Years: 1960-1963. LC 96-16561. (Journals of Thomas Merton: Vol. 4). 384p. 1997. pap. 15.00 (*0-06-065481-3*, Pub. by Harper SF) HarpC.
Merton, Thomas & Lax, Robert. A Catch of Anti-Letters. LC 94-1262. (Illus.). 128p. (Orig.). 1994. pap. 9.95 (*1-55612-712-X*, LL1712) Sheed & Ward WI.
***Merton, Thomas & Lax, Robert.** When Prophecy Still Had a Voice: The Letters of Thomas Merton & Robert Lax. Biddle, Arthur W., ed. 496p. 2001. 39.95 (*0-8131-2168-X*) U Pr of Ky.
Merton, Thomas & Milosz, Czeslaw. Striving Towards Being: The Letters of Thomas Merton & Czeslaw Milosz. Faggen, Robert, ed. LC 96-23827. 160p. 1997. 21.00 (*0-374-27100-3*) FS&G.
Merton, Thomas & Ruether, Rosemary Radford. At Home in the World: The Letters of Thomas Merton & Rosemary Radford Ruether. LC 95-10200. 110p. (Orig.). 1995. pap. text 13.00 (*1-57075-015-7*) Orbis Bks.
Merton, Thomas, jt. auth. see Arnold, Eberhard.
Merton, Thomas, jt. auth. see Niles, John J.
Merton, Thomas, ed. see Gandhi, Mohandas Karamchand.
Merton, Thomas, tr. see Augustine, Saint.
Merts, A. L., jt. ed. see Hauer, Allan.
Merttens, Ruth & Vass, Jeff. Sharing the Maths Cultures: IMPACT LEA Maths for Parents, Children & Teachers. 200p. 1990. pap. 29.95 (*1-85000-876-0*, Falmer Pr) Taylor & Francis.
Merttens, Ruth & Vass, Jeff, eds. Partnerships in Maths: Parents & Schools: the IMPACT Project. LC 92-42864. 256p. 1993. pap. 32.95 (*0-7507-0155-2*, Falmer Pr); boxed set 89.95 (*0-7507-0154-4*, Falmer Pr) Taylor & Francis.
Mertuago, Peter, ed. Dictionary of 1000 Russian Proverbs. LC 97-39302. (ENG & RUS.). 130p. (Orig.). 1997. pap. 11.95 (*0-7818-0564-3*) Hippocrene Bks.
Mertus, Julie. Kosovo: How Myths & Truths Started a War. LC 99-19044. 369p. 1999. pap. 19.95 (*0-520-21865-5*, Pub. by U CA Pr) Cal Prin Full Svc.
Mertus, Julie, et al, eds. The Suitcase: Refugee Voices from Bosnia & Croatia. Todosijevic, Jelica, tr. LC 96-18199. (Illus.). 256p. (C). 1997. pap. 16.95 (*0-520-20634-7*, Pub. by U CA Pr) Cal Prin Full Svc.
Mertus, Julie A. Kosovo: How Myths & Truths Started a War. LC 99-19044. 369p. 1999. 55.00 (*0-520-20962-1*, Pub. by U CA Pr) Cal Prin Full Svc.
— Meeting the Health Needs of Women: Survivors of the Balkan Conflict. unabridged ed. Pine, Rachel N., ed. 116p. 1993. pap. text 8.00 (*1-890671-14-2*) Center Reprod.
***Mertus, Julie A.** War's Offensive on Women: The Humanitarian Challenge in Bosnia, Kosovo & Afghanistan. 160p. 2000. 50.00 (*1-56549-118-1*); pap. 19.95 (*1-56549-117-3*) Kumarian Pr.
Mertvago, Peter. Dictionary of 1,000 French Proverbs. (ENG & FRE.). 131p. 1995. pap. 11.95 (*0-7818-0400-0*) Hippocrene Bks.
— Dictionary of 1,000 Spanish Proverbs. (ENG & SPA.). 131p. (Orig.). 1995. pap. 11.95 (*0-7818-0412-4*) Hippocrene Bks.
Mertvago, Peter, ed. Dictionary of 1000 German Proverbs. (ENG & GER.). 131p. (Orig.). 1997. pap. 11.95 (*0-7818-0471-X*) Hippocrene Bks.
— Dictionary of 1000 Italian Proverbs: With English Equivalents. LC 96-32952. (ENG & ITA.). 131p. (Orig.). 1997. pap. 11.95 (*0-7818-0458-2*) Hippocrene Bks.
— Dictionary of Russian Proverbs. (RUS.). 477p. 1996. pap. 35.00 (*0-7818-0424-8*) Hippocrene Bks.
Mertz. Trace Elements in Human & Animal Nutrition, 2 vols. 5th ed. 1988. 157.00 (*0-12-491253-2*) Acad Pr.
Mertz, Anne M. Morris Migration: A Saga of Forebears & Descendants. (Illus.). xvi, 476p. (Orig.). 1996. 40.00 (*0-7884-0516-0*, MERT) Heritage Bk.
— Morris Migration: A Saga of Forebears & Descendants. (Illus.). xii, 472p. (Orig.). 1996. pap. 30.00 (*0-7884-0550-0*, M167) Heritage Bk.
Mertz, Barbara. Temples, Tombs & Hieroglyphs: A Popular History of Ancient Egypt. LC 89-17911. (Illus.). 336p. 1990. pap. 15.95 (*0-87226-223-5*, 62235B, P Bedrick Books) NTC Contemp Pub Co.
Mertz, Barbara, see Michaels, Barbara, pseud.
Mertz, Barbara, see Peters, Elizabeth, pseud.
Mertz, Curtis A., jt. ed. see Stimson, Paul G.
Mertz, D. W. Moderate Realism & Its Logic. LC 95-44390. 310p. 1996. 40.00 (*0-300-06561-2*) Yale U Pr.
Mertz, Edwin T., ed. Quality Protein Maize. LC 92-71401. (Illus.). 294p. (Orig.). 1992. pap. 76.00 (*0-913250-75-9*) Am Assn Cereal Chem.
Mertz, Harold J., jt. ed. see Backaitis, Stanley H.
Mertz, James J., tr. see Murphy, John P., ed.
***Mertz, Joshua.** Machine Dreams. LC 00-104542. 304p. 2000. pap. 16.00 (*0-9661664-4-2*, Pub. by Bald Mtn Bks) Partners Pubs Grp.

M

Mertz, Karl C. Cinco: A "Kid's" Top-Five List, "If I Were President" (with Dedication to "Dave") LC 97-915752. (Illus.). 80p. 1997. 9.95 (*0-9658164-0-0*, 9701) Red Creek Pub.

— Duel Entendre: The Battle for Your Soul! LC 97-91753. (Illus.). 70p. 1997. 9.95 (*0-9658164-1-9*, 9702) Red Creek Pub.

Mertz, Lawrence N. Excursions in Astronomical Optics. LC 95-51497. 152p. 1996. 49.95 (*0-387-94664-0*) Spr-Verlag.

Mertz, Leslie A. Recent Advances & Issues in Biology. (Frontiers of Science Ser.). (Illus.). 292p. 2000. text 44.95 (*1-57356-234-3*) Oryx Pr.

Mertz, Steven. Sudden Death. (Orig.). 1995. mass mkt. 5.50 (*1-57297-032-4*) Blvd Books.

Mertz, Ursula R. Collector's Encyclopedia of American Composition Dolls 1900-1950: Identification & Values. LC 99-192994. 256p. 1998. 24.95 (*1-57432-080-7*) Collector Bks.

Mertz, Walter. Trace Elements in Human & Animal Nutrition, Vol. 1. 5th ed. 480p. 1987. text 104.00 (*0-12-491251-6*) Acad Pr.

— Trace Elements in Human & Animal Nutrition, Vol. 2. 5th ed. 1986. text 104.00 (*0-12-491252-4*) Acad Pr.

Mertz, Walter & Cornatzer, W. E., eds. Newer Trace Elements in Nutrition. LC 70-157834. (Illus.). 451p. reprint ed. pap. 139.90 (*0-608-30254-6*, 205501500007) Bks Demand.

Mertzlufft, Bonnie, et al. Learning Links for Language Arts. (Illus.). 128p. (Orig.). (J). (gr. 1-3). 1997. pap. 14.95 (*1-57612-005-8*, MM2034) Monday Morning Bks.

— Learning Links for Math. (Illus.). 128p. (Orig.). (J). (gr. 1-3). 1997. pap. 14.95 (*1-57612-006-6*) Monday Morning Bks.

Mertzlufft, F. O., jt. ed. see Zander, R.

***Mertzman, Robert.** Business & Sports: How Much Is Too Much? (C). 1999. pap. text 89.95 (*0-7872-6116-5*) Kendall-Hunt.

— The Current State of Sports Journalism. (C). 1999. pap. text 89.95 (*0-7872-6123-8*) Kendall-Hunt.

— Ethics & Management of Coaching. (C). 1999. pap. text 89.95 (*0-7872-6129-7*) Kendall-Hunt.

— Ethics & Management of Sports Agents & Athletes. (C). 1999. pap. text 89.95 (*0-7872-6131-9*) Kendall-Hunt.

— Homosexuality & Sports: Managing Personal & Social Values. (C). 1999. pap. text 89.95 (*0-7872-6130-0*) Kendall-Hunt.

— International Aspects of Sports: Managing a World of Sports. (C). 1999. pap. text 89.95 (*0-7872-6135-1*) Kendall-Hunt.

— Justice in Sports Management & Ownership. (C). 1999. pap. text 89.95 (*0-7872-6136-X*) Kendall-Hunt.

— Management Ethics in Sport: Excellence & Compliance. (C). 1999. pap. text 89.95 (*0-7872-6113-0*) Kendall-Hunt.

— Media & Sports: Watchdog or Lapdog? (C). 1999. pap. text 89.95 (*0-7872-6122-X*) Kendall-Hunt.

— Medicine & Sports: Peak Performance Vs. Optimum Health? (C). 1999. pap. text 89.95 (*0-7872-6120-3*) Kendall-Hunt.

— Race & Sports: Do Blacks Lose by Winning at Sports? (C). 1999. pap. text 89.95 (*0-7872-6134-3*) Kendall-Hunt.

— Science & Sports: Performance Enhancing Drugs. (C). 1999. pap. text 89.95 (*0-7872-6121-1*) Kendall-Hunt.

— Sports: A Summary Perspective. (C). 1999. pap. text 89.95 (*0-7872-6137-8*) Kendall-Hunt.

— Sports & Celebrity: Role Models or Marketing Vehicles? (C). 1999. pap. text 89.95 (*0-7872-6119-X*) Kendall-Hunt.

— Sports & Children: Training or Child Abuse? (C). 1999. pap. text 89.95 (*0-7872-6128-9*) Kendall-Hunt.

— Sports & Government S: Sport Subsides For Civic Interests? (C). 1999. pap. text 89.95 (*0-7872-6132-7*) Kendall-Hunt.

— Sports & Higher Education: Academics, Athletics & Financial Opportunity. (C). 1999. pap. text 89.95 (*0-7872-6124-6*) Kendall-Hunt.

— Sports & Justice: Title Ix & Gender Equality. (C). 1999. pap. text 89.95 (*0-7872-6117-3*) Kendall-Hunt.

— Sports & Life: Students, Athletes & Life Skills. (C). 1999. pap. text 89.95 (*0-7872-6126-2*) Kendall-Hunt.

— Sports & Primary & Secondary Education: Student Or Player Development? (C). 1999. pap. text 89.95 (*0-7872-6125-4*) Kendall-Hunt.

— Sports AssociationsI: Issues in the Ncaa's Management of Sport. (C). 1999. pap. text 89.95 (*0-7872-6133-5*) Kendall-Hunt.

— Sports Betting: Gaming's Effects on Games & Society. (C). 1999. pap. text 89.95 (*0-7872-6127-0*) Kendall-Hunt.

— Sports in Context: How Good Were The Good Old Days? (C). 1999. pap. text 89.95 (*0-7872-6114-9*) Kendall-Hunt.

— Sportsmanship, Gamesmanship & Character: Do Good Sports Make Good People? (C). 1999. pap. text 89.95 (*0-7872-6115-7*, 41611501) Kendall-Hunt.

— Violence & Aggression in Sports & Society. (C). 1999. pap. text 89.95 (*0-7872-6118-1*, 41611801) Kendall-Hunt.

— Voices in Sports & Society. 352p. (C). per. 45.95 (*0-7872-5816-4*) Kendall-Hunt.

— Voices in Sports & Society: Study Guide. 154p. (C). 1999. per. 24.95 (*0-7872-5817-2*) Kendall-Hunt.

***Mertzman, Robertx.** Welcome to the Virtual Summit on Sports & Society. (C). 1999. pap. text 89.95 (*0-7872-6112-2*, 41611201) Kendall-Hunt.

Mertzweiller, Joseph K., jt. ed. see Caillet, Marie.

Merullo, Roland. Leaving Losapas. 304p. 1992. pap. 10.00 (*0-380-71750-6*, Avon Bks) Morrow Avon.

***Merullo, Roland.** Passion for Golf: A Golfer's Quest for Meaning. (Illus.). 2000. 20.00 (*1-58574-162-0*) Lyons Pr.

Merullo, Roland. Revere Beach Boulevard: A Novel. LC 98-19908. 320p. 1998. 23.00 (*0-8050-6005-7*) H Holt & Co.

— Revere Beach Boulevard: A Novel. 336p. 1999. pap. 12.00 (*0-8050-6006-5*, Owl) H Holt & Co.

Merulo, Claudio. Claudio Merulo: Canzoni d'Intavolatura d'Organo. Cunningham, Walker & McDermott, Charles, eds. (Recent Researches in Music of the Renaissance Ser.: Vol. RRR90-91). (Illus.). xix, 184p. 1992. pap. 60.00 (*0-89579-272-9*) A-R Eds.

Merulo, Claudio, jt. auth. see Striggio, Alessandro.

Merunka. Tenis Pre Kazdeho. (SLO.). 160p. 1996. write for info. (*80-08-00302-2*, Pub. by Slov Pegagog Naklad) IBD Ltd.

Merusi, Donald. Windows NT 95 for Unix Professionals. LC 97-7962. 177p. 1997. pap. text 29.95 (*1-55558-181-1*, Digital DEC) Buttrwrth-Heinemann.

Merusi, Donald E. Software Implementation Techniques: VMS, UNIX, OS-2, MS-DOS. (Programmer's Ser.). (Illus.). 700p. 1992. pap. 39.95 (*1-55558-090-4*, EY-J822E-DP) DEC.

— Software Implementation Techniques: Writing Software in OpenVMS, OS/2, UNIX & Windows NT. 2nd ed. LC 95-14929. (Illus.). 567p. 1995. pap. 52.95 (*1-55558-134-X*, Digital DEC) Buttrwrth-Heinemann.

Merusi, Donald E., jt. auth. see Clarke, David L.

Merva, George E. Physical Principles of the Plant Biosystem. LC 95-79226. (Illus.). 272p. 1995. text 54.00 (*0-614-10659-1*, MO895) Am Soc Ag Eng.

Merva, George E., jt. auth. see Patterson, Dan.

Mervan, Leroy. Your First Gerbil. (Illus.). 32p. (Orig.). 1991. pap. 2.29 (*0-86622-063-1*, YF-107) TFH Pubns.

Mervin, Dana V. The 5 Minute Mutual Fund Investor: A Basic Guide to Investing in Mutual Funds. 240p. 1995. 19.95 (*0-9641819-0-8*) M Systs Pubng.

Mervin, David. George Bush & the Guardianship Presidency. 272p. 1996. text 39.95 (*0-312-12961-0*) St Martin.

— George Bush & the Guardianship Presidency. 1998. pap. 19.95 (*0-312-21199-6*) St Martin.

— Presidency Reagan. 1990. text 48.50 (*0-582-03487-6*, Pub. by Addison-Wesley) Longman.

— Ronald Reagan & the American Presidency. 237p. (C). 1990. pap. text 24.95 (*0-582-03493-0*, 78530) Longman.

Mervine, Pat, et al. I Can Cook, Too! (Illus.). 336p. (J). 1995. spiral bd. 49.00 (*1-884135-19-6*) Mayer-Johnson.

Mervine, Patricia L., et al. Art for Me, Too! (Illus.). 400p. (J). (ps-6). 1996. spiral bd. 34.00 (*1-884135-31-5*) Mayer-Johnson.

Mervyn, Fran, jt. auth. see Rich, Phil.

Mervyn, Len. Vitamin E Updated. Passwater, Richard A. & Mindell, Earl R., eds. (Good Health Guide Ser.). 32p. (Orig.). 1983. pap. 3.95 (*0-87983-274-6*, 32746K, Keats Publng) NTC Contemp Pub Co.

Mervyn, Leonard. Diccionario de Vitaminas. (CAT & SPA.). 240p. 1985. pap. 24.95 (*0-7859-4920-8*) Fr & Eur.

***Mervyn, Leonard.** Thorsons' Complete Guide to Vitamins & Minerals: All You Need to Know about Vitamins & Minerals. (Illus.). 2000. pap. 11.00 (*0-7225-3977-0*) Thorsons PA.

Merwald, Judith F., et al. The Christmas Tree Ship. (Illus.). 17p. (Orig.). (J). (gr. 2-6). 1993. pap. 10.00 (*0-9643859-0-2*, 1) True Story.

Merwe, Alwyn Van Der, see Van Der Merwe, Alwyn, ed.

Merwe, Alwyn Van Der, see Ferrero, Miguel & Van Der Merwe, Alwyn, eds.

Merwe, Alwyn Van Der, see Van Der Merwe, Alwyn, ed.

Merwe, Alwyn Van Der, see Tarozzi, Gino & Van Der Merwe, Alwyn, eds.

Merwe, Alwyn Van Der, see Barut, Asim O. & Van Der Merwe, Alwyn, eds.

Merwe, Anita Van der, see Andersen, Laurie H.

Merwe, C. G. Van Der, see Van Der Merwe, C. G.

Merwe, Christo H. Van Der, see Van Der Merwe, Christo H.

Merwe, D. Van Der, see Van Der Merwe, D.

Merwe, Dana va der, see van der Merwe, Dana.

Merwe, Derek van der, see Bradfield, Graham & van der Merwe, Derek, eds.

Merwe, Hendrik W. Van Der, see Hund, John & Van Der Merwe, Hendrik W.

Merwe, Nan Van Der, see Van Der Merwe, Nan.

Merwe, Petrus J. Van der, see Van der Merwe, Petrus J.

Merwe, R. Van Der, see Finnemore, M. & Van Der Merwe, R.

Merwe, S. Van Der, see Van Der Merwe, S.

Merwick, A. R., jt. ed. see Hutchison, J. W.

Merwick, Donna. Boston Priests, Eighteen Forty-Eight to Nineteen Ten: A Study in Social & Intellectual Change. LC 72-79309. 292p. 1973. 36.50 (*0-674-07975-2*) HUP.

— Death of a Notary: Conquest & Change in Colonial New York. LC 99-11943. 1999. 35.00 (*0-8014-3608-7*) Cornell U Pr.

— Possessing Albany, 1630-1710: The Dutch & English Experiences. (Illus.). 324p. (C). 1990. text 80.00 (*0-521-37386-7*) Cambridge U Pr.

Merwick, Katie. People Food for Dogs. (Illus.). 144p. 1998. pap. 14.95 (*0-9660341-0-4*) Blue-dog.

Merwin, Charles L. Financing Small Corporations in Five Manufacturing Industries: 1926-36. Bruchey, Stuart & Carosso, Vincent P., eds. LC 78-18970. (Small Business Enterprise in America Ser.). (Illus.). 1979. reprint ed. lib. bdg. 17.95 (*0-405-11473-7*) Ayer.

— Financing Small Corporations in Five Manufacturing Industries, 1926-36. (Financial Research Program III: Studies in Business Financing: No. 2). 189p. 1942. reprint ed. 50.00 (*0-87014-130-9*) Natl Bur Econ Res.

Merwin, Don, jt. auth. see Howells, John.

Merwin, Jack. Eskimo in a Cheap Suit. (Firelight Ser.). 64p. (Orig.). 1996. pap. 5.49 (*1-885962-68-1*) Lincoln Lrning.

— Spock in a Salad Bowl. (Firelight Ser.). 64p. (Orig.). 1996. pap. 5.49 (*1-885962-70-3*) Lincoln Lrning.

— Woodpecker in a Red Maserati. (Firelight Ser.). 64p. (Orig.). 1996. pap. 5.49 (*1-885962-69-X*) Lincoln Lrning.

Merwin, John. The Battenkill. (Illus.). 160p. 1993. 22.95 (*1-55821-208-6*) Lyons Pr.

— New American Trout Fishing. (Illus.). 320p. 1994. 30.00 (*0-02-584382-6*) Macmillan.

***Merwin, John.** New North American Trout Fishing. (Illus.). 2000. 9.99 (*0-7858-1192-3*) Bk Sales Inc.

Merwin, John. The Saltwater Tackle Box. Sullivan, Elizabeth V., ed. (Illus.). 128p. 1998. reprint ed. text 15.00 (*0-7881-5204-1*) DIANE Pub.

***Merwin, John.** Stillwater Trout. (Illus.). 224p. (Orig.). 2000. pap. 19.95 (*1-58574-042-X*) Lyons Pr.

— Streamer-Fly Fishing: A Practical Guide to the Best Patterns & Methods of Fishing the Streamer. (Illus.). 96p. 2000. pap. 14.95 (*1-58574-041-1*) Lyons Pr.

Merwin, John. Well Cast Lines. (Illus.). 160p. 1995. per. 10.00 (*0-684-81151-0*, Fireside) S&S Trade Pap.

Merwin, John, ed. see Wulff, Lee.

Merwin, Marjorie, jt. auth. see Granowsky, Alvin.

Merwin, Richard. Mega-Slank from Titanium. LC 92-12842. (Widgets Ser.). (J). (gr. 2). 1992. lib. bdg. 13.99 (*1-56239-151-8*) ABDO Pub Co.

Merwin, S. & Balonov, M. I., eds. The Chernobyl Papers: Doses to the Soviet Population & Early Health Effects Studies. xv, 427p. 1993. 75.00 (*1-883021-02-2*) Research Ent.

***Merwin, Samuel & Webster, Henry K.** Calumet "K" LC 99-33900. 1999. write for info. (*1-56114-145-3*) Second Renaissance.

Merwin, Samuel & Webster, Henry K. The Short-Line War. LC 67-29273. (Americans in Fiction Ser.). 340p. reprint ed. pap. text 8.95 (*0-89197-935-2*); reprint ed. lib. bdg. 32.50 (*0-8398-1256-6*) Irvington.

Merwin, Sandra. Evaluation: 10 Significant Ways for Measuring & Improving Training Impact. 80p. 19.95 (*0-7879-5123-4*, Pfffr & Co) Jossey-Bass.

Merwin, Sandra J. Real Self: The Inner Journey of Courage. 104p. (Orig.). 1991. pap. text 7.95 (*0-9628522-0-1*) TigerLily Pr.

Merwin, W. S. East Window: The Asian Translations. LC 98-40192. 340p. 1998. pap. 16.00 (*1-55659-091-1*) Copper Canyon.

***Merwin, W. S.** The First Four Books of Poems. 304p. 2000. pap. 16.00 (*1-55659-139-X*) Copper Canyon.

Merwin, W. S. The First Four Books of Poems: Including a Mask for Janus, the Dancing Bear, Green with Beasts, the Drunk in the Furnace. LC 89-12760. 1989. 45.00 (*0-02-584381-8*) Macmillan.

— Flower & Hand: Poems, 1977-1983. 250p. 1996. pap. text 15.00 (*1-55659-119-5*) Copper Canyon.

***Merwin, W. S.** The Folding Cliffs: A Narrative. LC 98-27434. 352p. 2000. pap. 16.95 (*0-375-70151-6*) Knopf.

Merwin, W. S. The Folding Cliffs: A Narrative in Verse. LC 98-27434. 336p. 1998. 25.00 (*0-375-40148-2*) Knopf.

— Houses & Travellers. 1995. pap. 12.95 (*0-8050-2872-2*) H Holt & Co.

— Mask for Janus. LC 76-144755. (Yale Series of Younger Poets: No. 49). reprint ed. 18.00 (*0-404-53849-5*) AMS Pr.

— The Miner's Pale Children. 1995. pap. 12.95 (*0-8050-2870-6*) H Holt & Co.

— Poem of the Cid. 1975. pap. 11.95 (*0-452-01060-8*, Mer) NAL.

— The Rain in the Trees. LC 87-46081. 96p. 1988. pap. 17.00 (*0-394-75858-7*) Knopf.

— The Real World of Manuel Cordova. 47p. 1995. 450.00 (*0-9614597-9-4*) Ninja Pr.

— The Restructuring of America: A Futurist Projection. 104p. (Orig.). 1997. pap. 12.95 (*0-932863-13-2*) Clarity Pr.

***Merwin, W. S.** The River Sound: Poems. LC 98-28255. 144p. 1999. 23.00 (*0-375-40486-4*) Knopf.

— The River Sound: Poems. 128p. 2000. pap. 15.00 (*0-375-70435-3*) Knopf.

Merwin, W. S. The Second Four Books of Poems. LC 92-39320. 320p. (Orig.). 1993. pap. 15.00 (*1-55659-054-7*, Pub. by Copper Canyon) Consort Bk Sales.

— Travels: Poems. 1994. pap. 17.00 (*0-679-75277-3*) Random.

— Unframed Originals: Recollections. LC 81-70063. 256p. 1983. 14.95 (*0-689-11284-X*) Atheneum Yung Read.

— Unframed Originals: Recollections. 89p. 1995. pap. 12.95 (*0-8050-2871-4*) H Holt & Co.

— The Vixen: Poems. 88p. 1997. pap. 15.00 (*0-679-76601-4*) Knopf.

Merwin, W. S., tr. The Satires of Persius. 112p. Date not set. pap. write for info. (*0-85646-019-2*, Pub. by Anvil Press) Dufour.

Merwin, W. S. & Wilson, Keith. Broadside. 1972. 30.00 (*0-941490-01-7*) Solo Pr.

Merwin, W. S., tr. see Alighieri, Dante.

Merwin, W. S., tr. see Euripides.

Merwin, W. S., tr. see Garcia Lorca, Federico.

Merwin, W. S., tr. see Neruda, Pablo.

Merwin-Webster. Calumet "K" LC 90-63345. (Illus.). 345p. 1993. reprint ed. 24.95 (*1-56114-146-1*) Second Renaissance.

Merxmuller, H. Prodromus Einer Flora Von Sudwestafrika. (C). 1988. text 720.00 (*0-7855-3159-9*, Pub. by Scientific) St Mut.

Mery, Gerardo. Sustainable Forestry Challenges for Developing Countries. Palo, Matti, ed. LC 96-27711. (Environmental Science & Technology Library). 400p. (C). 1996. text 144.00 (*0-7923-3738-7*) Kluwer Academic.

Mery, Michel. The Father, the Son & The Walkperson: And Other Sapiens-Fiction Stories. (Orig.). 1996. pap. 10.00 (*0-9622937-9-2*) III Pub.

— Pyrexia. 192p. (Orig.). 1997. pap. 10.00 (*1-886625-02-6*) III Pub.

Merydith, Connie. Bread Machine Baking for All Seasons: Delightful Recipes for Year-Round Pleasure. LC 96-39094. (Illus.). 192p. 1996. per. 12.00 (*0-7615-0794-9*) Prima Pub.

Merydith, Connie, jt. auth. see Foreman, George.

Meryl, Debra. Baby's Peek-a-Boo Album. (Illus.). 24p. (J). (ps-3). 1989. 13.99 (*0-448-15375-0*, G & D) Peng Put Young Read.

Meryll, Jane, ed. see Yelin, Joy.

Meryman, Richard. Andrew Wyeth. (First Impressions Ser.). (Illus.). 92p. 1991. 19.95 (*0-8109-3956-8*, Pub. by Abrams) Time Warner.

— Andrew Wyeth: A Secret Life. (Illus.). 464p. 1998. pap. 20.00 (*0-06-092921-9*, Perennial) HarperTrade.

— Andrew Wyeth (RI) A Secret Life. LC 96-16816. (Illus.). 416p. 1998. 35.00 (*0-06-017113-8*) HarpC.

— Louis Armstrong: A Self-Portrait, Special Edition. limited ed. LC 70-152507. (Illus.). 59p. 1996. boxed set 125.00 (*0-87130-026-5*, Pub. by Eakins) RAM Publications.

— Louis Armstrong - A Self Portrait. LC 70-152507. 1971. pap. 25.00 (*0-87130-027-3*) Eakins.

***Meryn, Siegfried, et al.** Men's Health & the Hormone Revolution. 350p. 2000. pap. 18.95 (*1-55321-103-0*, Pub. by NDE Pub) IPG Chicago.

Merz, Andrew K. Phillies Wit: Words of Wisdom from the Wild, Wacky, Wonderful '93 Phillies. Broussard, Anne E., ed. (Orig.). 1993. pap. 5.95 (*0-9640033-0-9*) Wit Press.

Merz, Blanche. Points of Cosmic Energy. (Illus.). 184p. (Orig.). pap. 20.95 (*0-8464-4271-X*) Beekman Pubs.

— Points of Cosmic Energy. 188p. (Orig.). 1988. pap. 15.95 (*0-85207-194-9*, Pub. by C W Daniel) Natl Bk Netwk.

Merz, Bob, jt. auth. see Jaffe, David S.

Merz, Carol & Furman, Gail. Community & Schools: Promise & Paradox. LC 96-50968. 128p. (C). 1997. text 38.00 (*0-8077-3617-1*); pap. text 17.95 (*0-8077-3616-3*) Tchrs Coll.

Merz, Carol, jt. auth. see Lutz, Frank.

Merz, Charles. Centerville, U. S. A. LC 78-160943. (Short Story Index Reprint Ser.). 1977. reprint ed. 20.95 (*0-8369-3922-0*) Ayer.

Merz, E. Ultrasound in Obstetrics & Gynecology. (Illus.). 343p. 1990. text 149.00 (*0-86577-376-9*) Thieme Med Pubs.

Merz, Eberhard. 3-D Ultrasound in Obstetrics & Gynecology. 170p. text 85.00 (*0-7817-1980-1*) Lppncott W & W.

Merz, Erich & Walter, Carl E. Advanced Nuclear Systems Consuming Excess Plutonium. LC 97-24674. (NATO ASI Series: Vol. 15). 362p. 1997. text 197.50 (*0-7923-4650-5*) Kluwer Academic.

Merz, Erich R. Federal Republic of Germany R & D Programme, Vol. 14. (Special Issue of the Journal Radioactive Waste Management & the Nuclear Fuel Cycle Ser.). 124p. 1986. pap. text 135.00 (*3-7186-0336-5*) Gordon & Breach.

Merz, Erich R., et al, eds. Mixed Oxide Fuel (MOX) Exploitation & Destruction in Power Reactors: Proceedings of the NATO Advanced Research Workshop, Obninsk, Russia, October 16-19, 1994. LC 95-12380. (NATO Advanced Sciences Institutes: Vol. 2). 320p. (C). 1995. text 173.50 (*0-7923-3473-6*) Kluwer Academic.

Merz, Erich R. & Walter, Carl E., eds. Disposal of Weapon Plutonium - Approaches & Prospects: Proceedings of the NATO Advanced Research Workshop, St. Petersburg, Russia, May 14-17, 1995. (NATO ASI: Partnership Sub-Series 1: Disarmament Technologies: Vol. 4). 339p. (C). 1996. text 232.00 (*0-7923-3841-3*) Kluwer Academic.

Merz, Eugene F., jt. auth. see Smith, Carol Ann.

Merz, John T. History of European Thought in the Nineteenth Century, Vol. 3 1990. 17.00 (*0-8446-2579-5*) Peter Smith.

Merz, K. M. & Roux, B., eds. Biological Membranes: A Molecular Perspective from Computation & Experiment. (Illus.). 500p. 1996. 99.50 (*0-8176-3827-X*) Birkhauser.

Merz, Kenneth M., Jr. & Le Grand, Scott M., eds. The Protein Folding Problem & Tertiary Structure Prediction. LC 93-41522. x, 581p. 1994. 87.50 (*0-8176-3693-5*) Birkhauser.

Merz, Kenneth M., Jr. & Roux, Benoit, eds. Biological Membranes: A Molecular Perspective from Computation & Experiment. 1996. write for info. (*3-7643-3827-X*) Birkhauser.

Merz, Marisa. Marisa Merz. (Illus.). 126p. 1999. pap. 32.95 (*88-7757-084-9*, Pub. by Hopefulmonster Editore) Dist Art Pubs.

Merz, Richard, jt. auth. see Kimball, Ralph.

Merz, T. Postscript & Acrobat/PDF: Applications, Trouble Shooting & Cross-Platform-Publishing. LC 96-42126. (Illus.). 424p. 1996. 69.50 (*3-540-60854-0*) Spr-Verlag.

***Merz, Thomas.** Postscript & Acrobat/PDF Bible: Applications, Troubleshooting & Cross-Platform-Publishing. 2nd ed. (Illus.). 650p. 1999. 64.95 (*3-540-65534-4*) Spr-Verlag.

Merz, Thomas. Web Publishing with Acrobat/PDF. LC 98-16265. 220p. 1998. pap. 44.95 incl. cd-rom (*3-540-63762-1*) Spr-Verlag.

Merz, Unther G., jt. ed. see Roth, Harald H.

Merzbach, E., jt. auth. see Ivanoff, B. G.

An Asterisk (*) at the beginning of an entry indicates that the title is appearing for the first time.

Merzbach, Ely, jt. auth. see Ivanoff, B. G.

Merzbach, Uta C., compiled by. Carl Friedrich Gauss: A Bibliography. LC 83-20345. 551p. 1984. lib. bdg. 100.00 (*0-8420-2169-8*) Scholarly Res Inc.

Merzbach, Uta C., jt. auth. see Davis, Audrey B.

Merzbach, Uta C., jt. ed. see Birkhoff, Garrett D.

Merzbacher, Eugen. Quantum Mechanics. 2nd ed. 640p. (C). 1969. text 95.95 (*0-471-59670-1*) Wiley.

— Quantum Mechanics. 3rd ed. LC 97-20756. 672p. 1997. text 103.95 (*0-471-88702-1*) Wiley.

Merzel, Dennis G. Beyond Sanity & Madness: The Way of Zen Master Dogen. 176p. (Orig.). 1994. pap. 14.95 (*0-8048-3035-5*) Tuttle Pubng.

Merzel, Dennis G. & Maezumi, Hakuyu T. The Eye Never Sleeps: Striking to the Heart of Zen. LC 90-52803. 176p. (Orig.). 1991. pap. 13.95 (*0-87773-569-7*, Pub. by Shambhala Pubns) Random.

Merzkirch, Wolfgang. Flow Visualization. 2nd ed. 260p. 1987. text 81.00 (*0-12-491351-2*) Acad Pr.

Merzlak, Regina. The Blue Door: A Book of Poems. LC 97-30837. 64p. 1998. pap. 14.95 (*0-7734-2842-9*, Mellen Poetry Pr) E Mellen.

— Earth Tones. LC 93-46363. 64p. 1994. pap. 14.95 (*0-7734-2722-8*, Mellen Poetry Pr) E Mellen.

— Underlight: Poems. LC 92-44220. 64p. 1993. pap. 14.95 (*0-7734-2770-8*, Mellen Poetry Pr) E Mellen.

Merzljakov, Ju. I., jt. auth. see Kargapolov, M. I.

Merzlyakov, N. S., jt. auth. see Yaroslavskii, Leonid P.

Mes, Li. What Italy Stands For. (Significant Issues Ser.). 89p. 1997. pap. text 15.95 (*0-89206-332-7*) CSIS.

Mesa-Bains, Amalia. Ceremony of Spirit: Nature & Memory in Contemporary Latino Art. LC 93-34619. (Illus.). 47p. 1993. 22.50 (*1-880508-02-8*) Mexican Museum.

Mesa-Bains, Amalia & Bettelheim, Judith. Adaline Kent Award Exhibition, 1991 - Mildred Howard: Ten Little Children Standing in a Line (One Got Shot, & Then There Were Nine) (Illus.). 1991. pap. 5.00 (*0-930495-10-1*) San Fran Art Inst.

Mesa-Bains, Amalia & Shulman, Judith H. A Facilitator's Guide to Diversity in the Classroom: A Casebook for Teachers & Teacher Educators. LC 94-7060. 1994. student ed. 21.00 (*0-8058-1688-7*); pap. 14.95 (*0-8058-1430-2*) L Erlbaum Assocs.

Mesa-Bains, Amalia, et al. Ceremony of Memory: Contemporary Hispanic Spiritual & Ceremonial Art. (Illus.). 48p. (Orig.). 1988. pap. text 15.00 (*0-929762-00-2*) CCA Santa Fe.

Mesa-Bains, Amalia, jt. auth. see Romo, Terezita.

Mesa-Bains, Amalia, jt. ed. see Shulman, Judith H.

Mesa, Cuevas. Spanish-English/English-Spanish Commercial Dictionary. (DUT & ENG.). 255p. 1993. 49.95 (*0-7859-9572-2*) Fr & Eur.

Mesa Group Staff. The Original Internet Address Book. LC 96-32050. 160p. (C). 1996. pap. text 5.95 (*0-13-260431-0*) P-H.

Mesa-Lago, Carmelo. Ascent to Bankruptcy: Financing Social Security in Latin America. LC 89-35475. (Latin American Ser.). 318p. 1990. text 49.95 (*0-8229-3600-3*) U of Pittsburgh Pr.

— Dialectica de la Revolucion Cubana del Idealism Carismatico al Pragmatismo Institucionalista. (SPA.). 244p. (C). 1979. pap. text 21.95 (*84-359-0203-X*) Transaction Pubs.

— The Economy of Socialist Cuba: A Two-Decade Appraisal. LC 80-54570. 251p. reprint ed. pap. 77.90 (*0-7837-5868-5*, 204558700006) Bks Demand.

— Health Care for the Poor in Latin America & the Caribbean. (PAHO Scientific Publications: No. 539). (ENG & SPA.). v, 234p. 1992. pap. text 56.00 (*92-75-11539-7*, 1610539) World Health.

***Mesa-Lago, Carmelo.** Market, Socialist & Mixed Economies: Comparative Policy & Performance: Chile, Costa Rica & Cuba LC 99-42559. 2000. 75.00 (*0-8018-6172-1*) Johns Hopkins.

Mesa-Lago, Carmelo. Social Security in Latin America: Pressure Groups, Stratification, & Inequality. LC 77-15732. (Pitt Latin American Ser.). 372p. reprint ed. pap. 115.40 (*0-7837-2474-8*, 204262800005) Bks Demand.

Mesa-Lago, Carmelo, ed. Cuba after the Cold War. LC 92-50847. (Latin American Ser.). 408p. (C). 1993. text 49.95 (*0-8229-3749-2*) U of Pittsburgh Pr.

— Cuban Studies, Vol. 16. LC 75-649635. 302p. 1986. text 39.95 (*0-8229-3540-6*) U of Pittsburgh Pr.

— Cuban Studies, Vol. 18. LC 75-649635. (Latin American Ser.). 261p. (C). 1988. text 39.95 (*0-8229-3593-7*) U of Pittsburgh Pr.

— Cuban Studies, Vol. 19. LC 75-649635. (Latin American Ser.). 384p. 1989. text 39.95 (*0-8229-3626-7*) U of Pittsburgh Pr.

— Cuban Studies, Vol. 20. LC 75-649635. (Latin American Ser.). 256p. 1990. text 39.95 (*0-8229-3649-6*) U of Pittsburgh Pr.

— Revolutionary Change in Cuba. LC 73-158190. 560p. reprint ed. pap. 173.60 (*0-7837-2473-X*, 204262700005) Bks Demand.

Mesa-Lago, Carmelo, et al, eds. Cuban Studies, Vol. 17. LC 75-649635. 255p. 1981. text 39.95 (*0-8229-3562-7*) U of Pittsburgh Pr.

Mesa-Lago, Carmelo & Beck, Carl, eds. Comparative Socialist Systems: Essays on Politics & Economics. LC 75-331585. 466p. reprint ed. pap. 144.50 (*0-8357-4638-0*, 203756900008) Bks Demand.

Mesa, Mario. Decidle Que Adolezco. (Aqui y Ahora Ser.). 1997. pap. 6.95 (*0-8477-0323-1*) U of PR Pr.

Mesa, Rosa Q. Argentina. LC 73-180800. (Latin American Serial Documents Ser.: Vol. 5). 726p. reprint ed. pap. 200.00 (*0-8357-5729-3*, 201354700087) Bks Demand.

— Bolivia. LC 73-180800. (Latin American Serial Documents Ser.: Vol. 6). 190p. reprint ed. pap. 58.90 (*0-8357-7336-1*, 201355200087) Bks Demand.

— Chile. LC 73-180800. (Latin American Serial Documents Ser.: Vol. 7). 359p. 1973. reprint ed. pap. 111.30 (*0-8357-0075-5*, 201354900087) Bks Demand.

— Colombia. LC 68-56197. (Latin American Serial Documents Ser.: Vol. 1). 150p. 1968. pap. 46.50 (*0-8357-0308-8*, 2013543) Bks Demand.

— Cuba. LC 70-79480. (Latin American Serial Documents Ser.: Vol. 3). 225p. 1969. reprint ed. pap. 69.80 (*0-8357-2178-7*, 201354500087) Bks Demand.

— Ecuador. LC 73-180800. (Latin American Serial Documents Ser.: Vol. 8). 174p. 1973. reprint ed. pap. 54.00 (*0-8357-0076-3*, 201355000087) Bks Demand.

— Paraguay. LC 73-180800. (Latin American Serial Documents Ser.: Vol. 9). 93p. 1973. reprint ed. pap. 30.00 (*0-8357-0077-1*, 201355100087) Bks Demand.

— Peru. LC 73-180800. (Latin American Serial Documents Ser.: Vol. 10). 307p. 1973. reprint ed. pap. 95.20 (*0-8357-0078-X*, 201354800087) Bks Demand.

— Uruguay. LC 73-180800. (Latin American Serial Documents Ser.: Vol. 11). 193p. 1973. reprint ed. pap. 59.90 (*0-8357-0079-8*, 201355300087) Bks Demand.

— Venezuela. LC 73-180800. (Latin American Serial Documents Ser.: Vol. 12). 337p. 1977. reprint ed. pap. 104.50 (*0-8357-0200-6*, 201355400087) Bks Demand.

Mesadieu, Rickter V. Scars of Slavery. LC 99-93008. (Illus.). 94p. 1999. pap. write for info. (*0-7392-0079-8*, P02940) Morris Pubng.

Mesangere, Pierre De La, see De La Mesangere, Pierre.

Mesaric, G. Black Magic Web: Unraveling the Mystery of the World Wide Web Technologies. 370p. 1997. pap. text 39.95 (*3-540-61063-4*) Spr-Verlag.

Mesarovic, M. D. & Takahara, Y. Abstract Systems Theory. (Lecture Notes in Control & Information Sciences: Vol. 116). viii, 439p. 1989. 79.95 (*0-387-50529-6*) Spr-Verlag.

Mesbah, Ali, et al. The Mystical Epistemology of Mulla Sadra. (Nur Ser.). 349p. (Orig.). 1997. pap. 17.00 (*1-883058-24-4*, Nur) Global Pubns.

Mesbah, M. T., et al. Status of Women in Islam. vi, 57p. 1990. text 10.95 (*0-685-35772-4*, Pub. by Radiant Pubs) S Asia.

Mesbahi, Mohiaddin, ed. Central Asia & the Caucasus after the Soviet Union: Domestic & International Dynamics. LC 94-16204. 344p. 1994. 49.95 (*0-8130-1307-0*) U Press Fla.

— Russia & the Third World in the Post-Soviet Era. 376p. (C). 1994. 49.95 (*0-8130-1270-8*); pap. 19.95 (*0-8130-1271-6*) U Press Fla.

Mesce, Bill, Jr. Four Day Shoot. 1993. pap. 7.95 (*0-9638760-0-7*) Generic Pubng.

***Mesce, Bill, Jr. & Szilagyi.** Angel Descendant. 2000. mass mkt. write for info. (*0-553-58197-X*) Bantam Dell.

***Mesce, Bill, Jr. & Szilagyi, Steve.** The Advocate. LC 00-39764. 320p. 2000. 23.95 (*0-553-80118-X*) Bantam.

Mesch, Abraham J., tr. see Hanover, Nathan.

Meschan, Isadore. An Atlas of Anatomy Basic to Radiology. 2nd ed. 1998. text. write for info. (*0-7216-3533-4*, W B Saunders Co) Harcrt Hlth Sci Grp.

Meschan, Isadore & Ott, David J. Introduction to Diagnostic Imaging. (Illus.). 416p. 1984. text 65.00 (*0-7216-6277-3*, W B Saunders Co) Harcrt Hlth Sci Grp.

MESCHBACH, KARL-HEINZ. Fabulous Finishes for Your Home, Step by Step. LC 99-14290. (Illus.). 128p. 1999. pap. 24.99 (*0-89134-921-9*, 31452, North Lght Bks) F & W Pubns Inc.

Meschel, Susan, jt. auth. see Handler, Andrew.

Meschel, Susan V., jt. auth. see Handler, Andrew.

Meschery, Joanne. Home & Away. 1994. 21.00 (*0-671-88419-0*) S&S Trade.

— Home & Away: A Novel. LC 97-31398. (California Fiction Ser.). 284p. 1998. 13.95 (*0-520-21342-4*, Pub. by U CA Pr) Cal Prin Full Svc.

***Meschery, Tom.** Nothing We Lose Can Be Replaced. (Rainshadow Editions Ser.). xii, 67p. 1999. pap. 12.00 (*1-891033-15-8*) Black Rock Pr.

Meschi, Bob. Antique Wicker from the Heywood-Wakefield Catalog. LC 94-65608. (Illus.). 60p. (Orig.). 1994. pap. 19.95 (*0-88740-618-1*) Schiffer.

Meschi, Edward J. Durand: The Man & His Glass. LC 99-167170. (Illus.). 192p. 1998. 39.95 (*1-57080-052-9*) Antique Pubns.

Meschiari, M., et al. Geometry Seminar "Luigi Bianchi" II 1984. (Lecture Notes in Mathematics Ser.: Vol. 1164). vi, 224p. 1985. 37.95 (*0-387-16048-5*) Spr-Verlag.

Meschinelli, Mark, tr. see Richards, James Henry & Richards, Patricia Lewis.

Meschino, James, et al. Break the Weight-Loss Barrier. LC 97-4342. 304p. (C). 1997. text 19.95 (*0-13-745407-4*) P-H.

Meschler, Maurice. St. Aloysius Gonzaga: Patron of Christian Youth. LC 84-52294. 348p. 1985. reprint ed. pap. 12.00 (*0-89555-275-2*) TAN Bks Pubs.

Meschter, Alfred T. The Ship St. Andrew, Galley: A Hypothesis. 1992. pap. 3.00 (*0-935980-08-3*) Schwenkfelder Lib.

Meschter, W. Kyrel. Twentieth-Century Schwenkfelders: A Narrative History. 1984. pap. 7.50 (*0-935980-03-2*) Schwenkfelder Lib.

Meschutt, David. A Bold Experiment: John Henri Isaac Browere's Life Masks of Prominent Americans. Tripp, Wendell, ed. 1988. pap. 5.95 (*0-917334-17-5*) NY Hist Assn.

Meschyan, S. R. Experimental Rheology of Clayey Soils. Mehta, N. K., tr. from RUS. LC 99-225738. (Geotechnika Ser.: No. 13). (Illus.). 460p. (C). 1996. text 126.00 (*90-5410-177-6*, Pub. by A A Balkema) Ashgate Pub Co.

Mescon, jt. auth. see Rachman.

Mescon Group Staff. Constructive Use of Power. (Performance Through Participation Ser.). 1996. text, teacher ed. 23.95 (*0-538-84935-5*); text, suppl. ed. 14.95 (*0-538-84934-7*) S-W Pub.

— Decision Making. (Performance Through Participation Ser.). 90p. 1996. text 14.95 (*0-538-84946-0*); text, teacher ed. 23.95 (*0-538-84947-9*) S-W Pub.

— Individual Behavior. (GC - Principles of Management Ser.). 1996. text, teacher ed. 23.95 (*0-538-84937-1*); text, suppl. ed. 14.95 (*0-538-84936-3*) S-W Pub.

— Making Meetings Productive. (Performance Through Participation Ser.). 1996. text, teacher ed. 23.95 (*0-538-84945-2*); text, suppl. ed. 14.95 (*0-538-84944-4*) S-W Pub.

— Managing Conflict in Teams. (Performance Through Participation Ser.). 90p. 1996. text 14.95 (*0-538-84942-8*); text, teacher ed. 23.95 (*0-538-84943-6*) S-W Pub.

— Managing in a Competitive Environment. (GC - Principles of Management Ser.). 1995. text, teacher ed. 25.95 (*0-538-85042-6*) S-W Pub.

— Planning & Goal Setting for Improved Performance. (GC - Principles of Management Ser.). 1995. text, teacher ed. 25.95 (*0-538-85038-8*) S-W Pub.

— Practicing Effective Leadership. (Performance Through Participation Ser.). 1996. text, teacher ed. 23.95 (*0-538-84939-8*); text, suppl. ed. 14.95 (*0-538-84938-X*) S-W Pub.

— Strengthening Teamwork: Trade Version. (GC - Principles of Management Ser.). 1995. text, teacher ed. 25.95 (*0-538-85041-8*) S-W Pub.

— Tapping Creativity. (GC - Principles of Management Ser.). 1996. text, suppl. ed. 14.95 (*0-538-84932-0*); text, suppl. ed. 23.95 (*0-538-84933-9*) S-W Pub.

— Techniques for Better Communication. (Performance Through Participation Ser.). 90p. 1996. text 14.95 (*0-538-84940-1*); text, teacher ed. 23.95 (*0-538-84941-X*) S-W Pub.

— Techniques for Problem Solving. (GC - Principles of Managment Ser.). 1995. text, teacher ed. 25.95 (*0-538-85039-6*) S-W Pub.

— Values: A Foundation for Success. (GC - Principles of Management Ser.). 1995. text, teacher ed. 25.95 (*0-538-85040-X*) S-W Pub.

Mescon, Michael H., et al. Business Today. 9th ed. LC 98-33629. 781p. (C). 1998. 82.00 (*0-13-080819-9*) P-H.

Mescon, Michael H., jt. auth. see Rachman, David J.

MESD School Health Services Staff. Practical Guidelines for Reducing the Risk of Communicable Disease in a School Setting. 1992. 7.50 (*1-880118-06-8*) MESD Pr.

MESD School Health Services Staff, jt. auth. see Bauer, Dee K.

Mesec, Andrea L. Serious Illness in the Classroom: An Educator's Resource. LC 96-41965. 140p. 1997. pap. text 22.50 (*1-56308-416-3*) Teacher Ideas Pr.

Meseck, Gerhard, ed. Handbuch der Seefischerei Nordeuropas, 11 vols. (GER.). 1967. pap. 851.00 (*3-510-42000-4*, Pub. by E Schweizerbartsche) Balogh.

Mesecke, Andrea & Scheer, Thorsten. Josef Paul Kleihues. LC 96-35949. (GER., Illus.). 296p. 1996. 65.00 (*3-7643-5387-2*, Pub. by Birkhauser) Princeton Arch.

Mesens, E. L. & Penrose, Roland, eds. London Bulletin, 1938 to 1940, 2 vols., Set. LC 77-96917. (Contemporary Art Ser.). (Illus.). 1970. reprint ed. 60.95 (*0-405-00733-7*) Ayer.

Mesera, F., et al, eds. Biomechanical Transport Processes. LC 90-4246. (NATO ASI Series A, Life Sciences: Vol. 193). (Illus.). 426p. (C). 1990. text 156.00 (*0-306-43676-0*) Plenum.

Meserole, Harrison T., ed. American Poetry of the Seventeenth Century. LC 85-21701. 576p. 1985. reprint ed. pap. 19.95 (*0-271-00418-5*) Pa St U Pr.

Meserole, Harrison T., jt. auth. see Bateson, Frederick W.

Meserole, Mike. 20th Century Sports: Images of Greatness. LC 99-63223. (Illus.). 256p. 1999. pap. 26.95 (*1-892129-12-4*) Total Sprts.

— The Ultimate Book of Sports Lists, 1999. LC 98-16678. 1999. 17.95 (*0-7894-3562-4*); pap. 17.95 (*0-7894-3753-8*) DK Pub Inc.

Meserve, Bruce E. Fundamental Concepts of Algebra. (Mathematics Ser.). 320p. 1982. reprint ed. pap. 9.95 (*0-486-61470-0*) Dover.

— Fundamental Concepts of Geometry. (Illus.). 352p. 1998. reprint ed. pap. 9.95 (*0-486-63415-9*) Dover.

Meserve, Bruce E., et al. Contemporary Mathematics. 4th ed. (Illus.). 720p. (C). 1986. text 57.80 (*0-13-170127-4*) P-H.

Meserve, Harry C. The Practical Meditator. LC 80-15631. 137p. 1981. 27.95 (*0-87705-506-8*, Kluwer Acad Hman Sci) Kluwer Academic.

Meserve, Mollie A. The Musical Theatre Cookbook: Recipes from Best Loved Musicals. 208p. 1993. pap. 9.95 (*0-937657-16-6*) Feedbk Theabks & Prospero.

Meserve, Mollie A., ed. The Playwright's Companion, 1998: A Practical Guide to Script Opportunities in the U. S. A. 14th rev. ed. 416p. 1998. pap. 20.95 (*0-937657-35-2*) Feedbk Theabks & Prospero.

Meserve, Mollie A. & Meserve, Walter J. The Theatre Lover's Cookbook: Recipes from 60 Favorite Plays. 208p. 1992. pap. 9.95 (*0-937657-11-5*) Feedbk Theabks & Prospero.

Meserve, Mollie A., jt. auth. see Meserve, Walter J.

Meserve, Mollie A., ed. see Barker, James N.

Meserve, Mollie A., ed. see Brougham, John.

Meserve, Mollie A., ed. see DeMille, William C.

Meserve, Mollie A., ed. see Foster, Charles.

Meserve, Mollie A., ed. see Lloyd, David & Rosenfeld, Sydney.

Meserve, Mollie A., ed. see Mathews, Cornelius.

Meserve, Mollie A., jt. ed. see Meserve, Walter J.

Meserve, Mollie A., ed. see Middleton, George.

Meserve, Mollie A., ed. see Sheldon, Edward.

Meserve, Mollie A., ed. see Smith, William H.

Meserve, Mollie A., ed. see Stowe, Harriet Beecher.

Meserve, Mollie Ann, jt. ed. see Meserve, Walter J.

Meserve, Ruth I., compiled by. Denis Sinor Bibliography. (Arcadia Bibliographica Virorum Eruditorum Ser.: Fasc. g). 64p. 1986. 18.00 (*0-931922-12-7*) Eurolingua.

Meserve, Ruth I., jt. ed. see Meserve, Walter M.

Meserve, Walter J. Heralds of Promise: The Drama of the American People During the Age of Jackson, 1829-1849, 86. LC 85-21846. (Contributions in American Studies: No.86). (Illus.). 282p. 1986. 59.95 (*0-313-23015-4*, MHP, Greenwood Pr) Greenwood.

— An Outline History of American Drama. 2nd ed. 416p. 1996. reprint ed. pap. 19.95 (*0-937657-18-2*) Feedbk Theabks & Prospero.

Meserve, Walter J., ed. On Stage America! A Selection of Distinctly American Plays. LC 96-85294. (Illus.). 576p. (Orig.). 1996. pap. 24.95 (*0-937657-20-4*) Feedbk Theabks & Prospero.

Meserve, Walter J., ed. Rip Van Winkle. (On Stage, America! Ser.). 47p. 1996. spiral bd. 4.95 (*0-937657-28-X*) Feedbk Theabks & Prospero.

Meserve, Walter J. & Meserve, Mollie A. A Chronological Outline of World Theatre. 144p. 1992. pap. 9.95 (*0-937657-12-3*) Feedbk Theabks & Prospero.

***Meserve, Walter J. & Meserve, Mollie A., eds.** When Conscience Trod the Stage: American Plays of Social Awareness. LC 98-70668. (Illus.). xii, 499 p. 1998. pap. 24.95 (*0-937657-36-0*) Feedbk Theabks & Prospero.

***Meserve, Walter J. & Meserve, Mollie Ann, eds.** Fateful Lightning: America's Civil War Plays. (Americana Ser.). (Illus.). 600p. (YA). (gr. 10-12). 2000. pap. 24.95 (*0-937657-50-6*) Feedbk Theabks & Prospero.

Meserve, Walter J., jt. auth. see Meserve, Mollie A.

Meserve, Walter J., ed. see Barker, James N.

Meserve, Walter J., ed. see Brougham, John.

Meserve, Walter J., ed. see DeMille, William C.

Meserve, Walter J., ed. see Foster, Charles.

Meserve, Walter J., ed. see Lloyd, David & Rosenfeld, Sydney.

Meserve, Walter J., ed. see Mathews, Cornelius.

Meserve, Walter J., ed. see Middleton, George.

Meserve, Walter J., ed. see Sheldon, Edward.

Meserve, Walter J., ed. see Smith, William H.

Meserve, Walter J., ed. see Stowe, Harriet Beecher.

Meserve, Walter J., ed. & intro. see Baker, Benjamin A.

Meserve, Walter J., ed. & intro. see Belasco, David.

Meserve, Walter J., ed. & intro. see Daly, Augustin.

Meserve, Walter J., ed. & intro. see Durivage, Oliver E.

Meserve, Walter J., ed. & intro. see Herne, James A.

Meserve, Walter J., ed. & intro. see Howard, Bronson.

Meserve, Walter J., ed. & intro. see Hoyt, Charles H.

Meserve, Walter J., ed. & intro. see Mowatt, Anna C.

Meserve, Walter J., ed. & intro. see Stone, John A.

Meserve, Walter J., ed. & intro. see Tyler, Royall.

Meserve, Walter M. & Meserve, Ruth I., eds. Modern Drama from Communist China. LC 77-92524. 368p. 1970. 24.95 (*0-8147-0302-X*) Boulevard.

Meserve, William N. Meserve Civil War Record: With the Intriguing War Story by Major William N. Meserve. Huebner, Richard A., ed. LC 87-23557. (Illus.). xxii, 290p. (C). 1988. 55.00 (*0-9619037-7-5*) RAH Pubns.

— Meserve Civil War Record: With the Intriguing War Story by Major William N. Meserve. deluxe limited ed. Huebner, Richard A., ed. LC 87-23557. (Illus.). xxii, 290p. (C). 1988. 85.00 (*0-9619037-6-7*) RAH Pubns.

***Mesetti, Marco.** Ducati: A History in Association with the Ducati Motor Museum. (Illus.). 288p. 2000. 39.95 (*1-85227-893-5*, 130257AE, Pub. by Virgin Bks) Motorbooks Intl.

Meseure, Anna. Macke. 1997. 12.99 (*3-8228-0671-4*) Benedikt Taschen.

Meseure, Anna. Macke. 1994. pap. 9.99 (*3-8228-0551-3*) Taschen Amer.

Meseure, Anna, jt. ed. see Wang, Wilfried.

Mesfin, Daniel J. Exotic Ethiopian Cooking. LC 87-90854. 213p. 1987. 18.95 (*0-317-57587-2*); pap. 14.95 (*0-9616345-0-2*) Ethiopian Ent.

— Exotic Ethiopian Cooking: Society, Culture, Hospitality & Tradition in Ethiopia. expanded ed. LC 89-81056. (Illus.). 310p. (Orig.). 1990. pap. 14.99 (*0-9616345-1-0*) Ethiopian Ent.

— Exotic Ethiopian Cooking: Society, Culture, Hospitality & Traditions in Ethiopia. enl. rev. ed. LC 89-81056. (Illus.). 352p. (C). 1993. pap. 15.99 (*0-9616345-2-9*) Ethiopian Ent.

Meshcherskii, I. & Romicki, R. Collection of Problems of Mechanics. LC 63-15496. (International Series of Monographs on Pure & Applied Mathematics: Vol. 65). 1965. 237.00 (*0-08-010145-3*, Pub. by Pergamon Repr) Franklin.

Meshenberg, Michael J. Documents of Our Ancestors: A Selection of Reproducible Genealogy Forms & Tips for Using Them. LC 96-24596. (Illus.). 148p. 1996. pap. 19.95 (*1-886223-01-7*) Avotaynu.

Mesher, Alan. The T Zone: The Path to Inner Power. 160p. 1997. pap. 14.95 (*0-9660295-3-4*) Beacon Ctr Pubns.

Meshii, M., ed. Mechanical Properties of BCC Metals: Proceedings of the U. S. - Japan Seminar. LC 82-81287. (Conference Proceedings Ser.). (Illus.). 253p. reprint ed. pap. 78.50 (*0-608-15985-9*, 205226700084) Bks Demand.

Meshinsky, Joanne. How to Choose a Nursing Home: A Guide to Quality Caring. 1991. pap. 7.95 (*0-380-76078-9*, Avon Bks) Morrow Avon.

Meshkinpour, Hooshang. Az Orshalim ta Orshalim: From Jerusalem to Jerusalem. (Bibliotheca Iranica Ser.: No. 11). (PER.). 312p. 1999. pap. 15.00 (*1-56859-088-1*) Mazda Pubs.

M

Meshko, Oksana. Between Death & Life. Moshinsky, George, tr. from UKR. (Illus.). 176p. 1981. 19.95 (*0-614-30269-2*) ZZYZX Pub.

*****Meshkov, Sydney, ed.** Gravitational Waves: Third Edoardo Amaldi Conference. LC 00-103506. (AIP Conference Proceedings Ser.: Vol. 523). (Illus.). xviii, 492p. 2000. 140.00 (*1-56396-944-0*) Am Inst Physics.

Meshorer, Yaakov. Ancient Jewish Coinage Vol. I: Persian Period Through Hasmoneans. (Illus.). 235p. 1982. lib. bdg. 80.00 (*1-886720-09-6*) S J Durst.

Meshorer, Ya'akov. Sylloge Nummorum Graecorum: The Collection of the American Numismatic Society: Palestine-South Arabia, Pt. 6. (Illus.). 54p. 1981. text 100.00 (*0-89722-187-7*) Am Numismatic.

Meshoulam, Ilan, jt. auth. see Bamberger, Peter.

Meshram, Pradip S. Early Caves of Maharashtra: A Cultural Study. (C). 1991. 46.00 (*81-85067-73-2*, Pub. by Sundeep Prak) S Asia.

Meshri, Indu D. & Ortoleva, Peter J., eds. Prediction of Reservoir Quality Through Chemical Modeling. (AAPG Memoir Ser.: No. 49). (Illus.). 175p. 1990. 15.00 (*0-89181-327-6*, 563) AAPG.

Mesiats, Gennadii A., et al. Pulsed Gas Lasers. LC 94-23266. Orig. Title: Impulsnye Gazovye Lazery. (ENG & RUS.). 1994. 85.00 (*0-8194-1709-2*, PM17) SPIE.

Mesibov, G. B., jt. auth. see Schopler, E.

Mesibov, Gary B., et al. Adolescent & Adult Psychoeducational Profile (AAPEP), Vol. IV. LC 78-13415. (Individualized Assessment & Treatment for Autistic & Developmentally Disabled Children Ser.). (Illus.). 150p. (Orig.). 1988. pap. 64.00 (*0-89079-152-X*, 1425) PRO-ED.

— Autism: Understanding the Disorder. LC 97-35645. (Clinical Child Psychology Library). (Illus.). 136p. (C). 1998. 45.00 (*0-306-45546-3*, Kluwer Plenum); pap. 25.00 (*0-306-45547-1*, Kluwer Plenum) Kluwer Academic.

Mesibov, Gary B., jt. auth. see Schopler, Eric.

Mesibov, Gary B., jt. ed. see Schopler, Eric.

Mesibov, Laurie L., compiled by. North Carolina Constitutional & Statutory Provisions with Respect to Higher Education. rev. ed. 403p. (C). 1988. pap. text 17.00 (*1-56011-110-0*, 88.08) Institute Government.

Mesic, Penelope. Buried Treasure. 1993. 15.95 (*0-226-52076-5*) U Ch Pr.

Mesic, Richard, jt. auth. see Harshberger, Edward R.

Mesic, Richard F. & Shaver, Russell D. Calculating the Utility of Attacks Against Ballistic Missile Transporter-Erector-Launchers. LC 95-4975. 80p. 1995. pap. text 15.00 (*0-8330-1626-1*, MR-469-AF) Rand Corp.

Mesick, Jane L. English Traveller in America, 1785-1835. 1971. reprint ed. 15.00 (*0-403-01106-X*) Scholarly.

— The English Traveller in America, 1785-1835. (BCL1 - U. S. History Ser.). 370p. 1991. reprint ed. lib. bdg. 89.00 (*0-7812-6376-X*) Rprt Serv.

Mesinai, Susan Y., jt. auth. see Carlebach, Shlomo.

Mesirov, Jill P., ed. Very Large Scale Computation in the Twenty-First Century. LC 91-20925. (Miscellaneous Bks.: No. 25). xviii, 327p. 1991. 60.25 (*0-89871-279-3*) Soc Indus-Appl Math.

Mesirow, Kip. The Care & Use of Japanese Woodworking Tools. LC 78-60055. (Illus.). 1982. reprint ed. pap. 9.95 (*0-918036-08-9*) Woodcraft Supply.

Mesit, Sydney Z., ed. see Watson, K. Rhydell.

Meske, Eunice B. & Rinehart, Carroll, compiled by. Individualized Instruction in Music. LC 75-10725. (Illus.). 168p. 1975. reprint ed. pap. 52.10 (*0-608-04213-7*, 206495300011) Bks Demand.

Meske, W., ed. Restructuring Science & Technology: Experience & Task in Economies in Transition. LC 97-75191. 375p. 1998. 97.00 (*90-5199-370-6*, 370-6) IOS Press.

Meskell, David. Racine: A Theatrical Reading. (Illus.). 284p. 1991. text 80.00 (*0-19-815161-6*) OUP.

Meskell, Lynn. Archaeologies of Social Life: Age, Sex, Class, Etcetera in Ancient Egypt. LC 99-27890. (Social Archaeology Ser.). (Illus.). 256p. 1999. text 59.95 (*0-631-21298-1*); pap. text 29.95 (*0-631-21299-X*) Blackwell Pubs.

Meskell, Lynne, ed. Archaeology under Fire: Nationalism, Politics & Heritage in the Eastern Mediterranean & Middle East. (Illus.). 240p. (C). 1999. 85.00 (*0-415-16470-2*, D6016); pap. 25.99 (*0-415-19655-8*, D6020) Routledge.

Meskens, Nadine & Roubens, Marc. Advances in Decision Analysis. LC 98-53210. (Mathematical Modelling--theory & Applications Ser.). 19p. 1999. write for info. (*0-7923-5563-6*) Kluwer Academic.

Meskill, Johanna M. A Chinese Pioneer Family: The Lins of Wu-Feng, Taiwan, 1729-1895. LC 78-70308. (Illus.). 392p. 1979. reprint ed. pap. 121.60 (*0-608-06478-5*, 206677500009) Bks Demand.

Meskill, John. Academies in Ming China: A Historical Essay. LC 81-24083. (Monographs: No. 39). xv, 203p. 1982. 19.00 (*0-8165-0771-6*) Assn Asian Studies.

— Gentlemanly Interests & Wealth on the Yangtze Delta. (Monographs: No. 49). (Illus.). vii, 208p. 1995. 29.00 (*0-924304-19-7*) Assn Asian Studies.

Meskill, John, tr. see Ch'oe, Pu.

Meskill, John T. An Introduction to Chinese Civilization. 699p. (C). 1973. pap. text 41.56 (*0-669-73502-7*) HM Trade Div.

Meskill, John T., intro. The Pattern of Chinese History: Cycles, Development or Stagnation. LC 82-18378. (Problems in Asian Civilizations Ser.). 108p. 1983. reprint ed. lib. bdg. 57.50 (*0-313-23739-5*, MEPC, Greenwood Pr) Greenwood.

Meskill, Tim. Current Market Outlook, 1998: World Market Demand & Airplane Supply Requirements. (Illus.). 60p. (C). 1999. pap. text 30.00 (*0-7881-7601-3*) DIANE Pub.

— Current Market Outlook, 1995: World Air Travel Demand & Airplane Supply Requirements. (Illus.). 43p. (Orig.). (C). 1995. pap. text 40.00 (*0-7881-0994-4*) DIANE Pub.

— Current Market Outlook, 1996: World Market Demand & Airplane Supply Requirements. (Illus.). 38p. (Orig.). (C). 1996. pap. text 40.00 (*0-7881-3035-8*) DIANE Pub.

— Current Market Outlook (1997) World Market Demand & Airplane Supply Requirements for Commercial Aircraft. (Illus.). 51p. (C). 1998. pap. text 35.00 (*0-7881-4930-X*) DIANE Pub.

Meskimmon, Marsha. The Art of Reflection: Women Artists' Self-Portraiture in the Twentieth Century. LC 96-14028. (Illus.). 224p. 1996. 52.00 (*0-231-10686-6*); pap. 19.50 (*0-231-10687-4*) Col U Pr.

— Engendering the City: Women Artists & Urban Space. LC 99-181257. 1997. pap. text 12.95 (*1-85727-098-3*, Pub. by Scarlet Pr) LPC InBook.

— We Weren't Modern Enough: Women Artists & the Limits of German Modernism. LC 99-30434. Vol. 25. 272p. 1999. 60.00 (*0-520-22133-8*, Pub. by U CA Pr); pap. 24.95 (*0-520-22134-6*, Pub. by U CA Pr) Cal Prin Full Svc.

Meskimmon, Marsha & West, Sherer, eds. Visions of the "Neue Frau" Women & the Visual Arts in Weimar Germany. (Illus.). 235p. (C). 1995. 78.95 (*1-85928-157-5*, Pub. by Scolar Pr) Ashgate Pub Co.

Meskin. 1998 Year Book of Dentistry. (Illus.). 528p. (C). (gr. 13). 1998. text 73.00 (*0-8151-7084-X*, 27509) Mosby Inc.

Meskin, Lawrence. 1997 Year Book of Dentistry. (Illus.). 552p. (C). (gr. 13). 1997. text 73.00 (*0-8151-7083-1*, 27508) Mosby Inc.

Mesko, Annah, ed. see Barr, William A.

*****Mesko, Jim.** Air War over Korea. (Illus.). 64p. 2000. pap. 11.95 (*0-89747-415-5*, 6082) Squad Sig Pubns.

Mesko, Jim. Amtracs in Action. (Armor in Action Ser.). (Illus.). 50p. 1993. pap. 9.95 (*0-89747-298-5*) Squad Sig Pubns.

— Armor in Vietnam: A Pictorial History. (Vietnam Studies Group). (Illus.). 80p. 1982. pap. 12.95 (*0-89747-126-1*, 6033) Squad Sig Pubns.

— F3H Demon in Action. LC 94-143231. (Aircraft in Action Ser.). (Illus.). 50p. 1994. pap. 9.95 (*0-89747-308-6*) Squad Sig Pubns.

— Ground War - Vietnam, Vol. 1. (Vietnam Studies Group). (Illus.). 64p. 1990. pap. 10.95 (*0-89747-251-9*, 6053) Squad Sig Pubns.

— Ground War - Vietnam, Vol. 2. (Vietnam Studies Group). (Illus.). 64p. 1992. pap. 10.95 (*0-89747-288-8*, 6057) Squad Sig Pubns.

— M-41 Walker Bulldog in Action. (Armor in Action Ser.). (Illus.). 50p. 1991. pap. 9.95 (*0-89747-262-4*, 2029) Squad Sig Pubns.

— M3 Half-Track in Action. (Armor in Action Ser.: No. 34). (Illus.). 50p. 1996. pap. 9.95 (*0-89747-363-9*, 2034) Squad Sig Pubns.

— M-3 Lee - Grant in Action. (Armor in Action Ser.). (Illus.). 50p. 1995. pap. 9.95 (*0-89747-346-9*) Squad Sig Pubns.

*****Mesko, Jim.** M4 Sherman Walk Around. (On Deck Ser.: Vol. 1). (Illus.). 80p. 2000. pap. 14.95 (*0-89747-410-4*) Squad Sig Pubns.

Mesko, Jim. OV-10 Bronco in Action. (Aircraft in Action Ser.). (Illus.). 50p. 1995. pap. 9.95 (*0-89747-340-X*) Squad Sig Pubns.

— U. S. Armored Cars in Action. LC 99-173461. (Armor in Action Ser.: Vol. 37). (Illus.). 50p. 1998. pap. 9.95 (*0-89747-391-4*, 2037) Squad Sig Pubns.

*****Mesko, Jim.** U. S. Self-Propelled Guns. (Armor in Action Ser.: Vol. 38). (Illus.). 50p. 1999. pap. 9.95 (*0-89747-403-1*) Squad Sig Pubns.

Mesko, Jim. U. S. Tank Destroyers in Action. (Armor in Action Ser.: Vol. 36). (Illus.). 50p. 1998. pap. 9.95 (*0-89747-385-X*, 2036) Squad Sig Pubns.

*****Mesko, Sabrina.** Healing Mudras: Yoga for Your Hands. (Illus.). 160p. 2000. pap. 18.00 (*0-345-43758-6*) Ballantine Pub Grp.

Meskoob, Shahrokh. Iranian Nationality & the Persian Language: Roles of Government, Religion, & Sufism in Persian Prose Writing. Perry, John, ed. Hillmann, Michael, tr. from PER. LC DK6225.M413 1992. 192p. 1992. 29.95 (*0-934211-21-3*) Mage Pubs Inc.

*****Meskouris, K., ed.** Baustatik - Baupraxis 7: Berichte der 7.Konferenz uber Baustatik- Baupraxis, Aachen, Deutschland, 18.-19. Marz 1999. (Illus.). 466p. (C). 1999. 105.00 (*90-5809-044-2*) A A Balkema.

Meskouris, K. & Wittek, U., eds. Aspects in Modern Computational Structural Analysis: Festschrift for Professor Kratzig. (Illus.). 510p. (C). 1997. text 126.00 (*90-5410-927-0*, Pub. by A A Balkema) Ashgate Pub Co.

Mesland, D. A., jt. ed. see Innocenti, L.

Mesle, C. Robert. Fire in My Bones: Reflection on Faith. 1984. pap. 19.00 (*0-8309-0387-9*) Herald Pub Hse.

Mesle, C. Robert & Cobb, John B., Jr. Process Theology: A Basic Introduction. LC 93-9204. 160p. (Orig.). 1993. pap. 12.99 (*0-8272-2945-3*) Chalice Pr.

Mesler, Craig R. & Flahive, Thomas J. The ISO 14000 Miniguide. 56p. 1997. pap. 4.50 (*0-527-76324-1*) Productivity Inc.

Mesler, Donald T., jt. auth. see Barenblat, Scot G.

Mesli, A., jt. auth. see Weber, J.

Meslier, Jean. Superstition in All Ages. Knoop, Anna, tr. from FRE. LC 77-161337. (Atheist Viewpoint Ser.). (Illus.). 346p. 1976. reprint ed. 25.95 (*0-405-03795-3*) Ayer.

— Superstition in All Ages: Last Will & Testament: Common Sense. Knoop, Anna, tr. 339p. 1996. reprint ed. pap. 17.95 (*1-56459-794-6*) Kessinger Pub.

— Le Testament, 3 vols. in 1. lxv, 1162p. 1974. reprint ed. write for info. (*3-487-05278-4*) G Olms Pubs.

Meslier, Jean & Knoop, Anna, trs. Superstition in All Ages: Last Will & Testament: Common Sense. 339p. 1974. reprint ed. spiral bd. 18.00 (*0-7873-0609-6*) Hlth Research.

Meslier, Jean, jt. auth. see D'Holbach, Paul H.

Meslin, F., et al, eds. Laboratory Techniques in Rabies. 2nd ed. LC 96-212237. (FRE.). 476p. (Orig.). (C). 1996. pap. text 115.00 (*92-4-154479-1*, 1150423) World Health.

Mesmer, Franz A. Mesmerism: The Discovery of Animal Magnetism (1779); A New Translation. Bouleur, Joseph, ed. & tr. by. from FRE. (Orig.). 1997. pap. 7.95 (*1-55818-382-5*) Holmes Pub.

Mesmer, Robert E., jt. auth. see Baes, Charles F., Jr.

*****Mesmer, Sharon.** The Empty Quarter. LC 99-52164. 103p. 2000. pap. 13.00 (*1-882413-66-0*, Pub. by Hanging Loose) SPD-Small Pr Dist.

Mesmer, Sharon. Half Angel, Half Lunch. 72p. 1998. pap. 12.95 (*1-889097-22-5*) Hard Pr MA.

Mesmer, Theodore. The Welsh Hills of Wauhesha County: A Photographic Study of Stewardship. (Illus.). 84p. 1997. pap. 15.95 (*0-9660501-0-X*) Celtic Ink.

Mesnard, P., jt. auth. see Margolin, J. C.

Mesnard, Pierre. Desarrollo De la Filosofia Politica en el Siglo XVI. (SPA.). 643p. 1956. 3.00 (*0-8477-2805-6*) U of PR Pr.

Mesnooh, Christopher J. Law & Business in France: A Guide to French Commercial & Corporate Law. LC 93-46936. 384p. (C). 1994. lib. bdg. 149.00 (*0-7923-2682-2*) Kluwer Academic.

Meso-American Indian Center Women's Committee, ed. Daughters of Abya Yala: Indigenous Women Regaining Control. LC 94-2780. (Illus.). 128p. 1994. 8.95 (*0-913990-09-4*) Book Pub Co.

Meson-, Photo-, & Electroproduction at Low & Inter. Proceedings of the Meson-, Photo-, & Electroproduction at Low & Intermediate Energies Symposium, Bonn, 1970. LC 25-9130. (Tracts in Modern Physics Ser.: Vol. 59). 1971. 71.95 (*0-387-05494-4*) Spr-Verlag.

Meson, Danusia L. Historia y Ficcion: El Caso 'Francisco' (SPA.). 1994. 12.00 (*950-515-375-9*) Edins Hispamerica.

Meson, Reg. Teach Yourself Photography. (Illus.). 224p. 1995. pap. 9.95 (*0-8442-3937-2*, Teach Yrslf) NTC Contemp Pub Co.

Mesquit, Teresa, tr. see Bech, Henning.

Mesquita, Bruce B. De, see De Mesquita, Bruce B., ed.

Mesquita, Stephen. Great Highways of the World. 1996. 29.95 (*0-614-97034-2*) Rand McNally.

Mesquitaabruyelle, Buenodo. Textiles & Clothing, Vol. I-3. (Single Market Review Ser.). 1998. 80.00 (*0-7494-2307-2*) Kogan Page Ltd.

Mesrobian, Armen Z. Magnificient Meditations of Assurance, Peace, & Wisdom. LC 97-95009. (Illus.). 238p. 1998. per. 14.00 (*0-9632735-2-3*) EPS Excel Pub.

— Prepare & Enjoy Creative Dental Retirement. LC 92-81607. (Illus.). 195p. 1992. spiral bd. 29.95 (*0-9632735-0-7*) EPS Excel Pub.

— Prepare & Enjoy Creative Retirement. LC 93-90246. (Illus.). 202p. (Orig.). 1993. pap. 17.95 (*0-9632735-1-5*) EPS Excel Pub.

Messadie, Gerald. Dictionary of Inventions. (Reference Library). 256p. 1998. pap. 6.95 (*1-85326-357-5*, 3575WW, Pub. by Wrdsworth Edits) NTC Contemp Pub Co.

— A History of the Devil. Urda, John, ed. Romano, Marc, tr. 384p. 1996. 27.00 (*1-56836-081-9*) Kodansha.

— A History of the Devil. Romano, Marc, tr. 384p. 1997. pap. 16.00 (*1-56836-198-X*, Kodansha Globe) Kodansha.

Message, Gordon M. Practical Aspects of Gas Chromotography-Mass Spectrometry. LC 83-23475. 368p. 1984. 195.00 (*0-471-06277-4*, Wiley-Interscience) Wiley.

Messager, Annette, jt. contrib. by see Conklin, Jo-Ann.

Messana, Jose. Euros 05. 1997. 16.95 (*3-86187-074-6*) B Gmunder.

Messaoudi, Khalida. Unbowed: An Algerian Woman Confronts Islamic Fundamentalism. Vila, Anne C., tr. from ENG. LC 98-12254. (Critical Authors & Issues Ser.). 184p. 1998. 35.00 (*0-8122-3449-9*); pap. 14.95 (*0-8122-1657-1*) U of Pa Pr.

Messaris, Paul. Visual "Literacy" Image, Mind & Reality. LC 93-26069. 224p. (C). 1994. pap. 25.00 (*0-8133-1937-4*, Pub. by Westview) HarpC.

— Visual Persuasion: The Role of Images in Advertising. LC 96-25184. 328p. 1996. 56.00 (*0-8039-7245-8*); pap. 24.95 (*0-8039-7246-6*) Sage.

Messe, Lawrence A., jt. auth. see Lane, Irving M.

Messec, Jerry. An Ordinary Life: L3. McConochie, Jean A., ed. (Regents Readers Ser.). (Illus.). 68p. (gr. 7-12). 1987. pap. text 3.50 (*0-13-639816-2*, 20886) Prentice ESL.

Messec, Jerry & Kranich, Roger. English Spoken Here Bk. 1: Getting Started. Schenk, Brian, ed. (English Spoken Here (ESL) Ser.). (Illus.). 160p. 1988. pap. text. write for info. (*0-8428-0850-7*) Cambridge Bk.

— English Spoken Here Bk. 3: Health & Safety. Schenk, Brian, ed. (English Spoken Here (ESL) Ser.). (Illus.). 128p. 1988. student ed. 3.95 (*0-8428-0856-6*) Cambridge Bk.

Messec, Jerry, et al. English Spoken Here Bk. 4: Life in the United States. (English Spoken Here (ESL) Ser.). (Illus.). 128p. 1988. student ed. 3.95 (*0-8428-0857-4*); 25.00 (*0-8428-0847-7*) Cambridge Bk.

Messec, Jerry, jt. auth. see Thiele, Margaret.

Messec, Jerry L., jt. auth. see Kranich, Roger E.

Messegue, Maurice. Die Krauterkuche: Ein Lexikon der Kuchenkrauter mit Uber 200 Franzoesichen Rezepten. (GER.). 19.95 (*0-7859-8425-9*, 3548349005) Fr & Eur.

— Of People & Plants: The Autobiography of Europe's Most Celebrated Herbal Healer. 336p. (Orig.). 1991. pap. 12.95 (*0-89281-437-3*) Inner Tradit.

Messel, Harry. Highlights in Science: Lectures for 24th Science School. 232p. 1988. pap. text 18.50 (*0-08-034430-5*, Pergamon Pr) Elsevier.

— Surveys of Tidal River Systems in the Northern Territory & Their Crocodile Populations. (Monographs: No. 15). (Illus.). 368p. 1982. 135.00 (*0-08-024831-4*, Pergamon Pr) Elsevier.

Messel, Harry, ed. The Biological Manipulation of Life. (Illus.). 352p. 1981. text 44.00 (*0-08-024825-X*, Pergamon Pr); pap. text 27.00 (*0-08-024824-1*, Pergamon Pr) Elsevier.

— Energy for Survival. (Illus.). 368p. 1979. text 22.00 (*0-08-024794-6*, Pergamon Pr); pap. text 17.00 (*0-08-024791-1*, Pergamon Pr) Elsevier.

— The Study of Populations. (Illus.). 266p. 1986. pap. text 26.00 (*0-08-029877-X*) Elsevier.

Messel, Harry, et al, eds. Surveys of Tidal River Systems in the Northern Territory & Their Crocodile Population: Monograph, No. 18. (Illus.). 308p. 1985. 135.00 (*0-08-029858-3*, Pergamon Pr) Elsevier.

Messel, Harry, et al. Survey of Tidal River Systems in the Northern Territory & Their Crocodile Populations: Monographs, Nos. 2-8. Incl. No. 2. Victoria & Fitzmaurice River Systems. 52p. 1979. pap. 28.00 (*0-08-023098-9*); No. 3. Adelaide, Daly & Moyle Rivers. 58p. 1979. pap. 28.00 (*0-08-023099-7*); No. 4. Alligator Region River System: Murgenella & Cooper's Creeks; East, South & West Alligator Rivers & Wildman River. 70p. 1979. pap. 28.00 (*0-08-024789-X*); No. 5. Goodmadeer & King River Systems: Majarie, Wurugoij & All Night Creeks. 62p. 1979. pap. 28.00 (*0-08-024790-3*); No. 6. Some Rivers & Creek Systems on Melville & Grant Islands: North & South Creeks on Grant Island. 64p. 1979. pap. 28.00 (*0-08-024784-9*); No. 7. Liverpool-Tomkinson River Systems & Nungbulgarri Creek. 84p. 1979. pap. 28.00 (*0-08-024785-7*); No. 8. Some Rivers & Creeks on the Western Shore of the Gulf of Carpentaria: Rose River, Muntak Creek; Hart, Walker & Koolatong Rivers. 40p. 1979. pap. 28.00 (*0-08-024786-5*); (Illus.). 1979. pap. write for info. (*0-318-55231-0*) Elsevier.

— Surveys of Tidal River Systems in the Northern Territory & Their Crocodile Population. (Monographs: No. 1). (Illus.). 464p. 1982. 155.00 (*0-08-024819-5*, G135, Pergamon Pr) Elsevier.

— Surveys of Tidal River Systems in the Northern Territory & Their Crocodile Populations. (Monographs: No. 17). (Illus.). 92p. 1981. pap. 28.00 (*0-08-024818-7*, Pergamon Pr) Elsevier.

— Surveys of Tidal River Systems in the Northern Territory of Australia: Resurveys of the Tidal Waterways of Van Diemen Gulf & the Southern Gulf of Carpentaria 1984 & 1985. (Surveys of Tidal Rivers Ser.: No. 19). (Illus.). 118p. 1986. 86.00 (*0-08-029882-6*) Elsevier.

— Surveys of Tidal Waterways in the Kimberley Region, Western Australia & Their Crocodile Populations: Monograph 20 - Tidal Waterways of the Kimberley Surveyed During 1977, 1978 & 1986. (Surveys of Tidal Rivers Ser.: No. 20). 357p. 1988. 83.00 (*0-08-034429-1*, Pergamon Pr) Elsevier.

Messel, Harry, jt. auth. see Elton, L. R.

Messell, J., jt. auth. see Guy, W.

Messena Essling, Andre P. Les Livres a Figures Venitiens: Etudes Sur l'Art de la Gravure Sur Lois a Venice, 6 vols. (FRE., Illus.). 2107p. 1995. reprint ed. 550.00 (*1-57898-026-7*) Martino Pubng.

Messenger, Ann. His & Hers: Essays in Restoration & Eighteenth-Century Literature. LC 86-7803. 288p. 1986. 34.95 (*0-8131-1575-2*) U Pr of Ky.

— Pastoral Tradition & the Female Talent: Studies in Augustan Poetry. LC 99-40174. (Studies in the Eighteenth Century: No. 25). 1999. write for info. (*0-404-63525-3*) AMS Pr.

— Woman & Poet in the Eighteenth Century: The Life of Mary Whateley Darwall (1738-1825) LC 94-821. (Studies in the Eighteenth Century: No. 27). xii, 273p. 1999. 59.50 (*0-404-63527-X*) AMS Pr.

Messenger, Ann, ed. Gender at Work: Four Women Writers of the Eighteenth Century. LC 89-21449. 166p. (C). 1990. text 29.95 (*0-8143-2147-X*) Wayne St U Pr.

Messenger, Ann, ed. see Knight, Ellis C.

Messenger, Betty. Picking up the Linen Threads: Life in Ulster's Mills. 265p. 1988. pap. 13.95 (*0-85640-415-2*, Pub. by Blackstaff Pr) Dufour.

Messenger, Bill. The Power of Music: A Complete Music Activities Program for Older Adults. LC 95-18826. 96p. 1995. spiral bd. 25.95 incl. audio (*1-878812-27-0*) Hlth Prof Pr.

Messenger, Bill, jt. auth. see Abrignani, Catherine.

*****Messenger, Charlene.** Secrets of the Third Little Pig: 7 Steps to Build a Child's Inner Strength. 2nd expanded rev. ed. LC 99-462515. (Illus.). 404p. 1999. pap. 14.00 (*0-9661904-4-0*) Brighter Pathways.

Messenger, Charlene. Secrets of the Third Little Pig: 7 Steps to Build a Child's Innerstrength. (Illus.). 367p. 1997. pap. 24.95 (*0-9661904-3-2*) Brighter Pathways.

Messenger, Charles. For Love of Regiment Vol. 1: A History of British Infantry, 1660-1993. (Illus.). 1994. 31.95 (*0-85052-371-0*, Pub. by Leo Cooper) Trans-Atl Phila.

— For Love of Regiment Vol. 2: A History of British Infantry, 1660-1993, Vol.2. (Illus.). 1995. 32.95 (*0-85052-422-9*, Pub. by Leo Cooper) Trans-Atl Phila.

— Hitler's Gladiator: The Life & Times of SS-Obergruppenfuhrer & General der Waffen-SS Sepp Dietrich. (Illus.). 245p. 1988. 32.95 (*0-08-031207-1*, Pub. by Brasseys) Brasseys.

*****Messenger, Charles.** Hitler's Gladiator: The Life & Wars of Panzer Army Commander Sepp Dietrich. 2000. pap. 22.95 (*1-57488-315-1*) Brasseys.

An Asterisk (*) at the beginning of an entry indicates that the title is appearing for the first time.

Messenger, Charles. The Last Prussian: A Biography of Field Marshal Gerd von Rundstedt 1875-1953. (Biography of Field Marshal Gerd von Rundstedt Ser.). 400p. 1991. 24.95 (*0-08-036707-0*, Pub. by Brasseys) Brasseys.

— The Pictorial History of World War II. (Illus.). 256p. 19.99 (*1-57215-244-3*, JG2443) World Pubns.

— The Second World War in the West. (Illus.). 224p. 1999. 29.95 (*0-304-35224-1*, Pub. by Cassell) Sterling.

— The Steadfast Gurkha Vol. 3: Historical Record of 6th Queen Elizabeth's Own Gurkha Rifles, 1948-1982. (Illus.). 147p. 1985. 24.95 (*0-436-27780-8*, Pub. by Leo Cooper) Trans-Atl Phila.

Messenger, Charles, ed. The Illustrated Book of World War II. LC 99-42024. (Illus.). 304p. 1999. 27.98 (*1-57145-217-6*, Thunder Bay) Advantage Pubs.

— Terriers in the Trenches: The Post Office Rifles at War, 1914-1918. 170p. (C). 1987. 100.00 (*0-7855-2168-2*, Pub. by Picton) St Mut.

Messenger, Charles, intro. Dictionary of Military Terms. 3rd ed. LC 95-13988. 512p. 1995. 44.95 (*1-85367-217-3*, Pub. by Greenhill Bks) Stackpole.

Messenger, Christian K. Sport & the Spirit of Play in Contemporary American Fiction. 456p. 1990. text 46.00 (*0-231-07094-2*) Col U Pr.

— Sports & the Spirit of Play in American Fiction: Hawthorne to Faulkner. LC 81-4843. 352p. 1981. text 57.50 (*0-231-05168-9*) Col U Pr.

— Sports & the Spirit of Play in American Fiction: Hawthorne to Faulkner. LC 81-4843. 352p. 1983. pap. text 23.00 (*0-231-05169-7*) Col U Pr.

Messenger, Dorothy, jt. auth. see Messenger, Orville J.

Messenger, E. C., tr. see Guiraud, Jean.

Messenger, Jack. Personal Excellence: A Guide to Getting the Most from Yourself & Others. LC 89-85531. 207p. 1989. 19.95 (*0-939975-04-1*) Exec Pr NC.

Messenger, Jannat. Twinkle, Twinkle, Little Star: A Lullaby Book with Twinkling Light & Musical Sound Chip. 1997. 9.95 (*1-888443-29-4*, Piggy Toes Pr) Intervisual Bks.

Messenger, John B., jt. auth. see Johnson, Sr., Rodney Lee.

Messenger, John C. Inis Beag: Isle of Ireland. 136p. 1983. reprint ed. pap. text 10.50 (*0-88133-051-5*) Waveland Pr.

— Inis Beag Revisited: The Anthropologist as Observant Participator. 154p. (C). 1988. reprint ed. pap. text 13.50 (*0-88133-408-1*) Sheffield WI.

Messenger, Ken. Clients As Individuals. (Skills for Caring Ser.). (Illus.). 48p. (Orig.). 1992. pap. text 9.95 (*0-443-04530-5*) Church.

Messenger, Michael. Coalport, 1795-1926. (Illus.). 424p. 1996. 89.50 (*1-85149-112-0*) Antique Collect.

Messenger, Norman. Making Faces. 11.95 (*0-394-22354-3*) Beginner.

— Making Faces. LC 92-52807. (Illus.). 20p. (J). 1993. 14.95 (*1-56458-111-X*) DK Pub Inc.

Messenger, Norman. Jack & the Beanstalk. LC 96-44201. (Nursery Classics Ser.). 32p. (J). (ps-k). 1996. 8.95 (*0-7894-1170-9*) DK Pub Inc.

— The Little Red Hen. LC 96-44203. (Nursery Classics Ser.). 32p. (J). (ps-k). 1997. 8.95 (*0-7894-1171-7*) DK Pub Inc.

Messenger, Orville J. & Messenger, Dorothy. Borrowed Time: A Surgeon's Struggle with Transfusion Induced AIDS. 160p. 1995. pap. 14.95 (*0-88962-582-4*) Mosaic.

Messenger, Phyllis M., jt. auth. see Desmond, Lawrence G.

Messenger, Phyllis Mauch, ed. The Ethics of Collecting Cultural Property: Whose Culture? Whose Property? 2nd enl. ed. LC 99-31907. (Illus.). 304p. 1999. pap. 19.95 (*0-8263-2125-9*) U of NM Pr.

Messenger, Ruth E. Ethical Teachings in the Latin Hymns of Medieval England. LC 30-20975. (Columbia University. Studies in the Social Sciences: No. 321). reprint ed. 20.00 (*0-404-51321-2*) AMS Pr.

***Messenger, Troy.** Holy Leisure: Recreation & Religion in God's Square Mile. (Illus.). 192p. 2000. pap. 17.95 (*1-56639-841-X*) Temple U Pr.

Messenger, Troy. Holy Leisure: Recreation & Religion in God's Square Mile. LC 98-51342. 1999. 29.95 (*0-8166-3253-7*); write for info. (*0-8166-3254-5*) U of Minn Pr.

Messent, Jan. Design Sources for Symbolism. (Design Ser.). (Illus.). 40p. 1993. pap. 12.50 (*1-874080-96-8*, 0968, Pub. by Crochet Design) A Schwartz & Co.

— Designing Worksheets. (Design Ser.). (Illus.). 40p. 1991. pap. 12.50 (*1-874080-05-4*, 0054, Pub. by Crochet Design) A Schwartz & Co.

— Have You Any Wool? The Creative Use of Yarn. rev. ed. (Illus.). 128p. 1987. pap. 19.95 (*0-85532-768-5*, 768-5, Pub. by Srch Pr) A Schwartz & Co.

— Knit an Enchanted Castle. (Craft Library). 48p. 1985. pap. 5.50 (*0-85532-600-X*, 600-X, Pub. by Srch Pr) A Schwartz & Co.

— Knit the Christmas Story. 1999. 8.95 (*0-85532-881-9*) Srch Pr.

— Knitted Gardens. (Illus.). 144p. 1992. pap. 22.50 (*0-85532-732-4*, 732-4, Pub. by Srch Pr) A Schwartz & Co.

— Wool 'n Magic: Creative Uses of Yarn...Knitting, Crochet, Embroidery. Dawson, Pam, ed. (Illus.). 144p. (YA). Date not set. pap. 22.95 (*0-85532-702-2*, 702-2, Pub. by Srch Pr) A Schwartz & Co.

Messent, Peter. Criminal Proceedings: The Contemporary American Crime Novel. LC 96-47828. 264p. 1997. 55.00 (*0-7453-1017-6*, Pub. by Pluto GBR) Stylus Pub VA.

— Criminal Proceedings: The Contemporary American Crime Novel. 264p. 1997. pap. 18.95 (*0-7453-1016-8*, Pub. by Pluto GBR) Stylus Pub VA.

Messent, Peter B. Ernest Hemingway. LC 92-9005. (Modern Novelists Ser.). 192p. 1992. text 29.95 (*0-312-08126-X*) St Martin.

— Mark Twain. LC 96-9831. (Modern Novelists Ser.). 248p. 1997. text 29.95 (*0-312-16479-3*) St Martin.

— New Readings of the American Novel: Narrative Theory & Its Application. LC 98-21410. 336p. 1998. pap. text 24.95 (*0-8173-0958-6*) U of Ala Pr.

Messer, Anne. Contemporary Images. 1989. 16.95 (*0-687-09505-0*) Abingdon.

Messer, Bonnie. Dealing with Change. (Lifesearch Ser.). 64p. 1996. pap. 4.95 (*0-687-01502-2*) Abingdon.

Messer, David & Dockrell, Julie, eds. Developmental Psychology: A Reader. (An Arnold Publication). (Illus.). 416p. 1998. text 80.00 (*0-340-70561-2*); pap. text 29.95 (*0-340-70562-0*) OUP.

Messer, David & Jones, Fiona. Psychology for Social Workers & Related Professionals. LC 97-40758. 1998. write for info. (*0-13-565417-3*) P-H.

Messer, David & Millar, Stuart. Exploring Developmental Psychology: From Infancy to Adolescence. (An Arnold Publication). 480p. 1999. pap. text 27.95 (*0-340-67682-5*, Pub. by E A) OUP.

***Messer, David & Millar, Stuart, eds.** Exploring Developmental Psychology: From Infancy to Adolescence. (An Arnold Publication). 480p. 1999. text 75.00 (*0-340-67683-3*, Pub. by E A) OUP.

***Messer, David J.** Psychology for Social Careers. LC 98-32273. 1999. pap. text 32.95 (*1-85302-762-6*) Taylor & Francis.

Messer, David W. Triumph II Vol. II: Philadelphia to Harrisburg, 1828-1998. Roberts, Charles S., ed. LC 98-71552. (Illus.). 400p. 1999. 65.00 (*0-934118-24-8*) Barnard Roberts.

Messer-Davidow, Ellen, et al, eds. Knowledges: Historical & Critical Studies in Disciplinarity. LC 92-46606. (Knowledge, Disciplinarity & Beyond Ser.). 465p. 1993. text 67.50 (*0-8139-1428-0*); pap. text 22.50 (*0-8139-1429-9*) U Pr of Va.

Messer-Davidow, Ellen, jt. ed. see Hartman, Joan E.

Messer, Donald E. Calling Church & Seminary into the 21st Century. 176p. 1995. 16.95 (*0-687-01351-8*) Abingdon.

Messer, Donald E., ed. Send Me? The Itineracy in Crisis. 208p. (Orig.). 1991. pap. 12.95 (*0-687-37155-4*) Abingdon.

Messer, Donald E., jt. auth. see Geis, Sally B.

Messer, Donald E., ed. see Abraham, William J.

Messer, Donald E., jt. ed. see Geis, Sally B.

Messer, Ellen & May, Kathryn E. Back Rooms: Voices from the Illegal Abortion Era. LC 93-49663. 258p. (C). 1994. pap. 18.95 (*0-87975-876-7*) Prometheus Bks.

Messer, Ellen & Uvin, Peter, eds. The Hunger Report 1995: The Alan Shawn Feinstein World Hunger Program, Brown University, Providence, Rhode Island. 256p. 1996. pap. text 14.00 (*90-5699-518-9*) Gordon & Breach.

Messer, Ellen, jt. ed. see Lambek, Michael.

***Messer, Gayle.** Audrain County, Missouri: Reflections of the Past, 1945-2000: A Pictorial History. LC 99-48833. (Illus.). 1999. write for info. (*1-57864-092-X*) Donning Co.

Messer, H. J. Able Seaman RNVR. (C). 1989. 60.00 (*0-86303-475-6*) St Mut.

Messer, Jane, ed. Bedlam: An Anthology of Sleepless Nights. 324p. (Orig.). 1997. pap. 14.00 (*1-86448-072-6*, Pub. by Allen & Unwin Pty) IPG Chicago.

Messer, Keith, ed. see Cole, Carlene.

Messer-Kruse, Timothy. The Yankee International: Marxism & the American Reform Tradition, 1848-1876. LC 97-36875. (Illus.). 336p. 1998. pap. 19.95 (*0-8078-4705-4*); lib. bdg. 59.95 (*0-8078-2403-8*) U of NC Pr.

Messer, Mitch & Anger Institute Staff. Soft Answers. 115p. 10.95 (*0-9636776-3-2*) Anger Inst.

***Messer, Mitchell H.** Allergic to Happiness: If You're So Smart, Why Aren't You Happy? 106p. 1999. pap. 18.95 (*0-9636776-7-5*) Anger Inst.

Messer, Mitchell H. Anger Intelligence: A Course in Anger Therapy. Greb, Richard, ed. (Emotional First Aid Ser.). 1999. spiral bd. 20.00 (*0-9636776-1-6*) Anger Inst.

— The Dictionary of Unsanity: A Guide to the Craziness of Everyday Life. Greb, Richard, ed. (Emotional First Aid Ser.). 1985. pap. 18.95 (*0-9636776-9-1*) Anger Inst.

— He Told Me He Loved Me: A Handbook for Staying Unpregnant. 1999. 18.95 (*0-9636776-4-0*) Anger Inst.

— Relieving the Manager's Internal Stress. Greb, Richard, ed. (Emotional First Aid Ser.). 1999. spiral bd. 20.00 (*0-9636776-8-3*) Anger Inst.

— The Suicide Dialogues: How to Talk to Your Child about Suicide. Greb, Richard, ed. (Emotional First Aid Ser.). 1995. 20.00 (*0-9636776-6-7*) Anger Inst.

***Messer, Mitchell H.** 21st Century Conflict Resolution. 60p. 1999. pap. 11.95 (*0-9636776-5-9*) Anger Inst.

— Yours, Mine, Ours: A Course in Marriages. Greb, Richard, ed. (Emotional First Aid Ser.). 1997. spiral bd. 20.00 (*0-9636776-2-4*) Anger Inst.

Messer, Mitchell H., et al. Managing Anger: A Handbook of Proven Techniques. (Illus.). 303p. 1992. pap. 14.95 (*0-9636776-0-8*) Anger Inst.

Messer, Mithcell, jt. auth. see Anger Clinic Staff.

Messer, Richard. Does God's Existence Need Proof? 170p. 1998. reprint ed. pap. text 19.95 (*0-19-826971-4*) OUP.

— Murder in the Family: Poems. 80p. (Orig.). 1995. pap. 8.95 (*0-933087-37-3*) Bottom Dog Pr.

Messer, Robert. Linear Algebra: Gateway to Mathematics. LC 93-21043. 560p. (C). 1997. 100.00 (*0-06-501728-5*) Addson-Wesley Educ.

Messer, Robert L. The End of an Alliance: James F. Byrnes, Roosevelt, Truman, & the Origins of the Cold War. LC 81-7618. 304p. reprint ed. pap. 94.30 (*0-7837-0307-4*, 204062900018) Bks Demand.

Messer, Sam & Red Lips. One Man by Himself: Portraits of Jon Serl. LC 95-34715. (Profile Ser.: No. 1). 48p. 1995. 39.95 (*0-9638433-6-2*) Hard Pr MA.

Messer, Stanley, jt. ed. see Arkowitz, Hal.

Messer, Stanley B., et al, eds. Hermeneutics & Psychological Theory, Vol. 2: Interpretative Perspectives on Personality, Psychotherapy, & Psychopathology. (Rutgers Symposia on Applied Psychology Ser.). 500p. (C). 1988. pap. text 20.00 (*0-8135-1292-1*) Rutgers U Pr.

Messer, Stanley B. & Warren, C. Seth. Models of Brief Psychodynamic Therapy: A Comparative Approach. LC 95-23628. 374p. 1995. lib. bdg. 39.95 (*1-57230-024-8*, 0024) Guilford Pubns.

— Models of Brief Psychodynamic Therapy: A Comparative Approach. 374p. 1998. pap. text 23.00 (*1-57230-340-9*) Guilford Pubns.

Messer, Stanley B., jt. ed. see Gurman, Alan S.

Messer, Stanley B., jt. ed. see Wachtel, Paul L.

Messer, Theron. Digging Deeper: Grace Discipleship Course. (Illus.). 68p. 1992. teacher ed., wbk. ed. 8.95 (*0-9622110-4-4*) Grace Minist.

— Grace Institute, Course 4. (Illus.). 253p. 1996. wbk. ed. 35.00 (*1-886965-03-X*) Grace Minist.

— I Wish: Marriage Enhancement Workbook. (Illus.). 98p. 1994. 11.95 (*0-9622110-6-0*) Grace Minist.

Messer, Theron & Hadden, Scott. Grace Institute, Course 1. (Illus.). 266p. 1995. wbk. ed. 35.00 (*1-886965-00-5*) Grace Minist.

— Grace Institute, Course 2. (Illus.). 217p. 1996. wbk. ed. 35.00 (*1-886965-01-3*) Grace Minist.

— Grace Institute, Course 3. (Illus.). 333p. 1996. wbk. ed. 35.00 (*1-886965-02-1*) Grace Minist.

— The Mystery of the Kingdom. (Illus.). 240p. (Orig.). 1997. pap. 9.95 (*1-886965-04-8*) Grace Minist.

Messer, Theron & Solomon, Charles. Solomon Institute in Spirituotherapy. (Illus.). 230p. 1993. wbk. ed. 25.00 (*0-9622110-5-2*) Grace Minist.

Messer, Thomas M. Acquisition Priorities: Aspects of Postwar Painting in Europe. LC 83-60337. (Illus.). 104p. (Orig.). 1983. pap. 12.95 (*0-89207-041-2*) S R Guggenheim.

— Fifty Years of Collecting: An Anniversary Selection. Painting Since World War II. (Fifty Years of Collecting: An Anniversary Selection: Vol. II). (Illus.). 147p. 1987. pap. 20.00 (*0-89207-066-8*) S R Guggenheim.

— Fifty Years of Collecting: An Anniversary Selection. Sculpture of the Modern Era. (Fifty Years of Collecting: An Anniversary Selection: Vol. III). (Illus.). 145p. (Orig.). 1987. pap. 20.00 (*0-89207-065-X*) S R Guggenheim.

— Kolar - Chiasmage: Selections from the Guggenheim. (Illus.). 20p. 1988. 4.00 (*0-685-45726-5*) Katonah Gal.

— Munch. (Masters of Art Ser.). (Illus.). 128p. 1986. 24.95 (*0-8109-1415-8*, Pub. by Abrams) Time Warner.

— Sixty Works: The Peggy Guggenheim Collection. (Illus.). 68p. 1982. pap. 5.95 (*0-89207-037-4*) S R Guggenheim.

— Vasily Kandinsky. LC 96-37573. (Masters of Art Ser.). (Illus.). 128p. 1997. 24.95 (*0-8109-1228-7*, Pub. by Abrams) Time Warner.

Messer, Thomas M., et al. Guida: Collezione Peggy Guggenheim. enl. rev. ed.Tr. of Handbook: Peggy Guggenheim Collection. (ITA., Illus.). 336p. (Orig.). 1986. 15.00 (*0-89207-054-4*) S R Guggenheim.

— Handbook: Peggy Guggenheim Collection. enl. rev. ed. (Illus.). 336p. (Orig.). 1986. 15.00 (*0-89207-053-6*) S R Guggenheim.

Messer, Thomas M., jt. intro. see Waldman, Diane.

Messere. Broadcast Internet Guide. LC 96-204714. 1996. mass mkt. 8.95 (*0-534-52578-4*) Course Tech.

Messere, Ken, ed. The Tax System in Industrialized Countries. LC 98-35493. (Illus.). 450p. 1999. text 115.00 (*0-19-829331-3*) OUP.

Messere, Ken, ed. see International Institute of Public Finance Congress.

Messerle, Hugo K. Magnetohydrodynamic Electrical Power Generation. LC 94-18580. (Energy Engineering Learning Package Ser.). 210p. 1995. pap. 79.95 (*0-471-94252-9*) Wiley.

Messerli, Bruno & Ives, Jack D. Mountains of the World: A Global Priority. LC 97-7699. (Illus.). 510p. 1997. 75.00 (*1-85070-781-2*) Prthnon Pub.

Messerli, Carlos R., jt. auth. see Pfatteicher, Philip H.

Messerli, Douglas. After. 130p. 1998. pap. 10.95 (*1-55713-353-0*) Sun & Moon CA.

***Messerli, Douglas.** Bow Down. (Littoral Bks.). 1999. pap. 12.95 (*1-928801-04-8*, Pub. by Sun & Moon CA) Consort Bk Sales.

Messerli, Douglas. Maxims from My Mother's Milk: Hymns to Him: A Dialogue. 72p. 1989. 12.95 (*1-55713-031-0*); pap. 8.95 (*1-55713-047-7*) Sun & Moon CA.

— Mr. Knife, Miss Fork, No. 2. Vol. 2. (Illus.). 196p. 1999. pap. 10.95 (*1-55713-401-4*, Pub. by Sun & Moon CA) Consort Bk Sales.

***Messerli, Douglas.** PIP Anthology of World Poetry of the 20th Century, Vol. 2. Vol. 2. (Illus.). 124p. 2000. pap. 15.95 (*1-892295-94-6*) Green Integer.

Messerli, Douglas. Silence All Round Marked: An Historical Play in Hysteria Writ. (Blue Corner Drama Ser.). 40p. (Orig.). 1991. pap. 5.95 (*1-55713-125-2*) Sun & Moon CA.

— The Walls Come True: An Opera for Spoken Voices (The Structure of Destruction, Pt. II) (Littoral Bks.). 200p. (Orig.). 1994. pap. 12.95 (*1-55713-180-5*) Sun & Moon CA.

Messerli, Douglas, ed. Fifty: A Celebration of Sun & Moon Classics, New Works by Friends. LC 95-199245. (Sun & Moon Classics Ser.: No. 50). 576p. 1994. pap. 13.95 (*1-55713-132-5*) Sun & Moon CA.

— Fifty: A Celebration of Sun & Moon Classics, New Works by Friends. LC 95-199245. (Sun & Moon Classics Ser.: Vol. 50). 576p. 1994. 24.95 (*1-55713-152-X*) Sun & Moon CA.

— From the Other Side of the Century: A New American Poetry 1960-1990. LC 94-210076. (Sun & Moon Classics Ser.: No. 47). 1136p. (Orig.). (C). 1994. pap. 29.95 (*1-55713-131-7*) Sun & Moon CA.

— The Gertrude Stein Awards in Innovative American Poetry 1993-1994, Vol. 1. 336p. (Orig.). 1995. pap. 13.95 (*1-55713-161-9*) Sun & Moon CA.

— The Gertrude Stein Awards in Innovative Poetry 1994-1995, Vol. 2. LC 96-50941. 336p. (Orig.). 1997. pap. 14.95 (*1-55713-274-7*) Sun & Moon CA.

— Mr. Knife, Miss Fork No. 1: A Biannual of International Poetry. 130p. 1998. pap. 10.95 (*1-55713-345-X*) Sun & Moon CA.

***Messerli, Douglas, ed.** The Pip Anthology of World Poetry of the 20th Century, Vol. 1. Vol. 1. (Illus.). 199p. 2000. pap. 15.95 (*1-892295-47-4*, Pub. by Green Integer) SPD-Small Pr Dist.

Messerli, Douglas, ed. The Sun & Moon Guide to Eating Through Literature & Art. LC 94-34013. (Illus.). 200p. 1994. 29.95 (*1-55713-178-3*) Sun & Moon CA.

Messerli, Douglas & Wellman, Mac, eds. From the Other Side of the Century II: A New American Drama, 1960-1995. (Sun & Moon Classics Ser.: No. 147). 1202p. 1998. pap. 29.95 (*1-55713-247-X*) Sun & Moon CA.

Messerli, Douglas, ed. see Barnes, Djuna.

Messerli, Franz H. ABCs of Antihypertensive Therapy. LC 94-177010. 288p. 1994. pap. text 53.00 (*1-881063-03-8*) Lppncott W & W.

— Current Cardiovascular Drug Therapy. 2nd ed. Zorab, Richard, ed. LC 95-1013. (Illus.). 1408p. 1996. text 115.00 (*0-7216-4814-2*, W B Saunders Co) Harcrt Hlth Sci Grp.

— Current Clinical Practice. (Illus.). 1000p. 1987. text 77.00 (*0-7216-1460-4*, W B Saunders Co) Harcrt Hlth Sci Grp.

Messerli, Franz H., ed. Cardiovascular Disease in the Elderly. (Developments in Cardiovascular Medicine Ser.). 1984. text 141.00 (*0-89838-596-2*) Kluwer Academic.

— Cardiovascular Disease in the Elderly. 3rd ed. LC 92-23628. 1992. text 225.50 (*0-7923-1859-5*) Kluwer Academic.

— Kidney in Essential Hypertension. (Developments in Cardiovascular Medicine Ser.). 1983. text 113.00 (*0-89838-616-0*) Kluwer Academic.

Messerli, Franz H. & Aepfelbacher, Franz C., eds. Hypertension in Postmenopausal Women. LC 95-39859. (Illus.). 312p. 1995. text 115.00 (*0-8247-9652-7*, RC685) Dekker.

Messerli, Franz H., jt. auth. see Opie, Lionel H.

Messerli, Joe, jt. auth. see Lewis, Jean.

Messerlin, Patrick, jt. auth. see Handley, Brian.

Messerlin, Patrick, jt. auth. see Hindley, Brian.

***Messerlin, Patrick A.** Measuring the Costs of Protection in Europe. 100p. 2000. pap. 15.95 (*0-88132-273-3*) Inst Intl Eco.

Messerly, John. Lock Block Logic. (Illus.). 90p. (J). (gr. 2-6). 1993. pap. text 15.95 (*0-9643700-0-X*) Elmwood Pr.

Messerly, John G. An Introduction to Ethical Theories. LC 94-23950. 200p. (Orig.). (C). 1994. pap. text 25.00 (*0-8191-9823-4*) U Pr of Amer.

Messerole. Varicose Veins. 1999. pap. 6.99 (*0-7615-1617-4*) Prima Pub.

Messerotti, Mauro, jt. auth. see Hanslmeier, Arnold.

Messerschmi. 9 Lives. LC 99-45726. 2000. 59.00 (*0-8133-6666-6*) Westview.

Messerschmid. 9 Lives. LC 99-45726. 2000. 20.00 (*0-8133-6667-4*) Westview.

Messerschmid, E. & Bertrand, R. Space Stations: Systems & Usage. LC 99 31031. (Illus.). 566p. 1999. 61.00 (*3-540-65464-X*) Spr-Verlag.

Messerschmidt, D. A. Moran of Kathmandu Priest, Educator & Ham Radio Voice of the Himalayas. 1997. pap. 87.00 (*0-7855-7438-7*, Pub. by Ratna Pustak Bhandar) St Mut.

Messerschmidt, Edwin, ed. see Billheimer, Paul E.

Messerschmidt, James. Capitalism, Patriarchy & Crime: Toward a Socialist Feminist Criminology. LC 86-15608. 224p. 1986. 60.00 (*0-8476-7496-7*) Rowman.

Messerschmidt, James, jt. auth. see Beirne, Piers.

Messerschmidt, James W. Crime as Structured Action: Gender, Race, Class & Crime in the Making. LC 96-35669. 144p. 1997. 39.95 (*0-7619-0717-3*); pap. 17.95 (*0-7619-0718-1*) Sage.

— Masculinities & Crime: Critique & Reconceptualization of Theory. LC 93-7809. 248p. (C). 1993. text 66.00 (*0-8476-7868-7*); pap. text 26.95 (*0-8476-7869-5*) Rowman.

Messerschmidt, Jim. The Trial of Leonard Peltier. LC 82-61152. 198p. 1983. 35.00 (*0-89608-164-8*) South End Pr.

Messerschmidt, Lowell. Bauern-Sensei. 1991. pap. 8.50 (*1-55673-311-9*, 7762, Fairway Pr) CSS OH.

Messerschmidt, Robert G. & Harthcock, Matthew A., eds. Infrared Microspectroscopy: Theory & Applications. LC 88-10850. (Practical Spectroscopy Ser.: Vol. 6). (Illus.). 302p. 1988. pap. 93.70 (*0-7837-8953-X*, 204966600002) Bks Demand.

Messerschmitt, David G. Networked Applications: A First Course on the New Computing Infrastructure. Clark, Dave, ed. LC 99-44481. (Networking Ser.). 500p. (C). 1999. text 69.95 (*1-55860-537-1*) Morgan Kaufmann.

— Networked Applications: A Guide to the New Computing Infrastructure. Clark, David, ed. LC 98-52772. (Networking Ser.). 416p. 1999. pap. text 34.95 (*1-55860-536-3*, Pub. by Morgan Kaufmann) Harcourt.

Messerschmitt, David G., jt. auth. see Hong, Micheal.

M

Messerschmitt, David G., jt. auth. see Lee, Edward A.
Messerschmitt, Henri. Encyclopedie Permanente d'Agriculture Biologique, 3 vols., Set. (FRE.). 660p. 1974. 250.00 (*0-8288-6041-6*, M6408) Fr & Eur.
Messersmith, Ann M. & Miller, Judy L. Forecasting in Foodservice. LC 00-91. 160p. 1991. 54.95 (*0-471-52916-8*) Wiley.
Messersmith, Dan W. The History of Mohave County to Nineteen Twelve. LC 91-62434. 230p. (C). 1991. pap. 15.95 (*0-9630125-0-9*) Mohave Cnty.
Messervy, Julie M. The Inward Garden: Creating a Place of Beauty & Meaning. LC 94-27802. (Illus.). 256p. (gr. 8). 1995. 40.00 (*0-316-56792-1*) Little.
— The Magic Land: Designing Your Own Enchanted Garden. LC 97-31531. (Illus.). 160p. 1998. 19.95 (*0-02-862091-7*) Macmillan Gen Ref.
Messet, David, ed. see Peck, Judith.
Messiaen, Oliver. The Technique of My Musical Language. 1987. reprint ed. lib. bdg. 39.00 (*0-685-14827-0*) Rprt Serv.
Messiah, A. Quantum Mechanics, Vol. 2. xvi, 632p. 1961. pap. 29.75 (*0-7204-0045-7*, North Holland) Elsevier.
Messiah, Albert. Quantum Mechanics. LC 99-55362. 1152p. 2000. pap. 29.95 (*0-486-40924-4*) Dover.
— Quantum Mechanics, Vol. I. 504p. 1961. pap. 61.75 (*0-7204-0044-9*, North Holland) Elsevier.
Messick, Blanche P. Fresh Roasted Ice Cream. (Illus.). 175p. (Orig.). 1988. 10.95 (*0-945913-17-6*); pap. 8.95 (*0-945913-16-8*) Publishers Ink.
Messick, Brinkley. The Calligraphic State: Textual Domination & History in a Muslim Society. 330p. 1996. 52.50 (*0-614-21101-8*, 120) Kazi Pubns.
— The Calligraphic State: Textual Domination & History in a Muslim Society. (Comparative Studies on Muslim Societies: No. 16). (C). 1992. 48.00 (*0-520-07605-2*, Pub. by U CA Pr) Cal Prin Full Svc.
— The Calligraphic State: Textual Domination & History in a Muslim Society. LC 91-44118. (Comparative Studies on Muslim Societies: No. 16). (Illus.). 324p. (C). 1996. pap. 19.95 (*0-520-20515-4*, Pub. by U CA Pr) Cal Prin Full Svc.
Messick, David M. & Cook, Karen S., eds. Equity Theory: Psychological & Sociological Perspectives. LC 82-18941. 336p. 1983. 45.00 (*0-275-91044-X*, C1044, Praeger Pubs) Greenwood.
Messick, David M. & Tenbrunsel, Ann E., eds. Codes of Conduct: Behavioral Research into Business Ethics. LC 96-3337. 409p. (C). 1996. text 49.50 (*0-87154-594-2*) Russell Sage.
Messick, David M., jt. auth. see Kramer, Roderick M.
Messick, David M., jt. auth. see Liebrand, Wim B.
Messick, Frederic M., compiled by. Primary Sources in European Diplomacy, 1914-1945: A Bibliography of Published Memoirs & Diaries, 6. LC 87-186. (Bibliographies & Indexes in World History Ser.: No. 6). 243p. 1987. lib. bdg. 69.50 (*0-313-24555-X*, MEU) Greenwood.
Messick, Hank. Lansky. Date not set. lib. bdg. 24.95 (*0-8488-1808-3*) Amereon Ltd.
— Razzle Dazzle. Date not set. lib. bdg. 29.95 (*0-8488-1812-1*) Amereon Ltd.
— Razzle Dazzle. (Illus.). 215p. 1995. 29.95 (*0-9650243-1-8*) For The Love Bks.
— The Silent Syndicate. Date not set. lib. bdg. 24.95 (*0-8488-1809-1*) Amereon Ltd.
— Syndicate in the Sun. Date not set. lib. bdg. 23.95 (*0-8488-1810-5*) Amereon Ltd.
— Syndicate Wife. Date not set. lib. bdg. 29.95 (*0-8488-1811-3*) Amereon Ltd.
— Syndicate Wife. 2nd ed. 214p. 1995. reprint ed. 29.95 (*0-9650243-0-X*) For The Love Bks.
Messick, Judith, tr. see Skram, Amalie.
Messick, Linda S. Through My Day with the 'L' Sound. (Illus.). 120p. (J). (gr. k-6). 1975. pap. text 8.95 (*0-87015-212-2*) Pacific Bks.
— Through My Day with the 'S' Sound. (Illus.). 120p. (J). (gr. k-6). 1975. pap. text 8.95 (*0-87015-214-9*) Pacific Bks.
— Through My Day with the 'SH' Sound. (Illus.). 112p. (J). (gr. k-6). 1975. pap. text 8.95 (*0-87015-215-7*) Pacific Bks.
Messick, Paul. Maximum MIDI: Music Applications in C++ LC 97-23268. (Illus.). 479p. 1997. pap. text 49.99 incl. cd-rom (*1-884777-44-9*) Manning Pubns.
Messick, Richard, ed. World Survey of Economic Freedom, 1995-1996. 220p. (Orig.). 1996. pap. text 29.95 (*1-56000-929-2*) Transaction Pubs.
Messick, Rosemary G., jt. auth. see Chapin, June R.
Messick, Samuel. Effectiveness of Coaching for the SAT: Review & Reanalysis from the Fifties to the FTC. 1988. 5.00 (*0-317-67894-9*) Educ Testing Serv.
— Individuality in Learning. LC 76-11886. 398p. reprint ed. pap. 123.40 (*0-608-12287-4*, 202377600034) Bks Demand.
Messick, Samuel, jt. ed. see Collins, Janet M.
Messick, Samuel, jt. ed. see Wainer, Howard.
Messick, Samuel J., ed. Issues of Access, Quality, Student Development & Public Policy. LC 98-25282. 400p. 1998. write for info. (*0-8058-2107-4*) L Erlbaum Assocs.
Messick, Tim. Cross Country Skiing in Yosemite. 2nd ed. (Illus.). 88p. 1994. pap. 9.95 (*0-934641-67-6*) Falcon Pub Inc.
Messick, Wayne D., jt. auth. see Jonovic, Donald J.
Messick, William, ed. see Luong Si Hang.
Messier, Andre. Auditing System Approach. 2nd ed. LC 98-49843. 848p. 1999. 90.31 (*0-07-290828-9*) McGraw.
Messier, J., et al, eds. Nonlinear Optical Effects in Organic Polymers. (C). 1989. text 202.50 (*0-7923-0132-3*) Kluwer Academic.
— Organic Molecules for Nonlinear Optics & Photonics. (C). 1991. text 257.50 (*0-7923-1181-7*) Kluwer Academic.
Messier, Mark, et al. Wayne Gretzky: The Making of a Great One. 128p. 1998. 19.95 (*1-887432-47-7*) Beckett Pubns.
Messier, Ronald A., jt. ed. see Dajani-Shareel, Hadia.
***Messier, William.** Auditing & Assurance Services: Ready Notes. 2nd ed. 176p. (C). 1999. pap. 15.31 (*0-07-290832-7*) McGrw-H Hghr Educ.
Messiha, F. S. & Tyner, G. S., eds. Endocrinological Aspects of Alcoholism. (Progress in Biochemical Pharmacology Ser.: Vol. 18). (Illus.). xii, 232p. 1981. 135.00 (*3-8055-2689-X*) S Karger.
Messiha, F. S., jt. ed. see Tyner.
Messik, Marilyn. East Coast - North America. (Welcome Directory of Selected Hotels & I Ser.). 1997. pap. text 14.95 (*0-9522508-2-9*) US Welcome.
— North America. (Welcome Directory of Selected Hotels & I Ser.). 1998. pap. text 16.95 (*0-9522508-7-X*) US Welcome.
Messimer, Dwight R. Escape. LC 93-11122. (Illus.). 288p. 1994. 29.95 (*1-55750-578-0*) Naval Inst Pr.
***Messimer, Dwight R.** Escape from Villingen, 1918. LC 00-25119. (C. A. Brannen Ser.: Vol. 5). (Illus.). 224p. 2000. 29.95 (*0-89096-956-6*) Tex A&M Univ Pr.
Messina. Tools for Business Process Redesign. 400p. 69.95 (*0-471-15460-1*) Wiley.
Messina, Annie. The Myrtle & the Rose. Bright, Jessie, tr. from ITA. & intro. by. LC 97-41902. 158p. (Orig.). 1997. pap. 12.50 (*0-934977-45-3*) Italica Pr.
Messina, Anthony M. Race & Party Competition in Britain. (Illus.). 214p. 1989. text 55.00 (*0-19-827534-X*) OUP.
Messina, Anthony M., et al, eds. Ethnic & Racial Minorities in Advanced Industrial Democracies, 29. LC 91-26374. (Contributions in Ethnic Studies: No. 29). 376p. 1992. 65.00 (*0-313-27259-X*, MEH/, Greenwood Pr) Greenwood.
***Messina, Antonino, ed.** Nuclear & Condensed Matter Physics: VI Regional CRRNSM Conference. LC 00-100717. (AIP Conference Proceedings Ser.: Vol. 513). (Illus.). 442p. 2000. 130.00 (*1-56396-929-7*, Pub. by Am Inst Physics) Spr-Verlag.
Messina, Calogero. Sicilians Wanted the Inquisition. LC 92-43674.Tr. of Volevano l'Inquisizione. 1993. pap. 10.00 (*1-881901-01-7*) LEGAS.
Messina, Christopher. Rhymes for a Reason. large type ed. (Illus.). 49p. (J). (gr. 1-7). 1995. 39.50 (*1-57529-005-7*) Kabel Pubs.
Messina, Constance G., jt. auth. see Messina, James J.
Messina, Edmund J. Cytology. LC 74-79836. (Allied Health Ser.). 1975. pap. 7.65 (*0-672-61382-4*, Bobbs) Macmillan.
Messina, Frank. A Window on Main Street. 219p. 1998. pap. 9.95 (*0-9656811-9-X*) Four Seasons.
Messina, G. & Hamza, M. H., eds. Computers & Their Applications for Development: Proceedings IASTED Symposium, Taormina, Italy, September 3-5, 1986. 222p. 1987. 55.00 (*0-88986-098-X*, 106) Acta Pr.
— Measurement, Signal Processing & Control - MECO '86: Proceedings IASTED Symposium, Taormina, Italy, September 3-5, 1986. 323p. 1986. 91.00 (*0-88986-096-3*, 105) Acta Pr.
Messina, James J., ed. Case Management Handbook. (Professional Handbook Ser.). 84p. (Orig.). 1982. pap. text 11.00 (*0-931975-18-2*) Advanced Dev Sys.
Messina, James J., pref. Advanced Communication Skills Handbook. (Professional Handbook Ser.). 61p. (Orig.). 1982. pap. text 10.00 (*0-931975-12-3*) Advanced Dev Sys.
— Basic Communication Skills Handbook. 53p. (Orig.). 1982. pap. text 10.00 (*0-931975-11-5*) Advanced Dev Sys.
— The Burnout & Stress Management Handbook: Professional Handbook Ser. 78p. (Orig.). 1982. pap. text 11.00 (*0-931975-14-X*) Advanced Dev Sys.
— Family Therapy Handbook. (Professional Handbook Ser.). 79p. (Orig.). 1982. pap. text 11.00 (*0-931975-19-0*) Advanced Dev Sys.
— The Group Leader's Handbook. (Professional Handbook Ser.). 45p. (Orig.). pap. text 7.00 (*0-931975-10-7*) Advanced Dev Sys.
— The Handbook of Readings for the Training of Consultants & Trainers. (Professional Handbook Ser.). 127p. (Orig.). 1982. pap. text 16.00 (*0-931975-08-5*) Advanced Dev Sys.
— The Handbook of Trainer's Activities. (Professional Handbook Ser.). 100p. (Orig.). 1982. pap. text 11.00 (*0-931975-09-3*) Advanced Dev Sys.
— The Human Services Counseling Skills. (Professional Handbook Ser.). 35p. (Orig.). 1982. pap. text 7.00 (*0-931975-17-4*) Advanced Dev Sys.
— Personal Values Analysis Handbook. (Professional Handbook Ser.). 26p. (Orig.). 1982. pap. text 7.00 (*0-931975-16-6*) Advanced Dev Sys.
— The Time Management Handbook. (Professional Handbook Ser.). 37p. (Orig.). 1982. pap. text 7.00 (*0-931975-15-8*) Advanced Dev Sys.
— Tools for Parents of Children with Developmental Disabilities. (Tools-for-Coping Ser.). 98p. (Orig.). 1987. pap. text 11.00 (*0-931975-07-7*) Advanced Dev Sys.
Messina, James J. & Messina, Constance G. Getting Parents Involved in the Exceptional Education Process. (Tools-for-Coping Ser.). 140p. (Orig.). 1988. pap. text 11.00 (*0-931975-24-7*) Advanced Dev Sys.
— Getting Parents Involved in the Exceptional Education Process a Leader's Guide. (Tools for Coping Ser.). 32p. (Orig.). 1988. pap. text 7.00 (*0-931975-25-5*) Advanced Dev Sys.
Messina, Jennifer. The Secrets of the Jennivine Restaurant Cookbook. 202p. 1992. pap. 12.95 (*0-9636478-0-6*) Jennivine.
***Messina, John.** Telecommunications Expense Management: How to Get the Best Telecom Services at the Lowest Price. 240p. 1999. pap. 29.95 (*1-57820-032-6*) Telecom Bks.
Messina, John L. Hand Motor Vehicle Treatise Only. LC 89-25234. 1990. ring bd. 105.00 (*0-685-59921-3*) West Group.
— Handling Motor Vehicle Accident Cases. LC 89-25234. 1990. ring bd. 135.00 (*0-685-58521-2*) West Group.
— Handling Motor Vehicle Accident Cases: Forms. LC 90-1377. 1990. ring bd. 135.00 (*0-685-34581-5*) West Group.
Messina, Kathlyn. The Sleeping Giant Reading Program. LC 82-83558. (Illus.). 160p. (Orig.). 1983. pap. 12.95 (*0-910569-00-2*) Hampton Court Pub.
Messina, Kathlyn & Dacquino, Vinny. Proud That I'm Still Me. (Illus.). 21p. (Orig.). (J). 1992. pap. 3.95 (*0-910569-03-7*); teacher ed. 5.00 (*0-910569-06-1*) Hampton Court Pub.
Messina-Kleinman, Deborah, jt. auth. see Kleinman, Lowell.
Messina, M. G. & Conner, William H. Southern Forested Wetlands: Ecology & Management. LC 97-41609. 640p. 1997. lib. bdg. 69.95 (*1-56670-228-3*) Lewis Pubs.
Messina, Maria. A House in the Shadows. Shepley, John, tr. from ITA. LC 89-60939. 133p. 1989. 25.95 (*0-910395-50-0*); pap. 9.95 (*0-910395-51-9*) Marlboro Pr.
Messina, Mark & Messina, Virginia. The Dietitian's Guide to Vegetarian Diets: Issues & Applications. LC 96-329. 528p. 1996. 49.00 (*0-8342-0635-8*) Aspen Pub.
Messina, Mark, et al. The Simple Soybean & Your Health: How Soyfoods Can Lower Your Cholesterol & Reduce Your Risk of Disease & Cancer. LC 93-43374. 272p. pap. 12.95 (*0-89529-611-X*, Avery) Penguin Putnam.
Messina, Mark, jt. auth. see Messina, Virginia.
***Messina, Noreen E.** Teen Work: Four Teens Tell All. (Illus.). (YA). (gr. 9-12). 2000. pap. text 13.28 (*1-56637-716-1*) Goodheart.
Messina, Paul C. & Murli, Almerico, eds. Practical Parallel Computing: Status & Prospects. fac. ed. LC 91-44139. 253p. 1991. reprint ed. pap. 78.50 (*0-7837-8279-9*, 204906000009) Bks Demand.
Messina, Paul C. & Sterling, Thomas A. System Software & Tools for High Performance Computing Environments. xix, 160p. 1993. pap. 5.00 (*0-89871-326-9*) Soc Indus-Appl Math.
Messina, Paul C., ed. see Fox, Mark.
***Messina, Paula & Stoffer, Phil Ward.** Geology of the NYC Metro Region. (Illus.). 416p. 2000. pap. text 23.00 (*0-945005-35-0*) U of Okla Pr.
Messina, Phillip. Anzio - Song of Destiny. 316p. 1992. pap. 5.95 (*0-935648-38-0*) Halldin Pub.
Messina, Robert J. The Covenant of 1996: Countdown the Last Seven Years. (Illus.). (Orig.). 1993. pap. text 8.00 (*0-685-65628-4*) Hse of Asher.
— For Signs & for Seasons: How Forty-Eight Ancient Celestial Signs Identify Our Messiah. 303p. 1992. pap. text. write for info. (*0-9633250-4-3*) Hse of Asher.
Messina, Susan S. Adolescents & the HIV-AIDS Epidemic: Stemming the Tide. 41p. 1993. 15.00 (*1-55516-646-6*, 6646) Natl Conf State Legis.
Messina, Virginia & Messina, Mark. The Vegetarian Way: Total Health for You & Your Family. LC 95-34599. 400p. 1996. pap. 24.00 (*0-517-88275-2*) Crown Pub Group.
***Messina, Virginia & Schumann, Kate.** Convenient Vegetarian: Quick & Easy Meatless Cooking. 192p. 1999. 14.00 (*0-02-862334-7*, Pub. by Macmillan) S&S Trade.
Messina, Virginia, jt. auth. see Messina, Mark.
Messina, Virginia, jt. auth. see Schumann, Kate.
***Messina, William S.** Statistical Process Control for Surface Mount Technology. (Illus.). 265p. (C). 1999. pap. 49.95 (*0-9675033-9-6*) Data Sleuths.
Messina, William S. Statistical Quality Control for Manufacturing Managers. LC 86-34022. (Engineering Management Ser.). 352p. 1987. 120.00 (*0-471-85774-2*) Wiley.
Messiner, C. Latin Phrasebook. Auden, H. W., tr. 338p. 1998. reprint ed. pap. 14.95 (*0-7818-0666-6*) Hippocrene Bks.
Messing, G. L., et al, eds. Ceramic Processing Science. (Ceramic Transactions Ser.: Vol. 83). (Illus.). 600p. 1998. 95.00 (*1-57498-056-4*, CT083) Am Ceramic.
Messing, Gary L., ed. see Ceramic Powder Science & Technology: Synthesis, Pr.
Messing, Gary L., ed. see International Conference on Ceramic Powder Process.
Messing, Gordon M. A Glossary of Greek Romany As Spoken in Agia Varvara (Athens) 175p. (Orig.). 1988. pap. 19.95 (*0-89357-187-3*) Slavica.
Messing, Gordon M., ed. see Smyth, Herbert W.
Messing, Joachim W., jt. auth. see Sussex, Ian M.
Messing, karen. One-Eyed Science: Occupational Health & Women Workers. LC 97-26885. 264p. 1998. 59.95 (*1-56639-597-6*) Temple U Pr.
Messing, Karen. One-Eyed Science: Occupational Health & Women Workers. LC 97-26885. 264p. 1998. pap. 22.95 (*1-56639-598-4*) Temple U Pr.
Messing, Karen, et al, eds. Invisible: Issues in Women's Occupational Health/La Sant'e des Travailleuses. LC 96-106063. (Illus.). 432p. 1995. pap. 25.95 (*0-921881-37-1*, Pub. by Gynergy-Ragweed) U of Toronto Pr.
***Messing, Lynn S. & Campbell, Ruth, eds.** Gesture, Speech & Sign. LC 99-18289. (Illus.). 256p. 1999. text 85.00 (*0-19-852451-X*) OUP.
Messing, Patricia, jt. auth. see Coyle, Rena.
Messing, Scott. Neoclassicism in Music: From the Genesis of the Concept Through the Schoenberg/Stravinsky Polemic. LC 96-430. 234p. (C). 1996. reprint ed. 65.00 (*1-878822-66-7*) Univ Rochester Pr.
Messing, Simon D. The Story of the Falashas: "Black Jews" of Ethiopia. (Illus.). 134p. 1982. pap. 12.50 (*0-9615946-9-1*) S D Messing.
Messing, Simon D., ed. Target of Health in Ethiopia: A Holistic Reader in Applied Anthropology. 285p. 1973. text 37.50 (*0-8422-5074-3*); pap. text 16.95 (*0-8422-0261-7*) Irvington.
Messinger, H. Langenscheidts Handworterbucher: Englisch. (DUT & ENG.). 760p. 1997. pap. write for info. (*3-468-04123-3*) Langenscheidt.
Messinger, H. & Langenscheidt-Redaktion. Langenscheidts Grobworterbucher: Deutsch-English. 1296p. 1997. pap. write for info. (*3-468-02125-9*) Langenscheidt.
Messinger, H., jt. auth. see Willman, H.
Messinger, Heinz. Langenscheidt Standard Dictionary German English-English German Thumb-Indexed, Thumb-Indexed. 1408p. 1993. 20.95 (*0-88729-044-2*) Langenscheidt.
Messinger, Jean G. & Rust, Mary J. Faith in High Places: Historic Country Churches of Colorado. 208p. (Orig.). 1995. pap. text 16.95 (*1-57098-013-6*) Roberts Rinehart.
Messinger, Lisa, jt. auth. see Paino, John.
Messinger, Lisa M. Abstract Expressionism: Works on Paper: Selections from the Metropolitan Museum of Art. LC 92-33802. (Illus.). 176p. 1993. 45.00 (*0-685-62556-7*) Abrams.
— Abstract Expressionism: Works on Paper: Selections from the Metropolitan Museum of Art. (Illus.). 176p. 1993. pap. 19.95 (*0-87099-657-6*) Metro Mus Art.
— James Brooks: A Quarter-Century of Work. LC 88-81869. (Illus.). 40p. (Orig.). 1988. pap. text 9.00 (*1-879195-02-X*) Heckscher Mus.
Messinger, Lisa M., et al. The Georgia O'Keeffe Museum. Hassrick, Peter H., ed. LC 97-7954. (Illus.). 144p. 1997. 35.00 (*0-8109-3685-2*, Pub. by Abrams) Time Warner.
***Messinger, Midge.** Freddie Q. Freckle. unabridged ed. Messinger, Robert, ed. LC 98-92167. (Illus.). 40p. (J). (ps-2). 1998. 12.95 (*1-893237-00-1*) Little Mai Pr.
Messinger, Milton A. Dare to Question! Teachership & Power Learning. LC 95-83813. (Illus.). 264p. (C). 1996. pap. text 22.00 (*1-888960-00-0*) Fine Print Pr.
Messinger, Paul R. The Marketing Paradigm: A Guide for General Managers. LC 94-41608. (C). 1995. 26.50 (*0-538-84494-9*) S-W Pub.
Messinger Press Staff, ed. see Ayers, Charles.
Messinger, Robert, ed. see Messinger, Midge.
Messinger, Sheldon L., ed. see Criminology Review Yearbook Staff.
Messinger, Thane J. The Young Lawyer's Jungle Book: A Survival Guide. LC 95-83497. 174p. 1996. pap. 18.95 (*1-888960-01-9*) Fine Print Pr.
Messinger, Thane Josef. The Young Lawyer's Jungle Book: A Survival Guide. 2nd ed. (Orig.). 1999. pap. text 18.95 (*1-888960-19-1*) Fine Print Pr.
Messingham, Simon. Fact Eater. (Doctor Who Ser.). 1999. mass mkt. 5.95 (*0-563-55569-6*) BBC Worldwide.
***Messingham, Simon.** The Tomb of Valdemar. (Doctor Who Ser.). 288p. 2000. mass mkt. 6.95 (*0-563-55591-2*, Pub. by BBC Bks) Genl Dist Srvs.
Messingham, Simon. Zeta Major. 1998. pap. 5.95 (*0-563-40597-X*) BBC.
***Messinis, Dimosthenis.** Table Tennis: From A to Z. Arsenis, William, tr. (Illus.). xviii, 166p. 2000. pap. 16.00 (*960-90743-1-6*) Dimosthenis Messinis.
Messite, Jacqueline, ed. see New York Academy of Medicine Staff.
Messiter, Arthur. History of the Choir & Music of Trinity Church. LC 72-137317. reprint ed. 37.50 (*0-404-04313-5*) AMS Pr.
Messler. Pharmacy Technology. 1999. pap. text. write for info. (*0-7216-7432-1*, W B Saunders Co) Harcrt Hlth Sci Grp.
— Real World Calculations. 1999. pap. text 26.95 (*0-7216-7556-5*, W B Saunders Co) Harcrt Hlth Sci Grp.
Messler, A. First Things in Old Somerset: Collection of Articles Relating to Somerset County. rev. ed. (Illus.). 172p. 1997. pap. 21.00 (*0-8328-6076-X*) Higginson Bk Co.
Messler, Abraham. Centennial History of Somerset County. (Illus.). 198p. 1997. reprint ed. lib. bdg. 26.50 (*0-8328-6077-8*) Higginson Bk Co.
Messler, Robert W., Jr. Joining of Advanced Materials. 560p. 1993. text 140.00 (*0-7506-9008-9*) Buttrwrth-Heinemann.
***Messler, Robert W., Jr.** Principles of Welding: Processes, Physics, Chemistry & Metallurgy. LC 98-34986. 662p. 1999. 135.00 (*0-471-25376-6*, Wiley-Interscience) Wiley.
Messler, Robert W., Jr., jt. auth. see Thomas, R. David.
Messler, W. Auditing. LC 96-14339. (C). 1996. text 70.74 (*0-07-041575-7*) McGraw.
Messley, John, et al. Groups for Children with A. D. H. D. Helping Children Learn Self-Control. (Illus.). 19p. 1997. pap. 14.95 (*0-9663152-0-0*) Kids on Track.
Messley, Karen & Norrell, Stephen A. Microbiology Lab Manual: Principles & Applications. 331p. (C). 1996. pap. text, lab manual ed. 51.00 (*0-13-255373-2*) P-H.
Messmacher, Genoves. Dinamica Maya. (SPA.). pap. 16.99 (*968-16-2491-2*, Pub. by Fondo) Continental Bk.
Messmann, Frank J. Richard Payne Knight: The Twilight of Virtuosity. 1974. text 38.50 (*90-279-2628-X*) Mouton.
Messmer. PC - Hardwarebuch. (GER.). (C). 1991. text. write for info. (*0-201-55985-4*) Addison-Wesley.
Messmer, Dale, ed. see Dalton, Robb E.
Messmer, Hans-Peter. Indispensable PC Hardware Book: Your Hardware Questions Answered. 3rd ed. 1408p. (C). 2000. pap. text 42.95 (*0-201-40399-4*) Addison-Wesley.

An Asterisk (*) at the beginning of an entry indicates that the title is appearing for the first time.

*Messmer, Hans-Peter. The Indispensable PC Hardware Book: Your Hardware Questions Answered. 4th ed. (C). 2000. pap. text. write for info. (0-201-59616-4) Addison-Wesley.

Messmer, Heinz, ed. Restorative Justice on Trial - Pitfalls & Potentials of Victim-Offender Mediation: International Research Perspectives - Proceedings of the NATO Advanced Research Workshop on Conflict, Crime & Reconciliation: The Organization of Welfare Interventions in the Field of Restitutive Justice, Held in Il Ciocco, Lucca, Italy 8-12 April, 1991. 608p. (C). 1992. lib. bdg. 281.00 (0-7923-1620-7) Kluwer Academic.

Messmer, K., ed. Capillary Functions & White Cell Interaction. (Progress in Applied Microcirculation Ser.: Vol. 18). (Illus.). x, 138p. 1991. 124.50 (3-8055-5397-8) S Karger.

— Compromised Perfusion: 13th Bodensee Symposium on Microcirculation, Lindau, June, 1995. (Progress in Applied Microcirculation Ser.: Vol. 22, 1996). (Illus.). x, 186p. 1996. 172.25 (3-8055-6225-X) S Karger.

— Microcirculation in Chronic Venous Insufficiency: 15th Bodensee Symposium on Microcirculation, June 1998. LC 99-30254. (Progress in Applied Microcirculation Ser.: Vol. 23, 1999). (Illus.). x, 216p. 1999. 149.75 (3-8055-6821-5) S Karger.

*Messmer, K., ed. Orthogonal Polarization Spectral Imaging (OPS Imaging) - a New Tool for the Observation & Measurement of the Human Microcirculation: 16th Bodensee Symposium on Microcirculation, Lindau, September 1999. (Progress in Applied Microcirculation Ser.: Vol. 24). (Illus.). 118p. 2000. 111.50 (3-8055-7065-1) S Karger.

Messmer, K., et al, eds. European Society Surgical Research, 16th Congress, Garmisch-Partenkirchen, April 1981. (Journal: European Surgical Research: Vol. 13, Suppl. 1). (Illus.). viii, 104p. 1981. pap. 35.75 (3-8055-2644-X) S Karger.

— Hemodilution & Flow Improvement: Bibliotheca Haematologica, No. 47. (Illus.). viii, 356p. 1982. pap. 164.50 (3-8055-2899-X) S Karger.

— Microcirculation in Organ Transplantation. (Progress in Applied Microcirculation Ser.: Vol. 21). (Illus.). x, 126p. 1994. 129.75 (3-8055-5849-X) S Karger.

— Mocrocirculation in Circulatory Disorders. (Illus.). 552p. 1988. 160.00 (0-387-70034-X) Spr-Verlag.

Messmer, K. & Fagrell, Bengt, eds. Mikrozirkulation und arterielle Verschlusskrankheiten, Muenchen, November 1980. (Illus.). vi, 222p. 1982. pap. 42.75 (3-8055-2417-X) S Karger.

Messmer, K. & Hammersen, F., eds. Entzuendung und Rheologie der Leukozyten. (GER., Illus.). x, 136p. 1985. pap. 61.75 (3-8055-4071-X) S Karger.

— Gastrointestinal Microcirculation. (Progress in Applied Microcirculation Ser.: Vol. 17). (Illus.). x, 222p. 1991. 195.00 (3-8055-5176-2) S Karger.

— Microcirculation & Inflammation: Vessel Wall, Inflammatory Cells, Mediator Interaction. (Progress in Applied Microcirculation Ser.: Vol. 12). xvi, 330p. 1987. pap. 130.50 (3-8055-4552-5) S Karger.

— Die Mikrozirkulation des Skelettmuskels. (Illus.). viii, 162p. 1985. pap. 64.50 (3-8055-3919-3) S Karger.

— Mikrozirkulation und Entzuendung: Beziehungen Zwischen Gefaesswand Entzuendungszellen und Mediatoren. (Illus.). xvi, 358p. 1988. pap. 130.50 (3-8055-4656-4) S Karger.

— Skeletal Muscle Microcirculation. (Mikrozirkulation in Forschung und Klinik; Progress in Applied Microcirculation Ser.: Vol. 5). (Illus.). vii, 148p. 1984. pap. 64.50 (3-8055-3920-7) S Karger.

— Struktur und Funktion Endothelialer Zellen. (Illus.). x, 150p. 1983. pap. 42.75 (3-8055-3712-3) S Karger.

— Vasomotion & Quantitative Kapillaroskopie. (Progress in Applied Microcirculation Ser.: Vol. 3). (Illus.). viii, 152p. 1984. pap. 71.50 (3-8055-3809-X) S Karger.

— White Cell Rheology & Inflammation. (Mikrozirkulation in Forschung und Klinik; Progress in Applied Microcirculation Ser.: Vol. 7). (Illus.). x, 124p. 1985. pap. 61.75 (3-8055-4040-X) S Karger.

Messmer, K. & Kuebler, W. M., eds. World Congress for Microcirculation: Abstracts. (Journal Ser.: Vol. 16, Supplement 1, 1996). (Illus.). x, 308p. 1996. pap. 77.50 (3-8055-6388-4) S Karger.

Messmer, K. & Menger, Michael D., eds. Liver Microcirculation & Hepatobiliary Function. (Progress in Applied Microcirculation Ser.: Vol. 19). (Illus.). viii, 172p. 1993. 161.75 (3-8055-5701-9) S Karger.

Messmer, K. & Stein, M., eds. Pathways in Applied Immunology: In Memoriam Walter Brendel. (Illus.). 152p. 1991. 38.95 (0-387-53989-1) Spr-Verlag.

Messmer, K., jt. ed. see Brendel, W.

Messmer, K., ed. see Hammersen, F.

Messmer, K., jt. ed. see Hammersen, F.

Messmer, Max. The Fast Forward MBA in Hiring: Finding & Keeping the Best People. LC 97-35609. (Fast Forward MBA Ser.). 256p. 1998. pap. 14.95 (0-471-24212-8) Wiley.

— Human Resources Kit for Dummies. LC 99-61322. 384p. 1999. pap. 24.99 incl. cd-rom (0-7645-5131-0) IDG Bks.

— Job Hunting for Dummies. (For Dummies Ser.). 400p. 1995. pap. 16.99 (1-56884-388-7) IDG Bks.

— Job Hunting for Dummies. 2nd ed. (For Dummies Ser.). 384p. 1999. pap. 16.99 (0-7645-5163-9, Dummies Trade Pr) IDG Bks.

*Messmer, Max. Managing Your Career for Dummies. (For Dummies (Lifestyles) Ser.). 384p. 2000. pap. 19.99 (0-7645-5253-8) IDG Bks.

Messmer, Otto. Nine Lives to Live: A Classic Felix Celebration. 144p. 1996. 39.95 (1-56097-308-0, Pub. by Fantagraph Bks) Seven Hills Bk.

Messmer, Sara E., ed. see Chavers-Wright, Madrue.

*Messmer, Wayne P. The Voice of Victory: One Man's Journey to Freedom Through Healing & Forgiveness. LC 99-91517. 264p. 1999. pap. 14.95 (0-9676588-0-2) W P M Pubg.

Messmore, Evelyn & Whitworth, Milli B. Twentieth Century Pioneer: Still Exploring. 60p. (Orig.). 1996. pap. text 12.95 (0-9643885-5-3) Personal Profiles.

Messnarz, Richard. Better Software Practice for Business Benefit: Principles & Experiences. 1999. pap. text 60.00 (0-7695-0049-8, IEEE Inst Elec) IEEE Comp Soc.

Messner & Rosenfeld. Crime & The American Dream. 3rd ed. (Criminal Justice Ser.). 2000. pap. text 22.00 (0-534-56277-9) Wadsworth Pub.

Messner, Abby, ed. see Downey, Martha Kate.

*Messner, Abby Ward. Captain Tommy. (Illus.). 28p. (J). (gr. 1-4). 1999. text 14.95 (1-885477-58-9) Fut Horizons.

Messner, Dirk & Deutsches Institute Staff. The Network Society: Economic Development & International Competitiveness As Problems of Social Governance. LC 97-23233. (German Development Institute Ser.). 413p. (C). 1997. pap. 39.95 (0-7146-4402-1, Pub. by F Cass Pubs) Intl Spec Bk.

Messner, Edward. Resilience Enhancement for the Resident Physician. 163p. 1993. pap. 7.95 (0-929240-57-X) EMIS.

Messner, Edward, et al, eds. What Therapists Learn about Themselves & How They Learn It: Autognosis. LC 93-74196. 166p. 1994. pap. 40.00 (1-56821-188-0) Aronson.

*Messner, Frank. Nachhaltiges Wirtschaften Mit Nicht-Erneuerbaren Ressourcen: Die Vier Ebenen einer Nachhaltigen Materialnutzung Am Beispiel von Kupfer und Seinen Substituten. (Europaische Hochschulschriften Ser.: Bd. 2533). 680p. 1999. 79.95 (3-631-35121-6) P Lang Pubng.

Messner, Fred. The Business-to-Business Communications Handbook. 1994. 44.95 (1-56318-001-4) Assn Natl Advertisers.

— Business to Business Communications Handbook. (Illus.). 320p. 59.95 (0-8442-3473-7) NTC Contemp Pub Co.

Messner, Julian, jt. auth. see Oz, Charles.

Messner-Loebs, William F. Epicurus: The Sage: The Many Loves of Zeus, Vol. 2. Nevelow, Mark, ed. (Illus.). 48p. 1991. pap. 9.95 (0-930289-91-9, Piranha Pr) DC Comics.

— Journey Saga Bk. 1: Tall Tales. (Illus.). 96p. (Orig.). 1987. pap. 9.95 (0-930193-28-8) Fantagraph Bks.

— The Journey Saga Bk. 2: Bad Weather. 96p. 1990. 9.95 (1-56097-029-4) Fantagraph Bks.

— Wonder Woman: Amazonia. Kupperberg, Paul, ed. (Illus.). 48p. 1998. pap. 7.95 (1-56389-301-0, Pub. by DC Comics) Time Warner.

— Wonder Woman: The Challenge of Artemis. LC 96-228591. (Illus.). 192p. 1996. mass mkt. 9.95 (1-56389-264-2, Pub. by DC Comics) Time Warner.

Messner, Michael, jt. auth. see Kimmel, Michael S.

Messner, Michael A. The Politics of Masculinities: Men in Movements. LC 96-35667. (Gender Lens Ser.). 128p. 1997. 35.00 (0-8039-5576-6); pap. 14.95 (0-8039-5577-4) Sage.

— Power at Play: Sports & the Problem of Masculinity. 256p. 1995. pap. 18.00 (0-8070-4105-X) Beacon Pr.

Messner, Michael A. & Sabo, Donald F., eds. Sport, Men, & the Gender Order: Critical Feminist Perspectives. LC 90-31880. (Illus.). 296p. 1992. pap. text 23.00 (0-87322-421-3, BMES0421) Human Kinetics.

Messner, Michael A., jt. auth. see Kimmel, Michael S.

Messner, Michael A., jt. ed. see Kimmel, Michael S.

Messner, Reinhold. All 14 Eight-Thousanders. 248p. 1999. 40.00 (0-89886-660-X) Mountaineers.

— All Fourteen Eight-Thousanders. Salkeld, Audrey, tr. from GER. (Illus.). 247p. 1988. 40.00 (0-938567-05-5) Mountaineers.

*Messner, Reinhold. Annapurna: 50 Years of Expeditions in the Death Zone. (Illus.). 204p. 2000. 24.95 (0-89886-738-X) Mountaineers.

Messner, Reinhold. Antarctica: Both Heaven & Hell. (Illus.). 383p. 1991. text 24.95 (0-89886-305-8) Mountaineers.

— The Crystal Horizon: Everest - The First Solo Ascent. rev. ed. Neate, Jill & Salkeld, Audrey, trs. from GER. LC 88-63854. (Illus.). 324p. 1998. pap. 24.95 (0-89886-574-3) Mountaineers.

— Everest: Expedition to the Ultimate. LC 99-38832. (Illus.). 288p. 1999. pap. 24.95 (0-89886-648-0) Mountaineers.

*Messner, Reinhold. My Quest for the Yeti: Confronting the Himalayas' Deepest Mystery. Constantine, Peter, tr. from GER. LC 99-55091. (Illus.). 192p. 2000. text 23.95 (0-312-20394-2) St Martin.

Messner, Reinhold. Reinhold Messner: Free Spirit - A Climber's Life. (Illus.). 256p. 1998. pap. 19.95 (0-89886-573-5) Mountaineers.

*Messner, Reinhold. To the Top of the World: Alpine Challenges in the Himalaya & Karakoram. (Illus.). 1999. pap. 24.95 (0-89886-677-4) Mountaineers.

*Messner, Reinhold, et al. Hermann Buhl: Climbing Without Compromise. LC 00-8990. (Illus.). 204p. 2000. 24.95 (0-89886-678-2) Mountaineers.

Messner, Roberta L. & Lewis, Susan J. Increasing Patient Satisfaction: A Guide for Nurses. LC 95-25628. (Illus.). 240p. 1996. 35.95 (0-8261-9250-5) Springer Pub.

Messner, Stephen D., et al. Marketing Investment Real Estate. 3rd ed. Berlin, Helene, ed. LC 81-86402. (Illus.). 546p. 1985. reprint ed. text 22.95 (0-913652-59-8, BK. 139) Realtors Natl.

— Real Estate Investment & Taxation. 4th ed. 464p. (C). 1990. text 54.80 (0-13-763053-0) P-H.

Messner, Stephen D., jt. ed. see Clapp, John M.

Messner, Steven F. & Rosenfeld, Richard. Crime & the American Dream. 130p. 1993. mass mkt. 13.75 (0-534-20106-7) Wadsworth Pub.

— Crime & the American Dream. 2nd ed. LC 96-3464. (Contemporary Issues in Crime & Justice Ser.). (Illus.). 124p. (C). 1996. 27.95 (0-534-51766-8) Wadsworth Pub.

Messner, Steven F. & Stark, Rodney. Criminology: An Introduction Using ExplorIt. 4th ed. (C). 1999. pap. text 18.00 (0-922914-33-8) Thomson Learn.

Messner, Steven F., jt. auth. see Liska, Allen E.

*Messner, William & Tilbury, Dawn. Control Tutorials for Matlab & Simulink: A Web-based Approach. 32p. 1998. pap. text 26.66 (0-201-47700-9) Addison-Wesley.

Messner, William A. Profitable Purchasing Management: A Guide for Small Business Owners-Managers. LC 81-69367. 317p. reprint ed. pap. 98.30 (0-608-12967-4, 202392200034) Bks Demand.

Messner, William C. Control Tutorials for Matlab & Simulink: A Web-Based Approach. 32p. (C). 1998. pap. text. write for info. (0-201-36194-9) Addison-Wesley.

*Messner, William J. Iron Passage. 216p. 1998. mass mkt. 15.95 (0-9653046-1-2) W J Messner.

Messner, Wm. J. Iron Fist. 2nd ed. 1996. pap. 11.95 (0-9653046-0-4) W J Messner.

Messner, Yvonne. Swimming Everyone. 2nd ed. (Everyone Ser.). 186p. 1992. pap. text 14.95 (0-88725-180-3) Hunter Textbks.

Messoner, Dale, ed. see Walter, Lori J.

Messonnier, Shawn. Acupuncture for Pets. (Pet Care Naturally Ser.). 64p. 1998. pap. 4.95 (0-87983-924-4, Keats Publng) NTC Contemp Pub Co.

*Messonnier, Shawn. Allergy Solution for Dogs. (Natural Vet Ser.). 208p. 2000. pap. 14.00 (0-7615-2672-2) Prima Pub.

— The Arthritis Solution for Dogs: Natural & Conventional Therapies to Ease Pain & Enhance... LC 00-23000. (Natural Vet Ser.). 208p. 2000. pap. 14.00 (0-7615-2622-6) Prima Pub.

Messonnier, Shawn. Be Your Own Boss: Starting Your Veterinary Practice. LC 94-71553. 196p. 1994. pap. text 29.95 (0-939674-55-6) Am Vet Pubns.

— Common Reptile Diseases & Treatments. (Illus.). 160p. (Orig.). 1996. pap. text 29.95 (0-86542-553-1) Blackwell Sci.

— 8 Weeks to a Healthy Cat. (Pet Care Naturally Ser.). 64p. 1998. pap. 4.95 (0-87983-970-8, Keats Publng) NTC Contemp Pub Co.

— 8 Weeks to a Healthy Dog. (Pet Care Naturally Ser.). 64p. 1998. pap. 4.95 (0-87983-969-4, Keats Publng) NTC Contemp Pub Co.

— Exotic Pets: A Veterinary Guide for Owners. LC 94-21728. 144p. 1994. pap. 8.95 (1-55622-381-1, Rep of TX Pr) Wordware Pub.

— Healthy Diet, Healthy Cat. (Pet Care Naturally Ser.). 64p. 1998. pap. 4.95 (0-87983-876-0, Keats Publng) NTC Contemp Pub Co.

— Healthy Diet, Healthy Dog. (Pet Care Naturally Ser.). 64p. 1998. pap. 4.95 (0-87983-875-2, Keats Publng) NTC Contemp Pub Co.

— Homeopathy for Pets. (Pet Care Naturally Ser.). 64p. 1998. pap. 4.95 (0-87983-925-2, Keats Publng) NTC Contemp Pub Co.

— Marketing Your Veterinary Practice. 168p. 1994. 29.95 (0-939674-56-4) Am Vet Pubns.

— Marketing Your Veterinary Practice, Vol. II. LC 96-37947. (Illus.). 176p. (gr. 13). 1997. pap. text 28.95 (0-8151-8583-9, 28819) Mosby Inc.

— Natural Supplements for Your Cat. (Pet Care Naturally Ser.). 64p. 1998. pap. 4.95 (0-87983-914-7, Keats Publng) NTC Contemp Pub Co.

— Natural Supplements for Your Dog. (Pet Care Naturally Ser.). 64p. 1998. pap. 4.95 (0-87983-913-9, Keats Publng) NTC Contemp Pub Co.

— Natural Therapy for Your Arthritic Cat. (Pet Care Naturally Ser.). 64p. 1998. pap. 4.95 (0-87983-880-9, Keats Publng) NTC Contemp Pub Co.

— Natural Therapy for Your Arthritic Dog. (Pet Care Naturally Ser.). 64p. 1998. pap. 4.95 (0-87983-879-5, Keats Publng) NTC Contemp Pub Co.

— Nutritional Therapy for Cat Diseases. (Pet Care Naturally Ser.). 64p. 1998. pap. 4.95 (0-87983-923-6, Keats Publng) NTC Contemp Pub Co.

— Nutritional Therapy for Dog Diseases. (Pet Care Naturally Ser.). 64p. 1998. pap. 4.95 (0-87983-922-8, Keats Publng) NTC Contemp Pub Co.

— Vaccination: What You Must Know Before You Vaccinate Your Cat. (Pet Care Naturally Ser.). 64p. 1998. pap. 4.95 (0-87983-912-0, Keats Publng) NTC Contemp Pub Co.

— Vaccination: What You Must Know Before You Vaccinate Your Dog. (Pet Care Naturally Ser.). 64p. 1998. pap. 4.95 (0-87983-911-2, Keats Publng) NTC Contemp Pub Co.

— Your Kitten's First Year. LC 96-48154. 144p. (Orig.). 1996. pap. 12.95 (1-55622-527-X, Seaside Pr) Wordware Pub.

— Your Puppy's First Year. LC 94-48892. 144p. 1995. pap. 12.95 (1-55622-386-2, Seaside Pr) Wordware Pub.

Messonnier, Shawn, jt. auth. see Gfeller.

*Messonnier, Shawn P. Veterinary Neurology. LC 99-44150. (The Practical Veterinarian Ser.). (Illus.). 210p. 1999. pap. text 25.00 (0-7506-7203-X) Buttrwrth-Heinemann.

Messora, Noemi. Cassell's Contemporary Italian: A Handbook of Grammar, Current Usage, & Word Power. LC 93-18041. (ITA., Illus.). 528p. 1993. pap. 25.00 (0-02-584375-3) Macmillan.

— Mastering Italian. (Mastering Languages Ser.). (Illus.). 341p. (Orig.). 1991. pap. 11.95 (0-87052-057-1); audio 12.95 (0-87052-066-0) Hippocrene Bks.

Messori, Marcello, ed. Financial Constraints & Market Failures: The Microfoundations of the New Keynesian Macroeconomics. LC 98-42882. 244p. 1999. 85.00 (1-85898-625-7) E Elgar.

*Messori, Vittorio. Los Desafíos del Catolico. 1999. 19.95 (84-08-02181-8) Planeta Edit.

Messori, Vittorio. Opus Dei: Leadership & Vision in Today's Catholic Church. Malsbary, Gerald, tr. from ITA. LC 97-28110. 186p. 1997. 27.50 (0-89526-450-1) Regnery Pub.

Messori, Vittorio, jt. auth. see Ratzinger, Joseph C.

Messori, Vittorio, ed. see Paul, John, II.

MESSQ Staff. The Middle East Military Balance, Vol. 1, Pt. 3. (Middle East Strategic Studies Quarterly: No. 8903). 176p. 1990. 40.50 (0-08-040375-1, Pergamon Pr) Elsevier.

*Messud, Claire. The Last Life. 480p. 2000. pap. 14.00 (0-15-601165-4) Harcourt.

Messud, Claire. The Last Life: A Novel. LC 99-25612. 368p. 1999. 24.00 (0-15-100471-4, Harvest Bks) Harcourt.

— When the World Was Steady. 270p. 1994. 19.95 (0-9645611-0-7) Granta.

— When the World Was Steady. 270p. 1995. reprint ed. pap. 11.95 (0-9645611-3-1) Granta.

Mestecky, J., et al. Advances in Mucosal Immunology Pts. A & B: Proceedings of the Seventh International Congress of Mucosal Immunology, Held in Prague, Czechoslovakia, August 16-21, 1992, Pts. A & B. (Advances in Experimental Medicine & Biology Ser.: Vol. 371). (Illus.). 1724p. (C). 1995. text 265.00 (0-306-45012-7, Kluwer Plenum) Kluwer Academic.

— Immunology of Milk & the Neonate. (Advances in Experimental Medicine & Biology Ser.: Vol. 310). (Illus.). 504p. (C). 1992. text 145.00 (0-306-44105-5, Kluwer Plenum) Kluwer Academic.

Mestecky, Jiri, et al, eds. Recent Developments in Mucosal Immunology, Pt. A: Cellular Interactions. LC 87-14129. (Illus.). 1866p. 1987. 135.00 (0-306-42614-5, Plenum Trade) Perseus Pubng.

— Recent Developments in Mucosal Immunology, Pt. B: Effector Functions. LC 87-14129. (Illus.). 1866p. 1987. 155.00 (0-306-42775-3, Plenum Trade) Perseus Pubng.

*Mestel, Leon. Stellar Magnetism. (International Series of Monographs on Physics). 658p. 1999. text 145.00 (0-19-851761-0) OUP.

Mestenhauser, Josef A. & Ellingboe, Brenda J. Reforming the Higher Education Curriculum: Internationalizing the Campus. LC 98-22654. (Ace/Oryx Series on Higher Education). 272p. (C). 1998. boxed set 34.95 (1-57356-173-8) Oryx Pr.

Mester, Cathy S. & Tauber, R. T. Oral Communication Skills for Vo-Tech Students: A Competency-Based Approach. (Orig.). 1991. pap. 10.75 (0-911168-79-6) Prakken.

Mester, Cathy S. & Tauber, Robert T. Tecnicas De Comunicacion Oral Para Estudiantes De Vocacional Tecnica: Metodo Basado en la Practica de Estas. Tellez, Francisco J. & De Paoli de Sales, Nanette, trs. from ENG. (SPA.). 160p. (Orig.). 1992. pap. text 10.75 (0-911168-83-4) Prakken.

Mester, Cathy S., jt. auth. see Tauber, Robert T.

Mester, Michael, jt. ed. see McIntire, Paul.

Mester, Terri A. Movement & Modernism: Yeats, Eliot, Williams & Early Twentieth-Century Dance. LC 96-29802. 1997. 30.00 (1-55728-455-5) U of Ark Pr.

Mesters, Carlos. God, Where Are You? An Introduction to the Bible. rev. ed. Drury, John & McDonagh, Francis, trs. from POR. LC 94-44034. 252p. 1995. reprint ed. pap. 15.00 (0-88344-998-6) Orbis Bks.

Mesters, V. Microcomputing Dictionary Spanish-English-French. (ENG, FRE & SPA.). 547p. 1996. pap. 50.00 (84-283-2328-3, Pub. by Paraninfo) IBD Ltd.

— Microcomputing Dictionary, Spanish-English-French. (ENG, FRE & SPA.). 1996. 50.00 (0-7859-9688-5) Fr & Eur.

Mesterton, Eric. The Waste Lands: Some Commentaries. LC 75-22205. (Studies in T. S. Eliot: No. 11). 1975. lib. bdg. 75.00 (0-8383-2085-6) M S G Haskell Hse.

Mesterton-Gibbons, Michael. A Concrete Approach to Mathematical Modelling. (Illus.). 624p. (C). 1989. 49.95 (0-201-12910-8); teacher ed. 14.95 (0-201-09099-6) Addison-Wesley.

— A Concrete Approach to Mathematical Modelling. 2nd ed. LC 94-35535. 624p. 1995. 84.95 (0-471-10960-6) Wiley.

Mesthene, Emmanuel. Mesthene: Technology & Social Change. LC 67-23043. (Orig.). (C). 1967. pap. write for info. (0-672-60900-2, CR14, Bobbs) Macmillan.

Mesthene, Emmanuel G. Technological Change: Its Impact on Man & Society. LC 76-106960. (Harvard Studies in Technology & Society). 127p. reprint ed. pap. 39.40 (0-7837-3851-X, 204367300010) Bks Demand.

Mesthrie, Rajend. English in Language Shift: The History, Structure & Sociolinguistics of South African Indian English. (Illus.). 272p. (C). 1993. text 69.95 (0-521-41514-4) Cambridge U Pr.

*Mesthrie, Rajend, et al. Introducing Sociolinguistics. LC 99-86981. (Illus.). 528p. 2000. 60.00 (1-55619-205-3); pap. 29.95 (1-55619-206-1) J Benjamins Pubng.

Mestmacker, Ernst J. Law & Economics of Transborder Telecommunications: A Symposium. (Law & Economics of International Telecommunications Ser.). 450p. 1987. 126.00 (3-7890-1368-4, Pub. by Nomos Verlags) Intl Bk Import.

Mestmacker, Ernst J., ed. Natural Gas in the Internal Market: A Review of Energy Policy. (International Energy & Resources Law & Policy Ser.). (C). 1993. lib. bdg. 145.50 (1-85333-795-1) Kluwer Academic.

Mestmacker, Ernst-Joachim, jt. ed. see Friedmann, Daniel.

Meston, Dougall, jt. auth. see Ilbert, Courtenay.

Meston, Dougall, jt. auth. see Wigan, C. R.

Meston, Michael C., ed. Cooper's Scottish Legal Tradition. (C). 1993. pap. 24.00 (0-85411-045-3, Pub. by Saltire Soc) St Mut.

Meston, Michael C., ed. see Lord Cooper.

M

Meston, Zach. The Legend of Zelda: A Link to the Past Game Secrets/NES. (Secrets of the Games Ser.). (Illus.). 224p. (Orig.). 1992. pap. 9.99 (*1-55958-204-9*) Prima Pub.
— Tekken 1 & 2 Survival Guide. (Gaming Mastery Ser.). (Illus.). 160p. (Orig.). 1996. pap. 12.95 (*1-884364-47-0*) Sandwich Islands.
***Meston, Zach.** Vanguard Bandits: Official Strategy Guide. Ireland, Victor & Shirley, Don, eds. (Illus.). 2000. 14.95 (*0-9662993-2-9*) Workg Designs.
Meston, Zach & Arnold, J. Douglas. Awesome Sega Genesis Secrets 4. (Gaming Mastery Ser.: No. 4). (Illus.). 352p. (YA). 1994. pap. 11.95 (*0-9624676-2-6*) Sandwich Islands.
— Awesome Super Nintendo Secrets. (Gaming Mastery Ser.: No. 2). (Illus.). 320p. (Orig.). 1993. pap. 11.95 (*0-9624676-7-7*) Sandwich Islands.
— Dungeon Master II: Skullkeep: The Official Strategy Guide. (Illus.). 144p. 1995. 12.95 (*1-884364-03-9*) Sandwich Islands.
— Heimdall: Official Strategy Guide. (Gaming Mastery Ser.). (Illus.). 120p. (Orig.). 1994. pap. 12.95 (*1-884364-02-0*) Sandwich Islands.
— Playstation Player's Guide, Vol. 2. (Gaming Mastery Ser.). 288p. (Orig.). (YA). (gr. 7 up). 1997. pap. 14.95 (*1-884364-49-7*) Sandwich Islands.
— Popful Mail. (Gaming Mastery Ser.). (Illus.). 160p. (Orig.). 1995. pap. 16.95 (*1-884364-18-7*) Sandwich Islands.
— Vay: The Official Strategy Guide. (Gaming Mastery Ser.). (Illus.). 120p. (Orig.). 1994. pap. 12.95 (*1-884364-10-1*) Sandwich Islands.
Meston, Zach & Ricciardi, John. Playstation Player's Guide. (Gaming Mastery Ser.). (Illus.). 320p. (Orig.). 1996. pap. 14.95 (*1-884364-22-5*) Sandwich Islands.
Meston, Zach, jt. auth. see Arnold, J. Douglas.
Meston, Zach, jt. auth. see DeMaria, Rusel.
Meston, Zach, ed. see Sandwich Islands Publishing Staff.
***Meston, Zack.** Dreamcast: Survival Guide. 1999. pap. text 14.95 (*1-884364-11-X*) Sandwich Islands.
Mestre, jt. auth. see Tuck.
Mestre, Ana, ed. The Complete Guide to Florida Foundations, 1996. 8th ed. 1996. per. 90.00 (*1-879543-15-X*) FL Fund Pubns.
***Mestre, Ani.** Mis Tres Adioses a Cuba: Diario de Dos Viajes. LC 98-62433. (SPA., Illus.). 213p. 1999. pap. 16.00 (*0-89729-895-0*) Ediciones.
Mestre, Ernesto. The Lazarus Rumba. LC 99-21857. 512p. 1999. text 27.50 (*0-312-19907-4*, Picador USA) St Martin.
***Mestre, Ernesto.** The Lazarus Rumba. 512p. 2000. pap. 15.00 (*0-312-26352-X*) St Martin.
Mestre, Jose P., jt. ed. see Cocking, Rodney R.
Mestre, Kenneth. The Power of Awareness. Levine, Joan & Levine, Newton, eds. Inlingua Translation Service Staff, tr. from SPA.Tr. of El Saber Es Poder. (Illus.). 110p. 1997. write for info. (*0-9654059-0-7*) Wrld Finan.
Mestre, Neville De, see De Mestre, Neville.
Mestrovi, C. & Stjepan, Gabriel. Anthony Giddens: The Last Modernist. LC 97-18129. 256p. (C). 1998. 80.00 (*0-415-09572-7*); pap. 24.99 (*0-415-09573-5*) Routledge.
Mestrovic, Stjepan, ed. see Debeljak, Ales.
Mestrovic, Stjepan, ed. see Sandelands, Lloyd.
Mestrovic, Stjepan G. The Balkanization of the West: The Confluence of Postmodernism & Postcommunism. LC 94-16377. 288p. (C). 1994. pap. 24.99 (*0-415-08755-4*, B3809) Routledge.
— Barbarian Temperament: Toward a Post-Modern Critical Theory. 326p. (C). 1993. pap. 27.99 (*0-415-10241-3*) Routledge.
— Durkheim & Postmodern Culture. (Communication & Social Order Ser.). 203p. 1992. pap. text 25.95 (*0-202-30440-X*); lib. bdg. 44.95 (*0-202-30439-6*) Aldine de Gruyter.
— Emile Durkheim & the Reformation of Sociology. LC 93-16886. 180p. (C). 1994. pap. 22.95 (*0-8476-7867-9*) Rowman.
— Postemotional Society. 224p. 1996. 69.95 (*0-7619-5128-8*); pap. 24.95 (*0-7619-5129-6*) Sage.
Mestrovic, Stjepan G., ed. The Conceit of Innocence: Losing the Conscience of the West in the War Against Bosnia. LC 97-17417. (Eastern European Studies: No. 4). 256p. 1997. 34.95 (*0-89096-770-9*) Tex A&M Univ Pr.
— Genocide After Emotion: The Postemotional Balkan War. LC 95-24241. 240p. (C). 1996. 80.00 (*0-415-12293-7*); pap. 18.95 (*0-415-12294-5*) Routledge.
Mestrovic, Stjepan G., et al. Habits of the Balkan Heart: Social Character & the Fall of Communism. LC 93-11072. 200p. 1993. 32.50 (*0-89096-556-0*); pap. 15.95 (*0-89096-593-5*) Tex A&M Univ Pr.
— The Road from Paradise: Prospects for Democracy in Eastern Europe. LC 92-32442. 224p. 1993. 29.95 (*0-8131-1827-1*) U Pr of Ky.
Mestrovic, Stjepan G., jt. ed. see Cushman, Thomas.
Mesulam, M. Marsel. Tracing Neural Connections with Horseradish Peroxidase. (IBRO Handbook Series: Methods in the Neurosciences). 268p. 1982. pap. 289.95 (*0-471-10029-3*, Wiley-Interscience) Wiley.
***Mesulam, M. Marsel, ed.** Principles of Behavioral & Cognitive Neurology. 2nd ed. LC 99-15581. (Illus.). 570p. 2000. text 79.95 (*0-19-513475-3*) OUP.
Mesyats, G. A. & Proskurovsky, D. I. Pulsed Electrical Discharge in Vacuum. (Atoms & Plasmas Ser.: Vol. 5). (Illus.). 310p. 1989. 106.95 (*0-387-50725-6*) Spr-Verlag.
Mesyats, Vadim. Guest in the Homeland: Selected Writings. Beylin, Tanya et al, trs. LC 97-34069. 1997. pap. 10.50 (*1-883689-45-7*) Talisman Hse.
***Meszaros, Erno.** Fundamentals of Atmospheric Aerosol Chemistry. (Illus.). 308p. 1999. 55.00 (*963-05-7624-4*, Pub. by Akade Kiado) Intl Spec Bk.
Meszaros, Erno. Global & Regional Changes in Atmospheric Composition. 192p. 1993. lib. bdg. 79.95 (*0-87371-662-0*, L662) Lewis Pubs.
Meszaros, Erno, et al. Atmospheric Particles & Nuclei. (Illus.). 273p. (C). 1991. 114.00 (*963-05-5682-0*, Pub. by Akade Kiado) St Mut.
Meszaros, Gary, jt. auth. see Platt, Carolyn V.
Meszaros, Istvan. Beyond Capital. 1020p. (C). 1996. 90.00 (*0-85036-454-X*, Pub. by MRLN) Paul & Co Pubs.
— Beyond Capital: Toward a Theory of Transition. 700p. 1995. 25.00 (*0-85345-881-2*, Pub. by Monthly Rev) NYU Pr.
— Marx's Theory of Alienation. 4th ed. (C). 1986. pap. write for info. (*0-85036-191-5*, Pub. by MRLN) Paul & Co Pubs.
— Necessity of Social Control. (C). 1972. pap. write for info. (*0-85036-153-2*, Pub. by MRLN) Paul & Co Pubs.
— The Power of Ideology. 640p. (C). 1990. pap. text 22.50 (*0-8147-5458-9*) NYU Pr.
— The Work of Sartre: Search for Freedom. (Modern Revivals in Philosophy Ser.). 288p. 1994. 61.95 (*0-7512-0272-X*, Pub. by Gregg Revivals) Ashgate Pub Co.
Meszaros, Mark W., ed. see Bilash, Borislaw, 2nd, et al.
Meszaros, Murray. The Best of Luck to You. 138p. (Orig.). 1996. pap. 9.99 (*0-9656687-0-3*) A M Media.
Meszaros, Peter. High-Energy Radiation from Magnetized Neutron Stars. LC 91-27376. (Theoretical Astrophysics Ser.). (Illus.). 546p. 1992. pap. text 46.00 (*0-226-52094-3*) U Ch Pr.
— High-Energy Radiation from Magnetized Neutron Stars. LC 91-27376. (Theoretical Astrophysics Ser.). (Illus.). 546p. 1992. lib. bdg. 113.00 (*0-226-52093-5*) U Ch Pr.
***Meszoly, Miklos.** Once There Was a Central Europe. 196p. 1999. pap. 21.00 (*963-13-3738-3*, Pub. by Corvina Bks) St Mut.
Met, Leon. Going Public: Quality Circles in the Public Sector, 2 vols., Set. 65p. 1984. 31.95 (*0-317-07126-2*) IAQC Pr.
Met, Philippe, tr. see Clark, Jim, et al.
Met, Philippe, tr. see Cole, Bruce K., ed.
Met, Philippe, tr. see Hoffman, Mark, et al.
Meta, Gruppo. Guido per l'Insegnante. (Illus.). 120p. 1996. pap. 47.95 (*0-521-57807-8*) Cambridge U Pr.
— Libro Degli Esecizi E Sintesi Di Grammatica. (Illus.). 210p. 1996. pap. 29.95 (*0-521-57808-6*) Cambridge U Pr.
— Libro Dello Studente. (Illus.). 243p. 1996. pap. 31.95 (*0-521-57809-4*) Cambridge U Pr.
Meta, Gruppo. Uno: Libro Degli Esercizi e Sintesi di Grammatica. (Illus.). 168p. (C). 1994. pap. text 19.95 (*0-521-46813-2*) Cambridge U Pr.
— Uno: Libro Dello Studente. (Illus.). 212p. (C). 1994. pap. text 22.95 (*0-521-46814-0*) Cambridge U Pr.
— Uno Nos. 1 & 2: Guida Per l'Insegnante. (Illus.). 170p. (C). 1994. pap. text 42.95 (*0-521-46812-4*); audio 28.95 (*0-521-46815-9*) Cambridge U Pr.
— Uno Nos. 3: Guida Per l'Insegnante, No. 3. (Illus.). 154p. (C). 1994. audio 17.95 (*0-521-46816-7*) Cambridge U Pr.
Metabooks, Inc. Staff. Escape, No. 3. (Orig.). 1986. pap. 2.25 (*0-685-43515-6*) Bantam.
Metaferia, Getachew & Shifferraw, Maigenet. The Ethiopian Revolution of 1974 & the Exodus of Ethiopia's Trained Human Resources. LC 91-48086. (African Studies: Vol. 24). 184p. 1992. lib. bdg. 79.95 (*0-7734-9458-8*) E Mellen.
Metailie, G. Dictionnaire d'Agriculture: Science de l'Animal (Chinois-Francais-Anglais) - Animal Science (Chinese-French-English)Tr. of Dictionary of Agriculture. 624p. Date not set. pap. 195.00 (*0-7859-9184-0*) Fr & Eur.
Metais, O. & Ferziger, J. H., eds. New Tools in Turbulence Modelling: Course Held in Les Houches, 21-31 May 1996. (Illus.). xvii, 298p. 1997. pap. 84.95 (*3-540-63090-2*) Spr-Verlag.
Metais, O. & Lesieur, Marcel, eds. Turbulence & Coherent Structures. (Fluid Mechanics & Its Applications Ser.). 640p. 1990. text 309.00 (*0-7923-0646-5*) Kluwer Academic.
Metakides, G., jt. auth. see Nerode, Anil.
***Metal, Amy.** Willow Springs Fairy Tales. (Illus.). 55p. 2000. mass mkt. 15.99 (*0-9674761-0-0*) Smiling Beagle.
Metal-Corbin, Josie, jt. auth. see Corbin, David.
Metal Powder Industries Federation Staff. Compendium on Metal Injection Molding. LC TN0695.C66. (Illus.). 137p. reprint ed. pap. 42.50 (*0-7837-5162-1*, 204489100004) Bks Demand.
— Copper Base Powder Metallurgy. Taubenblat, Pierre W., ed. LC 80-81464. (New Perspectives in Powder Metallurgy: Fundamentals, Methods, & Applications Ser.: No. 7). (Illus.). 227p. reprint ed. pap. 70.40 (*0-7837-5161-3*, 204489000004) Bks Demand.
— Forging of Powder Metallurgy Preforms. LC 73-1768. (New Perspectives in Powder Metallurgy; Fundamentals, Methods, & Applications Ser.: No. 6). 399p. reprint ed. pap. 123.70 (*0-7837-2044-0*, 204231200003) Bks Demand.
— Friction & Antifriction Materials. LC 74-127937. (Perspectives in Powder Metallurgy: Fundamentals, Methods, & Applications Ser.: No. 4). (Illus.). 350p. reprint ed. pap. 108.50 (*0-7837-5160-5*, 204488900004) Bks Demand.
— Iron Powder Metallurgy: With an Introductory Chapter by Kempton H. Roll & Peter K. Johnson. LC 67-17375. (Perspectives in Powder Metallurgy: Fundamentals, Methods, & Applications Ser.: No. 3). 387p. reprint ed. pap. 120.00 (*0-7837-2043-2*, 204231100003) Bks Demand.
— Metal Injection Molding: Preprint of a Seminar Held at the 1988 International Powder Metallurgy Conference, Orlando, Florida, June 7, 1988. LC TN0695.M44. (Illus.). 103p. reprint ed. pap. 32.00 (*0-7837-1563-5*, 204185500024) Bks Demand.
— Prevention & Detection of Cracks in Ferrous P - M Parts: Preprint of a Seminar Held at the 1988 International Powder Metallurgy Conference, Orlando, Florida, June 10, 1988. LC TN0695.P84. 128p. reprint ed. pap. 39.70 (*0-7837-1742-3*, 205727500024) Bks Demand.
— Properties, Evaluation & Testing of P-M Materials - Preprint of a Seminar Held at the 1988 International Powder Metallurgy Conference, Orlando, FL, June 8, 1988. LC TN0695.P651. (Illus.). 128p. reprint ed. pap. 39.70 (*0-7837-1564-1*, 204185600024) Bks Demand.
— Secondary Operations: Preprint of a Seminar Held at the 1988 International Powder Metallurgy Conference, Orlando, Florida, June 6, 1988, Seminar Chairman: Reynold Sansoucy. LC TN0695.S43. 66p. reprint ed. pap. 30.00 (*0-7837-2212-5*, 205727400003) Bks Demand.
Metal Powder Staff. Materials Standards for P-M Self-Lubricating Bearings. (Illus.). 20p. 1998. pap. 20.00 (*1-878954-66-0*) Metal Powder.
— Materials Standards for P-M Structural Parts. 1997. pap. 20.00 (*1-878954-62-8*, 1023) Metal Powder.
— Powder Metallurgy Design Manual. LC 98-37973. (Illus.). 175p. 1998. pap. 89.00 (*1-878954-67-9*, 5031) Metal Powder.
— Standard Test Methods for Metal Powders & Powder Metallurgy Products. (Illus.). 95p. 1998. pap. 40.00 (*1-878954-64-4*, 1038) Metal Powder.
Metalious, Grace. Peyton Place. LC 98-53350. 384p. 1999. pap. 14.95 (*1-55553-400-7*) NE U Pr.
— Peyton Place. 300p. 1991. reprint ed. lib. bdg. 38.95 (*0-89966-861-5*) Buccaneer Bks.
— Peyton Place: And Return to Peyton Place. LC 99-20443. (Illus.). 640p. 1999. 10.99 (*0-517-20477-0*) Random Hse Value.
Metallinos, Nikos. Television Aesthetics: Perceptual, Cognitive & Compositional Bases. (L E A's Communication Ser.). 250p. 1996. 69.95 (*0-8058-1221-0*); pap. text 29.95 (*0-8058-2218-6*) L Erlbaum Assocs.
Metallo, Frances R. The Abacus: Its History & Its Applications. (Hi Map Ser.: No. 17). 60p. pap. text 11.99 (*0-614-05309-9*, HM 5617) COMAP Inc.
Metallurgical Society of AIME, High Temperature Al. Superalloys, 1980: Proceedings of the Fourth International Symposium on Superalloys. LC 80-36888. 750p. reprint ed. pap. 200.00 (*0-608-11171-6*, 201549300094) Bks Demand.
Metallurgical Society of AIME Staff. Advanced Fibers & Composites for Elevated Temperatures: Proceedings of a Symposium Sponsored by the Metallurgical Society of AIME & the American Society for Metals Joint Composite Materials Committee at the 108th AIME Annual Meeting, New Orleans, Louisiana, February 20-21, 1979. Ahmad, I. & Noton, Bryan R., eds. LC 80-82650. (Metallurgical Society of AIME Conference Proceedings Ser.). 260p. reprint ed. pap. 80.60 (*0-8357-5124-4*, 202589900047) Bks Demand.
— Advanced Processing Methods for Titanium: Casting, Forming, Machining, Welding: Proceedings of a Symposium Held at the TMS Fall Meeting, Louisville, Kentucky, October 13-15, 1981. Hasson, Dennis F. & Hamilton, C. Howard, eds. LC 82-60584. (Conference Proceedings Ser.). 323p. reprint ed. pap. 100.20 (*0-8357-2595-2*, 205237500013) Bks Demand.
— Alternate Alloying for Environmental Resistance: Proceedings of the Symposium Sponsored by the Corrosion & Environmental Effects Committee of the Metallurgical Society of AIME & Held at the TMS-AIME Annual Meeting in New Orleans, Louisiana, from March 2-6, 1986. fac. ed. Smolik, G. R. & Banerji, S. K., eds. LC 86-31207. 497p. 1987. reprint ed. pap. 154.10 (*0-7837-8301-9*, 204908700010) Bks Demand.
— Amorphous Materials: Modeling of Structure & Properties: Proceedings of Symposium Held at the Fall Meeting of the Metallurgical Society of AIME, St. Louis, Missouri, October 25-26, 1982. Vitek, V., ed. LC 83-61432. 355p. reprint ed. pap. 110.10 (*0-8357-2596-0*, 205237600013) Bks Demand.
— Arsenic Metallurgy, Fundamentals & Applications: Proceedings of Symposium Sponsored by the TMS-AIME Physical Chemistry Committee & Mackay Mineral Research Institute, University of Nevada-Reno, at the 1988 TMS Annual Meeting & Exhibition, Phoenix, Arizona, January 25-28, 1988. Reddy, Ramana G. et al, eds. LC 87-43300. 544p. reprint ed. pap. 168.70 (*0-7837-1438-6*, 205241200016) Bks Demand.
— Calculation of Phase Diagrams & Thermochemistry of Alloy Phases: Proceedings of a Symposium Held at the Fall Meeting, Milwaukee, Wisconsin, September 17-18, 1979. Chang, Y. A. & Smith, J. Frederick, eds. LC 79-89675. 292p. reprint ed. pap. 90.60 (*0-8357-7966-1*, 202590700047) Bks Demand.
— Case Hardened Steels: Microstructural & Residual Stress Effects: Proceedings of the Symposium Held at the 112th AIME Annual Meeting, Atlanta, Georgia, March 9, 1983. Diesburg, Daniel E., ed. LC 83-63326. 247p. reprint ed. pap. 76.60 (*0-8357-2598-7*, 205237800013) Bks Demand.
— Chemical Metallurgy: A Tribute to Carl Wagner: Proceedings of a Symposium. Gokcen, Nev A., ed. LC 81-83779. (Conference Proceedings Ser.). 516p. reprint ed. pap. 160.00 (*0-608-17899-3*, 202912300058) Bks Demand.
— Chemistry & Physics of Rapidly Solidified Materials: Proceedings of a Symposium Sponsored by the Chemistry & Physics of Metals Committee of the Metallurgical Society of AIME, St. Louis MO, October 26-27, 1982. Berkowitz, B. J. & Scattergood, Ronald O., eds. LC 83-61484. (Illus.). 323p. reprint ed. pap. 100.20 (*0-8357-5537-1*, 203515100093) Bks Demand.
— Computer Control in Process Metallurgy: A Short Course Sponsored by TMS-AIME Held in Las Vegas, Nevada, February 20-21, 1976. LC TN0673.M4. 147p. reprint ed. pap. 45.60 (*0-608-11432-4*, 200430800041) Bks Demand.
— Computer Modeling of Phase Diagrams: Proceedings of a Symposium Held at the Fall Meeting of the Metallurgical Society in Toronto, Canada, October 13-17, 1985. Bennett, L. H., ed. LC 86-19174. 427p. reprint ed. pap. 132.40 (*0-8357-2599-5*, 205237900013) Bks Demand.
— Computer Modeling of Sheet Metal Forming Process: Theory, Verification, & Application, Proceedings of Symposium Sponsored by the Metallurgical Society & the TMS Detroit Section, Held at 12th Automotive Materials Symposium at Ann Arbor, Michigan, April 29-30, 1985. Wang, N. M. & Tang, S. C., eds. LC 85-26015. 302p. reprint ed. pap. 93.70 (*0-7837-1442-4*, 205241600016) Bks Demand.
— Computer Simulation of Microstructural Evolution: Proceedings of Symposium Sponsored by the American Society for Metals Materials Science Division Computer Simulation Technical Activity, Held at the Fall Meeting, Toronto, Canada, October 13-17, 1985. Srolovitz, David J., ed. LC 86-8687. 260p. reprint ed. pap. 80.60 (*0-7837-1441-6*, 205241500016) Bks Demand.
— Computer Usage in Materials Education: Proceedings of a Symposium. LC 85-18907. (Illus.). 149p. reprint ed. pap. 46.20 (*0-8357-4686-0*, 205234100008) Bks Demand.
— Computerized Metallurgical Databases: Proceedings of a Symposium, Held at the Fall Meeting of the Metallurgical Society in Cincinnati, Ohio, U. S. A., October 12-13, 1987. Cuthill, J. R. et al, eds. LC 87-43243. 205p. reprint ed. pap. 63.60 (*0-7837-1451-3*, 205242700018) Bks Demand.
— Copper & Nickel Converters: Proceedings of a Symposium on Converter Operating Practices Sponsored by the TMS-AIME Pyrometallurgy Committee at the 108th AIME Annual Meeting in New Orleans, LA, February 19-21, 1979. Johnson, Robert E., ed. LC 79-87441. (Illus.). 411p. reprint ed. pap. 127.50 (*0-8357-3202-9*, 205236200012) Bks Demand.
— Copper Smelting, an Update: Proceedings of a Symposium Held at the 111th AIME Annual Meeting, Dallas, Texas, February 14-18, 1982. George, David B. & Taylor, John C., eds. LC 81-86302. (Conference Proceedings Ser.). 353p. reprint ed. pap. 109.50 (*0-8357-2500-6*, 205238000013) Bks Demand.
— Corrosion-Erosion Behavior of Materials: Proceedings of a Symposium - Sponsored by the TMS-AIME Corrosion Resistant Metals Committee & the Oxidation Activity Committee of American Society for Metals at the Fall Meeting of the Metallurgical Society of AIME, St. Louis, Missouri, October 17-18, 1978. Natesan, K., ed. LC 80-81518. (Illus.). 320p. reprint ed. pap. 99.20 (*0-8357-7563-1*, 205232700001) Bks Demand.
— Corrosion of Metals Processed by Directed Energy Beams: Proceedings of a Symposium Sponsored by the Corrosion & Environmental Effects Committee. . . Held at the Fall Meeting of the Metallurgical Society of AIME, Louisville, KY, October 13, 1981. Clayton, Clive R. & Preece, Carolyn M., eds. LC 82-60586. (Conference Proceedings Ser.). (Illus.). 171p. reprint ed. pap. 53.10 (*0-8357-5538-X*, 203515200093) Bks Demand.
— Creep-Fatigue-Environment Interactions: Proceedings of a Symposium. Pelloux, R. M. & Stoloff, N. S., eds. LC 80-82904. (Conference Proceedings Ser.). (Illus.). 202p. reprint ed. pap. 62.70 (*0-8357-5605-X*, 205684500093) Bks Demand.
— Diffusion Analysis & Applications: Proceedings of a Symposium on Diffusion Analysis & Applications - Jointly Sponsored by the Minerals, Metals & Materials Society & the Atomic Transport Activities Committee of ASM, Held During the TMS Fall Meeting, September 25-29, 1988, Chicago, Illinois. Romig, A. D., Jr. & Dayananda, M. A., eds. LC 89-61029. 373p. reprint ed. pap. 115.70 (*0-7837-5640-2*, 205249200005) Bks Demand.
— Dislocations & Interfaces in Semiconductors: Proceedings of a Symposium "Dislocations & Interfaces in Semiconductors" Sponsored by the Electronic Device Materials Committee of TMS, Held at the 1988 TMS Annual Meeting, Phoenix, AZ, January 25-26, 1988. fac. ed. Rajan, Krishna et al, eds. LC 88-61505. (Illus.). 207p. 1988. pap. 64.20 (*0-7837-8603-4*, 205253400008) Bks Demand.
— Dispersion Strengthened Aluminum Alloys: Proceedings of the Six-Session Symposium Held at the 1988 TMS Annual Meeting, Phoenix, Arizona, January 25-29, 1988. Kim, Y. W. & Griffith, W. M., eds. LC 88-60117. (Illus.). 804p. reprint ed. pap. 200.00 (*0-7837-6062-0*, 205250800008) Bks Demand.
— Effects of Load & Thermal Histories on Mechanical Behavior of Materials: Proceedings of a Symposium Sponsored by the Mechanical Metallurgy & the Phase Transformation Committees of TMS-AIME, Held at the 1987 TMS-AIME Annual Meeting in Denver, Colorado, February 22-26, 1987. Liaw, Peter K. & Nicholas, T., eds. LC 87-42887. 307p. reprint ed. pap. 95.20 (*0-7837-5641-0*, 205249300005) Bks Demand.
— Electrometallurgy, Proceedings of the Extractive Metallurgy Division Symposium on Electrometallurgy Held in Cleveland, Ohio on December 2-3, 1968. LC TN0685. 368p. reprint ed. pap. 114.10 (*0-608-11168-6*, 200117100065) Bks Demand.
— The Electrorefining & Winning of Copper: Proceedings of

An Asterisk (*) at the beginning of an entry indicates that the title is appearing for the first time.

M

An Asterisk (*) at the beginning of an entry indicates that the title is appearing for the first time.

— Bible ABC. LC 97-38515. (Illus.). 32p. (J). (ps-2). 1998. 14.99 (*0-8499-1524-4*) Tommy Nelson.

— The Boy & the Whale: A Christmas Fairy Tale. (Illus.). 48p. 1994. 14.95 (*1-884506-15-1*) Third Story.

— David & Goliath. (Greatest Stories Ever Told Ser.). (Illus.). 40p. (J). (gr. k up). 1993. 19.95 incl. audio (*0-88708-295-5*, Rabbit Ears); 14.95 (*0-88708-294-7*, Rabbit Ears) Litle Simon.

— David & Goliath. (Illus.). (J). (gr. k up). 1996. pap. 10.95 (*0-614-97259-0*, Rabbit Ears) Litle Simon.

— Don't Believe It. (Illus.). 96p. 1996. pap. 9.95 (*0-312-14319-2*) St Martin.

— The Fool & the Flying Ship. LC 91-40669. (We All Have Tales Ser.). (Illus.). 40p. (J). (ps-3). 1992. 14.95 (*0-88708-228-9*, Rabbit Ears) Litle Simon.

— The Fool & the Flying Ship. LC 97-181678. (Illus.). 40p. (J). (ps up). 1997. mass mkt. 10.95 incl. audio (*0-689-81582-4*, Rabbit Ears) Litle Simon.

— The Fool & The Flying Ship, Set. LC 91-40669. (We All Have Tales Ser.). (Illus.). 36p. (J). (gr. k up). 1992. 19.95 incl. audio, sl. (*0-88708-229-7*, Rabbit Ears) Litle Simon.

— The Gardener's Apprentice. LC 96-36895. (Illus.). (J). 1997. lib. bdg. 20.00 (*1-56846-154-2*, Creative Eds) Creative Co.

M

— Jack & the Beanstalk. LC 91-14176. (Illus.). 40p. (J). (gr. k-3). 1997. pap. 10.95 incl. audio (*0-689-81583-2*, Rabbit Ears) Litle Simon.

— Jack & the Beanstalk. abr. adapted ed. LC 91-14176. (We All Have Tales Ser.). (Illus.). 40p. (J). (ps-3). 1991. 19.95 incl. audio (*0-88708-189-4*, Rabbit Ears) Litle Simon.

— King Midas. LC 91-40670. (We All Have Tales Ser.). (Illus.). 36p. (J). (gr. k up). 1992. 19.95 incl. audio (*0-88708-235-1*, Rabbit Ears) Litle Simon.

Metaxas, Eric. Peachboy: A Japanese Folktale. LC 91-15251. (Illus.). 36p. (J). (ps-3). 1995. pap. 19.95 (*0-689-80192-0*, Rabbit Ears) Litle Simon.

Metaxas, Eric. Princess Scargo & the Birthday Pumpkin: The Native American Legend. LC 95-36728. (Illus.). 48p. (J). (ps-3). 1996. pap. 19.95 incl. audio (*0-689-80231-5*) Aladdin.

— Puss in Boots. LC 92-7789. (We All Have Tales Ser.). (Illus.). 36p. (J). (gr. k-3). 1992. 19.95 incl. audio (*0-88708-286-6*, Rabbit Ears) Litle Simon.

— Puss in Boots. LC 92-7789. (We All Have Tales Ser.). (Illus.). 40p. (J). (ps-3). 1992. 14.95 (*0-88708-285-8*, Rabbit Ears) Litle Simon.

— Squanto & the First Thanksgiving. (Illus.). 48p. (J). (gr. k up). 1996. pap. 19.95 (*0-689-80234-X*) Macmillan.

— Squanto & the Miracle of Thanksgiving. LC 99-22912. (Illus.). 1999. 9.99 (*0-8499-5864-4*) Tommy Nelson.

Metaxas, Eric. Stormalong: The Legendary Sea Captain. LC 95-48132. (Illus.). 36p. (J). (gr. k up). 1995. pap. 19.95 incl. audio (*0-689-80194-7*, Rabbit Ears) Litle Simon.

Metaxas, Eric & Fraser, Douglas. David & Goliath. LC 92-36282. (Illus.). 40p. (J). (ps up). 1996. pap. 10.95 incl. audio (*0-689-80604-3*, Rabbit Ears) Litle Simon.

Metaxas, Eric & Peck, Everett. Mose the Fireman. LC 95-36725. (Illus.). 48p. (J). (ps up). 1996. pap. 19.95 (*0-689-80227-7*) Aladdin.

Metaxas, Eric, tr. & adapted by see Andersen, Hans Christian.

Metaxas, Eric, tr. & adapted by see Grimm, Jacob W. & Grimm, Wilhelm K.

Metaxas-Maranghidis, George, ed. Intellectual Property Laws of Europe. 664p. 1995. 215.95 (*0-471-95212-5*) Wiley.

Metaxas, P. Takis, ed. Introductory Lectures on Data Parallel Computing. (C). 1996. 54.00 incl. cd-rom (*1-56881-059-8*) AK Peters.

Metaxes, Eric. The Birthday ABC. LC 93-46896. (Illus.). 32p. (J). 1995. 15.00 (*0-671-88306-2*) S&S Bks Yung.

Metayer, Daniel Le, see Garlan, David & Le Metayer, Daniel, eds.

Metcald, jt. auth. see Metcalf.

Metcalf. Essentials of Writing. (C). 1994. pap. text, teacher ed. 33.75 (*0-15-502187-7*) Harcourt Coll Pubs.

— Research to the Point. 2nd ed. (C). 1994. pap. text, teacher ed. 33.75 (*0-15-502103-6*) Harcourt Coll Pubs.

— Research to the Point. 2nd rev. ed. (C). 1999. pap. text 21.50 (*0-15-503709-9*) Harcourt.

— Solution Focused Group Therapy. LC 98-26800. 256p. 1998. 29.95 (*0-684-84744-2*) S&S Trade.

Metcalf & Metcald. Living Anatomy. 1991. write for info. (*0-8151-5894-7*) Mosby Inc.

Metcalf & Eddy, Inc. Staff & Tchobanoglous, George. Wastewater Engineering: Collection & Pumping of Wastewater. (Water Resources & Engineering Ser.). (Illus.). 448p. (C). 1981. 111.25 (*0-07-041680-X*) McGraw.

— Wastewater Engineering: Treatment, Disposal & Reuse. 3rd ed. Burton, Franklin L., ed. (Water Resources & Environmental Engineering Ser.). 1024p. (C). 1991. 100.94 (*0-07-041690-7*) McGraw.

Metcalf, Alida C. Family & Frontier in Colonial Brazil: Santana de Parnaiba, 1580-1822. (C). 1992. 48.00 (*0-520-07574-9*, Pub. by U CA Pr) Cal Prin Full Svc.

***Metcalf, Allan A.** How We Talk: American Regional English Today. 208p. 2000. 24.00 (*0-618-04363-2*); pap. 14.00 (*0-618-04362-4*) HM.

Metcalf, Allan A. Poetic Diction in the Old English Meters of Boethius. LC 72-94487. (De Proprietatibus Litterarum, Ser. Practica: No. 50). 164p. 1973. pap. text 32.35 (*90-279-2537-2*) Mouton.

— Research to the Point. 2nd ed. 244p. (C). 1994. pap. text 24.00 (*0-15-501481-1*, Pub. by Harcourt Coll Pubs) Harcourt.

— The World in So Many Words: A Country-by-Country Tour of Words That Have Shaped Our Language. LC 99-29849. (Illus.). 320p. 1999. 19.00 (*0-395-95920-9*) HM.

Metcalf, Allan A. & Kerrigan, William J. Essentials of Writing to the Point. (Illus.). 125p. (Orig.). (C). 1994. pap. text 22.00 (*0-15-501709-8*, Pub. by Harcourt Coll Pubs) Harcourt.

Metcalf, Allan A., jt. auth. see Barnhart, David K.

Metcalf, Allen, jt. auth. see Kerrigan, William J.

Metcalf, Andy. Sexuality of Men. Humphries, Martin, ed. (C). pap. 16.95 (*0-86104-638-2*, Pub. by Pluto GBR) Stylus Pub VA.

***Metcalf, Anne.** Miller's Collector's Guides: Paperweights of the 19th & 20th Centuries. (Illus.). 64p. 2000. pap. 9.95 (*1-84000-309-X*, Pub. by Millers Pubns) Antique Collect.

Metcalf, B. W., et al. Cellular Adhesion: Molecular Definition to Therapeutic Potential. (New Horizons in Therapeutics Ser.: Vol. 22). (Illus.). 339p. (C). 1994. text 89.50 (*0-306-44685-5*, Kluwer Plenum) Kluwer Academic.

Metcalf, Barbara D. Perfecting Woman. 440p. 1996. pap. 17.50 (*0-614-21392-4*, 950) Kazi Pubns.

Metcalf, Barbara D., ed. Making Muslim Space in North America & Europe. LC 95-43429. (Comparative Studies on Muslim Societies: Vol. 22). (Illus.). 263p. (C). 1996. 55.00 (*0-520-20403-4*, Pub. by U CA Pr); pap. 22.50 (*0-520-20404-2*, Pub. by U CA Pr) Cal Prin Full Svc.

Metcalf, Barbara D., ed. Perfecting Women: Maulana Ashraf Ali Thanawi's Bihishti Zewar. 1990. 50.00 (*0-520-06491-7*, Pub. by U CA Pr) Cal Prin Full Svc.

Metcalf, Barbara D., tr. Perfecting Women: Maulana Ashraf Ali Thanawi's Bihishti. (C). 1992. pap. 18.95 (*0-520-08093-9*, Pub. by U CA Pr) Cal Prin Full Svc.

Metcalf, Bill. From Utopian Dreaming to Communal Reality: Co-Operative Lifestyle in Australia. LC 96-145185. (Illus.). 196p. 1995. pap. 29.95 (*0-86840-087-4*, Pub. by New South Wales Univ Pr) Intl Spec Bk.

***Metcalf, Bill.** The Gayndah Communes. 1998. pap. 25.95 (*1-875998-49-7*, Pub. by Central Queensland) Accents Pubns.

Metcalf, Bill. Shared Visions, Shared Lives: Communal Living Around the Globe. (Illus.). 192p. (Orig.). 1996. pap. 13.95 (*1-899171-01-0*, Pub. by Findhorn Pr) Words Distrib.

Metcalf, Bryce. Original Members & Other Officers Eligible to the Society of the Cincinnati 1783-1938. Davenport, Robert R., ed. 390p. 1994. text 45.00 (*1-885943-03-2*) Historic Trust.

Metcalf, C. W. Lighten Up: Let C. W. Metcalf Show You How to Be More Productive, Resilient, & Stress-Free by Taking Laughter Seriously. (Illus.). 256p. 1992. 19.95 (*0-201-56779-2*) Addison-Wesley.

Metcalf, C. W. & Felible, Roma. The Humor Option: Facilitator's Guide. 11p. (Orig.). 1987. student ed. 15.00 (*0-685-45029-5*) C W Metcalf.

— The Humor Option: Skills for Surviving & Thriving. 32p. (Orig.). 1987. student ed. 25.00 (*0-685-32630-6*) C W Metcalf.

— Lighten Up: Survival Skills for People under Pressure. (Illus.). 304p. 1993. pap. 14.00 (*0-201-62239-4*) Addison-Wesley.

Metcalf, D. M. An Atlas of Anglo-Saxon & Norman Coin Finds c.973-1086. (Illus.). 328p. 1998. 55.00 (*1-85444-110-8*, 1108, Pub. by Ashmolean Mus) A Schwartz & Co.

Metcalf, D. M. Coinage of Southeastern Europe. (Illus.). 376p. 1979. lib. bdg. 45.00 (*1-886720-06-1*) S J Durst.

Metcalf, D. M. Coinage of Southeastern Europe (820-1396 AD) (Illus.). 1979. lib. bdg. 45.00 (*0-932106-41-2*) S J Durst.

— Coinage of the Crusader & the Latin East in the Ashmolean Museum, Oxford. (Illus.). 1995. lib. bdg. 105.00 (*1-85444-062-4*) S J Durst.

— The Origins of the Anastasian Currency Reform. (Illus.). vii, 105p. 1969. text 36.50 (*0-317-54491-8*, Pub. by AM Hakkert) Coronet Bks.

— Sylloge of Coins of the British Isles: Ashmolean III, Henry VII. 1976. 19.98 (*0-19-725960-X*) David Brown.

— Thrymsas & Sceattas in the Ashmolean Museum, Vol. 1. LC 93-217365. (Illus.). 208p. 1993. 42.00 (*1-85444-047-0*, 047-1, Pub. by Ashmolean Mus) A Schwartz & Co.

— Thrymsas & Sceattas in the Ashmolean Museum, Vol. 2. (Illus.). 152p. 1994. 42.00 (*1-85444-066-7*, 066-7, Pub. by Ashmolean Mus) A Schwartz & Co.

— Thrymsas & Sceattas in the Ashmolean Museum, Vol. 3. (Illus.). 436p. 1995. 65.00 (*1-85444-067-5*, 067-5, Pub. by Ashmolean Mus) A Schwartz & Co.

Metcalf, David & Milner, Simon. New Perspectives on Industrial Disputes. 240p. (C). 1993. pap. 77.95 (*0-415-09151-9*) Thomson Learn.

Metcalf, Donald. The Molecular Control of Blood Cells. LC 88-605. (Illus.). 192p. 1988. 43.00 (*0-674-58157-1*) HUP.

***Metcalf, Donald.** Summon up the Blood: In Dogged Pursuit of the Blood Cell Regulators. (Illus.). 214p. 2000. 49.00 (*1-880854-27-9*); pap. 29.00 (*1-880854-28-7*) AlphaMed Pr.

Metcalf, Donald & Nicola, Nicos A. The Hemopoietic Colony-Stimulating Factors: From Biology to Clinical Applications. (Illus.). 352p. (C). 1995. text 85.00 (*0-521-46158-8*) Cambridge U Pr.

Metcalf, Doris H. African Americans: Their Impact on U. S. History. (Illus.). 240p. (J). (gr. 5-9). 1992. 17.99 (*0-86653-670-1*, GA1345) Good Apple.

— Portraits of African American Achievers. 144p. teacher ed. 13.99 (*0-86653-815-1*, GA1507) Good Apple.

— Portraits of Contemporary African Americans. 144p. teacher ed. 13.99 (*0-86653-723-6*, GA1442) Good Apple.

— Portraits of Exceptional African American Scientists. (Illus.). 144p. (J). (gr. 4-8). 1994. 13.99 (*0-86653-800-3*, GA1492) Good Apple.

— Portraits of Outstanding African American Women. 96p. 1996. teacher ed. 10.99 (*1-56417-717-3*, GA1548) Good Apple.

— Portraits of Outstanding Explorers. 96p. 1996. teacher ed. 11.99 (*1-56417-845-5*, GA1552) Good Apple.

— Thinking Upside Down. (Orig.). (J). (gr. 4-8). 1994. pap. text 12.97 (*0-937659-34-7*) GCT.

Metcalf, Doris H. & Marson, Ron. Rocks & Minerals. (Task Cards Ser.). (Illus.). 88p. 1989. teacher ed. 16.00 (*0-941008-23-1*) Tops Learning.

Metcalf Earney, Mary Katherine. First Find the Courthouse: An Anecdotal History of the 83rd Judicial District of Texas from 1917 to 1995. LC 97-76574. vii, 116p. 1997. write for info. (*0-9660550-0-4*) Listo Pub.

Metcalf, Eleanor M. Herman Melville, Cycle & Epicycle. LC 75-104230. 311p. 1970. reprint ed. lib. bdg. 65.00 (*0-8371-3340-8*, MEHM, Greenwood Pr) Greenwood.

Metcalf, Eugene, et al. Contemporary American Folk, Naive & Outsider Art: Into the Mainstream? LC 89-64503. (Illus.). 80p. (Orig.). 1990. pap. 15.00 (*0-940784-13-0*) Miami Univ Art.

Metcalf, Eugene W. Calligraphy Techniques & Uses. (Artist's Library). (Illus.). 64p. (Orig.). 1989. pap. 7.95 (*0-929261-10-0*, AL10) W Foster Pub.

***Metcalf, Eugene W. & Maresca, Frank, eds.** Ray Gun. LC 99-64972. (Illus.). 128p. 1999. 19.95 (*1-58418-004-8*) FotoFolio.

Metcalf, Eugene W., jt. auth. see Hall, Michael.

Metcalf, Eugene W., jt. ed. see Hall, Michael D.

Metcalf, Eva-Maria, jt. auth. see Zipes, Jack D.

Metcalf, Eva-Marie. Astrid Lindgren. LC 94-20503. (Twayne's World Authors Ser.: No. 851). 184p. 1994. 32.00 (*0-8057-4525-4*, Twyne) Mac Lib Ref.

Metcalf, Fay D. Teaching with Historic Places: A Series of Lesson Plans Produced by the National Park Service & the National Trust for Historic Preservation. LC 92-32149. 1992. write for info. (*0-89133-229-4*) Wiley.

Metcalf, Florence E. A Peek at Japan Vol. 1: A Lighthearted Look at Japan's Language & Culture. 2nd rev. ed. (Illus.). 133p. (Orig.). (J). (gr. 1-8). 1992. reprint ed. pap. 14.95 (*0-9631684-3-6*) Metco Pub.

Metcalf, Frank J. American Psalmody. 2nd ed. LC 68-13274. (Music Reprint Ser.). (Illus.). 1968. reprint ed. lib. bdg. 19.50 (*0-306-71132-X*) Da Capo.

Metcalf, Franz A. What Would Buddha Do? 101 Answers to Life's Daily Dilemmas. LC 99-41842. (Illus.). 160p. 1999. 15.00 (*1-56975-181-1*) Ulysses Pr.

Metcalf, Fred, ed. The Penguin Dictionary of Jokes. LC 96-140729. 240p. 1996. pap. 12.95 (*0-14-016602-5*, Penguin Bks) Viking Penguin.

— The Penguin Dictionary of Modern Humorous Quotations. 1988. pap. 13.95 (*0-14-007568-2*, Penguin Bks) Viking Penguin.

Metcalf, Gale, jt. auth. see Wallach, Joel.

Metcalf, George R. Fair Housing Comes of Age, 198. LC 87-17747. (Contributions in Political Science Ser.: No. 198). 254p. 1988. 59.95 (*0-313-24757-9*, MAH/, Greenwood Pr) Greenwood.

— From Little Rock to Boston: The History of School Desegregation, 8. LC 82-15581. (Contributions to the Study of Education Ser.: No. 8). 292p. 1983. 42.95 (*0-313-23470-1*, MDS/, Greenwood Pr) Greenwood.

Metcalf, Gilbert E., jt. auth. see Carraro, Carlo E.

Metcalf, Harlan G. The Pioneer Book of Nature Crafts. Orig. Title: Whittlin, Whistlin & Thingama Jigs. 1977. reprint ed. pap. 4.95 (*0-8065-0568-0*, Citadel Pr) Carol Pub Group.

Metcalf, Harold J. & Van der Straten, P. Laser Cooling & Trapping. Birman, J. L. et al, eds. LC 98-55408. (Graduate Texts in Contemporary Physics Ser.). (Illus.). 328p. 1999. text 69.95 (*0-387-98747-9*) Spr-Verlag.

— Laser Cooling & Trapping. Birman, J. L. et al, eds. LC 98-55408. (Graduate Texts in Contemporary Physics Ser.). (Illus.). 328p. 1999. pap. text 29.95 (*0-387-98728-2*) Spr-Verlag.

Metcalf, Harry L., jt. ed. see McGlynn, Thomas J.

Metcalf, Jane. Dowry of Uncommon Women: "She Married a Flying Officer & a Gentleman Which She Knew to Be an Enviable Thing." (Orig.). 1988. pap. 12.95 (*0-9619194-4-2*) X-Press Pubns.

Metcalf, Jane, jt. auth. see Curtis, Clive.

Metcalf, Jill. Marriage by Design, 1. 320p. 1999. mass mkt. 4.99 (*0-8439-4553-2*) Dorchester Pub Co.

Metcalf, Jim. Jim Metcalf: Collected Poems. LC 99-34687. 192p. 1999. pap. 15.95 (*1-56554-701-2*) Pelican.

Metcalf, John. Freedom from Culture: Selected Essays, 1982-92. 264p. 1994. pap. 17.95 (*1-55022-202-3*, Pub. by ECW) LPC InBook.

— Kayhut: A Warrior's Odyssey. (Illus.). 242p. 1998. pap. 15.00 (*0-9645173-4-5*) Four Dir Pub.

— The Lady Who Sold Furniture. 150p. (C). 1970. 20.00 (*0-920802-09-5*, Pub. by ECW) Genl Dist Srvs.

— Shooting the Stars. 256p. 1993. pap. write for info. (*0-88984-166-7*) Porcup Quill.

Metcalf, John, ed. The Bumper Book. 220p. (C). 1986. pap. text 12.00 (*0-920763-91-X*, Pub. by ECW) Genl Dist Srvs.

— The Bumper Book. (Illus.). 220p. (C). 1986. text 22.00 (*0-920763-92-8*, Pub. by ECW) Genl Dist Srvs.

— Carry on Bumping. 268p. (C). 1988. text 26.00 (*1-55022-079-9*, Pub. by ECW) Genl Dist Srvs.

— Carry on Bumping. (Illus.). 268p. (C). 1988. pap. text 13.00 (*1-55022-080-2*, Pub. by ECW) Genl Dist Srvs.

— The New Story Writers. 256p. 1992. pap. 18.95 (*1-55082-038-9*, Pub. by Quarry Pr) LPC InBook.

Metcalf, John & Struthers, J. R., eds. How Stories Mean. 360p. 1993. pap. write for info. (*0-88984-127-6*) Porcup Quill.

Metcalf, John, jt. ed. see Inkster, Tim.

Metcalf, John G., ed. Annals of the Town of Menden, Ma. 723p. 1993. reprint ed. lib. bdg. 72.00 (*0-8328-2885-8*) Higginson Bk Co.

Metcalf, John W., jt. auth. see Rayward, W. Boyd.

Metcalf, Joseph, 3rd, frwd. The U. S. Naval Railway Batteries in France. (Illus.). 97p. (C). 1995. reprint ed. pap. text 25.00 (*0-7881-2306-8*) DIANE Pub.

Metcalf, Julia A., et al. Laboratory Manual of Neutrophil Function. 206p. 1986. spiral bd. 38.00 (*0-88167-160-6*) Lppncott W & W.

— Laboratory Manual of Neutrophil Function. LC 85-25792. (Illus.). 205p. reprint ed. pap. 63.60 (*0-608-09729-2*, 206990600007) Bks Demand.

Metcalf, Keyes D. My Harvard Library Years, 1937-1955: A Sequel to Random Recollections of an Anachronism. Williams, Edwin E., ed. 320p. 1988. 25.00 (*0-674-59600-5*) HUP.

— Random Recollections of an Anachronism. 401p. 1980. 35.00 (*0-918414-02-4*) Readex Bks.

Metcalf, Lee. Council of Mutual Economic Assistance: The Failure of Reform. LC 97-61668. 250p. 1997. lib. bdg. 35.00 (*0-88033-382-0*, 485, Pub. by East Eur Monographs) Col U Pr.

Metcalf, Linda. Counseling Toward Solutions: A Practical Solution-Focused Program for Working with Students. 282p. 1994. pap. text 29.95 (*0-87628-267-2*) Ctr Appl Res.

— Parenting Toward Solutions: Positive Techniques to Help Parnets Use the Skills They Already Have to Raise Responsible, Loving Kids. LC 96-17949. 256p. 1996. text 27.95 (*0-13-269622-3*) P-H.

— Parenting Toward Solutions: Positive Techniques to Help Parnets Use the Skills They Already Have to Raise Responsible, Loving Kids. LC 96-26483. 256p. 1996. pap. text 19.95 (*0-13-269614-2*) P-H.

— Teaching Toward Solutions: Step by Step Strategies for Handling Academic, Behavior, & Family Issues in the Classroom. LC 98-34025. 1998. pap. text 28.95 (*0-87628-488-8*) Ctr Appl Res.

Metcalf, Michael. FORTRAN Optimization. rev. ed. (APIC Studies in Data Processing). 1985. text 81.00 (*0-12-492482-4*) Acad Pr.

Metcalf, Michael & Reid, John K. The F Programming Language. (Illus.). 254p. 1996. pap. text 29.95 (*0-19-850026-2*) OUP.

***Metcalf, Michael & Reid, John K.** Fortran 90/95 Explained. 2nd rev. ed. LC 99-15704. (Illus.). 358p. 1999. pap. text 32.00 (*0-19-850558-2*) OUP.

Metcalf, Michael D., jt. auth. see Madsen, David B.

Metcalf, P., jt. auth. see Bowles, D.

Metcalf, Paul. And Nobody Objected. 24p. 1996. pap. 5.00 (*0-945926-39-1*, Pub. by Paradigm RI) SPD-Small Pr Dist.

— And Nobody Objected. deluxe ed. 24p. 1996. pap. 20.00 (*0-945926-40-5*) Paradigm RI.

— Araminta & the Coyotes. (Illus.). 1990. pap. 10.00 (*0-912330-73-2*) Jargon Soc.

— The Assassination. 16p. 1979. pap. 10.00 (*0-930794-13-3*) Station Hill Pr.

— Both. LC 81-86062. 1982. 20.00 (*0-912330-49-X*) Jargon Soc.

— Genoa: A Telling of Wonders. LC 91-23293. 190p. 1991. reprint ed. pap. 8.95 (*0-8263-1300-0*) U of NM Pr.

— Louis the Torch. 56p. 1983. pap. 3.95 (*0-916696-20-0*) Cross Country.

— Mountaineers Are Always Free! 100p. 1991. pap. 9.50 (*0-917453-21-2*) Bamberger.

***Metcalf, Paul.** On Course for GCSE Maths Foundation & Intermediate Tiers. (Illus.). 208p. (YA). (gr. 9-11). 2000. pap. 19.95 (*0-7487-4511-4*, Pub. by S Thornes Pubs) Trans-Atl Phila.

Metcalf, Paul. Paul Metcalf Vol. 1: Collected Works, 1956-1976. LC 96-2777. Vol. 1. 550p. 1996. 35.00 (*1-56689-050-0*) Coffee Hse.

— Paul Metcalf Vol. II: Collected Works, 1976-1986. Vol. 2. 600p. 1997. 35.00 (*1-56689-056-X*) Coffee Hse.

— Paul Metcalf Vol. III: Collected Works, 1987-1997. 600p. 1997. 35.00 (*1-56689-062-4*) Coffee Hse.

— Three Plays. LC 92-85260. 138p. 1993. pap. 11.95 (*0-933598-46-7*) NC Wesleyan Pr.

— Three Plays. limited ed. LC 92-85260. 138p. 1993. pap. 20.00 (*0-933598-47-5*) NC Wesleyan Pr.

— U. S. Dept. of the Interior. LC 80-66485. (Illus.). 88p. (Orig.). 1980. pap. 10.50 (*0-917788-23-0*) Gnomon Pr.

— Will West. 2nd ed. 76p. 1973. reprint ed. pap. 10.00 (*0-912846-03-8*) Bookstore Pr.

***Metcalf, Paul, et al.** On Course for GCSE Maths Foundation & Intermediate Tiers with Answers. (Illus.). 208p. (YA). (gr. 9-11). 2000. pap. 19.95 (*0-7487-4512-2*, Pub. by S Thornes Pubs) Trans-Atl Phila.

— On Course for GCSE Maths Intermediate & Higher Tiers. (Illus.). 208p. (YA). (gr. 9-11). 2000. pap. 19.95 (*0-7487-4454-1*, Pub. by S Thornes Pubs) Trans-Atl Phila.

— On Course for GCSE Maths Intermediate & Higher Tiers with Answers. (Illus.). 208p. (YA). (gr. 9-11). 2000, pap. 19.95 (*0-7487-4455-X*, Pub. by S Thornes Pubs) Trans-Atl Phila.

Metcalf, Paul, et al. Three Times Three. LC 88-62647. 96p. (Orig.). 1989. pap. 10.00 (*0-933598-11-4*) NC Wesleyan Pr.

Metcalf, Paul, jt. auth. see Bowles, David.

Metcalf, Paul, jt. auth. see Faxon, Susan C.

Metcalf, Paul, jt. auth. see Spark, Clare.

Metcalf, Paula. Norma No Friends. 40p. (J). (gr. k-3). 1999. 15.95 (*1-902283-87-2*) Barefoot Bks NY.

Metcalf, Pauline C., ed. Ogden Codman & the Decoration of Houses. LC 88-71607. (Illus.). 240p. 1988. reprint ed. 60.00 (*0-87923-777-5*) Godine.

An Asterisk (*) at the beginning of an entry indicates that the title is appearing for the first time.

Metcalf, Peter. A Borneo Journey into Death: Berawan Eschatology from Its Rituals. LC 82-8460. (Symbol & Culture Ser.). 299p. reprint ed. pap. 92.70 (*0-8357-3322-X*, 203954600013) Bks Demand.

Metcalf, Peter & Huntington, Richard. Celebrations of Death: The Anthropology of Mortuary Ritual. 2nd ed. (Illus.). 252p. (C). 1991. pap. text 19.95 (*0-521-42375-9*) Cambridge U Pr.

Metcalf, Priscilla. James Knowles: Victorian Editor & Architect. (Illus.). 1980. 65.00 (*0-19-812626-3*) OUP.

Metcalf, Priscilla, jt. auth. see Harding, Vanessa.

***Metcalf, Robert.** The Successful Race Car Driver: A Career Development Handbook. LC 99-45955. 2000. write for info. (*0-7680-0497-7*) Soc Auto Engineers.

Metcalf, Robert L. Quaternary Environmental Chang. pap. text 65.00 (*0-471-98551-1*) Wiley.

Metcalf, Robert L. & Luckmann, William H., eds. Introduction to Insect Pest Management. 3rd ed. (Environmental Science & Technology Ser.). 672p. 1994. 125.00 (*0-471-58957-8*, Wiley-Interscience) Wiley.

Metcalf, Rosamond S. The Sugar Maple. LC 82-595. (Illus.). 40p. (J). (gr. 3-5). 1982. pap. 3.50 (*0-914016-87-3*) Phoenix Pub.

Metcalf, Slade R. & Bierstedt, Robin. Rights & Liabilities of Publishers, Broadcasters & Reporters, 2 vols. LC 82-16839. (Individual Rights Ser.). 1549p. 1982. text 200.00 (*0-07-041685-0*) Shepards.

Metcalf, Stephen, ed. & tr. see Nietzsche, Friedrich Wilhelm.

Metcalf, Thomas O. Prospecting for Gold: 101 Ways to Market Yourself & Strike Gold in Sales. (Illus.). 163p. 1999. pap. 14.95 (*1-55571-483-8*, Oasis Pr) PSI Resch.

Metcalf, Thomas R. Ideologies of the Raj. (New Cambridge History of India Ser.: Vol. III.4). (Illus.). 257p. (C). 1995. text 54.95 (*0-521-39547-X*) Cambridge U Pr.

— Ideologies of the Raj. (New Cambridge History of India Ser.: Vol. III.4). (Illus.). 256p. 1997. pap. text 22.95 (*0-521-58937-1*) Cambridge U Pr.

— An Imperial Vision: Indian Architecture & Britain's Raj. (Philip E. Lilienthal Imprint Ser.: No. 2). (Illus.). 316p. 1988. 55.00 (*0-520-06235-3*, Pub. by U CA Pr) Cal Prin Full Svc.

Metcalf, V. M., jt. auth. see Evans, D. R.

Metcalf, William E. The Cistophori of Hadrian. (Numismatic Studies: NS-15). (Illus.). 195p. 1980. 65.00 (*0-89722-004-8*) Am Numismatic.

Metcalf, William E., ed. America's Gold Coinage. (Coinage of the Americas Conference Ser.: No. 6). (Illus.). 132p. 1990. 15.00 (*0-89722-238-5*) Am Numismatic.

— Mnemata: Papers in Memory of Nancy M. Waggoner. (Illus.). 115p. 1991. 20.00 (*0-89722-243-1*) Am Numismatic.

Metcalf, William E., jt. ed. see Hahn, Wolfgang.

Metcalf, Woodbridge. Introduced Trees of Central California. (California Natural History Guides Ser.: No. 27). (Illus.). 1969. pap. 10.95 (*0-520-01548-7*, Pub. by U CA Pr) Cal Prin Full Svc.

— Native Trees of the San Francisco Bay Region. (California Natural History Guides Ser.: No. 4). (Orig.). 1959. pap. 10.00 (*0-520-00853-7*, Pub. by U CA Pr) Cal Prin Full Svc.

Metcalf, Zubie W., Jr. Career Planning Guide for the Allied Health Professions. 176p. 1997. pap. 14.95 (*0-683-30166-7*) Lppncott W & W.

Metcalfe. Accountancy. 1987. pap. 29.95 (*0-442-31749-2*) Chapman & Hall.

— Building a Speech. 2nd ed. (C). 1994. pap. text, teacher ed., suppl. ed. 49.75 (*0-15-501596-6*) Harcourt Coll Pubs.

— Building a Speech. 3rd ed. (C). 1997. pap. text, teacher ed. 28.00 (*0-15-503698-X*) Harcourt Coll Pubs.

— Building a Speech. 4th ed. (C). 2000. pap. text. write for info. (*0-15-506809-1*) Harcourt Coll Pubs.

Exercises & Experiments for Modern Chemistry 1986. 1986. pap., teacher ed. 35.75 (*0-03-001279-1*) H Holt & Co.

Metcalfe. Great Britain & Ghana. 808p. 1994. 148.95 (*0-7512-0145-6*) Ashgate Pub Co.

Metcalfe. Lab Experiments for Modern Chemistry, 1986. 1986. pap., student ed. 8.00 (*0-03-001307-0*) H Holt & Co.

— Modern Chemistry, 1986. 1986. pap., teacher ed. 79.75 (*0-03-001277-5*) H Holt & Co.

Metcalfe, A. V. Statistics in Engineering: A Practical Approach. 1994. pap. 39.95 (*0-412-49220-2*, Chap & Hall NY) Chapman & Hall.

Metcalfe, Andrew, jt. auth. see Game, Ann.

Metcalfe, Andrew V. Statistics in Civil Engineering. (Arnold Applications of Statistics Ser.). 408p. 1998. pap. text 45.00 (*0-340-67660-4*, Pub. by E A) OUP.

***Metcalfe, Andrew V.** Statistics in Management Science. 288p. 2000. pap. text 39.50 (*0-340-74075-2*) E A.

Metcalfe, Andrew V., jt. auth. see Hearn, Grant E.

Metcalfe, B., jt. auth. see Denning, Peter J.

***Metcalfe, Bob.** Internet Collapses & Other InfoWorld Punditry. 360p. 2000. pap. 19.99 (*0-7645-3503-X*) IDG Bks.

Metcalfe, Brent L., ed. New Approaches to the Book of Mormon: Explorations in Critical Methodology. LC 92-16269. (Illus.). 460p. 1993. 26.95 (*1-56085-017-5*) Signature Bks.

Metcalfe, C. R., ed. see Tomlinson, P. B.

Metcalfe, Dean D., et al. Food Allergy. 2nd ed. LC 96-43618. (Illus.). 600p. 1996. text 99.95 (*0-86542-432-2*) Blackwell Sci.

Metcalfe, Dean D., jt. ed. see Kaliner, Michael A.

Metcalfe, Fray & Long, Maria. The Art of Continental Knitting. (Illus.). 69p. (Orig.). 1986. pap. text 9.95 (*0-318-22298-1*) Merriway Co.

Metcalfe, H. Clark. Modern Chemistry. 1986. text 64.50 (*0-03-001274-0*) Holt R&W.

Metcalfe, Henry C., jt. auth. see Tead, Ordway, Jr.

Metcalfe, Howard H. Metcalfe Lineages. 2nd ed. 670p. 1995. reprint ed. pap. 99.50 (*0-8328-4882-4*); reprint ed. lib. bdg. 109.50 (*0-8328-4881-6*) Higginson Bk Co.

— Randolph Lineages, Being the Ancestry of Iris Patricia Follows from the Time of the Saxon Invasion of England Vol. I: The Southerners. (Illus.). 500p. 1995. reprint ed. pap. 75.00 (*0-8328-4936-7*); reprint ed. lib. bdg. 85.00 (*0-8328-4935-9*) Higginson Bk Co.

— Snowberger. Forty North: Lineages of Some Early Settlers among the 40th Parallel, Being the Ancestry of Barbara Lenore Snowberger, Including . . . Paul, Brumbaugh, Metzger, Covalt, Gustin, Cory, Davis . . . Barnes, Lee Wagoner, West, Lippincott, Keaffaber, Haupert & Shultz. (Illus.). 1074p. 1998. reprint ed. pap. 139.50 (*0-8328-9507-5*); reprint ed. lib. bdg. 149.50 (*0-8328-9506-7*) Higginson Bk Co.

***Metcalfe, I., ed.** Gondwana Dispersion & Asian Accretion. 361p. 1999. 90.00 (*90-5410-446-5*, Pub. by A A Balkema) Ashgate Pub Co.

Metcalfe, Ian S. Chemical Reaction Engineering: A First Course. LC 97-14900. (Oxford Chemistry Primers Ser.: No. 49). (Illus.). 96p. 1997. pap. text 12.95 (*0-19-856538-0*) OUP.

Metcalfe, J. C. Bible & the Human Mind. 1979. pap. 5.99 (*0-87508-913-5*) Chr Lit.

— Molded by the Cross. rev. ed. LC 97-185259. Orig. Title: In the Mould of the Cross. 144p. 1997. mass mkt. 5.99 (*0-87508-711-6*, 711) Chr Lit.

Metcalfe, J. S. Wealth from Diversity: Innovation, Structural Change & Finance for Regional Development in Europe. Vence-Deza, Xavier, ed. LC 96-8870. (Economics of Science, Technology & Innovation Ser.). 408p. (C). 1996. lib. bdg. 169.50 (*0-7923-4115-5*) Kluwer Academic.

Metcalfe, J. Stanley. Evolutionary Economics & Creative Destruction. LC 97-19056. 192p. (C). 1998. write for info. (*0-415-15868-0*) Routledge.

Metcalfe, James, et al. Burwell & Metcalfe's Heart Disease & Pregnancy: Physiology & Management. 2nd ed. 408p. 1986. 125.00 (*0-316-56797-3*, Little Brwn Med Div) Lppncott W & W.

Metcalfe, James J. Poem Portraits. 270p. 1992. reprint ed. lib. bdg. 29.95 (*0-89966-893-3*) Buccaneer Bks.

Metcalfe, Janet, ed. Metacognition: A Special Issue of the Personality & Social Psychology Review. 73p. 1998. pap. 20.00 (*0-8058-9840-9*) L Erlbaum Assocs.

Metcalfe, Janet & Shimamura, Arthur P., eds. Metacognition: Knowing about Knowing. (Illus.). 350p. 1994. 42.00 (*0-262-13298-2*, Bradford Bks) MIT Pr.

— Metacognition: Knowing about Knowing. (Illus.). 352p. 1996. reprint ed. pap. text 21.00 (*0-262-63169-5*, Bradford Bks) MIT Pr.

Metcalfe, Joannah. Pure Scents for Relaxation. LC 99-21362. (Illus.). 1999. pap. 12.95 (*0-8069-4845-0*) Sterling.

— Pure Scents for Romance. LC 99-14534. (Illus.). 1999. pap. 12.95 (*0-8069-4824-8*) Sterling.

***Metcalfe, Joannah.** Pure Scents for Vitality. 80p. 1999. pap. text 12.95 (*0-8069-4815-9*) Sterling.

Metcalfe, Joannah. Pure Scents for Well Being. LC 99-33942. 1999. pap. text 12.95 (*0-8069-4813-2*) Sterling.

Metcalfe, John. Smoking Leg, & Other Stories. LC 74-152950. (Short Story Index Reprint Ser.). 1977. reprint ed. 20.95 (*0-8369-3828-3*) Ayer.

***Metcalfe, Josie.** Be My Mummy. large type ed. 288p. 1999. 25.99 (*0-263-16024-6*, Pub. by Mills & Boon) Ulverscroft.

Metcalfe, Josie. Heart Surgeon. large type ed. (Mills & Boon Large Print Ser.). 288p. 1997. 23.99 (*0-263-15234-0*, Pub. by Mills & Boon) Ulverscroft.

— Hell on Wheels. large type ed. 288p. 1995. 23.99 (*0-263-14514-X*, Pub. by Mills & Boon) Ulverscroft.

***Metcalfe, Josie.** A Millennium Miracle. (Readers Choice Ser.). 2000. mass mkt. 4.50 (*0-373-51123-X*, 1511237) Harlequin Bks.

Metcalfe, Josie. No Alternative. large type ed. 288p. 1995. 23.99 (*0-263-14330-9*, Pub. by Mills & Boon) Ulverscroft.

— Promises to Keep. (Romance Ser.: Vol. 429). 1999. mass mkt. 3.50 (*0-373-17429-2*, 1-17429-1, Harlequin) Harlequin Bks.

— Second Chance. large type ed. (Mills & Boon Large Print Ser.). 288p. 1998. 24.99 (*0-263-15455-6*, Pub. by Mills & Boon) Ulverscroft.

— Secrets to Keep. large type ed. 288p. 1995. 23.99 (*0-263-14625-1*, Pub. by Mills & Boon) Ulverscroft.

— Seeing Eye to Eye. large type ed. 288p. 1996. 23.99 (*0-263-14520-4*, Pub. by Mills & Boon) Ulverscroft.

— Worth Waiting For. large type ed. (Mills & Boon Large Print Ser.). 288p. 1997. 22.50 (*0-263-14907-2*) Ulverscroft.

Metcalfe, Judith, ed. The Brain: Degeneration, Damage & Disorder. LC 97-42430. (Biology Ser.). (Illus.). 270p. 1998. 39.95 (*3-540-63796-6*) Spr-Verlag.

Metcalfe, Kathy & Olson, Myrle. Marginal & Footnote Poetry. 1977. pap. 3.95 (*0-910286-56-6*) Boxwood.

Metcalfe, Kevan. Understanding Cardiac Pacing: A Guide for Nurses. (Illus.). 197p. (C). 1992. pap. text 36.95 (*0-8385-9258-9*, A9258-3, Apple Lange Med) McGraw.

Metcalfe, Leon. Discovering Ghosts. (Handbook Ser.: No. 147). (Illus.). 88p. pap. 8.50 (*0-7478-0164-9*, Pub. by Shire Pubns) Parkwest Pubns.

Metcalfe, Les & Richards, Sue. Improving Public Management. 240p. (C). 1987. text 45.00 (*0-8039-8103-1*) Sage.

***Metcalfe, Mary.** Against All Odds. 36p. 1998. pap. 8.95 (*1-85856-093-4*, Trentham Bks) Stylus Pub VA.

Metcalfe, Mike. Business Research Through Argument. 160p. (C). 1995. lib. bdg. 103.00 (*0-7923-9616-2*) Kluwer Academic.

— Forecasting Profit. LC 94-22587. 368p. (C). 1995. lib. bdg. 133.00 (*0-7923-9482-8*) Kluwer Academic.

Metcalfe, Peter, et al. The Physics of Radiotherapy X-Rays from Linear Accelerators. LC 96-51445. (Illus.). 493p. 1997. text 119.95 (*0-944838-75-8*); pap. text 98.95 (*0-944838-76-6*) Med Physics Pub.

— The Q Book: The Physics of Radiotherapy X-Rays: Problems & Solutions. (Illus.). 100p. (C). 1998. pap. text, wbk. ed. 33.95 (*0-944838-86-3*) Med Physics Pub.

Metcalfe, Philip. 1933. LC 87-92040. 316p. 1988. 22.00 (*0-932966-87-X*) Permanent Pr.

***Metcalfe, R. & Rochelle, C., eds.** Chemical Containment of Waste in the Geosphere. (Special Publication Ser.: No. 157). 240p. 1999. 125.00 (*1-86239-040-1*, Pub. by Geol Soc Pub Hse) AAPG.

Metcalfe, Robert. Packet Communication. Salus, Peter H., ed. LC 96-204442. (Computer Classics Revisited Ser.). 224p. 1996. 39.95 (*1-57398-033-1*) Annabooks.

Metcalfe, Robert M., jt. auth. see Denning, Peter J.

Metcalfe, Sheldon. Building a Speech. 3rd ed. LC 97-70577. 576p. (C). 1997. pap. text 21.50 (*0-15-503697-1*) Harcourt Coll Pubs.

***Metcalfe, Syd.** One Speck of Humanity. large type ed. 376p. 2000. 31.99 (*0-7089-9130-0*) Ulverscroft.

Metcalfe, Terry. Union Pacific Freight Cars, 1936-1951. (Illus.). 200p. 1989. per. 24.95 (*0-9623347-0-7*) Metcalfe Pubns.

Metcalfe, William, et al, eds. Understanding Canada. 624p. (C). 1982. pap. text 22.50 (*0-8147-5383-3*) NYU Pr.

Metcalfe, William L. Contra Costa County Under the Vitascope. Tatam, Robert D., ed. (Illus.). 120p. 1994. pap. 14.99 (*0-9637954-1-4*) Highlnd Pubs.

Metchette, Glenna W. Catt & Willett Families of Sussex, England & British Columbia, Canada, 1905-1993. (Illus.). 132p. 1994. reprint ed. pap. 21.00 (*0-8328-4083-1*); reprint ed. lib. bdg. 31.00 (*0-8328-4082-3*) Higginson Bk Co.

Metchnikoff, Elie. The Nature of Man: Studies in Optimistic Philosophy. Kastenbaum, Robert J., ed. Mitchell, P. Chalmers, tr. LC 76-19582. (Death & Dying Ser.). (Illus.). 1977. reprint ed. lib. bdg. 31.95 (*0-405-09578-3*) Ayer.

— The Prolongation of Life: Optimistic Studies. Kastenbaum, Robert J., ed. Mitchell, P. Chalmers, tr. LC 76-19583. (Death & Dying Ser.). (Illus.). 1977. reprint ed. lib. bdg. 34.95 (*0-405-09579-1*) Ayer.

— Scientifically Soured Milk: Its Influence in Arresting Intestinal Putrefaction. 11p. 1996. reprint ed. spiral bd. 8.00 (*0-7873-0610-X*) Hlth Research.

***Metchnikoff, Elie, et al.** The Evolutionary-Biology Papers of Elie Metchnikoff. LC 99-49680. (Boston Studies in the Philosophy of Science). 2000. write for info. (*0-7923-6067-2*) Kluwer Academic.

Metchnikoff, Olga. Life of Elie Metchnikoff. LC 72-7248. (Select Bibliographies Reprint Ser.). 1977. reprint ed. 24.95 (*0-8369-6949-9*) Ayer.

Metcoff, Jill. Along the Wisconsin Riverway. LC 97-16357. (North Coast Bks.). (Illus.). 184p. 1997. 35.00 (*0-299-14140-3*) U of Wis Pr.

Meteer, Marie W. Expressibility & the Problem of Efficient Text Planning. LC 92-21879. 1992. 65.00 (*1-85567-022-4*) St Martin.

Metelka, Charles J. The Dictionary of Tourism. 3rd ed. Haller, Cynthia, ed. 328p. 1990. text 20.95 (*0-8273-3496-6*) Delmar.

Metellus, Jean. The Vortex Family: A Family Saga Set in Haiti. LC 95-206119. 235p. 1996. 30.00 (*0-7206-0948-8*, Pub. by P Owen Ltd) Dufour.

Metellus, Jerry, ed. & photos by see Marinakis, Maria M.

Metelmann, Velda P. Lua Getsiner: Herald of the Covenant. LC 97-182240. (Illus.). 250p. (Orig.). 1997. pap. 29.95 (*0-85398-416-6*) G Ronald Pub.

Metelsky, Robert M. Simplified Reef Keeping. Morris, Steve, ed. (Illus.). 275p. (Orig.). 1996. pap. text 39.95 (*0-9652843-0-1*) Shoreline Res.

Meteorite Research Symposium Staff. Meteorite Research: Proceedings of the Symposium, Vienna, Austria, Aug. 7-13, 1968. Millman, P. N., ed. (Astrophysic & Space Science Library: No.12). 941p. 1969. text 239.50 (*90-277-0132-6*) Kluwer Academic.

Meteorological Office Staff. Cloud Types for Observers. 38p. 1982. ring bd. 46.00 (*0-11-400334-3*, Pub. by Statnry Office) Balogh.

Meter, David A. Van, see Van Meter, David A.

Meter, David C. Van, see Kiely, Michael J. & Van Meter, David C.

Meter, Eddy J. Van, see Van Meter, Eddy J., ed.

Meter, Homer Van, see Van Meter, Homer.

Meter, J. H. The Literary Theories of Daniel Heinsius: A Study of the Development & Background of His Views on Literary Theory & Criticism During the Period from 1602 to 1612. LC 84-241833. (Republica Literaria Neerlandica Ser.). 433 p. 1985. 55.00 (*90-232-1892-2*, Pub. by Van Gorcum) Eisenbrauns.

Meter, Jennifer Van, see Van Meter, Jennifer.

Meter, Joyce Van, see Van Meter, Joyce.

Meter, Leo. Letters to Barbara. Agee, Joel, tr. (Illus.). 62p. 1996. pap. 16.95 (*0-87951-589-9*, Pub. by Overlook Pr) Penguin Putnam.

Meter McCoy, Sondra Van, see Van Meter McCoy, Sondra.

Meter, Paula Van, see Van Meter, Paula.

Meter, R. C. Van, see Van Meter, R. C.

Meter, Roz Van, see Van Meter, Roz.

Meteren, Emanuel Van, see Van Meteren, Emanuel.

Metes, George S. & Gundry, John. Agile Networks: New Models of Global Enterprise. LC 97-48538. 224p. (C). 1997. pap. 37.67 (*0-13-760125-5*) P-H.

Metes, George S., jt. auth. see Grenier, Raymond H.

Metes, Rozeta J., tr. see Focas, Spiridon G.

Metev, S. M. & Veiko, V. P. Laser-Assisted Microtechnology. 2nd ed. Gonser, U. et al, eds. LC 98-26049. (Series in Materials Science: Vol. 19). (Illus.). 250p. 1998. 69.95 (*3-540-63973-X*) Spr-Verlag.

Metev, Simeon M. & Veiko, Vadim P. Laser-Assisted Microtechnology. LC 94-25834. (Series in Material Science: Vol. 19). 1995. 75.95 (*0-387-53925-5*) Spr-Verlag.

Metevelis, Peter & Kawataba, Y. Tales with Two Souls: A Variety in Time & Culture. 96p. 1998. pap. 12.00 (*0-8059-4365-X*) Dorrance.

Metford, Beatrix. Where China Meets Burma: Life & Travel in the Burma-China Border Lands. LC 77-87047. reprint ed. 29.50 (*0-404-16844-2*) AMS Pr.

Metger, Bruce M. The Text of the New Testament: Its Transmission, Corruption & Restoration. 3rd enl. ed. (Illus.). 336p. (C). 1992. pap. text 24.95 (*0-19-507297-9*) OUP.

Metger, C. A., jt. auth. see Bryson, T. S.

Metghalchi, Hameed, et al, eds. Advanced Energy Systems Division, 1998: Proceedings ASME International Mechanical Engineering Congress & Exposition, Anaheim, CA. LC 99-188024. (AES Ser.: Vol. 38). 510p. 1998. 170.00 (*0-7918-1599-4*) ASME.

Meth, Clifford L. Crib Death & Other Bedtime Stories. (Illus.). 70p. (Orig.). 1995. pap. write for info. (*1-885591-76-4*) Morris Pubng.

— This Bastard Planet: Another Crib Death. 80p. (Orig.). 1995. pap. write for info. (*1-57502-026-2*) Morris Pubng.

Meth-Cohn, K. & Ree. Comprehensive Organic Functional Group Transformations, 7 vols., Vol. 1. 1996. write for info. (*0-08-042322-1*) Elsevier.

— Comprehensive Organic Functional Group Transformations, 7 vols., Vol. 2. 1996. write for info. (*0-08-042323-X*) Elsevier.

— Comprehensive Organic Functional Group Transformations, 7 vols., Vol. 3. 1996. write for info. (*0-08-042324-8*) Elsevier.

— Comprehensive Organic Functional Group Transformations, 7 vols., Vol. 4. 1996. write for info. (*0-08-042325-6*) Elsevier.

— Comprehensive Organic Functional Group Transformations, 7 vols., Vol. 5. 1996. write for info. (*0-08-042326-4*) Elsevier.

— Comprehensive Organic Functional Group Transformations, 7 vols., Vol. 6. 1996. write for info. (*0-08-042704-9*) Elsevier.

— Comprehensive Organic Functional Group Transformations, 7 vols., Vol. 7. 1996. write for info. (*0-08-042705-7*) Elsevier.

***Meth, Theodore.** Angels. 75p. 1999. pap. write for info. (*0-7392-0200-6*, PO3197) Morris Pubng.

Meth, Theodore. Castleton: A Sequence by Theodore Meth. 60p. (Orig.). 1996. pap. 11.95 (*1-57502-249-4*, P0929) Morris Pubng.

— Tell Me. 70p. (Orig.). 1996. pap. write for info. (*1-57502-309-1*) Morris Pubng.

— Trieste. LC 97-93440. 90p. 1997. pap. 12.50 (*1-57502-482-9*, PO1446) Morris Pubng.

***Metham, John.** Amoryus & Cleopes. LC 98-31520. 1999. pap. 11.00 (*1-58044-016-9*) Medieval Inst.

Metham, John. The Works of John Metham. Craig, H., ed. (EETS, OS Ser.: No. 132). 1974. 55.00 (*0-527-00129-5*) Periodicals Srv.

Methe, David T. Technological Competition in Global Industries: Marketing & Planning Strategies for American Industry. LC 90-8908. 248p. 1990. 59.95 (*0-89930-480-X*, MTG/, Quorum Bks) Greenwood.

Metheny, Karen B., jt. ed. see Yamin, Rebecca.

Metheny, Norma M., ed. Fluid & Electrolyte Balance: Nursing Considerations. 3rd ed. LC 95-49883. 480p. 1996. pap. text 28.95 (*0-397-55191-6*) Lppncott W & W.

***Metheny, Norma Milligan.** Fluid & Electrolyte Balance. 4th ed. LC 99-42877. 512p. 2000. pap. text. write for info. (*0-7817-2072-9*) Lppncott W & W.

***Metheny, Pat.** Pat Metheny Songbook. (Illus.). 448p. (J). 2000. pap. 29.95 (*0-634-00796-3*) H Leonard.

Metherell, Victoria, jt. auth. see Chirouze, Yves.

Methlie, Leif B., jt. auth. see Klein, Michel R.

Methodist Hospital Staff. Basic ECG Interpretation. 256p. (C). (gr. 13). 1986. pap. text 29.95 (*0-8016-3401-6*, 03401) Mosby Inc.

Methodius, Saint. St. Methodius, the Symposium: A Treatise on Chastity. Burghardt, Walter J. et al, eds. (Ancient Christian Writers Ser.: No. 27). 256p. 1958. 16.95 (*0-8091-0143-2*) Paulist Pr.

Methodology Committee American Classical League St, ed. Expertis Credite. 18p. 1991. 2.60 (*0-939507-29-3*, B19) Amer Classical.

Methold, Keith, et al. Cobb Davi Puzzle English, PEP 2. (English As a Second Language Bk.). 1978. pap. text 3.50 (*0-582-55258-3*) Longman.

— Pep Puzzles English, PEP 3. (English As a Second Language Bk.). 1978. pap. text 3.50 (*0-582-55259-1*) Longman.

— PUZZLES ENGLISH BOOK1, PEP 1. (English As a Second Language Bk.). 1978. pap. text 3.50 (*0-582-55260-5*) Longman.

— Understanding Technical English, 3 bks., Bk. 1. (English As a Second Language Bk.). (Illus.). 60p. 1975. pap. text 4.95 (*0-582-69032-3*) Longman.

— Understanding Technical English, 3 bks., Bk. 2. (English As a Second Language Bk.). (Illus.). 60p. 1975. pap. text 4.95 (*0-582-69035-8*) Longman.

— Understanding Technical English, 3 bks., Bk. 3. (English As a Second Language Bk.). (Illus.). 60p. 1980. pap. text 4.95 (*0-582-69036-6*) Longman.

M

Methorst-Kuiper, A. J. Krishnamurti: A Biography. 1974. lib. bdg. 250.00 (*0-87968-545-X*) Krishna Pr.
Methot, June. Blackman Revisited. 130p. (Orig.). 1995. pap. 15.00 (*0-941965-05-8*) Ocean Cnty Hist.
— Up & down the Beach. LC 88-51108. (Illus.). 208p. 1988. write for info. (*0-318-64042-2*) Whip Pubs.
***Methuen, C.** Time - Utopia - Eschatology Zeit - Utopie - Eschatologie Temps - Utopie - Eschatologie. Iv, 177p. 1999. 26.00 (*90-429-0775-4*, Pub. by Peeters Pub) Bks Intl VA.
Methuen, Charlotte. Kepler's Tubingen: Stimulus to a Theological Mathematics. LC 98-14850. (St. Andrews Studies in Reformation History). (Illus.). 280p. 1998. text 78.95 (*1-85928-397-7*, Q127.G3M475, Pub. by Ashgate Pub) Ashgate Pub Co.
***Methuen Historical Society Staff.** Methuen. (Images of America Ser.). 128p. 1999. pap. 18.99 (*0-7524-1264-7*) Arcadia Publng.
Methuen, Phillip. Haynes Volvo 260 Series Owners Workshop Manual, No. 400: 1975-1982. 17.95 (*1-85010-287-2*) Haynes Manuals.
Methven, Andrew. Agaricales of California 10 Vol. 10: Lactarius. 175p. 1998. pap. text 36.95 (*0-916422-85-2*) Mad River.
Methven, Andrew S. The Genus Clavariadelphus in North America. (Bibliotheca Mycologica: Vol. 138). (GER., Illus.). 192p. 1990. 48.00 (*3-443-59039-X*, Pub. by Gebruder Borntraeger) Balogh.
Methven, Barbara, ed. Cruising Guide to the Florida Keys. 6th ed. LC 81-176805. (Illus.). 240p. 1988. pap. 14.95 (*0-9619838-0-9*) F Papy Cruising Guide.
Methvin, J. J. Andele, the Mexican-Kiowa Captive: A Story of Real Life among the Indians. 133p. 1996. pap. 16.95 (*0-8263-1748-0*) U of NM Pr.
Methvin, Sharon W. Women's Choices & the Risk of Poverty: Case Studies of Breaking the Cycle. 2nd ed. LC 97-33179. (Children of Poverty Ser.). 240p. 1997. text 56.00 (*0-8153-3049-9*) Garland.
Metil, Luana. The Story of Karate: From Buddhism to Bruce Lee. (Illus.). 112p. (J). 1997. pap. text 10.95 (*0-8225-9770-5*) Lerner Pub.
Metil, Luana & Townsend, Jace. The Story of Karate: From Buddhism to Bruce Lee. LC 93-32006. (Sports Legacy Ser.). (Illus.). 112p. (YA). (gr. 5 up). 1995. lib. bdg. 23.93 (*0-8225-3325-1*, Lerner Publctns) Lerner Pub.
Metin, M. German/Turkish/German Dictionary Medicine. (GER & RUS.). 48p. 1994. 35.00 (*0-320-00567-4*) Fr & Eur.
Metis, Frank. At Your Fingertips: Blues. 1996. pap. 6.95 (*0-8256-1462-7*, AM92883) Music Sales.
Metis, Frank. At Your Fingertips: Boogie, Marches, & Ragtime. 1996. pap. 6.95 (*0-8256-1463-5*, AM92884) Music Sales.
— At Your Fingertips: First Classics. 1996. pap. 6.95 (*0-8256-1465-1*, AM92886) Music Sales.
— At Your Fingertips: Folk Songs Americana. 1996. pap. 6.95 (*0-8256-1466-X*, AM92887) Music Sales.
— At Your Fingertips: Sketches on Scales. 1996. pap. 6.95 (*0-8256-1464-3*, AM92885) Music Sales.
— Judy Collins Anthology. LC 89-753681. (Illus.). 192p. 1988. pap. 24.95 (*0-8256-2533-5*, AM 71200) Omnibus NY.
Metis, Frank, ed. The What'D'Ya Wanna Do? Songbook. (J). 1986. 11.00 (*1-877942-02-2*) Moose Schl Records.
Metis, Frank & Agay, Denes. The Joy of Irish Music. 80p. 1998. pap. text 11.95 (*0-8256-8098-0*, YK21793) Music Sales.
— The Joy of Italian Melodies. (Illus.). 79p. 1998. pap. text 11.95 (*0-8256-8099-9*, YK21801) Music Sales.
Metis, Frank, jt. see Agay, Denes.
Metivier, Michel. Semimartingales: A Course on Stochastic Processes. (Studies in Mathematics). 287p. 1982. 79.95 (*3-11-008674-3*) De Gruyter.
Metivier, Michel & Pardoux, E., eds. Stochastic Differential Systems. (Lecture Notes in Control & Information Sciences: Vol. 69). ix, 310p. 1985. 47.95 (*0-387-15176-1*) Spr-Verlag.
Metivier, Michel & Watanabe, S., eds. Stochastic Analysis. (Lecture Notes in Mathematics Ser.: Vol. 1322). 197p. 1988. 38.95 (*0-387-19352-9*) Spr-Verlag.
Metivier, Pamela, jt. auth. see Helmstetter, Greg.
Metken, Gunter. Spurensicherung: Eine Revision. (GER., Illus.). 240p. 1996. text 18.00 (*90-5705-019-6*) Gordon & Breach.
***Metland, Daphne.** Real Food from Your Food Processor. 128p. 2000. pap. 9.95 (*0-572-02608-0*) Foulsham UK.
Metlitskii, L. V., et al, eds. Controlled Atmosphere Storage of Fruits. Dhote, A. K., tr. from RUS. 209p. (C). 1983. text 76.00 (*90-6191-413-2*, Pub. by A A Balkema) Ashgate Pub Co.
Metlitzki, Dorothee. The Matter of Araby in Medieval England. LC 76-23678. 1977. 47.50 (*0-300-02003-1*) Yale U Pr.
Metlova-Kearns, Marie. Women Without A Country. LC 99-168542. 63 p. 1992. write for info. (*1-879966-01-8*) A O K Bks.
Metlzer, Hagen. Structure of Indecomposable Modules. 96p. (C). 1986. 60.00 (*0-685-46647-7*, Pub. by Collets) St Mut.
Metochites, Theodorus. Miscellanea Philosophica et Historia Graece. Muller, C., ed. 854p. 1921. reprint ed. lib. bdg. 95.00 (*0-685-13372-9*, Pub. by AM Hakkert) Coronet Bks.
Metos, Thomas H., jt. auth. see Belok, Michael V.
Metoyer, Betty, ed. see Hicks, Ralph.
Metoyer, Herbert & Williams, Karen, eds. Day's Dawn: A Short Story Anthology. LC 96-86230. (Illus.). 26p. (Orig.). 1996. pap. 15.00 (*1-888754-03-6*) Detroit Black.
Metoyer, Herbert R., ed. see Detroit Black Writer's Guild Staff.
Metoyer, Patrick G. I'm Rattle-Me-Bones III, Esquire. LC 87-90349. (Illus.). 24p. (Orig.). (J). (gr. 1-6). 1988. pap. 3.95 (*0-944523-02-1*) Western Slope Pubns.
— No Bones! No Bones! LC 87-90350. (Illus.). 24p. (Orig.). (J). (gr. k-2). 1988. pap. 3.95 (*0-944523-03-X*) Western Slope Pubns.
Metras, Gary. Destiny's Calendar. rev. ed. 75p. 1988. reprint ed. pap. 7.00 (*0-938566-39-3*) Adastra Pr.
— The Night Watches. 48p. 1981. pap. 10.00 (*0-938566-07-5*) Adastra Pr.
— The Night Watches. deluxe limited ed. 48p. 1981. 25.00 (*0-938566-08-3*) Adastra Pr.
— Seagull Beach. 35p. 1995. pap. 10.00 (*0-938566-69-5*) Adastra Pr.
Metras, Gary, ed. The Adastra Reader: The Collected Chapbooks. LC 87-70119. (Illus.). 248p. (Orig.). 1987. pap. 10.00 (*0-938566-32-6*) Adastra Pr.
Metraux, Alexandre, tr. see Merleau-Ponty, Maurice.
Metraux, Alfred. Ethnology of Easter Island. 1940. 42.00 (*0-527-02268-3*, B160K) Periodicals Srv.
— Myths of the Toba & Pilaga Indians of the Gran Chaco. LC 46-4565. (American Folklore Society Memoirs Ser.). 1974. reprint ed. 30.00 (*0-527-01092-8*) Periodicals Srv.
Metraux, Alfred. Voodoo in Haiti. 1989. pap. 11.96 (*0-8052-0894-1*) Schocken.
Metraux, Alfred, ed. Native Tribes of Eastern Bolivia & Western Matto Grosso. (Bureau of American Ethnology Bulletins Ser.). 182p. 1995. lib. bdg. 79.00 (*0-7812-4134-0*) Rprt Serv.
Metraux, Daniel A. Aum Shinrikyo & Japanese Youth. LC 99-27942. 144p. 1999. pap. 24.50 (*0-7618-1417-5*) U Pr of Amer.
***Metraux, Daniel A.** Aum Shinrikyo's Impact on Japanese Society. LC 00-35520. (Japanese Studies: Vol. 11). 196p. 2000. pap. 79.95 (*0-7734-7766-7*) E Mellen.
Metraux, Daniel A. The History As Theology of Soka Gakkai: A Japanese New Religion. LC 88-1613. (Studies in Asian Thought & Religion: Vol. 9). 200p. 1988. lib. bdg. 89.95 (*0-88946-055-8*) E Mellen.
— The Japanese Economy & the American Businessman. LC 89-9404. (Studies in Business: Vol. 5). 250p. 1989. lib. bdg. 89.95 (*0-88946-158-9*) E Mellen.
— The Lotus & the Maple Leaf: The Soka Gakkai Buddhist Movement in Canada. 160p. 1996. lib. bdg. 32.00 (*0-7618-0271-1*) U Pr of Amer.
— The Soka Gakkai Buddhist Movement in Quebec: The Lotus & the Fleur de Lys. LC 97-46185. (Canadian Studies: Vol. 20). 104p. 1997. text 59.95 (*0-7734-8472-8*) E Mellen.
— Taiwan's Political & Economic Growth in the Late Twentieth Century. LC 91-37670. 172p. 1991. lib. bdg. 79.95 (*0-7734-9636-X*) E Mellen.
Metraux, G., jt. auth. see Cotton, M. A.
Metraux, Guy P. Sculptors & Physicians in Fifth-Century Greece: A Preliminary Study. LC 96-222612. (Illus.). 184p. 1995. 55.00 (*0-7735-1231-4*, Pub. by McG-Queens Univ Pr) CUP Services.
Metraux, Rhoda, jt. ed. see Mead, Margaret.
Metraux, Ruth W., jt. auth. see Ames, Louise B.
Metreaux, Rhoda, jt. auth. see Abel, Theodora M.
Metress, Christopher, ed. The Critical Response to Dashiell Hammett, 15. LC 94-28713. (Critical Responses in Arts & Letters Ser.: No. 15). 304p. 1994. lib. bdg. 62.95 (*0-313-28938-7*) Greenwood.
Metress, Eileen K., jt. auth. see Fulton, Gene B.
Metress, Eileen K., jt. auth. see Fulton, Gere B.
Metress, Eileen M., jt. auth. see Kart, Cary S.
Metress, James F., jt. ed. see Brace, C. Loring.
Metress, Seamus P. The American Irish & Irish Nationalism: A Sociohistorical Introduction. 162p. 1995. 29.00 (*0-8108-3059-0*) Scarecrow.
— Outlines in Irish History: Eight Hundred Years of Struggle. LC 95-67850. 180p. (Orig.). 1995. pap. 8.95 (*0-9651836-0-2*) Connolly Bks.
***Metress, Seamus P. & Hardy-Johnston, Donna M., eds.** The Irish in North America: A Regional Bibliography. 227p. 1999. text 26.95 (*0-88835-009-0*) P D Meany.
Metrick, Sydney B. Crossing the Bridge: Creating Cermonies for Grieving & Healing from Life's Losses. 144p. (Orig.). 1995. pap. 11.95 (*0-89087-738-6*) Celestial Arts.
— I Do: A Guide to Creating Your Own Wedding Ceremony. 160p. 1995. pap. 11.95 (*0-89087-679-7*) Celestial Arts.
Metrick, Sydney B., jt. auth. see Beck, Renee.
Metro, Andre. Dictionnaire Forestier Multilingue. (FRE.). 434p. 1976. 125.00 (*0-8288-5651-6*, M6409) Fr & Eur.
Metro Deaf Senior Citizens, Inc. Staff. Health Care Delivery to Hearing Impaired Patients: An Instructional Guide for Hospitals on Developing Policies & Procedures. Thomas, Margaret R. & Ancheta, Jocelyn, eds. 112p. 1984. 70.00 (*0-9613623-0-8*) Metro Deaf Senior.
Metro Deaf Senior Citizens, Inc. Staff, et al. Hearcare: An Instructional Guide for Long Term Care Facilities on Developing Policies & Procedures. 112p. 1985. 47.50 (*0-9613623-1-6*) Metro Deaf Senior.
Metro Museum Staff. Metro Museum Journal 5. 1985. 35.00 (*0-226-52102-8*) U Ch Pr.
— Metro Museum Journal 4. 1985. 35.00 (*0-226-52100-1*) U Ch Pr.
— Metro Museum Journal 1. 1985. 35.00 (*0-226-52097-8*) U Ch Pr.
— Metro Museum Journal 3. 1985. 35.00 (*0-226-52099-4*) U Ch Pr.
— Metro Museum Journal 2. 1985. 35.00 (*0-226-52098-6*) U Ch Pr.
— Metropolitan Museum Journal 6. 1985. 35.00 (*0-226-52103-6*) U Ch Pr.
Metro Resource Publications Staff. Do It Yourself Job Search Manual. (Keep it Simple Ser.). (Illus.). 176p. (Orig.). pap. 11.95 (*0-945376-00-6*) Metro Resrc Pubns.
— The Flawless Resume Kit. (Keep it Simple Ser.). (Illus.). 67p. (Orig.). 1989. pap. 8.95 (*0-945376-01-4*) Metro Resrc Pubns.
— The Job Search Competency Review & Exam. (Illus.). 85p. (Orig.). pap. 10.00 (*0-945376-98-7*) Metro Resrc Pubns.
— Rctraining: Twenty-First Century Kcy to Success. (Keep it Simple Ser.). (Illus.). 132p. (Orig.). pap. 14.95 (*0-945376-99-5*) Metro Resrc Pubns.
***Metrobooks Staff.** Funny Faces. (Illus.). 8p. (ps-k). 2000. 8.99 (*1-58663-103-9*) M Friedman Pub Grp Inc.
— Hello Baby Duck. (Illus.). 8p. (J). (ps-k). 2000. 9.99 (*1-58663-106-3*) M Friedman Pub Grp Inc.
— My Puppy. (Illus.). 8p. (ps-k). 2000. 8.99 (*1-58663-104-7*) M Friedman Pub Grp Inc.
— Peek-A-Boo Park. (Illus.). 18p. (J). (ps-k). 2000. 9.99 (*1-58663-107-1*) M Friedman Pub Grp Inc.
— Satellite World Atlas. (Illus.). 224p. 2000. 19.98 (*1-58663-069-5*) M Friedman Pub Grp Inc.
— Spots & Stripes. (Illus.). 8p. (ps-k). 2000. 8.99 (*1-58663-105-5*) M Friedman Pub Grp Inc.
***Metropolis International Editors.** Athens for Less Compact Guide. (For Less Compact Guides Ser.). 2000. pap. text 9.95 (*1-901811-81-6*) Metropolis International.
— Boston for Less Compact Guide. (For Less Compact Guides Ser.). 2000. pap. text 9.95 (*1-901811-38-7*) Metropolis International.
— Bruges for Less Compact Guide. (For Less Compact Guides Ser.). 2000. pap. text 9.95 (*1-901811-76-X*) Metropolis International.
— Copenhagen for Less Compact Guide. (For Less Compact Guides Ser.). 2000. pap. text 9.95 (*1-901811-71-9*) Metropolis International.
— Dublin for Less Compact Guide. (For Less Compact Guides Ser.). 2000. pap. text 9.95 (*1-901811-86-7*) Metropolis International.
Metropolis International Editors. Hawaii for Less. 2000. pap. text 9.95 (*1-901811-41-7*) Metropolis International.
***Metropolis International Editors.** Iceland for Less Compact Guide. 72p. 2000. pap. 9.95 (*1-901811-24-7*, Pub. by Metropolis International) IPG Chicago.
— Istanbul for Less Compact Guide. (For Less Compact Guides Ser.). 2000. pap. text 9.95 (*1-901811-66-2*) Metropolis International.
Metropolis International Editors. Las Vegas for Less. 2000. pap. text 9.95 (*1-901811-56-5*) Metropolis International.
— Los Angeles for Less. 2000. pap. text 9.95 (*1-901811-51-4*) Metropolis International.
***Metropolis International Editors.** Munich for Less Compact Guide. (For Less Compact Guides Ser.). 2000. pap. text 9.95 (*1-901811-43-3*) Metropolis International.
Metropolis International Editors. San Francisco for Less: The Total Guidebook. 2000. pap. text 9.95 (*1-901811-61-1*) Metropolis International.
***Metropolis International Editors.** Washington D. C. for Less Compact Guide. 72p. 2000. pap. 9.95 (*1-901811-34-4*, Pub. by Metropolis International) IPG Chicago.
Metropolis, N., jt. auth. see Louck, J. D.
Metropolis, N. C., ed. see Applied Mathematics Symposium Staff.
Metropolis, Nicholas, et al, eds. A History of Computing in the Twentieth Century. LC 79-51683. 1980. text 100.00 (*0-12-491650-3*) Acad Pr.
Metropolit. The Christmas Story. (J). 1997. pap. 7.00 (*0-15-201555-8*, Harcourt Child Bks) Harcourt.
Metropolitan Anthony Khrapovitsky. The Christian Faith & War. (Orig.). 1973. pap. 0.50 (*0-317-30278-7*) Holy Trinity.
Metropolitan Court Judges Committee. Deprived Children: A Judicial Response: Seventy-Three Recommendations. 48p. 1986. 4.50 (*0-318-23300-2*) Natl Juv & Family Ct Judges.
Metropolitan Dade County, Historic Preservation Di & Chase, Charles E. Resourceful Rehab: A Guide for Historic Buildings in Dade County, Florida. (Illus.). (Orig.). 1987. pap. 9.95 (*0-9618373-0-6*) MDC-Hist Preserv Div.
Metropolitan Demetrios of Vresthena Staff, pref. see Saint Gregory of Nyssa.
Metropolitan Innocent of Moscow Staff. Indication of the Way into the Kingdom of Heaven. 48p. (Orig.). 1981. pap. 2.00 (*0-317-30275-2*) Holy Trinity.
Metropolitan Museum Art Staff. Metropolitan Museum Journal 15. 1985. 35.00 (*0-226-52112-5*) U Ch Pr.
— Metropolitan Museum Journal 14. 1985. 35.00 (*0-226-52111-7*) U Ch Pr.
— Metropolitan Museum Journal 16. 1986. 35.00 (*0-226-52113-3*) U Ch Pr.
— Metropolitan Museum Journal 13. 1985. 35.00 (*0-226-52110-9*) U Ch Pr.
Metropolitan Museum of Art (New York, N. Y.) Staff. From Van Eyck to Bruegel: Early Netherlandish Paintings in the Metropolitan Museum of Art. Ainsworth, Maryan W. & Christiansen, Keith, eds. LC 98-22196. (Illus.). 464p. 1998. 75.00 (*0-87099-870-6*) Metro Mus Art.
Metropolitan Museum of Art (New York, N. Y.) Staff, et al. From Van Eyck to Bruegel: Early Netherlandish Paintings in the Metropolitan Museum of Art. LC 98-22196. 1998. pap. 45.00 (*0-87099-871-4*) Metro Mus Art.
— Gerard David: Purity of Vision in an Age of Transition: Paintings in the Metropolitan Museum of Art. LC 98-30075. 347p. 1998. write for info. (*0-87099-877-3*) Metro Mus Art.
Metropolitan Museum of Art (New York, N. Y.) Staff, jt. auth. see Arnold, Dorothea.
Metropolitan Museum of Art (New York, N. Y.) Staff, jt. auth. see Cavallo, Adolph S.
Metropolitan Museum of Art (New York, N. Y.) Staff, jt. auth. see Laveissiere, Sylvain.
Metropolitan Museum of Art (New York, N. Y.) Staff, jt. auth. see Martin, Richard.
Metropolitan Museum of Art (New York, N. Y.) Staff, jt. auth. see Walker, Susan.
Metropolitan Museum of Art (New York, N. Y.) Staff, ed. see Voorsanger, Catherine Hoover & Howat, John K.
***Metropolitan Museum of Art (New York, NY) Staff.** Egyptian Art in the Age of the Pyramids. LC 99-22246. 1999. write for info. (*0-87099-907-9*) Metro Mus Art.
***Metropolitan Museum of Art (New York, NY) Staff, et al.** American Sculpture in the Metropolitan Museum of Art. LC 99-24636. 451p. 1999. 95.00 (*0-87099-914-1*) Metro Mus Art.
Metropolitan Museum of Art New York Staff, jt. auth. see Smith, Judith G.
Metropolitan Museum of Art Staff. Angels Postcard Book. (Illus.). 30p. 1995. 8.95 (*0-8212-2236-8*, Pub. by Bulfinch Pr) Little.
— Animalphabet: A Charming Alphabetical Menagerie from the Metropolitan Museum of Art. (Illus.). 60p. 1996. 9.95 (*0-8212-2286-4*, Pub. by Bulfinch Pr) Little.
***Metropolitan Museum of Art Staff.** Antonio Vivaldi: The Four Seasons. (Illus.). 60p. 1999. 16.95 (*0-8212-2617-7*, Pub. by Bulfinch Pr) Little.
Metropolitan Museum of Art Staff. Architectural Address Book. (Illus.). 144p. 1997. 22.50 (*0-8212-2337-2*, Pub. by Bulfinch Pr) Little.
***Metropolitan Museum of Art Staff.** Baby's Memory Book & Picture Frame. (Illus.). 32p. (J). 2000. per. 16.95 (*0-689-83364-4*) Litle Simon.
Metropolitan Museum of Art Staff. The Bulletin of the Metropolitan Museum of Art, New York: Old Series, Nov. 1905-June 1942. 1968. 7.78 (*0-405-02357-X*, 16013) Ayer.
— The Bulletin of the Museum of Modern Art. 1967. 15.95 (*0-405-18720-3*, 15626) Ayer.
— Cat Alphabet, Vol. 1. (Illus.). 60p. 1994. 9.95 (*0-8212-2129-9*, Pub. by Bulfinch Pr) Little.
— Computers & Their Potential Applications in Museums: A Conference. 23.95 (*0-405-00014-6*, 11652) Ayer.
— Contemporary Ceramics: Selections from the Collection in the Metropolitan Museum of Art. LC 98-45997. 1998. pap. write for info. (*0-87099-885-4*) Abrams.
— From Van Eyck to Bruegel: Early Netherlandish Painting in the Metropolitan Museum of Art. LC 98-22196. (Illus.). 452p. 1998. 75.00 (*0-8109-6528-3*, Pub. by Abrams) Time Warner.
— Gold. LC 98-6549. (Illus.). 64p. 1998. 24.50 (*0-684-85485-6*) S&S Trade.
***Metropolitan Museum of Art Staff.** Heel to Toe Address Book. 124p. 2000. 19.50 (*0-8212-2647-9*, Pub. by Bulfinch Pr) Little.
Metropolitan Museum of Art Staff. Help: A Record Book for Household Names, Notes & Numbers. 216p. 1997. 14.95 (*0-8212-2365-8*, Pub. by Bulfinch Pr) Little.
— Library Catalog of the Metropolitan Museum of Art. 2nd ed. 1994. 175.00 (*0-7838-2297-9*, G K Hall & Co) Mac Lib Ref.
— Library Catalog of the Metropolitan Museum of Art. 2nd rev. ed. 1980. 5985.00 (*0-8161-1470-6*, G K Hall & Co) Mac Lib Ref.
— Library Catalog of the Metropolitan Museum of Art, 3 vols., Suppl. 5. 2nd ed. 1994. 780.00 (*0-7838-2060-7*) Mac Lib Ref.
— Library Catalog of the Metropolitan Museum of Art, Supplement 3. 2nd ed. 1989. suppl. ed. 755.00 (*0-8161-1560-5*, G K Hall & Co) Mac Lib Ref.
— Library Catalog of the Metropolitan Museum of Art, Supplement 5. 1981. suppl. ed. 175.00 (*0-8161-1319-X*, G K Hall & Co) Mac Lib Ref.
— Library Catalog of the Metropolitan Museum of Art, Supplement 6. 1981. suppl. ed. 175.00 (*0-8161-1320-3*, G K Hall & Co) Mac Lib Ref.
— Life in America: A Special Loan Exhibition of Paintings Held During the Period of the New York World's Fair, April 24 to October 29. 1974. 18.95 (*0-405-02261-1*, 16138) Ayer.
— Lullabies: An Illustrated Songbook. (Illus.). 96p. (J). (gr. k up). 1997. 23.00 (*0-15-201728-3*) Harcourt.
***Metropolitan Museum of Art Staff.** Make Your Own Ornaments: Inspired by Medieval Stained Glass. (Illus.). 32p. (J). (ps-3). 2000. 16.99 (*0-670-89367-6*, Viking Child) Peng Put Young Read.
Metropolitan Museum of Art Staff. Masterpieces of the Metropolitan Museum of Art. (Illus.). 320p. 1998. pap. 35.00 (*0-8212-2509-X*, Pub. by Bulfinch Pr) Little.
— Metropolitan Museum Journal 1993, Vols. 1-30. Burn, Barbara, ed. (Illus.). 1993. lib. bdg. 60.00 (*0-226-52125-7*) U Ch Pr.
— Metropolitan Museum of Art: Hearts & Flowers Stamps with Book. 1998. text 14.99 (*0-670-87457-4*, PuffinBks) Peng Put Young Read.
— Monet Postcard Book, Vol. 1. (Illus.). 124p. 1994. 19.50 (*0-8212-2089-6*, Pub. by Bulfinch Pr); 9.95 (*0-8212-2088-8*, Pub. by Bulfinch Pr) Little.
— Monet's Years at Giverny: Beyond Impressionism. LC 95-1153. (Illus.). 182p. 1995. pap. 14.98 (*0-8109-8138-6*, Pub. by Abrams) Time Warner.
— The Music-Lovers's Birthday Book. (Illus.). 128p. 1987. boxed set 14.95 (*0-317-61333-2*) Abrams.
— New York, New York Address Book. (Illus.). 124p. 1998. 18.95 (*0-8212-2489-1*, Pub. by Bulfinch Pr) Little.
— New York, New York Postcard Book. (Illus.). 30p. 1998. pap. 9.95 (*0-8212-2488-3*, Pub. by Bulfinch Pr) Little.
— Pissarro, Vol. 1. (Illus.). 26p. 1998. 12.95 (*0-8212-2521-9*) Little.

An Asterisk (*) at the beginning of an entry indicates that the title is appearing for the first time.

— Publications of the Metropolitan Museum of Art on Microfiche, 1870 to the Present. (Monographs). 1800p. 1990. 5665.00 (*0-8161-1747-0*, G K Hall & Co) Mac Lib Ref.

— Time Line of Culture in the Nile Valley & Its Relationship to Other World Cultures. (Illus.). 70p. 1994. 10.95 (*0-8109-6474-0*, Pub. by Abrams) Time Warner.

— Van Gogh, Vol. 1. (Illus.). 124p. 1998. 19.95 (*0-8212-2558-8*) Little.

Metropolitan Museum of Art Staff, ed. Catalog of the Robert Goldwater Library of Primitive Art, 4 vols., Set. 1982. 520.00 (*0-8161-0381-X*, G K Hall & Co) Mac Lib Ref.

Metropolitan Museum of Art Staff & Mitchell, Carolyn B. Baby's Album: A Memory Book with Three-Dimensional Illustrations. (Illus.). 28p. 1994. 15.95 (*0-670-85438-7*, Viking Studio) Studio Bks.

— Egyptian Stamps. (J). 1996. pap. 14.99 (*0-670-87224-5*, Viking Child) Peng Put Young Read.

Metropolitan Museum of Art Staff & Priest, Alan. Chinese Sculpture in the Metropolitan Museum of Art. 1974. 40.95 (*0-405-02264-6*, 16141) Ayer.

Metropolitan Museum of Art Staff & Schnurnberger, Lynn E. Kings, Queens, Knights, & Jesters: Making Medieval Costumes. LC 77-25682. (Illus.). (J). (gr. 3 up). 1978. 14.95 (*0-06-025241-3*) HarpC Child Bks.

***Metropolitan Museum of Art Staff, et al.** Ancient Art from Cyprus: The Cesnola Collection in the Metropolitan Musem of Art. LC 99-56516. (Illus.). 400p. 2000. 60.00 (*0-8109-6552-6*, Pub. by Abrams) Time Warner.

Metropolitan Museum of Art Staff, et al. European Miniatures in the Metropolitan Museum of Art. LC 96-22153. 207p. 1996. 65.00 (*0-87099-808-0*) Metro Mus Art.

Metropolitan Museum of Art Staff, jt. auth. see Arnold, Dorothea.

Metropolitan Museum of Art Staff, jt. auth. see Lach, William.

Metropolitan Museum of Art Staff, jt. auth. see Smith, Dian G.

Metropolitan Museum of Art Staff, jt. auth. see Walker, Daniel S.

Metropolitan Museum of Art Staff (New York, N.Y.), jt. auth. see Larocca, Donald J.

Metropolitan Museum Staff. Curious Cats: In Art & Poetry. Lach, William, ed. LC 99-11663. (Illus.). 48p. (J). 1999. 16.00 (*0-689-83055-6*) Atheneum Yung Read.

Metropolitan Museum Staff. Metropolitan Museum Journal, Vol. 21. 1987. 50.00 (*0-226-52118-4*) U Ch Pr.

— Metropolitan Museum Journal, Vol. 23. 1989. lib. bdg. 60.00 (*0-226-52120-6*) U Ch Pr.

— Metropolitan Museum Journal 1989. 1989. lib. bdg. 75.00 (*0-226-52121-4*) U Ch Pr.

Metropolitan of Moscow, Philaret Staff. Christ is Risen: The Paschal Sermons of Metropolitan Philaret of Moscow. 1991. pap. 5.95 (*0-89981-118-3*) Eastern Orthodox.

Metropolitan Philaret of Moscow Staff. Catechism of the Orthodox Church. 1980. pap. 3.95 (*0-89981-009-8*) Eastern Orthodox.

— Comparison of the Differences in the Doctrines of Faith Between the Eastern & Western Churches. Pinkerton, Robert, tr. from RUS. 1974. reprint ed. pap. 1.25 (*0-89981-011-X*) Eastern Orthodox.

Metropolitan Staff, ed. see Saliba, Philip & Allen, Joseph J.

Metropolitan Staff, ed. see Yavorsky, Stefan.

***Metropolitan Toronto School Board Staff.** By Design: Technology Exploration & Integration: Activities for Grades 6-9. (Illus.). 176p. 1999. pap., teacher ed. 31.95 (*1-895579-78-3*, Pub. by Trifolium Inc) ACCESS Pubs Network.

Metropolitan Toronto School Board Staff. Challenging Ourselves: Towards Gender Equity & Violence-Free Relationships: A Handbook of Practical Activities. 109p. 1997. pap. write for info. (*1-85302-445-7*, Pub. by Jessica Kingsley) Taylor & Francis.

***Metropolitan Toronto School Board Teachers, ed.** All Aboard! Cross-Curricular Design & Technology Strategies & Activities. rev. ed. 170p. 1999. pap. 24.95 (*1-895579-86-4*, Pub. by Trifolium Inc) ACCESS Pubs Network.

Metropolitan Tulsa Chamber of Commerce Staff, jt. auth. see Hamill, John.

***Metropolitan Water District of Southern California Staff.** Demonstration-Scale Evaluation of Ozone & Peroxone. LC 99-462155. 2000. write for info. (*1-58321-059-8*) Am Water Wks Assn.

Metry. Drug Regimen Compliance. LC 98-28130. 212p. (C). 1999. 155.00 (*0-471-97122-7*) Wiley.

***Mets, David R.** The Air Campaign: John Warden & the Classical Airpower Theorists. LC 98-33838. (Illus.). 98p. 1999. pap. 6.50 (*1-58566-062-0*) Air Univ.

— Land-Based Airpower in Third World Crises. (Illus.). 171p. 1986. pap. 5.00 (*1-58566-000-0*) Air Univ.

Mets, David R. Master of Airpower: General Carl A. Spaatz. LC 88-5427. (Illus.). 448p. 1997. pap. 17.95 (*0-89141-639-0*) Presidio Pr.

Mets, David R., jt. ed. see Winton, Harold R.

Mets, Marilyn, jt. illus. see Ledwon, Peter.

Metsala, Jamie L. & Ehri, Linnea C., eds. Word Recognition in Beginning Literacy. LC 97-40338. 325p. 1998. write for info. (*0-8058-2898-2*); pap. write for info. (*0-8058-2899-0*) L Erlbaum Assocs.

Metsch, K. Linear Spaces with Few Lines. Dold, A. et al, eds. (Lecture Notes in Mathematics Ser.: Vol. 1490). xiii, 196p. 1991. 41.95 (*0-387-54720-7*) Spr-Verlag.

Metscher, Thomas, ed. see Beutin, Wolfgang.

Metscher, Thomas, jt. ed. see Herms, Dieter.

Metschikoff, Soia & Stotzky, Irwin. The Theory & Craft of American Law 1981. 1981. text 57.00 (*0-8205-3074-3*) Bender.

Metschl, John, ed. see Milwaukee Public Museum Staff.

Metso, Sarianna. The Textual Development of the Qumran Community Rule. LC 96-17974. (Studies on the Texts of the Desert of Judah). (Illus.). 200p. 1996. 84.00 (*90-04-10683-9*) Brill Academic Pubs.

Mett, Ida. The Kronstadt Uprising, 1921. LC DK0265.8.K7M. (Black Rose Bks.: Vol. 3). 100p. 1973. reprint ed. pap. 31.00 (*0-608-00455-3*, 206127400007) Bks Demand.

— The Kronstat Uprising. 93p. 1971. reprint ed. write for info. (*0-919618-19-7*); reprint ed. pap. write for info. (*0-919618-13-8*) Black Rose.

Mett, Percy, et al. The Specification & Design of Concurrent Systems. LC 93-44210. (McGraw-Hill International Series in Software Engineering). 1994. write for info. (*0-07-707966-3*) McGraw.

Metta, Vito, jt. auth. see Cotton, Delores.

Mette, Hans J. Urkunden Dramatischer Auffuehrungen in Griechenland. (Texte und Kommentare Ser.: Vol. 8). (C). 1977. 134.60 (*3-11-006782-X*) De Gruyter.

Mette, Norbert, jt. ed. see Greinacher, Norbert.

Mette, Norbette & Junker-Kenny, Maureen, eds. Little Children Suffer. (Concilium Ser.). 150p. (Orig.). 1996. pap. 15.00 (*1-57075-071-8*) Orbis Bks.

Mettee, Maurice F., et al. Fishes of Alabama & the Mobile Basin. LC 96-33100. (Illus.). 820p. 1996. write for info. (*0-8487-1485-7*) Oxmoor Hse.

Mettee, Stephen B., ed. The Portable Writers' Conference: Your Guide to Getting & Staying Published. LC 96-45131. 464p. 1997. pap. 19.95 (*1-884956-23-8*) Quill Driver.

Mettee, Stephen B., ed. see McCutcheon, Mark.

Metteer, Michael, tr. see Girard, Rene.

Metteer, Michael, tr. see Kittler, Friedrich A.

Mettenheim, Kurt Von, see Von Mettenheim, Kurt.

***Metter, Ellen.** Facts in a Flash: A Research Guide for Writers. LC 99-39517. 432p. 1999. 24.99 (*0-89879-910-4*, 10632, Wrtrs Digest Bks) F & W Pubns Inc.

Metter, Rose. Huevo. (SPA.). 13.00 (*84-348-3468-5*) SM Ediciones.

Metternich. Mongolian Folktales. LC 96-24687. (Illus.). 132p. 1996. pap. 19.95 (*0-937321-06-0*) Avery Pr CO.

Metternich, Clemens V. Memoirs of Prince Metternich, 1773-1835, 5 Vols, Set. LC 68-9611. 1970. reprint ed. 225.00 (*0-86527-128-3*) Fertig.

Mettes, L. & Zuman, Petr. Handbook Series in Organic Electrochemistry, 3 vols., Set. LC 77-24273. 931.00 (*0-8493-7220-8*, CRC Reprint) Franklin.

Mettger, Zak. Till Victory Is Won: Black Soldiers in the Civil War. (Young Readers' History of the Civil War Ser.). 1997. 14.19 (*0-606-12826-3*, Pub. by Turtleback) Demco.

Mettger, Zak, jt. auth. see Vlanton, Elias.

Mettigan, Nancy, ed. see Johnson, Loren G.

Metting, F. Blaine, ed. Soil Microbial Ecology: Applications in Agricultural & Environmental Management. LC 92-26049. (Books in Soils, Plants & the Environment: Vol. 25). (Illus.). 656p. 1992. text 199.00 (*0-8247-8737-4*) Dekker.

***Metting, Fred.** The Unbroken Circle: Tradition & Innovation in the Music of Ry Cooder & Taj Mahal. LC 00-38760. (American Folk Music & Folk Musicians Ser.). 2000. write for info. (*0-8108-3818-4*) Scarecrow.

Mettinger, Arthur. Aspects of Semantic Opposition in English. (Studies in Lexicography & Lexicology). 214p. 1994. text 45.00 (*0-19-824269-7*) OUP.

Mettinger, Tryggve N. The Dethronement of Sabaoth: Studies in the Shen & Kabod Theologies. (Coniectanea Biblica. Old Testament Ser.: No. 18). 158p. (Orig.). 1982. pap. 41.00 (*0-317-65792-5*) Coronet Bks.

— King & Messiah: The Civil & Sacred Legitimation of the Israelite Kings. (Coniectanea Biblica. Old Testament Ser.: No. 8). 342p. (Orig.). 1976. pap. 47.50 (*91-40-04349-5*, Pub. by Liber Gleerup) Coronet Bks.

— No Graven Image? Israelite Aniconism in Its Ancient Near Eastern Context. (Coniectanea Biblica, Old Testament Ser.: No. 42). 252p. 1995. pap. 52.50 (*91-22-01664-3*) Coronet Bks.

Mettler, Barbara. Basic Movement Exercises. 1973. 18.50 (*0-912536-06-3*) Mettler Studios.

— Creative Dance in Kindergarten. 1976. pap. 3.50 (*0-912536-08-X*) Mettler Studios.

— Dance As an Element of Life. 1985. 15.00 (*0-912536-12-8*) Mettler Studios.

— Group Dance Improvisations. 1975. 15.00 (*0-912536-07-1*) Mettler Studios.

— The Nature of Dance As a Creative Art Activity. 1980. 12.50 (*0-912536-11-X*) Mettler Studios.

Mettler, Barbara, ed. Materials of Dance As a Creative Art Activity. 5th ed. 1979. 18.50 (*0-912536-10-1*) Mettler Studios.

Mettler, Darlene D. Sound & Sense: Musical Allusion & Imagery in the Novels of Iris Murdoch. LC 90-22130. (American University Studies: English Language & Literature: Ser. IV, Vol. 127). XII, 169p. (C). 1991. text 34.95 (*0-8204-1462-X*) P Lang Pubng.

***Mettler, Elinor.** Fagan Sisters of Copake Falls. (Images of America Ser.). 128p. 1999. pap. 18.99 (*0-7385-0283-9*) Arcadia Publng.

Mettler, Felix. The Wild Boar. McCown, Edna, tr. from GER. 224p. 1995. 18.95 (*0-88064-134-7*); pap. 8.95 (*0-88064-153-3*) Fromm Intl Pub.

Mettler, Fred A., Jr. Essentials of Radiology. Bralow, Lisette, ed. LC 95-17721. (Illus.). 384p. 1995. pap. text 39.95 (*0-7216-6744-9*, W B Saunders Co) Harcrt Hlth Sci Grp.

— Imaging, Nineteen-Ninety. 1989. 125.00 (*0-316-56829-5*, Little Brwn Med Div) Lppncott W & W.

Mettler, Fred A. Radionuclide Imaging of the GI Tract. LC 85-21344. (Contemporary Issues in Nuclear Imaging Ser.: No. 2). (Illus.). 373p. 1986. reprint ed. pap. 115.70 (*0-7837-6811-7*, 204664300003) Bks Demand.

Mettler, Fred A., ed. Radionuclide Bone Imaging & Densitometry. (Contemporary Issues in Nuclear Imaging Ser.: Vol. 4). (Illus.). 344p. 1987. text 90.00 (*0-443-08546-3*) Church.

Mettler, Fred A., Jr., et al, eds. Medical Management of Radiation Accidents. 416p. 1989. boxed set 208.95 (*0-8493-4865-X*, RA1231) CRC Pr.

Mettler, Fred A. & Upton, Arthur C. Medical Effects of Ionizing Radiation. 2nd ed. 464p. 1995. text 140.00 (*0-7216-6646-9*, W B Saunders Co) Harcrt Hlth Sci Grp.

Mettler, Fred A., et al. Essentials of Nuclear Medicine Imaging. 4th ed. Bralow, Lisette, ed. LC 97-14400. (Illus.). 512p. 1997. text 69.00 (*0-7216-5121-6*, W B Saunders Co) Harcrt Hlth Sci Grp.

— Magnetic Resonance Imaging & Spectroscopy. fac. ed. LC 86-13620. (Illus.). 331p. 1986. reprint ed. pap. 102.70 (*0-7837-7823-6*, 204757900008) Bks Demand.

Mettler, Hans J., et al. Provence & Cote d'Azur. 2nd ed. (Travel Guides Ser.). (Illus.). 368p. 1998. pap. 21.95 (*2-89464-112-5*) Ulysses Travel.

***Mettler, Hans Jorg.** Provence & Cote D'Azur. 3rd ed. (Travel Guide Ser.). (Illus.). 2001. pap. 21.95 (*2-89464-327-6*) Ulysses Travel.

Mettler, Helen. The Co-Op & Condo Owner's Handbook: Everything You Have to Know about the Apartment You Own & Live In. LC 83-90305. 89p. (Orig.). 1983. pap. 7.95 (*0-9611254-0-3*) H R M Comm Inc.

Mettler, John J., Jr. Basic Butchering of Livestock & Game: Beef, Veal, Hogs, Lamb, Poultry, Rabbit, Venison. LC 85-70195. (Illus.). 208p. 1986. pap. 13.95 (*0-88266-391-7*, Garden Way Pub) Storey Bks.

— Horse Sense: A Complete Guide to Horse Selection & Care. Burns, Deborah, ed. LC 88-82753. (Illus.). 160p. (Orig.). 1989. 19.95 (*0-88266-549-9*, Garden Way Pub); pap. 14.95 (*0-88266-545-6*, Garden Way Pub) Storey Bks.

— Wild Turkeys: Hunting & Watching. LC 98-6392. (Illus.). 176p. 1998. pap. 14.95 (*1-58017-069-2*) Storey Bks.

Mettler, Lawrence E., et al. Population Genetics & Evolution. 2nd ed. (Illus.). 448p. (C). 1988. text 55.60 (*0-13-685678-0*) P-H.

Mettler, Michael. The Proper Care of Dwarf Rabbits. (Illus.). 256p. 1992. text 16.95 (*0-86622-443-2*, TW-121) TFH Pubns.

Mettler, Molly & Kemper, Donald W. Healthwise for Life: Medical Self-Care for People Age 50 or Better. 3rd rev. ed. LC 99-175289. (Illus.). 330p. 1998. pap. text 9.95 (*1-877930-60-1*) Healthwise.

Mettler, Molly, jt. auth. see FallCreek, Stephanie.

Mettler, Rene. Penguins. (First Discovery Book). 60p. (J). (ps-3). 1996. 11.95 (*0-590-73877-1*, Cartwheel) Scholastic Inc.

Mettler, Rene. Birds. LC 92-15956. (First Discovery Book). 24p. (J). (ps-3). 1993. 11.95 (*0-590-46367-5*) Scholastic Inc.

— Flowers. LC 92-15957. (First Discovery Book). 24p. (J). (ps-3). 1993. 11.95 (*0-590-46383-7*) Scholastic Inc.

Mettler, Rene, jt. auth. see Delafosse, Claude.

Mettler, Richard. Cognitive Learning Theory & Cane Travel Instruction: A New Paradigm. (Illus.). 170p. 1998. pap. text 35.00 (*0-7881-4883-4*) DIANE Pub.

— Cognitive Learning Theory & Cane Travel Instruction: A New Paradigm. LC 95-69567. 110p. 1995. pap. 10.00 (*0-9646058-0-5*) St NE DPI DRSVI.

Mettler, Shirley L. Disease Susceptibility: Medical Subject Analysis with Reference Bibliography. rev. ed. LC 85-48180. 150p. 1992. 47.50 (*1-55914-896-9*); pap. 44.50 (*1-55914-897-7*) ABBE Pubs Assn.

Mettler, Stephen C., jt. ed. see Hutcheson, Lynn D.

Mettler, Suzanne. Divided Citizens: Gender & Federalism in New Deal Public Policy. LC 98-18218. (Illus.). 272p. 1998. pap. 17.95 (*0-8014-8546-0*) Cornell U Pr.

***Mettler, Suzanne.** Divided Citizens: Gender & Federalism in New Deal Public Policy. LC 98-18218. (Illus.). 272p. 1998. text 49.95 (*0-8014-3329-0*) Cornell U Pr.

Mettling, Stephan R. & Cusic, David. Principles of Real Estate Practice. unabridged ed. (Illus.). 416p. (Orig.). 1996. pap. text 25.00 (*0-9652158-0-6*) Perfrmnce Pub.

Mettrop, P. J., jt. ed. see Musaph, H.

Metts, Sandra, jt. auth. see Cupach, William R.

Metts, Wallis C. How to Think As a Christian: The Blessing of Bias. 1997. 11.95 (*1-57558-015-2*) Hearthstone OK.

— Your Faith on Trial. 180p. (Orig.). 1979. pap. 5.49 (*0-89084-112-8*, 003707) Bob Jones Univ.

Metts, Wallis C., et al. Children's Book of the Bible. LC 97-75641. (Illus.). 320p. 1998. write for info. (*0-7853-2796-7*) Pubns Intl Ltd.

Mettzner, Susan, jt. auth. see Earle, Ralph.

Metuzals, J., ed. Electron Microscopy & Alzheimer's Disease. (Illus.). 1986. 20.00 (*0-911302-57-3*) San Francisco Pr.

Metz. Physical Chemistry. (C). 1999. text. write for info. (*0-03-022372-5*) Harcourt Coll Pubs.

***Metz, Alberta & Brannon, Ronald R.** Touching Tomorrow: The Story of Hephzibah Children's Home. 2nd ed. LC 99-191890. (Illus.). 1998. write for info. (*0-89827-196-7*) Wesleyan Pub Hse.

Metz, Alberta R. Francisco H. Soltero: Mexico. (Missionary Hero Ser.). (Illus.). 72p. (J). (gr. 4-7). 1981. pap. 3.99 (*0-89827-010-3*, BKB72) Wesleyan Pub Hse.

— God Found Kingsley Ridgway. (Family Missionary Ser.). (Illus.). 80p. (Orig.). (J). (gr. 4-7). 1985. pap. 5.99 (*0-89827-027-8*, BKB88) Wesleyan Pub Hse.

— Henry W. Johnston: Sierra Leone. (Missionary Hero Ser.). (Illus.). 72p. (J). (gr. 4-7). 1978. pap. 3.99 (*0-89827-000-6*, BKC25) Wesleyan Pub Hse.

— Herbert C. Sanders: South Africa. (Wesleyan Missionary Hero Ser.). (Illus.). 64p. (J). (gr. 4-7). 1979. pap. text 3.99 (*0-89827-004-9*, BKC26) Wesleyan Pub Hse.

— Maurice A.Gibbs: Japan. (Missionary Hero Ser.). (Illus.). 80p. (J). (gr. 4-7). 1980. pap. 3.99 (*0-89827-008-1*, BKD46) Wesleyan Pub Hse.

— Toughy. (Illus.). 94p. (Orig.). (J). (gr. 4-7). 1980. pap. 4.99 (*0-89827-009-X*, BKF63) Wesleyan Pub Hse.

— "Toughy" Learns to Fight. (Illus.). 101p. (Orig.). (J). (gr. 4-7). 1988. pap. 4.99 (*0-89827-056-1*, BKF64) Wesleyan Pub Hse.

***Metz, Alice.** Early American Pattern Glass. (Illus.). 1999. pap. text 17.95 (*1-57432-154-4*) Collector Bks.

— Much More Early American Pattern Glass: An Important American Heritage. (Illus.). 240p. 2000. pap. 17.95 (*1-57432-163-3*) Collector Bks.

Metz, Allan. A NAFTA Bibliography, 18. LC 96-32408. (Bibliographies & Indexes in Economics & Economic History: No. 18). 504p. 1996. lib. bdg. 105.00 (*0-313-29463-1*, Greenwood Pr) Greenwood.

Metz, Allan, compiled by. Bill Clinton's Pre-Presidential Career: An Annotated Bibliography, 27. LC 94-3017. (Bibliographies & Indexes in American History Ser.: Vol. 27). 248p. 1994. lib. bdg. 65.00 (*0-313-29285-X*, Greenwood Pr) Greenwood.

— National Service & AmeriCorps: An Annotated Bibliography, 26. LC 96-41280. (Bibliographies & Indexes in Law & Political Science: Vol. 26). 288p. 1997. lib. bdg. 72.95 (*0-313-30267-7*, Greenwood Pr) Greenwood.

Metz, Barbara & Burchill, John. The Enneagram & Prayer: Discovering Our True Selves Before God. 164p. 1987. pap. 14.95 (*0-87193-259-8*) Dimension Bks.

Metz, Christian. Film Language: A Semiotics of the Cinema. Taylor, Michael, tr. LC 73-90363. 288p. 1990. pap. text 18.00 (*0-226-52130-3*) U Ch Pr.

— The Imaginary Signifier: Psychoanalysis & the Cinema. Britton, Celia et al, trs. from FRE. LC 81-47551. 340p. 1986. pap. 19.95 (*0-253-20380-5*, MB-380) Ind U Pr.

— Language & Cinema. Umiker-Sebeok, Donna J., tr. 1974. text 64.65 (*90-279-2682-4*) Mouton.

Metz, Christopher, jt. auth. see Sackett, George C.

Metz, Christopher Y. IP Switching: Protocols & Architecture. LC 98-38791. (Series on Computer Communications). (Illus.). 464p. 1998. pap. 55.00 (*0-07-041953-1*) McGraw.

Metz, Clyde. Molecular Geometry & Bonding. Stanitski, C. L., ed. (Modular Laboratory Program in Chemistry Ser.). 16p. (C). 1998. pap. text 1.50 (*0-87540-409-X*, STRC 409) Chem Educ Res.

Metz, Clyde R. Models & the Crystalline State. Neidig, H. Anthony, ed. (Modular Laboratory Program in Chemistry Ser.). 16p. (C). 1988. pap. text 1.50 (*0-87540-351-4*, STRC 351-4) Chem Educ Res.

— Physical Chemistry. 896p. (C). 1999. text 87.50 (*0-03-097864-5*) SCP.

— Schaum's Outline for Physical Chemistry. 2nd ed. 512p. (C). 1987. pap. 15.95 (*0-07-041715-6*) McGraw.

— Statistical Analysis of Experimental Density Data. Neidig, H. Anthony, ed. (Modular Laboratory Program in Chemistry Ser.). 11p. (C). 1988. pap. text 1.50 (*0-87540-353-0*, PROP 353-0) Chem Educ Res.

— Study Guide, Physical Chemistry. (C). 2000. pap. text 19.50 (*0-03-097866-1*) Harcourt.

***Metz, Clyde R.** Studying the Temperature Dependence & Thermodynamics of Electrochemical Cells. (Modular Laboratory in Chemistry Ser.). 12p. (C). 1999. pap. text 1.50 (*0-87540-510-X*, ELEC 510X) Chem Educ Res.

Metz, Clyde R., et al. Experiments in Chemistry. 2nd ed. 300p. (C). 1991. pap. text, student ed. 49.00 (*0-03-053488-7*) SCP.

Metz, Dale, jt. auth. see Schlavettl, Nicholas.

Metz, Don. New Compact House Designs: 27 Award-Winning Plans, 1,250 Square Feet Or Less. Watson, Ben, ed. LC 90-50608. (Illus.). 192p. 1991. 27.95 (*0-88266-667-3*); pap. 19.95 (*0-88266-666-5*) Storey Bks.

Metz, Don, ed. The Compact House Book: Thirty-Three Prize Winning Designs One Thousand Square Feet or Less. 2nd ed. LC 83-8912. (Illus.). 208p. 1983. 27.95 (*0-88266-351-8*, Garden Way Pub); pap. 16.95 (*0-88266-323-2*, Garden Way Pub) Storey Bks.

Metz, Donald. Studies in Biblical Holiness. 292p. 1971. 21.99 (*0-8341-0117-3*) Beacon Hill.

Metz, Donald L. Running Hot: Structure & Stress in Ambulance Work. 252p. 1984. reprint ed. lib. bdg. 20.00 (*0-8191-4069-4*) U Pr of Amer.

Metz, Elizabeth, jt. auth. see Newman, Anabel P.

Metz, G. Harold. Shakespeare's Realist Tragedy: Studies in Titus Andronicus. LC 95-52067. (Illus.). 312p. 1996. 46.50 (*0-8386-3653-5*) Fairleigh Dickinson.

— Sources of Four Plays Ascribed to Shakespeare. LC 88-4793. (Illus.). 528p. 1989. text 48.00 (*0-8262-0690-5*) U of Mo Pr.

Metz, Harold. Business Builders: Success Strategies to Get Clients to Come to You. (Illus.). 208p. (Orig.). 1995. pap. text 39.00 (*0-89447-314-X*) Cypress.

Metz, Helen C., ed. Algeria: A Country Study. 4th ed. LC 94-43019. (DA Pam Area Handbook Ser.: No. 550-44). (Illus.). 440p. 1995. text 20.00 (*0-16-001650-9*, 008020013447) USGPO.

— Indian Ocean: Five Island Countries. 3rd ed. LC 95-16570. (Area Handbooks Ser.: DA Pam Ser.: Vol. 550-154). 412p. 1995. 22.00 (*0-8444-0857-3*) Lib Congress.

— Iran: A Country Study. 4th ed. LC 88-600484. (Area Handbook Ser.). (Illus.). 378p. 1989. text 17.00 (*0-16-001729-7*, S/N 008-020-01181-9) USGPO.

— Iraq: A Country Study. 4th ed. LC 89-13940. (Area Handbook Ser.). (Illus.). 332p. 1990. text 21.00 (*0-16-022052-1*, S/N 008-020-01206-8) USGPO.

— Persian Gulf States: A Country Study. (Illus.). 472p. (C). 1998. reprint ed. text 50.00 (*0-7881-7502-5*) DIANE Pub.

— Turkey: A Country Study. (Illus.). 458p. 1996. reprint ed. text 60.00 (*0-7881-3546-5*) DIANE Pub.

Metz, Helen C. & Merrill, Tim L. Nicaragua Country Studies: Area Handbook. 3rd ed. LC 94-43019. (Area Handbook DA Pam Ser.). 1994. write for info. (*0-8444-0831-X*) Lib Congress.

Metz, Helen C., ed. see Federal Research Division, Library of Congress Sta.

Metz, Helen C., ed. see Federal Research Division Staff.

Metz, Helen C., ed. see Library of Congress Federal Research Division Staff.

Metz, Helen Chapin. Algeria: A Country Study. 388p. 1995. boxed set 23.00 (*0-16-061170-9*) USGPO.

Metz, Helen Chapin. Nigeria: A Country Study. 428p. 1992. boxed set 28.00 (*0-16-040401-0*) USGPO.

Metz, Helen Chapin. Persian Gulf States: Country Studies. 502p. 1994. boxed set 29.00 (*0-16-061169-5*) USGPO.

— Saudi Arabia: A Country Study. 384p. 1993. boxed set 29.00 (*0-16-061157-1*) USGPO.

— Somalia: A Country Study. 320p. 1993. boxed set 25.00 (*0-16-061153-9*) USGPO.

— Sudan: A Country Study. 370p. 1992. boxed set 28.00 (*0-16-061149-0*) USGPO.

Metz, J. A. & Diekmann, O., eds. The Dynamics of Physiologically Structured Populations. (Lecture Notes in Biomathematics Ser.: Vol. 68). xii, 511p. 1986. 82.95 (*0-387-16786-2*) Spr-Verlag.

Metz, James. Oncotips. 256p. pap. text 19.95 (*0-7817-2564-X*) Lppncott W & W.

Metz, Jerred. Angels in the House: Poems by Jerred Metz. deluxe ed. (Illus.). 1978. 75.00 (*0-685-27838-7*) Heron Pr.

— Halley's Comet, Nineteen Ten: Fire in the Sky. (Illus.). (Orig.). 1985. 13.95 (*0-933439-00-8*); pap. 8.95 (*0-933439-01-6*) Singing Bone Pr.

Metz, Johan A. J., jt. ed. see Dieckmann, Ulf.

Metz, Johann B. Faith in History & Society. 148p. 1994. 30.00 (*0-86012-075-9*, Pub. by Srch Pr) St Mut.

— A Passion for God: The Mystical-Political Dimension of Christianity. Ashley, J. Matthew, ed. & tr. by. from GER. LC 97-36614. 224p. 1998. pap. 19.95 (*0-8091-3755-0*, 3755-0) Paulist Pr.

Metz, Johann B. & Haring, Hermann, eds. Resurrection or Reincarnation? (Concilium Ser.). 1993. 15.00 (*0-88344-872-6*) Orbis Bks.

Metz, Johann B., jt. ed. see Schillebeeckx, Edward.

Metz, Johannes B. Poverty of Spirit. rev. ed. Drury, John, tr. LC 97-49919. 64p. 1998. pap. 6.95 (*0-8091-3799-2*) Paulist Pr.

Metz, Johannes B., jt. ed. see Schillebeeckx, Edward.

Metz, John. The Fables of La Fontaine: Vocal Settings & Interpretations. LC 83-8272. (Juilliard Performance Guides Ser.: No. 2). 160p. 1986. lib. bdg. 54.00 (*0-918728-26-6*) Pendragon NY.

Metz, Judith. A Retreat with Elizabeth Seton: Meeting Our Grace. 98p. 1999. pap. 8.95 (*0-86716-304-6*, B3046) St Anthony Mess Pr.

Metz, Karen S. Information Sources in Power Engineering. LC 75-32096. 114p. 1976. lib. bdg. 42.95 (*0-8371-8538-6*, MPE/, Greenwood Pr) Greenwood.

Metz, Karen S., jt. auth. see Gabriel, Richard A.

Metz, Kim, jt. auth. see Roths, Regina.

***Metz, Lance E.** Sherman's Guide to Hugh Moore Park. 2nd ed. (Illus.). 1999. pap. 4.95 (*0-930973-22-4*) H M Historical.

Metz, Lance E. & Viest, Ivan, eds. The First Seventy-Five Years: A History of the Engineering Foundation. LC 90-85572. 512p. 1991. text 50.00 (*0-939204-44-4*) Eng Found.

Metz, Lance E., jt. auth. see Bartholomew, Craig L.

Metz, Leon C. Border: The U. S. - Mexico Line. LC 89-60730. (Illus.). 480p. 1989. 29.95 (*0-930208-27-7*) Mangan Books TX.

— Dallas Stoudenmire: El Paso Marshal. LC 70-79109. 1993. pap. 11.95 (*0-8061-2487-3*) U of Okla Pr.

— Desert Army: Fort Bliss on the Texas Border. LC 88-90910. (Illus.). (C). 1995. pap. 14.95 (*0-930208-36-6*) Mangan Books TX.

— El Paso: Guided Through Time. Mangan, Frank & Mangan, Judy, eds. LC 99-41812. (Illus.). 325p. 1999. 39.95 (*0-930208-37-4*) Mangan Books TX.

— El Paso Chronicles: A Record of Historical Events in El Paso, Texas. Mangan, Judy & Mangan, Frank, eds. LC 93-29521. (Illus.). 320p. (C). 1993. 24.95 (*0-930208-32-3*) Mangan Books TX.

— 400 Years in El Paso. (Illus.). 52p. 1997. 95.00 (*0-944551-25-4*) Sundance Pr TX.

— John Selman, Gunfighter. LC 79-6719. (Illus.). 272p. 1992. pap. 14.95 (*0-8061-2419-9*) U of Okla Pr.

— John Wesley Hardin: Dark Angel of Texas. Mangan, Judy & Mangan, Frank, eds. LC 96-11925. (Illus.). 320p. 1996. 39.95 (*0-930208-35-8*) Mangan Books TX.

— John Wesley Hardin: Dark Angel of Texas. LC 97-42244. (Illus.). xiv, 352p. 1998. pap. 16.95 (*0-8061-2995-6*) U of Okla Pr.

— Pat Garrett: The Story of a Western Lawman. LC 72-9261. (Illus.). 328p. 1983. pap. 14.95 (*0-8061-1838-5*) U of Okla Pr.

— Roadside History of Texas. Greer, Daniel, ed. LC 93-49677. (Roadside History Ser.). (Illus.). 464p. 1993. 30.00 (*0-87842-293-5*); pap. 18.00 (*0-87842-294-3*) Mountain Pr.

— Robert E. McKee Master Builder. Hamilton, Nancy, ed. (Illus.). 412p. 1998. 59.95 (*0-9646793-1-0*) R E McKee Fnd.

— The Shooters. LC 76-21578. (Illus.). 300p. 1976. 19.95 (*0-930208-04-8*) Mangan Books TX.

— The Shooters: A Gallery of Notorious Gunmen from the American West. LC 96-215375. 304p. 1996. pap. 13.00 (*0-425-15450-5*) Berkley Pub.

— Turning Points in El Paso, Texas. LC 85-60638. (Illus.). 128p. 1985. 19.95 (*0-930208-18-8*) Mangan Books TX.

Metz, Manfred, jt. auth. see Thomson, Anne.

Metz, Mary H. Different by Design: The Context & Character of Three Magnet Schools. 288p. 1986. 29.95 (*0-7102-0071-4*, Routledge Thoemms) Routledge.

Metz, Mary S. & Helstrom, Jo. Le Francais a Vivre. 4th ed. Rebisz, Jacqueline, ed. (Illus.). (gr. 9-12). 1978. text 29.92 (*0-07-041755-5*) McGraw.

Metz, Mary S., jt. auth. see Helstrom, Jo.

***Metz, Melinda.** The Case of the Rock Star's Secret: The Case of the Rock Star's Secret. (New Adventures of Mary-Kate & Ashley Ser.). (Illus.). 96p. (J). (gr. 4-7). 2000. mass mkt. 4.25 (*0-06-106589-7*) HarpC Child Bks.

Metz, Melinda. The Case of the Surprise Call. (New Adventures of Mary-Kate & Ashley Ser.). 86p. (J). (gr. 2-4). 1999. pap. 3.99 (*0-590-29403-2*) Scholastic Inc.

***Metz, Melinda.** The Dark One, No. 9. (Rosewell High Ser.: No. 9). 176p. (YA). (gr. 6 up). 2000. per. 5.99 (*0-671-03563-0*, Pocket Pulse) PB.

— The Intruder. (Rosewell High Ser.: No. 5). 176p. (YA). (gr. 6 up). 2000. per. 4.99 (*0-671-77459-X*, Archway) PB.

Metz, Melinda. The Outsider. (Rosewell High Ser.: No. 1). 170p. (YA). (gr. 7-12). 1998. mass mkt. 1.99 (*0-671-02374-8*, Archway) PB.

***Metz, Melinda.** The Outsider. (Rosewell High Ser.: No. 1). (YA). (gr. 7-12). 1999. per. 5.99 (*0-671-77466-2*, Pocket Books) PB.

Metz, Melinda. The Rebel. (Roswell High Ser.: No. 8). 176p. (YA). (gr. 8-12). 2000. per. 5.99 (*0-671-03562-2*) S&S Childrens.

***Metz, Melinda.** The Salvation. (Rosewell High Ser.: No. 10). 176p. (YA). (gr. 6 up). 2000. mass mkt. 5.99 (*0-671-03564-9*, Pocket Pulse) PB.

— The Seeker. (Rosewell High Ser.: No. 3). 176p. (YA). (gr. 6 up). 2000. mass mkt. 4.99 (*0-671-77464-6*, Pocket Pulse) PB.

Metz, Melinda. The Seeker, Vol. 3. (Rosewell High Ser.: No. 3). (YA). (gr. 6 up). 1999. mass mkt. 4.50 (*0-671-02376-4*) PB.

— The Stowaway. (Rosewell High Ser.: No. 6). 176p. (YA). (gr. 6 up). 2000. per. 4.99 (*0-671-02379-9*, Pocket Pulse) PB.

***Metz, Melinda.** Sweet Sixteen: Julia, No. 1. LC 99-66678. (Sweet Sixteen Ser.: No. 1'). 240p. (YA). (gr. 7-12). 2000. pap. 5.95 (*0-06-440814-0*, HarpTrophy) HarpC Child Bks.

— Sweet Sixteen: Sunny & Matt, No. 6. LC 99-66685. (Sweet Sixteen Ser.: No. 6). 224p. (YA). (gr. 12 up). 2000. pap. 5.95 (*0-06-440815-9*, HarpTrophy) HarpC Child Bks.

— The Vanished. (Rosewell High Ser.: No. 7). 176p. (YA). (gr. 6 up). 2000. per. 4.99 (*0-671-03561-4*, Pocket Pulse) PB.

Metz, Melinda. The Watcher. (Rosewell High Ser.: No. 3). (YA). (gr. 6 up). 1999. per. 4.50 (*0-671-02377-2*, Archway) PB.

***Metz, Melinda.** The Watcher. (Rosewell High Ser.: No. 4). 176p. (YA). (gr. 6 up). 2000. per. 4.99 (*0-671-77463-8*, Pocket Pulse) PB.

— The Wild One. (Rosewell High Ser.: No. 2). (YA). (gr. 6 up). 1999. mass mkt. 4.99 (*0-671-77465-4*, Pocket Books) PB.

Metz, Melinda. The Wild One, No. 2. (Rosewell High Ser.: No. 2). (YA). (gr. 6 up). 1998. pap. 3.99 (*0-671-02375-6*, Archway) PB.

Metz, Melinda, adapted by. Attack of the Mutant. (Goosebumps Presents Ser.: No. 12). (Illus.). 64p. (J). 1997. pap. text 3.99 (*0-590-93969-6*, Apple Paperbacks) Scholastic Inc.

— Attack of the Mutant. (Goosebumps Presents Ser.: No. 12). 1997. 9.19 (*0-606-11406-8*, Pub. by Turtleback) Demco.

Metz, P., ed. Stereoselective Heterocyclic Synthesis. LC 99-24586. (Desktop Editions in Chemistry Ser.). 180p. 1999. pap. 54.95 (*3-540-65554-9*) Spr-Verlag.

— Stereoselective Heterocyclic Synthesis I. (Topics in Current Chemistry Ser.: Vol. 189). (Illus.). 210p. 1997. 124.95 (*3-540-62678-6*) Spr-Verlag.

— Topics in Current Chemistry: Stereoselective Heterocyclic Synthesis II, Vol. 190. (Illus.). 180p. 1997. 109.00 (*3-540-62700-6*) Spr-Verlag.

Metz, Pamela K. The Creative Tao: Lao Tzu's Tao Te Ching Adapted for a New Age. Brand, Nancy, ed. LC 96-48365. (Illus.). (Orig.). 1997. lib. bdg. 27.95 (*0-89334-266-1*, Humanics Trade) Humanics Ltd.

— The Tao of Learning: Lao Tzu's Tao Te Ching Adapted for a New Age. LC 93-1945. (Illus.). 160p. 1994. lib. bdg. 27.95 (*0-89334-243-2*, 2432052) Humanics Ltd.

Metz, Pamela K. & Tobin, Jacqueline L. The Tao of Women. LC 95-14162. (Illus.). 192p. (Orig.). 1995. lib. bdg. 26.95 (*0-89334-245-9*, 2459X35) Humanics Ltd.

Metz, Patricia A. Determining Atomic Emission by Spectroscopy. (Modular Laboratory Program in Chemistry Ser.). 12p. (C). 1994. pap. text 1.50 (*0-87540-449-9*, STRC 449-9) Chem Educ Res.

Metz, Paul A. Metallogeny of the Fairbanks Mining District, Alaska & Adjacent Areas, 2 vols. LC 91-67232. (MIRL Reports: No. 90). (Illus.). 455p. (Orig.). (C). 1991. pap. text 24.00 (*0-911043-13-6*); pap. text 41.00 incl. fiche (*0-685-56388-X*) UAKF Min Ind Res Lab.

Metz, Randolph, ed. see Pfeiffer, Joseph.

Metz, Ray E. & Junion-Metz, Gail. Using the World Wide Web & Creating Home Pages: A How-to-Do-It Manual for Librarians. (Illus.). 290p. (Orig.). 1996. pap. 55.00 (*1-55570-241-4*) Neal-Schuman.

Metz, Rene, ed. see Cerdic Colloquium Staff.

Metz, Ricca L. Maudie: A Positive Nursing Home Experience. (Illus.). 144p. 1999. 9.95 (*0-8158-0535-7*) Chris Mass.

Metz, Robert, jt. auth. see Knotts, Don.

Metz, Robert A., ed. Applied Mining Geology: Problems of Sampling & Grade Control. LC 85-71945. 173p. reprint ed. pap. 53.70 (*0-8357-3414-5*, 203967100013) Bks Demand.

***Metz, Steven.** Armed Conflict in the 21st Century: The Information Revolution & Post-Modern Warfare. (Illus.). 133p. 2000. pap. write for info. (*1-58487-018-4*) SSI US Army.

— Refining American Strategy in Africa. 75p. 2000. pap. write for info. (*1-58487-014-1*) SSI US Army.

Metz, Warren. Change of Face & Pace. LC 82-90982. 1983. 12.95 (*0-87212-165-8*) Libra.

Metz, William D. & Hammond, Allen L. The Science Report on Solar Energy in America. LC 78-69957. (AAAS Publication: No. 78-10). 256p. reprint ed. pap. 79.40 (*0-7837-0070-9*, 204031700016) Bks Demand.

Metzbower, Edward A., ed. Lasers in Materials Processing. LC 83-72954. (Conference Proceedings - American Society for Metals Ser.). (Illus.). 276p. reprint ed. pap. 85.60 (*0-8357-6183-5*, 203431900089) Bks Demand.

Metzbower, Edward A., ed. see American Society for Metals Staff.

Metzbower, Edward A., jt. ed. see Hauser, D.

Metzdorf, R. F. The Tinker Library. (Illus.). 556p. 1995. reprint ed. 75.00 (*1-888262-66-4*) Martino Pubng.

Metzelaar, jt. auth. see Fox.

Metzelaar, Lawrence C. & Fox. Hands-on: MS DOS, Wordperfect 5.0 (includes version 4.2), dBASE III Plus, Lotus 1-2-3, 2.2 (includes version 2.01) 2nd ed. Apt, Alan, ed. (C). 1990. pap. text 34.95 (*0-8053-4503-5*) Benjamin-Cummings.

Metzelin, Ditmar, jt. auth. see Lange-Bertalot.

Metzeltin, Ditmar. Iconographia Diatomologica Vol. 5: Annotated Diatom Micrographs: Diversity - Taxonomy - Geobotany. Lange-Bertalot, Horst, ed. (Illus.). 695p. 1998. 225.00 (*3-87429-394-7*, Pub. by Koeltz Sci Bks) Lubrecht & Cramer.

Metzen, Gerhard, tr. see Amann, Herbert.

Metzenbaum, Shelley, jt. auth. see Coltman, Edward.

Metzer, Jacob. The Divided Economy of Mandatory Palestine. LC 97-38678. (Cambridge Middle East Studies: No. 11). (Illus.). 304p. (C). 1998. text 59.95 (*0-521-46550-8*) Cambridge U Pr.

— Some Economic Aspects of Railroad Development in Tsarist Russia. Bruchey, Stuart, ed. LC 77-77180. (Dissertations in European Economic History Ser.). 1978. lib. bdg. 20.95 (*0-405-10793-5*) Ayer.

Metzer, Patty. Keeper of the Light. 378p. (Orig.). 1996. pap. 12.95 (*1-885904-09-6*) Focus Pubng.

***Metzer, Patty.** Lights of the Veil. 2001. pap. 12.99 (*1-57673-627-X*) Multnomah Pubs.

Metzgar, J. D., jt. auth. see Hawley, W. M.

Metzgar, Jack. Striking Steel: Solidarity Remembered. LC 99-36085. (Critical Perspectives on the Past Ser.). (Illus.). 320p. 2000. 69.50 (*1-56639-738-3*); pap. 22.95 (*1-56639-739-1*) Temple U Pr.

Metzger. Immunotherapy Immune-Related Disease. 500p. 1997. write for info. (*0-12-492560-X*) Acad Pr.

Metzger, Alter B., tr. see Schneersohn, Joseph I.

Metzger, Andreas. Ghirlandaio. (Masters of Italian Art Ser.). (Illus.). 140p. 1998. 19.95 (*3-8290-0248-3*, 520528) Konemann.

Metzger, Anne Reynolds, see Reynolds Metzger, Anne.

Metzger, Barbara. An Angel for the Earl. (Orig.). 1994. mass mkt. 3.99 (*0-449-22215-2*) Fawcett.

— The Christmas Carrolls. 1997. mass mkt. 4.50 (*0-449-22510-0*) Fawcett.

— An Enchanted Affair. 1996. mass mkt. 4.50 (*0-449-22353-1*, Crest) Fawcett.

— Father Christmas. 1995. mass mkt. 4.50 (*0-449-22217-9*) Fawcett.

— Lady Whilton's Wedding. 1995. mass mkt. 4.50 (*0-449-22351-5*, Crest) Fawcett.

— Lord Heartless. 1998. mass mkt. 4.99 (*0-449-00171-7*, Crest) Fawcett.

— Miss Lockharte's Letters, No. 1. 1998. mass mkt. 4.99 (*0-449-00170-9*) Fawcett.

— The Primrose Path. 1997. mass mkt. 4.50 (*0-449-22509-7*, Crest) Fawcett.

***Metzger, Barbara.** The Primrose Path. LC 98-50509. 341 p. 1999. 27.95 (*0-7862-1764-2*) Thorndike Pr.

— Saved by Scandal. (Regency Romance Ser.). 224p. 2000. mass mkt. 4.99 (*0-451-20038-1*, Sig) NAL.

Metzger, Barbara. Snowdrops & Scandalbroth. 1997. mass mkt. 4.50 (*0-449-22506-2*, Crest) Fawcett.

— Snowdrops & Scandalbroth. large type ed. LC 97-50195. 272p. 1998. pap. 21.95 (*0-7838-8421-4*, G K Hall Lrg Type) Mac Lib Ref.

— A Suspicious Affair. (Orig.). 1994. mass mkt. 3.99 (*0-449-22216-0*) Fawcett.

— A Suspicious Affair. large type ed. LC 95-9788. 299p. (Orig.). 1995. reprint ed. pap. 19.95 (*0-7838-1297-3*, G K Hall Lrg Type) Mac Lib Ref.

— Valentines: A Trio of Regency Love Stories for Sweethearts'Day. 1996. mass mkt. 4.50 (*0-449-22352-3*) Fawcett.

***Metzger, Barbara.** Worthy Wife. (Regency Romance Ser.). 2000. mass mkt. 4.99 (*0-451-19961-8*, Sig) NAL.

Metzger, Barbara, jt. auth. see Schlank, Carol H.

***Metzger, Barry, ed.** Law & Development: A Record of the Procedures of the Roundtable Meeting of Chief Justices & Ministers Held in Manila, Philippines. 71p. (C). 1999. reprint ed. pap. text 20.00 (*0-7881-8243-9*) DIANE Pub.

Metzger, Bruce. Lexical Aids for Students of New Testament Greek. 100p. 1990. pap. 12.95 (*0-567-29182-0*, Pub. by T & T Clark) Bks Intl VA.

Metzger, Bruce M. Breaking the Code: Understanding the Book of Revelation. LC 93-5954. 112p. 1993. pap. 6.95 (*0-687-42807-6*); pap., teacher ed. 5.95 (*0-687-76973-6*) Abingdon.

— Breaking the Code: Understanding the Book of Revelation: Video Set. 1993. teacher ed. 39.95 incl. VHS (*0-687-76242-1*) Abingdon.

— The Canon of the New Testament: Its Origin, Development & Significance. 336p. 1997. reprint ed. pap. text 19.95 (*0-19-826954-4*) OUP.

— The Early Versions of the New Testament. 514p. 1977. text 45.00 (*0-19-826170-5*) OUP.

— Introduction to the Apocrypha. 286p. 1977. pap. text 22.95 (*0-19-502340-4*) OUP.

— Lexical Aids for Students of New Testament Greek. 3rd ed. LC 98-17400. 112p. (C). (gr. 8 up). 1998. pap. 7.99 (*0-8010-2180-4*) Baker Bks.

— Lexical Aids for Students of New Testament Greek. 3rd ed. xi, 100p. 1969. pap. text 5.65 (*0-9644891-0-4*) Princeton Theol Sem.

— Manuscripts of the Greek Bible: An Introduction to Paleography. (Illus.). 160p. (C). 1981. text 60.00 (*0-19-502924-0*) OUP.

— The New Testament: Its Background, Growth & Content. enl. ed. 310p. 1983. 21.95 (*0-687-27914-3*) Abingdon.

— Reminiscences of an Octogenarian. LC 97-28490. 242p. 1997. 24.95 (*1-56563-264-8*) Hendrickson MA.

Metzger, Bruce M. & Coogan, Michael D., eds. The Oxford Companion to the Bible. (Illus.). 932p. (C). 1993. 60.00 (*0-19-504645-5*) OUP.

Metzger, Bruce M. & Coogan, Michael David, eds. The Oxford Companion to the Bible. (Illus.). 1998. 45.00 (*0-19-511267-9*) OUP.

— The Oxford Companion to the Bible: Window's Version. (Illus.). 1996. 45.00 (*0-19-511266-0*) OUP.

***Metzger, Bruce Manning.** Breaking the Code: Understanding the Book of Revelation. 1999. pap. 7.95 (*0-687-08999-9*) Abingdon.

Metzger, Charles R. Emerson & Greenough: Transcendental Pioneers of an American Esthetic. LC 74-139140. 153p. (C). 1971. reprint ed. lib. bdg. 65.00 (*0-8371-5756-0*, MEEG, Greenwood Pr) Greenwood.

— F. Scott Fitzgerald's Psychiatric Novel: Nicole's Case, Dick's Case. (American University Studies: American Literature: Ser. XXIV, Vol. 13). XIV, 387p. (C). 1989. text 50.80 (*0-8204-1040-3*) P Lang Pubng.

— The Silent River: A Pastoral Elegy in the Form of a Recollection of Arctic Adventure. (Illus.). xi, 161p. (Orig.). 1984. pap. 7.95 (*0-9613094-0-7*) Omega LA.

Metzger, Christine. Germany. (Culineria Ser.). (Illus.). 460p. 2000. 39.95 (*3-89508-906-0*) Konemann.

Metzger-Court, Sarah & Pascha, Werner, eds. Japan's Socio-Economic Evolution: Continuity & Change. (Japan Library). 288p. (C). 1996. text 45.00 (*1-873410-39-5*, Pub. by Curzon Pr Ltd) UH Pr.

Metzger, D. E. & Crawford, M. E., eds. Fundamental & Applied Heat Transfer Research for Gas Turbines Engines. (HTD Ser.: Vol. 226). 96p. 1992. 30.00 (*0-7918-1071-2*, G00715) ASME.

Metzger, Daniel L. Electronic Circuit Behavior. 2nd ed. (Illus.). 400p. (C). 1983. student ed. 24.00 (*0-13-250191-0*) P-H.

— Electronics for Your Future. (Illus.). (C). 1994. pap. text 33.00 (*0-9639471-0-9*) Tech Trning.

Metzger, Daniel L. & Goodwin, Bernard. Electronic Pocket Handbook. 3rd ed. 352p. (C). 1998. pap. text 19.95 (*0-13-784190-6*) P-H.

Metzger, David. The Lost Cause of Rhetoric: The Relation of Rhetoric & Geometry in Aristotle & Lacan. LC 93-38231. 135p. (C). 1994. 31.95 (*0-8093-1855-5*) S Ill U Pr.

Metzger, Deborah A., et al. An Interested Approach to the Management of Chronic Pelvic Pain. LC 96-71489. 52p. (Orig.). 1996. pap. text 30.00 (*1-890076-00-7*, 96-001) Pharmedica Pr.

Metzger, Deena. Looking for the Faces of God. LC 89-23139. 96p. (Orig.). 1989. pap. 8.00 (*0-938077-23-6*) Parallax Pr.

— Sabbath among the Ruins: New Poems. 120p. 1992. pap. 10.00 (*0-938077-53-8*) Parallax Pr.

— Tree: Essays & Pieces. 3rd ed. LC 96-50153. 250p. (Orig.). 1997. pap. 15.95 (*1-55643-245-3*) North Atlantic.

— What Dinah Thought. 1999. pap. 7.95 (*0-14-012054-8*) Viking Penguin.

— Writing for Your Life: A Guide & Companion to the Inner Worlds. LC 91-55323. 272p. 1992. pap. 16.00 (*0-06-250612-9*, Pub. by Harper SF) HarpC.

Metzger, Edward C. Ralph, First Duke of Montagu, 1638-1709. LC 86-23797. (Studies in British History: Vol. 2). 450p. 1986. 109.95 (*0-88946-452-9*) E Mellen.

Metzger, Erika & Metzger, Mic. Reading Andreas Gryphius: Critical Trends, 1664-1993. LC 94-30027. (LCGERM Ser.). xii, 156p. 1994. 55.00 (*1-57113-005-5*) Camden Hse.

Metzger, Ernest. A New Outline of the Roman Civil Trial. 184p. 1998. text 87.00 (*0-19-826474-7*) OUP.

Metzger, Ernest, ed. A Companion to Justinian's "Institutes" LC 98-28017. 224p. 1998. 60.00 (*0-8014-3619-2*); pap. 25.00 (*0-8014-8584-3*) Cornell U Pr.

Metzger, G., tr. see Franke, H. W.

Metzger, Gustav. Damaged Nature, Auto Destructive Art. (Illus.). 111p. 1998. pap. 12.95 (*0-906630-05-3*, Pub. by Coracle Pr) Dist Art Pubs.

Metzger, Helene. Chemistry. Michael, Colette V., tr. from FRE. LC 91-16970. (Women in the Sciences Ser.: Vol. 1). 151p. (C). 1991. lib. bdg. 6.00 (0-933951-38-8) Locust Hill Pr.

Metzger, Henry, ed. FC Receptors & the Action of Antibodies. (Illus.). 368p. 1990. 49.00 (1-55581-016-0) ASM Pr.

Metzger, Jane, jt. ed. see Drazen, Erica.

Metzger, Jon. The Art & Language of Jazz Vibes. 366p. 1996. pap. 40.00 (0-939009-94-3) EPM Pubns.

***Metzger, Jordan S.** Lightning Fast Enlightenment: A Journey to the Secrets of Happiness. LC 98-91635. xii, 430p. 2000. pap. 18.95 (0-9665922-6-3) Profound Pr.

***Metzger, Joyce.** Nordland Haiku Revisited. (Illus.). 104p. 1999. pap. 8.95 (1-878116-95-9) JVC Bks.

— Once upon a Tourniquet: September in Europe. 88p. 1998. pap. 8.95 (1-878116-85-1) JVC Bks.

— Sudland Haiku. (Illus.). 104p. 1999. pap. 8.95 (1-878116-94-0) JVC Bks.

Metzger, Joyce, jt. auth. see Metzger, Wendell.

Metzger, Joyce, ed. see Locklin, Gerald.

Metzger, Joyce, ed. see Metzger, Wendell.

Metzger, Joyce, ed. see Phillips, Walt.

Metzger, Joyce, ed. see Silverman, Herschel.

Metzger, Joyce, ed. see Splake, T. K.

Metzger, Joyce, ed. see Winans, A. D.

Metzger, Joyce, ed. & photos by see Metzger, Wendell.

Metzger, Larry, jt. auth. see Page, Mary S.

Metzger, Linda, ed. Contemporary Authors. (New Revision Ser.: Vol. 18). 500p. 1986. text 150.00 (0-8103-1947-0) Gale.

— Contemporary Authors, Vol. 14. LC 81-640179. (New Revision Ser.). 500p. 1985. text 150.00 (0-8103-1943-8) Gale.

— Contemporary Authors, Vol. 15. LC 81-640179. (New Revision Ser.). 500p. 1985. text 150.00 (0-8103-1944-6) Gale.

Metzger, Linda & Ryan, Alan. Hispanic Writers: Sketches from CA. 2nd ed. 500p. 1999. 98.00 (0-8103-8377-2) Gale.

Metzger, Linda & Straub, Deborah A. Contemporary Authors, Vol. 16. rev. ed. LC 81-640179. (New Revision Ser.). 500p. 1985. text 150.00 (0-8103-1945-4) Gale.

Metzger, Linda & Straub, Deborah A., eds. Contemporary Authors. (New Revision Ser.: Vol. 19). 500p. 1986. text 150.00 (0-8103-1948-9) Gale.

— Contemporary Authors. (New Revision Ser.: Vol. 20). 500p. 1987. text 150.00 (0-8103-1949-7) Gale.

— Contemporary Authors. (New Revision Ser.: Vol. 21). 500p. 1987. text 150.00 (0-8103-1975-6) Gale.

— Contemporary Authors, Vol. 17. rev. ed. (New Revision Ser.). 500p. 1986. text 150.00 (0-8103-1946-2) Gale.

Metzger, Lois. Barry's Sister. LC 91-23738. 240p. (YA). (gr. 5 up). 1992. 15.95 (0-689-31521-X) Atheneum Yung Read.

— Ellen's Case. LC 95-2707. 208p. (YA). (gr. 5-9). 1995. 16.00 (0-689-31934-7) Atheneum Yung Read.

— Missing Girls. LC 98-18817. 208p. (YA). (gr. 5-9). 1999. 15.99 (0-670-87777-8) Viking Penguin.

Metzger, Marcel. History of the Liturgy: The Major Stages. Beaumont, Madeleine, tr. from FRE. LC 96-51700. 160p. 1997. pap. 16.95 (0-8146-2433-2) Liturgical Pr.

Metzger, Mary & Whittaker, Cinthya P. This Planet Is Mine: Teaching Environmental Awareness & Appreciation to Children. 256p. (Orig.). 1991. 17.00 (0-671-74817-3, Fireside) S&S Trade Pap.

Metzger, Melanie. Sign Language Interpreting: Deconstructing the Myth of Neutrality. 216p. 1998. 58.00 (1-56368-074-2) Gallaudet Univ Pr.

***Metzger, Melanie, ed.** Bilingualism & Identity in Deaf Communities. 2000. 55.00 (1-56368-095-5) Gallaudet Univ Pr.

Metzger, Melanie, jt. auth. see Bridges, Byron.

Metzger, Mic, jt. auth. see Metzger, Erika.

Metzger, Michael, et al. The Regional Welfare Effects of U. S. Import Restraints on Apparel, Petroleum, Steel & Textiles. LC 96-84411. 173p. 1996. 58.95 (1-85972-317-9, Pub. by Avebry) Ashgate Pub Co.

Metzger, Michael B., et al. Business Law & The Regulatory Environment. 9th ed. 250p. (C). 1994. text, student ed. 26.87 (0-256-14104-5, Irwn McGrw-H) McGrw-H Hghr Educ.

— Business Law & the Regulatory Environment: Concepts & Cases. 9th ed. LC 94-12503. (Irwin Legal Studies in Business Ser.). 1408p. (C). 1994. text 74.95 (0-256-14103-7, Irwn McGrw-H) McGrw-H Hghr Educ.

— Business Law & the Regulatory Environment: Concepts & Cases. 9th ed. LC 94-12503. (Legal Studies in Business). 1995. pap. write for info. (0-256-17191-2, Irwn McGrw-H) McGrw-H Hghr Educ.

Metzger, Michael M., ed. Fairy Tales as Ways of Knowing. (Germanic Studies in America Ser.: Vol. 41). 200p. 1981. pap. 14.00 (3-261-04883-2) P Lang Pubng.

Metzger, Nancy. Harpsichord Technique: A Guide to Expressivity. 2nd rev. ed. LC 97-76294. (Illus.). 112p. (Orig.). (C). 1998. pap. text 22.00 (0-9624934-1-4) Musica Dulce.

Metzger, Norman. The Health Care Supervisor's Handbook. 3rd ed. 272p. (C). 1988. 57.00 (0-87189-757-1) Aspen Pub.

Metzger, Norman, ed. Handbook of Health Care Human Resources Management. 2nd ed. 588p. 1990. 159.00 (0-8342-0094-5) Aspen Pub.

Metzger, Norman, jt. auth. see Bassett, Lawrence.

Metzger, Phil. The North Light Artist's Guide to Materials & Techniques. (Illus.). 192p. 1996. 29.99 (0-89134-675-9, North Lght Bks) F & W Pubns Inc.

— Perspective Without Pain. (Illus.). 144p. 1992. pap. 19.99 (0-89134-446-2, 30386, North Lght Bks) F & W Pubns Inc.

— Watercolor Basics: Perspective Secrets. LC 98-38014. (Warercolor Basics Ser.). (Illus.). 128p. 1999. pap. 18.99 (0-89134-880-8, North Lght Bks) F & W Pubns Inc.

Metzger, Philip W. Managing Programming People: A Personal View. (Illus.). 160p. write for info. (0-318-61856-7) P-H.

Metzger, Philip W. & Boddie, John. Managing a Programming Project: Process & People. 3rd ed. LC 95-44040. 400p. (C). 1995. 58.00 (0-13-554239-1) P-H.

Metzger, Philip W., jt. auth. see Brown, Michael D.

Metzger, R. Van Gogh. (SPA.). 1996. pap. 19.99 (3-8228-8849-4) Taschen Amer.

— Van Gogh. (Big Art Ser.). 1998. 19.99 (3-8228-7225-3) Taschen Amer.

***Metzger, R. & Walther, I. F.** Van Gogh. 1999. 19.99 (3-8228-7372-1) Taschen Amer.

Metzger, R. M., ed. Crystal Cohesion & Conformal Energies. (Topics in Current Physics Ser.: Vol. 26). (Illus.). 160p. 1981. 40.95 (0-387-10520-4) Spr-Verlag.

Metzger, R. M., et al, eds. Lower-Dimensional Systems & Molecular Electronics. (NATO ASI Ser.: Vol. 248). (Illus.). 756p. (C). 1990. text 198.00 (0-306-43826-7, Kluwer Plenum) Kluwer Academic.

Metzger, R. S. A Master of the Century Past. LC 93-37721. 288p. 1996. 17.95 (0-913720-87-9) Beil.

Metzger, Rainell M., ed. see Metzger, Thomas F.

Metzger, Rainer. Van Gogh. (Big Art Ser.). (Illus.). 1996. pap. text 19.99 (3-8228-8905-9) Taschen Amer.

***Metzger, Robert & Wen, Zhaofang.** Automatic Algorithm Recognition & Replacement. LC 99-88044. (Illus.). 233p. 2000. 40.00 (0-262-13368-7) MIT Pr.

Metzger, Robert M., ed. High Temperature Superconductivity: The First Two Years. (International Conference Ser., Tuscaloosa, Alabama, 11-13 April 1988). xxviii, 434p. 1989. text 137.00 (2-88124-299-5) Gordon & Breach.

Metzger, Robert O. Developing a Consulting Practice. (Survival Skills for Scholars Ser.: Vol. 3). (Illus.). 108p. (C). 1993. text 37.00 (0-8039-5046-2); pap. text 16.50 (0-8039-5047-0) Sage.

— Profitable Consulting: Helping American Managers Face the Future. 144p. 1988. 17.26 (0-201-09539-4) Addison-Wesley.

Metzger, Robert O., jt. auth. see Greiner, Larry E.

Metzger, Robert P. Reagan: American Icon. LC 89-60966. (Illus.). 144p. 1989. pap. 34.95 (0-8122-1302-5) U of Pa Pr.

Metzger, Robert P., ed. Transforming Texts: Classical Images in New Contexts. LC 91-58592. 1993. 24.50 (0-8387-5216-0) Bucknell U Pr.

Metzger, Stephen. Moon Handbooks: Colorado: Including Denver, Aspen, Mesa Verde & Rocky Mountain National Parks. 4th rev. ed. Vol. 4. (Illus.). 480p. 1999. pap. 17.95 (1-56691-145-1, Moon Handbks) Avalon Travel.

— Moon Handbooks: Santa Fe-Taos: Including Albuquerque. (Illus.). 180p. 1998. pap. 13.95 (1-56691-135-4, Moon Handbks) Avalon Travel.

***Metzger, Stephen.** Shifra Stein's Day Trips from Sacramento: Getaways Less Than Two Hours Away. (Shifra Stein's Day Trips Ser.). (Illus.). 256p. 2000. pap. 14.95 (0-7627-0717-8) Globe Pequot.

Metzger, Steve. I'm Having a Bad Day! LC 98-9301. (Dinofours Ser.). (Illus.). 32p. (J). (ps-1). 1998. 3.25 (0-590-03551-7) Scholastic Inc.

— I'm Not Your Friend! LC 95-49948. (Dinofours Ser.). (Illus.). 32p. (J). (ps-1). 1997. 2.99 (0-590-68991-6) Scholastic Inc.

***Metzger, Steve.** I'm So Grumpy! LC 99-89554. (Dinofours Ser.). (Illus.). (J). (ps-1). 2000. pap. write for info. (0-439-17959-9) Scholastic Inc.

Metzger, Steve. I'm Super Dino! LC 95-53228. (Dinofours Ser.). (Illus.). 32p. (J). (ps-1). 1997. 2.99 (0-590-68992-4) Scholastic Inc.

— I'm the Boss! LC 97-7315. (Dinofours Ser.). (Illus.). 32p. (J). (ps-1). 1998. pap. 2.99 (0-590-37458-3, Pub. by Scholastic Inc) Penguin Putnam.

***Metzger, Steve.** I'm the Winner! LC 99-10705. (Dinofours Ser.). (Illus.). (J). (ps-1). 1999. 3.25 (0-439-06327-2) Scholastic Inc.

Metzger, Steve. It's Apple Picking Day! LC 97-50574. (Dinofours Ser.). (Illus.). (J). (ps-1). 1998. 3.25 (0-590-03549-5) Scholastic Inc.

— It's Beach Day! LC 97-43277. (Dinofours Ser.). (Illus.). 32p. (J). (ps-1). 1998. 3.25 (0-590-03267-4) Scholastic Inc.

— It's Class Trip Day! LC 95-53229. (Dinofours Ser.). (Illus.). 32p. (J). (ps-1). 1997. 2.99 (0-590-68993-2) Scholastic Inc.

***Metzger, Steve.** It's Fall! LC 99-89563. (Dinofours Ser.). (Illus.). (J). (ps-1). 2000. pap. write for info. (0-439-17958-0) Scholastic Inc.

Metzger, Steve. It's Fire Drill Day! LC 97-7316. (Dinofours Ser.). (Illus.). 32p. (J). (ps-1). 1997. pap. 2.99 (0-590-37455-9, Pub. by Scholastic Inc) Penguin Putnam.

— It's Halloween! LC 98-47467. (Dinofours Ser.). (Illus.). (J). (ps-1). 1999. write for info. (0-439-06326-4) Scholastic Inc.

— It's Snowing. LC 98-9300. (Dinofours Ser.). (Illus.). (J). (ps-1). 1998. 3.25 (0-590-03550-9) Scholastic Inc.

— It's Time for School! LC 95-49949. (Dinofours Ser.). (Illus.). 32p. (J). (ps-1). 1997. 2.99 (0-590-68990-8) Scholastic Inc.

— It's Time-Out Time! LC 97-9117. (Dinofours Ser.). (Illus.). (J). (ps-1). 1998. 3.25 (0-590-37457-5) Scholastic Inc.

***Metzger, Steve.** It's Valentine's Day! LC 00-35813. (Dinofours Ser.). (Illus.). (J). (ps-1). 2001. pap. write for info. (0-439-17960-2) Scholastic Inc.

Metzger, Steve. Ladybug's Birthday. LC 97-48303. (Side-by-Side Ser.). (Illus.). (J). 1997. write for info. (0-590-10968-5); pap. 3.50 (0-590-02599-6) Scholastic Inc.

***Metzger, Steve.** Moon Handbooks: New Mexico: Santa Fe, Taos, Roswell & the Rio Grande. 5th rev. ed. (Illus.). 370p. 2000. pap. 15.95 (1-56691-203-2, Moon Handbks) Avalon Travel.

— No Girls Allowed! LC 99-10189. (Dinofours Ser.). (Illus.). (J). (ps-1). 2000. 20.01 (0-439-06328-0) Scholastic Inc.

Metzger, Steve. Where's Mommy? LC 97-9118. (Dinofours Ser.). (Illus.). (J). (ps-1). 1997. 3.25 (0-590-37456-7) Scholastic Inc.

***Metzger, Steve & Wilhelm, Hans.** Dinofours, We Love Bugs! LC 00-26576. (Dinofours Ser.). (Illus.). (J). 2001. pap. write for info. (0-439-17961-0) Scholastic Inc.

***Metzger, Sue McFarland & Roehrs, Susanne.** SAP R/3 Change & Transport Management: The Official SAP Guide. 496p. 2000. 49.95 incl. cd-rom (0-7821-2564-6) Sybex.

Metzger, T. Blood & Volts: Edison, Tesla, & the Electric Chair. (Illus.). 192p. 1996. pap. 12.00 (1-57027-060-0) Autonomedia.

Metzger, Thom. This Is Your Final Warning! 181p. Date not set. 7.00 (0-936756-88-8) Autonomedia.

Metzger, Thomas. Did Big Brother Give You Permission to Go Wee-Wee? LC 95-25313. (Illus.). 160p. (Orig.). 1995. pap. 12.95 (0-931892-98-8) B Dolphin Pub.

Metzger, Thomas A. Escape from Predicament: Neo-Confucianism & China's Evolving Political Culture. LC 76-25445. 303p. 1986. pap. text 20.00 (0-231-03980-8) Col U Pr.

— The Internal Organization of Ching Bureaucracy: Legal, Normative, & Communication Aspects. LC 72-96632. (Harvard Studies in East Asian Law: No. 7). 480p. reprint ed. pap. 148.80 (0-7837-2301-6, 205738900004) Bks Demand.

— "Transcending the West" Mao's Vision of Socialism & the Legitimization of Teng Hsiao-Ping's Modernization Program. LC 96-7880. (Hoover Essays Ser.: No. 15). 1996. pap. 5.00 (0-8179-3782-X) Hoover Inst Pr.

— The Unification of China & the Problem of Public Opinion in the Republic of China in Taiwan. LC 92-10214. (Essays in Public Policy Ser.: No. 32). 1992. pap. text 5.00 (0-8179-5372-8) Hoover Inst Pr.

— The Western Concept of a Civil Society in the Context of Chinese History. LC 97-49489. (Hoover Essays Ser.: No. 21). 1998. pap. 5.00 (0-8179-3842-7) Hoover Inst Pr.

Metzger, Thomas A., jt. ed. see Myers, Ramon H.

Metzger, Thomas F. Becoming a Political Pain in the Ass: How to Change Your Government Sensibly. LC 95-25300. (Illus.). 176p. (Orig.). 1995. pap. 12.95 (0-931892-99-6) B Dolphin Pub.

— Did Big Brother Give You Permission to Go Wee Wee? rev. ed. Metzger, Rainell M., ed. (Illus.). 144p. 1994. pap. 12.95 (0-9641789-0-7) Metzger Ent.

Metzger, W. James, jt. ed. see Page, Clive P.

Metzger, Walter P. Academic Freedom in the Age of the University. LC 61-2328. 232p. 1961. pap. text 20.00 (0-231-08512-5) Col U Pr.

Metzger, Walter P., ed. The Academic Profession Series, 40 vols., Set. (Illus.). 1977. reprint ed. lib. bdg. 1259.00 (0-405-10000-0) Ayer.

— The American Concept of Academic Freedom Information: A Collection of Essays & Reports-an Original Anthology. LC 76-55209. (Academic Profession Ser.). (Illus.). 1979. reprint ed. lib. bdg. 34.95 (0-405-10037-X) Ayer.

— The Constitutional Status of Academic Freedom. LC 76-55211. (Academic Profession Ser.). 1978. reprint ed. lib. bdg. 51.95 (0-405-10038-8) Ayer.

— The Constitutional Status of Academic Tenure: An Original Anthology. LC 76-52627. (Academic Profession Ser.). 1979. reprint ed. lib. bdg. 34.95 (0-405-09982-7) Ayer.

— Professors on Guard: The First AAUP Investigations. LC 76-55213. (Academic Profession Ser.). 1977. lib. bdg. 29.95 (0-405-10040-X) Ayer.

— Reader on the Sociology of the Academic Profession. LC 76-55212. (Academic Profession Ser.). 1979. reprint ed. lib. bdg. 56.95 (0-405-10039-6) Ayer.

Metzger, Walter P. & Reece, J. McGee. The Academic Marketplace. Caplow, Theodore & Barzun, Jacques, eds. LC 76-55171. (Academic Profession Ser.). (Illus.). 1977. reprint ed. lib. bdg. 26.95 (0-405-10002-7) Ayer.

Metzger, Walter P., jt. auth. see Yeomans, Henry A.

Metzger, Walter P., ed. see Annan, Noel G.

Metzger, Walter P., ed. see Berdahl, Robert O.

Metzger, Walter P., ed. see Bleuel, Hans P.

Metzger, Walter P., ed. see Bowman, Claude C.

Metzger, Walter P., ed. see Busch, Alexander.

Metzger, Walter P., ed. see Carnegie Foundation for the Advancement of Teachin.

Metzger, Walter P., ed. see Cattell, J. McKeen.

Metzger, Walter P., ed. see Cheyney, Edward P.

Metzger, Walter P., ed. see Elliott, Orrin L.

Metzger, Walter P., ed. see Ely, Richard T.

Metzger, Walter P., ed. see Flach, Johannes.

Metzger, Walter P., ed. see Hall, G. Stanley.

Metzger, Walter P., ed. see Hardy, Godfrey H.

Metzger, Walter P., ed. see Kluge, Alexander.

Metzger, Walter P., ed. see Kotsching, Walter M.

Metzger, Walter P., ed. see Lazarsfeld, Paul F. & Thielens, Wagner P., Jr.

Metzger, Walter P., ed. see McLaughlin, Mary M.

Metzger, Walter P., ed. see Mims, Edwin.

Metzger, Walter P., ed. see Mitsch, Wolfgang, et al.

Metzger, Walter P., ed. see Neumann, Franz L., et al.

Metzger, Walter P., ed. see Pattison, Mark.

Metzger, Walter P., ed. see Pollard, Lucille A.

Metzger, Walter P., ed. see Proctor, Mortimer R.

Metzger, Walter P., ed. see Quincy, Joseph.

Metzger, Walter P., ed. see Ross, Edward A.

Metzger, Walter P., ed. see Rudy, S. Willis.

Metzger, Walter P., ed. see Slosson, Edwin E.

Metzger, Walter P., ed. see Smith, Goldwin A.

Metzger, Walter P., ed. see Wiley, Malcolm W.

Metzger, Walter P., ed. see Winstanley, D. A.

Metzger, Wendell. Ain't Nobody Here but Us Typewriters. 48p. (Orig.). 1993. 4.95 (1-878116-29-0) JVC Bks.

***Metzger, Wendell.** Bone Slept Here: Arcadia Perfecto! Metzger, Joyce, ed. & photos by by. 96p. 1999. pap. 8.95 (1-878116-83-5) JVC Bks.

Metzger, Wendell. He & She. 60p. (Orig.). 1994. 5.95 (1-878116-23-1) JVC Bks.

— Hospital & Legalities: Two Plays. Carbone, Joyce, ed. (Illus.). 68p. (Orig.). 1995. pap. 6.95 (1-878116-49-5) JVC Bks.

***Metzger, Wendell.** Just for You. 1998. pap. 8.95 (1-878116-84-3) JVC Bks.

— Poeseys Forever. Carbone, Joyce, ed. 94p. 1997. pap. 6.95 (1-878116-73-8) JVC Bks.

Metzger, Wendell. Poeseys Only. Carbone, Joyce, ed. (Illus.). 52p. (Orig.). 1997. pap. 5.95 (1-878116-66-5) JVC Bks.

Metzger, Wendell. Poeseys Then but Mostly Now II. Carbone, Joyce, ed. 56p. 1997. pap. 5.95 (1-878116-80-0) JVC Bks.

— Seattle Style. Metzger, Joyce, ed. 64p. 1998. pap. 4.95 (1-878116-11-8) JVC Bks.

Metzger, Wendell. Troping the Triad. (Illus.). 60p. (Orig.). 1994. 5.95 (1-878116-24-X) JVC Bks.

— Two Plays. Carbone, Joyce, ed. (Illus.). 44p. (Orig.). 1995. pap. 4.95 (1-878116-44-4) JVC Bks.

— Two Travel Stories. Carbone, Joyce, ed. 48p. (Orig.). 1995. pap. 4.95 (1-878116-47-9) JVC Bks.

***Metzger, Wendell.** Vowels & Consonants. Metzger, Joyce, ed. 94p. 1999. pap. 8.95 (1-878116-98-3) JVC Bks.

— Whiskers. Metzger, Joyce, ed. & photos by by. 96p. 1999. pap. 8.95 (1-878116-96-7) JVC Bks.

Metzger, Wendell & Carbone, Joyce. Expose Numero Uno: Flanked by Small Press Hades. 52p. 1997. pap. 4.95 (1-878116-81-9) JVC Bks.

***Metzger, Wendell & Metzger, Joyce.** Easy Street. 64p. 1998. pap. 4.95 (1-878116-70-3) JVC Bks.

Metzger, Wendy. Problem Solving, Modeling, & Data Analysis Labs. 2nd ed. (C). 1997. pap. text 22.76 (0-669-41673-8) HM Trade Div.

Metzger, Will. Tell the Truth. 2nd ed. LC 83-25304. 191p. (Orig.). 1984. pap. 11.99 (0-87784-934-X, 934) InterVarsity.

Metzi, Francisco. The People's Remedy: The Struggle for Health Care in El Salvador's War of Liberation. Carroll, Jean, tr. from SPA. 224p. (C). 1988. pap. 10.00 (0-85345-775-1, Pub. by Monthly Rev) NYU Pr.

Metzidakis, Stamos. Repetition & Semiotics: Interpreting Prose Poems. LC 86-60801. 175p. 1986. 21.95 (0-917786-41-6) Summa Pubns.

Metzidakis, Stamos, ed. Understanding French Poetry: Essays for a New Millennium. LC 93-50527. (Illus.). 304p. 1994. text 15.00 (0-8153-0841-8, H1596) Garland.

Metzing, Dieter, ed. Frame Conceptions & Text Understanding. (Research in Text Theory Ser.: No. 5). 167p. (C). 1980. text 54.65 (3-11-008006-0) De Gruyter.

Metzinger, Sylvia V., compiled by. The Favrot Collection: A Catalogue of the Printed Material in the Howard-Tilton Memorial Library. 1978. pap. 4.00 (0-9603212-1-7) Tulane Univ.

***Metzinger, Thomas.** Neural Correlates of Consciousness: Empirical & Conceptual Questions. LC 99-87947. (Illus.). 367p. 2000. 50.00 (0-262-13370-9, Bradford Bks) MIT Pr.

Metzinger, Thomas, ed. Conscious Experience. 264p. 1995. 32.00 (0-907845-10-X, Pub. by Imprint Acad); pap. 16.00 (0-907845-05-3, Pub. by Imprint Acad) Philos Document.

Metzker, Issac. A Bintel Brief. 1990. pap. 12.00 (0-8052-0980-8) Schocken.

Metzker, Mary. Mary Metzker's Cooking Plain & Fancy. AmBroc, Charles, ed. (Illus.). 100p. (Orig.). 1988. pap. 8.95 (0-317-91230-5) Jam Prodns PA.

***Metzker, Ray K.** Landscapes. (Illus.). 168p. 2000. 50.00 (0-89381-911-5) Aperture.

Metzker, Ray K. Sand Creatures. (Illus.). 56p. 1979. pap. 14.95 (0-89381-051-7) Aperture.

Metzl, Jamie Frederic. Western Responses to Human Rights Abuses in Cambodia, 1975-80. 256p. 1996. text 65.00 (0-312-12849-5) St Martin.

Metzler. Appleton & Lange's Practice Test - Surgery. 2nd ed. (C). 1998. pap. text 19.95 (0-8385-0361-6) Appleton & Lange.

***Metzler.** 2000 Ways How to Build a Million Dollar Technology Consulting Practice. 320p. 1999. pap. text 119.00 (0-15-606303-4) Harcourt.

Metzler & Sebolt. Racquetball. 2nd ed. 160p. 1998. spiral bd. 33.95 (0-7872-4606-9, 41460601) Kendall-Hunt.

Metzler Baker, Joyce. Not by Might, nor by Power. LC 89-27002. (Illus.). 233p. 1990. pap. text 9.99 (0-87227-135-8, RBP5164) Reg Baptist.

***Metzler, David E.** Biochemistry. 2nd ed. 1250p. 1999. 79.95 (0-12-492540-5) Acad Pr.

Metzler, Eric H. Annotated Checklist & Distribution Maps of the Royal Moths & Giant Silkworm Moths (Lepidoptera: Saturniidae) in Ohio. (Biological Notes Ser.). 1980. pap. text 3.00 (0-86727-088-8) Ohio Bio Survey.

Metzler, Howard C., jt. auth. see Fink, Norman S.

Metzler, Jack. Picacho Gold. Eaton, Gillian, ed. 336p. (Orig.). (YA). 1995. pap. 8.95 (1-888445-00-9) Sonstar Pubns.

— Tachechana. (Serenade Super Saga Ser.: No. 2). 252p. 1986. pap. 6.95 (0-310-47511-2, 15597P) Zondervan.

Metzler, James A. Layer 3 Switching: A Guide for IT Professionals. LC 99-199263. 280p. 1998. 58.00 (0-13-919838-5) P-H.

***Metzler, James C.** How to Build a Million Dollar Technology Consulting Practice with CD-ROM. 320p. 2000. pap. 129.00 incl. cd-rom (0-15-607221-1) Harcourt Prof.

Metzler, John J. Divided Dynamism: The Diplomacy of Separated Nations: Germany, Korea, China. 240p. 1996. pap. 24.50 (0-7618-0625-3) U Pr of Amer.

— Divided Dynamism: The Diplomacy of Separated Nations: Germany, Korea, China. LC 95-49760. (Germany, Korea, China). 240p. (C). 1996. lib. bdg. 52.50 (0-7618-0235-5) U Pr of Amer.

Metzler, Ken. Creative Interviewing: The Writer's Guide to Gathering Information by Asking Questions. 3rd ed. LC 96-12079. 238p. 1996. pap. text 36.00 (0-205-26258-9) Allyn.

— Newswriting. 2nd ed. (Illus.). 208p. (C). 1987. pap. text 38.20 (0-13-611641-8) P-H.

Metzler, Kenneth J. & Tiner, Ralph W. Wetlands of Connecticut. (Report of Investigations Ser.: No. 13). (Illus.). 113p. (Orig.). 1992. pap. text 14.95 (0-942081-03-X) CT DEP CGNHS.

Metzler, Kenneth T., et al. Yesterday's Adventure: A Photographic History of Lane County, Oregon. LC 99-158254. (Lane County Histories Ser.: No. 1). (Illus.). 128p. 1998. 27.95 (0-9648434-2-0); pap. 17.95 (0-9648434-1-2) Lane Cnty Hist.

Metzler, Lloyd A. Collected Papers. LC 79-184108. (Economic Studies: No. 140). (Illus.). 614p. 1973. 35.00 (0-674-13775-2) HUP.

Metzler, Lloyd A. & Haberler, Gottfried. International Monetary Policies. Wilkins, Mira, ed. LC 78-3938. (International Finance Ser.). 1979. reprint ed. lib. bdg. 17.95 (0-405-11239-4) Ayer.

Metzler, Michael. Medical Examination Review: Surgery (MEPC) 11th ed. 317p. (C). 1996. pap. text 21.95 (0-8385-6195-0, A6195-0, Apple Lange Med) McGraw.

Metzler, Michael & Sebolt, Don. The Interactive Learning Approach: Student Personal Workbook for Golf. (The Personalized Sport Instruction Ser.). 144p. (C). 1994. pap. text, spiral bd. 15.95 (0-8403-9948-0, 40994801) Kendall-Hunt.

— The Interactive Learning Approach: Student Personal Workbook for Racquetball. (The Personalized Sport Instruction Ser.). 176p. (C). 1994. spiral bd. 14.95 (0-8403-9954-5) Kendall-Hunt.

— The Interactive Learning Approach: Student Personal Workbook for Tennis. (The Personalized Sport Instruction Ser.). 144p. (C). 1994. pap. text, spiral bd. 17.95 (0-8403-9949-9, 40994901) Kendall-Hunt.

Metzler, Michael, et al. Volleyball. (Personalized Sport Instructional Ser.). 144p. (C). 1996. pap. text, ring bd. 23.95 (0-7872-2675-0, 41267501) Kendall-Hunt.

Metzler, Michael W. Instructional Models for Physical Education. LC 99-36589. 388p. (C). 1999. pap. text 45.00 (0-205-26418-2, Macmillan Coll) P-H.

— Instructional Supervision for Physical Education. LC 89-7461. (Illus.). 272p. 1990. text 24.00 (0-87322-254-7, BMET0254) Human Kinetics.

Metzler, R. J., jt. auth. see Woldman, N. E.

Metzler, Rosemary. Snooty the Fox & the Mysterious Black Box. large type ed. LC 98-67721. (Illus.). 84p. (YA). (gr. 3 up). 1998. pap. 10.95 (0-88100-106-6) Natl Writ Pr.

Metzler, Rosemary M. Snooty the Fox. 28p. (J). 1993. pap. write for info. (0-9637381-0-0) Snooty Prods.

— Snooty the Fox Meets Dead-Eye Dick. (Illus.). 48p. (J). (gr. 3-4). 1995. lib. bdg. 6.95 (0-9637381-1-9) Snooty Prods.

Metzler, Susan & Metzler, Van. Texas Mushrooms: A Field Guide. LC 91-2239. (Corrie Herring Hooks Ser.: No. 18). (Illus.). 358p. 1992. 39.95 (0-292-75125-7); pap. 19.95 (0-292-75126-5) U of Tex Pr.

Metzler, Van, jt. auth. see Metzler, Susan.

Metzloff, Thomas B., ed. Professional Responsibility: Anthology. LC 94-15848. 267p. 1994. pap. 29.95 (0-87084-573-X) Anderson Pub Co.

Metzloff, Thomas B., jt. auth. see Patterson, L. Ray.

***Metzman, Fran & Stocke, Joy E.** Ugly Cookies. 304p. 2000. pap. 14.95 (0-918618-77-0) Pella Pub.

Metzner, Clifton G., Jr., ed. Water Quality Issues of the California-Baja California Border Region. (Border Issue Ser.). 84p. 1989. 10.00 (0-925613-02-9) SDSU Inst Reg Studies.

Metzner, Edward P. More Than a Soldier's War: Pacification in Vietnam. LC 95-18482. (Texas A&M University Military History Ser.: No. 47). (Illus.). 224p. (C). 1995. 29.95 (0-89096-666-4) Tex A&M Univ Pr.

Metzner, H. Die Ascorbinsaeure in der Pflanzenzelle. (Protoplasmatologia Ser.: Vol. 2B, Pt. 2b). (ENG & GER., Illus.). iv, 159p. 1957. 44.30 (0-387-80453-6) Spr-Verlag.

Metzner, Joan. A Personal Psalm Journal. LC 97-60533. 120p. 1998. pap. 9.95 (0-89622-733-2) Twenty-Third.

Metzner, John J. Reliable Data Communication. LC 97-35787. (Telecommunications Ser.). (Illus.). 350p. 1997. text 85.00 (0-12-491740-2) Morgan Kaufmann.

Metzner, P. & Thuillier, A., eds. Sulphur Reagents in Organic Synthesis. (Best Synthetic Methods Ser.). (Illus.). 224p. 1994. text 79.00 (0-12-690770-6) Acad Pr.

Metzner, Paul. Crescendo of the Virtuoso: Spectacle, Skill, & Self-Promotion in Paris During the Age of Revolution. LC 97-43167. (Studies on the History of Society & Culture). 371p. 1998. 50.00 (0-520-20684-3, Pub. by U CA Pr) Cal Prin Full Svc.

Metzner, Ralph. Green Psychology: Cultivating a Spiritual Connection with the Natural World. LC 99-20490. 240p. 1999. 14.95 (0-89281-798-4, Park St Pr) Inner Tradit.

***Metzner, Ralph.** The Spell. 2000. pap. 15.20 (5-550-00550-6) Nairi.

Metzner, Ralph. The Unfolding Self: Varieties of Transformative Experience. rev. ed. LC 97-19672. (Illus.). 336p. 1998. pap. 14.95 (1-57983-000-5) Origin Pr CA.

Metzner, Ralph, ed. Ayahuasca: Hallucinogens, Consciousness, & the Spirit of Nature. LC 99-12425. (Illus.). 294p. 1999. pap. 14.95 (1-56025-160-3, Thunders Mouth) Avalon NY.

Metzner, Seymour. One-Minute Game Guide. LC 67-29157. (J). (gr. 1-6). 1968. pap. 6.99 (0-8224-5070-4) Fearon Teacher Aids.

Metzner, Seymour, jt. auth. see Sharp, Richard M.

Metzner, Sheila. Color. 172p. 1991. 50.00 (0-944092-15-2) Twin Palms Pub.

— Color. limited ed. 172p. 1991. 150.00 (0-944092-16-0) Twin Palms Pub.

— Inherit the Earth. (Illus.). 136p. 2000. 75.00 (0-8212-2586-3); 75.00 (0-8212-2601-0) Bulfinch Pr.

Meucci, Antonella, jt. auth. see Nardi, Adriano.

Meude-Monpas, J. J. De, see De Meude-Monpas, J. J.

Meude-Monpas, Jean J. De, see De Meude-Monpas, Jean J.

Meudell, Karen & Callen, Tony. Management & Organisational Behaviour: A Student Workbook. 2nd ed. 224p. 1995. pap. 34.50 (0-273-61929-2) F T P-H.

Meudt, Edna. Promised Land, the Life & Times of Henry Dodge, First Territorial Governor of Wisconsin: A Historical Drama. Westburg, John E., ed. LC 80-54737. 56p. 1980. pap. 8.00 (0-87423-026-8) Westburg.

— The Rose Jar: The Autobiography of Edna Meudt. LC 90-7204. (Illus.). 352p. 1990. 17.50 (0-944133-07-X) Nrth Cntry Pr.

Meudt, R., jt. auth. see Lutz, H.

Meudt, Werner J., ed. Strategies of Plant Reproduction. LC 82-11594. (Beltsville Symposia in Agricultural Research Ser.: No. 6). (Illus.). 400p. 1983. text 66.50 (0-86598-054-3) Rowman.

Meuel, David. Islands in the Sky. unabridged ed. 78p. (Orig.). 1997. pap. 10.00 (0-9658374-0-8) D Meuel Communs.

Meuer, Teresa & Abramson, Betsy. A Family's Guide to Selecting, Financing & Asserting Rights in a Nursing Home. 31p. 1986. 15.00 (0-932622-09-7) Ctr Public Rep.

Meulders, Daniaele, jt. auth. see Gustafsson, Siv.

Meulders, Daniele, et al. Atypical Employment in the EC. (Illus.). 280p. (C). 1994. text 72.95 (1-85521-426-1, Pub. by Dartmth Pub) Ashgate Pub Co.

— Position of Women on the Labour Market in the European Community. 216p. 1993. 72.95 (1-85521-419-9, Pub. by Dartmth Pub) Ashgate Pub Co.

Meulders, Daniele, jt. ed. see Capros, Pantelis.

Meulemans, W. The Genetics of Dizygotic Twinning. No. 84. 167p. (Orig.). 1994. pap. 38.50 (90-6186-609-X, Pub. by Leuven Univ) Coronet Bks.

Meulemeester, Katie De, see De Meulemeester, Katie.

Meulen, A. Ter, ed. Studies in Modeltheoretic Semantics. (Groningen-Amsterdam Studies in Semantics). x, 206p. 1983. pap. 36.95 (90-70176-80-7) Mouton.

Meulen, Alice G. Ter, see Reuland, Eric J. & Ter Meulen, Alice G.

Meulen, Alice G. Ter, see Ter Meulen, Alice G.

Meulen, Alice G. Ter, see Van Benthem, Johan F. & Ter Meulen, Alice G., eds.

Meulen, Alice G. Ter, see Ter Meulen, Alice G.

Meulen, Alice Ter, jt. ed. see Van Benthem, Johan.

Meulen, B. F. Van Der, see De Jong-Gierveld, J. & Hox, J. J.

Meulen, D. Van der, see Van der Meulen, D.

***Meulen, David L. Vander, ed.** Studies in Bibliography. Vol. 52. 300p. 2000. 50.00 (0-8139-2010-8) U Pr of Va.

Meulen, F. Van der, see Van der Meulen, F.

Meulen, Jan Van Der, see Van Der Meulen, Jan.

Meulen, Marjon van der, see Van Der Meulen, Marjon.

***Meulen, Meine van.** Definitions for Hardware & Software Safety Engineers. LC 99-89562. 190p. 2000. pap. text (1-85233-175-5) Spr-Verlag.

Meulen, P. R. Van der, see Van der Meulen, P. R., ed.

Meulen, V. Ter & Billeter, M. A., eds. Measles Virus, No. 191. (Currents Topics in Microbiology & Immunology Ser.: Vol. 191). 319p. 1995. 124.00 (0-387-57389-5) Spr-Verlag.

Meulen, V. Ter & Katz, M. B., eds. Slow Virus Infections of the Central Nervous System. LC 77-1570. 1977. 136.00 (0-387-90188-4) Spr-Verlag.

Meulen, Van Der & Gruss, Joseph. Colour Atlas & Text of Ocular Plastic Surgery. 1995. 215.00 (0-7234-1924-8) Mosby Inc.

Meulenbeld, G. Jan & Wujastyk, Dominik, eds. Studies on Indian Medical History: Papers Presented at the International Workshop on the Study of Indian Medicine Held at the Wellcome Institute for the History of Medicine, Sept. 2-4, 1985. (Groningen Oriental Studies: Vol. II). 247p. (Orig.). (C). 1987. pap. 46.00 (90-6980-015-2, Pub. by Egbert Forsten) Hod1der & Stoughton.

Meulenbelt, Anja, et al, eds. A Creative Tension: Key Issues of Socialist Feminism. Couling, Della, tr. 152p. (Orig.). 1984. 30.00 (0-89608-237-7); pap. 8.50 (0-89608-236-9) South End Pr.

Meulendyk, Phyllis. Mother Goose Teaches the Ten Commandments. 23p. 1989. pap. text 10.00 (1-58302-051-9, BPS-02) One Way St.

Meulenkamp, Wim, jt. auth. see Headley, Gwyn.

Meuli, Judith, jt. auth. see Carabillo, Toni.

Meunch, David, photos by. Colorado II. LC 86-83242. (Illus.). 160p. 1987. 39.95 (0-932575-31-5) Gr Arts Ctr Pub.

— National Parks of America. (Illus.). 208p. 1993. 50.00 (1-55868-124-8) Gr Arts Ctr Pub.

— Utah. LC 89-81615. (Illus.). 160p. 1990. 39.95 (1-55868-024-1) Gr Arts Ctr Pub.

***Meunier, A.** Sam Generations. (C). 1999. pap. text 41.50 (0-03-030941-7) Harcourt.

***Meunier, B., et al, eds.** Metal-Oxo & Metal-Peroxo Species in Catalytic Oxidations. (Structure & Bonding Ser.: 97). x, 294p. 2000. (3-540-66943-4) Spr-Verlag.

Meunier, Bernard, ed. Biomimetic Oxidations Catalyzed by Transition Metal Complexes. LC 99-36713. 500p. 1998. 88.00 (1-86094-098-6, Pub. by Imperial College) World Scientific Pub.

— DNA & RNA Cleavers & Chemotherapy of Cancer & Viral Diseases. (NATO ASI Ser.: Series C, Vol. 479). 372p. 1996. text 217.50 (0-7923-4025-6) Kluwer Academic.

Meunier, C., jt. auth. see Lochak, P.

Meunier, Christiane. Big 'n Easy Miniature Quilts. Hearn, Deborah & Feece, Debra, eds. LC 97-48883. (Illus.). 32p. 1998. pap. 12.95 (1-885588-18-6) Chitra Pubns.

***Meunier, Christiane.** Colorful Quilts for Kids. Feece, Debra, ed. (Illus.). 32p. 1999. pap. 12.95 (1-885588-29-1) Chitra Pubns.

— Easy Art Quilts: Amazing Designs Based on Tradition. Feece, Debra & Campbell, Elsie, eds. (Illus.). 32p. 2000. pap. 14.95 (1-885588-34-8) Chitra Pubns.

Meunier, Christiane. Easy Traditional Quilts: Log Cabins. Campbell, Elsie, ed. (Illus.). 32p. 1999. pap. 12.95 (1-885588-26-7) Chitra Pubns.

***Meunier, Christiane.** Easy Traditional Quilts: Stars. Feece, Debra & Hearn, Deborah, eds. LC 98-28543. (Illus.). 32p. 1999. pap. 12.95 (1-885588-23-2) Chitra Pubns.

Meunier, J. Physics of Amphiphilic Layers. Langevin, D. & Boccara, Nino, eds. (Proceedings in Physics Ser.: Vol. 21). (Illus.). 410p. 1987. 78.95 (0-387-18255-1) Spr-Verlag.

Meunier, Jacques & Savarin, A. M. The Amazonian Chronicles. rev. ed. Christensen, Carol, tr. LC 93-12724. 192p. 1994. reprint ed. 20.00 (1-56279-053-6) Mercury Hse Inc.

Meunier, Pamela S. The Obsidian Trials: Seven Spiritual Steps for Overcoming Our Fears. 194p. 1999. pap. 14.95 (0-9669095-0-X, Pub. by Galactica Pr) ACCESS Pubs Network.

Meunier-Tardif, Ghislaine. Eye People, Ear People: Getting Along. Baxter, Edward, tr. from FRE. 144p. (Orig.). 1988. pap. 9.95 (1-55021-009-2, Pub. by NC Ltd) U of Toronto Pr.

Meuninck, jt. auth. see Philip.

Meuninck, Jill, ed. see Meuninck, Jim.

Meuninck, Jim. Diving Opportunities for Fun & Profit: Over 100 Ways to Make Money Diving. Gunter, Claude & Meuninck, Jill, eds. (Illus.). 216p. (Orig.). 1986. pap. 9.95 (0-939865-00-9) Meunincks Media.

— Edible Wild Plants Handbooks. 2nd ed. LC 99-19357. (Illus.). 64p. 1999. pap. text 7.95 (0-7627-0479-9) Globe Pequot.

***Meurant, G., ed.** Computer Solution of Large Linear Systems. (Studies in Mathematics & Its Applications: Vol. 28). 776p. 1999. 149.50 (0-444-50169-X, North Holland) Elsevier.

Meurant, Georges. Shoowa Design. (Illus.). 205p. 1986. 60.00 (0-500-97331-8) Michigan Mus.

— Shoowa Design: African Textiles from the Kingdom of Kuba. (Illus.). 200p. 1986. 60.00 (0-500-59733-2) Thames Hudson.

Meurant, Georges & Tho, Robert F. Mbuti Design: Paintings by Pygmy Women of the Ituri Rainforest. LC 95-78910. (Illus.). 224p. 1996. 60.00 (0-500-97430-6, Pub. by Thames Hudson) Norton.

Meurant, Gloria. My Worship Planner & Organizer. 1992. pap. 8.50 (1-55673-439-5, 9242) CSS OH.

***Meurer, Dave.** Boyhood Daze. 176p. 1999. pap. 9.99 (1-55661-209-5) Bethany Hse.

— Daze of Our Wives. LC 99-51017. 192p. 2000. pap. 9.99 (0-7642-2342-9) Bethany Hse.

***Meurer, Hans Joachim.** Cinema & National Identity in a Divided Germany, 1979-1989: The Split Screen. LC 00-41823. (Studies in History & Criticism of Film). (Illus.). 2000. write for info. (0-7734-7640-7) E Mellen.

Meurer, K. A. Mineralocorticoids & Hypertension. Kaufman, W. et al, eds. (International Boehringer Mannheim Symposia Ser.). (Illus.). 225p. 1983. 56.95 (0-387-12391-1) Spr-Verlag.

Meurer, Michael R. Sealed Battery Selection for Designers & Users. 1996. text 55.00 (0-07-041824-1) McGraw.

Meurer, Susan, jt. auth. see Sobel, David.

Meurers, Reinald Von, see Von Meurers, Reinald.

Meurig, Arthwyr A., tr. see Seals, David.

Meurig, H. & Thomas, W. O. Y Geiriadur Mawr: The Complete Welsh-English, English-Welsh Dictionary. Williams, S. J., ed. (ENG & WEL.). 859p. 1981. 75.00 (0-8288-4684-7, M-9434) Fr & Eur.

Meuris, Jacques. Klimt. (Big Art Ser.). 1998. 19.99 (3-8228-7213-X) Taschen Amer.

— Magritte. Underwood, J. A., tr. (Illus.). 236p. 1990. 85.00 (0-87951-409-4, Pub. by Overlook Pr) Penguin Putnam.

— Magritte. 1994. pap. 19.99 (3-8228-0546-7) Taschen Amer.

— Magritte. (SPA.). 1996. pap. 19.99 (3-8228-0666-8) Taschen Amer.

— Magritte. (Big Art Ser.). 1998. 19.99 (3-8228-7215-6) Taschen Amer.

***Meuris, Jacques.** Magritte. 1999. 19.99 (3-8228-7368-3) Taschen Amer.

Meurman, Arne. Annihilating Fields of Standard Modules of Sl(2, C) & Combinatorial Identities. LC 98-45652. (Memoirs of the American Society Ser.). 1999. write for info. (0-8218-0923-7) Am Math.

Meurn, Robert J. Survival Guide for the Mariner. LC 93-7990. (Illus.). 240p. 1993. text 25.00 (0-87033-444-1) Cornell Maritime.

— Watchstanding Guide for the Merchant Marine. LC 89-71208. (Illus.). 256p. 1990. text 27.50 (0-87033-409-3) Cornell Maritime.

Meurn, Robert J., jt. auth. see Sauerbier, Charles L.

Meurois-Givaudan, Anne & Meurois-Givaudan, Daniel. Way of the Essenes: Christ's Hidden Life Remembered. 383p. 1993. reprint ed. pap. 16.95 (0-89281-322-9, Destiny Bks) Inner Tradit.

Meurois-Givaudan, Daniel, jt. auth. see Meurois-Givaudan, Anne.

Meuron, De, see Zaugg, Remy & De Meuron.

Meurs, A. Van, see Saris, Willem E. & Van Meurs, A.

Meurs, Mieke, ed. Many Shades of Red: State Policy & Collective Agriculture. LC 98-41936. 320p. 1998. 62.00 (0-8476-9038-5); pap. 21.95 (0-8476-9039-3) Rowman.

Meursault, Martin. Enjoy! The Authoritative Guide to the Restaurants of the Monterey Peninsula. LC 97-191759. 256p. (Orig.). 1997. pap. 15.95 (0-9657404-0-4, 101) Sanford Frederick.

Meusebach, Karl H. Von, see Von Meusebach, Karl H.

Meusel, Heinrich. Grundschule der Leibesubungen. (GER.). 288p. 1956. write for info. (3-296-80800-0, Pub. by Weidmann) Lubrecht & Cramer.

Meusel, Heinrich, ed. Caesar - Lexicon Caesarianum, Vol. I. vi, 772p. 1958. write for info. (3-296-11201-4) G Olms Pubs.

— Caesar - Lexicon Caesarianum, Vol. II, 1. xi, 648p. 1958. write for info. (3-296-11202-2) G Olms Pubs.

— Caesar - Lexicon Caesarianum, Vol. II, 2. 674p. 1958. write for info. (3-296-11203-0) G Olms Pubs.

Meusel, Johann G. Lexikon der Vom Jahre 1750-1800 Verstorbenen Teutschen Schriftsteller, 15 vols., Set. 1968. reprint ed. write for info. (0-318-71929-0) G Olms Pubs.

— Teutsches Kunstlerlexikon, 3 vols. reprint ed. write for info. (0-318-71930-4) G Olms Pubs.

Meusel, Johann G., jt. auth. see Hamberger, Georg C.

Meuser, F., et al, eds. Plant Polymeric Carbohydrates. 295p. 1993. 105.00 (0-85186-645-X) CRC Pr.

***Meuser, Mark.** Class Encounters. LC 99-55107. 185p. 2000. 17.95 (1-58141-015-8) Rivercross Pub.

Meuss, A. R., tr. see Schilcher, Heinz.

Meuss, A. R., tr. see Steiner, Rudolf.

Meuss, Anna R., tr. see Masters, Brien.

Meuss, Anna R., tr. see Society for Cancer Research Staff.

Meuss, Anna R., tr. see Steiner, Rudolf.

Meuss, Anna R., tr. see Wolff, Otto.

***Meussen, Gerard T.** The Principle of Equality in European Taxation. 2nd ed. LC 99-16460. (Eucotax Series on European Taxation). 1999. 135.00 (90-411-9693-5) Kluwer Law Intl.

Meutsch, Dietrich & Viehoff, Reinhold, eds. Comprehension of Literary Discourse: Results & Problems of Interdisciplinary Approaches. (Research in Text Theory Ser.: No. 13). vi, 259p. (C). 1988. lib. bdg. 103.10 (3-11-011111-X) De Gruyter.

Meuzelaar, H. L. Computer-Enhanced Analytical Spectroscopy, Vol. 2. LC 87-15883. (Modern Analytical Chemistry Ser.). (Illus.). 340p. (C). 1990. text 89.50 (0-306-43276-5, Kluwer Plenum) Kluwer Academic.

Meuzelaar, H. L., ed. Advances in Coal Spectroscopy. (Modern Analytical Chemistry Ser.). (Illus.). 440p. (C). 1991. text 115.00 (0-306-43796-1, Kluwer Plenum) Kluwer Academic.

Meuzelaar, H. L. & Isenhour, T. L. Computer-Enhanced Analytical Spectroscopy, Vol. 1. LC 87-15883. (Modern Analytical Chemistry Ser.). (Illus.). 288p. (C). 1988. text 89.50 (0-306-42644-7, Kluwer Plenum) Kluwer Academic.

Mevers, Frank C. Composite Index to Volumes 14-17 (Revolutionary War Rolls) of the New Hampshire State Papers. 343p. (Orig.). 1993. pap. 24.00 (1-55613-824-5) Heritage Bk.

Meville, Herman. Lauter American Literature IV & Moby Dick, 3 vols. 3rd ed. Lauter, ed. (American Heritage Library). (C). Date not set. 51.56 (0-395-90168-5) HM.

Meville, Peter. Do Cats Need Shrinks? 1994. 6.99 (0-7858-0158-8) Bk Sales Inc.

Mevlendyke, Eve, jt. auth. see Lipman, Jean.

Mew. The Law of Limitations. 382p. 1991. boxed set 77.00 (0-409-80909-8, MICHIE) LEXIS Pub.

Mew, Charlotte. Collected Poems & Selected Prose. 156p. 1998. pap. 14.95 (1-85754-363-7, Pub. by Carcanet Pr) Paul & Co Pubs.

Mew Group Staff. Exploring Statistics, Set. (Illus.). 86p. 1993. teacher ed., student ed., ring bd. 110.00 (0-340-53158-4, Pub. by Hodder & Stought Ltd) Lubrecht & Cramer.

***Mewaldt, Richard A., et al, eds.** Acceleration & Transport of Energetic Particles Observed in the Heliosphere: Ace 2000 Symposium. LC 00-105240. (AIP Conference Proceedings Ser.: Vol. 528). (Illus.). xv, 472p. 2000. 170.00 (1-56396-951-3) Am Inst Physics.

***Mewborn, Willie.** All about Exodus. 45p. 2000. pap. write for info. (1-930070-62-4) Words of Faith.

— All about Joseph & the Children of Israel. 40p. Date not set. pap. write for info. (1-930070-63-2) Words of Faith.

— All about Joshua & Moses. (Illus.). 50p. 2000. pap. write for info. (1-930070-13-6) Words of Faith.

— Explain the Terms... Genesis to Revelations. 85p. Date not set. pap. write for info. (1-930070-08-X) Words of Faith.

— The God of All Comfort. 52p. 2000. write for info. (1-930070-02-0) Words of Faith.

— The Life, Death, Burial & Resurrection of Jesus Christ. Date not set. pap. write for info. (1-930070-28-4) Words of Faith.

— Psalms in the Time of Trouble. 110p. Date not set. pap. write for info. (1-930070-37-3) Words of Faith.

An Asterisk (*) at the beginning of an entry indicates that the title is appearing for the first time.

— Resting in God's Love. 80p. 2000. write for info. (*1-930070-01-2*) Words of Faith.
— A Study Guide to Abraham, Isaac & Jacob. 52p. 2000. write for info. (*1-930070-44-6*) Words of Faith.
— Test Your Bible Power. 85p. Date not set. pap. write for info. (*1-930070-36-5*) Words of Faith.
— Through the Storms & Through the Rain. 110p. 1999. mass mkt. 9.95 (*1-930070-00-4*) Words of Faith.
— Wise Counseling from Proverbs. 56p. Date not set. pap. write for info. (*1-930070-34-9*) Words of Faith.
Mewes, Gail E. Sailing Thru Menopause: 100 Tips on Coping with 'The Change' (Illus.). v, 102p. 1998. spiral bd. 14.95 (*0-9665789-0-2*) ArtzToGo.
Mewes, Julia, jt. auth. see Farhar, Barbara C.
Mewhorter, Lucille. Countdown to Christmas: A Tree Trimming Service. 16p. (Orig.). 1997. pap. 5.25 (*0-7880-1044-1*) CSS OH.
Mewis, J. J., et al, eds. Loss Prevention & Safety Promotion in the Process Industries; Proceedings of the 8th International Symposium, Antwerp, Belgium, June 6-9, 1995, 2 vols. LC 95-6875. 1500p. 1995. 376.75 (*0-444-82136-8*) Elsevier.
— Loss Prevention & Safety Promotion in the Process Industries: Proceedings of the 8th International Symposium, Antwerp, Belgium, June 6-9, 1995, Vol. 1. LC 95-6875. 1995. 359.50 (*0-444-82131-7*) Elsevier.
— Loss Prevention & Safety Promotion in the Process Industries: Proceedings of the 8th International Symposium, Antwerp, Belgium, June 6-9, 1995, Vol. 2. LC 95-6875. 1995. write for info. (*0-444-82134-1*) Elsevier.
Mews, Constant J. The Lost Love Letters of Heloise & Abelard: Perceptions of Dialogue in Twelfth-Century France. Chiavaroli, Neville, tr. from LAT. LC 98-39073. 302p. 1999. text 49.95 (*0-312-21604-1*) St Martin.
Mews, Siegfried. Critical Essays on Bertolt Brecht. (Critical Essays on World Literature Ser.). 280p. 1989. 49.00 (*0-8161-8844-0*, G K Hall & Co) Mac Lib Ref.
— Essays on Brecht. LC 78-31157. (North Carolina. University. Studies in the Germanic Languages & Literatures: No. 79). reprint ed. 27.00 (*0-404-50954-1*) AMS Pr.
— Guenter Grass & His Critics. (Literary Criticism in Perspective Ser.). 2002. 55.00 (*1-57113-062-4*) Camden Hse.
Mews, Siegfried, ed. A Bertolt Brecht Reference Companion. LC 95-44785. 448p. 1997. lib. bdg. 95.00 (*0-313-29266-3*, Greenwood Pr) Greenwood.
— The Fisherman & His Wife: Gunter Grass's The Flounder in Critical Perspective. LC 81-69878. (Studies in Modern Literature: No. 12). (Illus.). 1983. 32.50 (*0-404-61582-1*) AMS Pr.
Mews, Siegfried & Hardin, James. Dictionary of Literary Biography: 20th Century Italian Poets, Vol. 128. (Second Ser.). 400p. 1993. text 155.00 (*0-8103-5387-3*) Gale.
Mews, Stuart, ed. Religion in Politics: A World Guide. 332p. 1990. 75.00 (*1-55862-051-6*) St James Pr.
Mewshaw, Michael. Money to Burn. 480p. 1988. mass mkt. 4.50 (*1-55817-060-X*, Pinncle Kensgtn) Kensgtn Pub Corp.
— Money to Burn. 1990. mass mkt. 4.95 (*1-55817-408-7*, Pinncle Kensgtn) Kensgtn Pub Corp.
Mexican American Cultural Center Staff, tr. see Galeron, Soledad, et al, eds.
Mexican Museum Staff. Leonora Carrington: The Mexican Years, 1943-1985. Draher, Patricia, ed. 48p. 1991. 20.00 (*1-880508-00-1*) Mexican Museum.
Mexican Writers Staff, jt. auth. see Vargas, Javier.
Mexicanos Editores Staff. Album de Oro Del Declamador Universal. (SPA.). 1997. pap. text 10.98 (*968-15-0380-5*) Ed Mex.
— Civismo, Verdadera Speracion. (SPA.). 1997. pap. text 8.98 (*968-409-915-0*) Edamex.
— Declamador Sin Maestro. (SPA.). 1997. pap. text 5.98 (*968-15-0693-6*) Ed Mex.
— Hombre Mediocre. (SPA.). 1997. pap. text 4.98 (*968-15-0174-8*) Ed Mex.
— Lo Mejor de la Cocina Mexicana. (SPA.). 1997. pap. text 5.98 (*968-15-0844-0*) Ed Mex.
— Poemas de Amor. (SPA.). 1997. pap. text 4.98 (*968-15-0446-1*) Ed Mex.
— Recetario Completo de Sopas y Consomes. (SPA.). 1997. pap. text 4.98 (*968-15-0852-1*) Ed Mex.
— Vertigo del Erotismo. (SPA.). 1997. pap. text 14.98 (*968-409-891-X*) Edit Diana.
Mey, Chris, jt. auth. see Meyer, Trish.
Mey, Dennis L. De, see De Mey, Dennis L.
Mey, Holger H., jt. auth. see Laird, Robbin F.
Mey, J. G. De, see De Mey, J. G.
Mey, J. L. Concise Encyclopedia of Pragmatics. LC 98-34937. 1100p. 1998. 179.50 (*0-08-042992-0*, Pergamon Pr) Elsevier.
Mey, Jacob L. An Introduction to Pragmatics. LC 93-19925. 336p. 1993. pap. 26.95 (*0-631-18691-3*) Blackwell Pubs.
— When Voices Clash A Study in Literary Pragmatics. LC 98-41964. 1998. pap. 40.00 (*3-11-015821-3*) De Gruyter.
***Mey, Jacob L.** When Voices Clash: A Study in Literary Pragmatics. LC 98-41964. (Trends in Linguistics, Studies & Monographs). 1998. 143.45 (*3-11-015820-5*) De Gruyter.
Mey, Jacob L. Whose Language: A Study in the Linguistic-Pragmatics. LC 85-6123. (Pragmatics & Beyond Companion Ser.: Vol. 3). ix, 412p. 1985. 84.00 (*0-915027-61-5*); pap. 27.95 (*0-915027-57-7*) J Benjamins Pubng Co.
Mey, Jacob L., ed. Language & Discourse: Test & Protest. A Festschift for Petr Sgall. LC 86-6882. (Linguistic & Literary Studies in Eastern Europe: Vol. 19). xiii, 611p. 1986. 127.00 (*90-272-1525-1*) J Benjamins Pubng Co.
— Pragmalinguistics: Theory & Practice. (Janua Linguarum, Series Major: No. 85). 1979. text 80.80 (*90-279-7757-7*) Mouton.
Mey, Vander Brenda J. & Neff, Ronald L. Incest As Child Abuse: Research & Applications. LC 86-91536. 229p. 1986. 59.95 (*0-275-92114-X*, C2114, Praeger Pubs) Greenwood.
Meyanathan, Saha D., ed. Industrial Structures & the Development of Small & Medium Enterprise Linkages: Examples from East Asia. LC 94-20988. (EDI Seminar Ser.). 166p. 1994. pap. 22.00 (*0-8213-2876-X*) World Bank.
— Managing Restructuring in the Textile & Garment Subsector: Examples from Asia. LC 93-50881. (EDI Seminar Ser.). 210p. 1994. pap. 22.00 (*0-8213-2768-2*, 12768) World Bank.
Meybeck, M., jt. ed. see Lerman, A.
Meybeck, Michel, et al, eds. Water Quality Assessment of the Former Soviet Union. LC 98-36760. (Illus.). 612p. (C). (gr. 13). 1998. 125.00 (*0-419-23920-0*, D6628, E & FN Spon) Routledge.
Meybloom, Paul G. The Nile Mosaic of Palestrina: Early Evidence of Egyptian Religion in Italy. 424p. 1994. text 152.00 (*90-04-10137-3*) Brill Academic Pubs.
Meyding, Thomas, jt. auth. see Dannemann, Gerhard.
Meyen, Edward L. Exceptional Children in Today's Schools. 3rd rev. ed. 576p. (C). 1996. text 56.00 (*0-89108-237-9*, 9501) Love Pub Co.
Meyen, Edward L., et al, eds. Challenges Facing Special Education. LC 92-74810. 404p. 1993. pap. 37.00 (*0-89108-229-8*, 9305) Love Pub Co.
— Educating Students with Mild Disabilities: Strategies & Methods. 2nd ed. 500p. (C). 1998. pap. text 49.00 (*0-89108-253-0*, 9704) Love Pub Co.
— Effective Instructional Strategies for Exceptional Children. LC 87-83464. 522p. 1988. pap. text 40.00 (*0-89108-201-8*) Love Pub Co.
— Strategies for Teaching Exceptional Children in Inclusive Settings. 528p. (Orig.). (C). 1996. pap. text 49.00 (*0-89108-244-1*, 9603) Love Pub Co.
Meyen, Edward L. & Skrtic, Thomas M., eds. Special Education & Student Disability: Traditional, Emerging, & Alternative Perspectives. 4th ed. LC 92-74811. Orig. Title: Exceptional Children & Youth. (Illus.). 830p. 1995. text 58.00 (*0-89108-231-X*) Love Pub Co.
Meyen, Franz J., 3rd. Outlines of the Geography of Plants: Native Country, the Culture, & the Uses of the Principal Cultivated Plants on Which the Prosperity of Nations Is Based. Egerton, Frank N., ed. LC 77-74239. (History of Ecology Ser.). 1978. reprint ed. lib. bdg. 39.95 (*0-405-10408-1*) Ayer.
Meyen, Sergei V. Geography of Macroevolution in Higher Plants. (Soviet Scientific Reviews Ser.). 76p. 1992. pap. text 69.00 (*3-7186-5215-3*, Harwood Acad Pubs) Gordon & Breach.
Meyen, Victor B. & Dundee, Mark. Qualified Domestic Relations Order Answer Book. 608p. boxed set 118.00 (*1-56706-358-6*, S294) Panel Pubs.
— Qualified Domestic Relations Order Answer Book. annuals 616p. 1996. 116.00 (*1-56706-175-3*) Panel Pubs.
— Qualified Domestic Relations Order Answer Book. annuals 2nd ed. LC 98-129925. 608p. 1996. boxed set 118.00 (*1-56706-433-7*, 64337) Panel Pubs.
Meyendorff, Alexander F., jt. auth. see Kohn, S.
Meyendorff, Elizabeth, tr. see Ouspensky, Leonid.
Meyendorff, John. The Byzantine Legacy in the Orthodox Church. LC 82-797. 268p. (Orig.). 1982. pap. 11.95 (*0-913836-90-7*) St Vladimirs.
— Byzantine Theology: Historical Trends & Doctrinal Themes. 2nd rev. ed. LC 72-94167. viii, 243p. 1987. pap. 17.00 (*0-8232-0967-9*) Fordham.
— Byzantium & the Rise of Russia. LC 89-28011. 326p. 1989. reprint ed. pap. 16.95 (*0-88141-079-9*) St Vladimirs.
— Catholicity & the Church. LC 83-20218. (Illus.). 160p. (Orig.). 1983. pap. 10.95 (*0-88141-006-3*) St Vladimirs.
— Christ in Eastern Christian Thought. LC 75-31977. Orig. Title: Le Christ Dans la Theologie Byzantine. 248p. 1975. pap. 13.95 (*0-913836-27-3*) St Vladimirs.
— Gregory Palamas, The Triads. (Classics of Western Spirituality Ser.). 192p. 1997. reprint ed. pap. 19.95 (*0-8091-2447-5*) Paulist Pr.
— Imperial Unity & Christian Divisions, Vol. II: The Church 450-680 AD. LC 87-31433. (Illus.). 402p. 1990. 29.95 (*0-88141-056-X*); pap. 17.95 (*0-88141-055-1*) St Vladimirs.
— Living Tradition. LC 78-2031. 202p. 1970. pap. 9.95 (*0-913836-48-6*) St Vladimirs.
— Marriage: An Orthodox Perspective. LC 75-14241. 144p. 1975. pap. 9.95 (*0-913836-05-2*) St Vladimirs.
— The Orthodox Church: Its Past & Its Role in the World Today. 3rd ed. LC 81-4978. 196p. 1996. reprint ed. pap. 11.95 (*0-913836-81-8*) St Vladimirs.
— Rome, Constantinople, Moscow: Historical & Theological Studies. 3457th ed. 208p. 1996. pap. 11.95 (*0-88141-134-5*) St Vladimirs.
— St. Gregory Palamas & Orthodox Spirituality. LC 96-23233. (Illus.). 184p. 1996. pap. 11.95 (*0-913836-11-7*) St Vladimirs.
— A Study of Gregory Palamas. LC 98-36076. 245p. 1964. 12.95 (*0-913836-14-1*) St Vladimirs.
— Vision of Unity. LC 87-23495. 192p. (Orig.). 1987. pap. 8.95 (*0-88141-068-3*) St Vladimirs.
— Witness to the World. LC 87-23493. 262p. (Orig.). 1987. pap. 9.95 (*0-88141-069-1*) St Vladimirs.
Meyendorff, John, et al, eds. The Legacy of St. Vladimir: Byzantium, Russia, America. LC 90-32389. 324p. 1990. pap. 11.95 (*0-88141-078-0*) St Vladimirs.
Meyendorff, John, jt. auth. see Fahey, Michael J.
Meyendorff, M. F. Vospominanija: Memoirs. (Illus.). 432p. 1990. 18.00 (*0-9616413-6-3*) Multilingual.
Meyendorff, Paul. Russia, Ritual, & Reform: The Liturgical Reforms of Nikon in the 17th Century. LC 91-36886. 256p. (Orig.). 1991. pap. 14.95 (*0-88141-090-X*) St Vladimirs.
Meyendorff, Paul, tr. see Aslanoff, Catherine, ed.
Meyendorff, Paul, tr. see Ement, Oliver C.
Meyendorff, Paul, tr. see St. Germanus of Constantinople.
Meyenn, K. V., ed. Wolfgang Pauli: Scientific Correspondence with Bohr, Einstein, Heisenberg a. o. Part II: 1930-1939. (Sources in the History of Mathematics & Physical Sciences Ser.: Vol. 6). 800p. 1985. 280.00 (*0-387-13609-6*) Spr-Verlag.
Meyenn, K. V., jt. ed. see Hermann, A.
Meyenn, K. V., jt. ed. see Pauli, W.
Meyer. The Awakening. (Bedford Introduction to Literature Ser.). 2000. pap. text 35.55 (*0-312-13883-0*) St Martin.
***Meyer.** Compact Bedford Introduction to Literature. 5th ed. 1999. pap. text 42.95 (*0-312-17137-4*); pap. text 45.95 (*0-312-24950-0*) St Martin.
— Compact Bedford Introduction to Literature. 4th ed. 1999. pap. text 42.95 (*0-312-24801-6*) St Martin.
Meyer. The Complete Bedford Introduction to Literature. 3rd ed. 1993. pap. text 1.64 (*0-312-10155-4*) St Martin.
— Dead. (Bedford Introduction to Literature Ser.). 2000. pap. text 34.65 (*0-312-13890-3*) St Martin.
— Encore des Exercises! 3rd ed. 1998. 7.74 (*0-07-228239-8*) McGraw.
— Expert Witnesses Explaining & Understanding Science. LC 99-186621. 256p. 1998. boxed set 84.95 (*0-8493-1197-7*) CRC Pr.
— Frankenstein. (Bedford Introduction to Literature Ser.). 2000. pap. text 35.55 (*0-312-13884-9*) St Martin.
— Great Expectations. (Bedford Introduction to Literature Ser.). 1995. pap. text 36.00 (*0-312-13885-7*) St Martin.
— Gulliver's Travels. (Bedford Introduction to Literature Ser.). 2000. pap. text 35.55 (*0-312-13886-5*) St Martin.
— Gustav Adolfs Page. (GER.). (C). 1984. 3.95 (*0-8442-2799-4*, X2799-4) NTC Contemp Pub Co.
— Handbook of Ornament. 4th ed. (Illus.). 548p. pap. 10.95 (*0-486-20302-6*) Dover.
— Heart of Darkness. (Bedford Introduction to Literature Ser.). 2000. pap. text 35.55 (*0-312-13888-1*) St Martin.
— The House of Mirth. (Bedford Introduction to Literature Ser.). 1995. pap. text 36.00 (*0-312-13889-X*) St Martin.
***Meyer.** Huckleberry Finn. (Bedford Introduction to Literature Ser.). 2000. pap. text 35.55 (*0-312-13882-2*) St Martin.
Meyer. Human Development. 7th ed. 1996. pap. text, student ed. 27.40 (*0-13-233156-X*) P-H.
— Life 3. 7th ed. 1996. text 74.49 (*0-13-233131-4*) P-H.
— Lifetime Encyclopedia of Letters. 3rd ed. LC 98-27538. (C). 1999. text 34.95 (*0-13-921065-2*) P-H.
— 100 Best Films to Rent. 1999. text. write for info. (*0-312-18031-4*) St Martin.
— Poetry. (Bedford Introduction to Literature Ser.). 2000. pap. text 52.20 (*0-312-13896-2*) St Martin.
— Poetry: An Introduction. 1994. pap. text, teacher ed. 10.00 (*0-312-11712-4*) St Martin.
— Poetry Introduction. 2nd ed. LC 97-72374. 1997. pap. text 39.95 (*0-312-14835-6*) St Martin.
— Portrait of a Lady. (Bedford Introduction to Literature Ser.). 2000. pap. text 35.10 (*0-312-13891-1*) St Martin.
— Risk Management. (FP - Risk Management Ser.). 2002. mass mkt. 58.95 (*0-538-86415-X*) S-W Pub.
— The Scarlet Letter. (Bedford Introduction to Literature Ser.). 1995. pap. text 35.10 (*0-312-13892-X*) St Martin.
— Der Schuss Von der Kanzel. unabridged ed. (World Classic Literature Ser.). (GER.). pap. 7.95 (*3-89507-032-7*, Pub. by Bookking Intl) Distribks Inc.
— The Turn of the Screw. (Bedford Introduction to Literature Ser.). 1995. pap. text 35.10 (*0-312-13893-8*) St Martin.
— Voices & Visions. 1995. pap. text, teacher ed. 27.50 (*0-312-08383-1*), pap. text, teacher ed. 5.00 (*0-312-08384-X*) St Martin.
— Wuthering Heights. (Bedford Introduction to Literature Ser.). 2000. pap. text 36.00 (*0-312-13894-6*) St Martin.
— Yachting. 1999. pap. 12.50 (*0-312-89529-1*) St Martin.
— Z-Im Poetry Intro. 2nd ed. 1997. pap. text 10.00 (*0-312-14836-4*) St Martin.
Meyer & Brown. Practicing Public Management. 3rd ed. pap. text. write for info. (*0-312-06745-3*) St Martin.
Meyer & Krueger. A Minitab Guide Statistics. LC 97-227381. 416p. (C). 1997. pap. text 26.40 (*0-13-784232-5*) P-H.
Meyer, jt. auth. see Ciccione.
Meyer, jt. auth. see Cushenbery, D.
Meyer, jt. auth. see Jackins, Harvey.
Meyer, ed. see Moliere.
Meyer, Gerhard, et al. Glucksspiel & Delinquenz: Eine Empirische Untersuchung. (GER., Illus.). 179p. 1998. 28.95 (*3-631-33295-5*) P Lang Pubng.
Meyer, Rudolph X. Elements of Space Technology. LC 98-52665. (Illus.). 352p. (C). 1999. text 79.95 (*0-12-492940-0*) Acad Pr.
Meyer & Meyer Verlag Staff. Physical Education & Sport Changes & Challenges. pap. 29.00 (*3-89124-320-0*) Meyer & Meyer.
Meyer, A. Voltaire. 1972. 59.95 (*0-8490-1268-6*) Gordon Pr.
***Meyer, A. & Johnson, T.** Gear Refurbishment, an Economical Approach for Aerospace Overhaul & Repair. (Technical Papers: Vol. 98FTM12). 19p. 1998. pap. 30.00 (*1-55589-730-4*) AGMA.
Meyer, A. & Orlando, S. German-Italian, Italian-German Technical Dictionary: Dizionario Tecnico Italiano-Tedesco-Italiano. 6th ed. (ITA.). 2912p. 1981. 125.00 (*0-8288-2122-4*, M8446) Fr & Eur.
— German-Italian Technical Dictionary of Architecture Nuclear Weapons & Civil Engineering: Technisches Worterbuch: Architektur, Atomwaffen, Bauwesen, Vol. 2. 6th ed. (GER & ITA.). 1567p. 1981. 95.00 (*0-8288-0883-X*, M7652) Fr & Eur.
— Italian-German Technical Dictionary of Architecture - Nuclear Weapons & Civil Engineering: Technisches Woerterbuch: Architektur, Atomwaffen, Bauwesen, Vol. 1. 6th ed. (GER & ITA.). 1345p. 1981. 95.00 (*0-8288-0882-1*, M7651) Fr & Eur.
Meyer, A. E., ed. The Hamburg Short Psychotherapy Comparison Experiment. (Psychotherapy & Psychosomatics Ser.: Vol. 35, Nos. 2-3, 1981). (Illus.). 136p. 1981. 34.00 (*3-8055-3435-3*) S Karger.
Meyer, A. G. Transmission Development of TEXTRON Lycoming's Geared Fan Engines. (Nineteen Eighty-Eight Fall Technical Meeting Ser.: Vol. 88FTM11). (Illus.). 10p. 1988. pap. text 30.00 (*1-55589-519-0*) AGMA.
Meyer, A. R. & Taitslin, M. A., eds. Logic at Botik Eighty-Nine. (Lecture Notes in Computer Science Ser.: Vol. 363). x, 289p. 1989. 37.00 (*0-387-51237-3*) Spr-Verlag.
Meyer, Aaron D., jt. auth. see Meyer, June V.
Meyer-Abich, Klaus M. Revolution for Nature: From the Environment to the Connatural World. Armstrong, Matthew, tr. (Philosophy & the Environment Ser.: No. 3). 145p. 1993. 25.00 (*0-929398-70-X*); pap. 15.95 (*0-929398-69-6*) UNTX Pr.
Meyer, Adolf. The Commonsense Psychiatry of Dr. Adolf Meyer: Fifty-Two Selected Papers. Lief, Alfred, ed. LC 73-2406. (Mental Illness & Social Policy; the American Experience Ser.). 1973. reprint ed. 46.95 (*0-405-05216-2*) Ayer.
Meyer, Adolph E. Development of Education in the Twentieth Century. 2nd ed. LC 75-97332. 609p. 1969. reprint ed. lib. bdg. 85.00 (*0-8371-2838-2*, MEET, Greenwood Pr) Greenwood.
— Modern European Educators & Their Work. LC 73-152197. (Essay Index Reprint Ser.). 1977. reprint ed. 20.95 (*0-8369-2246-8*) Ayer.
Meyer, Adrian, jt. auth. see Jolles, Adrian.
Meyer, Agnes E. Out of These Roots. Baxter, Annette K., ed. LC 79-8801. (Signal Lives Ser.). (Illus.). 1980. reprint ed. lib. bdg. 46.95 (*0-405-12848-7*) Ayer.
Meyer, Al. Miner's Rule - A More Definitive Approach. (Technical Papers: Vol. 95FTM8). (Illus.). 6p. 1995. pap. text 30.00 (*1-55589-657-X*) AGMA.
Meyer, Alain. La Condition Humaine de Malraux. (FRE.). 254p. 1991. pap. 15.95 (*0-7859-4530-X*, 207038442X) Fr & Eur.
Meyer, Albert J. & Vassiliou, Simos G. The Economy of Cyprus. LC 62-8183. (Harvard Middle Eastern Studies: No. 5). (Illus.). 125p. reprint ed. pap. 38.80 (*0-7837-1522-6*, 204179900024) Bks Demand.
Meyer, Albert R., et al, eds. Research Directions in Computer Science: An MIT Perspective. 516p. 1991. 49.50 (*0-262-13257-5*) MIT Pr.
Meyer, Alcie, jt. ed. see Meyer, David.
***Meyer, Aleta L.** Promoting Nonviolence in Early Adolescence: Responding in Peaceful & Positive Ways. LC 00-29629. 2000. pap. write for info. (*0-306-46386-5*) Plenum.
Meyer, Alfred G. The Feminism & Socialism of Lily Braun. LC 84-43077. (Illus.). 256p. 1986. 35.00 (*0-253-32169-7*) Ind U Pr.
Meyer, Alfred G., jt. ed. see Wolchik, Sharon L.
Meyer, Alfred W., jt. auth. see Speidel, Richard E.
Meyer, Alice, jt. ed. see Meyer, David.
Meyer, Andrea S., jt. auth. see Harper, David R.
Meyer, Anita. The Bride & the Bodyguard. 1996. per. 3.99 (*0-373-07754-8*, 1-07754-4) Silhouette.
Meyer, Anja. Elfriede Jelinek in der Geschlechterpresse. (Germanistische Texte und Studien: Vol. 44). (GER.). ix, 168p. 1994. write for info. (*3-487-09887-3*) G Olms Pubs.
Meyer, Anne & Rose, David. Learning to Read in the Computer Age. (Illus.). 110p. 1999. pap. 9.95 (*1-57129-070-2*) Brookline Bks.
Meyer, Annette E. Evolution of United States Budgeting: Changing Fiscal & Financial Concepts, 95. LC 89-1890. 193p. 1989. 52.95 (*0-313-25868-6*, MEV, Greenwood Pr) Greenwood.
Meyer, Annie N., ed. Woman's Work in America. LC 72-2615. (American Women Ser.: Images & Realities). 462p. 1980. reprint ed. 26.95 (*0-405-04469-0*) Ayer.
Meyer, Anthony J. P. Oceanic Art, 2 Vols. LC 97-137042. (ENG, FRE & GER., Illus.). 640p. 1998. boxed set 49.95 (*3-89508-080-2*, 810033) Konemann.
Meyer-Arendt, Jurgen R. Introduction to Classical & Modern Optics. 4th ed. LC 94-30562. 480p. 1994. 83.33 (*0-13-124356-X*) P-H.
Meyer-Arendt, Jurgen R., ed. Selected Papers on Schlieren Optics. LC 92-29545. (Milestone Ser.: Vol. MS 61). 1992. pap. 45.00 (*0-8194-1048-9*) SPIE.
— Selected Papers on Schlieren Optics. LC 92-29545. (Milestone Ser.: Vol. MS 61/HC). 1992. 55.00 (*0-8194-1049-7*) SPIE.
Meyer-Arendt, Klaus & Hartmann, Rudi, eds. Casino Gambling in America: Origins, Trends, & Impacts. LC 97-32874. (Tourism Dynamics Ser.). (Illus.). xi, 270 p. 1998. pap. text 30.00 (*1-882345-17-7*) Cognizant Comm.
Meyer-Arendt, Klaus J. & Hartmann, Rudi, eds. Casino Gambling in America: Origins, Trends, & Impacts. LC 97-32874. (Tourism Dynamics Ser.). (Illus.). 270p. 1998. text 38.00 (*1-882345-16-9*) Cognizant Comm.
Meyer, Arline. Apostles in England: Sir James Thornhill & the Legacy of Raphael's Tapestry Cartoons. LC 96-61308. (Illus.). 112p. (Orig.). (C). 1997. pap. 25.00 (*1-884919-02-2*) Wallach Art Gallery.
Meyer-Arlt, Regine. Nach Dem Ende: Posthistoire und die Dramen Thomas Bernhards. (Germanistische Texte und Studien Ser.: Bd. 56). (GER.). viii, 218p. 1997. 40.00 (*3-487-10480-6*) G Olms Pubs.

M

Meyer, Art & Meyer, Jocele. Earthkeepers: Environmental Perspectives on Hunger, Poverty, & Injustice. LC 90-24473. 264p. (Orig.). 1991. pap. 13.99 (*0-8361-3544-X*) Herald Pr.

Meyer, Arthur L. Baking Across America. LC 98-15165. (Illus.). 496p. 1998. 45.00 (*0-292-75216-4*); pap. 24.95 (*0-292-75222-9*) U of Tex Pr.

— Texas Tortes: A Collection of Recipes from the Heart ... of Texas. LC 96-9422. (Illus.). 120p. 1997. 17.95 (*0-292-75201-6*) U of Tex Pr.

Meyer, Arthur W. The Rise of Embryology. LC 40-3220. (Illus.). 391p. 1939. reprint ed. pap. 30.00 (*0-608-08332-1*, 203313200084) Bks Demand.

Meyer, B. Indoor Air Quality. 1982. text. write for info. (*0-201-05094-3*) Addison-Wesley.

***Meyer, B.** Intertemporal Asset Pricing: Evidence from Germany. LC 98-46205. (Illus.). 287p. 1999. pap. 67.00 (*3-7908-1159-9*) Spr-Verlag.

Meyer, B., et al, eds. Formaldehyde Release from Wood Products. LC 86-14194. (ACS Symposium Ser.: No. 316). (Illus.). 240p. 1986. 54.95 (*0-8412-0982-0*) Am Chemical.

— Formaldehyde Release from Wood Products. LC 86-14194. (ACS Symposium Ser.: Vol. 316). 248p. 1986. reprint ed. pap. 76.90 (*0-608-03520-3*, 206423900008) Bks Demand.

Meyer, B. E., tr. see Hoffding, Harald.

Meyer, B. J., et al. Human Physiology: Chemical, Physical, & Physiological Principles. (Illus.). 550p. (C). 1994. pap. text 60.00 (*0-7021-2949-6*, Pub. by Juta & Co) Intl Spec Bk.

Meyer, Baber. Computers in Your Future 1998. 520p. (C). 1998. 80.00 (*1-57576-838-0*) Que Educ & Trng.

Meyer-Baer, Kathi. Music of the Spheres & the Dance of Death. LC 83-18905. (Music Reprint Ser.). (Illus.). 376p. 1984. reprint ed. lib. bdg. 47.50 (*0-306-76224-2*) Da Capo.

Meyer, Balthasar H. History of Transportation in the United States Before 1860. 678p. 1993. reprint ed. lib. bdg. 149.00 (*0-7812-5217-2*) Rprt Serv.

— Railway Legislation in the United States. LC 73-2523. (Big Business; Economic Power in a Free Society Ser.). 1973. reprint ed. 23.95 (*0-405-05102-6*) Ayer.

Meyer, Barb, ed. see Phillips, Laurel & Stahl, Barbara.

Meyer, Barbara, jt. auth. see Katz, Lori.

Meyer, Barbara F. & Cato, Bob. The Great Garlic Cookbook. LC 91-43496. (Illus.). 160p. 1992. pap. 14.95 (*0-87131-673-0*) M Evans.

***Meyer, Barbara M.** More Sketches: Carmel to Orcas Island. 100p. 1999. pap. 24.95 (*1-888345-17-9*) Paper Jam.

Meyer, Barbara M. Sketching in the San Juans: And a Bit Beyond. 100p. 1996. pap. 24.95 (*1-888345-01-2*) Paper Jam.

Meyer, Beat. Urea-Formaldehyde Resins. (Illus.). 1979. text. write for info. (*0-201-04558-3*) Addison-Wesley.

Meyer, Ben F. Christus Faber: The Master-Builder & the House of God. (Princeton Theological Monographs: No. 29). (Orig.). 1992. pap. 24.00 (*1-55635-014-7*) Pickwick.

— Critical Realism in the New Testament. LC 88-31722. (Princeton Theological Monographs: No. 17). 225p. (Orig.). 1989. pap. 19.95 (*0-915138-97-2*) Pickwick.

— Five Speeches That Changed the World. 144p. (Orig.). 1994. pap. 9.95 (*0-8146-2282-8*) Liturgical Pr.

— One Loaf, One Cup: Ecumenical Studies of 1 Cor 11 & Other Eucharistic Texts. (New Gospel Studies: No. 6). 180p. 1992. 25.00 (*0-86554-398-4*, MUP/H324) Mercer Univ Pr.

— Reality & Illusion in the New Testament Scholarship: A Primer in Critical Realist Hermeneutics. 256p. (Orig.). 1995. pap. text 16.95 (*0-8146-5771-0*, M Glazier) Liturgical Pr.

Meyer, Ben F., jt. ed. see McEvenue, Sean E.

Meyer, Bernard. Bernard Meyer's East Coast Cuisine: Regional Cooking with French Flair. 138p. 1988. pap. 6.95 (*0-88780-063-7*, Pub. by Formac Publ Co) Formac Dist Ltd.

Meyer, Bernard S. Botany at the Ohio State University: The First One Hundred Years. LC 84-60410. (Bulletin New Ser.: Vol. 6, No. 2). 177p. 1983. pap. text 10.00 (*0-86727-096-9*) Ohio Bio Survey.

— Judicial Retirement Laws of the Fifty States & the District of Columbia. LC 99-28273. 306p. 1999. 40.00 (*0-8232-1925-9*, Pub. by Fordham); pap. 20.00 (*0-8232-1926-7*, Pub. by Fordham) BookMasters.

Meyer, Bernd E., jt. auth. see Linnhoff-Popien, Claudia.

Meyer, Bernd E., jt. ed. see Marriott, Kim.

***Meyer, Bertrand.** Design by Contract. 2000. pap. 39.99 (*0-13-088921-0*) P-H.

Meyer, Bertrand. Eiffel: The Language. (Object-Oriented Ser.). (Illus.). 300p. 1990. pap. 45.00 (*0-13-247925-7*) P-H.

— Intro Theory of Programming Languages. 550p. 1988. boxed set 37.00 (*0-318-37858-2*) P-H.

— Object-Oriented Software Construction. 2nd ed. LC 97-2407. 1296p. (C). 1997. pap. 70.00 (*0-13-629155-4*) P-H.

— Object Success: A Manager's Guide to Object Orientation, It's Impact on the Corporation, & It's Use for Re-engineering. 250p. 1995. 63.00 (*0-13-192833-3*) P-H.

Meyer, Bertrand & Beziven, Jean. Tools 4: Technology of Object-Oriented Languages & Systems. 415p. (C). 1991. pap. text 115.00 (*0-13-923160-9*, 270609) P-H.

Meyer, Bertrand, jt. ed. see Mingins, Christine.

Meyer, Beryl, jt. auth. see Klensch, Elsa.

Meyer, Beth, ed. see Moss, Maureen.

Meyer, Bette E. Fort George Wright: Not Only When the Band Played. LC 93-32422. 1993. 22.50 (*0-87770-543-7*); pap. 14.95 (*0-87770-525-9*) Ye Galleon.

Meyer, Bill. Anuak: Mission to Danger. (Illus.). 330p. (Orig.). 1997. pap. 14.25 (*0-9658377-2-6*) Perc Pr.

— Cash Flow: A Practical Guide for the Entrepreneur. LC 98-67318. 255p. 1998. pap. 16.75 (*0-9658377-4-2*) Perc Pr.

— Combat Medic: The 79th EVAC. 280p. 1998. pap. 14.25 (*0-9658377-3-4*) Perc Pr.

— Cotoc: Anatomy of a Start-Up. LC 97-67686. 333p. (Orig.). 1997. pap. 14.75 (*0-9658377-1-8*) Perc Pr.

Meyer, Bill, ed. Defining Drug Courts: The Key Components. 43p. (C). 1998. pap. text 15.00 (*0-7881-7428-2*) DIANE Pub.

***Meyer, Birgit.** Translating the Devil: Religion & Modernity among the Ewe in Ghana LC 99-37739. 1999. pap. write for info. (*0-86543-798-X*) Africa World.

Meyer, Birgit & Geschiere, Peter, eds. Globalization & Identity: Dialectics of Flow & Closure. LC 98-52219. 240p. 1999. pap. 24.95 (*0-631-21238-8*) Blackwell Pubs.

Meyer, Blaire, et al, eds. The Road of Life. (Illus.). 70p. (Orig.). 1987. pap. 5.00 (*0-9615214-1-4*) Barton Cty Comm.

Meyer-Blanck, Michael. Leben, Leib & Liturgie: Die Praktische Theologie Wilhelm Staehlins. (Arbeiten zur Praktischen Theologie Ser.: Vol. 6). (GER.). xiv, 465p. (C). 1994. lib. bdg. 152.35 (*3-11-014364-X*) De Gruyter.

— Wort und Antwort: Geschichte und Gestaltung der Konfirmation am Beispiel der Ev.-luth. Landeskirche Hannovers. (Arbeiten zur Praktischen Theologie Ser.: Bd. 2). (GER.). xii, 338p. (C). 1992. lib. bdg. 106.15 (*3-11-013258-3*, 248-91) De Gruyter.

Meyer, Bobby. Topiary for Everyone, 1. (Illus.). 96p. 1999. pap. 24.95 (*0-85532-882-7*, Pub. by Srch Pr) A Schwartz & Co.

Meyer, Bonney, jt. auth. see Grey, John.

Meyer, Bonnie J., et al. Memory Improved: Reading & Memory Enhancement Across the Life Span Through Strategic Text Structure. 264p. 1988. 49.95 (*0-8058-0111-1*) L Erlbaum Assocs.

Meyer-Botnaerescue, Helen, jt. auth. see Machado, Jeanne M.

Meyer-Botnarescue, Helen, jt. auth. see Machado, Jeanne M.

Meyer-Breiting, E., jt. auth. see Burkhardt, A.

Meyer, Brian. Buffalo Bluff: A Regional Trivia Game. 1988. pap. 13.95 (*0-9620314-5-3*) WNY Wares.

— Quotable Cuomo: The Mario Years. (Illus.). 120p. 1991. pap. 5.95 (*1-879201-03-8*) WNY Wares.

— The World According to Griffin: End of an Era. (Illus.). 117p. 1993. pap. 5.95 (*1-879201-11-9*) WNY Wares.

Meyer, Brian & Connolly, Tom. Hometown Heroes: Western New Yorkers in Desert Storm. (Illus.). 120p. 1991. pap. 5.95 (*1-879201-04-6*) WNY Wares.

— Hometown Heroes: Western New Yorkers in Desert Storm. (Illus.). 120p. 1992. pap. 5.95 (*1-879201-07-0*) WNY Wares.

Meyer, Brian & Finkel, Anna. A-to-Z Bus Tour of Buffalo: A Kid's Guide. (Kid's Guide Ser.). (Illus.). 36p. (J). 1993. pap. 3.50 (*1-879201-10-0*) WNY Wares.

Meyer, Brian & Marren, Joe. Buffalo's Brush with the Arts: From Huck Finn to Murphy Brown. (Illus.). 112p. 1998. pap. 7.95 (*1-879201-24-0*) WNY Wares.

Meyer, Brian, jt. auth. see Gromosiak, Paul.

Meyer, Bruce. Goodbye Mr. Spalding. 228p. 1996. pap. text 16.95 (*0-88753-282-9*) Black Moss.

— The Presence. LC 98-55995. 60p. 1999. pap. 10.95 (*1-885266-75-8*, Pub. by Story Line) Consort Bk Sales.

Meyer, Bruce & O'Riordan, Brian. In Their Words: Interviews with Fourteen Canadian Writers. (Illus.). 211p. (Orig.). 1984. pap. 12.95 (*0-88784-142-2*, Pub. by Hse of Anansi Pr) Genl Dist Srvs.

Meyer, Bruce F., jt. auth. see Missair, Alfredo R.

Meyer, Bruce L. Data Communications Practice. rev. ed. LC 73-85629. (ABC of the Telephone Ser.: Vol. 11). (Illus.). 64p. (C). 1988. pap. text 24.95 (*1-56016-010-1*) ABC TeleTraining.

Meyer, Bruce S., jt. auth. see Wise, Aaron N.

Meyer, C., ed. Modelling & Analysis of Reinforced Concrete Structures for Dynamic Loading. (CISM International Centre for Mechnical Sciences Ser.: Suppl. 346). (Illus.). ix, 250p. 1998. pap. 67.00 (*3-211-82919-9*) Spr-Verlag.

Meyer, C. A. Thermodynamic & Transport Properties of Steam. LC 67-3043. 363p. reprint ed. pap. 112.60 (*0-608-11664-5*, 201101100072) Bks Demand.

Meyer, C. D., jt. auth. see Sagan, Hans.

Meyer, C. K., et al. The Guide to South Dakota Grant Assistance & Technical Services. 1975. 5.00 (*1-55614-044-4*) U of SD Gov Res Bur.

Meyer, C. Kenneth & Brown, Charles H. Practicing Public Management: A Casebook. 2nd ed. LC 88-60537. 250p. (C). 1988. pap. text 34.95 (*0-312-00329-3*) St Martin.

Meyer, C. Kenneth, et al. An Assessment of Grant Information & Tracking Systems: A Look at Selected Agencies of South Dakota State Government. 1978. 5.00 (*1-55614-021-5*) U of SD Gov Res Bur.

— Direct Democracy in South Dakota: The People Conducting Their Own Business. 1979. 10.00 (*1-55614-033-9*) U of SD Gov Res Bur.

— Social Indicators: An Aid to Public Policy Evaluation in State Government. 1979. 1.00 (*1-55614-114-9*) U of SD Gov Res Bur.

Meyer, C. P., jt. auth. see Charlier, R. H.

Meyer-Camberg, Ernst. Das Praktische Lexikon der Naturheilkunde: Practical Lexicon of Natural Healing. (GER.). 1977. pap. 45.00 (*0-8288-5514-5*, M7594) Fr & Eur.

***Meyer, Carl.** Matrix Analysis & Applied Linear Algebra. (Miscellaneous Titles in Applied Mathematics Ser.: No. 71). (Illus.). 695p. 2000. 75.00 incl. audio compact disk (*0-89871-454-0*, OT0071) Soc Indus-Appl Math.

Meyer, Carl D. & Plemmons, Richard J., eds. Linear Algebra, Markov Chains, & Queueing Models. LC 93-2100. (IMA Volumes in Mathematics & Its Applications Ser.: Vol. 48). (Illus.). 1993. 69.95 (*0-387-94085-5*); write for info. (*3-540-94085-5*) Spr-Verlag.

Meyer, Carl H. & Matyas, Stephen M. Cryptography: A New Dimension in Computer Data Security: A Guide for the Design & Implementation of Secure Systems. LC 82-2831. 755p. 1982. text 195.00 (*0-471-04892-5*) Wiley.

Meyer, Carl S., ed. Moving Frontiers. 524p. 1986. pap. 26.00 (*0-570-04461-8*, 12-3069) Concordia.

Meyer, Carol. Glass from Quseir al-Qadim & the Indian Ocean Trade. LC 92-61543. (Studies in Ancient Oriental Civilization: No. 53). (Illus.). xxvi, 201p. 1991. pap. 35.00 (*0-918986-87-7*) Orient Inst.

— Make It Simpler: A Practical Guide to Problem Solving in Mathematics. 1983. text 19.95 (*0-201-20036-8*) Addison-Wesley.

Meyer, Carol H. Assessment in Social Work Practice. 192p. (C). 1993. text 36.50 (*0-231-07556-1*) Col U Pr.

Meyer, Carol H., ed. Social Work with the Aging. rev. ed. LC 75-27193. (Readings in Social Work Ser.). 257p. 1986. pap. text 21.95 (*0-87101-139-5*) Natl Assn Soc Wkrs.

Meyer, Carol H. & Mattaini, Mark A., eds. Foundations of Social Work Practice: A Graduate Text. 310p. (C). 1995. lib. bdg. 34.95 (*0-87101-237-5*, 2375) Natl Assn Soc Wkrs.

***Meyer, Carolyn.** Anastasia: Last Grand Duchess, Russia, 1914. LC 00-20399. (Royal Diaries Ser.). (Illus.). 224p. (YA). (gr. 4-7). 2000. 10.95 (*0-439-12908-7*) Scholastic Inc.

Meyer, Carolyn. Christmas Crafts. LC 74-2608. (Illus.). 160p. (J). (gr. 5 up). 1974. 13.95 (*0-06-024197-7*) HarpC Child Bks.

— Drummers of Jericho. LC 94-36105. 336p. (YA). (gr. 7 up). 1995. 11.00 (*0-15-200441-6*, Gulliver Bks); pap. 5.00 (*0-15-200190-5*, Gulliver Bks) Harcourt.

Meyer, Carolyn. Drummers of Jericho. 1995. 10.10 (*0-606-10997-8*, Pub. by Turtleback) Demco.

Meyer, Carolyn. Gideon's People. LC 95-37917. (Gulliver Bks.). 320p. (J). (gr. 4-7). 1996. 12.00 (*0-15-200303-7*); pap. 6.00 (*0-15-200304-5*, Gulliver Bks) Harcourt.

— In a Different Light: Growing up in a Yup'ik Eskimo Village in Alaska. LC 95-31140. (Illus.). 196p. (J). (gr. 4-7). 1996. 17.00 (*0-689-80146-7*) McElderry Bks.

***Meyer, Carolyn.** Isabel: Jewel of Castilla, Spain, 1466. LC 99-16805. (Royal Diaries Ser.). (Illus.). 240p. (J). (gr. 4-7). 2000. 10.95 (*0-439-07805-9*) Scholastic Inc.

Meyer, Carolyn. Jubilee Journey. LC 96-44563. (J). (gr. 5-9). 1997. 13.00 (*0-15-201377-6*); pap. 6.00 (*0-15-201591-4*) Harcourt.

— Mary Bloody Mary. LC 99-21185. 256p. 1999. 16.00 (*0-15-201906-5*) Harcourt.

— Mary Bloody Mary. 2001. pap. write for info. (*0-15-201905-7*) Harcourt.

— The Real World of Engineering: Case History, No. 44. LC 87-199. 224p. 3.50 (*0-614-05213-0*, CHN0445913.5M) ASFE.

— The Real World of Engineering: Case History, No. 45. LC 92-2578. 192p. 3.50 (*0-614-05214-9*, CHN04505913.5M) ASFE.

— The Real World of Engineering: Case History, No. 46. LC 92-2578. 192p. 3.50 (*0-614-05215-7*, CHN04605913.5M) ASFE.

— Rio Grande Stories. 1994. 9.10 (*0-606-09791-0*, Pub. by Turtleback) Demco.

— A Voice from Japan: An Outsider Looks In. LC 88-2286. (Illus.). 240p. (YA). (gr. 7 up). 1988. 14.95 (*0-15-200633-8*, Gulliver Bks) Harcourt.

— A Voice from Japan: An Outsider Looks In. LC 88-2286. 240p. (YA). (gr. 7 up). 1992. pap. 9.95 (*0-15-200634-6*, Gulliver Bks) Harcourt.

— Voices of Northern Ireland: Growing up in a Troubled Land. LC 87-199. (Illus.). 224p. (YA). (gr. 7 up). 1987. 15.95 (*0-15-200635-4*, Gulliver Bks) Harcourt.

— Voices of Northern Ireland: Growing up in a Troubled Land. LC 86-45059. 288p. (YA). (gr. 7 up). 1992. pap. 9.95 (*0-15-200638-9*) Harcourt.

— Voices of Northern Ireland: Growing up in a Troubled Land. LC 87-199. (Illus.). 224p. (YA). 1992. pap. 9.95 (*0-15-200636-2*) Harcourt.

— Voices of South Africa: Growing up in a Troubled Land. LC 86-45059. 244p. (J). (gr. 7 up). 1986. 16.95 (*0-15-200637-0*) Harcourt.

— Where the Broken Heart Still Beats: The Story of Cynthia Ann Parker. LC 92-257. (Great Episodes Ser.). 192p. (J). (gr. 3-7). 1992. 16.95 (*0-15-200639-7*, Gulliver Bks); pap. 7.00 (*0-15-295602-6*, Gulliver Bks) Harcourt.

Meyer, Carolyn. Where the Broken Heart Still Beats: The Story of Cynthia Ann Parker. 1992. 12.10 (*0-606-06148-7*, Pub. by Turtleback) Demco.

Meyer, Carolyn. White Lilacs. LC 92-30503. (Illus.). 256p. (J). (gr. 3-7). 1993. 12.00 (*0-15-200641-9*, Gulliver Bks); pap. 6.00 (*0-15-295876-2*, Gulliver Bks) Harcourt.

— White Lilacs. large type ed. (J). 1993. 63.00 (*0-614-09861-0*, L-34182-00) Am Printing Hse.

Meyer, Carolyn, compiled by. Rio Grande Stories. LC 93-33639. (Illus.). 224p. (J). (gr. 3-7). 1994. 12.00 (*0-15-200548-X*, Gulliver Bks); pap. 6.00 (*0-15-200066-6*, Gulliver Bks) Harcourt.

Meyer, Carolyn & Gallenkamp, Charles. The Mystery of the Ancient Maya. rev. ed. (Illus.). 192p. (J). (gr. 7 up). 1995. mass mkt. 15.00 (*0-689-50619-8*) McElderry Bks.

Meyer, Carolyn & Pickens, Kel. Multicultural Sing & Learn: Folk Songs & Monthly Activities. (Illus.). 144p. (J). (gr. k-5). 1994. 13.99 (*0-86653-830-5*, GA1522) Good Apple.

— Sing & Learn. (Illus.). 144p. (J). (ps-3). 1989. student ed. 13.99 (*0-86653-476-8*, GA1078) Good Apple.

Meyer, Carolyn J. Human Development. 4th ed. 288p. (C). 1986. student ed. write for info. (*0-317-44275-9*) P-H.

Meyer, Carolyn M. Group Lesson for Suzuki Violin & Viola. 84p. 1993. pap. text 12.95 (*0-87487-435-1*) Summy-Birchard.

Meyer, Carrie A. The Economics & Politics of NGOS in Latin America. LC 98-56629. 216p. 1999. 59.95 (*0-275-96621-6*, Praeger Pubs) Greenwood.

***Meyer, Carrie A.** The Economics & Politics of NGOs in Latin America. 2000. pap. write for info. (*0-275-97099-X*, Praeger Trade) Greenwood.

Meyer, Carrie A. Land Reform in Latin America: The Dominican Case. LC 88-39661. 142p. 1989. 49.95 (*0-275-93202-8*, C3202, Praeger Pubs) Greenwood.

Meyer, Catherine L. They Are My Children, Too: A Mother's Struggle for Her Sons. LC 99-18192. 352p. 1999. 23.00 (*1-891620-15-0*, Pub. by PublicAffairs NY) HarpC.

Meyer, Charles. Beside the Still Waters. (Reverend Lucas Holt Mystery Ser.). 232p. 1997. pap. 6.50 (*0-9631149-4-8*) Stone Angel.

— Blessed Are the Merciless. 2nd ed. (Reverend Lucas Holt Mystery Ser.). 266p. 1997. reprint ed. pap. 6.50 (*0-9631149-5-6*) Stone Angel.

— Deathangel. LC 99-52237. 288p. 1999. 24.95 (*0-9651879-7-7*) Boaz Pubng.

— A Good Death: Challenges, Choices & Care Options. LC 98-60132. 64p. 1998. pap. 6.95 (*0-89622-923-8*) Twenty-Third.

— The Saints of God Murders. 256p. (Orig.). 1995. mass mkt. 5.99 (*0-425-14869-6*, Prime Crime) Berkley Pub.

— Surviving Death: A Practical Guide to Caring for the Dying & the Bereaved. rev. ed. LC 91-65169. 200p. 1991. pap. 9.95 (*0-89622-486-4*) Twenty-Third.

Meyer, Charles & Kilbourn, W. Douglas, Jr. Accounting for Lawyers. 1994. student ed. 30.00 (*1-55917-002-6*, 4318); audio 135.00 (*1-55917-000-X*) Natl Prac Inst.

Meyer, Charles, et al. The Living Light Vol. 34, No. 4: Special Feature: Death, Burial, & Bereavement. Marthaler, Berard, ed. 96p. (C). 1998. pap. 8.95 (*1-57455-157-4*) US Catholic.

Meyer, Charles A., jt. ed. see Kao, Deborah M.

Meyer, Charles E. Rituals of the First Four Grades Societatis Rosicruciana. 68p. 1993. reprint ed. pap. 9.95 (*1-56459-364-9*) Kessinger Pub.

Meyer, Charles F. Apposition in Contemporary English. (Studies in English Language). (Illus.). 166p. (C). 1992. text 47.95 (*0-521-39475-9*) Cambridge U Pr.

Meyer, Charles F., jt. ed. see Aarts, Bas.

Meyer, Charles H. Accounting & Finance for Lawyers in a Nutshell. (Paralegal). 423p. (C). 1995. pap. text 17.00 (*0-314-04763-8*) West Pub.

— Securities Exchange Act of 1934: Analyzed & Explained. 251p. 1994. reprint ed. 45.00 (*0-8377-2447-3*, Rothman) W S Hein.

Meyer, Charles R. Art of Scrimshaw. 1976. 23.95 (*0-8488-0293-4*) Amereon Ltd.

— How to Be a Clown. 1976. 16.95 (*0-8488-0295-0*); pap. 10.95 (*0-8488-0294-2*) Amereon Ltd.

— How to Be a Juggler. 1976. 16.95 (*0-8488-0297-7*); pap. 12.95 (*0-8488-0296-9*) Amereon Ltd.

— How to Be a Magician. 1976. 16.95 (*0-8488-0299-3*); pap. 12.95 (*0-8488-0298-5*) Amereon Ltd.

— How to Be an Acrobat. 1976. 16.95 (*0-8488-0301-9*); pap. 12.95 (*0-8488-0300-0*) Amereon Ltd.

Meyer, Charles W. & Wolff, Nancy. Social Security & Individual Equity: Evolving Standards of Equity & Adequacy, 15. LC 92-25739. (Studies in Social Welfare Policies & Programs: No. 15). 208p. 1993. 49.95 (*0-313-26459-7*, MYC, Greenwood Pr) Greenwood.

Meyer, Cheryl. The Wandering Uterus: Politics & the Reproductive Rights of Women. LC 96-35694. 208p. (C). 1997. text 45.00 (*0-8147-5563-1*); pap. text 17.50 (*0-8147-5562-3*) NYU Pr.

Meyer, Christian. Design of Concrete Structures. LC 95-24569. 576p. (C). 1995. 100.00 (*0-13-203654-1*) P-H.

Meyer, Christian & Okamura, Hajime, eds. Finite Element Analysis of Reinforced Concrete Structures. (Seminar Proceedings Ser.). 696p. 1986. 60.00 (*0-87262-549-4*) Am Soc Civil Eng.

Meyer, Christian, jt. auth. see Lockley, Martin.

Meyer, Christiane. Animal Welfare Legislation in Canada & Germany: A Comparison. (European University Studies, Series 2: Vol. 2007). (Illus.). 285p. 1996. pap. 54.95 (*3-631-30733-0*) P Lang Pubng.

— Animal Welfare Legislation in Canada & Germany: A Comparison. (European University Studies, Series 2: Vol. 2007). (Illus.). 285p. 1996. pap. 54.95 (*0-8204-3214-8*) P Lang Pubng.

Meyer, Christine & Moosang, Faith. Living with the Land: Communities Restoring the Earth. (New Catalyst Bioregional Ser.). 144p. 1992. pap. 9.95 (*0-86571-251-4*) New Soc Pubs.

Meyer, Christopher. Fast Cycle Time: How to Align Purpose, Strategy & Structure for Speed. 288p. 1993. 35.00 (*0-02-921181-6*) Free Pr.

— Knowledge Advantage: Leveraging Knowledge Into Marketplace Success. 1999. 24.95 (*1-84112-067-7*) Capstone Pub NH.

— Relentless Growth: How Silicon Valley's Innovation Secrets Can Work for Your Business. LC 97-30740. (Illus.). 224p. 1997. 27.00 (*0-684-83446-4*) Free Pr.

Meyer, Christopher, jt. auth. see Davis, Stan.

***Meyer, Chuck.** Dying Church, Living God: A Call to Begin Again. 160p. 2000. pap. 16.95 (*1-896836-39-9*, Pub. by NStone Publ) Logos Prods.

Meyer, Chuck. The Eighth Day Letters, Poems & Parables. 175p. (Orig.). 1991. pap. 8.95 (*0-9631149-1-3*) Stone Angel.

M

— Fast, Funny & Forty. 170p. (Orig.). 1994. pap. 9.95 (*0-9631149-3-X*) Stone Angel.
— God's Laughter & Other Heresies. 2nd ed. 238p. 1992. pap. 9.95 (*0-9631149-0-5*) Stone Angel.
— The Gospel According to Bubba. (Illus.). 192p. (Orig.). 1992. pap. 9.95 (*0-9631149-2-1*) Stone Angel.
***Meyer, Chuck.** Twelve Smooth Stones: A Father Writes to His Daughter about Money, Sex, Spirituality & Other Things That Really Matters. 192p. 1999. pap. 14.95 (*1-896836-27-5*) NStone Publ.
Meyer, Clarence. American Folk Medicine. LC 85-155364. 320p. 1985. reprint ed. pap. 9.95 (*0-916638-10-3*) Meyerbooks.
— Herbal Aphrodisiacs from World Sources. enl. ed. Meyer, David, ed. (Illus.). 148p. (Orig.). 1993. pap. 8.95 (*0-916638-23-5*) Meyerbooks.
— The Herbalist Almanac: Fifty Years of Herbal Knowledge. Meyer, David C., ed. (Illus.). 1977. pap. 9.95 (*0-916638-02-2*) Meyerbooks.
— Old Ways Rediscovered. Meyer, David C., ed. (Illus.). 156p. (Orig.). 1988. pap. 8.95 (*0-916638-18-9*) Meyerbooks.
— Onions: Condiment, Nutrient, Medicine. Meyer, David C., ed. (Illus.). 115p. (Orig.). 1993. pap. 8.95 (*0-916638-16-2*) Meyerbooks.
— Vegetarian Medicines. Meyer, David C., ed. (Illus.). 96p. (Orig.). 1981. pap. 5.95 (*0-916638-06-5*) Meyerbooks.
Meyer, Clarence, compiled by. Herbal Recipes. (Illus.). 1978. pap. 3.95 (*0-916638-04-9*) Meyerbooks.
— Sachets, Potpourri & Incense Recipes. (Illus.). 96p. (Orig.). 1986. pap. 3.95 (*0-916638-13-8*) Meyerbooks.
Meyer, Clarence. Essential Oils of Herbs & Flowers: A Guide & Recipe Book. 100p. (Orig.). Date not set. pap. write for info. (*0-916638-14-6*) Meyerbooks.
Meyer, Claudia. Donald Teague: A Life in Color. deluxe ed. (Illus.). 144p. 1988. 300.00 (*0-9620327-1-9*) Nygard Pub.
Meyer, Conrad F. Plautus in the Convent. Howard, William G., tr. LC 62-17089. xiv, 133p. 1964. pap. 3.95 (*0-8044-6503-7*) Continuum.
— The Saint: A Fictional Biography of Thomas Becket. Twaddell, W. F., tr. from GER. LC 77-7038. 137p. reprint ed. pap. 42.50 (*0-608-17696-6*, 203002700067) Bks Demand.
— The Tempting of Pescara. Bell, C., tr. LC 75-4902. 184p. 1975. reprint ed. 35.00 (*0-86527-313-8*) Fertig.
Meyer, Corky & Ginter, Steve. Grumman Swing-Wing XF10F-1 Jaguar. (Naval Fighters Ser.: No. 26). (Illus.). 34p. (Orig.). 1993. pap. text 7.95 (*0-942612-26-4*) Naval Fighters.
Meyer, Corwin. Naval Fighters No. 44: Grumman's Mach-2 International F11F1F Supertiger. Ginter, Steve, ed. (Illus.). 48p. 1998. pap. 10.95 (*0-942612-44-2*, NF44) Naval Fighters.
Meyer, Corwin & Ginter, Steve. Naval Fighters Vol. 40: Grumman F11F Tiger. (Illus.). 144p. 1998. pap. 22.95 (*0-942612-40-X*, NF40) Naval Fighters.
Meyer, Cynthia A., ed. see Knox, Carol R.
Meyer, D. L., jt. auth. see Ingraham, L. L.
Meyer, Dan. Account for Your Own Success: Everything You Need to Manage Your Own Business & Personal Finances. (Illus.). 176p. 1993. pap. 16.95 (*0-932150-04-7*) MCS.
— Union Square Cafe Cookbook Ri. LC 94-1110. (Illus.). 336p. 1995. 32.50 (*0-06-017013-1*) HarperTrade.
Meyer, Dan M. ECMO Extracorporeal Membrane Oxigenation. (Vademecum Ser.). 2000. spiral bd. 45.00 (*1-57059-575-5*) Landes Bioscience.
Meyer, Daniel. Stephen A. Douglas & the American Union. LC 94-2381. (Illus.). 48p. 1994. pap. 10.00 (*0-943056-21-7*) Univ Chi Lib.
Meyer, Daniel E., et al, eds. Chemical Structure Software for Personal Computers. LC 88-8153. (ACS Professional Reference Bk.). (Illus.). xiv, 107p. 1988. pap. text 26.00 (*0 8412 1539 1*, Pub. by Am Chemical) OUP.
— Chemical Structure Software for Personal Computers. LC 88-8153. (ACS Professional Reference Bk.). (Illus.). xiv, 107p. 1988. 39.95 (*0-8412-1538-3*) Am Chemical.
Meyer, Dave. Dave's Nuggets. pap. 2.00 (*0-944834-07-8*) Life Word-Meyer Ministries.
— Nuggets of Life. 160p. (Orig.). 1996. mass mkt. 5.99 (*0-89274-974-1*, HH-974) Harrison Hse.
Meyer, David. A Collector's Tale. (Illus.). 8p. (Orig.). 1995. pap. 5.00 (*0-941543-09-9*) Sun Dog Pr.
— Examinando los Pretextos para el Recasamiento de Personas Divorciadas. 12p. 1996. pap. 0.50 (*0-9624603-9-7*) Comt Restoration Fam.
Meyer, David, compiled by. Howard Thurston's Card Tricks: An Illustrated & Descriptive Checklist of Various Editions Covering a 50 Year Period. (Illus.). 48p. (Orig.). 1991. pap. 9.50 (*0-916638-75-8*) Meyerbooks.
Meyer, David & Meyer, Alcie, eds. The Temptations of Jesus: An Illustrated Bible Passage for Young Children. LC 93-60713. (Illus.). 40p. (Orig.). (J). (ps-4). 1996. pap. 12.95 incl. audio (*1-879099-08-X*) Thy Word.
Meyer, David & Meyer, Alice, eds. The Beatitudes: An Illustrated Bible Passage for Young Children. LC 93-60712. (Illus.). 32p. (Orig.). (J). (ps-4). 1993. pap. 12.95 incl. audio (*1-879099-07-1*) Thy Word.
— First Corinthians Thirteen: An Illustrated Bible Chapter for Young Children. LC 90-71555. (Illus.). 48p. (Orig.). (J). (ps-4). 1990. pap. 12.95 incl. audio (*1-879099-01-2*) Thy Word.
— Isaiah 53: An Illustrated Bible Chapter for Young Children. LC 91-90827. (Illus.). 40p. (Orig.). (J). (ps-4). 1992. pap. 12.95 incl. audio (*1-879099-06-3*) Thy Word.
— Isaiah 53/Psalm 139. 24p. (Orig.). 1997. pap. 12.95 (*1-879099-28-4*) Thy Word.
— The Lord's Prayer: An Illustrated Bible Passage for Young Children. LC 91-90826. (Illus.). 32p. (Orig.). (J). (ps-4). 1991. pap. 12.95 incl. audio (*1-879099-05-5*) Thy Word.
— Matthew 4:1-11/Psalm 91. 16p. (Orig.). 1997. pap. 12.95 (*1-879099-27-6*) Thy Word.
— I Corinthians 12 & 13. 32p. 1999. pap. 12.95 (*1-879099-29-2*) Thy Word.
— Psalm 91: An Illustrated Bible Chapter for Young Children. LC 90-71556. (Illus.). 48p. (Orig.). (J). (ps-4). 1991. pap. 12.95 incl. audio (*1-879099-04-7*) Thy Word.
— Psalm 139: An Illustrated Bible Chapter for Young Children. LC 91-90825. (Illus.). 48p. (Orig.). (J). (ps-4). 1991. pap. 12.95 incl. audio (*1-879099-03-9*) Thy Word.
— Psalm 23: An Illustrated Bible Chapter for Young Children. (Illus.). 32p. (J). (ps-4). 1990. pap. 12.95 incl. audio (*1-879099-00-4*) Thy Word.
— The Ten Commandments: An Illustrated Bible Passage for Young Children. LC 90-71557. (Illus.). 40p. (Orig.). (J). (ps-4). 1991. pap. 12.95 incl. audio (*1-879099-02-0*) Thy Word.
— The Ten Commandments/The Beatitudes. 16p. 1997. pap. 12.95 (*1-879099-26-8*) Thy Word.
Meyer, David & Tarrow, Sidney, eds. The Social Movement Society: Contentious Politics for a New Century. LC 97-30586. (Illus.). 282p. 1997. pap. 24.95 (*0-8476-8541-1*); text 68.50 (*0-8476-8540-3*) Rowman.
Meyer, David, ed. see Houdini, Harry & Thurston, Howard.
Meyer, David, ed. see Meyer, Clarence.
Meyer, David B. Laboratory Guide for Human Histology. rev. ed. LC 85-15296. 133p. (Orig.). reprint ed. pap. 41.30 (*0-608-10582-1*, 207120300009) Bks Demand.
Meyer, David B., tr. see Drews, Ulrich.
Meyer, David C., ed. see Meyer, Clarence.
Meyer, David E. & Kornblum, Sylvan, eds. Attention & Performance XIV: Synergies in Experimental Psychology, Artificial Intelligence, & Cognitive Neuroscience a Silver Jubilee Volume. (Illus.). 937p. 1993. 82.50 (*0-262-13284-2*, Bradford Bks) MIT Pr.
***Meyer, David J.** Rabbinic Driving Manual. (Illus.). 64p. (YA). (gr. 10-12). 1998. pap. write for info. (*0-933873-94-8*) Torah Aura.
Meyer, David N. A Girl & a Gun: The Complete Renter's Guide to Film Noir. LC 97-34771. 288p. 1998. pap. 14.00 (*0-380-79067-X*, Avon Bks) Morrow Avon.
— The 100 Best Films to Rent You've Never Heard Of: Neglected Classics, Hits from By-Gone Eras & Hidden Treasures. 3rd ed. LC 96-32865. (Illus.). 224p. 1996. pap. 11.95 (*0-312-15042-3*) St Martin.
Meyer, David P. Underemployment from a Human Perspective. 63p. 1985. 6.25 (*0-317-01303-3*, IN303) Ctr Educ Trng Employ.
***Meyer, David R.** Hong Kong as a Global Metropolis. LC 99-32285. (Cambridge Studies in Historical Geography: No. 30). (Illus.). 297p. (C). 2000. 64.95 (*0-521-64344-9*) Cambridge U Pr.
Meyer, David R. Spatial Variation of Black Urban Households. LC 72-129455. (University of Chicago, Department of Geography, Research Paper Ser.: No. 129). 144p. reprint ed. pap. 44.70 (*0-7837-0404-6*, 204072500018) Bks Demand.
Meyer, David S. A Winter of Discontent: The Nuclear Freeze & American Politics. LC 89-26588. 320p. 1990. 65.00 (*0-275-93305-9*, C3305, Praeger Pubs); pap. 22.95 (*0-275-93306-7*, B3306, Praeger Pubs) Greenwood.
Meyer, David S., jt. auth. see Rochon, Thomas R.
Meyer de Schauensee, Rodolphe. A Guide to the Birds of South America. 463p. 1982. pap. 25.00 (*0-87098-027-0*) U KS Nat Hist Mus.
***Meyer, Debbie.** Good Friends Great Tastes: A Celebration of Life, Food & Friendship. (Illus.). 224p. 2000. 22.95 (*0-9676269-0-0*, Pub. by Good Friends) Wimmer Cos.
Meyer, Debbie. Nutcracker - the Musical. (Illus.). 26p. (Orig.). 1996. pap. 4.50 (*0-88680-418-3*) I E Clark.
Meyer, Deke. Advanced Fly Fishing for Steelhead. (Illus.). 160p. 1992. pap. 29.95 (*1-878175-10-6*) F Amato Pubns.
— Float Tube Fly Fishing. (Illus.). 125p. (Orig.). 1989. pap. 11.95 (*0-936608-71-4*) F Amato Pubns.
— Saltwater Flies: Over 700 of the Best. (Illus.). 120p. 1995. pap. 24.95 (*1-57188-020-8*) F Amato Pubns.
— Tying Bass Flies: 12 of the Best. (Illus.). 32p. 1995. pap. 9.95 (*1-57188-041-0*) F Amato Pubns.
— Tying Saltwater Flies: 12 of the Best. (Illus.). 32p. 1996. 9.95 (*1-57188-066-6*) F Amato Pubns.
— Tying Trout Flies: 12 of the Best. (Illus.). 32p. 1993. pap. 9.95 (*1-878175-40-8*) F Amato Pubns.
— Tying Trout Nymphs: 12 of the Best. LC 95-126895. (Illus.). 32p. 1994. pap. 9.95 (*1-878175-87-4*) F Amato Pubns.
Meyer-Denkmann, Gertrud. Experiments in Sound: New Directions in Musical Education for Young Children. Paynter, Elizabeth & Paynter, John, eds. LC 50-26923.Tr. of Klangexperimente Und Gestaltungsversuche Im Kindesalter. 1977. pap. 25.00 (*0-900938-49-8*, UE26923) Eur-Am Music.
Meyer, Dennie J. & Harvey, John W. Veterinary Laboratory Medicine: Interpretation & Diagnosis. 2nd ed. Kersey, Ray, ed. LC 97-7725. (Illus.). 352p. 1997. pap. text 39.00 (*0-7216-6222-6*, W B Saunders Co) Harcrt Hlth Sci Grp.
***Meyer, Diana & Fromm, David.** Metropolitan Life Foundation Awards: Round II Winners in Supportive Housing & Property & Asset Management. (Illus.). 52p. 1998. pap. 15.00 (*0 942901-15-0*) Enterprise Fnd.
Meyer, Dieter, jt. auth. see Markl, Hermann.
Meyer-Dinkgrafe, Daniel. Consciousness & the Actor: A Reassessment of Western & Indian Approaches to the Actor's Emotional Involvement from the Perspective of Vedic Psychology. LC 96-11751. (European University Studies, Series XXX: Vol. 67). 203p. 1996. pap. 42.95 (*0-8204-3180-X*, PN2071) P Lang Pubng.
***Meyer-Dinkgrhafe, Daniel.** Approaches to Acting: Past & Present. LC 00-43136. (Illus.). 2001. pap. write for info. (*0-8264-4901-8*) Continuum.
— Who's Who in Contemporary World Theatre. LC 99-47437. 304p. 2000. 44.95 (*0-415-14161-3*) Routledge.
Meyer, Don, jt. auth. see Cannon, Casey.
Meyer, Donald, ed. Uncommon Fathers: Reflections on Raising a Child with a Disability. LC 95-8651. 206p. (Orig.). (C). 1995. pap. 14.95 (*0-933149-68-9*) Woodbine House.
Meyer, Donald B. The Protestant Search for Political Realism, 1919-1941. 2nd ed. LC 88-17509. 519p. reprint ed. pap. 160.90 (*0-608-09091-3*, 206972500005) Bks Demand.
— Sex & Power: The Rise of Women in America, Russia, Sweden, & Italy. LC 87-6080. 749p. 1987. reprint ed. pap. 200.00 (*0-608-02312-4*, 206295300004) Bks Demand.
Meyer, Donald J. Living with a Brother or Sister with Special Needs: A Book for Sibs. 2nd expanded rev. ed. LC 96-7020. (Illus.). 144p. (ps up). 1996. pap. 14.95 (*0-295-97547-4*) U of Wash Pr.
Meyer, Donald J., ed. Views from Our Shoes: Growing up with a Brother or Sister with Special Needs. LC 97-18351. (Illus.). 113p. (J). (gr. 3 up). 1997. pap. 14.95 (*0-933149-98-0*) Woodbine House.
Meyer, Donald W., jt. auth. see Shroeder, E. M.
Meyer, Doris. Speaking for Themselves: Neomexicano Cultural Identity & the Spanish-Language Press, 1880-1920. LC 96-4526. (Paso por Aqui Ser.). 279p. 1996. pap. 29.95 (*0-8263-1749-9*) U of NM Pr.
Meyer, Doris, ed. Reinterpreting the Spanish American Essay: Women Writers of the 19th & 20th Centuries. LC 94-17119. (Texas Pan American Ser.). 272p. (C). 1995. text 37.50 (*0-292-75167-2*) U of Tex Pr.
— Rereading the Spanish American Essay: Translations of 19th & 20th Century Women's Essays. LC 95-3564. (Texas Pan American Ser.). (Illus.). 320p. (Orig.). 1995. 40.00 (*0-292-75179-6*); pap. 19.95 (*0-292-75182-6*) U of Tex Pr.
Meyer, Doris & Fernandez-Olmos, Margarite, eds. Introductory Essays. (Contemporary Women Authors of Latin America Ser.: Vol. I). 103p. 1984. pap. 9.50 (*0-930888-20-0*) Brooklyn Coll Pr.
— New Translations. (Contemporary Women Authors of Latin America Ser.: Vol. II). 331p. 1984. pap. 12.50 (*0-930888-21-9*) Brooklyn Coll Pr.
Meyer, Doris, tr. see Campobello, Nellie.
Meyer, Douglas E. Two Good Friday Tenebrae Services: Paradoxes of the Passion - What Shall I Do, Then, - With Jesus Who Is Called Christ? 36p. 1999. pap. 4.95 (*0-7880-1314-9*) CSS OH.
***Meyer, Douglas K.** Making the Heartland Quilt. LC 99-41235. (Illus.). 384p. 2000. 49.95 (*0-8093-2289-7*) S Ill U Pr.
Meyer, Duane G. The Highland Scots of North Carolina, 1732-1776. LC 61-66281. xi, 218p. 1987. reprint ed. pap. 14.95 (*0-8078-4199-4*) U of NC Pr.
Meyer, Dwain. Today Is the First Day of the Rest of Your Layout. LC 97-188451. 80p. (Orig.). 1997. pap. 9.95 (*0-89024-321-2*, 12193, Kalmbach Books) Kalmbach.
Meyer, E. & Ziehnski, Donald D. Future Options Unlimited, Bk. 2. Date not set. teacher ed. 14.95 (*0-910857-71-7*, 071-7AP) Educ Impress.
Meyer, E. Gerald, jt. ed. see Niederhauser, Warren D.
Meyer, E. M., et al, eds. Novel Approaches to the Treatment of Alzheimer's Disease. LC 89-26615. (Advances in Behavioral Biology Ser.: No. 36). (Illus.). 400p. 1989. 110.00 (*0-306-43402-4*, Plenum Trade) Perseus Pubng.
Meyer, E. M., et al. Treatment of Dementias: A New Generation of Progress. (Advances in Behavioral Biology Ser.: Vol. 40). (Illus.). 448p. (C). 1992. text 130.00 (*0-306-44228-0*, Kluwer Plenum) Kluwer Academic.
Meyer, Earl C. & Allen. Entrepreneurship & Small Business Management. (Illus.). 192p. (YA). (gr. 6-12). 1999. student ed., wbk. ed. 8.10 (*0-02-675122-4*) Glencoe.
— Entrepreneurship & Small Business Management. annot. ed. 1999. teacher ed. 40.70 (*0-02-675121-6*) Glencoe.
Meyer, Earl C. & Allen, Kathleen R. Entrepreneurship & Small Business Management. (Illus.). 384p. (YA). (gr. 6-12). 1993. text, student ed. 32.75 (*0-02-675119-4*) Glencoe.
Meyer, Eduard. Forschungen Zur Alten Geschichte, 2 vols. xiv, 879p. 1966. reprint ed. write for info. (*0-318-70784-5*) G Olms Pubs.
— Forschungen Zur Alten Geschichte, Bd. I: Zur Alteren Geschichte. xiv, 879p. 1966. reprint ed. write for info. (*0-318-70785-3*) G Olms Pubs.
— Forschungen Zur Alten Geschichte, Bd. II: Zur Geschichte des 5. Jahrh v. Chr. xiv, 879p. 1966. reprint ed. write for info. (*0-318-70786-1*) G Olms Pubs.
— Theopompus Hellenika. xii, 291p. 1966. reprint ed. write for info. (*0-318-70976-7*) G Olms Pubs.
Meyer, Edward, ed. see Slager, Christina Joie.
Meyer, Edward C., et al. Who Will Lead? Senior Leadership in the United States Army. LC 94-34319. 296p. 1995. 65.00 (*0-275-95041-7*, Praeger Pubs) Greenwood.
***Meyer, Edward H.** Nine Easy Hymn Preludes, Bk. 3. 36p. 1998. pap. 13.50 (*0-8100-0957-9*) Northwest Pub.
Meyer, Edward H. Samm Level 2: Accompaniment Songbook. 1998. 25.00 (*0-8100-0781-9*) Northwest Pub.
— Samm Level 2: Student Songbook. 1998. 7.50 (*0-8100-0782-7*) Northwest Pub.
— Samm Level 2: Teacher's Guide. 1998. teacher ed. 225.00 (*0-8100-0783-5*) Northwest Pub.
Meyer, Edward N. Giant Strides: The Legacy of Dick Wellstood. LC 98-39905. (Studies in Jazz: No. 32). (Illus.). 280p. 1999. 45.00 (*0-8108-3564-9*) Scarecrow.
***Meyer, Eleanor Walsh.** The Keeper of Ugly Sounds. (Illus.). 32p. (J). (gr. k-3). 1998. 16.95 (*1-890817-02-3*, Pub. by Winslow Pr) Publishers Group.
Meyer, Elisa. Feeding Your Allergic Child. 1996. pap. 10.95 (*0-614-19387-7*) St Martin.
— Feeding Your Allergic Child. LC 96-45969. 160p. 1997. pap. 11.95 (*0-312-14612-4*) St Martin.
***Meyer, Elisa.** Feeding Your Allergic Child: Happy Food for Healthy Kids. 179p. 1999. reprint ed. pap. text 12.00 (*0-7881-6472-4*) DIANE Pub.
Meyer, Ellen H., jt. ed. see DeMaria, Robert.
Meyer, Emily & Smith, Louise Z. The Practical Tutor. (Illus.). 368p. 1987. pap. text 29.95 (*0-19-503865-7*) OUP.
***Meyer, Eric A.** Cascading Style Sheets: The Definitive Guide. Koman, Richard, ed. LC 00-35694. (Illus.). 480p. 2000. pap. 34.95 (*1-56592-622-6*) OReilly & Assocs.
Meyer, Eric K. Designing Infographics. LC 96-78595. 336p. 1997. 39.99 (*1-56830-339-4*) Hayden.
Meyer, Ernest A., jt. ed. see Erlandsen, Stanley L.
Meyer, Ernest L. Hey Yellowbacks: The War Diary of a Conscientious Objector. LC 75-143432. (Peace Movement in America Ser.). x, 209p. 1972. reprint ed. lib. bdg. 29.95 (*0-89198-080-6*) Ozer.
— Hey! Yellowbacks: The War Diary of a Conscientous Objector. (American Biography Ser.). 209p. 1991. reprint ed. lib. bdg. 69.00 (*0-7812-8284-5*) Rprt Serv.
Meyer, Ernst H. English Chamber Music. LC 71-127181. (Music Ser.). (Illus.). 1971. reprint ed. lib. bdg. 39.50 (*0-306-70037-9*) Da Capo.
Meyer, Ernst Von, see Von Meyer, Ernst.
Meyer, Esther da Costa. The Work of Antonio Sant'Elia: Retreat into the Future. LC 94-39125. (Publications in the History of Art). 1995. 47.50 (*0-300-04309-0*) Yale U Pr.
Meyer, Eugen. Humes und Berkeleys Philosophie der Mathematik Vergleichend und Kritisch Dargestellt. (GER.). 1997. reprint ed. 19.80 (*3-487-06769-2*) G Olms Pubs.
Meyer, Eugene. Chemistry Hazardous Materials. 2nd ed. 1989. 67.00 (*0-89303-133-X*, Medical Exam) Appleton & Lange.
— Chemistry of Hazardous Materials. 3rd ed. LC 97-39821. 624p. 1997. 74.00 (*0-8359-5175-8*) P-H.
Meyer, Eugene & Brady, Joseph V., eds. Research in the Psychobiology of Human Behavior. LC 78-24710. (Illus.). 160p. reprint ed. pap. 49.60 (*0-8357-8303-0*, 203415200088) Bks Demand.
***Meyer, Eugene L.** Maryland Lost & Found... Again. expanded rev. ed. LC 99-89771. (Illus.). 240p. 2000. pap. write for info. (*1-891521-08-X*) Woodholme Hse.
Meyer, Eve R., ed. see Carr, Banjamin.
Meyer, Eve R., ed. see Gassmann, Florian L.
Meyer, F. A., ed. see Weizman Institute of Science Staff.
Meyer, F. B. Abraham Friend of God. 1997. pap. 7.99 (*0-907927-86-6*) Emerald House Group Inc.
— Blessed Ar Ye: Talks on the Beatitudes. 142p. 1998. pap. 8.99 (*1-84030-021-3*) Emerald House Group Inc.
— The Blessed Life. (Heritage Ser.). 1997. pap. 1.99 (*0-87509-606-9*) Chr Pubns.
— Dedicated Life. 1997. pap. text 8.99 (*1-898787-88-3*) Emerald House Group Inc.
— Devotional Commentary on Exodus. LC 78-9530. 480p. 1978. pap. 16.99 (*0-8254-3244-8*, Kregel Class) Kregel.
— Great Thoughts from the Upper Room. 160p. 1983. reprint ed. pap. 6.95 (*0-310-44601-5*, 12364P) Zondervan.
— Great Verses Through the Bible. 144p. 1982. pap. 14.45 (*0-310-29131-3*, 10212P) Zondervan.
— Israel: A Prince with God. Chao, Lorna, tr. from CHI. (Meyer's Bible Characters Ser.). 1987. pap. write for info. (*0-941598-37-3*) Living Spring Pubns.
— Joseph: Beloved, Hated, Exalted. Chen, Ruth T., tr. from CHI. (Meyer's Bible Characters Ser.). 1987. pap. write for info. (*0-941598-38-1*) Living Spring Pubns.
— The Life of Abraham: The Obedience of Faith. Wubbels, Lance, ed. (Bible Character Ser.). 192p. 1996. pap. 9.99 (*1-883002-34-6*) Emerald WA.
— The Life of David: The Man after God's Own Heart. Wubbles, Lance, ed. (Bible Character Ser.). 182p. 1995. pap. 9.99 (*1-883002-21-4*) Emerald WA.
— The Life of Joseph: Beloved, Hated, & Exalted. Wubbels, Lance, ed. (Bible Character Ser.). 149p. 1995. pap. 9.99 (*1-883002-23-0*) Emerald WA.
— The Life of Moses: The Servant of God. Wubbels, Lance, ed. (Bible Character Ser.). 170p. 1996. pap. 9.99 (*1-883002-35-4*) Emerald WA.
— The Life of Paul: A Servant of Jesus Christ. Wubbels, Lance, ed. (Bible Character Ser.). 179p. 1995. pap. 9.99 (*1-883002-22-2*) Emerald WA.
— The Life of Peter: Fisherman, Disciple, Apostle. Wubbels, Lance, ed. (Bible Character Ser.). 192p. 1996. pap. 9.99 (*1-883002-36-2*) Emerald WA.
— O Profeta da Esperanca. Orig. Title: The Prophet of Hope. (POR.). 112p. 1987. pap. 5.95 (*0-8297-1607-6*) Vida Pubs.
— Old Testament Men of Faith. (World Classic Reference Library). 575p. 1995. reprint ed. 19.99 (*0-529-10423-7*, OTMF) World Publng.
— Our Daily Walk. 16.99 (*1-85792-048-1*, Pub. by Christian Focus) Spring Arbor Dist.
— Our Daily Walk. 1982. pap. 9.95 (*0-310-29141-0*) Zondervan.
— Our Glorious Lord. large type ed. 6.99 (*1-85792-103-8*, Pub. by Christian Focus) Spring Arbor Dist.
— Paz, Perfecta Paz. large type ed.Tr. of Peace, Perfect Peace. (SPA.). 56p. 1990. pap. 2.99 (*1-56063-339-5*, 494021) Editorial Unilit.
— Pocketbook of Daily Prayers. 1997. pap. text 2.99 (*0-87788-620-2*, H Shaw Pubs) Waterbrook Pr.
— Power for Living. 126p. 1997. pap. 8.99 (*1-84030-006-X*) Emerald House Group Inc.
— Prophet of Hope. 1997. pap. 8.99 (*1-898787-28-X*) Emerald House Group Inc.

An Asterisk (*) at the beginning of an entry indicates that the title is appearing for the first time.

— The Secret of Guidance. Taniguchi, Ruth W., tr. from ENG. (CHI.). 1984. pap. write for info. (*0-941598-07-1*) Living Spring Pubns.

— The Secret of Guidance. LC 97-199562. (Classics Ser.). 128p. 1997. mass mkt. 4.99 (*0-8024-6398-3*, 395) Moody.

— Some Secrets of Christian Living. 144p. (Orig.). 1985. pap. 6.70 (*0-310-38721-3*, 17076P) Zondervan.

Meyer, Faith, ed. see Piche, Thomas E.

Meyer, F.B. Christ In You. (Moody Classics Ser.). (Orig.). 1998. mass mkt. 4.99 (*0-8024-5431-3*) Moody.

Meyer, Fernand, ed. see Parfionovitch, Yuri.

Meyer, Francis. Resources for Teaching Poetry, Vol. 1. Date not set. pap. text. write for info. (*0-312-11633-0*) St Martin.

Meyer, Francis D. Exercise Designed for the Aging. (Exercise & Care of Aging Body Ser.). (Illus.). 181p. 1985. pap. text 5.95 (*0-9615720-0-0*) FDM Distributor.

Meyer, Frank. Line of Duty. Costa, Gwen, ed. LC 90-43991. 1992. pap. 15.95 (*0-87949-332-1*) Ashley Bks.

Meyer, Frank S. In Defense of Freedom & Related Essays. LC 95-39943. 1996. 15.00 (*0-86597-139-0*); pap. 7.50 (*0-86597-140-4*) Liberty Fund.

Meyer, Frank S., ed. African Nettle. LC 78-121488. (Essay Index Reprint Ser.). 1977. 24.95 (*0-8369-1764-2*) Ayer.

Meyer, Frank S., et al. Left, Right & Center: Essays on Liberalism & Conservatism in the United States. Goldwin, Robert A., ed. LC 70-156679. (Essay Index Reprint Ser.). 1977. reprint ed. 20.95 (*0-8369-2777-X*) Ayer.

M

Meyer, Franz O. Lonely Planet Diving & Snorkeling Guide to Belize. 2nd ed. (Illus.). 96p. 1998. pap. 15.95 (*0-86442-575-9*) Lonely Planet.

***Meyer, Franziska.** Avantgarde in Hinterland: Caroline Schlegel-Schelling in der DDR-Literatur. (German Life & Civilization Ser.: Vol. 25). XIII, 258p. (C). 1999. text 52.95 (*0-8204-3924-X*) P Lang Pubng.

Meyer, Fred & Baker, Ralph, eds. Law Enforcement & Police Policy. (C). 1979. pap. 15.00 (*0-918592-31-3*) Pol Studies.

— State Policy Problems. 1992. pap. 15.00 (*0-944285-28-7*) Pol Studies.

Meyer, Frederic B. Atlas of Operative Neurosurgery. Zorab, Richard, ed. LC 98-18407. (Illus.). 480p. (C). 1998. text 295.00 (*0-443-08951-5*, M2039) Church.

Meyer, Frederick A. Life Is a Trust. (Religious Ser.). 95p. 1986. 8.95 (*0-935087-09-5*) Wright Pub Co.

Meyer, Frederick B. Daily Prayers: A Classic Collection. LC 95-7979. Orig. Title: My Daily Prayer. 144p. 1995. 12.99 (*0-87788-169-3*, H Shaw Pubs) Waterbrook Pr.

***Meyer, Frederick B.** Psalms. (Classics Ser.). (Illus.). 190p. 1999. pap. 9.99 (*1-84030-056-6*) Emerald House Group Inc.

***Meyer, Frederick G.** Great Herbal of Leonhart Fuchs, 2 Vol. De Historia Stirpium Commentarii Insignes, 1542 (notable. LC 98-53007. 1999. 299.50 (*0-8047-3803-3*) Stanford U Pr.

***Meyer, Frederick G., et al.** The Great Herbal of Leonhart Fuchs. LC 98-53007. 1999. write for info. (*0-8047-3757-6*) Stanford U Pr.

Meyer, Frederick G., et al. The Great Herbal of Leonhart Fuchs: De Historia Stirpium Commentarii Insignes, 1542 (Notable Commentaries on the History of Plants) LC 98-53007. 895p. 1999. write for info. (*0-8047-1631-5*) Stanford U Pr.

Meyer, Frederick V., et al. Problems of a Mature Economy: A Text for Students of the British Economy. LC 79-123635. xii, 627p. 1970. write for info. (*0-333-04240-9*) Macmillan.

Meyer, Fredric B., ed. Sundt's Occlusive Cerebrovascular Disease. 2nd rev. ed. LC 94-18063. 1994. text 175.00 (*0-7216-4911-4*, W B Saunders Co) Harcrt Hlth Sci Grp.

Meyer, Fredrich, et al, eds. Theory of Accretion Disks: Proceedings of the NATO Advanced Research Workshop Held in Garching, FRG March 6-10, 1989. (C). 1989. text 255.50 (*0-7923-0453-5*) Kluwer Academic.

Meyer, Friedrich. Maler Muller-Bibliographie. viii, 175p. 1974. reprint ed. write for info. (*3-487-05286-5*) G Olms Pubs.

Meyer, Fritzjuergen. Das Trophische Parenchym. (Handbuch der Pflanzenanatomie Encyclopedia of Plant Anatomy - Traite d' Anatomie Vegetale Ser.: Band IV, Teil 7). (Illus.). x, 188p. 1962. 52.00 (*3-443-39007-2*, Pub. by Gebruder Borntraeger) Balogh.

Meyer, G. & Morss, L. R., eds. Synthesis of Lanthanide & Actinide Compounds. (C). 1991. text 226.50 (*0-7923-1018-7*) Kluwer Academic.

Meyer, G., jt. ed. see Petry, S.

Meyer, G. Curt, jt. ed. see Hall, Linda K.

***Meyer, G. Dale & Heppard, Kurt A.** Entrepreneurship as Strategy: Competing on the Entrepreneurial Edge. LC 00-8076. (Entrepreneurship & the Management of Growing Enterprises Ser.). 2000. pap. write for info. (*0-7619-1580-X*) Sage.

Meyer, G. J. Executive Blues. LC 95-11984. 1995. 21.95 (*1-879957-22-1*, Franklin Sq Pr) Harpers Mag Found.

— Executive Blues: Down & Out in Corporate America. (Illus.). 1995. 21.95 (*0-614-15415-4*, Franklin Sq Pr) Harpers Mag Found.

Meyer, G. J., jt. auth. see Searson, P. C.

Meyer, Gabriel. The Gospel of Joseph: A Father's Story. 172p. 1994. 19.95 (*0-8245-1406-8*) Crossroad NY.

— In the Shade of the Terebinth: Tales of a Night Journey. (Illus.). 143p. 1994. 10.95 (*0-939516-23-3*) Forest Peace.

Meyer, Gabriel, jt. auth. see Snyder, Elizabeth.

Meyer, Gail M., jt. auth. see Grant, Gregory J.

Meyer, Galen. First & Second Thessalonians: Longing for the Lord. (Revelation Ser.). 1995. pap., teacher ed. 6.75 (*1-56212-089-1*) CRC Pubns.

— Hebrews: Glimpsing the Glory. LC 93-14321. (Revelation Series for Adults). 1993. pap., student ed. 4.95 (*1-56212-044-1*) CRC Pubns.

— The Stories of Abraham: Trusting the God Who Calls. (Revelation Ser.). 1993. pap., teacher ed. 6.75 (*1-56212-088-3*) CRC Pubns.

Meyer, Gary J. Automating Personnel Operations: The Human Resource Manager's Guide to Computerization. 1984. ring bd. 76.50 (*1-55645-416-3*) Busn Legal Reports.

Meyer, George E. & DeShazer, James A., eds. Optics in Agriculture, Forestry & Biological Processing II, Vol. 2907. 284p. 1996. 66.00 (*0-8194-2309-2*) SPIE.

— Precision Agriculture & Biological Quality, Vol. 3543. 176p. 1999. 89.00 (*0-8194-3005-6*) SPIE.

***Meyer, George E. & DeShazer, James A., eds.** Precision Agriculture & Biological Quality. LC 99-208071. 400p. 1999. pap. text 89.00 (*0-8194-3155-9*) SPIE.

Meyer, George H. American Folk Art Canes: Personal Sculpture. LC 92-9714. (Illus.). 252p. 1992. 65.00 (*0-295-97200-9*) U of Wash Pr.

Meyer, George W., ed. see Wordsworth, William.

Meyer, Gerald. Progress in Inorganic Chemistry: Molecular Level Artificial Photosynthetic Materials, Vol. 44. LC 59-13035. (Progress in Inorganic Chemistry Ser.). 421p. 1996. 175.00 (*0-471-12535-0*) Wiley.

— Vito Marcantonio: Radical Politician, 1902-1954. LC 88-31669. (SUNY Series in American Labor History). 303p. (C). 1989. text 64.50 (*0-7914-0082-4*); pap. text 21.95 (*0-7914-0083-2*) State U NY Pr.

Meyer, Gerry. Help Unwanted. Date not set. write for info. (*0-8050-4910-X*) H Holt & Co.

Meyer, Gladys C. Softball for Girls & Women. (Illus.). 320p. 1984. pap. 11.95 (*0-684-18140-1*) S&S Trade.

Meyer, Gretchen, ed. see Simms, Darrell D.

Meyer, H. J., jt. auth. see Heidrich, H.

Meyer, H. O. The Interaction Between Medium Energy Nucleons in Nuclei, Indiana University Cyclotron Facility, 1982. LC 83-70649. (AIP Conference Proceedings Ser.: No. 97). 433p. 1983. lib. bdg. 38.50 (*0-88318-196-7*) Am Inst Physics.

Meyer, H. O., jt. ed. see Boyd, F. R.

Meyer, H. O., jt. ed. see Schwandt, P.

***Meyer, Hans.** The Book of Wood Names. 582p. 2000. reprint ed. pap. 35.00 (*0-941936-62-7*, Pub. by Linden Pub Fresno) IPG Chicago.

Meyer, Hans G. Eine Sabbatampel Im Erfurter Dom. (Studien Zur Kunstgeschichte Ser.: Bd. 16). (GER.). 175p. 1982. write for info. (*3-487-07294-7*) G Olms Pubs.

***Meyer, Hans-Otto & Schwandt, Peter, eds.** Nuclear Physics at Storage Rings: Fourth International Conference: STORI99. LC 00-102026. (AIP Conference Proceedings Ser.: Vol. 512). (Illus.). xv, 436p. 2000. 130.00 (*1-56396-928-9*, Pub. by Am Inst Physics) Spr-Verlag.

Meyer, Harding. That All May Be One: Perceptions & Models of Ecumenicity. LC 98-53603. 176p. 1999. pap. 18.00 (*0-8028-4348-4*) Eerdmans.

Meyer, Harding, jt. ed. see Vischer, Lukas.

Meyer, Harold E. Credit & Collection Letters That Get Results. 2nd ed. 272p. (C). 1994. pap. text 14.95 (*0-13-123704-7*) P-H.

— Lifetime Encyclopedia of Letters. expanded rev. ed. 430p. (C). 1996. 49.95 incl. 3.5 hd (*0-13-256801-2*) P-H.

— Lifetime Encyclopedia of Letters. rev. expanded ed. 430p. 1991. text 34.95 (*0-13-529546-7*) P-H.

— Lifetime Encyclopedia of Letters. 2nd rev. ed. 464p. (C). 1997. pap. text 18.95 (*0-13-894874-7*) P-H.

— Lifetime Encyclopedia of Letters. 3rd rev. expanded ed. LC 98-27538. 496p. 1999. 35.00 (*0-7352-0034-3*) PH Pr.

— Streetwise Lifetime Encyclopedia. 464p. (C). 1991. pap. 15.00 (*0-13-461906-4*) P-H.

Meyer, Harvey K. & Meyer, Jessie H. Historical Dictionary of Honduras. LC 93-49521. (Latin American Historical Dictionaries Ser.: No. 25). (Illus.). 736p. 1994. 81.50 (*0-8108-2845-6*) Scarecrow.

Meyer, Hazel. The Gold in Tin Pan Alley. LC 77-7039. 258p. 1977. reprint ed. lib. bdg. 65.00 (*0-8371-9694-9*, MEGO, Greenwood Pr) Greenwood.

Meyer, Heinz. Das Aesthetische Urteil. (Studien und Materialien Zur Geschichte der Philosophie Ser.: Bd. 10). (GER.). 444p. 1990. write for info. (*3-487-09202-6*) G Olms Pubs.

— Alienation, Entfremdung und Selbstverwirklichung. (Studien und Materialien Zur Geschichte der Philosophie Ser.: Bd. 8). (GER.). 223p. 1984. write for info. (*3-487-07481-8*) G Olms Pubs.

— Mensch und Pferd: Zur Kultursoziologie einer Mensch-Tier-Assoziation. (GER., Illus.). vi, 306p. 1975. write for info. (*3-487-08099-0*) G Olms Pubs.

— Reiten und Ausbilden. (Nova Hippologica Ser.). (Illus.). 186p. 1996. write for info. (*3-487-08254-3*) G Olms Pubs.

— Wahrheit und Sittlichkeit. (Studien und Materialien Zur Geschichte der Philosophie Ser.: Bd. 9). (GER.). 434p. 1989. write for info. (*3-487-09011-2*) G Olms Pubs.

***Meyer, Heinz-Dieter & Boyd, William L.** Education Between State, Markets & Civil Society: Comparative Perspectives. LC 00-42696. 2000. write for info. (*0-8058-3195-9*) L Erlbaum Assocs.

Meyer, Helen C., jt. auth. see Machado, Jeanne M.

Meyer, Helga. The Contemporary Craft of Paper Mache: Techniques - Projects - Inspirations. Taylor, Carol, ed. LC 96-22299. (Illus.). 128p. 1996. pap. 29.95 (*1-887374-11-6*, Pub. by Lark Books) Random.

Meyer, Henry C. Drang Nach Osten: Gortunes of a Slogan-Concept in German-Slavic Relations, 1849-1990. (GER.). 142p. 1996. 29.95 (*3-906755-93-2*) P Lang Pubng.

Meyer, Henry I. The Face of Business. LC 79-55064. 282p. reprint ed. pap. 87.50 (*0-608-13025-7*, 202355100033) Bks Demand.

— The Moving Force. LC 81-66231. 333p. reprint ed. pap. 103.30 (*0-608-11908-3*, 202357200033) Bks Demand.

Meyer, Henry J., et al. Girls at Vocational High: An Experiment in Social Work Intervention. LC 65-16221. 212p. 1965. 29.95 (*0-87154-601-9*) Russell Sage.

Meyer, Henry J., jt. auth. see Litwak, Eugene.

Meyer, Henye. The Exiles of Crocodile Island. (ArtScroll Youth Ser.). (Illus.). 224p. (YA). (gr. 6-12). 1984. 14.99 (*0-89906-772-7*); pap. 11.99 (*0-89906-773-5*) Mesorah Pubns.

Meyer, Herb. A Kaskaskia Chronology. 8p. 1995. pap. 2.50 (*0-913415-05-7*) Am Kestrel Pr.

Meyer, Herb, jt. auth. see McNerney, Michael J.

Meyer, Herbert E. Hard Thinking: The Fusion of Politics & Sciences. 72p. 1993. 9.95 (*0-935166-08-4*) Storm King Pr.

— Real-World Intelligence: Organized Information for Executives. 102p. 1991. 19.95 (*0-935166-05-X*) Storm King Pr.

Meyer, Herbert E. & Meyer, Jill M. How to Write: Communicating Ideas & Information - New Edition. 2nd ed. 1993. pap. 6.95 (*0-935166-07-6*) Storm King Pr.

Meyer, Herbert W. & Manchester, Steven R. The Oligocene Bridge Creek Flora of the John Day Formation, Oregon. LC 97-31080. (University of California Publications in Geological Sciences). 364p. 1998. 50.00 (*0-520-09816-1*) Univ of California Angeles Ctr.

Meyer, Herman. The Poetics of Quotation in the European Novel. LC 65-17152. 288p. reprint ed. pap. 89.30 (*0-8357-3701-2*, 203642500003) Bks Demand.

Meyer-Hofmeister, E., et al, eds. Accretion Disks - New Aspects: Proceedings of the EARA Workshop Held in Garching, Germany, 21-23 October, 1996. LC 97-17624. (Lecture Notes in Physics Ser.: No. 487). xii, 356p. 1997. 79.00 (*3-540-62866-5*) Spr-Verlag.

Meyer, Howard L. The First Book of Attorney Abuse & Bench Bashing. (Illus.). 1991. 9.95 (*1-879201-01-1*) WNY Wares.

***Meyer, Howard N., ed.** The Magnificent Activist: The Writings of Thomas Wentworth Higginson (1823-1911) 600p. 2000. pap. text 22.50 (*0-306-80954-0*) Da Capo.

Meyer, I. Hotel & Restaurant Dictionary: Fachworterbuch Gaststatten-und Hotelwesen. 2nd ed. (ENG, FRE, GER & RUS.). 208p. 1981. 39.95 (*0-8288-1478-3*, M15242) Fr & Eur.

Meyer, Ian & Huggett, Richard J. Geography: Theory in Practice, Bks. 1-3. 208p. (C). 1979. pap. write for info. (*0-7855-2594-7*) St Mut.

— Geography: Theory in Practice, Bks. 1-3, Bk. 1. 208p. (C). 1979. pap. 32.00 (*0-06-318096-0*) St Mut.

— Geography: Theory in Practice, Bks. 1-3, Bk. 2. 208p. (C). 1979. pap. 32.00 (*0-06-318166-5*) St Mut.

— Geography: Theory in Practice, Bks. 1-3, Bk. 3. 208p. (C). 1979. pap. 32.00 (*0-7855-7063-2*) St Mut.

***Meyer-Ilse, Werner, et al, eds.** X-Ray Microscopy: Proceedings of the Sixth International Conference. LC 00-101916. (AIP Conference Proceedings Ser.: Vol. 507). (Illus.). 756p. 2000. pap. 165.00 (*1-56396-926-2*) Am Inst Physics.

Meyer, Ingolf, jt. auth. see Schick, Walter.

***Meyer, Ingrid.** Your Own Two Feet. LC 00-27367. 224p. 2000. pap. 12.95 (*0-312-24134-8*) St Martin.

Meyer, Isaac. Oldest Books in the World: An Account of the Religion, Wisdom, Philosophy, Ethics, Psychology, Manners, Proverbs, Sayings, Refinement, etc., of the Ancient Egyptians (1900) 540p. 1995. reprint ed. pap. 33.00 (*1-56459-486-6*) Kessinger Pub.

— Scarabs: The History, Manufacture, & Religious Symbolism of the Scarabaeus, in Ancient Egypt, Phoenicia, Sardinia, Etruria, Etc. 205p. 1995. reprint ed. pap. 17.95 (*1-56459-491-2*) Kessinger Pub.

Meyer, Ivan H., jt. auth. see Fox, William.

***Meyer, J.** Belleza en Lugar de Cenizas.Tr. of Beauty for Ashes. (SPA.). 2000. 8.99 (*0-7899-0384-9*, 550099) Editorial Unilit.

— El Campo de Batalla de la Mente.Tr. of Battlefield of the Mind. (SPA.). 2000. 8.99 (*0-7899-0385-7*, 550100) Editorial Unilit.

— La Decision Mas Importante Nunca Antes Hecha.Tr. of Most Important Decision. (SPA.). 1.99 (*0-7899-0382-2*, 550097) Editorial Unilit.

— Espera un Mover de Dios... Repentinamente.Tr. of Expect a Move of God... Suddenly. (SPA.). 1.29 (*0-7899-0383-0*, 550095) Editorial Unilit.

— Hazlo con Temor.Tr. of Do It! Afraid. (SPA.). 1.29 (*0-7899-0381-4*, 550096) Editorial Unilit.

Meyer, J. Life in the Word Devotional. LC 99-192638. 219 p. 1998. 14.99 (*1-57794-038-5*) Harrison Hse.

Meyer, J Sanidad para el Corazon Herido.Tr. of Healing the Broken Hearted. (SPA.). 1.99 (*0-7899-0386-5*, 550098) Editorial Unilit.

Meyer, J., et al, eds. Advances in Noninvasive Cardiology. (Developments in Cardiovascular Medicine Ser.). 1983. text 141.50 (*0-89838-576-8*) Kluwer Academic.

— Improvement of Myocardial Perfusion. (Developments in Cardiovascular Medicine Ser.). 1985. lib. bdg. 193.00 (*0-89838-748-5*) Kluwer Academic.

Meyer, J., jt. ed. see Vaeth, J. M.

Meyer, J. F., et al, eds. Dependable Computing for Critical Applications 2. (Dependable Computing & Fault-Tolerant Systems Ser.: Vol. 6). (Illus.). xvi, 442p. 1992. 124.95 (*0-387-82330-1*) Spr-Verlag.

***Meyer, J. J. C. & Schobbens, P. Y., eds.** Formal Models of Agents: ESPRIT Project ModelAge Final Report. (Lecture Notes in Computer Science Ser.: Vol. 1760). vii, 253p. 2000. pap. 52.00 (*3-540-67027-0*) Spr-Verlag.

***Meyer, J. L., ed.** Radiation Therapy of Benign Disease: New Applications of Radiotherapy Technology. (Frontiers of Radiation Therapy & Oncology Ser.: Vol. 35). (Illus.). x, 200p. 2000. 174.00 (*3-8055-7063-5*) S Karger.

Meyer, J. L. & Vaeth, J. M., eds. Cancer & the Elderly. (Frontiers of Radiation Therapy & Oncology Ser.: Vol. 20). (Illus.). viii, 202p. 1986. 161.00 (*3-8055-4145-7*) S Karger.

— The Lymphatic System & Cancer: Mechanisms & Clinical Management. (Frontiers of Radiation Therapy & Oncology Ser.: Vol. 28). (Illus.). x, 240p. 1994. 205.25 (*3-8055-5889-9*) S Karger.

— Organ Conservation in Curative Cancer Treatment: Indications, Contraindications, Methods. (Frontiers of Radiation Therapy & Oncology Ser.: Vol. 27). (Illus.). xii, 256p. 1993. 216.75 (*3-8055-5663-2*) S Karger.

Meyer, J. L., jt. ed. see Vaeth, J. M.

Meyer, Jack. Common Sense Union: An Agenda for Social & Political Reform. 55p. (Orig.). 1994. pap. 6.00 (*0-9631727-2-7*) CSU Pubns.

— The In-Between: A Vision of World Peace. LC 92-70265. (Illus.). 325p. 1992. 22.00 (*0-9631727-0-0*) CSU Pubns.

***Meyer, Jack.** Mind of God. 1999. 20.00 (*0-9672197-0-1*) CrocusplusDBR.

Meyer, Jack. The Odyssey of the Western Spirit: An Account of Human Reality. (Illus.). 365p. 1998. pap. 30.00 (*0-9631727-3-5*) CSU Pubns.

***Meyer, Jack.** Our Fathers & Mothers: A Family Story, 1800-2000 A. D. (Illus.). 125p. 2000. pap. 10.00 (*0-9672197-1-X*) CrocusplusDBR.

Meyer, Jack. Washington, D. C. Monuments in Architectural & Historical Review. (Illus.). 21p. (Orig.). 1993. pap. 4.00 (*0-9631727-1-9*) CSU Pubns.

Meyer, Jack A. South Carolina in the Mexican War: A History of the Palmetto Regiment of Volunteers 1846-1917. (Illus.). 316p. 1996. 25.00 (*1-880067-35-8*) SC Dept of Arch & Hist.

— Wage-Price Standards & Economic Policy. LC 82-8810. (AEI Studies: No. 358). 88p. reprint ed. pap. 30.00 (*0-8357-4543-0*, 203744000008) Bks Demand.

Meyer, Jack A., compiled by. An Annotated Bibliography of the Napoleonic Era: Recent Publications, 1945-1985, 8. LC 87-7605. (Bibliographies & Indexes in World History Ser.: No. 8). 305p. 1987. lib. bdg. 75.00 (*0-313-24901-6*, MNF, Greenwood Pr) Greenwood.

Meyer, Jack A., ed. Market Reforms in Health Care: Current Issues, New Directions, Strategic Decisions. LC 82-22678. (AEI Symposia Ser.: No. 82F). 352p. reprint ed. pap. 109.20 (*0-8357-4503-1*, 203735900008) Bks Demand.

Meyer, Jack A., et al. From Health Care to Health: A New Approach to Resource Allocation. 44p. (Orig.). 1993. pap. write for info. (*0-9629870-4-2*) Milbank Memorial.

— Passing the Health Care Buck: Who Pays the Hidden Cost? LC 83-12296. (AEI Ser.: No. 386). 63p. reprint ed. pap. 30.00 (*0-8357-4521-X*, 203738000008) Bks Demand.

— Setting New Priorities in Health Care. (Illus.). 60p. (Orig.). 1993. pap. text. write for info. (*0-9629870-2-6*) Milbank Memorial.

Meyer, Jacky, tr. see Drechsel, Willem, et al, eds.

***Meyer, James.** Minimalism: Themes & Movements. 2000. 69.95 (*0-7148-3460-2*) Phaidon Pr.

Meyer, James. Thirty Changing Meter Duets for Treble Clef Instruments. 41p. 1984. pap. 9.95 (*0-938170-05-8*) Wimbledon Music.

Meyer, James & Hardick, Lothar. Words of St. Francis. rev. ed. 434p. 1982. pap. 15.00 (*0-8199-0833-9*, Frncscn Herld) Franciscan Pr.

Meyer, James, jt. text see Hickey, David.

***Meyer, Jan.** Parachuting Manual with Log for Accelerated FreeFall: With a Summary of the First Jump Course. 4th rev. ed. LC 91-6811. (Illus.). 36p. 2000. pap. 3.95 (*1-56860-068-2*) Para Pub.

Meyer, Jan-Waalke. Untersuchungen zu den Tonlebermodellen aus dem Alten Orient. (Alter Orient und Altes Testament Ser.: Vol. 39). (GER.). ix, 333p. 1987. text 85.00 (*3-7887-1271-6*) NeukirchenerV.

Meyer, Jane, ed. Vocational Biographies Series B: 175 Titles, 7 bks. (Series B98). (Illus.). 728p. 1998. lib. bdg. 306.25 (*0-87063-705-3*); spiral bd. 245.00 (*0-87063-704-5*) Vocational Biographies.

Meyer, Jane, jt. auth. see Bowen, Asta.

Meyer, Janet L. Crimes of a Guilty Land. 34p. (YA). (gr. 7-12). 1997. pap. 10.00 (*1-890852-01-5*) Inst SW Pub.

***Meyer, Janet L.** Sydney Pollack: A Critical Filmography. LC 98-25890. (Illus.). 248p. 1998. lib. bdg. 38.50 (*0-7864-0486-8*) McFarland & Co.

Meyer, Janet L. Visual Parables. Vol. 1: Engaging the Spiritual Elements of Film - a Text for Christian Parents, Educators & Clergy. LC 97-72830. 160p. (Orig.). 1997. pap. 15.95 (*1-890852-02-3*) Inst SW Pub.

Meyer, Jean. Plant Galls & Gall Inducers. Cheskin, Suellen, tr. (Handbuch der Pflanzenanatomie Encyclopedia of Plant Anatomy - Traite d' Anatomie Vegetale Ser.). (Illus.). viii, 291p. 1987. 88.00 (*3-443-01023-7*, Pub. by Gebruder Borntraeger) Balogh.

Meyer, Jean & Maresquelle, H. J. Anatomie des Galles. (Handbuch der Pflanzenanatomie Encyclopedia of Plant Anatomy - Traite d' Anatomie Vegetale Ser.: Band XIII, Teil 1). (GER., Illus.). xvi, 662p. 1983. 176.00 (*3-443-14013-0*, Pub. by Gebruder Borntraeger) Balogh.

Meyer, Jean A. The Cristero Rebellion: The Mexican People Between Church & State, 1926-1929. LC 75-35455. (Cambridge Latin American Studies: No. 24). 272p. reprint ed. pap. 77.60 (*0-608-15753-8*, 2031692) Bks Demand.

An Asterisk (*) at the beginning of an entry indicates that the title is appearing for the first time.

***Meyer, Jean-Arcady, et al, eds.** From Animals to Animats Vol. 6: Proceedings of the Sixth International Conference on Simulation of Adaptive Behavior. (Complex Adaptive Systems Ser.). 500p. 2000. 65.00 (*0-262-63200-4*, Bradford Bks) MIT Pr.

Meyer, Jean-Arcady, jt. ed. see Roitblat, Herbert L.

Meyer, Jean-Christophe. Barron's Junior Illustrated Dictionary - French-English. (ENG & FRE., Illus.). 180p. (J). (gr. 2 up). 1994. 16.95 (*0-8120-6458-5*) Barron.

Meyer, Jean-Claude, jt. text see Dolz, Joaquim.

Meyer, Jeffrey D., jt. auth. see Shook, Michael.

***Meyer, Jeffrey F.** Myths in Stone: Religious Dimensions of Washington, D. C. LC 00-20172. 2001. write for info. (*0-520-21481-1*) U CA Pr.

***Meyer, Jennifer.** Cracking the NCLEX 2000-2001. 2000. pap. 25.00 (*0-375-75542-X*) Random.

Meyer, Jerome. The Bonsai Book of Practical Facts Plus Addenda. 5th ed. LC 90-38869. (Illus.). 128p. 1992. 17.95 (*0-945487-00-2*) Purchase Pub.

Meyer, Jerry. The Clay-Target Handbook. 224p. 1995. pap. 16.95 (*1-55821-415-1*) Lyons Pr.

— The Sporting Clays Handbook. (Illus.). 144p. 1990. pap. 15.95 (*1-55821-066-0*) Lyons Pr.

Meyer, Jessie H., jt. auth. see Meyer, Harvey K.

Meyer, Jill M., jt. auth. see Meyer, Herbert E.

Meyer, Jimmy E., jt. ed. see Van Tassel, David D.

Meyer, Joachim E. Death & Neurosis. Nunberg, Margarete, tr. LC 73-19951. 147p. (C). 1975. 35.00 (*0-8236-1130-2*) Intl Univs Pr.

Meyer, Joann, jt. auth. see Sawyer, Ben.

Meyer, Jocele, jt. auth. see Meyer, Art.

***Meyer, Joe.** Beat Peculiar. 1999. pap. 12.95 (*0-9662984-6-2*) Landwaster Bks.

Meyer, Johann J. Sexual Life in Ancient India. 1989. reprint ed. 32.00 (*81-208-0638-7*, Pub. by Motilal Bnarsidass) S Asia.

***Meyer, John.** Our Voices, Our Visions. (Teenink Ser.). (YA). 2000. pap. 12.95 (*1-55874-816-4*) Health Comm.

Meyer, John. Studies on the Augsburg Confession. 1995. 27.99 (*0-8100-0571-9*, 15N0572) Northwest Pub.

Meyer, John, jt. auth. see Amato, Joseph A.

Meyer, John A. Lung Cancer Chronicles. LC 89-11000. (Illus.). 250p. (Orig.). 1990. 35.00 (*0-8135-1492-4*); pap. 12.95 (*0-8135-1493-2*) Rutgers U Pr.

Meyer, John C. Christian Beliefs & Teachings. 2nd ed. LC 97-20085. 144p. (Orig.). (C). 1997. 44.00 (*0-7618-0802-7*); pap. 24.50 (*0-7618-0803-5*) U Pr of Amer.

Meyer, John C., Jr. Complaints of Police Corruption. (Criminal Justice Center Monographs). 1977. pap. text 3.25 (*0-318-37489-7*) John Jay Pr.

Meyer, John G., Jr. Company Command: The Bottom Line. 235p. (Orig.). (C). 1995. pap. text 40.00 (*0-7881-2153-7*) DIANE Pub.

Meyer, John J., et al. Health Care Fraud & Abuse: Enforcement & Compliance. (BNA's Health Law & Business Ser.: No. 2600). 1997. 125.00 (*1-55871-356-5*) BNA.

Meyer, John-Jules & Van der Hoek, Wiebe. Epistemic Logic for AI & Computer Science. (Tracts in Theoretical Computer Science Ser.: No. 41). (Illus.). 368p. (C). 1995. text 64.95 (*0-521-46014-X*) Cambridge U Pr.

Meyer, John-Jules C. & Wieringa, Roel J., eds. Deontic Logic in Computer Science: Normative System Specification. LC 93-8781. (Illus.). 331p. 1993. reprint ed. pap. 102.70 (*0-608-05266-3*, 206580400001) Bks Demand.

Meyer, John L., ed. Radiation Injury: Advances in Management & Prevention, 32nd San Francisco Cancer Symposium, San Francisco, Calif., March 1997. LC 99-24336. (Frontiers of Radiation Therapy & Oncology Ser.: Vol. 32). (Illus.). x, 200p. 1999. pap. 174.00 (*3-8055-6802-9*) S Karger.

Meyer, John L. & Shadle, Carolyn C. The Changing Outplacement Process: New Methods & Opportunities for Transition Management. LC 94-2988. 312p. 1994. 65.00 (*0-89930-890-2*, Quorum Bks) Greenwood.

Meyer, John P. & Allen, Natalie J. Commitment in the Workplace: Theory, Research & Application. LC 96-45780. (Advanced Topics in Organizational Behavior Ser.: Vol. 1). 180p. (C). 1997. 34.00 (*0-7619-0104-3*, 01043); pap. 15.95 (*0-7619-0105-1*, 01051) Sage.

Meyer, John R., ed. Techniques of Transport Planning Vol. 1: Pricing & Project Evaluation. LC 79-108833. (Transport Research Program Ser.). 343p. 1971. 17.95 (*0-8157-5690-9*) Brookings.

— Techniques of Transport Planning Vol. 2: Systems Analysis & Simulation Models, Transport Research Program. LC 79-108833. 1971. 22.95 (*0-8157-5040-4*) Brookings.

Meyer, John R. & Foster, Carol F. A Guide to the Frogs & Toads of Belize. LC 95-30424. (Illus.). 96p. (C). 1996. text 24.50 (*0-89464-963-9*) Krieger.

Meyer, John R. & Gomez-Ibanez, Jose A. Autos, Transit, & Cities. LC 81-6477. (Twentieth Century Fund Report Ser.). 370p. reprint ed. pap. 114.70 (*0-7837-1523-4*, 204180000024) Bks Demand.

Meyer, John R. & Oster, Clinton V., Jr. Deregulation & the Future of Innercity Passenger Travel. (Regulation of Economic Activity Ser.: No. 15). (Illus.). 366p. 1987. 39.95 (*0-262-13225-7*) MIT Pr.

Meyer, John R. & Weinberg, Daniel H. On the Classification of Economic Fluctuations. (Explorations in Economic Research Two Ser.: No. 2). 36p. 1975. reprint ed. 35.00 (*0-685-66195-4*) Natl Bur Econ Res.

Meyer, John R., Jr., et al. Airline Deregulation: The Early Experience. LC 81-3620. 307p. 1981. 49.95 (*0-86569-078-2*, Auburn Hse) Greenwood.

Meyer, John R., et al. Economics of Competition in the Transportation Industries. LC 59-6160. (Economic Studies: No. 107). (Illus.). 377p. 1959. 27.00 (*0-674-23251-8*) HUP.

***Meyer, John R., et al.** Essays in Transportation Economics & Policy: A Handbook in Honor of John R. Meyer. LC 98-40260. 1999. pap. text 22.95 (*0-8157-3181-7*) Brookings.

Meyer, John R., et al. Moving to Market: Restructuring Transport in the Former Soviet Union. Strong, John S., ed. (Studies in International Development; Institute for International Development Ser.). 232p. 1996. 30.00 (*0-674-58814-2*) HUP.

— Urban Transportation Problem. LC 65-13848. (Rand Corporation Research Studies). (Illus.). 427p. 1965. pap. 18.00 (*0-674-93121-1*) HUP.

Meyer, John R., jt. auth. see Gomez-Ibanez, Jose A.

Meyer, John R., jt. ed. see Kain, John F.

***Meyer, John Stirling, et al, eds.** Vascular Dementia. (Illus.). 300p. 2000. write for info. (*0-87993-425-5*) Futura Pub.

Meyer, John W. No Turning Back: On the Loose in China & Tibet. (Illus.). 328p. (Orig.). 1991. pap. 10.95 (*0-911627-13-8*) Neither-Nor Pr.

Meyer, John W. & Hannan, Michael T., eds. National Development & the World System: Educational, Economic, & Political Change, 1950-1970. LC 78-26986. 1995. lib. bdg. 32.50 (*0-226-52136-2*) U Ch Pr.

— National Development & the World System: Educational, Economic, & Political Change, 1950-1970. LC 78-26986. 344p. reprint ed. pap. 106.70 (*0-608-09022-0*, 206965700005) Bks Demand.

Meyer, John W. & Scott, W. Richard. Organizational Environments: Ritual & Rationality. LC 91-18467. 308p. 1992. pap. 95.50 (*0-608-07788-7*, 205266300010) Bks Demand.

— Organizational Environments: Ritual & Rationality. (Illus.). 312p. (C). 1992. 48.00 (*0-8039-4468-3*); pap. 23.50 (*0-8039-4469-1*) Sage.

Meyer, John W., jt. ed. see Scott, W. Richard.

Meyer, Jon & Downing, Troy. Java Virtual Machine. Shulmann, Andrew, ed. LC 97-146808. (Computer Science). 452p. 1997. pap. 32.95 (*1-56592-194-1*) Thomson Learn.

Meyer, Jon K., et al, eds. Clinical Management of Sexual Disorders. 2nd ed. LC 86-20620. (Illus.). 405p. reprint ed. pap. 125.60 (*0-8357-4757-3*, 203768300009) Bks Demand.

Meyer, Jon'a & Jesilow, Paul. Doing Justice in the People's Court: Sentencing by Municipal Court Judges. LC 96-3774. (SUNY Series in New Directions in Crime & Justice Studies). 192p. (C). 1996. text 49.50 (*0-7914-3137-1*); pap. text 16.95 (*0-7914-3138-X*) State U NY Pr.

Meyer, Jona F. Inaccuracies in Children's Testimony: Memory, Suggestibility, or Obedience to Authority? LC 96-51807. (Illus.). 164p. 1997. 39.95 (*0-7890-0167-5*); pap. 14.95 (*0-7890-0237-X*) Haworth Pr.

Meyer, Jone, ed. A-7, Low-Tech Careers in a High-Tech World: 25 Titles. (Series A97: Vol. 7). (Illus.). 104p. 1997. lib. bdg. 46.88 (*0-87063-701-0*); spiral bd. 37.50 (*0-87063-674-X*) Vocational Biographies.

— B-7, Work & Home - How Women Cope: New Feminism: Equilibrium Unseats Equality, 25 titles. (Series B98: Vol. 7). (Illus.). 104p. 1998. lib. bdg. 46.88 (*0-87063-707-X*); spiral bd. 37.50 (*0-87063-706-1*) Vocational Biographies.

— College Careers: 350 Titles, 14 bks. rev. ed. (Education for Success Ser.: No. CC99). (Illus.). 1999. spiral bd. 475.00 (*0-87063-718-5*) Vocational Biographies.

— College Careers, Health Careers, Trade, Industrial & Technical Careers: 700 Titles, 28 bks. rev. ed. (Education for Success Ser.). 1997. spiral bd. 925.00 (*0-87063-724-X*) Vocational Biographies.

— Health Careers: 175 titles, 7 bks. rev. ed. (Education for Success Ser.: No. HC99). (Illus.). 1999. spiral bd. 245.00 (*0-87063-720-7*) Vocational Biographies.

— Trade, Industrial & Technical Careers: 175 Titles, 7 bks. rev. ed. (Education for Success Ser.: No. TI97). (Illus.). 1997. spiral bd. 245.00 (*0-87063-722-3*) Vocational Biographies.

— Vocational Biographies C-7: Computer Careers: Computers-Redefining Work. (Illus.). 104p. 1999. lib. bdg. 46.88 (*0-87063-711-8*, Series C99) Vocational Biographies.

— Vocational Biographies C-7: Computers-Redefining Work: Computer Careers. (Series C99). (Illus.). 104p. 1999. spiral bd. 37.50 (*0-87063-710-X*, Series C99) Vocational Biographies.

— Vocational Biographies - Series D-00: 175 Titles, 7 vols. (Illus.). 2000. lib. bdg. 318.75 (*0-87063-781-9*, D-00); spiral bd. 255.00 (*0-87063-780-0*, D-00) Vocational Biographies.

— Vocational Biographies Budget Career Library - Series Z, A, B, C: 700 Titles, 28 bks. (Illus.). 1999. lib. bdg. 1187.50 (*0-87063-799-1*); spiral bd. 950.00 (*0-87063-798-3*) Vocational Biographies.

— Vocational Biographies Career Library - Series Y, Z, A, B, C: 877 Titles, 35 bks. (Illus.). 1999. lib. bdg. 1493.75 (*0-87063-797-5*); spiral bd. 1195.00 (*0-87063-796-7*) Vocational Biographies.

— Vocational Biographies Series A: 175 Titles, 7 bks. (Series A97). (Illus.). 1997. lib. bdg. 306.25 (*0-87063-673-1*); spiral bd. 245.00 (*0-87063-672-3*) Vocational Biographies.

— Vocational Biographies Series C: 175 Titles, 7 vols. (Series C99). (Illus.). 1999. lib. bdg. 318.75 (*0-87063-709-6*); spiral bd. 255.00 (*0-87063-708-8*) Vocational Biographies.

— Vocational Biographies Series Y: 177 Titles, 7 bks. (Series Y95). (Illus.). 1995. lib. bdg. 306.25 (*0-87063-562-X*); spiral bd. 245.00 (*0-87063-554-9*) Vocational Biographies.

— Vocational Biographies Series Z: 175 Titles, 7 bks. (Series Z96). (Illus.). 1996. lib. bdg. 306.25 (*0-87063-659-6*); spiral bd. 245.00 (*0-87063-651-0*) Vocational Biographies.

— Vocational Biographies Starter Career Library - Series B-C: 350 Titles, 14 bks. (Illus.). 1999. lib. bdg. 593.75 (*0-87063-801-7*); spiral bd. 475.00 (*0-87063-800-9*) Vocational Biographies.

— X-7, Your Career in Small Business: 25 Titles. (Series X94: Vol. 7). (Illus.). 104p. 1994. lib. bdg. 46.88 (*0-87063-481-X*); spiral bd. 37.50 (*0-87063-473-9*) Vocational Biographies.

— Y-7, Information Age Careers: 27 Titles. (Series Y95: Vol. 7). (Illus.). 112p. 1995. lib. bdg. 46.88 (*0-87063-569-7*); spiral bd. 37.50 (*0-87063-561-1*) Vocational Biographies.

— Z-7, Not for Profit: People Helping People Opportunities, 25 titles. (Series Z96: Vol. 7). (Illus.). 104p. 1996. lib. bdg. 46.88 (*0-87063-700-2*); spiral bd. 37.50 (*0-87063-660-X*) Vocational Biographies.

Meyer, Jorgen C. Pre-Republican Rome: An Analysis of the Cultural & Chronological Relations, 1000-500 B.C. (Analecta Romana Ser.: Suppl. XI). 210p. (Orig.). 1983. pap. 43.50 (*87-7492-434-6*, Pub. by Odense Universitets Forlag) Coronet Bks.

Meyer, Joseph. Protection: "The Sealed Book" 10th annot. ed. Mead, Daniel R., ed. & illus. by. LC 94-74310. 192p. 1999. pap. 12.95 (*0-934422-08-7*, BKS-100587) Mead Pub Corp.

Meyer, Joseph E. The Herbalist. rev. ed. (Illus.). 304p. 1986. pap. text 11.95 (*0-916638-00-6*) Meyerbooks.

— The Old Herb Doctor. 2nd rev. ed. (Illus.). 176p. 1984. pap. 8.95 (*0-916638-08-1*) Meyerbooks.

Meyer, Joseph R., ed. Analysis & Design of Pile Foundations: Proceedings of a Symposium. LC 84-72087. (Illus.). 418p. 1984. reprint ed. pap. 129.60 (*0-608-04426-1*, 205966100012) Bks Demand.

Meyer, Josh, jt. auth. see Willis, Dan.

Meyer, Joyce. Battlefield of the Mind How to Win the War in Your Mind. 1999. pap. text 14.99 (*1-57794-169-1*) Harrison Hse.

***Meyer, Joyce.** Battlefield of the Mind: Winning the Battle in Your Mind. 1999. pap. 12.99 (*1-57794-185-3*) Dake Pub.

Meyer, Joyce. Battlefield of the Mind: Winning the Battle in Your Mind. LC 96-114494. 259p. 1995. pap. 12.99 (*0-89274-778-1*, HH-778) Harrison Hse.

— Be Anxious for Nothing. 1999. 17.99 (*1-57794-106-3*) Dake Pub.

***Meyer, Joyce.** Be Healed in Jesus' Name. 1999. pap. text 7.99 (*1-57794-173-X*) Harrison Hse.

Meyer, Joyce. Beauty for Ashes: Receiving Emotional Healing. LC 94-220563. 176p. 1994. pap. 8.99 (*0-89274-679-3*, HH-679) Harrison Hse.

***Meyer, Joyce.** Como Tener Exito Siendo Usted Mismo. (SPA.). 2000. pap. 9.99 (*0-7899-0786-0*) Spanish Hse Distributors.

Meyer, Joyce. Do It Afraid! 48p. 1996. 1.25 (*0-89274-933-4*, HH-933) Harrison Hse.

— Don't Dread. pap. 1.50 (*1-57794-028-8*) Harrison Hse.

— Eat & Stay Thin. 199p. 1999. 16.99 (*1-57794-144-6*) Harrison Hse.

— Enjoying Where You Are on the Way to Where You Are Going. LC 96-224031. 224p. 1996. pap. 11.99 (*0-89274-948-2*, HH-948) Harrison Hse.

— Expect a Move of God... Suddenly. 64p. 1996. 1.50 (*0-89274-932-6*, HH-932) Harrison Hse.

— Grief & Loneliness. 96p. 1998. pap. 6.99 (*1-57794-016-4*) Harrison Hse.

— Healing the Brokenhearted: Experience Restoration Through the Power of God's Word. 128p. 1997. pap. 4.99 (*0-89274-968-7*) Harrison Hse.

— Help Me - I'm Frustrated. pap. 6.99 (*1-57794-012-1*) Rounder Records.

— Help Me! I'm Afraid. (Help Me! Ser.). 160p. 1999. pap. 5.99 (*1-57794-035-0*) Dake Pub.

— Help Me! I'm Depressed. (Help Me! Ser.). 160p. 1999. pap. 5.99 (*1-57794-040-7*) Dake Pub.

— Help Me! I'm Discouraged. (Help Me! Ser.). 160p. 1999. pap. 5.99 (*1-57794-013-X*) Dake Pub.

— Help Me! I'm Insecure. 160p. 1999. pap. 5.99 (*1-57794-042-3*) Dake Pub.

***Meyer, Joyce.** Help Me, I'm Married. 2000. 19.99 (*1-57794-156-X*) Harrison Hse.

Meyer, Joyce. Help Me! I'm Stressed. 160p. 1999. pap. 5.99 (*1-57794-011-3*, HH2-011-3) Dake Pub.

— Help Me! I'm Worried. 160p. 1999. pap. 5.99 (*1-57794-010-5*) Dake Pub.

***Meyer, Joyce.** How to Succeed at Being Yourself: Finding The Confidence to Fulfill Your Destiny. 1999. 19.99 (*1-57794-164-0*) Harrison Hse.

Meyer, Joyce. If Not for the Grace of God. LC 96-163998. 208p. (Orig.). 1995. pap. 12.99 (*0-89274-796-X*, HH-796) Harrison Hse.

— Life in the Word Devotional. 272p. pap. 24.99 (*1-57794-048-2*, HH2-038-5) Harrison Hse.

— Life in the Word Gift Book. LC 97-224549. 160p. 1997. pap. 5.99 (*1-57794-004-0*) Harrison Hse.

— Life in the Word Gift Set. boxed set 14.99 (*1-57794-044-X*, IW-044) Harrison Hse.

— Life in the Word Journal. 160p. 7.99 (*1-57794-046-6*, HH2-046-6) Harrison Hse.

— Life in the Word Journal. 1999. 9.99 (*1-57794-170-5*) Harrison Hse.

— Life Without Strife: How God Can Heal & Restore Broken Relationships. 1995. pap. 12.99 (*0-88419-408-6*) Creation House.

***Meyer, Joyce.** Life Without Strife: How God Can Heal & Restore Troubled Relationships. 197p. 2000. pap. 12.99 (*0-88419-734-4*) Creation House.

Meyer, Joyce. Managing Your Emotions Instead of Your Emotions Managing You. 288p. 1997. 17.99 (*1-57794-026-1*, HH2-026) Harrison Hse.

— Me & My Big Mouth! Your Answer Is Right under Your Nose. LC 97-141734. 288p. pap. 13.99 (*0-89274-969-5*) Harrison Hse.

***Meyer, Joyce.** Me & My Big Mouth Study Guide. 2000. pap. 12.99 (*1-57794-218-3*) Harrison Hse.

Meyer, Joyce. The Most Important Decision You'll Ever Make. 80p. (Orig.). 1996. mass mkt. 4.99 (*0-89274-940-7*, HH-940) Harrison Hse.

— The Most Important Decision You'll Ever Make. (Orig.). pap. 3.00 (*0-944834-02-7*) Life Word-Meyer Ministries.

***Meyer, Joyce.** Palabra, el Mombre, la Sangre. (SPA.). 1999. pap. 8.99 (*958-9269-66-4*) Spanish Hse Distributors.

Meyer, Joyce. Peace. 80p. 1995. mass mkt. 4.99 (*0-89274-924-5*, HH-924) Harrison Hse.

— Prepare to Prosper. 64p. 1997. pap. text 1.50 (*0-89274-996-2*) Harrison Hse.

***Meyer, Joyce.** Reduce Me to Love. 2000. 19.99 (*1-57794-262-0*) Harrison Hse.

Meyer, Joyce. Root of Rejection. LC 95-172832. 112p. 1994. pap. 6.99 (*0-89274-738-2*, HH-738) Harrison Hse.

***Meyer, Joyce.** Seeking Faithfulness: Journey to A Deeper Life in The Spirit. 1999. pap. text 6.99 (*1-57794-179-9*) Harrison Hse.

— Seeking Goodness: Journey to A Deeper Life in The Spirit. 1999. pap. text 6.99 (*1-57794-180-2*) Harrison Hse.

— Seeking Humility: Journey to A Deeper Life in The Spirit. 1999. pap. text 6.99 (*1-57794-176-4*) Harrison Hse.

— Seeking Joy: Journey to A Deeper Life in The Spirit. 1999. pap. text 6.99 (*1-57794-178-0*) Harrison Hse.

— Seeking Kindness: Journey to A Deeper Life in The Spirit. 1999. pap. text 6.99 (*1-57794-175-6*) Harrison Hse.

— Seeking Love: Journey to A Deeper Life in The Spirit. 1999. pap. text 6.99 (*1-57794-174-8*) Harrison Hse.

— Seeking Patience: Journey to A Deeper Life in The Spirit. 1999. pap. text 6.99 (*1-57794-177-2*) Harrison Hse.

— Seeking Peace: Journey to A Deeper Life in The Spirit. 1999. pap. text 6.99 (*1-57794-181-0*) Harrison Hse.

— Seeking Self-control: Journey to A Deeper Life in The Spirit. 1999. pap. text 6.99 (*1-57794-183-7*) Harrison Hse.

— Seeking Spiritual Growth: Journey to A Deeper Life in The Spirit. 1999. pap. text 6.99 (*1-57794-184-5*) Harrison Hse.

— Si No Fuera Por la Gracia de Dios. (SPA.). 2000. pap. 8.99 (*5-550-02889-1*) Nairi.

Meyer, Joyce. Tell Them I Love Them. 80p. (Orig.). 1995. mass mkt. 4.99 (*0-89274-783-8*, HH-783) Harrison Hse.

— Tell Them I Love Them. 52p. (Orig.). 1988. pap. 3.00 (*0-944834-00-0*) Life Word-Meyer Ministries.

— Weary Warriors, Fainting Saints. 144p. 1997. mass mkt. 5.99 (*1-57794-027-X*, HH2-027-X) Harrison Hse.

— When, God, When? 64p. (Orig.). mass mkt. 4.99 (*0-89274-846-X*, HH-846) Harrison Hse.

— Why, God, Why? 64p. (Orig.). mass mkt. 4.99 (*0-89274-845-1*, HH-845) Harrison Hse.

— Word, the Name, the Blood. LC 96-112901. 139p. 1995. 14.99 (*0-89274-827-3*) Harrison Hse.

— Word the Name the Blood. 1998. pap. text 12.99 (*1-57794-118-7*) Harrison Hse.

Meyer, Joyce A. Steak Lovers' Guide to Indiana: As You Wander Indiana You Won't Wonder Where to Go for Great Steak. LC 98-70619. 1998. pap. 13.95 (*0-9662694-0-3*) IN Beef Cattle.

Meyer, Judith L. The Spirit of Yellowstone: The Cultural Evolution of a National Park. LC 96-15567. 176p. 1996. lib. bdg. 26.95 (*0-8476-8248-X*) Rowman.

Meyer, Judith W. Diffusion of an American Montessori Education. LC 74-80719. (University of Chicago, Department of Geography, Research Paper Ser.: No. 160). 111p. 1975. reprint ed. pap. 31.70 (*0-608-02277-2*, 2062918) Bks Demand.

***Meyer, Judy.** The Animal Connection: A Guide to Intuitive Communication with Your Pet. LC 99-49878. (Illus.). 208p. 2000. pap. 10.95 (*0-452-28174-1*, Plume) Dutton Plume.

Meyer, June V. & Meyer, Aaron D. June Meyer's Authentic Hungarian Heirloom Recipes. 2nd ed. LC 98-162177. 195p. 1998. pap. 20.00 (*0-9665062-0-0*) Meyer & Assoc.

Meyer, Jurgen. Acoustics & the Performances of Music. Bowsher, John & Westphal, Sibylle, trs. from GER. (Illus.). 260p. 1978. 129.95 (*0-933224-28-1*, 1001) Bold Strummer Ltd.

Meyer, K. Wie Sagt Man in der Schweiz? (Duden-Taschenbucher Ser.: No. 22). (GER.). 380p. 1989. pap. 20.00 (*3-411-04131-5*) Bibliogr Inst Brockhaus.

Meyer, K. De, see De Meyer, K., ed.

Meyer, K. R. & Hall, G. R. Introduction to Hamiltonian Dynamical Systems & the N-Body Problem. (Applied Mathematical Sciences Ser.: Vol. 90). (Illus.). xii, 292p. 1991. 54.95 (*0-387-97637-X*) Spr-Verlag.

Meyer, K. R., jt. auth. see Hale, Jack.

Meyer, K. R., jt. auth. see Markus, Lawrence.

Meyer, K. R., jt. ed. see Saari, D.

***Meyer, Karl & Brysac, Shareen.** Tournament of Shadows. 2000. reprint ed. pap. 17.50 (*1-58243-106-X*, Pub. by Counterpt DC) HarpC.

Meyer, Karl & Brysac, Shareen Blair. The Tournament of Shadows: The Race for Empire in Central Asia. Bessie, Cornelia & Bessie, Michael, eds. LC 99-35250. 672p. 1999. text 35.00 (*1-58243-028-4*, Pub. by Counterpt DC) HarpC.

M

An Asterisk (*) at the beginning of an entry indicates that the title is appearing for the first time.

M

Meyer, Karl H. Altkirchenslavisch-Griechisches Worterbuch des Codex Supraliensis. (GRE.). 35.00 (*0-685-71713-5*) J J Augustin.

Meyer, Katharine M. & McElroy, Martin P., eds. Detroit Architecture: AIA Guide. rev. ed. LC 80-132260. (Illus.). 266p. 1980. pap. 15.95 (*0-8143-1651-4*) Wayne St U Pr.

Meyer, Katherine, jt. auth. see Seidler, John.

Meyer, Kathleen. How to Shit in the Woods: An Environmentally Sound Approach to a Lost Art. 2nd rev. ed. LC 94-18053. 112p. 1994. pap. 6.95 (*0-89815-627-0*) Ten Speed Pr.

Meyer, Kathleen A. Bear, Your Manners Are Showing. Beegle, Shirley, ed. (Happy Day Bks.). (Illus.). 24p. (J). (ps-3). 1994. reprint ed. pap. 1.99 (*0-7847-0251-9*, 24-04201) Standard Pub.

— God's Gifts, 5 vols. Incl. Vol. 1. Seeing. 1986. (*0-687-15307-7*); Vol. 2. Hearing. 1986. (*0-687-15306-9*); Vol. 3. Smelling. 1986. (*0-687-15308-5*); Vol. 4. Tasting. 1986. (*0-687-15309-3*); Vol. 5. Touching. 1986. (*0-687-15310-7*); 16p. (Orig.). (J). (gr. 1-3). 1986. pap. write for info. (*0-318-60470-1*) Abingdon.

— I Have a New Friend. LC 95-5803. (Illus.). 32p. (J). 1995. 10.95 (*0-8120-6532-8*); pap. 4.95 (*0-8120-9408-5*) Barron.

Meyer, Kathryn & Parssinen, Terry. Power & Profit: A History of the International Drug Trade. LC 98-23716. (State & Society in East Asia Ser.). 304p. 1998. pap. 19.95 (*0-8476-9017-2*) Rowman.

— Webs of Smoke: Smugglers, Warlords, Spies & the History of the International Drug Trade. LC 98-23716. (State & Society in East Asia Ser.). 304p. 1998. 29.95 (*0-8476-9016-4*, Pub. by Rowman) Natl Bk Netwk.

Meyer, Kathy, ed. Reach for the Stars' - Success Secrets' LC 97-75590. 256p. 1998. pap. 19.00 (*0-9658893-0-0*) James & Brookfield.

Meyer, Katrina A. Faculty Workload Studies: Perspectives, Needs & Future Directions. Fife, Jonathan D., ed. LC 98-84054. (ASHE-ERIC Higher Education Report Ser.: Vol. 26). 100p. 1998. pap. 24.00 (*1-878380-81-8*, 26-1) GWU Grad Schl E&HD.

Meyer, Kay. Life in the Sandwich Generation: Life in the Sandwich Generation. (Family Life Issues Ser.). 1995. pap. 4.50 (*0-570-09490-9*, 20-2702) Concordia.

Meyer, Kay, ed. see Cota-Robles, Patricia D.

Meyer, Kay E. The Road to Harmony . . . Day-by-Day. (Illus.). 398p. (Orig.). 1993. 17.00 (*0-9637023-0-0*) Grp Avatar.

Meyer, Keith G. Agricultural Law. Date not set. pap. text, teacher ed. write for info. (*0-314-90261-9*) West Pub.

Meyer, Keith G., et al. Agricultural Law: Cases & Materials. LC 84-19692. (American Casebook Ser.). 931p. (C). 1984. 65.00 (*0-314-85082-1*) West Pub.

Meyer, Keith G., jt. auth. see Pedersen, Donald B.

***Meyer, Ken.** Approaching Ambidexterity. 84p. 1999. 12.95 (*0-7866-4521-0*, 98202) Mel Bay.

— Solid Time Tool Kit. 104p. 1999. pap. 22.95 (*0-7866-4034-0*, 97339BCD) Mel Bay.

Meyer, Kenneth, et al. An Analysis of Social Indicator & Quality of Life Research. 10.00 (*1-55614-018-5*) U of SD Gov Res Bur.

— An Operation of State & Regional Indicators in Public Policy & Quality of Life Evaluation. 10.00 (*1-55614-075-4*) U of SD Gov Res Bur.

— Public Employee Turnover in State Government: Costs & Beneifits. 1978. 1.00 (*1-55614-100-9*) U of SD Gov Res Bur.

— Robbery-Related Assaults on Police: An Empirical Analysis of National Incidents. 1979. 1.00 (*1-55614-109-2*) U of SD Gov Res Bur.

— Simpco Land Use Planning Information System Design: What to Do When the Data Arrives. (Technical Reports: No. 1). 1978. 5.00 (*1-55614-113-0*) U of SD Gov Res Bur.

Meyer, Kenneth, jt. auth. see Beville, Mitchel J.

Meyer, Kenneth, jt. auth. see Clem, Alan L.

Meyer, Kenneth M. Minister's Guide to Financial Planning. 160p. 1987. pap. 7.95 (*0-310-34621-5*, 18421P) Zondervan.

***Meyer, Kenneth R.** Periodic Solutions of the N-Body Problem. LC 99-49591. (Lecture Notes in Mathematics Ser.: Vol. 1719). ix, 144p. 2000. pap. 36.80 (*3-540-66630-3*) Spr-Verlag.

Meyer, Kenton T. The Crumhorn: Its History, Design, Repertory, & Technique. LC 83-3463. (Studies in Musicology: No. 66). (Illus.). 295p. reprint ed. pap. 91.50 (*0-8357-1406-3*, 207051100097) Bks Demand.

Meyer, Kirstine B. Die Entwickelung de Temperaturbegriffs Im Laufe der Zeiten (the Discovery of Temperature in the Course of Time) Cohen, I. Bernard, ed. LC 80-2134. (Development of Science Ser.). (GER., Illus.). 1981. reprint ed. lib. bdg. 18.95 (*0-405-13886-5*) Ayer.

Meyer, Klaus. Direct Investment in Economies in Transition. LC 98-13453. 320p. 1998. 95.00 (*1-85898-736-9*) E Elgar.

Meyer, Klaus D., jt. auth. see Kruse, Rudolf.

Meyer-Krahmer, Frieder. Science & Technology in the Federal Republic of Germany. (Guides to World Science & Technology Ser.). 480p. 1990. 115.00 (*0-582-05439-7*, 076418-99584) Longman.

Meyer-Krahmer, Frieder, ed. Innovation & Sustainable Development: Lessons for Innovation Policies. LC 97-39317. (Technology, Innovation & Policy Ser.: Vol. 6). (Illus.). viii, 206p. 1997. pap. 63.00 (*3-7908-1038-X*) Spr-Verlag.

Meyer-Krahmer, Frieder, jt. ed. see Krull, Wilhelm.

Meyer-Kung, Heidi. Die Grosse Kuche Italiens: Meisterrezepte der Besten Restaurants Zwischen Piemont und Sizilien. (GER., Illus.). 168p. (C). 1985. 40.00 (*3-8170-0005-7*, Pub. by Knstvrlag Weingrtn) Intl Bk Import.

Meyer, Kuno. Ancient Irish Poetry. LC 94-174554. 115p. 1998. reprint ed. pap. 13.95 (*0-09-473380-5*, Pub. by Constable & Co) Trafalgar.

— Bibliography of the Works of John Strachan on Celtic Language & Literature. 1996. pap. 3.00 (*0-89979-078-X*) British Am Bks.

— Learning in Ireland in the Fifth Century & the Transmission of Letters. 1998. pap. 7.50 (*0-89979-104-2*) British Am Bks.

— Loan Words in Early Irish from Old Norse, Anglo-Saxon, Early English, Latin & Early French. 1996. pap. 10.00 (*0-89979-080-1*) British Am Bks.

— Miscellanea Hibernica. 1998. pap. 10.00 (*0-89979-100-X*) British Am Bks.

— A Primer of Irish Metrics. LC 78-72640. (Celtic Language & Literature Ser.: Goidelic & Brythonic). 88p. 1984. reprint ed. 27.50 (*0-404-17569-4*) AMS Pr.

— Ueber die Aelteste Irische Dichtung. LC 78-72641. (Celtic Language & Literature Ser.: Goidelic & Brythonic). reprint ed. 57.50 (*0-404-17574-0*) AMS Pr.

Meyer, Kuno, ed. Cain Adamnain. (Anecdota Oxoniensia Ser.: No. 12). 1988. reprint ed. 37.50 (*0-404-63962-3*) AMS Pr.

— Cath Finntraga. (Anecdota Oxoniensia Ser.: No. 4). 1988. reprint ed. 47.50 (*0-404-63954-2*) AMS Pr.

— The Death Tales of the Ulster Heroes. LC 78-72612. (Royal Irish Academy. Todd Lecture Ser.: Vol. 14). reprint ed. 27.50 (*0-404-60574-5*) AMS Pr.

— Hail Brigit: An Old-Irish Poem on the Hill of Alenn. 1987. pap. 4.95 (*0-89979-040-2*) British Am Bks.

— Hibernica Minora. (Anecdota Oxoniensia Ser.: No. 8). 1988. reprint ed. 49.50 (*0-404-63958-5*) AMS Pr.

— The Instructions of King Cormac Mac Airt. LC 78-72613. (Royal Irish Academy. Todd Lecture Ser.: Vol. 15). reprint ed. 27.50 (*0-404-60575-3*) AMS Pr.

— Life of Colman Son of Luachan. LC 78-72616. (Royal Irish Academy. Todd Lecture Ser.: Vol. 17). reprint ed. 27.50 (*0-404-60577-X*) AMS Pr.

— The Triads of Ireland. LC 78-72688. (Royal Irish Academy. Todd Lecture Ser.: Vol. 13). reprint ed. 27.50 (*0-404-60573-7*) AMS Pr.

Meyer, Kuno, tr. Selections from Ancient Irish Poetry. LC 75-28829. reprint ed. 27.50 (*0-404-13819-5*) AMS Pr.

Meyer, Kuno, tr. see Imran Brain.

Meyer, Kurt. Bitches, Bastards & Lovers. LC 81-83570. 1983. 9.95 (*0-87212-157-7*) Libra.

— Duden Taschenbucher: Woerterbuch der Schweizerischen. (GER.). 380p. 1989. 29.95 (*0-7859-8350-3*, 3411041315) Fr & Eur.

***Meyer, Kurt.** Stardust. (Illus.). 330p. 2000. pap. 17.95 (*1-58151-057-8*, Pub. by BookPartners) Midpt Trade.

Meyer, Kurt. They Called Her Jewgirl. LC 99-70096. 240p. 1999. 21.95 (*1-57197-158-0*) Pentland Pr.

Meyer, Kurt W. Mahabharata: The Tharu Barka Naach. Tharu, Ashok & Rai, Dinesh, trs. (Illus.). 124p. 1998. 18.00 (*0-9666742-2-7*); pap. 10.00 (*0-9666742-0-0*) Rusca Pr.

Meyer, L. A. Sheet Metal. 1995. student ed. 11.96 (*0-8269-1908-1*) Am Technical.

Meyer, Larry L. The Complete Works of Marcus Uteris. LC 87-10325. 176p. 1987. 15.00 (*0-942273-03-6*) Calafia Pr.

— My Summer with Molly: The Journal of a Second Generation Father. LC 89-840. (Illus.). 192p. 1989. 16.95 (*0-942273-04-4*) Calafia Pr.

Meyer, Larry L. & Meyer, Paula. Santa's Favorite Questions from Kids. Kramer, Cheryl, ed. LC 95-94434. 60p. (Orig.). (J). pap. write for info. (*0-9646762-0-6*) Captain Blys.

Meyer-Larsen, Werner. Germany, Inc. The Challenge to America & How It Will Change World Business. Thornton, Thomas, tr. from GER. LC 99-33865. 256p. 1999. 27.50 (*0-471-35357-4*) Wiley.

Meyer, Laura, jt. auth. see Jones, Amelia.

Meyer, Laure. Arts & Crafts of Africa: Everyday Life, Rituals, & Court Art. (Illus.). 208p. 1997. pap. text 27.50 (*2-87939-098-2*) Stewart Tabori & Chang.

— Black Africa: Masks, Sculpture & Jewelry. (Illus.). 224p. 1997. pap. text 27.50 (*2-87939-035-4*) Stewart Tabori & Chang.

Meyer, Laurence H., ed. Improving Money Stock Control: Problems, Solutions & Consequences. 1982. lib. bdg. 73.50 (*0-89838-115-0*) Kluwer Academic.

Meyer, Leisa D. Creating G. I. Jane: Sexuality & Power in the Women's Army Corps During World War II. (Illus.). 288p. 1998. pap. 19.50 (*0-231-10145-7*) Col U Pr.

— Creating GI-Jane: Sexuality & Power in the Women's Army Corps. (Illus.). 288p. 1996. 31.00 (*0-231-10144-9*) Col U Pr.

Meyer, Leo, jt. auth. see Wray, Lynn.

Meyer, Leo A. Atomic Energy in Industry: A Guide for Tradesmen & Technicians. LC 62-21342. 128p. reprint ed. pap. 39.70 (*0-8357-5854-0*, 200458100043) Bks Demand.

— Sheet Metal. (Illus.). 298p. 1995. teacher ed. 10.96 (*0-8269-1909-X*); wbk. ed. pap. 29.96 (*0-8269-1907-3*) Am Technical.

Meyer, Leonard B. Emotion & Meaning in Music. LC 56-9130. 318p. 1961. pap. text 12.00 (*0-226-52139-7*, P56) U Ch Pr.

— Explaining Music: Essays & Explorations. LC 77-90968. 1994. reprint ed. pap. text 14.00 (*0-226-52142-7*, P769) U Ch Pr.

— Music, the Arts, & Ideas. LC 67-25515. 1993. pap. text 12.95 (*0-226-52141-9*, P336) U Ch Pr.

— Music, the Arts, & Ideas: Patterns & Predictions in Twentieth-Century Culture. LC 93-45855. xii, 354p. 1994. pap. text 20.00 (*0-226-52143-5*) U Ch Pr.

— Spheres of Music: A Gathering of Essays. LC 99-34400. 312p. 1998. pap. text 22.00 (*0-226-52154-0*); lib. bdg. 55.00 (*0-226-52153-2*) U Ch Pr.

— Style & Music: Theory, History, & Ideology. LC 96-17957. xii, 376p. 1997. pap. text 17.95 (*0-226-52152-4*) U Ch Pr.

Meyer, Leonard B., jt. auth. see Cooper, Grosvenor.

Meyer, Linda. I See Myself Changing. 1998. pap. 12.95 (*0-9615995-6-1*) Recover Comns.

— John Meyer Pants-on-Fire: Pilot Adventures. LC 94-65977. (Illus.). 15p. (J). (gr. k-2). 1994. pap. 14.95 (*0-9640577-0-0*) Sunshine Advent.

— Teenspeak: A Bewildered Parent's Guide to Teenagers. LC 94-21338. 144p. 1994. pap. 8.95 (*1-56079-338-4*) Petersons.

— Why Is It So Hard To Take Care Of My Parent? 1999. pap. text 13.95 (*1-891874-05-5*) Recover Comns.

Meyer, Linda, ed. Rules & Reasoning. 201p. 1998. 54.00 (*1-901362-98-1*) Hart Pub.

Meyer, Linda D. Safety Zone. (Illus.). 32p. (J). 1985. pap. 3.50 (*0-446-38238-8*) Warner Bks.

Meyer, Lisa. Quotes for Kids: Today's Interpretations of Timeless Quotes Designed to Nurture the Young Spirit. LC 97-69588. (Illus.). 160p. (J). 1998. 13.95 (*0-9660148-0-4*) Reach Pr.

Meyer, Lois, et al. Transcription Skills for Business. 5th ed. LC 97-18746. 250p. (C). 1997. pap. text 36.60 (*0-13-639550-3*) P-H.

Meyer, Lorenzo. The Mexican Revolution & the Anglo-American Powers: The End of Confrontation & the Beginning of Negotiation. (Research Reports: No. 34). 40p. (Orig.). (C). 1985. pap. 5.00 (*0-935391-33-9*, RR-34) UCSD Ctr US-Mex.

Meyer, Lorenzo, jt. auth. see Camin, Aguilar.

Meyer, Lorenzo, jt. auth. see Vazquez, Josefina Z.

Meyer, Louis, ed. Eminent Hebrew Christians of the Nineteenth Century: Brief Biographical Sketches. LC 83-22013. (Texts & Studies in Religion: Vol. 17). 184p. 1983. lib. bdg. 79.95 (*0-88946-806-0*) E Mellen.

Meyer, Louis & Moyer, Ruth C. Transcription Skills for Business. 3rd ed. 1988. pap. text 296.75 (*0-471-82151-9*) P-H.

Meyer, Louise, jt. auth. see Ahiagble, Gilbert.

Meyer, Luanna H. Making Friends: The Influences of Culture & Development. LC 97-29475. (Children, Youth & Change Ser.). 425p. 1997. 48.95 (*1-55766-301-7*) P H Brookes.

Meyer, Luanna H., jt. auth. see Scotti, Joseph R.

Meyer, Lucy, ed. see Fowler, Alex D.

Meyer-Luebke, Wilhelm. Grammatik Der Romanischen Sprachen, 4 vols., Set. lxvi, 2391p. 1972. reprint ed. write for info. (*3-487-04236-3*) G Olms Pubs.

— Romanisches Etymologisches Woerterbuch. 5th ed. (GER & ITA.). 1204p. 1992. 395.00 (*0-8288-6419-5*, M-7604) Fr & Eur.

Meyer Lyons. Projecting Environmental Trends. 59.95 (*1-84014-194-8*) Ashgate Pub Co.

Meyer, Lysle E. The Farther Frontier: Six Case Studies of Americans & Africa, 1848-1936. LC 90-50770. (Illus.). 272p. 1992. 45.00 (*0-945636-19-9*) Susquehanna U Pr.

Meyer, M. Meyer's Manual on Louisiana Real Estate. 1991. 90.00 (*0-87511-913-1*) Claitors.

Meyer, M. & Miller, E. Urban Transportation Planning. 524p. (C). 1984. 101.56 (*0-07-041752-0*) McGraw.

Meyer, M. & Piiper, J., eds. Pulmonary Gas Exchange. (Progress in Respiratory Research Ser.: Vol. 21). (Illus.). xiv, 274p. 1986. 216.75 (*3-8055-4330-1*) S Karger.

Meyer, M. & Schaap, J., eds. Historiography of Women's Cultural Traditions. (Women's Studies). viii, 196p. 1986. pap. 46.15 (*90-6765-276-8*) Mouton.

Meyer, M. W. Change in Public Bureaucracies. LC 76-47193. (Illus.). 256p. 1979. text 74.95 (*0-521-22670-8*) Cambridge U Pr.

Meyer, M. Wilhelm. The End of the World: The Destiny of Man & Our Planet. Wagner, Margaret, tr. from GER. (Science for the Workers Ser.). (Illus.). 140p. 1984. 12.95 (*0-88286-087-9*) C H Kerr.

Meyer, Madeleine & Pontikis, Vassilis, eds. Computer Simulation in Materials Science: Intermatomic Potentials, Simulation Techniques & Applications. 560p. (C). 1991. text 264.50 (*0-7923-1455-7*) Kluwer Academic.

Meyer, Maggi H. Changing. LC 84-62316. 90p. 1984. pap. 6.00 (*0-915727-10-2*) im-Press.

— Come Along: Well, a Semi-Autobiography of Prose & Poems. 90p. 1998. per. 10.00 (*0-915727-14-5*) im-Press.

— Et Cetera. 28p. 1995. write for info. (*0-614-13522-2*) im-Press.

— In Thrall. 60p. 1992. per. 5.00 (*0-915727-12-9*) im-Press.

— Maggi: Three Faces of Poetry. 176p. 1988. per. 10.00 (*0-915727-11-0*) im-Press.

Meyer, Maggi H., ed. see McDaniel, Wilma E.

***Meyer, Mahlon.** Taiwan Personalities LC 99-204194. 171p. 1998. write for info. (*957-586-759-9*, Pub. by Bookman Bks) Bookman Bks.

***Meyer, Majel.** The Gentle Revolution: Solution to Moral Deterioration & War. 185p. 1999. pap. 12.00 (*0-9651740-4-2*) Stndrd of Zion.

Meyer, Majel & Wood, J. A. Perfect Love with Sequel, 2 vols. in 1. abr. ed. 217p. 1996. reprint ed. pap. 10.00 (*0-9651740-0-X*) Stndrd of Zion.

Meyer, Manfred. Educational Television. LC 98-127358. 1997. 32.00 (*1-86020-528-3*, Pub. by U of Luton Pr) Bks Intl VA.

Meyer, Manfred, ed. Constraint Programming: Selected Papers. 1995. write for info. (*0-387-59479-5*) Spr-Verlag.

— Constraint Programming: Selected Papers. 1995. 49.00 (*3-540-59479-5*) Spr-Verlag.

Meyer, Marc. The Search for Order Vol. 1: Landmarks of World Civilization. LC 93-73093. 432p. (C). 1994. text 14.95 (*1-56134-230-0*, Dshkn McG-Hill) McGrw-H Hghr Educ.

— The Search for Order Vol. 2: Landmarks of World Civilization. LC 93-73095. 448p. (C). 1994. text 14.95 (*1-56134-231-9*, Dshkn McG-Hill) McGrw-H Hghr Educ.

Meyer, Marc A. Course Kit: The Search for Order: Volumes I & II. (C). 1995. text. write for info. (*0-697-31350-6*) Brown & Benchmark.

Meyer, Marc A., ed. The Culture of Christendom: Essays in Medieval History in Commemoration of Denis L. T. Bethell. LC 93-16356. 328p. 1993. 60.00 (*1-85285-064-7*) Hambledon Press.

Meyer, Maria M. The Comfort of Home: An Illustrated Step-by-Step Guide for Caregivers. LC 98-92954. (Illus.). 364p. 1998. pap. 23.00 (*0-9664767-0-0*) CareTrust Pubns.

Meyer, Marian. A Century of Progress: History of the New Mexico School for the Deaf. LC 88-63785. (Illus.). 1989. text. write for info. (*0-318-64812-1*) NM School Deaf.

— Mary Donoho: New First Lady of the Santa Fe Trail. LC 90-56218. (Illus.). 150p. 1991. pap. 12.95 (*0-941270-69-6*) Ancient City Pr.

Meyer, Marianne. Metal Heads: The Case of the Rival Robots. LC 97-209963. (Kinetic City Super Crew Ser.: No. 5). (Illus.). 192p. (J). (gr. 3-5). 1998. pap. 4.25 (*0-07-006386-9*, Lrning Triangle) McGraw.

— Snow Problem: The Case of the Mushing Madness. (Kinetic City Super Crew Ser.: No. 9). (Illus.). 160p. (J). (gr. 3-5). 1998. pap. 4.25 (*0-07-006693-0*) McGraw.

Meyer, Marilyn. Instructor's Manual with Test Bank & Transparency Masters to Accompany Martin - Parker, Mastering Today's Software, Spreadsheets with Quattro Pro 4.0. 2nd ed. 140p. (C). 1994. pap. text, teacher ed. 84.00 (*0-03-002904-X*) Dryden Pr.

Meyer, Marilyn & Baber, Robert. Computers in Your Future. 2nd annot. ed. (Illus.). 500p. (C). 1996. pap. text, teacher ed. 80.00 (*1-57576-488-1*) Que Educ & Trng.

Meyer, Marilyn & Baber, Roberta. Computers in Your Future. 2nd rev. ed. LC 96-69173. (Illus.). 500p. (C). 1996. pap. text 80.00 (*1-57576-480-6*) Que Educ & Trng.

Meyer, Marilyn, jt. auth. see Martin, Edward G.

Meyer, Marjorie. One Man's Vision: The Life of Automotive Pioneer Ralph R. Teetor. LC 95-77508. (Illus.). 225p. 1995. pap. 16.95 (*1-878208-67-5*) Guild Pr IN.

Meyer, Mark. Racin' The NASCAR/Winston Cup Stock Car Racing Series. LC 88-62456. (Illus.). 200p. 1989. 45.00 (*0-943231-18-3*) Howell Pr VA.

— Wings. LC 83-51813. (Illus.). 144p. 1984. 19.98 (*0-934738-05-X*); pap. 12.98 (*0-934738-62-9*) Lickle Pubng.

Meyer, Mark H. & Lehnerd, Alvin P. The Power of Product Platforms: Creating & Sustaining Robust Corporations. LC 96-33508. 288p. 1997. 34.50 (*0-684-82580-5*) Free Pr.

Meyer, Marlyn. Computers in Your Future. 2nd ed. 1997. pap. text, student ed. 24.00 (*1-57576-537-3*) Que Educ & Trng.

Meyer, Marshall, et al. Limits to Bureaucratic Growth. (Studies in Organization: No. 3). x, 259p. 1985. 52.95 (*3-11-009865-2*) De Gruyter.

Meyer, Marshall W. Theory of Organizational Structure. LC 76-56415. (Studies in Sociology). 1977. pap. text 3.95 (*0-672-61193-7*, Bobbs) Macmillan.

Meyer, Marshall W. & Zucker, Lynne G. Permanently Failing Organizations. 180p. (C). 1989. text 38.95 (*0-8039-3258-8*); pap. text 19.50 (*0-8039-3259-6*) Sage.

Meyer, Marshall W., et al. Environments & Organizations. LC 76-50706. (Jossey-Bass Social & Behavioral Science Ser.). 423p. reprint ed. pap. 131.20 (*0-8357-4996-7*, 203792900009) Bks Demand.

Meyer, Martin A. History of the City of Gaza from the Earliest Times to the Present. LC 07-29749. (Columbia University. Oriental Studies: No. 5). reprint ed. 29.50 (*0-404-50495-7*) AMS Pr.

Meyer, Marvin. The Secret Teachings of Jesus: Four Gnostic Gospels. 1986. pap. 10.00 (*0-394-74433-0*) Vin Bks.

Meyer, Marvin & Mirecki, Paul A., eds. Ancient Magic & Ritual Power. (Religions in the Graeco-Roman World Ser.: Vol. 129). 1995. 165.00 (*90-04-10406-2*) Brill Academic Pubs.

Meyer, Marvin C. & Olsen, O. Wilford. Essentials of Parasitology. 6th ed. 304p. (C). 1997. spiral bd. write for info. (*0-07-114981-3*, WCB McGr Hill) McGrw-H Hghr Educ.

Meyer, Marvin C., et al. Essentials of Parasitology. 5th ed. 320p. (C). 1991. text. write for info. (*0-697-12310-3*, WCB McGr Hill) McGrw-H Hghr Educ.

— Essentials of Parasitology. 6th ed. 320p. (C). 1995. text 46.40 (*0-697-15983-3*, WCB McGr Hill) McGrw-H Hghr Educ.

Meyer, Marvin W. Ancient Mysteries A Sourcebook of Sacred Texts. LC 99-13435. 1999. pap. text 19.95 (*0-8122-1692-X*) U of Pa Pr.

— The Unknown Sayings of Jesus. LC 97-49693. 128p. 1998. 18.00 (*0-06-065588-7*, Pub. by Harper SF) HarpC.

— Who Do People Say I Am? The Interpretation of Jesus in the New Testament Gospels. LC 82-24229. 95p. reprint ed. pap. 30.00 (*0-608-14506-8*, 202533700043) Bks Demand.

Meyer, Marvin W., tr. The Gospel of Thomas: The Hidden Sayings of Jesus. LC 91-58913. 144p. 1992. 19.00 (*0-06-065581-X*, Pub. by Harper SF) HarpC.

Meyer, Marvin W. & Smith, Richard. Ancient Christian Magic: Coptic Texts of Ritual Power. LC 98-33163. 1999. 17.95 (*0-691-00458-7*, Pub. by Princeton U Pr) Cal Prin Full Svc.

Meyer, Mary. Fahrenheit 451: A Study Guide. (Novel-Ties Ser.). (YA). (gr. 9-12). 1984. pap. text, teacher ed. 15.95 (*0-88122-114-7*) Lrn Links.

An Asterisk (*) at the beginning of an entry indicates that the title is appearing for the first time.

Meyer, Mary & Booker, Jane. Eliciting & Analyzing Expert Judgment: A Practical Guide. (Knowledge Based Systems Ser.: Vol. 5). (Illus.). 452p. (C). 1991. text 69.95 (*0-12-493230-4*) Acad Pr.

Meyer, Mary C. Walking with Jesus. LC 92-10912. (Illus.). 80p. (Orig.). (J). (ps-5). 1992. pap. 11.99 (*0-8361-3574-1*) Herald Pr.

Meyer, Mary C., et al. Sexual Harassment at Work. (Illus.). 256p. 1981. text 17.50 (*0-89433-156-6*) Petrocelli.

Meyer, Mary C., ed. see Bender, Carrie.

Meyer, Mary K., ed. Gender Politics in Global Governance. 336p. 1998. pap. 26.95 (*0-8476-9161-6*) Rowman.

Meyer, Mary K. & Prugl, Elisabeth, eds. Gender Politics in Global Governance. 336p. 1998. 69.00 (*0-8476-9160-8*) Rowman.

Meyer, Mary K., jt. ed. see Filby, P. William.

Meyer, Matt, jt. auth. see Sutherland, Bill.

Meyer, Matthias. Feuerbach und Zinzendorf. (Theologische Texte und Studien: Bd. 1). (GER.). xx, 242p. 1992. write for info. (*3-487-09599-8*) G Olms Pubs.

Meyer, Matthias, jt. auth. see Beyreuther, Erich.

Meyer, Max, ed. & tr. see Ebbinghaus, Hermann.

Meyer, Melissa L. The White Earth Tragedy: Ethnicity & Dispossession at a Minnesota Anishinaabe Reservation, 1889-1920. LC 93-23456. (Illus.). xviii, 333p. (C). 1994. text 60.00 (*0-8032-3154-7*) U of Nebr Pr.

— The White Earth Tragedy: Ethnicity & Dispossession at a Minnesota Anishinaabe Reservation, 1889-1920. LC 93-23456. (Illus.). 333p. 1994. pap. text 16.00 (*0-8032-8256-7*) U of Nebr Pr.

Meyer, Mercer. Just Grandma & Me. (J). (gr. 1 up). 1994. pap. 23.75 incl. cd-rom (*1-57135-002-0*) Living Bks.

— What Do You Do with a Kangaroo? (J). (ps-3). 1993. pap. 199.51 (*0-590-21034-3*) Scholastic Inc.

Meyer, Merle E., jt. auth. see Altmaier, Elizabeth M.

Meyer, Mich. Jewish Identity Modern World. LC 89-70707. (Samuel & Althea Stroum Lectures in Jewish Studies). 120p. 1990. pap. 20.00 (*0-295-97000-6*) U of Wash Pr.

Meyer, Michael. Bedford Introduction to Literature. 1992. 19.95 (*0-614-32375-4*) St Martin.

— Bedford Introduction to Literature. 3rd ed. 1992. pap. text, teacher ed. 2.60 (*0-312-07498-0*) St Martin.

— Bedford Introduction to Literature. 4th ed. 384p. 1995. pap. text, teacher ed. 10.00 (*0-312-11958-5*) St Martin.

— Bedford Introduction to Literature: Reading, Thinking & Writing. 5th ed. LC 98-85194. 1999. 37.50 (*0-312-17140-4*) Bedford Bks.

— Bedford's Introduction to Literature: Frankenstein. 1991. pap. text 43.20 (*0-312-13671-4*) St Martin.

— Building Client/Server Applications with Visual Basic. (Illus.). 1000p. (Orig.). 1998. 49.99 (*0-7897-0623-7*) Que.

— The Compact Bedford Introduction to Literature: Reading, Thinking, & Writing. 4th ed. LC 96-85012. 1600p. 1996. pap. text 42.95 (*0-312-13263-8*) St Martin.

— Hamlet. (Bedford Introduction to Literature Ser.). 1995. pap. text 35.10 (*0-312-13887-3*) St Martin.

— Of Problematology: Philosophy, Science & Language. Jamison, David, tr.Tr. of De la Problematologie. 318p. 1995. pap. text 18.95 (*0-226-52151-6*) U Ch Pr.

— The Politics of Music in the Third Reich. (American University Studies: History: Ser. IX, Vol. 49). (Illus.). XIV, 434p. 1993. text 69.95 (*0-8204-0805-0*) P Lang Pubng.

— Several More Lives to Live: Thoreau's Political Reputation in America, 29. LC 76-56622. (Contributions in American Studies: No. 29). 216p. 1977. 49.95 (*0-8371-9477-6*, MES/, Greenwood Pr) Greenwood.

— Thinking & Writing about Literature. 201p. (C). 1995. pap. text 22.95 (*0-312-11166-5*) St Martin.

— Visual Basic 4 Developer's Handbook. 1996. pap. 34.99 (*0-7821-1605-1*) Sybex.

— Willensverneinung und Lebensbejahung: Zur Bedeutung von Schopenhauer und Nietzsche im Werk Ricarda Huchs. Schonert, Jorg, ed. (Hamburger Beitraege Zur Lebensbejahung: Bd. 25). (Illus.). 255p. 1998. pap. 45.95 (*3-631-33302-1*) P Lang Pubng.

Meyer, Michael, ed. Armed Conflict & the New Law Vol. 1: Aspects of the 1977 Geneva Protocols & the 1980 Weapons Convention. 298p. 1989. pap. 60.00 (*0-903067-30-7*, Pub. by Brit Inst ICL) St Mut.

— Armed Conflict & the New Law Vol. 2: Effecting Compliance. 256p. 1993. pap. 90.00 (*0-903067-36-6*, Pub. by Brit Inst ICL) St Mut.

Meyer, Michael, ed. From Metaphysics to Rhetoric. 216p. (C). 1989. lib. bdg. 142.00 (*90-277-2814-3*, Pub. by Kluwer Academic) Kluwer Academic.

Meyer, Michael, tr. The Plays of Ibsen, Vols. III, IV. 1986. pap. 4.95 (*0-317-43114-5*) PB.

Meyer, Michael & Stipdonk, Paul. The Luftwaffe: From Training School to the Front - An Illustrated Study, 1933-1945. (Illus.). 288p. (C). (gr. 13). 1996. 39.95 (*0-88740-924-5*) Schiffer.

Meyer, Michael, et al. Resources for Teaching "The Compact Bedford Introduction to Literature" 4th ed. 384p. 1996. pap., spiral bd. 13.33 (*0-312-13264-6*) St Martin.

Meyer, Michael, jt. auth. see Cournand, Andre.

Meyer, Michael, jt. auth. see Plaut, W. Gunther.

Meyer, Michael, ed. see Douglass, Frederick.

Meyer, Michael, ed. see Keyes, Sidney.

Meyer, Michael, ed. & tr. see Fried, Hedi.

Meyer, Michael, tr. see Ibsen, Henrik.

Meyer, Michael, tr. see Strindberg, August.

Meyer, Michael, tr. & intro. see Ibsen, Henrik.

Meyer, Michael, tr. & intro. see Strindberg, August.

Meyer, Michael A. Hebrew Union College - Jewish Institute of Religion: A Centennial History, 1875-1975. 2nd rev. ed. (Illus.). 306p. 1993. reprint ed. pap. 20.00 (*0-87820-109-2*) Hebrew Union Coll Pr.

— The Origins of the Modern Jew: Jewish Identity & European Culture in Germany, 1749-1824. LC 67-12384. (Waynebooks Ser.: No. 32). 250p. (C). 1972. reprint ed. pap. 16.95 (*0-8143-1470-8*) Wayne St U Pr.

— Response to Modernity: A History of the Reform Movement in Judaism. LC 94-45560. 510p. 1995. reprint ed. pap. text 19.95 (*0-8143-2555-6*) Wayne St U Pr.

Meyer, Michael A., ed. German-Jewish History in Modern Times: Tradition & Enlightenment 1600-1780. (Illus.). 416p. 1996. 52.50 (*0-231-07472-7*) Col U Pr.

Meyer, Michael A., ed. Ideas of Jewish History. LC 87-13810. 374p. 1987. reprint ed. pap. 18.95 (*0-8143-1951-3*) Wayne St U Pr.

Meyer, Michael A., ed. Ideas of Jewish History. LC 87-13810. 374p. reprint ed. pap. 116.00 (*0-608-10566-X*, 2071186) Bks Demand.

Meyer, Michael A. & Jersch-Wenzel, Stefi. German-Jewish History in Modern Times: Emancipation & Acculturation, 1870-1871, Vol. 2. 392p. (Orig.). 1997. pap. 52.50 (*0-231-07474-3*) Col U Pr.

Meyer, Michael C. Huerta: A Political Portrait. LC 70-162343. 290p. reprint ed. pap. 89.90 (*0-7837-4653-9*, 204437700002) Bks Demand.

— Mexican Rebel: Pascual Orozco & the Mexican Revolution, 1910-1915. LC 67-10667. (Illus.). 198p. 1967. reprint ed. pap. 61.40 (*0-7837-6758-7*, 205915700011) Bks Demand.

— Water in the Hispanic Southwest: A Social & Legal History, 1550-1850. LC 83-24276. 209p. 1996. pap. 17.95 (*0-8165-1595-6*) U of Ariz Pr.

***Meyer, Michael C. & Beezley, William H., eds.** The Oxford History of Mexico. LC 99-56044. (Illus.). 768p. 2000. write for info. (*0-19-511228-8*) OUP.

Meyer, Michael C., et al. The Course of Mexican History. 6th ed. LC 98-13289. (Illus.). 744p. (C). 1998. text 62.00 (*0-19-511000-5*); pap. text 36.95 (*0-19-511001-3*) OUP.

Meyer, Michael C., jt. ed. see Esquenazi-Mayo, Roberto.

Meyer, Michael C., jt. ed. see Greenleaf, Richard E.

Meyer, Michael D. & Institute of Transportation Engineers Staff. A Toolbox for Alleviating Traffic Congestion & Enhancing Mobility. LC 98-4839. (Illus.). iii, 355p. 1997. pap. text 40.00 (*0-935403-12-4*, IR-054B) Inst Trans Eng.

***Meyer, Michael J., ed.** The Betrayal of Brotherhood in the Work of John Steinbeck. LC 99-53133. (Studies in American Literature: Vol. 33). 576p. 2000. 119.95 (*0-7734-7835-3*) E Mellen.

Meyer, Michael J. & Hayashi, Tetsumaro. The Hayashi Steinbeck Bibliography, 1982-1996. LC 98-22003. (Scarecrow Author Bibliographies Ser.: No. 99). 448p. 1998. 59.00 (*0-8108-3482-0*) Scarecrow.

Meyer, Michael J. & Parent, William A., eds. The Constitution of Rights: Human Dignity & American Values. LC 91-55535. (Start to Read! Library Edition Ser.). 256p. 1992. pap. text 16.95 (*0-8014-9950-X*) Cornell U Pr.

Meyer, Michael L. & Gissing, George R. The Odd Women: A Play LC 94-204567. 68 p. 1993. pap. write for info. (*0-573-01852-9*) French.

Meyer, Michael M. & Fienberg, Stephen E., eds. Assessing Evaluation Studies: The Case of Bilingual Education. LC 92-64011. 138p. 1992. reprint ed. pap. 42.80 (*0-608-02337-X*, 206297800004) Bks Demand.

Meyer, Michael T. & Thurman, E. M., eds. Herbicide Metabolites in Surface Water & Groundwater, Vol. 630. LC 96-20170. (ACS Symposium Ser.: No. 630). (Illus.). 330p. 1996. text 105.00 (*0-8412-3405-1*, Pub. by Am Chemical) OUP.

Meyer, Michel. From Logic to Rhetoric. LC 86-26346. (Pragmatics & Beyond Ser.: Vol. VII:3). ix, 147p. 1986. pap. 47.00 (*1-55619-002-6*) J Benjamins Pubng Co.

— Meaning & Reading: A Philosophical Essay On Language & Literature. (Pragmatics & Beyond Ser.: Vol. IV: 3). ix, 176p. 1983. 53.00 (*90-272-2515-X*) J Benjamins Pubng Co.

— Of Problematology: Philosophy, Science & Language. Jamison, David, tr. from FRE. LC 94-46783.Tr. of De la Problematologie. 318p. 1995. lib. bdg. 49.95 (*0-226-52150-8*) U Ch Pr.

— Rhetoric, Language, & Reason. LC 92-41696. (Literature & Philosophy Ser.). 192p. (C). 1994. 35.00 (*0-271-01057-6*); pap. text 16.95 (*0-271-01058-4*) Pa St U Pr.

Meyer, Michel, ed. Questions & Questioning. (Foundations of Communication & Cognition Ser.). vi, 392p. (C). 1988. lib. bdg. 129.25 (*3-11-010680-9*) De Gruyter.

Meyer, Mike, jt. intro. see Singer, E. A.

Meyer, Milford J. Pennsylvania Vehicle Code Annotated. 2nd ed. Zanan, Arthur S., ed. LC 94-72323. 1999. ring bd. 109.50 (*1-887024-07-7*) Bisel Co.

Meyer, Milford J. & Zanan, Arthur S. Handbook of Civil Procedure in the State & Federal Courts of Pennsylvania. LC 82-71145. 1993. text 63.00 (*1-887024-33-6*) Bisel Co.

— Pennsylvania Trial Advocacy. 288p. 1999. text 59.50 (*1-887024-65-4*) Bisel Co.

Meyer, Milford J., jt. auth. see Zanan, Arthur S.

Meyer, Milton W. Asia: A Concise History. LC 95 44450. 608p. (C). 1996. lib. bdg. 64.50 (*0-8476-8068-1*) Rowman.

— Asia: A Concise History. 620p. (C). 1996. pap. text 24.95 (*0-8476-8063-0*) Rowman.

— China: A Concise History. 2nd rev. ed. 368p. (C). 1994. pap. text 16.95 (*0-8226-3033-8*); lib. bdg. 50.00 (*0-8476-7953-5*) Rowman.

— South Asia: A Short History of the Subcontinent. 2nd ed. (Quality Paperback Ser.: No. 34). 268p. (Orig.). 1976. pap. 10.00 (*0-8226-0034-X*) Littlefield.

Meyer, Moe, ed. The Politics & Poetics of Camp. LC 93-18913. (Illus.). 240p. (C). 1993. pap. 25.99 (*0-415-08248-X*) Routledge.

Meyer, N. Dean. Decentralization: Fantasies, Failings & Fundamentals. 125p. (Orig.). 1998. pap. 8.95 (*0-9641635-3-5*) NDMA Pubng.

Meyer, N. Dean. The Internal Economy: Applying Market Economics within Corporations to Eliminate Backlog & Turn Bureaucrats into Entrepreneurs. 350p. 17.95 (*1-892606-13-5*) NDMA Pubng.

Backlogs... Unreasonable expectations... Poor returns on investments... Decentralization just to give business units control over staff's priorities. All of these symptoms point to a dysfunctional internal economy. Dean Meyer coined the term "internal economy" to describe the resource-management processes within organizations. It comprises the budgeting, priority-setting, pricing & resource-tracking mechanisms that manage the flow of money & time through corporations. Internal economics involves much more than accounting which only reports what has already happened. Meyer shows how these critical governance processes determine what each department will do in service of others in the corporation. If you think of each department as a business within a business, all staff serve as a marketplace (the rest of the corporation) that is hungry for help but can only afford a limited amount of service. Unfortunately, according to Meyer, most corporations are run by a "central soviet," making it difficult to balance supply & demand & to set proper priorities. This book pioneers the application of economics within corporations. A balance of theory, practical guidelines & insightful case studies, it gives leaders the tools they need to replace politics & bureaucracy with sensible, business like market mechanisms.
Publisher Paid Annotation.

Meyer, N. Dean. Outsourcing. 106p. (Orig.). 1999. pap. 8.95 (*1-892606-04-6*) NDMA Pubng.

Outsourcing promises tantalizing benefits: cost savings, improved responsibilities & fewer distractions. Unfortunately, those claims don't hold up under the harsh test of reality. The ugly truth is that outsourcing is often the last resort for executives frustrated with staff departments. But does it make sense to get rid of management headaches by eliminating an entire department? This book offers practical guidelines that answer the fundamental questions: When is outsourcing appropriate & when is it just throwing too much money at the problem?
Publisher Paid Annotation.

— RoadMap: How to Understand, Diagnose & Transform Organizations. 2nd rev. ed. (Illus.). 141p. (Orig.). 1998. pap. 8.95 (*0-9641635-2-7*) NDMA Pubng.

— Structural Cybernetics: An Overview. (Orig.). 1995. pap. 8.95 (*0-9641635-1-9*) NDMA Pubng.

Meyer, N. Dean & Boone, Mary E. The Information Edge. 2nd ed. (Illus.). 406p. 1995. reprint ed. pap. 19.95 (*0-9641635-0-0*) NDMA Pubng.

Meyer, N. L., et al. Taxonomic Literature of Southern African Plants. (Strelitzia Ser.: Vol. V). (Illus.). 164p. 1977. 40.00 (*1-874907-35-8*, Pub. by Natl Botanical Inst) Balogh.

Meyer, Nan. The Inter-Faith Family Seder Book: How to Celebrate a Jewish Passover Supper with Christian In-Laws & Non-Jewish Friends. (Illus.). iv, 33p. 1998. 13.95 (*0-9663305-0-1*) Heritage New York.

Meyer, Nancy. Endangered Species Coloring-Learning Books Adventure Series. (Illus.). (J). (ps-3). 1993. write for info. (*1-883408-05-9*) Meyer Pub FL.

Meyer, Naomi. The Journey with Joshua: Educating My Autistic Child. 250p. 1994. 21.95 (*1-56062-256-3*) CIS Comm.

Meyer, Nathan M. The Patmos Prediction. LC 89-63537. 261p. (Orig.). 1989. pap. 9.95 (*0-941241-04-1*) Prophecy Pubns.

Meyer, Nicholas. Canary Trainer: From the Memoirs of John H. Watson. 224p. 1995. pap. 10.00 (*0-393-31241-0*) Norton.

— The Seven-Percent Solution. large type ed. 1977. 27.99 (*0-7089-0052-6*) Ulverscroft.

— The West End Horror. large type ed. 1978. 27.99 (*0-7089-0098-4*) Ulverscroft.

— The West End Horror: From the Memoris of John H. Watson. 1994. pap. 8.95 (*0-393-31153-8*) Norton.

Meyer, Nicholas, ed. The Seven-Percent Solution: Being a Reprint from the Reminiscences of John H. Watson, M.D. LC 93-5779. 256p. 1993. pap. 9.95 (*0-393-31119-8*) Norton.

Meyer, Nicholas E. The Biographical Dictionary of Hispanic Americans. LC 95-36140. (Illus.). 256p. (YA). (gr. 5-12). 1996. 26.95 (*0-8160-3280-7*) Facts on File.

— Magic in the Dark: A Young Viewer's History of the Movies. LC 85-13004. (Illus.). 284p. reprint ed. pap. 88.10 (*0-7837-5335-7*, 204507500005) Bks Demand.

Meyer-Nieberg, P. Banach Lattices. (Universitext Ser.). xv, 395p. 1991. 69.95 (*0-387-54201-9*) Spr-Verlag.

Meyer, O. & Klauser, R. Clavis Mediaevalis: Kleines Woerterbuch der Mittelalterforschung. (GER.). 312p. 1966. 75.00 (*0-8288-6699-6*, M-7323) Fr & Eur.

Meyer-Ohle, Hendrick, jt. auth. see Legewie, Jochen.

Meyer-Ortmanns, H. & Klumper, A., eds. Field Theoretical Tools for Polymer & Particle Physics. LC 98-13619. (Lecture Notes in Physics: Vol. 508). xvi, 258p. 1998. 73.00 (*3-540-64308-7*) Spr-Verlag.

Meyer-Ortmanns, Hildegard & Reisz, Thomas. Phase Transitions in Particle Physics: The Phase Structure of QCD. 200p. 1999. 28.00 (*981-02-3441-4*) World Scientific Pub.

Meyer, P. Energy Systems Analysis for Developing Countries. (Lecture Notes in Economics & Mathematical Systems Ser.: Vol. 222). vi, 344p. 1984. 41.00 (*0-387-12879-4*) Spr-Verlag.

Meyer, P., ed. Gene Silencing in Higher Plants & Related Phenomena in Other Eukaryotes. (Currents Topics in Microbiology & Immunology Ser.: Vol. 197). 240p. 1995. 140.95 (*0-387-58236-3*) Spr-Verlag.

Meyer, P. & Furnivall, F. J., eds. Curial Made by Maystere Alain Charretier. (EETS Extra Ser.: Vol. 54). 1965. reprint ed. 20.00 (*0-19-722516-0*, Pub. by EETS) Boydell & Brewer.

Meyer, P. A. Quantum Probability for Probabilists. Dold, A. et al, eds. (Lecture Notes in Mathematics Ser.: Vol. 1538). 297p. 1993. pap. 43.00 (*0-387-56476-4*) Spr-Verlag.

Meyer, P. A., jt. ed. see Azema, J.

Meyer, P. A., ed. see Seminaire Pierre Lelong Staff.

Meyer, P. D. Uncertainty Analyses of Infiltration & Subsurface Flow & Transport for SDMP Sites. 158p. 1997. per. 16.00 (*0-16-062863-6*) USGPO.

Meyer, Pamela. Quantum Creativity: Nine Principles for a Life of Possibility. LC 97-91009. x, 175p. 1997. pap. 19.95 (*0-9660114-0-6*, Yezand Pr) Meyer Creativity.

***Meyer, Pamela.** Quantum Creativity: Nine Principles to Transform the Way You Work. LC 99-57946. 224p. 2000. pap. 16.95 (*0-8092-2439-9*, 243990, Contemporary Bks) NTC Contemp Pub Co.

Meyer, Patricia, ed. see Lempfrit, Honore-Timothee.

Meyer, Patricia A. The Teachings of the Angel of North America Bk. 1: How to Save Your Soul & Your Society. 160p. 1996. pap. 10.95 (*0-9646601-0-5*) Oaklea Pr.

Meyer, Paul A. Quantum Probability for Probabilists, Vol. X. 2nd ed. Dold, A et al, eds. LC 95-37123. (Lecture Notes in Mathematics Ser.: Vol. 1538). 312p. 1995. 62.95 (*3-540-60270-4*) Spr-Verlag.

Meyer, Paul J. & Chesser, Barbara J. I Inherited a Fortune! LC 97-4570. xv, 266 p. 1997. 22.95 (*1-56530-243-5*, Pub. by Summit TX) BookWorld.

Meyer, Paul J., et al. Bridging the Leadership Gap: The Keys to Success. LC 98-9018. 248p. 1998. 24.99 (*1-56530-279-6*) Summit TX.

Meyer, Paul M. Juristische Papyri. 440p. 1980. 50.00 (*0-89005-188-7*) Ares.

Meyer, Paul M., jt. ed. see Mommsen, Theodor.

Meyer, Paul R., Jr., ed. Surgery of Spine Trauma. LC 88-23790. (Illus.). 879p. 1989. reprint ed. pap. 200.00 (*0-7837-9590-4*, 206033900005) Bks Demand.

Meyer, Paula, jt. auth. see Meyer, Larry L.

Meyer, Pedro. Truths & Fictions: A Journey from Documentary to Digital Photography. LC 94-79645. (Illus.). 136p. 1995. 60.00 (*0-89381-608-6*) Aperture.

Meyer, Peter. Awarding College Credit for Non-College Learning. LC 74-28918. (Jossey-Bass Series in Higher Education). 223p. reprint ed. pap. 69.20 (*0-8357-4952-5*, 203788400009) Bks Demand.

— Blind Love: The True Story of the Texas Cadet Murders, Vol. 1. LC 98-120464. 256p. 2000. mass mkt. 6.50 (*0-312-96412-9*, St Martins Paperbacks) St Martin.

— Cocteau - Feydeau: 13 Monologues. (Oberon Bks.). 72p. 1997. 16.95 (*1-870259-62-9*) Theatre Comm.

***Meyer, Peter.** Getting Started in Computer Consulting. LC 99-29705. 258p. 1999. pap. 18.95 (*0-471-34813-9*) Wiley.

— Warp-Speed Growth: Managing the Fast-Track Business Without Sacrificing Time, People & Money. LC 99-87908. 215p. 2000. 25.00 (*0-8144-0526-6*) AMACOM.

Meyer, Peter & Fasenfest, David, eds. The Comparative Politics of Local Economic Development. (Orig.). 1991. pap. 15.00 (*0-944285-26-0*) Pol Studies.

Meyer, Peter, tr. see Adamov, Arthur.

Meyer, Peter, tr. see Feydeau, Georges.

Meyer, Peter B. Jews in the Soviet Satellites. LC 79-97297. 1971. reprint ed. lib. bdg. 59.75 (*0-8371-2621-5*, MEJS, Greenwood Pr) Greenwood.

Meyer, Peter B., ed. Comparative Studies in Local Economic Development: Problems in Policy Implementation, 144. LC 92-35599. (Contributions in Economics & Economic History Ser.: No. 144). 240p. 1993. 65.00 (*0-313-28820-8*, GM8820, Greenwood Pr) Greenwood.

Meyer, Peter B., et al. Contaminated Land: Reclamation, Redevelopment & Re-Use in the United States & the European Union. LC 95-19495. (Illus.). 240p. 1995. 85.00 (*1-85898-243-X*) E Elgar.

Meyer, Peter K. Medicalese: A Humorous Medical Dictionary. Graves, Catherine, ed. LC 93-74044. (Illus.). 96p. (Orig.). 1994. pap. 9.95 (*0-9628186-1-5*) Avian Cetacean.

— Nature Guide to the Carolina Coast: Common Birds, Crabs, Shells, Fish, & Other Entities of the Coastal Environment. LC 90-85396. (Illus.). (Orig.). 1991. pap. 13.95 (*0-9628186-0-7*) Avian Cetacean.

Meyer, Philip. Ethical Journalism: A Guide for Students, Practitioners, & Consumers. 272p. (C). 1993. reprint ed. pap. text 25.00 (*0-8191-8332-6*) U Pr of Amer.

— Precision Journalism: A Reporter's Introduction to Social Science Methods. 2nd ed. LC 79-2172. (Illus.). 444p. reprint ed. pap. 137.70 (*0-8357-6688-8*, 205686800094) Bks Demand.

Meyer, Philip, et al. The Newspaper Survival Book: An Editor's Guide to Marketing Research. LC 84-48042. (Illus.). 183p. reprint ed. pap. 56.80 (*0-608-09350-5*, 205409600002) Bks Demand.

Meyer, Philip E. Mastering Inventory. 2nd unabridged ed. 218p. 1996. pap. text 49.00 (*1-884826-29-6*) AIPB.

Meyer, Philip E., jt. auth. see Shillinglaw, Gordon.

Meyer, Philippe & Marche, Pierre, eds. Blood Cells & Arteries in Hypertension & Atherosclerosis. LC 88-26425. (Atherosclerosis Reviews Ser.: No. 19). (Illus.). 299p. reprint ed. pap. 92.70 (*0-608-00588-6*, 206117500007) Bks Demand.

***Meyer, Philippe.** A Parisian's Paris. 268p. 2000. pap. 16.95 (*2-08-013664-X*, Pub. by Flammarion) Abbeville Pr.

Meyer-Plath & Schneider, A. M. Die Landmauer von Konstantinopel Pt. 2: Aufnahme, Beschreibung und Geschichte. (Denkmaeler Antiker Architektur Ser.: Vol. 8). (GER., Illus.). x, 170p. (C). 1978. reprint ed. 229.25 (*3-11-004992-9*) De Gruyter.

Meyer, Poul. Systemic Aspects of Public Administration. LC 73-178907. 183 p. 1973. write for info. (*87-12-57198-9*) GAD.

Meyer, Priscilla, ed. Essays on Gogol: Logos & the Russian Word. (Studies in Russian Literature & Theory). 300p. 1992. 49.95 (*0-8101-1009-1*) Northwestern U Pr.

Meyer, Priscilla, jt. ed. see Fusso, Susanne.

Meyer, R., et al. Alcohol Reinforcement. 1991. 92.50 (*0-8176-3463-0*) Birkhauser.

Meyer, R., jt. auth. see Denecke, H. J.

Meyer, R., jt. auth. see Kempt, K.

Meyer, R. A. & Paar, Vladimir, eds. Nuclear Structure, Reactions & Symmetries: Proceedings of the International Conference on Nuclear Structure, Reactions & Symmetries Dubrovnik, Yugoslavia 5-14 June 1986, 2 vols. 309p. 1986. text 164.00 (*9971-5-0141-4*) World Scientific Pub.

Meyer, R. A., ed. see National Congress on Pressure Vessels & Piping Sta.

Meyer, R. Daniel, jt. auth. see Klotz, Jerome H.

Meyer, R. M. Essential Mathematics for Applied Fields. (Universitext Ser.). (Illus.). 555p. 1979. 79.95 (*0-387-90450-6*) Spr-Verlag.

Meyer, R. M., ed. Fisheries Resource Utilization & Policy: Proceedings of the World Fisheries Congress, Athens, Theme 2. 500p. (C). 1996. text 120.00 (*1-886106-27-4*) Science Pubs.

Meyer, R. Wilton. Clumber Spaniel: AKC Rank #124. (Rare Breed Ser.). (Illus.). 96p. 1997. 19.95 (*0-7938-0764-6*, RX-114) TFH Pubns.

Meyer, Ralph, jt. ed. see Beck, William C.

Meyer, Randall K. Digging up the Past. (Illus.). 595p. (Orig.). 1994. write for info. (*0-9641984-0-1*) NAP AL.

Meyer, Raymond, tr. see Ingarden, Roman.

Meyer, Raymond, tr. see Kautsky, Karl.

Meyer, Raymond F. Backwoods Jazz in the Twenties. LC 88-64118. 120p. (Orig.). 1989. pap. 9.95 (*0-934426-19-8*) NAPSAC Reprods.

Meyer, Raymond W. Handbook of Polyester Molding Compounds & Molding Technology. 300p. 1987. text 45.00 (*0-412-00771-1*, 9199, Chap & Hall NY) Chapman & Hall.

— Handbook of Pultrusion Technology. 220p. 1985. 32.50 (*0-412-00761-4*, NO. 9201, Chap & Hall NY) Chapman & Hall.

Meyer, Rene, ed. see Ryle, Gilbert.

Meyer, Richard. Stories from the Heart: Teachers & Students Researching Their Literacy Lives. 176p. 1996. pap. 15.50 (*0-8058-8044-5*) L Erlbaum Assocs.

Meyer, Richard, ed. Dos Profetas Poderosos.Tr. of Two Powerful Prophets. (SPA., Illus.). 91p. 1996. pap., teacher ed. 5.50 (*1-879892-58-8*, SI-885-M) Editorial Bautista.

— Escalones Hacia el Exito.Tr. of Stepping Stones to Success. (SPA., Illus.). 1997. pap., teacher ed. 5.50 (*1-879892-61-8*, SI-888) Editorial Bautista.

— Josue: Reclama tu Herencia.Tr. of Joshua: Claim the Inheritence. (SPA., Illus.). 89p. 1996. pap., teacher ed. 4.40 (*1-879892-56-1*, SS-953) Editorial Bautista.

— Libertadores Osados.Tr. of Daring Deliverers. (SPA., Illus.). 87p. 1997. pap., teacher ed. 5.50 (*1-879892-60-X*, SI-887) Editorial Bautista.

— Libres en Cristo, Vol. 1.Tr. of Free in Christ (Romans 1-7). (SPA., Illus.). 100p. 1997. pap., teacher ed. 4.40 (*1-879892-63-4*, SS-961) Editorial Bautista.

— Libres en Cristo, Vol. 2.Tr. of Free in Christ (Romans 1-7). (SPA., Illus.). 99p. 1997. pap., teacher ed. 4.40 (*1-879892-64-2*, SS-962) Editorial Bautista.

— Que Sabes? (SPA., Illus.). 87p. 1997. pap., teacher ed. 5.50 (*1-879892-59-6*, SI-886) Editorial Bautista.

— Reglamentos! A Quien le Hacen Falta?Tr. of Rules! Who Needs Them?. (SPA., Illus.). 88p. 1996. pap., teacher ed. 5.50 (*1-879892-52-9*, SI-883) Editorial Bautista.

— Temas Desconcertantes.Tr. of Perplexing Problems. (SPA., Illus.). 83p. 1996. pap., teacher ed. 5.50 (*1-879892-53-7*, SI-884) Editorial Bautista.

— Tu Eres el Christo.Tr. of Thou Art the Christ. (SPA., Illus.). 104p. 1996. pap., teacher ed. 4.40 (*1-879892-57-X*, SS-954) Editorial Bautista.

Meyer, Richard, et al. Composing a Teacher Study Group: Learning about Inquiry in Primary Classrooms. LC 97-31515. 208p. 1998. write for info. (*0-8058-2699-8*); pap. write for info. (*0-8058-2700-5*) L Erlbaum Assocs.

Meyer, Richard, jt. auth. see McDowell, Peggy.

Meyer, Richard, ed. see Anderson, Donald K.

Meyer, Richard, ed. see Button, C. Lloyd.

Meyer, Richard, ed. see Gower, David M.

Meyer, Richard, ed. see Gromacki, Robert G.

Meyer, Richard, ed. see Hartog, John, III.

Meyer, Richard, ed. see Hartog, John, II.

Meyer, Richard, ed. see Houghton, Myron J., et al.

Meyer, Richard, ed. see Master, John R.

Meyer, Richard, ed. see Nettleton, David.

Meyer, Richard, ed. see Pickering, Ernest.

Meyer, Richard, ed. see Porter, Charles.

Meyer, Richard, ed. see Reder, Timothy S.

Meyer, Richard, ed. see Regular Baptist Press Staff.

Meyer, Richard, ed. see Wagner, Charles U.

Meyer, Richard, ed. see Walton, Arthur B.

Meyer, Richard, ed. see Warren, Dave & Warren, Pat.

Meyer, Richard, ed. see Welch, W. Wilbert.

Meyer, Richard A. & Brenner, Daeg S., eds. Nuclei off the Line of Stability. LC 86-25905. (ACS Symposium Ser.: No. 324). (Illus.). xvi, 518p. 1986. 104.95 (*0-8412-1005-5*, PA 414) Am Chemical.

— Nuclei off the Line of Stability. LC 86-25905. (ACS Symposium Ser.: Vol. 324). 552p. 1986. reprint ed. pap. 171.20 (*0-608-03528-9*, 206424700008) Bks Demand.

Meyer, Richard A. & Paar, Vladimir. Symmetries & Nuclear Structure. (Nuclear Science Research Conference Ser.: Vol. 13). xx, 620p. 1987. text 240.00 (*3-7186-0400-0*) Gordon & Breach.

Meyer, Richard C. One Anothering Vol. 1: Biblical Building Blocks for Small Groups. LC 90-46181. 160p. (Orig.). 1998. pap. 12.95 (*0-931055-73-3*) Innisfree Pr.

— One Anothering Vol. 2: Building Spiritual Community in Small Groups. LC 90-46181. 160p. 1999. pap. 12.95 (*1-880913-35-6*) Innisfree Pr.

Meyer, Richard D., jt. ed. see Holmberg, Kenneth.

Meyer, Richard E. Introduction to Mathematical Fluid Dynamics. 192p. 1982. reprint ed. pap. 7.95 (*0-486-61554-5*) Dover.

Meyer, Richard E., ed. Cemeteries & Gravemarkers: Voices of American Culture. LC 92-31114. (Illus.). 347p. (C). 1992. reprint ed. pap. text 23.95 (*0-87421-160-3*) Utah St U Pr.

— Ethnicity & the American Cemetery. LC 92-74504. 239p. (C). 1993. 48.95 (*0-87972-600-8*) Bowling Green Univ Popular Press.

— Markers: The Journal of the Association for Gravestone Studies, No. 10. LC 81-642903. (Illus.). 256p. 1992. pap. 25.00 (*1-878381-03-2*) Assn Gravestone Studies.

— Markers: The Journal of the Association for Gravestone Studies, No. 11. LC 81-642903. (Illus.). 233p. 1993. pap. 25.00 (*1-878381-04-0*) Assn Gravestone Studies.

— Markers: The Journal of the Association for Gravestone Studies, No. 13. LC 81-642903. (Illus.). 243p. 1996. pap. 25.00 (*1-878381-06-7*) Assn Gravestone Studies.

— Markers: The Journal of the Association for Gravestone Studies, Vol. 15. LC 81-642903. (Illus.). 356p. 1998. 42.00 (*1-878381-08-3*) Assn Gravestone Studies.

Meyer, Richard E., et al, eds. Markers: The Journal of the Association for Gravestone Studies, Vol. 8. LC 81-642903. (Illus.). 352p. (C). 1991. 25.00 (*1-878381-01-6*) Assn Gravestone Studies.

Meyer, Richard F., ed. Exploration for Heavy Crude Oil & Natural Bitumen: Research Conference. LC 87-3491. (AAPG Studies in Geology: Vol. 25). 744p. 1987. reprint ed. pap. 200.00 (*0-608-03022-8*, 206347200006) Bks Demand.

Meyer, Richard K., et al. MechWarrior. (BattleTech Ser.). (Illus.). 144p. (Orig.). 1991. pap. 15.00 (*0-931787-58-0*) FASA Corp.

***Meyer, Richard L.** Rural Financial Markets in Asia: Paradigms, Policies, & Performance. (A Study of Rural Asia: Vol. 3). 368p. 2000. pap. 29.95 (*0-19-592451-7*); text 55.00 (*0-19-592450-9*) OUP.

Meyer, Richard M. Altgermanische Religionsgeschichte: History of Ancient Germanic Religion. Bolle, Kees W., ed. LC 77-79143. (Mythology Ser.). (GER.). 1978. reprint ed. lib. bdg. 54.95 (*0-405-10552-5*) Ayer.

Meyer, Richard N. Glass Oasis: And Other Love - Hate Poetry about Los Angeles. LC 91-90267. 57p. 1991. pap. 6.00 (*0-9629451-0-2*) R M Concepts.

***Meyer, Rick.** Master Guide for Passing the Respiratory Care Credentialing Exams. 4th ed. 566p. 1999. pap. text 53.33 (*0-13-013832-0*) P-H.

***Meyer, Rick, et al.** Master Guide for Passing the Respiratory Care Credentialing Exams. 4th ed. LC 99-43212. (Cancer Chemotherapy Annual Ser.). 632p. 2000. 195.00 (*0-444-50074-X*) Elsevier.

Meyer, Robert. Paleoalterites & Paleosols: Imprints of Terrestrial Processes in Sedimentary Rocks. (Illus.). 162p. (C). 1997. text 94.00 (*90-5410-724-3*, Pub. by A A Balkema) Ashgate Pub Co.

Meyer, Robert A. Assessment of Carbon-Carbon Composite Research in the Far East. 58p. (Orig.). (C). 1992. pap. text 40.00 (*1-56806-021-1*) DIANE Pub.

— Life's Tapestry: A Collection of Poems. (Illus.). 164p. 1993. 12.95 (*0-931541-14-X*) Mancorp Pub.

Meyer, Robert E. Managing Rural Development. (Bibliographies in Technology & Social Change Ser.: No. 2). (Illus.). 40p. (C). 1988. pap. 6.00 (*0-945271-05-0*) ISU-CIKARD.

Meyer, Robert G. Abnormal Behavior & the Criminal Justice System. 312p. 1992. 37.00 (*0-669-24450-3*) Lxngtn Bks.

— Case Studies in Abnormal Behavior. 4th ed. LC 98-4459. 312p. 1998. pap. 44.00 (*0-205-28624-0*) Allyn.

***Meyer, Robert G.** Case Studies in Abnormal Behavior. 5th ed. LC 00-38998. 320p. 2000. pap. text 40.00 (*0-205-32429-0*) Allyn.

Meyer, Robert G. Cases in Developmental Psychology & Psychopathology. 410p. 1989. pap. text 28.00 (*0-205-11907-7*, H19078) Allyn.

— Preparation for Board Certification & Licensing Examinations in Psychology: The Professional, Legal & Ethical Components. 184p. 1992. 29.00 (*0-9634417-0-1*) Monkestee Pr.

— Preparation for Licensing & Board Certification Examinations in Psychology: The Professional, Legal, & Ethical Components. 2nd ed. LC 94-23369. (Continuing Education in Psychiatry & Psychology Ser.: No. 4). 224p. 1995. pap. 24.95 (*0-87630-767-5*, 7675) Brunner-Mazel.

Meyer, Robert G. & Deitsch, Sarah E. The Clinician's Handbook: Integrated Diagnostics, Assessment, & Intervention in Adult & Adolescent Psychopathology. 4th ed. 528p. (C). 1995. 95.00 (*0-205-17181-8*) Allyn.

Meyer, Robert G., jt. auth. see Gray, Paul R.

Meyer, Robert G., jt. auth. see Salmon, Paul G.

Meyer, Robert G., jt. auth. see Smith, Steven R.

Meyer, Robert H., jt. auth. see Teske, Raymond H.

Meyer, Robert T., ed. Palladius: Dialogue on the Life of St. John Chrysostom. (Ancient Christian Writers Ser.: No. 45). 1985. 16.95 (*0-8091-0358-3*) Paulist Pr.

Meyer, Roberta. Listen to the Heart: Creating Intimate Families Through the Power of Unconditional Love. LC 88-40603. 208p. 1990. mass mkt. 8.95 (*0-446-39134-4*, Pub. by Warner Bks) Little.

Meyer, Robin, jt. ed. see Robertson, David W.

Meyer, Rochelle W. Exploresorts. (Hi Map Ser.: No. 16). (Illus.). 60p. teacher ed. 11.99 (*0-614-05310-2*, HM 5616) COMAP Inc.

Meyer, Rochelle W. & Meyer, Walter J. Play It Again Sam: Recurrence Equations & Recursion in Mathematics & Computer Science. Malkevitch, Joseph, ed. (Explorations in Mathematics Ser.). (Illus.). 114p. (Orig.). 1990. pap. text 12.95 (*0-912843-17-9*) COMAP Inc.

Meyer-Rochow, V. B. & Tiang, K. M. Zoologica Band XLV, Heft 134: The Eye of E - Jasus Edwardsii (Crustacea, Decapoda, Palinuridae): Electrophysiology, Histology & Behaviour. (Publications in Zoology). (Illus.). iv, 61p. 1984. pap. 51.00 (*3-510-55020-X*) Balogh.

Meyer, Roger E., ed. Psychopathology & Addictive Disorders. LC 85-30547. 384p. 1986. lib. bdg. 47.50 (*0-89862-680-3*) Guilford Pubns.

Meyer, Roger E. & McLaughlin, Christopher J. Between Mind, Brain, & Managed Care: The Now & Future World of Academic Psychiatry. 340p. 1998. pap. text 39.00 (*0-88048-815-8*, 8815) Am Psychiatric.

***Meyer, Roger N.** Asperger Employment Guide: A Workbook for Individuals on the Autistic Spectrum & Their Families. LC 99-41650. 1999. pap., wbk. ed. 24.95 (*1-85302-796-0*) Jessica Kingsley.

Meyer, Rolf, jt. auth. see Pejcic, Bogdan.

Meyer, Ron. The Portobello Mushroom Cookbook. (Illus.). 78p. 1999. pap. 11.95 (*0-9671074-0-7*) R Meyer.

Meyer, Ron & De Wit, Bob. Strategy: Process, Content, Context - Executive Edition. 256p. 1999. pap. 22.99 (*1-86152-317-3*, Pub. by ITBP) Thomson Learn.

***Meyer, Ron, et al.** Center: The Power of Aikido. LC 99-50135. (Illus.). 150p. 2000. pap. text 14.95 (*1-58394-012-X*) Frog Ltd CA.

Meyer, Ron, jt. auth. see De Wit, Bob.

Meyer, Ron, jt. ed. see Stone, John.

Meyer, Ronald, ed. see Akhmatova, Anna Andreevena.

Meyer, Ronald, ed. see Gogol, Nikolai Vasilevich.

Meyer, Roy W. Everyone's Country Estate: A History of Minnesota's State Parks. LC 91-14407. (Illus.). xviii, 357p. 1991. 34.95 (*0-87351-265-0*); pap. 19.95 (*0-87351-266-9*) Minn Hist.

— History of the Santee Sioux: United States Indian Policy on Trial. rev. ed. LC 93-34329. (Illus.). xx, 507p. 1993. pap. 17.95 (*0-8032-8203-6*, Bison Books) U of Nebr Pr.

— The Middle Western Farm Novel in the Twentieth Century. LC 64-17221. 272p. 1965. reprint ed. pap. 84.40 (*0-608-02142-3*, 206281100003) Bks Demand.

— The Village Indians of the Upper Missouri: The Mandans, Hidatsas, & Arikaras. LC 77-4202. 392p. reprint ed. pap. 121.60 (*0-7837-3034-9*, 204290300006) Bks Demand.

Meyer, Rudolf. The Wisdom of Fairy Tales. 267p. 1988. 19.95 (*0-88010-192-X*) Anthroposophic.

— The Wisdom of Fairy Tales. pap. 16.95 (*0-86315-208-2*, 1872, Pub. by Floris Bks) Anthroposophic.

Meyer, Rudolf & Kohler, J. Explosives. 4th rev. expanded ed. 457p. 1992. 198.00 (*3-527-28506-7*, Wiley-VCH) Wiley.

Meyer, Rudolph. Beitraege zur Geschichte von Text & Sprache des Alten Testaments Gesammelte Aufsaetze. (Beiheft zur Zeitschrift fuer die Alttestamentliche Wissenschaft Ser.: Bd 209). (GER.). viii, 259p. (C). 1993. lib. bdg. 129.25 (*3-11-013695-3*) De Gruyter.

— Hebraische Grammatik: Mit Einem Bibliographischen Nachwort von Udo Rutersworden. (Studienbuch Ser.). (GER.). iv, 552p. (Orig.). (C). 1992. pap. text 36.95 (*3-11-013694-5*) De Gruyter.

Meyer, Russ, see Schwartz, Adolph A., pseud.

Meyer, Russell J. The Faerie Queene: Educating the Reader. (Twayne's Masterworks Ser.: No. 73). 168p. 1991. 23.95 (*0-8057-8076-9*); pap. 13.95 (*0-8057-8122-6*) Macmillan.

***Meyer, Ruth.** Minitab Guide to Statistics. 2nd ed. 403p. 2001. pap. 24.00 (*0-13-014156-9*) P-H.

Meyer, Ruth K. David Black: An American Sculptor. (Illus.). (Orig.). 1985. pap. 3.00 (*0-915577-06-2*) Taft Museum.

— The Pines: Brad Davis. (Illus.). 10p. (Orig.). 1984. pap. 3.00 (*0-915577-04-6*) Taft Museum.

Meyer, Ruth K. & Krueger, David D. A Course in Modern Business Statistics, Minitap Computer Supplement. 2nd ed. (C). 1995. pap. text 22.40 (*0-02-380837-3*, Macmillan Coll) P-H.

— Statistics for Business & Economics, Minitab Computer Supplement. 6th ed. 416p. (C). 1994. pap. text 24.00 (*0-02-380840-3*, Macmillan Coll) P-H.

Meyer, Ruth K., jt. auth. see O'Hara, Catherine L.

MEyer, Ruth K., jt. auth. see Shanes, Eric.

Meyer, Ruth K., ed. see Chapman, Laura H.

Meyer, S. Animal Pests & How to Get the Upper Hand on 'Em. (Illus.). 175p. 1993. pap. text 9.95 (*1-878488-91-0*) Quixote Pr IA.

Meyer-Sabellek, W., et al. Blood Pressure Measurements. 340p. 1990. 80.00 (*0-387-91332-7*, 1915) Spr-Verlag.

Meyer, Salome, jt. auth. see Comely, Peter.

Meyer, Sam. Paradoxes of Fame: The Francis Scott Key Story. LC 95-60983. (Illus.). 144p. 1995. 15.95 (*1-885457-06-5*) Eastwind MD.

Meyer, Sandy. The Strange Journey of Byron & Cyros: Exploratory Guide. LC 96-90385. (Woods-in-the-Round Ser.). (Illus.). 20p. (J). (ps-6). 1997. pap., wbk. ed. 4.75 (*1-889928-01-1*) Wood-in-the-Round Pub.

— The Strange Journey of Byron & Cyrus, Incls. Parent-Teacher Exploratory Guide. LC 96-90385. (Woods-in-the-Round Ser.: Vol. 1). (Illus.). 48p. (J). (ps-6). 1997. lib. bdg. 17.95 (*1-889928-00-3*) Wood-in-the-Round Pub.

***Meyer-Schaffer, Christina.** Handbook to Understanding Literature. 2000. pap. text 14.95 (*0-7641-1240-6*) Barron.

Meyer, Scott. The Guys' Guide to Guys' Videos. LC 97-16675. (Illus.). 400p. 1997. pap. 12.00 (*0-380-78705-9*, Avon Bks) Morrow Avon.

— 100 Jobs in Words. (100 Jobs Ser.). 1996. 14.95 (*0-02-861432-1*) Macmillan.

— Totally Roses. (Totally Flowers Ser.). (Illus.). 96p. 1996. pap. 5.95 (*0-89087-781-5*) Celestial Arts.

Meyer, Scott B. Proper Care of Marine Aquaria. (TW Ser.). (Illus.). 256p. 1992. 16.95 (*0-86622-347-9*, TW117) TFH Pubns.

***Meyer, Scott B.** Proper Care of Marine Aquarium. (Illus.). 2000. 12.95 (*0-7938-3156-3*) TFH Pubns.

Meyer, Shannon, jt. auth. see Landres, Peter.

Meyer-Spasche, R. Pattern Formation in Viscous Flows: The Taylor-Couette Problem & Rayleigh-Benard Convection. 2nd ed. LC 99-211198. (International Series in Numerical Mathematics: Vol. 28). 196p. 1999. 69.50 (*3-7643-6047-X*) Birkhauser.

Meyer-Stamer, Jorg & Deutsches Institut fur Entwicklungspolitik Staff. Technology, Competitiveness & Radical Policy Change: The Case of Brazil. LC 97-8178. (German Development Institute Book Ser.: Vol. 9). 336p. 1997. pap. 34.50 (*0-7146-4379-3*, Pub. by F Cass Pubs) Intl Spec Bk.

***Meyer, Stefen G.** The Experimental Arabic Novel: Post-Colonial Literary Modernism in the Levant. (C). 2000. pap. text 23.95 (*0-7914-4734-0*) State U NY Pr.

— The Experimental Arabic Novel: Post-Colonial Literary Modernism in the Levant. (C). 2000. text 71.50 (*0-7914-4733-2*) State U NY Pr.

Meyer-Stein, Goldie P., et al. Bilingualism among American Slovaks; Use of the DAE & the DA of Schele de Vere's Manuscript Notes; A Cleburne County, Arkansas, Word List; Low German in Mexico. (Publications of the American Dialect Society: No. 46). 39p. 1966. pap. 5.05 (*0-8173-0646-3*) U of Ala Pr.

Meyer, Stephen, III. The Five Dollar Day: Labor Management & Social Control in the Ford Motor Company, 1908-1921. LC 80-22795. 249p. (C). 1981. text 49.50 (*0-87395-508-0*); pap. text 19.95 (*0-87395-509-9*) State U NY Pr.

Meyer, Stephen. Stalin over Wisconsin: The Making & Unmaking of Militant Unionism, 1900-1950. LC 91-32610. 275p. (C). 1992. text 45.00 (*0-8135-1798-2*) Rutgers U Pr.

***Meyer, Stephen, ed.** Alexander Bioscience Directory: 2000 San Diego County Edition. 9th rev. ed. 222p. 1999. pap. 59.95 (*1-885062-16-8*, Pub. by Tech Directory) Sunbelt Pubns.

— Alexander Technology Directory: 2000 Los Angeles County Edition. 2nd rev. ed. 555p. 1999. pap. 79.95 (*1-885062-14-1*, Pub. by Tech Directory) Sunbelt Pubns.

— Alexander Technology Directory: 2000 Orange County Edition. 2nd rev. ed. 555p. 1999. pap. 79.95 (*1-885062-15-X*, Pub. by Tech Directory) Sunbelt Pubns.

***Meyer, Stephen, frwd.** Alexander Technology Directory: 2000 San Diego County Edition. 9th rev. ed. 555p. 1999. pap. 79.95 (*1-885062-13-3*, Pub. by Tech Directory) Sunbelt Pubns.

Meyer, Stephen, jt. ed. see Lichtenstein, Nelson.

Meyer, Stephen A. Baseline Sampling for Netware. 512p. 1995. 59.95 (*0-8493-9446-5*, 9446) CRC Pr.

***Meyer, Stephen G.** As Long as They Don't Move Next Door: Segregation & Racial Conflict in American Neighborhoods. LC 99-34669. 400p. 2000. 29.95 (*0-8476-9700-2*, Pub. by Rowman) Natl Bk Netwk.

Meyer, Stephen M. The Dynamics of Nuclear Proliferation. LC 83-17893. (Illus.). xvi, 244p. (C). 1986. pap. text 11.00 (*0-226-52149-4*) U Ch Pr.

— The Dynamics of Nuclear Proliferation. LC 83-17893. (Illus.). xvi, 230p. (C). 1993. lib. bdg. 20.00 (*0-226-52148-6*) U Ch Pr.

— Soviet Defense Decisionmaking: What Do We Know & What Do We Understand? (CISA Working Papers: No. 33). 72p. (Orig.). 1982. pap. 15.00 (*0-86682-041-8*) Ctr Intl Relations.

— A Statistical Risk Model for Forecasting Nuclear Proliferation. (CISA Working Papers: No. 41). 29p. (Orig.). 1983. pap. 15.00 (*0-86682-053-1*) Ctr Intl Relations.

Meyer, Steven M., jt. auth. see McCafferty, Michael D.

Meyer, Stewart. The Lotus Crew. (Midnight Classics Ser.). 150p. 1996. reprint ed. pap. 10.99 (*1-85242-417-6*) Serpents Tail.

Meyer, Stuart. The New York State Drunk Driving Penalties & Sanctions Handbook. LC 97-72029. 99p. 1997. text 49.95 (*0-8318-0770-9*) Am Law Inst.

Meyer, Stuart L. Data Analysis for Scientists & Engineers. 513p. (C). 1992. reprint ed. text 85.00 (*0-9635027-1-9*); reprint ed. pap. text 55.00 (*0-9635027-0-0*) Peer Mgmt Cnslts.

An Asterisk (*) at the beginning of an entry indicates that the title is appearing for the first time.

M

Meyer, Susan. America's Great Illustrators. 1988. 24.98 (*0-88365-645-0*) Galahad Bks.
— Imperialism at Home: Race & Victorian Women's Fiction. LC 95-49466. (Reading Women Writing Ser.). 232p. (C). 1996. text 39.95 (*0-8014-3132-8*) Cornell U Pr.
— Imperialism at Home: Race & Victorian Women's Fiction. (Reading Women Writing Ser.). 232p. 1996. pap. text 15.95 (*0-8014-8255-0*) Cornell U Pr.
Meyer, Susan, jt. ed. see Harman, Barbara.
Meyer, Susan E. Edgar Degas. LC 94-8420. (First Impressions Ser.). (Illus.). 92p. (J). 1994. 19.95 (*0-8109-3220-2*, Pub. by Abrams) Time Warner.
— Mary Cassatt. (First Impressions Ser.). (Illus.). 80p. (YA). (gr. 7 up). 1990. 19.95 (*0-8109-3154-0*, Pub. by Abrams) Time Warner.
— Norman Rockwell's World War II: Impressions from the Homefront. 96p. 1991. pap. 20.00 (*0-9631011-0-2*) USAA.
— A Treasury of the Great Children's Book Illustrators. (Illus.). 272p. 1997. pap. 24.95 (*0-8109-2694-6*, Pub. by Abrams) Time Warner.
Meyer, Susan E., jt. auth. see Demoney, Jerry.
Meyer, Susan E., ed. see Guptill, Arthur L.
Meyer, Susan E., ed. see Kinstler, Everett R.
Meyer, Susan M. Survival Guide for the Beginning Speech-Language Clinician. LC 98-27314. 245p. 1998. 44.00 (*0-8342-1116-5*) Aspen Pub.
Meyer, Sylvan & Nash, Seymour C. Prostate Cancer: Making Survival Decisions. 284p. 1994. 19.95 (*0-226-56857-1*) U Ch Pr.
Meyer, Sylvia. Professional Table Service. (Illus.). 464p. 1991. text 52.95 (*0-442-23982-3*, VNR) Wiley.
Meyer, Sylvia, et al. Professional Table Service. Holtmann, Heinz, tr. 464p. 1990. 64.95 (*0-471-28926-4*, VNR) Wiley.
Meyer, T. H. Clairvoyance & Consciousness: The Tao Impulse in Evolution. Wood, John M., tr. (Illus.). 80p. 1991. pap. 14.95 (*0-904693-28-7*, Pub. by Temple Lodge) Anthroposophic.
— D. N. Dunlop: A Man of Our Time. Bass, Ian, tr. (Illus.). 512p. 1992. 39.95 (*0-904693-38-4*, Pub. by Temple Lodge) Anthroposophic.
Meyer, T. H. & Vreede, Elizabeth. The Bodhisattva Question: Krishnamurti, Rudolf Steiner, Annie Besant, Valentin Tomberg, & the Mystery of the Twentieth Century Master. Wood, John M., tr. (Illus.). 200p. 1993. pap. 18.95 (*0-904693-50-3*, Pub. by Temple Lodge) Anthroposophic.
Meyer, T. H., jt. auth. see Fortner, Brand.
Meyer, T. H., ed. see Steiner, Rudolf.
Meyer, Ted. Body Count. 166p. 1997. pap. 7.50 (*0-9611140-1-0*) Mey-Hse Bks.
— The Citizens Club. 224p. (Orig.). 1983. pap. 4.50 (*0-9611140-0-2*) Mey-Hse Bks.
Meyer, Theresa. Guide to Evaluations with Forms for the Physical Therapist. 125p. 1994. spiral bd. 29.95 (*1-55642-476-0*) SLACK Inc.
— Review Book for the Physical Therapist Assistant, 2 vols. 4th ed. LC 00-26536. (C). 2000. pap. text 64.95 (*1-55642-475-2*) SLACK Inc.
— Review Book for the Physical Therapy Licensing Exam, 2 vols. LC 00-27002. (Illus.). (C). 2000. pap. text 75.00 (*1-55642-474-4*) SLACK Inc.
Meyer, Thomas. At Dusk Iridescent: A Gathering of Poems, 1972-1997. LC 98-87784. 272p. 1999. 100.00 (*0-912330-82-1*); pap. 40.00 (*0-912330-81-3*) Jargon Soc.
— Bang Book. LC 76-137212. (Illus.). 1971. 20.00 (*0-912330-19-8*); pap. 12.50 (*0-912330-20-1*) Jargon Soc.
— Fourteen Poems. 24p. (Orig.). 1989. pap. 10.00 (*0-317-93709-X*) French Broad.
— Fourteen Poems. deluxe ed. 24p. (Orig.). 1989. 35.00 (*0 317 93710 3*) French Broad.
— Fourteen Poems. limited ed. 24p. (Orig.). 1989. 50.00 (*0-685-25581-6*) French Broad.
— Staves Calends Legends. 1979. 20.00 (*0-912330-36-8*); pap. 12.50 (*0-912330-37-6*) Jargon Soc.
Meyer, Thomas, et al. Donald Anderson. (Illus.). 46p. (Orig.). 1987. pap. 12.00 (*0-943107-00-8*) ND Mus Art.
Meyer, Thomas R., ed. The Case for Mars IV - The International Exploration of Mars: Considerations for Sending Humans. LC 97-156474. (Science & Technology Ser.: Vol. 90). (Illus.). 502p. 1997. 35.00 (*0-87703-420-6*, Am Astronaut Soc); pap. 22.50 (*0-87703-421-4*, Am Astronaut Soc) Univelt Inc.
— The Case for Mars IV - The International Exploration of Mars: Mission Strategy & Architectures. LC 97-154329. (Science & Technology Ser.: Vol. 89). (Illus.). 790p. 1997. 40.00 (*0-87703-418-4*, Am Astronaut Soc); pap. 27.50 (*0-87703-419-2*, Am Astronaut Soc) Univelt Inc.
Meyer-Thoss, Christiane. Meret Oppenheim, the Book of Ideas: Sketches & Design for Fashion & Jewelry. 192p. 1996. 65.00 (*3-906127-51-6*, Pub. by Gachnang & Springer) Dist Art Pubs.
Meyer, Timothy P., jt. auth. see Anderson, James A.
Meyer, Tommye Q., jt. auth. see Quarles, Mary D.
***Meyer, Trish & Mey, Chris.** Creating Motion Graphics with after Effects: High Impact Animation for Video & Film. (Illus.). 352p. 2000. pap. 49.95 incl. cd-rom (*0-87930-606-8*) Miller Freeman.
Meyer, Ulrich. Biblical Quotation & Allusion in the Cantata Libretti of Johann Sebastian Bach. LC 97-9567. (Studies in Liturgical Musicology: No. 5). 223p. 1997. 48.00 (*0-8108-3329-8*) Scarecrow.
Meyer, Urs, et al, eds. Anti-diabetic Agents, Vol. 27. (Illus.). 240p. 1996. text 80.00 (*0-12-013327-X*) Acad Pr.
Meyer, Urs A., jt. auth. see Jucker, Ernst.
Meyer, Urs A., jt. ed. see Testa, Bernard.
Meyer, Ursula & Wolfson, Alice. Abenteur in Deutschland. (Illus.). (J). (gr. 9-12). 1976. pap. text 4.75 (*0-88345-276-6*, 18485) Prentice ESL.
— Workbook in Everyday German. (J). (gr. 9-10). 1976. pap. text 4.75 (*0-88345-277-4*, 18600) Prentice ESL.
Meyer, Ursula, jt. auth. see Kind, Uwe.
Meyer, Valerie. Candle-Making Is Fun. 1998. pap. text 14.00 (*0-627-01725-8*, Pub. by J L Van Schaik) BHB Intl.
— Easy Festive Candles. 1998. pap. text 20.00 (*0-627-01850-5*) J L Van Schaik.
Meyer-Veden, Hans. Espana. LC 98-195398. 131 p. 1997. 98.00 (*3-930698-80-3*) Natl Audubon.
Meyer, Velma. Robby: The True Story of an Incredible Friendship Between a Robin & his Human Family. 96p. (Orig.). 1998. pap. 7.99 (*0-8280-1291-1*) Review & Herald.
Meyer, Verne, jt. auth. see Sebranek, Patrick.
Meyer, Viktor E. & Black, Michael J., eds. Microsurgical Procedures. (Illus.). 268p. 1991. text 149.00 (*0-443-03463-X*) Church.
Meyer, Vivian, jt. auth. see Martin, Elizabeth.
Meyer, W. Geologie der Eifel. xv, 618p. 1994. 52.00 (*3-510-65161-8*, Pub. by E Schweizerbartsche) Balogh.
Meyer, W., ed. Principles & Practice of Mathematics. (Textbooks in Mathematical Sciences Ser.). 686p. 1996. 64.95 (*0-387-94612-8*) Spr-Verlag.
Meyer, W., et al, eds. High Energy Spin Physics Workshops, Vol. 2: Proceedings of the International Symposium, 9th, Bonn, FRG, September 6-15, 1990. (Illus.). xiii, 393p. 1991. 75.95 (*0-387-54073-3*) Spr-Verlag.
Meyer, W., jt. ed. see Althoff, K. H.
Meyer, W. E. & Reichert, J., eds. Surface Characteristics of Roadways: International Research & Technologies, STP 1031. LC 90-35195. (Special Technical Publication (STP) Ser.). (Illus.). 600p. 1990. text 99.00 (*0-8031-1391-9*, STP1031) ASTM.
Meyer, W. E. & Walter, J. D., eds. Frictional Interaction of Tire & Pavement - STP 793. LC 82-72886. 330p. 1983. text 30.00 (*0-8031-0231-3*, STP793) ASTM.
Meyer, Wade. Conversations. 71p. 1999. pap. 9.95 (*0-7414-0104-5*) Buy Books.
***Meyer, Walter.** Tomorrow Will Be Better: Surviving Nazi Germany. LC 98-50224. (Illus.). 224p. 1999. pap. 19.95 (*0-8262-1217-4*) U of Mo Pr.
Meyer, Walter J. Geometry & Its Applications. LC 98-28224. 531p. 1999. 64.95 (*0-12-493270-3*) Acad Pr.
Meyer, Walter J., jt. auth. see Meyer, Rochelle W.
Meyer, Warren G., et al. Retail Marketing: For Employees, Managers & Entrepreneurs. 1988. pap. text 7.68 (*0-07-002457-X*); pap. text 7.68 (*0-07-002458-8*) McGraw.
— Retail Marketing: For Employees, Managers & Entrepreneurs. 8th ed. 1988. text 21.80 (*0-07-041698-2*) McGraw.
— Retailing Principles & Practices. 7th ed. LC 80-24885. (Illus.). 560p. (gr. 11-12). 1982. text 25.16 (*0-07-041693-1*) McGraw.
***Meyer, Wayne.** Clinton on Clinton: A Portrait of the President in His Own Words. LC 99-33499. 288p. 1999. pap. 12.50 (*0-380-80279-1*, Avon Bks) Morrow Avon.
Meyer, Wilhelm & Stets, Johannes. Das Rheintal Zwischen Bingen und Bonn. (Sammlung Geologischer Fuehrer Ser.: Band 89). (GER., Illus.). xii, 386p. 1996. spiral bd. 32.00 (*3-443-15069-1*, Pub. by Gebruder Borntraeger) Balogh.
Meyer, Wilhelm J. Die Franzosischen Drucker- und Verlegerzeichen des Fifteenth Jahrhunderts. 171p. 1970. reprint ed. write for info. (*0-318-71463-9*) G Olms Pubs.
— Die Franzosischen Drucker- und Verlegerzeichen des XV Jahrhunderts, Vol. 2. 171p. 1970. reprint ed. write for info. (*0-318-71846-4*) G Olms Pubs.
— Gesammelte Abhandlungen zur Mittellateinischen Rhythmik, 3 vols., Set. 1181p. 1970. reprint ed. write for info. (*0-318-71268-7*) G Olms Pubs.
Meyer, William. Native Americans: The New Indian Resistance. LC 71-163221. (Little New World Paperbacks Ser.). 96p. reprint ed. pap. 30.00 (*0-608-13783-9*, 202063500018) Bks Demand.
***Meyer, William B.** Americans & Their Weather. LC 99-33193. (Illus.). 304p. 2000. 35.00 (*0-19-513182-7*) OUP.
Meyer, William B. Human Impact on the Earth. (Illus.). 248p. (C). 1996. pap. text 27.95 (*0-521-55847-6*) Cambridge U Pr.
Meyer, William B. & Turner, B. L., II, eds. Changes in Land Use & Land Cover: A Global Perspective. (Illus.). 380p. (C). 1994. 49.95 (*0-521-47085-4*) Cambridge U Pr.
Meyer, William F. Life & Health Insurance Law. LC 72-76891. 1972. 125.00 (*0-685-59870-5*) West Group.
Meyer, William G. Colorado Rules of Evidence with Objections. 2nd ed. LC 98-231342. 211p. 1998. 25.95 (*1-55681-613-8*) Natl Inst Trial Ad.
Meyer, William H. Human Rights & International Political Economy in Third World Nations: Multinational Corporations, Foreign Aid & Repression. LC 98-4940. 264p. 1998. 65.00 (*0-275-96172-9*, Praeger Pubs); pap. 22.95 (*0-275-96280-6*, Praeger Pubs) Greenwood.
— Transnational Media & Third World Development: The Structure & Impact of Imperialism, 11. LC 88-10239. (Contributions to the Study of Mass Media & Communications Ser.: No. 11). 146p. 1988. 57.95 (*0-313-26264-0*, MYN/, Greenwood Pr) Greenwood.
Meyer, William K. Advanced PICK Programming. (Illus.). 320p. 1989. 29.95 (*0-8306-2999-8*) McGraw-Hill Prof.
Meyer, William W. Nice Things about Growing Older. 68p. (Orig.). 1990. pap. 7.75 (*1-877871-11-7*, 3530) Ed Ministries.
Meyer, Yves. Wavelets. (Studies in Advanced Mathematics: No. 37). 239p. (C). 1993. text 74.95 (*0-521-42000-8*) Cambridge U Pr.
Meyer, Yves. Wavelets: Algorithms & Applications. LC 93-15100. (Miscellaneous Bks.: No. 38). xi, 133p. 1993. pap. 24.50 (*0-89871-309-9*) Soc Indus-Appl Math.
— Wavelets & Operators. (Cambridge Studies in Advanced Mathematics: No. 37). 240p. (C). 1995. pap. text 32.95 (*0-521-45869-2*) Cambridge U Pr.
— Wavelets, Vibrations, & Scalings. LC 97-34730. (CRM Monograph Ser.). 133p. 1997. text 29.00 (*0-8218-0685-8*) Am Math.
Meyer, Yves, et al, eds. Wavelets & Applications: Proceedings of the International Conference Marseille, France, May 1989. (Recherches en Mathematiques Appliquees - Research Notes in Applied Mathematics Ser.: Vol. 20). (Illus.). xii, 450p. 1992. 96.95 (*0-387-54516-6*) Spr-Verlag.
***Meyer, Yves & Coifman, Ronald.** Wavelets: Calderon-Zygmund & Multilinear Operators. (Studies in Advanced Mathematics: Vol. 48). 320p. (C). 2000. pap. write for info. (*0-521-79473-0*) Cambridge U Pr.
Meyer, Yves & Coifman, Ronald. Wavelets Vol. 2: Calderon-Zygmund Operators & Multilinear Operators. Salinger, David, tr. (Studies in Advanced Mathematics: Vol. 48). (Illus.). 333p. (C). 1997. text 64.95 (*0-521-42001-6*) Cambridge U Pr.
Meyer, Yves, jt. auth. see Jaffard, Stephane.
Meyer Zur Capellen, Jurg. Raphael in Florence. (Illus.). 264p. 1996. 58.00 (*1-898592-08-X*, Pub. by Art Bks Intl) Partners Pubs Grp.
Meyerbeer, Giacomo. Excerpts from the Early Italian Operas: Romilda e Constanza, 1817, Semiramide riconosciuta, 1819, Emma di Resburgo, 1819, Mrgherita d'Anjou, 1820 & L'esule di Granata, 1822, Vol. 23. LC 91-754851. (Italian Opera 1810-1840 Ser.). 308p. 1992. text 30.00 (*0-8240-6572-7*) Garland.
***Meyerbeer, Giacomo & Le Tellier, Robert Ignatius.** The Diaries of Giacomo Meyerbeer: 1791-1839. LC 98-52129. (Illus.). 576p. 1999. 65.00 (*0-8386-3789-2*) Fairleigh Dickinson.
Meyerbroker, Helga. Rose Windows & How to Make Them. unabridged ed. 77p. (J). (gr. 2-6). 1994. pap. 12.95 (*0-86315-196-5*, 28194, Pub. by Floris Bks) Gryphon Hse.
Meyerding, Jane. Everywhere House. LC 93-41740. 256p. (Orig.). 1994. pap. 9.95 (*0-934678-42-1*) New Victoria Pubs.
Meyerhof, Walter E. Elements of Nuclear Physics. (C). 1967. text 71.00 (*0-07-041745-8*) McGraw.
Meyerhof, Walter E., jt. auth. see Eichler, Jorg.
Meyerhofer, Nicholas J. Germany & the United States Facing the Post-Communist World. (ENG & GER.). (Orig.). pap. write for info. (*0-910973-06-7*) Arrowhead AZ.
Meyerhofer, Nicholas J., ed. The Fiction of the I: Contemporary Austrian Writers & Autobiography. LC 98-54312. (Studies in Austrian Literature, Culture & Thought). 288p. 1999. pap. 29.50 (*1-57241-080-9*) Ariadne CA.
Meyerhofer, Nicholas J., jt. ed. see Webb, Karl E.
Meyerhofer, Nicholas J., tr. see Frischmuth, Barbara.
Meyerhoff, A. A., jt. auth. see Khudoley, K. M.
Meyerhoff, Arthur A. Surge Tectonics: A New Hypothesis of Global Geodynamics. (Solid Earth Science Library). 340p. (C). 1996. text 176.50 (*0-7923-4156-2*) Kluwer Academic.
Meyerhoff, Arthur A., et al, eds. Phanerozoic Faunal & Floral Realms of the Earth: The Intercalary Relations of the Malvinokaffric & Gondwana Faunal Realms with the Tethyan Faunal Realm. (Memoir Ser.: No. 189). (Illus.). 69p. 1996. 40.00 (*0-8137-1189-4*) Geol Soc.
Meyerhoff, Arthur A., et al. China: Stratigraphy, Paleogeography & Tectonics. (C). 1991. text 215.00 (*0-7923-0972-3*) Kluwer Academic.
Meyerhoff, Dirk. Traditioneller Stoff und Individuelle Gestaltung, Untersuchungen Zu Alkaios und Sappho. (Beitrage Zur Altertumswissenschaft Ser.: Band 3). (GER.). viii, 264p. 1984. write for info. (*3-487-07463-X*) G Olms Pubs.
Meyerhoff, Hans, tr. see Friedlander, Paul.
Meyerhoff, Paul, 2nd. Sabotage Flight. LC 94-37177. (Illus.). 200p. (Orig.). (J). (gr. 5-9). 1995. pap. 9.95 (*0-931625-24-6*) DIMI Pr.
Meyerhoff, Robert W., ed. Manufacture of Superconducting Materials: An International Conference, 8-10 November, 1976, Port Chester, New York, Proceedings. LC 77-11148. (Materials-Metalworking Technology Ser.). (Illus.). 239p. reprint ed. pap. 74.10 (*0-608-10721-2*, 201947800013) Bks Demand.
Meyerhoff, Roland & Gillespie, George H., eds. Supernovae Spectra: La Jolla Institute, 1980. (AIP Conference Proceedings Ser.: No. 63). 173p. 1980. lib. bdg. 18.25 (*0-88318-162-2*) Am Inst Physics.
Meyerhoff, William L. Otolaryngology: Head/Neck Surgery. (C). 1992. text 215.00 (*0-7216-3623-3*) Harcourt.
Meyerhoff, William L. & Roland, Peter. Hearing Loss. (Illus.). 288p. 1996. text 69.00 (*0-86577-623-7*) Thieme Med Pubs.
Meyerhoff, William L., ed. see Paparella, Michael M. & Shumrick, Donald A.
***Meyerholz, Linda.** Codependency Sucks. 216p. 1999. pap. 14.95 (*1-57087-434-4*) Prof Pr NC.
Meyerhuber, Carl I., Jr. Less Than Forever: The Rise & Decline of Union Solidarity in Western Pennsylvania, 1914-1948. LC 86-62504. 240p. 1987. 39.50 (*0-941664-27-9*) Susquehanna U Pr.
Meyering, Robert A. Who Am I? LC 95-49452. (Open Door Bks.). 1996. pap. 3.95 (*1-56212-151-0*) CRC Pubns.
— Who Is Jesus? LC 93-49845. 1993. pap. 3.95 (*1-56212-035-2*) CRC Pubns.
Meyering, Robert A., jt. auth. see Vander Berg, Edward.
Meyering, Sheryl L. A Reader's Guide to the Short Stories of Willa Cather. LC 93-10381. (Reference Ser.). 304p. 1993. 65.00 (*0-8161-1834-5*, Hall Reference) Macmillan.
— Sylvia Plath: A Reference Guide, 1973-1988. (Reference Guides to Literature Ser.). 288p. 1989. 45.00 (*0-8161-8929-3*, Hall Reference) Macmillan.
Meyering, Theo C. Historical Roots of Cognitive Science. 270p. (C). 1989. lib. bdg. 142.00 (*0-7923-0349-0*, Pub. by Kluwer Academic) Kluwer Academic.
Meyerink, George. Appliance Service Handbook. 2nd ed. (Illus.). 497p. 1987. 88.00 (*0-13-038902-1*) P-H.
Meyerink, Kory. Printed Sources: A Guide to Published Genealogical Records. LC 98-10852. (Illus.). 839p. 1998. 49.95 (*0-916489-70-1*) Ancestry.
Meyeroff, Stephen. Washington, Adams, & Jefferson: The Building of a New Nation. (Student's Guide Through American History Ser.). (Illus.). (YA). (gr. 8-12). 1998. write for info. (*0-9646602-2-9*) Oak Tree Pubs.
Meyerowitz. A Summer's Day. 1987. 17.95 (*0-07-541243-8*) McGraw.
Meyerowitz, Elliot M., ed. Arabidopsis. (Monographs: No. 27). (Illus.). 1270p. (C). 1994. 130.00 (*0-87969-428-9*) Cold Spring Harbor.
Meyerowitz, Jacob. Before the Beginning of Time. LC 93-86657. (Illus.). 336p. 1994. 35.00 (*0-9607034-1-1*) RRP Pub.
Meyerowitz, Joanne, ed. Not June Cleaver: Women & Gender in the Postwar America, 1945-1960. LC 93-26987. (Critical Perspectives on the Past Ser.). 368p. (C). 1994. pap. 22.95 (*1-56639-171-7*); text 69.95 (*1-56639-170-9*) Temple U Pr.
Meyerowitz, Joanne J. Women Adrift: Independent Wage Earners in Chicago, 1880-1930. (Women in Culture & Society Ser.). (Illus.). xxiv, 248p. 1988. 35.95 (*0-226-52197-4*) U Ch Pr.
— Women Adrift: Independent Wage Earners in Chicago, 1880-1930. LC 87-22449. (Women in Culture & Society Ser.). (Illus.). xxiv, 248p. 1991. pap. text 14.95 (*0-226-52198-2*) U Ch Pr.
Meyerowitz, Joel. At the Water's Edge. LC 96-83223. (Illus.). 120p. 1996. 12.95 (*0-8212-2310-0*, Pub. by Bulfinch Pr) Little.
— Cape Light: Color Photographs by Joel Meyerowitz. MacDonald, Bruce K. & Ackley, Clifford S., eds. 112p. 1979. pap. 29.95 (*0-87846-131-0*, Pub. by Bulfinch Pr) Little.
— George Balanchine's the Nutcracker. (Illus.). 86p. 1999. text 30.00 (*0-7881-6052-4*) DIANE Pub.
— A Summer's Day. LC 84-40642. (Illus.). 156p. 1985. pap. 750.00 (*0-8129-1195-4*, Times Bks) Crown Pub Group.
— A Summer's Day. limited ed. LC 84-40642. (Illus.). 156p. 1985. 750.00 (*0-8129-1194-6*, Times Bks); 750.00 (*0-8129-1196-2*, Times Bks) Crown Pub Group.
Meyerowitz, Joel, jt. auth. see Westerbeck, Colin.
Meyerowitz, Patricia. And a Little Child: Stories of Anyone. Strobel, Peter, tr. LC 81-52891. (ENG & GER.). 52p. 1982. pap. 5.00 (*0-9607034-0-3*) RRP Pub.
Meyerowitz, Rael. Transferring to America: Jewish Interpretations of American Dreams. LC 94-43358. (SUNY Series in Psychoanalysis & Culture). 302p. (C). 1995. text 59.50 (*0-7914-2607-6*); pap. text 19.95 (*0-7914-2608-4*) State U NY Pr.
***Meyerowitz, Rick.** Return of the Nose Masks. LC 98-38993. (Illus.). 1998. pap. 7.95 (*0-7611-1244-8*) Workman Pub.
Meyerowitz, Steve. Food Combining & Digestion: A Rational Approach to Combining What You Eat to Maximize Digestion & Health. 110p. 1996. pap. 7.95 (*1-878736-57-4*, Pub. by Sproutman) Book Pub Co.
— Juice Fasting & Detoxification: Use the Healing Power of Fresh Juice to Feel Young & Look Great. LC 99-90265. 156p. 1999. pap. 10.95 (*1-878736-65-5*, Pub. by Sproutman) Book Pub Co.
— Kitchen Garden Cookbook: Sprout Breads, Cookies, Soups, Salads & 250 Other Low Fat, Dairy-Free Vegetarian Recipes. 5th rev. ed. LC 99-90518. (Illus.). 336p. 1999. pap. 14.95 (*1-878736-86-8*, Pub. by Sproutman) Book Pub Co.
***Meyerowitz, Steve.** Power Juices, Power Drinks: Quick & Delicious Recipes to Prevent & Reverse Disease. 2000. pap. 16.00 (*1-57566-528-X*, Knsington) Kensgtn Pub Corp.
Meyerowitz, Steve. Sproutman's Kitchen Garden Cookbook: Sprout Breads, Cookies, Salads, Soups & 250 Other Low Fat, Dairy-Free, Vegetarian Recipes. (Illus.). 320p. 1994. pap. 14.95 (*1-878736-84-1*, Pub. by Sproutman) Book Pub Co.
— Sprouts: The Miracle Food. LC 99-90521. 224p. 1999. pap. 12.95 (*1-878736-04-3*, Pub. by Sproutman) Book Pub Co.
— Wheatgrass: Nature's Finest Medicine. Flaxman, Nancy, ed. LC 99-90355. (Illus.). 216p. 1999. pap. 12.95 (*1-878736-97-3*, Pub. by Sproutman) Book Pub Co.
Meyerowitz, Theresa B. Israeli Journal. LC 92-54528. (C). 1994. 30.00 (*0-8453-4845-0*, Cornwall Bks) Assoc Univ Prs.
— The Journal. LC 90-55330. (Illus.). 136p. 1992. 30.00 (*0-8453-4830-2*, Cornwall Bks) Assoc Univ Prs.
— The Poetic Canvas. LC 87-46429. (Illus.). 128p. 1989. 30.00 (*0-8453-4817-5*, Cornwall Bks) Assoc Univ Prs.
— William Meyerowitz: The Artist Speaks. LC 84-45010. (Illus.). 192p. 1986. 40.00 (*0-87982-513-8*) Art Alliance.
— William Meyerowitz: The Artist Speaks. LC 84-45010. (Illus.). 192p. 1986. 40.00 (*0-8453-4768-3*, Cornwall Bks) Assoc Univ Prs.
Meyers. The A+ Certification Exam Guide. 1999. teacher ed. write for info. (*0-07-135100-0*) McGraw.
***Meyers.** Encyclopedia of Enivornmental Analysis & Remediation, Vol. 2. 1998. 312.50 (*0-471-16639-1*) Wiley.

— Encyclopedia of Environmental Analysis & Remediation, Vol. 1. 672p. 1998. 312.50 (0-471-16642-1) Wiley.
— Encyclopedia of Environmental Analysis & Remediation, Vol. 3. 1998. 312.50 (0-471-16640-5) Wiley.
— Encyclopedia of Environmental Analysis & Remediation, Vol. 4. 1998. 312.50 (0-471-16636-7) Wiley.
— Encyclopedia of Environmental Analysis & Remediation, Vol. 5. 1998. 312.50 (0-471-16635-9) Wiley.
— Encyclopedia of Environmental Analysis & Remediation, Vol. 6. 1998. 312.50 (0-471-16632-4) Wiley.
— Encyclopedia of Environmental Analysis & Remediation, Vol. 7. 1998. 312.50 (0-471-16631-6) Wiley.
— Encyclopedia of Environmental Analysis & Remediation, Vol. 8. 1998. 312.50 (0-471-16629-4) Wiley.

Meyers. Encyclopedia of Physical Science & Technology, Vols. 10-18, Carton Vol. 2. 2nd ed. 1992. 1449.00 (0-12-226929-2) Acad Pr.
— Meyers Enzyklopaedisches Lexikon, 25 vols. (GER.). 1973. 3995.00 (0-8288-6321-0, M-7558) Fr & Eur.
— Meyers Grosses Handlexikon. 14th ed. (GER.). 1072p. 1985. 75.00 (0-8288-1962-9, M15509) Fr & Eur.
— Meyers Grosses Taschenlexikon, 24 vols. 5th ed. (GER.). 1995. 395.00 (0-320-00102-4) Fr & Eur.
— Meyers Kontinente und Meere-Daten, Karten die Enzyklopadie der Erde, 8 vols. (GER.). 1973. 625.00 (0-7859-0118-3, M7560) Fr & Eur.
— Meyers Large Pocket Lexicon: Meyers Grosses Taschenlexikon des Gesamten Wissens. 2nd ed. (GER.). 8640p. 1987. 350.00 (0-8288-1963-7, M15512) Fr & Eur.
— Meyers Physik-Lexikon: Meyers Physics Lexicon. (GER.). 1973. 85.00 (0-8288-6323-7, M-7561) Fr & Eur.
— Meyers Standardlexikon des Gesamtes Wissesns. 2nd ed. (GER.). 1118p. 1980. 45.00 (0-8288-1964-5, M7562) Fr & Eur.
— Techical Analysis. 2nd rev. ed. 1994. 14.23 (0-07-134963-4) McGraw.
— Ultrasonography for Surgeons. 1999. text. write for info. (0-7216-7236-1, W B Saunders Co) Harcrt Hlth Sci Grp.
— Writing with Confidence. 6th ed. LC 99-11746. 514p. 1999. pap. text 50.00 (0-321-03801-0) Addson-Wesley Educ.

Meyers, jt. auth. see Lowry.

Meyers, Cindy L., compiled by. Index of Bible Citations by Puritan & Contemporary Authors. unabridged ed. 248p. 1996. pap. 10.50 (1-58339-168-1, E5) Triangle Press.

Meyers, A. W. & Craighead, W. E. Cognitive Behavior Therapy with Children. LC 83-16116. (Applied Clinical Psychology Ser.). (Illus.). 514p. (C). 1984. 85.00 (0-306-41291-8, Plenum Trade) Perseus Pubng.

Meyers, Alan. Cocaine: A Treatment Guide for Counselors. 120p. (Orig.). 1988. pap. 9.95 (0-937119-01-6) Meyers Pub.

***Meyers, Alan.** Composing with Confidence. LC 99-14236. 416p. (C). 1999. write for info. (0-321-04449-5) Addison-Wesley.

Meyers, Alan. Composing with Confidence. 4th ed. LC 96-18208. 1996. text. write for info. (0-673-99708-1) Addison-Wesley Educ.

***Meyers, Alan.** Composing with Confidence. 5th ed. LC 99-14236. (Illus.). 542p. (C). 1999. pap. text 49.00 (0-321-03802-9) Addison-Wesley.

Meyers, Alan. Custom Composing with Confidence: Spiral Edition CB. (C). 1997. spiral bd. 46.00 (0-321-02052-9) Addison-Wesley.
— Staff Development Training Program for Nursing Homes & ACLF's. 150p. 1995. wbk. ed. 89.95 (0-937119-03-2) Meyers Pub.
— Writing with Confidence. 4th ed. (C). 1992. text, teacher ed. write for info. (0-321-40633-8) Addson-Wesley Educ.

Meyers, Albert. Immigration of the Irish Quakers Into Pennsylvania, 1682-1750: With Their Early History in Ireland. LC 77-92027. (Illus.). xxii, 477p. 1994. reprint ed. 30.00 (0-8063-0252-6, 3980) Genealog Pub.

Meyers, Albert, ed. Organic Synthesis, Vol. 70. 336p. 1992. 74.95 (0-471-57743-X) Wiley.

Meyers, Allen. Jewish Community of South Philadelphia. LC 98-86766. (Images of America Ser.). (Illus.). 128p. 1998. pap. 16.99 (0-7524-1202-7) Arcadia Publng.

Meyers, Amanda L. Rachael's Rainbow. (Illus.). 16p. (J). (gr. k-6). 1999. pap. 13.00 (0-8059-4760-4) Dorrance.

Meyers, Amy, ed. After Midnight Stories, Bk. 4. large type ed. 1990. 27.99 (0-7089-2290-2) Ulverscroft.

Meyers, Amy R., ed. Art & Science in America: Issues of Representation. LC 98-14245. 208p. 1998. pap. 15.00 (0-87328-172-1) Huntington Lib.

Meyers, Amy R. & Pritchard, Margaret B., eds. Empire's Nature: Mark Catesby's New World Vision. LC 98-23257. (Published for the Omohundro Institute of Early American History & Culture, Williamsburg, Virginia Series). (Illus.). 296p. 1999. 60.00 (0-8078-2459-3); pap. 24.95 (0-8078-4762-3) U of NC Pr.

Meyers-Anderson, Maribeth, jt. auth. see Gordon, David.

Meyers, Anna. National Summary of State Medicaid Managed Care Programs: Program Descriptions as of June 30, 1995. 182p. 1996. pap. 13.00 (0-16-048860-5) USGPO.

Meyers, Annette. The Big Killing. 270p. 1998. reprint ed. lib. bdg. 29.95 (0-7351-0035-7) Replica Bks.
— The Deadliest Option. 354p. 1998. reprint ed. lib. bdg. 29.95 (0-7351-0036-5) Replica Bks.
— Free Love. LC 99-14589. (Greenwich Village Historical Ser.). 256p. 1999. 23.95 (0-89296-694-7, Pub. by Mysterious Pr) Little.

***Meyers, Annette.** Free Love. 2001. mass mkt. write for info. (0-446-60921-8) Warner Bks.

Meyers, Annette. The Groaning Board: A Smith & Wetzon Mystery. 352p. 1998. mass mkt. 5.99 (0-553-56977-5) Bantam.
— Murder: The Musical. 370p. 1998. reprint ed. lib. bdg. 29.95 (0-7351-0034-9) Replica Bks.

***Meyers, Annette.** Murder Me Now. 288p. 2001. 23.95 (0-89296-695-5) Mysterious Pr.

Meyers, Annette. Tender Death. 288p. 1998. reprint ed. lib. bdg. 29.95 (0-7351-0037-3) Replica Bks.

Meyers, Arlen D. Biological Basis of Facial Plastic Surgery. (American Academy of Facial Plastic & Reconstructive Surgery Monograph). (Illus.). 216p. 1993. text 69.00 (0-86577-443-9) Thieme Med Pubs.

Meyers, Arthur. The Cheyenne. (First Bks.). (Illus.). 64p. (J). (gr. 5-8). 1992. pap. 6.95 (0-531-15636-2) Watts.

Meyers, Arthur, jt. auth. see Slattery, Thomas.

Meyers, Augustus. Ten Years in the Ranks U. S. Army. Kohn, Richard H., ed. LC 78-22387. (American Military Experience Ser.). 1980. reprint ed. lib. bdg. 26.95 (0-405-11864-3) Ayer.

Meyers, Bensel. Literary Culture: Read & Write Literary Arguments. 638p. 1998. pap. 34.60 (0-536-01629-1) Pearson Custom.

Meyers, Bert. The Wild Olive Tree, 2 vols. in one. 118p. 1982. reprint ed. pap. 6.95 (0-915572-67-2) Panjandrum.

Meyers, Betty & Fellers, Frederick P., compiled by. Discographies of Commercial Recordings of the Cleveland Orchestra (1924-1977) & the Cincinnati Symphony Orchestra (1917-1977) LC 78-3122. 211p. 1978. lib. bdg. 42.95 (0-313-20375-X, MDI/) Greenwood.

Meyers, Bill. The Haunting: There's No Escape From. (Forbidden Doors Ser.: Vol. 4). (J). 1995. pap. 5.99 (0-8423-1727-9) Tyndale Hse.

***Meyers, Bruce F.** Fortune Favors the Brave: The Story of First Force Recon. LC 99-56896. (Special Warfare Ser.). (Illus.). 240p. 2000. 32.95 (1-55750-548-9) Naval Inst Pr.

Meyers, Bruce F., ed. Alternate Dispute Resolution Deskbook: Arbitration & Mediation in Washington. 2nd rev. ed. LC 95-60632. 550p. 1995. pap., ring bd. write for info. (0-88129-245-1) Wash Bar CLE.

Meyers, Bryan. Desktop Guide to CL Programming. LC 94-33312. (News 3X/400 Technical Reference Ser.). 205p. 1994. pap. 34.95 (1-882419-07-3) News Four-Hund.

Meyers, Bryan & Riehl, Dan. Control Language Programming for the AS/400. 2nd ed. LC 97-33820. 522p. 1997. pap. text 65.00 (1-882419-76-6) News Four-Hund.

Meyers, Bryan & Sutherland, Jef. VisualAge for RPG by Example. LC 98-8985. 300p. 1998. pap. 69.00 (1-882419-83-9) News Four-Hund.

***Meyers, Bryan & Yaeger, Judy.** Programming in RPG IV. 2nd ed. (Illus.). 450p. 2000. pap. text 65.00 (1-58304-074-9) News Four-Hund.

***Meyers, Burt R.** Antimicrobial Therapy Guide. 3rd ed. LC 98-74078. 1999. pap. 24.95 (1-884065-35-X) Assocs in Med.

Meyers, Byran. RPG IV Jump Start: Moving Ahead with the New RPG. 2nd rev. ed. LC 96-51286. 214p. 1997. pap. 39.95 (1-882419-67-7) News Four-Hund.

Meyers, C. E., et al. Primary Abilities at Mental Age Six. (SRCD M Ser.: Vol. 27, No. 1). 1962. pap. 25.00 (0-527-01592-X) Periodicals Srv.

***Meyers, Carol, et al, eds.** Women in Scripture: A Dictionary of Named & Unnamed Women in the Hebrew Bible, the Aprocryphal/Deuterocanonical Books & the New Testament. LC 99-89577. (Illus.). 572p. 2000. 45.00 (0-395-70936-9) HM.

Meyers, Carol L. Discovering Eve: Ancient Israelite Women in Context. 256p. 1991. reprint ed. pap. text 12.95 (0-19-506581-6) OUP.

Meyers, Carol L. & Meyers, Eric M. Haggai, Zechariah 1-8, Vol. 25B. LC 85-20924. (Anchor Bible Ser.). (Illus.). 576p. 1987. 40.00 (0-385-14482-2) Doubleday.
— Zechariah Nine-Fourteen: A New Translation with Introduction & Commentary. LC 92-34535. (Anchor Bible Ser.: Vol. 25C). 576p. 1993. 40.00 (0-385-14483-0, Anchor NY) Doubleday.

Meyers, Carol L. & O'Connor, M., eds. The Word of the Lord Shall Go Forth: Essays in Honor of David Noel Freedman in Celebration of His Sixtieth Birthday. LC 83-20589. (American Schools of Oriental Research Special Volume Ser.: No. 1). xviii, 742p. 1983. text 59.50 (0-931464-19-6) Eisenbrauns.

Meyers, Carol L., jt. ed. see Carter, Charles.

Meyers, Carole T. How to Organize a Babysitting Cooperative & Get Some Free Time Away from the Kids. LC 76-12660. (Illus.). 88p. (Orig.). 1976. pap. 6.95 (0-917120-00-0) Carousel Pr.
— Miles of Smiles: 101 Great Car Games & Activities. LC 91-458885. (Illus.). 128p. (Orig.). (J). (ps-11). 1992. pap. 8.95 (0-917120-11-6) Carousel Pr.
— Weekend Adventures in Northern California. 6th ed. LC 96-47236. (Illus.). 416p. (Orig.). 1997. pap. 17.95 (0-917120-15-9) Carousel Pr.

Meyers, Carole T., ed. The Family Travel Guide: An Inspiring Collection of Family-Friendly Vacations. LC 94-74893. (Illus.). 432p. (Orig.). 1995. pap. 16.95 (0-917120-14-0) Carousel Pr.

Meyers, Carole T., ed. see Barrus, Pamela L.

Meyers, Carolyn & Ernst, Edward W., eds. Restructuring Engineering Education: A Focus on Change. (Illus.). 57p. (C). 1996. reprint ed. pap. text 25.00 (0-7881-3688-7) DIANE Pub.

Meyers, Casey. Walking: A Complete Guide to the Complete Exercise. 1992. pap. 12.00 (0-679-73777-4) Vin Bks.

Meyers, Charles J., jt. auth. see Williams, H. R.

Meyers, Charles J., jt. auth. see Williams, Howard R.

Meyers, Chet & Jones, Thomas. Promoting Active Learning: Strategies for the College Classroom. LC 92-41685. (Higher & Adult Education Ser.). 224p. 1993. text 28.95 (1-55542-524-0) Jossey-Bass.

Meyers, Cindy. Rolling along with Goldilocks & the Three Bears. LC 99-10648. (J). (ps-2). 1999. pap. text 14.95 (1-890627-12-7) Woodbine House.

Meyers, Craig, jt. auth. see Schroeder, Frederick.

Meyers, D. Mark. Dealing with Dilemmas: Coaching Students in Decision Making. (Illus.). 144p. 1998. pap. 13.95 (0-673-36369-4) Addson-Wesley Educ.

***Meyers, Daniel.** Tales from the Pits. 256p. 2000. 24.95 (0-06-105882-3) HARP Ent.

Meyers, David W. The Human Body & the Law. 2nd ed. LC 90-71394. 368p. 1991. 47.50 (0-8047-1885-7) Stanford U Pr.

Meyers, Deborah, jt. ed. see Liggett, Stephen B.

Meyers, Del, ed. see McGorray, Judy.

Meyers, Diana T. Subjection & Subjectivity: Psychoanalytic Feminism & Moral Philosophy. LC 94-20584. (Thinking Gender Ser.). 256p. (C). 1994. 70.00 (0-415-90471-4, A6579); pap. 19.99 (0-415-90508-7, A6583) Routledge.

Meyers, Diana T., ed. Feminist Ethics & Social Theory: A Sourcebook. LC 96-41609. 772p. 1997. pap. 35.00 (0-415-91537-6) Routledge.
— Feminist Ethics & Social Theory: A Sourcebook. LC 96-41609. 772p. (C). 1997. 85.00 (0-415-91536-8) Routledge.
— Feminists Rethink the Self. LC 96-43121. (Feminist Theory & Politics Ser.). 1996. pap. 75.00 (0-8133-2082-8, Pub. by Westview) HarpC.

Meyers, Diana T., et al. Kindred Matters: Rethinking the Philosophy of the Family. LC 92-54970. 336p. 1993. text 45.00 (0-8014-2594-8); pap. text 17.95 (0-8014-9909-7) Cornell U Pr.

Meyers, Diana T., jt. ed. see Kipnis, Kenneth.

Meyers, Diana T., jt. ed. see Kittay, Eva F.

Meyers, Diana Tietjens, ed. Feminists Rethink the Self. LC 96-43121. (Feminist Theory & Politics Ser.). 288p. (C). 1996. pap. 26.00 (0-8133-2083-6, Pub. by Westview) HarpC.

Meyers, Diane. Disaster Response & Recovery: A Handbook for Mental Health Professionals. (Illus.). 144p. (C). 1996. reprint ed. pap. text 40.00 (0-7881-3126-5) DIANE Pub.

Meyers, Donald I., jt. ed. see Glick, Robert A.

Meyers, Donna. Client Teaching Guides for Home Health Care. 2nd ed. 225p. 1997. 89.00 incl. disk (0-8342-1054-1, 10541) Aspen Pub.
— Client Teaching Guides for Home Health Care. 2nd rev. ed. LC 97-18555. 225p. 1997. spiral bd. 59.00 (0-8342-0968-3, 20968) Aspen Pub.

Meyers, Douglas, jt. auth. see Smith, Maggy.

Meyers, E. C. Basic Bush Survival. (Illus.). 160p. (Orig.). 1997. pap. 14.95 (0-88839-399-7) Hancock House.

Meyers, Edward C. Thunder in the Morning Calm: The Royal Canadian Navy in Korea, 1950-1955. (Illus.). 248p. 1992. 19.95 (0-920277-71-3, Pub. by Howell Pr VA) Howell Pr VA.

Meyers, Edward M. Public Opinion & the Political Future of the Nation's Capital. LC 96-11860. 288p. 1996. 60.00 (0-87840-622-0); pap. 23.95 (0-87840-623-9) Georgetown U Pr.

Meyers, Eleanor S., ed. Envisioning the New City: A Reader on Urban Ministry. 336p. (Orig.). 1992. pap. 32.95 (0-664-25315-6) Westminster John Knox.

Meyers, Elizabeth, ed. see Green, Robert K.

Meyers, Ellen, ed. Experienced Teachers Handbook. (Illus.). 68p. (Orig.). 1993. pap. 12.00 (0-939229-04-8) Teachers Ntwrk.
— Teacher-Parent Partnerships Handbook. (Illus.). 64p. 1989. pap. 10.95 (0-939229-02-1) Teachers Ntwrk.

Meyers, Ellen & McIsaac, Paul, eds. How Teachers Are Changing Schools. (By Teachers, for Teachers Ser.). (Illus.). 100p. (Orig.). 1994. pap. 16.90 (0-939229-05-6) Teachers Ntwrk.
— How We Are Changing Schools Collaboratively. 83p. (Orig.). 1995. pap. 16.90 (0-939229-07-2) Teachers Ntwrk.
— Teacher's Guide to Cyberspace. (Illus.). 86p. (Orig.). 1996. pap. 19.95 (0-939229-08-0) Teachers Ntwrk.

Meyers, Eric M. Galilee Through the Centuries: Confluence of Cultures. LC 99-25995. (Duke Judaic Studies : Vol. 1). xii, 436p. 1999. text 42.50 (1-57506-040-X) Eisenbrauns.

Meyers, Eric M., ed. The Oxford Encyclopedia of Archaeology in the Near East, 5 vols., Set, Vols. 1-4. LC 96-17152. (Illus.). 2608p. 1996. text 595.00 (0-19-506512-3) OUP.

Meyers, Eric M. & Alford, Ricker. T-Shirts for Fun or Profit. (Illus.). 88p. (Orig.). (YA). (gr. 6 up). 1996. pap. 12.95 (0-9653537-6-1) True North.

Meyers, Eric M., et al. Excavations at Ancient Meiron, Upper Galilee, Israel, 1971-72, 1974-75, 1977. (American Schools of Oriental Research Excavation Reports). 276p. 1981. 75.00 (0-89757-204-1, Pub. by Sheffield Acad) CUP Services.
— Excavations at the Ancient Synagogue of Gush Halav: Meiron Excavation Project Reports 5. LC 90-47594. (Meiron Excavation Project Reports: No. 5). xx, 292p. 1990. text 50.00 (0-931464-59-5) Eisenbrauns.
— Sepphoris. viii, 63p. 1992. pap. text 14.95 (0-9602686-9-3, Pub. by Center Judaic Studies) Eisenbrauns.

Meyers, Eric M., jt. auth. see Meyers, Carol L.

Meyers, Eytan. International Immigration Policy: A Political Economy Analysis. text. write for info. (0-312-23143-1) St Martin.

Meyers, Frank M. The Commanches. 400p. 1987. reprint ed. 35.00 (0-942211-95-2) Olde Soldier Bks.

Meyers, Frank S., jt. auth. see Holloway, Harry.

Meyers, Fred E. Motion & Time Study: Improving Work Methods & Management. 2nd ed. LC 97-52133. 334p. (C). 1998. 77.00 (0-13-897455-1) P-H.

***Meyers, Fred E. & Stephens, Matthew P.** Manufacturing Facilities Design & Material Handling. 2nd ed. LC 99-19587. (Illus.). 415p. 1999. 98.00 (0-13-674821-X) P-H.

Meyers, Frederic. European Coal Mining Unions: Structure & Function. (Monograph & Research Ser.: No. 7). 161p. 1961. 5.00 (0-89215-009-2) U Cal LA Indus Rel.
— Mexican Industrial Relations Viewed from the Perspective of the Mexican Labor Court. (Monograph & Research Ser.: No. 24). 103p. 1979. 5.00 (0-89215-104-8) U Cal LA Indus Rel.
— Ownership of Jobs: A Comparative Study. (Monograph & Research Ser.: No. 11). 114p. 1964. 5.00 (0-89215-012-2) U Cal LA Indus Rel.
— State & Government Employee Unions in France. LC 73-634398. (Comparative Studies in Public Employment Labor Relations Ser.). 1971. 10.00 (0-87736-007-3); pap. 5.00 (0-87736-008-1) U of Mich Inst Labor.
— Training in European Enterprises. (Monograph & Research Ser.: No. 14). 173p. 1969. 5.00 (0-89215-015-7) U Cal LA Indus Rel.

Meyers, Frederic, jt. ed. see Hildebrand, George H.

Meyers, Frederic, tr. see Watillon, Leon.

Meyers, Frederick H. & Gean, Constantine J. Pocket Drug Guide. 3rd ed. LC 98-13760. 265p. 1998. pap. 24.95 (0-683-30597-2) Lppncott W & W.

Meyers, Frederick H., jt. auth. see Gean, Constantine J.

Meyers, Gary D. The Carpenter's Toolbox Manual. (On-the-Job Reference Ser.). 384p. 1999. pap. text 11.00 (0-13-115296-3) P-H.

***Meyers, Gerald C. & Meyers, Susan.** Dealers, Healers, Brutes & Saviros: Eight Winning Styles for Solving Giant Business Crises. LC 99-44839. (Illus.). 256p. 2000. text 27.95 (0-471-34782-5) Wiley.

Meyers, Glenn G. Miguel Delibes: An Annotated Critical Bibliography. LC 98-52551. (Author Bibliographies Ser.: No. 102). (Illus.). 352p. 1999. 50.00 (0-8108-3626-2) Scarecrow.

Meyers, Grove E. Aerospace Power: The Case for Indivisible Application. (Illus.). 96p. 1986. pap. 4.75 (1-58566-013-2) Air Univ.

Meyers, H. Alan. Cocaine: The Users Guide to Self-Help Treatment. rev. ed. 1985. pap. 9.95 (0-937119-00-8) Meyers Pub.

Meyers, H. H. With Cloak & Dagger. 213p. (Orig.). 1995. pap. 9.95 (0-923309-28-4) Hartland Pubns.

***Meyers, Harold B.** Reservations. LC 99-11760. 281p. 1999. 24.95 (0-87081-524-5) Univ Pr Colo.

Meyers, Helen C., ed. Between Analyst & Patient: New Dimensions in Countertransference & Transference. 280p. 1986. text 45.00 (0-88163-043-8) Analytic Pr.

Meyers, Herbert M. & Lubliner, Murray J. The Marketer's Guide to Successful Package Design. LC 97-50260. (Illus.). 304p. 1998. 49.95 (0-8442-3438-9, NTC Business Bks) NTC Contemp Pub Co.

Meyers, J. Gordon & Lawyer, John. A Guidebook for Problem-Solving in Group Settings. (Illus.). 38p. 1986. pap. text 2.95 (0-934134-62-6) Sheed & Ward WI.

Meyers, J. Thomas. Chert Resources of the Lower Illinois Valley. (Reports of Investigations: No. 18). (Illus.). 42p. 1970. pap. 2.00 (0-89792-042-2) Ill St Museum.

Meyers, James H. Segmentation & Positioning for Strategic Marketing Decisions. LC 96-16461. 358p. 1996. 49.95 (0-87757-259-3) Am Mktg.

Meyers, James P. The Educational System of Kenya, Vol. 93B. (ECE Presents Ser.). (Illus.). 100p. (Orig.). (C). 1993. pap. text 21.00 (1-883971-03-9) Educ Credential.

Meyers, Jan, ed. Small Business & Entry-Level Employees - How to Increase Take-Home Pay & Keep America Working: Hearing Before the Committee on Small Business, U. S. House of Representatives. 88p. (C). 1998. pap. text 25.00 (0-7881-7065-1) DIANE Pub.

Meyers, Jane. Magic Child: All about Love & Power from the Inside Out. LC 98-74025. (Illus.). 332p. 1999. pap. 19.95 (1-58151-020-9) BookPartners.

Meyers, Jason. Lessons from Leaders Vol. 1: Politicians. (Illus.). 1985. pap. 4.95 (0-913290-83-1) Camaro Pub.

Meyers, Jean O., ed. see O'Gara, W. H.

***Meyers, Jeff.** Hereafter. 82p. 2000. pap. 9.95 (1-882550-26-9, Pub. by Quiet Lion Pr) SPD-Small Pr Dist.

Meyers, Jeffery. Bogart: A Life in Hollywood. (Illus.). 384p. 1999. pap. 16.00 (0-88064-234-3) Fromm Intl Pub.

***Meyers, Jeffery.** Robert Frost: A Biography. 462p. 1999. 31.95 (0-7351-0140-X) Replica Bks.

Meyers, Jeffrey. The Biographer's Art. 191p. (C). 1989. 30.00 (0-941533-52-2, NAB) I R Dee.
— Bogart: A Life in Hollywood. LC 96-39308. (Illus.). 369p. 1997. 30.00 (0-395-77399-7) HM.
— D. H. Lawrence: A Biography. 445p. 24.95 (0-685-39477-8) Knopf.
— D. H. Lawrence & the Experience of Italy. LC 82-60261. 207p. reprint ed. pap. 64.20 (0-7837-3006-3, 204293500006) Bks Demand.
— Early Frost. 1999. 8.99 (0-7858-1129-X) Bk Sales Inc.

***Meyers, Jeffrey.** Edgar Allan Poe: His Life & Legacy. 2000. reprint ed. pap. 17.95 (0-8154-1038-7, Pub. by Cooper Sq) Natl Bk Netwk.
— Gary Cooper: An American Hero. LC 97-49959. 288p. 1998. 26.00 (0-688-15494-8, Wm Morrow) Morrow Avon.

Meyers, Jeffrey. Hemingway: A Biography. LC 98-54965. (Illus.). 688p. 1999. mass mkt. 17.95 (0-306-80890-0, Pub. by Da Capo) HarpC.

***Meyers, Jeffrey.** Hemingway: Life into Art. 2000. 27.95 (0-8154-1078-6, Pub. by Cooper Sq) Natl Bk Netwk.

An Asterisk (*) at the beginning of an entry indicates that the title is appearing for the first time.

Meyers, Jeffrey. Homosexuality & Literature: 1890-1930. 1977. lib. bdg. 32.95 (*0-7735-0300-5*, Pub. by McG-Queens Univ Pr) CUP Services.
— Homosexuality & Literature 1890-1930. 200p. (C). 1987. reprint ed. pap. 15.00 (*0-485-12054-2*, Pub. by Athlone Pr) Humanities.
***Meyers, Jeffrey.** Orwell: Wintry Conscience of a Generation. (Illus.). 320p. 2000. 27.95 (*0-393-04792-X*) Norton.
— Privileged Moments: Encounters with Writers. LC 00-8609. 2000. 24.95 (*0-299-16940-5*) U of Wis Pr.
Meyers, Jeffrey. Robert Frost: A Biography. (Illus.). 448p. 1997. pap. 15.00 (*0-395-85603-5*, Mariner Bks) HM.
***Meyers, Jeffrey.** Scott Fitzgerald. 2000. pap. 18.95 (*0-8154-1036-0*) Cooper Sq.
Meyers, Jeffrey. The Spirit of Biography. Litz, A. Walton, ed. LC 89-33823. (Studies in Modern Literature: No. 102). 315p. reprint ed. 97.70 (*0-8357-2001-2*, 207074500004) Bks Demand.
— Wyndham Lewis: A Revaluation. 1980. 55.00 (*0-7735-0516-4*, Pub. by McG-Queens Univ Pr) CUP Services.
Meyers, Jeffrey, ed. American Novelists: Ernest Hemingway. (Critical Heritage Ser.). 628p. (C). 1997. 160.00 (*0-415-15934-2*) Routledge.
— D. H. Lawrence & Tradition. LC 84-16175. 176p. 1985. lib. bdg. 25.00 (*0-87023-464-1*) U of Mass Pr.
— George Orwell. (Critical Heritage Ser.). 406p. (C). 1997. 140.00 (*0-415-15923-7*) Routledge.
— George Orwell: The Critical Heritage. (Critical Heritage Ser.). 432p. 1975. 69.50 (*0-7100-8255-X*, Routledge Thoemms) Routledge.
— Robert Lowell: Interviews & Memoirs. 384p. 1988. text 42.50 (*0-472-10089-0*, 10089) U of Mich Pr.
Meyers, Jeffrey, ed. see Campbell, Roy.
Meyers, Jeffrey, ed. see Frost, Robert.
Meyers, Jessica. Fall's Gems. 12p. 1996. pap. 3.00 (*0-945926-41-3*, Pub. by Paradigm RI) SPD-Small Pr Dist.
Meyers, Jim. How to Earn Money on Your Utility Bills. LC 93-78049. 85p. 1993. pap. 10.95 (*0-9636969-0-4*) ICDI Pubns.
Meyers, Jim, ed. see Otto, Helen T.
Meyers, Joel, et al. Mental Health Consultation in the Schools: A Comprehensive Guide for Psychologists, Social Workers, Psychiatrists, Counselors, Educators, & Other Human Service Professionals. LC 79-83567. (Social & Behavioral Science Ser.). 262p. 1979. text 38.95 (*0-87589-400-3*) Jossey-Bass.
Meyers, Joel, jt. auth. see Parsons, Richard D.
Meyers, Judith. Practical Vocabulary. LC 97-47189. (Basics Made Easy Ser.). 208p. 1998. pap. 13.95 (*1-57685-082-X*) LrningExprss.
***Meyers, Judith.** Secrets of Taking Any Test: Learn the Techniques Successful Test-Takers Know. 2nd ed. (Illus.). 2000. pap. text. write for info. (*1-57685-307-1*, Pub. by LrningExprss) Natl Bk Netwk.
Meyers, Judith. The Secrets of Taking Any Test in 20 Minutes a Day. Gish, Jim, ed. LC 97-21550. (Basics Made Easy Ser.). 192p. 1997. pap. 13.95 (*1-57685-071-4*) LrningExprss.
— Vocabulary & Spelling Skills for College Students. LC 97-43619. (Learning Express Basic Skills for College Students Ser.). 186p. (C). 1997. pap. text 20.40 (*0-13-080255-7*) P-H.
— Vocabulary & Spelling Success in 20 Minutes a Day. LC 98-17968. 192p. 1998. pap. 16.00 (*1-57685-127-3*) LrningExprss.
Meyers, Kent. Light in the Crossing. LC 99-22069. 1999. text 21.95 (*0-312-20337-3*) St Martin.
***Meyers, Kent.** Light in the Crossing: Stories. 240p. 2000. pap. 12.95 (*0-312-26758-4*) St Martin.
Meyers, Kent. The River Warren: A Novel. LC 99-26983. 280p. 1999. pap. 13.00 (*0-15-601062-3*, Harvest Bks) Harcourt.
***Meyers, Kent.** The River Warren: A Novel. LC 98-71627. 271p. 1998. 21.00 (*1-886913-23-4*) Ruminator Bks.
Meyers, Kent. The Witness of Combines. 248p. 1998. pap. 16.95 (*0-8166-3105-0*) U of Minn Pr.
— The Witness of Combines. LC 98-12898. 248p. 1998. 17.95 (*0-8166-3104-2*) U of Minn Pr.
Meyers, Larry F. Tax Tips & Strategies: Income Tax Hints Every Taxpayer Should Know, 1994. 2nd ed. LC 94-164985. (Illus.). 1993. pap. 14.95 (*0-9639166-0-2*) L Meyers Pubng.
— Tax Tips & Strategies: 1995 Edition. (Illus.). 160p. 1995. pap. 13.95 (*0-9639166-1-0*) L Meyers Pubng.
Meyers, Larry S. Baseball Blackbook, 1992: The Winning Edge for Serious Rotisserie. rev. ed. (Illus.). 224p. 1992. pap. 12.99 (*1-55958-141-7*) Prima Pub.
Meyers, Lawrence, ed. see Shafton, Lori A.
Meyers, Lewis. Crosscurrents: Writing on the Stream of Reading. 462p. (C). 1992. pap. text 36.76 (*0-669-21458-2*); teacher ed. 33.96 (*0-669-21459-0*) HM Trade Div.
— Findings: Readings for Critical Writing. (C). 1996. text, teacher ed. 31.56 (*0-669-33044-2*); pap. text 30.36 (*0-669-33042-6*) HM Trade Div.
Meyers, M. A. Dynamic Radiology of the Abdomen. (Illus.). 592p. 1988. 134.00 (*0-387-96624-2*) Spr-Verlag.
— Dynamic Radiology of the Abdomen: Normal & Pathologic Anatomy. 4th ed. (Illus.). 680p. 1993. write for info. (*3-540-94022-7*) Spr-Verlag.
Meyers, M. A., ed. Computed Tomography of the Gastrointestinal Tract. (Illus.). xiv, 279p. 1986. 200.00 (*0-387-96232-8*) Spr-Verlag.
Meyers, M. A. & Ghahremani, G. G., eds. Iatrogenic Gastrointestinal Complications. (Radiology of Iatrogenic Disorders Ser.). (Illus.). 307p. 1981. 172.00 (*0-387-90505-7*) Spr-Verlag.
Meyers, M. F. Doctors' Marriages: A Look at the Problems & Their Solutions. 2nd ed. (Illus.). 284p. (C). 1994. text 39.00 (*0-306-44618-9*, Kluwer Plenum) Kluwer Academic.
Meyers, Madeleine, intro. Cherokee Nation: Life Before the Tears. LC 93-70437. (Perspectives on History Ser.). (Illus.). 64p. (YA). (gr. 5-12). 1993. pap. 6.95 (*1-878668-26-9*) Disc Enter Ltd.
— Forward into Light: The Struggle for Women's Suffrage. LC 93-70436. (Perspectives on History Ser.). (Illus.). 64p. (YA). (gr. 5-12). 1994. pap. 6.95 (*1-878668-25-0*) Disc Enter Ltd.
Meyers, Marc A. Dynamic Behavior of Materials. 688p. 1994. 140.00 (*0-471-58262-X*) Wiley.
Meyers, Marc A. & Chawla, Krishan K. Mechanical Behavior of Materials. LC 98-22454. 680p. (C). 1998. 105.00 (*0-13-262817-1*) P-H.
Meyers, Marc A., et al. Metallurgical Applications of Shock-Wave & High-Strain Rate Phenomena. (Mechanical Engineering Ser.: Vol. 52). (Illus.). 1136p. 1986. text 280.00 (*0-8247-7612-7*) Dekker.
— Shock-Wave & High-Strain-Rate Phenomena in Materials. (Mechanical Engineering Ser.: Vol. 77). (Illus.). 1184p. 1992. text 299.00 (*0-8247-8579-7*) Dekker.
Meyers, Marc Andre, et al, eds. Mechanics & Materials: Fundamentals & Linkages. LC 98-29974. 648p. 1999. 135.00 (*0-471-24317-5*) Wiley.
Meyers, Margaret. Swimming in the Congo. LC 95-17162. 280p. (Orig.). 1995. pap. 13.95 (*1-57131-006-1*) Milkweed Ed.
Meyers, Mari. Gourmet Gringo. LC 96-15424. 1996. pap. 14.95 (*1-885590-16-4*) Golden West Pub.
Meyers, Marian. News Coverage of Violence Against Women: Engendering Blame. LC 96-25357. 148p. 1996. 38.95 (*0-8039-5635-5*); pap. 18.95 (*0-8039-5636-3*) Sage.
***Meyers, Marian, ed.** Mediated Women: Representations in Popular Culture. LC 99-29090. (Communication Ser.). 400p. (C). 1999. 85.00 (*1-57273-239-3*); pap. 34.50 (*1-57273-240-7*) Hampton Pr NJ.
Meyers, Mark, jt. auth. see Perelman, Richard B.
***Meyers, Martin.** Koordination Als Konstituente des Stils Diderots: Untersuchungen Zu Seinem Dramatischen Werk. XI, 318p. 1999. 51.95 (*3-631-34414-7*) P Lang Pubng.
Meyers, Marvin. Jacksonian Persuasion: Politics & Belief. 2nd rev. ed. viii, 232p. 1960. pap. 12.95 (*0-8047-0506-2*) Stanford U Pr.
Meyers, Marvin, ed. see Madison, James.
Meyers, Marvin H., ed. The Multiply Injured Patient with Complex Fractures. LC 83-9333. (Illus.). 435p. reprint ed. pap. 134.90 (*0-7837-1490-4*, 205718600023) Bks Demand.
Meyers, Mary. Teaching to Diversity. 144p. 1994. pap. text 27.26 (*0-201-55547-6*) Addison-Wesley.
— Teaching to Diversity: Teaching & Learning in the Multi-Ethnic Classroom. LC 94-137. 1994. pap. write for info. (*0-7725-1958-7*) Addison-Wesley.
Meyers, Mary A. A New World Jerusalem: The Swedenborgian Experience in Community Construction, 65. LC 82-11997. (Contributions in American Studies: No. 65). (Illus.). 217p. 1983. 55.00 (*0-313-23602-X*, MNJ/, Greenwood Pr) Greenwood.
Meyers, Matt. Take Home Poems. LC 95-90080. 72p. (Orig.). 1995. pap. 4.95 (*0-9646336-0-4*) M Meyers.
Meyers, Melanie & Angelo, Frank. An Octagon for the Curriers. (Illus.). 112p. (Orig.). 1995. pap. 29.95 (*0-8143-2643-9*) Wayne St U Pr.
— An Octagon for the Curriers LC 95-69824. 111p. 1995. write for info. (*0-9645916-0-X*) Post Pub.
Meyers, Melba. Naked Emotions. 72p. 1984. pap. 6.00 (*0-9612296-0-8*) Williams SC.
Meyers, Michael & Schwarz, Brian. Network+ All-In-One Certification Exam Guide. 512p. 1999. 54.99 (*0-07-134563-9*) McGraw.
Meyers, Michael, jt. auth. see Myers, Michael.
***Meyers, Michael J.** A+ All-in-One Certification Exam Guide. 2nd ed. 966p. 1999. pap. text 59.99 (*0-07-212266-8*) McGraw.
Meyers, Mike. Network Troubleshooting & Repair. 1100p. 1999. 59.95 (*0-07-913737-7*) McGraw.
Meyers, Mike & McCullers, Michael. Austin Powers: How to Be an International Man of Mystery. LC 97-168263. 112p. 1997. pap. 10.00 (*1-57297-317-X*) Blvd Books.
Meyers, Morton. Diagnosis & Staging of Neoplasms of the Digestive Tract. LC 97-26538. 350p. 1997. text 165.00 (*0-397-51757-2*) Lppncott W & W.
Meyers, Morton A. Dynamic Radiology of the Abdomen: Normal & Pathologic Anatomy. 4th ed. LC 93-16236. (Illus.). 680p. 1996. 169.00 (*0-387-94022-7*) Spr-Verlag.
***Meyers, Morton A.** Dynamic Radiology of the Abdomen: Normal & Pathologic Anatomy. 5th ed. LC 99-28933. (Illus.). 656p. 1999. 179.00 (*0-387-98845-9*) Spr-Verlag.
Meyers, Odette. Doors to Madame Marie. LC 96-28470. (McLellan Bks.). (Illus.). 400p. 1997. 24.95 (*0-295-97576-8*) U of Wash Pr.
— The Enchanted Umbrella: With a Short History of the Umbrella. (Illus.). 28p. (J). (ps-3). 1988. 13.95 (*0-15-200448-3*, Gulliver Bks) Harcourt.
Meyers, P. & Hickman, T. R. Oasis of White Palm. 1983. 6.00 (*0-394-53153-1*) Random Bks Yng Read.
Meyers, Pat, ed. see King, Heather.
Meyers, Patricia, jt. auth. see Cabrera, Roberto.
Meyers, Patrick. Feedlot. 1984. pap. 5.25 (*0-8222-0395-2*) Dramatists Play.
— K-2. 1983. pap. 5.25 (*0-8222-0606-4*) Dramatists Play.
Meyers, Paul. HTML 3.2 Web Classroom. LC 98-22465. 306p. (C). 1998. pap. 42.00 (*0-13-796111-1*) P-H.
Meyers, Perla. Fresh from the Garden: Cooking & Gardening Throughout the Season. 288p. 1996. 30.00 (*0-517-59357-2*) C Potter.
— Perla Meyers' Art of Seasonal Cooking. Knide, Judy, ed. (Illus.). 527p. 1998. text 27.00 (*0-7881-5291-2*) DIANE Pub.
***Meyers, Perla.** Spur of the Moment Cook: Spontaneous & Flavorful Meals for the Busiest Days of the Week. LC 93-33690. 320p. 1999. pap. 15.00 (*0-688-17010-2*, Wm Morrow) Morrow Avon.
Meyers, Philip. Series 7 Stockbroker Exam. 5th ed. 464p. 1998. 50.00 (*0-02-862196-4*, Arc) IDG Bks.
Meyers, Philip, jt. auth. see Discovery Books Staff.
Meyers, Phillip. Registered Representative: Stockbroker's Exam. 2nd ed. (Illus.). 448p. 1992. pap. 35.00 (*0-13-770702-9*, Arco) Macmillan Gen Ref.
Meyers, Pieter, jt. ed. see Scott, David A.
Meyers, R. A., ed. Encyclopedia of Molecular Biology & Molecular Medicine, Vol. 3. 544p. 1996. 460.00 (*3-527-28473-7*) Wiley.
— Molecular Biology & Biotechnology: A Comprehensive Desk Reference. 1072p. 1995. 235.00 (*0-471-18571-X*); pap. 125.00 (*0-471-18634-1*) Wiley.
Meyers, R. E. & Torrance, E. P. Imagining: Invitations to Think about the Future for Intermediate Grades. 64p. 1986. pap. 14.95 (*0-936386-37-1*) Creative Learning.
Meyers, Rawley. Daily Readings in Catholic Classics. LC 92-71959. 332p. (Orig.). 1992. pap. 14.95 (*0-89870-389-1*) Ignatius Pr.
Meyers, Ray. The Saturn Profile. 350p. 1998. pap. 12.95 (*1-57502-887-5*, PO 2437) Morris Pubng.
Meyers, Reva. Winning Career Strategies: For Student in Hospitality, Travel & Tourism. Parkerson, Janet & Witzman, Joseph E., eds. (Orig.). 1988. pap. write for info. (*0-935423-06-0*) Educ Pubns.
Meyers, Ric. Murder on the Air: Television's Great Mystery Series. (Illus.). 240p. 1989. pap. 12.95 (*0-89296-977-6*) Mysterious Pr.
Meyers, Richard. Great Martial Arts Movies: From Bruce Lee to Jackie Chan . . . & More. rev. ed. LC 99-30571. (Illus.). 288p. 1998. pap. 19.95 (*0-8065-2026-4*, Citadel Pr) Carol Pub Group.
— How to Ace Any College-Level Problem-Solving Course: A Holistic Approach to Academic Excellence. LC 96-95209. viii, 264p. (Orig.). 1997. pap. text 17.95 (*0-9654805-6-9*) LLP Press.
Meyers, Richard, et al. From Bruce Lee to Ninja: Martial Arts Movies. (Illus.). 256p. 1986. reprint ed. pap. 14.95 (*0-8065-1009-9*, Citadel Pr) Carol Pub Group.
Meyers, Richard A. Pascal: The Software Fundamentals of Computer Science. 848p. (C). 1992. pap. 65.00 (*0-13-725623-X*) P-H.
Meyers, Richard E. The Journey's Loom: Collected Poems, Vol. 1. LC 99-71721. 100p. 1999. pap. 12.50 (*1-882260-14-7*) Carrier Pigeon.
Meyers, Richard S. Murder in Halruaa. LC 95-62254. (Forgotten Realms Ser.). 280p. 1996. 18.99 (*0-7869-0521-2*, 8657, Pub. by TSR Inc) Random.
Meyers, Rick, jt. auth. see Erb, Michael R.
Meyers, Robert A. Coal Desulfurization. LC 77-9928. (Illus.). 270p. reprint ed. pap. 83.70 (*0-8357-6059-6*, 203455200090) Bks Demand.
***Meyers, Robert A.** Encyclopedia of Analytical Chemistry: Applications, Theory & Instrumentation. LC 00-42282. (Illus.). 2000. write for info. (*0-471-97670-9*) Wiley.
Meyers, Robert A. Encyclopedia of Environmental Analysis & Remediation, 8 vols. LC 97-41586. (Encyclopedia Series in Environmental Science). 5488p. 1998. 2000.00 (*0-471-11708-0*, Wiley-Interscience) Wiley.
— The Encyclopedia of Environmental Pollution & Cleanup, 2 vols. Set. LC 99-17884. 1936p. 1999. 200.00 (*0-471-31612-1*) Wiley.
Meyers, Robert A., ed. Coal Handbook. LC 81-7824. (Energy, Power, & Environment Ser.: No. 11). (Illus.). 868p. reprint ed. pap. 200.00 (*0-7837-5175-3*, 204490500004) Bks Demand.
— Encyclopedia of Lasers & Optical Technology. 764p. 1990. text 108.00 (*0-12-226693-5*) Acad Pr.
— Encyclopedia of Modern Physics. 773p. 1989. text 122.00 (*0-12-226692-7*) Acad Pr.
— Encyclopedia of Molecular Biology & Molecular Medicine, 6 vols., Vol. 6. Incl. Vol. 4. Encyclopedia of Molecular Biology & Molecular Medicine Vol. 4: Mass Spectrometry High Speed DNA Fragment Sizing - Plasma Liproprotein. (Illus.). 528p. 1996. 460.00 (*3-527-28474-5*, Wiley-VCH); Vol. 5. Encyclopedia Of Molecular Biology Vol. 5: Plasmids - Synthetic Peptide & Nonpeptide Combinatorial Libraries. (Illus.). 544p. 1997. 460.00 (*3-527-28475-3*, Wiley-VCH); Vol. 6. Encyclopedia of Molecular Biology & Molecular Medicine Vol. 6. (Illus.). 512p. 1997. 460.00 (*3-527-28476-1*, Wiley-VCH); Vol. 1. Vol. 1: Achilles' Cleavage to Cytoskeleton-Plasma Membrane Interactions. (Illus.). 480p. 1995. 460.00 (*3-527-28471-0*, Wiley-VCH); Vol. 2. Vol. 2: Denaturation of DNA - Growth Factors. (Illus.). 496p. 1996. 460.00 (*3-527-28472-9*, Wiley-VCH); 1p. 1997. 2760.00 (*3-527-28478-8*, Wiley-VCH) Wiley.
— Encyclopedia of Physical Science & Technology, Set, Vols. 1-18. 2nd ed. (Illus.). 14080p. 1992. text 2895.00 (*0-12-226930-6*) Acad Pr.
— Encyclopedia of Telecommunications. 525p. 1988. text 100.00 (*0-12-226691-9*) Acad Pr.
— Molecular Biology & Biotechnology: A Comprehensive Desk Reference. LC 95-9063. (Illus.). xxxviii, 1046p. 1995. 149.95 (*1-56081-569-8*, Wiley-VCH); pap. 59.95 (*1-56081-925-1*, Wiley-VCH) Wiley.
— The Petroleum Refining Process Handbook. 2nd ed. LC 96-26991. (Illus.). 848p. 1996. 105.00 (*0-07-041796-2*) McGraw.
Meyers, Robert G. The Likelihood of Knowledge. 187p. (C). 1988. text 106.00 (*90-277-2671-X*, D Reidel) Kluwer Academic.
Meyers, Robert J. & Smith, Jane Ellen. Clinical Guide to Alcohol Treatment: The Community Reinforcement Approach. LC 95-546. (Substance Abuse Ser.). 211p. 1995. lib. bdg. 31.00 (*0-89862-857-1*) Guilford Pubns.
Meyers, Robin R. Morning Sun on a White Piano. LC 97-23082. (Illus.). 144p. 1998. 16.95 (*0-385-48954-4*) Doubleday.
***Meyers, Robin R.** Morning Sun on a White Piano: Simple Pleasures & the Sacramental Life. 144p. 2000. pap. 9.95 (*0-385-49869-1*) Doubleday.
Meyers, Robin R. With Ears to Hear: Preaching As Self-Persuasion. LC 92-42040. 176p. (Orig.). 1993. pap. 12.95 (*0-8298-0951-1*) Pilgrim OH.
Meyers, Rochelle, jt. auth. see Ray, Michael L.
Meyers, Ron. Big Ds - Little d's for a Lifetime of Health. Andrecht, Summer, ed. 32p. (Orig.). 1997. pap. 3.95 (*0-941903-28-1*) Ransom Hill.
Meyers, Ron & Farricielli, Susan. CADD Desktop Tutor: Advanced AutoCAD Release 14. 2nd unabridged ed. Angelini, Mike, tr. (Illus.). 175p. 1997. wbk. ed. 249.00 incl. cd-rom (*1-891502-05-0*, R14ADVA97) Tech Learn Co.
Meyers, Ron & Kane, Bill. AutoCAD 2000 - 3D Modeling: Instructor Manual. 2nd unabridged ed. Allen, Richard & Martz, Laura, eds. (Illus.). 230p. 1999. pap. text, teacher ed., spiral bd. 75.00 (*1-891502-59-X*, A153DIM) Tech Learn Co.
— AutoCAD 2000 - 3D Modeling: Student Manual. 2nd unabridged ed. Allen, Richard & Martz, Laura, eds. (Illus.). 230p. 1999. pap. text, student ed., spiral bd. 75.00 (*1-891502-60-3*, A153DSM) Tech Learn Co.
Meyers, Ron, ed. see Allen, Richard.
Meyers, Ronald & Eric Clearinghouse on Assessment & Evaluation Publ. Developing & Implementing Local Education Standards. LC 98-41103. 1998. write for info. (*1-886047-02-2*) ERIC Assess & Eval.
Meyers, Roy T. Strategic Budgeting. LC 94-3056. 248p. (C). 1994. text 49.50 (*0-472-10362-8*, 10362) U of Mich Pr.
— Strategic Budgeting. LC 94-3056. 248p. (C). 1996. pap. text 23.95 (*0-472-08414-3*, 08414) U of Mich Pr.
Meyers, Roy T., ed. Handbook of Government Budgeting. LC 98-40393. (Business & Management Ser.). 784p. 1998. 65.00 (*0-7879-4292-8*) Jossey-Bass.
Meyers, Ruth A. Continuing the Reformation: Re-Visioning Baptism in the Episcopal Church. LC 97-38357. 250p. 1997. 29.95 (*0-89869-195-8*) Church Pub Inc.
Meyers, Ruth A., ed. Baptism & Ministry: Liturgical Studies One. 112p. 1994. pap. 10.95 (*0-89869-241-5*) Church Pub Inc.
— Children at the Table: A Collection of Essays on Children & the Eucharist. 210p. 1995. pap. 12.95 (*0-89869-199-0*) Church Pub Inc.
— How Shall We Pray: Expanding Our Language about God, Liturgical Studies Two. 160p. 1994. pap. 12.95 (*0-89869-242-3*) Church Pub Inc.
Meyers, Samuel L., Jr. Civil Rights & Race Relations in the Post Reagan-Bush Era. LC 96-37730. 288p. 1997. 59.95 (*0-275-95621-0*, Praeger Pubs) Greenwood.
Meyers, Samuel M., ed. see Bradbury, William C.
Meyers, Scott. Effective C++ 50 Simple Ways to Improve Your Programs & Designs. (Illus.). 224p. (C). 1991. pap. text 39.95 (*0-201-56364-9*) Addison-Wesley.
***Meyers, Scott.** Effective C++CD: Eighty-Five Specific Ways to Improve Your Program & Designs. 1998. cd-rom 29.95 (*0-201-31015-5*) Addison-Wesley.
Meyers, Scott. More Effective C++ Thirty-Five New Ways to Improve Your Programs & Designs. 336p. (C). 1995. pap. text 39.95 (*0-201-63371-X*) Addison-Wesley.
Meyers, Scott D. Effective C++ 50 Specfic Ways to Improve Your Programs & Designs. 2nd ed. LC 97-24041. (Professional Computing Ser.). 288p. (C). 1997. pap. text 38.95 (*0-201-92488-9*) Peachpit Pr.
Meyers, Sharen. Regaining Faith after Boston: An Insider's Views. 83p. (Orig.). 1997. pap. 6.95 (*1-56794-119-2*, C-2438) Star Bible.
Meyers, Spike, jt. auth. see Duchow, Paul G.
Meyers Staff. Bildwoerterbuch German-English-French, Vol. 29 Grosses Lexikon. (ENG, FRE & GER.). 937p. 1981. 275.00 (*0-7859-6917-9*) Fr & Eur.
— Deutsches Woerterbuch A-F: Meyers Enzyklopaedisches Lexikon, Vol. 30. (GER.). 928p. 1979. 275.00 (*0-7859-6918-7*) Fr & Eur.
— Deutsches Woerterbuch G-N: Meyers Enzyklopaedisches Lexikon, Vol. 31. 983p. 1980. 275.00 (*0-7859-6919-5*) Fr & Eur.
— Deutsches Woerterbuch O-Z: Meyers Enzyklopaedisches Lexikon, Vol. 32. (GER.). 1087p. 1981. 275.00 (*0-7859-7098-3*) Fr & Eur.
Meyers, Stephen, jt. auth. see Sathaye, Jayant.
Meyers, Stephen F. Swaps. 480p. 1997. mass mkt. 107.95 (*0-412-61160-0*) Chapman & Hall.
Meyers, Stephen L. Breezers: A Lighthearted History of the Open Trolley Car in America. Harris, Marion, ed. LC 93-33978. (Illus.). 184p. 1993. text 56.00 (*0-933449-20-8*) Transport Trails.
Meyers, Steve, ed. & intro. see Anka, Darryl J.
Meyers, Steven J. Lime Creek Odyssey. LC 88-32705. (Illus.). 124p. 1989. 14.95 (*1-55591-037-8*) Fulcrum Pub.
— San Juan River Chronicle. (Illus.). 160p. 1994. 19.95 (*1-55821-277-9*) Lyons Pr.
— San Juan River Chronicle: Personal Remembrances of One of America's Best-Inown Trout Streams. 2nd ed. 160p. 1997. reprint ed. pap. 14.95 (*1-55821-600-6*) Lyons Pr.
Meyers, Susan. Amy's Haunted House. (J). 1995. pap. 2.95 (*0-8167-3576-X*) Troll Communs.
— Amy's Haunted House. (Always Friends Club Ser.). 1995. 8.05 (*0-606-07189-X*, Pub. by Turtleback) Demco.
— Beautiful Brittany. (J). 1995. pap. 2.95 (*0-8167-3575-1*) Troll Communs.

— Beautiful Brittany. (Always Friends Club Ser.). (J). 1995. 8.05 (*0-606-07271-3*, Pub. by Turtleback) Demco.
— Cricket Goes to the Dogs. (Always Friends Club Ser.). 1995. 8.05 (*0-606-07402-3*, Pub. by Turtleback) Demco.
— Meg & the Secret Scrapbook. (Always Friends Club Ser.). (J). 1995. 8.05 (*0-606-07857-6*, Pub. by Turtleback) Demco.

Meyers, Susan & Lakin, Joan. Who Will Take the Children? A New Custody Option for Divorced Mothers & Fathers. LC 82-17847. 228p. 1983. write for info. (*0-672-52739-1*) Macmillan.

Meyers, Susan, jt. auth. see Meyers, Gerald C.

Meyers, Susan, ed. see Koosman, Jerry.

***Meyers, Terence M. & DeSherer, Dorinda D.** Business Owner's Tax Savings & Financing Deskbook with CD-ROM. 700p. 2000. pap. 89.00 incl. cd-rom (*0-15-607227-0*) Harcourt Prof.

***Meyers, Terence M., et al.** Business Owner's Reporting & Compliance Manual. 400p. 2000. pap. 89.00 (*0-15-607225-4*) Harcourt Prof.

Meyers, Terry L. The Sexual Tensions of William Sharp: A Study of the Birth of Fiona Macleod, Incorporating Two Lost Works, "Ariadne in Naxos" & "Beatrice" LC 94-29463. (Studies in Nineteenth-Century British Literature: Vol. 2). 132p. (C). 1996. 37.95 (*0-8204-2637-7*) P Lang Pubng.

Meyers, Thomas & Denies, Mark. Longterm & Peakscan: Neutron Activation Analysis Computer Programs. (Technical Reports Ser.: No. 2). (Illus.). 1972. pap. 1.00 (*0-932206-11-5*) U Mich Mus Anthro.

Meyers, Thomas A. The Technical Analysis Course: A Winning Program for Investors & Traders. rev. ed. LC 94-107063. 250p. 1993. text 47.50 (*1-55738-523-8*, Irwn Prfssnl) McGraw-Hill Prof.

Meyers, Thomas A., jt. auth. see Colby, Robert W.

Meyers, W. & Hayes, M. V., eds. China Policy: New Priorities & Alternatives. viii, 88p. 1972. text 123.00 (*0-677-12210-1*) Gordon & Breach.

Meyers, Walter Dean, et al. One More River to Cross: An African American Photograph Album. LC 95-3839. (Illus.). 176p. (J). (gr. 4-7). 1999. reprint ed. pap. 18.00 (*0-15-202021-7*, Harcourt Child Bks) Harcourt.

Meyers, Warren B. Who Is That? (Illus.). 1976. pap. 7.95 (*0-8065-0535-4*, Citadel Pr) Carol Pub Group.

***Meyers, William.** Nonviolence & Its Violent Consequences. 20p. 2000. pap. 2.00 (*1-886625-07-7*, Pub. by III Pub) Left Bank.

Meyers, William. Vampires or Gods? 192p. (Orig.). 1993. pap. 15.00 (*0-9622937-5-X*) III Pub.

Meyers, William C. & Jones, Scott R. Textbook of Liver & Biliary Surgery. LC 89-13907. (Illus.). 508p. 1990. reprint ed. pap. 157.50 (*0-608-05869-6*, 205983600007) Bks Demand.

Meyers, William H., et al, eds. Lithuania's Accession to the European Union: Successes & Challenges for a Rural Economy in Transition. LC 98-44966. (Illus.). 238p. 1999. text 49.95 (*0-8138-1973-3*) Iowa St U Pr.

Meyers, William R. The Evaluation Enterprise: A Realistic Appraisal of Evaluation Careers, Methods & Applications. LC 81-81961. (Jossey-Bass Social & Behavioral Science Ser.). 284p. reprint ed. pap. 88.10 (*0-8357-4997-5*, 203793000009) Bks Demand.

***Meyersohn, Maxwell.** Riding the Heavens: Stories & Seminars to Inspire Your Faith. LC 99-59300. 2000. 14.99 (*0-310-23333-X*) Zondervan.

Meyerson, Arthur T., ed. Barriers to Treating the Chronic Mentally Ill. LC 87-646993. (New Directions for Mental Health Services Ser.: No. MHS 33). 1987. pap. 25.00 (*1-55542-966-1*) Jossey-Bass.

Meyerson, B. & Ostertag, C., eds. Advances in Stereotactic & Functional Neurosurgery 11, No. 64. (Acta Neurochirugica Ser.: Vol. 64). 152p. 1996. 140.00 (*3-211-82720-X*) Spr-Verlag.

Meyerson, Bjorn A., jt. auth. see European Society For Stereotactic & Functional Neu.

Meyerson, Denise. False Consciousness. (Oxford Philosophical Monographs). (Illus.). 194p. 1991. text 65.00 (*0-19-824819-9*, 11953) OUP.
— Rights Limited. LC 98-189269. xxviii, 185p. 1998. pap. 22.50 (*0-7021-4396-0*, Pub. by Juta & Co) Gaunt.

Meyerson, E. Identity & Reality. (Classics in the History & Philosophy of Science Ser.: Vol. 4). ii, 496p. 1989. pap. text 69.00 (*2-88124-349-5*) Gordon & Breach.

Meyerson, Emile. Explanation in the Sciences. 648p. (C). 1991. lib. bdg. 267.50 (*0-7923-1129-9*, Pub. by Kluwer Academic) Kluwer Academic.
— The Relativistic Deduction: Epistemological Implications of the Theory of Relativity with a Review by Albert Einstein. Sipfle, David A. & Sipfle, Mary A., trs. 290p. 1985. text 147.00 (*90-277-1699-4*, D Reidel) Kluwer Academic.

Meyerson, Eva M. The Impact of Ownership Structure & Executive Team Composition on Firm Performance: The Resolution of a Leadership Paradox. (Industrial Institute for Economic & Social Research Report Ser.). (Illus.). 170p. (Orig.). 1992. pap. 44.50 (*91-7204-395-4*) Coronet Bks.

Meyerson, Harvey & Simonelli, Danelle K. Launchpad for the 21st Century: Yearbook of the International Space Year. LC 99-490718. (Advances in the Astronautical Sciences Ser.). (Illus.). 412p. 1995. pap. text, suppl. ed. 50.00 (*0-87703-394-3*, Am Astronaut Soc) Univelt Inc.
— Launchpad for the 21st Century: Yearbook of the International Space Year. 2nd ed. LC 99-490718. (Advances in the Astronautical Sciences Ser.). (Illus.). 412p. 1995. lib. bdg., suppl. ed. 70.00 (*0-87703-393-5*, Am Astronaut Soc) Univelt Inc.

Meyerson, Joel, ed. Measuring Institutional Performance in Higher Education. LC 93-6403. 141p. (C). 1993. 29.95 (*1-56079-331-7*) Petersons.

Meyerson, Joel, jt. auth. see Hanson, Katherine H.

Meyerson, Joel W. New Thinking on Higher Education: Creating a Context for Change. (Forum Ser.: Vol. 1). 208p. 1998. 34.95 (*1-882982-23-1*) Anker Pub.

Meyerson, Joel W. & Anderson, Richard, eds. New Models for Higher Education. LC 98-161257. 144p. 1997. 34.95 (*1-56079-808-4*) Petersons.
— Productivity & Higher Education: Improving the Effectiveness of Faculty, Facilities, & Financial Resources. LC 91-22290. 144p. 1991. 27.95 (*1-56079-090-3*) Petersons.

Meyerson, Joel W., jt. auth. see Anderson, Richard E.

Meyerson, Joel W., jt. ed. see Anderson, Richard E.

Meyerson, Joel W., jt. ed. see Massy, William F.

Meyerson, Julia. Tambo: Life in an Andean Village. (Illus.). 297p. 1990. pap. 18.95 (*0-292-78078-8*) U of Tex Pr.

Meyerson, Mark D. The Muslims of Valencia in the Age of Fernando & Isabel. 370p. 1996. 49.95 (*0-614-21628-1*, 861) Kazi Pubns.
— The Muslims of Valencia in the Age of Fernando & Isabel: Between Coexistence & Crusade. LC 90-35502. (Illus.). 382p. 1991. 58.00 (*0-520-06888-2*, Pub. by U CA Pr) Cal Prin Full Svc.

Meyerson, Mark D. & English, Edward D., eds. Christians, Muslims, & Jews in Medieval & Early Modern Spain: Interaction & Cultural Change. LC 99-35905. (Conferences in Medieval Studies: No. VIII). 352p. 2000. 45.00 (*0-268-02250-X*, Pub. by U of Notre Dame Pr) Chicago Distribution Ctr.

***Meyerson, Mark D. & English, Edward D., eds.** Christians, Muslims, & Jews in Medieval & Early Modern Spain: Interaction & Cultural Change. rev. ed. LC 99-35905. (Notre Dame Conference in Medieval Studies: Vol. VIII). 344p. 2000. pap. 26.00 (*0-268-02263-1*, Pub. by U of Notre Dame Pr) Chicago Distribution Ctr.

Meyerson, Martin & Banfield, Edward C. Boston: The Job Ahead. LC 66-14449. (Publication of the Joint Center for Urban Studies of the Massachusetts Institute of Technology & Harvard University). 128p. reprint ed. pap. 39.70 (*0-7837-4479-X*, 204418700001) Bks Demand.

Meyerson, Martin & Winegrad, Dilys P. Gladly Learn & Gladly Teach: Franklin & His Heirs at the University of Pennsylvania, 1740-1976. LC 77-82383. 270p. 1978. 37.95 (*0-8122-7735-X*) U of Pa Pr.

Meyerson, Mitch & Ashner, Laurie. Six Keys to Creating the Life You Desire. LC 98-67408. 330p. 1999. pap. 19.95 (*1-57224-125-X*) New Harbinger.

Meyerson, Mitch, jt. auth. see Ashner, Laurie.

Meyerstein, E. H., ed. see Royal Society of Literature, United Kingdom Staff.

Meyerstein, F. Walter, ed. Foundations of Big Bang Cosmology. 368p. (C). 1989. text 99.00 (*9971-5-0755-2*) World Scientific Pub.

Meyerstein, F. Walter, jt. auth. see Brisson, Luc.

***Meyhofer, Dirk.** The Architecture of Wine: Bordeaux & Napa Valley. (Illus.). 236p. 2000. 59.95 (*1-58423-033-9*) Gingko Press.

Meyhofer, Dirk. Contemporary European Architects, Vol. 2. 1994. pap. 24.99 (*3-8228-9455-9*) Taschen Amer.
— Contemporary European Architects, Vol. 2. (SPA.). 1996. pap. 24.99 (*3-8228-0758-3*) Taschen Amer.
— Contemporary Japanese Architects. (SPA.). 1996. pap. 24.99 (*3-8228-0755-9*) Taschen Amer.
— Contemporary Japanese Architects, Vol. 1. LC 95-227199. (SPA.). 1994. pap. 24.99 (*3-8228-9442-7*) Taschen Amer.

Meyjes, G. H. Jean Gerson, Apostle of Unity: His Church Politics & Ecclesiology. LC 99-29699. 436p. 1999. 138.50 (*90-04-11296-0*) Brill Academic Pubs.

Meylach, Martin & Whited, Charles. Diving to a Flash of Gold. LC 73-116234. (Florida Classics Ser.). (Illus.). 382p. (Orig.). 1987. reprint ed. pap. 15.95 (*0-912451-16-5*) Florida Classics.

Meylan, B. A. & Butterfield, B. G. Three-Dimensional Structure of Wood: A Scanning Electron Microscope Study. (Illus.). 80p. (C). 1972. pap. text 34.50 (*0-8156-5030-2*) Syracuse U Pr.

Meylan, Claude. L' Option Nucleaire et les Entreprises Suisses. (European University Studies: Economics & Management: Ser. 5, Vol. 446). (FRE.). XIV, 272p. 1983. 35.80 (*3-261-03281-2*) P Lang Pubng.

Meylan, G. & Crane, P., eds. OPSO Absorption Lines: Proceedings of the ESO Workshop Held at Garching, Germany, 21-24 November 1994, Vol. XXIII. (ESO Astrophysics Symposia, European Southern Observatory Ser.). 471p. 1995. 39.95 (*3-540-60152-X*) Spr-Verlag.

Meylan, G., jt. ed. see Djorgovski, S. G.

Meylan, William M., jt. auth. see Howard, Philip H.

Meyland, August L., III. Better Than Money Can Buy: The New Volunteers. 168p. (Orig.). 1996. pap. 10.95 (*0-931029-01-5*) Innersearch.

Meyler, John & Roberson, Geoffrey. The Ocular Disease Manual. (Manual Ser.). (Illus.). 224p. 1998. pap. 60.00 (*0-7506-1816-7*) Buttrwrth-Heinemann.

Meyn, Barbara. The Abalone Heart. Trusky, Tom, ed. LC 88-71465. (Ahsahta Press Modern & Contemporary Poets of the West Ser.). 75p. (Orig.). 1988. pap. 6.95 (*0-916272-37-0*) Ahsahta Pr.

Meyn, S. P. & Tweedie, R. L. Markov Chains & Stochastic Stability. (Communications & Control Engineering Ser.). (Illus.). xvi, 548p. 1996. 119.95 (*0-387-19832-6*) Spr-Verlag.

Meynard, Yves. The Book of Knights. LC 97-34387. 256p. 1998. 21.95 (*0-312-86482-5*, Pub. by Tor Bks) St Martin.
— The Book of Knights. 2nd ed. LC 99-12198. 1999. pap. 13.95 (*0-312-86831-6*) St Martin.

Meynell, Alice C. Ceres' Runaway & Other Essays. LC 67-30223. (Essay Index Reprint Ser.). 1977. 17.95 (*0-8369-0704-3*) Ayer.
— The Colour of Life & Other Essays on Things Seen & Heard. 1977. 11.95 (*0-8369-7231-7*, 8030) Ayer.
— Essays. LC 70-100251. 267p. 1970. reprint ed. lib. bdg. 65.00 (*0-8371-2984-2*, MEES, Greenwood Pr) Greenwood.
— Hearts of Controversy. LC 68-57332. (Essay Index Reprint Ser.). 1977. 17.95 (*0-8369-0705-1*) Ayer.
— Prose & Poetry. LC 76-117824. (Essay Index Reprint Ser.). 1977. 20.95 (*0-8369-1983-1*) Ayer.
— Rhythm of Life: And Other Essays. LC 78-37794. (Essay Index Reprint Ser.). 1977. reprint ed. 17.95 (*0-8369-2613-7*) Ayer.
— Second Person Singular, & Other Essays. LC 68-55851. (Essay Index Reprint Ser.). 1977. 17.95 (*0-8369-0706-X*) Ayer.

Meynell, E. Portrait of William Morris. 1972. 59.95 (*0-8490-0881-6*) Gordon Pr.

Meynell, Everard. The Life of Francis Thompson. (BCL1-PR English Literature Ser.). 360p. 1992. reprint ed. lib. bdg. 89.00 (*0-7812-7504-0*) Rprt Serv.
— The Life of Francis Thompson. (Illus.). 1971. reprint ed. 18.00 (*0-403-01107-8*) Scholarly.

Meynell, Hugo. The Art of Handel's Operas. LC 86-5406. (Studies in the History & Interpretation of Music: Vol. 1). 264p. 1986. lib. bdg. 89.95 (*0-88946-425-1*) E Mellen.
— An Introduction to the Philosophy of Bernard Lonergan. 236p. 1991. text 35.00 (*0-8020-5869-8*); pap. text 16.95 (*0-8020-6792-1*) U of Toronto Pr.
— Is Christianity True? LC 93-47617. 149p. (C). 1994. pap. text 14.95 (*0-8132-0804-1*) Cath U Pr.

Meynell, Hugo, jt. ed. see McLean, George F.

Meynell, Hugo, jt. ed. see Stoeber, Michael.

Meynell, Hugo A. The Nature of Aesthetic Value. LC 85-2742. 158p. (C). 1986. text 29.50 (*0-88706-118-4*) State U NY Pr.

***Meynell, Hugo A.** Postmodernism & the New Enlightenment. LC 99-17999. 1999. 39.95 (*0-8132-0946-3*) Cath U Pr.

Meynell, Hugo A. Postmodernism & the New Enlightenment. LC 99-17999. 2000. pap. 19.95 (*0-8132-0947-1*) Cath U Pr.
— Redirecting Philosophy: The Nature of Knowledge from Plato to Lonergan. LC 99-189141. 336p. 1998. text 70.00 (*0-8020-4314-3*); pap. text 21.95 (*0-8020-8140-1*) U of Toronto Pr.
— The Theology of Bernard Lonergan. (Studies in Religion). 235p. (C). 1986. pap. 15.95 (*1-55540-016-7*, 01 00 42, Pub. by OUP) OUP.

Meynell, Laurence. The Affair at Barwold. large type ed. 1990. 27.99 (*0-7089-2142-6*) Ulverscroft.
— Don't Stop for Hooky Hefferman. 1990. mass mkt. 3.50 (*0-373-26053-9*) Harlequin Bks.
— The Fairly Innocent Little Man. (Mystery Ser.: No. 102). 1992. per. 3.99 (*0-373-26102-0*) Harlequin Bks.
— Hooky Gets the Wooden Spoon. 1991. reprint ed. per. 3.95 (*0-373-26077-6*) Harlequin Bks.
— The Secret of the Pit. large type ed. 336p. 1985. 27.99 (*0-7089-1328-8*) Ulverscroft.
— Silver Guilt. large type ed. 1989. 27.99 (*0-7089-2060-8*) Ulverscroft.

Meynell, Viola. Alice Meynell. LC 79-145182. (Illus.). 1971. reprint ed. 49.00 (*0-403-00804-2*) Scholarly.

Meynell, W., ed. see Thompson, Francis.

Meynell, Wilfred, ed. see Thompson, Francis.

Meynen. International Cartographic Association Bibliography: 1956-1972. (International Cartographic Association Ser.). 1985. pap. 39.50 (*1-85166-207-3*, Pergamon Pr) Elsevier.

Meynen, Emil. International Geographical Glossary. (ENG, FRE & GER.). 1479p. (Orig.). 1985. 350.00 (*0-8288-0957-7*, M 7600) Fr & Eur.

Meyners, Eckart. Fit for Riding: Exercises for Riders & Vaulters. Herrmann, Elke, tr. from GER. LC 92-34931. (Illus.). 164p. 1992. pap. 18.95 (*0-939481-29-4*) Half Halt Pr.

***Meynet, Roland.** Rhetorical Analysis: An Introduction to Biblical Rhetoric. Racaut, Luc, tr. LC 98-145470. (JSOT Supplement Ser.: No. 256). 392p. 1998. 85.00 (*1-85075-870-0*, Pub. by Sheffield Acad) CUP Services.

Meynier, Gil, tr. see Daniel-Rops, Henry.

Meyns, Bart. Ventricular Support with Miniature Rotary Blood Pumps: An Experimental Study. (Acta Biomedica Lovaniensia Ser.: Vol. 145). (Illus.). 119p. 1997. pap. 49.50 (*90-6186-804-1*, Pub. by Leuven Univ) Coronet Bks.

***Meyr-Harting, Ursula.** Techniques of Drawing. 48p. 1999. pap. 12.95 (*1-85444-113-2*, 1132, Pub. by Ashmolean Mus) A Schwartz & Co.

Meyr, Heinrich & Ascheid, Gerd. Synchronization in Digital Communications Vol. 1: Phase-, Frequency-Locked Loops, & Amplitude Control, Vol. 1, Phase-, Frequency-Locked Loops, and Amplit. LC 89-22445. (Series in Telecommunications). 528p. 1990. 149.00 (*0-471-50193-X*) Wiley.

Meyr, Heinrich, et al. Digital Communication Receivers: Synchronization, Channel Estimation & Signal Process, Vol. 2, Synchronization, Channel Estimation, and S. LC 97-17108. (Series in Telecommunications & Signal Processing). 864p. 1997. 105.00 (*0-471-50275-8*) Wiley.

Meyrick, Bette. Cockies Is Convenient. 160p. (C). 1981. pap. 20.00 (*0-85088-615-5*, Pub. by Gomer Pr) St Mut.
— Invasion! 70p. (YA). 1991. pap. 23.00 (*0-86383-773-5*, Pub. by Gomer Pr) St Mut.
— Invasion. (J). (gr. 4). 1991. pap. 7.95 (*0-8464-4879-3*, Gomer Pr) Beekman Pubs.

Meyrick, Gustav. Wapurgisnacht. Mitchell, Michael, tr. (Studies in Austrian Literature, Culture, & Thought. Translation Ser.). 1993. pap. 12.50 (*0-929497-71-6*) Ariadne CA.

Meyrick, Kathryn. Hazel's Healthy Halloween. LC 90-46517. 32p. (J). 1989. 13.99 (*0-85953-296-8*); pap. 6.99 (*0-85953-308-5*) Childs Play.
— The Lost Music: Gustav Mole's War on Noise. LC 91-33555. (Illus.). 32p. (J). (ps-5). 1992. 13.99 (*0-85953-304-2*); pap. 6.99 (*0-85953-327-1*) Childs Play.

Meyrick, Kathryn. The Lost Music: Gustav Mole's War on Noise. unabridged ed. (Theatre Ser.). (Illus.). (J). (ps-5). 1992. audio 6.99 (*0-85953-378-6*) Childs Play.

Meyrick, Kathryn. Musical Life of Gustav Mole. (GRE.). (J). 1990. pap. 6.99 (*0-85953-802-8*); pap. 6.99 (*0-85953-550-9*) Childs Play.
— Musical Life of Gustav Mole. LC 90-49100. 32p. (J). (ps-3). 1990. 13.99 (*0-85953-303-4*); pap. 6.99 (*0-85953-347-6*) Childs Play.

***Meyrick, Kathryn.** The Musical Life of Gustav Mole. (Child's Play Library). (J). 1999. pap. 13.99 incl. audio (*0-85953-333-6*) Childs Play.

Meyrick, Kathryn. The Musical Life of Gustav Mole. unabridged ed. (Theatre Ser.). (J). (gr. k-5). 1990. audio 6.99 (*0-85953-376-X*) Childs Play.

Meyrick, Robert. The Etchings & Engravings of Edgar Holloway. LC 96-15208. (Illus.). 114p. 1996. 86.95 (*1-85928-304-7*, Pub. by Scolar Pr) Ashgate Pub Co.
— The Etchings & Engravings of Edgar Holloway. limited ed. LC 96-15208. 114p. 1996. 253.95 (*1-85928-306-3*, Pub. by Scolar Pr) Ashgate Pub Co.

Meyrier, Chantal. Lexi-Hotel Francais-Anglais. 144p. 1993. pap. 22.95 (*0-7859-5637-9*, 2713512441) Fr & Eur.

Meyrink, Gustav. The Angel of the West Window. Mitchell, Mike, tr. from GER. & intro. by. (Studies in Austrian Literature, Culture, & Thought. Translation Ser.). 421p. 1991. pap. 17.00 (*0-929497-44-9*) Ariadne CA.
— The Angel of the West Window. Mitchell, Mike, ed. 421p. 2000. pap. write for info. (*0-946626-65-0*, Pub. by Dedalus) Hippocrene Bks.
— The Golem. Mitchell, Michael, tr. from GER. (Studies in Austrian Literature, Culture, & Thought. Translation Ser.). 262p. 1995. pap. 14.95 (*1-57241-014-0*) Ariadne CA.
— The Golem. (Illus.). 224p. 1985. reprint ed. pap. 7.95 (*0-486-25025-3*) Dover.
— The Golem. 2nd ed. Irwin, Robert, ed. Mitchell, Mike, tr. from GER. 262p. 2000. pap. write for info. (*1-873982-91-7*, Pub. by Dedalus) Hippocrene Bks.
— The Green Face. Mitchell, Mike, tr. (Studies in Austrian Literature, Culture, & Thought. Translation Ser.). 224p. 1993. pap. 14.99 (*0-929497-37-6*) Ariadne CA.
— The Opal & Other Stories. Mitchell, Michael, tr. (Studies in Austrian Literature, Culture, & Thought. Translation Ser.). 222p. 1994. pap. 14.95 (*0-929497-89-9*) Ariadne CA.
— The White Dominican. Mitchell, Michael, tr. (Studies in Austrian Literature, Culture, & Thought. Translation Ser.). 1994. pap. 12.95 (*0-929497-88-0*) Ariadne CA.

Meyrowitz, Alan L., ed. Foundations of Knowledge Acquisition: Machine Learning. (International Series in Engineering & Computer Science, VLSI, Computer Architecture, & Digital Screen Processing). 352p. (C). 1993. text 120.00 (*0-7923-9278-7*) Kluwer Academic.

Meyrowitz, Alan L., jt. ed. see Chipman, Susan.

Meyrowitz, Elliott L. The Prohibition of Nuclear Weapons: The Relevance of International Law. 350p. 1990. 75.00 (*0-941320-53-7*) Transnatl Pubs.

Meyrowitz, Joshua. No Sense of Place: The Impact of Electronic Media on Social Behavior. 431p. 1986. pap. text 15.95 (*0-19-504231-X*) OUP.

Meyrowitz, Michael R., jt. auth. see Mauro, Joseph V.

Meys, Marie-Jose, jt. auth. see Charra, Pierre-Jean.

Meyskens, Frank L., Jr. & Prasad, Kedar N., eds. Vitamins & Cancer: Human Cancer Prevention by Vitamins & Micronutrients. LC 85-27134. (Experimental Biology & Medicine Ser.: Vol. 10). 481p. 1986. 119.50 (*0-89603-094-6*) Humana.

Meyskens, Frank L., jt. ed. see Prasad, K. N.

Meyskens, Frank L., Jr., jt. ed. see Prasad, Kedar N.

Meystel, A. Autonomous Mobile Robots: Vehicle with Cognitive Control. (Series in Automation: Vol. 1). 600p. 1991. text 87.00 (*9971-5-0088-4*); pap. text 41.00 (*9971-5-0089-2*) World Scientific Pub.

***Meystel, A. M.** International Conference on Intelligent Systems & Semiotics: A Learning Perspective, Isas '97, Gaithersburg, Maryland, September 22-25. 609p. 1998. per. 54.00 (*0-16-060863-5*) USGPO.

Meystel, A. M., ed. Proceedings of the 1997 International Conference on Intelligent Systems & Semiotics: A Learning Perspective, ISAS '97. 587p. 1997. pap. write for info. (*1-886843-02-3*, PB 98122880) Ntl Inst Stndrds.

Meystel, Alex M., jt. auth. see Albus, James S.

Meystre, P., jt. ed. see Letokhov, V. S.

Meystre, Pierre. Elements of Quantum Optics. (Illus.). xiv, 484p. 1990. 44.50 (*0-387-52160-7*, 3867) Spr-Verlag.

Meystre, Pierre, ed. Nonclassical Effects in Quantum Optics. 464p. 1991. 89.95 (*0-88318-784-1*) Spr-Verlag.

Meystre, Pierre & Sargent, M., III. Elements of Quantum Optics. 3rd ed. LC 98-26050. (Illus.). 350p. 1998. pap. 59.95 (*3-540-64220-X*) Spr-Verlag.

Meystre, Pierre & Scully, Marian O., eds. Quantum Optics, Experimental Gravitation, & Measurement Theory. LC 83-4159. (NATO ASI Series B, Physics: Vol. 94). (Illus.). 712p. 1983. 145.00 (*0-306-41354-X*, Plenum Trade) Perseus Pubng.

Meystre, Pierre, jt. auth. see Sargent, Murray, III.

Meyyappan, M., ed. Computational Modeling in Semiconductor Processing. LC 94-17563. 1994. 37.00 (*0-89006-707-4*) Artech Hse.

Meyyappan, M., et al, eds. Process Control, Diagnostics & Modeling in Semiconductor Manufacturing I. LC 97-211633. (Proceedings Ser.: Vol. 97-9). 348p. 1997. 75.00 (*1-56677-136-6*) Electrochem Soc.

An Asterisk (*) at the beginning of an entry indicates that the title is appearing for the first time.

Meyyappan, M., et al. Process Control, Diagnostics & Modeling in Semiconductor Manufacturing I. LC 95-60437. (Proceedings Ser.: Vol. 95-2). 630p. 1995. pap. 62.00 (*1-56677-096-3*) Electrochem Soc.

Meyyappan, M., jt. ed. see Mathad, G. S.

Mez, Adam. Die Renaissance des Islams. iv, 492p. 1968. reprint ed. write for info. (*0-318-71533-3*) G Olms Pubs.

— The Renaissance of Islam. Bukhsl, Salahuddin K. & Margoliovth, D. S., trs. LC 70-180361. reprint ed. 45.00 (*0-404-56293-0*) AMS Pr.

Mez, Carl. Lauraceae Americaneae Monographice Descrips. 1963. reprint ed. 64.00 (*3-7682-0171-6*) Lubrecht & Cramer.

***Meza-Compean, Juan Antonio.** Revolution Reborn. 95p. 1998. pap. 10.00 (*1-877603-53-8*) Pecan Grove.

Meza, Fernando A., compiled by. Percussion Discography: An International Compilation of Solo & Chamber Percussion Music, 36. LC 89-28647. (Discographies Ser.: No. 36). 117p. 1990. lib. bdg. 49.95 (*0-313-26867-3*, MPQ/, Greenwood Pr) Greenwood.

Meza, Isaura. Maquinas Vivientes. (Ciencia para Todos Ser.). (SPA.). pap. 6.99 (*968-16-4988-5*, Pub. by Fondo) Continental Bk.

Meza, L. M. De La, see De la Meza, L. M., ed.

Mezaki, R. & Inoue, H., eds. Rate Equations of Solid-Catalyzed Reactions. 420p. 1991. text 140.00 (*0-86008-481-7*, Pub. by U of Tokyo) Col U Pr.

***Mezaki, Reiji, et al.** Engineering Data on Mixing. LC 99-55646. 1999. write for info. (*0-444-82802-8*) Elsevier.

Mezard, M., et al. Spin Glass Theory & Beyond. (Lecture Notes in Physics Ser.: Vol. 9). 476p. 1987. text 99.00 (*9971-5-0115-5*); pap. text 55.00 (*9971-5-0116-3*) World Scientific Pub.

Mezei, Balazs M. World & Life-World: Aspects of the Philosophy of Edmund Husserl. LC 95-4145. (European University Studies: Ser. 20, Vol.457). VIII, 199p. 1995. pap. 37.95 (*3-631-48344-9*) P Lang Pubng.

Mezei, Kathy, ed. Ambiguous Discourse: Feminist Narratology & British Women Writers. LC 95-26584. 288p. (C). 1996. pap. 18.95 (*0-8078-4599-X*) U of NC Pr.

— Ambiguous Discourse: Feminist Narratology & British Women Writers. LC 95-26584. 288p. (C). (gr. 13). 1996. lib. bdg. 49.95 (*0-8078-2290-6*) U of NC Pr.

Mezek, Karen & Leimert, Karen M. Goodnight Blessings. LC 93-41583. (J). (ps-2). 1994. 10.99 (*0-8499-1134-6*) Word Pub.

Mezel, Kathy, jt. ed. see Gerson, Carole.

Mezereny, Eugene. Cross Country Skiing in Southern California: A Skiing Guide to the Southern California Area. LC 93-38527. (Illus.). 160p. 1993. pap. 14.00 (*1-879415-08-9*) Mtn n Air Bks.

Mezerik, Avrahm G., jt. ed. see Bliven, Bruce, Jr.

***Mezey, Gillian C. & King, Michael, eds.** Male Victims of Sexual Assault. 2nd ed. 176p. 2000. text 39.95 (*0-19-262932-8*) OUP.

Mezey, L., jt. auth. see Dezsenyi-Szemzo, P.

Mezey, Mathy D., et al, eds. Nursing Homes & Nursing Care: Lessons from the Teaching Nursing Homes. 176p. 1988. 23.95 (*0-8261-6210-X*) Springer Pub.

Mezey, Mathy D. & McGivern, Diane O., eds. Nurses, Nurse Practitioners: Evolution to Advanced Practice. LC 93-13719. 400p. 1993. 32.95 (*0-8261-7770-0*) Springer Pub.

Mezey, Mathy D. & O'Neill-McGivern, Diane. Nurses, Nurse Practitioners: Evolution to Advanced Practice. 2nd ed. LC 98-26293. (Series on Advanced Practice Nursing). 1998. 39.95 (*0-8261-7771-9*) Springer Pub.

Mezey, Mathy D., et al. Health Assessment of the Older Individual, Vol. 2. 2nd rev. ed. LC 92-49574. (Geriatric Nursing Ser.). 256p. 1993. 29.95 (*0-8261-2902-1*) Springer Pub.

Mezey, Mathy D., jt. auth. see Gould, David A.

Mezey, Michael L., jt. ed. see Olson, David M.

Mezey, P. G., jt. ed. see Carbo-Dorca, Ramon.

Mezey, Paul G. Shape in Chemistry: An Introduction to Molecular Shape & Topology. 224p. 1993. 99.95 (*0-471-18741-0*) Wiley.

Mezey, Paul G. Shape in Chemistry: An Introduction to Molecular Shape & Topology. LC 93-15622. 1993. 75.00 (*0-89573-727-2*, Wiley-VCH) Wiley.

Mezey, Paul G., ed. New Developments in Molecular Chirality. 300p. (C). 1991. text 155.50 (*0-7923-1021-7*) Kluwer Academic.

Mezey, Paul G., jt. auth. see Carbo-Dorca, R.

Mezey, Phiz. Multi-Image Design & Production. 176p. 1988. pap. text 52.95 (*0-240-51740-7*, Focal) Buttrwrth-Heinemann.

Mezey, Robert, jt. ed. see Berg, Stephen.

Mezey, Robert, ed. see Coulette, Henri.

Mezey, Robert, ed. & intro. see Hardy, Thomas.

Mezey, Susan G. Children in Court: Public Policymaking & Federal Court Decisions. LC 95-21045. 206p. (C). 1996. text 59.50 (*0-7914-2961-X*); pap. text 19.95 (*0-7914-2962-8*) State U NY Pr.

— No Longer Disabled: The Federal Courts & the Politics of Social Security Disability, 7. LC 87-31783. (Studies in Social Welfare Policies & Programs: No. 7). 208p. 1988. 55.00 (*0-313-25424-9*, MNL/, Greenwood Pr) Greenwood.

***Mezey, Susan Gluck.** Pitiful Plaintiffs: Child Welfare Litigation & the Federal Courts. LC 99-50679. 288p. 2000. pap. 19.95 (*0-8229-5717-5*); text 45.00 (*0-8229-4116-3*) U of Pittsburgh Pr.

Mezger, Gabi. The Jesse Owens Story. LC 98-194404. (Cover-to-Cover Chapter Bks.). 55 p. 1997. write for info. (*0-7807-6690-3*) Perfection Learn.

Mezger, Ann S., ed. see Pluto, Terry.

Mezger, Dorothea. Copper in the World Economy. LC 79-3883. 282p. 1980. 28.00 (*0-85345-544-9*, Pub. by Monthly Rev) NYU Pr.

Mezger, Uwe. Biomonitoring Mit Epilithischen und Epiphytischen Flechten in Einem Belastungsgebiet (Berlin) Ein Verfahrensvergleich. (Bibliotheca Lichenologica: No. 63). 164p. 1996. 53.10 (*3-443-58042-4*, Pub. by Gebruder Borntraeger) Balogh.

Mezhenina, E. P. Dictionary of Eponymic Names of Diseases & Syndromes. 182p. 1982. 19.95 (*0-8288-1858-4*, M15443) Fr & Eur.

Mezhenkov, V. & Skelley, E., eds. Soviet Scene, 1988: A Selection of Articles & Interviews from the Soviet Press. (C). 1987. pap. 45.00 (*0-569-09093-8*, Pub. by Collets) St Mut.

Mezhikovskii, Semjon M. Physico-Chemical Principles for Processing of Oligomeric Blends. (Polymer Science & Engineering Monographs, a State-of-the-Art Tutorial Ser.: Vol. 4). 224p. 1998. text 90.00 (*90-5699-661-4*) Gordon & Breach.

Mezias, Stephen J. & Chung, Seungwha. Due Process & Participation at the FASB: A Study of the Comment Period. LC 89-85780. 34p. 1989. pap. 20.00 (*0-910586-77-2*, 085-89) Finan Exec.

Mezias, Stephen J. & Scarselletta, Mario. Agenda-Setting at the FASB. LC 91-73315. 42p. (Orig.). 1994. pap. 20.00 (*0-910586-84-5*) Finan Exec.

Mezick, Dan. Visual Basic 5 Bootcamp: Everything You Need to Pass Microsoft's Visual Basic 5 Certification. LC 97-41798. (Illus.). 640p. 1997. 54.95 incl. cd-rom (*0-07-913671-0*) Osborne-McGraw.

***Mezick, Dan & Hillier, Scot.** MTS Programming with Visual Basic. LC 98-86702. (Illus.). 488p. 1999. pap. 29.99 incl. cd-rom (*0-672-31425-8*) Sams.

Mezick, Dan, et al. Visual Basic 6 (Bootcamp) Certification Exam Guide. 788p. 1999. 59.99 incl. cd-rom (*0-07-134534-5*) McGraw.

Mezieres, Philippe De, see De Mezieres, Philippe.

Mezines, Basil J. Trade Associations & the Antitrust Laws. 2nd ed. (Corporate Practice Ser.: No. 32). 1993. 95.00 (*1-55871-298-4*) BNA.

Mezines, Basil J., et al. Administrative Law, 6 vols. 1977. ring bd. 1200.00 incl. cd-rom (*0-8205-1301-6*) Bender.

Mezini, Mira. Variational Object-Oriented Programming Beyond Classes & Inheritance. LC 98-42589. (Kluwer International Series in Engineering & Computer Science). 1998. 129.95 (*0-7923-8313-3*) Kluwer Academic.

***Mezirow, Jack.** Learning as Transformation: Critical Perspectives on a Theory in Progress. LC 00-9158. (Higher & Adult Education Ser.). 2000. 38.95 (*0-7879-4845-4*) Jossey-Bass.

— Transformative Dimensions of Adult Learning. LC 90-24155. (Higher & Adult Education Ser.). 269p. 1998. text 34.45 (*1-55542-339-6*) Jossey-Bass.

Mezirow, Jack, et al. Fostering Critical Reflection in Adulthood: A Guide to Transformative & Emancipatory Learning. LC 89-39667. (Higher & Adult Education - Adult & Continuing Education Ser.). 416p. 1990. text 38.95 (*1-55542-207-1*) Jossey-Bass.

— Last Gamble on Education. 206p. 1988. 10.95 (*0-318-36404-2*, AEA-1) A A A C E.

— Last Gamble on Education: Dynamics of Adult Basic Education - New Dimensions in Program Analysis. 206p. 1975. 13.00 (*0-88379-010-6*) A A A C E.

Mezo, Kathryn, jt. auth. see Mezo, Merle.

Mezo, Merle & Mezo, Kathryn. Inventors Patent Information Guide. LC 87-82938. 103p. 1987. spiral bd., vinyl bd. 24.95 (*0-9619923-0-1*) Inventrs Motiv Enterp.

Mezo, Richard E. A Study of B. Traven's Fiction: The Journey to Solipaz. LC 92-46178. 212p. 1993. text 89.95 (*0-7734-9838-9*) E Mellen.

Mezrich, Ben. Fertile Ground. 2000. mass mkt. 6.99 (*0-06-109798-5*) HarpC.

— Fertile Ground: A Novel. LC 99-22560. (Illus.). 288p. 1999. 24.00 (*0-06-018752-2*) HarpC.

***Mezrich, Ben.** Skin: The X-Files. large type ed. LC 99-43526. (X-Files Ser.). 1999. 25.95 (*0-7838-8778-7*, G K Hall & Co) Mac Lib Ref.

Mezrich, Ben. Threshold. 352p. 1997. mass mkt. 6.99 (*0-446-60521-2*, Pub. by Warner Bks) Little.

— X-Files: Skin. abr. ed. LC 98-49471. 272p. 1999. 23.95 (*0-06-105041-5*) HarpC.

Mezu, Rose U. Songs of the Hearth. 64p. (Orig.). 1994. 35.00 (*0-87831-065-7*); pap. 20.00 (*0-87831-066-5*) Blck Acad Pr.

— Women in Chains: Abandonment in Love Relationships in the Fiction of Selected West African Writers. 252p. (Orig.). (C). 1994. text 50.00 (*0-87831-169-6*); pap. text 25.00 (*0-87831-170-X*) Blck Acad Pr.

Mezu, S. Okechukwu. Leopold Sedar Senghor et la Defense et Illustration de la Civilisation Noire. 19.50 (*0-685-36567-0*) Fr & Eur.

Mezvinsky, Norton, jt. auth. see Shahak, Israel.

Mezzacappa, Anthony. Stellar Evolution, Stellar Explosions & Galactic Chemical Evolution: Proceedings of the 2nd Oak Ridge Symposium on Atomic & Nuclear Astrophysics, Oak Ridge, Tennessee, 2-6 December 1997. LC 98-38895. 737p. 1998. 310.00 (*0-7503-0555-X*) IOP Pub.

Mezzacappa, K. The Link Between HR & Customer Bonding. (Financial Times Management Briefings Ser.). 1997. pap. 94.50 (*0-273-63256-6*, Pub. by F T P-H) Trans-Atl Phila.

Mezzatesta, Michael P. Henri Matisse-Sculptor-Painter: A Formal Analysis of Selected Works. LC 84-80456. (Illus.). 150p. 1984. 38.00 (*0-912804-16-5*); pap. 19.95 (*0-912804-15-7*) Kimbell Art.

***Mezzatesta, Philip & DeFazio, Christine, texts.** Houdon. (Illus.). 85p. 1998. 45.00 (*1-58821-043-X*) Salander OReilly.

Mezzetti, M., et al, eds. Large Scale Structure & Motions in the Universe. (C). 1988. text 237.50 (*0-7923-0082-3*) Kluwer Academic.

Mezzich, J. E. & Schmolke, M., eds. Comprehensive Diagnosis, Ethics & Quality of Life. (Psychopathology Ser.: Vol. 32, No. 3 (1999)). (Illus.). 56p. 1999. pap. 25.25 (*3-8055-6839-8*) S Karger.

Mezzich, Juan E., ed. Clinical Care & Information Systems in Psychiatry. LC 86-1193. (Clinical Insights Ser.). 145p. reprint ed. pap. 45.00 (*0-8357-7851-7*, 203622800002) Bks Demand.

Mezzich, Juan E., et al, eds. Culture & Psychiatric Diagnosis: A DSM-IV Perspective. 432p. 1996. text 57.00 (*0-88048-553-1*, 8553) Am Psychiatric.

— Psychiatric Diagnosis: A World Perspective. LC 93-46006. 1994. 125.00 (*0-387-94221-1*) Spr-Verlag.

Mezzich, Juan E., et al, eds. Psychiatric Epidemiology: Assessment Concepts & Methods. LC 93-13621. (Series in Psychiatry & Neuroscience). 560p. (C). 1994. text 86.00 (*0-8018-4615-3*) Johns Hopkins.

Mezzich, Juan E. & Von Cranach, Michael, eds. International Classification in Psychiatry: Unity & Diversity. (Illus.). 412p. 1988. text 99.95 (*0-521-32754-7*) Cambridge U Pr.

Mezzich, Juan E. & Zimmer, Ben A. Emergency Psychiatry. LC 88-13599. 475p. 1990. 67.50 (*0-8236-1647-9*) Intl Univs Pr.

Mezzo & Pirus. Armed & Dangerous. 48p. 1995. pap. 9.95 (*0-87816-361-1*) Kitchen Sink.

Mezzullo, Louis A. An Estate Planner's Guide to Family Limited Partnerships & Limited Liability Companies. LC 97-47044. 1997. write for info. (*1-57073-496-8*) Amer Bar Assn.

***Mezzullo, Louis A.** An Estate Planner's Guide to Life Insurance. LC 00-25274. 2000. write for info. (*1-57073-823-8*) Amer Bar Assn.

Mezzullo, Louis A. An Estate Planner's Guide to Qualified Retirement Benefits. 2nd ed. LC 97-47020. 1997. 89.95 (*1-57073-495-X*) Amer Bar Assn.

Mezzullo, Louis A. & Woolpert, Mark. Advising the Elderly Client, 3 vols., Set. LC 92-72717. 1992. ring bd. 395.00 (*0-685-59858-6*) West Group.

MFOA Committee Staff. Public Employee Retirement Administration. 134p. 1977. 15.00 (*0-686-84367-3*) Municipal.

Mfume, Kweisi. No Free Ride. 1996. 24.00 (*0-614-95690-0*) Ballantine Pub Grp.

— No Free Ride. LC 97-92949. 1997. pap. 12.00 (*0-345-41364-4*) Ballantine Pub Grp.

Mgalobelov, Yu B., jt. auth. see Landau, Yu A.

Mgaloblishvili, Tamila, ed. Ancient Christianity in the Caucasus. 288p. 1997. 65.00 (*0-7007-0633-X*, Pub. by Curzon Pr Ltd) Paul & Co Pubs.

M'Gillivray, Duncan. The Fur Trade Journal of Duncan M'Gillivray, 1794-1795. 200p. 1989. 24.95 (*0-87770-470-8*) Ye Galleon.

M'Gonigle, R. Michael, jt. auth. see Gale, Fred P.

M'Gowan, George, tr. see Von Meyer, Ernst.

M.H. Publications Staff. The Comedie of Errors. 138p. 1990. 95.00 (*1-872680-13-5*, Pub. by M H Pubns) St Mut.

— The Life & Death of King Richard II. 1990. 95.00 (*1-872680-16-X*, Pub. by M H Pubns) St Mut.

— The Life of Henry the Fifth. 242p. 1990. 95.00 (*1-872680-07-0*, Pub. by M H Pubns) St Mut.

— Measure for Measure. 1990. 95.00 (*1-872680-15-1*, Pub. by M H Pubns) St Mut.

— Much Ado about Nothing. 196p. 1990. 175.00 (*1-872680-04-6*, Pub. by M H Pubns) St Mut.

— The Tragedie of Anthonie, & Cleopatra. 300p. 1990. 175.00 (*1-872680-06-2*, Pub. by M H Pubns) St Mut.

— The Tragedie of Hamlet, Prince of Denmarke. 272p. 1990. 175.00 (*1-872680-01-1*, Pub. by M H Pubns) St Mut.

— The Tragedie of Julius Caesar. 280p. 1990. 175.00 (*1-872680-09-7*, Pub. by M H Pubns) St Mut.

— The Tragedie of King Lear. 225p. 1990. 175.00 (*1-872680-10-0*, Pub. by M H Pubns) St Mut.

— The Tragedie of Romeo & Juliet. 238p. 1990. 125.00 (*1-872680-05-4*, Pub. by M H Pubns) St Mut.

— The Tragedie of Troylus & Cressida. 1990. 95.00 (*1-872680-17-8*, Pub. by M H Pubns) St Mut.

M.H. Publications Staff, ed. see Shakespeare, William.

***Mhalkhonen, Eino.** Forest Condition in a Changing Environment: The Finnish Case. LC 00-28155. (Forestry Sciences Ser.). 2000. write for info. (*0-7923-6228-4*) Kluwer Academic.

Mhaskar, H. N. Weighted Polynomial Approximation. (Series on Decompositions & Approximation). 300p. 1997. text 74.00 (*981-02-1312-3*) World Scientific Pub.

Mheara, Roisin N. In Search of Irish Saints. LC 94-178997. (Illus.). 128p. 1994. pap. 15.00 (*1-85182-138-4*, Pub. by Four Cts Pr) Intl Spec Bk.

Mhina, A. K. & Munishi, G. K. Understanding Africa'a Food Problems: Social Policy Perspectives. (African Social Challenges Ser.: No. 1). 259p. 1991. lib. bdg. 60.00 (*0-905450-39-6*, Pub. by H Zell Pubs) Seven Hills Bk.

Mhire, Herman, ed. Rhythms du Monde Francophone: Festival International de Louisiano. (Illus.). 120p. (Orig.). 1996. 50.00 (*0-9651622-0-6*); pap. 30.00 (*0-614-14976-2*) Festival Intl.

Mhire, Herman, et al. Robert Russett: A Retrospective Survey. (Illus.). 84p. (Orig.). 1989. pap. 20.00 (*0-936819-05-7*) USL Art Museum.

Mhire, Herman, ed. see Grootkerk, Paul.

Mhlanga, Bonny. The Colour of English Justice: A Multivariate Analysis. LC 96-79369. 224p. 1997. text 59.95 (*1-85972-495-7*, Pub. by Avebry) Ashgate Pub Co.

Mhlanga, Constance C., jt. ed. see Obudho, Robert A.

Mhley, Rita R. Woodmont Country Club: A Proud Tradition for the Nation's Capital. LC 88-50441. (Illus.). 168p. 1988. 30.00 (*0-9620503-0-X*) Woodmont Cntry Club.

Mhller, Claus. Analysis of Spherical Symmetries in Euclidean Spaces, Vol. 129. Marsden, J. E. et al, eds. LC 97-14536. (Applied Mathematical Sciences Ser.: No. 129). (Illus.). 300p. 1997. 59.95 (*0-387-94949-6*) Spr-Verlag.

Mhlophe, Gcina, et al. Have You Seen Zandile? LC 90-33908. 77p. (Orig.). (C). 1990. pap. 9.95 (*0-435-08600-6*, 08600) Heinemann.

Mho Works Staff. Cricket in the Telephone (at Sunset) Poems from the Fessenden Review. LC 98-37182. 75p. 1998. 100.00 (*0-917320-14-X*) Mho & Mho.

— A Cricket in the Telephone (At Sunset) Poetry from the Fessenden Review. Lark, Lolita, ed. LC 98-37182. 64p. 1999. pap. 10.00 (*0-917320-13-1*) Mho & Mho.

Mhohwald, H., jt. auth. see Lvov, Yurij.

Mhone, Buy C. The Political Economy of a Dual Labor Market in Africa: The Copper Industry & Dependency in Zambia, 1929-1969. LC 80-70184. (Illus.). 256p. 1982. 34.50 (*0-8386-3063-4*) Fairleigh Dickinson.

Mhonnich, Uwe, jt. auth. see Kolb, Hans-Peter.

MHS Library & Archives Staff. Genealogical Resources of the Minnesota Historical Society: A Guide. 2nd ed. LC 89-3305. (Illus.). xii, 63p. 1993. pap. 6.95 (*0-87351-240-5*) Minn Hist.

MHS Staff. Split Rock Lighthouse. rev. ed. LC 92-8341. (Minnesota Historic Sites Pamphlet Ser.: No. 15). Orig. Title: Split Rock. (Illus.). 32p. 1993. pap. 7.50 (*0-87351-275-8*) Minn Hist.

Mhuhlhoff, Claudia, jt. auth. see Galli, Mirko.

Mhuller-Graff, Peter C., et al. Poland & the European Union: Between Association & Membership. LC 97-178367. (ECSA Ser.). 320p. 1997. write for info. (*3-7890-4652-3*) Nomos Verlags.

Mhuller-Isberner, Rhudiger, jt. auth. see Hodgins, Sheilagh.

Mhuller, Manfred W., jt. auth. see International Dortmund Meeting Staff.

Mhuller, P., jt. auth. see Van Regenmortel, M. H. V.

***Mhuller, Silvia M. & Paul, Wolfgang J.** Computer Architecture: Complexity & Correctness. LC 00-33827. (Illus.). 2000. write for info. (*3-540-67481-0*) Spr-Verlag.

Mhyre, Noel L. Testing for Electrical Safety in Hospitals. (Illus.). 27p. 1975. 2.00 (*0-917054-03-2*) Med Communications.

Mi, Bill, jt. auth. see Geanuracos, John.

Mi, Hung-Fu. The Systematic Classic of Acupuncture, MoxiBustion. LC 91-72854. 800p. 1994. 89.95 (*0-936185-29-5*) Blue Poppy Pr.

Mi Kim, Myung. Under Flag. 2nd ed. LC 91-23725. (Illus.). 46p. 1998. reprint ed. pap. 9.00 (*0-932716-49-0*) Kelsey St Pr.

Mi-La-Ras-Pa Staff. The Hundred Thousand Songs of Milarepa. LC 98-43692. 1999. 55.00 (*1-57062-476-3*) Random Hse Chldrns.

Mi Mi Khaing, Daw. Burmese Family. LC 76-6607. (Illus.). reprint ed. 32.50 (*0-404-15291-0*) AMS Pr.

Mi-pham, Lama. Calm & Clear. LC 73-79058. (Tibetan Translation Ser.: Vol. 1). (Illus.). 127p. 1973. pap. 12.95 (*0-913546-02-X*) Dharma Pub.

MI Technoligies Staff. Computer Monitor Troubleshooting Tips, 1999 Ed. 299p. 1999. pap. text 49.95 incl. cd-rom (*0-7906-1179-1*) Prompt Publns.

Mi, Y. Three-Dimensional Analysis of Crack Growth. LC 95-71358. (Topics in Engineering Ser.: Vol. 28). 204p. 1996. text 128.00 (*1-56252-355-4*, 4451) Computational Mech MA.

Mialaret, Gaston. Lexicon of Education: Lexique d'Education. (FRE.). 168p. 1981. pap. 12.95 (*0-8288-1389-2*, M14201) Fr & Eur.

— Vocabulaire de L'Education: Vocabulary of Education. (FRE.). 488p. 1979. 125.00 (*0-8288-4842-4*, M6410) Fr & Eur.

Mialaret, Gerald. Dancing with Dragons. Zysk, Veronica, ed. 1996. pap. 19.95 (*1-885477-30-9*) Fut Horizons.

Miall, Andrew D. Analysis of Fluvial Depositional Systems. LC TN0870.A45. (Education Course Note Ser.: Vol. 20). (Illus.). 79p. reprint ed. pap. 30.00 (*0-608-08731-9*, 206937000004) Bks Demand.

— The Geology of Fluvial Deposits: Sedimentary Facies, Basin Analysis & Petroleum Geology. LC 96-31798. (Illus.). 592p. 1996. 79.00 (*3-540-59186-9*) Spr-Verlag.

— The Geology of Sequence Stratigraphy. LC 98-36659. 433p. 1996. 49.50 (*3-540-59348-9*) Spr-Verlag.

— The Geology of Stratigraphic Sequences. LC 96-26786. 1996. write for info. (*0-387-59348-9*) Spr-Verlag.

— Principles of Sedimentary Basin Analysis. (Illus.). 550p. 1985. 48.50 (*0-387-90941-9*) Spr-Verlag.

— Principles of Sedimentary Basin Analysis. 2nd ed. (Illus.). 424p. 1997. 74.95 (*0-387-97119-X*) Spr-Verlag.

***Miall, Andrew D.** Principles of Sedimentary Basin Analysis. 3rd enl. ed. LC 99-36198. (Illus.). xv, 672p. 1999. 79.95 (*3-540-65790-8*) Spr-Verlag.

Miall, Andrew D., et al. Cretaceous & Tertiary Sediments of Eclipse Trough, Bylot Island Area, Arctic Canada & Their Regional Setting. LC 80-509459. (Geological Survey; 79-23 Ser.). (ENG & FRE.). 20 p. 1980. write for info. (*0-660-10582-9*, Pub. by Can7 Govern Pub) Intl Spec Bk.

***Miall, Antony & Milsted, David.** The Xenophobe's Guide to the English. (Xenophobe's Guides Ser.). 64p. 1999. pap. 5.95 (*1-902825-26-8*) Oval Bks.

Miall, B., tr. see Garcia-Calderon, F.

Miall, Bernard, jt. auth. see D'Ollone, Vicomte.

Miall, Bernard, tr. see Bernstein, Eduard.

Miall, Bernard, tr. see Cabaton, Antoine.

Miall, Bernard, tr. see Fabre, Jean H.

Miall, Bernard, tr. see Hamburger, Max.

M

An Asterisk (*) at the beginning of an entry indicates that the title is appearing for the first time.

Miall, Bernard, tr. see Rolland, Romain.

Miall, Bernard, tr. see Salvatorelli, Luigi.

***Miall, David S., ed.** Empirical Studies of Literature: Selected Papers from IGEL '98. A Special Issue of Discourse Processes. 86p. 1999. pap. 20.00 (0-8058-9782-8) L Erlbaum Assocs.

Miall, David S., ed. Humanities & the Computer: New Directions. 232p. 1990. text 55.00 (0-19-824244-1) OUP.

Miall, Hugh, ed. Redefining Europe: New Patterns of Conflict & Cooperation. LC 94-15091. 1994. pap. 22.95 (1-85567-258-8) Bks Intl VA.

— Redefining Europe: New Patterns of Conflict & Cooperation. LC 94-15091. 320p. 1994. 55.00 (1-85567-257-X) Bks Intl VA.

Miall, Hugh, et al. Contemporary Conflict Resolution: The Prevention, Management & Transformation of Deadly Conflict. LC 98-52193. 256p. 1999. 59.95 (0-7456-2034-5); pap. 24.95 (0-7456-2035-3) Blackwell Pubs.

Miall, Laurence M., jt. auth. see Miall, Stephen.

Miall, Stephen & Miall, Laurence M. Chemistry, Matter, & Life. LC 70-39099. (Essay Index Reprint Ser.). 1977. reprint ed. 23.95 (0-8369-2703-6) Ayer.

Miamee, A. G. Nonstationary Stochastic Processes & Their Applications: Proceedings of the Workshop. 296p. 1992. text 95.00 (981-02-1076-0) World Scientific Pub.

M

Miami Dade Community College Staff. Social Environmental Anthology. 2nd ed. 482p. 1998. pap. text 40.00 (0-536-01339-X) Pearson Custom.

***Miami Dolphins.** Miami Dolphins. CWC Sports Inc., ed. (NFL Team Yearbooks Ser.). (J). (gr. 1-12). 1998. pap. 9.99 (1-891613-13-8) Everett Sports.

Miami Hearld Staff. The Miami Herald 1995 South Florida Outdoor Guide. Millman, Ken, ed. (Illus.). 262p. 1994. pap. 12.95 (0-8362-8080-6) Andrews & McMeel.

Miami Herald Staff. Florida's Best Golf Courses: A Guide to the Top-Ranked Courses You Can Play. LC 95-37350. 202p. 1995. pap. 9.95 (0-8362-0568-5) Andrews & McMeel.

— Miami: In Our Own Words. Ancrum, Nancy & Bard, Richard, eds. (Illus.). 212p. 1995. pap. 15.95 (0-8362-0572-3) Andrews & McMeel.

— Una Vida de Novela: Eva Peron, Marilyn Monroe, Grace Kelly. 160p. 1995. pap. 7.95 (0-8362-7036-3) Andrews & McMeel.

Miami Herald Staff & El Nuevo Herald Staff, eds. Hurricanes: How to Prepare & Recover. (Illus.). 128p. (Orig.). 1993. pap. 9.95 (0-8362-1718-7) Andrews & McMeel.

Miami Herald Staff & Gressette, Felicia. The Miami Herald Guide to South Florida's Best Restaurants. LC 95-44801. 176p. 1995. pap. 7.95 (0-8362-0785-8) Andrews & McMeel.

Miami Herald Staff & Owen, Allison. The Papal Visit: John Paul II in Miami. (SPA., Illus.). 112p. (Orig.). 1987. pap. 18.95 (0-942084-67-5) SeaSide Pub.

Miami Herald Staff, et al. The Papal Visit: John Paul II in Miami. (Illus.). 112p. (Orig.). 1987. pap. 18.95 (0-942084-66-7) SeaSide Pub.

Miami University, Hispanic American Institute Staf. University of Miami Hispanic-American Studies. McNicoll, R. E. & Owre, J. R., eds. LC 70-117825. (Essay Index Reprint Ser.). 1977. 23.95 (0-8369-1997-1) Ayer.

Miami Valley Career Tech Ctr Staff & Price, Sharon M. Tuning in to My Child's Future: A Roadmap for Career Exploration & Success-3 Book Program. (Illus.). 135p. (J). (gr. 6-10). 1998. pap. 19.95 (0-9660694-4-7) PrepWorks Pub.

Mian, M. A. Petroleum Engineering Handbook for the Practicing Engineer. 627p. 1992. 99.95 (0-87814-370-X, P4445) PennWell Bks.

— Petroleum Engineering Handbook for the Practicing Engineer, Vol. 2. 688p. 1992. 109.95 (0-87814-379-3, P4510) PennWell Bks.

Mian, Q. Javed & Lerrick, Alison. Saudi Business & Labor Law: Its Interpretation & Application. 2nd ed. 450p. 1987. lib. bdg. 407.50 (0-86010-573-3) G & T Inc.

Mianbe Betoudji, Denis. Le Dieu Supreme et le Dieu Des Patriarches (Genesis 14, 18-20) (Religionswissenschaftliche Texte und Studien: No. 1). (FRE.). iv, 290p. 1986. write for info. (3-487-07760-4) G Olms Pubs.

***Miannay, D. P.** Advances in Mechanical Behaviour, Plasticity & Damage: Proceedings of Euromat 2000. 2000. 495.00 (0-08-042815-0, Pergamon Pr) Elsevier.

Miannay, D. P. Fracture Mechanics. Ling, F. F., ed. LC 97-10651. (Mechanical Engineering Ser.). (Illus.). 288p. 1997. 69.95 (0-387-98242-6) Spr-Verlag.

Miano, John. C++ Builder: How to... LC 97-13749. 848p. 1997. 49.99 (1-57169-109-X) Sams.

***Miano, John.** Compressed Image File Formats: JPEG, PNG, GIF, XBM, BMP. LC 99-15179. 288p. (C). 1999. pap. text 44.95 (0-201-60443-4) Addison-Wesley.

***Miano, Lou.** Russ Columbo: The Amazing Life & Mysterious Death of a Hollywood Singer. (Illus.). 224p. 2000. pap. 19.95 (0-9677970-1-2) Silver Tone.

***Miano, Mark.** Dead of Summer. LC 98-67477. 224p. 1999. text 20.00 (1-57566-404-6) Kensgtn Pub Corp.

Miano, Mark. Flesh & Stone. LC 96-77849. 288p. 1997. 18.95 (1-57566-128-4, Knsington) Kensgtn Pub Corp.

— Flesh & Stone: A Michael Carpo Mystery. 288p. 1998. pap. 5.99 (1-57566-273-6) Kensgtn Pub Corp.

***Miano, Mark.** Street Where. (Michael Carpo Mystery Ser.). 1999. mass mkt. 5.99 (1-57566-407-0, Knsington) Kensgtn Pub Corp.

Miano, Mark. The Street Where She Lived: A Michael Carpo Mystery. LC 97-73470. 320p. 1998. 20.00 (1-57566-270-1, Knsington) Kensgtn Pub Corp.

Miano, T. M., ed. see Sixth International Meeting of the International H.

Mianogue, Ethel. Irish Country Cooking. 1995. 6.98 (0-7858-0504-4) Bk Sales Inc.

Mianyu, Q. & Changlong, Y., eds. China's Sports Medicine. (Medicine & Sport Science Ser.: Vol. 28). (Illus.). viii, 120p. 1989. 86.25 (3-8055-4806-0) S Karger.

Miao, Gong, et al, eds. China Coal Industry Yearbook: Nineteen Eighty-Three. Zunfang, Chen et al, trs. from CHI. (China Coal Industry Yearbooks Ser.). (Illus.). 304p. 1984. text 50.00 (0-918062-61-6, Pub. by Economic Info) Random House.

— China Coal Industry Yearbook Nineteen Eighty-Two. (China Coal Industry Yearbooks Ser.). (Illus.). 336p. 1983. text 40.00 (0-918062-60-8, Pub. by Economic Info) Random House.

***Miao, Jiawen.** Simple Fitness Exercises: Traditional Chinese Movements for Health & Rejuvenation. LC 00-30650. 2000. 17.95 (1-56718-495-2) Llewellyn Pubns.

— The Tao of Health & Fitness. (Illus.). 136p. 2000. pap. 12.95 (1-892515-19-9, Pub. by Multi-Media Commns) Unique Pubns.

Miarka, Judy M. Classy Cat - Astrological Annotated Categorized Catalogue. 140p. 1993. 11.00 (0-86690-395-X, M3130-014) Am Fed Astrologers.

***Miarka, Tobias.** Financial Intermediation & Deregulation: A Critical Analysis of Japanese Bank-Firm Relationships. LC 00-41695. (Contributions to Economics Ser.). 2000. pap. write for info. (3-7908-1307-9) Physica-Verlag.

Miasek, Meryl A., ed. see Miller, Heather S.

Miasek, Meryl A., ed. see Schofield, Eileen.

Miaskowski, Christine. Clinical Manual for Pain Management. 1999. pap. text 29.95 (0-7216-6073-8, W B Saunders Co) Harcrt Hlth Sci Grp.

— Oncology Nursing: An Essential for Patient Care. Cullen, Barbara N., ed. (Illus.). 329p. 1996. pap. text 32.00 (0-7216-6041-X, W B Saunders Co) Harcrt Hlth Sci Grp.

— Pain Management: Principles. 1999. text 65.00 (0-7216-6040-1, W B Saunders Co) Harcrt Hlth Sci Grp.

Miaskowski, Christine, ed. Oncology Nursing. LC 94-32089. (Plans of Care for Specialty Practice Ser.). 260p. (C). 1995. pap. 45.95 (0-8273-6118-1) Delmar.

Miaskowski, Christine & Buschsel, Patricia. Oncology Nursing: Assessment & Clinical Care. (Illus.). 1700p. 1999. text 95.00 (0-8151-6990-6, 27463) Mosby Inc.

Miaskowski, Christine, et al. The Year Book of Oncology Nursing, 1994. 320p. 1994. 39.95 (0-8151-6140-9) Mosby Inc.

— The Year Book of Oncology Nursing, 1995. 320p. 1995. 39.95 (0-8151-6141-7) Mosby Inc.

— The Year Book of Oncology Nursing, 1996. 320p. 1996. 39.95 (0-8151-6142-5) Mosby Inc.

Miasnikov, V. Ch'ing Empire & the Russian State in the 17th Century. 342p. (C). 1985. 80.00 (0-7855-3890-9) St Mut.

Miatello, A. International Nuclear Agreements: A Quadra-Lingual Glossary. (ENG, FRE, GER & ITA.). 391p. 1988. 110.00 (0-8288-7898-6) Fr & Eur.

***Miau, Jiun-Jih & Holdaway, Richard.** Reducing the Cost of Spacecraft Ground Systems & Operations. LC 99-86806. 460p. 2000. 195.00 (0-7923-6174-1) Kluwer Academic.

Miazek, Bonifacy, ed. Adam Mickiewicz - Leben und Werk. (Illus.). 414p. 1998. pap. 56.95 (3-631-32063-9) P Lang Pubng.

Miazga, Donna. The Reintegration Resource: Compensatory Bridges to Independence. 1995. pap. 35.00 (0-930599-42-X) Thinking Pubns.

Miazga, Mike, ed. see Fleury, Robert E.

MIB, Inc. Staff & SOA/ AAIM/ HOLUA-IHOU Mortality & Morbidity Liaison Committee. Multiple Medical Impairment Study. LC 98-39856. 1998. 95.00 (0-9665356-0-X) CMAS Bks.

Mibashan, David. Still...Life. 196p. 1994. pap. 12.95 (0-88962-539-5) Mosaic.

Mibrathu, Yohanis, jt. auth. see Aboubaker Alwan, Daoud.

Mica, Daniel A., ed. see Chien, Frederick F.

***Mica, John L., ed.** Federal Hiring from the Welfare Rolls: Congressional Hearings. 173p. (C). 1999. reprint ed. pap. text 30.00 (0-7881-8296-X) DIANE Pub.

Micacci, Gustavo, jt. auth. see Scharff, Paul.

Micale, F. J., jt. auth. see Sharma, M. K.

Micale, Frances. Not Another Meeting: A Practical Guide for Facilitating Effective Meetings. LC 99-20270. (Illus.). xvi, 163p. 1999. pap. 17.95 (1-55571-480-3, Oasis Pr) PSI Resch.

Micale, Mark S. Approaching Hysteria: Disease & Its Interpretations. LC 94-16596. 327p. 1995. text 35.00 (0-691-03717-5, Pub. by Princeton U Pr) Cal Prin Full Svc.

***Micale, Mark S.** Enlightenment, Passion, Modernity: Historical Essays in European Thought & Culture. LC 99-39589. 1999. pap. text 24.95 (0-8047-3117-9) Stanford U Pr.

Micale, Mark S., ed. Beyond the Unconscious: Essays of Henri F. Ellenberger in the History of Psychiatry. Dubor, Francoise, tr. 488p. 1993. text 49.50 (0-691-08550-1, Pub. by Princeton U Pr) Cal Prin Full Svc.

Micale, Mark S & Porter, Roy, eds. Discovering the History of Psychiatry. LC 93-12244. 480p. 1994. text 49.50 (0-19-507739-3) OUP.

Micali, A., ed. Clifford Algebras & Their Applications in Mathematical Physics. 536p. (C). 1992. lib. bdg. 204.50 (0-7923-1623-1) Kluwer Academic.

Micallef, A. M. Texas Safari: World Class Big Game Hunting in the State of Texas. (Illus.). 256p. 1986. 25.00 (0-9616868-0-4) CF Ranch.

Micallef, Mary. Floods & Droughts. (Natural Disaster Ser.). (Illus.). 48p. (J). (gr. 4-8). 1985. student ed. 7.99 (0-86653-323-0, GA 632) Good Apple.

— Listening: The Basic Connection. (Illus.). 96p. (J). (gr. 3-8). 1984. student ed. 11.99 (0-86653-188-2, GA 555) Good Apple.

— Storms & Blizzards. (Natural Disaster Ser.). (Illus.). 48p. (J). (gr. 4-8). 1985. student ed. 7.95 (0-86653-321-4, GA 683) Good Apple.

Micarelli, William F. History of the 1992 Economic Census. (Illus.). 472p. (C). 1998. pap. text 50.00 (0-7881-4939-3) DIANE Pub.

Micarelli, William F. & United States Staff. History of the 1987 Economic Censuses. LC 92-212020. 1992. write for info. (0-16-037887-7) USGPO.

Micchelli, C. A., jt. auth. see Dikshit, H. P.

Micchelli, Charles A. Mathematical Aspects of Geometric Modeling. LC 94-10478. (CBMS-NSF Regional Conference Series in Applied Mathematics: Vol. 65). ix, 256p. 1994. pap. 42.50 (0-89871-331-5) Soc Indus-Appl Math.

Micchelli, Charles A., jt. ed. see Gasca, Mariano.

Miccinello, Angela, ed. see Romanillos, Jose L.

Miccio-Fonseca, L. C. Personal Sentence Completion Inventory. Hewat, A., ed. 88p. (Orig.). 1997. pap. 50.00 (1-884444-47-4) Safer Soc.

Miccio, Susan. Tibetan Spaniel. (Rare Breed Ser.). (Illus.). 96p. 1997. 19.95 (0-7938-0760-3, RX110) TFH Pubns.

Miccio, Susan W. The Tibetan Spaniel: A Gift from the Roof of the World. LC 96-13302. (Illus.). 256p. 1996. 39.95 (0-940269-12-0) OTR Pubns.

Micco, Jerry. 100 Years of Front Page News: From the 1st Century of the Daily Press. LC 95-38670. 1995. pap. write for info. (0-8092-3199-9) NTC Contemp Pub Co.

Micco, Mary & O'Neil, Therese. Using the Internet. 184p. (C). 1996. pap. text 19.96 (0-395-77057-2) HM.

Micek, Greg & Carter, Lee. The Great White Horse. (Dad & Me Ser.). (Illus.). 64p. (J). (gr. k-4). 1998. pap. 6.95 (1-888237-15-5) Baxter Pr.

Micek, Joseph G. Orchids in the Mud: Personal Accounts by Veterans of the 132nd Infantry Regiment. Muehrcke, Robert C., ed. (Illus.). 464p. 1985. 22.00 (0-9615127-0-9) J G Micek.

Micek, Tomas, photos by. Magnificent Horses of the World, 6 bks. Incl. Andalusian Horses. LC 95-16322. (Illus.). (J). (gr. 3 up). 1995. lib. bdg. 23.93 (0-8368-1366-9); Arabian Horses. LC 95-16321. (Illus.). 48p. (J). (gr. 3 up). 1995. lib. bdg. 23.93 (0-8368-1367-7); Friesian Horses. LC 95-16320. (Illus.). 48p. (J). (gr. 3 up). 1995. lib. bdg. 23.93 (0-8368-1368-5); Icelandic Ponies. LC 95-16315. (Illus.). 48p. (J). (gr. 3 up). 1995. lib. bdg. 23.93 (0-8368-1370-7); Lipizzaner Horses. Kellner, Elisabeth, photos by. LC 95-16313. (Illus.). 48p. (J). (gr. 3 up). 1995. lib. bdg. 23.93 (0-8368-1371-5); Palimino Horses: Austria's Haflingers. Kellner, Elisabeth, photos by. LC 95-16336. (Illus.). (J). (gr. 3 up). 1995. lib. bdg. 23.93 (0-8368-1369-3); (Illus.). (J). 1995. Set lib. bdg. 143.60 (0-8368-1365-0) Gareth Stevens Inc.

Miceli, A. P. Man with the Red Umbrella. 1974. 22.95 (0-87511-603-5) Claitors.

Miceli, Andrew. Wireless Technician's Handbook. LC 99-45832. 1999. 59.00 (1-58053-005-2) Artech Hse.

Miceli, Eve, jt. auth. see Lazar, Elysa.

Miceli, Marcia P. & Near, Janet P. Blowing the Whistle: The Organizational & Legal Implications for Companies & Their Employees. 332p. 1992. 28.95 (0-669-19599-5) Lxngtn Bks.

Miceli, Michael A., ed. see American Institue of Certified Public Accountants.

Miceli, Michael A., ed. see American Institute of Certified Public Accountants.

Miceli, Stacey, ed. see Lapan, Glenda, et al.

Miceli, Stacey, ed. see Lappan, Glenda, et al.

Miceli, Thomas J. Economics of the Law: Torts, Contracts, Property, & Litigation. (Illus.). 256p. 1997. text 39.95 (0-19-510390-4) OUP.

Miceli, Thomas J. & Segerson, Kathleen. Compensation for Regulatory Takings: An Economic Analysis with Applications. LC 96-14557. (Economics of Legal Relationships Ser.: Vol. 1). 253p. 1996. 73.25 (0-7623-0112-0) Jai Pr.

Miceli, Vincent P. The Antichrist. 297p. 1991. pap. 17.95 (0-912141-02-6) Roman Cath Bks.

— The Roots of Violence. LC 88-70610. 1989. 19.95 (0-8158-0449-0) Chris Mass.

Miceli, William J. Radar Processing, Technology, & Applications II. LC 98-122605. 32p. 1997. pap. 69.00 (0-8194-2583-4) SPIE.

Miceli, William J., ed. Radar Processing, Technology & Applications, Vol. 2845. 380p. 1996. 76.00 (0-8194-2233-9) SPIE.

— Radar Processing, Technology & Applications III, Vol. 3462. LC 99-182528. 1998. 80.00 (0-8194-2917-1) SPIE.

***Miceli, William J., ed.** Radar Processing, Technology & Applications IV. 1999. pap. text 72.00 (0-8194-3296-2) SPIE.

Micelis, Marco De, see Dal Co, Francesco & De Micelis, Marco, notes.

Micelli, Vincent P. The Gods of Atheism. 490p. 1983. reprint ed. 24.95 (0-912141-00-X) Roman Cath Bks.

Micelotta, Jeanette, et al. Get Rid of Your Butt: Tighter Buns, Thinner Thighs in 75 Minutes a Week. (Illus.). 60p. 1998. reprint ed. pap. text 5.00 (0-7881-5207-6) DIANE Pub.

Micevych, Paul E. & Hammer, Ronald P., Jr., eds. Neurobehavioral Effects of Sex Steroid Hormones. (Illus.). 464p. (C). 1995. text 90.00 (0-521-45430-1) Cambridge U Pr.

Micgiel, John, ed. Perspectives on Political & Economic Transitions after Communism. LC 97-73639. xiv, 267p. (C). 1997. pap. 19.95 (0-9654520-1-8) Col U Inst E Cntrl Eur.

***Micgiel, John S.** Coercion & the Establishment of Communist. 1999. text. write for info. (0-312-10167-8) St Martin.

Micgiel, John S., ed. State & Nation Building in East Central Europe. xxii, 369p. (Orig.). (C). 1996. pap. 19.95 (0-9654520-0-X) Col U Inst E Cntrl Eur.

Micha, Alexandre, jt. auth. see Chretien de Troyes.

Micha, D. A., jt. auth. see Levin, F. S.

Micha, David A., ed. Few-Body Systems & Multiparticle Dynamics. LC 87-72594. (AIP Conference Proceedings Ser.: No. 162). 304p. 1987. lib. bdg. 60.00 (0-88318-362-5) Am Inst Physics.

Michaaud, Michael, jt. auth. see Turino, Ken.

Michael. Finding Your Soul Mate. LC 92-20660. (Illus.). 128p. (Orig.). 1992. pap. 9.95 (0-87728-765-1) Weiser.

Michael, et al. Reform in Administrator Preparation Programs: Individual Perspectives. Wendel, Frederick C. & Bryant, Miles T., eds. 83p. (Orig.). (C). 1990. pap. text 7.00 (1-55996-143-0) Univ Council Educ Admin.

Michael, A. M. Irrigation: Theory & Practice. 801p. 1982. 90.00 (0-7069-1513-5) St Mut.

***Michael, Aloysius.** American Virtues & Cultural Values from the 1820's to 1990's: Virtuous Materialism. LC 99-86142. 296p. 2000. text 89.95 (0-7734-7775-6) E Mellen.

Michael, Aloysius. Radhakrishna on Hindu Moral Life & Action. 1979. 17.50 (0-8364-0334-7) S Asia.

***Michael, Angie.** Best Impressions in Hospitality: Your Professional Image for Excellence. LC 99-49977. 214p. 1999. 31.95 (0-7668-1584-6) Delmar.

Michael, Angie, jt. auth. see Amiel, Ilene.

Michael, Angie, jt. ed. see Pooser, Doris.

Michael, Arnold. Blessed among Women. reprint ed. write for info. (0-318-61348-4); reprint ed. pap. 8.95 (0-318-21242-0) Gray Pubns CA.

Michael, Bill, ed. see Adams, Ansel.

Michael, Burlingame, ed. see Hay, John.

Michael C. Carlos Museum Staff. Handbook to the Michael C. Carlos Museum. 151p. 1996. pap. 12.00 (0-9638169-8-5) M C Carlos Mus.

Michael, Chester P. & Norrisey, Marie C. Arise: A Christian Psychology of Love. 160p. (Orig.). 1981. pap. 3.95 (0-940136-00-7) Open Door Inc.

— Prayer & Temperament: Different Prayer Forms for Different Personality Types. rev. ed. 208p. (Orig.). 1991. pap. 7.95 (0-940136-02-3) Open Door Inc.

Michael, Christine. Looking down from the Mountain Top: The Story of One Woman's Fight Against All Odds. Plaut, Mary, ed. LC 91-62562. (Illus.). 300p. 1992. pap. 24.95 (0-9630571-0-3) Spirit of Success.

Michael, Christopher & Ismail, Mohammed I. Statistical Modeling for Computer-Aided Design of MOS VLSI Circuits. LC 92-35702. (Kluwer International Series in Engineering & Computer Science). 208p. (C). 1993. text 104.50 (0-7923-9299-X) Kluwer Academic.

Michael, Colette V. Sade: His Ethics & Rhetoric. (American University Studies: Romance Languages & Literature: Ser. II, Vol. 106). XIV, 249p. (C). 1989. text 37.95 (0-8204-0884-0) P Lang Pubng.

Michael, Colette V., tr. see Metzger, Helene.

Michael, D. J., ed. see Topical Conference on Ferritic Alloys for Use in N.

Michael, Dames. Avebury Cycle. 1996. pap. 16.95 (0-500-27139-9) Thames Hudson.

Michael, David, jt. auth. see Mills, Dick.

Michael, Diana L. Vows of Silence. 208p. 1993. pap. 12.95 (0-9634910-4-0) Samara Anjelae.

Michael Digest Group Staff. The Michael Game: One Hundred & One Questions to Ask a Channel & More. 160p. 1988. pap. 7.95 (0-941109-01-1) Warwick Pr CA.

Michael, Donald N. Learning to Plan - & Planning to Learn. 2nd ed. LC HN17.5.M5. 416p. 1997. 44.95 (0-917917-10-3); pap. 29.95 (0-917917-08-1) Miles River.

— On Learning to Plan & Planning to Learn. LC 73-7153. (Jossey-Bass Behavioral Science Ser.). 359p. reprint ed. pap. 111.30 (0-8357-4701-8, 205235600008) Bks Demand.

Michael, Donald N., ed. The Future Society. 131p. 1970. 34.95 (0-87855-068-2); pap. text 21.95 (0-87855-565-X) Transaction Pubs.

Michael, Dorian. Open Tuning for Solo Guitar: 14 Songs, 9 Tuning. (Illus.). 80p. 1997. pap. 19.95 incl. cd-rom (1-57424-050-1) Centerstream Pub.

Michael, Douglas C. Legal Accounting Principles & Applications. LC 97-9147. (Paralegal). 556p. 1997. text 36.50 (0-314-21136-5) West Pub.

Michael, Duncan. How Skyscrapers Are Made. (How It Is Made Ser.). (Illus.). 32p. (YA). (gr. 5-12). 1987. 14.95 (0-8160-1692-5) Facts on File.

Michael, E. Handbuch fuer Pilzfreunde: Volume 4: Blaetterilze-Dunkelblaettler. 3rd ed. Kreisel, H, ed. (Illus.). 472p. 1985. text 34.80 (3-437-30349-X) Lubrecht & Cramer.

***Michael, E.** In & Out. 2000. write for info. (0-688-17711-5, Wm Morrow) Morrow Avon.

Michael, E., et al. Handbuch der Pilzfreunde, Vol. 1: Die Wichtigsten und Haeufigsten Pilze Mit Besonderer Beruecksichtigung der Giftpilze. (GER., Illus.). 408p. 1978. lib. bdg. 45.00 (3-437-30436-4) Balogh.

— Handbuch Fuer Pilzfreunde Vol. 5: Blaetterpilze - Milchkinge und Taeublinge. 2nd ed. (GER., Illus.). 408p. 1983. lib. bdg. 48.00 (3-437-30750-9) Balogh.

— Handbuch Fuer Pilzfreunde, Vol. 6: Die Gattungen der Grosspilze Europas. Bestimmungsschluessel und Gesamt-Register to Vols. 1-5. 2nd ed. (GER., Illus.). 310p. 1988. lib. bdg. 30.00 (3-437-30352-X) Balogh.

An Asterisk (*) at the beginning of an entry indicates that the title is appearing for the first time.

Michael, E. A. Locally Multiplicatively-Convex Topological Algebras. LC 52-42839. (Memoirs Ser.: No. 1/11). 82p. 1971. reprint ed. pap. 16.00 (*0-8218-1211-4*, MEMO/1/11) Am Math.

Michael, E. J. Queen of the Sun: A Modern Revelation. 2nd rev. ed. (Illus.). 250p. 1995. pap. 12.95 (*0-9642147-8-4*) Mtn Rose Pubng.

Michael, E. J., tr. see Bethlem, Jaap & Knobbout, Charlotte E.

Michael, Emory J. Queen of the Sun: A Modern Revelation. LC 95-18437. (Illus.). (Orig.). 1995. pap. 10.00 (*0-06-251356-7*) Harper SF.

Michael, Emory John. Alchemy of Sacred Living: Creating a Culture of Light. 263p. 1998. pap. 14.95 (*0-9642147-2-5*) Mtn Rose Pubng.

Michael, Erika & Freitag, Wolfgang. Hans Holbein the Younger: A Guide to Research. LC 97-19462. (Artist Resource Manuals Ser.: No. 2). 770p. 1997. text 100.00 (*0-8153-0389-0*, H1480) Garland.

Michael, Ernest D., jt. auth. see Burke, Edmund J.

***Michael, Evan.** Big & Small. 2000. write for info. (*0-688-17712-3*, Wm Morrow) Morrow Avon.

Michael, F. & Sisavic, Irene. The Ultimate Travel Journal. LC 87-81868. 128p. (Orig.). 1987. 19.95 (*0-9619093-1-5*); 44.95 (*0-9619093-2-3*); pap. 9.95 (*0-9619093-0-7*) Florian Group.

Michael, Fersoun. G P S Waypoint Colin Idaho. 1999. 12.95 (*1-892182-16-5*) Glassford Pub.

Michael, Franz. China Through the Ages: History of a Civilization. 278p. (C). 1986. pap. 28.00 (*0-86531-726-7*, Pub. by Westview) HarpC.

— The Taiping Rebellion: Documents & Comments. Chang, Chung-Li, ed. Incl. Vol. 2. LC 66-13538. 756p. 1971. 35.00 (*0-295-73959-2*); Vol. 3. LC 66-13538. 1107p. 1971. 35.00 (*0-295-73960-6*); LC 66-13538. (Publications on Asia of the Institute for Comparative & Foreign Area Studies: No. 14, Pt. 2). 1971. write for info. (*0-318-56165-4*) U of Wash Pr.

Michael, Gayl, ed. see Lancaster, Clay.

Michael, Gene E. His Voice. 1998. pap. write for info. (*1-57553-962-4*) Watermrk Pr.

Michael, Gene Y. Environmental Data Bases: Design, Implementation & Maintenance. 112p. 1991. boxed set 79.95 (*0-87371-422-9*, L422) Lewis Pubs.

***Michael, George.** George Michael. (Illus.). 1999. pap. 15.95 (*0-7119-7891-3*) Music Sales.

Michael, George. The Overlook Treasury of Federal Antiques. 1988. pap. 19.95 (*0-87951-268-7*, Pub. by Overlook Pr) Penguin Putnam.

***Michael, George.** Wolves. LC 98-36871. (Nature Books Ser.). (Illus.). 32p. (gr. 1-3). 1998. lib. bdg. 22.79 (*1-56766-584-5*) Childs World.

Michael, H. N., tr. see Kushnareva, Karen K.

Michael, Harlan. Discover the Moment. LC 95-78224. 96p. (Orig.). 1996. per. 10.00 (*0-9647785-0-5*) Autumn Lane Bks.

Michael, Henry N. Lieutenant Zagoskin's Travels in Russian America. (ENG.). 358p. 1967. text 50.00 (*1-57833-015-7*) Todd Commns.

Michael, Henry N., ed. The Archaeology & Geomorphology of Northern Asia: Selected Works. LC 65-1456. (Arctic Institute of North America-Anthropology of the North; Translation from Russian Sources Ser.: No. 5). 528p. reprint ed. pap. 163.70 (*0-8357-5715-3*, 201917400011) Bks Demand.

Michael, Henry N., ed. see Levin, Maksim G.

Michael, Henry N., ed. see Zagoskin, Lavrentii A.

Michael, Henry N., tr. see Dolitsky, Alexander B., ed.

Michael, Henry N., tr. see Masson, V. M.

Michael, I. M. & Unwin, R. A. Employment Creation in the United States & the United Kingdom: An Econometric Comparison. LC HD5713.. (Bank of England - Discussion Papers: No. 27). (Illus.). 81p. 1986. reprint ed. pap. 30.00 (*0-608-03148-8*, 206360100007) Bks Demand.

Michael, Ian. The Teaching of English: From the Sixteenth Century to 1870. (Illus.). 644p. 1987. text 99.95 (*0-521-24196-0*) Cambridge U Pr.

Michael, Ib. Prince. Haveland, Barbara, tr. from DAN. LC 99-32515. 352p. 1999. text 25.00 (*0-374-23723-9*) FS&G.

Michael, Iris A. Healthy Breasts: Every Woman's Birthright! (Illus.). 151p. (Orig.). 1991. pap. text 16.95 (*0-9627883-0-9*) Clarke Pub.

Michael, J. P., ed. & tr. see Reutov, Oleg A., et al.

***Michael, Jack.** Modigliani. (Reveries Ser.). (Illus.). 120p. 2000. 14.95 (*1-85995-705-6*, Pub. by Parkstone Pr) Bks Intl VA.

Michael, Jack, jt. auth. see Ewers, Randolph L.

Michael, Jack D., Jr. The Best Way to Know God's Will. 2nd rev. ed. 96p. 1998. reprint ed. pap. 5.00 (*0-9629844-5-0*) J M Outreach Min.

— The Christ Conspiracy. (Illus.). 288p. (Orig.). 1994. pap. 10.00 (*0-9629844-3-4*) J M Outreach Min.

— Deception in the End Times. 2nd ed. 176p. 1998. pap. 7.00 (*0-9629844-6-9*) J M Outreach Min.

***Michael, Jack D., Jr.** Foundation Building: A Study Guide for Christians. large type ed. (Illus.). 144p. 2000. spiral bd. 12.00 (*0-9629844-8-5*) J M Outreach Min.

Michael, Jack D., Jr. Grievous Wolves: Hindering Spirits That Challenge & Oppose Spiritual Leadership. (Illus.). 112p. 1998. pap. 6.00 (*0-9629844-7-7*) J M Outreach Min.

— Will God Supply All Your Needs? (Illus.). 80p. (Orig.). 1995. pap. 5.00 (*0-9629844-2-6*) J M Outreach Min.

Michael, James. The Politics of Secrecy. 1979. 20.00 (*0-901108-80-4*, Pub. by NCCL) St Mut.

— Privacy & Human Rights: An International & Comparative Study, with Special Reference to Developments in Information Technology. LC 94-11932. 208p. 1994. 48.95 (*1-85521-381-8*, Pub. by Dartmth Pub) Ashgate Pub Co.

Michael, James J. From A to Z39.50: A Networking Primer. 176p. 1994. pap. 29.50 (*0-88736-766-6*) Mecklermedia.

Michael, Joel A. Problem Solving in Physiology. 400p. (C). 1998. pap. text 36.67 (*0-13-244104-7*) P-H.

***Michael, John.** Anxious Intellects: Academic Professionals, Public Intellectuals & Enlightenment Values. LC 99-48726. 248p. 2000. pap. 17.95 (*0-8223-2496-2*) Duke.

Michael, John. Emerson & Skepticism: The Cipher of the World. LC 87-30267. 208p. 1988. reprint ed. pap. 64.50 (*0-608-06712-1*, 206690900009) Bks Demand.

— The Last Nightmare. 118p. (Orig.). 1988. pap. 7.95 (*0-945644-00-0*) Intl Pub Inc.

Michael, John, ed. National Art Education Association: Our History Celebrating 50 Years, 1947-1997. (Illus.). 254p. 1997. pap. 25.00 (*1-890160-00-8*, 267) Natl Art Ed.

Michael, John A. Art & Adolescence: Teaching Art at the Secondary Level. LC 83-4147. 240p. (C). 1983. pap. text 18.95 (*0-8077-2743-1*) Tchrs Coll.

Michael, John A., ed. The Lowenfeld Lectures: Viktor Lowenfeld on Art Education & Therapy. LC 80-29265. (Illus.). 420p. (C). 1982. text 40.00 (*0-271-00283-2*) Pa St U Pr.

— Visual Arts Teacher Resource Handbook: A Practical Guide for Teaching K-12 Visual Arts. LC 93-15855. (Teacher Resource Handbook Ser.). (Illus.). 420p. 1993. pap. 34.95 (*0-8039-6375-0*) Corwin Pr.

Michael, Joi, ed. see Roquemore, Erma.

Michael, Judith, pseud. Acts of Love. 1998. mass mkt. 7.99 (*0-8041-1787-X*) Ivy Books.

***Michael, Judith, pseud.** A Certain Smile. 2000. mass mkt. 7.99 (*0-449-22426-0*) Ballantine Pub Grp.

Michael, Judith, pseud. A Certain Smile. LC 98-52333. 352p. 1999. 25.00 (*0-517-70325-4*) Crown Pub Group.

— A Certain Smile. large type ed. LC PS3563.I254C47 1999. 1999. pap. 24.95 (*0-375-70678-X*) Random.

— Deceptions. 1994. mass mkt. 6.99 (*0-671-89954-6*) PB.

— Inheritance. Grose, Bill, ed. 1989. mass mkt. 6.50 (*0-671-68885-5*) PB.

— Inheritance. 1994. per. 6.99 (*0-671-89955-4*) PB.

— Judith Michael, 3 vols. 1989. boxed set 15.40 (*0-671-92230-0*) PB.

— Judith Michael, 3 vols. 1990. boxed set 17.40 (*0-671-96370-8*) S&S Trade.

— Possessions. Grose, Bill, ed. 1989. mass mkt. 6.50 (*0-671-69383-2*) PB.

— Possessions. 1994. per. 6.99 (*0-671-89956-2*) PB.

— Pot of Gold. 1994. pap. 209.70 (*0-671-99160-4*); mass mkt. 6.99 (*0-671-88629-0*) PB.

— Pot of Gold. LC 93-14336. 1993. 23.00 (*0-671-70704-3*) S&S Trade.

Michael, Judith, pseud. Pot of Gold. abr. ed. 1993. 17.00 incl. audio (*0-671-87586-8*) S&S Audio.

Michael, Judith, pseud. Pot of Gold. large type ed. LC 94-6739. 1994. 26.95 (*1-56895-060-8*) Wheeler Pub.

— Private Affairs. 1994. mass mkt. 6.99 (*0-671-89957-0*) PB.

— A Ruling Passion. 1994. mass mkt. 6.99 (*0-671-89958-9*) PB.

— Sleeping Beauty. 640p. 1994. mass mkt. 6.99 (*0-671-89959-7*) PB.

— Sleeping Beauty. Grose, Bill, ed. 640p. 1992. reprint ed. mass mkt. 5.99 (*0-671-78252-5*) PB.

— A Tangled Web. Rubenstein, Julie, ed. 1995. mass mkt. 6.50 (*0-671-52548-4*) PB.

— A Tangled Web. 592p. 1995. per. 6.99 (*0-671-53288-X*) PB.

— A Tangled Web. 464p. 1994. 23.00 (*0-671-79879-0*) S&S Trade.

— A Tangled Web. large type ed. LC 95-2007. (Large Print Bks.). 1995. 25.95 (*1-56895-201-5*) Wheeler Pub.

Michael, Ken. Terror Within. LC 96-215435. 414p. 1996. pap. 12.95 (*1-85756-178-3*, Pub. by Janus Pubng) Paul & Co Pubs.

Michael, Laura, tr. see Shukshin, Vasily.

Michael, Linda. Big As Texas: The A to Z Tour of Texas Cities & Places. LC 87-36793. (Illus.). 64p. (J). (ps-3). 1988. pap. 6.95 (*0-937460-34-6*) Hendrick-Long.

Michael, Livi. Their Angel Reach. 240p. 1995. pap. 9.99 (*0-7493-2163-6*) Buttrwrth-Heinemann.

Michael, Lord, et al. The Spiritual Laws & Lessons of the Universe. (Illus.). 148p. 1999. pap. 16.95 (*0-9640104-6-1*) Bridger Hse.

Michael, M. A., tr. see Hoff, Trygve J.

Michael, M. Luisa. House for Sale. 352p. 1991. pap. text 21.95 (*0-89420-282-0*, 344044, Halcyon) Natl Book.

Michael, Magali C. Feminism & the Postmodern Impulse: Post-World War II Fiction. LC 95-41406. 275p. (C). 1996. text 65.50 (*0-7914-3015-4*); pap. text 21.95 (*0-7914-3016-2*) State U NY Pr.

Michael, Marjorie & Baron, Virginia. A Woman's Journey. 30p. 1992. pap. 12.95 (*0-9634822-0-3*) MTwo Media.

Michael, Mark. Preserving Wildlife: An International Perspective. LC 99-38312. 275p. 1999. pap. 21.95 (*1-57392-727-9*, Humanity Bks) Prometheus Bks.

Michael, Marvin. A Passion for Flying: Exciting Stories of a Boeing Test Pilot. LC 96-230331. 192p. (Orig.). 1996. pap. 10.95 (*1-883893-59-3*) WinePress Pub.

Michael, Mary J. Futrtools - A Journeybook: A Diary for the Journey Through Your Mind. (Virtual Gym Ser.). 1996. spiral bd. 19.95 (*0-9651947-0-1*) MXM Inc.

Michael, Matto, ed. see Davies, Michael.

Michael, Maureen, jt. auth. see McGilp, Jacqueline.

Michael, Maurice A. Traveller's Quest: Original Contributions Towards a Philosophy of Travel. LC 72-5673. (Essay Index Reprint Ser.). 1977. reprint ed. 24.95 (*0-8369-7297-X*) Ayer.

Michael, Michaelis, ed. Philosophy in Mind: The Place of Philosophy in the Study of Mind. (Philosophical Studies). 332p. (C). 1994. lib. bdg. 140.00 (*0-7923-3143-5*, Pub. by Kluwer Academic) Kluwer Academic.

Michael, Michele. The New Apartment Book. 1996. pap. 30.00 (*0-517-88759-2*) C Potter.

Michael, Mike. Constructing Identities. 192p. (C). 1996. pap. 15.99 (*0-8039-8952-0*) Sage.

— Constructing Identities: The Social, the Nonhuman & Change. 192p. (C). 1996. 45.00 (*0-8039-8951-2*) Sage.

***Michael, Mike.** Reconnecting Culture, Technology & Nature: From Society to Heterogeneity. LC 00-36887. (International Library of Sociology Ser.). 2000. pap. write for info. (*0-415-20117-9*) Routledge.

Michael Nagler & Associates Staff. Gandhi. (For Beginners Ser.). (Illus.). 192p. 1998. pap. 11.00 (*0-86316-278-9*) Writers & Readers.

Michael, Nancy. Don't Sweat It -- Paint It. (Illus.). 32p. (Orig.). 1987. pap. 6.95 (*0-941284-42-5*) J Shaw Studio.

Michael, Nelson & Kim, Jerome H. HIV Protocols. LC 98-27244. (Methods in Molecular Medicine Ser.: Vol. 17). (Illus.). 432p. 1999. 89.50 (*0-89603-369-4*) Humana.

***Michael Nelson & Associates Staff, ed.** Alive at the Core: Exemplary Approaches to General Education in the Humanities. 320p. 2000. 36.95 (*0-7879-4760-1*, Pfiffr & Co) Jossey-Bass.

Michael, Nicholas. Armies of Medieval Burgundy 1364-1477. (Men-at-Arms Ser.: No. 144). (Illus.). 48p. pap. 11.95 (*0-85045-518-9*, 9076, Pub. by Ospry) Stackpole.

Michael, Norma, jt. auth. see Burton, Celia.

Michael of Ephesus, jt. auth. see Aristotle.

***Michael Omara Books U. K. Staff, ed.** Love Checks. 80p. 2000. pap. 5.95 (*1-57071-519-X*) Sourcebks.

Michael, P. D. & Maguire, J. European Fuel Cells R&D Review (Sept. 1994) (Fuel Cell Information Ser.: Vol. V). (Illus.). 62p. 1996. lib. bdg. 105.00 (*0-89934-312-0*, BT963) Bus Tech Bks.

Michael, Pamela. Rowing Partners: 101 Ways to Build Community Partnerships. (Illus.). 20p. 1998. 5.00 (*0-9662771-1-2*) Intl Riv Ntwrk.

***Michael, Pamela, ed.** The Gift of Rivers: True Stories of Life on the Water. 256p. 2000. pap. 14.95 (*1-885211-42-2*, 42-2, Pub. by Trvlers Tale) Publishers Group.

Michael, Pamela & Bond, Marybeth, eds. A Mother's World: Journeys of the Heart. 233p. 1998. pap. 14.95 (*1-885211-26-0*, 26-0) Trvlers Tale.

Michael, Pamela, jt. ed. see Bond, Marybeth.

Michael, Payne. Intermediate Algebra. (Illus.). 541p. 1985. text 54.75 (*0-314-85285-9*) West Pub.

Michael, Peter P. Multiple Sclerosis: A Dragon with a Hundred Heads. LC 79-10954. 1981. 22.95 (*0-87949-170-1*) Ashley Bks.

***Michael, R.** Development & Repair of Cataract Induced by Ultraviolet Radiation. (Opthalmologica Ser.: Vol. 32, Suppl. 1 (2000)). (Illus.). vi, 120p. 2000. pap. 34.00 (*3-8055-7044-9*) S Karger.

Michael, R. Blake. Origins of Virasaiva Sects: A Typological Analysis of Ritual & Associational Patterns in the Sunyasampadane. (C). 1992. 25.00 (*81-208-0776-6*, Pub. by Motilal Bnarsidass) S Asia.

Michael, Robert. The Holocaust: A Chronology & Documentary. LC 97-27120. 360p. 1998. 40.00 (*0-7657-5984-5*) Aronson.

Michael, Robert J. The Educator's Guide to Students with Epilepsy. LC 95-16962. (Illus.). 174p. 1995. 44.95 (*0-398-06537-3*); pap. 30.95 (*0-398-06538-1*) C C Thomas.

Michael, Robert T. The Effect of Education on Efficiency in Consumption. (Occasional Papers: No. 116). 149p. 1972. 38.80 (*0-87014-242-9*) Natl Bur Econ Res.

Michael, Robert T., jt. auth. see Lazear, Edward P.

Michael, Robert T., ed. see National Research Council, Panel on Poverty & Fami.

Michael, Robert T., ed. see National Research Council Staff.

Michael, Ronald L., jt. ed. see Egan, Geoff.

Michael, Russ. The Birth of Earth As a Star. Bennett, G. M., ed. (Illus.). 220p. 1997. pap. 15.98 (*1-882786-36-X*) New Dawn NY.

— Mental Room of Mirrors: Self-Therapy Technique. Bennett, G. M., ed. (Illus.). 210p. 1997. pap. 15.98 (*1-882786-31-9*) New Dawn NY.

— Tales of the Ram. 160p. (Orig.). 1989. pap. 9.95 (*0-945127-04-9*) Upword Pr.

Michael S. Knapp & Associates Staff. Paths to Partnership: University & Community As Learners in Interprofessional Education. LC 98-21269. 278p. 1998. 60.00 (*0-8476-8875-5*); pap. 24.95 (*0-8476-8876-3*) Rowman.

Michael, S. M. Culture & Urbanization. (C). 1989. 60.00 (*81-210-0231-1*, Pub. by Inter-India Pubns) S Asia.

— Dalits in Modern India: Vision & Values. LC 98-37909. 1998. write for info. (*0-7619-9290-1*) Sage.

— Untouchable: Dalits in Modern India. LC 99-11837. 190p. 1999. lib. bdg. 47.00 (*1-55587-697-8*) L Rienner.

Michael, Sarah. Three Consort Songs, for Soprano & Treble, Tenor & Bass Viols. (Contemporary Consort Ser.: No. 6). 22p. 1994. pap. text 12.00 (*1-56571-094-0*) PRB Prods.

Michael, Scott W. Aquarium Sharks & Rays: An Essential Guide to Their Selection, Keeping & Natural History. Date not set. 34.95 (*1-890087-57-2*) Microcosm Ltd.

***Michael, Scott W.** Marine Fishes: 500 Essential-to-Know Aquarium Species. LC 99-35858. (PocketExpert Guide Ser.: Vol. 1). (Illus.). 448p. 1999. pap. 24.95 (*1-890087-38-6*) Microcosm Ltd.

Michael, Scott W. Reef Fishes: A Guide to Their Identification, Behavior & Captive Care. LC 98-34408. 1998. 69.95 (*1-890087-21-1*) Microcosm Ltd.

— Reef Sharks & Rays of the World: A Guide to Their Identification, Behavior, & Ecology. Hashagen, Ken & Bertsch, Hans, eds. LC 92-46402. (Illus.). 112p. (Orig.). (C). 1993. pap. 24.95 (*0-930118-18-9*, 188M) Sea Chall.

Michael, Sherif A. Succeed with Solomon's Principles: The Higher Power Approach. LC 97-62499. (Illus.). 256p. 1998. pap. 11.95 (*1-57921-085-6*, Pub. by WinePress Pub) BookWorld.

Michael, T. Anthony. Auscultation of the Heart. 2000. pap. 165.00 incl. cd-rom (*0-07-864292-2*) McGraw.

— Auscultation of the Heart: A Cardiophonetic Approach. LC 97-15124. (Illus.). 504p. 1997. text, pap. text 39.95 incl. disk (*0-07-018005-9*) McGraw-Hill HPD.

***Michael, Toni.** Greetings, Cousins! Family History Publishing: A Guide to Family History for Fun & Profit. (Illus.). 32p. 1999. pap. 12.95 (*0-9672348-0-8*) Win Win Commns.

Michael, Valerie. The Leatherworking Handbook: A Practical Illustrated Sourcebook of Techniques & Projects. (Illus.). 128p. 1995. pap. 19.95 (*0-304-34511-3*, Pub. by Cassell) Sterling.

Michael, Veronica & Caole, Frances. Ayuqucinka. large type ed.Tr. of My Feelings. (ESK., Illus.). 8p. (J). (gr. k-3). 1999. pap. text 6.00 (*1-58084-055-8*); pap. text 6.00 (*1-58084-117-1*) Lower Kuskokwim.

— Mihigimanitka. large type ed.Tr. of My Feelings. (ESK., Illus.). 8p. (J). (gr. k-3). 1999. pap. text 6.00 (*1-58084-130-9*) Lower Kuskokwim.

— My Feelings. large type ed. (Illus.). 8p. (J). (gr. k-3). 1999. pap. text 6.00 (*1-58084-054-X*) Lower Kuskokwim.

— Qanuqitpit. large type ed.Tr. of My Feelings. (ESK., Illus.). 8p. (J). (gr. k-3). 1999. pap. text 6.00 (*1-58084-123-6*) Lower Kuskokwim.

— Qanuqitpit. large type ed.Tr. of My Feelings. (ESK., Illus.). 8p. (J). (gr. k-3). 1999. pap. text 6.00 (*1-58084-138-4*) Lower Kuskokwim.

Michael, Veronica, jt. auth. see Caole, Francis.

Michael, Vilot. TEC Course - Advanced C++ Workshop. 1991. ring bd. write for info. (*0-201-41899-1*) Addison-Wesley.

Michael, Waldstein & Wisse, Frederik. The Apocryphon of John: A Synopsis of Nag Hammadi Codices II, 1, III, 1, & IV, 1 with BG 8502,2. LC 95-19459. (Nag Hammadi & Manichaean Studies, Vol. 33; The Copticgnostic Library). 1995. 103.50 (*90-04-10395-3*) Brill Academic Pubs.

Michael, Walther P. Measuring International Capital Movements. LC 74-160315. (National Bureau of Economic Research, Occasional Paper Ser.: No. 114). 160p. reprint ed. pap. 49.60 (*0-608-30153-1*, 200622000055) Bks Demand.

— Measuring International Capital Movements. (Occasional Papers: No. 114). 160p. 1971. reprint ed. 40.00 (*0-87014-229-1*) Natl Bur Econ Res.

Michael, Wendy A., et al. FDDI: An Introduction to Fiber Distributed Data Interface. (Networking & Data Communications Ser.). (Illus.). 209p. 1992. pap. 29.95 (*1-55558-093-9*, EY-J840E-DP, Digital DEC) Buttrwrth-Heinemann.

Michael, William B., ed. Teaching for Creative Endeavor: Bold New Venture. LC 76-6603. reprint ed. 45.00 (*0-404-15292-9*) AMS Pr.

Michael, William B., jt. auth. see Isaac, Stephen.

Michael Wolff & Co. Staff. Net Mac. 1996. pap. 22.00 (*0-679-77385-1*) Random.

Michael Wolff & Company, Inc. Staff. Net Girl. 1997. pap. 22.00 (*0-679-77383-5*) Random.

— Net Out. 400p. 1997. pap. 22.00 (*0-679-77171-9*) Fodors Travel.

Michael, Wolfgang F. Das Deutsche Drama Des Mittelalters. (Grundriss der Germanischen Philologie Ser.: Vol. 20). 304p. (C). 1971. 119.25 (*3-11-003310-0*) De Gruyter.

— England under George I, 2 vols. LC 79-123757. reprint ed. 115.00 (*0-404-04314-3*) AMS Pr.

Michaelesson, Magnus. Congenital Heart Malformations in Mammals. 1999. write for info. (*1-86094-158-3*, Pub. by Imperial College) World Scientific Pub.

Michaeli, David. Momentary Reflection on Movement: The Spirit of T'ai Chi. (Illus.). 112p. 1998. mass mkt. 8.95 (*965-494-003-5*, Pub. by Astrolog Pub) Assoc Pubs Grp.

— No. large type ed. 242p. 1998. mass mkt. 7.50 (*965-494-002-7*, Pub. by Astrolog Pub) Assoc Pubs Grp.

— Yes. large type ed. 242p. 1998. mass mkt. 7.50 (*965-494-001-9*, Pub. by Astrolog Pub) Assoc Pubs Grp.

Michaeli, Walter. Extrusion Dies. 1986. 89.95 (*0-02-949550-4*) Free Pr.

— Extrusion Dies for Plastics & Rubber: Design & Engineering Computations. 2nd ed. 340p. 1992. 98.50 (*1-56990-063-9*) Hanser-Gardner.

— Plastics Processing: An Introduction. 211p. 1995. pap. 49.95 (*1-56990-144-9*) Hanser-Gardner.

***Michaeli, Walter.** Training in Plastics Technology: A Text & Workbook. 2nd ed. LC 99-48717. (Illus.). (C). 1999. pap., wbk. ed. write for info. (*1-56990-293-3*) Hanser-Gardner.

Michaeli, Walter, et al. Introduccion a la Tecnologia de los Plasticos. 174p. (C). 1992. pap. write for info. (*1-56990-175-9*) Hanser-Gardner.

— Tecnologia de los Composites-Plasticos Reforzados. 182p. 1992. pap. write for info. (*1-56990-171-6*) Hanser-Gardner.

— Training in Injection Molding. Alex, Kurt, tr. from GER. LC 95-11657.Tr. of Technologie des Spritzgiessens. 172p. 1995. pap. 34.95 (*1-56990-135-X*) Hanser-Gardner.

M

— Training in Plastics Technology. LC 95-11658.Tr. of Technologie der Kuntstoffe. 172p. 1995. pap. 34.95 (*1-56990-134-1*) Hanser-Gardner.

Michaeli, Walter, jt. auth. see Potsch, Gerd.

Michaelis. Basic Michaelis English-Portuguese, Portuguese-English Dictionary: Dicionario Basico Michaelis Ingles-Portugues-Ingles. (ENG & POR.). 856p. 1985. 75.00 (*0-8288-0493-1*, M9285) Fr & Eur.

***Michaelis.** Dicionario Melhoramentos Practico Da Lingua Portuguesa. 1999. 69.95 (*85-06-01707-6*) Midwest European Pubns.

— Dicionario Mini Melhoramentos Da Lingua Portuguesa. 1999. pap. 13.95 (*85-06-01675-4*) Midwest European Pubns.

Michaelis. Michaelis Business English - Portuguese Dictionary. 5th ed. 407p. 1992. 125.00 (*0-7859-8713-4*) Fr & Eur.

— Mini Michaelis Dicionario: English-Portuguese. 1999. pap. 13.95 (*85-06-01595-2*) Midwest European Pubns.

***Michaelis.** Mini Michaelis Dicionario Frances-Portugues/Portugues-Frances. 1999. pap. 13.95 (*85-06-01725-4*) Midwest European Pubns.

Michaelis. New Illustrated Michaelis English-Portuguese Dictionary: Novo Michaelis Dicionario Ilustrado, Vol. 1. 41st ed. (ENG & POR., Illus.). 1151p. 1986. 95.00 (*0-8288-0494-X*, M14123) Fr & Eur.

— New Michaelis Portuguese-English Illustrated Dictionary: Novo Michaelis Dicionario Ilustrado, Vol. 2. 40th ed. (ENG & POR., Illus.). 1327p. 1986. 95.00 (*0-8288-0495-8*, M14122) Fr & Eur.

***Michaelis.** Pequeno Michaelis Dicionario Alemao-Portugues/Portugues-Alemao. 1999. pap. 18.95 (*85-06-01622-3*) Midwest European Pubns.

— Pequeno Michaelis Dicionario Espanhol-Portugues/Portugues-Espanhol. 1999. pap. 18.95 (*85-06-01344-5*) Midwest European Pubns.

— Pequeno Michaelis Dicionario Frances-Portugues/Portugues-Frances. 1999. pap. 18.95 (*85-06-01674-6*) Midwest European Pubns.

— Pequeno Michaelis Dicionario Italiano-Portugues/Portugues-Italiano. 1999. pap. 18.95 (*85-06-01621-5*) Midwest European Pubns.

Michaelis. Pocket Dictionary Michaelis: English-Portuguese/Portuguese-English. 1999. pap. 8.95 (*85-06-01486-7*) Midwest European Pubns.

— Small Michaelis English-Portuguese, Portuguese-English Dictionary: Pequeno Dicionario Michaelis: Ingles-Portugues, Portugues-Ingles. (ENG & POR.). 642p. 1980. pap. 22.95 (*0-8288-0496-6*, M9282) Fr & Eur.

Michaelis, Adolf, jt. auth. see Jahn, Otto.

Michaelis, Anthony R., ed. Interdisciplinary Science Reviews Essay Annual: Volume 5, 1981. LC Q 0001.I576. 350p. reprint ed. pap. 108.50 (*0-608-16175-6*, 202254300027) Bks Demand.

***Michaelis, Bill & O'Connell, John M.** The Game & Play Leaders' Handbook: Facilitating Fun & Positive Interaction. LC 98-88948. (Illus.). 208p. 2000. pap. 19.95 (*1-892132-02-8*, PLH113) Venture Pub PA.

Michaelis, David. N. C. Wyeth: A Biography. LC 98-6143. (Illus.). 555p. 1998. 40.00 (*0-679-42626-4*) Random.

Michaelis De Vasconcellos, Carolina. Cancioneiro Da Ajuda, 2 vols., Set. xxviii, 1925p. 1979. reprint ed. write for info. incl. 3.5 hd (*3-487-06924-5*) G Olms Pubs.

***Michaelis, Dean.** The Complete .50-Caliber Sniper Course: Hard-Target Interdiction. (Illus.). 576p. 2000. pap. 60.00 (*1-58160-068-2*, 10011336) Paladin Pr.

Michaelis, Elaine, jt. auth. see Hirst, Cyntha C.

Michaelis, Johann D. Dissertation on the Influence of Opinions on Language & of Language on Opinions. LC 72-147981. reprint ed. pap. 37.50 (*0-404-08236-X*) AMS Pr.

Michaelis, John U. Social Studies for Children: A Guide to Basic Instruction. 9th ed. (Illus.). 448p. (C). 1988. text 24.00 (*0-13-818832-7*) P-H.

Michaelis, John U. & Garcia, Jesus. Social Studies for Children: A Guide to Basic Instruction. 11th ed. 448p. 1995. 77.00 (*0-205-17537-6*) Allyn.

— Social Studies for Children: A Guide to Basic Instruction. 11th ed. (C). 1996. pap., teacher ed. write for info. (*0-205-18890-7*, H8890-9) Allyn.

***Michaelis, K., et al.** Evaluation of Wear, Scuffing & Pitting Capacity of Gear Lubricants. (Technical Papers: Vol. 98FTM8). 10p. 1998. pap. 30.00 (*1-55589-726-6*) AGMA.

Michaelis, K., jt. auth. see Winter, Hans.

Michaelis, Karen L. Reporting Child Abuse: A Guide to Mandatory Requirements for School Personnel. Herman, Jerry J. & Herman, Janice L., eds. LC 93-28246. (Road Maps to Success Ser.). 72p. 1993. pap. 14.95 (*0-8039-6100-6*) Corwin Pr.

Michaelis, Karin. The Dangerous Age. 215p. 1991. reprint ed. 25.95 (*0-8101-1015-6*); reprint ed. pap. 12.95 (*0-8101-1040-7*) Northwestern U Pr.

Michaelis, Laura A. Aspectual Grammar & Past-Time Reference. LC 97-11820. 320p. (C). 1998. 90.00 (*0-415-15678-5*) Routledge.

Michaelis, Mark, jt. auth. see Schildt, Herbert.

Michaelis, P. & Stahler, F., eds. Recent Policy Issues in Environmental & Resource Economics. LC 98-30591. (Contributions to Economics Ser.). (Illus.). viii, 193p. 1998. pap. 63.00 (*3-7908-1137-8*) Spr-Verlag.

Michaelis, Richard. Looking Further Forward: An Answer to Looking Backward. LC 72-154452. (Utopian Literature Ser.). 1971. reprint ed. 16.95 (*0-405-03534-9*) Ayer.

Michaelis, Rolf. SS-Heimwehr Danzig 1939: An Ephemeral Paramilitary Formation - Poland 1939. 76p. 1998. pap. write for info. (*1-899765-01-8*) Intl Spec Bk.

Michaelis, W. Air Pollution: Dimensions, Trends & Interactions with a Forest Ecosystem. LC 96-49480. (Illus.). 170p. 1997. 99.95 (*3-540-61323-4*) Spr-Verlag.

Michaelis, Walfried, jt. ed. see Kausch, Hartmut.

***Michaelowa, Axel & Dutschke, Michael, eds.** Climate Policy & Development: Flexible Instruments & Developing Countries. LC 99-87674. 288p. 2000. 95.00 (*1-84064-331-5*) E Elgar.

Michaels. Baby, You're Mine! 1997. per. 3.25 (*0-373-15709-6*) Harlequin Bks.

— Essentials of Business Law. 1994. 17.25 (*0-07-042155-2*) McGraw.

— The Fake Fiance. large type ed. 1997. per. 3.25 (*0-373-15724-X*, Harlequin) Harlequin Bks.

— Family Secrets, Kids & Kisses. large type ed. 1994. per. 2.99 (*0-373-15570-0*) Harlequin Bks.

— The Husband Project (Finding Mr. Right) large type ed. (Large Print Ser.). 1998. per. 3.50 (*0-373-15750-9*, Harlequin) Harlequin Bks.

— The Perfect Divorce. large type ed. 1997. per. 3.25 (*0-373-15690-1*, Harlequin) Harlequin Bks.

— The Playboy Assignment. large type ed. (Finding Mr. Right Ser.). 1998. per. 3.50 (*0-373-15746-0*, Harlequin) Harlequin Bks.

— Sacred & Profane. mass mkt. write for info. (*0-312-90057-0*) Tor Bks.

— A Singular Honeymoon. 1994. per. 2.99 (*0-373-15546-8*) Harlequin Bks.

Michaels, Abbe, jt. auth. see Howard-Howard, Margo.

Michaels, Alan. Suffix Obsession: A Dictionary of All Words Ending in Annual, Ennial, Anthropy, Archy, Cracy, Cide, Culture, Gamy, Gon, Hedron, Lagnia, Latry, Theism, Loquy, Machy, Mancy, Mania, Nym, Phagous, Vorous, Phany, Philia & Phobia. LC 92-50941. 196p. 1993. lib. bdg. 32.50 (*0-89950-674-7*) McFarland & Co.

Michaels, Alan S. Structured Strategic Planning: A Practical Guide to Formulating & Implementing Corporate, Business Unit & Cost Center Strategies. LC 94-96085. (Illus.). 324p. (Orig.). 1994. pap. 85.00 (*0-9641122-0-5*) A S Michaels.

Michaels, Albert L., jt. auth. see Reisem, Richard O.

Michaels, Albert L., jt. ed. see Wilkie, James W.

Michaels, Andrew, et al. Saint-Frances Guide to Cardiology. 220p. 21.95 (*0-683-30660-X*) Lppncott W & W.

Michaels, Anne. Fugitive Pieces. (Illus.). 294p. 1998. pap. 12.00 (*0-679-77659-1*) Vin Bks.

— Fugitive Pieces. large type ed. LC 97-24456. 384p. 1997. 24.95 (*0-7862-1200-4*) Thorndike Pr.

— Poems: The Weight of Oranges, Miner's Pond, Skin Divers. LC 99-47105. 192p. 2000. 25.00 (*0-375-40140-7*) Knopf.

Michaels, Art & Fox, Joe. Kick Boxing Basics. LC 98-30846. (Illus.). 128p. 1998. pap. 9.95 (*0-8069-9781-8*) Sterling.

Michaels, Art, jt. auth. see Fox, Joe.

Michaels, Augusta. Sweeter Than Wine. limited num. ed. 230p. 1999. pap. 6.99 (*1-893108-03-1*) Neighbrhd Pr Pubng.

Michaels, Axel, et al, eds. Wild Goddesses in India & Nepal: Proceedings of an International Symposium. Berne & Zurich, November 1994. (Studia Religiosa Helvetica. Jahrbuch: Vol. 2). 574p. (C). 1996. pap. text 62.95 (*3-906756-04-1*, Pub. by P Lang) P Lang Pubng.

Michaels, Barbara L. Gertrude Kasebier. (Illus.). 208p. 1992. 45.00 (*0-8109-3505-8*, Pub. by Abrams) Time Warner.

Michaels, Barbara, pseud. Ammie, Come Home. 256p. 1987. mass mkt. 6.99 (*0-425-09949-0*) Berkley Pub.

— Be Buried in the Rain. 336p. 1997. mass mkt. 5.99 (*0-06-101010-3*, Harp PBks) HarpC.

— Be Buried in the Rain. 336p. 1999. mass mkt. 6.50 (*0-06-104469-5*) HarpC.

— Black Rainbow. 1991. mass mkt. 7.50 (*0-425-12481-9*) Berkley Pub.

— The Crying Child. 1989. mass mkt. 6.99 (*0-425-11584-4*) Berkley Pub.

— The Crying Child. large type ed. (Americana Series). 329p. 1995. 21.95 (*0-7862-0353-6*) Thorndike Pr.

— The Dancing Floor. 464p. 1998. mass mkt. 6.99 (*0-06-109254-1*) HarpC.

— The Dancing Floor. large type ed. LC 97-2200. (Basic Ser.). 557p. 1997. 27.95 (*0-7862-1058-3*) Thorndike Pr.

— The Dancing Floor. large type ed. LC 97-2200. 1998. pap. 25.95 (*0-7862-1059-1*) Thorndike Pr.

Michaels, Barbara, pseud. The Dancing Floor: Rosenblat,&Barbara. abr. ed. 1997. audio. write for info. (*0-694-51783-6*, CPN 2625, Pub. by HarperAudio) Lndmrk Audiobks.

Michaels, Barbara, pseud. The Dark on the Other Side. 1988. mass mkt. 6.99 (*0-425-10928-3*) Berkley Pub.

— The Grey Beginning. 304p. 1995. mass mkt. 5.50 (*0-06-100725-0*) HarpC.

— The Grey Beginning. 304p. 1999. mass mkt. 6.50 (*0-06-104471-7*) HarpC.

— The Grey Beginning. 1988. mass mkt. 4.50 (*0-8125-3031-4*, Pub. by Tor Bks) St Martin.

— The Grey Beginning. large type ed. (Charnwood Large Print Ser.). 352p. 1995. 27.99 (*0-7089-8842-3*, Charnwood) Ulverscroft.

— The Grey Beginning. 288p. 1994. reprint ed. 20.00 (*0-7278-4538-1*) Severn Hse.

— Greygallows. 352p. 1993. mass mkt. 7.50 (*0-425-13794-5*) Berkley Pub.

— Here I Stay. 1988. mass mkt. 4.99 (*0-8125-2140-4*, Harp PBks) HarpC.

— Here I Stay. 352p. 1994. mass mkt. 5.99 (*0-06-100726-9*, Harp PBks) HarpC.

— Here I Stay. 352p. 1999. mass mkt. 6.50 (*0-06-104470-9*) HarpC.

— House of Many Shadows. 304p. (Orig.). 1996. mass mkt. 6.50 (*0-425-15189-1*) Berkley Pub.

— House of Many Shadows. large type ed. (Orig.). 1981. pap. 12.00 (*0-7089-0666-4*) Ulverscroft.

— Houses of Stone. large type ed. LC 93-40498. 556p. 1994. lib. bdg. 23.95 (*0-8161-5936-X*) Thorndike Pr.

— Houses of Stone. large type ed. LC 93-40498. 556p. 1995. 18.95 (*0-8161-5937-8*) Thorndike Pr.

— Houses of Stone. 400p. 1994. reprint ed. mass mkt. 6.99 (*0-425-14306-6*) Berkley Pub.

— Into the Darkness. 1991. mass mkt. 6.99 (*0-425-12892-X*) Berkley Pub.

— The Master of Blacktower. 304p. 1995. mass mkt. 6.50 (*0-425-14941-2*) Berkley Pub.

***Michaels, Barbara, pseud.** Other Worlds: Rosenblat,&Barbara. abr. ed. 1999. audio 18.00 (*0-694-52082-9*, 396222, Pub. by HarperAudio) Lndmrk Audiobks.

Michaels, Barbara, pseud. Other Worlds: The Bell Witch & the Stratford Haunting. LC 98-39204. 224p. 1999. 23.00 (*0-06-019235-6*) HarpC.

***Michaels, Barbara, pseud.** Other Worlds: The Bell Witch & the Stratford Haunting. 304p. 2000. mass mkt. 6.99 (*0-06-109749-7*) HarpC.

— Other Worlds: The Bell Witch & the Stratford Haunting. large type ed. LC 98-53490. (Paperback Bestsellers Ser.). 280p. 1950. pap. 27.95 (*0-7838-8557-1*, G K Hall Lrg Type) Mac Lib Ref.

Michaels, Barbara, pseud. Other Worlds: The Bell Witch & the Stratford Haunting. large type ed. LC 98-53490. 1999. 29.95 (*0-7838-8556-3*, G K Hall Lrg Type) Mac Lib Ref.

— Other Worlds: The Bell Witch & the Stratford Haunting. large type ed. LC 98-53490. 1999. write for info. (*0-7862-1770-7*) Thorndike Pr.

— Patriot's Dream. 352p. 1994. mass mkt. 6.99 (*0-425-13355-9*) Berkley Pub.

— Prince of Darkness. 240p. 1988. mass mkt. 6.99 (*0-425-10853-8*) Berkley Pub.

— Scattered Blossoms. 1992. 20.00 (*0-685-53583-5*) S&S Trade.

— Search the Shadows. 1988. mass mkt. 6.99 (*0-425-11183-0*) Berkley Pub.

— Search the Shadows. 416p. 1997. mass mkt. 6.50 (*0-06-101009-X*, Harp PBks) HarpC.

— Search the Shadows RI. 416p. 1999. mass mkt. 6.50 (*0-06-104472-5*) HarpC.

— Shattered Silk. 320p. 1996. mass mkt. 6.50 (*0-06-101008-1*, Harp PBks) HarpC.

— Shattered Silk RI. 320p. 1999. mass mkt. 6.50 (*0-06-104473-3*) HarpC.

— Smoke & Mirrors. 1990. mass mkt. 6.99 (*0-425-11911-4*) Berkley Pub.

— Someone in the House. 1976. 20.95 (*0-8488-0834-7*) Amereon Ltd.

— Someone in the House. 1989. mass mkt. 6.99 (*0-425-11389-2*) Berkley Pub.

— Sons of the Wolf. 1989. mass mkt. 6.99 (*0-425-11687-5*) Berkley Pub.

— Sons of the Wolf. 1994. reprint ed. lib. bdg. 20.00 (*0-7278-4665-5*) Severn Hse.

— Stitches in Time. 400p. 1996. mass mkt. 6.99 (*0-06-109253-3*, Harp PBks) HarpC.

— Stitches in Time RI. 400p. 1999. mass mkt. 6.99 (*0-06-104474-1*) HarpC.

— Vanish with the Rose. 432p. 1993. mass mkt. 6.99 (*0-425-13898-4*) Berkley Pub.

Michaels, Barbara, pseud. Vanish with the Rose. abr. ed. 1992. 17.00 incl. audio (*0-671-75594-3*) S&S Audio.

Michaels, Barbara, pseud. Wait for What Will Come. 1990. mass mkt. 6.99 (*0-425-12005-8*) Berkley Pub.

— The Walker in Shadows. 1992. mass mkt. 6.99 (*0-425-13399-0*) Berkley Pub.

— Wings of the Falcon. 1988. mass mkt. 6.99 (*0-425-11045-1*) Berkley Pub.

— Wings of the Falcon. 230p. 1995. reprint ed. 20.00 (*0-7278-4722-8*) Severn Hse.

— Witch. 1989. mass mkt. 6.99 (*0-425-11831-2*) Berkley Pub.

— The Wizard's Daughter. 336p. 1995. mass mkt. 6.99 (*0-425-14642-1*) Berkley Pub.

— The Wizard's Daughter. large type ed. LC 96-53155. (Americana Series). 479p. 1997. 24.95 (*0-7862-1025-7*) Thorndike Pr.

— The Wizard's Daughter. 336p. 1996. reprint ed. 24.00 (*0-7278-4917-4*) Severn Hse.

***Michaels, Bill.** Bulsabar's Bad Day. (Pokemon Junior Ser.: Vol. 4). (Illus.). 112p. (J). (gr. k-4). 2000. pap. 3.99 (*0-439-15427-8*) Scholastic Inc.

— Meowth, the Big Mouth. (Pokemon Junior Ser.: Bk. 2). (Illus.). 48p. (J). (gr. k-4). 2000. mass mkt. 3.99 (*0-439-15417-0*) Scholastic Inc.

— Surf's up, Pikachu! (Pokemon Junior Ser.: Bk. 1). (Illus.). 48p. (J). (gr. k-4). 2000. mass mkt. 3.99 (*0-439-15405-7*) Scholastic Inc.

Michaels, Bill. Witchcraft. 288p. 1997. mass mkt. 4.99 (*0-8217-5601-X*, Zebra Kensgtn) Kensgtn Pub Corp.

Michaels, Carolyn. Children's Book Collecting. LC 92-35088. (Illus.). xii, 202p. (C). 1993. lib. bdg. 35.00 (*0-208-02267-8*, Lib Prof Pubns) Shoe String.

Michaels, Carolyn & Leopold, Dennette C. Library Literacy Means Lifelong Learning. LC 84-10705. 388p. 1985. 36.00 (*0-8108-1719-5*) Scarecrow.

Michaels, Cathleen. Uncork It!!! How to Be a Wine Expert Overnight. (Illus.). 88p. (Orig.). 1996. pap. 8.95 (*0-9652389-0-3*) Core Pubng.

Michaels, Charles & Cohen, Ruth. Four-Three-Two-One Bridge Student Text. 5th rev. ed. 1986. pap. 4.95 (*0-87643-008-6*) Barclay Bridge.

Michaels, Charlie & Brown, Mike. Avoiding Wedding Aftershock or I Like You Even Better Now That I Know You. LC 90-81456. (Illus.). 160p. 1990. pap. 14.95 (*0-9626525-0-4*) Carmichael Ventures.

Michaels, Craig, et al. Transition to Employment. LC 97-47019. (Series on Transition). 75p. 1998. pap. text 9.00 (*0-89079-783-8*, 8572) PRO-ED.

Michaels, Craig A., ed. Transition Strategies for Persons with Learning Disabilities. LC 94-2164. (Illus.). 312p. (Orig.). (C). 1994. pap. text 39.95 (*1-56593-165-3*, 0476) Thomson Learn.

Michaels, David D. Basic Refraction Techniques. LC 88-18541. 186p. 1988. reprint ed. pap. 57.70 (*0-608-04712-0*, 206543300004) Bks Demand.

Michaels, Dia L., jt. auth. see Bumslag, Naomi.

Michaels, Eileen. When Are You Entitled to New Underwear & Other Major Financial Decisions: Making Your Money Dreams Come True. LC 96-43277. 272p. 1997. 23.50 (*0-684-81534-6*) S&S Trade.

— When Are You Entitled to New Underwear & Other Major Financial Decisions: Making Your Money Dreams Come True. large type ed. LC 97-2317. 459p. 1997. 24.95 (*0-7838-8116-9*, G K Hall Lrg Type) Mac Lib Ref.

Michaels, Elizabeth. Illicit. 1995. pap. 4.99 (*0-8217-5167-0*) NAL.

— Lord Barton's Honour. (Regency Romance Ser.). 1993. mass mkt. 2.99 (*0-373-31201-6*, 1-31201-6) Harlequin Bks.

Michaels, Elizabeth A. From a Silver Heart. Tolley, Carolyn, ed. 576p. (Orig.). 1993. mass mkt. 4.99 (*0-671-76096-3*) PB.

— Illicit. 320p. 1996. pap. 2.99 (*0-8217-5489-0*) Kensgtn Pub Corp.

— Illicit. large type ed. (Black Satin Romance Ser.). 337p. 1997. 27.99 (*1-86110-032-9*) Ulverscroft.

— A Jewel So Rare. Tolley, Carolyn, ed. 336p. (Orig.). 1992. mass mkt. 4.99 (*0-671-72730-3*) PB.

— Of Sapphire Dreams. 320p. 1997. mass mkt. 4.99 (*0-8217-5540-4*, Zebra Kensgtn) Kensgtn Pub Corp.

— Til There Was You. 320p. 1998. mass mkt. 4.99 (*0-8217-5821-7*, Zebra Kensgtn) Kensgtn Pub Corp.

Michaels, Elsa. The Vegetarian Menu Cookbook. LC 73-5514. 191p. 1973. write for info. (*0-87749-516-5*) Crescent Pubng.

Michaels, Eric. Bad Aboriginal Art & Other Essays: Tradition, Media, & Technological Horizons. LC 93-5132. (Theory out of Bounds Ser.: No. 3). 296p. 1993. pap. 21.95 (*0-8166-2341-4*) U of Minn Pr.

— Unbecoming. Foss, Paul, ed. LC 97-7920. (Illus.). xxv, 129p. 1997. pap. 13.95 (*0-8223-2014-2*); lib. bdg. 39.95 (*0-8223-2005-3*) Duke.

Michaels, Evelyn B., jt. auth. see Holub, Alexander S.

Michaels, Evelyne. Encyclopedia of Health & Aging: Complete Guide to Health & Well Being in Your Later Years. LC 96-37274. 288p. 1997. per. 16.00 (*0-7615-0856-2*) Prima Pub.

Michaels, Fern. All She Can Be. 192p. 1987. mass mkt. 3.50 (*0-345-34812-5*) Ballantine Pub Grp.

— All She Can Be. large type ed. 230p. 1996. 22.95 (*0-7862-0296-3*) Thorndike Pr.

— Annie's Rainbow, 1. 384p. 1999. mass mkt. 6.99 (*0-8217-6173-0*) Kensgtn Pub Corp.

— Annie's Rainbow. 306p. 1999. 26.00 (*0-7278-5477-1*) Severn Hse.

— Annie's Rainbow. large type ed. LC 99-15673. 472p. 1950. pap. 30.00 (*0-7838-8670-5*, G K Hall Lrg Type) Mac Lib Ref.

***Michaels, Fern.** Annie's Rainbow. large type ed. LC 99-15673. (Core Ser.). 1999. pap. 30.00 (*0-7838-8669-1*, G K Hall Lrg Type) Mac Lib Ref.

Michaels, Fern. Automatic Transmissions & Transaxles. 3rd rev. ed. (Illus.). 848p. 1980. pap. text 1.50 (*0-671-57015-3*) Chek-Chart.

— Beyond Tomorrow Best of the Best. 1994. per. 4.50 (*0-373-48302-3*, 5-48302-9) Silhouette.

— Captive Innocence. 384p. 1998. 25.00 (*0-7278-5390-2*) Severn Hse.

E. 1994. per. 4.50 (*0-373-48302-3*, 5-48302-9) Silhouette.

— Captive Innocence. 384p. 1998. 25.00 (*0-7278-5390-2*) Severn Hse.

— Captive Passions. LC 76-56142. 1987. mass mkt. 5.95 (*0-345-34683-1*) Ballantine Pub Grp.

— Captive Passions. large type ed. LC 99-18675. 608p. 1999. write for info. (*0-7838-8585-7*, G K Hall & Co) Mac Lib Ref.

— Captive Secrets. large type ed. (General Ser.). 415p. (Orig.). 1992. lib. bdg. 21.95 (*0-8161-5360-4*, G K Hall Lrg Type) Mac Lib Ref.

— Captive Splendors. 400p. 1983. mass mkt. 6.99 (*0-345-31648-7*, Ballantine) Ballantine Pub Grp.

***Michaels, Fern.** Captive Splendors. 2000. mass mkt. 6.99 (*0-345-91633-6*) Ballantine Pub Grp.

Michaels, Fern. Captive Splendors. (Captives Ser.). 1994. 22.00 (0-7278-4605-1) Severn Hse.
***Michaels, Fern.** Captive Splendors. large type ed. LC 99-53132. 2000. 30.00 (0-7838-8834-1, G K Hall Lrg Type) Mac Lib Ref.
Michaels, Fern. Celebration. LC 98-67474. 368p. 1999. 24.00 (1-57566-402-X) Kensgtn Pub Corp.
***Michaels, Fern.** Celebration. 2000. mass mkt. 6.99 (0-8217-6452-7, Zebra Kensgtn) Kensgtn Pub Corp.
Michaels, Fern. Celebration. large type ed. LC 99-25117. 594p. 1999. 29.95 (0-7838-8626-8, G K Hall & Co) Mac Lib Ref.
***Michaels, Fern.** Celebration. large type ed. LC 99-25117. (Paperback Bestsellers Ser.). 576p. 2000. pap. 27.95 (0-7838-8627-6, G K Hall Lrg Type) Mac Lib Ref.
Michaels, Fern. Cinders to Satin. 1999. mass mkt. 5.99 (0-345-33952-5) Ballantine Pub Grp.
***Michaels, Fern.** Cinders to Satin. 1999. mass mkt. 6.99 (0-345-91570-4) Ballantine Pub Grp.
Michaels, Fern. Dear Emily. 512p. 1995. mass mkt. 5.99 (0-8217-4952-8, Zebra Kensgtn) Kensgtn Pub Corp.
— Dear Emily. 448p. 1996. pap. 6.99 (0-8217-5676-1, Zebra Kensgtn) Kensgtn Pub Corp.
— Dear Emily. large type ed. LC 95-34680. (Large Print Bks.). 1995. 25.95 (1-56895-254-6, Compass) Wheeler Pub.
— Dear Emily. 448p. 1996. reprint ed. 22.00 (0-7278-4802-X) Severn Hse.
— The Delta Ladies. 336p. 1995. per. 5.99 (0-671-79917-7) PB.
— The Delta Ladies. large type ed. 344p. 1995. lib. bdg. 24.95 (1-57490-028-5, Beeler LP Bks) T T Beeler.
— Desperate Measures. 1996. mass mkt. 6.99 (0-614-15941-5); mass mkt. 6.99 (0-8041-1536-2) Ivy Books.
— Desperate Measures. 1996. pap. 6.99 (0-614-98032-1, Avon Bks) Morrow Avon.
— Desperate Measures. large type ed. LC 94-34299. 588p. 1995. lib. bdg. 23.95 (0-7862-0337-4) Thorndike Pr.
— Finders Keepers. LC 98-65171. 352p. 1998. 24.00 (1-57566-323-6, Knsington) Kensgtn Pub Corp.
— Finders Keepers. 432p. 1999. mass mkt. 6.99 (0-8217-6307-5, Zebra Kensgtn) Kensgtn Pub Corp.
— Finders Keepers. LC 98-44852. 1998. 26.95 (1-56895-693-2) Wheeler Pub.
— For All Their Lives. 1992. mass mkt. 5.99 (0-345-36592-5) Ballantine Pub Grp.
— For All Their Lives. large type ed. LC 92-14410. (General Ser.). 1992. pap. 17.95 (0-8161-5362-0, G K Hall Lrg Type) Mac Lib Ref.
— Free Spirit. (Love & Life Ser.). 224p. (Orig.). 1983. mass mkt. 5.99 (0-345-30840-9) Ballantine Pub Grp.
— Golden Lasso. 1994. per. 4.50 (0-373-48297-3, 5-48297-1) Silhouette.
***Michaels, Fern.** The Guest List. 2000. mass mkt. 6.99 (0-8217-6657-0, Zebra Kensgtn) Kensgtn Pub Corp.
— Heart of the Home. 25.95 (0-7862-1491-0) Five Star.
— Listen to Your Heart. 214p. 2000. 20.00 (1-57566-572-7) Kensgtn Pub Corp.
— Listen to Your Heart. large type ed. 2000. 26.95 (1-56895-876-5) Wheeler Pub.
Michaels, Fern. Nightstar. 1998. per. 5.50 (1-55166-458-5, 1-66458-0, Mira Bks) Harlequin Bks.
— Nightstar. (Best of the Best Ser.). 1993. per. 4.50 (0-373-48274-4, 5-48274-0) Silhouette.
— Paint Me Rainbows. 256p. 1994. per. 4.99 (1-55166-003-2, 1-66003-4, Mira Bks) Harlequin Bks.
— Paint Me Rainbows. 2000. mass mkt. 5.99 (0-373-48398-8, 1-48398-1) Harlequin Bks.
— Paint Me Rainbows. 1994. mass mkt. 4.50 (0-373-48316-3, 5-48316-9) Silhouette.
Michaels, Fern. Picture Perfect. (Illus.). 256p. 25.00 (0-7278-5515-8) Severn Hse.
Michaels, Fern. Sara's Song. 416p. 1998. pap. 6.99 (0-8217-5856-X, Zebra Kensgtn) Kensgtn Pub Corp.
***Michaels, Fern.** Sara's Song. 416p. 1999. 26.00 (0-7278-2266-7, Pub. by Severn Hse) Chivers N Amer.
Michaels, Fern. Sara's Song. large type ed. LC 98-22309. 1998. 27.95 (0-7862-1524-0) Thorndike Pr.
***Michaels, Fern.** Sea Gypsy. 2000. per. 5.99 (1-55166-605-7, Mira Bks) Harlequin Bks.
Michaels, Fern. Sea Gypsy. (Best of the Best Ser.). (C). 1993. per. 4.50 (0-373-48275-2, 5-48275-7) Silhouette.
— Seasons of Her Life. 1994. mass mkt. 5.99 (0-345-36591-7) Ballantine Pub Grp.
— Serendipity. 1997. mass mkt. 6.99 (0-449-14982-X) Fawcett.
— Sins of Omission. 512p. 1989. mass mkt. 5.99 (0-345-34120-1) Ballantine Pub Grp.
***Michaels, Fern.** Sins of the Flesh. large type ed. LC 99-46178. (Romance Ser.). 1999. 28.95 (0-7838-8785-X, G K Hall & Co) Mac Lib Ref.
Michaels, Fern. Sins of the Flesh. 448p. 1995. reprint ed. 22.00 (0-7278-4754-6) Severn Hse.
***Michaels, Fern.** Split Second. 1999. 25.00 (0-7278-5431-3, Pub. by Severn Hse) Chivers N Amer.
Michaels, Fern. Tender Warrior. 384p. (Orig.). 1982. mass mkt. 5.99 (0-345-30358-X) Ballantine Pub Grp.
— Tender Warrior. 384p. (Orig.). 25.00 (0-7278-5220-5) Severn Hse.
— Texas Fury. 512p. 1989. mass mkt. 5.99 (0-345-31375-5, Ballantine) Ballantine Pub Grp.
— Texas Fury. large type ed. LC 93-13197. 792p. 1993. lib. bdg. 22.95 (1-56054-754-5) Thorndike Pr.
— Texas Heat. 640p. 1986. mass mkt. 5.99 (0-345-33100-1) Ballantine Pub Grp.
— Texas Heat. large type ed. LC 92-42500. 681p. 1993. lib. bdg. 20.95 (1-56054-660-3) Thorndike Pr.
— Texas Rich. 640p. 1987. mass mkt. 5.95 (0-345-33540-6) Ballantine Pub Grp.
— Texas Sunrise. 1994. mass mkt. 6.99 (0-345-36593-3) Ballantine Pub Grp.
— Texas Sunrise. large type ed. LC 93-13194. 480p. 1994. lib. bdg. 22.95 (1-56054-755-3) Thorndike Pr.
— To Taste the Wine. (Orig.). 1987. mass mkt. 5.95 (0-345-30360-1) Ballantine Pub Grp.
— Valentina. 1983. mass mkt. 5.99 (0-345-31126-4, Ballantine) Ballantine Pub Grp.
— Valentina. 448p. 1998. 25.00 (0-7278-5331-7) Severn Hse.
— Vegas Heat. LC 96-77850. 400p. 1997. 25.00 (1-57566-138-1, Knsington) Kensgtn Pub Corp.
— Vegas Heat. 480p. 1997. mass mkt. 6.99 (0-8217-5758-X, Zebra Kensgtn) Kensgtn Pub Corp.
— Vegas Rich. 512p. 1996. 25.00 (1-57566-057-1, Knsington) Kensgtn Pub Corp.
— Vegas Rich. 1997. 188.73 (0-8217-8721-7); pap. 6.99 (0-8217-5594-3, Zebra Kensgtn) Kensgtn Pub Corp.
— Vegas Rich, Vol. 1. large type ed. LC 96-3208. 1996. 26.95 (1-56895-370-4, Compass) Wheeler Pub.
— Vegas Sunrise. LC 96-80347. 384p. 1997. 25.00 (1-57566-214-0, Knsington) Kensgtn Pub Corp.
— Vegas Sunrise. 480p. 1998. pap. 6.99 (0-8217-5983-3, Zebra Kensgtn) Kensgtn Pub Corp.
— Vegas Sunrise. large type ed. 1998. 27.95 (1-56895-571-5, Compass) Wheeler Pub.
***Michaels, Fern.** Vixen in Velvet. large type ed. 303p. 2000. lib. bdg. 27.95 (1-58547-051-1) Ctr Point Pubg.
— What You Wish For. 2000. 24.00 (1-57566-573-5, Knsington) Kensgtn Pub Corp.
Michaels, Fern. Whisper My Name. 1999. per. 5.50 (1-55166-473-9, 1-66473-9, Mira Bks) Harlequin Bks.
— Whisper My Name. (Best of the Best Ser.). 1993. mass mkt. 4.50 (0-373-48273-6, 5-48273-2) Silhouette.
— Whitefire. LC 97-23467. (Five Star Romance Ser.). 369p. 1997. lib. bdg. 25.95 (0-7862-1208-X) Five Star.
— Whitefire. 352p. 1997. mass mkt. 6.99 (0-8217-5638-9, Zebra Kensgtn) Kensgtn Pub Corp.
— Wild Honey. Tolley, Carolyn, ed. 336p. 1992. mass mkt. 5.99 (0-671-79390-X) PB.
— Wild Honey. large type ed. (Large Print Ser.). 352p. 1996. lib. bdg. 24.95 (1-57490-041-2, Beeler LP Bks) T T Beeler.
— Wish List. (Five Star Romances Ser.). 1996. lib. bdg. 23.95 (0-7862-0851-1) Five Star.
— Wish List. 352p. 1996. pap. 6.99 (0-8217-5228-6, Zebra Kensgtn) Kensgtn Pub Corp.
— Wish List. large type ed. LC 96-15056. (Large Print Bks.). 1996. 25.95 (1-56895-336-4) Wheeler Pub.
***Michaels, Fern.** Yesterday. 1999. 24.00 (1-57566-467-4, Knsington) Kensgtn Pub Corp.
— Yesterday. LC 99-52170. 1999. 26.95 (1-56895-797-1, Wheeler) Wheeler Pub.
***Michaels, Fern, et al.** Five Golden Rings. 464p. 2000. mass mkt. 6.99 (0-8217-7062-4, Zebra Kensgtn) Kensgtn Pub Corp.
Michaels, Fern, et al. Heart of the Home. 1997. mass mkt. 5.99 (0-614-27797-3, Topaz) NAL.
— Homecoming. large type ed. LC 97-52118. 482p. 1998. 26.95 (0-7838-8433-8, G K Hall & Co) Mac Lib Ref.
— A Joyous Season. 352p. 1996. mass mkt. 6.99 (0-8217-5440-8, Zebra Kensgtn) Kensgtn Pub Corp.
***Michaels, Fern, et al.** Pet Pals: Authors & Their Pets. (Author Scrapbks.: Vol. 1). (Illus.). 38p. 1999. pap. 5.00 (1-58365-038-5, Indigo Publicatns) BT Pub.
Michaels, G. J. Tip of the Spear: U.S. Marine Light Armor in the Gulf War. LC 97-51651. (Illus.). 272p. 1998. 29.95 (1-55750-599-3) Naval Inst Pr.
Michaels, Gerald Y., jt. auth. see Goldstein, Arnold P.
Michaels, Grant. Body to Dye For. LC 90-28597. Vol. 1. 241p. 1991. pap. 11.95 (0-312-05825-X) St Martin.
— Dead As a Doornail. LC 97-48908. 256p. 1998. text 22.95 (0-312-18077-2) St Martin.
— Dead As a Doornail. 256p. 1999. pap. 12.95 (0 312 20644 5) St Martin.
— Love You to Death. LC 92-37742. (Stonewall Inn Mysteries Ser.). 1993. text 8.95 (0-312-08841-8) St Martin.
— Mask for a Diva. LC 95-39343. 304p. 1996. pap. 9.95 (0-312-14120-3) St Martin.
— Time to Check Out: A Stan Kraychik Mystery. LC 97-8807. 256p. 1997. pap. 11.95 (0-312-15673-1) St Martin.
Michaels, Ian, ed. see Shaw, George Bernard.
Michaels, Ian, ed. see Wilde, Oscar.
Michaels, J. Ramsey. I Peter. (Biblical Commentary Ser.: Vol. 49). 29.99 (0-8499-0248-7) Word Pub.
— Interpreting the Book of Revelation. LC 92-16597. (Guides to New Testament Exegesis Ser.). 160p. 1998. pap. 14.99 (0-8010-6293-4) Baker Bks.
— John. (New International Biblical Commentary Ser.). 386p. 1989. pap. 11.95 (0-943575-14-1) Hendrickson MA.
— Revelation. LC 97-5276. (IVP New Testament Commentary Ser.: Vol. 20). 300p. 1997. 17.99 (0-8308-1820-0, 1820) InterVarsity.
Michaels, Jack V. Understanding the Time Value of Money. (Illus.). 382p. (Orig.). 1996. pap. 29.95 (0-9649133-0-5) Mgmt Sci FL.
Michaels, Jack V. & Wood, William P. Design to Cost. LC 88-31936. 432p. 1989. 175.00 (0-471-60900-5) Wiley.
Michaels, Jenevy. Tuesday's Child. 256p. 1996. mass mkt. 4.99 (0-7860-0339-1, Pinncle Kensgtn) Kensgtn Pub Corp.
Michaels, Jennifer E. Franz Jung: Expressionist, Dadaist, Revolutionary Outsider. (American University Studies: Germanic Languages & Literature: Ser. I, Vol. 70). X, 238p. (C). 1988. text 35.50 (0-8204-0758-5) P Lang Pubng.
— Franz Werfel & the Critics. (LCGERM Ser.). x, 178p. 1994. 55.00 (1-879751-99-2) Camden Hse.
Michaels, Joanne. The Joy of Divorce. LC 94-78914. (Illus.). 100p. 1995. 9.95 (0-9619429-2-4) JMB NY.
— Nun in the Closet. LC 94-2197. 200p. (Orig.). 1994. pap. 9.95 (0-934678-43-X) New Victoria Pubs.
Michaels, Joanne & Barile, Mary. Famous Woodstock Cooks: And Their Favorite Recipes. 2nd ed. (Illus.). 143p. (Orig.). 1994. pap. 14.95 (0-9619429-0-8) JMB NY.
Michaels, Joanne & Barile, Mary-Margaret. The Best of the Hudson Valley & Catskill Mountains: An Explorer's Guide. 3rd ed. LC 97-44270. (Explorer's Guide Ser.). (Illus.). 272p. 1998. pap. 16.00 (0-88150-396-7, Pub. by Countryman) Norton.
Michaels, Joe. A-6 Intruder in Action. (Aircraft in Action Ser.). (Illus.). 50p. 1993. pap. 9.95 (0-89747-302-7) Squad Sig Pubns.
Michaels, Joe, et al. Prime of Your Life. LC 80-21205. 366p. reprint ed. pap. 113.50 (0-608-12288-2, 202515900042) Bks Demand.
Michaels, Joe, ed. see Roquemore, Erma.
Michaels, John G. & Rosen, Kenneth H. Applications of Discrete Mathematics. 352p. (C). 1991. 31.25 (0-07-041823-3) McGraw.
Michaels, John G., jt. auth. see Bloch, Norman J.
Michaels, John H., jt. auth. see Meader, Greg.
Michaels, Jon. The Official Anti Rush Limburger Handbook. 144p. (Orig.). 1995. pap. 14.95 (0-9649839-0-7) Gadfly Prodns.
— You Know He's a Two-Timing Egomaniacal, Womanizing Slimeball When . . . Carle, Cliff, ed. (Illus.). 120p. (Orig.). 1997. pap. 5.95 (1-57644-045-1) CCC Pubns.
Michaels, Jonathan. Personal Finance on the Web: The Interactive Guide. LC 97-2919. (Illus.). 316p. 1997. pap. 24.95 (0-471-16385-6) Wiley.
Michaels, Joshua. Cheap Sex. LC 86-3311. 1988. 18.95 (0-87949-244-9) Ashley Bks.
***Michaels, Judith.** A Certain Smile. 2000. mass mkt. 6.99 (0-449-00681-6, Crest) Fawcett.
Michaels, Judith. Risking Intensity: Reading & Writing Poetry with High School Students. LC 98-47499. 188p. 1999. 15.95 (0-8141-4171-4) NCTE.
Michaels, Judith E. The President's Call: Executive Leadership from FDR to George Bush. LC 97-4562. (Policy & Institutional Studies). 348p. 1997. pap. 22.00 (0-8229-5628-4); text 50.00 (0-8229-3977-0) U of Pittsburgh Pr.
Michaels, Judy, jt. auth. see Stevens, Jared.
Michaels, Julia, tr. see Nilton, Bonder.
Michaels, Kasey. The Anonymous Miss Addams. 192p. (Orig.). 1989. pap. 2.95 (0-380-75668-4, Avon Bks) Morrow Avon.
— Baby Fever. (Silhouette Promo Ser.). (Orig.). 1999. per. 5.99 (0-373-48380-5, 1-48380-9, Harlequin) Harlequin Bks.
— The Belligerent Miss Boynton. 224p. (Orig.). 1982. pap. 2.95 (0-380-77073-3, Avon Bks) Morrow Avon.
— The Bride of the Unicorn. 384p. 1993. mass mkt. 5.99 (0-671-73181-5, Pocket Star Bks) PB.
***Michaels, Kasey.** Can't Take My Eyes Off of You. 2000. mass mkt. 5.99 (0-8217-6522-1, Zebra Kensgtn) Kensgtn Pub Corp.
— Can't Take My Eyes Off of You. large type ed. LC PS3563.I2725C36 2000. 2000. 25.95 (1-57490-265-2, Beeler LP Bks) T T Beeler.
— Carried Away: Logan Assents, Ryan Objects. 2000. per. 3.50 (0-373-19438-2) Harlequin Bks.
Michaels, Kasey. The Chaotic Miss Crispino. 192p. (Orig.). 1991. mass mkt. 3.99 (0-380-76300-1, Avon Bks) Morrow Avon.
***Michaels, Kasey.** Come Near Me. 384p. 2000. mass mkt. 6.50 (0-446-60583-2, Pub. by Warner Bks) Little.
Michaels, Kasey. The Dad Next Door. 1995. per. 2.99 (0-373-19108-1, 1-19108-9) Silhouette.
— The Dubious Miss Dalrymple. 192p. 1990. pap. 2.95 (0-380-89908-6, Avon Bks) Morrow Avon.
— Escapade. 338p. (Orig.). 1999. mass mkt. 6.50 (0-446-60683-9, Pub. by Warner Bks) Little.
— Five's a Crowd. (Love & Laughter Ser.). 1996. per. 3.50 (0-373-44003-0, 1-44003-1) Harlequin Bks.
— The Haunted Miss Hampshire. 192p. (Orig.). 1992. mass mkt. 3.99 (0-380-76301-X, Avon Bks) Morrow Avon.
— The Homecoming. 324p. 1996. mass mkt. 5.99 (0-671-50123-2, PB Trade Paper) PB.
— Husbands Don't Grow on Trees. 1995. per. 3.50 (0-373-52008-5) Silhouette.
— The Illusions of Love. Zion, Claire, ed. 368p. 1994. mass mkt. 5.50 (0-671-79340-3, Pocket Star Bks) PB.
— Indiscreet. 369p. 1998. mass mkt. 6.50 (0-446-60582-4, Pub. by Warner Bks) Little.
***Michaels, Kasey.** Indiscreet. large type ed. LC 99-86685. 2000. 25.95 (1-56895-843-9) Wheeler Pub.
— Jessie's Expecting. (Romance Ser.: Bk. 1475). 2000. mass mkt. 3.50 (0-373-19475-7, 1-19475-2) Silhouette.
Michaels, Kasey. The Legacy of the Rose. Zion, Claire, ed. 448p. (Orig.). 1992. mass mkt. 5.99 (0-671-73180-7) PB.
— The Lurid Lady Lockport. 208p. (Orig.). 1984. pap. 2.95 (0-380-86231-X, Avon Bks) Morrow Avon.
— Marriage in a Suitcase. (Romance Ser.). 1993. pap. 2.75 (0-373-08949-X, 5-08949-5) Silhouette.
***Michaels, Kasey.** Marrying Maddy. (Silhouette Romance Ser.: Vol. 1469). 2000. mass mkt. 3.50 (0-373-19469-2, 1-19469-5) Harlequin Bks.
Michaels, Kasey. A Masquerade in the Moonlight. 1994. mass mkt. 5.50 (0-671-79339-X) PB.
— The Mischievous Miss Murphy. (Regency Romance Ser.). 176p. 1987. pap. 2.95 (0-380-89907-8, Avon Bks) Morrow Avon.
— Passion of an Angel. 400p. 1995. mass mkt. 5.99 (0-671-79342-X) S&S Trade.
— Playful Lady Penelope. 192p. 1988. pap. 2.95 (0-380-75297-2, Avon Bks) Morrow Avon.
— Prenuptial Agreement. (Romance Ser.). 1992. pap. 2.69 (0-373-08898-1, 5-08898-4) Silhouette.
— Prenuptial Agreement. large type ed. 215p. 1993. reprint ed. lib. bdg. 13.95 (1-56054-614-X) Thorndike Pr.
— Promise. 1997. per. 5.99 (0-671-50114-3, Pocket Books) PB.
— The Questioning Miss Quinton. 176p. 1987. pap. 2.95 (0-380-75296-4, Avon Bks) Morrow Avon.
***Michaels, Kasey.** Raffling Ryan. (Romance Ser.: Bk. 1481). 2000. mass mkt. 3.50 (0-373-19481-1, 1-19481-0) Silhouette.
Michaels, Kasey. The Rambunctious Lady Royston. 224p. 1982. pap. 2.95 (0-380-81448-X, Avon Bks) Morrow Avon.
— Romeo in the Rain, Bk. 30. (Born in the U. S. A. Ser.). 1997. per. 4.50 (0-373-47180-7, 1-47180-4) Harlequin Bks.
— The Secrets of the Heart. Zion, Claire, ed. 384p. (Orig.). 1995. mass mkt. 5.99 (0-671-79341-1) PB.
***Michaels, Kasey.** The Sheikh's Secret Son. (Fortunes of Texas Ser.). 2000. per. 4.50 (0-373-65036-1) Harlequin Bks.
Michaels, Kasey. Strange Bedfellows. (36 Hours Ser.: Vol. 2). 1997. per. 4.50 (0-373-65007-8) Harlequin Bks.
— The Tenacious Miss Tamerlane. 192p. 1982. pap. 2.95 (0-380-79889-1, Avon Bks) Morrow Avon.
— Timely Matrimony. (Silhouette Romance Ser.). 1994. per. 2.75 (0-373-19030-1, 1-19030-5) Harlequin Bks.
— To Marry at Christmas. 1996. pap. 4.99 (0-614-16982-8) Harlequin Bks.
— Uncle Daddy. (Romance Ser.). 1993. pap. 2.69 (0-373-08916-3, 5-08916-4) Silhouette.
— The Untamed. 307p. 1996. per. 5.99 (0-671-50115-1) PB.
— The Wagered Miss Winslow. 192p. (Orig.). 1992. mass mkt. 3.99 (0-380-76302-8, Avon Bks) Morrow Avon.
***Michaels, Kasey.** Waiting for You. 2000. mass mkt. 6.99 (0-446-60584-0) Warner Bks.
Michaels, Kasey, et al. Key to My Heart: Love, Emmaline; Knock Three Times; Remington & Juliet, 3 bks. in 1. (Promo Ser.: No. 83349). 1998. per. 5.99 (0-373-83349-0, 1-83349-0) Harlequin Bks.
Michaels, Kasey, jt. auth. see McAllister, Anne.
Michaels, Kasey, jt. auth. see Richards, Emilie.
Michaels, Katherine. Crashing into the Wall of Vanity: Cosmetic Surgery Is It for You? 160p. 1992. pap. 6.95 (0-9634948-0-5, TX3346596) Reality Matrix.
Michaels, Kay. Christmas Is Coming: A Fold-Around Pop-up Book Featuring Mickey Mouse & Friends. LC 94-68595. (Illus.). 10p. (J). 1995. 11.95 (0-7868-3039-5, Pub. by Disney Pr) Little.
Michaels, Kenneth. K M. 514p. mass mkt. 5.99 (1-55197-175-5) Picasso Publ.
Michaels, Kevin. AIDS Crisis: Impact On the Gay Subculture, Pt. 1. 130p. 1986. ring bd. 11.95 (0-939020-77-7) MLP Ent.
— AIDS Crisis: Impact on the Gay Subculture, Pt. 2. 110p. 1987. ring bd. 12.95 (0-939020-79-3) MLP Ent.
— The Gay Book of Etiquette. rev. ed. 113p. 1984. pap. 11.95 (0-939020-76-9) MLP Ent.
— The Heterosexual Trap. 120p. 1987. ring bd. 12.50 (0-939020-80-7) MLP Ent.
— Michaels on Gay Life, Vol. 1. 140p. (Orig.). 1986. pap., ring bd. 11.95 (0-939020-78-5) MLP Ent.
— Michaels on Gay Life, Vol. 2. 140p. (Orig.). 1987. ring bd. 12.95 (0-939020-81-5) MLP Ent.
Michaels, Kristin. Voyage to Love. (Orig.). (YA). 1981. mass mkt. 2.75 (0-451-09983-4, W9983, Sig) NAL.
— Voyage to Love. (Orig.). 1982. mass mkt. 2.50 (0-451-11525-2, AE1525, Sig) NAL.
Michaels, L. Atlas of Ear, Nose & Throat Pathology. (C). 1990. text 287.50 (0-7923-8934-4) Kluwer Academic.
Michaels, Larry R. East Side Story: People & Places in the History of East Toledo. (Illus.). 208p. 1993. pap. 9.95 (1-883829-12-7) Bihl Hse Pub.
— Treasures of East Toledo: A History of the Schools, Churches, Houses, & Other Landmarks of the East Side. (Illus.). 164p. 1997. 15.00 (1-883829-15-1); pap. 10.00 (1-883829-17-8) Bihl Hse Pub.
***Michaels, Larry R., ed.** That New World: Selected Poems of Sarah Piatt, 1861-1911. 272p. 1999. pap. 11.95 (1-883829-07-0) Bihl Hse Pub.
***Michaels, Laura.** Symphony of the Stars: A Spiritual Adventure. Chadwick, Gloria, ed. LC 99-70521. 80p. 2000. pap. 11.00 (1-883717-93-0) Myst Mndscapes.
Michaels, Leigh. Atout Coeur. (Horizon Ser.). (FRE.). 1997. pap. 3.50 (0-373-39439-X, 1-39439-4) Harlequin Bks.
— Baby, You're Mine! (Romance Ser.: No. 3463). 1997. per. 3.25 (0-373-03463-6, 1-03463-6) Harlequin Bks.
— The Best Made Plans. (Romance Ser.: No. 214). 1992. per. 2.89 (0-373-03214-5) Harlequin Bks.
— The Billionaire Date. (Romance Ser.). 1998. per. 3.50 (0-373-03496-2, 1-03496-6) Harlequin Bks.
— The Billionaire Date. large type ed. 1998. per. 3.50 (0-373-15742-8, Harlequin) Harlequin Bks.
— The Boss & the Baby. anniversary ed. (Romance Ser.: No. 3552). 1999. per. 3.50 (0-373-03552-7, 1-03552-6) Harlequin Bks.
— The Boss & the Baby. anniversary large type ed. (Romance Ser.: No. 3552). 1999. per. 3.50 (0-373-15798-3, 1-15798-1) Harlequin Bks.
***Michaels, Leigh.** Boss's Bride, Vol. 455. large type ed. Vol. 455. 2000. mass mkt. 3.50 (0-373-15855-6) Harlequin Bks.
— The Bridal Swap. 288p. 2000. 26.99 (0-263-16446-2, Pub. by Mills & Boon) Ulverscroft.
— Bride on Loan. (Romance Ser.: Vol. 3604). 2000. per. 3.50 (0-373-03604-3) Harlequin Bks.

M

— Bride on Loan. large type ed. (Harlequin Romance Ser.: No. 450). 2000. per. 3.50 (*0-373-15850-5*, Harlequin) Harlequin Bks.

Michaels, Leigh. The Daddy Trap. (Romance Ser.). 1996. per. 3.25 (*0-373-03411-3*, 1-03411-5) Harlequin Bks.

— Dating Games. (Romance Ser.). 1993. per. 2.99 (*0-373-03290-0*, 1-03290-3) Harlequin Bks.

— Defi Amoureux. (Horizon Ser.: Bk. 495). 1999. mass mkt. 3.50 (*0-373-39495-0*, 1-39495-6) Harlequin Bks.

— Un Duo Romantique. (Horizon Ser.). (FRE.). 1994. pap. 3.50 (*0-373-39289-3*, 1-39289-3) Harlequin Bks.

***Michaels, Leigh.** Exclusively Yours. 2000. mass mkt. 4.50 (*0-373-82213-8*, 1-82213-9) Harlequin Bks.

Michaels, Leigh. The Fake Fiance. 1997. per. 3.25 (*0-373-03478-4*, 1-03478-4) Harlequin Bks.

— Family Secrets. (Promo Ser.). 1999. per. 4.50 (*0-373-21961-X*, 1-21961-7) Harlequin Bks.

— Family Secrets: (Kids & Kisses) (Romance Ser.). 1994. per. 2.99 (*0-373-03324-9*, 1-03324-0) Harlequin Bks.

— Her Husband-to-Be. (Romance Ser.: No. 3541). 1999. per. 3.50 (*0-373-03541-1*, 1-03541-9) Harlequin Bks.

— Her Husband-to-Be. large type ed. (Romance Ser.: No. 387). 1999. 3.50 (*0-373-15787-8*, 1-15787-4) Harlequin Bks.

— House of Dreams. (Larger Print Ser.). 1995. pap. 2.99 (*0-373-15589-1*, 1-15589-4); per. 2.99 (*0-373-03343-5*, 1-03343-0) Harlequin Bks.

— The Husband Project. (Romance Ser.). 1998. per. 3.50 (*0-373-03504-7*, 1-03504-7) Harlequin Bks.

***Michaels, Leigh.** The Husband Project. large type ed. 1999. 25.99 (*0-263-15987-6*, Pub. by Mills & Boon) Ulverscroft.

Michaels, Leigh. An Imperfect Love. large type ed. (Magna Large Print Ser.). 265p. 1998. 29.99 (*0-7505-1210-5*, Pub. by Mgna Lrg Print) Ulverscroft.

— Invitation to Love. large type ed. (Harlequin Romance Ser.). 1995. 19.95 (*0-263-14215-9*) Mac Lib Ref.

— Invitation to Love: Sealed with a Kiss. (Romance Ser.). 1995. per. 2.99 (*0-373-03352-4*, 1-03352-1) Harlequin Bks.

— Kiss Yesterday Goodbye. 1994. per. 3.59 (*0-373-45165-2*) Harlequin Bks.

— The Lake Effect. (Romance Ser.). 1993. per. 2.99 (*0-373-03275-7*, 1-03275-4) Harlequin Bks.

— Let Me Count the Ways. (Romance Ser.: No. 3023). 1989. per. 2.50 (*0-373-03023-1*) Harlequin Bks.

— Let Me Count the Ways. large type ed. (Magna Large Print Ser.). 287p. 1996. 27.99 (*0-7505-0989-9*, Pub. by Mgna Lrg Print) Ulverscroft.

— Marrying the Boss! (Romance Ser.). 1996. per. 3.25 (*0-373-03423-7*, 1-03423-0) Harlequin Bks.

— Marrying the Boss! large type ed. (Harlequin Romance Ser.). 1997. 20.95 (*0-263-15124-7*) Mac Lib Ref.

— A Matter of Principal. large type ed. 277p. 1996. 11.50 (*0-7505-0856-6*, Pub. by Mgna Lrg Print) Ulverscroft.

— A Matter of Principle. (Romance Ser.: No. 3070). 1990. per. 2.50 (*0-373-03070-3*) Harlequin Bks.

— Old School Ties. (Romance Ser.: No. 184). 1992. per. 2.89 (*0-373-03184-X*, 1-03184-8) Harlequin Bks.

— Once & for Always. large type ed. 1995. 11.50 (*0-7505-0827-2*, Pub. by Mgna Lrg Print) Ulverscroft.

— The Only Man for Maggie: Holding Out for a Hero. LC 96-718. (Romance Ser.). 186p. 1996. per. 3.25 (*0-373-03401-6*, 1-03401-6) Harlequin Bks.

— The Perfect Divorce! (Romance Ser.). 1997. per. 3.25 (*0-373-03444-X*, 1-03444-6) Harlequin Bks.

— The Playboy Assignment. (Romance Ser.). 1998. per. 3.50 (*0-373-03500-4*, 1-03500-5) Harlequin Bks.

***Michaels, Leigh.** The Playboy Assignment. large type ed. 1999. 25.99 (*0-263-15935-3*, Pub. by Mills & Boon) Ulverscroft.

Michaels, Leigh. Le Plus Fou Des Paris. (Horizon Ser.: No. 487). (FRE.). 1998. mass mkt. 3.50 (*0-373-39487-X*, 1-39487-3) Harlequin Bks.

— Promise Me Tomorrow. (Romance Ser.: No. 141). 1991. per. 2.75 (*0-373-03141-6*) Harlequin Bks.

— Une Rencontre Explosive. (Horizon Ser.: No. 474). (FRE.). 1998. pap. 3.50 (*0-373-39474-8*, 1-39474-1) Harlequin Bks.

— Safe in My Heart. (Romance Ser.). 1993. per. 2.89 (*0-373-03248-X*, 1-03248-1) Harlequin Bks.

— A Singular Honeymoon. (Romance Ser.). 1994. per. 2.99 (*0-373-03300-1*, 1-03300-0) Harlequin Bks.

— A Singular Honeymoon. (Promo Ser.). 1999. per. 4.50 (*0-373-21983-0*, 1-21983-1) Harlequin Bks.

— Taming a Tycoon. LC 95-13542. (Romance Ser.). 186p. 1995. per. 2.99 (*0-373-03367-2*, 1-03367-9) Harlequin Bks.

— Taming a Tycoon. large type ed. 288p. 1996. 19.95 (*0-263-14669-3*) Thorndike Pr.

— A Taste of Love: Recipes from Romance. 190p. (Orig.). 1995. pap. 12.95 (*0-9641275-1-2*) PBL Ltd.

— Temporary Measures. (Romance Ser.: No. 3160). 1991. per. 2.79 (*0-373-03160-2*) Harlequin Bks.

— Ties That Bind. (Romance Ser.). 1993. per. 2.89 (*0-373-03263-3*, 1-03263-0) Harlequin Bks.

— Traveling Man. 1994. per. 2.99 (*0-373-03311-7*) Harlequin Bks.

***Michaels, Leigh.** The Tycoon's Baby. large type ed. 288p. 1999. 25.99 (*0-263-16209-5*, Pub. by Mills & Boon) Ulverscroft.

Michaels, Leigh. The Tycoon's Baby: Daddy Boom. (Romance Ser.: No. 3574). 1999. per. 3.50 (*0-373-03574-8*, 1-03574-0) Harlequin Bks.

— The Tycoon's Baby: Daddy Boom. large type ed. (Larger Print Ser.: No. 420). 1999. per. 3.50 (*0-373-15820-3*, 1-15820-3) Harlequin Bks.

— An Uncommon Affair. (Romance Ser.: No. 3119). 1991. per. 2.75 (*0-373-03119-X*) Harlequin Bks.

— The Unexpected Landlord. (Romance Ser.). 1992. per. 2.89 (*0-373-03233-1*, 1-03233-3) Harlequin Bks.

— The Unlikely Santa. LC 96-296. 189p. 1995. per. 2.99 (*0-373-03388-5*, 1-03388-5) Harlequin Bks.

— Wednesday's Child. (Family Continuity Program Ser.: No. 12). 1999. mass mkt. 4.50 (*0-373-82160-3*, 1-82160-2) Harlequin Bks.

***Michaels, Leigh.** Wife on Approval, Vol. 454. large type ed. Vol. 454. 2000. mass mkt. 3.50 (*0-373-15854-8*) Harlequin Bks.

— Wife on Approval: Hiring Ms. Right. (Romance Ser.: Bk. 3608). 2000. per. 3.50 (*0-373-03608-6*, 1-03608-6) Harlequin Bks.

Michaels, Leigh. With No Reservations. large type ed. 1990. lib. bdg. 18.95 (*0-263-12355-3*) Mac Lib Ref.

— Writing the Romance Novel. 190p. 1996. pap. 13.95 (*0-9641275-2-0*) PBL Ltd.

***Michaels, Leigh.** Writing the Romance Novel. 2nd rev. ed. 280p. 1999. pap. 21.95 (*1-892689-01-4*) PBL Ltd.

Michaels, Leonard. A Girl with a Monkey: New & Selected Stories. LC 99-86600. 240p. 2000. pap. text 14.95 (*1-56279-120-6*) Mercury Hse Inc.

— The Men's Club. LC 92-45612. 200p. 1993. pap. 10.00 (*1-56279-039-0*) Mercury Hse Inc.

— Sylvia. LC 92-16541. 144p. 1992. 10.00 (*1-56279-029-3*) Mercury Hse Inc.

***Michaels, Leonard.** Time Out of Mind. 2000. pap. 13.00 (*1-57322-819-2*, Riverhd Trade) Berkley Pub.

Michaels, Leonard. Time Out of Mind: The Diaries of Leonard Michaels, 1961-1995. LC 99-19020. (Illus.). 214p. 1999. 24.95 (*1-57322-142-2*, Riverhead Books) Putnam Pub Group.

— To Feel These Things. LC 92-45611. 160p. (Orig.). 1993. pap. 12.00 (*1-56279-040-4*) Mercury Hse Inc.

Michaels, Leonard, et al, eds. West of the West: Imagining California: An Anthology. 1995. 15.95 (*0-520-20164-7*, Pub. by U CA Pr) Cal Prin Full Svc.

Michaels, Leonard, jt. ed. see Ricks, Christopher.

Michaels, Leslee A., ed. Kids for Kids: Messages of Hope & Love from the Nation's Children. LC 96-80051. (Illus.). 64p. (J). 1977. pap. 12.95 (*1-890059-68-4*) Happy Hrt Pr.

— Reaching for the Stars: If It Is to Be, It Is up to Me! LC 96-80052. (Illus.). 64p. (Orig.). (J). 1997. pap. 12.95 (*1-890059-66-8*) Happy Hrt Pr.

Michaels, Leslie & Chissick, Seymour S., eds. Asbestos: Properties, Applications, & Hazards, Vol. 1. LC 78-16535. (Illus.). 572p. reprint ed. pap. 177.40 (*0-8357-5782-X*, 205225200001) Bks Demand.

Michaels, Lisa. Split: A Counterculture Childhood. LC 98-11867. 320p. 1998. 23.00 (*0-395-83739-1*) HM.

— Split: A Counterculture Childhood. 307p. 1999. pap. 13.00 (*0-395-95788-5*) HM.

Michaels, Lloyd. The Phantom of the Cinema: Character in Modern Film. LC 97-11383. (Cultural Studies in Cinema - Video). (Illus.). 191p. (C). 1997. pap. text 19.95 (*0-7914-3568-7*) State U NY Pr.

— The Phantom of the Cinema: Character in Modern Film. LC 97-11383. (Cultural Studies in Cinema - Video). (Illus.). 191p. (C). 1997. text 59.50 (*0-7914-3567-9*) State U NY Pr.

***Michaels, Lloyd, ed.** Ingmar Bergman's Persona. LC 99-10290. (Film Handbks.). (Illus.). 224p. 1999. pap. 16.95 (*0-521-65698-2*) Cambridge U Pr.

— Ingmar Bergman's Persona. (Film Handbks.). (Illus.). 224p. (C). 1999. 49.95 (*0-521-65175-1*) Cambridge U Pr.

Michaels, Lorna. La Belle et le Voyou. (Rouge Passion Ser.). (FRE.). 1997. pap. 3.50 (*0-373-37440-2*, 1-37440-4) Harlequin Bks.

— The Great Chili Caper. (Temptation Ser.). 1996. per. 3.50 (*0-373-25684-1*, 1-25684-1) Harlequin Bks.

— The Reluctant Bodyguard. LC 95-7113. (Superromance Ser.). 299p. 1995. mass mkt. 3.75 (*0-373-70633-2*, 1-70633-2) Harlequin Bks.

— The Reluctant Hunk. LC 95-4579. (Temptation Ser.: No. 523). 219p. 1995. per. 2.99 (*0-373-25623-X*, 1-25623-9) Harlequin Bks.

— The Trouble with Tonya. 1997. per. 3.50 (*0-373-25732-5*, 1-25732-8) Harlequin Bks.

Michaels, Lynn. Aftershock. (Temptation Ser.). 1994. per. 2.99 (*0-373-25581-0*, 1-25581-9) Harlequin Bks.

— Molly & the Phantom. LC 97-10523. 219p. 1994. mass mkt. 2.99 (*0-373-25611-6*, 1-25611-4) Harlequin Bks.

— Nightwing. LC 95-13947. (Temptation Ser.). 218p. 1995. per. 3.25 (*0-373-25642-6*, 1-25642-9) Harlequin Bks.

Michaels, Margie. Beloved Pirate. large type ed. LC 82-7387. (Second Chance At Love Ser.). 302p. 1982. write for info. (*0-89340-519-1*) Chivers N Amer.

***Michaels, Marianne.** The Toilet Paper Chronicles: Gallows Humor from the Y2K Underground. (Illus.). (C). 1999. pap. write for info. (*0-9674927-1-8*) S C I.

Michaels, Marion. The Little Cowboy: Pursuing Dana's Dream. viii, 120p. 1998. pap. 12.95 (*0-9661615-0-5*, 00132545, A Genius) Michaels News.

Michaels, Marion C. In the Morning Sky: Poetry & Puzzles. 90p. 1999. pap. 12.00 (*0-9661615-1-3*, 00132545, A Genius) Michaels News.

Michaels, Marissa. The Hunchback of Notre Dame Gargoyles Joke Book. LC 96-83597. (Illus.). 64p. (J). (gr. 1-4). 1996. pap. 2.95 (*0-7868-4099-4*, Pub. by Disney Pr) Time Warner.

Michaels, Marissa, jt. auth. see Shymalan, M. Night.

Michaels, Mark. Blues Riffs for Guitar. (Illus.). 48p. 1978. pap. 12.95 (*0-8256-2203-4*, AM23532) Music Sales.

— Original Jeff Beck. (Illus.). 80p. 1985. pap. 14.95 (*0-8256-2340-5*, AM38357) Music Sales.

— Teach Yourself Rhythm Guitar. 64p. pap. 12.95 (*0-8256-2201-8*, AM21650) Music Sales.

Michaels, Melisa. Sister to the Rain. 304p. 1998. mass mkt. 5.99 (*0-451-45730-7*, ROC) NAL.

Michaels, Melisa C. Cold Iron. 368p. 1997. mass mkt. 5.99 (*0-451-45654-8*, ROC) NAL.

— Far Harbor. 256p. 1989. pap. 3.95 (*0-8125-4581-8*, Pub. by Tor Bks) St Martin.

— Floater Factor. 288p. 1988. pap. 3.50 (*0-8125-4578-8*, Pub. by Tor Bks) St Martin.

***Michaels, Melisa C.** Through the Eyes of the Dead. 2001. mass mkt. 5.99 (*0-373-26370-8*, 1-26370-6) Harlequin Bks.

— Through the Eyes of the Dead. 192p. 1989. 17.95 (*0-8027-5718-9*) Walker & Co.

Michaels, Mickey. Survival Guide for Parents: How to Avoid Screwing up Your Kids or Losing Your Own Sanity. LC 94-74608. 125p. 1995. pap. 9.95 (*0-9644761-1-8*) Possibility Pr.

Michaels, Monica. Single in Orange County: Resource Directory & Guidebook. (Illus.). 176p. (Orig.). 1996. pap. 19.95 (*1-890144-44-4*) Page Pub.

Michaels, Morgan & Teitelbaum, Michael. Where Is Carmen Sandiego? License Plate Sticker Book. (Illus.). 64p. (Orig.). (J). (gr. 2-7). 1996. pap. 3.95 (*0-8167-3965-X*) Troll Communs.

Michaels, Nancy. Helping Women Recover from Abortion. LC 88-10447. 192p. (Orig.). 1988. pap. 8.99 (*0-87123-621-4*) Bethany Hse.

***Michaels, Nancy & Karpowicz, Debbi J.** Off the Wall Marketing Ideas. LC 99-27506. 224p. 1999. pap. 10.95 (*1-58062-205-4*) Adams Media.

Michaels, Neal. How to Use, Compile, Maintain, & Sell Mailing Lists. 32p. 1992. pap. 12.00 (*0-915665-27-1*) Premier Publishers.

Michaels, Neal, jt. auth. see Bates, Owen.

Michaels, Neal, jt. auth. see Stilson, Galen.

Michaels, Patrick J. Sound & Fury: The Science & Politics of Global Warming. 196p. 1992. 21.95 (*0-932790-90-9*) Cato Inst.

***Michaels, Patrick J. & Balling, Robert C., Jr.** The Satanic Gases: Clearing the Air about Global Warming. 224p. 2000. 19.95 (*1-882577-91-4*, Pub. by Cato Inst); pap. 10.95 (*1-882577-92-2*, Pub. by Cato Inst) Natl Bk Netwk.

Michaels, Paul, et al. Case Histories of Geophysics Applied to Civil Engineering & Public Policy: Proceedings of Sessions Sponsored by the Geophysical Engineering Committee of the ASCE Geotechnical Engineering Division in Conjunction with the ASCE National Convention in Washington, D. C., November 10-14, 1996. LC 96-36648. (Geotechnical Special Publications). 128p. 1996. 24.00 (*0-7844-0208-6*) Am Soc Civil Eng.

Michaels, Peter. We Come As Friends: True Tales of Positive Alien Encounters. LC 98-93307. 288p. 1999. mass mkt. 6.50 (*0-380-79907-3*, Avon Bks) Morrow Avon.

Michaels, Ragini E. Facticity: A Door to Mental Health & Beyond. (Illus.). 256p. (Orig.). 1991. pap. 16.95 (*0-9628686-0-4*) Facticity Tr.

— Storytelling the Truth. 2000. pap. 19.95 (*0-9628686-2-0*) Facticity Tr.

Michaels, Richard M. Transportation Planning & Policy Decision Making: Behavioral Science Contributions. LC 79-24820. 250p. 1980. 65.00 (*0-275-90524-1*, C0524, Praeger Pubs) Greenwood.

Michaels, Roger B. & Hintze, Lehi F. Geologic Map of the Scipio Pass Quadrangle, Millard County, Utah. (Map of the Utah Geological Survey Ser.: Vol. 164). (Illus.). 25p. 1994. pap. 6.00 (*1-55791-566-0*, M-164) Utah Geological Survey.

Michaels, Scott, jt. auth. see Barrett, Warrick L.

Michaels, Sharon A. How to Give Yourself the Power to Succeed: Learning to Recognize the Things You're Doing that Keep You from the Things You Want. LC 96-96795. 176p. (Orig.). 1996. pap., mass mkt. 12.95 (*1-888972-00-9*) Empowering Publns.

***Michaels, Shauna.** Hold onto the Night. 192p. 2000. pap. 9.95 (*1-893896-11-0*) Ima Jinn.

Michaels, Shirley, ed. see Craig, Rebecca T. & Wright, Barbara.

Michaels, Ski. Felix, the Funny Fox. LC 85-14097. (Illus.). 48p. (Orig.). (J). (gr. 1-3). 1997. pap. 3.95 (*0-8167-0591-7*) Troll Communs.

— One Hundred Two Creepy, Crawly Bug Jokes. LC 91-42737. (Illus.). 64p. (J). (gr. 2-6). 1996. pap. 2.95 (*0-8167-2745-7*) Troll Communs.

— One Hundred Two Haunted House Jokes. LC 91-21891. (Illus.). 64p. (J). (gr. 2-6). 1997. pap. 2.95 (*0-8167-2578-0*) Troll Communs.

Michaels, Stase. The Bedside Guide to Dreams. 1996. mass mkt. 5.99 (*0-449-22384-1*) Fawcett.

Michaels, Steve. Homespun Insight: A Collection of Short Stories with down Home Values Brought to Life for Today's Business Person. (Illus.). 139p. 1998. pap. 9.95 (*0-966851-0-2*) TAS Mrktg.

***Michaels-Surface, Donna.** I'm Living It...Not Dieting! A Journal. (Illus.). 11p. 2000. pap. 7.95 (*1-882330-59-5*) Magni Co.

***Michaels-Surface, Donna & Snyder, Gary S.** Fit, Fabulous & Fifty: The Revolutionary Live It or Diet System. (Illus.). 362p. 2000. 27.95 (*1-882330-58-7*) Magni Co.

Michaels, Susan. An Infamous Fiasco. 1989. mass mkt. 3.95 (*0-446-35373-6*) Warner Bks.

— Sightings. LC 96-583. (Illus.). 256p. 1996. pap. 11.00 (*0-684-82369-1*, Fireside) S&S Trade Pap.

— Sightings UFO. LC 97-19475. (Illus.). 256p. 1997. pap. 11.00 (*0-684-83630-0*, Fireside) S&S Trade Pap.

Michaels, Suzanne. Magic Merlin Preschool. LC 96-70796. (Illus.). xx, 324p. (Orig.). 1997. pap. 24.95 (*0-9654779-1-6*) A-Parent Love.

— Raising Children to Be Gifted. LC 96-70797. (Illus.). xx, 212p. (Orig.). 1997. pap. 12.95 (*0-9654779-0-8*) A-Parent Love.

***Michaels, Tee. Accuser of the Brethren, Part 1. 244p. 2000. 12.95 (*0-9678574-0-6*) T Michaels.**

After escaping a near-death experience at the tender age of sixteen & dysfunctional family life, twenty-five-year-old Celeste Tyler is finally on her way to achieving success in both her professional & personal life. She has acquired a nice home, an exciting career, devoted friends & even dares to give her heart away for the very first time. Finally securing the peace & happiness that evaded her for so long, life seems just about perfect. Then, without warning, the gates of hell are opened & her perfect life begins to crumble. A race begins between life & death as Celeste desperately tries to outwit a madman, who constantly remains one step ahead & always appears around every corner. With time running out & only a stranger to turn to, Celeste comes face to face with the most unbelievable nightmare of all time. A nightmare that will change her life & all the lives of those around her forever. Covenant Signature Publishing, P.O. Box 2742, Lafayette, LA. 70596-2743, 888-330-7066 *Publisher Paid Annotation.*

Michaels, Theresa. A Corner of Heaven. (Family Continuity Program Ser.: No. 36). 1999. mass mkt. 4.50 (*0-373-82184-0*, 1-82184-2) Harlequin Bks.

— Fire & Sword. 1994. per. 3.99 (*0-373-28843-3*, 1-28843-0) Harlequin Bks.

— The Merry Widows - Catherine. (Historical Ser.: No. 400). 1998. per. 4.99 (*0-373-29000-4*, 1-29000-6) Harlequin Bks.

— The Merry Widows - Mary. (Historical Ser.: No. 372). 1997. per. 4.99 (*0-373-28972-3*, 1-28972-7) Harlequin Bks.

— The Merry Widows--Sarah: The Merry Widows. (Historical Ser.: Bk. 469). 1999. per. 4.99 (*0-373-29069-1*, 1-29069-1) Harlequin Bks.

***Michaels, Theresa.** Once a Hero. (Historical Ser.: Vol. 505). 2000. per. 4.99 (*0-373-29105-1*) Harlequin Bks.

Michaels, Theresa. Once a Lawman. (Historical Ser.). 1996. per. 4.99 (*0-373-28916-2*, 1-28916-4) Harlequin Bks.

— Once a Maverick. LC 95-19046. (Historical Ser.). 296p. 1995. per. 4.50 (*0-373-28876-X*, 1-28876-0) Harlequin Bks.

— Once an Outlaw. LC 96-709. 296p. 1995. per. 4.50 (*0-373-28896-4*, 1-28896-8) Harlequin Bks.

Michaels, Tilde. Rabbit Spring. LC 87-18107. (Illus.). 85p. (J). (gr. 2-6). 1989. 11.95 (*0-15-200568-4*, Gulliver Bks) Harcourt.

Michaels, Twin. Millenishocks: Abandoning the Chase: Hints on How the Turn of the Century Will Reorient Our Priorities. LC 98-88308. (Illus.). 144p. 1998. pap. 19.99 (*0-9667846-6-9*, HRH326) Metro Ventures.

Michaels, Walter B. The Gold Standard & the Logic of Naturalism: American Literature at the Turn of the Century. 257p. (Orig.). (C). 1987. pap. 15.95 (*0-520-05982-4*, Pub. by U CA Pr) Cal Prin Full Svc.

— Our America: Nativism, Modernism, & Pluralism. LC 95-12117. (Post-Contemporary Interventions Ser.). 208p. 1995. text 29.95 (*0-8223-1700-1*) Duke.

— Our America: Nativism, Modernism, & Pluralism. LC 95-12117. (Post-Contemporary Interventions Ser.). 200p. 1997. pap. text 12.95 (*0-8223-2064-9*) Duke.

Michaels, Walter B. & Pease, Donald E., eds. The American Renaissance Reconsidered. LC 84-47940. (Selected Papers from the English Institute; 1982-83, New Ser.: No. 9). 231p. reprint ed. pap. 71.70 (*0-8357-8020-1*, 203411800088) Bks Demand.

— The American Renaissance Reconsidered. LC 84-47940. (Selected Papers from the English Institute; 1982-83, New Ser.: No. 9). 208p. 1989. reprint ed. pap. text 15.95 (*0-8018-3937-8*) Johns Hopkins.

Michaels, Wanda I., jt. auth. see Ross, Ronald G.

Michaels, Wendy. Playbuilding Shakespeare. LC 96-15738. (Illus.). 175p. (C). 1997. pap. 19.95 (*0-521-57025-5*) Cambridge U Pr.

Michaels, Wendy, jt. auth. see Tarlington, Carole.

Michaels, William. The Beaverdale Flyer. (Illus.). 80p. 1998. pap. 10.00 (*1-892282-02-X*) Perry Pub WA.

— Clare & Her Shadow. LC 90-8487. (Illus.). 32p. (J). (ps-k). 1991. lib. bdg. 16.50 (*0-208-02301-1*, Linnet Bks) Shoe String.

Michaelsen, Helen. Die Entwicklung und die Konsequenzen Westlicher Einflusse auf die Zeitgenossische Kunst in Thailand. (Europaische Hochschulschriften, Reihe 28: Bd. 266). (GER.). 381p. 1996. 63.95 (*3-631-49734-2*) P Lang Pubng.

Michaelsen, J. La Guerra Espiritual. (Serie Actualidades - Actualities Ser.).Tr. of Spirit Wars. (SPA.). 1982. 2.29 (*1-56063-185-6*, 498125); pap. write for info. (*0-614-27050-2*) Editorial Unilit.

Michaelsen, Johanna. The Beautiful Side of Evil. LC 82-82240. 224p. 1982. pap. 9.99 (*0-89081-322-1*) Harvest Hse.

***Michaelsen, Johanna.** El Lado Bello del Mal (The Beautiful Side of Evil) (SPA & ENG.). 215p. 1999. 9.99 (*0-88113-535-6*) Caribe Betania.

Michaelsen, O. V. Words at Play: Quips, Quirks & Oddities. LC 97-23519. 256p. 1998. pap. 12.95 (*0-8069-9791-5*) Sterling.

An Asterisk (*) at the beginning of an entry indicates that the title is appearing for the first time.

Michaelsen, Scott. The Limits of Multiculturalism: Interrogating the Origins of American Anthropology. 280p. 1999. pap. 19.95 (*0-8166-3247-2*, Pub. by U of Minn Pr); lib. bdg. 49.95 (*0-8166-3246-4*, Pub. by U of Minn Pr) Chicago Distribution Ctr.

Michaelsen, Scott & Johnson, John E. Border Theory: The Limits of Cultural Politics. LC 97-3356. 1997. pap. 21.95 (*0-8166-2963-3*); text 54.95 (*0-8166-2962-5*) U of Minn Pr.

Michaelsen, William B. Creating the American Presidency, 1775-1789. 208p. (Orig.). (C). 1987. pap. text 22.50 (*0-8191-5807-0*) U Pr of Amer.

Michaelson. Toronto's Best Kept Secrets. 1994. pap. text. write for info. (*0-7730-5207-0*) Addison-Wesley.

Michaelson, Arthur M., jt. auth. see Blattmachr, Jonathan G.

***Michaelson, Carol.** Gilded Dragons: Buried Treasures from China's Golden Ages. (Illus.). 160p. 1999. pap. 29.95 (*0-7141-1489-8*, Pub. by British Mus Pr) Art Media Resources.

Michaelson, Connie O. & Greenberg, Michael R. New Jersey Toward the Year 2000: Employment Projections. 190p. 1978. pap. text 18.95 (*0-88285-051-2*) Transaction Pubs.

Michaelson, Gerald. 50 Ways to Close a Sale: And Keep the Customer for Life. abr. ed. 1995. audio 12.00 (*0-694-51563-9*, CPN 10059) HarperAudio.

Michaelson, Gerald A. Elementary Standard. 1995. 39.95 (*0-387-94621-7*) Spr-Verlag.

***Michaelson, Gerald A.** Sun Tzu: The Art of War for Managers. 224p. 2000. pap. 10.95 (*1-58062-459-6*) Adams Media.

Michaelson, Gerald A. Sun Tzu: The Art of War for Managore: New Translation & Business Commentary. Research Society of Sun Tzu Staff, tr. from CHI. LC 98-50037. (Illus.). 1998. pap. 14.95 (*1-883999-09-X*) Pressmark Intl.

— Winning the Marketing War: A Field Manual for Business Leaders. 272p. 1995. pap. 12.95 (*1-883999-04-9*) Pressmark Intl.

Michaelson, Gerald A., jt. auth. see Sun-Tzu.

Michaelson, Herbert B. How to Write & Publish Engineering Papers & Reports. 3rd ed. LC 90-36209. 240p. 1990. pap. 19.95 (*0-89774-650-3*) Oryx Pr.

Michaelson, James B. Puppies As a New Pet. 64p. 1991. pap. 6.95 (*0-86622-616-8*, TU-008) TFH Pubns.

Michaelson, Karen L., ed. And the Poor Get Children: Radical Perspectives on Population Dynamics. LC 81-38389. 272p. 1981. pap. 10.00 (*0-85345-553-8*, Pub. by Monthly Rev) NYU Pr.

Michaelson, Karen L., et al. Childbirth in America: Anthropological Perspectives. LC 87-37490. 313p. 1988. 55.00 (*0-89789-136-8*, Bergin & Garvey) Greenwood.

Michaelson, L. W. On My Being Dead & Other Stories. LC 83-81251. (Orig.). 1984. pap. 4.00 (*0-913123-02-1*) Galileo.

Michaelson, Menachem. Zvi Ribak: A Jewish Artist. Grant, Murray, ed. LC 91-52500. (Illus.). 162p. 1991. 80.00 (*0-88734-615-4*) Players Pr.

Michaelson, Mike. Chicago's Best-Kept Secrets. LC 90-63162. (Illus.). 320p. (Orig.). 1994. pap. 9.95 (*0-8442-9636-8*, Passprt Bks) NTC Contemp Pub Co.

— The Complete Idiot's Travel Guide to Chicago. (Complete Idiot's Travel Guide Ser.). (Illus.). 320p. 1999. pap. 15.95 (*0-02-863415-2*) Macmillan.

— Exploring the Capitol: A Self-Guided Tour Through the Halls of Congress. 48p. 1992. pap. 7.95 (*1-881846-03-2*) C-Span.

Michaelson, Peter. Freedom from Self-Sabotage: The Intelligent Reader's Guide to Success & Self-Fulfillment. LC 97-68491. 200p. 1997. pap. 14.95 (*1-882631-29-3*) Prospect NM.

— Secret Attachments: Exposing the Roots of Addictions & Compulsions. LC 92-83750. 208p. 1993. pap. 14.95 (*1-882631-26-9*) Prospect NM.

— See Your Way to Self-Esteem: An In-Depth Study of the Causes & Cures of Low Self-Esteem. LC 92-62627. 210p. (Orig.). 1993. pap. 14.95 (*1-882631-25-0*) Prospect NM.

Michaelson, S. M. & Lin, J. C. Biological Effects & Health Implications of Radiofrequency Radiation. (Illus.). 688p. (C). 1987. text 155.00 (*0-306-41580-1*, Kluwer Plenum) Kluwer Academic.

Michaelson, Sandra. The Emotional Catering Service: The Quest for Emotional Independence. LC 93-83821. 264p. 1993. pap. 15.95 (*1-882631-27-7*) Prospect NM.

— Is Anyone Listening? Repairing Broken Lines in Couples Communication. (Illus.). 160p. 1997. pap. 12.95 (*1-882631-30-7*) Prospect NM.

— LoveSmart: Transforming the Emotional Patterns That Sabotage Relationships. (Illus.). 280p. (Orig.). 1996. pap. 15.95 (*1-882631-28-5*) Prospect NM.

Michaelson, Sherryl E. Report of the Good Ol' Boys Roundup Policy Review: Department of the Treasury. (Illus.). 219p. 1998. reprint ed. pap. text 35.00 (*0-7881-4645-9*) DIANE Pub.

Michaelson, Sidney, jt. auth. see Morton, A. Q.

Michaely, Michael. Balance-of-Payments Adjustment Policies: Japan, Germany, & the Netherlands. (Occasional Papers: No. 106). 122p. 1968. reprint ed. 31.80 (*0-87014-492-8*) Natl Bur Econ Res.

— Israel. LC 75-323600. (Foreign Trade Regimes & Economic Development Ser.: No. 3). 239p. reprint ed. pap. 74.10 (*0-8357-7579-8*, 205690000096) Bks Demand.

— Israel. (Special Conference Series on Foreign Trade Regimes & Economic Development: No. 3). 239p. 1975. reprint ed. 62.20 (*0-87014-503-7*) Natl Bur Econ Res.

— The Responsiveness of Demand Policies to Balance of Payments: Postwar Patterns. (Studies in International Economic Relations: No. 5). 317p. 1971. reprint ed. 82.50 (*0-87014-221-6*) Natl Bur Econ Res.

— Theory of Commercial Policy: Trade & Protection. LC 77-21657. 256p. reprint ed. pap. 79.40 (*0-608-09481-1*, 205428100005) Bks Demand.

Michailakis, Dimitris. Legislating Death: Socio-Legal Studies on the Brain Death Controversy in Sweden. (Studia Sociologica Upsaliensia: No. 40). 254p. 1995. pap. 47.50 (*91-554-3500-9*) Coronet Bks.

Michaios, A. C. Global Report on Student Well-Being, Vol. II: Family, Friends, Living Partner & Self-Esteem. (Recent Research in Psychology Ser.). x, 288p. 1991. 79.95 (*0-387-97666-3*) Spr-Verlag.

Michal, Dan, jt. auth. see Moore, Lance.

***Michal, Gerhard, ed.** Biochemical Pathways: An Atlas of Biochemistry & Molecular Biology. LC 98-33226. 277p. 1998. 115.00 (*0-471-33130-9*) Wiley.

Michalak, Beth, et al. High Performance Teamwork. 48p. (Orig.). 1994. pap. text 5.95 (*0-87425-991-6*) HRD Press.

Michalak, Donald F. Competing Conceptions of American Foreign Policy. 352p. (C). 1997. pap. text 53.00 (*0-06-044431-2*) Addson-Wesley Educ.

Michalak-Gray, Joanna, jt. auth. see Gotteri, Nigel.

Michalak, Laurence O. & Salacuse, Jeswald W., eds. Social Legislation in the Contemporary Middle East. LC 86-18613. (Research Ser.: No. 64). (Illus.). xii, 381p. (C). 1986. pap. text 15.50 (*0-87725-164-9*) U of Cal IAS.

Michalak, Patricia S. Herbs. LC 92-32758. (Rodale's Successful Organic Gardening Ser.). 1993. pap. 14.95 (*0-87596-558-X*); text 24.95 (*0-87596-557-1*) Rodale Pr Inc.

Michalak, Patricia S. & Gilkeson, Linda A. Controlling Pests & Diseases. LC 93-6103. (Rodale's Successful Organic Gardening Ser.). 1994. pap. 14.95 (*0-87596-612-8*) Rodale Pr Inc.

Michalak, Patricia S. & Peterson, Cass. Vegetables. LC 92-31890. (Rodale's Successful Organic Gardening Ser.). (Illus.). 1993. pap. 14.95 (*0-87596-564-4*) Rodale Pr Inc.

Michalak, Paul, jt. illus. see Marx, David F.

Michalakias, John, jt. auth. see Birney, Bill.

Michalakopoulos, T. N., jt. ed. see Panagiotou, G. N.

Michalczyk, John J. Andre Malraux's Espoir: The Propaganda-Art Film & the Spanish Civil War. LC 77-7308. (Romance Monographs: No. 27). 1977. 25.00 (*84-399-6811-6*) Romance.

— Costa-Gavras: The Political Fiction Film. (Illus.). 296p. 1984. 48.50 (*0-87982-029-2*) Art Alliance.

— The French Literary Filmmakers. LC 78-75171. (Illus.). 230p. 1980. 38.50 (*0-87982-027-6*) Art Alliance.

Michalczyk, John J., ed. Medicine, Ethics & the Third Reich: Historical & Contemporary Issues. LC 94-25916. (Illus.). 240p. (Orig.). 1994. pap. 19.95 (*1-55612-752-9*, LL1752) Sheed & Ward WI.

— Resisters, Rescuers, & Refugees: Historical & Ethical Issues. LC 97-33127. (Illus.). 352p. 1997. pap. 21.95 (*1-55612-970-X*, LL1970) Sheed & Ward WI.

Michaleas, George. A Time to Honor: A Selective History of Massachusetts. 56p. 1998. pap. 8.00 (*0-8059-4461-3*) Dorrance.

Michalec, G. W. Analysis & Comparison of Total Composite Error & Position Error in Gears. (Technical Papers: Vol. P239.07). (Illus.). 15p. 1958. pap. text 30.00 (*1-55589-304-X*) AGMA.

— Methods of Specifying Precision of Spur Gears. (Technical Papers: Vol. P319.01). (Illus.). 29p. 1956. pap. text 30.00 (*1-55589-386-4*) AGMA.

— Over-Pin Measurement Tolerances for Various AGMA Classes of Fine-Pitch Gears. (Technical Papers: Vol. P239.04). (Illus.). 20p. 1957. pap. text 30.00 (*1-55589-301-5*) AGMA.

Michalec, G. W., jt. auth. see Karsch, A. F.

Michalek, George C. & Fader, Barbara M. Blessed Are Those Who Mourn: Personalized Prayers of the Faithful for the Funeral Rite. LC 98-4034. 104p. 1998. pap. 17.95 (*0-87793-654-4*) Ave Maria.

Michalenko, Seraphim, jt. auth. see Flynn, Vinny.

Michalenko, Seraphim, tr. see Kowalska, Faustina.

***Michalenko, Sophia.** The Life of Faustina Kowalska: The Authorized Biography. LC 99-17574. 1999. pap. 12.99 (*1-56955-153-7*) Servant.

Michaletzky, G., et al. Representability in Stochastic Systems. 228p. 1999. 52.00 (*963-05-7546-9*, Pub. by Akade Kiado) Intl Spec Bk.

Michaletzky, Gyorgy, jt. auth. see Csiszar, Imre.

Michalewics, Maciej, jt. auth. see Ras, Zbigniew W.

Michalewicz, Bogumila & Turkington, Carol. Learn Spanish: The Lazy Way. (Lazy Way Ser.). 352p. 1999. pap. 12.95 (*0-02-862650-8*) Macmillan Gen Ref.

Michalewicz, M. T. Humans to Proteins No. 2: Advances on Computational Life Sciences Series. (Illus.). 220p. 1997. 89.95 (*0-643-06033-2*, Pub. by CSIRO) Accents Pubns.

Michalewicz, Zbigniew. Genetic Algorithms + Data Structures = Evolution Programs. 3rd expanded rev. ed. 387p. 1996. text 44.95 (*3-540-60676-9*) Spr-Verlag.

— Genetic Algorithms Plus Data Structures Equal Evolution Programs. 2nd ed. LC 94-25886. (Illus.). 340p. 1994. 39.00 (*3-540-58090-5*) Spr-Verlag.

— Genetic Algorithms Plus Data Structures Equals Evolution Programs. Loveland, D. W. et al, eds. LC 92-19925. (Symbolic Computation - Artificial Intelligence Ser.). (Illus.). xiv, 250p. 1993. 49.00 (*0-387-55387-8*) Spr-Verlag.

— Genetic Algorithms Plus Data Structures Equals Evolution Programs. 2nd expanded ed. LC 94-25886. 1994. 39.00 (*0-387-58090-5*) Spr-Verlag.

Michalewicz, Zbigniew, ed. Statistical & Scientific Database Management. (Lecture Notes in Computer Science Ser.: Vol. 420). v, 256p. 1990. 35.00 (*0-387-52342-1*) Spr-Verlag.

***Michalewicz, Zbigniew & Fogel, David B.** How to Solve It: Modern Heuristics. LC 99-37542. (Illus.). xi, 469p. 1999. 42.00 (*3-540-66061-5*) Spr-Verlag.

Michalewicz, Zbigniew, jt. auth. see Dasgupta, D.

Michalewicz, Zbigniew, tr. see Bork, B. A., ed.

Michalewiz, M. T. Plants to Ecosystems. (Advances in Computational Life Sciences Ser.). (Illus.). 133p. 1997. 64.95 (*0-643-05942-3*, Pub. by CSIRO) Accents Pubns.

Michalidou, Nicolaou I. Prosopography of Ptolemaic Cyprus. (Studies in Mediterranean Archaeology: Vol. XLIV). 165p. (Orig.). 1976. pap. 29.50 (*91-85058-70-X*) P Astroms.

Michalik, G., jt. auth. see Mielczarski, Wladyslaw.

Michalik, K., tr. see Bezwinska, J. & Czech, Danuta, eds.

Michalik, Wieslaw, jt. ed. see Gibb, Richard.

Michalk, D., jt. auth. see Huxtable, R. J.

Michalka, Wolfgang, jt. auth. see Lee, Marshall M.

Michalko, Michael. Cracking Creativity: (The Secrets of Creative Genius) LC 97-39273. 352p. 1998. 24.95 (*0-89815-913-X*) Ten Speed Pr.

— Thinkertoys: A Handbook of Creativity in Business. (Illus.). 335p. (Orig.). 1991. pap. 17.95 (*0-89815-408-1*) Ten Speed Pr.

— Thinkpak. 61p. 1994. pap. 16.95 (*0-89815-607-6*) Ten Speed Pr.

Michalko, Rod. The Mystery of the Eye & the Shadow of Blindness. 224p. 1998. pap. text 17.95 (*0-8020-8093-6*) U of Toronto Pr.

— The Two-in-One: Walking with Smokie, Walking with Blindness. LC 98-20119. (Animals, Culture & Society Ser.). 256p. 1998. text 44.95 (*1-56639-648-4*); pap. text 16.95 (*1-56639-649-2*) Temple U Pr.

Michalkow, Janina. Nicholas Poussin. (GER.). 164p. 1980. 99.00 (*0-7855-1600-X*, Pub. by Collets) St Mut.

Michalopoulos, Andre. Homer. (World Authors Ser.). 224p. 1966. 28.95 (*0-8057-2432-X*) Macmillan.

Michalopoulos, Andre, tr. see Averoff-Tossizza, Evangelos.

Michalopoulos, Constantine. Trade Issues in the New Independent States. LC 93-22695. (Studies of Economics in Transformation: No. 7). 39p. 1993. pap. 22.00 (*0 8213 2483 7*, 12483) World Bank.

Michalopoulos, Constantine & Tarr, David G. Trade in the New Independent States. (Studies of Economies in Transformation: No. 13). (RUS.). 274p. 1995. 17.95 (*0-8213-3236-8*, 13236) World Bank.

— Trade Performance & Policy in the New Independent States. LC 96-12272. (Directions in Development Ser.). 36p. 1996. pap. 22.00 (*0-8213-3615-0*, 13615) World Bank.

— Trade Performance & Policy in the New Independent States: Russian Edition. 52p. 1996. pap. 22.00 (*0-8213-3687-8*, 13687) World Bank.

Michalopoulos, Constantine & Tarr, David G., eds. Trade in the New Independent States. LC 94-35297. (Studies of Economies in Transformation: No. 15). 294p. 1995. pap. 22.00 (*0-8213-3077-2*, 13077) World Bank.

Michalos, Alex C. Global Report on Student Well-Being: Employment, Finances, Housing & Transportation. (Recent Research in Psychology Ser.: Vol. 3). x, 306p. 1992. 79.95 (*0-387-97948-4*) Spr-Verlag.

— Global Report on Student Well-Being: Religion, Education, Recreation & Health. (Recent Research in Psychology Ser.: Vol. 4). x, 304p. 1992. 79.95 (*0-387-97949-2*) Spr-Verlag.

— Global Report on Student Well-Being, Vol. One: Life Satisfaction & Happiness. (Recent Research in Psychology Ser.). (Illus.). x, 253p. 1991. pap. 39.00 (*0-387-97460-1*) Spr-Verlag.

— North American Social Report: Economics, Religion, & Morality, Vol. 5. 1982. pap. text 84.00 (*90-277-1358-8*) Kluwer Academic.

— North American Social Report Vol. 1: A Comparative Study of the Quality of Life in Canada & Theusa from 1964 to 1974: Foundations, Populations & Health. 280p. 1980. pap. text 101.00 (*90-277-1058-9*) Kluwer Academic.

— North American Social Report Vol. 3: A Comparative Study of the Quality of Life in Canada & the U. S. A. from 1964 to 1974. 212p. 1981. pap. text 95.50 (*90-277-1257-3*) Kluwer Academic.

— Popper-Carnap Controversy. 133p. 1971. pap. text 71.00 (*90-247-5127-6*) Kluwer Academic.

— A Pragmatic Approach to Business Ethics. LC 94-45244. 248p. 1995. text 36.95 (*0-8039-7084-6*); pap. text 17.95 (*0-8039-7085-4*) Sage.

Michalos, Alex C., ed. see Philosophy of Science Association Staff.

Michalove, Ed, jt. auth. see Delson, Donn.

Michalove, Sharon D. & Reeves, A. Compton, eds. Estrangement, Enterprise & Education in 15th Century England. (Fifteenth Century Ser.). 192p. 1998. 74.95 (*0-7509-1384-3*, Pub. by Sutton Pub Ltd) Intl Pubs Mktg.

Michalowicz, Jerzy, tr. see Kahane, David.

Michalowicz, Jerzy, tr. see Tory, Avraham.

Michalowski. Order, Law & Crime. 1985. 14.50 (*0-07-553915-2*) McGraw.

***Michalowski, Kevin.** You Cook It! The Guys Guide to Game Cookery. LC 99-67512. (Illus.). 208p. 2000. spiral bd. 14.95 (*0-87341-861-1*, YCI) Krause Pubns.

Michalowski, Kevin, ed. Bowhunter's Digest. 4th ed. LC 83-91589. 256p. 1999. pap. 19.95 (*0-87341-758-5*) Krause Pubns.

Michalowski, P., tr. see Amsterdamski, Stefan.

Michalowski, Piotr. The Lamentation over the Destruction of Sumer & Ur. LC 88-33386. (Mesopotamian Civilizations Ser.: Vol. 1). (Illus.). xvi, 219p. (C). 1989. text 42.50 (*0-931464-43-9*) Eisenbrauns.

Michalowski, Radoslaw L., ed. Cold Regions Engineering. 408p. 1989. 6.00 (*0-87262-680-6*) Am Soc Civil Eng.

Michalowski, Raymond J. Order, Law & Crime. 512p. (C). 1985. pap. 56.56 (*0-07-554450-4*) McGraw.

Michalowski, Sabine & Woods, Lorna. German Constitutional Law: The Protection of Civil Liberties. LC 99-25091. 370p. 1999. text 96.95 (*1-85521-920-4*, Pub. by Ashgate Pub) Ashgate Pub Co.

Michalowski, Stefan, jt. auth. see Harvey, John.

Michals, Duane. Album: The Portraits of Duane Michals, 1958-1988. (Illus.). 144p. 1988. 55.00 (*0-942642-31-7*) Twelvetrees Pr.

— Eros & Thanatos. (Illus.). 64p. 1992. 50.00 (*0-944092-20-9*) Twin Palms Pub.

— Eros & Thanatos. limited ed. (Illus.). 64p. 1992. 150.00 (*0-944092-21-7*) Twin Palms Pub.

— Sleep & Dreams. (Illus.). 64p. 1984. pap. 11.95 (*0-912810-46-7*) Lustrum Pr.

— Upside down, Inside Out, & Backwards. 80p. (J). 1994. pap. 19.95 (*0-9638863-0-4*) Sonny Boy Bks.

Michals, Duane, photos by. Salute, Walt Whitman. (Illus.). 112p. 1996. 50.00 (*0-944092-34-9*) Twin Palms Pub.

— Salute, Walt Whitman. limited ed. (Illus.). 96p. 1996. 150.00 (*0-944092-35-7*) Twin Palms Pub.

Michalsen, Karen, ed. see Stoliar, Marda.

Michalske, Terry A. & Wendman, Mark A., eds. Micromachining & Imaging, Vol. 3009. 158p. 1997. 59.00 (*0-8194-2420-X*) SPIE.

M

Michalski. American Humor. 1998. pap. 63.75 (*0-07-431288-X*) McGraw.

— Temperature Measurement. 2nd ed. Date not set. text. write for info. (*0-471-86779-9*) Wiley.

Michalski, Anna & Wallace, Helen. The European Community: The Challenge of Enlargement. 1993. pap. 15.95 (*0-905031-56-3*) Brookings.

***Michalski, Anthony R., ed.** The Master Key System by Charles F. Haanel. LC 98-88742. x, 195p. 2000. pap. 19.95 (*0-9678514-0-8*) Kallisti Pubng.

Michalski, Carol A. Don't Blame God. 1996. pap. text 7.95 (*0-89228-112-X*) Impact Christian.

Michalski, Krzysztof. Logic & Time: An Essay on Husserl's Theory of Meaning. Czerniawski, Adam, tr. from POL. LC 96-19684. (Boston Studies in the Philosophy of Science: NO. 185). 176p. (C). 1996. text 100.50 (*0-7923-4082-5*) Kluwer Academic.

Michalski, Melvin. The Relationship Between the Universal Priesthood of the Baptized & the Ministerial Priesthood of the Ordained in Vatican II & in Subsequent Theology No. 10: Understanding "Essentia et Non Gradu," Lumen Gentium. LC 95-39806. (Understanding "Essentia Et Non Gradu Tantum," Lumen Gentium Ser.: No. 10). 290p. 1996. write for info. (*0-7734-2264-1*) E Mellen.

Michalski, Ryszard, et al, eds. Machine Learning & Data Mining: Methods & Applications. 456p. 1998. 84.99 (*0-471-97199-5*) Wiley.

Michalski, Ryszard S., ed. Multistrategy Learning. LC 93-22647. (International Series in Engineering & Computer Science, VLSI, Computer Architecture, & Digital Screen Processing). 166p. (C). 1993. text 157.50 (*0-7923-9374-0*) Kluwer Academic.

Michalski, Ryszard S., et al, eds. Machine Learning: An Artificial Intelligence Approach, Vol. II. LC 82-10654. (Illus.). 738p. 1986. text 53.95 (*0-934613-00-1*) Morgan Kaufmann.

Michalski, Ryszard S. & Tecuci, George, eds. Machine Learning: A Multi-Strategy Approach, Vol. 4. 782p. (Orig.). (C). 1993. text 63.95 (*1-55860-251-8*) Morgan Kaufmann.

Michalski, Ryszard S. & Wnek, Janusz, eds. Proceedings of the Third International Workshop on Multistrategy Learning. 348p. 1996. pap. text 40.00 (*1-57735-010-3*) AAAI Pr.

Michalski, Ryszard S., jt. ed. see Kodratoff, Yves.

Michalski, Sergiusz. Public Monuments: Art in Political Bondage, 1870-1997. (Essays in Art & Culture Ser.). (Illus.). 256p. 1998. pap. 24.95 (*1-86189-025-7*, Pub. by Reaktion Bks) Consort Bk Sales.

Michalski, W., ed. The Future of Industrial Societies: Problems, Prospects, Solutions. 313p. 1978. lib. bdg. 80.00 (*90-286-0257-7*) Kluwer Academic.

Michalski, Walter J. 40 Tools for Cross-Functional Teams: Building Synergy for Breakthrough Creativity. LC 98-34170. (Illus.). 160p. 1998. pap. text 30.00 (*1-56327-198-2*) Productivity Inc.

— 40 Top Tools for Manufacturers: A Guide for Implementing Powerful Improvement. LC 97-48352. (Illus.). 160p. 1998. pap. 25.00 (*1-56327-197-4*) Productivity Inc.

Michalson, Edgar L., et al. Conservation Farming in the United States: The Methods of Accomplishments of the Steep Program. LC 98-32081. 256p. 1998. boxed set 54.95 (*0-8493-1185-3*) CRC Pr.

Michalson, Gordon E., Jr. Fallen Freedom: Kant on Radical Evil & Moral Regeneration. 184p. 1990. text 59.95 (*0-521-38397-8*) Cambridge U Pr.

— Kant & the Problem of God. LC 98-33148. 216p. 1999. 62.95 (*0-631-21219-1*); pap. 26.95 (*0-631-21220-5*) Blackwell Pubs.

— Lessing's "Ugly Ditch" A Study of Theology & History. LC 84-42991. 224p. (C). 1985. 29.50 (*0-271-00385-5*) Pa St U Pr.

***Michalson, Karen.** Enemy Glory. 2001. text 25.95 (*0-312-89061-3*) St Martin.

Michalson, Karen. Victorian Fantasy Literature: Literary Battles with Church & Empire. LC 90-19302. (Studies in British Literature: Vol. 10). 308p. 1990. lib. bdg. 99.95 (*0-88946-378-6*) E Mellen.

Michalson, Linda, jt. ed. see Lewis, Michael.

Michalun, M. Varinia, jt. auth. see Michalun, Natalia.

***Michalun, Natalia.** Cosmetic Ingredients Dictionary. 2nd ed. 2001. pap. 25.75 (*1-56253-660-5*) Thomson Learn.

Michalun, Natalia & Michalun, M. Varinia. Milady's Skin Care & Cosmetic Ingredients Dictionary. LC 93-33822. (Career Development Ser.). 328p. 1994. pap. 22.50 (*1-56253-125-5*) Thomson Learn.

Michard, Jean-Guy. The Reign of the Dinosaurs. (Discoveries Ser.). (Illus.). 144p. 1992. pap. 12.95 (*0-8109-2808-6*, Pub. by Abrams) Time Warner.

Michard, L., jt. auth. see Lagarde, A.

Michas, Nicholas, jt. auth. see Reynolds, Lloyd G.

Michas, Peter A., et al. The Rod of an Almond Tree in God's Master Plan. LC 97-60123. 224p. 1997. pap. 12.00 (*1-57921-007-4*, Pub. by WinePress Pub) BookWorld.

Michas, Yia-Yia Sophia & Sarlas-Fontana, Jane. The Golden Cobwebs. (Illus.). 24p. 1998. pap. 9.95 (*0-9638336-4-2*) Spero & Me.

Michasiw, Kim I., ed. & intro. see Dacre, Charlotte.

Michaud, Achille, jt. auth. see Cormier, Michel.

***Michaud, Cassandra.** Sites & Insights: Archaeological Discoveries at the Jefferson Patterson Park & Museum. (Jefferson Patterson Park & Museum Studies in Archaeology Ser.: Vol. 2). (Illus.). 40p. 2000. 5.00 (*1-878399-78-0*) Div Hist Cult Progs.

Michaud, David L., jt. auth. see Macdonald, John M.

***Michaud, Debbie.** Healing Traditions & Spiritual Practices of Wicca. LC 00-21042. 160p. 2000. pap. 11.95 (*0-658-00386-0*, 003860, Keats Publng) NTC Contemp Pub Co.

***Michaud, Dominique.** Recombinant Protease Inhibitors in Plants. 307p. 2000. 99.00 (*1-58706-007-8*, Pub. by Eurekah) Landes Bioscience.

Michaud, Dominique. Recombinant Protease Inhibitors in Plants. LC 99-27038. (Biotechnology Intelligence Unit Ser.). 307p. 1999. 89.00 (*1-57059-626-3*) Landes Bioscience.

Michaud, E. Guillaume de Champeaux et les Ecoles de Paris. 2nd ed. (Medieval Studies Reprint). (FRE.). reprint ed. lib. bdg. 48.00 (*0-697-00011-7*) Irvington.

Michaud, Ellen, et al. Boost Your Brainpower. 472p. 1993. 9.98 (*1-56731-026-5*, MJF Bks) Fine Comms.

— Total Health for Women: From Allergies & Back Pain to Overweight & PMS, the Best Preventive & Curative Advice for Over 110 Women's Health Problems. LC 95-9810. 1995. 31.95 (*0-87596-311-0*) Rodale Pr Inc.

— Total Health for Women: From Allergies & Back Pain to Overweight & PMS, the Best Preventive & Curative Advice for over 110 Women's Health Problems. LC 97-8823. 608p. 1997. pap. 15.95 (*0-87596-463-X*) Rodale Pr Inc.

Michaud, G. Guide France. 14.95 (*0-685-36082-2*) Fr & Eur.

— Nouveau Guide France: Manuel de Civilisation Francaise. (Hachette Ser.). (FRE.). pap. 26.95 (*2-01-015387-1*) Schoenhof.

— Nouveau Guide France: Manuel de Civilization Francaise. write for info. (*0-318-63623-9*) Fr & Eur.

— Nouveau Guide France: Manuel de Civilization Francaise. 2nd rev. ed. 1992. 34.95 (*0-8288-7899-4*, F695) Fr & Eur.

Michaud, G. & Tutukov, A., eds. Evolution of Stars: The Photospheric Abundance Connection. (C). 1991. pap. text 73.00 (*0-7923-1128-0*); lib. bdg. 157.50 (*0-7923-1127-2*) Kluwer Academic.

Michaud, Gene, jt. ed. see Dittmar, Linda.

Michaud, J., ed. History of Mysore under Hyder Ali & Tippoo Sultan. Menon, Raman V. K., tr. from FRE. 290p. 1986. reprint ed. 22.00 (*0-8364-1733-X*, Pub. by Manohar) S Asia.

Michaud, Jean & Ovesen, Jan. Turbulent Times & Enduring People: Mountain Minorities in the South-East Asian Massif. 350p. (C). 1999. text 55.00 (*0-7007-1180-5*, Pub. by Curzon Pr Ltd) UH Pr.

Michaud, Joseph F. Bibliotheque des croisades, 4 vols., Set. LC 76-29846. (FRE.). reprint ed. 325.00 (*0-404-15450-6*) AMS Pr.

— History of the Crusades, 3 vols. Robson, W., tr. LC 72-172729. reprint ed. 195.00 (*0-404-04320-8*) AMS Pr.

Michaud, Joy. The Uranus-Neptune Influence. LC 94-16827. (Illus.). 208p. (Orig.). 1994. pap. 11.95 (*0-87728-806-2*) Weiser.

Michaud, Leon A. The Legend of Simon of Cyrene. 224p. (Orig.). 1995. pap. 15.95 (*1-885001-07-X*) Via Press.

Michaud, Margaret A. Dead End: Homeless Teenagers: A Multi-Service Approach. (Illus.). 137p. (Orig.). 1988. pap. 14.95 (*0-920490-81-6*) Temeron Bks.

Michaud, Marie-Christine. Migration World Magazine Cumulative Index, 1973-1995. 43p. 1996. lib. bdg. 9.95 (*0-934733-99-6*) CMS.

Michaud, Michael, jt. auth. see McFadden, Christine.

Michaud, Michael A. Reaching for the High Frontier: The American Pro-Space Movement, 1972-84. LC 86-91456. 462p. 1986. 59.95 (*0-275-92151-4*, C2151, Praeger Pubs) Greenwood.

Michaud, Michael G. Bedtime Stories. LC 97-75654. (Illus.). 28p. 1998. pap. 10.00 (*1-882585-04-6*) MGM Pr.

— Bedtime Stories. limited ed. LC 97-75654. (Illus.). 28p. 1998. 40.00 (*1-882585-05-4*) MGM Pr.

— Cardinal Winds. limited ed. LC 92-81452. (Illus.). 28p. (Orig.). (C). 1992. pap. 24.00 (*0-9620574-6-0*) MGM Pr.

— Flames of Hate in the City of Angels. (Illus.). 20p. (Orig.). (C). 1992. pap. 4.95 (*0-9620574-7-9*) MGM Pr.

— Giraffes on Horseback Salad. LC 94-96658. (Illus.). 48p. (Orig.). (C). 1994. pap. 7.95 (*1-882585-01-1*) MGM Pr.

— The Land of Open Hands. (Illus.). 20p. (Orig.). (C). 1991. pap. 25.00 (*0-9620574-4-4*) MGM Pr.

— Moribundo. LC 92-96944. (Illus.). 32p. (Orig.). (C). 1992. pap. 9.95 (*0-9620574-9-5*) MGM Pr.

— Moribundo. deluxe limited ed. LC 92-96944. (Illus.). 32p. (Orig.). (C). 1992. pap. 50.00 (*0-9620574-8-7*) MGM Pr.

— Seven Deadly Sins: or How I Spent My Summer Vacation. (Illus.). 8p. (Orig.). 1995. pap. 10.00 (*1-882585-03-8*) MGM Pr.

— Silly Me. LC 89-92010. 123p. (Orig.). 1989. pap. 8.95 (*0-9620574-1-X*) MGM Pr.

— Uncle Mike's Totally Cool Way Excellent Tasty Sweet & Real Fattening Heirloom Dessert Recipes in No Particular Order & Some Candy Recipes Too, Cookbook. LC 93-80824. (Illus.). 165p. (Orig.). (C). 1993. spiral bd. 25.00 (*1-882585-00-3*) MGM Pr.

— The World According to Natasha. (Illus.). 28p. (Orig.). (C). 1991. pap. 20.00 (*0-9620574-3-6*) MGM Pr.

— The World of Mirth. 31p. (Orig.). 1988. pap. 5.95 (*0-9620574-0-1*) MGM Pr.

Michaud, Michael G., ed. see Wood, Beatrice.

Michaud, Patrick A. Accident Prevention & OSHA Compliance. 320p. 1995. boxed set 94.95 (*1-56670-150-3*, L1150) Lewis Pubs.

Michaud, Paul J., jt. auth. see Norian, Nicole A.

Michaud, Regis. The American Novel To-Day: A Social & Psychological Study. LC 77-2571. 1977. reprint ed. lib. bdg. 59.75 (*0-8371-9553-5*, MIAN, Greenwood Pr) Greenwood.

— The American Novel To-Day: A Social & Psychological Study. LC 77-2571. 1977. reprint ed. fiche. write for info. (*0-8371-9606-X*, Greenwood Pr) Greenwood.

— The American Novel To-Day: A Social & Psychological Study. LC 77-2571. 1977. reprint ed. write for info. incl. fiche (*0-8371-9605-1*, Greenwood Pr) Greenwood.

— The American Novel To-Day: A Social & Psychological Study. (BCL1-PS American Literature Ser.). 293p. 1992. reprint ed. lib. bdg. 79.00 (*0-7812-6641-6*) Rprt Serv.

— Emerson, the Enraptured Yankee. Boas, George, tr. LC 74-5374. reprint ed. 42.50 (*0-404-11538-1*) AMS Pr.

— Modern Thought & Literature in France. LC 67-23248. (Essay Index Reprint Ser.). 1977. 18.95 (*0-8369-0707-8*) Ayer.

Michaud, Richard O. Efficient Asset Management: A Practical Guide to Stock Portfolio Optimization & Asset Allocation. LC 98-5193. (Financial Management Association Survey & Synthesis Ser.). 152p. 1998. 35.00 (*0-87584-743-9*) Harvard Busn.

Michaud, Roland & Michaud, Sabrina. Afghanistan. LC 89-51869. (Illus.). 132p. 1990. reprint ed. pap. 17.95 (*0-500-27393-6*, Pub. by Thames Hudson) Norton.

Michaud, Ronald W., ed. see Arthur Andersen & Co. Staff & Pilko Associates Staff.

Michaud, Rosemary. Sherlock Holmes & the Somerset Hunt. 200p. 1993. 25.00 (*0-86025-276-0*, Pub. by I Henry Pubns) Empire Pub Srvs.

Michaud, Sabrina, jt. auth. see Michaud, Roland.

Michaud, Scott. The Life & Times of Gustav Likan. (Illus.). 192p. 1994. 49.95 (*1-880092-15-8*) Bright Bks TX.

Michaud, Stephen G. Lethal Shadow: The Inside Story of America's Most Dangerous Criminal. 360p. (Orig.). 1994. mass mkt. 6.50 (*0-451-40530-7*, Onyx) NAL.

Michaud, Stephen G. & Aynesworth, Hugh. If You Love Me, You Will Do My Will: The Stranger-than-Fiction Saga of a Trappist Monk, a Texas Widow, & Her Half-Billion Dollar Fortune. (Illus.). 1990. 19.95 (*0-393-02762-7*) Norton.

***Michaud, Stephen G. & Hazelwood, Roy.** The Evil That Men Do: FBI Profiler Roy Hazelwood's Journey into the Minds of Sexual Predators. (Illus.). 336p. 1999. mass mkt. 6.99 (*0-312-97060-9*, St Martins Paperbacks) St Martin.

Michaud, Stephen G., jt. auth. see Hazelwood, Roy.

Michaud, Stephen G., jt. auth. see Weathers, Beck.

Michaud, Susan, ed. see Lovecraft, H. P.

***Michaud, Terry.** Buying & Selling Teddy Bears: Price Guide. (Illus.). 2000. pap. 19.95 (*0-942620-38-0*) Portfolio Pr.

Michaud, Thomas C. Foot Orthoses & Other Forms of Conservative Foot Care. (Illus.). 270p. 1993. 80.00 (*0-683-05974-2*) Lppncott W & W.

Michaux, Agnes. Dictionnaire Misogyne. (FRE.). 1993. pap. 45.00 (*0-7859-5635-2*, 2709612585) Fr & Eur.

Michaux, Francois A. Travels to the West of the Allegheny Mountains in the States of Ohio, Kentucky & Tennessee. 1993. reprint ed. lib. bdg. 89.00 (*0-7812-5390-X*) Rprt Serv.

Michaux, Henri. Aileurs. (FRE.). 1986. pap. 11.95 (*0-7859-2802-2*) Fr & Eur.

— Barbare en Asie. (Imaginaire Ser.). (FRE.). 238p. 1986. pap. 15.95 (*2-07-070622-2*) Schoenhof.

— A Barbarian in Asia. Beach, Sylvia, tr. from FRE. LC 86-5362. (New Directions Classics Ser.). 192p. 1986. reprint ed. pap. 7.95 (*0-8112-0991-1*, NDP622, Pub. by New Directions) Norton.

— By Surprise. Hough, Randolph, tr. from FRE. 112p. (Orig.). 1987. pap. 5.95 (*0-937815-05-5*) Hanuman Bks.

— Connaissance par les Gouffre. (FRE.). 1988. pap. 14.95 (*0-7859-2811-1*) Fr & Eur.

— Darkness Moves: An Henri Michaux Anthology, 1927-1984. Ball, David, tr. LC 92-12925. 1994. 38.00 (*0-520-07231-6*, Pub. by U CA Pr) Cal Prin Full Svc.

— Darkness Moves: An Henri Michaux Anthology, 1927-1984. 1997. pap. text 19.95 (*0-520-21229-0*, Pub. by U CA Pr) Cal Prin Full Svc.

— Epreuves Exorcismes, 1940-44. (FRE.). 1989. pap. 10.95 (*0-7859-2815-4*) Fr & Eur.

— Face aux Verroux. (FRE.). 1992. pap. 14.95 (*0-7859-3383-2*) Fr & Eur.

— Meidosems: Poems & Lithographs. Jackson, Elizabeth R., tr. from FRE. & intro. by. LC 92-27205. (Illus.). 184p. (Orig.). 1993. pap. 24.95 (*0-939952-13-0*) Moving Parts.

— Miserable Miracle: La Mescaline. (FRE.). 1991. pap. 10.95 (*0-7859-3381-6*) Fr & Eur.

— Plume: Lointain Interieur. (FRE.). 1985. pap. 14.95 (*0-7859-3379-4*) Fr & Eur.

— Selected Writings of Henri Michaux. Ellmann, Richard, tr. LC 68-25545. (ENG & FRE.). 1990. pap. 13.95 (*0-8112-0105-8*, NDP264, Pub. by New Directions) Norton.

— Spaced, Displaced/Deplacements,Degagements. Constantine, David & Constantine, Helen, trs. (Contemporary French Poets Ser.). (ENG & FRE.). 192p. 1993. pap. 19.95 (*1-85224-135-7*, Pub. by Bloodaxe Bks) Dufour.

— Tent Posts. Hoggard, Lynn, tr. (Green Integer Ser.: No. 4). 176p. 1997. pap. 10.95 (*1-55713-328-X*) Green Integer.

— La Vie dans les Plis. (FRE.). 1989. pap. 16.95 (*0-7859-2822-7*) Fr & Eur.

Michaux, Henri, et al. Translations: Experiments in Reading. Wellman, Don et al, eds. Simic, Charles et al, trs. from CHI. (Illus.). 272p. (Orig.). 1983. pap. 12.00 (*0-942030-03-6*) O ARS.

Michaux, Henri, jt. auth. see Pound.

Michaux, J. P. Elsevier's Dictionary of Transports & Logistics. 500p. 1998. write for info. (*0-444-82929-6*) Elsevier.

— French-English - English-French Dictionary of Machine Tools. 179p. pap. 33.00 (*2-7080-0444-1*) IBD Ltd.

Michaux, Jean-Pierre. Dictionnaire de l'Outillage et de la Machine Outil: French-English, English-French. (ENG & FRE.). 1976. pap. 22.95 (*0-7859-7928-X*, 2708004441) Fr & Eur.

— Dictionnaire Selectif des arbres, des Plantes et des Fleurs. (FRE.). 1979. 19.95 (*0-7859-7929-8*, 2-7080-0463-8) Fr & Eur.

Michaux, Louis A. Christmas: Make-Believe Or Discovery. Davies, Evan, ed. LC 88-92481. (Illus.). 65p. (Orig.). 1989. pap. 7.50 (*0-317-93408-2*) L A Michaux.

Michaux, Phyllis. The Unknown Ambassadors: A Saga of Citizenship. LC 95-83659. 175p. (Orig.). 1996. pap. 15.95 (*0-9639260-2-0*) Aletheia.

***Miche, Mary.** Weaving Music into Young Minds. (C). 2000. pap. 29.95 (*0-7668-0019-9*) Thomson Learn.

Micheals, Fern. Heart & Home. 1997. mass mkt. 6.99 (*0-451-19168-4*, Sig) NAL.

Micheals, Lee, ed. Briers Way. 69p. (C). 1990. 35.00 (*0-7223-2424-3*, Pub. by A H S Ltd) St Mut.

Micheaux, Oscar. The Case of Mrs. Wingate. 6th ed. LC 73-18593. (Illus.). reprint ed. 69.50 (*0-404-11404-0*) AMS Pr.

— The Conquest: The Story of a Negro Pioneer. LC 75-89391. (Black Heritage Library Collection). 1977. 30.95 (*0-8369-8632-6*) Ayer.

— The Conquest: The Story of a Negro Pioneer. LC 94-6243. (Illus.). xxi, 332p. 1994. pap. 9.95 (*0-8032-8209-5*, Bison Books) U of Nebr Pr.

— The Homesteader: A Novel. LC 94-6203. (Illus.). ix, 533p. 1994. pap. 12.95 (*0-8032-8208-7*, Bison Books) U of Nebr Pr.

— The Masquerade: An Historical Novel. LC 73-18595. reprint ed. 49.50 (*0-404-11406-7*) AMS Pr.

— The Wind from Nowhere. LC 72-4810. (Black Heritage Library Collection). 1977. reprint ed. 35.95 (*0-8369-9109-5*) Ayer.

Michejda, Christopher J., jt. ed. see Loeppky, Richard N.

Michel, ed. Histoire de l'Art, 8 tomes en 15. write for info. (*0-8288-7900-1*) Fr & Eur.

— Histoire de l'Art, 8 tomes en 15, Set. 175.00 (*0-685-36014-8*) Fr & Eur.

Michel & Company Staff. Happy Ever After! (Illus.). 32p. 1994. 6.95 (*0-8362-4714-0*) Andrews & McMeel.

— Happy Wishes Birthday Girl. (Illus.). 80p. 1994. 4.95 (*0-8362-3083-3*) Andrews & McMeel.

— A Mother Knows Just What to Do. (Illus.). 32p. 1995. 6.95 (*0-8362-4738-8*) Andrews & McMeel.

— Small Lullabies. (Illus.). 80p. 1994. 4.95 (*0-8362-3082-5*) Andrews & McMeel.

— Two Little Ladies. (Illus.). 32p. 1994. 6.95 (*0-8362-4715-9*) Andrews & McMeel.

Michel, A. N., et al. Associative Memory Using Artificial Neural Networks. 300p. 1995. text 74.00 (*981-02-1581-9*) World Scientific Pub.

Michel, A. R. Clinical Biology of Sodium: The Physiology & Pathophysiology of Sodium in Mammals. LC 95-2407. 1995. write for info. (*0-08-840842-6*, Pergamon Pr) Elsevier.

Michel, Aime. Flying Saucers & the Straight-Line Mystery. LC 58-8787. (Illus.). 1958. 48.95 (*0-87599-077-0*) S G Phillips.

Michel, Albert, jt. auth. see Loth, Bernard.

Michel, Albin. Humanism in Islam. Boisard, Marcel A., tr. 322p. 1996. 19.95 (*0-614-21511-0*, 470) Kazi Pubns.

Michel Albin Staff. Dictionnaire National des Communes de France. 40th ed. (FRE.). 1342p. 1992. 150.00 (*0-8288-6917-0*, 2226057242) Fr & Eur.

Michel, Aloys A. The Indus Rivers: A Study of the Effects of Partition. LC 67-13444. 624p. reprint ed. pap. 193.50 (*0-608-14023-6*, 202202100024) Bks Demand.

Michel, Andreas. Theologies aus der Peripherie. 432p. 1997. text 145.35 (*3-11-015689-X*) De Gruyter.

Michel, Andreas, tr. see Lyotard, Jean-Francois.

Michel, Andree. The Modernization of North African Families in the Paris Area. LC 72-184752. (New Babylon Studies in the Social Sciences: No. 16). (Illus.). 387p. (Orig.). 1974. pap. text 34.75 (*90-279-7312-1*) Mouton.

Michel, Anthony, jt. auth. see Antsaklis, Panos.

Michel, Anthony M. & Herget, Charles J. Applied Algebra & Functional Analysis. LC 93-15006. Orig. Title: Mathematical Foundations in Engineering & Science. (Illus.). xi, 484p. 1993. reprint ed. pap. 10.95 (*0-486-67598-X*) Dover.

Michel, Anthony N. & Kaining Wang. Qualitative Theory for Dynamical Systems. LC 94-35418. (Pure & Applied Mathematics Ser.: Vol. 186). (Illus.). 472p. 1994. text 175.00 (*0-8247-9420-6*) Dekker.

Michel, Anthony N., jt. auth. see Liu, Derong.

Michel, Barbara. Beyond Eden: Leah's Hope Is Sorely Tried When Shunning Overshadows Peter Johni. Monsholl, Evelyn, ed. (Eden Ser.: Vol. 4). 256p. 1998. pap. 9.95 (*0-936369-63-9*) Son-Rise Pubns.

— Dawn of Eden: Love Sustains Rachel When Tragedy Shatters Her Dreams. Minshull, Evelyn, ed. (Eden Ser.: Vol. 3). 256p. 1997. pap. 9.95 (*0-936369-96-5*) Son-Rise Pubns.

— Return to Eden: Elizabeth's Search for Answers. (Eden Ser.: Vol. 3). 240p. (Orig.). 1995. pap. 9.95 (*0-936369-65-5*) Son-Rise Pubns.

— Search for Eden: Rebecca Searches for True Meaning in Life. 2nd ed. Minshull, Evelyn, ed. (Eden Ser.: Vol. 1). 244p. 1996. reprint ed. pap. 9.95 (*0-936369-90-6*) Son-Rise Pubns.

Michel, Barbara N., jt. auth. see Michel, John L.

Michel-Beyerle, M. E., ed. Antennas & Reaction Centers of Photosynthetic Bacteria: Structure, Interactions & Dynamics. (Chemical Physics Ser.: Vol. 42). (Illus.). 384p. 1985. 71.00 (*0-387-16154-6*) Spr-Verlag.

— The Reaction Center of Photosynthetic Bacteria: Feldafing-II-Meeting. (Biophysics Ser.: Vol. 6). (Illus.). xiv, 469p. 1991. 135.95 (*0-387-53420-2*) Spr-Verlag.

— The Reaction Center of Photosynthetic Bacteria: Structure & Dynamics. LC 96-15841. (Illus.). 438p. 1996. 119.00 (*3-540-61075-8*) Spr-Verlag.

Michel, C. Recueil d'Inscriptions Grecques: Supplements, 1912-1927. 227p. 1976. 25.00 (*0-89005-110-0*) Ares.

Michel, C. Charles, jt. ed. see Renkin, Eugene M.

Michel, C. Randall. Justice Gone Awry: The Arrest & Trials of Jesus Christ. LC 96-121632. (Illus.). 72p. (Orig.). 1995. pap. 7.95 (*1-883893-08-9*) WinePress Pub.

Michel, Charles. Recueil d'Inscriptions Grecques. (Subsidia Epigraphica Ser.). (GER.). xxvi, 1000p. 1976. reprint ed. write for info. (*3-487-05634-8*) G Olms Pubs.

— Recueil d'Inscriptions Grecques: Supplement. (Subsidia Epigraphica Ser.). (GER.). 106p. 1976. reprint ed. write for info. (*3-487-06140-6*) G Olms Pubs.

Michel, Christian. Kleines Psychologisches Woerterbuch. (GER.). 39.95 (*0-7859-8368-6*, 3451040549) Fr & Eur.

Michel, Claude, jt. auth. see Vurpas, Anne-Marie.

Michel, Dan. Ayenbite of Inwyt Vol. II: Introduction, Notes & Glossary, Vol. II, Intro., Notes & Glossary. Gradon, Pamela, ed. (OS 278 Ser.). 338p. 1979. 23.00 (*0-19-722280-3*) OUP.

***Michel, David.** Telling the Story. 2000. pap. 10.99 (*0-87148-946-5*) Pathway Pr.

Michel, De Trez. American Warriors: Pictorial History of the American Paratroopers Prior to Normandy. 1994. text 69.00 (*2-9600176-0-9*, 017609) Combined Pub.

— At the Point of No Return: Pictorial History of the American Paratroopers in the Invasion of Normandy. 1994. text 69.00 (*2-9600176-1-7*, 017617) Combined Pub.

Michel, Dieter, jt. auth. see Engelhardt, Gunter.

Michel, Diethelm. Untersuchungen zur Eigenart des Buches Qohelet. (Beiheft zur Zeitschrift fuer die Alttestamentliche Wissenschaft Ser.: No. 183). vii, 329p. (C). 1989. lib. bdg. 95.40 (*3-11-012161-1*) De Gruyter.

Michel, Donald E. Music Therapy: An Introduction, Including Music in Special Education. 2nd ed. (Illus.). 152p. (C). 1985. 29.95 (*0-398-05063-5*) C C Thomas.

Michel, Donald E. & Jones, Janet L. Music for Developing Speech & Language Skills in Children: A Guide for Parents & Therapists. (MMB Horizon Ser.: No. 9). 56p. (Orig.). 1991. pap. 9.95 (*0-918812-69-0*, ST 233) MMB Music.

Michel, Edouard. Flemish Painting in the Seventeenth Century. (Illus.). 45p. 1939. lib. bdg. 35.00 (*0-8288-3981-6*) Fr & Eur.

***Michel, Elizabeth.** An Orchestra of Voices: Making the Argument for Greater Speech & Press Freedom in the People's Republic of China. Xupei, Sun C., ed. LC 00-32375. 2000. write for info. (*0-275-96956-8*, Praeger Pubs) Greenwood.

Michel, Emile. Rembrandt, 2 vols. 1972. 200.00 (*0-8490-0943-X*) Gordon Pr.

Michel, Eric, ed. ADEC 98 International Art Price Annual. 2704p. 1998. 69.00 (*2-907129-12-0*, Pub. by ADEC Diffusion) New Eng Gallery.

— ADEC 92 International Art Price Annual: Annuaire Des Cotes. 1992. 69.00 (*2-907129-04-X*, Pub. by ADEC Diffusion) New Eng Gallery.

— ADEC 93 International Art Price Annual: Annuaire Des Cotes. 2526p. 1993. 69.00 (*2-907129-05-8*, Pub. by ADEC Diffusion) New Eng Gallery.

— ADEC 94 International Art Price Annual: Annuaire Des Cotes. 2640p. 1994. 69.00 (*2-907129-06-6*, Pub. by ADEC Diffusion) New Eng Gallery.

— ADEC 95 International Art Price Annual: Annuaire Des Cotes. 2718p. 1995. 69.00 (*2-907129-07-4*, Pub. by ADEC Diffusion) New Eng Gallery.

— ADEC 96 International Art Price Annual: Annuaire Des Cotes. 2350p. 1996. 69.00 (*2-907129-08-2*, Pub. by ADEC Diffusion) New Eng Gallery.

Michel, Ernest. Promises to Keep. LC 93-13550. (Illus.). 320p. 1993. 22.00 (*0-9623032-4-0*) Barricade Bks.

Michel, F. Curtis. Theory of Neutron Star Magnetospheres. (Theoretical Astrophysics Ser.). (Illus.). 532p. 1990. pap. text 42.00 (*0-226-52331-4*); lib. bdg. 96.00 (*0-226-52330-6*) U Ch Pr.

Michel, France. English - French Vocabulary of Electronic Data Interchange. (ENG & FRE.). 37p. 1991. pap. 19.95 (*0-8288-9406-X*) Fr & Eur.

— Vocabulary of Cooking Utensils. (ENG & FRE.). 39p. 1990. pap. 29.95 (*0-8288-9379-9*) Fr & Eur.

Michel, France, jt. auth. see Boivin, Gilles.

Michel, Freda. The Machiavellian Marquess. 1979. mass mkt. 1.75 (*0-449-50014-4*, Coventry) Fawcett.

An Asterisk (*) at the beginning of an entry indicates that the title is appearing for the first time.

Michel, Genevieve. The Rulers of Tikal: An Historical Reconstruction & Field Guide to the Stelae. (Illus.). 148p. (Orig.). (C). 1989. pap. 13.00 (0-9626221-1-7) Vista Pubns FL.

Michel, George F. & Moore, Celia L. Developmental Psychobiology: An Interdisciplinary Science. LC 94-47023. (Illus.). 532p. 1995. 66.00 (0-262-13312-1, Bradford Bks) MIT Pr.

Michel, George J. Building Schools: The New School & Community Relations. LC 96-61024. 320p. 1996. pap. text 39.95 (1-56676-460-2) Scarecrow.

Michel, Gert. Mineral- und Thermalgewasser - Allgemeine Balneogeologie, Band 7. (Lehrbuch der Hydrogeologie Ser.). xii, 397p. 1998. 88.00 (3-443-01011-3, Pub. by Gebruder Borntraeger) Balogh.

Michel, Gwyneth, ed. The Essential Wedding Collection. 40p. (C). 1997. pap. text 6.95 (0-7692-1619-6, WBHB9710) Wrner Bros.

Michel, Gwyneth, ed. see Marcus, Linda & Schram, Ruth E.

Michel, Hartmut. Crystallization of Membrane Proteins. 208p. 1990. 104.00 (0-8493-4816-1, QP552) CRC Pr.

Michel, Henry J. Basic Frank Lloyd Wright: Legend & Fact about America's Most Creative Architect. Wetterberg, D. A., ed. LC 99-70549. (Illus.). 64p. 1999. pap. 9.95 (0-9652237-2-8, One Palm Bks) Michel Pub Servs.

Michel, Irene C. 50 Years of Hi, Honey, I'm Home. (Illus.). 128p. 1996. pap. 9.95 (0-9652692-0-5) I C Michel.

Michel, Irene C., ed. see Boudreaux, Warren L.

Michel, J., et al, eds. Defects in Electronic Materials II. LC 97-6020. (Materials Research Society Symposium Proceedings Ser.: No. 442). 710p. 1997. text 75.00 (1-55899-346-0) Materials Res.

Michel, J. P., et al, eds. Geriatric Programs & Departments: Around the World. 496p. 1998. pap. 45.95 (0-8261-1198-X) Springer Pub.

***Michel, J. P. & Hof, P. R., eds.** Management of Aging: The University of Geneva Experience. LC 99-32982. (Interdisciplinary Topics in Gerontology Ser.: Vol. 30). (Illus.). 268p. 1999. 172.25 (3-8055-6860-6) S Karger.

Michel, J. P., et al. Dictionary of Earth Sciences: English-French - French-English. 3rd ed. 364p. 1997. pap. 110.00 (0-471-96603-7) Wiley.

Michel, J. P., jt. auth. see Fairbridge, Rhodes W.

Michel, James. Development Cooperation Report, 1997: Efforts & Policies of the Members of the Development Assistance Committee, 1998 Edition. 224p. 1998. pap. 30.00 (92-64-16019-1, 43-98-01-1-P, Pub. by Org for Econ) OECD.

Michel, James H. Development Cooperation Report, 1996. 290p. (Orig.). 1997. pap. 35.00 (92-64-15400-0, 43-97-01-1, Pub. by Org for Econ) OECD.

Michel, Jean, jt. auth. see Digne, Francois.

Michel, Jean-Pierre. Dictionary of Earth Sciences, English/French-French/English. 3rd ed. (ENG & FRE.). 368p. 1997. pap. 150.00 (0-7859-9503-X) Fr & Eur.

Michel, John J. Mr. Michel's War: From Manila to Mukden: An American Naval Officer's War with the Japanese, 1941-1945. LC 97-28805. (Illus.). 352p. 1998. 26.95 (0-89141-643-9) Presidio Pr.

Michel, John L. & Michel, Barbara N. Antiquing New York. 1995. 46.00 (0-231-10012-4) Col U Pr.

Michel, John L. & Michel, Barbara N. Antiquing New York: The Guide to the Antique Dealers of New York. (Illus.). 342p. 1995. pap. 18.95 (0-231-10013-2) Col U Pr.

Michel, Joyce H. I Can Jump! My Little Kindergarten Practice Reader. 2nd rev. ed. (I Can! Bks.). (Illus.). 20p. (J). (gr. k). 1991. reprint ed. 1.75 (0-9647262-0-3) I Can Bks.

— I Can Ride! A Practice Reader. 2nd rev. ed. (I Can! Bks.). 20p. (J). (gr. k-3). 1993. reprint ed. 1.75 (0-9647262-1-1) I Can Bks.

Michel, Ken. Love Is Shown in Little Ways. LC 96-148300. (Illus.). 80p. 1995. 4.95 (0-8362-3126-0) Andrews & McMeel.

Michel, L., et al, eds. Spontaneous Symmetry Breakdown & Related Subjects: XXI Karpacz Winter School on Theoretical Physics, Poland, 1985. 504p. 1985. 78.00 (9971-978-54-7) World Scientific Pub.

Michel, Laurence A. & Sewall, Richard B., eds. Tragedy: Modern Essays in Criticism. LC 77-13779. 340p. 1978. reprint ed. lib. bdg. 55.00 (0-8371-9876-3, MITR, Greenwood Pr) Greenwood.

Michel, Lou. Light: The Shape of Space: Designing with Space & Light. (Architecture Ser.). 277p. 1995. 69.95 (0-471-28618-4, VNR) Wiley.

Michel, Louis. Light - The Shape of Space: Designing with Space & Light. (Illus.). 288p. 1995. text 59.95 (0-442-01804-5, VNR) Wiley.

Michel, M., tr. see Guigou, Jean-Louis.

Michel, Maher, et al. Essays Plans for Anaesthesia Exams. (Illus.). 192p. (Orig.). 1993. pap. text 39.95 (0-443-04395-7) Church.

Michel, Marc. La Mission Marchand, 1895 to 1899. (Monde d'Outre Mer Passe & Present, Etudes Ser.: No. 36). (Illus.). 1972. pap. 49.25 (90-279-7153-6) Mouton.

Michel, Marianne R. Chardin. McCarthy, Eithne, tr. (Illus.). 296p. 1996. 125.00 (0-8109-4041-8, Pub. by Abrams) Time Warner.

Michel, Mark. The Beginner's Guide to Real Estate Wealth. 1986. pap. 9.95 (0-939383-04-7) Omnibus Pr.

Michel, Marshall. Clashes: Air Combat over North Vietnam, 1965-1972. LC 97-9279. (Illus.). 352p. 1997. 32.95 (1-55750-585-3) Naval Inst Pr.

Michel, Mary E., jt. ed. see Broman, Sarah H.

Michel, Norbert, et al. Monaco. (Illus.). 440p. 1998. 39.95 (3-8290-0658-6) MBI Pubg.

Michel, Pamela A. The Child's View of Reading: Understandings for Teachers & Parents. LC 93-24104. 192p. (C). 1993. pap. text 41.00 (0-205-13784-9, Longwood Div) Allyn.

***Michel, Patrick J.** Five. (Illus.). 224p. 2000. 44.95 (1-893263-17-7) Ipso Facto.

Michel, Paula, ed. see Milne, Drucilla.

Michel, Peter. The Dawn of a New Time: A Spiritual Novel. LC 99-21432. 192p. 1999. pap. 13.95 (1-885394-38-1, Pub. by Bluestar Communs) ACCESS Pubs Network.

— Faith & Dogma: What the Pope Didn't Say. LC 95-17818. 160p. 1995. pap. 10.95 (1-885394-13-6) Bluestar Communs.

— Krishnamurti - Love & Freedom: Approaching a Mystery. 208p. 1995. pap. 10.95 (1-885394-00-4) Bluestar Communs.

Michel, Petra, ed. The Synthesis Approach to Digital System Design. (International Series in Engineering & Computer Science, VLSI, Computer Architecture, & Digital Screen Processing). 432p. (C). 1992. text 152.50 (0-7923-9199-3) Kluwer Academic.

Michel, Petra, tr. see Andersen, Hans Christian.

Michel, Pierre. James Gould Cozzens: An Annotated Checklist. LC 75-169068. (Serif Series: Bibliographies & Checklists: No. 22). 123p. reprint ed. pap. 38.20 (0-7837-0565-4, 204090900019) Bks Demand.

Michel, Pierre, ed. see Rabelais, Francois.

Michel, Pierre A. Mandatory Financial Information & Capital Market Equilibrium in Belgium. (Accounting Thought & Practice Ser.). 225p. 1987. text 10.00 (0-8240-7852-7) Garland.

Michel, Pierre-Frank. Jugendstilglasmalerei in der Schweiz. (GER., Illus.). 160p. (C). 1986. 118.00 (3-8170-2006-6, Pub. by Knstvrlag Weingrtn) Intl Bk Import.

Michel, R., et al, eds. Unsteady Turbulent Shear Flows: Proceedings. (International Union of Theoretical & Applied Mechanics Symposia Ser.). 450p. 1982. 76.95 (0-387-11099-2) Spr-Verlag.

Michel, R. & Arnal, D., eds. Laminar-Turbulent Transition: IUTAM Symposium, Toulouse, France, September 11-15, 1989. (International Union of Theoretical & Applied Mechanics Symposia Ser.). (Illus.). 704p. 1991. 174.95 (0-387-52196-8) Spr-Verlag.

Michel, Richard C., jt. auth. see Levy, Frank S.

Michel, Richard C., jt. auth. see Lewis, Gordon H.

Michel, Rodolphe, jt. auth. see Shirai, Tetsuya.

Michel, Sally. Drawing Animals & Pets. (Understand How to Draw Ser.: No. 6). (Illus.). 32p. pap. 4.95 (0-85532-574-7, 574-7, Pub. by Srch Pr) A Schwartz & Co.

— Painting Animals in Watercolour. (Illus.). 128p. pap. 22.50 (0-85532-648-4, 648-4, Pub. by Srch Pr) A Schwartz & Co.

— Painting Cats in Watercolour. (Leisure Arts Ser.: No. 26). (Illus.). 32p. pap. 4.95 (0-85532-558-5, 558-5, Pub. by Srch Pr) A Schwartz & Co.

Michel, Sandra S. Visions to Keep. Syrja, Steven, ed. 320p. (Orig.). 1990. pap. 14.95 (0-917178-20-3) Lenape Pub.

Michel, Sandra S., ed. see Smith, Viola B.

Michel, Sandy. No More Someday. (Illus.). 1973. pap. 2.00 (0-917178-16-5) Lenape Pub.

***Michel, Sonya.** Children's Interests/Mothers' Rights: The Shaping of America's Child Care Policy. LC 98-34830. 432p. 2000. 40.00 (0-300-05951-5); pap. 18.00 (0-300-08551-6) Yale U Pr.

Michel, Sonya & Muncy, Robyn. Engendering America: A Documentary History, 1865-the Present. LC 98-29229. (Illus.). 408p. 1999. pap. 18.00 (0-07-044361-0, McGrw-H College) McGrw-H Hghr Educ.

Michel, Sonya, jt. ed. see Koven, Seth.

Michel, Steve. The Bob Dylan Concordance. 153p. 1992. pap. 29.95 (0-9635031-0-3) Rolling Tomes.

Michel, Theresa H., jt. ed. see Wittink, Harriet.

Michel-Thiriet, Philippe. Marcel Proust Lexikon. (GER.). 514p. 1992. 125.00 (0-7859-8407-0, 3518403907) Fr & Eur.

Michel, Thomas F., tr. see Taymiya, Ibn.

Michel, Trudi. Inside Tin Pan Alley. (American Autobiography Ser.). 172p. 1995. reprint ed. lib. bdg. 69.00 (0-7812-8593-3) Rprt Serv.

***Michelaard, B.** The Pegasus Project. 368p. 2000. pap. 5.50 (0-8439-4707-1, Leisure Bks) Dorchester Pub Co.

Michelassi, F. & Milsom, J. W., eds. Operative Strategies in Inflammatory Bowel Disease. LC 97-20702. (Illus.). 568p. 1999. 150.00 (0-387-94966-6) Spr-Verlag.

Michele, A. D. The Mollifier. (Chapbook Ser.). (Illus.). 15p. 1996. pap. 10.00 (0-9652505-1-2) Synaesthesia.

Michele C. Solitary Traveller. 20p. (Orig.). 1990. pap. 3.00 (0-916397-13-0) Manic D Pr.

Michele, Murray. Hymns in the Style of Masters Piano. 1997. pap. 10.95 (0-634-00342-9) H Leonard.

***Michelen, Abraham.** Digital Electronics Lab Manual. 304p. (C). 2000. pap. 49.00 (0-13-087418-3, Prentice Hall) P-H.

***Micheler, Eva & Prentice, D. D., eds.** Joint Ventures in English & German Law. 304p. 2000. 80.00 (1-84113-106-7, Pub. by Hart Pub) Intl Spec Bk.

Michelet, Jon. Orion's Belt. large type ed. 528p. 1987. 27.99 (0-7089-1689-9) Ulverscroft.

Michelet, Jules. Histoire de la Revolution Francaise, 2 vols., Vol. 1. Walter, ed. (Pleiade Ser.). (FRE.). 74.95 (2-07-010356-0) Schoenhof.

— Histoire de la Revolution Francaise, 2 vols., Vol. 2. Walter, ed. (Pleiade Ser.). (FRE.). 78.95 (2-07-010357-9) Schoenhof.

— History of the French Revolution. Wright, Gordon, ed. Cocks, Charles, tr. from FRE. LC 67-15315. (Classic European Historians Ser.). xxii, 476p. (C). 1997. reprint ed. pap. text 16.95 (0-226-52333-0) U Ch Pr.

— Jeanne d'Arc. (FRE.). 1974. pap. 10.95 (0-7859-4011-1) Fr & Eur.

— Jeanne d'Arc. (Folio Ser.: No. 441). (FRE.). 320p. 1974. pap. 8.95 (2-07-036441-0) Schoenhof.

— Joan of Arc. Guerard, Albert, tr. 152p. 1967. pap. text 13.95 (0-472-06122-4, 06122, Ann Arbor Bks) U of Mich Pr.

— Mer. (Folio Ser.: No. 1470). (FRE.). 416p. 1983. pap. 13.95 (2-07-037470-X) Schoenhof.

— The People. 1973. 200.00 (0-8490-0810-7) Gordon Pr.

— Witchcraft, Sorcery & Superstition. Allinson, A. R., tr. from FRE. LC 95-9367. Orig. Title: Satanism & Witchcraft. 352p. 1995. pap. 12.95 (0-8065-1686-0, Citadel Pr) Carol Pub Group.

Micheletti, Emma. Ghirlandaio. Brierley, Anthony, tr. from ITA. LC 98-158510. (Library of Great Masters). (Illus.). 80p. 1990. pap. 12.99 (1-878351-08-7) Riverside NY.

— Ghirlandaio. (Grandes Maestros del Arte Ser.). (SPA., Illus.). 80p. 1992. pap. 12.99 (1-878351-27-3) Riverside NY.

***Micheletti, Eric.** Commandement Des Operations Speciales. 1998. 37.95 (2-908182-80-7, 182807) Histoire.

— French Special Forces. 1999. pap. 44.95 (2-908182-83-1) Histoire.

— Second Foreign Legion Paratroop Regiment. (Illus.). 2000. 37.95 (2-913903-06-1, Pub. by Histoire) Combined Pub.

Micheletti, G. F., ed. Flexible Manufacturing Systems. (Illus.). 420p. 1988. 174.95 (0-387-18524-0) Spr-Verlag.

Micheletti, Michele. Civil Society & State Relations in Sweden. 224p. (C). 1995. 79.95 (1-85972-037-4, Pub. by Avebry) Ashgate Pub Co.

— The Swedish Farmers' Movement & Government Agricultural Policy. LC 89-16206. 225p. 1990. 59.95 (0-275-93398-9, C3398, Praeger Pubs) Greenwood.

Micheletti, Robert. The 15 Minute Gourmet Cookbook. 4th ed. iv, 90p. 1995. 16.95 (0-9674265-0-2, 15MGVI) Fifteen Min Gourmet.

Michelfeld. Ethical Issues in Cyberspace. (C). 1999. pap. text. write for info. (0-15-507957-3) Harcourt Coll Pubs.

Michelfelder, Diane P. & Palmer, Richard E., eds. Dialogue & Deconstruction: The Gadamer-Derrida Encounter. LC 88-24792. (SUNY Series in Contemporary Continental Philosophy). 352p. (C). 1989. pap. text 21.95 (0-7914-0009-3) State U NY Pr.

Micheli, L. French - English Dictionary of Home Automation. (ENG & FRE.). 260p. 1991. pap. 40.00 (2-85608-042-1) IBD Ltd.

— French-English Dictionary of Home Automation: Dictionnaire de la Domotique. (ENG & FRE.). 250p. 1991. pap. 59.95 (0-8288-6969-3, 2856080421) Fr & Eur.

Micheli, Lyle J. Pediatric & Adolescent Sports Medicine. 218p. 1984. 62.95 (0-316-56949-6, Little Brwn Med Div) Lppncott W & W.

Micheli, Lyle J., et al, eds. Soviet-American Dance Medicine: Proceedings of the 1990 Glasnost Dance Medicine Conference & Workshops. (Illus.). 113p. (Orig.). 1991. pap. text 10.00 (0-88314-512-X) AAHPERD.

Micheli, Lyle J. & Jenkins, Mark. Healthy Runner's Handbook. LC 95-26222. (Illus.). 264p. (Orig.). 1996. pap. 16.95 (0-88011-524-6, PMIC0524) Human Kinetics.

— Sports Medicine Bibl: Prevent, Detect, & Treat Your Sports Injuries Through the Latest Medical Techn. LC 95-2316. (Illus.). 352p. 1995. pap. 21.00 (0-06-273143-2, Harper Ref) HarpC.

Micheli, Maria R. & Bova, Rodolfo. Fingerprinting Methods Based on PCR. LC 96-30117. 441p. 1997. pap. 99.50 (3-540-61229-7) Spr-Verlag.

***Micheli-Tzanakou, Evangelia.** Supervised & Unsupervised Pattern Recognition: Feature Extraction & Computational Intelligence. LC 99-43495. (Industrial Electronics Ser.). 392p. 1999. boxed set 99.95 (0-8493-2278-2) CRC Pr.

Michelin. Benelux Hotel & Restaurant Guide 1998. (ENG, FRE, GER & ITA.). 448p. 1998. 24.95 (0-7859-9608-7) Fr & Eur.

— Europe Hotel & Restaurant Guide 1998. (ENG, FRE, GER, ITA & JPN.). 1998. 24.95 (0-7859-9609-5) Fr & Eur.

— France, Camping & Caravaning 1998. (FRE.). 1998. pap. 19.95 (0-7859-9612-5) Fr & Eur.

— France Hotel & Restaurant Guide 1998. (ENG, FRE, GER & ITA.). 1998. 25.95 (0-7859-9602-8) Fr & Eur.

— Germany Hotel & Restaurant Guide 1998. (ENG, FRE, GER & ITA.). 1998. 25.95 (0-7859-9604-4) Fr & Eur.

— Great Britain Hotel & Restuarant Guide 1998. (ENG, FRE, GER & ITA.). 1998. 25.95 (0-7859-9606-0) Fr & Eur.

— Ireland Hotel & Restaurant Guide 1998. (ENG, FRE, GER & ITA.). 1998. 11.95 (0-7859-9614-1) Fr & Eur.

— Itlay Hotel & Restaurant Guide 1998. (ENG, FRE, GER & ITA.). 1998. 25.95 (0-7859-9603-6) Fr & Eur.

— London Hotel & Restaurant Guide 1998. (ENG, FRE, GER & ITA.). 1998. 11.95 (0-7859-9611-7) Fr & Eur.

— Paris Hotel & Restaurant Guide 1998. (ENG, FRE, GER & ITA.). 1998. 11.95 (0-7859-9610-9) Fr & Eur.

— Portugal Hotel & Restaurant Guide 1998. (ENG, FRE, GER, ITA & POR.). 1998. 11.95 (0-7859-9613-3) Fr & Eur.

— Spain & Portugal Hotel & Restaurant Guide 1998. (ENG, FRE, GER, ITA & POR.). 1998. 25.95 (0-7859-9605-2) Fr & Eur.

— Switzerland Hotel & Restaurant Guide 1998. (ENG, FRE, GER & ITA.). 1998. 24.95 (0-7859-9607-9) Fr & Eur.

Michelin, ed. Michelin Benelux Hotel & Restaurant Guide, 1997. (ENG, FRE, GER & ITA.). 1997. 26.95 (0-7859-9386-X) Fr & Eur.

— Michelin Hotel & Restaurant Guide to Benelux, 1997. 1997. 24.95 (0-7859-9460-2) Fr & Eur.

— Michelin Hotel & Restaurant Guide to Germany, 1997. 1997. 25.95 (0-7859-9461-0) Fr & Eur.

Michelin Staff. Albi/Rodez/Nimes. 1998. 6.95 (2-06-700080-2) Michelin.

— Algeria/Tunisia Map. 1994. 10.95 (2-06-700958-3, 958) Michelin.

— Alpes du Nord Green Guide. 2nd ed. (FRE.). 1996. pap. 19.95 (0-7859-9150-6) Fr & Eur.

— Alps (of France) Green Guide: France (Regional Guides) 1998. per. 20.00 (2-06-130101-0, 1301) Michelin.

— Alsace et Lorraine Green Guide: France (Guides Regionaux) 6th ed. (Green Guide Ser.). (FRE., Illus.). 1997. per. 20.00 (2-06-037206-2, 372) Michelin.

— Alsace et Lorraine Green Guide--Vosges. 4th ed. (FRE.). 1997. pap. 19.95 (0-7859-9151-4) Fr & Eur.

— Amsterdam. 1999. pap. text 9.95 (2-06-655101-5) Michelin.

— Amsterdam. 1999. pap. text 18.00 (2-06-054701-6); pap. text 9.95 (2-06-660301-5) Michelin.

***Michelin Staff.** Amsterdam. 1999. pap. 18.00 (2-06-454701-0) Michelin.

— Amsterdam. 1999. pap. text 18.00 (2-06-154701-X) Michelin.

Michelin Staff. Amsterdam in Your Pocket Guide. (In Your Pocket Guide Ser.). 1996. per. 9.95 (2-06-650101-8, 6501) Michelin.

***Michelin Staff.** Atlantic Coast: Loire to Pyrenees. 2nd ed. 1998. pap., pap. text 20.00 (2-06-138002-6) Michelin.

Michelin Staff. Atlas Great Britain & Ireland. 6th ed. 1995. pap., spiral bd. 39.95 (0-7859-9118-2) Fr & Eur.

— Atlas of Mammography. 368p. 1997. text. write for info. (0-412-56020-8) Chapman & Hall.

***Michelin Staff.** Austria. 15th ed. 1998. write for info. (2-06-092603-3) Michelin.

Michelin Staff. Austria Green Guide. 1997. pap. 19.95 (0-7859-7183-1, 2067015079) Fr & Eur.

***Michelin Staff.** Austria Green Guide. (Green Guide Ser.). (SPA., Illus.). 1998. per. 20.00 (2-06-450801-5, 4508) Michelin.

Michelin Staff. Austria Green Guide: Europe (Country Guides) 2nd ed. (Illus.). 1997. per. 20.00 (2-06-150702-6, 1507) Michelin.

— Auvergne - The Valley Green Guide: France (Regional Guides) 2nd ed. (Green Guides Ser.). (Illus.). 1997. per. 20.00 (2-06-130402-8, 1304) Michelin.

— Auvergne Green Guide French Edition. (FRE.). 1996. pap. 19.95 (0-7859-7220-X, 2067003046) Fr & Eur.

— Barcelona. 1999. pap. text 9.95 (2-06-660501-8) Michelin.

— Belgique Green Guide French Edition. (FRE.). 1996. pap. 19.95 (0-7859-7208-0, 2060411011) Fr & Eur.

***Michelin Staff.** Belgium - Luxembourg, Vol. 909. 2nd ed. 1999. 8.95 (2-06-090903-1) Michelin.

Michelin Staff. Belgium Green Guide: Europe (City & Regional Guides) (Illus.). 1997. per. 20.00 (2-06-151402-2, 1514) Michelin.

***Michelin Staff.** Benelux, No. 907. 2nd ed. 1998. write for info. (2-06-090703-9) Michelin.

Michelin Staff. Benelux (Hotel & Restaurant Guide) 1996. (ENG, FRE, GER & ITA.). 1996. 24.95 (0-7859-9911-6) Fr & Eur.

***Michelin Staff.** Benelux Hotels & Restaurants: 2000 Edition. 100th ed. (Red Guide Benelux Ser.). (Illus.). 1999. pap. text. write for info. (2-06-960023-8) Michelin.

Michelin Staff. Benelux Red Guide. 1994. 24.95 (0-7859-7164-5, 2060060494) Fr & Eur.

— Berlin in Your Pocket Guide. (In Your Pocket Guide Ser.). 1998. per. 9.95 (2-06-652401-8, 6524) Michelin.

— Berry Limousin Green Guide. 2nd ed. 1996. pap. 19.95 (0-7859-9133-6) Fr & Eur.

— Berry Limousin Green Guide: France (Guides Regionaux) (Green Guide Ser.). (FRE., Illus.). 1998. per. 20.00 (2-06-030504-7) Michelin.

— Bourgogne Green Guide. 3rd ed. 1994. pap. 18.95 (0-7859-9119-0) Fr & Eur.

— Bourgogne Green Guide: France (Guides Regionaux) 4th ed. (FRE., Illus.). 1996. per. 20.00 (2-06-030704-X, 307) Michelin.

— Bourgogne Green Guide French Edition. (FRE.). pap. 17.95 (0-7859-7222-6, 2067003070) Fr & Eur.

— Bretagne Green Guide. 3rd ed. (FRE.). 1991. pap. 18.95 (0-7859-9159-X) Fr & Eur.

— Bretagne Green Guide: France (Guides Regionaux) 6th ed. (FRE.). 1996. per. 20.00 (2-06-030906-9, 309) Michelin.

— Bretagne Green Guide French Edition. (FRE.). pap. 17.95 (0-7859-7223-4, 2060030943) Fr & Eur.

— Brittany Green Guide English Edition. 1997. pap. 19.95 (0-7859-7200-5, 2067013149) Fr & Eur.

— Brittany in Your Pocket Guide. (In Your Pocket Guides Ser.). 1996. per. 9.95 (2-06-630101-9, 6301) Michelin.

***Michelin Staff.** Bruxelles/Brussel-Oostende-Liege #213. 26th ed. 1999. 8.95 (2-06-000213-3) Michelin.

Michelin Staff. Budapest. 1999. pap. text 9.95 (2-06-660601-4) Michelin.

— Burgundy Green Guide English Edition. 1995. pap. 19.95 (0-7859-7201-3, 2067013084) Fr & Eur.

***Michelin Staff.** California. 1999. 20.00 (2-06-159803-X) Michelin.

Michelin Staff. California Green Guide. 1997. pap. 19.95 (0-7859-9120-4) Fr & Eur.

— California Green Guide French Edition. (FRE.). 1996. pap. 19.95 (0-7859-7177-7, 2061598013) Fr & Eur.

***Michelin Staff.** Camping & Caravanning France: 2000 Edition. (Red Guide France Ser.). (Illus.). 2000. pap. text. write for info. (2-06-961044-6) Michelin.

Michelin Staff. Camping Caravaning France 1996 Edition. (FRE.). 1996. 15.95 (0-7859-9901-9) Fr & Eur.

— Canada Green Guide. 5th ed. (FRE.). 1995. pap. 19.95 (0-7859-9160-3); pap. 19.95 (0-7859-9161-1) Fr & Eur.

***Michelin Staff.** Cataluna Green Guide. (Green Guide Ser.). (SPA., Illus.). 1998. per. 20.00 (2-06-453001-0) Michelin.

M

An Asterisk (*) at the beginning of an entry indicates that the title is appearing for the first time.

Michelin Staff. Champagne-Ardennes Green Guide. 2nd ed. (FRE.). 1995. pap. 19.95 (*0-7859-9134-4*) Fr & Eur.

— Chateaux de la Loire Green Guide: France (Guides Regionaux) (FRE., Illus.). 1997. per. 20.00 (*2-06-031705-3*, 317) Michelin.

***Michelin Staff.** Chateaux of the Loire. 1999. pap. 20.00 (*2-06-132205-0*) Michelin.

Michelin Staff. Chateaux of the Loire Green Guide. 2nd ed. (Orig.). 1996. pap. 19.95 (*0-7859-9162-X*) Fr & Eur.

***Michelin Staff.** Chicago. 2nd ed. (Green Guide Ser.). 1999. pap. 18.00 (*2-06-159402-6*) Michelin.

Michelin Staff. Corse Green Guide: France (Guides Regionaux) (FRE., Illus.). 1997. per. 20.00 (*2-06-031903-X*, 319) Michelin.

— Corse Green Guide French Edition. (FRE.). 1997. pap. 19.95 (*0-7859-7226-9*) Fr & Eur.

— Cote D'Azur Green Guide. 2nd ed. 1994. pap. 18.95 (*0-7859-9121-2*) Fr & Eur.

— Cote D'Azur Green Guide: France (Guides Regionaux) 4th ed. (FRE.). 1997. per. 20.00 (*2-06-032004-6*, 320) Michelin.

— Cote d'Azur Green Guide French Edition. (FRE.). pap. 17.95 (*0-7859-7227-7*, 2067003208) Fr & Eur.

***Michelin Staff.** Deutschland Hotels & Restaurants 2000. (Red Guide Deutschland). (Illus.). 1999. pap. 26.00 (*2-06-962037-9*) Michelin.

Michelin Staff. Deutschland Red Guide. 1994. 26.95 (*0-7859-7165-3*, 2060062497) Fr & Eur.

— Dordogne Green Guide English Edition. 1994. pap. 19.95 (*0-7859-7203-X*, 2067013238) Fr & Eur.

— England: West Country Green Guide. 3rd ed. 1995. pap. 18.95 (*0-7859-9104-2*) Fr & Eur.

— England-West Green Guide English Edition. pap. 17.95 (*0-7859-7184-X*, 2061562035) Fr & Eur.

— Epinal/Nancy/Strasbourg. 1991. pap. text 6.95 (*2-06-700062-4*) Michelin.

***Michelin Staff.** Espana & Portugal Hotels & Restaurants. 100th ed. (Michelin Red Guide Espana/Portugal Ser.). 1999. pap. text 26.00 (*2-06-963028-5*) Michelin.

Michelin Staff. Espana Green Guide Spanish Edition. (SPA.). pap. 19.95 (*0-7859-7249-8*, 2067045261) Fr & Eur.

— Espana-Portugal Red Guide. (SPA.). 1994. 24.95 (*0-7859-7166-1*, 2060063493) Fr & Eur.

— Euro-Disney Green Guide English Edition. pap. 17.95 (*0-7859-7195-5*, 2067014811) Fr & Eur.

***Michelin Staff.** Europe, No. 970. 10th ed. 1999. write for info. (*2-06-097011-3*) Michelin.

Michelin Staff. Europe Atlas. 1994. pap., spiral bd. 39.95 (*0-7859-9135-2*) Fr & Eur.

— Europe (Hotel & Restaurant Guide) 1996. 1996. 24.95 (*0-7859-9903-5*) Fr & Eur.

***Michelin Staff.** Europe Main Cities Hotels & Restaurants: 2000 Edition. 100th ed. (Red Guide Europe (Main Cities) Ser.). (Illus.). 2000. pap. text. write for info. (*2-06-970019-4*) Michelin.

Michelin Staff. Europe Road Atlas. (FRE.). pap. 29.95 (*0-7859-7253-6*, 060057749X); pap., spiral bd. 29.95 (*0-7859-7252-8*, 060057749X) Fr & Eur.

— Flanders Picardy Green Guide. 1995. pap. 19.95 (*0-7859-9136-0*) Fr & Eur.

— Flandres-Artois-Picardie Green Guide. 3rd ed. (FRE.). 1996. pap. 19.95 (*0-7859-9163-8*) Fr & Eur.

— Florida. 2nd ed. (Green Guides Ser.). 343p. 1999. pap. 20.00 (*2-06-152802-3*) Michelin.

— Florida in Your Pocket Guide. (In Your Pocket Guides Ser.). 1996. per. 9.95 (*2-06-650201-6*, 6502) Michelin.

— Floride Green Guide: Amerique du Nord. (FRE., Illus.). 1997. per. 20.00 (*2-06-052801-1*, 528) Michelin.

***Michelin Staff.** Floride/Florida. 1999. pap. 20.00 (*2-06-052802-X*) Michelin.

Michelin Staff. France. (FRE.). pap. 29.95 (*0-7859-7255-2*, 206700915X); pap., spiral bd. 14.95 (*0-7859-7254-4*, 206700915X) Fr & Eur.

— France Green Guide. (FRE.). (Orig.). 1996. pap. 19.95 (*0-7859-9164-6*) Fr & Eur.

— France Green Guide French Edition. (FRE.). 1996. pap. 19.95 (*0-7859-7210-2*, 2060039010) Fr & Eur.

— France (Hotel & Restaurant Guide) 1996. 1996. 25.95 (*0-7859-9907-8*) Fr & Eur.

***Michelin Staff.** France Hotels & Restaurants: 2000 Edition. 100th ed. (Red Guide France Ser.). (Illus.). 2000. pap. text. write for info. (*2-06-964091-4*) Michelin.

Michelin Staff. France Red Guide. (Orig.). 1994. 24.95 (*0-7859-7168-8*, 2060664497) Fr & Eur.

***Michelin Staff.** France, Reversible. 1999. pap. 8.95 (*2-06-091628-3*) Michelin.

— France, Route Planning. 1999. write for info. (*2-06-091116-8*) Michelin.

— Francia Green Guide. (Green Guide Ser.). (SPA., Illus.). 1998. per. 20.00 (*2-06-449402-2*) Michelin.

Michelin Staff. French Michelin Green Guide Alpes du Sud. (FEM.). 1995. pap. 18.95 (*0-7859-9069-0*) Fr & Eur.

— French Michelin Green Guide Chateaux de la Loire. 1995. pap. 18.95 (*0-7859-9070-4*) Fr & Eur.

— French Michelin Green Guide Corse. 1995. pap. 19.95 (*0-7859-9071-2*) Fr & Eur.

— French Michelin Green Guide Maroc. 1995. pap. 19.95 (*0-7859-9072-0*) Fr & Eur.

— French Riviera Green Guide. 2nd ed. 1995. pap. 19.95 (*0-7859-9138-7*) Fr & Eur.

— Germany Green Guide. 1997. pap. 19.95 (*0-7859-9139-5*) Fr & Eur.

— Germany (Hotel & Restaurant Guide) 1996. 1996. 25.95 (*0-7859-9900-0*) Fr & Eur.

— Gorges du Tarn Green Guide. 2nd ed. 1996. pap. 19.95 (*0-7859-9123-9*) Fr & Eur.

— Gorges du Tarn Green Guide: France (Guides Regionaux) 3rd ed. (FRE.). 1996. per. 20.00 (*2-06-033703-8*, 337) Michelin.

***Michelin Staff.** Grand Duche de Luxembourg. 2nd ed. 1999. write for info. (*2-06-092403-0*) Michelin.

— Great Britain. (Illus.). 1999. pap. text 36.00 (*4-408-01316-1*) Michelin.

— Great Britain & Ireland. 1999. 10.95 (*2-06-098618-4*) Michelin.

— Great Britain & Ireland Hotels & Restaurants: 2000 Edition. 100th ed. (Red Guide Great Britain Ser.). (Illus.). 1999. pap. text. write for info. (*2-06-965027-8*) Michelin.

Michelin Staff. Great Britain & Ireland Red Guide. 1994. 24.95 (*0-7859-7169-6*, 2060065496) Fr & Eur.

— Great Britain & Ireland Road Atlas. (FRE.). pap. 29.95 (*0-7859-7256-0*, 2061122051); pap., spiral bd. 29.95 (*0-7859-7257-9*, 2061122051) Fr & Eur.

— Great Britain Green Guide: English Edition. pap. 17.95 (*0-7859-7186-6*, 2067015419) Fr & Eur.

— Great Britain (Hotel & Restaurant Guide) 1996. 1996. 24.95 (*0-7859-9908-6*) Fr & Eur.

— Greater London Red Guide. 1994. pap. 12.95 (*0-7859-7173-4*, 2060066492) Fr & Eur.

— Grecia. (Green Guides Ser.). 1999. pap. text 20.00 (*2-06-451901-7*) Michelin.

— Greece Green Guide: English Edition. 2nd ed. 1991. pap. 17.95 (*0-7859-7187-4*, 520) Fr & Eur.

— Greece Green Guide: Japanese Edition. (JPN.). pap. 36.00 (*0-7859-7241-2*, 4408013080) Fr & Eur.

Michelin Staff. Greek Islands of the Aegean in Your Pocket Guide. (In Your Pocket Guides Ser.). 1996. per. 9.95 (*2-06-650301-0*, 6503) Michelin.

Michelin Staff. Green Guide Canada. 1994. pap. 19.95 (*0-7859-9105-0*) Fr & Eur.

— Hollande Green Guide. 5th ed. (FRE.). 1993. pap. 19.95 (*0-7859-9140-9*) Fr & Eur.

— Hollande Green Guide: Europe (Guides Pays) (FRE., Illus.). 1997. pap. 20.00 (*2-06-052902-6*, 529) Michelin.

***Michelin Staff.** Hungary No. 925. 2nd ed. 1999. 8.95 (*2-06-092502-9*) Michelin.

Michelin Staff. Ile-De-France Green Guide: France (Guides Regionaux) 3rd ed. (FRE., Illus.). 1997. per. 20.00 (*2-06-032603-6*, 326) Michelin.

— Ile de France Green Guide French Edition. (FRE.). 1997. 19.95 (*0-614-00376-8*, 2063261X) Fr & Eur.

— Ireland Green Guide. pap. 17.95 (*0-7859-7188-2*, 2067015354) Fr & Eur.

— Ireland Green Guide: Europe (Country Guides) 3rd ed. (Illus.). 1997. pap. 20.00 (*2-06-153503-8*, 1535) Michelin.

— Ireland (Hotel & Restaurant Guide), 1996. 1996. 11.95 (*0-7859-9910-8*) Fr & Eur.

***Michelin Staff.** Ireland Hotels & Restaurants: 2000 Edition. 100th ed. (Red Guide Ireland Ser.). (Illus.). 1999. pap. text. write for info. (*2-06-971009-2*) Michelin.

Michelin Staff. Ireland Red Guide. 1994. pap. 12.95 (*0-7859-7175-0*, 2060071496) Fr & Eur.

***Michelin Staff.** Italia Hotels & Restaurants. 100th ed. (Red Guide Italia Ser.). 1999. pap. text 26.00 (*2-06-967045-7*) Michelin.

Michelin Staff. Italia Red Guide. 1994. 24.95 (*0-7859-7170-X*, 2060067499) Fr & Eur.

— Italy Green Guide. 1995. pap. 19.95 (*0-7859-9153-0*) Fr & Eur.

— Italy Green Guide: Europe (Country Guides) (Green Guide Ser.). (Illus.). 1998. per. 20.00 (*2-06-153405-8*, 1534) Michelin.

— Jura-Franche-Comte Green Guide French Edition. (FRE.). 1995. pap. 19.95 (*0-7859-7231-5*, 2060034019) Fr & Eur.

***Michelin Staff.** Languedoc-Gorges du Tarn Cevennes. (FRE.). 1999. pap. text 20.00 (*2-06-033704-6*) Michelin.

Michelin Staff. London Green Guide. 1997. pap. 19.95 (*0-7859-9127-1*) Fr & Eur.

— London Hotel & Restaurant Guide, 1996. 1996. 11.95 (*0-7859-9874-8*) Fr & Eur.

***Michelin Staff.** London Hotels & Restaurants: 2000 Edition. 100th ed. (Red Guide London Ser.). (Illus.). 1999. pap. text. write for info. (*2-06-966026-5*) Michelin.

Michelin Staff. Madrid. 1999. pap. text 9.95 (*2-06-660901-3*) Michelin.

— Malta. 1999. pap. text 9.95 (*2-06-652601-0*) Michelin.

— Maroc. (FRE.). 24.95 (*0-8288-6146-3*) Fr & Eur.

— Maroc Green Guide. 6th ed. (FRE.). 1995. pap. 19.95 (*0-7859-9141-7*) Fr & Eur.

— Maroc Green Guide: Afrique. 2nd ed. (FRE., Illus.). 1997. pap. 20.00 (*2-06-054402-5*, 544) Michelin.

— Mexico Green Guide. 2nd ed. (SPA.). 1996. pap. 19.95 (*0-7859-9172-7*) Fr & Eur.

— Mexico Guatemala Belize Green Guide. (SPA.). 1998. per. 20.00 (*2-06-457801-3*, 4578) Michelin.

— Mexico Guatemala Belize Green Guide: North America. 1998. per. 20.00 (*2-06-157801-2*, 1578) Michelin.

***Michelin Staff.** Michelin Atlas France. 8th ed. (Illus.). 1999. pap. text 9.00 (*2-06-091528-7*) Michelin.

Michelin Staff. Michelin France. (Illus.). 256p. 1995. 40.00 (*0-8212-2219-8*, Pub. by Bulfinch Pr) Little.

— Michelin France Road Atlas. 1995. pap., spiral bd. 39.95 (*0-7859-9073-9*) Fr & Eur.

— Michelin Green Atlantic Coast, France Green Guide. 1995. 18.95 (*0-7859-9102-6*) Fr & Eur.

— Michelin Green-Dordogne: France (Regional Guides) (Green Guides for All Ser.). 1998. 20.00 (*2-06-132501-7*) Michelin.

— Michelin Green Guide - Alpes du Nord. (FRE.). 14.95 (*0-8288-6171-4*) Fr & Eur.

— Michelin Green Guide - Alpes du Sud. (FRE.). 14.95 (*0-8288-6172-2*) Fr & Eur.

— Michelin Green Guide - Alsace et Lorraine (Vosges) (FRE.). 14.95 (*0-8288-6173-0*) Fr & Eur.

— Michelin Green Guide - Austria. 14.95 (*0-8288-6117-X*) Fr & Eur.

— Michelin Green Guide - Auvergne. (FRE.). 14.95 (*0-8288-6174-9*) Fr & Eur.

— Michelin Green Guide - Belgium - Luxemburg. (FRE.). 14.95 (*0-8288-6142-0*) Fr & Eur.

— Michelin Green Guide - Berry-Limousin. (FRE.). 14.95 (*0-8288-6176-5*) Fr & Eur.

— Michelin Green Guide - Bourgogne. (FRE.). 14.95 (*0-8288-6175-7*) Fr & Eur.

— Michelin Green Guide - Bretagne. (FRE.). 14.95 (*0-8288-6177-3*) Fr & Eur.

— Michelin Green Guide - Brittany. 14.95 (*0-8288-6133-1*) Fr & Eur.

— Michelin Green Guide - Burgundy. 14.95 (*0-8288-6134-X*) Fr & Eur.

— Michelin Green Guide - Canada. 14.95 (*0-8288-6103-X*); 14.95 (*0-8288-6143-9*) Fr & Eur.

— Michelin Green Guide - Champagne-Ardennes. (FRE.). 14.95 (*0-8288-6178-1*) Fr & Eur.

— Michelin Green Guide - Chateaux de la Loire. (FRE.). 14.95 (*0-8288-6179-X*) Fr & Eur.

— Michelin Green Guide - Chateaux of the Loire. 14.95 (*0-8288-6135-8*) Fr & Eur.

— Michelin Green Guide - Corse. (FRE.). 14.95 (*0-8288-6180-3*) Fr & Eur.

— Michelin Green Guide - Cote d'Azur. (FRE.). 14.95 (*0-8288-6181-1*) Fr & Eur.

— Michelin Green Guide - Dordogne. 14.95 (*0-8288-6136-6*) Fr & Eur.

— Michelin Green Guide - England - West Country. 14.95 (*0-8288-6118-8*) Fr & Eur.

— Michelin Green Guide - Espana. (SPA.). 14.95 (*0-8288-6194-3*) Fr & Eur.

— Michelin Green Guide - Flandres - Artois - Picardie. (FRE.). 14.95 (*0-8288-6182-X*) Fr & Eur.

— Michelin Green Guide - France. 14.95 (*0-8288-6119-6*); 14.95 (*0-8288-6144-7*) Fr & Eur.

— Michelin Green Guide - French Riviera. 14.95 (*0-8288-6137-4*) Fr & Eur.

— Michelin Green Guide - Germany. 14.95 (*0-8288-6120-X*) Fr & Eur.

— Michelin Green Guide - Gorges du Tarn. (FRE.). 14.95 (*0-8288-6183-8*) Fr & Eur.

— Michelin Green Guide - Holland. (FRE.). 14.95 (*0-8288-6145-5*) Fr & Eur.

— Michelin Green Guide - Ile de France. 14.95 (*0-8288-6138-2*); 14.95 (*0-8288-6184-6*) Fr & Eur.

— Michelin Green Guide - Jura - Franche Comte. (FRE.). 14.95 (*0-8288-6185-4*) Fr & Eur.

— Michelin Green Guide - London. 14.95 (*0-8288-6130-7*) Fr & Eur.

— Michelin Green Guide - Mexico. 14.95 (*0-8288-6114-5*); 14.95 (*0-8288-6195-1*) Fr & Eur.

— Michelin Green Guide - New England. 14.95 (*0-8288-6101-3*); 14.95 (*0-8288-6147-1*) Fr & Eur.

— Michelin Green Guide - New York. (FRE.). 14.95 (*0-8288-6149-8*) Fr & Eur.

— Michelin Green Guide - New York City. 14.95 (*0-8288-6113-7*) Fr & Eur.

— Michelin Green Guide - Normandie Cotentin. (FRE.). 14.95 (*0-8288-6186-2*) Fr & Eur.

— Michelin Green Guide - Normandie Vallee Seine. (FRE.). 14.95 (*0-8288-6187-0*) Fr & Eur.

— Michelin Green Guide - Normandy Cotentin. 14.95 (*0-8288-6139-0*) Fr & Eur.

— Michelin Green Guide - Normandy Seine Valley. 14.95 (*0-8288-6140-4*) Fr & Eur.

— Michelin Green Guide - Paris. (FRE.). 14.95 (*0-8288-6170-6*) Fr & Eur.

— Michelin Green Guide - Perigord-Ouercy. (FRE.). 14.95 (*0-8288-6188-9*) Fr & Eur.

— Michelin Green Guide - Poitou-Vendee-Charente. (FRE.). 14.95 (*0-8288-6189-7*) Fr & Eur.

— Michelin Green Guide - Portugal. (SPA.). 14.95 (*0-8288-6196-X*) Fr & Eur.

— Michelin Green Guide - Provence. 14.95 (*0-8288-6141-2*); 14.95 (*0-8288-6190-0*) Fr & Eur.

— Michelin Green Guide - Pyrenees-Aquitaine. (FRE.). 14.95 (*0-8288-6191-9*) Fr & Eur.

— Michelin Green Guide - Pyrenees-Roussillon. (FRE.). 14.95 (*0-8288-6192-7*) Fr & Eur.

— Michelin Green Guide - Quebec Province. 14.95 (*0-8288-6115-3*); 14.95 (*0-8288-6148-X*) Fr & Eur.

— Michelin Green Guide - Scotland. 14.95 (*0-8288-6127-7*) Fr & Eur.

— Michelin Green Guide - Vallee du Rhone. (FRE.). 14.95 (*0-8288-6193-5*) Fr & Eur.

— Michelin Green Guide - Washington D. C. 14.95 (*0-8288-6116-1*) Fr & Eur.

— Michelin Green Guide Belgium. 1994. pap. 19.95 (*0-7859-9106-9*) Fr & Eur.

— Michelin Green Guide Brittany. 1995. pap. 18.95 (*0-7859-9074-7*) Fr & Eur.

— Michelin Green Guide Canada. 7th ed. 1999. pap. text 20.00 (*2-06-151707-2*) Michelin.

— Michelin Green Guide Chateaux of the Loire. 1994. pap. 18.95 (*0-7859-9107-7*) Fr & Eur.

— Michelin Green Guide Dordogne. 1994. pap. 18.95 (*0-7859-9111-5*) Fr & Eur.

— Michelin Green Guide France. 1994. pap. 19.95 (*0-7859-9108-5*); pap. 19.95 (*0-7859-9109-3*) Fr & Eur.

— Michelin Green Guide Netherlands. 1994. pap. 19.95 (*0-7859-9110-7*) Fr & Eur.

— Michelin Green Guide Normandy. 1994. pap. 18.95 (*0-7859-9112-3*) Fr & Eur.

— Michelin Green Guide Portugal. 1995. 19.95 (*0-7859-9093-3*) Fr & Eur.

— Michelin Green Guide Pyrenees Roussillon. 1994. pap. 18.95 (*0-7859-9113-1*) Fr & Eur.

— Michelin Green Guide To London. 2nd ed. (Illus.). 1997. per. 18.00 (*2-06-159002-0*, 1590) Michelin.

— Michelin Green Guide to Washington D. C., Vol. 1. 1999. pap. 18.00 (*2-06-157704-0*) Michelin.

— Michelin Green Guide Washington D. C. 2nd ed. 1964. pap. 18.95 (*0-7859-9114-X*) Fr & Eur.

— Michelin Green Guides - Great Britain. 14.95 (*0-8288-6121-8*) Fr & Eur.

— Michelin Green Guides - Greece. 14.95 (*0-8288-6122-6*) Fr & Eur.

— Michelin Green Guides - Ireland. 14.95 (*0-8288-6123-4*) Fr & Eur.

— Michelin Green Guides - Italy. 14.95 (*0-685-66129-6*) Fr & Eur.

— Michelin Green Guides - Netherlands. 14.95 (*0-8288-6125-0*) Fr & Eur.

— Michelin Green Guides - Paris. 14.95 (*0-8288-6131-5*) Fr & Eur.

— Michelin Green Guides - Portugal. 14.95 (*0-8288-6126-9*) Fr & Eur.

— Michelin Green Guides - Rome. 14.95 (*0-8288-6132-3*) Fr & Eur.

— Michelin Green Guides - Spain. 14.95 (*0-8288-6128-5*) Fr & Eur.

— Michelin Green Guides - Switzerland. 14.95 (*0-8288-6129-3*) Fr & Eur.

— Michelin Green Paris. 2nd ed. (Michelin Green Guides (foreign Language) Ser.). 1998. pap. text 18.00 (*2-06-435902-8*) Michelin.

— Michelin Guide No. 301: Alpes du Nord. (Green Guides Ser.). (FRE.). 1988. pap. 16.95 (*0-7859-0217-1*, 2067003011) Fr & Eur.

— Michelin Guide No. 302: Alpes du Sud. (Green Guides Ser.). (FRE.). 1988. pap. 16.95 (*0-7859-0218-X*, 2060030218) Fr & Eur.

— Michelin Guide No. 304: Auvergne. (Green Guides Ser.). (FRE.). 1992. pap. 18.95 (*0-7859-0219-8*, 2067003046) Fr & Eur.

— Michelin Guide No. 305: Berry-Limousin. (Green Guides Ser.). (FRE.). 1990. pap. 16.95 (*0-7859-0220-1*, 2067003054) Fr & Eur.

— Michelin Guide No. 307: Bourgogne. (Green Guides Ser.). (FRE.). 1988. pap. 16.95 (*0-7859-0221-X*, 2067003070) Fr & Eur.

— Michelin Guide No. 308: Burgundy. (Green Guides Ser.). 1992. pap. 19.95 (*0-7859-0222-8*, 2067013084) Fr & Eur.

— Michelin Guide No. 309: Bretagne. (Green Guides Ser.). (FRE.). 1986. pap. 16.95 (*0-7859-0223-6*, 2060030943) Fr & Eur.

— Michelin Guide No. 314: Brittanny. (Green Guides Ser.). 1992. pap. 18.95 (*0-7859-0224-4*, 2067013149) Fr & Eur.

— Michelin Guide No. 316: Champagne-Ardennes. (Green Guides Ser.). (FRE.). 1992. pap. 19.95 (*0-7859-0225-2*, 2060031621) Fr & Eur.

— Michelin Guide No. 317: Chateaux de la Loire. (Green Guides Ser.). (FRE.). 1990. pap. 16.95 (*0-7859-0226-0*, 2067003178) Fr & Eur.

— Michelin Guide No. 319: Corse. (Green Guides Ser.). (FRE.). 1989. pap. 16.95 (*0-7859-0227-9*, 2060031915) Fr & Eur.

— Michelin Guide No. 320: Cote d'Azur. (Green Guides Ser.). (FRE.). 1987. pap. 16.95 (*0-7859-0228-7*, 2060032016) Fr & Eur.

— Michelin Guide No. 322: Chateaux of the Loire. (Green Guides Ser.). 1989. pap. 14.95 (*0-7859-0229-5*, 206701322X) Fr & Eur.

— Michelin Guide No. 323: Dordogne - Description & Travel. (Green Guides Ser.). 1992. pap. 18.95 (*0-7859-0230-9*, 2067013238) Fr & Eur.

— Michelin Guide No. 326: Ile de France - Descripton & Travel. (Green Guides Ser.). (FRE.). 1992. pap. 18.95 (*0-7859-0231-7*, 206003261X) Fr & Eur.

— Michelin Guide No. 335: French Riviera. (Green Guides Ser.). 1988. pap. 14.95 (*0-7859-0232-5*, 2067013351) Fr & Eur.

— Michelin Guide No. 337: Gorges du Tarn. (Green Guides Ser.). (FRE.). 1989. pap. 16.95 (*0-7859-0233-3*, 2060033721) Fr & Eur.

— Michelin Guide No. 338: Flandres-Artois-Picardie. (Green Guides Ser.). (FRE.). 1988. pap. 16.95 (*0-7859-0234-1*, 2067003380) Fr & Eur.

— Michelin Guide No. 340: Jura-Franche Comte. (Green Guides Ser.). (FRE.). 1992. pap. 18.95 (*0-7859-0235-X*, 2060034019) Fr & Eur.

— Michelin Guide No. 341: Ile de France. (Green Guides Ser.). 1990. pap. 14.95 (*0-7859-0236-8*, 2060134110) Fr & Eur.

— Michelin Guide No. 346: Normandie Cotentin. (Green Guides Ser.). (FRE.). 1988. pap. 16.95 (*0-7859-0237-6*, 2060034612) Fr & Eur.

— Michelin Guide No. 347: Normandie Vallee de la Seine. (Green Guides Ser.). (FRE.). 1988. pap. 16.95 (*0-7859-0238-4*, 206003471X) Fr & Eur.

— Michelin Guide No. 349: Normandy Cotentin. (Green Guides Ser.). 1989. pap. 14.95 (*0-7859-0239-2*, 2060134919) Fr & Eur.

— Michelin Guide No. 350: Normandy Seine Valley. (Green Guides Ser.). 1989. pap. 14.95 (*0-7859-0240-6*, 206013501X) Fr & Eur.

— Michelin Guide No. 352: Paris. (Green Guides Ser.). (FRE.). 1989. pap. 16.95 (*0-7859-0241-4*, 2067003526) Fr & Eur.

— Michelin Guide No. 355: Paris. (Green Guides Ser.). 1990. pap. 14.95 (*0-7859-0242-2*, 2060135516) Fr & Eur.

— Michelin Guide No. 362: Provence. (Green Guides Ser.). (FRE.). 1988. pap. 16.95 (*0-7859-0243-0*, 2060036216) Fr & Eur.

An Asterisk (*) at the beginning of an entry indicates that the title is appearing for the first time.

— Michelin Guide No. 367: Pyrenees-Aquitaine. (Green Guides Ser.). (FRE.). 1989. pap. 16.95 (*0-7859-0244-9*, 2060036720) Fr & Eur.

— Michelin Guide No. 368: Pyrenees-Roussillon. (Green Guides Ser.). (FRE.). 1989. pap. 16.95 (*0-7859-0245-7*, 2067003682) Fr & Eur.

— Michelin Guide No. 370: Perigord-Quercy. (Green Guides Ser.). (FRE.). 1990. pap. 18.95 (*0-7859-0246-5*, 2067003704) Fr & Eur.

— Michelin Guide No. 371: Poitou-Vendee-Charente. (Green Guides Ser.). (FRE.). 1990. pap. 16.95 (*0-7859-0247-3*, 2067003712) Fr & Eur.

— Michelin Guide No. 372: Alsace et Lorraine, Vosges. (Green Guides Ser.). (FRE.). 1989. pap. 16.95 (*0-7859-0248-1*, 2060037247) Fr & Eur.

— Michelin Guide No. 373: Vallee du Rhone. (Green Guides Ser.). (FRE.). 1989. pap. 16.95 (*0-7859-0249-X*, 2067003739) Fr & Eur.

— Michelin Guide No. 375: Provence. (Green Guides Ser.). 1989. pap. 14.95 (*0-7859-0250-3*, 2067013750) Fr & Eur.

— Michelin Guide No. 390: France. (Green Guides Ser.). (FRE.). 1989. pap. 16.95 (*0-7859-0251-1*, 2060039010) Fr & Eur.

— Michelin Guide No. 481: Euro-Disney. (Green Guides Ser.). 1992. pap. 18.95 (*0-7859-0276-7*, 2067014811) Fr & Eur.

— Michelin Guide No. 491: France. (Green Guides Ser.). 1992. pap. 19.95 (*0-7859-0277-5*, 2067014919) Fr & Eur.

— Michelin Guide No. 503: Germany. (Green Guides Ser.). 1987. pap. 16.95 (*0-7859-0278-3*, 2060150337) Fr & Eur.

— Michelin Guide No. 507: Austria. (Green Guides Ser.). 1992. pap. 19.95 (*0-7859-0279-1*, 2067015079) Fr & Eur.

— Michelin Guide No. 510: Belgique-Luxembourg, French Edition. (Green Guides Ser.). (FRE.). 1992. pap. 19.95 (*0-7859-0280-5*, 2060051044) Fr & Eur.

— Michelin Guide No. 517: Canada. (Green Guides Ser.). 1990. pap. 16.95 (*0-7859-0282-1*, 2060151732) Fr & Eur.

— Michelin Guide No. 520: Greece. (Green Guides Ser.). 1992. pap. 19.95 (*0-7859-0283-X*, 2067015206) Fr & Eur.

— Michelin Guide No. 521: Spain. (Green Guides Ser.). 1987. pap. 16.95 (*0-7859-0284-8*, 2060152135) Fr & Eur.

— Michelin Guide No. 534: Italy. (Green Guides Ser.). 1989. pap. 16.95 (*0-7859-0286-4*, 2067015346) Fr & Eur.

— Michelin Guide No. 535: Ireland. (Green Guides Ser.). 1992. pap. 19.95 (*0-7859-0287-2*, 2067015354) Fr & Eur.

— Michelin Guide No. 541: Great Britain. (Green Guides Ser.). 1992. pap. 19.95 (*0-7859-0288-0*, 2067015419) Fr & Eur.

— Michelin Guide No. 543: London. (Green Guides Ser.). 1990. pap. 14.95 (*0-7859-0289-9*, 2060154359) Fr & Eur.

— Michelin Guide No. 545: Maroc. (Green Guides Ser.). (FRE.). 1988. pap. 16.95 (*0-7859-0290-2*, 2060054532) Fr & Eur.

— Michelin Guide No. 548: New York. (Green Guides Ser.). (FRE.). 1989. pap. 16.95 (*0-7859-0291-0*, 2067005480) Fr & Eur.

— Michelin Guide No. 551: New York City. (Green Guides Ser.). 1992. pap. 19.95 (*0-7859-0292-9*) Fr & Eur.

— Michelin Guide No. 553: Hollande. (Green Guides Ser.). (FRE.). 1992. pap. 19.95 (*0-7859-0293-7*, 2060055342) Fr & Eur.

— Michelin Guide No. 555: Netherlands. (Green Guides Ser.). 1990. pap. 19.95 (*0-7859-0294-5*, 2060155517) Fr & Eur.

— Michelin Guide No. 557: Portugal. (Green Guides Ser.). 1989. pap. 16.95 (*0-7859-0295-3*, 2060155738) Fr & Eur.

— Michelin Guide No. 559: Rome. (Green Guides Ser.). 1985. pap. 14.95 (*0-7859-0296-1*, 2067015591) Fr & Eur.

— Michelin Guide No. 562: England-The West Country. (Green Guides Ser.). 1990. pap. 14.95 (*0-7859-0297-X*, 206015622X) Fr & Eur.

— Michelin Guide No. 563: Switzerland. (Green Guides Ser.). 1988. pap. 16.95 (*0-7859-0298-8*, 206701563X) Fr & Eur.

— Michelin Guide No. 565: Portugal. (Green Guides Ser.). (SPA.). 1988. pap. 19.95 (*0-7859-0299-6*, 2067045652) Fr & Eur.

— Michelin Guide No. 568: Nouvelle Angleterre. (Green Guides Ser.). (FRE.). 1988. pap. 16.95 (*0-7859-0300-3*, 2060056829) Fr & Eur.

— Michelin Guide No. 569: New England. (Green Guides Ser.). 1988. pap. 14.95 (*0-7859-0301-1*, 2067015699) Fr & Eur.

— Michelin Guide No. 572: Province de Quebec. (Green Guides Ser.). (FRE.). 1992. pap. 19.95 (*0-7859-0302-X*, 2980083348) Fr & Eur.

— Michelin Guide No. 573: Quebec Province. (Green Guides Ser.). 1992. pap. 19.95 (*0-7859-0303-8*, 2980083356) Fr & Eur.

— Michelin Guide No. 575: Scotland. (Green Guides Ser.). 1990. pap. 16.95 (*0-7859-0304-6*, 2060157528) Fr & Eur.

— Michelin Guide No. 577: Washington, D. C. (Green Guides Ser.). 1988. pap. 14.95 (*0-7859-0305-4*, 206701577X) Fr & Eur.

— Michelin Guide No. 579: Mexico. (Green Guides Ser.). 1990. pap. 19.95 (*0-7859-0306-2*, 2060157919) Fr & Eur.

— Michelin Guide No. 580: Mexico. (Green Guides Ser.). (SPA.). 1988. pap. 19.95 (*0-7859-0307-0*, 2060458013) Fr & Eur.

— Michelin Guide No. 603: Benelux. (Red Guides Ser.). 1993. 23.95 (*0-7859-0310-0*, 2060060397) Fr & Eur.

— Michelin Guide No. 613: Camping, France. (Green Guides Ser.). 1993. pap. 17.95 (*0-7859-0311-9*, 2060061393) Fr & Eur.

— Michelin Guide No. 623: Deutschland. (Red Guides). 1993. 25.95 (*0-7859-0312-7*, 206006239X) Fr & Eur.

— Michelin Guide No. 633: Espana-Portugal. (Red Guides). 1993. 23.95 (*0-7859-0313-5*, 2060063396) Fr & Eur.

— Michelin Guide No. 643: France. (Red Guides). 1993. 24.95 (*0-7859-0314-3*, 2060064392) Fr & Eur.

— Michelin Guide No. 653: Great Britain & Ireland. (Red Guides). 1993. 23.95 (*0-7859-0315-1*, 5060065399) Fr & Eur.

— Michelin Guide No. 663: Greater London. (Red Guides). 1993. pap. 12.95 (*0-7859-0316-X*, 2060066395) Fr & Eur.

— Michelin Guide No. 673: Italia. (Red Guides). 1993. 23.95 (*0-7859-0317-8*, 2060067391) Fr & Eur.

— Michelin Guide No. 683: Paris & Environs. (Red Guides). 1993. pap. 12.95 (*0-7859-0318-6*, 2060068398) Fr & Eur.

— Michelin Guide No. 703: Europe, Main Cities. (Red Guides). 1993. 24.95 (*0-685-63826-X*, 2030070392) Fr & Eur.

— Michelin Guide No. 713: Ireland. (Red Guides). 1993. pap. 12.95 (*0-7859-0320-8*, 2060071399) Fr & Eur.

— Michelin Map No. 11: Paris Atlas. (Main Roads Maps with Useful Addresses Ser.). 1988. pap. 14.95 (*0-7859-0130-2*, 206700011X) Fr & Eur.

— Michelin Map No. 14: Paris Atlas with Metro & Regional Connections. (Main Roads Maps Ser.). 1992. pap. 14.95 (*0-7859-0132-9*, 2067000144) Fr & Eur.

— Michelin Map No. 15: Paris by Arrondissements. (Main Roads Maps Ser.). 1992. pap. 19.95 (*0-7859-0133-7*, 2067000152) Fr & Eur.

— Michelin Map No. 30: Lyon. (Specialized Maps Ser.). 1992. pap. 9.95 (*0-7859-0134-5*, 2067000306) Fr & Eur.

— Michelin Map No. 31: Lyon with Index. (Specialized Maps Ser.). 1992. pap. 9.95 (*0-7859-0135-3*, 2067000314) Fr & Eur.

— Michelin Map No. 40: Barcelona. (Main Roads Maps Ser.). 1992. pap. 9.95 (*0-7859-0136-1*, 2067040405) Fr & Eur.

— Michelin Map No. 41: Barcelona with Index. (Main Roads Maps Ser.). 1992. pap. 9.95 (*0-7859-0137-X*, 2067040413) Fr & Eur.

— Michelin Map No. 51: Calais - Lille - Bruxelles. (Road Maps with Tourist Index Ser.). 1992. pap. 7.95 (*0-7859-0138-8*, 2067000519) Fr & Eur.

— Michelin Map No. 52: Le Havre - Dieppe - Amiens. (Road Maps with Tourist Index Ser.). 1992. pap. 7.95 (*0-7859-0139-6*, 2067000527) Fr & Eur.

— Michelin Map No. 53: Arras - Char. - Mex. - St. Quentin. (Road Maps with Tourist Index Ser.). 1992. pap. 7.95 (*0-7859-0140-X*, 2067000535) Fr & Eur.

— Michelin Map No. 54: Cherbourg - Caen - Rouen. (Road Maps with Tourist Index Ser.). 1992. pap. 7.95 (*0-7859-0141-8*, 2067000543) Fr & Eur.

— Michelin Map No. 55: Caen - Rouen - Paris. (Road Maps with Tourist Index Ser.). 1992. pap. 7.95 (*0-7859-0142-6*, 2067000551) Fr & Eur.

— Michelin Map No. 56: Paris - Rheims - Chalons-sur-Marne. (Road Maps with Tourist Index Ser.). 1992. pap. 7.95 (*0-7859-0143-4*, 206700056X) Fr & Eur.

— Michelin Map No. 57: Verdun - Metz - Wissembourg. (Road Maps with Tourist Index Ser.). 1992. pap. 7.95 (*0-7859-0144-2*, 2067000578) Fr & Eur.

— Michelin Map No. 58: St. Brieuc - St. Malo - Rennes. 1992. pap. 7.95 (*0 7859 0145 0*, 2067000586) Fr & Eur.

— Michelin Map No. 59: Brest - Quimper - St. Brieuc. (Road Maps with Tourist Index Ser.). 1992. pap. 7.95 (*0-7859-0146-9*, 2067000594) Fr & Eur.

— Michelin Map No. 60: Le Mans - Chartres - Paris. 1992. pap. 7.95 (*0-7859-0147-7*, 2067000608) Fr & Eur.

— Michelin Map No. 61: Paris - Troyes - Chaumont. (Road Maps with Tourist Index Ser.). 1992. pap. 7.95 (*0-7859-0148-5*, 2067000616) Fr & Eur.

— Michelin Map No. 62: Epinal - Nancy - Strasbourg. (Road Maps with Tourist Index Ser.). 1992. pap. 7.95 (*0-7859-0149-3*, 2067000624) Fr & Eur.

— Michelin Map No. 63: Vannes - Le Baule - Angers. (Road Maps with Tourist Index Ser.). 1992. pap. 7.95 (*0-7859-0150-7*, 2067000632) Fr & Eur.

— Michelin Map No. 64: Angers - Tours - Orleans. (Road Maps with Tourist Index Ser.). 1992. pap. 7.95 (*0-7859-0151-5*, 2067000640) Fr & Eur.

— Michelin Map No. 65: Montargis - Auxerre - Dijon. (Road Maps with Tourist Index Ser.). 1992. pap. 7.95 (*0-7859-0152-3*, 2067000659) Fr & Eur.

— Michelin Map No. 66: Dijon - Besancon - Mulhouse. (Road Maps with Tourist Index Ser.). 1992. pap. 7.95 (*0-7859-0153-1*, 2067000667) Fr & Eur.

— Michelin Map No. 67: Nantes - Les Sables-de l'O. - Poitiers. (Road Maps with Tourist Index Ser.). 1992. pap. 7.95 (*0-7859-0154-X*, 2067000675) Fr & Eur.

— Michelin Map No. 68: Niort - Poitiers - Chateauroux. (Road Maps with Tourist Index Ser.). 1992. pap. 7.95 (*0-7859-0155-8*, 2067000683) Fr & Eur.

— Michelin Map No. 69: Bourges - Nevers - Macon. (Road Maps with Tourist Index Ser.). 1992. pap. 7.95 (*0-7859-0156-6*, 2067000691) Fr & Eur.

— Michelin Map No. 72: Angouleme - Limoges - Gueret. 1992. pap. 7.95 (*0-7859-0157-4*, 2067000721) Fr & Eur.

— Michelin Map No. 73: Clermont-FD - Vichy - Lyon. (Road Maps with Tourist Index Ser.). 1992. pap. 7.95 (*0-7859-0158-2*, 206700073X) Fr & Eur.

— Michelin Map No. 74: Lyon - Chambery - Geneve. (Road Maps with Tourist Index Ser.). 1992. pap. 7.95 (*0-7859-0159-0*, 2067000748) Fr & Eur.

— Michelin Map No. 75: Bordeaux - Perigueux - Tulle. 1992. pap. 7.95 (*0-7859-0160-4*, 2067000756) Fr & Eur.

— Michelin Map No. 76: Aurillac - le Puy - St. Etienne. (Road Maps with Tourist Index Ser.). 1992. pap. 7.95 (*0-7859-0161-2*, 2067000764) Fr & Eur.

— Michelin Map No. 77: Valence - Grenoble - Gap. (Road Maps with Tourist Index Ser.). 1992. pap. 7.95 (*0-7859-0162-0*, 2067000772) Fr & Eur.

— Michelin Map No. 78: Bordeaux - Dax - Biarritz. (Road Maps with Tourist Index Ser.). 1992. pap. 7.95 (*0-7859-0163-9*, 2067000780) Fr & Eur.

— Michelin Map No. 79: Bordeaux - Agen - Montauban. (Road Maps with Tourist Index Ser.). 1992. pap. 7.95 (*0-7859-0164-7*, 2067000799) Fr & Eur.

— Michelin Map No. 80: Albi - Rodez - Nimes. (Road Maps with Tourist Index Ser.). 1992. pap. 7.95 (*0-7859-0165-5*, 2067000802) Fr & Eur.

— Michelin Map No. 81: Montelimar - Avignon - Digne. (Road Maps with Tourist Index Ser.). 1992. pap. 7.95 (*0-7859-0166-3*, 2067000810) Fr & Eur.

— Michelin Map No. 82: Mont-de-Marsan - Pau - Toulouse. (Road Maps with Tourist Index Ser.). 1992. pap. 7.95 (*0-7859-0167-1*, 2067000829) Fr & Eur.

— Michelin Map No. 83: Carcassone - Montpellier - Nimes. (Road Maps with Tourist Index Ser.). 1992. pap. 7.95 (*0-7859-0168-X*, 2067000837) Fr & Eur.

— Michelin Map No. 84: Marseille - Toulon - Nice. (Road Maps with Tourist Index Ser.). 1992. pap. 7.95 (*0-7859-0169-8*, 2067000845) Fr & Eur.

— Michelin Map No. 85: Biarritz - Lourdes - Luchon. (Road Maps with Tourist Index Ser.). 1992. pap. 7.95 (*0-7859-0170-1*, 2067000853) Fr & Eur.

— Michelin Map No. 86: Luchon - Andorre - Perpignan. (Road Maps with Tourist Index Ser.). 1992. pap. 7.95 (*0-7859-0171-X*, 2067000861) Fr & Eur.

— Michelin Map No. 87: Vosges - Alsace. (Road Maps with Tourist Index Ser.). 1992. pap. 7.95 (*0-7859-0172-8*, 206700087X) Fr & Eur.

— Michelin Map No. 88: Clermont - Ferrand - Lyon - St. Etienne. 1992. pap. 7.95 (*0-7859-0173-6*, 2067000888) Fr & Eur.

— Michelin Map No. 90: Corse. (Road Maps with Tourist Index Ser.). 1992. pap. 7.95 (*0-7859-0174-4*, 206700090X) Fr & Eur.

— Michelin Map No. 92: France. (Road Atlases Ser.). 1992. spiral bd. 39.95 (*0-7859-0175-2*, 600569179) Fr & Eur.

— Michelin Map No. 96: France. (Road Atlases Ser.). 1992. pap. 39.95 (*0-7859-0176-0*, 600571653) Fr & Eur.

— Michelin Map No. 98: France. (Road Atlases Ser.). 1992. 39.95 (*0-7859-0177-9*, 060057167X) Fr & Eur.

— Michelin Map No. 101: Outskirts of Paris. (Main Roads Maps: France Ser.). 1992. pap. 9.95 (*0-7859-0178-7*, 2067001019) Fr & Eur.

— Michelin Map No. 102: Battle of Normandy. (WW Two Battlefields Ser.). 1992. pap. 12.95 (*0-7859-0179-5*, 206700102X) Fr & Eur.

— Michelin Map No. 106: Environs of Paris. (Main Roads Maps: France Ser.). 1992. pap. 9.95 (*0-7859-0180-9*, 206700102X) Fr & Eur.

— Michelin Map No. 115: Cote d'Azur. (Main Roads Maps: France Ser.). 1992. pap. 9.95 (*0-7859-0181-7*, 2067001159) Fr & Eur.

— Michelin Map No. 121: Great Britain & Ireland. (Road Atlases Ser.). pap. 39.95 (*0-7859-0339-9*, 2067011219) Fr & Eur.

— Michelin Map No. 122: Great Britain & Ireland. (Road Atlases Ser.). spiral bd. 39.95 (*0-7859-0182-5*, 2067011227) Fr & Eur.

— Michelin Map No. 129: Europe. (Road Atlases Ser.). 1992. spiral bd. 39.95 (*0-7859-0183-3*, 2067001299) Fr & Eur.

— Michelin Map No. 133: Europe. (Road Atlases Ser.). 1992. 39.95 (*0-7859-0184-1*, 600571637) Fr & Eur.

— Michelin Map No. 134: Europe. large type ed. (Road Atlases Ser.). 1992. pap. 39.95 (*0-7859-0185-X*, 600572595) Fr & Eur.

— Michelin Map No. 135: Europe. (Road Atlases Ser.). 1992. pap. 39.95 (*0-7859-0186-8*, 600573214) Fr & Eur.

— Michelin Map No. 170: Beaune - Macon - Evian. (Road Maps with Tourist Index Ser.). 1992. pap. 7.95 (*0-7859-0187-6*, 2067001701) Fr & Eur.

— Michelin Map No. 171: La Rochelle - Royan - Bordeaux. 1992. pap. 7.95 (*0-7859-0188-4*, 206700171X) Fr & Eur.

— Michelin Map No. 189: Evian - Annecy - Briancon. (Road Maps with Tourist Index Ser.). 1992. pap. 7.95 (*0-7859-0189-2*, 2067001892) Fr & Eur.

— Michelin Map No. 212: Brugge - Rotterdam - Antwerpen. (Road Maps with Tourist Index Ser.). 1990. pap. 7.95 (*0-7859-0190-6*, 2067002120) Fr & Eur.

— Michelin Map No. 213: Brussel - Oostende - Liege. (Road Maps with Tourist Index Ser.). 1992. pap. 7.95 (*0-7859-0340-2*, 2067002139) Fr & Eur.

— Michelin Map No. 214: Mons - Dinant - Luxembourg. (Road Maps with Tourist Index Ser.). 1990. pap. 7.95 (*0-7859-0191-4*, 2067002147) Fr & Eur.

— Michelin Map No. 215: Luxembourg. (Road Maps with Tourist Index Ser.). 1992. pap. 7.95 (*0-7859-0192-2*, 2067002155) Fr & Eur.

— Michelin Map No. 216: Neuchatel - Basel - St. Gallen. (Road Maps with Tourist Index Ser.). 1992. pap. 7.95 (*0-7859-0193-0*, 2067002163) Fr & Eur.

— Michelin Map No. 217: Geneve - Bern - Andermatt. (Road Maps with Tourist Index Ser.). 1992. pap. 7.95 (*0-7859-0194-9*, 2067002171) Fr & Eur.

— Michelin Map No. 218: Andermatt - St. Moritz - Bolzano-Bozen. (Road Maps with Tourist Index Ser.). 1992. pap. 7.95 (*0-7859-0195-7*, 206700218X) Fr & Eur.

— Michelin Map No. 219: Aosta - Aoste - Zermatt - Milano. (Road Maps with Tourist Index Ser.). 1992. pap. 7.95 (*0-7859-0196-5*, 2067002199) Fr & Eur.

— Michelin Map No. 230: Bretagne. (Main Roads Maps: France Ser.). 1990. pap. 9.95 (*0-7859-0197-3*, 2067002309) Fr & Eur.

— Michelin Map No. 231: Normandie. (Main Roads Maps: France Ser.). 1990. pap. 9.95 (*0-7859-0198-1*, 2067002317) Fr & Eur.

— Michelin Map No. 232: Loire Region (Pays de Loire) (Main Roads Maps: France Ser.). 1990. pap. 9.95 (*0-7859-0199-X*, 2067002325) Fr & Eur.

— Michelin Map No. 233: Poitou-Charentes. (Main Roads Maps: France Ser.). 1990. pap. 9.95 (*0-7859-0200-7*, 2067002333) Fr & Eur.

— Michelin Map No. 234: Aquitaine. (Main Roads Maps: France Ser.). 1990. pap. 9.95 (*0-7859-0201-5*, 2067002341) Fr & Eur.

— Michelin Map No. 235: Midi Pyrenees. (Main Roads Maps: France Ser.). 1990. pap. 9.95 (*0-7859-0202-3*, 206700235X) Fr & Eur.

— Michelin Map No. 236: Nord de la France. (Main Roads Maps: France Ser.). 1990. pap. 9.95 (*0-7859-0203-1*, 2067002368) Fr & Eur.

— Michelin Map No. 237: Ile de France. (Main Roads Maps: France Ser.). 1988. pap. 9.95 (*0-7859-0204-X*, 2067002376) Fr & Eur.

— Michelin Map No. 238: Centre France. (Main Roads Maps: France Ser.). 1990. pap. 9.95 (*0-7859-0205-8*, 2067002374) Fr & Eur.

— Michelin Map No. 239: Auvergne-Limousin. (Main Roads Maps: France Ser.). 1990. pap. 9.95 (*0-7859-0206-6*, 2067002392) Fr & Eur.

— Michelin Map No. 240: Languedoc - Roussillon. 1990. pap. 9.95 (*0-7859-0207-4*, 2067002406) Fr & Eur.

— Michelin Map No. 241: Champagne-Ardennes. (Main Roads Maps: France Ser.). 1990. pap. 9.95 (*0-7859-0208-2*, 2067002414) Fr & Eur.

— Michelin Map No. 242: Alsace et Lorraine. (Main Roads Maps: France Ser.). 1990. pap. 9.95 (*0-7859-0209-0*, 2067002422) Fr & Eur.

— Michelin Map No. 243: Bourgogne-Franche Comte. (Main Roads Maps: France Ser.). 1990. pap. 9.95 (*0-7859-0210-4*, 2067002430) Fr & Eur.

— Michelin Map No. 244: Rhone - Alpes. 1990. pap. 9.95 (*0-7859-0211-2*, 2067002449) Fr & Eur.

— Michelin Map No. 245: Provence-Cote d'Azur. (Main Roads Maps: France Ser.). 1988. pap. 9.95 (*0-685-64752-8*, 2067002457) Fr & Eur.

— Michelin Map No. 246: Vallee du Rhone. (Main Roads Maps: France Ser.). 1990. pap. 9.95 (*0-7859-0213-9*, 2067002465) Fr & Eur.

— Michelin Map No. 263: Battle of Provence. (WW Two Battlefields Ser.). 1992. pap. 12.95 (*0-7859-0214-7*, 2067002635) Fr & Eur.

— Michelin Map No. 264: Battle of Alsace. (WW Two Battlefields Ser.). 1992. pap. 12.95 (*0-7859-0215-5*, 2067002643) Fr & Eur.

— Michelin Map No. 265: Victory Road. (WW Two Battlefields Ser.). 1992. pap. 12.95 (*0-7859-0216-3*, 2067002651) Fr & Eur.

— Michelin Map No. 401: Scotland. (Main Roads Maps, Great Britain & Ireland Ser.). 1988. pap. 9.95 (*0-7859-0252-X*, 2067004018) Fr & Eur.

— Michelin Map No. 402: Midlands-The North. (Main Roads Maps, Great Britain & Ireland Ser.). 1988. pap. 9.95 (*0-7859-0253-8*, 2067004026) Fr & Eur.

— Michelin Map No. 403: Wales-West Country-Midlands. (Main Roads Maps, Great Britain & Ireland Ser.). 1988. pap. 9.95 (*0-7859-0254-6*, 2067004034) Fr & Eur.

— Michelin Map No. 404: South East-Midlands-East Anglia. (Main Roads Maps, Great Britain & Ireland Ser.). 1992. pap. 9.95 (*0-7859-0255-4*, 2067004042) Fr & Eur.

— Michelin Map No. 405: Ireland. (Main Roads Maps, Great Britain & Ireland Ser.). 1992. pap. 9.95 (*0-7859-0256-2*, 2067004050) Fr & Eur.

— Michelin Map No. 407: Benelux. (Main Roads Maps Ser.). 1992. pap. 9.95 (*0-7859-0257-0*, 2067004077) Fr & Eur.

— Michelin Map No. 408: Netherlands. (Main Roads Maps Ser.). 1989. pap. 9.95 (*0-7859-0258-9*, 2067004085) Fr & Eur.

— Michelin Map No. 409: Belgium-Luxemburg. (Main Roads Maps Ser.). 1992. pap. 9.95 (*0-7859-0259-7*, 2067004093) Fr & Eur.

— Michelin Map No. 411: Northern Germany. (Main Roads Maps Ser.). 1988. pap. 9.95 (*0-7859-0260-0*, 2067004115) Fr & Eur.

— Michelin Map No. 412: Central Germany. (Main Roads Maps Ser.). 1990. pap. 9.95 (*0-7859-0261-9*, 2067004123) Fr & Eur.

— Michelin Map No. 413: Bavaria, Southern Germany. (Main Roads Maps Ser.). 1992. pap. 9.95 (*0-7859-0262-7*, 2067004131) Fr & Eur.

— Michelin Map No. 428: North West Italy. (Main Roads Maps Ser.). 1990. pap. 9.95 (*0-7859-0263-5*, 206700428X) Fr & Eur.

— Michelin Map No. 429: North East Italy. (Main Roads Maps Ser.). 1990. pap. 9.95 (*0-7859-0264-3*, 2067004298) Fr & Eur.

— Michelin Map No. 430: Central Italy. (Main Roads Maps Ser.). 1992. pap. 9.95 (*0-7859-0265-1*, 2067004301) Fr & Eur.

— Michelin Map No. 431: South Italy. (Main Roads Maps Ser.). 1992. pap. 9.95 (*0-7859-0266-X*, 206700431X) Fr & Eur.

M

— Michelin Map No. 432: Sicily. (Main Roads Maps Ser.). 1992. pap. 9.95 (*0-7859-0267-8*, 2067004328) Fr & Eur.
— Michelin Map No. 433: Sardinia. (Main Roads Maps Ser.). 1992. pap. 9.95 (*0-7859-0268-6*, 2067004336) Fr & Eur.
— Michelin Map No. 441: North West Spain. (Main Roads Maps Ser.). 1990. pap. 9.95 (*0-7859-0269-4*, 2067004417) Fr & Eur.
— Michelin Map No. 442: Northern Spain. (Main Roads Maps Ser.). 1990. pap. 9.95 (*0-7859-0270-8*, 2067004425) Fr & Eur.
— Michelin Map No. 443: North East Spain. (Main Roads Maps Ser.). 1990. pap. 9.95 (*0-7859-0271-6*, 2067004433) Fr & Eur.
— Michelin Map No. 444: Central Spain. (Main Roads Maps Ser.). 1990. pap. 9.95 (*0-7859-0272-4*, 2067004441) Fr & Eur.
— Michelin Map No. 445: Central-Eastern Spain. (Main Roads Maps Ser.). 1990. pap. 9.95 (*0-7859-0273-2*, 206700445X) Fr & Eur.
— Michelin Map No. 446: Southern Spain. (Main Roads Maps Ser.). 1990. pap. 9.95 (*0-7859-0274-0*, 2067004468) Fr & Eur.
— Michelin Map No. 450: Canary Islands. (Main Roads Maps Ser.). 1990. pap. 9.95 (*0-7859-0275-9*, 2067004501) Fr & Eur.
— Michelin Map No. 585: Valley of the Kings. (France Historical Ser.). 1992. pap. 9.95 (*0-7859-0308-9*, 2067005855) Fr & Eur.
— Michelin Map No. 588: Treasure Houses of the Sun King. (France Historical Ser.). 1992. pap. 9.95 (*0-7859-0309-7*, 206700588X) Fr & Eur.
— Michelin Map No. 918: Northern France. (Specialized Maps Ser.). 1992. pap. 7.95 (*0-7859-0321-6*, 2067009184) Fr & Eur.
— Michelin Map No. 919: Southern France. (Specialized Maps Ser.). 1992. pap. 7.95 (*0-7859-0322-4*, 2067009192) Fr & Eur.
— Michelin Map No. 953: Africa, North & West. (Main Roads Maps Ser.). 1988. pap. 9.95 (*0-7859-0323-2*, 2067009532) Fr & Eur.
— Michelin Map No. 954: Africa, NE Including Egypt & Arabia. (Main Roads Maps Ser.). 1988. pap. 9.95 (*0-7859-0324-0*, 2067009540) Fr & Eur.
— Michelin Map No. 955: Africa, Central & South Madagascar. (Main Roads Maps Ser.). 1988. pap. 9.95 (*0-7859-0325-9*, 2067009559) Fr & Eur.
— Michelin Map No. 969: Morocco. (Main Roads Maps Ser.). 1992. pap. 9.95 (*0-7859-0326-7*, 2067009699) Fr & Eur.
— Michelin Map No. 970: Europe. (Main Roads Maps Ser.). 1990. pap. 9.95 (*0-7859-0327-5*, 2067009702) Fr & Eur.
— Michelin Map No. 972: Algeria-Tunisia. (Main Roads Maps Ser.). 1990. pap. 9.95 (*0-7859-0328-3*, 2067009729) Fr & Eur.
— Michelin Map No. 975: Ivory Coast. (Main Roads Maps Ser.). 1990. pap. 9.95 (*0-7859-0329-1*, 2067009753) Fr & Eur.
— Michelin Map No. 980: Greece. (Main Roads Maps Ser.). 1992. pap. 9.95 (*0-7859-0330-5*, 206700980X) Fr & Eur.
— Michelin Map No. 984: Germany. (Main Roads Maps Ser.). 1988. pap. 9.95 (*0-7859-0331-3*, 2067009842) Fr & Eur.
— Michelin Map No. 985: Scandinavia & Finland. (Main Roads Maps Ser.). 1988. pap. 9.95 (*0-7859-0332-1*, 2067009850) Fr & Eur.
— Michelin Map No. 986: Great Britain & Ireland. (Main Roads Maps Ser.). 1992. pap. 9.95 (*0-7859-0333-X*, 2067009869) Fr & Eur.
— Michelin Map No. 987: Germany - Austria - Benelux. (Main Roads Maps Ser.). 1992. pap. 9.95 (*0-7859-0334-8*, 2067009877) Fr & Eur.
— Michelin Map No. 988: Italy. (Main Roads Maps Ser.). 1992. pap. 9.95 (*0-7859-0335-6*, 2067009885) Fr & Eur.
— Michelin Map No. 989: France. (Main Roads Maps Ser.). 1992. pap. 9.95 (*0-7859-0336-4*, 2067009893) Fr & Eur.
— Michelin Map No. 990: Spain & Portugal. (Main Roads Maps Ser.). 1992. pap. 9.95 (*0-7859-0337-2*, 2067009907) Fr & Eur.
— Michelin Map No. 991: Yugoslavia. (Main Roads Maps Ser.). 1988. pap. 9.95 (*0-7859-0338-0*, 2067009915) Fr & Eur.
— Michelin Red Travel Guide - Camping - France. (ENG, FRE, GER & ITA.). 1992. 14.95 (*0-685-66128-8*) Fr & Eur.
— Michelin Red Travel Guide - Greater London. 1992. 8.95 (*0-8288-6110-2*) Fr & Eur.
— Michelin Road Atlas - Europe. pap. 19.95 (*0-8288-6200-1*) Fr & Eur.
— Michelin Road Atlas - Europe. large type ed. pap. 19.95 (*0-8288-6201-X*) Fr & Eur.
— Michelin Road Atlas - France. 29.95 (*0-8288-6199-4*) Fr & Eur.
— Michelin Road Atlas - France. large type ed. pap. 19.95 (*0-8288-6198-6*) Fr & Eur.
— Michelin Road Atlas - Great Britain - Ireland. 19.95 (*0-8288-6197-8*) Fr & Eur.
— Michelin Road Atlas - Italy. 1994. pap., spiral bd. 39.95 (*0-7859-9115-8*) Fr & Eur.
***Michelin Staff.** Michelin Tourist & Motoring Atlas: Europe. 3rd ed. (Illus.). 2000. pap. 20.00 (*2-06-113503-X*); pap. 20.00 (*2-06-113603-6*) Michelin.
— Michelin Tourist & Motoring Atlas: France. (Illus.). 1999. pap. 20.00 (*2-06-109203-9*) Michelin.
Michelin Staff. Michelin Tourist & Motoring Atlas Europe. 2nd ed. 1999. pap. text 20.00 (*2-06-113602-8*) Michelin.
***Michelin Staff.** Michelin Tourist & Motoring Atlas Europe. 3rd ed. (Illus.). 2000. pap. 20.00 (*2-06-112903-X*) Michelin.
— Michelin Tourist & Motoring Atlas Italy. 6th ed. (Illus.). 2000. pap. text. write for info. (*2-06-146506-4*) Michelin.
— Michelin Tourist & Motoring Atlas Spain & Portugal. 7th ed. (Illus.). 2000. pap. text. write for info. (*2-06-146007-0*) Michelin.
Michelin Staff. Michelin's France Hotel & Restaurant Guide, 1997. (ENG, FRE & GER.). 1997. pap. 26.95 (*0-7859-9390-8*) Fr & Eur.
— Michelin's Great Britain & Ireland Hotel & Restaurant Guide, 1997. (ENG, FRE & GER.). 1997. pap. 26.95 (*0-7859-9391-6*) Fr & Eur.
— Michelin's Guide to Scandinavia & Finland. 1997. pap. 19.95 (*0-7859-9399-1*) Fr & Eur.
— Michelin's Portugal Hotel & Restaurant Guide, 1997. (ENG, FRE & GER.). 1997. 14.95 (*0-7859-9394-0*) Fr & Eur.
— Michelin's Switzerland Hotel & Restaurant Guide, 1997. (ENG, FRE & GER.). 1997. pap. 26.95 (*0-7859-9395-9*) Fr & Eur.
— Morocco Map. 1997. 10.95 (*2-06-700959-1*, 959) Michelin.
— Motoring Atlas France. 10th ed. 192p. 1996. 39.95 (*0-7859-9747-4*) Fr & Eur.
***Michelin Staff.** Netherlands, No. 908. 2nd ed. 1999. 8.95 (*2-06-090803-5*) Michelin.
Michelin Staff. Netherlands Green Guide: English Edition. 1995. pap. 19.95 (*0-7859-7190-4*, 20600155517) Fr & Eur.
***Michelin Staff.** New England. 9th ed. (Green Guide to New England). (Illus.). 1999. 20.00 (*2-06-156909-9*) Michelin.
Michelin Staff. New England Green Guide. 6th ed. 1995. pap. 19.95 (*0-7859-9142-5*) Fr & Eur.
***Michelin Staff.** New York City Green Guide. 1999. pap. 18.00 (*2-06-155113-0*) Michelin.
Michelin Staff. New York City Green Guide. 11th ed. 1997. pap. 19.95 (*0-7859-9128-X*) Fr & Eur.
— New York City Green Guide French Edition. (FRE.). 1997. pap. 19.95 (*0-7859-7215-3*, 2067005480) Fr & Eur.
Michelin Staff. New York in Your Pocket Guide. (In Your Pocket Guides Ser.). 1996. per. 9.95 (*2-06-650401-7*, 6504) Michelin.
Michelin Staff. New York/New Jersey/Pennsylvania Green Guide: North America. 1998. per. 20.00 (*2-06-154901-2*, 1549) Michelin.
— Normandie Vallee de la Seine Green Guide: France (Guides Regionaux) 3rd ed. (FRE., Illus.). 1996. per. 20.00 (*2-06-034703-3*, 347) Michelin.
— Normandy Green Guide: English Edition. 1996. pap. 19.95 (*0-7859-7206-4*, 2061348017) Fr & Eur.
— Northern France & Paris Region Green Guide: France (Regional Guides) 3rd ed. (Green Guides Ser.). (Illus.). 1997. per. 20.00 (*2-06-134403-8*, 1344) Michelin.
— Nouvelle Angleterre Green Guide: French Edition. (FRE.). 1997. pap. 19.95 (*0-7859-7213-7*, 2060056829) Fr & Eur.
— Nueva York. 1999. pap. text 9.95 (*2-06-661101-8*) Michelin.
***Michelin Staff.** Outskirts of Paris. 1999. 8.95 (*2-06-010125-5*) Michelin.
Michelin Staff. Parid & Environs Red Guide. 1994. pap. 12.95 (*0-7859-7174-2*, 2060068495) Fr & Eur.
— Paris. 1999. pap. text 9.95 (*2-06-661201-4*) Michelin.
***Michelin Staff.** Paris & Environs Hotels & Restaurants: 2000 Edition. 100th ed. (Red Guide Paris Ser.). (Illus.). 2000. pap. text. write for info. (*2-06-968049-5*) Michelin.
Michelin Staff. Paris Atlas by Arrondissements. 6th ed. 1994. pap. 29.95 (*0-7859-9145-X*) Fr & Eur.
— Paris Atlas by Arrondissements. 8th ed. 1997. per. 15.00 (*2-06-700015-2*, 015) Michelin.
— Paris Atlas Par Arrondissements. 16th ed. 1999. pap. text 12.95 (*2-06-001601-0*) Jonathan Cape.
— Paris Atlas with Metro & Regional. 13th ed. 1994. pap. write for info. (*0-7859-9129-8*) Fr & Eur.
— Paris Green Guide. 2nd ed. 1996. pap. 19.95 (*0-7859-9147-6*) Fr & Eur.
— Paris Green Guide French Edition. (FRE.). 1996. pap. 19.95 (*0-7859-7216-1*, 2067003526) Fr & Eur.
— Paris (Hotel & Restaurant Guide), 1996. 1996. 11.95 (*0-7859-9905-1*) Fr & Eur.
Michelin Staff. Paris in Your Pocket Guide. (In Your Pocket Guides Ser.). 1996. per. 9.95 (*2-06-630201-5*, 6302) Michelin.
Michelin Staff. Paris Northeast Map with Index. 11th ed. (Orig.). 1996. pap. 12.95 (*2-06-700020-9*, 20) Michelin.
— Paris Northwest Map with Index. 11th ed. (Orig.). 1996. pap. 12.95 (*2-06-700018-7*, 18) Michelin.
***Michelin Staff.** Paris Plan Poche, 1. 1999. 2.95 (*2-06-000003-3*) Michelin.
Michelin Staff. Paris Southeast Map with Index. 9th ed. (Orig.). 1996. pap. 12.95 (*2-06-700024-1*, 24) Michelin.
— Paris Southwest Map with Index. 10th ed. (Orig.). 1996. pap. text 12.95 (*2-06-700022-5*, 22) Michelin.
— Paris Street Atlas with Index & Practical Information. 20th ed. 1997. per. 12.00 (*2-06-700011-X*, 011) Michelin.
— Perigord-Quercy Green Guide. (FRE.). 252p. 1989. pap. 17.95 (*0-7859-7234-X*, 2067003704) Fr & Eur.
— Perigord-Quercy Green Guide: France (Guides Regionaux) 4th ed. (Green Guides Ser.). (FRE., Illus.). 1997. per. 20.00 (*2-06-037004-3*, 370) Michelin.
— Plan Paris. 14th ed. 1995. pap. 14.95 (*0-7859-9130-1*) Fr & Eur.
— Poitou-Vendee-Charentes Green Guide. 3rd ed. (FRE.). 1995. pap. 19.95 (*0-7859-9155-7*) Fr & Eur.
— Portugal. 2nd ed. 1998. pap. text 20.00 (*2-06-456702-X*) Michelin.
***Michelin Staff.** Portugal, Vol. 940. 2nd ed. 1999. write for info. (*2-06-094003-6*) Michelin.
Michelin Staff. Portugal Green Guide. 5th ed. 1995. pap. 19.95 (*0-7859-7191-2*, 557) Fr & Eur.
— Portugal (Hotel & Restaurant Guide), 1996. 1996. 11.95 (*0-7859-9909-4*) Fr & Eur.
***Michelin Staff.** Portugal Hotels & Restaurants. 100th ed. 1999. pap. text 12.00 (*2-06-972006-3*) Michelin.
— Prague in Your Pocket Guide. (In Your Pocket Guides Ser.). 1996. per. 9.95 (*2-06-650501-3*, 6505) Michelin.
Michelin Staff. Provence Green Guide. (FRE.). 1996. pap. 19.95 (*0-7859-9168-9*) Fr & Eur.
— Pyrenees-Aquitaine Green Guide. 3rd ed. (FRE.). 1992. pap. 18.95 (*0-7859-9156-5*) Fr & Eur.
— Pyrenees-Aquitaine Green Guide: France (Guides Regionaux) (FRE., Illus.). 1997. per. 20.00 (*2-06-036705-0*, 367) Michelin.
— Pyrenees-Aquitaine Green Guide French Edition. (FRE.). pap. 17.95 (*0-7859-7237-4*, 2067003674) Fr & Eur.
— Pyrenees-Roussillon Green Guide. 3rd ed. (FRE.). 1992. pap. 18.95 (*0-7859-9157-3*) Fr & Eur.
— Pyrenees-Roussillon Green Guide French Edition. (FRE.). pap. 17.95 (*0-7859-7238-2*, 2067003682) Fr & Eur.
— Quebec Green Guide French Edition. (FRE.). 1996. pap. 19.95 (*0-7859-7214-5*, 2067005723) Fr & Eur.
— Quebec (Province) Green Guide English Edition. 1996. pap. 19.95 (*0-7859-7181-5*, 2067015737) Fr & Eur.
— Rhone-Alpes Map. 1997. per. 8.95 (*2-06-700244-9*, 244) Michelin.
— Roma. 1999. pap. text 9.95 (*2-06-661401-7*) Michelin.
***Michelin Staff.** Roma. (Michelin Green Guides (foreign Language) Ser.). 1999. pap. 18.00 (*2-06-453901-8*) Michelin.
— Rome. (Illus.). 1999. pap. text 36.00 (*4-408-01315-3*) Michelin.
Michelin Staff. Rome Green Guide. 2nd ed. 1995. pap. 19.95 (*0-7859-9158-1*) Fr & Eur.
Michelin Staff. Rome in Your Pocket Guide. (In Your Pocket Guides Ser.). 1996. per. 9.95 (*2-06-650601-X*, 6506) Michelin.
Michelin Staff. San Francisco. 1999. pap. text 9.95 (*2-06-658001-5*) Michelin.
— San Francisco. 1999. pap. text 9.95 (*2-06-653001-8*) Michelin.
— San Francisco. 2nd ed. 1999. pap. text 18.00 (*2-06-159502-2*) Michelin.
Michelin Staff. Scandinavia/Finland Green Guide: Europe (Country Guides) (Illus.). 1996. per. 20.00 (*2-06-156701-0*, 1567) Michelin.
Michelin Staff. Scotland Green Guide. 2nd ed. 1996. pap. 19.95 (*0-7859-9132-8*) Fr & Eur.
— Sicily Green Guide: Europe (City & Regional Guides) 1998. per. 20.00 (*2-06-157601-X*, 1576) Michelin.
Michelin Staff. South of France in Your Pocket Guide: Riviera. (In Your Pocket Guides Ser.). 1996. per. 9.95 (*2-06-630301-1*, 6303) Michelin.
— Southern Spain in Your Pocket Guide. (In Your Pocket Guides Ser.). 1996. per. 9.95 (*2-06-650701-6*, 6507) Michelin.
Michelin Staff. Spain & Portugal Atlas. 1993. spiral bd. 39.95 (*0-7859-9148-4*) Fr & Eur.
— Spain Green Guide. 1993. pap. 19.95 (*0-7859-9149-2*) Fr & Eur.
— Spain (Hotel & Restaurant Guide), 1996. 1996. 24.95 (*0-7859-9904-3*) Fr & Eur.
— Spanish Michelin Espana Green Guide. 1995. pap. 19.95 (*0-7859-9103-4*) Fr & Eur.
— St. Petersburg. 1999. pap. text 9.95 (*2-06-657501-1*) Michelin.
— St. Petersburg. 1999. pap. text 9.95 (*2-06-652501-4*) Michelin.
***Michelin Staff.** Suisse-Schweiz-Svizzera Hotels & Restaurants. 100th ed. 1999. pap. text 25.00 (*2-06-969007-5*) Michelin.
— Suiza/Switzerland. 1999. pap. 20.00 (*2-06-456001-7*) Michelin.
Michelin Staff. Switzerland Green Guide. 1995. pap. 19.95 (*0-7859-9169-7*) Fr & Eur.
— Switzerland Green Guide: Europe (Country Guides) 3rd ed. (Green Guides Ser.). (Illus.). 1997. per. 20.00 (*2-06-156303-1*, 1563) Michelin.
— Switzerland (Hotel & Restaurant Guide) 1996. 1996. 24.95 (*0-7859-9902-7*) Fr & Eur.
— Thailand Green Guide: Asia. 1997. per. 20.00 (*2-06-159601-0*, 1596) Michelin.
— Tuscany Green Guide: Europe (City & Regional Guides) 1999. pap. 20.00 (*2-06-159702-5*) Michelin.
— Tuscany in Your Pocket Guide. (In Your Pocket Guides Ser.). 1996. per. 9.95 (*2-06-650801-2*, 6508) Michelin.
— Valle del Loira. 1999. pap. text 9.95 (*2-06-661501-3*) Michelin.
— Valle du Rhone Green Guide French Edition. (FRE.). pap. 17.95 (*0-7859-7239-0*, 2067003739) Fr & Eur.
— Vallee des Rois (Valley of the Kings) Map.Tr. of Valley of the Kings. (FRE & ENG.). 1997. per. 8.95 (*2-06-700266-X*, 266) Michelin.
— Vallee du Rhone Green Guide. 2nd ed. (FRE.). 1996. pap. 19.95 (*0-7859-9170-0*) Fr & Eur.
— Vallee du Rhone Green Guide: France (Guides Regionaux) (FRE., Illus.). 1996. per. 20.00 (*2-06-037303-4*, 373) Michelin.
— Venecia. 1999. pap. text 9.95 (*2-06-661601-X*) Michelin.
Michelin Staff. Venice Green Guide: Europe (City & Regional Guides) (Illus.). 1996. per. 18.00 (*2-06-158701-1*, 1587) Michelin.
— Venice in Your Pocket Guide. (In Your Pocket Guides Ser.). 1996. per. 9.95 (*2-06-650901-9*, 6509) Michelin.
Michelin Staff. Venise Green Guide: Europe (Guides Villes et Regionaux) (FRE., Illus.). 1996. per. 18.00 (*2-06-058701-8*, 587) Michelin.
— Washington, D. C. Green Guide. 1997. pap. 19.95 (*0-7859-9171-9*) Fr & Eur.
Michelin Staff, ed. Alpes du Nord Green Guide: France (Guides Regionaux) 4th ed. (Green Guide Ser.). (FRE., Illus.). 1996. per. 20.00 (*2-06-030104-1*, 301) Michelin.
— Alpes du Sud Green Guide: France (Guides Regionaux) 4th ed. (Green Guide Ser.). (FRE.). 1997. per. 20.00 (*2-06-030204-8*, 302) Michelin.
— Alsace Vosges Champagne Green Guide: France (Regional Guides) 1998. per. 20.00 (*2-06-130301-3*, 1303) Michelin.
— Auvergne Green Guide: France (Guides Regionaux) 3rd ed. (FRE.). 1996. per. 20.00 (*2-06-030403-2*, 304) Michelin.
— Barcelona in Your Pocket Guide. (In Your Pocket Guides Ser.). 1998. per. 9.95 (*2-06-652001-2*, 6520) Michelin.
— Belgique Green Guide: Europe (Guides Villes et Regionaux) (FRE., Illus.). 1996. per. 20.00 (*2-06-051102-X*, 511) Michelin.
— Brittany Green Guide: France (Regional Guides) 4th ed. 1997. per. 20.00 (*2-06-131404-X*, 1314) Michelin.
— Brussels Green Guide: Europe (City & Regional Guides) (Illus.). 1996. per. 18.00 (*2-06-151301-8*, 1513) Michelin.
Michelin Staff, ed. Bruxelles Green Guide: Europe (Guides Villes et Regionaux) (FRE., Illus.). 1996. per. 18.00 (*2-06-051301-4*, 513) Michelin.
Michelin Staff, ed. Chateaux de la Loire Green Guide: Europe. (JPN.). 1991. per. 36.00 (*4-408-01303-X*, 9317) Michelin.
Michelin Staff, ed. Danemark/Norvege/Suede/Finlande Green Guide: Europe (Guides Pays) (FRE., Illus.). 1996. per. 20.00 (*2-06-056701-7*, 567) Michelin.
— Disneyland Paris Green Guide. 2nd ed. (Orig.). 1995. per. 20.00 (*2-06-148102-7*, 1481) Michelin.
Michelin Staff, ed. Ecosse Green Guide: Europe (Guides Pays) (FRE.). 1996. per. 20.00 (*2-06-055001-7*, 550) Michelin.
Michelin Staff, ed. Espana Green Guide. 3rd ed. (SPA.). 1997. per. 20.00 (*2-06-452603-X*, 4526) Michelin.
— Europe Green Guide: Europe (Country Guides) 1996. per. 20.00 (*2-06-159101-9*, 1591) Michelin.
— Europe Green Guide: Europe (Guides Pays) (FRE.). 1996. per. 20.00 (*2-06-059101-5*, 591) Michelin.
Michelin Staff, ed. Flandres - Artois - Picardie Green Guide: France (Guides Regionaux) 4th ed. (FRE.). 1996. per. 20.00 (*2-06-033804-2*, 338) Michelin.
Michelin Staff, ed. Florence et Toscane Green Guide: Europe (Guides Villes et Regionaux) (FRE.). 1997. per. 20.00 (*2-06-059702-1*, 597) Michelin.
Michelin Staff, ed. France Green Guide. (JPN.). (Orig.). 1993. per. 36.00 (*4-408-01305-6*, 9499) Michelin.
— France Green Guide. 3rd ed. (Green Guides Ser.). (FRE., Illus.). (Orig.). 1996. per. 20.00 (*2-06-149103-0*, 1491) Michelin.
— French Riviera Green Guide: France (Regional Guides) 3rd ed. 1997. per. 20.00 (*2-06-133503-9*, 1335) Michelin.
Michelin Staff, ed. Germany Green Guide: Europe (Country Guides) 1996. per. 20.00 (*2-06-150402-7*, 1504) Michelin.
— Greece Green Guide: Europe (Country Guides) 3rd ed. 1997. per. 20.00 (*2-06-152003-0*, 1520) Michelin.
— Ile de France Green Guide. (JPN.). 1992. per. 36.00 (*4-408-01302-1*, 9326) Michelin.
— Italia Green Guide. 2nd ed. (SPA.). (Orig.). 1997. per. 20.00 (*2-06-453302-8*, 4533) Michelin.
Michelin Staff, ed. Italy (Hotel & Restaurant Guide) 1996 Edition. 1996. 24.95 (*0-7859-9906-X*) Fr & Eur.
— Italy Lake District in Your Pocket Guide. (In Your Pocket Guide Ser.). 1998. per. 9.95 (*2-06-652101-9*, 6521) Michelin.
— Lisbon in Your Pocket Guide. (In Your Pocket Guide Ser.). 1998. per. 9.95 (*2-06-652301-1*, 6523) Michelin.
— Londres Green Guide. (SPA.). 1998. per. 18.00 (*2-06-459001-3*, 4590) Michelin.
— Mexico Guatemala Belize Green Guide: Amerique du Nord. (FRE.). 1998. per. 20.00 (*2-06-057801-9*, 578) Michelin.
***Michelin Staff, ed.** Michelin Alsace, Lorraine, Champagne Green Guide. 1999. pap. 19.95 (*0-320-03746-0*) Fr & Eur.
— Michelin Amsterdam Green Guide. 1999. pap. 19.95 (*0-320-03760-6*) Fr & Eur.
— Michelin Atlantic Coast Green Guide. 1999. pap. 19.95 (*0-320-03765-7*) Fr & Eur.
— Michelin Austria Green Guide. 1999. pap. 19.95 (*0-320-03753-3*) Fr & Eur.
— Michelin Auvergne & Rhone Valley Green Guide. 1999. pap. 19.95 (*0-320-03764-9*) Fr & Eur.
— Michelin Belgium, Luxembourg Green Guide. 1999. pap. 19.95 (*0-320-03758-4*) Fr & Eur.
— Michelin Benelux Hotel & Restaurant Red Guide. 2000. 24.95 (*0-320-03725-8*) Fr & Eur.
— Michelin Brittany Green Guide. 1999. pap. 19.95 (*0-320-03762-2*) Fr & Eur.
— Michelin California Green Guide. 1999. pap. 19.95 (*0-320-03770-3*) Fr & Eur.
— Michelin Canada Green Guide. 1999. pap. 19.95 (*0-320-03771-1*) Fr & Eur.
— Michelin Chateaux de la Loire Green Guide. 1999. pap. 19.95 (*0-320-03737-1*) Fr & Eur.
— Michelin Dordogne, Berry, Limousin Green Guide. 1999. pap. 19.95 (*0-320-03747-9*) Fr & Eur.
— Michelin Espana Green Guide. (SPA.). 1999. pap. 19.95 (*0-320-03767-3*) Fr & Eur.
— Michelin France Green Guide. 1999. pap. 19.95 (*0-320-03728-2*) Fr & Eur.
— Michelin French Riviera Green Guide. 1999. pap. 19.95 (*0-320-03736-3*) Fr & Eur.

An Asterisk (*) at the beginning of an entry indicates that the title is appearing for the first time.

— Michelin Germany Green Guide. 1999. pap. 19.95 (*0-320-03740-1*) Fr & Eur.
— Michelin Germany Hotel & Restaurant Red Guide. 1248p. 2000. 25.95 (*0-320-03722-3*) Fr & Eur.
— Michelin Great Britain & Ireland Hotel & Restaurant Red Guide. 2000. 259.95 (*0-320-03743-6*) Fr & Eur.
— Michelin Great Britain Green Guide. 1999. pap. 19.95 (*0-320-03752-5*) Fr & Eur.
— Michelin Great Britain Hotel & Restaurant Red Guide. 2000. 25.95 (*0-320-03726-6*) Fr & Eur.
— Michelin Greece Green Guide. 1999. pap. 19.95 (*0-320-03756-8*) Fr & Eur.
— Michelin Ireland Green Guide. 1999. pap. 19.95 (*0-320-03749-5*) Fr & Eur.
— Michelin Italy Green Guide. 1999. pap. 19.95 (*0-320-03729-0*) Fr & Eur.
— Michelin London Green Guide. 1999. pap. 19.95 (*0-320-03739-8*) Fr & Eur.
— Michelin London Hotel & Restaurant Red Guide. 2000. 11.95 (*0-320-03724-X*) Fr & Eur.
— Michelin Netherlands Green Guide. 1999. pap. 19.95 (*0-320-03761-4*) Fr & Eur.
— Michelin New England Green Guide. 1999. pap. 19.95 (*0-320-03759-2*) Fr & Eur.
— Michelin New York City Green Guide. 1999. pap. 19.95 (*0-320-03727-4*); pap. 19.95 (*0-320-03734-7*) Fr & Eur.
— Michelin New York Green Guide. (FRE.). 1999. pap. 24.95 (*0-320-03772-X*) Fr & Eur.
— Michelin New York, New Jersey & Pennsylvania Green Guide. 1999. pap. 19.95 (*0-320-03769-X*) Fr & Eur.
— Michelin Paris Green Guide. 2000. pap. 19.95 (*0-320-03733-9*) Fr & Eur.
Michelin Staff, ed. Michelin Paris Hotel & Restaurant Guide, 1997. (ENG, FRE & GER.). 1997. pap. 14.95 (*0-7859-9398-3*) Fr & Eur.
***Michelin Staff, ed.** Michelin Portugal Green Guide. 1999. pap. 19.95 (*0-320-03755-X*) Fr & Eur.
— Michelin Provence Green Guide. 1999. pap. 19.95 (*0-320-03732-0*) Fr & Eur.
— Michelin Red France Hotels & Restaurants 2000. 100th ed. (Red Guide France Ser.). (Illus.). 2000. pap. 26.00 (*2-06-864091-0*) Michelin.
— Michelin Rome Green Guide. pap. 19.95 (*0-320-03744-4*) Fr & Eur.
— Michelin Scandinavia Green Guide. 1999. pap. 19.95 (*0-320-03751-7*) Fr & Eur.
— Michelin Scotland Green Guide. 1999. pap. 19.95 (*0-320-03748-7*) Fr & Eur.
— Michelin Sicily Green Guide. 1999. pap. 19.95 (*0-320-03745-2*) Fr & Eur.
— Michelin Spain Green Guide. 1999. pap. 19.95 (*0-320-03730-4*) Fr & Eur.
— Michelin Spain Hotel & Restaurant Red Guide. 2000. 25.95 (*0-320-03738-X*) Fr & Eur.
— Michelin Switzerland Green Guide. 1999. pap. 19.95 (*0-320-03731-2*) Fr & Eur.
— Michelin Switzerland Hotel & Restaurant Red Guide. 468p. 2000. 24.95 (*0-320-03723-1*) Fr & Eur.
— Michelin Tourist & Motoring Atlas Great Britain & Ireland. 11th ed. (Illus.). 1999. pap. 20.00 (*2-06-112211-6*) Michelin.
— Michelin Tuscany Green Guide. 1999. pap. 19.95 (*0-320-03741-X*) Fr & Eur.
— Michelin Venice Green Guide. 1999. pap. 19.95 (*0-320-03754-1*) Fr & Eur.
— Michelin Vienna Green Guide. 1999. pap. 19.95 (*0-320-03763-0*) Fr & Eur.
— Michelin Washington, D. C. Green Guide. 1999. pap. 19.95 (*0-320-03757-6*) Fr & Eur.
— Michelin West Country of England Green Guide. 1999. pap. 19.95 (*0-320-03766-5*) Fr & Eur.
Michelin Staff, ed. Michelin's Europe Hotel & Restaurant Guide, 1997. (ENG, FRE & GER.). 1997. pap. 26.95 (*0-7859-9389-4*) Fr & Eur.
— Michelin's Germany Hotel & Restaurant Guide, 1997. (ENG, FRE & GER.). 1997. pap. 26.95 (*0-7859-9387-8*) Fr & Eur.
— Michelin's Guide to Venice. 1997. pap. 19.95 (*0-7859-9401-7*) Fr & Eur.
— Michelin's Guide to Wales. 1997. pap. 19.95 (*0-7859-9400-9*) Fr & Eur.
— Michelin's Ireland Hotel & Restaurant Guide, 1997. (ENG, FRE & GER.). 1997. pap. 14.95 (*0-7859-9392-4*) Fr & Eur.
— Michelin's Italy Hotel & Restaurant Guide, 1997. (ENG, FRE & GER.). 1997. pap. 26.95 (*0-7859-9393-2*) Fr & Eur.
— Michelin's London Hotel & Restaurant Guide, 1997. (ENG, FRE & GER.). 1997. pap. 14.95 (*0-7859-9397-5*) Fr & Eur.
— Michelin's Spain-Portugal Hotel & Restaurant Guide, 1997. (ENG, FRE & GER.). 1997. pap. 26.95 (*0-7859-9388-6*) Fr & Eur.
— Normandy Green Guide: France (Regional Guides) 2nd ed. 1996. per. 20.00 (*2-06-134802-5*, 1348) Michelin.
— Paris Green Guide: Europe. (JPN.). 1991. per. 36.00 (*4-408-01301-3*, 9353) Michelin.
— Paris Green Guide: France (Guides Regionaux) 4th ed. (FRE.). 1997. per. 18.00 (*2-06-035204-5*, 352) Michelin.
Michelin Staff, ed. Paris Green Guide: France (Regional Guides) 3rd ed. (Illus.). 1996. per. 18.00 (*2-06-135503-X*, 1355) Michelin.
Michelin Staff, ed. Provence Green Guide: France (Regional Guides) 3rd ed. 1996. per. 20.00 (*2-06-137503-0*, 1375) Michelin.
***Michelin Staff, ed.** Rome. 3rd ed. (Green Guide Ser.). (Illus.). 2000. 18.00 (*2-06-153903-3*) Michelin.
— Rome Green Guide: Europe (City & Regional Guides) 2nd ed. 1997. per. 18.00 (*2-06-153902-5*, 1539) Michelin.
Michelin Staff, ed. San Francisco Green Guide: Amerique du Nord. (Guides Verts Ser.). (FRE.). 1998. per. 18.00 (*2-06-059501-0*, 595) Michelin.
— Sicily in Your Pocket Guide. (In Your Pocket Guide Ser.). 1998. per. 9.95 (*2-06-652201-5*, 6522) Michelin.
Michelin Staff, ed. Spain Green Guide. (JPN.). 1996. per. 36.00 (*4-408-01310-2*, 9526) Michelin.
Michelin Staff, ed. Switzerland Green Guide: Europe. (JPN.). 1991. per. 36.00 (*4-408-01306-4*, 9564) Michelin.
— Vienna in Your Pocket Guide. (In Your Pocket Guide Ser.). 1998. per. 9.95 (*2-06-651901-4*, 6519) Michelin.
Michelin Staff, ed. Wales Green Guide: Europe (City & Regional Guides) 1996. per. 20.00 (*2-06-151001-9*, 1510) Michelin.
***Michelin Staff.** Michelin Europe Red Guide, Hotels & Restaurants: 2000 Edition. 708p. 2000. pap. 25.00 (*0-320-03718-5*) Fr & Eur.
— Michelin France Red Guide, Hotels & Restaurants: 2000 Edition. 1488p. 2000. 26.00 (*0-320-03719-3*) Fr & Eur.
— Michelin Italy Red Guide, Hotels & Restaurants: 2000 Edition. 924p. 1999. 26.00 (*0-320-03721-5*) Fr & Eur.
— Michelin Northern France & Paris Region Green Guide. 1999. pap. 19.95 (*0-320-03773-8*) Fr & Eur.
— Michelin Paris Red Guide, Hotels & Restaurants: 2000 Edition. 384p. 2000. pap. 12.00 (*0-320-03720-7*) Fr & Eur.
***Michelin Travel Publication Staff.** Alemania. (Illus.). 2000. 20.00 (*2-06-450101-0*) Michelin.
— Barcelona Atlas. (Illus.). 2000. pap. 12.95 (*2-06-204000-8*) Michelin.
— Berlin Atlas. (Illus.). 2000. pap. 12.95 (*2-06-203300-1*) Michelin.
— Brussels. (In Your Pocket Guides Ser.). 2000. 9.95 (*2-06-651001-7*) Michelin.
— Bruxelles. (In Your Pocket Guides Ser.). 2000. 9.95 (*2-06-656001-4*) Michelin.
— California. 1999. pap. text 36.00 (*4-408-01318-8*) Michelin.
— France Atlas. 2nd ed. 2000. pap. text 8.95 (*2-06-009502-6*) Michelin.
— Madrid Atlas. (Illus.). 2000. pap. 12.95 (*2-06-204200-0*) Michelin.
— Michelin Green Guide Le Quebec. 3rd ed. 1999. pap. text 20.00 (*2-06-057203-7*) Michelin.
— Michelin Green Guide to Costa Azul. 2000. 20.00 (*2-06-432001-6*) Michelin.
— Michelin Green Guide to Estados Unidos Oeste. (Illus.). 2000. 20.00 (*2-06-455901-9*) Michelin.
— Michelin Green Guide to Nueva York. (Michelin Green Guide Ser.). (Illus.). 2000. 20.00 (*2-06-000058-0*) Michelin.
— Michelin Neos Guide Cuba. 2000. 22.00 (*2-06-855201-9*) Michelin.
— Michelin Neos Guide Guatemala, Belize. 2000. 22.00 (*2-06-855801-7*) Michelin.
— Michelin Neos Guide Indonesia. 2000. 26.00 (*2-06-855701-0*) Michelin.
— Michelin Neos Guide Rajasthan. 2000. 22.00 (*2-06-855901-3*) Michelin.
— Michelin Neos Guide Reunion, Mauritius, Seychelles. 2000. 24.00 (*2-06-855301-5*) Michelin.
— Michelin Neos Guide Sri Lanka, Maldives. 2000. 24.00 (*2-06-856001-1*) Michelin.
— Michelin Neos Guide Syria, Jordan. 2000. 24.00 (*2-06-855401-1*) Michelin.
— Michelin Neos Guide Tunisia. 2000. 22.00 (*2-06-855501-8*) Michelin.
— Michelin Neos Guide Turkey. 2000. 26.00 (*2-06-855601-4*) Michelin.
— Munich & the Royal Castles of Bavaria. (In Your Pocket Guides Ser.). 2000. 9.95 (*2-06-653201-0*) Michelin.
— Munich et les Chateaux Royaux de Baviere. (In Your Pocket Guides Ser.). 2000. 9.95 (*2-06-658201-8*) Michelin.
— Naples, Pompei, Capri, Ischia, Sorrento et la Cote Amalfitaine. (In Your Pocket Guides Ser.). 2000. 9.95 (*2-06-658301-4*) Michelin.
— Naples, Pompeii, Capri, Sorrento & the Amalfi Coast. (In Your Pocket Guides Ser.). 2000. 9.95 (*2-06-653301-7*) Michelin.
— Nouvelle Angleterre. 6th ed. (Michelin Green Guides Ser.). 1999. pap. text 20.00 (*2-06-056806-4*) Michelin.
— Rome Atlas. (Illus.). 2000. pap. 12.95 (*2-06-203800-3*) Michelin.
***Michelin Travel Publication Staff, ed.** Cuba. (Illus.). 2000. 22.00 (*2-06-850201-1*) Michelin.
— Guatemala/Belize. (Illus.). 2000. 22.00 (*2-06-850801-X*) Michelin.
— Indonesie. (Illus.). 2000. 26.00 (*2-06-850701-3*) Michelin.
— Michelin Green Bourgogne. 5th ed. (Illus.). 2000. pap. 18.00 (*2-06-030705-8*) Michelin.
— Michelin Green Corse. 4th ed. (Illus.). 2000. pap. 20.00 (*2-06-319048-8*) Michelin.
— Michelin Green Guide Languedoc Roussillon Tarn Gorges. 2nd ed. (Illus.). 1998. pap. 20.00 (*2-06-136602-3*) Michelin.
— Michelin Green Guide to Andalucia. (Illus.). 2000. 20.00 (*2-06-458301-7*) Michelin.
— Michelin Green Guide to Bruselas. (Illus.). 2000. 18.00 (*2-06-451301-9*) Michelin.
— Michelin Green Guide to Budapest et la Hongrie. (Illus.). 2000. 20.00 (*2-06-054201-4*) Michelin.
— Michelin Green Guide to Escocia. (Illus.). 2000. 20.00 (*2-06-457501-4*) Michelin.
— Michelin Green Guide to Estados Unidos Este. (Illus.). 2000. 20.00 (*2-06-455701-6*) Michelin.
— Michelin Green Guide to Florencia y la Toscana. (Illus.). 2000. 20.00 (*2-06-459701-8*) Michelin.
— Michelin Green Guide to Gran Bretana. (Illus.). 2000. 20.00 (*2-06-450501-6*) Michelin.
— Michelin Green Guide to Hungary/Budapest. (Illus.). 2000. 20.00 (*2-06-154201-8*) Michelin.
— Michelin Green Guide to Pacific Northwest. (Illus.). 2000. 20.00 (*2-06-158401-2*) Michelin.
— Michelin Green Guide to Praga. (Illus.). 2000. 18.00 (*2-06-456501-9*) Michelin.
— Michelin Green Guide to Prague. (Illus.). 2000. 18.00 (*2-06-056501-4*); 18.00 (*2-06-156501-8*) Michelin.
— Michelin Green Guide to U. S. A. (Illus.). 2000. 20.00 (*2-06-055701-1*) Michelin.
— Michelin Green Guide to U. S. A. East. (Illus.). 2000. 20.00 (*2-06-155701-5*) Michelin.
— Michelin Green Guide to U. S. A. Ouest. (Illus.). 2000. 20.00 (*2-06-055901-4*) Michelin.
— Michelin Green Guide to U. S. A. West. (Illus.). 2000. 20.00 (*2-06-155901-8*) Michelin.
— Michelin Green Guide to Venicia. (Illus.). 2000. 18.00 (*2-06-458701-2*) Michelin.
— Michelin Green Normandie Vallee de Seine Gg. 4th ed. (FRE., Illus.). 2000. pap. 20.00 (*2-06-037304-2*) Michelin.
— Michelin Green Paris. 5th ed. (FRE., Illus.). 2000. pap. 18.00 (*2-06-035205-3*) Michelin.
— Michelin Green Vallee du Rhone. 4th ed. (FRE., Illus.). 2000. pap. 20.00 (*2-06-034703-7*) Michelin.
— Michelin Neos Guide to Rajasthan. (Illus.). 2000. 22.00 (*2-06-850901-6*) Michelin.
— Michelin Red Guide Suisse/Schweiz/Svizzera 1998: Hotels & Restaurants. (Michelin Red Guide Ser.). (Illus.). 1999. 25.00 (*2-06-969999-4*) Michelin.
— Reunion/Maurice/Seychelles. (Illus.). 2000. 24.00 (*2-06-850301-8*) Michelin.
— Syrie/Jordanie. (Illus.). 2000. 24.00 (*2-06-850401-4*) Michelin.
— Tunisie. (Illus.). 2000. 22.00 (*2-06-850501-0*) Michelin.
— Turquie. (Illus.). 2000. 26.00 (*2-06-850601-7*) Michelin.
***Michelin Travel Publications Staff.** Dublin. (Michelin in Your Pocket Guides Ser.). (Illus.). 2000. 9.95 (*2-06-653101-4*); 9.95 (*2-06-658101-1*) Michelin.
— Michelin London. (Illus.). 2000. 12.95 (*2-06-002034-4*) Michelin.
Micheline, Jack. Imaginary Conversation with Jack Kerouac. 24p. (Orig.). 1989. pap. 5.00 (*0-929730-07-0*) Zeitgeist Pr.
— Last House in America. 1976. pap. 15.00 (*0-915016-06-0*) Second Coming.
— Outlaw of the Lowest Planet. (Orig.). pap. 5.00 (*0-929730-47-X*) Zeitgeist Pr.
— River of Red Wine. 60p. 1986. reprint ed. pap. 9.95 (*0-934953-04-X*) Water Row Pr.
— Skinny Dynamite & Other Short Stories. Winans, A. D., ed. LC 79-63969. 96p. 1980. pap. 20.00 (*0-915016-27-3*) Second Coming.
Micheline, Jack, et al. Bad, Mad & Dying. (Chapbook Ser.). (Illus.). 15p. 1997. pap. 10.00 (*0-9652505-5-5*) Synaesthesia.
Michelini, Ann N. Euripides & the Tragic Tradition. LC 86-40057. (Wisconsin Studies in Classics). 400p. 1987. reprint ed. pap. 124.00 (*0-7837-9788-5*, 206051700005) Bks Demand.
Michelinie, David. Invasion of the Spider-Slayers. (Illus.). 112p. 1995. pap. 15.95 (*0-7851-0100-4*) Marvel Entrprs.
— Spider-Man: Carnage. (Illus.). 80p. 1993. pap. 6.95 (*0-87135-971-5*) Marvel Entrprs.
— Spider-Man: Maximum Carnage. (Illus.). 336p. 1994. 24.95 (*0-7851-0038-5*) Marvel Entrprs.
— Spider-Man: The Return of Sinister Six. (Spider-Man Ser.). (Illus.). 144p. 1994. pap. 15.95 (*0-7851-0043-1*) Marvel Entrprs.
— Spider-Man: Venom Returns. (Illus.). 112p. 1993. pap. 12.95 (*0-87135-966-9*) Marvel Entrprs.
— Spider-Man vs. Doctor Doom. (Illus.). 64p. 1995. pap. 5.95 (*0-7851-0110-1*) Marvel Entrprs.
— Spiderman: Carnage in New York. (J). 1995. mass mkt. 6.50 (*0-425-16703-8*) Berkley Pub.
— Venom: Lethal Protector. (Illus.). 144p. 1995. pap. 15.95 (*0-7851-0107-1*) Marvel Entrprs.
Michelinie, David & McFarlane, Todd. Spider-Man vs. Venom. 112p. 1992. pap. 12.95 (*0-87135-616-3*) Marvel Entrprs.
Michelinie, David & Smith, Dean W. Spider-Man: Carnage in New York. (Orig.). 1995. mass mkt. 5.99 (*1-57297-019-7*) Blvd Books.
Michelis, Dennis. Ten Greek Popes. 1987. pap. 7.95 (*0-937032-54-9*) Light&Life Pub Co MN.
Michelis, Giorgio De, see De Michelis, Giorgio, ed.
Michelis, Michael. Tubular Disease. Date not set. write for info. (*0-938607-33-2*) Field & Wood Inc Medical.
Michell. Clinical Biology of Mammalian Sodium Metabolism. 370p. 1995. 173.00 (*0-08-040842-7*, Pergamon Pr) Elsevier.
— Growing up in Smoke. (C). pap. 11.95 (*0-7453-0446-X*, Pub. by Pluto GBR) Stylus Pub VA.
Michell, ed. Fundamental Mathematics for Economic Analysis: Instructor's Solution Manual. (C). 1999. pap. text, student ed. write for info. (*0-321-40069-0*) Addison-Wesley.
Michell, A. R. The Advancement of Veterinary Science Vol. 1: Veterinary Medicine Beyond 2000, Vol. 1. (Advancement of Veterinary Science Ser.). (Illus.). 288p. 1993. text 100.00 (*0-85198-759-1*) OUP.
— The Advancement of Veterinary Science Vol. 2: Veterinary Education - The Future, Vol. 2. (Advancement of Veterinary Science Ser.). (Illus.). 240p. 1993. text 100.00 (*0-85198-760-5*) OUP.
Michell, A. R., ed. The Advancement of Veterinary Science Vol. 3: History of the Healing Professions, Vol. 3. (Advancement of Veterinary Science Ser.). (Illus.). 160p. 1993. text 80.00 (*0-85198-761-3*) OUP.
— The Advancement of Veterinary Science, Vol. 4: Veterinary Science - Growth Points & Comparative Medicine, Vol. 4. (Illus.). 240p. 1993. text 100.00 (*0-85198-762-1*) OUP.
***Michell, A. R. & Ewbank, R.** Ethics, Welfare, Law & Market Forces: The Veterinary Interface. 235p. 1998. pap. 80.00 (*0-900767-99-5*, Pub. by Univs Fed Animal Welfare) St Mut.
Michell, David. A Boys War. 1988. pap. 6.95 (*9971-972-71-9*) OMF Bks.
Michell, Dorothy. More Australian Tales of Ghost & Fantasy. 207p. (C). 1990. 50.00 (*0-947333-00-2*, Pub. by Pascoe Pub) St Mut.
— Slave by Marriage. 179p. (C). 1990. 50.00 (*0-947333-15-0*, Pub. by Pascoe Pub) St Mut.
Michell, Dorothy, ed. Commie-The Girl Who Married the Butler: A Novella of the 19th Century Australia, 1953-93. 184p. (C). 1990. 36.00 (*0-947333-01-0*, Pub. by Pascoe Pub) St Mut.
Michell, E. B. Art & Practice of Hawking. (Illus.). 303p. 1983. pap. 25.00 (*0-87556-656-1*) Saifer.
Michell, Edward B. Siamese-English Dictionary. (ENG & THA.). 1977. reprint ed. 43.95 (*0-518-19004-8*) Ayer.
Michell, Frank. Annals of an Ancient Cornish Town: Redruth. (C). 1989. 65.00 (*0-907566-85-5*, Pub. by Dyllansow Truran) St Mut.
Michell, George. Architecture & Art of Southern India: Vijayanagara & the Successor States, 1350-1750. (New Cambridge History of India Ser.: No. I:6). (Illus.). 324p. (C). 1995. text 90.00 (*0-521-44110-2*) Cambridge U Pr.
— Blue Guide Southern India. 500p. 1998. pap. 25.95 (*0-393-31748-X*) Norton.
***Michell, George.** Hindu Art & Architecture. LC 00-100590. (World of Art Ser.). (Illus.). 224p. 2000. pap. 14.95 (*0-500-20337-7*, Pub. by Thames Hudson) Norton.
Michell, George. The Hindu Temple: An Introduction to Its Meaning & Forms. (Illus.). 194p. 1988. pap. 17.95 (*0-226-53230-5*) U Ch Pr.
— The Royal Palaces of India. LC 93-60425. (Illus.). 232p. 1999. reprint ed. pap. 39.95 (*0-500-27964-0*, Pub. by Thames Hudson) Norton.
— The Vijayanagara Courtly Style. (C). 1992. 44.00 (*81-85425-29-9*, Pub. by Manohar) S Asia.
Michell, George, ed. Architecture of the Islamic World: Its History & Social Meaning. LC 84-50341. (Illus.). 288p. 1995. pap. 29.95 (*0-500-27847-4*, Pub. by Thames Hudson) Norton.
***Michell, George, ed.** Eternal Kaveri. (Illus.). 124p. 1999. 60.00 (*81-85026-45-9*, Pub. by Marg Publns) Art Media Resources.
Michell, George, ed. Temple Towns of Tamil Nadu. (Illus.). (C). 1993. 68.00 (*81-85026-21-1*, Pub. by Marg Publns) Art Media Resources.
Michell, George & Zebrowski, Mark. Architecture & Art of the Deccan Sultanates. LC 98-24737. (New Cambridge History of India Ser.: Vol. I:7). (Illus.). 320p. (C). 1999. 85.00 (*0-521-56321-6*) Cambridge U Pr.
Michell, George, jt. auth. see Eaton, Richard M.
Michell, George, ed. see McCutchion, David.
Michell, Humphrey. Sparta: To Kryton tes Politeias ton Lakedaimonoin. LC 85-12537. 348p. 1985. reprint ed. lib. bdg. 59.75 (*0-313-24955-5*, MISP, Greenwood Pr) Greenwood.
Michell, J. An Introduction to the Logic of Psychological Measurement. 200p. (C). 1990. text 55.00 (*0-8058-0566-4*) L Erlbaum Assocs.
Michell, J. E., tr. see Scheidemann, Philip.
Michell, Joel. Measurement in Psychology: A Critical History of a Methodological Concept. LC 98-39566. (Ideas in Context Ser.: No. 53). 256p. (C). 1999. text 54.95 (*0-521-62120-8*) Cambridge U Pr.
Michell, John. The Earth Spirit: Its Ways, Shrines, & Mysteries. (Art & Imagination Ser.). (Illus.). 1989. pap. 15.95 (*0-500-81011-7*, Pub. by Thames Hudson) Norton.
— Eccentric Lives & Peculiar Notions. 248p. 1999. pap. 14.95 (*0-932813-67-4*) Adventures Unltd.
— Megalithomania: Artists, Antiquarians & Archaeologists at the Old Stone Monuments. LC 81-69643. (Illus.). 168p. 1982. 37.50 (*0-8014-1479-2*) Cornell U Pr.
— Secrets of the Stones: New Revelations of Astro-Archaeology & the Mystical Science of Antiquity. (Illus.). 128p. 1989. pap. 10.95 (*0-89281-337-7*, Destiny Bks) Inner Tradit.
***Michell, John.** The Temple at Jerusalem: A Revelation. (Illus.). 80p. 2000. pap. 12.95 (*1-57863-199-8*) Weiser.
Michell, John. Who Wrote Shakespeare? LC 95-62460. (Illus.). 272p. 1999. pap. 17.95 (*0-500-28113-0*, Pub. by Thames Hudson) Norton.
Michell, John & Rhone, Christine. Twelve-Tribe Nations & the Science of Enchanting the Landscape. LC 91-26915. (Illus.). 192p. (Orig.). 1991. pap. 17.95 (*0-933999-49-6*) Phanes Pr.
***Michell, Keith.** Keith Michell's Practically Macrobiotic Cookbook. LC 99-40745. 240p. 2000. pap. 25.00 (*0-89281-848-4*, Inner Trad Espanol) Inner Tradit.
Michell, Lewis. The Life & Times of the Right Honourable Cecil John Rhodes, 1853-1902, 2 vols. Wilkins, Mira, ed. LC 76-29768. (European Business Ser.). 1977. reprint ed. lib. bdg. 63.95 (*0-405-09782-4*) Ayer.
Michell, Monica. Teacher's Guide to the Great American West. (Illus.). 24p. (Orig.). 1985. pap. 4.95 (*0-935213-09-0*) J S Blanton Mus.
Michell, R. B., jt. auth. see Bradley, Robert F.
Michell, Richard, tr. see Prokofieff, Sergei O.
Michell, Robert. Golden Eagles. 313p. (C). 1990. pap. 48.00 (*0-646-09558-7*, Pub. by Boolarong Pubns) St Mut.
Michell, Robert H., et al, eds. Inositol Lipids in Cell Signalling. 534p. 1989. text 157.00 (*0-12-493860-4*) Acad Pr.

M

Michell, Ronald. The Carews of Beddington. 129p. 1989. pap. 29.00 (*0-317-47426-X*, Pub. by Sutton Libs & Arts) St Mut.

Michell, Ronald H. The Carews of Beddington. (C). 1985. pap. 29.00 (*0-907335-02-0*, Pub. by Sutton Libs & Arts) St Mut.

Michell, Tony. From a Developing to a Newly Industrialized Country: The Republic of Korea, 1961-82. (Employment, Adjustment & Industrialisation Ser.: No. 6). xii, 180p. (Orig.). 1988. pap. 24.00 (*92-2-106396-8*) Intl Labour Office.

Michelle, jt. auth. see Morrison.

Michelle, Amber, ed. see Rose, Andrea.

Michelle, Andree. Caught in a Trap. 294p. 1999. pap. text 8.95 (*1-885478-87-9*, Pub. by Genesis Press) BookWorld.

Michelle, Lonnie. How Kids Make Friends: Secrets for Making Lots of Friends, No Matter How Shy You Are. LC 95-60589. (Illus.). 64p. (Orig.). (J). (gr. 2-6). 1995. pap. 9.95 (*0-9638152-1-0*) Freedom Pubng.

Michelle, Lorin, jt. auth. see Biederman, Jerry.

Michelli, Dena. Successful Assertiveness. LC 96-32472. 1997. pap. 6.95 (*0-7641-0071-8*) Barron.

— Successful Networking. LC 97-11498. (Barron's Business Success Ser.). 96p. 1997. pap. 6.95 (*0-7641-0059-9*) Barron.

Michelli, Joseph A. Humor, Play, & Laughter: Stress-Proofing Life with Your Kids. LC 97-36458. 208p. 1998. pap. 11.95 (*0-944634-49-4*, Love & Logic Pr) Cline-Fay Inst.

Michello, Dennis, jt. auth. see Pose, Frederick.

Michello, Janet, jt. auth. see Tausig, Mark.

Michelman, Barbara, jt. auth. see Bregman, Rita.

Michelman, Fran & Weiner, Sue. Shopping Bag Secrets: The Most Irresistible Bags from the World's Most Unique Stores. (Illus.). 144p. 1999. 25.00 (*0-7893-0235-7*, Pub. by Universe) St Martin.

Michelman, Frank I. Brennan & Democracy. LC 98-43565. 176p. 1999. 24.95 (*0-691-00715-2*, Pub. by Princeton U Pr) Cal Prin Full Svc.

Michelman, Hans J. & Soldatos, Panayotis, eds. European Integration: Theories & Approaches. LC 94-984. 118p. (Orig.). (C). 1994. pap. text 24.50 (*0-8191-9455-7*) U Pr of Amer.

***Michelman, Irving.** The March to Capitalism in the Transition Countries. LC 98-71401. (Avebury Series in Philosophy). 130p. 1998. text 59.95 (*1-84014-101-8*) Ashgate Pub Co.

Michelman, Irving S. The Crisis Meters: Business Response to Social Crises. LC 73-4914. (Illus.). xviii, 418p. 1973. lib. bdg. 45.00 (*0-678-01320-9*) Kelley.

— The Moral Limitations of Capitalism. (Avebury Series in Philosophy). 184p. 1994. 72.95 (*1-85628-877-3*, Pub. by Avebry) Ashgate Pub Co.

Michelman, Jeffrey E. Lotus 1-2-3 Release 2.3 for Accounting: Principles. (Illus.). 400p. (C). 1992. disk 53.35 (*1-878748-81-5*); disk 53.35 (*1-878748-82-3*); disk 24.95 (*1-878748-83-1*); disk 24.95 (*1-878748-84-X*) Course Tech.

— Lotus 1-2-3 Release 2.2 for Accounting. (Illus.). 568p. (C). 1990. disk 56.75 (*1-878748-00-9*); disk 56.75 (*1-878748-01-7*); disk 31.00 (*1-878748-56-4*); disk 31.00 (*1-878748-57-2*) Course Tech.

Michelmann, Hans J. Organisational Effectiveness in a Multinational Bureaucracy. LC 78-60532. 271p. 1979. 55.00 (*0-275-90394-X*, C0394, Praeger Pubs) Greenwood.

Michelmann, Hans J. & Soldatos, Panayotis. Federalism & International Relations: The Role of Subnational Units. (Illus.). 334p. 1991. text 85.00 (*0-19-827491-2*) OUP.

Michelot, Christian, jt. auth. see Durier, Roland.

Michelotti, Leo. Intermediate Classical Dynamics with Applications to Beam Physics. LC 93-9418. 352p. 1995. 95.95 (*0-471-55384-0*) Wiley.

Michelove, Leon D., ed. see International SAMPE Technical Conference Staff.

Michelow, Bryan J., jt. auth. see Hartrampf, Carl R., Jr.

Michelozzi, Betty Neville. Coming Alive from Nine to Five: The Career Search Handbook. 6th ed. LC 98-53450. 1999. pap. text 29.95 (*0-7674-0216-2*) Mayfield Pub.

Michels. Basic Math Approach to Concepts of Chemistry. (Chemistry Ser.). 1979. mass mkt. 13.50 (*0-8185-0273-8*) Brooks-Cole.

Michels. Math Approach to Chemistry. (Chemistry Ser.). 1997. 36.25 (*0-534-49836-1*) Brooks-Cole.

— Molecular Genetic Analysis. 1969. text. write for info. (*0-471-89919-4*); pap. text. write for info. (*0-471-89921-6*) Wiley.

Michels, A., jt. ed. see Freymann, J. R.

Michels, Caroll. How to Survive & Prosper As an Artist: A Complete Guide to Career Management. 3rd rev. ed. (Illus.). 288p. 1995. pap. 11.95 (*0-8050-1953-7*, Owl) H Holt & Co.

— How to Survive & Prosper As an Artist: Selling Yourself Without Selling Your Soul. 4th ed. LC 97-16240. 304p. 1997. 14.95 (*0-8050-5504-5*) H Holt & Co.

Michels, Christine. Beyond Betrayal. 368p. 1998. mass mkt. 5.50 (*0-505-52264-0*, Love Spell) Dorchester Pub Co.

— In Destiny's Arms. 400p. 1996. mass mkt. 5.50 (*0-505-52095-8*, Love Spell) Dorchester Pub Co.

— A Season of Miracles: Try to Remember. (Intimate Moments Ser.: No. 900). 1998. per. 4.25 (*0-373-07900-1*, 1-07900-3) Silhouette.

***Michels, Christine.** Undercover with the Enemy. (Intimate Moments Ser.: Bk. 1013). 2000. per. 4.50 (*0-373-27083-6*, 1-27083-4) Silhouette.

Michels, Dia L., jt. auth. see Baumslag, Naomi.

Michels, Georg B. At War with the Church: Religious Dissent in Seventeenth-Century Russia. LC 98-48248. 1999. 60.00 (*0-8047-3358-9*) Stanford U Pr.

Michels, Gerald J., Jr., jt. auth. see Rush, Charles M.

Michels, Gloria. How to Make Yourself Famous: Secrets of a Professional Publicist. 2nd ed. 304p. 1994. pap. 12.95 (*0-8038-9359-0*) Hastings.

***Michels, Greg.** Governments of Alabama 1999. (Governments of Your State Ser.). (Illus.). 2000. text 150.00 (*1-55507-965-2*) Municipal Analysis.

Michels, Greg. Governments of Alabama, 1989. (Governments of Your State Ser.). (Illus.). 1989. text 150.00 (*1-55507-312-3*) Municipal Analysis.

***Michels, Greg.** Governments of Arkansas 1999. (Governments of Your State Ser.). (Illus.). 2000. text 150.00 (*1-55507-966-0*) Municipal Analysis.

Michels, Greg. Governments of Arkansas, 1989. (Governments of Your State Ser.). (Illus.). 1989. text 150.00 (*1-55507-313-1*) Municipal Analysis.

***Michels, Greg.** Governments of California 1999. (Governments of Your State Ser.). (Illus.). 2000. text 150.00 (*1-55507-967-9*) Municipal Analysis.

Michels, Greg. Governments of California, 1989. (Governments of Your State Ser.). (Illus.). 1989. text 150.00 (*1-55507-314-X*) Municipal Analysis.

***Michels, Greg.** Governments of Colorado 1999. (Governments of Your State Ser.). (Illus.). 2000. text 150.00 (*1-55507-968-7*) Municipal Analysis.

Michels, Greg. Governments of Colorado, 1989. (Governments of Your State Ser.). (Illus.). 1989. text 150.00 (*1-55507-315-8*) Municipal Analysis.

***Michels, Greg.** Governments of Connecticut 1999. (Governments of Your State Ser.). (Illus.). 2000. text 150.00 (*1-55507-882-6*) Municipal Analysis.

Michels, Greg. Governments of Connecticut, 1989. (Governments of Your State Ser.). (Illus.). 1989. text 150.00 (*1-55507-316-6*) Municipal Analysis.

***Michels, Greg.** Governments of Florida 1999. (Governments of Your State Ser.). (Illus.). 2000. text 150.00 (*1-55507-969-5*) Municipal Analysis.

Michels, Greg. Governments of Florida, 1989. (Governments of Your State Ser.). (Illus.). 1989. text 150.00 (*1-55507-317-4*) Municipal Analysis.

***Michels, Greg.** Governments of Georgia 1999. (Governments of Your State Ser.). (Illus.). 2000. text 150.00 (*1-55507-970-9*) Municipal Analysis.

Michels, Greg. Governments of Georgia, 1989. (Governments of Your State Ser.). (Illus.). 1989. text 150.00 (*1-55507-318-2*) Municipal Analysis.

***Michels, Greg.** Governments of Illinois 1999. (Governments of Your State Ser.). (Illus.). 2000. text 150.00 (*1-55507-971-7*) Municipal Analysis.

— Governments of Indiana 1999. (Governments of Your State Ser.). (Illus.). 2000. text 150.00 (*1-55507-972-5*) Municipal Analysis.

— Governments of Iowa 1999. (Governments of Your State Ser.). (Illus.). 2000. text 150.00 (*1-55507-973-3*) Municipal Analysis.

— Governments of Kansas 1999. (Governments of Your State Ser.). (Illus.). 2000. text 150.00 (*1-55507-974-1*) Municipal Analysis.

— Governments of Kentucky 1999. (Governments of Your State Ser.). (Illus.). 2000. text 150.00 (*1-55507-976-8*) Municipal Analysis.

— Governments of Louisiana 1999. (Governments of Your State Ser.). (Illus.). 2000. text 150.00 (*1-55507-977-6*) Municipal Analysis.

— Governments of Maine 1999. (Governments of Your State Ser.). (Illus.). 2000. text 150.00 (*1-55507-978-4*) Municipal Analysis.

— Governments of Massachusetts 1999. (Governments of Your State Ser.). (Illus.). 2000. text 150.00 (*1-55507-979-2*) Municipal Analysis.

— Governments of Michigan 1999. (Governments of Your State Ser.). (Illus.). 2000. text 150.00 (*1-55507-980-6*) Municipal Analysis.

— Governments of Minnesota 1999. (Governments of Your State Ser.). (Illus.). 2000. text 150.00 (*1-55507-981-4*) Municipal Analysis.

— Governments of Mississippi 1999. (Governments of Your State Ser.). (Illus.). 2000. text 150.00 (*1-55507-982-2*) Municipal Analysis.

— Governments of Missouri 1999. (Governments of Your State Ser.). (Illus.). 2000. text 150.00 (*1-55507-983-0*) Municipal Analysis.

— Governments of Nebraska 1999. (Governments of Your State Ser.). (Illus.). 2000. text 150.00 (*1-55507-984-9*) Municipal Analysis.

— Governments of New Jersey 1999. (Governments of Your State Ser.). (Illus.). 2000. text 150.00 (*1-55507-985-7*) Municipal Analysis.

— Governments of New York 1999. (Governments of Your State Ser.). (Illus.). 2000. text 150.00 (*1-55507-986-5*) Municipal Analysis.

— Governments of North Dakota 1999. (Governments of Your State Ser.). (Illus.). 2000. text 150.00 (*1-55507-885-0*) Municipal Analysis.

— Governments of Ohio 1999. (Governments of Your State Ser.). (Illus.). 2000. text 150.00 (*1-55507-987-3*) Municipal Analysis.

— Governments of Oklahoma 1999. (Governments of Your State Ser.). (Illus.). 2000. text 150.00 (*1-55507-988-1*) Municipal Analysis.

— Governments of Pennsylvania 1999. (Governments of Your State Ser.). (Illus.). 2000. text 150.00 (*1-55507-989-X*) Municipal Analysis.

— Governments of South Dakota 1999. (Governments of Your State Ser.). (Illus.). 2000. text 150.00 (*1-55507-990-3*) Municipal Analysis.

— Governments of Tennessee 1999. (Governments of Your State Ser.). (Illus.). 2000. text 150.00 (*1-55507-991-1*) Municipal Analysis.

— Governments of Texas 1999. (Governments of Your State Ser.). (Illus.). 2000. text 150.00 (*1-55507-992-X*) Municipal Analysis.

— Governments of the Carolinas 1999. (Governments of Your State Ser.). (Illus.). 2000. text 150.00 (*1-55507-996-2*) Municipal Analysis.

— Governments of the Northeast 1999. (Governments of Your State Ser.). (Illus.). 2000. text 150.00 (*1-55507-998-9*) Municipal Analysis.

— Governments of the Northwest 1999. (Governments of Your State Ser.). (Illus.). 2000. text 150.00 (*1-55507-997-0*) Municipal Analysis.

— Governments of the West 1999. (Governments of Your State Ser.). (Illus.). 2000. text 150.00 (*1-55507-886-9*) Municipal Analysis.

— Governments of U. S. Largest Cities, Counties & States 1999. (Governments of Your State Ser.). (Illus.). 2000. text 235.00 (*1-55507-999-7*) Municipal Analysis.

— Governments of Vermont 1999. (Governments of Your State Ser.). (Illus.). 2000. text 150.00 (*1-55507-883-4*) Municipal Analysis.

— Governments of Virginia 1999. (Governments of Your State Ser.). (Illus.). 2000. text 150.00 (*1-55507-993-8*) Municipal Analysis.

— Governments of Washington 1999. (Governments of Your State Ser.). (Illus.). 2000. text 150.00 (*1-55507-994-6*) Municipal Analysis.

— Governments of West Virginia 1999. (Governments of Your State Ser.). (Illus.). 2000. text 150.00 (*1-55507-995-4*) Municipal Analysis.

— Governments of Wisconsin 1999. (Governments of Your State Ser.). (Illus.). 2000. text 150.00 (*1-55507-884-2*) Municipal Analysis.

Michels, Greg, ed. Alabama Government's Performance Standards, 1990. (Governments Performance Standards Ser.). (Illus.). 150p. 1990. text 125.00 (*1-55507-474-X*) Municipal Analysis.

— Arkansas Governments Performance Standards, 1990. (Governments Performance Standards Ser.). (Illus.). 150p. 1990. text 125.00 (*1-55507-475-8*) Municipal Analysis.

— California Governments Performance Standards, 1990. (Governments Performance Standards Ser.). (Illus.). 150p. 1990. text 125.00 (*1-55507-476-6*) Municipal Analysis.

— The Carolinas Governments Performance Standards, 1990. (Governments Performance Standards Ser.). (Illus.). 150p. 1990. text 125.00 (*1-55507-508-8*) Municipal Analysis.

— Colorado Governments Performance Standards, 1990. (Governments Performance Standards Ser.). (Illus.). 150p. 1990. text 125.00 (*1-55507-477-4*) Municipal Analysis.

— Connecticut Governments Performance Standards, 1990. (Governments Performance Standards Ser.). (Illus.). 150p. 1990. text 125.00 (*1-55507-478-2*) Municipal Analysis.

— Florida Governments Performance Standards, 1990. (Governments Performance Standards Ser.). (Illus.). 150p. 1990. text 125.00 (*1-55507-479-0*) Municipal Analysis.

— Georgia Governments Performance Standards, 1990. (Governments Performance Standards Ser.). (Illus.). 150p. 1990. text 125.00 (*1-55507-480-4*) Municipal Analysis.

— Governments of Alabama, 1985. (Governments of Your State Ser.). 1984. 150.00 (*1-55507-041-8*); text 150.00 (*0-317-38176-8*) Municipal Analysis.

— Governments of Alabama, 1986. (Governments of Your State Ser.). 1985. text 150.00 (*1-55507-086-8*) Municipal Analysis.

— Governments of Alabama 1989: Expert Edition. (Governments of Your State: Expert Ser.). (Illus.). 400p. 1989. text 325.00 (*1-55507-350-6*) Municipal Analysis.

— Governments of Alabama, 1990. (Governments of Your State Ser.). (Illus.). 400p. 1990. text 150.00 (*1-55507-398-0*) Municipal Analysis.

— Governments of Alabama, 1990: Expert Edition. (Governments of Your State: Expert Ser.). (Illus.). 400p. 1990. text 325.00 (*1-55507-436-7*) Municipal Analysis.

— Governments of Alabama, 1991. (Governments of Your State Ser.). (Illus.). 400p. 1991. text 150.00 (*1-55507-522-3*) Municipal Analysis.

— Governments of Arkansas, 1985. (Governments of Your State Ser.). 1984. text 150.00 (*1-55507-042-6*) Municipal Analysis.

— Governments of Arkansas, 1986. (Governments of Your State Ser.). 1985. text 150.00 (*1-55507-087-6*) Municipal Analysis.

— Governments of Arkansas 1989: Expert Edition. (Governments of Your State: Expert Ser.). (Illus.). 400p. 1989. text 325.00 (*1-55507-351-4*) Municipal Analysis.

— Governments of Arkansas, 1990. (Governments of Your State Ser.). (Illus.). 400p. 1990. text 150.00 (*1-55507-399-9*) Municipal Analysis.

— Governments of Arkansas, 1990: Expert Edition. (Governments of Your State: Expert Ser.). (Illus.). 400p. 1990. text 325.00 (*1-55507-437-5*) Municipal Analysis.

— Governments of Arkansas, 1991. (Governments of Your State Ser.). (Illus.). 400p. 1991. text 150.00 (*1-55507-523-1*) Municipal Analysis.

— Governments of California, 1985. (Governments of Your State Ser.). 1984. text 150.00 (*1-55507-043-4*) Municipal Analysis.

— Governments of California, 1986. (Governments of Your State Ser.). 1985. text 150.00 (*1-55507-088-4*) Municipal Analysis.

— Governments of California, 1989: Expert Edition. (Governments of Your State: Expert Ser.). (Illus.). 400p. 1989. text 325.00 (*1-55507-352-2*) Municipal Analysis.

— Governments of California, 1990. (Governments of Your State Ser.). (Illus.). 400p. 1990. text 150.00 (*1-55507-400-6*) Municipal Analysis.

— Governments of California, 1990: Expert Edition. (Governments of Your State: Expert Ser.). (Illus.). 400p. 1990. text 325.00 (*1-55507-438-3*) Municipal Analysis.

— Governments of California, 1991. (Governments of Your State Ser.). (Illus.). 400p. 1991. text 150.00 (*1-55507-524-X*) Municipal Analysis.

— Governments of Colorado, 1985. (Governments of Your State Ser.). 1984. text 150.00 (*1-55507-044-2*) Municipal Analysis.

— Governments of Colorado, 1986. (Governments of Your State Ser.). 1985. text 150.00 (*1-55507-089-2*) Municipal Analysis.

— Governments of Colorado, 1989: Expert Edition. (Governments of Your State: Expert Ser.). (Illus.). 400p. 1989. text 325.00 (*1-55507-353-0*) Municipal Analysis.

— Governments of Colorado, 1990. (Governments of Your State Ser.). (Illus.). 400p. 1990. text 150.00 (*1-55507-401-4*) Municipal Analysis.

— Governments of Colorado, 1990: Expert Edition. (Governments of Your State: Expert Ser.). (Illus.). 400p. 1990. text 325.00 (*1-55507-473-1*) Municipal Analysis.

— Governments of Colorado, 1991. (Governments of Your State Ser.). (Illus.). 400p. 1991. text 150.00 (*1-55507-525-8*) Municipal Analysis.

— Governments of Connecticut, 1985. (Governments of Your State Ser.). 1984. text 150.00 (*1-55507-045-0*) Municipal Analysis.

— Governments of Connecticut, 1986. (Governments of Your State Ser.). 1985. text 150.00 (*1-55507-090-6*) Municipal Analysis.

— Governments of Connecticut, 1989: Expert Edition. (Governments of Your State: Expert Ser.). (Illus.). 400p. 1989. text 325.00 (*1-55507-354-9*) Municipal Analysis.

— Governments of Connecticut, 1990. (Governments of Your State Ser.). (Illus.). 400p. 1990. text 150.00 (*1-55507-402-2*) Municipal Analysis.

— Governments of Connecticut, 1990: Expert Edition. (Governments of Your State: Expert Ser.). (Illus.). 400p. 1990. text 325.00 (*1-55507-439-1*) Municipal Analysis.

— Governments of Connecticut, 1991. (Governments of Your State Ser.). (Illus.). 400p. 1991. text 150.00 (*1-55507-526-6*) Municipal Analysis.

— Governments of Florida, 1985. (Governments of Your State Ser.). 1984. text 150.00 (*1-55507-046-9*) Municipal Analysis.

— Governments of Florida, 1986. (Governments of Your State Ser.). 1985. text 150.00 (*1-55507-091-4*) Municipal Analysis.

— Governments of Florida, 1989: Expert Edition. (Governments of Your State: Expert Ser.). (Illus.). 400p. 1989. text 325.00 (*1-55507-355-7*) Municipal Analysis.

— Governments of Florida, 1990. (Governments of Your State Ser.). (Illus.). 400p. 1990. text 150.00 (*1-55507-403-0*) Municipal Analysis.

— Governments of Florida, 1990: Expert Edition. (Governments of Your State: Expert Ser.). (Illus.). 400p. 1990. text 325.00 (*1-55507-440-5*) Municipal Analysis.

— Governments of Florida, 1991. (Governments of Your State Ser.). (Illus.). 400p. 1991. text 150.00 (*1-55507-527-4*) Municipal Analysis.

— Governments of Georgia, 1985. (Governments of Your State Ser.). 1984. text 150.00 (*1-55507-047-7*) Municipal Analysis.

— Governments of Georgia, 1986. (Governments of Your State Ser.). 1985. text 150.00 (*1-55507-092-2*) Municipal Analysis.

— Governments of Georgia, 1989: Expert Edition. (Governments of Your State: Expert Ser.). (Illus.). 400p. 1989. text 325.00 (*1-55507-356-5*) Municipal Analysis.

— Governments of Georgia, 1990. (Governments of Your State Ser.). (Illus.). 400p. 1990. text 150.00 (*1-55507-404-9*) Municipal Analysis.

— Governments of Georgia, 1990: Expert Edition. (Governments of Your State: Expert Ser.). (Illus.). 400p. 1990. text 325.00 (*1-55507-441-3*) Municipal Analysis.

— Governments of Georgia, 1991. (Governments of Your State Ser.). (Illus.). 400p. 1991. text 150.00 (*1-55507-528-2*) Municipal Analysis.

— Governments of Illinois, 1985. (Governments of Your State Ser.). 1984. text 150.00 (*1-55507-048-5*) Municipal Analysis.

— Governments of Illinois, 1986. (Governments of Your State Ser.). 1985. text 150.00 (*1-55507-093-0*) Municipal Analysis.

— Governments of Illinois, 1989. (Governments of Your State Ser.). (Illus.). 1989. text 150.00 (*1-55507-319-0*) Municipal Analysis.

— Governments of Illinois, 1989: Expert Edition. (Governments of Your State: Expert Ser.). (Illus.). 400p. 1989. text 325.00 (*1-55507-357-3*) Municipal Analysis.

— Governments of Illinois, 1990. (Governments of Your State Ser.). (Illus.). 400p. 1990. text 150.00 (*1-55507-405-7*) Municipal Analysis.

— Governments of Illinois, 1990. (Governments of Your State: Expert Ser.). (Illus.). 1990. text 325.00 (*1-55507-442-1*) Municipal Analysis.

— Governments of Illinois, 1991. (Governments of Your State Ser.). (Illus.). 400p. 1991. text 150.00 (*1-55507-529-0*) Municipal Analysis.

— Governments of Indiana, 1985. (Governments of Your State Ser.). 1984. text 150.00 (*1-55507-049-3*) Municipal Analysis.

— Governments of Indiana, 1986. (Governments of Your State Ser.). 1985. text 150.00 (*1-55507-094-9*) Municipal Analysis.

— Governments of Indiana, 1989. (Governments of Your State Ser.). (Illus.). 1989. text 150.00 (*1-55507-320-4*) Municipal Analysis.

— Governments of Indiana, 1989: Expert Edition. (Governments of Your State: Expert Ser.). (Illus.). 400p. 1989. text 325.00 (*1-55507-358-1*) Municipal Analysis.

An Asterisk (*) at the beginning of an entry indicates that the title is appearing for the first time.

— Governments of Indiana, 1990. (Governments of Your State Ser.). (Illus.). 400p. 1990. text 150.00 (*1-55507-406-5*) Municipal Analysis.

— Governments of Indiana, 1990: Expert Edition. (Governments of Your State: Expert Ser.). (Illus.). 400p. 1990. text 325.00 (*1-55507-443-X*) Municipal Analysis.

— Governments of Indiana, 1991. (Governments of Your State Ser.). (Illus.). 400p. 1991. text 150.00 (*1-55507-530-4*) Municipal Analysis.

— Governments of Iowa, 1985. (Governments of Your State Ser.). 1984. text 150.00 (*1-55507-050-7*) Municipal Analysis.

— Governments of Iowa, 1986. (Governments of Your State Ser.). 1985. text 150.00 (*1-55507-095-7*) Municipal Analysis.

— Governments of Iowa, 1989. (Governments of Your State Ser.). (Illus.). 1989. text 150.00 (*1-55507-321-2*) Municipal Analysis.

— Governments of Iowa, 1989: Expert Edition. (Governments of Your State: Expert Ser.). (Illus.). 400p. 1989. text 325.00 (*1-55507-359-X*) Municipal Analysis.

— Governments of Iowa, 1990. (Governments of Your State Ser.). (Illus.). 400p. 1990. text 150.00 (*1-55507-407-3*) Municipal Analysis.

— Governments of Iowa, 1990: Expert Edition. (Governments of Your State: Expert Ser.). (Illus.). 400p. 1990. text 325.00 (*1-55507-444-8*) Municipal Analysis.

— Governments of Iowa, 1991. (Governments of Your State Ser.). (Illus.). 400p. 1991. text 150.00 (*1-55507-531-2*) Municipal Analysis.

— Governments of Kansas, 1985. (Governments of Your State Ser.). 1984. text 150.00 (*1-55507-051-5*) Municipal Analysis.

— Governments of Kansas, 1986. (Governments of Your State Ser.). 1985. text 150.00 (*1-55507-096-5*) Municipal Analysis.

— Governments of Kansas, 1989. (Governments of Your State Ser.). (Illus.). 1989. text 150.00 (*1-55507-322-0*) Municipal Analysis.

— Governments of Kansas, 1989: Expert Edition. (Governments of Your State: Expert Ser.). (Illus.). 400p. 1989. text 325.00 (*1-55507-360-3*) Municipal Analysis.

— Governments of Kansas, 1990. (Governments of Your State Ser.). (Illus.). 400p. 1990. text 150.00 (*1-55507-408-1*) Municipal Analysis.

— Governments of Kansas, 1990: Expert Edition. (Governments of Your State: Expert Ser.). (Illus.). 400p. 1990. text 325.00 (*1-55507-445-6*) Municipal Analysis.

— Governments of Kansas, 1991. (Governments of Your State Ser.). (Illus.). 400p. 1991. text 150.00 (*1-55507-532-0*) Municipal Analysis.

— Governments of Kentucky, 1985. (Governments of Your State Ser.). 1984. text 150.00 (*1-55507-052-3*) Municipal Analysis.

— Governments of Kentucky, 1986. (Governments of Your State Ser.). 1985. text 150.00 (*1-55507-097-3*) Municipal Analysis.

— Governments of Kentucky, 1989. (Governments of Your State Ser.). (Illus.). 1989. text 150.00 (*1-55507-323-9*) Municipal Analysis.

— Governments of Kentucky, 1989: Expert Edition. (Governments of Your State: Expert Ser.). (Illus.). 400p. 1989. text 325.00 (*1-55507-361-1*) Municipal Analysis.

— Governments of Kentucky, 1990. (Governments of Your State Ser.). (Illus.). 400p. 1990. text 150.00 (*1-55507-409-X*) Municipal Analysis.

— Governments of Kentucky, 1990: Expert Edition. (Governments of Your State: Expert Ser.). (Illus.). 400p. 1990. text 325.00 (*1-55507-446-4*) Municipal Analysis.

— Governments of Kentucky, 1991. (Governments of Your State Ser.). (Illus.). 400p. 1991. text 150.00 (*1-55507-533-9*) Municipal Analysis.

— Governments of Louisiana, 1985. (Governments of Your State Ser.). 1984. text 150.00 (*1-55507-053-1*) Municipal Analysis.

— Governments of Louisiana, 1986. (Governments of Your State Ser.). 1985. text 150.00 (*1-55507-098-1*) Municipal Analysis.

— Governments of Louisiana, 1989. (Governments of Your State Ser.). (Illus.). 1989. text 150.00 (*1-55507-324-7*) Municipal Analysis.

— Governments of Louisiana, 1989: Expert Edition. (Governments of Your State: Expert Ser.). (Illus.). 400p. 1989. text 325.00 (*1-55507-362-X*) Municipal Analysis.

— Governments of Louisiana, 1990. (Governments of Your State Ser.). (Illus.). 400p. 1990. text 150.00 (*1-55507-410-3*) Municipal Analysis.

— Governments of Louisiana, 1990: Expert Edition. (Governments of Your State: Expert Ser.). (Illus.). 400p. 1990. text 325.00 (*1-55507-447-2*) Municipal Analysis.

— Governments of Louisiana, 1991. (Governments of Your State Ser.). (Illus.). 400p. 1991. text 150.00 (*1-55507-534-7*) Municipal Analysis.

— Governments of Maine, 1985. (Governments of Your State Ser.). 1984. text 150.00 (*1-55507-054-X*) Municipal Analysis.

— Governments of Maine, 1986. (Governments of Your State Ser.). 1985. text 150.00 (*1-55507-099-X*) Municipal Analysis.

— Governments of Maine, 1989. (Governments of Your State Ser.). (Illus.). 1989. text 150.00 (*1-55507-325-5*) Municipal Analysis.

— Governments of Maine, 1989: Expert Edition. (Governments of Your State: Expert Ser.). (Illus.). 400p. 1989. text 325.00 (*1-55507-363-8*) Municipal Analysis.

— Governments of Maine, 1990. (Governments of Your State Ser.). (Illus.). 400p. 1990. text 150.00 (*1-55507-411-1*) Municipal Analysis.

— Governments of Maine, 1990: Expert Edition. (Governments of Your State: Expert Ser.). (Illus.). 400p. 1990. text 325.00 (*1-55507-448-0*) Municipal Analysis.

— Governments of Maine, 1991. (Governments of Your State Ser.). (Illus.). 400p. 1991. text 150.00 (*1-55507-535-5*) Municipal Analysis.

— Governments of Massachusetts, 1986. (Governments of Your State Ser.). 1985. text 150.00 (*1-55507-100-7*) Municipal Analysis.

— Governments of Massachusetts, 1989. (Governments of Your State Ser.). (Illus.). 1989. text 150.00 (*1-55507-326-3*) Municipal Analysis.

— Governments of Massachusetts, 1989: Expert Edition. (Governments of Your State: Expert Ser.). (Illus.). 400p. 1989. text 325.00 (*1-55507-364-6*) Municipal Analysis.

— Governments of Massachusetts, 1990. (Governments of Your State Ser.). (Illus.). 400p. 1990. text 150.00 (*1-55507-412-X*) Municipal Analysis.

— Governments of Massachusetts, 1990: Expert Edition. (Governments of Your State: Expert Ser.). (Illus.). 400p. 1990. text 325.00 (*1-55507-449-9*) Municipal Analysis.

— Governments of Massachusetts, 1991. (Governments of Your State Ser.). (Illus.). 400p. 1991. text 150.00 (*1-55507-536-3*) Municipal Analysis.

— Governments of Massachusetts,1985. (Governments of Your State Ser.). 1984. text 150.00 (*1-55507-055-8*) Municipal Analysis.

— Governments of Michigan, 1985. (Governments of Your State Ser.). 1984. text 150.00 (*1-55507-056-6*) Municipal Analysis.

— Governments of Michigan, 1986. (Governments of Your State Ser.). 1985. text 150.00 (*1-55507-101-5*) Municipal Analysis.

— Governments of Michigan, 1989. (Governments of Your State Ser.). (Illus.). 1989. text 150.00 (*1-55507-327-1*) Municipal Analysis.

— Governments of Michigan, 1989: Expert Edition. (Governments of Your State: Expert Ser.). (Illus.). 400p. 1989. text 325.00 (*1-55507-365-4*) Municipal Analysis.

— Governments of Michigan, 1990. (Governments of Your State Ser.). (Illus.). 400p. 1990. text 150.00 (*1-55507-413-8*) Municipal Analysis.

— Governments of Michigan, 1990: Expert Edition. (Governments of Your State: Expert Ser.). (Illus.). 400p. 1990. text 325.00 (*1-55507-450-2*) Municipal Analysis.

— Governments of Michigan, 1991. (Governments of Your State Ser.). (Illus.). 400p. 1991. text 150.00 (*1-55507-537-1*) Municipal Analysis.

— Governments of Minnesota, 1985. (Governments of Your State Ser.). 1984. text 150.00 (*1-55507-057-4*) Municipal Analysis.

— Governments of Minnesota, 1986. (Governments of Your State Ser.). 1985. text 150.00 (*1-55507-102-3*) Municipal Analysis.

— Governments of Minnesota, 1989. (Governments of Your State Ser.). (Illus.). 1989. text 150.00 (*1-55507-328-X*) Municipal Analysis.

— Governments of Minnesota, 1989: Expert Edition. (Governments of Your State: Expert Ser.). (Illus.). 400p. 1989. text 325.00 (*1-55507-366-2*) Municipal Analysis.

— Governments of Minnesota, 1990. (Governments of Your State Ser.). (Illus.). 400p. 1990. text 150.00 (*1-55507-414-6*) Municipal Analysis.

— Governments of Minnesota, 1990: Expert Edition. (Governments of Your State: Expert Ser.). (Illus.). 400p. 1990. text 325.00 (*1-55507-451-0*) Municipal Analysis.

— Governments of Minnesota, 1991. (Governments of Your State Ser.). (Illus.). 400p. 1991. text 150.00 (*1-55507-538-X*) Municipal Analysis.

— Governments of Missisippi, 1989. (Governments of Your State Ser.). (Illus.). 1989. text 150.00 (*1-55507-329-8*) Municipal Analysis.

— Governments of Mississippi, 1985. (Governments of Your State Ser.). 1984. text 150.00 (*1-55507-058-2*) Municipal Analysis.

— Governments of Mississippi, 1986. (Governments of Your State Ser.). 1984. text 150.00 (*1-55507-103-1*) Municipal Analysis.

— Governments of Mississippi, 1989: Expert Edition. (Governments of Your State: Expert Ser.). (Illus.). 400p. 1989. text 325.00 (*1-55507-367-0*) Municipal Analysis.

— Governments of Mississippi, 1990. (Governments of Your State Ser.). (Illus.). 400p. 1990. text 150.00 (*1-55507-415-4*) Municipal Analysis.

— Governments of Mississippi, 1990: Expert Edition. (Governments of Your State: Expert Ser.). (Illus.). 400p. 1990. text 325.00 (*1-55507-452-9*) Municipal Analysis.

— Governments of Mississippi, 1991. (Governments of Your State Ser.). (Illus.). 400p. 1991. text 150.00 (*1-55507-539-8*) Municipal Analysis.

— Governments of Missouri, 1986. (Governments of Your State Ser.). 1985. text 150.00 (*1-55507-104-X*) Municipal Analysis.

— Governments of Missouri, 1989. (Governments of Your State Ser.). (Illus.). 1989. text 150.00 (*1-55507-330-1*) Municipal Analysis.

— Governments of Missouri, 1989: Expert Edition. (Governments of Your State: Expert Ser.). (Illus.). 400p. 1989. text 325.00 (*1-55507-368-9*) Municipal Analysis.

— Governments of Missouri, 1990. (Governments of Your State Ser.). (Illus.). 400p. 1990. text 150.00 (*1-55507-416-2*) Municipal Analysis.

— Governments of Missouri, 1990: Expert Edition. (Governments of Your State: Expert Ser.). (Illus.). 400p. 1990. text 325.00 (*1-55507-453-7*) Municipal Analysis.

— Governments of Missouri, 1991. (Governments of Your State Ser.). (Illus.). 400p. 1991. text 150.00 (*1-55507-540-1*) Municipal Analysis.

— Governments of Nebraska, 1985. (Governments of Your State Ser.). 1984. text 150.00 (*1-55507-060-4*) Municipal Analysis.

— Governments of Nebraska, 1986. (Governments of Your State Ser.). 1985. text 150.00 (*1-55507-105-8*) Municipal Analysis.

— Governments of Nebraska, 1989. (Governments of Your State Ser.). (Illus.). 1989. text 150.00 (*1-55507-331-X*) Municipal Analysis.

— Governments of Nebraska, 1989: Expert Edition. (Governments of Your State: Expert Ser.). (Illus.). 400p. 1989. text 325.00 (*1-55507-369-7*) Municipal Analysis.

— Governments of Nebraska, 1990. (Governments of Your State Ser.). (Illus.). 400p. 1990. text 150.00 (*1-55507-417-0*) Municipal Analysis.

— Governments of Nebraska, 1990: Expert Edition. (Governments of Your State: Expert Ser.). (Illus.). 400p. 1990. text 325.00 (*1-55507-454-5*) Municipal Analysis.

— Governments of Nebraska, 1991. (Governments of Your State Ser.). (Illus.). 400p. 1991. text 150.00 (*1-55507-541-X*) Municipal Analysis.

— Governments of New Jersey, 1985. (Governments of Your State Ser.). 1984. text 150.00 (*1-55507-061-2*) Municipal Analysis.

— Governments of New Jersey, 1986. (Governments of Your State Ser.). 1985. text 150.00 (*1-55507-106-6*) Municipal Analysis.

— Governments of New Jersey, 1989. (Governments of Your State Ser.). (Illus.). 1989. text 150.00 (*1-55507-332-8*) Municipal Analysis.

— Governments of New Jersey, 1989: Expert Edition. (Governments of Your State: Expert Ser.). (Illus.). 400p. 1989. text 325.00 (*1-55507-370-0*) Municipal Analysis.

— Governments of New Jersey, 1990. (Governments of Your State Ser.). (Illus.). 400p. 1990. text 150.00 (*1-55507-418-9*) Municipal Analysis.

— Governments of New Jersey, 1990: Expert Edition. (Governments of Your State: Expert Ser.). (Illus.). 400p. 1990. text 325.00 (*1-55507-455-3*) Municipal Analysis.

— Governments of New Jersey, 1991. (Governments of Your State Ser.). (Illus.). 400p. 1991. text 150.00 (*1-55507-542-8*) Municipal Analysis.

— Governments of New York, 1985. (Governments of Your State Ser.). 1984. text 150.00 (*1-55507-062-0*) Municipal Analysis.

— Governments of New York, 1986. (Governments of Your State Ser.). 1985. text 150.00 (*1-55507-107-4*) Municipal Analysis.

— Governments of New York, 1989. (Governments of Your State Ser.). (Illus.). 1989. text 150.00 (*1-55507-333-6*) Municipal Analysis.

— Governments of New York, 1989: Expert Edition. (Governments of Your State: Expert Ser.). (Illus.). 400p. 1989. text 325.00 (*1-55507-371-9*) Municipal Analysis.

— Governments of New York, 1990. (Governments of Your State Ser.). (Illus.). 400p. 1990. text 150.00 (*1-55507-419-7*) Municipal Analysis.

— Governments of New York, 1990: Expert Edition. (Governments of Your State: Expert Ser.). (Illus.). 400p. 1990. text 325.00 (*1-55507-456-1*) Municipal Analysis.

— Governments of New York, 1991. (Governments of Your State Ser.). (Illus.). 400p. 1991. text 150.00 (*1-55507-543-6*) Municipal Analysis.

— Governments of North Dakota, 1985. (Governments of Your State Ser.). 1984. text 150.00 (*1-55507-063-9*) Municipal Analysis.

— Governments of North Dakota, 1986. (Governments of Your State Ser.). 1985. text 150.00 (*1-55507-108-2*) Municipal Analysis.

— Governments of North Dakota, 1989. (Governments of Your State Ser.). (Illus.). 1989. text 150.00 (*1-55507-334-4*) Municipal Analysis.

— Governments of North Dakota, 1989: Expert Edition. (Governments of Your State: Expert Ser.). (Illus.). 400p. 1989. text 325.00 (*1-55507-396-4*) Municipal Analysis.

— Governments of North Dakota, 1990. (Governments of Your State Ser.). (Illus.). 400p. 1990. text 150.00 (*1-55507-420-0*) Municipal Analysis.

— Governments of North Dakota, 1990: Expert Edition. (Governments of Your State: Expert Ser.). (Illus.). 400p. 1990. text 325.00 (*1-55507-457-X*) Municipal Analysis.

— Governments of North Dakota, 1991. (Governments of Your State Ser.). (Illus.). 400p. 1991. text 150.00 (*1-55507-544-4*) Municipal Analysis.

— Governments of Ohio, 1985. (Governments of Your State Ser.). 1984. text 150.00 (*1-55507-064-7*) Municipal Analysis.

— Governments of Ohio, 1986. (Governments of Your State Ser.). 1985. text 150.00 (*1-55507-109-0*) Municipal Analysis.

— Governments of Ohio, 1989. (Governments of Your State Ser.). (Illus.). 1989. text 150.00 (*1-55507-335-2*) Municipal Analysis.

— Governments of Ohio, 1989: Expert Edition. (Governments of Your State: Expert Ser.). (Illus.). 400p. 1989. text 325.00 (*1-55507-372-7*) Municipal Analysis.

— Governments of Ohio, 1990. (Governments of Your State Ser.). (Illus.). 400p. 1990. text 150.00 (*1-55507-421-9*) Municipal Analysis.

— Governments of Ohio, 1990: Expert Edition. (Governments of Your State: Expert Ser.). (Illus.). 400p. 1990. text 325.00 (*1-55507-458-8*) Municipal Analysis.

— Governments of Ohio, 1991. (Governments of Your State Ser.). (Illus.). 400p. 1991. text 150.00 (*1-55507-545-2*) Municipal Analysis.

— Governments of Oklahoma, 1985. (Governments of Your State Ser.). 1984. text 150.00 (*1-55507-065-5*) Municipal Analysis.

— Governments of Oklahoma, 1986. (Governments of Your State Ser.). 1985. text 150.00 (*1-55507-110-4*) Municipal Analysis.

— Governments of Oklahoma, 1989. (Governments of Your State Ser.). (Illus.). 1989. text 150.00 (*1-55507-336-0*) Municipal Analysis.

— Governments of Oklahoma, 1989: Expert Edition. (Governments of Your State: Expert Ser.). (Illus.). 400p. 1989. text 325.00 (*1-55507-373-5*) Municipal Analysis.

— Governments of Oklahoma, 1990. (Governments of Your State Ser.). (Illus.). 400p. 1990. text 150.00 (*1-55507-422-7*) Municipal Analysis.

— Governments of Oklahoma, 1990: Expert Edition. (Governments of Your State: Expert Ser.). (Illus.). 400p. 1990. text 325.00 (*1-55507-459-6*) Municipal Analysis.

— Governments of Oklahoma, 1991. (Governments of Your State Ser.). (Illus.). 400p. 1991. text 150.00 (*1-55507-546-0*) Municipal Analysis.

— Governments of Pennsylvania, 1985. (Governments of Your State Ser.). 1984. text 150.00 (*1-55507-066-3*) Municipal Analysis.

— Governments of Pennsylvania, 1986. (Governments of Your State Ser.). 1985. text 150.00 (*1-55507-111-2*) Municipal Analysis.

— Governments of Pennsylvania, 1989. (Governments of Your State Ser.). (Illus.). 1989. text 150.00 (*1-55507-337-9*) Municipal Analysis.

— Governments of Pennsylvania, 1989: Expert Edition. (Governments of Your State: Expert Ser.). (Illus.). 400p. 1989. text 325.00 (*1-55507-374-3*) Municipal Analysis.

— Governments of Pennsylvania, 1990. (Governments of Your State Ser.). (Illus.). 400p. 1990. text 150.00 (*1-55507-423-5*) Municipal Analysis.

— Governments of Pennsylvania, 1990. (Governments of Your State: Expert Ser.). (Illus.). 1990. text 325.00 (*1-55507-460-X*) Municipal Analysis.

— Governments of Pennsylvania, 1991. (Governments of Your State Ser.). (Illus.). 400p. 1991. text 150.00 (*1-55507-547-9*) Municipal Analysis.

— Governments of South Dakota, 1985. (Governments of Your State Ser.). 1984. text 150.00 (*1-55507-067-1*) Municipal Analysis.

— Governments of South Dakota, 1986. (Governments of Your State Ser.). 1985. text 150.00 (*1-55507-112-0*) Municipal Analysis.

— Governments of South Dakota, 1989. (Governments of Your State Ser.). (Illus.). 1989. text 150.00 (*1-55507-338-7*) Municipal Analysis.

— Governments of South Dakota, 1989: Expert Edition. (Governments of Your State: Expert Ser.). (Illus.). 400p. 1989. text 325.00 (*1-55507-375-1*) Municipal Analysis.

— Governments of South Dakota, 1990. (Governments of Your State Ser.). (Illus.). 400p. 1990. text 150.00 (*1-55507-424-3*) Municipal Analysis.

— Governments of South Dakota, 1990: Expert Edition. (Governments of Your State: Expert Ser.). (Illus.). 400p. 1990. text 325.00 (*1-55507-461-8*) Municipal Analysis.

— Governments of South Dakota, 1991. (Governments of Your State Ser.). (Illus.). 400p. 1991. text 150.00 (*1-55507-548-7*) Municipal Analysis.

— Governments of Tennessee, 1985. (Governments of Your State Ser.). 1984. text 150.00 (*1-55507-068-X*) Municipal Analysis.

— Governments of Tennessee, 1986. (Governments of Your State Ser.). 1985. text 150.00 (*1-55507-113-9*) Municipal Analysis.

— Governments of Tennessee, 1989. (Governments of Your State Ser.). (Illus.). 1989. text 150.00 (*1-55507-339-5*) Municipal Analysis.

— Governments of Tennessee, 1989: Expert Edition. (Governments of Your State: Expert Ser.). (Illus.). 400p. 1989. text 325.00 (*1-55507-376-X*) Municipal Analysis.

— Governments of Tennessee, 1990. (Governments of Your State Ser.). (Illus.). 400p. 1990. text 150.00 (*1-55507-425-1*) Municipal Analysis.

— Governments of Tennessee, 1990: Expert Edition. (Governments of Your State: Expert Ser.). (Illus.). 400p. 1990. text 325.00 (*1-55507-462-6*) Municipal Analysis.

— Governments of Tennessee, 1991. (Governments of Your State Ser.). (Illus.). 400p. 1991. text 150.00 (*1-55507-549-5*) Municipal Analysis.

— Governments of Texas, 1985. (Governments of Your State Ser.). 1984. text 150.00 (*1-55507-069-8*) Municipal Analysis.

— Governments of Texas, 1986. (Governments of Your State Ser.). 1985. text 150.00 (*1-55507-114-7*) Municipal Analysis.

— Governments of Texas, 1989. (Governments of Your State Ser.). (Illus.). 1989. text 150.00 (*1-55507-340-9*) Municipal Analysis.

— Governments of Texas, 1989: Expert Edition. (Governments of Your State: Expert Ser.). (Illus.). 400p. 1989. text 325.00 (*1-55507-377-8*) Municipal Analysis.

— Governments of Texas, 1990. (Governments of Your State Ser.). (Illus.). 400p. 1990. text 150.00 (*1-55507-426-X*) Municipal Analysis.

— Governments of Texas, 1990: Expert Edition. (Governments of Your State: Expert Ser.). (Illus.). 400p. 1990. text 325.00 (*1-55507-463-4*) Municipal Analysis.

— Governments of Texas, 1991. (Governments of Your State Ser.). (Illus.). 400p. 1991. text 150.00 (*1-55507-550-9*) Municipal Analysis.

— Governments of the Carolinas, 1985. (Governments of Your State Ser.). 1984. text 150.00 (*1-55507-075-2*) Municipal Analysis.

— Governments of the Carolinas, 1986. (Governments of Your State Ser.). 1985. text 150.00 (*1-55507-120-1*) Municipal Analysis.

— Governments of the Carolinas, 1989. (Governments of Your State Ser.). (Illus.). 1989. text 150.00 (*1-55507-346-8*) Municipal Analysis.

— Governments of the Carolinas, 1989: Expert Edition. (Governments of Your State: Expert Ser.). (Illus.). 400p. 1989. text 325.00 (*1-55507-383-2*) Municipal Analysis.

— Governments of the Carolinas, 1990. (Governments of Your State Ser.). (Illus.). 400p. 1990. text 150.00 (*1-55507-432-4*) Municipal Analysis.

— Governments of the Carolinas, 1990: Expert Edition. (Governments of Your State: Expert Ser.). (Illus.). 400p. 1990. text 325.00 (*1-55507-469-3*) Municipal Analysis.

— Governments of the Carolinas, 1991. (Governments of Your State Ser.). (Illus.). 400p. 1991. text 150.00 (*1-55507-556-8*) Municipal Analysis.
— Governments of the Northeast, 1985. (Governments of Your State Ser.). 1984. text 150.00 (*1-55507-076-0*) Municipal Analysis.
— Governments of the Northeast, 1986. (Governments of Your State Ser.). 1985. text 150.00 (*1-55507-123-6*) Municipal Analysis.
— Governments of the Northeast, 1989. (Governments of Your State Ser.). (Illus.). 1989. text 150.00 (*1-55507-349-2*) Municipal Analysis.
— Governments of the Northeast, 1989: Expert Edition. (Governments of Your State: Expert Ser.). (Illus.). 400p. 1989. text 325.00 (*1-55507-384-0*) Municipal Analysis.
— Governments of the Northeast, 1990. (Governments of Your State Ser.). (Illus.). 400p. 1990. text 150.00 (*1-55507-435-9*) Municipal Analysis.
— Governments of the Northeast, 1990: Expert Edition. (Governments of Your State: Expert Ser.). (Illus.). 400p. 1990. text 325.00 (*1-55507-472-3*) Municipal Analysis.
— Governments of the Northeast, 1991. (Governments of Your State Ser.). (Illus.). 400p. 1991. text 150.00 (*1-55507-558-4*) Municipal Analysis.
— Governments of the Northwest, 1985. (Governments of Your State Ser.). 1984. text 150.00 (*1-55507-078-7*) Municipal Analysis.
— Governments of the Northwest, 1986. (Governments of Your State Ser.). 1985. text 150.00 (*1-55507-121-X*) Municipal Analysis.
— Governments of the Northwest, 1989. (Governments of Your State Ser.). (Illus.). 1989. text 150.00 (*1-55507-347-6*) Municipal Analysis.
— Governments of the Northwest, 1989: Expert Edition. (Governments of Your State: Expert Ser.). (Illus.). 400p. 1989. text 325.00 (*1-55507-386-7*) Municipal Analysis.
— Governments of the Northwest, 1990. (Governments of Your State Ser.). (Illus.). 400p. 1990. text 150.00 (*1-55507-433-2*) Municipal Analysis.
— Governments of the Northwest, 1990: Expert Edition. (Governments of Your State: Expert Ser.). (Illus.). 400p. 1990. text 325.00 (*1-55507-470-7*) Municipal Analysis.
— Governments of the Northwest, 1991. (Governments of Your State Ser.). (Illus.). 400p. 1991. text 150.00 (*1-55507-557-6*) Municipal Analysis.
— Governments of the West, 1985. (Governments of Your State Ser.). 1984. text 150.00 (*1-55507-077-9*) Municipal Analysis.
— Governments of the West, 1986. (Governments of Your State Ser.). 1985. text 150.00 (*1-55507-122-8*) Municipal Analysis.
— Governments of the West, 1989. (Governments of Your State Ser.). (Illus.). 1989. text 150.00 (*1-55507-348-4*) Municipal Analysis.
— Governments of the West, 1989: Expert Edition. (Governments of Your State: Expert Ser.). (Illus.). 400p. 1989. text 325.00 (*1-55507-385-9*) Municipal Analysis.
— Governments of the West, 1990. (Governments of Your State Ser.). (Illus.). 400p. 1990. text 150.00 (*1-55507-434-0*) Municipal Analysis.
— Governments of the West, 1990: Expert Edition. (Governments of Your State: Expert Ser.). (Illus.). 400p. 1990. text 325.00 (*1-55507-471-5*) Municipal Analysis.
— Governments of the West, 1991. (Governments of Your State Ser.). (Illus.). 400p. 1991. text 150.00 (*1-55507-559-2*) Municipal Analysis.
— Governments of Vermont, 1985. (Governments of Your State Ser.). 1984. text 150.00 (*1-55507-070-1*) Municipal Analysis.
— Governments of Vermont, 1986. (Governments of Your State Ser.). 1985. text 150.00 (*1-55507-115-5*) Municipal Analysis.
— Governments of Vermont, 1989. (Governments of Your State Ser.). (Illus.). 1989. text 150.00 (*1-55507-341-7*) Municipal Analysis.
— Governments of Vermont, 1989: Expert Edition. (Governments of Your State: Expert Ser.). (Illus.). 400p. 1989. text 325.00 (*1-55507-378-6*) Municipal Analysis.
— Governments of Vermont, 1990. (Governments of Your State Ser.). (Illus.). 400p. 1990. text 150.00 (*1-55507-427-8*) Municipal Analysis.
— Governments of Vermont, 1990: Expert Edition. (Governments of Your State: Expert Ser.). (Illus.). 400p. 1990. text 325.00 (*1-55507-464-2*) Municipal Analysis.
— Governments of Vermont, 1991. (Governments of Your State Ser.). (Illus.). 400p. 1991. text 150.00 (*1-55507-551-7*) Municipal Analysis.
— Governments of Virginia, 1985. (Governments of Your State Ser.). 1984. text 150.00 (*1-55507-071-X*) Municipal Analysis.
— Governments of Virginia, 1986. (Governments of Your State Ser.). 1985. text 150.00 (*1-55507-116-3*) Municipal Analysis.
— Governments of Virginia, 1989. (Governments of Your State Ser.). (Illus.). 1989. text 150.00 (*1-55507-342-5*) Municipal Analysis.
— Governments of Virginia, 1989: Expert Edition. (Governments of Your State: Expert Ser.). (Illus.). 400p. 1989. text 325.00 (*1-55507-379-4*) Municipal Analysis.
— Governments of Virginia, 1990. (Governments of Your State Ser.). (Illus.). 400p. 1990. text 150.00 (*1-55507-428-6*) Municipal Analysis.
— Governments of Virginia, 1990: Expert Edition. (Governments of Your State: Expert Ser.). (Illus.). 400p. 1990. text 325.00 (*1-55507-465-0*) Municipal Analysis.
— Governments of Virginia, 1991. (Governments of Your State Ser.). (Illus.). 400p. 1991. text 150.00 (*1-55507-552-5*) Municipal Analysis.
— Governments of Washington, 1985. (Governments of Your State Ser.). 1984. text 150.00 (*1-55507-072-8*) Municipal Analysis.
— Governments of Washington, 1986. (Governments of Your State Ser.). 1985. text 150.00 (*1-55507-117-1*) Municipal Analysis.
— Governments of Washington, 1989. (Governments of Your State Ser.). (Illus.). 1989. text 150.00 (*1-55507-343-3*) Municipal Analysis.
— Governments of Washington, 1989: Expert Edition. (Governments of Your State: Expert Ser.). (Illus.). 400p. 1989. text 325.00 (*1-55507-380-8*) Municipal Analysis.
— Governments of Washington, 1990. (Governments of Your State Ser.). (Illus.). 400p. 1990. text 150.00 (*1-55507-429-4*) Municipal Analysis.
— Governments of Washington, 1990: Expert Edition. (Governments of Your State: Expert Ser.). (Illus.). 400p. 1990. text 325.00 (*1-55507-466-9*) Municipal Analysis.
— Governments of Washington, 1991. (Governments of Your State Ser.). (Illus.). 400p. 1991. text 150.00 (*1-55507-553-3*) Municipal Analysis.
— Governments of West Virginia, 1985. (Governments of Your State Ser.). 1984. text 150.00 (*1-55507-073-6*) Municipal Analysis.
— Governments of West Virginia, 1986. (Governments of Your State Ser.). 1985. text 150.00 (*1-55507-118-X*) Municipal Analysis.
— Governments of West Virginia, 1989. (Governments of Your State Ser.). (Illus.). 1989. text 150.00 (*1-55507-344-1*) Municipal Analysis.
— Governments of West Virginia, 1989: Expert Edition. (Governments of Your State: Expert Ser.). (Illus.). 400p. 1989. text 325.00 (*1-55507-381-6*) Municipal Analysis.
— Governments of West Virginia, 1990. (Governments of Your State Ser.). (Illus.). 400p. 1990. text 150.00 (*1-55507-430-8*) Municipal Analysis.
— Governments of West Virginia, 1990: Expert Edition. (Governments of Your State: Expert Ser.). (Illus.). 400p. 1990. text 325.00 (*1-55507-467-7*) Municipal Analysis.
— Governments of West Virginia, 1991. (Governments of Your State Ser.). (Illus.). 400p. 1991. text 150.00 (*1-55507-554-1*) Municipal Analysis.
— Governments of Wisconsin, 1986. (Governments of Your State Ser.). 1985. text 150.00 (*1-55507-119-8*) Municipal Analysis.
— Governments of Wisconsin, 1989. (Governments of Your State Ser.). (Illus.). 1989. text 150.00 (*1-55507-345-X*) Municipal Analysis.
— Governments of Wisconsin, 1989: Expert Edition. (Governments of Your State: Expert Ser.). (Illus.). 400p. 1989. text 325.00 (*1-55507-382-4*) Municipal Analysis.
— Governments of Wisconsin, 1990. (Governments of Your State Ser.). (Illus.). 400p. 1990. text 150.00 (*1-55507-431-6*) Municipal Analysis.
— Governments of Wisconsin, 1990: Expert Edition. (Governments of Your State: Expert Ser.). (Illus.). 400p. 1990. text 325.00 (*1-55507-468-5*) Municipal Analysis.
— Governments of Wisconsin, 1991. (Governments of Your State Ser.). (Illus.). 400p. 1991. text 150.00 (*1-55507-555-X*) Municipal Analysis.
— Illinois Governments Performance Standards, 1990. (Governments Performance Standards Ser.). (Illus.). 150p. 1990. text 125.00 (*1-55507-481-2*) Municipal Analysis.
— Indiana Governments Performance Standards, 1990. (Governments Performance Standards Ser.). (Illus.). 150p. 1990. text 125.00 (*1-55507-482-0*) Municipal Analysis.
— Iowa Government's Performance Standards, 1990. (Governments Performance Standards Ser.). (Illus.). 150p. 1990. text 125.00 (*1-55507-483-9*) Municipal Analysis.
— Kansas Governments Performance Standards, 1990. (Governments Performance Standards Ser.). (Illus.). 150p. 1990. text 125.00 (*1-55507-484-7*) Municipal Analysis.
— Kentucky Governments Performance Standards, 1990. (Governments Performance Standards Ser.). (Illus.). 150p. 1990. text 125.00 (*1-55507-485-5*) Municipal Analysis.
— Louisiana Governments Performance Standards, 1990. (Governments Performance Standards Ser.). (Illus.). 150p. 1990. text 125.00 (*1-55507-486-3*) Municipal Analysis.
— Maine Governments Performance Standards, 1990. (Governments Performance Standards Ser.). (Illus.). 150p. 1990. text 125.00 (*1-55507-487-1*) Municipal Analysis.
— Massachusetts Governments Performance Standards, 1990. (Governments Performance Standards Ser.). (Illus.). 150p. 1990. text 125.00 (*1-55507-488-X*) Municipal Analysis.
— Michigan Governments Performance Standards, 1990. (Governments Performance Standards Ser.). (Illus.). 150p. 1990. text 125.00 (*1-55507-489-8*) Municipal Analysis.
— Minnesota Governments Performance Standards, 1990. (Governments Performance Standards Ser.). (Illus.). 150p. 1990. text 125.00 (*1-55507-490-1*) Municipal Analysis.
— Mississippi Governments Performance Standards, 1990. (Governments Performance Standards Ser.). (Illus.). 150p. 1990. text 125.00 (*1-55507-491-X*) Municipal Analysis.
— Missouri Governments Performance Standards, 1990. (Governments Performance Standards Ser.). (Illus.). 150p. 1990. text 125.00 (*1-55507-492-8*) Municipal Analysis.
— Nebraska Governments Performance Standards, 1990. (Governments Performance Standards Ser.). (Illus.). 150p. 1990. text 125.00 (*1-55507-493-6*) Municipal Analysis.
— New Jersey Governments Performance Standards, 1990. (Governments Performance Standards Ser.). (Illus.). 150p. 1990. text 125.00 (*1-55507-494-4*) Municipal Analysis.
— New York Government's Performance Standards, 1990. (Governments Performance Standards Ser.). (Illus.). 150p. 1990. text 125.00 (*1-55507-495-2*) Municipal Analysis.
— North Dakota Governments Performance Standards, 1990. (Governments Performance Standards Ser.). (Illus.). 150p. 1990. text 125.00 (*1-55507-496-0*) Municipal Analysis.
— The Northeast Governments Performance Standards, 1990. (Governments Performance Standards Ser.). (Illus.). 150p. 1990. text 125.00 (*1-55507-511-8*) Municipal Analysis.
— The Northwest Governments Performance Standards, 1990. (Governments Performance Standards Ser.). (Illus.). 150p. 1990. text 125.00 (*1-55507-509-6*) Municipal Analysis.
— Ohio Governments Performance Standards, 1990. (Governments Performance Standards Ser.). (Illus.). 150p. 1990. text 125.00 (*1-55507-497-9*) Municipal Analysis.
— Oklahoma Governments Performance Standards, 1990. (Governments Performance Standards Ser.). (Illus.). 150p. 1990. text 125.00 (*1-55507-498-7*) Municipal Analysis.
— Pennsylvania Governments Performance Standards, 1990. (Governments Performance Standards Ser.). (Illus.). 150p. 1990. text 125.00 (*1-55507-499-5*) Municipal Analysis.
— South Dakota Governments Performance Standards, 1990. (Governments Performance Standards Ser.). (Illus.). 150p. 1990. text 125.00 (*1-55507-500-2*) Municipal Analysis.
— Tennessee Governments Performance Standards, 1990. (Governments Performance Standards Ser.). (Illus.). 150p. 1990. text 125.00 (*1-55507-501-0*) Municipal Analysis.
— Texas Governments Performance Standards, 1990. (Governments Performance Standards Ser.). (Illus.). 150p. 1990. text 125.00 (*1-55507-502-9*) Municipal Analysis.
— Vermont Governments Performance Standards, 1990. (Governments Performance Standards Ser.). (Illus.). 150p. 1990. text 125.00 (*1-55507-503-7*) Municipal Analysis.
— Virginia Governments Performance Standards, 1990. (Governments Performance Standards Ser.). (Illus.). 150p. 1990. text 125.00 (*1-55507-504-5*) Municipal Analysis.
— Washington Governments Performance Standards, 1990. (Governments Performance Standards Ser.). (Illus.). 150p. 1990. text 125.00 (*1-55507-505-3*) Municipal Analysis.
— The West Governments Performance Standards, 1990. (Governments Performance Standards Ser.). (Illus.). 150p. 1990. text 125.00 (*1-55507-510-X*) Municipal Analysis.
— West Virginia Governments Performance Standards, 1990. (Governments Performance Standards Ser.). (Illus.). 150p. 1990. text 125.00 (*1-55507-506-1*) Municipal Analysis.
— Wisconsin Governments Performance Standards, 1990. (Governments Performance Standards Ser.). (Illus.). 150p. 1990. text 125.00 (*1-55507-507-X*) Municipal Analysis.

Michels, Heide. Monet's House. Ivor, Helen, tr. from FRE. LC 97-210585. (Illus.). 144p. 1997. 35.00 (*0-517-70667-9*) C Potter.
Michels, Jeanne & Murphy, Phyllis. The Queen of Bingo. LC 95-186019. 1994. pap. 5.25 (*0-8222-1417-2*) Dramatists Play.
Michels, Joanne, ed. see Baums, Roosevelt.
Michels, Kenneth M., jt. ed. see deHaven-Smith, Lance.
Michels, Leo. Basic Math Approach To Concepts Of Chem. 3rd ed. LC 84-17493. (Chemistry). 274p. (C). 1985. mass mkt. 21.75 (*0-534-04656-8*) Brooks-Cole.
— Basic Math Approach To Concepts Of Chem. 4th ed. (Chemistry). 320p. (C). 1990. mass mkt. 36.50 (*0-534-12978-1*) Brooks-Cole.
— A Basic Mathematical Approach to the Concepts of Chemistry. 6th ed. (Chemistry Ser.). 333p. 1995. mass mkt. 52.95 (*0-534-26574-X*) Brooks-Cole.
Michels, Leo, jt. auth. see Roberts, Keith.
Michels, Linda & Thompson, Catherine. The Rottweiler: Sentinel Supreme. 256p. 1998. 27.95 (*0-87605-084-4*) Howell Bks.
***Michels, Natalie.** Umweltschutz und Entwicklungspolitik: Mechanismen Zur Berucksichtigung von Entwicklungslandern in Internationalen Umweltschutzubereinkommen. (Europaische Hochschulschriften Ser: Bd. 2750). lix, 395p. 1999. 68.95 (*3-631-35363-4*) P Lang Pubng.
Michels, Patrick. Fortizymo: The Time Has Come. 164p. (Orig.). 1997. pap. 9.95 (*1-880710-05-6*) Monterey Pacific.
Michels, Robert. First Lectures in Political Sociology. De Grazia, Alfred, tr. LC 73-14172. (Perspectives in Social Inquiry Ser.). 184p. 1978. reprint ed. 16.95 (*0-405-05515-3*) Ayer.
— Political Parties. LC 98-27094. 379p. 2000. pap. 29.95 (*0-7658-0469-7*) Transaction Pubs.
— Il Proletariato e la Borghesia Nel Movimento Socialista Italiano: Saggio Di Scienza Sociografico-Politica: Proletariat & Bourgeoisie Within the Socialist Movement: a Sociographic Political Essay. LC 74-25769. (European Sociology Ser.). 404p. 1975. reprint ed. 33.95 (*0-405-06523-X*) Ayer.
Michels, Robert, jt. auth. see MacKinnon, Roger A.
Michels, Ronald G. Vitreous Surgery. (Illus.). 126p. 1982. 25.00 (*0-317-94081-3*) Am Acad Ophthal.
Michels, Tilde. At the Frog Pond. Ignatowicz, Nina, tr. from GER. LC 88-37835.Tr. of Am Froschweiher. (Illus.). 32p. (J). (ps-4). 1989. 11.95 (*0-397-32314-X*); lib. bdg. 11.89 (*0-397-32315-8*) HarpC Child Bks.
— Gustavo Va a la Escuela (Gustavo Goes to School) (SPA., Illus.). (J). (gr. 3-4). 1995. pap. 5.99 (*968-16-4726-2*, Pub. by Fondo) Continental Bk.
— Sophie the Rag Picker. (Illus.). (J). (gr. k-1). 1962. 10.95 (*0-8392-3036-2*) Astor-Honor.
— What a Beautiful Day! (Illus.). (J). (ps-3). 1992. lib. bdg. 19.95 (*0-87614-739-2*, Carolrhoda) Lerner Pub.
— Who's That Knocking at My Door? (Illus.). 28p. (J). (ps-3). 1986. 10.95 (*0-8120-5732-5*) Barron.
— Who's That Knocking at My Door? (Illus.). 28p. (J). (ps-3). 1992. pap. 4.95 (*0-8120-1486-3*) Barron.
***Michels, Tom.** Antique Maps: The Vatican Collection. (Tempons Ser.). (Illus.). 220p. 2000. 55.00 (*1-85995-750-1*) Parkstone Pr.
Michelsen, Ari M., et al. Effectiveness of Residential Water Conservation Price & Nonprice Programs. LC 98-4507. xxiii, 128 p. 1998. write for info. (*0-89867-954-0*) Am Water Wks Assn.
— Residential Water Use, Rate, Revenue & Nonprice Conservation Program Database: For the Research Project on Effectiveness of Residential Water Conservation Price & Nonprice Programs in Urban Areas in the Western U. S. LC 98-6425. xix, 158p. 1998. write for info. (*0-89867-955-9*) Am Water Wks Assn.
Michelsen, David. Blues Harmonica Classics. 108p. 1995. spiral bd. 12.95 (*0-7866-0080-2*, 95260) Mel Bay.
— Dr. Midnight's Blues Harp. audio 9.98 (*0-7866-0053-5*, 95051C) Mel Bay.
— Dr. Midnight's Blues Harp. 96p. 1994. spiral bd. 9.95 (*0-7866-0025-X*, 95051) Mel Bay.
— Dr. Midnight's Blues Harp Songbook. 1994. pap., spiral bd. 18.95 incl. audio (*0-7866-1190-1*, 95051P) Mel Bay.
Michelsen, Gerd, jt. auth. see Fischer, Hubertus.
Michelsen, Neil F. The American Ephemeris: 1991-2000. (American Ephemeris Ser.). 128p. (Orig.). 1996. pap. 12.95 (*0-917086-21-X*) ACS Pubns.
— The American Ephemeris for the 20th Century at Midnight. 5th rev. ed. (American Ephemeris Ser.). 608p. 1996. pap. 21.95 (*0-935127-19-4*) ACS Pubns.
— The American Ephemeris for the 20th Century at Noon. 5th rev. ed. (American Ephemeris Ser.). 608p. 1996. pap. 26.95 (*0-935127-20-8*) ACS Pubns.
— The American Ephemeris for the 21st Century 2000-2050 at Midnight. 2nd ed. 304p. 1997. pap. 18.95 (*0-935127-59-3*) ACS Pubns.
— The American Ephemeris for the 21st Century at Noon. 2nd ed. 304p. (Orig.). 1997. pap. 18.95 (*0-935127-58-5*) ACS Pubns.
Michelsen, Neil F. The American Ephemeris, 2001-2010. 128p. 1997. pap. 12.95 (*0-935127-51-8*) ACS Pubns.
Michelsen, Neil F. The American Heliocentric Ephemeris, 2001-2050. (American Ephemeris Ser.). 303p. (Orig.). 1996. pap. 29.95 (*0-935127-42-9*) ACS Pubns.
— The American Midpoint Ephemeris, 1991-1995. (American Ephemeris Ser.). 60p. 1985. pap. 9.95 (*0-935127-17-8*) ACS Pubns.
— The American Midpoint Ephemeris, 1996-2000. 64p. 1995. pap. 15.95 (*0-935127-47-X*) ACS Pubns.
— The American Sidereal Ephemeris, 2001-2025. (American Ephemeris Ser.). 292p. (Orig.). 1996. pap. 29.95 (*0-935127-43-7*) ACS Pubns.
— The American Sidereal Ephemeris, 1976-2000. 2nd ed. 292p. (Orig.). 1996. pap. 29.95 (*0-935127-48-8*) ACS Pubns.
— The Asteroid Ephemeris, 1900-2050. 208p. 1999. pap. 26.95 (*0-935127-66-6*) ACS Pubns.
— Search for the Christmas Star. 23p. 1987. pap. 5.00 (*0-935127-07-0*) ACS Pubns.
— Tables of Planetary Phenomena. 2nd rev. ed. 249p. 1990. pap. 29.95 (*0-935127-31-3*) ACS Pubns.
Michelsen, Neil F., et al. The Michelsen Book of Tables: Placidus & Koch Tables of Houses. 176p. (Orig.). 1997. pap. 15.95 (*0-935127-60-7*) ACS Pubns.
Michelsen, Sofus S., jt. auth. see Watermeyer, Basil.
Michelsohn, Arie M., jt. ed. see Raizen, Senta A.
Michelsohn, Marie-Louise, jt. auth. see Lawson, H. Blaine, Jr.
Michelson. Color Atlas of Uveitis Diagnosis. 2nd ed. (Illus.). 158p. (C). (gr. 13). 1992. text 83.00 (*0-8151-5872-6*, 21944) Mosby Inc.
— The Eye in Clinical Medical. 1995. 54.95 (*0-7234-2147-1*) Mosby Inc.
Michelson, A. A. Studies in Optics. unabridged ed. LC 95-10180. (Illus.). 208p. 1995. reprint ed. pap. text 8.95 (*0-486-68700-7*) Dover.
Michelson, A. M. & Bannister, J. V., eds. Life Chemistry Reports, Vol. 1, Part 1. 56p. 1982. pap. text 106.00 (*3-7186-0185-0*) Gordon & Breach.
— Life Chemistry Reports, Vol. 1, Part 2. 108p. 1982. pap. text 82.00 (*3-7186-0186-9*) Gordon & Breach.
— Life Chemistry Reports, Vol. 2. 96p. 1983. pap. text 77.00 (*3-7186-0199-0*) Gordon & Breach.
— Life Chemistry Reports, Vol. 2. 84p. 1984. pap. text 69.00 (*3-7186-0220-2*) Gordon & Breach.
Michelson, A. M., jt. ed. see Bannister, J. V.
Michelson, A. R., ed. Defect Recognition & Image Processing in Semiconductors, 1995: Proceedings of the Sixth International Conference, Held in Boulder, CO, 3-6 December 1995. LC 96-11246. (Institute of Physics Conference Ser.: Vol. 149). 436p. 1996. 243.00 (*0-7503-0372-7*) IOP Pub.
Michelson, Albert A. Studies in Optics. 1992. pap. text 2.45 (*0-226-52388-5*, P514) U Ch Pr.

An Asterisk (*) at the beginning of an entry indicates that the title is appearing for the first time.

Michelson, Annette. Drawing into Film: Directors' Drawings. LC 93-83854. (Illus.). 104p. (Orig.). 1993. pap. write for info. (*1-878283-30-8*) PaceWildenstein.

Michelson, Annette, ed. see Vertov, Dziga.

Michelson, Arnold M. & Levesque, Allen H. Error-Control Techniques for Digital Communication. LC 84-15327. 488p. 1985. 165.00 (*0-471-88074-4*, Wiley-Interscience) Wiley.

Michelson, Bruce. American Literature. 5th ed. Date not set. pap. write for info. (*0-393-95875-2*) Norton.

***Michelson, Bruce.** Literary Wit. 2000. pap. 15.95 (*1-55849-274-7*) U of Mass Pr.

Michelson, Bruce. Mark Twain on the Loose: A Comic Writer & the American Self. LC 94-37579. 280p. 1995. pap. 18.95 (*0-87023-967-8*) U of Mass Pr.

— Wilbur's Poetry: Music in a Scattering Time. LC 90-20353. 272p. (C). 1991. lib. bdg. 35.00 (*0-87023-741-1*) U of Mass Pr.

Michelson, Carmen & Davis, Mary-Ann. The Knitters Guide to Sweater Design. LC 87-46352. (Illus.). 398p. 1904. 29.95 (*0-934026-33-5*) Interweave.

Michelson, Court. Michelson's Book of World Baseball Records. 184p. (Orig.). 1985. pap. 9.95 (*0-934175-00-4*) Sports Rec.

Michelson, D. Electrostatic Atomization. (Illus.). 164p. 1990. 95.00 (*0-85274-235-5*) IOP Pub.

Michelson, Derrick O. Fachworterbuch Textil. (ENG & GER.). 136p. 49.95 (*3-87150-106-9*, M-7404) Fr & Eur.

Michelson, Derrick O. & Wagner, G. Textile Dictionary: Fachwoerterbuch Textil. 4th ed. (FRE & GER.). 120p. 1987. 49.95 (*0-8288-0744-2*, M 7404) Fr & Eur.

Michelson, Greg, jt. ed. see Hammond, Kevin.

Michelson, John L., ed. see Technical Association of the Pulp & Paper Industry.

Michelson, Karin. A Comparative Study of Lake-Iroquoian Accent. (C). 1988. text 173.50 (*1-55608-054-9*) Kluwer Academic.

Michelson, Karin, jt. ed. see Gerdts, Donna B.

Michelson, L., et al. Social Skills Assessment & Training with Children: An Empirically Based Handbook. (Illus.). 282p. (C). 1983. 65.00 (*0-306-41234-9*, Plenum Trade) Perseus Pubng.

Michelson, L., jt. auth. see Edelstein, B. A.

Michelson, Larry K. & Ray, William J., eds. Handbook of Dissociation: Theoretical, Empirical, & Clinical Perspectives. (Illus.). 615p. (C). 1996. 110.00 (*0-306-45150-6*, Plenum Trade) Perseus Pubng.

Michelson, M. J., ed. Comparative Pharmacology, 2 vols., Set. 1008p. (C). 1973. 452.00 (*0-08-016389-0*, Pub. by Pergamon Repr) Franklin.

Michelson, Maureen R. Rose Hills, a Place to Remember. Maze, Dessie L. & Durko, Sandy V., eds. LC 89-90901. 112p. 1989. 60.00 (*0-9622358-1-4*) Rose Hills Pubns.

— Rose Hills, a Place to Remember. limited ed. Maze, Dessie L. & Durko, Sandy V., eds. LC 89-90901. 112p. 1989. 200.00 (*0-9622358-0-6*) Rose Hills Pubns.

— Women & Work: In Their Own Words. 2nd ed. 192p. 1994. pap. 14.95 (*0-939165-23-6*) NewSage Press.

Michelson, P. F. & Hu En-ke, eds. Experimental Gravitational Physics: Proceedings of the Int'l Symposium on Experimental Gravitational Physics. 570p. (Orig.). (C). 1988. pap. 66.00 (*9971-5-0516-9*); text 138.00 (*9971-5-0515-0*) World Scientific Pub.

Michelson, Paul E. Conflict & Crisis: Romanian Political Development, 1861-1871. (Modern European History Ser.). 336p. 1987. text 15.00 (*0-8240-8029-7*) Garland.

***Michelson, Paul E.** Romanian Politics, 1859-1871: From Prince Cuza to Prince Carol. LC 98-161666. 344p. 1998. 50.00 (*973-98091-9-7*, Pub. by Ctr Romanian Studies) Intl Spec Bk.

Michelson, Paul E. & Bodea, Cornelia, eds. The Revolution of 1848 in the Romanian Lands: An Introduction & Guide. (Illus.). 320p. 2001. 58.00 (*973-98391-3-4*, Pub. by Ctr Romanian Studies) Intl Spec Bk.

Michelson, Paul E., ed. & pref. see Zub, Alexandru.

Michelson, Peter. Speaking the Unspeakable: A Poetics of Obscenity. LC 91-46954. (SUNY Series, The Margins of Literature). 312p. (C). 1992. pap. text 24.95 (*0-7914-1224-5*) State U NY Pr.

***Michelson, Peter, ed.** The Extant Poetry & Prose of Max Michelson, Imagist (1880-1953) LC 99-89194. (Studies in American Literature: Vol. 34). 132p. 2000. text 69.95 (*0-7734-7806-X*) E Mellen.

Michelson, Peter, pref. Pacific Plainsong, Vols. I-XIII. LC 77-95077. (Illus.). 1978. pap. 4.95 (*0-89681-000-3*) Brillig Works.

Michelson, Peter, tr. Many Mountains Moving Vol. 1 No. 3: Feature: Poets from India. (Illus.). 176p. 1995. pap. 6.50 (*1-886976-02-3*) Many Mntns.

Michelson, Richard. Animals That Ought to Be: Poems about Imaginary Pets. LC 95-26262. (Illus.). 32p. (J). (ps-3). 1996. per. 16.00 (*0-689-80635-3*) S&S Trade.

— A Book of Flies Real or Otherwise. LC 98-46894. (Illus.). 56p. (J). (gr. 4-7). 1999. 18.95 (*0-7614-5050-5*, Cav Child Bks) Marshall Cavendish.

— Did You Say Ghosts? LC 92-30134. (Illus.). 32p. (J). (gr. 1 up). 1993. lib. bdg. 14.95 (*0-02-766915-7*, Mac Bks Young Read) S&S Childrens.

— Grandpa's Gamble. LC 97-52633. (Illus.). 32p. (J). (ps-3). 1999. 15.95 (*0-7614-5034-3*, Cav Child Bks) Marshall Cavendish.

— Tap Dancing for the Relatives. LC 85-9166. (University of Central Florida Contemporary Poetry Ser.). 69p. 1985. 14.95 (*0-8130-0827-1*) U Press Fla.

Michelson, Richard S., jt. auth. see Maher, Patrick T.

Michelson, Seth, ed. Mathematical Modeling in Tumor Growth & Progression. (Invasion & Metastasis Ser.: Vol. 16, No. 4-5, 1997). (Illus.). 100p. 1997. pap. 48.75 (*3-8055-6548-8*) S Karger.

Michelson, Seth & Schofield, Timothy. The Biostatistics Cookbook: The Most User-Friendly Guide for the Bio/Medical Scientist. 1996. lib. bdg. 87.00 (*0-7923-3884-7*) Kluwer Academic.

Michelson, Sonia. New Dimensions in Classical Guitar for Children. 104p. (J). 1995. spiral bd. 8.95 (*1-56222-115-9*, 94537) Mel Bay.

Michelson, Sonia. Young Beginners First Repertoire for Classic Guitar. 48p. 1996. pap. 8.95 (*0-7866-0484-0*, 95466) Mel Bay.

Michelson, Steven K. Getting Started with High School Choir. (Getting Started Ser.). 64p. 1994. pap. 11.00 (*1-56545-046-9*, 1628) MENC.

Michelson, Stuart. Investment Management. 200p. (C). 1993. pap. text, teacher ed. 13.00 (*0-03-030033-9*) Dryden Pr.

Michelson, Truman. Contributions to Fox Ethnology. (Bureau of American Ethnology Bulletins Ser.). 168p. 1995. lib. bdg. 79.00 (*0-7812-4085-9*) Rprt Serv.

— Contributions to Fox Ethnology. reprint ed. 39.00 (*0-403-03571-6*) Scholarly.

— Contributions to Fox Ethnology - II. (Bureau of American Ethnology Bulletins Ser.). 183p. 1995. lib. bdg. 79.00 (*0-7812-4095-6*) Rprt Serv.

— Fox Miscellany. (Bureau of American Ethnology Bulletins Ser.). 124p. 1995. lib. bdg. 79.00 (*0-7812-4114-6*) Rprt Serv.

— Fox Miscellany. reprint ed. 29.00 (*0-403-08986-7*) Scholarly.

— Notes on the Buffalo-Head Dance of the Bear Gens of the Fox Indians. reprint ed. 29.00 (*0-403-03668-2*) Scholarly.

— Notes on the Buffalo-Head Dance of the Thunder Gens of the Fox Indians. (Bureau of American Ethnology Bulletins Ser.). 94p. 1995. lib. bdg. 79.00 (*0-7812-4087-5*) Rprt Serv.

— Notes on the Fox Wapanowiweni. (Bureau of American Ethnology Bulletins Ser.). 195p. 1995. lib. bdg. 79.00 (*0-7812-4105-7*) Rprt Serv.

— Owl Sacred Pack of the Fox Indians. (Bureau of American Ethnology Bulletins Ser.). 83p. 1995. lib. bdg. 79.00 (*0-7812-4072-7*) Rprt Serv.

Michelson, Truman, ed. Observations on the Thunder Dance of the Bear Gens of the Fox Indians. (Bureau of American Ethnology Bulletins Ser.). 73p. 1995. lib. bdg. 79.00 (*0-7812-4089-1*) Rprt Serv.

— Ojibwa Texts, 2 vols. LC 73-3542. (American Ethnological Society Publications: No. 7). reprint ed. 96.50 (*0-404-58157-9*) AMS Pr.

Michelson, Truman, tr. Kickapoo Tales. LC 73-3544. (American Ethnological Society Publications: No. 9). reprint ed. 31.50 (*0-404-58159-5*) AMS Pr.

Michelson, William, ed. Public Policy in Temporal Perspective. 1978. pap. text 28.50 (*90-279-7824-7*) Mouton.

Michelson, William, et al. The Child in the City: Vol. 2: Changes & Challenges. 1979. pap. 15.95 (*0-8020-6338-1*) U of Toronto Pr.

***Michelsson, Elisabeth.** Appropriating King Arthur: The Arthurian Legend in English Drama & Entertainment, 1485-1625. (Studia Anglistica Upsaliensia Ser.: Vol. 109). (Illus.). 328p. 1999. pap. 57.50 (*91-554-4615-9*, Pub. by Uppsala Univ Acta Univ Uppsaliensis) Coronet Bks.

Michelutti, Dorina. Loyalty to the Hunt. 56p. pap. 5.00 (*0-919349-70-6*) Guernica Editions.

Michener. Social Psychology. 4th ed. (C). 1997. text. write for info. (*0-15-508312-0*) Harcourt Coll Pubs.

Michener, Andrew H. Small Group Processes. (Social Psychology Ser.). 240p. 2000. pap. 60.00 (*0-8133-3111-0*); pap. 25.00 (*0-8133-3112-9*) Westview.

Michener, Anna J. Becoming Anna: The Autobiography of a Sixteen-Year-Old. LC 98-11049. 256p. 1999. pap. 12.00 (*0-226-52403-5*) U Ch Pr.

***Michener, Anna J.** Becoming Anna: The Autobiography of a Sixteen-Year Old. LC 98-11049. 255p. 1998. 22.00 (*0-226-52401-9*) U Ch Pr.

Michener, Carolee K. Oil, Oil, Oil! (Illus.). 128p. 1997. pap. 18.75 (*0-9662225-0-4*) Venango Co Hist Soc.

Michener, Carolee K., ed. Venango Heritage Cookbook. (Illus.). 396p. 1985. pap. 14.50 (*0-9662225-2-0*) Venango Co Hist Soc.

— The Year the Freshet Didn't Come. (Illus.). 98p. 1984. pap. 7.00 (*0-9662225-1-2*) Venango Co Hist Soc.

Michener, Charles. Stone Roberts: Paintings & Drawings. LC 93-6930. (Illus.). 64p. 1993. pap. 24.95 (*0-8109-2550-8*, Pub. by Abrams) Time Warner.

— Stone Roberts: Paintings & Drawings. LC 93-6930. 1993. write for info. (*0-8109-3773-5*) Abrams.

Michener, Charles D. The Social Behavior of the Bees. LC 73-87379. 464p. 1974. 49.95 (*0-674-81175-5*) Belknap Pr.

Michener, Charles D., et al. The Bee Genera of North & Central America (Hymenoptera: Apoidea) LC 92-31000. (Illus.). 304p. (C). 1994. text 45.00 (*1-56098-256-X*) Smithsonian.

Michener, Chris. From Then into Now: William Kennedy's Albany Cycle. LC 97-36308. 1997. 24.95 (*0-940866-70-6*); pap. 18.95 (*0-940866-71-4*) U Scranton Pr.

Michener, Dorothy. Creating Connections: Learning to Appreciate Diversity. Britt, Leslie, ed. (Illus.). 96p. (Orig.). 1995. pap. text, teacher ed. 10.95 (*0-86530-310-X*, IP310-0) Incentive Pubns.

— The Green Team: Winning Ideas & Activities to Promote Environmental Awareness. Britt, Leslie, ed. (Illus.). 160p. (Orig.). (J). (gr. 3-6). 1993. pap. text, teacher ed. 14.95 (*0-86530-271-5*, 269-9) Incentive Pubns.

— Health & Success: Active Learning Strategies to Promote Student Wellness. (Illus.). 96p. (J). (gr. 4-8). 1999. pap. 10.95 (*0-86530-412-2*, IP 412-2) Incentive Pubns.

— What's News? High Interest, Skills-Based Activities to Strengthen Reading Interest & Global Awareness. Quinn, Anna, ed. (Illus.). 96p. (Orig.). (J). (gr. 4-7). 1995. pap. text 10.95 (*0-86530-337-1*, IP 337-1) Incentive Pubns.

Michener, Dorothy & Muschlitz, Beverly. Bulletin Board Bonanza. (Illus.). 96p. (J). (gr. 2-6). 1981. pap. 10.95 (*0-86530-028-3*, IP-283) Incentive Pubns.

— Filling the Gaps. LC 83-80963. (Illus.). 96p. (gr. 2-6). 1983. pap. text 10.95 (*0-86530-076-3*, IP-763) Incentive Pubns.

— Teacher's Gold Mine II: More Ideas & Activities for Creative Teaching. (Illus.). 160p. (Orig.). (J). (gr. 1-6). 1992. pap. text 14.95 (*0-86530-150-6*, 83-9) Incentive Pubns.

Michener, Ezra. A Retrospect of Early Quakerism: Being Extracts from the Records of Philadelphia Yearly Meeting & the Meetings Composing It. LC 91-66330. 434p. 1991. text 35.00 (*0-9629841-0-8*) Oneonta Pr.

Michener, Gail R., jt. ed. see Murie, Jan O.

Michener, H. Andrew. Social Psychology. 3rd ed. (C). 1994. pap. text, teacher ed., suppl. ed. 33.75 (*0-15-500764-5*) Harcourt Coll Pubs.

— Social Psychology. 4th ed. (C). 1997. pap. text, teacher ed. 42.00 (*0-15-504129-0*) Harcourt.

— Social Psychology. 4th ed. LC 98-87316. (C). 1998. text 76.00 (*0-15-504128-2*) Harcourt.

— South Pacific. 1992. 100.00 (*0-15-200615-X*) Harcourt.

Michener, H. Andrew & DeLamater, John D. Social Psychology. 3rd ed. (Illus.). 688p. (C). 1993. text 77.50 (*0-15-500760-2*) Harcourt Coll Pubs.

Michener, James A. Alaska. 1088p. 1989. mass mkt. 7.99 (*0-449-21726-4*, Crest) Fawcett.

— The Bridge at Andau. 224p. 1985. mass mkt. 5.99 (*0-449-21050-2*, Crest) Fawcett.

— The Bridges at Toko-Ri. 128p. 1984. mass mkt. 5.95 (*0-449-20651-3*, Crest) Fawcett.

— The Bridges at Toko-Ri. 1982. 11.05 (*0-606-00430-0*, Pub. by Turtleback) Demco.

— Caravans. 448p. 1986. mass mkt. 6.95 (*0-449-21380-3*, Crest) Fawcett.

— Caribbean. 448p. 1991. mass mkt. 6.99 (*0-449-21749-3*, Crest) Fawcett.

— Centennial. 1088p. 1987. mass mkt. 6.99 (*0-449-21419-2*, Crest) Fawcett.

— A Century of Sonnets. LC 96-54228. 260p. 1997. 24.95 (*1-880510-50-2*) State House Pr.

— A Century of Sonnets. limited ed. LC 96-54228. 260p. 1997. 200.00 (*1-880510-51-0*) State House Pr.

— Chesapeake. 1083p. 1986. mass mkt. 6.99 (*0-449-21158-4*, Crest) Fawcett.

— The Covenant. 1248p. 1987. mass mkt. 6.99 (*0-449-21420-6*, Crest) Fawcett.

— Creatures of the Kingdom. large type ed. LC 93-44109. 1994. 25.95 (*1-56895-054-3*) Wheeler Pub.

— The Drifters. 768p. 1986. mass mkt. 6.99 (*0-449-21353-6*) Fawcett.

— The Eagle & the Raven. LC 90-9684. (Illus.). 228p. 1990. 19.95 (*0-938349-57-0*) State House Pr.

— The Eagle & the Raven. 1991. mass mkt. 4.95 (*0-8125-1301-0*, Pub. by Tor Bks) St Martin.

Michener, James A. Eagle & the Raven, a Novel. 1991. 10.05 (*0-606-11284-7*, Pub. by Turtleback) Demco.

Michener, James A. Fires of Spring. 480p. 1987. mass mkt. 6.99 (*0-449-21470-2*) Fawcett.

— The Floating World. (Illus.). 472p. 1983. reprint ed. pap. 18.95 (*0-8248-0873-8*) UH Pr.

— Hawaii. 1140p. 1986. mass mkt. 7.99 (*0-449-21335-8*, Crest) Fawcett.

— Hawaii. 1995. reprint ed. lib. bdg. 39.95 (*1-56849-612-5*) Buccaneer Bks.

— Iberia: Spanish Travels & Reflections. (Illus.). 960p. 1984. reprint ed. mass mkt. 7.99 (*0-449-20733-1*, Crest) Fawcett.

— James A. Michener on the Social Studies. (Bulletin Ser.: No. 85). 118p. 1991. pap. 14.95 (*0-87986-060-X*) Nat Coun Soc Studies.

— Journey. 256p. 1994. mass mkt. 5.99 (*0-449-21847-3*) Fawcett.

— Journey. large type ed. LC 89-48690. 1990. lib. bdg. 11.95 (*0-89621-976-3*) Thorndike Pr.

— Legacy. 288p. 1988. mass mkt. 6.99 (*0-449-21641-1*, Crest) Fawcett.

— Literary Reflections. 1995. pap. 4.99 (*0-8125-5052-8*, Pub. by Forge NYC) St Martin.

— Literary Reflections: Michener on Michener, Hemingway, Capote, & Others. LC 93-32356. (Illus.). 224p. 1993. 21.95 (*1-880510-06-5*) State House Pr.

— Mexico. 1994. mass mkt. 7.99 (*0-449-22187-3*, Crest) Fawcett.

— Miracle in Seville. LC 94-10187. (Illus.). 1995. 25.00 (*0-685-72068-3*) Random.

— My Lost Mexico. LC 92-26953. (Illus.). 176p. 1992. 24.95 (*0-938349-93-7*) State House Pr.

— My Lost Mexico. 224p. 1993. mass mkt. 4.99 (*0-8125-3437-9*, Pub. by Tor Bks) St Martin.

— My Lost Mexico. limited ed. LC 92-26953. (Illus.). 176p. 1992. 125.00 (*0-938349-94-5*) State House Pr.

— The Novel. 448p. 1992. mass mkt. 5.99 (*0-449-22143-1*, Crest) Fawcett.

— Poland. 768p. 1984. mass mkt. 6.99 (*0-449-20587-8*, Crest) Fawcett.

— The Quality of Life. 1994. reprint ed. lib. bdg. 24.95 (*1-56849-311-8*) Buccaneer Bks.

— Rascals in Paradise. 384p. 1987. mass mkt. 6.99 (*0-449-21459-1*, Crest) Fawcett.

— Recessional. 1995. mass mkt. 7.99 (*0-449-22345-0*) Fawcett.

— Return to Paradise. 416p. 1984. mass mkt. 6.99 (*0-449-20650-5*, Crest) Fawcett.

— Sayonara. 1983. mass mkt. 6.99 (*0-449-20414-6*, Crest) Fawcett.

— The Source. (Illus.). 1078p. 1976. mass mkt. 6.99 (*0-449-21147-9*, Crest) Fawcett.

— The Source. 1995. reprint ed. lib. bdg. 49.95 (*1-56849-611-7*) Buccaneer Bks.

— South Pacific. LC 91-28934. (Performing Arts Ser.). (Illus.). 40p. (J). 1992. 16.95 (*0-15-200618-4*, Gulliver Bks) Harcourt.

— Space. 864p. 1983. mass mkt. 6.99 (*0-449-20379-4*, Crest) Fawcett.

— Tales of the South Pacific. lib. bdg. 26.95 (*0-8488-2103-3*) Amereon Ltd.

— Tales of the South Pacific. 384p. 1984. mass mkt. 6.99 (*0-449-20652-1*, Crest) Fawcett.

— Tales of the South Pacific. 336p. 1987. 35.00 (*0-02-584540-3*) S&S Trade.

— Texas. 1344p. 1987. mass mkt. 6.99 (*0-449-21092-8*, Crest) Fawcett.

Michener, James A., ed. Hokusai Sketchbooks: Selections from the Manga. LC 58-9983. (Illus.). 286p. 1958. 65.00 (*0-8048-0252-1*) Tuttle Pubng.

Michener, James A. & Kings, John. Six Days in Havana. (Illus.). 144p. 1989. 24.95 (*0-292-77629-2*) U of Tex Pr.

Michener, James A., jt. auth. see Hemingway, Ernest.

Michener, John. The Back to the City Movement & the Possibilities of Increasing Racial & Economic Integration. 50p. 1978. 3.50 (*0-318-15819-1*) Natl Neighbors.

Michener, John W., Jr. Managing Your Law Practice: The Big Picture Perspective, Developing a Long-Term Strategy for the Legal Industry. Miles, C. Joseph, ed. LC 96-78021. 250p. 1996. pap. text. write for info. (*0-7620-0081-3*) West Group.

Michener, Marian. Dreaming under a Ton of Lizards. LC 99-31973. 160p. (Orig.). 1999. pap. 12.00 (*1-883523-34-6*, Pub. by Spinsters Ink) SPD-Small Pr Dist.

Michener, R., jt. auth. see Lajtha, K.

Michener, Roger, ed. The Balance of Freedom: Political Economy, Law, & Learning. LC 94-38254. 288p. (C). 1995. text 24.95 (*0-943852-73-0*) Prof World Peace.

— The Balance of Freedom: Political Economy, Law & Learning. LC 94-38254. 288p. (C). 1995. pap. text 14.95 (*0-943852-74-9*) Prof World Peace.

— Nationality, Patriotism, & Nationalism. LC 93-36087. 256p. (C). 1994. pap. text 14.95 (*0-943852-66-8*) Prof World Peace.

— Nationality, Patriotism & Nationalism. LC 93-36087. 256p. 1994. text 24.95 (*0-943852-65-X*) Prof World Peace.

Michener, William K., et al, eds. Environmental Information Management & Analysis: Ecosystem to Global Scales. LC 94-1213. (Applications in Geographic Information Systems Ser.). 516p. 1994. 99.00 (*0-7484-0123-7*, Pub. by Tay Francis Ltd) Taylor & Francis.

***Michener, William K. & Brunt, James W.** Ecological Data: Design, Management & Processing. LC 99-42236. (Methods in Ecology Ser.). (Illus.). 2000. pap. 59.95 (*0-632-05231-7*) Blackwell Sci.

Michenfelder, John D. Anesthesia & the Brain: Clinical, Functional, Metabolic, & Vascular Correlates. (Illus.). 215p. 1988. text 89.00 (*0-443-08628-1*) Church.

Michet, Heather. The Jump Journal. 90p. 1997. pap. 10.00 (*0-9659884-0-6*) Living Simply.

Michette, A. G. Optical Systems for Soft X-Rays. (Illus.). 344p. (C). 1986. text 110.00 (*0-306-42320-0*, Kluwer Plenum) Kluwer Academic.

Michette, A. G., jt. auth. see Duke, P. J.

Michette, Alan G. & Buckley, C., eds. X-Ray Science & Technology. LC 93-1839. (Illus.). 376p. 1993. 78.00 (*0-7503-0233-X*) IOP Pub.

Michette, Alan G., jt. auth. see Schawlow, Arthur L.

Michetti, Piere, ed. see Smith, Phillip D., et al.

Michi, Josef, ed. Modular Chemistry: Proceedings of the NATO Advanced Research Workshop, Aspen Lodge near Estes Park, Colorado, USA, September 9-12, 1995. LC 97-33655. (NATO Advanced Science Institute Ser.: No. 499). 21p. 1997. text 314.50 (*0-7923-4730-7*) Kluwer Academic.

Michie. Development London Financial. 1600p. 2000. text 625.00 (*1-86064-334-5*, Pub. by I B T) St Martin.

— Political Economy of South Africa's Transition. (ITBP Reference Ser.). 1998. pap. 18.99 (*1-86152-455-2*) Thomson Learn.

Michie (Firm) Staff, jt. auth. see Fletcher, Ann C.

Michie, A. Coordination of Building Services: Design Stage Methods. (C). 1982. 50.00 (*0-86022-150-4*, Pub. by Build Servs Info Assn) St Mut.

Michie, A. & Wix, J. Computer Draughting. (C). 1983. 63.00 (*0-86022-111-3*, Pub. by Build Servs Info Assn) St Mut.

— An Overview of Computers in the Building Service Industry. (C). 1983. 80.00 (*0-86022-106-7*, Pub. by Build Servs Info Assn) St Mut.

Michie, Allan A. & Graebner, Walter, eds. Their Finest Hour: The War in the First Person. LC 41-2009. 213p. reprint ed. pap. 66.10 (*0-608-13760-X*, 205168200001) Bks Demand.

Michie, Allen. Richardson & Fielding: The Dynamics of a Critical Rivalry. LC 99-25685. 264p. 1999. 42.50 (*0-8387-5419-8*) Bucknell U Pr.

Michie, Aruna N., ed. Rural Poverty & Public Policy in the United States. (Orig.). 1986. pap. 15.00 (*0-918592-93-3*) Pol Studies.

Michie Butterworth Editorial Staff. Consolidated Index: Consolidated Index 1994. (New Hampshire Practice Ser.). 432p. 1992. pap. 49.50 (*1-56257-269-5*, MICHIE) LEXIS Pub.

— Hawaii Court Rules Annotated, 1994 Edition. annot. ed. 1994. pap. 30.00 (*1-55834-041-6*, 42197-10, MICHIE) LEXIS Pub.

M

An Asterisk (*) at the beginning of an entry indicates that the title is appearing for the first time.

— Illinois Criminal Practice Law & Rules Annotated, 1993 Edition. 104p. pap. 30.00 (*0-614-05844-9*, MICHIE) LEXIS Pub.
— Illinois Federal Court Rules Annotated, 1994 Edition. 192p. pap. 20.00 (*0-614-05845-7*, MICHIE) LEXIS Pub.
— Illinois State Court Rules Annotated, 1994 Edition. 152p. 1994. pap. 25.00 (*0-614-05847-3*, MICHIE) LEXIS Pub.
— Instructions for Virginia & West Virginia. 3rd ed. 168p. 1987. 120.00 (*0-614-05857-0*, MICHIE) LEXIS Pub.
— Instructions for Virginia & West Virginia, 3 vols., Set. 3rd ed. (Illus.). 32p. 1987. 135.00 (*0-614-05856-2*, MICHIE) LEXIS Pub.
— Maryland Rules, 1994 Edition, 2 vols., Set. pap. 50.00 (*1-55834-043-2*, MICHIE) LEXIS Pub.
— Michie on Banks & Banking, 1955-1992, 13 vols., Set. 1994. suppl. ed. 440.00 (*0-87215-034-8*, 74600-10, MICHIE) LEXIS Pub.
— North Dakota Court Rules Annotated, 1994-95 Edition. 55.00 (*0-87473-870-9*, MICHIE) LEXIS Pub.
— Rhode Island Court Rules Annotated, 1994 Edition. 45.00 (*1-55834-089-0*, MICHIE) LEXIS Pub.
— South Dakota Court Rules, 1994 Edition. pap. 52.50 (*1-55834-144-7*, MICHIE) LEXIS Pub.
— Tennessee Jurisprudence, 29 vols., Set. 1991. 1800.00 (*0-87215-503-X*, 77370-10, MICHIE) LEXIS Pub.
— Tennessee Private Acts Index. 652p. 1984. 75.00 (*0-614-05976-3*, MICHIE) LEXIS Pub.
— Washington Rules of Court Annotated, 1994 Edition. 50.00 (*1-55834-178-1*, MICHIE) LEXIS Pub.
— West Virginia Court Rules, 1994 Edition. pap. 55.00 (*1-55834-050-5*, MICHIE) LEXIS Pub.

M

Michie Butterworth Editorial Staff & Harriman, D. P. Wyoming Court Rules Annotated. 973p. 1991. spiral bd. 85.00 (*0-87473-733-8*, MICHIE) LEXIS Pub.

Michie Butterworth Editorial Staff & Munger, J. P. Michie's Jurisprudence of Virginia & West Virginia with 1991 Cumulative Supplement, 50 vols., Set. rev. ed. 1993. 1200.00 (*0-87215-128-X*, 74700-10, MICHIE) LEXIS Pub.

***Michie, Chris.** Name Droppings: It's All about Me, Isn't It. 128p. 2000. pap. 18.00 (*0-7388-2227-2*) Xlibris Corp.

Michie Company Editorial Staff. Code of Virginia, 1950, 25 vols. write for info. (*0-318-54327-3*, MICHIE) LEXIS Pub.
— Code of Virginia, 1950, 25 vols., Set. write for info. (*0-87215-137-9*, MICHIE) LEXIS Pub.
— Colorado Court Rules, Incl. updates thru March, 1997. 1989. spiral bd. 70.00 (*0-87473-469-X*, 41033-10, MICHIE) LEXIS Pub.
— Delaware Code Annotated, Revised 1974, 21 vols. write for info. (*0-318-54328-1*, MICHIE) LEXIS Pub.
— Delaware Code Annotated, Revised 1974, 21 vols., Set. write for info. (*0-87215-247-2*, MICHIE) LEXIS Pub.
— Drugs in Litigation: Damage Awards Involving Prescription & Nonprescription Drugs, 1995. LC KF801.A7C565 1995. 936p. 1995. pap. 62.00 (*1-55834-226-5*, 71208-12, MICHIE) LEXIS Pub.
— General Statutes of North Carolina, Annotated, 24 vols., Set. write for info. (*0-87215-132-8*, 46405-10, MICHIE) LEXIS Pub.
— Indiana Alcoholic Beverage Law & Rules, 1992: Annotated. 313p. 1992. pap. 12.50 (*0-685-62337-8*, MICHIE) LEXIS Pub.
— Indiana Criminal & Traffic Law Manual. 1001p. 1992. pap. 22.50 (*0-685-62338-6*, MICHIE) LEXIS Pub.
— Maryland Code of 1957, 37 vols., Set. write for info. (*0-87215-129-8*, MICHIE) LEXIS Pub.

***Michie Company Editorial Staff.** North Carolina Juvenile Code & Related Statutes Annotated: 1999-2000 Cumulative Supplement. (C). 2000. pap. 13.00 (*1-56011-371-5*) Institute Government.

Michie Company Editorial Staff. Police, Crimes & Offenses & Motor Vehicle Laws of Virginia, 2 vols. 1992. 80.00 (*0-685-62339-4*, MICHIE); 80.00 (*0-685-62355-6*, MICHIE) LEXIS Pub.
— Rhode Island Court Rules Annotated, 1991-92. 1216p. pap. 45.00 (*0-87473-729-X*, MICHIE) LEXIS Pub.
— Tennessee Private Acts Index, Incl. 1991 Suppl. 652p. 1984. 75.00 (*0-87215-812-8*, 48441-10, MICHIE) LEXIS Pub.
— West Virginia Court Rules Annotated. 1309p. 1992. 45.00 (*0-87473-879-2*, MICHIE) LEXIS Pub.

Michie Company Editorial Staff, compiled by. Maine Probate Forms. rev. ed. 290p. 1991. ring bd. 55.00 (*0-89442-116-6*, 81670, MICHIE) LEXIS Pub.

Michie Company Editorial Staff, ed. Instructions for Virginia & West Virginia. 3rd ed. 1996. suppl. ed. 45.00 (*0-614-25257-1*, 73075-13, MICHIE) LEXIS Pub.

***Michie Company Editorial Staff, prod.** Administrative & Financial Laws for Local Government in North Carolina: 1999 Cumulative Supplement. (C). 2000. pap. 25.00 (*1-56011-370-7*) Institute Government.

Michie Company Editorial Staff, jt. auth. see Indiana Judges Association, Civil Instructions Com.

Michie Company Editorial Staff, jt. auth. see Publisher's Staff.

Michie Company Editorial Staff, ed. see Publisher's Editorial Staff.

Michie, Donald. Expert Systems in a Microelectronic Age. 287p. 1984. 60.00 (*0-85224-493-2*, Pub. by Edinburgh U Pr) Col U Pr.
— Machine Intelligence & Related Topics. xii, 316p. 1982. text 161.00 (*0-677-05560-9*) Gordon & Breach.

Michie, Donald, ed. Introductory Readings in Expert Systems. (Studies in Cybernetics: Vol. 1). xviii, 238p. 1982. text 75.00 (*0-677-16350-9*) Gordon & Breach.

Michie, Donald, et al, eds. Machine Intelligence 14: Applied Machine Intelligence. (Illus.). 470p. (C). 1996. text 115.00 (*0-19-853860-X*) OUP.

Michie Editor Staff. U. S. District Court for the District of Puerto Rico: Local Rules. 155p. 1994. 25.00 (*0-327-01037-1*, 82900, MICHIE) LEXIS Pub.

Michie Editorial Staff. Florida Rules of Court Service, 4 vols. 1972. ring bd. 280.00 (*0-327-03955-8*, 80779, MICHIE) LEXIS Pub.
— Laws of Puerto Rico Annotated, 41 vols. (SPA.). Date not set. 1309.00 (*0-327-01022-3*, 47530, MICHIE) LEXIS Pub.
— Local Rules of the Superior Court: Washington State, 2 vols. 1981. ring bd. 95.00 (*0-327-00954-3*, 82823, MICHIE) LEXIS Pub.
— Local Rules of the Superior Court, 1981-1993: Washington State, 2 vols., Set. 1100p. Date not set. ring bd. 95.00 (*0-409-20200-2*, 82823-10, MICHIE) LEXIS Pub.

Michie Editorial Staff. Tennessee Jurisprudence, 31 vols. 1800.00 (*0-327-00825-3*, MICHIE) LEXIS Pub.

Michie Editorial Staff, ed. Florida Criminal Defense Trial Manual, 5 vols., Set. 2000p. Date not set. 350.00 (*0-409-26032-0*, 80614-10, MICHIE) LEXIS Pub.

***Michie Editorial Staff, ed.** Pennsylvania Law Encyclopedia, Vol. 7. 2nd ed. 600p. 2000. write for info. (*0-327-04944-8*) LEXIS Pub.

Michie Editorial Staff, ed. see England, Arthur J. & Simon.

Michie Editors Staff. Leyes de Puerto Rico: Puerto Rico Session Laws. (SPA.). 1993. ring bd. 85.00 (*0-327-01025-8*, 47578, MICHIE) LEXIS Pub.
— Leyes de Puerto Rico Anotadas: Laws of Puerto Rico Annotated, 41 vols. annot. ed. (SPA.). 1994. 1319.00 (*0-327-01024-X*, 47460, MICHIE) LEXIS Pub.
— Maine Probate Forms. rev. ed. 1991. ring bd. 55.00 (*0-327-00985-3*, 81670, MICHIE) LEXIS Pub.

Michie, Elsie B. Outside the Pale: Cultural Exclusion, Gender Difference, & the Victorian Woman Writer. LC 93-2458. (Reading Women Writing Ser.). 208p. 1993. pap. text 14.95 (*0-8014-8085-X*) Cornell U Pr.

***Michie, Gregory.** Holler If You Hear Me: The Education of a Teacher & His Students. LC 99-44218. (Teaching & Social Justice Ser.). 216p. 1999. 44.00 (*0-8077-3889-1*); pap. 19.95 (*0-8077-3888-3*) Tchrs Coll.

Michie, Helena. Sororophobia: Differences among Women in Literature & Culture. (Illus.). 224p. 1992. text 55.00 (*0-19-507387-8*) OUP.

Michie, Helena & Cahn, Naomi. Confinements: Fertility & Infertility in Contemporary Culture. LC 97-1779. 224p. (C). 1997. text 50.00 (*0-8135-2432-6*); pap. text 17.95 (*0-8135-2433-4*) Rutgers U Pr.

Michie, James & Kavanagh, Patrick J., eds. The Oxford Book of Short Poems. 1986. pap. 9.95 (*0-685-10547-4*) OUP.

Michie, James, jt. ed. see Kavanagh, Patrick J.

Michie, James, tr. see Catullus, Gaius Valerius.

Michie, James, tr. see Horace.

Michie, James L. Richmond Hill Plantation, 1810-1868: The Discovery of Antebellum Life on a Waccamaw Rice Plantation. LC 89-24298. (Illus.). xx, 204p. 1990. 24.95 (*0-87152-441-4*) Reprint.

***Michie, Jonathan.** Global Instability The Political Economy of World Economic Governance. LC 98-42021. 1999. 90.00 (*0-415-20222-1*); pap. 27.99 (*0-415-20223-X*) Routledge.

Michie, Jonathan. Wages in the Business Cycle: An Empirical & Methodological Analysis. 194p. 1992. 45.00 (*0-86187-686-5*) St Martin.

Michie, Jonathan, ed. The Economic Legacy 1979-1992. (Illus.). 391p. 1993. pap. text 39.95 (*0-12-494061-7*) Acad Pr.

Michie, Jonathan, ed. The Economics of Restructuring & Intervention. 240p. 1991. text 90.00 (*1-85278-346-X*) E Elgar.

***Michie, Jonathan, ed.** Reader's Guide to the Social Sciences, 2 vols. 2000p. 2000. 250.00 (*1-57958-091-2*) Fitzroy Dearborn.

***Michie, Jonathan & Kitson, Michael.** The Political Economy of Competitiveness: Essays on Employment, Public Policy & Corporate Performance. LC 99-57353. 1999. write for info. (*0-415-20495-X*) Routledge.
— The Political Economy of Competitiveness: Essays on Employment, Public Policy & Corporate Performance. LC 99-57353. (Contemporary Political Economy Ser.). 1999. pap. write for info. (*0-415-20496-8*) Routledge.

Michie, Jonathan & Reati, Angelo, eds. Employment, Technology & Economic Needs: Theory, Evidence & Public Policy. LC 97-52043. 384p. 1998. 100.00 (*1-85898-680-X*) E Elgar.

Michie, Jonathan & Smith, James G., eds. Managing the Global Economy. (Illus.). 370p. 1995. text 75.00 (*0-19-828969-3*); pap. text 26.00 (*0-19-828968-5*) OUP.

Michie, Jonathan & Smith, John G., eds. Creating Industrial Capacity: Towards Full Employment. (Illus.). 342p. (C). 1996. pap. text 28.00 (*0-19-829030-6*) OUP.
— Employment & Economic Performance: Jobs, Inflation, Growth. (Illus.). 278p. 1997. text 85.00 (*0-19-829094-2*); pap. text 32.00 (*0-19-829093-4*) OUP.
— Globalization, Growth, & Governance: Creating an Innovative Economy. LC 99-172049. (Illus.). 292p. 1998. text 79.00 (*0-19-829345-3*); pap. text 29.95 (*0-19-829344-5*) OUP.

Michie, Jonathan, ed. see Adcock, Fleur.

Michie, Jonathan, jt. ed. see Archibugi, Daniele.

Michie, Jonathan, jt. ed. see Buckley, Peter.

Michie, Jonathan, jt. ed. see Deakin, Simon.

Michie, Jonathan, jt. ed. see Howells, Jeremy.

Michie, Jonathon & Smith, John G., eds. Creating Industrial Capacity: Towards Full Employment. (Illus.). 342p. (C). 1996. text 80.00 (*0-19-829029-2*) OUP.
— Unemployment in Europe. LC 94-202908. (Illus.). 384p. 1994. pap. text 39.95 (*0-12-494065-X*) Acad Pr.

Michie, Lindsay W. Portrait of an Appeaser: Robert Hadow, First Secretary in the British Foreign Office, 1931-1939. LC 95-42503. 184p. 1996. 59.95 (*0-275-95369-6*, Praeger Pubs) Greenwood.

Michie, Michael. An Enlightenment Tory in Victorian Scotland: The Career of Sir Archibald Alison. LC 99-220209. 240p. 1997. text 60.00 (*0-7735-1025-7*, Pub. by McG-Queens Univ Pr) CUP Services.

Michie, Peter S. The Life & Letters of Emory Upton. Kohn, Richard H., ed. LC 78-22388. (American Military Experience Ser.). 1980. reprint ed. lib. bdg. 40.95 (*0-405-11865-1*) Ayer.

***Michie, Ranald C.** The London Stock Exchange: A History. LC 99-25367. (Illus.). 688p. 2000. text 110.00 (*0-19-829508-1*) OUP.

***Michie Staff.** Missouri Criminal & Traffic Law Manual, 1999-2000. annuals 992p. 2000. text 32.00 (*0-327-10429-5*, MICHIE) LEXIS Pub.

Michie Staff. New Hampshire Statutes Pertaining to Health & Human Services: 1997-98 Edition. Date not set. 42.50 (*1-55834-866-2*, 28819-13, MICHIE) LEXIS Pub.
— Texas Rules of Civil Procedure. 1986. ring bd. 39.50 (*0-327-00952-7*, 82642, MICHIE) LEXIS Pub.
— Texas Rules of Civil Procedure, 1984-1990. 400p. Date not set. ring bd. 39.50 (*0-409-25020-1*, 82642, MICHIE) LEXIS Pub.

***Michiels, Luc & Motmans, Kris, eds.** Cancer Immunotherapy Protocols. 375p. 2000. 99.50 (*0-89603-829-7*) Humana.

Michielssen, Eric, jt. ed. see Rahmat-Samii, Yahya.

Michie's Editorial Staff. North Dakota Century Code Annotated, Court Rules: 1998-99 Edition. 1,141p. pap. 55.00 (*0-327-11944-6*) LEXIS Pub.

***Michigan & NILS Publishing Company.** Michigan Related Laws to the Insurance Laws. LC 98-61115. 1999. write for info. (*0-89246-503-4*) NILS Pub.

Michigan Association of Municipal Attorneys Staff, jt. auth. see Michigan Municipal League Staff.

***Michigan Historical Commission Staff, ed.** Michigan Biographies, 2 vols. 966p. 1999. pap. 65.00 (*0-8063-4930-1*) Clearfield Co.

Michigan Intercollegiate Athletic Association Staf. Celebrating a Century of the Student Athlete: A 100-Year History of the Oldest Collegiate Athletic Conference in the United States. Renner, Thomas L., ed. (Illus.). 206p. (Orig.). (C). 1988. 20.00 (*0-9634061-2-4*); pap. 15.00 (*0-9634061-4-0*) MI IAA.

Michigan Judicial Institute Staff. Michigan Criminal Procedure Benchbook. LC 92-74196. 276p. 1992. ring bd. 85.00 (*0-685-65664-0*, 92-024) U MI Law CLE.

Michigan Judicial Institute Staff & Michigan Probate Judges, Blue-Ribbon Committee Sta. Probate Court Benchbooks, 3 vols., 1. LC 90-84059. 1032p. 1990. pap. 65.00 (*0-685-39000-4*, 90-031) U MI Law CLE.
— Probate Court Benchbooks, 3 vols., 2. LC 90-84059. 1032p. 1990. pap. 65.00 (*0-685-39001-2*, 90-032) U MI Law CLE.
— Probate Court Benchbooks, 3 vols., 3. LC 90-84059. 1032p. 1990. pap. 65.00 (*0-685-39002-0*, 90-033) U MI Law CLE.

Michigan Legal Services Staff & National Health Law Program Staff. Health Law: Training of Trainers. 706p. 1985. 35.00 (*0-685-23177-1*, 41,209) NCLS Inc.

Michigan Legislative Council Staff. Michigan Administrative Code, 1979: 1989 Annual Supplement. Peters, Roger W., ed. 1071p. 1990. pap. 26.50 (*1-878210-02-5*) Legis Serv Bur.
— Michigan Administrative Code, 1979: 1990 Annual Supplement. Peters, Roger W., ed. 1991. pap. 30.00 (*1-878210-03-3*) Legis Serv Bur.
— Michigan Administrative Code, 1979: 1992 Annual Supplement. Peters, Roger W., ed. 1993. pap. 36.00 (*1-878210-05-X*) Legis Serv Bur.
— Michigan Administrative Code, 1979: 1993 Annual Supplement. Peters, Roger, ed. 1994. pap. 33.00 (*1-878210-07-6*) Legis Serv Bur.
— Michigan Administrative Code, 1979: 1994 Annual Supplement. Peters, Roger, ed. 1995. pap. write for info. (*1-878210-08-4*) Legis Serv Bur.
— Michigan Administrative Code 1979 1997 Annual Supplement. Peters, Roger, ed. pap. write for info. (*1-878210-11-4*) Legis Serv Bur.
— Michigan Manual, 1995-1996. Peters, Roger W., ed. (Illus.). 1176p. 1995. 20.00 (*1-878210-06-8*) Legis Serv Bur.
— Michigan Manual, 1991-1992. rev. ed. (Illus.). 1135p. 1991. 15.00 (*1-878210-04-1*) Legis Serv Bur.

Michigan Livestock Exchange Staff, jt. auth. see Kramer, Carl E.

Michigan Municipal League Staff. Directory of Michigan Municipal Officials. 1995. 36.00 (*0-318-19475-9*) MI Municipal.
— Glossary of Municipal Terms. 1995. 15.00 (*0-317-05702-2*) MI Municipal.
— Junk Yard & Second-Hand Dealers Ordinance Analysis. (Ordinance Analysis Ser.: No. 8). 1986. pap. 5.00 (*0-317-00870-6*) MI Municipal.
— Meetings: Minutes & Agendas. 1995. 15.00 (*0-317-05704-9*) MI Municipal.
— Salaries & Wages in Michigan Municipalities over 1,000 Population. (Information Bulletin Ser.: No. 109). 1995. 50.00 (*0-318-19474-0*) MI Municipal.

Michigan Municipal League Staff & Michigan Association of Municipal Attorneys Staff. Handbook for Municipal Attorneys in Michigan. 1994. 100.00 (*0-317-05716-2*) MI Municipal.

Michigan Municipal League Staff, ed. see Hannah, Susan B.

Michigan Papyri Staff. Michigan Papyri (P. Mich. XII) LC 71-649942. (American Studies in Papyrology: No. 14). 142p. reprint ed. pap. 44.10 (*0-7837-5486-8*, 204525100005) Bks Demand.
— Michigan Papyri XIV. McCarren, Vincent P., ed. LC 71-649942. (American Studies in Papyrology: No. 22). 110p. reprint ed. pap. 34.10 (*0-7837-5491-4*, 204525600005) Bks Demand.

Michigan Press Staff. Greek-English Dictionary of Science & Technological Terms. (ENG & GRE.). 569p. 95.00 (*0-7859-9054-2*) Fr & Eur.

Michigan Probate Judges, Blue-Ribbon Committee Sta, jt. auth. see Michigan Judicial Institute Staff.

Michigan Sea Grant Staff. Lightning & Boats. (Illus.). 9p. 1995. pap. 1.00 (*1-885756-00-3*, MICHU-SG89-700) MI Sea Grant.

Michigan State Bar Special Committee on Standard C. Michigan Criminal Jury Instructions, 3 vols. 2nd ed. LC 89-82310. 1500p. 1991. suppl. ed. 75.00 (*0-685-58877-7*, 92-030); disk. write for info. (*0-318-68094-7*) U MI Law CLE.
— Michigan Criminal Jury Instructions, 3 vols., Set. 2nd ed. LC 89-82310. 1500p. 1991. ring bd., suppl. ed. 210.00 (*0-685-38202-8*, 76-010) U MI Law CLE.

Michigan State University, Institute of Public Utilities Staff. Adjusting to Regulatory, Pricing & Marketing Realities: Proceedings of the Institute of Public Utilities Annual Conference, 14th, Williamsburg, VA, 1982. LC 83-62894. (MSU Public Utilities Papers). 781p. reprint ed. pap. 200.00 (*0-8357-5100-7*, 202940500060) Bks Demand.
— Alternatives to Traditional Regulation: Options for Reform: Proceedings of the Institute of Public Utilities Nineteenth Annual Conference. Trebing, Harry M. & Mann, Patrick C., eds. LC 88-83141. (MSU Public Utilities Papers: No. 1987). 616p. reprint ed. pap. 191.00 (*0-7837-6268-2*, 204598000010) Bks Demand.
— Assessing New Pricing Concepts in Public Utilities: Proceedings of the Institute of Public Utilities Ninth Annual Conference. Trebing, Harry M., ed. LC 78-620031. (MSU Public Utilities Papers). (Illus.). 528p. reprint ed. pap. 163.70 (*0-8357-5805-2*, 205638300063) Bks Demand.
— Award Papers in Public Utility Economics & Regulations. LC 82-83703. (MSU Public Utilities Papers: Vol. 1982). (Illus.). 371p. reprint ed. pap. 115.10 (*0-608-20502-8*, 207175400002) Bks Demand.
— Changing Patterns in Regulation, Markets & Technology: The Effect on Public Utility Pricing: Proceedings of the Institute of Public Utilities Fifteenth Annual Conference, Williamsburg, VA, 1983. Mann, Patrick C. & Trebing, Harry M., eds. LC 84-60967. (MSU Public Utilities Papers: Vol. 1984). (Illus.). 794p. reprint ed. pap. 200.00 (*0-608-20498-6*, 207175000002) Bks Demand.
— Diversification, Deregulation & Increased Uncertainty in the Public Utilities Industries: Proceedings of the Institute of Public Utilities Thirteenth Annual Conference, Williamsburg, VA, 1981. LC 82-83704. (MSU Public Utilities Papers: Vol. 1983). (Illus.). 610p. reprint ed. pap. 189.10 (*0-608-20503-6*, 207175500002) Bks Demand.
— Energy & Communications in Transition: Proceedings of the Institute of Public Utilities Eleventh Annual Conference, Williamsburg, VA, 1979. LC 80-83982. (MSU Public Utilities Papers: Vol. 1981). (Illus.). 591p. reprint ed. pap. 183.30 (*0-608-20504-4*, 207175600002) Bks Demand.
— The Impact of Deregulation & Market Forces on Public Utilities: The Future Role of Regulation: Proceedings of the Institute of Public Utilities Sixteenth Annual Conference, Williamsburg, VA, 1984. Mann, Patrick C. & Trebing, Harry M., eds. LC 85-81789. (MSU Public Utilities Papers: Vol. 1985). (Illus.). 592p. reprint ed. pap. 183.60 (*0-608-20501-X*, 207175300002) Bks Demand.
— Issues in Public Utility Regulation: Proceedings of the Institute of Public Utilities Tenth Annual Conference. Trebing, Harry M., ed. LC 79-88890. (MSU Public Utilities Papers: 1979). 582p. 1979. reprint ed. pap. 180.50 (*0-608-03811-3*, 206466100009) Bks Demand.
— New Challenges to Public Utility Management: Proceedings of the Sixth Annual Conference, 24-25 April, 1973. LC 74-620096. (MSU Public Utilities Papers: Vol. 1974). (Illus.). 271p. reprint ed. pap. 84.10 (*0-608-20505-2*, 207175700002) Bks Demand.
— New Regulatory & Management Strategies in a Changing Market Environment: Proceedings of the Institute of Public Utilities Eighteenth Annual Conference, Williamsburg, VA, 1986. Trebing, Harry M. & Mann, Patrick C., eds. LC 87-73267. (MSU Public Utilities Papers: Vol. 1987). (Illus.). 661p. reprint ed. pap. 200.00 (*0-608-20499-4*, 207175100002) Bks Demand.
— Public Utility Regulation in an Environment of Change: Proceedings of the Institute of Public Utilities Seventeenth Annual Conference, Williamsburg, VA, 1985. Mann, Patrick C. & Trebing, Harry M., eds. LC 87-81826. (MSU Public Utilities Papers: Vol. 1987). 605p. reprint ed. pap. 187.60 (*0-608-20500-1*, 207175200002) Bks Demand.
— Regulatory Responses to Continuously Changing Industry Structures: Proceedings of the Institute of Public Utilities Twenty-Third Annual Conference, Williamsburg, VA, 1991. LC 93-80037. (MSU Public Utilities Papers: Vol. 1991). (Illus.). 472p. reprint ed. pap. 146.40 (*0-608-20506-0*, 207175800002) Bks Demand.

Michigan State University, Project Physnet Staff. Introduction to Physics, Vol. I. (C). 1993. pap. text 30.00 (*1-881592-34-0*) Hayden-McNeil.
— Introduction to Physics, Vol. II. (C). 1993. pap. text 30.00 (*1-881592-21-9*) Hayden-McNeil.

An Asterisk (*) at the beginning of an entry indicates that the title is appearing for the first time.

M

An Asterisk (*) at the beginning of an entry indicates that the title is appearing for the first time.

— One Must Wait. 304p. 1999. pap. 6.50 (*0-312-97186-9*, St Martins Paperbacks) St Martin.

*Mickelbury, Penny. The Step Between. LC 99-42199. 240p. 2000. 22.00 (*0-684-85990-4*) S&S Trade.

Mickelbury, Penny. Where to Choose. LC 98-47703. 255p. 1999. 22.00 (*0-684-83742-0*) Simon & Schuster.

***Mickelbury, Penny.** Where to Choose. 2001. reprint ed. pap. write for info. (*0-312-97708-5*, St Martins Paperbacks) St Martin.

Mickelen, Alvera. How to Write Missionary Letters. 6th rev. ed. (Illus.). 56p. (Orig.). 1995. pap. 4.95 (*0-9623741-1-3*) Media Assocs Intl.

Mickels, Kathy, jt. auth. see McKeever, Audrey.

Mickelsen, A. Berkeley & Mickelsen, Alvera M. Understanding Scripture: How to Read & Study the Bible. LC 92-7905. 142p. 1992. pap. 9.95 (*0-943575-84-2*) Hendrickson MA.

Mickelsen, Alvera, ed. Women, Authority & the Bible. LC 86-7158. 304p. (Orig.). 1986. pap. 16.99 (*0-87784-608-1*, 608) InterVarsity.

Mickelsen, Alvera & Mickelsen, Berkley. Family Bible Encyclopedia, 2 vols. Incl. Vol. 1. A - K. LC 78-55384. 1978. 9.95 (*0-89191-100-6*); Vol. 2. L - Z. LC 78-55384. 1978. 9.95 (*0-89191-127-8*); LC 78-55384. (Illus.). 1978. 12.95 (*0-89191-201-0*) Cook.

Mickelsen, Alvera M., jt. auth. see Mickelsen, A. Berkeley.

Mickelsen, Berkley, jt. auth. see Mickelsen, Alvera.

M

Mickelsen, Carol. Camping Your Way Through Europe: The Dream Trip You Thought You Couldn't Afford. (Illus.). 275p. Date not set. pap. 14.95 (*0-9652421-0-2*) Affordable Travel.

Mickelsen, William C. & Riemann, Hugo. Hugo Riemann's Theory of Harmony Bk. III: A Study & History of Music Theory. LC 76-15366. 279p. reprint ed. pap. 86.50 (*0-8357-7772-3*, 203613200002) Bks Demand.

Mickelson, Alan R. Guided Wave Optics. 1993. text 64.95 (*0-442-00715-9*, VNR) Wiley.

— Physical Optics. (Illus.). 320p. 1992. text 64.95 (*0-442-00614-4*, VNR) Wiley.

— Theory of Optical Communications. 1992. text. write for info. (*0-442-00714-0*, VNR) Wiley.

Mickelson, Belle. Animals of the Seas & Wetlands: Alaska Sea Week Curriculum Series, Grade 1. (Alaska Sea Grant Report: No. 85-11). (Illus.). 220p. 1985. teacher ed., ring bd. 12.00 (*1-56612-015-2*) AK Sea Grant CP.

— Discovery, an Introduction: Alaska Sea Week Curriculum Series, Grade Kindergarten. (Alaska Sea Grant Report: No. 83-06). (Illus.). 130p. (Orig.). 1983. reprint ed. pap., teacher ed. 6.50 (*1-56612-019-5*) AK Sea Grant CP.

— Marine Mammals, Coastal & River Issues. (Alaska Sea Week Curriculum Ser.). (Illus.). 186p. 1994. reprint ed. teacher ed., ring bd. 12.50 (*1-56612-023-3*) AK Sea Grant CP.

Mickelson, Belle, jt. auth. see Barr, N.

Mickelson, Bonnie S. Hollyhocks & Radishes: Mrs. Chard's Almanac Cookbook. LC 89-90856. (Illus.). 307p. 1989. 26.95 (*0-9622412-1-0*); pap. 19.95 (*0-9622412-0-2*) Pickle Point.

Mickelson, Bonnie S., ed. The Overlake School Cookbook: The Little Blue Book of Great Recipes. rev. ed. (Illus.). 182p. 1993. reprint ed. 13.95 (*0-9622412-6-1*) Pickle Point.

— Private Collection, 2 vols., Set. 1994. boxed set 35.95 (*0-685-65601-2*) Pickle Point.

— A Recipe Treasury. (Illus.). 80p. 1992. ring bd. 19.95 (*0-9622412-2-9*) Pickle Point.

Mickelson, Bonnie S., ed. see Junior League of Palo Alto Staff.

Mickelson, Bonnie S., ed. see Overlake School Staff.

***Mickelson, David M., et al.** Glacial Processes, Past & Present. LC 99-50399. 1999. write for info. (*0-8137-2337-X*) Geol Soc.

Mickelson-Gaughan, Joan, ed. Milestones in Western Civilization Vol. 1: Selected Readings: Ancient Greece Through the Middle Ages. LC 90-46171. (Illus.). 447p. 1990. 52.00 (*0-8108-2188-5*) Scarecrow.

— Milestones in Western Civilization Vol. III: Selected Readings: 1815 to the Present. (Illus.). 552p. 1998. 57.50 (*0-8108-3205-4*) Scarecrow.

Mickelson-Gaughan, Joan, intro. Milestones in Western Civilization Vol. 2: Selected Readings: The Renaissance Through Waterloo. LC 90-46171. 439p. 1991. 52.00 (*0-8108-2508-2*) Scarecrow.

Mickelson, James S., jt. auth. see Haynes, Karen S.

***Mickelson, Joy-Ruth.** Our Sons Were Labeled Behavior Disordered: Here Are the Stories of Our Lives. LC 99-58211. 224p. 2000. 48.00 (*1-891928-06-6*); pap. 23.95 (*1-891928-05-8*) Educ Intl Pr.

Mickelson, Marlys. Biking in Vikingland. rev. ed. 1993. pap. 7.95 (*0-934860-00-9*) Adventure Pubns.

— Biking Vikingland's Rail & Trails. 106p. 1997. pap. text 9.95 (*1-885061-20-X*) Adventure Pubns.

— Seat Yourself: A Complete Guide to Twin Cities Arenas, Auditoriums & Theaters. 2nd ed. (Illus.). 76p. 1990. reprint ed. pap. 8.95 (*0-934860-75-0*) Adventure Pubns.

Mickelson, Paul. Gospel Flute. 80p. 1995. pap. 9.95 (*0-7866-0505-7*, 95476) Mel Bay.

— Gospel Trumpet. 80p. 1995. pap. 9.95 (*0-7866-0506-5*, 95477) Mel Bay.

Mickelson, Peter G. Natural History of Alaska's Prince William Sound & How to Enjoy It. (Illus.). 210p. (Orig.). (C). 1989. pap. 9.95 (*0-317-93866-5*) AK Wild Wings.

***Mickelson, Robert P., et al.** Transportation Development Process. LC 98-67634. (Synthesis of Highway Practice Ser.). 48p. 1998. write for info. (*0-309-06820-7*) Natl Acad Pr.

***Mickelson, Roslyn A.** Children on the Streets of the Americas: Globalization, Homelessness Education in Brazil, Cuba & the United States. LC 99-22989. 300p. 1999. pap. 22.99 (*0-415-92322-0*) Routledge.

***Mickelson, Roslyn Arlin, ed.** Children on Streets of the Americas: Globalization Homelessness & Education in United States Brazil & China. LC 99-22989. 304p. (C). 2000. text. write for info. (*0-415-92321-2*) Routledge.

Mickelson, Sig. America's Other Voice: The Story of Radio Free Europe & Radio Liberty. LC 83-13659. 269p. 1983. 55.00 (*0-275-91722-3*, C1722, Praeger Pubs) Greenwood.

***Mickelson, Sig.** The Decade That Shaped Television News: CBS in the 1950s. LC 97-32044. 264p. 1998. 39.95 (*0-275-95567-2*, Praeger Pubs) Greenwood.

Mickelson, Sig. From Whistle Stop to Sound Bite: Four Decades of Politics & Television. LC 89-3554. 196p. 1989. 55.00 (*0-275-92351-7*, C2351, Praeger Pubs); pap. 19.95 (*0-275-92632-X*, B2632, Praeger Pubs) Greenwood.

Mickelson, Sig & Teran, Elena M., eds. The First Amendment - The Challenge of New Technology. LC 88-19037. 132p. 1989. 39.95 (*0-275-93088-2*, C3088, Praeger Pubs) Greenwood.

Mickelsson, J. Current Algebras & Groups. (Monographs in Nonlinear Physics). (Illus.). 332p. (C). 1989. text 95.00 (*0-306-43363-X*, Kluwer Plenum) Kluwer Academic.

Mickelsson, J. & Pekonen, O., eds. Topological & Geometrical Methods in Field Theory: Proceedings of the 2nd International Symposium, Turku, Finland, 26 May-1 June 1991. 448p. 1992. text 109.00 (*981-02-0961-4*) World Scientific Pub.

Mickelthwait, Lucy, selected by. I Spy a Freight Train: Transportation in Art. LC 95-36429. (Illus.). 32p. (J). (ps-3). 1996. 19.00 (*0-688-14700-3*, Grenwillow Bks) HarpC Child Bks.

Mickelton, Coleman T. & Stephen, White C. Early Childhood Education: Building a Philosophy for Teaching. LC 99-11342. (Illus.). 416p. (C). 1999. teacher ed. 52.00 (*0-02-427222-1*, Macmillan Coll) P-H.

Mickens, Allison C., ed. see Valerio, Maurice.

Mickens, Ed. The One Hundred Best Companies for Gay Men & Lesbians. Isaacson, Dana, ed. 288p. (Orig.). 1994. per. 12.00 (*0-671-87479-9*) PB.

Mickens, June, et al. Making Good Decisions about Kinship Care. LC 96-39922. 1997. 19.95 (*1-57073-380-5*) Amer Bar Assn.

***Mickens, Ronald E.** Applications of Nonstandard Finite Difference Schemes. LC 00-28292. 2000. write for info. (*981-02-4133-X*) World Scientific Pub.

Mickens, Ronald E. Difference Equations Theory & Applications. 2nd ed. 448p. (gr. 13). 1991. ring bd. 73.95 (*0-442-00136-3*, Chap & Hall CRC) CRC Pr.

— Nonstandard Finite Difference Models of Differential Equations. 250p. 1993. text 61.00 (*981-02-1458-8*) World Scientific Pub.

— Oscillations in Planar Phase-Space Dynamic Systems. LC 95-44982. (Series on Advances in Mathematics for Applied Sciences). 250p. 1996. text 48.00 (*981-02-2292-0*) World Scientific Pub.

Mickens, Ronald E., ed. Mathematics & Science. 352p. (C). 1990. pap. 32.00 (*981-02-0234-2*); text 101.00 (*981-02-0233-4*) World Scientific Pub.

Mickey, M. P. Cowrie Shell Miao of Kweichow. (Harvard University Peabody Museum of Archaeology & Ethnology Papers). 1972. reprint ed. pap. 25.00 (*0-527-01282-3*) Periodicals Srv.

Mickey Old Coyote, Lloyd G. & Smith, Helene. Apsaalooka: The Crow Nation Then & Now. rev. ed. Snyder, Catherine, ed. LC 92-82527. (Illus.). 251p. (Orig.). 1993. pap. 29.95 (*0-945437-11-0*) MacDonald-Sward.

— Flag & Emblem of the Apsaalooka Native. Snyder, Catherine, ed. LC 94-48414. (Illus.). 75p. (Orig.). 1995. pap. 14.95 (*0-945437-17-X*) MacDonald-Sward.

Mickey, Paul A. Breaking Free from Wedlock Deadlock: Popular Myths That Cause, Christian Truths That Cure. LC 88-72131. 192p. (Orig.). 1988. pap. 7.95 (*0-917851-16-1*) Bristol Hse.

***Mickey, Paul A.** Twelve Keys to a Better Marriage. Orig. Title: Tough Marriage. 224p. 1998. reprint ed. pap. 9.95 (*1-885224-16-8*) Bristol Hse.

Mickey, Paul A. & Proctor, William. Twelve Keys to a Better Marriage. Orig. Title: Tough Marriage. 224p. 1990. pap. 8.99 (*0-310-53981-1*) Zondervan.

Mickey, Paul A., jt. auth. see Ashmore, Ginny.

Mickey, Paul A., jt. auth. see Ashmore, Ginny W.

Mickey, Robert S., jt. auth. see Cunningham, Peter S.

Mickey, Thomas J. Sociodrama: An Interpretive Theory for the Practice of Public Relations. 136p. (Orig.). (C). Date not set. lib. bdg. 42.00 (*0-7618-0027-1*) U Pr of Amer.

— Sociodrama: An Interpretive Theory for the Practice of Public Relations. 136p. (Orig.). (C). 1995. pap. text 22.00 (*0-7618-0028-X*) U Pr of Amer.

Mickiewicz, A., jt. auth. see Blaszak, Maaiej.

Mickiewicz, Adam. Pan Tadeus. Mackenzie, Kennety R., tr. from POL. LC 93-195891. (Illus.). 598p. 1992. pap. 19.95 (*0-7818-0033-1*) Hippocrene Bks.

Mickiewicz, Ellen P. Changing Channels: Television & the Struggle for Power in Russia. (Illus.). 368p. 1997. 35.00 (*0-19-510163-4*) OUP.

— International Security & Arms Control. Koldowicz, Roman, ed. LC 86-15073. 183p. 1986. 55.00 (*0-275-92186-7*, C2186, Praeger Pubs) Greenwood.

— Media & the Russian Public. LC 80-21544. 156p. 1981. 42.95 (*0-275-90682-5*, C0682, Praeger Pubs) Greenwood.

***Mickiewicz, Ellen Propper.** Changing Channels: Television & the Struggle for Power in Russia. rev. ed. LC 99-28624. 416p. 1999. pap. 19.95 (*0-8223-2463-6*) Duke.

***Mickiewicz, Ellen Propper & Roselle, Laura.** Democracy on the Air. LC 99-52026. 1999. pap. write for info. (*0-9673605-0-1*) Duke U De Wit.

***Mickiewicz, Ellen Propper, et al.** Television & Elections. 2nd ed. LC 99-52029. 1999. pap. write for info. (*0-9673605-1-X*) Duke U De Wit.

Micklas, Sebastian. Verses in a Minor Chord. (Illus.). 83p. 1985. pap. 1.95 (*0-8199-0888-6*, Frncscn Herld) Franciscan Pr.

Mickle, James E. Taxonomy of Specimens of the Pennsylvanian-Age Marattialean Fern Psaronius from Ohio & Illinois. (Scientific Papers: Vol. XIX). (Illus.). vii, 64p. (Orig.). 1984. pap. 5.00 (*0-89792-101-1*) Ill St Museum.

***Mickle, Kathryn.** Journey to Mastery: Feng Shui for Life. (Illus.). 161p. 2000. pap. 14.95 (*1-889890-03-0*) Wellness Inst of Res.

Mickle, M. M. & Da Costa, Francisco. Say It in Portuguese. (Orig.). 1955. pap. 3.95 (*0-486-20809-5*) Dover.

Mickle, Shelley F. The Queen of October. (Front Porch PB Ser.). 320p. 1992. pap. 8.95 (*1-56512-003-5*, 72003) Algonquin Bks.

— Replacing Dad. 266p. 1993. 16.95 (*1-56512-017-5*) Algonquin Bks.

***Mickle, Shelley Fraser.** The Kids Are Gone, the Dog Is Depressed & Mom's on the Loose. LC 00-101312. 240p. 2000. 17.95 (*0-9672788-1-3*, SFM-2) Alachua Pr.

Mickleburgh, John. Consumer Protection. 1979. pap. 30.00 (*0-903486-49-0*, UK, MICHIE) LEXIS Pub.

Micklem, Caryl, et al. Duty & Delight: Routley Remembered. Leaver, Robin A. et al, eds. LC 85-60220. 310p. 1985. 29.95 (*0-916642-27-5*, 782) Hope Pub.

Micklem, Nathaniel. National Socialism & the Roman Catholic Church. LC 78-63696. (Studies in Fascism: Ideology & Practice). (Illus.). 280p. reprint ed. 31.00 (*0-404-16957-0*) AMS Pr.

— The Theology of Politics. 1977. 13.95 (*0-8369-7119-1*, 7953) Ayer.

Micklem, Niel. The Nature of Hysteria. LC 95-18320. 144p. (C). 1995. 45.00 (*0-415-12186-8*) Routledge.

Mickler, Ernest M. White Trash Cooking. LC 85-80302. (Illus.). 134p. 1986. spiral bd. 19.95 (*0-89815-189-9*) Ten Speed Pr.

— White Trash Cooking II. LC 96-48635. (Illus.). 138p. 1996. spiral bd. 19.95 (*0-89815-892-3*) Ten Speed Pr.

Mickler, Michael L. A History of the Unification Church in America 1959-1974: Emergence of a National Movement. LC 93-27146. (Cults & Nonconventional Religious Groups Ser.). 240p. 1993. 56.00 (*0-8153-1138-9*) Garland.

Mickler, R. A. & Fox, S., eds. The Productivity & Sustainability of Southern Forest Ecosystems in a Changing Environment. LC 97-10648. (Ecological Studies: Vol. 128). (Illus.). 944p. 1998. 164.00 (*0-387-94851-1*) Spr-Verlag.

Mickler, Renee. Feeling Lost at Work: Understanding the Impact of Corporate Change on Your Life. 1995. pap. 14.95 (*0-9646983-0-7*) Media Futura.

Mickler, Robert A., jt. ed. see Fox, Susan.

Mickler, Robert A., ed. see Hom, John L.

Mickler, Steve. The Myth of Privilege: Aboriginal Status, Media Visions & Public Ideas. 346p. 1998. 19.95 (*1-86368-249-X*, Pub. by Fremantle Arts) Intl Spec Bk.

Mickles, Morgan, jt. auth. see Breitling, Wolf.

***Micklethwait, David.** Noah Webster & the American Dictionary. LC 99-39094. (Illus.). 358p. 2000. lib. bdg. 49.95 (*0-7864-0640-2*) McFarland & Co.

Micklethwait, John & Wooldridge, Adrian. The Witch Doctors: Making Sense of the Management Gurus. LC 96-6793. 272p. 1996. 25.00 (*0-8129-2833-4*, Times Bks) Crown Pub Group.

— The Witch Doctors: Making Sense of the Management Gurus. 304p. 1998. pap. 15.00 (*0-8129-2988-8*, Times Bks) Crown Pub Group.

***Micklethwait, John & Woolridge, Adrian.** Future Perfect: The Challenge & Hidden Pursuit of Globalization. LC 99-54251. 416p. 2000. 27.50 (*0-8129-3096-7*, Times Bks) Crown Pub Group.

Micklethwait, Lucy. A Child's Book of Play in Art: Great Pictures Great Fun. (Illus.). 48p. 1996. 16.95 (*0-7894-1003-6*) DK Pub Inc.

Micklethwait, Lucy. I Spy: An Alphabet in Art. 64p. (J). (ps-3). 1996. pap. 9.95 (*0-688-14730-5*, Wm Morrow) Morrow Avon.

— I Spy Two Eyes: Numbers in Art. (Illus.). (J). 1999. 15.15 (*0-606-15581-3*) Turtleback.

Micklethwait, Lucy. Spot a Cat. LC 94-44797. (Illus.). 32p. (J). (ps-7). 1995. 9.95 (*0-7894-0144-4*, 5-70595) DK Pub Inc.

— Spot a Dog: A Child's Book of Art. LC 94-48608. (Illus.). 32p. (J). (ps-7). 1995. 9.95 (*0-7894-0145-2*, 5-70596) DK Pub Inc.

Micklethwait, Lucy, compiled by. A Child's Book of Art: Discover Great Paintings. LC 98-37537. (J). 1999. 16.95 (*0-7894-4283-3*) DK Pub Inc.

Micklethwait, Lucy, creator. I Spy Two Eyes: Numbers in Art. LC 92-35641. (Illus.). 48p. (J). (ps-3). 1993. 19.00 (*0-688-12640-5*, Grenwillow Bks) HarpC Child Bks.

Micklethwait, Lucy, selected by. A Child's Book of Art: Great Pictures, First Words. LC 92-54320. (Illus.). 64p. (J). (gr. k up). 1993. 16.95 (*1-56458-203-5*) DK Pub Inc.

— I Spy: An Alphabet in Art. LC 91-42212. (Illus.). 64p. (J). (ps-3). 1992. 19.00 (*0-688-11679-5*, Grenwillow Bks) HarpC Child Bks.

— I Spy a Lion: Animals in Art. LC 93-30017. 48p. (J). (ps-3). 1994. 19.00 (*0-688-13230-8*, Grenwillow Bks) HarpC Child Bks.

***Micklethwaite, Lucy.** I Spy Two Eyes: Numbers in Art. (Illus.). 48p. (J). (gr. k-3). 1998. pap. 9.95 (*0-688-16158-8*, Wm Morrow) Morrow Avon.

Micklethwaite Peterson, Dawn, jt. auth. see Connor, Richard C.

Micklewright, M., jt. auth. see Atkinson, A. B.

Mickley, Linda D., jt. ed. see Fox, M. W.

Mickley, Linda D., ed. see Fox, Michael A.

Mickley, M. F. Mickley: Genealogy of the Mickley Family of America, with a Brief General Record of the Michelet Family of Metz & Some Interesting & Valuable Correspondence, Biographical Sketches, Obits & History Memorabilia. (Illus.). 182p. 1991. reprint ed. pap. 27.50 (*0-8328-1708-2*); reprint ed. lib. bdg. 37.50 (*0-8328-1707-4*) Higginson Bk Co.

Micklin, Lee. Born Cree: The Life of Pete Hawley, of Sitting Horse Drum. (Illus.). 1998. pap. 17.95 (*0-9632138-2-2*) Seattle Indian.

Micklin, M. & Poston, D. L. Continuities in Sociological Human Ecology. LC 97-38054. (Series on Demographic Methods & Population Analysis). (Illus.). 390p. (C). 1998. 49.50 (*0-306-45610-9*, Plenum Trade) Perseus Pubng.

Micklin, Michael, jt. ed. see Olsen, Marvin E.

Micklin, Philip P. Water & the New States of Central Asia. 60p. 1997. pap. 12.95 (*1-86203-000-6*, Pub. by Royal Inst Intl Affairs) Brookings.

Micklin, Philip P., ed. see North Atlantic Treaty Organization Staff, et al.

Micklitsch, Christine N. & Ryan-Mitlyng, Theresa A. Physician Performance Management: Tool for Survival & Success. (Illus.). 122p. (Orig.). 1996. pap. 75.00 (*1-56829-078-0*, 4928) Med Group Mgmt.

Micklitz, Hans W. & Reich, Norbert. Legal Aspects of European Space Policy. 151p. 1989. pap. 36.00 (*3-7890-1875-9*, Pub. by Nomos Verlags) Intl Bk Import.

Micklitz, Hans W. & Weatherill, Stephen. European Economic Law. LC 97-18967. (TEMPUS Ser.). 576p. 1997. pap. 48.95 (*1-85521-562-4*, Pub. by Dartmth Pub); text 96.95 (*1-85521-557-8*, Pub. by Dartmth Pub) Ashgate Pub Co.

Micklo, Stephen J., jt. auth. see Helton, Sonia M.

Micklos, David A. & Freyer, Greg A. DNA Science: A First Course in Recombinant DNA Technology. (Illus.). 477p. 1990. pap. 32.95 (*0-89278-411-3*) Carolina Biological.

***Micklos, John.** Daddy Poems. (Illus.). (J). 2000. pap. 8.95 (*1-56397-870-9*) Boyds Mills Pr.

***Micklos, John, Jr., ed.** Mommy Poems. (Illus.). 32p. (J). 2000. 15.95 (*1-56397-849-0*); pap. 8.95 (*1-56397-908-X*, Wordsong) Boyds Mills Pr.

Micklus, Robert. The Comic Genius of Dr. Alexander Hamilton. LC 89-22468. 232p. 1990. text 28.00 (*0-87049-633-6*) U of Tenn Pr.

Micklus, Robert, ed. see Hamilton, Alexander.

Mickolus, Edward F. International Terrorism: Attributes of Terrorist Events, 1968-1977 (ITERATE 2) LC 82-82385. 1982. write for info. (*0-89138-927-X*, ICPSR 7947) ICPSR.

— Terrorism, 1988-1991: A Chronology of Events & a Selectively Annotated Bibliography, 6. LC 92-46525. (Bibliographies & Indexes in Military Studies: No. 6). 928p. 1993. lib. bdg. 165.00 (*0-313-28970-0*, GR8970, Greenwood Pr) Greenwood.

— Transnational Terrorism: A Chronology of Events, 1968-1979. LC 79-6829. 967p. 1980. lib. bdg. 145.00 (*0-313-22206-1*, MTT/, Greenwood Pr) Greenwood.

Mickolus, Edward F., compiled by. The Literature of Terrorism: A Selectively Annotated Bibliography. LC 80-541. 553p. 1980. lib. bdg. 125.00 (*0-313-22265-7*, MLT/, Greenwood Pr) Greenwood.

Mickolus, Edward F. & Flemming, Peter A., eds. Terrorism, 1980-1987: A Selectively Annotated Bibliography, 8. LC 87-32275. (Bibliographies & Indexes in Law & Political Science Ser.: No. 8). 323p. 1988. lib. bdg. 99.50 (*0-313-26248-9*, MKT) Greenwood.

Mickolus, Edward F. & Simmons, Susan L. Terrorism, 1992-1995: A Chronology of Events & a Selectively Annotated Bibliography, 9. LC 97-9149. (Bibliographies & Indexes in Military Studies: vOL. 9). 980p. 1997. lib. bdg. 145.00 (*0-313-30468-8*, Greenwood Pr) Greenwood.

Mickolus, Edward F., et al. International Terrorism in the 1980s Vol. 2, 1984-1985: A Chronology of Events. LC 88-19891. 794p. 1989. reprint ed. pap. 200.00 (*0-608-06857-8*, 206706300002) Bks Demand.

Micks, Marianne H. Deep Waters: An Exploration of Baptism. 107p. (Orig.). 1996. pap. 9.95 (*1-56101-126-6*) Cowley Pubns.

— Future Present: The Phenomenon of Christian Worship. LC 75-103844. 1984. 6.95 (*0-8164-2109-9*) Harper SF.

— Loving the Questions: An Exploration of the Nicene Creed. LC 93-22816. 134p. 1993. pap. 9.95 (*1-56101-081-2*) Cowley Pubns.

— Loving the Questions: An Exploration of the Nicene Creed. LC 93-22816. 144p. (C). 1993. pap. 11.00 (*1-56338-072-2*) TPI PA.

Mickulecky, Bea. Basic Reading Power. LC 97-146721. 176p. 1996. pap. text 22.77 (*0-201-84673-X*) Addison-Wesley.

— Reading Power. 2nd ed. 304p. 1997. pap. text 22.40 (*0-201-84674-8*) Addison-Wesley.

Mickunas, Algis & Pilotta, Joseph. Technocracy vs. Democracy: Issues in the Politics of Communication. LC 97-46115. (Communication Ser.). 224p. (C). 1998. text 42.50 (*1-57273-106-0*); pap. text 18.95 (*1-57273-107-9*) Hampton Pr NJ.

Mickunas, Algis, jt. auth. see Pilotta, Joseph J.

Mickunas, Algis, jt. auth. see Stewart, David.

Mickunas, Algis, jt. intro. see Kramer, Eric M.

Mickunas, Algis, tr. see Gebser, Jean.

Mickunas, Algis, tr. see Stroker, Elisabeth.

Mickunes, Algis, jt. auth. see Stewart, David.

An Asterisk (*) at the beginning of an entry indicates that the title is appearing for the first time.

Mickwitz, Gunnar. Geld und Wirtschaft im Romischen Reich des vierten Jahrhunderts N. Chr. Finley, Moses, ed. LC 79-4991. (Ancient Economic History Ser.). (GER.). 1979. reprint ed. lib. bdg. 25.95 (*0-405-12380-9*) Ayer.

Mickwitz, Per. Implementation of Key Environmental Principles: Experiences from the Baltic Sea Nord 1998:2. LC 99-183778. 161p. 1998. pap. 20.00 (*92-893-0142-2*, NC1422, Pub. by Nordic Coun Minsters) Bernan Associates.

Miclet, Laurent & De La Higuera, Colin. Grammatical Inference: Learning Syntax from Sentences:Third International Colloquium, ICGI-96, Montpellier, France, September 1996 Proceedings, Vol. 114. LC 96-43282. (Lecture Notes on Artificial Intelligence). viii, 327p. 1996. 56.00 (*3-540-61778-7*) Spr-Verlag.

Mico, Jose, tr. see Reuter, Paul.

Micocci, Harriet. Captain Orkle's Treasure. (Illus.). (J). (gr. 3-7). 1961. 10.95 (*0-8392-3003-6*) Astor-Honor.

Micoch, Jan. Frantisek Drtikol: Photographs 1901-1914. 1999. 30.00 (*80-86217-08-6*) Kant.

Micolean, Tyler, jt. auth. see Moore, James.

Micolo, Anthony M. Practical Supervision: How to Organize for Effectiveness. Bruce, Stephen E., ed. 322p. 1987. ring bd. 63.71 (*1-55645-427-9*, 427) Busn Legal Reports.

Micon. Song for Healing. 1994. 15.98 (*1-885394-02-0*) Bluestar Communs.

Micone, Marco. Beyond the Ruins. MacDougall, Jill, tr. (Drama Ser.: No. 10). 78p. 1995. pap. 8.00 (*0-920717-86-1*) Guernica Editions.

— Gens du Silence. (FRE.). 1991. pap. write for info. (*2-89135-026-X*) Guernica Editions.

— Two Plays. 180p. 1988. pap. 10.00 (*0-919349-72-2*) Guernica Editions.

Micoref Educational Systems Staff. Lotus 1-2-3 with Template. 1986. pap. 19.95 (*0-913365-05-X*) Microref Educ Systs.

— Microref for MS & PC-DOS. 1986. pap. 19.95 (*0-913365-09-2*) Microref Educ Systs.

— Quattro Pro 1.O - 2.O Quick Ref. 1991. pap. 19.95 (*0-913365-89-0*) Microref Educ Systs.

— WordPerfect for Windows Quick Reference. 1992. pap. 19.95 (*1-56351-072-3*) Microref Educ Systs.

— WordPerfect for Windows Quick Reference Version 5.1 & 5.2. 1993. pap. 14.95 (*1-56351-207-6*) Microref Educ Systs.

— WordStar 4.0-6.0 Quick Reference Guide. 1990. pap. 19.95 (*0-01-336561-4*) Microref Educ Systs.

***Micou, Paul.** Last Word. 2000. pap. 9.95 (*0-552-99502-9*, Pub. by Transworld Publishers Ltd) Trafalgar.

Micou, Paul. The Music Programme. 1990. 16.95 (*1-55972-023-9*, Birch Ln Pr) Carol Pub Group.

***Micou, Paul.** Rotten Times. 2000. pap. 9.95 (*0-552-99501-0*, Pub. by Transworld Publishers Ltd) Trafalgar.

Micovic, P. Health Planning & Management Glossary. (SEARO Regional Health Papers: No. 2). 316p. 1984. pap. text 10.00 (*92-9022-171-2*) World Health.

***Micozzi.** Fundamentals of Comparative & Alternative Medicine. 2000. pap. text. write for info. (*0-323-01192-6*) Mosby Inc.

Micozzi, Marc S. Current Review of Complementary Medicine. LC 99-12780. 1999. 49.95 (*1-57340-129-3*) Current Med.

***Micozzi, Marc S.** Doctors Advice on Alternative Medicine. 2000. pap. text 29.95 (*0-9670772-9-X*) Integratv Med Commn.

Micozzi, Marc S. Postmortem Change in Human & Animal Remains: A Systematic Approach. (Illus.). 136p. 1991. pap. 23.95 (*0-398-06288-9*); text 34.95 (*0-398-05747-8*) C C Thomas.

Micozzi, Marc S., ed. Fundamentals of Complementary & Alternative Medicine. LC 95-39128. (Complementary & Alternative Medicine Ser.). 303p. 1995. pap. text 44.00 (*0-443-05355-3*) Church.

Micozzi, Marc S. & Moon, Thomas E. Macronutrients: Investigating Their Role in Cancer. (Illus.). 496p. 1992. text 210.00 (*0-8247-8593-2*) Dekker.

Micozzi, Marc S., jt. auth. see Moon, Thomas E.

Micro Analysis & Design Staff. Micro SAINT User's Guide. (Version 2.0 Ser.). 1986. text 50.00 (*0-937197-01-7*) Micro Analysis.

— Micro SAINT User's Guide. rev. ed. (Version 2.2 Ser.). 1986. text 50.00 (*0-937197-05-X*) Micro Analysis.

— Micro SAINT User's Guide: Version 2.1. 1986. 50.00 (*0-937197-03-3*) Micro Analysis.

— Micro SAINT User's Guide: Version 3.0. 1987. 60.00 (*0-317-64493-9*) Micro Analysis.

Micro House Staff. Network Technical Guide. LC 98-131562. 1997. pap. text 49.95 incl. cd-rom (*1-880252-31-7*) Micro Hse.

Micro House Staff, jt. auth. see Mueller, Scott.

Micro Magazine Staff. Exploring Assembly Language Programming on Your Commodore 64. write for info. (*0-318-58227-9*) P-H.

— Exploring Character Graphics on Your Commodore 64. write for info. (*0-318-58228-7*) P-H.

— Mastering Your Atari Through 8 BASIC Projects. write for info. (*0-318-58229-5*) P-H.

— Mastering Your Commodore 64 Through Eight BASIC Projects. write for info. (*0-318-58230-9*) P-H.

Micro Modeling Associates, Inc. Staff. Microsoft Web Commerce Solutions. LC 99-10307. 800p. 1999. pap. 49.99 (*0-7356-0579-3*) Microsoft.

Micro Modeling Associates Staff. Microsoft Intranet Solutions. LC 97-7687. 500p. 1997. pap. text 39.99 (*1-57231-509-1*) Microsoft.

Micro Reference Staff. Shortcuts Windows 95. 60p. Date not set. pap. 2.95 (*1-56351-248-3*) Microref Educ Systs.

— Super Shortcuts Access 97. 80p. 1997. pap. 4.95 (*1-56351-347-1*) Microref Educ Systs.

— Super Shortcuts Excel 97. 80p. 1997. pap. 4.95 (*1-56351-345-5*) Microref Educ Systs.

— Super Shortcuts Outlook 97. 80p. 1997. pap. 4.95 (*1-56351-373-0*) Microref Educ Systs.

— Super Shortcuts Power Point 97. 80p. 1997. pap. 4.95 (*1-56351-372-2*) Microref Educ Systs.

— Super Shortcuts Word 97. 80p. 1997. pap. 4.95 (*1-56351-344-7*) Microref Educ Systs.

Microbiological Standardization, Permanent Section, ed. Brucellosis: Proceedings of the International Symposium on Standardization & Control of Vaccines & Reagents, 24, Tunise & Bourse du Travail, 1968. (Immunobiological Standardization Symposia Ser.: Vol. 12). 1970. 26.25 (*3-8055-0634-1*) S Karger.

MicroCase Corporation Staff. American Government: An Introduction Using MicroCase. 1997. pap. 21.00 (*0-15-504039-1*) Harcourt Coll Pubs.

Microcase Corporation Staff. MicroCase Analysis System Reference Manual: Version 3. (Illus.). 400p. 1994. pap. 24.95 (*0-922914-14-1*) MicroCase.

MicroCase Corporation Staff, jt. auth. see Stark, Rodney.

Microcase Staff. American Government: An Introduction to Using Microcase. 1996. pap. text 24.00 (*0-15-503939-3*, Pub. by Harcourt Coll Pubs) Harcourt.

Microcosmos-B. U. Staff. The Microcosmos Curriculum Guide to Exploring Microbial Space. 480p. 1994. boxed set 44.95 (*0-8403-8515-3*) Kendall-Hunt.

Microfax Staff. Microfax Gallimimus. (J). 1997. pap. text 0.99 (*0-7894-2125-9*) DK Pub Inc.

Microfax Staff, ed. The Lost World. (J). 1997. pap. text 2.95 (*0-7894-2117-8*) DK Pub Inc.

Microlytics, Inc. Staff. Pocket Word Finder Thesaurus. 1990. mass mkt. 4.99 (*0-671-68613-5*) PB.

MicroMax International A.S. Staff. Prof. MicroMax Internet: CD Rom with activity book, IBM. 49.95 incl. cd-rom (*0-8219-1657-2*) EMC-Paradigm.

— Prof. MicroMax Windows 95: CD Rom with teacher's guide, IBM. 49.95 incl. cd-rom (*0-8219-1660-2*) EMC-Paradigm.

Micropal Staff. The Individual Investor's Guide to Low-Load Mutual Funds, 1997. 16th ed. LC 95-75595. 1997. pap. text 24.95 (*1-883328-00-4*) Am Assn Indiv Investors.

Microprocessor Report Newsletter Staff. Understanding RISC Microprocessors. 564p. 1993. pap. 79.95 (*1-56276-159-5*, Ziff-Davis Pr) Que.

— Understanding X86 Microprocessors. 318p. 1993. pap. 49.95 (*1-56276-158-7*, Ziff-Davis Pr) Que.

Microref Educational Systems Staff. Microref, 1993 Guide Series. (Illus.). (Orig.). 1993. pap., spiral bd. 99.75 (*1-56351-098-7*) Microref Educ Systs.

— WordPerfect Quick Reference Guide. 1997. pap. text 14.95 (*1-56351-146-0*) Microref Educ Systs.

Micros, Marianne. Al Purdy: An Annotated Bibliography. 277p. (C). 1980. pap. 9.00 (*0-920763-61-8*, Pub. by ECW) Genl Dist Srvs.

***Microsoft Certified Trainers Staff.** MCSE Core Requirements. 3rd ed. (MCSE Exam Preparation Guide Ser.). (Illus.). 1999. pap. 149.96 (*0-7821-2699-5*) Sybex.

Microsoft Consulting Services Staff. Deploying Microsoft Exchange Server 5.5. LC 98-20388. 330p. 39.99 incl. cd-rom (*0-7356-0528-9*) Microsoft.

— Managing & Maintaining Microsoft Exchange Server 5.5. LC 98-22195. 300p. 39.99 incl. cd-rom (*0-7356-0529-7*) Microsoft.

***Microsoft Corporation.** Microsoft Windows 2000 Server Resource Kit. LC 99-45616. 2000. 299.99 incl. cd-rom (*1-57231-805-8*) Microsoft.

***Microsoft Corporation Staff.** ALS Networking Essentials Plus. 3rd ed. 950p. 2000. boxed set 55.00 (*0-7356-0912-8*) Microsoft Pr.

— Analyzing Requirements & Designing Solution Architectures MCSD Training: For Exam; 70-100. LC 99-33881. (Training Guide Ser.). (Illus.). 1999. pap. 69.99 (*0-7356-0854-7*) Microsoft.

Microsoft Corporation Staff. Automation Programmer's Reference. LC 97-4202. 450p. 1997. pap. text 24.99 (*1-57231-584-9*) Microsoft.

— Building Applications with Microsoft Outlook 2000. LC 99-20170. 528p. 1999. pap. 49.99 (*0-7356-0581-5*) Microsoft.

— Building Applications with Microsoft Outlook 98. LC 98-2769. 550p. 39.99 incl. cd-rom (*1-57231-718-3*) Microsoft.

— Computing Starts Here (gr. 8). 1997. cd-rom 29.99 (*1-57231-738-8*) Little.

— Computing Starts Here (gr. 8). 1998. cd-rom 29.99 (*1-57231-745-0*) Little.

— Deploying Microsoft Office 2000 Notes from the Field. LC 99-46114. 1999. pap. text 39.99 (*0-7356-0727-3*) Microsoft.

— Deploying Microsoft SQL Server 7.0 Notes from the Field. LC 99-23817. (Notes from the Field Ser.). (Illus.). 570p. 1999. pap. 39.99 (*0-7356-0726-5*) Microsoft.

— Developing for Microsoft Agent. LC 97-38025. 320p. 29.99 incl. cd-rom (*1-57231-720-5*) Microsoft.

— Dynamic HTML Reference & Software Development Kit / LC 98-55331. 700p. 1999. pap. 49.99 (*0 7356 0638-2*) Microsoft.

***Microsoft Corporation Staff.** Ecommerce Development. 1999. pap. text 49.95 (*0-7356-0891-1*) Microsoft.

Microsoft Corporation Staff. Encarta, Single User License. (NO - Novell/Wordperfect Ser.). 1995. 57.95 (*0-538-65623-9*) S-W Pub.

***Microsoft Corporation Staff.** Enterprise Development Using Microsoft Visual Basic 6.0. LC 99-33875. (Microsoft Mastering Ser.). 1999. pap. 49.99 (*0-7356-0901-2*) Microsoft.

Microsoft Corporation Staff. Foxpro for Windows. 1994. pap. 26.95 (*0-06-502442-7*) Addson-Wesley Educ.

— Home Essentials At a Glance. 1998. pap. write for info. (*1-57231-729-9*) Microsoft.

***Microsoft Corporation Staff.** Inside Microsoft Windows Media Technologies. 1999. pap. 39.99 (*0-7897-2225-9*) Que.

Microsoft Corporation Staff. Introducing Windows 95. LC 96-197907. (Professional Editions Ser.). 368p. 1995. pap. 12.95 (*1-55615-860-2*) Microsoft.

— Kit de Ressources Techniques Windows 95. (FRE.). 1552p. 1995. 195.00 (*0-7859-9848-9*) Fr & Eur.

— Learn Visual Basic 5 Now. 1998. pap. write for info. (*1-57231-445-1*) Microsoft.

— Managing a Microsoft Windows NT Network: Notes from the Field. LC 98-52142. 400p. 1999. pap. 39.99 (*0-7356-0647-1*) Microsoft.

***Microsoft Corporation Staff.** MCSE Online Training Kit, Microsoft Windows Network Infrastructure Administration 2000. 2000. pap. text 99.99 (*0-7356-0952-7*) Microsoft.

— MCSE Online Training Kit, Microsoft Windows Professional 2000. (IT-Training Kits Ser.). 2000. pap. text 99.99 (*0-7356-0953-5*) Microsoft.

— MCSE Online Training Kit, Microsoft Windows Server 2000. (IT-Training Kits Ser.). 2000. pap. 99.99 (*0-7356-0954-3*) Microsoft.

— MCSE Online Training Kit Windows Active Directory Services 2000. (IT-Training Kits Ser.). (Illus.). 2000. pap. text 99.99 (*0-7356-1008-8*) Microsoft.

Microsoft Corporation Staff. MCSE Readiness Review; Designing & Implementing Databases with Microsoft SQL Serve: Exam 70-026. LC 99-45690. 1999. pap. text 29.99 (*0-7356-0673-0*) Microsoft.

— MCSE Readiness Review Exam 70-058 Networking Essentials. LC 98-39270. 350p. 1998. 29.99 incl. cd-rom (*0-7356-0536-X*) Microsoft.

— MCSE Readiness Review Exam 70-073 Windows NT Workstation 4.0. LC 98-39269. 350p. 1998. 29.99 incl. cd-rom (*0-7356-0537-8*) Microsoft.

— MCSE Readiness Review Exam 70-067 Windows NT Server 4.0. LC 98-39271. 350p. 1999. 29.99 incl. cd-rom (*0-7356-0538-6*) Microsoft.

— MCSE Readiness Review Exam 70-059 TCP/IP. LC 99-20169. 350p. 1999. 29.99 incl. cd-rom (*0-7356-0540-8*) Microsoft.

***Microsoft Corporation Staff.** MCSE Readiness Review Exam 70-210 Installing, Configuring & Administering Microsoft Windows Pr. (MCSE Readiness Review Ser.). 2000. pap. text 24.99 (*0-7356-0949-7*) Microsoft.

— MCSE Readiness Review Exam 70-216: Implementing & Administrating a Microsoft Windows Network I. 2000. pap. 24.99 (*0-7356-0950-0*) Microsoft.

— MCSE Readiness Review Exam 70-215: Installing, Configuring & Administering Microsoft Windows SE. 2000. pap. 24.99 (*0-7356-0948-9*) Microsoft.

— MCSE Readiness Review Holiday. 1999. pap. text 99.99 (*0-7356-0923-3*) Microsoft.

— MCSE Training Kit: Microsoft Windows 2000 Infrastructure Administration. LC 00-24946. (Illus.). 520p. 2000. pap. 59.99 (*1-57231-904-6*) Microsoft.

Microsoft Corporation Staff. Microsoft BackOffice Resource Kit. 2nd ed. LC 98-2588. 2706p. 1998. 199.99 incl. cd-rom (*1-57231-632-2*, 868458) S&S Childrens.

— Microsoft BackOffice Resource Kit Pt. 2: Microsoft SQL Server, Pt. 2. LC 97-831. 500p. 1997. pap. text 79.99 incl. cd-rom (*1-57231-534-2*) Microsoft.

***Microsoft Corporation Staff.** Microsoft Backoffice Server 5.0 Integration & Interoperability Technical. 2000. 49.99 (*0-7356-1036-3*) Microsoft.

— Microsoft BackOffice Small Business Server 4.5 Resource Kit. LC 99-13774. 1000p. 1999. pap. 69.99 (*0-7356-0577-7*) Microsoft.

Microsoft Corporation Staff. Microsoft BackOffice 4.5 Resource Kit. LC 99-13771. 2500p. 1999. boxed set 199.99 (*0-7356-0583-1*) Microsoft.

— Microsoft Bookshelf, Single User License. (NO - Novell/Wordperfect Ser.). 1995. 44.95 (*0-538-65626-3*) S-W Pub.

— Microsoft Certified Professional + Internet Training Kit. LC 98-6122. 2224p. 299.99 incl. cd-rom (*1-57231-906-2*) Microsoft.

— Microsoft Certified Systems Engineer Core Requirements Training Kit. LC 98-6123. 2280p. 329.99 incl. cd-rom (*1-57231-905-4*) Microsoft.

— Microsoft Excel - Visual Basic Programmer's Guide for Windows 95: The Guide to Increasing Productivity with Microsoft Excel/Visual Basic. (Professional Editions Ser.). 368p. 1995. 24.95 (*1-55615-819-X*) Microsoft.

— Microsoft Excel - Visual Basic Reference: For Microsoft Excel for Windows 95 & for Microsoft Excel for Windows 3.1 & Macintosh Systems. 2nd ed. (Professional Editions Ser.). 848p. 1995. 29.95 (*1-55615-920-X*) Microsoft.

— Microsoft Excel Developer's Kit: For Microsoft Excel for Windows 95, & for Microsoft Excel for Windows 3.1 & Macintosh Systems. 3rd ed. (Professional Editions Ser.). 450p. 1996. 49.95 incl. cd-rom (*1-55615-879-3*) Microsoft.

— Microsoft Excel Worksheet Function Reference. 3rd ed. LC 96-33464. 312p. 1996. pap. text 24.95 (*1-57231-341-2*) Microsoft.

— Microsoft Excel Worksheet Function Reference: For Microsoft Excel for Windows 95, & for Microsoft Excel for Windows 3.1 & Macintosh Systems. 2nd ed. (Professional Editions Ser.). 344p. 1995. 22.95 (*1-55615-878-5*) Microsoft.

— Microsoft Exchange Server Gateway Programmer's Guide. (gr. 8). 1998. pap. 24.95 (*1-55615-859-9*) Little.

— Microsoft Exchange Server Training. LC 98-3872. 600p. 1997. 99.99 incl. cd-rom (*1-57231-709-4*) Microsoft.

***Microsoft Corporation Staff.** Microsoft Exchange Server 5.5: Resource Guide. (IT Resource Kits Ser.). (Illus.). 1999. pap. 49.99 (*0-7356-0896-2*) Microsoft.

Microsoft Corporation Staff. Microsoft Internet Information Server. 1999. boxed set 55.00 (*0-7356-0521-1*) Little.

— Microsoft Internet Information Server. LC 97-53095. (Academic Learning Ser.). (Illus.). 379p. 1998. 99.99 incl. cd-rom (*1-57231-731-0*) Microsoft.

— Microsoft Internet Information Server Resource Kit. LC 97-48754. 1200p. 1998. pap. text 99.99 (*1-57231-638-1*) Microsoft.

***Microsoft Corporation Staff.** Microsoft Internet Information Server 5.0 Documentation. LC 99-50192. 1999. pap. text 49.99 (*0-7356-0652-8*) Microsoft.

Microsoft Corporation Staff. Microsoft Jet Database Engine Programmer's Guide: The Essential Reference for the Database Engine Used in Microsoft Windows-Based Applications & Programming Environments. 2nd ed. LC 97-15488. (Professional Editions Ser.). 700p. 1997. pap. 39.95 incl. cd-rom (*1-57231-342-0*) Microsoft.

— MicroSoft LAN Manager for Windows NT. LC 92-37697. 1993. pap. 39.95 (*1-55615-543-3*) Microsoft.

— Microsoft Manual of Style for Technical Publications. 3rd ed. LC 98-14000. 336p. 29.99 incl. cd-rom (*1-57231-890-2*) Microsoft.

— Microsoft NT Server Resource Kit. 912p. 1996. pap. text, boxed set 149.95 incl. cd-rom (*1-57231-344-7*) Microsoft.

— Microsoft ODBC 3.0 Software Development Kit & Programmer's Reference, 2 vols. 2nd ed. LC 96-45660. 1488p. 1997. 99.99 (*1-57231-516-4*) Microsoft.

— Microsoft Office 97: Developer Edition Resource Library. 2000p. 99.99 incl. cd-rom (*1-57231-606-3*) Microsoft.

— Microsoft Office 97 Resource Kit. LC 96-45661. 1997. pap. text 59.99 incl. disk (*1-57231-329-3*) Microsoft.

— Microsoft Office Resource Kit. rev. ed. LC 97-38787. 1360p. 59.99 incl. cd-rom (*1-57231-640-3*) Microsoft.

— Microsoft Office 97-Visual Basic Language Reference, 5 vols. LC 97-3521. 4192p. 1997. pap. text 129.99 (*1-57231-339-0*) Microsoft.

— Microsoft Office 97-Visual Basic Programmer's Guide. LC 96-29988. 700p. 1997. pap. text 34.99 (*1-57231-340-4*) Microsoft.

***Microsoft Corporation Staff.** Microsoft Office 2000 Development. LC 99-33883. (Microsoft Mastering Ser.). 1999. pap. 49.99 (*0-7356-0899-7*) Microsoft.

Microsoft Corporation Staff. Microsoft Office 2000 Resource Kit With CDROM. LC 99-19168. (Resource Kit Ser.). (Illus.). 875p. 1999. pap. 59.99 (*0-7356-0555-6*) Microsoft.

— Microsoft Office 2000 Starts Here. 1999. cd-rom 29.99 (*0-7356-0506-8*) Microsoft.

— Microsoft Office 97 Small Business Edition 1997. cd-rom 29.99 (*1-57231-735-3*) Microsoft.

— Microsoft OLE DB Software Development Kit & Programmer's Reference. LC 97-7697. 784p. 1997. 39.99 incl. cd-rom (*1-57231-612-8*) Microsoft.

— Microsoft OLE DB 2.0 Programmer's Reference & Data Access Software Development Kit. LC 98-39268. 1000p. 1998. pap. 49.99 (*0-7356-0590-4*) Microsoft.

— Microsoft Press Computer Dictionary. 4th ed. LC 99-20168. 1999. pap. 34.99 (*0-7356-0615-3*) Microsoft.

— Microsoft Press Computer User's Dictionary. LC 98-13998. 416p. 14.99 (*1-57231-862-7*) Microsoft.

— Microsoft Project/Visual Basic Reference. 2nd ed. LC 97-31955. 700p. 1997. 39.99 (*1-57231-680-2*) Microsoft.

— Microsoft Publisher, Single User License. (NO - Novell/Wordperfect Ser.). 1995. 46.95 (*0-538-65237-3*) S-W Pub.

— Microsoft SNA Server Training Kit. LC 98-40875. 450p. 1998. 217.99 incl. cd-rom (*1-57231-932-1*) Microsoft.

***Microsoft Corporation Staff.** Microsoft SNA Server 4.0 Resource Guide. (IT Resource Kits Ser.). (Illus.). 1999. pap. 69.99 (*0-7356-0927-6*) Microsoft.

Microsoft Corporation Staff. Microsoft Solutions Framework Programmers Guide. pap. write for info. (*1-57231-223-8*) Microsoft.

— Microsoft Sourcebook for the Help Desk. 2nd ed. LC 97-832. 400p. 1997. pap. text 49.99 incl. cd-rom (*1-57231-582-2*) Microsoft.

***Microsoft Corporation Staff.** Microsoft SQL Server 7.0 Database Implementation Online Training Kit. 1999. pap. 99.99 incl. cd-rom (*0-7356-0679-X*) Microsoft.

Microsoft Corporation Staff. Microsoft SQL Server Training: Hands-on Self-Paced Training Kit for Version 6.5, 2 vols. LC 96-18665. 1400p. 1996. 199.95 (*1-55615-930-7*) Microsoft.

***Microsoft Corporation Staff.** Microsoft SQL Server 7.0 Data Warehousing Online Training. 2000. pap., boxed set 99.99 incl. cd-rom (*0-7356-0782-6*) Microsoft Pr.

Microsoft Corporation Staff. Microsoft SQL Server 7.0 Database Implementation Training Kit: Exam #70-029. LC 99-13770. (Training Kit Ser.). 800p. 1999. pap. 99.99 incl. cd-rom (*1-57231-826-0*) Microsoft.

— Microsoft SQL Server 7.0 System Administration Training Kit. LC 99-13556. 800p. 1999. 99.99 incl. cd-rom (*1-57231-827-9*) Microsoft.

***Microsoft Corporation Staff.** Microsoft SQL 7.0 Resource Guide. (Illus.). 1999. pap. 59.99 (*0-7356-0894-6*) Microsoft.

Microsoft Corporation Staff. Microsoft Systems: Management Server Training. LC 97-36002. 500p. 1997. 99.99 incl. cd-rom (*1-57231-614-4*) Microsoft.

***Microsoft Corporation Staff.** Microsoft Systems Management Server 2.0 Resource Guide. (IT Resource Kits Ser.). (Illus.). 1999. pap. 79.99 (*0-7356-0928-4*) Microsoft.

Microsoft Corporation Staff. Microsoft Systems Management Server 2.0 Training Kit. LC 99-13364. 500p. 1998. 99.99 incl. cd-rom (*1-57231-834-1*) Microsoft.

M

— Microsoft TCP/IP Training: Hands-On, Self-Paced Training for Internetworking Microsoft TCP/IP on Microsoft Windows NT 4.0. LC 97-20760. 500p. 1997. 99.99 incl. cd-rom (1-57231-623-3) Microsoft.

— Microsoft Visual Basic Deluxe Learning Edition Version 5.0. 384p. 1997. pap. text 129.99 incl. cd-rom (1-57231-551-2) Microsoft.

— Microsoft Visual Basic 5.0: Programmer's Guide. LC 97-828. 912p. 1997. 29.99 (1-57231-604-7) Microsoft.

*__Microsoft Corporation Staff.__ Microsoft Visual Basic 6.0 Development. LC 99-33876. (Microsoft Mastering Ser.). 1999. pap. 49.99 (0-7356-0900-4) Microsoft.

__Microsoft Corporation Staff.__ Microsoft Visual Basic 6.0 Programmer's Guide: Programmer's Guide. LC 98-14786. 960p. 39.99 (1-57231-863-5) Microsoft.

*__Microsoft Corporation Staff.__ Microsoft Visual Basic 6.0 Programming/Mastering Solution Set: Complete Two-in-One Learning Solution. (Illus.). 1999. pap. 99.99 incl. audio compact disk (0-7356-0812-1) Microsoft.

__Microsoft Corporation Staff.__ Microsoft Visual Basic 5 Language Reference Volume 2: ActiveX Controls, Vol. 2. LC 97-3523. 600p. 1997. pap. text 24.99 (1-57231-508-3) Microsoft.

— Microsoft Visual Basic 6.0, Deluxe Learning Edition. LC 98-15687. 1390p. 139.99 incl. cd-rom (1-57231-873-2) Microsoft.

*__Microsoft Corporation Staff.__ Microsoft Visual Basic 6.0 Fundamentals. LC 99-33884. (Microsoft Mastering Ser.). (Illus.). 1999. pap. 49.99 (0-7356-0898-9) Microsoft.

__Microsoft Corporation Staff.__ Microsoft Visual Basic 6.0 Reference Library: Reference Library. LC 98-14787. 3284p. 89.99 (1-57231-864-3) Microsoft.

— Microsoft Visual C++ 6.0 Reference Library: Reference Library. LC 98-14785. 4729p. 149.99 (1-57231-865-1) Microsoft.

— Microsoft Visual C++ Language Reference. LC 97-2404. 750p. 1997. pap. text 29.99 (1-57231-521-0) Microsoft.

— Microsoft Visual C++ MFC Library Reference, Pt. 1. LC 97-2421. 1000p. 1997. pap. text 39.99 (1-57231-518-0) Microsoft.

— Microsoft Visual C++ MFC Library Reference, Pt. 2. 1000p. 1997. pap. text 39.99 (1-57231-519-9) Microsoft.

— Microsoft Visual C++ Programmer's References, 6 vols., Set. 2nd ed. (Professional Editions Ser.). 1995. pap. 159.95 (1-55615-901-3) Microsoft.

— Microsoft Visual C++ Run-Time Library Reference. LC 97-2405. 1000p. 1997. pap. text 29.99 (1-57231-520-2) Microsoft.

— Microsoft Visual C++ 6.0 Deluxe: Learning Ed., 3. LC 99-13360. 1440p. 1999. boxed set 139.99 (0-7356-0636-6) Microsoft.

— Microsoft Visual FoxPro 6.0 Programmer's Guide. LC 98-15689. 832p. 29.99 (1-57231-868-6) Microsoft.

— Microsoft Visual FoxPro 6.0 Language Reference. LC 98-7484. 1166p. 39.99 (1-57231-870-8) Microsoft.

— Microsoft Visual InterDev 6.0 Web Technologies Reference: Web Reference. LC 98-7485. 1575p. 39.99 (1-57231-871-6) Microsoft.

— Microsoft Visual InterDev 6.0 Programmer's Guide. LC 98-18207. 464p. 24.99 (1-57231-867-8) Microsoft.

— Microsoft Visual J++ 6.0 Reference Library: Reference Library. LC 98-30054. 1800p. 99.99 (1-57231-872-4) Microsoft.

— Microsoft Visual J++ 6.0 Programmer's Guide: Programmer's Guide. LC 98-30056. 500p. 27.99 (1-57231-869-4) Microsoft.

— Microsoft Visual J++ 6.0 Deluxe Learning Edition. deluxe ed. LC 98-30055. 992p. 1998. 139.99 incl. cd-rom (1-57231-930-5) Microsoft.

— Microsoft Visual Studio 6.0 Core Reference Set. LC 98-6655. 3576p. 129.99 (1-57231-884-8) Microsoft.

— Microsoft Windows Architecture Training. LC 97-53090. 500p. 1997. 79.99 incl. cd-rom (1-57231-708-6) Microsoft.

— Microsoft Windows CE Programmers Guide. LC 97-43824. 848p. 1997. pap. text 49.99 incl. cd-rom (1-57231-643-8) Microsoft.

— Microsoft Windows 98 Training Kit. LC 98-22197. 1350p. 99.99 incl. cd-rom (1-57231-730-2) Microsoft.

— Microsoft Windows 95 Resource Kit. LC 96-175225. (Resource Kit Ser.). 1376p. 1995. pap. 67.95 incl. cd-rom (1-55615-678-2) Microsoft.

— Microsoft Windows 95 Training Kit, Deluxe Multimedia Edition. deluxe ed. 1200p. 1998. 199.99 incl. cd-rom (1-57231-830-9) Microsoft.

— Microsoft Windows 95 Training: Hands-On, Self-Paced Training for Supporting Windows 95, 2 vols. LC 95-36241. (Training Kit Ser.). 1200p. 1995. pap. 199.95 incl. cd-rom (1-55615-931-5) Microsoft.

— Microsoft Windows NT 4.0 Network Administrator's Training. LC 97-829. 800p. 1997. 99.99 (1-57231-439-7) Microsoft.

— Microsoft Windows NT 4.0 Upgrade Training. 49.99 (1-57231-528-8) Microsoft.

— Microsoft Windows NT Resource Kit Version 3.51 Update with CD-ROM. (Resource Kit Ser.). 272p. 1995. pap. 39.95 incl. cd-rom (1-55615-929-3) Microsoft.

— Microsoft Windows NT Server Enterprise Training. 1999. boxed set 55.00 (0-7356-0520-3) Little.

— Microsoft Windows NT Server Enterprise Training. LC 97-43134. 900p. 1997. 99.99 incl. cd-rom (1-57231-710-8) Microsoft.

— Microsoft Windows NT Server 4.0 One Step at a Time. (Independent Ser.). 275p. pap. 22.95 (1-57231-449-4) Microsoft.

— Microsoft Windows NT Server Resource Kit: Supplement Four. (Resource Kit Ser.). 1998. pap. text 49.99 (1-57231-806-6) Microsoft.

— Microsoft Windows NT Technical Support Training. LC 97-830. (Training Kit Ser.). 800p. 1997. pap. 99.99 incl. cd-rom (1-57231-373-0) Microsoft.

— Microsoft Windows NT Training, International Version: Interactive Self-Paced Training & Preparation for the Microsoft Certified Professional Exams. (Training Kit Ser.). boxed set 199.95 (1-57231-278-5) Microsoft.

— Microsoft Windows NT Workstation 4.0 Starts Here. (gr. 8). 1997. cd-rom 29.99 (1-57231-737-X) Little.

— Microsoft Windows NT Workstation Resource Kit. 1408p. 1996. pap. text 69.95 incl. cd-rom (1-57231-343-9) Microsoft.

*__Microsoft Corporation Staff.__ Microsoft Windows 2000 Beta Upgrade Training Kit. LC 99-33261. 1999. pap. 79.99 (1-57231-894-5) Microsoft.

— Microsoft Windows 2000 Professional Resource Kit. LC 99-88818. (Illus.). 1808p. 2000. pap. text 69.99 incl. cd-rom (1-57231-808-2) Microsoft.

__Microsoft Corporation Staff.__ Microsoft Windows User Experience: Official Guidelines for User Interface Developers & Designers. LC 99-36326. 864p. 1999. pap. 49.99 (0-7356-0566-1) Microsoft.

*__Microsoft Corporation Staff.__ Microsoft Windows 95 Corporate Migration Kit. 1998. boxed set 99.95 (1-57231-266-1) Microsoft.

__Microsoft Corporation Staff.__ Microsoft Windows 98 Resource Kit. LC 98-2768. 1766p. 1998. 69.99 incl. cd-rom (1-57231-644-6) Microsoft.

*__Microsoft Corporation Staff.__ Microsoft Works Suite 2001 Step by Step. 240p. 2000. 19.99 (0-7356-1035-5) Microsoft.

__Microsoft Corporation Staff.__ Microsoft XML 2.0 Programmer's Guide & Software Development Kit. (Microsoft Programming Series Ser.). 1999. pap. text 49.99 (0-7356-0639-0) Microsoft.

— Networking Essentials. 2nd ed. LC 97-34595. 800p. 1997. pap. text 99.99 (1-57231-527-X) Microsoft.

*__Microsoft Corporation Staff.__ Networking Essentials. 3rd ed. LC 99-41069. 1999. pap. 59.99 (1-57231-902-X) Microsoft Pr.

__Microsoft Corporation Staff.__ Networking Essentials, Deluxe Multimedia Edition. 2nd deluxe ed. 850p. 199.00 incl. cd-rom (1-57231-831-7) Microsoft.

— OLE 2 Programmer's Reference Library, 2 vols., Set. 2nd ed. (Professional Editions Ser.). 1499p. 1995. pap. 50.00 (1-55615-749-5) Microsoft.

— OLE 2 Programmer's Reference Library: Working with 32-Bit Windows Objects, 1. 2nd ed. 1100p. 1995. pap. 29.95 (1-55615-850-5) Microsoft.

— Optimizing Network Traffic: Notes from the Field. LC 98-52138. 400p. 1999. pap. 39.99 (0-7356-0648-X) Microsoft.

— Optimizing Windows NT, Vol. 4. 608p. write for info. incl. disk (1-55615-655-3) Microsoft.

— Programmer's Guide to Pen Services for Microsoft Windows 95. LC 95-1474. (Professional Editions Ser.). 544p. 1995. 27.95 (1-55615-835-1) Microsoft.

__Microsoft Corporation Staff.__ Quick Course Office 97: Professional Edition. 1997. pap. text 53.99 (1-57231-879-1) Microsoft.

— Running Microsoft Office 2000: Premium Edition. (Running Ser.). 1999. pap. text. write for info. (0-7356-0819-9) Microsoft.

__Microsoft Corporation Staff.__ Supporting Windows 98. 1999. 99.99 (0-7356-0612-9) Microsoft.

— TCP/IP for Microsoft Windows NT. 1998. boxed set 55.00 (0-7356-0522-X) Little.

— User's Guide, Windows Office Pro V4.3 Academic Edition 3.5. (NO - Novell/Wordperfect Ser.). 1995. text 121.95 (0-538-66027-9) S-W Pub.

*__Microsoft Corporation Staff.__ Web Application Development Using Microsoft Visual InterDev 6. LC 99-39053. (Microsoft Mastering Ser.). 1999. pap. 49.99 (0-7356-0902-0) Microsoft.

__Microsoft Corporation Staff.__ Windows NT Resource Guide, Vol. 1. LC 94-45564. 1024p. Date not set. write for info. incl. 3.5 hd (1-55615-653-7) Microsoft.

*__Microsoft Corporation Staff, ed.__ Building an Enterprise Active Directory. LC 99-57855. (Illus.). 2000. 39.99 (0-7356-0860-1) Microsoft.

— Distributed Applications with Microsoft Visual C++ 6.0. (DV-MCSD Training Kits Ser.). 2000. pap. text 69.99 (0-7356-0926-8) Microsoft.

__Microsoft Corporation Staff, ed.__ Embedded Systems. 1999. 59.99 (1-57231-962-3) Microsoft.

*__Microsoft Corporation Staff, ed.__ Microsoft Office 2000 Technical Support Training Kit. LC 99-33882. 800p. (C). (gr. 8). 1999. boxed set 99.99 (0-7356-0669-2) Little.

__Microsoft Corporation Staff, ed.__ Microsoft Windows NT Workstation. 1998. 29.99 (1-57231-915-1) Microsoft.

— Net Essentials. 2nd ed. 650p. 1998. boxed set 55.00 (1-57231-909-7) Microsoft.

__Microsoft Corporation Staff & Semick, James.__ Microsoft Internet Information Server 4.0: Exam 70-087. LC 99-13776. (MCSE Readiness Review Ser.). (Illus.). 463p. 1999. pap. 29.99 (0-7356-0541-6) Microsoft.

__Microsoft Corporation Staff, et al.__ MCSE Readiness Review Exam 70-068 Windows NT Server 4.0 in the Enterprise: MCSE Readiness Review, Exam 70-068. LC 99-21358. 350p. 1999. 29.99 incl. cd-rom (0-7356-0539-4) Microsoft.

— PC 98 System Design Guide. LC 97-37612. 672p. 29.99 (1-57231-716-7) Microsoft.

__Microsoft Corporation Staff, jt. auth. see Catapult, Inc., Staff.__

__Microsoft Corporation Staff, jt. auth. see Intel Corporation Staff.__

__Microsoft Corporation Staff, ed. see Vies, John.__

__Microsoft Educational Services Staff.__ Microsoft Windows NT Training: Interactive Self-Paced Training & Preparation for the Microsoft Certified Professional Exams, 2 vols. LC 97-178163. (Training Kit Ser.). 1320p. 1996. boxed set 199.95 (1-55615-864-5) Microsoft.

*__Microsoft Press Interactive Staff.__ Designing of Scalability with Microsoft Windows DNA. (DV-MPS General Ser.). (Illus.). 2000. pap. 49.99 (0-7356-0968-3) Microsoft.

— Microsoft Mastering MFC Development Using Microsoft Visual C++ (DV-DLT Mastering Ser.). (Illus.). 2000. pap. 49.99 (0-7356-0925-X) Microsoft.

__Microsoft Press Interactive Staff.__ Microsoft Office 97 Starts Here. 1997. pap. text 29.95 (1-57231-607-1) Microsoft.

— Microsoft Windows 95 & Internet Explorer 4.0 Starts Here. 1997. pap. text 29.99 (1-57231-523-7) Microsoft.

— Microsoft Windows NT Workstation 4.0 Starts Here. 1997. pap. text 29.99 incl. cd-rom (1-57231-522-9) Microsoft.

*__Microsoft Press Interactive Staff.__ Upgrading to Microsoft Windows 2000. LC 99-45521. (Illus.). 1999. pap. 59.99 (0-7356-0940-3) Microsoft.

— Web Database Development Fundamentals. LC 00-20240. (DV-DLT Fundamentals Ser.). (Illus.). 450p. 2000. pap. 49.99 (0-7356-0966-7) Microsoft.

*__Microsoft Press Staff.__ Developing XML Solutions: Programming for the Business Internet with Mircosoft Windows DNA. (DV-MPS General Ser.). (Illus.). 2000. pap. text 49.99 (0-7356-0796-6) Microsoft.

— Inside Microsoft Windows 2000. (Illus.). 2000. pap. text 49.99 (0-7356-1021-5) Microsoft.

— MCSE Online Training Kit, Networking Essentials Plus. 1999. pap. 99.99 incl. cd-rom (0-7356-0881-4) Microsoft Pr.

— Microsoft Application Center Resource Kit. (IT Resource Kits Ser.). (Illus.). 2000. pap. 69.99 (0-7356-1023-1) Microsoft.

— Microsoft Exchange 2000 Server Administrator's Pocket Consultant. (IT-Administrator's Companion Ser.). (Illus.). 2000. pap. text 29.99 (0-7356-0962-4) Microsoft.

— Microsoft Management Console Design & Development Kit. LC 00-23796. (DV-MPE Software Development Kits Ser.). (Illus.). 829p. 2000. pap. text 59.99 (0-7356-1038-X) Microsoft.

— Microsoft Mastering: E-Commerce Development: Business-to-Business. (DV-DLT Mastering Ser.). (Illus.). 2000. pap. text. write for info. (0-7356-1043-6) Microsoft.

— Microsoft Windows CE Resource Kit. (IT Resource Kits Ser.). (Illus.). 2000. pap. text 59.99 (0-7356-0969-1) Microsoft.

— Microsoft Windows 2000 MCSE Core Requirements Training Kit. (IT-Training Kits Ser.). (Illus.). 2000. pap. 199.99 (0-7356-1130-0) Microsoft.

— Programming Microsoft Outlook & Microsoft Exchange. 2nd ed. LC 00-28169. (DV-MPS Programming Ser.). (Illus.). 2000. pap. text 49.99 (0-7356-1019-3) Microsoft.

— XML Step by Step. (DV-DLT Fundamentals Ser.). (Illus.). 2000. pap. text 49.99 (0-7356-1020-7) Microsoft.

__Microsoft Product Support Services Staff.__ Ask Microsoft about Excel for Windows 95. 400p. 1999. pap. 24.99 (0-7897-0806-X) Que.

— Ask Microsoft about Microsoft Office for Windows 95. 600p. 1996. pap. text 24.99 (0-7897-0819-1) Que.

— Ask Microsoft about Windows 95. 600p. 1996. pap. text 24.99 (0-7897-0805-1) Que.

— Ask Microsoft about Word for Windows 95. 400p. 1999. pap. 24.99 (0-7897-0804-3) Que.

__Microsoft Site Builder Network Staff.__ How the Web Was Won. LC 98-22938. 265p. 29.99 (1-57231-917-8) Microsoft.

*__Microsoft Staff.__ Inside Out: Microsoft, Who Do We Think We Are. 224p. 2000. 45.00 (0-446-52739-4) Warner Bks.

*__Microsoft Staff, ed.__ Computer Dictionary: English-Portuguese/Portuguese-English. (ENG & POR.). 805p. 1998. pap. 150.00 (0-320-03625-1) Fr & Eur.

__Microsymposium Staff.__ Radiological Aspects of Renal Transplantation: Proceedings of the Microsymposium, Nymegen, 1977. Penn, William, ed. (Radiologia Clinica et Biologica Ser.: Vol. 47, No. 1). (Illus.). 1977. 17.00 (3-8055-2844-2) S Karger.

__Microteac Staff.__ The Psychology Experimenter. (C). 1986. 295.00 (0-15-572674-9, Pub. by Harcourt Coll Pubs) Harcourt.

__Microtrend Inc. Staff.__ C Language on the IBM PC. 1984. 14.95 (0-685-08090-0) P-H.

__Microwave Theory & Techniques Society, Lasers & El.__ Digest of the 1996 International Topical Meeting on Microwave Photonics. Institute of Electrical & Electronics Engineers, I, ed. 200p. 1996. pap. write for info. (0-614-10965-5, 96TH8153) Inst Electrical.

__Microys, Helmut, et al, eds.__ Cast-in-Place Concrete in Tall Building Design & Construction. 320p. 1992. text 54.00 (0-07-012536-8) McGraw.

__Micta, Andrew A., ed. see Freidzon, Sergei.__

__Micucci, Charles.__ The Life & Times of the Apple. LC 90-22779. (Illus.). 32p. (J). (gr. k-3). 1996. pap. 5.95 (0-531-07067-0) Orchard Bks Watts.

— Life & Times of the Apple. 1995. 11.15 (0-606-08798-2, Pub. by Turtleback) Demco.

— Life & Times of the Honeybee. (J). 1997. pap. text 93.32 (0-395-86149-7) HM.

— The Life & Times of the Honeybee. LC 93-8135. (Illus.). 32p. (J). (gr. k-3). 1997. reprint ed. pap. 5.95 (0-395-86139-X) HM.

— Life & Times of the Peanut. LC 96-1290. (Illus.). 32p. (J). (gr. k-3). 1997. 16.00 (0-395-72289-6) HM.

*__Micucci, Charles.__ Life & Times of the Peanut. (Illus.). (J). 2000. 11.40 (0-606-18211-X) Turtleback.

— The Life & Times of the Peanut. (Illus.). 32p. (J). 2000. pap. 5.95 (0-618-03314-9) HM.

__Micucci, Charles.__ Life & Times of the Honeybee. LC 93-8135. 32p. (J). (gr. k-3). 1995. 15.00 (0-395-65968-X) Ticknor & Flds Bks Yng Read.

*__Micucci, Dana.__ Artists in Residence: A Guide to the Homes & Studios of Eight 19th-Century Painters. (Illus.). 2001. pap. write for info. (1-892145-00-6) Little Bkrm.

__Micucci, Joseph A.__ The Adolescent in Family Therapy: Breaking the Cycle of Conflict & Control. LC 98-37859. (Family Therapy Ser.). 336p. 1998. 35.00 (1-57230-389-1) Guilford Pubns.

*__Micucci, Joseph A.__ The Adolescent in Family Therapy: Breaking the Cycle of Conflict & Control. (Family Therapy Ser.). 336p. 2000. pap. 19.95 (1-57230-588-6, 0588) Guilford Pubns.

*__Micula, Gheorghe & Micula, Sanda.__ Handbook of Splines. LC 98-49063. (Mathematics & Its Applications Series: Vol. 462). 604p. 1999. 297.00 (0-7923-5503-2) Kluwer Academic.

__Micula, Gheorghe & Pavel, Paraschiva.__ Differential & Integral Equations Through Practical Problems & Exercises. LC 92-22561. (Kluwer Texts in Mathematical Sciences Ser.: Vol. 7). 408p. (C). 1992. text 226.50 (0-7923-1890-0) Kluwer Academic.

__Micula, Sanda, jt. auth. see Micula, Gheorghe.__

*__Miculka.__ Speaking for Success. (Business Communications Ser.). 1998. pap. text 34.95 (0-538-68655-3) Thomson Learn.

__Miculka, Jean H.__ Speaking American English. (PS - Communication/English Ser.). (C). 1991. mass mkt. 20.25 (0-538-70328-8) S-W Pub.

__Miculka, Jones.__ Speaking American English. (C). 1991. 245.00 (0-538-70329-6) Thomson Learn.

*__Miczah, Marie Anakee.__ Mehndi: Rediscovering Henna Body Art. (Miczak Exotic Treasures Ser.). (Illus.). 199p. 1999. pap. 14.95 (0-7414-0280-7) Buy Books.

__Miczak, Marie.__ Nature's Weeds, Native Medicines: Native American Herbal Secrets. LC 98-75821. 1999. pap. 10.95 (0-914955-48-9) Lotus Pr.

__Miczak, Marie A.__ Secret Potions, Elixirs & Concoctions: Botanical & Aromatic Recipes for Mind, Body & Soul. (Illus.). 130p. 1999. pap. 10.95 (0-914955-45-4) Lotus Pr.

__Miczo, Alexander.__ Digital Logic Testing & Simulation. 480p. (C). 1985. pap. text, suppl. ed. 10.00 (0-471-60422-4) Wiley.

__Mid.__ Merrymeeting Merry Eating. 1988. pap. 15.95 (0-9620094-0-7) Mid Coast Hosp.

__Mid-America Spectroscopy Symposium (16th: 1965, Ch.__ Developments in Applied Spectroscopy Vol. 5: Proceedings of the Sixteenth Annual Mid-America Spectroscopy Symposium Held in Chicago, IL, June 14-17, 1965. Pearson, L. R. & Grove, E. L., eds. LC 61-17720. 516p. 1966. reprint ed. pap. 160.00 (0-608-08163-9, 202629300005) Bks Demand.

__Mid-Atlantic Center for the Arts Staff, ed.__ Cape May Fare. (Illus.). 236p. 1987. reprint ed. pap. 12.95 (0-9663295-1-1) Mid-Atl Ctr Arts.

__Mid-South Fly Fishers Staff.__ Home Waters: Guide to Fishing Northern Arkansas, Southern Missouri & Western Tennessee. (Illus.). 128p. 1993. pap. 17.95 (1-882626-15-X) Impress Ink.

__Midant, Jean-Paul.__ Dictionnaire de l'Architecture du Xxeme Siecle. (FRE.). 1012p. 1997. 350.00 (0-7859-9498-X) Fr & Eur.

__Midant-Reynes, Beatrix.__ The Prehistory of Egypt. Shaw, Ian, tr. LC 99-33594. 320p. 1999. 64.95 (0-631-20169-6); pap. 29.95 (0-631-21787-8) Blackwell Pubs.

__Midda, Sara.__ Growing up & Other Vices. LC 94-17826. (Illus.). 32p. 1994. 13.95 (1-56305-728-X, 3728) Workman Pub.

— In & Out of the Garden. LC 81-40501. (Illus.). 128p. 1981. 22.50 (0-89480-193-7, 344) Workman Pub.

— Sara Midda Baby Book. 1999. 22.95 (0-7611-1229-4) Workman Pub.

— Sara Midda's Book of Days from the South of France: A Sketch Book. LC 90-50369. 96p. 1990. 13.95 (1-56305-367-5, 3367F) Workman Pub.

__Middaugh, Dallas.__ Turok 2: Seeds of Evil. LC 98-65459. 96p. 1998. per. 12.99 (0-7615-1588-7) Prima Pub.

*__Middaugh, Michael F.__ Understanding Faculty Productivity: Standards & Benchmarks for Colleges & Universities. LC 00-9571. (Higher & Adult Education Ser.). 2001. 32.95 (0-7879-5022-X) Jossey-Bass.

__Middaugh, Michael F., et al.__ Strategies for the Practice of Institutional Research: Concepts, Resources, & Applications. 124p. (C). 1994. pap. text 14.95 (1-882393-04-X) Assn Instl Res.

__Middaugh, Robert C., Jr.__ Exercises in Celestial Navigation. (Illus.). 60p. (Orig.). (C). 1994. pap. text 17.50 (1-879778-24-6, BK-0312) Marine Educ.

— Exercises in Coastwise Navigation. (Illus.). 48p. 1986. pap. text 17.50 (1-879778-33-5, BK-556) Marine Educ.

__Midddleton, David.__ Beyond the Chandeleurs. 88p. 1999. pap. 12.95 (0-8071-2378-1) La State U Pr.

__Middeke, Martin & Huber, Werner, eds.__ Biofictions: The Rewriting of Romantic Lives in Contemporary Fiction & Drama. LC 98-52965. (GERM Ser.). 1999. 55.00 (1-57113-123-X) Camden Hse.

__Middelburg, Cornelis A.__ Logic & Specifiction: Extending VDM-SL for Advanced Formal Specification. LC 92-38105. 1993. pap. 61.95 (0-412-48680-6) Chapman & Hall.

__Middeldorp, A., ed. see Fuji International Symposium on Functional & Logic Programming Staff, et al.__

__Middeldyk, R. A. Van, see Van Middeldyk, R. A.__

__Middelhoek, S., jt. ed. see Ciureanu, P.__

An Asterisk (*) at the beginning of an entry indicates that the title is appearing for the first time.

Middelton-Moz, Jane. Children of Trauma: Rediscovering Your Discarded Self. 104p. (Orig.). 1989. pap. 9.95 (1-55874-014-7) Health Comm.
— Shame & Guilt: Masters of Disguise. 1990. pap. 8.95 (1-55874-072-4) Health Comm.
***Middelton-Moz, Jane.** Welcoming Our Children to a New Millennium: A Day Book of Hopes & Wishes for the Future. LC 99-42104. 1999. pap. 12.95 (1-55874-742-7) Health Comm.
Middendorf, jt. auth. see Thorpe, James F.
Middendorf, Jesse C., ed. The Church Rituals Handbook. LC 97-12067. 240p. 1997. kivar 14.99 (0-8341-1627-8) Beacon Hill.
Middendorf, John, jt. auth. see Long, John.
***Middendorf, Jon.** Worship-Centered Youth Ministry: A Compass for Guiding Youth into God's Story. 2000. pap. 14.99 (0-8341-1826-2) Beacon Hill.
Middendorf, Jon. You Might Be a Youth Worker If . . . LC 97-12063. (Illus.). 96p. (Orig.). 1997. pap. 8.99 (0-8341-1668-5) Beacon Hill.
Middendorf, Michael P. The "I" in the Storm: A Study of Romans 7. LC 97-27932. 1997. 19.95 (0-570-04261-5, 53-1021) Concordia.
Middendorf, William H. What Every Engineer Should Know about Inventing. (What Every Engineer Should Know Ser.: Vol. 7). (Illus.). 168p. 1981. text 59.75 (0-8247-7497-3) Dekker.
Middendorf, William H. & Engelmann, Richard H. Design of Devices & Systems. 3rd ed. LC 97-41590. (Illus.). 584p. 1997. text 69.75 (0-8247-9924-0) Dekker.
Middendorf, William H., jt. auth. see Engelmann.
Middendorff, Wolf. Effectiveness of Punishment Especially in Relation to Traffic Offenses. (N. Y. U. Criminal Law Education & Research Center Publications: Vol. 5). xii, 129p. 1968. reprint ed. 22.50 (0-8377-0826-5, Rothman) W S Hein.
Middendorp, Kooiman-van, jt. auth. see Maria, Gerarda.
Middione, Carlo. Carlo Middione's Traditional Pasta. (Illus.). 128p. (Orig.). 1996. pap. 15.95 (0-89815-805-2) Ten Speed Pr.
— The Food of Southern Italy. LC 87-15406. (Cookbook Library). (Illus.). 330p. 1987. 35.00 (0-688-05042-5, Wm Morrow) Morrow Avon.
— La Vera Cucina: Traditional Recipes from the Homes & Farms of Italy. 416p. 1996. 35.00 (0-684-81206-1) Simon & Schuster.
Middle East Executive Reports, Ltd. Staff. Arab Investors Sourcebook. Hearn, William C., ed. 650p. 1989. pap. 220.50 (0-915797-01-1) Intl Exec Reports.
Middle East Watch Staff. Empty Reforms: Saudi Arabia's New Basic Laws. Human Rights Watch Staff, ed. LC 92-18857. 68p. (Orig.). 1992. pap. 7.00 (1-56432-068-5) Hum Rts Watch.
— Genocide in Iraq: The Anfal Campaign Against the Kurds. Human Rights Watch Staff, ed. 400p. (Orig.). 1993. pap. 20.00 (1-56432-108-8) Hum Rts Watch.
— Hidden Death: Land Mines & Civilian Casualties in Iraqi Kurdistan. Human Rights Watch Staff, ed. LC 92-19398. 78p. (Orig.). 1992. pap. 7.00 (1-56432-067-7) Hum Rts Watch.
— Israel & Israeli-Occupied Territories: The Israeli Army & the Intifoda: Policies That Contribute to the Killings. LC 90-83440. 240p. (Orig.). 1990. pap. 15.00 (0-929692-66-7, M E Watch) Hum Rts Watch.
Middle East Water Information Network Staff, ed. Mewin Directory of Individuals & Organizations Specializing in Water Resources in the Middle East. 333p. (Orig.). 1996. pap. 27.00 (0-9639821-2-5) Osage.
Middle Georgia Girl Scout Council Staff. Middle Georgia on My Mind. (Illus.). 1990. 10.00 (0-87197-282-4) Favorite Recipes.
Middle Georgia Historical Society, Inc. Members. Macon: An Architectural & Historical Guide. Orig. Title: A Guide to Macon's Architectural & Historical Heritage. (Illus.). 132p. (Orig.). 1996. 25.00 (0-9651017-1-1); pap. 10.00 (0-9651017-0-3) Middle Georgia.
Middle, Hara G., jt. auth. see Middle, Howard.
Middle, Howard & Middle, Hara G. Conversational Greek in Seven Days. (Language in Seven Days Ser.). (GRE., Illus.). 96p. 1995. pap. 8.95 (0-8442-4503-8, 45038, Passprt Bks) NTC Contemp Pub Co.
Middle, Howard & Middle, Hara G. Conversational Greek in Seven Days. (Language in 7 Days Ser.). (Illus.). 96p. 1995. 12.95 incl. audio (0-8442-4502-X, 326228, Passprt Bks) NTC Contemp Pub Co.
***Middlebrook, Ann N. & Tolbert, Margaret A.** Stratospheric Ozone Depletion. LC 99-58346. (Global Change Instruction Program Ser.). (Illus.). 42p. 2000. pap. text. write for info. (1-891389-10-6) Univ Sci Bks.
Middlebrook, Christina. Seeing the Crab: A Memoir of Dying Before I Do. LC 97-26082. 224p. 1997. pap. 12.95 (0-385-48865-3, Anchor NY) Doubleday.
***Middlebrook, David.** Seven Legal Survival Skills Every Church Needs. 228p. 2000. pap. 12.99 (0-88419-722-0) Creation House.
Middlebrook, Diane W. Anne Sexton: A Biography. LC 92-50093. 1992. pap. 17.00 (0-679-74182-8) Vin Bks.
— Gin Considered As a Demon. LC 82-84116. 70p. (Orig.). 1983. pap. 3.95 (0-941692-04-3) Elysian Pr.
— Suits Me: The Double Life of Billy Tipton. 320p. 1999. pap. 14.00 (0-395-95789-3) HM.
Middlebrook, Diane W. & Yalom, Marilyn, eds. Coming to Light: American Women Poets in the Twentieth Century. (Women & Culture Ser.). 288p. 1985. pap. text 17.95 (0-472-08061-X, 08061) U of Mich Pr.
Middlebrook, Diane W., jt. auth. see Lippard, Lucy.
Middlebrook, Diane W., ed. see Sexton, Anne.
***Middlebrook, Kevin J.** Conservative Parties, the Right & Democracy in Latin America. LC 99-87435. (Illus.). 464p. 2000. 59.95 (0-8018-6385-6) Johns Hopkins.
— Conservative Parties, the Right & Democracy in Latin America. LC 99-87435. 464p. 2000. pap. 17.95 (0-8018-6386-4) Johns Hopkins.
Middlebrook, Kevin J. Electoral Observation & Democratic Transitions in Latin America. LC 98-35686. (U.S.-Mexico Contemporary Perspectives Ser.). 1998. pap. 14.95 (1-878367-38-2) UCSD Ctr US-Mex.
— The Paradox of Revolution: Labor, the State, & Authoritarianism in Mexico. LC 94-29470. 424p. 1995. text 59.95 (0-8018-4922-5) Johns Hopkins.
— The Paradox of Revolution: Labor, the State & Authoritarianism in Mexico. LC 94-29470. 424p. 1995. pap. text 18.95 (0-8018-5148-3) Johns Hopkins.
— Political Liberalization in an Authoritarian Regime: The Case of Mexico. (Research Reports: No. 41). 36p. (Orig.). (C). 1985. pap. 5.00 (0-935391-40-1, RR-41) UCSD Ctr US-Mex.
Middlebrook, Kevin J., et al, eds. Politics of Economic Restructuring in Mexico: State-Society Relations & Regime Change in Mexico. (U. S. - Mexico Contemporary Perspectives Ser.: No. 7). 351p. 1994. pap. 21.95 (1-878367-18-8) UCSD Ctr US-Mex.
Middlebrook, L. F. Register of the Middlebrook Family, Descendants of Joseph Middlebrook of Fairfield, Connecticut. (Illus.). 411p. 1989. reprint ed. pap. 61.50 (0-8328-0871-7); reprint ed. lib. bdg. 69.50 (0-8328-0870-9) Higginson Bk Co.
Middlebrook, Mark & Tanzillo, Tony. Maximizing AutoLISP Release 13 & 14. 960p. (C). 1997. pap. 44.95 incl. cd-rom (0-8273-7994-3) Delmar.
Middlebrook, Martin. Arnheim 1944: The Airbourne Battalion. 1995. pap. 17.95 (0-14-014342-4, Pub. by Pnguin Bks Ltd) Trafalgar.
— Battleship. 1994. pap. 17.95 (0-14-023469-1, Pub. by Pnguin Bks Ltd) Trafalgar.
— Berlin Raids: RAF Bomber Command Winter, 1943-1944. (Military Classics). 2000. pap. 9.95 (0-304-35347-7) Continuum.
Middlebrook, Martin. Boston at War. (C). 1989. text 35.00 (0-902662-62-7, Pub. by R K Pubns); pap. text 21.00 (0-7855-6992-8, Pub. by R K Pubns) St Mut.
— The Catholic Church in Boston. (C). 1989. text 35.00 (0-902662-65-1, Pub. by R K Pubns); pap. text 30.00 (0-7855-6989-8, Pub. by R K Pubns) St Mut.
Middlebrook, Martin. Convoy. 1992. pap. 19.95 (0-14-016695-5, Pub. by Pnguin Bks Ltd) Trafalgar.
— The First Day on the Somme: 1 July 1916. 1992. pap. 19.95 (0-14-017134-7, Pub. by Pnguin Bks Ltd) Trafalgar.
— Kaiser's Battle: 21 March 1918. 1994. pap. 17.95 (0-14-017135-5, Pub. by Pnguin Bks Ltd) Trafalgar.
Middlebrook, Martin. The Peenemunde Raid. LC 82-17850. (Illus.). 272p. 1983. write for info. (0-672-52759-6) Macmillan.
Middlebrook, Martin. Somme Battlefields: A Comprehensive Guide from Crecy to the Two World Wars. pap. 24.95 (0-14-012847-6, Pub. by Pnguin Bks Ltd) Trafalgar.
— Your Country Needs You: Expansion of the British Army Divisions: 1914-1918. (Illus.). 2000. 29.95 (0-85052-711-2, Pub. by Leo Cooper) Combined Pub.
***Middlebrook, Phyllis Wat.** The Fish Soup Bowl Expedition. 88p. 2000. pap. write for info. (1-930330-00-6) Ten Pell Bks.
Middlebrook, Ron. Backpacker's Songbook. (Illus.). 106p. 1994. pap. 5.50 (0-931759-85-4) Centerstream Pub.
— Bass Guitar Chord Chart. 4p. 1985. pap. 2.50 (0-931759-01-3, 286) Centerstream Pub.
— E 9th Pedal Steel Chord Chart, Vol. 1. (Illus.). 8p. 1987. pap. 3.00 (0-931759-22-6) Centerstream Pub.
— 5 String Banjo Chart, Vol. 1. (Illus.). 4p. 1985. pap. 2.50 (0-931759-04-8) Centerstream Pub.
— 5 String Banjo Natural Style, Vol. 1. (Illus.). 36p. 1980. pap. 6.95 (0-931759-63-3) Centerstream Pub.
— Guitar Chords Chart. 4p. 1995. pap. text 2.95 (1-57424-004-8) Centerstream Pub.
— Guitar Chords Plus: A Comprehensive Study of Chords, Tuning, Keys, Transposing. 88p. (Orig.). 1996. pap. 11.95 (1-57424-026-9) Centerstream Pub.
— Guitar Tablature Manuscript. 100p. 1992. pap. 3.95 (0-931759-25-0) Centerstream Pub.
Middlebrook, Ron. Guitar Tuning for the Complete Idiot. (Illus.). 32p. 1981. pap. 5.95 (1-57424-079-X) Centerstream Pub.
Middlebrook, Ron. It's a Banjo Christmas for 5 String Banjo. (Illus.). 36p. 1995. pap. text 5.95 (1-57424-002-1) Centerstream Pub.
— It's a Guitar Christmas. (Illus.). 36p. 1995. pap. text 5.95 (1-57424-003-X) Centerstream Pub.
Middlebrook, Ron. Left Hand Chord Chart. (Illus.). 4p. 1982. pap. 2.50 (1-57424-078-1) Centerstream Pub.
Middlebrook, Ron. Mandolin Chords, Plus. 8p. 1995. pap. text 3.95 (1-57424-007-2) Centerstream Pub.
— Open Guitar Tunings: A Guide to over 75 Tunings, Vol. 1. (Illus.). 8p. 1991. pap. 4.95 (0-931759-47-1) Centerstream Pub.
— Pick & Grin Patterns for Guitar. 4p. 1995. pap. text 2.00 (1-57424-005-6) Centerstream Pub.
— Power Rhythm Chording. rev. ed. (Illus.). 56p. (YA). (gr. 8 up). 1995. pap. text 17.95 incl. audio compact disk (0-931759-96-X) Centerstream Pub.
Middlebrook, Ron. Scale Power: A Study of Modes for the Guitar. (Illus.). 28p. 1980. pap. 5.95 (1-57424-090-0) Centerstream Pub.
— Scales & Modes in the Beginning. (Illus.). 136p. 1982. pap. 11.95 (1-57424-077-3) Centerstream Pub.
Middlebrook, Ron. Songs Around the Campfire: Western Songs. (Illus.). 168p. 1994. pap. 24.95 (0-931759-86-2) Centerstream Pub.
— Songs for Little Cowpokes. 1998. pap. 15.95 incl. audio compact disk (1-57424-054-4) Centerstream Pub.
— Songs of the Cowboy: Western Songs. 96p. (Orig.). 1990. pap. 12.95 (0-931759-46-3) Centerstream Pub.
— Songs of the Trail: Western Songs. (Illus.). 112p. (Orig.). 1992. pap. 14.95 (0-931759-67-6, 00000152) Centerstream Pub.
— Tenor Banjo Chord Chart. 4p. 1995. pap. text 2.00 (1-57424-008-0) Centerstream Pub.
— 300 Fiddle Tunes: Jigs, Reels, Hornpies, Waltzs. (Illus.). 96p. 1998. pap. 9.95 (1-57424-056-0) Centerstream Pub.
***Middlebrook, Ron.** Ukelele Songbook: Play 50 Popular Songs in Music Notation or Tablature. (Illus.). 80p. 1999. pap. 9.95 (1-57424-072-2) Centerstream Pub.
Middlebrook, Ron. Ukulele Chords. (Illus.). 4p. 1999. pap. 2.95 (1-57424-070-6) Centerstream Pub.
***Middlebrook, Ron, ed.** Hawaiian Ukelele: The Early Methods. abr. ed. (Illus.). 416p. 1998. pap. 35.00 (1-57424-052-8) Centerstream Pub.
Middlebrook, Ron, ed. Marvin's Favorite Halloween Songs. 36p. (C). 1985. pap. text 5.95 (0-931759-07-2) Centerstream Pub.
***Middlebrook, Ron D.** Aloha Collection of Hawaiian Songs: 43 Hawaiian Songs with Ukulele Chono Chart. (Illus.). 96p. 2000. pap. 11.95 (1-57424-084-6, Centerbrook Publishing) Centerstream Pub.
Middlebrook, Stanley M. & Pinnick, Alfred W. How Malaya Is Governed. 2nd ed. LC 73-179225. (Illus.). reprint ed. 34.50 (0-404-54852-0) AMS Pr.
***Middlebrook, Val Middler.** Val's Victory: Defeat Was Never an Option. (Illus.). 336p. 2000. pap. 19.95 (0-9700305-0-9) Ardem Assocs.
Middlebrook, William T. How to Estimate the Building Needs of a College or University: A Demonstration of Methods Developed At the University of Minnesota. LC 56-11614. 181p. reprint ed. pap. 56.20 (0-608-18646-5, 205589100039) Bks Demand.
Middlebrooks, Anthony E. Are We There Yet? The Quality Journey from Mission Through Performance. LC 98-90392. (Illus.). 130p. 1998. pap. 21.95 (0-9665039-0-2) WI Youth.
— Behavior Quicks On-the-Spot Behavior Management Resource. 72p. 1998. pap. 9.95 (0-9665039-1-0) WI Youth.
Middlebrooks, Anthony E., ed. see After School Inc. Staff.
Middlebrooks, Arthur & Terrill, Craig. Market Leadership Strategies for Service Companies: Creating Growth, Profits & Customer Loyalty. LC 99-10338. 288p. 1999. 39.95 (0-8442-2441-3, 24413, Natl Textbk Co) NTC Contemp Pub Co.
Middlebrooks, Donna, jt. auth. see Gordon, Judy.
Middlebrooks, Florence L. Blue Ribbon Cookbook. LC 79-15295. 1980. 22.95 (0-87949-160-4) Ashley Bks.
Middlebrooks-Hutcherson, Gracie. How Many Vehicles Can You Name? I Can Name These Objects! Can You? What Animals Do You See?, 3 vols. Clowney, Earle D., tr. (ENG & SPA., Illus.). (Orig.). (J). 1992. audio. write for info. (1-882485-06-8) Enhance Your Chlds.
— How Many Vehicles Can You Name? I Can Name These Objects! Can You? What Animals Do You See?, 3 vols., Set. Clowney, Earle D., tr. (ENG & SPA., Illus.). (Orig.). (J). 1992. 25.00 (1-882485-05-X); pap. 12.00 (1-882485-07-6) Enhance Your Chlds.
Middlebrooks, Sally. Getting to Know City Kids: Understanding Their Thinking, Imagining & Socializing. LC 97-40580. 1998. 40.00 (0-8077-3686-4); pap. 19.95 (0-8077-3685-6) Tchrs Coll.
Middlebury College Staff, jt. auth. see Heartney, Eleanor.
Middlecamp, C., jt. auth. see Kean, E.
Middlechild, Zachia. A Journey into Earth, Art & Higher Consciousness. 26p. 1995. pap. 9.95 (0-9651177-0-7) Cherifco Middlechild.
Middlecoff, Cary. Advanced Golf. LC 98-51039. (Illus.). 240p. 1999. pap. 16.95 (1-58080-025-4, Pub. by Burford Bks) Natl Bk Netwk.
— The Golf Swing. LC 98-51038. (Illus.). 256p. 1999. pap. 18.95 (1-58080-074-2, Pub. by Burford Bks) Natl Bk Netwk.
Middleditch, Alison, jt. auth. see Oliver, Jean.
Middleditch, B. S. Analytical Artifacts: GS., MS, HPLC, TLC, & PC. 1030p. 1989. 421.00 (0-444-87158-6) Elsevier.
Middleditch, Brian S., et al. Mass Spectrometry of Priority Pollutants. LC 80-14953. 320p. 1981. 75.00 (0-306-40505-9, Plenum Trade) Perseus Pubng.
Middleditch, Leigh B., Jr. & Sinclair, Kent. Virginia Civil Procedure. 3rd ed. LC 98-88479. 1012p. 1998. 105.00 (0-327-00592-0, 60659-11) LEXIS Pub.
— Virginia Civil Procedure, 1992. 2nd ed. 998p. 1993. text 90.00 (1-55834-003-3, 60659-10, MICHIE) LEXIS Pub.
Middleditch, Leigh B., Jr., jt. auth. see Sinclair, Kent.
***Middleditch, Michael.** Amsterdam Mapguide: The Essential Guide to the Tolerant City. (Mapguides Ser.). 2000. pap. 8.95 (0-14-028452-4) Penguin Putnam.
Middleditch, Michael. The New York Mapguide: The Essesntial Guide to Manhattan. 64p. 1998. pap. 8.95 (0-14-026562-7) Viking Penguin.
— The Paris Mapguide. 64p. 1995. pap. 8.95 (0-14-046962-1, Penguin Bks) Viking Penguin.
***Middleditch, Michael.** The Penguin London Mapguide. 4th ed. 64p. 2000. pap. 8.95 (0-14-027948-2, Penguin Bks) Viking Penguin.
Middleditch, Michael. The Penguin London Mapguide: The Essential Guide. rev. ed. (Illus.). 48p. 1993. pap. 7.95 (0-14-046954-0, Penguin Bks) Viking Penguin.
— The Penguin Map of Europe. 1993. pap. 9.95 (0-14-051286-1) Viking Penguin.
Middlehurst, Barbara M. & Aller, Lawrence H., eds. Nebulae & Interstellar Matter. LC 66-13879. (Stars & Stellar Systems Ser.: Vol. 7). (Illus.). 1995. lib. bdg. 72.00 (0-226-45959-4) U Ch Pr.
Middlehurst, Barbara M., jt. ed. see Kuiper, Gerard P.
Middlehurst, Robin. Leading Academics. LC 93-14563. 192p. 1994. 123.00 (0-335-09989-0); pap. 41.95 (0-335-09988-2) OpUniv Pr.
Middlekauff. International Food Regulation Handbook: Policy - Science - Law. Shubik, Philippe, ed. (Food Science & Technology Ser.: Vol. 34). (Illus.). 600p. 1989. text 225.00 (0-8247-7909-6) Dekker.
Middlekauff, Robert. Ancients & Axioms: Secondary Education in Eighteenth-Century New England. LC 79-165725. (American Education Ser, No. 2). 1979. reprint ed. 23.95 (0-405-03713-9) Ayer.
— Benjamin Franklin & His Enemies. LC 95-30917. (Illus.). 275p. (C). 1996. 40.00 (0-520-20268-6, Pub. by U CA Pr) Cal Prin Full Svc.
— Benjamin Franklin & His Enemies. 274p. 1998. pap. text 15.95 (0-520-21378-5, Pub. by U CA Pr) Cal Prin Full Svc.
— The Glorious Cause: The American Revolution, 1763 to 1789. (Oxford History of the United States Ser.). (Illus.). 736p. 1982. text 45.00 (0-19-502921-6) OUP.
— The Glorious Cause: The American Revolution, 1763 to 1789. 2nd ed. (Oxford History of the United States Ser.). (Illus.). 736p. 1985. pap. text 19.95 (0-19-503575-5) OUP.
— Mathers: Three Generations of Puritan Intellectuals,1596-1728. LC 98-50840. 450p. 1999. pap. 16.95 (0-520-21930-9, Pub. by U CA Pr) Cal Prin Full Svc.
Middlekauff, Woodrow S. & Lane, Robert S. Adult & Immature Tabanidae (Diptera) of California. LC 78-66042. (Bulletin of the California Insect Survey Ser.: No. 22). (Illus.). 105p. reprint ed. pap. 32.60 (0-8357-5119-8, 203289700081) Bks Demand.
Middlekauff, Woodrow W. A Revision of the Sawfly Family Orussida for North & Central America (Hymenoptera: Symphyta, Orussidae) LC 83-1397. (University of California Publications in Entomology: No. 101). 58p. 1983. pap. 30.00 (0-7837-7493-1, 204921500010) Bks Demand.
Middleman. Fundamentals of Polymer Processing. 1977. student ed. 22.75 (0-07-041852-7) McGraw.
Middleman, Dan. Pain. (Illus.). 226p. 1998. pap. 17.50 (0-911521-52-6) Tafnews.
Middleman, Jo-Ann. Till a Hundred & Twenty Years: A Memoir. LC 95-94698. 224p. 1995. pap. 12.95 (0-9647771-0-X) EMESS Pr.
Middleman, Louis I. Environmental Restoration & Waste Management (Dept. of Energy) Five-Year Plan, Fiscal Years 1992-1996. (Illus.). 622p. (C). 1996. reprint ed. pap. text 60.00 (0-7881-3202-4) DIANE Pub.
Middleman, Ruth R. A Study Guide for ACSW Certification. 1995. pap. 15.95 (0-87101-264-2) Natl Assn Soc Wkrs.
Middleman, Ruth R., ed. Activities & Action in Groupwork. LC 83-309. (Social Work with Groups Ser.: Vol. 6, No. 1). 105p. 1983. text 39.95 (0-86656-228-1) Haworth Pr.
Middleman, Ruth R. & National Association of Social Workers Staff. A Study Guide for ACSW Certification. 4th ed. LC 98-36653. 1998. write for info. (0-87101-299-5) Natl Assn Soc Wkrs.
Middleman, Ruth R. & Wood, Gale G. Skills for Direct Practice in Social Work. 176p. 1990. pap. text 22.00 (0-231-05509-9) Col U Pr.
Middleman, Ruth R. & Wood, Gale G., eds. Teaching Secrets: The Technology in Social Work Education. LC 91-27072. (Journal of Teaching in Social Work: Vol. 5, No. 2). (Illus.). 138p. 1992. 49.95 (1-56024-213-2) Haworth Pr.
— Teaching Secrets: The Technology in Social Work Education. LC 91-27072. 138p. 1996. pap. 19.95 (0-7890-6045-0) Haworth Pr.
Middleman, Ruth R., jt. auth. see Wood, Gale G.
Middleman, Stanley. The Flow of High Polymers: Continuum & Molecular Rheology. LC 67-29460. 255p. reprint ed. pap. 79.10 (0-608-16938-2, 205629800056) Bks Demand.
— An Introduction to Fluid Dynamics: Principles of Analysis & Design. LC 97-9530. 528p. 1997. text 109.95 (0-471-18209-5) Wiley.
— An Introduction to Mass & Heat Transfer: Principles of Analysis & Design. LC 97-9531. 696p. 1997. text 114.95 (0-471-11176-7) Wiley.
— Modeling Axisymmetric Flows: Dynamics of Films, Jets, & Drops. LC 95-2196. (Illus.). 299p. 1995. text 63.00 (0-12-494950-9) Acad Pr.
Middleman, Stanley & Hochberg, Arthur K. Process Engineering Analysis in Semiconductor Device Fabrication. (Illus.). 672p. (C). 1993. 98.75 (0-07-041853-5) McGraw.
Middlemas, Keith. Diplomacy of Illusion: The British Government & Germany, 1937-1939. (Modern Revivals in History Ser.). 510p. 1992. 64.95 (0-7512-0009-3, Pub. by Gregg Revivals) Ashgate Pub Co.
— Power, Competition & the State: Britain in Search of Balance, 1940-1961, Vol. 1. (Publication Ser.: No. 349). 404p. (C). 1987. text 14.78 (0-8179-8491-7) Hoover Inst Pr.
Middlemas, Robert K. The Clydesiders: A Left-Wing Struggle for Parliamentary Power. LC 66-2916. (Illus.). 307p. 1965. 39.50 (0-678-08040-2) Kelley.
Middlemass, Robert & Holworthy Hall Staff. The Valiant. unabridged ed. Landes, William-Alan, ed. LC 97-41680. 55p. 1997. pap. 6.00 (0-88734-753-3) Players Pr.
***Middlemiss, Bob.** A Common Glory. LC 00-9799. 2000. write for info. (0-916078-52-3) Iris Pr.
Middlemiss, Howard, jt. auth. see Cockshott, Peter.
Middlemist, Dennis R. Organizational Behavior. Date not set. pap. text, student ed. 20.00 (0-314-79361-5) West Pub.
Middlemore, S. G., tr. see Burckhardt, Jacob.

M

An Asterisk (*) at the beginning of an entry indicates that the title is appearing for the first time.

Middlemost, Eric A. Magmas, Rocks & Planetary Development: A Survey of Magma/Igneous Rock Systems. 288p. (C). 1997. pap. text 42.19 (0-582-23089-6, Drumbeat) Longman.

Middles, Mick. From Joy Division to New Order: The Factory Story. (Illus.). 320p. (Orig.). 1996. pap. 17.95 (0-7535-0041-8, Pub. by Virgin Bks) London Brdge.

*Middles, Mick. Ian McCulloch: King of Cool. 2000. pap. text 15.95 (1-897783-13-2) Indep Music Pr.

Middles, Mick. Oasis: Round Their Way. 126p. (Orig.). (YA). pap. 17.95 (1-897783-10-8, MRSS627, Pub. by Indep Music Pr) Music Sales.

*Middles, Mick. Shaun Ryder: Happy Mondays, Black Grape & other Traumas. 2000. pap. text 15.95 (1-897783-11-6) Indep Music Pr.

Middles, Mick. Shaun Ryder: In His Own Words. (Illus.). 102p. 1998. pap. text 15.95 (0-7119-6815-2) Omnibus NY.

— The Smiths: The Complete Story. 128p. 1988. pap. 14.95 (0-8464-4925-0) Beekman Pubs.

*Middles, Mick. The Stone Roses: Breaking into Heaven; The Rise & Fall. (Illus.). 250p. 1999. 19.95 (0-7119-7546-9) Omnibus NY.

Middlesworth, E. M. & Massoud, H. ULSI Science & Technology: 5th International Symposium. (Proceedings Ser.: Vol. 95-5). 534p. 1995. 59.00 (1-56677-099-8) Electrochem Soc.

*Middlesworth, Mike. Manic Street Preachers Biography. 2000. pap. 19.95 (0-7119-7738-0) Omnibus NY.

Middletn, David L., jt. auth. see Caldwell, Harry B.

Middleton. Avionic System. 1989. text. write for info. (0-582-01881-1, Pub. by Addison-Wesley) Longman.

— Changeling. LC 97-47409. 150p. 1998. pap., student ed. 9.95 (0-7190-4481-2) St Martin.

Middleton. Child Sexual Abuse. text. write for info. (0-471-49150-0); pap. text. write for info. (0-471-49151-9) Wiley.

Middleton. Data Analysis of Earth Science. LC 99-21690. 260p. 1999. pap. text 46.67 (0-13-393505-1) P-H.

— Encyclopedia of Sub-Saharan Africa. 1997. 395.00 (0-13-279936-7) P-H.

— Encyclopedia of Sub Saharan Africa, Vol. 1. LC 97-31364. 1998. 120.00 (0-684-80467-0) S&S Trade.

— Encyclopedia of Sub Saharan Africa, Vol. 2. 1998. 120.00 (0-684-80468-9) S&S Trade.

— Encyclopedia of Sub Saharan Africa, Vol. 3. 1998. 120.00 (0-684-80469-7) S&S Trade.

— Encyclopedia of Sub Saharan Africa, Vol. 4. 1998. 120.00 (0-684-80470-0) S&S Trade.

— Simon & Schuster Crostics, 118. 1997. pap. 8.00 (0-684-83502-9) S&S Trade.

— Super Crostics. 5th ed. 224p. 1999. per. 10.00 (0-684-84364-1) S&S Trade.

Middleton, et al. Tears of the Crocodile: From Rio to Reality in the Developing World. LC 93-5266. 228p. (C). 70.00 (0-7453-0764-7); pap. 19.95 (0-7453-0765-5, Pub. by Pluto GBR) Stylus Pub VA.

Middleton, Alex L., jt. ed. see Perrins, Christopher M.

Middleton, Alex L. A. American Goldfinch. LC 98-12766. (Wild Bird Guide Ser.). (Illus.). 112p. 1998. pap. 19.95 (0-8117-2687-8) Kitch Keepsakes.

Middleton, Andrew. Rugs & Carpets: Techniques, Traditions & Designs. (Illus.). 192p. 1996. 30.00 (1-85732-634-2, Pub. by Reed Illust Books) Antique Collect.

Middleton, Arthur. Globes of the Western World. (Illus.). 224p. 1993. 95.00 (0-85667-395-1) Sothebys Pubns.

— Towards a Renewed Priesthood. 139p. (Orig.). 1996. pap. 12.95 (0-85244-273-4, Pub. by Gracewing) Morehouse Pub.

Middleton, Arthur P. Annapolis on the Chesapeake. (Illus.). 80p. (Orig.). 1988. 29.95 (0-933101-13-9); pap. 15.95 (0-933101-14-7) Legacy Pubns.

*Middleton, Barbara, ed. The Heritage of Butler County, Alabama. (Heritage of Alabama Ser.: Vol. 7). 320p. 2001. 50.00 (1-891647-38-5) Herit Pub Consult.

Middleton, Bernadette. The Feng Shui Primer & Workbook. large type ed. (Illus.). 108p. (Orig.). 1997. mass mkt., wbk. ed. 18.00 (0-9662034-0-2) MidKam Corp.

Middleton, Bernard C. A History of English Craft Bookbinding Technique. 328p. (C). 1988. 130.00 (0-946323-13-5, Pub. by New5 Holland) St Mut.

— A History of English Craft Bookbinding Technique. 4th ed. LC 96-3342. 1996. 55.00 (1-884718-28-0) Oak Knoll.

*Middleton, Bernard C. Recollections: An Autobiography of Bernard C. Middleton. LC 99-88180. 2000. write for info. (1-58456-016-9) Oak Knoll.

Middleton, Bernard C. Restoration of Leather Bindings. 3rd ed. LC 98-6705. (Illus.). 200p. 1998. 39.95 (1-884718-50-7, 50322) Oak Knoll.

*Middleton, Beth. Wetland Restoration, Flood Pulsing, & Disturbance Dynamics. LC 98-4512. (Illus.). 400p. 1998. 69.95 (0-471-29263-X) Wiley.

Middleton, Betty J. Special Times: Honoring Our Jewish & Christian Heritages for Grades 1 & 2. LC 95-113806. 208p. 1994. pap. 30.00 (1-55896-281-6) Unitarian Univ.

Middleton, C. The Famous Historie of Chinon of England. (EETS, OS Ser.: No. 165). 1972. reprint ed. 45.00 (0-527-00162-7) Periodicals Srv.

Middleton, C & Garza-Falcon, Leticia M., trs. Andalusian Poems. 120p. 1993. 40.00 (0-87923-887-9) Godine.

*Middleton, Carl H. Quotation Overture: A History of Ideas Through the Best Quotations. LC 99-32055. 1999. 34.00 (1-56072-697-0, Nova Kroshka Bks) Nova Sci Pubs.

*Middleton, Charlotte. Tabitha's Terrifically Tough Tooth. LC 99-88849. (Illus.). (J). 2001. write for info. (0-8037-2583-3) Peng Put Young Read.

Middleton, Christopher. Anasphere: Poems. deluxe limited ed. (Burning Deck Poetry Chapbooks Ser.). 1978. 20.00 (0-930900-54-5) Burning Deck.

*Middleton, Christopher. Faint Harps & Silver Voices: Selected Translations. 220p. 2000. pap. 35.00 (1-85754-355-6, Pub. by Carcanet Pr) Paul & Co Pubs.

Middleton, Christopher. The Historie of Heaven. LC 76-57400. (English Experience Ser.: No. 816). 1977. reprint ed. lib. bdg. 20.00 (90-221-0816-3) Walter J Johnson.

— In the Mirror of the Eighth King. (Green Integer Ser.: No. 11). 96p. 1999. pap. 11.95 (1-55713-331-X, Pub. by Green Integer) Consort Bk Sales.

— Intimate Chronicles. LC 96-17207. 104p. (Orig.). 1996. pap. 12.95 (1-878818-47-3, Pub. by Sheep Meadow) U Pr of New Eng.

— Jackdaws Jiving: Selected Essays on Poetry & Translation. LC 99-195331. 240p. 1998. pap. 29.95 (1-85754-351-3, Pub. by Carcanet Pr) Paul & Co Pubs.

— Munich up Close. (Illus.). 144p. 1994. pap. 12.95 (0-8442-9454-3, Passprt Bks) NTC Contemp Pub Co.

— Nonsequences: Self Poems. (Orig.). (C). 1966. pap. 2.00 (0-393-04228-6) Norton.

— Some Dogs. 24p. 1993. pap. 7.95 (1-870612-93-0, Pub. by Enitha Pr) Dufour.

— Woden Dog: Poems. deluxe ed. (Burning Deck Poetry Ser.). 32p. 1982. pap. 20.00 (0-930901-06-1) Burning Deck.

Middleton, Christopher, ed. see Goethe, Johann Wolfgang Von.

Middleton, Christopher, ed. see Gustafsson, Lars.

Middleton, Christopher, ed. see Nietzsche, Friedrich Wilhelm.

Middleton, Christopher, ed. & tr. see Gustafsson, Lars.

Middleton, Christopher, tr. see Benn, Gottfried.

Middleton, Christopher, tr. see Grass, Gunter.

Middleton, Christopher, tr. see Hofmann, Gert.

Middleton, Christopher, tr. see Kuoni, Carin & Walser, Robert.

Middleton, Christopher, tr. see Wolf, Christa.

Middleton, Christopher, tr. & intro. see Walser, Robert.

Middleton, D., jt. ed. see Dyer, P.

Middleton, D. H., ed. Airspeed: The Company & Its Aeroplanes. 216p. 1990. 50.00 (0-86138-009-6, Pub. by T Dalton) St Mut.

Middleton, Darren J., jt. ed. see Bien, Peter A.

*Middleton, Darren J. N. Novel Theology: Nikos Kazantzakis' Encounter with Whiteheadian Process Theism. 2000. 39.95 (0-86554-624-X, H521) Mercer Univ Pr.

Middleton, David. Beyond the Chandeleurs. LC 99-33409. 88p. 1999. text 19.95 (0-8071-2377-3) La State U Pr.

— The Burning Fields. LC 90-49724. 64p. 1991. pap. 7.95 (0-8071-1639-4) La State U Pr.

— An Introduction to Statistical Communication Theory. LC 96-11241. 1184p. 1996. 99.95 (0-7803-1178-7, PC5648) Inst Electrical.

— An Introduction to Statistical Communication Theory. LC 58-8042. 1140p. 1987. reprint ed. 73.95 (0-932146-15-5) Peninsula CA.

— Time to Unite: What God's Word Teaches on the Church & the Churches. 1997. pap. text 1.99 (0-85234-002-8, Pub. by Evangelical Pr) P & R Pubng.

— Topics in Communications Theory. LC 64-25001. 126p. 1987. reprint ed. 19.95 (0-932146-14-7) Peninsula CA.

Middleton, David & Edwards, Derek, eds. Collective Remembering. (Inquiries in Social Construction Ser.). 240p. (C). 1990. text 47.50 (0-8039-8234-8); pap. text 18.95 (0-8039-8235-6) Sage.

Middleton, David & Heller, Joseph. Joseph Heller: An Interview, No. 5. LC 88-23455. (Contemporaries Ser.). 1988. write for info. (0-935061-42-8) Contemp Res.

Middleton, David, jt. auth. see Finlay, John.

Middleton, David, jt. auth. see Pearson, David.

Middleton, David, jt. ed. see Engestrom, Yrjo.

Middleton, David, ed. see Finlay, John.

Middleton, David, ed. see Olshevskii, Viktor V.

*Middleton, David L. Toni Morrison's Fiction: Contemporary Criticism. (Critical Studies in Black Life & Culture: 30). 344p. 1999. pap. 24.95 (0-8153-3588-1) Garland.

Middleton, David L. & Trotman, C. James, eds. Toni Morrison's Fiction: Contemporary Criticism. LC 96-43555. (Critical Studies in Black Life & Culture: Vol. 30). 344p. 1996. text 65.00 (0-8153-0869-8) Garland.

Middleton, David L., jt. auth. see Richmond, Kent D.

Middleton, David N., ed. QS-9000: Automotive Quality Standard Explained. 1997. 19.95 (1-891578-02-2) INFORM VA.

Middleton, Deborah, ed. see Nunez, Nicolas.

Middleton, DeWight. The Challenge of Human Diversity: Mirrors, Bridges, & Chasms. 116p. (C). 1998. pap. text 10.50 (0-88133-986-5) Waveland Pr.

Middleton, Don. Cheetahs. LC 97-48445. (Big Cats Ser.). 24p. (J). (gr. k-4). 1999. 17.27 (0-8239-5212-6, PowerKids) Rosen Group.

— Dealing with Competitiveness. LC 98-22633. (Conflict Resolution Library). 24p. (J). 1999. 17.26 (0-8239-5267-3, PowerKids) Rosen Group.

— Dealing with Discrimination. LC 98-11549. (Conflict Resolution Library). 24p. (J). 1999. 17.26 (0-8239-5270-3, PowerKids) Rosen Group.

— Dealing with Feeling Left Out. LC 98-5642. (Conflict Resolution Library). 24p. (J). 1999. 17.26 (0-8239-5269-X, PowerKids) Rosen Group.

— Dealing with Secrets. LC 98-22631. (Conflict Resolution Library). 24p. (J). 1999. 17.26 (0-8239-5265-7, PowerKids) Rosen Group.

— Dealing with Someone Who Is Selfish. LC 98-5641. (Conflict Resolution Library). 24p. (J). 1999. 17.26 (0-8239-5268-1, PowerKids) Rosen Group.

— Dealing with Tattling. LC 98-22632. (Conflict Resolution Library). 24p. (J). 1999. 17.26 (0-8239-5266-5, PowerKids) Rosen Group.

*Middleton, Don. Jaguars. LC 97-45034. (Big Cats Ser.). (Illus.). 24p. (J). (gr. k-4). 1999. lib. bdg. 18.60 (0-8239-5210-X) Rosen Group.

Middleton, Don. Leopards. LC 97-44840. 24p. (J). (gr. k-4). 1999. 15.93 (0-8239-5209-6, PowerKids) Rosen Group.

— Lions. LC 97-32690. (Big Cats Ser.). 24p. (J). (gr. k-4). 1998. 17.27 (0-8239-5208-8) Rosen Group.

— Tigers. LC 97-38706. (Big Cats Ser.). 24p. (J). (gr. k-4). 1999. 15.93 (0-8239-5213-4, PowerKids) Rosen Group.

*Middleton, Don. Winning PR in the Wired World. (Illus.). 2000. 24.95 (0-07-136342-4) McGraw.

Middleton, Don C. Dealing with Competition. (Conflict Resolution Library). (Illus.). 24p. (J). (gr. k-4). 1998. pap. 6.95 (1-56838-269-3) Hazelden.

— Dealing with Feeling Left Out. (Conflict Resolution Library). (Illus.). 24p. (J). (gr. k-4). 1998. pap. 6.95 (1-56838-270-7) Hazelden.

— Dealing with Secrets. (Conflict Resolution Library). (Illus.). 24p. (J). (gr. k-4). 1998. pap. 6.95 (1-56838-271-5) Hazelden.

Middleton, Donald. Tests of Character: Epic Flights by Legendary Test Pilots. 224p. 1995. 35.00 (1-56091-671-0, R-149) Soc Auto Engineers.

Middleton, Dorothy. Victorian Lady Travellers. (Illus.). 189p. 1993. reprint ed. pap. 11.00 (0-89733-063-3) Academy Chi Pubs.

Middleton, Drew, intro. Air War in Vietnam. 18.95 (0-405-11519-9) Ayer.

Middleton, Drew & Brown, Gene. Southeast Asia. (Great Contemporary Issues Ser.). 27.95 (0-405-13399-5) Ayer.

Middleton, Elliott, Jr. Allergy: Principles & Practice, 2 vols. 5th ed. LC 98-173984. (Illus.). 2016p. (C). (gr. 13). 1998. text 265.00 (0-8151-0072-8, 27204) Mosby Inc.

Middleton Elya, Susan. Say Hola to Spanish. LC 95-478. (ENG & SPA., Illus.). 32p. (J). (ps-5). 1996. 15.95 (1-880000-29-6) Lee & Low Bks.

Middleton, Fiona. Seal: People of the Sea. (Illus.). 192p. 1996. 35.00 (1-85158-744-6, Pub. by Mainstream Pubng) Trafalgar.

Middleton, Gayle. The Christmas Spirit. (Illus.). 16p. 1989. pap. 12.95 (0-685-29047-6, 51034) Willitts Designs.

— The Legend of Catlantis. (Illus.). 112p. 1989. text 24.95 (0-685-29046-8, 47025) Willitts Designs.

Middleton, George. Diana Does It. 1961. pap. 5.25 (0-8222-0306-5) Dramatists Play.

— Embers & Other One-Act Plays: With the Failures, the Gargoyle, in His House, Madonna, the Man Masterful. LC 77-70359. (One-Act Plays in Reprint Ser.). 1977. reprint ed. 20.00 (0-8486-2020-8) Roth Pub Inc.

— Nowadays. Meserve, Walter J. & Meserve, Mollie A., eds. (When Conscience Trod the Stage Ser.). 1998. pap., spiral bd. 4.95 (0-937657-46-8) Feedbk Theabks & Prospero.

— These Things Are Mine. (American Autobiography Ser.). 448p. 1995. reprint ed. lib. bdg. 99.00 (0-7812-8594-1) Rprt Serv.

Middleton, Gerard V., ed. Primary Sedimentary Structures & Their Hydrodynamic Interpretation: A Symposium. LC 76-219474. (Society of Economic Paleontologists & Mineralogists, Special Publication Ser.: No. 12). 272p. reprint ed. pap. 84.40 (0-608-12955-0, 202473800038) Bks Demand.

Middleton, Gerard V. & Southard, John B. Mechanics of Sediment Movement: Lecture Notes for Short Course No. 3, Sponsored by the Eastern Section of the Society of Economic Paleontologists & Mineralogists, & Given in Providence, Rhode Island, March 13-14, 1984. 2nd ed. LC TC0175.2.M54. (SEPM Short Course Ser.: No. 3, 1984). 411p. reprint ed. pap. 127.50 (0-7837-2417-9, 204255400005) Bks Demand.

Middleton, Gerard V. & Wilcock, Peter R. Mechanics in the Earth & Environmental Sciences. (Illus.). 475p. (C). 1994. pap. text 42.95 (0-521-44669-4) Cambridge U Pr.

Middleton, Gerard V., et al. Nonlinear Dynamics & Fractals: New Numerical Techniques for Sedimentary Data. (Short Course Notes Ser.: No. 36). (Illus.). 180p. (Orig.). 1995. pap. 55.00 (1-56576-021-2) SEPM.

Middleton, Gordon K., Jr. Good News for Hurting Hearts: Breaking the Code. 64p. (Orig.). (YA). 1994. pap. 4.95 (0-9641534-0-8) GKM Pubng.

Middleton, Grace, et al. Report Writing for Speech-Language Pathologists. 173p. 1998. pap. text 44.00 (0-12-784563-1) Acad Pr.

— Report Writing for Speech-Language Pathologists. 173p. 1992. pap. text 46.00 (0-7616-7797-6) Commun Skill.

Middleton, Grace, jt. auth. see Pannbacker, Mary.

Middleton, Grace F. & Pannbacker, Mary. Cleft Palate & Related Disorders. Anderson, Kirsteen, ed. LC 97-74552. (Illus.). 302p. 1997. ring bd. 58.50 (1-883315-25-5, 7431) Imaginart Intl.

*Middleton, Harry. The Bright Country: A Fisherman's Return to Trout, Wild Water & Himself. 304p. 2000. pap. 18.00 (0-87108-904-1) Pruett.

Middleton, Harry. The Earth Is Enough: Growing up in a World of Flyfishing, Trout & Old Men. LC 95-43024. 206p. 1996. pap. 18.00 (0-87108-874-6) Pruett.

— On the Spine of Time: A FlyFisher's Journey among Mountain People, Streams & Trout. LC 97-36183. 179p. 1997. pap. 18.00 (0-87108-892-4) Pruett.

— Rivers of Memory. LC 92-38119. 89p. 1993. 18.95 (0-87108-835-5) Pruett.

Middleton, Haydn. Ancient Olympic Games. LC 99-24332. (Olympics Ser.). (Illus.). 32p. (J). (gr. 4-8). 1999. lib. bdg. 15.95 (1-57572-450-2) Heinemann Lib.

— Captain Cook: The Great Ocean Explorer. (What's Their Story? Ser.). (Illus.). 32p. (J). 1998. lib. bdg. 12.95 (0-19-521433-1) OUP.

— Cleopatra: The Queen of Dreams. LC 97-27366. (What's Their Story? Ser.). (Illus.). 32p. (J). (gr. 1-4). 1998. lib. bdg. 12.95 (0-19-521404-8) OUP.

*Middleton, Haydn. Crises at the Olympics. LC 99-22709. (Olympics Ser.). (Illus.). 32p. (J). (gr. 4-8). 1999. 15.95 (1-57572-452-9) Heinemann Lib.

Middleton, Haydn. Diana, Princess of Wales. LC 97-49616. (Lives & Times Ser.). 1998. 19.92 (1-57572-715-3) Heinemann Lib.

— Diana, Princess of Wales. LC 98-23294. (Profiles Ser.). (Illus.). (J). 1998. 22.79 (1-57572-716-1) Heinemann Lib.

— Great Olympic Moments. LC 99-24331. (Olympics Ser.). 1999. lib. bdg. write for info. (1-57572-451-0) Heinemann Lib.

— Henry Ford: The People's Carmaker. LC 97-27370. (What's Their Story? Ser.). (Illus.). 32p. (J). (gr. 3-4). 1998. lib. bdg. 12.95 (0-19-521406-4) OUP.

— Island of the Mighty. (Oxford Myths & Legends Ser.). 80p. (YA). (gr. 5-12). 1987. 20.00 (0-19-274133-0) OUP.

*Middleton, Haydn. Modern Olympic Games. LC 99-24273. (Olympics Ser.). 1999. lib. bdg. 22.79 (1-57572-453-7) Heinemann Lib.

— Mother Teresa. LC 99-89881. 2000. lib. bdg. write for info. (1-57572-227-5) Heinemann Lib.

Middleton, Haydn. Thomas Edison. LC 97-27373. (What's Their Story?). (Illus.). 32p. (J). (gr. 1-4). 1998. lib. bdg. 12.95 (0-19-521401-3) OUP.

— William Shakespeare: The Master Playwright. LC 97-32049. (What's Their Story? Ser.). (Illus.). 32p. (J). (gr. 2 up). 1998. lib. bdg. 12.95 (0-19-521430-7) OUP.

Middleton, Helen. Healthy Heart Cookbook: Simple, Tasty & Nutritious Recipes Low in Salt, Fat & Cholesterol, 1. 1999. 12.95 (1-85967-885-8) Anness Pub.

Middleton, Henry. The Last East Indian Voyage. LC 74-25700. (English Experience Ser.: No. 307). 1971. reprint ed. 20.00 (90-221-0307-2) Walter J Johnson.

*Middleton, Ian. I See a Voice. LC 98-119312. 179 p. 1998. 16.95 (1-86950-270-1) HarpC.

Middleton, J., ed. Computer Methods in Biomechanics & Biomedical Engineering. 850p. 1998. text 220.00 (90-5699-206-6) Gordon & Breach.

Middleton, J., et al, eds. Computer Methods in Biomechanics & Biomedical Engineering. 576p. 1996. text 72.00 (2-919875-00-0) Gordon & Breach.

Middleton, J. & Pande, G. N., eds. Numeta 85, Numerical Methods in Engineering, Theory & Applications: Proceedings of an International Conference Swansea, UK, 7-11 January 1985, 2 vols., Set. 1084p. (C). 1985. text 388.00 (90-6191-577-5, Pub. by A A Balkema) Ashgate Pub Co.

Middleton, J., jt. ed. see Pande, G. N.

Middleton, J. E., tr. see Tindall, Adrienne, ed.

Middleton, J. Richard, jt. auth. see Walsh, Brian J.

Middleton, James A. & Goepfert, Polly. Inventive Strategies for Teaching Mathematics: Implementing Standards for Reform, No. 6. LC 96-13468. (Psychology in the Classroom Ser.). 165p. (Orig.). 1996. pap. text 17.95 (1-55798-368-2) Am Psychol.

Middleton, Jeff. Illustrated DOS Computing. (Illus.). 48p. (Orig.). 1990. pap. 29.95 (0-8464-4322-8) Beekman Pubs.

Middleton, Jennie, ed. see Davis, Akie.

Middleton, Jeremy. Coming Alive. 1999. pap. text 9.99 (0-946068-71-2) Spring Arbor Coll.

Middleton, Jo A. Willa Cather's Modernism: A Study of Style & Technique. LC 89-45407. 178 p. 1990. 36.50 (0-8386-3385-4) Fairleigh Dickinson.

Middleton, John. The Central Tribes of the North-Eastern Bantu. LC 76-44758. reprint ed. 27.50 (0-404-15952-4) AMS Pr.

— Encyclopedia of Africa: South of the Sahara, 4 vols. LC 97-31364. 1755p. 1997. 475.00 (0-684-80466-2) Mac Lib Ref.

— The Lugbara of Uganda. 2nd ed. (Orig.). (C). 1992. pap. text 23.50 (0-15-500622-3) Harcourt Coll Pubs.

— Lugbara Religion: Ritual & Authority among an East African People. LC 60-51074. 294p. reprint ed. pap. 91.20 (0-608-13679-4, 205538700017) Bks Demand.

*Middleton, John. Smart Things to Know about Your Career. (Smart Things to Know about... Ser.). 2000. pap. 16.95 (1-84112-114-2) Capstone Pub NH.

Middleton, John. The World of the Swahili: An African Mercantile Civilization. (Illus.). 320p. (C). 1992. 37.50 (0-300-05219-7) Yale U Pr.

— The World of the Swahili: An African Mercantile Civilization. (Illus.). 266p. 1994. pap. 18.00 (0-300-06080-7) Yale U Pr.

*Middleton, John & Beidelman, Thomas O. Lugbara Religion. 344p. 1999. 56.95 (3-8258-4034-4); pap. 29.95 (3-8258-4033-6, Pub. by CE24) Transaction Pubs.

Middleton, John & Campbell, Jane. Zanzibar, Its Society & Politics. LC 84-29046. (Illus.). 71p. 1985. reprint ed. lib. bdg. 55.00 (0-313-24739-0, MIZA, Greenwood Pr) Greenwood.

Middleton, John & Kershaw, Greet. The Central Tribes of the North-Eastern Bantu: The Kikuyu Including Embu, Meru, Mere, Chuka, Mwimbi, Tharaka, & the Kamba of Kenya. LC 76-351844. (Ethnographic Survey of Africa: East Central Africa Ser.: Pt. 5). 108p. pap. 33.50 (0-8357-6962-3, 203902200009) Bks Demand.

Middleton, John & Waltham, Tony. The Underground Atlas: A Gazetteer of the World's Cave Regions. (Illus.). 239p. 1999. reprint ed. text 30.00 (0-7881-6134-2) DIANE Pub.

Middleton, John, et al. Skills Training for Productivity: Vocational Education & Training in Developing Countries. (World Bank Publications). (Illus.). 374p. 1993. text 49.95 (0-19-520887-0, 60887) OUP.

Middleton, John, jt. auth. see Adhikarya, Ronny.

Middleton, John, ed. see De Vere Allen, James.

An Asterisk (*) at the beginning of an entry indicates that the title is appearing for the first time.

M

An Asterisk (*) at the beginning of an entry indicates that the title is appearing for the first time.

— Simon & Schuster's Super Crostics Book, No. 3. 224p. 1995. per. 9.00 (*0-671-51132-7*, Fireside) S&S Trade Pap.

— Super Crostics Book, Vol. 4. 224p. 1997. per. 9.00 (*0-684-81340-8*) S&S Trade.

— The Witch c. 1613, Vol. 8. (Malone Society Ser.). (Illus.). 112p. 1948. text 39.95 (*0-19-729007-8*) OUP.

Middleton, Thomas H., ed. Simon & Schuster Crostics, No. 112. 1994. pap. 7.00 (*0-671-89711-X*, Fireside) S&S Trade Pap.

Middleton, Tim, jt. auth. see Giles, Judy.

Middleton, Tim, jt. ed. see Giles, Judy.

Middleton, Tom. The Book of Maidenhead. 1977. 50.00 (*0-86023-006-6*) St Mut.

— New York Times Acrostic Crossword Puzzles, Vol. 7. 1997. pap. 10.00 (*0-8129-2704-4*, Times Bks) Crown Pub Group.

Middleton, Victor. Marketing in Travel & Tourism. 2nd ed. LC 94-240552. 480p. 1994. pap. 36.95 (*0-7506-0973-7*) Buttrwrth-Heinemann.

***Middleton, Victor T. C.** Marketing in Travel & Tourism. 394p. 2000. pap. 37.95 (*0-7506-4471-0*) Buttrwrth-Heinemann.

Middleton, W. E. The Experimenters: A Study of the Accademia del Cimento. LC 77-142816. (ITA., Illus.). 431p. reprint ed. pap. 133.70 (*0-8357-9271-4*, 201569200095) Bks Demand.

— The History of the Barometer. (Illus.). 512p. 1997. 49.50 (*0-948382-08-2*, Pub. by Baros Bks) Antique Collect.

— Scientific Revolution. 88p. 1965. pap. 11.95 (*0-87073-851-8*) Schenkman Bks Inc.

Middleton, W. E., tr. see Bouguer, Pierre.

Middleton, William, et al. Web Programming with Perl 5: Internet Programming with Perl. LC 96-67955. 365p. 1997. 29.99 (*1-57521-112-2*) Sams.

Middleton, William D. From Bullets to Bart: Bulletin No. 127. Carlson, Norman, ed. LC 88-70491. (Bulletin Ser.: No. 127). (Illus.). 176p. 1989. 35.00 (*0-915348-27-6*) Central Electric.

***Middleton, William D.** Landmarks on the Iron Road: Two Centuries of North American Railroad Engineering. LC 98-55475. (Railroads Past & Present Ser.). 1999. 39.95 (*0-253-33559-0*) Ind U Pr.

Middleton, William D. South Shore: The Last Interuban. 2nd rev. ed. LC 98-55983. (Railroads Past & Present Ser.). (Illus.). 192p. 1999. text 35.00 (*0-253-33533-7*) Ind U Pr.

— Traction Classics: The High Speed & Deluxe Interurban Cars, Vol. 2. LC 83-18482. (Illus.). 230p. 1985. 20.00 (*0-87095-089-4*) Gldn West Bks.

***Middleton, William D.** Yet There Isn't a Train I Wouldn't Take: Railway Journeys by William D. Middleton. LC 99-46002. (Railroads Past & Present Ser.). (Illus.). 256p. 2000. 39.95 (*0-253-33699-6*) Ind U Pr.

Middleton, William D. & Lawson, Thomas L., eds. Anatomy & MRI of the Joints: A Multiplanar Atlas. (Illus.). 316p. 1989. text 166.00 (*0-88167-455-9*) Lppncott W & W.

Middleton, William D., jt. auth. see Kurtz, Alfred B.

Middleton, William E. The History of the Barometer. LC 64-10942. 511p. reprint ed. pap. 158.50 (*0-608-30409-3*, 200388700037) Bks Demand.

— A History of the Theories of Rain & Other Forms of Precipitation. LC 66-15982. (Watts History of Science Library). 231p. reprint ed. pap. 71.70 (*0-608-12565-2*, 202405900035) Bks Demand.

— A History of the Thermometer & Its Use in Meteorology. LC 66-23978. 262p. reprint ed. pap. 81.30 (*0-608-15188-2*, 202737600055) Bks Demand.

— Invention of the Meteorological Instruments. LC 68-31640. (Illus.). 377p. reprint ed. pap. 116.90 (*0-608-14707-9*, 202585300046) Bks Demand.

— Vision Through the Atmosphere. LC QC0976.T7M5. 264p. reprint ed. pap. 81.90 (*0-608-10101-X*, 201436600089) Bks Demand.

Middleton, William J. Garden Rubaiyat: An Illustrated Collection of Flower Poetry. LC 96-90632. (Illus.). 52p. (Orig.). 1996. pap. 4.50 (*1-886467-10-2*) WJM Press.

— Half Borrowed Couplets: The Poet & the Jester. LC 98-96079. (Illus.). 52p. 1998. pap. 5.00 (*1-886467-32-3*) WJM Press.

— It's about Time. 47p. 1994. pap. 4.00 (*1-886467-00-5*) WJM Press.

***Middleton, William J.** Limerick 101: A Concise Collegiate Course for Constructing Comic Limericks, with 101 Examples. LC 98-96855. (Illus.). 76 p. 1999. pap. 5.00 (*1-886467-42-0*) WJM Press.

Middleton, William J. Limerick Tyme. (Orig.). 1996. pap. 3.50 (*1-886467-11-0*) WJM Press.

— Little Songs: A Collection of Sonnets & Villanelles. LC 96-90477. (Illus.). 52p. (Orig.). 1996. pap. 5.00 (*1-886467-08-0*) WJM Press.

— Moon Dancing: Poems. LC 98-96000. (Illus.). 60p. 1998. pap. 5.50 (*1-886467-30-7*) WJM Press.

— My Color. LC 96-90743. (Illus.). 52p. (Orig.). 1996. pap. 5.00 (*1-886467-14-5*) WJM Press.

— Professor McGee's Solution: And Other Light & Whimsical Verse. 2nd rev. ed. LC 98-96253. (Illus.). 56p. 1998. pap. 5.00 (*1-886467-35-8*) WJM Press.

***Middleton, William J.** Pun in Cheek: A Collection of Punny Limericks. LC 99-61132. (Illus.). 76p. 1999. pap. 6.00 (*1-886467-47-1*) WJM Press.

— Puns upon a Rhyme: A Collection of Punny Limericks. LC 00-100113. (Illus.). 71p. 2000. pap. 6.00 (*1-886467-56-0*) WJM Press.

Middleton, William J., ed. When Pigs Fly: An Omnium-Gatherum of Double Dactyls (Poems in Dactylic Meter) LC 97-90229. (Illus.). 64p. (Orig.). 1997. pap. 6.00 (*1-886467-16-1*) WJM Press.

Middleton, William J. & Stanbrough, Harvey E. Partners in Rhyme. LC 95-90023. 65p. 1995. pap. 5.50 (*1-886467-04-8*) WJM Press.

Middleton, William J., jt. auth. see Land, Marybelle S.

Middleton, William S. Values in Modern Medicine. LC 72-1379. (Illus.). 321p. reprint ed. pap. 99.60 (*0-8357-4751-4*, 203767300009) Bks Demand.

Middletonb. Restoration Wetlands. (General Science Ser.). 1998. text 54.95 (*0-442-02583-1*, VNR) Wiley.

***Middletown, Thomas.** A Mad World, My Masters. 1999. pap. 15.00 (*0-87830-099-6*) Routledge.

Middlewood, David, jt. ed. see Bush, Tony.

Middour, Jay W., et al, eds. Spaceflight Mechanics 1998. (Advances in the Astronautical Sciences Ser.: 99). 1638p. 1998. lib. bdg. 280.00 (*0-87703-450-8*, Am Astronaut Soc) Univelt Inc.

Midelfort, H. C. Mad Princes of Renaissance Germany. LC 93-39116. (Studies in Early Modern German History). (Illus.). 224p. (C). 1994. text 30.00 (*0-8139-1500-7*) U Pr of Va.

— Mad Princes of Renaissance Germany. 1996. pap. 14.50 (*0-8139-1501-5*) U Pr of Va.

Midelfort, H. C., tr. see Behringer, Wolfgang.

Midelfort, H. Erik. A History of Madness in Sixteenth-Century Germany. LC 98-16558. 558p. 1999. 55.00 (*0-8047-3334-1*) Stanford U Pr.

— Witch Hunting in Southwestern Germany, 1562-1684: The Social & Intellectual Foundations. LC 75-183891. 320p. 1972. 42.50 (*0-8047-0805-3*) Stanford U Pr.

Midelfort, H. Erik, ed. see Weyer, Johann.

Midence, Kenny & Elander, James. Sickle Cell Disease: A Psychosocial Approach. 1994. 39.95 (*1-870905-14-8*, Radcliffe Med Pr) Scovill Paterson.

Midence, Kenny, jt. ed. see Myers, Lynn.

Midenhall. Flights of Fancy. mass mkt. 6.95 (*0-7472-5215-7*, Pub. by Headline Bk Pub) Trafalgar.

Midfeldt, Linda J. Green As in Springtime. LC 94-66793. 128p. (Orig.). (J). 1994. pap. 7.99 (*0-8100-0526-3*, 17N1626) Northwest Pub.

Midford, Paul, jt. auth. see Youtz, David.

Midge, Tiffany. Outlaws, Renegades & Saints: Diary of a Mixed-Up Halfbreed. 1996. pap. 12.95 (*0-912678-93-3*) Greenfld Rev Lit.

Midgeley, Magdelina. TRB Culture: The First Farmers of the North European Plain. (Illus.). 424p. 1993. 102.00 (*0-7486-0348-4*, Pub. by Edinburgh U Pr) Col U Pr.

Midgely, Derek & Torrance, Kenneth E. Potentiometric Water Analysis. LC 77-7213. 421p. reprint ed. pap. 130.60 (*0-608-17653-2*, 203051200069) Bks Demand.

— Potentiometric Water Analysis. 2nd ed. LC 90-25307. 600p. 1991. 495.00 (*0-471-92983-2*) Wiley.

Midgett, Andrea. Against All Odds. 160p. 1990. pap. 8.99 (*0-310-71101-0*) Zondervan.

Midgett, Douglas, ed. see Midgett, Kent.

Midgett, Kent. Traces on the Landscape. Midgett, Douglas, ed. (Illus.). 166p. 1998. pap. 13.00 (*0-931209-80-3*) Mid-Prairie Bks.

Midgett, Steve. Mokume Gane in the Small Shop: The Complete Guide to Diffusion Welded Mokume. LC 96-83701. (Illus.). 128p. (Orig.). Date not set. pap. 16.95 (*0-9651650-8-6*) Earthshine Pr.

Midgette, Nancy S. To Foster the Spirit of Professionalism: Southern Scientists & State Academies of Science. LC 91-7765. (History of American Science & Technology Ser.). 248p. (C). 1991. text 34.95 (*0-8173-0549-1*) U of Ala Pr.

Midgette, Sally. The Navajo Progressive in Discourse: A Study in Temporal Semantics. (History & Language Ser.: Vol. 6). XIV, 252p. (C). 1995. text 47.95 (*0-8204-2536-2*) P Lang Pubng.

Midgley. Gender & Imperialism. LC 97-20338. 256p. 1998. pap. 29.95 (*0-7190-4820-6*, Pub. by Manchester Univ Pr); text 79.95 (*0-7190-4819-2*, Pub. by Manchester Univ Pr) St Martin.

Midgley & Pia. Fields & Methods of Social Change. 1984. text 49.95 (*0-435-82583-6*) Ashgate Pub Co.

Midgley, Amy, jt. auth. see McClister, M. T.

Midgley, Clare. Women Against Slavery: The British Campaigns 1780-1870. (Illus.). 296p. (C). 1995. pap. 25.99 (*0-415-12708-4*) Routledge.

Midgley, David. New Directions in Transactional Analysis Counselling: An Explorer's Handbook. (Illus.). 200p. pap. 25.00 (*1-85343-429-9*) Free Assoc Bks.

— New Directions in Transactional Analysis Counselling: An Explorer's Handbook. (Illus.). 14p. 1999. 55.00 (*1-85343-430-2*, Pub. by Free Assoc Bks) Intl Spec Bk.

— Writing Weimar: Critical Realism in German Literature, 1918-1933. LC 99-55510. (Illus.). 280p. 2000. text 65.00 (*0-19-815179-9*) OUP.

Midgley, David, ed. The German Novel in the Twentieth Century: Beyond Realism. 207p. 1993. text 49.95 (*0-312-10062-0*) St Martin.

Midgley, David A. & Lefton, Phillip. How to Prepare for SAT II: American History & Social Studies. 10th rev. ed. LC 98-9574. 430p. 1998. pap. 13.95 (*0-7641-0460-8*) Barron.

Midgley, E. B. The Ideology of Max Weber: A Thomist Critique. LC 82-16445. 182p. (C). 1983. text 42.00 (*0-389-20343-2*, 07187) B&N Imports.

Midgley, E. G., ed. see Bunyan, John.

Midgley, Elizabeth. Compounds & Contractions. (Basic Skills Ser.). (Illus.). 32p. (J). (gr. 2). 1997. pap. text 4.95 (*0-88724-409-2*, CD-2109) Carson-Dellos.

Midgley, Gillian, et al. Diagnosis in Color: Medical Mycology. 155p. 1997. text 22.95 (*0-7234-2450-0*, Pub. by Wolfe Pub) Mosby Inc.

Midgley, Graham. Snug in Their Mouldy Cells: University Life in Eighteenth-Century Oxford. LC 96-19288. (Illus.). 256p. 1996. 32.00 (*0-300-06813-1*) Yale U Pr.

Midgley, Graham, ed. see Bunyan, John.

Midgley, J. R. Lawyers' Professional Liability. 208p. 1992. pap. write for info. (*0-7021-2675-6*, Pub. by Juta & Co) Gaunt.

Midgley, J. R., jt. auth. see Van Der Walt, J. C.

Midgley, James. Social Development. 192p. (C). 1995. 69.95 (*0-8039-7772-7*); pap. 23.95 (*0-8039-7773-5*) Sage.

— Social Security: Inequality & the Third World. LC 84-5188. (Social Development in the Third World Ser.). 235p. reprint ed. pap. 72.90 (*0-608-05265-5*, 206580300001) Bks Demand.

— Social Welfare in Global Context. LC 96-51210. 1997. 52.00 (*0-7619-0787-4*) Sage.

Midgley, James & Glennerster, Howard, eds. The Radical Right & the Welfare State. 208p. (C). 1991. text 59.00 (*0-389-20976-7*) B&N Imports.

Midgley, James & Sherraden, Michael W. Alternatives to Social Security: An International Inquiry. LC 96-41484. 168p. 1997. 52.95 (*0-86569-245-9*, Auburn Hse) Greenwood.

Midgley, James, et al. Community Participation, Social Development & the State. 200p. 1986. 42.50 (*0-416-39820-0*, 1014) Routledge.

Midgley, James, jt. auth. see Hardiman, Margaret.

Midgley, James, jt. ed. see Hokenstad, M. C.

Midgley, James, jt. ed. see Karger, Howard J.

Midgley, James B. & Tracy, Martin B., eds. Challenges to Social Security: An International Exploration. LC 95-34275. 176p. 1996. 55.00 (*0-86569-244-0*, Auburn Hse) Greenwood.

Midgley, Jane. The Women's Budget. (Illus.). 1987. 3.00 (*0-9506968-0-3*) WILPF.

Midgley, Jane W. Southeastern Wildflowers: Your Complete Guide to Plant Communities, Identification, Culture, Propagation, Traditional Uses. LC 98-50028. 304p. 1999. 19.95 (*1-57587-106-8*) Crane Hill AL.

Midgley, John. The Great Victorian Cookbook. 248p. 1995. write for info. (*1-57215-047-5*) World Pubns.

Midgley, John, jt. auth. see Wood, Stephen.

Midgley, John M. & Vollmer Midgley, Susan. Decision to Love: A Marriage Preparation Program Guide. LC 92-61349. 166p. 1992. pap., teacher ed. 9.95 (*0-89622-538-0*) Twenty-Third.

Midgley, Jon, jt. auth. see Mays, Elaine.

Midgley, L. M. Ministers' Accounts II of the Earldom of Cornwall, 1296-7. (Camden Third Ser.). 35.00 (*0-86193-068-1*) David Brown.

Midgley, Leslie. How Many Words Do You Want? Richardson, Stewart, ed. 320p. 1989. 19.95 (*1-55972-015-8*, Birch Ln Pr) Carol Pub Group.

Midgley, Mary. Animals & Why They Matter. 160p. 1998. reprint ed. pap. 15.00 (*0-8203-2041-2*) U of Ga Pr.

— Beast & Man: The Roots of Human Nature. LC 95-7506. 424p. (C). (gr. 13). 1995. pap. 20.99 (*0-415-12740-8*) Routledge.

— Beast & Man: The Roots of the Human Nature. 400p. 1995. pap. 17.95 (*0-415-10445-9*, C0560) Routledge.

— Biological & Cultural Evolution. 23p. 1984. pap. 6.00 (*0-904674-08-8*, Pub. by Octagon Pr) ISHK.

— Can't We Make Moral Judgements? (Mind Matters Ser.). 192p. (C). 1993. pap. 16.95 (*0-312-08726-8*) St Martin.

— The Ethical Primate: Humans, Freedom & Morality. LC 94-8485. 208p. (C). (gr. 13). 1994. 50.00 (*0-415-09530-1*, B0130) Routledge.

— The Ethical Primate: Humans, Freedom, & Morality. LC 95-26200. 208p. (C). 1996. pap. 17.99 (*0-415-13224-X*) Routledge.

— Evolution As a Religion: Strange Hopes & Stranger Fears. 192p. (C). 1985. pap. 20.99 (*0-416-39660-7*, 9513) Routledge.

— Science As Salvation: A Modern Myth & Its Meaning. LC 91-30984. 256p. (C). (gr. 13). 1992. 65.00 (*0-415-06271-3*, A7063) Routledge.

— Science As Salvation: A Modern Myth & Its Meaning. 256p. (C). 1994. pap. 18.99 (*0-415-10773-3*) Routledge.

— Utopias, Dolphins, & Computers: Some Problems in Philosophical Plumbing. 192p. (C). 1996. 32.99 (*0-415-13377-7*) Routledge.

— Wickedness. 232p. 1986. pap. 9.95 (*0-7448-0053-6*, 0053W) Routledge.

— Wickedness: A Philosophical Essay. 208p. 1984. 35.00 (*0-7100-9759-X*, Routledge Thoemms) Routledge.

— Wickedness: Philosophical Essay. 224p. (C). 1987. pap. 17.99 (*0-415-08409-1*) Routledge.

— Wisdom, Information & Wonder: What Is Knowledge For? 272p. 1989. 27.50 (*0-415-02829-9*) Routledge.

— Wisdom, Information & Wonder: What is Knowledge For? 288p. (C). 1991. pap. 20.99 (*0-415-02830-2*, A5460) Routledge.

Midgley, Michael. Butterworths Taxation Library, 3 vols., Set. ring bd. write for info. (*0-409-66128-7*, NZ, MICHIE) LEXIS Pub.

Midgley, Michael & Andrew, Lee. Butterworths Commercial Service, 2 vols., Set. ring bd. write for info. (*0-409-68100-8*, NZ, MICHIE) LEXIS Pub.

Midgley, Susan V., jt. auth. see Vollmer, John M.

Midgley, Susan Vollmer, see Midgley, John M. & Vollmer Midgley, Susan.

Midha, Kamal K. Bio-International Bioavailability, Bioequivalance/Pharmacokinetic. Blume, Henning H., ed. 1993. 73.00 (*3-88763-019-X*) CRC Pr.

Midhat, Ali H. The Life of Midhat Pasha. LC 73-6290. (Middle East Ser.). 1973. reprint ed. 24.95 (*0-405-05348-7*) Ayer.

MIDI Staff. Interactive Blues Jam for Keyboard. (Illus.). 1993. pap. 14.95 (*0-8256-1361-2*, AM91302) Music Sales.

— Interactive Rock Jams for Keyboard. (Illus.). 1993. pap. 14.95 (*0-8256-1365-5*, AM91247) Music Sales.

Midkiff, Mary D. Fitness, Performance & the Female Equestrian. LC 96-22537. 1996. 24.95 (*0-87605-945-0*) Howell Bks.

Midkiff, Ruby B. & Thomasson, Rebecca D. A Practical Approach to Using Learning Styles in Math Instruction. LC 93-5643. (Illus.). 132p. 1993. pap. 25.95 (*0-398-06289-7*) C C Thomas.

— A Practical Approach to Using Learning Styles in Math Instruction. LC 93-5643. (Illus.). 132p. (C). 1993. text 36.95 (*0-398-05888-1*) C C Thomas.

Midlam, Don S. Flight of the Lucky Lady. (Illus.). 216p. 1954. 12.95 (*0-8323-0091-8*) Binford Mort.

***Midlands Invitational Staff, et al.** Midlands Invitational 2000: Works on Paper. LC 00-30192. 2000. pap. write for info. (*0-936364-29-7*) Joslyn Art.

Midlands Technical College Staff. Managing Your Institution's Effectiveness: A User Guide. (AACC Strategies & Solutions Ser.). (Illus.). 102p. 1997. pap. 35.00 (*0-87117-299-2*, 1392) Comm Coll Pr Am Assn Comm Coll.

Midlarksy, Elizabeth & Kahana, Eva. Altruism & the Elderly. (Library of Social Research: Vol. 196). 320p. 1994. 59.95 (*0-8039-2768-1*); pap. 26.00 (*0-8039-2769-X*) Sage.

Midlarsky, Manus I. The Evolution of Inequality: War, State Survival & Democracy in Comparative Perspective. LC 98-35062. 364p. 1998. 45.00 (*0-8047-3376-7*) Stanford U Pr.

Midlarsky, Manus I., ed. Handbook of War Studies. 352p. 1989. text 55.00 (*0-04-497055-2*) Routledge.

— Handbook of War Studies. LC 92-46397. 406p. 1993. pap. text 20.95 (*0-472-08224-8*, 08224) U of Mich Pr.

Midlarsky, Manus I., ed. Handbook of War Studies II. (Illus.). 518p. (C). text 69.50 (*0-472-09724-5*, 09724); pap. text 29.95 (*0-472-06724-9*, 06724) U of Mich Pr.

Midlarsky, Manus I., ed. Inequality & Contemporary Revolutions. (Monograph Series in World Affairs: Vol. 22, Bk. 2). (Illus.). 184p. (Orig.). 1986. pap. 9.95 (*0-87940-081-1*) Monograph Series.

— Inequality, Democracy, & Economic Development. LC 96-40356. 380p. (C). 1998. text 64.95 (*0-521-57191-X*); pap. text 24.95 (*0-521-57675-X*) Cambridge U Pr.

Midlarsky, Manus I. & Vasquez, John A. From Rivalry Cooperatn: Soviet & American Perspectives on the Post Cold War Era. 300p. (C). 1997. pap. text 34.60 (*0-06-501081-7*) Addson-Wesley Educ.

Midlen, Alex & Redding, Theresa. Environmental Management for Aquaculture. (Aquaculture Ser.). 240 p. 1998. write for info. (*0-412-59500-1*) Kluwer Academic.

Midler, Christopher, jt. auth. see Lundin, Rolf A.

***Midmarch Arts Press Staff.** How to Publish Your Own Book. 6p. 1999. pap. 2.50 (*1-877675-33-4*) Midmarch Arts.

Midmore, P. & Harrison-Mayfield, L., eds. Rural Economic Modelling: An Input-Output Approach. LC 96-219748. 128p. 1996. text 55.00 (*0-85199-112-2*) OUP.

Midmore, Peter. Input-Output Models & the Agricultural Sector. 148p. 1991. text 82.95 (*1-85628-223-6*, Pub. by Avebry) Ashgate Pub Co.

Midness, Anna, et al. Reading Between the Signs: Intercultural Communication for Sign Language Interpreters. LC 99-10959. 252p. 1999. pap. 21.95 (*1-877864-73-0*) Intercult Pr.

Midolle, et al. Florid & Unusual Alphabets. LC 75-30175. (Pictorial Archive Ser.). 89p. 1976. reprint ed. pap. 7.95 (*0-486-23304-9*) Dover.

Midori, Fetish. The Beauty of Fetish. (Illus.). 144p. 1998. 49.95 (*3-908161-19-3*) Abbeville Pr.

Midroni, Gyl & Bilbao, Juan. Biopsy Diagnosis of Peripheral Neuropathy. 477p. 1995. text 170.00 (*0-7506-9552-8*) Buttrwrth-Heinemann.

Midttun, Atle. European Electricity Systems in Transition: A Comparative Analysis. LC 96-44349. (Elsevier Global Energy Policy & Economics Ser.). 350p. 1997. 115.50 (*0-08-042994-7*, Pergamon Pr) Elsevier.

Midttun, Atle, jt. auth. see Baumgartner, Thomas.

Midura, Daniel W. & Glover, Donald R. The Competition-Cooperation Link: Games for Developing Respectful Competitors. LC 98-22391. (Illus.). 160p. 1998. pap. 16.00 (*0-88011-850-4*, BMID0850) Human Kinetics.

— More Team Building Challenges. LC 95-8965. (Illus.). 120p. (Orig.). 1995. pap. text 14.95 (*0-87322-785-9*, BMID0785) Human Kinetics.

Midura, Daniel W., jt. auth. see Glover, Donald R.

Midwest Living Magazine Living Staff. Weekend Getaways. LC 99-161130. (Midwest Living Ser.). (Illus.). 144p. 1998. pap. 14.95 (*0-696-20820-2*) Meredith Bks.

Midwest Plan Service Engineers Staff. Beef Housing & Equipment Handbook. 4th ed. MWPS Staff, ed. LC 85-28358. (Illus.). 1987. pap. 7.00 (*0-89373-068-8*, MWPS-6) MidWest Plan Serv.

— Conservation Tillage Systems & Management. LC 92-37291. (Illus.). (Orig.). 1992. pap. 15.00 (*0-89373-088-2*, MWPS-45) MidWest Plan Serv.

— Designs for Glued Trusses. 4th ed. LC 80-39547. (Illus.). 84p. 1981. pap. 7.00 (*0-89373-051-3*, MWPS-9) MidWest Plan Serv.

— Farm Buildings Wiring Handbook. 2nd ed. LC 91-21159. (Illus.). 63p. 1992. pap. 10.00 (*0-89373-085-8*, MWPS-28) MidWest Plan Serv.

— Farm Shop Plans Book. rev. ed. LC 94-38735. (Illus.). 32p. (Orig.). 1994. pap. 10.00 (*0-89373-091-2*, MWPS-26) MidWest Plan Serv.

— Grain Drying, Handling & Storage Handbook. 2nd ed. MWPS Staff, ed. LC 86-12751. (Illus.). 1987. pap. 7.00 (*0-89373-071-8*, MWPS-13) MidWest Plan Serv.

— Heating, Cooling & Tempering Air for Livestock Housing. LC 90-34153. 1991. pap. 6.00 (*0-89373-076-9*, MWPS-34) MidWest Plan Serv.

— Home & Yard Improvements Handbook. LC 78-4505. (Illus.). 100p. 1978. pap. 9.00 (*0-89373-034-3*, MWPS-21) MidWest Plan Serv.

An Asterisk (*) at the beginning of an entry indicates that the title is appearing for the first time.

— Horse Housing & Equipment Handbook. (Illus.). 60p. 1971. pap. 7.00 (*0-89373-009-2*, MWPS-15) MidWest Plan Serv.

— Livestock Waste Facilities Handbook. 3rd ed. Church, Glenn A., II, ed. LC 93-7384. (Illus.). 112p. 1993. pap. 8.00 (*0-89373-089-0*, MWPS-18) MidWest Plan Serv.

— Low Temperature & Solar Grain Drying Handbook. LC 80-12869. (Illus.). 86p. 1980. pap. 6.00 (*0-89373-048-3*, MWPS-22) MidWest Plan Serv.

— Natural Ventilating Systems for Livestock Housing. Midwest Plan Service Personnel Staff, ed. LC 89-14544. (Illus.). 32p. 1989. pap. 5.00 (*0-89373-074-2*, MWPS-33) MidWest Plan Serv.

— Onsite Domestic Sewage Disposal Handbook. LC 81-18994. (Illus.). 40p. (Orig.). (C). 1982. pap. 6.00 (*0-89373-053-X*, MWPS-24) MidWest Plan Serv.

— Private Water Systems Handbook. 4th ed. LC 79-19040. (Illus.). 72p. 1979. pap. 7.00 (*0-89373-045-9*, MWPS-14) MidWest Plan Serv.

— Solar Livestock Housing Handbook. LC 82-20889. (Illus.). 88p. (Orig.). 1983. pap. 7.00 (*0-89373-056-4*, MWPS-23) MidWest Plan Serv.

— Swine Housing & Equipment Handbook. 4th ed. LC 82-2292. (Illus.). 112p. 1983. pap. 8.00 (*0-89373-054-8*, MWPS-8) MidWest Plan Serv.

Midwest Plan Service Personnel Staff, ed. see Friday, William H., et al.

Midwest Plan Service Personnel Staff, ed. see Midwest Plan Service Engineers Staff.

Midwest Research Institute Staff. Development of Heat-Stable Electrocoating Resins with Improved Insulation Properties. 49p. 1970. 7.35 (*0-317-34512-5*, 170) Intl Copper.

— New Applications for Copper & Copper Compounds. 109p. 1974. 16.35 (*0-317-34538-9*, 229) Intl Copper.

— Studies to Evaluate the Potential for Improvements in Biological & Chemical Characteristics of Potable Water Transported in Copper Pipe. 26p. 1984. write for info. (*0-318-60414-0*) Intl Copper.

Midwestern Food & Social Policy Conference Staff. Food & Social Policy No. 1: Proceedings of the 1976 Midwestern Food & Social Policy Conference. Dull, Kay E. & Koerselman, Gary H., eds. LC 78-111470. (Illus.). 414p. 1978. reprint ed. pap. 128.40 (*0-608-00174-0*, 206095600006) Bks Demand.

Midwestern Mechanics Conference. Developments in Mechanics: Proceedings of the Midwestern Mechanics Conference, 7th, Michigan State University, 1961, Vol. 1. Lay, J. E. & Malvern, Lawrence E., eds. LC 61-17719. 636p. reprint ed. pap. 197.20 (*0-608-10168-0*, 201938700001) Bks Demand.

Midwifery Today Magazine Staff. Life of a Midwife: A Celebration of Midwifery. LC 98-198139. (Illus.). 92p. 1997. pap. 25.00 (*1-890446-05-X*) Midwifery Today.

— Tricks of the Trade, Vol. 1. 2nd ed. 56p. 1997. reprint ed. pap. 20.00 (*1-890446-02-5*) Midwifery Today.

Midwifery Today Staff. Paths to Becoming a Midwife: Getting an Education. 4th ed. (Illus.). 332p. 1998. pap. 29.95 (*1-890446-00-9*) Midwifery Today.

— Wisdom of the Midwives Vol. 2: Tricks of the Trade. LC 99-186623. (Illus.). 96p. 1997. pap. 25.00 (*1-890446-03-3*) Midwifery Today.

Midwinter, Arthur & Monaghan, Claire. From Rates to Poll Tax: Local Government Finance in the Thatcher Era. 176p. 1993. text 68.00 (*0-7486-0402-2*, Pub. by Edinburgh U Pr); pap. text 30.00 (*0-7486-0397-2*, Pub. by Edinburgh U Pr) Col U Pr.

Midwinter, Arthur F. & McVicar, Murray. The Size & Efficiency Debate: Public Library Authorities in a Time of Change. LC Z 0791.M53. (British Library R&D Report: Vol. 6143). 106p. reprint ed. pap. 32.90 (*0-608-20965-1*, 207183700002) Bks Demand.

Midwinter, Eric. The Development of Social Welfare in Britain. LC 93-21335. (C). 1994. pap. 33.95 (*0-335-19104-5*) OpUniv Pr.

Midwinter, John E. Optical Fibers for Transmission. LC 91-4636. 428p. 1992. reprint ed. 66.50 (*0-89464-595-1*) Krieger.

Midwinter, John E., ed. Photonics in Switching, 2 vols. LC 92-38764. (Quantum Electronics - Principles & Applications Ser.). (Illus.). 674p. 1993. text 164.00 (*0-12-496050-2*) Acad Pr.

— Photonics in Switching, 2 vols., Vol. 1. LC 92-38764. (Quantum Electronics - Principles & Applications Ser.). (Illus.). 322p. 1993. text 82.00 (*0-12-496051-0*) Acad Pr.

— Photonics in Switching, 2 vols., Vol. 2. LC 92-38764. (Quantum Electronics - Principles & Applications Ser.). (Illus.). 352p. 1993. text 82.00 (*0-12-496052-9*) Acad Pr.

Midwinter, John E., jt. auth. see Zernike, Frits.

Midwinter Staff. Pensioned Off: Retirement & Income Examined. LC 96-39951. (Rethinking Aging Ser.). 1997. pap. 29.95 (*0-335-19682-9*) OpUniv Pr.

Midwood, Bart. The World in Pieces. LC 97-23559. 224p. 1998. 24.00 (*1-57962-008-6*) Permanent Pr.

Miebs, Von U. & Vehovirta, L. Gramatik/Glossar Spanisch. (Kontakt Deutsch Ser.). (GER.). 64p. 1997. pap. write for info. (*3-468-90523-8*) Langenscheidt.

— Kursbuch: Textbook. (Kontakt Deutsch Ser.). (GER., Illus.). 160p. 1997. pap. 24.50 (*3-468-90520-3*) Langenscheidt.

— Redemittelbuch: Redemittelbuch. (Kontakt Deutsch Ser.). (GER.). 200p. 1997. pap. 19.95 (*3-468-90521-1*) Langenscheidt.

Mieczkowski, Bogdan. Dysfunctional Bureaucracy: A Comparative & Historical Perspective. 312p. (Orig.). (C). 1991. pap. text 29.50 (*0-8191-8394-6*); lib. bdg. 57.00 (*0-8191-8393-8*) U Pr of Amer.

— The Rot at the Top: Dysfunctional Bureaucracy in Academia. 252p. (Orig.). (C). 1995. pap. text 29.50 (*0-8191-9845-5*); lib. bdg. 52.50 (*0-8191-9844-7*) U Pr of Amer.

— Social Services for Women in Eastern Europe. (ASN Series in Issues Studies (U. S. S. R. & East Europe): No. 3). 128p. (Orig.). (C). 1982. pap. 9.50 (*0-910895-00-7*) Assn Study Nat.

— Transportation in Eastern Europe. (East European Monographs: No. 38). 221p. 1978. text 60.00 (*0-914710-31-1*, Pub. by East Eur Monographs) Col U Pr.

Mieczkowski, Bogdan, ed. Eastern European Transportation: Systems & Modes. (Developments in Transportation Studies: No. 2). 366p. 1980. lib. bdg. 132.00 (*90-247-2390-6*) Kluwer Academic.

Mieczkowski, Bogdan & Zinam, Oleg. Bureaucracy, Technology, Ideology: Quality of Life East & West. LC 84-71093. (Issue Studies (U. S. S. R. & East Europe): No. 5). 463p. (Orig.). 1984. pap. 28.00 (*0-910895-02-3*) Assn Study Nat.

Mieczkowski, Rondo, ed. Sundays at Seven: Choice Words from a Different Light's Gay Writers Series. LC 95-83537. 144p. (Orig.). 1996. pap. 12.00 (*1-886360-01-4*) Alamo Sq Pr.

Mieczkowski, Tammy A., jt. auth. see Timm, Neil H.

Mieczkowski, Tom. Drug Testing Methods Assessment & Evaluation. LC 98-51465. (Methods in Analytical Toxicology Ser.). 1999. boxed set 69.95 (*0-8493-7884-2*) CRC Pr.

***Mieczkowski, Yanek.** The Routledge Historical Atlas of Presidential Elections. (Atlases of American History Ser.). (Illus.). 2001. 40.00 (*0-415-92133-3*); pap. 17.95 (*0-415-92139-2*) Routledge.

Mieczkowski, Zbigniew. Environmental Issues of Tourism & Recreation. LC 95-9062. (Illus.). 566p. (Orig.). (C). 1995. 74.50 (*0-8191-9994-X*); pap. 45.00 (*0-8191-9995-8*) U Pr of Amer.

***Miedaner, Talane.** Coach Yourself to Success: 101 Tips for Reaching Your Goals at Work & in Life. LC 99-31866. 256p. 2000. 22.95 (*0-8092-2536-0*, 253600, Contemporary Bks) NTC Contemp Pub Co.

Miedema, F., jt. auth. see Schuitemaker, Hanneke.

Miedema, Rienk & Mermut, Ahmed R., eds. Annotated Bibliography on Soil Micromorphology, 1968-1986. 250p. (Orig.). 1990. pap. text 60.00 (*0-85198-681-1*) OUP.

Miedema, Siebren, et al, eds. The Politics of Human Science. 229p. 1995. pap. 19.95 (*90-5487-095-8*) Paul & Co Pubs.

Mieder, Wolfgang. As Strong As a Moose: New England Expressions. (Illus.). 88p. (Orig.). 1997. pap. 6.95 (*1-881535-24-X*) New Eng Pr VT.

Mieder, Wolfgang. As Sweet As Apple Cider: Vermont Expressions. LC 88-12464. (Illus.). 72p. (Orig.). 1988. pap. 6.95 (*0-933050-58-5*) New Eng Pr VT.

Mieder, Wolfgang. Howl like a Wolf: Animal Proverbs. LC 93-86688. (Illus.). 95p. (Orig.). 1993. pap. 6.95 (*1-881535-08-8*) New Eng Pr VT.

— Illuminating Wit, Inspiring Wisdom: Proverbs from Around the World. 1998. 16.00 (*0-7352-0001-7*) PH Pr.

— International Proverb Scholarship: An Annotated Bibliography, Supplement I, 1800-1981. LC 90-3049. (Folklore Bibliographies Ser.: Vol. 15). 454p. 1990. text 20.00 (*0-8240-4037-6*, 1230) Garland.

— International Proverb Scholarship: An Annotated Bibliography Supplement II, 1982-1991. LC 90-3049. (Folklore Bibliographies Ser.: Vol. 20). 959p. 1993. text 30.00 (*0-8153-1133-8*, H1655) Garland.

— Love: Proverbs of the Heart. LC 89-63662. (Illus.). 80p. (Orig.). 1989. pap. 6.95 (*0-933050-63-1*) New Eng Pr VT.

— Not by Bread Alone: Proverbs of the Bible. LC 90-63099. (Illus.). 80p. (Orig.). 1990. pap. 6.95 (*0-933050-86-0*) New Eng Pr VT.

— The Politics of Proverbs: From Traditional Wisdom to Proverbial Stereotypes. LC 96-41944. (Illus.). 288p. 1997. 52.95 (*0-299-15450-5*); pap. 19.95 (*0-299-15454-8*) U of Wis Pr.

***Mieder, Wolfgang.** The Proverbial Abraham Lincoln: An Index to Proverbs in the Works of Abraham Lincoln. LC 99-52371. 224p. 2000. text 49.95 (*0-8204-4955-5*) P Lang Pubng.

Mieder, Wolfgang. Salty Wisdom: Proverbs of the Sea. LC 90-52966. (Illus.). 64p. (Orig.). 1990. pap. 6.95 (*0-933050-82-8*) New Eng Pr VT.

— Talk Less & Say More: Vermont Proverbs. LC 86-50974. (Illus.). 64p. (Orig.). 1986. pap. 6.95 (*0-933050-42-9*) New Eng Pr VT.

— Yankee Wisdom: New England Proverbs. LC 89-61223. (Illus.). 72p. (Orig.). 1989. pap. text 6.95 (*0-933050-73-9*) New Eng Pr VT.

Mieder, Wolfgang, compiled by. Wise Words: Essays on the Proverb. LC 94-3960. (Folklore Casebks.: Vol. 6). 608p. 1994. text 25.00 (*0-8153-0942-2*, H1638) Garland.

Mieder, Wolfgang, ed. American Proverbs: A Study of Texts & Contexts. (Sprichworterforschung Ser.: Vol. 13). (Illus.). 394p. 1990. pap. 57.00 (*3-261-03975-2*) P Lang Pubng.

— Disenchantments: An Anthology of Modern Fairy Tale Poetry. LC 84-40592. 223p. reprint ed. pap. 69.20 (*0-608-03569-6*, 205965400009) Bks Demand.

— Friedrich Petri (Peters) Der Teutschen Weissheit. (Nachancke deutscher Literature des 17. Jahrhunderts Ser.: Vol. 46). (GER.). 1126p. 1983. 90.00 (*3-261-03246-4*) P Lang Pubng.

— Illuminating Wit, Inspiring Wisdom: Proverbs from Around the World. 2nd ed. LC 97-49520. 256p. (C). 1998. mass mkt. 16.00 (*0-13-906264-5*) P-H.

— Prentice Hall Encyclopedia of World Proverbs. 582p. 1996. reprint ed. 12.98 (*1-56731-126-1*, MJF Bks) Fine Comms.

Mieder, Wolfgang, et al, eds. Dictionary of American Proverbs. 736p. 1991. 65.00 (*0-19-505399-0*) OUP.

— A Dictionary of American Proverbs. 1996. pap. 17.95 (*0-614-20456-9*) OUP.

— A Dictionary of American Proverbs. 736p. 1996. reprint ed. pap. 19.95 (*0-19-511133-8*) OUP.

Mieder, Wolfgang & Bryan, George, eds. The Proverbial Harry S. Truman: An Index to Proverbs in the Works of Harry S. Truman. LC 96-49836. XI, 247p. (C). 1997. text 39.95 (*0-8204-3748-4*) P Lang Pubng.

Mieder, Wolfgang & Bryan, George B., eds. The Proverbial Charles Dickens: An Index to Proverbs in the Works of Charles Dickens. LC 97-13446. (Dickens' Universe Ser.: Vol. 4). 319p. (C). 1997. text 39.95 (*0-8204-3837-5*) P Lang Pubng.

— The Proverbial Winston S. Churchill: An Index to Proverbs in the Works of Sir Winston Churchill, 38. LC 95-2464. (Bibliographies & Indexes in World History Ser.: Vol. 38). 448p. 1995. lib. bdg. 85.00 (*0-313-29433-X*, Greenwood Pr) Greenwood.

— Proverbs in World Literature: A Bibliography. XIV, 305p. (C). 1997. text 42.95 (*0-8204-3499-X*) P Lang Pubng.

Mieder, Wolfgang & Dundes, Alan, eds. The Wisdom of Many: Essays on the Proverb. LC 94-16235. 346p. 1994. reprint ed. 45.00 (*0-299-14360-0*); reprint ed. pap. 19.95 (*0-299-14364-3*) U of Wis Pr.

Mieder, Wolfgang & Kingsbury, Mildred. Weather Wisdom. VIII, 478p. (C). 1996. text 49.95 (*0-8204-3326-8*) P Lang Pubng.

***Mieder, Wolfgang & Sobieski, Janet.** Proverb Iconography: An International Bibliography. LC 98-52124. (Illus.). xix, 225p. (C). 1999. text 49.95 (*0-8204-4198-8*) P Lang Pubng.

Mieder, Wolfgang, jt. compiled by see Bryan, George B.

Mieder, Wolfgang, jt. ed. see Bryan, George B.

Mieder, Wolfgang, ed. see Cornette, James C., Jr.

Mieder, Wolfgang, tr. see Rilke, Phia.

Mieder, Wolfgang, tr. see Von Ebner-Eschenbach, Marie.

Miedzgova. Zaklady Etiky. (SLO.). 110p. 1996. write for info. (*80-08-01729-5*, Pub. by Slov Pegagog Naklad) IBD Ltd.

Miedzian, Myriam. Boys Will Be Boys: Breaking the Link Between Masculinity & Violence. 384p. 1992. pap. 14.00 (*0-385-42254-7*, Anchor NY) Doubleday.

Miedzian, Myriam & Malinovich, Alisa. Generations: A Century of Women Speak about Their Lives. 592p. 1998. pap. 16.95 (*0-385-33325-0*) Dell.

— Generations: A Century of Women Speak about Their Lives. LC 97-9353. 592p. 1997. 27.50 (*0-87113-678-3*, Atlntc Mnthly) Grove-Atltic.

Miedzinski, Charles & Bogzaran, Fariba. Gordon Onslow Ford: Paintings of the Inner-Worlds, Exhibition Catalogue. (Illus.). 24p. 1993. pap. 15.00 (*0-8150-0005-7*) Wittenborn Art.

Miedzyrzecka, Daniela, tr. see Kott, Jan.

Mieg, Harald A. & Ubersetzer, Gunter S. Computers As Experts? On the Nonexistence of Expert Systems. LC 92-36725. (Psychology of Decisions & Conflict Ser.: Vol. 5). VIII, 163p. 1992. 40.00 (*3-631-42748-4*) P Lang Pubng.

Miehe, Georg. Langtang Himal: Flora und Vegetation Als Klimazeiger und -Zeugen Im Himalaya (A Prodromus of the Vegetation Ecology of the Himalayas) (Dissertationes Botanicae Ser.: Band 158). (ENG & GER.). xxviii, 530p. 1990. 130.00 (*3-443-64070-2*, Pub. by Gebruder Borntraeger) Balogh.

Miehe, Georg, jt. auth. see Beug, Hans-Jurgen.

Miehe, George. Vegetationsgeographische Untersuchungen im Dhaulagiri-und Annapurna-Himalaya, 2 vols. (Dissertationes Botanicae Ser.: No. 66). (Illus.). 500p. 1982. lib. bdg. 128.00 (*3-7682-1356-0*) Lubrecht & Cramer.

Miehe, Patrick K., compiled by. The Robert Lowell Papers at the Houghton Library, Harvard University: A Guide to the Collection, 12. LC 90-45082. (Bibliographies & Indexes in American Literature Ser.: No. 12). 240p. 1990. lib. bdg. 89.50 (*0-313-27692-7*, HLW, Greenwood Pr) Greenwood.

Miehe, Sabine. Vegetation Ecology of the Jebel Marra Massif in the Semiarid Sudan. (Dissertationes Botanicae Ser.: Band 113). (Illus.). xiv, 205p. 1988. pap. 77.00 (*3-443-64025-7*, Pub. by Gebruder Borntraeger) Balogh.

Miekisz, Jacek. Quasicrystals: Microscopic Models of Nonperiodic Structures. (Notes in Mathematical & Theoretical Physics, Series A: Vol. 5). 106p. (Orig.). 1993. pap. 36.50 (*90-6186-573-5*, Pub. by Leuven Univ) Coronet Bks.

Miel, Alice, et al. Individualizing Reading Practices. LC 58-8337. (Practical Suggestions for Teaching Ser.: No. 14). 101p. reprint ed. pap. 31.40 (*0-8357-2761-0*, 203988600014) Bks Demand.

Miel, Jan. Pascal & Theology. LC 75-93822. 236p. reprint ed. pap. 73.20 (*0-608-15870-4*, 203074600070) Bks Demand.

Mielche, Paul De, see De Mielche, Paul.

Mielczarek, Eugenie V., et al, eds. Biological Physics. LC 93-3280. (Key Papers in Physics). 1993. 69.95 (*0-88318-855-4*) Spr-Verlag.

***Mielczarek, Eugenie Vorborger & McGrayne, Sharon Bertsch.** Iron, Nature's Universal Element: Why People Need Iron & Animals Make Magnets. LC 99-56540. (Illus.). 240p. 2000. 30.00 (*0-8135-2831-3*) Rutgers U Pr.

***Mielczarek, Zygmunt.** Flucht und Dissidenz: Außenseiter und Neurotiker in der Deutschschweizer Literatur Unter Mitwirkung von Robert Rduch. 1999. 32.95 (*3-631-35666-8*) P Lang Pubng.

Mielczarski, Wladyslaw, ed. Fuzzy Logic Techniques in Power Systems. LC 97-42010. (Studies in Fuzziness & Soft Computing: Vol. 11). (Illus.). x, 456p. 1997. 108.00 (*3-7908-1044-4*) Spr-Verlag.

Mielczarski, Wladyslaw & Michalik, G. Competitive Electricity Markets. LC 98-35198. 1998. 69.00 (*1-56072-603-2*) Nova Sci Pubs.

Mields, Hugh. Federally Assisted New Communities: New Dimensions in Urban Development. LC 73-78874. (Urban Land Institute, ULI Landmark Reports). 287p. reprint ed. pap. 89.00 (*0-608-11924-5*, 202324200032) Bks Demand.

Miele, A. & Salvetti, A. Applied Mathematics in Aerospace Science & Engineering. (Mathematical Concepts & Methods in Science & Engineering Ser.: Vol. 44). (Illus.). 526p. (C). 1994. 125.00 (*0-306-44754-1*, Plenum Trade) Perseus Pubng.

Miele, Carole. From Nursing Assistant to Clinical Care Associate. LC 98-23249. 512p. 1998. pap. text 43.93 (*0-8359-5108-1*) Allyn.

Miele, Chris, ed. William Morris on Architecture. (SAP Literature Ser.). 100p. 1996. pap. 9.95 (*1-85075-612-0*, Pub. by Sheffield Acad) CUP Services.

***Miele, H. S.** From Nursing Assistant to Clinical Care: Associate Workbook. 272p. 1998. pap. text, wbk. ed. 23.60 (*0-8359-5117-0*) P-H.

Miele, Joseph P. New Jersey Comprehensive Statewide Master Plan for Alcoholism, Tobacco & Other Drug Abuse. (Illus.). 243p. (C). 1998. pap. text 30.00 (*0-7881-4899-0*) DIANE Pub.

***Miele, Joseph P., ed.** Women's Addictions: New Jersey AD HOC Committee on Women & Addictions (1996) 102p. 2000. reprint ed. pap. text 20.00 (*0-7881-8519-5*) DIANE Pub.

Miele, Louis. 21 Century Italian, Vol. I. (ITA., Illus.). 480p. 1997. pap. 24.95 (*0-9666298-0-9*) Intl Univ.

Miele, Mark. The Dumbbell Book: Fitness Without a Gym. 112p. 1992. pap. 11.95 (*1-880680-01-7*) Sand Dllr Fl.

Miele, Robert, jt. auth. see Martenz, Arden.

Mieli, Aldo. Science Arabe & Son Role dans l'Evolution Scientifique Mondiale. (Medieval Studies Reprint). (FRE.). reprint ed. lib. bdg. 47.00 (*0-697-00044-3*) Irvington.

Mieli, Paola. Being Human: The Technological Extensions of the Boundaries of the Body. 240p. 1999. 27.95 (*1-56886-052-8*, Pub. by Marsilio Pubs); pap. text 14.95 (*1-56886-053-6*, Pub. by Marsilio Pubs) Consort Bk Sales.

Mielikainen, K., jt. ed. see Spiecker, Heinrich.

Mielke, A. Hamiltonian & Lagrangian Flows on Center Manifolds: With Applications to Elliptic Variational Problems. Dold, A. et al, eds. (Lecture Notes in Mathematics Ser.: Vol. 1489). (Illus.). x, 140p. 1991. 31.95 (*0-387-54710-X*) Spr-Verlag.

Mielke, A. & Hoopes. Anthropology. 2nd ed. 448p. 1995. pap. text, student ed. 23.80 (*0-13-301581-5*) P-H.

Mielke, A., jt. auth. see Kirchgassner, K.

Mielke, Arthur J. Christians, Feminists, & the Culture of Pornography. 154p. (C). 1994. pap. text 28.50 (*0-8191-9765-3*); lib. bdg. 48.50 (*0-8191-9764-5*) U Pr of Amer.

Mielke, Bruce. Integrated Computer Graphics. Westby, ed. 419p. (C). 1991. text 67.00 (*0-314-78431-4*) West Pub.

Mielke, Dan & Holstedt, Peggy. Alcohol & Drug Abuse Prevention Education in Oregon: K-12 Infused Lesson Guide. (Illus.). 762p. (Orig.). (C). 1993. pap. text 50.00 (*0-7881-0081-5*) DIANE Pub.

Mielke, Howard. Patterns of Life: Biogeography of a Changing World. (Illus.). 370p. 1989. 75.00 (*0-04-574032-1*); pap. 29.95 (*0-04-574033-X*) Routledge.

Mielke, James H., jt. ed. see Crawford, Michael H.

Mielke, Judy. Native Plants for Southwestern Landscapes. LC 93-12092. (Illus.). 384p. (Orig.). (C). 1993. pap. 24.95 (*0-292-75147-8*); text 39.95 (*0-292-75553-8*) U of Tex Pr.

Mielke, Paul W., jt. auth. see Brown, Timothy J.

Mielke, Randall G. Road to Box Office: The Seven Film Comedies of Bing Crosby, Bob Hope & Dorothy Lamour, 1940-1962. LC 96-52179. (Illus.). 171p. 1997. lib. bdg. 34.50 (*0-7864-0162-1*) McFarland & Co.

Mielke, Robert. The Riddle of the Painful Earth: Suffering & Society in W. D. Howell's Major Writings of the Early 1890s. (Illus.). 214p. (Orig.). 1994. lib. bdg. 40.00 (*0-943549-16-7*) Truman St Univ.

Miell, Dorothy. Doing Social Psychology: Laboratory & Field Exercises. LC 99-171335. 330p. 1998. write for info. (*0-7619-6049-X*) Sage.

Miell, Dorothy & Dallos, Rudi, eds. Social Interaction & Personal Relationships. LC 96-160572. 392p. 1996. 45.00 (*0-7619-5035-4*); pap. 16.99 (*0-7619-5036-2*) Sage.

***Miell, Dorothy & Wetherell, Margaret, eds.** Doing Social Psychology. LC 99-171335. 256p. 1998. pap. 24.95 (*0-7619-6050-3*) Sage.

Mielnik, Edward M. Metalworking Science & Engineering. 848p. (C). 1991. 98.75 (*0-07-041904-3*); pap. text, teacher ed. 18.75 (*0-07-041905-1*) McGraw.

Mielziner, Moses. Introduction to the Talmud. 4th ed. LC 68-29908. 1969. reprint ed. 27.50 (*0-8197-0156-4*); reprint ed. pap. 19.95 (*0-8197-0015-0*) Bloch.

Mienert, J., jt. ed. see Henriet, J.-P.

Mienville, Lisa, jt. auth. see Robeson, Bonnie.

Mier, Martha. The Best of Martha Mier, Bk. 1. 16p. 1996. pap. 5.95 (*0-7390-0861-7*, 16610) Alfred Pub.

— Christmas Cheer, Bk. 1. 24p. 1993. pap. 5.95 (*0-7390-0611-8*, 6680) Alfred Pub.

— Christmas Kaleidoscope, Vol. 2. 24p. 1998. pap. 5.95 (*0-7390-0563-4*, 18754) Alfred Pub.

— Ding Dong Merrily on High, Piano Duet. 8p. 1999. pap. 2.95 (*0-7390-0372-0*, 18977) Alfred Pub.

— Frontier Frolic. 4p. Date not set. pap. 2.50 (*0-7390-0722-X*, 19704) Alfred Pub.

— Fuzzy Wuzzy Worm, Level A. (Basic Piano Library). 4p. 1993. pap. 2.50 (*0-7390-0885-4*, 6193) Alfred Pub.

— Gypsy Celebration. (Alfred Ensemble Ser.). 8p. 1993. pap. 5.95 (*0-7390-0773-4*, 5447) Alfred Pub.

— Jazz, Rags, & Blues, Bk. 2. 24p. 1993. pap. 5.95 (*0-7390-0850-1*, 6643) Alfred Pub.

— Jazz, Rags & Blues, Bk. 3. 24p. 1996. pap. 5.95 (*0-7390-0893-5*, 16871) Alfred Pub.

— Jazz, Rags & Blues, Bk. 4. 24p. 1998. pap. 5.95 (*0-7390-0550-2*, 18770) Alfred Pub.

— Just Imagine!, Bk. 1. 16p. 1993. pap. 5.95 (*0-7390-0542-1*, 6684) Alfred Pub.

— Just Imagine Bk. 2: 7 Late Elementary Piano Solos That Encourage Expressive Playing. 16p. 1994. pap. 5.95 (*0-7390-0679-7*, 11706) Alfred Pub.

— Keyboard Kaleidoscope Bk. 1: 7 Delightful Late Elementary Solos in Various Styles, Moods & Colors. 16p. 1995. pap. 4.95 (*0-7390-0497-2*, 14683) Alfred Pub.

— Ladybug Boogie. 4p. 1994. pap. 2.50 (*0-7390-0761-0*, 5498) Alfred Pub.

— Petite Gavotte. 4p. 1994. pap. 2.50 (*0-7390-0845-5*, 12883) Alfred Pub.

— Reflections of the Heart. 4p. 1999. pap. 2.50 (*0-7390-0390-9*, 18531) Alfred Pub.

— Romantic Impressions, Bk. 1. 24p. 1993. pap. 5.95 (*0-7390-0617-7*, 6688) Alfred Pub.

— Treasures for Two, Bk. 1. 32p. 1994. pap. 6.50 (*0-7390-0332-1*, 11753) Alfred Pub.

Mier, Martha, jt. auth. see Montgomery, June.

Mier, Avinoam. International Aspects of Rural & Urban Metropolitan Systems. Stern, Eliahu & Krakover, Shaul, eds. (Geography Research Forum Ser.: Vol. 9). 149p. (Orig.). 1988. pap. 29.95 (*0-88738-732-2*) Transaction Pubs.

Mier, Edwin E. & Yocom, Betsy. Taking ATM to Task: 1988 Edition. 4th rev. ed. (Illus.). 400p. 1998. spiral bd. 495.00 (*1-891869-00-0*) Mier Communs.

***Mier, Edwin E., et al.** Getting VoIP to Work, 1999. 220p. 1999. 995.00 (*1-891869-03-5*) Mier Communs.

Mier, J. G., et al. Fracture Processes in Concrete, Rock & Ceramics: Proceedings of the International RILEM-ESIS Conference. 1100p. 1991. write for info. (*0-412-43080-0*, E & FN Spon) Routledge.

Mier, James W., jt. auth. see Atkins, Michael B.

Mier-Jedrzejowicz, W. A. A Guide to HP Handheld Calculators & Computers. 3rd rev. ed. LC 97-61853. (Illus.). 154p. 1997. pap. 24.95 (*1-888840-30-7*) Wilson-Barnett.

Mier-Jedrzejowicz, Wlodek. A Guide to HP Handheld Calculators & Computers. 2nd rev. ed. LC 96-60698. (Illus.). 98p. 1996. pap. 22.95 (*1-888840-00-5*, WL0296) Wilson-Barnett.

— Tips & Programs for the HP-32S. (Illus.). 81p. (Orig.). (C). 1988. pap. text 7.95 (*0-937637-05-X*, 2014) Interfab Corp.

Mier, Kenneth. God's Miracle Power Suddenly Begins Working with a Simple Prayer. 1998. pap. write for info. (*1-889505-29-3*) White Wing Pub.

Mier, Martha. Christmas Kaleidoscope, Bk. 1. 24p. 1996. pap. 5.95 (*0-7390-0358-5*, 16878) Alfred Pub.

— Firefly Waltz. 1999. pap. 2.50 (*0-7390-0302-X*, 18536) Alfred Pub.

— Hymns for Meditation. 1999. pap. 5.95 (*0-7390-0321-6*, 17603) Alfred Pub.

— Midnight Shadows. 4p. 1999. pap. 2.50 (*0-7390-0288-0*, 18519) Alfred Pub.

— Musical Snapshots. 24p. 1999. pap. 5.95 (*0-7390-0336-4*, 18199) Alfred Pub.

— Rhapsody: For the Left Hand Alone. 1999. pap. 2.50 (*0-7390-0319-4*, 18996) Alfred Pub.

***Mier, Naomi & Daniel, Becky.** Sensory Stimulation Through Imagination Vacation. (Illus.). 44p. 1998. pap. text 7.95 (*1-56490-104-1*) G Grimm Assocs.

Mier, Paul D. & Van de Kerkhof, Peter C., eds. Textbook of Psoriasis. LC 85-16669. (Illus.). 292p. 1986. text 156.00 (*0-443-03210-6*) Church.

Mier, R. J. & Brower, T. J. Pediatric Orthopedics: A Guide for the Primary Care Physician. (Illus.). 340p. (C). 1994. text 49.50 (*0-306-44796-7*, Kluwer Plenum) Kluwer Academic.

Mier, Robert. Social Justice & Local Development Policy. (Illus.). 256p. 1993. 52.00 (*0-8039-4947-2*); pap. 24.50 (*0-8039-4948-0*) Sage.

Mier, Robert, jt. auth. see Bingham, Richard D.

Mier, Robert, jt. ed. see Bingham, Richard D.

***Mierau, Christina B.** Accept No Substitutes! The History of American Advertising. LC 99-27580. (People's History Ser.). (Illus.). 88p. (YA). (gr. 6-9). 2000. 22.60 (*0-8225-1742-6*, Lerner Publctns) Lerner Pub.

Miermont, Jacques. A Dictionary of Family Therapy. Jenkins, Hugh, ed. Turner, Chris, tr. from FRE. (Illus.). 600p. (C). 1995. text 111.95 (*0-631-17048-0*) Blackwell Pubs.

Miernowska, Ewa. Le Dialogue des Discours dans les Romans d'Albert Cohen, Vol. 22. LC 97-10689. (Francophone Cultures & Literatures Ser.). X, 162p. (C). 1998. text 41.95 (*0-8204-3807-3*) P Lang Pubng.

Miernowski, Jan. Le Dieu Nant: Thologies Ngatives l'Aube des Temps Modernes. LC 97-38232. (Studies in the History of Christian Thought, 0081-8607: No. 82). (FRE., Illus.). 176p. 1997. 66.25 (*90-04-10915-3*) Brill Academic Pubs.

Miernyk, William H. Illusions of Conventional Economics. 185p. 1982. pap. 12.00 (*0-937058-14-9*) West Va U Pr.

Mierop, L. H. Van, see Van Mierop, L. H., ed.

***Mierow, Dorothy.** Thirty Years in Pokhara You Must Have Seen a Lot of Changes. 1999. pap. 160.00 (*0-7855-7648-7*) St Mut.

Miers, Charles, jt. ed. see Trecker, Jim.

Miers, David. Compensation for Criminal Injuries. 300p. 1990. text 95.00 (*0-406-12324-1*, UK, MICHIE) LEXIS Pub.

— State Compensation for Criminal Injuries. 319p. 1997. pap. 54.00 (*1-85431-505-6*, Pub. by Blackstone Pr) Gaunt.

Miers, David, jt. auth. see Twining, William.

Miers, Earl S. Lincoln Day-by-Day: A Chronology, 1809-1865. rev. ed. 1164p. 1988. reprint ed. 45.00 (*0-89029-542-5*) Morningside Bkshop.

— The Web of Victory: Grant at Vicksburg. LC 84-9717. (Illus.). 320p. 1984. pap. 16.95 (*0-8071-1199-6*) La State U Pr.

Miers, Earl S. & Brown, Richard A., eds. Gettysburg. LC 96-1729. (American History Through Literature Ser.). 258p. (C). (gr. 13). 1996. 70.95 (*1-56324-696-1*); pap. 24.95 (*1-56324-697-X*) M E Sharpe.

Miers, Earl S. & Ellis, Richard, eds. Bookmaking & Kindred Amenities. LC 70-80392. (Essay Index Reprint Ser.). xiii, 147p. 1977. 20.95 (*0-8369-1045-1*) Ayer.

Miers, Earl S., ed. see LeConte, Emma.

***Miers, Earl Schenck.** Pirate Chase. 2nd ed. (YA). 1998. pap. 4.95 (*0-87935-203-5*) Colonial Williamsburg.

Miers, Horst E. Lexikon des Geheimwissens. (GER.). 125.00 (*0-8288-7901-X*, M7214) Fr & Eur.

— Lexikon des Geheimwissens. deluxe ed. (GER.). 125.00 (*3-7626-0028-7*, M-7214) Fr & Eur.

Miers, John. Travels in Chili & La Plata, 2 vols. LC 76-128416. reprint ed. 115.00 (*0-404-04317-8*) AMS Pr.

***Miers, Mary.** Doors & Windows: One Hundred Period Details. (Illus.). 108p. 2000. pap. 24.95 (*1-85410-686-4*, Pub. by Aurum Pr) London Brdge.

Miers, Richenda. Scotland: Cadogan Books. 5th ed. (Cadogan Guides Ser.). (Illus.). 608p. 1998. pap. text 18.95 (*1-86011-073-8*, Pub. by Cadgn Bks) Globe Pequot.

— Scotland: Highlands & Islands. 2nd ed. (Cadogan Guides Ser.). 304p. 1998. text 17.95 (*1-86011-018-5*, Pub. by Cadgn Bks) Macmillan.

***Miers, Richenda.** Scotland: Highlands & Islands. 3rd ed. (City Guides Ser.). (Illus.). 2000. pap. 17.95 (*1-86011-951-4*) Cadgn Bks.

Miers, Suzanne & Klein, Martin A. Slavery & Colonial Rule in Africa. LC 98-27601. (Studies in Slave & Post-Slave Societies & Cultures). 312p. 1999. 59.50 (*0-7146-4884-1*, Pub. by F Cass Pubs); pap. 26.50 (*0-7146-4436-6*, Pub. by F Cass Pubs) Intl Spec Bk.

Miers, Suzanne & Kopytoff, Igor, eds. Slavery in Africa: Historical & Anthropological Perspectives. LC 76-53653. 492p. reprint ed. pap. 152.60 (*0-608-20454-4*, 207170700002) Bks Demand.

Miers, Suzanne & Roberts, Richard L., eds. End of Slavery in Africa. LC 88-40192. 448p. 1988. pap. text 22.95 (*0-299-11554-2*) U of Wis Pr.

Miers, Suzanne, jt. ed. see Jaschok, Maria.

Mierse, William E. Temples & Towns in Roman Iberia: The Social & Architectural Dynamics of Sanctuary Designs from the Third Century B. C. to the Third Century A. D. LC 97-46951. 391p. 1999. 65.00 (*0-520-20377-1*, Pub. by U CA Pr) Cal Prin Full Svc.

Mierse, William E., jt. auth. see Hanfmann, George M.

Mierswa, Richard, jt. auth. see Mierswa, Ruth.

Mierswa, Ruth & Mierswa, Richard. Ray-Centered Astrology. LC 84-90404. 1986. 16.00 (*0-87212-185-2*) Libra.

Mierswa, Ruth M. Who You Are & Why You Are Here: Find Your Life Purpose & Personality Type. LC 97-92639. (Illus.). 312p. 1998. pap. 16.00 (*0-9661080-0-0*) Rainbow Gate.

Miert, Karel Von, see Von Miert, Karel.

Miertschin, Susan L., jt. auth. see Goodson, Carole E.

Miertshcin, Susan L., jt. auth. see Goodson, C. E.

***Miertus, Stanislav & Fassina, Giorgio.** Combinatorial Chemistry & Technology: Principles, Methods & Applications LC 99-15461. (Illus.). 448p. 1999. text 165.00 (*0-8247-1960-3*) Dekker.

Mierzecki, R. The Historical Development of Chemical Concepts. 296p. (C). 1991. text 234.00 (*0-7923-0915-4*) Kluwer Academic.

Mierzejewski, Alfred C. The Collapse of the German War Economy, 1944-1945: Allied Air Power & the German National Railway. LC 88-4777. xxi, 285p. (C). 1988. 55.00 (*0-8078-1792-9*) U of NC Pr.

***Mierzejewski, Alfred C.** The Most Valuable Asset of The Reich: A History of The German National Railway 1920-1932, Vol. 1. LC 98-53440. (Illus.). 656p. 1999. 85.00 (*0-8078-2496-8*) U of NC Pr.

— The Most Valuable Asset of the Reich: A History of the German National Railway Vol. 2: 1933-1945. (Illus.). 368p. 2000. 45.00 (*0-8078-2574-3*) U of NC Pr.

Mierzejewski, D. L. Fundamentals of Chemistry. (Illus.). 410p. 1982. ring bd. 149.50 (*0-87683-212-5*) GP Courseware.

Mierzwa, Joseph W. The Twenty-First Century Family Legal Guide. 448p. 1994. pap. 19.95 (*0-9637285-0-4*) Prose Assocs.

Mierzwa, Ronald B. Child Church: Homily Outlines for Preaching to Children. LC 95-52994. 128p. (Orig.). 1996. pap., teacher ed. 10.95 (*0-89390-370-1*) Resource Pubns.

Mies, Maria. Patriarchy & Accumulation on a World Scale: Women in the International Division of Labour. 260p. (C). 1986. pap. 22.50 (*0-86232-342-8*, Pub. by St Martin) St Martin.

— Patriarchy & Accumulation on a World Scale: Women in the International Division of Labour. 260p. (C). 1986. text 49.95 (*0-86232-341-X*, Pub. by Zed Books) St Martin.

***Mies, Maria.** Patriarchy & Accumulation on a World Scale; Women in the International Division of Labour. 1999. text 65.00 (*1-85649-734-8*) Zed Books.

— Patriarchy & Accumulation on a World Scale; Women in the International Division of Labour. 2nd ed. 1999. pap. 22.50 (*1-85649-735-6*) St Martin.

Mies, Maria & Shiva, Vandana. Ecofeminism: Reconnecting a Divided World. 336p. (C). 1993. text 22.50 (*1-85649-156-0*, Pub. by Zed Books) St Martin.

Mies, Paul. Beethoven's Sketches: An Analysis of His Style Based on a Study of His Sketch-Books. 198p. 1990. reprint ed. lib. bdg. 59.00 (*0-7812-9044-9*) Rprt Serv.

Miescher, Peter A., ed. Systemic Lupus Erythematosus. LC 95-1128. 240p. 1995. 92.00 (*0-387-59039-0*) Spr-Verlag.

Miescher, Peter A., jt. ed. see Muller-Eberhard, H. J.

Miescke, Lori. Safety Smart--Intermediate: Teaching Responsibility for Personal & Home Safety. Mitchell, Judy & Clerico, Don, eds. (Illus.). 144p. (Orig.). (J). (gr. 4-6). 1995. pap., teacher ed. 13.95 (*1-57310-016-1*) Teachng & Lrning Co.

***Miescke, Lori.** Toe Ticklers. 64p. 1999. pap. 8.99 (*0-570-05381-1*) Concordia.

Miesel, Sandra. Against Time's Arrow: The High Crusade of Poul Anderson. LC 78-14913. (Milford Series: Popular Writers of Today: Popular Writers of Today: Vol. 18). 64p. 1978. pap. 13.00 (*0-89370-224-2*) Millefleurs.

Miesel, Victor. Ludwig Meidner: An Expressionist Master. (Illus.). 71p. 1978. pap. 6.00 (*0-912303-16-6*) Michigan Mus.

Miesel, William P. The Creative Card Magic of William P. Miesel. LC 80-80275. (Illus.). 178p. 1980. 20.00 (*0-9604016-0-1*) Unikorn Magik.

Miesen. Dementia in Close Up. LC 98-23238. 248p. (C). 1999. 75.00 (*0-415-12884-6*) Routledge.

— Dementia in Close-up. LC 98-23238. 248p. (C). 1999. pap. 24.99 (*0-415-12885-4*) Routledge.

Miesen, M. Bere, jt. ed. see Jones, Gemma M.

***Miesfeld, Roger L.** Applied Molecular Genetics. LC 98-29973. 293p. 1999. pap. 49.95 (*0-471-15676-0*) Wiley.

Miesner, Joseph M., Sr., jt. auth. see Brandes-Miesner, Marta.

Miesse, Frank. Chinese Herbs Made Easy. 20p. Date not set. pap. 2.95 (*0-913923-64-8*) Woodland UT.

Miessler. Inorganic Chemistry. 2nd ed. 1999. pap. text, student ed. 15.75 (*0-13-919242-5*) P-H.

Miessler, Gary L. Inorganic Chemistry. 2nd ed. LC 98-29946. 642p. 1998. 105.00 (*0-13-841891-8*) P-H.

Miessmer, Andreas. Fabulous Fruit Cooking: A Gourmet Guide to Great Fruit Dishes from Soup to Sorbet. rev. ed. Morgenthal, Deborah, ed. LC 96-4215. (Illus.). 144p. 1996. 19.95 (*1-887374-07-8*) Lark Books.

Miessner, B. F. On the Early History of Radio Guidance. (Illus.). 1964. 15.00 (*0-911302-00-X*) San Francisco Pr.

Mieszkowski, Gretchen. The Reputation of Criseyde, 1155-1500. (Connecticut Academy of Arts & Sciences Ser., Trans.: Vol. 43). 1971. pap. 39.50 (*0-685-22886-X*) Elliots Bks.

Mieszkowski, Peter. Taxes, Public Goods & Urban Economics: The Selected Essays of Peter Mieszkowski. LC 99-38554. (Studies in Fiscal Federalism & State-Local Finance). 544p. 2000. 100.00 (*1-85898-897-7*) E Elgar.

Mieszkowski, Peter & Straszheim, Mahlon R., eds. Current Issues in Urban Economics. LC 78-14947. 605p. reprint ed. pap. 187.60 (*0-7837-4780-2*, 204453500003) Bks Demand.

Mieszkowski, Peter, jt. ed. see McLure, Charles E., Jr.

Mieth, Annemarie, jt. auth. see Beisbart, Ortwin.

Mieth, Dietmar & Cahill, Lisa S., eds. Migrants & Refugees: The Moral Challenge. (Concilium Ser.). 1993. 15.00 (*0-88344-873-4*) Orbis Bks.

Mieth, Dietmar & Theobald, Christoph, eds. Unanswered Questions. 150p. 1999. pap. 15.00 (*1-57075-225-7*) Orbis Bks.

Mieth, Dietmar, jt. auth. see Hildt, Elisabeth.

Mieth, Dietmar, jt. ed. see Cahill, Lisa S.

Mieth, Dietmar, jt. ed. see Pohier, Jacques.

Miethe, Beverly, jt. auth. see Miethe, Terry L.

Miethe, Terance D. Whistleblowing at Work: Tough Choices in Exposing Fraud, Waste & Abuse on the Job. LC 98-43034. (Crime & Society Ser.). 252p. 1998. pap. 30.00 (*0-8133-3549-3*, Pub. by Westview) HarpC.

Miethe, Terance D. & McCorkle, Richard C. Crime Profiles: The Anatomy of Dangerous Persons, Places, & Situations. LC 97-23654. (Illus.). 275p. (Orig.). (C). 1998. pap. text. write for info. (*0-935732-94-2*) Roxbury Pub Co.

Miethe, Terance D. & Meier, Robert F. Crime & Its Social Context: Toward an Integrated Theory of Offenders, Victims, & Situations. LC 93-24503. (SUNY Series in Deviance & Social Control). 209p. (C). 1994. pap. text 19.95 (*0-7914-1902-9*) State U NY Pr.

***Miethe, Terence D. & McCorkle, Richard C.** Crime Profiles: The Anatomy of Dangerous Persons, Places & Situations. 2nd ed. (Illus.). 276p. (C). 2001. pap. text. write for info. (*1-891487-54-X*) Roxbury Pub Co.

Miethe, Terry L. Augustinian Bibliography, 1970-1980: With Essays on the Fundamentals of Augustinian Scholarship. LC 82-6173. 218p. 1982. lib. bdg. 59.95 (*0-313-22629-6*, MIA/, Greenwood Pr) Greenwood.

Miethe, Terry L. Compact Dictionary of Doctrinal Words. LC 88-12161. 224p. (Orig.). 1988. reprint ed. pap. 9.99 (*0-87123-678-8*, 210678) Bethany Hse.

***Miethe, Terry L.** C.S. Lewis' Miracles. LC 99-37901. (Shepherd's Notes Ser.). 1999. 5.95 (*0-8054-9394-8*) Broadman.

Miethe, Terry L. Living Your Faith: Closing the Gap Between Mind & Heart. 185p. (Orig.). (C). 1993. pap. 9.99 (*0-89900-620-5*) College Pr Pub.

Miethe, Terry L. & Bourke, Vernon J., compiled by. Thomistic Bibliography, 1940-1978. LC 80-1195. 318p. 1980. lib. bdg. 49.95 (*0-313-21991-5*, MTH/, Greenwood Pr) Greenwood.

Miethe, Terry L. & Miethe, Beverly. Serving Christ: A Family Affair. LC 95-140. 1995. pap. 12.99 (*0-89900-730-9*) College Pr Pub.

Miethe, Terry L., jt. auth. see Gould, Dana.

Miething, Andreas. The Establishment of Spermatogenesis in the Seminiferous: Epithelium of the Pubertal Golden Hamster (Mesocricetus Auratus) LC 97-42016. (Advances in Anatomy, Embryology & Cell Biology Ser.: Vol. 140). (Illus.). 104p. 1998. pap. 89.00 (*3-540-63655-2*) Spr-Verlag.

Miettinen, Asko, jt. auth. see Donckels, Rik.

Miettinen, H. E., jt. ed. see Bonner, B. E.

Miettinen, Jukka O. Classical Dance & Theatre in South-East Asia. (Illus.). 196p. 1993. text 80.00 (*0-19-588595-3*) OUP.

Miettinen, Kaisa. Nonlinear Multiobjective Optimization. LC 98-37888. (International Series in Operations Research & Management Science). 1998. write for info. (*0-7923-8278-1*) Kluwer Academic.

Miettinen, Reijo, jt. auth. see Engestrom, Yrjo.

Mietus, Norbert J., jt. auth. see Adamson.

Mietus, Norbert J., jt. auth. see Adamson, John E.

Mietz, J., ed. Electrochemical Rehabilitation Methods for Reinforced Concrete Structures: A State of the Art Report. (European Federation of Corrosion Publications Ser.: No. 24). (Illus.). 70p. 1998. pap. 50.00 (*1-86125-082-7*, Pub. by Inst Materials) Ashgate Pub Co.

Mietz, J., et al, eds. Corrosion of Reinforcement in Concrete - Monitoring, Prevention & Rehabilitation: Papers from Eurocorr '97. (European Federation of Corrosion Publications Ser.: No. 25). (Illus.). 228p. 1998. 90.00 (*1-86125-083-5*, Pub. by Inst Materials) Ashgate Pub Co.

Mietzer, Dick. The Subsidized Muse: Public Support for the Arts in the United States. (Modern Revivals in Economics Ser.). 300p. 1993. 61.95 (*0-7512-0142-1*, Pub. by Gregg Pub) Ashgate Pub Co.

Mieusset, R., jt. auth. see Hamamah, S.

***Mieville, China.** King Rat. 320p. 2000. pap. 14.95 (*0-312-89072-9*) St Martin.

— King Rat. LC 99-26657. 320p. 1999. 23.95 (*0-312-89073-7*, Pub. by Tor Bks) St Martin.

Miewald, Robert, jt. ed. see Welch, Susan.

Miewald, Robert D., ed. Nebraska Government & Politics. LC 83-3684. (Politics & Governments of the American States Ser.). xiv, 230p. 1984. text 15.00 (*0-8032-3078-8*); pap. text 12.95 (*0-8032-8113-7*) U of Nebr Pr.

Miewald, Robert D. & Longo, Peter J. The Nebraska State Constitution: A Reference Guide, 13. LC 92-21359. (Reference Guides to the State Constitutions of the United States Ser.: No. 13). 240p. 1993. lib. bdg. 75.00 (*0-313-27947-0*, MNG, Greenwood Pr) Greenwood.

Miezala, Lorraine. Collector's Guide to Barbie Doll Paper Dolls: Identification & Values. LC 97-190246. (Collector's Guide to Ser.). (Illus.). 144p. 1997. pap. 16.95 (*0-89145-771-2*, 4859) Collector Bks.

Miezitis, S. Creating Alternatives to Depression in Our Schools: Assessment, Intervention & Prevention. LC 91-861. (Illus.). 457p. 1992. pap. text 37.00 (*0-88937-039-7*) Hogrefe & Huber Pubs.

Miezo, Peggy M. Parenting Children with Disabilities. 1983. 49.75 (*0-8247-1090-8*) Phoenix Soc.

Miffleton, Jack. God Be in My Heart Children's Book. (J). 1998. pap. 6.95 (*0-915531-85-2*) OR Catholic.

— Sunday's Child: A Planning Guide for Liturgies with Both Children & Adults. 64p. 1989. pap. 7.95 (*0-912405-62-7*, Pastoral Press) OR Catholic.

Mifflin, Houghton. Integrated Math, vol. 1. 1994. text, teacher ed. 91.96 (*0-395-64427-5*); text, student ed. 59.32 (*0-395-64426-7*) HM.

— Integrated Math, vol. 2. 1994. text, student ed. 61.56 (*0-395-64439-9*) HM.

Mifflin, Margot. Bodies of Subversion: A Secret History of Women & Tattoo. LC 97-28410. 1997. pap. text 23.95 (*1-890451-00-2*) Juno Bks.

Mifflin, Ray, jt. auth. see Weeks-Mifflin, Mary.

Mifflin, Theodore E., et al. Diagnostic Molecular Biology. 1993. text 47.50 (*0-07-041933-7*) McGraw.

Miflin, B. J. Oxford Surveys of Plant Molecular Biology, Vol. 7. (Illus.). 342p. 1991. pap. 55.00 (*0-19-857750-8*) OUP.

Miflin, B. J., ed. Oxford Surveys of Plant Molecular & Cell Biology, Vol. 3: 1986. (Illus.). 482p. (Orig.). 1987. pap. 48.00 (*0-19-854202-X*) OUP.

— Oxford Surveys of Plant Molecular & Cell Biology, Vol. 5: 1988. (Illus.). 224p. (Orig.). 1989. pap. 48.00 (*0-19-854238-0*) OUP.

— Oxford Surveys of Plant Molecular & Cell Biology, 1989, Vol. 6. (Illus.). 322p. 1990. pap. 48.00 (*0-19-857735-4*) OUP.

Miflin, B. J., et al, eds. The Biochemistry of Plants Vol. 16: A Comprehensive Treatise, Intermediary Nitrogen Metabolism. 402p. 1990. text 146.00 (*0-12-675416-0*) Acad Pr.

Miflin, B. J. & Miflin, H. F., eds. Oxford Surveys of Plant Molecular & Cell Biology, Vol. 4: 1987. (Illus.). 376p. (Orig.). 1988. pap. 48.00 (*0-19-854233-X*) OUP.

Miflin, H. F., jt. ed. see Miflin, B. J.

Mifsud, Alfred. Knights Hospitallers of the Venerable Tongue of England in Malta. LC 78-63348. (Crusades & Military Orders Ser.: Second Series). (Illus.). reprint ed. 59.50 (*0-404-17009-9*) AMS Pr.

Mifsud, Manwel. Loan Verbs in Maltese: A Descriptive & Comparative Study. LC 94-43608. (Studies in Semitic Languages & Linguistics: Vol. 21). xvii, 339p. 1994. 124.00 (*90-04-10091-1*) Brill Academic Pubs.

Migachyov, Dina. Mathematics for Little Ones: How to Make Your Child Successful in Math. (Illus.). viii, 183p. (J). (gr. k-3). 1999. pap. 19.95 (*0-9672535-0-0*) Quaternion.

Migaki, George, jt. ed. see Montali, Richard J.

Migaki, George, jt. ed. see Ribelin, William E.

An Asterisk (*) at the beginning of an entry indicates that the title is appearing for the first time.

Migala, Joseph. Polish Radio Broadcasting in the United States. 309p. 1987. text 55.50 (*0-88033-112-7*, 216, Pub. by East Eur Monographs) Col U Pr.

Migaly, Peter. The Best Cartoons for Health & Fitness: (Cartoons Only Version) 100p. (Orig.). Date not set. pap. 4.65 (*0-9647363-3-0*) P Migaly.

— The Lighter Side of Overweight: A Self-Help Book for Weight Control (with Cartoons) (Smokeless Side: No. 2). (Illus.). 100p. (Orig.). Date not set. pap. 15.95 (*0-9647363-1-4*) P Migaly.

— Pain Free: A Self-Help Guide & Program Description for Becoming Pain Free Again. (Illus.). 100p. (Orig.). Date not set. pap. 15.95 (*0-9647363-2-2*) P Migaly.

— The Smokeless Side: Humor to Reverse Your Urge to Smoke & the Effects of Ads & Peer Pressure. The Original Cartoon Book for Smoking Cessation, Vol. 1. LC 95-94397. 112p. 1995. pap. 15.95 (*0-9647363-0-6*) P Migaly.

Migas, Abraham I. Kevod Elohim. 1979. 30.95 (*0-405-12616-6*) Ayer.

Migayrou, Frederic, jt. auth. see Saee, Michele.

***Migdal, A. B.** Qualitative Methods in Quantum Theory. (Illus.). 256p. 2000. pap. text 39.00 (*0-7382-0302-5*) Perseus Pubng.

Migdal, A. B., tr. see Krylov, Nikolai S.

Migdal, Arkadii B. Qualitative Methods in Quantum Theory. Leggett, Anthony J., tr. (Advanced Book Classics Ser.). 1977. 29.95 (*0-8053-7064-1*) Addison-Wesley.

Migdal, Joel S. Peasants, Politics, & Revolution: Pressures Toward Political & Social Change in the Third World. LC 74-2972. 311p. reprint ed. pap. 96.50 (*0-8357-7889-4*, 203630800002) Bks Demand.

— Strong Societies & Weak States: State-Society Relations & State Capabilities in the Third World. (Illus.). 344p. 1988. pap. text 17.95 (*0-691-01073-0*, Pub. by Princeton U Pr) Cal Prin Full Svc.

Migdal, Joel S., et al, eds. State Power & Social Forces: Domination & Transformation in the Third World. LC 93-48757. (Cambridge Studies in Comparative Politics). 347p. (C). 1994. text 64.95 (*0-521-46166-9*); pap. text 20.95 (*0-521-46734-9*) Cambridge U Pr.

Migdal, Joel S., et al. Palestinian Society & Politics. LC 79-84002. 308p. reprint ed. pap. 95.50 (*0-8357-2553-7*, 204024400015) Bks Demand.

Migdal, Joel S., jt. auth. see Kimmerling, Baruch.

Migdal, Stehen, ed. see Hughes, Richard.

Migdal, Stehen, jt. ed. see Hughes, Richard.

Migdal, Sy, jt. auth. see Stallone, James.

Migdalas, Athanasios, et al, eds. Multilevel Optimization: Algorithms & Applications. LC 97-42021. (Nonconvex Optimization & Its Applications Ser.). 406p. 1998. text 214.00 (*0-7923-4693-9*, D Reidel) Kluwer Academic.

Migdalas, Athanasios, et al. Parallel Computing in Optimization. LC 97-14126. (Applied Optimization Ser.). 1997. lib. bdg. 260.00 (*0-7923-4583-5*) Kluwer Academic.

Migdall, Alan L. Spectroradiometric Detector Measurements Pt. 3: Infrared Detectors. 59p. 1999. pap. 5.25 (*0-16-056785-8*) USGPO.

Migdalski, Edward C. The Inquisitive Angler. 280p. 1991. 27.95 (*1-55821-132-2*) Lyons Pr.

Migdalski, Tom. The Complete Book to Shotgunning Games. LC 97-28446. (Illus.). 328p. (Orig.). 1997. pap. 16.95 (*1-57028-142-4*, 81424H, Mstrs Pr) NTC Contemp Pub Co.

Migdol, Gary. Stanford: Home of Champions. 273p. 1997. 39.95 (*1-57167-116-1*) Sports Pub.

Migdoll, Ivor. Butterflies of Southern Africa. 1998. pap. 24.95 (*1-86825-624-3*, Pub. by New5 Holland) Sterling.

— Field Guide to the Butterflies of Southern Africa. (C). 1988. 110.00 (*1-85368-002-8*, 314, Pub. by New5 Holland) St Mut.

Migdow, Jeffery, jt. auth. see Loehr, James.

Migel, Parmenia. Great Ballet Prints of the Romantic Era. (Illus.). 1990. 19.50 (*0-8446-5905-3*) Peter Smith.

— Great Ballet Prints of the Romantic Era: 109 Illustrations, Including 9 in Full Color. (Illus.). 128p. (Orig.). 1981. pap. 9.95 (*0-486-24050-9*) Dover.

Migel, Parmenia, ed. see Picasso, Pablo.

Migeod, Frederick W. The Languages of West Africa. 1977. 34.95 (*0-405-30129-4*); 34.95 (*0-405-30130-8*) Ayer.

— The Languages of West Africa, 2 vols. LC 72-3001. (Black Heritage Library Collection). 1977. reprint ed. 69.95 (*0-8369-9076-5*) Ayer.

Miggins, Edward M., jt. ed. see Campbell, Thomas F.

***Mighall, Robert.** A Geography of Victorian Gothic Fiction: Mapping History's Nightmares. (Illus.). 344p. 2000. text 74.00 (*0-19-818472-7*) OUP.

Mighall, Robert, ed. Oscar Wilde. (Everyman's Poetry Ser.). 116p. 1997. pap. 1.95 (*0-460-87803-4*, Everyman's Classic Lib) Tuttle Pubng.

Mighell, John. Miller's Antiques Checklist: Clocks. LC 96-139075. (Illus.). 192p. 1993. 15.95 (*1-85732-945-7*, Pub. by Millers Pubns) Antique Collect.

Mighell, Ronald L. & Black, J. D. Interregional Competition in Agriculture: With Special Reference to Dairy Farming in the Lake States & New England. LC 51-11577. (Economic Studies: No. 89). (Illus.). 334p. 1951. 22.50 (*0-674-46050-2*) HUP.

Mighetto, Lisa. Wild Animals & American Environmental Ethics. LC 91-16910. (Illus.). 209p. (Orig.). 1991. pap. 19.95 (*0-8165-1266-3*); lib. bdg. 39.95 (*0-8165-1160-8*) U of Ariz Pr.

***Might, Jennie.** Beaded Baltimore: Album Blocks & Quilt. (Illus.). 20p. 2000. pap. 12.95 (*0-9665853-2-1*) Black Giraffe.

Might, Jennie. Beaded Favors: Design for Needlecases & Treasure Bags. (Illus.). 50p. 1999. 16.95 (*0-9665853-1-3*, BF-1) Black Giraffe.

— Beaded Needlecases: A Book of Instruction & Design. (Illus.). 26p. 1998. pap. 14.95 (*0-9665853-0-5*) Black Giraffe.

Might Magazine Editors. For the Love of Cheese. LC 96-194047. 160p. 1996. pap. 12.00 (*1-57297-153-3*) Blvd Books.

Might Magazine Staff. Shiny Adidas Tracksuits & the Death of Camp: And Other Essays from Might Magazine. LC 98-217139. 243p. 1998. pap. 14.00 (*0-425-16477-2*) Blvd Books.

Mighton, John. Little Years. LC 97-124269. 72p. 1997. pap. text 11.95 (*0-88754-548-3*) Theatre Comm.

***Mighton, John.** Possible Worlds: Acting Edition. 80p. 1998. pap. 10.00 (*0-929741-43-9*) Playsmith.

Migiel, Marilyn. Gender & Genealogy in Tasso's "Gerusalemme Liberata" LC 93-32355. 204p. 1993. text 89.95 (*0-7734-9392-1*) E Mellen.

Migiel, Marilyn & Schiesari, Juliana, eds. Refiguring Woman: Perspectives on Gender & the Italian Renaissance. LC 90-55736. 304p. 1991. text 42.50 (*0-8014-2538-7*); pap. text 16.95 (*0-8014-9771-X*) Cornell U Pr.

***Miglani, Gurbachan S.** Dictionary of Plant Genetics & Molecular Biology: A Dictionary of Terms. LC 97-20226. (Illus.). 348p. (C). 1998. 89.95 (*1-56022-871-7*) Haworth Jrnl Co-Edits.

Migliaccio, Eric, ed. see Thompson, Bobi.

Migliaccio, Janice C. Follow Your Heart's Vegetarian Soup Cookbook. LC 82-21822. (Illus.). 128p. (Orig.). 1983. pap. 7.95 (*0-88007-131-1*) Woodbridge Pr.

***Migliaccio, Puccio.** Glass for the Table: XIX Century Murano Glass Tableware. (Illus.). 2000. pap. text 19.95 (*88-7743-213-6*) Arsenale Editrice.

Migliardi, Robert D. HU-16 Albatross in Action. (Aircraft in Action Ser.). (Illus.). 50p. 1996. pap. 9.95 (*0-89747-354-X*, 1161) Squad Sig Pubns.

Migliaresi, C. Biomedical Applications of Composites. 246p. 1995. spiral bd. 84.95 (*0-8493-6548-1*) CRC Pr.

Migliaro, Al & Jain, Chaman L. An Executive's Guide to Econometric Forecasting. 74p. (C). 1983. pap. 26.95 (*0-932126-10-3*) Graceway.

Migliaro, Al & Jain, Chaman L., eds. Understanding Business Forecasting: A Manager's Guide. 234p. (Orig.). 1985. pap. 27.95 (*0-932126-12-X*) Graceway.

Migliaro, Al, jt. auth. see Jain, Chaman L.

Migliaro, Marco W. Glossary of Stationary Battery Terminology. Alber, Glenn, ed. (Illus.). 56p. (Orig.). 1992. 18.95 (*0-9635109-0-8*) Alber Technol.

Miglierini, Marcel & Petridis, Dimitris. Mossbauer Spectroscopy in Materials Science. LC 99-13873. (Nato Science Ser.). 1999. write for info. (*0-7923-5640-3*) Kluwer Academic.

Miglin, Marilyn. Marilyn Miglin. 192p. 2000. write for info. (*1-886094-68-3*) Chicago Spectrum.

Miglinas, Skirmante, ed. see Budrys, Milda.

Miglio, Paige. Bear's Baby. 32p. 15.95 (*0-06-029240-7*) HarpC.

— Bear's Baby. 32p. (ps up). pap. 5.95 (*0-06-443741-8*); lib. bdg. 15.89 (*0-06-029241-5*) HarpC.

Miglioli, P., et al, eds. Theorem Proving with Analytic Tableaux & Related Methods: Proceedings of the 5th International Workshop, Tableaux '96, Terrasini, Palermo, Italy, 15-17th, 1996. LC 96-17235. (Lecture Notes in Artificial Intelligence Ser.: Vol. 107). 329p. 1996. pap. 56.00 (*3-540-61208-4*) Spr-Verlag.

Migliore, Josephine & Whitaker, Dave. And I Loved Them: Voices & Memories from a Prison Ministry. LC 99-19738. 200p. 1999. pap. 14.95 (*1-56625-116-8*) Bonus Books.

Migliore, Daniel L. Faith Seeking Understanding: An Introduction to Christian Theology. LC 91-13551. xiv, 326p. (C). 1991. pap. 22.00 (*0-8028-0601-5*) Eerdmans.

Migliore, Daniel L., jt. auth. see Billman, Kathleen D.

Migliore, Herman M. Flexible Automation & Intelligent Manufacturing, 1998: Proceedings of the Eighth International FAIM Conference, School of Engineering & Applied Science, Portland State University, July 1-3, 1998. LC 98-20519. 1998. 225.00 (*1-56700-118-1*) Begell Hse.

Migliore, J. C. Introduction to Liaison Theory & Deficiency Modules. LC 98-15680. (Progress in Mathematics Ser.: Vol. 165). 300p. 1998. 49.50 (*0-8176-4027-4*) Birkhauser.

Migliore, Leonard, ed. Laser Materials Processing. (Manufacturing Engineering & Materials Processing Ser.: Vol. 46). (Illus.). 336p. 1996. text 150.00 (*0-8247-9714-0*) Dekker.

Migliore, Leonard R. & Schaeffer, Ronald D., eds. Lasers as Tools for Manufacturing II, Vol. 2993. LC 97-200950. 262p. 1997. 69.00 (*0-8194-2404-8*) SPIE.

Migliore, Marilyn & Ross, Philip. The Hunger Within: A Twelve-Week Self-Guided Journey from Compulsive Eating to Recovery. 224p. 1998. pap. 15.95 (*0-385-48758-4*, Main St Bks) Doubleday.

Migliore, R. Henry, et al. Church & Ministry Strategic Planning: From Concept to Success. LC 93-17360. (Illus.). 161p. 1994. 49.95 (*1-56024-346-5*) Haworth Pr.

— Strategic Planning for Not-for-Profit Organizations. LC 94-10900. (Illus.). 200p. 1994. 39.95 (*1-56024-919-6*) Haworth Pr.

Migliore, Sam. Mal'uocchiu: Ambiguity, Evil Eye & the Language of Distress. LC 97-169892. (Anthropological Horizons Ser.). (Illus.). 144p. 1997. pap. text 16.95 (*0-8020-7922-9*) U of Toronto Pr.

— Mal'Uocchiu: Ambiguity, Evil Eye, & the Languages of Distress. (Anthropological Horizons Ser.: No. 10). (Illus.). 40.00p. 1997. text 40.00 (*0-8020-0959-X*) U of Toronto Pr.

Migliori. Enucleation, Evisceration & Exenteration of the Eye. LC 98-50637. 256p. 1999. text 95.00 (*0-7506-9495-5*) Buttrwrth-Heinemann.

Migliori, Albert & Sarrao, John L. Resonant Ultrasound Spectroscopy: Applications to Physics, Materials Measurements & Non-Destructive Evaluation. LC 96-29930. 201p. 1997. 89.95 (*0-471-12360-9*) Wiley.

Migliorini, Mario. Kennel Building & Management. LC 87-21435. (Illus.). 208p. 1987. 27.95 (*0-87605-656-7*) Howell Bks.

— Yorkshire Terriers. LC 75-126573. 76p. 1971. write for info. (*0-668-02388-0*, ARCO) Macmillan.

Migliorini, Paola. Scienza e Terminologia Medica Nella Letteratura Latina di eta Neroniana: Seneca, Lucano, Persio, Petronio. (Studien Zur Klassischen Philologie Ser.: Bd. 104). 229p. 1997. 44.95 (*3-631-31229-6*) P Lang Pubng.

Migliorini, Paola, jt. auth. see Caponi, Laura.

Mignani, Rigo, ed. see Herbert, George.

Mignano, Andrew J., Jr., jt. auth. see Weinstein, Carol S.

Mignault, Robert L., jt. auth. see Baldwin, David A.

Mignerey, A., jt. auth. see Bauer, W.

Mignerey, Sharon. Cassidy's Courtship. (Intimate Moments Ser.). 1998. per. 4.25 (*0-373-07864-1*, 1-07864-1) Silhouette.

— His Tender Touch. (Intimate Moments Ser.: No. 935). 1999. per. 4.25 (*0-373-07935-4*, 1-07935-9) Silhouette.

Mignery, Herb. Best of Mignery. Cornhuskers Press Staff, ed. LC 85-70978. 1985. pap. text 15.95 (*0-933909-01-2*) Cornhusker Pr.

— 14 Carrot Mignery. Daniels, Jeremy L., ed. (Illus.). 109p. 1990. 29.95 (*0-933909-04-7*); pap. 15.95 (*0-933909-05-5*) Cornhusker Pr.

— Western Horseman Collection of Mignery Cartoons. Cornhusker Press Staff, ed. LC 90-86357. 1991. pap. 24.95 (*0-933909-06-3*) Cornhusker Pr.

Mignery, Sharon. A Sacred Trust. 320p. 1997. mass mkt. 5.50 (*0-8217-5566-8*, Zebra Kensgtn) Kensgtn Pub Corp.

Mignie, Sophie, tr. see Smarandache, Florentin.

Mignin, Robert J., jt. ed. see Reed, Keith A.

Mignini, Robert J., jt. ed. see Reed, Keith A.

***Mignola, Mike.** Hellboy: Odd Jobs. (Illus.). (J). 2000. pap. 14.95 (*1-56971-440-1*) Dark Horse Comics.

Mignola, Mike. Hellboy: Seeds of Destruction. 1998. pap. 17.95 (*1-56971-316-2*) Dark Horse Comics.

— Hellboy: Wake the Devil. 1997. pap. text 17.95 (*1-56971-226-3*) Dark Horse Comics.

— Hellboy Bk. 1: Seed of Destruction. (Illus.). 128p. 1994. pap. 17.95 (*1-56971-038-4*) Dark Horse Comics.

— Hellboy Bk. 1: Seed of Destruction. deluxe limited ed. (Illus.). 136p. 1995. 99.95 (*1-56971-051-1*) Dark Horse Comics.

Mignolli, Marisa. Hosanna to You, Jesus! A Palm Sunday Experience. (Illus.). 32p. (Orig.). (J). (ps-3). 1993. pap. 3.95 (*0-8198-3368-1*) Pauline Bks.

Mignolo, Walter D. The Darker Side of the Renaissance: Literacy, Territoriality, & Colonization. 448p. (C). 1997. pap. 22.95 (*0-472-08437-2*, 08437) U of Mich Pr.

***Mignolo, Walter D.** Local Histories/Global Designs: Coloniality, Subaltern Knowledges, & Border Thinking. LC 99-32342. 296p. 2000. 55.00 (*0-691-00139-1*, Pub. by Princeton U Pr); pap. 18.95 (*0-691-00140-5*, Pub. by Princeton U Pr) Cal Prin Full Svc.

Mignolo, Walter D., jt. ed. see Boone, Elizabeth H.

Mignon, Charles W., ed. see Cather, Willa.

Mignon, Charles W., ed. see Taylor, Edward.

Mignon, M. & Jensen, Randall T., eds. Endocrine Tumors of the Pancreas. (Frontiers of Gastrointestinal Research Ser.: Vol. 23). (Illus.). xii, 482p. 1994. 323.50 (*3-8055-5953-4*) S Karger.

Mignon, Molly R. Dictionary of Concepts in Archaeology, 13. LC 92-43151. (Reference Sources for the Social Sciences & Humanities Ser.: No. 13). 384p. 1993. lib. bdg. 99.50 (*0-313-24659-9*, MID, Greenwood Pr) Greenwood.

Mignon, Molly R. & Boxberger, Daniel L., eds. Native North Americans: An Ethnohistorical Approach. 2nd ed. LC 97-71354. 508p. (C). 1997. pap. 42.95 (*0-7872-3607-1*) Kendall-Hunt.

Mignone, Emilio F. Witness to the Truth: The Complicity of Church & Dictatorship in Argentina. Berryman, Phillip, tr. from SPA. LC 88-1448. 180p. reprint ed. pap. 55.80 (*0-8357-2686-X*, 204022200015) Bks Demand.

Mignone, Mario B. Italy Today: A Country in Transition. LC 94-5280. (Studies in Modern European History: Vol. 16). 272p. (C). 1995. pap. text 29.95 (*0-8204-2659-8*) P Lang Pubng.

— Italy Today: At the Crossroads of the New Millenium, Vol. 16. 3rd rev. ed. LC 98-12025. (Studies in Modern European History). (Illus.). XVIII, 464p. (C). 1998. pap. text 33.95 (*0-8204-4041-8*) P Lang Pubng.

Mignonneau, Laurent, jt. ed. see Sommerer, Christa.

Mignosa, Charles, ed. see McGill, Ormond.

Mignot, Claude. The Pocket Louvre: A Vistor's Guide to 500 Works. LC 99-18384. (Illus.). 540p. (J). 2000. 19.95 (*0-7892-0578-5*, Abbeville Kids) Abbeville Pr.

Mignotte, M. Mathematics for Computer Algebra. xiv, 346p. 1991. 62.95 (*0-387-97675-2*) Spr-Verlag.

Mignotte, M. & Stefanescu, D. Polynomials: An Algorithmic Approach. (Series in Discrete Mathematics & Theoretical Computer Science). 320p. 1999. pap. 49.00 (*981-4021-51-2*) Spr-Verlag.

Migon, Helio & Gamerman, Dani. Statistical Inference: An Integrated Approach. (Illus.). 224p. 1999. text 55.00 (*0-340-74059-0*, Pub. by E A) OUP.

Migone, L., ed. Urinary Proteins. (Contributions to Nephrology Ser.: Vol. 26). (Illus.). viii, 124p. 1981. pap. 29.75 (*3-8055-1848-X*) S Karger.

Migrenne, Jean, tr. see Emanuel, James A.

Migsch, Herbert. Jeremias Ackerkauf: Eine Untersuchung von Jeremia 32. (Osterreichische Biblische Studien Ser.: Bd. 15). (GER., Illus.). 455p. 1996. 69.95 (*3-631-49152-2*) P Lang Pubng.

Migueis, Jose Rodrigues. A Man Smiles at Death with Half a Face. Monteiro, George, tr. & intro. by. LC 90-38976. 109p. 1990. reprint ed. pap. 33.80 (*0-608-02325-6*, 206296600004) Bks Demand.

— Steerage & Ten Other Stories. LC 82-84530. (Illus.). 224p. (Orig.). 1983. pap. 6.00 (*0-943722-06-3*) Gavea-Brown.

Miguel, Byron. Seis Dias de Noviembre: El Fusilamiento de los Estudiantes de Medicina. LC 90-84963. (Coleccion Cuba y sus Jueces). (SPA., Illus.). 96p. (Orig.). 1990. pap. 9.95 (*0-89729-586-2*) Ediciones.

Miguel Carmona, Soledad San, see Balster, Brigitte.

Miguel, Elias M. Ladron de La Mente, Vol. 2. 128p. (C). 1995. pap. 20.00 (*0-07-044312-2*) McGraw.

Miguel, Guadalupe San, see San Miguel, Guadalupe.

Miguel, J. M. de, see De Miguel, J. M.

Miguel, M. San, see Bastero, J. & San Miguel, M., eds.

Miguel-Munoz, Elias. En Estas Tierras: In This Land. LC 88-64102. 142p. 1989. pap. 13.00 (*0-916950-92-1*) Biling Rev-Pr.

Miguel, Pedro San, see San Miguel, Pedro.

Miguel Say, Pedro. Cuentos Miguelenos: Ik'ti' Yuu Naj Pel Mekel Ana. (MYN & SPA., Illus.). 160p. (Orig.). 1996. pap. 8.95 (*1-886502-10-2*, Ediciones Yax Te) Yax Te Found.

Miguelez, Roberto. L' Analyse des Formations Sociales. (FRE.). 634p. 1992. 39.95 (*0-921252-20-X*) LEGAS.

Miguens, Jose E., jt. ed. see Turner, Frederick C.

Miguet, Serge, et al. Discrete Geometry for Computer Imagery: 6th International Workshop, DGCI '96, Lyon, France, November 13-15, 1996: Proceedings. LC 96-48647. (Lecture Notes in Computer Science Ser.: Vol. 1176). 349p. 1996. text 62.00 (*3-540-62005-2*) Spr-Verlag.

— Parallel Image Analysis: Tools & Models. LC 98-216411. (Series in Machine Perception & Artificial Intelligence: Vol. 31). 130p. 1998. 22.00 (*981-02-3458-9*) World Scientific Pub.

***Mih, Walter C.** The Fascinating Life & Theory of Albert Einstein. LC 00-25990. (Illus.). 139p. 2000. lib. bdg. 27.95 (*1-56072-786-1*) Nova Sci Pubs.

Mihailescu, Calin-Andrei & Hamarneh, Walid, eds. Fiction Updated: Theories of Fictionality in Contemporary Criticism. (Theory - Culture Ser.). 384p. 1995. text 60.00 (*0-8020-0576-4*); pap. text 24.95 (*0-8020-6995-9*) U of Toronto Pr.

Mihailescu, I., jt. auth. see Mendras, H.

Mihailidi, A. English-Serbocroat Dictionary of Chemical Technology. 2nd rev. ed. 544p. (C). 1985. 195.00 (*0-7855-6457-8*, Pub. by Collets) St Mut.

Mihailidi, Agapi. English-Serbocroatian Dictionary of Chemical Engineering: Hemijsko-Tehnoloski Recnik Englesko-Srpskohrvatski. (ENG & SER.). 544p. 1985. 49.95 (*0-8288-0174-6*, F108040) Fr & Eur.

Mihailov, V. P., ed. Boundary for Differential Equations, Vol. 3. (Proceedings of the Steklov Institute of Mathematics Ser.). 256p. 1975. 84.00 (*0-8218-3026-0*, STEKLO126) Acad Pr.

Mihailov, V. P., ed. see Steklov Institute of Mathematics Staff.

Mihailovic, Alexandar. Corporeal Words: Mikhail Bakhtin's Theology of Discourse. LC 97-13576. (Studies in Russian Literature & Theory). 1997. 59.95 (*0-8101-1459-3*) Northwestern U Pr.

Mihailovic, Alexandar, ed. Tchaikovsky & His Contemporaries: A Centennial Symposium, 49. LC 98-21979. (Contributions to the Study of Music & Dance: Vol. 49). 432p. 1999. 69.50 (*0-313-30825-X*, Greenwood Pr) Greenwood.

Mihailovich, Vasa D. First Supplement to a Comprehensive Bibliography of Yugoslav Literature in English 1981-1985. 338p. (Orig.). 1989. pap. 22.95 (*0-89357-188-1*) Slavica.

— Second Supplement to "A Comprehensive Bibliography of Yugoslav Literature in English" 1986-1990. 301p. (Orig.). 1992. pap. 22.95 (*0-89357-230-6*) Slavica.

Mihailovich, Vasa D., ed. Contemporary Yugoslav Poetry. LC 77-22865. (Iowa Translations Ser.). 290p. reprint ed. pap. 89.90 (*0-608-15062-2*, 202593600047) Bks Demand.

— White Stones & Fir Trees: An Anthology of Contemporary Slavic Literature. LC 74-32519. 603p. 1977. 50.00 (*0-8386-1194-X*) Fairleigh Dickinson.

Mihailovich, Vasa D., et al, eds. Modern Slavic Literatures. Incl. Vol. 2. Bulgarian, Czechoslovak, Polish, Ukrainian, & Yugoslav Literatures. LC 64-20047. 1976. 60.00 (*0-8044-3177-9*); Vol. 1. LC 75-10105. (Orig.). 1972. 60.00 (*0-8044-3176-0*); LC 76-15658. (Library of Literary Criticism). 1972. 120.00 (*0-8044-3175-2*) Continuum.

Mihailovich, Vasa D. & Matejic, Mateja. A Comprehensive Bibliography of Yugoslav Literature in English, 1593-1980. xii, 586p. 1984. 34.95 (*0-89357-136-9*) Slavica.

Mihailovich, Vasa D., jt. auth. see Holton, Milne.

Mihailovich, Vasa D., jt. auth. see Milivojevic, Dragan D.

Mihailovich, Vasa D., jt. ed. see Holton, Milne.

Mihailovich, Vasa D., ed. & tr. see Njegos, Petar Petrovic.

Mihaiu, George. Seaports of the Americas, 1998 Edition: The AAPA Directory. 160p. 1998. pap. 79.00 (*1-888817-08-9*) Compass NAmer.

Mihajlov, Mihajlo, et al. Underground Notes. 2nd ed. Ivusic, Maria M. & Ivusic, Christopher, trs. from CRO. LC 80-65723. 208p. 1982. reprint ed. pap. 6.95 (*0-89241-131-7*); reprint ed. lib. bdg. 20.00 (*0-89241-132-5*) Caratzas.

Mihalakis, Diana & Bertrand, Marlene C. Kindercize. (Illus.). 69p. 1987. pap. 22.00 (*0-9618696-0-7*) Kindercize Mktg.

M

Mihalap, Hope. Where There's Hope: There's Life & Laughter. Johnson, Judith A., ed. LC 95-80174. (Illus.). 215p. (Orig.). 1994. pap. 15.00 (*0-9611354-6-8*) T Knox Pub.

Mihalas, Dimitri. Cantata for Six Lives & Continuo. Pursifull, Carmen M., ed. (Hawk Production Ser.). 41p. (Orig.). 1992. pap. 5.00 (*0-932884-98-9*) Red Herring.

— Depression & Spiritual Growth. LC 96-69501. 1996. write for info. (*0-87574-327-7*) Pendle Hill.

— A Distant Summons. Pursifull, Carmen, ed. & intro. by. 30p. (YA). (gr. 10-12). 1998. pap. 5.00 (*1-881900-05-3*) Hawk Prods.

— Dream Shadows. Pursifull, Carmen M., ed. 53p. (Orig.). 1994. pap. 5.00 (*1-881900-02-9*) Hawk Prods.

— Foundation of Radiation Hydrodynamics. LC 99-42987. 736p. 1999. pap. text 22.95 (*0-486-40925-2*) Dover.

— If I Should Die Before I Wake. Pursifull, Carmen M., ed. 43p. (Orig.). pap. 5.00 (*1-881900-00-2*) Hawk Prods.

— Life Matters. Pursifull, Carmen M., ed. 63p. (Orig.). 1995. pap. 5.00 (*1-881900-03-7*) Hawk Prods.

Mihalas, Dimitri, jt. ed. see Winkler, Karl-Heinz A.

Mihalas, Dimitri M. & Binney, James J. Galactic Astronomy: Structure & Kinematics. 2nd ed. LC 81-1612. (Illus.). 597p. (C). 1981. text 40.00 (*0-7167-1280-6*) W H Freeman.

Mihalcin, Ron, ed. Army Research Laboratory: Annual Review 1996. (Illus.). 68p. (C). 1998. pap. text 30.00 (*0-7881-7429-0*) DIANE Pub.

Mihalic, Frank J. The Art of Bonsai "Made Easy" (Illus.). 38p. 1990. pap. 4.95 (*0-9700533-0-4*) Ichiban Prods.

— The Art of Bonsai "Made Easy" 1996. pap. 21.95 incl. VHS (*0-9700533-3-9*) Ichiban Prods.

Mihalic, Slavko. Atlantis: Selected Poems, Nineteen Fifty-Three to Nineteen Eighty-Two. Simic, Charles & Kastmiler, Peter, trs. LC 83-81610. 48p. 1984. pap. 5.00 (*0-912678-61-5*, Greenfld Rev Pr) Greenfld Rev Lit.

Mihalich, Joseph C. Existentialism & Thomism. (Quality Paperback Ser.: No. 170). 91p. (Orig.). (C). 1969. reprint ed. pap. 6.95 (*0-8226-0170-2*) Littlefield.

***Mihalick, Roseanna.** Collecting Handkerchiefs. (Illus.). 144p. 2000. pap. 24.95 (*0-7643-1131-X*) Schiffer.

Mihalik, Michael & Tschantz, Steven T. Semistability of Amalgamated Products & HNN-Extensions. LC 92-10061. (Memoirs Ser.: No. 471). 86p. 1992. pap. 24.00 (*0-8218-2531-3*, MEMO/98/471) Am Math.

Mihalik, Paul, Sr. The Final Warning. LC 97-69915. 64p. 1997. pap. 4.95 (*1-57918-043-4*, 3691) Queenship Pub.

— Virgin Mary: Fr. Gobbi & the Year 2000. 1999. pap. text 3.95 (*1-57918-106-6*) Queenship Pub.

Mihaljek, Dubravko, jt. auth. see Dodsworth, John.

Mihalkanin, Edward S., jt. auth. see Gorman, Robert F.

Mihalko, Carolyn, ed. Donor Recruitment/Public Relations Manual, Vol. 2. (Illus.). 1992. pap. text 25.00 (*1-56395-017-0*) Am Assn Blood.

Mihalko, Carolyn, jt. ed. see Botos, Leslie.

Mihaly, Laszlo & Martin, Michael C. Solid State Physics: Problems & Solutions. LC 96-6184. 280p. 1996. pap. 40.95 (*0-471-15287-0*) Wiley.

Mihaly, Lauren, ed. New York Party Directory. 2nd ed. (Illus.). 72p. 1986. 9.95 (*0-933255-00-4*) NY Party Pub Ass.

Mihaly, Mary E., jt. auth. see Gottlieb, Mark.

***Mihalyfy, Ilona, et al.** Hungarian Basic Course Level Two. (Multilingual Books Intensive Cassette Foreign Language Ser.). 306p. 1999. pap. text 240.00 (*1-58214-033-2*) Mltilingl Bks.

— Hungarian Complete Course with 50 Cassettes: FSI Hungarian Level 182 Combined. (Multilingual Books Intensive Cassette Foreign Language Ser.). 606p. 1999. pap. text 395.00 (*1-58214-065-0*) Mltilingl Bks.

Mihalyfy, Ilona, jt. auth. see Koski, August A.

Mihalyi, Louis. More Nature, Nuture, Nostalgia: Gleaned fro "Black River Journal" 1990. pap. 9.95 (*0-932052-79-7*) North Country.

Mihalyi, Martha. The Woman in the Glass House Speaks. (Illus.). 40p. (Orig.). (C). 1989. pap. write for info. (*0-318-65553-5*) Stone & Water Pr.

Mihalyi, Peter. Socialist Investment Cycles: Analysis in Retrospect. LC 92-31351. (International Studies in Economics & Econometrics). 1992. lib. bdg. 155.50 (*0-7923-1973-7*) Kluwer Academic.

***Mihalyi, Victoria.** Tribe of Star Bear. 238p. 1998. pap. 14.95 (*0-88887-832-X*) Borealis.

Mihalyka, Jean M. Loose Papers & Sundry Chancery Causes. 1997. pap. 28.00 (*1-886706-22-0*) Hickory Hse.

Mihalyka, Jean M. Marriages: Northampton County, VA. (1660-1854 Ser.). 177p. (Orig.). 1995. reprint ed. pap. text 16.50 (*0-7884-0166-1*) Heritage Bk.

***Mihalyka, Jean M.** Marriages Northampton County, Virginia 1660-1854. 168p. 2000. pap. 20.50 (*0-7884-1506-9*, 1506) Heritage Bk.

Mihalyka, Jean M., jt. auth. see Wilson.

Mihalyo, Daniel. Wood Burners. LC 97-976. (Illus.). 112p. (Orig.). 1997. pap. 19.95 (*1-56898-104-X*) Princeton Arch.

Mihanovich, Clement S. Americanization of the Croats in St. Louis, Missouri During the Past Thirty Years. LC 75-146895. 1971. reprint ed. pap. 10.00 (*0-88247-122-8*) Ragusan Pr.

Mihanovich, Clement S., jt. compiled by see Werth, Alvin.

Mihara, Katsuyoshi, jt. ed. see Hamasaki, Naotaka.

Mihara, Sam & Hogue, Vicki. Sam Mihara's Fly Fishing Alaska: A Guide to Enjoying Alaska's Waters & Saving Money. (Illus.). 1997. pap. 19.95 (*0-9656258-0-X*, 100) Eskay Pub.

Mihara, Yoshiaki, ed. Agricultural Meteorology of Japan. LC 74-78859. (East-West Center Bk.), 225p. reprint ed. pap. 69.80 (*0-7837-3985-0*, 204381500011) Bks Demand.

Mihashi, H. Size Effects in Concrete Structures. 568p. 1994. mass mkt. 161.95 (*0-419-19040-6*, E & FN Spon) Routledge.

Mihashi, H., et al, eds. Fracture Toughness & Fracture Energy Test Methods for Concrete & Rock: Proceedings of the International Workshop Sendai, 12 - 14 October 1988. (Illus.). 640p. (C). 1989. text 207.00 (*90-6191-988-6*, Pub. by A A Balkema) Ashgate Pub Co.

Mihelcic, James R. Fundamentals of Environmental Engineering. LC 98-39323. 352p. 1998. pap. 61.95 (*0-471-24313-2*) Wiley.

Mihelic, Duesan. The Political Element in the Port Geography of Trieste. LC 69-18024. (University of Chicago, Department of Geography, Research Paper Ser.: No. 120). (Illus.). 117p. reprint ed. pap. 36.30 (*0-7837-0397-X*, 204071800018) Bks Demand.

Mihelich, Edward P. Hidden Memories. (Illus.). xi, 275p. (Orig.). 1996. pap. 18.00 (*1-883228-13-1*) Invictus MI.

— Vintage Memories. (Illus.). 110p. 1998. pap. 14.95 (*1-883228-21-2*) Invictus MI.

Mihelick, J. R. & Rafferty, R. C. Investigations of an E. P. Lubricant for Wormgearing. (Technical Papers: Vol. P254.29). (Illus.). 17p. 1967. pap. text 30.00 (*1-55589-357-0*) AGMA.

Mihesuah, Devon A. American Indians: Stereotypes & Realities. LC 97-163158. 1998. reprint ed. pap. 14.95 (*0-932863-22-1*) Clarity Pr.

— Cultivating the Rosebuds: The Education of Women at the Cherokee Female Seminary, 1851-1909. 240p. Date not set. pap. text 17.95 (*0-252-06677-4*) U of Ill Pr.

***Mihesuah, Devon A.** The Roads of My Relations. LC 99-50808. (Sun Tracks Ser.). 240p. 2000. 35.00 (*0-8165-2040-2*); pap. 17.95 (*0-8165-2041-0*) U of Ariz Pr.

Mihesuah, Devon A., ed. Natives & Academics: Research & Writing about American Indians. LC 97-30298. xi, 213p. 1998. pap. text 15.00 (*0-8032-8243-5*) U of Nebr Pr.

***Mihesuah, Devon A., ed.** Repatriation Reader: Who Owns American Indian Remains? LC 00-36380. (Illus.). 328p. 2000. pap. 20.00 (*0-8032-8264-8*, Bison Books) U of Nebr Pr.

Mihevc, John. The Market Tells Them So: The World Bank & Economic Fundamentalism in Africa. LC 95-13678. (Illus.). 320p. (C). 1996. text 25.00 (*1-85649-328-8*, Pub. by Zed Books) St Martin.

Mihevic, Demetra. When the Barred Owl Calls. 189p. (Orig.). (YA). 1995. pap. 9.99 (*0-88092-131-5*) Royal Fireworks.

Mihich, E. & Eckhardt, S., eds. Design of Cancer Chemotherapy. (Antibiotics & Chemotherapy Ser.: Vol. 28). (Illus.). x, 194p. 1980. 77.50 (*3-8055-0411-X*) S Karger.

Mihich, E., jt. auth. see Hemler, M. E.

Mihich, Enrico, ed. Biological Responses in Cancer: Progress Toward Potential Applications, Vol. 1. LC 82-18041. 322p. 1982. 85.00 (*0-306-41146-6*, Plenum Trade) Perseus Pubng.

— Biological Responses in Cancer: Progress Toward Potential Applications, Vol. 2. LC 82-18041. 258p. 1984. 85.00 (*0-306-41583-6*, Plenum Trade) Perseus Pubng.

— Biological Responses in Cancer: Progress Toward Potential Applications; Vol. 4. LC 82-18041. 270p. 1985. 79.50 (*0-306-42044-9*, Plenum Trade) Perseus Pubng.

Mihich, Enrico, et al, eds. Normal, Malignant Hematopoiesis & New Advances: Proceedings of the Sixth Pezcoller Symposium Held in Rovereto, Italy, June 29-July 1, 1994, Vol. 6. LC 95-37107. (Pezcoller Foundation Symposium Ser.: Vol. 6). (Illus.). 260p. 1995. 95.00 (*0-306-45136-0*, Kluwer Plenum) Kluwer Academic.

Mihich, Enrico & Croce, Carlo, eds. The Biology of Tumors: Proceedings of the 9th Annual Pezcoller Symposium Held in Rovereto, Italy, June 4-7, 1997. (Pezcoller Foundation Symposia Ser.: No. 9). (Illus.). 364p. 1998. 125.00 (*0-306-45932-9*, Kluwer Plenum) Kluwer Academic.

Mihich, Enrico & Hartwell, Leland, eds. Genomic Instability & Immortality in Cancer: Proceedings of the Eighth Annual Pezcoller Symposium Held in Trento, Italy, June 17-19, 1996. LC 97-29967. (Pezcoller Foundation Symposia Ser.). 262p. 1998. 89.50 (*0-306-45700-8*, Kluwer Plenum) Kluwer Academic.

Mihich, Enrico & Housman, David, eds. Cancer Genes: Functional Aspects; Proceedings of the Seventh Pezcoller Symposium Held in Trento, Italy, June 14-16, 1995. LC 96-41755. (Pezcoller Foundation Symposia Ser.: Vol. 7). 300p. 1997. 95.00 (*0-306-45482-3*, Kluwer Plenum) Kluwer Academic.

Mihich, Enrico & Sakurai, Yoshio, eds. Biological Responses in Cancer: Progress Toward Potential Applications, Vol. 3: Immunomodulation by Anticancer Drugs. LC 84-18041. 230p. 1985. 85.00 (*0-306-41879-7*, Plenum Trade) Perseus Pubng.

Mihm, J. Christopher. Decennial Census: Overview of Historical Census Issues. 52p. 1999. pap. text 20.00 (*0-7881-7979-9*) DIANE Pub.

— Managing for Results: An Agenda to Improve the Usefulness of Agencies' Annual Performance Plans. 48p. (C). 1999. pap. text 20.00 (*0-7881-7631-5*) DIANE Pub.

Mihm, Madelyn T. Sentence by Sentence: A Basic Rhetoric, Reader & Grammar. 375p. (C). 1988. pap. text 37.00 (*0-15-579672-0*, Pub. by Harcourt Coll Pubs) Harcourt.

Mihm, Martin C., Jr. & Googe, Paul. Problematic Pigmented Lesions: A Case Method Approach. LC 89-12216. (Illus.). 543p. 1990. text 98.00 (*0-8121-1261-X*) Lppncott W & W.

Mihopoulos, Effie. Languid Love Lyrics. (Offset Offshoot Ser.: No. 16). 70p. 1993. pap. 8.00 (*0-941240-18-5*) Ommation Pr.

— The Moon Cycle. (Offset Offshoot Ser.: No. 14). 8.00 (*0-941240-17-7*) Ommation Pr.

Mihopoulos, Effie, ed. Dancers: Eight Stories about the Dance. (Illus.). 1986. 4.00 (*0-941240-08-8*) Ommation Pr.

— Dancers II: Eight Stories about the Dance. (Dialogues on Dance Ser.: No. 8). 70p. 1987. 6.00 (*0-941240-10-X*) Ommation Pr.

Mihoubi, Bachir, tr. see Atias, Christian.

Mihura, Miguel. Melocoton en Almibar - Ninette y un Senor de Murcia. 7th ed. (SPA.). 204p. 1989. pap. 11.95 (*0-7859-5136-9*) Fr & Eur.

— Tres Sombreros de Copa. Tordera, Antonio, ed. (Nueva Austral Ser.: Vol. 63). (SPA.). 1991. pap. text 11.95 (*84-239-1863-7*) Elliots Bks.

— Tres Sombreros de Copa. 15th ed. (SPA.). 136p. 1991. pap. 11.95 (*0-7859-5135-0*) Fr & Eur.

— Tres Sombreros de Copa - Maribel y la Extrana Familia. 11th ed. (SPA.). 206p. 1988. pap. 10.95 (*0-7859-5137-7*) Fr & Eur.

Mihyo, Paschal, jt. auth. see Ogbu, Osito M.

Miido, Helis. The Integrated Medical Library. (Illus.). 200p. 1991. lib. bdg. 89.95 (*0-8493-0182-3*, Z65) CRC Pr.

Miikkulainen, Risto. Subsymbolic Natural Language Processing: An Integrated Model of Scripts, Lexicon, & Memory. LC 92-37285. (Neural Network Modeling & Connectionism Ser.). 422p. (C). 1993. 52.50 (*0-262-13290-7*, Bradford Bks) MIT Pr.

Mijakovs'kyj, Volodymyr. Unpublished & Forgotten Writings: Editor's Text in English. Antonovych, Marc, ed. (Sources of Modern History of the Ukraine Ser.). (UKR., Illus.). 516p. 1984. 30.00 (*0-916381-02-1*) Ukrainian Arts Sci.

Mijalkovic, S., jt. auth. see Joppich, W.

Mijares, Sharon G. The Babysitter's Manual. (Illus.). 60p. (J). (gr. 6-9). 1983. spiral bd. 4.98 (*0-911925-00-7*) Grace Pubns.

***Mijares, Tomas C., et al.** The Management of Police Specialized Tactical Units. LC 00-27308. 2000. pap. write for info. (*0-398-07070-9*) C C Thomas.

Mijatovic, Elodie L. Serbian Folklore. Denton, W., ed. LC 68-56477. 1972. reprint ed. 24.95 (*0-405-08788-8*, Pub. by Blom Pubns) Ayer.

Mijatovic, M. Hadronic Mechanics & Nonpotential Interaction. 371p. 1989. 175.00 (*0-941743-72-1*) Nova Sci Pubs.

Mijatovic, Mijat, jt. auth. see Dimitrovski, Dragan.

Mijeski, Kenneth J., ed. The Nicaraguan Constitution of 1987: English Translation & Commentary. LC 90-47132. (Monographs in International Studies, Latin America Ser.: No. 17). 355p. (Orig.). (C). 1991. pap. 25.00 (*0-89680-165-9*) Ohio U Pr.

Mijia, A., jt. ed. see Bankowski, Z.

***Mijkesenaar, Paul & Westendorp, Piet.** Open Here: The Art of Instructional Design. (Illus.). 144p. 1999. pap. 29.95 (*1-55670-962-5*) Stewart Tabori & Chang.

Mijksenaar, Paul. Visual Function: An Introduction to Information Design. (Illus.). 56p. (Orig.). 1997. pap. 14.95 (*1-56898-118-X*) Princeton Arch.

Mijksenaar, Paul & Westendorp, Piet. Open Here! The Art of Instructional Design. LC 97-33247. 1998. write for info. (*1-55670-617-0*) Stewart Tabori & Chang.

Mijnhardt, Wijnand W., jt. ed. see Jacob, Margaret C.

Mijoga, Hilary B. The Pauline Notion of Deeds of the Law. LC 98-20475. 200p. 1998. 74.95 (*1-57309-321-1*, U Pr W Africa); pap. 54.95 (*1-57309-320-3*, U Pr W Africa) Intl Scholars.

Mijolla, Elizabeth De, see De Mijolla, Elizabeth.

Mijs, W. J. New Methods for Polymer Synthesis. (Illus.). 336p. (C). 1992. text 85.00 (*0-306-43871-2*, Kluwer Plenum) Kluwer Academic.

Mijs, W. J. & De Jonge, C. R. H., eds. Organic Syntheses by Oxidation with Metal Compounds. (Illus.). 936p. (C). 1986. text 222.00 (*0-306-41999-8*, Kluwer Plenum) Kluwer Academic.

Mijs, W. J., jt. auth. see Nijenhuis, K. T.

Mijs, Wim, jt. ed. see Muller, Sam.

Mijuskovic, B. L. Achilles of Rationalist Arguments: The Simplicity, Unity & the Identity of Thought & Soul from the Cambridge Platonists to Kant: A Study in the History of Argument. (Archives Internationales D'Histoire des Idees Ser.: No. 13). 142p. 1974. pap. text 44.00 (*90-247-1597-0*, Pub. by M Nijhoff) Kluwer Academic.

Mijuskovic, Ben. Contingent Immaterialism: Meaning, Freedom, Time & Mind. 214p. (Orig.). 1984. pap. 30.00 (*90-6032-254-1*, Pub. by B R Gruner) Humanities.

Mijuskovic, Vera, jt. auth. see Fiser, Ana.

Mika, Andre. Prince of Egypt: Read Along Story book & Tape. (Illus.). 32p. 1998. pap. text 8.99 (*0-14-088862-4*, PuffinBks) Peng Put Young Read.

Mika, J. R. & Banasiak, J. Singularly Perturbed Evolution Equations with Applications to Kinetic Theory. (Series on Advances in Mathematics for Applied Sciences). 250p. 1995. text 61.00 (*981-02-2125-8*) World Scientific Pub.

Mika, Jim. Writing with Confidence: A Composition Program for High School Juniors & Seniors. (Illus.). 160p. 1993. pap. text 11.95 (*0-9639717-0-0*) Jennifer Pubng.

Mika, Jozsef & Torok, Tibor. Analytical Emission Spectroscopy: Fundamentals. enl. rev. ed. Floyd, P. A., ed. Nemes, Laszlo, tr. from HUN. LC 74-196239. (Illus.). 533p. reprint ed. pap. 165.30 (*0-8357-5455-3*, 202572400046) Bks Demand.

Mika, Kristine L. Program Outcome Evaluation: A Step-by-Step Handbook. LC 96-44909. 106p. 1996. pap. 16.95 (*0-87304-286-7*) Manticore Pubs.

Mika, Stephen. Microcomputers for Building Surveyors. (C). 1986. text 50.00 (*0-85406-309-9*, Pub. by Surveyors Pubns) St Mut.

Mikael'an, Galina, jt. auth. see Akhmanova, Olga.

Mikaelian, A. Women Who Mean Business: Success Stories of Women over Forty. LC 99-27429. (Illus.). 368p. 1999. 24.00 (*0-688-15677-0*, Wm Morrow) Morrow Avon.

Mikaelian, Andrei L. Optical Methods for Information Technologies. LC 94-11785. 1994. 125.00 (*0-89864-070-9*) Allerton Pr.

Mikaelian, Andrei L., ed. Optical Information Science & Technology (OIST97) Vol. 3347: Optical Recording Mechanisms & Media. LC 98-172299. 432p. 1998. 89.00 (*0-8194-2794-2*) SPIE.

— Optical Information Science & Technology (OIST97) Vol. 3348: Computer & Holographic Optics & Image Processing. LC 98-172301. 368p. 1998. 80.00 (*0-8194-2795-0*) SPIE.

— Optical Information Science & Technology (OIST97) Vol. 3402: Optical Memory & Neural Networks. LC 98-172300. 532p. 1998. 99.00 (*0-8194-2852-3*) SPIE.

Mikaelsen, Ben. Countdown. LC 96-19998. (Illus.). 256p. (J). (gr. 4-7). 1996. 15.95 (*0-7868-0252-9*, Pub. by Hyprn Child) Time Warner.

— Countdown. (Illus.). 256p. (J). (gr. 4-8). 1996. lib. bdg. 15.89 (*0-7868-2207-4*, Pub. by Hyprn Child) Little.

— Countdown. (J). 1997. 11.05 (*0-606-13292-9*, Pub. by Turtleback) Demco.

— Countdown. LC 96-19998. 256p. (J). (gr. 4-8). 1997. reprint ed. pap. 5.95 (*0-7868-1208-7*, Pub. by Hyprn Ppbks) Little.

***Mikaelsen, Ben.** Mikaelson Untitled. (J). 2001. write for info. (*0-380-97745-1*) Morrow Avon.

Mikaelsen, Ben. Petey. 256p. (J). 1998. lib. bdg. 16.49 (*0-7868-2376-3*, Pub. by Disney Pr) Little.

— Petey. LC 98-10183. 256p. (YA). (gr. 7 up). 1998. 15.95 (*0-7868-0426-2*, Pub. by Disney Pr) Time Warner.

***Mikaelsen, Ben.** Petey. LC 98-10183. 256p. (YA). (gr. 5-9). 2000. pap. 5.99 (*0-7868-1336-9*, Pub. by Hyprn Child) Time Warner.

Mikaelsen, Ben. Rescue Josh McGuire. LC 91-71386. 272p. (J). (gr. 7 up). 1991. lib. bdg. 14.89 (*1-56282-100-8*, Pub. by Hyprn Child) Little.

— Rescue Josh McGuire. LC 91-71386. 272p. (YA). (gr. 5-9). 1993. pap. 5.95 (*1-56282-523-2*, Pub. by Hyprn Child) Time Warner.

— Rescue Josh McGuire. (J). 1993. 9.60 (*0-606-05987-3*, Pub. by Turtleback) Demco.

— Sparrow Hawk Red. LC 92-53458. 224p. (YA). (gr. 5-9). 1993. 14.95 (*1-56282-387-6*, Pub. by Hyprn Child) Time Warner.

— Sparrow Hawk Red. (J). 1994. 9.60 (*0-606-06758-2*, Pub. by Turtleback) Demco.

— Stranded. LC 94-27069. 256p. (J). (gr. 4-8). 1995. 15.95 (*0-7868-0072-0*, Pub. by Hyprn Child) Time Warner.

— Stranded. LC 94-27069. 256p. (J). (ps-3). 1995. lib. bdg. 15.89 (*0-7868-2059-4*, Pub. by Hyprn Child) Little.

— Stranded. LC 94-27069. 288p. (J). (gr. 4-8). 1996. pap. 4.95 (*0-7868-1109-9*, Pub. by Hyprn Ppbks) Little.

— Stranded. LC 94-27069. (J). 1996. 10.05 (*0-606-08882-2*, Pub. by Turtleback) Demco.

***Mikaelsen, Ben.** Touching Spirit Bear. (J). 2001. write for info. (*0-380-97744-3*, Wm Morrow) Morrow Avon.

Mikail. Moh's Micrographic Surgery. (Illus.). 432p. 1991. text 170.00 (*0-7216-3415-X*, W B Saunders Co) Harcrt Hlth Sci Grp.

Mikal, Alan. Exploring Boston Harbor. (Illus.). 128p. 1973. 10.95 (*0-8158-0303-6*) Chris Mass.

Mikal, Elizabeth J. Until Darkness Holds No Fear: The Healing of a Multiple Personality. Rydlun, Judith, ed. LC 95-80336. (Illus.). 304p. (Orig.). 1995. pap. 16.95 (*1-883862-08-6*) Bks Beyond Brdrs.

Mikalac, Miriam, jt. auth. see Carter, Eneida.

Mikalachki, Albert. Change Process in Sport & Physical Education Management. Zeigler, Earle F. & Leyshon, Glynn A., eds. (Monograph Series on Sport & Physical Education Management). 37p. (Orig.). 1988. pap. text 3.80 (*0-87563-317-X*) Stipes.

Mikalachki, Jodi. The Legacy of Boadicea: Gender & Recovery of Native Origins in Early Modern England. LC 97-39148. (Illus.). 218p. (C). (gr. 13). 1998. 75.00 (*0-415-18263-8*); pap. 24.99 (*0-415-18264-6*) Routledge.

Mikalson, Jon D. Athenian Popular Religion. LC 82-25616. xiv, 142p. (C). 1987. reprint ed. pap. 17.95 (*0-8078-4194-3*) U of NC Pr.

— Honor Thy Gods: Popular Religion in Greek Tragedy. LC 91-50282. xvi, 360p. (C). 1992. 55.00 (*0-8078-2005-9*); pap. 19.95 (*0-8078-4348-2*) U of NC Pr.

***Mikalson, Jon D.** Religion in Hellenistic Athens. LC 97-35407. (Hellenistic Culture & Society Ser.). 385p. 1998. 48.00 (*0-520-21023-9*, Pub. by U CA Pr) Cal Prin Full Svc.

Mikalson, Jon D. The Sacred & Civil Calendar of the Athenian Year. LC 74-25622. 240p. reprint ed. pap. 74.40 (*0-8357-2784-X*, 203991000014) Bks Demand.

Mikalson, Jon D., ed. see Mackendrick, Paul L.

Mikami, Riichiro, ed. see International Symposium on Sarcoidosis Staff.

Mikami, T. Let's Try Sumi Painting. 1996. 23.95 (*4-07-972938-3*) Shufu No.

— Sumi Painting. 1996. pap. 12.95 (*4-07-971229-4*) Shufu No.

Mikami, Y. The Development of Mathematics in China & Japan. 2nd ed. LC 74-6716. 383p. 1974. text 29.50 (*0-8284-0149-7*) Chelsea Pub.

Mikanagi, K., et al, eds. Purine & Pyrimidine Metabolism in Man VI, 2 pts., Pt. A. (Illus.). 574p. 1989. 120.00 (*0-306-43233-1*, Plenum Trade) Perseus Pubng.

— Purine & Pyrimidine Metabolism in Man VI, 2 pts., Pt. B. (Illus.). 566p. 1989. 120.00 (*0-306-43234-X*, Plenum Trade) Perseus Pubng.

— Purine & Pyrimidine Metabolism in Man VI, 2 pts., Set. (Illus.). 1989. 210.00 (*0-685-44617-4*, Plenum Trade) Perseus Pubng.

M

An Asterisk (*) at the beginning of an entry indicates that the title is appearing for the first time.

Mikanagi, Yumiko. Japan's Trade Policy: Action or Reaction? LC 95-23841. (Studies in the Growth Economies of Asia Ser.: Vol. 4). 184p. (C). 1996. 85.00 (*0-415-13735-7*) Routledge.

Mikasinovich, Branko, ed. Modern Yugoslav Satire. LC 79-83730. (Illus.). (Orig.). 1979. 20.00 (*0-89304-029-0*, CCC117); pap. 12.00 (*0-89304-030-4*) Cross-Cultrl NY.

Mikasinovich, Branko, jt. ed. see Barkan, Stanley H.

Mikasinovich, Branko, tr. see Popa, Vasco.

Mikatavage, Raimonda. Imigranti I Izbjeglice: Stvorite Novi Zivot U Americi. World Relief Corporation Staff, tr. LC 99-70112. (Pioneer Living Ser.). (SER & CRO., Illus.). 208p. 1999. pap. 14.95 (*0-9647213-4-1*) Melodija Bks.

— Immigrants & Refugees: Create Your New Life in America. 2nd ed. LC 98-65061. Orig. Title: Satisfaction in the Land of Opportunity. 208p. 1998. pap. 14.95 (*0-9647213-5-X*) Melodija Bks.

— Immigranty y Bezhentsy: Kak Ustroit Vashu Novuyu Zhizn V Amerike. World Relief Corporation Staff, tr. LC 99-70111. (Pioneer Living Ser.). (RUS., Illus.). 224p. 1999. pap. 14.95 (*0-9647213-2-5*) Melodija Bks.

— Inmigrantes y Refugiados: Como Crear Su Neuva Vida en los Estados Unidos. Lopez, Nora L., tr. LC 99-70110. (Pioneer Living Ser.). (SPA., Illus.). 224p. 1999. pap. 14.95 (*0-9647213-3-3*) Melodija Bks.

— Satisfaction in the Land of Opportunity: Answers for U. S. Immigrants & Refugees. LC 97-93344. (Pioneer Living Ser.). (Illus.). 192p. (Orig.). 1997. pap. 19.95 (*0-9647213-6-8*) Melodija Bks.

— Your Journey to Success: A Guide for Young Lithuanians. LC 95-77918. (Illus.). 192p. (Orig.). 1996. pap. 14.95 (*0-9647213-8-4*) Melodija Bks.

Mikdadi, Faysal. Gamal Abdel Nasser: A Bibliography, 5. LC 91-21168. (Bibliographies of World Leaders Ser.: No. 5). 164p. 1991. lib. bdg. 65.00 (*0-313-28119-X*, MKG, Greenwood Pr) Greenwood.

— Margaret Thatcher: A Bibliography, 18. LC 92-38071. (Bibliographies of British Statesmen Ser.: No. 18). 288p. 1993. lib. bdg. 89.50 (*0-313-28288-9*, MKE/) Greenwood.

Mike, jt. auth. see A. Jay.

Mike Brynes & Associates Staff. Bumper to Bumper: The Diesel Mechanics Student's Guide to Tractor Trailer Operations. (Illus.). x, 242p. (Orig.). (C). 1993. pap. text 23.95 (*0-9621687-4-2*, MSG) M Byrnes & Assocs.

Mike Byrnes & Associates Staff. Bumper to Bumper: La Guia Completa Para Operaciones de Autotransporte de Carga. Pedrero, Manuel, tr. from ENG. (SPA., Illus.). xii, 610p. (Orig.). (C). 1993. pap. text 41.95 (*0-9621687-3-4*, GUIA) M Byrnes & Assocs.

Mike, Jan. Juan Bobo & the Horse of Seven Colors: A Puerto Rican Legend. LC 95-11765. (Legends of the World Ser.). (Illus.). 32p. (J). (gr. 2-5). 1995. pap. 4.95 (*0-8167-3746-0*) Troll Communs.

— Juan Bobo & the Horse of Seven Colors: A Puerto Rican Legend. LC 95-11765. (Legends of the World Ser.). (Illus.). 32p. (J). (gr. 2-6). 1997. lib. bdg. 18.60 (*0-8167-3745-2*) Troll Communs.

Mike, Jan & Mike, Samuel. Desert Seasons. 32p. (J). (gr. k-8). 1991. pap. 7.95 (*0-918080-49-5*, 20975) Treas Chest Bks.

Mike, Jan M. The Bird Maiden: A Serbian Legend. (Legends of the World Ser.). (Illus.). 32p. (J). (gr. 2-5). 1996. pap. 4.95 (*0-8167-4023-2*) Troll Communs.

— The Bird Maiden: A Serbian Legend. (Legends of the World Ser.). (J). 1996. 10.15 (*0-606-09077-0*, Pub. by Turtleback) Demco.

— Clever Karlis: A Latvian Legend. (Legends of the World Ser.). (Illus.). 32p. (J). (gr. 2-5). 1996. pap. 4.95 (*0-8167-4024-0*) Troll Communs.

— Clever Karlis: A Latvian Legend. (Legends of the World Ser.). 1996. 10.15 (*0-606-09152-1*, Pub. by Turtleback) Demco.

— Gift of the Nile: An Ancient Egyptian Legend. LC 92-5826. (Legends of the World Ser.). (Illus.). 32p. (J). (gr. 2-5). 1996. pap. 4.95 (*0-8167-2814-3*) Troll Communs.

— Gift of the Nile: An Ancient Egyptian Legend. LC 92-5826. (Legends of the World Ser.). (Illus.). 32p. (J). (gr. 2-5). 1997. lib. bdg. 18.60 (*0-8167-2813-5*) Troll Communs.

— Juan Bobo & el Caballo de Siete Colores. (Leyendas del Mundo Ser.).Tr. of Juan Bobo & the Horse of Seven Colors. (SPA., Illus.). 32p. (Orig.). (J). (gr. 2-6). 1996. pap. 4.95 (*0-8167-4174-3*) Troll Communs.

— Juan Bobo & the Horse of Seven Colors: A Puerto Rican Legend. (Legends of the World Ser.). 1995. 9.15 (*0-606-07753-7*, Pub. by Turtleback) Demco.

— New Mexico, Land of Enchantment Alphabet Book. (Illus.). 32p. (Orig.). (J). (gr. k-5). 1993. pap. 7.95 (*0-918080-55-X*) Treas Chest Bks.

— Opossum & the Great Firemaker: A Mexican Legend. LC 92-36459. (Legends of the World Ser.). (Illus.). 32p. (J). (gr. 2-5). 1993. pap., teacher ed. 1.95 (*0-8167-3056-3*) Troll Communs.

— Opossum & the Great Firemaker: A Mexican Legend. LC 92-36459. (Legends of the World Ser.). (Illus.). 32p. (J). (gr. 2-5). 1997. lib. bdg. 18.60 (*0-8167-3055-5*) Troll Communs.

— Opossum & the Great Firemaker: A Mexican Legend. (Legends of the World Ser.). (J). 1993. 9.15 (*0-606-05526-6*, Pub. by Turtleback) Demco.

— La Zariguerya y el Gran Creador de Fuego - Opossum & the Great Filmmaker: Una Leyenda Mexicana. LC 92-36459. (SPA.). (J). (gr. 2-5). 1997. pap. 4.95 (*0-8167-3073-3*) Troll Communs.

— La Zarigueya y el Gran Creador de Fuego: Una Leyenda Mexicana. (Leyendas del Mundo Ser.). (SPA.). 1993. 9.15 (*0-606-05406-5*, Pub. by Turtleback) Demco.

Mike, Jan M. & Lowmiller, Cathie. Bizagolaa: An Apache Girl. (Illus.). 32p. (Orig.). (J). (gr. k-6). 1989. pap. 3.95 (*0-918080-46-0*, 20976) Treas Chest Bks.

Mike, John. Brilliant Babies, Powerful Adults: Awaken the Genius Within. 176p. 1997. pap. 14.95 (*0-9644294-2-X*) Satori Pr.

Mike, Samuel, jt. illus. see Mike, Jan.

Mikel, et al. AFIP Advanced Laboratory Methods in Histology & Pathology. (Illus.). 254p. 1994. pap. text 45.00 (*1-881041-13-1*) Am Registry Path.

Mikell, Gwendolyn. Cocoa & Chaos in Ghana. 288p. 1992. pap. 18.95 (*0-88258-153-8*) Howard U Pr.

— Cocoa & Chaos in Ghana. LC 87-25795. (Illus.). 284p. 1989. 29.95 (*0-943852-39-0*) Prof World Peace.

Mikell, Gwendolyn, ed. African Feminism: The Politics of Survival in Sub-Saharan Africa. LC 97-6260. 392p. 1997. text 39.95 (*0-8122-3349-2*); pap. text 19.95 (*0-8122-1580-X*) U of Pa Pr.

Mikels, Elaine. Just Lucky I Guess: From Closet Lesbian to Radical Dyke. LC 93-71778. 385p. (Orig.). 1993. pap. text 12.95 (*0-9637257-1-8*) Desert Crone.

— Just Lucky I Guess: From Closet Lesbian to Radical Dyke. 2nd ed. (Orig.). 1994. pap. 12.95 (*0-9637257-2-6*) Desert Crone.

***Mikels, Jennifer.** The Bridal Quest. (Special Edition Ser.: Bk. 1360). 2000. mass mkt. 4.50 (*0-373-24360-X*, 1-24360-9) Silhouette.

Mikels, Jennifer. Child of Mine. 1995. mass mkt. 3.75 (*0-373-09993-2*, 1-09993-6) Silhouette.

— A Daddy for Devin. (Special Edition Ser.: No. 1150). 1998. per. 3.99 (*0-373-24150-X*, 1-24150-4) Silhouette.

— Denver's Lady. (Special Edition Ser.). 1994. per. 3.50 (*0-373-09870-7*, 5-09870-2) Silhouette.

— Expecting Baby. 1996. per. 3.99 (*0-373-24023-6*, 1-24023-3) Silhouette.

— Forever Mine. (Special Edition Ser.: No. 1265). 1999. per. 4.25 (*0-373-24265-4*, 1-24265-0) Silhouette.

— Jake Ryker's Back in Town. (Special Edition Ser.). 1994. per. 3.50 (*0-373-09929-0*, 1-09929-0) Silhouette.

— A Job for Jack. (Special Edition Ser.: No. 735). 1992. per. 3.39 (*0-373-09735-2*, 5-09735-7) Harlequin Bks.

— Just the Three of Us: Family Arch. (Special Edition Ser.: No. 1251). 1999. per. 4.25 (*0-373-24251-4*, 1-24251-0) Silhouette.

— Le Lien d'Amour. (Amours d'Aujourd'Hui Ser.: Vol. 321). (FRE.). 1999. mass mkt. 4.99 (*0-373-38321-5*, 1-38321-5) Harlequin Bks.

— The Marriage Bargain. 1998. per. 4.25 (*0-373-24168-2*, 1-24168-6) Silhouette.

— Married . . . With Twins! (Special Edition Ser.). 1996. per. 3.99 (*0-373-24054-6*, 1-24054-8) Silhouette.

— Remember Me? (Special Edition Ser.: No. 1107). 1997. per. 3.99 (*0-373-24107-0*, 1-24107-4) Silhouette.

***Mikels, Jennifer.** Sara's Father. 2000. mass mkt. 4.50 (*0 373 82227-8*, 1-82227-9) Harlequin Bks.

Mikels, Jennifer. Sara's Father. (Special Edition Ser.). 1995. per. 3.75 (*0-373-09947-9*, 1-09947-2) Silhouette.

— Temporary Daddy. (Special Edition Ser.). 1998. per. 4.25 (*0-373-24192-5*, 1-24192-6) Silhouette.

— Your Child, My Child. 1993. per. 3.39 (*0-373-09807-3*, 5-09807-4) Silhouette.

Mikenda, W., jt. ed. see Schuster, P.

Mikes, Anthony P. Lifeblood: A 365 Days-a-Year New Business Plan for Small Agencies. 6th rev. ed. (Illus.). 288p. 1998. pap. 59.95 (*0-9626971-4-1*) Second Wind.

— The Small Agency Survival Manual: How to Emerge Victorious from the Advertising Battleground. 515p. (Orig.). 1995. pap. 79.95 (*0-9626971-3-3*) Second Wind.

Mikes, Antonios G., et al, eds. Biomaterials for Drug & Cell Delivery Vol. 331: Materials Research Society Symposium Proceedings. LC 94-9650. 289p. 1994. text 83.00 (*1-55899-230-8*) Materials Res.

Mikes, George. How to Be a Brit: A Mikes Minibus, 3 vols. in 1. (Illus.). 1984. 19.95 (*0-233-97724-4*, Pub. by Andre Deutsch) Trafalgar.

— How to Be Poor. (Illus.). 144p. 1984. 17.95 (*0-233-97541-1*, Pub. by Andre Deutsch) Trafalgar.

Mikes, Jay. Basketball FundaMENTALS: A Complete Mental Training Guide. LC 86-19133. 272p. 1987. pap. 17.95 (*0-88011-442-8*, PMIK0442) Human Kinetics.

Mikes, Keleman. Letters from Turkey. Adams, Bernard, tr. from HUN. LC 97-51369. 61p. 1998. 110.00 (*0-7103-0610-5*, Pub. by Kegan Paul Intl) Col U Pr.

Mikes, O. High-Performance Liquid Chromatography of Biopolmers & Bioligomers, Part A: Principles, Materials, & Techniques. (Journal of Chromatography Library: Vol. 41A). 380p. 1988. 230.75 (*0-444-42951-4*) Elsevier.

— High-Performance Liquid Chromatography of Biopolymers & Biooligomers: Part B - Separation of Individual Compound Classes. (Journal of Chromatography Library: No. 41B). 722p. 1988. 291.25 (*0-444-43034-2*) Elsevier.

Mikes, Petr. In the Tracks of the Dead. Keys, Kerry S. & Boeke, Wanda, trs. from CZE. (Illus.). 33p. 1993. pap. 10.00 (*0-930502-08-6*) Pine Pr.

Mikes, Steven. Sistema X Window. (SPA.). (C). 1993. pap. text 17.00 (*0-201-60124-9*) Addison-Wesley.

— UNIX for INS-DOS Programmers. (C). 1992. pap. text. write for info. (*0-201-55642-1*) Addison-Wesley.

— Visual Programming Tools for X. 500p. (C). 2000. pap. text 34.00 (*0-13-954132-2*) P-H.

— X Window Program Design & Development. (C). 1991. pap. text 26.95 (*0-201-55077-6*) Addison-Wesley.

— X Windows Developer's Technical Reference. 800p. 1989. pap. text 34.95 (*0-201-52370-1*) Addison-Wesley.

Mikesell. Fiscal Administration. 4th ed. (C). 1993. text, teacher ed. 28.00 (*0-534-24607-9*) Harcourt.

— Fundamentals of Manufacturing Processes. (Mechanical Technology Ser.). 1996. 60.95 (*0-8273-7542-5*) Delmar.

Mikesell, Janice H. Fate Worse Than Death: And Other Hospital Stories. LC 95-16217. 50p. 1995. pap. 8.00 (*0-929925-30-0*) Hens Teeth.

— Some People Don't Know That Barns Have Faces: A Book for Prairie Children. LC 98-93564. (Illus.). 40p. (J). (gr. k-4). 1999. pap. 10.00 (*0-9621112-4-4*) H Smith.

Mikesell, John L. Fiscal Administration. 5th ed. LC 98-72197. (C). 1998. text 71.00 (*0-15-505528-3*) Harcourt Coll Pubs.

— Fiscal Administration: Analysis & Applications for the Public Sector. 4th ed. LC 94-4547. 594p. (C). 1994. text 71.00 (*0-534-24606-0*) Harcourt.

Mikesell, John L., jt. auth. see Due, John F.

Mikesell, Marvin W. Northern Morocco: A Cultural Geography. LC 84-29028. 135p. 1985. reprint ed. lib. bdg. 57.50 (*0-313-23865-0*, MNOR, Greenwood Pr) Greenwood.

Mikesell, Marvin W., ed. Geographers Abroad: Essays on the Problems & Prospects of Research in Foreign Areas. LC 73-87829. (Research Papers: No. 152). 296p. 1973. pap. text 14.50 (*0-89065-059-4*) U Ch Pr.

Mikesell, Marvin W., jt. ed. see Wagner, Philip L.

Mikesell, Raymond F. The Bretton Woods Debates: A Memoir. LC 94-8984. (Essays in International Finance Ser.: No. 192). 68p. 1994. pap. 10.00 (*0-88165-099-4*) Princeton U Int Finan Econ.

— Foreign Investment in Copper Mining: Case Studies of Mines in Peru & Papua New Guinea. LC 75-11356. (Resources for the Future Ser.). (Illus.). 166p. 1975. 18.00 (*0-8018-1750-1*) Johns Hopkins.

— Foreign Investment in Copper Mining: Case Studies of Mines in Peru & Papua New Guinea. LC 75-11356. 166p. reprint ed. pap. 51.50 (*0-608-12068-5*, 202415000035) Bks Demand.

— Foreign Investment in the Petroleum & Mineral Industries: Case Studies of Investor-Host Country Relations. LC 79-123860. 477p. reprint ed. pap. 147.90 (*0-608-12387-0*, 205211300034) Bks Demand.

— The Global Copper Industry: Problems & Prospects. 176p. 1988. lib. bdg. 65.00 (*0-7099-3508-0*) Routledge.

— New Patterns of World Mineral Development. LC 79-90054. (British-North American Committee Ser.). 116p. 1980. 5.00 (*0-89068-049-3*) Natl Planning.

— Nonfuel Minerals: Foreign Dependence & National Security. LC 86-27247. (Illus.). 269p. reprint ed. pap. 83.40 (*0-7837-4719-5*, 205907100003) Bks Demand.

— Petroleum Company Operations & Agreements in the Developing Countries. LC 83-43265. 148p. 1984. pap. text 20.00 (*0-915707-07-1*) Resources Future.

— Revisiting Bretton Woods: Proposals for Reforming the International Monetary Institutions. (Public Policy Brief Ser.: Vol. 24). 44p. (Orig.). 1996. write for info. (*0-941276-15-5*) J Levy.

— The World Copper Industry: Structure & Economic Analysis. LC 79-4581. 393p. 1979. pap. 19.95 (*0-8018-2270-X*, Pub. by Resources Future) Johns Hopkins.

Mikesell, Raymond F. & Furth, J. Herbert. Foreign Dollar Balances & the International Role of the Dollar. (Studies in International Economic Relations: No. 8). 141p. 1974. 36.70 (*0-87014-262-3*) Natl Bur Econ Res.

Mikesell, Raymond F., jt. auth. see Auty, Richard M.

Mikesell, Richard H., et al, eds. Integrating Family Therapy: Handbook of Family Psychology & Systems Theory. LC 95-3106. 645p. 1995. text 69.95 (*1-55798-280-5*, 431-7450) Am Psychol.

Mikesell, Robert E., Jr., jt. auth. see Baker, MeeCee.

Mikesell, Sarah. Opportunities in Veterinary Medicine. LC 92-43493. (Opportunities In . . . Ser.). (Illus.). 160p. 1993. pap. 11.95 (*0-8442-4060-5*, 40605, VGM Career) NTC Contemp Pub Co.

— Opportunities in Veterinary Medicine. LC 92-43493. (Opportunities in...Ser.). (Illus.). 160p. 1994. 14.95 (*0-8442-4059-1*, 40591, VGM Career) NTC Contemp Pub Co.

Mikesell, Shirley K. Early Settlers of Indiana's "Gore" (Illus.). 405p. (Orig.). 1995. pap. text 29.50 (*0-7884-0254-4*) Heritage Bk.

— Early Settlers of Montgomery County, Ohio: Genealogical Abstracts from Common Pleas Court Records. 317p. (Orig.). 1992. pap. 25.00 (*1-55613-601-3*) Heritage Bk.

— Early Settlers of Montgomery County, Ohio: Genealogical Abstracts from Land Records, Tax Lists, & Biographical Sketches. viii, 241p. (Orig.). 1991. pap. 21.50 (*1-55613-495-9*) Heritage Bk.

— Early Settlers of Montgomery County, Ohio Vol. III: Genealogical Abstracts from Marriage & Divorce Records, 1803-1827, Early Deeds Recorded Late, Election Abstracts, Obituary of an Early Settler. viii, 208p. (Orig.). 1993. pap. text 19.00 (*1-55613-751-6*) Heritage Bk.

***Mikesell, Stephen.** Class, State & Struggle in Nepal: Writings, 1989-1995. 1999. 36.00 (*81-7304-267-5*, Pub. by Manohar) S Asia.

Mikesell, Suzanne, ed. see Mutke, Peter H.

Mikeseu, Shirley K. Butler County, Ohio Land Records Vol. 2: 1816-1823. viii, 300p. 1997. pap. 23.00 (*0-7884-0698-1*, M358) Heritage Bk.

— Butler County, Ohio Land Resources, 1803-1816. LC 97-183775. (Illus.). vii, 287p. 1997. pap. 23.00 (*0-7884-0666-3*, M348) Heritage Bk.

Mikesh, Robert. Martin B-57 Canberra. 0.00 (*0-88740-772-2*) Schiffer.

Mikesh, Robert. Restoring Museum Aircraft. 1998. 64.95 (*1-85310-875-8*) Specialty Pr.

Mikesh, Robert C. Excalibur III: The Story of a P-51 Mustang. (Illus.). 76p. 1998. pap. text 20.00 (*0-7881-5269-6*) DIANE Pub.

— Japanese Aircraft Code Names & Designations. LC 92-85346. (Illus.). 192p. (Orig.). 1993. pap. 14.95 (*0-88740-447-2*) Schiffer.

— Japanese Aircraft Interiors, 1940-1945. (Illus.). 256p. 1999. write for info. (*0-914144-61-8*) Monogram Aviation.

— Zero: Combat & Development History of Japan's Legendary Mitsubishi A6M Zero Fighter. LC 94-26701. (Illus.). 128p. 1994. pap. 19.95 (*0-87938-915-X*) MBI Pubg.

Mikesh, Robert C. & Abe, Shorzoe. Japanese Aircraft, 1910-1941. (Putnam Aviation Ser.). (Illus.). 320p. 1990. 55.00 (*1-55750-563-2*) Naval Inst Pr.

Mikesky, jt. auth. see Getchell.

Miketta, Patricia L. Rape: How to Fight, Prevent, Use Protective Psychology or Later Identify Rapists. 3rd rev. ed. LC 90-56286. 230p. 1995. 47.50 (*0-7883-0454-2*); pap. 44.50 (*0-7883-0455-0*) ABBE Pubs Assn.

Mikhail, E. H. Brendan Behan: An Annotated Bibliography of Criticism. 117p. 1980. text 44.00 (*0-06-494826-9*, N6595) B&N Imports.

— Contemporary British Drama, 1950-1976. 147p. 1976. 10.00 (*0-87471-854-6*) Rowman.

— Sean O'Casey & His Critics: An Annotated Bibliography, 1916-1982. LC 84-14166. (Author Bibliographies Ser.: No. 67). 362p. 1985. 34.50 (*0-8108-1747-0*) Scarecrow.

Mikhail, E. H., compiled by. An Annotated Bibliography of Modern Anglo-Irish Drama. LC 80-51874. x, 300p. 1981. 20.00 (*0-87875-201-3*) Whitston Pub.

Mikhail, E. H., compiled by. John Galsworthy the Dramatist: A Bibliography of Criticism. LC 76-155722. vi, 91p. 1971. 15.00 (*0-87875-009-6*) Whitston Pub.

— Lady Gregory: An Annotated Bibliography of Criticism. LC 81-50702. xii, 258p. (C). 1982. 45.00 (*0-87875-216-1*) Whitston Pub.

— A Research Guide to Modern Irish Dramatists. LC 78-69874. xii, 104p. 1979. 25.00 (*0-87875-166-1*) Whitston Pub.

Mikhail, E. H., ed. The Abbey Theatre: Interviews & Recollections. LC 86-3407. 220p. 1986. 59.00 (*0-389-20616-4*, N8174) B&N Imports.

Mikhail, E. H., ed. see Behan, Brendan.

Mikhail, Edward M., jt. auth. see Anderson, J. M.

Mikhail, Hanna. Politics & Revelation: Mawardi & After. (Islamic Surveys Ser.). 128p. 1995. 50.00 (*0-7486-0519-3*, Pub. by Edinburgh U Pr) Col U Pr.

Mikhail, Labib. God's Last Messenger. LC 99-172249. 1998. pap. 10.00 (*1-890297-07-0*) Blessed Hope Ministry.

— I Surrender All. 1999. 15.00 (*1-890297-14-3*) Blessed Hope Ministry.

— Islam, Muhammad & the Koran: A Documented Analysis. 188p. (Orig.). 1996. pap. 12.00 (*1-890297-09-7*) Blessed Hope Ministry.

Mikhail, Mona N. Mafouz & Idris: Studies in Arabic Short Fiction. 272p. (C). 1992. text 45.00 (*0-8147-5474-0*) NYU Pr.

Mikhail, Nagy, jt. auth. see Raskova, Jana.

Mikhail, Raouf S. & Robens, Erich. Microstructure & Thermal Analysis of Solid Surfaces. LC 82-17507. (Wiley Heyden Publication). 506p. reprint ed. pap. 156.90 (*0-7837-3237-6*, 204325600007) Bks Demand.

Mikhail, Rauof S., jt. auth. see Mikhailov, G. K.

Mikhailov, A. S. Foundations of Synergetics: Distributed Active Systems. LC 93-43340. (Synergetics Ser.: Vol. 51). 1994. write for info. (*3-540-57299-6*) Spr-Verlag.

— Foundations of Synergetics: Distributed Active Systems. 2nd ed. LC 93-43340. (Synergetics Ser.: Vol. 51). 1994. write for info. (*0-387-57299-6*) Spr-Verlag.

— Foundations of Synergetics One: Distributed Active Systems. Haken, H., ed. (Synergetics Ser.: Vol. 51). (Illus.). 208p. 1990. 69.00 (*0-387-52775-3*) Spr-Verlag.

Mikhailov, A. S. & Loskutov, A. Yu. Foundations of Synergetics II: Complex Patterns. 2nd enl. rev. ed. Haken, H., ed. (Springer Series in Synergetics: No. 52). xii, 280p. 1996. 99.50 (*3-540-61066-9*) Spr-Verlag.

— Foundations of Synergetics Two: Complex Patterns. Haken, H., ed. (Synergetics Ser.: Vol. 52). (Illus.). viii, 210p. 1991. 79.00 (*0-387-53448-2*) Spr-Verlag.

Mikhailov, A. S., jt. ed. see Haken, H.

Mikhailov, A. V., jt. auth. see Ivanov-Kholodny, G. S.

Mikhailov, Andrey, jt. auth. see Bergstrom, Christer.

Mikhailov, B. M. & Bubnov, Yu N. Organoboron Compounds in Organic Synthesis. xxxiv, 781p. 1984. text 634.00 (*3-7186-0113-3*) Gordon & Breach.

Mikhailov, Boris. Boris Mikhailov: Les Miserables: Homeless People in Ukraine. (Illus.). 256p. 1999. 49.95 (*3-908247-09-8*, 910061, Pub. by Scalo Pubs) Dist Art Pubs.

Mikhailov, G. A. Minimization of Computational Costs of Non-Analogue Monte Carlo Methods. 220p. (C). 1992. text 43.00 (*981-02-0707-7*) World Scientific Pub.

— New Monte Carlo Methods with Estimating Derivatives. 202p. 1995. 145.00 (*90-6764-190-1*, Pub. by VSP) Coronet Bks.

— Optimization of Weighted Monte Carlo Methods. Glowinski, Roland et al, eds. Sabelfeld, K. K., tr. from RUS. (Computational Physics Ser.). 220p. 1992. 103.95 (*0-387-53005-3*) Spr-Verlag.

***Mikhailov, G. A.** Parametric Estimates by the Monte Carlo Method. 196p. 1999. 145.00 (*90-6764-297-5*, Pub. by VSP) Coronet Bks.

Mikhailov, G. K. & Mikhail, Rauof S. Applied Mechanics Vol. 4: Soviet Review. 1994. write for info. (*0-8493-9329-9*) CRC Pr.

Mikhailov, G. K. & Parton, V. Z. Fluid Mechanics. (Applied Mechanics: Soviet Reviews Ser.: Vol. 3). 500p. 1991. 145.00 (*0-89116-719-6*) CRC Pr.

Mikhailov, K. V., et al. Polymer Concretes & Their Structural Uses. Parameswaran, V. S., ed. (Russian Translation Ser.: No. 91). (Illus.). 326p. (C). 1991. text 123.00 (*90-6191-110-9*, Pub. by A A Balkema) Ashgate Pub Co.

M

An Asterisk (*) at the beginning of an entry indicates that the title is appearing for the first time.

Mikhailov, M. D. & Ozisik, M. Necati. Unified Analysis & Solutions of Heat & Mass Diffusion. LC 93-34237. (Illus.). 544p. 1994. reprint ed. pap. text 15.95 (0-486-67876-8) Dover.

Mikhailov, Mikhail D. & Kryzhanowsky, Iliya I. Chalcogenide Inorganic Photoresists Holography & Microlithography. (Laser & Optical Science & Technology Ser.). Date not set. 179.95 (0-8493-3784-4, 3784) CRC Pr.

Mikhailov, N. A. Pavel Korin. 102p. 1982. pap. 35.00 (0-7855-1647-6) St Mut.

***Mikhailov, V. N., ed.** Catalog of Worldwide Nuclear Testing. LC 99-25847. 129p. 1999. 108.00 (1-56700-131-9) Begell Hse.

Mikhailova, Tatyana A., jt. auth. see Rozhkov, Anatoly S.

Mikhailovich, Sergei, jt. auth. see Serkovski, Belo T.

Mikhailovich, Vladimir, et al. Conservation of the Biological Diversity As a Prerequisite for Sustainable Development in the Black Sea Region: International NATO Advanced Research Workshop, Tblisi - Kobuleti, Repbulic of Georgia, 5-12 October, 1996. LC 98-20375. (NATO Science Ser.). 1998. 227.00 (0-7923-5113-4) Kluwer Academic.

Mikhailovskii, A. B. Electromagnetic Instabilities in an Inhomogeneous Plasma. (Plasma Physics Ser.). (Illus.). 320p. 1992. 147.00 (0-7503-0182-1) IOP Pub.

— Instabilities in a Confined Plasma. LC 98-3932. (Plasma Physics Ser.). 462p. 1998. 200.00 (0-7503-0532-0) IOP Pub.

— Theory of Plasma Instabilities, 2 vols. Incl. Vol. 1. Instabilities of a Homogeneous Plasma. LC 73-83899. 308p. 1974. 59.50 (0-306-17181-3, Kluwer Plenum); Vol. 2. Instabilities of an Inhomogeneous Plasma. LC 73-83899. 332p. 1974. 59.50 (0-306-17182-1, Kluwer Plenum); LC 73-83899. (Studies in Soviet Science, Physical Sciences Ser.). 1974. write for info. (0-318-55302-3, Kluwer Plenum) Kluwer Academic.

Mikhailovsky, V. Uchenije o Pravoslavnom Bogosluzhenii.Tr. of Teachings of the Orthodox Divine Services. 146p. reprint ed. pap. text 6.00 (0-317-30287-6) Holy Trinity.

Mikhalchishin, Adrian. Hanging Pawns. (Illus.). 200p. 1999. pap. text 19.95 (1-879479-77-X) ICE WA.

***Mikhalchishin, Adrian.** Isolated Pawn. (Illus.). 200p. 2000. pap. 19.95 (1-879479-82-6) ICE WA.

Mikhalchishin, Adrian & Pein, Malcolm. The Exchange Grunfeld. 160p. 1995. pap. 19.95 (1-85744-005-6, Pub. by Cadgn Bks) Macmillan.

Mikhalev, Alexander A. & Zolotykh, Andrej A. Combinatorial Aspects of Lie Superalgebras. LC 95-15995. 272p. 1995. pap. 134.95 (0-8493-8960-7, 8960) CRC Pr.

Mikhaylov, Boris. Unfinished Dissertation. (Illus.). 224p. 1998. 45.00 (3-931141-97-7, Pub. by Scalo Pubs) Dist Art Pubs.

Mikheev, M. I., jt. ed. see Karvonen, M.

***Mikheev, Vasily V.** A Spy-Game. LC 97-91418. 1999. pap. 12.95 (0-533-12667-3) Vantage.

Mikheeva, G. V., ed. see Nitkina, N. V.

Mikhejev, A. V., jt. auth. see Frumkina, R. M.

Mikheyev, Dimitry. The Rise & Fall of Gorbachev. 178p. (Orig.). (C). 1992. pap. text 12.95 (1-55813-041-1) Hudson Instit IN.

— Russia Transformed. LC 96-206835. (Hudson Institute Bk.). 288p. (Orig.). (C). 1996. pap. 12.95 (1-55813-054-3) Hudson Instit IN.

Mikheyev, Sergei M., tr. see Berezhkov, Valentin M.

Mikheyev, Vadim. Sikorsky - S-16 No. 1. LC 97-220413. (Great War Aircraft in Profile Ser.: No. 1). (Illus.). 32p. (Orig.). 1997. pap. 19.95 (0-9637110-8-3) Flying Machines.

Mikhin, N. M., jt. auth. see Kragel'skii, I. V.

Mikhin, V. Western Expansionism in the Persian Gulf. (C). 1988. 17.50 (0-8364-2448-4, Pub. by Allied Pubs) S Asia.

***Mikhlin, Alexander S.** Death Penalty in Russia. LC 99-196143. 183 p. 1999. 65.00 (90-411-9312-X) Kluwer Law Intl.

Mikhlin, Solomon G. Linear Integral Equations. (Russian Monographs & Texts on the Physical Sciences). viii, 224p. 1961. text 195.00 (0-677-20320-9) Gordon & Breach.

Mikhlin, Solomon G., jt. auth. see Whyte, W.

Miki, Mihoko, jt. compiled by see Makino, Yasuko.

Miki, Roy. The Prepoetice of William Carlos Williams: Kora in Hell. LC 83-15551. (Studies in Modern Literature: No. 32). (Illus.). 223p. reprint ed. pap. 69.20 (0-8357-1476-4, 207056300001) Bks Demand.

— Random Access File. LC 95-168600. (Writing West Series). 96p. 1995. pap. 8.95 (0-88995-130-6, Pub. by Red Deer) Genl Dist Srvs.

— Saving Face. 1997. pap. 7.95 (0-88801-155-5, Pub. by Turnstone Pr) Genl Dist Srvs.

Miki, Roy, ed. Tracing the Paths: Reading Isn't Equal Writing the Martyrology. 344p. 1988. pap. 21.95 (0-88922-256-8, Pub. by Talonbks) Genl Dist Srvs.

Miki, Roy & Kobayashi, Cassandra. Justice in Our Time: The Japanese Canadian Redress Settlement. LC 92-204010. 160p. 1991. 26.95 (0-88922-292-4, Pub. by Talonbks) Genl Dist Srvs.

Miki, Roy, ed. see Kiyooka, Roy K.

Mikic. International Trade. LC 97-44293. (Illus.). 512p. 1998. 24.95 (0-312-21312-3); text 69.95 (0-312-21311-5) St Martin.

Mikics, David. The Limits of Moralizing: Pathos & Subjectivity in Spenser & Milton. 1994. 42.50 (0-8387-5285-3) Bucknell U Pr.

Mikimoto, Haruhiko. Haruhiko Mikimoto Illustrations. 96p. 1993. pap. 24.95 (0-945814-51-8) US Renditions.

Mikio Sumiya & Koji Taira, eds. An Outline of Japanese Economic History, 1603-1940: Major Works & Research Findings. LC 79-670232. 386p. reprint ed. pap. 119.70 (0-7837-6270-4, 204598200010) Bks Demand.

Mikiro, Sasaki. Demented Flute: Selected Poems, 1967-1986. Fitzsimmons, Thomas, ed. Elliott, William I. et al, trs. from JPN. (Asian Poetry in Translation Ser.: No. 9). (Illus.). 64p. 1988. pap. 15.00 (0-942668-14-6); text 25.00 (0-942668-15-4) Katydid Bks.

Mikita, Michael A., jt. ed. see Wershaw, Robert L.

Mikitani, Ryoichi, jt. ed. see Posen, Adam S.

Mikitiuk, I. V., jt. auth. see Prikarpatskii, A. V.

Mikiuscak. 12 Step Approach to Healing in Nursing. (Professional Reference - Nursing Ser.). 2002. pap. 20.95 (0-8273-6604-3) Delmar.

Mikkalsen, Stacy, jt. ed. see Edwards, Henry.

Mikke, jt. auth. see Mikkelsen.

Mikkeli. Europe as an Idea & Identity. LC 97-27133. 224p. 1998. text 65.00 (0-312-21039-6) St Martin.

Mikkelsen. Susan Cooper. LC 97-35453. 1998. 32.00 (0-8057-7813-6, Twyne) Mac Lib Ref.

Mikkelsen & Mikke. Words & Pictures: Lessons in Children's Literature & Literacies. LC 99-24055. 512p. 1999. pap. 42.80 (0-697-39357-7) McGraw.

Mikkelsen, Britha. Industrial Labour in Africa: Annotated Bibliography. 59p. 1979. write for info. (91-7106-158-4, Pub. by Nordic Africa) Transaction Pubs.

— Methods for Development Work & Research: A Guide for Practioners. LC 95-5373. (Illus.). 250p. 1995. 35.00 (0-8039-9229-7); pap. 16.95 (0-8039-9230-0) Sage.

Mikkelsen, Britha, jt. auth. see Eriksen, Tore L.

Mikkelsen, Edwin J., jt. auth. see Brown, Phil.

Mikkelsen, John. Hoping Against Hope: A Selection of Modern Day Healing Miracles. LC 93-84110. (Orig.). 1993. pap. 12.95 (0-9636935-0-6) Step Stone NY.

Mikkelsen, Kurt V., jt. auth. see Billing, Gert D.

***Mikkelsen, Markella.** Lonely Planet Greek Phrasebook. 2nd ed. (Lonely Planet Phrasebooks). (ENG & GRE., Illus.). 320p. 2000. pap. 7.95 (0-86442-683-6) Lonely Planet.

Mikkelsen, Michael A. The Bishop Hill Colony. LC 78-63808. (Johns Hopkins University. Studies in the Social Sciences. Thirtieth Ser. 1912: 1). reprint ed. 27.50 (0-404-61071-4) AMS Pr.

— The Bishop Hill Colony: A Religious, Communistic Settlement in Henry County, Illinois. LC 72-187466. (American Utopian Adventure Ser.). 167p. 1972. reprint ed. lib. bdg. 35.00 (0-87991-014-3) Porcupine Pr.

Mikkelsen, Nina. Virginia Hamilton. LC 94-621. (Twayne's United States Authors Ser.). 200p. 1994. 32.00 (0-8057-4010-4, Twyne) Mac Lib Ref.

Mikkelsen, Paula M., jt. ed. see Bieler, Rudiger.

Mikkelsen, Peter. Journey into One: The Final Unity. LC 98-228028. 234p. 1998. pap. 12.95 (0-9664816-0-7) Parnassus CA.

Mikkelsen, Tom, et al, eds. Brain Tumor Invasion: Biological, Clinical & Therapeutic Considerations. LC 97-29119. 464p. 1998. 119.95 (0-471-15452-0, Wiley-Liss) Wiley.

Mikkelson, Britha, jt. auth. see Eriksen, Tore L.

Mikkelson, Gerald, tr. see Rasputin, Valentin.

Mikkelson, Holly. Using the Mandarin Tape Set with the Interpreter's Edge Generic Edition, 3 cass. 103p. (C). 1997. spiral bd. 35.00 incl. audio (1-880594-17-X) ACEBO.

— Using the Russian Tape Set with the Interpreter's Edge Generic Edition, 3 cass. 96p. (C). 1996. spiral bd. 35.00 incl. audio (1-880594-15-3) ACEBO.

— Using the Vietnamese Tape Set with the Interpreter's Edge Generic Edition, 3 cass. 98p. (C). 1996. spiral bd. 35.00 incl. audio (1-880594-16-1) ACEBO.

Mikkelson, Holly M. The Interpreter's Companion. 3rd ed. (Illus.). 472p. 1996. pap. text 38.00 (1-880594-14-5, IC3) ACEBO.

— The Interpreter's Edge: Practical Exercises in Court Interpreting. 3rd ed. (Illus.). 434p. 1995. pap. text 80.00 (1-880594-13-7, IE3) ACEBO.

— The Interpreter's Edge Turbo Supplement: Advanced Exercises in Court Interpreting. Willis, Jim & Alvarez, Norma, eds. (ENG & SPA.). 94p. (Orig.). (C). 1993. pap. text 50.00 (1-880594-08-0, IET) ACEBO.

— The Interpreter's RX: A Training Program for Spanish/English Medical Interpreting. (SPA., Illus.). 262p. (C). 1994. pap. 60.00 (1-880594-11-0, 1RX) ACEBO.

— Using the Cantonese Tape Set with the Interpreter's Edge Generic Edition, 3 cass. 122p. (C). 1994. spiral bd. 35.00 incl. audio (1-880594-12-9) ACEBO.

— Using the Korean Tape Set with the Interpreter's Edge Generic Edition, 3 cass. (KOR.). 92p. (C). 1994. spiral bd. 35.00 incl. audio (1-880594-10-2) ACEBO.

Mikkelson, Holly M., jt. auth. see Willis, Jim.

Mikkelson, Shirley, ed. Dusting off Dreams, Vol. I. (Illus.). 152p. (Orig.). 1994. pap. 24.95 (0-943536-81-2) Quill Bks.

Mikkelson, Shirley J., ed. All My Tomorrows, Vol. I. (Illus.). 148p. (Orig.). 1993. pap. 24.95 (0-943536-73-1) Quill Bks.

— All My Tomorrows, Vol. II. (Illus.). 148p. (Orig.). 1993. pap. 24.95 (0-943536-74-X) Quill Bks.

— All My Tomorrows, Vol. III. (Illus.). 148p. (Orig.). 1993. pap. 24.95 (0-943536-75-8) Quill Bks.

— Dusting off Dreams, Vol. II. (Illus.). 152p. (Orig.). 1994. pap. 24.95 (0-943536-82-0) Quill Bks.

— Dusting off Dreams, Vol. III. (Illus.). 152p. (Orig.). 1994. pap. 24.95 (0-943536-83-9) Quill Bks.

— Echoes from the Silence, Vol. I. (Illus.). 156p. (Orig.). 1995. pap. 24.95 (0-943536-94-4) Quill Bks.

— Echoes from the Silence, Vol. II. (Illus.). 156p. (Orig.). 1995. pap. 24.95 (0-943536-95-2) Quill Bks.

— Echoes from the Silence, Vol. III. (Illus.). 156p. (Orig.). 1995. pap. 24.95 (0-943536-96-0) Quill Bks.

— Treasure the Moment. (Orig.). 1996. pap. 24.95 (0-943536-84-7) Quill Bks.

Mikkelson, Tim & Pherigo, Suzanne. Practical Software Configuration. 1997. pap. 39.00 incl. cd-rom (0-614-28521-6) P-H.

— Practical Software Configuration Management: The Latenight Developer's Handbook. LC 97-173384. 336p. (C). 1997. pap. text 44.99 (0-13-240854-6) P-H.

Mikker, Max L. Sports - the Importance of Oxygen & Anaerobic Thresholds in Training, Performance & Competition: Index of New Information with Authors, Subjects, Research Categories & References. 166p. 1997. 47.50 (0-7883-1518-8); pap. 44.50 (0-7883-1519-6) ABBE Pubs Assn.

— Sports Encyclopedia: Index & Reference Books of New Information Vol. 1: Anaerobic Thresholds, Vol. 1. Bartone, John C., ed. 150p. 1996. 44.50 (0-7883-1077-1); pap. 39.50 (0-7883-1078-X) ABBE Pubs Assn.

Mikkers, Bote. Pendulum Workbook. (Illus.). 176p. 1990. reprint ed. pap. text 29.95 (1-85398-036-6, Pub. by Ashgrove Pr) Words Distrib.

Mikkola, Donald E., jt. ed. see Schlesinger, Mark E.

Mikkola, Heimo. Owls of Europe. LC 83-71804. (Illus.). 400p. 1983. 40.00 (0-931130-10-7) Harrell Bks.

Miklas, Christine L., ed. see American Indian Lawyer Training Program, Inc., Sta & American Indian Resources Institute Staff.

Miklas, Heinz, comment. Berlinski Sbornik. fac. ed. (Codices Selecti B Ser.: Vol. LXXIX). (GER.). 276p. 1989. 93.00 (3-201-01477-X, Pub. by Akademische Druck-und) Balogh.

Miklausen, Anthony J. The Brown Algal Origin of Land Plants & the Algal Origin of Life on Earth & in the Universe. LC 97-22068. 1997. 60.00 (1-57249-095-0, Ragged Edge) White Mane Pub.

Miklautsch, Lydia, jt. auth. see Greenfield, John.

Miklavele, Milan. Applied Functional Analysis & Partial Differential Equations. 300p. 1998. 38.00 (981-02-3535-6) World Scientific Pub.

Miklavicic, Damijan, jt. auth. see Klauenberg, B. Jon.

Mikles, J., jt. auth. see Huba, M.

Miklich, Carol L. Feeding the New American Family. (Illus.). 475p. (Orig.). 1996. pap. 24.95 (0-9640966-0-9) B & C Pubng.

Miklitsch, Robert. From Hegel to Madonna: Towards a General Economy of "Commodity Fetishism" LC 97-32814. (SUNY Series in Postmodern Culture). (Illus.). 224p. (C). 1997. pap. text 18.95 (0-7914-3540-7) State U NY Pr.

— From Hegel to Madonna: Towards a General Economy of "Commodity Fetishism" (SUNY Series in Postmodern Culture). 224p. (C). 1998. text. write for info. (0-7914-3539-3) State U NY Pr.

— Psycho-Marxism: Marxism & Psychoanalysis Late in the 20th Century. 1998. pap. 12.00 (0-8223-6460-3) Duke.

Miklos, George, jt. auth. see John, Bernard.

Miklos, Stephen J. How to Prepare for the New Law School Admission Test (LSAT) 369p. 1983. pap. 9.95 (0-15-600032-6) Harcourt.

Miklosi, Judit. The Authentic Hungarian Cookbook. 72p. 1989. 75.00 (963-13-4085-6, Pub. by Corvina Bks) St Mut.

Miklovic, Daniel T. Real-Time Control Networks. LC 93-13670. (Resources for Measurement & Control Ser.). 277p. 1993. 50.00 (1-55617-231-1) ISA.

Miklowitz, David J. & Goldstein, Michael J. Bipolar Disorder: A Family-Focused Treatment Approach. LC 97-26189. 318p. 1997. lib. bdg. 36.00 (1-57230-283-6) Guilford Pubns.

Miklowitz, Gloria. Standing Tall, Looking Good. 1990. 17.95 (0-385-30338-6) Bantam.

Miklowitz, Gloria D. After the Bomb. (Orig.). (YA). (gr. 6-9). 1987. pap. 2.50 (0-590-40568-3) Scholastic Inc.

— Anything to Win. (J). 1990. mass mkt. write for info. (0-440-80222-9) Dell.

— Anything to Win. (J). 1989. 9.09 (0-606-04608-9, Pub. by Turtleback) Demco.

— Camouflage. LC 97-18053. 166p. (YA). (gr. 7-12). 1998. 16.00 (0-15-201467-5) Harcourt.

— Masada: The Last Fortress. LC 98-17756. 198p. (YA). (gr. 7-12). 1999. pap. 7.00 (0-8028-5168-1, Eerdmans Bks) Eerdmans.

— Masada: The Last Fortress. LC 98-17756. 198p. (YA). (gr. 7 up). 1999. 16.00 (0-8028-5165-7, Eerdmans Bks) Eerdmans.

— Past Forgiving. 160p. (YA). (gr. 7 up). 1995. per. 16.00 (0-671-88442-5) S&S Bks Yung.

— The War Between the Classes. 176p. (YA). (gr. 6 up). 1986. mass mkt. 4.99 (0-440-99406-3, LLL BDD) BDD Bks Young Read.

Miklowitz, Gloria D. The War Between the Classes. (Laurel-Leaf Contemporary Fiction Ser.). (J). 1985. 9.60 (0-606-03078-6, Pub. by Turtleback) Demco.

Miklowitz, Julius, ed. Wave Propagation in Solids. LC 72-101230. 189p. reprint ed. pap. 58.60 (0-608-30878-1, 201012500068) Bks Demand.

Miklowitz, Paul S. Metaphysics to Metafictions: Hegel, Nietzsche, & the End of Philosophy. LC 97-35112. (Series in Hegelian Studies). 256p. (C). 1998. text 57.50 (0-7914-3877-5); pap. text 18.95 (0-7914-3878-3) State U NY Pr.

Miklukho-Maklai, N. D., ed. Persidiskie i Tadzhikskie Rukopisi Instituta Vostokovedeniia Rossiiskoi Akademii Nauk: Kratkii (Alfavitnyi Katalog), Vol. 1. LC 95-25791. (PER & RUS.). 1998. lib. bdg. 220.00 (0-88354-140-8) N Ross.

Miknis, Francis P. & McKay, John F., eds. Geochemistry & Chemistry of Oil Shales. LC 83-11801. (ACS Symposium Ser.: No. 230). 576p. 1983. lib. bdg. 65.95 (0-8412-0799-2) Am Chemical.

— Geochemistry & Chemistry of Oil Shales. LC 83-11801. (ACS Symposium Ser.: Vol. 230). 575p. 1983. reprint ed. pap. 178.30 (0-608-03079-1, 206353200007) Bks Demand.

Miko Hino. Water Quality & Its Control. LC 99-227618. (Hydraulic Structures Design Manual Ser.: Vol. 5). (Illus.). 262p. 1994. text 142.00 (90-5410-123-7, Pub. by A A Balkema) Ashgate Pub Co.

Miko, Stephen J. Toward Women in Love: The Emergence of a Lawrentian Aesthetic. LC 73-151583. (Yale Studies in English: No. 177). 309p. reprint ed. pap. 95.80 (0-8357-8354-5, 203382700087) Bks Demand.

Mikoff, Eli C. & Baker, Pamela J. Biology Today: An Issues Approach. LC 95-81972. 495p. (C). 1996. pap. 53.44 (0-07-042629-5) McGraw.

***Mikofsky, Bernard.** Proverbs about Family & Nations. 1999. pap. write for info. (1-58235-307-7) Watermrk Pr.

Mikohailov, G. K. Super-Hypersonic Aerodynamic & Heat Transfer. 352p. 1992. lib. bdg. 210.00 (0-8493-9309-4, TL571) CRC Pr.

Mikojkovic-Djuric, Jelena. Aspects of Soviet Culture: Voices of Glasnost 1960-1990. 180p. 1991. text 33.50 (0-88033-204-2, Pub. by East Eur Monographs) Col U Pr.

Mikol, Bob. Temperature Directed Fishing: How to Reduce Bycatch & Increase Productivity. (Marine Advisory Bulletin Ser.: Vol. 48). (Illus.). 43p. 1997. pap. 4.00 (1-56612-051-9) AK Sea Grant CP.

Mikolaj, Alan A. Drug Dosage Calculations for the Emergency Care Provider. LC 96-16998. 156p. 1996. pap. text 43.00 (0-8359-4994-X) P-H.

Mikolajczyk, Marian, Jr., et al. Chiral Sulfur Reagents: Applications in Asymmetric & Stereoselective Synthesis. LC 96-6162. (New Directions in Organic & Biological Chemistry Ser.). 288p. 1997. boxed set 104.95 (0-8493-9120-2) CRC Pr.

Mikolajczyk, N. Andrzej. Sylloge of Coins of the British Isles: Polish Museums, Vol. 37. (Sylloge of Coins of the British Isles: Vol. 37). (Illus.). 88p. 1988. 65.00 (0-19-726063-2) OUP.

Mikolajczyk, Stanislaw. The Rape of Poland. LC 73-141282. (Illus.). 309p. 1972. reprint ed. lib. bdg. 65.00 (0-8371-5879-6, MIRP, Greenwood Pr) Greenwood.

***Mikolajewska, Barbara.** Chrzciny Marysi. (Live Art Ser.).Tr. of Baptising Marisia. (POL., Illus.). 110p. 1999. pap. 24.95 (0-9659529-9-1) Lintons Vid Pr.

Mikolajewska, Barbara. Desire Came upon That One in the Beginning... Creation Hymns of the Rig Veda. 23p. (Orig.). 1997. pap. 5.00 (0-9659529-0-8) Lintons Vid Pr.

— Desire Came upon That One in the Beginning... Creation Hymns of the Rig Veda. 2nd ed. 64p. (Orig.). 1999. pap. 9.50 (0-9659529-1-6) Lintons Vid Pr.

***Mikolajewska, Barbara.** This Is Us Vol. 1: Doing Math: Category Theorists at Buffalo (Full Color Edition) (Live Art Ser.). (Illus.). 108p. 1999. pap. 34.95 (0-9659529-7-5) Lintons Vid Pr.

— This Is Us Vol. 1: Doing Math: Category Theorists at Buffalo (Grayscale Edition) (Live Art Ser.). (Illus.). 108p. 1999. pap. 14.95 (0-9659529-3-2) Lintons Vid Pr.

— This Is Us Vol. 2: Symposium: Celebrating (with) Saunders. (Live Art Ser.). (Illus.). 170p. 1999. pap. 34.95 (1-929865-01-5) Lintons Vid Pr.

— This Is Us Vol. 3: Facing Off. (Live Art Ser.). (Illus.). 82p. 1999. pap. 20.00 (1-929865-00-7) Lintons Vid Pr.

Mikolajewska, Barbara & Lewenstein, Barbara. Zjawisko Wspolnoty: Wybor Tekstow. 2nd rev. enl. ed.Tr. of Phenomenon of Community: Selected Writings. (POL.). 482p. (C). 1999. pap. text 40.00 (0-9659529-2-4) Lintons Vid Pr.

Mikolajewska, Joanna, et al, eds. The Symbiotic Phenomenon. (C). 1988. text 211.50 (90-277-2723-6) Kluwer Academic.

Mikolajski, Andrew. Clematis: A Step-by-Step Handbook for Cultivation & Care. (New Plant Library). (Illus.). 64p. 1997. 9.95 (1-85967-511-5, Lorenz Bks) Anness Pub.

— Climbing Roses: A Step-by-Step Handbook for Cultivation & Care. (New Plant Library). (Illus.). 64p. 1997. 9.95 (1-85967-512-3, Lorenz Bks) Anness Pub.

— Conifers: A Step-by-Step Handbook for Cultivation & Care. (New Plant Library). (Illus.). 64p. 1997. 9.95 (1-85967-513-1, Lorenz Bks) Anness Pub.

— Fuschias. (The New Plant Library). (Illus.). 64p. 1997. 9.95 (1-85967-387-2, Lorenz Bks) Anness Pub.

— Heathers: A Step-by-Step Handbook for Cultivation & Care. (New Plant Library). (Illus.). 64p. 1997. 9.95 (1-85967-514-X, Lorenz Bks) Anness Pub.

— Hostas: At-a-Glance Guide to Varieties, Cultivation & Care. (The New Plant Library). (Illus.). 64p. 1997. 9.95 (1-85967-388-0, Lorenz Bks) Anness Pub.

— Old Roses: At-a-Glance Guide to Varieties, Cultivation & Care. Hawthorne, Lin, ed. (The New Plant Library). (Illus.). 64p. 1997. 9.95 (1-85967-389-9, Lorenz Bks) Anness Pub.

***Mikolajski, Andrew.** Orchids. (New Plant Library). 1999. 11.95 (0-7548-0125-X, Lorenz Bks) Anness Pub.

Mikolajski, Andrew. Water Plants: At-a-Glance Guide to Varieties, Cultivation & Care. McHoy, Peter, ed. (The New Plant Library). (Illus.). 64p. 1997. 9.95 (1-85967-390-2, Lorenz Bks) Anness Pub.

***Mikolanis & HADG Staff.** Coding Guide for Breast Procedures & Surgeries. 2000. pap. 89.00 (0-8342-1722-8) Aspen Pub.

Mikolas, Barbara S. Pool of Water: New Age Reflections. (Illus.). 128p. (Orig.). 1989. pap. 7.95 (1-877633-01-1) Luthers.

An Asterisk (*) at the beginning of an entry indicates that the title is appearing for the first time.

Mikolas, Mark. Nature Walks in Southern Vermont: Nature-Rich, Easy to Moderate Walks in the Green Mountain State. (AMC Nature Walks Guides Ser.). (Illus.). 384p. 1995. pap. 12.95 (*1-878239-47-3*) AMC Books.

Mikolas, Miklos. Real Functions, Abstract Spaces & Orthogonal Series. LC 95-169801. 400p. 1994. pap. 150.00 (*963-05-6652-4*, Pub. by Akade Kiado) St Mut.

Mikolaycak, Charles. Orpheus. abr. ed. LC 91-27440. (Illus.). 32p. (YA). (gr. 7 up). 1992. 19.95 (*0-15-258804-3*, Harcourt Child Bks) Harcourt.

Mikolaycak, Charles. Bearhead: A Russian Folktale. LC 91-55026. 32p. (J). (gr. k-3). 1991. lib. bdg. 16.95 (*0-8234-0902-3*) Holiday.

— A Gift from Saint Nicholas. LC 87-8797. 32p. (J). (gr. k-3). 1988. lib. bdg. 16.95 (*0-8234-0674-1*) Holiday.

— He Is Risen: The Easter Story. LC 84-15869. 32p. (J). (gr. 4-6). 1985. lib. bdg. 16.95 (*0-8234-0547-8*) Holiday.

— The Rumor of Pavel & Paali: A Ukrainian Folktale. LC 87-19958. 32p. (J). (gr. 1-3). 1988. 13.95 (*0-06-023277-3*) HarpC Child Bks.

Mikoletsky, Loren, ed. Allgemeines Verwaltungsarchiv, Archiv der Republik, Vienna. LC 94-45841. (Archives of the Holocaust Ser.: Vol. 21). (GER.). 480p. 1995. text 138.00 (*0-8240-6465-8*) Garland.

Mikoljksi, Andrew. Primulas. (The New Plant Library). (Illus.). 64p. 1998. 9.95 (*1-85967-595-6*, Lorenz Bks) Anness Pub.

Mikolowski, Ken. Big Enigmas. 77p. (Orig.). 1990. pap. 8.00 (*0-9622474-4-8*) Past Tents Pr.

Mikolowski, Ken & Vranich, Mick. Dispatch Detroit: Anthology. Monhollen, Christine, ed. (Illus.). 88p. 1998. pap. 10.00 (*1-884118-02-X*) Doorjamb Pr.

Mikolyzk, Thomas A., compiled by. Langston Hughes: A Bio-Bibliography, 2. LC 90-3613. (Bio-Bibliographies in Afro-American & African Studies: No. 2). 312p. 1990. lib. bdg. 45.00 (*0-313-26895-9*, MLK/, Greenwood Pr) Greenwood.

— Oscar Wilde: An Annotated Bibliography, 38. LC 93-14052. (Bibliographies & Indexes in World Literature Ser.: No. 38). 512p. 1993. lib. bdg. 85.00 (*0-313-27597-1*, MOT/, Greenwood Pr) Greenwood.

Mikos, Antonios G., et al, eds. Polymers in Medicine & Pharmacy: Materials Research Society Symposium Proceedings. (MRS Symposium Proceedings Ser.: Vol. 394). 208p. 1995. text 90.00 (*1-55899-297-9*, 394) Materials Res.

Mikos, Michael J. Polish Baroque & Enlightenment Literature: An Anthology. (Illus.). 382p. 1996. 29.95 (*0-89357-266-7*) Slavica.

— Polish Renaissance Literature: An Anthology. (Illus.). 275p. 1995. 24.95 (*0-89357-257-8*) Slavica.

Mikos, Michael J., tr. from POL. Medieval Literature of Poland: An Anthology. LC 91-24676. (Library of Medieval Literature: Vol. 82B). (Illus.). 286p. 1992. text 19.00 (*0-8153-0408-0*, GLML82B) Garland.

Mikos, Pal. The Collections of the Budapest Museum of Applied Arts. 376p. 1981. 180.00 (*0-7855-1523-2*) St Mut.

Mikosch, Falk. Interoperability of Standards for Robotics in Cime. LC 96-44419. (Research Reports ESPRIT). 140p. 1996. text 28.00 (*3-540-61884-8*) Spr-Verlag.

Mikosch, Thomas. Elementary Stochastic Calculus, with Finance in View. LC 98-26351. (Advanced Series on Statistical Science & Applied Probability). 1998. 34.00 (*981-02-3543-7*) World Scientific Pub.

Mikoshiba, Nobuo, ed. see International Conference on Internal Friction & Ul.

Mikotowicz, Tom. Oliver Smith: A Bio-Bibliography, 43. LC 93-21635. (Bio-Bibliographies in the Performing Arts Ser.: No. 43). 264p. 1993. lib. bdg. 69.50 (*0-313-28709-0*, Greenwood Pr) Greenwood.

Mikotowicz, Tom, ed. Theatrical Designers: An International Biographical Dictionary. LC 91-28086. 408p. 1992. lib. bdg. 73.00 (*0-313-26270-5*, MZT/, Greenwood Pr) Greenwood.

***Mikoyan, Stepan Anastasovich.** Stepan Anastasovich Mikoyan: Memoirs of Military Test-Flying & Life with the Kremlin's Elite. 1999. 45.00 (*1-85310-916-9*) Naval Inst Pr.

Miksa, Elizabeth J., jt. auth. see Herr, Sarah.

Miksa, Francis L. The DDC, the Universe of Knowledge, & the Post-Modern Library. LC 97-41719. 99p. 1998. pap. 20.00 (*0-910608-64-4*) OCLC Forest Pr.

Miksanek, Tony. Murmurs: The Story of a Stethoscope. 113p. 1995. 12.95 (*0-9646089-0-1*) Illusions Pr.

Miksche, Ferdinand O. The Failure of Atomic Strategy & a New Proposal for the Defence of the West. LC 76-27852. 224p. 1977. reprint ed. lib. bdg. 59.50 (*0-8371-9023-1*, MIFA, Greenwood Pr) Greenwood.

— Secret Forces: The Technique of Underground Movements. LC 73-110273. (Illus.). 181p. 1971. reprint ed. lib. bdg. 55.00 (*0-8371-4499-X*, MISF, Greenwood Pr) Greenwood.

Miksche, Jerome P., jt. auth. see Berlyn, Graeme P.

Miksic, John. Borobudur. (Illus.). 160p. 1991. 69.50 (*0-945971-31-1*) Periplus.

— Borobudur: Golden Tales of the Buddhas. (Illus.). 160p. 1990. 45.00 (*0-945971-15-X*) Periplus.

— Borobudur: Golden Tales of the Buddhas. (Illus.). 1995. pap. 29.95 (*0-945971-90-7*) Periplus.

— The Mysteries of Borobudur. (Asia's Cultural Attractions Ser.). (Illus.). 32p. 2000. 9.95 (*962-593-198-8*) Tuttle Pubng.

— Vertellingen Van de Buddha: Borobudur. (Illus.). 160p. 1991. 4.95 (*0-945971-25-7*) Periplus.

Miksovsky, Katja, jt. auth. see Koju, Stephan.

Miksovsky, Katja, jt. ed. see Koja, Stephan.

Mikul, Suzanne. Surviving the 60's: From the Hog Farm to the Father's House. (Illus.). 128p. 1998. pap. 10.00 (*1-57502-970-7*, PO2659) Morris Pubng.

Mikula, G., jt. auth. see Lerner, M. J.

Mikula, Mark F., et al, eds. Great American Court Cases, 4 vols. LC 99-11419. 2644p. (J). 1998. 350.00 (*0-7876-2947-2*, 00158804) Gale.

Mikula, Patrick. Gann's Scientific Methods Unveiled, 2 vols. Incl. Vol. 2. LC 96-189308. (Illus.). 208p. 1996. 200.00 (*0-9650518-1-1*, 208B); Vol. 1. 292p. 1995. 150.00 (*0-9650518-0-3*); 300.00 (*0-9650518-2-X*, 500-C) Austin Financial Grp.

***Mikula, Patrick.** Homestead Journals. (Illus.). 2000. pap. text 20.00 (*0-9679977-0-4*) Mikul Prodns.

Mikula, Poldi. Pilot's Guide to Recreational Destinations: Eastern United States. LC 99-90433. (Illus.). 350p. 1999. pap. 26.95 (*0-9671785-0-9*) Beyond Clouds.

***Mikula, Rick.** The Family Butterfly Book: Raise Your Own Butterflies! Create a Butterfly Habitat - 15 Projects & Activities - Close-Ups of 40 Favorite North American Butterflies. (Illus.). 176p. 2000. 29.95 (*1-58017-335-7*, 67335); pap. 16.95 (*1-58017-292-X*, 67292) Storey Bks.

Mikula, Rick. Garden Butterflies of North America: A Gallery of Garden Butterflies & How to Attract Them. LC 97-8246. (Illus.). 143p. 1997. 29.50 (*1-57223-086-X*, 086X) Willow Creek Pr.

Mikula-Toth, Agnes, jt. auth. see Brown, Melanie.

Mikulan, K., jt. auth. see Thomas, N.

***Mikulan, Krunoslav.** Enemies on All Sides: The Croation Armed Forces in World War II, 1941-1945. Munoz, Antonio J., ed. 2000. pap. write for info. (*1-891227-22-X*, Axis Europa Bks) Axis Europa.

***Mikulas.** The Complete Counselor. 2000. 30.00 (*0-534-52517-2*) Wadsworth Pub.

Mikulecky, Bea. Constructing Job Ads. 1990. mass mkt. 9.00 (*0-13-852286-3*) P-H.

— A Short Course in Teaching Reading Skills. (Illus.). 176p. 1990. pap. text 29.73 (*0-201-50079-5*) Addison-Wesley.

— Workplace Resources: Banking Note-Taking for Training Programs & Meeting. 1990. mass mkt. 9.00 (*0-13-852302-9*) P-H.

Mikulecky, Bea & Jeffries, Linda. Reading Power. (Illus.). 304p. (C). 1986. pap. text 23.52 (*0-201-15865-5*) Addison-Wesley.

Mikulecky, Bea, jt. auth. see Jeffries.

Mikulecky, Donald C. Applications of Network Thermodynamics to Problems in Biomedical Engineering. LC 92-30771. (Monographs in Biomedical Engineering). (C). 1993. text 80.00 (*0-8147-5490-2*) NYU Pr.

Mikulecky, Donald C. & Clarke, Alexander M., eds. Biomedical Engineering: Opening Doors, Set. (Monographs in Biomedical Engineering). 298p. (C). 1990. text 85.00 (*0-8147-7908-5*) NYU Pr.

Mikulecky, Larry. Balancing the Cash Drawer. 1990. mass mkt. 9.00 (*0-13-852229-4*) P-H.

— Cross Selling Using Brochures & Tables. 1990. mass mkt. 9.00 (*0-13-852237-5*) P-H.

— Developing Internal Correspondence. 1990. mass mkt. 9.00 (*0-13-852294-4*) P-H.

— Performing Complex Calculations. 1990. mass mkt. 9.00 (*0-13-852245-6*) P-H.

— Preparing Customer Correspondence. 1990. mass mkt. 9.00 (*0-13-852278-2*) P-H.

— Proofreading Written Work. 1990. mass mkt. 9.00 (*0-13-852260-X*) P-H.

— Reading Job Ads. 1990. mass mkt. 9.00 (*0-13-852211-1*) P-H.

— Studying Training Materials. 1990. mass mkt. 9.00 (*0-13-852328-2*) P-H.

— Workplace Resources, Building Communication Skills: Strategic Skill Builders. 1990. mass mkt. 9.00 (*0-13-852310-X*) P-H.

Mikulecky, Larry & Drew, Rad A. On the Job, Bk. 1. (On the Job Ser.). 144p. (Orig.). 1988. pap. text 6.00 (*0-8428-0160-X*) Cambridge Bk.

— On the Job, Bk. 3. (On the Job Ser.). 144p. (Orig.). 1988. pap. text 6.00 (*0-8428-0162-6*) Cambridge Bk.

— On the Job: Activity Book II. (On the Job Ser.). 80p. (Orig.). 1988. pap. text 4.00 (*0-8428-0164-2*) Cambridge Bk.

Mikulecky, Larry, jt. auth. see Stricht, Thomas G.

Mikulecky, Paul, jt. auth. see Karlins, Dave.

Mikulincer, M. Human Learned Helplessness: A Coping Perspective. (Series in Social/Clinical Psychology). (Illus.). 324p. (C). 1994. 49.50 (*0-306-44743-6*, Plenum Trade) Perseus Pubng.

Mikulsky, K. Lenin's Teaching on the World Economy. Riordan, Jim, tr. from RUS. 1975. pap. 25.00 (*0-8464-0560-1*) Beekman Pubs.

Mikuni, Akio. Japan: The Road to Recovery. (Occasional Paper Ser.: Vol. 55). 43p. 1998. pap. 10.00 (*1-56708-104-5*) Grp of Thirty.

Mikuriya, Tod. Excerpts from the Indian Hemp Commission Report. 48p. 1995. 9.95 (*0-86719-420-0*) Last Gasp.

Mikus, Karen, jt. auth. see Fialka, Janice.

Mikusinski, Jan. Operational Calculus, Vol. 1. 2nd ed. (International Series on Pure & Applied Mathematics: Vol. 109). (Illus.). 320p. 1983. 151.00 (*0-08-025071-8*, Pub. by Pergamon Repr) Franklin.

Mikusinski, Jan & Mikusinski, Piotr. An Introduction to Analysis: From Number to Integral. LC 92-42751. 290p. 1993. text 87.95 (*0-471-58988-8*) Wiley.

Mikusinski, Jan, jt. auth. see Hartman, S.

Mikusinski, Piotr, jt. auth. see Debnath, Lokenath.

Mikusinski, Piotr, jt. auth. see Mikusinski, Jan.

Mikusinski, Piotr, jt. ed. see Debnath, Lokenath.

Mikusko, M. Brady. Sourcebook of Oral Histories of Trade Union & Working in the United States. (Program on Workers Culture Ser.). 94p. 1982. pap. 6.50 (*0-87736-348-X*) U of Mich Inst Labor.

Mikva, Abner J. Legislative Process. LC 94-74421. 1104p. 1995. 62.00 (*0-316-56987-9*) Aspen Pub.

Mikva, Abner J. & Lane, Eric. An Introduction to Statutory Interpretation & the Legislative Process. LC 97-23133. 1997. pap. text 18.95 (*1-56706-612-7*) Aspen Law.

— Legislative Process. 1104p. 1995. teacher ed. write for info. (*0-316-56968-2*, 69682) Aspen Law.

Mikva, Rachel S., ed. Broken Tablets: Restoring the Ten Commandments & Ourselves. LC 99-40417. 192p. 1999. 21.95 (*1-58023-066-0*) Jewish Lights.

***Mikwright.** Happy Birthday...Blah, Blah, Blah. 2000. 7.95 (*0-7407-0492-3*) Andrews & McMeel.

— Hey, Girl! 2000. 7.95 (*0-7407-0493-1*) Andrews & McMeel.

***Mikwright Ltd., Staff.** Big, Bigger, Just Right. (Illus.). 2000. 10.95 (*0-7407-0692-6*) Andrews & McMeel.

— Say No More. 2000. 10.95 (*0-7407-0693-4*) Andrews & McMeel.

Mila, R. L., tr. see Aristophanes.

Milacic, V. R. & McWaters, J. F. Diagnostic & Preventive Maintenance Strategies in Manufacturing Systems. 252p. 1988. 90.00 (*0-444-70382-9*, North Holland) Elsevier.

Miladinovic, Tomislav. Woerterbuch der Elektrotechnik und Elektronik: German & Russian Dictionary of Electronics & Electrical Engineering. (GER & RUS.). 1970. 175.00 (*0-8288-6561-2*, M-7016) Fr & Eur.

Milady. Standard System of Salon Skills. 2nd abr. rev. ed. 688p. 1998. text, teacher ed. 100.00 (*1-56253-399-1*) Milady Pub.

***Milady.** Texto General de Cosmetologia. 3rd ed. 1999. 58.95 (*1-56253-474-2*) Thomson Learn.

Milady Editors. Exam Reviews in Hair Structure & Chemistry. 1977. pap. 12.95 (*0-87350-135-7*) Milady Pub.

— Practical Beauty Culture Workbook. (Illus.). 1984. pap. 16.00 (*0-87350-378-3*) Milady Pub.

— Practical Beauty Culture Workbook. 2nd ed. (Illus.). 1988. pap., teacher ed. 23.95 (*0-87350-351-1*) Milady Pub.

— Standard Textbook of Professional Barber Styling. 1983. text 34.50 (*0-87350-501-8*) Milady Pub.

— Teacher Training System. (Massage Ser). 2000. pap. text 52.75 (*1-56253-582-X*) Thomson Learn.

***Milady Editors.** Texto General De Cosm. 3rd ed. (SPA.). 2000. pap. 19.50 (*1-56253-705-9*) Milady Pub.

Milady Editors. Texto General de Cosmetologia. (SPA.). 1989. pap., student ed. 6.50 (*0-87350-879-3*) Milady Pub.

— Van Dean Manual. rev. ed. (Illus.). 1990. text 36.95 (*0-87350-516-6*) Milady Pub.

— Van Dean Practical Workbook. (Illus.). 1990. teacher ed. 30.95 (*0-87350-524-7*); pap. 22.95 (*0-87350-518-2*) Milady Pub.

— Van Dean Theory Workbook. (Illus.). 1990. teacher ed. 26.95 (*0-87350-523-9*); pap. 22.95 (*0-87350-519-0*) Milady Pub.

— Workbook for Professional Barber Styling. 1984. teacher ed. 26.95 (*0-87350-500-X*) Milady Pub.

— Workbook for Professional Barber Styling. 1990. pap. 17.95 (*0-87350-503-4*) Milady Pub.

Milady Inc. Staff. Nail Technology: Answer Key. 3rd ed. (Cosmetology Ser.). 1992. pap., teacher ed., wbk. ed. 26.95 (*1-56253-091-7*) Milady Pub.

— Van Dean Manual. (Cosmetology Ser.). 1987. text 36.95 (*0-87350-368-6*) Milady Pub.

— Van Dean Practical: Answer Key. (Cosmetology Ser.). 1975. wbk. ed. 26.95 (*0-87350-064-4*, VNR) Wiley.

— Van Dean Review Questions & Answers. (Cosmetology Ser.). 1990. pap. 2.50 (*0-87350-296-5*, VNR) Wiley.

— Van Dean Theory. (Cosmetology Ser.). 1975. wbk. ed. 15.50 (*0-87350-358-9*, VNR) Wiley.

— Van Dean Theory: Answer Key. (Cosmetology Ser.). 1975. wbk. ed. 34.84 (*0-87350-065-2*, VNR) Wiley.

Milady Inc. Staff & Lewis, Donna. 1998-1999 Guide to Cosmetology Licensing. 192p. pap. 50.00 (*1-56253-446-7*, Pub. by Delmar) Thomson Learn.

Milady Publishing Company Staff. Salonovations Cosmetology Dictionary. 2nd rev. ed. LC 94-23230. (Career Development Ser.). 512p. 1995. pap. 14.95 (*1-56253-214-6*) Thomson Learn.

***Milady Publishing Co. Staff.** Standard Exam Review. 166p. 1999. 18.95 (*1-56253-472-6*) Milady Pub.

— Standard Practical Workbook. 316p. 1999. wbk. ed. 25.95 (*1-56253-469-6*) Thomson Learn.

— Standard Textbook of Cosmetology. 704p. 1999. pap. 51.95 (*1-56253-467-X*) Milady Pub.

— Standard Theory Workbook. 176p. 1999. pap., wbk. ed. 25.95 (*1-56253-468-8*) Thomson Learn.

Milady Publishing Company Staff. Answers to Milady's Professional Barber-Styling Workbook. 2nd rev. ed. 193p. 1992. 29.95 (*1-56253-147-6*) Milady Pub.

— Answers to Milady's Workbook for Hair Structure & Chemistry Simplified. 2nd rev. ed. 86p. 1993. 28.50 (*1-56253-152-2*) Milady Pub.

— Art & Science Nail Tech Workbook. 2nd ed. (NAILS). 1997. pap., wbk. ed. 20.75 (*1-56253-327-4*) Thomson Learn.

— Art & Science of Nail Technology. 3rd ed. (Nails Ser.). 1992. text 31.45 (*1-56253-117-4*) Milady Pub.

— Art & Science of Nail Technology. 3rd ed. (Cosmetology Ser.). 1992. pap., wbk. ed. 17.95 (*1-56253-090-9*, VNR) Wiley.

— Art & Science of Nail Technology Course Management. 3rd ed. (Cosmetology Ser.). 1992. 43.95 (*1-56253-092-5*, VNR) Wiley.

— Art/Science Nail: Tech-Spanish Exam Review. (NAILS). (SPA.). 65p. 1993. pap. 14.50 (*1-56253-181-6*) Thomson Learn.

— Art/Science Nail Tech. 2nd ed. LC 96-35281. (NAILS). 1997. 46.95 (*1-56253-326-6*) Thomson Learn.

— Clairol Professional 28 Black Styles & Hair Color Tips. LC 95-30578. (Cosmetology Ser.). 1996. pap. 4.50 (*1-56253-323-1*) Milady Pub.

— Cosmetology State Board Exam Review. (Standard Texts of Cosmetology Ser.). 1988. pap. 18.25 (*0-87350-365-1*, VNR) Wiley.

— Electrology Curriculum Guide. (Cosmetology Ser.). 1988. 2.50 (*0-87350-750-9*, VNR) Wiley.

— Hair Structure & Chemistry: Lectures & LP. 2nd ed. (Cosmetology Ser.). 1993. 59.95 (*1-56253-150-6*, VNR) Wiley.

— Hair Structure & Chemistry: Simple Workbook. 2nd rev. ed. (HAIR). 86p. 1993. 21.60 (*1-56253-151-4*) Thomson Learn.

— Hair Structure & Chemistry Exam Review. 2nd ed. Morehouse, Jayne, ed. 55p. 1993. pap. 13.50 (*1-56253-153-0*) Milady Pub.

— Lesson Plans to Accompany Milady's Standard Textbook of Cosmetology. 404p. 1995. text, teacher ed. 49.95 (*1-56253-234-0*) Milady Pub.

— Marinello Haircutting Manual. (Cosmetology Ser.). 1969. pap. 23.50 (*0-87350-486-0*, VNR) Wiley.

— Milady's Art & Science of Nail Technology. (SPA.). 224p. 1994. pap. 32.45 (*1-56253-156-5*) Milady Pub.

— Milady's Flash Cosmetology Dictionary. 1996. 19.95 (*1-56253-372-X*) Milady Pub.

— Milady's Standard Textbook of Cosmetology. LC 99-19654. 716p. 1999. 57.95 (*1-56253-466-1*) Thomson Learn.

— Milady's Standard Textbook of Cosmetology: Practical Workbook-Answer Key. rev. ed. 273p. 1995. text, teacher ed. 28.00 (*1-56253-219-7*) Milady Pub.

— Milady's Standard Textbook of Cosmetology: Theory Workbook-Answer Key. rev. ed. 130p. 1995. text, teacher ed. 29.95 (*1-56253-221-9*) Milady Pub.

— Milady's Standard Textbook of Cosmetology, 1991. 1980. pap. 13.50 (*1-56253-018-6*) Delmar.

— Milady's Standard Textbook of Cosmetology, 1991. 544p. 1991. student ed. 26.95 (*1-56253-008-9*) Delmar.

— Milady's Standard Textbook of Cosmetology, 1991. 544p. 1991. pap. 32.45 (*1-56253-003-8*) Delmar.

— Milady's Standard Textbook of Cosmetology, 1991. 544p. 1991. pap. 12.50 (*1-56253-059-3*) Delmar.

— Milady's Standard Textbook of Cosmetology, 1991. 1982. VHS 160.00 (*0-87350-659-6*) Milady Pub.

— Milady's Standard Textbook of Cosmetology, 1991. 1991. pap. 15.95 (*0-87350-443-7*) Milady Pub.

— Milady's Standard Textbook of Cosmetology, 1991. 2nd ed. 1991. pap. 1.00 (*1-56253-004-6*) Delmar.

— Milady's Standard Textbook of Cosmetology, 1991. 2nd ed. 544p. 1991. text 35.45 (*1-56253-001-1*) Delmar.

— Practical Beauty Culture, No. I. (Standard Texts of Cosmetology Ser.). (SPA.). 1990. pap. 24.95 (*0-87350-384-8*, VNR) Wiley.

— Revision Del Examen De Estado De Cosmetologia - State Exam Review for Cosmetology. (SPA.). 1992. pap., student ed. 14.95 (*1-56253-099-2*) Milady Pub.

— Salonovations Encyclopedia. (Cosmetology Ser.). Date not set. text 49.95 (*1-56253-364-9*) Milady Pub.

— Smart Tutor/Smart Tester. (Standard Texts of Cosmetology Ser.). 1989. teacher ed. 10.00 (*0-87350-806-8*, VNR) Wiley.

— Spanish Language Glossary - Cosmetology. (Career Development Ser.). (SPA.). 1985. pap. 13.95 (*0-87350-414-3*) Thomson Learn.

— Standard Perm Waving Manual. (Cosmetology Ser.). 1997. pap. text 18.95 (*1-56253-365-7*) Milady Pub.

— Standard Practical Workbook. 91st ed. (Standard Texts of Cosmetology Ser.). 1991. pap. 20.25 (*1-56253-007-0*) Delmar.

— Standard Test Bank. (Standard Texts of Cosmetology Ser.). 1993. 49.95 (*1-56253-202-2*, VNR) Wiley.

— Standard Textbook for Professional Barber-Styling: Lesson Plans. rev. ed. 184p. 1993. 49.95 (*1-56253-163-8*) Milady Pub.

— Standard Textbook of Cosmetology. 9th deluxe ed. (Standard Texts of Cosmetology Ser.). 1992. text 41.95 (*1-56253-173-5*) Milady Pub.

— State Exam Review for Nail Technology. 63p. 1993. pap. 13.50 (*1-56253-170-0*) Milady Pub.

— Std Practical Workbook 95 Ed. rev. ed. (STANDARD TEXTS OF COSMETOLOGY). 273p. 1994. pap. 20.75 (*1-56253-218-9*) Thomson Learn.

— Std Theory Workbook. rev. ed. (STANDARD TEXTS OF COSMETOLOGY). 130p. 1994. pap. 20.75 (*1-56253-220-0*) Thomson Learn.

— Std Txt Prof Barber Styl-Exam Review 2e. 2nd rev. ed. (HAIR). 152p. 1993. pap. text 13.50 (*1-56253-144-1*) Thomson Learn.

— Std Txtbk Cosmetology Exam Rev 95 Ed. (STANDARD TEXTS OF COSMETOLOGY). 126p. 1994. pap. 15.25 (*1-56253-237-5*) Thomson Learn.

— Student Aptitude Test: Barber. (Cosmetology Ser.). 1983. pap. 6.50 (*0-87350-867-X*, VNR) Wiley.

— Student Aptitude Test: Cosmetology. (Cosmetology Ser.). 1973. pap. 6.50 (*0-87350-878-5*, VNR) Wiley.

— Student Recruitment/Retention Pocket Guide. (Cosmetology Ser.). 1988. pap. 9.95 (*0-87350-448-8*, VNR) Wiley.

— Successful Salon Management. (Cosmetology Ser.). 1975. 34.50 (*0-87350-067-9*, VNR) Wiley.

— Texto General De Cosm-Exam Rev 96. (STANDARD TEXTS OF COSMETOLOGY). (SPA.). 144p. 1995. pap., student ed. 18.50 (*1-56253-256-1*) Thomson Learn.

— Texto General de Cosm-Practical Workbook. 2nd ed. (STANDARD TEXTS OF COSMETOLOGY). (SPA.). 288p. 1995. pap. 21.50 (*1-56253-257-X*) Milady Pub.

— Texto General De Cosmetologia. 2nd ed. LC 95-2982. (STANDARD TEXTS OF COSMETOLOGY). (ENG & SPA.). 656p. 1995. pap. 46.50 (*1-56253-254-5*) Thomson Learn.

— Texto General de Cosmetologia, Respuestas a las

M

Preguntas de Repaso.Tr. of Milady's Standard Textbook of Cosmetology. (SPA.). 19p. 1993. pap., teacher ed. write for info. (*1-56253-143-3*) Milady Pub.

— Texto General de Cosmetologia: Answers Practical. (SPA.). 288p. 1996. teacher ed. 29.95 (*1-56253-258-8*) Milady Pub.

— Texto General de Cosmetologia: Answers to Theory Workbook. (SPA.). 144p. 1996. 29.95 (*1-56253-260-X*) Milady Pub.

— Texto General de Cosmetology 96: Theory. 2nd rev. ed. (STANDARD TEXTS OF COSMETOLOGY). (SPA.). 144p. 1995. pap. 21.50 (*1-56253-259-6*) Milady Pub.

— Van Dean Lesson Plans. rev. ed. (Cosmetology Ser.). 1991. pap. 51.95 (*0-87350-520-4*, VNR) Wiley.

Milady Publishing Company Staff, jt. auth. see Howe.

Milady Publishing Company Staff, jt. auth. see Janssen, Marybeth.

Milady Publishing Company Staff, jt. auth. see Sheahan, Maura.

Milady Publishing Company Staff, jt. auth. see Wurdinger, Victoria.

***Milady Publishing Staff.** Cosmetology. (Illus.). 1999. 65.21 (*1-56253-461-0*) Milady Pub.

Milady Publishing Staff. Standard System Salon Skills: Hairdressing. LC 98-7543. (Hair Ser.). 1998. pap. 56.25 (*1-56253-398-3*) Thomson Learn.

Milady Staff. Answers to Milady's Professional Barber-Styling Workbook. 3rd ed. (Cosmetology Ser.). 240p. 1998. student ed., wbk. ed. 49.95 (*1-56253-368-1*) Milady Pub.

— Lesson Plans for Milady's Professional Barber-Styling. 3rd ed. (Cosmetology Ser.). 216p. (C). 1998. student ed. 74.95 (*1-56253-369-X*) Milady Pub.

***Milady Staff.** Milady's Cosmetology Dictionary. 3rd ed. 2001. pap. 14.50 (*1-56253-667-2*) Milady Pub.

Milady Staff. Std Prof Barber Styling-Exam Review. 3rd ed. LC 98-219608. (HAIR). 200p. (C). 1998. suppl. ed. 18.95 (*1-56253-370-3*) Thomson Learn.

— Std Prof Barber Styling Wkbk. 3rd ed. (HAIR). 240p. 1998. wbk. ed. 25.95 (*1-56253-367-3*) Thomson Learn.

***Milady Staff.** Texto General De Cosm. 3rd ed. (SPA.). 2000. pap., wbk. ed. 19.50 (*1-56253-706-7*) Milady Pub.

Milakovich, Michael E. Improving Service Quality: Achieving High Performance in the Public & Private Sectors. LC 94-46379. 280p. 1995. boxed set 54.95 (*1-884015-45-X*) St Lucie Pr.

— Public Administration in America. 5th ed. 1995. pap. text, teacher ed. 5.00 (*0-312-11992-5*) St Martin.

Milakovich, Michael E., jt. auth. see Humphrey, John A.

Milam, D., et al, eds. 17th Heat Treating Society Conference Proceedings Including the 1st International Induction Heat Treating Symposium. (Illus.). 1400p. 1997. 197.00 (*0-87170-610-5*, 6634) ASM.

Milam, Douglas F., jt. ed. see Smith, Joseph A., Jr.

Milam, Edward E. & Crumbley, D. Larry. Estate Planning, after the 1976 Tax Reform Act. LC 78-970. 240p. reprint ed. pap. 74.40 (*0-608-12133-9*, 202389600034) Bks Demand.

Milam, Edward E., jt. auth. see Crumbley, D. L.

Milam, Edward E., jt. auth. see Crumbley, D. Larry.

Milam, Erin E., jt. auth. see Potter, Melody M.

Milam, James R. & Ketcham, Katherine. Under the Influence: A Guide to the Myths & Realities of Alcoholism. 256p. 1984. mass mkt. 6.99 (*0-553-27487-2*) Bantam.

Milam, June M. Big Decisions. Gilmer, Chris & Nelson, Laura L., eds. (Drugless Douglass Tales Ser.). (Illus.). 20p. (J). (ps-k). 1994. pap. text 32.95 (*1-884307-15-9*); pap. text, student ed. 6.95 (*1-884307-16-7*) Dev Res Educ.

— Big Decisions. Daley, Charlotte C., ed. Miranda, Carmen, tr. (Drugless Douglass Tales Ser.). (SPA., Illus.). 24p. (Orig.). (J). (ps). 1997. pap. 32.95 (*1-884307-34-5*); pap. 6.95 (*1-884307-35-3*) Dev Res Educ.

— Flying Around. Nelson, Laura L. & Gilmer, Chris, eds. (Drugless Douglass Tales Ser.). (Illus.). 20p. (J). (ps-k). 1994. pap. text 32.95 (*1-884307-17-5*); pap. text, student ed. 6.95 (*1-884307-18-3*) Dev Res Educ.

— Flying Around. Daley, Charlotte C., ed. Miranda, Carmen, tr. (Drugless Douglass Tales Ser.). (SPA., Illus.). 24p. (Orig.). (J). (ps). 1997. pap. 32.95 (*1-884307-36-1*); pap. 6.95 (*1-884307-37-X*) Dev Res Educ.

— I've Got an Idea. Gilmer, Chris, ed. (Drugless Douglass Tales Ser.). (Illus.). 20p. (J). (ps). 1994. pap. text 32.95 (*1-884307-07-8*); student ed. 6.95 (*1-884307-08-6*) Dev Res Educ.

— I've Got an Idea! Daley, Charlotte C., ed. Miranda, Carmen, tr. (Drugless Douglass Tales Ser.). (SPA., Illus.). 24p. (Orig.). (J). (ps). 1997. pap. 32.95 (*1-884307-26-4*); pap., student ed. 6.95 (*1-884307-27-2*) Dev Res Educ.

— Just a Little Lie. Daley, Charlotte C., ed. Miranda, Carmen, tr. (Drugless Douglass Tales Ser.). (SPA., Illus.). 24p. (Orig.). (J). (ps). 1997. pap. 32.95 (*1-884307-22-1*); pap., student ed. 6.95 (*1-884307-23-X*) Dev Res Educ.

— Rainy Days. Gilmer, Chris & Peaster, Laura L., eds. (Drugless Douglass Tales Ser.). (Illus.). 20p. (Orig.). (J). (ps). 1994. student ed. 6.95 (*1-884307-12-4*); pap. 32.95 (*1-884307-11-6*) Dev Res Educ.

— Rainy Days. Daley, Charlotte C., ed. Miranda, Carmen, tr. (Drugless Douglass Tales Ser.). (SPA., Illus.). 24p. (Orig.). (J). (ps). 1997. pap. 32.95 (*1-884307-30-2*); pap. 6.95 (*1-884307-31-0*) Dev Res Educ.

— The Short Cut. Gilmer, Chris, ed. (Drugless Douglass Tales Ser.). (Illus.). 20p. (J). (ps). 1994. pap. text 32.95 (*1-884307-05-1*); student ed. 6.95 (*1-884307-06-X*) Dev Res Educ.

— The Short Cut. Daley, Charlotte C., ed. Miranda, Carmen, tr. (Drugless Douglass Tales Ser.). (SPA., Illus.). 24p. (J). (ps). 1997. pap. 32.95 (*1-884307-24-8*); pap., student ed. 6.95 (*1-884307-25-6*) Dev Res Educ.

— A Terrible Thing. Nelson, Laura L. & Gilmer, Chris, eds. (Drugless Douglass Tales Ser.). (Illus.). 20p. (J). (ps-k). 1994. pap. text 32.95 (*1-884307-13-2*) Dev Res Educ.

— A Terrible Thing. Daley, Charlotte C., ed. Miranda, Carmen, tr. (Drugless Douglass Tales Ser.). (SPA., Illus.). 24p. (Orig.). (J). (ps). 1997. pap. 32.95 (*1-884307-32-9*); pap. 6.95 (*1-884307-33-7*) Dev Res Educ.

Milam, June M. & Gaston, Kathy. All by Myself. Gilmer, Chris & Wilson, Amy L., eds. (Drugless Douglass Tales Ser.). (Illus.). 24p. (Orig.). (J). (ps). 1993. pap. text 32.95 (*1-884307-00-0*); student ed. 6.95 (*1-884307-01-9*) Dev Res Educ.

Milam, June M., et al. Create-a-Book. Daley, Charlotte C., ed. (Drugless Douglass Tales Ser.). (Illus.). 39p. (Orig.). (J). (ps). 1997. pap., wbk. ed. 4.95 (*1-884307-19-1*) Dev Res Educ.

Milam, June M., jt. auth. see Gilmer, Chris.

Milam, Lorenzo W. Cripple Liberation Front Marching Band Blues. 222p. 1992. 14.95 (*0-917320-10-7*); pap. 9.95 (*0-917320-09-3*) Mho & Mho.

— CripZen: A Manual for Survival. 254p. 1993. 17.95 (*0-917320-02-6*); pap. 12.95 (*0-917320-03-4*) Mho & Mho.

— The Radio Papers: From KRAB to KCHU-Essays on the Art & Practice of Radio Transmission. (Twenty-Five Years of Community Broadcasting Ser.). (Illus.). 224p. 1986. pap. 9.95 (*0-917320-19-0*) Mho & Mho.

— Sex & Broadcasting: A Handbook on Building a Radio Station for the Community. (Illus.). 375p. 1988. pap. 12.95 (*0-917320-01-8*) Mho & Mho.

Milam, Lorenzo W., jt. auth. see Gallant, Jonathan.

Milam, Mary A. Right Side Up. 239p. (Orig.). 1991. pap. 5.95 (*0-9631187-0-6*) Marigold Pub.

— Right Side Up. 54p. (Orig.). 1994. pap. 3.95 (*0-9631187-1-4*) Marigold Pub.

***Milam, Mary Kay.** Meet Zippyr the Zebra-Key. 2nd ed. (Illus.). 24p. (J). (ps-k). 1999. reprint ed. pap. 15.95 (*1-58597-008-5*) Leathers Pub.

— The Waiting Place. (Illus.). 32p. (J). 2000. pap. 8.95 (*1-58597-027-1*) Leathers Pub.

— The Zooming Star Babies. Date not set. pap. write for info. (*1-890622-65-6*) Leathers Pub.

Milam, Melody J., jt. auth. see Harris, Jerry L.

Milamed, Susan, jt. auth. see Schwartz, Rosaline.

Milan. Develop Reading Skills. 4th ed. 1994. teacher ed. 10.93 (*0-07-041928-0*) McGraw.

Milan, A. B., tr. see Ardito, Stefano.

Milan, Albert R. Breast Self-Examination. LC 79-56529. (Illus.). 128p. 1980. pap. 3.50 (*0-89480-124-4*, 419) Workman Pub.

Milan, Anthony. Miracles Do Happen! Monthly Meditations for African Americans. rev. ed. 48p. 1994. pap. 6.95 (*0-913543-41-1*) African Am Imag.

Milan, Deanne K. Developing Reading Skills. 4th ed. LC 94-7827. 576p. (C). 1994. pap. 36.56 (*0-07-041914-0*) McGraw.

— Improving Reading Skills. 3rd ed. LC 95-14560. 512p. (C). 1995. pap. 35.94 (*0-07-041930-2*) McGraw.

Milan, Edward E., jt. auth. see Crumbley, D. Larry.

Milan, Garth, jt. auth. see Bales, Donnie.

Milan, Henrietta C., tr. see Levin, Rob, ed.

Milan, June M. Just a Little Lie. Gilwer, Chris, ed. (Drugless Douglass Tales Ser.). (Illus.). 20p. (J). (ps). 1993. pap. text 32.95 (*1-884307-03-5*); student ed. 6.95 (*1-884307-04-3*) Dev Res Educ.

Milan, June M., et al. All by Myself. Daley, Charlotte C., ed. Miranda, Carmen, tr. (Drugless Douglass Tales Ser.). (SPA., Illus.). 24p. (Orig.). (J). (ps). 1997. pap. 32.95 (*1-884307-20-5*); pap., student ed. 6.95 (*1-884307-21-3*) Dev Res Educ.

Milan, Luys. Libro de Musica de Vihuela de Mano Intitulado el Maestro. (Publikationen Alterer Musik Ser.: No. II). xxx, 382p. 1976. reprint ed. write for info. (*3-487-00629-4*) G Olms Pubs.

Milan, Michael A., jt. auth. see Ayllon, Teodoro.

Milan-Spears, Deanne. Developing Critical Reading Skills. 5th ed. LC 97-43782. 640p. 1998. pap. 36.56 (*0-07-041960-4*) McGraw.

Milan, Tony B. Cuentos de un Continente Invisible. LC 96-86112. (SPA.). 103p. 1996. pap. 7.95 (*0-9642290-1-3*) Fly Machine.

— Tales from an Invisible Continent. LC 94-72513. 110p. (Orig.). 1994. pap. 8.95 (*0-9642290-0-5*) Fly Machine.

Milan, Victor. Battletech 25. 1996. mass mkt. 6.99 (*0-451-45388-3*, ROC) NAL.

— Black Dragon. (Battletech Ser.: Vol. 29). 400p. 1996. mass mkt. 5.99 (*0-451-45528-2*, ROC) NAL.

— CLD (Collective Landing Detachment) 304p. 1995. mass mkt. 5.50 (*0-380-77734-7*, Avon Bks) Morrow Avon.

— CLD (Collective Landing Detachment) 1997. mass mkt. 5.99 (*0-380-78533-1*, Avon Bks) Morrow Avon.

— Dangerous Games. 1996. pap. 5.99 (*0-7869-0524-7*, Pub. by TSR Inc) Random.

— From the Depths. (Star Trek Ser.: No. 66). 288p. 1993. mass mkt. 5.50 (*0-671-86911-6*) PB.

— Hearts of Chaos. (Battletech Ser.: No. 26). 1996. mass mkt. 5.99 (*0-451-45523-1*, ROC) NAL.

— Red Sands. 416p. (Orig.). 1993. mass mkt. 4.99 (*0-446-35840-1*, Pub. by Warner Bks) Little.

— Sword Play. (Forgotten Realms Arcane Age Netheril Trilogy Ser.: Bk. 1). 1996. pap. 5.99 (*0-7869-0492-5*, Pub. by TSR Inc) Random.

— War in Tethyr. (The Nobles Ser.). 320p. (Orig.). 1995. pap. 5.99 (*0-7869-0184-5*, Pub. by TSR Inc) Random.

Milan, Victor & Snodgrass, Melinda M. Runespear. 288p. 1987. mass mkt. 3.50 (*0-445-20247-5*, Pub. by Warner Bks) Little.

Milan, Virginia E., jt. auth. see Meredith, Howard L.

Milanese, M., et al, eds. Robustness in Identification & Control. (Applied Information Technology Ser.). (Illus.). 350p. 1989. 85.00 (*0-306-43251-X*, Plenum Trade) Perseus Pubng.

Milanese, M., et al. Bounding Approaches to System Identification. LC 96-18485. (Illus.). 586p. (C). 1996. 162.00 (*0-306-45021-6*, Plenum Trade) Perseus Pubng.

Milanesi, Enza. Bulfinch Guide to Carpets: How to Identify, Classify, & Evaluate Antique Carpets & Rugs. (Illus.). 192p. 1993. 23.50 (*0-8212-2057-8*, Pub. by Bulfinch Pr) Little.

***Milanesi, Enza.** The Carpet: Origins, Art & History. DeChene, Charlotte, ed. Giammanco, Rosanna M., tr. (Illus.). 200p. 1999. text 50.00 (*1-55209-438-3*) Firefly Bks Ltd.

Milanesio, Antonion. An Inexplicable Image. 1996. pap. 39.95 (*0-85439-535-0*, Pub. by St Paul Pubns) St Mut.

Milani, A., et al, eds. Asteroids, Comets, & Meteors 1993: Proceedings of the 160th Symposium of the International Astronomical Union, Held in Belgirate, Italy, June 14-18, 1993. LC 94-16936. (International Astronomical Union Symposia Ser.). 503p. (C). 1994. lib. bdg. 176.50 (*0-7923-2880-9*) Kluwer Academic.

Milani, A., et al. Non-gravitational Perturbations & Satellite Geodesy. (Illus.). 136p. 1987. 92.00 (*0-85274-538-9*) IOP Pub.

Milani, Abbas. The Persian Sphinx: Amir-Abbas Hoveyda & the Riddle of the Iranian Revolution. (Illus.). 2000. 29.95 (*0-934211-61-2*) Mage Pubs Inc.

— Tales of Two Cities: A Persian Memoir. LC DS318.84 M55 1996. (Illus.). 264p. 1996. 24.95 (*0-934211-47-7*) Mage Pubs Inc.

— Tales of Two Cities: A Persian Memoir. LC 96-46049. (Illus.). 272p. 1997. reprint ed. pap. 15.00 (*1-56836-167-X*, Kodansha Globe) Kodansha.

Milani, Abbas, tr. see Irani, Manuchehr.

***Milani, Brian.** Designing the Green Economy: The Post-Industrial Alternative to Corporate Globalization. 256p. 2000. 65.00 (*0-8476-9189-6*); pap. 19.95 (*0-8476-9190-X*) Rowman.

Milani, Farzaneh. Veils & Words: The Emerging Voices of Iranian Women Writers. LC 91-28640. (Contemporary Issues in the Middle East Ser.). 320p. 1992. pap. 17.95 (*0-8156-0266-9*); text 39.95 (*0-8156-2557-X*) Syracuse U Pr.

Milani, Farzaneh, tr. see Behbahani, Simin.

Milani, Michael. It Happens Every Morning. Blair, Kathryn, ed. (Illus.). 375p. 1996. 29.95 (*0-9648973-0-X*) Papas Pubng.

Milani, Mohsen M. The Making of Iran's Islamic Revolution: From Monarchy to Islamic Republic. 2nd ed. LC 94-14600. 268p. (C). 1994. pap. 29.00 (*0-8133-8476-1*, Pub. by Westview) HarpC.

Milani, Myrna. Catsmart. LC 97-26730. 432p. 1998. 19.95 (*0-8092-3024-0*, 302400, Contemporary Bks) NTC Contemp Pub Co.

— Dogsmart. LC 97-10646. 432p. 1997. 19.95 (*0-8092-3150-6*, 315060, Contemporary Bks) NTC Contemp Pub Co.

— Dogsmart. 400p. 1998. pap. 14.95 (*0-8092-2947-1*, 294710, Contemporary Bks) NTC Contemp Pub Co.

— Preparing for the Loss of Your Pet: The Complete Guide to Helping Your Family Accept the Inevitable. LC 98-38778. 356p. 1998. per. 15.95 (*0-7615-1648-4*) Prima Pub.

Milani, Myrna M. The Art of Veterinary Practice: A Guide to Client Communication. LC 94-40919. 294p. 1995. 29.95 (*0-8122-3260-7*) U of Pa Pr.

— Cats Body Language. 1993. pap. 13.00 (*0-688-12840-8*, Quil) HarperTrade.

— Dogs Body Language. 1993. pap. 12.00 (*0-688-12841-6*, Quil) HarperTrade.

Milani, Myrna M. & Smith, Brian R. A Primer of Rotational Physics. LC 84-13518. (Rational Physics Ser.). (Illus.). (Orig.). 1985. 15.00 (*0-943290-02-3*); pap. 10.00 (*0-943290-01-5*) Fainshaw Pr.

— Rotational Physics: The Principles of Energy. LC 85-16305. (Rational Physics Ser.). (Illus.). (Orig.). 1986. pap. 12.00 (*0-943290-03-1*) Fainshaw Pr.

Milani, Myrna M., jt. auth. see Smith, Brian R.

Milani, P. & Iannotta, S. Cluster Beam Synthesis of Nanostructured Materials. LC 98-52462. (Illus.). 200p. 1999. 89.95 (*3-540-64370-2*) Spr-Verlag.

Milani, Terrence E. & Johnston, J. William, eds. The College Union in the Year Two Thousand. LC 85-644751. (New Directions for Student Services Ser.: No. SS 58). 100p. 1992. pap. 22.00 (*1-55542-762-6*) Jossey-Bass.

Milanich, Jerald & Proctor, Samuel, eds. Tacachale: Essays on the Indians of Florida & Southwestern Georgia During the Historic Period. LC 77-20051. (Ripley P. Bullen Monographs in Anthropology & History Ser.: Vol. 1). 229p. 1978. reprint ed. pap. 71.00 (*0-608-04496-2*, 206524100001) Bks Demand.

Milanich, Jerald T. Archaeology of Pre-Columbian Florida. LC 93-36888. (Illus.). 496p. (C). 1994. 49.95 (*0-8130-1272-4*); pap. 24.95 (*0-8130-1273-2*) U Press Fla.

***Milanich, Jerald T.** Famous Florida Sites: Mount Royal & Crystal River. LC 98-52049. (Southeastern Classics in Archaeology, Anthropology, & History Ser.). 1999. 29.95 (*0-8130-1694-0*) U Press Fla.

Milanich, Jerald T. Florida Indians & the Invasion from Europe. (Illus.). 304p. 1998. reprint ed. pap. 19.95 (*0-8130-1636-3*) U Press Fla.

— Florida's Indians from Ancient Times to the Present. LC 97-45841. (Native People, Cultures & Places of the Southeastern United States Ser.). (Illus.). 224p. 1998. 39.95 (*0-8130-1598-7*); pap. 19.95 (*0-8130-1599-5*) U Press Fla.

— Laboring in the Fields of the Lord: Spanish Missions & Southeastern Indians. (Illus.). 208p. 1999. 26.95 (*1-56098-940-8*) Smithsonian.

— The Timucua. LC 95-40289. (Peoples of America Ser.). (Illus.). 256p. (C). 1996. 31.95 (*1-55786-488-8*) Blackwell Pubs.

***Milanich, Jerald T.** The Timucua. (Peoples of America Ser.). 256p. 1999. pap. 27.95 (*0-631-21864-5*) Blackwell Pubs.

Milanich, Jerald T., ed. Earliest Hispanic - Native American Interactions in the American Southeast. LC 91-17734. (Spanish Borderlands Sourcebooks Ser.: Vol. 12). 528p. 1991. text 30.00 (*0-8240-1951-2*) Garland.

— The Hernando de Soto Expedition. LC 90-29269. (Spanish Borderlands Sourcebooks Ser.: Vol. 11). 496p. 1991. text 25.00 (*0-8240-1950-4*) Garland.

Milanich, Jerald T. & Hudson, Charles. Hernando de Soto & the Indians of Florida. LC 92-22868. (Columbus Quincentenary Series - Ripley P. Bullen). (Illus.). 312p. 1993. 39.95 (*0-8130-1170-1*) U Press Fla.

Milanich, Jerald T. & Milbrath, Susan, eds. First Encounters: Spanish Explorations in the Caribbean & the United States, 1492-1570. (Ripley P. Bullen Monographs: No. 9). (Illus.). 232p. 1989. 49.95 (*0-8130-0946-4*); pap. 24.95 (*0-8130-0947-2*) U Press Fla.

Milanich, Jerald T. & Proctor, Samuel, eds. Tacachale: Essays on the Indians of Florida & Southeastern Georgia During the Historic Period. LC 94-6039. (Ripley P. Bullen Monographs). 232p. 1994. pap. 18.95 (*0-8130-1297-X*) U Press Fla.

Milanich, Jerald T., et al. Archaeology of Northern Florida A.D. 200-900: The McKeithen Weeden Island Culture. LC 97-12249. (Illus.). 224p. 1997. pap. 29.95 (*0-8130-1538-3*) U Press Fla.

Milano, Camelo A., jt. auth. see Clary, Bryan M.

Milano, Carol. Hers: The Wise Woman's Guide to Starting a Business on 2,000 Dollars or Less. LC 91-71885. 208p. (Orig.). 1991. pap. 14.95 (*0-9607118-7-2*) Allworth Pr.

— Hers: The Wise Woman's Guide to Starting a Business on $2,000 or Less. 2nd rev. ed. LC 96-79672. 192p. 1997. pap. text 16.95 (*1-880559-67-6*) Allworth Pr.

Milano, Dominic, ed. Synthesizer Programming. (Keyboard Magazine Synthesizer Library). (Illus.). 120p. (Orig.). 1987. pap. 14.95 (*0-88188-550-9*, HL00183703) H Leonard.

Milano, Duane R., jt. auth. see Research & Education Association Staff.

Milano, Geraldine B., jt. auth. see Mayott, Clarence W.

Milano, James V. & Brogan, Patrick. Soldiers, Spies, & the Rat Line: America's Undeclared War Against the Soviets. 264p. 1995. 23.95 (*1-57488-050-0*) Brasseys.

***Milano, James V. & Brogran, Patrick.** Soldiers, Spies & the Rat Line. 2000. reprint ed. pap. 17.95 (*1-57488-304-6*) Brasseys.

Milano, L. Mozan No. 2: The Epigraphic Finds of the Sixth Season. (Mesopotamian Studies: No. 5-1). (Illus.). 34p. (C). 1991. pap. text 9.00 (*0-89003-276-9*) Undena Pubns.

Milano, Michael & Ullius, Diane. Designing Powerful Training: The Sequential-Iterative Model. LC 97-49624. (Illus.). 340p. 1998. 49.95 (*0-7879-0966-1*) Jossey-Bass.

***Milano, Phillip J. & Lane, Larry.** Why Do White People Smell Like Wet Dogs When They Come Out of the Rain? And Other Questions Worth a Smack on the Head from Mom. LC 99-91353. 210p. 1999. pap. 9.95 (*0-9675971-0-2*) Y Forum.

***Milano, Randy.** Learn Piano & Organ Chords in Only One Minute! LC 98-92323. (Illus.). 2000. pap. 21.95 (*0-9679989-0-5*) Empire Pubng Grp.

***Milano, Sam.** Maestro. (Nexus Ser.). 2000. mass mkt. 10.95 (*0-352-33511-4*) Virgin Bks.

Milano, Susan Murphy. Defending Our Lives: Protecting Yourself from Stalking & Domestic Violence. 1995. 18.95 (*1-879360-41-1*) Noble Pr.

***Milano, Valerie.** Gwyneth Paltrow. (Illus.). 220p. 2000. pap. 16.95 (*1-55022-407-7*, Pub. by ECW) LPC InBook.

Milanova, D. Swedish-Russian Dictionary. (RUS & SWE.). 760p. 1973. 59.95 (*0-8288-6331-8*, M-9077) Fr & Eur.

Milanovic, Branko. Income, Inequality, & Poverty During the Transition from Planned to Market Economy. LC 97-32776. (Regional & Sectoral Studies). 256p. 1998. pap. 30.00 (*0-8213-3994-X*, 13994) World Bank.

— Liberalization & Entrepreneurship: Dynamics of Reform in Socialism & Capitalism. LC 89-4196. 200p. (gr. 13). 1989. text 79.95 (*0-87332-568-0*) M E Sharpe.

Milanovic, Branko, jt. ed. see Hillman, Arye L.

Milanovic, Michael. Studies in Language Testing 3: Performance Testing, Cognition & Assessment. (Studies in Language Testing). 313p. 1996. text 64.95 (*0-521-48169-4*) Cambridge U Pr.

Milanovic, Petar J. Karst Hydrogeology. LC 80-54287. 1981. 40.00 (*0-918334-36-5*) WRP.

Milanovich, Norma. Modeling Equitable Behavior in the Classroom: Training Module V. (Illus.). 53p. 1995. pap. text 8.50 (*1-878550-14-4*) Inter Dev Res Assn.

Milanovich, Norma J. & McCune, Shirley. The Light Shall Set You Free. Date not set. wbk. ed. write for info. (*0-9627417-1-X*) Athena NM.

— The Light Shall Set You Free. LC 94-78618. 1996. pap. 17.95 (*0-9627417-7-9*) Athena NM.

Milanowski, Stephen & Tarte, Bob. Duplicity. LC 91-65127. (Illus.). 42p. 1992. 22.95 (*0-942159-11-X*) U of Wash Pr.

Milarch, Christopher G. Day by Day in Advent: Devotions for the Season. LC 90-29126. (Illus.). 48p. (Orig.). 1991. pap. 5.99 (*0-8066-2556-2*, 10-25562) Augsburg Fortress.

Milard, A. & Chisholm, J. Early Civilizations. (Illustrated World History Ser.). (Illus.). 96p. (YA). (gr. 6 up). 1992. pap. 12.95 (*0-7460-0328-5*) EDC.

An Asterisk (*) at the beginning of an entry indicates that the title is appearing for the first time.

— Early Civilizations. (Illustrated World History Ser.). (Illus.). 194p. (YA). (gr. 6 up). 1999. lib. bdg. 20.95 (*0-88110-438-8*) EDC.

***Milardo, Robert M.** Families as Relationships. 2000. pap. write for info. (*0-471-49152-7*) Wiley.

Milardo, Robert M., ed. Families & Social Networks. LC 87-20462. (New Perspectives on Family Ser.). 237p. reprint ed. pap. 73.50 (*0-7837-6595-9*, 204616000011) Bks Demand.

Milarepa. Drinking the Mountain Stream: Songs of Tibet's Beloved Saint, Milarepa. Rinpoche, Kunga & Cutillo, Brian, trs. from TIB. LC 93-35945. (Illus.). 192p. 1995. reprint ed. pap. 14.95 (*0-86171-063-0*) Wisdom MA.

***Milarn, Don, Jr.** The Lost Passions of Jesus. 2000. pap. 11.99 (*0-9677402-0-7*, Pub. by Mercy Place) Destiny Image.

Milas, Gene H. Teambuilding & Total Quality: A Guidebook to TQM Success. LC 97-13900. (Illus.). 240p. 1997. 29.95 (*0-89806-173-3*, MILTQM) Eng Mgmt Pr.

Milavec, Aaron. Exploring Scriptural Sources: Rediscovered Discipleship. LC 94-25512. 224p. (Orig.). 1994. pap. 19.95 (*1-55612-706-5*) Sheed & Ward WI.

— A Pilgrim Experiences the World's Religions. LC 84-9024. (Mellen Lives Ser.: Vol. 1). 96p. 1984. pap. 34.95 (*0-88946-010-8*) E Mellen.

— To Empower As Jesus Did: Acquiring Spiritual Power through Apprenticeship. LC 82-6466. (Toronto Studies in Theology: Vol. 9). 345p. (C). 1982. lib. bdg. 99.95 (*0-88946-966-0*) E Mellen.

Milazzo, Dino. Getting the Most Out of Your VCR & Planning Your Home Entertainment System. (Illus.). 192p. (Orig.). 1992. pap. 12.95 (*0-9633138-3-5*) Inamar.

Milazzo, G., et al, eds. Bioelectrochemistry of Cells & Tissues. LC 95-8558. (Biochemistry Ser.: Vol. 2). 1996. 178.00 (*0-8176-5085-7*) Birkhauser.

Milazzo, G. & Blank, Martin, eds. Bioelectrochemistry 3: Charge Separation Across Biomembranes. (Ettore Majorana International Science Ser., Life Sciences: Vol. 51). (Illus.). 348p. (C). 1990. text 126.00 (*0-306-43606-X*, Kluwer Plenum) Kluwer Academic.

Milazzo, G., ed. see Blank, Martin.

Milazzo, G., jt. ed. see Brabec, V.

Milazzo, G., jt. ed. see Graver, P.

Milazzo, Giulio, ed. Topics in Bioelectrochemistry & Bioenergetics, 2 vols., 4. LC 76-18231. 356p. reprint ed. pap. 101.50 (*0-608-17588-9*, 2030431) Bks Demand.

— Topics in Bioelectrochemistry & Bioenergetics, 2 vols., 5. LC 76-18231. 319p. 1983. reprint ed. pap. 98.90 (*0-608-08512-X*, 203043100005) Bks Demand.

Milazzo, Giulio, jt. auth. see Lenaz, Giorgio.

Milazzo, Guilio & Caroli, Sergio. Tables of Standard Electrode Potentials. LC 77-8111. 437p. reprint ed. pap. 135.50 (*0-608-17691-5*, 203041100069) Bks Demand.

Milazzo, Guilio, jt. auth. see Graber, Peter.

Milazzo, Lee, ed. Conversations with Joyce Carol Oates. LC 89-16673. (Literary Conversations Ser.). 144p. 1989. text 39.50 (*0-87805-411-1*) U Pr of Miss.

Milazzo, Matteo. Subsidies in World Fisheries: A Reexamination. LC 98-16921. (Technical Paper Ser.: No. 406). 98p. 1998. pap. 22.00 (*0-8213-4216-9*, 14216) World Bank.

Milazzo, Matteo J. The Chetnik Movement & the Yugoslav Resistance. LC 74-24383. 219p. reprint ed. pap. 67.90 (*0-7837-2187-0*, 204252500004) Bks Demand.

Milazzo, Richard, ed. Beauty & Critique. LC 82-50165. 176p. (Orig.). 1983. pap. text 8.00 (*0-939858-01-0*) T S L Pr.

Milazzo, Richard, jt. auth. see Collins, Tricia.

Milazzo, Richard, ed. see Ball, Pam, et al.

Milazzo, Richard, ed. see Gillespie, Abraham L.

Milazzo, Richard, ed. see Marsicano, Ed.

***Milbank.** Customized Campaign. 2000. 25.00 (*0-465-04590-1*, Pub. by Basic) HarpC.

Milbank, Alison. Dante & the Victorians. LC 98-18296. (Illus.). 328p. 1998. text 79.95 (*0-7190-3700-X*, Pub. by Manchester Univ Pr) St Martin.

Milbank, Alison, ed. see Radcliffe, Ann.

Milbank, Caroline R. Couture: The Great Designers. LC 85-2827. (Illus.). 432p. 1997. reprint ed. 90.00 (*0-941434-51-6*) Stewart Tabori & Chang.

— New York Fashion: The Evolution of American Style. (Illus.). 304p. 1996. pap. text 29.95 (*0-8109-2647-4*, Pub. by Abrams) Time Warner.

Milbank, John. The Mercurial Wood: Sites, Tales, Qualities. LC 99-201828. xiv, 69p. 1998. pap. 15.95 (*3-7052-0113-1*, Pub. by Poetry Salzburg) Intl Spec Bk.

— The Religious Dimension in the Thought of Giambattista Vico, 1668-1744: Language, Law & History, Vol. 11. LC 91-32629. 292p. 1993. text 89.95 (*0-7734-9215-1*) E Mellen.

— The Religious Dimension in the Thought of Giambattista Vico, 1668-1744: The Early Metaphysics. LC 91-32629. (Studies in the History of Philosophy: Vol. 23). 364p. 1991. lib. bdg. 99.95 (*0-7734-9694-7*) E Mellen.

— Theology & Social Theory: Beyond Secular Reason. (Signposts in Theology Ser.). 448p. 1993. pap. text 31.95 (*0-631-18948-3*) Blackwell Pubs.

— The Word Made Strange: Theology, Language & Culture. LC 96-17201. 300p. (C). 1996. 66.95 (*0-631-20335-4*); pap. 30.95 (*0-631-20336-2*) Blackwell Pubs.

Milbank, John, et al, eds. Radical Orthodoxy: A New Theology. LC 98-19444. 277p. 1999. pap. 25.99 (*0-415-19699-X*, D6355) Routledge.

— Radical Orthodoxy: A New Theology. LC 98-19444. (Radical Orthodoxy Ser.). 288p. (C). (gr. 13). 1999. 75.00 (*0-415-19698-1*, D6351) Routledge.

Milbank Memorial Fund Staff, ed. The Milbank Memorial Fund at Ninety. LC 96-150103. 144p. (Orig.). 1995. pap. write for info. (*1-887748-02-4*) Milbank Memorial.

Milbank, Samuel L. & Fox, Daniel M., frwds. Enhancing the Accountability of Alternative Medicine. (Illus.). 44p. 1998. pap. write for info. (*1-887748-18-0*) Milbank Memorial.

— 1997 Robert H. Ebert Memorial Lecture. 32p. 1997. pap. write for info. (*1-887748-16-4*) Milbank Memorial.

Milbank, Tweed, Hadley & McCloy Law Firm Staff. Creditors Workout Strategies. 195.00 (*0-685-69622-7*, BBWR) Warren Gorham & Lamont.

Milbank, Tweed, Hadley & McCloy Staff. The Guide to Financing International Oil & Gas Projects. (Project Finance Strategy Reports). 1996. 225.00 (*1-85564-550-5*, Pub. by Euromoney) Am Educ Systs.

Milbauer. An Introduction to Geography. 1998. pap. text, student ed. write for info. (*0-13-923756-9*) P-H.

Milbauer, Asher Z. Transcending Exile: Conrad, Nabokov, I. B. Singer. LC 84-22104. 155p. 1985. 49.95 (*0-8130-0815-8*) U Press Fla.

Milberg, William, ed. The Megacorp & Macrodynamics: Essays in Memory of Alfred Eichner. LC 90-26733. 230p. (C). (gr. 13). 1992. text 75.95 (*0-87332-782-9*) M E Sharpe.

Milberg, William, ed. The Megacorp & Macrodynamics: Essays in Memory of Alfred Eichner. LC 90-26733. 230p. (C). (gr. 13). 1992. pap. text 40.95 (*0-87332-783-7*) M E Sharpe.

Milberg, William, jt. auth. see Heilbroner, Robert.

Milberg, William, jt. auth. see Heilbroner, Robert L.

Milberry, Larry & Halliday, Hugh. The Royal Canadian Air Force at War, 1939-1945. (Illus.). 480p. 1996. 65.00 (*0-921022-04-2*, Pub. by Vanwell Publ) Howell Pr VA.

Milbert, Jacques. Picturesque Itinerary of the Hudson River & Peripheral Parts of North America. LC 67-29606. (American Environmental Studies). 1971. reprint ed. 26.95 (*0-405-02678-1*) Ayer.

***Milbery, James F. & Greenwald, Richard E.** Making the Technical Sale: A Handbook for Technical Sales Professionals. 2000. pap. text 34.95 (*0-9662889-9-8*) Muska Lipman.

Milbourn, Evelyn, jt. auth. see Milbourn, Maurice.

Milbourn, Maurice. Understanding Miniature British Pottery & Porcelain, 1730 - the Present Day. (Illus.). 229p. 1995. 29.50 (*1-85149-237-2*) Antique Collect.

Milbourn, Maurice & Milbourn, Evelyn. Understanding Miniature British Pottery & Porcelain, 1730 - the Present Day. (Understanding Ser.). (Illus.). 184p. 1983. 29.50 (*0-907462-30-8*) Antique Collect.

***Milbourne, Anna.** Windows 98 for Beginners. (Usborne Computer Guides Ser.). (Illus.). 80p. (gr. 5-9). 2000. 18.95 (*1-58086-263-2*) EDC.

***Milbourne, Anna, ed.** Windows 98 for Beginners. (Computer Guides Ser.). (Illus.). 80p. (J). (gr. 5-9). 2000. pap. 10.95 (*0-7460-3638-8*, Pub. by Usbrne Pbng UK) EDC.

Milbourne, Christopher. Houdini. LC 97-48805. 224p. 1998. 14.99 (*0-517-18903-8*) Random Hse Value.

Milbourne, Luke. Notes on Dryden's Virgil (1698) LC 74-16036. (Life & Times of Seven Major British Writers Ser.). 232p. 1974. write for info. (*0-8240-1236-4*) Garland.

Milbourne, Paul, ed. Revealing Rural 'Others' Representation, Power & Identity in the British Countryside. LC 96-9773. (Rural Studies). (Illus.). 224p. 1997. 95.00 (*1-85567-424-6*) Bks Intl VA.

Milbrandt, Ben. EDI (Electronic Data Interchange) - Making Business More Efficient. LC 87-2669. 80p. (Orig.). (C). 1987. pap. 25.00 (*0-944952-00-3*) EDI in Busn.

Milbrath, Constance. Patterns of Artistic Development: Comparative Studies of Talent. LC 97-32148. (Illus.). 438p. (C). 1998. text 59.95 (*0-521-44313-X*) Cambridge U Pr.

Milbrath, Lester W. Environmentalists: Vanguard for a New Society. LC 83-24250. (SUNY Series in Environmental Public Policy). 180p. (C). 1985. text 59.50 (*0-87395-887-X*); pap. text 19.95 (*0-87395-888-8*) State U NY Pr.

— Envisioning a Sustainable Society: Learning Our Way Out. LC 88-37558. (SUNY Series in Environmental Public Policy). 403p. (C). 1989. text 64.50 (*0-7914-0162-6*); pap. text 21.95 (*0-7914-0163-4*) State U NY Pr.

— Learning to Think Environmentally: While There Is Still Time. LC 95-34640. (Illus.). 136p. (C). 1996. text 32.50 (*0-7914-2953-9*); pap. text 9.95 (*0-7914-2954-7*) State U NY Pr.

— The Washington Lobbyists. LC 76-5789. (Illus.). 431p. 1976. reprint ed. lib. bdg. 105.00 (*0-8371-8802-4*, MIWL, Greenwood Pr) Greenwood.

— Washington Lobbyists Survey, 1956-1957. 1972. write for info. (*0-89138-054-X*) ICPSR.

Milbrath, Lester W., et al, eds. The Politics of Environmental Policy. LC 75-27013. (Sage Contemporary Social Science Issues Ser.: No. 18). 136p. reprint ed. pap. 42.20 (*0-608-10739-5*, 202193200026) Bks Demand.

Milbrath, Susan. Star Gods of the Maya: Astronomy in Art, Folklore, & Calendars. LC 99-6136. (Linda Schele Series in Maya & Pre-columbian Studies). 352p. 2000. pap. 24.95 (*0-292-75226-1*) U of Tex Pr.

***Milbrath, Susan.** Star Gods of the Maya: Astronomy in Art, Folklore & Calendars. 352p. 2000. 55.00 (*0-292-75225-3*) U of Tex Pr.

Milbrath, Susan. Study of Olmec Sculptural Chronology. LC 79-89248. (Studies in Pre-Columbian Art & Archaeology: No. 23). (Illus.). 75p. 1979. pap. 10.00 (*0-88402-093-2*) Dumbarton Oaks.

Milbrath, Susan, jt. ed. see Milanich, Jerald T.

Milburn, A., et al. Polishing Wear. (Nineteen Ninety Fall Technical Meeting Ser.: Vol. 90FTM5). (Illus.). 13p. 1990. pap. text 30.00 (*1-55589-557-3*) AGMA.

Milburn, B. A. Curious Cases: A Collection of American & English Decisions Selected for Their Readability. (Illus.). xvi, 441p. reprint ed. 37.50 (*0-8377-0819-2*, Rothman) W S Hein.

***Milburn, David.** Digital Photography Bible. LC 00-35001. (Bible Ser.). (Illus.). 696p. 2000. 39.99 (*0-7645-3394-0*) IDG Bks.

Milburn, Diane. The Deutschlandbild of A. R. Orage & the New Age Circle. LC 95-52058. (Illus.). 299p. 1996. pap. 57.95 (*0-8204-2957-0*, 68643) P Lang Pubng.

Milburn, Douglas. Alarm Clocks! Weird & Wonderful Exercises for English Language Learners. (Illus.). 1998. pap. text. write for info. (*1-882483-56-1*) Alta Bk Ctr.

***Milburn, Douglas.** Alarm Clocks! Teacher's Tips & Answer Key: Weird & Wonderful Exercises for English Language Learners. (Illus.). 66p. 1998. pap. text, teacher ed. 14.95 (*1-882483-57-X*) Alta Bk Ctr.

Milburn, G. J., jt. auth. see Walls, D. F.

Milburn, Geoffrey, jt. auth. see Barrow, Robin.

Milburn, George. Catalogue. LC 87-5432. 312p. 1987. reprint ed. lib. bdg. 18.95 (*0-940827-00-X*) Davenport NYC.

— No More Trumpets & Other Stories. LC 79-134968. (Short Story Index Reprint Ser.). 1977. 20.95 (*0-8369-3699-X*) Ayer.

— Oklahoma Town. LC 72-134969. (Short Story Index Reprint Ser.). 1977. 15.95 (*0-8369-3700-7*) Ayer.

***Milburn, Gerard J.** The Feynman Processor: Quantum Entanglement & the Computing Revolution. 240p. 1999. pap. text 13.00 (*0-7382-0173-1*, Pub. by Perseus Pubng) HarpC.

Milburn, Gerard J. Shrodinger's Machines: The Quantum Technology Reshaping Everyday Life. LC 96-51024. 188p. 1997. pap. text 21.95 (*0-7167-3106-1*) W H Freeman.

***Milburn, J. A. & Skinner, Ross.** Accounting Standards in Evolution: Trade Version. 2nd ed. 672p. 2000. 74.95 (*0-13-088846-X*) P-H.

***Milburn, J. A. & Skinner, Ross M.** Accounting Standards in Evolution. 2nd ed. 672p. 2000. 99.93 (*0-13-088015-9*) P-H.

Milburn, J. A., jt. ed. see Zimmermann, M. H.

Milburn, JoAnn F., jt. auth. see Cartledge, Gwendolyn.

Milburn, JoAnne F., jt. ed. see Cartledge, Gwendolyn.

Milburn, Josephine F. British Business & Ghanaian Independence. LC 76-50681. 166p. reprint ed. pap. 51.50 (*0-8357-6741-8*, 203539600095) Bks Demand.

Milburn, Josephine F. & Doyle, William. New England Political Parties. LC 82-17059. (Illus.). 282p. 1983. reprint ed. pap. 87.50 (*0-608-05341-4*, 206504600012) Bks Demand.

Milburn, Josephine F. & Schuck, Victoria, eds. New England Politics. LC 80-14530. (Illus.). 333p. 1986. reprint ed. pap. 103.30 (*0-608-05337-6*, 206504200012) Bks Demand.

Milburn, Kate. I Only Ask for Yesterday's Encore. (Illus.). 70p. (Orig.). 1994. pap. 10.00 (*0-9638316-0-7*); pap. text 10.00 (*0-614-29817-2*) Renais Pr.

Milburn, Ken. Designing Web Pages with FrontPage 97. LC 96-37701. 720p. 1996. 44.99 (*1-56205-697-2*) New Riders Pub.

— Designing Web Pages with Frontpage 98. 1997. 45.00 (*1-56205-812-6*) New Riders Pub.

***Milburn, Ken.** Flash 4 Web Animation F/X & Design. LC 99-49093. (Illus.). 1999. pap. 49.99 (*1-57610-555-5*) Coriolis Grp.

— Master Photoshop 5 Visually. LC 99-10950. 640p. 2000. pap. 39.99 (*0-7645-6045-X*) IDG Bks.

— Photoshop 5.5 Professional Results. (Illus.). 2000. pap. 29.99 (*0-07-212299-4*) McGrw-H Intl.

— Taking & Sharing Digital Photographs. (Illus.). 128p. 2000. pap. 8.99 (*0-7645-8633-5*, CPG Pr) IDG Bks.

Milburn, Ken & Warner, Janine. Designing Web Pages with Pagemill 2.0. LC 97-146804. 544p. 1997. 44.99 (*1-56205-711-1*) New Riders Pub.

Milburn, Leigh H. Progressed Horoscope Simplified. 180p. 1936. 17.00 (*0-86690-131-0*, M1339-014) Am Fed Astrologers.

Milburn, Lonna. Building a Cancer Information Network in Texas: A Demonstration in the Heart of Texas Region. (Special Project Reports). 277p. 1989. pap. 10.00 (*0-89940-864-8*) LBJ Sch Pub Aff.

Milburn, Michael & Oelbermann, Maren. Electromagnetic Fields & Your Health. 208p. 1994. pap. 12.00 (*0-921586-30-2*, Pub. by New Star Bks) Genl Dist Srvs.

Milburn, Michael A. & Conrad, Sheree D. The Politics of Denial. (Illus.). 304p. 1998. reprint ed. pap. text 15.00 (*0-262-63184-9*) MIT Pr.

— The Politics of Denial: Reactionary Rage. LC 96-16100. (Illus.). 304p. 1996. 30.00 (*0-262-13330-X*) MIT Pr.

***Milburn, Pat.** Journey to Wonderland. 190p. 2000. pap. 11.95 (*1-891929-46-1*) Four Seasons.

Milburn, Reggie. Crazy Hercules Game. (Crazy Games Ser.). (J). (gr. 1 up). 1997. pap. 2.95 (*0-8431-7918-X*, Price Stern) Peng Put Young Read.

Milburn, Robert L. Early Christian Art & Architecture. (Illus.). 336p. 1991. pap. 28.00 (*0-7045-0597-5*) Ashgate Pub Co.

— Early Christian Interpretations of History. LC 79-21671. 221p. 1980. reprint ed. lib. bdg. 59.50 (*0-313-22157-X*, MIEA, Greenwood Pr) Greenwood.

Milburn, Thomas W. & Watman, Kenneth H., eds. On the Nature of Threat: A Social Psychological Analysis. LC 80-20814. 148p. 1981. 45.00 (*0-275-90683-3*, C0683, Praeger Pubs) Greenwood.

***Milburn, William.** Oriental Commerce Vol. 1: Containing a Geographical Description of the Principal Places in the East Indies, China & Japan. 2nd ed. (Illus.). 1150p. 1999. reprint ed. 137.50 (*81-215-0895-9*, Pub. by M Manoharial) S Asia.

— Oriental Commerce Vol. 2: Containing a Geographical Description of the Principal Places in the East Indies, China & Japan. 2nd ed. 1999. reprint ed. 99.50 (*81-215-0896-7*, Pub. by M Manoharial) S Asia.

***Milby, Brian.** Installing, Configuring, & Customizing Red Hat Linux 6. 1999. pap. 39.99 (*0-7615-2306-5*) Prima Pub.

Milby, June. The Jade Frog. 26p. Date not set. 3.95 (*1-879934-26-4*) St Andrews NC.

Milby, T. H., jt. auth. see Johnson, Forrest L.

Milcak, Peter, jt. auth. see Valek, Miroslav.

Milch, David & Clark, Bill. True Blue. 256p. 1997. mass mkt. 6.99 (*0-380-72505-3*, Avon Bks) Morrow Avon.

Milch, Jerome, jt. auth. see Feldman, Elliot J.

Milch, Robert. Aeneid Notes. (Cliffs Notes Ser.). 80p. 1963. pap. 4.95 (*0-8220-0119-5*, Cliff) IDG Bks.

— Aeschylus' Agamemnon Notes. (Cliffs Notes Ser.). 72p. 1965. pap. 4.95 (*0-8220-0128-4*, Cliff) IDG Bks.

— Aristotle's Ethics Notes. (Cliffs Notes Ser.). 112p. (Orig.). 1966. pap. 4.95 (*0-8220-0889-0*, Cliff) IDG Bks.

— Faust I & II Notes, Pts. I & II. (Cliffs Notes Ser.). 72p. 1965. pap. 4.95 (*0-8220-0479-8*, Cliff) IDG Bks.

— Oedipus the King, Oedipus at Colonus & Antigone Notes. (Cliffs Notes Ser.). 64p. (Orig.). 1965. pap. 4.95 (*0-8220-0708-8*, Cliff) IDG Bks.

Milch, Robert A. Palliative Pain & Symptom Management for Children & Adolescents. 29p. 1985. pap. 7.95 (*0-317-61842-3*) Child Hospice VA.

Milch, Robert J. Euripides' Electra & Medea Notes. (Cliffs Notes Ser.). 72p. 1965. pap. 4.95 (*0-8220-0424-0*, Cliff) IDG Bks.

— Idylls of the King Notes. (Cliffs Notes Ser.). 72p. 1964. pap. 4.95 (*0-8220-0636-7*, Cliff) IDG Bks.

— The Iliad, Notes. (Cliffs Notes Ser.). 72p. 1962. pap. 4.95 (*0-8220-0645-6*, Cliff) IDG Bks.

— Odyssey Notes. (Cliffs Notes Ser.). 72p. 1963. pap. 4.95 (*0-8220-0921-8*, Cliff) IDG Bks.

Milchard, Les J. To Heaven Via Walthamstow. (C). 1989. pap. 35.00 (*0-7223-2268-2*, Pub. by A H S Ltd) St Mut.

Milchard, M., jt. auth. see Hone, A.

Milchhoefer, A. Ancient Athens, Piraeus & Phaleron: Schriftquellen Zur Topographie Von Athen. 156p. 1977. pap. 20.00 (*0-89005-215-8*) Ares.

Milchman, Alan & Rosenberg, Alan, eds. Martin Heidegger & the Holocaust. 288p. (C). 1996. text 60.00 (*0-391-03925-3*) Humanities.

— Martin Heidegger & the Holocaust. LC 95-21824. 288p. (C). 1997. pap. 17.50 (*0-391-04015-4*) Humanities.

Milchman, Alan, ed. see Nicholson, Graeme.

Milchovich, Sue K. & Dunn-Long, Barbara. Diabetes Mellitus: A Practical Handbook. 7th ed. LC 99-13739. (Illus.). 212p. 1999. pap. 14.95 (*0-923521-47-X*) Bull Pub.

Milco, Michael R. Ethical Dilemmas in Church Leadership: Case Studies in Biblical Decisionmaking. LC 96-52011. 192p. 1997. pap. 11.99 (*0-8254-3197-2*) Kregel.

Mild, Mary L., ed. Songs of Miriam: A Women's Book of Devotions. LC 93-45872. 1994. pap. 7.00 (*0-8170-1207-9*) Judson.

— Women at the Well: Meditations on Healing & Wholeness. 424p. 1996. pap. 16.00 (*0-8170-1245-1*) Judson.

Mild, Rosemary. Miriam's Gift: A Mother's Blessing - Then & Now. LC 98-40757. (Illus.). 176p. 1999. pap. 12.95 (*1-56474-295-4*) Fithian Pr.

Mild, Warren. Joseph Highmore of Holborn Row: Biography of 18th Century British Portrait Painter. LC 90-91935. (Illus.). 490p. 1990. 48.00 (*0-9627517-0-7*) Mild Assocs.

Milday Staff. Milady's Standard Textbook of Cosmetology. rev. ed. 634p. 1994. pap. write for info. (*1-56253-210-3*); pap. write for info. (*1-56253-213-8*) Milady Pub.

— Milday's Art & Science of Nail Technology. rev. ed. 272p. 1997. pap. write for info. (*1-56253-330-4*); pap., teacher ed., wbk. ed. write for info. (*1-56253-328-2*) Milady Pub.

Milde, Kurt. Neorenaissance in der Deutschen Architektur des 19 Jahrhunderts. (GER.). 352p. 1981. 168.00 (*0-7855-1598-4*) St Mut.

Milde, M. H., et al, eds. Index Annual Report-Northern Nut Growers Association, 1910-1975. 152p. 1983. 7.50 (*0-9602248-1-5*) N Nut Growers.

Milde, W. & Schuder, Werner, eds. De Captu Lectoris: Wirkungen Des Buches in 15. und 16. Jahrhundert Dargestellt an Ausgewahlten Handschriften und Drucken. xii, 313p. (C). 1988. lib. bdg. 161.55 (*3-11-009989-6*) De Gruyter.

Mildenball, Cheryl. Summer of Enlightment. (Black Lace Ser.). 1995. mass mkt. 5.95 (*0-352-32937-8*, Pub. by Virgin Bks) London Brdge.

Mildenberg, Leo. Vestigia Leonis: Studien zur Antiken Numismatik Israels, Palastinas und der Ostlichen Mittelmeerwelt. LC 98-154776. (Novum Testamentum et Orbis Antiquus Ser.: Vol. 36). (GER & FRE.). xxi, 400p. 1998. text 98.00 (*3-7278-1155-2*, Pub. by Ed Univ Fri) Eisenbrauns.

Mildenberg, Leo & Hurter, Silvia, eds. The Arthur S. Dewing Collection of Greek Coins, 2 vols. (ACNAC (American Coins in North American Collections)). (Illus.). 336p. 1985. boxed set 120.00 (*0-89722-206-7*) Am Numismatic.

Mildenberg, R., et al. Hydrocarbon Resins. LC 97-175735. 191p. 1997. 195.00 (*3-527-28617-9*, Wiley-VCH) Wiley.

Mildenberger, Friedrich. Theorie der Theologie: Enzyklopaedie als Methodenlehre. (GER.). 164p. 1972. 19.95 (*0-8288-6424-1*, M-7094) Fr & Eur.

Mildenhall, C. Fortune's Tide. 1997. mass mkt. 6.95 (*0-7472-5388-9*, Pub. by Headline Bk Pub) Trafalgar.

— Intimate Strangers. mass mkt. 6.95 (*0-7472-5126-6*, Pub. by Headline Bk Pub) Trafalgar.

— Liaison Family Affair. mass mkt. 6.95 (*0-7472-5387-0*) Headline Bk Pub.

M

— Liaison Intimate Disclosures. 1997. mass mkt. 6.95 (*0-7472-5589-X*, Pub. by Headline Bk Pub) Trafalgar.
— Liaison Pleasure Points. 1997. mass mkt. 6.95 (*0-7472-5590-3*, Pub. by Headline Bk Pub) Trafalgar.
— Liaison Voyeurs. 1998. mass mkt. 6.95 (*0-7472-5814-7*, Pub. by Headline Bk Pub) Trafalgar.
— Private lessons. mass mkt. 6.95 (*0-7472-5125-8*, Pub. by Headline Bk Pub) Trafalgar.
— Second Chance. mass mkt. 6.95 (*0-7472-5214-9*, Pub. by Headline Bk Pub) Trafalgar.
Mildenhall, Cheryl. By Any Means. 1998. mass mkt. 5.95 (*0-352-33221-2*, Pub. by BLA4) London Brdge.
— The Lure of Satyria. (Black Lace Ser.). 1995. mass mkt. 5.95 (*0-352-32994-7*, Pub. by Virgin Bks) London Brdge.
— Pulling Power. 256p. (Orig.). 1997. mass mkt. 5.95 (*0-352-33139-9*, Pub. by BLA4) London Brdge.
— A Sense of Entitlement. (Black Lace Ser.). 272p. (Orig.). 1996. mass mkt. 5.95 (*0-352-33053-8*, Pub. by Virgin Bks) London Brdge.
Milder, Ben. The Good Book Says. 147p. 1995. pap. 14.50 (*1-56809-014-5*) Time Being Bks.
— The Good Book Says . . . Light Verse to Illuminate the Old Testament. LC 95-5159. 147p. 1995. 20.95 (*1-56809-013-7*) Time Being Bks.
***Milder, Benjamin.** The Good Book Also Says... Numerous Humorous Poems Inspired by the New Testament. LC 99-49121. (Illus.). 149p. 1999. 25.00 (*1-56809-060-9*); pap. 15.95 (*1-56809-061-7*) Time Being Bks.
Milder, Benjamin & Rubin, Melvin L. The Fine Art of Prescribing Glasses Without Making a Spectacle of Yourself. 2nd ed. (Illus.). 544p. 1991. text 78.00 (*0-937404-02-0*) Triad Pub FL.
Milder, John, jt. auth. see Snow, Robbie.
Milder, N. David. Niche Strategies for Downtown Revitalization. LC 97-65110. 140p. 1997. pap. 69.95 (*0-915910-40-3*) Downtown Res.
Milder, Robert. Reimagining Thoreau. (Cambridge Studies in American Literature & Culture: No. 85). 256p. (C). 1995. text 64.95 (*0-521-46149-9*) Cambridge U Pr.
Milder, Robert, jt. ed. see Bryant, John.
Milder, Robert, ed. see Melville, Herman.
Milder, Robert, ed. & intro. see Melville, Herman.
Mildmay, Eroica. Lucker & Tiffany Peel Out. 192p. 1994. pap. 12.99 (*1-85242-285-8*) Serpents Tail.
Mildmay, Grace. With Faith & Physic: The Life of a Tudor Gentlewoman - Lady Grace Mildmay, 1552-1620. Pollock, Linda, ed. 179p. 1994. 55.00 (*1-85585-071-0*, Pub. by Collins & Br) Trafalgar.
Mildner, Gerard C., jt. auth. see Salins, Peter D.
Mildon, Marsha. Fighting for Air. LC 95-19144. 185p. (Orig.). 1995. pap. text 10.95 (*0-934678-69-3*) New Victoria Pubs.
— Stalking the Goddess Ship. LC 98-51841. 210p. 1999. pap. 10.95 (*1-892281-02-3*) New Victoria Pubs.
Mildr, Steven J. Cottonwood House. 125p. 1997. 19.95 (*1-881168-34-4*) Red Danceflr.
Mildred, M., jt. ed. see Dukes, Gramham.
Mildred, Mark & Wade, Evans B., eds. Product Liability: Law & Insurance. ring bd. 185.00 (*1-85044-595-8*) LLP.
Mildren, Ken & Hicks, Peter, eds. Information Sources in Engineering. 3rd ed. 600p. 1996. 110.00 (*1-85739-057-1*) Bowker-Saur.
Mildvan, Donna, jt. auth. see Mandell, Gerald L.
Milea, Ioan, tr. see Freud, Sigmund.
Mileaf. Electricity 1- 7. 2nd rev. ed. 1997. text 53.27 (*0-13-889585-6*) P-H.
Mileaf, Harry & Pearson, A. J. Electricity One-Seven. 3rd rev. ed. LC 98-2722. 1998. text 90.00 (*0-13-917857-0*) P-H.
Mileage, Judith. Chinese Gods & Myths. 1999. 7.99 (*0-7858-1078-1*) Bk Sales Inc.
— Indian Gods & Myths. 1999. 7.99 (*0-7858-1079-X*) Bk Sales Inc.
— Japanese Gods & Myths. 1999. 7.99 (*0-7858-1080-3*) Bk Sales Inc.
— Myths & Legends of the Vikings. 1999. 7.99 (*0-7858-1077-3*) Bk Sales Inc.
— Viking Gods. 1999. 7.99 (*0-7858-1081-1*) Bk Sales Inc.
Milech, Barbara H., jt. auth. see Jolley, Elizabeth.
Mileck, Joseph. Hermann Hesse: Life & Art. LC 76-48020. 1978. pap. 15.95 (*0-520-04152-6*, Pub. by U CA Pr) Cal Prin Full Svc.
Mileck, Joseph. Hermann Hesse: Life, Work & Criticism. (Authoritative Studies in World Literature). 49p. 1984. pap. 13.82 (*0-919966-39-X*) York Pr Ltd.
Mileck, Joseph. Hermann Hesse & His Critics. LC 72-10899. (North Carolina. University. Studies in the Germanic Languages & Literatures: No. 21). reprint ed. 34.00 (*0-404-50921-5*) AMS Pr.
— Samatimerisch Phonetik Grammatik Lexikographie: Geschichte der Mundart der Deutschen Gemeinde Sanktmartin am Nordlichen Rand des Rumanischen Banats. (Berkeley Models of Grammars Ser.: Vol. 3). XII, 373p. (C). 1997. text 58.95 (*0-8204-3655-0*) P Lang Pubng.
***Mileck, Joseph.** Zum Exodus der Rumaniendeutschen: Banater Sanktmartiner in Deutschland, Osterreich und Ubersee. (Berkeley Insights in Linguistics & Semiotics Ser.: Vol. 39). XII, 367p. (C). 1999. text 63.00 (*0-8204-4446-4*) P Lang Pubng.
Mileham, James W. The Conspiracy Novel: Structure & Metaphor in Balzac's Comedie Humaine. LC 81-68004. (French Forum Monographs: No. 31). 142p. (Orig.). 1982. pap. 9.95 (*0-917058-30-5*) French Forum.
Mileham, Patrick. The Scottish Regiments, 1633-1996. 352p. 1997. 45.00 (*1-873376-45-6*, Pub. by Spellmnt Pubs) St Mut.
— The Scottish Regiments, 1633-1996. 2nd rev. ed. (Illus.). 328p. 1996. 45.00 (*1-885119-24-0*) Sarpedon.
Mileham, Patrick & Spacey, Keith. Transforming Corporate Leadership. (Illus.). 225p. 1996. 25.00 (*0-273-61457-6*) F T P-H.
Mileiko, S. T. Metal & Ceramic Based Composites. 1996. write for info. (*0-614-17929-7*) Elsevier.
— Metal & Ceramic Based Composites. LC 97-49108. (Composite Materials Ser.: Vol. 12). 704p. 1997. 301.50 (*0-444-82814-1*) Elsevier.
Mileikovskii, I. E. & Trushin, S. I. Analysis of Thin-Walled Structures. LC 99-227324. (Russian Translation Ser.: No. 108). (ENG., Illus.). 196p. (C). 1994. 110.00 (*90-5410-250-0*, Pub. by A A Balkema) Ashgate Pub Co.
Milekic, Slavko, jt. auth. see Weisler, Steven E.
Milella, Nicholas. Vest Pocket Italian. LC 89-15366. (ENG & ITA.). 1986. pap. 5.95 (*0-8489-5104-2*) Inst Lang Study.
Milelr, Clara G. Harding, Ancestry of President Harding & Its Relation to the Hardings of Wyoming Valley & Clifford, Pennsylvania. 50p. 1997. reprint ed. pap. 10.00 (*0-8328-8962-8*); reprint ed. lib. bdg. 20.00 (*0-8328-8961-X*) Higginson Bk Co.
Milener, Eugene D. Oneonta: The Development of a Railroad Town. 2nd rev. ed. (Illus.). 600p. 1997. 62.95 (*0-9662095-0-8*) Hartwick Coll.
Milenkovic. Operating Systems. 2nd ed. 1992. student ed. 27.50 (*0-07-041923-X*) McGraw.
Milenkovic, Dragen, jt. auth. see Mori, Takeo.
Milenkovic, Milan, jt. ed. see Furht, Borko.
Milenkovic, Zora, jt. auth. see Lunt, Susie.
Milenkovitch, Deborah D. Plan & Market in Yugoslav Economic Thought. LC 78-140534. (Russian & East European Studies: No. 9). 333p. reprint ed. 103.30 (*0-8357-9440-7*, 201110400074) Bks Demand.
Milenkovitch, Michael M. Milovan Djilas: An Annotated Bibliography, 1928-1975. LC 76-20364. 50p. reprint ed. pap. 30.00 (*0-608-11434-0*, 201649900026) Bks Demand.
Milenski, Paul & Grande, Marilyn. Sexual Rhythms. 107p. 1990. pap. 11.95 (*0-9625313-0-8*) Mntn Pr MA.
Miler, I. The Immunity of the Foetus & Newborn Infant. 1983. text 135.00 (*90-247-2610-7*) Kluwer Academic.
Miler, Judy K., jt. ed. see Rabolt, Nancy.
Milera, Laura. The Flavor of Cuba: Traditional Recipes from the Cuban Kitchen. (Illus.). 200p. 1995. pap. 23.95 (*0-9642941-7-6*) Royal Palm Pr.
Miles. The Beatles: In Their Own Words. (In Their Own Words Ser.). (Illus.). 128p. pap. 15.95 (*0-86001-540-8*, OP 40419, Pub. by Bobcat) Omnibus NY.
— Chekov & Britain. Date not set. 49.50 (*0-85496-847-4*, Pub. by Berg Pubs) NYU Pr.
— Ciprofloxacin Product Information Monograph: Compendium of Preclinical & Clinical Data. 160p. 1988. text 100.00 (*0-8247-8020-5*) Dekker.
— Frank Zappa: Visual Documentary. (Illus.). 112p. pap. 24.95 (*0-7119-3099-6*, OP 47102) Omnibus NY.
— Oranizational Behav Lect Guide. 1998. pap. 12.50 (*0-07-234134-3*) McGraw.
— The Rolling Stones: A Visual Documentary. (Illus.). 160p. pap. 24.95 (*0-7119-3460-6*, OP 47318) Omnibus NY.
— The Three Little Pigs. LC 97-16007. (Ready-to-Read Ser.). (Illus.). 32p. (J). (gr. k-1). 1998. per. 15.00 (*0-689-81788-6*) S&S Childrens.
***Miles.** Uses of Decoration: Essays in the Architectural Everyday. LC 99-58869. 2000. text. write for info. (*0-471-48962-X*) Wiley.
— Uses of Decoration: Essays in the Architectural Everyday. LC 99-58869. 2000. pap. text. write for info. (*0-471-48963-8*) Wiley.
Miles, ed. European Community & the Nordic Countries. 328p. (C). 1996. 90.00 (*0-415-12422-0*); pap. 27.99 (*0-415-12423-9*) Routledge.
Miles & Mabbett, Andy. Pink Floyd: 21st Anniversary Edition. 25th anniversary ed. LC 95-234243. (Illus.). 156p. 1988. pap. 24.95 (*0-7119-4109-2*, OP40583) Omnibus NY.
Miles, jt. auth. see Amato.
Miles, jt. auth. see Bracegirdle.
Miles, A. E. & Grigson, C., eds. Colyer's Variations & Diseases of the Teeth of Animals. 2nd ed. (Illus.). 686p. 1990. text 395.00 (*0-521-25273-3*) Cambridge U Pr.
Miles, A. J. Tournament Chess, Vol. 6. 176p. 1983. pap. 21.95 (*0-08-029721-8*, Pergamon Pr) Elsevier.
Miles, A. J., ed. see Chandler, M.
Miles, A. J., jt. ed. see Chandler, M.
Miles, A. Marie. Bible: Bible Chain of Truth. 168p. (YA). (gr. 5 up). pap. 3.00 (*0-686-29101-8*) Faith Pub Hse.
Miles, Agnes. Women, Health & Medicine. 224p. 1991. pap. 34.95 (*0-335-09905-X*) OpUniv Pr.
***Miles, Al.** Domestic Violence: What Every Clergy Member Needs to Know. LC 99-51589. 2000. pap. 17.00 (*0-8006-3175-7*, Fortress Pr) Augsburg Fortress.
Miles, Alan. Dictionary of Classical Ballet in Labanotation. (Illus.). 108p. 1976. pap. text 15.00 (*0-932582-17-6*, Pub. by Dance Notation) Princeton Bk Co.
— Labanotation Workbook, Vol. II. 64p. 1970. pap. 12.00 (*0-317-56647-4*) Princeton Bk Co.
— Labanotation Workbook, Vols. I & II. 64p. (C). 1995. pap. 12.00 (*0-932582-18-4*, Pub. by Dance Notation) Princeton Bk Co.
Miles, Albert S. College Law. LC 87-61790. (Illus.). 121p. (Orig.). (C). 1987. pap. 25.00 (*0-943487-01-3*) Sevgo Pr.
Miles, Alfred H., ed. Poets & the Poetry of the Nineteenth Century, 12 vols. rev. ed. LC 16-2291. reprint ed. 780.00 (*0-404-05120-0*) AMS Pr.
Miles, Allan. Labanotation Workbook, Vol. II. 64p. (C). 1984. pap. 12.00 (*0-932582-19-2*) Dance Notation.
Miles, Andrew. Social Mobility in Nineteenth & Early Twentieth-Century England. LC 98-44283. 220p. 1999. text 65.00 (*0-312-22045-6*) St Martin.
Miles, Andrew, et al, eds. Melatonin: Clinical Perspectives. (Illus.). 304p. 1988. 80.00 (*0-19-261652-8*) OUP.
Miles, Andrew & Lygon, Myriam. Effective Clinical Practice. 224p. (Orig.). 1996. pap. text 32.95 (*0-632-03908-6*) Blackwell Sci.
Miles, Andrew, jt. auth. see Savage, Mike.
***Miles, Angela.** If I Could Change the Weather. 18p. 2000. 9.00 (*0-9678635-0-3*) Painted Bridge.
Miles, Angela. Integrative Feminisms: Building a Global Vision, 1960s to 1990s. LC 92-33164. (Perspectives on Gender Ser.). 208p. (C). 1995. pap. 18.99 (*0-415-90757-8*, B0256) Routledge.
Miles, Angela & Finn, Geraldine, eds. Feminism. 2nd rev. ed. 443p. 1989. 48.99 (*0-921689-23-3*, Pub. by Black Rose); pap. 19.99 (*0-921689-22-5*, Pub. by Black Rose) Consort Bk Sales.
— Feminism in Canada: From Pressure to Politics. 315p. 1982. write for info. (*0-919619-02-9*); pap. write for info. (*0-919619-00-2*) Black Rose.
Miles, Ann, et al. Women & Economic Change: Andean Perspectives. LC 97-3481. (Society for Latin American Anthropology Publication Ser.). 1997. write for info. (*0-913167-80-0*) Am Anthro Assn.
Miles, Anthony. First Steps to Winning Chess. 136p. 1992. pap. 12.95 (*0-945806-08-6*) Summit CA.
***Miles, Archie, ed.** Silva: British Trees. (Illus.). 416p. 1999. 60.00 (*0-09-186788-6*, Pub. by Ebury Pr) Trafalgar.
Miles, Austin. Don't Call Me Brother: A Ringmaster's Escape from the Pentacostal Church. LC 89-60074. (Illus.). 331p. (C). 1989. 26.95 (*0-87975-507-5*) Prometheus Bks.
— Setting the Captives Free: Victims of the Church Tell Their Stories. LC 90-41249. 239p. (C). 1990. 25.95 (*0-87975-617-9*) Prometheus Bks.
Miles, Barbara. Play with Me: Crafts for Preschoolers. (Illus.). (Orig.). (ps). 1990. pap. 13.98 (*0-88290-367-5*) Horizon Utah.
***Miles, Barry.** The Beat Hotel: Ginsberg, Burroughs & Corso in Paris, 1957-1963. LC 00-20187. (Illus.). 304p. 2000. 24.00 (*0-8021-1668-X*, Pub. by Grove-Atltic) Publishers Group.
Miles, Barry. The Beatles: A Diary. Charlesworth, Charles, ed. (Illus.). 360p. 1998. 39.95 (*0-7119-6315-0*) Omnibus NY.
— Jack Kerouac: King of the Beats: A Portrait. LC 98-35289. (Illus.). 332p. 1999. 25.00 (*0-8050-6043-X*); 15.00 (*0-8050-6044-8*, Owl) H Holt & Co.
— John Lennon: In His Own Words. (In Their Own Words Ser.). (Illus.). 128p. pap. 15.95 (*0-86001-816-4*, OP 41060, Pub. by Bobcat) Omnibus NY.
— Paul McCartney: Many Years from Now. LC 98-105657. (Illus.). 512p. 1997. 27.50 (*0-8050-5248-8*) H Holt & Co.
— Paul McCartney: Many Years from Now. (Illus.). 696p. 1998. pap. 16.95 (*0-8050-5249-6*, Owl) H Holt & Co.
— William Burroughs: El Hombre Invisible. LC 92-38285. (Illus.). 272p. (J). 1994. pap. 12.45 (*0-7868-8018-X*, Pub. by Hyperion) Time Warner.
***Miles, Barry & Stead, Gertrude.** Cemeteries of the City of Newport News, Formerly Warwick Co., Virginia. LC 99-230468. (Illus.). 145p. 1999. 55.00 (*0-7884-1179-9*, M340) Heritage Bk.
***Miles, Barry W.** Cemeteries of the City of Hampton, Virginia: Formerly Elizabeth City County. (Illus.). 293p. 1999. 111.00 (*0-7884-1287-6*, M364) Heritage Bk.
***Miles, Barry W. & Miles, Moody K., III.** Abstracts of the Wills & Administrations of Accomack County, Virginia 1800-1860. 773p. 2000. 45.50 (*0-7884-1507-7*, 1507) Heritage Bk.
Miles, Barry W. & Miles, Moody K., III. Marriage Records of Accomack County, VA, 1854-1895. LC 97-210564. vi, 414p. 1997. 29.00 (*0-7884-0680-9*, M353) Heritage Bk.
Miles, Barry W., et al. Tombstone Inscriptions of Upper Accomack Co., VA. (Illus.). 372p. (Orig.). 1995. 27.50 (*0-7884-0223-4*) Heritage Bk.
Miles, Bebe. Wildflower Perennials for Your Garden: A Detailed Guide to Years of Bloom from America's Native Heritage. (American Garden Classics Ser.). (Illus.). 320p. 1996. pap. 18.95 (*0-8117-2660-6*) Stackpole.
Miles, Benard J. Hydroxybenzoic Acids--Index of New Information & Medical Research Bible. 150p. 1994. 47.50 (*0-7883-0094-6*); pap. 44.50 (*0-7883-0095-4*) ABBE Pubs Assn.
Miles, Bernard. Favorite Tales from Shakespeare. (Illus.). 128p. (J). (gr. 4-7). 1993. reprint ed. 14.95 (*1-56288-257-0*) Checkerboard.
— Robin Hood: His Life & Legend. LC 79-64615. (Illus.). 128p. (J). (gr. 4 up). 12.95 (*1-56288-412-3*) Checkerboard.
— Well-Loved Tales from Shakespeare. LC 85-63829. (Illus.). 128p. (J). (gr. 2 up). 1986. 12.95 (*0-528-82758-8*) Checkerboard.
Miles, Betty. Goldilocks. LC 97-16008. (Illus.). 32p. (J). (ps-3). 1998. per. 3.99 (*0-689-81786-X*) S&S Childrens.
— Goldilocks & the Three Bears Ready to Read. LC 97-16008. (Ready-to-Read Ser.). (Illus.). 32p. (J). (gr. k-1). 1998. mass mkt. 15.00 (*0-689-81787-8*) S&S Childrens.
— The Hare & the Tortoise. LC 97-17355. (Illus.). 32p. (J). 1998. per. 3.99 (*0-689-81793-2*) S&S Childrens.
Miles, Betty. Hey! I'm Reading! A How-To-Read Book for Beginners. 1995. 17.20 (*0-606-07640-9*, Pub. by Turtleback) Demco.
Miles, Betty. I Would If I Could. 120p. (J). (gr. 3-6). 1983. pap. 2.95 (*0-380-63438-4*, Avon Bks) Morrow Avon.
— Just the Beginning. 148p. (J). (gr. 3 up). 1978. pap. 2.50 (*0-380-01913-2*, Avon Bks) Morrow Avon.
— Maudie & Me & the Dirty Book. 140p. (J). (gr. 4-7). 1981. pap. 2.95 (*0-380-55541-7*, Avon Bks) Morrow Avon.
— The Real Me. 124p. (J). (gr. 4-7). 1978. pap. 2.75 (*0-380-00347-3*, Avon Bks) Morrow Avon.
— The Secret Life of the Underwear Champ. LC 80-15651. (Books for Young Readers Ser.). (Illus.). 128p. (J). (gr. 3-7). 1981. pap. 4.99 (*0-394-84563-3*, Pub. by Random Bks Yng Read) Random.
Miles, Betty. The Secret Life of the Underwear Champ. (J). 1981. 10.09 (*0-606-02731-9*, Pub. by Turtleback) Demco.
Miles, Betty. Sink or Swim. 208p. (YA). (gr. 3-7). 1987. pap. 2.95 (*0-380-69913-3*, Avon Bks) Morrow Avon.
— The Sky Is Falling. LC 97-17351. (Ready-to-Read Ser.). (Illus.). 32p. (J). (ps-4). 1998. per. 15.00 (*0-689-81790-8*) S&S Childrens.
— Sky is Falling, Level 1. (Ready-to-Read Ser.). 1998. 9.19 (*0-606-13777-7*, Pub. by Turtleback) Demco.
— The Sky Is Falling Ready To Read. LC 97-17351. 32p. (J). 1998. per. 3.99 (*0-689-81791-6*) S&S Childrens.
— The Three Little Pigs. LC 97-16007. (Illus.). 32p. (J). (ps-3). 1998. per. 3.99 (*0-689-81789-4*) S&S Childrens.
Miles, Betty, jt. auth. see Aesop.
Miles, Betty T., et al. The Miles Chart Display, 2 vols. 1980. 163.95 (*0-405-19072-7*, 19805) Ayer.
— Miles Chart Display of Popular Music, 1955-1970 Vol. 1: Top 100. 3rd ed. (Illus.). 1979. reprint ed. lib. bdg. 95.00 (*0-913920-03-7*) Convex Indus.
Miles, Beverly, ed. see Walter, Alan C.
Miles-Blackard, Lisa, ed. see Miles, Leslie H., Jr., et al.
Miles-Brown, John. Acting: A Drama Studio Source Book. 110p. 1987. pap. 14.95 (*0-7206-0632-2*, Pub. by P Owen Ltd) Dufour.
— Directing Drama. LC 87-60978. (Illus.). 168p. 1994. pap. 25.00 (*0-7206-0688-8*, Pub. by P Owen Ltd) Dufour.
— Speech for the Speaker. LC 89-81770. 128p. 1989. pap. 18.95 (*0-7206-0726-4*, Pub. by P Owen Ltd) Dufour.
Miles, C., jt. auth. see Fallding, H.
Miles, C. Joseph, ed. see Michener, John W., Jr.
Miles, C. W., jt. auth. see Seabrooke, W.
Miles, Calvin. Calvin's Christmas Wish. LC 93-60591. 1996. 10.19 (*0-606-10153-5*, Pub. by Turtleback) Demco.
— When Dreams Came True. Literacy Volunteers of New York City Staff, ed. (New Writers' Voices Ser.). (Illus.). 64p. (Orig.). 1990. pap. text 3.50 (*0-929631-18-8*, Signal Hill) New Readers.
Miles, Candice, ed. see Golden, Harris.
Miles, Cara. Lord of the Night. 384p. (Orig.). 1993. mass mkt. 4.50 (*0-380-76453-9*, Avon Bks) Morrow Avon.
— Love Me with Fury. 384p. (Orig.). 1991. mass mkt. 4.50 (*0-380-76450-4*, Avon Bks) Morrow Avon.
— Promise Me Forever. 1992. mass mkt. 4.50 (*0-380-76451-2*, Avon Bks) Morrow Avon.
— Surrender to the Fury. 384p. (Orig.). 1992. mass mkt. 4.50 (*0-380-76452-0*, Avon Bks) Morrow Avon.
Miles, Cassie. Are You Lonesome Tonight? (Intrigue Ser.). 1994. per. 2.99 (*0-373-22269-6*, 1-22269-4) Harlequin Bks.
— Borrowed Time. LC 95-6908. (American Romance Ser.). 250p. 1995. per. 3.50 (*0-373-16574-9*, 1-16574-5) Harlequin Bks.
— Buffalo McCloud. (American Romance Ser.). 1995. per. 3.50 (*0-373-16567-6*, 1-16567-9) Harlequin Bks.
— Don't Be Cruel. (Intrigue Ser.). 1994. per. 2.99 (*0-373-22285-8*, 1-22285-0) Harlequin Bks.
— Father, Lover, Bodyguard: Captive Hearts. (Intrigue Ser.: Bk. 521). 1999. per. 3.99 (*0-373-22521-0*, 1-22521-8) Harlequin Bks.
— Forget Me Not: Rocky Mountain Rescue. (Intrigue Ser.: No. 449). 1998. per. 3.75 (*0-373-22449-4*, 1-22449-2) Harlequin Bks.
— Guarded Moments. (Intrigue Ser.). 1996. per. 3.75 (*0-373-22391-9*, 1-22391-6) Harlequin Bks.
— Heartbreak Hotel. (Intrigue Ser.). 1993. per. 2.99 (*0-373-22237-8*, 1-22237-1) Harlequin Bks.
— The Impostor (Avenging Angels) (Intrigue Ser.). 249p. 1996. per. 3.75 (*0-373-22363-3*, 1-22363-5) Harlequin Bks.
— A New Year's Conviction. 1997. per. 3.75 (*0-373-22402-8*, 1-22402-1) Silhouette.
— A Real Angel. 1997. per. 3.75 (*0-373-22443-5*, 1-22443-5) Harlequin Bks.
— A Risky Proposition. (Temptation Ser.: No. 394). 1992. per. 2.99 (*0-373-25494-6*, 1-25494-5) Harlequin Bks.
— Rule Breaker. (Intrigue Ser.). 1996. per. 3.75 (*0-373-22381-1*, 1-22381-7) Harlequin Bks.
— The Safe Hostage. (Intrigue Ser.). 1999. mass mkt. 3.99 (*0-373-22529-6*, 1-22529-1) Harlequin Bks.
— The Suspect Groom. LC 96-650. (Intrigue Ser.). 250p. 1995. per. 3.50 (*0-373-22332-3*, 1-22332-0) Harlequin Bks.
— Un Temoin Tres Suspect. (Rouge Passion Ser.: No. 522). (FRE.). 1999. mass mkt. 3.99 (*0-373-37522-0*, 1-37522-9) Harlequin Bks.
***Miles, Cassie.** Undercover Protector. (Intrigue Ser.: Vol. 584). 2000. mass mkt. 4.25 (*0-373-22584-9*, 1-22584-6) Harlequin Bks.
Miles, Chris. Business Traveler's Atlas. (Illus.). 208p. 1992. pap. 12.95 (*0-13-095217-6*, H M Gousha) Prntice Hall Bks.
***Miles, Christopher.** Love in the Ancient World. 2000. pap. 21.95 (*1-84188-010-8*) Seven Dials.
Miles, Christopher & Norwich, John Julius. Love in the Ancient World. LC 98-125216. 1997. text 27.50 (*0-312-17988-X*) St Martin.
Miles, Claudia, ed. see Curry, Jerri.
Miles, Clement A. Christmas Customs & Traditions: Their History & Significance. (Illus.). 1990. 23.50 (*0-8446-5484-1*) Peter Smith.
— Christmas Customs & Traditions: Their History & Significance. LC 76-9183. (Illus.). 400p. 1976. reprint ed. pap. 8.95 (*0-486-23354-5*) Dover.

An Asterisk (*) at the beginning of an entry indicates that the title is appearing for the first time.

— Christmas in Ritual & Tradition: Christian & Pagan. LC 89-29299. (Illus.). 400p. 1990. reprint ed. lib. bdg. 42.00 (1-55888-896-9) Omnigraphics Inc.

***Miles College Staff.** Miles College: A Journey into Academic Excellence. 314p. (C). 1999. per. 34.95 (0-7872-6247-1, 41624701) Kendall-Hunt.

— Stepping Stones to Success: Learning Across the Curriculum. 108p. (C). 1999. per. 37.95 (0-7872-6387-7, 41638701) Kendall-Hunt.

Miles, Curtis. The Mindful Worker: Learning & Working into the 21st Century. LC 94-78037. 246p. (Orig.). 1994. pap. text 19.95 (0-943202-46-9) H & H Pub.

— Studying Work in College: A Guide for Work-Study Students. 34p. (Orig.). 1995. pap. text 9.95 (0-943202-53-1) H & H Pub.

Miles, Curtis, jt. auth. see Foster, Donna.

Miles, D. Constructive Change: Managing International Technology Transfer. LC 95-236054. (International Construction Management Ser.: Vol. 5). 1995p. 1995. pap. 13.50 (92-2-108750-6) Intl Labour Office.

— International Project Marketing. LC 96-113427. (International Construction Management Ser.: Vol. 6). xv, 143p. (Orig.). 1995. pap. 13.50 (92-2-108745-X) Intl Labour Office.

Miles, D. & Neale, Richard H. Building for Tomorrow: International Experience in Construction Industry Development. vii, 238p. (Orig.). 1991. pap. 27.00 (92-2-107284-3) Intl Labour Office.

Miles, D., et al. Pricing & Bidding: Handbook & Workbook. (Improve Your Construction Business Ser.: Vol. 1). 112p. 1994. pap. 24.75 (92-2-109160-0) Intl Labour Office.

— Site Management: Handbook & Workbook. LC 97-129342. (Improve Your Construction Business Ser.: Vol. 2). 112p. 1996. pap. 24.75 (92-2-109315-8) Intl Labour Office.

Miles, D. C. & Briston, J. H. Polymer Technology. 3rd ed. (Illus.). 720p. 1996. 155.00 (0-8206-0344-9) Chem Pub.

Miles, D. K., jt. auth. see Chowdhury, G.

Miles, D. K., jt. auth. see Hall, S. G.

Miles, Dale A., et al. Basic Principles of Oral & Maxillofacial Radiology. (Illus.). 240p. 1992. pap. text 42.00 (0-7216-3471-0, W B Saunders Co) Harcrt Hlth Sci Grp.

— Oral & Maxillofacial Radiology: Radiologic - Pathologic Correlations. (Illus.). 352p. 1991. text 65.00 (0-7216-3070-7, W B Saunders Co) Harcrt Hlth Sci Grp.

— Radiographic Imaging for Dental Auxiliaries. 2nd ed. LC 92-17230. (Illus.). 336p. 1993. pap. text 43.00 (0-7216-6729-5, W B Saunders Co) Harcrt Hlth Sci Grp.

— Radiographic Imaging for Dental Auxiliaries. 3rd ed. Kuhn, Shirley, ed. LC 98-27545. (Illus.). 380p. 1999. pap. text 35.00 (0-7216-8016-X, W B Saunders Co) Harcrt Hlth Sci Grp.

Miles, Daniel J., jt. auth. see Mukes, Martin J.

Miles, David, jt. auth. see Corkish, Jo.

Miles, David, jt. auth. see Cunliffe, Barry.

Miles, David, jt. auth. see Mackie, Karl.

Miles, David H. Hofmannsthal's Novel, Andreas: Memory & Self. LC 70-155001. (Princeton Essays in European & Comparative Literature Ser.). 242p. reprint ed. pap. 75.10 (0-8357-3425-0, 203968300013) Bks Demand.

— Testing for Short-Termism in the U. K. Stock Market. fac. ed. LC HG5431.. 42p. 1992. reprint ed. pap. 30.00 (0-7837-8335-3, 204912200010) Bks Demand.

Miles, Derek. Accounting & Book-Keeping for the Small Building Contractor. (Small Building Contractor Ser.). 190p. 1979. pap. 21.00 (0-903031-54-X, Pub. by Intermed Tech) Stylus Pub VA.

— Appropriate Technology for Rural Development: The ITDG Experience. (ITDG Occasional Papers). 32p. 1982. pap. 12.00 (1-85339-367-3, Pub. by Intermed Tech) Stylus Pub VA.

— Financial Planning for the Small Building Contractor. (Small Building Contractor Ser.). (Illus.). 188p. 1979. pap. 21.00 (0-903031-55-8, Pub. by Intermed Tech) Stylus Pub VA.

Miles, Derek, jt. auth. see Edmonds, G. A.

Miles, Dillwyn, ed. The Description of Pembrokeshire George Owen. LC 94-221556. 324p. 1994. 53.00 (1-85902-120-4, Pub. by Gomer Pr) St Mut.

Miles, Dilwyn. Description of Pembrokeshire: George Owen. 1998. 52.95 (0-8464-4828-9) Beekman Pubs.

Miles, Don C., et al. Trackside: Preserving Railroad Station Warehouse Districts: A Comparative Study of Seven Cities. Kreisman, Lawrence, ed. (Illus.). 140p. (Orig.). 1988. pap. write for info. (0-9621572-0-1) City Tacoma Hist Preserv.

Miles, Don E. Signs of the Nineties: The Poet. (Illus.). 108p. (Orig.). 1992. pap. 12.50 (0-9635478-0-1) Marked Tree.

Miles, Don G., jt. ed. see Fox, Karl A.

Miles, Donald. Broadcast News Handbook. LC 75-2550. 1975. teacher ed. 2.75 (0-672-21198-X, Bobbs); pap. 9.95 (0-672-21183-1, Bobbs) Macmillan.

***Miles, Donald F. & Goff, Charles E.** Laying a Foundation to Introduce Evidence (Preparing & Using Evidence at Trial) Part 1, 2 - Winter 2000 Action Guide, 2 vols. Compton, Linda, ed. 112p. 2000. pap. text 58.00i (0-7626-0394-1, CP-11236) Cont Ed Bar-CA.

Miles, Donald G. Understanding Depression Facilitator's Guide: Overcoming Despair Through Christ. 127p. 1998. pap., teacher ed. 12.00 (1-58119-018-2) T P Min.

— Understanding Depression Member's Guide: Overcoming Despair Through Christ. 106p. 1998. pap., student ed. 10.00 (1-58119-017-4) T P Min.

Miles, Dorothy. Church of Our Fathers: The Story of Old St. Michaels. 2nd ed. MacDonald, Alexander, ed. 112p. (Orig.). 1984. reprint ed. pap. write for info. (0-318-65391-5) D Miles.

— Dreams of Glory: A Family Saga. 300p. (Orig.). 1989. 15.00 (0-9623631-0-3); pap. 8.00 (0-9623631-1-1) D Miles.

— Gestures-Poetry in Sign Language. Joyce, John, ed. LC 76-55854. (Illus.). 1976. pap. 14.95 (0-917002-12-1) Joyce Media.

— The Revival of a Marblehead Mansion. MacDonald, Alexander, ed. 35p. 1982. reprint ed. pap. write for info. (0-318-65392-3) D Miles.

Miles, Douglas G., jt. auth. see Ryan, Tim.

Miles, Douglas L., ed. Water-Rock Interaction (WRI-Six) Proceedings of the International Symposium, Malvern, UK, 3 - 8 August 1989. (Illus.). 838p. (C). 1989. text 168.00 (90-6191-970-3, Pub. by A A Balkema) Ashgate Pub Co.

***Miles, Edward H., ed.** The Executive Guide to Medicare Managed Care. 185p. 1998. spiral bd. 172.50 (1-882364-37-6, Amer Busn Pub) Hlth Res Pub.

— Grant Funding for Elderly Health Services. 2nd ed. 139p. 1996. spiral bd. 81.50 (1-882364-08-2, Amer Busn Pub) Hlth Res Pub.

— The Healthcare IS/IT Market Yearbook. 498p. 1999. per. 433.50 (1-882364-36-8, Amer Busn Pub) Hlth Res Pub.

— The Hospice Reimbursement & Financing Guide. 2nd ed. 224p. 1997. spiral bd. 133.00 (1-882364-22-8, Amer Busn Pub) Hlth Res Pub.

Miles, Edward L. Global Ocean Politics: The Decision Process at the Third United Nations Conference on the Law of the Sea, 1973-1982. LC 97-43948. 568p. 1998. 177.00 (90-411-0448-8) Kluwer Law Intl.

— Organizational Arrangements to Facilitate Global Management of Fisheries. LC 73-20844. (Resources for the Future, Program of International Studies of Fishery Arrangements, Paper: No. 4). 35p. reprint ed. pap. 30.00 (0-608-12542-3, 202380800034) Bks Demand.

Miles, Edward L., ed. The Management of World Fisheries: Implications of Extended Coastal State Jurisdiction. 344p. 1990. 30.00 (0-295-96854-0) U of Wash Pr.

Miles, Edward L., et al, eds. Natural Resources Economics & Policy Applications: Essays in Honor of James A. Crutchfield. 448p. 1986. 30.00 (0-295-96345-X) U of Wash Pr.

Miles, Edward L. & Allen, S., eds. The Law of the Sea & Ocean Development Issues in the Pacific Basin: 15th Annual Conference Proceeding. 638p. 1983. 18.00 (0-911189-06-8) Law Sea Inst.

Miles, Edward L. & Treves, Tullio, eds. The Law of the Sea: New Worlds, New Discoveries, 26th Conference Proceedings. 500p. 58.00 (0-911189-26-2) Law Sea Inst.

Miles, Edward L., et al. Atlas of Marine Use in the North Pacific Region. LC 81-675743. (Illus.). 107p. 1982. 195.00 (0-520-04433-9, Pub. by U CA Pr) Cal Prin Full Svc.

Miles, Edward L., jt. ed. see Kuribayashi, Tadao.

Miles, Edwin A. Jacksonian Democracy in Mississippi. LC 78-107415. (American Scene Ser.). 1970. reprint ed. lib. bdg. 29.50 (0-306-71884-7) Da Capo.

Miles, Elaine. The Bangor Dyslexia Teaching System. 2nd ed. 96p. 1992. pap. 29.99 (1-879105-72-1, 0427) Thomson Learn.

— Many Hands: Making a Communal Quilt. (Illus.). 75p. (Orig.). 1982. 6.95 (0-936810-02-5) M & M.

Miles, Elaine, jt. auth. see Miles, T. R.

Miles, Elaine, jt. ed. see Miles, T. R.

Miles, Elaine T. Patchwork Year: A Datebook. (Illus.). 128p. 1983. pap. 4.95 (0-936810-03-3) M & M.

Miles, Elizabeth. Feng Shui Cookbook: Creating Health & Harmony in Your Kitchen. LC 98-6446. (Illus.). 176p. 1998. 15.95 (1-55972-465-X, Birch Ln Pr) Carol Pub Group.

— Tune Your Brain: Using Music to Manage Your Mind, Body, & Mood. LC 98-102956. 240p. 1997. pap. 12.00 (0-425-16017-3) Berkley Pub.

Miles, Elizabeth. Goldilocks & the Three Bears. (Children's Classics Ser.). 32p. (J). 1991. 6.95 (0-8362-4900-3) Andrews & McMeel.

Miles, Elizabeth B. The Elizabeth B. Miles Collection: English Silver. LC 75-37418. (Illus.). 145p. 1976. pap. 12.00 (0-317-13587-2) Wadsworth Atheneum.

***Miles, Ellen.** Cheer Fever. (Illus.). 144p. (J). (gr. 4-7). 2000. pap. 4.99 (0-439-19454-7) Scholastic Inc.

— Flinstones in Viva Rock Vegas: Digest Edition. (Illus.). 80p. (J). (gr. 4-7). 2000. pap. 3.99 (0-439-17303-5) Scholastic Inc.

— Superstars of Womens Tennis. (Illus.). (J). (gr. 4-6). 2000. pap. 5.99 (0-689-83959-6) Aladdin.

Miles, Ellen G. George & Martha Washington: Portraits from the Presidential Years. LC 98-47395. (Illus.). 64p. 1999. pap. 17.95 (0-8139-1886-3) U Pr of Va.

— Memorials of Great & Good Men Who Were My Friends: Portraits in the Life of Oliver Wolcott, Jr. (Illus.). 55p. 1998. reprint ed. pap. 8.50 (0-944026-88-5) Am Antiquarian.

— Saint-Memin & the Neoclassical Profile Portrait in America. LC 94-15239. (Illus.). 512p. 1994. text 95.00 (1-56098-411-2) Smithsonian.

Miles, Ellen G., et al, contrib. by. American Paintings of the Eighteenth Century. LC 94-37473. (National Gallery of Art USA Publication). (Illus.). 440p. 1996. 85.00 (0-89468-210-5) OUP.

Miles, Ellen G., ed. The Portrait in Eighteenth-Century America. LC 90-50995. (Illus.). 168p. (C). 1993. 49.50 (0-87413-437-4) U Delaware Pr.

Miles, Elton. Tales of the Big Bend. LC 76-17977. (Illus.). 200p. 1995. pap. 13.95 (0-89096-360-6) Tex A&M Univ Pr.

Miles, Emerett S., jt. auth. see Sanford, Winifred M.

Miles, Emily L., jt. auth. see Beanland, Ame.

Miles, Emma B. Spirit of the Mountains. LC 75-19222. (Tennesseana Editions Ser.). (Illus.). 250p. 1975. reprint ed. pap. 17.00 (0-87049-465-1) U of Tenn Pr.

Miles, Eustace. Life after Life: The Theory of Reincarnation. 180p. 1985. pap. 16.50 (0-89540-126-6, SB-126) Sun Pub.

Miles, F. A. & Wallman, J., eds. Visual Motion & Its Role in the Stabilization of Gaze. LC 92-32805. (Reviews of Oculomotor Research Ser.: Vol. 5). 418p. 1992. 296.50 (0-444-81195-8) Elsevier.

Miles, Fern H. Captive Community: Life in a Japanese Internment Camp, 1941-1945. LC 87-61092. viii, 192p. (Orig.). 1987. pap. 8.95 (0-9618895-0-0) Mossy Creek Pr.

Miles, Gary. Inside Hockey. LC 96-39798. (Illus.). 160p. 1997. 24.98 (1-56799-421-0) M Friedman Pub Grp Inc.

***Miles, Gary.** Inside Hockey: Players, Pucks & Penalty Boxes. rev. ed. LC 00-27469. 160p. 2000. 19.98 (1-58663-004-0, MetroBooks) M Friedman Pub Grp Inc.

Miles, Gary, et al. Inside Hockey: Players, Pucks & Penalty Boxes. LC 98-20188. 1998. 24.98 (1-56799-702-3, MetroBooks) M Friedman Pub Grp Inc.

Miles, Gary B. Livy: Reconstructing Early Rome. 256p. 1995. text 39.95 (0-8014-3060-7) Cornell U Pr.

— Livy: Reconstructing Early Rome. 264p. 1996. pap. 15.95 (0-8014-8426-X) Cornell U Pr.

Miles, Geoffrey. Classical Mythology in English Literature: A Critical Anthology. LC 98-43914. 1999. 80.00 (0-415-14754-9); pap. 24.99 (0-415-14755-7) Routledge.

— Shakespeare & the Constant Romans. (Oxford English Monographs). 226p. (C). 1996. text 55.00 (0-19-811771-X) OUP.

Miles, George. Go West & Grow up with the Country: An Exhibition of Nineteenth-Century Guides to the American West in the Collections of the American Antiquarian Society. (Illus.). 47p. (Orig.). 1991. pap. 13.00 (0-944026-30-3) Am Antiquarian.

— Wills, Probate & Administration. 200p. 1993. 34.00 (1-85431-295-2, Pub. by Blackstone Pr) Gaunt.

Miles, George, ed. Foundations for the LPC. (Legal Practice Course Guides Ser.). 411p. 1997. pap. 38.00 (1-85431-701-6, Pub. by Blackstone Pr) Gaunt.

— Foundations for the LPC, 1998-99. 2nd ed. (Legal Practice Course Guides Ser.). 415p. 1998. pap. 40.00 (1-85431-788-1) Gaunt.

Miles, George & Denyer, Paulene. Wills, Probate & Administration, 1996/97. 4th ed. (Legal Practice Course Guides Ser.). 367p. 1996. pap. 36.00 (1-85431-546-3, Pub. by Blackstone Pr) Gaunt.

Miles, George C. The Coinage of the Arab Amirs of Crete. (Numismatic Notes & Monographs: 160). (Illus.). 95p. 1960. pap. 12.00 (0-89722-059-5) Am Numismatic.

Miles, George H. A Review of Hamlet. LC 77-172730. reprint ed. 29.50 (0-404-04324-0) AMS Pr.

***Miles, George K.** Jones Genealogical Notes: Joseph & Lydfia (Roberts) Jones of Gwynedd, Philadelphia Co. 67p. 1999. reprint ed. 23.50 (0-7404-0010-X) Higginson Bk Co.

Miles, George K. Jones. Genealogical Notes: Joseph & Lydia Robert Jones of Gwynedd, Philadelphia County, Pa.; John & Mary Stall Jones of Vincent Township, Chester County, Pa; Jesse & Elizabeth Frick Jones of Vincent Township, Chester County, Pa. (Illus.). 67p. 1997. reprint ed. pap. 13.50 (0-8328-9355-2); reprint ed. lib. bdg. 23.50 (0-8328-9354-4) Higginson Bk Co.

Miles, H., tr. see Bunin, Ivan A.

Miles, Hal V. A Personal Guide to Achieving Winning Pick 3 Numbers: The Big Three. (Illus.). 115p. (Orig.). Date not set. pap. text 24.95 (0-9654845-0-5) Miles Intl Assn.

Miles, Hamish, et al. The Paintings of James McNeill Whistler, 2 vols. LC 80-5214. (Studies in British Art). (Illus.). 567p. 1980. 275.00 (0-300-02384-7) Yale U Pr.

Miles, Hamish, ed. see Painter, William M.

Miles, Hamish, tr. see Maurois, Andre.

Miles, Hamish, tr. see Villiers De l'Isle-Adam, Jean M.

Miles, Harold. Bad Ol' Boy. LC 93-2059. 375p. 1993. 22.50 (0-89603-267-1) Humana.

Miles, Henry A. Lowell, As It Was, & As It Is. LC 72-5063. (Technology & Society Ser.). (Illus.). 234p. 1976. reprint ed. 18.95 (0-405-04714-2) Ayer.

Miles, I. & Irvine, J., eds. The Poverty of Progress: Changing Ways of Life in Industrial Societies. LC 81-17779. (Illus.). 275p. 1982. 161.00 (0-08-028906-1, K110, Pub. by Pergamon Repr) Franklin.

Miles, Ian. Home Informatics: Information Technology & the Transformation of Everyday Life. 224p. 1992. 49.00 (0-86187-975-9) St Martin.

Miles, Ian, jt. auth. see Boden, Mark.

Miles, Ian, jt. auth. see Cole, Sam.

Miles, Ian, jt. auth. see Whitaker, Marian.

Miles, J. The 1989 Conference Issue. 74p. 1990. text 76.00 (3-7186-5103-3, Harwood Acad Pubs) Gordon & Breach.

— Ships, Sailors & the Sea. 1989. lib. bdg. 15.95 (0-88110-365-9, Usborne) EDC.

— Ships, Sailors & the Sea. (gr. 2 up). 1989. pap. 8.95 (0-7460-0285-8, Usborne) EDC.

Miles, J., et al, eds. Temporal & Spatial Patterns of Vegetation Dynamics. (Advances in Vegetation Science Ser.). (C). 1989. text 266.50 (0-7923-0103-X) Kluwer Academic.

Miles, J. & Walton, D. W., eds. Primary Succession on Land. LC 92-35652. 309p. 1993. 65.00 (0-632-03547-1) Blackwell Sci.

Miles, J. C. First Book of the Keyboard. (First Music Ser.). (Illus.). 64p. (J). (gr. 1-4). 1993. pap. 10.95 (0-7460-0962-3); lib. bdg. 18.95 (0-88110-622-4) EDC.

Miles, Jack. Blood of the Lamb. 1999. write for info. (0-375-40014-1) Knopf.

— Blood of the Lamb. 1999. pap. write for info. (0-679-78160-9) Vin Bks.

— God: A Biography. LC 94-30153. 446p. 1995. 30.00 (0-679-41833-4) Knopf.

— God: A Biography. 1996. pap. 15.00 (0-679-74368-5) Vin Bks.

Miles, Jacob R., 3rd, ed. see Williams, Bob.

Miles, James. Comprehensive Index to Oregon Statutes, 1994. 1200p. 1994. pap. 100.50 (0-614-05794-9, MICHIE) LEXIS Pub.

Miles, James A. The Legacy of Tiananmen: China in Disarray. LC 95-52804. (China in Disarray Ser.). 408p. 1996. 37.50 (0-472-10731-3, 10731) U of Mich Pr.

— The Legacy of Tiananmen: China in Disarray. 408p. (C). 1997. pap. 19.95 (0-472-08451-8, 08451) U of Mich Pr.

***Miles, James A. & Woobridge, J. Randall.** Spin-Offs & Equity Carve-Outs: Achieving Faster Growth & Better Performance. LC 98-73869. 117p. 1999. pap. 39.75 (1-885065-14-0, 099-01, Pub. by Finan Exec) E Elgar.

Miles, James G. Congresses, Presidents & the $5 1/2 Trillion National Debt. LC 98-34358. 112p. 1998. pap. 12.95 (1-58141-005-0) Rivercross Pub.

— Pay Any Price. 288p. 1989. 19.95 (0-9627006-0-6, TXU 350 632) J G Miles.

Miles, James M. Georgia Civil War Sites. (Illus.). 140p. (Orig.). 1987. pap. 8.95 (0-941907-00-7) J & R Graphics.

Miles, James W., jt. ed. see Laird, Marshall.

Miles, Jeff. Tigers. (Scots Plaid Press Fine Poetry Ser.: No. 3). 36p. 1998. pap. 12.00 (1-879009-31-5) Old Barn Entrprs.

Miles, Jennifer A. Illustrated Glossary of Petroleum Geochemistry. (Illus.). 146p. 1994. reprint ed. pap. text 21.95 (0-19-854849-4) OUP.

Miles, Jerry L. Sir Walter Raleigh: A Reference Guide. (Reference Guides to Literature Ser.). 148p. (C). 1986. 45.00 (0-8161-8596-4, Hall Reference) Macmillan.

Miles, Jim. Civil War Sites in Georgia. LC 96-4597. (Illus.). 224p. 1996. pap. text 8.95 (1-55853-405-9) Rutledge Hill Pr.

— Fields of Glory: A History & Tour Guide of the Atlanta Campaign. LC 89-6389. (Illus.). 192p. 1989. pap. 14.95 (1-55853-023-1) Cumberland Hse.

***Miles, Jim.** Fields of Glory: A History & Tour Guide of the Atlanta Campaign. (Illus.). 192p. 1999. pap. 14.95 (1-58182-072-0, Cumberland Hearthside) Cumberland Hse.

— Forged in Fire: A History & Tour Guide of the War in the East, from Manassas to Antietam, 1861-1862. (Illus.). 608p. 2000. pap. 24.95 (1-58182-089-5, Cumberland Hearthside) Cumberland Hse.

— Kingfisher Young People's Pocket Altas. (Illus.). (J). 1997. 15.30 (0-606-18235-7) Turtleback.

— Paths to Victory: A History & Tour Guide of the Stones River, Chickamauga, Chattanooga, Knoxville. (Illus.). 192p. 1999. pap. 12.95 (1-58182-074-7, Cumberland Hearthside) Cumberland Hse.

Miles, Jim. Paths to Victory: A History & Tour Guide of the Stone's River, Chickamauga, Chattanooga, Knoxville, & Nashville Campaigns. LC 91-29167. (Illus.). 224p. (Orig.). 1991. pap. 12.95 (1-55853-126-2) Cumberland Hse.

— Piercing the Heartland. LC 95-50653. (Illus.). 224p. (Orig.). 1991. pap. 12.95 (1-55853-104-1) Cumberland Hse.

***Miles, Jim.** Piercing the Heartland: A History & Tour Guide of the Fort Donelson, Shiloh & Perryville Campaigns. 176p. 1999. pap. 12.95 (1-58182-075-5, Cumberland Hearthside) Cumberland Hse.

— A River Unvexed: A History & Tour Guide of HTE Campaign for the Mississippi River. 608p. 1999. pap. 24.95 (1-58182-076-3, Cumberland Hearthside) Cumberland Hse.

Miles, Jim. A River Unvexed: A History & Tour Guide to the Campaign for the Mississippi River. LC 93-35025. (Illus.). 596p. 1994. pap. 24.95 (1-55853-210-2) Cumberland Hse.

***Miles, Jim.** To the Sea: A History & Tour Guide of Sherman's March. (Illus.). 336p. 1999. pap. 18.95 (1-58182-073-9, Cumberland Hearthside) Cumberland Hse.

Miles, Jim, ed. The Kingfisher Young People's Pocket Atlas. (Illus.). 192p. (J). (gr. 4-8). 1997. pap. 10.95 (0-7534-5064-X) LKC.

Miles, John. Infectious Diseases: Colonising the Pacific? LC 97-198317. 112p. 1997. pap. 29.95 (1-877133-26-4, Pub. by Univ Otago Pr) Intl Spec Bk.

— A Most Deadly Retirement. 1997. per. 4.99 (0-373-26252-3, 1-26252-6, Wrldwide Lib) Harlequin Bks.

— A Most Deadly Retirement: A Laura Michaels Mystery. 246p. 1995. 22.95 (0-8027-3258-5) Walker & Co.

— Murder in Retirement. (Worldwide Library Mysteries: No. 243). 1997. per. 4.99 (0-373-26243-4, 1-26243-5, Wrldwide Lib) Harlequin Bks.

— Murder in Retirement: A Laura Michaels Mystery. LC 93-25234. 1994. 19.95 (0-8027-3246-1) Walker & Co.

— A Permanent Retirement. (Worldwide Library Mysteries). 256p. 1997. per. 4.99 (0-373-26228-0, 1-26228-6, Wrldwide Lib) Harlequin Bks.

— A Permanent Retirement. LC 92-12985. 230p. 1992. 19.95 (0-8027-1243-6) Walker & Co.

***Miles, John.** The President's Bodyguard. 2000. pap. 11.95 (1-891929-59-3) Four Seasons.

Miles, John. Stoppers: How to Put an End to Meetings, Monologues, Conferences, Discussions, Telephone Calls, Debates, Filibusters, Boring Parties, & Anything That Lasts Too Long. LC 93-6277. 64p. (Orig.). 1994. pap 3.98 (0-687-39639-5) Abingdon.

— Tenoclock Scholar: A Johnnie Baker Mystery. LC 95-30752. 252p. 1996. 22.95 (0-8027-3273-9) Walker & Co.

Miles, John & Moore, Carolynne. Practical Knowledge Based Systems in Conceptual Design. LC 92-46682. 1993. 142.95 (0-387-19823-7) Spr-Verlag.

Miles, John & Morris, Tom. Operation Nightfall. LC 74-17665. 224p. 1975. 6.95 (0-672-52085-0, Bobbs) Macmillan.

M

An Asterisk (*) at the beginning of an entry indicates that the title is appearing for the first time.

M

Miles, John A. R. Public Health Progress. 1984. lib. bdg. 107.50 (*90-277-9085-X*) Kluwer Academic.
Miles, John C. Guardians of the Parks: A History of the National Park & Conservation Association. 1995. 29.95 (*0-614-10447-5*, L115) Natl Parks & Cons.
— Guardians of the Parks: A History of the National Parks & Conservation Association. LC 95-134. 363p. 1995. 36.95 (*1-56032-446-5*) Taylor & Francis.
Miles, John C., ed. Impressions of the North Cascades: Essays about a Northwest Landscape. (Illus.). 224p. (Orig.). 1996. pap. 14.95 (*0-89886-484-4*) Mountaineers.
— Treasury of Animal Stories. LC 90-11158. (Illus.). 96p. (J). (gr. 2-5). 1991. lib. bdg. 20.65 (*0-8167-2240-4*) Troll Communs.
— Treasury of Animal Stories. LC 90-11158. (Illus.). 96p. (J). (gr. 2-5). 1997. pap. 7.95 (*0-8167-2241-2*) Troll Communs.
— Treasury of Christmas. LC 90-39372. (Illus.). 96p. (J). (gr. 2-5). 1991. lib. bdg. 20.65 (*0-8167-2236-6*) Troll Communs.
— Treasury of Christmas. LC 90-39372. (Illus.). 96p. (J). (gr. 2-5). 1997. pap. 7.95 (*0-8167-2237-4*) Troll Communs.
Miles, John C. & Priest, Simon. Adventure Education. LC 90-71690. 473p. 1991. pap. 31.95 (*0-910251-39-8*) Venture Pub PA.
***Miles, John C. & Priest, Simon, eds.** Adventure Programming. LC 99-66066. 540p. 1999. text 39.95 (*1-892132-09-5*, APR110) Venture Pub PA.
Miles, John C., jt. auth. see O'Brien, Eileen.
Miles, John C., ed. see Dempsey, Michael.
Miles, John G. The Law Officer's Pocket Manual. LC 91-169764. 1999. 15.95 (*0-87179-648-1*) BNA Books.
— The Law Officer's Pocket Manual, 1999 Edition. 162p. 1998. spiral bd. 15.95 (*1-57018-059-8*, 1106) BNA Books.
Miles, John J. Health Care & Antitrust Law, 4 vols., Set. LC 92-5626. (Health Law Ser.). 1992. ring bd. 475.00 (*0-87632-831-1*) West Group.
Miles, John W. The Potential Theory of Unsteady Supersonic Flow. LC 59-564. (Cambridge Monographs on Mechanics & Mathematics). 234p. reprint ed. pap. 66.70 (*0-608-11117-1*, 2050772) Bks Demand.
***Miles, Johnnie H.** African Americans Book Lists. LC 00-37305. 2000. write for info. (*0-13-084364-4*) P-H.
Miles, Jonathan. Eric Gill & David Jones at Capel-Y-Ffin. 172p. 1992. pap. 15.95 (*1-85411-052-7*) Dufour.
— Eric Gill & David Jones at Capel-Y-Ffin. 172p. 1993. 35.00 (*1-85411-051-9*) Dufour.
Miles, Jonathan & Shiel, Derek. David Jones: The Maker Unmade. LC 96-154496. (Illus.). 328p. 1996. 65.00 (*1-85411-134-5*, Pub. by Seren Bks) Dufour.
Miles, Josephine. Civil Poems. 1966. pap. 1.00 (*0-685-29875-2*) Oyez.
— Collected Poems, 1930-1983. LC 82-11014. 280p. 1983. text 24.95 (*0-252-01017-5*) U of Ill Pr.
— Collected Poems, 1930-1983. 280p. 1999. pap. text 19.95 (*0-252-06767-3*) U of Ill Pr.
— Coming to Terms. Poems. LC 79-18235. 80p. 1979. 9.95 (*0-252-00768-9*) U of Ill Pr.
— Fields of Learning. 1968. pap. 1.00 (*0-685-04667-2*) Oyez.
— The Primary Language of Poetry in the 1740's & 1840's. LC 83-45454. reprint ed. 27.50 (*0-404-20177-6*) AMS Pr.
— The Primary Language of Poetry in the 1640's, Vol. 19, No. 1. LC 78-11614. (Univ. of California Publications in English: Vol. 19, No. 1). (Illus.). 160p. 1979. reprint ed. lib. bdg. 38.50 (*0-313-20661-9*, MIPP, Greenwood Pr) Greenwood.
Miles, Joyce B., jt. auth. see Craig, Betty L.
Miles, Julia, ed. Playwriting Women: 7 Plays from the Women's Project. 325p. (C). 1993. pap. 17.95 (*0-435-08617-0*, 08617) Heinemann.
— Women Heroes: Six Short Plays from the Women's Project. 256p. 1988. pap. 8.95 (*0-936839-22-8*) Applause Theatre Bk Pubs.
— Women's Project Two: Five New Plays by Women. LC 84-81624. 1984. 21.95 (*0-933826-73-7*) PAJ Pubns.
— Womenswork: Five New Plays from the Women's Project. 356p. 1989. pap. 11.95 (*1-55783-029-0*) Applause Theatre Bk Pubs.
Miles, Julia, ed. & intro. see Women's Project (New York, N.Y.) Staff.
Miles, Kathy, ed. see Reed, John.
Miles, Keith. Double Eagle. large type ed. 355p. 1992. 11.50 (*0-7505-0337-8*) Ulverscroft.
— Murder in Perspective: An Architectural Mystery. LC 96-35898. 246p. 1997. 21.95 (*0-8027-3298-4*) Walker & Co.
***Miles, Keith.** Saint's Rest. LC 98-52922. (Merlin Richards Mystery Ser.). 312p. 1999. 23.95 (*0-8027-3332-8*) Walker & Co.
Miles, Keith A. Flagstick. large type ed. 333p. 1994. 27.99 (*0-7505-0601-6*) Ulverscroft.
Miles-Kubota, Mitzi, ed. West Wind Review Vol. 15: Sites, Vol. 15. 15th ed. (Illus.). 224p. (YA). (gr. 10 up). 1996. pap. 10.00 (*0-9630694-5-4*) So Oregon.
Miles, L. Hotshots - Flags. (Illus.). 32p. (J). (gr. 2 up). 1997. pap. 2.95 (*0-7460-2793-1*, Usborne) EDC.
Miles, L. W., ed. Textile Printing. 2nd ed. 1994. pap. 70.00 (*0-901956-57-0*, Pub. by Textile Inst) St Mut.
Miles-LaGrange, Vicki, jt. auth. see Burke, Bob.
Miles, Laughton E. & Broughton, Roger J., eds. Medical Monitoring in the Home & Work Environment. LC 89-24228. 352p. 1990. reprint ed. pap. 109.20 (*0-608-03431-2*, 206413200008) Bks Demand.
Miles, LaVerne. Do-It-Yourself Poetry. (Illus.). 32p. (Orig.). 1997. pap. text, wbk. ed. 9.95 (*1-891098-02-0*, 97-0702, Paper Tools) Think Publ.
Miles, Lawrence. Alien Bodies. 8th ed. (Doctor Who Ser.). 1998. pap. 5.95 (*0-563-40577-5*) BBC.
— Christmas on a Rational Planet. (Dr. Who New Adventures Ser.). 280p. 1996. mass mkt. 5.95 (*0-426-20476-X*, Pub. by Virgin Bks) London Brdge.
***Miles, Lawrence.** Dead Romance. (New Adventures Ser.). 1999. mass mkt. 6.95 (*0-426-20532-4*) London Brdge.
Miles, Lawrence. Down. (Orig.). 1997. mass mkt. 5.95 (*0-426-20512-X*, Pub. by Virgin Bks) London Brdge.
Miles, Lawrence W., Jr. The California Auto Dealer Legal Manual. 200p. 1993. pap. 75.00 (*0-9635978-0-9*) Clairidge Pr.
— Law of the Car: Everything You Ever Wanted to Know about Buying, Owning, & Selling a Vehicle. 175p. 1993. pap. text. write for info. (*0-9635978-1-7*) Clairidge Pr.
Miles, Lee. Sweden & European Integration. LC 97-13479. (Illus.). 352p. 1997. text 77.95 (*1-85521-629-9*, Pub. by Ashgate Pub) Ashgate Pub Co.
***Miles, Lee.** Sweden & the European Union Evaluated. LC 00-31400. 2000. pap. write for info. (*0-8264-4869-0*) Continuum.
Miles, Lee A. Fine Tuning Air Conditioning Systems & Heat Pumps. Turpin, Joanna, ed. LC 94-30563. (Illus.). 104p. (Orig.). 1995. pap. 14.95 (*0-912524-96-0*) Busn News.
Miles, Lena. Country Reds. 90p. 1994. write for info. (*0-9642054-0-8*) High Ridge.
Miles, Leo W. High Pressure: A Pipeliner's Story. (Illus.). 179p. (C). 1988. 17.95 (*0-9622105-0-1*) Raton Bks.
Miles, Leslie H., Jr., et al. Dimensions of Value. 6th rev. ed. Miles-Blackard, Lisa, ed. (Illus.). 451p. 1997. pap. text 40.00 (*0-9661733-0-9*) MB Valuations.
Miles, Linda. His Girl Monday to Friday. (Romance Ser.: Vol. 428). 1999. mass mkt. 3.50 (*0-373-17428-4*, 1-17428-3, Harlequin) Harlequin Bks.
— Husband-to-Be. 1998. pap. 3.50 (*0-373-17402-0*, 1-17402-8) Harlequin Bks.
***Miles, Linda.** Last-Minute Bridegroom. 1999. mass mkt. 3.50 (*0-373-17439-X*) Harlequin Bks.
Miles, Linda. Linda Miles Practice Dynamics. 160p. 1986. 29.95 (*0-87814-301-7*) PennWell Bks.
Miles, Linda & Hailey, Walter. Your Key to the Practice. Gordon, Kirpal, ed. (Illus.). 96p. (Orig.). 1995. pap. text 19.95 (*1-882306-06-6*) Planned Mktg.
***Miles, Linda & Miles, Robert.** The New Marriage: Transcending the Happily-Ever-After Myth: How to Put Your Relationship Back on Track. 144p. 2000. pap. 19.95 (*1-879384-39-6*) Cypress Hse.
Miles, Linda L. The Rise & Fall of Managed Care. McCullough, Virginia, ed. 96p. 1997. pap. 12.95 (*0-9658409-0-5*) Link Pub VA.
Miles, Lion G., ed. The Hessians of Lewis Miller. (Illus.). 66p. 1983. pap. 15.00 (*0-939016-07-9*) Johannes Schwalm Hist.
Miles, Lisa. Atlas of 20th Century. (History Atlases Ser.). (Illus.). 64p. (J). (gr. 4-7). 1997. 12.95 (*0-7460-2499-1*, Usborne) EDC.
Miles, Lisa. Atlas of World History. (Illus.). 96p. (J). (gr. 4-7). 1996. 16.95 (*0-7460-1728-6*, Usborne) EDC.
***Miles, Lisa.** Encyclopedia of Ancient Greece. (Usborne Encyclopedia Ser.). (Illus.). 160p. (gr. 4-7). 2000. 27.95 (*1-58086-259-4*) EDC.
Miles, Lisa. First Words Sticker Book. (Sticker Learning Bks.). (Illus.). 18p. 1999. pap. 6.95 (*0-7460-3334-6*, Usborne) EDC.
— Hair Braiding. (How to Make Ser.). (Illus.). 32p. (J). (gr. 3-7). 1996. lib. bdg. 14.95 (*0-88110-821-9*, Usborne) EDC.
— Hotshot Computers. (Hotshots Ser.). (Illus.). 32p. (J). (gr. 2-5). 1997. pap. 2.95 (*0-7460-2782-6*, Usborne) EDC.
— Hotshot History of Britain. (Hotshots Ser.). (Illus.). 32p. (J). (gr. 2-5). 1997. pap. 2.95 (*0-7460-2787-7*, Usborne) EDC.
— Hotshot Secret Codes. (Hotshots Ser.). (Illus.). 32p. (J). (gr. 2-5). 1997. pap. 2.95 (*0-7460-2794-X*, Usborne) EDC.
— Hotshot Swimming. (Hotshots Ser.). (Illus.). 32p. (J). (gr. 2-5). 1997. pap. 2.95 (*0-7460-2558-0*, Usborne) EDC.
— Hotshot World History Dates. (Hotshots Ser.). (Illus.). 32p. (J). (gr. 2-5). 1997. pap. 2.95 (*0-7460-2797-4*, Usborne) EDC.
— Hotshots Lettering. (Hotshots Ser.). (Illus.). 32p. (J). (gr. 2 up). 1995. pap. 2.95 (*0-7460-2274-3*, Usborne) EDC.
— Hotshots Rocks & Minerals. (Hotshots Ser.). (Illus.). 32p. (J). (gr. 2-5). 1997. pap. 2.95 (*0-7460-2790-7*, Usborne) EDC.
— Hotshots Spying for Beginners. (Hotshots Ser.). (Illus.). 32p. (J). (gr. 2 up). 1996. pap. 2.95 (*0-7460-2549-1*, Usborne) EDC.
***Miles, Lisa.** Libro de Pegatinas Banderas (Flags Sticker Book) (Spotter's Guides Sticker Bks.). (SPA., Illus.). 32p. (gr. 2 up). 1999. pap. 7.95 (*0-7460-3644-2*, Usborne) EDC.
— Libro de Pegatinas Gatos (Cats Sticker Book) (Spotter's Guide Sticker Bks.). (ENG & SPA., Illus.). 32p. (YA). (gr. 2 up). 2000. pap. 7.95 (*0-7460-3884-4*, Usborne) EDC.
— Libro de Pegatinas Rocas y Minerales. (Spotter's Guides Sticker Bks.). (SPA., Illus.). 32p. (gr. 2 up). 1999. pap. 7.95 (*0-7460-3642-6*, Usborne) EDC.
Miles, Lisa. Starting to Read Sticker Book. (Sticker Learning Bks.). (Illus.). 18p. 1999. pap. text 6.95 (*0-7460-3408-3*, Usborne) EDC.
Miles, Lisa, ed. Flags Sticker Book. (Spotter's Guides Sticker Bks.). 24p. (J). (gr. 2 up). 1998. pap. 7.95 (*0-7460-3151-3*) EDC.
— Flowers Sticker Book. (Spotter's Guides Sticker Bks.). (Illus.). 24p. (J). (gr. 2 up). 1998. pap. 7.95 (*0-7460-2997-7*) EDC.
— Letters to Copy. (Sticker Learning Bks.). (Illus.). 18p. (J). (ps-3). 1999. pap. 6.95 (*0-7460-3110-6*, Usborne) EDC.
— Starting to Write Sticker Book. (Sticker Learning Bks.). (Illus.). (J). (ps-3). 1999. pap. text 6.95 (*0-7460-3108-4*, Usborne) EDC.
***Miles, Lisa, ed.** Time Sticker Book. (Sticker Learning Book Ser.). (Illus.). 18p. (J). (ps-k). 2000. pap. 6.95 (*0-7460-3726-0*, Pub. by Usbne Pbng UK) EDC.
— Words to Write Sticker Learning Book. (Sticker Learning Bks.). (Illus.). 18p. (YA). (ps-k). 2000. pap. write for info. (*0-7460-3727-9*, Pub. by Usbne Pbng UK) EDC.
***Miles, Lisa & Cartwright, Stephen.** Counting to Ten. (Sticker Learning Bks.). (Illus.). 18p. (J). (ps-3). 1999. pap. 6.95 (*0-7460-3407-5*, Usborne) EDC.
***Miles, Lisa & Reid, Struan, eds.** Encyclopedia of Ancient Greece. (Encyclopedias Ser.). (Illus.). 160p. (YA). (gr. 4-7). 2000. 19.95 (*0-7460-3403-2*, Pub. by Usbrne Pbng UK) EDC.
Miles, Lisa & Smith, Alastair. Astronomy & Space. (Complete Books Ser.). (J). (gr. 3 up). 1998. lib. bdg. 22.95 (*1-58086-130-X*, Usborne) EDC.
— Astronomy & Space. (Complete Books Ser.). (Illus.). 96p. (J). (gr. 3-4). 1998. pap. 14.95 (*0-7460-3104-1*, Usborne) EDC.
Miles, Lisa & Watt, Fiona M. Hair Braiding. (How to Make Ser.). (Illus.). 32p. (J). (gr. 3-7). 1996. pap. 6.95 (*0-7460-2321-9*, Usborne) EDC.
— Hotshots Hair Braiding. (Hotshots Ser.). (Illus.). 32p. (J). (gr. 2 up). 1996. pap. 2.95 (*0-7460-2664-1*, Usborne) EDC.
Miles, Lisa, ed. see O'Brien, Eileen & Riddell, Diana.
Miles, Lisaj, jt. auth. see Watt, Fiona.
Miles, M. B., jt. auth. see Huberman, A. M.
Miles, M. Scott. Someone in My Corner. LC 96-133591. 144p. 1995. pap. 1.30 (*1-56476-409-5*, 6-3409, Victor Bks) Chariot Victor.
— When the Walls Are Closing In. 132p. (Orig.). 1993. pap. 6.50 (*1-56476-104-5*, 6-3104, Victor Bks) Chariot Victor.
Miles, Malcolm. Art for Public Places: Critical Essays. (Illus.). 244p. 1991. pap. 18.95 (*0-9506783-8-4*, Pub. by Winchester Schl Art Pr) Paul & Co Pubs.
— Public Art in the City. LC 96-48742. (Illus.). 280p. (C). 1997. pap. 27.99 (*0-415-13943-0*) Routledge.
— Public Art in the City. LC 96-48742. (Illus.). 280p. (C). 1997. 85.00 (*0-415-13942-2*) Routledge.
***Miles, Malcolm, et al.** City Cultures Reader. LC 99-16477. 304p. 2000. pap. 29.99 (*0-415-20734-7*) Routledge.
Miles, Marc A. Devaluation, the Trade Balance, & the Balance of Payments. LC 78-7550. (Business Economics & Finance Ser.: No. 11). 160p. reprint ed. pap. 49.60 (*0-7837-0632-4*, 204097600019) Bks Demand.
***Miles, Margaret.** No Rest for the Dove. 336p. 2000. mass mkt. 5.99 (*0-553-57864-2*) Bantam Dell.
Miles, Margaret. Too Soon for Flowers. 320p. 1999. mass mkt. 5.99 (*0-553-57863-4*) Bantam.
— A Wicked Way to Burn. 336p. 1998. mass mkt. 5.50 (*0-553-57862-6*) Bantam.
Miles, Margaret M. The City Eleusinion. LC 97-32514. (Athenian Agora Ser.: Vol. 31). 1998. 75.00 (*0-87661-231-1*) Am Sch Athens.
Miles, Margaret R. Carnal Knowing: Female Nakedness & Religious Meaning in the Christian West. 272p. 1994. 45.00 (*0-86012-182-8*, Pub. by Srch Pr) St Mut.
— Carnal Knowing: Female Nakedness & Religious Meaning in the Christian West. LC 90-55679. 272p. 1991. pap. 15.00 (*0-679-73401-5*) Vin Bks.
***Miles, Margaret R.** Plotinus on Body & Beauty: Society, Philosophy & Religion in 3rd Century Rome. LC 99-32105. 224p. 1999. 64.95 (*0-631-21274-4*); pap. text 26.95 (*0-631-21275-2*) Blackwell Pubs.
Miles, Margaret R. Reading for Life: Beauty, Pluralism, & Responsibility. LC 96-40925. 228p. 1997. 29.95 (*0-8264-1009-X*) Continuum.
— Seeing & Believing: Religion & Values in the Movies. LC 95-24927. 272p. 1997. pap. 15.00 (*0-8070-1031-6*) Beacon Pr.
— The Vaughan Pride. large type ed. (Linford Romance Library). 288p. 1997. pap. 16.99 (*0-7089-5012-4*, Linford) Ulverscroft.
Miles, Margaret R., ed. see Johnston, Ralph C., Jr.
Miles, Margaret R., ed. see Wilkins, Walter J.
Miles, Margot. The Old Tennant. 127p. (C). 1988. 49.00 (*0-7316-4200-7*) St Mut.
Miles, Marianne W. Quick Reference for Psychiatric Nursing. 64p. 1994. pap. text 8.95 (*0-8151-8919-2*) Mosby Inc.
Miles, Marshall. Stronger Competitive Bidding. LC 92-70047. 324p. (Orig.). 1992. pap. 14.95 (*1-877908-03-7*) Lawrence & Leong Pub.
Miles, Martin J. Real Estate Investor's Complete Handbook. LC 82-351. 572p. 1982. 49.95 (*0-13-763086-7*, Busn) P-H.
Miles, Mary. Nantucket Etcetera. (Illus.). 196p. (Orig.). 1989. pap. 12.00 (*0-9623188-1-7*) Yesterdays Island.
— Nantucket Gam. LC 93-71134. 192p. 1993. write for info. (*0-9636885-1-0*); pap. write for info. (*0-9636885-2-9*) Faraway Pub.
— What's So Special about Nantucket? LC 98-71418. (Illus.). 36p. (J). (ps up). 1993. lib. bdg. 17.00 (*0-9636885-0-2*) Faraway Pub.
— Yesterday's & Today's Island. (Illus.). 200p. (Orig.). 1989. pap. write for info. (*0-318-65208-0*) Yesterdays Island.
Miles, Mary A., ed. see Zabel, Craig.
Miles, Mary D. Stress. (Lifesearch Ser.). 64p. (Orig.). 1994. pap. 4.95 (*0-687-77876-X*) Abingdon.
Miles, Matthew B. Learning to Work in Groups: A Practical Guide for Members & Trainers. 2nd ed. LC 98-70680. (Illus.). 360p. (C). 1998. pap. text 32.95 (*0-9658339-8-4*) Educ Intl Pr.
— Learning to Work in Groups: A Practical Guide for Members & Trainers. 2nd ed. LC 80-18150. 357p. 1981. reprint ed. pap. 110.70 (*0-608-02750-2*, 205255800007) Bks Demand.
Miles, Matthew B. & Huberman, A. Michael. Qualitative Data Analysis: An Expanded Sourcebook. 2nd ed. 352p. (C). 1994. text 75.00 (*0-8039-4653-8*); pap. text 34.00 (*0-8039-5540-5*) Sage.
Miles, Matthew B., jt. auth. see Gold, Barry A.
Miles, Matthew B., jt. auth. see Louis, Karen S.
Miles, Matthew B., jt. auth. see Weitzman, Eben.
Miles, Michael. Counterpoint/Clawhammer Banjo. 24p. 1996. pap. 17.95 incl. audio compact disk (*0-7866-0549-9*, 95550BCD) Mel Bay.
Miles, Mike E., jt. auth. see Wurtzebach, Charles H.
Miles, Miska. Ani y la Anciana.Tr. of Annie & the Old One. (SPA.). 1992. 12.99 (*968-16-3748-8*) Fondo.
— Annie & the Old One. (Illus.). 44p. (J). (gr. k-3). 1972. 16.95 (*0-316-57117-2*, Joy St Bks) Little.
— Annie & the Old One. (J). 1971. 12.90 (*0-606-03336-X*, Pub. by Turtleback) Demco.
— Annie & the Old One. (Illus.). 44p. (J). (gr. k-3). 1985. reprint ed. pap. 7.95 (*0-316-57120-2*) Little.
— Gertrude's Pocket. (Illus.). (J). (gr. 2-5). 1984. 15.75 (*0-8446-6164-3*) Peter Smith.
Miles, Moody K., III, jt. auth. see Miles, Barry W.
Miles, Morgan P., jt. ed. see Hills, Gerald E.
Miles, Murray. Insight & Inference: Descartes's Founding Principle & Modern Philosophy. (Toronto Studies in Philosophy). 600p. 1998. text 120.00 (*0-8020-4315-1*) U of Toronto Pr.
Miles, Nelson A. The Civil War: A Firsthand Look. unabridged ed. 1986. pap. 7.95 incl. audio (*1-882071-15-8*, 017) B&B Audio.
— Personal Recollections & Observations of General Nelson A. Miles, 2 Vols. Incl. Vol. 1. Personal Recollections & Observations of General Nelson A. Miles. Wooster, Robert, contrib. by. LC 91-39603. (Illus.). 319p. Date not set. reprint ed. pap. 11.95 (*0-8032-8180-3*, Bison Books); Vol. 2. Personal Recollections & Observations of General Nelson A. Miles. LC 91-39603. (Illus.). 272p. Date not set. reprint ed. pap. 11.95 (*0-8032-8181-1*, Bison Books); LC 91-39603. Date not set. reprint ed. Set pap. 23.90 (*0-8032-8182-X*, Bison Books) U of Nebr Pr.
— Personal Recollections & Observations of General Nelson A. Miles. rev. ed. LC 68-23812. (American Scene Ser.). (Illus.). 1969. reprint ed. lib. bdg. 69.50 (*0-306-71020-X*) Da Capo.
— Serving the Republic: Memoirs of the Civil & Military Life of Nelson A. Miles. LC 74-147786. (Select Bibliographies Reprint Ser.). 1977. reprint ed. 28.95 (*0-8369-5632-X*) Ayer.
Miles, Octavia, ed. see Yancey, Antronette K.
Miles, P., et al, eds. Reflections on the 1988-1990 March of the Living. (Illus.). 139p. (Orig.). 1991. pap. 25.00 (*0-930029-04-6*) Central Agency.
Miles, P. G., jt. auth. see Shu-Ting Chang.
Miles, Pamela S., et al. Obstetrics & Gynecology. LC 94-3805. (Oklahoma Notes Ser.). (Illus.). 240p. 1994. 16.95 (*0-387-94184-3*) Spr-Verlag.
— Obstetrics & Gynecology. 2nd rev. ed. (Oklahoma Notes Ser.). (Illus.). 218p. 1996. pap. text 17.95 (*0-387-94632-2*) Spr-Verlag.
Miles, Patricia H., jt. auth. see Bracegirdle, Brian.
Miles, Patrick, ed. Chekhov on the British Stage. LC 92-26037. (Illus.). 270p. (C). 1993. text 69.95 (*0-521-38467-2*) Cambridge U Pr.
Miles, Patrick, jt. auth. see Westfall, Tanja.
Miles, Patrick, tr. see Smeliansky, Anatoly.
Miles, Patrick, tr. see Vampilov, Aleksandr.
Miles, Paul L., jt. auth. see Venzon, Anne C.
Miles, Peggy. Internet World Guide to Webcasting. LC 97-52093. 448p. 1998. pap. 29.99 (*0-471-24217-9*) Wiley.
Miles, Peter. A Gift of Observation. 92p. (C). 1988. 75.00 (*0-7212-0794-4*, Pub. by Regency Pr GBR) St Mut.
— The Teachings of Osiris. 144p. 1997. reprint ed. pap. 19.95 (*0-7661-0045-6*) Kessinger Pub.
***Miles, Peter.** Wow Wow: Sites Unseen/The Internet Review. 2000. pap. text 14.95 (*3-8238-5450-X*) te Neues.
Miles, Peter & Smith, Malcolm. Cinema, Literature & Society: Elite & Mass Culture in Interwar Britain. (Film Ser.). 272p. 1987. lib. bdg. 35.00 (*0-7099-3363-0*, Pub. by C Helm) Routldge.
***Miles, Peter, et al.** Fuel 3000. (Illus.). 160p. 2000. 45.00 (*3-8238-5462-3*) te Neues.
Miles, Peter, ed. see Smollett, Tobias George.
Miles, Peter, ed. see Trollope, Anthony.
Miles, Preston. Speech Power. Pei, Mario A., ed. 59p. pap. text 99.95 incl. audio (*1-55678-024-9*, 1804) Learn Inc.
Miles, R., et al, eds. Research & Development in Expert Systems XV: Proceedings of ES98, the 18th Annual International Conference of the British Computer Society Specialist Group on Expert Systems, Cambridge, December, 1998. x, 225p. 1999. pap. (*1-85233-086-4*) Spr-Verlag.
Miles, R. E. & Chalmers, A. Progress in Transputer & Occam Research. LC 94-75912. 229p. (gr. 12). 1994. pap. 70.00 (*90-5199-163-0*) IOS Press.
Miles, R. E., jt. ed. see Chamberlain, J. M.
Miles, R. E., jt. ed. see Snowden, C. M.
Miles, R. Glen. Between Gloom & Glory: Sermons for Advent/Christmas/Epiphany. (First Lessons Ser.). 1998. 8.95 (*0-7880-1227-4*); pap. 8.95 (*0-7880-1226-6*) CSS OH.
— Between Glory & Gloom: Sermons for Advent/Christmas/Epiphany. LC 98-15099. (First Lessons Ser.). 1998. pap. 8.95 (*0-7880-1225-8*) CSS OH.
***Miles, R. Margaret.** Maiden & Mother: Devotions to the Blessed Virgin Mary Throughout the Year. 208p. 2000. pap. 14.95 (*0-89870-780-3*, Pub. by Ignatius Pr) Midpt Trade.

An Asterisk (*) at the beginning of an entry indicates that the title is appearing for the first time.

Miles, R. S., et al. The Design of Educational Exhibits. (Illus.). 224p. (C). 1982. text 44.95 (*0-04-069002-4*) Routledge.

Miles, Ray. King of the Wildcatters: The Life & Times of Tom Slick, 1883-1930. LC 96-20128. (Kenneth E. Montague Series in Oil & Business History: No. 9). (Illus.). 160p. 1996. 29.95 (*0-89096-715-6*) Tex A&M Univ Pr.

— Offering Meditations. LC 97-43297. 1998. 5.99 (*0-8272-2709-4*) Chalice Pr.

Miles, Raymond E. & Snow, Charles C. Fit, Failure & the Hall of Fame: How Companies Succeed or Fail. (Illus.). 224p. 1994. 24.95 (*0-02-921265-0*) Free Pr.

— Organizational Strategy: Structure & Process. (Management Ser.). (Illus.). (C). 1978. text 66.00 (*0-07-041932-9*) McGraw.

***Miles, Rebekah L.** The Pastor as Moral Guide. LC 98-48893. (Creative Pastoral Care & Counseling Ser.). 128p. 1999. pap. 14.00 (*0-8006-3136-6*, 1-3136, Fortress Pr) Augsburg Fortress.

Miles, Richard. Constructing Identities in Late Antiquity. LC 98-37614. 1999. 75.00 (*0-415-19406-7*) Routledge.

— Elizabeth Keith: The Printed Works, 1917-1939: A Catalogue Raisonne. (Illus.). 80p. 1991. pap. 27.50 (*1-877921-07-6*) Pacific Asia.

— Prints of Paul Jacoulet. (Illus.). 140p. (C). 1982. pap. text 50.00 (*0-903697-13-0*) Pacific Asia.

Miles, Richard. The Prints of Paul Jacoulet. LC 82-81033. (Illus.). 140p. 1982. 75.00 (*1-877921-28-9*) Pacific Asia.

Miles, Richard. Watercolors of Paul Jacoulet. (Illus.). 84p. 1989. pap. 38.00 (*1-877921-01-7*) Pacific Asia.

Miles, Richard, jt. auth. see Traub, Roger D.

Miles, Richard, ed. see Blocher, Larry, et al.

Miles, Richard B., jt. auth. see Blocher, Larry R.

Miles, Robert. Anne Radcliffe: The Great Enchantress. 208p. 1995. text 79.95 (*0-7190-3828-6*, Pub. by Manchester Univ Pr); text 24.95 (*0-7190-3829-4*, Pub. by Manchester Univ Pr) St Martin.

— Capitalism & Unfree Labor: Anomaly or Necessity? 256p. 1987. lib. bdg. 49.50 (*0-422-61730-X*) Routledge.

— Capitalism & Unfree Labor: Anomaly or Necessity? 256p. 1989. 55.00 (*0-422-79250-0*, A0712); pap. 18.95 (*0-685-26092-5*, A3795) Routledge.

— Racism. 175p. (C). 1989. pap. 16.99 (*0-415-01809-9*) Routledge.

— Racism after 'Race' Relations. LC 92-47079. 256p. (C). 1993. pap. 24.99 (*0-415-10034-8*) Routledge.

— Racism & Migrant Labour: A Critical Text. 206p. (Orig.). 1983. pap. 14.95 (*0-7100-9212-1*, Routledge Thoemms) Routledge.

Miles, Robert & Thranhardt, Dietrich. Migration & European Integration: The Dynamics of Inclusion & Exclusion. 224p. 1995. 38.50 (*0-8386-3613-6*) Fairleigh Dickinson.

Miles, Robert, et al. Prose Style: A Contemporary Guide. 2nd ed. 224p. (C). 1990. pap. text 31.60 (*0-13-713181-X*) P-H.

Miles, Robert, jt. auth. see Miles, Linda.

Miles, Robert, jt. ed. see Monteith, Moira.

Miles, Robert H. Leading Corporate Transformation: An Executive Briefing. LC 96-51317. (Jossey-Bass Business & Management Ser.). 1997. mass mkt. 25.00 (*0-7879-0327-2*) Jossey-Bass.

Miles, Robert H. & Randolph, W. Alan. Organization Game. 2nd ed. (C). 1985. text 25.00 (*0-673-16654-6*) Addson-Wesley Educ.

***Miles, Robert P.** The World's Greatest Investment: 101 Reasons to Own Berkshire Hathaway. 2nd expanded ed. 247p. 1999. pap. 19.95 (*0-9672302-1-7*) R P Miles.

Miles, Robert W. Eyes Forward: Messages for Today from Yesterday. LC 99-38113. 224p. 1999. pap. 18.95 (*0-86534-296-2*) Sunstone Pr.

— That Frenchman, John Calvin. LC 83-45625. reprint ed. 29.00 (*0-404-19843-0*) AMS Pr.

Miles, Roger & Zavala, Lauro. Towards the Museum of the Future: New European Perspectives. LC 93-12788. 204p. (C). (gr. 13). 1994. 65.00 (*0-415-09498-4*) Routledge.

Miles, Roger E. Symetric Bends: How to Join Two Lengths of Cord. (Series on Knots & Everything). 150p. 1995. text 32.00 (*981-02-2194-0*) World Scientific Pub.

Miles, Roger J. & Nicholas, Robin A. J., eds. Mycoplasma Protocols. LC 98-4288. (Methods in Molecular Biology Ser.). (Illus.). 336p. 1998. 89.50 (*0-89603-525-5*) Humana.

Miles, Rogers B. Science, Religion & Belief: The Clerical Virtuosi of the Royal Society of London, 1663-1687. LC 91-16763. (American University Studies: Theology & Religion: Ser. VII, Vol. 106). 207p. 1992. 41.95 (*0-8204-1564-2*) P Lang Pubng.

Miles, Rosalind. Act of Passion. large type ed. (Black Satin Romance Ser.). 432p. 1996. 27.99 (*1-86110-002-7*) Ulverscroft.

— Ben Jonson: His Craft & Art. 272p. (C). 1990. text 70.50 (*0-389-20944-9*) B&N Imports.

— Ben Jonson: His Craft & Art. 256p. 1990. 55.00 (*0-415-05578-4*, A4913) Routledge.

— Ben Jonson: His Life & Work. 288p. 1986. 55.00 (*0-7102-0838-3*, 08383, Routledge Thoemms) Routledge.

— Guenevere: Queen of the Summer Country. LC 98-27659. 432p. 1999. 24.00 (*0-609-60362-0*) Crown Pub Group.

***Miles, Rosalind.** Guenevere: Queen of the Summer Country. 528p. 2000. pap. text 9.95 (*0-609-80650-5*) Crown Pub Group.

— The Knight of the Sacred Lake. LC 99-40177. 432p. 2000. 24.00 (*0-609-60623-9*, FIC014000, Crown) Crown Pub Group.

— The Problem of Measure for Measure: A Historical Investigation LC 75-35037. 349 p. 1976. 22.50 (*0-06-494824-2*) HarpC.

Miles, Ruth H., jt. auth. see Morrow, Jean.

Miles, Sadie M. Anthology I, a Collection of Plays, Short Stories & Poetry: Incidents in the Life of a Slave Girl. Woolfolk, Thomas, Jr., ed. LC 99-1287. 200p. 1999. pap. 20.00 (*1-886098-04-2*, 1554) Woolfolk Pubns.

Miles, Sally. Crisis at Crabtree. LC 95-82211. (Illus.). 32p. (J). (gr. 3-5). 1996. 11.95 (*0-7188-2651-5*, Lutterworth-Parkwest) Parkwest Pubns.

Miles, Sam. Guilt Free Gourmet: Food That Tastes "Too Good" to Be "Good for You" over 1,200 Recipes, Vol. 1. 422p. 1997. 49.95 (*0-9641843-0-3*) Wellness.

***Miles, Sara.** How to Hack a Party Line: The Democrats & Silicon Valley. 256p. 2001. 24.00 (*0-374-17714-7*) FS&G.

Miles, Sara & Rofes, Eric E. Opposite Sex: Gay Men on Lesbians, Lesbians on Gay Men. LC 97-33960. 288p. 1998. text 55.00 (*0-8147-7476-8*); pap. text 17.00 (*0-8147-7477-6*) NYU Pr.

Miles, Sara, ed. see Jordan, June.

Miles, Sara, tr. see Rugama, Leonel, et al.

***Miles, Sian.** Simone Weil. 304p. 2000. pap. 13.50 (*0-8021-3729-6*, Grove) Grove-Atltic.

Miles, Sian, ed. from FRE. Simone Weil: An Anthology. LC 86-9242. 304p. 1986. pap. 12.95 (*1-55584-021-3*, Grove) Grove-Atltic.

Miles, Simon. Reasons Why. (C). 1989. 24.95 (*1-871058-04-X*, Pub. by Dragonheart Pr) St Mut.

Miles, Steven. Consumerism: As a Way of Life. LC 98-60536. viii, 174p. 1998. write for info. (*0-7619-5214-4*) Sage.

***Miles, Steven.** Youth Lifestyles in a Changing World. LC 99-56818. 2000. pap. write for info. (*0-335-20099-0*) OpUniv Pr.

Miles, Susan G. Adoption Literature for Children & Young Adults: An Annotated Bibliography, 21. LC 91-31854. (Bibliographies & Indexes in Sociology Ser.: No. 21). 232p. 1991. lib. bdg. 49.95 (*0-313-27606-4*, MBK/, Greenwood Pr) Greenwood.

Miles, T. R. Help for Dyslexic Children. 116p. (C). 1983. pap. 14.99 (*0-415-04570-3*) Routledge.

— Speaking of God: Theism, Atheism & the Magnus Image. 160p. 1999. pap. 60.00 (*1-85072-202-1*, Pub. by W Sessions) St Mut.

Miles, T. R., ed. Understanding Dyslexia. (C). 1988. 65.00 (*1-871458-07-2*, Pub. by Bath Educ Pubs) St Mut.

Miles, T. R. & Miles, Elaine. Dyslexia: A Hundred Years On. 2nd ed. LC 98-27637. 192p. 1999. pap. 28.95 (*0-335-20034-6*) OpUniv Pr.

— Help for Dyslexic Children. 116p. 1983. pap. 9.95 (*0-416-33740-6*, NO. 3829) Routledge.

Miles, T. R. & Miles, Elaine, eds. Dyslexia & Mathematics. 144p. (C). 1991. pap. 20.99 (*0-415-04987-3*, A5962) Routledge.

Miles, T. R. & Varma, V., eds. Dyslexia & Stress. 145p. 1995. pap. 45.00 (*1-56593-593-4*, 1214) Singular Publishing.

Miles, T. R., jt. auth. see Harzem, Peter.

Miles, T. R., jt. ed. see Pavlidis, George T.

Miles, Thomas H. Critical Thinking & Writing for Science & Technology. 345p. (C). 1989. pap. text 43.00 (*0-15-516156-3*) Harcourt Coll Pubs.

— Critical Thinking & Writing for Science & Technology. 345p. (C). 1990. pap. text, teacher ed. 2.75 (*0-15-516157-1*) Harcourt Coll Pubs.

— Guide to Building Sensible Phrases with Noun Strings & Unit Modifiers. 59p. 1994. pap. text 20.00 (*0-914548-78-6*, 154-94) Soc Tech Comm.

Miles, Thomas J. Mathematics. LC 96-29496. 650p. 1997. mass mkt. 76.95 (*0-314-09576-4*) West Pub.

— Mathematics: One of the Liberal A. (Mathematics Ser.). (C). 1997. pap., student ed. 21.95 (*0-314-20973-5*) Brooks-Cole.

Miles, Thomas R., jt. auth. see Gilroy, Dorothy E.

Miles, Thomas S. Death on Request U. S. A. 104p. 1999. pap. 11.00 (*0-8059-4573-3*) Dorrance.

Miles, Timothy R. Dyslexia at College. 160p. 1987. 12.95 (*0-416-39670-4*) Routledge.

***Miles, Tony & Ford, Martin.** Practical Fishing Encyclopedia. 256p. 2000. 40.00 (*0-7548-0283-3*) Anness Pub.

Miles, Victoria. Bald Eaglets. (Illus.). 24p. (Orig.). (J). (gr. 1-4). 1995. pap. 5.95 (*1-55143-028-2*) Orca Bk Pubs.

***Miles, Victoria.** La Cena del Cachorro.Tr. of Pup's Supper. (SPA., Illus.). 12p. (J). (ps-k). 1998. bds. 5.95 (*1-878244-26-4*) Monterey Bay Aquarium.

Miles, Victoria. Cougar Kittens. (Illus.). 24p. (Orig.). (J). (gr. 1-4). 1995. pap. 5.95 (*1-55143-026-6*) Orca Bk Pubs.

— Pup's Supper. LC 98-30062. (Illus.). (J). 1998. bds. 5.95 (*1-878244-22-1*) Monterey Bay Aquarium.

— Sea Otter Pup. (Illus.). 24p. (Orig.). (J). (gr. 1-4). 1993. pap. 5.95 (*1-55143-002-9*) Orca Bk Pubs.

— Spotted Owlets. (Illus.). 24p. (Orig.). (J). (gr. 1-4). 1993. pap. 5.95 (*1-55143-004-5*) Orca Bk Pubs.

Miles, Virginia G. & DeBaugh, R. Adam. The UFMCC Mission Statement. 30p. 1990. pap. 2.50 (*1-888493-07-0*) Chi Rho Pr.

Miles, Walter R., et al. Science in Progress. Baitsell, George A., ed. LC 78-37534. (Essay Index Reprint Ser.: 4). 1977. reprint ed. 46.95 (*0-8369-2529-7*) Ayer.

Miles, Wilfred. Military Operations, France & Belgium, 1916, Vol. II. (Great War Ser.: No. 19). (Illus.). 654p. reprint ed. 49.95 (*0-89839-169-5*) Battery Pr.

Miles, Wilfrid. Military Operations, France & Belgium, 1916 Vol. II: Maps & Appendices. (Great War Ser.: No. 34). 135p. 1994. reprint ed. 39.95 (*0-89839-207-1*) Battery Pr.

— Military Operations, France & Belgium, 1917: The Battle of Cambrai, Vol. III. (Great War Ser.: No. 13). (Illus.). 432p. reprint ed. 49.95 (*0-89839-162-8*) Battery Pr.

Miles, William. The Image Makers: A Bibliography of American Presidential Campaign Biographies. LC 79-19472. 272p. 1979. 26.50 (*0-8108-1252-5*) Scarecrow.

— Songs, Odes, Glees & Ballads: A Bibliography of American Presidential Campaign Songsters, 27. LC 90-44938. (Music Reference Collection: No. 27). 256p. 1990. lib. bdg. 62.95 (*0-313-27697-8*, MGI, Greenwood Pr) Greenwood.

Miles, William, compiled by. The People's Voice: An Annotated Bibliography of American Presidential Campaign Newspapers, 1828-1984, 6. LC 87-11969. (Bibliographies & Indexes in American History Ser.: No. 6). 259p. 1987. lib. bdg. 75.00 (*0-313-23976-2*, MPN/) Greenwood.

Miles, William, jt. auth. see Burns, Khephra.

Miles, William D., tr. see Kirmani, Mir Hussain Ali Khan.

Miles, William F. Bridging Mental Boundaries in a Postcolonial Microcosm: Identity & Development in Vanuatu. LC 98-9698. (Illus.). 288p. 1998. text 47.00 (*0-8248-1979-9*); pap. text 22.95 (*0-8248-2048-7*) UH Pr.

— Elections & Ethnicity in French Martinique: A Paradox in Paradise. LC 85-16737. 302p. 1985. 65.00 (*0-275-90031-2*, C0031, Praeger Pubs) Greenwood.

— Hausaland Divided: Colonialism & Independence in Nigeria & Niger. LC 93-31669. (Wilder House Series in Politics, History, & Culture). (Illus.). 392p. 1994. text 49.95 (*0-8014-2855-6*) Cornell U Pr.

— Imperial Burdens: Countercolonialism in Former French India. LC 93-50213. 255p. 1994. lib. bdg. 47.00 (*1-55587-511-4*) L Rienner.

Miles, Wyndham D., ed. American Chemists & Chemical Engineers. LC 76-192. 544p. 1976. text 34.00 (*0-8412-0278-8*, Pub. by Am Chemical) OUP.

Milesi-Ferretti, Gian M. & Razin, Assaf. Current-Account Sustainability. LC 96-46436. (Princeton Studies in International Finance: Vol. 81). 78p. 1996. pap. 13.50 (*0-88165-253-9*) Princeton U Int Finan Econ.

Milesius, Timotheus. Die Perser. (Wissenschaftliche Veroffentlichungen der Deutschen Orient-Gesellschaft Ser.: Heft 3). 126p. 1973. reprint ed. write for info. (*3-487-05049-8*) G Olms Pubs.

Milestone Media Inc. Staff, jt. auth. see Dingle, Derek T.

Milestone, Wayne D., ed. Reliability, Stress Analysis & Failure Prevention Methods in Mechanical Design: International Conference on Reliability, Stress Analysis & Failure Prevention, 1980, San Francisco, CA. LC 80-66039. 327p. reprint ed. pap. 101.40 (*0-608-15564-0*, 205639300064) Bks Demand.

***Milet Limited Publishing Staff.** Carrying. 2000. pap. 9.95 (*1-84059-122-6*); pap. 9.95 (*1-84059-123-4*); pap. 9.95 (*1-84059-124-2*); pap. 9.95 (*1-84059-125-0*); pap. 9.95 (*1-84059-126-9*), pap. 9.95 (*1-84059-127-7*); pap. 9.95 (*1-84059-128-5*); pap. 9.95 (*1-84059-129-3*) Milet Ltd.

— Celebrating. 2000. pap. 9.95 (*1-84059-130-7*); pap. 9.95 (*1-84059-131-5*); pap. 9.95 (*1-84059-132-3*); pap. 9.95 (*1-84059-133-1*); pap. 9.95 (*1-84059-134-X*); pap. 9.95 (*1-84059-135-8*); pap. 9.95 (*1-84059-136-6*); pap. 9.95 (*1-84059-137-4*) Milet Ltd.

— Eating. 2000. pap. 9.95 (*1-84059-138-2*); pap. 9.95 (*1-84059-139-0*); pap. 9.95 (*1-84059-140-4*); pap. 9.95 (*1-84059-141-2*); pap. 9.95 (*1-84059-142-0*); pap. 9.95 (*1-84059-143-9*); pap. 9.95 (*1-84059-144-7*); pap. 9.95 (*1-84059-145-5*) Milet Ltd.

— Smiling. 2000. pap. 9.95 (*1-84059-114-5*); pap. 9.95 (*1-84059-115-3*); pap. 9.95 (*1-84059-116-1*); pap. 9.95 (*1-84059-117-X*); pap. 9.95 (*1-84059-118-8*); pap. 9.95 (*1-84059-119-6*); pap. 9.95 (*1-84059-120-X*); pap. 9.95 (*1-84059-121-8*) Milet Ltd.

Mileti, Dennis. Disasters by Design: A Reassessment of Natural Hazards in the United States. LC 99-29511. (Natural Hazards & Disasters Ser.). 376p. 1999. 47.95 (*0-309-06360-4*, Joseph Henry Pr) Natl Acad Pr.

Mileti, Dennis S., et al. Earthquake Prediction Response & Options for Public Policy. (Program on Environment & Behavior Monograph Ser.: No. 31). 190p. (Orig.). (C). 1981. pap. 20.00 (*0-685-28105-1*) Natural Hazards.

Miletic, Antun. Coverup: The Political Protection of Kurt Waldheim, Nazi War Criminal & Public Statesman. 1996. pap. text 19.95 (*0-935016-39-2*) Arrowood Pr.

***Miletic, Milan.** Insomnia. LC 00-91316. 2000. pap. 10.95 (*0-533-13543-5*) Vantage.

Miletich, John J. Acid Rain in Canada: A Selected Bibliography. LC 83-15159. (CPL Bibliographies Ser.: No. 124). 1983. 6.00 (*0-86602-124-8*, Sage Prdcls Pr) Sage.

— AIDS: A Multimedia Sourcebook. LC 92-39121. 232p. 1993. pap. 21.95 (*0-89789-362-X*, Greenwood Pr) Greenwood.

— Depression in the Elderly: A Multimedia Sourcebook, 36. LC 97-16238. (Bibliographies & Indexes in Gerontology Ser.: Vol. 36). 248p. 1997. lib. bdg. 69.50 (*0-313-30113-1*, Greenwood Pr) Greenwood.

— Retirement-Planning & Adjustment: A Selected Bibliography. (CPL Bibliographies Ser.: No. 117). 53p. 1983. 10.00 (*0-86602-117-5*, Sage Prdcls Pr) Sage.

— Treatment of Cocaine Abuse: An Annotated Bibliography, 9. LC 91-35403. (Bibliographies & Indexes in Medical Studies: No. 9). 256p. 1992. lib. bdg. 59.95 (*0-313-27839-3*, MTQ/, Greenwood Pr) Greenwood.

Miletich, John J., compiled by. AIDS: A Multimedia Sourcebook, 10. LC 93-10830. (Bibliographies & Indexes in Medical Studies: No. 10). 288p. 1993. lib. bdg. 65.00 (*0-313-28669-8*) Greenwood.

— Airline Safety: An Annotated Bibliography, 7. LC 90-13988. (Bibliographies & Indexes in Psychology Ser.: No. 7). 240p. 1990. lib. bdg. 65.00 (*0-313-27391-X*, MRS/, Greenwood Pr) Greenwood.

— Depression: A Multimedia Sourcebook, 11. LC 95-4194. (Bibliographies & Indexes in Medical Studies: No. 11). 240p. 1995. lib. bdg. 75.00 (*0-313-29374-0*, Greenwood Pr) Greenwood.

— Police, Firefighter & Paramedic Stress: An Annotated Bibliography, 6. LC 89-28649. (Bibliographies & Indexes in Psychology Ser.: No. 6). 239p. 1990. lib. bdg. 65.00 (*0-313-26682-4*, MOF/, Greenwood Pr) Greenwood.

— Retirement: An Annotated Bibliography, 2. LC 86-9933. (Bibliographies & Indexes in Gerontology Ser.: No. 2). 164p. 1986. lib. bdg. 47.95 (*0-313-24815-X*, MRI/, Greenwood Pr) Greenwood.

— States of Awareness: An Annotated Bibliography, 5. LC 88-24733. (Bibliographies & Indexes in Psychology Ser.). 306p. 1988. lib. bdg. 59.95 (*0-313-26194-6*, MSR, Greenwood Pr) Greenwood.

— Work & Alcohol Abuse: An Annotated Bibliography, 12. LC 87-23619. (Bibliographies & Indexes in Sociology Ser.: No. 12). 280p. 1987. lib. bdg. 59.95 (*0-313-25689-6*, MWR/, Greenwood Pr) Greenwood.

Miletich, John S. The Bugarstica: Bilingual Anthology of the Earliest Extant South Slavic Folk Narrative Song. (Illinois Medieval Monographs: No. III). 384p. 1990. text 34.95 (*0-252-01711-0*) U of Ill Pr.

M

Miletich, Leo N. Broadway's Prize-Winning Musicals: An Annotated Guide for Libraries & Audio Collectors. LC 92-4125. (Illus.). 255p. 1993. lib. bdg. 49.95 (*1-56024-288-4*) Haworth Pr.

— Broadway's Prize-Winning Musicals: An Annotated Guide for Libraries & Audio Collectors. LC 92-4125. 255p. 1993. pap. 29.95 (*1-56023-018-5*, Harrington Park) Haworth Pr.

— Dan Stuart's Fistic Carnival. (Illus.). 264p. 1994. 29.50 (*0-89096-614-1*); pap. 14.95 (*0-89096-615-X*) Tex A&M Univ Pr.

Miletski, Hani. Mother-Son Incest: The Unthinkable Broken Taboo: An Overview of Findings. Bear, Euan et al, eds. LC HV6570.7.M5 1997. 46p. 1995. pap. 10.00 (*1-884444-31-8*) Safer Soc.

Miletsky & Hewlett, Packar. Fat Free. 7th ed. 1999. student ed. 34.95 (*0-13-011847-8*) P-H.

Miletsky, Jason. Digital Publishing to Go. LC 99-55290. (To Go Ser.). 300p. 1999. pap. text 34.99 (*0-13-013536-4*) P-H.

***Miletsky, Jason.** Photoshop Five Point Five to Go. 320p. 2000. pap. 34.99 (*0-13-027018-0*) P-H.

— Web Photoshop Five Point Five to Go. 2000. pap. 34.99 (*0-13-027008-3*) P-H.

— Web Photoshop 5 to Go. LC 99-26471. (To Go Ser.). 320p. 1999. pap. text 34.99 (*0-13-011848-6*) P-H.

Miletta, Maureen. A Multiage Classroom: Choice & Possibility. LC 96-5491. 121p. (Orig.). 1996. pap. text 18.00 (*0-435-08889-0*, 08889) Heinemann.

Mileur, James J., jt. ed. see Milkis, Sidney M.

Mileur, Jean-Pierre. The Critical Romance: The Critic As Reader, Writer, Hero. LC 89-40533. 272p. 1990. pap. text 15.00 (*0-299-12414-2*) U of Wis Pr.

Mileur, Jerome M., ed. Polity: The Journal of the Northeastern Political Science Association. (Illus.). 200p. 1992. lib. bdg. 50.00 (*0-317-00292-9*) Polity NE Poli Sci.

Mileur, Jerome M. & Sulzner, George T. Campaigning for the Massachusetts Senate: Electioneering Outside the Political Limelight. LC 73-85898. 208p. 1974. pap. 16.95 (*0-87023-140-5*) U of Mass Pr.

Mileur, Jerome M., jt. auth. see Crotty, William.

Mileur, Jerome M., jt. ed. see White, John K.

Mileusky, Uziel, comment. The Ohr Somayach Haggadah. 180p. 1998. 16.95 (*1-56871-137-9*, Pub. by Targum Pr) Feldheim.

Milev, Geo. The Road to Freedom: Poems & Prose Poems. Osers, Ewald, tr. LC 87-82775. (Illus.). 66p. 1990. reprint ed. pap. 16.95 (*0-948259-45-0*, Pub. by Forest Bks) Dufour.

Milevsky, Moshe A. Money Logic: Financial Strategies for the Smart Investor. 1999. text 28.95 (*0-7737-3171-7*, Pub. by Stoddart Publ) Genl Dist Srvs.

Milewska, Maria I., ed. Slownik Geograficzno - Krajoznawczy Polski. (POL., Illus.). 896p. 1994. 26.00 (*83-01-09822-8*) Szwede Slavic.

Milewski, B. Supersymmetry & Supergravity, 1983: Proceedings of the XIX Winter School & Workshop on Theoretical Physics, Karpacz, Poland, February 14-26, 1983. 588p. (C). 1983. 98.00 (*9971-950-23-5*); pap. 52.00 (*9971-950-97-9*) World Scientific Pub.

Milewski, John V., ed. see Adams, John, et al.

Milewski, Ron & Lang, Rick. Pocket Guide for Documentation: EMT-B Skills. LC 98-38471. 1998. 13.00 (*0-7637-0879-8*) Jones & Bartlett.

Milewski, Stanley E., jt. auth. see Swastek, Joseph.

Milewski, Tadeusz. Introduction to the Study of Language. 1973. pap. text 63.10 (*90-279-2598-4*) Mouton.

Miley. The Social Work Field Experience. (C). 1999. pap. text 26.67 (*0-205-29020-5*, Longwood Div) Allyn.

Miley, Charles H., jt. ed. see Renzetti, Claire M.

Miley, David A., ed. see Birch, John E.

Miley, Dianne Haynes. Time to Enjoy Your Blessings. LC 98-45942. 144p. 1999. pap. 9.99 (*0-570-05347-1*) Concordia.

Miley, George H. Fusion Energy Conversion. LC 75-44554. (Nuclear Science Technology Ser.). (Illus.). 1976. text 53.00 (*0-89448-008-1*, 300009) Am Nuclear Soc.

Miley, George H., ed. Laser Interaction & Related Plasma Phenomena. (AIP Conference Proceedings Ser.: No. 318). 696p. 1994. text 150.00 (*1-56396-324-8*) Am Inst Physics.

Miley, George H. & Campbell, E. Michael, eds. Laser Interaction & Related Plasma Phenomena: 13th International Conference. LC 97-76763. (Conference Proceedings Ser.: Vol. 406). (Illus.). liv, 708p. 1997. 185.00 (*1-56396-696-4*) Am Inst Physics.

Miley, George H. & Hora, Heinrich, eds. Laser Interaction & Related Plasma Phenomena, Vol. 10. (Illus.). 700p. (C). 1993. 186.00 (*0-306-44353-8*, Plenum Trade) Perseus Pubng.

Miley, George H., jt. auth. see Nakai, Sadao.

Miley, George H., jt. ed. see Hora, Heinrich.

Miley, Jeanie. Becoming Fire: Experience the Presence of Jesus Every Day. LC 98-17457. 288p. 1998. pap. 16.00 (*1-57312-193-2*) Smyth & Helwys.

— ChristHeart: A Way of Knowing Jesus. LC 99-28462. 304p. 1999. pap. 20.00 (*1-57312-285-8*) Smyth & Helwys.

— The Spiritual Art of Creative Silence: Lessons in Christian Meditation. 192p. 1996. pap. 9.99 (*0-87788-140-5*, H Shaw Pubs) Waterbrook Pr.

— Women at Midlife Vol. 1: Embracing the Challenges. 80p. 1999. pap. text 4.99 (*0-87788-858-2*, H Shaw Pubs) Waterbrook Pr.

Miley, Jerry D. Night Is Colder Than Autumn. (Original Poetry Ser.). 20p. 1991. 3.00 (*0-916397-18-1*) Manic D Pr.

— Standing in Line. 20p. (Orig.). 1990. pap. 3.00 (*0-916397-08-4*) Manic D Pr.

***Miley, Karla K. & O'Melia, Michael.** Generalist Social Work Practice: An Empowering Approach. 3rd ed. 544p. 2000. pap. text 50.00 (*0-205-31951-3*) Allyn.

Miley, Karla K. & O'Melia, Micheal. Generalist Social Work Practice: An Empowering Approach. 2nd ed. LC 97-11908. 509p. 1997. pap. text 53.00 (*0-205-26740-8*) Allyn.

Miley, Karla K., jt. auth. see Dubois, Brenda.

Miley, Michael. StuffIt Deluxe User's Guide 3.0. Schargel, David, ed. (Illus.). 290p. 1992. 120.00 (*1-878777-03-3*) Aladdin Systs.

Miley, Michael & Schargel, David. StuffIt SpaceSaver User's Guide 1.0. (Illus.). 36p. 1992. 59.95 (*1-878777-04-1*) Aladdin Systs.

Miley, W. N. & Oosterhuis, D. M., eds. Nitrogen Nutrition of Cotton: Practical Issues. 115p. 1990. 15.00 (*0-89118-105-9*) Am Soc Agron.

Miley, William M. The Psychology of Well Being. LC 98-44533. 280p. 1999. 65.00 (*0-275-96275-X*, Praeger Pubs) Greenwood.

Milford, Annette. Collective Decision-Making: Social Choice & Political Economy. Schofield, Norman, ed. LC 96-28939. (Recent Economic Thought Ser.). 448p. (C). 1996. lib. bdg. 151.50 (*0-7923-9711-8*) Kluwer Academic.

Milford, Bryan, jt. auth. see Coen, Patricia.

Milford Conference Staff. Social Case Work, Generic & Specific: An Outline: a Report of the Milford Conference. LC 74-83097. (Studies in the Practice of Social Work: No. 2). 102p. reprint ed. pap. 31.70 (*0-7837-5365-9*, 204512900005) Bks Demand.

Milford, H. S., ed. see Cowper, William.

Milford, H. S., ed. see Hunt, Leigh.

Milford, Homer, ed. see De Onate, Juan.

Milford, Humphrey S., ed. Selected Modern English Essays, 406. LC 80-29398. (World's Classics, Second Ser.). 342p. 1981. reprint ed. lib. bdg. 69.50 (*0-313-22763-2*, MISE, Greenwood Pr) Greenwood.

Milford-Lutzker, Mary-Ann. A Celebration of Independence: Women Artists of India. (Orig.). 1977. pap. write for info. (*0-9638030-2-6*) Mills Art Gal.

***Milford, Phil.** Delaware Trivia. LC 99-36038. 1999. pap. 6.95 (*1-55853-780-5*) Rutledge Hill Pr.

Milford, Tommy M., jt. auth. see Kardas, Edward P.

Milfull, Inge G. The Hymns of the Anglo-Saxon Church: A Study & Edition of the "Durham Hymnal" (Cambridge Studies in Anglo-Saxon England: No. 17). (Illus.). 510p. (C). 1997. text 95.00 (*0-521-46252-5*) Cambridge U Pr.

Milfull, John. Why Germany? National Socialist Antisemitism & the European Context. 264p. 1993. 46.50 (*0-85496-315-4*) Berg Pubs.

Milfull, John, ed. The Attractions of Fascism: Social Psychology & Aesthetics of the "Triumph of the Right" LC 89-28950. 326p. 1990. 40.00 (*0-85496-613-7*) Berg Pubs.

— Britain in Europe: Prospects for Change. LC 98-74841. 286p. 1999. text 70.95 (*0-7546-1044-6*) Ashgate Pub Co.

***Milgaard, Joyce & Edwards, Peter.** A Mother's Story: My Battle to Free David Milgaard. 288p. 1999. 24.95 (*0-385-25807-0*) BDD Bks Young Read.

***Milgate, Michael.** Alliances, Outsourcing, & the Lean Organization. 2001. write for info. (*1-56720-365-5*) Greenwood.

Milgate, Murray. Political Class Economy. pap. 0.00 (*0-691-00390-4*) Princeton U Pr.

— Ricardian Politics. pap. 0.00 (*0-691-00387-4*) Princeton U Pr.

Milgate, Murray, ed. Critical Issues in Social Thought. 244p. 1989. text 84.00 (*0-12-496248-3*) Acad Pr.

Milgate, Murray & Stimson, Shannon C. Ricardian Politics. 176p. 1992. text 45.00 (*0-691-04278-0*, Pub. by Princeton U Pr) Cal Prin Full Svc.

Milgate, Murray, ed. see Eatwell, John.

Milgram, Arthur J. & Rantala, M. L., eds. Cloning: For & Against. LC 98-50289. (Series for & Against: Vol. 3). 300p. 1998. 42.95 (*0-8126-9374-4*); pap. 19.95 (*0-8126-9375-2*) Open Court.

Milgram, Arthur N., jt. auth. see Artin, Emil.

Milgram, B. Lynne, jt. ed. see Grimes, Kimberly M.

Milgram, Gail G. Alcohol Education Materials: Annotated Bibliographies. Incl. Literature of 1980-1981. 1981. 10.00 (*0-911290-13-3*); Literature of 1950-1973. 1975. 20.00 (*0-911290-44-3*); Literature of 1978-1979. Page, Penny B. 1979. 10.00 (*0-911290-10-9*); Literature of 1979-1980. 1980. 10.00 (*0-911290-11-7*); Literature of 1973-1978. Keller, Mark. 1980. 20.00 (*0-911290-06-0*); write for info. (*0-318-55564-6*) Rutgers Ctr Alcohol.

Milgram, James R., ed. Algebraic & Geometric Topology, 2 pts., Pt. 1. 3rd ed. LC 78-14304. (Proceedings of Symposia in Pure Mathematics Ser., Humboldt State University, Arcata, CA, July 29-August 16, 1974: Vol. 32). 412p. 1989. pap. 36.00 (*0-8218-1432-X*, PSPUM/32.1) Am Math.

— Algebraic & Geometric Topology, 2 pts., Pt. 2. 3rd ed. LC 78-14304. (Proceedings of Symposia in Pure Mathematics Ser., Humboldt State University, Arcata, CA, July 29-August 16, 1974: Vol. 32). 322p. 1989. pap. 36.00 (*0-8218-1433-8*, PSPUM/32.2) Am Math.

— Algebraic & Geometric Topology, 2 pts., Set. 3rd ed. LC 78-14304. (Proceedings of Symposia in Pure Mathematics Ser., Humboldt State University, Arcata, CA, July 29-August 16, 1974: Vol. 32). 734p. 1989. pap. 60.00 (*0-8218-1473-7*, PSPUM/32) Am Math.

Milgram, James W. Abraham Lincoln Illustrated Envelopes & Letter Paper. (Illus.). 272p. 1984. 21.95 (*0-9614018-0-X*) Northbrook Pub.

Milgram, James W. Presidential Campaign Illustrated Envelopes & Letter Paper 1840-1872. 1994. 42.50 (*0-9614018-2-6*) D G Phillips.

Milgram, James W. Radiologic & Histologic Pathology of Nontumorous Diseases of Bones & Joints, 2 vols. Gruhn, John G., ed. (Illus.). 1382p. 1990. 199.00 (*0-9614018-1-8*) Northbrook Pub.

***Milgram, James W.** United States Registered Mail, 1845-1870. LC 98-65975. 1998. pap. 29.95 (*1-877998-04-4*) D G Phillips.

Milgram, Judah, ed. & tr. see Thomas, Fred.

Milgram, Lynne. Managing Smart: 325 High-Performance Tips Every Manager Must Know. LC 99-13625. 400p. 1998. 26.95 (*0-88415-752-0*, 5752) Gulf Pub.

Milgram, Morris. The Challenge of Open Housing: Good Neighborhood. 248p. 1977. 8.00 (*0-318-15820-5*, O-2) Natl Neighbors.

Milgram, R. James, jt. auth. see Madsen, Ib H.

Milgram, Richard J., jt. auth. see Adem, Alejandro.

Milgram, Robert M. & Runco, Mark A., eds. Counseling Gifted & Talented Children: A Guide for Teachers, Counselors, & Parents. (Creativity Research Ser.). 288p. 1991. pap. 39.50 (*0-89391-773-7*) Ablx Pub.

Milgram, Roberta M. Teaching Gifted & Talented Learners in Regular Classrooms. (Illus.). 316p. 1989. pap. 41.95 (*0-398-06290-0*) C C Thomas.

— Teaching Gifted & Talented Learners in Regular Classrooms. (Illus.). 316p. (C). 1989. text 66.95 (*0-398-05557-2*) C C Thomas.

Milgram, Roberta M., et al, eds. Teaching & Counseling Gifted & Talented Adolescents: An International Learning Style Perspective. LC 92-35348. 296p. 1993. 65.00 (*0-275-93640-6*, C3640, Praeger Pubs) Greenwood.

Milgram, Roberta M. & Runco, Mark A., eds. Counseling Gifted & Talented Children: A Guide for Teachers, Counselors, & Parents. (Creativity Research Ser.). 288p. 1991. text 73.25 (*0-89391-724-9*) Ablx Pub.

Milgram, Roberta M., jt. auth. see Hong, Eunsook.

Milgram, Roger. Milgrim on Licensing, 4 vols. 1991. ring bd. 250.00 (*0-8205-1743-7*) Bender.

Milgram, Stanley. Obedience to Authori. 256p. 1983. pap. 14.50 (*0-06-131983-X*, TB1983, Torch) HarpC.

Milgram, Stanley, et al. The Individual in a Social World: Essays & Experiment. 2nd ed. 320p. (C). 1992. pap. 27.19 (*0-07-041936-1*) McGraw.

***Milgrim, David.** Cows Can't Fly. (Picture Puffin Ser.). (Illus.). 32p. (J). (ps-3). 2000. pap. 5.99 (*0-14-056721-6*, PuffinBks) Peng Put Young Read.

Milgrim, David. Here in Space. LC 97-11373. (Illus.). 32p. (J). 1997. 15.95 (*0-8167-4393-2*) BrdgeWater.

— Here in Space. (Illus.). 32p. (J). (ps-2). 1998. pap. 5.95 (*0-8167-4462-9*) Troll Communs.

— Why Benny Barks. LC 93-47102. (Step into Reading Ser.: A Step 1 Book). (Illus.). 32p. (J). (ps-1). 1994. lib. bdg. 11.99 (*0-679-96157-7*, Pub. by Random Bks Yng Read) Random.

— Why Benny Barks. LC 93-47102. (Step into Reading Ser.: A Step 1 Book). (Illus.). 32p. (J). (ps-3). 1994. pap. 3.99 (*0-679-86157-2*, Pub. by Random Bks Yng Read) Random.

Milgrim, David. Why Benny Barks. (Step into Reading Ser.: A Step 1 Book). (J). (ps-1). 1994. 9.19 (*0-606-06877-5*, Pub. by Turtleback) Demco.

Milgrim, David. Cows Can Fly. LC 97-25434. 32p. (ps-3). 1998. 15.99 (*0-670-87475-2*) Viking Penguin.

Milgrim, Roger M. Milgrim on Trade Secrets, 4 vols., Set. 1967. ring bd. 1020.00 (*0-8205-1738-0*) Bender.

Milgrim, Sally-Anne. Plays to Play with in Class. LC 85-60244. (Illus.). 208p. 1991. pap. 10.95 (*0-89390-060-5*, Pub. by Resource Pubns) Empire Pub Srvs.

Milgrim, Shirley. Haym Salomon: Liberty's Son. LC 75-17349. (Illus.). 120p. (J). (gr. 5-8). 1975. pap. 7.95 (*0-8276-0073-9*) JPS Phila.

— Pathways to Independence: Discovering Independence National Historical Park. LC 73-89767. (Illus.). 128p. 1975. 16.95 (*0-85699-101-5*) Chatham Pr.

***Milgrom.** Practical Allergy. 2001. pap. text. write for info. (*0-323-01236-1*) Mosby Inc.

— Treating Post-Natal Depression. text 55.00 (*0-471-98108-7*) Wiley.

Milgrom. Treating Post-Natal Depression. LC 99-45635. 292p. 2000. pap. 39.95 (*0-471-98645-3*) Wiley.

Milgrom, Elie, jt. ed. see Joosen, Wouter.

Milgrom, Felix, et al, eds. Antibodies: Protective, Destructive & Regulatory Role: International Convocation on Immunology, Amherst, N.Y., June 1984. (Illus.). xiv, 462p. 1985. 326.25 (*3-8055-3990-8*) S Karger.

— Principles of Immunological Diagnosis in Medicine. LC 80-20724. (Illus.). 536p. reprint ed. pap. 166.20 (*0-8357-7650-6*, 205697600096) Bks Demand.

Milgrom, Felix & Flanagan, Thomas D., eds. Medical Microbiology. LC 82-1261. (Illus.). 762p. reprint ed. pap. 200.00 (*0-7837-2581-7*, 204274000006) Bks Demand.

Milgrom, Felix, ed. see International Convocation on Immunology Staff.

Milgrom, Jacob. The JPS Torah Commentary: Numbers. 520p. 1990. 60.00 (*0-8276-0329-0*) JPS Phila.

— Leviticus 17-27. LC 99-89367. (Anchor Bible Ser.). 2000. write for info. (*0-385-41255-X*) Doubleday.

***Milgrom, Jacob.** Leviticus 23-27. LC 99-86528. (Anchor Bible Ser.). 2000. 50.00 (*0-385-50035-1*) Doubleday.

Milgrom, Jacob. Leviticus 1-16, Vol. 3. 1184p. 1998. 55.00 (*0-385-11434-6*) Doubleday.

— Studies in Levitical Terminology Vol. 1: Vol. 1, The Encroacher & the Levite. The Term Aboda. LC 76-626141. (Univeraity of California Publications. Near Eastern Studies: Vol. 14). 120p. reprint ed. pap. 37.20 (*0-608-11083-3*, 202138000021) Bks Demand.

Milgrom, Lionel R. The Colours of Life: An Introduction to the Chemistry of Porphyrins & Related Compounds. (Illus.). 256p. 1997. pap. text 39.95 (*0-19-855962-3*) OUP.

— The Colours of Life: An Introduction to the Chemistry of Porphyrins & Related Compounds. (Illus.). 255p. (C). 1997. text 95.00 (*0-19-855380-3*) OUP.

Milgrom, Paul. Auction Theory for Privatization. (Churchill Lectures in Economics). (Illus.). 160p. (C). 1999. text 24.95 (*0-521-55184-6*) Cambridge U Pr.

Milgrom, Paul & Roberts, John. Economics, Organization & Management. 600p. 1992. 100.00 (*0-13-224650-3*) P-H.

Milgrom, Peter & Weinstein, Philip. Early Childhood Caries: A Team Approach to Prevention & Treatment. (Illus.). 200p. 1998. pap. text 39.95 (*1-880291-02-9*) Cont Dental Educ.

Milgroom, Mike, ed. Visual Elements Three: Marks & Patterns. (Design Sourcebook Ser.). (Illus.). 1990. pap. 19.99 (*0-935603-40-9*, 30212) Rockport Pubs.

Milhailovich, Vasa D., ed. DLB 147: South Slavic Writers Before World War II. LC 94-79482. 368p. 1994. text 155.00 (*0-8103-5708-9*) Gale.

Milham, Charles G. Gallant Pelham. 250p. 1988. reprint ed. 25.00 (*0-942211-63-4*) Olde Soldier Bks.

— Gallant Pelham, American Extraordinary. 1976. 22.95 (*0-8488-1099-6*) Amereon Ltd.

Milham, Mary E., ed. Platina: On Right Pleasure & Good Health (A Critical Edition & Translation of De Honesta Voluptate et Valetudine) LC 97-30151. (Medieval & Renaissance Texts & Studies: No. 168). 528p. 1998. 35.00 (*0-86698-208-6*, MR168) MRTS.

***Milham, Mary E., ed. from LAT.** On Right Pleasure & Good Health, Vol. 37. LC 98-55450. 200p. 1999. pap. text 12.95 (*1-889818-12-7*) Pegasus Pr.

Milhaud, Darius, jt. auth. see Weill, Kurt.

Milhaud, Gaston. Les Philosophes - Geometres de la Grece: Platon & Ses & Predecesseurs. LC 75-13280. (History of Ideas in Ancient Greece Ser.). (FRE.). 1976. reprint ed. 26.95 (*0-405-07323-2*) Ayer.

Milhaven, J. Giles. Good Anger. LC 89-61217. 224p. 1989. pap. 12.95 (*1-55612-264-0*) Sheed & Ward WI.

Milhaven, John G. Hadewijch & Her Sisters: Other Ways of Loving & Knowing. LC 92-31369. (SUNY Series, The Body in Culture, History, & Religion). 171p. (C). 1993. text 57.50 (*0-7914-1541-4*); pap. text 18.95 (*0-7914-1542-2*) State U NY Pr.

Milheim, William D. Computer-Based Simulations in Education & Training: A Selected Bibliography. LC 92-32545. (Educational Technology Selected Bibliography Ser.: Vol. 8). 60p. (Orig.). 1992. pap. 24.95 (*0-87778-254-7*) Educ Tech Pubns.

Milheim, William D., compiled by. Artificial Intelligence & Instruction: A Selected Bibliography. LC 89-23662. (Educational Technology Selected Bibliography Ser.: Vol. 1). 55p. 1989. pap. 24.95 (*0-87778-220-2*) Educ Tech Pubns.

Milheim, William D., ed. Authoring-Systems Software for Computer-Based Training. LC 93-40880. (Illus.). 200p. 1994. 44.95 (*0-87778-274-1*) Educ Tech Pubns.

Milheim, William D., ed. see Clemente, Rebecca & Bohlin, Roy M.

Milheim, William D., ed. see Huyvaert, Sarah H. & Huyvaert, Thomas R.

Milheim, William D., ed. see Lamb, Annette.

Milheim, William D., ed. see Maddux, Cleborne D.

Milheim, William D., ed. see McLellan, Hilary.

Milheim, William D., ed. see Tennyson, Robert D. & Anderson, Ronald O.

Milholland, Charlotte. The Girl Pages: A Handbook of Resources for Growing Strong, Confident, Creative Girls. 448p. (J). 1999. pap. 14.95 (*0-7868-8109-7*, Pub. by Hyperion) Time Warner.

***Milholland, Dennis.** Degrees of Retribution: A Novel of Contempt. LC 00-190861. 416p. 2000. 25.00 (*0-7388-2044-X*) Xlibris Corp.

— Degrees of Retribution: A Novel of Contempt. 1999th ed. LC 00-190861. 416p. 2000. pap. 18.00 (*0-7388-2045-8*) Xlibris Corp.

Milhomme, Janet, jt. auth. see Broukal, Milada.

Milhorat, Thomas H. Cerebrospinal Fluid & the Brain Edemas. (Illus.). 172p. (C). 1987. 45.00 (*0-944809-00-6*) NeuroSci Soc NY.

Milhorn, H. T., Jr. Chemical Dependence: Diagnosis, Treatment & Prevention. (Illus.). 352p. 1990. 125.00 (*0-387-97292-7*) Spr-Verlag.

— Drug & Alcohol Abuse: The Authoritative Guide for Parents, Teachers, & Counselors. LC 94-97. (Illus.). 412p. (C). 1994. 27.95 (*0-306-44640-5*, Plenum Trade) Perseus Pubng.

Milhous, Enid, jt. auth. see Refnes, Vera.

Milhous, Judith. Thomas Betterton & the Management of Lincoln's Inn Fields, 1695-1708. LC 78-21017. 318p. 1979. 31.95 (*0-8093-0906-8*) S Ill U Pr.

Milhous, Judith & Hume, Robert D., eds. Producible Interpretation: Eight English Plays, 1675-1707. LC 84-5634. (Illus.). 352p. 1985. text 36.95 (*0-8093-1167-4*) S Ill U Pr.

— Vice Chamberlain Coke's Theatrical Papers, 1706-1715. LC 81-5616. 319p. 1982. 31.95 (*0-8093-1024-4*) S Ill U Pr.

***Milhous, Judith, et al.** Italian Opera in Late Eighteenth Century London: The Pantheon Opera & Its Aftermath 178, Vol. 2. (Illus.). 896p. 2000. text 130.00 (*0-19-816716-4*) OUP.

Milhous, Katherine. Egg Tree. LC 50-6817. (Illus.). 32p. (J). (gr. 1-4). 1971. 15.00 (*0-684-12716-4*) Scribner.

— Egg Tree. 2nd ed. LC 91-15854. (Illus.). 32p. (J). (gr. k-3). 1992. mass mkt. 5.95 (*0-689-71568-4*) Aladdin.

— Egg Tree. 2nd ed. 1992. 11.15 (*0-606-01570-1*, Pub. by Turtleback) Demco.

Mili, Ali. Structured Specifying: Techniques & Applications. (Information Technology Ser.). 1990. text 39.95 (*0-470-21527-5*) P-H.

Mili, Ali, et al. Computer Program Construction. (Illus.). 400p. (C). 1994. text 71.95 (*0-19-509236-8*) OUP.

Miliaeva, Liudmilla. Ukrainian Icon from 11th-18th Centuries: From Byzantine Sources to the Baroque. (Temporis Ser.). (Illus.). 239p. 1996. 55.00 (*1-85995-241-0*) Parkstone Pr.

Milian, Marta, jt. ed. see Camps, Anna.

Milianowicz, Stanislaw A. Redshift Connection: Concerning the Gravitational Interaction of Mass with Electromagnetic Radiation. LC 95-81001. (Illus.). ix, 237p. (Orig.). 1995. pap. 48.00 (*0-9652987-3-6*) Arysutt AMS.

Miliaras, E. S., ed. see American Society of Mechanical Engineers Staff.

Miliband, David, ed. Reinventing the Left. 250p. 1994. pap. text 26.95 (*0-7456-1391-8*) Blackwell Pubs.

Miliband, Ralph. Capitalist Democracy in Britain. 174p. (C). 1984. pap. 15.95 (*0-19-285137-3*) OUP.

— Divided Societies: Class Struggle in Contemporary Capitalism. (Illus.). 286p. 1990. text 55.00 (*0-19-827535-8*) OUP.

— Divided Societies: Class Struggle in Contemporary Capitalism. 288p. 1991. reprint ed. pap. text 17.95 (*0-19-285234-5*, 9048) OUP.

Miliband, Ralph. Social Register '83. 1983. pap. text 10.00 (*0-85345-641-0*) Monthly Rev.

— Social Register'91 Communist Regimes. 1991. pap. text 18.00 (*0-85345-826-X*) Monthly Rev.

Miliband, Ralph. Socialism for a Skeptical Age. LC 95-120599. 200p. (C). 1994. pap. 19.00 (*1-85984-057-4*, C0495, Pub. by Verso) Norton.

Miliband, Ralph, et al, eds. Revolution Today: Aspirations & Realities: Socialist Register 1989. 336p. (Orig.). (C). 1989. pap. 15.00 (*0-85345-784-0*, Pub. by Monthly Rev) NYU Pr.

Miliband, Ralph & Panitch, Leo, eds. Between Globalism & Nationalism: Socialist Register 1994. 288p. (Orig.). (C). 1994. pap. text 18.00 (*0-85345-907-X*, Pub. by Merlin) Monthly Rev.

— New World Order? Socialist Register, 1992. 360p. (C). 1992. pap. text 18.00 (*0-85345-855-3*, Pub. by Monthly Rev) NYU Pr.

Miliband, Ralph & Saville, John, eds. The Socialist Register, 1978. 338p. 1978. pap. 10.00 (*0-85345-453-1*) Monthly Rev.

Miliband, Ralph, jt. ed. see Saville, John.

Milic-Emili, J. Applied Physiology in Respiratory Mechanics. LC 97-34796. 120p. 1997. 98.00 (*3-540-75041-X*) Spr-Verlag.

Milicevic, Barbara. Your Spiritual Child. (Illus.). 96p. 1984. pap. 7.00 (*0-87516-528-1*) DeVorss.

Milicevic, Jovan. English-Serbocroat Dictionary of Engineering. 266p. (C). 1986. 180.00 (*0-7855-6755-0*, Pub. by Collets) St Mut.

— English-Serbocroatian Dictionary of Mechanical Engineering. (ENG & SER.). 266p. 1986. 29.95 (*0-8288-0657-8*, F 14124) Fr & Eur.

— Serbian/English/Serbian Accounting Dictionary. (CRO, ENG & SER.). 326p. 1997. 95.00 (*0-320-00051-6*) Fr & Eur.

— Serbocroatian-English Dictionary of Mechanical Engineering. (ENG & SER.). 250p. 1986. 39.95 (*0-8288-0656-X*, F 14125) Fr & Eur.

Milich, E., et al. European Communities Oil & Gas Technological Development Projects: Second Status Report. 264p. 1984. lib. bdg. 108.00 (*0-86010-616-0*) G & T Inc.

Milich, Edzia F. God Had a Reason. (Illus.). 116p. 1993. pap. 20.00 (*0-9636347-0-4*) Rose Pub CA.

Milich, Klaus J. & Peck, Jeffrey M., eds. Multiculturalism in Transit: A German-American Exchange. LC 98-26838. (International Political Currents Ser.: No. 3). 304p. 1998. 59.95 (*1-57181-163-X*) Berghahn Bks.

Milich, Melissa. Miz Fannie Mae's Fine New Easter Hat. LC 96-14233. (Illus.). 32p. (J). (gr. k-3). 1997. 14.95 (*0-316-57159-8*) Little.

Milich, Paul. Courtroom Handbook on Georgia Evidence. 600p. (C). 1996. pap. text. write for info. (*0-314-09941-7*) West Pub.

An Asterisk (*) at the beginning of an entry indicates that the title is appearing for the first time.

Milich, Zorka. A Stranger's Supper: An Oral History of Centenarian Women in Montenegro. 192p. 1995. pap. 15.95 (*0-8057-9132-9*, Twyne) Mac Lib Ref.

— A Stranger's Supper: An Oral History of Centenarian Women in Montenegro. 192p. 1995. 29.95 (*0-8057-9131-0*, Twyne) Mac Lib Ref.

Milidantri, Mary Ann. Hurray for Today, Level 1. 1979. pap. 4.50 (*0-8497-5601-4*, WE1.) Kjos.

— Hurray for Today, Level 2. 1979. pap. 4.50 (*0-8497-5602-2*, WE2) Kjos.

Milik, Jozef R., et al, eds. Les "Petites Grottes" de Qumran: Textes. (Discoveries in the Judaean Desert Ser.: No. III). 336p. 1997. text 105.00 (*0-19-826946-3*) OUP.

Milik, Jozef T. & Barthelemy, D., eds. Qumran Cave 1. (Discoveries in the Judaean Desert Ser.: No. I). (Illus.). 176p. 1997. text 95.00 (*0-19-826301-5*) OUP.

Milik, Jozef T., jt. auth. see De Vaux, Roland.

***Miliken, W., et al.** Yanomami a Forest People - Advances in Amazonian Ethobotany. (Illus.). 1999. pap. write for info. (*1-900347-73-3*, Pub. by Royal Botnic Grdns) Balogh.

Milikides, E. Industrial Wastewater Treatment & Disposal. (Water Science & Technology Ser.: Vol. 25). 200p. 1992. 84.75 (*0-08-041858-9*, Pergamon Pr) Elsevier.

Milikowski, Clara & Berman, Irwin. Color Atlas of Basic Histopathology. (Illus.). 615p. (Orig.). (C). 1996. 54.95 (*0-8385-1382-4*, A1382-9, Apple Lange Med) McGraw.

Milikowski, Karen. Airway Care. (Respiratory Care Workbook Ser.: Vol. 8). 24p. (gr. 13). 1995. text, wbk. ed. 8.95 (*0-8151-6311-8*, 26029) Mosby Inc.

— Basic Patient Assessment, Vol. 2. (Respiratory Care Workbook Ser.). 24p. (gr. 13). 1995. text, wbk. ed. 8.95 (*0-8151-6305-3*, 26023) Mosby Inc.

— Clinical Blood Gases, Vol. 7. (Respiratory Care Workbook Ser.). 24p. (C). (gr. 13). 1995. text, wbk. ed. 8.95 (*0-8151-6310-X*, 26028) Mosby Inc.

— Mechanical Ventilation, Vol. 4. (Respiratory Care Workbook Ser.). 24p. (gr. 13). 1995. text, wbk. ed. 8.95 (*0-8151-6307-X*, 26025) Mosby Inc.

— Mosby's Respiratory Care Workbook Series: Comprehensive. (Illus.). 272p. (C). (gr. 13). 1995. pap. text 46.00 (*0-8151-6313-4*, 26030) Mosby Inc.

— Mosby's Respiratory Care Workbook Series: Introduction to Respiratory Care. 24p. (gr. 13). 1995. text 8.95 (*0-8151-6303-7*, 26022) Mosby Inc.

— Neonatal & Pediatric Respiratory Care, Vol. 6. (Respiratory Care Workbook Ser.). 24p. (gr. 13). 1995. text, wbk. ed. 8.95 (*0-8151-6309-6*, 26027) Mosby Inc.

— Pulmonary Function Testing, Vol. 3. (Respiratory Care Workbook Ser.). 24p. (gr. 13). 1994. text 8.95 (*0-8151-6306-1*, 26024) Mosby Inc.

— Respiratory Care Pharmacology & Aerosol, Vol. 4. (Respiratory Care Workbook Ser.). 24p. (gr. 13). 1994. text 8.95 (*0-8151-6308-8*, 26026) Mosby Inc.

Milin, Irene & Milin, Mike. How to Buy & Manage Rental Property: The Milin Method of Real Estate Management for the Small Investor. 272p. 1988. pap. 12.00 (*0-671-64423-8*) S&S Trade Pap.

Milin, Isaak M. Univalent Functions & Orthonormal Systems. LC 77-1198. (Translations of Mathematical Monographs: Vol. 49). 202p. 1977. text 62.00 (*0-8218-1599-7*, MMONO/49) Am Math.

Milin, Mike, jt. auth. see Milin, Irene.

Milinar, Zdravji. Local Government & Rural Development in Yugoslavia. (Special Series on Rural Local Government: No. 18). 136p. pap. 3.50 (*0-86731-104-5*) Cornell CIS RDC.

Milinchuk, V. K. & Tupikov, V. I., eds. Organic Radiation Chemistry. 1989. text 185.00 (*0-470-21452-X*) P-H.

Milindapanha. The Milindapanho, Being Dialogues Between King Milinda & the Buddhist Sage: The Pali Text to Which Has Now Been Appended a General Index...& An Index of Gathas. reprint ed. 42.00 (*0-404-17348-9*) AMS Pr.

Miline, Rebecca. Investigative Interviewing: A Guidebook for Professional Practice. LC HV8073.M56 1999. 240p. (C). 1999. 55.00 (*0-471-98728-X*) Wiley.

Milingo, Emmanuel. The World in Between: Christian Healing & the Struggle for Spiritual Survival. LC 84-191633. 144p. (Orig.). reprint ed. pap. 44.70 (*0-7837-5520-1*, 204529000005) Bks Demand.

Milinki, Andrea K., ed. Cases in Qualitative Research: Research Reports for Discussion & Evaluation. 183p. (C). 1999. pap. text 23.95 (*1-884585-17-5*) Pyrczak Pub.

***Milinki, Andrea K., ed.** A Cross Section of Psychological Research: Journal Articles for Discussion & Evaluation. rev. ed. (Illus.). 170p. 1999. 24.95 (*1-884585-13-2*) Pyrczak Pub.

Milinowski, Marta. Teresa Carreno "By the Grace of God" LC 76-58931. (Music Reprint Ser.). 1977. reprint ed. lib. bdg. 45.00 (*0-306-70870-1*) Da Capo.

Milio, Frank R. & Loffredo, William M. Qualitative Testing for Lipids. Neidig, H. Anthony, ed. (Modular Laboratory Program in Chemistry Ser.). 16p. (C). 1994. pap. text 1.50 (*0-87540-447-2*, REAC 447-2) Chem Educ Res.

Milio, Frank R., jt. auth. see Loffredo, William M.

Milio, Frank R., jt. auth. see Wagner.

Milio, Nancy. Engines of Empowerment: Using Information Technology to Create Healthy Communities & Challenge Public Policy. LC 95-43993. 304p. 1996. pap. 22.00 (*1-56793-038-7*, 0973) Health Admin Pr.

Milio, Nancy. 9226 Kercheval: The Storefront that Did Not Burn, New Edition. (Illus.). 224p. (C). pap. text 16.95 (*0-472-08695-2*, 08695) U of Mich Pr.

Milio, Nancy. Ninety-Two Twenty-Six Kercheval: The Storefront That Did Not Burn. 224p. 1970. pap. text 17.95 (*0-472-06180-1*, 06180, Ann Arbor Bks) U of Mich Pr.

— Nutrition Policy for Food-Rich Countries: A Strategic Analysis. LC 89-43482. 240p. reprint ed. pap. 74.40 (*0-608-08796-3*, 206943500004) Bks Demand.

***Milio, Nancy.** Public Health in the Market: Facing Managed Care, Lean Government & Health Disparities. LC 99-50720. 432p. 2000. text 42.50 (*0-472-11136-1*, 11136) U of Mich Pr.

***Milione, Ronnie P.** Administering Windows 2000. (Administering Ser.). (Illus.). 2000. pap. 44.99 (*0-07-212625-6*) Osborne-McGraw.

Milioni, B., jt. auth. see Toledo, F.

Milionis, Steve. Dealing with Adolescent Conflict: A Parent's Practical Guide to Effective Communication Skills. Colwell, Lynn, ed. LC 96-94140. (Illus.). xi, 146p. (Orig.). 1996. pap. 12.95 (*1-889104-00-0*) Milionis Educ.

Milios, Rita. Anorexia & Bulimia. 87p. (YA). (gr. 7-12). 1993. pap. 6.95 (*1-57515-030-1*) PPI Pubng.

— Bears, Bears Everywhere. (Rookie Readers Ser.). 32p. (J). (ps-2). 1988. lib. bdg. 17.00 (*0-516-02085-4*) Childrens.

— Bears, Bears Everywhere. (Rookie Readers Ser.). 32p. (J). (ps-3). 1988. pap. 4.95 (*0-516-42085-2*) Childrens.

— Dreams Journal. 48p. 1995. ring bd. 9.95 (*0-9641657-2-4*) Tools for Transform.

— The Hungry Billy Goat. LC 88-673. (Rookie Readers Ser.). (Illus.). 32p. (J). (gr. k-2). 1989. pap. 4.95 (*0-516-42090-9*); lib. bdg. 17.00 (*0-516-02090-0*) Childrens.

— I Am. LC 87-5163. (Rookie Readers Ser.). (Illus.). 32p. (J). (ps-3). 1987. pap. 4.95 (*0-516-42081-X*) Childrens.

— Imagi-Size: Activities to Exercise Your Students' Imaginations. (Illus.). 80p. 1993. pap. 9.95 (*1-880505-05-3*, CLC0160) Pieces of Lrning.

— Intuition Log Book. 96p. 1995. ring bd. 9.95 (*0-9641657-3-2*) Tools for Transform.

— Planetary Initiation. LC 94-60531. 128p. 1995. pap. 9.95 (*0-9641657-0-8*) Tools for Transform.

— Shopping Savvy. Rosen, Ruth C., ed. (Life Skills Library). (Illus.). 48p. (YA). (gr. 7-12). 1992. lib. bdg. 14.95 (*0-8239-1455-0*) Rosen Group.

— Tools for Transformation. LC 94-60530. 128p. 1995. pap. 9.95 (*0-9641657-1-6*) Tools for Transform.

— Working Together Against Racism. LC 94-1023. (Library of Social Activism). (Illus.). 64p. (YA). (gr. 7-12). 1995. lib. bdg. 16.95 (*0-8239-1840-8*) Rosen Group.

— Yo Soy (I Am) LC 87-5163. (Spanish Rookie Readers Ser.). (SPA., Illus.). 32p. (J). (gr. k-2). 1990. pap. 3.50 (*0-516-52081-4*) Childrens.

Milios, Rita & King, Marcia. Cigarette Smoking. 88p. (YA). (gr. 7-12). 1994. pap. 6.95 (*1-57515-044-1*) PPI Pubng.

Milis, Ludo J. Angelic Monks & Earthly Men: Monasticism & Its Meaning to Medieval Society. (Illus.). 184p. (C). 1992. 60.00 (*0-85115-303-8*) Boydell & Brewer.

— Angelic Monks & Earthly Men: Monasticism & Its Meaning to Medieval Society. (Illus.). 184p. 1999. pap. 29.95 (*0-85115-737-8*) Boydell & Brewer.

Milis, Ludo J., ed. The Pagan Middle Ages. LC 98-40431. 168p. 1998. 55.00 (*0-85115-638-X*, Boydell Pr) Boydell & Brewer.

Milisauskas, Sarunas. Early Neolithic Settlement & Society at Olszanica. (Memoirs Ser.: No. 19). xx, 320p. (Orig.). 1986. pap. 20.00 (*0-915703-03-3*) U Mich Mus Anthro.

Military & Police Uniform Assoc. Staff, ed. The Military & Police Uniform Association. (Gay Men in Uniform Ser.). (Illus.). 80p. (Orig.). 1997. pap. 30.00 (*0-614-04388-3*) L Wendruck.

Military History Institute Staff, jt. auth. see Spallone, Joseph.

Military History Magazine Staff. Military History's Magazine Tenth Anniversary Index. Kelly, C. Brian, ed. (Illus.). (Orig.). (C). 1994. pap. text 21.95 (*1-884641-03-2*) Cowles Enthusiast.

***Military History Section, Headquarters, Army Forces Far East Staff.** Pearl Harbor Operations: General Outline of Orders & Plans. (World War II Monograph Ser.: Vol. 32). (Illus.). 30p. 1999. pap. 4.50 (*1-57638-156-0*, 32-S) Merriam Pr.

Militello, Frederick C. & Davis, Henry A. The Empowered Organization: Redefining the Roles & Practices of Finance. LC 94-70916. (Illus.). 225p. (Orig.). 1994. pap. 35.00 (*0-910586-95-0*, 094-03) Finan Exec.

— Foreign Exchange Risk Management: A Survey of Corporate Practices. LC 94-70913. 175p. (Orig.). 1995. pap. text 35.00 (*0-910586-94-2*, 094-11) Finan Exec.

Militello, Joseph. Winning with the Thoroughbreds: "A Race Fans' Guide to Handicapping & History" LC 94-6141. (Illus.). 283p. (Orig.). 1995. pap. 14.95 (*0-9641634-0-3*) J Militello.

Militky, J., et al. Modified Polyester Fibres. (Textile Science & Technology Ser.: Vol. 10). 262p. 1991. 205.00 (*0-444-98735-5*) Elsevier.

***Milito, John.** Ultimate Golf Puzzles. 96p. 2000. pap. 5.95 (*1-55054-755-0*, Greystone) DGL.

Milito, John. Ultimate Hockey Puzzles: Crosswords & More. 1998. pap. 5.95 (*1-55054-647-3*, Pub. by DGL) Sterling.

Militz, Annie R. Concentration. 84p. 1996. reprint ed. spiral bd. 8.50 (*0-7873-0614-2*) Hlth Research.

— Concentration. 84p. 1996. reprint ed. pap. 8.00 (*1-56459-863-2*) Kessinger Pub.

— Primary Lessons in Christian Living & Healing (1918) 180p. 1998. reprint ed. pap. 19.95 (*0-7661-0307-2*) Kessinger Pub.

— The Renewal of the Body. 166p. 1996. reprint ed. spiral bd. 16.00 (*0-7873-0613-4*) Hlth Research.

— The Renewal of the Body. 166p. 1996. reprint ed. pap. 14.95 (*1-56459-862-4*) Kessinger Pub.

Miliukov, P. N., et al. S.A. Muromtsev I Pervaia Duma: Sbornik State I. Muromcew, Cyril, ed. LC 98-40379. (RUS.). 174p. 1998. pap. 14.00 (*1-55779-114-7*) Hermitage Pubs.

Miliukov, Paul N. Outlines of Russian Culture: The Origins of Ideology. Wieczynski, Joseph L., tr. from RUS. LC 74-81632. (Russian Ser.: Vol. 19, Pt. 1). 1974. 24.50 (*0-87569-056-4*) Academic Intl.

Milius, Greta. Music Was Our Passport. Thayer, Lydia, ed. & pref. by. LC 96-85964. (Illus.). (Orig.). 1996. pap. 12.95 (*0-9603832-8-X*) Anthony Pub Co.

Milius, John. The Wind & Lion. 18.95 (*0-88411-454-6*) Amereon Ltd.

Milius, Patti, ed. West of the Rockies: From Campfire to Candlelight. (Illus.). 360p. 1994. 17.95 (*0-9641314-0-4*) JSLOGJ.

Miliutin, A. A. & Osmolovskii, N. P. Calculus of Variations & Optimal Control. LC 98-29674. (Translations of Mathematical Monographs: Vol. 180). 372p. 1998. 129.00 (*0-8218-0753-6*) Am Math.

***Milivojevic, Dragan.** Leo Tolstoy & the Oriental Religious Heritage: Influences & Parallels. 200p. 1998. text 28.00 (*0-88033-416-9*, 518, Pub. by East Eur Monographs) Col U Pr.

Milivojevic, Dragan D. Current Russian Phonemic Theory, 1952-1962. LC 75-108142. (Janua Linguarum, Ser. Minor: No. 78). (Orig.). 1970. pap. text 16.15 (*3-10-800273-2*) Mouton.

Milivojevic, Dragan D. & Mihailovich, Vasa D. Yugoslav Linguistics in English: A Bibliography, 1900-1980. 122p. (Orig.). 1990. pap. 18.95 (*0-89357-213-6*) Slavica.

Milivojevic, Dragan D., jt. auth. see Matejic, Mateja.

***Milivojevic, Joann.** Puerto Rico. LC 99-39109. (Ticket to Ser.). (Illus.). 48p. (J). 2000. lib. bdg. 22.60 (*1-57505-144-3*, Carolrhoda) Lerner Pub.

Milivojevic, Joann. Puerto Rico. LC 98-54648. (Globe-Trotters Club Ser.). (Illus.). 48p. (J). (gr. 3-5). 2000. lib. bdg. 22.60 (*1-57505-119-2*, Carolrhoda) Lerner Pub.

— Serbia. LC 98-19256. (Enchantment of the World Ser.). 144p. (YA). (gr. 5-10). 1999. 32.00 (*0-516-21196-X*) Childrens.

Milivojevic, Marko. Descent into Chaos: Yugoslavia's Worsening Crisis. (C). 1989. 35.00 (*0-907967-08-6*, Pub. by Inst Euro Def & Strat) St Mut.

Milivojevic, Marko, et al, eds. Yugoslavia's Security Dilemmas: Army Forces, National Defence & Foreign Policy. LC 87-23081. 332p. 1988. 72.00 (*0-85496-149-6*) Berg Pubs.

Milivojevic, Marko & Maurer, Pierre. Swiss Neutrality & Security: Armed Forces, National Defence & Foreign Policy. LC 89-28949. 272p. 1991. 55.00 (*0-85496-608-0*) Berg Pubs.

Miljan, Toivo. The Political Economy of North-South Relations. 712p. 1987. pap. 29.95 (*0-921149-11-5*) Broadview Pr.

Miljan, Toivo, et al. Food & Agriculture in Global Perspective: Discussions in the Committee of the Whole of the United States. (Illus.). 260p. 1980. 74.00 (*0-08-025550-7*, Pergamon Pr) Elsevier.

Miljkovic, Tajana. Student's Russian & Serbocroatian Pocket Dictionary: Ruso-Hrvatski Ili Srpski I Hrvatsko Ili Srpskoruski Dzepni Rjecnik Za Osnovn. (RUS & SER.). 496p. 1984. pap. 19.95 (*0-8288-1641-7*, F114890) Fr & Eur.

Milk, Chocolate. Dr. Chocolate Milk's Get Fat Quick Diet. LC 95-82232. 76p. 1996. pap. 5.95 (*1-56352-289-6*) Longstreet.

Milke, J., jt. auth. see Klote, J.

***Milken, Mike.** Taste for Living World Cookbook: More of Mike Milken's Favorite Recipes for Fighting Cancer & Heart Disease. (Illus.). 1999. 27.50 (*0-9673655-0-3*) CAP.

***Milkereit, Joanne.** Discovery Drafting Strategy. (Paralegal Ser.). (C). 2000. pap. 16.95 (*0-8273-8226-X*) Delmar.

Milkereit, Joanne & Higdon, Hal. The Runner's Cookbook. LC 78-58058. (Illus.). 324p. 1979. spiral bd. 16.95 (*0-89037-145-8*) Anderson World.

Milkias, Paulos. Ethiopia: A Comprehensive Bibliography. (Reference Bks.). 650p. 1989. 90.00 (*0-8161-9066-6*, Hall Reference) Macmillan.

***Milkis, Landy.** American Government. 2002. 36.00 (*0-07-238319-4*) McGraw.

Milkis, Sidney M. Political Parties & American Democracy. LC 99-14370. (Interpreting American Politics Ser.). 364p. 1999. 49.50 (*0-8018-6194-2*) Johns Hopkins.

— Political Parties & American Democracy: Remaking American Democracy. LC 99-14370. (Interpreting American Politics Ser.). 364p. 1999. pap. 17.95 (*0-8018-6195-0*) Johns Hopkins.

— The President & the Parties: The Transformation of the American Party System since the New Deal. LC 92-42965. 424p. (C). 1993. pap. text 24.95 (*0-19-508425-X*) OUP.

Milkis, Sidney M. & Mileur, James J., eds. Progressivism & the New Democracy. LC 99-19459. (Political Development of the American Nation Ser.). 312p. 1999. 50.00 (*1-55849-192-9*); pap. 16.95 (*1-55849-193-7*) U of Mass Pr.

Milkis, Sidney M. & Nelson, Michael. The American Presidency: Origins & Development, 1776-1993. 2nd ed. LC 93-43358. 489p. (C). 1994. pap. text 29.95 (*0-87187-766-X*) Congr Quarterly.

— The American Presidency: Origins & Development, 1776-1993. 2nd ed. LC 93-43358. 489p. 1994. 44.95 (*0-87187-949-2*) Congr Quarterly.

— The American Presidency: Origins & Development 1776-1998. 3rd ed. LC 98-54458. 474p. 1999. pap. 31.95 (*1-56802-432-0*) Congr Quarterly.

Milkis, Sidney M., jt. auth. see Harris, Richard A.

Milkis, Sidney M., jt. auth. see Landy, Marc.

Milkman, Harvey & Sunderwirth, Stanley. Craving for Ecstasy: How Our Passions Become Addictions & What We Can Do about Them. LC 98-21171. 224p. 1998. reprint ed. pap. 18.95 (*0-7879-4132-8*) Jossey-Bass.

Milkman, Harvey, et al. Project Self Discovery: Artistic Alternatives for High Risk Youth. 200p. 1996. pap. 49.95 (*0-471-16241-8*) Wiley.

Milkman, Harvey B. & Sederer, Lloyd I., eds. Treatment & Choices for Alcoholism & Substance Abuse. 395p. 1990. 51.00 (*0-669-20019-0*) Lxngtn Bks.

Milkman, Harvey B. & Shaffer, Howard J., eds. The Addictions: Multidisciplinary Perspectives & Treatments. LC 84-47871. 204p. 1984. 39.95 (*0-669-08739-4*) Lxngtn Bks.

Milkman, Harvey B., jt. auth. see Wanberg, Kenneth W.

Milkman, Paul. PM: A New Deal in Journalism. LC 97-5675. (Illus.). 240p. 1997. text 45.00 (*0-8135-2434-2*) Rutgers U Pr.

Milkman, Ruth. Farewell to the Factory: Autoworkers in the Late Twentieth Century. LC 96-22684. (Illus.). 240p. 1997. pap. 15.95 (*0-520-20678-9*, Pub. by U CA Pr) Cal Prin Full Svc.

Milkman, Ruth. Gender at Work: The Dynamics of Job Segregation by Sex During World War II. LC 86-7001. (Working Class in American History Ser.). 232p. 1987. pap. text 15.95 (*0-252-01357-3*) U of Ill Pr.

— Japan's California Factories: Labor Relations & Economic Globalization. (Monograph & Research Ser.: No. 55). 130p. 1991. pap. 11.00 (*0-89215-171-4*) U Cal LA Indus Rel.

***Milkman, Ruth, ed.** Organizing Immigrants: The Challenge for Unions in Contemporary California. LC HD6490.O72U657 2000. 200p. pap. 18.95 (*0-8014-8617-3*) Cornell U Pr.

Milkman, Ruth, ed. Women, Work & Protest: A Century of U. S. Women's History. 320p. (Orig.). 1985. pap. 14.95 (*0-7100-9940-1*, Routledge Thoemms) Routledge.

***Milkman, Ruth & Wong, Kent.** Voices from the Front Lines: Organizing Immigrant Workers in Los Angeles. Rabadan, Luis Escala, tr. (ENG & SPA., Illus.). 92p. 2000. 5.00 (*0-89215-188-9*) U Cal LA Indus Rel.

M

Milkon, Phyllis A. Cooking Healthy with BCV's Shortcuts: Delicious Recipes Lower in Fat - Cholesterol - Sodium with No Refined Sugar Plus Nutrient Data. LC 91-73959. 250p. 1991. pap. 19.00 (*0-9630025-1-1*) Burgess Creat.

— Earthly Angels: David Chen's Survival of Famine & Persecution. LC 99-94318. (Illus.). 152p. 1999. pap. 12.00 (*0-9630025-2-X*) Burgess Creat.

Milkov, Nikolay. The Varieties of Understanding Vols. 1 & 2: English Philosophy since 1898, 3 vols. 1996. pap. 127.95 (*0-8204-3222-9*) P Lang Pubng.

— The Varieties of Understanding Vols. 1 & 2: English Philosophy since 1898, 2 vols., Vols. 1 & 2. xxxii, 893p. 1997. 127.95 (*3-631-48508-5*) P Lang Pubng.

Milkovich. Compensation. 6th ed. 672p. 1998. 87.81 (*0-256-25965-8*) McGraw.

— Human Resource Management. 9th ed. 1999. 63.25 (*0-07-237392-X*) McGraw.

***Milkovich, Barbara A.** It's Gone, Did You Notice? A History of the Mesabi Range Village of Franklin 1892-1994. unabridged ed. LC 00-102330. (Illus.). 170p. (C). 2000. pap. 21.95 (*0-9679984-0-9*) J J Milkovich.

Milkovich, Barbara A. & Cramer, Esther, eds. Early Businesses in Orange County: A Selection of Stories about the Creators of County Commerce. (Orange Countiana Ser.: Vol. V). (Illus.). 256p. 1992. 17.97 (*1-881860-00-0*); pap. 13.17 (*1-881860-01-9*); text 29.95 (*0-685-60658-9*); pap. text 21.95 (*0-685-60659-7*) Orange Cnty Hist.

Milkovich, Carolyn, jt. auth. see Milkovich, George T.

Milkovich, George & Boudreau, John. CPS Human Resource Management: Creating & Leading Effective Organizations. 7th ed. 288p. (C). 1995. text 25.95 (*0-256-21474-3*, Irwn McGrw-H) McGrw-H Hghr Educ.

— Direccion y Administracion de Recursos Humanos. 6th ed. (SPA.). (C). 1996. text 29.00 (*0-8151-6406-8*, Irwn McGrw-H) McGrw-H Hghr Educ.

Milkovich, George, jt. auth. see Newman, Jerry M.

Milkovich, George T. Administracion de los Recursos Humanos. 6th ed. (SPA.). (C). 1994. pap. text. write for info. (*0-201-60126-5*) Addison-Wesley.

Milkovich, George T., et al, eds. Pay for Performance: Evaluating Performance Appraisal & Merit Pay. 224p. 1991. pap. text 24.95 (*0-309-04427-8*) Natl Acad Pr.

Milkovich, George T. & Boudreau, John W. Human Resource Management. 8th ed. LC 96-17944. 768p. (C). 1996. text 66.50 (*0-256-19354-1*, Irwn McGrw-H) McGrw-H Hghr Educ.

Milkovich, George T. & Milkovich, Carolyn. Cases in Compensation. 7th ed. 100p. (C). 1999. pap. text 26.50 (*0-945601-04-2*) Compensation.

Milkovich, George T., et al. Cases in Compensation. 5th ed. 100p. (C). 1994. pap. text. write for info. (*0-945601-02-6*) Compensation.

— Cases in Compensation. 6th ed. 100p. (C). 1997. pap. write for info. (*0-945601-03-4*) Compensation.

— Compensation. 5th ed. LC 95-16253. 656p. (C). 1995. text 69.75 (*0-256-14145-2*, Irwn Prfssnl) McGraw-Hill Prof.

Milkowski, Bill. Jaco: The Extraordinary & Tragic Life of Jaco Pastorius. (Illus.). 264p. 1995. 22.95 (*0-87930-361-1*) Miller Freeman.

— Jaco: The Extraordinary & Tragic Life of Jaco Pastorius. (Illus.). 264p. 1996. pap. 14.95 (*0-87930-426-X*) Miller Freeman.

— Rockers, Jazzbos, Visionaries. LC 98-19249. 1998. 21.95 (*0-8230-7833-7*) Watsn-Guptill.

Milkowski, Jandra, jt. auth. see Zulauf, Sander W.

Milks, Mary J., compiled by. United States Catholic Elementary & Secondary Schools 1996-97. (Data Bank Ser.). (Illus.). 41p. 1997. pap. 18.00 (*1-55833-190-5*) Natl Cath Educ.

Milks, Mary J., jt. auth. see Savage, Frank X.

Mill. Resorts. 2001. text 41.00 (*0-471-36188-7*) Wiley.

An Asterisk (*) at the beginning of an entry indicates that the title is appearing for the first time.

Mill & Morrison. The Tourism System. 3rd ed. LC 97-76576. 398p. 1997. per. 49.95 (*0-7872-3327-7*, 41332701) Kendall-Hunt.

Mill, Anna J. Medieval Plays in Scotland. LC 68-56497. 353p. 1972. reprint ed. 26.95 (*0-405-08789-6*, Pub. by Blom Pubns) Ayer.

Mill, Anna J., jt. ed. see D'Evelyn, C.

***Mill, Cherry.** Managing for the First Time. 96p. 2000. pap. 17.95 (*0-8464-5179-4*) Beekman Pubs.

Mill, Christine. Norman Collie - A Life in Two Worlds: Mountain Explorer & Scientist, 1859-1942. (Aberdeen University Press Bks.). (Illus.). 256p. 1987. text 30.00 (*0-08-032456-8*, Pub. by Aberdeen U Pr) Macmillan.

Mill, Elizabeth, tr. see Beuchot, Mauricio.

Mill, G. J. Van, see Van Mill, G. J.

Mill, Harriet Taylor, jt. auth. see Mill, John Stuart.

Mill Hunk Herald Editors. Overtime: Ten Years of Punching Out with the Mill Hunk Herald (1977-87) 208p. (Orig.). 1990. pap. 12.95 (*0-931122-55-4*) West End.

Mill, James. Analysis of the Phenomena of the Human Mind, 2 vols. in 1. Findlater, A. et al, eds. xxvii, 856p. 1982. reprint ed. 128.70 (*3-487-07243-2*) G Olms Pubs.

— Analysis of the Phenomena of the Human Mind, 2 vols. 2nd ed. 1986. reprint ed. pap. 41.95 (*0-935005-54-4*) Lincoln-Rembrandt.

— Elements of Political Economy. 3rd ed. 311p. 1971. reprint ed. 48.10 (*3-487-04192-8*) G Olms Pubs.

— Elements of Political Economy. 3rd ed. 1986. reprint ed. pap. 27.95 (*0-935005-56-0*); reprint ed. lib. bdg. 44.95 (*0-935005-55-2*) Lincoln-Rembrandt.

— An Essay of the Impolicy of a Bounty on the Exportation of Grain & on the Principles Which Ought to Regulate the Commerce of Grain. LC 66-19693. 70p. 1966. reprint ed. 25.00 (*0-678-00152-9*) Kelley.

— Essay on Government. Shields, Currin V., ed. (gr. 9 up). 1955. pap. 2.95 (*0-672-60215-6*, LLA47, Bobbs) Macmillan.

— Essays on Government, Jurisprudence, Liberty of the Press & Law of Nations Reprinted from the Supplement to the Encyclopaedia Britannica. LC 86-7454. 140p. 1986. reprint ed. 35.00 (*0-678-00297-5*) Kelley.

— Political Writings. Ball, Terence, ed. (Cambridge Texts in the History of Political Thought Ser.). 356p. (C). 1992. text 59.95 (*0-521-38323-4*); pap. text 19.95 (*0-521-38748-5*) Cambridge U Pr.

— Schools for All: 1812 Edition. Stern, Jeffrey, ed. & intro. by. (Classics in Education Ser.). 88p. 1996. reprint ed. 65.00 (*1-85506-294-1*) Bks Intl VA.

Mill, Jan Van, see Van Mill, Jan, ed.

Mill, Jan Van, see Husek, Miroslav & Van Mill, Jan, eds.

Mill, Jean S. Guide to Owning a Bengal Cat. LC 99-26496. (Illus.). 64p. 1999. 19.95 (*0-7910-5459-4*) Chelsea Hse.

— Guide to Owning a Bengal Cat. (Illus.). 64p. 1997. pap. 6.95 (*0-7938-2168-1*, RE-401) TFH Pubns.

Mill, John Stuart. Additional Letters of John Stuart Mill. Filipiuk, Marion et al, eds. 1991. text 110.00 (*0-8020-2768-7*) U of Toronto Pr.

— Auguste Comte & Positivism: 1865 Edition. (Key Texts Ser.). 202p. 1996. reprint ed. pap. 28.95 (*1-85506-219-4*) Bks Intl VA.

— Autobiography. Robson, John M., ed. & intro. by. 240p. 1990. pap. 11.95 incl. 5.25 hd (*0-14-043316-3*, Penguin Classics) Viking Penguin.

— Autobiography of John Stuart Mill. LC 24-27691. 240p. (C). 1960. pap. text 19.00 (*0-231-08506-0*) Col U Pr.

Mill, John Stuart. Autobiography of John Stuart Mill, 001. Stillinger, Jack, ed. (C). 1957. pap. 13.96 (*0-395-05120-7*, RivEd) HM.

Mill, John Stuart. Considerations on Representative Government. LC 90-63889. (Great Books in Philosophy). 365p. 1991. pap. 6.95 (*0-87975-670-5*) Prometheus Bks.

— Dissertations & Discussions, 2 vols. LC 72-94. (Studies in Philosophy: No. 40). 1972. reprint ed. lib. bdg. 150.00 (*0-8383-1400-7*) M S G Haskell Hse.

— Earlier Letters, 1812-1848, 2 Vols, Set. Mineka, Francis E., ed. LC 65-109962. (Collected Works of John Stuart Mill). 1963. text 75.00 (*0-8020-5123-5*) U of Toronto Pr.

— The Early Draft of John Stuart Mill's Autobiography. Stillinger, Jack, ed. LC 61-62769. 226p. reprint ed. pap. 70.10 (*0-608-10010-2*, 201333300086) Bks Demand.

— Essays on Economics & Society, 2 vols., Vol. 1. Robson, J. M., ed. LC 68-56473. (Collected Works of John Stuart Mill: No. 4-5). 460p. 1975. reprint ed. pap. 142.60 (*0-608-08216-3*, 202640700001) Bks Demand.

— Essays on Economics & Society, 2 vols., Vol. 2. Robson, J. M., ed. LC 68-56473. (Collected Works of John Stuart Mill: No. 4-5). 450p. 1975. reprint ed. pap. 139.50 (*0-608-08217-1*, 202640700002) Bks Demand.

— Essays on England, Ireland & the Empire. Robson, John M., ed. (Collected Works of John Stuart Mill: Vol. 6). 744p. 1982. text 75.00 (*0-8020-5572-9*) U of Toronto Pr.

— Essays on Equality, Law & Education. Robson, John M., ed. (Collected Works of John Stuart Mill: No. XXI). 592p. 1984. text 70.00 (*0-8020-5629-6*) U of Toronto Pr.

— Essays on Ethics, Religion & Society. Robson, J. M., ed. LC BJ1008.M54. (Collected Works of John Stuart Mill: Vol. 10). 720p. reprint ed. pap. 200.00 (*0-608-14711-7*, 203764800009) Bks Demand.

— Essays on French History & Historians. Robson, John M., ed. (Collected Works of John Stuart Mill: No. 20). 656p. 1985. text 75.00 (*0-8020-2490-4*) U of Toronto Pr.

— Essays on Philosophy & the Classics. Robson, J. M., ed. LC 63-25976. (Collected Works of John Stuart Mill: No. 11). (Illus.). 680p. reprint ed. pap. 200.00 (*0-8357-4732-8*, 203764900009) Bks Demand.

— Essays on Some Unsettled Questions of Political Economy. 2nd ed. LC 68-25642. (Reprints of Economic Classics Ser.). vi, 164p. 1968. reprint ed. 35.00 (*0-678-00390-4*) Kelley.

— Essays on Some Unsettled Questions of Political Economy: 1844 Edition. (Key Texts Ser.). 172p. 1996. reprint ed. pap. 19.95 (*1-85506-160-0*) Bks Intl VA.

— An Examination of Sir William Hamilton's Philosophy. Robson, John M., ed. LC 63-25976. (Collected Works of John Stuart Mill). 1979. text 60.00 (*0-8020-2329-0*) U of Toronto Pr.

— J. S. Mill Early Monographs, 8 vols., Set. 1488p. (C). 1990. 620.00 (*0-415-07767-2*) Routledge.

— John Mill's Boyhood Visit to France: Being a Journal & Notebook. LC 60-4877. 165p. reprint ed. pap. 51.20 (*0-608-09948-1*, 201436700090) Bks Demand.

— John Stuart Mill's Social & Political Thought: Critical Assessments, 4 vols., Set. Smith, G. W., ed. & intro. by. LC 97-16803. 1696p. (C). 1998. 700.00 (*0-415-14073-0*) Routledge.

— John Stuart Mill's Social & Political Thought: Critical Assessments, Vol. 1. Smith, G. W., ed. & intro. by. LC 97-16803. 1998. write for info. (*0-415-14328-4*) Routledge.

— John Stuart Mill's Social & Political Thought: Critical Assessments, Vol. 2. Smith, G. W., ed. & intro. by. LC 97-16803. 1998. write for info. (*0-415-14329-2*) Routledge.

— John Stuart Mill's Social & Political Thought: Critical Assessments, Vol. 3. Smith, G. W., ed. & intro. by. LC 97-16803. 1998. write for info. (*0-415-14330-6*) Routledge.

— John Stuart Mill's Social & Political Thought: Critical Assessments, Vol. 4. Smith, G. W., ed. & intro. by. LC 97-16803. 1998. write for info. (*0-415-14331-4*) Routledge.

— John Stuart Mill's "The Subjection of Women" His Contemporary & Modern Critics. Jacobs, Lesley A. & Vandewetering, Richard, eds. LC 99-13420. 1999. write for info. (*0-88206-093-7*) Caravan Bks.

— Journals & Debating Speeches, 2 vols. Robson, John M., ed. (Collected Works of John Stuart Mill: Nos. 26 & 27). 900p. 1988. text 135.00 (*0-8020-2674-5*) U of Toronto Pr.

— Later Letters, 1849-1870, 4 vols, Set. Mineka, Francis E. & Lindley, Dwight N., eds. LC 75-163833. (Collected Works of John Stuart Mill). 1972. text 125.00 (*0-8020-5261-4*) U of Toronto Pr.

— Mill: Texts, Commentaries. expanded rev. ed. Ryan, Alan, ed. & selected by. LC 96-7642. 365p. (C). 1996. pap. text 11.25 (*0-393-97009-4*) Norton.

— Mill on Bentham & Coleridge. LC 82-15854. 168p. (C). 1983. reprint ed. lib. bdg. 42.50 (*0-313-23740-9*, MIOB, Greenwood Pr) Greenwood.

— Mill on Liberty. (C). 1997. pap. text. write for info. (*0-321-02591-1*) Addson-Wesley Educ.

— Miscellaneous Writings. Robson, John M., ed. & intro. by. (Collected Works of John Stuart Mill: Vol. 31). 462p. 1989. text 85.00 (*0-8020-2728-8*) U of Toronto Pr.

***Mill, John Stuart.** On Liberty. Himmelfarb, Gertrude, ed. & intro. by. 192p. (C). 1998. pap. 5.33 (*0-14-043207-8*) Addson-Wesley Educ.

— On Liberty. Alexander, Edward, ed. (Literary Texts Ser.). 294p. 1999. pap. 5.95 (*1-55111-199-3*) Broadview Pr.

Mill, John Stuart. On Liberty. Rapaport, Elizabeth, ed. & intro. by. LC 77-26848. (HPC Classics Ser.). 139p. (C). 1978. pap. text 4.95 (*0-915144-43-3*); lib. bdg. 24.95 (*0-915144-44-1*) Hackett Pub.

— On Liberty. Castell, Alburey, ed. LC 47-3494. (Crofts Classics). 128p. (C). 1947. pap. text 4.95 (*0-88295-056-8*) Harlan Davidson.

— On Liberty. Shields, Currin V., ed. & intro. by. LC 96-209150. 176p. (C). 1956. pap. text 5.80 (*0-02-409690-3*, Pub. by P-H) S&S Trade.

— On Liberty. LC 85-63408. (Great Books in Philosophy). 129p. 1986. pap. 5.95 (*0-87975-336-6*) Prometheus Bks.

— On Liberty: With the Subjection of Women & Chapters on Socialism. Collini, Stefan, ed. (Cambridge Texts in the History of Political Thought Ser.). 328p. (C). 1989. pap. text 9.95 (*0-521-37917-2*) Cambridge U Pr.

— On Liberty: With the Subjection of Women & Chapters on Socialism. Collini, Stefan, ed. (Cambridge Texts in the History of Political Thought Ser.). 260p. (C). 1989. 21.95 (*0-521-37015-9*) Cambridge U Pr.

— On Liberty & Other Essays. Gray, John, ed. & intro. by. (Oxford World's Classics Ser.). 628p. 1998. pap. 8.95 (*0-19-283384-7*) OUP.

— On Liberty & Utilitaranism. 1992. 15.00 (*0-679-41329-4*) Everymns Lib.

— On Liberty & Utilitarianism. 240p. 1993. mass mkt. 5.95 (*0-553-21414-4*) Bantam.

— On Socialism. LC 87-61246. (Great Books in Philosophy). 146p. (Orig.). 1976. pap. 7.95 (*0-87975-404-4*) Prometheus Bks.

— Principles of Political Economy: And Chapters on Socialism. Riley, Jonathan, ed. & intro. by. (Oxford World's Classics Ser.). 512p. 1999. pap. 10.95 (*0-19-283672-2*) OUP.

— Principles of Political Economy: With Some of their Applications to Social Philosophy. Ashley, William J., ed. & intro. by. (Reprints of Economic Classics Ser.). iiii, 1013p. 1987. reprint ed. 57.50 (*0-678-00073-5*); reprint ed. pap. 29.95 (*0-678-01453-1*) Kelley.

— Public & Parliamentary Speeches, 2 vols. Robson, John M. & Kinzer, Bruce L., eds. (Collected Works of John Stuart Mill: Nos. XXVIII-XXIX). 760p. 1988. text 135.00 (*0-8020-2693-1*) U of Toronto Pr.

— Sobre la Libertad & Comentarios a Tocqueville. Negro, Pavon D., ed. Garcia Cay, Cristina, tr. (Nueva Austral Ser.: Vol. 183). (SPA.). 1991. pap. text 24.95 (*84-239-1983-8*) Elliots Bks.

— The Subjection of Women. Okin, Susan Moller, ed. & intro. by. LC 88-1762. (HPC Classics Ser.). 128p. (C). 1988. pap. text 4.95 (*0-87220-054-X*); lib. bdg. 24.95 (*0-87220-055-8*) Hackett Pub.

— The Subjection of Women. Mansfield, Sue, ed. LC 76-3318. (Crofts Classics). 136p. (C). 1980. pap. text 44.95 (*0-88295-116-5*) Harlan Davidson.

— The Subjection of Women. 1970. pap. text 9.95 (*0-262-63038-9*) MIT Pr.

— The Subjection of Women. LC 85-63407. (Great Books in Philosophy). 106p. 1986. pap. 5.95 (*0-87975-335-8*) Prometheus Bks.

— The Subjection of Women. LC 96-39387. (Dover Thrift Editions Ser.). 112p. 1997. reprint ed. pap. text 1.50 (*0-486-29601-6*) Dover.

— System of Logic. 8th ed. 1986. reprint ed. pap. 52.95 (*0-935005-34-X*); reprint ed. lib. bdg. 69.95 (*0-935005-29-3*) Lincoln-Rembrandt.

— Theism. Taylor, Richard, ed. 1957. pap. 2.25 (*0-672-60238-5*, Bobbs) Macmillan.

— Three Essays on Religion. LC 98-15124. 267p. 1998. pap. text 7.95 (*1-57392-212-9*) Prometheus Bks.

— Three Essays on Religion. LC 76-130995. reprint ed. 23.45 (*0-404-04325-9*) AMS Pr.

— Utilitarianism. Sher, George, ed. & intro. by. LC 78-74450. (HPC Classics Ser.). 80p. (C). 1979. pap. text 3.95 (*0-915144-41-7*) Hackett Pub.

— Utilitarianism. 1974. pap. 11.95 (*0-452-00970-7*, Mer) NAL.

— Utilitarianism. Crisp, Roger, ed. LC 97-31037. (Oxford Philosophical Texts Ser.). 164p. (C). 1998. pap. text 11.95 (*0-19-875163-X*) OUP.

— Utilitarianism. Crisp, Roger, ed. LC 97-31037. (Oxford Philosophical Texts Ser.). 164p. (C). 1998. text 29.95 (*0-19-875162-1*) OUP.

— Utilitarianism. LC 86-62704. (Great Books in Philosophy). 83p. 1987. pap. 5.95 (*0-87975-376-5*) Prometheus Bks.

— Utilitarianism, On Liberty, Considerations on Representative Government, Remarks on Bentham's Philosophy. Williams, Geraint, ed. 512p. 1993. pap. 6.95 (*0-460-87346-6*, Everyman's Classic Lib) Tuttle Pubng.

— Writings on India. Robson, John M. et al, eds. (Collected Works of John Stuart Mill: Vol. 30). 340p. 1990. text 90.00 (*0-8020-2717-2*) U of Toronto Pr.

Mill, John Stuart & Comte, Auguste. The Correspondence of John Stuart Mill & Auguste Comte. Haac, Oscar A., tr. from FRE. & frwd. by. LC 93-33297. 376p. (C). 1994. 54.95 (*1-56000-148-8*) Transaction Pubs.

Mill, John Stuart & Mill, Harriet Taylor. Essays on Sex Equality. Rossi, Alice S., ed. LC 78-133381. 251p. 1970. pap. 12.95 (*0-226-52546-5*, P420) U Ch Pr.

Mill, John Stuart, et al. Sexual Equality: Writings by John Stuart Mill, Harriet Taylor Mill, & Helen Taylor. Robson, Ann P. & Robson, John M., eds. 409p. 1994. text 60.00 (*0-8020-0513-6*); pap. text 19.95 (*0-8020-6949-5*) U of Toronto Pr.

— Utilitarianism & Other Essays. Ryan, Alan, ed. 352p. 1987. pap. 16.99 (*0-14-043272-8*, Penguin Classics) Viking Penguin.

Mill, Kristin L. A Is for Aesop. unabridged ed. Landes, William-Alan, ed. LC 97-36393. 48p. (J). (gr. 1-7). 1997. pap. 10.00 (*0-88734-520-4*) Players Pr.

Mill, Peter J. & McQuaid, C. D., eds. Advances in Littorinid Biology: Proceedings of the Fourth International Symposium Held in Roscoff, France, 19-25 September 1995. (Developments in Hydrobiology Ser.: Vol. 3). 200p. (C). 1995. text 166.00 (*0-7923-3733-6*) Kluwer Academic.

Mill-Price, Jamie. Between the Vine, Vol. 1. (Illus.). 70p. (Orig.). 1997. pap. 9.50 (*1-56770-400-X*) S Scheewe Pubns.

Mill, R. R., jt. ed. see Dickson, J. H.

Mill, Robert C. Restaurant Management: Customers, Operations & Employees. LC 97-30345. 388p. 1997. 69.00 (*0-13-201774-1*) P-H.

***Mill, Robert C.** Restaurant Management: Customers, Operations & Employees. 2nd ed. 448p. 2000. 64.00 (*0-13-027364-3*) P-H.

Mill, Robert C., ed. Human Factors in the Process Operations. 108p. 1992. 30.00 (*0-85295-294-5*, 9CH7) Gulf Pub.

Millage, Philip J. & Rousopoulos, Deno. The Owner's Guide to the Construction Process. 96p. 1999. pap. 12.95 (*0-9669315-0-5*) Educ Media.

Millais, John E. The Parables of Our Lord & Savior Jesus Christ. 1990. 12.50 (*0-8446-5225-3*) Peter Smith.

Millais, John G. Life & Letters of Sir John Everett Millais, President of the Royal Academy, 2 vols. LC 72-148280. reprint ed. 124.50 (*0-404-04326-7*) AMS Pr.

Millais, Malcolm. Structures for Buildings. (Illus.). 368p. 1996. pap. 39.99 (*0-419-21970-6*, E & FN Spon) Routledge.

Millais, Raoul. Elijah & Pin-Pin. LC 91-20032. (Illus.). 48p. (J). (ps-1). 1992. pap. 14.00 (*0-671-75543-9*) S&S Bks Yung.

Millam, Michael J. Reaction Guide for Organic Chemistry. 204p. (C). 1989. pap. text 17.96 (*0-669-13248-9*) HM Trade Div.

— Reaction Guide for the Brief Organic Chemistry Course. 185p. (C). 1989. pap. text 16.76 (*0-669-13247-0*) HM Trade Div.

Millam, Rosalind. Anti-Discriminatory Practice in Childcare & Education. LC 96-335. (Practical Childcare Ser.). (Illus.). 160p. 1996. pap. 27.95 (*0-304-33413-8*); text 70.00 (*0-304-33412-X*) Continuum.

Millan, Alonso. Plan Manzanares. (SPA.). 85p. 1967. 1.00 (*0-8288-7154-X*) Fr & Eur.

Millan, Carlos. Canciones Mas Famosas Accompaniamneto Guitarra P/hombre O Mujer/ (SPA.). 927p. 1997. pap. text 59.98 (*968-13-3111-7*) Edit Diana.

Millan, Eduardo S., compiled by. Dicc. de Compositores Mexicanos de Musica de Concierto. (SPA.). pap. 14.99 (*968-16-4900-1*, Pub. by Fondo) Continental Bk.

Millan, Eric, jt. auth. see Grard, Oliver.

Millan, Gonzalo, tr. see Geddes, Gary.

Millan, Gordon. The Best of the First Ten Years of the Irish Wolfhound Quarterly. (Illus.). 272p. 1995. 80.00 (*0-614-04541-X*) Donald R Hoflin.

— A Throw of the Dice: The Life of Stephane Mallarme. LC 93-40180. 1994. 35.00 (*0-374-27707-9*) FS&G.

Millan, Jim. Serpent Kills: Play. LC 95-130601. 116p. 1997. pap. text 11.95 (*0-88754-528-9*) Theatre Comm.

Millan, M. M., jt. auth. see Gryning, S. E.

Millan, Victor. Mexico Reborn. 1976. 59.95 (*0-8490-2250-9*) Gordon Pr.

Millan, W. H., jt. auth. see Rogers, J. W.

Milland, Pacelli, jt. auth. see Armstrong, Regis J.

Millane, Pacelli, jt. auth. see Armstrong, Regis J.

Millang, John A., ed. see Millang, Theresa N.

Millang, Steve, jt. auth. see Scelsa, Greg.

***Millang, Theresa.** Birds of New York Field Guide. (Illus.). 125p. 1999. pap. 11.95 (*1-885061-75-7*) Adventure Pubns.

— The Great Minnesota Hot Dish. 1999. pap. 9.95 (*1-885061-25-0*) Adventure Pubns.

Millang, Theresa, ed. see McDaniel, Effie.

Millang, Theresa N. Beau & CJ Jokes: Collection of Cajun Jokes. Millang, John A., ed. (Illus.). 44p. 1996. write for info. (*0-9624584-1-4*) id Pub.

— Best of Cajun-Creole Recipes. 108p. 1992. pap. 5.95 (*0-934860-93-9*) Adventure Pubns.

— The Best of Chili Recipes. 108p. 1998. spiral bd. 5.95 (*0-934860-08-4*) Adventure Pubns.

— I Love Cheesecake. 108p. (Orig.). 1995. pap. 7.95 (*1-885061-07-2*) Adventure Pubns.

— I Love Pies You Don't Bake. 113p. 1999. spiral bd. 8.95 (*0-9624584-2-2*) id Pub.

Millar, Alan. Reasons & Experience. 238p. 1991. text 80.00 (*0-19-824270-0*) OUP.

Millar, Alejandra, tr. see Zollars, Jean A.

***Millar, Andree.** Orchids of Papua New Guinea. LC 99-38929. (Illus.). 128p. 1999. 34.95 (*0-88192-438-5*) Timber.

***Millar, Ann, ed.** The Biographical Dictionary of the Australian Senate, 1901-1929. 500p. 2000. 69.95 (*0-522-84921-0*, Pub. by Melbourne Univ Pr) Paul & Co Pubs.

Millar, Ann, ed. Medical Management of HIV & AIDS. LC 95-40049. (Illus.). 260p. 1995. 132.00 (*3-540-19958-6*) Spr-Verlag.

Millar, Annie, et al. Monitoring the Outcome of Social Services, 2 vols. Incl. Vol. 1. Preliminary Suggestions. 1977. 6.50 (*0-87766-194-4*); Vol. 2. Review of Past Research & Test Activities. 88p. 1977. 6.50 (*0-87766-200-2*); 1977. write for info. (*0-318-56305-3*) Urban Inst.

Millar, Bill. Global Treasury Management: Key Strategies for Bottom-Line Results in Today's Global Financial Markets. 224p. 1991. 39.95 (*0-88730-469-9*, HarpBusn) HarpInfo.

***Millar, Bonnie.** The Siege of Jerusalem in Its Physical, Literary & Historical Contexts. 224p. 2000. 65.00 (*1-85182-506-1*, Pub. by Four Cts Pr) Intl Spec Bk.

Millar, Bryan. Of Other Gods. 416p. mass mkt. 4.99 (*1-896329-27-6*) Picasso Publ.

Millar, C. E., jt. ed. see Hall, D. A.

Millar, Cam. Ice Skating Basics. LC 98-21163. (Illus.). 96p. (YA). (gr. 4 up). 1999. 17.95 (*0-8069-9517-3*) Sterling.

— In-Line Skating Basics. LC 95-30965. (Illus.). 96p. (Orig.). 1996. 17.95 (*0-8069-3849-8*) Sterling.

— In-Line Skating Basics. (Orig.). 1996. 18.15 (*0-606-12737-2*, Pub. by Turtleback) Demco.

— Roller Hockey. (Illus.). 96p. (J). 1997. pap. 12.95 (*0-8069-4376-9*) Sterling.

***Millar, Carla C. J. M., et al.** International Business: Emerging Issues & Emerging Markets. LC 99-49413. 272p. 2000. text 69.95 (*0-312-22945-3*) St Martin.

Millar, D. D., jt. auth. see Cram, L. E.

Millar, D. D., jt. ed. see Brennan, M. H.

Millar, Dan P., jt. auth. see Irvine, Robert B.

Millar, Delia. Victorian Watercolours & Drawings: In the Collection of Her Majesty the Queen. (Illus.). 1056p. 1995. 250.00 (*0-85667-436-2*) Sothebys Pubns.

— Victorian Watercolours & Drawings: In the Collection of Her Majesty the Queen, 2 vols., Set. (Illus.). 1056p. 1995. 250.00 (*0-302-00650-8*, Pub. by Zwemmer Bks) Intl Spec Bk.

Millar, Donald. The Messel Era. 1988. pap. text 13.00 (*0-08-034431-3*, Pergamon Pr) Elsevier.

— The Messel Era: The History of the School of Physics & its Science Foundation with the University of Sydney 1952-1987. 176p. 1987. 11.75 (*0-317-66359-3*, Pergamon Pr) Elsevier.

Millar, Donald, jt. auth. see Swash, Mary.

***Millar, Elaine & Walsh, Mark.** Mental Health Matters in Primary Care. (Illus.). 160p. 2000. pap. 34.95 (*0-7487-4528-9*, Pub. by S Thornes Pubs) Intl Spec Bk.

***Millar, Elisabeth.** The Fragrant Veil: Scents for the Sensuous Woman. 2000. pap. 14.95 (*1-56718-491-X*) Llewellyn Pubns.

Millar, Ernest, tr. see Mukasa, Ham.

Millar, Fergus. The Crowd in Rome in the Late Republic. (Thomas Spencer Jerome Lectures). (Illus.). 256p. (C). 1998. text 47.50 (*0-472-10892-1*, 10892) U of Mich Pr.

— The Emperor in the Roman World. LC 76-20059. 696p. 1977. 79.95 (*0-8014-1058-4*) Cornell U Pr.

— The Emperor in the Roman World. LC 76-20059. 696p. 1992. pap. 27.50 (*0-8014-8049-3*) Cornell U Pr.

— The Roman Near East, 31 B. C. - A. D. 337. LC 93-18174. 624p. 1993. 51.50 (*0-674-77885-5*) HUP.

Millar, Fergus, ed. The Roman Empire & Its Neighbours. 2nd ed. LC 81-326. 376p. 1981. 49.50 (*0-8419-0711-0*) Holmes & Meier.

An Asterisk (*) at the beginning of an entry indicates that the title is appearing for the first time.

Millar, Fergus & Segal, Erich, eds. Caesar Augustus: Seven Aspects. LC 83-20976. (Illus.). 232p. 1984. pap. text 26.00 (*0-19-814858-5*) OUP.

Millar, Fergus G. The Roman Near East, 31 B. C. - A. D. 337. (Illus.). 624p. 1995. pap. text 24.50 (*0-674-77886-3*, MILROX) HUP.

Millar, Gabriel B., ed. Thresholds: Near-Life Experiences. (Illus.). 192p. 1995. pap. 18.95 (*1-869890-68-X*, Pub. by Hawthorn Press) Anthroposophic.

Millar, Garnet W. E. Paul Torrance: "The Creativity Man": An Authorized Biography. (Illus.). 387p. 1995. pap. 42.50 (*1-56750-166-4*); text 78.50 (*1-56750-165-6*) Ablx Pub.

***Millar, Gary J.** Now Choose Life: Theology & Ethics in Deuteronomy. LC 99-28294. (New Studies in Biblical Theology). 216p. 1999. pap. 24.00 (*0-8028-4407-3*) Eerdmans.

Millar Gault, S. Diccionario Ilustrado en Color de Arbustos: Shrub Dictionary in Color. (SPA.). 210p. 1978. 75.00 (*0-7859-5062-1*) Fr & Eur.

Millar, Geoffrey T., jt. auth. see Dhillon, Baljean.

Millar, Gilbert J. Tudor Mercenaries & Auxiliaries, 1485-1547. LC 79-22164. 239p. reprint ed. pap. 74.10 (*0-608-08556-1*, 206907900002) Bks Demand.

Millar, Graham, jt. auth. see Percy, John.

Millar, H. R., jt. auth. see Nesbit, E.

Millar Hayes, Margaret. Reconstructed Marriage Records of Owsley County, Kentucky, 1843-1910, Pt. 1, (A-L) LC 99-201827. 432p. 1999. pap. 36.50 (*0-7884-1058-X*, H100) Heritage Bk.

Millar, Heather. Spain in the Age of Exploration. LC 97-2090. (Cultures of the Past Ser.). (YA). (gr. 5-12). 1998. lib. bdg. 28.50 (*0-7614-0303-5*, Benchmark NY) Marshall Cavendish.

Millar, Heather, jt. auth. see Millar, Myrna.

Millar, I. Liam Neeson. 1998. mass mkt. 6.99 (*0-340-62831-6*) Hodder & Stought Ltd.

Millar, Ian, et al, eds. The Cambridge Dictionary of Scientists. (Illus.). 399p. (C). 1996. pap. 16.95 (*0-521-56718-1*) Cambridge U Pr.

***Millar, J.** Screaming at the World. 1999. pap. write for info. (*1-58235-267-4*) Watermrk Pr.

Millar, J., et al. Practical Anaesthesia & Analgesia for Day Surgery. (Illus.). 256p. (Orig.). 1997. pap. 39.90 (*1-85996-081-2*, Pub. by Bios Sci) Bks Intl VA.

Millar, J. G., jt. auth. see McConville, J. Gordon.

Millar, James R. The ABCs of Soviet Socialism. LC 80-24196. 230p. 1981. reprint ed. pap. 71.30 (*0-7837-8080-X*, 204783300008) Bks Demand.

— The Soviet Economic Experiment. 352p. 1990. pap. text 16.95 (*0-252-06088-1*) U of Ill Pr.

Millar, James R., ed. Cracks in the Monolith: Party Power in the Brezhnev Era. LC 92-9300. (Contemporary Soviet - Post Soviet Politics Ser.). 256p. (gr. 13). 1992. text 85.95 (*0-87332-885-X*) M E Sharpe.

— Politics, Work, & Daily Life in the U. S. S. R. A Survey of Former Soviet Citizens. (Illus.). 444p. 1987. pap. text 33.95 (*0-521-34890-0*) Cambridge U Pr.

Millar, James R. & Wolchik, Sharon L., eds. Social Legacies of Communism. (Woodrow Wilson Center Press Ser.). 420p. (C). 1994. text 80.00 (*0-521-46182-0*); pap. text 22.95 (*0-521-46748-9*) Cambridge U Pr.

Millar, Jane. Poverty & the Lone-Parent Family: The Challenge to Social Policy. 216p. 1989. text 63.95 (*0-566-05770-0*) Ashgate Pub Co.

Millar, Jane, jt. ed. see Jones, Helen.

***Millar, Jay.** The Ghosts of Jay Millar. 160p. 1999. pap. 22.95 (*1-55245-043-0*, Pub. by Coach Hse Bks) SPD-Small Pr Dist.

***Millar, Jeremy.** Jane & Louise Wilson. (Illus.). 128p. 2000. pap. 22.00 (*1-84166-027-2*) Relaxtn Co.

Millar, Jim. Handbook of Hawaiian Machine - Made Soda Bottles. (Illus.). 114p. (Orig.). 1988. pap. 14.00 (*1-56046-211-6*) Interact Pubs.

Millar, Jocelyn G. & Haynes, Kenneth F. Methods in Chemical Ecology: Bioassay Mehods, Vol. 2. LC 97-39820. (Illus.). 416p. 1998. pap. write for info. (*0-412-08041-9*) Kluwer Academic.

— Methods in Chemical Ecology: Chemical Methods, Vol. 1. LC 97-39820. 416p. 1998. write for info. (*0-412-08071-0*) Kluwer Academic.

Millar, John. An Historical View of the English Government: From the Settlement of the Saxons in Britain to the Revolution in 1688 to Which Are Subjoined Some Dissertations Connected with the History of the Government from the Revolution to the Present Time. 3rd ed. 1801p. 1997. reprint ed. 450.00 (*1-85506-506-1*) Thoemmes Pr.

— Observations Concerning the Distinction of Ranks in Society. LC 78-67536. reprint ed. 34.50 (*0-404-17199-0*) AMS Pr.

— The Origin of the Distinction of Ranks: 1806 Edition. 450p. 1996. reprint ed. 75.00 (*1-85506-080-9*) Bks Intl VA.

Millar, John F. Classical Architecture in Renaissance Europe: 1419-1585. LC 86-50560. (Illus.). 250p. (Orig.). 1987. pap. 24.00 (*0-934943-06-0*) Thirteen Colonies Pr.

— A Complete Life of Christ. LC 85-51584. (Illus.). 180p. (Orig.). 1986. 16.00 (*0-934943-04-4*); pap. 9.00 (*0-934943-01-X*) Thirteen Colonies Pr.

— Handbook on the Founding of Australia 1788. LC 87-50807. (Illus.). 128p. 1987. pap. 16.00 (*0-934943-19-2*) Thirteen Colonies Pr.

— Ships of the American Revolution. Knill, Harry, ed. (Illus.). 48p. (Orig.). 1976. pap. 3.95 (*0-88388-036-9*) Bellerophon Bks.

Millar, John R., jt. auth. see Liberti, Lorenzo.

Millar, Judy. Basic Drama Sketches. (Scene Bks.). 58p. (YA). (gr. 8-12). 1996. pap. 8.95 (*1-57514-012-8*, 6007) Encore Perform Pub.

— Basic Drama Sketches, Short Plays for Teen Audiences Vol. 2: 5 Plays. 1994. pap. 8.95 (*1-57514-019-5*) Encore Perform Pub.

— Classroom Drama: The Most Fun You'll Ever Have. (Three Week Unit for Introducing Drama to Teens Ser.). (Illus.). 45p. (Orig.). 1996. pap. text 12.95 (*1-57514-017-9*, 5018); pap. text, student ed., wbk. ed. 5.95 (*1-57514-018-7*, 5018T) Encore Perform Pub.

Millar, Kenneth, see MacDonald, Ross, pseud.

Millar, Kirsta & Sher, Jonathan P. Raising North Carolina: Assessing the Needs & Resources for NC Smart Start Population. (Illus.). 250p. 1999. pap. write for info. (*0-9665180-2-0*) NC Child.

Millar, Margaret. An Air That Kills. 250p. 1985. pap. 4.95 (*0-930330-23-4*) Intl Polygonics.

— Ask Me for Tomorrow. 184p. 1991. pap. 8.95 (*1-55882-115-5*) Intl Polygonics.

— Beast in View. 160p. 2000. mass mkt. 5.95 (*0-7867-0667-8*) Carroll & Graf.

***Millar, Margaret.** The Cannibal Heart. LC 99-55483. 2000. 26.95 (*0-7862-2335-9*) Thorndike Pr.

Millar, Margaret. The Devil Loves Me. large type ed. LC 99-18837. 1999. 25.95 (*0-7862-1908-4*) Thorndike Pr.

— Fire Will Freeze. (Library of Crime Classics). 162p. 1987. pap. 4.95 (*0-930330-59-5*) Intl Polygonics.

***Millar, Margaret.** How Like an Angel. 288p. 2000. mass mkt. 5.95 (*0-7867-0706-2*) Carroll & Graf.

Millar, Margaret. The Iron Gates. large type ed. LC 98-51091. 1999. 26.95 (*0-7862-1779-0*) Thorndike Pr.

— The Listening Walls. 236p. 1986. pap. 5.95 (*0-930330-52-8*) Intl Polygonics.

— Mermaid. 216p. 1991. pap. 8.95 (*1-55882-114-7*) Intl Polygonics.

— Mermaid LC 82-16198. 317p. 1982. write for info. (*0-89340-543-4*) Chivers N Amer.

— The Murder of Miranda. 22.95 (*0-89190-156-6*) Amereon Ltd.

— Rose's Last Summer. 223p. 1985. pap. 4.95 (*0-930330-26-9*) Intl Polygonics.

— A Stranger in My Grave. 308p. 1990. reprint ed. pap. 7.95 (*1-55882-066-3*) Intl Polygonics.

— Vanish in an Instant. LC 89-85721. 248p. 1990. reprint ed. pap. 7.95 (*1-55882-051-5*, Lib Crime Classics) Intl Polygonics.

— Wall of Eyes. 224p. 1986. pap. 4.95 (*0-930330-42-0*) Intl Polygonics.

Millar, Martin. Milk, Sulphate & Alby Starvation. LC 95-149417. 152p. 1989. pap. 13.95 (*1-85702-214-9*) Trafalgar.

Millar, Mary. Assessing Information Needs Module 1: Facilitator's Guide. (Primary Health Care Management Advancement Programme (PHC MAP) Modules Ser.). 55p. 1993. pap. text. write for info. (*1-882839-08-0*) Aga Khan Fnd.

— Assessing the Quality of Management Module 7: Facilitator's Guide. (Primary Health Care Management Advancement Programme (PHC MAP) Modules Ser.). 47p. 1993. pap. text. write for info. (*1-882839-13-7*) Aga Khan Fnd.

— Cost Analysis Module 8: Facilitator's Guide. (Primary Health Care Management Advancement Programme (PHC MAP) Modules Ser.). 53p. 1993. pap. text. write for info. (*1-882839-14-5*) Aga Khan Fnd.

— Sustainability Analysis Module 9: Facilitator's Guide. (Primary Health Care Management Advancement Programme (PHC MAP) Modules Ser.). 55p. 1993. pap. text. write for info. (*1-882839-16-1*) Aga Khan Fnd.

Millar, Melanie S. Cracking the Gender Code: Who Rules the Wired World? LC 99-177852. 225p. 1998. pap. 16.95 (*1-896764-14-2*, Pub. by Sec Story Pr) LPC InBook.

Millar, Myrna & Millar, Heather. The Toxic Labyrinth: A Family's Successful Battle Against Environmental Illness. (Illus.). 304p. 1996. pap. 14.00 (*0-9699245-0-X*) B & T International.

Millar, Paul, jt. see Baxter, James K.

Millar, Perry S. & Baar, Carl. Judicial Administration in Canada. LC 82-173244. (Canadian Public Administration Ser.). 476p. reprint ed. Apple II 147.60 (*0-7837-1019-4*, 204133000020) Bks Demand.

Millar, Peter. Stealing Thunder. 288p. 1999. 23.95 (*1-58234-016-1*) Bloomsbury Pubg.

***Millar, Peter.** Stealing Thunder. 2000. pap. 13.95 (*1-58234-071-4*) Bloomsbury Pubg.

***Millar, Peter W.** Iona. 64p. 2000. pap. text 6.50 (*1-85311-166-X*) Canterbury Press Norwich.

Millar, Rob, et al. Professional Interviewing. (International Series on Communication Skills). (Illus.). 224p. (C). 1991. pap. 27.99 (*0-415-04085-X*, A6297) Routledge.

Millar, Robert. Policing the Miners Strike. Fine, Ben, ed. (C). 1985. pap. 19.50 (*0-85315-633-6*, Pub. by Lawrence & Wishart); text 52.50 (*0-85315-632-8*, Pub. by Lawrence & Wishart) NYU Pr.

Millar, Robert L., et al. Women & Political Participation in Northern Ireland. 304p. (C). 1996. 72.95 (*1-85628-991-5*, Pub. by Avebry) Ashgate Pub Co.

Millar, Robert W., ed. & tr. see Engelmann, Arthur, et al.

Millar, Robert W., tr. see Garofalo, Raffaele.

***Millar, Robin, et al.** Improving Science Education: The Contribution of Research. LC 00-33989. 2000. pap. write for info. (*0-335-20645-X*, Pub. by OpUniv Pr) Taylor & Francis.

Millar, Roderick. Doing Business with France. 1998. pap. text 35.00 (*0-7494-2564-4*) Kogan Page Ltd.

Millar, Roderick, ed. London As an International Business Centre. 256p. 1998. pap. 35.00 (*0-7494-2543-1*) Kogan Page Ltd.

Millar, Roderick & Chandramouli, M. S. Doing Business with India. 1999. pap. text 65.00 (*0-7494-2924-0*, Pub. by Kogan Page Ltd) LPC InBook.

Millar, Roderick & Reuvid, Jonathan. Doing Business with Germany. 2nd ed. 1999. pap. text 32.95 (*0-7494-2951-8*, Pub. by Kogan Page Ltd) LPC InBook.

Millar, Stuart, jt. auth. see Messer, David.

Millar, Stuart, jt. ed. see Messer, David.

Millar, Susan B. Bugis Weddings: Rituals of Social Location in Modern Indonesia. LC 89-62006. (Monographs: No. 29). (Illus.). 236p. (Orig.). (C). 1989. pap. 17.50 (*0-944613-06-3*) UC Berkeley Ctrs SE Asia.

Millar, Susanna. Understanding & Representing Space: Theory & Evidence from Experiments with Blind & Sighted Children. LC 94-10299. (Illus.). 324p. 1994. text 85.00 (*0-19-852142-1*) OUP.

Millar, T. B. Australia in Peace & War. (Australian National Universtity Press Ser.). 1996. text. write for info. (*0-08-032999-3*, Pergamon Pr); pap. text. write for info. (*0-08-032998-5*, Pergamon Pr) Elsevier.

Millar, T. B. & Walter, James, eds. Asian-Pacific Security after the Cold War. 144p. (Orig.). 1993. pap. 24.95 (*1-86373-398-1*, Pub. by Allen & Unwin Pty) Paul & Co Pubs.

Millar, T. J. & Raga, A. C., eds. Shocks in Astrophysics: Proceedings of the International Conference on Shocks in Astrophysics. 336p. (C). 1996. lib. bdg. 195.00 (*0-7923-3899-5*) Kluwer Academic.

Millar, T. J. & Williams, David A., eds. Rate Coefficients in Astrochemistry. (C). 1988. text 195.50 (*90-277-2752-X*) Kluwer Academic.

Millar, T. J., jt. auth. see Cherchneff, I.

Millar, T. J., jt. ed. see James, R. A.

Millar, T. J., jt. ed. see Williams, D. A.

***Millar, Thomas P.** Biochemistry Explained: A Practical Guide to Learning Biochemistry. 212p. 2000. text 58.00 (*90-5702-474-8*, Harwood Acad Pubs); pap. text 24.00 (*90-5702-475-6*, Harwood Acad Pubs) Gordon & Breach.

Millar, W. P., jt. auth. see Gidney, R. D.

Millar, Will. Messing about in Boats: The Nautical Confessions of an Unsinkable Irishman. (Illus.). 192p. 1997. pap. 16.95 (*1-55110-620-5*) Whitecap Bks.

Millard, jt. auth. see Bungey, John H.

Millard, A. J. A Technological Lag: Diffusion of Electrical Technology in England, 1879-1914. (Modern European History Ser.). 264p. 1987. text 15.00 (*0-8240-7823-3*) Garland.

***Millard, A. R.** Reading & Writing in the Time of Jesus. LC 99-58496. 2000. text 35.00 (*0-8147-5637-9*) NYU Pr.

— Reading & Writing in the Time of Jesus. (Biblical Seminar Ser.: No. 69). 200p. 2000. pap. 24.50 (*1-84127-070-9*, Pub. by Sheffield Acad) CUP Services.

Millard, A. R., et al, eds. Faith, Tradition & History: Old Testament Historiography in Its Near Eastern Context. LC 94-2529. xiv, 354p. 1994. text 37.50 (*0-931464-82-X*) Eisenbrauns.

Millard, Alan. Equality: A Man's Claim. abr. ed. 580p. (Orig.). 1995. pap. 14.95 (*1-56901-342-X*) A Millard.

— First Kings - Second Chronicles. (Bible Study Commentaries Ser.). 126p. 1985. pap. 4.95 (*0-87508-155-X*) Chr Lit.

Millard, Alan. The Great Salt Lake Guidebook. (Illus.). pap. write for info. (*0-88290-689-5*) Horizon Utah.

Millard, Allan. The Eponyms of the Assyrian Empire 910-612 B. C. (State Archives of Assyria Ser.: Vol. 2). xvi, 155p. 1994. pap. text 36.50 (*951-45-6715-3*, Pub. by Neo-Assyrian Text) Eisenbrauns.

Millard, Andre. America on Record: A History of Recorded Sound. (Illus.). 425p. (C). 1995. pap. text 18.95 (*0-521-47556-2*) Cambridge U Pr.

— Edison & the Business of Innovation. (Johns Hopkins Studies in the History of Technology; New Ser.). 408p. (C). 1993. reprint ed. pap. text 24.95 (*0-8018-4730-3*) Johns Hopkins.

Millard, Ann V., jt. auth. see Howard, Mary T.

Millard, Anne. The Age of Revolutions. (Picture History Ser.). (Illus.). (J). (gr. 3-7). 1979. pap. 6.95 (*0-86020-263-1*, Usborne); lib. bdg. 14.95 (*0-88110-112-5*, Usborne) EDC.

— Crusaders, Aztecs & Samurai. (Picture History Ser.). (Illus.). 32p. (J). (gr. 3-7). 1978. pap. 6.95 (*0-86020-194-5*, Usborne); lib. bdg. 14.95 (*0-88110-110-9*, Usborne) EDC.

— Eric the Red: The Vikings Sail the Atlantic. LC 93-26113. (Beyond the Horizons Ser.). 48p. (J). 1994. lib. bdg. 24.26 (*0-8114-7252-3*) Raintree Steck-V.

— Eyewitness Atlas of Ancient Worlds. (Illus.). 64p. (J). (gr. 5 up). 1994. write for info. (*1-56458-679-0*) DK Pub Inc.

— The First Civilization. (Picture History Ser.). (Illus.). 32p. (J). (gr. 3-7). 1977. pap. 6.95 (*0-86020-138-4*, Usborne); lib. bdg. 14.95 (*0-88110-107-9*, Usborne) EDC.

— How People Lived. LC 92-54315. (See & Explore Library). (Illus.). 64p. (J). (gr. 3-7). 1993. 12.95 (*1-56458-237-X*) DK Pub Inc.

— Lost Civilizations. LC 96-20486. (Mysteries of...Ser.). (Illus.). 40p. (J). (gr. 4-6). 1996. lib. bdg. 22.90 (*0-7613-0534-3*, Copper Beech Bks) Millbrook Pr.

— New Book of Pharaohs. LC 98-15579. 32p. (J). (gr. 4-6). 1998. 24.90 (*0-7613-0859-8*, Copper Beech Bks); pap. 9.95 (*0-7613-0778-8*, Copper Beech Bks) Millbrook Pr.

— Pyramids. LC 95-39660. (Story Library). (Illus.). 64p. (J). (gr. 3-7). 1996. 16.95 (*1-85697-674-2*) LKC.

— Pyramids. LC 95-13269. (Mysteries Of-- Ser.). (J). 1995. 12.15 (*0-606-09659-0*, Pub. by Turtleback) Demco.

— The Pyramids: The Latest Secrets Revealed in the Light of Recent Scientific Discoveries. (Mysteries of...Ser.). (Illus.). 40p. (J). (gr. 4-6). 1995. pap. 6.95 (*1-56294-194-1*, Copper Beech Bks) Millbrook Pr.

— Round the World Cookbook. (Illus.). 48p. (J). (gr. 2-6). 1993. pap. 8.95 (*0-7460-0966-6*, Usborne) EDC.

Millard, Anne. Stuarts. (Illus.). (J). 1995. pap. write for info. (*0-237-51603-9*) EVN1 UK.

Millard, Anne. The Usborne Book of World History. (Picture History Ser.). (Illus.). 195p. (J). (gr. 3-7). 1986. 24.95 (*0-86020-959-8*) EDC.

— Warriors & Seafarers. (Picture History Ser.). (Illus.). (J). (gr. 3-7). 1977. lib. bdg. 14.95 (*0-88110-108-7*, Usborne) EDC.

— The World of the Pharaoh. LC 98-28851. (World of Ser.). (Illus.). 48p. (J). (gr. 4-6). 1998. 19.95 (*0-87226-292-8*, P Bedrick Books) NTC Contemp Pub Co.

Millard, Anne & Evans, Cheryl. Greek Myths & Legends. (Myths & Legends Ser.). (Illus.). 64p. (J). (gr. 6 up). 1999. lib. bdg. 17.95 (*0-88110-224-5*) EDC.

Millard, Anne & Peach, S. The Greeks. (Illustrated World History Ser.). (Illus.). 96p. (YA). (gr. 6 up). 1990. pap. 12.95 (*0-7460-0342-0*) EDC.

— The Greeks. (Illustrated World History Ser.). (Illus.). 194p. (YA). (gr. 6 up). 1999. lib. bdg. 20.95 (*0-88110-415-9*) EDC.

Millard, Anne, et al. Ancient World. (Illustrated World History Ser.). (Illus.). 288p. (YA). (gr. 6 up). 1992. pap. 24.95 (*0-7460-1233-0*) EDC.

Millard, Anne, jt. auth. see Chisholm, Jane.

Millard, Anne, jt. auth. see Evans, Cheryl.

Millard, Bob. Country Music: 75 Years of America's Favorite Music. LC 98-48219. (Illus.). 384p. 1999. reprint ed. mass mkt. 22.95 (*0-306-80903-6*, Pub. by Da Capo) HarpC.

Millard, Brian. Winning on the Stock Market. 2nd ed. LC 97-41438. 208p. 1998. pap. 34.95 (*0-471-97053-0*) Wiley.

Millard, Brian J. Channels & Cycles: A Tribute to J. M. Hurst. (Illus.). 248p. 1999. 45.00 (*0-934380-50-3*, 1401) Traders Pr.

— Millard on Channel Analysis: The Key to Share Price Prediction. LC 96-46490. 212p. 1997. pap. 48.50 (*0-471-96845-5*) Wiley.

— Millard on Profitable Charting Techniques. 2nd ed. LC 96-47782. 222p. 1997. pap. 48.50 (*0-471-96846-3*) Wiley.

— Millard on Traded Options. 2nd ed. LC 96-46656. 212p. 1997. pap. 48.50 (*0-471-96780-7*) Wiley.

— Traded Options Simplified. LC 98-13965. 190p. 1998. pap. 42.50 (*0-471-96658-4*) Wiley.

Millard, C. S., jt. auth. see Mason, Stuart.

Millard, Catherine. A Children's Companion Guide to America's History. LC 93-78892. (Illus.). 96p. 1993. pap., student ed. 11.99 (*0-88965-102-7*, Pub. by Horizon Books) Chr Pubns.

— Christian Heritage of Our Nation History Curriculm: National Landmarks. 1998. pap. text 29.95 (*0-9658616-0-0*) Christ Herit.

— Christian Heritage of Our Nation History Curriculum: National Memorials. 1998. pap. 29.95 (*0-9658616-1-9*) Christ Herit.

— Great American Statesmen & Heroes. (Illus.). 302p. 1995. pap. 14.99 (*0-88965-120-5*, 0021205, Pub. by Horizon Books) Chr Pubns.

Millard, D. O. Applied Anatomy of the Lymphatics. 278p. 1997. reprint ed. pap. 22.00 (*0-7873-0615-0*) Hlth Research.

Millard, D. Ralph, Jr. Cleft, 3 vols., Set. 2964p. 1980. text 662.00 (*0-316-57148-2*) Lppncott W & W.

— Cleft Craft: Alveolar & Palatal Deformities, Vol. III. 1980. text 235.00 (*0-316-57139-3*, Little Brwn Med Div) Lppncott W & W.

— Cleft Craft: Bilateral & Rare Deformities, Vol. 2. 1976. text 235.00 (*0-316-57138-5*, Little Brwn Med Div) Lppncott W & W.

— Cleft Craft - The Evolution of Its Surgery Vol. 1: The Unilateral Deformity, Vol. 1. 1976. text 235.00 (*0-316-57137-7*) Lppncott W & W.

— Principalization of Plastic Surgery. 1986. 235.00 (*0-316-57153-9*, Little Brwn Med Div) Lppncott W & W.

— A Rhinoplasty Tetrology: Corrective, Secondary, Congenital, Reconstructive. LC 96-1014. 1000p. 1996. text 415.00 (*0-316-57156-3*, Little Brwn Med Div) Lppncott W & W.

Millard, David L. The Joy of Watercolor. (Illus.). 144p. 1992. reprint ed. pap. 18.95 (*0-8230-2566-7*, Watson-Guptill Bks) Watsn-Guptill.

Millard, Edward. Export Marketing for a Small Handicraft Business. 2nd ed. 184p. 1996. pap. 19.50 (*1-85339-352-5*, Pub. by Intermed Tech) Stylus Pub VA.

Millard, Elaine. Differently Literate: Boys, Girls & the Schooling of Literacy. LC 97-204761. 216p. 1997. 79.95 (*0-7507-0660-0*, Falmer Pr); pap. 27.95 (*0-7507-0661-9*, Falmer Pr) Taylor & Francis.

Millard, Elaine, jt. auth. see Clark, Ann.

Millard, Elizabeth. Criminal Trial Preparation. (Illus.). 204p. 1992. pap. 35.00 (*0-685-14628-6*) NJ Inst CLE.

***Millard, F.** Polish Politics & Society. LC 99-12745. 1999. write for info. (*0-415-15903-2*) Routledge.

Millard, Frances. The Anatomy of the New Poland: Post-Communist Politics in Its First Phase. (Studies of Communism in Transition). 272p. 1994. 95.00 (*1-85278-924-7*) E Elgar.

Millard, Gregory. Geechies. 1992. pap. 5.95 (*0-88378-092-5*) Third World.

***Millard, H. Dean & Mason, David, eds.** Perspectives on 3rd World Workshop on Oral Medicine, 1998. 392p. 2000. pap. text 65.00 (*0-9645852-1-9*) UMI Schl Dentsy.

Millard, J. M. Yang-Baxter Equations in Paris: Proceedings of the Conference. 300p. 1993. text 95.00 (*981-02-1343-3*) World Scientific Pub.

Millard, James. Chesapeake & Ohio Streamliners: Second to None: The Cars. (Illus.). 121p. 1996. 29.95 (*0-939487-21-7*) Ches & OH Hist.

Millard, Kenneth. Edwardian Poetry. (Oxford English Monographs). 208p. 1992. text 65.00 (*0-19-812225-X*) OUP.

M

An Asterisk (*) at the beginning of an entry indicates that the title is appearing for the first time.

Millard, Kent. Spiritual Gifts. (Lifesearch Ser.). 64p. (Orig.). 1994. pap. 4.95 (*0-687-77866-2*) Abingdon.

Millard, Kerry. Gordon's Biscuit. 1998. 16.00 (*0-207-18748-7*) HarpC.

— Gordon's Biscuit. 1999. pap. 6.95 (*0-207-19145-X*) HarpC.

Millard, Kevin D., et al. Federal Gift, Estate, & Generation-Skipping Transfer Taxation of Life Insurance. 2nd ed. LC 98-4873. (Insurance Counselor Ser.). 1998. 64.95 (*1-57073-536-0*) Amer Bar Assn.

Millard, L. Adult Learners: Study Skills & Teaching Methods. (C). 1981. 40.00 (*1-85041-010-0*, Pub. by Univ Nottingham) St Mut.

Millard, Mary. Shattered Secrets. 408p. (Orig.). 1992. pap. 16.95 (*0-9624022-5-7*) Venture Bk Pubns.

***Millard, Mike.** Leaving Japan: Observations of the Dysfunctional U. S.- Japan Relationship. LC 00-41290. (Illus.). 2000. write for info. (*0-7656-0660-7*) M E Sharpe.

— Leaving Japan: Observations on a Dysfunctional U.S.-Japan Relationship. 200p. 2000. text 37.95 (*0-7656-0659-3*, East Gate Bk) M E Sharpe.

Millard, P., tr. see Adzhemyan, L. T., et al.

Millard, P., tr. see Belokurov, V. V. & Shirov, D. V.

Millard, Patricia. Trade Associations & Professional Bodies of the United Kingdom. 8th ed. 600p. 1987. 78.00 (*0-08-033390-7*, Pergamon Pr) Elsevier.

— Trade Associations & Professional Bodies of the United States. 7th ed. 1984. 46.00 (*0-08-023024-5*, Pergamon Pr) Elsevier.

Millard, Patricia, ed. Trade Associations & Professional Bodies of the United Kingdom. 9th ed. LC 88-19516. (Trade Association & Professional Bodies Ser.). 530p. 1988. 40.00 (*0-08-034876-9*, Pergamon Pr) Elsevier.

Millard, Richard J., jt. ed. see Ware, Mark E.

Millard, Rodney J. The Master Spirit of the Age: Canadian Engineers & the Politics of Professionalism, 1887-1922. 236p. 1988. text 37.50 (*0-8020-2652-4*) U of Toronto Pr.

Millard, S. P. Environmental Stats for S-PLUS: User's Manual for Windows & UNIX, Version 1.1. LC 98-4685. 400p. 1998. pap. 59.95 (*0-387-98486-0*) Spr-Verlag.

Millard, Scott, jt. auth. see Johnson, Eric A.

Millard, Scott, ed. see Johnson, Eric A.

Millard, Scott, ed. see Walheim, Lance.

***Millard, Steven P.** Environmental Statistics. 416p. 1999. 79.95 (*0-8493-7168-6*) CRC Pr.

Millard, Sue. Creative Candlewicking for the Home. (Illus.). 96p. (C). 1988. 100.00 (*1-85368-069-9*, Pub. by New5 Holland) St Mut.

Millard, Susan. Against the Odds. 273p. 1995. pap. 35.00 (*0-85131-630-1*, Pub. by J A Allen) St Mut.

Millardet, Pierre M. The Discovery of Bordeaux Mixture. Schneiderhan, F. J., tr. (Phytopathological Classics Ser.). 25p. 1933. 22.00 (*0-89054-004-7*) Am Phytopathol Soc.

Millares. Applied Drug Information. LC 98-193486. 1998. 40.00 (*0-915486-28-8*) Applied Therapeutics.

Millares, Carlo. Historia de la Literatura Latina. (Breviarios Ser.). (SPA.). pap. 9.99 (*968-16-0744-9*, Pub. by Fondo) Continental Bk.

Millares, Carlos A. Tratado de Paleografia Espanola, 3 vols., 2-Laminas. 3rd ed. 1176p. 1989. write for info. (*0-318-65349-4*) Elliots Bks.

— Tratado de Paleografia Espanola, 3 vols., 3-Laminas. 3rd ed. 1176p. 1989. write for info. (*0-318-65350-8*) Elliots Bks.

— Tratado de Paleografia Espanola, 3 vols., Set. 3rd ed. 1176p. 1989. 975.00 (*84-239-4986-9*) Elliots Bks.

Millares Carlos, Agustin. Tratado de Paleografia Espanola, 3 vols., 1-Texto. 3rd ed. 1176p. 1989. write for info. (*0-318-65348-6*) Elliots Bks.

***Millares, Selena.** Dialogues of the Air & the Sea. Reyes, Carlos, tr. from SPA.Tr. of Dialogos Del Aire y el Mar. 32p. 2000. pap. 7.00 (*0-932264-28-X*) Trask Hse Bks.

Millares Vazquez, Manuel, tr. see McNeill, William H.

Millas. Papel Mojado: Level C. text 8.95 (*0-88436-999-4*) EMC-Paradigm.

Millas, Aristides J. Seventy Years of Miami Architecture: Commercial & Institutional Architecture in Dade County. LC 91-70266. (Illus.). 96p. (Orig.). 1991. pap. 14.95 (*1-880511-01-0*) Bass Museum.

Millas, Juan J. El Desorden de Tu Nombre (The Disorder of Your Name) 176p. 1995. pap. 12.50 (*0-679-76091-1*) Vin Bks.

Millas, Juan J., adapted by. El Desorden de Tu Nombre, Level 3. (Leer en Espanol Ser.). (SPA.). (C). 1998. pap. 5.95 (*84-294-3485-2*) Santillana.

— Letra Muerta, Level 4. (Leer en Espanol Ser.). (SPA.). (C). 1998. pap. 6.95 (*84-294-3487-9*) Santillana.

Millasich, James, see Britton, James, pseud.

Millat, Jurgen, et al, eds. Transport Properties of Fluids: Their Correlation, Prediction & Estimation. (Illus.). 497p. (C). 1996. text 100.00 (*0-521-46178-2*) Cambridge U Pr.

Millau, Christian. Guide Gault Millau France 1994: French Edition. (FRE.). 799p. 1994. 69.95 (*0-614-00404-7*, 2902968701) Fr & Eur.

— Guide Gault Millau Paris 1994: French Edition. (FRE.). 720p. 1994. 59.95 (*0-614-00403-9*, 2902968396) Fr & Eur.

Millau, Gault. Gault Millau Guide to Paris 1998. (FRE.). 1998. 79.95 (*0-7859-9556-0*) Fr & Eur.

Millau, Gault, ed. Gault Millau Guide to France: French Edition. (FRE.). 1997. 79.95 (*0-7859-9318-5*) Fr & Eur.

— Gault Millau Guide to France 1998. 1998. 79.95 (*0-7859-9557-9*) Fr & Eur.

Millay, Edna St. Vincent. Collected Lyrics. LC 75-6348. 304p. 1981. pap. 14.00 (*0-06-090863-7*, CN863, Perennial) HarperTrade.

— Collected Poems. LC 75-6348. 1992. reprint ed. lib. bdg. 59.95 (*0-89968-266-9*, Lghtyr Pr) Buccaneer Bks.

— Collected Poems of E. Millay, Norma, ed. LC 75-6348. 768p. 1981. reprint ed. pap. 22.50 (*0-06-090889-0*, CN-889, Perennial) HarperTrade.

— Collected Sonnets. rev. expanded ed. LC 83-48369. 224p. 1988. pap. 13.00 (*0-06-091091-7*, CN 1091, Perennial) HarperTrade.

— Early Poems. Peppe, Holly, ed. & intro. by. LC 98-23165. (Penguin Twentieth-Century Classics Ser.). 173p. 1998. pap. 12.95 (*0-14-118054-4*) Viking Penguin.

— Edna St. Vincent Millay's Poems Selected for Young People. LC 77-25671. (Illus.). 120p. (YA). (gr. 7 up). 1979. 14.00 (*0-06-024218-3*) HarpC Child Bks.

***Millay, Edna St. Vincent.** First Fig & Other Poems. LC 99-53136. 2000. pap. 1.50 (*0-486-41104-4*) Dover.

Millay, Edna St. Vincent. Renascence & Other Poems. LC 72-3092. (Granger Index Reprint Ser.). 1977. reprint ed. pap. 13.95 (*0-8369-8245-2*) Ayer.

— Renascence & Other Poems. (Thrift Editions Ser.). (Illus.). 64p. 1991. reprint ed. pap. 1.00 (*0-486-26873-X*) Dover.

— Selected Poems: Perennial Classics Edition. LC 91-55102. 192p. 1999. pap. 12.00 (*0-06-093168-X*) HarpC.

Millay, Edna St. Vincent, et al. Selected from Twentieth-Century American Poetry: An Anthology. Literacy Volunteers of New York City Staff, ed. (Writers' Voices Ser.). 64p. (Orig.). 1991. pap. text 3.95 (*0-929631-29-3*, Signal Hill) New Readers.

Millay, Norma, ed. see Millay, Edna St. Vincent.

Millberg, Karen. Flight Against the Wind. (American Autobiography Ser.). 182p. 1995. reprint ed. lib. bdg. 69.00 (*0-7812-8595-X*) Rprt Serv.

***Millbower, Lenn.** Training with a Beat: The Teaching Power of Music. LC 00-22195. (Illus.). 224p. 2000. 29.95 (*1-57922-000-2*) Stylus Pub VA.

Millbrook, Minnie Dubbs, see Leland, Ottilie M. & Dubbs Millbrook, Minnie.

Millbrook, Press. Soft Sorts Water Babies. 1998. 9.95 (*0-7613-0393-6*) Millbrook Pr.

Millbrook Press Staff. Assorted Animal Fun. 1998. pap. 9.95 (*0-7613-1102-5*) Millbrook Pr.

— Assorted Crocodile/Tiger. 1998. pap. text 7.95 (*0-7613-1103-3*) Millbrook Pr.

— Assorted Lift the Flap. 1998. pap. text 8.45 (*0-7613-1116-5*) Millbrook Pr.

— Cars & Trucks. (Soft Sorts Ser.). 10p. (J). (ps-k). 1998. 10.95 (*0-7613-0394-4*, Copper Beech Bks) Millbrook Pr.

***Millbrook Society Staff.** Hatboro. LC 99-69057. (Images of America Ser.). (Illus.). 128p. 2000. pap. 18.99 (*0-7385-0342-8*) Arcadia Publng.

***Millbrooke, Anne M.** Aviation History. LC 99-16561. 636p. 1999. write for info. (*0-88487-235-1*) Jeppesen Sanderson.

***Millburn, John R.** The Adams of Fleet Street, Instrument Makers to King George: The History of a London Business, 1735-1830. LC 99-56586. 320p. 2000. text 104.95 (*0-7546-0080-7*, Pub. by Ashgate Pub) Ashgate Pub Co.

Mille, Agnes De, see De Mille, Agnes.

Mille, Anna G. De, see De Mille, Anna G.

Mille, Carol E. Which Translation Do You Prefer. 1975. pap. 1.95 (*0-915374-52-8*, 52-8) Rapids Christian.

Mille, James De, see De Mille, James.

Milledge, A., jt. auth. see Whittome, S.

Millegan, Patrick S., jt. ed. see Gibson, Richard I.

***Milleker, Elizabeth J.** The Year One: Art of the Ancient World East & West. (Illus.). 300p. 2000. 50.00 (*0-300-08514-1*) Yale U Pr.

Millen, Bruce H. The Political Role of Labor in Developing Countries. LC 79-29735. 148p. 1980. reprint ed. lib. bdg. 59.50 (*0-313-22286-X*, MIPO, Greenwood Pr) Greenwood.

Millen, C. M. The Low-Down Laundry Line Blues. LC 97-41117. (Illus.). 32p. (J). (ps-3). 1999. 15.00 (*0-395-87497-1*) HM.

— A Symphony for the Sheep. LC 95-43097. (Illus.). 32p. (J). 1996. 14.95 (*0-395-76503-X*) HM.

Millen, Cynthia. The Right to Privacy. 150p. 1998. 76.50 (*1-901657-11-6*); pap. 51.00 (*1-901657-10-8*) Gaunt.

Millen, John. Kanji Power: A Workbook for Mastering Japanese Characters. (Tuttle Lanaguage Library). (JPN.). 184p. (Orig.). 1992. pap., student ed. 14.95 (*0-8048-1725-1*) Tuttle Pubng.

Millen, Nina. Children's Games from Many Lands. LC 65-24039. (Illus.). 194p. reprint ed. pap. 60.20 (*0-7837-1952-3*, 204216900001) Bks Demand.

Millen, Patricia E. Bare Trees: Zadock Pratt, Master Tanner & the Story of What Happened to the Catskill Mountain Forests. LC 95-24109. (Illus.). 112p. 1995. pap. 11.95 (*1-883789-05-2*) Blk Dome Pr.

Millen, Rochelle L., et al, eds. New Perspectives on the Holocaust: A Guide for Teachers & Scholars. (C). 1996. pap. text 19.50 (*0-8147-5540-2*) NYU Pr.

— New Perspectives on the Holocaust: A Guide for Teachers & Scholars. 420p. (C). 1996. text 55.00 (*0-8147-5539-9*) NYU Pr.

Millender, Daruthula H. Louis Armstrong. LC 96-24544. (Illus.). 192p. 1997. 4.99 (*0-689-80881-X*) S&S Bks Yung.

— Louis Armstrong, Young Music Maker. (Childhood of Famous Americans Ser.). (J). 1997. 10.09 (*0-606-11582-X*, Pub. by Turtleback) Demco.

Millender, Dharathula H. Crispus Attucks: Black Leader of Colonial Patriots. LC 86-10779. (Childhood of Famous Americans Ser.). (Illus.). 192p. (J). (gr. 3-7). 1986. reprint ed. mass mkt. 4.95 (*0-02-041810-8*) Macmillan.

Millender, Dharathula H. Crispus Attucks, Black Leader of Colonial Patriots. (Childhood of Famous Americans Ser.). (J). 1982. 10.05 (*0-606-03186-3*, Pub. by Turtleback) Demco.

Millender, Dharathula H. Martin Luther King, Jr. Young Man with a Dream. (Childhood of Famous Americans Ser.). (J). 1986. 10.05 (*0-606-03247-9*, Pub. by Turtleback) Demco.

— Martin Luther King, Jr. Young Man with a Dream. LC 86-10739. (Childhood of Famous Americans Ser.). (Illus.). 192p. (J). (gr. 3-7). 1986. reprint ed. mass mkt. 4.95 (*0-02-042010-2*) Macmillan.

Millender, Franchelle C. South Carolina Elder Law. 415p. 1995. ring bd. 89.95 (*0-943856-68-X*, 540) SC Bar CLE.

Millender, Lewis H., et al, eds. Occupational Disorders of the Upper Extremity. (Illus.). 308p. 1991. text 83.00 (*0-443-08797-0*) Church.

Millenig, Virginia, et al, eds. Family Nurse Practitioner Set, 3 vols. 2nd ed. 1998. pap. text 130.00 (*1-878028-24-3*) Hlth Lead Assoc.

***Millennium Books Editors.** America's Heartland, 2001-2002. (Pets Welcome Ser.). 272p. 2000. pap. 15.95 (*1-888820-10-1*, Pub. by Millennium Calif) Andrews & McMeel.

— Great Lakes, 2001-2002. (Pets Welcome Ser.). 272p. 2000. pap. 15.95 (*1-888820-09-8*, Pub. by Millennium Calif) Andrews & McMeel.

— National Edition, 2001-2002. (Pets Welcome Ser.). 516p. 2000. pap. 19.95 (*1-888820-11-X*, Pub. by Millennium Calif) Andrews & McMeel.

Millennium Info Group Staff. Year 2000 Survival Checklists & Workbook. pap., wbk. ed. 25.00 (*0-89540-425-7*) Sun Pub.

Millennium Info Group Staff. Year 2000 Survival Checklists & Workbook: A Y2K Millennium Bug Resource Guide. (YTwoK Ser.). 1998. wbk. ed. 35.00 (*0-89540-417-6*) Sun Pub.

Millenson, J. R. Mind Matters: Psychological Medicine in Holistic Practice. LC 94-61963. (Illus.). 337p. (Orig.). (C). 1995. pap. text 29.95 (*0-939616-21-1*) Eastland.

Millenson, Michael L. Demanding Medical Excellence: Doctors & Accountability in the Information Age. LC 97-16677. 434p. 1997. 24.95 (*0-226-52587-2*) U Ch Pr.

— Demanding Medical Excellence: Doctors & Accountability in the Information Age. LC 99-39141. 2000. pap. 16.00 (*0-226-52588-0*) U Ch Pr.

Millenson, Susan F. Sir John Soane's Museum. LC 86-24926. (Architecture & Urban Design Ser.: No. 18). (Illus.). 202p. reprint ed. pap. 62.70 (*0-8357-1766-6*, 207061100005) Bks Demand.

Miller. ACA: Pain Management, Vol. 6. 1998. text 195.00 (*0-443-07513-1*, W B Saunders Co) Harcrt Hlth Sci Grp.

— ACA: Pediatric Anesthesia, Vol. 7. LC 98-21386. 1998. text 135.00 (*0-443-07964-1*) Harcourt.

— ACA: Subspecialty Care, Vol. 5. LC 97-47123. (C). 1998. text 135.00 (*0-443-07905-6*, W B Saunders Co) Harcrt Hlth Sci Grp.

— Air Conditioners: Home & Commercial. 1986. 15.95 (*0-02-501930-9*) Macmillan.

— Aix"Isms" for Unix Professionals. LC 98-24750. 184p. (C). 1998. pap. 45.00 (*0-13-757246-8*) P-H.

— Algebra Mentor. (Mathematics Ser.). 1990. pap., student ed. 17.95 (*0-534-14040-8*) Brooks-Cole.

— America at Odds. LC 97-44927. 1998. 38.00 (*0-534-53631-X*) Brooks-Cole.

— America at Odds. (Political Science Ser.). 1998. student ed. 15.25 (*0-534-53632-8*) Wadsworth Pub.

— American Drama Between the Wars. 1997. pap. 18.00 (*0-8057-1622-X*, Twyne) Mac Lib Ref.

— Atlas Clinical Anesthesia. 1999. text 750.00 (*0-443-07907-2*) Church.

— Basic College Mathematics Worktext. 5th ed. (C). 1998. pap. text. write for info. (*0-201-41735-9*) Addison-Wesley.

— Batman: Dark Knight. 12.95 (*0-446-38672-3*, Pub. by Warner Bks) Little.

— Becoming Laura Ingalls Wilder: The Woman Behind the Legend. large type ed. LC 98-42031. 1999. 25.95 (*0-7862-1690-5*) Thorndike Pr.

— Beginning Algebra with Graphics Calculator. (Mathematics Ser.). 2000. mass mkt. 55.95 (*0-534-93660-1*) PWS Pubs.

***Miller.** Broadsides: The Age of Fighting Sail, 1775-1815. LC 99-52346. (Illus.). 400p. 2000. 30.00 (*0-471-18517-5*) Wiley.

Miller. Business Law: Planning Guide. 6th ed. 1995. pap., suppl. ed. write for info. (*0-314-07886-X*) West Pub.

— Business Law: Text & Exercises. 2nd ed. LC 98-12717. (LA - Business Law Ser.). (C). 1998. pap. 65.95 (*0-538-88545-9*) S-W Pub.

— Business Law Alternatives. 6th ed. Date not set. pap. text, teacher ed. write for info. (*0-314-07885-1*) West Pub.

— Business Law Text. Date not set. pap. text, teacher ed. write for info. (*0-314-08930-6*) West Pub.

— Business Law Today. 3rd ed. (LA - Business Law Ser.). 1994. pap. 15.00 (*0-314-03635-0*) West Pub.

— California Economy: Case Study. 9th ed. (C). 1997. 13.80 (*0-673-97619-X*) Addison-Wesley.

— Can We Unravel Scientific Creativity? A Special Double Issue of the "Creativity Research Journal", Vol. 9, Nos. 2 & 3, 1996. 1996. pap. 20.00 (*0-8058-9910-3*) L Erlbaum Assocs.

— Career. Date not set. text, teacher ed. 42.95 (*0-314-69754-3*) West Pub.

Miller. Career Adventure: Exploring & Planning for Tomorrow. 2nd ed. 1994. text 41.00 (*0-314-02591-X*, Pub. by West Pub) Thomson Learn.

Miller. Chemistry: A Basic Introduction. (Chemistry Ser.). 1978. pap. 17.50 (*0-534-00527-6*); pap., student ed. 5.50 (*0-534-00577-2*); pap., student ed. 7.00 (*0-534-00623-X*) Wadsworth Pub.

— Chemistry: A Basic Introduction. 2nd ed. (Chemistry Ser.). 1981. pap., student ed. 7.75 (*0-534-00893-3*) Wadsworth Pub.

— Chemistry: A Basic Introduction. 3rd ed. 1984. pap. 32.50 (*0-534-02764-4*) Wadsworth Pub.

— Chemistry: A Contemporary Approach. 2nd ed. (Chemistry Ser.). 1987. pap., student ed. 14.00 (*0-534-07201-1*) Wadsworth Pub.

— Chemistry: Basic Introduction. 3rd ed. 1984. pap., teacher ed. write for info. (*0-534-02766-0*); pap., student ed. 12.00 (*0-534-02765-2*) Wadsworth Pub.

— Chemistry: Basic Introduction. 3rd ed. 1984. pap. 9.00 (*0-534-03232-X*) Wadsworth Pub.

***Miller.** Classics of Public Budgeting. 2000. 71.00 (*0-8133-9773-1*, Pub. by Westview) HarpC.

Miller. Classroom Projects, Your Career Adventure. 2nd ed. (Career Development). 1998. pap. 21.00 (*0-538-42776-0*) S-W Pub.

— Connaissances & Reactions. (Secondary French Ser.). (FRE.). 1994. mass mkt. 53.95 (*0-8384-4950-6*); mass mkt., wbk. ed. 17.95 (*0-8384-4951-4*) Heinle & Heinle.

— Consumer Economics in Action. (Principles of Economics Ser.). 1993. mass mkt., wbk. ed. 17.25 (*0-314-01025-4*) West Pub.

***Miller.** Cracking Toefl with Cd, 2001. 2000. pap. 20.00 (*0-375-76161-6*) Random.

Miller. Criminal Justice in Action. LC 99-22187. (Criminal Justice Ser.). 1999. pap. 76.95 (*0-534-56808-4*) Wadsworth Pub.

— Critical Care Neurology. LC 98-54233. (Blue Books of Practical Neurology: Vol. 21). 440p. 1999. text 95.00 (*0-7506-9968-X*) Buttrwrth-Heinemann.

— Critical Thinking & Writing Business Law Today. 4th ed. (SWC-Business Law Ser.). 1997. 21.25 (*0-314-20708-2*) Sth-Wstrn College.

— Critical Thinking for Environmental Science. (Biology Ser.). 1996. mass mkt. 2.50 (*0-534-50619-4*) Wadsworth Pub.

— Critical Thinking Gde-america At Odds. (Political Science). 1998. 8.75 (*0-534-53634-4*) Wadsworth Pub.

— Cultural Anthropology. LC 98-22358. 496p. 1998. pap. text 62.00 (*0-205-16396-3*) Allyn.

***Miller.** Culture Interpersonal Moralty. 2000. pap. 16.95 (*0-8133-1856-4*, Pub. by Westview) HarpC.

Miller. The Developmentally Appropriate Inclusive Classroom in Early Education. (Special Education Ser.). 48p. 1996. teacher ed. 13.95 (*0-8273-6705-8*) Delmar.

— Dictionary of Dreams. (Reference Library). 640p. 1997. pap. 6.95 (*1-85326-325-7*, 3257WW, Pub. by Wrdsworth Edits) NTC Contemp Pub Co.

— Dimensions of Community Health. 6th ed. 2001. 42.22 (*0-07-231982-8*) McGraw.

— ECON TODAY MICRO93 SG PK. 9th ed. (C). 1997. 65.95 (*0-321-80050-8*) Addison-Wesley.

— Economic Education for Consumers. (Principles of Economics Ser.). 1999. 57.95 (*0-538-68686-3*) S-W Pub.

— Economic Education for Consumers. (Principles of Economics Ser.). 1999. wbk. ed. 10.00 (*0-538-68687-1*) S-W Pub.

— Economic Issue. 7th ed. (Miscellaneous/Catalogs Ser.). 1994. pap., student ed. 20.95 (*0-314-03592-3*) S-W Pub.

— Economic Issues Consumers. 8th ed. (Health Sciences Ser.). (C). 1997. student ed. 15.75 (*0-314-20928-X*) Wadsworth Pub.

***Miller.** Economics: Today & Tomorrow. 1999. teacher ed. write for info. (*0-02-823596-7*) Glencoe.

— Economics Today. 1999. 58.00 (*0-201-63582-8*) Addison-Wesley.

Miller. Economics Today. 9th ed. (C). 1998. write for info. (*0-201-39149-X*) Addison-Wesley.

Miller. Economics Today: Macro & Your Economic Life. 9th ed. 1997. text, teacher ed., suppl. ed. 23.66 (*0-673-97617-3*) Addson-Wesley Educ.

Miller. Economics Today: MicroView & Your Economic Life. 8th ed. 592p. (C). 1997. pap. 45.00 (*0-06-502272-6*) HarpC.

— Economy Today. 9th ed. (C). 1997. 105.00 (*0-321-80103-2*) Addison-Wesley.

***Miller.** Electronic Devices & Circuit Theory. (Student Material TV Ser.). (C). 2001. pap. 59.25 (*0-7668-0677-4*) Delmar.

Miller. An Enemy of the People. (Longman Literature Ser.). 1993. pap. text. write for info. (*0-582-09717-7*, Pub. by Addison-Wesley) Longman.

— Energy: Electricity & Electronics. (Tech & Industrial Education Ser.). (C). 1982. teacher ed. 11.95 (*0-538-33502-5*); trans. 430.95 (*0-538-33505-X*) S-W Pub.

***Miller.** Environmental Microbiology. 608p. 2000. 99.95 (*0-12-497570-4*) Acad Pr.

Miller. Environmental Science. 3rd ed. (Biology Ser.). 1990. mass mkt. write for info. (*0-534-13459-9*) Wadsworth Pub.

— Environmental Science. 4th ed. (Biology Ser.). 1993. teacher ed. 35.00 (*0-534-17810-3*) Wadsworth Pub.

— Environmental Science. 6th ed. (Biology Ser.). 1997. pap. 58.25 (*0-534-50615-1*) Wadsworth Pub.

— Environmental Science. 7th ed. (Biology Ser.). 1998. mass mkt. 58.50 (*0-534-53546-1*) Wadsworth Pub.

***Miller.** Environmental Science. 8th ed. (Biology Ser.). 2000. text 19.00 (*0-534-37882-X*) Brooks-Cole.

Miller. Environmental Science: International Version. 8th ed. LC 99-42986. (Biology Ser.). 118p. 2000. pap. 78.95 (*0-534-37614-2*) Brooks-Cole.

— Environmental Science with Infotrac 8th ed. LC 99-42986. (Biology Ser.). 2000. pap. 58.50 (*0-534-37613-4*) Brooks-Cole.

— The Essential's-West's America Government. 2nd ed. 1998. mass mkt. 35.00 (*0-538-42536-9*) S-W Pub.

— Experiences Along the Way, Your Career Adventure: Explore & Plan. 2nd ed. (Career Development Ser.). 1998. pap., wbk. ed. 29.95 (*0-538-42376-5*) S-W Pub.

M

An Asterisk (*) at the beginning of an entry indicates that the title is appearing for the first time.

— Experiences with Electrons. (Tech & Industrial Education Ser.). 1983. text 27.95 (*0-538-33520-3*); teacher ed. 8.00 (*0-538-33522-X*) S-W Pub.

— Exploring Career Choices: Your Career Adventure. 2nd ed. (Career Development Ser.). 1998. mass mkt. 2.75 (*0-538-42377-3*) S-W Pub.

***Miller.** Footnote to Plato: Introduction to Western Philosophy. 512p. 1998. pap. text 53.96 (*0-536-01887-1*) Pearson Custom.

Miller. Fundamentals of Business Law. 3rd ed. Date not set. pap. text, teacher ed. write for info. (*0-314-07884-3*) West Pub.

— Fundamentals of Management. Date not set. pap. text, teacher ed. write for info. (*0-314-08978-0*) West Pub.

— General & Oral Pathology for the Dental Hygienist. (C). (gr. 13). 1995. teacher ed. write for info. (*0-8151-6952-3*) Mosby Inc.

— Global Change. (C). 1996. pap. text, teacher ed. write for info. (*0-15-505358-2*) Harcourt Coll Pubs.

***Miller.** Golfing in the Zone. 160p. 2000. 6.98 (*1-56731-379-5*, MJF Bks) Fine Comms.

Miller. Guide to Florida Clast Mathematical Compentency. 8th ed. 384p. (C). 1997. pap., suppl. ed. 28.00 (*0-673-98438-9*) Addison-Wesley.

— Handbook on Critical Thinking: Fundamentals of Business Law. 4th ed. (SWC-Business Law). 1998. pap. 5.00 (*0-324-00624-1*) S-W Pub.

— A History of the Information Age. 1995. 30.00 (*0-8161-1982-1*, G K Hall & Co) Mac Lib Ref.

Miller. The Human Quest. 1995. 19.95 (*0-87973-735-2*) Our Sunday Visitor.

Miller. Immunology/Gastrointestinal Tract, Vol. II. 144p. 1987. 85.00 (*0-8493-4312-7*, CRC Reprint) Franklin.

— The Informed Argument. 4th ed. (C). 1995. pap. text, teacher ed. 33.75 (*0-15-502146-X*) Harcourt Coll Pubs.

— Informed Argument. 5th ed. (C). 1997. pap. text, teacher ed. 28.00 (*0-15-503810-9*) Harcourt Coll Pubs.

— Informix Basics. LC 98-36692. 1998. pap. 49.99 (*0-13-080799-0*) S&S Trade.

— Intermediate Macroeconomics 01. LC 97-28402. (HD - Intermediate Macroeconomics Ser.: No. 1). 1997. mass mkt. 86.95 (*0-538-87534-8*) S-W Pub.

— Introduction to AutoCAD. 1995. pap. text 19.00 (*0-8053-6420-X*) Benjamin-Cummings.

— Introduction to Critical Thinking & Writing in the Legal Environment of Business. (SWC-Business Law). 1995. pap. 5.75 (*0-314-08759-1*) West Pub.

— An Introduction to Environmental Science. (Biology Ser.). 1986. pap. write for info. (*0-534-05354-8*) Wadsworth Pub.

— An Introduction to Environmental Science. 2nd ed. (Biology Ser.). 1988. pap. write for info. (*0-534-09067-2*) Wadsworth Pub.

— Learning Language Addiction Counseling. LC 98-29190. 243p. 1998. pap. text 46.00 (*0-205-26318-6*) P-H.

— Legal Environment. Date not set. pap. text, student ed. 10.25 (*0-314-01947-2*); pap. text, suppl. ed. write for info. (*0-314-02160-4*) West Pub.

— Legal Environment: Answers. Date not set. pap. text, suppl. ed. write for info. (*0-314-02069-1*) West Pub.

— Legal Environment: Printouts. Date not set. pap. text. write for info. (*0-314-02070-5*) West Pub.

— Legal Environment Handbook. Date not set. pap. text 5.75 (*0-314-02071-3*); pap. text. write for info. (*0-314-02072-1*) West Pub.

— The Legal Environment Today. Date not set. pap. text, teacher ed. write for info. (*0-314-08863-6*) West Pub.

— Legal Environmental Business Answers. Date not set. pap. text. write for info. (*0-314-09147-5*) West Pub.

— Legal Environmental Business Statistics Handbook. Date not set. pap. text. write for info. (*0-314-09154-8*) West Pub.

— Letters to Callie. 1999. pap. write for info. (*0-671-52103-9*) S&S Trade.

Life of Harold Sellers Colton. 15.95 (*0 912586 70 2*) Dine College Pr.

— Living in Environment. (Biology Ser.). 1975. pap., student ed. 1.00 (*0-534-00454-7*) Wadsworth Pub.

— Living in the Environmt, 3rd. 3rd ed. (Biology Ser.). 1981. pap. write for info. (*0-534-02015-1*) Wadsworth Pub.

***Miller.** Living Now: Strategies for Success & Fulfillment. 2nd ed. 1999. pap. text 45.50 (*0-538-42954-2*) Thomson Learn.

— Living Now: Strategies, Success & Fulfillment. 1996. 12.00 (*0-314-20313-3*, Pub. by West Pub) Thomson Learn.

Miller. Living Now Academics. (Skills Life & Living Now Ser.). 1996. mass mkt. write for info. (*0-314-09793-7*) West Pub.

— Living Now Action Book. (Skills Life & Living Now Ser.). 1996. mass mkt. 24.00 (*0-314-09794-5*) West Pub.

— Living Now Careers. (Skills Life & Living Now Ser.). 1996. mass mkt. write for info. (*0-314-09792-9*) West Pub.

— Living Now Student. 1996. mass mkt., wbk. ed. write for info. (*0-314-09735-X*) West Pub.

— Living Now Work & Family. (Skills Life & Living Now Ser.). 1996. mass mkt. 24.00 (*0-314-09797-X*) West Pub.

— Mark Miller's Networking Libra. 1997. 145.00 (*1-55851-575-5*, M&T Bks) IDG Bks.

— Marketing & Modernity. LC 98-119929. 1997. 55.00 (*1-85973-991-1*, Pub. by Berg Pubs) NYU Pr.

— Mastering Legal Environment. Date not set. pap. text 20.00 (*0-314-02201-5*) West Pub.

Miller. Math Teachers Problem Solving Study Guide. 4th ed. 488p. 1997. pap., student ed. 31.95 (*0-471-36868-7*) Wiley.

Miller. Mathematical Ideas: Custom Book (8th Edition) 8th ed. 970p. (C). 1997. pap. text 75.00 (*0-321-01303-4*) Addson-Wesley Educ.

***Miller.** Mathematics for Elementary Teachers A Contemporary Approach. 5th ed. 2000. pap. text 31.95 (*0-471-36862-8*) Wiley.

Miller. Microeconomics: Economy Today. 9th ed. (C). 1998. 85.80 (*0-321-80186-5*) Addison-Wesley.

— Microsoft NT Workstation 5.0. (Computer Applications Ser.). 2000. pap., student ed. write for info. (*0-538-68911-0*) Thomson Learn.

— Microsoft Windows 2000 Professional. LC 99-59927. (Computer Applications Ser.). 2000. pap. 46.95 (*0-538-68910-2*) Thomson Learn.

— Money, Banking & Financial Markets. (SWC-Finance Ser.). 2000. pap. 90.95 (*0-324-01562-3*) Thomson Learn.

— Monsters. (World of the Unknown Ser.). (Illus.). 32p. (J). (gr. k-6). 1977. text 6.95 (*0-86020-146-5*) EDC.

— Nationalists & Nomads. LC 98-33698. 1999. lib. bdg. 46.00 (*0-226-52803-0*) U Ch Pr.

— Nationalists & Nomads. LC 98-33698. (Illus.). 248p. 1999. pap. text 19.00 (*0-226-52804-9*) U Ch Pr.

— Notorious. 1987. mass mkt. 3.95 (*0-445-73484-1*, Pub. by Warner Bks) Little.

— Novel. Date not set. 23.00 (*0-8050-6012-X*) H Holt & Co.

— Obstetric Decision Making. (C). 2000. pap. text. write for info. (*0-7216-8274-X*, W B Saunders Co) Harcrt Hlth Sci Grp.

— 101 Favorite Stories from the Bible. 1996. 12.99 (*1-885270-00-3*) Christian Aid.

— Optical Fiber Telecommunications, 2 vols. 1998. 229.00 (*0-12-497349-3*) Acad Pr.

***Miller.** Optimization: Foundations & Applications. LC 99-21921. 653p. 1999. pap. 89.95 (*0-471-35169-5*) Wiley.

Miller. Optimization: Foundations & Applications, 1. LC 99-21921. 570p. 1999. text 150.00 (*0-471-32242-3*) Wiley.

***Miller.** Order by Accident. 176p. 2000. 60.00 (*0-8133-6794-8*, Pub. by Westview) HarpC.

— Organizational Communication. 3rd ed. 2001. text 39.25 (*0-534-56144-6*) Thomson Learn.

Miller. Paralegal Today Essentials. Date not set. pap. text, teacher ed. write for info. (*0-314-06150-9*); pap. text, student ed. 13.75 (*0-314-06151-7*) West Pub.

— People & Their Planet: A Textbook of Environmental Science. (Illus.). 640p. 1991. pap. text 39.95 (*0-8016-3301-X*) Mosby Inc.

— Personal Law Handbook. LC 94-156023. Date not set. pap. text 9.00 (*0-314-03031-X*) West Pub.

— PH Reader Quiz Book. 4th ed. 1995. pap. text. write for info. (*0-13-164906-X*) Allyn.

— Physics for Scientists & Engineers. 2nd ed. 1996. pap. text, student ed. 25.20 (*0-13-231697-8*) P-H.

***Miller.** Picture History. (Illus.). 2000. pap. 14.95 (*0-486-40967-8*) Dover.

Miller. Pockets of Pride. 1994. 17.95 (*0-02-921690-7*) S&S Trade.

— Positive Child Guidance. (Early Childhood Education Ser.). 1990. 28.95 (*0-8273-3383-8*, VNR) Wiley.

— Positive Child Guidance Instructor's Guide. 2nd ed. (Early Childhood Education Ser.). 1996. 14.00 (*0-8273-5879-2*, VNR) Wiley.

— Power Journalism. LC 97-73100. (C). 1997. pap. text 21.00 (*0-15-503976-8*, Pub. by Harcourt Coll Pubs) Harcourt.

— Principles of Everyday Behavior Analysis. (Psychology Ser.). 1975. 14.75 (*0-8185-0141-3*) Brooks-Cole.

***Miller.** Quick Review on Civil Procedure. 4th ed. (Sum & Substance Quick Review Ser.). 1999. pap. 19.95 (*0-314-24289-9*) West Pub.

— Race to Save the Planet: 2001 Edition. 2000. pap. 18.00 (*0-534-37807-2*) Brooks-Cole.

— Race to Save the Planet: 2002 Edition. 2001. pap. 19.00 (*0-534-38105-7*) Brooks-Cole.

Miller. Radiographic Anatomy & Positioning. (C). 1999. 40.00 (*0-8385-8251-6*, Apple Lange Med) McGraw.

— Readings In Organizational Communication. (Speech & Theater). 2000. pap. 29.95 (*0-534-52083-9*) Wadsworth Pub.

— Reteaching , Living Now. (Career Development Ser.). 1996. text, wbk. ed. 22.50 (*0-314-20317-6*) West Pub.

— Review of Orthopaedics. 3rd ed. LC 99-16737. (C). 2000. pap. text. write for info. (*0-7216-8153-0*, W B Saunders Co) Harcrt Hlth Sci Grp.

— Sabbath Shiurim, Vol. II. 1979. 19.95 (*0-87306-404-6*) Feldheim.

Miller. Saint-Exupery's Le Petit Prince: Educational Edition, 001. rev. ed. (FRE.). 110p. (C). 1975. pap. 26.76 (*0-395-24005-0*) HM.

Miller. Science & Dissent in Post-Mao: The Politics of Knowledge. LC 95-24846. (Illus.). 366p. 1996. pap. 18.95 (*0-295-97532-6*) U of Wash Pr.

Miller. Screenwriting for Film & Television. LC 97-33479. 276p. 1997. pap. 33.00 (*0-205-27299-1*) P-H.

Miller. The Sea Aflame: A Naval History of World War II. 1995. 30.00 (*0-02-584995-6*) Macmillan.

— Sentencing. (Nutshell Ser.). Date not set. pap. text. write for info. (*0-314-06587-3*) West Pub.

— Stops Along the Way, Your Career Adventure: Explore & Plan. 2nd ed. (Career Development Ser.). 1999. pap., wbk. ed. 29.95 (*0-538-42375-7*) S-W Pub.

— Story of Easter. 1999. text 2.29 (*0-307-98902-X*) Gldn Bks Pub Co.

— Strategic Management (Brief) 2nd ed. 560p. 1996. pap. 50.94 (*0-07-042991-X*) McGraw.

— Strategic Selling. 1988. mass mkt. 10.95 (*0-446-38922-6*, Pub. by Warner Bks) Little.

— Students with Learning Disabilities. 1998. pap. text 18.95 (*0-536-01771-9*) Pearson Custom.

— Study Guide Fundamentals Of Business Law 3. 3rd ed. (SWC-Business Law). 1995. pap., student ed. 21.00 (*0-314-07893-2*) West Pub.

— Surgical Atlas of Sports Medicine. 1999. text. write for info. (*0-7216-7307-4*, W B Saunders Co) Harcrt Hlth Sci Grp.

— Sustaining the Earth. 3rd ed. (Biology Ser.). 1997. 36.25 (*0-534-52890-2*) Wadsworth Pub.

— Sustaining the Earth: An Integrated Approach. 4th ed. LC 99-21140. (Biology Ser.). 4p. 1999. pap. text 32.75 (*0-534-37108-6*) Brooks-Cole.

— Sustaining the Earth: An Integrated Approach. 4th ed. (Biology Ser.). 1999. 37.00 (*0-534-56286-8*) Wadsworth Pub.

Miller. Theories of Developmental Psychology. pap. text. write for info. (*0-7167-2846-X*) Worth.

— Theories of Developmental Psychology. 1998. text. write for info. (*0-7167-2847-8*) Worth.

— Third World in Merchant Shipping. 59.95 (*1-85972-548-1*) Ashgate Pub Co.

— West Paralegal Today. (Paralegal Ser.). (C). 1995. pap. 10.25 (*0-314-05437-5*) Brooks-Cole.

— West Paralegal Today. 2nd ed. (Paralegal Ser.). (C). 1999. pap., suppl. ed. 7.00 (*0-7668-1012-7*); pap., suppl. ed. 7.00 (*0-7668-1013-5*) Delmar.

Miller. West Paralegal Today-Handbook Court Cases. (Paralegal). (C). 1995. pap. text 6.75 (*0-314-06039-1*) West Pub.

***Miller.** West Paralegal Today, NY. 2nd ed. (Paralegal Ser.). (C). 1999. pap. 7.00 (*0-7668-1014-3*) Delmar.

Miller. West Paralegal Today Ny Supp. (Paralegal). (C). 1995. 9.00 (*0-314-05434-0*) Delmar.

***Miller.** West Paralegal Today, TX. 2nd ed. (Paralegal Ser.). (C). 1999. pap., suppl. ed. 7.00 (*0-7668-1015-1*) Delmar.

Miller. West's American Government. 2nd ed. (Social Studies). 1998. mass mkt. 51.50 (*0-314-14116-2*) S-W Pub.

— West's Paralegal Today: Complete Study Guide. (C). 1995. pap., student ed. 19.25 (*0-314-07610-7*) Delmar.

— Why You Can't Be Whatever You Want to Be. LC 99-18579. 2000. 19.99 (*0-310-22647-3*) Zondervan.

— Writing Reaction Mechanisms in Organic Chemistry. 2nd ed. 480p. (C). 1999. pap. text 48.50 (*0-12-496712-4*) Acad Pr.

— Your Career Adventure. Date not set. text 42.50 (*0-314-69753-5*) West Pub.

— Your Career Adventure. 2nd ed. 1998. mass mkt. 40.00 (*0-314-22322-3*) Wadsworth Pub.

Miller, ed. Basic College Mathematics: Instructor's Solution Manual. 4th ed. 1997. pap. text, teacher ed. 24.00 (*0-673-55466-X*, GoodYrBooks) Addson-Wesley Educ.

Miller, ed. Basic College Mathematics & Measurements. (C). 1997. text 72.00 (*0-673-67541-6*) Addison-Wesley.

— Basic Mth Choice Mccc CB. (C). 1995. text 45.00 (*0-673-67535-1*) Addison-Wesley.

— Geometry. (C). 1997. pap. text 9.60 (*0-673-67567-X*) Addison-Wesley.

Miller, ed. Texas Supply Economics Today. 8th ed. 1994. pap. text 11.00 (*0-06-501473-1*) S&S Trade.

Miller & Chynoweth, Alan G. Optical Fiber Telecommunications. 1996. 79.50 (*0-614-18457-6*, B01027) Info Gatekeepers.

***Miller & Cross.** Study Guide with Quicken Business Law Partner 3.0 Cd-Rom to Accompany the Legal Environment Today: Business in Its Ethical, Regualtory & international. 2nd ed. (SWC -Business Law Ser.). 1998. pap. 23.00 (*0-538-88536-X*) Sth-Wstrn College.

Miller & Felszeghy. Engineering Features of the Santa Barbara Earthquake of August 13, 1978. 129p. 1978. pap. 12.00 (*0-685-14399-6*) Earthquake Eng.

Miller & Forseth. Graphics for Architecture. 2nd ed. (Architecture Ser.). 1997. pap. 32.95 (*0-442-02210-7*, VNR) Wiley.

Miller & Gauvain, Mary. Reading on Development of Children. 1993. 34.40 (*0-7167-2582-7*) W H Freeman.

Miller & Harley. Zoology. 3rd ed. 1995. teacher ed. 25.62 (*0-697-24377-X*, WCB McGr Hill) McGrw-H Hghr Educ.

— Zoology. 3rd ed. 1995. teacher ed. 34.68 (*0-697-24375-3*, WCB McGr Hill) McGrw-H Hghr Educ.

Miller & Heinze-Fry. Sustaining the Earth. 2nd ed. 1995. teacher ed. 62.25 (*0-534-23923-4*) Brooks-Cole.

***Miller & Hollowell.** Business Law Text & Exercises. 3rd ed. 2001. pap. 46.75 (*0-324-06192-7*) Sth-Wstrn College.

Miller & Jaques. How to Know the Trees. 4th ed. 1999. pap. text 15.00 (*0-697-05114-5*) McGraw.

***Miller & Jentz.** Fundamentals of Business Law. 4th ed. LC 98-13273. (SWC-Business Law Ser.). 1998. pap. 75.95 (*0-538-88657-9*) S-W Pub.

— Web Tutor on WEBTC to Accompany BLT-Comprehensive Bus Law. 5th ed. (SWC-Business Law Ser.). 1999. pap. 34.25 (*0-324-05274-X*) Sth-Wstrn College.

Miller & Kurland. Introduction to Internet. 1996. mass mkt. 5.00 (*0-534-50620-8*) Brooks-Cole.

— Introduction to the Internet for Environment Science & Lite. 2nd ed. (Biology Ser.). (C). 1997. mass mkt. 5.00 (*0-534-51918-0*) Wadsworth Pub.

Miller & Nicholson. The Ultrasonics Business, What's It All about? Where Are the Opportunities. LC 95-213826. (Illus.). 182p. 1995. 2650.00 (*1-56965-222-8*, GB123) BCC.

Miller & Post. How Theory Shapes Technique: Perspectives on a Self-Psychological Clinical Presentation. (Psychoanalytic Inquiry Ser.: Vol. 10, No. 4). 1990. 20.00 (*0-88163-952-4*) Analytic Pr.

Miller & Price. Dimensions of Community Health. 5th ed. LC 97-41027. 576p. 1997. pap. 56.56 (*0-697-29447-1*) McGraw.

Miller & Pulsinelli. Economics Today. 8th ed. 368p. (C). 1997. pap., student ed. 25.00 (*0-06-501467-7*) Addson-Wesley Educ.

— Economics Today. 8th rev. ed. (C). 1997. pap., student ed. 27.00 (*0-06-502248-3*) Addson-Wesley Educ.

Miller & Rockett. Environmental Science & Living Environment & Sustaining Earth. 4th ed. (Biology Ser.). 1993. lab manual ed. 11.50 (*0-534-17809-X*) Wadsworth Pub.

Miller & Ryan. Stops along the Way, Your Career. (CA - Career Development Ser.). (C). 1994. mass mkt., wbk. ed. 25.95 (*0-314-03562-1*) S-W Pub.

***Miller & Stafford.** Economic Issues for Consumers. 9th ed. (Health Sciences Ser.). 2000. 59.50 (*0-534-55236-6*) Wadsworth Pub.

Miller & Starekow. Haute off the Press. LC 95-133076. (ENG & SPA.). 244p. 1996. write for info. (*0-918481-11-2*) TDF Pub.

Miller & Telljohan. Health Education in the Elementary School. 3rd ed. 352p. 2000. pap. 50.31 (*0-697-29433-1*) McGraw.

***Miller & Van Hoose.** Macroeconomics Theory Policy. 2nd ed. 2000. pap., student ed. 20.00 (*0-324-05498-X*) Sth-Wstrn College.

— Money, Banking & Financial Markets. (SWC-General Business Ser.). (C). 2000. text 20.25 (*0-324-05891-8*) Sth-Wstrn College.

Miller & Whicker. Handbook of Research Methods in Public Administration. LC 98-37295. (Illus.). 704p. 1998. text 225.00 (*0-8247-0213-1*) Dekker.

Miller & Wynn. Chemistry: A Basic Introduction. (Chemistry Ser.). 1978. pap., lab manual ed. 8.50 (*0-534-00529-2*) Wadsworth Pub.

— Chemistry: A Basic Introduction. 2nd ed. (Chemistry Ser.). 1980. pap., lab manual ed. write for info. (*0-534-01785-1*) Thomson Learn.

— Chemistry: Basic Introduction. 4th ed. (Chemistry Ser.). 1987. pap., lab manual ed. 33.75 (*0-534-06915-0*) Wadsworth Pub.

Miller, et al. Basc Coll Math Ans Custm. 4th ed. (C). 1998. teacher ed. 2.00 (*0-201-43516-0*) Addison-Wesley.

***Miller, et al.** Classics of Public Budgeting. 350p. 2000. pap. 29.00 (*0-8133-9774-X*, Pub. by Westview) HarpC.

Miller, et al. Custom Business Math. 7th ed. (C). 1998. pap. text 51.00 (*0-201-38822-7*) Addison-Wesley.

— Electronic Calculator. 6th ed. 176p. 1997. pap., wbk. ed. 21.00 (*0-673-38902-2*) Addison-Wesley.

Miller, et al. Experiences along the Way, Your Career Adventure: Explore & Plan. rev. ed. (Career Education). 1994. pap., wbk. ed. 24.00 (*0-314-04031-5*) West Pub.

Miller, et al. Fundamentals of College Algebra. (C). 1990. pap. text, student ed. 23.33 (*0-673-38958-8*) Addson-Wesley Educ.

— Handbook on Strategic Management. (Public Administration & Public Policy Ser.: Vol. 38). (Illus.). 496p. 1989. text 245.00 (*0-8247-8089-2*) Dekker.

— Lab Experiments - Chem: Basic Intro. 3rd ed. 1984. pap. text 18.50 (*0-534-02818-7*) Wadsworth Pub.

— Laboratory Evaluation of Pulmonary Function. 1987. 26.50 (*0-397-58574-8*) Lppncott W & W.

— Laboratory Manual for Concepts of Physical Activity. 7th ed. 106p. (C). 1998. spiral bd. 18.95 (*0-7872-5163-1*, 41516301) Kendall-Hunt.

***Miller, et al.** Web Tutor on Webct to Accompany Business Law Today-standard. 5th ed. 1999. pap. 19.00 (*0-534-76560-2*) Wadsworth Pub.

Miller, jt. auth. see Ayres.

Miller, jt. auth. see Brown.

Miller, jt. auth. see Canavos.

Miller, jt. auth. see Clarkson.

Miller, jt. auth. see Cross.

Miller, jt. auth. see Finkelman.

Miller, jt. auth. see Garlick.

Miller, jt. auth. see Jackson.

Miller, jt. auth. see Jentz.

Miller, jt. auth. see Jentz, Gaylord A.

Miller, jt. auth. see Levine.

Miller, jt. auth. see Lial.

Miller, jt. auth. see Macey.

Miller, jt. auth. see Robinson.

Miller, jt. auth. see Robinson, Stanley L.

Miller, jt. auth. see Stoker.

Miller, ed. see Avienus, Lucius F.

Miller, jt. ed. see Harne.

Miller, jt. ed. see Johnson.

Miller, Cleve. Oh, America. 93p. 1999. pap. 10.95 (*0-9669179-5-2*) Fifth Wrld.

***Miller, James.** American Slavery. LC 00-39332. (Illus.). 2000. lib. bdg. write for info. (*0-7377-0424-1*) Greenhaven.

— Flowers in the Dustbin: The Rise of Rock & Roll, 1947-1977. 416p. 2000. pap. 15.00 (*0-684-86560-2*, Fireside) S&S Trade Pap.

— Flowers in the Dustbin: The Rise of Rock & Roll 1947-1977. LC 99-21077. (Illus.). 416p. 1999. 25.50 (*0-684-80873-0*) Simon & Schuster.

— The Passion of Michel Foucault. 2000. pap. 24.95 (*0-674-00157-5*) HUP.

Miller, James, ed. Foreign Relations of the United States, 1964-1968 Vol. 17: Eastern Europe. 1996. boxed set 29.00 (*0-16-048091-4*) USGPO.

Miller, Leroy & Miller, Roger. Pocket Guide to Economics Today Printed & Electronic Supplements (the 1999-2000 Edition) 10th ed. 112p. 1998. pap. text 145.00 (*0-321-03364-7*) Addison-Wesley.

Miller, Leroy, jt. auth. see Miller, Roger.

***Miller, Roger & Lessard, Donald R.** The Strategic Management of Large Engineering Projects: Shaping Institutions, Risks & Governance. (Illus.). 240p. (C). 2001. 34.95 (*0-262-12236-7*) MIT Pr.

Miller, Roger & Miller, Leroy. Economic Experiments T/a Econ Today, The 1999-2000 Edition. 10th ed. 1999. pap. text 130.31 (*0-321-03366-3*) Addison-Wesley.

M

Miller, Roger, jt. auth. see Miller, Leroy.

Miller, Roger, ed. & photos by see Pilling, Ron.

Miller & Fairmont Press Staff. Industrial Forecast 1998 to 2000. LC 97-20008. 396p. (C). 1997. pap. text 135.00 (*0-13-647231-1*) P-H.

Miller, A. B. Cervical Cancer Screening Programmes: Managerial Guidelines. (FRE & SPA., Illus.). viii, 50p. 1992. pap. text 12.00 (*92-4-154447-3*, 1150390) World Health.

Miller, A. B., ed. Diet & the Aetiology of Cancer. (ESO Monographs). (Illus.). 84p. 1989. 73.95 (*0-387-50681-0*) Spr-Verlag.

Miller, A. B., et al, eds. Cancer Screening. 456p. (C). 1991. text 105.00 (*0-521-41041-X*) Cambridge U Pr.

Miller, A. Carolyn & Punsalan, Victoria J., compiled by. Refereed & Nonrefereed Economic Journals: A Guide for Publishing Opportunities. LC 87-25158. 269p. 1988. lib. bdg. 65.00 (*0-313-25857-0*, MPB/, Greenwood Pr) Greenwood.

Miller, A. G., rev. The Boatswain's Manual. rev. ed. (C). 1987. 84.00 (*0-85174-475-3*) St Mut.

Miller, A. G. & Cope, T. A., eds. Flora of the Arabian Peninsula & Socotra, Vol. 1. (Illus.). 536p. 1996. 160.00 (*0-7486-0475-8*, Pub. by Edinburgh U Pr) Col U Pr.

Miller, A. I., ed. Sixty-Two Years of Uncertainty: Historical, Philosophical & Physical Inquiries into the Foundations of Quantum Mechanics. (NATO ASI Ser.: Vol. 226). (Illus.). 320p. (C). 1990. text 138.00 (*0-306-43608-6*, Kluwer Plenum) Kluwer Academic.

M

Miller, A. M. From Delos to Delphi: A Literary Study of the Homeric Hymn to Apollo. (Mnemosyne Ser.: Supplement 93). xii, 130p. 1986. pap. 36.50 (*90-04-07674-3*) Brill Academic Pubs.

Miller, A. Robin & Browning, Sandra. Till Death Do Us Part: A Multicultural Approach to Marriage. LC 99-26127. (Contemporary Studies in Sociology: Vol. 14). 1999. 78.50 (*0-7623-0263-1*) Jai Pr.

Miller, A. T., jt. auth. see Durand, John.

Miller, A. V., tr. see Hegel, Georg Wilhelm Friedrich.

Miller, Aaron D. The Arab States & the Palestine Question: Between Ideology & Self-Interest, 120. LC 86-931. (Washington Papers: No. 120). 114p. 1986. 49.95 (*0-275-92215-4*, C2215, Praeger Pubs); pap. 18.95 (*0-275-92216-2*, B2216, Praeger Pubs) Greenwood.

— Search for Security: Saudi Arabian Oil & American Foreign Policy, 1939-1949. LC 79-18144. 340p. 1980. reprint ed. pap. 105.40 (*0-608-00199-6*, 206098200006) Bks Demand.

Miller, Abbie. Why Cats Meow. LC 98-10143. 23p. (J). (gr. 4-7). 1996. pap. 1.95 (*1-56763-166-5*) Ozark Pub.

Miller, Abraham H. Terrorism & Hostage Negotiations. LC 79-3288. (Special Studies in National & International Terrorism). 134p. 1983. text 28.00 (*0-89158-856-6*) Westview.

Miller, Abraham H., ed. Terrorism, the Media, & the Law. LC 82-11020. 232p. 1982. lib. bdg. 30.00 (*0-941320-04-9*) Transnatl Pubs.

Miller Accounting Staff. Miller's Comprehensive GAAS Guide, 1987. 1987. 42.00 (*0-317-64875-6*); pap. 32.00 (*0-317-64876-4*) Harcourt.

Miller, Adam, jt. auth. see Card, Emily.

Miller, Adam D. Apocalypse Is My Garden. LC 96-62097. 80p. (Orig.). (C). 1997. pap. 10.95 (*0-9656576-0-4*) Eshu Hse Pub.

— Forever Afternoon: Poems. LC 94-3903. (Lotus Poetry Ser.: Vol. 2). 1994. pap. 10.00 (*0-87013-354-3*) Mich St U Pr.

Miller-Adams, Michelle. World Bank: New Agendas in a Changing World. LC 98-42331. 1999. 75.00 (*0-415-19353-2*) Routledge.

Miller, Adolph. Converting for Flexible Packaging: A Primer. LC 93-61005. 185p. 1993. pap. text 59.95 (*1-56676-061-5*) Technomic.

Miller, Agnes, jt. auth. see Stapledon, Olaf.

***Miller, Al.** Tin Stackers: The History of the Pittsburgh Steamship Company. LC 98-55159. (Illus.). 1999. 34.95 (*0-8143-2832-6*, Great Lks Bks) Wayne St U Pr.

Miller, Alain O., ed. Advanced Research on Animal Cell Technology. (NATO Advanced Science Institutes Series C: Mathematical & Physical Sciences). (C). 1988. text 245.00 (*0-7923-0031-9*) Kluwer Academic.

Miller, Alan. Environmental Problem Solving: Psychosocial Barriers to Adaptive Change. Alexander, D., ed. LC 98-11430. (Springer Series in Environmental Management). (Illus.). 264p. 1998. 89.95 (*0-387-98499-2*) Spr-Verlag.

Miller, Alan, jt. auth. see Moore, Curtis.

Miller, Alan C., et al. The Disposable Woman. Ashton, Sylvia, ed. LC 77-77865. 1977. 22.95 (*0-87949-077-2*) Ashley Bks.

Miller, Alan D., et al, eds. Neural Control of the Respiratory Muscles. LC 96-8017. 320p. 1996. boxed set 169.95 (*0-8493-4001-2*) CRC Pr.

Miller, Alan D., jt. auth. see Yates, Bill J.

Miller, Alan J. Standard & Poor's 401K Planning Guide: Every Employee's Guide to Making 401K Decisions. LC 94-40808. 244p. 1994. pap. 12.95 (*0-07-042197-8*) McGraw.

Miller, Alan L., ed. see Hori, Ichiro.

***Miller, Alan N., II.** East Tennessee's Forgotten Children: Apprentices from 1778 to 1911. 207p. 2000. pap. 24.00 (*0-8063-4966-2*, Pub. by Clearfield Co) ACCESS Pubs Network.

Miller, Alan R., jt. auth. see Robbins, Judd.

Miller, Alan S. Gaia Connections: An Introduction to Ecology, Ecoethics, & Economics. 288p. (C). 1991. pap. text 17.95 (*0-8476-7656-0*) Rowman.

Miller, Alan W. The Atlas of Virginia Statewide Elections, 1980 Through 1994. LC 95-75541. (Illus.). 137p. (Orig.). 1995. spiral bd. 29.95 (*0-9645318-0-1*) Klipsan Pr.

— God of Daniel S: In Search of the American Jew. (Brown Classics in Judaica Ser.). 260p. 1986. reprint ed. pap. text 26.00 (*0-8191-5047-9*) U Pr of Amer.

Miller, Alan W., ed. Atlas of California Presidential Elections, 1932-1996. LC 97-75671. (Illus.). 153p. 1997. spiral bd. 34.95 (*0-9645318-6-0*) Klipsan Pr.

— Atlas of Idaho General Elections by County, 1994 & 1996. LC 97-75670. (Illus.). 126p. 1997. spiral bd. 34.95 (*0-9645318-7-9*) Klipsan Pr.

— Atlas of Oregon Gubernatorial Elections by County: 1934-1994. LC 96-77123. (Illus.). 139p. (Orig.). 1996. spiral bd. 29.95 (*0-9645318-4-4*) Klipsan Pr.

— Atlas of the 1994 California General Election: Statewide Offices & Measures by County. LC 95-77910. (Illus.). 133p. (Orig.). 1995. spiral bd. 29.95 (*0-9645318-1-X*) Klipsan Pr.

— Atlas of United States Presidential Elections: 1932-1996. LC 97-71234. (Illus.). 122p. (Orig.). 1997. spiral bd. 34.95 (*0-9645318-5-2*) Klipsan Pr.

Miller, Albert, et al. Elements of Meteorology. 4th ed. LC 82-61242. (Illus.). 443p. reprint ed. pap. 137.40 (*0-608-15993-X*, AU0036700082) Bks Demand.

Miller, Albert G. Captain Whopper. (Illus.). (J). (gr. 3-7). 1968. 10.95 (*0-8392-3058-3*) Astor-Honor.

— More Captain Whopper Tales. (Illus.). (J). (gr. 3-7). 1968. 10.95 (*0-8392-3060-5*) Astor-Honor.

Miller, Alden H., jt. auth. see Grinnell, Joseph.

***Miller, Alex.** Conditions of Faith: A Novel. LC 99-57116. 352p. 2000. 25.00 (*0-684-86935-7*) Scribner.

Miller, Alex. Philosophy of Language. 300p. 1998. text 60.00 (*0-7735-1708-1*, Pub. by McG-Queens Univ Pr); pap. text 19.95 (*0-7735-1709-X*, Pub. by McG-Queens Univ Pr) CUP Services.

— Strategic Management. 3rd ed. LC 97-22814. 1088p. (C). 1997. 88.44 (*0-07-043014-4*) McGraw.

Miller, Alex & Dess, Gregory G. Strategic Management. 2nd ed. LC 95-36996. (Management Ser.). (C). 1995. text 98.30 (*0-07-042791-7*) McGraw.

Miller, Alfred. An Honest Angler: The Best of Sparse Grey Hackle. Sherwood, Patricia M., ed. LC 97-30931. 272p. 1998. 30.00 (*1-55821-624-3*) Lyons Pr.

Miller, Alfred C. Descendants & Related Families of Kerrs Creek, Rockbridge County, Virginia, Vol. 1. 1991. lib. bdg. write for info. (*0-9624215-1-0*) A C Miller.

— Descendants & Related Families of Kerrs Creek, Rockbridge County, Virginia, Vol. 2. 1991. lib. bdg. write for info. (*0-9624215-2-9*) A C Miller.

— Descendants & Related Families of Kerrs Creek, Rockbridge County, Virginia, Vol. 3. 1991. lib. bdg. write for info. (*0-9624215-3-7*) A C Miller.

— Grandmother's Touring Sedan, Vol. 1. unabridged ed. 35p. (Orig.). 1995. pap. 6.00 (*0-9624215-6-1*) A C Miller.

— One Time Around & Beyond. 591p. 1990. 46.50 (*0-9624215-0-2*) A C Miller.

— Reaching Out Vol. 1: Ross Bible Church History. unabridged ed. (Illus.). 36p. (Orig.). 1992. pap. 7.00 (*0-9624215-4-5*) A C Miller.

— Threads of Life Vol. 1: A History of Kerrs Creek Baptist Church. unabridged ed. (Illus.). 301p. 1996. pap. 20.00 (*0-9624215-5-3*) A C Miller.

Miller, Alice. Banished Knowledge: Facing Childhood injury. 224p. 1991. pap. 12.95 (*0-385-26762-2*, Anchor NY) Doubleday.

— Breaking Down the Wall of Silence: The Liberating Experience of Facing the Painful Truth. rev. ed. Worrall, Simon, tr. LC 96-34165. 1997. pap. 12.95 (*0-452-01173-6*, Mer) NAL.

Miller, Alice. Drama of the Gifted Child: Walker,&Kathryn, Set. abr. ed. 1992. audio 18.00 (*1-55994-429-3*, CPN 2235) HarperAudio.

Miller, Alice. For Your Own Good: Hidden Cruelty in Child-Rearing & the Roots of Violence. Hannum, Hildegarde & Hannum, Hunter, trs. 282p. 1990. pap. 13.00 (*0-374-52269-3*) FS&G.

— Index to the Works of Immanuel Velikovsky, Vol. 1. 1977. 25.00 (*0-917994-08-6*) Kronos Pr.

— Paths of Life: Seven Scenarios. LC 98-17578. 208p. 1998. 23.00 (*0-375-40379-5*) Pantheon.

— Paths of Life: Seven Scenarios. 1999. pap. 12.00 (*0-375-70345-4*) Vin Bks.

— Pictures of a Childhood: Sixty-Six Watercolours & an Essay. rev. ed. Hannum, Hildegarde, tr. (Illus.). 178p. 1999. pap. text 15.00 (*0-7881-6200-4*) DIANE Pub.

— Prisoners of Childhood. 128p. 1996. reprint ed. 20.00 (*0-465-06287-3*, Pub. by Basic) HarpC.

— Thou Shalt Not Be Aware: Society's Betrayal of the Child. Hannum, Hildegarde & Hannum, Hunter, trs. from GER. 336p. 1998. pap. 14.00 (*0-374-52543-9*, Noonday) FS&G.

— Thou Shalt Not Be Aware: Society's Betrayal of the Child. LC 85-32084. 336p. 1991. pap. 13.95 (*0-452-00929-4*, Mer) NAL.

— Untouched Key: Tracing Childhood Trauma in Creativity & Destructiveness. 192p. 1991. pap. 13.95 (*0-385-26764-9*, Anchor NY) Doubleday.

Miller, Alice D. All Our Lives. 1994. reprint ed. lib. bdg. 21.95 (*1-56849-519-6*) Buccaneer Bks.

— Not for Love. 1994. reprint ed. lib. bdg. 21.95 (*1-56849-518-8*) Buccaneer Bks.

— Welcome Home. 1994. reprint ed. lib. bdg. 21.95 (*1-56849-524-2*) Buccaneer Bks.

— The White Cliffs. 74p. Date not set. 16.95 (*0-8488-2369-9*) Amereon Ltd.

— The White Cliffs. 74p. 1987. reprint ed. lib. bdg. 19.95 (*0-89966-615-9*) Buccaneer Bks.

Miller, Alice E. Cecil County: A Study in Local History. (Illus.). 173p. 1998. reprint ed. lib. bdg. 29.00 (*0-8328-9736-1*) Higginson Bk Co.

Miller, Alistair W. & Hanretty, Kevin P. Obstetrics Illustrated. 5th ed. LC 97-28645. 1997. pap. text 42.00 (*0-443-05041-4*) Church.

Miller, Allan. Mad Amadeus Sued a Madam. LC 97-3303. (Illus.). 64p. (Orig.). 1997. pap. 10.01 (*1-56792-077-2*) Godine.

— A Passion for Acting: Exploring the Creative Process. Weiler, Fred, ed. (Illus.). 189p. (Orig.). (C). 1995. pap. 16.95 (*0-9644844-0-4*) Dynmic Prod.

***Miller, Allan, ed.** Model Railroad Resources Handbook: A Where-to-Find-It Guide for the Hobbyist. (Illus.). 192p. 2000. pap. 16.95 (*0-87341-887-5*) Krause Pubns.

Miller, Allan, ed. see Larson, Russ & Horowitz, Mark.

Miller, Allan R. Yankee on the Prairie: Howard R. Barnard, Pioneer Educator. (Illus.). 216p. 1995. pap. 15.95 (*0-89745-184-8*) Sunflower U Pr.

Miller, Allen, ed. see Dowben, Peter A.

Miller, Allen O. & Osterhaven, M. Eugene, trs. Heidelberg Catechism. LC 62-20891. 128p. 1963. pap. 4.95 (*0-8298-0060-3*) Pilgrim OH.

Miller, Alyce. The Nature of Longing. 240p. 1995. pap. 10.00 (*0-393-31379-4*, Norton Paperbks) Norton.

— The Nature of Longing: Stories by Alyce Miller. LC 94-7582. (Flannery O'Connor Award for Short Fiction Ser.). 264p. 1994. 19.95 (*0-8203-1674-1*) U of Ga Pr.

— Stopping for Green Lights. LC 98-28610. 304p. 1999. 23.95 (*0-385-48944-7*) Doubleday.

Miller, Amelia F., jt. auth. see McGowan, Susan.

Miller, Amy B. Shaker Medicinal Herbs: A Compendium of History, Lore & Uses. rev. ed. LC 97-50602. (Illus.). 224p. 1998. 35.00 (*1-58017-040-4*, Garden Way Pub) Storey Bks.

Miller, Amy J. The Pioneer Doctor in the Ozarks White River Country. rev. ed. (Illus.). 165p. 1994. pap. 15.80 (*0-9643894-0-1*) Delphi Assocs.

Miller, Anastasia M. Frommer's Vancouver & Victoria. 4th ed. (Frommer's Travel Guides Ser.). 256p. 1998. pap. 14.95 (*0-02-862052-6*, Frommer) Macmillan Gen Ref.

***Miller, Anastasia M. & Brown, Jarred.** What Logos Do. 2000. pap. 20.00 (*1-56496-705-0*) Rockport Pubs.

Miller, Anastatia R. & Brown, Jared M. Design Sense: Limited Budget Solutions That Work. (Illus.). 160p. 1998. pap. 35.00 (*1-56496-461-2*) Rockport Pubs.

Miller, Andrea, ed. see Shurr, Timothy D.

Miller, Andrew. Casanova in Love. LC 98-19565. 288p. (C). 1998. 23.00 (*0-15-100409-9*) Harcourt.

— Casanova in Love. 288p. 2000. pap. 13.00 (*0-15-600769-X*, Harvest Bks) Harcourt.

— Ingenious Pain: A Novel. LC 96-47341. 352p. (C). 1997. 24.00 (*0-15-100258-4*) Harcourt.

— Ingenious Pain: A Novel. 337p. (C). 1998. pap. 13.00 (*0-15-600600-6*, Harvest Bks) Harcourt.

Miller, Andrew, et al. Rethinking Work Experience. 280p. 1991. 79.95 (*1-85000-895-7*, Falmer Pr); pap. 34.95 (*1-85000-896-5*, Falmer Pr) Taylor & Francis.

Miller, Andrew, jt. ed. see Coughlan, Andrew.

Miller, Andrew, jt. ed. see Lane, David A.

Miller, Andrew B. Church History Publishing Kit. 80p. 1994. ring bd. 25.00 (*1-881576-28-0*) Providence Hse.

Miller, Andrew D. The Great Static Cross. 245p. 1999. pap. 15.95 (*0-7414-0056-1*) Buy Books.

Miller, Andrew H. Novels Behind Glass: Commodity Culture & Victorian Narrative. (Literature, Culture, Theory Ser.: No. 17). (Illus.). 254p. (C). 1995. text 59.95 (*0-521-47133-8*) Cambridge U Pr.

Miller, Andrew H. & Adams, James E., eds. Sexualities in Victorian Britain. LC 96-5128. (Illus.). 256p. 1996. text 39.95 (*0-253-33066-1*) Ind U Pr.

Miller, Andrew J. & Gupta, Avijit. Varieties of Fluvial Form. LC 98-36750. 538p. 1999. 155.00 (*0-471-97351-3*) Wiley.

***Miller, Andrew J., et al.** Treatment of the Uncomplicated Aural Cholesteatoma. 2nd rev. ed. LC 99-38642. (Self-Instructional Ser.). (Illus.). 60p. 1999. pap. text 25.00 (*1-56772-025-0*) AAO-HNS.

Miller, Andrew M. Plato: Ion. 2nd ed. 1984. pap. text 6.00 (*0-929524-27-6*) Bryn Mawr Commentaries.

Miller, Andrew W., tr. Greek Lyric: An Anthology in Translation. LC 95-45733. 280p. 1996. pap. text 9.95 (*0-87220-291-7*); lib. bdg. 34.95 (*0-87220-292-5*) Hackett Pub.

Miller, Andy. Pupil Behavior & Teacher Culture. (Introduction to Education Ser.). (Illus.). 176p. 1997. pap. 33.95 (*0-304-33683-1*); text 90.00 (*0-304-33684-X*) Continuum.

Miller, Andy, jt. auth. see McCullough, Darryl.

Miller, Anesa. A Road Beyond Loss: 3 Cycles of Poems & an Epilogue. (Illus.). 64p. (Orig.). 1995. per. 7.00 (*0-9647642-0-2*) Mem Fnd Lost Chldrn.

Miller, Angela. The Empire of the Eye: Landscape Representation & American Cultural Politics, 1825-1875. (Illus.). 312p. 1996. pap. text 24.95 (*0-8014-8338-7*) Cornell U Pr.

Miller, Angela, jt. auth. see Norman, David.

Miller, Angelyn. The Enabler: When Helping Harms the Ones You Love. 128p. (Orig.). 1990. mass mkt. 4.95 (*0-345-36848-7*) Ballantine Pub Grp.

Miller, Anistasia R. Complete Astrological Handbook. 1998. write for info. (*0-8052-4148-5*) Schocken.

Miller, Anistatia & Brown, Jared. Shaken Not Stirred. 1997. 14.00 (*0-614-28088-5*, Harper Ref) HarpC.

***Miller, Anistatia, et al.** Champagne Cocktails. (Illus.). 128p. 1999. 12.00 (*0-06-099613-7*, ReganBks) HarperTrade.

Miller, Anistatia, et al. Champagne Cocktails: Includes recipes, quotes, lore, & a directory of the world's poshest lounges. (Illus.). 128p. 1999. pap. 12.00 (*0-06-039292-4*, ReganBks) HarperTrade.

Miller, Anistatia, ed. see Spinrad, Leonard & Spinrad, Thelma.

Miller, Anistatia R. Shaken Not Stirred: A Celebration of the Martini. LC 97-2496. 160p. 1997. pap. 10.00 (*0-06-273488-1*, Harper Ref) HarpC.

Miller, Anistatia R. & Brown, Jared M. The Complete Astrological Handbook for the 21st Century. LC 99-17725. 612p. 1999. pap. 19.95 (*0-8052-1086-5*) Schocken.

— Graphic Design Speak: A Visual Dictionary for Designers. 1999. 40.00 (*1-56496-602-X*) Rockport Pubs.

— Optometry in America: A History of the Illinois College of Optometry (1872-1997) LC 96-77258. (Illus.). 160p. 1996. 45.00 (*0-9652759-1-4*) IL Coll Optometry.

Miller, Anistatia R., jt. auth. see Brown, Jared.

Miller, Anita. Uncollecting Cheever: The Family of John Cheever vs. Academy Chicago Publishers. LC 98-7425. 264p. 1998. 27.95 (*0-8476-9076-8*, Pub. by Rowman) Natl Bk Netwk.

Miller, Anita, ed. Complete Transcripts of the Clarence Thomas-Anita Hill Hearings: October 11, 12, 13, 1991. 150p. 1994. pap. 22.95 (*0-89733-408-6*) Academy Chi Pubs.

Miller, Anita, ed. Four Classic Ghostly Tales. 250p. 1993. pap. 10.00 (*0-89733-398-5*) Academy Chi Pubs.

Miller, Anita & Greenberg, Hazel, eds. The Equal Rights Amendment: A Bibliographic Study. LC 76-24999. 367p. 1976. lib. bdg. 85.00 (*0-8371-9058-4*, ERA/, Greenwood Pr) Greenwood.

Miller, Anita, jt. auth. see Weimann, Jeanne M.

Miller, Anita, ed. see Hare, Augustus.

Miller, Anita, tr. see Haasse, Hella S.

Miller, Ann. Creativity. (Handbooks for Language Teachers Ser.). (Illus.). 36p. 1995. pap. 24.00 (*0-7487-1814-1*, Pub. by S Thornes Pubs) Trans-Atl Phila.

— Guilty Pleasures. 384p. 1988. mass mkt. 4.95 (*0-445-20648-9*, Pub. by Warner Bks) Little.

***Miller, Ann.** Microsoft Office 2000. (Marquee Ser.). 2001. 44.00 (*0-7638-0359-6*) EMC-Paradigm.

Miller, Ann. Star Struck. 352p. (Orig.). 1989. mass mkt. 3.95 (*0-445-20777-9*, Pub. by Warner Bks) Little.

— Wild Nights. 496p. 1987. mass mkt. 3.95 (*0-445-20374-9*, Pub. by Warner Bks) Little.

Miller, Ann K. Engineering Quality Software. LC 92-16345. 1992. pap. text 10.95 (*0-201-63432-5*) Addison-Wesley.

Miller, Ann R., et al, eds. Work, Jobs, & Occupations: A Critical Review of the Dictionary of Occupational Titles. LC 80-24653. 455p. reprint ed. pap. 141.10 (*0-7837-1639-7*, 204193200024) Bks Demand.

Miller, Anna M. The Buyer's Guide to Affordable Antique Jewelry: How to Find, Buy, & Care for Fabulous Antique Jewelry. LC 92-37557. 1993. 9.95 (*0-8065-1411-6*) Carol Pub Group.

— Cameos Old & New. LC 90-47269. (Illus.). 168p. (gr. 13). 1991. text 52.95 (*0-442-00278-5*) Chapman & Hall.

— Cameos Old & New. 2nd rev. ed. LC 98-9343. (Illus.). 288p. 1998. pap. 19.95 (*0-943763-17-7*) GemStone Pr.

— Gems & Jewelry Appraising: Techniques of Professional Practice. (Illus.). 208p. 1988. mass mkt. 51.95 (*0-442-26467-4*) Chapman & Hall.

***Miller, Anna M.** Gems & Jewelry Appraising: Techniques of Professional Practice. 2nd rev. ed. LC 99-29596. (Illus.). 240p. 1999. 39.95 (*0-943763-10-X*) GemStone Pr.

Miller, Anna M. Illustrated Guide to Jewelry Appraising. 1989. text 42.95 (*0-442-31944-4*) Chapman & Hall.

— Illustrated Guide to Jewelry Appraising: Antique, Period & Modern. 1989. mass mkt. 62.95 (*0-412-98931-X*, Chap & Hall NY) Chapman & Hall.

***Miller, Anna M.** The Illustrated Guide to Jewelry Appraising: Antique, Period & Modern. 2nd rev. ed. LC 99-37593. (Illus.). 216p. 1999. 39.95 (*0-943763-23-1*) GemStone Pr.

Miller, Anna M. & Sinkankas, John. Standard Catalog of Gem Values. 2nd ed. LC 94-76638. (Illus.). 288p. 1995. pap. 24.00 (*0-945005-16-4*) Geoscience Pr.

Miller, Anne. 365 Sales Tips for Winning Business. LC 98-5782. 240p. 1998. pap. 11.00 (*0-399-52419-3*, Perigee Bks) Berkley Pub.

Miller, Anne, jt. auth. see Heynes, Michael.

Miller, Anne I. The Independent Theatre in Europe, 1887 to the Present. LC 65-27914. 445p. 1972. 30.95 (*0-405-08790-X*, Pub. by Blom Pubns) Ayer.

Miller, Anne K., jt. auth. see Heynes, Michael.

Miller, Anthony, et al. Appleton & Lange's Review for the Physician Assistant. 3rd ed. (Illus.). 400p. (C). 1997. pap. 34.95 (*0-8385-0279-2*, A-0279-8) McGraw.

Miller, Anthony A., jt. auth. see Simon, Albert F.

Miller, Anthony B., ed. Advances in Cancer Screening. LC 97-17047. (Cancer Treatment & Research Ser.: Vol. 86). (Illus.). 208p. (C). 1996. text 212.00 (*0-7923-4019-1*) Kluwer Academic.

Miller, Anthony R. Pupil Transportation Management: School Bus Operations, Personnel Management for Transportation Managers & Supervisors. LC 88-61377. 210p. (Orig.). (C). 1988. pap. text 15.75 (*0-929298-00-4*) Ramsburg & Roth Pubs.

Miller, Arlene, jt. auth. see Shelly, Judith A.

Miller, Arlene B., jt. auth. see Shelly, Judith A.

Miller, Arnold. From Ritual to Repertoire: A Systems Approach to Cognitive Development with Disordered Children. LC 89-5809. (Personality Processes Ser.). 544p. 1989. 150.00 (*0-471-84897-2*) Wiley.

Miller, Arnold W. Descriptive Set Theory & Forcing: How to Prove Theorems about Borel Sets the Hard Way, Vol. IV. Buss, S. R. et al, eds. (Lecture Notes in Logic Ser.: Vol. 4). 130p. 1995. 46.95 (*3-540-60059-0*) Spr-Verlag.

Miller, Arthur. After the Fall. 1964. pap. 5.25 (*0-8222-0010-4*) Dramatists Play.

— After the Fall. (Plays Ser.). 128p. 1980. pap. 9.95 (*0-14-048162-1*, Penguin Bks) Viking Penguin.

— All My Sons. 1948. pap. 5.25 (*0-8222-0016-3*) Dramatists Play.

***Miller, Arthur.** All My Sons. (Classics Ser.). 2000. pap. 9.00 (*0-14-118546-5*) Penguin Putnam.

An Asterisk (*) at the beginning of an entry indicates that the title is appearing for the first time.

M

An Asterisk (*) at the beginning of an entry indicates that the title is appearing for the first time.

*Miller, Barbara J.** Regrets. large type ed. (Falls Bend Mystery Ser.: Vol. 4). 199p. 1998. pap. 7.00 (*1-893151-13-1*) Weavers Old.

Miller, Barbara J. Relics. large type ed. (Falls Bend Mysteries Ser.: Vol. 3). 221p. 1997. pap. 7.00 (*1-893151-09-3*) Weavers Old.

— Rendezvous. large type ed. (Falls Bend Mysteries Ser.: Vol. 2). 174p. 1996. pap. 7.00 (*1-893151-03-4*) Weavers Old.

Miller, Barbara L. Colorado Coffee Grounds: Your Traveling Companion to Colorado Coffeehouses. LC 97-94816. (Illus.). 288p. 1997. pap. 14.95 (*0-9661635-7-5*) Charted Grnds.

Miller, Barbara S. Gitagovinda of Jayadeva: Love Songs of the Dark Lord. (C). 1992. reprint ed. 11.50 (*0-685-54515-6*, Pub. by Motilal Bnarsidass) S Asia.

— Love Song of the Dark Lord: Jayadeva's Gitagovinda. 131p. 1997. pap. 17.50 (*0-231-11097-9*) Col U Pr.

Miller, Barbara S., comment. Yoga: Disipline of Freedom. 160p. (C). 1996. 18.95 (*0-520-20190-6*, Pub. by U CA Pr) Cal Prin Full Svc.

Miller, Barbara S., ed. Masterworks of Asian Literature in Comparative Perspective: A Guide for Teaching. LC 93-24473. (Columbia Project on Asia in the Core Curriculum Ser.). 616p. (C). (gr. 13). 1994. text 93.95 (*1-56324-257-5*, East Gate Bk); pap. text 31.95 (*1-56324-258-3*, East Gate Bk) M E Sharpe.

M

— The Powers of Art: Patronage in Indian Culture. (Illus.). 364p. 1992. text 19.95 (*0-19-562842-X*) OUP.

Miller, Barbara S., et al, eds. The Theater of Memory: Three Plays of Kalidasa. LC 83-26362. (Translations from the Oriental Classics Ser.). 384p. (Orig.). 1984. text 68.50 (*0-231-05838-1*); pap. text 27.00 (*0-231-05839-X*) Col U Pr.

Miller, Barbara S., tr. The Bhagavad-Gita: Krishna's Counsel in Time of War. LC 86-13725. (Illus.). 176p. 1986. text 34.50 (*0-231-06468-3*) Col U Pr.

— Phantasies of a Love-Thief: The Caurapancasika Attributed to Bilhana. LC 77-122947. (Studies in Oriental Culture: No. 6). 233p. 1971. text 57.50 (*0-231-03451-2*) Col U Pr.

Miller, Barbara S., tr. The Bhagavad-Gita. 176p. (Orig.). 1986. mass mkt. 5.95 (*0-553-21365-2*, Bantam Classics) Bantam.

Miller, Barbara S., jt. auth. see Gordon, Leonard A.

Miller, Barbara S., jt. auth. see Pata, Njali.

Miller, Barbara S., ed. see Kramrisch, Stella.

*Miller, Barbara Stoler.** The Plays of Kalidasa: Theater of Memory. Gerow, Edwin, ed. 387p. 1999. pap. 125.00 (*81-208-1681-1*, Pub. by Motilal Bnarsidass) St Mut.

Miller, Barnett. The Palace School of Muhammad the Conqueror. LC 73-6291. (Middle East Ser.). 1973. reprint ed. 20.95 (*0-405-05349-5*) Ayer.

Miller, Barnette. Beyond the Sublime Porte. LC 79-111774. reprint ed. 62.50 (*0-404-04329-1*) AMS Pr.

Miller, Barry. A Most Unlikely God: A Philosophical Enquiry. LC 95-50518. 224p. (C). 1996. text 27.00 (*0-268-01422-1*) U of Notre Dame Pr.

Miller, Barry A., ed. Racial/Ethnic Patterns of Cancer in the United States, 1988-1992. (Illus.). 138p. (C). 1997. pap. text 25.00 (*0-7881-4592-4*) DIANE Pub.

Miller, Barry I., jt. auth. see Miller, Kathryn S.

Miller, Basil. Charles G. Finney. LC 77-2813. (Men of Faith Ser.). 144p. 1973. mass mkt. 4.99 (*0-87123-061-5*) Bethany Hse.

— Florence Nightingale. LC 87-71602. (Women of Faith Ser.). 128p. 1987. reprint ed. mass mkt. 4.99 (*0-87123-985-X*) Bethany Hse.

— George Muller. (Men of Faith Ser.). 16p. 1972. reprint ed. mass mkt. 4.99 (*0-87123-182-4*) Bethany Hse.

— The Holy Spirit. 1990. reprint ed. pap. 6.99 (*0-88019-259-3*) Schmul Pub Co.

— John Wesley. (Men of Faith Ser.). 144p. 1973. reprint ed. mass mkt. 4.99 (*0-87123-272-3*) Bethany Hse.

— Mary Slessor. LC 85-71477. 144p. 1985. reprint ed. mass mkt. 4.99 (*0-87123-849-7*) Bethany Hse.

— William Carey. LC 85-71476. (Men of Faith Ser.). 16p. 1985. reprint ed. mass mkt. 4.99 (*0-87123-850-0*) Bethany Hse.

Miller, Basil, compiled by. Beautiful Poems on Jesus. LC 68-58826. (Granger Index Reprint Ser.). 1977. 19.95 (*0-8369-6029-7*) Ayer.

Miller, Beatrice. Musically Mixed. 32p. 1995. pap. text 5.95 (*0-87487-746-6*) Summy-Birchard.

Miller, Beatrice, ed. Bach - Jesu, Joy of Man's Desiring. 4p. 1993. pap. 2.95 (*0-7390-0842-0*, 6389) Alfred Pub.

Miller, Becky, jt. auth. see Miller, Steve.

Miller, Ben, ed. The Advanced Card & Identification Technology Sourcebook, 1997. 286p. (Orig.). 1996. pap. 195.00 (*1-878413-03-1*) Personal Identification.

Miller, Ben, jt. auth. see Basinger, J. Martin.

*Miller, Benjamin.** Fat of the Land: Garbage in New York - The Last 200 Years. 425p. 2000. pap. 18.00 (*1-56858-172-6*, Pub. by FWEW) Publishers Group.

Miller, Benjamin. When Opponents Cooperate: Great Power Conflict & Collaboration in World Politics. 368p. 1995. text 52.50 (*0-472-10458-6*, 10458) U of Mich Pr.

Miller, Benjamin F. Miller-Keane Encyclopedia & Dictionary of Medicine, Nursing & Allied Health. 5th ed. 1992. text 25.95 (*0-7216-3456-7*, W B Saunders Co) Harcrt Hlth Sci Grp.

— Poems: Partly Medical. (Countway Library Associates Historical Publication: No. 4). 85p. 1978. 9.95 (*0-686-23786-2*) F A Countway.

Miller, Benjamin S. Ranch Life in Southern Kansas & the Indian Territory, As Told by a Novice: How a Fortune Was Made in Cattle. LC 75-111. (Mid-American Frontier Ser.). 1975. reprint ed. 19.95 (*0-405-06878-6*) Ayer.

Miller, Benjamin S. & Singewald, Joseph T. The Deposits of South America. Wilkins, Mira, ed. LC 76-29758. (European Business Ser.). (Illus.). 1977. reprint ed. lib. bdg. 51.95 (*0-405-09773-5*) Ayer.

Miller, Berkeley & Canak, William L. New Labor, New Laws: Public Sector Collective Bargaining Laws. 200p. (C). 1999. pap. 35.00 (*0-8133-0689-2*) Westview.

*Miller-Bernal, Leslie.** Separate by Degree: Women Students' Experiences in Single-Sex & Coeducational Colleges. LC 98-54164. (History of Schools & Schooling Ser.: Vol. 9). 400p. (C). 2000. pap. text 29.95 (*0-8204-4412-X*) P Lang Pubng.

Miller, Bernard. Advanced Organic Chemistry: Reactions & Mechanisms. LC 97-11855. 338p. 1997. 71.00 (*0-13-373275-4*) P-H.

Miller, Bernard, ed. see International Conference on Thermal Analysis Staff.

Miller, Bertha M., et al, eds. Illustrators of Children's Books: 1946-1956, Vol. 2. LC 57-31264. (Illus.). 229p. 1958. 28.95 (*0-87675-016-1*) Horn Bk.

Miller, Bertha M. & Field, Elinor W., eds. Newbery Medal Books, 1922-1955. LC 55-13968. (Illus.). 458p. 1955. 22.95 (*0-87675-396-9*) Horn Bk.

Miller, Bessie M., jt. auth. see Doris, Lillian.

Miller, Beth A., jt. auth. see Prior, Jennifer Overend.

Miller, Bette L., jt. auth. see Rapoza, Lydia L.

Miller, Bettina, ed. From Flappers to Flivvers...We Helped Make the '20s Roar. LC 95-69124. 164p. 1995. 14.95 (*0-89821-149-2*, 20101) Reiman Pubns.

Miller, Bettina, ed. see Reiman Publications Staff.

Miller, Betty. The Amish in Switzerland & Other European Countries. 1978. pap. 1.50 (*0-685-46025-8*) O R Miller.

— Exposing Satan's Devices. (Overcoming Life Ser.). 104p. 1991. pap. 5.00 (*1-57149-008-6*) Christ Unltd.

— Exposing Satan's Devices Workbook. (Overcoming Life Ser.). 213p. 1993. pap. 10.00 (*1-57149-009-4*) Christ Unltd.

— Extremes or Balance? (Overcoming Life Ser.). 52p. 1994. pap. 5.00 (*1-57149-014-0*) Christ Unltd.

— Extremes or Balances? (Overcoming Life Ser.). 1995. pap., wbk. ed. 10.00 (*1-57149-015-9*) Christ Unltd.

— Healing of the Spirit, Soul & Body. (Overcoming Life Ser.). 60p. 1994. pap. 5.00 (*1-57149-010-8*) Christ Unltd.

— Healing of the Spirit, Soul & Body Workbook. (Overcoming Life Ser.). 1995. pap. 10.00 (*1-57149-011-6*) Christ Unltd.

— Keys to the Kingdom. (Overcoming Life Ser.). 56p. 1994. pap. 5.00 (*1-57149-006-X*) Christ Unltd.

— Keys to the Kingdom Workbook. (Overcoming Life Ser.). 1995. pap. 10.00 (*1-57149-007-8*) Christ Unltd.

— Mark of God or Mark of the Beast. (End Times Ser.). 112p. 1991. pap. 5.00 (*1-57149-019-1*) Christ Unltd.

— Neither Male nor Female. (Overcoming Life Ser.). 70p. 1994. pap. 5.00 (*1-57149-012-4*) Christ Unltd.

— Neither Male nor Female Workbook. (Overcoming Life Ser.). 1995. pap. 10.00 (*1-57149-013-2*) Christ Unltd.

— The Pathway into the Overcomer's Walk Workbook. (Overcoming Life Ser.). 92p. 1994. pap. 5.00 (*1-57149-016-7*) Christ Unltd.

— The Pathway into the Overcomer's Walk Workbook. (Overcoming Life Ser.). 1995. pap. 10.00 (*1-57149-017-5*) Christ Unltd.

— Personal Spiritual Warfare. (End Times Ser.). 92p. 1991. pap. 5.00 (*1-57149-018-3*) Christ Unltd.

— Prove All Things. (Overcoming Life Ser.). 44p. 1994. pap. 5.00 (*1-57149-000-0*) Christ Unltd.

— Prove All Things Workbook. (Overcoming Life Ser.). 1995. pap. 10.00 (*1-57149-001-9*) Christ Unltd.

— The True God. (Overcoming Life Ser.). 46p. 1994. pap. 5.00 (*1-57149-002-7*) Christ Unltd.

— The True God Workbook. (Overcoming Life Ser.). 1995. pap. 10.00 (*1-57149-003-5*) Christ Unltd.

— The Will of God. (Overcoming Life Ser.). 50p. 1994. pap. 5.00 (*1-57149-004-3*) Christ Unltd.

— The Will of God Workbook. (Overcoming Life Ser.). 1995. pap. 10.00 (*1-57149-005-1*) Christ Unltd.

Miller, Betty A. Amish Pioneers of the Walnut Creek Valley. 1978. pap. 2.50 (*0-685-87375-7*) O R Miller.

Miller, Betty A. & Miller, Oscar R. Bixel Family History: Descendants of Abraham Bixel & Magdalena Schumacher, 1843-1984. (Illus.). 94p. 1984. pap. 7.50 (*0-317-17479-7*) O R Miller.

— Cornelius Jansen Family History, 1822-1973. (Illus.). 73p. 1974. pap. 4.50 (*0-685-64818-4*) O R Miller.

Miller, Betty D., jt. auth. see Miller, Kent.

*Miller, Betty Davis.** The Last Thing You Get to Know. 2000. pap. 9.95 (*1-930454-05-8*) Swan Scythe.

*Miller, Betty G.** Deaf & Sober: Journeys Through Recovery. (Illus.). 196p. 1998. pap. 24.95 (*0-913072-86-9*, DE026) Natl Assn Deaf.

Miller, Beverly, jt. auth. see Bradbury, Jim.

Miller, Bill. Alley Strewn Phrases. 56p. (Orig.). 1986. pap. 5.00 (*0-940584-04-2*) Gull Bks.

— Sacramento, D. C. A Political Lampoon. LC 88-30886. 192p. 1988. 15.95 (*0-929473-00-0*); pap. 8.95 (*0-317-91079-5*) Erin Pr Inc.

— The Ways of Wisdom: Great Thoughts from Great Thinkers. 64p. 1992. pap. 4.95 (*0-9630439-4-3*) Bayrock.

Miller, Bill & Caligiuri, Tony. Modern Bird Hunting. LC 89-63989. (Hunter's Information Ser.). 328p. 1990. write for info. (*0-914697-27-7*) N Amer Outdoor Grp.

Miller, Bill, jt. auth. see Ayers, Shirley.

Miller, Bill, ed. see Burch, Monte.

Miller, Bill, jt. ed. see Cohn, Howard.

Miller, Bill, ed. see Helgeland, Glenn.

Miller, Bill, ed. see Lapinski, Mike, et al.

Miller, Bill, ed. see Sandford, R. Loren.

Miller, Billie M. Soo Ling: The Story of the Silkworm. Luna, Rose Mary, tr. (ENG & SPA., Illus.). 12p. (J). 1991. 12.00 (*1-878742-01-9*); pap. 6.00 (*1-878742-02-7*) Kidship Assoc.

*Miller, Billy.** Ultimate Snowboarding. 1999. pap. 16.95 (*1-85868-513-3*, Pub. by Carlton Bks Ltd) Natl Bk Netwk.

Miller, Bjorn & Voronkov, Lev, eds. Defence Doctrines & Conversion. (Illus.). 176p. 1996. text 77.95 (*1-85521-709-0*, Pub. by Dartmth Pub) Ashgate Pub Co.

Miller, Blair. American Silent Film Comedies: An Illustrated Encyclopedia of Persons, Studios & Terminology. LC 94-38777. (Illus.). 292p. 1995. lib. bdg. 45.00 (*0-89950-929-0*) McFarland & Co.

Miller, Bob. Bob Miller's Algebra for the Clueless. LC 98-32281. (Illus.). 176p. 1998. pap., student ed. 10.95 (*0-07-043425-5*) McGraw.

— Bob Miller's Calc for the Clueless: Calculus I. 2nd ed. 176p. 1997. pap. 76.65 (*0-07-913706-7*) McGraw.

*Miller, Bob.** Bob Miller's Geometry for the Clueless. (Illus.). 176p. 2000. pap. text 10.95 (*0-07-136109-X*, Schaums Outlne) McGraw-Hill Prof.

Miller, Bob. Calc I. 2nd ed. LC 97-43438. (Bob Miller's Calc for the Clueless Ser.). (Illus.). 176p. (C). 1997. pap. text, student ed. 10.95 (*0-07-043408-5*, Schaums Outlne) McGraw-Hill Prof.

— Calc III. LC 97-43440. (Bob Miller's Calc for the Clueless Ser.). (Illus.). 176p. (C). 1997. pap. text, student ed. 10.95 (*0-07-043410-7*, Schaums Outlne) McGraw-Hill Prof.

— Calc II. 2nd ed. LC 97-43439. (Bob Miller's Calc for the Clueless Ser.). (Illus.). 176p. (C). 1997. pap. text, student ed. 10.95 (*0-07-043409-3*, Schaums Outlne) McGraw-Hill Prof.

— Conversations with God. 3rd large type ed. LC 92-85047. (Illus.). 106p. (Orig.). 1992. pap. 5.95 (*0-9634161-0-3*) Vanquish Pubns.

— One Hundred Personal Effectiveness Traps & Their Solutions. Morgan, Jane, ed. (Illus.). 206p. (Orig.). 1987. pap. 15.00 (*0-942227-01-8*) Universal Lrn Ctr.

— One Thousand One Tips to Increase Your Effectiveness. Morgan, Jane, ed. 184p. (Orig.). 1987. pap. 20.00 (*0-942227-00-X*) Universal Lrn Ctr.

— One Thousand One Tips to Increased Effectiveness: PracticalTips Techniques & Ideas to Save You Time & Get More Done in Your Busy Day. Morgan, Jane, ed. 192p. (Orig.). 1987. pap. 20.00 (*0-318-22828-9*) Universal Lrn Ctr.

— Precalc . . . Including Trigonometry. 2nd ed. LC 97-43437. (Bob Miller's Calc for the Clueless Ser.). (Illus.). 176p. (C). 1997. pap. text, student ed. 10.95 (*0-07-043407-7*, Schaums Outlne) McGraw-Hill Prof.

— SAT Math for the Clueless. LC 99-165915. (Illus.). 160p. 1998. pap. 10.95 (*0-07-043432-8*) McGraw.

— Searching for Kenny: Searching for God. LC 96-94008. 352p. 1996. 15.00 (*0-9650373-0-4*) Lewis Creek.

— You Have My Word on It. large type ed. Allen, Kathleen, ed. LC TXU 660-807. (Illus.). 85p. (Orig.). 1994. pap. 4.95 (*0-9634161-1-1*) Vanquish Pubns.

Miller, Bob, et al, eds. The Amish-Country Cookbook, Vol. 3. (Illus.). 308p. 1993. spiral bd. 12.99 (*0-934998-49-3*) Evangel Indiana.

*Miller, Bob & Miller, Sue.** Amish-Country Cookbook, Vol. 2. 304p. 1999. pap. 12.99 (*1-891314-05-X*, Pub. by Jordan IN) BookWorld.

— Amish-Country Cookbook, Vol. 3. 308p. 1999. pap. 12.99 (*1-891314-06-8*, Pub. by Jordan IN) BookWorld.

Miller, Bob W., et al, eds. Leadership in Higher Education: A Handbook for Practicing Administrators. LC 82-15579. 585p. 1983. lib. bdg. 99.50 (*0-313-22263-0*, MHE/, Greenwood Pr) Greenwood.

Miller, Bobby. Fabulous: A Photographic Diary of Studio 54. LC 98-26377. (Illus.). 144p. 1998. pap. 24.95 (*0-312-19567-2*) St Martin.

Miller, Bondell, ed. see Campondonica, Carol.

Miller, Bonnie R. Fifty on Fifty: Wisdom from Accomplished Women at the Half Century Mark. (Illus.). 128p. 1998. 29.95 (*0-446-91237-9*) Warner Bks.

Miller, Boyd. Copy Editing: Making Good Writing Better. 64p. 1992. pap. text 5.95 (*0-9615971-1-9*) Wordpix Serv.

— Veteran's Return to a Battlefield: Where 29th Division Fought near Aachen. (Illus.). 36p. 1985. 4.00 (*0-9615971-0-0*) Wordpix Serv.

Miller, Bradford. Returning to Seneca Falls - the First Women's Rights Convention & Its Meaning for Men Today: A Journey into the Historical Soul of America. 225p. 1995. pap. 17.95 (*0-940262-71-1*, Lindisfarne) Anthroposophic.

Miller, Branda, jt. ed. see Irmas, Deborah.

Miller, Brandon M. Buffalo Gals: Women of the Old West. (Illus.). 88p. (YA). (gr. 5 up). 1995. lib. bdg. 21.27 (*0-8225-1730-2*) Lerner Pub.

— Buffalo Gals: Women of the Old West. (Illus.). 88p. (J). (gr. 5-8). 1997. pap. text 8.95 (*0-8225-9772-1*) Lerner Pub.

— Dressed for the Occasion: What Americans Wore, 1620-1970. LC 98-22668. 88p. (YA). (gr. 6-9). 1999. 22.60 (*0-8225-1738-8*, Carolrhoda) Lerner Pub.

— Just What the Doctor Ordered: The History of American Medicine. LC 95-51491. 88p. (J). 1997. lib. bdg. 21.27 (*0-8225-1737-X*, Lerner Publctns) Lerner Pub.

*Miller, Brent C.** Families Matter: A Research Synthesis of Family Influences on Adolescent Pregnancy. 53p. 1998. pap. 15.00 (*1-58671-012-5*) Natl Cpgn Teen Preg.

Miller, Brent C. Family Research Methods. LC 86-964. (Family Studies Text Ser.: Vol. 4). (Illus.). 160p. (Orig.). (C). 1986. text 42.00 (*0-8039-2143-8*) Sage.

— Family Research Methods, No. 4. LC 86-964. (Family Studies Text Ser.: Vol. 4). (Illus.). 160p. (Orig.). (C). 1986. pap. text 18.95 (*0-8039-2144-6*) Sage.

Miller, Brent C., et al, eds. Preventing Adolescent Pregnancy: Model Programs & Evaluations. (Focus Editions Ser.: Vol. 140). (Illus.). 304p. 1992. 59.95 (*0-8039-4390-3*) Sage.

— Preventing Adolescent Pregnancy: Model Programs & Evaluations. LC 91-45070. (Sage Focus Editions Ser.: No. 140). (Illus.). 304p. reprint ed. pap. 94.30 (*0-608-09625-3*, 205278300007) Bks Demand.

— Preventing Adolescent Pregnancy: Model Programs & Evaluations, No. 140. (Focus Editions Ser.: Vol. 140). (Illus.). 304p. 1992. pap. 26.00 (*0-8039-4391-1*) Sage.

Miller, Brent C. & Olson, David H., eds. Family Studies Review Yearbook, Vol. 3. LC 83-643783. (Illus.). 616p. 1985. reprint ed. pap. 191.00 (*0-7837-1128-X*, 204165800003) Bks Demand.

Miller, Brett C., jt. ed. see Parini, Jay.

Miller, Brian. Gold Mines: The Psychology of Winning in Sport. (Illus.). 160p. 1998. pap. 29.95 (*1-86126-100-4*, Pub. by Crolwood) Trafalgar.

Miller, Brian, et al. Prairie Night: Black-Footed Ferrets & the Recovery of Endangered Species. (Illus.). 320p. 1996. 37.50 (*1-56098-603-4*) Smithsonian.

Miller, Brian, jt. see Reading, Richard P.

Miller, Brian, jt. photos by see Thomas, Bill.

Miller, Brian E. Poetry from Heaven. Trezise, Rene, ed. (Illus.). 50p. 1998. pap. 15.00 (*0-9664602-0-0*) Vic Crown Pub.

Miller, Brian J. South Wales Railways at the Grouping. 96p. (C). 1989. 75.00 (*0-905928-55-5*, Pub. by D Brown & Sons Ltd) St Mut.

Miller, Bruce. Dr. Bruce Miller's "The Nutrition Guarantee" LC 97-45347. 480p. 1998. pap. 17.99 (*1-56530-283-4*, Pub. by Summit TX) BookWorld.

Miller, Bruce A. Children at the Center: Implementing the Multiage Classroom. LC 94-34054. xii, 123p. 1994. pap. 15.95 (*0-86552-130-1*) U of Oreg ERIC.

Miller, Bruce A. & Hahn, Karen. Finding Their Own Place: Youth from Three Small Rural Communities Take Part in Instructive School-to-Work Experiences. LC 97-30278. 114p. 1997. pap. 12.00 (*1-880785-18-8*) ERIC-CRESS.

Miller, Bruce E. The Arts & the Basis of Education. 134p. (Orig.). (C). 1993. pap. text 19.50 (*0-8191-9128-0*); lib. bdg. 47.00 (*0-8191-9127-2*) U Pr of Amer.

Miller, Bruce I., ed. see Sullivan, Arthur & Gilbert, W. S.

*Miller, Bruce J.** The Actor as Storyteller: An Introduction to Acting. LC 99-13025. xiv, 289p. 1999. text 39.95 (*0-7674-0605-2*, 0605-2) Mayfield Pub.

Miller, Bruce J., jt. ed. see Anderson-Miller, Julia.

Miller, Bruce K., jt. auth. see Wolf, Arthur D.

Miller, Bruce L. & Cummings, Jeffrey L., eds. The Human Frontal Lobes: Functions & Disorders. LC 98-36944. (The Science & Practice of Neuropsychology Series). 661p. 1998. 80.00 (*1-57230-390-5*) Guilford Pubns.

Miller, Bruce W., III. Chumash: A Picture of Their World. (Illus.). 136p. (Orig.). 1988. pap. 8.95 (*0-944627-51-X*) Sand River Pr.

— The Gabrielino: A Southern California Indian Tribe. 132p. (Orig.). 1991. pap. 7.95 (*0-944627-90-0*) Sand River Pr.

Miller, Bruce W. Hotdocs in One Hour for Lawyers. LC 98-72617. 1999. pap. 34.95 (*1-57073-580-8*) Amer Bar Assn.

Miller, Bruce W. & Widess, Jim. The Caner's Handbook: A Descriptive Guide . . . to Restoring Cane, Rush, Splint, Danish Cord, Rawhide & Wicker Furniture. LC 91-60690. (Illus.). 144p. 1991. pap. 18.95 (*0-937274-60-7*) Lark Books.

Miller, Bryan. The New York Times Guide to Restaurants in New York City. LC 86-5896. 448p. 1987. pap. 12.95 (*0-8129-1313-2*, Times Bks) Crown Pub Group.

— The New York Times Guide to Restaurants in New York City. 1992. pap. 15.00 (*0-8129-2089-9*, Times Bks) Crown Pub Group.

— The New York Times Guide to Restaurants in New York City. rev. ed. (Illus.). 448p. 1988. pap. 12.95 (*0-8129-1735-9*, Times Bks) Crown Pub Group.

— The New York Times Guide to Restaurants in New York City, 1993-1994. 1992. 15.00 (*0-8129-1859-2*, Times Bks) Crown Pub Group.

Miller, Bryan & Rama, Marie. Cooking for Dummies. (For Dummies Ser.). 432p. 1996. pap. 19.99 (*0-7645-5002-0*) IDG Bks.

Miller, Bryan, jt. auth. see Franey, Pierre.

Miller, Bryan, jt. auth. see Miller, Light.

Miller, Bryan, jt. auth. see Yosses, Bill.

Miller, Burnett, jt. auth. see Zimmer, William.

Miller-Busschau, Kristin. Flirting with Frypans: Cook Book for Men. (Illus.). (C). 1993. pap. text 14.95 (*1-881116-21-2*) Black Forest Pr.

Miller, Butch & Smith, Steve. Short Track Driving Techniques. (Illus.). 80p. 1989. pap. text 16.95 (*0-936834-65-X*) S S Autosports.

Miller, Buzz & Marriett, Jane. Not for Love Alone: Labanotation Score. (Educational Performance Collection). 80p. 1986. pap. write for info. (*0-932582-50-8*) Dance Notation.

Miller, Byron & West, Richard. Embedded Systems Design Primer. Paetznick, Ryan, ed. (Illus.). 200p. 1999. pap. 42.00 (*0-9636637-1-2*) Impatience Pubns.

Miller, Byron, ed. see Schwalbe, Donna.

*Miller, Byron A.** Geography & Social Movements: Comparing Antinuclear Activism in the Boston Area. (Social Movements, Protest & Contention Ser.: Vol. 12). 2000. 54.95 (*0-8166-2950-1*); pap. text 21.95 (*0-8166-2951-X*) U of Minn Pr.

Miller, Byron E. The Design & Development of Fuzzy Logic Controllers. Parker, James, ed. (Illus.). 224p. (Orig.). 1996. pap. 52.00 (*0-9636637-0-4*) Impatience Pubns.

An Asterisk (*) at the beginning of an entry indicates that the title is appearing for the first time.

— Object Oriented Design Made Easy! LC 93-78275. (Illus.). 1993. pap. 19.95 (*0-9636637-6-3*) Impatience Pubns.

Miller, C. Clinical Epidemiology & Biostatistics. (National Medical Ser.). (Illus.). 435p. 1992. 26.00 (*0-683-06206-9*) Lppncott W & W.

— Ion Channel Reconstitution. LC 86-4900. (Illus.). 600p. (C). 1986. text 144.00 (*0-306-42136-4*, Kluwer Plenum) Kluwer Academic.

Miller, C. & Neogi, P. Interfacial Phenomena: Equilibrium & Dynamic Effects. (Surfactant Science Ser.: Vol. 17). (Illus.). 368p. 1985. text 199.00 (*0-8247-7490-6*) Dekker.

Miller, C. & Parks, J. E., eds. Resonance Ionization Spectroscopy, 1992: Proceedings of the 6th International Symposium on Resonance Ionization Spectroscopy & Its Applications, Santa Fe, New Mexico, 24-29 May 1992. (Institute of Physics Conference Ser.: No. 128). (Illus.). 376p. 1992. 189.00 (*0-7503-0230-5*) IOP Pub.

Miller, C., et al. Mysteries of Unknown (B - U) (World of the Unknown Ser.). (Illus.). 96p. (YA). (gr. 6 up). 1992. pap. 12.95 (*0-86020-492-8*) EDC.

Miller, C., jt. ed. see Juhasz, S.

Miller, C. Arden. Maternal Health & Infant Survival. 2nd ed. LC 91-62010. 52p. 1991. reprint ed. pap. text 7.50 (*0-943657-14-8*) ZERO TO THREE.

Miller, C. Arden & Moos, Merry K., eds. Local Health Departments: Fifteen Case Studies. LC 81-68703. 528p. 1981. 12.00 (*0-87553-094-X*, 061) Am Pub Health.

Miller, C. Arden & Williams, Bret C. Preventive Health Care for Young Children: Findings from a 10-Country Study & Directions for United States Policy. LC 91-61824. 80p. (Orig.). 1991. pap. 9.50 (*0-943657-16-4*) ZERO TO THREE.

Miller, C. Arden, et al. Monitoring Children's Health: Key Indicators. 2nd ed. 176p. 1989. 17.50 (*0-87553-162-8*) Am Pub Health.

Miller, C. C. The Adventures of the Streetsboro Bear. LC 95-94104. (Illus.). 47p. (Orig.). (J). (gr. k-3). 1995. pap. 4.95 (*0-9645652-0-X*) Bright Side Bks.

Miller, C. C., jt. auth. see Cummings, M. F.

Miller, C. D. EMT Basic National Standards Review Self Test. 239p. 1992. pap. 29.33 (*0-89303-875-X*) Appleton & Lange.

— Food Values of Poi, Taro & Limu. (BMB Ser.: No. 37). 1969. reprint ed. pap. 25.00 (*0-527-02140-7*) Periodicals Srv.

Miller, C. D. & Hafen, Brent Q. EMT-B National Standards Review Self Test. 2nd ed. LC 97-37172. 464p. 1997. pap. text 36.40 (*0-8359-5155-3*) P-H.

Miller, C. D. & White, David. EMT Basic National Standards Review Self Test. 208p. 1992. pap. text. write for info. (*0-318-68768-2*) P-H.

Miller, C. H. Erasmi Opera Omnia, Vol. IV-3. 224p. 1979. 262.50 (*0-444-85383-9*, North Holland) Elsevier.

Miller, C. H., ed. The Praise of Folie by Sir Thomas Chaloner. (EETS Original Ser.: Vol. 257). 1965. 30.00 (*0-19-722257-9*, Pub. by EETS) Boydell & Brewer.

***Miller, C. J.** Consumer & Trading Law: Text, Cases & Materials. 2nd ed. 810p. 1998. pap. text 52.00 (*0-19-876478-2*) OUP.

Miller, C. J. Contempt of Court. 2nd ed. (Illus.). 552p. 1991. reprint ed. pap. text 49.95 (*0-19-825684-1*) OUP.

***Miller, C. J.** Contempt of Court. 3rd ed. 750p. 2000. text 165.00 (*0-19-825697-3*) OUP.

— United Kingdom National Committee of Comparative Law Vol. 6: Comparative Product Liability. 198p. 1986. pap. 44.00 (*0-903067-28-5*, Pub. by Brit Inst ICL) St Mut.

Miller, C. J., et al, eds. Consumer & Trading Law. 2nd ed. 810p. 1998. text 92.00 (*0-19-876479-0*) OUP.

Miller, C. J. & Harvey, Brian W. Consumer & Trading Law - Cases & Materials. 1985. 100.00 (*0-406-01260-1*, UK, MICHIE); pap. 64.00 (*0-406-01261-X*, U.K., MICHIE) LEXIS Pub.

Miller, C. J., et al. Miller: Product Liability & Safety Encyclopaedia. ring bd. write for info. (*0-406-00758-6*, MPLSISET, MICHIE) LEXIS Pub.

Miller, C. John. Outgrowing the Ingrown Church. 176p. 1986. pap. 12.99 (*0-310-28411-2*, 12815P) Zondervan.

— Powerful Evangelism for the Powerless. 2nd rev. ed. LC 97-6827. Orig. Title: Evangelism & Your Church. 176p. 1997. pap. 9.99 (*0-87552-383-8*) P & R Pubng.

— Repentance & Twentieth Century Man. (Orig.). 1993. pap. 5.99 (*0-87508-334-X*) Chr Lit.

Miller, C. John & Juliani, Barbara M. Come Back, Barbara. 2nd expanded ed. LC 97-16981. 176p. 1997. reprint ed. pap. 9.99 (*0-87552-384-6*) P & R Pubng.

Miller, C. John & Miller, Barbara. Come Back, Barbara. 176p. 1988. mass mkt. 9.99 (*0-310-37471-5*, 11670P) Zondervan.

Miller, C. Kenneth. Multicast Networking & Applications. LC 98-29715. 304p. (C). 1998. 39.95 (*0-201-30979-3*) Addison-Wesley.

Miller, C. L. Depression Era Dime Store Glass. LC 98-89996. (Illus.). 144p. 1999. pap. 12.95 (*0-7643-0665-0*) Schiffer.

— Door-to-Door Collectibles: Salves, Lotions, Pills & Potions from W. T. Rawleigh. LC 97-31799. 1998. pap. 29.95 (*0-7643-0331-7*) Schiffer.

— Jewel Tea: Sales & Housewares Collectibles. LC 95-35253. (Illus.). 280p. 1995. 49.95 (*0-88740-898-2*) Schiffer.

— The Jewel Tea Company: Its History & Products. LC 94-65854. (Illus.). 288p. 1994. 39.95 (*0-88740-634-3*) Schiffer.

— Jewel Tea Grocery Products. LC 96-6042. (Illus.). 240p. (YA). (gr. 10-13). 1996. write for info. (*0-88740-984-9*) Schiffer.

Miller, C. L., ed. Eet Smakelijk, 12 bks., Set. 2nd ed. LC 96-83765. (Illus.). 589p. 14.95 (*0-9612710-0-0*) Holland Jr Welfare.

Miller, C. William. Benjamin Franklin's Philadelphia Printing: A Descriptive Bibliography. LC 72-83464. (Memoirs Ser.: Vol. 102). 1974. 50.00 (*0-87169-102-7*, M102-MIC) Am Philos.

Miller, Calvin. Apples, Snakes, & Bellyaches. LC 96-44522. (Illus.). (J). 1996. 18.99 (*0-87788-016-6*, H Shaw Pubs) Waterbrook Pr.

— The Book of Jesus. 576p. 1998. per. 15.00 (*0-684-83150-3*) S&S Trade.

— The Book of Jesus: A Treasury of the Greatest Stories & Writings about Christ. 608p. 1996. 30.00 (*0-684-81559-1*) S&S Trade.

***Miller, Calvin.** Book of Jesus: A Treasury of the Greatest Stories & Writings about Christ. 1999. pap. 15.00 (*0-8054-2051-7*) Broadman.

Miller, Calvin. A Covenant for All Seasons: The Marriage Journey. LC 95-7593. 192p. 1995. 14.99 (*0-87788-386-6*, H Shaw Pubs) Waterbrook Pr.

***Miller, Calvin.** The Devine Symphony. LC 00-8166. (Illus.). 304p. 2000. pap. 12.99 (*0-7642-2170-1*) Bethany Hse.

Miller, Calvin. Disarming the Darkness: A Guide to Spiritual Warfare. LC 96-44160. (Spiritual Directions Ser.). 160p. 1997. 16.99 (*0-310-20196-9*) Zondervan.

— The Empowered Leader: 10 Keys to Servant Leadership. 1997. pap. 10.99 (*0-8054-1098-8*) Broadman.

— The First Christmas. LC 97-22292. (Illus.). 32p. (J). (ps-3). 1997. write for info. (*0-7814-0050-3*, Chariot Bks) Chariot Victor.

***Miller, Calvin.** Into the Depths of God. LC 00-8429. 256p. 1999. text 16.99 (*0-7642-2172-8*) Bethany Hse.

— The Jesus We Knew: A 31-Day Journey Through the Gospels. LC 99-59711. 216p. 2000. 16.99 (*0-8054-9415-4*) Broadman.

— El Lider Con Poder.Tr. of Empowered Leader. (SPA.). 224p. 1999. pap. text 11.50 (*0-311-46163-8*, Edit Mundo) Casa Bautista.

Miller, Calvin. Marketplace Preaching: How to Return the Sermon to Where It Belongs. LC 94-32754. 192p. 1995. pap. 12.99 (*0-8010-6320-5*) Baker Bks.

— My Friend, My King: John's Vision of Our Hope of Heaven. LC 99-28723. 1999. 14.99 (*0-7814-3315-0*) Chariot Victor.

— My Lord & My God: Thomas' Incredible Account of Jesus' Resurrection. LC 97-44952. (Illus.). (J). 1998. 14.99 (*0-7814-3032-1*) Chariot Victor.

— An Owner's Manual for the Unfinished Soul. LC 96-37642. 176p. 1997. 15.99 (*0-87788-554-0*, H Shaw Pubs) Waterbrook Pr.

— The Philippian Fragment: Chinese Edition. Kam, May-Chun, tr. (CHI.). 139p. 1985. pap. 6.50 (*1-56582-080-0*) Christ Renew Min.

— The Singer. LC 74-20097. (Illus.). 152p. (Orig.). 1975. pap. 9.99 (*0-87784-639-1*, 639) InterVarsity.

— The Singer Trilogy. (Illus.). 496p. 1992. reprint ed. pap. 19.99 (*0-8308-1321-7*, 1321) InterVarsity.

— Snow. 16p. (YA). (gr. 8 up). 1998. text 11.99 (*0-7642-2152-3*) Bethany Hse.

— Unchained Soul: A Devotional Walk on the Journey into Christlikeness. 288p. 1999. pap. 10.99 (*0-7642-2169-8*) Bethany Hse.

— Walking with Saints: Through the Best & Worst Times of Our Lives. LC 94-32745. 1995. pap. 16.99 (*0-7852-8006-5*) Nelson.

***Miller, Calvin.** Wind. (Illus.). 160p. 2000. 11.99 (*0-7642-2362-3*) Bethany Hse.

Miller, Calvin, intro. Images of Heaven: Reflections on Glory. 168p. 1996. 15.99 (*0-87788-388-2*, H Shaw Pubs) Waterbrook Pr.

Miller, Calvin, jt. auth. see Kinkade, Thomas.

Miller, Calvin A. Until He Comes: Daily Inspirations for Those Who Await the Savior. LC 98-24500. 384p. 1998. 19.00 (*0-8054-1654-4*) Broadman.

Miller, Calvin C. Boris Yeltsin: First President of Russia. LC 94-16562. (Champions of Freedom Ser.). (Illus.). 192p. (YA). (gr. 5 up). 1995. lib. bdg. 18.95 (*1-883846-08-0*) M Reynolds.

***Miller, Calvin C.** Mary Wollstonecraft & the Rights of Women. LC 99-13519. (World Writers Ser.). (Illus.). 112p. (YA). (gr. 5 up). 1999. lib. bdg. 18.95 (*1-883846-41-2*) M Reynolds.

Miller, Calvin C. Pete Sampras. LC 97-48344. (Great Athletes Ser.). (Illus.). 64p. (YA). (gr. 3 up). 1998. lib. bdg. 17.95 (*1-883846-26-9*) M Reynolds.

— Spirit Like a Storm: The Story of Mary Shelley. LC 95-53826. (World Writers Ser.). (Illus.). 112p. (YA). (gr. 5 up). 1996. lib. bdg. 18.95 (*1-883846-13-7*) M Reynolds.

Miller, Calvin M. Optical Fiber Splices & Connectors. 1996. 119.00 (*0-614-18458-4*, B25006) Info Gatekeepers.

Miller, Calvin M., et al. Optical Fiber Splices & Connectors: Theory & Methods. LC 86-1439. (Optical Engineering Ser.: No. 10). (Illus.). 440p. reprint ed. pap. 136.40 (*0-7837-4424-2*, 205248400012) Bks Demand.

Miller, Cam. In-Line Skating Basics. (Illus.). 96p. (Orig.). 1996. pap. 12.95 (*0-8069-3851-X*) Sterling.

Miller, Cameron & Falla, Dominique. Woodlore. LC 94-27987. (Illus.). 32p. (J). (gr. k-4). 1995. 14.95 (*0-395-72034-6*) Ticknor & Flds Bks Yng Read.

Miller Canfield Paddock Staff. Employment Law Handbook: Guide for Michigan Employers. 3rd ed. 368p. 1999. pap. 119.00 (*1-893318-00-1*) Michigan Cham Com.

Miller, Carey & Beaumont, eds. United Kingdom National Committee of Comparative Law: The Option of Litigating in Europe, Vol. 14. 181p. 1993. pap. 75.00 (*0-904281-04-3*, Pub. by UK Natl Committee) St Mut.

Miller, Carey D. Food Values of Breadfruit, Taro Leaves, Coconut, & Sugar Cane, 1929. pap. 18.00 (*0-527-02170-9*, BO64K) Periodicals Srv.

Miller, Carl. Stages of Desire: Male & Female Homosexuality in British & American Theatre. Date not set. pap. 21.95 (*0-304-32817-0*, Pub. by Cassell) LPC InBook.

— Stages of Desire: Male & Female Homosexuality in British & American Theatre. LC 96-176861. (Lesbian & Gay Studies). 256p. 1995. 69.95 (*0-304-32815-4*, Pub. by Cassell) LPC InBook.

Miller, Carl F. Archaeological Investigations at the Hosterman Site (39PO7), Oake Reservoir Area, Potter County, South Dakota, 1956, Vol. 35. fac. ed. (Smithsonian Institution, Bureau of American Ethnology Ser.: Bulletin 189). (Illus.). 154p. (C). 1964. reprint ed. pap. text 16.88 (*1-55567-704-5*) Coyote Press.

Miller, Carl H. Breweries of Cleveland. (Illus.). 296p. 1998. 26.95 (*0-9662084-0-4*) Schnitzelbank Pr.

Miller, Carlene. Killing at the Cat: A Lexy Hyatt Mystery. LC 98-25229. 200p. 1998. pap. 10.95 (*0-934678-95-2*) New Victoria Pubs.

— Mayhem at the Marina: A Lexy Hyatt Mystery. LC 99-25699. 200p. 1999. pap. 11.95 (*1-892281-05-8*) New Victoria Pubs.

Miller, Carli K., ed. see Kistler, Vivian.

***Miller, Carlos Ledson.** Belize: A Novel. 430p. 2000. 25.00 (*0-7388-0716-8*); pap. 18.00 (*0-7388-0717-6*) Xlibris Corp.

— Panama: A Novel. 2000. 25.00 (*0-7388-0714-1*); pap. 18.00 (*0-7388-0715-X*) Xlibris Corp.

Miller, Carman. Painting the Map Red: Canada & the South African War, 1899-1902. (Illus.). 542p. 1998. pap. 29.95 (*0-7735-1750-2*, Pub. by McG-Queens Univ Pr) CUP Services.

— Painting the Map Red: Canada & the South African War, 1899-1902. 592p. 1993. 49.95 (*0-7735-0913-5*) U of Toronto Pr.

Miller, Carmen. Painting the Map Red Vol. 2: Canada & the South African War, 1899-1902. (Illus.). 557p. 1999. pap. 25.50 (*0-86980-939-3*) Univ Natal Pr.

Miller, Carol. Laboratory Manual for Concepts of Physical Activity. 6th ed. 96p. (C). 1995. pap. text, spiral bd. 14.95 (*0-8403-9559-0*) Kendall-Hunt.

***Miller, Carol.** The Other Side of Yesterday: The China Maya Connection. LC 00-190632. 116p. 2000. 25.00 (*0-7388-1870-4*); pap. 18.00 (*0-7388-1871-2*) Xlibris Corp.

— Travels in the Maya World. LC 00-190747. 239p. 2000. 25.00 (*0-7388-1971-9*); pap. 18.00 (*0-7388-1972-7*) Xlibris Corp.

Miller, Carol. What Students Can Tell Us about the Multicultural Classroom. Bridwell-Bowles, Lillian & Batchelder, Susan, eds. (Technical Reports: No. 1). 7p. (Orig.). (C). 1992. pap. 2.00 (*1-881221-04-0*) U Minn Ctr Interdis.

Miller, Carol & Razavi, Shahra, eds. Missionaries & Mandarins: Feminist Engagement with Development Institutions. 96p. 1998. pap. 17.50 (*1-85339-434-3*, Pub. by Intermed Tech) Stylus Pub VA.

Miller, Carol & Rivera, Guadalupe. The Winged Prophet from Hermes to Quetzalcoatl: An Introduction to the Mesoamerican Deities Through the Tarot. LC 94-18281. (Illus.). 448p. (Orig.). 1994. pap. 17.95 (*0-87728-799-6*) Weiser.

Miller, Carol, jt. auth. see Evans, Carolyn.

Miller, Carol, jt. auth. see Martin, Deirdre.

Miller, Carol, jt. auth. see Wirtshafter, Donald.

Miller, Carol A. Nursing Care for Older Adults: Theory & Practice. 2nd ed. LC 94-10140. 624p. 1994. pap. text 34.95 (*0-397-55086-3*) Lppncott W & W.

— Nursing Care of Older Adults: Theory & Practice. 3rd ed. LC 98-45982. 19p. 1998. pap. text. write for info. (*0-7817-1623-3*) Lppncott W & W.

Miller, Carol E. Disciples of Jesus, Beginner-Primary Teacher. 1984. pap. 2.25 (*0-915374-47-1*) Rapids Christian.

— Teaching Junior High. 1980. pap. 3.50 (*0-915374-23-4*) Rapids Christian.

— Teaching Toddlers. 88p. 1996. reprint ed. pap. text, teacher ed. 3.50 (*0-915374-22-6*, 22-6) Rapids Christian.

— The Ten Commandments: Youth & Adult Student. 1971. pap. 1.00 (*0-915374-45-5*) Rapids Christian.

— Ten Commandments: Youth & Adult Teacher. 1991. pap. 2.50 (*0-915374-37-4*) Rapids Christian.

— Under the Sun & in the Heavenlies: Youth & Adult Teacher. 1985. pap. 2.25 (*0-915374-49-8*) Rapids Christian.

Miller, Carol J., ed. International Association of Logopaedics & Phoniatrics, 19th Congress, Edinburgh 1983: Abstracts. (Journal: Folia Phoniatrica: Vol. 35, No. 3-4). 96p. 1983. pap. 31.50 (*3-8055-3730-1*) S Karger.

Miller, Carol P. & Wheeler, Robert. Cleveland: A Concise History, 1796-1996. 2nd ed. LC 97-9916. (Encyclopedia of Cleveland History Ser.). 1997. 35.00 (*0-253-33336-9*); pap. 14.95 (*0-253-21147-6*) Ind U Pr.

Miller, Carole A., ed. see Seklemian, M.

Miller, Caroline. Lamb in His Bosom. 1991. lib. bdg. 35.95 (*1-56849-057-7*) Buccaneer Bks.

— Lamb in His Bosom. LC 92-38286. (Modern Southern Classics Ser.). 368p. 1993. 24.95 (*1-56145-074-X*); pap. 14.95 (*1-56145-075-8*) Peachtree Pubs.

Miller, Caroline, ed. see Krasner, A. M.

***Miller, Carolyn.** Soulmates: Following Inner Guidance to the Relationship of Your Dreams. LC 99-47400. 276p. 2000. pap. 12.95 (*0-915811-86-3*, Pub. by H J Kramer Inc) Publishers Group.

***Miller, Carolyn & Smith, Sharon.** Savoring San Francisco: Recipes from the City's Neighborhood Restaurants. 192p. 2000. pap. 18.95 (*1-57061-236-6*) Sasquatch Bks.

Miller, Carolyn, ed. see Brown, Ellen.

Miller, Carolyn, ed. see DeMers, John.

Miller, Carolyn, ed. see Philpotts, Kaui.

Miller, Carolyn, ed. see Ryan, Nancy R.

Miller, Carolyn G. Creating Miracles: Understanding the Experience of Divine Intervention. Carleton, Nancy, ed. LC 94-48620. 372p. 1995. pap. 12.95 (*0-915811-62-6*) H J Kramer Inc.

Miller, Carolyn G., contrib. by. The Home Office: Markets for Equipment, Supplies & Services. 112p. 1995. 2650.00 (*1-56965-073-X*, G-189) BCC.

Miller, Carolyn Greene. Computer Software Market Development. LC 98-143434. 148p. 1997. 2750.00 (*1-56965-081-0*, G-032N) BCC.

***Miller, Carolyn R.** 50 Writing Lessons That Work! Motivating Prompts & Easy Activities That Develop the Essentials of Strong Writing. 64p. (J). 1999. pap. 9.95 (*0-590-52212-4*) Scholastic Inc.

Miller, Carolynne L. Indiana Sources for Genealogical Research in the Indiana State Library. 199p. 1984. 20.00 (*0-87195-079-0*) Ind Hist Soc.

Miller, Casper J. Faith Healers in the Himalaya. 1997. pap. 77.00 (*0-7855-7395-X*, Pub. by Ratna Pustak Bhandar) St Mut.

Miller-Catchpole, Robin, jt. auth. see Bezkorovainy, Anatoly.

Miller, Catherine, ed. see McHugh, Fenton.

Miller, Catherine G. Carscape: A Parking Handbook. (Illus.). 121p. (Orig.). 1988. pap. 30.00 (*0-945387-00-8*, TL175.M55) Wshngtn St Pr.

Miller, Cathleen, jt. auth. see Dirie, Waris.

Miller, Cathy. Harvesting, Preserving & Arranging. 1998. 30.00 (*0-676-57320-7*) Random.

— Harvesting, Preserving, & Arranging Dried Flowers. LC 97-15287. (Illus.). 208p. 1997. 30.00 (*1-885183-51-8*) Artisan.

— Sights & Insights: A Guide to the Findhorn Foundation Community. 1995. pap. text 4.00 (*1-899171-50-9*, Pub. by Findhorn Pr) Words Distrib.

***Miller, Cecilia.** The Mantra Is a Prayer to God. (Illus.). 24p. (J). 2000. reprint ed. 12.95 (*0-911307-92-3*, 205426, Pub. by SYDA Found) Words Distrib.

— Walking the Path with Neela: An Alphabet of Siddha Yoga Meditation. LC 99-220191. (Illus.). 48p. (J). 1998. pap. 10.95 (*0-911307-66-4*, Pub. by SYDA Found) Words Distrib.

Miller Center Commission. Transferring Responsibility: The Dangers of Transition: Report of the Miller Center Commission on Presidential Transitions & Foreign Policy. LC 86-5536. 9.00 (*0-8191-5344-3*) U Pr of Amer.

Miller, Chaim, jt. auth. see Shear, Eli M.

Miller, Char. Selected Writings of Hiram Bingham - Missionary to the Hawaiian Islands, 1814-1869: To Raise the Lord's Banner. LC 88-11790. (Studies in American Religion: Vol. 31). 550p. 1988. lib. bdg. 119.95 (*0-88946-675-0*) E Mellen.

Miller, Char, ed. American Forests: Nature, Culture, & Politics. LC 97 14811. (Development of Western Resources Ser.). 288p. 1997. 35.00 (*0-7006-0848-6*); pap. 17.95 (*0-7006-0849-4*) U Pr of KS.

— Missions & Missionaries in the Pacific. LC 85-5074. (Symposium Ser.: Vol. 14). 136p. 1986. lib. bdg. 69.95 (*0-88946-705-6*) E Mellen.

***Miller, Char, ed.** Water in the West: A High Country News Reader. (Illus.). 320p. 2000. pap. 29.95 (*0-87071-480-5*) Oreg St U Pr.

Miller, Char & Grantham, Stephanie. Organized at Last Vol. I: Step by Step. 2nd rev. ed. 118p. 1996. pap. text 7.95 (*0-9636982-0-6*, 9270) G & R Pub.

Miller, Char & Rothman, Hal, eds. Out of the Woods: Essays in Environmental History. LC 97-4747. 368p. 1997. pap. 22.95 (*0-8229-5631-4*); text 50.00 (*0-8229-3982-7*) U of Pittsburgh Pr.

***Miller, Char & Stabler, Rebecca.** The Greatest Good. LC 99-41539. 1999. write for info. (*0-939970-80-5*) Soc Am Foresters.

***Miller, Charles.** Gift of the World: An Introduction to the Theology of Dumitru Staniloae. 128p. 2000. 34.95 (*0-567-08696-8*) T&T Clark Pubs.

Miller, Charles. Love in Vain. (Illus.). 50p. (Orig.). (C). 1997. pap. 20.00 (*0-935645-16-0*) AJFP.

— Praying the Eucharist: Reflections on the Eucharistic Experience of God. LC 96-3465. 128p. 1996. pap. 9.95 (*0-8192-1670-4*) Morehouse Pub.

— Valve Radio & Audio Repair Handbook. 2nd ed. (Illus.). 176p. 2000. pap. 37.95 (*0-7506-3995-4*, Newnes) Buttrwrth-Heinemann.

Miller, Charles, jt. auth. see Greer, James K.

Miller, Charles, jt. auth. see Swaddling, David.

Miller, Charles A. A Catawba Assembly. LC 73-84983. (Illus.). 250p. 1973. pap. 10.00 (*0-9606522-0-5*) Trackaday.

— Isn't That Lewis Carroll? LC 83-51809. (Illus.). 126p. 1984. pap. 4.00 (*0-9606522-1-3*) Trackaday.

— Jefferson & Nature. 320p. (C). 1993. reprint ed. pap. text 16.95 (*0-8018-4729-X*) Johns Hopkins.

Miller, Charles C., ed. History of Allen County, Ohio & Representative Citizens. (Illus.). 872p. 1993. reprint ed. lib. bdg. 89.00 (*0-8328-2784-3*) Higginson Bk Co.

Miller, Charles D. Abundant Life. LC 97-75131. xlv, 172p. 1997. pap. 14.95 (*0-9660624-1-8*) AUM Pub.

— Basic College Math: Solutions Manual. 5th ed. (C). 1998. pap. text, student ed. 21.56 (*0-321-01317-4*) Addson-Wesley Educ.

— Basic College Mathematics. 4th ed. (C). 1994. teacher ed. write for info. (*0-673-55467-8*) Addson-Wesley Educ.

— Deny Thyself. xxiv, 110p. 1998. pap. 14.95 (*0-9660624-3-4*) AUM Pub.

— Economics Today. 7th ed. (C). 1997. pap. 72.00 (*0-06-044501-7*) Addson-Wesley Educ.

— Family Values. LC 98-92117. 208p. 1998. pap. 14.95 (*0-9660624-5-0*) AUM Pub.

M

— Mathematical Ideas: Solutions Manual. 8th ed. 464p. (C). 1997. pap. text, student ed. 25.00 (0-673-98371-4) Addison-Wesley.

Miller, Charles D., ed. Basic College Math Brief. (C). 1997. text 54.00 (0-673-67502-5) Addison-Wesley.

Miller, Charles D. & Salzman, Stanley A. Business Mathematics. 5th ed. Hoelzle, Louis F., ed. (C). 1997. pap. text 54.00 (0-673-38901-4) Addson-Wesley Educ.

— Business Mathematics: A Programmed Approach, Bk. 2. (C). 1981. pap. text 22.50 (0-673-15426-2) Addson-Wesley Educ.

— Business Mathematics: A Programmed Approach, Bk. 1. (C). 1980. pap. text 25.33 (0-673-15347-9) Addson-Wesley Educ.

Miller, Charles D., et al. Algebra for College Students. (C). 1991. text 59.00 (0-673-46469-5) Addson-Wesley Educ.

— Algebra for College Students. (C). 1991. 18.50 (0-673-46470-9) Addson-Wesley Educ.

— Basic College Mathematics. Date not set. pap. text. write for info. (0-673-55866-5) Addson-Wesley Educ.

— Basic College Mathematics. 4th ed. Date not set. pap., teacher ed. write for info. (0-673-46950-6) Addson-Wesley Educ.

— Basic College Mathematics. 5th ed. LC 96-52938. (Illus.). 716p. (C). 1997. pap. text 78.00 (0-321-01265-8) Addson-Wesley Educ.

— Basic College Mathematics: Student's Solution Manual, 4e. 4th ed. (C). 1995. pap. text, student ed. 22.50 (0-673-99064-8) Addson-Wesley Educ.

— Beginning Algebra. (C). 1991. pap. text 21.00 (0-673-46461-X); 18.50 (0-673-46460-1) Addson-Wesley Educ.

— Beginning Algebra. 6th ed. (C). 1991. text 57.50 (0-673-46459-8) Addson-Wesley Educ.

— Business Mathematics. 6th ed. LC 93-22140. 636p. (C). 1997. teacher ed. 11.00 (0-673-99052-4) Addson-Wesley Educ.

— Business Mathematics. 7th ed. LC 96-657. 656p. (C). 1997. pap. text 72.00 (0-673-99551-8) Addson-Wesley Educ.

— Business Mathematics. 8th ed. LC 98-48200. 712p. (C). 1999. pap. text 78.00 (0-321-04503-3) Addison-Wesley.

— Business Mathematics, Bk. 1: A Programmed Approach. LC 79-24513. 223p. reprint ed. pap. 69.20 (0-7837-4050-6, 204388000001) Bks Demand.

— College Algebra. 6th ed. (C). 1997. pap. text, student ed. 26.00 (0-673-46816-X) Addson-Wesley Educ.

— College Algebra: A Student's Solution Manual. 6th ed. (C). 1993. pap. text, teacher ed. 23.44 (0-673-46817-8) Addson-Wesley Educ.

— The Economics of Public Issues. 9th ed. 272p. (C). 1997. pap. 26.00 (0-06-501336-0) Addson-Wesley Educ.

— Finite Mathematics. 5th ed. (C). 1993. pap. text, student ed. 26.50 (0-673-46756-2) Addson-Wesley Educ.

— Fundamental Trigonometry 290. 2nd ed. 432p. (C). 1997. 90.00 (0-673-38961-8) Addson-Wesley Educ.

— Fundamentals of College Algebra. 4th ed. 528p. (C). 1997. 88.00 (0-673-46743-0) Addson-Wesley Educ.

— Fundamentals of College Algebra: A Student's Solution Manual. 4th ed. (C). 1997. pap. text, teacher ed. 32.00 (0-673-46992-1) Addson-Wesley Educ.

— Intermediate Algebra. 5th ed. LC 94-11108. (C). 1995. text 64.69 (0-673-46744-9) Addson-Wesley Educ.

— Intermediate Algebra. 6th ed. (C). 1991. pap., suppl. ed. 18.50 (0-673-46465-2) Addson-Wesley Educ.

— Intermediate Algebra. 7th ed. (C). Date not set. pap. text, student ed. 9.00 (0-673-55940-8) Addson-Wesley Educ.

— Intermediate Algebra: A Student's Solution Manual. 5th ed. (C). 1994. pap. text, student ed. 12.50 (0-673-99063-X) Addson-Wesley Educ.

— Intermediate Algebra: A Text Workbook. 4th ed. (C). 1997. text 61.00 (0-673-46272-2) Addson-Wesley Educ.

— Intermediate Algebra with Early Functions & Graphing. 5th ed. LC 94-12271. (C). 1995. pap. text 64.69 (0-673-99313-2) Addson-Wesley Educ.

— Introduction to Algebra: A Student's Solution Manual. 5th ed. (C). 1994. pap. text, student ed. 12.50 (0-673-99062-1) Addson-Wesley Educ.

— Mathematical Ideas. 7th ed. LC 93-1955. 828p. (C). 1993. 14.50 (0-673-99095-8) Addson-Wesley Educ.

— Mathematical Ideas. 8th ed. LC 96-25478. 928p. (C). 1997. 86.00 (0-673-99893-2) Addson-Wesley Educ.

— Student's Solution Manual to Accompany Calculus With Applications & Calculus With Applications Brief Version. 5th ed. (C). 1993. pap. text 23.00 (0-673-46755-4) Addson-Wesley Educ.

— Trigonometry. 5th ed. (C). 1992. student ed. 14.00 (0-673-46815-1) Addson-Wesley Educ.

Miller, Charles D., jt. auth. see Lial, Margaret L.

Miller, Charles E. Airlift Doctrine. (Illus.). 447p. 1988. pap. 17.00 (1-58566-019-1) Air Univ.

Miller, Charles E. As Rain That Falls: Homiletic Reflections for the Weekdays of Advent & Lent. LC 88-13963. 157p. 1988. pap. 7.95 (0-8189-0535-2) Alba.

***Miller, Charles E.** The Celebration of the Eucharist. (Liturgy for the People of God Ser.: Vol. 2). 206p. (YA). 2000. pap. 14.95 (0-8189-0879-3, Saint Pauls) Alba.

— Foundations of Vatican II Liturgy, 3, 1. (Liturgy for the People of God Ser.: Vol. 1). 125p. (YA). 2000. pap. 10.95 (0-8189-0878-5, Saint Pauls) Alba.

— Liturgy for the People of God: A Trilogy, 3 vols. (Liturey For the People of God). (YA). 2000. pap. 36.95 (0-8189-0881-5, Saint Pauls) Alba.

Miller, Charles E. Making Holy the Day: A Commentary in the Liturgy of the Hours. 1976. 1.50 (0-89942-410-4, 410/04) Catholic Bk Pub.

— Mother & Disciple: A Devout Discourse on the Blessed Virgin Mary. LC 89-32761. 108p. (Orig.). 1989. pap. 4.95 (0-8189-0548-4) Alba.

— Opening the Treasures: A Book of Daily Homily Meditations. LC 81-19095. (Illus.). 557p. 1982. pap. 19.95 (0-8189-0424-0) Alba.

— Ordained to Preach: A Theology & Practice of Preaching. LC 92-16295. 236p. (Orig.). 1992. pap. 12.95 (0-8189-0637-5) Alba.

— Random Reminiscences of Sixty Years of Law Practice. 144p. 2000. 19.95 (1-58244-022-0) Rutledge Bks.

***Miller, Charles E.** Sacraments & Other Matters Liturgical, 3, 3. (Liturgy for the People of God Ser.: Vol. 3). 214p. 2000. pap. 14.95 (0-8189-0880-7, Saint Pauls) Alba.

Miller, Charles E. Sunday Preaching: Brief Homilies for the Sundays of the Three Cycles. LC 97-7378. 1997. pap. 18.95 (0-8189-0782-7) Alba.

Miller, Charles E., ed. Together in Prayer: Learning to Love the Liturgy of the Hours. LC 94-23025. 124p. (Orig.). 1994. pap. 9.95 (0-8189-0712-6) Alba.

Miller, Charles F., III. On Group-Theoretic Decision Problems & Their Classification. LC 70-146647. (Annals of Mathematics Studies: No. 68). 116p. 1971. reprint ed. pap. 36.00 (0-608-06492-0, 206678900009) Bks Demand.

Miller, Charles R., III. Illustrated Guide to the National Electrical Code. 2nd rev. abr. ed. LC 98-28423. 448p. (C). 1999. mass mkt. 42.95 (0-7668-0529-8) Delmar.

Miller, Charles W., Jr. The Automobile Gold Rushes & Depression Era Mining. LC 97-11450. 1998. 29.95 (0-89301-195-9) U of Idaho Pr.

— Stake Your Claim! The Tale of America's Enduring Mining Laws. (Illus.). 1991. 34.95 (0-87026-080-4) Westernlore.

Miller, Charles W. Today's Technology in Bible Prophecy. (Illus.). 512p. (Orig.). 1990. pap. 10.00 (0-9627032-0-6) TIP MI.

Miller, Charles W., ed. see DOE Technical Information Center Staff.

Miller, Charly D. EMT Paramedic National Standards. 3rd ed. LC 96-38269. 411p. 1996. pap. text 36.40 (0-8359-5102-2) P-H.

— Jems EMS Pocket Guide. (Illus.). 152p. (C). (gr. 13). 1996. spiral bd. 12.95 (0-8151-7283-4, 28041) Mosby Inc.

Miller, Charly D. & White, David. EMT-Basic National Standards Review Self Test. 2nd ed. LC 94-12398. (C). 1994. pap. 27.00 (0-89303-002-3) Appleton & Lange.

— EMT-Paramedic National Standards Review Self Test. LC 92-49915. write for info. (0-89303-955-1) Brady Pub.

***Miller, Chinle.** Salt Lake City: Jewel of the Wasatch. LC 99-91688. (Illus.). 16p. 2000. pap. 7.95 (0-9655961-3-3, Pub. by Yellow Cat) Books West CO.

Miller, Chris. Public Service Trade Unionism & Radical Politics. LC 95-39634. (Illus.). 312p. 1996. 79.95 (1-85521-641-8, Pub. by Dartmth Pub) Ashgate Pub Co.

Miller, Chris & Hale, Mary. Immune Support Cookbook: Easy Delicious Recipes to Support Your Health If You're HIV Positive or Suffer From CFIDS, Cancer or Other Degenerative Diseases. 224p. 1995. 18.95 (1-55972-310-6, Birch Ln Pr) Carol Pub Group.

***Miller, Chris, et al.** Microsoft Windows 2000 Server Unleashed. (Unleashed Ser.). 800p. 2000. pap. 49.99 (0-672-31739-7) Sams.

Miller, Chris, jt. auth. see Hale, Mary.

Miller, Chris, jt. auth. see Turcotte, Bryan R.

Miller, Chris, tr. see Monneret, Sophie.

Miller, Chris H. & Palenik, Charles John. Infection Control & Management of Hazardous Materials for the Dental Team. 2nd ed. LC 98-13526. (Illus.). 376p. (C). (gr. 13). 1998. pap. text 29.00 (0-8151-5688-X, 29798) Mosby Inc.

Miller, Christian. A Childhood in Scotland. LC 80-2449. 1982. 12.95 (0-385-17474-8) Doubleday.

Miller, Christina G. & Berry, Louise A. Air Alert: Rescuing the Earth's Atmosphere. LC 95-21295. (Illus.). 128p. (YA). (gr. 5-9). 1996. 16.00 (0-689-31792-1) Atheneum Yung Read.

Miller, Christine. Choosing a Package Holiday: How to Plan & Prepare for a Disaster-Free Experience. (Family Reference Ser.). 142p. 1997. pap. 19.95 (1-85703-332-9, Pub. by How To Bks) Trans-Atl Phila.

— Unemployment: The Turning of the Tide?: A Bibliography on the Social & Economic Impacts of Unemployment, 1984-1988 LC 90-184638. v, 195 p. 1989. write for info. (0-946655-30-8) Tech Comm.

Miller, Christine M. & McKinney, Bruce C., eds. Governmental Commission Communication. LC 93-17118. (Praeger Series in Political Communication). 248p. 1993. 62.95 (0-275-94223-6, C4223, Praeger Pubs) Greenwood.

Miller, Christine M., jt. auth. see Ancell, R. Manning.

Miller, Christopher. Environmental Rights: Critical Perspectives. LC 97-51719. (Illus.). 248p. (C). 1998. 85.00 (0-415-17064-8) Routledge.

Miller, Christopher & Fricker, Claire. Planning & Hazard. (Progress in Planning Ser.: Vol. 40). 260p. 1994. 56.25 (0-08-042474-0, Pergamon Pr) Elsevier.

Miller, Christopher L. Blank Darkness: Africanist Discourse in French. LC 85-1157. (Illus.). xii, 288p. 1986. pap. text 13.95 (0-226-52622-4) U Ch Pr.

— Blank Darkness: Africanist Discourse in French. LC 85-1157. (Illus.). xii, 288p. 1986. lib. bdg. 36.00 (0-226-52621-6) U Ch Pr.

— Prophetic Worlds: Indians & Whites on the Columbia Plateau. 180p. (C). 1985. text 35.00 (0-8135-1084-8) Rutgers U Pr.

— Theories of Africans: Francophone Literature & Anthropology in Africa. (Black Literature & Culture Ser.). (Illus.). 338p. 1990. pap. text 19.95 (0-226-52802-2) U Ch Pr.

— Theories of Africans: Francophone Literature & Anthropology in Africa. (Black Literature & Culture Ser.). (Illus.). 352p. 1990. lib. bdg. 60.00 (0-226-52801-4) U Ch Pr.

***Miller, Christopher W.** Developing New Product Concepts: A Workbook for Innovation. Pennsylvania Chamber of Business & Industry Educational Foundation Staff, ed. (Illus.). 151p. 1999. pap. 70.00 (1-929744-04-8) Penn Chamber of Bus.

Miller, Chuck. How in the Morning: Poems 1962-1988. Sklar, Morty, ed. LC 88-16062. (Outstanding Author Ser.: No. 5). 80p. 1988. 12.75 (0-930370-32-5); pap. 7.00 (0-930370-33-3) Spirit That Moves.

— How in the Morning: Poems 1962-1988, Signed A-Z. limited ed. Sklar, Morty, ed. LC 88-16062. (Outstanding Author Ser.: No. 5). 80p. 1988. 25.00 (0-930370-34-1) Spirit That Moves.

— Northern Fields: New & Selected Poems. LC 93-26007. 128p. (Orig.). 1994. pap. 11.95 (1-56689-014-4) Coffee Hse.

— Now That I'm a Christian, Vol. 1. 64p. (Orig.). 1974. pap. 5.95 (0-8307-0425-6, 5201918, Regal Bks) Gospel Lght.

Miller, Chuck, ed. see King, Stephen.

***Miller, Cindy.** Character Counts: An Interactive Bible Study. 64p. 1999. pap. write for info. (0-7392-0319-3, PO3472) Morris Pubng.

***Miller, C.L.** Depression Era Dime Store: Kitchen, home & Garden. (Illus.). 144p. 1999. pap. 12.95 (0-7643-1050-X) Schiffer.

Miller, Claire S., jt. auth. see Reischl, Dennis.

***Miller, Clara M.** Echoes of a Haunting: A House in the Country. LC 99-91451. 2000. 25.00 (0-7388-0802-4); pap. 18.00 (0-7388-0803-2) Xlibris Corp.

Miller, Clarence H., ed. see More, Thomas.

Miller, Clarence W. The Funeral Book. Jacobs, Pamela D., ed. LC 94-18601. 96p. 1994. pap. 7.95 (1-885003-02-1) R D Reed Pubs.

Miller, Clark. He Always Puts It to the Right: A Historical, Scientific, Anecdotal Analysis of the Penalty Kick. (Illus.). 256p. 1998. 29.95 (0-575-06587-7, Pub. by V Gollancz) Trafalgar.

Miller-Clark, Denise, ed. New Chicago Photographers. (Illus.). 32p. 1984. 10.00 (0-932026-13-3) Columbia College Chi.

Miller-Clark, Denise, pref. Linda Connor: Spiral Journey: Photographs, 1967-1990. 70p. 1990. pap. 25.00 (0-932026-21-4) Columbia College Chi.

Miller, Claude. Fat & Fed Up: Challenge to Weight Control. 1970. 5.95 (0-8184-0031-5) Carol Pub Group.

Miller, Claudia A. Shannon Miller: My Child, My Hero. LC 98-39127. 292p. 1999. 19.95 (0-8061-3110-1) U of Okla Pr.

Miller, Claudia S., jt. auth. see Ashford, Nicholas A.

Miller, Clem. Some Things You Never Forget: 5 Battle Stars from Tunisia to the Poe Valley. 290p. (Orig.). 1996. pap. 15.95 (1-886028-19-2) Savage Pr.

***Miller, Cleve.** Hawk. 40p. 1999. pap. 5.95 (0-9669179-6-0) Fifth Wrld.

Miller, Clifford, jt. auth. see Pearson, Hilary.

Miller, Clinton E. How Insurance Companies Settle Cases. 356p. 1989. ring bd. 119.00 (0-938065-43-2) James Pub Santa Ana.

Miller, Clive & Domoney, Lynette. Unemployment & Social Services. (C). 1988. 60.00 (0-7855-3744-9, Pub. by Natl Inst Soc Work) St Mut.

Miller, Clive & Scott, Tony. Strategies & Tactics: Planning & Decision Making in Social Services Fieldwork Teams. (C). 1984. 55.00 (0-7855-3736-8, Pub. by Natl Inst Soc Work); 59.00 (0-7855-5898-5, Pub. by Natl Inst Soc Work); 75.00 (0-7855-0073-1, Pub. by Natl Inst Soc Work); pap. 35.00 (0-902789-32-5, Pub. by Natl Inst Soc Work) St Mut.

Miller, Clive, et al. Everyday Community Care: A Manual for Mangers. (C). 1991. pap. 38.00 (0-902789-73-2, Pub. by Natl Inst Soc Work) St Mut.

Miller, Clive, jt. auth. see Flynn, Norman.

Miller, Clive, jt. auth. see Scott, Tony.

Miller, Clive, jt. ed. see Flynn, Norman.

Miller, Clyde. Commentary on First & Second Kings. LC 88-72271. (Living Word Ser.). 416p. 1992. 27.95 (0-89112-188-9) Abilene Christ U.

Miller, Clyde L., tr. see DeCusa, Nicolas.

Miller, Clyde L., tr. see Gerson, Jean.

Miller, Colin, ed. see Christian Parenting Staff.

Miller, Connie. Feminist Research Methods: An Annotated Bibliography, 13. LC 91-3792. (Bibliographies & Indexes in Women's Studies: No. 13). 288p. 1991. lib. bdg. 65.00 (0-313-26029-X, MFT, Greenwood Pr) Greenwood.

Miller, Constance & Campbell, Kay. From the Ashes: A Head Injury Self-Advocacy Guide. 100p. (Orig.). 1987. pap. write for info. (0-318-62771-X) Phoenix Seattle.

— From the Ashes: A Head Injury Self-Advocacy Guide. (Illus.). 107p. (Orig.). 1987. student ed. 23.00 (0-9636594-0-5) Phoenix Seattle.

Miller, Constance, ed. see Dalai Lama XIV.

Miller, Constance O. Gazehounds: The Search for Truth. deluxe ed. (Illus.). 184p. 1995. pap. 30.00 (0-614-04524-X) Donald R Hoflin.

Miller, Constance O. & Gilbert, Edward M., Jr. The New Complete Afgan Hound. 4th rev. ed. (Illus.). 288p. 1988. pap. 25.95 (0-87605-001-1) Howell Bks.

Miller, Cookie, ed. see Blumin, Barbara.

Miller, Corki & Snodgrass, Mary Ellen. Storytellers: A Biographical Directory of 120 English-Speaking Performers Worldwide. LC 97-49075. (Illus.). 336p. 1998. boxed set 55.00 (0-7864-0470-1) McFarland & Co.

Miller, Corliss. Creative Ideas in Machine Embroidery. 96p. 1996. 19.95 (0-9629056-4-X) Quilters Res.

Miller, Corrine. Special Welcomes No. 3: Crazy about Crafting. 72p. 1994. pap. 10.50 (1-56770-309-7) S Scheewe Pubns.

Miller, Craig, ed. see Kenner, Corrine.

Miller, Craig K. Baby Boomer Spirituality: Ten Essential Values of a Generation. LC 91-72143. 192p. 1992. pap. 12.95 (0-88177-106-6, DR106) Discipleship Res.

— Encounters with Jesus: A Group Study in Baby Boomer Spirituality. LC 92-70576. 88p. 1992. pap. 9.95 (0-88177-113-9, DR113) Discipleship Res.

— PostModerns: The Beliefs, Hopes & Fears of Young Americans (1965-81) LC 95-83705. 192p. 1997. pap. 19.95 (0-88177-157-0, DR157) Discipleship Res.

Miller, Craig K. & Benedict, Daniel T. Contemporary Worship for the 21st Century: Worship or Evangelism? LC 94-68463. 136p. 1994. pap. 15.95 (0-88177-138-4, DR138) Discipleship Res.

***Miller, Craig K. & Icaza-Willetts, Lia.** Culture Shifts: A Group Bible Study for Postmodern Times. LC 97-77098. 112p. 1998. pap. 15.95 (0-88177-241-0, DR241) Discipleship Res.

***Miller, Craig Kennet.** Next Church. Now: Creating New Faith Communities. LC 99-68755. 192p. 2000. pap. text 21.95 (0-88177-293-3, DR293) Discipleship Res.

Miller, Craig R. & Shumway, Larry V. Social Dance in the Mormon West. Edison, Carol A., ed. 96p. 1998. pap. write for info. (0-9623975-4-7) Utah Arts Council.

Miller, Craig S., jt. auth. see Langlais, Robert P.

***Miller, Crane S. & Hysolp, Richard S.** California, the Geography of Diversity. 2nd rev. ed. viii, 295p. (C). 1999. pap. 40.95 (0-7674-1345-8) Mayfield Pub.

Miller, Cristanne. Emily Dickinson: A Poet's Grammar. 256p. 1987. pap. 16.00 (0-674-25036-2) HUP.

— Marianne Moore: Questions of Authority. LC 95-7167. 320p. (C). 1995. 43.00 (0-674-54862-0) HUP.

Miller, Cristanne, jt. ed. see Keller, Lynn.

Miller, Crow. Let's Get Growing: A Dirt-under-the-Nails Primer on Raising Vegetables, Fruits & Flowers Organically. (Illus.). 388p. 1995. 23.95 (0-87596-640-3) Rodale Pr Inc.

Miller, Crow, jt. auth. see Miller, Elizabeth.

Miller, Cynthia, tr. & illus. see Molina, Felipe S., ed.

Miller, Cynthia A., ed. Journal of the Senate of Virginia Session of 1798-1799. v, 92p. 1977. 10.00 (0-88490-010-X) Library of VA.

Miller, Cynthia D. Canine Adventures: Fun Things to Do with Your Dog. 1998. pap. text 19.95 (0-9649413-0-9) Animalia Pub.

— Creating a Peaceable Kingdom: How to Live with More Than One Pet. LC 95-83688. (Illus.). 242p. 1997. 24.95 (0-9649413-6-8) Animalia Pub.

Miller, Cynthia D., jt. ed. see Hart, John.

Miller, Cynthia L., ed. The Verbless Clause in Biblical Hebrew: Linguistic Approaches. LC 98-45884. (Linguistic Studies in Ancient West Semitic: Vol. 1). xii, 368p. 1999. text 39.50 (1-57506-036-1) Eisenbrauns.

Miller, Cynthia P. Challenges of the Heart. LC 90-21432. (Illus.). 144p. (Orig.). (YA). 1991. pap. 3.99 (0-932581-79-X) Word Aflame.

Miller, Cyral & Levack, Nancy. A Paraprofessional's Handbook for Working with Students Who Are Visually Impaired. LC 97-4158. 1997. write for info. (1-880366-21-5) TSBVI.

Miller, D. Above a Common Soldier: Frank & Mary Clark in the American West & Civil War from Letters, 1847-1872. rev. ed. LC 97-4686. 222p. 1997. 55.00 (0-8263-1799-5) U of NM Pr.

***Miller, D.** Grandma Emma's Cookbook. (Illus.). 47p. 1999. spiral bd. 4.95 (0-9670704-3-0) Abana Bks.

— Miller Family Cookbook. (Illus.). 167p. 1999. spiral bd. 9.95 (0-9670704-2-2) Abana Bks.

Miller, D. Soviet Navy. LC 88-11327. (Soviet Military Power Ser.). (Illus.). 48p. (J). (gr. 3-8). 1988. lib. bdg. 13.95 (0-685-58300-7) Rourke Corp.

— Soviet Navy. LC 88-11327. (Soviet Military Power Ser.). (Illus.). 48p. (J). (gr. 3-8). 1988. lib. bdg. 18.60 (0-86625-336-X) Rourke Pubns.

— Soviet Rocket Forces. LC 88-11367. (Soviet Military Power Ser.). (Illus.). 48p. (J). (gr. 3-8). 1988. lib. bdg. 13.95 (0-685-58297-3) Rourke Corp.

— Soviet Rocket Forces. LC 88-11367. (Soviet Military Power Ser.). (Illus.). 48p. (J). (gr. 3-8). 1988. lib. bdg. 18.60 (0-86625-333-5) Rourke Pubns.

— Soviet Submarines. (Soviet Military Power Ser.). (Illus.). 48p. (J). (gr. 3-8). 1987. lib. bdg. 13.95 (0-685-58296-5) Rourke Corp.

— Soviet Submarines. (Soviet Military Power Ser.). (Illus.). 48p. (J). (gr. 3-8). 1987. lib. bdg. 18.60 (0-86625-332-7) Rourke Pubns.

Miller, D., ed. Clinical Light Damage to the Eye. (Illus.). 180p. 1987. 199.00 (0-387-96451-7) Spr-Verlag.

***Miller, D. A.** Place for Us: Essay on the Broadway Musical. 160p. 2000. pap. 14.00 (0-674-00388-8) HUP.

Miller, D. A. Bringing Out Roland Barthes. 1992. pap. 14.95 (0-520-07948-5, Pub. by U CA Pr) Cal Prin Full Svc.

— Forbidden Knowledge... or Is It. 3rd ed. 256p. 1998. pap. 11.95 (0-939513-89-7) Joy Pub SJC.

— The Novel & the Police. 1988. pap. 15.95 (0-520-06746-0, Pub. by U CA Pr) Cal Prin Full Svc.

— Place for Us: Essay on the Broadway Musical. LC 98-15685. (Illus.). 160p. 1998. 22.00 (0-674-66990-8) HUP.

Miller, D. A., jt. auth. see Barthes, Roland.

Miller, D. Douglas & Highsmith, Anne L., compiled by. Heinrich Schutz: A Bibliography of the Collected Works & Performing Editions, 9. LC 86-7610. (Music Reference Collection: No. 9). 295p. 1986. lib. bdg. 55.00 (0-313-24884-2, MHZ/) Greenwood.

Miller, D. F. & Aubin, L. X. St. Alphonsus Liguori: Bishop, Confessor, Founder of the Redemptorist & Doctor of the Church. LC 87-51071. Orig. Title: Saint Alphonsus Mary de' Liquori - Founder, Bishop, & Doctor (1696-1780). 388p. 1992. reprint ed. pap. 16.50 (0-89555-329-5) TAN Bks Pubs.

An Asterisk (*) at the beginning of an entry indicates that the title is appearing for the first time.

Miller, D. Gary. Ancient Scripts & Phonological Knowledge. LC 94-28635. (Current Issues in Linguistic Theory Ser.: No. 116). xvi, 139p. 1994. lib. bdg. 35.00 (*1-55619-570-2*) J Benjamins Pubng Co.
— Complex Verb Formation. LC 92-34479. (Current Issues in Linguistic Theory Ser.: No. 95). xx, 381p. 1993. 83.00 (*1-55619-156-1*) J Benjamins Pubng Co.
Miller, D. Larry. God's Vitamin "C" for the Spirit of Men: "Tug-at-the-Heart" Stories to Encourage & Strengthen Your Spirit. LC 96-68838. 304p. 1996. pap. 12.95 (*0-914984-81-0*) Starburst.
— Men of the Bible: God's Word for the Biblically-Inept. Richards, Larry, ed. (God's Word for the Biblically-Inept Ser.: Vol. 5). (Illus.). 352p. 2000. pap. 16.95 (*1-892016-07-9*) Starburst.
Miller, D. Larry, jt. auth. see Miller, Kathy C.
Miller, D. Larry, jt. compiled by see Miller, Kathy Collard.
Miller, D. Larry, jt. compiled by see Miller, Kathy C.
Miller, D. M. The Evolution of God. LC 97-90302. 1997. pap. 12.95 (*0-533-12357-7*) Vantage.
Miller, D. Patrick. The Book of Practical Faith. 75p. 1999. reprint ed. pap. 12.95 (*0-9656809-2-4*) Fearless Bks.
— The Book of Practical Faith: A Path of Useful Spirituality. LC 95-16502. 88p. 1995. 14.95 (*0-8050-4179-6*) H Holt & Co.
— The Complete Story of the Course: The History, the People, & the Controversies Behind "A Course in Miracles" LC 97-60088. 240p. (Orig.). 1997. per. 15.95 (*0-9656809-0-8*) Fearless Bks.
Miller, D. Patrick. The Complete Story of the Course: The History, the People & the Controversies Behind "A Course in Miracles", Set. abr. ed. 1997. pap. 16.95 incl. audio (*1-55927-453-0*) Audio Renaissance.
Miller, D. Patrick. A Little Book of Forgiveness: Challenges & Meditations for Anyone with Something to Forgive. 90p. 1999. reprint ed. pap. 12.95 (*0-9656809-1-6*) Fearless Bks.
***Miller, D. Patrick.** Love after Life. 240p. 2000. pap. 14.95 (*0-9656809-3-2*) Fearless Bks.
Miller, D. Patrick, jt. auth. see Rusk, Tom.
Miller, D. Quentin, ed. Re-Viewing James Baldwin: Things Not Seen. LC 99-33993. (Illus.). 312p. 2000. 69.50 (*1-56639-736-7*); pap. 22.95 (*1-56639-737-5*) Temple U Pr.
Miller, D. S. Discharge Characteristics. LC 99-227542. (Hydraulic Structures Design Manual Ser.: Vol. 8). (Illus.). 270p. (C). 1994. 142.00 (*90-5410-180-6*, Pub. by A A Balkema) Ashgate Pub Co.
— Internal Flow Systems. 2nd rev. ed. 364p. (C). 1990. 79.00 (*0-947711-77-5*, Pub. by BHRA Fluid) U of Ill Pr.
Miller, Dale. Dale Miller/Country, Blues & Ragtime Guitar Styles. 44p. 1996. pap. 17.95 incl. audio compact disk (*0-7866-2711-5*, 96557BCD) Mel Bay.
— Fingers Don't Fail Me Now: Intermediate Level. 96p. 1997. pap. 19.95 incl. audio compact disk (*0-7866-2658-5*, 96514BCD) Mel Bay.
Miller, Dale, ed. Logic Programming: Proceedings of the '93 International Symposium, Vancouver, British Columbia, October 26-29, 1993, Reports & Notes. (Logic Programming Ser.). (Illus.). 708p. 1993. pap. text 82.50 (*0-262-63152-0*) MIT Pr.
Miller, Dale & Miller, Patricia. The Gospel of Mark As Midrash on Earlier Jewish & New Testament Sacred Literature. LC 90-32887. (Studies in Bible & Early Christianity: Vol. 21). 408p. 1990. lib. bdg. 109.95 (*0-88946-621-1*) E Mellen.
Miller, Dale, jt. ed. see Prentice, Deborah.
Miller, Dale E. Rhymes Without Reason. Wightman, Heather, ed. (Illus.). 90p. 1997. pap. write for info. (*1-888911-04-2*) Benson Smythe.
Miller, Dale E., jt. auth. see Ching, Francis D. K.
Miller, Dan. 48 Days to the Work You Love. Miller, Joanne, ed. 85p. 1996. write for info. (*0-9659072-0-1*) Busn Source.
— Living, Laughing & Loving Life. LC 97-60589. 128p. 1997. pap. 9.95 (*1-57921-020-1*, Pub. by WinePress Pub) BookWorld.
— Look with the Heart. 365p. 1998. 24.95 (*0-9653086-2-6*) Phoenix Images.
***Miller, Dan.** Xing Yi Nei Gong. (Illus.). 200p. 1999. pap. 19.95 (*0-86568-174-0*) Unique Pubns.
***Miller, Dan, ed.** Flatpicking Collection - 1997 Annual Edition. 80p. 1998. pap. 19.95 incl. audio compact disk (*0-7866-3867-2*, 97342BCD) Mel Bay.
Miller, Dan, et al, eds. Critical Paths: Blake & the Argument of Method. LC 87-13514. (Illus.). xii, 382p. (C). 1987. text 59.95 (*0-8223-0751-0*); pap. text 24.95 (*0-8223-0792-8*) Duke.
Miller, Dan & Nam, Park B. The Fundamentals of Pa Kua Chang: The Methods of Lu Shui-Tien As Taught by Park Bok Nam. 204p. 1993. pap. 19.95 (*1-883175-01-1*) High View Pubns.
Miller, Dan, jt. auth. see Cartnell, Tim.
Miller, Dan, jt. auth. see Nelson, Bradley J.
Miller, Dan, jt. auth. see Weibel, Michael R.
Miller, Dan E., et al, eds. Constructing Complexity: Symbolic Interaction & Social Forms. LC 98-205519. (Studies in Symbolic Interaction: Supplement 3). 1997. 73.25 (*0-7623-0251-8*) Jai Pr.
***Miller, Dana R., et al, trs. from ENG.** Miracles & Monasteries of 17th-Century Ukraine. (Harvard Library of Early Ukrainian Literature: Vol. 10). 350p. (C). 2000. text 39.95 (*0-916458-81-4*) Harvard Ukrainian.
Miller, Dana R., ed. see Kopystens'kyj, Zaxarija.
Miller, Daniel. Capitalism: An Ethnographic Approach. LC 96-35850. (Explorations in Anthropology Ser.). 384p. 1997. 60.00 (*1-85973-123-6*, Pub. by Berg Pubs); pap. 24.95 (*1-85973-128-7*, Pub. by Berg Pubs) NYU Pr.
— Forging Political Compromise: Antonin Svehla & the Czechoslovak Republican Party, 1918-1933. LC 99-6111. (Pitt Series in Russian & East European Studies). (Illus.). 454p. 1999. text 45.00 (*0-8229-4091-4*) U of Pittsburgh Pr.
— Material Cultures: Why Some Things Matter. LC 97-31175. 256p. 1998. pap. 22.00 (*0-226-52601-1*); lib. bdg. 45.00 (*0-226-52600-3*) U Ch Pr.
— Modernity - An Ethnographic Approach: Dualism & Mass Consumption in Trinidad. LC 93-23406. 340p. 1994. 49.50 (*0-85496-916-0*, Pub. by Berg Pubs); pap. 19.50 (*0-85496-917-9*, Pub. by Berg Pubs) NYU Pr.
— Shopping, Place, & Identity. LC 97-35292. 240p. (C). 1998. pap. 27.99 (*0-415-15461-8*) Routledge.
— Shopping, Place, & Identity. LC 97-35292. (Illus.). 232p. (C). 1998. 85.00 (*0-415-15460-X*) Routledge.
— Starting a Small Restaurant: A Guide to Excellence in the Purveying of Public Victuals. rev. ed. LC 83-6188. 224p. (Orig.). 1983. pap. 12.95 (*0-916782-37-9*) Harvard Common Pr.
— A Theory of Shopping. LC 97-51720. 180p. 1998. text 39.95 (*0-8014-3555-2*); pap. text 16.95 (*0-8014-8551-7*) Cornell U Pr.
Miller, Daniel, ed. Acknowledging Consumption. LC 94-37293. (Material Cultures Ser.). (Illus.). 304p. (C). 1995. pap. 29.99 (*0-415-10689-3*, C0227) Routledge.
— Unwrapping Christmas. (Oxford Studies in Social & Cultural Anthropology). (Illus.). 250p. 1995. pap. text 22.00 (*0-19-828066-1*) OUP.
— Worlds Apart: Modernity Through the Prism of the Local. LC 94-46805. (Uses of Knowledge Ser.). 240p. (C). 1995. pap. 27.99 (*0-415-10789-X*) Routledge.
— Worlds Apart: Modernity Through the Prism of the Local. LC 94-46805. (Uses of Knowledge Ser.). 240p. (C). (gr. 13). 1995. 85.00 (*0-415-10788-1*) Routledge.
Miller, Daniel, et al, eds. Domination & Resistance. LC 95-274. (One World Archaeology Ser.). (Illus.). 352p. (C). 1995. pap. 34.99 (*0-415-12254-6*, C0587) Routledge.
***Miller, Daniel & Slater, Don.** The Internet: An Ethnographic Approach. 224p. 2000. 65.00 (*1-85973-384-0*, Pub. by Berg Pubs); pap. 19.50 (*1-85973-389-1*, Pub. by Berg Pubs) NYU Pr.
Miller, Daniel, jt. auth. see Dethy, Ray C.
Miller, Daniel, jt. ed. see Carrier, James G.
Miller, Daniel E. & Qiu, Li, eds. Topics in Control & Its Applications: A Tribute to Edward J. Davison. LC 98-52347. 212p. 1999. 84.00 (*1-85233-150-X*) Spr-Verlag.
Miller, Daniel J. & Lea, Robert N. Guide to the Coastal Marine Fishes of California. 249p. 1972. reprint ed. pap. 9.50 (*0-931876-13-3*, 4065) ANR Pubns CA.
Miller, Daniel R., ed. Coming of Age: Protestantism in Contemporary Latin America. (Calvin College Ser.: Vol. I). 265p. (Orig.). lib. bdg. 56.50 (*0-8191-9406-9*) U Pr of Amer.
— Coming of Age: Protestantism in Contemporary Latin America. (Calvin College Ser.: Vol. I). 265p. (Orig.). 1994. pap. text 27.50 (*0-8191-9407-7*) U Pr of Amer.
Miller, Daniel W. The Unseen Universe: Of Mind & Matter. 2nd rev. ed. 330p. (Orig.). 1996. reprint ed. pap. 12.95 (*0-9638055-1-7*) Beyond Realm.
— The Web & the Cloth: The Making of Homeodynamic Systems. Rogers, Marion, ed. LC 98-92941. (Unseen Universe Ser.: No. 2). Orig. Title: The Homeodynamic Universe. (Illus.). 275p. (Orig.). 1998. pap. 12.95 (*0-9638055-2-5*) Beyond Realm.
Miller, Danny. The Icarus Paradox: How Exceptional Companies Bring about Their Own Downfall. 256p. 1990. 19.95 (*0-88730-453-2*, HarpBusn) HarpInfo.
— Icarus Paradox: How Exceptional Companies Bring about Their Own Downfall. LC 90-5039. 320p. 1992. pap. 12.00 (*0-88730-524-5*, HarpBusn) HarpInfo.
Miller, Danny, jt. auth. see Kets de Vries, Manfred F.
Miller, Danny, jt. auth. see Quintana, Kathy.
Miller, Danny L. Wingless Flights: Appalachian Women in Fiction. LC 96-30729. (Illus.). 187p. 1996. 35.95 (*0-87972-717-9*); pap. 21.95 (*0-87972-718-7*) Bowling Green Univ Popular Press.
Miller, Danny L., ed. & intro. see Pace, Mildred M.
Miller, Darcy. Enhancing Adolescent Competence: Strategies for Classroom Management. LC 97-32400. (C). 1997. 48.95 (*0-534-53843-6*) Wadsworth Pub.
Miller, Darcy, jt. auth. see Miller, Kathy C.
Miller, Dare. Dog Master System. LC 75-36106. 1997. 19.95 (*0-686-22367-5*); pap. 9.95 (*0-686-22368-3*) Dog Master.
Miller, Darla. First Steps Toward Cultural Difference: Socialization in Infant-Toddler Day Care. 112p. 1989. 8.50 (*0-87868-351-8*) Child Welfare.
Miller, Darla F. Positive Child Guidance. 2nd ed. 312p. (C). 1995. pap. 29.75 (*0-8273-5878-4*) Delmar.
Miller, Darla F. Positive Child Guidance. 3rd ed. LC 99-34456. (Early Childhood Education Ser.). 366p. (C). 1999. pap. 37.95 (*0-7668-0360-0*) Delmar.
Miller, Darlene. Your Shape, Your Clothes & You: Secrets of a Successful Wardrobe. rev. ed. (Illus.). 80p. 1994. 14.95 (*0-9642936-0-9*) Clothes For You.
Miller, Darlis A. Across the Plains in 1864 with Additional Paymaster Samuel C. Staples. 96p. 1980. pap. text 27.95 (*0-89126-098-6*) MA-AH Pub.
— Captain Jack Crawford: Buckskin Poet, Scout, & Showman. LC 93-8611. (Illus.). 385p. reprint ed. pap. 119.40 (*0-608-04115-7*, 206484800011) Bks Demand.
Miller, Darrow L. Discipling Nations: The Power of Truth to Transform Cultures. 306p. 1998. pap. 14.99 (*1-57658-015-6*) YWAM Pub.
Miller, Daryl E., jt. auth. see Burton, Allen W.
Miller, Dave. Brewing the World's Great Beers: A Step-By-Step Guide. Watson, Ben, ed. LC 91-50605. (Illus.). 160p. 1992. 22.95 (*0-88266-776-9*); pap. 12.95 (*0-88266-775-0*) Storey Bks.
— The Complete Handbook of Home Brewing. Clarkson, Sarah M., ed. LC 87-46447. (Illus.). 248p. 1988. 19.95 (*0-88266-522-7*, Garden Way Pub); pap. 12.95 (*0-88266-517-0*, Garden Way Pub) Storey Bks.
— Continental Pilsener. (Classic Beer Style Ser.). 101p. 1990. pap. 11.95 (*0-937381-20-9*) Brewers Pubns.
— Dave Miller's Homebrewing Guide: Everything You Need To know to Make Great Tasting Beer. LC 95-13385. 296p. 1995. pap. 16.95 (*0-88266-905-2*) Storey Bks.
— Singing & New Testament Worship. 1994. pap. 5.45 (*0-89137-144-3*) Quality Pubns.
Miller, Dave & Blum, Kenneth. Overload: Attention Deficit Disorder & the Addictive Brain. 224p. 1995. pap. 10.95 (*0-8362-0460-3*) Andrews & McMeel.
Miller, Dave, ed. see St. Claire, Mary.
Miller, David. Appearance & Event. 32p. 1997. pap. 5.00 (*0-945926-49-9*, Pub. by Paradigm RI) SPD-Small Pr Dist.
— Art & Disclosure: Seven Essays. LC 99-218968. 1998. 11.95 (*1-900152-30-4*, Pub. by Stride Pubns) SPD-Small Pr Dist.
***Miller, David.** Brassey's Book of the Crusades. (Illus.). 2001. 29.95 (*1-57488-292-9*) Brasseys.
— Citizenship & National Identity. LC 99-58780. 240p. 2000. text 59.95 (*0-7456-2393-X*, Pub. by Polity Pr); pap. text 27.95 (*0-7456-2394-8*, Pub. by Polity Pr) Blackwell Pubs.
— Cold War: A Military History. LC 99-46757. 480p. 1999. text 27.95 (*0-312-24183-6*) St Martin.
Miller, David. Collected Poems. 109p. 1997. pap. 14.95 (*3-7052-0971-X*, Pub. by Poetry Salzburg) Intl Spec Bk.
***Miller, David.** Commentaries, Vol. II. 10p. 2000. pap. 5.00 (*1-57141-052-X*) Runaway Spoon.
Miller, David. Commodore One Twenty-Eight File Programming. (Illus.). 300p. (Orig.). (C). 1987. 21.95 (*0-8306-0205-4*, 2805) McGraw-Hill Prof.
— Commodore 128 Data File Program. 1991. 24.95 (*0-8306-6429-7*) McGraw-Hill Prof.
— Critical Rationalism: A Restatement & Defence. 277p. 1994. 44.95 (*0-8126-9197-0*); pap. 19.95 (*0-8126-9198-9*) Open Court.
— Cup Magic. LC 81-144073. 1981. write for info. (*0-283-98697-2*) S1 & J.
— Dark Eden: The Swamp in Nineteenth-Century American Culture. (Cambridge Studies in American Literature & Culture: No. 43). (Illus.). 337p. (C). 1990. text 69.95 (*0-521-37553-3*) Cambridge U Pr.
— Don't Mention the War: Northern Ireland, Propaganda & the Media. 280p. (C). 1994. 59.95 (*0-7453-0835-X*, Pub. by Pluto GBR); pap. 17.95 (*0-7453-0836-8*, Pub. by Pluto GBR) Stylus Pub VA.
***Miller, David.** Dying to Care? Work, Stress & Burnout in HIV/AIDS Carers. LC 99-42155. (Social Aspects of AIDS Ser.). 2000. write for info. (*1-85728-821-1*, Pub. by UCL Pr Ltd) Taylor & Francis.
— The Illustrated Directory of Tanks & Fighting Vehicles. (Illus.). 480p. 2000. pap. 11.95 (*0-7603-0892-6*, 130173AP, Pub. by MBI Pubg) Motorbooks Intl.
— Just Like You & Me. LC 00-22707. (Illus.). (J). 2001. write for info. (*0-8037-2586-8*, Dial Yng Read) Peng Put Young Read.
— Lady De Lancey's Narrative: A Story of Duty & Devotion. 224p. 2000. 80.00 (*1-86227-082-1*, Pub. by Spellmnt Pubs) St Mut.
— Lord of Bellavista: The Dramatic Story of a Prison Transformed. 1999. pap. text 10.95 (*0-281-05128-3*) Abingdon.
Miller, David. Macintosh Data Files. (Illus.). 232p. 14.95 (*0-685-09444-8*) P-H.
— Market, State, & Community: Theoretical Foundations of Market Socialism. 370p. 1991. pap. text 35.00 (*0-19-827864-0*) OUP.
— On Nationality. (Oxford Political Theory Ser.). 220p. 1997. reprint ed. pap. text 19.95 (*0-19-829356-9*) OUP.
— Primavera: Poems. deluxe ed. (Burning Deck Poetry Chapbooks Ser.). 1979. pap. 15.00 (*0-930900-63-4*) Burning Deck.
— Principles of Social Justice. LC 99-21281. 384p. 1999. 45.00 (*0-674-70628-5*) HUP.
— Rethink Northern Ireland. LC 98-28732. 344p. (C). 1998. pap. text 34.60 (*0-582-30287-0*) Longman.
***Miller, David.** Samurai Warriors. (Illus.). 128p. 1999. 24.95 (*0-312-24167-4*) St Martin.
Miller, David. Seals & Sea Lions. LC 97-44771. (WorldLife Library). (Illus.). 84p. (Orig.). (YA). (gr. 5 up). 1998. pap. 16.95 (*0-89658-371-6*) Voyageur Pr.
— Social Justice. 376p. 1979. pap. text 28.00 (*0-19-824621-8*) OUP.
***Miller, David.** Special Forces: The Men, the Weapons & the Operations. 1999. 29.95 (*1-84065-021-4*) Salamander.
Miller, David. Stromata: Poems. (Poetry Ser.). 64p. 1994. pap. 8.00 (*0-930901-96-7*, PR9619.3.M47S77) Burning Deck.
— Stromata: Poems. limited ed. (Poetry Ser.). 64p. 1994. pap. 15.00 (*0-930901-97-5*) Burning Deck.
Miller, David. Submarines of the World LC 99-177982. 189p. 1991. write for info. (*0-86101-562-2*, Pub. by Salamander) Combined Pub.
— U-Boats: A Comprehensive Illustrated History. (Illus.). 2000. 27.95 (*1-57488-246-5*) Brasseys.
— U-Boats: The Illustrated History of the Raiders of the Deep. (Illus.). 192p. 1999. 19.98 (*0-7624-0527-9*) Running Pr.
Miller, David. Unity. 32p. (Orig.). 1981. pap. 3.00 (*0-935162-03-8*) Singing Horse.
— Web Multimedia Development. 600p. 1996. 44.99 (*1-56205-683-2*) New Riders Pub.
***Miller, David.** The Wisdom of the Eye. 275p. 2000. 49.95 (*0-12-496860-0*) Acad Pr.
Miller, David. The Wreck of the Isabella. LC 95-67721. (Illus.). 272p. 1995. 27.95 (*1-55750-768-6*) Naval Inst Pr.
— The Wreck of the Isabella: Naval Actions During the Napoleonic Wars. (Illus.). 259p. 1995. 42.50 (*0-85052-456-3*, Pub. by Leo Cooper) Trans-Atl Phila.
— You Can Do Thousands of Things with String. 48p. (J). (gr. 3-7). 1996. pap. text 6.95 (*1-86373-959-9*) IPG Chicago.
— You Can Make Paper Sculptures. (Illus.). 48p. (Orig.). (J). (gr. 3-7). 1996. pap. 6.95 (*1-86373-863-0*, Pub. by Allen & Unwin Pty) IPG Chicago.
Miller, David, ed. Blackwell Encyclopedia of Political Thought. 1991. pap. 35.95 (*0-631-17944-5*) Blackwell Pubs.
***Miller, David, ed.** Illustrated Book of Guns: An Illustrated Directory of over 1000 Military & Sporting Firearms. (Illus.). 2000. pap. 34.95 (*1-84065-172-5*, Pub. by Salamander) Combined Pub.
Miller, David, ed. Liberty. (Oxford Readings in Politics & Government Ser.). 232p. 1991. 65.00 (*0-19-878041-9*, 12225) OUP.
Miller, David & Effler, James M. Dynamic Airbrush. (Illus.). 176p. 1996. pap. 24.99 (*0-89134-699-6*, North Lght Bks) F & W Pubns Inc.
Miller, David & Martin, Diana. Getting Started in Airbrush. LC 93-682. (Illus.). 128p. 1993. pap. 24.99 (*0-89134-479-9*, 30514, North Lght Bks) F & W Pubns Inc.
***Miller, David & Spick, Mike.** Battle-Winning Weapons of World War II. (Illus.). 272p. 2000. 29.95 (*0-7603-0968-X*, 130747AP, Pub. by MBI Pubg) Motorbooks Intl.
Miller, David & Walzer, Michael, eds. Pluralism, Justice, & Equality. (Illus.). 318p. 1995. pap. text 21.00 (*0-19-828008-4*) OUP.
Miller, David & Woodford Publishing Editors. Atlanta '96: The Official Commemorative Book of the Centennial Olympic Games. LC 96-60617. (Illus.). 208p. 1996. 25.95 (*0-942627-29-6*) Woodford Pubng.
Miller, David, jt. auth. see Bennett, Lydia.
Miller, David, jt. auth. see Miller, Merlene.
Miller, David, jt. auth. see Random House Value Publishing Staff.
Miller, David, jt. auth. see Stegmaier, Mark J.
Miller, David, jt. ed. see Bonasso, Pete.
Miller, David, ed. see Chambers, Maggie.
Miller, David, ed. see Popper, Karl R.
Miller, David, ed. see Rolston, Bill.
Miller, David, tr. see Cuza-Male, Belkis.
Miller, David A. Die Schwertertraeger der Wehrmacht: Recipients of the Knight's Cross with Oakleaves & Swords. 3rd rev. ed. (World War II Monograph: Vol. 298). 62p. 1997. 16.95 (*1-57638-073-4*, M298H); pap. 6.95 (*1-57638-025-4*, M298S) Merriam Pr.
Miller, David A., 2nd. The First 100 Years of the Lutheran Home at Topton: A Gift of Love. 304p. 1995. lib. bdg. 19.95 (*0-9648388-0-X*) Lutheran Home.
Miller, David A. Prophetic Secrets & the New World Order. LC 97-60986. 192p. 1997. per. 7.95 (*1-57258-089-5*) Teach Servs.
Miller, David C. American Iconology: New Approaches to Nineteenth Century Art & Literature. 1995. pap. 19.00 (*0-300-06514-0*) Yale U Pr.
Miller, David C., ed. American Iconology: New Approaches to Nineteenth-Century Art & Literature. LC 92-46082. (Illus.). 360p. 1993. 45.00 (*0-300-05478-5*) Yale U Pr.
Miller, David D. Open VMS Operating System Concepts. 2nd ed. LC 97-7963. 541p. 1997. pap. text 49.95 (*1-55558-157-9*, Digital DEC) Buttrwrth-Heinemann.
Miller, David E. Great Salt Lake: Past & Present. 5th rev. ed. Eckman, Lawrence L. & Eckman, Anne M., eds. (Illus.). 50p. (Orig.). 1994. pap. 5.00 (*0-9639924-0-6*) Utah Hist Atlas.
— Hole In the Rock. Eckman, Lawrence L. & Eckman, Anne M., eds. (Illus.). 231p. (C). reprint ed. pap. 12.95 (*0-9639924-1-4*) Utah Hist Atlas.
— Hole in the Rock: An Epic in the Colonization of the Great American West. 2nd ed. LC 66-22142. (Illus.). 261p. reprint ed. pap. 81.00 (*0-8357-6426-5*, 203579400097) Bks Demand.
— Living Trust Handbook. 216p. 1991. pap. 20.00 (*0-9627178-0-0*) D E Miller Law.
— Occupational Safety, Health, & Fire Index: A Source Guide to Voluntary & Obligatory Regulations, Codes Standards & Publications. LC 76-12285. (Occupational Safety & Health Ser.: Vol. 1). 224p. reprint ed. pap. 69.50 (*0-608-16736-3*, 202782300054) Bks Demand.
— The Ten Commands of Christian Parenting. (Illus.). 182p. (Orig.). 1996. pap. 8.95 (*1-883928-15-X*) Longwood.
Miller, David E. & Miller, Della S. Nauvoo: The City of Joseph. 2nd ed. (Illus.). 280p. Date not set. reprint ed. pap. 14.95 (*0-9639924-2-2*) Utah Hist Atlas.
Miller, David G. The Word Made Flesh Made Word: The Failure & Redemption of Metaphor in Edward Taylor's Christographia. LC 95-18468. 152p. 1995. 29.50 (*0-945636-85-7*) Susquehanna U Pr.
Miller, David H. The Alaska Treaty. (Alaska History Ser.: No. 18). (Illus.). 1981. 18.00 (*0-919642-95-0*) Limestone Pr.
— Custer's Fall: The Indian Side of the Story. 288p. 1992. pap. 13.95 (*0-452-01095-0*, Mer) NAL.
— The Drafting of the Covenant, 2 vols. 1412p. 1998. reprint ed. 285.00 (*1-56169-427-4*) Gaunt.
— Snow Cover & Climate in the Sierra Nevada, California. LC 55-9597. (University of California Publications in Social Welfare: Vol. 11). 226p. reprint ed. pap. 70.10 (*0-608-18653-8*, 202127100022) Bks Demand.
— Water at the Surface of the Earth: Student Edition. LC 82-13769. (International Geophysics Ser.). (C). 1982. pap. text 78.00 (*0-12-496752-3*) Acad Pr.

M

Miller, David H., et al. Magnetic Resonance in Multiple Sclerosis. LC 96-21044. (Illus.). 210p. (C). 1997. text 90.00 (*0-521-47325-X*) Cambridge U Pr.

Miller, David J., et al. Photon, '95: Gamma-Gamma Collisions: Proceedings of the IXth International Workshop. LC 95-41305. 470p. 1995. 112.00 (*981-02-2473-7*) World Scientific Pub.

Miller, David J. & Hersen, Michel, eds. Research Fraud in the Behavioral & Biomedical Sciences. LC 91-21625. 272p. 1992. 99.95 (*0-471-52068-3*) Wiley.

Miller, David K. Measurement by the Physical Educator: Why & How. 2nd ed. 400p. (C). 1993. text. write for info. (*0-697-16621-X*) Brown & Benchmark.

— Measurement by the Physical Educator: Why & How. 3rd ed. LC 97-187893. 352p. (C). 1997. text. write for info. (*0-697-29488-9*) Brown & Benchmark.

Miller, David K. & Allen, T. Earl. Fitness: A Lifetime Commitment. 5th ed. LC 93-45699. (Illus.). 352p. (C). 1994. pap. text 26.00 (*0-02-381292-3*, Macmillan Coll) P-H.

Miller, David L. George Herbert Mead: Self, Language & the World. LC 80-14725. 324p. 1993. pap. text 7.95 (*0-226-52613-5*, P910) U Ch Pr.

***Miller, David L.** Introduction to Collective Behavior & Collective Action. 2nd ed. 504p. (C). 2000. pap. 37.95 (*1-57766-105-2*) Waveland Pr.

Miller, David L. Patient or Profit. LC 97-91262. 1998. 8.95 (*0-533-12614-2*) Vantage.

— The Poem's Two Bodies: The Poetics of the 1590 Faerie Queene. LC PR2358.M48. 311p. 1991. reprint ed. pap. 96.50 (*0-608-02541-0*, 206318500004) Bks Demand.

Miller, David L., et al, eds. The Production of English Renaissance Culture. (Illus.). 336p. 1994. text 42.50 (*0-8014-2961-7*); pap. text 16.95 (*0-8014-8201-1*) Cornell U Pr.

Miller, David L. & Dunlop, Alexander, eds. Approaches to Teaching Spenser's The Faerie Queene. LC 94-5713. (Approaches to Teaching World Literature Ser.: Vol. 50). ix, 207p. (Orig.). 1994. pap. 18.00 (*0-87352-724-0*, AP50P); lib. bdg. 37.50 (*0-87352-723-2*, AP50C) Modern Lang.

Miller, David L., jt. ed. see Jay, Gregory S.

Miller, David L., ed. see Mead, George Herbert.

Miller, David L., jt. ed. see Puligandla, Ramakrishma.

Miller, David M. Frank Herbert. Schlobin, Roger C., ed. LC 80-20880. (Starmont Reader's Guide Ser.: Vol. 5). 70p. 1980. pap. 13.00 (*0-916732-07-X*) Millefleurs.

— John Milton: Poetry. (English Authors Ser.: No. 242). 200p. 1978. 28.95 (*0-8057-6724-X*) Macmillan.

Miller, David M., et al, eds. Tectonic & Stratigraphic Studies in the Eastern Great Basin. LC 83-5632. (Geological Society of America Ser.: Vol. 157). (Illus.). 334p. 1983. reprint ed. pap. 103.60 (*0-608-07709-7*, 206779700010) Bks Demand.

Miller, David M. & Busby, Cathy, eds. Jurassic Magmatism & Tectonics of the North American Cordillera. LC 95-20090. (Special Papers: No. 299). (Illus.). 425p. 1995. pap. 95.00 (*0-8137-2299-3*) Geol Soc.

Miller, David M. & Lush, Andrew P. Geologic Map of the Pilot Peak Quadrangle, Box Elder County, Utah & Elko County, Nevada. (Map of the Utah Geological Survey Ser.: Vol. 160). (Illus.). 25p. 1994. pap. 6.00 (*1-55791-562-8*, M-160) Utah Geological Survey.

Miller, David M. & Wertz, Dorothy C. Hindu Monastic Life: The Monks & Monasteries of Bhubaneswar. 1996. 52.00 (*81-7304-156-3*, Pub. by Manohar) S Asia.

Miller, David N. Bibliography of Isaac Bashevis Singer, 1924-1949. LC 83-47647. 315p. (Orig.). (C). 1984. pap. text 28.95 (*0-8204-0002-5*) P Lang Pubng.

— Recovering the Canon: Essays on Isaac Bashevis Singer. (Studies in Judaism in Modern Times: Vol. 8). xxii, 154p. 1986. 49.00 (*90-04-07681-6*) Brill Academic Pubs.

Miller, David N., jt. ed. see Lambropoulos, Vassilis.

Miller, David P. & Reill, Peter H., eds. Visions of Empire: Voyages, Botany, & Representations of Nature. (Illus.). 387p. (C). 1996. text 64.95 (*0-521-48303-4*) Cambridge U Pr.

Miller, David S., et al. Directory of Archival & Manuscript Repositories in the Delaware Valley. 2nd ed. LC 98-86652. xii, 36 p. 1998. write for info. (*0-9665984-0-7*) City of Philly Dept Records.

Miller, David S., jt. auth. see Keyes, Thomas R.

Miller, David W. Church, State, & Nation in Ireland, 1898-1921. LC 72-95453. 589p. reprint ed. pap. 182.60 (*0-608-15676-0*, 203199200077) Bks Demand.

— The Courts' View of Regulation at the Federal Energy Regulatory Commission, 2 vols. LC 89-147208. 1048p. 1988. ring bd. 170.00 (*0-685-29078-6*) Norland Pr.

— Dead Lawyers & Other Pleasant Thoughts. LC 92-56804. 96p. 1993. pap. 10.95 (*0-679-74441-X*) Random.

— Fitting Frequency Distributions: Philosophy & Practice, 2 vols., Set. 825p. (Orig.). 1995. pap., spiral bd. 70.00 (*0-9653534-3-5*) Miller Ideas.

— Fitting Frequency Distributions: Philosophy & Practice, Vol. 1: Discrete Distributions. 359p. (Orig.). 1995. pap., spiral bd. write for info. (*0-9653534-1-9*) Miller Ideas.

— Fitting Frequency Distributions: Philosophy & Practice, Vol. 2: Continuous Distributions. (Orig.). 1995. pap., spiral bd. write for info. (*0-9653534-2-7*) Miller Ideas.

***Miller, David W.** Second Only to Grant: Quartermaster General Montgomery C. Meigs. (Illus.). 352p. 2000. 40.00 (*1-57249-212-0*, WM Books) White Mane Pub.

Miller, David W. & Starr, Martin K. Structure of Human Decisions. (Orig.). 1967. pap. text 13.95 (*0-13-854687-8*) P-H.

Miller, David W., jt. auth. see Yerkes, Kenneth J.

Miller, David W., jt. ed. see Brown, Stewart J.

Miller, Davina. Export or Die: Britain's Defence Trade with Iran & Iraq. LC 96-41707. 247p. 1996. 89.50 (*0-304-33852-4*) Continuum.

***Miller, Davis.** The Tao of Bruce Lee: A Martial Arts Memoir. LC 99-87697. (Illus.). 240p. 2000. 23.00 (*0-609-60477-5*, BIO005000) Harmony Bks.

— The Tao of Muhammad Ali. LC 98-56510. 336p. 1999. pap. 14.00 (*0-609-80453-7*, Three Riv Pr) Crown Pub Group.

Miller, Dawn. David Robinson: Backboard Admiral. (Illus.). 64p. (J). (gr. 4-9). 1991. pap. 4.95 (*0-8225-9600-8*, First Ave Edns); lib. bdg. 18.60 (*0-8225-0494-4*, Lerner Publctns) Lerner Pub.

— The Journal of Callie Wade. 336p. 1996. 20.00 (*0-671-52100-4*) PB.

— The Journals of Callie Wade. 288p. 1998. mass mkt. 6.50 (*0-671-52101-2*) S&S Trade.

— Letters to Callie. 1999. 25.01 (*0-671-52102-0*) S&S Trade.

Miller, Dayton C. Catalogue of Books & Literary Material Relating to the Flute & Other Musical Instruments. 1988. reprint ed. lib. bdg. 59.00 (*0-7812-0679-0*) Rprt Serv.

— Catalogue of Books & Literary Material Relating to the Flute & Other Musical Instruments, with Annotations. LC 72-181210. 29.00 (*0-403-01621-5*) Scholarly.

— The Science of Musical Sounds. 286p. 1990. reprint ed. lib. bdg. 69.00 (*0-7812-9127-5*) Rprt Serv.

— The Science of Musical Sounds. 2nd ed. LC 76-181211. 286p. 1926. reprint ed. 59.00 (*0-403-01622-3*) Scholarly.

Miller, Dayton C., tr. see Boehm, Theobold.

Miller, Dean. State Parks on the Great Lakes. 370p. 1997. pap. 15.95 (*1-881139-17-4*) Glovebox Guidebks.

***Miller, Dean A.** The Epic Hero. LC 99-39582. 2000. 52.00 (*0-8018-6239-6*) Johns Hopkins.

Miller, Dean F. Dimensions of Community Health. 4th ed. 512p. (C). 1994. text. write for info. (*0-697-15262-6*) Brown & Benchmark.

— Safety: Principles & Issues. LC 94-71726. 320p. (C). 1994. text. write for info. (*0-697-10943-7*) Brown & Benchmark.

Miller, Dean F. & Telljohann, Susan. Health Education in the Elementary School. 2nd ed. LC 95-77539. 372p. (C). 1995. text 47.77 (*0-697-15256-1*) Brown & Benchmark.

Miller, Debbie. Flight of the Golden Plover: The Amazing Migration Between Hawaii & Alaska. LC 95-47349. (Illus.). 32p. (J). (gr. 2 up). 1996. 15.95 (*0-88240-474-1*, Alaska NW Bks) Gr Arts Ctr Pub.

***Miller, Debbie.** Midnight Wilderness: Journeys in Alaska's Arctic National Wildlife Refuge. LC 00-38039. 2000. pap. 14.95 (*0-88240-517-9*, Alaska NW Bks) Gr Arts Ctr Pub.

Miller, Debbie S. Animal Parade. (Illus.). 32p. (J). 1997. write for info. (*0-316-57384-1*) Little.

— A Caribou Journey. LC 93-9777. (Illus.). 32p. (J). (gr. k-3). 1994. 15.95 (*0-316-57380-9*) Little.

***Miller, Debbie S.** A Caribou Journey. 32p. (J). (ps-3). 2000. pap. 5.95 (*0-316-57174-1*) Little.

— Caribou Journey. (Illus.). (J). 2000. 11.40 (*0-606-18255-1*) Turtleback.

Miller, Debbie S. Disappearing Lake: Nature's Magic in Denali National Park. LC 96-35107. (Illus.). 32p. (J). (gr. 2-5). 1997. 15.95 (*0-8027-8474-7*); lib. bdg. 16.85 (*0-8027-8475-5*) Walker & Co.

— Disappearing Lake: Nature's Magic in Denali National Park. (Illus.). 32p. (J). (gr. 1-4). 1999. reprint ed. pap. 6.95 (*0-8027-7558-6*) Walker & Co.

— A Polar Bear Journey. LC 96-42284. (Illus.). 32p. (J). (gr. k-3). 1997. 15.95 (*0-316-57244-6*) Little.

— A Woolly Mammoth Journey. LC 99-42428. 2001. write for info. (*0-316-57212-8*) Little.

***Miller, Debbie S. & Van Zyle, Jon.** River of Life. LC 99-38350. 32p. (J). (gr. k-3). 2000. 15.00 (*0-395-96790-2*, Clarion Bks) HM.

Miller, Debbie S., jt. auth. see MacArthur, Loren.

Miller, Debby, et al. Sound Patterns for Primary Children. (Illus.). 98p. 1988. teacher ed., spiral bd. 8.95 (*1-886131-29-5*, SP) Math Lrning.

Miller, Debora J., jt. auth. see Nelson, John D.

Miller, Deborah. Coping When a Parent Is Gay. Rosen, Ruth C., ed. (Coping Ser.). (YA). (gr. 7-12). 1992. lib. bdg. 17.95 (*0-8239-1404-6*) Rosen Group.

***Miller, Deborah.** Corel Draw 9 Bible. LC 99-32152. (Bible Ser.). 1008p. 1999. pap. 39.99 (*0-7645-3315-0*) IDG Bks.

Miller, Deborah. Coreldraw 8 Bible. LC 97-77545. (Bible Ser.). 992p. 1998. pap. 39.99 (*0-7645-3183-2*) IDG Bks.

— Fins & Scales: A Kosher Tale. LC 90-24388. (Illus.). 32p. (J). (gr. k-4). 1992. pap. 6.95 (*0-929371-26-7*) Kar-Ben.

***Miller, Deborah, ed.** Sacred Fire: Torah from the Years of Fury, 1939-1942. Worch, J. Hershy, tr. from HEB. LC 99-48146. 360p. 2001. 30.00 (*0-7657-6127-0*) Aronson.

***Miller, Deborah & Dennis, Mary L.** The Pigman. 32p. (YA). (gr. 7-8). 1999. 11.95 (*1-56137-390-7*) Novel Units.

Miller, Deborah & Kelly, Pat. Coping with Incest. rev. ed. (YA). (gr. 7-12). 1995. lib. bdg. 17.95 (*0-8239-1949-8*) Rosen Group.

Miller, Deborah & Shi, Shannon. 1995 China Medical Market Report Vol. 1: An Indepth Market Study on China's Pharmaceutical, Biotechnology & Medical Device Markets. 100p. (Orig.). 1995. pap. 79.95 (*0-9657889-0-3*) Golden Tri Org.

Miller, Deborah U. My Siddur. (Illus.). 35p. (J). (gr. k-2). 1984. pap. text 4.95 (*0-87441-389-3*) Behrman.

— Only Nine Chairs-A Tall Tale for Passover. LC 82-80035. (Illus.). 40p. (J). (ps-4). 1982. pap. 5.95 (*0-930494-13-X*) Kar-Ben.

Miller, Debra L. Principles for Health Care Reform. (CSIS Panel Reports). 34p. (Orig.). (C). 1994. pap. 10.95 (*0-89206-269-X*) CSIS.

Miller, Debra M. Out of the Shadow: Artists of the Warhol Circle, Then & Now. 100p. 1996. pap. 20.00 (*1-887421-01-7*) Univ Gall U of DE.

Miller, Debra S. Independent Women: Creating Our Lives, Living Our Visions. LC 98-28248. 240p. 1998. pap. 16.95 (*1-885171-25-0*) PageMill Pr.

***Miller-Degenfeld, Marie-Therese, ed.** The Poet & the Countess: Hugo Von Hofmannsthal's Correspondence with Countess Ottonie Degenfeld. (Studies in German Literature, Linguistics & Culture). 384p. 2000. 65.00 (*1-57113-030-6*, Pub. by Camden Hse) Boydell & Brewer.

Miller, Delbert C. Handbook of Research Design & Social Measurement. 5th ed. 400p. (C). 1991. 95.00 (*0-8039-4219-2*); pap. 44.00 (*0-8039-4220-6*) Sage.

— International Community Power Structures: Comparative Studies of Four World Cities. LC 74-85093. (Illus.). 342p. reprint ed. 106.10 (*0-8357-9219-6*, 205521100011) Bks Demand.

Miller, Della S., jt. auth. see Miller, David E.

Miller, Dennis. Ranting Again. 224p. 1999. pap. 11.95 (*0-385-48853-X*) Broadway BDD.

— Ranting Again. LC 97-44475. 224p. 1998. 21.95 (*0-385-48852-1*) Doubleday.

— The Rants. 224p. 1997. pap. 12.95 (*0-385-47802-X*, Main St Bks) Doubleday.

***Miller, Dennis.** Rants III. LC 99-55833. 224p. 2000. 21.95 (*0-385-49535-8*) Doubleday.

Miller, Dennis & Hunt, Amelia. Changing Lives: A Practical Guide to a Spiritually Powerful Youth Ministry. Prin, John, ed. (Illus.). 280p. (Orig.). (C). 1989. pap. text 26.95 (*0-9627730-0-X*) CD Publshng.

Miller, Dennis, et al. Just Between Us. 180p. (Orig.). (C). 1997. reprint ed. spiral bd. 6.95 (*0-945105-09-6*) Yoest Expressions.

Miller, Dennis D. Food Chemistry: A Laboratory Manual. LC 97-31762. 176p. 1998. pap., lab manual ed. 43.95 (*0-471-17543-9*, Wiley-Interscience) Wiley.

***Miller, Denny.** Le Ministere de Puissance: Un Manuel pour les Predicateurs Pentecotistes. (Discovery Ser.).Tr. of Power Ministry. (FRE.). 142p. 1999. pap. text. write for info. (*2-912377-07-2*, Editions SAFT) Africa Theolog Trng.

— Power Ministry: A Handbook for Pentecostal Preachers. (Discovery Ser.). 134p. 1999. pap. text. write for info. (*1-891110-06-3*, ATTS Pubns) Africa Theolog Trng.

Miller, Derek. The Age Between: Adolescence & Therapy. rev. ed. LC 83-3893. 456p. 1986. 50.00 (*0-87668-639-0*) Aronson.

— Age Between Adolescence & Therapy. LC 83-3893. 1995. pap. text 50.00 (*1-56821-732-3*) Aronson.

— Attack on the Self: Adolescent Behavioral Disturbances & Their Treatment. LC 86-17418. 340p. 1986. 55.00 (*0-87668-927-6*) Aronson.

— Attack on the Self: Adolescent Behavioral Disturbances & Their Treatment. LC 93-74780. 352p. 1994. pap. 45.00 (*1-56821-214-3*) Aronson.

Miller, Derek, et al. Miller, Reiter & Robbins: Three New Poets. 1991. 15.00 (*0-914610-96-1*); pap. 9.00 (*0-914610-95-3*) Hanging Loose.

Miller, Deyanne F., jt. auth. see Braund, Kathryn.

Miller, Diana. Pelargoniums: A Gardener's Guide to the Species & Their Hybrids & Cultivars. LC 96-18242. (Illus.). 208p. 1996. 29.95 (*0-88192-363-X*) Timber.

Miller, Diana C., jt. auth. see Magee, Maggie.

Miller, Diane & Wright, Donna, eds. Leading an Empowered Organization Manual. 4th rev. ed. 73p. 1997. pap. text 35.00 (*1-886624-07-0*) Creat Hlthcare.

Miller, Diane, et al. Dental Office Hazard Communication. 2nd rev. ed. (Illus.). 103p. (C). 1989. ring bd. 95.00 (*0-317-93906-8*) Hascom Inc.

Miller, Diane, ed. see Tracy, Denise D.

Miller, Diane H. Freedom to Differ: The Shaping of the Gay & Lesbian Struggle for Civil Rights. LC 98-13816. 220p. 1998. text 55.00 (*0-8147-5595-X*); pap. text 18.50 (*0-8147-5596-8*) NYU Pr.

Miller, Diane M. & Miller, Virgil E. Become a Success Magnet: Success for the Mind, Body & Soul. LC BF637.S8M55 1997. 148p. 1998. pap. 13.95 (*1-890865-15-X*, KHB15X) Knight Hse.

— Enlightment 101: An Awakening for the Soul. 110p. 1999. 16.00 (*1-890865-18-4*, KHB184) Knight Hse.

Miller, Dickinson S. Philosophical Analysis & Human Welfare. Easton, Loyd D., ed. LC 75-4832. (Philosophical Studies: No. 3). 343p. 1975. text 171.00 (*90-277-0566-6*, D Reidel) Kluwer Academic.

Miller, Divina. Export or Die: Britain's Defence Trade with Iran & Iraq. LC 96-41707. 1996. pap. 21.95 (*0-304-33853-2*) Continuum.

Miller, Dolores E., jt. auth. see Miller, Jerome H.

Miller, Don. Calculator Explorations & Problems. (J). 1995. pap. 10.95 (*0-201-48038-7*) Addison-Wesley.

— Calculator Explorations & Problems. 108p. (J). (gr. 5-12). 1979. pap. text 10.95 (*0-914040-75-8*) Cuisenaire.

— Euphoria vs. Ecstasy. 175p. 1992. pap. 13.95 (*0-9635165-3-1*) Gate Prods.

— I Love Chocolate. LC 88-83286. (Illus.). 130p. (Orig.). 1988. pap. 8.95 (*0-938711-06-7*) Tecolote Pubns.

— The Intrepid Journey of a Timid Tourist. LC 91-90034. 160p. 1991. pap. 11.95 (*0-9628975-1-5*) Eldon Pr.

— Mental Math & Estimation. 80p. (J). (gr. 3-8). 1992. pap. text 10.95 (*0-938587-30-7*) Cuisenaire.

— Pet Owner's Guide to the English Springer Spaniel. (Pet Owner's Guide Ser.). (Illus.). 80p. 1997. 8.00 (*1-86054-020-1*, Pub. by Ringpr Bks) Seven Hills Bk.

***Miller, Don.** Prayer & the Art of Volkswagen Maintenance. LC 99-41916. 300p. 2000. pap. 10.99 (*0-7369-0160-4*) Harvest Hse.

— Problem Solving Explorations. 1997. pap. 86.95 (*0-471-36659-5*) Wiley.

Miller, Don & Miller, Kathleen. Bible Memory Verse Games for Children: 50 Fun & Creative Activities to Help Kids Learn - & Remember - God's Word. 68p. (J). 1995. pap. 8.99 (*0-8341-1539-5*) Beacon Hill.

Miller, Don & Naraine, Bishnu. Problem Solving Challenges. 114p. pap. text 12.00 (*1-883547-06-7*) Tricon Pub.

Miller, Don, et al. The Hollywood Corral: A Comprehensive B-Western Roundup. Smith, M. P. & Hulse, Ed, eds. (Illus.). 600p. 1992. 59.95 (*1-880756-03-X*) Riverwood Pr.

Miller, Don A. & Beaver, Marion L. Clinical Social Work Practice with the Elderly: Primary, Secondary, & Tertiary Intervention. 280p. (C). 1985. pap. 19.50 (*0-534-10991-8*) Brooks-Cole.

Miller, Don A., jt. auth. see Beaver, Marion L.

Miller, Don C., jt. auth. see Cohen, Stan B.

Miller, Don E. Drug Wars: The Final Battle: Rescuing America from Drug Violence. LC 94-66003. (Illus.). 406p. (Orig.). 1994. pap. 9.95 (*0-9640695-0-4*) Speranza Prods.

Miller, Don M., jt. auth. see Canavos, George C.

***Miller, Donald.** Aaronel: The Art of Aaronel deRoy Gruber. (Illus.). 128p. 1999. lib. bdg. 49.95 (*0-9660955-2-9*, Centaur Editions) D Miller.

Miller, Donald. The Architecture of Benno Janssen. LC 98-185741. (Illus.). 180p. 1999. 49.95 (*0-9660955-0-2*, Pub. by D Miller); pap. 29.95 (*0-9660955-1-0*, Pub. by D Miller) Madison Bks UPA.

— What about Those Who Are Left? pap. 1.99 (*0-87509-743-X*) Chr Pubns.

Miller, Donald & De Roo, Gert, eds. Integrating City Planning & Environmental Improvement: Practicable Strategies for Sustainable Urban Development. LC 98-74513. 7p. 1999. text 69.95 (*1-84014-983-3*) Ashgate Pub Co.

— Urban Environmental Planning: Policies, Instruments & Methods in an International Perspective. 336p. 1997. 91.95 (*1-85972-593-7*, Pub. by Avebry) Ashgate Pub Co.

Miller, Donald A. Concepts of Family Life in Modern Catholic Theology: From Vatican II Through "Christifideles Laici" (Distinguished Research Ser.). 272p. 1996. 69.95 (*1-57309-105-7*, Cath Scholar Pr) Intl Scholars.

— Concepts of Family Life in Modern Catholic Theology: From Vatican II Through "Christifideles Laici" (Distinguished Research Ser.). 272p. 1996. pap. 54.95 (*1-57309-104-9*, Cath Scholar Pr) Intl Scholars.

— Medicine for Depression. (Christian Living Ser.). 33p. 1994. pap. 1.59 (*0-87509-571-2*) Chr Pubns.

— Songs in the Night: How to Have Peace under Pressure. 1992. pap. 1.59 (*0-87509-489-9*) Chr Pubns.

Miller, Donald C. Ghost Towns of Montana. LC 72-95496. (Illus.). 177p. 1981. pap. 18.95 (*0-87108-606-9*) Pruett.

— Ghosts of the Black Hills. LC 79-87462. (Illus.). 72p. 1979. pap. 3.95 (*0-933126-07-7*) Pictorial Hist.

Miller, Donald C., jt. auth. see Cohen, Stan B.

Miller, Donald C., jt. auth. see Davis, Arnold R.

Miller, Donald E. The Gospel & Mother Goose. fac. ed. LC 87-5180. (Illus.). 133p. (Orig.). 1994. pap. 41.30 (*0-7837-7345-5*, 204729800007) Bks Demand.

— Reinventing American Protestantism: Christianity in the New Millennium. LC 96-35140. 262p. 1997. 27.50 (*0-520-20938-9*, Pub. by U CA Pr) Cal Prin Full Svc.

— Reinventing American Protestantism: Christianity in the New Millennium. 262p. 1999. pap. 17.95 (*0-520-21811-6*, Pub. by U CA Pr) Cal Prin Full Svc.

— A Self-Instruction Guide Through Brethren History. fac. ed. LC BX7815.. (Church of the Brethren, Heritage Learning Program Ser.). 108p. 1976. pap. 33.50 (*0-7837-7346-3*, 204729900007) Bks Demand.

Miller, Donald E. & Miller, Lorna T. Survivors: An Oral History of the Armenian Genocide. LC 92-18439. 274p. 1993. 40.00 (*0-520-07984-1*, Pub. by U CA Pr) Cal Prin Full Svc.

Miller, Donald E. & Relkin, Donald B. Improving Credit Practice. LC 70-119384. 367p. reprint ed. pap. 113.80 (*0-608-10876-6*, 205151700086) Bks Demand.

Miller, Donald E., jt. auth. see Seltser, Barry J.

Miller, Donald E., jt. auth. see Seymour, Jack L.

***Miller, Donald Eugene.** Survivors: An Oral History of the Armenian Genocide. 274p. 1999. pap. 17.95 (*0-520-21956-2*, Pub. by U CA Pr) Cal Prin Full Svc.

Miller, Donald F. The Reason of Metaphor: A Study in Politics. 268p. (C). 1992. text 29.95 (*0-8039-9410-9*) Sage.

Miller, Donald G. On This Rock: A Commentary on First Peter. LC 93-30951. (Princeton Theological Monographs: No. 34). 1993. pap. 25.00 (*1-55635-020-1*) Pickwick.

— The Scent of Eternity: The Life of Harris Elliott Kirk. LC 89-35945. (Illus.). xvi, 730p. (C). 1990. 31.95 (*0-86554-332-1*, MUP/H246) Mercer Univ Pr.

Miller, Donald G., ed. The Hermeneutical Quest: Essays in Honor of James Luther Mays on His Sixty-Fifth Birthday. LC 86-833. (Princeton Theological Monographs: No. 4). 1986. pap. 20.00 (*0-915138-86-7*) Pickwick.

Miller, Donald G., et al. P. T. Forsyth: The Man, the Preacher's Theologian & Prophet for the Twentieth Century. (Pittsburgh Theological Monographs: No. 36). 1981. pap. 15.00 (*0-915138-48-4*) Pickwick.

Miller, Donald G., tr. see Bovon, Francois & Rouiller, Gregoire, eds.

Miller, Donald L. City of the Century. 704p. 1997. per. 17.00 (*0-684-83138-4*) S&S Trade Pap.

— City of the Century: The Epic of Chicago & the Making of America. (Illus.). 480p. 1996. 35.00 (*0-684-80194-9*) S&S Trade.

— Lewis Mumford: A Life. LC 91-29646. (Illus.). 672p. 1992. pap. 24.95 (*0-8229-5907-0*) U of Pittsburgh Pr.

— Lewis Mumford: A Life. 628p. 1999. reprint ed. pap. text 23.00 (*0-7881-6271-3*) DIANE Pub.

An Asterisk (*) at the beginning of an entry indicates that the title is appearing for the first time.

M

Miller, Edward J. & Wolensky, Robert P., eds. The Small City & Regional Community: Proceedings of the 1979 Conference, Vol. II. (Orig.). 1979. pap. text 16.50 (*0-932310-01-X*) U of Wis-Stevens Point.

— The Small City & Regional Community: Proceedings of the 1981 Conference, Vol. IV. LC 79-644450. viii, 550p. (Orig.). (C). 1981. pap. text 16.50 (*0-932310-03-6*) U of Wis-Stevens Point.

— The Small City & Regional Community: Proceedings of the 1984 Conference, Vol. VI. LC 79-644450. viii, 450p. (Orig.). (C). 1985. pap. text 16.50 (*0-932310-06-0*) U of Wis-Stevens Point.

Miller, Edward J., jt. auth. see Wolensky, Robert P.

Miller, Edward J., jt. ed. see Wolensky, Robert P.

Miller, Edward M. U. S. S. Monitor: The Ship that Launched a Modern Navy. 1978. 24.95 (*0-915268-10-8*) Ayer.

Miller, Edward P. Letters to the Thirsty: For Vision... For Life... For Rest. 208p. 1998. 14.95 (*1-57856-047-0*) Waterbrook Pr.

Miller, Edward S. Civil War Sea Battles. (Illus.). 288p. 1995. 24.95 (*0-938289-52-7*, 289527) Combined Pub.

— War Plan Orange: The U. S. Strategy to Defeat Japan, 1897-1945. LC 91-14361. (Illus.). 509p. 1991. 34.95 (*0-87021-759-3*) Naval Inst Pr.

Miller, Edwin E. & Yocom, Betsy. The Switch Book: 1977 Edition. 3rd rev. ed. (Illus.). 310p. 1997. spiral bd. 495.00 (*1-891869-01-9*) Mier Communs.

Miller, Edwin H. Salem Is My Dwelling Place: A Life of Nathaniel Hawthorne. LC 91-14543. (Illus.). 648p. 1991. pap. 21.00 (*0-87745-381-0*); text 37.95 (*0-87745-332-2*) U of Iowa Pr.

— Walt Whitman's "Song of Myself" A Mosaic of Interpretations. LC 88-38069. 209p. 1989. pap. text 19.95 (*0-87745-345-4*) U of Iowa Pr.

Miller, Edwin H., ed. see Whitman, Walt.

Miller, Eileen. The Edinburgh International Festival 1947-1996. 400p. (C). 1996. text 86.95 (*1-85928-153-2*, Pub. by Scolar Pr) Ashgate Pub Co.

Miller, Elaine. Windy City Kitchens: Recipes from Chicago's Favorite Restaurants. Miller, John, ed. (Illus.). 84p. 1997. pap. 19.95 (*0-9659678-0-8*, Pub. by Eleni Pub) Partners Pubs Grp.

Miller, Elaine, jt. ed. see Miller, Kimball.

Miller, Elaine, tr. see Perissinotto, Giorgia, ed.

Miller, Eldon. Stdt Sol V1 - Calc & Analy Geom, Vol. I. (Math). 208p. (C). 1982. mass mkt. 8.25 (*0-534-00980-8*) PWS Pubs.

Miller, Eleanor M. Street Woman. (Women in the Political Economy Ser.). 216p. 1987. pap. 19.95 (*0-87722-509-5*) Temple U Pr.

Miller, Elinor & Genovese, Eugene D., eds. Plantation, Town, & County: Essays on the Local History of American Slave Society. LC 73-20359. 463p. reprint ed. pap. 143.60 (*0-608-10894-4*, 202277800029) Bks Demand.

Miller, Elinor, tr. see Butor, Michel.

Miller, Elinor S., tr. see Oppenheim, Lois, ed.

Miller, Elisa & Stefanopoulos, Soula, eds. The Russian Far East: A Business Reference Guide. 275p. 1997. pap. 59.00 (*0-9641286-2-4*) Russian Far East.

Miller, Elisa B. & Karp, Alexander. The Russian Far East: A Business Reference Guide 1999-2000. 4th ed. (Illus.). 270p. 1998. pap. text 49.00 (*0-9641286-3-2*) Russian Far East.

***Miller, Elizabeth.** Internet Resource Directory 2000/2001: K-12 Teachers & Librarians. 2000. pap. 27.50 (*1-56308-839-8*) Libs Unl.

Miller, Elizabeth. 16th-Century Italian Ornament Prints. 1999. 95.00 (*1-85177-263-4*) V&A Ent.

Miller, Elizabeth, ed. Dracula: The Shade & the Shadow: Papers Presented at "Dracula 97" a Centenary Celebration at Los Angeles, August 1997. 256p. 1998. 29.95 (*1-874287-10-4*, Pub. by Desert Island Bks) Firebird Dist.

Miller, Elizabeth & Miller, Crow. Smith & Hawken Hands-On Gardener: The Organic Management of Pests. LC 99-86923. (Smith & Hawken Ser.). (Illus.). 128p. 1999. pap. 11.95 (*0-7611-1401-7*) Workman Pub.

Miller, Elizabeth, jt. ed. see Casey, G. J.

Miller, Elizabeth B. The Internet Resource Directory for K-12 Teachers & Librarians. 450p. 1999. pap. 27.50 (*1-56308-812-6*) Libs Unl.

***Miller, Elizabeth D.** Read It! Draw It! (Illus.). (J). (gr. k). 1999. pap., wbk. ed. 4.95 (*0-7690-0156-4*) Seymour Pubns.

— Read It! Draw It! (Illus.). (J). (gr. 1). 1999. pap., wbk. ed. 4.95 (*0-7690-0157-2*) Seymour Pubns.

— Read It! Draw It! (Illus.). (J). (gr. 2). 1999. pap., wbk. ed. 4.95 (*0-7690-0158-0*) Seymour Pubns.

— Read It! Draw It! (Illus.). (J). (gr. 3). 1999. pap., wbk. ed. 4.95 (*0-7690-0159-9*) Seymour Pubns.

Miller, Elizabeth D. Read It! Draw It! Solve It! (Illus.). 192p. (J). (gr. 3). 1997. pap. text 15.95 (*1-57232-436-8*) Seymour Pubns.

— Read It! Draw It! Solve It! - Grade 1: Problem Solving for Primary Grades. Anderson, Catherine et al, eds. (Illus.). 180p. (Orig.). 1996. pap., teacher ed. 16.95 (*1-57232-434-1*, 33800) Seymour Pubns.

— Read It! Draw It! Solve It! - Grade 2: Problem Solving for Primary Grades. Anderson, Catherine et al, eds. (Illus.). 180p. (Orig.). 1996. pap., teacher ed. 16.95 (*1-57232-435-X*, 33801) Seymour Pubns.

Miller, Elizabeth G., tr. see Balcells, Jacqueline.

Miller, Elizabeth G., tr. see Lindo, Hugo.

Miller, Elizabeth I. Just Like Home. LC 98-52519.Tr. of Como en Mi Tierra. (Illus.). 32p. (J). (gr. 1-3). 1999. lib. bdg. 15.95 (*0-8075-4068-4*) A Whitman.

Miller, Elizabeth L. Get Rolling: The Beginner's Guide to In-Line Skating. LC 92-81185. (Illus.). 128p. (Orig.). 1992. pap. 10.00 (*0-9632196-2-6*) Pix & Pts.

Miller, Elizabeth W., ed. The Negro in America: A Bibliography. 2nd enl. rev. ed. 373p. (C). 1970. pap. 18.50 (*0-674-60702-3*) HUP.

Miller, Elizabeth W., ed. see Mather, Cotton.

Miller, Elizabeth D. Read It! Draw It! Solve It!, Animal Book. (Illus.). (J). 1997. pap. text 15.95 (*1-57232-437-6*) Seymour Pubns.

Miller, Ellen. Like Being Killed. 352p. 1999. pap. 12.95 (*0-452-27929-1*, Plume) Dutton Plume.

— Like Being Killed. 352p. 1998. 24.95 (*0-525-94372-2*) NAL.

— Mosby's Review for the Clinical Competency Test: Small Animal Medicine & Surgery. LC 98-231811. 264p. (C). (gr. 13). 1997. pap. text 39.95 (*0-8151-4379-6*, 31125) Mosby Inc.

— Video: A Guide for Lawyers. LC 83-80276. 142p. 1983. 29.75 (*0-88238-063-X*) Law Arts.

Miller, Ellen, jt. auth. see Hansen, Orval.

Miller, Ellen C. Eastern Sketches: Notes of Scenery, Schools, & Tent Life in Syria & Palestine. Davis, Moshe, ed. (America & the Holy Land Ser.). 1977. reprint ed. lib. bdg. 23.95 (*0-405-10269-0*) Ayer.

Miller, Ellen K. Escherichia Coli 0157: Bibliography. January 1993-December 1993. 64p. (Orig.). (C). 1995. pap. text 35.00 (*0-7881-2179-0*) DIANE Pub.

Miller, Elliot. A Crash Course on the New Age Movement: Describing & Evaluating a Growing Social Force. (Christian Research Institute Ser.). 264p. 1989. pap. 12.99 (*0-8010-6248-9*) Baker Bks.

Miller, Elliot & Samples, Kenneth B. The Cult of the Virgin: Catholic Mariology & the Apparitions of Mary. LC 92-4273. (Christian Research Institute Ser.). 192p. 1992. pap. 9.99 (*0-8010-6291-8*) Baker Bks.

Miller, Elliott. The Jews of Sandor. (Illus.). 25p. (Orig.). (C). 1975. pap. 1.50 (*0-935982-21-3*, SMJ-01) Spertus Coll.

Miller, Elmer I. Legislature of the Province of Virginia. LC 08-1371. (Columbia University. Studies in the Social Sciences: No. 76). reprint ed. 32.50 (*0-404-51076-0*) AMS Pr.

Miller, Elmer S. Nurturing Doubt: From Missionary to Anthropologist in the Argentine Chaco. LC 94-30791. 248p. (C). 1995. pap. text 17.50 (*0-252-06455-0*) U of Ill Pr.

Miller, Elmer S., ed. Nurturing Doubt: From Missionary to Anthropologist in the Argentine Chaco. LC 94-30791. 248p. 1995. text 44.95 (*0-252-02155-X*) U of Ill Pr.

— Peoples of the Gran Chaco. LC 98-41385. (Native Peoples of the Americas Ser.). 184p. 1999. 65.00 (*0-89789-532-0*, Bergin & Garvey) Greenwood.

Miller, Elspeth, jt. ed. see Findlay, Margaret.

Miller, Elvina E. Captured in Africa. LC 97-61002. 192p. 1997. pap. 6.95 (*1-57921-043-0*) WinePress Pub.

Miller, Emery P., ed. User's Guide to Powder Coating. LC 85-71675. (Illus.). 176p. (Orig.). 1975. reprint ed. pap. 54.60 (*0-8357-6481-8*, 203585200097) Bks Demand.

— User's Guide to Powder Coating. 2nd fac. ed. LC 87-61422. (Illus.). 176p. (Orig.). 1987. reprint ed. pap. 54.60 (*0-7837-8189-X*, 204789400008) Bks Demand.

***Miller, Emil.** Introduction to Applied Technical Mathematics. (Illus.). 263p. (C). 1999. pap. text 30.00 (*0-923231-35-8*) Mohican Pub.

Miller, Emily, ed. see Business of Your Own Staff.

Miller, Emma G. Clatsop County, Oregon: Its History, Legends & Industries. LC 57-13209. (Illus.). 334p. 1978. reprint ed. 14.95 (*0-8323-0034-9*) Binford Mort.

Miller, Emmanuel. Glossaire Grec-Latin de la Bibliotheque de Laon. 230p. reprint ed. write for info. (*0-318-72054-X*) G Olms Pubs.

Miller, Emmett E. Deep Healing: The Essence of Mind/Body Medicine. LC 96-13953. 400p. 1997. pap. 12.95 (*1-56170-336-2*, 197) Hay House.

***Miller, Eric.** Song of the Vulgar Starling. 120p. 1999. pap. 11.25 (*0-921411-93-6*) Genl Dist Srvs.

Miller, Eric & Miller, Walden. Discovering CD-I. Davis, David F., ed. (Illus.). 178p. (Orig.). (C). 1991. pap. text. write for info. (*0-918035-02-3*, DCD68NA68BK) Microware Systs.

Miller, Eric D., jt. ed. see Harvey, John H.

***Miller, Eric E.** Why Am I Still Eating Crumbs: You're Living Beneath Your Privileges! 47p. 2000. pap. 10.00 (*0-9678926-0-0*) E E Miller.

Miller, Eric J., ed. Task & Organization. LC 75-12606. (Wiley Series on Individuals, Groups & Organizations). 397p. reprint ed. pap. 123.10 (*0-608-15935-2*, 203092800072) Bks Demand.

Miller, Eric John & Tavistock Institute of Human Relations Staff. The Tavistock Institute Contribution to Job & Organizational Design, 2 vols., Vols. I & II. LC 98-33169. 950p. 1999. 333.95 (*1-84014-407-6*) Ashgate Pub Co.

Miller, Erica T. Salonovations' Day Spa Operations. (SKIN). (Illus.). 176p. 1996. pap. 37.95 (*1-56253-255-3*) Thomson Learn.

— Salonovations' Day Spa Techniques. (SKIN). (Illus.). 228p. 1996. pap. 37.95 (*1-56253-261-8*) Thomson Learn.

— Salonovations' Shiatsu Massage: The Oriental Approach to Beauty Enhancement. 2nd rev. ed. (MASSAGE). 160p. 1995. pap. 15.95 (*1-56253-264-2*) Thomson Learn.

Miller, Ericka M. The Other Reconstruction: Where Violence & Womanhood Meet in the Writings of Ida B. Wells-Barnett, Angelina Weld Grimke, & Nella Larsen. rev. ed. LC 99-29874. (Studies in African American History & Culture). 176p. 1999. 48.00 (*0-8153-3495-8*) Garland.

Miller, Erika T. Guide to Collections in the Archives & Special Collections on Women in Medicine at the Medical College of Pennsylvania. 69p. (Orig). (C). 1987. 10.00 (*0-944542-00-X*) Med Coll PA ASCWM.

Miller, Erin-Aine, jt. ed. see Hinman, Felicitas.

Miller, Ernest. The Holy Spirit. 140p. 1999. pap. text 12.95 (*1-887653-11-2*) Papito.

Miller, Ernest C., ed. Conference Leadership: A Manual to Assist in the Development of Conference Leaders. rev. ed. LC 72-86426. (Illus.). 124p. reprint ed. pap. 38.50 (*0-608-10767-0*, 205034400060) Bks Demand.

Miller, Ernest G., jt. auth. see Lyden, Fremont J.

***Miller, Ernestine G.** The Babe Book: George Herman Ruth, the All-Time Greatest Baseball Player. LC 00-29945. 176p. 2000. 19.95 (*0-7407-1012-5*) Andrews & McMeel.

Miller, Errol. Blue Atlantis. (Illus.). iii, 29p. 1997. pap. 5.00 (*1-893035-01-8*) Encircle Pubns.

— Downward Glide. LC 98-72190. 104p. 1998. per. 10.50 (*0-9663047-0-5*) BGB Pr.

— Education for All: Caribbean Perspectives & Imperatives. 273p. (C). 1992. pap. text 18.50 (*0-940602-45-8*) IADB.

— Educational Reform in the Commonwealth Caribbean. LC 98-35796. (Educational Ser.). 1998. write for info. (*0-8270-3640-X*) OAS.

— Forever Beyond Us. LC 97-65922. 70p. 1997. 10.00 (*0-9657687-0-8*) Sulphur River.

— 4-Runners. 40p. 1999. pap. 4.95 (*0-9647373-4-5*) Marimbo Commun.

***Miller, Errol.** Magnolia Hall. Baratier, David, ed. 72p. 2000. pap. 8.00 (*1-886350-51-5*, Pub. by Pavement Saw) SPD-Small Pr Dist.

Miller, Errol. A Succession of Fine Lives. Bixby, Robert, ed. 36p. 1993. pap. 6.00 (*1-882983-04-1*) March Street Pr.

***Miller, Errol.** These Nights Nothing Can Keep Us In. 24p. 2000. pap. 4.95 (*1-930935-08-0*) Phony Lid Pubns.

Miller, Erston V. & Munger, James I. Good Fruits & How to Buy Them. (Illus.). (Orig.). 1967. 4.95 (*0-910286-22-1*); pap. 3.95 (*0-910286-04-3*) Boxwood.

Miller, Esther Lay, see Lay Miller, Esther.

Miller, Ethel B., tr. see Pichot, Pierre.

Miller, Ethel H. Story of Quailwood. (Illus.). 48p. 1952. 4.95 (*0-912142-07-3*); pap. 2.00 (*0-912142-04-9*) White S Bks.

— White Saddle. (J). 1934. 5.95 (*0-912142-02-2*); pap. 3.95 (*0-912142-03-0*); lib. bdg. 6.95 (*0-912142-01-4*) White S Bks.

Miller, Ethel M. Bibliography of Ohio Botany. (Bulletin Ser.: No. 27). 1932. pap. text 3.00 (*0-86727-026-8*) Ohio Bio Survey.

***Miller, Eugene.** Guide to Graduate Business Schools. 11th ed. 736p. 1999. pap. 16.95 (*0-7641-0846-8*) Barron.

Miller, Eugene, jt. auth. see Thomas, Edmund J.

Miller, Eugene D. A Holy Alliance? The Church & the Left in Costa Rica, 1932-1948. LC 96-21909. (Perspectives on Latin America & the Caribbean Ser.). 242p. (gr. 13). 1996. text 85.95 (*1-56324-910-3*) M E Sharpe.

Miller, Eugene E. Voice of a Native Son: The Poetics of Richard Wright. LC 89-37374. 275p. 1990. text 35.00 (*0-87805-399-9*) U Pr of Miss.

Miller, Eugene F., ed. see Hume, David.

Miller, Ev. Close the Door So It Can't Get in Your Room: What Makes a Good Teacher. (Illus.). 52p. 1986. pap. 4.00 (*0-88680-265-2*) I E Clark.

— Crying from the Earth. unabridged ed. Landes, William-Alan, ed. LC 97-6300. 59p. (Orig.). 1997. pap. 6.00 (*0-88734-702-9*) Players Pr.

— Dickerson for Senate. 1983. pap. 3.00 (*0-686-39594-8*) Eldridge Pub.

— A Dusty Echo. LC 88-93078. 42p. (Orig.). 1989. pap. 6.00 (*0-88734-219-1*) Players Pr.

— The Girl Who Was Asked to Turn Blue. 28p. (YA). 1986. pap. 3.50 (*0-87129-674-8*, G47) Dramatic Pub.

— Morning Shows the Day. LC 93-48187. 60p. (Orig.). 1994. pap. 6.00 (*0-88734-246-9*) Players Pr.

— A Nice Day in the Park. 1984. pap. 1.75 (*0-912963-03-4*) Eldridge Pub.

— The Visitor. 33p. 1995. pap. 4.00 (*1-57514-137-X*, 1096) Encore Perform Pub.

— The Wonderful Western Hat. 1985. pap. 3.50 (*0-87129-372-2*, W61) Dramatic Pub.

Miller, Ev & Landes, William-Alan. World Without End. LC 97-6520. 63p. 1997. pap. 6.00 (*0-88734-714-2*) Players Pr.

Miller, Evelyn. Airedale Terriers. (Illus.). 1997. pap. 9.95 (*0-7938-2380-3*, KW-165S) TFH Pubns.

— Budgies As a Hobby. (Save Our Planet Ser.). (Illus.). 96p. 1991. pap. 8.95 (*0-86622-416-5*, TT002) TFH Pubns.

— Fox Terriers. 192p. 1994. 9.95 (*0-7938-1103-1*, KW-185) TFH Pubns.

— Miniature Pinschers, AKC Rank No. 23. (KW Dog Ser.). (Illus.). 1996. pap. 9.95 (*0-7938-2358-7*, KW162S) TFH Pubns.

— Reading & Language Arts for All Students: A Practical Guide for Content Area Teachers. 504p. (C). 1996. per. 54.95 (*0-7872-2093-0*) Kendall-Hunt.

Miller, F. A., jt. auth. see Heilbronner, E.

Miller, F. B. Miller Family: Descendants of Frank Miller. (Illus.). 174p. 1991. reprint ed. pap. 37.00 (*0-8328-2087-3*); reprint ed. lib. bdg. 47.00 (*0-8328-2086-5*) Higginson Bk Co.

Miller, F. D. & Kureth, E. C. Reflections of a Warrior. McCarthy, Paul, ed. 256p. 1992. reprint ed. mass mkt. 5.50 (*0-671-75396-7*) PB.

Miller, F. J. Handbook of Russian Prepositions. (Texts Ser.). 240p. 1991. pap. 24.95 (*0-941051-27-7*) Focus Pub-R Pullins.

— Handbook of Russian Prepositions Exercise Key. (Texts Ser.). 1991. pap. 9.95 (*0-941051-32-3*) Focus Pub-R Pullins.

Miller, F. J., et al. Reading & Speaking about Russian Newspapers. 3rd ed. (Focus Texts Ser.). (RUS.). 246p. (C). 1995. pap. 32.95 (*0-941051-11-0*) Focus Pub-R Pullins.

— Reading & Speaking about Russian Newspapers: Workbook. 3rd ed. (Focus Texts Ser.). (RUS.). 98p. (C). 1995. pap., wbk. ed. 12.95 (*0-941051-12-9*) Focus Pub-R Pullins.

Miller, F. L., ed. see Thomas, D. V.

Miller, F. P., et al, eds. Land Use Planning, Techniques & Policies. (Special Publications: No. 12). 123p. 1984. pap. 8.40 (*0-89118-772-3*) Soil Sci Soc Am.

Miller, F. R., jt. auth. see Curtis, W. D.

Miller, F. Thornton. Juries & Judges vs. the Law: Virginia's Provincial Legal Perspective, 1783-1828. (Illus.). 192p. (C). 1994. text 25.00 (*0-8139-1486-8*) U Pr of Va.

Miller, F. Thornton, ed. see Taylor, John.

Miller, Faren. The Illusionists. 1991. mass mkt. 4.95 (*0-446-36131-3*, Pub. by Warner Bks) Little.

Miller, Faye Y. & Coffey, Wayne. Winning Basketball for Girls: New Edition. (Illus.). 160p. 1992. 28.95 (*0-8160-2769-2*); pap. 16.95 (*0-8160-2776-5*) Facts on File.

Miller, Florence & Rotella, Alexis K. Eleven Renga. (Illus.). 40p. 1993. pap. 13.00 (*0-917951-27-1*) Jade Mtn.

— A String of Monarchs. 25p. 1995. pap. 13.00 (*0-614-07899-7*) Jade Mtn.

Miller, Florence, jt. auth. see Rotella, Alexis K.

***Miller, Florence Foley.** The Misty Trail: Life in the Early Years of This Century. LC 99-91222. 322p. 1999. 25.00 (*0-7388-0680-3*); pap. 18.00 (*0-7388-0681-1*) Xlibris Corp.

Miller, Florence M. Millere. Sketch of Miller (English) & Calhoun-Miller (Scotch-Irish) Families, with Their Genealogy. 196p. 1996. reprint ed. pap. 29.50 (*0-8328-5244-9*); reprint ed. lib. bdg. 39.50 (*0-8328-5243-0*) Higginson Bk Co.

Miller, Florence S. A Legacy of Learning: The History of the West Chester Area Schools. LC 94-60393. 339p. 1994. text 25.00 (*0-9640745-0-8*) W Chester Area.

Miller, Floyd C. Gods Maintenance Program for the New Creature. Biebel, Kenneth, ed. (Illus.). 61p. (Orig.). 1988. write for info. (*0-318-63719-7*) Prevailing Word Pubns.

Miller, Floyd J. The Search for a Black Nationality: Black Emigration & Colonization, 1787-1863. LC 75-4650. (Blacks in the New World Ser.). 311p. reprint ed. pap. 96.50 (*0-608-11508-8*, 202024700016) Bks Demand.

Miller, Floyd J., ed. see Delany, Martin R.

Miller, Forestt A. Dmitrii Miliutin & the Reform Era in Russia. LC 68-20545. 256p. 1968. reprint ed. pap. 79.40 (*0-608-01829-5*, 206247800003) Bks Demand.

Miller, Fracis M. How to Think about Health Care Reform: Disasters of Price-Fixing & Cost Shifting Can't Be Cured by More of the Same. (Issue Papers: No. 4-93). 6p. 1993. pap. text 8.00 (*1-57655-078-8*) Independ Inst.

***Miller, Frances D.** Gaze at God, Glance at All Else. Rowland, K. Nicole, ed. 160p. (C). 2000. 18.99 (*0-9665424-4-4*) Mst Design.

Miller, Francesca. Latin American Women & the Search for Social Justice. LC 91-50371. (Illus.). 342p. 1991. pap. 22.95 (*0-87451-558-0*) U Pr of New Eng.

Miller, Francis P. Man from the Valley: Memoirs of a Twentieth Century Virginian. LC 71-132255. (Illus.). 280p. reprint ed. pap. 86.80 (*0-8357-3867-1*, 203659900004) Bks Demand.

Miller, Francis T. Lindbergh: His Story in Pictures. Gilbert, James B., ed. LC 79-7286. (Flight: Its First Seventy-Five Years Ser.). (Illus.). 1980. reprint ed. lib. bdg. 36.95 (*0-405-12195-4*) Ayer.

— Lindbergh: His Story in Pictures. (Illus.). 318p. 1989. reprint ed. pap. 14.95 (*0-910667-14-4*) USM.

— Portrait Life of Lincoln. LC 76-133528. (Select Bibliographies Reprint Ser.). 1977. reprint ed. 28.95 (*0-8369-5560-9*) Ayer.

Miller, Francis W. Smart Investors: Picking the Right Stock Broker for Maximum Profits. LC 96-18822. 1996. pap. text 16.95 (*0-935016-43-0*) Zinn Pub Grp.

Miller, Frank. Batman: Dark Knight. Date not set. mass mkt. write for info. (*0-446-38673-1*, Pub. by Warner Bks) Little.

— Batman: The Dark Knight Returns. 10th anniversary ed. Kahan, Bob, ed. (Illus.). 224p. 1996. 45.00 (*1-56389-341-X*) DC Comics.

— Batman: The Dark Knight Returns 10th Anniversary. 10th ed. (Illus.). 224p. 1997. pap. text 14.95 (*1-56389-342-8*, Pub. by DC Comics) Time Warner.

Miller, Frank. Batman: Year One. Bruning, Richard, ed. (Illus.). 208p. 1997. mass mkt. 9.95 (*0-930289-33-1*, Pub. by Warner Bks) Little.

Miller, Frank. Big Fat Kill. (Sin City Ser.). 1996. pap. 15.00 (*1-56971-171-2*) Dark Horse Comics.

***Miller, Frank.** Big Guy & Rusty the Boy Robot. 1999. pap. text 14.95 (*1-56971-201-8*) Dark Horse Comics.

Miller, Frank. Daredevil: Born Again. 176p. 1987. pap. 16.95 (*0-87135-297-4*) Marvel Entrprs.

— Daredevil: Man Without Fear. (Illus.). 160p. 1994. pap. 15.95 (*0-7851-0046-6*) Marvel Entrprs.

— Elektra No. 16: Assassin. deluxe limited ed. Duffy, Jo, ed. (Illus.). 255p. 1989. ring bd. 39.95 (*0-936211-14-8*) Graphitti Designs.

— Give Me Liberty, Bk. 1. deluxe limited ed. (Illus.). 224p. 1995. 114.95 (*1-56971-045-7*) Dark Horse Comics.

— Give Me Liberty, Bk. 1. 2nd ed. (Illus.). 208p. 1994. pap. 19.95 (*1-56971-067-8*) Dark Horse Comics.

— Hard Boiled, Bk. 1. deluxe limited ed. (Illus.). 144p. 1995. 99.95 (*1-56971-049-X*) Dark Horse Comics.

***Miller, Frank.** Martha Washington Saves the World. 112p. 1999. pap. 12.95 (*1-56971-384-7*) Dark Horse Comics.

— MGM Posters: The Golden Years. 192p. 15.99 (*1-57215-269-9*) World Pubns.

Miller, Frank. Ronin. 302p. 1987. mass mkt. 12.95 (*0-446-38674-X*, Pub. by Warner Bks) Little.

— Ronin. Marx, Barry, ed. (Illus.). 302p. 1995. mass mkt. 19.95 (*0-930289-21-8*, Pub. by Warner Bks) Little.

— Sin City. rev. ed. (Illus.). 208p. 1992. pap. 15.00 (*1-878574-59-0*) Dark Horse Comics.
— Sin City: A Dame to Kill For. 2nd ed. (Illus.). 208p. 1994. pap. 15.00 (*1-56971-068-6*) Dark Horse Comics.
— Sin City: Booze, Broads, & Bullets. 160p. 1999. pap. 15.00 (*1-56971-366-9*) Dark Horse Comics.
— Sin City: Family Values. 128p. 1997. pap. 10.00 (*1-56971-313-8*) Dark Horse Comics.
— Sin City: That Yellow Bastard. 1997. 25.00 (*1-56971-187-9*); pap. text 15.00 (*1-56971-225-5*) Dark Horse Comics.
— Sin City: The Big Fat Kill. (Illus.). 184p. 1995. 25.00 (*1-56971-076-7*) Dark Horse Comics.
— Sin City Bk. 1: A Dame to Kill For. rev. ed. Prosser, Jerry, ed. (Illus.). 208p. 1994. 25.00 (*1-56971-036-8*) Dark Horse Comics.
— Spawn & Batman. (Illus.). 52p. 1994. pap. 9.95 (*1-58240-019-9*) Image Comics.
***Miller, Frank.** 300. 88p. 2000. 30.00 (*1-56971-402-9*) Dark Horse Comics.
Miller, Frank & Darrow, Geof. Hard Boiled. Prosser, Jerry, ed. (Illus.). 128p. 1993. pap. 14.95 (*1-878574-58-2*) Dark Horse Comics.
Miller, Frank & Gibbons, Dave. Martha Washington Goes to War. (Illus.). 144p. 1995. pap. 17.95 (*1-56971-090-2*) Dark Horse Comics.
Miller, Frank & Mazzucchelli, David. Batman: Year One. 1988. mass mkt. 10.95 (*0-446-38923-4*, Pub. by Warner Bks) Little.
Miller, Frank, et al. Daredevil: Gang War. (Illus.). 112p. 1992. pap. 14.95 (*0-87135-880-8*) Marvel Entrprs.
Miller, Frank, jt. auth. see Kagan, Olga.
Miller, Frank, tr. see Ivanov, Vsevolod.
Miller, Frank B. Miller Family: An Address Delivered Before the Miller Re-Union at N. Waldoboro, Maine, Sept. 7, 1904, with Genealogy. (Illus.). 47p. 1995. reprint ed. pap. 10.00 (*0-8328-4562-0*); reprint ed. lib. bdg. 20.00 (*0-8328-4561-2*) Higginson Bk Co.
***Miller, Frank B.** Soldiers & Sailors of the Plantation of Lower St. Georges. 66p. 1999. pap. 12.00 (*0-8063-4924-7*) Clearfield Co.
Miller, Frank C. BPR for HVAC. (Blueprint Reading & Drafting Ser.). 32p. 1995. text, teacher ed. 10.95 (*0-8273-6873-9*) Delmar.
Miller, Frank C. & Miller, Wilma B. Blueprint Reading for Heating, Ventilating & Air Conditioning. LC 95-1920. 256p. 1996. pap., teacher ed. 48.95 (*0-8273-6872-0*) Delmar.
***Miller, Frank E.** Genealogy of the Family of Millers, from 1570 to 1925. fac. ed. 378p. 1999. reprint ed. pap. 58.00 (*0-7404-0019-3*) Higginson Bk Co.
— Genealogy of the Family of Millers, from 1570 to 1925. fac. ed. (Illus.). 378p. 1999. reprint ed. 68.00 (*0-7404-0018-5*) Higginson Bk Co.
Miller-Frank, Felicia. The Mechanical Song: Women, Voice, & the Artificial in Nineteenth-Century French Narrative. LC 94-34279. 223p. 1995. 35.00 (*0-8047-2381-8*) Stanford U Pr.
Miller, Frank J. Folklore for Stalin: Russian Folklore & Pseudofolklore in the Stalin Era. LC 90-21540. 192p. (gr. 13). 1990. text 79.95 (*0-87332-668-7*) M E Sharpe.
— A Handbook of Russian Verbs: Spravochnik po Russkim Glagolam. (ENG & RUS.). (Orig.). (C). 1989. pap. text 18.95 (*0-87501-052-0*) Ardis Pubs.
Miller, Frank J., tr. Metamorphoses, Bks. 1-8. (Loeb Classical Library: No. 42-43). 484p. 1916. text 18.95 (*0-674-99046-3*) HUP.
— Metamorphoses, Bks. 9-15. (Loeb Classical Library: No. 42-43). 510p. 1916. text 18.95 (*0-674-99047-1*) HUP.
Miller, Frank L. Gifford Pinchot: An American Conservationist. Date not set. 22.95 (*0-465-02665-6*, Pub. by Basic); pap. write for info. (*0-465-02664-8*) Basic.
Miller, Frank N. Pathology, Review for New National Boards. LC 93-79828. 222p. 1993. pap. text 25.00 (*0-9632873-3-8*) J & S Pub VA.
Miller, Frank W., et al. Criminal Justice Administration: Cases & Materials On. 4th ed. (University Casebook Ser.). 1265p. 1991. text 45.50 (*0-88277-860-9*) Foundation Pr.
— Criminal Justice Administration: Cases & Materials, 1994 Supplement. 4th ed. (University Casebook Ser.). 129p. 1994. 7.95 (*1-56662-209-3*) Foundation Pr.
— Criminal Justice Administration: 1997 Supplement to Cases & Materials. 4th ed. (University Casebook Ser.). 217p. (C). 1997. pap. text. write for info. (*1-56662-520-3*) Foundation Pr.
— Criminal Justice Administration, 1996. 4th ed. (University Casebook Ser.). 175p. 1996. pap. text, suppl. ed. write for info. (*1-56662-393-6*) Foundation Pr.
— The Juvenile Justice Process. 3rd ed. LC 85-10268. (University Casebook Ser.). 1020p. 1985. text 39.95 (*0-88277-243-0*) Foundation Pr.
— 1998 Supplement to Cases & Materials on Criminal Justice Administration. 4th ed. (University Casebook Ser.). 236p. 1998. pap. text, suppl. ed. 10.50 (*1-56662-677-3*) Foundation Pr.
— 1995 Supplement to Cases & Materials on Criminal Justice Administration. 4th ed. (University Casebook Ser.). 142p. 1995. pap. text 8.50 (*1-56662-301-4*) Foundation Pr.
— The Police Function. 5th ed. 640p. 1991. pap. text 23.95 (*0-88277-881-1*) Foundation Pr.
— Prosecution & Adjudication. 4th ed. 1260p. 1991. pap. text 23.25 (*0-88277-882-X*) Foundation Pr.
Miller, Franklin D., Jr., et al. College Physics. 6th ed. 869p. (C). 1987. pap. text, teacher ed. 24.50 (*0-15-511747-5*) SCP.
***Miller, Franklin G., ed.** Frontiers in Bioethics: Essays Dedicated to John C. Fletcher. 224p. 2000. pap. 19.95 (*1-55572-075-7*) Univ Pub Group.
Miller, Franklin G., jt. auth. see Fletcher, John C.
Miller, Fred. Studio Recording for Musicians. (Illus.). 144p. pap. 17.95 (*0-8256-4204-3*, AM32681) Music Sales.
Miller, Fred & Milroy, Steven J. They Call Me Fred--The Landlord. LC 98-51. (Illus.). 293p. 1999. 12.32 (*1-55212-232-8*) Trafford Pub.
Miller, Fred, jt. auth. see Goss, David.
Miller, Fred D., Jr. Nature, Justice, & Rights in Aristotle's Politics. (Illus.). 442p. 1997. pap. text 24.95 (*0-19-823726-X*) OUP.
Miller, Fred D. Out of the Mouths of Babes: The Infant Formula Controversy. 98p. 1983. pap. 16.95 (*0-912051-01-9*) Transaction Pubs.
Miller, Fred H. & Harrell, Alvin C. Law of Modern Payment Systems & Notes. 2nd ed. LC 92-22178. 844p. 1992. pap. 42.95 (*0-87084-562-4*) Anderson Pub Co.
Miller, Fred H., et al. Consumer Law: Cases, Problems & Materials. LC 98-19530. 494p. 1998. boxed set 80.00 (*0-89089-869-3*) Carolina Acad Pr.
Miller, Fred L. The Biddle Street Bridge: The Bittersweet Life of Growing up in East Baltimore Circa 1950's. LC 98-96841. 192p. 1999. (*0-9668962-1-1*); pap. (*0-9668962-0-3*) Slingshot Publ.
— How to Calm down Even If You're Absolutely, Totally Nuts: A Simple Guide to Relaxation. 112p. 1999. pap. 9.00 (*0-9665275-9-3*) Namaste Pr CA.
Miller, Fred P. Christian Attitudes & Racial Problems. rev. ed. 60p. 1993. pap. 4.95 (*1-883116-03-1*) Moellerhaus.
— Revelation: A Panorama of the Gospel Age. 404p. 1991. pap. 19.95 (*1-883116-01-5*) Moellerhaus.
— Revelation: A Panorama of the Gospel Age. 2nd rev. ed. 424p. 1993. pap. text 19.95 (*1-883116-00-7*) Moellerhaus.
— Thinking on Drinking: A New Look at an Old Question. 32p. 1990. pap. 3.50 (*1-883116-04-X*) Moellerhaus.
— Zechariah & Jewish Renewal: From Gloom to Glory. 255p. 1992. pap. 15.95 (*1-883116-02-3*) Moellerhaus.
***Miller, Frederick H. & Hastie, Cindy D.** The ABC's of the UCC. LC 99-13909. 1999. write for info. (*1-57073-491-7*) Amer Bar Assn.
Miller, Frederick H., et al. Practitioner's Guide to the Oklahoma Uniform Consumer Credit Code, 1990-1992. 490p. 1990. ring bd. 95.00 (*0-409-25146-1*, MICHIE) LEXIS Pub.
Miller, Frederick H., jt. auth. see Stockton, John M.
Miller, Frederick L. Una Guia Para la Confesion. 15p. 1989. 0.25 (*0-911988-80-7*, 38058) AMI Pr.
— A Guide to Confession. 20p. 1997. 0.25 (*1-56036-105-0*, 38050) AMI Pr.
— The Marian Spirituality of Pope John Paul II. (Queen of Apostles Ser.: Vol. XII). 19p. 1992. pap. 0.65 (*1-56036-050-X*, 49743) AMI Pr.
— Mary: Catechist at Fatima. 25p. 1991. 1.50 (*1-56036-010-0*, 38611) AMI Pr.
— The Significance of Fatima: A Seventy-Five Year Perspective. 45p. 1993. 0.65 (*1-56036-078-X*, 35003) AMI Pr.
— The Trial of Faith of St. Therese of Lisieux. LC 97-23190. 240p. (Orig.). 1998. pap. 12.95 (*0-8189-0799-1*) Alba.
Miller, Fredric M. Arranging & Describing Archives & Manuscripts. (Archival Fundamentals Ser.). 132p. 1990. pap. 27.00 (*0-931828-75-9*) Soc Am Archivists.
Miller, Fredric M. & Gillette, Howard, Jr. Washington Seen: A Photographic History, 1875-1965. LC 95-2948. (Illus.). 288p. 1995. 35.95 (*0-8018-4979-9*) Johns Hopkins.
Miller, Fredric M., et al. Philadelphia Stories: A Photographic History, 1920-1960. (Illus.). 336p. (C). 1988. 27.95 (*0-87722-551-6*) Temple U Pr.
— Still Philadelphia: A Photographic History, 1890-1940. LC 82-19227. 312p. 1983. 24.95 (*0-87722-306-8*) Temple U Pr.
Miller, Freeman & Bachrach, Steven J. Cerebral Palsy: A Complete Guide for Caregiving. 2nd ed. (Johns Hopkins Press Health Bks.). 488p. 1998. reprint ed. pap. 18.95 (*0-8018-5949-2*) Johns Hopkins.
Miller, Freeman, et al. Cerebral Palsy: A Complete Guide for Caregiving. LC 95-8826. (Health Bks.). (Illus.). 488p. 1995. 35.95 (*0-8018-5091-6*) Johns Hopkins.
Miller, Fremont. Growing up with Wyoming: Eighty Years of Memories. Christensen, Eugenia, ed. (Illus.). 400p. 1998. pap. 15.00 (*0-9658855-1-8*) Mortimore Pub.
Miller, G. Drugs & the Law: Detection, Recognition & Investigation. 2nd ed. 770p. 1994. pap. 44.95 (*0-87526-398-4*) Gould.
— God Can Be Trusted. large type ed. 5.99 (*1-871676-55-X*, Pub. by Christian Focus) Spring Arbor Dist.
Miller, G. A. Nucleon Resonances & Nucleon Structures: Institute for Nuclear Theory 1st Summer School. 400p. 1992. text 95.00 (*981-02-0954-1*) World Scientific Pub.
***Miller, G. H.** 10,000 Dreams Interpreted. 304p. 2000. 14.98 (*1-58663-095-4*) M Friedman Pub Grp Inc.
Miller, G. M., compiled by. Thudding Drums. LC 79-76948. (Granger Index Reprint Ser.). 1977. 19.95 (*0-8369-6030-0*) Ayer.
Miller, G. S., Jr. Characters & Probable History of the Hawaiian Rat. (BMB Ser.). 1972. reprint ed. pap. 25.00 (*0-527-02117-2*) Periodicals Srv.
— The Families & Genera of Bats. 1967. reprint ed. 80.00 (*3-7682-0534-7*) Lubrecht & Cramer.
Miller, G. S. What, How & Do It! 205p. (C). 1989. text 70.00 (*1-872795-41-2*, Pub. by Pentland Pr) St Mut.
Miller, G. Tyler, Jr. Chemistry: A Basic Introduction. 4th ed. 561p. (C). 1986. pap. 53.75 (*0-534-06912-6*) Wadsworth Pub.
— Environmental Science: An Introduction. 448p. (C). 1985. pap. 28.00 (*0-534-05352-1*) Wadsworth Pub.
— Environmental Science: An Introduction. 2nd ed. 407p. (C). 1988. pap. 36.75 (*0-534-09066-4*) Wadsworth Pub.
— Environmental Science: Sustaining the Earth. 3rd ed. 465p. (C). 1990. mass mkt. 39.00 (*0-534-13458-0*) Wadsworth Pub.
— Environmental Science: Sustaining the Earth. 4th ed. 470p. (C). 1992. pap. 44.25 (*0-534-17808-1*) Wadsworth Pub.
— Environmental Science: Working with the Earth. 5th ed. LC 94-1534. 540p. 1994. mass mkt. 49.00 (*0-534-21588-2*) Wadsworth Pub.
— Environmental Science: Working with the Earth. 6th ed. LC 94-1534. (Biology Ser.). 517p. (C). 1996. pap. 58.25 (*0-534-50616-X*) Wadsworth Pub.
***Miller, G. Tyler, Jr.** Environmental Science: Working with the Earth. 7th ed. (Illus.). 566p. 1999. write for info. (*0-534-80545-0*) Brooks-Cole.
Miller, G. Tyler. Environmental Science: Working with the Earth. 7th ed. LC 97-14111. (Wadsworth Biology Ser.). 1998. 58.50 (*0-534-53541-0*) Wadsworth Pub.
Miller, G. Tyler, Jr. Living in the Environment. (Biology Ser.). 1975. pap. 14.75 (*0-534-00347-8*) Wadsworth Pub.
— Living in the Environment. 2nd ed. (Biology Ser.). 1979. pap. 20.75 (*0-534-00684-1*) Wadsworth Pub.
— Living in the Environment. 4th ed. (Biology Ser.). Date not set. pap., teacher ed. write for info. (*0-534-04334-8*) Wadsworth Pub.
— Living in the Environment. 5th ed. (Biology). 1987. pap., teacher ed. write for info. (*0-534-08053-7*) Wadsworth Pub.
— Living in the Environment. 6th ed. (Biology Ser.). 1990. mass mkt., teacher ed. write for info. (*0-534-12223-X*) Wadsworth Pub.
Miller, G. Tyler. Living in the Environment. 7th ed. (Biology Ser.). 1992. pap. write for info. (*0-534-16561-3*) Wadsworth Pub.
— Living in the Environment. 8th ed. (Biology Ser.). Date not set. 39.40 (*0-534-33085-1*) Wadsworth Pub.
— Living in the Environment. 8th ed. (Biology Ser.). 1993. pap., teacher ed. 37.75 (*0-534-19952-6*) Wadsworth Pub.
— Living in the Environment. 9th ed. (Biology Ser.). 1995. pap. text, teacher ed. 57.00 (*0-534-23901-3*) Wadsworth Pub.
***Miller, G. Tyler.** Living in the Environment. 11th ed. LC 99-17666. (Biology Ser.). 1999. 59.75 (*0-534-56268-X*) Wadsworth Pub.
***Miller, G. Tyler, Jr.** Living in the Environment. 11th ed. (Biology Ser.). 2000. text 19.00 (*0-534-37753-X*) Brooks-Cole.
— Living in the Environment. 11th ed. 1999. pap. 56.00 (*0-534-37608-8*) Thomson Learn.
— Living in the Environment. 12th ed. 2001. pap. 62.00 (*0-534-37697-5*) Thomson Learn.
Miller, G. Tyler, Jr. Living in the Environment: An Introduction to Environmental Science. 4th ed. 460p. (C). 1984. pap. 34.50 (*0-534-04332-1*) Wadsworth Pub.
— Living in the Environment: An Introduction to Environmental Science. 5th ed. 603p. (C). 1987. pap. 35.50 (*0-534-08052-9*) Wadsworth Pub.
— Living in the Environment: An Introduction to Environmental Science. 6th ed. 620p. (C). 1989. pap. 43.25 (*0-534-12222-1*) Wadsworth Pub.
— Living in the Environment: An Introduction to Environmental Science. 7th ed. 705p. (C). 1991. pap. 55.95 (*0-534-16560-5*) Wadsworth Pub.
— Living in the Environment: Principles, Connections, & Solutions. 8th ed. 701p. (C). 1993. pap. 49.25 (*0-534-19950-X*) Wadsworth Pub.
— Sustaining the Earth: An Integrated Approach. 360p. 1994. text 28.75 (*0-534-21432-0*) Wadsworth Pub.
— Sustaining the Earth: An Integrated Approach. 2nd ed. LC 95-18546. (Biology Ser.). 325p. (C). 1995. text 38.95 (*0-534-23922-6*) Wadsworth Pub.
— Sustaining the Earth: An Integrated Approach. 3rd ed. LC 97-384. (Biology). (C). 1997. pap. 36.25 (*0-534-52884-8*) Wadsworth Pub.
Miller, G. Tyler, Jr. & Janiskee. Living in the Environment. 4th ed. 1984. student ed. 8.75 (*0-534-04333-X*) Brooks-Cole.
Miller, G. Tyler, Jr., et al. Chemistry: A Contemporary Approach. 2nd ed. 638p. (C). 1987. pap. 41.50 (*0-534-07200-3*) Wadsworth Pub.
Miller, G. Wayne. King of Hearts: The True Story of the Maverick Who Pioneered Open Heart Surgery. LC 99-38264. 352p. 2000. 25.00 (*0-8129-3003-7*, Times Bks) Crown Pub Group.
— Toy Wars: The Epic Struggle Between G. I. Joe & the Companies That Make Them. LC 98-45468. 368p. 1999. pap. text 12.95 (*1-58062-104-X*) Adams Media.
— Toy Wars: The Epic Struggle Between G. I. Joe, Barbie & the Companies That Make Them. LC 97-18248. 1998. 25.00 (*0-8129-2984-5*, Times Bks) Crown Pub Group.
***Miller, G. Wayne.** The Work of Human Hands. rev. ed. 356p. 1999. pap. 14.95 (*1-880325-27-6*, Pub. by BorderInds NH) Allnce Hse.
Miller, G. William, ed. Regrowing the American Economy. LC 83-3171. 192p. 1983. 11.95 (*0-13-771022-4*); pap. 4.95 (*0-13-771014-3*) Am Assembly.
Miller, Gabriel. Critical Essays on Clifford Odets. (Critical Essays on American Literature Ser.). 288p. (C). 1991. 47.00 (*0-8161-7300-1*, Hall Reference) Macmillan.
***Miller, Gabriel.** The Films of Martin Ritt: Fanfare for the Common Man. (Illus.). 272p. 2000. pap. 18.00 (*1-57806-277-2*); lib. bdg. 45.00 (*1-57806-276-4*) U Pr of Miss.
Miller, Gale. Becoming Miracle Workers: Language & Meaning in Brief Therapy. LC 97-3300. (Social Problems & Social Issues Ser.). 250p. 1997. pap. text 21.95 (*0-202-30571-6*); lib. bdg. 43.95 (*0-202-30570-8*) Aldine de Gruyter.
— Enforcing the Work Ethic: Rhetoric & Everyday Life in a Work Incentive Program. LC 89-26319. (SUNY Series in the Sociology of Work). (Illus.). 252p. (C). 1991. pap. text 21.95 (*0-7914-0424-2*) State U NY Pr.
Miller, Gale, ed. Studies in Organizational Sociology Vol. 10: Essays in Honor of Charles K. Warriner. LC 91-28828. (Contemporary Studies in Sociology: Vol. 10). 239p. 1991. 78.50 (*1-55938-372-0*) Jai Pr.
Miller, Gale & Dingwall, Robert, eds. Context & Method in Qualitative Research. 240p. 1997. 75.00 (*0-8039-7631-3*); pap. 25.95 (*0-8039-7632-1*) Sage.
Miller, Gale & Holstein, J. Perspectives on Social Problems, Vol. 9. 1998. 78.50 (*0-7623-0296-8*) Jai Pr.
Miller, Gale & Holstein, James A. Constructionist Controversies: Issues in Social Problems Theory. LC 92-36979. (Social Problems & Social Issues Ser.). 231p. 1993. pap. text 26.95 (*0-202-30457-4*) Aldine de Gruyter.
Miller, Gale & Holstein, James A., eds. Social Problems in Everyday Life: Studies of Social Problems Work. LC 97-28996. 260p. 1997. 25.75 (*0-7623-0297-6*) Jai Pr.
Miller, Gale, jt. ed. see Holstein, James A.
***Miller, Gareth.** International Aspects of Succession. LC 99-46212. 330p. 2000. text 78.95 (*1-85521-838-0*, Pub. by Ashgate Pub) Ashgate Pub Co.
Miller, Gary. Mind Bogglers for Juniors. 38p. (J). 1991. student ed. 1.95 (*1-882449-00-2*) Messenger Pub.
Miller, Gary, jt. auth. see Grentz, Theresa.
Miller, Gary E. The Meaning of General Education: The Emergence of a Curriculum Paradigm. LC 87-26739. 224p. reprint ed. pap. 69.50 (*0-7837-0988-9*, 204129400020) Bks Demand.
Miller, Gary J. Managerial Dilemmas: The Political Economy of Hierarchy. (Political Economy of Institutions & Decisions Ser.). (Illus.). 272p. (C). 1992. text 59.95 (*0-521-37281-X*) Cambridge U Pr.
— Managerial Dilemmas: The Political Economy of Hierarchy. (Political Economy of Institutions & Decisions Ser.). (Illus.). 272p. (C). 1993. pap. text 18.95 (*0-521-45769-6*) Cambridge U Pr.
Miller, Gary J., jt. auth. see Knott, Jack H.
Miller, Gary M. Modern Electronic Communication. 2nd ed. (Illus.). 592p. (C). 1983. text 42.00 (*0-13-593152-5*) P-H.
— Modern Electronic Communication. 6th ed. LC 98-11895. 794p. 1998. pap. text 100.00 (*0-13-859828-2*) P-H.
Miller, Gene. God's Saving Power. (Eagle Bible Ser.). 1989. pap. 0.99 (*0-87162-499-0*, D9151) Warner Pr.
Miller, Gene H. Microcomputer Engineering. 2nd ed. LC 98-24745. 544p. 1998. pap. 100.00 (*0-13-895368-6*) P-H.
Miller, Genevieve. Bibliography of the History of Medicine of the United States & Canada, 1939-1960. 1979. 37.95 (*0-405-10616-5*) Ayer.
— A Bibliography of the Writings of Henry E. Sigerist. LC 66-19764. 123p. reprint ed. pap. 38.20 (*0-8357-7205-5*, 202383100034) Bks Demand.
Miller, Genevieve, ed. Letters of Edward Jenner & Other Documents Concerning the Early History of Vaccination. LC 82-21295. (Henry E. Sigerist Supplements to the Bulletin of the History of Medicine, New Ser.). 176p. (C). 1983. text 28.50 (*0-8018-2962-3*) Johns Hopkins.
Miller, Geoffrey. Straits: British Policy Towards the Ottoman Empire & the Origins of the Dardanelles Campaign. (Illus.). 300p. 1998. 27.95 (*0-85958-655-3*, Pub. by Univ of Hull Pr) Paul & Co Pubs.
— Superior Force: The Conspiracy Behind the Escape of Goeben & Breslau. (Illus.). 400p. 1996. pap. 25.00 (*0-85958-635-9*, Pub. by Univ of Hull Pr) Paul & Co Pubs.
Miller, Geoffrey & Clark, Gary. The Cerebral Palsies: Causes, Consequences, & Management. (Illus.). 384p. 1998. text 77.00 incl. audio (*0-7506-9964-7*) Buttrwrth-Heinemann.
Miller, Geoffrey & Ramer, Jeanette C., eds. Static Encephalopathies of Infancy & Childhood. LC 91-37166. (Illus.). 384p. reprint ed. pap. 119.10 (*0-608-07191-9*, 206741600009) Bks Demand.
***Miller, Geoffrey F.** The Mating Mind: How the Sexual Choice Shaped the Evolution of Human Nature. LC 00-22673. 352p. 2000. 27.50 (*0-385-49516-1*) Doubleday.
Miller, Geoffrey P., jt. auth. see Amihud, Yakov.
Miller, Geoffrey P., jt. auth. see Macey, Jonathan R.
Miller, George, II. Born to Die. 300p. 1998. 48.00 (*1-901647-05-6*, Pub. by Othila Pr); pap. 23.95 (*1-901647-06-4*, Pub. by Othila Pr) Intl Spec Bk.
— Landscaping with Native Plants of Texas & the Southwest. LC 90-44298. (Illus.). 128p. (Orig.). 1991. pap. 19.95 (*0-89658-138-1*) Voyageur Pr.
— Prentice Hall Reader. 5th ed. LC 97-40656. 628p. 1997. pap. text 37.00 (*0-13-627902-3*) P-H.
***Miller, George.** The Prentice Hall Reader. 6th ed. LC 00-31347. 656p. 2000. pap. 35.33 (*0-13-022563-0*) P-H.
Miller, George, II. Residential Real Estate Appraisal. 3rd ed. LC 97-10358. 526p. 1997. 49.00 (*0-13-460635-3*) P-H.
Miller, George, II, compiled by. The Prentice Hall Reader. 4th ed. LC 94-32237. 593p. 1994. pap. text 33.00 (*0-13-079302-7*) P-H.
Miller, George, II, ed. Giving Children a Chance: The Case for More Effective National Policies. (Orig.). write for info. (*0-318-67253-7*) Ctr National Policy.
— Giving Children a Chance: The Case for More Effective National Policies. LC 88-35188. 246p. (Orig.). (C). 1989. pap. text 21.00 (*0-944237-28-2*); lib. bdg. 37.25 (*0-944237-27-4*) Ctr National Policy.
Miller, George, II & Matthews, Hugoe. Richard Jefferies: A Bibliographical Study. 832p. 1993. 139.95 (*0-85967-918-7*, Pub. by Scolar Pr) Ashgate Pub Co.
Miller, George & Noonan, Chris. A Little Pig Goes a Long Way. LC 98-30342. (Babe Ser.). 48p. (J). (gr. k-3). 1999. lib. bdg. 11.99 (*0-375-90110-8*) Random.

M

An Asterisk (*) at the beginning of an entry indicates that the title is appearing for the first time.

Miller, George, II & Smith, Frank, eds. Genesis of Language: A Psycholinguistic Approach. 1968. pap. text 16.50 (*0-262-69022-5*) MIT Pr.

Miller, George, II, jt. auth. see Stueart, Robert D.

Miller, George A. Psychology: The Science of Mental Life. 3rd ed. LC 98-12443. (Illus.). 388p. 1998. reprint ed. pap. text 29.95 (*0-937431-06-0*) Adams Bannister Cox.

— The Science of Words. (Illus.). 267p. (C). 1996. pap. text 19.95 (*0-7167-6016-9*) W H Freeman.

Miller, George A. & Johnson-Laird, Philip N. Language & Perception. 773p. 1987. pap. 17.95 (*0-674-50948-X*) Belknap Pr.

Miller, George A., et al. Plans & the Structure of Behavior. (Illus.). 226p. (C). 1986. reprint ed. text 24.95 (*0-937431-00-1*) Adams Bannister Cox.

Miller, George A., jt. auth. see Chomsky, Noam.

Miller, George A., jt. ed. see Grusky, Oscar.

Miller, George A., jt. intro. see James, William.

Miller, George B., Jr., et al, compiled by. Puppetry Library: An Annotated Bibliography Based on the Batchelder-McPharlin Collection at the University of New Mexico. LC 80-23474. 171p. 1981. lib. bdg. 47.95 (*0-313-21359-3*, HPL/, Greenwood Pr) Greenwood.

Miller, George E. Educating Medical Teachers. (Commonwealth Fund Publications). (Illus.). 243p. 1980. 26.95 (*0-674-23775-7*) HUP.

Miller, George F. Academy System of the State of New York. LC 76-89205. (American Education: Its Men, Institutions, & Ideas. Series 1). 1977. reprint ed. 18.95 (*0-405-01443-0*) Ayer.

Miller, George H. Railroads & the Granger Laws. LC 75-138059. 308p. reprint ed. pap. 95.50 (*0-8357-4752-2*, 203767400009) Bks Demand.

Miller, George H., jt. auth. see Ashley, Robert.

Miller, George H., ed. see Dagostino, Frank R. & Gallagher, Katy.

Miller, George J., jt. ed. see Reed, H. Clay.

***Miller, George K.** Project Documentation: Debt Finance. 120p. 2000. pap. text 350.00 (*1-85564-789-3*, Pub. by Euromoney) Am Educ Systs.

Miller, George L. Tantalum & Niobium. LC TN0799.T3M5. (Metallurgy of the Rarer Metals Ser.: 6). 789p. reprint ed. pap. 200.00 (*0-608-14824-5*, 202573400046) Bks Demand.

Miller, George N. The Strike of a Sex & Zugassent's Discovery: After the Sex Struck. LC 73-20636. (Sex, Marriage & Society Ser.). 124p. 1974. reprint ed. 19.95 (*0-405-05812-8*) Ayer.

Miller, George N., ed. see Noyes, John H.

Miller, George O., photos by. The Ozarks: The People, the Mountains, the Magic. LC 95-36141. (Illus.). 96p. 1996. pap. 4.95 (*0-89658-281-7*) Voyageur Pr.

Miller, George O., jt. auth. see Tull, Delena.

***Miller, Georges.** Cracking the Toefl Cbt 2000. 540p. 1999. pap. 30.00 incl. audio compact disk (*0-375-75469-5*, Pub. by PRP NY) Random.

Miller, Gerald J. Government Financial Management Theory. (Public Administration & Public Policy Ser.: Vol. 43). (Illus.). 272p. 1991. text 125.00 (*0-8247-7910-X*) Dekker.

— Handbook of Debt Management. (Public Administration & Public Policy Ser.: Vol. 60). (Illus.). 984p. 1996. text 215.00 (*0-8247-9388-9*) Dekker.

Miller, Gerald R. Introduction to Speech Communication. 2nd ed. LC 78-173982. 1972. pap. text 3.95 (*0-672-61298-4*, SC7, Bobbs) Macmillan.

Miller, Gerald R. & Stiff, James B. Deceptive Communication: Many Questions & a Few Answers. (Series in Interpersonal Communication: Vol. 14). (Illus.). 160p. 1993. 52.00 (*0-8039-3484-X*); pap. 24.50 (*0-8039-3485-8*) Sage.

Miller, Gerald R., jt. auth. see Fontes, Norman E.

Miller, Gerald R., jt. ed. see Knapp, Mark L.

Miller, Gerald R., jt. ed. see Roloff, Michael E.

Miller, Gerald V. The Gay Male's Odyssey in the Corporate World: From Disempowerment to Empowerment. LC 94-47539. (C). 1995. pap. 14.95 (*1-56023-867-4*); lib. bdg. 39.95 (*1-56024-942-0*) Haworth Pr.

Miller, Gereon. Incomplete Category Fronting: A Derivational Approach to Remnant Movement in German. LC 97-38345. (Studies in Natural Language & Linguistic Theory). 339p. 1997. text 120.50 (*0-7923-4837-0*) Kluwer Academic.

Miller, Gerlinde F. Die Bedeutu ng des Entwicklungsbeqriffs fuer Menschenbild und Dichtungstheorie bei Gottfried Benn. (New York University Ottendorfer Ser.: Vol. 29). (GER.). X, 291p. 1990. text 47.80 (*0-8204-0835-2*) P Lang Pubng.

***Miller, Gerrit S.** The Families & Genera of Bats. (Illus.). 282p. 2000. reprint ed. 64.95 (*1-930665-02-4*) Blackburn Pr.

Miller, Gilbert H. & Crooks, Alan F., eds. Major Modern Essayists. 2nd ed. LC 93-20970. 487p. 1994. pap. text 38.80 (*0-13-497983-4*) P-H.

Miller, Girard. Effective Budgetary Presentations: The Cutting Edge. LC 82-81886. (Illus.). 230p. 1982. 15.00 (*0-685-06405-0*); pap. 18.50 (*0-686-84269-3*); pap. 23.50 (*0-686-84268-5*) Municipal.

Miller, Girard, jt. auth. see Government Finance, Officers Association Staff.

Miller, Girard, jt. auth. see Municipal Finance Officers Association Staff.

Miller, Glen H. Basic Chemistry. (C). 1930. text. write for info. (*0-06-383625-4*) S&S Trade.

Miller, Glen M., jt. auth. see Phipps, Lloyd J.

Miller, Glenn. Customer Service & Innovation in Libraries. 93p. 1996. pap. 19.00 (*0-917846-39-7*, 95614) Highsmith Pr.

— Human Geography. 160p. (C). 1995. pap., per. 20.95 (*0-7872-1547-3*) Kendall-Hunt.

— Mommy, Why Can't Grandma Remember Me? (Illus.). 24p. (J). (gr. k-3). 1996. pap. 9.00 (*0-8059-3841-9*) Dorrance.

Miller, Glenn A. & Pender, Robert H. Golf: A Target Sport. 3rd ed. (Illus.). 108p. (Orig.). 1997. pap. text 11.95 (*0-89641-242-3*) American Pr.

Miller, Glenn I. Hosea Model for Marriage. LC 98-4015. 84p. 1998. pap. 7.95 (*1-57249-121-3*, Ragged Edge) White Mane Pub.

Miller, Glenn R., ed. see Seo, Myung-Seok.

Miller, Glenn T. The Modern Church: The Dawn of the Reformation to the Eve of the Third Millennium. LC 97-7866. 312p. 1996. pap. 18.95 (*0-687-00605-8*) Abingdon.

— Piety & Intellect: The Aims & Purposes of Ante-Bellum Theological Education. 458p. 1990. write for info. (*1-55540-470-7*) Assn of Theol Schls.

Miller, Glenn W. & Skaggs, Jimmy M., eds. Metropolitan Wichita: Past, Present, & Future. LC 77-16690. x, 194p. 1978. pap. 12.95 (*0-7006-0169-4*) U Pr of KS.

***Miller, Glennie T.** Think on These Things: Living to See Three Centuries & Still Ticking... (Illus.). xix,279p. 2000. Price not set. (*0-9629264-1-8*) M E Kurtz.

Miller, Gloria. Above All, Don't Flush: Adventures in Valorous Living. LC 81-22035. 160p. (Orig.). 1982. pap. 7.95 (*0-916930-03-3*) Wistaria Pr.

Miller, Gloria B. Figure Sculpture in Wax & Plaster. Miller, Richard M., ed. (Illus.). 176p. 1987. reprint ed. pap. 9.95 (*0-486-25354-6*) Dover.

— The Gift of Wine: A Straightforward Guide to the Wine Experience. (Illus.). 320p. 1996. 25.00 (*1-55821-444-5*, 14445) Lyons Pr.

— Thousand Recipe Chinese Cookbook. 944p. 1984. pap. 21.00 (*0-671-50993-4*, Fireside) S&S Trade Pap.

Miller, Gloria Bley, ed. see Baxter, Freddie Mae.

***Miller, Gordon.** The Career Coach: Winning Strategies for Getting Ahead in Today's Job Market. 240p. 2001. 24.95 (*0-385-49600-1*) Doubleday.

Miller, Gordon. Quit Your Job & Get Big. 112p. 1998. pap. 9.95 (*0-385-49593-5*) Doubleday.

— Quit Your Job Often: And Get Big Raises. (Illus.). 90p. 1998. pap. 9.95 (*0-9665230-5-9*) Q Y J O.

Miller, Gordon, ed. Wisdom of the Earth: Visions of an Ecological Faith. LC 95-77679. (Wisdom of the Earth Ser.: Vol. 1). (Illus.). 176p. (Orig.). 1997. pap. 19.95 (*0-9647007-1-9*) Green Rock.

— Wisdom of the Earth: Visions of an Ecological Faith, 2 vols., Set. (Wisdom of the Earth Ser.: Vol. 1). (Illus.). (Orig.). pap. write for info. (*0-9647007-0-0*) Green Rock.

Miller, Gordon, jt. auth. see Dann, Kevin.

Miller, Gordon L. The History of Science. (Magill Bibliographies Ser.). 193p. 1992. 42.00 (*0-8108-2795-6*) Scarecrow.

***Miller, Gordon L., ed.** Nature's Fading Chorus: Classic & Contemporary Writings on Amphibians. (Illus.). 250p. 2000. 45.00 (*1-55963-793-5*); pap. 19.95 (*1-55963-794-3*) Island Pr.

Miller, Grace P. Call of Duty: A Montana Girl in World War II. LC 98-44086. (Illus.). 152p. 1999. 24.95 (*0-8071-2343-9*) La State U Pr.

Miller, Grady. The Legal & Economic Basis of International Trade. LC 95-44348. 256p. 1996. 67.95 (*0-89930-918-6*, Quorum Bks) Greenwood.

Miller, Graham. Calvin's Wisdom. 392p. 1992. 35.99 (*0-85151-624-6*) Banner of Truth.

— Treasury of His Promises. 386p. (Orig.). 1986. pap. 18.99 (*0-85151-472-3*) Banner of Truth.

Miller, Granville, jt. auth. see Armour, Frank.

Miller, Greg. Aggressive Whitetail Hunting. LC 94-73155. (Illus.). 208p. 1995. pap. 14.95 (*0-87341-336-9*, AWH01) Krause Pubns.

— Iron Wheel. LC 97-12904. 80p. 1998. pap. 11.00 (*0-226-52798-0*); lib. bdg. 21.00 (*0-226-52797-2*) U Ch Pr.

— Proven Whitetail Tactics. LC 97-73037. (Illus.). 224p. 1997. pap. 19.95 (*0-87341-509-4*, AWII02) Krause Pubns.

— Rub-Line Secrets. Durkin, Patrick, ed. LC 99-61147. 208p. 1999. pap. 19.95 (*0-87341-812-3*) Krause Pubns.

Miller, Gregory, jt. auth. see Connell, Des W.

Miller, Gregory A., ed. The Behavioral High-Risk Paradigm in Psychopathology. LC 95-6678. (Series in Psychopathology). (Illus.). 304p. 1995. 118.00 (*0-387-94504-0*) Spr-Verlag.

Miller, Gregory D., et al. Handbook of Dairy Foods & Nutrition. 288p. 1994. boxed set 85.00 (*0-8493-8505-9*, 8505) CRC Pr.

***Miller, Gregory D., et al.** Handbook of Dairy Foods & Nutrition. 2nd ed. LC 99-32183. (Modern Nutrition Ser.). 448p. 1999. boxed set 89.95 (*0-8493-8731-0*) CRC Pr.

Miller, Gustav. Interpretados de los Suenos. 1998. pap. write for info. (*0-942272-55-2*) Original Pubns.

Miller, Gustavus H. Dictionary of Dreams. 640p. 1985. per. 14.00 (*0-671-76261-3*) S&S Trade.

— Dictionary of Dreams. 1994. 9.98 (*1-85326-943-3*, Pub. by Wrdsworth Edits) NTC Contemp Pub Co.

Miller, Gwynelle W., jt. auth. see Miller, Sherman N.

Miller, H. Sales Training: ASTD Trainer's Sourcebook. 437p. 1995. pap. 39.95 (*0-07-053436-5*) McGraw.

Miller, H. & McGuire, G. Evaluating Liberal Adult Education. 1961. 2.50 (*0-87060-034-6*, REP 125) Syracuse U Cont Ed.

Miller, H. & Rosenfeld, U., eds. Tenth Symposium on Latin-American Geosciences, Berlin 1986. (Zentralblatt Fuer Geologie Ser.). (Illus.). 368p. 1987. pap. 92.40 (*0-945345-26-7*) Lubrecht & Cramer.

Miller, H., et al. A Short Textbook of Radiotherapy. 4th ed. (Illus.). 299p. 1979. 52.00 (*0-443-01389-6*) Church.

Miller, H. A. Electrical Installation Practice. 5th ed. LC 93-7062. 1993. pap. 24.95 (*0-632-03524-2*) Blackwell Sci.

Miller, H. A. & Whittier, H. O. Prodromus Florae Hepaticarum Polynesiae. (Bryophytorum Bibliotheca Ser.: Vol. 25). 422p. 1983. lib. bdg. 128.00 (*3-7682-1373-0*) Lubrecht & Cramer.

Miller, H. A., et al. Bryoflora of the Atolls of Micronesia. (Illus.). 1963. pap. 32.00 (*3-7682-5411-9*) Lubrecht & Cramer.

— Prodromus Florae Muscorum Polynesiae with a Key to Genera. 1978. lib. bdg. 65.00 (*3-7682-1115-0*) Lubrecht & Cramer.

Miller, H. G., et al. OSHA & State Employee Hazard Communications Program, 2 vols., Vols. 1-2. Knowles-McFarland, ed. 622p. 1985. 395.00 (*0-940394-16-2*) Labelmaster.

Miller, H. Lyman. Science & Disssent in Post-Mao China: The Politics of Knowledge. LC 95-24846. (Illus.). 366p. 1996. 38.00 (*0-295-97505-9*) U of Wash Pr.

***Miller, H. Peter R.** Millionaires' Handbook: Sage Advice for Success in Business & Life. 196p. 2000. pap. 9.95 (*0-915009-70-6*, Pub. by World Leis Corp) Midpt Trade.

Miller, H. R., et al, eds. Blazar Continuum Variability, Vol. 110. (ASP Conference Series Proceedings). 512p. 1996. 34.00 (*1-886733-30-9*) Astron Soc Pacific.

Miller, H. R. & Ravenel, D. C., eds. Algebraic Topology. Vol. 1286. (Lecture Notes in Mathematics Ser.). vii, 341p. 1987. 49.95 (*0-387-18481-3*) Spr-Verlag.

Miller, H. R. & Witta, P. J., eds. Active Galactic Nuclei. (Lecture Notes in Physics Ser.: Vol. 307). xi, 438p. 1988. 59.95 (*0-387-19492-4*) Spr-Verlag.

Miller, H. S., jt. ed. see Shephard, Roy J.

Miller, Hal. The Abandoned Middle: The Ethics & Politics of Abortion in America. LC 88-90864. 92p. (Orig.). (C). 1988. pap. text 7.95 (*0-929645-00-6*) Penumbra MA.

Miller, Hannah E. Films in the Classroom: A Practical Guide. LC 78-21941. 313p. reprint ed. pap. 97.10 (*0-608-15231-5*, 202749600055) Bks Demand.

Miller, Harlan. Arguments, Arrows, Trees & Truth: A First Book in Logic & Language. 2nd ed. 242p. (C). 1980. pap. text 8.65 (*0-89894-036-2*) Advocate Pub Group.

Miller, Harlan B. & Williams, William H., eds. Ethics & Animals. LC 82-21387. (Contemporary Issues in Biomedicine, Ethics, & Society Ser.). 400p. 1983. pap. 29.95 (*0-89603-053-9*) Humana.

Miller, Harland. Make Yourself Ready: Study Guide. 214p. 1997. spiral bd. 12.95 (*0-9661146-0-4*) Eternal Hope.

Miller, Harland W. Make Yourself Ready: Preparing to Meet the King. LC 96-79609. 224p. (Orig.). 1998. pap. 11.99 (*0-933451-36-9*) Prescott Pr.

Miller, Harley. Zoology. 4th ed. 1998. student ed., spiral bd. 21.25 (*0-697-34558-0*) McGraw.

— Zoology. 4th ed. LC 98-12999. 1998. pap. text 52.00 (*0-697-34555-6*) McGraw.

— Zoology. 4th ed. 1999. text 64.00 (*0-697-34556-4*) McGraw.

— Zoology. 5th ed. 2002. 53.25 (*0-07-029411-9*) McGraw.

Miller-Harley. Zoology Web Page. 4th ed. 1998. write for info. (*0-07-228380-7*) McGraw.

Miller, Harold D., jt. ed. see Zimmerman, Sherwood E.

Miller, Harold G. New Zealand, 32. LC 82-24157. (British Empire History Ser.). 155p. 1983. reprint ed. lib. bdg. 55.00 (*0-313-22997-X*, MINZ, Greenwood Pr) Greenwood.

— Race Conflict in New Zealand, 1814-1865. LC 81-20183. (Illus.). 238p. 1982. reprint ed. lib. bdg. 52.50 (*0-313-23443-4*, MIRC, Greenwood Pr) Greenwood.

Miller, Harold L., ed. Wisconsin Progressives: The Charles McCarthy Papers: Guide to a Microfilm Edition. 38p. 1986. pap. write for info. (*0-87020-235-9*) Chadwyck-Healey.

— Wisconsin Progressives: The John R. Commons Papers: Guide to a Microfilm Edition. 48p. 1986. pap. write for info. (*0-87020-236-7*) Chadwyck-Healey.

— Wisconsin Progressives: The Richard T. Ely Papers: Guide to a Microfilm Edition. 78p. 1986. pap. write for info. (*0-87020-233-2*) Chadwyck-Healey.

Miller, Harold L. & Aber, Lynn B., eds. Wisconsin Progressives: The Edward A. Ross Papers: Guide to a Microfilm Edition. 51p. 1986. pap. write for info. (*0-87020-234-0*) Chadwyck-Healey.

Miller, Harold L., jt. ed. see Albert, Peter J.

Miller, Harold R. The Aqualine Chase. 360p. 1998. mass mkt. 6.99 (*1-893181-00-6*) Le Gesse Stevens.

— The Emerald Head Chase. LC 99-62091. 400p. 1998. mass mkt. write for info. (*1-893181-01-4*, Simon & Northrop) Le Gesse Stevens.

***Miller, Harold R.** The Phillipine Chase. LC 99-62090. 400p. 1998. mass mkt. write for info. (*1-893181-02-2*, Simon & Northrop) Le Gesse Stevens.

Miller, Harold R. Sand Cay Chase. 410p. 1998. mass mkt. 6.99 (*1-893181-03-0*, Simon & Northrop) Le Gesse Stevens.

Miller, Harrice S. Cc Costume Jewelry. 2nd ed. 344p. 1994. pap. 16.00 (*0-380-77078-4*, Avon Bks) Morrow Avon.

Miller, Harrice S. Instant Expert: Collecting Costume Jewelry. (Illus.). 130p. 1997. pap. 14.00 (*0-9641509-4-8*) Allian Pubng.

Miller, Harrice S., jt. auth. see Lane, Kenneth Jay.

Miller, Harriet P. Pioneer Colored Christians. LC 73-37313. (Black Heritage Library Collection). 1977. reprint ed. 22.95 (*0-8369-8950-3*) Ayer.

Miller, Harriett P., jt. auth. see Bell, Charles B.

Miller, Harry. Common Sense Book. 304p. 1987. mass mkt. 6.50 (*0-553-27789-8*) Bantam.

— Common Sense Book of Kitten & Cat Care. 272p. (Orig.). 1984. mass mkt. 5.99 (*0-553-26805-8*) Bantam.

Miller, Harry, ed. see National Passive Solar Conference Staff.

Miller, Harry D. & Starr, Marvin B. Miller & Starr California Real Estate Desk Set. 2nd ed. LC 98-131973. 1997. write for info. (*0-8321-0087-0*) West Group.

Miller, Harry E. Banking Theories in the U. S. Before 1860. LC 78-182194. (Library of Money & Banking History). xi, 240p. 1972. reprint ed. lib. bdg. 39.50 (*0-678-00886-8*) Kelley.

Miller, Harry L. Choosing College Major in Education. 1979. 10.95 (*0-679-50957-7*) McKay.

— Understanding Group Behavior: A Discussion Guide. rev. ed. LC BF0199. 99p. reprint ed. pap. 30.70 (*0-608-11360-3*, 200063700036) Bks Demand.

Miller, Harry S. The Basic Pattern of Nature: The Universal Code. abr. ed. (Illus.). 180p. (Orig.). 1996. pap. 29.00 (*0-9657604-1-3*) Uniscience Educ.

— The Ecocom, the Ultimate Community: Multipurpose Solution, Municipal Problems. abr. ed. (Illus.). 200p. (Orig.). Date not set. pap. 29.00 (*0-9657604-3-X*) Uniscience Educ.

— The Total Scheme of Things: Totalistic Science. abr. ed. (Illus.). 450p. (Orig.). 1996. pap. 45.00 (*0-9657604-0-5*) Uniscience Educ.

— TSOT. COM-Articles: Book of Articles, Ultimate Knowledge. abr. ed. (Illus.). 250p. (Orig.). Date not set. pap. 29.00 (*0-9657604-2-1*) Uniscience Educ.

Miller, Harvey R. & Cook, Michael L. A Practical Guide to the Bankruptcy Reform Act, 2 vols. 1400p. 1979. write for info. (*0-318-65476-8*, C00191) P-H.

Miller, Haskell M. Prayers for the Age of Technology. LC 97-29583. 64p. 1998. pap. 7.50 (*0-7880-1172-3*) CSS OH.

— Prayers for the Age of Technology. 1998. pap. 7.50 (*0-7880-1175-8*) CSS OH.

***Miller, Haskell M.** Social Ministry: An Urgent Agenda for Pastors & Churches. 152p. 2000. pap. 9.99 (*0-8361-9138-2*) Herald Pr.

— Strangers in Our Mist. 1999. pap. write for info. (*0-7880-1432-3*) CSS OH.

Miller, Haynes R., et al, eds. Proceedings of the Northwestern Homotopy Theory Conference. LC 83-9941. (Contemporary Mathematics Ser.: Vol. 19). 454p. 1983. pap. 42.00 (*0-8218-5020-2*, CONM/19) Am Math.

***Miller, Hazel.** Pathways of Poetry. 2000. write for info. (*1-58235-573-8*) Watermrk Pr.

***Miller, Heather.** My Chickens. (Welcome Bks.). (Illus.). (J). 2000. 13.50 (*0-516-23105-7*) Childrens.

— My Chickens. LC 00-24385. (My Farm Ser.). (Illus.). 24p. (J). (ps-2). 2000. pap. write for info. (*0-516-23030-1*) Childrens.

— My Cows. LC 00-24386. (My Farm Ser.). (Illus.). 24p. (J). (ps-2). 2000. pap. 4.95 (*0-516-23031-X*) Childrens.

— My Cows. (Welcome Bks.). (Illus.). (J). 2000. 13.50 (*0-516-23106-5*) Childrens.

— My Goats. (Welcome Bks.). (Illus.). (J). 2000. 13.50 (*0-516-23107-3*) Childrens.

— My Goats. LC 00-24384. (My Farm Ser.). (Illus.). 24p. (J). (ps-2). 2000. pap. write for info. (*0-516-23032-8*) Childrens.

— My Horses. LC 00-20922. (My Farm Ser.). (Illus.). 24p. (J). (ps-2). 2000. pap. 4.95 (*0-516-23033-6*) Childrens.

— My Horses. (Welcome Bks.). (Illus.). (J). 2000. 13.50 (*0-516-23108-1*) Childrens.

— My Pigs. LC 00-24625. (My Farm Ser.). (Illus.). 24p. (J). (ps-2). 2000. pap. 4.95 (*0-516-23034-4*) Childrens.

— My Pigs. (Welcome Bks.). (Illus.). (J). 2000. 13.50 (*0-516-23109-X*) Childrens.

— My Sheep. (Welcome Bks.). (Illus.). (J). 2000. 13.50 (*0-516-23110-3*) Childrens.

— My Sheep. LC 00-24363. (My Farm Ser.). (Illus.). 24p. (J). (ps-2). 2000. pap. write for info. (*0-516-23035-2*) Childrens.

Miller, Heather, tr. see Barish, Wendy & Jeunesse, Gallimard.

Miller, Heather, tr. see Delafosse, Claude, et al.

Miller, Heather G., et al, eds. AIDS: The Second Decade. 512p. 1990. pap. 39.95 (*0-309-04287-9*) Natl Acad Pr.

Miller, Heather R. Champeen. LC 99-42722. 296p. (YA). 1999. 19.95 (*0-87074-446-1*, Pub. by SMU Press) Tex A&M Univ Pr.

— Friends & Assassins: Poems. LC 92-35984. 64p. (C). 1993. pap. 10.95 (*0-8262-0829-0*); text 18.95 (*0-8262-0828-2*) U of Mo Pr.

— Hard Evidence: Poems. LC 90-35051. 64p. 1990. 18.95 (*0-8262-0754-5*); pap. 10.95 (*0-8262-0751-0*) U of Mo Pr.

— In the Funny Papers: Stories. LC 95-21678. 168p. (C). 1995. pap. 17.95 (*0-8262-1031-7*) U of Mo Pr.

***Miller, Heather Ross.** Crusoe's Island: The Story of a Writer & a Place. 214p. 2000. 19.95 (*1-928556-04-3*) Coastal NC.

Miller, Heather Ross. Days of Love & Murder. Trowbridge, William et al, eds. (Missouri Chapbook Ser.). 34p. 1999. pap. 7.50 (*1-887240-04-7*, Pub. by GreenTower Pr) Spring Church Bk Co.

Miller, Heather S. Children & Gardens: An Annotated Bibliography of Children's Garden Books, 1829-1988. Miasek, Meryl A., ed. (CBHL Plant Bibliography Ser.). 60p. (Orig.). (J). 1991. pap. write for info. (*0-9621791-1-6*) CBHL Inc.

— Managing Acquisitions & Vendor Relations: A How-to-Do-It Manual. (How-to-Do-It Ser.). 196p. 1992. 49.95 (*1-55570-111-6*) Neal-Schuman.

Miller, Helen H. The Case for Liberty. LC 65-16295. (Illus.). 270p. reprint ed. pap. 83.70 (*0-8357-3051-4*, 203930700012) Bks Demand.

— George Mason, Gentleman Revolutionary. LC 75-1377. (Illus.). 404p. reprint ed. pap. 125.30 (*0-8357-3873-6*, 203660500004) Bks Demand.

M

An Asterisk (*) at the beginning of an entry indicates that the title is appearing for the first time.

— Passage to America: Ralegh's Colonists Take Ship for Roanoke. (America's 400th Anniversary Ser.). (Illus.). xiv, 84p. 1986. reprint ed. pap. 6.00 (*0-86526-202-0*) NC Archives.

Miller, Helen L. Everyday Plays for Boys & Girls. LC 86-8884. (Orig.). (J). (gr. 1-6). 1986. pap. 12.95 (*0-8238-0274-4*) Kalmbach.

— First Plays for Children. LC 60-8933. 295p. (J). (gr. 1-3). 1985. pap. 12.95 (*0-8238-0268-X*) Kalmbach.

— Special Plays for Holidays. LC 86-9332. (Orig.). (J). (gr. 1-6). 1986. pap. 12.95 (*0-8238-0275-2*) Kalmbach.

Miller, Helen P. The Frog with the Grumpy Jump. unabridged ed. (Illus.). 20p. (J). (ps-4). 1997. pap. 6.95 (*0-9653084-4-8*) Mtn Hse Pub.

— The Holidays of Hilda Hippopotamus. unabridged ed. (Illus.). 28p. (J). (ps-5). 1997. pap. 6.95 (*0-9653084-2-1*) Mtn Hse Pub.

— PopPaw's Magic Garden. unabridged ed. (Illus.). 28p. (J). (ps-3). 1997. pap. 6.95 (*0-9653084-3-X*) Mtn Hse Pub.

Miller, Helen S. America's First Black: "Professional Nurse" 1986. write for info. (*0-935087-13-3*) Wright Pub Co.

Miller, Helena. The Magic Box. Grishaver, Joel Lurie, ed. (Illus.). (Orig.). (J). (gr. k up). 1996. pap. text 18.95 (*0-933873-92-1*) Torah Aura.

Miller, Henri. Free Trade Versus Protectionism. LC 96-8676. (Reference Shelf Ser.). 1996. pap. 25.00 (*0-8242-0889-7*) Wilson.

Miller, Henry. The Air-Conditioned Nightmare. LC 45-11390. 1970. pap. 11.95 (*0-8112-0106-6*, NDP302, Pub. by New Directions) Norton.

— Aller Retour New York. LC 91-4029. (New Directions Classics Ser.). 96p. 1991. reprint ed. 9.95 (*0-8112-1193-2*, Pub. by New Directions) Norton.

— Big Sur & the Oranges of Hieronymus Bosch. LC 57-5542. 1964. pap. 12.95 (*0-8112-0107-4*, NDP161, Pub. by New Directions) Norton.

— Black Spring. LC 63-11077. 244p. 1989. pap. 12.00 (*0-8021-3182-4*, Grove) Grove-Atltic.

— Book of Friends. 1978. 42.50 (*0-911156-73-9*) Bern Porter.

— The Books in My Life. LC 71-88728. 1969. reprint ed. pap. 12.95 (*0-8112-0108-2*, NDP280, Pub. by New Directions) Norton.

— California Missions: The Earliest Series of Views Made in 1856. Knill, Harry, ed. (Illus.). 64p. (Orig.). 1985. pap. 5.95 (*0-88388-119-5*) Bellerophon Bks.

— The Colossus of Maroussi. LC 58-9511. 1958. pap. 10.95 (*0-8112-0109-0*, NDP75, Pub. by New Directions) Norton.

Miller, Henry. The Cosmological Eye. LC 75-88729. 1961. reprint ed. pap. 14.95 (*0-8112-0110-4*, NDP109, Pub. by New Directions) Norton.

Miller, Henry. Crazy Cock: A Novel. LC 91-9244. 240p. 1992. pap. 12.00 (*0-8021-3293-6*, Grove) Grove-Atltic.

— A Devil in Paradise. LC 93-16389. (Bibelot Ser.). 128p. (Orig.). 1993. reprint ed. pap. 7.50 (*0-8112-1244-0*, NDP765, Pub. by New Directions) Norton.

***Miller, Henry.** From Tropic of Cancer: Previously Unpublished Sections. Jackson, Roger, ed. (Illus.). 114p. 1999. 125.00 (*1-893918-00-9*) R Jackson.

Miller, Henry. From Your Capricorn Friend: Henry Miller & the Stroker, 1978-1980. LC 83-17460. 101p. 1984. pap. 8.95 (*0-8112-0891-5*, NDP568, Pub. by New Directions) Norton.

— Henry Miller, 3 vols. Incl. Black Spring. 1979. Tropic of Cancer. 1979. Tropic of Capricorn. 1979. 1979. Set pap. 13.85 (*0-394-17094-6*, B430) Grove-Atltic.

— Henry Miller - Stories, Essays, Travel Sketches. Fine, Antony, ed. (Illus.). 1994. 12.98 (*1-56731-009-5*, MJF Bks) Fine Comms.

— Henry Miller - The Paintings: A Centennial Retrospective. Johansen, Deborah, ed. & intro. by. LC 91-30032. (Illus.). 128p. (Orig.). 1991. pap. 25.00 (*0-9600554-2-8*) Coast Pub.

— Henry Miller on Writing. Moore, Thomas H., ed. LC 64-10675. 1964. pap. 9.95 (*0-8112-0112-0*, NDP151, Pub. by New Directions) Norton.

— Henry Miller Reader. Durrell, Lawrence, ed. LC 73-38712. (Essay Index Reprint Ser.). 1977. reprint ed. 22.95 (*0-8369-2664-1*) Ayer.

— Henry Miller Reader. Durrell, Lawrence, ed. LC 59-15022. 1969. reprint ed. pap. 13.95 (*0-8112-0111-2*, NDP269, Pub. by New Directions) Norton.

— Henry Miller's Book of Friends: A Trilogy. LC 86-31691. 320p. (Orig.). 1987. pap. 9.95 (*0-88496-256-3*) Capra Pr.

— Horoscope: Two Essays with Introduction by Henry Miller. Herman, Jeanine et al, trs. from FRE. (Illus.). 32p. (Orig.). 1996. pap. 12.95 (*1-885983-18-2*, 620191, Turtle Pt) Turtle Point Pr.

— Into the Heart of Life: Henry Miller at 100. Turner, Fredrick, ed. LC 91-29996. 224p. (Orig.). 1991. pap. 10.95 (*0-8112-1185-1*, NDP728, Pub. by New Directions) Norton.

— Just Wild about Harry. LC 62-17269. 1979. pap. 7.95 (*0-8112-0724-2*, NDP479, Pub. by New Directions) Norton.

— Letters By Henry Miller to Hoki Tokuda Miller. Howard, Joyce, ed. LC 86-8874. 208p. 1987. 19.95 (*0-88191-038-4*) Freundlich.

— Letters to Anais Nin. 1996. pap. 14.00 (*0-15-600387-2*) Harcourt.

— The Mezzotints. Jackson, Roger, ed. (Illus.). 40p. (C). 1993. 40.00 (*0-9634136-2-7*) R Jackson.

— Moloch, or, This Gentile World. LC 92-10327. 288p. 1993. pap. 12.00 (*0-8021-3372-X*, Grove) Grove-Atltic.

— Nexus: The Rosy Crucifixion III, Vol. III. LC 87-16. 320p. 1987. pap. 12.95 (*0-8021-5178-7*, Grove) Grove-Atltic.

— Nothing but the Marvelous: The Wisdoms of Henry Miller. 2nd rev. expanded ed. Fielding, Blair, ed. (Illus.). 143p. 1999. pap. 12.95 (*0-88496-440-X*, Pub. by Capra Pr) Consort Bk Sales.

— Plexus. 1987. pap. 9.95 (*0-394-62370-3*) Random.

— Plexus: The Rosy Crucifixion II, Vol. II. LC 86-33722. 640p. 1987. pap. 14.95 (*0-8021-5179-5*, Grove) Grove-Atltic.

— Printemps Noir. (FRE.). 1975. pap. 11.95 (*0-7859-4042-1*) Fr & Eur.

— Quiet Days in Clichy. LC 87-12377. 160p. 1987. pap. 11.00 (*0-8021-3016-X*, Grove) Grove-Atltic.

— The Rosy Crucifixion. Incl. Nexus. LC 80-8064. 1980. pap. Plexus. LC 80-8064. 1980. pap. Sexus. LC 80-8064. 1980. pap. LC 80-8064. 1600p. 1980. Set boxed set 12.85 (*0-394-17774-6*, B 449) Grove-Atltic.

— Sextet. LC 77-20795. (Illus.). 188p. 1977. pap. 7.95 (*0-88496-111-7*) Capra Pr.

— Sextet. 1994. 14.95 (*0-7145-3828-0*); pap. 9.95 (*0-7145-3844-2*) Riverrun NY.

— Sextet: Six Essays. LC 95-9979. (I.O. Evans Studies in the Philosophy & Criticism of Literature, 0271-9061: Vol. 29). 192p. 1995. pap. 21.00 (*0-8095-1903-8*) Millefleurs.

— Sexus: The Rosy Crucifixion I, Vol. I. LC 86-35723. 512p. 1987. pap. 13.95 (*0-8021-5180-9*, Grove) Grove-Atltic.

— The Smile at the Foot of the Ladder. LC 58-11829. (Illus.). 64p. 1975. pap. 6.95 (*0-8112-0556-8*, NDP386, Pub. by New Directions) Norton.

— Stand Still Like the Hummingbird. LC 62-10408. 1967. reprint ed. pap. 10.95 (*0-8112-0322-0*, NDP236, Pub. by New Directions) Norton.

***Miller, Henry.** Time. (Collins Gem Ser.). (Illus.). 256p. 2000. pap. 7.95 (*0-00-472472-0*, Pub. by HarpC) Trafalgar.

Miller, Henry. The Time of the Assassins: A Study of Rimbaud. LC 55-12452. 1962. pap. 9.95 (*0-8112-0115-5*, NDP115, Pub. by New Directions) Norton.

***Miller, Henry.** To Your Health: A Proposal to Reform the Food & Drug Administration. 2000. pap. 14.95 (*0-8179-9902-7*) Hoover Inst Pr.

Miller, Henry. Tropic of Cancer. LC 61-15597. 352p. 1987. pap. 11.95 (*0-8021-3178-6*, Grove) Grove-Atltic.

— Tropic of Cancer. 288p. 1995. mass mkt. 6.95 (*0-451-52605-8*, Sig) NAL.

— Tropic of Cancer. 1987. pap. 7.95 (*0-394-62375-4*) Random.

— Tropic of Capricorn. LC 86-33510. 352p. 1987. pap. 13.00 (*0-8021-5182-5*, Grove) Grove-Atltic.

— Tropic of Capricorn. 1987. pap. 7.95 (*0-394-62379-7*) Random.

— Tropique du Cancer. (FRE.). 1972. pap. 13.95 (*0-7859-3997-0*) Fr & Eur.

— Under the Roofs of Paris. LC 84-73204. Orig. Title: Opus Pistorum. 288p. 1985. pap. 12.00 (*0-8021-3183-2*, Grove) Grove-Atltic.

— Wisdom of the Heart. LC 41-28118. 1967. pap. 10.95 (*0-8112-0116-3*, NDP94, Pub. by New Directions) Norton.

— The World of Lawrence. 1996. pap. 14.95 (*0-7145-3867-1*) Riverrun NY.

Miller, Henry & Fowlie, Wallace. Letters of Henry Miller & Wallace Fowlie, 1943-1972 LC 74-24859. 184 p. 1975. 9.50 (*0-394-49737-6*) Random.

Miller, Henry & Laughlin, James. Henry Miller & James Laughlin: Selected Letters. Wickes, George, ed. LC 95-8079. 304p. 1995. 27.50 (*0-393-03864-5*) Norton.

Miller, Henry & Nin, Anais. A Literate Passion: Letters of Anais Nin & Henry Miller, 1932-1953. Stuhlmann, Gunther, ed. 1987. 19.95 (*0-15-152729-6*) Harcourt.

Miller, Henry & Schnellock, Emil. Letters to Emil. Wickes, George, ed. LC 88-36470. 192p. 1989. reprint ed. 21.95 (*0-8112-1092-8*, Pub. by New Directions) Norton.

— Letters to Emil. Wickes, George, ed. LC 88-36470. 192p. 1991. reprint ed. pap. 12.95 (*0-8112-1170-3*, NDP717, Pub. by New Directions) Norton.

Miller, Henry, et al. New York Practice Guide: Negligence, 4 vols. 1989. ring bd. 510.00 (*0-8205-1521-3*) Bender.

— Why Abstract? LC 74-6407. (Studies in Comparative Literature: No. 35). 1974. lib. bdg. 75.00 (*0-8383-1837-1*) M S G Haskell Hse.

Miller, Henry, jt. auth. see Durrell, Lawrence.

Miller, Henry, jt. auth. see Nin, Anais.

Miller, Henry Arthur, jt. auth. see Puckering, R. D.

Miller, Henry C. State Coinage of Connecticut. (Illus.). 1981. reprint ed. lib. bdg. 35.00 (*0-915262-64-9*) S J Durst.

Miller, Henry D. The Management of Change in Universities: Universities, State & Economy in Australia, Canada & the United Kingdom. LC 94-44549. 208p. 1994. 123.00 (*0-335-19089-8*) OpUniv Pr.

Miller, Henry G. Settlement. (Art of Advocacy Ser.). 1983. 160.00 (*0-8205-1041-6*) Bender.

Miller, Henry I. Is the Biodiversity Treaty a Bureaucratic Time Bomb? LC 94-43957. (Essays in Public Policy Ser.: No. 56). 1994. pap. text 5.00 (*0-8179-5612-3*) Hoover Inst Pr.

— Policy Controversy in Biotechnology: An Insider's View. 1997. text 69.95 (*0-12-496725-6*) Acad Pr.

— Policy Controversy in Biotechnology: An Insider's View. LC 96-35982. (Biotechnology Intelligence Unit Ser.). 1996. write for info. (*1-57059-408-2*) Chapman & Hall.

Miller, Henry I., jt. auth. see Anderson, Terry Lee.

Miller, Henry K., ed. see Fielding, Henry.

Miller, Henry M., et al. The Archaeology of Sixteenth- & Seventeenth-Century British Colonization in the Caribbean, United States, & Canada No. 4: Guides to Historical Archaeological Literature. LC 97-206882. 120p. (Orig.). 1996. 15.00 (*1-886818-02-9*) Society Hist Arch.

***Miller, Herb.** Church Personality Matters! How to Build Positive Patterns. LC 98-43550. 1999. 16.99 (*0-8272-0477-9*) Chalice Pr.

Miller, Herb. Connecting with God: Fourteen Ways Churches Can Help People Grow Spiritually. LC 94-6697. (Effective Church Ser.). 144p. (Orig.). 1994. pap. 12.95 (*0-687-09405-4*) Abingdon.

— Consecration Sunday Stewardship Program Book: Estimate of Giving Card. pap. 9.00 (*0-687-00940-5*) Abingdon.

— Consecration Sunday Stewardship Program Book: Guest Leader's Book, Guest Leader's Book. 1996. pap. text 10.00 (*0-687-00923-5*) Abingdon.

— Discovery Sunday: A Spiritual Growth Experience for Individuals & Congregations. 96p. 1996. pap. 10.00 (*0-8358-0767-3*) Upper Room Bks.

— Jesus' Twenty Megatruths. LC 98-17309. 144p. 1998. pap. 12.99 (*0-8272-1712-9*) Chalice Pr.

— Leadership Is the Key: Unlocking Your Effectiveness in Ministry. LC 96-51887. (Leadership Insight Ser.). 176p. 1997. pap. 14.95 (*0-687-01375-5*) Abingdon.

— Money Is Everything: What Jesus Said about the Spiritual Power of Money. LC 94-70012. 72p. 1994. pap. 8.95 (*0-88177-132-5*, DR132) Discipleship Res.

— The Vital Congregation: Ten Basic Measurements. LC 90-31095. (Effective Church Ser.). 1990. pap. 12.95 (*0-687-43796-2*) Abingdon.

Miller, Herb, ed. see Arnold, Jeffrey.

Miller, Herb, ed. see Bauknight, Brian K.

Miller, Herb, ed. see Cueni, Robert.

Miller, Herb, ed. see Grimm, Eugene.

Miller, Herb, ed. see Lee, Robert A.

Miller, Herb, ed. see Mundey, Paul.

Miller, Herb, ed. see Nelson, Alan E.

Miller, Herb, ed. see Owens, Bill.

Miller, Herb, ed. see Ramey, Robert H., Jr.

Miller, Herb, ed. see Wright, Timothy.

Miller, Herbert. Evangelism's Open Secrets. 2nd ed. LC 77-23468. 112p. 1985. pap. 7.99 (*0-8272-0805-7*) Chalice Pr.

— Fishing on the Asphalt: Effective Evangelism in Main Line Denominations. LC 83-10006. 208p. (Orig.). 1983. pap. 8.99 (*0-8272-1011-6*) Chalice Pr.

— Tools for Active Christians. LC 79-14795. (P.A.C.E. Ser.). (Orig.). 1979. pap. 9.99 (*0-8272-3624-7*) Chalice Pr.

Miller, Herbert A. School & the Immigrant. LC 71-129507. (American Immigration Collection. Series 2). 1980. reprint ed. 13.95 (*0-405-00561-X*) Ayer.

Miller, Herbert A., jt. auth. see Park, Robert Ezra.

Miller, Herbert C. & Mattioli, Leone, eds. Clinical Problems in Pediatrics. LC 77-89459. 251p. reprint ed. pap. 77.90 (*0-8357-6760-4*, 203542100095) Bks Demand.

Miller, Herbert C. & Merritt, T. Allen. Fetal Growth in Humans. LC 79-9974. (Illus.). 192p. reprint ed. pap. 59.60 (*0-608-18482-9*, 203300100082) Bks Demand.

Miller, Herbert E. & Mead, George C. CPA Review Manual. 5th ed. (Illus.). 1979. 38.50 (*0-685-03807-6*); text 28.95 (*0-685-03808-4*) P-H.

Miller, Herman. Herman Miller Inc. Building & Beliefs. (Illus.). 192p. 1995. 30.00 (*1-55835-132-9*) AIA Press.

Miller, Herman L. Lumbering in Early Twentieth Century Michigan: The Kneeland-Bigelow Company Experience. (Illus.). 86p. (Orig.). 1995. pap. 19.95 (*0-9645716-0-9*) Walnut Hll Pr.

Miller, Hess. The Police in the Community. 3rd ed. (Criminal Justice Ser.). 2001. pap. text 55.75 (*0-534-53946-7*) Brooks-Cole.

***Miller-Heyl, Janet L., et al.** Dare to Be You: A Systems Approach to the Early Prevention of Problem Behaviors. LC 00-35239. (Prevention in Practice Library). 2000. pap. write for info. (*0-306-46393-8*, Kluwer Plenum) Kluwer Academic.

Miller, Hildy & Ashcroft, Mary E. Strong, Typical, & Weak College Writers Vol. 5: Twenty-Two Case Studies. Bridwell-Bowles, Lillian & Olson, Mark, eds. (Monographs: Vol. 5). 211p. (Orig.). 1996. pap. 16.00 (*1-881221-11-3*) U Minn Ctr Interdis.

Miller, Hobart G., et al. OSHA & State Employee Hazard Communications Program. rev. ed. 325p. 1988. teacher ed. 295.00 (*0-940394-29-4*) Labelmaster.

Miller, Holly. How to Add More Than Pennies to Your Thoughts. 1990. pap. 3.99 (*0-87162-501-6*, D4318) Warner Pr.

Miller, Holly G., jt. auth. see Hensley, Dennis E.

Miller, Hope. Hope's Mushroom Cookbook: A Guide to the Practical Application of Botany. rev. ed. (Illus.). 212p. (Orig.). 1993. pap. 24.95 (*0-916422-79-8*) Mad River.

Miller, Hope H. & Miller, Orson K., Jr. Gasteromycetes: Morphological & Developmental Features. 150p. 1987. pap. 14.95 (*0-916422-74-7*) Mad River.

Miller, Howard. Abraham Lincoln's Flag: We Won't Give up a Star. (Illus.). 26p. (J). (gr. 4-6). 1990. pap. text 4.95 (*0-939631-19-9*) Thomas Publications.

— Trees. 3rd ed. (Pictured Key Nature Ser.). 276p. (C). 1978. text. write for info. (*0-697-04896-9*, WCB McGr Hill) McGrw-H Hghr Educ.

Miller, Howard A. & Lamb, Samuel H. Oaks of North America. LC 83-25042. (Illus.). 328p. 1984. pap. 12.95 (*0-87961-137-5*) Naturegraph.

Miller, Howard S. The Eads Bridge. 2nd ed. LC 99-17885. (Illus.). 160p. 1999. text 29.95 (*1-883982-29-4*, Pub. by MO Hist Soc) U of Mo Pr.

Miller, Howard S., jt. auth. see Corbett, Katharine T.

Miller, Howard W. How to Automate Your Computer Center: Achieving Unattended Operations. 339p. 1993. pap. 49.95 (*0-471-58427-4*, GA3187) Wiley.

— Reengineering Legacy Software Systems. LC 97-30947. 250p. 1997. pap. 39.95 (*1-55558-195-1*, Digital DEC) Buttrwrth-Heinemann.

Miller, Hub. Laminated Wood Boatbuilder: A Step-by-Step Guide for the Backyard Builder. 1993. pap. 24.95 (*0-87742-386-5*) Intl Marine.

Miller, Hubert. Vergleichende Studien an Praemesozoischen Gesteinen Chilesunter Besonderer Beruecksichtigung Ihrer Kleintektonik. (Geotektonische Forschungen Ser.: Vol. 36). (GER.). ii, 64p. 1970. pap. 23.00 (*3-510-50002-4*, Pub. by E Schweizerbartsche) Balogh.

Miller, Hubert J. Padre Miguel Hidalgo: Father of Mexican Independence. 77p. (Orig.). 1986. pap. text 5.00 (*0-938738-05-4*) U TX Pan Am Pr.

***Miller, Hugh.** Alistair MacLean's Unaco: Prime Target. 230p. 1998. mass mkt. 10.95 (*0-00-649934-1*, Pub. by HarpC) Trafalgar.

Miller, Hugh. Ballykissangel: A Sense of Place. 1999. pap. 10.95 (*0-912333-63-4*) BB&T Inc.

— Ballykissangel: The New Arrival. LC 97-49050. 1998. pap. 10.95 (*0-912333-62-6*) BB&T Inc.

— Borrowed Time. large type ed. LC 98-15545. 1998. 20.00 (*0-7862-1495-3*) Thorndike Pr.

Miller, Hugh. Seaforth BBC Tie In, Vol. 2. 272p. Date not set. pap. 9.95 (*0-14-024191-4*, Pub. by Pnguin Bks Ltd) Trafalgar.

Miller, Hugh. Skin Deep. large type ed. 293p. 1993. 27.99 (*0-7505-0446-3*) Ulverscroft.

— Traces of Guilt: Forensic Science & the Fight Against Crime. (Illus.). 192p. 1997. pap. 14.95 (*0-563-36964-7*, BBC-Parkwest) Parkwest Pubns.

***Miller, Hugh.** Traces of Guilt: Forensic Science & the Fight Against Crime. (Illus.). 192p. 1999. reprint ed. pap. text 14.00 (*0-7881-6570-4*) DIANE Pub.

— What the Corpse Revealed: Murder & the Science of Forensic Detection. 2000. mass mkt. 6.99 (*0-312-97573-2*) St Martin.

Miller, Hugh. What the Corpse Revealed: Murder & the Science of Forensic Detection. 3rd ed. LC 99-20223. (Illus.). 256p. 1999. text 23.95 (*0-312-20546-5*) St Martin.

Miller, Hugh, ed. Best One-Act Plays of 1958-59. 255p. 1960. 16.95 (*0-910278-83-0*) Boulevard.

Miller, Hugh G. Isthmian Highway: A Review of the Problems of the Caribbean. LC 76-111725. (American Imperialism: Viewpoints of United States Foreign Policy, 1898-1941 Ser.). 1970. reprint ed. 26.95 (*0-405-02039-2*) Ayer.

— The Old Red Sandstone: or New Walks in an Old Field. Albritton, Claude C., Jr., ed. LC 77-6531. (History of Geology Ser.). (Illus.). 1978. reprint ed. lib. bdg. 37.95 (*0-405-10451-0*) Ayer.

— Scenes & Legends of the North of Scotland: Traditional History of Cromarty. 2nd rev. ed. Dorson, Richard M., ed. (International Folklore Ser.). 1977. reprint ed. lib. bdg. 41.95 (*0-405-10110-4*) Ayer.

— The Testimony of the Rocks: or Geology in Its Bearings on Two Theologies, Natural & Revealed. Gould, Stephen Jay, ed. LC 79-8336. (History of Paleontology Ser.). (Illus.). 1980. reprint ed. lib. bdg. 46.95 (*0-405-12720-0*) Ayer.

Miller, Hugh M., et al. HCO Hist of Western. 5th ed. LC 90-56020. (College Outline Ser.). (Illus.). 320p. 1991. pap. 15.00 (*0-06-467107-0*, Harper Ref) HarpC.

Miller, Hugh S., et al. Instructions for Obstetric & Gynecologic Patients. 2nd ed. Schmitt, William, ed. LC 97-7620. 272p. 1997. pap. text 45.00 (*0-7216-7368-6*, W B Saunders Co) Harcrt Hlth Sci Grp.

Miller, Hugh S., jt. auth. see Griffith, H. Winter.

Miller, Hugh T. & Alkadra, Mohamad. These Things Happen: Stories from the Public Sector. LC 98-9021. 1998. pap. write for info. (*1-57420-063-1*) Chatelaine.

Miller, Hugh T. & Fox, Charles J., eds. Postmodernism, "Reality" & Public Administration: A Discourse. LC 96-35674. 213p. (Orig.). 1997. pap. 25.95 (*1-57420-060-7*) Chatelaine.

Miller, Hugh T., jt. auth. see Fox, Charles F.

Miller, Hunter, ed. U. S. Treaties . . . Digests . . . Miller: Treaties & Other International Acts of the United States of America, 8 vols., Set. LC 31-28952. 1977. reprint ed. 425.00 (*1-57588-373-2*, 201240) W S Hein.

***Miller, Hurley B.** Once in a Lifetime. LC 99-74704. 128p. 2000. pap. 11.95 (*1-57197-195-5*, Pub. by Pentland Pr) Assoc Pubs Grp.

Miller, I., jt. auth. see Agopian, L.

Miller, I. Pickering. Life Immortal (1898) 386p. 1998. reprint ed. pap. 27.95 (*0-7661-0632-2*) Kessinger Pub.

Miller, Ian. Guitar Manual 1. Stang, Aaron, ed. 100p. (C). 1993. pap. text 18.95 (*0-7692-1356-1*, GF0579) Wrner Bros.

Miller, Ian, jt. auth. see Harrison, M. John.

Miller, Ian J. Gemini. 1986. 30.00 (*0-7223-2057-4*, Pub. by A H S Ltd) St Mut.

Miller, Ian M. & Brodelius, Peter, eds. Plant Membrane Biology. (Proceedings of the Phytochemical Society of Europe Ser.: Vol. 38). (Illus.). 310p. (C). 1996. text 135.00 (*0-19-857776-1*, Clarendon Pr) OUP.

Miller, Inabeth, jt. ed. see Willie, Charles V.

Miller, Ingrid W. Afro-Hispanic Literature: An Anthology of Hispanic Writers of Hispanic Ancestry. LC 91-84525. (Coleccion Ebano y Canela). 143p. (Orig.). 1991. pap. 19.00 (*0-89729-582-X*) Ediciones.

Miller, Iona, jt. auth. see Miller, Richard.

Miller, Iona, jt. auth. see Miller, Richard A.

Miller, Ira, jt. auth. see Fitzpatrick, Dan.

Miller, Irby H. The Ozark Clan of Elkhead Creek: Early Life in Northwest Colorado. 2nd rev. ed. LC 96-61963. (Illus.). 336p. 1997. pap. 15.95 (*0-9655961-0-9*) Yellow Cat.

Miller, Iris. Visions of Washington: Composite Plan of Urban Interventions. 1992. 68.00 (*0-9635710-0-1*) Iris Miller.

Miller, Iris & Busser, Robert A., eds. Urban Design: Visions & Reflections. 160p. (Orig.). (C). 1991. pap. text. write for info. (*0-9635710-1-X*) Iris Miller.

M

Miller, Iris & Grim, Ronald E., eds. Capital Visions: Reflections on a Decade of Urban Design & a Look Ahead. (Illus.). v, 52p. (Orig.). (C). 1995. pap. text. write for info. (*0-8444-0882-4*) Lib Congress.

Miller, Irving. Burns for Bairns. (Illus.). (C). 1989. pap. text 35.00 (*0-907526-46-2*, Pub. by Alloway Pub) St Mut.

Miller, Irwin. American Health Care Blues: Blue Cross, HMOs, & Pragmatic Reform. 160p. 1996. text 32.95 (*1-56000-265-4*) Transaction Pubs.

***Miller, Irwin.** American Health Care Blues: Blue Cross, HMOs & Pragmatic Reform since 1960. 148p. 2000. pap. 21.95 (*0-7658-0723-8*) Transaction Pubs.

Miller, Irwin & Miller, Marylees. Statistical Methods for Quality: With Applications to Engineering & Management. LC 94-4684. 416p. 1994. 66.00 (*0-13-013749-9*) P-H.

Miller, Irwin, et al. Probability & Statistics for Engineers. 5th ed. LC 93-24611. 640p. 1993. text 96.00 (*0-13-721408-1*) P-H.

Miller, Isabel. A Dooryard Full of Flowers. 160p. 1993. pap. 9.95 (*1-56280-029-9*) Naiad Pr.

— Laurel. 144p. (Orig.). 1996. pap. 10.95 (*1-56280-146-5*) Naiad Pr.

— The Love of Good Women. 224p. 1986. pap. 8.95 (*0-930044-81-9*) Naiad Pr.

— Side by Side. 256p. 1990. pap. 9.95 (*0-941483-77-0*) Naiad Pr.

Miller, Isobel, jt. auth. see Miller, Kentalle.

Miller, Ivan. Nightdreams & Daymares: Introspection from the Inner City. Barnett, Shia, ed. 1999. pap. 12.00 (*0-9655430-2-1*) Blckberry Bks.

Miller, Ivan J. What Managed Care Is Doing to Outpatient Mental Health: A Look Behind the Veil of Secrecy. 49p. 1994. pap. 6.00 (*0-9645263-0-1*) Boulder Psychother.

Miller, J. A Fortune Found. 1990. pap. 25.00 (*0-7220-3570-5*) St Mut.

— Grassroots to God. 1990. pap. 21.00 (*0-7220-3770-8*) St Mut.

— Improve Your Reading, Improve Your Job: Basic Reading Skills for the Working Adult. Shotwell, Nancy, ed. LC 90-84075. (Fifty-Minute Ser.). (Illus.). 120p. (Orig.). 1991. pap. 10.95 (*1-56052-086-8*) Crisp Pubns.

— Religion in the Popular Prints, 1600-1832. LC 85-5938. (English Satirical Print Ser.). 372p. 1986. lib. bdg. 100.00 (*0-85964-170-8*) Chadwyck-Healey.

***Miller, J., et al, eds.** Evolvable Systems - From Biology to Hardware: Proceedings, Third International Conference, ICES 2000, Edinburgh, Scotland, U. K., April 17-19, 2000. (Lecture Notes in Computer Science Ser.: Vol. 1801). x, 286p. 2000. pap. 52.00 (*3-540-67338-5*) Spr-Verlag.

Miller, J., ed. see Gass, Tyler E. & Bennett, T.

Miller, J., jt. ed. see Morel, T.

Miller, J. A., jt. ed. see Crow, D. E.

Miller, J. Abbott. Dimensional Typography No. 1: Words in Space Kiosk Report. LC 98-117891. (Illus.). 64p. (Orig.). 1996. pap. 11.95 (*1-56898-089-2*) Princeton Arch.

Miller, J. Abbott & Tarr, Patsy, eds. Dance Ink: Photographs. LC 97-11244. 1997. pap. 35.00 (*0-8118-1855-1*) Chronicle Bks.

Miller, J. Abbott, jt. auth. see Lupton, Ellen.

Miller, J. Abbott, ed. see Jacobs, Laura, et al.

Miller, J. Allen. Christian Doctrine: Lectures & Sermons. 1946. 1.75 (*0-934970-01-7*) Brethren Church.

Miller, J. Anthony. Texas vs. Johnson: The Flag-Burning Case. LC 96-34850. (Landmark Supreme Court Cases Ser.). (Illus.). 112p. (YA). (gr. 6 up). 1997. lib. bdg. 20.95 (*0-89490-858-8*) Enslow Pubs.

Miller, J. C. Estadistica para Quimica Analitica. (SPA.). (C). 1993. pap. text 19.66 (*0-201-60140-0*) Addison-Wesley.

Miller, J. C. & Haglund, R. F., Jr., eds. Laser Ablation, Mechanisms & Applications: Proceedings of a Workshop Held in Oak Ridge, Tennessee, U. S. A., 8-10 April 1991. (Lecture Notes in Physics Ser.: Vol. 389). viii, 362p. 1991. 58.00 (*0-387-97731-7*) Spr-Verlag.

***Miller, J. C. & Miller, J. N.** Statistics & Chemometrics for Analytical Chemistry. 4th ed. LC 00-22435. (Illus.). 2000. pap. write for info. (*0-13-022888-5*) P-H.

Miller, J. C. & Miller, J. N. Statistics for Analytical Chemistry. 2nd ed. LC 87-22604. (Mathematics & Its Applications Ser.). 227p. 1988. text 44.95 (*0-470-20902-X*) P-H.

Miller, J. D. Commonwealth in the World. 3rd ed. LC 65-8789. (Illus.). 304p. 1965. 34.95 (*0-674-14700-6*) HUP.

— Questions Most Asked about Anxiety & Phobias: A Lively, Down to Earth Guide for Overcoming Panic. 166p. (Orig.). 1996. pap. 10.50 (*0-9654873-0-X*) Pretext Pr.

Miller, J. D., et al, eds. Advances in Brain Resuscitation. (Illus.). 344p. 1991. 141.00 (*0-387-70067-6*) Spr-Verlag.

Miller, J. D. & Vincent, R. J., eds. Order & Violence: Hedley Bull & International Relations. (Illus.). 228p. 1990. text 59.00 (*0-19-827555-2*) OUP.

Miller, J. D., jt. auth. see Carsten, M. E.

Miller, J. D., jt. auth. see Parekh, B. K.

Miller, J. D., jt. ed. see Evans, L. T.

Miller, J. D., jt. ed. see Howard, D. H.

Miller, J. D., ed. see International Symposium on Hydrometallurgy Staff.

Miller, J. D., jt. ed. see Teasdale, G. M.

Miller, J. Dale. 1000 Spanish Idioms. 2nd ed. LC 71-180253. xii, 173p. (C). 1971. pap. text 8.95 (*0-8425-1513-5*, Friends of the Library) Brigham.

Miller, J. David & Trenholm, Locksley, eds. Mycotoxins in Grain: Compounds Other Than Aflatoxin. LC 93-73623. (Illus.). 552p. 1994. 159.00 (*0-9624407-5-2*) Eagan Pr.

Miller, J. David, jt. auth. see Glanville, Jerry.

Miller, J. E. & Schmidt, F. E., Jr., eds. Slurry Erosion: Uses, Applications, & Test Methods. LC 87-920. (Special Technical Publication Ser.: No. 946). (Illus.). 274p. 1987. text 48.00 (*0-8031-0941-5*, STP946) ASTM.

Miller, J. E., Jr., ed. see Whitman, Walt.

Miller, J. G. Family Property & Financial Provision. 3rd ed. 600p. 1993. 75.00 (*0-85459-750-6*, Pub. by Tolley Pubng) St Mut.

Miller, J. Gareth. The Machinery of Succession. 2nd ed. (Illus.). 400p. 1996. text 96.95 (*1-85521-442-3*, Pub. by Dartmth Pub) Ashgate Pub Co.

Miller, J. H., et al, eds. Gorbachev at the Helm: A New Era in Soviet Politics? 320p. 1987. lib. bdg. 47.50 (*0-7099-5506-5*, Pub. by C Helm) Routldge.

Miller, J. Hillis. Ariadne's Thread: Story Lines. 320p. (C). 1992. 42.50 (*0-300-05216-2*) Yale U Pr.

— Ariadne's Thread: Story Lines. 1995. pap. 20.00 (*0-300-06309-1*) Yale U Pr.

***Miller, J. Hillis.** Black Holes. LC 98-41706. (Cultural Memory in the Present Ser.). 537p. 1999. 65.00 (*0-8047-3243-4*) Stanford U CFREES.

— The Disappearance of God: Five Nineteenth-Century Writers. 392p. 2000. 16.95 (*0-252-06910-2*) U of Ill Pr.

Miller, J. Hillis. Fiction & Repetition: Seven English Novels. LC 81-6733. 260p. 1982. 25.00 (*0-674-29925-6*) HUP.

— Fiction & Repetition: Seven English Novels. 260p. 1982. pap. 15.00 (*0-674-29926-4*) HUP.

— The Form of Victorian Fiction. 151p. 1980. 20.00 (*0-934958-00-9*) Bellflower.

— Illustration. (Essays in Art & Culture Ser.). (Illus.). 160p. 1992. 39.00 (*0-674-44357-8*) HUP.

— Illustration. (Illus.). 160p. 1994. pap. 23.95 (*0-674-44358-6*) HUP.

— Reading Narrative. LC 98-5734. (Oklahoma Project for Discourse & Theory Ser.: No. 18). (Illus.). 304p. 1998. 28.95 (*0-8061-3097-0*); pap. 28.95 (*0-8061-3098-9*) U of Okla Pr.

— Theory Now & Then. LC 90-44884. 420p. 1991. text 54.95 (*0-8223-1112-7*) Duke.

— Topographies. LC 94-25351. (Meridian: Crossing Aesthetics Ser.). xv , 378p. 1995. 49.50 (*0-8047-2378-8*); pap. 16.95 (*0-8047-2379-6*) Stanford U Pr.

— Tropes, Parables, Performatives: Essays on Twentieth-Century Literature. LC 90-44886. 288p. 1991. text 54.95 (*0-8223-1111-9*) Duke.

— Victorian Subjects. LC 90-44885. 336p. 1991. text 54.95 (*0-8223-1110-0*) Duke.

Miller, J. Hillis & Asensi, Manuel. Black Holes. LC 98-41706. (Cultural Memory in the Present Ser.). 1999. 19.95 (*0-8047-3244-2*) Stanford U Pr.

Miller, J. Hillis, et al. Narrative Endings. LC PN3378.N3. (Ninteenth-Century Studies: Vol. 33, No. 1). 160p. reprint ed. pap. 49.60 (*0-608-18291-5*, 203154100075) Bks Demand.

Miller, J. J., et al. Fitted Numerical Methods for Singularity Perturbation Problems: Error Estimates in the Maximum Norm for Linear Problems in One & Two Dimensions. 165p. 1996. text 28.00 (*981-02-2462-1*, McaPmCpMf-B2933) World Scientific Pub.

Miller, J. Jefferson, II. English Yellow-Glazed Earthenware. LC 73-21328. (Illus.). 126p. 1974. 35.00 (*0-87474-150-5*, MIEY) Smithsonian.

Miller, J. K., intro. Official Fair-Use Guidelines: Complete Texts of Four Official Documents Arranged for Use by Educators. 3rd ed. 1987. pap. 5.95 (*0-914143-11-5*, Copy Info Svc) Assn Ed Comm Tech.

Miller, J. Keith. Compelled to Control: Recovering Intimacy in Broken Relationships. rev. ed. LC 97-5376. 250p. 1997. pap. 11.95 (*1-55874-461-4*) Health Comm.

— A Hunger for Healing: The Twelve Steps as a Classic Model for Christian Spiritual Growth. LC 90-55295. 288p. 1992. pap. 14.00 (*0-06-065767-7*, Pub. by Harper SF) HarpC.

— A Hunger for Healing Workbook. LC 94-123011. 160p. 1992. pap., student ed. 16.00 (*0-06-065721-9*, Pub. by Harper SF) HarpC.

— Secret Life of the Soul. LC 97-26017. 1997. 19.99 (*0-8054-6375-5*) Broadman.

Miller, J. Lane & Miller, Madeleine S. Harper's Encyclopedia of Bible Life. 440p. 1996. 10.98 (*0-7858-0726-8*) Bk Sales Inc.

Miller, J. Lawrence. Some Things Against the Churches: A Wake-Up Call to the Congregational Churches. unabridged ed. 116p. (Orig.). 1996. pap. 7.95 (*0-9651142-9-5*) Scroll Pubs.

Miller, J. M. The Big Lie: A Weatherby Mystery. LC 93-27309. 1994. pap. 10.99 (*0-8407-6357-3*) Nelson.

— Extreme Methods. LC 99-54990. 256p. (C). 2000. pap. 26.67 (*0-321-05487-3*) Addison-Wesley.

Miller, J. M. & Spelman, F. A., eds. Cochlear Implants. (Illus.). 350p. 1989. 168.95 (*0-387-97033-9*, 2956) Spr-Verlag.

Miller, J. M., jt. auth. see Shintani, Terry.

Miller, J. M., jt. ed. see Hamburger, Joel I.

Miller, J. Martin, et al. Needle Biopsy of the Thyroid: Current Concepts. LC 82-16667. 289p. 1983. 89.50 (*0-275-91403-8*, C1403, Praeger Pubs) Greenwood.

Miller, J. Maxwell. The History of Israel: An Essential Guide. 128p. 1997. pap. 14.95 (*0-687-00083-1*) Abingdon.

Miller, J. Maxwell, ed. Archaeological Survey of the Kerak Plateau: Conducted During 1978-1982 under the Direction of J. Maxwell Miller. (Archaeological Reports: Vol. 1). (Illus.). 354p. (C). 1991. reprint ed. 69.00 (*1-55540-642-4*, 85 00 01, Pub. by Am Sch Orient Res) David Brown.

Miller, J. Maxwell, jt. auth. see Hayes, John H.

Miller, J. Maxwell, jt. ed. see Hayes, John H.

***Miller, J. Michael.** From Shanghai to Corregidor: Marines in the Defense of the Philippines. (Illus.). 44p. (C). 1999. pap. text 15.00 (*0-7881-7326-X*) DIANE Pub.

— From Shanghai to Corregidor: Marines in the Defense of the Philippines. 44p. 1998. pap. 4.25 (*0-16-061350-7*) USGPO.

Miller, J. Michael. A Guide to Specimen Management. 2nd rev. ed. LC 98-36019. (Illus.). 200p. 1998. pap. 29.95 (*1-55581-138-8*) ASM Pr.

— The North Anna Campaign "Even to Hell Itself" May 21-26, 1864. (Virginia Civil War Battles & Leaders Ser.). (Illus.). 188p. 1989. 19.95 (*0-930919-71-8*) H E Howard.

Miller, J. Michael & Wentworth, Berttina B., eds. Methods for Quality Control in Diagnostic Microbiology. LC 85-3991. 368p. 1985. 45.00 (*0-87553-121-0*) Am Pub Health.

Miller, J. Michael, ed. see Burke, Pat.

Miller, J. Michael, ed. & intro. see John Paul, II, pseud.

Miller, J. N., jt. auth. see Miller, J. C.

Miller, J. P. Days of Wine & Roses. 1973. pap. 5.25 (*0-8222-0281-6*) Dramatists Play.

— Days of Wine & Roses. (Script Publishing Project Ser.: Vol. I). iv, 143p. 1999. 19.95 (*0-9671345-1-X*) Harvest Moon Pubg.

— Follow Me. (J). 1998. 3.25 (*0-679-88662-1*) Random Bks Yng Read.

— Good Night, Little Rabbit. LC 85-62017. (Board Bks.). (Illus.). 7p. (J). (ps). 1986. 4.99 (*0-394-87992-9*, Pub. by Random Bks Yng Read) Random.

***Miller, J. P.** The Holistic Curriculum. 140p. 1998. pap. 29.50 (*0-7744-0320-9*) OISE.

Miller, J. P. Numbers in Presence & Absence: A Study of Husserl's Philosophy of Mathematics. (Phaenomenologica Ser.: Vol. 90). 157p. 1982. lib. bdg. 99.50 (*90-247-2709-X*, Pub. by M Nijhoff) Kluwer Academic.

— The People Next Door. 1969. pap. 5.25 (*0-8222-0884-9*) Dramatists Play.

— Yoo-Hoo Little Rabbit. LC 85-61529. (Illus.). (J). (ps). 1986. 4.99 (*0-394-87884-1*, Pub. by Random Bks Yng Read) Random.

Miller, J. P., et al, eds. From Reaction to Cognition: 5th European Workshop on Modelling Autonomous Agents in a Multi-Agent World, MAAMAW '93, Neuchatel, Switzerland, August 25-27, 1993, Selected Papers, Vol. VI. LC 95-34609. (Lecture Notes in Artificial Intelligence: Vol. 957). 254p. 1995. 43.00 (*3-540-60155-4*) Spr-Verlag.

***Miller, J. Philip.** We All Sing with the Same Voice. (J). 2001. lib. bdg. write for info. (*0-06-029364-0*) HarpC Child Bks.

— We All Sing with the Same Voice. 32p. (J). (ps-2). 2001. 15.95 incl. audio (*0-06-027475-1*) HarpC Child Bks.

Miller, J. R. Beautiful Living. 208p. 1998. 14.99 (*1-56292-543-1*) Honor Bks OK.

— Devotional Hours with the Bible. LC 97-74613. (Walk in the Word Ser.). 608p. 1997. reprint ed. pap. 24.99 (*0-89957-219-7*) AMG Pubs.

— Equal Rights: The Jesuits' Estates Act Controversy. (Illus.). 1979. 55.00 (*0-7735-0302-1*, Pub. by McG-Queens Univ Pr) CUP Services.

— Fillet & Root Design Considerations. (Technical Papers: Vol. P109.26). (Illus.). 21p. 1971. pap. text 30.00 (*1-55589-183-7*) AGMA.

— The Freethinker's Little Handbook: Ammunition in the Battle for Truth. 104p. 1995. spiral bd. 9.95 (*0-9636500-1-7*) Flying M Grp.

— How Professional Gamblers Beat the Pro Football Pointspread: A Step-by-Step Textbook Guide. (Illus.). 130p. 1993. student ed., spiral bd. 34.95 (*0-9636500-0-9*) Flying M Grp.

— Mini-Guide to the Contents of the Books of the Bible. pap. 0.99 (*0-87377-163-X*) GAM Pubns.

— The Nine Hundred One Best Jokes There Ever Was. LC 91-24866. (Illus.). 192p. (Orig.). 1991. pap. 6.95 (*1-55853-122-X*) Rutledge Hill Pr.

— Roulette for the Weekend Gambler: How to Get in, Make Your Hit & Get Out a Winner. 86p. 1995. spiral bd. 7.95 (*0-9636500-2-5*) Flying M Grp.

— Shingwauk's Vision: A History of Native Residential Schools. (Illus.). 700p. 1996. text 70.00 (*0-8020-0833-X*) U of Toronto Pr.

— Shingwauk's Vision: A History of Native Residential Schools. (Illus.). 700p. 1996. pap. text 29.95 (*0-8020-7858-3*) U of Toronto Pr.

— Skyscrapers Hide the Heavens: A History of Indian-White Relations in Canada. 2nd rev. ed. (Illus.). 408p. 1991. pap. text 22.95 (*0-8020-6869-3*) U of Toronto Pr.

— Strength of a Gentle Heart. 1994. 4.99 (*0-310-96289-7*) Zondervan.

Miller, J. R. Whom the Lord Loveth. 192p. 1996. pap. 6.50 (*0-7399-0205-9*, 2328) Rod & Staff.

Miller, J. R., ed. Sweet Promises: A Reader in Indian-White Relations in Canada. 448p. 1991. pap. text 24.95 (*0-8020-6818-9*) U of Toronto Pr.

Miller, J. R. & Miller, Nita Q. 100 Classic Folk & Bluegrass Songs: Words to Your Favorite Old Time Mountain Music. large type ed. (Illus.). 128p. (Orig.). 1997. pap., spiral bd. 15.00 (*0-9636500-3-3*) Flying M Grp.

Miller, J. R. & Miller, T. A., eds. Insect-Plant Interactions: Plant Interactions. (Experimental Entomology Ser.). (Illus.). 350p. 1990. 119.95 (*0-387-96260-3*) Spr-Verlag.

Miller, J. Ronald. Prophet in the House. LC 93-73155. 171p. (Orig.). 1993. pap. 10.00 (*0-9638451-0-1*) Commun Church.

Miller, J. S. Astrophysics of Active Galaxies & Quasi-Stellar Objects. 519p. (C). 1985. text 30.00 (*0-935702-21-0*) Univ Sci Bks.

Miller, J. S., ed. Ferromagnetic & High Spin Molecular Based Materials. (Molecular Crystals & Liquid Crystals Ser.). viii, 562p. 1989. pap. text 1352.00 (*2-88124-402-5*) Gordon & Breach.

Miller, J. T., ed. see Oberdorfer, Don.

***Miller, J. Wesley, ed.** The Reports of Sir Edward Coke, Knt. in Verse. LC 99-63255. 1999. reprint ed. 58.00 (*1-57588-493-3*) W S Hein.

Miller, J. William. Modern Playwrights at Work, Vol. 1. 1968. 12.00 (*0-573-69018-9*) French.

Miller, Jack. A Faith Worth Sharing: A Lifetime of Conversations about Christ. LC 99-28900. 144p. 1999. pap. 8.99 (*0-87552-391-9*) P & R Pubng.

— The Important Steps That Take You to Health, Wealth & Happiness. 120p. 1992. 19.95 (*1-882434-00-5*) Grp Commun.

Miller, Jack, ed. Jews in Soviet Culture. 325p. 1983. 44.95 (*0-87855-495-5*) Transaction Pubs.

Miller, Jack E. Menu Pricing & Strategy. 4th ed. LC 96-17742. (Hospitality, Travel & Tourism Ser.). (Illus.). 224p. 1996. text 42.95 (*0-442-02209-3*, VNR) Wiley.

Miller, Jack E. & Drummond, Karen E. Your Hospitality Field Experience: A Student Workbook. LC 95-12109. 304p. 1995. pap. 64.95 (*0-471-05327-9*) Wiley.

Miller, Jack E. & Hayes, David K. Basic Food & Beverage Cost Control. 400p. 1993. 54.95 (*0-471-57918-1*); pap. text, teacher ed. write for info. (*0-471-30619-3*) Wiley.

Miller, Jack E. & Pavesic, David V. Menu Pricing & Strategy: Why We Can't Keep Up with What Happens in the World & What We Can Do About It. 4th ed. (Hospitality, Travel & Tourism Ser.). 228p. 1996. pap. 49.95 (*0-471-28747-4*, VNR) Wiley.

Miller, Jack E., et al. Supervision in the Hospitality Industry. 2nd ed. 160p. 1992. pap. write for info. (*0-471-57820-7*) Wiley.

— Supervision in the Hospitality Industry. 3rd ed. LC 98-2774. 456p. 1998. 59.95 (*0-471-19420-4*) Wiley.

Miller, Jack R. & Harrison, George R. Completing the Uniform Residential Appraisal Report. 20p. (Orig.). 1993. pap. 15.00 (*0-614-23693-2*) Todd Pub.

Miller, Jack W., ed. Addressing the Problems of Youth At-Risk: Approaches That Work. 237p. (Orig.). 1994. pap. 10.00 (*0-9640143-0-0*) GSU Coll Educ.

Miller, Jacob. Memories of a Forty-Eighter: Sketches from the German-American Period of Storm & Stress in the 1850s. LC 96-26678. (Werner D. Mueller Reprint Ser.). 244p. 1996. 17.95 (*0-911704-46-9*) Western Res.

***Miller, Jacob.** The Yorkville Anthology of New Writers. LC 99-91281. 249p. 1999. 25.00 (*0-7388-0724-9*); pap. 18.00 (*0-7388-0725-7*) Xlibris Corp.

Miller, Jacob, jt. auth. see Fiorini, Gene.

Miller, Jacqueline, jt. auth. see Canfield, Jack.

Miller, Jacqueline Y., ed. The Common Names of North American Butterflies. 177p. (Orig.). 1998. pap. text 16.00 (*0-7881-5551-2*) DIANE Pub.

Miller, Jacques-Alain, ed. On Feminine Sexuality, the Limits of Love & Knowledge, Vol. 20. Fink, Bruce, tr. LC 97-43225. (The Seminar of Jacques Lacan Ser.). 192p. 1998. 30.00 (*0-393-04573-0*) Norton.

— The Seminar of Jacques Lacan Bk. 1: Freud's Papers on Technique, 1953-1954. Forrester, John, tr. & notes by. 1991. pap. 16.95 (*0-393-30697-6*) Norton.

— The Seminar of Jacques Lacan Bk. 2: The Ego in Freud's Theory & in the Technique of Psychoanalyis, 1954-1955. Tomaselli, Sylvana, tr. 1991. pap. 17.95 (*0-393-30709-3*) Norton.

Miller, Jacques-Alain, ed. see Lacan, Jacques.

Miller, Jacques F., et al, eds. Advances in Molecular & Cell Biology Vol. 5: Molecular Immunology. 264p. 1992. 128.50 (*1-55938-517-0*) Jai Pr.

***Miller, Jake.** Looneyville Zip Code 25259 Lore: Applachian Mountains Folklore - Popular Etmology - Colloquial Speech. LC 99-91441. 2000. 25.00 (*0-7388-0782-6*); pap. 18.00 (*0-7388-0783-4*) Xlibris Corp.

Miller, Jake. Round Trip, Looneyville - Tokyo Via U. S. S. George F. Elliott Lines: Memoirs & Thoughts of a 70 Year Old War Veteran & His Surviving Comrades. LC 98-92638. (Illus.). 186p. 1998. pap. 13.95 (*1-57502-754-2*, P02091) Morris Pubng.

Miller, Jake C. Building a Better World. LC 96-69275. 118p. (Orig.). 1996. pap. text 10.95 (*1-883122-06-6*) Pearce Pub.

Miller, James. Democracy Is in the Streets: From Port Huron to the Siege of Chicago. LC 94-15547. 432p. 1994. pap. 14.95 (*0-674-19725-9*, MILDEX) HUP.

— The Detroit Yiddish Theater, 1920 to 1937. LC 67-16851. 196p. reprint ed. pap. 60.80 (*0-7837-3796-3*, 204361600010) Bks Demand.

— Drilltype Two: Number & Special Character Drills. LC 77-80579. 1978. spiral bd. 9.96 (*0-02-830700-3*) Glencoe.

— Fluid Exchanges: Artists & Critics in the Age of AIDS. 496p. 1992. pap. 22.95 (*0-8020-6824-3*); text 50.00 (*0-8020-5892-2*) U of Toronto Pr.

— Harlequin-Horace: or The Art of Modern Poetry. LC 92-25505. (Augustan Reprints Ser.: No. 178). 1976. reprint ed. 14.50 (*0-404-70178-7*, PR3549) AMS Pr.

— History & Human Existence: From Marx to Merleau-Ponty. LC 78-51747. 1979. pap. 15.95 (*0-520-04779-6*, Pub. by U CA Pr) Cal Prin Full Svc.

— Measures of Wisdom: The Cosmic Dance in Classical & Christian Antiquity. 672p. 1986. text 60.00 (*0-8020-2553-6*) U of Toronto Pr.

— Rousseau: Dreamer of Democracy. LC 83-17396. (Illus.). 274p. (C). 1995. reprint ed. pap. text 12.95 (*0-300-03518-7*) Hackett Pub.

Miller, James, tr. see Saumjan, S. K.

An Asterisk (*) at the beginning of an entry indicates that the title is appearing for the first time.

Miller, James A. Quarternary History of the Sangamon River Drainage System, Central Illinois. (Reports of Investigations: No.27). (Illus.). 36p. 1973. pap. 2.00 (*0-89792-051-1*) Ill St Museum.

Miller, James A., ed. Approaches to Teaching Wright's Native Son. LC 96-40462. (Approaches to Teaching World Literature Ser.: No. 58). x, 141p. 1997. pap. 18.00 (*0-87352-740-2*, AP58P); lib. bdg. 37.50 (*0-87352-739-9*, AP58C) Modern Lang.

Miller, James A. & Macintyre, Ian G. Field Guidebook to the Reefs of Belize. (Third International Symposium on Coral Reefs Ser.). (Illus.). 36p. 1977. pap. 5.00 (*0-932981-41-0*) Univ Miami A R C.

Miller, James A., jt. auth. see Westbrook, Charles.

Miller, James A., ed. see Smith, Morgan & Smith, Marvin.

Miller, James B. Best Boss - Worst Boss: Lessons & Laughs from the International Best Boss/Worst Boss Contest. LC 98-18606. (Illus.). 224p. 1998. per. 11.00 (*0-684-84639-X*) S&S Trade.

***Miller, James B.** Brady's New Curriculum Course Guide for Paramedics. 8p. 2000. cd-rom 39.99 (*0-13-087223-7*) P-H.

Miller, James C. The Economist As Reformer: Revamping the FTC, 1981-1985. LC 89-6504. (AEI Studies: No. 489). 110p. (C). 1989. lib. bdg. 16.25 (*0-8447-3684-8*) U Pr of Amer.

Miller, James C., III. Fix the U. S. Budget! Reflections of an "Abominable No-Man" LC 93-40600. (Publication Ser.: No. 413). 176p. (C). 1994. pap. 19.95 (*0-8179-9212-X*) Hoover Inst Pr.

— Monopoly Politics. LC 99-23021. (Publication Ser.: Vol. 457). 152p. 1999. pap. 17.95 (*0-8179-9652-4*) Hoover Inst Pr.

Miller, James C., III & Yandle, Bruce, eds. Benefit-Cost Analyses of Social Regulation: Case Studies from the Council on Wage & Price Stability. LC 79-876. 183p. reprint ed. pap. 56.80 (*0-8357-4436-1*, 203727000008) Bks Demand.

Miller, James D. The Pastoral Letters As Composite Documents. (Society for New Testament Studies Monograph Ser.: Vol. 93). 224p. (C). 1997. text 54.95 (*0-521-56048-9*) Cambridge U Pr.

Miller, James E., Jr. The American Quest for a Supreme Fiction: Whitman's Legacy in the Personal Epic. LC 78-15176. 1979. lib. bdg. 25.00 (*0-226-52611-9*) U Ch Pr.

— The American Quest for a Supreme Fiction: Whitman's Legacy in the Personal Epic. LC 78-15176. 1996. pap. text 14.95 (*0-226-52612-7*) U Ch Pr.

Miller, James E. The American Quest for a Supreme Fiction: Whitman's Legacy in the Personal Epic. LC 78-15176. 376p. reprint ed. pap. 116.60 (*0-608-09482-X*, 205428200005) Bks Demand.

— Autumn Wisdom: Finding Meaning in Life's Later Years. LC 95-21562. (Willowgreen Ser.). 64p. 1995. pap. 14.99 (*0-8066-2834-0*, 9-2834) Augsburg Fortress.

— Caregiver's Book: Caring for a Loved One, Caring for Yourself. 64p. 1996. pap. 14.99 (*0-8066-2985-1*, 9-2985, Augsburg) Augsburg Fortress.

***Miller, James E.** Foreign Relations of the United States, 1964- 1968, Cyprus, Greece & Turkey, Vol. 16. 836p. 2000. boxed set 49.00 (*0-16-045085-3*) USGPO.

Miller, James E. From Elite to Mass Politics: Italian Socialism in the Giolittian Era, 1900-1914. LC 89-20043. 277p. 1990. 32.00 (*0-87338-395-8*) Kent St U Pr.

— Helping the Bereaved Celebrate the Holidays: A Sourcebook for Planning Educational & Remembrance Events. 96p. (Orig.). 1997. pap. text 7.95 (*1-885933-25-8*) Willowgreen Pubng.

***Miller, James E.** How Can I Help? 12 Things to Do When Someone You Know Suffers a Loss. rev. ed. 64p. 2000. pap. text 6.95 (*1-885933-19-3*) Willowgreen Pubng.

Miller, James E. How Will I Get Through the Holidays? 12 Ideas for Those Whose Loved One Has Died. LC 95-91007. 64p. (Orig.). 1996. pap. 6.95 (*1-885933-22-3*) Willowgreen Pubng.

— Italian Foreign Policy: The Regional Politics of an Intermediate State. LC 85-17958. 1986. 18.75 (*0-8191-4968-3*); pap. 7.75 (*0-8191-4969-1*) U Pr of Amer.

Miller, James E., Jr. Leaves of Grass: America's Lyric-Epic of Self & Democracy. (Masterwork Studies). 160p. 1992. 29.00 (*0-8057-8089-0*, Twyne); pap. 14.95 (*0-8057-8565-5*, Twyne) Mac Lib Ref.

Miller, James E. Little Book for Preachers: 101 Ideas for Better Sermons. 112p. 1996. pap. 6.99 (*0-8066-2991-6*, 9-2991, Augsburg) Augsburg Fortress.

— Myth & Method: Modern Theories of Fiction. LC 60-12941. (Bison Book Ser.: No. BB105). 177p. reprint ed. pap. 54.90 (*0-608-18779-8*, 202982100065) Bks Demand.

— One You Love Is Dying: 12 Ideas to Guide You on the Journey. LC 97-60134. (Illus.). 64p. (Orig.). 1997. pap. text 6.95 (*1-885933-23-1*) Willowgreen Pubng.

— A Reader's Guide to Herman Melville. LC 97-43462. 1998. pap. 19.95 (*0-8156-0495-5*) Syracuse U Pr.

***Miller, James E.** The Rewarding Practice of Journal Writing: A Guide for Starting & Keeping Your Personal Journal. LC 98-90456. 62p. 1998. pap. 6.95 (*1-885933-28-2*) Willowgreen Pubng.

— Seasons of Grief & Healing: A Guide for Those Who Mourn. LC 99-53044. 2000. pap. text 5.99 (*0-8066-4036-7*) Augsburg Fortress.

Miller, James E. T. S. Eliot's Personal Waste Land: Exorcism of the Demons. LC 76-40424. 1977. 28.50 (*0-271-01237-4*) Pa St U Pr.

— The United States & Italy, 1940-1950: The Politics & Diplomacy of Stabilization. LC 85-10035. xv, 356p. 1986. 45.00 (*0-8078-1673-6*) U of NC Pr.

— The United States & Italy, 1940-1950: The Politics & Diplomacy of Stabilization. LC 85-10035. 372p. reprint ed. pap. 115.40 (*0-608-06007-0*, 206633500008) Bks Demand.

— Welcoming Change: Discovering Hope in Life's Transitions. LC 97-21457. (The Willowgreen Ser.). 64p. 1997. pap. 14.99 (*0-8066-3338-7*, 9-3338, Augsburg) Augsburg Fortress.

— The Western Paradise: Greek & Hebrew Traditions. LC 96-44823. (Non Series Monograph). 144p. 1996. 69.95 (*1-57309-127-8*); pap. 49.95 (*1-57309-126-X*) Intl Scholars.

— What Will Help Me?/How Can I Help? 12 Things to Remember When You Have Suffered a Loss/12 Things to Do When Someone You Know Suffers a Loss. LC 94-96346. 64p. 1994. reprint ed. pap. 6.95 (*1-885933-20-7*) Willowgreen Pubng.

— When a Man Faces Grief/A Man You Know is Grieving: How to Plan, Design, Facilitate, & Enjoy Them. LC 97-91154. 64p. 1998. pap. 6.95 (*1-885933-26-6*) Willowgreen Pubng.

— When You Know You're Dying: 12 Thoughts to Guide You Through the Days Ahead. LC 97-60133. (Illus.). 64p. (Orig.). 1997. pap. text 6.95 (*1-885933-24-X*) Willowgreen Pubng.

— When You're Ill or Incapacitated/When You're the Caregiver: 12 Things to Remember in Times of Sickness, Injury or Disability/12 Things to Do if Someone You Care For is Ill or Incapacitated. LC 95-90163. 64p. 1995. reprint ed. pap. 6.95 (*1-885933-21-5*) Willowgreen Pubng.

— Winter Grief, Summer Grace: Returning to Life after a Loved One Dies. LC 95-22489. 64p. 1995. pap. 14.99 (*0-8066-2833-2*) Augsburg Fortress.

Miller, James E. & Golden, Thomas. Effective Support Groups: How to Plan, Design, Facilitate, & Enjoy Them. LC 98-90047. 64p. 1998. pap. 6.95 (*1-885933-27-4*) Willowgreen Pubng.

Miller, James E., Jr. & Regenstein, Helen. Walt Whitman. rev. ed. (Twayne's United States Authors Ser.: No. 20). 176p. (C). 1990. 32.00 (*0-8057-7600-1*) Macmillan.

Miller, James E., et al. Start with the Sun: Studies in the Whitman Tradition. LC 60-5493. (Bison Bk.: No. 165). 269p. reprint ed. pap. 83.40 (*0-7837-7047-2*, 204685800004) Bks Demand.

Miller, James E., Jr., jt. auth. see Farrell, Edmund J.

Miller, James E., jt. auth. see Jevne, Ronna F.

Miller, James E., tr. see Shaumyan, Sebastian K.

Miller, James G. Living Systems. (Illus.). 1152p. (C). 1992. pap. text 49.95 (*0-87081-363-3*) Univ Pr Colo.

— The Pharmacology & Clinical Usefulness of Carisoprodol: A Symposium Sponsored by Wayne State University College of Medicine & the University of Michigan Medical School, Department of Postgraduate Medicine, held in Detroit, Michigan, July 1, 1959. LC 59-15115. 192p. reprint ed. pap. 59.60 (*0-7837-3656-8*, 204352700009) Bks Demand.

Miller, James G., jt. auth. see Swanson, G. A.

Miller, James G., jt. ed. see Uhr, Leonard M.

Miller, James H. Grounding. 2nd ed. (ABC Pocket Guide for the Field Ser.). (Illus.). 36p. (C). 1988. pap. 7.95 (*1-56016-027-6*) ABC TeleTraining.

— History of Summers County: From the Earliest Settlement to the Present Time. (Illus.). 838p. 1997. reprint ed. lib. bdg. 85.00 (*0-8328-6955-4*) Higginson Bk Co.

— History of Summers County, West Virginia from the Earliest Settlement to Present Time. xiv, 1039p. 1997. reprint ed. pap. 62.50 (*0-7884-0696-5*, M359) Heritage Bk.

— Self-Supporting Scenery for Children's Theatre & Grown-Ups' Too: A Scenic Workbook for the Open Stage. 5th rev. ed. Zapel, Arthur L., ed. LC 81-84402. (Illus.). 128p. (C). 1993. reprint ed. pap. 15.95 (*0-916260-91-7*, B105) Meriwether Pub.

Miller, James H. Small Stage Sets on Tour: A Practical Guide to Portable Stage Sets. 2nd ed. Zapel, Arthur L. & Zapel, Theodore O., eds. LC 87-42872. 128p. 1987. pap. 15.95 (*0-916260-46-1*, B102) Meriwether Pub.

Miller, James H. Stage Lighting in the Boondocks. 4th rev. ed. Zapel, Arthur L., ed. LC 95-22366. (Illus.). 144p. 1995. pap. 12.95 (*1-56608-017-7*, B141) Meriwether Pub.

— Stagecraft for Christmas & Easter Plays: A Method of Simplified Staging for the Church. Zapel, Arthur L. & Zapel, Theodore O., eds. LC 89-49383. (Illus.). 96p. (Orig.). 1989. pap. 9.95 (*0-916260-64-X*, B170) Meriwether Pub.

— Station Protectors. (ABC Pocket Guide for the Field Ser.). 40p. (Orig.). (C). 1983. pap. 7.95 (*1-56016-026-8*) ABC TeleTraining.

Miller, James I. Reflections: A Perspective on Brotherhood. LC 97-72335. 133 p. 1999. 7.95 (*0-88053-090-1*) Macoy Pub.

Miller, James J. An Environmental History of Northeast Florida. LC 97-43564. (Florida Museum of Natural History Ser.). (Illus.). 320p. 1998. 49.95 (*0-8130-1600-2*) U Press Fla.

Miller, James M. Chromatography: Concepts & Contrasts. LC 87-16084. 320p. 1988. 94.95 (*0-471-84821-2*) Wiley.

— Genesis of Culture in the Ohio Valley, 1800-1825. 1993. reprint ed. lib. bdg. 89.00 (*0-7812-5391-8*) Rprt Serv.

— Genesis of Western Culture: The Upper Ohio Valley, 1800-1825. LC 77-87420. (American Scene Ser.). 1969. reprint ed. lib. bdg. 29.50 (*0-306-71566-X*) Da Capo.

— Separation Methods in Chemical Analysis. LC 74-13781. (Illus.). 319p. reprint ed. pap. 98.90 (*0-608-17419-X*, 205645400067) Bks Demand.

***Miller, James M. & Crowther, Jonathan.** Analytical Chemistry in a GMP Environment: A Practical Guide. 512p. 2000. 115.00 (*0-471-31431-5*) Wiley.

Miller, James M., et al. Instructions & Warnings: The Annotated Bibliography. LC 89-23362. (Warnings Ser.: Vol. 3). 395p. 1990. 45.00 (*0-940537-06-0*); disk 150.00 (*0-685-26954-X*) Fuller Tech.

Miller, James M., jt. auth. see Lehto, Mark R.

Miller, James M., jt. auth. see McNair, Harold M.

Miller, James N., jt. auth. see Miller, Jane C.

Miller, James Q. & Fountain, Nathan B. Neurology Recall. LC 97-2668. (Recall Ser.). 340p. 1997. pap. 27.00 (*0-683-18216-1*) Lppncott W & W.

Miller, James R. A Life of Character. rev. ed. 1998. pap. 14.99 (*0-89957-239-1*) AMG Pubs.

Miller, James Russell, jt. auth. see Braselmane.

Miller, James V. Best Boss, Worst Boss: Lessons & Laughs from the International "Best Boss, Worst Boss" Contest. LC 96-10081. 262p. 1996. 22.95 (*1-56530-201-X*) Summit TX.

— Big Bear: (Mistahimusqua) LC 96-156221. (Illus.). 133p. 1996. pap. 14.95 (*1-55022-272-4*, Pub. by ECW) Genl Dist Srvs.

— The Big Fifty. large type ed. (Linford Western Library). 272p. (Orig.). 1988. pap. 16.99 (*0-7089-6602-0*, Linford) Ulverscroft.

— The Brass Boy. large type ed. (Linford Western Library). 1990. pap. 16.99 (*0-7089-6803-1*, Linford) Ulverscroft.

— Campaigning. large type ed. (Linford Western Library). 304p. (Orig.). 1988. pap. 16.99 (*0-7089-6487-7*, Linford) Ulverscroft.

— Carston's Law. Grad, Doug, ed. (Ex-Rangers Ser.: No. 9). 224p. (Orig.). 1993. pap. 3.50 (*0-671-74827-0*) PB.

— The Ex-Rangers No. 11: South of the Border, No. 11. 224p. (Orig.). 1993. mass mkt. 3.99 (*0-671-74829-7*) PB.

— Hell with the Hide Off. large type ed. LC 93-42948. 1994. pap. 16.95 (*0-8161-5933-5*, G K Hall Lrg Type) Mac Lib Ref.

— Mister Henry. large type ed. (Linford Western Library). 277p. (Orig.). 1989. pap. 16.99 (*0-7089-6679-9*, Linford) Ulverscroft.

— Orphan's Preferred. large type ed. (Linford Western Library). 304p. 1988. pap. 16.99 (*0-7089-6493-1*, Linford) Ulverscroft.

— Salt in the Blood: The Fishing Communities of Scotland. 1999. pap. 25.00 (*0-86241-836-4*) Interlink Pub.

— Shootout in Sendero. Grad, Doug, ed. (Ex-Rangers Ser.: No. 8). 224p. (Orig.). 1992. pap. 3.50 (*0-671-74826-2*) PB.

— The Six Hundred Mile Stretch. Grad, Doug, ed. (Ex-Rangers Ser.: No. 6). 224p. (Orig.). 1992. pap. 3.50 (*0-671-74824-6*) PB.

— Spencer's Revenge. large type ed. (Linford Western Library). 237p. 1989. pap. 16.99 (*0-7089-6671-3*, Linford) Ulverscroft.

— Stranger from Nowhere. Grad, Doug, ed. (Ex-Rangers Ser.: No. 10). 224p. (Orig.). 1993. mass mkt. 3.99 (*0-671-74828-9*) PB.

— That Damn Single Shot. large type ed. 1990. pap. 16.99 (*0-7089-6864-3*) Ulverscroft.

Miller, James V. & Weinert, Regina. Spontaneous Spoken Language: Syntax & Discourse. LC 97-39156. (Illus.). 472p. 1998. text 115.00 (*0-19-823656-5*) OUP.

Miller, James V., jt. auth. see Brown, Keith.

Miller, James V., jt. auth. see Newman, Standford J.

Miller, James W. Beyond My Canopy. Asher, Ken, ed. LC 80-82869. 64p. (Orig.). 1980. write for info. (*0-9620151-0-5*); pap. write for info. (*0-9620151-1-3*) J W Miller.

Miller, James W., ed. & tr. see Gerstacker, Friedrich.

***Miller, Jamie C.** Heavenly Miracles. large type ed. 2000. 20.00 (*0-06-019915-6*, HarpCollins) HarperTrade.

Miller, Jamie C. 10-Minute Life Lessons for Kids: 52 Fun & Simple, Games & Activities to Teach Your Children Games & Honesty, Trust, Love, & Other Important Values. LC 98-18484. (Illus.). 240p. 1998. pap. 10.00 (*0-06-095255-5*, Perennial) HarperTrade.

Miller, Jamie C., et al, eds. Christmas Miracles: Magical True Stories of Modern-Day Miracles. LC 97-15524. 192p. 1997. 15.00 (*0-688-15588-X*, Quil) HarperTrade.

— The Magic of Christmas Miracles: An All-New Collection of Inspiring True Stories. LC 98-23939. 192p. 1998. 15.00 (*0-688-16456-0*, Wm Morrow) Morrow Avon.

***Miller, Jamie C. & Laur, Lewis.** Heavenly Miracles: Magical True Stories of Guardian Angels & Answered Prayers. 192p. 2000. 16.00 (*0-688-17370-5*, Wm Morrow) Morrow Avon.

***Miller, Jamie C., et al.** A Gift of Miracles: Magical True Stories To Touch Your Family's Heart. LC 99-44823. 192p. 1999. 15.00 (*0-688-17369-1*, Wm Morrow) Morrow Avon.

Miller, Jamie C., et al. Mothers' Miracles: Magical True Stories of Maternal Love & Courage. LC 98-43268. (Illus.). 192p. 1999. 16.00 (*0-688-16622-9*, Wm Morrow) Morrow Avon.

Miller, Jan. Die Europaische Union der Zwei Geschwindigkeiten: Grundlagen und Wirkungen einer Differenzierten Wahrungsunion. (Europaische Hochschulschriften: Reihe 5: Bd. 1962). (GER., Illus.). 322p. 1996. pap. 57.95 (*3-631-30580-X*) P Lang Pubng.

Miller, Jan W. Retouching Your Photographs. (Illus.). 144p. 1986. pap. 22.50 (*0-8174-3832-7*, Amphoto) Watsn-Guptill.

Miller, Jana, jt. auth. see Stich, Sally.

Miller, Jane. Birth of a Foal. LC 76-5402. (J). (gr. k-3). 1977. 12.95 (*0-397-31702-6*) HarpC Child Bks.

— The Farm Alphabet Book. (Illus.). 32p. (J). (ps-2). 1987. pap. 2.99 (*0-590-31991-4*) Scholastic Inc.

Miller, Jane. Farm Alphabet Book. 1981. 8.19 (*0-606-01014-9*, Pub. by Turtleback) Demco.

Miller, Jane. Farm Counting Book. (Illus.). 24p. (J). (ps-1). 1992. lib. bdg. 5.95 (*0-671-66552-9*) S&S Bks Yung.

— Memory at These Speeds: New & Selected Poems. 224p. 1996. pap. text 15.00 (*1-55659-118-7*) Copper Canyon.

— Seductions: Studies in Reading & Culture. (Convergences Ser.). 208p. (C). 1991. 28.00 (*0-674-79679-9*) HUP.

***Miller, Jane.** Wherever You Lay Your Head. LC 99-6032. 96p. 1999. pap. 14.00 (*1-55659-128-4*, Pub. by Copper Canyon) SPD-Small Pr Dist.

Miller, Jane, ed. Eccentric Propositions: Literature & the Curriculum. 224p. (Orig.). pap. 17.95 (*0-7100-9987-8*, Routledge Thoemms) Routledge.

Miller, Jane, ed. see Kimball, Helen.

Miller, Jane A., jt. auth. see Benson, Dale S.

Miller, Jane A., ed. see Woodke, Dale.

Miller, Jane Ann, tr. see Gaidar, Yegor.

Miller, Jane C. & Miller, James N. Statistics for Analytical Chemistry. 3rd ed. LC 93-4521. 256p. (C). 1993. pap. text 90.00 (*0-13-030990-7*) P-H.

Miller, Jane E. Rebel Women: Feminism, Modernism & the Edwardian Novel. LC 96-38641. 1996. pap. text 15.95 (*0-226-52677-1*) U Ch Pr.

Miller, Jane F. Your Child Needs a Champion: Mastering the A. D. D. Challenge by Making the Right Choices. LC 97-93086. (Illus.). 224p. 1997. pap. 16.95 (*0-9658190-0-0*) JMA Pubns.

Miller, Jane R. August Zero. LC 93-4137. 96p. 1993. 22.00 (*1-55659-060-1*); pap. 11.00 (*1-55659-061-X*) Copper Canyon.

— Working Time: Essays on Poetry, Culture, & Travel. LC 91-45197. (Poets on Poetry Ser.). 168p. (C). 1992. text 39.50 (*0-472-09480-7*, 09480) U of Mich Pr.

— Working Time: Essays on Poetry, Culture, & Travel. LC 91-45197. (Poets on Poetry Ser.). 168p. (C). 1992. pap. 13.95 (*0-472-06480-0*, 06480) U of Mich Pr.

Miller, Janeen, jt. auth. see Kueter, Roger A.

Miller, Janet L. Creating Spaces & Finding Voices: Teachers Collaborating for Empowerment. LC 89-36216. (SUNY Series, Teacher Preparation & Development). 204p. (C). 1990. text 64.50 (*0-7914-0281-9*); pap. text 21.95 (*0-7914-0282-7*) State U NY Pr.

Miller, Janet R., jt. auth. see Gutknecht, Douglas B.

Miller, Janice. Family Planning Management Terms: A Pocket Glossary in Arabic, French & English. Bouzidi, Med, ed. LC 96-161343. (ARA, ENG & FRE.). 270p. (Orig.). 1997. pap. 12.00 (*0-913723-34-7*) Mgmt Sci Health.

— Family Planning Management Terms: A Pocket Glossary in Bangla & Englis. Sayeed, Abu, ed. 190p. (Orig.). 1996. pap. 12.00 (*0-614-30038-X*) Mgmt Sci Health.

— Family Planning Management Terms: A Pocket Glossary in Three Languages. Bahanon, Claire, ed. (ENG, FRE & SPA.). 270p. (Orig.). 1995. pap. 12.00 (*0-614-30037-1*) Mgmt Sci Health.

Miller, Janice, et al, eds. Strategies de Gestion pour Ameliorer les Services de Planification Familiale: Un Compendium du Mangement de la Planification Familiale. (FRE., Illus.). 434p. (Orig.). 1997. pap. 25.00 (*0-913723-39-8*) Mgmt Sci Health.

Miller, Janice & Wolff, James A., eds. Management Strategies for Improving Family Planning Services: The Family Planning Manager Compendium. (Illus.). 431p. 1996. spiral bd. 25.00 (*0-913723-37-1*) Mgmt Sci Health.

Miller, Janice, et al. Estrategias Gerenciales para Mejorar los Servicios de Planificacion Familiar: Un Compendio de Actualidad Gerencial en Planificacion Familiar. Bahaun, Claire et al, eds. (SPA., Illus.). 434p. (Orig.). 1997. pap. 25.00 (*0-913723-43-6*) Mgmt Sci Health.

Miller, Janice J. & Kilpatrick, John. Issues for Managers: An International Perspective. 5th (C). 1987. teacher ed. write for info. (*0-256-05763-X*, Irwn McGrw-H) McGrw-H Hghr Educ.

Miller, Janice J., jt. auth. see Miller, Robert.

Miller, Janice M., jt. auth. see Ayres, H. Joseph.

Miller, Jason. Barrymore's Ghost. LC 98-104347. 1997. pap. 5.25 (*0-8222-1563-2*) Dramatists Play.

— That Championship Season. 1972. pap. 5.25 (*0-8222-1126-2*) Dramatists Play.

— Three One Act Plays by Jason Miller. 1972. pap. 5.25 (*0-8222-0759-1*) Dramatists Play.

***Miller, Jason & Hinkle, Elizabeth.** Expert Advice for Federal Contractors. 2nd ed. LC 99-71169. 1999. write for info. (*0-914176-84-6*) Wash Busn Info.

Miller, Jay. American Indian Families. LC 96-15164. (True Bk.). 48p. (J). 1996. lib. bdg. 21.00 (*0-516-20133-6*) Childrens.

— American Indian Families. (True Bks.). 48p. (J). 1997. pap. 6.95 (*0-516-26089-8*) Childrens.

— American Indian Festivals. LC 96-13475. (True Bks.). 48p. (J). 1996. lib. bdg. 21.00 (*0-516-20134-4*) Childrens.

— American Indian Festivals. (True Bks.). 48p. (J). 1997. pap. 6.95 (*0-516-26090-1*) Childrens.

— American Indian Foods. LC 96-13476. (True Bks.). (J). 1996. lib. bdg. 21.00 (*0-516-20135-2*) Childrens.

— American Indian Foods. (True Bks.). 48p. (J). 1997. pap. 6.95 (*0-516-26091-X*) Childrens.

— American Indian Games. LC 96-13477. (True Bks.). 48p. (J). 1996. lib. bdg. 21.00 (*0-516-20136-0*) Childrens.

— American Indian Games. (True Bks.). 48p. (J). 1997. pap. 6.95 (*0-516-26092-8*) Childrens.

— Convair B-58 Hustler: The World's First Supersonic Bomber. 1998. pap. text 27.95 (*1-85780-058-3*) Specialty Pr.

— Lockheed Martin's Skunk Works: The Official History. rev. ed. (Illus.). 216p. 1995. pap. 29.95 (*1-85780-037-0*, Pub. by Midland Pubng) Specialty Pr.

— Lushootseed Culture & the Shamanic Odyssey: An Anchored Radiance. LC 98-38249. (Illus.). 334p. 1999. text 45.00 (*0-8032-3200-4*) U of Nebr Pr.

— Native Americans. (New True Books Ser.). (Illus.). 48p. (J). (gr. 2-4). 1993. pap. 5.50 (*0-516-41192-6*) Childrens.

M

— Native Americans. LC 93-3442. (New True Books Ser.). (Illus.). 48p. (J). (ps-3). 1993. lib. bdg. 21.00 (0-516-01192-8) Childrens.

— Soviet Space. LC 91-65880. (Orig.). 1991. 35.00 (0-9629867-0-4); pap. 15.00 (0-9629867-3-9) Ft Worth Mus Sci Hist.

— Tsimshian Culture: A Light Through the Ages. LC 96-35895. (Illus.). 204p. 1997. text 50.00 (0-8032-3192-X) U of Nebr Pr.

***Miller, Jay.** Tsimshian Culture: A Light Through the Ages. (Illus.). 204p. 2000. pap. text 24.00 (0-8032-8266-4, Bison Books) U of Nebr Pr.

— Writings in Indian History: 1985-1990. 216p. 1999. pap. text 12.95 (0-8061-2796-1) U of Okla Pr.

Miller, Jay, et al, compiled by. Writings in Indian History, 1985-1990. LC 95-8776. (D'Arcy McNickle Center Bibliographies in American Indian History Ser.: Vol. 2). 232p. 1995. 28.95 (0-8061-2759-7) U of Okla Pr.

Miller, Jay, ed. Mourning Dove: A Salishan Autobiography. LC 89-14780. (American Indian Lives Ser.). (Illus.). xl, 267p. 1990. pap. 12.95 (0-8032-8207-9, Bison Books) U of Nebr Pr.

Miller, Jay & Vane, Sylvia B. Shamanic Odyssey: The Lushootseed Salish Journey to the Land of the Dead. LC 88-16761. (Anthropological Papers: No. 32). (Illus.). 215p. 1988. pap. 28.95 (0-87919-112-0) Ballena Pr.

Miller, Jay, jt. auth. see Butowski, Piotr.

Miller, Jay, jt. auth. see Gordon, Yefim.

Miller, Jay, ed. see Mourning Dove.

Miller, Jayna. Too Much Trick or Treat. Thatch, Nancy R., ed. LC 91-14930. (Books for Students by Students). (Illus.). 26p. (J). (gr. k-4). 1991. lib. bdg. 15.95 (0-933849-37-0) Landmark Edns.

Miller, Jean. The Island of Greasy Luck LC 97-215046. (Illus.). 105p. (J). 1995. write for info. (0-9647211-0-4) Meadow Creek Pr.

— Prophets of Joy: A Spirituality for the Baptized. 1990. pap. 9.95 (0-87193-268-7) Dimension Bks.

***Miller, Jean & Stiver, Irene.** The Healing Connection: How Women Form Relationships in Therapy & in Life. Hooks, Tisha, ed. 1998. pap. 15.00 (0-8070-2921-1) Beacon Pr.

Miller, Jean, jt. auth. see Foerster, Sharon.

Miller, Jean, jt. auth. see Frederick, John.

Miller, Jean B. Toward a New Psychology of Women. 2nd ed. LC 86-47553. 192p. 1987. reprint ed. pap. 14.00 (0-8070-2909-2) Beacon Pr.

Miller, Jean-Chris. The Body Art Book: A Complete, Illustrated Guide to Tattoos, Piercings, & Other Body. LC 97-227194. (Illus.). 192p. 1997. pap. 12.00 (0-425-15985-X) Berkley Pub.

Miller, Jean-Chris, jt. auth. see Zuckerman, Roy.

Miller, Jean R. & Janosik, Ellen. Family Focused Care. (Illus.). 1979. text 32.95 (0-07-042060-2) McGraw.

Miller, Jean W. Power Plus Assertiveness: Step-by-Step with the Magic Communication Wand. (Illus.). 192p. 1998. pap. 12.00 (0-9663030-0-8) Commun Ents.

Miller, Jeanine, jt. auth. see Feuerstein, Georg.

Miller, Jeanne. Perfectly Safe Home. 1991. pap. 9.95 (0-671-70580-6, Fireside) S&S Trade Pap.

Miller, Jeannette L., jt. auth. see Schager, Elisabeth.

Miller, Jeff. Alleluia! Sing a Song. 1.75 (0-687-07095-3) Abingdon.

— Beds: Nine Outstanding Projects from One of America's Best Craftsmen. LC 99-15009. 1999. pap. 24.95 (1-56158-254-9) Taunton.

Miller, Jeff. Chairmaking & Design. LC 97-16538. (Illus.). 208p. 1997. pap. 24.95 (1-56158-158-5, 070290) Taunton.

***Miller, Jeff.** COM+ Programming Bible. (Bible Ser.). (Illus.). 1000p. 2001. pap. text 39.99 (0-7645-4666-X) IDG Bks.

— Hear My Prayer. 1.50 (0-687-06208-X) Abingdon.

— Hymn of Love. 1.25 (0-687-02730-6) Abingdon.

— Rejoice, Praise the Lord & Sing. 1.25 (0-687-07215-8) Abingdon.

— Unto Us. 1.25 (0-687-08144-0) Abingdon.

Miller, Jeff R., ed. see Gifford, Robert L.

Miller, Jeffery, ed. CWA at Fifty. (Illus.). 64p. 1988. pap. text 5.00 (0-9621092-0-7) CWA.

Miller, Jeffery, ed. see Bowles, Paul.

Miller, Jeffrey. Paul Bowles: A Descriptive Bibliography. LC 84-10967. (Illus.). 327p. 1986. 50.00 (0-87685-609-1) Black Sparrow.

Miller, Jeffrey & Koford, Kenneth J., eds. Social Norms & Economic Institutions. 264p. (C). 1991. text 57.50 (0-472-10242-7, 10242) U of Mich Pr.

Miller, Jeffrey, ed. see Bowles, Paul.

Miller, Jeffrey, ed. see Fulcanelli.

Miller, Jeffrey, jt. ed. see Jones, Derek C.

Miller, Jeffrey, ed. see Suzuki, David T. & Griffiths, Tony.

Miller, Jeffrey A. The Childhood Depression Sourcebook. 288p. 1998. pap. 16.00 (0-7373-0001-9, 00019W) NTC Contemp Pub Co.

Miller, Jeffrey A., ed. see Lochmandy, Paula.

Miller, Jeffrey G. & Colosi, Thomas R. Fundamentals of Negotiation. 75p. 1989. pap. 28.00 (0-911937-28-5) Environ Law Inst.

Miller, Jeffrey G. & Johnston, Craig N. The Law of Hazardous Waste Disposal & Remediation: Cases, Legislation, Regulations, Policies (American Casebook Series) LC 96-8765. (Paralegal). 85p. (C). 1996. text 42.25 (0-314-06584-9) West Pub.

Miller, Jeffrey G., et al. Benchmarking Global Manufacturing: Understanding International Suppliers, Customers, & Competitors. (APICS Ser.). 443p. 1992. 47.50 (1-55623-674-3, Irwn Prfssnl) McGraw-Hill Prof.

Miller, Jeffrey H. Discovering Molecular Genetics: A Case Study Course with Problems & Scenarios. (Illus.). 672p. (C). 1995. pap., wbk. ed. 9.95 (0-87969-482-3); text 59.00 (0-87969-475-0) Cold Spring Harbor.

— A Short Course in Bacterial Genetics: A Laboratory Manual & Handbook for Escherichia Coli & Related Bacteria, 2 vols., Set. (Illus.). 876p. 1992. student ed. 80.00 (0-87969-349-5) Cold Spring Harbor.

Miller, Jeffrey H., et al, eds. Bacterial Genetic Systems. (Methods in Enzymology Ser.: Vol. 204). (Illus.). 706p. 1991. text 125.00 (0-12-182105-6) Acad Pr.

Miller, Jeffrey H. & Calos, Michele P., eds. Gene Transfer Vectors for Mammalian Cells. LC 87-149603. (Current Communications in Molecular Biology Ser.). 179p. reprint ed. pap. 55.50 (0-7837-1998-1, 204227200002) Bks Demand.

Miller, Jeffrey H. & Reznikoff, William S., eds. The Operon. 2nd ed. LC 80-15490. (Cold Spring Harbor Monographs). 479p. 1980. reprint ed. pap. 148.50 (0-608-01813-9, 206246200003) Bks Demand.

Miller, Jeffrey K., jt. ed. see Brenner, Sydney.

Miller, Jeffrey M. & Chambers, Larry. The Four Hundred One (k) Plan Management Handbook: A Guide for Sponsors & Their Advisors. 300p. 1992. 50.00 (1-55738-465-7, Irwn Prfssnl) McGraw-Hill Prof.

Miller, Jeffrey M. & Phillips, Maureen M. The 401(k) Plan Management Handbook: A Guide for Sponsors & Their Advisors. 2nd rev. ed. LC 96-3992. (Illus.). 269p. 1996. text 55.00 (0-7863-0982-2, Irwn Prfssnl) McGraw-Hill Prof.

***Miller, Jeffrey S.** The Horror Spoofs of Abbott & Costello: A Critical Assessment of the Comedy Team's Monster Films. LC 99-52498. 251p. 1999. lib. bdg. 39.95 (0-7864-0642-9) McFarland & Co.

Miller, Jeffrey S. Something Completely Different: British Television & American Culture. LC 99-40614. 208p. 1999. pap. 17.95 (0-8166-3241-3, Pub. by U of Minn Pr); lib. bdg. 44.95 (0-8166-3240-5, Pub. by U of Minn Pr) Chicago Distribution Ctr.

Miller, Jenifer. Healing Center & Retreats: Healthy Getaways for Every Body & Budget. LC 98-25847. (Illus.). 240p. 1998. pap. 16.95 (1-56261-404-5) Avalon Travel.

Miller, Jennie Brand, et al. The Glucose Revolution: The Authoritative Guide to the Glycemic Index - The Groundbreaking Medical Discovery. LC 98-56156. (Illus.). 304p. 1999. pap. 14.95 (1-56924-660-2) Marlowe & Co.

Miller, Jennifer. Baby's First Animal Songs. LC 97-216197. (Illus.). 1997. write for info. (0-7853-2319-8) Pubns Intl Ltd.

— Baby's First Bedtime Songs. LC 97-216120. (Illus.). (J). 1997. write for info. (0-7853-2317-1) Pubns Intl Ltd.

— Coastal Affair. (Southern Exposure Ser.). (Illus.). 120p. (Orig.). 1982. pap. 4.00 (0-943810-13-2) Inst Southern Studies.

Miller, Jentz. Business Law Essentials: Study Guide. 5th ed. 1999. pap. 16.75 (0-324-00856-2) Thomson Learn.

— Business Law Today. 5th ed. (SWC-Business Law Ser.). 1999. pap., student ed. 16.75 (0-324-00845-7) Thomson Learn.

— Business Law Today & the Cpa Exam. 5th ed. 1999. 16.75 (0-324-02230-1) Thomson Learn.

— Fundamentals of Business Law. 2nd ed. (LA - Business Law Ser.). (C). 1993. pap., student ed. 19.95 (0-314-01674-0) S-W Pub.

— Handbook Selected Statutes & Cases Busines Law Today Stan. 5th ed. (SWC-Business Law Ser.). 1999. pap. 14.95 (0-324-02742-7) Sth-Wstrn College.

Miller, Jerome A. In the Throe of Wonder: Intimations of the Sacred in a Post-Modern World. LC 91-12723. 222p. (C). 1992. text 19.50 (0-7914-0953-8) State U NY Pr.

Miller, Jerome G. Last One over the Wall: The Massachusetts Experiment in Closing Reform Schools. 2nd ed. LC 98-8556. 300p. 1998. pap. text 17.95 (0-8142-0758-8) Ohio St U Pr.

— Search & Destroy: African American Males in the Criminal Justice System. (Illus.). 318p. (C). 1996. text 29.95 (0-521-46021-2) Cambridge U Pr.

— Search & Destroy: African American Males in the Criminal Justice System. (Illus.). 318p. 1997. pap. 16.95 (0-521-59858-3) Cambridge U Pr.

Miller, Jerome H. & Miller, Dolores E. Gettysburg for Walkers Only: Four Auto-Free Tours of the Battlefield. (Illus.). 64p. (C). 1991. pap. text 3.95 (0-939631-38-5) Thomas Publications.

Miller, Jerome K. Church Copyright Seminar. 1987. 24.87 incl. audio (0-914143-15-8, Copy Info Svc) Assn Ed Comm Tech.

— Using Copyrighted Videocassettes in Classrooms, Libraries, & Training Centers. 2nd ed. LC 87-24572. (Copyright Information Bulletin Ser.: No. 3). 131p. 1988. 19.95 (0-914143-14-X, Copy Info Svc) Assn Ed Comm Tech.

— Video Copyright Permissions: A Guide to Securing Permission to Retain, Perform, & Transmit Television Programs Videotaped off the Air. (Copyright Information Bulletin Ser.: No. 5). 140p. 1989. 29.95 (0-914143-13-1, Copy Info Svc) Assn Ed Comm Tech.

Miller, Jerry L. Compliance Training Core Product. 1995. ring bd. 295.00 (0-7602-0065-3, Irwn Prfssnl) McGraw-Hill Prof.

— Guide to Preparing Board Reports. 1990. ring bd. 49.00 (1-55520-127-X, Irwn Prfssnl) McGraw-Hill Prof.

Miller, Jerry L., jt. auth. see Coyne, John.

Miller, Jerry P., ed. Millennium Intelligence: Understanding & Conducting Competitive Intelligence in the Digital Age. 2000. pap. 29.95 (0-910965-28-5, CyberAge Bks) Info Today Inc.

***Miller, Jessel.** The Calico Cat. (Illus.). 24p. (ps-3). 1999. 18.95 (0-9660381-8-5) Jessel Gallery.

Miller, Jessel. Mustard: A Story about Soft Love & Strong Values. Gamble, Carolynne, ed. (Soft Love Strong Values Ser.). (Illus.). 48p. (J). (ps-6). 1998. 24.00 (0-9660381-7-7) Jessel Gallery.

— Mustard Bk. II: A Journey to Love. Gamble, Carolynne, ed. (Illus.). 48p. (J). (ps-6). 1998. 24.95 (0-9660381-1-8) Jessel Gallery.

***Miller, Jessel.** Mustard Bk. III: Lessons from Old Souls. Gamble, Carolynne, ed. (Illus.). 48p. (ps-6). 1999. 24.95 (0-9660381-5-0) Jessel Gallery.

Miller, Jewel. Whisper of Love. LC 91-30828. 176p. (Orig.). 1991. pap. 7.99 (0-8361-3570-9) Herald Pr.

Miller, Jill. Happy As a Dead Cat. 120p. (Orig.). 1997. pap. 9.95 (0-7043-3898-X, Pub. by Womens Press) Trafalgar.

Miller, Jim W. The Brier Poems. LC 97-72322. 176p. 1997. pap. 14.50 (0-917788-62-1) Gnomon Pr.

— Copperhead Cane. O'Dell, Mary E., ed. Dorsett, Thomas, tr. from ENG. (Library Poetry Ser.). (GER.). 80p. 1995. 17.50 (0-9623666-5-X); pap. 11.95 (0-9623666-6-8) Green Rvr Writers.

— His First, Best Country. LC 92-75360. 224p. 1993. 22.50 (0-917788-54-0) Gnomon Pr.

— His First, Best Country. 224p. 1995. pap. 13.50 (0-917788-55-9) Gnomon Pr.

— The Mountains Have Come Closer. LC 80-80456. 1980. pap. 9.95 (0-913239-19-4) Appalach Consortium.

— Newfound. rev. ed. LC 96-77903. 214p. (J). 1996. reprint ed. pap. 13.50 (0-917788-59-1) Gnomon Pr.

— Round & Round with Kahlil Gibran. LC 90-30378. 10p. (Orig.). 1990. pap. 4.00 (0-926487-05-1) Rowan Mtn Pr.

Miller, Jo, ed. see Long, Jeanne, et al.

Miller, Jo, jt. ed. see Miller, Ray.

Miller, Jo A., jt. ed. see Knudsen, Dean D.

Miller, Joan. Before Baby Arrives. 128p. 1995. pap. 6.95 (0-572-01655-7, Pub. by Foulsham UK) Assoc Pubs Grp.

— Culture & Interpersonal Morality. (New Directions in Social Psychology Ser.). 2000. 54.95 (0-8133-1855-6) Westview.

— One Girl's War. 156p. 1989. 15.95 (0-312-03410-5) St Martin.

— Taking the "Ouch" out of Headaches. (Taking the "Ouch" out of Headaches Ser.). 1983. 24.95 incl. audio (0-9613786-0-3) J Miller.

— Your Baby's Development. 128p. 1995. pap. 6.95 (0-572-01657-3, Pub. by Foulsham UK) Assoc Pubs Grp.

***Miller, Joan, et al.** Beyond Bingo. LC 99-63262. 192p. 2000. pap. 13.95 (0-88739-284-9) Creat Arts Bk.

Miller, Joan E., jt. auth. see Schwartz, Sue.

Miller, Joan H. & Jones, Norman. Organic & Compost-Based Growing Media for Tree Seedling Nurseries. LC 94-23707. (Technical Papers: No. 264). 90p. 1995. pap. 22.00 (0-8213-3039-X, 13039) World Bank.

Miller, Joan I. & Taylor, Bruce J. The Punctuation Handbook. 96p. (Orig.). 1989. pap. 4.95 (0-937473-14-6) Alcove Pub Co OR.

Miller, Joan M., et al. BASIC Programming for the Classroom & Home Teacher. 262p. (C). 1982. pap. text 17.95 (0-8077-2728-8) Tchrs Coll.

Miller, JoAnn, ed. see Persky, Margaret.

Miller, JoAnn, ed. see Wagner, James K.

Miller, JoAnn, ed. see Williams, Karen F. & Terrell, Lloyd P.

Miller, JoAnn E., ed. see Jones, Doris M.

Miller, JoAnn E., ed. see Knight, Janet R. & Gilliam, Lynn W.

Miller, Joanne. Moon Handbooks: Pennsylvania: Including Pittsburgh, the Poconos, Philadelphia, Gettysburg & the Dutch Country. (Illus.). 450p. 1998. pap. 18.95 (1-56691-110-9, Moon Handbks) Avalon Travel.

Miller, Joanne, jt. auth. see Jaderstrom, Susan.

Miller, Joanne, ed. see de Garmo, Joan Askew.

Miller, Joanne, ed. see Miller, Dan.

Miller, Joanne L., et al, eds. Papers in Speech Communication: Speech Perception, 3 vols., Vol. 2. LC 91-32651. 874p. 1991. text 46.00 (0-88318-959-3) Acoustical Soc Am.

Miller, Joanne L. & Eimas, Peter D., eds. Speech, Language, & Communication. 2nd ed. LC 94-39355. (Handbook of Perception & Cognition Ser.). (Illus.). 415p. 1995. text 65.00 (0-12-497770-7) Acad Pr.

Miller, Joanne L., jt. ed. see Eimas, Peter D.

Miller, Joaquin. The Complete Poetical Works of Joaquin Miller. LC 72-4967. (Romantic Tradition in American Literature Ser.). 356p. 1978. reprint ed. 31.95 (0-405-04638-3) Ayer.

— Forty Nine: The Gold-Seekers of the Sierras. LC 78-104527. reprint ed. lib. bdg. 27.50 (0-8398-1258-2) Irvington.

— Illustrated History of the State of Montana: From the Earliest Period of Its Discovery to the Present Time, Together with Glimpses of Its Auspicious Future; ...Biographical Mention of Many of Its Pioneers & Prominent Citizens. (Illus.). 822p. 1997. reprint ed. lib. bdg. 86.50 (0-8328-6860-4) Higginson Bk Co.

— Joaquin Miller's Poems (The Bear Edition), 6 vols., Set. LC 74-5238. reprint ed. 425.00 (0-404-11530-6) AMS Pr.

— Life Amongst the Modocs: Unwritten History. LC 85-52081. 447p. 1987. 19.95 (0-913522-13-9) Urion Pr CA.

— Life Amongst the Modocs: Unwritten History. 457p. 1996. reprint ed. pap. 15.95 (0-930588-79-7) Heyday Bks.

— Life Amongst the Modocs: Unwritten History. LC 68-57540. (Muckrakers Ser.). 460p. reprint ed. lib. bdg. 27.50 (0-8398-1259-0) Irvington.

— Life Amongst the Modocs: Unwritten History. (Muckrakers Ser.). 460p. 1984. reprint ed. pap. 6.95 (0-8290-1565-5) Irvington.

— Poetical Works. (BCL1-PS American Literature Ser.). 587p. 1992. reprint ed. lib. bdg. 99.00 (0-7812-6798-6) Rprt Serv.

— Selected Writings of Joaquin Miller. Rosenus, Alan, ed. LC 73-88918. (Primary Source Bks.). (Illus.). 1976. 18.95 (0-913522-05-8); pap. 14.95 (0-913522-06-6) Urion Pr CA.

— Songs of the Sierras. LC 71-104528. 309p. reprint ed. lib. bdg. 36.50 (0-8398-1260-4) Irvington.

Miller, Jody A., ed. see Maxson, Cheryl L. & Klein, Malcolm W.

Miller, Joe. Burst of Speed: Five Proven Techniques to Increase Your Speed. (Illus.). 144p. 1984. 15.95 (0-89651-705-5) Hardwood Pr.

— If the Earth... Were a Few Feet in Diameter. LC 98-19053. (Illus.). 32p. (J). (ps-3). 1999. 16.95 (0-86713-054-7, 85131) Greenwich Wrkshop.

— The Nuts & Bolts a Novice Needs to Wire His New Home: The Bundle Saved Will Be His. (Illus.). 65p. (Orig.). 1986. pap. 9.95 (0-9616542-0-1) Joe Miller Pub.

— Take It Outside: Hiking in the Triangle. Hughes, Karen, ed. (Illus.). 200p. (C). (up). 1998. pap. 10.00 (0-935400-30-3) News & Observer.

Miller, Joe A., ed. see Institute of Labor & Industrial Relations Staff.

Miller, Joel E., jt. auth. see Parella, Robert E.

Miller, Joel S., ed. Chemically Modified Surfaces in Catalysis & Electrocatalysis. LC 82-8731. (ACS Symposium Ser.: Vol. 192). 311p. 1982. reprint ed. pap. 96.50 (0-608-03117-8, 206357000007) Bks Demand.

— Chemically Modified Surfaces in Catalysis & Electrolysis. LC 82-8731. (ACS Symposium Ser.: No. 192). 301p. 1982. lib. bdg. 43.95 (0-8412-0727-5) Am Chemical.

— Extended Linear Chain Compounds, Vol. 1. LC 81-17762. 498p. (C). 1981. 125.00 (0-306-40711-6, Plenum Trade) Perseus Pubng.

— Extended Linear Chain Compounds, Vol. 2. LC 81-17762. 532p. 1981. 125.00 (0-306-40712-4, Plenum Trade) Perseus Pubng.

— Extended Linear Chain Compounds, Vol. 3. LC 81-17762. 580p. 1983. 125.00 (0-306-40941-0, Plenum Trade) Perseus Pubng.

***Miller, John.** After the Civil Wars: Government in the Reign of Charles II. LC 00-42426. 2000. pap. write for info. (0-582-29899-7) Longman.

Miller, John. Beauty. LC 96-44525. 1997. pap. 14.95 (0-8118-1340-1) Chronicle Bks.

— The Berkshires: A History & Guide. pap. write for info. (0-318-58334-8) Random.

— Christmas Stories. LC 92-46110. 224p. 1993. 17.95 (0-8118-0345-7) Chronicle Bks.

— Cutdown: A Claude McCutcheon Novel. LC 98-153330. 1997. 22.00 (0-671-56904-X) PB.

— Dream Catcher: A Nighttime Journal. 160p. 1994. 17.95 (0-8118-0754-1) Chronicle Bks.

— Early Victorian New Zealand: A Study of Racial Tensions & Social Attitudes 1839-1852. LC 86-22845. (Illus.). 227p. 1986. reprint ed. lib. bdg. 65.00 (0-313-25283-1, MIEV, Greenwood Pr) Greenwood.

— Egotopia: Narcissism & the New American Landscape. LC 97-10770. 200p. 1997. 29.95 (0-8173-0901-2) U of Ala Pr.

— Egotopia: Narcissism & the New American Landscape. 512p. 1999. pap. 16.95 (0-8173-0993-4) U of Ala Pr.

— An Englishman's Home. 208p. 1987. 45.00 (0-905392-46-9) St Mut.

***Miller, John.** Friendship: Great Minds on the Deepest Bond. LC 99-41557. 144p. 1999. 15.00 (0-688-17273-3, Wm Morrow) Morrow Avon.

Miller, John. History of Erie County, Pennsylvania: A Narrative Account of Its Historical Progress, Its People & Its Principal Interests, 2 vols., Vol. I. (Illus.). 897p. 1992. reprint ed. lib. bdg. 89.00 (0-8328-1424-5) Higginson Bk Co.

— History of Erie County, Pennsylvania: A Narrative Account of Its Historical Progress, Its People & Its Principal Interests, 2 vols., Vol. II. (Illus.). 709p. 1992. reprint ed. lib. bdg. 78.50 (0-8328-1425-3) Higginson Bk Co.

— Inquiry into the Present State of the Civil Law of England. viii, 533p. 1994. reprint ed. 57.50 (0-8377-2449-X, Rothman) W S Hein.

***Miller, John.** James II. (Illus.). 304p. 2000. 17.00 (0-300-08728-4) Yale U Pr.

— Judi Dench: With a Crack in Her Voice: The Biography. LC 99-52489. (Illus.). 336p. 1999. 24.95 (1-56649-111-8) Welcome Rain.

Miller, John. Korea, 1951-1953. 336p. 1996. per. 12.00 (0-16-001927-3) USGPO.

— Memoirs of General Miller, in the Service of the Republic of Peru, 2 vols. 2nd ed. reprint ed. 135.00 (0-404-04339-9) AMS Pr.

— Minnesota Civil Practice. 2nd ed. 1995. text 73.75 (0-86678-862-X, 81740-10, MICHIE) LEXIS Pub.

— Minnesota Legal Form for Commercial Real Estate. 1995. ring bd. 69.95 (0-917126-89-0, 81772-10, MICHIE) LEXIS Pub.

— New Orleans Stories: Great Writers on the City. 224p. 1992. pap. 12.95 (0-8118-0059-8) Chronicle Bks.

— New York Considered & Improved, from the Original Mss. in the British Museum. Paltsits, Victor H., ed. & intro. by. (Illus.). 135p. 1997. reprint ed. pap. 18.50 (0-8328-6092-1); reprint ed. lib. bdg. 28.50 (0-8328-6091-3) Higginson Bk Co.

— On the Present Unsettled Condition of the Law & Its Administration. iv, 172p. 1995. reprint ed. 30.00 (0-8377-2478-3, Rothman) W S Hein.

— Ralph Richardson: The Authorized Biography. (Illus.). 392p. 1997. pap. 9.95 (0-330-34780-2, Pub. by Pan) Trafalgar.

— Ralph Richardson: The Authorized Biography. LC 96-156527. (Illus.). 399p. 1995. 42.50 (0-283-06237-1, Pub. by S1 & J) Trans-Atl Phila.

— Restoration & the England of Charles II. 2nd ed. LC 96-50299. 152p. (C). 1997. pap. 15.93 (*0-582-29223-9*) Longman.

*__Miller, John.__ Revolution: Faces of Change. 2000. pap. text 22.95 (*1-56025-261-8*, Thunders Mouth) Avalon NY.

Miller, John. A Spiritual Journey to the End of the Rainbow. (Illus.). 74p. (Orig.). 1996. pap. 11.95 (*0-9656531-0-2*) Rainbow Pr ID.

— Trail of Ambigious Picture Postcards. 1998. pap. text 24.00 (*4-7713-3401-3*, Pub. by Korinsha) Dist Art Pubs.

— Treasure in Louisiana: Treasure Hunters Guide to the Bayou State. 290p. (Orig.). 1996. pap. 18.95 (*1-57502-237-0*, P0911) Morris Pubng.

Miller, John, contrib. by. When down Is Up: The Desublimating Impluse. (Illus.). 180p. 1998. text 50.00 (*90-5701-012-7*, 810582); pap. text 22.95 (*90-5701-052-6*, 810583) Gordon & Breach.

Miller, John, ed. Apocalypse 2000: The Book of Revelation. LC 98-19378. (Illus.). 152p. 1998. 17.95 (*1-56975-138-2*) Ulysses Pr.

— Bail VI: Proceedings of the Sixth International Conference on Boundary & Interior Layers - Computational & Asymptotic Methods. (Orig.). (C). 1992. pap. 125.00 (*0-9631678-1-2*) Inst Computation.

— The Best of Southwold. (Illus.). 128p. 1998. pap. 17.95 (*0-7509-1864-0*, Pub. by Sutton Pub Ltd) Intl Pubs Mktg.

— Fish Tales: Stories from the Sea. LC 93-2665. (Illus.). 160p. 1993. 30.00 (*0-8117-0619-2*) Stackpole.

— Legends: Women Who Have Changed the World Through the Eyes of Great Women Writers. LC 98-16225. (Illus.). 128p. 1998. 29.95 (*1-57731-042-X*) New Wrld Lib.

— Life: A User's Manual. LC 98-3733. 144p. 1998. 15.00 (*1-57731-067-5*) New Wrld Lib.

— Los Angeles Stories. 176p. (Orig.). 1991. pap. 11.95 (*0-87701-822-7*) Chronicle Bks.

— Nasecode IX: Proceedings of the 9th International Conference on the Numerical Analysis of Semiconductors Devices & Integrated Circuits. 110p. (Orig.). 1993. pap. 75.00 (*0-9631678-2-0*) Inst Computation.

— Nasecode VII: Proceedings of the 7th International Conference on the Numerical Analysis of Semiconductor Devices & Integrated Circuits. x, 280p. (Orig.). (C). 1991. pap. 95.00 (*0-9631678-0-4*) Inst Computation.

— On Suicide: Great Writers on the Ultimate Question. 224p. 1993. pap. 10.95 (*0-8118-0231-0*) Chronicle Bks.

— San Francisco Stories. 312p. 24.95 (*0-8488-2682-5*) Amereon Ltd.

— San Francisco Stories: Great Writers on the City. LC 89-25337. 304p. (Orig.). 1990. pap. 12.95 (*0-87701-669-0*) Chronicle Bks.

Miller, John, et al, eds. Berlin: Tales of the City. LC 95-40878. (Chronicles Abroad Ser.). 224p. 1996. 13.95 (*0-8118-1081-X*) Chronicle Bks.

— European Dinantian Environments. fac. ed. LC 86-13323. (Geological Journal Special Issue Ser.: No. 12). (Illus.). 412p. 1987. pap. 127.80 (*0-7837-7657-8*, 204741000007) Bks Demand.

— Real World Banking. 3rd ed. (Real World Readers Ser.). (Illus.). 64p. (C). Date not set. pap. text 8.50 (*1-878585-57-6*) Dollars & Sense.

Miller, John, photos by. The Old Stone House Museum: Brownington, Vermont. (Illus.). 26p. (Orig.). 1996. pap. 5.00 (*0-614-30163-7*) Orleans.

Miller, John & Anderson, Genevieve, eds. Chicago Stories: Great Writers on the City. LC 92-20490. 256p. 1993. pap. 12.95 (*0-8118-0164-0*) Chronicle Bks.

Miller, John & Clark, Susannah, eds. Havana: Tales of the City. LC 95-41208. (Chronicles Abroad Ser.). 244p. 1996. 13.95 (*0-8118-1058-5*) Chronicle Bks.

*__Miller, John & Kenedi, Aacon.__ Lovers: Great Romances of Our Time Through the Eyes of Legendary Writers. (Illus.). 128p. 1999. 29.95 (*0-8212-2612-6*, Pub. by Bulfinch Pr) Little.

*__Miller, John & Kenedi, Aaron.__ Healing Hearts: Compassionate Writers on Breaking Up. LC 99-49324. 144p. 2000. 16.00 (*0-688-17274-1*, Wm Morrow) Morrow Avon.

*__Miller, John & Kenedi, Aaron, eds.__ God's Breath: Sacred Scriptures of the World - The Essential Texts of Buddhism, Christianity, Judaism, Islam, Hinduism, Sufism, & Taoism. 2000. reprint ed. pap. 16.95 (*1-56924-618-1*) Marlowe & Co.

Miller, John & Miller, Kirsten. Istanbul. LC 94-34514. (Chronicles Abroad Ser.). 208p. 1995. 13.95 (*0-8118-0823-8*) Chronicle Bks.

Miller, John & Miller, Kirsten, eds. Alaska Stories: Tales from the Wild Frontier. LC 94-15574. 192p. 1995. pap. 11.95 (*0-8118-0675-8*) Chronicle Bks.

— Cairo: Tales of the City. LC 93-1815. (Chronicles Abroad Ser.). 192p. 1994. 12.95 (*0-8118-0492-5*) Chronicle Bks.

— Hong Kong. LC 93-48091. (Chronicles Abroad Ser.). 256p. 1994. 12.95 (*0-8118-0680-4*) Chronicle Bks.

— In the Garden. LC 93-34672. (Illus.). 160p. 1994. 30.00 (*0-8117-0906-X*) Stackpole.

— Lust: Lascivious Love Stories & Passionate Poems. LC 93-28053. (Illus.). 144p. 1994. 14.95 (*0-8118-0691-X*) Chronicle Bks.

— Prague. LC 93-48953. (Chronicles Abroad Ser.). (Illus.). 256p. 1994. 12.95 (*0-8118-0649-9*) Chronicle Bks.

Miller, John & Smith, Tim, eds. Cape Cod Stories: Tales from Cape Cod, Nantucket, & Martha's Vineyard. 224p. 1996. pap. 12.95 (*0-8118-1080-1*) Chronicle Bks.

— The Moon Box: Legends, Mystery, & Lore from Luna, 4 vols. (Illus.). 160p. 1995. pap. 29.95 (*0-8118-1060-7*) Chronicle Bks.

— San Francisco Thrillers: True Crimes & Dark Mysteries from the City by the Bay. LC 95-12957. (Illus.). 272p. 1995. pap. 14.95 (*0-8118-1043-7*) Chronicle Bks.

Miller, John, Jr. & Tackley, Margaret E. Korea, 1951-1953. (Illus.). 328p. 1996. reprint ed. pap. text 45.00 (*0-7881-3387-X*) DIANE Pub.

Miller, John, jt. auth. see Browne, Sheila.

Miller, John, jt. auth. see Clapham, Mark.

Miller, John, jt. auth. see De Young, Jim.

Miller, John, jt. auth. see Dosani, Majid.

Miller, John, jt. auth. see Gielgud, John.

Miller, John, jt. auth. see Kelley, Mike.

Miller, John, jt. auth. see Manoff, Tom.

Miller, John, jt. auth. see McAllister, Dawson.

Miller, John, jt. auth. see Pilates, Joseph H.

Miller, John, ed. see Haley, Alex, et al.

Miller, John, ed. see Hemingway, Ernest.

Miller, John, ed. see Koral, Randall.

Miller, John, ed. see Kuhlewind, Georg.

Miller, John, ed. see Miller, Elaine.

Miller, John, ed. see Moore, Thomas.

Miller, John A. Causes Of Action. 256p. 1999. 23.00 (*0-671-02331-4*) S&S Trade.

— Causes of Action. 320p. 1999. per. 6.99 (*0-671-02332-2*) PB.

— Cutdown: A Claude McCutcheon Novel. 288p. 1998. mass mkt. 6.50 (*0-671-56905-8*) S&S Trade.

— Implementing Activity-Based Management in Daily Operations: Organizational Guide to Imlementation. LC 95-20153. 256p. 1995. 39.95 (*0-471-04003-7*) Wiley.

— Jackson Street: And Other Soldier Stories. LC 94-61157. 178p. 1995. 18.95 (*0-9642949-3-1*) Orloff Pr.

— Jackson Street: And Other Soldier Stories. LC 96-38541. 1997. per. 11.00 (*0-671-56906-6*) PB.

— Master Builders of Sixty Centuries. LC 70-37524. (Essay Index Reprint Ser.). (Illus.). 1977. reprint ed. 23.95 (*0-8369-2566-1*) Ayer.

Miller, John A., Jr. Pink. 216p. mass mkt. 4.99 (*1-55197-173-9*) Picasso Publ.

Miller, John A., ed. Proceedings, 26th Annual Simulation Symposium. LC 71-149514. 352p. 1993. pap. text 80.00 (*0-8186-3620-3*, ANSS-26) Soc Computer Sim.

Miller, John B. Floods: People at Risk, Strategies for Prevention. (Illus.). 93p. 1998. pap. text 40.00 (*0-7881-7105-4*) DIANE Pub.

— Floods - People at Risk, Strategies for Prevention. (Illus.). 93p. 32.00 (*92-1-132021-6*, GB1399) UN.

Miller, John C. Crisis in Freedom. 257p. 22.95 (*0-8488-2571-3*) Amereon Ltd.

— The Federalist Era, 1789-1801. (Illus.). 304p. (C). 1998. pap. text 13.95 (*1-57766-031-5*) Waveland Pr.

— The First Frontier: Life in Colonial America. 284p. 1986. reprint ed. pap. text 19.00 (*0-8191-4977-2*) U Pr of Amer.

— Origins of the American Revolution: With a New Introduction & Bibliography. 2nd ed. (Illus.). xxii, 530p. 1959. 67.50 (*0-8047-0593-3*); pap. 18.95 (*0-8047-0594-1*) Stanford U Pr.

— Sam Adams: Pioneer in Propaganda. (Illus.). 437p. 1936. 52.50 (*0-8047-0024-9*) Stanford U Pr.

— Sam Adams: Pioneer in Propaganda. LC 60-7699. (Illus.). 447p. reprint ed. pap. 30.00 (*0-608-20213-4*, 207146700012) Bks Demand.

— Triumph of Freedom, 1775-1783. LC 78-23672. (Illus.). 718p. 1979. reprint ed. lib. bdg. 79.50 (*0-313-20779-8*, MITF, Greenwood Pr) Greenwood.

— Triumph of Freedom, 1775-1783. (History - United States Ser.). 718p. 1993. reprint ed. lib. bdg. 109.00 (*0-7812-4833-7*) Rprt Serv.

— The Wolf by the Ears: Thomas Jefferson & Slavery. 336p. 1991. reprint ed. pap. text 16.50 (*0-8139-1365-9*) U Pr of Va.

Miller, John C., ed. Laser Ablation: Principles & Aplications. LC 94-5045. (Series in Material Science: Vol. 48). 1994. 64.95 (*0-387-57571-5*) Spr-Verlag.

— Poe's Helen Remembers. LC 79-742. (Illus.). 528p. 1980. text 40.00 (*0-8139-0771-3*) U Pr of Va.

Miller, John C. & Geohegan, David, eds. Laser Ablation: Mechanism & Applications-II. (AIP Conference Proceedings Ser.: No. 288). (Illus.). 456p. 1993. text 150.00 (*1-56396-226-8*, AIP Pr) Spr-Verlag.

Miller, John D. Fast Steps for the Canon EOS 5/A2/A2E. 40p. 1995. pap. 25.00 (*0-9649037-0-9*) Advant One.

Miller, John D., jt. ed. see Rigby, Thomas H.

Miller, John E. Becoming Laura Ingalls Wilder: The Woman Behind the Legend. Foley, William E., ed. LC 97-51348. (Biography Ser.). (Illus.). 320p. 1998. 29.95 (*0-8262-1167-4*) U of Mo Pr.

— How to Start a Business Without a Bankroll. 128p. (Orig.). 1986. 55.00 (*0-933203-00-4*) Miller Money Mgmt.

— Laura Ingalls Wilder's Little Town: Where History & Literature Meet. (Illus.). 220p. 1995. pap. 14.95 (*0-7006-0713-7*) U Pr of KS.

— The Reciprocating Pump: Theory, Design & Use. 2nd ed. LC 91-2639. 484p. (C). 1994. lib. bdg. 82.50 (*0-89464-599-4*) Krieger.

— South Dakota: A Journey Through Time. LC 98-61431. (Illus.). 120p. (Orig.). (YA). (gr. 3 up). 1998. pap. text 12.00 (*1-57579-130-7*) Pine Hill Pr.

Miller, John E. & Halvorson, Mark J. The Way They Saw Us: The South Dakota State Historical Society Collection of Images from the Nineteenth-Century Illustrated Press. Koupal, Nancy T., ed. LC 89-50608. (Illus.). 64p. (Orig.). 1989. pap. 5.00 (*0-9622621-0-2*) SD State Hist Soc.

Miller, John E., jt. auth. see Pawson, David L.

Miller, John F. Ovid Fasti, Vol. II. (Latin Commentaries Ser.). 102p. (Orig.). (C). 1985. pap. text 7.00 (*0-929524-46-2*) Bryn Mawr Commentaries.

Miller, John G. The Battle to Save the Houston. McCarthy, Paul, ed. 264p. 1992. reprint ed. mass mkt. 4.99 (*0-671-78621-0*) PB.

— The Bridge at Dong Ha. (Bluejacket Bks.). (Illus.). 216p. 1996. pap. 15.95 (*1-55750-587-X*) Naval Inst Pr.

*__Miller, John G.__ Personality Accountability: Powerful & Practical Ideas for You & Your Organization. 1998. 25.00 (*0-9665832-0-5*) DeVere Pr.

— Personality Accountability: Powerful & Practical Ideas for You & Your Organization. 1998. pap. 15.00 (*0-9665832-1-3*) Denver Pr.

*__Miller, John Grider.__ The Co-Vans: U. S. Marine Advisors in Vietnam. LC 00-33922. (Illus.). 184p. 2000. 24.95 (*1-55750-549-7*) Naval Inst Pr.

*__Miller, John H.__ Called by Love: Reflections on God's Intervention in Human History. 229p. 2000. reprint ed. pap. 10.00 (*1-887567-14-3*) CBCCU Amer.

Miller, John H. Love Come of Age: Reflections on Christian Spirituality. 135p. 1998. pap. 10.00 (*1-887567-11-9*) CBCCU Amer.

— Love Responds: Reflections on Christian Morality. 149p. (Orig.). 1990. pap. 7.00 (*0-9626257-0-1*) CBCCU Amer.

Miller, John H., ed. Advances in Chemical Physics: Single Perturbation Problems in Chemical Physics, Vol. 97. 373p. 1997. 195.00 (*0-471-11531-2*) Wiley.

Miller, John H., intro. Curing World Poverty: The New Role of Property. LC 94-175798. (Illus.). 310p. (Orig.). 1994. pap. 15.00 (*0-9626257-5-2*) CBCCU Amer.

Miller, John H. & Gelfand, Michael, eds. Pediatric Nuclear Imaging. LC 93-38091. 1994. text 115.00 (*0-7216-3685-3*, W B Saunders Co) Harcrt Hlth Sci Grp.

Miller, John H., jt. auth. see Bergstrom, Theodore C.

Miller, John H., jt. auth. see Hatfield, William E.

Miller, John H., tr. see Poupard, Paul.

Miller, John H., tr. see Schooyans, Michael.

Miller, John H., tr. see Schooyans, Michel.

Miller, John H., tr. & pref. see Schooyans, Michel.

Miller, John J. The Unmaking of Americans: How Multiculturalism Has Undermined the Assimilation Ethic. LC 97-38208. 320p. 1998. 25.00 (*0-684-83622-X*) Free Pr.

Miller, John J., III, ed. Juvenile Rheumatoid Arthritis. LC 78-55290. (Illus.). 280p. 1979. 35.00 (*0-88416-189-7*) Mosby Inc.

Miller, John J., III, jt. auth. see Isenberg, David A.

Miller, John J., jt. auth. see Leigh, Stephen.

Miller, John J., ed. see Metallurgical Society of AIME Staff.

Miller, John Lester & Friedman, Ed. Photonics Rules of Thumb: Optics, Electro-Optics, Fiber Optics, & Lasers. (Illus.). 423p. 1996. 55.00 (*0-07-044329-7*) McGraw.

Miller, John M. Deer Camp: Last Light in the Northeast Kingdom. Ostrum, Meg, ed. 129p. 1992. 30.00 (*0-262-13283-4*) MIT Pr.

— Minnesota Legal Forms: Commercial Real Estate. Date not set. lib. bdg. 69.95 (*0-327-01029-0*, 81772, MICHIE) LEXIS Pub.

— Minnesota Legal Forms: Commercial Real Estate. 180p. 1982. ring bd. 69.95 incl. disk (*0-917126-88-2*, MICHIE) LEXIS Pub.

— Minnesota Legal Forms: Commercial Real Estate. 180p. 1993. ring bd. 69.95 incl. disk (*0-614-05900-3*, MICHIE); ring bd., suppl. ed. 35.00 (*0-614-03156-7*, MICHIE); suppl. ed. 35.00 (*0-685-70860-8*, MICHIE) LEXIS Pub.

Miller, John M., jt. ed. see Lundgren, Claes.

Miller, John N. & Clark, Raymond C., eds. The World: The 1990s from the Pages of a Real Small-Town Daily Newspaper - A Multi-Level Reader. (Illus.). 112p. (Orig.). 1993. pap. text 12.00 (*0-86647-078-6*) Pro Lingua.

Miller, John P. The Contemplative Practitioner: Meditation in Education & the Professions. LC 94-4767. 184p. 1994. 52.95 (*0-89789-401-4*, Bergin & Garvey) Greenwood.

— Creating Academic Settings: High Craft & Low Cunning: Memoirs. LC 91-90125. 247p. 1991. 17.00 (*0-9629010-0-8*) J Simcon Pr.

*__Miller, John P.__ Education & the Soul: Toward a Spiritual Curriculum. LC 99-31605. 224p. (C). 1999. text 44.50 (*0-7914-4341-8*); pap. text 14.95 (*0-7914-4342-6*) State U NY Pr.

Miller, John P. Pricing of Military Procurements. (Yale Studies in National Policy: No. 2). 1949. 89.50 (*0-685-69842-4*) Elliots Bks.

Miller, John R. The Last Family: A Suspense Novel. 480p. 1997. reprint ed. mass mkt. 6.99 (*0-553-57496-5*) Bantam.

Miller, John R., jt. auth. see Campbell, Luther.

Miller, John T. Ideology & Enlightenment: The Political & Social Thought of Samuel Taylor Coleridge. (Modern European History Ser.). 336p. 1987. text 15.00 (*0-8240-7824-1*) Garland.

Miller, John W. Calling God "Father" Essays on the Bible, Fatherhood & Culture. 2nd ed. LC 99-36566. 208p. 1999. pap. 16.95 (*0-8091-3897-2*) Paulist Pr.

— The Definition of the Thing: With Some Notes on Language. 192p. (C). 1980. reprint ed. 20.00 (*0-393-01377-4*) Norton.

— The Definition of the Thing: With Some Notes on Language. 1983. reprint ed. pap. 12.95 (*0-393-30059-5*) Norton.

— In Defense of the Psychological. 192p. 1985. reprint ed. pap. 6.50 (*0-393-30226-1*) Norton.

— Jesus at Thirty: A Psychological & Historical Perspective. LC 97-23723. 160p. 1997. 18.00 (*0-8006-3107-2*, Fortress Pr) Augsburg Fortress.

— Meet the Prophets: A Beginner's Guide to the Books of the Biblical Prophets. 288p. 1987. pap. 14.95 (*0-8091-2899-3*) Paulist Pr.

— The Midworld of Symbols & Functioning Objects. 192p. 1982. reprint ed. 20.00 (*0-393-01579-3*) Norton.

— The Midworld of Symbols & Functioning Objects. 192p. 1984. reprint ed. pap. 6.95 (*0-393-30156-7*) Norton.

— The Origins of the Bible: Rethinking Canon History. LC 94-33902. (Theological Inquiries Ser.). 272p. 1995. pap. 18.95 (*0-8091-3522-1*) Paulist Pr.

— The Paradox of Cause & Other Essays. 1990. pap. 10.95 (*0-393-30731-X*) Norton.

— The Philosophy of History with Reflections & Aphorisms. LC 80-29179. 192p. (C). 1981. reprint ed. 22.25 (*0-393-01464-9*) Norton.

— The Philosophy of History with Reflections & Aphorisms. LC 80-29179. 192p. 1983. reprint ed. pap. 12.95 (*0-393-30060-9*) Norton.

*__Miller, John W., et al, eds.__ Machine Vision Systems for Inspection & Metrology VIII. 260p. 1999. pap. text 72.00 (*0-8194-3429-9*) SPIE.

Miller, John W. & McKenna, Michael C., eds. Literacy Education in the 21st Century: A Special Double Issue of the Peabody Journal of Education. 392p. 1999. pap. 45.00 (*0-8058-9804-2*) L Erlbaum Assocs.

Miller, John W., tr. see Goldoni, Carlo.

Miller, Johnny, jt. auth. see Gorden, Bill.

Miller, Jon. Confessions of a Baseball Purist: What's Right--& Wrong--with Baseball, As Seen from the Best. LC 98-5285. 272p. 1998. 24.00 (*0-684-84518-0*) S&S Trade.

— Pathways in the Workplace: The Effect of Race & Gender on Access to Organzational Resources. (American Sociological Assn. Rose Monographs). (Illus.). 128p. 1986. text 54.95 (*0-521-32365-7*) Cambridge U Pr.

— The Social Control of Religious Zeal: A Study of Organizational Contradictions. LC 93-6030. (Arnold & Caroline Rose Monograph Series of the American Sociological Association). 240p. (C). 1994. text 48.00 (*0-8135-2060-6*) Rutgers U Pr.

Miller, Jon, ed. Research on Child Language Disorders: A Decade of Progress. 1990. pap. 32.00 (*0-316-57220-9*) Little.

Miller, Jon, photos by. Frank Lloyd Wright Home & Studio, Oak Park. (Opus Ser.: Vol. 23). (Illus.). 60p. 1996. 42.00 (*3-930698-23-4*, Pub. by E J Wasmuth) Dist Art Pubs.

*__Miller, Jon & Hyman, Mark.__ Confessions of a Baseball Purist: What's Right & Wrong with Baseball, as Seen from the Best Seat in the House. LC 99-39409. 2000. pap. 15.95 (*0-8018-6316-3*) Johns Hopkins.

Miller, Jon F. Assessing Language Production: Experimental Procedures. (Illus.). 186p. (C). 1991. pap. text 57.00 (*0-205-13546-3*) Allyn.

Miller, Jon F., et al, eds. Communication Development in Children with Down Syndrome. LC 98-18258. 1998. pap. 34.95 (*1-55766-350-5*, 3505) P H Brookes.

Miller, Jon F. & Paul, Rhea. The Clinical Assessment of Language Comprehension. LC 94-35065. 208p. 1994. spiral bd. 34.95 (*1-55766-176-6*) P H Brookes.

Miller, Jon F., jt. auth. see Leadholm, Barbara J.

Miller, Jonathan. The Afterlife of Plays. (Distinguished Graduate Research Lectures: No. 5). 48p. 1992. 12.50 (*1-879691-12-4*) SDSU Press.

— Darwin for Beginners. 176p. 1990. pap. 11.00 (*0-679-72511-3*) McKay.

— Don Giovanni: Myths of Seduction & Betrayal. 1991. pap. 11.95 (*0-8018-4332-4*) Johns Hopkins.

— Goalkeeping. (Soccer School Ser.). (Illus.). 32p. (J). (gr. 3 up). 1998. pap. 5.95 (*0-7460-2907-1*, Usborne); lib. bdg. 13.95 (*1-58086-131-8*, Usborne) EDC.

*__Miller, Jonathan.__ On Reflection. LC 98-66560. (Illus.). 224p. 1998. pap. 40.00 (*1-85709-236-8*) Nat Gallery Pubns.

Miller, Jonathan. On Reflection. (Illus.). 224p. 1998. 40.00 (*0-300-07713-0*) Yale U Pr.

Miller, Jonathan, ed. Training & Fitness. (Soccer School Ser.). (Illus.). 32p. (YA). (gr. 5 up). 1999. pap. text 5.95 (*0-7460-2909-8*, Usborne); lib. bdg. 13.95 (*1-58086-134-2*, Usborne) EDC.

Miller, Jonathan & Van Loon, Boris. Darwin for Beginners. 12.95 (*0-906495-95-4*) Writers & Readers.

Miller, Jonathan, jt. auth. see Lurie, Joe.

Miller, Jonathan, jt. auth. see Pelham, David.

Miller, Jonathan, jt. ed. see Durant, John.

Miller, Jonathon D. A Better Life: Improving Self & World. (Illus.). 100p. 2000. 17.98 (*0-935815-09-0*) Lifecircle.

— Business Success: A Complete Manual for Enjoyable Success of Your Small Business. large type ed. 117p. 1999. ring bd. 19.95 (*0-935815-08-2*) Lifecircle.

— Candida Yeast & Other Parasites: The Battle in Your Body. rev. ed. (Orig.). Date not set. pap. 4.98 (*0-935815-03-1*) Lifecircle.

— The Fountain of Youth: Secrets of Health, Rejuvenation & Long Life. 2000. pap. 6.98 (*0-935815-05-8*) Lifecircle.

— Healing the Whole Person. (Orig.). Date not set. pap. 9.98 (*0-935815-04-X*) Lifecircle.

— Herbs & Iridology. 3rd rev. ed. (Illus.). (Orig.). Date not set. pap. 6.98 (*0-935815-01-5*) Lifecircle.

— Nutrition, Health & Harmony: A Handbook of Natural Health. rev. ed. (Illus.). (Orig.). 1980. pap. 5.98 (*0-935815-00-7*) Lifecircle.

— Stress Control: Save Your Life from Distress the Real Disease. 1999. pap. 4.98 (*0-935815-06-6*) Lifecircle.

Miller, Joni. True Grits: The Southern Foods Mail-Order Catalog. LC 88-51583. (Illus.). 384p. (Orig.). 1990. pap. 10.95 (*0-89480-344-1*, 1344) Workman Pub.

Miller, Jordan Y. The Health Introduction to Drama. 3rd ed. LC 87-80582. 1047p. (C). 1988. pap. text 32.76 (*0-669-14812-1*) HM Trade Div.

— The Heath Introduction to Drama. 5th ed. 1114p. (C). 1996. pap. text 32.76 (*0-669-35506-2*) HM Trade Div.

Miller, Jordan Y. & Frazer, Winifred L. American Drama Between the Wars: A Critical History. (Twayne's Critical History of American Drama Ser.). 280p. 1991. 33.00 (*0-8057-8950-2*, Twyne) Mac Lib Ref.

M

An Asterisk (*) at the beginning of an entry indicates that the title is appearing for the first time.

Miller, Joseph. The Descendants of Captain Thomas Carter of "Lyford", Lancaster County, Virginia, with Allied Families. (Illus.). 430p. 1989. reprint ed. pap. 67.50 (*0-8328-0377-4*); reprint ed. lib. bdg. 77.50 (*0-8328-0376-6*) Higginson Bk Co.
— Discovering Life in Christ. (Illus.). 62p. (C). 1989. teacher ed. 2.99 (*0-87227-137-4*, RBP5167); student ed. 2.99 (*0-87227-136-6*, RBP5165) Reg Baptist.
— Discovering Life in the Church. 94p. 1990. student ed. 2.99 (*0-87227-141-2*, RBP5170); pap., teacher ed. 2.99 (*0-87227-142-0*, RBP5169) Reg Baptist.
— Singer & Songs of the Church. reprint ed. lib. bdg. 75.00 (*0-7812-0770-3*) Rprt Serv.

Miller, Joseph B. Relief at Last: Neutralization for Food Allergy & Other Illnesses. (Illus.). 352p. 1987. pap. text 45.95 (*0-398-06643-4*) C C Thomas.
— Relief at Last: Neutralization for Food Allergy & Other Illnesses. (Illus.). 352p. (C). 1987. text 60.95 (*0-398-05283-2*) C C Thomas.

Miller, Joseph C. Way of Death: Merchant Capitalism & the Angolan Slave Trade, 1730-1830. LC 87-40368. (Illus.). 800p. (Orig.). 1997. pap. 32.95 (*0-299-11564-X*) U of Wis Pr.

Miller, Joseph C., ed. Slavery & Slaving in World History: A Bibliography, 1900-1991, Vol. 1. 2nd ed. LC 97-32908. 604p. (gr. 13). 1998. text 115.95 (*0-7656-0279-2*) M E Sharpe.
— Slavery & Slaving in World History: A Bibliography, 1900-1991, 1992-1996, Vol. 1 & 2. LC 97-32908. 828p. (gr. 13). 1998. text 183.95 (*0-7656-0281-4*) M E Sharpe.
— Slavery & Slaving in World History: A Bibliography, 1992-1996, Volume 2 (supplement) LC 97-32908. 266p. (C). (gr. 13). 1998. text, suppl. ed. 89.95 (*0-7656-0280-6*) M E Sharpe.

Miller, Joseph C., jt. ed. see Finkelman, Paul.

Miller, Joseph H. The Linguistic Moment: From Wordsworth to Stevens. LC 84-42894. 467p. 1985. reprint ed. pap. 144.80 (*0-608-02504-6*, 206314800004) Bks Demand.

Miller, Joseph L., Jr. How to Destroy God's Kingdom & Democracy at the Same Time: Case Study: Water Supply of Portland, Oregon. 59p. 1989. pap. text 3.45 (*0-9614887-1-9*) DRC Graphics Serv.
— What Good Is Free Speech in a Closet? A Story of Cover-up in Planning for Our Grandchildren's Drinking Water. (Illus.). 68p. 1985. pap. 4.75 (*0-9614887-0-0*) DRC Graphics Serv.

Miller, Joseph M., et al, eds. Readings in Medieval Rhetoric. LC 73-77857. 319p. reprint ed. pap. 98.90 (*0-8357-6690-X*, 205687000094) Bks Demand.

Miller, Joseph S., jt. ed. see Osterbrock, Donald E.

Miller, Joseph T. The Politics of Chinese Trotskyism. 200p. (C). 1990. pap. text 29.00 (*0-8133-7875-3*) Westview.

Miller, Joshua. The MAO Game. LC 97-5847. 224p. 1998. pap. 12.00 (*0-380-73182-7*, Avon Bks) Morrow Avon.
— The Mao Game. LC 97-5847. 224p. 1997. 21.00 (*0-06-039185-5*, ReganBks) HarperTrade.
— The Rise & Fall of Democracy in Early America, 1630-1789: The Legacy for Contemporary Politics. 128p. 1991. 29.50 (*0-271-00744-3*) Pa St U Pr.

Miller, Joshua I. Democratic Temperament: The Legacy of William James. LC 96-51864. (American Political Thought Ser.). 178p. 1997. 29.95 (*0-7006-0831-1*) U Pr of KS.

Miller, Joy. Addictive Relationships: Reclaiming Your Boundaries. (Orig.). 1989. pap. 7.95 (*1-55874-003-1*) Health Comm.

***Miller, Joy Erlichman.** Love Carried Me Home: Women Surviving Auschwitz. 250p. 2000. pap. 11.95 (*1-55874-824-5*, Simcha Press) Health Comm.

Miller, Joyce. A Home for Grandma. (Illus.). 280p. (YA). (gr. 7-10). 1983. 9.85 (*0-7399-0105-2*, 2282) Rod & Staff.
— War-Torn Velley. (Illus.). 256p. 1990. 9.40 (*0-7399-0159-1*, 2459) Rod & Staff.

Miller, Joyce, et al. Review Questions for Ultrasound: A Sonographer's Exam Guide. LC 97-42674. (Review Questions Ser.). (Illus.). 190p. 1998. pap. 39.95 (*1-85070-704-9*) Prthnon Pub.

Miller, Judi. Courtney Gets Crazier. MacDonald, Pat, ed. 160p. (Orig.). (J). (gr. 4-6). 1993. pap. 2.99 (*0-671-73821-6*, Minstrel Bks) PB.
— Courtney Gets Crazier. (My Crazy Cousin Ser.). (Orig.). (YA). 1997. mass mkt. 3.50 (*0-671-00279-1*, Minstrel Bks) PB.
— Cry in the Night. 224p. 1990. pap. 3.95 (*0-380-75699-4*, Avon Bks) Morrow Avon.

Miller, Judi. How to be Friends with a Boy - How to be Friends with a Girl. 128p. (YA). (gr. 4-7). 1990. pap. 2.50 (*0-590-42806-3*) Scholastic Inc.

Miller, Judi. How to Be Friends with a Boy - How to be Friends With a Girl. (J). 1990. 7.60 (*0-606-04697-6*, Pub. by Turtleback) Demco.
— My Crazy Cousin Courtney Comes Back. MacDonald, Pat, ed. 160p. (J). 1994. pap. 3.50 (*0-671-88734-3*, Minstrel Bks) PB.
— My Crazy Cousin Courtney Comes Back. 1993. 8.09 (*0-606-11650-8*, Pub. by Turtleback) Demco.
— My Crazy Cousin Courtney Comes Back. 1994. 8.60 (*0-606-11651-6*, Pub. by Turtleback) Demco.
— My Crazy Cousin Courtney Gets Crazier. (Crazy Courtney Ser.). 1997. 8.60 (*0-606-11652-4*, Pub. by Turtleback) Demco.
— My Crazy Cousin Courtney Returns Again. MacDonald, Pat, ed. 160p. (Orig.). 1995. pap. 3.50 (*0-671-88733-5*, Minstrel Bks) PB.
— My Crazy Cousin Courtney Returns Again. (Orig.). 1995. 8.60 (*0-606-11653-2*, Pub. by Turtleback) Demco.
— Purple Is My Game, Morgan Is My Name. 119p. (J). (gr. 4-7). 1998. per. 3.99 (*0-671-00280-5*) PB.

Miller, Judi, jt. auth. see Weber, Eric.

Miller, Judi B., jt. auth. see Taylor, Anita.

Miller, Judith. Care & Repair of Everyday Treasures. LC 97-5506. (Illus.). 256p. 1997. 29.95 (*0-89577-924-2*, Pub. by RD Assn) Penguin Putnam.
— Classic Style. LC 98-18915. (Illus.). 176p. 1998. 35.00 (*0-684-84997-6*, S&S Edns) Simon & Schuster.
— Country Finishes & Effect: A Creative Guide to Decorating Techniques. LC 96-71421. (Illus.). 176p. 1997. 37.50 (*0-8478-2017-3*, Pub. by Rizzoli Intl) St Martin.
— God Has Ninety-Nine Names: A Reporter's Journey Through a Militant Middle East. 1997. per. 15.00 (*0-684-83228-3*, Touchstone) S&S Trade Pap.

***Miller, Judith.** Judith Miller's Color: Period & Regional Style from Around the World. LC 00-39980. (Illus.). 252p. 2000. 40.00 (*0-609-60784-7*) C Potter.

Miller, Judith. Judith Miller's Guide to Period-Style Curtains & Soft Furnishings. LC 96-18133. (Illus.). 176p. 1996. 37.50 (*0-87951-688-7*, Pub. by Overlook Pr) Penguin Putnam.

***Miller, Judith.** Judith Miller's Guide to Period-Style Curtains & Soft Furnishings. (Illus.). 2000. pap. 29.95 (*1-58567-054-5*, Pub. by Overlook Pr) Penguin Putnam.

Miller, Judith. Miller's Collectables Price Guide, 1995-1996, Vol. VI. (Illus.). 497p. 1995. 25.00 (*1-85732-542-7*, Pub. by Reed Illust Books) Antique Collect.
— Miller's Collector's Cars, 1995-1996. (Illus.). 352p. 1995. 35.00 (*1-85732-559-1*, Pub. by Reed Illust Books) Antique Collect.
— Miller's International Antiques Price Guide, 1998. (Illus.). 808p. 1997. 35.00 (*1-84000-039-2*, Pub. by Mitchell Beazley) Antique Collect.

Miller, Judith. Miller's Pocket Antiques Fact File: Essential Information for Dealers, Collectors & Enthusiasts. (Illus.). 192p. 1994. 12.95 (*0-85533-689-7*) Mitchell Beazley.

Miller, Judith. Miller's Traditional English Christmas. LC 96-173386. 160p. 1997. 19.95 (*1-85732-995-3*, Pub. by Millers Pubns) Antique Collect.
— More Period Details: The House Renovator's Bible. 1999. 40.00 (*0-609-60410-4*) Random Hse Value.
— Period Fireplaces: A Practical Guide to Period-Style Decorating. (Illus.). 128p. 1995. 27.95 (*1-85732-397-1*, Pub. by Reed Illust Books) Antique Collect.
— Period Kitchens: A Practical Guide to Period-Style Decorating. (Illus.). 128p. 1995. 27.95 (*1-85732-398-X*, Pub. by Reed Illust Books) Antique Collect.
— The Style Sourcebook: The Definitive Illustrated Directory of Fabrics, Paints, Wallpaper, Tiles, Flooring. LC 97-41166. (Illus.). 400p. 1998. 60.00 (*1-55670-631-6*) Stewart Tabori & Chang.
— Wooden Houses: A Comprehensive Guide to Wood's Natural Beauty in Architecture & Interiors. LC 97-8672. (Illus.). 192p. 1997. 45.00 (*1-55670-610-3*) Stewart Tabori & Chang.

Miller, Judith, ed. Miller's Antiques Encyclopedia: The Definitive Reference on Antiques & Collectibles. (Illus.). 560p. 1998. 70.00 (*1-85732-747-0*, Pub. by Millers Pubns) Antique Collect.

Miller, Judith & Miller, Martin. Miller's Art Nouveau & Art Deco: Buyer's Guide. LC 96-147591. (Illus.). 400p. 1995. 29.95 (*1-85732-685-7*, Pub. by Millers Pubns) Antique Collect.
— Miller's Classic Motorcycles Price Guide, 1996. (Illus.). 176p. 1996. 17.95 (*1-85732-658-X*, Pub. by Reed Illust Books) Antique Collect.
— Miller's Collectables Price Guide, 1996-1997. (Illus.). 496p. 1996. 25.00 (*1-85732-752-7*) Antique Collect.
— Miller's International Antiques Price Guide, 1996. (Illus.). 808p. 1995. 35.00 (*1-85732-746-2*, Pub. by Millers Pubns) Antique Collect.
— Miller's International Antiques Price Guide, 1997. (Illus.). 808p. 1996. 35.00 (*1-85732-892-2*, Pub. by Reed Illust Books) Antique Collect.
— Miller's Picture Price Guide, 1996. (Illus.). 400p. 1995. 30.00 (*1-85732-609-1*, Pub. by Reed Illust Books) Antique Collect.
— Miller's Pine & Country Furniture: Buyer's Guide. (Illus.). 400p. 1995. 29.95 (*1-85732-684-9*, Pub. by Reed Illust Books) Antique Collect.
— Miller's Pocket Dictionary of Antiques: An Authoritative Reference Guide for Dealers, Collectors, & Enthusiasts. (Illus.). 160p. 1990. 10.95 (*0-85533-760-5*, Pub. by Millers Pubns) Antique Collect.
— Miller's Understanding Antiques. rev. ed. (Antique Collectors' Club Ser.). (Illus.). 256p. 1997. 27.95 (*1-85732-857-4*, Pub. by Mitchell Beazley) Antique Collect.
— Period Finishes & Effects. LC 92-5471. (Illus.). 180p. 1992. 40.00 (*0-8478-1569-2*, Pub. by Rizzoli Intl) St Martin.
— Victorian Style. (Antique Collectors' Club Ser.). (Illus.). 240p. 1997. pap. 29.95 (*1-85732-955-4*, Pub. by Mitchell Beazley) Antique Collect.

Miller, Judith & Miller, Martin, eds. Miller's Understanding Antiques. (Illus.). 272p. 1993. pap. 19.95 (*1-85732-001-8*, Pub. by Millers Pubns) Antique Collect.
— Victorian Style: Creating Period Interiors for Contemporary Living. (Illus.). 240p. 1993. 45.00 (*1-85732-098-0*, Pub. by Millers Pubns) Antique Collect.

Miller, Judith & Selby, Dave. Miller's Collector's Cars Price Guide, 1998-1999. (Illus.). 352p. 1997. 35.00 (*1-84000-008-2*, Pub. by Millers Pubns) Antique Collect.

Miller, Judith & Walker, Mick. Miller's Classic Motorcycles Price Guide, 1998-1999. (Illus.). 176p. 1997. 19.95 (*1-84000-009-0*, Pub. by Millers Pubns) Antique Collect.

***Miller, Judith, et al.** Perspectives on Nonprofit Board Diversity. 60p. 1999. pap. text 19.99 (*0-925299-91-X*) Natl Ctr Nonprofit.

Miller, Judith, ed. see Bly, John.

Miller, Judith, ed. see Davidson, Richard.

Miller, Judith, ed. see Knowles, Eric.

Miller, Judith, ed. see Lang, Gordon.

Miller, Judith A. Community-Based Long-Term Care. (Illus.). 320p. 1991. 45.00 (*0-8039-3918-3*); pap. 21.95 (*0-8039-3919-1*) Sage.
— Community-Based Long-Term Care: Innovative Models. LC 90-9223. 263p. 1991. reprint ed. pap. 81.60 (*0-608-02769-3*, 206383500007) Bks Demand.
— Mastering the Market: The State & the Grain Trade in Northern France, 1700-1860. LC 98-20682. (Illus.). 288p. (C). 1998. text 49.95 (*0-521-62129-1*) Cambridge U Pr.

Miller, Judith D., jt. auth. see Jacobus, Lee A.

Miller, Judith F. Coping with Chronic Illness: Overcoming Powerlessness. 3rd ed. LC 99-14320. (Illus.). 573p. (C). 1999. pap. text 37.95 (*0-8036-0298-7*) Davis Co.

Miller, Judith G. Francoise Sagan. (World Authors Ser.: No. 797). 152p. 1988. text 22.95 (*0-8057-8228-1*) Macmillan.
— Theater & Revolution in France since 1968. LC 76-47500. (French Forum Monographs: No. 4). 169p. (Orig.). 1977. pap. 10.95 (*0-917058-03-8*) French Forum.

Miller, Judith G., jt. ed. see Makward, Christiane P.

Miller, Judith G., tr. see Drai, Martine, et al.

Miller, Judith McCoy. Woven Threads. 1997. mass mkt. 1.99 (*1-57748-196-8*) Barbour Pub.

***Miller, Judith McCoy, et al.** American Dream: Four Inspirational Love Stories from America's Past. 352p. 2000. pap. 4.97 (*1-57748-727-3*) Barbour Pub.

***Miller, Judith S.** Direct Connection: Transformation of Consciousness. LC 99-69142. 244p. 2000. pap. 19.95 (*1-58244-077-8*) Rutledge Bks.

Miller, Judy. Abstracts. (Illus.). 92p. (Orig.). 1988. pap. 11.96 (*0-912833-11-4*) J Miller Pubns.
— Birds & Flowers. (Illus.). 112p. (Orig.). 1987. pap. 7.96 (*0-912833-00-9*) J Miller Pubns.
— Carousel. (Illus.). 68p. (Orig.). 1990. pap. 7.16 (*0-912833-13-0*) J Miller Pubns.
— Climb up to the Sunshine. 244p. 1993. 8.95 (*0-942341-06-6*) Dawn Pubns TX.
— Cups Running Over. 235p. 1985. 8.95 (*0-89225-278-2*) Dawn Pubns TX.
— Gifts for All Occasions. (Illus.). 104p. (Orig.). 1983. pap. 7.96 (*0-912833-01-7*) J Miller Pubns.
— Gifts II: For All Occasions. (Illus.). 104p. (Orig.). 1985. pap. 7.96 (*0-912833-03-3*) J Miller Pubns.
— God in My Day. 151p. 1994. 7.95 (*0-942341-09-0*) Dawn Pubns TX.
— Grilled Cheese at Four O'Clock in the Morning. (Illus.). 104p. (J). (gr. 3-7). 1996. pap. 6.95 (*0-945448-02-3*, 4904-01, Pub. by Am Diabetes) NTC Contemp Pub Co.
— Grilled Cheese at Four O'Clock in the Morning. LC 96-68. 1996. 12.15 (*0-606-09370-2*, Pub. by Turtleback) Demco.
— Heart Against a Thorn. 60p. 1990. pap. 6.95 (*0-942341-03-1*) Dawn Pubns TX.
— Heritage. LC 98-126346. 260p. 1997. pap. 10.95 (*0-942341-13-9*) Dawn Pubns TX.
— Hold Gently This Bright Hour. 130p. (Orig.). 1988. pap. 5.95 (*0-942341-01-5*) Dawn Pubns TX.
— Holidays. (Illus.). 68p. 1990. pap. 7.16 (*0-912833-14-9*) J Miller Pubns.
— House Tours. (Illus.). 112p. (Orig.). 1984. pap. 7.96 (*0-912833-02-5*) J Miller Pubns.
— House Tours II. (Illus.). 96p. (Orig.). 1985. pap. 7.96 (*0-912833-04-1*) J Miller Pubns.
— House Tours III: International. (Illus.). 112p. (Orig.). 1987. pap. 12.76 (*0-912833-10-6*) J Miller Pubns.
— House Tours IV: International. (Illus.). 96p. (Orig.). pap. 12.76 (*0-912833-12-2*) J Miller Pubns.
— It Only Takes a Spark. 167p. (Orig.). 1987. pap. 7.95 (*0-942341-00-7*) Dawn Pubns TX.
— Judy Miller Presents: Pattern Book 1. (Illus.). 80p. (Orig.). 1986. pap. 6.36 (*0-912833-06-8*) J Miller Pubns.
— Judy Miller Presents: Pattern Book 2. (Illus.). 80p. (Orig.). 1986. pap. 6.36 (*0-912833-07-6*) J Miller Pubns.
— Judy Miller Presents: Pattern Book 3. (Illus.). 80p. (Orig.). 1987. pap. 6.36 (*0-912833-08-4*) J Miller Pubns.
— Judy Miller Presents: Pattern Book 4. (Illus.). 80p. (Orig.). 1989. pap. 6.36 (*0-912833-09-2*) J Miller Pubns.
— New Day Dawning. 350p. (Orig.). 1989. pap. 10.95 (*0-942341-02-3*) Dawn Pubns TX.
— Northstar: Focus on Reading: Writing Advanced Tests. 48p. 1999. ring bd. 13.27 (*0-201-45825-X*) Addison-Wesley.
— The Power of Names: A Fascinating Study in the Psychology of Names. Bernard, Barry, ed. 211p. (Orig.). 1992. per. 11.95 (*0-9631327-0-9*) Cascade Spec.
— Ripples on the Water. 150p. (Orig.). 1990. pap. 7.95 (*0-942341-04-X*) Dawn Pubns TX.
— Seasons of Celebration. 146p. 1994. 6.95 (*0-614-04220-8*) Dawn Pubns TX.
— Seasons of the Heart. 126p. 1984. 6.95 (*0-89225-272-3*) Dawn Pubns TX.
— SideLights. (Illus.). 72p. 1986. pap. 7.96 (*0-912833-05-X*) J Miller Pubns.
— Songs in the Night. 500p. 1995. 12.95 (*0-942341-10-4*) Dawn Pubns TX.

Miller, Judy & Parker, Farris. Faithfully Yours. 159p. 1991. 7.95 (*0-942341-05-8*) Dawn Pubns TX.

Miller, Judy, jt. auth. see Daley, Dennis.

Miller, Judy, jt. auth. see Daley, Dennis C.

Miller, Judy A. The Self Publisher's Guide: Your Personal Consultant Through the Self Publishing Process. Bernard, Barry & Linder, David, eds. LC 97-91795. x, 116p. (Orig.). 1997. per. 9.95 (*0-9631327-1-7*) Cascade Spec.

Miller, Judy L., jt. auth. see Messersmith, Ann M.

Miller, Julano. Life Line Series, 5 in 1 set, Set. (Illus.). 48p. (J). (gr. 3-9). 1985. pap. 17.00 (*0-87879-484-0*) High Noon Bks.

Miller, Jule P., 3rd. Using Self Psychology in Child Psychotherapy. LC 95-22943. 1996. pap. 45.00 (*1-56821-492-8*) Aronson.

Miller, Julia K. Wild Animals: 1000 or More Places to See & Photograph Birds & Wildlife in the United States & Canada. (Illus.). 400p. 1990. pap. 18.95 (*0-937480-11-8*) Intl Resources.

Miller, Julia R., jt. auth. see Mitstifer, Dorothy I.

Miller, Julia W., jt. auth. see Feldman, Douglas A.

Miller, Julian H. A Monograph of the World Species of Hypoxylon. LC 61-15571. 250p. reprint ed. pap. 77.50 (*0-608-15797-X*, 203104600073) Bks Demand.

Miller, Julian J., ed. CRC Handbook of Ototoxicity. LC 84-20032. 336p. 1985. 187.00 (*0-8493-3215-X*, RF285, CRC Reprint) Franklin.

Miller, Julian S., ed. Isaac Watts Merrill's Journal, 1828-1878, 3 vols. (Illus.). 2500p. Date not set. 100.00 (*1-878651-13-7*) HPL Pr.
— Isaac Watts Merrill's Journal, 1828-1878, 3 vols. (Illus.). 2500p. 1991. pap. 65.00 (*1-878651-17-X*) HPL Pr.

***Miller, Julie.** Always Faithful. (Angel's Touch Ser.). 368p. 2000. mass mkt. 5.50 (*0-505-52374-4*, Love Spell) Dorchester Pub Co.
— Business Writing That Counts. 2nd ed. 2000. pap. 19.95 (*1-883697-75-1*) Hara Pub.

Miller, Julie. How Would You Vote? A Play about Guns in School. 1997. 10.00 (*1-57960-003-4*) Disc Enter Ltd.

***Miller, Julie.** One Good Man. (Intrigue Ser.: Bk. 588). 2000. mass mkt. 4.25 (*0-373-22588-1*, 1-22588-7) Harlequin Bks.

Miller, Julie. Shadow of the Hawk, 1 vol. (Love Spell Ser.). 320p. 1999. mass mkt. 4.99 (*0-505-52322-1*) Dorchester Pub Co.

Miller, Julie, ed. Business Writing That Counts! How to Write Quickly & Clearly in Three Easy Steps. LC 98-93336. x, 250p. 1999. pap. 22.95 (*0-9663670-0-6*) Fitz Pr.

Miller, Juliet V. The Family-Career Connection: A New Framework for Career Development. 49p. 1984. 5.50 (*0-318-22103-9*, IN288) Ctr Educ Trng Employ.

Miller, Juliet V. & Musgrove, Mary L., eds. Issues in Adult Career Counseling. LC 85-644750. (New Directions for Adult & Continuing Education Ser.: No. ACE 32). (Orig.). 1986. pap. 22.00 (*1-55542-983-1*) Jossey-Bass.

Miller, Julius E., jt. auth. see Justin, Lawrence G.

Miller, K. Ruth Hanna McCormick: A Life in Politics, 1880-1944. LC 91-28230. 339p. 1992. 13.95 (*0-8263-1333-7*) U of NM Pr.

Miller, K., et al. Principles & Practice of Immunotoxicology. (Illus.). 392p. 1991. 195.00 (*0-632-02563-8*) Blackwell Sci.
— Second Year Evaluation of the Florida Public Guardianship Pilot Program. 1984. write for info. (*0-318-58137-X*) FSU CSP.

Miller, K., jt. auth. see Lindsey, S.

Miller, K. D. A Litany in Time of Plague. LC 95-108751. 160p. 1994. pap. write for info. (*0-88984-145-4*) Porcup Quill.

Miller, K. J. & Brown, M. W., eds. Multiaxial Fatigue - STP 853. LC 85-7376. 750p. 1985. text 88.00 (*0-8031-0444-8*, STP853) ASTM.

Miller, K. J. & Smith, R. F. Mechanical Behaviour of Materials. 1980. 781.00 (*0-08-024739-3*, Pub. by Pergamon Repr) Franklin.

Miller, Kamae A, ed. see St. Denis, Ruth.

***Miller, Kara E.** The Shop Teacher. (Illus.). 25p. 2000. pap. write for info. (*0-7541-0977-1*, Pub. by Minerva Pr) Unity Dist.

Miller, Karen. Ages & Stages: Developmental Descriptions & Activities, Birth Through Eight Years. LC 85-25175. (Illus.). 153p. (C). 1985. pap. 14.95 (*0-910287-05-8*, RJ131.M54) TelShare Pub Co.
— Assembly Language Programming: The Intel Pentium. (Illus.). 352p. (C). 1999. text 67.00 (*0-19-512376-X*) OUP.

Miller, Karen. Many Danes, Some Norwegians: Karen Miller's Diary, 1894. (Illus.). xviii, 173p. 1997. pap. 14.95 (*0-930697-02-2*) Lur Pubns.

Miller, Karen. More Things to Do with Toddlers & Twos. LC 90-70984. (Illus.). 212p. (Orig.). (C). 1990. pap. 14.95 (*0-910287-08-2*) TelShare Pub Co.
— The Outside Play & Learning Book: Activities for Young Children. Charner, Kathleen, ed. LC 88-82595. (Illus.). 253p. (Orig.). 1989. pap. 14.95 (*0-87659-117-9*) Gryphon Hse.
— A Programmer's View of Computer Architecture: With Assembly Language Examples from the MIPS RISC Architecture. (Illus.). 132p. (C). 1993. pap. write for info. (*0-03-006314-0*) OUP.
— Reiki I Manual. 2nd ed. 88p. (Orig.). 1993. spiral bd. 12.95 (*0-9630439-5-1*) Bayrock.
— Reiki II Manual. 2nd ed. (Illus.). 124p. (Orig.). 1993. spiral bd. 12.95 (*0-9630439-6-X*) Bayrock.
— Simple Steps: Developmental Activities for Infants, Toddlers & Two-Year-Olds. LC 99-26411. (Illus.). 304p. (J). (ps). 1999. pap. 24.95 (*0-87659-204-3*, 18274, Pub. by Gryphon Hse) Consort Bk Sales.
— Things to Do with Toddlers & Twos. LC 92-184870. (Illus.). 168p. (C). 1984. pap. 14.95 (*0-910287-04-X*) TelShare Pub Co.

Miller, Karen, et al. The Crisis Manual for Early Childhood Teachers: How to Handle the Really Difficult Problems. (Illus.). 382p. 1996. pap. 29.95 (*0-87659-176-4*) Gryphon Hse.

Miller, Karen, jt. auth. see Goodman, James.

Miller, Karen, jt. auth. see Miller, Kevin.

An Asterisk (*) at the beginning of an entry indicates that the title is appearing for the first time.

Miller, Karen A. Secrets of the Food Pyramid. (Illus.). 116p. (J). (gr. 4-6). 1998. teacher ed., spiral bd. 29.95 incl. VHS (*1-891608-01-0*) Edutain Ala.

***Miller, Karen A. J.** Populist Nationalism: Republican Insurgency & American Foreign Policy Making, 1918-1925. 69. LC 98-41419. (Contributions in American History Ser.: Vol. 183). 216p. 1999. 57.95 (*0-313-30776-8*, Greenwood Pr) Greenwood.

Miller, Karen M. Poetry to My Lovers. 34p. (Orig.). 1996. pap. 9.43 (*0-9654907-0-X*) kilo mike bks.

Miller, Karen M., jt. auth. see Poertner, Shirley.

Miller, Karen M., ed. see Baer, Jeanne.

Miller, Karen M., ed. see Banks, Lydia.

Miller, Karen M., ed. see Cadwell, Charles M.

Miller, Karen M., ed. see Caroselli, Marlene.

Miller, Karen M., ed. see Deblieux, Mike.

Miller, Karen M., ed. see Deems, Richard S. & Warner, K. C.

Miller, Karen M., ed. see DuPont, Kay.

Miller, Karen M., ed. see Ford, Lisa.

Miller, Karen M., ed. see Holcomb, Jane.

Miller, Karen M., ed. see Knapp, Bonnie.

Miller, Karen M., ed. see Lawson, Karen.

Miller, Karen M., ed. see Lebedun, Jean.

Miller, Karen M., ed. see Mallory, Charles.

Miller, Karen M., ed. see Nichols, Geoff.

Miller, Karen M., ed. see Pope, Carla B. & Whitver, Kathryn S.

Miller, Karen M., ed. see Wood, Hal.

Miller, Karen Massetti, jt. auth. see Weinstein, Elizabeth.

Miller, Karen Massetti, ed. see Deviney, David E.

Miller, Karen P., ed. see National Association of Insurance Commissioners St.

Miller, Karen S. The Voice of Business: Hill & Knowlton & Postwar Public Relations. LC 98-11935. (Luther Hartwell Hodges Series on Business, Society, & the State). (Illus.). 280p. 1999. 39.95 (*0-8078-2439-9*) U of NC Pr.

Miller, Karl, ed. The Three Hostages. LC 94-29801. (Illus.). 330p. 1995. pap. (*0-19-282419-8*) OUP.

Miller, Karl, ed. see Stevenson, Robert Louis.

Miller, Karl V., jt. auth. see Marchinton, R. Larry.

Miller, Kate. First Book of WordPerfect for Windows. 1993. 14.95 (*1-56761-132-X*, Alpha Ref) Macmillan Gen Ref.

— 10 Minute Guide to cc: Mail with cc: Mail Mobile. LC 94-72769. 176p. (Orig.). 1994. 10.99 (*1-56761-587-2*, Alpha Ref) Macmillan Gen Ref.

— 10 Minute Guide to cc: Mobile. (Illus.). (Orig.). 1995. pap. text 10.99 (*0-614-07357-X*, Alpha Ref) Macmillan Gen Ref.

Miller, Katherine. My Apple Tree & Me. (Food & Fun for the Mind, Body, & Soul Ser.: No. 3). (Illus.). 32p. (Orig.). (J). (gr. k-3). 1996. pap. 8.95 (*0-9653035-1-9*) Huckleberry CT.

— Organizational Communication: Approaches & Processes. LC 94-28667. 353p. 1994. pap. 36.25 (*0-534-20790-1*) Wadsworth Pub.

— Organizational Communication: Approaches & Processes. 2nd ed. LC 98-16390. 1998. pap. 56.95 (*0-534-52227-0*) Wadsworth Pub.

Miller, Katherine B., et al. Strategies for Managing Ozone-Depleting Refrigerants: Confronting the Future. LC 94-32043. 134p. 1995. pap. 34.95 (*0-935470-84-0*) Battelle.

***Miller, Katherine J. & Mizes, J. Scott.** Comparative Treatments of Eating Disorders. LC 00-27400. 2000. write for info. (*0-8261-1358-3*) Springer Pub.

***Miller, Kathleen.** Advanced Legal Research Exercise Manual. (Paralegal Ser.). (C). 2000. pap. 17.25 (*0-7668-2024-6*) Thomson Learn.

Miller, Kathleen. Fair Share Divorce for Women. (Illus.). 318p. (Orig.). 1995. pap. 19.95 (*0-9644549-0-4*) Miller Advisors.

— Restraining the American Workforce. 1989. 30.00 (*0-201-11585-9*) Addison-Wesley.

Miller, Kathleen, jt. auth. see Miller, Don.

***Miller, Kathleen Ann.** Tera, My Journey Home: Seichem, Shamanism, Symbology, Herbs & Reincarnation. 2nd rev. ed. (Healing Art Ser.). (Illus.). 308p. 1999. per. 21.95 (*1-886903-12-3*) K Milner.

Miller, Kathleen N. Mathematics for Business: College Course. 6th ed. 1987. text 37.95 (*0-07-042061-0*) McGraw.

Miller, Kathleen N., jt. auth. see Peterson, David R.

Miller, Kathryn. Haunted Houses. 46p. 1986. reprint ed. pap. 3.95 (*0-87129-026-X*, H57) Dramatic Pub.

— A Thousand Cranes. 28p. 1990. pap. 5.50 (*0-87129-004-9*, T80) Dramatic Pub.

Miller, Kathryn C. Fayette County, Pennsylvania: Gleanings. 98p. 1990. per. 9.00 (*1-55856-029-7*, 027) Closson Pr.

— Records from the Past - Funeral Home Records: Fairchance, PA. LC 97-66980. 176p. 1997. per. 16.00 (*1-55856-253-2*, 246) Closson Pr.

— Some Fayette County, PA Cemeteries. 239p. 1996. per. 19.95 (*1-55856-222-2*, 026) Closson Pr.

Miller, Kathryn M. Did My First Mother Love Me? A Story for an Adopted Child. (Illus.). 48p. (J). (ps-2). 1994. 12.95 (*0-930934-85-7*); pap. 5.95 (*0-930934-84-9*) Morning Glory.

Miller, Kathryn S. Amelia Earhart. 1993. pap. 5.60 (*0-87129-291-2*, A54) Dramatic Pub.

— Poe! Poe! Poe! A Play Based on the Life & Writings of Edgar Allan Poe. (Illus.). 24p. (J). (gr. 4-12). 1984. pap. 3.25 (*0-88680-224-5*) I E Clark.

— The Red Badge of Courage. (YA). 1995. pap. 6.50 (*0-87602-336-7*) Anchorage.

— The Shining Moment: (Musical) (J). 1989. 6.00 (*0-87602-286-7*) Anchorage.

— You Don't See Me. 22p. 1986. reprint ed. pap. 3.95 (*0-87129-022-7*, Y15) Dramatic Pub.

Miller, Kathryn S. & Miller, Barry I. I'm A Celebrity! A Play About Daydreams. (Illus.). 32p. 1983. pap. 4.00 (*0-88680-088-9*) I E Clark.

Miller, Kathryn Schultz. Blue Horses. 41p. 1990. pap. 3.95 (*1-58342-003-7*, B63) Dramatic Pub.

***Miller, Kathy.** Psalms: God's Abundance for Living. 240p. 2000. 19.95 (*1-892016-30-3*) Starburst.

Miller, Kathy, jt. auth. see Sanna, Lucy.

Miller, Kathy A., et al. Stress: Facilitator's Manual. (Well Aware About Health Risk Reduction Ser.). (Illus.). (Orig.). 1983. 35.00 (*0-943562-53-8*) Well Aware.

— Stress: Participant Workbook. (Well Aware About Health Risk Reduction Ser.). (Illus.). 120p. (Orig.). 1982. student ed. 8.75 (*0-943562-54-6*) Well Aware.

Miller, Kathy A., jt. auth. see Dunton, Sabina.

Miller, Kathy C. God's Chewable Vitamin "C" for the Spirit of Moms: A Dose of God's Insight, One Bite at a Time. LC 96-72367. (Illus.). 160p. 1997. pap. 6.95 (*0-914984-94-2*) Starburst.

— God's Chewable Vitamin "C" for the Spirit: A Dose of God's Wisdom One Bite at a Time. LC 95-71944. 160p. 1996. pap. 6.95 (*0-914984-84-5*) Starburst.

— God's Vitamin "C" for the Spirit of Women: "Tug-at-the-Heart" Stories to Inspire & Delight Your Spirit. LC 96-72368. (Illus.). 304p. 1997. pap. 12.95 (*0-914984-93-4*) Starburst.

— Speaking Professionally: Advanced Skills for Powerful Speaking. (Training Ser.). 80p. 1998. pap. text 29.95 (*1-884061-15-X*) Womens Minist.

***Miller, Kathy C.** Through His Eyes: A Woman's Guide to Living with an Eternal Perspective. LC 99-38117. 192p. 1999. pap. 13.00 (*1-57683-117-5*) NavPress.

Miller, Kathy C. The Useful Proverbs. LC 97-60494. 224p. 1997. pap. 9.99 (*0-529-10771-6*, TUP) World Publng.

— When Counting to 10 Isn't Enough: Defusing Anger. LC 96-3838. 96p. 1996. pap. 7.99 (*0-87788-745-4*, H Shaw Pubs) Waterbrook Pr.

— Writing Professionally: Practical Instruction for Getting Your Message into Print. (Training Ser.). 80p. 1998. pap. text 29.95 (*1-884061-19-2*) Womens Minist.

— Your View of God . . . God's View of You: Inspirational Devotions for Women. LC 93-192039. 136p. 1992. pap. 9.99 (*0-8341-1431-3*) Beacon Hill.

Miller, Kathy C., compiled by. God's Vitamin "C" for the Hurting Spirit: Tug-at-the-Heart Stories to Comfort & Strengthen Your Spirit. LC 97-68724. (God's Vitamin C for the Spirit Ser.: Vol. 4). (Illus.). 256p. 1997. pap. 12.95 (*0-914984-69-1*) Starburst.

Miller, Kathy C., ed. God's Abundance for Women: Devotions for a More Meaningful Life. (God's Abundance Ser.). 320p. 1999. 19.95 (*1-892016-14-1*, Pub. by Starburst) Natl Bk Netwk.

***Miller, Kathy C., ed.** Proverbs: God's Abundance for Living. 240p. 2000. 19.95 (*1-892016-31-1*) Starburst.

Miller, Kathy C. & Miller, D. Larry. When the Honeymoon's Over: Building a Real-Life Marriage. LC 97-10278. 1997. 9.99 (*0-87788-565-6*, H Shaw Pubs) Waterbrook Pr.

Miller, Kathy C. & Miller, D. Larry, compiled by. God's Vitamin "C" for the Christmas Spirit: Tug-at-the-Heart Traditions & Inspirations to Warm the Heart. LC 96-68840. 192p. 1996. 14.95 (*0-914984-85-3*) Starburst.

Miller, Kathy C. & Miller, Darcy. Staying Friends with Your Kids. LC 97-2827. 96p. 1997. 7.99 (*0-87788-800-0*, H Shaw Pubs) Waterbrook Pr.

Miller, Kathy Collard. Promises of God's Abundance for a More Meaningful Life. LC 98-86023. (God's Abundance Ser.). 208p. 1998. pap. 9.95 (*0-914984-09-8*, Pub. by Starburst) Natl Bk Netwk.

— Since Life Isn't a Game, These Are God's Rules: Finding Joy & Happiness in God's Ten Commandments. 208p. 1999. 17.95 (*1-892016-15-X*, Pub. by Starburst) Natl Bk Netwk.

***Miller, Kathy Collard.** Why Do I Put So Much Pressure on Myself? Confessions of a Recovering Perfectionist. 260p. 2000. 10.00 (*1-56955-127-8*, Vine Bks) Servant.

Miller, Kathy Collard. Women of the Bible. Richards, Larry, ed. LC 98-83165. (God's Word for the Biblically-Inept Ser.: Vol. 5). (Illus.). 352p. 1999. pap. 16.95 (*0-914984-06-3*, Pub. by Starburst) Natl Bk Netwk.

Miller, Kathy Collard, compiled by. God's Unexpected Blessings: What to Expect from God When You Least Expect It. LC 97-80889. (Illus.). 336p. 1998. 18.95 (*0-914984-07-1*) Starburst.

— Stories of God's Abundance: For a More Joyful Life. (God's Abundance Ser.). 304p. 1999. pap. 12.95 (*1-892016-06-0*) Starburst.

— Why Fret That God Stuff? Learn to Let Go & Let God Take Control. LC 98-86025. 304p. 1998. pap. 12.95 (*0-914984-50-0*, Pub. by Starburst) Natl Bk Netwk.

Miller, Kathy Collard, ed. God's Abundance: 365 Days to a Simpler Life. LC 97-68720. 496p. 1997. 19.95 (*0-914984-97-7*) Starburst.

— More God's Abundance: Joyful Devotions for Every Season. (God's Abundance Ser.). 320p. 1999. 19.95 (*1-892016-13-3*, Pub. by Starburst) Natl Bk Netwk.

Miller, Kathy Collard & Miller, D. Larry, compiled by. God's Vitamin "C" for the Spirit: "Tug-at-the-Heart" Stories to Fortify & Enrich Your Life. LC 95-71943. 304p. 1996. pap. 12.95 (*0-914984-83-7*) Starburst.

Miller, Kathy H. In the Interstices of the Tate: Edith Wharton's Narrative Strategies. LC 92-29801. (American University Studies: American Literature: Ser. XXIV, Vol. 47). 155p. (C). 1993. text 38.95 (*0-8204-2041-7*) P Lang Pubng.

Miller, Keith. Automobile Accident Law & Practice, 4 vols. 1988. ring bd. 580.00 (*0-8205-1158-7*, 158) Bender.

— Highway Home Through Texas. LC 93-84638. 86p. 1993. pap. 12.95 incl. audio (*1-55725-064-2*) Paraclete MA.

— A Second Touch: Chinese Edition. Kao, Samuel E., tr. (CHI.). 202p. 1997. pap. 5.00 (*1-56582-090-8*) Christ Renew Min.

— Simple Surveying. (C). 1977. 21.00 (*0-907649-58-0*, Pub. by Expedit Advisory Ctr) St Mut.

— The Taste of New Wine. LC 93-82109. 128p. 1993. pap. 9.95 (*1-55725-059-6*, 930-026, Pub. by Paraclete MA) BookWorld.

Miller, Keith, jt. auth. see Baldwin, Michael.

Miller, Keith D. Voice of Deliverance: The Language of Martin Luther King, Jr. & Its Sources. LC 98-10324. 280p. 1998. reprint ed. pap. 17.95 (*0-8203-2013-7*) U of Ga Pr.

Miller, Keith H. Prudhoe Bay Governor: Alaska's Keith Miller. LC 97-60349. (Illus.). 296p. 1997. 24.95 (*1-878100-99-8*) Todd Commns.

***Miller, Keith J. & McDowell, David L., eds.** Mixed-Mode Crack Behavior. LC 99-37767. (STP Ser.: Vol. 1359). (Illus.). 335p. 1999. pap. text 150.00 (*0-8031-2602-6*, STP 1359) ASTM.

Miller, Keith W., jt. auth. see Roth, Sheldon H.

Miller, Kelly. Appeal to Conscience: America's Code of Caste, a Disgrace to Democracy. LC 71-89390. (Black Heritage Library Collection). 1977. 11.95 (*0-8369-8633-4*) Ayer.

— Appeal to Conscience: America's Code of Caste a Disgrace to Democracy. LC 69-18553. (American Negro: His History & Literature. Series 2). 1968. reprint ed. 11.95 (*0-405-01881-9*) Ayer.

— As to the Leopard's Spots. (African-American Chapbook Ser.). (Illus.). 32p. (Orig.). 1989. reprint ed. pap. 16.95 (*0-685-26488-2*) Dreamkeeper Pr.

— The Everlasting Stain. 1990. 25.00 (*0-87498-030-5*) Assoc Pubs DC.

— Out of the House of Bondage. LC 69-18554. (American Negro: His History & Literature. Series 2). 1969. reprint ed. 11.95 (*0-405-01882-7*) Ayer.

— Race Adjustment. Incl. Essays on the Negro in America. LC 68-29012. 1968. Everlasting Stain. LC 68-29012. 1968. LC 68-29012. (American Negro: His History & Literature, Ser. 1). 688p. 1969. reprint ed. 19.95 (*0-405-01831-2*) Ayer.

— Race Adjustment: Essays on the Negro in America. LC 77-89389. (Black Heritage Library Collection). 1977. 18.95 (*0-8369-8634-2*) Ayer.

Miller, Kelly S., et al. Initial Public Offerings Annual, 1989. 969p. 1990. lib. bdg. 175.00 (*1-55888-314-2*) Omnigraphics Inc.

Miller, Ken. Eclipse Hawaii: Guide to the Eclipse of July 11, 1991. (Illus.). 48p. 1991. pap. 4.95 (*0-930897-50-1*) Bishop Mus.

— The Hamptons: Long Island's East End. (Illus.). 208p. 1993. 45.00 (*0-8478-1694-X*, Pub. by Rizzoli Intl) St Martin.

— Have You Kicked Your Horseshoer Today? A Consumer's Guide to Horseshoeing. LC 91-188948. (Illus.). 105p. 1992. 17.45 (*0-685-57468-7*) Treeline Pub.

— Open All Night Ken Miller. (Illus.). 118p. 1995. 40.00 (*0-87951-571-6*, Pub. by Overlook Pr) Penguin Putnam.

Miller, Ken, photos by. The Hamptons: Long Island's East End. (Illus.). 176p. 1998. pap. 35.00 (*0-8478-2146-3*, Pub. by Rizzoli Intl) St Martin.

Miller, Ken, jt. auth. see Vollmann, William T.

Miller, Kenn. Six Silent Men: 101st LRP, Rangers, Book 2, Bk. 2. 1997. mass mkt. 5.99 (*0-8041-1564-8*) Ivy Books.

Miller, Kenn, jt. auth. see Chambers, Larry.

Miller, Kenneth. To Be Damned. LC 96-36149. 477p. mass mkt. 6.99 (*1-896329-29-2*) Picasso Publ.

Miller, Kenneth & Ross, Bertram. An Introduction to the Fractional Calculus & Fractional Differential Equations. LC 93-9500. 384p. 1993. 135.00 (*0-471-58884-9*, Wiley-Interscience) Wiley.

Miller, Kenneth E. Anthology of Songs for the Solo Voice. 3rd ed. 320p. (C). 1994. pap. text 43.00 (*0-13-720558-9*) P-H.

— Friends & Rivals: Coalition Politics in Denmark, 1901-1995. 306p. (C). 1995. lib. bdg. 46.50 (*0-7618-0187-1*) U Pr of Amer.

— Greenland. LC 92-122448. (World Bibliographical Ser.). 134p. 1991. lib. bdg. 55.00 (*1-85109-139-4*) ABC-CLIO.

— Principles of Singing: A Textbook for Voice Class or Studio. 2nd ed. 288p. (C). 1989. pap. text 45.00 (*0-13-712712-X*) P-H.

***Miller, Kenneth L.** Evening of Pale Sunshine. LC 99-90581. 280p. 1999. pap. 16.00 (*0-9672569-1-7*) KLM Litry Svs.

Miller, Kenneth L. Objective-Based Safety Training. LC 97-52715. 269p. 1998. boxed set 59.95 (*1-56670-286-0*) Lewis Pubs.

Miller, Kenneth L. & Weidner, William A., eds. Handbook of Management of Radiation Protection Programs. 536p. 1986. 280.00 (*0-8493-3769-0*, RA569, CRC Reprint) Franklin.

— Handbook of Management of Radiation Protection Programs. 2nd ed. 496p. 1992. boxed set 208.95 (*0-8493-3770-4*, RA569) CRC Pr.

Miller, Kenneth R. Finding Darwin's God: A Scientist's Search for Common Ground Between God & Evolution. LC 99-16754. 352p. 1999. 25.00 (*0-06-017593-1*, Cliff Street) HarperTrade.

— Finding Darwin's God: A Scientist's Search For Common Ground Between God & Evolution. 288p. 2000. pap. 14.00 (*0-06-093049-7*, Cliff Street) HarperTrade.

Miller, Kenneth R., jt. auth. see Levine, Joseph.

Miller, Kenneth R., jt. auth. see Levine, Joseph S.

Miller, Kenneth R., ed. see Bittar, E. Edward.

Miller, Kenneth S. Complex Stochastic Processes: An Introduction to Theory & Application. LC 73-18094. 252p. reprint ed. pap. 78.20 (*0-608-15310-9*, 205632800059) Bks Demand.

— Partial Differential Equations. LC 87-16930. 262p. (C). 1987. reprint ed. lib. bdg. 27.50 (*0-89464-234-0*) Krieger.

— Partial Differential Equations in Engineering Problems. 1953. 47.00 (*0-13-650408-6*) P-H.

— Some Eclectic Matrix Theory. LC 85-18454. 140p. (C). 1987. lib. bdg. 16.00 (*0-89874-895-X*) Krieger.

Miller, Kenneth S. & Leskiw, Donald M. An Introduction to Kalman Filtering with Applications. LC 85-12606. 128p. 1986. lib. bdg. 21.50 (*0-89874-824-0*) Krieger.

Miller, Kenneth S. & Walsh, J. B. Advanced Trigonometry. abr. ed. LC 76-7918. 116p. (C). 1977. 13.00 (*0-88275-391-6*) Krieger.

Miller, Kenneth S., jt. auth. see Murray, Francis J.

Miller, Kenny. Kenny Cooks America. (Illus.). 192p. 1998. pap. 19.95 (*1-85375-272-X*) Prion.

Miller, Kenny & Vaughan, Donald. Kenny Miller: Surviving Teenage Werewolves, Puppet People & Hollywood. LC 98-53567. (Illus.). 224p. 1999. pap. 28.50 (*0-7864-0641-0*) McFarland & Co.

Miller, Kent & Miller, Betty D. To Kill & Be Killed - Case Studies from Florida's Death Row. LC 88-32360. 118p. 1989. pap. 9.95 (*0-932727-23-9*); lib. bdg. 16.95 (*0-932727-24-7*) Hope Pub Hse.

Miller, Kent C. Ministry to the Homebound. (Healing Presence Ser.). 176p. (Orig.). (C). 1995. pap. text 29.95 (*0-89390-268-3*) Resource Pubns.

Miller, Kent S. & Radelet, Michael L. Executing the Mentally Ill: The Criminal Justice System of the Case of Alvin Ford. (Illus.). 200p. 1993. 44.00 (*0-8039-5149-3*); pap. 19.50 (*0-8039-5150-7*) Sage.

Miller, Kentalle & Miller, Isobel. Retraining & Tradition: Skilled Worker in an Era of Change. 192p. 1975. pap. 27.95 (*0-8464-1127-X*) Beekman Pubs.

Miller, Kenton R. Balancing the Scales: Managing Biodiversity at the Bioregional Level. large type ed. LC 95-62391. 150p. 1996. pap. 20.00 (*0-915825-85-6*, MIBSP) World Resources Inst.

Miller, Kenton R. & Lanou, Steven M. National Biodiversity Planning: Guidelines Based on Early Experiences Around the World. 160p. 1995. pap. 25.00 (*1-56973-025-3*) World Resources Inst.

Miller, Kenton R., jt. auth. see Reid, Walter V.

Miller, Kenton R., jt. ed. see McNeely, Jeffrey A.

Miller, Kerby & Wagner, Paul. Out of Ireland: The Story of Irish Emigration to America. (Illus.). 132p. 1997. 29.95 (*1-57098-179-5*); pap. 19.95 (*1-57098-180-9*) Roberts Rinehart.

Miller, Kerby A. Emigrants & Exiles: Ireland & the Irish Exodus to North America. 704p. 1988. pap. text 19.95 (*0-19-505187-4*) OUP.

Miller, Kerby A., jt. ed. see Donnelly, J. S., Jr.

Miller, Kevin. Everywhere Was Far by Kevin Miller. (Shadowmark Poetry Ser.: Vol. 5). (Illus.). 104p. 1998. pap. 13.00 (*0-911287-28-0*) Blue Begonia.

— Professional NT Services. 450p. 1998. pap. 49.99 (*1-86100-130-4*, Pub. by Wrox Press) Wrox Pr Inc.

Miller, Kevin & Miller, Karen. More Than You & Me: Touching Others Through the Strength of Your Marriage. LC 94-1740. 270p. 1994. pap. 9.99 (*1-56179-217-9*) Focus Family.

Miller, Kevin, jt. auth. see Osborne, Rick.

***Miller, Kim.** Handbook for Multi-Sensory Worship. LC 99-39677. 1999. pap. text 39.00 (*0-687-06860-6*) Abingdon.

Miller, Kimball & Miller, Elaine, eds. Making Sense of Managed Care Vol. I: Building Blocks & Fundamentals. LC 97-70473. 141p. 1997. 32.00 (*0-924674-51-2*) Am Coll Phys Execs.

— Making Sense of Managed Care Vol. II: Strategic Positioning. LC 97-70473. 185p. 1997. 32.00 (*0-924674-52-0*) Am Coll Phys Execs.

— Making Sense of Managed Care Vol. III: Operational Issues & Practical Answers. LC 97-70473. 199p. 1997. 32.00 (*0-924674-53-9*) Am Coll Phys Execs.

Miller, Kirk & Polis, Michael. HIV Resident Pocket Survival Guide. 100p. (C). 1999. pap. 9.95 (*1-883205-35-2*) Intl Med Pub.

***Miller, Kirk M.** Tort Actions under the General Municipal Law in N. Y. C. 2000, ring bd. 29.95 (*0-930137-79-5*) Looseleaf Law.

Miller, Kirsten, jt. auth. see Miller, John.

Miller, Kirsten, jt. ed. see Miller, John.

Miller, Klara & Nicklin, Stephen, eds. Immunology of the Gastrointestinal Tract, 2 vols., Set. 336p. 1987. 259.90 (*0-8493-4310-0*, RC817) CRC Pr.

Miller, Klara, jt. auth. see Liddell, F. D.

Miller, Klara, jt. ed. see Leonard, Brian E.

Miller, Kristie. Ruth Hanna McCormick: A Life in Politics, 1880-1944. LC 91-28230. (Illus.). 353p. reprint ed. pap. 109.50 (*0-608-07276-1*, 206750400009) Bks Demand.

Miller, Kristin. The Careless Quilter: Decide-As-You-Sew, Design-As-You-Go Quiltmaking. LC 94-7377. (Illus.). 260p. (Orig.). 1994. pap. 18.95 (*1-55853-296-X*) Rutledge Hill Pr.

Miller, Kristine, ed. see Brackney, David J.

Miller, Kristine, ed. see Brown, Sandy S.

Miller, Kristine, ed. see Brown, Sandy S., et al.

Miller, Kristine, ed. see Dickich, Nadja.

Miller, Kristine, ed. see Lugenbuchl, Michael.

Miller, Kristine, ed. see Lugenbuehl, Michael & Brown, Sandy S.

Miller, Kristine, ed. see Palmer, Norma E.

Miller-Kritsberg, Ceci, jt. auth. see Lee, John.

Miller, Kyle, ed. Great Quotes from Great Sports Heroes. rev. ed. LC 96-51724. (Successories Ser.). Orig. Title: Great American Sports Heroes: 270 of the Greatest Quotes about Sports. (Illus.). 128p. 1997. pap. 7.99 (*1-56414-287-6*) Career Pr Inc.

M

An Asterisk (*) at the beginning of an entry indicates that the title is appearing for the first time.

Miller, L. Concurrent Engineering Design: Integrating Best Practices for Process Improvement. LC 92-85526. 319p. 1993. 12.95 (*0-87263-433-7*) SME.

Miller, L. & Grenz, Stanley J., eds. Fortress Introduction to Contemporary Theologies. LC 98-34169. 192p. 1998. pap. 17.00 (*0-8006-2981-7*, 1-2981, Fortress Pr) Augsburg Fortress.

Miller, L. Ann, jt. auth. see Ketcham, Katherine.

Miller, L. D., et al, eds. Remote Sensing & Geoinformation Systems as Related to Regional Planning of Health Services. (CPL Bibliographies Ser.: No. 51). 76p. 1981. 10.00 (*0-86602-051-9*, Sage Prdcls Pr) Sage.

Miller, L. Keith. Principles of Everyday Behavior Analysis. 2nd ed. LC 79-27797. 512p. (C). 1980. pap. 30.75 (*0-8185-0373-4*) Brooks-Cole.

Miller, L. Keith. Principles of Everyday Behavior Analysis. 3rd ed. LC 96-2625. (Psychology Ser.). 4448p. (C). 1996. mass mkt. 60.95 (*0-534-16146-4*) Brooks-Cole.

Miller, L. Keith. Principles of Everyday Behavior Analysis. 3rd ed. (C). 1997. pap. text, teacher ed. write for info. (*0-534-34313-9*) Brooks-Cole.

Miller, L. L., et al, eds. Parallel Architectures for Data Knowledge-Based Systems. LC 94-15104. 616p. 1994. 58.00 (*0-8186-6352-9*, BP06352) IEEE Comp Soc.

Miller, L. R. Small Farmer's Journal Index: The First Twenty Years. 63p. 1997. pap. 9.00 (*1-885210-04-3*) Small Farmers.

— Training Workhorses: Training Teamsters. (Illus.). 352p. (Orig.). 1994. pap. 24.95 (*1-885210-00-0*) Small Farmers.

Miller, L. S. & Mullin, J. B. Electronic Materials: From Silicon to Organics. (Illus.). 566p. (C). 1991. 135.00 (*0-306-43655-8*, Plenum Trade) Perseus Pubng.

Miller, L. Scott. Accelerating the Educational Advancement of Minorities: A Nation-Building & Region-Building Imperative for America's Third Century. LC 94-31669. 393p. 1995. 42.00 (*0-300-05793-8*) Yale U Pr.

— American Imperative: Accelerating Minority Educational Advancement. 416p. 1997. pap. text 18.00 (*0-300-07279-1*) Yale U Pr.

Miller-Lachman, Lyn. Educating Children in a Diverse Society. (Teaching Methods Ser.). 1995. teacher ed. 19.00 (*0-8273-5958-6*) Delmar.

— Schools for All: Educating Children in a Diverse Society. LC 94-26265. (Illus.). 402p. (C). 1995. pap. 61.95 (*0-8273-5957-8*) Delmar.

Miller-Lachmann, Lyn. Hiding Places. 206p. (Orig.). (YA). (gr. 9-12). 1987. pap. 4.95 (*0-938961-00-4*, Stamp Out Sheep Pr) Sq One Pubs.

— Our Family, Our Friends, Our World: An Annotated Guide to Significant Multicultural Books for Children & Teenagers. 710p. 1992. 46.00 (*0-8352-3025-2*) Bowker.

Miller-Lachmann, Lyn, compiled by. Global Voices, Global Visions: A Core Collection of Multicultural Books. 875p. 1995. 55.00 (*0-8352-3291-3*) Bowker.

Miller, Lafe, ed. see Burnette, Alma.

Miller, LaMar P., ed. Equality of Educational Opportunity: A Handbook for Research. LC 73-9244. (Studies in Education: No. 1). 1974. lib. bdg. 37.50 (*0-404-10535-1*) AMS Pr.

Miller, LaMar P., jt. ed. see Lagemann, Ellen C.

***Miller, Larissa.** Dim & Distant Days: Stories from My Life. (Glas Ser.: Vol. 25). (Illus.). 200p. 2000. pap. 14.95 (*1-56663-338-9*, Pub. by I R Dee) Natl Bk Netwk.

Miller, Larry. Beyond Golf Vol. 1: How to Transform Your Game & Your Life. LC 96-69115. 208p. 1996. pap. 12.95 (*1-883478-18-9*) Stillpoint.

— God's Chewable Vitamin "C" for the Spirit of Dads: A Dose of Godly Character, One Bite at a Time. LC 96-68839. 160p. 1996. pap. 6.95 (*0-914984-82-9*) Starburst.

***Miller, Larry.** Holographic Golf: Uniting the Mind & Body to Improve Your Game. 2nd ed. LC 00-35973. (Illus.). (J). 2000. write for info. (*1-56554-716-0*) Pelican.

Miller, Larry. King Odorant & His Flies. Anderson, David & Tronslin, Andrea, eds. LC 95-200709. (Illus.). 157p. (J). (ps up). 1995. pap. 8.95 (*0-9641330-7-5*) Portunus Pubng.

— Selling in Agribusiness. Lee, Jasper S., ed. (Career Preparation for Agriculture-Agribusiness Ser.). (Illus.). 1979. text 16.96 (*0-07-041962-0*) McGraw.

Miller, Larry & Braswell, Michael. Human Relations & Police Work. 4th ed. LC 97-205440. 232p. (C). 1996. pap. text 15.95 (*0-88133-919-9*) Waveland Pr.

Miller, Larry & Quilici, Alexander E. The Turbo C Survival Guide. LC 88-25880. (Illus.). 553p. 1989. pap. 29.95 (*0-471-61708-3*) Wiley.

***Miller, Larry & Redfield, James.** Exploring the "Zone" LC 00-38531. 2000. 19.95 (*1-56554-717-9*) Pelican.

Miller, Larry, jt. auth. see Kent, George C.

Miller, Larry L. Ohio Place-Names. LC 95-14555. 320p. 1996. 25.95 (*0-253-32932-9*) Ind U Pr.

***Miller, Larry S.** Hardness of Heart/Hardness of Life: The Stain of Human Infanticide. LC 99-51880. 640p. 2000. pap. 48.50 (*0-7618-1578-3*) U Pr of Amer.

— Vapours. 322p. mass mkt. 5.99 (*1-55197-109-7*) Picasso Publ.

Miller, Larry S. & Sansone, Sam J. Police Photography. 4th ed. LC 98-18745. 270p. 1998. pap. 35.95 (*0-87084-816-X*) Anderson Pub Co.

Miller, Larry S. & Whitehead, John T. Introduction to Criminal Justice Research & Statistics. LC 94-73246. 482p. (C). 1995. pap. text 45.95 (*0-87084-567-5*) Anderson Pub Co.

Miller, Larry S., et al. Student Workbook to Accompany Introduction to Criminal Justice Research & Statistics. 221p. (C). 1995. wbk. ed. 17.95 (*0-87084-566-7*) Anderson Pub Co.

Miller, Laura. 101 Proven Ways to Make Your School Studies Easier. (Illus.). x, 70p. 1998. pap. 6.95 (*0-9665522-0-2*) EduSource.

Miller, Laura, jt. auth. see Bartz, David.

Miller, Laura, ed. see Garner, Dwight L.

***Miller, Laura Brylawski.** The Square at Vigevano. (Stories & Half Stories Ser.: Vol. 2). 260p. 2000. 24.95 (*0-931846-57-9*); pap. 14.95 (*0-931846-54-4*) Wash Writers Pub.

Miller, Laura J., ed. Postpartum Mood Disorders. LC 98-24929. (Clinical Practice Ser.). 280p. 1998. text 39.50 (*0-88048-929-4*, 8929) Am Psychiatric.

Miller, Laurence. Freud's Brain: Neuropsychodynamic Foundations of Psychoanalysis. LC 91-16480. 276p. 1991. lib. bdg. 35.00 (*0-89862-762-1*) Guilford Pubns.

— Psychotherapy of the Brain-Injured Patient: Reclaiming the Shattered Self. 256p. (C). 1993. 29.95 (*0-393-70158-1*) Norton.

— Shocks to the System: Psychotherapy of Traumatic Disability Syndromes. LC 98-14545. 256p. 1998. 40.00 (*0-393-70256-1*) Norton.

***Miller, Laurence, intro.** City Stills: The Photography of Ray K. Metzker. LC 99-18301. (Illus.). 108p. 1999. 39.95 (*3-7913-2002-5*, Pub. by Prestel) te Neues.

Miller, Laurence H., jt. ed. see Goy, Peter A.

Miller, Laurie, jt. auth. see Krumn, Rob.

Miller, LaVella. Where to Fish: Successful Fishing in Heavenly Northern California. LC 97-93577. (Illus.). 72p. 1997. spiral bd. write for info. (*1-57579-065-3*) Pine Hill Pr.

Miller, Lavina L., jt. auth. see Miller, Roger L.

Miller, Lavina Leed & Miller, Roger Leroy. Living Now: Strategies for Success & Fulfillment. 2nd ed. 1999. pap. 189.00 (*0-538-43010-9*) Thomson Learn.

Miller, Lawrence. Samuel Beckett: The Expressive Dilemma. LC 91-45795. 192p. 1992. text 45.00 (*0-312-07960-5*) St Martin.

— Whole System Architecture: Beyond Reengineering: A Guidebook for Designing Work Processes & Human Systems for High Performance Capabilities. 2nd ed. (Illus.). 320p. 1994. student ed., spiral bd. 49.95 (*0-9629679-2-0*) Miller Howard Cnslt.

Miller, Lawrence, jt. auth. see Howard, Jennifer.

Miller, Lawrence H. Advanced Programming: Design & Structure Using PASCAL. 624p. (C). 1986. write for info. (*0-318-61095-7*) Addison-Wesley.

— Programming & Problem Solving: A Second Course with Pascal. 624p. (C). 1986. teacher ed. write for info. (*0-201-05579-1*); text 39.75 (*0-201-05531-7*) Addison-Wesley.

Miller, Lawrence H. & Quilici, Alexander E. C Programming Language: An Applied Perspective. LC 85-17848. 340p. 1987. pap. 27.95 (*0-471-82560-3*) Wiley.

— The Joy of C: Programming in C. 3rd ed. LC 96-52028. 816p. 1997. pap. text 67.95 incl. disk (*0-471-12933-X*) Wiley.

Miller, Lawrence M. American Spirit: Visions of a New Corporate Culture. 256p. 1985. mass mkt. 3.95 (*0-446-32710-7*) Warner Bks.

Miller, Lawrence M. & Uhlfelder, Helene F. Change Management: Creating the Dynamic Organization Through Whole System Architecture. (Illus.). 432p. 1997. pap. 49.95 (*0-9629679-6-3*) Miller Howard Cnslt.

— The Leader's Guide to Change Management: Creating & Sustaining a Dynamic Organization. 160p. 1997. pap. 16.95 (*0-9629679-7-1*) Miller Howard Cnslt.

***Miller, Lawrence McK.** Witness for Humanity: The Biography of Clarence E. Pickett. LC 99-45120. 1999. 20.00 (*0-87574-934-8*) Pendle Hill.

Miller, Lee. Success Is an Inside Job: The Secrets to Getting Anything You Want. LC 98-73383. 264p. 1996. pap. 12.95 (*1-57174-119-4*) Hampton Roads Pub Co.

Miller, Lee, ed. From the Heart: Voices of the American Indian. 1996. pap. 15.00 (*0-679-76891-2*) Random.

— From the Heart: Voices of the American Indian. 1996. pap. 13.00 (*0-614-97867-X*) Vin Bks.

Miller, Lee, jt. auth. see Cattell, Hudson.

Miller, Lee E. Get More Money on Your Next Job: 25 Proven Strategies for Getting More Money, Better Benefits & Greater Job Security. LC 97-14974. 182p. 1997. pap. 14.95 (*0-07-043146-9*) McGraw.

Miller, Lee E., jt. auth. see Warner, Michael A.

Miller, Lee G. Story of Ernie Pyle. LC 78-100169. 439p. 1970. reprint ed. lib. bdg. 75.00 (*0-8371-3743-8*, MIEP, Greenwood Pr) Greenwood.

***Miller, Lee K.** The Book. 96p. 2000. 20.00 (*1-56167-572-5*) Am Literary Pr.

***Miller, Lee S.** Welcome to the Wonderful World of Leebo. 208p. 2000. pap. 13.00 (*1-56167-610-1*) Am Literary Pr.

Miller, Lee S., jt. auth. see Cattell, Hudson.

Miller, Lee T. Medical Student's Guide to Successful Residency Matching, 1994-1995. (Illus.). 112p. 1994. 9.95 (*0-683-05996-3*) Lppncott W & W.

Miller, Lee T. & Donowitz, Leigh G. 1998-1999 Medical Student's Guide to Successful Residency Matching. 102p. 1998. pap. 14.95 (*0-683-30613-8*) Lppncott W & W.

Miller, Lee T. & Donowitz, Leigh G. 1999-2000 Medical Student's Guide to Successful Residency Matching. 112p. pap. text 14.95 (*0-7817-2163-6*) Lppncott W & W.

Miller, Lee T. & Donowitz, Leigh G. 1997-1998 Medical Student's Guide to Successful Residency Matching. 101p. 1997. pap. 14.95 (*0-683-30207-8*) Lppncott W & W.

— 1996-1997 Medical Student's Guide to Successful Residency Matching. 87p. (Orig.). 1996. pap. 14.95 (*0-683-18043-6*) Lppncott W & W.

Miller, Lee T. & Donowitz, Leigh G. 2000-2001 Medical Student's Guide to Successful Residency Matching. 120p. pap. text 14.95 (*0-7817-2576-3*) Lppncott W & W.

Miller, Len. Gambling Times Guide to Casino Games. (Illus.). 170p. (Orig.). 1983. pap. text 5.95 (*0-685-01829-6*) Carol Pub Group.

— Gambling Times Guide to Casino Games. 1990. (Illus.). (Orig.). 1983. pap. 9.95 (*0-89746-071-5*) Gambling Times.

Miller, Lenore H. The Nature Specialist: A Complete Guide to Program & Activities. 170p. 1986. pap. 24.95 (*0-87603-087-8*) Am Camping.

Miller, Lenore H., jt. auth. see Walter, Carol.

Miller, Leo. Ghost Stories. Costa, Gwen, ed. LC 91-33874. (YA). 1992. pap. 13.95 (*0-87949-358-5*) Ashley Bks.

— John Milton's Writings in the Anglo-Dutch Negotiations, 1651-1654. LC 92-33554. (Duquesne Studies: Language & Literature Ser.: Vol. 13). 368p. (C). 1992. text 48.00 (*0-8207-0232-3*) Duquesne.

Miller, Leon C. How to Direct the High School Play. 1968. pap. 12.95 (*0-87129-366-8*, H33) Dramatic Pub.

Miller, Leon H., jt. auth. see Dickey, John W.

Miller, Leon K. Musical Savants: Exceptional Skill in Mentally Retarded. 272p. (C). 1989. text 49.95 (*0-8058-0034-4*) L Erlbaum Assocs.

Miller, Leonard A., et al, eds. Essentials of Basic Science in Surgery. LC 92-17502. 416p. 1993. pap. text 39.00 (*0-397-51168-X*) Lppncott W & W.

Miller, Leonard A., jt. auth. see Gallagher, Lynn M.

Miller, Leonard P., ed. Stroke Therapy: Basic, Preclinical, & Clinical Directions. LC 98-22640. 456p. 1998. 135.00 (*0-471-18347-4*, Wiley-Liss) Wiley.

Miller, Leroy, ed. The Amish-Mennonites at Kempsville, Virginia, 1900-1970: A Collection of Stories & Photos from a Time & Place, Gone Forever, Yet Living in our Memories of a Good & Pleasant Land. LC 95-44305. 1996. write for info. (*0-89865-954-X*) Donning Co.

Miller, Leroy, jt. auth. see Bergey, Mary T.

Miller, LeRoy, ed. & illus. see Sunday, Patricia A.

Miller, Lesley. Cristobal Balenciaga. (Fashion Designers Ser.). (Illus.). 96p. (Orig.). 1993. pap. 25.95 (*0-8419-1344-7*) Holmes & Meier.

Miller, Leslie. Secret Wish. LC 98-5282. 35p. (J). (ps-3). 1996. pap. 1.95 (*1-56763-167-3*) Ozark Pub.

Miller, Leslie, et al, eds. Literature & Politics in Central Europe: Studies in Honour of Marketa Goetz-Stankewicz. LC 93-1490. (GERM Ser.). 158p. 1993. 60.00 (*1-879751-68-2*) Camden Hse.

Miller, Leslie, et al. Activities Guide for Teachers: Brain Comparisons. rev. ed. (BrainLink Ser.: Vol. 1). (Illus.). vi, 32p. 1997. pap. write for info. (*1-888997-21-4*) Baylor Coll Med.

Miller, Leslie, et al. Brain Comparisons: Activities Guide for Teachers. (BrainLink Ser.: Vol. 1). (Illus.). vi, 32p. 1992. pap., teacher ed. write for info. (*1-888997-00-1*) Baylor Coll Med.

— Brain Comparisons: Activities Guide for Teachers. rev. ed. (BrainLink Ser.: Vol. 1). (Illus.). vi, 32p. 1993. pap., teacher ed. write for info. (*1-888997-01-X*) Baylor Coll Med.

Miller, Leslie, jt. ed. see Emery, Robert W.

***Miller, Leslie A.** Annie's Second Chance: A Second Chance at Life Offers a Second Chance at Love. (Illus.). 48p. (J). (gr. 3-6). 2000. 17.95 (*1-929407-00-9*) Treasure Text.

Miller, Leslie A. The Secret Wish. LC 98-5282. (J). 1998. write for info. (*1-56763-286-6*) Ozark Pub.

— Staying up for Love. LC 89-61327. 68p. (Orig.). (C). 1990. pap. 11.95 (*0-88748-096-9*) Carnegie-Mellon.

— Ungodliness. LC 93-73475. (Poetry Ser.). 80p. (Orig.). 1994. 20.95 (*0-88748-172-8*); pap. 11.95 (*0-88748-173-6*) Carnegie-Mellon.

— Yesterday Had a Man in It. LC 97-65559. (Poetry Ser.). 88p. 1998. 24.95 (*0-88748-269-4*); pap. 11.95 (*0-88748-271-6*) Carnegie-Mellon.

***Miller, Leslie A. & Rose, Paul A.** Suicide. (Current Controversies Ser.). 320p. (YA). 2000. pap. 13.96 (*0-7377-0317-2*) Greenhaven.

— Suicide. LC 99-53091. (Current Controversies Ser.). 320p. (YA). 2000. 17.45 (*0-7377-0318-0*) Greenhaven.

Miller, Lester. The Best Gift.Tr. of Beste Geschenk. (GER.). 32p. (YA). (gr. 4-9). 1997. pap. 1.70 (*0-7399-0304-7*, 2363.2) Rod & Staff.

— Boys & Girls of the Bible. 32p. (J). (gr. 1-5). 1994. pap. 1.55 (*0-7399-0187-7*, 2945) Rod & Staff.

— The Broken Crayon.Tr. of Zerbrochenen Buntstifte. (GER.). 32p. (YA). (gr. 4-9). 1997. pap. 1.70 (*0-7399-0303-9*, 2461.2) Rod & Staff.

— Dot to Dot Coloring Book God Gave Us. 32p. (J). (gr. 1-4). 1987. pap. 1.90 (*0-7399-0176-1*, 1987) Rod & Staff.

— The Good Bargan.Tr. of Gute Kauf. (GER.). 32p. (YA). (gr. 4-9). 1997. pap. 1.70 (*0-7399-0305-5*, 2364.2) Rod & Staff.

— The Hungry Cat.Tr. of Die Hungrige Katze. (GER.). 32p. 1997. pap. 1.70 (*0-7399-0302-0*, 2278.2) Rod & Staff.

— Poems for Memorization. 199p. (J). (gr. 1-10). 1988. pap. 6.75 (*0-7399-0166-4*, 2354) Rod & Staff.

— Princess in Calico. (Still Waters Ser.). 92p. 1989. pap. 4.65 (*0-7399-0141-9*, 2362) Rod & Staff.

— The 23rd Psalm Coloring Book. 28p. (J). (gr. 3-5). 1986. pap. 1.55 (*0-7399-0174-5*, 2934) Rod & Staff.

— The 23rd Psalm Coloring Book. (SPA.). 26p. (J). (gr. 3-5). 1995. pap. 1.20 (*0-7399-0175-3*, 2934.1) Rod & Staff.

— The Wedded Life.Tr. of Vida Matrimonial. (SPA.). 83p. 1979. reprint ed. pap. 2.85 (*0-7399-0212-1*, 2465.1) Rod & Staff.

— The Wedded Life.Tr. of Vida Matrimonial. (GER.). 95p. 1981. reprint ed. pap. 3.00 (*0-7399-0232-6*, 2465.2) Rod & Staff.

Miller, Leta E. & Lieberman, Frederic. Lou Harrison: Composing a World. (Illus.). 416p. 1998. 35.00 (*0-19-511022-6*) OUP.

Miller, Leta E., jt. auth. see Cohn, Albert.

Miller, Leta E., ed. see Caimo, Gioseppe.

Miller, Leta E., ed. see De Villiers, Pierre, et al.

Miller, Leta E., ed. see Harrison, Lou.

Miller, Levi. Ben's Wayne. LC 89-32436. 168p. 1989. 14.95 (*0-934672-77-6*) Good Bks PA.

— Ben's Wayne. LC 89-32436. 168p. 1992. pap. 9.95 (*1-56148-061-4*) Good Bks PA.

— Our People: The Amish & Mennonites in Ohio. rev. ed. LC 91-76519. (Illus.). 64p. 1992. pap. 4.99 (*0-8361-3582-2*) Herald Pr.

Miller, Lew. Miracles Can Happen to You: Power of Visual Imagery. 3rd ed. LC 85-61118. 72p. (Orig.). 1986. reprint ed. pap. 5.45 (*0-9615752-0-4*) Milbeck Pr.

Miller, Lewis. Nursing in America. (C). 1989. 32.00 (*0-7223-2389-1*, Pub. by A H S Ltd) St Mut.

— Psychology of Interviewing. (C). 1989. 60.00 (*0-7223-2388-3*, Pub. by A H S Ltd) St Mut.

Miller-Lewis, S. Jill. Dressing Successfully, Vol. 1, No. 1. rev. ed. (Illus.). 52p. (Orig.). 1987. pap. 10.00 (*0-934155-00-3*) Miller Des.

— Fashions Throughout the Years, Vol. 1. (Illus.). 65p. (Orig.). 1987. pap. 10.00 (*0-934155-01-1*) Miller Des.

— How to Become a Fashion Designer: A Guide on the Ins & Outs of Fashion Designing, Vol. 1, No. 1. (Illus.). 60p. (Orig.). 1987. pap. 10.00 (*0-934155-02-X*) Miller Des.

— Making Yourself Even More Beautiful, Vol. I, No. 1. (Illus.). 46p. (Orig.). 1987. pap. 8.00 (*0-934155-03-8*) Miller Des.

— Silk: The Luxurious Fabric, Vol. 1, No. 1. (Illus.). 34p. (Orig.). 1987. pap. text 8.00 (*0-934155-04-6*) Miller Des.

Miller, Liam, jt. auth. see Hanley, Mary.

Miller, Libby, jt. auth. see Rothlein, Liz C.

Miller Lieber, Carol, et al. Conflict Resolution in the High School: 36 Lessons. 338p. 1998. pap. text 38.00 (*0-942349-11-3*) Eductrs Soc Respons.

***Miller, Light.** Ayurvedic Remedies for the Whole Family. (Illus.). 448p. 2000. pap. 24.95 (*0-914955-80-2*) Lotus Pr.

Miller, Light & Miller, Bryan. Ayurveda & Aromatherapy: The Earth Essential Guide to Ancient Wisdom & Modern Healing. LC 95-80409. (Illus.). 368p. (Orig.). 1995. pap. 21.95 (*0-914955-20-9*) Lotus Pr.

Miller, Lillian B. In Pursuit of Fame: Rembrandt Peale, 1778-1860. LC 92-18207. (Illus.). 320p. 1993. 60.00 (*0-295-97243-2*) U of Wash Pr.

Miller, Lillian B., ed. The Peale Family: Creation of a Legacy, 1770-1870. LC 96-13975. (Illus.). 320p. 1996. pap. 48.00 (*0-7892-0248-4*) Abbeville Pr.

Miller, Lillian B., et al, eds. The Selected Papers of Charles Wilson Peale & His Family. LC 82-20155. (Illus.). 576p. 1997. 110.00 (*0-300-06180-3*) Yale U Pr.

Miller, Lillian B., ed. see Library of Congress Staff.

Miller, Lillian B., ed. see Peale, Charles W.

Miller, Lillian S., ed. see Peale, Charles W.

***Miller, Linda.** Courting Susannah. 320p. 2000. per. 7.99 (*0-671-00400-X*) PB.

Miller, Linda. Towards Reading: Literacy Development in the Pre-School Years. LC 95-14679. (Re-Thinking Reading Ser.). 144p. 1995. text 104.95 (*0-335-19216-5*) OpUniv Pr.

Miller, Linda, et al. Manual of Laboratory Immunology. 2nd ed. LC 89-13712. (Illus.). 427p. 1991. pap. text 45.50 (*0-8121-1319-5*) Lppncott W & W.

Miller, Linda, jt. auth. see Hess, Karen M.

Miller, Linda, ed. see Chambers, Maggie.

Miller, Linda, ed. see St. Claire, Mary.

Miller, Linda B. Shadow & Substance: Jimmy Carter & the Camp David Accords. (Pew Case Studies in International Affairs). 50p. (C). 1992. pap. text 3.50 (*1-56927-433-9*) Geo U Inst Dplmcy.

— World Order & Local Disorder: The United Nations & Internal Conflicts. LC 67-16953. 245p. reprint ed. pap. 76.00 (*0-8357-7078-8*, 203338200085) Bks Demand.

Miller, Linda D. Time Out for Love. 150p. 1996. mass mkt. 5.00 (*0-9634431-5-1*) C Y Pub Grp.

Miller, Linda F. An Introduction to the Literature & Personalities of the Bible. 89p. (YA). (gr. 9-12). 1985. teacher ed. 16.00 (*1-881678-10-5*) CSEE.

Miller, Linda Lael. Angelfire. Marrow, Linda, ed. 352p. 1991. per. 5.99 (*0-671-73765-1*) PB.

— Banner O'Brian. Marrow, Linda, ed. 1991. mass mkt. 6.99 (*0-671-73766-X*) PB.

— Banner O'Brien. 1995. mass mkt. 5.99 (*0-671-53422-X*) PB.

— Banner O'Brien. 1998. per. 3.99 (*0-671-02012-9*) PB.

***Miller, Linda Lael.** Bridget. (Women of Primrose Creek Ser.: Vol. 1). 160p. 2000. mass mkt. 3.99 (*0-671-04244-0*, Sonnet Bks) PB.

Miller, Linda Lael. Caroline & the Raider. Marrow, Linda, ed. 368p. 1992. mass mkt. 6.99 (*0-671-67638-5*) PB.

— Christy. (Women of Primrose Creek Ser.: No. 2). 176p. 2000. per. 3.99 (*0-671-04245-9*, Sonnet Bks) PB.

— Corbin's Fancy. Marrow, Linda, ed. 320p. 1991. mass mkt. 5.99 (*0-671-73767-8*) PB.

— Corbin's Fancy. 1995. mass mkt. 5.99 (*0-671-53421-1*) PB.

— Daniel's Bride. Marrow, Linda, ed. 400p. 1992. per. 6.99 (*0-671-73166-1*) PB.

— Daring Moves. (Mira Bks.). 1996. per. 5.50 (*1-55166-098-9*, 1-66098-4, Mira Bks) Harlequin Bks.

***Miller, Linda Lael.** Daring Moves. LC 00-30299. 2001. write for info. (*0-7862-2619-6*) Thorndike Pr.

Miller, Linda Lael. Desire & Destiny. Marrow, Linda, ed. 320p. 1990. per. 6.99 (*0-671-70635-7*) PB.

— Emma & the Outlaw. Marrow, Linda, ed. 384p. 1991. mass mkt. 6.99 (*0-671-67637-7*) PB.

— Escape from Cabriz. 1999. pap. 5.99 (*1-55166-550-6*, 1-66550-4, Mira Bks) Harlequin Bks.

— Fletcher's Woman. (Tapestry Romance Ser.). 1991. mass mkt. 5.99 (*0-671-73768-6*) PB.

M

— Fletcher's Woman. 1997. mass mkt. 3.99 (*0-671-01004-2*) PB.

— Forever & the Night. large type ed. LC 93-39749. 507p. 1994. lib. bdg. 20.95 (*0-7862-0068-5*) Thorndike Pr.

— Glory, Glory. 1997. per. 5.50 (*1-55166-179-9*, 1-66179-2, Mira Bks) Harlequin Bks.

— Here & Then. 1997. per. 5.50 (*1-55166-304-X*, Mira Bks) Harlequin Bks.

— Here & Then. (Special Edition Ser.: No. 762). 1992. per. 3.39 (*0-373-09762-X*) Silhouette.

— In Our Dreams. 320p. (Orig.). 1998. mass mkt. 6.99 (*0-8217-5997-3*, Zebra Kensgtn) Kensgtn Pub Corp.

— Jessica. (Springwater Seasons Ser.: Bk. 4). 151p. 1999. mass mkt. 3.99 (*0-671-02687-9*) PB.

***Miller, Linda Lael.** Jessica. large type ed. LC 99-33700. 1999. 27.95 (*0-7862-2160-7*) Thorndike Pr.

Miller, Linda Lael. Just Kate. 1995. per. 4.99 (*1-55166-055-5*, Mira Bks) Harlequin Bks.

***Miller, Linda Lael.** Just Kate. 256p. 2000. mass mkt. 5.99 (*1-55166-631-6*, 1-66631-2, Mira Bks) Harlequin Bks.

Miller, Linda Lael. Knights. 304p. 1996. 22.00 (*0-671-52850-5*, PB Hardcover) PB.

— Knights. 1996. per. 6.99 (*0-671-87317-2*) PB.

— Knights. large type ed. LC 96-45014. 1996. 25.95 (*1-56895-391-7*, Compass) Wheeler Pub.

— Lauralee. Marrow, Linda, ed. 1990. mass mkt. 5.99 (*0-671-70634-9*) PB.

— The Legacy. Marrow, Linda, ed. 336p. 1994. mass mkt. 6.99 (*0-671-79792-1*, Pocket Star Bks) PB.

— The Legacy. large type ed. LC 94-29353. 488p. 1995. 20.95 (*0-7862-0326-9*) Thorndike Pr.

— Lily & the Major. Marrow, Linda, ed. 384p. 1990. mass mkt. 5.50 (*0-671-67636-9*) PB.

***Miller, Linda Lael.** Megan. (Women of Primrose Creek Ser.: No. 4). 320p. 2000. mass mkt. 5.99 (*0-671-04247-5*, Sonnet Bks) PB.

Miller, Linda Lael. Memory's Embrace. Marrow, Linda, ed. 320p. 1991. per. 6.99 (*0-671-73769-4*) PB.

— Memory's Embrace. 1995. mass mkt. 5.99 (*0-671-53420-3*) PB.

— Miranda. (Springwater Seasons Ser.: Bk. 3). 1999. mass mkt. 3.99 (*0-671-02686-0*) PB.

***Miller, Linda Lael.** Miranda: Springwater Seasons, Bk. 3. large type ed. LC 99-36091. (Thorndike Americana Ser.). 1999. 26.95 (*0-7862-2159-3*) Thorndike Pr.

Miller, Linda Lael. Mixed Messages. 1996. per. 5.50 (*1-55166-164-0*, Mira Bks) Harlequin Bks.

— Moonfire. Marrow, Linda, ed. 384p. 1991. mass mkt. 5.99 (*0-671-73770-8*) PB.

— My Darling Melissa. Marrow, Linda, ed. 336p. 1991. mass mkt. 6.99 (*0-671-73771-6*) PB.

— My Darling Melissa. 1995. mass mkt. 5.99 (*0-671-53419-X*) PB.

— My Outlaw. 320p. 1997. per. 6.99 (*0-671-87318-0*) PB.

***Miller, Linda Lael.** One Wish. 368p. 2000. per. 6.99 (*0-671-53786-5*, Pocket Star Bks) PB.

— One Wish. large type ed. LC 00-39917. 2000. write for info. (*1-56895-878-1*) Wheeler Pub.

Miller, Linda Lael. Only Forever. LC 96-2314. 248p. 1995. per. 4.99 (*1-55166-073-3*, 1-66073-7, Mira Bks) Harlequin Bks.

— Part of the Bargain. (Men Made in America Ser.). 1994. per. 3.59 (*0-373-45176-8*, 1-45176-4) Harlequin Bks.

***Miller, Linda Lael.** Part of the Bargain. 1999. per. 5.99 (*1-55166-512-3*, 1-66512-4, Mira Bks) Harlequin Bks.

— Part of the Bargain. LC 00-30292. 2001. write for info. (*0-7862-2621-8*) Thorndike Pr.

Miller, Linda Lael. Pirates. 336p. 1996. per. 6.50 (*0-671-87316-4*, PB Trade Paper) PB.

— Pirates. large type ed. LC 95-34858. (Large Print Bks.). 1995. 24.95 (*1-56895-249-X*, Compass) Wheeler Pub.

— Princess Annie. Marrow, Linda, ed. 480p. 1994. mass mkt. 5.99 (*0-671-79793-X*, Pocket Star Bks) PB.

— Rachel. (Springwater Seasons Ser.: Bk. 1). 145p. 1999. mass mkt. 3.99 (*0-671-02684-4*) PB.

***Miller, Linda Lael.** Rachel. large type ed. LC 99-36089. 1999. 26.95 (*0-7862-2157-7*) Thorndike Pr.

Miller, Linda Lael. Ragged Rainbows. 1994. mass mkt. 4.50 (*0-373-48300-7*, 5-48300-3, Mira Bks) Harlequin Bks.

— Ragged Rainbows. 1998. per. 5.50 (*1-55166-467-4*, 1-66467-1, Mira Bks) Harlequin Bks.

***Miller, Linda Lael.** Ragged Rainbows. large type ed. LC 00-39641. 2001. write for info. (*0-7838-9052-4*, G K Hall Lrg Type) Mac Lib Ref.

Miller, Linda Lael. Savannah. (Springwater Seasons Ser.: Bk. 2). 144p. 1999. mass mkt. 3.99 (*0-671-02685-2*) PB.

***Miller, Linda Lael.** Savannah. large type ed. LC 99-36090. 1999. 26.95 (*0-7862-2158-5*) Thorndike Pr.

— Skye. (Women of Primrose Creek Ser.: No. 3). 176p. 2000. per. 3.99 (*0-671-04246-7*, Sonnet Bks) PB.

Miller, Linda Lael. Snowflakes on the Sea. (Mira Bks.). 1998. per. 5.50 (*1-55166-428-3*, 1-66428-3, Mira Bks) Harlequin Bks.

— Snowflakes on the Sea. 1994. mass mkt. 4.50 (*0-373-48303-1*, 5-48303-7) Silhouette.

***Miller, Linda Lael.** Snowflakes on the Sea. LC 00-34399. 2001. write for info. (*0-7862-2615-3*) Thorndike Pr.

Miller, Linda Lael. Springwater. 1998. mass mkt. 6.99 (*0-671-02751-4*) PB.

***Miller, Linda Lael.** Springwater. LC 99-46171. 1999. 25.95 (*1-56895-786-6*, Wheeler) Wheeler Pub.

Miller, Linda Lael. A Springwater Christmas. 1999. per. 6.99 (*0-671-02752-2*) PB.

***Miller, Linda Lael.** Springwater Omnibus. 608p. 2000. 7.99 (*0-7434-0362-2*) PB.

Miller, Linda Lael. State Secrets. 256p. 1994. per. 4.99 (*1-55166-014-8*, Mira Bks) Harlequin Bks.

— State Secrets. 2000. mass mkt. 5.99 (*0-373-48402-X*, 1-48402-1) Harlequin Bks.

— State Secrets. 1994. mass mkt. 4.50 (*0-373-48307-4*, 5-48307-8) Silhouette.

— Taming Charlotte. Marrow, Linda, ed. 352p. 1993. mass mkt. 5.99 (*0-671-73754-6*, Pocket Star Bks) PB.

— There & Now. 1997. per. 5.50 (*1-55166-283-3*, 1-66283-2, Mira Bks) Harlequin Bks.

— There & Now. (Special Ser.: No. 754). 1992. per. 3.39 (*0-373-09754-9*) Silhouette.

— Time Without End. 368p. (Orig.). 1995. mass mkt. 5.99 (*0-425-15042-9*) Berkley Pub.

— Together. 384p. (Orig.). 1996. mass mkt. 5.99 (*0-380-78405-X*, Avon Bks) Morrow Avon.

— Tonight & Always. 352p. (Orig.). 1996. mass mkt. 6.50 (*0-425-15541-2*) Berkley Pub.

***Miller, Linda Lael.** Two Brothers: The Lawman. large type ed. LC 99-31382. 1999. write for info. (*1-56895-747-5*) Wheeler Pub.

— Two Brothers: The Lawman & the Gunslinger. 2001. mass mkt. write for info. (*0-7434-1154-4*, Pocket Star Bks) PB.

— Two Brothers: The Lawman & the Gunslinger. LC 98-230261. 320p. 1998. mass mkt. 12.00 (*0-671-00401-8*) S&S Trade.

Miller, Linda Lael. Used-to-Be Lovers. 249p. 1995. per. 4.99 (*1-55166-037-7*, 1-66037-2, Mira Bks) Harlequin Bks.

— The Vow. 339p. 1998. mass mkt. 6.99 (*0-671-00399-2*) PB.

— Wanton Angel. Marrow, Linda, ed. 352p. 1991. mass mkt. 5.99 (*0-671-73772-4*) PB.

— Wild about Harry. LC 95-21494. 187p. 1995. mass mkt. 5.99 (*0-373-15310-4*, 1-15310-5) Harlequin Bks.

— Wild about Harry. 1996. mass mkt. 5.99 (*0-373-48340-6*, 1-48340-3) Harlequin Bks.

— Wild about Harry. 2000. per. 5.99 (*1-55166-575-1*) Harlequin Bks.

— Willow. Marrow, Linda, ed. 320p. 1991. mass mkt. 5.99 (*0-671-73773-2*) PB.

— Yankee Wife. Marrow, Linda, ed. 368p. 1993. mass mkt. 6.99 (*0-671-73755-4*, Pocket Star Bks) PB.

Miller, Linda Lael, et al. Avon Books Presents: Haunting Love Stories. 480p. (Orig.). 1991. mass mkt. 4.99 (*0-380-76659-0*, Avon Bks) Morrow Avon.

— Everlasting Love. 400p. 1995. per. 6.99 (*0-671-52150-0*, Pocket Star Bks) PB.

— Heatwave. (Promo Ser.). 1998. per. 9.99 (*0-373-83402-0*, 1-83402-7) Harlequin Bks.

***Miller, Linda Lael, et al.** Heatwave. 1999. per. 12.95 (*0-373-83441-1*) Harlequin Bks.

— Heatwave: Part of the Bargain, The Dream Unfolds, Whistleblower. 2000. per. 9.99 (*0-373-83459-4*, 1-83459-7) Harlequin Bks.

Miller, Linda Lael, jt. auth. see Krentz, Jayne Ann.

Miller, Linda M., ed. The Impact of the Media on Collective Bargaining. LC 80-65636. 92p. 1980. pap. 4.00 (*0-943001-16-1*) Am Arbitration.

Miller, Linda M., et al, eds. ABA Book Buyer's Returns Handbook, 1994-1995. 342p. 1994. 50.00 (*1-879556-15-4*) ABA.

Miller, Linda P., ed. Letters from the Lost Generation: Gerald & Sara Murphy & Friends. LC 90-42139. (Illus.). 362p. 1993. pap. 16.95 (*0-8135-1966-7*) Rutgers U Pr.

Miller, Linda P., jt. ed. see Miller, Randall M.

Miller, Linda Patterson, jt. ed. see Miller, Randall M.

Miller, Linda R. Planning a Christian Wedding. 82p. 1992. ring bd. 12.95 (*0-940883-05-8*) Calvary Pubns.

Miller, Linda S. & Hess, Karen M. The Police in the Community: Strategies in the 21st Century. 2nd ed. LC 97-37745. (C). 1997. 77.95 (*0-534-53789-8*) Wadsworth Pub.

Miller, Lindsay, jt. auth. see Gardner, David.

Miller, Lindsay, jt. ed. see Gardner, David.

Miller, Lindsay, jt. ed. see Garnder, David.

Miller, Lindsay, jt. ed. see Nunan, David.

Miller, Lisa. Understanding Your Baby. Osborne, Elsie, ed. (Understanding Your Child Ser.: Vol. 1). 80p. (Orig.). 1997. pap. 8.95 (*1-894020-00-6*) Warwick Publ.

Miller, Lisa. Understanding Your 8 Year Old. Osborne, Elsie, ed. (Understanding Your Child Ser.: Vol. 9). 96p. 1997. pap. 8.95 (*1-894020-08-1*) Warwick Publ.

— Understanding Your 4 Year Old. (Understanding Your Child Ser.: Vol. 5). 96p. 1997. pap. 8.95 (*1-894020-04-9*) Warwick Publ.

Miller, Lisa, jt. ed. see Palestrant, Ellen.

Miller, Lise, jt. auth. see Toothaker, Larry E.

Miller, Lise M., jt. auth. see Seranne, Ann.

Miller, Liz. Advanced In-Line Skating. LC 99-86503. (Illus.). 144p. 2000. pap. 14.95 (*0-07-135448-4*) McGraw.

— Get Rolling. 2nd ed. LC 97-39353. (Illus.). 144p. 1998. pap. 13.95 (*0-07-043258-9*) McGraw.

— Memorabilia: The Regional Prints of Jane Dunning Baldwin. 20p. 1989. pap. 2.95 (*0-910524-14-9*) Eastern Wash.

Miller, Lloyd. Music & Song in Persia: The Art of Avaz. (Illus.). 400p. 1997. 79.95 (*0-7007-0664-X*, Pub. by Curzon Pr Ltd) Paul & Co Pubs.

***Miller, Lloyd.** Music & Song in Persia: The Art of Avaz. LC 99-19892. (Illus.). 360p. 1999. 60.00 (*0-87480-614-3*) U of Utah Pr.

Miller, Lloyd E., Jr. The Profaners. rev. ed. 175p. (Orig.). 1995. pap. 4.95 (*0-9639322-1-7*) Literary Prods.

— Soul of the Shepherd. 175p. (Orig.). 1995. pap. 4.95 (*0-9639322-2-5*) Literary Prods.

— Tenth Stay at Midnight. 104p. 1994. reprint ed. pap. 4.95 (*0-9639322-0-9*) Literary Prods.

— Trail to El Paso. (Western Classic Premier Bks.). 225p. (Orig.). 1995. pap. 4.95 (*0-9639322-3-3*) Literary Prods.

Miller, Lois. The Story of the Wright Brothers & Their Sister. (Illus.). 160p. (J). (gr. 3). 1995. pap. text 6.00 (*1-930092-33-4*, CLP29640) Christian Liberty.

Miller, Lois K., ed. The Baculoviruses. LC 97-17668. (Viruses Ser.). 468p. (C). 1997. text 110.00 (*0-306-45641-9*, Kluwer Plenum) Kluwer Academic.

Miller, Lois K. & Ball, L. A., eds. The Insect Viruses. LC 98-27923. (Viruses Ser.). (Illus.). 434p. (C). 1998. text 125.00 (*0-306-45881-0*, Kluwer Plenum) Kluwer Academic.

Miller, Lois N. Abstracts of Deeds, 1830-1838: Deed Book A, Washington County, AR. 166p. 1990. 31.50 (*1-878193-14-7*); pap. 25.00 (*1-878193-15-5*) L N Miller Geog Pubns.

— Index to Wills, 1828-1931 & Index to Probate Records A-K Book, 1836-1901. 165p. 1985. reprint ed. 30.00 (*1-878193-12-0*); reprint ed. pap. 22.00 (*1-878193-13-9*) L N Miller Geog Pubns.

— Marriages of Washington County, Arkansas, 1845-71. 118p. (Orig.). 1982. 31.50 (*1-878193-00-7*); pap. 25.00 (*1-878193-01-5*) L N Miller Geog Pubns.

— Marriages of Washington County, Arkansas, 1871-91. 194p. 1985. 27.00 (*1-878193-02-3*); pap. 22.00 (*1-878193-03-1*) L N Miller Geog Pubns.

— Marriages of Washington County, Arkansas, 1930-41. 260p. 1990. 37.50 (*1-878193-10-4*); pap. 30.00 (*1-878193-11-2*) L N Miller Geog Pubns.

— Tax Records for Washington County, Arkansas, Real Estate & Personal Property, 1890. 317p. 1990. 42.50 (*1-878193-16-3*); pap. 34.00 (*1-878193-17-1*) L N Miller Geog Pubns.

Miller, Lois N., et al. Marriages of Washington County, Arkansas, 1901-10. 166p. 1990. 31.50 (*1-878193-04-X*); pap. 25.00 (*1-878193-05-8*) L N Miller Geog Pubns.

— Marriages of Washington County, Arkansas, 1911-21. 218p. 1990. 31.50 (*1-878193-06-6*); pap. 25.00 (*1-878193-07-4*) L N Miller Geog Pubns.

— Marriages of Washington County, Arkansas, 1922-30. 156p. 1990. 31.50 (*1-878193-08-2*); pap. 25.00 (*1-878193-09-0*) L N Miller Geog Pubns.

Miller, Loren. Bishops: The Eternal Crusade. (Primal Order Ser.). 128p. 1994. pap. 12.95 (*1-880992-19-1*) Wizards Coast.

Miller, Lori, jt. auth. see Fried, Gil.

Miller, Lori K. Sport Business Management. LC 97-7553. 1997. 49.00 (*0-8342-0942-X*) Aspen Pub.

Miller, Lorna T., jt. auth. see Miller, Donald E.

***Miller, Lorna Touryan.** Witch. 1999. pap. text 9.95 (*1-899866-21-3*) Slab-O-Concrete Pubns.

Miller, Lorraine, jt. auth. see Conner, Daniel.

Miller, Lorraine O. Dear Diary: A Story about Child Abuse. LC 96-79867. 16p. (Orig.). (J). (gr. 4-8). 1997. pap. 5.95 (*1-57543-026-6*) Mar Co Prods.

Miller, Louis. Beacons of Light: Profiles of Ecclesiastical Writers Cited in the Catechism. LC 94-79997. 64p. 1995. pap. 4.95 (*0-89243-784-7*) Liguori Pubns.

Miller, Louis & Einstein, Stanley, eds. Drugs & Society: Contemporary Social Issues. 317p. 1976. 34.95 (*0-87855-273-1*) Transaction Pubs.

Miller, Louis W. & Abell, John B. DRIVE (Distribution & Repair in Variable Environments) Design & Operation of the Ogden Prototype. LC 92-13079. 1992. pap. text 7.50 (*0-8330-1243-6*, R-4158-AF) Rand Corp.

— Evaluations of Alternative Approaches to Central Stock Leveling. LC 95-2391. (MR-546-AF Ser.). 95p. 1995. pap. text 15.00 (*0-8330-1632-6*, MR-546-AF) Rand Corp.

Miller, Louise. Animals. LC 93-49056. (VGM Career Portraits Ser.). (Illus.). 96p. (J). 1994. 13.95 (*0-8442-4359-0*, 43590, VGM Career) NTC Contemp Pub Co.

— Careers for Animal Lovers: And Other Zoological Types. LC 90-50725. (Careers for You Ser.). (Illus.). 128p. (YA). (gr. 7 up). 1995. pap. 9.95 (*0-8442-8125-5*, 81255, VGM Career) NTC Contemp Pub Co.

— Careers for Animal Lovers: And Other Zoological Types. (VGM Careers for You Ser.). (Illus.). 128p. 1995. 14.95 (*0-8442-8107-7*, 81077, VGM Career) NTC Contemp Pub Co.

***Miller, Louise.** Careers for Animal Lovers & Other Zoological Types. 2nd ed. (Careers for You Ser.). 2000. 14.95 (*0-658-00458-1*, VGM Career) NTC Contemp Pub Co.

— Careers for Animal Lovers & Other Zoological Types. 2nd ed. LC 00-40417. (VGM Careers for You Ser.). (Illus.). 2000. pap. write for info. (*0-658-00463-8*, Passprt Bks) NTC Contemp Pub Co.

Miller, Louise. Careers for Nature Lovers: And Other Outdoor Types. (Careers for You Ser.). (Illus.). 136p. 1993. 14.95 (*0-8442-8132-8*, 81328, VGM Career) NTC Contemp Pub Co.

— Careers for Nature Lovers: And Other Outdoor Types. (Illus.). 136p. 1994. pap. 9.95 (*0-8442-8133-6*, 81336, VGM Career) NTC Contemp Pub Co.

— Careers for Night Owls & Other Insomniacs. LC 94-28733. (VGM Careers for You Ser.). (Illus.). 160p. 1995. 14.95 (*0-8442-4115-6*, 41156, VGM Career); pap. 9.95 (*0-8442-4116-4*, 41164, VGM Career) NTC Contemp Pub Co.

***Miller, Lowell.** The Single Best Investment. 288p. 2000. pap. 12.95 (*1-58062-269-0*) Adams Media.

Miller, Lowell. The Single Best Investment: Achieve Lasting Wealth with Low-Risk, Steady Growth Stocks. LC 98-50810. (Illus.). 288p. 1999. 21.95 (*1-58062-134-1*) Adams Media.

Miller, Lucien. Masks of Fiction in Dream of the Red Chamber: Myth, Mimesis, & Persona. fac. ed. LC 75-23643. (Association for Asian Studies, Monographs & Papers: No. 28). 359p. 1994. pap. 111.30 (*0-7837-7674-8*, 204742700007) Bks Demand.

Miller, Lucien, ed. South of the Clouds: Tales of Yunnan. Xu, Guo et al, trs. LC 93-36563. (McLellan Bks.). 342p. (C). 1994. 40.00 (*0-295-97293-9*); pap. 19.95 (*0-295-97348-X*) U of Wash Pr.

Miller, Lucille. Heidi. (J). 1936. 6.00 (*0-87602-136-4*) Anchorage.

Miller, Lucinda G. & Murray, Wallace J., eds. Herbal Medicinals: A Clinician's Guide. LC 98-12043. 383p. 1998. pap. 39.95 (*0-7890-0467-4*, Pharmctl Prods) Haworth Pr.

— Herbal Medicinals: A Clinician's Guide. LC 98-12043. (Illus.). 13p. 1998. 59.95 (*0-7890-0466-6*, Hawrth Medical) Haworth Pr.

Miller, Lucy. KidTech: Hands-On Problem Solving with Design Technology for Grades 5-8. Anderson, Catherine & Gideon, Joan, eds. (Illus.). 124p. (Orig.). (J). (gr. 5-8). 1997. pap. text 17.95 (*1-57232-541-0*, 29705) Seymour Pubns.

Miller, Lucy J., ed. Developing Norm-Referenced Standardized Tests. LC 88-36502. (Physical & Occupational Therapy in Pediatrics Ser.: Vol. 9, No. 1). (Illus.). 205p. 1989. text 49.95 (*0-86656-883-2*) Haworth Pr.

Miller, Luke, jt. auth. see Dennis, Clue T.

Miller, Lula, jt. auth. see Yoder, Elmina.

Miller, Lura L., ed. see Miller, Rita A.

Miller, Luree. Literary Hills of San Francisco. LC 91-44656. (Literary Cities Ser.). (Illus.). 72p. (Orig.). 1992. pap. 8.95 (*0-913515-76-0*, Starrhill Press) Black Belt Communs.

— Literary Villages of London. LC 88-36889. (Literary Cities Ser.). (Illus.). 80p. (Orig.). 1989. pap. 8.95 (*0-913515-41-8*, Starrhill Press) Black Belt Communs.

— On Top of the World: Five Women Explorers in Tibet. LC 84-16619. (Illus.). 224p. 1984. reprint ed. pap. 12.95 (*0-89886-097-0*) Mountaineers.

Miller, Lyle. The Stress Solution. 1994. mass mkt. 5.99 (*0-671-75311-8*) PB.

Miller, Lyle H., et al. Stress & Marriage: The Conflict-Reducing, Intimacy-Enhancing, Problem-Solving Guide to a Better Marriage. 318p. 1998. pap. text 14.00 (*0-7881-5858-9*) DIANE Pub.

Miller, Lyle L. Developing Reading Efficiency. 4th ed. LC 79-55778. 1980. 24.00 (*0-8087-3958-1*) Pearson Custom.

Miller, Lyle L. Increasing Reading Efficiency. 5th ed. 1997. pap. 41.50 (*0-15-517669-2*) Harcourt.

Miller, Lyle L. Increasing Reading Efficiency. 5th ed. 352p. (C). 1984. pap. text 29.75 (*0-03-062049-X*) Harcourt Coll Pubs.

— Personalizing Reading Efficiency. 2nd ed. (C). 1981. pap. text. write for info. (*0-8087-3990-5*) Pearson Custom.

***Miller, Lynda.** Bird & His Ring. (Illus.). 20p. (J). (gr. k-7). 1999. 10.00 (*0-9636140-4-5*, Neon Rose) Smart Alternat.

Miller, Lynda. The Smart Profile: A Qualitative Approach of Describing Learners & Designing Instruction. 94p. 1993. pap. 24.00 (*0-9636140-0-2*) Smart Alternat.

***Miller, Lynda.** Two Friends. (Illus.). 20p. (J). (gr. k-5). 1999. 10.00 (*0-9636140-3-7*, Neon Rose) Smart Alternat.

Miller, Lynda. What We Call Smart: A New Narrative for Intelligence & Learning. LC 92-40680. (School-Age Children Ser.). (Illus.). 182p. (Orig.). (C). 1993. pap. 39.95 (*1-879105-44-6*, 0228) Thomson Learn.

— Your Personal Smart Profile: A Qualitative Approach for Describing Yourself in Your Everyday Life. 134p. 1993. pap. 29.00 (*0-9636140-1-0*) Smart Alternat.

Miller, Lynda & Newbill, Chris. Section 504 in the Classroom: How to Design & Implement Accommodation Plans. LC 97-35305. 120p. 1998. pap. text 13.00 (*0-89079-748-X*, 8645) PRO-ED.

Miller, Lynda, et al. Cultural Cobblestones: Teaching Cultural Diversity. (School Library Media Ser.: No. 4). (Illus.). 216p. (Orig.). 1994. 26.50 (*0-8108-2966-5*) Scarecrow.

Miller, Lynda, jt. auth. see Wallach, Geraldine P.

Miller, Lynn. Did You Say Baby? (Yours Truly Ser.). 1999. per. 3.50 (*0-373-52088-3*, 1-52088-1) Harlequin Bks.

— The Hand That Holds the Camera: Interviews with Women Film & Video Directors. LC 87-32871. 271p. 1988. text 10.00 (*0-8240-8530-2*) Garland.

— Is There a Husband in the House? 1997. per. 3.50 (*0-373-52054-9*, 1-52054-3) Silhouette.

Miller, Lynn A. Firstfruits Living: Giving God Our Best. LC 90-48699. 96p. (Orig.). 1991. pap. 7.99 (*0-8361-3543-1*) Herald Pr.

— Just in Time: Stories of God's Extravagance. LC 97-954. 112p. (Orig.). 1997. pap. 8.99 (*0-8361-9067-X*) Herald Pr.

Miller, Lynn C. Travis of Travis Heights: A Real Shaggy Dog Story. (Illus.). 35p. (J). (gr. 2-12). 1997. pap. 17.95 (*0-9636140-2-9*) Smart Alternat.

Miller, Lynn C., jt. ed. see Read, Stephen J.

Miller, Lynn E. Managing Human Service Organizations. LC 88-35682. 256p. 1989. 62.95 (*0-89930-305-6*, MMN/, Quorum Bks) Greenwood.

Miller, Lynn F., jt. auth. see Comtois, M. F.

Miller, Lynn F., jt. ed. see Boos, Florence.

Miller, Lynn H. Global Order: Values & Power in International Relations. 4th ed. LC 98-5797. 336p. (C). 1998. pap. text 29.00 (*0-8133-6880-4*, Pub. by Westview) HarpC.

Miller, Lynn H., jt. auth. see Jensen, Lloyd.

Miller, Lynn H., jt. auth. see Jenson, Lloyd.

Miller, Lynn H., jt. auth. see Schuster, Jack H.

Miller, Lynn R. Buying & Setting up Your Small Farm or Ranch. (Illus.). 195p. 1997. pap. 19.95 (*1-885210-06-X*) Small Farmers.

M

***Miller, Lynn R.** Horsedrawn Plows & Plowing. (Illus.). 368p. 2000. 50.00 (1-885210-09-4); pap. 32.95 (1-885210-08-6) Small Farmers.
Miller, Lynn R. Thought Small. (Illus.). 150p. 1997. 24.50 (1-885210-07-8) Small Farmers.
— Training Workhorses: Training Teamsters. (Illus.). 352p. 1994. pap. 24.95 (1-885210-01-9) Small Farmers.
— Why Farm. 95p. 1997. pap. 11.00 (1-885210-05-1) Small Farmers.
— Work Horse Handbook. (Illus.). 224p. 1983. pap. 14.95 (0-9607268-0-2) Small Farmers.
Miller, Lynn R., ed. see Morris, Edmund.
***Miller, Lynn Ruth.** Starving Hearts. 177p. 2000. pap. 17.95 (0-615-11671-X) Excentrix Pr.
Miller, Lynne, jt. auth. see Lieberman, Ann.
Miller, Lynne, jt. ed. see Lieberman, Ann.
Miller, Lynne D., jt. ed. see Dottin, Erskine S.
Miller, M. Quick & Easy Math. 48p. (J). 1997. pap. 8.95 (0-590-96374-0) Scholastic Inc.
— Yom Tov Shiurim. LC 94-6787. 1994. 16.95 (0-87306-673-1) Feldheim.
Miller, M., ed. Control Technologies for Air Pollution. (C). 1991. text 350.00 (0-89771-590-X, Pub. by Intl Bk Distr) St Mut.
— Environmental Monitoring. (C). 1991. text 350.00 (0-89771-591-8, Pub. by Intl Bk Distr) St Mut.
— The Logic of Language Development in Early Childhood. King, R. T., tr. from GER. (Language & Communication Ser.: Vol. 3). (Illus.). 1979. 39.95 (0-387-09606-X) Spr-Verlag.
Miller, M. C., ed. Excerpta de Historia Macedonia Bks. VII-XII: Epitoma Historiarum Philippicarum. (Illus.). xxiii, 132p. (C). 1992. text 15.00 (0-89005-410-X) Ares.
— Supplementum Inscriptionum Atticarum VI: The Latin Inscriptions of Athens & Attica. (Inscriptiones Atticae Ser.). (LAT., Illus.). viii, 189p. (C). 1992. text 35.00 (0-89005-532-7) Ares.
Miller, M. C., III, et al. Mathematical Models in Medical Diagnosis. LC 81-5170. 187p. 1981. 62.95 (0-275-91349-X, C1349, Praeger Pubs) Greenwood.
Miller, M. C., jt. auth. see De Voto, J.
Miller, M. C., ed. see Barber, G. L.
Miller, M. C., ed. see Hanno the Carthaginian.
***Miller, M. C. J.** The Origins of the Professional Roman Soldier. (Illus.). 250p. 2000. write for info. (0-89005-584-X) Ares.
***Miller, M. C. J., ed.** Abbreviations in Latin. (Illus.). 514p. 1999. pap. 30.00 (0-89005-568-8) Ares.
Miller, M. C. J., ed. see Hondius, J. J.
Miller, M. C. J., ed. see Newby, J. D.
Miller, M. Catherine. Flooding the Courtrooms: Law & Water in the Far West. LC 92-33048. (Law in the American West Ser.: Vol. 4). (Illus.). x, 256p. 1993. text 60.00 (0-8032-3153-9) U of Nebr Pr.
Miller, M. E. The Comprehensive Classification of Fractures. 300p. 1994. 135.00 (0-387-14150-2) Spr-Verlag.
— The Comprehensive Classification of Fractures. 300p. 1997. text 135.00 (0-387-14156-1) Spr-Verlag.
Miller, M. H., jt. ed. see Artis, M. J.
Miller, M. I., jt. auth. see Snyder, D. L.
***Miller, M. K.** Atom Probe Tomography: Analysis at the Atomic Level. LC 00-34894. 2000. write for info. (0-306-46415-2, Kluwer Plenum) Kluwer Academic.
Miller, M. K. & Smith, G. D. Atom Probe Microanalysis: Principles & Applications to Materials Problems. (Monograph). 278p. 1989. text 17.50 (0-931837-99-5) Materials Res.
Miller, M. K., et al. Atom Probe Field Ion Microscopy. (Monographs on the Physics & Chemistry of Materials). (Illus.). 520p. 1996. text 120.00 (0-19-851387-9) OUP.
Miller, M. M., jt. ed. see Harwood, D. S.
Miller, M. R. & Davies, E. Key Facts in Infection. 38p. 1993. spiral bd. write for info. (0-443-04993-9) Church.
Miller, Mabel R. Ellen: The Girl with Two Angels. LC 95-26698. 94p. (J). 1996. pap. 6.99 (0-8163-1325-3) Pacific Pr Pub Assn.
***Miller, Mabel R.** Grandma Ellen & Me. Thomas, Jerry D., ed. (Illus.). 86p. 2000. pap. 6.99 (0-8163-1691-0) Pacific Pr Pub Assn.
Miller, Madelaine H. Ernie: Hemingway's Sister "Sunny" Remembers. (Illus.). 1999. reprint ed. pap. 19.95 (1-882376-68-4) Thunder Bay Pr.
Miller, Madeleine S. Harper's Bible Dictionary. 8th ed. 1973. 18.65 (0-06-065673-5) HarpC.
Miller, Madeleine S., jt. auth. see Miller, J. Lane.
Miller, Madge. Alice in Wonderland. (J). 1953. 6.00 (0-87602-104-6) Anchorage.
— Hansel & Gretel. (J). 1954. 6.00 (0-87602-135-6) Anchorage.
— The Land of the Dragon. (J). 1946. 6.00 (0-87602-148-8) Anchorage.
— OPQRS, Etc. (J). (gr. 4 up). 1984. pap. 6.00 (0-87602-246-8) Anchorage.
— The Pied Piper of Hamelin. (J). 1951. 6.00 (0-87602-174-7) Anchorage.
— Pinocchio. (J). 1954. 6.00 (0-87602-175-5) Anchorage.
— The Princess & the Swineherd. (J). 1946. 6.00 (0-87602-181-X) Anchorage.
— Puss in Boots: Miniature Play. 37p. (J). 1954. 6.00 (0-87602-184-4) Anchorage.
— The Unwicked Witch. (J). (gr. 1-7). 1964. 6.00 (0-87602-216-6) Anchorage.
Miller, Madge, jt. auth. see Crusoe, Robinson.
Miller, Malcolm. Chartres Cathedral. 2nd rev. ed. (Illus.). 96p. (Orig.). 1998. pap. 19.99 (1-878351-54-0) Riverside NY.
***Miller, Manya Delon.** Complete Fertility Organizer: A Guidebook & Record-Keeper for Women. 243p. 1999. pap. 16.95 (0-471-34799-X) Wiley.
***Miller, Mara.** Encyclopedia of Ethical, Moral, Conduct, & Honor Codes. 2000. lib. bdg. 65.00 (0-87436-941-X) ABC-CLIO.
Miller, Mara. The Garden As an Art. LC 92-8162. 233p. (C). 1993. text 64.50 (0-7914-1377-2); pap. text 21.95 (0-7914-1378-0) State U NY Pr.
Miller, Marc. The Color Mac. 2nd ed. 500p. 1995. 50.00 (1-56830-126-X) Hayden.
— Fundamental Tennis. LC 93-48385. (Fundamental Sports Ser.). (Illus.). 64p. (J). (gr. 5-9). 1995. lib. bdg. 21.27 (0-8225-3450-9, Lerner Publctns) Lerner Pub.
Miller, Marc, ed. Elections: Grassroots Strategies for Change. (Southern Exposure Ser.). (Illus.). 120p. (Orig.). 1984. pap. 4.00 (0-943810-17-5) Inst Southern Studies.
— Liberating Our Past. (Illus.). 120p. 1984. pap. 4.00 (0-943810-18-3) Inst Southern Studies.
Miller, Marc, intro. Waging Peace. (Southern Exposure Ser.). (Illus.). 120p. (Orig.). 1982. pap. 3.00 (0-943810-14-0) Inst Southern Studies.
Miller, Marc & Smith, Lester. Marc Miller's Traveller. rev. ed. Lee, Tony, ed. (Traveller Ser.). (Illus.). (YA). (gr. 9 up). pap. 25.00 (0-614-18941-1) Imperium Games.
Miller, Marc & Wright, Ronald. Criminal Procedures: The Police Cases, Statutes, & Executive Materials. LC 98-42138. 1998. pap. text 52.95 (0-7355-0266-8) Panel Pubs.
Miller, Marc, ed. see Carrell, Ross & Detz, Jim.
Miller, Marc L. & Auyong, Jan, eds. Proceedings of the 1996 World Congress on Coastal & Marine . . . Experiences in Management & Development. LC 98-85252. (Illus.). 336p. 1998. pap. text 35.00 (0-934539-17-0, WSGWO98-02WASHU) Wash Sea Grant.
Miller, Marc L. & Wright, Ronald F. Criminal Procedures. LC 98-14160. ii, 1866 p. 1998. boxed set 60.00 (1-56706-645-3) Aspen Law.
***Miller, Marc L. & Wright, Ronald F.** Criminal Procedures: Cases, Statutes, & Executive Materials, 2000 Case Supplement. 328p. 2000. pap., suppl. ed. write for info. (0-7355-1325-2, 13252) Panel Pubs.
Miller, Marc L. & Wright, Ronald F. Criminal Procedures, the Adjudicative Process. LC 98-33180. 1174 p. 1999. pap. text 52.95 (0-7355-0329-X, Aspen Law & Bus) Aspen Pub.
Miller, Marc L., jt. auth. see Kirk, Jerome.
Miller, Marc S. The Irony of Victory: World War II & Lowell, Massachusetts. LC 87-27212. 248p. 1988. text 24.95 (0-252-01505-3) U of Ill Pr.
— Seattle - Tacoma Health Care Choices: The Families U. S. A. Guide to Quality & Cost. (Illus.). 240p. (Orig.). 1996. pap. 10.95 (0-9617893-1-X) Fam USA Found.
Miller, Marc S., ed. Bay Area Health Care Choices: The Families U. S. A. Guide to Quality & Cost. (Illus.). 240p. 1996. pap. 10.95 (0-9617893-3-6) Fam USA Found.
— Chicago Area Health Care Choices: The Families U. S. A. Guide to Quality & Cost. (Illus.). 240p. (Orig.). 1996. pap. 10.95 (0-9617893-2-8) Fam USA Found.
Miller, Marc S. & Families United for Senior Action Foundation Staff. Health Care Choice for Today's Consumer: Families U. S. A. Guide to Quality & Cost. rev. expanded ed. LC 96-35919. (Illus.). 480p. 1997. pap. 17.95 (0-471-17090-9) Wiley.
Miller, Marc S. & Grover, Martha S. Health Care Choices in the Boston Area: Families U. S. A. Guide to Quality & Cost. (Illus.). 212p. (Orig.). 1995. pap. 10.95 (1-879326-24-8) Fam USA Found.
Miller, Marc S., ed. see Families U. S. A. Staff.
Miller, Marc S., ed. see Grover, Martha S.
Miller, Marc W. Mega Traveller: Imperial Encyclopedia. Fugate, Joe, Sr. & Thomas, Gary L., eds. (Illus.). 96p. (Orig.). 1987. pap. 15.00 (0-943580-48-X) Game Designers.
— Mega Traveller: Player's Manual. Fugate, Joe, Sr. & Thomas, Gary L., eds. (Illus.). 104p. (Orig.). 1987. pap. 10.00 (0-943580-38-2) Game Designers.
— Mega Traveller: Referee's Manual. Fugate, Joe, Sr. & Thomas, Gary L., eds. (Illus.). 104p. (Orig.). 1987. pap. 10.00 (0-943580-47-1) Game Designers.
— Rebellion Sourcebook. (MegaTraveller Ser.). (Illus.). 96p. (Orig.). 1988. pap. 15.00 (0-943580-63-3) Game Designers.
— Referee's Companion: For Mega Traveller. (MegaTraveller Ser.). (Illus.). 96p. (Orig.). 1988. pap. 15.00 (0-943580-71-4) Game Designers.
***Miller, Marcia.** The Big Book of Ready-To-Go Writing Activities: 50 Engaging Writing Activities with Reproducible Graphic Organizer That Teach Kids How to Tell a Story, Convey Information. (Illus.). 128p. (J). (gr. 3-6). 2000. pap. 21.99 (0-439-07747-8) Scholastic Inc.
Miller, Marcia. Every Day of the School Year Math Problems. 112p. 1999. pap. 14.95 (0-590-64407-6) Scholastic Inc.
— Times Tunes: 12 Super-Fun Songs & Hands-On Activities That Teach the Multiplication Facts. (Illus.). 32p. 1998. pap. text 9.95 (0-590-49943-2) Scholastic Inc.
Miller, Marcia & Lee, Martin. Investigating with Pattern Blocks. 72p. (J). (gr. k-3). 1995. pap. text 9.50 (0-938587-78-1) Cuisenaire.
Miller, Marcia & Ridout, Orlando, eds. Architecture in Annapolis: A Field Guide. LC 98-52009. (Illus.). 215p. 1998. pap. 20.00 (1-878399-73-X) Div Hist Cult Progs.
Miller, Marcia, jt. auth. see Lee, Martin.
Miller, Marcia M. Post Card Views & Other Souvenirs: Poems. (Illus.). 64p. 1973. pap. 2.95 (0-913270-24-5) Sunstone Pr.
Miller, Marcus. Exchange Rate Management among the G-7/G-3. 2001. pap. 16.95 (0-88132-281-4) Inst Intl Eco.
Miller, Marcus, jt. ed. see Krugman, Paul R.
Miller, Marcy & Palmer, Patti. The Business of Teaching Sewing. (Illus.). 128p. 1996. pap. 29.95 (0-935278-39-7) Palmer-Pletsch.
Miller, Mardith K. Building & Builders in Hispanic California 1769-1850. (Illus.). 231p. (Orig.). 1995. pap. 37.00 (0-915076-12-8) SW Mission.
Miller, Marek. Arystokracja. (POL., Illus.). 270p. 1994. 24.00 (0-614-02646-6) Szwede Slavic.
Miller, Margaret. Baby Faces. (Illus.). 14p. (J). (ps-4). 1998. bds. 4.99 (0-689-81911-0) Litle Simon.
***Miller, Margaret.** Baby Food. (Look Baby! Bks.). (Illus.). 14p. (J). (ps-k). 2000. pap. 5.99 (0-689-83190-0) Litle Simon.
Miller, Margaret. Big & Little. LC 97-17242. (Illus.). 24p. (J). (ps-3). 1998. 15.95 (0-688-14748-8, Grenwillow Bks) HarpC Child Bks.
***Miller, Margaret.** Big & Little. LC 97-17242. (Illus.). 24p. (J). (ps-3). 1998. 14.93 (0-688-14749-6, Grenwillow Bks) HarpC Child Bks.
Miller, Margaret. Can You Guess? LC 92-29406. (Illus.). 40p. (J). (ps up). 1993. 15.00 (0-688-11180-7, Grenwillow Bks) HarpC Child Bks.
Miller, Margaret. Can You Guess. LC 92-29406. (Illus.). 40p. (J). (ps up). 1993. 14.93 (0-688-11181-5, Grenwillow Bks) HarpC Child Bks.
Miller, Margaret. Get Ready, Baby. (Look Baby! Bks.). (Illus.). 14p. (J). (ps-k). 2000. pap. 5.99 (0-689-83189-7) Litle Simon.
— Guess Who? LC 93-26704. (Illus.). 40p. (J). (ps up). 1994. 15.00 (0-688-12783-5, Grenwillow Bks) HarpC Child Bks.
Miller, Margaret. Guess Who? LC 93-26704. (Illus.). 40p. (J). (ps-3). 1994. lib. bdg. 14.93 (0-688-12784-3, Wm Morrow) Morrow Avon.
Miller, Margaret. Here We Go. (Super Chubby Board Bks.). (Illus.). 26p. (J). (ps-k). 1998. 4.99 (0-689-80041-X) Litle Simon.
— I Can Help. (Super Chubby Board Bks.). (Illus.). 26p. (J). (ps-k). 1998. 4.99 (0-689-80044-4) Litle Simon.
***Miller, Margaret.** I Love Colors, Vol. 1. (Illus.). 14p. (J). (ps-3). 1999. bds. 4.99 (0-689-82356-8, 076714004993) S&S Childrens.
Miller, Margaret. I'm Grown Up. (Super Chubby Board Bks.). (Illus.). 26p. (J). (ps-k). 1998. 4.99 (0-689-80043-6) Litle Simon.
— Lets Pretend. (Super Chubby Board Bks.). (Illus.). 26p. (J). (ps-k). 1998. 4.99 (0-689-80042-8) Litle Simon.
— Look Baby Board Books What's on My Head? (Illus.). 14p. (J). (ps-4). 1998. 4.99 (0-689-81912-9) Litle Simon.
— Me & My Bear. (Illus.). 14p. (J). (ps-3). 1999. bds. 4.99 (0-689-82355-X, 076714004993) Litle Simon.
— My Five Senses. (Illus.). 24p. (J). 1998. per. 5.99 (0-689-82009-7) Aladdin.
— My Five Senses. LC 93-1956. (Illus.). 24p. (J). (ps up). 1994. 16.00 (0-671-79168-0) S&S Bks Yung.
— My Five Senses. 1998. 11.19 (0-606-13631-2, Pub. by Turtleback) Demco.
— Now I'm Big. LC 95-17774. (Illus.). 32p. (J). (ps up). 1996. 15.00 (0-688-14077-7, Grenwillow Bks); lib. bdg. 14.93 (0-688-14078-5, Grenwillow Bks) HarpC Child Bks.
— Some People: Photographs by Pefer Foe. (Illus.). 42p. Date not set. pap. text 8.00 (1-879293-09-9) Contemp Art Mus.
— Super Chubby: I Can Make It! (Illus.). 26p. (J). (ps). 1997. 4.99 (0-689-80048-7) S&S Childrens.
— Super Chubby: Let's Play! (Illus.). 26p. (J). (ps). 1997. 4.99 (0-689-80047-9) S&S Childrens.
— Super Chubby: Water Play. (Illus.). 12p. (J). (ps). 1997. 4.99 (0-689-80046-0) S&S Childrens.
— Super Chubby: Wheels Go 'Round. (Illus.). 24p. (J). (ps-k). 1997. 4.99 (0-689-80045-2) S&S Childrens.
— A Vessel of Honor. LC 97-93383. 254p. 1997. 23.00 (0-9657389-5-7) Herit Pub Hse.
— Where Does It Go? LC 91-30160. (Illus.). 40p. (J). (ps-4). 1992. 16.00 (0-688-10928-4, Grenwillow Bks) HarpC Child Bks.
— Where Does It Go. LC 91-30160. (Illus.). 40p. (J). (ps-3). 1998. mass mkt. 4.95 (0-688-15851-X, Wm Morrow) Morrow Avon.
Miller, Margaret. Who Uses This. LC 89-30456. (Illus.). 40p. (J). (ps-k). 1990. 15.93 (0-688-08279-3, Grenwillow Bks) HarpC Child Bks.
— Who Uses This. 40p. (J). 1999. mass mkt. 5.95 (0-688-17057-9, Wm Morrow) Morrow Avon.
Miller, Margaret. Whose Hat? LC 86-18324. (Illus.). 40p. (J). (ps-3). 1988. 16.00 (0-688-06906-1, Grenwillow Bks) HarpC Child Bks.
— Whose Hat? 1997. 10.85 (0-606-12092-0, Pub. by Turtleback) Demco.
— Whose Hat. LC 86-18324. (Illus.). 40p. (ps-3). 1997. mass mkt. 4.95 (0-688-15279-1, Wm Morrow) Morrow Avon.
— Whose Shoe? LC 90-38491. (Illus.). 40p. (J). (ps-k). 1991. 16.00 (0-688-10008-2, Grenwillow Bks) HarpC Child Bks.
Miller, Margaret, photos by. At the Shore. LC 96-157692. (Illus.). 12p. (J). (ps-k). 1996. 4.99 (0-689-80052-5) S&S Bks Yung.
— Family Time. (Super Chubby Board Bks.). (Illus.). 12p. (J). (ps). 1996. 4.99 (0-689-80051-7) Litle Simon.
— Happy Days. LC 96-157694. (Super Chubby Board Bks.). (Illus.). 24p. (J). (ps-k). 1996. 4.99 (0-689-80050-9) Litle Simon.
— I Can Make It. (Super Chubby Board Bks.). (Illus.). (J). (ps-k). 1997. 4.99 (0-614-29105-4) Litle Simon.
— Let's Play! (Illus.). (J). (ps-k). 1997. 4.99 (0-614-29106-2) Litle Simon.
— My Best Friends. LC 96-157695. (Super Chubby Board Bks.). (Illus.). 12p. (J). (ps). 1996. 4.99 (0-689-80049-5) Litle Simon.
— Water Play. (Illus.). (J). (ps-k). 1997. 4.99 (0-614-29107-0) Litle Simon.
— Wheels Go Round. (Illus.). (J). (ps-k). 1997. 4.99 (0-614-29108-9) Litle Simon.
Miller, Margaret, et al. Human Development. LC 92-13561. (Skills for Caring Ser.). (Illus.). 40p. (Orig.). 1992. pap. text 9.00 (0-443-04531-3) Church.
Miller, Margaret, jt. auth. see Scott, Elaine.
Miller, Margaret A. Restructuring in Virginia: A Case in Point. 1995. 10.00 (0-614-13551-6) SHEEO.
Miller, Margaret C. Athens & Persia in the Fifth Century B. C. A Study in Cultural Receptivity. LC 98-14077. (Illus.). xiv, 331p. (C). 1996. write for info. (0-521-49598-9) Cambridge U Pr.
Miller, Margaret I. Here Am I, Lord. 1998. 10.95 (0-9661305-0-2) Ampelos Pr.
Miller, Margaret J. Blockbender Quilts. LC 95-4634. 1995. pap. 26.95 (1-56477-107-5, B224) Martingale & Co.
— Easy Pieces: Creative Color Play with Two Simple Quilt Blocks. LC 98-6315. (Illus.). 144p. 1998. pap. 27.95 (1-57120-051-7, 10175) C & T Pub.
***Miller, Margaret J.** Smashing Sets: Exciting Ways to Arrange Quilt Blocks. Aneloski, Liz & Philp, Stephanie, eds. LC 00-8346. (Illus.). 96p. 2000. pap. 23.95 (1-57120-110-6, Pub. by C & T Pub) Watsn-Guptill.
Miller, Margaret J. Strips That Sizzle. Weiland, Barbara, ed. LC 92-8798. (Illus.). 112p. (Orig.). 1997. reprint ed. pap. 24.95 (1-56477-009-5, B141, That Patchwrk Pl) Martingale & Co.
Miller, Margarette S. Twenty-Three Words: A Biography of Francis Bellamy, Author of the Pledge of Allegiance. LC 79-9478. (Illus.). 400p. 1976. 15.00 (0-686-15626-9) Natl Bellamy.
Miller, Margery. Sound Business Bites: A Common Sense Approach to Customer Service & Management. LC 94-22154. 100p. (Orig.). 1994. pap. 10.00 (1-884363-04-0) Odenwald Pr.
Miller, Margery S. & Allan, Karen K. Reading the Newspaper: Middle Level. (Illus.). 160p. (Orig.). 1987. pap. text 14.56 (0-89061-480-6, Jamestwn Pub) NTC Contemp Pub Co.
Miller, Margery S., jt. auth. see Allan, Karen K.
Miller, Margery S., jt. auth. see Allen, Karen K.
Miller, Marguerite, jt. auth. see Kern, R. Fred.
Miller, Marguerite L., jt. auth. see Cochrane, Ruth T.
Miller, Marian A. The Third World in Global Environmental Politics. LC 94-36484. 182p. 1995. pap. text 17.95 (1-55587-423-1) L Rienner.
— The Third World in Global Environmental Politics. 224p. 1995. 9.00 (0-335-19501-6); pap. 2.00 (0-335-19500-8) OpUniv Pr.
Miller, Marianne M. Too Busy: A Days of the Week Story. Wray, Rhonda, ed. LC 93-11657. (Illus.). 36p. (J). (gr. k-3). 1993. pap. 4.95 (0-916260-96-8, B114) Meriwether Pub.
Miller, Marie. Just Learning to Color. (SPA., Illus.). 32p. (J). (gr. k). 1996. pap. 0.80 (0-7399-0170-2, 2940.1) Rod & Staff.
Miller, Marie F., jt. auth. see Miller, W. R.
Miller, Marie F., jt. auth. see Miller, Wilbur R.
Miller, Marie S. New Dimensions in Floral Design. (Illus.). 173p. (Orig.). (C). 1981. text 29.95 (0-9606424-0-4) M S Miller.
Miller, Marilyn. At the Airport. (Behind the Scenes Ser.). (Illus.). 32p. (ps-4). 1996. lib. bdg. 21.40 (0-8172-4086-1) Raintree Steck-V.
— At the Airport. (Behind the Scenes Ser.). 32p. (J). (gr. k-4). 1996. pap. text 5.95 (0-8172-6475-2) Raintree Steck-V.
Miller, Marilyn. Behind the Scenes: At the Shopping Mall. 32p. (J). (gr. k-4). 1996. pap. text 5.95 (0-8172-6477-9) Raintree Steck-V.
Miller, Marilyn. The Bridge at Selma. LC 84-40379. (Turning Points in American History Ser.). (Illus.). 64p. (J). (gr. 5 up). 1984. lib. bdg. 14.95 (0-382-06826-2) Silver Burdett Pr.
— The Bridge at Selma. LC 84-40379. (Turning Points in American History Ser.). (Illus.). 64p. (YA). (gr. 5 up). 1984. pap. 7.95 (0-382-06973-0) Silver Burdett Pr.
— The Hospital. LC 95-8868. (Behind the Scenes Ser.). (Illus.). 32p. (J). (ps-4). 1996. lib. bdg. 22.83 (0-8172-4087-X) Raintree Steck-V.
— Thanksgiving. LC 97-27926. (World of Holidays Ser.). (Illus.). 32p. (J). (gr. 2-5). 1998. pap. 7.95 (0-8172-8106-1) Raintree Steck-V.
— The Trans-Continental Railroad. LC 85-40167. (Turning Points in American History Ser.). (Illus.). 64p. (YA). (gr. 5 up). 1985. pap. 7.95 (0-382-09912-5) Silver Burdett Pr.
— The TV News Studio. LC 95-19525. (Behind the Scenes Ser.). (Illus.). 32p. (J). (ps-4). 1996. lib. bdg. 21.40 (0-8172-4089-6) Raintree Steck-V.
— Words That Built a Nation: A Young Person's Collection of Historic American Documents. LC 98-31415. (Illus.). 172p. (YA). (gr. 4-9). 1999. 18.95 (0-590-29881-X, Pub. by Scholastic Inc) Penguin Putnam.
Miller, Marilyn F. At the Shopping Mall. LC 95-31336. (Behind the Scenes Ser.). (Illus.). 32p. (J). (ps-4). 1996. lib. bdg. 21.40 (0-8172-4088-8) Raintree Steck-V.
— Thanksgiving. LC 97-27926. (World of Holidays Ser.). (J). 1998. 22.83 (0-8172-4612-6) Raintree Steck-V.
Miller, Marilyn J. & Sorehon Glen Assoc. Staff. Body & Soul: Storytelling as Healing Practice. (New Perspectives in Folklore Ser.). 250p. 1998. text 37.00 (0-8153-2370-0) Garland.
Miller, Marilyn L., et al, eds. School Library Journal's Best: A Reader for Children's, Young Adult, & School Librarians. LC 96-23856. 475p. 1997. pap. 45.00 (1-55570-203-1) Neal-Schuman.
Miller, Marilyn M. & Shapiro, Michael J. Retinopathy of Prematurity. 1995. 86.00 (90-6299-125-4) Kugler Pubns.

An Asterisk (*) at the beginning of an entry indicates that the title is appearing for the first time.

M

An Asterisk (*) at the beginning of an entry indicates that the title is appearing for the first time.

Miller, Mary, et al. Opportunities in Fitness Careers. 2nd ed. LC 96-48293. (Opportunities in... Ser.). (Illus.). 160p. pap. 11.95 (*0-8442-4687-5*, 46875, Natl Textbk Co) NTC Contemp Pub Co.

Miller, Mary A. & Babcock, Dorothy E. Critical Thinking Applied to Nursing. teacher ed. write for info. (*0-8151-6960-4*) Mosby Inc.

— Critical Thinking Applied to Nursing. LC 95-37174. (Illus.). 368p. (C). (gr. 13). 1995. pap. text 25.00 (*0-8151-6962-0*, 27243) Mosby Inc.

Miller, Mary Ann. Childbearing Family, No. 2. 1983. 30.50 (*0-316-57338-8*, Little Brwn Med Div) Lppncott W & W.

Miller, Mary B., jt. auth. see Ancona, George.

Miller, Mary B., jt. auth. see Charlip, Remy.

Miller, Mary C. Color for Interior Architecture. LC 96-47402. 162p. 1997. pap. 54.95 (*0-471-12736-1*) Wiley.

— Devotions for Living with Loss. 1991. 7.95 (*0-910452-72-5*) Covenant.

— Lost Mansions of Mississippi. LC 95-51855. (Illus.). 192p. (C). 1996. 35.00 (*0-87805-888-5*) U Pr of Miss.

***Miller, Mary C. & Carter, Mary R.** Written in the Bricks: A Visual & Historical Tour of 15 Mississippi Hometowns. LC 99-39583. (Illus.). 1999. pap. 39.95 (*1-893062-09-0*) Quail Ridge.

Miller, Mary Carol. Marshall County, MS: From the Collection of Chesley Thorne Smith. (Images of America Ser.). (Illus.). 128p. 1998. pap. 16.99 (*0-7524-1211-6*) Arcadia Publng.

Miller, Mary E. The Art of MesoAmerica: From Olmec to Aztec. 2nd rev. ed. LC 95-70510. (World of Art Ser.). (Illus.). 240p. 1996. pap. 14.95 (*0-500-20290-7*, Pub. by Thames Hudson) Norton.

Miller, Mary Ellen. Maya Art & Architecture. LC 99-70938. (World of Art Ser.). (Illus.). 240p. (Orig.). 1999. pap. 14.95 (*0-500-20327-X*, Pub. by Thames Hudson) Norton.

Miller, Mary Ellen, jt. auth. see Schele, Linda.

Miller, Mary F. How to Get a Job with a Cruise Line: Adventure, Travel, Romance: How to Sail Around the World on Luxury Cruise Ships & Get Paid for It. 4th ed. LC 96-54282. 208p. 1997. pap. 14.95 (*0-9624019-8-6*) Ticket Adventure.

***Miller, Mary Fallon.** How to Get a Job with a Cruise Line: Adventure Travel Romance: How to Sail the World on Luxury Cruise Ships & Get Paid for It. 5th ed. 240p. 2000. pap. 16.95 (*0-9624019-3-5*) Ticket Adventure.

Miller, Mary Fallon, et al. 2001Cruise Chooser: Buyers Guide to Cruise Vacation Values, Bargains, Discounts & Deals. (Illus.). 448p. (Orig.). 1999. pap. 16.95 (*0-9624019-2-7*) Ticket Adventure.

Miller, Mary J. Fast Forward. 1999. pap. 3.95 (*0-14-034992-8*, Viking) Viking Penguin.

— Rewind & Search: Conversations with the Makers & Decision-Makers of CBC Television Drama. LC 97-117924. 472p. 1996. 60.00 (*0-7735-1365-5*, Pub. by McG-Queens Univ Pr) CUP Services.

***Miller, Mary Jane.** Women, God Wants to Get Personal with You. (Illus.). 24p. 2000. pap. 7.00 (*0-8059-4859-7*) Dorrance.

Miller, Mary K. Mathematics for Nurses with Clinical Applications. LC 80-26040. 390p. (Orig.). (C). 1981. pap. 31.00 (*0-8185-0429-3*) Brooks-Cole.

Miller, Mary R. Children of the Salt River. LC 76-45149. (Language Science Monographs: Vol. 16). 1977. pap. 16.00 (*0-87750-206-4*) Res Inst Inner Asian Studies.

— The Women of Candelaria. LC 96-26463. (Illus.). 128p. (Orig.). 1996. pap. 31.95 (*0-7649-0005-6*) Pomegranate Calif.

Miller, Mary S. No Visible Wounds: Identifying Nonphysical Abuse of Women by Their Men. 320p. 1996. pap. 12.00 (*0-449-91079-2*) Fawcett.

Miller, Maryann. Coping with Weapons & Violence in School & on Your Streets, 7 vols. Rosen, Ruth C., ed. (Coping Ser.). 192p. (YA). (gr. 7-12). 1996. lib. bdg. 17.95 (*0-8239-2267-7*) Rosen Group.

— Drugs & Date Rape. LC 94-37824. (Drug Abuse Prevention Library). (Illus.). 64p. (YA). (gr. 7-12). 1995. lib. bdg. 17.95 (*0-8239-2064-X*) Rosen Group.

— Drugs & Gun Violence. LC 95-5910. (Drug Abuse Prevention Library). (Illus.). 64p. (YA). (gr. 7-12). 1996. lib. bdg. 17.95 (*0-8239-2060-7*) Rosen Group.

— Drugs & Violent Crime, 8 vols. LC 95-26264. (Drug Abuse Prevention Library). (Illus.). 64p. (Orig.). (YA). (gr. 7-12). 1996. lib. bdg. 17.95 (*0-8239-2282-0*) Rosen Group.

— Everything You Need to Know about Dealing with the Police. LC 94-18526. (Need to Know Library). (Illus.). 64p. (YA). (gr. 7-12). 1995. lib. bdg. 17.95 (*0-8239-1875-0*) Rosen Group.

— Your Best Foot Forward: Winning Strategies for the Job Interview. LC 93-44347. (Lifeskills Library). (Illus.). 48p. (YA). (gr. 7-12). 1994. lib. bdg. 14.95 (*0-8239-1697-9*) Rosen Group.

Miller, Maryjane. Going Distance. 1999. pap. 3.95 (*0-14-036353-X*, Viking) Viking Penguin.

Miller, Marylees, jt. auth. see Miller, Irwin.

***Miller, Matt.** Captain Cuffs on the Beat. (Action Tool Books Ser.). (Illus.). 12p. (J). (ps-k). 2000. bds. 5.99 (*1-57584-423-0*) Rdrs Digest.

Miller, Matt, jt. auth. see Fisher-Price Staff.

Miller, Matthew J., jt. auth. see Singer, Naomi E.

Miller, Maureen. The Formation of a Medieval Church: Ecclesiastical Change in Verona, 950-1150. LC 92-54971. (Illus.). 264p. 1993. text 39.95 (*0-8014-2837-8*) Cornell U Pr.

***Miller, Maureen C.** The Bishop's Palace: Architecture & Authority in Medieval Italy. LC 00-22380. (Conjunctions of Religion & Power in the Medieval Past Ser.). (Illus.). 2000. pap. write for info. (*0-8014-8539-8*) Cornell U Pr.

— The Bishop's Palace: Architecture & Authority in Medieval Italy. (Illus.). 2000. 49.95 (*0-8014-3535-8*) Cornell U Pr.

Miller, Maurice. Hearing Aids. LC 72-190707. (Studies in Communicative Disorders). (C). 1972. pap. write for info. (*0-672-61284-4*, Bobbs) Macmillan.

Miller, Max J. & Love, Edgar J., eds. Parasitic Diseases: Treatment & Control. 352p. 1989. lib. bdg. 195.00 (*0-8493-4922-2*, RC119) CRC Pr.

Miller, Max J., et al. Diagnosis & Treatment of Prevalent Diseases of North American Indian Populations. (American Indian Health Ser.: Vol. 2). 250p. 1974. text 27.50 (*0-8422-7216-X*) Irvington.

Miller, Maxine. God Is Pro-Choice. LC 97-90421. 1997. pap. 8.95 (*0-533-12397-6*) Vantage.

Miller, Maxwell. The Universal Tarot Package. (Illus.). 144p. (Orig.). 1996. pap. 25.00 (*0-87728-840-2*) Weiser.

Miller, May. The Clearing & Beyond. LC 73-93070. 1974. 7.50 (*0-910350-08-6*) Charioteer.

— Collected Poems. LC 88-83172. 235p. (YA). (gr. 7-12). 1989. 18.00 (*0-916418-70-7*) Lotus.

— Dust of Uncertain Journey. LC 75-40977. 67p. (YA). (gr. 9-12). 1975. pap. 5.00 (*0-916418-05-7*) Lotus.

— Halfway to the Sun. LC 81-50427. (Series Six). (Illus.). 50p. (Orig.). (J). (gr. 6). 1981. pap. text 7.00 (*0-931846-17-X*) Wash Writers Pub.

— Halfway to the Sun. (Illus.). 52p. (Orig.). (J). (gr. 2-5). 1988. reprint ed. pap. 5.00 (*0-916418-75-8*) Lotus.

— Not That Far. 1973. 6.85 (*0-941490-12-2*) Solo Pr.

— The Ransomed Wait. LC 82-83856. 77p. (YA). (gr. 9-12). 1983. per. 5.00 (*0-916418-40-5*) Lotus.

Miller, May T., jt. auth. see Burton, Susan B,.

Miller, Maynard M. & Marston, Richard A., eds. Environment & Society in the Manaslu-Ganesh Region of the Central Nepal Himalaya. (UW Publications Ser.). (Illus.). 110p. 1989. pap. 10.00 (*0-941570-10-X*) U of Wyoming.

Miller-McLemore, Bonnie J. Also a Mother: Work & Family As Theological Dilemma. LC 93-44713. 224p. (Orig.). 1994. pap. 19.95 (*0-687-11020-3*) Abingdon.

— Death, Sin & the Moral Life: Contemporary Cultural Interpretations of Death. LC 87-28872. (American Academy of Religion Academy Ser.). 357p. 1988. 31.95 (*1-55540-202-X*, 01 01 59); pap. 20.95 (*1-55540-203-8*) OUP.

Miller, Melinda J. & Rachfalski, Jane. Rainbow Dancer: Positive Thought, Imagery & Exercise for Self-Esteem, Inner Peace & Caring for the Earth. Van Wert, Johanna, ed. LC 92-80720. (Illus.). 119p. (Orig.). 1991. pap. 19.95 (*0-9631046-0-8*) Rainbow Dancer.

Miller, Melissa. Cat I. Q. Test. (Illus.). 208p. 1996. pap. 8.95 (*0-14-025735-7*, Penguin Bks) Viking Penguin.

— The Dog I.Q. Test: For Dogs & Their Owners. 192p. 1994. pap. 9.95 (*0-14-024020-9*, Penguin Bks) Viking Penguin.

Miller, Melissa A. Family Violence: The Compassionate Church Responds. LC 93-80269. 184p. (Orig.). 1994. pap. 11.99 (*0-8361-3654-3*) Herald Pr.

Miller, Melton. AutoCAD R13 for Engineers. (Illus.). 1997. teacher ed. write for info. (*0-8053-6424-2*) Benjamin-Cummings.

Miller, Melton. AutoCAD R13 for Engineers: Toolkit. rev. ed. (Illus.). 190p. 1997. pap. 21.33 (*0-8053-6423-4*) Benjamin-Cummings.

— AutoCAD R12 for Engineers: Toolkit. (Illus.). 192p. 1995. pap. 21.00 (*0-8053-6421-8*) Benjamin-Cummings.

Miller, Melvia. An Apple a Day. (Illus.). 1990. 9.95 (*0-685-45575-0*) Mothership Pubns.

— A Picture Speaks a Thousand Words. pap. 25.00 (*0-685-74228-8*) Mothership Pubns.

Miller, Melville D., Jr. & Goldhill, Nancy. You & the Law in New Jersey: A Resource Guide. 384p. 1988. text 38.00 (*0-8135-1342-1*) Rutgers U Pr.

Miller, Melville D., Jr., et al. You & the Law in New Jersey: A Resource Guide. 2nd ed. LC 97-43070. 448p. 1998. pap. 19.00 (*0-8135-2532-2*); text 50.00 (*0-8135-2531-4*) Rutgers U Pr.

Miller, Melvin D. Principles & a Philosophy for Vocational Education. 250p. 1985. 17.00 (*0-318-17790-0*, SN48) Ctr Educ Trng Employ.

Miller, Melvin E., et al, eds. Spirituality, Ethics & Relationship in Adulthood: Clinical & Theoretical Explorations. LC 99-39480. 260p. 2000. 62.50 (*1-887841-29-6*, 66125, Psychosocial) Intl Univs Pr.

Miller, Melvin E. & Cook-Greuter, Susanne, eds. Transcendence & Mature Thought in Adulthood: The Further Reaches of Adult Development. 300p. (C). 1994. pap. text 27.95 (*0-8476-7919-5*); lib. bdg. 69.50 (*0-8476-7918-7*) Rowman.

***Miller, Melvin E. & Cook-Greuter, Susanne R.** Creativity, Spirituality & Transcendence: Paths to Integrity & Wisdom in the Mature Self. LC 99-29746. (Publications in Creativity Research). 261p. 1999. write for info. (*1-56750-461-2*) Ablx Pub.

Miller, Melvin E., jt. auth. see Young-Eisendrath, Polly.

Miller, Melvin R. That Woman I Married. 104p. 1986. pap. 3.95 (*0-88144-061-2*) Christian Pub.

***Miller, Merl K., et al.** The Personal Robot Navigator. (Illus.). 198p. 1998. pap. 44.95 (*1-888193-00-X*) AK Peters.

Miller, Merle. Plain Speaking: An Oral Biography of Harry S. Truman. 480p. 1986. mass mkt. 6.99 (*0-425-09499-5*) Berkley Pub.

Miller, Merle & Cogley, John. Blacklisting: Two Key Documents. LC 78-161171. (History of Broadcasting: Radio to Television Ser.). 1980. reprint ed. 35.95 (*0-405-03579-9*) Ayer.

***Miller, Merle L.** Designing the New Generation John Deere Tractors. LC 99-72167. (Illus.). 144p. 1999. pap. 17.95 (*1-892769-04-2*, H0199) Am Soc Ag Eng.

Miller, Merlene. Recovery Education: A Guide for Teaching Chemically Dependent People. 1992. pap. 4.00 (*0-8309-0565-0*) Herald Pub Hse.

Miller, Merlene & Gorski, Terence. Lowering the Risk: A Self-Care Plan for Relapse Prevention. 31p. 1991. pap. 4.00 (*0-8309-0609-6*) Herald Pub Hse.

Miller, Merlene & Gorski, Terence T. Family Recovery: Growing Beyond Addiction. 1982. pap. 6.50 (*0-8309-0369-0*) Herald Pub Hse.

Miller, Merlene & Miller, David. Reversing the Weight Gain Spiral: The Groundbreaking Program for Lifelong Weight Management. 2nd ed. (Illus.). 334p. Date not set. reprint ed. pap. text 14.00 (*0-9661604-0-1*) Harrison Pub.

Miller, Merlene, et al. Learning to Live Again: A Guide for Recovery from Chemical Dependency. rev. ed. 1992. pap. text 12.50 (*0-8309-0619-3*) Herald Pub Hse.

Miller, Merlene, jt. auth. see Gorski, Terence T.

Miller, Merlene, jt. auth. see Gorski, Terrence.

Miller, Merry. Beauty Secrets: A Daily Guide of Beauty Basics. Caton, Patrick, ed. 365p. 1996. pap., spiral bd. 6.50 (*1-56245-231-2*) Great Quotations.

Miller, Merton H. Financial Innovations & Market Volatility. (Illus.). 288p. 1991. text 40.95 (*1-55786-252-4*) Blackwell Pubs.

— Merton Miller on Derivatives. LC 97-210562. 240p. 1997. 34.95 (*0-471-18340-7*) Wiley.

Miller, Merton H. & Upton, Charles W. Macroeconomics: A Neoclassical Introduction. LC 73-90598. xvi, 384p. (C). 1986. pap. text 17.00 (*0-226-52623-2*) U Ch Pr.

Miller, Merton H., jt. auth. see Fama, Eugene F.

Miller, Merton H., ed. see Kessel, Reuben A.

Miller, Merton L. A Preliminary Study of the Pueblo of Taos, New Mexico. LC 74-7992. reprint ed. 31.50 (*0-404-11879-8*) AMS Pr.

Miller, Mervyn. Raymond Unwin: Architect & Planner - A Biography. (Illus.). 240p. 1992. text 59.00 (*0-7185-1363-0*, Pub. by Leicester U Pr) Cassell & Continuum.

Miller, Miamon. The Balkan Folkdance Music Gig Book. 30p. (J). 1994. student ed. 11.00 (*0-9626468-4-9*) Fuge Imaginea.

— How to Play Romanian Folk Violin. Fraenkel, Eran, ed. (Illus.). 31p. (Orig.). 1990. student ed. 20.00 (*0-9626468-0-6*) Fuge Imaginea.

Miller, Miamon & Cerael, Larche. How to Play Romanian Folk Violin, Vol. 2. (Illus.). 29p. (Orig.). 1994. pap. 20.00 (*0-9626468-3-0*) Fuge Imaginea.

Miller, Miamon, ed. see Apan, Valeria.

Miller, Miamon, ed. see Saunders, Lawrence.

***Miller, Michael.** Complete Idiot's Guide to Fixing Your #$ @ PC Problems. (Complete Idiot's Guide Ser.). 416p. 1999. pap. text 16.99 (*0-7897-2092-2*) Que.

— Complete Idiot's Guide to Home Theater Systems. (Complete Idiot's Guides (Lifestyle) Ser.). (Illus.). 312p. 2000. pap. 16.95 (*0-02-863939-1*, Alpha Ref) Macmillan Gen Ref.

— The Complete Idiot's Guide to Online Auctions. 331p. 1999. 16.99 (*0-7897-2057-4*) Que.

Miller, Michael. Complete Idiot's Guide to Surfing the Internet with WebTV. (Complete Idiot's Guides (Computers) Ser.). 350p. 1999. pap. 16.99 (*0-7897-2041-8*) Que.

***Miller, Michael.** The Complete Idiot's Guide to Yahoo! LC 99-67105. 339p. 2000. pap. 19.99 (*0-7897-2277-1*) Que.

Miller, Michael. Development of the Central Nervous System: Effects of Alcohol & Opiates. LC 91-22912. 360p. 1991. 295.00 (*0-471-56125-8*, Wiley-Liss) Wiley.

— Easy Internet. 2nd ed. LC 97-65528. 272p. 1997. 24.99 (*0-7897-1219-9*) Que.

— Easy Internet with Netscape. 1996. pap. text 24.99 incl. disk (*0-7897-0752-7*) Que.

— Intimate Terrorism: The Crisis of Love in an Age of Disillusion. 256p. 1996. pap. 13.00 (*0-393-31532-0*) Norton.

— Jackhammer. deluxe limited ed. 16p. 1972. pap. 10.00 (*0-914496-01-8*) Helikon NY.

***Miller, Michael.** Mastering Word 2000: Premium Edition. 2nd ed. 2000. pap. 39.99 (*0-7821-2662-6*) Sybex.

— Official Printmaster Guide. (Illus.). 1999. pap. 17.99 (*0-7897-2081-7*) Que.

— PowerPoint 2000! I Didn't Know You Could Do That... 2000. pap. 19.99 (*0-7821-2787-8*) Sybex.

Miller, Michael. Red, White & Green. LC 97-62482. Vol. 107. 227p. 1998. pap. 15.00 (*0-87404-278-X*) U of Tex Pr.

— Teach Yourself More Windows 98 in 24 Hours. LC 98-85067. (Teach Yourself Ser.). 1998. pap. 19.99 (*0-672-31343-X*) Sams.

***Miller, Michael.** Using Windows 98, Preview ed. (Using... Ser.). 1998. pap. 9.99 (*0-7897-1651-8*) Que.

Miller, Michael. What Are They Saying about Papal Primacy? (What Are They Saying about...Ser.). 128p. 1983. pap. 4.95 (*0-8091-2501-3*) Paulist Pr.

Miller, Michael & Vogel, Robert A. The Practice of Coronary Disease Prevention. LC 95-45490. (Illus.). 352p. 1996. pap. 24.95 (*0-683-18045-2*) Lppncott W & W.

Miller, Michael A. Digital Electronics. LC 96-22291. (C). 1996. mass mkt. 81.95 (*0-314-20151-3*) West Pub.

— Introduction to Data & Network Communications. LC 99-36709. (Electronics Technology Ser.). 522p. 1999. pap. 63.95 (*0-7668-1100-X*) Delmar.

— Introduction to Digital & Data Communications. Conty, ed. 435p. (C). 1992. text 46.50 (*0-314-93371-9*) West Pub.

— The 68000 Family Microprocessor. 2nd ed. 1992. 71.20 (*0-02-381560-4*, Macmillan Coll) P-H.

Miller, Michael A., jt. ed. see Holt, Roy J.

Miller, Michael B. The Bon Marche: Bourgeois Culture & the Department Store. LC 80-36797. (Illus.). 295p. reprint ed. pap. 91.50 (*0-8357-8819-9*, 203265000085) Bks Demand.

— Bon Marche: Bourgeois Culture & the Department Store, 1869-1920. 304p. (C). 1994. pap. text 17.95 (*0-691-03494-X*, Pub. by Princeton U Pr) Cal Prin Full Svc.

— Shanghai on the Metro: Spies, Intrigue, & the French Between the Wars. LC 93-34114. (C). 1994. 42.50 (*0-520-08519-1*, Pub. by U CA Pr) Cal Prin Full Svc.

Miller, Michael B., tr. see Arguerta, Manlio.

Miller, Michael D. Camelot the True Story. Cooper, Edith, ed. (Illus.). 380p. 1998. pap. 14.95 (*0-9651484-1-6*) Rideout Pub.

— Marine War Risks. 2nd ed. 621p. 1994. 185.00 (*1-85044-516-8*) LLP.

Miller, Michael E. False Apostle. 205p. mass mkt. 4.99 (*1-55197-011-2*) Picasso Publ.

Miller, Michael F. Classical Greek & Roman Coins: The Investor's Handbook. LC 81-69260. (Illus.). 224p. 1982. 22.95 (*0-9607106-0-4*) Altara Group.

Miller, Michael J., et al, eds. Satellite Communications: Mobile & Fixed Services. LC 93-10183. (International Series in Engineering & Computer Science, VLSI, Computer Architecture, & Digital Screen Processing). 432p. (C). 1993. lib. bdg. 120.50 (*0-7923-9333-3*) Kluwer Academic.

Miller, Michael J., jt. ed. see Flug, Phyllis O.

***Miller, Michael K.** Enfield. (Images of America Ser.). 1999. pap. 16.99 (*0-7385-0002-X*) Arcadia Publng.

Miller, Michael L., jt. auth. see Dorpat, Theodore L.

Miller, Michael M. North Dakota Centennial Newspaper Index. 130p. 1991. write for info. (*0-9629777-0-5*) ND State Univ.

Miller, Michael O. & Sales, Bruce D. The Law & Mental Health Professionals: Arizona. LC 86-10780. 357p. 1986. 59.95 (*0-912704-50-0*) Am Psychol.

Miller, Michael O., ed. see Brant, Jonathan.

Miller, Michael S. & Tiley, Larry P. Manual of Canine & Feline Cardiology. 2nd ed. (Illus.). 528p. 1994. pap. text 65.00 (*0-7216-5940-3*, W B Saunders Co) Harcrt Hlth Sci Grp.

Miller, Michael T. Responsive Academic Decision-Making: Involving Faculty in Higher Education Governance. 170p. 1999. 19.95 (*1-58107-020-9*, Pub. by New Forums) Booksource.

Miller, Michaela. Cats. LC 97-16614. (Pet Ser.). (Illus.). 24p. (J). 1998. 18.50 (*1-57572-572-X*) Heinemann Lib.

— Dogs. LC 97-11983. (Pet Ser.). (Illus.). 24p. (J). 1998. 18.50 (*1-57572-573-8*) Heinemann Lib.

— Goldfish. LC 97-16615. (Pet Ser.). (Illus.). 24p. (J). 1998. 18.50 (*1-57572-574-6*) Heinemann Lib.

***Miller, Michaela.** Guinea Pigs. LC 97-11985. (Pet Ser.). (Illus.). 24p. (J). (gr. k-2). 1998. 18.50 (*1-57572-575-4*) Heinemann Lib.

Miller, Michaela. Hamsters. LC 97-11984. (Pet Ser.). (Illus.). 24p. (J). 1998. 18.50 (*1-57572-576-2*) Heinemann Lib.

— Rabbits. LC 97-11986. (Pet Ser.). (Illus.). 24p. (J). 1998. 18.50 (*1-57572-577-0*) Heinemann Lib.

Miller, Michaerl, ed. see Felder, Linda & Powell, Robert.

Miller, Michele G., jt. auth. see Brantley, Clarice P.

Miller, Michele G., jt. auth. see Hulbert, Jack E.

Miller, Michelle. Hunger in the First Person Singular: Stories of Desire & Power. LC 92-72299. (Illus.). 176p. (Orig.). 1993. pap. 9.00 (*0-938513-15-X*) Amador Pubs.

Miller, Michelle, et al. Adolescent Relationships & Drug Use. LC 99-34292. (Volume in LEA's Communication Ser.). 224p. 1999. write for info. (*0-8058-3435-4*) L Erlbaum Assocs.

***Miller, Michelle, et al.** Adolescent Relationships & Drug Use. LC 99-34292. (Volume in LEA's Communication Ser.). 224p. 1999. pap. write for info. (*0-8058-3436-2*) L Erlbaum Assocs.

Miller, Michelle A., jt. auth. see Miller, Thomas I.

Miller, Mike. Hootie: How the Blowfish Put Pop Back into Pop Rock. LC 97-2711. (Illus.). 224p. 1997. 29.95 (*1-887714-11-1*); pap. 10.00 (*1-887714-12-X*) Summerhse Pr.

— Lycos Personal Internet Guide. LC 98-86987. 1998. pap. text 12.99 (*0-7897-1831-6*) Que.

— Missouri Gardener's Guide: The What, Where, When, How & Why of Gardening in Missouri. (Illus.). 424p. 1998. pap. 19.95 (*1-888608-50-1*) Cool Springs Pr.

***Miller, Mike.** Month by Month Gardening in Missouri. (Illus.). 320p. 2000. pap. 18.95 (*1-888608-25-0*) Cool Springs Pr.

— My Missouri Garden: A Gardener's Journal. (Illus.). 128p. 2000. spiral bd. 19.95 (*1-930604-08-4*) Cool Springs Pr.

Miller, Mike. Teach Yourself Netscape Netcenter in 10 Minutes. (Teach Yourself . . . Ser.). (Illus.). 238p. 1999. pap. 12.99 (*0-672-31637-4*) Sams.

— Using CompuServe. 3rd ed. (Illus.). 400p. 1996. 24.99 (*0-7897-0595-8*) Que.

— Using Windows 98: Preview Edition. LC 97-80710. 1997. 19.99 (*0-7897-1543-0*, Que New Media) MCP SW Interactive.

— Webster's New World Vocabulary of Success. 400p. 1998. pap. text 8.95 (*0-02-862328-2*, Pub. by Macmillan) S&S Trade.

— You're on the Air with Mike Miller. LC 74-78647. (Illus.). 155p. (Orig.). 1975. pap. 3.95 (*0-88435-001-0*) Chateau Pub.

An Asterisk (*) at the beginning of an entry indicates that the title is appearing for the first time.

Miller, Mike, et al. Alaska: A Golden Past, a Rich Future. (Illus.). 320p. (C). 1995. text 49.95 (*0-9634100-3-2*) Wyndham Pubns.

Miller, Mildred B. & Snyder, Bascha G. Kosher Gourmet Cookbook. LC 94-1531. (Illus.). 320p. 1994. reprint ed. pap. 7.95 (*0-486-28155-8*) Dover.

Miller, Mildred Farkash. A World Split Open. LC 98-89257. (Illus.). 128p. 1999. pap. 10.00 (*0-9668450-0-5*) Powderhorn Writers.

Miller, Millie & Nelson, Cyndi. Chanterelle: A Rocky Mountain Mushroom Book. (Pocket Nature Guides Ser.). (Illus.). 1986. pap. 5.95 (*0-933472-97-8*) Johnson Bks.

— Desert Critters: Plants & Animals of the Southwest. LC 96-219349. (Pocket Nature Guides Ser.). (Illus.). (Orig.). 1996. pap. 5.95 (*1-55566-172-6*) Johnson Bks.

— The Early Birds: Common Backyard Birds. (Pocket Nature Ser.). (Illus.). 1997. pap. 5.95 (*1-55566-205-6*) Johnson Bks.

— Hummers: Hummingbirds of North America. (Pocket Nature Guides Ser.). (Illus.). 1987. pap. 5.95 (*1-55566-012-6*) Johnson Bks.

— Painted Ladies: Butterflies of North America. (Illus.). (Orig.). 1993. pap. 5.95 (*1-55566-103-3*) Johnson Bks.

***Miller, Millie & Nelson, Cyndi.** The United States of America: A State-by-State Guide. LC 98-40926. (Illus.). 64p. (J). (gr. 3-7). 1999. 14.95 (*0-590-04374-9*, Pub. by Scholastic Inc) Penguin Putnam.

Miller, Milo H. Ellis: History & Genealogy of the John Ellis Family, 1797-1935. (Illus.). 165p. 1997. reprint ed. pap. 29.00 (*0-8328-8470-7*); reprint ed. lib. bdg. 39.50 (*0-8328-8469-3*) Higginson Bk Co.

Miller, Miranda. A Thousand & One Coffee Mornings: Scenes from Arabia. LC 89-81667. 142p. 1990. 29.95 (*0-7206-0761-2*, Pub. by P Owen Ltd) Dufour.

Miller, Miriam. A History of the Early Years of the Roman Catholic Diocese of Charlotte. LC 84-9645. (Illus.). 208p. 1984. 20.95 (*0-9624488-1-8*) Laney-Smith.

Miller, Miriam Y. & Chance, Jane, eds. Approaches to Teaching Sir Gawain & the Green Knight. LC 85-21548. (Approaches to Teaching World Literature Ser.: No. 9). xii, 256p. 1986. pap. 18.00 (*0-87352-492-6*, AP09P); lib. bdg. 37.50 (*0-87352-491-8*, AP09C) Modern Lang.

Miller, Mitchell H., Jr. Plato's Parmenides: The Conversion of the Soul. 314p. 1991. pap. 16.95 (*0-271-00803-2*) Pa St U Pr.

Miller, Mitchell H. Plato's Parmenides: The Conversion of the Soul. LC 85-43301. 314p. 1986. reprint ed. pap. 97.40 (*0-608-06477-7*, 206677400009) Bks Demand.

Miller, Mitchell W., jt. auth. see Cohen, Arnold B.

Miller, Mitra, et al. Managing the Corporate Intranet. LC 97-41086. 427p. 1998. pap. 39.99 (*0-471-19978-8*) Wiley.

Miller, Moira. Sandy MacStovie's Monster. (Illus.). 1994. pap. 21.00 (*1-899827-27-7*) St Mut.

— Whuppity Stoorie. (Illus.). 1994. pap. 21.00 (*1-899827-26-9*) St Mut.

Miller, Mona. Barbie Freckles! LC 93-73617. (Golden Super Shape Bks.). (Illus.). 24p. (J). (ps-k). 1997. pap. 3.29 (*0-307-10049-9*, 10049, Goldn Books) Gldn Bks Pub Co.

— Barbie Practice Makes Perfect. LC 96-77298. (Super Shape Bks.). (Illus.). (J). 3.29 (*0-307-10087-1*, 10087, Goldn Books) Gldn Bks Pub Co.

— Disney's Bambi. LC 97-74419. (Super Shape Bks.). (Illus.). 24p. (J). (ps-3). 1997. 3.29 (*0-307-10055-3*, 10055, Goldn Books) Gldn Bks Pub Co.

Miller, Morris. Debt & Environment: Converging Crises. 347p. pap. 19.95 (*92-1-100457-8*) UN.

Miller, Morris & Janis, Arthur. Modern Bookkeeping & Accounting. 2nd ed. LC 72-109961. (gr. 10-12). 1973. teacher ed. 8.48 (*0-02-830820-4*) Glencoe.

— Modern Bookkeeping & Accounting. 2nd ed. LC 72-109961. (YA). (gr. 10-12). 1973. student ed. 48.76 (*0-02-830830-1*) Glencoe.

Miller, Morton A. Reading & Writing Short Essays. 3rd ed. 416p. (C). 1986. pap. text 31.50 (*0-07-554763-5*) McGraw.

— Reading & Writing Short Essays. 3rd ed. 405p. 1986. pap. text. write for info. (*0-318-55406-2*) Random.

Miller, Moshe, tr. Tomer Devorah. 1994. 16.95 (*0-944070-99-X*) Targum Pr.

— Tzipisa Leyeshua. 1993. 13.95 (*0-944070-97-3*) Feldheim.

Miller, Moshe, tr. see Cordevero, Moshe.

Miller, Moshe L., tr. see Steinberg, Shalom D.

Miller, Muriel M. The Chintz Collectors Handbook. (Illus.). 150p. 1998. pap. 24.95 (*1-870703-03-0*, Pub. by Francis Jos Pubns) Krause Pubns.

***Miller, Muriel M.** Royal Winton Collectors Handbook from 1925: Cottage Ware, Art Deco, Lustre Ware, Pastels, Etc., Vol. 1. LC 99-216628. 1999. pap. 19.95 (*1-870703-23-5*) Krause Hse.

Miller, Myron, jt. auth. see Dispezio, Michael A.

Miller, N. Tacitus: Annals XV, Annals XV. (Latin Texts Ser.). (LAT.). 1994. pap. 22.95 (*1-85399-434-0*, Pub. by Brist Class Pr) Focus Pub-R Pullins.

Miller, N., ed. Tacitus: Annals I. (Bristol Latin Texts Ser.). (LAT.). 1989. pap. 20.95 (*1-85399-358-1*, Pub. by Brist Class Pr) Focus Pub-R Pullins.

Miller, N. S. The Pharmacology of Alcohol & Drugs of Abuse & Addiction. (Illus.). 312p. 1990. 99.00 (*0-387-97383-4*) Spr-Verlag.

Miller, N. S. & Gold, M. S. Alcohol, Vol. 2. LC 91-2391. (Drugs of Abuse: Vol. 2). (Illus.). 290p. (C). 1991. text 51.00 (*0-306-43641-8*, Kluwer Plenum) Kluwer Academic.

***Miller, Nadine.** Barbarian Earl. (Signet Regency Romance Ser.). 224p. 1999. mass mkt. 4.99 (*0-451-19887-5*) NAL.

Miller, Nadine. Unlikely Angel. 224p. 1998. mass mkt. 4.99 (*0-451-19467-5*, Sig) NAL.

***Miller, Nancy.** Bible Pictures & Stories. Sisters, Yoder, tr.Tr. of Dibujos e Historias de la Biblia. (SPA., Illus.). 64p. (J). (ps-3). 1998. pap. 2.15 (*0-7399-0318-7*, 2492.1) Rod & Staff.

Miller, Nancy. Clutterology: Getting Rid of Clutter & Getting Organized! LC 97-94722. (Illus.). 192p. 1999. pap. 19.95 (*0-9629944-0-5*) CPM Systems.

— Subject to Change: Women's Writing--Feminist Reading. (Gender & Culture Ser.). 185p. 1989. pap. text 18.50 (*0-231-06661-9*) Col U Pr.

Miller, Nancy, jt. auth. see Rounds, Michael F.

Miller, Nancy, ed. see Bosakowski, Thomas.

Miller, Nancy, ed. see Chase, Harold S.

Miller, Nancy, ed. see Dekker, Dick.

Miller, Nancy, ed. see Krantz, Grover S.

Miller, Nancy, ed. see Mazonson, Peter.

Miller, Nancy B. Dance Me along the Path: A Collection of Poems. LC 96-71669. (Illus.). 96p. (Orig.). 1997. pap. 11.00 (*1-881539-15-6*) Tabby Hse Bks.

— Nobody's Perfect: Living & Growing with Children Who Have Special Needs. LC 93-2556. (Illus.). 272p. 1993. pap. 21.00 (*1-55766-143-X*) P H Brookes.

Miller, Nancy B. & Sammons, Catherine C. Everybody's Different: Understanding & Changing Our Reactions to Disabilities. LC 98-51018. 384p. 1999. pap. 21.95 (*1-55766-359-9*, 3599) P H Brookes.

Miller, Nancy B., jt. auth. see Falk, R. Frank.

Miller, Nancy E. Cost-effectiveness of Psychotherapy: A Guide for Practitioners, Researchers, & Policymakers. LC 97-43075. (Illus.). 384p. 1999. text 55.00 (*0-19-511458-2*) OUP.

— File Structures: With Ada. Apt, Alan, ed. (Illus.). 600p. (C). 1990. teacher ed. write for info. (*0-318-63300-0*); disk. write for info. (*0-8053-0441-X*) Benjamin-Cummings.

Miller, Nancy E. File Structures Using Pascal. LC 86-21641. 487p. (C). 1987. 62.00 (*0-8053-7082-X*) Benjamin-Cummings.

Miller, Nancy E. File Structures with ADA. Apt, Alan, ed. (Illus.). 600p. (C). 1990. 62.00 (*0-8053-0440-1*) Benjamin-Cummings.

Miller, Nancy E. & Cohen, Gene D., eds. Clinical Aspects of Alzheimer's Disease & Senile Dementia. LC 80-39741. (Aging Ser.: No. 15). 371p. 1981. reprint ed. pap. 115.10 (*0-608-00592-4*, 206117900007) Bks Demand.

Miller, Nancy E., jt. auth. see Petersen, Charles G.

Miller, Nancy H. & Taylor, Craig B. Lifestyle Management for Patients with Coronary Heart Disease. LC 95-177. (Current Issues in Cardiac Rehabilitation Ser.: Monograph No. 2). 144p. (Orig.). 1995. pap. text 24.00 (*0-87322-441-8*, BHOU0441) Human Kinetics.

***Miller, Nancy K.** Bequest & Betrayal: Memoirs of a Parent's Death. LC 99-48635. (Illus.). 208p. 2000. pap. 14.95 (*0-253-21379-7*) Ind U Pr.

Miller, Nancy K. French Dressing: Women, Men, & Ancient Regime Fiction. LC 94-16707. 250p. (C). 1994. pap. 24.99 (*0-415-90322-X*, A4597) Routledge.

— Getting Personal: Feminist Occasions & Other Autobiographical Acts. 180p. (C). 1991. pap. 20.00 (*0-415-90324-6*, A4604) Routledge.

Miller, Nancy K., ed. Bequest & Betrayal: Memoirs of a Parent's Death. (Illus.). 208p. 1996. 23.00 (*0-19-509130-2*) OUP.

Miller, Nancy K., ed. The Poetics of Gender. LC 85-29904. (Gender & Culture Ser.). 272p. 1987. pap. text 21.00 (*0-231-06311-3*) Col U Pr.

Miller, Nancy K., ed. see Awkward, Michael.

Miller, Nancy K., jt. ed. see DeJean, Joan.

Miller, Nancy K., ed. see Heilbrun, Carolyn G.

Miller, Nancy K., ed. see Schor, Naomi.

***Miller, Naomi.** Mapping Cities. (Illus.). 92p. 2000. pap. 20.00 (*1-881450-13-9*) U of Wash Pr.

Miller, Naomi & Morgan, Keith. Boston Architecture, 1975-1990. (Illus.). 272p. 1996. pap. 29.95 (*3-7913-1679-6*, Pub. by Prestel) te Neues.

***Miller, Naomi & Yavneh, Naomi, eds.** Maternal Measures: Figuring Caregiving in the Early Modern Period. LC 99-55005. (Women & Gender in Early Modern England, 1500-1750 Ser.). (Illus.). 400p. 2000. text 70.95 (*0-7546-0031-9*, Pub. by Ashgate Pub) Ashgate Pub Co.

Miller, Naomi F. The Archaeology of Garden & Field. 248p. (C). 1998. pap. text 14.95 (*0-8122-1641-5*) U of Pa Pr.

Miller, Naomi F. & Gleason, Kathryn L., eds. The Archaeology of Garden & Field. (Illus.). 248p. (C). 1994. text 29.95 (*0-8122-3244-5*) U of Pa Pr.

Miller, Naomi J. Changing the Subject: Mary Wroth & Figurations of Gender in Early Modern England. (Studies in the English Renaissance). 256p. 1996. text 34.95 (*0-8131-1964-2*) U Pr of Ky.

Miller, Naomi J. & Waller, Gary, eds. Reading Mary Wroth: Representing Alternatives in Early Modern England. LC 91-390. 256p. (C). 1991. pap. text 20.00 (*0-87049-710-3*) U of Tenn Pr.

Miller, Natalie. The Statue of Liberty. LC 91-44647. (Cornerstones to Freedom Ser.). (Illus.). 32p. (J). (gr. 4-7). 1992. lib. bdg. 19.50 (*0-516-06655-2*) Childrens.

— The Statue of Liberty. LC 91-44647. (Cornerstones to Freedom Ser.). (Illus.). 32p. (J). (gr. 4-7). 1993. pap. 5.95 (*0-516-46655-0*) Childrens.

Miller, Nathan. The Naval Air War, 1939-1945. 21.95 (*0-405-13277-8*) Ayer.

***Miller, Nathan.** Spying for America: The Hidden History of U. S. Intelligence. (Illus.). 491p. 1999. reprint ed. pap. text 15.00 (*0-7881-6304-3*) DIANE Pub.

Miller, Nathan. Spying for America: The Hidden History of U. S. Intelligence. 2nd ed. LC 98-159944. 512p. 1997. pap. text 14.95 (*1-56924-721-8*) Marlowe & Co.

— Star-Spangled Men: America's Ten Worst Presidents. LC 97-35655. (Illus.). 272p. 1998. 22.50 (*0-684-83610-6*) S&S Trade.

— Star-Spangled Men: America's Ten Worst Presidents. 272p. 1999. pap. 13.00 (*0-684-85206-3*, Touchstone) S&S Trade Pap.

— Theodore Roosevelt: A Life. 1994. pap. 17.00 (*0-688-13220-0*, Quil) HarperTrade.

— The U. S. Navy: A History. 3rd ed. LC 97-26244. (Illus.). 328p. 1997. pap. 22.95 (*1-55750-595-0*) Naval Inst Pr.

— War at Sea: A Naval History of World War II. 576p. 1995. 32.50 (*0-684-80380-1*) S&S Trade.

— War at Sea: A Naval History of World War II. (Illus.). 608p. 1997. reprint ed. pap. 19.95 (*0-19-511038-2*) OUP.

Miller, Neal E. & Dollard, John. Social Learning & Imitation. LC 78-23728. (Illus.). 341p. 1979. reprint ed. lib. bdg. 35.00 (*0-313-20714-3*, MISL, Greenwood Pr) Greenwood.

Miller, Ned. Emmett's Snowball. LC 89-77787. (Illus.). 40p. (J). (ps-2). 1995. 14.95 (*0-8050-1394-6*, Bks Young Read) H Holt & Co.

— Emmett's Snowball. (Illus.). 32p. (J). (gr. k-2). 1999. reprint ed. pap. 5.95 (*0-8050-4455-8*) H Holt & Co.

Miller, Ned, ed. see Clarke, Richard.

Miller, Neil. Conversation in Portuguese: Points of Departure. 2nd rev. ed. LC 80-83025. (Illus.). (Orig.). (C). 1980. pap. text 11.95 (*0-9601444-2-0*) N Miller.

— Ecology Simulations for Use in the Introductory Biology Laboratory. 37p. (C). 1992. pap. text 6.76 (*0-669-29739-9*) HM Trade Div.

— Gay Life. 1992. write for info. (*0-679-41241-7*) McKay.

Miller, Neil & Newman, Nancy. Walsh & Hoyt's Clinical Neuro-Ophthalmology, 5 vols. (Illus.). 1997. write for info. (*0-683-06034-1*) Lppncott W & W.

Miller, Neil R,. Walsh & Hoyt's Clinical Neuro-Ophthalmology, Vol. 1. 4th ed. (Illus.). 382p. 1982. lib. bdg. 115.00 (*0-683-06020-1*) Lppncott W & W.

Miller, Neil R. Walsh & Hoyt's Clinical Neuro-Ophthalmology, Vol. 2. 4th ed. (Illus.). 750p. 1984. 135.00 (*0-683-06021-X*) Lppncott W & W.

— Walsh & Hoyt's Clinical Neuro-Ophthalmology: Infections & Inflammation of the Central Nervous System & Non-organic (Functional) Neuro-Opthalmologic Disease, Vol. 5, Pts. 1 & 2. 4th ed. (Illus.). 2693p. 1994. 225.00 (*0-683-06024-4*) Lppncott W & W.

— Walsh & Hoyt's Clinical Neuro-Ophthalmology Vol. 4: Vascular Disease, Vol. 4. 4th ed. (Illus.). 947p. 1991. 170.00 (*0-683-06023-6*) Lppncott W & W.

Miller, Neil R., ed. Walsh & Hoyt's Clinical Neuro-Ophthalmology, Vol. 3. 4th ed. 734p. 1987. 140.00 (*0-683-06022-8*) Lppncott W & W.

Miller, Neil R. & Newman, Nancy J. The Essentials: Walsh & Hoyt's Clinical Neuro-Opthalmology. 5th ed. LC 98-21736. 820p. 1998. pap. 69.00 (*0-683-30682-0*) Lppncott W & W.

Miller, Neil R., et al. Walsh & Hoyt's Clinical Neuro-Ophthalmology, Vol. 1. 5th ed. LC 96-50372. 1816p. 1997. 175.00 (*0-683-30230-2*) Lppncott W & W.

— Walsh & Hoyt's Clinical Neuro-Ophthalmology, Vol. 2. 5th ed. LC 96-50372. 1110p. 1997. 175.00 (*0-683-30231-0*) Lppncott W & W.

— Walsh & Hoyt's Clinical Neuro-Ophthalmology, Vol. 3. 5th ed. LC 96-50372. 1088p. 1998. 175.00 (*0-683-30232-9*) Lppncott W & W.

— Walsh & Hoyt's Clinical Neuro-Ophthalmology, Vol. 4. 5th ed. LC 96-50372. 1022p. 1998. 175.00 (*0-683-30233-7*) Lppncott W & W.

— Walsh & Hoyt's Clinical Neuro-Ophthalmology, Vol. 5, Pts. 1 & 2. 5th ed. LC 96-50372. 819p. 1998. 175.00 (*0-683-30234-5*) Lppncott W & W.

Miller, Neil Z. Immunization Theory vs. Reality: Expose on Vaccinations. LC 95-69726. (Illus.). 160p. (Orig.). 1995. pap. 12.95 (*1-881217-12-4*) New Atlantean.

— Immunizations: The People Speak! Questions, Comments, & Concerns about Vaccinations. LC 95-72728. (Illus.). 80p. (Orig.). 1996. pap. 8.95 (*1-881217-16-7*) New Atlantean.

— Vaccine Roulette: Gambling with Your Child's Life. 32p. (Orig.). 1995. pap. 5.95 (*1-881217-09-4*) New Atlantean.

— Vaccine Seminar: Critical Data for New Parents & Health Practitioners. 40p. (Orig.). 1995. pap. 6.95 (*1-881217-08-6*) New Atlantean.

— Vaccines: Are They Really Safe & Effective? 8th rev. ed. LC 92-81105. (Illus.). 80p. 1998. pap. 8.95 (*1-881217-10-8*) New Atlantean.

Miller, Neva F., et al, eds. Analytical Lexicon of the Greek New Testament. (Greek Testament Library). 504p. 2000. 44.99 (*0-8010-2135-9*) Baker Bks.

Miller, Newton W. & Navarre, Monty, eds. The Airguide Manual. 2nd ed. 1207p. 1987. pap. write for info. (*0-934754-01-2*) Airguide Pubns.

Miller, Newton W., jt. auth. see Goldstein, Avram.

Miller, Nicholas J. Between Nation & State: Serbian Politics in Croatia, Before the First World War. LC 97-4821. (Series in Russian & East European Studies). (Illus.). 280p. 1998. text 45.00 (*0-8229-3989-4*) U of Pittsburgh Pr.

Miller, Nicholas R. Committees, Agendas, & Voting. LC 94-6282. (Fundamentals of Pure & Applied Economics Ser.). x, 162p. 1995. pap. text 26.00 (*3-7186-5569-1*) Gordon & Breach.

Miller, Nicola. In the Shadow of the State: Intellectuals & the Quest for National Identity in Twentieth-Century Spanish America. 1999. 60.00 (*1-85984-738-2*, Pub. by Verso); pap. text 20.00 (*1-85984-205-4*, Pub. by Verso) Norton.

Miller, Nicole M. Curiosity Shop: Amazing Fish. 17p. 1998. 39.95 (*1-878631-43-8*) S Kovalik.

Miller, Niela. Counseling in Genderland: A Guide for You & Your Transgendered Client. (Illus.). 200p. (Orig.). 1996. pap. 29.95 (*0-9626262-6-0*) Different Path Pr.

Miller, Nina. Heart of Hulda: A Biography. (Illus.). 142p. (Orig.). reprint ed. pap. 12.95 (*0-940151-07-3*) Statesman-Exam.

— Making Love Modern: The Intimate Public Worlds of New York's Literary Women. LC 97-44487. 304p. 1999. pap. 18.95 (*0-19-511605-4*) OUP.

Miller, Nita Q., jt. auth. see Miller, J. R.

Miller, Nod, jt. auth. see Boud, David.

Miller, Norbert & Salaquarda, Jorg, eds. Nietzsche - Briefweshsel, Kritische Gesamtausgabe: I, Abtielung, Vierter Band Nachbericht Zu Abteilung I: Briefe Von und An Friedrich Nietzsche Oktober 1849-April 1869. (GER.). viii, 960p. 1993. lib. bdg. 276.95 (*3-11-012277-4*) De Gruyter.

Miller, Norbert, ed. see Alexis, Willibald.

Miller, Norma. Swingin' at the Savoy: The Memoir of a Jazz Dancer. LC 96-20104. (Illus.). 310p. 1996. 29.95 (*1-56639-494-5*) Temple U Pr.

Miller, Norma, jt. auth. see Walton, Stuart.

Miller, Norma, tr. & intro. see Menander.

Miller, Norma L., ed. The Healthy School Handbook: Conquering the Sick Building Syndrome & Other Environmental Hazards in & Around Your School. LC 95-6345. 1995. pap. 21.95 (*0-8106-1863-X*, NEA Prof Lib) NEA.

Miller, Norman, ed. AIDS in Africa: The Social Impact & Policy Issues. LC 88-12750. (Studies in African Health & Medicine: Vol. 1). 350p. 1989. lib. bdg. 99.95 (*0-88946-187-2*) E Mellen.

Miller, Norman, et al, eds. Principles of Addiction Medicine: ASAM Review Course Syllabus. 1000p. 1994. 140.00 (*1-880425-02-5*) Am Soc Addict Med.

Miller, Norman & Brewer, Marilynn B. Intergroup Relations. Manstead, Anthony S., ed. (Mapping Social Psychology Ser.). 160p. 1996. 9.00 (*0-335-09261-6*); pap. 2.00 (*0-335-09260-8*) OpUniv Pr.

Miller, Norman & Yeager, Rodger. Kenya: The Quest for Prosperity. 2nd ed. (Profiles - Nations of Contemporary Africa Ser.). 254p. (C). 1993. pap. 27.00 (*0-8133-8202-5*, Pub. by Westview) HarpC.

Miller, Norman, et al. Group Process, Group Decision, Group Action. Manstead, Anthony S., ed. (Mapping Social Psychology Ser.). 256p. 1992. pap. 30.95 (*0-335-09862-2*) OpUniv Pr.

Miller, Norman, jt. ed. see Hertz-Lazarowitz, Rachel.

Miller, Norman C. Garcia Lorca's Poema del Cante Jondo. (Monografias A Ser.: Vol. LXV). 226p. (C). 1977. 51.00 (*0-7293-0048-X*, Pub. by Tamesis Bks Ltd) Boydell & Brewer.

Miller, Norman G. & Goebel, Paul R. The Buyer, Seller & Broker's Guide to Creative Home Finance. (Illus.). 464p. 1986. 14.95 (*0-13-109413-0*) P-H.

Miller, Norman G., jt. auth. see Geltner, David.

Miller, Norman G., jt. auth. see Goebel, Paul R.

Miller, Norman J., jt. auth. see Sanden, John H.

Miller, Norman M. & Cave, Hugh B. I Took the Sky Road. LC 79-21830. 1980. reprint ed. 19.95 (*0-89201-089-4*) Zenger Pub.

Miller, Norman N., jt. ed. see Yeager, Rodger.

Miller, Norman S. Addiction Psychiatry: Current Diagnosis & Treatment. LC 94-32386. 300p. 1995. 84.50 (*0-471-56201-7*) Wiley.

Miller, Norman S., ed. Comprehensive Handbook of Drug & Alcohol Addiction. (Illus.). 1360p. 1991. text 99.75 (*0-8247-8474-X*) Dekker.

— The Principles & Practice of Addictions in Psychitry. LC 95-20662. (Illus.). 589p. 1997. 73.00 (*0-7216-5211-5*, W B Saunders Co) Harcrt Hlth Sci Grp.

— Treating Coexisting Psychiatric & Addictive Disorders: A Practical Guide. LC 94-4696. 1994. 24.95 (*0-89486-972-8*, 1499) Hazelden.

Miller, Norman S., ed. Treatment of the Addictions: Applications of Outcome Research for Clinical Management. LC 94-22157. (Alcoholism Treatment Quarterly Ser.: Vol. 12, No. 2). (Illus.). 135p. 1994. lib. bdg. 39.95 (*1-56024-686-3*) Haworth Pr.

Miller, Norman S., et al, eds. Manual of Therapeutics for Addictions. LC 96-30946. 364p. 1997. pap. 67.50 (*0-471-56176-2*) Wiley.

Miller, Norman S., intro. Treatment of the Addictions: Applications of Outcome Research for Clinical Management. LC 94-22157. (Alcoholism Treatment Quarterly Ser.: Vol. 12, No. 2). (Illus.). 135p. 1994. pap. 14.95 (*1-56023-064-9*, Harrington Park) Haworth Pr.

Miller, Norman S. & Gold, Mark S., eds. Pharmacological Therapies for Drug & Alcohol Addictions. LC 94-3755. (Illus.). 480p. 1994. text 165.00 (*0-8247-8979-2*) Dekker.

Miller, Norman S. & Stimmel, Barry, eds. The Integration of Pharmacological & Nonpharmacological Treatments in Drug - Alcohol Addictions. LC 97-31682. (Journal of Addictive Diseases Monograph Ser.: Vol. 16, No. 4). 122p. 1997. 39.95 (*0-7890-0375-9*, Pharmctl Prods) Haworth Pr.

Miller, Norton G., ed. Bryophyte Systematics. (Advances in Bryology Ser.: Vol. 4). (GER., Illus.). viii, 264p. 1991. 95.00 (*3-443-52002-2*, Pub. by Gebruder Borntraeger) Balogh.

— Bryophyte Ultrastructure: Publication of the International Association of Bryologists. (Advances in Bryology Ser.: Vol. 3). (GER., Illus.). vii, 281p. 1988. 71.00 (*3-443-52001-4*, Pub. by Gebruder Borntraeger) Balogh.

Miller, Norton G., et al, eds. Biology of Sphagnum. (Advances in Bryology Ser.: Vol. 5). (GER., Illus.). viii, 338p. 1993. 106.00 (*3-443-52003-0*, Pub. by Gebruder Borntraeger) Balogh.

Miller, Nyle H. & Snell, Joseph W. Great Gunfighters of the Kansas Cowtowns, 1867-1886. LC 63-63480. (Illus.). v, 498p. 1967. pap. 19.95 (*0-8032-5137-8*, Bison Books) U of Nebr Pr.

Miller, O. D. Har-Moad, or The Mountain of the Assembly: A Series of Esoteric Archaelogical Studies. (Illus.). 445p. 1998. reprint ed. pap. 39.95 (*1-55818-459-7*) Holmes Pub.
Miller, O. Victor. One Man's Junk. George, Roberta & Phillips, Nancy, eds. 159p. (Orig.). 1995. pap. 10.00 (*0-9638364-1-2*) Snake Nation.
Miller, O. Victor & Hotz, James A. Where Remedies Lie. Emond, Louis, ed. LC 98-125966. (Illus.). x, 320p. 1997. 29.95 (*0-9658029-0-6*) Caduceus Pr.
Miller, Oaky. One Hundred One Ways to Dump on Your Ex! The All-Purpose Get Even! Book. (Illus.). 108p. (Orig.). 1986. pap. 5.95 (*0-930753-01-1*) Spect Ln Pr.
Miller, Olin, compiled by. 4000 Errors & Unfavorable Bible Verses. 34p. 1996. reprint ed. spiral bd. 8.00 (*0-7873-1308-4*) Hlth Research.
Miller, Olive B. Heroes, Outlaws & Funny Fellows of America. LC 72-96306. (Illus.). 332p. 1973. reprint ed. lib. bdg. 46.00 (*0-8154-0468-9*) Cooper Sq.
Miller, Olive T. Bird-Lover in the West. LC 76-125753. (American Environmental Studies). 1971. reprint ed. 19.95 (*0-405-02679-X*) Ayer.
***Miller, Orlando J. & Therman, Eeva.** Human Chromosomes. 4th ed. LC 00-44007. 2000. pap. write for info. (*0-387-95046-X*) Spr-Verlag.
Miller, Orlando W. The Frontier in Alaska & the Matanuska Colony. LC 74-82747. (Yale Western Americana Ser.: No. 26). 340p. reprint ed. pap. 105.40 (*0-7837-3303-8*, 205770500006) Bks Demand.
Miller, Orson K., Jr., jt. auth. see Miller, Hope H.
Miller, Oscar, Jr. Employee Turnover in the Public Sector. rev. ed. LC 95-52899. (Garland Studies in the History of American Labor). 126p. 1996. text 47.00 (*0-8153-2403-0*) Garland.
Miller, Oscar J. & Schwartz, Mortimer D. Recommended Publications for Legal Research, 1981. LC 87-10106. 1987. 37.50 (*0-8377-2533-X*, Rothman) W S Hein.
— Recommended Publications for Legal Research, 1983. LC 87-4837. 1987. 37.50 (*0-8377-2531-3*, Rothman) W S Hein.
— Recommended Publications for Legal Research, 1984. LC 86-3253. 1986. 37.50 (*0-8377-2528-3*, Rothman) W S Hein.
— Recommended Publications for Legal Research, 1985. LC 86-31543. 1987. 37.50 (*0-8377-2530-5*, Rothman) W S Hein.
— Recommended Publications for Legal Research, 1986. LC 87-12723. 1987. 37.50 (*0-8377-2532-1*, Rothman) W S Hein.
Miller, Oscar J. & Schwartz, Mortimer D., compiled by. Recommended Publications for Legal Research, 1979. 1985. pap. text 37.50 (*0-8377-2527-5*, Rothman) W S Hein.
Miller, Oscar J., et al. Recommended Publications for Legal Research, 1980. LC 86-17669. 1986. 37.50 (*0-8377-2529-1*, Rothman) W S Hein.
Miller, Oscar R., jt. auth. see Miller, Betty A.
Miller, Owen J., jt. ed. see Valdes, Mario J.
Miller, P. The Cooperative Extension Service: Paradoxical Servant. LC 73-8308. (Landmark Ser.: No. 2). 1973. pap. text 2.00 (*0-87060-060-5*, LNH 2) Syracuse U Cont Ed.
— The Gardener's Dictionary. 1969. reprint ed. 120.00 (*3-7682-0613-0*) Lubrecht & Cramer.
Miller, P. & Loates, M. Collins Pocket Guide: Fish of Britain & Europe. (Illus.). 288p. 1997. pap. 24.95 (*0-00-219945-9*, Pub. by HarpC) Trafalgar.
Miller, P. & McBride, J. R., eds. Oxidant Air Pollution Impacts in the Montane Forests of Southern California: The San Bernadino Mountain Case Study. LC 98-11498. (Ecological Studies: Vol. 134). (Illus.). 464p. 1998. 139.00 (*0-387-98493-3*) Spr-Verlag.
Miller, P. B. L. A.'s 99 Best Hole-in-the-Wall Restaurants: A Paul Wallach Guide. Ramirez, Lynette, ed. 1989. 6.95 (*0-9619156-2-5*) P Wallach.
Miller, P. C., ed. Resource Use by Chaparral & Matorral: A Comparison of Vegetation Function in Two Mediterranean Type Ecosystems. (Ecological Studies: Vol. 39). (Illus.). 416p. 1981. 156.00 (*0-387-90556-1*) Spr-Verlag.
***Miller, P. E.** Implementing IPV 6: Supporting the Next Generation. 2nd ed. LC 99-51488. 432p. 2000. pap. 49.99 (*0-7645-4589-2*) IDG Bks.
Miller, P. L., ed. Selected Topics in Medical Artificial Intelligence. (Computers & Medicine Ser.). (Illus.). 220p. 1988. 74.00 (*0-387-96701-X*) Spr-Verlag.
Miller, P. L., ed. see Society for Experimental Biology (Great Britain).
Miller, P. R. & Pollard, H. L., eds. Multilingual Compendium of Plant Diseases, Vol. 2. LC 75-46932. 434p. 1977. 48.00 (*0-89054-020-9*) Am Phytopathol Soc.
Miller, P. Schuyler. Alicia in Blunderland. 1983. 10.00 (*1-880418-22-3*) D M Grant.
Miller, Paddy J. Cash, Credit, or Murder Accepted. 376p. (Orig.). 1996. pap. 16.95 (*0-89896-268-4*) Larksdale.
— Lies in the Family Album. 288p. 1994. pap. 12.95 (*0-89896-291-9*) Larksdale.
Miller, Page P. A Claim to New Roles. LC 85-2249. (American Theological Library Association Monograph: No. 22). 253p. 1985. 26.50 (*0-8108-1809-4*) Scarecrow.
Miller, Page P., ed. Reclaiming the Past: Landmarks of Women's History. LC 91-46604. (Illus.). 239p. reprint ed. pap. 74.10 (*0-608-09351-3*, 205409700002) Bks Demand.
Miller, Pam. Farmer McFee. (Whole-Language Big Bks.). (Illus.). 16p. (Orig.). (J). (ps-2). 1994. pap. 16.95 (*1-56784-069-8*) Newbridge Educ.
— El Granjero Garces. Palacios, Argentina, tr. (Spanish Whole Language Big Bks.).Tr. of Farmer McFee. (SPA., Illus.). 16p. (Orig.). (J). (ps-2). 1994. pap. 14.95 (*1-56784-096-5*) Newbridge Educ.
Miller, Pamela. Fast Little Shoes. 40p. (Orig.). 1986. pap. 3.00 (*0-942582-11-X*) Erie St Pr.
— The McCord Museum Archives. (Illus.). 32p. 1993. pap. 29.95 (*0-7735-0965-8*, Pub. by McG-Queens Univ Pr) CUP Services.
— The Vision Care Assistant: An Introductory Handbook. 3rd ed. Corngold, Sally M., ed. 144p. 1999. lib. bdg. 22.00 (*0-929780-01-9*) VisionExtension.
Miller, Pamela, ed. Eighteen Seventy Census Index to Hamilton County, Ohio Including Cincinnati. (Illus.). 400p. 1988. lib. bdg. 235.00 (*0-945302-00-2*) Egeon Enterprises.
Miller, Pamela, et al. The McCord Family: A Passionate Vision. (Illus.). 144p. 1993. pap. 44.95 (*0-7735-0971-2*, Pub. by McG-Queens Univ Pr) CUP Services.
Miller, Pamela, ed. see Ching Hai, Suma.
Miller, Pamela C., jt. auth. see Anderson, Kathleen.
Miller, Pamela J. A Handbook for the Ophthalmic Practice: Documentation & Record Keeping Made Easy. LC 97-20888. 124p. (Orig.). 1997. pap. 25.00 (*0-943599-91-1*) OEPF.
— The Introductory Handbook for the Contact Lens Assistant. Corngold, Sally M., ed. LC 95-13939. (Illus.). 114p. (C). 1995. lib. bdg. 19.50 (*0-929780-06-X*) VisionExtension.
Miller, Pat. Gabby Gourmet. 10th ed. 1992. pap. 7.95 (*0-918481-09-0*) TDF Pub.
Miller, Pat, et al. The Serendipity Cookbook: The Best from New York's Incredible Dessert Emporium. LC 94-20351. (Illus.). 240p. 1994. pap. 14.95 (*0-8065-1541-4*, Citadel Pr) Carol Pub Group.
Miller, Pat P. Script Supervising & Film Continuity. 2nd ed. (Illus.). 228p. 1990. pap. 32.95 (*0-240-80018-4*, Focal) Buttrwrth-Heinemann.
— Script Supervising & Film Continuity. 3rd ed. 236p. 1999. pap. 24.95 (*0-240-80294-2*, Focal) Buttrwrth-Heinemann.
Miller, Patrice M., jt. ed. see Demick, Jack.
Miller, Patricia. Provisioning (How-To for Pleasure Boaters) 2000. 12.95 (*0-9638470-2-3*) Pt Loma Pubng.
Miller, Patricia, compiled by. Connecticut 18th Century Epitaphs. 2nd ed. (Illus.). 90p. 1999. reprint ed. pap. 14.95 (*0-930194-23-3*) Ctr Thanatology.
Miller, Patricia, jt. auth. see Miller, Dale.
Miller, Patricia, jt. auth. see Rains, John.
Miller, Patricia A., et al. American Health Line 50-State Report. Knoll, Sara R., ed. 134p. (C). 1996. write for info. (*0-614-14544-9*) APN Inc.
Miller, Patricia C. Dreams in Late Antiquity: Studies in the Imagination of a Culture. LC 93-40363. 288p. 1994. text 49.50 (*0-691-07422-4*, Pub. by Princeton U Pr); pap. text 16.95 (*0-691-05835-0*, Pub. by Princeton U Pr) Cal Prin Full Svc.
***Miller, Patricia C.** Dresden: A Poem. 8p. 1999. pap. 3.00 (*1-884235-23-9*) Helicon Nine Eds.
Miller, Patricia C. Westport: Missouri's Port of Many Returns. LC 83-17523. (Illus.). 128p. 1983. 15.00 (*0-913504-82-3*) Lowell Pr.
Miller, Patricia C. & Robertson, John, eds. Rockhurst Review: A Fine Arts Journal. 120p. (Orig.). 1997. pap. 6.00 (*1-886761-09-4*) Rockhurst Col.
Miller, Patricia D., ed. Fitness Programming & Physical Disability: A Publication for Disabled Sports U. S. A. LC 94-4961. 232p. 1995. pap. text 30.00 (*0-87322-434-5*, BMIL0434) Human Kinetics.
Miller, Patricia H. Theories of Development Psychology. 3rd ed. LC 92-37252. (C). 1993. text 28.00 (*0-7167-2308-5*) W H Freeman.
— Theories of Development Psychology. 3rd ed. LC 92-37252. 498p. (C). 1998. pap. 38.95 (*0-7167-2309-3*) W H Freeman.
***Miller, Patricia H. & Scholnick, Ellin K.** Toward Feminist Developmental Psychology. LC 99-33632. 320p. 2000. text 80.00 (*0-415-92177-5*) Routledge.
***Miller, Patricia H. & Scholnick, Ellin Kofsky, eds.** Toward Feminist Developmental Psychology. LC 99-33632. 320p. (C). 2000. pap. 23.99 (*0-415-92178-3*) Routledge.
Miller, Patricia M. Sex Is Not a Four-Letter Word! Talking Sex with Children Made Easier. 176p. (Orig.). 1994. pap. 14.95 (*0-8245-1437-8*) Crossroad NY.
Miller, Patricia S. & McDowelle, James O. Administering Preschool Programs in Public Schools: Practitioner's Handbook. LC 92-20133. (Illus.). 298p. (Orig.). (C). 1992. pap. text 39.95 (*1-879105-78-0*, 0341) Thomson Learn.
Miller, Patrick. Psalms. (Interpreting Biblical Texts Ser.). 2001. 18.95 (*0-687-00845-X*) Abingdon.
Miller, Patrick, jt. auth. see Falk, Charles.
Miller, Patrick, ed. see Brueggemann, Walter.
Miller, Patrick D. Deuteronomy. (Interpretation: a Bible Commentary for Preaching & Teaching Ser.). 276p. 1990. text 25.00 (*0-8042-3105-2*) Westminster John Knox.
Miller, Patrick D., Jr. Interpreting the Psalms. LC 85-16258. 176p. 1986. pap. 17.00 (*0-8006-1896-3*, 1-1896, Fortress Pr) Augsburg Fortress.
***Miller, Patrick D.** Religion of Ancient Israel. (Library of Ancient Israel). 264p. 2000. 39.95 (*0-664-22145-9*) Westminster John Knox.
Miller, Patrick D. They Cried to the Lord: The Form & Theology of Biblical Prayer. LC 94-10750. 480p. 1994. pap. 28.00 (*0-8006-2762-8*, 1-2762, Fortress Pr) Augsburg Fortress.
Miller, Patrick D. & Roberts, J. M. The Hand of the Lord: A Reassessment of the "Ark Narrative" of Samuel. LC 76-48737. (Johns Hopkins Near Eastern Studies). 128p. reprint ed. pap. 39.70 (*0-608-12635-7*, 201095900072) Bks Demand.
Miller, Patrick D., jt. auth. see Brueggemann, Walter.
Miller, Patrick D., ed. see Bartlett, David L.
Miller, Patrick D., ed. see Brueggemann, Walter.
Miller, Patrick D., ed. see Craddock, Fred B.
Miller, Patrick D., ed. see Mann, Thomas W.
Miller, Patrick D., ed. see Ringe, Sharon H.
Miller, Patrick J. Tyler Rose - The Earl Campbell Story. (Illus.). vi, 250p. 1997. 24.95 (*0-9659563-0-X*) Schuromil Prodns.
***Miller, Patrick W.** Grant Writing: Strategies for Developing Winning Proposals. LC 99-96197. (Illus.). 160p. (C). 2000. pap. text 29.95 (*0-9673279-2-X*) P Miller Assoc.
— How to Write Tests for Students. (Aspects of Learning Ser.). (Illus.). 1990. pap. 13.75 (*0-8106-3008-7*) NEA.
— Nonverbal Communication in the Classroom. LC 99-93528. (Illus.). 48p. 2000. pap. text 6.95 (*0-9673279-0-3*) P Miller Assoc.
— Nonverbal Communication in the Workplace. LC 99-93527. (Illus.). 48p. 2000. pap. text 6.95 (*0-9673279-1-1*) P Miller Assoc.
Miller, Patrizia & Fairbanks, Linda C. The Cat & the Old Rat. Barbee, S. Diane, ed. 24p. 1986. 20.00 (*0-938364-03-0*) Orirana Pr.
Miller, Patti. Writing Your Life: A Journey of Discovery. 144p. 1995. pap. 11.95 (*1-86373-641-7*) IPG Chicago.
Miller, Paul. Christmas on Stage: An Anthology of Royalty-Free Christmas Plays for All Ages. (Orig.). 1993. pap. 5.50 (*0-00-546342-4*) Lillenas.
— Christmas Program Builder, No. 46. 26p. 1993. pap. 4.50 (*0-8341-9427-9*, MC-146) Nazarene.
— Christmas Program Builder, No. 47. 35p. 1994. 4.99 (*0-8341-9104-0*, MC-147) Lillenas.
— Christmas Program Builder, No. 48. 1995. pap. 4.50 (*0-8341-9355-8*, MC-148) Nazarene.
— Christmas Program Builder, No. 49. 1996. pap. 4.50 (*0-8341-9531-3*, MC-149) Nazarene.
— Don't Miss the Pageant. 1991. pap. 4.99 (*0-00-528508-9*) Lillenas.
— Home for Christmas: Program Resources. 1991. pap. 4.50 (*0-00-528487-2*) Lillenas.
— 365 Days of Spiritual Growth. pap. 14.00 (*0-687-08166-1*) Dimen for Liv.
— Troubled in Toyland. 54p. 1992. pap. text 5.99 (*0-8341-9733-2*) Lillenas.
Miller, Paul & Wyatt, Jeff. The Psalms in Worship. LC 98-155786. 1995. pap. 9.99 (*0-8341-9432-5*, MP-754) Nazarene.
Miller, Paul, jt. auth. see Wyatt, Jeff.
Miller, Paul, tr. see Kawano, Martin.
Miller, Paul A. & Wood, Diane S., eds. Recapturing the Renaissance: New Perspectives on Humanism, Dialogue & Texts. 224p. (Orig.). 1996. pap. text 22.95 (*1-886935-14-9*) New Prdigm Pr.
Miller, Paul B. & Larson, Kermit D. CPS Fundamental Accounting Principles Class Computer Problems. 13th ed. 24p. (C). 1995. text 4.00 (*0-256-21081-0*, Irwn McGrw-H) McGrw-H Hghr Educ.
— Financial Accounting Ready Notes. 6th ed. 288p. (C). 1995. text 23.12 (*0-256-19654-0*, Irwn McGrw-H) McGrw-H Hghr Educ.
— Financial Accounting with Working Papers. 6th ed. 1,240p. (C). 1994. text 49.95 (*0-256-18535-2*, Irwn McGrw-H) McGrw-H Hghr Educ.
— Financial Accounting Working Papers. 6th ed. (C). 1994. text 26.25 (*0-256-13340-9*, Irwn McGrw-H) McGrw-H Hghr Educ.
— Fundamental Accounting Principles: Chapters 1-13. 1994. text 18.00 (*0-256-16419-3*, Irwn McGrw-H) McGrw-H Hghr Educ.
— Fundamental Accounting Principles: Chapters 1-19. 13th ed. (C). 1993. text, suppl. ed. 33.12 (*0-256-15851-7*, Irwn McGrw-H) McGrw-H Hghr Educ.
— Fundamental Accounting Principles: Working Papers 1-6. 13th ed. (C). 1994. text, suppl. ed. 13.50 (*0-256-18356-2*, Irwn McGrw-H) McGrw-H Hghr Educ.
— Fundamental Accounting Principles Students Integrated Learning System 2: Chapters 14-27. 13th ed. 1544p. (C). 1993. text 43.95 (*0-256-11543-5*, Irwn McGrw-H) McGrw-H Hghr Educ.
Miller, Paul B., et al. The FASB: The People, the Process, & the Politics. 3rd ed. LC 93-5703. 208p. (C). 1993. text 22.95 (*0-256-08276-6*, Irwn McGrw-H) McGrw-H Hghr Educ.
— The FASB: The People, the Process & the Politics. 4th ed. LC 97-22277. 1997. write for info. (*0-256-20741-0*, Irwn Prfssnl) McGraw-Hill Prof.
Miller, Paul B., jt. auth. see Larson, Kermit.
Miller, Paul B., jt. auth. see Larson, Kermit D.
Miller, Paul B., jt. auth. see Nelson, A. Thomas.
Miller, Paul D. Both Swords & Plowshares: Military Roles in the 1990s. LC 92-44040. 1992. 7.50 (*0-89549-095-1*) Inst Foreign Policy Anal.
— Digital Exorcism. (Angry Women in Rock Ser.: Vol. 2). 200p. 1999. pap. text 24.99 (*1-890451-01-0*) Juno Bks.
— The Inter-Agency Process: Engaging America's Full National Security Capabilities. LC 93-17575. (National Security Papers: No. 11). 1993. 7.50 (*0-89549-097-8*) Inst Foreign Policy Anal.
— Leadership in a Transnational World: The Challenge of Keeping the Peace. LC 93-25820. (National Security Papers: No. 12). 1993. write for info. (*0-89549-098-6*) Inst Foreign Policy Anal.
***Miller, Paul D.** New Perspectives on Benign Prostatic Hypertrophy (BPH) (New Perspectives Ser.). (Illus.). 2001. pap. text 19.95 (*1-873413-62-9*) Merit Pub Intl.
Miller, Paul E. Down Beat's Yearbook of Swing. LC 78-6152. 183p. 1978. reprint ed. lib. bdg. 35.00 (*0-313-20476-4*, MIYS, Greenwood Pr) Greenwood.
Miller, Paul E., ed. Esquire's Jazz Book: 1944-1946, 3 vols. (Roots of Jazz Ser.). 1979. reprint ed. lib. bdg. 75.00 (*0-306-79528-0*); reprint ed. lib. bdg. 27.50 (*0-685-73546-X*); reprint ed. lib. bdg. 27.50 (*0-306-79525-6*); reprint ed. lib. bdg. 27.50 (*0-306-79526-4*); reprint ed. lib. bdg. 27.50 (*0-306-79527-2*) Da Capo.
Miller, Paul E. & Cole-Dai, Phyllis. My Daily Walk, 1999 & 365 Days of Spiritual Growth. 1998. pap. 21.00 (*0-687-05726-4*) Dimen for Liv.
Miller, Paul E., jt. auth. see Dai, Phyllis C.
Miller, Paul J., tr. see Della Mirandola, Pico.
Miller, Paul M. Christmas Comes to Lone Star Gulch. 72p. (J). 1989. 5.99 (*0-8341-9157-1*, MP-67) Lillenas.
— Christmas Program Builder Resources for the Creative Program Director, Vol. 52. (Christmas Program Builders Ser.). 1999. pap. text 4.99 (*0-8341-9976-9*) Lillenas.
— Developing the Church Drama Ministry. (Drama Topics Ser.). 55p. 1994. 9.99 (*0-8341-9127-X*, MP-513) Lillenas.
— Dinner Theatre: Entertaining Outreach. (Drama Topics Ser.). 53p. 1994. 9.99 (*0-8341-9056-7*, MP-510) Lillenas.
— Ebenezer, Jr. 1985. 10.99 (*0-685-68495-4*, TA-9064C) Lillenas.
— The Missing Jesus. 57p. 1984. 4.99 (*0-8341-9373-6*, MC-262) Lillenas.
— Stewardship Program Builder, Vol. 1. 44p. 1992. pap. text 5.50 (*0-8341-9826-6*) Nazarene.
Miller, Paul M., compiled by. Christmas Program Builder, No. 38. 40p. 1984. 4.99 (*0-8341-9143-1*, MC-138) Lillenas.
— Christmas Program Builder, No. 41. 37p. 1987. 4.99 (*0-8341-9144-X*, MC-141) Lillenas.
— Christmas Program Builder, No. 42. 46p. 1988. 4.99 (*0-8341-9145-8*, MC-142) Lillenas.
— Christmas Program Builder, No. 43. 38p. 1989. 4.99 (*0-8341-9522-4*, MC-143) Lillenas.
— Christmas Program Builder, No. 44. 53p. 1991. 4.99 (*0-8341-9521-6*, MC-144) Lillenas.
— The Christmas Script Book. 53p. 1988. 5.99 (*0-8341-9374-4*, MC-270) Lillenas.
— Easter Program Builder No.19. 48p. 1986. pap. 4.50 (*0-8341-9711-1*) Nazarene.
— Evangelistic Program Builder, No. 1. 1987. 5.50 (*0-685-74873-1*, MP-615) Lillenas.
— Evangelistic Program Builder, No. 2. 52p. 1994. 5.99 (*0-8341-9026-5*, MP-616) Lillenas.
— Lenten & Easter Drama Resources. 1982. 4.99 (*0-685-68678-7*, ME-227) Lillenas.
— Missionary Program Builder, No. 4. 36p. 1990. pap. 4.50 (*0-8341-9747-2*, MP-204) Nazarene.
— Mother's Day & Father's Day Program Builder, No. 7. 55p. 1985. pap. 4.50 (*0-8341-9405-8*, MP-307) Nazarene.
— Mother's Day & Father's Day Program Builder, No. 9. Vol. 9. 23p. 1934. pap. 4.50 (*0-8341-9493-7*, MP-309) Nazarene.
— Senior Adult Program Builder, No. 1. 60p. 1984. 5.99 (*0-8341-9632-8*, MP-627) Lillenas.
— Senior Adult Program Builder, No. 2. 32p. 1992. 5.99 (*0-8341-9827-4*, MP-502) Lillenas.
— A Shepherd, a Wish, & Three Wisemen: Dramatic Resources for Christmas. 28p. 1981. pap. 4.50 (*0-8341-9732-4*) Nazarene.
— Special Events in the Church Program Builder, No. 2. 48p. 1982. 5.99 (*0-8341-9111-3*, MP-612) Lillenas.
— Special Worship Resources. 1982. 5.50 (*0-685-68737-6*, MP-613) Lillenas.
— Special Worship Resources. 60p. 1983. pap. text 5.50 (*0-8341-9862-2*) Nazarene.
— Women's Program Builder, No. 2. 48p. 1985. 5.99 (*0-8341-9250-0*, MP-632) Lillenas.
Miller, Paul M., ed. Star Quest. 1989. 6.99 (*0-685-68459-8*, MC-71) Lillenas.
Miller, Paul M., jt. auth. see Wyatt, Jeff.
Miller, Paul M., jt. compiled by see Stargel, Scott.
***Miller, Paul R., et al.** Evaluating Ozone Air Pollution Effects on Pines in the Western United States. (Illus.). 79p. 2000. reprint ed. pap. text 25.00 (*0-7881-8920-4*) DIANE Pub.
Miller, Paul W., ed. Seven Minor Epics of the English Renaissance. LC 67-10125. 304p. 1977. 50.00 (*0-8201-1034-5*) Schol Facsimiles.
Miller, Paula, jt. auth. see Chateu, Kathy.
Miller, Paula J. Marriage - The Sacrament of Divine-Human Communion: A Commentary on St. Bonaventures Breviloquium. (Illus.). 268p. 1996. pap. 24.95 (*0-8199-0967-X*) Franciscan Pr.
— Members of One Body: Prophets, Priests & Kings: An Ecclesiology of Mission. LC 98-30621. 300p. 1999. pap. text 14.95 (*0-8189-0854-8*) Alba.
Miller, Paule M. Parlons de Tout: Livre Pour Cours de Conversation Francaise. 278p. (C). 1990. reprint ed. 34.00 (*0-89464-495-5*) Krieger.
Miller, Paulette, tr. see Gaarder, Jostein.
Miller, Pavla. Transformations of Patriarchy in the West, 1500-1900. LC 98-35746. (Interdisciplinary Studies in History). 400p. 1999. 35.00 (*0-253-33469-1*) Ind U Pr.
Miller, Payton, ed. see Hollis, Durwood.
Miller-Pedersen, P. & Koestler, A. G. Hydrocarbon Seals: Importance for Exploration & Production. LC 97-48379. (Norwegian Petroleum Society (NPF) Special Publication Ser.). 226p. 1997. 200.75 (*0-444-82825-7*) Elsevier.
***Miller, Peggy.** Martha Contemplates the Universe. 28p. 1999. pap. 6.00 (*0-9648232-8-4*) Frith Pr.
Miller, Peggy, jt. auth. see Miller, Ron.
Miller, Peggy J. Amy, Wendy & Beth: Learning Language in South Baltimore. LC 81-11656. 208p. (C). 1982. text 22.95 (*0-292-70357-0*) U of Tex Pr.
Miller, Peggy J., jt. auth. see Haight, Wendy L.
Miller, Peggy J., jt. ed. see Corsaro, William A.

An Asterisk (*) at the beginning of an entry indicates that the title is appearing for the first time.

M

Miller, Rathe & Brothers, Chet, eds. Dream Girls 1996: A Titillating Guide to the Best Topless Bars & Men's Clubs Across America. (Dream Girls Ser.: Vol. 1). 250p. (Orig.). 1995. pap. 14.95 (*0-9650289-5-X*) Horn Dance.

Miller, Ray. Beat the Clock Sports. (Illus.). 24p. (J). 1999. pap. 6.95 (*1-58295-014-8*, Pub. by Pace Prods) Andrews & McMeel.

— Building a Home Darkroom. 4th ed. LC 96-68474. (Kodak Workshop Ser.). (Illus.). 96p. (C). 1998. pap. 17.95 (*0-87985-746-3*, KW-14, Kodak) Saunders Photo.

— Camaro! Chevy's Classy Chassis. (Chevy Chase Ser.: Vol. 4). (Illus.). 320p. 1981. 44.95 (*0-913056-10-3*) Evergreen Pr.

— Chevrolet: The Coming of Age: An Illustrated History of Chevrolet's Passenger Cars, 1911-1942. (Illus.). 1995. pap. 29.95 (*0-913056-08-1*) Evergreen Pr.

— Chevrolet USA-1: An Illustrated History of Chevrolet's Passenger Cars 1946-1959. LC 76-12000. (Chevy Chase Ser.: Vol. 2). (Illus.). 320p. 1977. 44.95 (*0-913056-07-3*) Evergreen Pr.

— Dream Catcher Miniatures. (Illus.). 8p. (J). 1997. pap. 6.95 (*1-880592-72-X*, Pub. by Pace Prods) Andrews & McMeel.

— Falcon: Wish You Were Here. LC 82-90194. (Ford Road Ser.: Vol. 7). (Illus.). 320p. 1983. 44.95 (*0-913056-11-1*) Evergreen Pr.

— Magic Tricks. (Illus.). 8p. (J). 1997. pap. 6.95 (*1-880592-70-3*, Pub. by Pace Prods) Andrews & McMeel.

— Man Kidnapped by UFO for Third Time. Bixby, Robert, ed. 39p. 1994. pap. text 6.00 (*0-9624453-6-3*) March Street Pr.

— Mustang Does It. LC 77-78278. (Ford Road Ser.: Vol. 6). (Illus.). 320p. 1978. lib. bdg. 44.95 (*0-913056-09-X*) Evergreen Pr.

***Miller, Ray.** On the Road to Alaska (Fiction by Ray Miller) 33p. 2000. pap. 6.00 (*1-882983-48-3*) March Street Pr.

Miller, Ray. San Antonio-Border. 2nd ed. (Eyes of Texas Travel Guides Ser.). (Illus.). 252p. 1988. pap. 10.95 (*0-88415-234-0*, 5234) Gulf Pub.

— Sloppy Slimy Sticky Soggy Dripping Moving Science. 24p. (gr. 3-7). 1999. pap. 7.95 (*0-590-18725-2*) Scholastic Inc.

Miller, Ray & Embree, Glenn. Henry's Lady: An Illustrated History of the Model A Ford. LC 72-77244. (Ford Road Ser.: Vol. 2). (Illus.). 320p. 1972. 44.95 (*0-913056-03-0*) Evergreen Pr.

— The Nifty 'Fifties' Fords: An Illustrated History of the Early Post-War Fords. LC 73-93879. (Ford Road Ser.: Vol. 5). (Illus.). 320p. 1974. 44.95 (*0-913056-05-7*) Evergreen Pr.

— The Real Corvette: An Illustrated History of Chevrolet's Sports Car. LC 75-8100. (Chevy Chase Ser.: Vol. 3). (Illus.). 320p. 1975. 24.98 (*0-913056-06-5*) Evergreen Pr.

— Thunderbird! An Illustrated History of the Ford T-Bird. LC 73-75630. (Ford Road Ser.: Vol. 4). (Illus.). 300p. 1973. 44.95 (*0-913056-04-9*) Evergreen Pr.

— The V-Eight Affair: An Illustrated History of the Pre-War Ford V-8. LC 70-174898. (Ford Road Ser.: Vol. 3). (Illus.). 303p. 1972. pap. 29.95 (*0-913056-02-2*) Evergreen Pr.

Miller, Ray & Miller, Jo, eds. Catalina - Wish You Were Here. LC 93-71599. (Illus.). 96p. (Orig.). 1993. pap. 19.95 (*0-913056-13-8*) Evergreen Pr.

— Hawaii! - Wish You Were Here. LC 93-91067. (Illus.). 96p. (Orig.). 1994. pap. 19.95 (*0-913056-14-6*) Evergreen Pr.

Miller, Ray, Jr., jt. auth. see McCloy, James F.

Miller, Ray, Jr., ed. & tr. see Bayer, Hans.

Miller, Ray H. Fun Facts. (About Farm History Ser.). (Illus.). iii, 29p. (J). (gr. 2 up). 1995. boxed set 6.95 (*1-887327-03-7*); boxed set 6.95 (*1-887327-00-2*) Ertl Co.

Miller, Ray H., jt. auth. see Benanti, Carol.

Miller, Raymond, ed. New Zealand Politics in Transition, Vol. 1. LC 97-223557. (Illus.). 464p. 1997. pap. text 65.00 (*0-19-558339-6*) OUP.

Miller, Raymond, jt. auth. see Pace Products Staff.

Miller, Raymond C., ed. Twentieth-Century Pessimism & the American Dream. LC 79-26081. (Franklin Memorial Lectures Ser.: No. 8). 118p. reprint ed. pap. 33.70 (*0-7837-3802-1*, 2043622) Bks Demand.

— Twentieth-Century Pessimism & the American Dream, VIII. LC 79-26081. (Franklin Memorial Lectures Ser.: Vol. VIII). (Illus.). 104p. 1980. reprint ed. lib. bdg. 38.50 (*0-313-22122-7*, MITW, Greenwood Pr) Greenwood.

Miller, Raymond W. & Gardiner, Duane T. Soils in Our Environment. 8th ed. LC 96-53481. 736p. 1997. 105.00 (*0-13-610882-2*) P-H.

***Miller, Raymond W. & Gardiner, Duane T.** Soils in Our Environment. 9th ed. LC 99-88996. 656p. 2000. 96.00 incl. cd-rom (*0-13-020036-0*) P-H.

Miller-Rebec. Intro to Psychology. 1999. 46.50 (*0-697-07840-X*) McGraw.

— Introduction to Psyc. 1999. 13.00 (*0-697-10348-X*) McGraw.

Miller, Reese P., tr. see Descartes, Rene.

Miller, Reese P., jt. tr. see Miller, Valentine R.

Miller, Reg T. Pyramid Truth Gateway Universe: The Purpose, Intent & Overview of Extraterrestrial Visitations. (Illus.). 380p. 1998. pap. 24.95 (*0-9651546-4-5*) Med Bear.

Miller, Reggie & Wojciechowski, Gen. I Love Being the Enemy: A Season on the Court with the NBA'S Best Shooter & Sharpest Tongue. (Illus.). 320p. 1995. 23.00 (*0-684-81389-0*) Simon & Schuster.

Miller, Regina. The Developmentally Appropriate Inclusive Childhood Classroom. LC 95-13337. (C). 1919. mass mkt. 45.00 (*0-8273-7071-7*) Delmar.

— The Developmentally Appropriate Inclusive Classroom in Early Education. (Special Education Ser.). 416p. (C). 1995. mass mkt. 66.95 (*0-8273-6704-X*) Delmar.

Miller, Regina & Mixer, Jennifer. Don't Pay Retail! Indiana's Discount Buying Guide. 275p. 1994. pap. 9.95 (*1-878208-54-3*) Guild Pr IN.

Miller, Reinhard, jt. auth. see Mobius, D.

Miller, Rex. Basic Electricity. (gr. 9-12). 1978. pap. 10.45 (*0-02-662570-9*) Glencoe.

— Basic Electricity. (gr. 9-12). 1978. 10.64 (*0-02-662580-6*) Glencoe.

— Butcher. Grad, Doug, ed. 320p. 1994. mass mkt. 5.50 (*0-671-86882-9*) PB.

— Chaingang. Grad, Doug, ed. 320p. 1992. mass mkt. 4.99 (*0-671-74847-5*) PB.

***Miller, Rex.** Chaingang. ed. 2000. 6.99 (*1-58586-236-3*) E-Rgts E-Reads.

— Electrician's Pocket Manual. (Pocket Reference Ser.). (Illus.). 420p. 2000. pap. text 24.95 (*0-07-136026-3*) McGraw-Hill Prof.

Miller, Rex. The Electrician's Toolbox Manual. 352p. 1989. pap. 12.95 (*0-13-247701-7*) P-H.

— Electricity & Electronics. 2nd ed. 1991. pap. 35.95 (*0-8273-4419-8*) Delmar.

— Electricity & Electronics. 2nd ed. 1991. teacher ed. 14.95 (*0-8273-4420-1*) Delmar.

— Electricity for Heating, Air Conditioning & Refrigeration. 369p. (C). 1988. pap. text 66.50 (*0-15-520947-7*, Pub. by SCP) Harcourt.

— Electricity for Heating, Air Conditioning & Refrigeration. 369p. (C). 1988. pap. text 4.00 (*0-15-520948-5*) SCP.

— Fractional Horsepower Electric Motors. 1984. text 15.95 (*0-672-23410-6*) Macmillan.

— Industrial & Residential Electricity. write for info. (*0-02-676360-5*) Glencoe.

— Industrial Electricity. rev. ed. (gr. 9-12). 1982. text 33.88 (*0-02-664730-3*) Glencoe.

— The Investor's Guide to Vintage Character Collectibles. LC 98-84628. (Illus.). 176p. 1998. pap. 19.95 (*0-87341-609-0*, VCC01) Krause Pubns.

— Machinists Library: Basic Machine Shop, 3 vols., Set. 4th ed. 1983. 57.95 (*0-672-23380-0*, Bobbs) Macmillan.

— Refrigeration & Air-Conditioning Technology. 1983. text 36.47 (*0-02-665540-3*) Glencoe.

— Residential Electrical Wiring. (Illus.). 300p. 1981. student ed. 9.52 (*0-02-665640-X*) Glencoe.

— St. Louis Blues. limited ed. 160p. 1995. boxed set 40.00 (*0-940776-30-8*) Maclay Assoc.

— Small Electric Motors. 3rd ed. 436p. 1993. 30.00 (*0-02-584975-1*, Aude IN) IDG Bks.

— Small Gasoline Engines. 3rd ed. 681p. 1993. 30.00 (*0-02-584991-3*) Macmillan.

Miller, Rex & Baker, Glenn E. Carpentry & Construction. 2nd ed. 548p. 1991. pap. 34.95 (*0-07-157668-1*) McGraw.

— Carpentry & Construction. 2nd ed. (Illus.). 656p. 1991. 42.95 (*0-8306-8678-9*, 3678) McGraw-Hill Prof.

Miller, Rex & Miller, Mark R. Electric Motor Controls. 464p. (C). 1991. text 57.00 (*0-13-249376-4*) P-H.

— Electronics the Easy Way. 3rd ed. LC 94-46445. (Illus.). 416p. 1995. pap. 12.95 (*0-8120-9144-2*) Barron.

Miller, Rex & Miller, Mark R., eds. Electrician: Electrician's Helper. 8th ed. LC 98-88862. (Illus.). 256p. 1998. 19.95 (*0-02-862818-7*, Arc) IDG Bks.

Miller, Rex & Miller, Martin R. Mathematics for Electricians & Electronics Technicians. 1985. text 14.95 (*0-8161-1700-4*) Macmillan.

Miller, Rex & Morrisey, Thomas J. Metal Technology. LC 74-77817. 1976. 22.39 (*0-672-97623-4*, Bobbs); 5.99 (*0-672-97624-2*, Bobbs); teacher ed. 3.67 (*0-672-97625-0*, Bobbs) Macmillan.

Miller, Rex, et al. Carpentry & Construction. 3rd ed. LC 98-42540. (Illus.). 560p. 1999. 87.95 (*0-07-042053-X*) McGraw.

— Carpentry & Construction. 3rd ed. (Illus.). 560p. 1999. pap. 44.95 (*0-07-042052-1*) McGraw-Hill Prof.

Miller, Rex, jt. auth. see Baker, Glenn E.

Miller, Rex, jt. auth. see Fuller, Nelson.

Miller, Rex, ed. see Anderson, Edwin P.

Miller, Rich & Anderson, Neil. Reality Check: Winning the Mind Game. (Freedom in Christ for Teens Ser.: 2). 150p. (YA). 1996. pap. 8.99 (*1-56507-409-2*) Harvest Hse.

Miller, Rich, jt. auth. see Anderson, Neil.

Miller, Rich, jt. auth. see Anderson, Neil T.

Miller, Rich, jt. auth. see McAllister, Dawson.

Miller, Richard. California Traveler: Ghost Towns of California - Remnants of the Mining Days. (American Traveler Ser.: Vol. 19). (Illus.). 48p. 1999. pap. 6.95 (*1-55838-124-4*) R H Pub.

— Introduction to Differential Equations. 2nd ed. 640p. (C). 1991. text 57.80 (*0-13-478264-X*) P-H.

— Mosca: A Factual Fiction. unabridged ed. LC 97-91845. (Illus.). iv, 237p. 1997. pap. 16.00 (*0-9658423-0-4*, DFI Bks) Dada Found.

— National Schools of Singing: English, French, German & Italian Techniques of Singing Revisited. LC 96-35557. 1997. 39.00 (*0-8108-3237-2*) Scarecrow.

— On the Art of Singing. (Illus.). 336p. 1996. 30.00 (*0-19-509825-0*) OUP.

***Miller, Richard.** Singing Schumann: An Interpretive Guide for Performers. LC 98-31645. (Illus.). 264p. 1999. 35.00 (*0-19-511904-5*) OUP.

Miller, Richard. The Structure of Singing: System & Art in Vocal Technique. (Illus.). 372p. 1986. 39.00 (*0-02-872660-X*, Schirmer Books) Mac Lib Ref.

***Miller, Richard.** Training Soprano Voices. LC 99-27828. (Illus.). 224p. 2000. 25.00 (*0-19-513018-9*) OUP.

***Miller, Richard, et al, eds.** The Placenta from Implantation to Trophoblastic Disease Vol. 13: Apoptosis, Proliferation, Invasion & Pathology. LC 99-44470. (Illus.). 548p. 1999. 120.00 (*1-58046-064-X*, Pub. by Univ Rochester Pr) Boydell & Brewer.

Miller, Richard, tr. from FRE. A Modest Proposal. LC 94-78232.Tr. of Y'a Bon Bamboula. 80p. (Orig.). 1994. pap. 8.95 (*0-913745-43-X*) Ubu Repertory.

Miller, Richard & Miller, Iona. The Modern Alchemist: A Guide to Personal Transformation. (Illus.). 300p. (Orig.). 1994. pap. 14.95 (*0-933999-37-2*) Phanes Pr.

Miller, Richard, tr. see Barthes, Roland.

Miller, Richard, tr. see Cesaire, Aime.

Miller, Richard, tr. see Cobb, Margaret G., ed.

Miller, Richard, tr. see Le Guerer, Annick.

Miller, Richard A. Beating Bad Breath: Your Complete Guide to Eliminating & Preventing Halitosis. (Illus.). 64p. (Orig.). 1995. pap. 8.95 (*1-56167-202-5*) Am Literary Pr.

— The Magical & Ritual Use of Aphrodisiacs. LC 92-7672. (Illus.). 176p. (Orig.). 1992. pap. 10.95 (*0-89281-402-0*, Destiny Bks) Inner Tradit.

— The Magical & Ritual Use of Herbs. LC 92-4925. (Illus.). 128p. 1992. pap. 10.95 (*0-89281-401-2*, Destiny Bks) Inner Tradit.

— The Potential of Herbs As a Cash Crop. 2nd ed. 230p. 1998. pap. 20.00 (*0-911311-55-6*) Acres USA.

— El Uso Magico y Ritual de las Hierbas (The Magic & Ritual Use of Herbs) (SPA., Illus.). 111p. 1995. pap. 12.95 (*0-89281-467-5*) Inner Tradit.

— El Uso Magico y Ritual de los Afrodisiacos (The Magical & Ritual Use of Aphrodisiacs) (SPA., Illus.). 140p. 1996. pap. 10.95 (*0-89281-581-7*, Inner Trad Espanol) Inner Tradit.

Miller, Richard A. & Miller, Iona. The Magical & Ritual Use of Perfumes. LC 88-32020. (Illus.). 183p. 1990. pap. 12.95 (*0-89281-210-9*, Destiny Bks) Inner Tradit.

Miller, Richard B. Bankers Almanac 1985. LC HG1611.B36. (Bankers Reference Ser.). 464p. reprint ed. pap. 143.90 (*0-8357-5962-8*, 205218100053) Bks Demand.

— Casuistry & Modern Ethics: A Poetics of Practical Reasoning. 336p. 1996. pap. text 18.95 (*0-226-52637-2*); lib. bdg. 48.00 (*0-226-52636-4*) U Ch Pr.

— Interpretations of Conflict: Ethics, Pacificism, & the Just-War Tradition. LC 91-3044. 306p. 1991. pap. text 22.00 (*0-226-52796-4*) U Ch Pr.

— Interpretations of Conflict: Ethics, Pacificism, & the Just-War Tradition. LC 91-3044. 296p. 1994. lib. bdg. 48.00 (*0-226-52795-6*) U Ch Pr.

— Super Banking: Innovative Management Strategies That Work. 250p. 1988. 50.00 (*1-55623-114-8*, Irwn Prfssnl) McGraw-Hill Prof.

Miller, Richard B., ed. War in the Twentieth Century: Sources in Theological Ethics. LC 92-2318. (Library of Theological Ethics). 320p. 1992. pap. 26.00 (*0-664-25323-7*) Westminster John Knox.

Miller, Richard C. & Solverson, John F. Student Lamps of the Victorian Era. (Illus.). 176p. 1992. pap. 34.95 (*0-915410-86-9*, 4012) Antique Pubns.

— Student Lamps of the Victorian Era. limited ed. (Illus.). 176p. 1992. 49.95 (*0-915410-87-7*, 4013) Antique Pubns.

***Miller, Richard Copeland & Levine, Philip.** Passage Europe. deluxe ed. 2000. 500.00 (*1-888899-06-9*) Lodima.

Miller, Richard Copeland, jt. auth. see Levine, Philip.

Miller, Richard D., jt. auth. see Frech, H. E.

Miller, Richard E. As If Learning Mattered: Reforming Higher Education. LC 97-39221. 264p. 1998. text 39.95 (*0-8014-3483-1*); pap. text 15.95 (*0-8014-8528-2*) Cornell U Pr.

Miller, Richard E., jt. ed. see McClellan, Keith.

Miller, Richard F. & Mooney, Robert F. The Civil War: The Nantucket Experience. Oldham, Elizabeth, ed. (Illus.). 216p. (Orig.). 1994. pap. 14.95 (*0-9627851-1-3*) Wesco Pub MA.

Miller, Richard H., ed. The Evolution of the Cold War: From Confrontation to Containment. LC 79-4258. (American Problem Studies). 144p. 1979. reprint ed. pap. text 10.50 (*0-88275-935-3*) Krieger.

Miller, Richard I. The Assessment of College Performance. LC 79-83575. (Jossey-Bass Series in Higher Education). (Illus.). 392p. reprint ed. pap. 121.60 (*0-8357-4912-6*, 203784200009) Bks Demand.

— Developing Programs for Faculty Evaluation: A Sourcebook for Higher Education. LC 73-12063. (Jossey-Bass Higher Education Ser.). 260p. reprint ed. pap. 80.60 (*0-608-16939-0*, 202776300056) Bks Demand.

— Evaluating Faculty Performance. LC 70-184958. (Jossey-Bass Higher Education Ser.). 161p. reprint ed. pap. 50.00 (*0-608-17771-7*, 205655600072) Bks Demand.

Miller, Richard I., ed. Applying the Deming Method to Higher Education. 133p. 1991. 27.00 (*0-910402-98-1*) Coll & U Personnel.

Miller, Richard I., et al. Evaluating, Improving & Judging Faculty Performance in Two-year Colleges. LC 99-22083. 208p. 2000. 55.00 (*0-89789-692-0*, Bergin & Garvey) Greenwood.

Miller, Richard K. Artificial Intelligence Applications for Business Management. LC 86-46130. 300p. 1987. text 110.00 (*0-88173-032-7*) Fairmont Pr.

— Artificial Intelligence Applications for Manufacturing. LC 86-46129. 500p. 1987. text 110.00 (*0-88173-031-9*) Fairmont Pr.

— Design for Manufacturability - Assembly. 219p. 1990. pap. text 955.00 (*0-89671-111-0*) SEAI Tech Pubns.

— Directory of Technical Magazines & Directories. 1982. text 45.00 (*0-915586-33-9*) Fairmont Pr.

Miller, Richard K. Electric Utilities & Independent Power: Impact of Deregulation. LC 95-22855. 209p. 1995. 69.95 (*0-87814-632-6*) PennWell Bks.

Miller, Richard K. Electric Utilities & Independent Power: Impact of Deregulation. LC 95-22855. 209p. 1995. 95.00 (*0-88173-233-8*) PennWell Bks.

— Energy & Noise. 39.00 (*0-915586-40-1*) Fairmont Pr.

— Energy Conservation Marketing Handbook. 1982. text 42.50 (*0-915586-65-7*) Fairmont Pr.

— Guide to the Noise Control Literature. 39.00 (*0-915586-09-6*) Fairmont Pr.

— Handbook of Selling to the U. S. Military. 1982. text 39.00 (*0-915586-63-0*) Fairmont Pr.

— Industrial Robot Handbook: Case Histories of Effective Robot Use in 70 Industries. (Illus.). 686p. (gr. 13). 1989. text 126.95 (*0-442-23733-2*) Chapman & Hall.

— Manufacturing Simulation. LC 89-17111. 178p. 1989. pap. text 95.00 (*0-88173-104-8*) Fairmont Pr.

— Municipal Water Environmental Markets. (Illus.). 299p. 1997. spiral bd. 185.00 (*1-881503-68-2*) R K Miller Assocs.

— Neural Networks. LC 89-17158. 302p. 1989. pap. text 95.00 (*0-88173-100-5*) Fairmont Pr.

— The 1997 Travel & Tourism Market Research Handbook. 400p. 1997. 275.00 (*1-881503-79-8*) R K Miller Assocs.

— Optical Computers: The Next Frontier in Computing, 2 vols. (Illus.). 276p. 1991. pap. text 285.00 (*0-89671-113-7*) SEAI Tech Pubns.

— Remote Sensing, Noncontact Sensing, & Image Processing. 966p. 1991. pap. text 485.00 (*0-89671-109-9*) SEAI Tech Pubns.

— Superconductors: Electronics & Computer Applications. LC 89-17028. 270p. 1989. pap. text 95.00 (*0-88173-103-X*) Fairmont Pr.

— Waterjet Cutting. LC 88-45797. 154p. 1990. text 62.95 (*0-88173-068-8*) Fairmont Pr.

Miller, Richard K., compiled by. Energy Conservation & Utilization in Foundries. 45.00 (*0-915586-44-4*) Fairmont Pr.

— Energy Conservation & Utilization in the Glass Industry. 45.00 (*0-915586-48-7*) Fairmont Pr.

Miller, Richard K., ed. Fifth Generation Computers. LC 86-45549. 220p. 1986. text 54.95 (*0-88173-050-5*) Fairmont Pr.

Miller, Richard K. & Fairmont Press Staff. Manufacturing Simulation. 186p. (C). 1989. pap. 95.00 (*0-13-555517-5*) P-H.

— Neural Networks. 312p. (C). 1989. pap. text 95.00 (*0-13-615477-8*) P-H.

— Superconductors. 280p. (C). 1989. pap. text 95.00 (*0-13-876616-9*) P-H.

Miller, Richard K. & Gunter, Christy H. Air Duct Cleaning Services. (Market Research Survey Ser.: No. 306). 50p. 1996. 200.00 (*1-55865-330-9*) Future Tech Surveys.

— Air Quality Instrumentation. (Market Research Survey Ser.: No. 296). 50p. 1996. 200.00 (*1-55865-320-1*) Future Tech Surveys.

— Asbestos Abatement. (Market Research Survey Ser.: No. 310). 50p. 1996. 200.00 (*1-55865-334-1*) Future Tech Surveys.

— Bioremediation. (Market Research Survey Ser.: No. 290). 50p. 1996. 200.00 (*1-55865-314-7*) Future Tech Surveys.

— Canadian Water & Wastewater Markets. (Market Research Survey Ser.: No. 320). 50p. 1996. 200.00 (*1-55865-342-2*) Future Tech Surveys.

— Commercial Lighting. (Market Research Survey Ser.: No. 329). 50p. 1997. pap. 200.00 (*1-55865-350-3*) Future Tech Surveys.

— Consulting Engineering Services to the Electric Utility Industry. (Market Research Survey Ser.: No. 347). 50p. 1997. pap. 200.00 (*1-55865-362-7*) Future Tech Surveys.

— Demand Side Management. (Market Research Survey Ser.: No. 348). 50p. 1997. pap. 200.00 (*1-55865-363-5*) Future Tech Surveys.

— Electric Utilities: Executive Outlook. (Market Research Survey Ser.: No. 324). 50p. 1997. pap. 200.00 (*1-55865-346-5*) Future Tech Surveys.

— Electric Vehicles, Report 326. (Market Research Survey Ser.: No. 326). 50p. 1997. pap. 200.00 (*1-55865-348-1*) Future Tech Surveys.

— Electrotechnologies. (Market Research Survey Ser.: No. 337). 50p. 1997. pap. 200.00 (*1-55865-356-2*) Future Tech Surveys.

— Energy Management in Commercial Buildings. (Market Research Survey Ser.: No. 338). 50p. 1997. pap. 200.00 (*1-55865-357-0*) Future Tech Surveys.

— Energy Management Systems. (Market Research Survey Ser.: No. 341). 50p. 1997. pap. 200.00 (*1-55865-360-0*) Future Tech Surveys.

— Energy Service Companies. (Market Research Survey Ser.: No. 333). 50p. 1997. pap. 200.00 (*1-55865-352-X*) Future Tech Surveys.

— Environmental Emergency Response. (Market Research Survey Ser.: No. 301). 50p. 1996. 200.00 (*1-55865-325-2*) Future Tech Surveys.

— Environmental Engineering Services. (Market Research Survey Ser.: No. 297). 50p. 1996. 200.00 (*1-55865-321-X*) Future Tech Surveys.

— Environmental Equipment Rental. (Market Research Survey Ser.: No. 315). 50p. 1996. 200.00 (*1-55865-338-4*) Future Tech Surveys.

— Environmental Laboratory Services. (Market Research Survey Ser.: No. 303). 50p. 1996. 200.00 (*1-55865-327-9*) Future Tech Surveys.

— Environmental Legal Services. (Market Research Survey Ser.: No. 304). 50p. 1996. 200.00 (*1-55865-328-7*) Future Tech Surveys.

An Asterisk (*) at the beginning of an entry indicates that the title is appearing for the first time.

— Environmental Risk Assessment. (Market Research Survey Ser.: No. 299). 50p. 1996. 200.00 (*1-55865-323-6*) Future Tech Surveys.
— Environmental Site Assessments. (Market Research Survey Ser.: No. 300). 50p. 1996. 200.00 (*1-55865-324-4*) Future Tech Surveys.
— Environmental Software. (Market Research Survey Ser.: No. 302). 50p. 1996. 200.00 (*1-55865-326-0*) Future Tech Surveys.
— Environmental Training & Continuing Education. (Market Research Survey Ser.: No. 311). 50p. 1996. 200.00 (*1-55865-335-X*) Future Tech Surveys.
— Federal Environmental Markets. (Market Research Survey Ser.: No. 298). 50p. 1996. 200.00 (*1-55865-322-8*) Future Tech Surveys.
— Fuel Cells. (Market Research Survey Ser.: No. 334). 50p. 1997. pap. 200.00 (*1-55865-353-8*) Future Tech Surveys.
— Goundwater Remediation. (Market Research Survey Ser.: No. 288). 50p. 1996. 200.00 (*1-55865-309-0*) Future Tech Surveys.
— Hazardous Waste Off-Site Services. (Market Research Survey Ser.: No. 307). 50p. 1996. 200.00 (*1-55865-331-7*) Future Tech Surveys.
— Independent Power Production. (Market Research Survey Ser.: No. 330). 50p. (Orig.). 1997. pap. 200.00 (*1-55865-351-1*) Future Tech Surveys.
— Indoor Air Monitors. (Market Research Survey Ser.: No. 322). 50p. 1996. 200.00 (*1-55865-344-9*) Future Tech Surveys.
— Industrial Air Pollution Control Equipment. (Market Research Survey Ser.: No. 293). 50p. 1996. 200.00 (*1-55865-317-1*) Future Tech Surveys.
— Industrial Air Pollution Monitoring Services. (Market Research Survey Ser.: No. 295). 50p. 1996. 200.00 (*1-55865-319-8*) Future Tech Surveys.
— Industrial Energy Management, Report 339. (Market Research Survey Ser.: No. 339). 50p. 1997. pap. 200.00 (*1-55865-358-9*) Future Tech Surveys.
— Industrial Stormwater Management. (Market Research Survey Ser.: No. 292). 50p. 1996. 200.00 (*1-55865-316-3*) Future Tech Surveys.
— Industrial Water Reuse & Recycling. (Market Research Survey Ser.: No. 321). 50p. 1996. 200.00 (*1-55865-343-0*) Future Tech Surveys.
— Interstate Waste Transport Services. (Market Research Survey Ser.: No. 313). 50p. 1996. 200.00 (*1-55865-336-8*) Future Tech Surveys.
— Leaking Underground Storage Tank Remediation. (Market Research Survey Ser.: No. 289). 50p. 1996. 200.00 (*1-55865-313-9*) Future Tech Surveys.
— Medical Waste Management. (Market Research Survey Ser.: No. 285). 50p. 1996. 200.00 (*1-55865-310-4*) Future Tech Surveys.
— Municipal Sludge Management. (Market Research Survey Ser.: No. 323). 50p. 1996. 200.00 (*1-55865-345-7*) Future Tech Surveys.
— Municipal Solid Waste Management. (Market Research Survey Ser.: No. 308). 50p. 1996. 200.00 (*1-55865-332-5*) Future Tech Surveys.
— Municipal Stormwater Management. (Market Research Survey Ser.: No. 291). 50p. 1996. 200.00 (*1-55865-315-5*) Future Tech Surveys.
— Natural Gas: Executive Outlook. (Market Research Survey Ser.: No. 325). 50p. 1997. pap. 200.00 (*1-55865-347-3*) Future Tech Surveys.
— Natural Gas Vehicles. (Market Research Survey Ser.: No. 327). 50p. 1997. pap. 200.00 (*1-55865-349-X*) Future Tech Surveys.
— Nuclear Power. (Market Research Survey Ser.: No. 346). 50p. 1997. pap. 200.00 (*1-55865-361-9*) Future Tech Surveys.
— Opportunities of ISO 14,000. (Market Research Survey Ser.: No. 314). 50p. 1996. 200.00 (*1-55865-337-6*) Future Tech Surveys.
— Photovoltaics. (Market Research Survey Ser.: No. 335). 50p. 1997. pap. 200.00 (*1-55865-354-6*) Future Tech Surveys.
— Pollution Prevention. (Market Research Survey Ser.: No. 305). 50p. 1996. 200.00 (*1-55865-329-5*) Future Tech Surveys.
— Remediation Equipment. (Market Research Survey Ser.: No. 287). 50p. 1996. 200.00 (*1-55865-312-0*) Future Tech Surveys.
— Septic Tanks. (Market Research Survey Ser.: No. 317). 50p. 1996. 200.00 (*1-55865-340-6*) Future Tech Surveys.
— Site Remediation. (Market Research Survey Ser.: No. 286). 50p. 1996. 200.00 (*1-55865-311-2*) Future Tech Surveys.
— Sorbents. (Market Research Survey Ser.: No. 309). 50p. 1996. 200.00 (*1-55865-333-3*) Future Tech Surveys.
— Trenchless Technology. (Market Research Survey Ser.: No. 316). 50p. 1996. 200.00 (*1-55865-339-2*) Future Tech Surveys.
— Variable Frequency Motor Drives, Report 340. (Market Research Survey Ser.: No. 340). 50p. 1997. pap. 200.00 (*1-55865-359-7*) Future Tech Surveys.
— Voc Control Equipment. (Market Research Survey Ser.: No. 294). 50p. 1996. 200.00 (*1-55865-318-X*) Future Tech Surveys.
— Water & Industrial Tanks. (Market Research Survey Ser.: No. 318). 50p. 1996. 200.00 (*1-55865-341-4*) Future Tech Surveys.
— Wind Power. (Market Research Survey Ser.: No. 336). 50p. 1997. pap. 200.00 (*1-55865-355-4*) Future Tech Surveys.

Miller, Richard K. & Montone, Wayne V. Handbook of Acoustical Enclosures & Barriers. 33.00 (*0-915586-06-1*) Fairmont Pr.

Miller, Richard K. & Rupnow, Marcia E. Aboveground Storage Tanks. (Survey on Technology & Markets Ser.: No. 215). 50p. 1994. pap. text 200.00 (*1-55865-246-9*) Future Tech Surveys.
— Air Doors & Air Curtains. LC 90-83931. (Survey on Technology & Markets Ser.: No. 136). 50p. 1991. pap. text 200.00 (*1-55865-161-6*) Future Tech Surveys.
— Air Duct Cleaning Services. (Survey on Technology & Markets Ser.: No. 221). 50p. 1993. pap. text 200.00 (*1-55865-252-3*) Future Tech Surveys.
— Air Pollution Instrumentation. LC 90-83884. (Survey on Technology & Markets Ser.: No. 180). 50p. 1991. pap. text 200.00 (*1-55865-204-3*) Future Tech Surveys.
— Asbestos Abatement Equipment. LC 90-83848. (Survey on Technology & Markets Ser.: No. 143). 50p. 1991. pap. text 200.00 (*1-55865-168-3*) Future Tech Surveys.
— Asbestos Contracting Services. LC 90-83847. (Survey on Technology & Markets Ser.: No. 142). 50p. 1991. pap. text 200.00 (*1-55865-167-5*) Future Tech Surveys.
— Asbestos Laboratory Services. LC 90-83849. (Survey on Technology & Markets Ser.: No. 144). 50p. 1991. pap. text 200.00 (*1-55865-169-1*) Future Tech Surveys.
— Asphalt Recycling. LC 90-84379. (Survey on Technology & Markets Ser.: No. 173). 50p. 1991. pap. text 200.00 (*1-55865-225-6*) Future Tech Surveys.
— Balers. LC 90-83888. (Survey on Technology & Markets Ser.: No. 184). 50p. 1991. pap. text 200.00 (*1-55865-208-6*) Future Tech Surveys.
— Bioenergy Systems. LC 90-83926. (Survey on Technology & Markets Ser.: No. 126). 50p. 1991. pap. text 200.00 (*1-55865-149-7*) Future Tech Surveys.
— CFC Alternatives. LC 90-83916. (Survey on Technology & Markets Ser.: No. 110). 50p. 1991. pap. text 200.00 (*1-55865-133-0*) Future Tech Surveys.
— CFC Recovery & Recycling Equipment. LC 90-83934. (Survey on Technology & Markets Ser.: No. 140). 50p. 1991. pap. text 200.00 (*1-55865-165-9*) Future Tech Surveys.
— Chemical Storage Buildings. LC 90-83882. (Survey on Technology & Markets Ser.: No. 178). 50p. 1991. pap. text 200.00 (*1-55865-202-7*) Future Tech Surveys.
— Chemical Storage Drums. (Survey on Technology & Markets Ser.: No. 156). 50p. 1991. 200.00 (*1-55865-226-4*) Future Tech Surveys.
— Chromatography, Gas. LC 90-83897. (Survey on Technology & Markets Ser.: No. 193). 50p. 1991. pap. text 200.00 (*1-55865-217-5*) Future Tech Surveys.
— Cogeneration. (Survey on Technology & Markets Ser.: No. 207). 50p. 1993. pap. text 200.00 (*1-55865-238-8*) Future Tech Surveys.
— Commercial Air Cleaning Systems. LC 90-83895. (Survey on Technology & Markets Ser.: No. 191). 50p. 1991. pap. text 200.00 (*1-55865-215-9*) Future Tech Surveys.
— Commercial Lighting. (Survey on Technology & Markets Ser.: No. 209). 50p. 1993. pap. text 200.00 (*1-55865-240-X*) Future Tech Surveys.
— Cooling Towers. LC 90-83921. (Survey on Technology & Markets Ser.: No. 117). 50p. 1991. pap. text 200.00 (*1-55865-140-3*) Future Tech Surveys.
— Dataloggers. LC 90-83898. (Survey on Technology & Markets Ser.: No. 194). 50p. 1991. pap. text 200.00 (*1-55865-218-3*) Future Tech Surveys.
— Demand Side Management. (Survey on Technology & Markets Ser.: No. 220). 50p. 1993. pap. text 200.00 (*1-55865-251-5*) Future Tech Surveys.
— Electric & Magnetic Field Recovery. LC 90-83933. (Survey on Technology & Markets Ser.: No. 139). 50p. 1991. pap. text 200.00 (*1-55865-164-0*) Future Tech Surveys.
— Electric Utilities: Executive Outlook. (Survey on Technology & Markets Ser.: No. 202). 50p. 1993. pap. text 200.00 (*1-55865-233-7*) Future Tech Surveys.
— Emergency Lighting. LC 89-85437. (Survey on Technology & Markets Ser.: No. 129). 50p. 1991. pap. text 200.00 (*1-55865-152-7*) Future Tech Surveys.
— Energy Efficient Motors. (Survey on Technology & Markets Ser.: No. 212). 50p. 1993. pap. text 200.00 (*1-55865-243-4*) Future Tech Surveys.
— Energy Management & HVAC Software. LC 90-83908. (Survey on Technology & Markets Ser.: No. 103). 50p. 1991. pap. text 200.00 (*1-55865-126-8*) Future Tech Surveys.
— Energy Management Consulting Services. LC 90-83914. (Survey on Technology & Markets Ser.: No. 106). 50p. 1991. pap. text 200.00 (*1-55865-129-2*) Future Tech Surveys.
— Energy Management in Commercial Buildings. LC 90-83913. (Survey on Technology & Markets Ser.: No. 105). 50p. 1991. pap. text 200.00 (*1-55865-128-4*) Future Tech Surveys.
— Energy Management, Industrial. LC 90-83912. (Survey on Technology & Markets Ser.: No. 104). 50p. 1991. pap. text 200.00 (*1-55865-127-6*) Future Tech Surveys.
— Energy Management Systems. (Survey on Technology & Markets Ser.: No. 208). 50p. 1993. pap. text 200.00 (*1-55865-239-6*) Future Tech Surveys.
— Energy Project Financing. LC 90-83924. (Survey on Technology & Markets Ser.: No. 120). 50p. 1991. pap. text 200.00 (*1-55865-143-8*) Future Tech Surveys.
— Environmental & Waste Management Robotics. LC 90-83894. (Survey on Technology & Markets Ser.: No. 190). 50p. 1991. pap. text 200.00 (*1-55865-214-0*) Future Tech Surveys.
— Environmental Consulting Services. (Survey on Technology & Markets Ser.: No. 219). 50p. 1993. pap. text 200.00 (*1-55865-250-7*) Future Tech Surveys.
— Environmental Immunoassays. (Survey on Technology & Markets Ser.: No. 169). 50p. 1991. pap. text 200.00 (*1-55865-231-0*) Future Tech Surveys.
— Environmental Legal Services. (Survey on Technology & Markets Ser.: No. 223). 50p. 1993. pap. text 200.00 (*1-55865-253-1*) Future Tech Surveys.
— Environmental Noise Control. LC 90-83904. (Survey on Technology & Markets Ser.: No. 200). 50p. 1991. pap. text 200.00 (*1-55865-224-8*) Future Tech Surveys.
— Environmental Software. (Survey on Technology & Markets Ser.: No. 217). 50p. 1993. pap. text 200.00 (*1-55865-248-5*) Future Tech Surveys.
— Expert Systems. LC 90-83860. (Survey on Technology & Markets Ser.: No. 153). 50p. 1991. pap. text 200.00 (*1-55865-180-2*) Future Tech Surveys.
— Fluidized Bed Boilers. LC 89-85439. (Survey on Technology & Markets Ser.: No. 131). 50p. 1991. pap. text 200.00 (*1-55865-154-3*) Future Tech Surveys.
— Fuel Cells. LC 90-83923. (Survey on Technology & Markets Ser.: No. 119). 50p. 1991. pap. text 200.00 (*1-55865-142-X*) Future Tech Surveys.
— Fume Hoods. LC 90-83928. (Survey on Technology & Markets Ser.: No. 133). 50p. 1991. pap. text 200.00 (*1-55865-158-6*) Future Tech Surveys.
— Global Positioning Systems. LC 90-83857. (Survey on Technology & Markets Ser.: No. 152). 50p. 1991. pap. text 200.00 (*1-55865-177-2*) Future Tech Surveys.
— Hearing Protective Devices. LC 90-83902. (Survey on Technology & Markets Ser.: No. 198). 50p. 1991. pap. text 200.00 (*1-55865-222-1*) Future Tech Surveys.
— Heat Pumps. LC 89-85430. (Survey on Technology & Markets Ser.: No. 122). 50p. 1991. pap. text 200.00 (*1-55865-145-4*) Future Tech Surveys.
— Heat Recovery Equipment. LC 89-85431. (Survey on Technology & Markets Ser.: No. 123). 50p. 1991. pap. text 200.00 (*1-55865-146-2*) Future Tech Surveys.
— HVAC - R CFC Recovery Equipment. (Survey on Technology & Markets Ser.: No. 210). 50p. 1993. pap. text 200.00 (*1-55865-241-8*) Future Tech Surveys.
— HVAC & Energy Systems Water Treatment. LC 90-83929. (Survey on Technology & Markets Ser.: No. 134). 50p. 1991. pap. text 200.00 (*1-55865-159-4*) Future Tech Surveys.
— Indoor Air Quality. (Survey on Technology & Markets Ser.: No. 218). 50p. 1993. pap. text 200.00 (*1-55865-249-3*) Future Tech Surveys.
— Industrial Air Pollution Control Equipment. LC 90-83885. (Survey on Technology & Markets Ser.: No. 181). 50p. 1991. pap. text 200.00 (*1-55865-205-1*) Future Tech Surveys.
— Infrared Heaters. LC 89-85433. (Survey on Technology & Markets Ser.: No. 125). 50p. (Orig.). 1991. pap. text 200.00 (*1-55865-148-9*) Future Tech Surveys.
— Intelligent Buildings. LC 90-83911. (Survey on Technology & Markets Ser.: No. 102). 50p. (Orig.). 1991. pap. text 200.00 (*1-55865-125-X*) Future Tech Surveys.
— Landfill Design & Construction. LC 90-83887. (Survey on Technology & Markets Ser.: No. 183). 50p. 1991. pap. text 200.00 (*1-55865-207-8*) Future Tech Surveys.
— Landfill Methane Gas Recovery. LC 90-83892. (Survey on Technology & Markets Ser.: No. 188). 50p. 1991. pap. text 200.00 (*1-55865-212-4*) Future Tech Surveys.
— Landfill Privatization. LC 90-83886. (Survey on Technology & Markets Ser.: No. 182). 50p. 1991. pap. text 200.00 (*1-55865-206-X*) Future Tech Surveys.
— Lead Paint Abatement. LC 90-83850. (Survey on Technology & Markets Ser.: No. 145). 50p. 1991. pap. text 200.00 (*1-55865-170-5*) Future Tech Surveys.
— Leak Detectors. (Survey on Technology & Markets Ser.: No. 216). 50p. 1993. pap. text 200.00 (*1-55865-247-7*) Future Tech Surveys.
— Lechate Collection & Treatment Systems. LC 90-83891. (Survey on Technology & Markets Ser.: No. 187). 50p. 1991. pap. text 200.00 (*1-55865-211-6*) Future Tech Surveys.
— Lining Systems & Containment Membranes. LC 90-83853. (Survey on Technology & Markets Ser.: No. 148). 50p. 1991. pap. text 200.00 (*1-55865-173-X*) Future Tech Surveys.
— Medical Waste Management. LC 90-83866. (Survey on Technology & Markets Ser.: No. 161). 50p. 1991. pap. text 200.00 (*1-55865-186-1*) Future Tech Surveys.
— Meteorological Instruments. LC 90-83899. (Survey on Technology & Markets Ser.: No. 195). 50p. 1991. pap. text 200.00 (*1-55865-219-1*) Future Tech Surveys.
— Municipal & Industrial Composting. LC 90-83868. (Survey on Technology & Markets Ser.: No. 163). 50p. 1991. pap. text 200.00 (*1-55865-188-8*) Future Tech Surveys.
— Natural Gas: Executive Outlook. (Survey on Technology & Markets Ser.: No. 204). 50p. 1993. pap. text 200.00 (*1-55865-235-3*) Future Tech Surveys.
— Natural Gas Vehicles. (Survey on Technology & Markets Ser.: No. 205). 50p. 1993. pap. text 200.00 (*1-55865-236-1*) Future Tech Surveys.
— Neural Network. LC 90-83861. (Survey on Technology & Markets Ser.: No. 154). 50p. 1991. pap. text 200.00 (*1-55865-181-0*) Future Tech Surveys.
— Occupancy Sensors. LC 89-85424. (Survey on Technology & Markets Ser.: No. 116). 50p. 1991. pap. text 200.00 (*1-55865-139-X*) Future Tech Surveys.
— Oil Spill Prevention & Clean-Up. LC 90-83867. (Survey on Technology & Markets Ser.: No. 162). 50p. 1991. pap. text 200.00 (*1-55865-187-X*) Future Tech Surveys.
— Outdoor Lighting Systems. LC 89-85436. (Survey on Technology & Markets Ser.: No. 128). 50p. 1991. pap. text 200.00 (*1-55865-151-9*) Future Tech Surveys.
— Packaged Cogeneration Systems. LC 90-83915. (Survey on Technology & Markets Ser.: No. 108). 50p. 1991. pap. text 200.00 (*1-55865-131-4*) Future Tech Surveys.
— Paper Recycling. LC 90-83878. (Survey on Technology & Markets Ser.: No. 174). 50p. 1991. pap. text 200.00 (*1-55865-198-5*) Future Tech Surveys.
— PCBs. LC 90-83852. (Survey on Technology & Markets Ser.: No. 147). 50p. 1991. pap. text 200.00 (*1-55865-172-1*) Future Tech Surveys.
— Pet Recycling. LC 90-83876. (Survey on Technology & Markets Ser.: No. 171). 50p. 1991. pap. text 200.00 (*1-55865-196-9*) Future Tech Surveys.
— Petroleum: Strategic Planning & Future Trends. LC 90-83932. (Survey on Technology & Markets Ser.: No. 138). 50p. 1991. pap. text 200.00 (*1-55865-163-2*) Future Tech Surveys.
— Photovoltaics. LC 89-85417. (Survey on Technology & Markets Ser.: No. 109). 50p. 1991. pap. text 200.00 (*1-55865-132-2*) Future Tech Surveys.
— PID Controllers. LC 89-85429. (Survey on Technology & Markets Ser.: No. 121). 50p. 1991. pap. text 200.00 (*1-55865-144-6*) Future Tech Surveys.
— Protective Clothing. LC 90-83903. (Survey on Technology & Markets Ser.: No. 199). 50p. 1991. pap. text 200.00 (*1-55865-223-X*) Future Tech Surveys.
— Radon. LC 90-83851. (Survey on Technology & Markets Ser.: No. 146). 50p. 1991. pap. text 200.00 (*1-55865-171-3*) Future Tech Surveys.
— Respiratory Protection. LC 90-83901. (Survey on Technology & Markets Ser.: No. 197). 50p. 1991. pap. text 200.00 (*1-55865-221-3*) Future Tech Surveys.
— Secondary Containment Systems. (Survey on Technology & Markets Ser.: No. 157). 50p. 1991. 200.00 (*1-55865-227-2*) Future Tech Surveys.
— Site Remediation. (Survey on Technology & Markets Ser.: No. 227). 50p. 1994. pap. text 200.00 (*1-55865-258-2*) Future Tech Surveys.
— Sludge Management Equipment. LC 90-83900. (Survey on Technology & Markets Ser.: No. 196). 50p. 1991. pap. text 200.00 (*1-55865-220-5*) Future Tech Surveys.
— Solar Screen Window Films. LC 90-83927. (Survey on Technology & Markets Ser.: No. 130). 50p. 1991. pap. text 200.00 (*1-55865-153-5*) Future Tech Surveys.
— Solvent Recovery Equipment. LC 90-83881. (Survey on Technology & Markets Ser.: No. 177). 50p. 1991. pap. text 200.00 (*1-55865-201-9*) Future Tech Surveys.
— Sorbents. LC 90-83873. (Survey on Technology & Markets Ser.: No. 168). 50p. 1991. pap. text 200.00 (*1-55865-193-4*) Future Tech Surveys.
— Spectroscopy in Environmental & Occupational Health Applications. LC 90-83875. (Survey on Technology & Markets Ser.: No. 170). 50p. 1991. pap. text 200.00 (*1-55865-195-0*) Future Tech Surveys.
— Standby Power Systems. LC 90-83920. (Survey on Technology & Markets Ser.: No. 115). 50p. 1991. pap. text 200.00 (*1-55865-138-1*) Future Tech Surveys.
— Steam Traps. LC 89-85440. (Survey on Technology & Markets Ser.: No. 132). 50p. 1991. pap. text 200.00 (*1-55865-155-1*) Future Tech Surveys.
— Stormwater Management. (Survey on Technology & Markets Ser.: No. 225). 50p. 1993. pap. text 200.00 (*1-55865-255-8*) Future Tech Surveys.
— Thermal Energy Storage. (Survey on Technology & Markets Ser.: No. 206). 50p. 1993. pap. text 200.00 (*1-55865-237-X*) Future Tech Surveys.
— Underground Storage Tanks. (Survey on Technology & Markets Ser.: No. 214). 50p. 1994. pap. text 200.00 (*1-55865-245-0*) Future Tech Surveys.
— UNIX Workstations. LC 90-83862. (Survey on Technology & Markets Ser.: No. 155). 50p. 1991. pap. text 200.00 (*1-55865-182-9*) Future Tech Surveys.
— Used Tire Recycling & Resource Recovery. LC 90-83879. (Survey on Technology & Markets Ser.: No. 175). 50p. 1991. pap. text 200.00 (*1-55865-199-3*) Future Tech Surveys.
— Utility Meter Reading Systems. LC 89-85445. (Survey on Technology & Markets Ser.: No. 137). 50p. 1991. pap. text 200.00 (*1-55865-162-4*) Future Tech Surveys.
— Utility-Scale Energy Storage. LC 90-83919. (Survey on Technology & Markets Ser.: No. 114). 50p. 1991. pap. text 200.00 (*1-55865-137-3*) Future Tech Surveys.
— Variable Frequency Motor Drives. (Survey on Technology & Markets Ser.: No. 211). 50p. 1993. pap. text 200.00 (*1-55865-242-6*) Future Tech Surveys.
— Vibration Isolators. LC 90-83930. (Survey on Technology & Markets Ser.: No. 135). 50p. 1991. pap. text 200.00 (*1-55865-160-8*) Future Tech Surveys.
— Virtual Reality. (Survey on Technology & Markets Ser.: No. 201). 50p. 1991. pap. text 200.00 (*1-55865-232-9*) Future Tech Surveys.
— Waste Compactors. LC 90-83890. (Survey on Technology & Markets Ser.: No. 186). 50p. 1991. pap. text 200.00 (*1-55865-210-8*) Future Tech Surveys.
— Waste Minimization & Pollution Prevention. (Survey on Technology & Markets Ser.: No. 224). 50p. 1993. pap. text 200.00 (*1-55865-254-X*) Future Tech Surveys.
— Waste Oil Recycling & Resource Recovery. LC 90-83880. (Survey on Technology & Markets Ser.: No. 176). 50p. 1991. pap. text 200.00 (*1-55865-200-0*) Future Tech Surveys.
— Waste Shredders. LC 90-83889. (Survey on Technology & Markets Ser.: No. 185). 50p. 1991. pap. text 200.00 (*1-55865-209-4*) Future Tech Surveys.
— Waste-to-Energy. (Survey on Technology & Markets Ser.: No. 213). 50p. 1994. pap. text 200.00 (*1-55865-244-2*) Future Tech Surveys.
— Water Quality Instrumentation. LC 90-83896. (Survey on Technology & Markets Ser.: No. 192). 50p. 1991. pap. text 200.00 (*1-55865-216-7*) Future Tech Surveys.
— Wind Power. LC 90-83925. (Survey on Technology & Markets Ser.: No. 124). 50p. 1991. pap. text 200.00 (*1-55865-147-0*) Future Tech Surveys.

Miller, Richard K. & Sell, George R. Volterra Integral Equations & Topological Dynamics. LC 52-42839. (Memoirs Ser.: No. 1/102). 67p. 1979. reprint ed. pap. 19.00 (*0-8218-1802-3*, MEMO/1/102) Am Math.

M

Miller, Richard K. & Supnow, Marcia E. Electric Vehicles. (Survey on Technology & Markets Ser.: No. 203). 50p. 1994. pap. text 200.00 (*1-55865-234-5*) Future Tech Surveys.

Miller, Richard K. & Thiede, Henry A., eds. HIV, Prenatal Infections & Therapy: The Role of the Placenta. (Trophoblast Research Ser.: Vol. 8). (Illus.). 632p. 1995. 135.00 (*1-878822-45-4*) Univ Rochester Pr.

— Molecular Biology & Cell Regulation of the Placenta. (Trophoblast Research Ser.: Vol. 5). (Illus.). 488p. (C). 1991. 85.00 (*0-9630864-0-5*) Verav Med.

Miller, Richard K. & Thumann, Albert. Fundamentals of Noise Control Engineering. 2nd ed. 292p. 1989. text 68.00 (*0-88173-091-2*) Fairmont Pr.

Miller, Richard K. & Walker, Matthew, eds. Superconductivity Update. LC 88-45796. 220p. 1990. pap. text 95.00 (*0-88173-071-8*) Fairmont Pr.

Miller, Richard K. & Walker, Terri C. Active Noise Control. LC 88-81665. (Survey on Technology & Markets Ser.: No. 74). 50p. 1989. pap. text 200.00 (*1-55865-073-3*) Future Tech Surveys.

— AI Programming Systems. LC 88-81893. (Survey on Technology & Markets Ser.: No. 95). 50p. 1989. pap. text 200.00 (*1-55865-095-4*) Future Tech Surveys.

— Aquaculture. LC 88-80910. (Survey on Technology & Markets Ser.: No. 27). 50p. 1989. pap. text 200.00 (*1-55865-026-1*) Future Tech Surveys.

— Array Processors. LC 88-81632. (Survey on Technology & Markets Ser.: No. 41). 50p. 1989. pap. text 200.00 (*1-55865-040-7*) Future Tech Surveys.

— Artificial Neural Systems: A Survey on Technology & Markets, No. 11. LC 88-80489. 44p. 1989. pap. text 200.00 (*1-55865-010-5*) Future Tech Surveys.

— Automated Guided Vehicles: A Survey on Technology & Markets. LC 88-80495. 50p. 1989. pap. text 200.00 (*1-55865-002-4*) Future Tech Surveys.

— Automotive Sensors: A Survey on Technology & Markets. LC 88-84057. (Survey on Technology & Markets Ser.: No. 67). 50p. 1989. pap. text 200.00 (*1-55865-109-8*) Future Tech Surveys.

— Autonomous Vehicle Guidance Systems. LC 88-81887. (Survey on Technology & Markets Ser.: No. 90). 50p. 1989. pap. text 200.00 (*1-55865-089-X*) Future Tech Surveys.

— Bioprocessing. LC 88-80910. (Survey on Technology & Markets Ser.: No. 26). 50p. 1989. pap. text 200.00 (*1-55865-025-3*) Future Tech Surveys.

— Biosensors: A Survey on Technology & Markets. LC 88-80900. (Survey on Technology & Markets Ser.: No. 16). 50p. 1989. pap. text 200.00 (*1-55865-015-6*) Future Tech Surveys.

— Biotechnology in Animal Agriculture. LC 88-80913. (Survey on Technology & Markets Ser.: No. 25). 50p. 1989. pap. text 200.00 (*1-55865-024-5*) Future Tech Surveys.

— Biotechnology in Plant Agriculture. LC 88-80908. (Survey on Technology & Markets Ser.: No. 24). 50p. 1989. pap. text 200.00 (*1-55865-023-7*) Future Tech Surveys.

— Canadian CIM Markets. LC 88-84067. (Survey on Technology & Markets Ser.: No. 72). 50p. 1989. pap. text 200.00 (*1-55865-119-5*) Future Tech Surveys.

— CD-ROM. LC 88-80905. (Survey on Technology & Markets Ser.: No. 21). 50p. 1989. pap. text 200.00 (*1-55865-020-2*) Future Tech Surveys.

— Cellular Telephones. LC 88-81674. (Survey on Technology & Markets Ser.: No. 83). 50p. 1989. pap. text 200.00 (*1-55865-082-2*) Future Tech Surveys.

— Chaos Fractals & Non-Linear Dynamic Systems. LC 88-80491. (Survey on Technology & Markets Ser.: No. 12). 50p. 1989. pap. text 200.00 (*1-55865-011-3*) Future Tech Surveys.

— CIM Systems Integrators. LC 88-81657. (Survey on Technology & Markets Ser.: No. 66). 50p. 1989. pap. text 200.00 (*1-55865-065-2*) Future Tech Surveys.

— Clean Room Robotics. LC 88-81637. (Survey on Technology & Markets Ser.: No. 46). 50p. 1989. pap. text 200.00 (*1-55865-045-8*) Future Tech Surveys.

— Color Sensors & Instrumentation. LC 88-84060. (Survey on Technology & Markets Ser.: No. 85). 50p. 1989. pap. text 200.00 (*1-55865-112-8*) Future Tech Surveys.

— Computer-Aided Software Engineering. LC 88-81631. (Survey on Technology & Markets Ser.: No. 40). 50p. 1989. pap. text 200.00 (*1-55865-039-3*) Future Tech Surveys.

— Computer Integrated Manufacturing. LC 88-72187. (Survey on Technology & Markets Ser.: No. 34). 50p. 1989. pap. text 200.00 (*1-55865-099-7*) Future Tech Surveys.

— Computer Workstations: A Survey on Technology & Markets, No. 7. LC 88-80485. 50p. 1988. pap. text 200.00 (*1-55865-006-7*) Future Tech Surveys.

— Computers for Artificial Intelligence. LC 88-84063. (Survey on Technology & Markets Ser.: No. 91). 50p. 1989. pap. text 200.00 (*1-55865-115-2*) Future Tech Surveys.

— Coordinate Measuring Machines. LC 88-81668. (Survey on Technology & Markets Ser.: No. 77). 50p. 1989. pap. text 200.00 (*1-55865-076-8*) Future Tech Surveys.

— Database Engines. LC 88-81633. (Survey on Technology & Markets Ser.: No. 42). 50p. 1989. pap. text 200.00 (*1-55865-041-5*) Future Tech Surveys.

— Decision Support Systems. LC 88-81884. (Survey on Technology & Markets Ser.: No. 93). 50p. 1989. pap. text 200.00 (*1-55865-092-X*) Future Tech Surveys.

— Dextrous Robotic Hands. LC 88-80903. (Survey on Technology & Markets Ser.: No. 19). 50p. 1989. pap. text 200.00 (*1-55865-018-0*) Future Tech Surveys.

— Diamond Films: A Survey on Technology & Markets, No. 14. LC 88-80492. 34p. 1989. pap. text 200.00 (*1-55865-013-X*) Future Tech Surveys.

— Environmental Markets: 1991-93. 435p. 1991. 285.00 (*0-89671-118-8*) SEAI Tech Pubns.

— Expert Systems in Manufacturing. LC 88-81886. (Survey on Technology & Markets Ser.: No. 92). 50p. 1989. pap. text 200.00 (*1-55865-091-1*) Future Tech Surveys.

— Fault-Tolerant Computers. LC 88-81635. (Survey on Technology & Markets Ser.: No. 44). 50p. 1989. pap. text 200.00 (*1-55865-043-1*) Future Tech Surveys.

— Fiber Optic LANS. LC 88-81643. (Survey on Technology & Markets Ser.: No. 52). 50p. 1989. pap. text 200.00 (*1-55865-051-2*) Future Tech Surveys.

— Fiber Optic Sensors. LC 88-81651. (Survey on Technology & Markets Ser.: No. 60). 50p. 1989. pap. text 200.00 (*1-55865-059-8*) Future Tech Surveys.

— Flat Panel Displays. LC 88-81655. (Survey on Technology & Markets Ser.: No. 64). 50p. 1989. pap. text 200.00 (*1-55865-063-6*) Future Tech Surveys.

— Flexible Manufacturing Systems. LC 88-81645. (Survey on Technology & Markets Ser.: No. 54). 50p. 1989. pap. text 200.00 (*1-55865-053-9*) Future Tech Surveys.

— Flow Sensors. LC 88-84053. (Survey on Technology & Markets Ser.: No. 32). 50p. 1989. pap. text 200.00 (*1-55865-105-5*) Future Tech Surveys.

— FMS-CIM Systems Integration Handbook. LC 88-45791. 520p. 1989. pap. text 95.00 (*0-88173-067-X*) Fairmont Pr.

— Four Eighty-Six Microprocessor Impact. LC 88-84066. (Survey on Technology & Markets Ser.: No. 96). 50p. 1989. pap. text 200.00 (*1-55865-118-7*) Future Tech Surveys.

— Fuzzy Controllers. 82p. 1991. 285.00 (*0-89671-117-X*) SEAI Tech Pubns.

— Fuzzy Sets & Systems. LC 88-81895. (Survey on Technology & Markets Ser.: No. 94). 50p. 1989. pap. text 200.00 (*1-55865-093-8*) Future Tech Surveys.

— Gallium Arsenide. LC 88-81650. (Survey on Technology & Markets Ser.: No. 59). 50p. 1989. pap. text 200.00 (*1-55865-058-X*) Future Tech Surveys.

— Global Positioning System Applications. 156p. 1991. 285.00 (*0-89671-125-0*) SEAI Tech Pubns.

— High-Tc Superconductor Applications: A Survey on Technology & Markets, No. 4. LC 88-80490. 49p. 1988. pap. text 200.00 (*1-55865-003-2*) Future Tech Surveys.

— Holography. LC 88-81642. (Survey on Technology & Markets Ser.: No. 51). 50p. 1989. pap. text 200.00 (*1-55865-050-4*) Future Tech Surveys.

— Image Compression. 87p. 1991. 285.00 (*0-89671-122-6*) SEAI Tech Pubns.

— Indoor Air Quality. 244p. 1991. 285.00 (*0-89671-116-1*) SEAI Tech Pubns.

— Industrial Bioelectronics. LC 88-80907. (Survey on Technology & Markets Ser.: No. 23). 50p. 1989. pap. text 200.00 (*1-55865-022-9*) Future Tech Surveys.

— Industrial Heat Processing Equipment. LC 88-80493. (Survey on Technology & Markets Ser.: No. 78). 50p. 1989. pap. text 200.00 (*1-55865-077-6*) Future Tech Surveys.

— Industrial Noise Control Markets. LC 88-84059. (Survey on Technology & Markets Ser.: No. 68). 50p. 1989. pap. text 200.00 (*1-55865-067-9*) Future Tech Surveys.

— Industrial Robots. LC 88-81646. (Survey on Technology & Markets Ser.: No. 55). 50p. 1989. pap. text 200.00 (*1-55865-054-7*) Future Tech Surveys.

— Infrared Thermography. LC 88-84058. (Survey on Technology & Markets Ser.: No. 73). 50p. 1989. pap. text 200.00 (*1-55865-110-1*) Future Tech Surveys.

— Integrated Optical Circuits. LC 88-81644. (Survey on Technology & Markets Ser.: No. 53). 50p. 1989. pap. text 200.00 (*1-55865-052-0*) Future Tech Surveys.

— Interactive Multi-Media. 138p. 1991. 285.00 (*0-89671-121-8*) SEAI Tech Pubns.

— Knowledge-Based Systems: A Survey on Technology & Markets. LC 88-80493. 50p. 1989. pap. text 200.00 (*1-55865-000-8*) Future Tech Surveys.

— Laboratory Robots. LC 88-81638. (Survey on Technology & Markets Ser.: No. 47). 50p. 1989. pap. text 200.00 (*1-55865-046-6*) Future Tech Surveys.

— Laser Sensors. LC 88-72189. (Survey on Technology & Markets Ser.: No. 80). 50p. 1989. pap. text 200.00 (*1-55865-097-0*) Future Tech Surveys.

— Learning & Automated Discovery in AI Systems. LC 88-81889. (Survey on Technology & Markets Ser.: No. 88). 50p. 1989. pap. text 200.00 (*1-55865-087-3*) Future Tech Surveys.

— Machine Translation. LC 88-80494. (Survey on Technology & Markets Ser.: No. 2). 50p. 1989. pap. text 200.00 (*1-55865-001-6*) Future Tech Surveys.

— Machine Vision. LC 88-80902. (Survey on Technology & Markets Ser.: No. 18). 50p. 1989. pap. text 200.00 (*1-55865-017-2*) Future Tech Surveys.

— Magnetic Refrigeration: A Survey on Technology & Markets. LC 88-80922. (Survey on Technology & Markets Ser.: No. 38). 50p. 1989. pap. text 200.00 (*1-55865-037-7*) Future Tech Surveys.

— Manufacturing Simulation. LC 88-72190. (Survey on Technology & Markets Ser.: No. 35). 50p. 1989. pap. text 200.00 (*1-55865-096-2*) Future Tech Surveys.

— Manufacturing Software. LC 88-81640. (Survey on Technology & Markets Ser.: No. 49). 50p. 1989. pap. text 200.00 (*1-55865-048-2*) Future Tech Surveys.

— Map & Industrial LANS. LC 88-81647. (Survey on Technology & Markets Ser.: No. 56). 50p. 1989. pap. text 200.00 (*1-55865-055-5*) Future Tech Surveys.

— Medical-Clinical Bioelectronics. LC 88-80906. (Survey on Technology & Markets Ser.: No. 22). 50p. 1989. pap. text 200.00 (*1-55865-021-0*) Future Tech Surveys.

— Molecular Electronics. LC 88-81636. (Survey on Technology & Markets Ser.: No. 45). 50p. 1989. pap. text 200.00 (*1-55865-044-X*) Future Tech Surveys.

— Multi-Sensor & Data Fusion. LC 88-81634. (Survey on Technology & Markets Ser.: No. 43). 50p. 1989. pap. text 200.00 (*1-55865-042-3*) Future Tech Surveys.

— Natural Language & Voice Processing. LC 89-17105. 259p. 1989. pap. text 95.00 (*0-88173-102-1*) Fairmont Pr.

Miller, Richard K. & Walker, Terri C. Natural Language & Voice Processing. 269p. (C). 1989. pap. text 95.00 (*0-13-610734-6*, Macmillan Coll) P-H.

Miller, Richard K. & Walker, Terri C. Natural Language Understanding. LC 88-81661. (Survey on Technology & Markets Ser.: No. 70). 50p. 1989. pap. text 200.00 (*1-55865-069-5*) Future Tech Surveys.

— Non-Industrial Robotic Markets, No. 9. LC 88-80487. (Survey on Technology & Markets Ser.). 52p. 1989. pap. text 200.00 (*1-55865-008-3*) Future Tech Surveys.

— Occupational Safety & Industrial Hygiene Markets. 3rd rev. ed. 426p. 1997. 485.00 (*1-881503-77-1*) R K Miller Assocs.

— Optical Computing. LC 88-81641. (Survey on Technology & Markets Ser.: No. 50). 50p. 1989. pap. text 200.00 (*1-55865-049-0*) Future Tech Surveys.

— Optical Encoders & Resolvers. LC 88-84061. (Survey on Technology & Markets Ser.: No. 86). 50p. 1989. pap. text 200.00 (*1-55865-113-6*) Future Tech Surveys.

— Parallel Processing. LC 89-17155. 284p. 1989. pap. text 95.00 (*0-88173-101-3*) Fairmont Pr.

— Parallel Processing. 200p. 1991. 285.00 (*0-89671-128-5*) SEAI Tech Pubns.

— Parallel Processing: A Survey on Technology & Markets, No. 8. LC 88-80486. 32p. 1988. pap. text 200.00 (*1-55865-007-5*) Future Tech Surveys.

— Pressure Sensors. LC 88-84054. (Survey on Technology & Markets Ser.: No. 48). 50p. 1989. pap. text 200.00 (*1-55865-106-3*) Future Tech Surveys.

— Programmable Controllers. LC 88-81656. (Survey on Technology & Markets Ser.: No. 65). 50p. 1989. pap. text 200.00 (*1-55865-064-4*) Future Tech Surveys.

— Radiation Detectors. LC 88-84052. (Survey on Technology & Markets Ser.: No. 31). 50p. 1989. pap. text 200.00 (*1-55865-104-7*) Future Tech Surveys.

— Remote Sensing. LC 88-84059. (Survey on Technology & Markets Ser.: No. 81). 50p. 1991. pap. text 200.00 (*1-55865-111-X*) Future Tech Surveys.

— RISC Architectures. LC 88-81639. (Survey on Technology & Markets Ser.: No. 87). 50p. 1989. pap. text 200.00 (*1-55865-086-5*) Future Tech Surveys.

— Robotic Applications in Non-Industrial Environments. 311p. 1991. 285.00 (*0-89671-119-6*) SEAI Tech Pubns.

— Robotic, Vision & AI Applications in Agriculture. LC 88-81667. (Survey on Technology & Markets Ser.: No. 76). 50p. 1989. pap. text 200.00 (*1-55865-075-X*) Future Tech Surveys.

— Sensor Markets, 1991-95. 235p. 1991. 485.00 (*0-89671-115-3*) SEAI Tech Pubns.

— Shape Memory Alloys. LC 88-81888. (Survey on Technology & Markets Ser.: No. 89). 50p. 1989. pap. text 200.00 (*1-55865-100-4*) Future Tech Surveys.

— Silicon Micromachining & Microstructures. LC 88-80901. (Survey on Technology & Markets Ser.: No. 17). 50p. 1989. pap. text 200.00 (*1-55865-016-4*) Future Tech Surveys.

— Smart Cards. LC 88-80899. (Survey on Technology & Markets Ser.: No. 15). 50p. 1989. pap. text 200.00 (*1-55865-014-8*) Future Tech Surveys.

— Smart Homes & Home Automation. LC 88-80904. (Survey on Technology & Markets Ser.: No. 20). 50p. 1989. pap. text 200.00 (*1-55865-019-9*) Future Tech Surveys.

— Smart Power Chips. LC 88-81670. (Survey on Technology & Markets Ser.: No. 79). 50p. 1989. pap. text 200.00 (*1-55865-078-4*) Future Tech Surveys.

— Smart Sensors. LC 88-81654. (Survey on Technology & Markets Ser.: No. 63). 50p. 1989. pap. text 200.00 (*1-55865-062-8*) Future Tech Surveys.

— Solid State Cameras. LC 88-81662. (Survey on Technology & Markets Ser.: No. 71). 50p. 1989. pap. text 200.00 (*1-55865-070-9*) Future Tech Surveys.

— Spatial Light Modulators. LC 88-80482. (Survey on Technology & Markets Ser.: No. 13). 50p. 1989. pap. text 200.00 (*1-55865-012-1*) Future Tech Surveys.

— SQUID Sensors. LC 88-81653. (Survey on Technology & Markets Ser.: No. 62). 50p. 1989. pap. text 200.00 (*1-55865-061-X*) Future Tech Surveys.

— Supercomputers. LC 88-82059. (Survey on Technology & Markets Ser.: No. 37). 50p. 1989. pap. text 200.00 (*1-55865-036-9*) Future Tech Surveys.

— Superconductor Magnetic Energy Storage. LC 88-80923. (Survey on Technology & Markets Ser.: No. 39). 50p. 1989. pap. text 200.00 (*1-55865-038-5*) Future Tech Surveys.

— Surface Mount Technology. LC 88-81649. (Survey on Technology & Markets Ser.: No. 58). 50p. 1989. pap. text 200.00 (*1-55865-057-1*) Future Tech Surveys.

— Tactile Sensors: A Survey on Technology & Markets, No. 6. LC 88-80484. 54p. 1988. pap. text 200.00 (*1-55865-005-9*) Future Tech Surveys.

— Temperature Sensors. LC 88-72188. (Survey on Technology & Markets Ser.: No. 30). 50p. 1989. pap. text 200.00 (*1-55865-098-9*) Future Tech Surveys.

— Thin Film Sensors. LC 88-84057. (Survey on Technology & Markets Ser.: No. 61). 50p. 1989. pap. text 200.00 (*1-55865-107-1*) Future Tech Surveys.

— Three-D Computing: Modeling, Image Processing, & Visualization. 246p. 1991. 285.00 (*0-89671-130-7*) SEAI Tech Pubns.

— Underground Storage Tanks. 226p. 1991. 285.00 (*0-89671-120-X*) SEAI Tech Pubns.

— UNIX. LC 88-82060. (Survey on Technology & Markets Ser.: No. 84). 50p. 1989. pap. text 200.00 (*1-55865-083-0*) Future Tech Surveys.

— Vibration Sensors & Analyzers. LC 88-81666. (Survey on Technology & Markets Ser.: No. 75). 50p. 1989. pap. text 200.00 (*1-55865-074-1*) Future Tech Surveys.

— Voice & Speech Processing. 293p. 1991. 285.00 (*0-89671-126-9*) SEAI Tech Pubns.

— Voice Processing. LC 88-81660. (Survey on Technology & Markets Ser.: No. 69). 50p. 1989. pap. text 200.00 (*1-55865-068-7*) Future Tech Surveys.

— Waterjet Cutting: A Survey on Technology & Markets, No. 5. LC 88-80483. 36p. 1988. pap. text 200.00 (*1-55865-004-0*) Future Tech Surveys.

— Workstation Trends of the 1990s. 212p. 1991. 285.00 (*0-89671-114-5*) SEAI Tech Pubns.

— X-Ray Machine Vision & Computed Tomography: A Survey on Technology & Markets, No. 10. LC 88-80488. 36p. 1988. pap. text 200.00 (*1-55865-009-1*) Future Tech Surveys.

Miller, Richard K. & Walker, Terri C., eds. Environmental Markets: 1992-1995. (Orig.). 1992. pap. text 485.00 (*1-881503-00-3*) R K Miller Assocs.

— Sensor & Instrumentation Markets, 1992-1995. (Orig.). 1992. pap. text 485.00 (*1-881503-01-1*) R K Miller Assocs.

Miller, Richard K., et al. Analytical Laboratory Services: Water. (Market Research Survey Ser.: No. 276). 50p. 1996. 200.00 (*1-55865-295-7*) Future Tech Surveys.

— Commercial & Residential Water Environmental Markets. 155p. 1997. 135.00 (*1-881503-66-6*) R K Miller Assocs.

— Contract Operations & Municipal Water/Wastewater Privatization. (Market Research Survey Ser.: No. 274). 50p. 1996. 200.00 (*1-55865-298-1*) Future Tech Surveys.

— Environmental Consulting Services: Water & Wastewater. (Market Research Survey Ser.: No. 273). 50p. 1996. 200.00 (*1-55865-297-3*) Future Tech Surveys.

— Environmental Markets: Alabama. 130p. 1996. 185.00 (*1-881503-39-9*) R K Miller Assocs.

— Environmental Markets: Arizona. 130p. 1996. 185.00 (*1-881503-44-5*) R K Miller Assocs.

— Environmental Markets: Arkansas. 130p. 1996. 185.00 (*1-881503-43-7*) R K Miller Assocs.

— Environmental Markets: California. 130p. 1996. 185.00 (*1-881503-29-1*) R K Miller Assocs.

— Environmental Markets: Colorado. 130p. 1996. 185.00 (*1-881503-32-1*) R K Miller Assocs.

— Environmental Markets: Connecticut. 130p. 1996. 185.00 (*1-881503-42-9*) R K Miller Assocs.

— Environmental Markets: Georgia. 130p. 1996. 185.00 (*1-881503-28-3*) R K Miller Assocs.

— Environmental Markets: Illinois. 130p. 1996. 185.00 (*1-881503-49-6*) R K Miller Assocs.

— Environmental Markets: Indiana. 130p. 1996. 185.00 (*1-881503-40-2*) R K Miller Assocs.

— Environmental Markets: Iowa. 130p. 1996. 185.00 (*1-881503-45-3*) R K Miller Assocs.

— Environmental Markets: Kansas. 130p. 1996. 185.00 (*1-881503-46-1*) R K Miller Assocs.

— Environmental Markets: Kentucky. 130p. 1996. 185.00 (*1-881503-47-X*) R K Miller Assocs.

— Environmental Markets: Louisiana. 130p. 1996. 185.00 (*1-881503-35-6*) R K Miller Assocs.

— Environmental Markets: Maryland. 130p. 1996. 185.00 (*1-881503-48-8*) R K Miller Assocs.

— Environmental Markets: Massachusetts. 130p. 1996. 185.00 (*1-881503-33-X*) R K Miller Assocs.

— Environmental Markets: Michigan. 130p. 1996. 185.00 (*1-881503-41-0*) R K Miller Assocs.

— Environmental Markets: Minnesota. 130p. 1996. 185.00 (*1-881503-50-X*) R K Miller Assocs.

— Environmental Markets: Mississippi. 130p. 1996. 185.00 (*1-881503-59-3*) R K Miller Assocs.

— Environmental Markets: Missouri. 130p. 1996. 185.00 (*1-881503-51-8*) R K Miller Assocs.

— Environmental Markets: Nebraska. 130p. 1996. 185.00 (*1-881503-60-7*) R K Miller Assocs.

— Environmental Markets: Nevada. 130p. 1996. 185.00 (*1-881503-56-9*) R K Miller Assocs.

— Environmental Markets: New Jersey. 130p. 1996. 185.00 (*1-881503-31-3*) R K Miller Assocs.

— Environmental Markets: New York. 130p. 1996. 185.00 (*1-881503-30-5*) R K Miller Assocs.

— Environmental Markets: North Carolina. 130p. 1996. 185.00 (*1-881503-54-2*) R K Miller Assocs.

— Environmental Markets: Ohio. 130p. 1996. 185.00 (*1-881503-37-2*) R K Miller Assocs.

— Environmental Markets: Oklahoma. 130p. 1996. 185.00 (*1-881503-61-5*) R K Miller Assocs.

— Environmental Markets: Oregon. 130p. 1996. 185.00 (*1-881503-55-0*) R K Miller Assocs.

— Environmental Markets: Pennsylvania. 130p. 1996. 185.00 (*1-881503-34-8*) R K Miller Assocs.

— Environmental Markets: South Carolina. 130p. 1996. 185.00 (*1-881503-62-3*) R K Miller Assocs.

— Environmental Markets: Tennessee. 130p. 1996. 185.00 (*1-881503-57-7*) R K Miller Assocs.

— Environmental Markets: Texas. 130p. 1996. 185.00 (*1-881503-36-4*) R K Miller Assocs.

— Environmental Markets: Utah. 130p. 1996. 185.00 (*1-881503-63-1*) R K Miller Assocs.

— Environmental Markets: Virginia. 130p. 1996. 185.00 (*1-881503-38-0*) R K Miller Assocs.

— Environmental Markets: Washington. 130p. 1996. 185.00 (*1-881503-52-6*) R K Miller Assocs.

— Environmental Markets: West Virginia. 130p. 1996. 185.00 (*1-881503-58-5*) R K Miller Assocs.

— Environmental Markets: Wisconsin. 130p. 1996. 185.00 (*1-881503-64-X*) R K Miller Assocs.

— Ergonomics. (Market Research Survey Ser.: No. 243). 50p. 1996. 200.00 (*1-55865-278-7*) Future Tech Surveys.

— Eye & Face Protection. (Market Research Survey Ser.: No. 248). 50p. 1996. 200.00 (1-55865-274-4) Future Tech Surveys.
— Eye & Face Washes & Emergency Showers. (Market Research Survey Ser.: No. 269). 50p. 1996. 200.00 (1-55865-293-0) Future Tech Surveys.
— Fall Protection. (Market Research Survey Ser.: No. 258). 50p. 1996. 200.00 (1-55865-286-8) Future Tech Surveys.
— Foot Protection. (Market Research Survey Ser.: No. 253). 50p. 1996. 200.00 (1-55865-285-X) Future Tech Surveys.
— Fume Hoods. (Market Research Survey Ser.: No. 264). 50p. 1996. 200.00 (1-55865-289-2) Future Tech Surveys.
— Hand & Arm Protection. (Market Research Survey Ser.: No. 251). 50p. 1996. 200.00 (1-55865-284-1) Future Tech Surveys.
— Hazardous Chemical Containment & Storage Equipment. (Market Research Survey Ser.: No. 256). 50p. 1996. 200.00 (1-55865-291-4) Future Tech Surveys.
— Head Protection. (Market Research Survey Ser.: No. 249). 50p. 1996. 200.00 (1-55865-294-9) Future Tech Surveys.
— Hearing Protection. (Market Research Survey Ser.: No. 247). 50p. 1996. 200.00 (1-55865-276-0) Future Tech Surveys.
— IAQ Consulting Services. (Market Research Survey Ser.: No. 244). 50p. 1996. 200.00 (1-55865-277-9) Future Tech Surveys.
— Industrial Air Filtration. (Market Research Survey Ser.: No. 266). 50p. 1996. 200.00 (1-55865-290-6) Future Tech Surveys.
— Industrial Audiometric Testing. (Market Research Survey Ser.: No. 246). 50p. 1996. 200.00 (1-55865-275-2) Future Tech Surveys.
— Industrial Hygiene & Safety Engineering Consulting Services. (Market Research Survey Ser.: No. 237). 50p. 1996. 200.00 (1-55865-268-X) Future Tech Surveys.
— Industrial Hygiene Laboratory Services. (Market Research Survey Ser.: No. 238). 50p. 1996. 200.00 (1-55865-269-8) Future Tech Surveys.
— Industrial Medical Surveillance. (Market Research Survey Ser.: No. 245). 50p. 1996. 200.00 (1-55865-280-9) Future Tech Surveys.
— Industrial Noise Control. (Market Research Survey Ser.: No. 236). 50p. 1996. 200.00 (1-55865-267-1) Future Tech Surveys.
— Industrial Water & Wastewater. (Market Research Survey Ser.: No. 271). 50p. 1996. 200.00 (1-55865-301-5) Future Tech Surveys.
— Industrial Water Environmental Markets. (Illus.). 180p. 1997. 185.00 (1-881503-67-4) R K Miller Assocs.
— Lead-Based Paint Abatement. (Market Research Survey Ser.: No. 263). 50p. 1996. 200.00 (1-55865-288-4) Future Tech Surveys.
— Liquid/Solid Separation Equipment. (Market Research Survey Ser.: No. 283). 50p. 1996. 200.00 (1-55865-306-6) Future Tech Surveys.
— Membrane Separation Equipment. (Market Research Survey Ser.: No. 282). 50p. 1996. 200.00 (1-55865-308-2) Future Tech Surveys.
— Municipal Water & Wastewater. (Market Research Survey Ser.: No. 272). 50p. 1996. 200.00 (1-55865-296-5) Future Tech Surveys.
— Natural Gas Cooling. (Market Research Survey Ser.: No. 239). 50p. 1996. 200.00 (1-55865-270-1) Future Tech Surveys.
— Neural Net Applications & Products. 347p. 1990. pap. 285.00 (0-89671-107-2) SEAI Tech Pubns.
— Ozone Disinfection in Municipal Water & Wastewater. (Market Research Survey Ser.: No. 279). 50p. 1996. 200.00 (1-55865-300-7) Future Tech Surveys.
— Proective Clothing. (Market Research Survey Ser.: No. 252). 50p. 1996. 200.00 (1-55865-282-5) Future Tech Surveys.
— Pumps in Municipal Water & Wastewater Applications. (Market Research Survey Ser.: No. 281). 50p. 1996. 200.00 (1-55865-299-X) Future Tech Surveys.
— Radon Abatement. (Market Research Survey Ser.: No. 262). 50p. 1996. 200.00 (1-55865-287-6) Future Tech Surveys.
— Respiratory Proection. (Market Research Survey Ser.: No. 250). 50p. 1996. 200.00 (1-55865-283-3) Future Tech Surveys.
— Safety & Health Training. (Market Research Survey Ser.: No. 240). 50p. 1996. 200.00 (1-55865-272-8) Future Tech Surveys.
— Safety Signs, Tags, & Labels. (Market Research Survey Ser.: No. 257). 50p. 1996. 200.00 (1-55865-281-7) Future Tech Surveys.
— Safety Training Materials. (Market Research Survey Ser.: No. 241). 50p. 1996. 200.00 (1-55865-271-X) Future Tech Surveys.
— SCADA/Control Systems in Municipal Water & Wastewater Facilities. (Market Research Survey Ser.: No. 284). 50p. 1996. 200.00 (1-55865-303-1) Future Tech Surveys.
— Seismic Protection. (Market Research Survey Ser.: No. 234). 50p. 1996. 200.00 (1-55865-265-5) Future Tech Surveys.
— Software for Industrial Safety & Health. (Market Research Survey Ser.: No. 242). 50p. 1996. 200.00 (1-55865-292-2) Future Tech Surveys.
— Toxic Gas Monitors. (Market Research Survey Ser.: No. 255). 50p. 1996. 200.00 (1-55865-273-6) Future Tech Surveys.

***Miller, Richard K., et al.** U. S. Environmental Markets, 1998-2001: An In-Depth Assessment of Environmental Market Trends, Market Drivers, Emerging Markets & Business Opportunities LC 99-197341. 358p. 1998. write for info. (1-881503-85-2) R K Miller Assocs.
Miller, Richard K., et al. U. S. Environmental Markets, 1997-2000. 8th rev. ed. 481p. 1997. 485.00 (1-881503-74-7) R K Miller Assocs.
— Ultraviolet Disinfection in Municipal Water & Wastewater. (Market Research Survey Ser.: No. 280). 50p. 1996. 200.00 (1-55865-307-4) Future Tech Surveys.
— Vibration Isolators. (Market Research Survey Ser.: No. 235). 50p. 1996. 200.00 (1-55865-266-3) Future Tech Surveys.
— Water Environmental Markets: State-by-State. 340p. 1997. 185.00 (0-614-29518-1) R K Miller Assocs.
— Water Environmental Markets: State-by-State. 220p. 1997. 185.00 (1-881503-78-X) R K Miller Assocs.
— Water Pipe/Sewer Maintenance Services. (Market Research Survey Ser.: No. 275). 50p. 1996. 200.00 (1-55865-304-X) Future Tech Surveys.
— Water Quality Instrumentation. (Market Research Survey Ser.: No. 277). 50p. 1996. 200.00 (1-55865-305-8) Future Tech Surveys.
— Water Resources Environmental Markets. 245p. 1997. 185.00 (1-881503-65-8) R K Miller Assocs.
— Water Treatment Chemicals. (Market Research Survey Ser.: No. 278). 50p. 1996. 200.00 (1-55865-302-3) Future Tech Surveys.
Miller, Richard K., jt. auth. see Barr, David F.
Miller, Richard K., jt. auth. see Morrish, Donald.
Miller, Richard K., jt. auth. see Oviatt, Mark D.
Miller, Richard K., jt. auth. see Pursell, Joshua R.
Miller, Richard K., jt. auth. see Rupnow, Marcia E.
Miller, Richard K., jt. auth. see Rupow, Marcia E.
Miller, Richard K., jt. auth. see Walker, Terri C.
Miller, Richard K., jt. auth. see Zeuch, Nello.
Miller, Richard K., ed. see Industrial Heating Equipment Association Staff.
Miller, Richard K., & Associates Staff & Griffith, Karen P. Industrial Forecast, 1998-2000. LC 97-20008. 300p. 1997. pap. 135.00 (0-88173-275-3) Fairmont Pr.
***Miller, Richard Kendall.** Engineering-Related E-Commerce. LC 00-31691. (Illus.). 2000. write for info. (0-88173-348-2) Fairmont Pr.
Miller, Richard Kendall & Walker, Terri C. Suvey on Cad/Cam, CAE. LC 88-81648. (Survey on Technology & Markets Ser.: No. 57). 50p. 1989. pap. text 200.00 (1-55865-056-3) Future Tech Surveys.
Miller, Richard L. A Brief Guide to Meteorological Data for Environmental & Safety Professionals. (Illus.). 68p. 1997. pap. text 16.95 (1-881043-04-5) Legis Corp.
— The Case for Legalizing Drugs. LC 90-7379. 264p. 1991. 35.00 (0-275-93459-4, C3459, Praeger Pubs) Greenwood.
— Drug Warriors & Their Prey: From Police Power to Police State. LC 95-9306. 272p. 1996. 24.95 (0-275-95042-5, Praeger Pubs) Greenwood.
— Environmental Projects in Eastern Europe: Laying the Groundwork. Shaw, Kim L., ed. Saet, Yuli, tr. (Illus.). 150p. 1997. pap. text 24.95 (1-881043-02-9) Legis Corp.
— Environmental Short Shorts: Two Thousand Facts Arranged for Rapid Learning. 224p. (Orig.). (C). 1991. pap. 24.95 (1-881043-00-2) Legis Corp.
— Evaluating the Nuclear Fallout Background in Environmental Investigations. unabridged ed. Shaw, Kim L., ed. (Illus.). 220p. 1997. pap. text 85.00 (1-881043-03-7) Legis Corp.
— Heritage of Fear: Illusion & Reality in the Cold War. 1988. 24.95 (0-8027-1021-2) Walker & Co.
— Nazi Justiz: Law of the Holocaust. LC 94-46176. 248p. 1995. 45.00 (0-275-94912-5, Praeger Pubs) Greenwood.
— The Top 100 Formulas for Industrial Hygiene & Safety. unabridged ed. Shaw, Kim L., ed. 126p. 1997. pap. text 24.95 (1-881043-01-0) Legis Corp.
Miller, Richard L., et al. General & Oral Pathology for the Dental Hygienist. (Illus.). 400p. (C). (gr. 13). 1995. pap. text 43.00 (0-8016-7024-1, 07024) Mosby Inc.
Miller, Richard M., ed. see Miller, Gloria B.
Miller, Richard N. Multinational Direct Marketing: The Methods & the Markets. LC 95-18495. 354p. 1995. 44.95 (0-07-042356-3) McGraw.
Miller, Richard T., jt. auth. see Henry, Robert G.
Miller, Richard U., et al. The Impact of Collective Bargaining on Hospitals. LC 79-9401. 244p. 1979. 62.95 (0-275-90395-8, C0395, Praeger Pubs) Greenwood.
Miller, Richard W. Flow Measurement Engineering Handbook. 3rd ed. (Illus.). 1168p. 1996. 135.00 (0-07-042366-0) McGraw.
— Moral Differences: Truth, Justice & Conscience in a World of Conflict. 416p. 1992. pap. text 19.95 (0-691-02092-2, Pub. by Princeton U Pr) Cal Prin Full Svc.
— Mountain Directory East for Truckers, RV, & Motorhome Drivers. (Illus.). 85p. (Orig.). 1997. pap. 12.95 (0-9646805-2-1) R&R Pub.
— Mountain Directory East for Truckers, RV & Motorhome Drivers. 2nd rev. ed. (Illus.). 92p. 1999. pap. 12.95 (0-9646805-5-6) R&R Pub.
— Mountain Directory for Truckers, RV, & Motorhome Drivers. 3rd rev. ed. (Illus.). 119p. 1996. pap. 12.95 (0-9646805-1-3) R&R Pub.
***Miller, Richard Wilson.** Mountain Directory West for Truckers, RV & Motorhome Drivers. 4th rev. ed. (Illus.). 152p. 2000. pap. 14.95 (0-9646805-6-4) R&R Pub.
***Miller, Rick.** Sam Bass & Gang. LC 99-34248. (Illus.). 424p. 1999. 34.95 (1-880510-65-0); pap. 21.95 (1-880510-66-9) State House Pr.
— Sam Bass & Gang. limited ed. LC 99-34248. (Illus.). 424p. 1999. 150.00 (1-880510-67-7) State House Pr.

Miller, Rick. The Train Robbing Bunch. LC 82-22204. (Early West Ser.). (Illus.). 175p. 1983. 21.95 (0-932702-25-2); pap. 10.95 (0-932702-27-9) Creative Texas.
Miller, Rickey. Kitchen Memories from My Childhood. (Illus.). 110p. 1994. text 14.95 (0-9641543-0-7) Millers Three.
Miller, Rima. Team Planning for Educational Leaders. 79p. 1987. pap. 21.95 (1-56602-017-4) Research Better.
— Your Leadership Style. 62p. 1987. pap. 17.95 (1-56602-019-0) Research Better.
Miller, Rima, jt. auth. see Woods-Houston, Michele A.
***Miller, Rita A.** Requiem I - Remus: House of Moon & Metamorphosis. Miller, Lura L., ed. (Illus.). vi, 100p. 1998. pap. 10.00 (0-9678399-0-4) Ajuga Pr.
Miller, Rita E., jt. auth. see Frangipane, Leo G., Jr.
Miller, Rita R. & Bailey, Joseph R. Quality Assurance Activities for Stat Laboratories. 220p. 1996. ring bd. 60.00 (0-915274-81-7, 202671) Am Assn Clinical Chem.
Miller, Rita S., ed. Brooklyn, U. S. A. (Brooklyn College Studies on Society in Change: No. 7). (Illus.). 1979. 20.00 (0-930888-02-2) Brooklyn Coll Pr.
Miller, Riva, jt. auth. see Bor, Robert.
***Miller, Rob.** Name Your Pet! Over 3500 Names. (Illus.). 160p. 1999. pap. 7.95 (1-86436-431-9, Pub. by New Holland) BHB Intl.
Miller, Rob, ed. Implementing Architecture: Exposing the Paradigm Surrounding the Implements & the Implementation of Architecture. 1988. 50.00 (0-932526-25-X) Nexus Pr.
Miller, Rob H. Shanghai Creek Fire. Bayes, Ronald H., ed. (Illus.). 1979. pap. 5.00 (0-932662-30-7) St Andrews NC.
Miller, Robbie. Clueless & Called: Discipleship & the Gospel of Mark. (Generation Why Ser.: Vol. 1:5). 44p. (YA). (gr. 9-12). 1995. pap. 12.95 (0-87303-261-6) Faith & Life.
***Miller, Robbie R.** Faith That Works: Serving God's Vision. (Generation Why Ser.: Vol. 4:7). 41p. (YA). (gr. 9-12). 1999. pap. 12.95 (0-87303-287-X) Faith & Life.
Miller, Robert. Axonal Conduction Time & Human Cerebral Laterality: A Psychobiological Theory. 304p. 1996. text 57.00 (3-7186-5865-8) Gordon & Breach.
— Buffalo Soldiers. (Reflections of a Black Cowboy Ser.). (Illus.). 104p. (J). (gr. 4-7). 1992. pap. 4.95 (0-382-24085-5) Silver Burdett Pr.
— Buffalo Soldiers, Bk. 2. (Reflections of a Black Cowboy Ser.). (Illus.). 104p. (J). (gr. 4-7). 1992. lib. bdg. 12.95 (0-382-24080-4) Silver Burdett Pr.
— Calc I Helper. (C). 1991. pap. 8.95 (0-07-042257-5) McGraw.
— Calc II Helper. (C). 1991. pap. 9.95 (0-07-042258-3) McGraw.
— Cowboys. (Reflections of a Black Cowboy Ser.). (Illus.). 104p. (J). (gr. 4-7). 1992. pap. 4.95 (0-382-24084-7) Silver Burdett Pr.
— Cowboys, Bk. 1. (Reflections of a Black Cowboy Ser.). (Illus.). 104p. (J). (gr. 4-7). 1992. lib. bdg. 12.95 (0-382-24079-0) Silver Burdett Pr.
— Liability or Asset? A Policy for the Falkland Islands. (C). 1990. 45.00 (0-907967-80-9, Pub. by Inst Euro Def & Strat) St Mut.
— M. I. Hummel Album. 320p. 1994. 19.98 (0-88365-878-X) Galahad Bks.
— Mountain Men. (Reflections of a Black Cowboy Ser.). (Illus.). 104p. (J). (gr. 4-7). 1991. pap. 4.95 (0-382-24087-1) Silver Burdett Pr.
— Mountain Men, Bk. 4. (Reflections of a Black Cowboy Ser.). (Illus.). 104p. (J). (gr. 4-7). 1991. lib. bdg. 12.95 (0-382-24082-0) Silver Burdett Pr.
— Pioneers. (Reflections of a Black Cowboy Ser.). (Illus.). 104p. (J). (gr. 4-7). 1991. pap. 4.95 (0-382-24086-3) Silver Burdett Pr.
— Pioneers, Bk. 3. (Reflections of a Black Cowboy Ser.). (Illus.). 104p. (J). (gr. 4-7). 1991. lib. bdg. 12.95 (0-382-24081-2) Silver Burdett Pr.
— Reflections of a Black Cowboy Series. 4 vols. (Illus.). 416p. (J). (gr. 4-7). 1991. pap. 19.80 (0-382-24083-9); lib. bdg. 51.80 (0-382-24078-2) Silver Burdett Pr.
— The Story of Jean Baptiste Du Sable. (Illus.). 32p. (J). (gr. 4-8). 1994. pap. 12.95 (0-382-24397-8) Silver Burdett Pr.
***Miller, Robert, et al, eds.** Complex Brain Functions: Conceptual Advances in Russian Neuroscience. (Conceptual Advances in Brain Research Ser.: Vol. 2). 432p. 2000. text 120.00 (90-5823-021-X, Harwood Acad Pubs) Gordon & Breach.
Miller, Robert & Basten, Fred. Gringo. LC 14-251. 1980. 10.95 (0-9603490-0-6) Noble Hse.
***Miller, Robert & Hrycyniak, Stephen J.** GriefQuest: Men Coping with Loss. 168p. 1999. pap. 9.95 (0-88489-597-1) St Marys.
Miller, Robert & Keeler, Ellisa. Internet Direct: Connecting Through SLIP & PPP. LC 95-233. 1995. pap. 24.95 (1-55828-432-X, MIS Pr) IDG Bks.
Miller, Robert & Miller, Janice J. Introduction to Business: An International Perspective. 61p. (C). 1987. teacher ed. write for info. (0-256-05762-1, Irwn McGrw-H) McGrw-H Hghr Educ.
Miller, Robert & Population Council Staff. The Situation Analysis Approach to Assessing Family Planning & Reproductive Health Services: A Handbook. LC 97-5428. 1997. write for info. (0-87834-090-4) Population Coun.
***Miller, Robert & Wickens, Jeffrey, eds.** Brain Dynamics & the Striatal Complex. (Conceptual Advances in Brain Research Ser.: Vol. 1). 324p. 2000. text 80.00 (90-5702-478-0, Harwood Acad Pubs) Gordon & Breach.

Miller, Robert & Wilson, Kenneth. Making & Enjoying Telescopes: 6 Complete Projects & a Stargazer's Guide. (Illus.). 160p. 1997. pap. 14.95 (0-8069-1278-2) Sterling.
***Miller, Robert, et al.** Les Missions de Paix et le Canada: Enseignements des Conflits au Nicaragua, Cambodge et en Somalie. (FRE.). 1999. pap. 17.50 (0-88936-872-4, Pub. by IDRC Bks) Stylus Pub VA.
Miller, Robert, jt. auth. see Keeler, Ellisa.
Miller, Robert, jt. auth. see Robinson, Jerry.
Miller, Robert, jt. auth. see Semple, Stephen J.
Miller, Robert, jt. auth. see Weber, Gerard P.
Miller, Robert, jt. ed. see Mindel, Adrian.
Miller, Robert, jt. ed. see Wirick, Gregory.
Miller, Robert A. The Federal Role in Education: New Directions in the Eighties. 192p. 1980. pap. 9.50 (0-318-03020-9); lib. bdg. 15.00 (0-318-03019-5) Inst Educ Lead.
Miller, Robert B. Minitab Handbook for Business & Economics. 628p. (C). 1987. pap. 18.50 (0-87150-092-2, 36G01210) PWS Pubs.
Miller, Robert B., compiled by. Cemetery Inscriptions from Shrub Oak Cemetery, Westchester County. 99p. 1997. reprint ed. pap. 15.00 (0-8328-6276-2) Higginson Bk Co.
— Cemetery Inscriptions from Westchester County (Including Mt. Kisco, Bedford, Elmsford, Groton Village, Poundridge, New Canaan, Hastings-on-Hudson) 214p. 1997. reprint ed. pap. 25.00 (0-8328-6274-6) Higginson Bk Co.
— Cemetery Inscriptions from Westchester County (Including Towns of Unionville, Greenville, Hartsdale, Mamaroneck, Harrison, Ossining) 145p. 1997. reprint ed. pap. 19.00 (0-8328-6275-4) Higginson Bk Co.
Miller, Robert B. & Wichern, Dean W. Intermediate Business Statistics: Analysis of Variance, Regression, & Time Series. 525p. (C). 1995. pap. 63.00 (0-534-51083-3) Wadsworth Pub.
Miller, Robert B., et al. Conceptual Selling. 320p. 1989. mass mkt. 14.99 (0-446-38906-4, Pub. by Warner Bks) Little.
Miller, Robert B., et al. Strategic Selling. 320p. 1988. mass mkt. 14.99 (0-446-38627-8, Pub. by Warner Bks) Little.
— Successful Large Account Management. 240p. 1995. 25.00 (0-8050-1304-0) H Holt & Co.
— Successful Large Account Management. 240p. 1992. reprint ed. mass mkt. 12.95 (0-446-39356-8, Pub. by Warner Bks) Little.
Miller, Robert B., jt. auth. see Cryer, Jonathan D.
Miller, Robert D. Spelling Games & Puzzles for Junior High. (Makemaster Bk.). (J). (gr. 6-8). 1976. pap. 9.99 (0-8224-6460-8) Fearon Teacher Aids.
— Tommy the Toothbrush. (Illus.). 16p. (J). (gr. 2-4). 1982. write for info. (0-318-56644-3) Miller OH.
***Miller, Robert D. & Hutton, Rebecca C.** Problems in Health Care Law. 8th ed. LC 99-47599. 2000. write for info. (0-8342-1602-7) Aspen Pub.
Miller, Robert D., jt. auth. see Kaplan, Leonard V.
Miller, Robert F. Careers with Out College, Travel. LC 93-4638. (Tech Prep Ser.). xiii, 96p. (YA). (gr. 10-12). 1993. pap. 7.95 (1-56079-249-3) Petersons.
— One Hundred Thousand Tractors: The MTS & the Development of Controls in Soviet Agriculture. LC 70-95929. (Russian Research Center Studies: No. 60). (Illus.). 439p. 1970. 37.00 (0-674-63875-1) HUP.
Miller, Robert F., ed. Development of Civil Society in Communist Systems. 176p. 1992. pap. text 19.95 (1-86373-171-7, Pub. by Allen & Unwin Pty) Paul & Co Pubs.
Miller, Robert F. & Pincus, Marilyn. Running a Meeting That Works. 2nd ed. LC 96-46273. (Barron's Business Success Ser.). 1997. pap. 6.95 (0-8120-9823-4) Barron.
Miller, Robert G. Statistical Prediction by Discriminant Analysis. (Meteorological Monograph: Vol. 4. No. 25). (Illus.). 54p. (Orig.). 1962. pap. 17.00 (0-933876-13-0) Am Meteorological.
Miller, Robert H. Buffalo Soldiers: The Story of Emanuel Stance. LC 94-28640. (Stories of the Forgotten West Ser.). (Illus.). 32p. (J). (gr. k-3). 1994. 12.95 (0-382-24400-1); lib. bdg. 14.95 (0-382-24391-9) Silver Burdett Pr.
— Buffalo Soldiers: The Story of Emanuel Stance. LC 94-28640. (Stories of the Forgotten West Ser.). (Illus.). 32p. (J). (ps-3). 1994. pap. 5.95 (0-382-24395-1) Silver Burdett Pr.
— Graham Greene: A Descriptive Catalog. LC 77-92925. 85p. reprint ed. pap. 30.00 (0-7837-5810-3, 204547700006) Bks Demand.
***Miller, Robert H.** Law School Confidential: A Complete Guide to the Law School Experience. LC 00-27851. 352p. 2000. pap. 17.95 (0-312-24309-X, St Martin Griffin) St Martin.
Miller, Robert H. A Pony for Jeremiah. LC 96-3473. (Illus.). 64p. (J). 1996. pap. 4.95 (0-382-39460-7); lib. bdg. 12.95 (0-382-39459-3) Silver Burdett Pr.
— Power System Operation. 3rd ed. 271p. 1994. 60.00 (0-07-041977-9) McGraw.
— Reflections of a Black Cowboy. (Field Guides Ser.: Vol. I). (Illus.). 9p. (J). (gr. 5-7). 1988. pap. text 9.95 (0-929592-01-8) Waterline Prodns.
— Reflections of a Black Cowboy. 2nd ed. (Illus.). (J). 1998. write for info. (0-382-39806-8); 22.00 (0-382-39807-6); 10.00 (0-382-39808-4); 22.00 (0-382-39809-2); 10.00 (0-382-39810-6); lib. bdg. 22.00 (0-382-39805-X) Silver Burdett Pr.
— Reflections of a Black Cowboy. 2nd ed. (Pioneers Ser.). (Illus.). (J). 1999. 10.00 (0-382-39804-1); 22.00 (0-382-39803-3) Silver Burdett Pr.
— The Story of Jean Baptiste Du Sable. LC 94-28634.

M

(Stories of the Forgotten West Ser.). (Illus.). 32p. (J). (gr. k-3). 1994. 12.95 (*0-382-24402-8*); lib. bdg. 14.95 (*0-382-24392-7*) Silver Burdett Pr.

— The Story of Nat Love. LC 93-46287. (Stories of the Forgotten West Ser.). (Illus.). 32p. (J). (gr. k-3). 1994. 12.95 (*0-382-24398-6*); pap. 5.95 (*0-382-24393-5*); lib. bdg. 14.95 (*0-382-24389-7*) Silver Burdett Pr.

— The Story of "Stagecoach" Mary Fields. (Stories of the Forgotten West Ser.). (Illus.). 32p. (J). (gr. k-3). 1994. 12.95 (*0-382-24399-4*); pap. 5.95 (*0-382-24394-3*); lib. bdg. 14.95 (*0-382-24390-0*) Silver Burdett Pr.

— U. S. & Vietnam, 1787-1941. (Illus.). 324p. (Orig.). (C). 1994. pap. text 40.00 (*0-7881-0810-7*) DIANE Pub.

Miller, Robert H., ed. United States & Vietnam, 1787-1941, 2 vols. (Illus.). 334p. 1990. pap. text 50.00 (*1-57979-151-4*) DIANE Pub.

Miller, Robert H. & Malinowski, James H. Power System Operation. 3rd ed. 271p. 1997. 50.00 (*0-7803-3461-2*, PC5720-QOE) Inst Electrical.

Miller, Robert H. & Opie, Christine A. Back Pain Relief: The Ultimate Guide: A Comprehensive Pain Management Program. LC 96-47953. (Illus.). 224p. (Orig.). 1997. pap. 14.95 (*0-88496-418-3*) Capra Pr.

Miller, Robert J. The Complete Gospels. annot. ed. LC 94-34585. 480p. 1994. pap. 20.00 (*0-06-065587-9*, Pub. by Harper SF) HarpC.

M

***Miller, Robert J.** Falling into Faith. LC 00-41016. (Lecto Divina Ser.: Cycle C). 268p. 2000. 16.95 (*1-58051-078-7*) Sheed & Ward WI.

Miller, Robert J. GriefQuest: Reflections for Men Coping with Loss. LC 96-84091. (Illus.). 242p. 1996. pap. 10.95 (*0-87029-293-5*, 20161) Abbey.

***Miller, Robert J.** The Jesus Seminar & Its Critics. LC 99-47547. 1999. 17.00 (*0-944344-78-X*) Polebridge Pr.

Miller, Robert J., ed. The Complete Gospels: Annotated Scholars Version. 3rd expanded rev. ed. LC 94-34585. 480p. 1995. pap. 18.00 (*0-944344-49-6*) Polebridge Pr.

— The Complete Gospels: Annotated Scholars Version. 3rd expanded rev. ed. LC 94-34585. 480p. (C). 1995. 28.00 (*0-944344-45-3*) Polebridge Pr.

Miller, Robert J., jt. auth. see Hrycyniak, Stephen J.

Miller, Robert K. Carlyle's Life of John Sterling: A Study in Victorian Biography. LC 86-25062. (Nineteenth-Century Studies). 113p. reprint ed. pap. 35.10 (*0-8357-1782-8*, 207056400001) Bks Demand.

— The Informed Argument: A Multidisciplinary Reader & Guide. 5th ed. LC 97-72225. 730p. (C). 1997. pap. text 40.00 (*0-15-503809-5*, Pub. by Harcourt Coll Pubs) Harcourt.

— The Informed Argument: Brief Edition. 384p. (C). 1998. pap. text 23.00 (*0-15-503185-6*, Pub. by Harcourt Coll Pubs) Harcourt.

***Miller, Robert K.** Motives for Writing. 3rd ed. LC 98-48744. 695p. 1999. pap. text 31.95 (*1-55934-924-7*, 924-7) Mayfield Pub.

Miller, Robert L. Linguistic Relativity Principle & Humboldtian Ethnolinguistics. LC 68-13340. (Janua Linguarum, Ser.). 1968. pap. text 44.60 (*90-279-0595-9*) Mouton.

— M. I. Hummel: The Golden Anniversary Album. 1989. 19.98 (*0-88365-745-7*) Galahad Bks.

***Miller, Robert L.** M. I. Hummel Figurines, Plates, Miniatures & More Price Guide. 8th ed. (Illus.). 2000. pap. 24.95 (*0-942620-35-6*) Portfolio Pr.

Miller, Robert L. Number One Price Guide to M. I. Hummel. 5th ed. 1992. pap. 15.95 (*0-88486-068-X*) Arrowood Pr.

Miller, Robert L., Jr. Three Faces. (Illus.). 28p. 1998. pap. 6.00 (*0-9666777-0-6*) Voice of Truths.

Miller, Robert L., et al. Acoustic Charge Transport: Device Technology & Applications. LC 92-10502. (Microwave Library). 606p. 1992. text 75.00 (*0-89006-520-9*) Artech Hse.

Miller, Robert L., jt. auth. see Weber, Gerard P.

Miller, Robert L., jt. ed. see Wilford, Rick.

Miller, Robert M. Bishop G. Bromley Oxnam: Paladin of Liberal Protestantism. LC 90-42071. 608p. 1990. 34.95 (*0-687-03564-3*) Abingdon.

— Health Problems of the Horse. Vorhes, Gary, ed. (Illus.). 144p. (Orig.). 1987. pap. 12.95 (*0-911647-13-9*) Western Horseman.

— How Shall They Hear Without a Preacher? The Life of Ernest Fremont Tittle. LC 74-149031. 538p. reprint ed. pap. 166.80 (*0-7837-0284-1*, 204060500018) Bks Demand.

— Imprint Training of the Newborn Foal: Of the Newborn Foal. (Illus.). 149p. (Orig.). 1991. pap. 12.95 (*0-911647-22-8*) Western Horseman.

— Star Myths: Show-Business Biographies on Film. LC 83-14292. 416p. 1983. 40.00 (*0-8108-1643-1*) Scarecrow.

***Miller, Robert M.** Understanding the Ancient Secrets of the Horse's Mind. LC 99-46591. 1999. 29.95 (*0-929346-65-3*) R Meerdink Co Ltd.

Miller, Robert M., jt. auth. see Byrge, Duane.

Miller, Robert N. Miracles in the Making: Scientific Evidence for the Effectiveness of Prayer. 1996. 13.95 (*0-89804-097-3*); pap. 9.95 (*0-89804-096-5*) Ariel GA.

Miller, Robert P., ed. Chaucer: Sources & Backgrounds. (Illus.). 524p. (C). 1977. text 24.95 (*0-19-502167-3*) OUP.

Miller, Robert R. Juan Alvarado, Governor of California, 1836-1842. LC 98-17589. (Illus.). 232p. 1998. 29.95 (*0-8061-3077-6*) U of Okla Pr.

— Mexico: A History. LC 84-28105. (Illus.). 384p. 1989. pap. 17.95 (*0-8061-2178-5*) U of Okla Pr.

— Shamrock & Sword: The Saint Patrick's Battalion in the U. S. - Mexican War. LC 89-5252. (Illus.). 148p. 1997. pap. 14.95 (*0-8061-2964-6*) U of Okla Pr.

Miller, Robert R., jt. auth. see Daly, John A.

Miller, Robert R., ed. see Zeh, Frederick.

***Miller, Robert Ryal.** Juan Alvarado: Governor of California, 1836-1842. LC 98-17589. (Illus.). 232p. 1999. pap. text 12.95 (*0-8061-3101-2*) U of Okla Pr.

Miller, Robert T. & Flowers, R. Barri, eds. Toward Benevolent Neutrality: Church, State, & the Supreme Court, 2 vols. 5th ed. LC 96-18086. 895p. 1996. 75.00 (*0-918954-63-0*) Baylor Univ Pr.

Miller, Robert W. Horse Discourse. (Illus.). 100p. 1999. pap. 15.00 (*0-9649807-1-1*) R W Miller.

— Scores. (Illus.). 47p. (Orig.). 1995. pap. 7.95 (*0-9649807-0-3*) R W Miller.

— Urban Forestry. 2nd ed. 480p. (C). 1996. 105.00 (*0-13-458522-4*) P-H.

— Western Horse Behavior & Training. 304p. 1975. pap. 17.95 (*0-385-08181-2*) Doubleday.

Miller, Roberta B. City & Hinterland: A Case Study of Urban Growth & Regional Developments, 77. LC 78-55340. (Contributions in American History Ser.: No. 77). (Illus.). 179p. 1979. 45.00 (*0-313-20524-8*, MCH/, Greenwood Pr) Greenwood.

Miller, Roberta R., jt. ed. see Shimosato, Yukio.

Miller, Robin. Talks with Jonathon Bk. I: A Guide to Transformation. 156p. (Orig.). 1993. pap. 14.95 (*1-881343-04-9*) Channel One.

Miller, Robin F. The Brothers Karamazov: Worlds of the Novel. (Masterwork Studies). 160p. (C). 1992. 23.95 (*0-8057-8060-2*, Twyne) Mac Lib Ref.

— The Brothers Karamazov: Worlds of the Novel. (Masterwork Studies: No. 83). 160p. (C). 1992. pap. 13.95 (*0-8057-8118-8*, Twyne) Mac Lib Ref.

— Dostoevsky & The Idiot: Author, Narrator & Reader. LC 80-29496. 305p. 1981. 36.95 (*0-674-21490-0*) HUP.

Miller, Robin F., ed. see Feuer, Katherine B.

Miller, Robin F., jt. ed. see Jones, Malcolm V.

Miller, Robin J., see Scribbles, R. J., pseud.

Miller, Robyn, jt. auth. see Wingrove, David.

Miller, Rodney E. Institutionalizing Music: The Administration of Music Programs in Higher Education. LC 93-19769. (Illus.). 216p. 1993. pap. 31.95 (*0-398-06292-7*) C C Thomas.

— Institutionalizing Music: The Administration of Music Programs in Higher Education. LC 93-19769. (Illus.). 216p. (C). 1993. text 44.95 (*0-398-05874-1*) C C Thomas.

Miller, Roger. Economics Today 1999-2000 with Economics in Action: Version 2. 10th ed. (C). 2000. pap. text 71.00 (*0-321-06891-2*) Addson-Wesley Educ.

— Maryland: A Portrait. 4th rev. ed. (Illus.). 168p. 1998. 39.95 (*0-911897-45-3*) Image Ltd.

Miller, Roger, ed. & photos by see Swisher, Joe A.

Miller, Roger C. The Complete Barbel Angler. (Illus.). 192p. 1997. pap. 45.00 (*1-85223-980-8*, Pub. by Crolwood) Trafalgar.

Miller, Roger C., photos by. Baltimore: A Portrait. 3rd rev. ed. LC 93-61093. (Illus.). 160p. 1993. 39.95 (*0-911897-23-2*) Image Ltd.

Miller, Roger C. & VanHoose, David D. Essentials of Money, Banking, & Financial Markets. LC 96-13104. 498p. (C). 1997. pap. 73.00 (*0-673-98126-6*) Addson-Wesley Educ.

***Miller, Roger G.** To Save a City: The Berlin Airlift, 1948-1949. LC 00-32617. (Illus.). 288p. 2000. 34.95 (*0-89096-967-1*) Tex A&M Univ Pr.

— To Save a City: The Berlin Airlift, 1948-1949. 136p. 1998. per. 8.00 (*0-16-061377-9*) USGPO.

Miller, Roger L. Business Law Today. 4th ed. (SWC-Business Law). (C). 1996. mass mkt., student ed. 20.95 (*0-314-20678-7*) S-W Pub.

— Business Law Today. 4th ed. (SWC-Business Law Ser.). 1997. pap., student ed. 20.50 (*0-314-20795-3*) Thomson Learn.

— Economic Issues for Consumers. 5th ed. LC 86-24722. (Illus.). 526p. (C). 1987. text 41.00 (*0-314-30391-X*) West Pub.

— Economics Today. 8th ed. LC 93-8233. (C). 1994. text 42.00 (*0-06-501465-0*) Addson-Wesley Educ.

— Economics Today. 8th ed. LC 95-8149. (C). 1995. pap. 31.00 (*0-06-502544-X*) Addson-Wesley Educ.

— Economics Today. 8th rev. ed. 928p. (C). 1997. pap., suppl. ed. 59.00 (*0-06-502581-4*) Addson-Wesley Educ.

— Economics Today: Micro View. 8th ed. LC 93-8234. (C). 1994. text 30.00 (*0-06-501877-X*) Addson-Wesley Educ.

— Economics Today: The Macro View. 9th ed. LC 96-16629. (C). 1996. write for info. (*0-673-98056-1*) Addson-Wesley Educ.

— Economics Today: The Macro View. 10th ed. LC 98-20220. 560p. (C). 1998. pap. text 67.00 (*0-201-36014-4*) Addison-Wesley.

— Economics Today: The Micro View. 9th ed. LC 96-2363. (Series in Economics). (C). 1996. pap. 74.00 (*0-673-98055-3*) Addson-Wesley Educ.

***Miller, Roger L.** Economics Today: The Micro View. 10th ed. LC 98-22981. 608p. (C). 1998. pap. text 70.00 (*0-201-36013-6*) Addison-Wesley.

Miller, Roger L. Economics Today: 1999-2000. 10th ed. 480p. (C). 1998. pap. text 33.00 (*0-321-03350-7*) Addison-Wesley.

— Economics Today: 1999-2000. 10th ed. 304p. (C). 1998. pap. text, student ed. 18.00 (*0-321-03354-X*) Addison-Wesley.

— Economics Today Newsletter. 9th ed. (C). 1997. pap. text. write for info. (*0-321-01773-0*) Addison-Wesley.

— Economics Today, the Macro View 1999-2000. 8th ed. LC 93-8235. (C). 1994. text 30.00 (*0-06-501878-8*) Addson-Wesley Educ.

— Economics Today, the Macro View 1999-2000. 1999th ed. 1998. pap. 62.81 (*0-321-04663-3*) Addson-Wesley Educ.

— Economics Today with Your Economic Life. 8th ed. 576p. (C). 1997. 67.00 (*0-06-502294-7*) Addson-Wesley Educ.

— The Legal Environment Today: Business in Its Ethical, Regulatory & International Setting. (SWC-Business Law). 1996. pap., student ed. 19.00 (*0-314-08915-2*) West Pub.

— Your Economic Life: Economics Today. 10th ed. 32p. (C). 1998. write for info. (*0-321-03363-9*) Addison-Wesley.

Miller, Roger L., ed. Economics Today: Study Guide. 9th ed. (C). 1997. pap. text, student ed. 32.81 (*0-673-98057-X*) Addson-Wesley.

Miller, Roger L. & Cross, Frank B. The Legal & Regulatory Environment Today: Changing Perspectives for Business. LC 92-18824. 650p. (C). 1993. text 68.50 (*0-314-01046-7*) West Pub.

— The Legal Environment Today: Business in Its Ethical, Regulatory & International Setting. (SWC-Business Law). 700p. (C). 1996. pap. 69.75 (*0-314-06425-7*) West Pub.

— The Legal Environment Today: Business in Its Ethical, Regulatory & International Setting. 2nd ed. LC 98-5809. 1998. pap. 98.95 (*0-538-88534-3*) S-W Pub.

Miller, Roger L. & Crout, George C. Middletown. LC 98-86558. (Images of America Ser.). (Illus.). 128p. 1998. pap. 16.99 (*0-7524-1287-6*) Arcadia Publng.

Miller, Roger L. & Hollowell, William E. Business Law: Text & Exercises. (C). 1995. pap. 45.25 (*0-314-07091-5*) West Pub.

Miller, Roger L. & Jentz, Gaylord A. Business Law Today: Text, Summarized Cases, Legal, Ethical, Regulatory, & International Environment. 4th ed. LC 96-15501. 1996. pap. 70.25 (*0-314-09488-1*) West Pub.

— Business Law Today, Comprehensive Edition 4/e. 4th ed. LC 96-46400. (SWC-Business Law). 1996. mass mkt. 73.50 (*0-314-20490-3*) West Pub.

— Business Law Today: Text, Summarized. 3rd ed. Perlee, Clyde, ed. LC 93-25927. (SWC-Business Law). 850p. (C). 1993. text 72.50 (*0-314-02582-0*) West Pub.

— Business Law Today, The Alternate Essentials Edition: Text A. 4th ed. LC 96-51497. (SWC-Business Law). 1997. pap. 76.95 (*0-314-21350-3*) West Pub.

— Business Law Today, The Essentials 4/e. 4th ed. LC 96-51496. (SWC-Business Law). 1997. pap. 70.95 (*0-314-20491-1*) West Pub.

— Business Law Today: The Essentials, Text. 3rd ed. Perlee, Clyde, ed. LC 93-37600. (SWC-Business Law). 620p. (C). 1994. pap. 45.75 (*0-314-02852-8*) West Pub.

— Fundamentals Of Business Law. 2d. 2nd ed. Perlee, Clyde, ed. LC 92-20019. (SWC-Business Law). 760p. (C). 1992. reprint ed. pap. text 44.25 (*0-314-01004-1*) West Pub.

— Fundamentals Of Business Law. 3/e. 3rd ed. LC 95-522. (SWC-Business Law). 700p. (C). 1995. pap. 50.75 (*0-314-06148-7*) West Pub.

Miller, Roger L. & Miller, Lavina L. Living Now: Strategies for Success & Fulfillment. LC 96-268. 1996. pap. 47.50 (*0-314-04919-3*) West Pub.

Miller, Roger L. & Pulsinelli, eds. Economics Today. 8th rev. ed. 400p. (C). 1997. pap., student ed. 25.00 (*0-06-501468-5*) Addson-Wesley Educ.

Miller, Roger L. & Pulsinelli, Robert W. Understanding Economics. (Illus.). 457p. (C). 1983. text 52.00 (*0-314-69669-5*); pap. text, teacher ed. write for info. (*0-314-71114-7*) West Pub.

Miller, Roger L. & Stafford, Alan D. Economic Issues for Consumers. 8th ed. LC 96-48300. 500p. 1996. 83.95 (*0-314-09772-4*) West Pub.

Miller, Roger L. & Sttafford, Alan D. Economic Issues for Consumers. 7th ed. Perlee, Clyde, ed. LC 93-8170. 500p. (C). 1993. mass mkt. 49.75 (*0-314-02261-9*) West Pub.

Miller, Roger L. & Urisko, Mary S. West Paralegal Today-hc. LC 94-37650. (Paralegal). 900p. (C). 1995. mass mkt. 79.95 (*0-314-04360-8*) West Pub.

Miller, Roger L. & VanHoose, David D. Modern Money & Banking. 3rd ed. LC 92-12189. (C). 1993. text 69.00 (*0-07-042335-0*); text, student ed. 26.25 (*0-07-042338-5*) McGraw.

Miller, Roger L., et al. Economics of the Public Issues. 11th ed. LC 98-20508. 240p. (C). 1998. pap. 34.60 (*0-321-03068-0*) Addson-Wesley Educ.

— Personal Finance Today. (Illus.). 446p. (C). 1983. pap. text, teacher ed. write for info. (*0-314-71112-0*) West Pub.

Miller, Roger L., jt. auth. see Cross, Frank B.

Miller, Roger L., jt. ed. see Manne, Henry G.

***Miller, Roger Leroy.** Business Law Today: The Essentials: Text & Summarized Cases--Legal, Ethical, Regulatory & International Environment. 5th ed. LC 99-26246. 600p. 1999. pap. text 78.95 (*0-324-00416-8*) Sth-Wstrn College.

Miller, Roger Leroy. Consumer Economics in Action. 10th ed. (HB - Economics Ser.). (C). 1992. mass mkt. 39.75 (*0-314-00330-4*) West Pub.

— Economics: East Coast Case Study (9th Edition) 9th ed. (C). 1997. pap. text 13.00 (*0-673-97860-5*) Addison-Wesley.

— Economics Today. 8th ed. 592p. (C). 1997. pap., student ed. 34.00 (*0-06-501466-9*) Addson-Wesley Educ.

— Economics Today. 10th ed. LC 98-22980. 880p. (C). 1998. 94.00 (*0-201-31689-7*) Addison-Wesley.

— Economics Today. 10th ed. LC 98-22980. 1p. 1999. write for info. (*0-321-04664-1*) Addison-Wesley.

— Economics Today: Texas Economics Case Studies. 9th ed. 152p. (C). 1997. pap. text 13.00 (*0-673-97618-1*) Addison-Wesley.

— Economics Today: The Micro View. 9th ed. 1997. text 63.00 (*0-673-98540-7*) Addison-Wesley.

— Economics Today: The 1999-2000 Edition. 10th ed. 880p. (C). 1998. text 90.00 (*0-321-04674-9*) Addison-Wesley Educ.

— Economics Today : With Your Economic Life: The Practical Applications of Economics (9th Ed) 9th ed. (C). 1997. text 100.00 (*0-673-98539-3*) Addison-Wesley.

— Economics Today 1999-2000. 10th ed. 1998. pap. text 62.81 (*0-321-04662-5*) Addson-Wesley Educ.

— Economics Today, the Micro View 1999-2000. 10th ed. 1998. 94.00 (*0-321-04661-7*) Addison-Wesley.

***Miller, Roger LeRoy.** Economics Today 2001-2002. LC 00-38120. 2000. pap. write for info. (*0-321-07817-9*); pap. write for info. (*0-321-07818-7*) Addson-Wesley Educ.

Miller, Roger Leroy. Essentials of Money, Banking & Financial Markets. (C). 1997. pap. text, student ed. 25.00 (*0-673-98267-X*) Addison-Wesley.

— The Macro View of Economics Today. 10th ed. 288p. (C). 1998. pap. text, student ed. 24.00 (*0-321-03351-5*) Addison-Wesley.

— The Micro View of Economics Today. 10th ed. 320p. (C). 1998. pap. text, student ed. 24.00 (*0-321-03352-3*) Addson-Wesley Educ.

— Understanding Business. 1991. mass mkt. 46.50 (*0-314-80042-5*) West Pub.

Miller, Roger Leroy, ed. Student Learning Guide to Accompany Economics Today: The MacRo View. 9th ed. (C). 1997. pap. text, student ed. 23.44 (*0-673-98059-6*) Addison-Wesley.

— Student Learning Guide to Accompany Economics Today: The Micro View. 9th ed. (C). 1997. pap. text, student ed. 23.44 (*0-673-98058-8*) Addison-Wesley.

***Miller, Roger LeRoy & Urisko, Mary Meinzinger.** West's Paralegal Today: The Essentials, the Legal Team at Work. 2nd ed. LC 99-51373. 336p. 2000. 65.95 (*0-7668-1016-X*) Delmar.

Miller, Roger LeRoy, jt. auth. see Cross, Frank B.

Miller, Roger Leroy, jt. auth. see Miller, Lavina Leed.

Miller, Roger R., ed. see Institute on Research Toward Improving Race Relati.

Miller, Roland E. Mappila Muslims of Kerala: A Study of Islamic Trends. 2nd enl. rev. ed. 389p. 1992. 22.00 (*0-86311-270-6*, Pub. by Sangam Bks Ltd) S Asia.

***Miller, Roland E.** Mission Agendas in the New Century: A Summary of the Congress on the World Mission of the Church - St. Paul '98. 80p. 2000. pap. text 3.50 (*1-886513-31-7*) Kirk Hse Pubs.

Miller, Roland E. Muslim Friends: Their Faith & Feeling. 1996. 19.00 (*0-570-04624-6*, 12-3205) Concordia.

Miller, Roland H., III. Supplemental Security Income: Action Needed on Long-Standing Problems Affecting Program Integrity. (Illus.). 64p. 1999. pap. text 20.00 (*0-7881-7970-5*) DIANE Pub.

Miller, Roland H., III, et al. Social Security Advocacy: Organizations That Mail Fund-Raising Letters. (Illus.). 81p. (C). 1998. pap. text 25.00 (*0-7881-4777-3*) DIANE Pub.

Miller, Roman & Brubaker, Beryl, eds. Bioethics & the Beginning of Life: An Anabaptist Perspective. LC 89-15266. 224p. (Orig.). 1989. pap. 15.99 (*0-8361-3502-4*) Herald Pr.

***Miller, Ron.** Bradamant: The Iron Tempest. Dore, Gustave, ed. (Illus.). 334p. 2000. pap. 16.95 (*1-58752-027-3*) Timberwolf Pr.

Miller, Ron. The Dream Machines: An Illustrated History of the Spaceship in Art, Science, & Literature. 744p. (Orig.). 1993. 112.50 (*0-89464-039-9*) Krieger.

— Extraordinary Voyages. 1976. 21.95 (*0-8488-0712-X*) Amereon Ltd.

— History of Rockets. (Venture Books-Science). 1999. pap. text 9.95 (*0-531-15962-0*) Watts.

***Miller, Ron.** The History of Science Fiction. LC 00-36823. 2001. write for info. (*0-531-11866-5*) Watts.

Miller, Ron. Mystery! A Celebration: Stalking Public Television's Greatest Sleuths. LC 96-42130. (Illus.). 320p. 1996. pap. 27.95 (*0-912333-89-8*) BB&T Inc.

— Rockets. LC 97-49808. (Venture Book Ser.). (J). 1999. 25.00 (*0-531-11430-9*) Watts.

— What Are Schools For? Holistic Education in American Culture. 3rd rev. ed. LC 97-35897. 208p. (Orig.). (C). 1997. pap. 18.95 (*0-9627232-0-7*) Psychology Pr.

Miller, Ron, ed. Educational Freedom for a Democratic Society: A Critique of National Standards, Goals & Curriculum. 260p. (Orig.). 1995. pap. text 18.95 (*1-885580-01-0*, Resrce Ctr Redesign Educ) Psychology Pr.

Miller, Ron, intro. New Directions in Education: Selections from Holistic Education Review. 400p. (Orig.). (C). 1991. pap. 12.95 (*0-9627232-1-5*) Psychology Pr.

Miller, Ron & Hartmann, William K. The Grand Tour: A Traveler's Guide to the Solar System. rev. ed. LC 80-54620. (Illus.). 208p. 1993. 25.95 (*1-56305-511-2*, 3511); pap. 15.95 (*1-56305-031-5*, 3031) Workman Pub.

Miller, Ron & Miller, Peggy. Mines of the Mojave. 1996. pap. 4.50 (*0-87505-414-5*) Borden.

Miller, Ron & Verne, Jules. 20,000 Leagues under the Sea: Jules Verne's Classic Tale. LC 98-10624. (Eyewitness Classics Ser.). (Illus.). 64p. (J). 1998. 14.95 (*0-7894-3428-8*) DK Pub Inc.

***Miller, Ron, et al.** Challenging the Giant Vols. 1-4: The Best of Skole: The Journal of Alternative Education. Leue, Mary M., ed. & intro. by. (Illus.). 503p. 2000. pap. 14.95 (*1-878115-13-8*) Dwn-To-Erth Bks.

Miller, Ron, jt. auth. see Haddock, Durwood.

MIller, Ron, jt. auth. see Hartmann, William K.

Miller, Ronald, jt. auth. see Colangelo, Robert.

Miller, Ronald, jt. auth. see Deaton, Angus.

Miller, Ronald B., ed. The Restoration of Dialogue: Readings in the Philosophy of Clinical Psychology. 654p. 1992. 59.95 (*1-55798-157-4*) Am Psychol.

Miller, Ronald B., ed. The Restoration of Dialogue: Readings in the Philosophy of Clinical Psychology. 654p. 1992. pap. 29.95 (*1-55798-166-3*) Am Psychol.

An Asterisk (*) at the beginning of an entry indicates that the title is appearing for the first time.

Miller, Ronald D. Anesthesia. 5th ed. Ross, Allan, ed. LC 99-19722. (Illus.). 2525p. 1999. text. write for info. (*0-443-07988-9*, W B Saunders Co) Harcrt Hlth Sci Grp.
— 1998 Year Book of Plastic & Reconstructive Surgery. 2nd ed. (Illus.). 352p. (C). (gr. 13). 1998. text 82.00 (*0-8151-9728-4*, 25015) Mosby Inc.
— 1997 Year Book of Plastic & Reconstructive Surgery. (Illus.). 480p. (C). (gr. 13). 1997. text 82.00 (*0-8151-9727-6*, 25014) Mosby Inc.
— Paul Bailey & the Westernlore Press: The 1st 40 Years, with Annotated Bibliography. LC 83-51162. (Illus.). 1984. 25.00 (*0-930704-16-9*) Sagebrush Pr.
— Shady Ladies of the West. LC 64-25860. (Illus.). 18.95 (*0-87026-023-5*) Westernlore.
Miller, Ronald D., ed. Anesthesia, 3 vols., Vol. 1. 2nd ed. LC 85-17446. 898p. reprint ed. pap. 200.00 (*0-8357-4657-7*, 203758900001) Bks Demand.
— Anesthesia, 3 vols., Vol. 2. 2nd ed. LC 85-17446. 921p. reprint ed. pap. 200.00 (*0-8357-4658-5*, 203758900002) Bks Demand.
— Anesthesia, 3 vols., Vol. 3. 2nd ed. LC 85-17446. 899p. reprint ed. pap. 200.00 (*0-8357-4659-3*, 203758900003) Bks Demand.
Miller, Ronald D., jt. auth. see Stoelting, Robert K.
Miller, Ronald E. Further Results on Inter-Regional Feedback Effects in Input-Output Models: Supplement. (Discussion Papers: No. 7). 1966. pap. 10.00 (*1-55869-049-2*) Regional Sci Res Inst.
— Interregional Feedback Effects in Input-Output Models: Some Preliminary Results. (Discussion Papers: No. 7). 1965. pap. 10.00 (*1-55869-061-1*) Regional Sci Res Inst.
Miller, Ronald E. & Dossani, Nazir G. A Note on Degeneracy & Multiple Optima in Linear Programs. (Discussion Papers: No. 17). 1967. pap. 10.00 (*1-55869-080-8*) Regional Sci Res Inst.
Miller, Ronald S., jt. auth. see New Age Journal Editors.
Miller, Ronald S., jt. auth. see Schachter-Shalomi, Zalman.
Miller, Ronald W. Planning for Success: A 10-Step Process for Setting & Achieving Your Goals in Life. (Illus.). 120p. (Orig.). 1990. pap. write for info. (*0-9625695-0-X*) New Pers Pub.
Miller, Ronni. Dance with the Elephants: Free Your Creativity & Write. LC 96-95189. 171p. (Orig.). 1996. pap., per. 12.00 (*0-9655391-0-5*) Write It Out.
Miller, Ronnie. Following the Americans to the Persian Gulf: Canada, Australia, & the Development of the New World Order. LC 92-55107. 1994. 32.50 (*0-8386-3536-9*) Fairleigh Dickinson.
— From Lebanon to the Intifada: The Jewish Lobby & Canadian Middle East Policy. 128p. (Orig.). (C). 1990. pap. text 23.00 (*0-8191-7985-X*); lib. bdg. 40.50 (*0-8191-7984-1*) U Pr of Amer.
Miller, Ronnie K. & McIntire, Paul, eds. ASNT Nondestructive Testing Handbook, Vol. 5: Acoustic Emission Testing. (Illus.). 604p. 1987. 121.25 (*0-931403-02-2*, 130) Am Soc Nondestructive.
Miller, Rory. Britain & Latin America in the Nineteenth & Twentieth Centuries. LC 92-35634. (Studies in Modern History). 228p. (C). 1993. text 56.50 (*0-582-21877-2*, 79639) Longman.
— Britain & Latin American 19TH & 20TH Centuries. LC 92-35634. (Studies in Modern History). 228p. (C). 1995. pap. 51.00 (*0-582-49721-3*, 79638) Longman.
***Miller, Rory.** Divided Against Zion: Anti-Zionist Opposition in Britain to a Jewish State in Palestine, 1945-1948. LC 00-35899. (Israeli History, Politics & Society Ser.). 2000. pap. write for info. (*0-7146-8102-4*, Pub. by F Cass Pubs) Intl Spec Bk.
— Divided Against Zion: Anti-Zionist Opposition in Britain to a Jewish State in Palestine, 1945-1948. (Israeli History, Politics & Society Ser.). 288p. 2000. 54.50 (*0-7146-5051-X*, Pub. by F Cass Pubs) Intl Spec Bk.
Miller, Rory, jt. ed. see Davila, Carlos.
Miller, Rosalie J. & Walker, Kay F. Perspectives on Theory for the Practice of Occupational Therapy. 2nd ed. Orig. Title: Six Perspectives on Theory for the Practice of Occupational Therapy. 320p. 1993. 51.00 (*0-8342-0358-8*, 20358) Aspen Pub.
Miller, Rosalind & Terwillegar, Jane. Commonsense Cataloging: A Cataloger's Manual. 4th rev. ed. 182p. 1990. 29.00 (*0-8242-0789-0*) Wilson.
Miller, Rose. The Old Barn. LC 92-35283. (Publish-a-Book Contest Ser.). (Illus.). 32p. (J). (gr. 1-6). 1992. lib. bdg. 22.83 (*0-8114-3581-4*) Raintree Steck-V.
Miller, Rose M. From Fear to Freedom: Living As Sons & Daughters of God. LC 94-13660. 176p. 1994. pap. 9.99 (*0-87788-259-2*, H Shaw Pubs) Waterbrook Pr.
Miller, Rose M., jt. auth. see Stone, J. David.
***Miller, Roselyn Ogden.** Poor as Church Mice. LC 00-34070. (Illus.). 2000. write for info. (*1-886225-57-5*) MG-Hill OH.
Miller, Ross. American Apocalypse: The Great Fire & the Myth of Chicago. LC 89-20338. (Illus.). 298p. 1997. 29.95 (*0-226-52599-6*) U Ch Pr.
— The Drum Set Crash Course. Testa, Joe, ed. 92p. (Orig.). 1996. pap. text 24.95 (*1-57623-522-X*, PERC9611CD) Wrner Bros.
***Miller, Ross.** The Great Chicago Fire. 304p. 2000. 17.50 (*0-252-06914-5*) U of Ill Pr.
Miller, Ross. Here's the Deal: The Buying & Selling of the Great American Cities. LC 95-17004. (Illus.). 336p. 1996. 27.50 (*0-394-58999-8*) Knopf.
Miller, Rowland S. Embarrassment: Poise & Peril in Everyday Life. LC 96-21200. (Emotions & Social Behavior Ser.). 232p. 1996. lib. bdg. 39.95 (*1-57230-127-9*) Guilford Pubns.
— Embarrassment: Poise & Peril in Everyday Life. (Emotions & Social Behavior Ser.). 232p. 1997. pap. text 22.00 (*1-57230-247-X*, 0247) Guilford Pubns.
Miller, Roy A. The Footprints of the Buddha: An Eighth-Century Old Japanese Poetic Sequence. (American Oriental Ser.: Vol. 58). x, 185p. 1975. pap. 15.00 (*0-940490-58-7*) Am Orient Soc.
— Japan Country Living Postcard: Country Living. (Illus.). 1993. pap. 8.95 (*0-8048-1925-4*) Tuttle Pubng.
— Japanese & Other Altaic Languages. LC 79-151129. (History & Structure of Languages Ser.). 1993. lib. bdg. 26.00 (*0-226-52719-0*) U Ch Pr.
— Japanese Reader: Graded Lessons in the Modern Language. LC 62-9359. (JPN.). 250p. 1963. pap. 16.95 (*0-8048-1647-6*) Tuttle Pubng.
— Nihongo: In Defence of Japanese. LC 85-23007. 260p. (C). 1986. text 45.00 (*0-485-11251-5*, Pub. by Athlone Pr) Humanities.
Miller, Roy Andrew. Studies in the Grammatical Tradition in Tibet. (Studies in the History of Linguistics: No. 6). xix, 142p. 1976. 39.00 (*90-272-0897-2*) J Benjamins Pubng Co.
Miller, Roy L., Sr., jt. auth. see Lawyer, Eunice L.
Miller, Ruby M., jt. auth. see Miller, E. Willard.
Miller, Rudy M., jt. auth. see Miller, E. Willard.
Miller, Rupert, Jr. Survival Analysis. (Wiley Classics Library). 238p. 1998. pap. 54.95 (*0-471-25548-3*) Wiley.
Miller, Rupert G., Jr. Simultaneous Statistical Inference. (Series in Statistics). (Illus.). 299p. 1991. 82.95 (*0-387-90548-0*) Spr-Verlag.
***Miller, Russ.** Algorithms Sequential & Parallel: A Unified Approach. LC 99-47207. (Illus.). 336p. 1999. 66.00 (*0-13-086373-4*) P-H.
Miller, Russ. Oddly Enough. (Illus.). 64p. 1998. pap. 8.95 (*0-941613-99-2*, Caliber Comics) Stabur Pr.
Miller, Russ & Stout, Quentin F. Parallel Algorithms for Regular Architectures: Meshes & Pyramids. (Illus.). 336p. 1996. 42.00 (*0-262-13233-8*) MIT Pr.
Miller, Russell. Bare-Faced Messiah: A Biography of L. Ron Hubbard. 1995. 19.95 (*0-8050-0654-0*) H Holt & Co.
— The Larger Hope, Vol. 2. 1991. pap. 25.00 (*0-933840-25-X*) Unitarian Univ.
— The Larger Hope: The Universalist Church in America, Vol. 1. 1991. pap. 25.00 (*0-933840-00-4*) Unitarian Univ.
— Magnum: Fifty Years at the Front Line of History. LC 97-49040. (Illus.). 336p. 1998. 26.00 (*0-8021-1631-0*, Grove) Grove-Atltic.
— Magnum: Fifty Years at the Front Lines of History. (Illus.). 336p. 1999. pap. 15.00 (*0-8021-3653-2*, Grove) Grove-Atltic.
— Nothing Less Than Victory. 1998. pap. 15.00 (*0-688-16845-0*, Quil) HarperTrade.
***Miller, Russell R.** Doing Business in Newly Privatized Markets: Global Opportunities & Challenges. LC 99-59831. 310p. 2000. 70.00 (*1-56720-260-8*, Q260, Quorum Bks) Greenwood.
Miller, Russell R. Selling to Newly Emerging Markets. LC 97-13401. 288p. 1998. 65.00 (*1-56720-044-3*, Quorum Bks) Greenwood.
Miller, Russell R., jt. auth. see Shuster, Albert H.
Miller, Russell V. Annotated Trade Practices Act, 1991. 12th ed. liv, 520p. 1991. pap. 39.00 (*0-455-21042-X*, Pub. by LawBk Co) Gaunt.
— Annotated Trade Practices Act, 1993. 14th ed. 770p. 1993. pap. 45.00 (*0-455-21186-8*, Pub. by LawBk Co) Gaunt.
— Annotated Trade Practices Act, 1994. 15th ed. LC 95-148784. 678p. 1994. pap. 45.00 (*0-455-21239-2*, Pub. by Sweet & Maxwll) Gaunt.
— Annotated Trade Practices Act, 1995. 16th ed. LC 95-151541. 680p. 1995. pap. 45.00 (*0-455-21312-7*, Pub. by LawBk Co) Gaunt.
***Miller, Russell V.** Miller's Annotated Competition Law. 800p. 2000. pap. 66.50 (*0-455-21707-6*, Pub. by LBC Info Servs) Gaunt.
— Miller's Annotated Trade Practices Act. 21st ed. 1300p. 2000. pap. 60.00 (*0-455-21706-8*, Pub. by LBC Info Servs) Gaunt.
Miller, Russell V. Miller's Annotated Trade Practices Act, 1997. 18th ed. 834p. 1997. pap. 48.00 (*0-455-21481-6*, Pub. by LawBk Co) Gaunt.
Miller-Russo, Linda & Miller-Russo, Peter. Angelic Enlightenment: A Personal Process. LC 99-22349. 240p. 1999. pap. 12.95 (*1-56718-482-0*) Llewellyn Pubns.
Miller-Russo, Peter, jt. auth. see Miller-Russo, Linda.
***Miller, Ruth.** I Went to the Bay. (Illus.). 32p. (J). (ps-2). 2000. pap. 5.95 (*1-55074-789-4*) Kids Can Pr.
Miller, Ruth. I Went to the Bay. unabridged ed. (Illus.). 24p. (J). (ps-2). 1999. 12.95 (*1-55074-498-4*, Pub. by Kids Can Pr) Genl Dist Srvs.
— Our Trip to Mesa Verde, 1922. LC 97-193038. (Illus.). 52p. (Orig.). 1997. pap. 6.95 (*1-890437-04-2*) Western Reflections.
***Miller, Ruth & Gurth, Per-Henrik.** I Went to the Farm. (Illus.). 24p. (J). (ps-k). 2000. 14.95 (*1-55074-705-3*, Pub. by Kids Can Press) Genl Dist Srvs.
Miller, Ruth & Parks, Sandy. Success Through Color Charisma. LC 83-73079. 133p. (Orig.). 1983. pap. 12.00 (*0-916359-38-7*) Color Charisma.
Miller, Ruth H., jt. ed. see Gorman, G. E.
Miller, Ruth M. & Lennor, Linda A. The Angel Oak Story. (Illus.). 1989. 5.00 (*0-937684-26-0*) Tradd St Pr.
Miller, Ruth R. California Divorce: Through the Legal Maze. 2nd rev. ed. LC 97-73589. (Illus.). 120p. 1997. pap. 13.95 (*0-9620223-1-4*) Beier & Assocs.
Miller, Ryder, jt. ed. see Daniels, Keith Allen.
Miller, Ryle, tr. see Pichot, Pierre.
Miller, Ryle L., Jr. How to Write for the Professional Journals: A Guide for Technically Trained Managers. LC 87-32592. 189p. 1988. 52.95 (*0-89930-254-8*, MHT/, Quorum Bks) Greenwood.
Miller, S. Arete: Ancient Writers, Papyri, & Inscriptions on the History & Ideals of Greek Athletics & Games. 120p. 1979. pap. 12.50 (*0-89005-313-8*) Ares.
— Handbook of Agrohydrology. 280p. 1994. pap. 90.00 (*0-85954-389-7*, Pub. by Nat Res Inst) St Mut.
Miller, S., jt. auth. see Gregory, J.
Miller, S., jt. auth. see Maxwell, D.
Miller, S., jt. ed. see Lewis, M.
Miller, S. A., ed. Nutrition & Behavior. 320p. 1981. pap. 65.00 (*0-89859-735-8*) L Erlbaum Assocs.
Miller, S. Dennis. How to Write a Police Report. LC 92-36440. 148p. (C). 1993. pap. 30.95 (*0-8273-4728-6*) Delmar.
Miller, Sally, jt. ed. see Millonig, Virginia L.
Miller, Sally D. Mourning & Dancing: A Memoir of Grief & Recovery. LC 99-10952. 215p. 1999. pap. 10.95 (*1-55874-671-4*) Health Comm.
***Miller, Sally Downham.** Mourning & Dancing for Schools: A Grief & Recovery Sourcebook for Students, Teachers & Parents. 200p. 2000. pap. 10.95 (*1-55874-775-3*) Health Comm.
Miller, Sally K. Adult Nurse Practitioner Certification Study Question Book. LC 99-22641. 300p. 1999. pap. text 35.00 (*1-878028-20-0*) Hlth Lead Assoc.
— Family Nurse Practitioner Certification Study Question Book Set, 3 vols. 900p. 1999. pap. text 70.00 (*1-878028-26-X*) Hlth Lead Assoc.
Miller, Sally K., ed. Acute Care Nurse Practitioner Certification Study Question Book. LC 99-10079. 300p. 1998. pap. text 35.00 (*1-878028-25-1*) Hlth Lead Assoc.
Miller, Sally M. From Prairie to Prison: The Life of Social Activist Kate Richards O'Hare. LC 93-12223. (Missouri Biography Ser.). (Illus.). 280p. (C). 1993. 34.95 (*0-8262-0898-3*) U of Mo Pr.
— Victor Berger & the Promise of Constructive Socialism, 1910-1920, 24. LC 72-175609. (Contributions in American History Ser.: No. 24). 275p. 1973. 59.95 (*0-8371-6264-5*, MVB/, Greenwood Pr) Greenwood.
Miller, Sally M., ed. American Labor in the Era of World War II. LC 94-24570. 240p. 1995. pap. 21.95 (*0-275-95185-5*, Praeger Pubs) Greenwood.
— The Ethnic Press in the United States: A Historical Analysis & Handbook. LC 85-31699. 459p. 1987. lib. bdg. 99.50 (*0-313-23879-0*, MIE/, Greenwood Pr) Greenwood.
— Flawed Liberation: Socialism & Feminism, 19. LC 80-1050. (Contributions in Women's Studies: No. 19). 214p. 1981. 55.00 (*0-313-21401-8*, MFL/, Greenwood Pr) Greenwood.
— John Muir: Life & Work. LC 93-10925. (Illus.). 324p. 1993. reprint ed. pap. 18.95 (*0-8263-1594-1*) U of NM Pr.
***Miller, Sally M., ed.** John Muir in Historical Perspective. 280p. 1999. pap. text 29.95 (*0-8204-4008-6*) P Lang Pubng.
Miller, Sally M., ed. Race, Ethnicity, & Gender in Early Twentieth-Century American Socialism. LC 95-40447. (Garland Reference Library of Social Science: Vol. 880). 303p. 1996. text 66.00 (*0-8153-1163-X*) Garland.
Miller, Sally M. & Cornford, Daniela. American Labor in the Era of World War II, 45. LC 94-24570. (Contributions in Labor Studies: Vol. 45). 240p. 1995. 65.00 (*0-313-29074-1*) Greenwood.
Miller, Sally M. & Latham, A. J. Studies in the Economic History of the Pacific Rim. LC 96-50306. 272p. (C). 1997. 90.00 (*0-415-14819-7*) Routledge.
Miller, Sally M., ed. see O'Hare, Kate R.
Miller, Sam. Searching the World Wide Web: An Introductory Curriculum for Using Search Engines. McMannis, Christy, ed. (Illus.). 55p. 1997. spiral bd. 14.95 (*1-56484-123-5*) Intl Society Tech Educ.
***Miller, Sam, et al.** Keyboard Success. 2nd ed. 150p. (J). (gr. 3-9). 1999. teacher ed., spiral bd. 29.95 (*1-56484-152-9*) Intl Society Tech Educ.
— Keyboard Success Student Flip Book. 2nd ed. 60p. 1999. spiral bd. 8.00 (*1-56484-153-7*) Intl Society Tech Educ.
Miller, Sam F. Design Process: A Primer for Architectural & Interior Design. 240p. 1995. pap. 39.95 (*0-442-01394-9*, VNR) Wiley.
Miller, Sam F. Design Process: A Primer for Architectural & Interior Design. (Architecture Ser.). 229p. 1995. 49.95 (*0-471-28549-8*, VNR) Wiley.
Miller, Sammy. Sammy Miller on Trials. (Illus.). 1971. 5.95 (*0-393-60015-7*) Norton.
Miller, Samuel. The Life of the Soul. large type ed. (Large Print Inspirational Ser.). 208p. 1986. pap. 12.95 (*0-8027-2551-1*) Walker & Co.
— Thoughts on Public Prayer. 1992. 19.99 (*0-87377-927-4*) GAM Pubns.
Miller, Samuel, jt. auth. see Crean, Hugh.
Miller, Samuel, tr. see Del Rio Garcia, Eduardo.
Miller, Samuel D. An Aerospace Bibliography. (Reference Ser.). 341p. 1986. reprint ed. pap. text. write for info. (*0-912799-22-6*) AFH & MP.
Miller, Samuel D., jt. auth. see Olson, Mary W.
Miller, Samuel F. Lectures on the Constitution of the United States. xxi, 765p. 1981. reprint ed. 52.00 (*0-8377-0836-2*, Rothman) W S Hein.
Miller, Samuel H. Religion in a Technical Age. LC 68-17628. 158p. reprint ed. pap. 49.00 (*0-7837-3848-X*, 204367000010) Bks Demand.
Miller, Samuel H. & Wright, G. Ernest, eds. The Roman Catholic-Protestant Colloquium, Ecumenical Dialogue at Harvard. LC 64-19583. 396p. 1964. 35.00 (*0-674-23700-5*) Belknap Pr.
Miller, Samuel L. History of the Town of Waldoboro, Maine. (Illus.). 281p. 1988. reprint ed. lib. bdg. 33.00 (*0-8328-0034-1*, ME0007) Higginson Bk Co.
Miller, Samuel O., jt. auth. see Dane, Barbara O.
Miller, Sandra E., et al. Rural Resource Management: Problem Solving for the Long Term. LC 93-38131. (Illus.). 340p. (C). 1994. pap. text 39.95 (*0-8138-0686-0*) Iowa St U Pr.
Miller, Sandra L., ed. see Libby, Gary R.
Miller, Sandra L., ed. see Poyner, Robin.
Miller, Sandra S. Smart Choices for Health: A Self-Paced Program That Puts You in Charge of Your Weight. Eberle, Suzanne G., ed. (Illus.). 150p. 1999. pap. text 24.95 (*0-9672735-3-6*) Providence Hlth.
Miller, Sandra W. & Tulloch, Charlotte R., eds. Teaching Basic Skills Through Home Economics. 75p. (C). 1989. pap. text 8.00 (*0-911365-29-X*, A261-08474) Family & Consumer Sci Educ.
Miller, Sandro, photos by. American Bikers. (Illus.). 160p. 1998. 40.00 (*3-8238-0369-7*) te Neues.
Miller, Sandy. Cerro Gordo, Illinois. (Illus.). 140p. 1989. 52.50 (*0-88107-145-5*) Curtis Media.
Miller, Sandy, ed. see Butler-Moore, Nylea L. & Krau, Carol F.
Miller, Sanford & Mocanu, P. T. Differential Subordinations. LC 99-48720. (Pure & Applied Mathematics Ser.). 459p. 1999. write for info. (*0-8247-0029-5*) Dekker.
Miller, Sanford, jt. auth. see Van Der Heijden, C. A.
Miller, Sanford S., ed. see State University of New York Conference on Complex.
***Miller, Sara.** Colors All Around. (Barbie Ser.). (Illus.). 12p. (J). (ps-1). 2000. bds. 5.99 (*1-57584-656-X*, Pub. by Rdrs Digest) S&S Trade.
— Happy Birthday, Girl. (Barbie Birthday Bk.). (Illus.). 52p. (J). (gr. k-4). 2001. 11.99 (*1-57584-729-9*, Pub. by Rdrs Digest) S&S Trade.
— Just for Fun: The Essential Get-Together Book for Girls. (Barbie Ser.). (Illus.). 12p. (J). (gr. 1-4). 2000. bds. 11.99 (*1-57584-651-9*, Pub. by Rdrs Digest) S&S Trade.
— Learn & Grow. (Illus.). 8p. (J). (ps-1). 1999. bds. 15.99 (*1-57584-348-X*, RDYF) Rdrs Digest.
Miller, Sara. Memory Keeper. (Barbie Generation Girl Ser.). (Illus.). 12p. (J). (gr. 4-6). 2000. pap. 12.99 (*1-57584-411-7*, Pub. by Rdrs Digest) S&S Trade.
***Miller, Sara.** Merry Christmas, Snowden! (Snowden & Friends Ser.). 12p. (J). (ps-1). 1999. bds. 3.99 (*1-57584-418-4*, Pub. by Rdrs Digest) S&S Trade.
— Snowden's Magical Christmas. (Snowden & Friends Ser.). 10p. (J). 1999. bds. 4.99 (*1-57584-419-2*, Pub. by Rdrs Digest) S&S Trade.
Miller, Sara & Balducci, Rita. I Can Snap ! (I Can Do It! Bks.: Vol. 4). (Illus.). 10p. (J). (gr. k-3). 1999. bds. 4.99 (*1-57584-278-5*, Pub. by Rdrs Digest) Random.
— I Can Zip! (I Can Do It! Bks.: Vol. 3). (Illus.). 10p. (J). (gr. k-3). 1999. bds. 4.99 (*1-57584-277-7*, Pub. by Rdrs Digest) Random.
***Miller, Sara, et al.** Keyboard Success Curriculum Kit, Set. 1999. teacher ed., student ed. 44.95 (*1-56484-158-8*) Intl Society Tech Educ.
Miller, Sara S. Better Than TV. LC 96-34385. (Illus.). 48p. (J). 1998. pap. 3.99 (*0-440-41355-9*) Dell.
***Miller, Sara S.** Chickens. LC 99-30130. (True Bks.). (J). 2000. 22.00 (*0-516-21576-0*) Childrens.
— Cows. LC 99-30138. (True Bks.). (J). 2000. 22.00 (*0-516-21577-9*) Childrens.
Miller, Sara S. Flies: From Flower Flies to Mosquitoes. LC 97-24035. (Animals in Order Ser.). (Illus.). 48p. (J). (gr. 3-5). 1999. pap. text 6.95 (*0-531-15919-1*) Watts.
***Miller, Sara S.** Goats. LC 99-30139. (True Bks.). (J). 2000. 22.00 (*0-516-21578-7*) Childrens.
— Horses & Rhinos: What They Have in Common. LC 98-8205. (Animals in Order Ser.). 47p. (J). (gr. 3-5). 1999. 23.00 (*0-531-11586-0*) Watts.
Miller, Sara S. If It Flies, Is It a Fly? LC 97-24035. (Animals in Order Ser.). (J). 1999. 23.00 (*0-531-11486-4*) Watts.
— Perching Birds: Singing in the Trees. LC 97-51591. (Animals in Order Ser.). (J). 1999. 23.00 (*0-531-11520-8*) Watts.
— Piggy in the Parlor: And Other Tales, Vol. 1. unabridged ed. (Illus.). 53p. (J). (gr. 1-5). 1997. 19.50 (*1-57529-057-X*) Kabel Pubs.
***Miller, Sara S.** Pigs. LC 99-30129. (True Bks.). (J). 2000. 22.00 (*0-516-21579-5*) Childrens.
Miller, Sara S. Rodents: From Mice to Muskrats. (Illus.). 48p. 1998. pap. 6.95 (*0-531-15920-5*) Watts.
— Rodents: From Mice to Muskrats. LC 97-24034. (Animals in Order Ser.). (J). 1998. 23.00 (*0-531-11488-0*) Watts.
***Miller, Sara S.** Sheep. LC 99-32312. (True Bks.). (J). 2000. 22.00 (*0-516-21580-9*) Childrens.
— Snakes & Lizards: What They Have in Common LC 99-30417. (Animals in Order Ser.). 2000. 23.00 (*0-531-11594-1*) Watts.
Miller, Sara S. Three Stories You Can Read to Your Cat. LC 96-51. (Illus.). 48p. (J). (gr. 2-5). 1997. 13.95 (*0-395-78831-5*) HM.
— Three Stories You Can Read to Your Dog. LC 93-38856. (Illus.). 48p. (J). (gr. 2-5). 1995. 13.95 (*0-395-69938-X*) HM.
— Three Stories You Can Read to Your Dog. LC 93-38856. (Illus.). 48p. (J). (ps-3). 1997. reprint ed. pap. 5.95 (*0-395-86135-7*) HM.
— True Bugs: When Is a Bug Really a Bug? LC 97-15720. (Animals in Order Ser.). (J). 1998. 22.00 (*0-531-11479-1*) Watts.
— True Bugs: When Is a Bug Really a Bug? LC 97-15720. (Animals in Order Ser.). (Illus.). 48p. (J). (gr. 3-5). 1999. pap. text 6.95 (*0-531-15922-1*) Watts.
***Miller, Sara S.** Waterfowl: From Swans to Screamers. LC 98-8204. (Animals in Order Ser.). 47p. (J). 1999. 22.00 (*0-531-11584-4*) Watts.
Miller, Sara Swan. Better Than TV. (First Choice Chapter Book Ser.). (J). 1998. 9.19 (*0-606-13199-X*, Pub. by Turtleback) Demco.
— Cicadas & Aphids: What They Have in Common. LC 98-2703. (Animals in Order Ser.). (J). 1999. 23.00 (*0-531-11519-4*) Watts.
— Cicadas & Aphids: What They Have in Common. 1999. pap. text 6.95 (*0-531-15944-2*) Watts.

M

*Miller, Sara Swan. Frogs & Toads: What They Have in Common. LC 99-42710. (Animals in Order Ser.). (Illus.). 2000. 23.00 (0-531-11632-8) Watts.

— Horses & Rhinos: What They Have in Common. (Animals in Order Ser.). (Illus.). (J). 2000. pap. 6.95 (0-531-16401-2) Watts.

Miller, Sara Swan. Perching Birds of North America. (Animals in Order Ser.). 1999. pap. text 6.95 (0-531-15946-9) Watts.

*Miller, Sara Swan. Salamanders: Secret, Silent Lives. (Animals in Order Ser.). (Illus.). (J). 2000. pap. 6.95 (0-531-16402-0) Watts.

— Snakes & Lizards: What They Have in Common. (Animals in Order Ser.). (Illus.). (J). 2000. pap. 6.95 (0-531-16448-9) Watts.

— Three More Stories You Can Read to Your Dog. LC 99-39880. (Illus.). 48p. (J). (ps-3). 2000. 14.00 (0-395-92293-3) HM.

Miller, Sara Swan. Turtles: Life in a Shell. 1999. pap. text 6.95 (0-531-15947-7) Watts.

*Miller, Sara Swan. Wading Birds: From Herons to Hammerheads. LC 99-57535. (Animals in Order Ser.). (Illus.). (J). 2001. write for info. (0-531-11630-1) Watts.

— Waterfowl: From Swans to Screamers. (Animals in Order Ser.). (Illus.). (J). 2000. pap. 6.95 (0-531-16403-9) Watts.

M

*Miller, Sara Swan, et al. Birds of Prey: From Falcons to Vultures. LC 99-59415. (Animals in Order Ser.). (J). 2001. write for info. (0-531-11631-X) Watts.

*Miller, Sara Swan & Savage, Steve. Owls, the Silent Hunters. LC 99-42008. (Animals in Order Ser.). (Illus.). 2000. 23.00 (0-531-11595-X) Watts.

— Shorebirds: From Stilts to Sanderlings. LC 99-42009. (Animals in Order Ser.). (Illus.). 2000. 23.00 (0-531-11596-8) Watts.

Miller, Sarah, jt. auth. see Early, Gill.

Miller, Sarah W. & Madaris, Don L. Count on Us. Montgomery, Charles, ed. 44p. 1984. reprint ed. pap. 3.95 (0-916043-00-2) Light Hearted Pub Co.

Miller, Sasha. Ladylord. 1997. mass mkt. 5.99 (0-8125-4949-X, Pub. by Tor Bks) St Martin.

*Miller, Sasha & Norton, Andre. To the King a Daughter. 320p. 2000. text 25.95 (0-312-87336-0) St Martin.

Miller, Saul & Maass Hill, Peggy. Sports Psychology for Cyclists. LC 99-37808. (Illus.). 1999. pap. 16.95 (1-884737-68-4) VeloPress.

Miller-Schroeder, Patricia. Blue Whales. LC 97-11465. (Untamed World Ser.). (Illus.). 64p. (J). (gr. 5-9). 1998. lib. bdg. 27.12 (0-8172-4570-7) Raintree Steck-V.

— Blue Whales. (Untamed World Ser.). 1998. pap. 8.95 (0-8172-8011-1) Raintree Steck-V.

— Gorillas. LC 96-21248. (Untamed World Ser.). (Illus.). 64p. (J). (gr. 5-9). 1997. lib. bdg. 27.17 (0-8172-4562-6) Raintree Steck-V.

*Miller-Schroeder, Patricia. Scales, Slime & Salamanders: The Science of Reptiles & Amphibians. LC 99-40878. (Science at Work Ser.). (J). (gr. 4-7). 2000. lib. bdg. 25.69 (0-7398-0141-4) Raintree Steck-V.

— Wings, Wheels & Keels: The Science of Transportation. LC 99-26889. (Science@work Ser.). (J). 2000. lib. bdg. 25.69 (0-7398-0139-2) Raintree Steck-V.

*Miller, Scott. Deconstructing Harold Hill: The Insider's Guide to Musical Theatre. LC 99-50311. 256p. 1999. pap. 18.95 (0-325-00166-9) Heinemann.

Miller, Scott. Escape from Babel: Toward a Unifying Language for Psychotherapy Practice. 256p. 1996. 32.00 (0-393-70219-7) Norton.

— From Assassins to West Side Story: The Director's Guide to Musical Theatre. LC 96-3248. 242p. (Orig.). 1996. pap. 19.95 (0-435-08699-5, 08699) Heinemann.

— Loon Journal. (Illus.). 40p. (Orig.). (J). (gr. 4 up). 1989. pap. 5.98 (0-926147-01-3) Loonfeather.

— The Miracle Method: A Radically New Approach to Problem Drinking. 192p. 1996. pap. 13.00 (0-393-31533-9) Norton.

Miller, Scott, jt. ed. see Braham, Randolph L.

Miller, Scott A. Developmental Research Methods. 2nd ed. LC 96-51752. 338p. 1997. 61.00 (0-13-398892-9) P-H.

Miller, Scott D., et al, eds. Handbook of Solution-Focused Brief Therapy. (Psychology Ser.). 400p. 1996. 41.95 (0-7879-0217-9) Jossey-Bass.

Miller, Scott D. & Berg, Insoo K. The Miracle Method: A Radically New Approach to Problem Drinking. 160p. 1995. 19.95 (0-393-03740-1) Norton.

Miller, Scott D., jt. auth. see Berg, Insoo K.

Miller, Scott E., jt. ed. see Keast, Allen.

Miller, Scott S. & Guy, Thomas. Dealing with the IRS. (Illus.). 70p. 1992. pap. 8.95 (0-9631941-0-0) Creek Bend Pub.

Miller, Sean. The Naysayer's Yearbook. 184p. 1997. pap. 16.95 (0-9658099-0-0) Presence Pr.

Miller, Seumas, et al. Police Ethics. LC 97-200044. 256p. 1998. pap. 29.95 (1-86448-308-3, Pub. by Allen & Unwin Pty) Paul & Co Pubs.

Miller, Shannon. Invested with Meaning: Raleigh Circle in the New World. LC 98-10974. (New Cultural Studies). (Illus.). 248p. 1998. 37.50 (0-8122-3442-1) U of Pa Pr.

Miller, Shannon & Richardson, Nancy A. Winning Every Day: Gold Medal Advice for a Happy, Healthy Life! LC 98-10059. 144p. (J). (gr. 5 up). 1998. pap. 12.95 (0-553-09776-8) Bantam.

*Miller, Shari, et al. Reflections: Precolumbian Inspiration in Mexican Silver Design, 1930-1970. LC 99-71417. (Illus.). 32p. 1999. pap. 15.00 (0-911611-17-7) Tucson Mus Art.

Miller, Sharilynne. Stamp Art: The Elegant Art of Rubber Stamping. 1999. pap. 21.99 (1-56496-583-X) Rockport Pubs.

Miller, Sharon L., jt. ed. see Chaves, Mark.

*Miller, Shawn William. Fruitless Trees: Portuguese Conservation & Brazil's Colonial Timber. LC 99-33182. 1999. 55.00 (0-8047-3396-1) Stanford U Pr.

Miller, Sheila. Ian & the Gigantic Leafy Obstacle. 1983. pap. 2.95 (9971-83-790-0) OMF Bks.

— My Book about Hudson. 1975. pap. 2.95 (9971-972-20-4) OMF Bks.

Miller, Sheila & Murray, Ian. The Gods Must Be Angry. (Illus.). 34p. (J). (gr. 1-4). 1990. 2.95 (9971-972-93-X) OMF Bks.

Miller, Sheila, jt. ed. see Szur, Rolene.

Miller, Sheila W. Gifts for Your Soul: A Book of Daily Devotions. LC 97-9222. 224p. 1997. 15.99 (0-310-20975-7) Zondervan.

Miller, Sheldon. Stealth Management: With Shared Goals They Will Hardly Know You Are Leading Them. LC 92-90895. (Illus.). 300p. 1993. 27.95 (0-9635316-0-3) Stealth Mgmt.

Miller, Sheldon I., jt. ed. see Frances, Richard J.

Miller, Shelley, compiled by. Serial Publications Available by Exchange: Mexico, Central America & Panama. (Bibliography & Reference Ser.: No. 29). vii, 86p. (Orig.). 1992. pap. 22.00 (0-917617-28-2) SALALM.

Miller, Shelley & Sonntag-Grigera, Gabriela. Serial Publications Available by Exchange: Caribbean Area. (Bibliography & Reference Ser.: No. 36). 48p. (Orig.). 1994. pap. 19.50 (0-917617-45-2) SALALM.

Miller, Sherman N. The Quick White Paper. (Illus.). 130p. (C). 1998. reprint ed. pap. 19.95 (0-9640915-3-4) S N M Pubng.

Miller, Sherman N. & Miller, Gwynelle W. Wedlock . . . The Common Sense Marriage. 224p. (Orig.). 1994. pap. 12.95 (0-9640915-6-9) S N M Pubng.

Miller, Sherod, ed. Marriages & Families: Enrichment Through Communication. LC 75-27012. (Sage Contemporary Social Science Issues Ser.: No. 20). 126p. reprint ed. pap. 39.10 (0-608-10113-3, 202193300026) Bks Demand.

Miller, Sherod & Miller, Phyllis. Collaborative Team Skills. (Illus.). 1994. teacher ed., ring bd. 65.00 (0-917340-21-3) Interpersonal Comm.

— Collaborative Team Skills. (Illus.). 135p. (C). 1994. pap. text 20.00 (0-917340-20-5) Interpersonal Comm.

Miller, Sherod, et al. Working Together: Productive Communication on the Job. (Illus.). 200p. 1985. text, teacher ed. 40.00 (0-917340-14-0); ring bd. 40.00 (0-917340-11-6) Interpersonal Comm.

Miller, Sherry C. The Day Happy E. Bunny Lost His Cotton Tail. (Illus.). 16p. (Orig.). (J). (gr. k-5). 1983. pap. 0.49 (0-685-43303-X) Double M Pub.

— Lost in the Arctic with Pal Bear. (Molly Character - Color Me Ser.: No. 2). (Illus.). 32p. (Orig.). (J). (gr. k-5). 1984. pap. 1.95 (0-913379-01-8) Double M Pub.

— Santa's Helper. LC 83-72493. (Molly Character - Color Me Ser.: No. 1). (Illus.). 32p. (Orig.). (J). (gr. k-5). 1983. pap. 1.95 (0-913379-00-X) Double M Pub.

— Snowharry Takes a Vacation (with Arctic Friends) (Molly Character - Color Me Ser.: No. 4). (Illus.). 32p. (J). (gr. k-5). 1985. pap. write for info. (0-913379-03-4) Double M Pub.

— Snowskate Goes for Gold. (Molly Character - Color Me Ser.: No. 3). (Illus.). 32p. (Orig.). (J). (gr. k-5). 1984. pap. 1.95 (0-913379-02-6) Double M Pub.

Miller, Sheryl Krieger, ed. see Cox, James A.

Miller, Shirley, et al. Training Manager Competencies: The Standards. 128p. 1989. ring bd. 125.00 (1-881326-05-5) IBSTPI.

Miller, Shirley A. The Covenant: A Promise Written in the Stars. (Illus.). 182p. 1998. pap. 19.95 (1-892967-00-6) Lampholder Pubns.

— Tempera Mysticism: Exploding the Temperament Theory. LC 91-65106. 176p. 1991. pap. 9.95 (0-914984-30-6) Lampholder Pubns.

*Miller, Shirley Ann. Countdown to Eternity... The 7,000 Year Time-Line in the Book of Revelation. 180p. 1998. pap. 18.95 (1-892967-01-4) Lampholder Pubns.

Miller, Shirley J. Billy. (Illus.). 60p. (Orig.). (J). (gr. 2-6). 1993. pap. 6.95 (1-878580-92-2) Asylum Arts.

— My House, Your House. (Illus.). 60p. (Orig.). (J). (gr. 2-6). 1993. pap. 6.95 (1-878580-91-4) Asylum Arts.

— School Days. (Illus.). 80p. (Orig.). (J). (gr. 2-6). 1993. pap. 6.95 (1-878580-90-6) Asylum Arts.

Miller, Shirley M., compiled by. Webster's New World Speller - Divider: Based upon Webster's New World Dictionary of the American Language, College Edition. 3rd ed. 1992. write for info. (0-318-69384-4, Webstrs New) Macmillan Gen Ref.

Miller, Sigmund. One Bright Day. 1952. pap. 5.25 (0-8222-0852-0) Dramatists Play.

Miller, Skip. Tidewater Fishing. 256p. 1996. pap. 11.95 (0-8092-3018-6) NTC Contemp Pub Co.

— Tidewater Fishing: The Complete Guide to Eastern Virginia Waters. LC 93-9061. 256p. 1993. pap. 11.95 (1-56943-007-1) NTC Contemp Pub Co.

Miller-Slade, Donna. Liability Issues in Perinatal Nursing. LC 98-27994. 416p. 1998. pap. text 39.95 (0-397-55276-9) Lppncott W & W.

Miller, Somi A. & Lake, Patricia. Thai Cooking Class. (Illus.). 96p. (Orig.). 1993. pap. 7.00 (0-685-66882-7) HarpC.

Miller, Stacey J., jt. auth. see Birkel, J. Damian.

Miller, Stanford & Bleach, Yvonne. Putting the Heart Back into Teaching: A Manual for Junior Primary Teachers. pap. 22.95 (0-9583885-5-5, 2009, Pub. by Novalis Trust) Anthroposophic.

Miller, Stanford & Shepherd, Ralph. Standing on the Brink: An Education for the 21st Century. LC 95-206980. pap. 15.95 (0-9583885-1-2, 2007, Pub. by Novalis Trust) Anthroposophic.

Miller, Stanford M. Two Thousand Hard to Locate Latin Forms. (LAT.). 18p. 1992. spiral bd. 2.45 (0-939507-21-8, B104) Amer Classical.

Miller, Stanley. Freehand: The Art of Stanley Mouse. deluxe limited ed. Williams, Roger, ed. (Illus.). 128p. 1998. 250.00 (0-943389-24-0, SLG Bks) Snow Lion-SLG Bks.

Miller, Stanley, jt. auth. see Jakes, T. D.

Miller, Stanley J. & Maloney, Mary E. Cutaneous Oncology. LC 97-7305. 1997. 295.00 (0-86542-517-5) Blackwell Sci.

Miller, Stanton S. Environmental Monitoring. LC 76-54966. (ACS Reprint Collection Ser.). 207p. reprint ed. pap. 64.20 (0-7837-1453-X, 205242900021) Bks Demand.

Miller, Stella G. Two Groups of Thessalian Gold. LC 77-80473. (University of California Publications in Social Welfare: No. 18). (Illus.). 126p. reprint ed. pap. 39.10 (0-608-18310-5, 203158100075) Bks Demand.

Miller, Stephen. Excellence & Equity: The National Endowment for the Humanities. LC 83-21861. 202p. reprint ed. pap. 62.70 (0-7837-5789-1, 204545500006) Bks Demand.

— Misguiding Lights? (Dialog Ser.). 44p. 1991. pap., teacher ed. 5.50 (0-8341-1279-5); pap., student ed. 6.50 (0-8341-1280-9) Beacon Hill.

— Present Moments. LC 99-11113. 1999. pap. 4.97 (1-56955-055-7) Servant.

— Protecting Restaurant Profits. 1988. pap. 36.95 (0-86730-252-6) Lebhar Friedman.

— Special Interest Groups in American Politics. LC 83-4691. 160p. 1983. 34.95 (0-87855-485-8) Transaction Pubs.

Miller, Stephen, ed. Spiritual Zest: Finding It & Keeping It. (Dialog Ser.). 44p. 1992. pap., teacher ed. 5.50 (0-8341-1447-X); pap., student ed. 6.50 (0-8341-1448-8) Beacon Hill.

Miller, Stephen, ed. Partings at Dawn: An Anthology of Japanese Gay Literature. (Illus.). 352p. 1996. 50.00 (0-940567-17-2); pap. 19.95 (0-940567-18-0) Gay Sunshine.

Miller, Stephen, jt. ed. see Perez, Janet.

Miller, Stephen, ed. see Shakespeare, William.

Miller, Stephen A. General Zoology. 3rd ed. 352p. (C). 1993. text, lab manual ed. write for info. (0-697-13703-1, WCB McGr Hill) McGrw-H Hghr Educ.

Miller, Stephen A. Zoology. 3rd ed. 148p. (C). 1995. spiral bd., lab manual ed. write for info. (0-697-31405-7, WCB McGr Hill) McGrw-H Hghr Educ.

Miller, Stephen A. & Harley, John P. Zoology. 60p. (C). 1991. write for info. (0-697-14072-5, WCB McGr Hill) McGrw-H Hghr Educ.

— Zoology. 2nd ed. 744p. (C). 1993. per. write for info. (0-697-13704-X, WCB McGr Hill) McGrw-H Hghr Educ.

— Zoology. 2nd ed. 744p. (C). 1993. text. write for info. (0-697-16952-9, WCB McGr Hill); text, student ed. 24.37 (0-697-13706-6, WCB McGr Hill) McGrw-H Hghr Educ.

— Zoology. 3rd ed. LC 94-73690. 752p. (C). 1995. text 80.47 (0-697-24373-7, WCB McGr Hill) McGrw-H Hghr Educ.

— Zoology. 3rd ed. LC 94-73690. 752p. (C). 1995. text 80.47 (0-697-24374-5, WCB McGr Hill) McGrw-H Hghr Educ.

— Zoology. 3rd ed. 776p. (C). 1997. pap. text. write for info. (0-07-114983-X, WCB McGr Hill) McGrw-H Hghr Educ.

— Zoology. 4th ed. LC 98-12999. 1998. 7.68 (0-07-115810-3) McGraw.

— Zoology, 1. 2nd ed. 744p. (C). 1993. text. write for info. (0-697-16953-7, WCB McGr Hill) McGrw-H Hghr Educ.

— Zoology, 4. 2nd ed. 744p. (C). 1993. text. write for info. (0-697-20486-3, WCB McGr Hill) McGrw-H Hghr Educ.

— Zoology: The Animal Kingdom. 400p. (C). 1995. per. write for info. (0-697-29036-0, WCB McGr Hill) McGrw-H Hghr Educ.

— Zoology: The Animal Kingdom. 400p. (C). 1997. per. write for info. (0-07-114982-1, WCB McGr Hill) McGrw-H Hghr Educ.

Miller, Stephen A. & Templin, Jay M. Student Study Guide to Accompany Zoology. 3rd ed. 256p. (C). 1995. text, student ed. 24.37 (0-697-26068-2, WCB McGr Hill) McGrw-H Hghr Educ.

*Miller, Stephen B. Historical Sketches of Hudson: Embracing the Settlement of the City, City Government, Etc. 120p. 2000. 29.50 (0-7404-0042-8) Higginson Bk Co.

— Historical Sketches of Hudson NY. 2000. pap. 19.50 (0-7404-0043-6) Higginson Bk Co.

Miller, Stephen B. Historical Sketches of Hudson NY. 140p. 1985. reprint ed. 12.50 (0-932334-75-X, NY11031); reprint ed. pap. 8.95 (0-932334-77-6, NY11030) Hrt of the Lakes.

Miller, Stephen E. The Woman in the Yard. LC 98-43849. 304p. 1999. text 23.00 (0-312-19962-7, Picador USA) St Martin.

*Miller, Stephen E. The Woman in the Yard. 2000. pap. 13.00 (0-312-26414-3) St Martin.

Miller, Stephen G. Arete: Greek Sports from Ancient Sources. LC 90-28646. (Illus.). 239p. 1991. 48.00 (0-520-07508-0, Pub. by U CA Pr); pap. 17.95 (0-520-07509-9, Pub. by U CA Pr) Cal Prin Full Svc.

— Nemea: A Guide to the Site & Museum. 1990. 45.00 (0-520-06590-5, Pub. by U CA Pr); pap. 16.95 (0-520-06799-1, Pub. by U CA Pr) Cal Prin Full Svc.

Miller, Stephen G., tr. see Valavanis, Kimon P.

Miller, Stephen J. Parson's Diseases of the Eye. 18th ed. (Illus.). 442p. 1990. text 59.95 (0-443-04230-6) Church.

Miller, Stephen M. Beacon Small-Group Bible Studies, II Corinthians, Galatians: Reckless Freedom, Responsible Living. Wolf, Earl C., ed. 96p. (Orig.). 1985. pap. 4.99 (0-8341-0957-3) Beacon Hill.

— Christians in a Crooked World. (Dialog Ser.). 40p. 1988. pap., teacher ed. 5.50 (0-8341-1204-3) Beacon Hill.

— How to Improve Your Prayer Life. (Dialog Ser.). 44p. 1987. pap., teacher ed. 5.50 (0-8341-1158-6); pap., student ed. 6.50 (0-8341-1159-4) Beacon Hill.

— Jessica. 26p. 1997. pap. 7.95 (0-944754-40-6) Pudding Hse Pubns.

— Lord Methuen & the British Army: Failure & Redemption in South Africa. LC 98-24089. 288p. 1999. 39.50 (0-7146-4904-X, Pub. by F Cass Pubs); pap. 17.50 (0-7146-4460-9, Pub. by F Cass Pubs) Intl Spec Bk.

— Turning Points. 40p. 1992. pap., teacher ed. 5.50 (0-8341-1400-3); pap., student ed. 6.50 (0-8341-1401-1) Beacon Hill.

Miller, Stephen M., ed. Clean Living in a Dirty World. (Dialog Ser.). 44p. 1991. pap., teacher ed. 5.50 (0-8341-1277-9); pap., student ed. 6.50 (0-8341-1278-7) Beacon Hill.

— How to Live the Holy Life. (Dialog Ser.). 128p. 1986. pap. 6.50 (0-8341-1103-9) Beacon Hill.

— What Jesus Said About. (Dialog Ser.). 44p. 1989. pap., teacher ed. 5.50 (0-8341-1221-3) Beacon Hill.

— What Jesus Said About. (Dialog Ser.). 112p. 1989. pap., student ed. 6.50 (0-8341-1171-3) Beacon Hill.

— When Life Gets Rough. (Dialog Ser.). 108p. 1986. pap., student ed. 6.50 (0-8341-1116-0) Beacon Hill.

Miller, Stephen M. & MIller, Stephen M., eds. When Life Gets Rough. 44p. 1986. pap., teacher ed. 5.50 (0-8341-1117-9) Beacon Hill.

MIller, Stephen M., jt. ed. see Miller, Stephen M.

Miller, Stephen P. An Act of God: Memories of Vietnam. rev. ed. 32p. (Orig.). (C). 1987. reprint ed. pap. 5.00 (0-943285-00-3) Blarney Pub.

— Art Is Boring for the Same Reason We Stayed in Vietnam. (Post- & Pre-Everything Ser.). 120p. 1992. pap. 9.00 (0-934450-50-1) Unmuzzled Ox.

— Culture as Surveillance: The Seventies Now. LC 98-47225. 1999. pap. text 19.95 (0-8223-2166-1) Duke.

— Seventies Now: Culture as Surveillance. LC 98-47225. (Illus.). 432p. 1999. 59.95 (0-8223-2154-8) Duke.

Miller, Stephen Paul, jt. ed. see Diggory, Terence.

Miller, Stephen R. Daniel. (New American Commentary Ser.: Vol. 18). 576p. 1994. 27.99 (0-8054-0118-0) Broadman.

— Daniel. LC 97-37019. (Shepherd's Notes Ser.). 1997. 5.95 (0-8054-9015-9) Broadman.

— Kay Sage: Surrealist. (Illus.). 100p. (Orig.). Date not set. pap. 25.00 (0-9648856-0-3) Nelmar Pr.

Miller, Stephen R., ed. see Shakespeare, William.

Miller, Stephen W. Cardiac Angiography. 430p. 1984. 105.00 (0-316-57367-1, Little Brwn Med Div) Lppncott W & W.

— Cardiac Radiology - The Requisites. (Illus.). 466p. (C). (gr. 13). 1996. text 85.00 (0-8016-6478-0, 06478) Mosby Inc.

Miller, Steve. The Art of the Weathervane. LC 83-51742. (Illus.). 160p. 1984. 35.00 (0-88740-005-1) Schiffer.

— Avengers: Kree War. 1998. 8.95 (0-7869-1232-4, Pub. by TSR Inc) Random.

— Contemporary Christian Music Debate: Worldly Compromise Or Agent of Renewal? 261p. 1993. reprint ed. pap. 9.99 (1-884543-09-X) O M Lit.

*Miller, Steve. Debate de la Musica Cristiana Contemporanea. (SPA.). 2000. mass mkt. 9.99 (0-7899-0465-9) Editorial Unilit.

Miller, Steve. The Doomgrinder. 1998. 11.95 (0-7869-1252-9, Pub. by TSR Inc) Random.

— Experimental Design & Statistics. 2nd ed. (New Essential Psychology Ser.). 192p. 1984. pap. 8.95 (0-416-34940-4, NO. 9014) Routledge.

— Experimental Design Statistics. 2nd ed. 192p. (C). 1984. pap. 14.99 (0-415-04011-6) Routledge.

— How to Get into the Bible. LC 97-7843. 464p. 1998. 12.99 (0-7852-1135-7) Nelson.

*Miller, Steve. How to Get the Most Out of Trade Shows. 3rd ed. 176p. 2000. pap. 14.95 (0-658-00939-7, 009397) NTC Contemp Pub Co.

— How to Get the Most out of Trade Shows. 3rd rev. ed. LC 98-46786. 176p. 1999. 29.95 (0-8442-2347-6) NTC Contemp Pub Co.

Miller, Steve. Multivariate Design & Statistics. (New Essential Psychology Ser.). 224p. 1986. pap. 7.95 (0-416-34930-7, 1019) Routledge.

*Miller, Steve. Psychedelic Memoirs. Yarak, Jo Ann, ed. (Illus.). 57p. 1998. pap. 9.95 (1-893963-01-2) YarakWorks Pub.

Miller, Steve & Altenburg, Tom. Steve Miller's Bible Memorization Flash Cards. (Genesis Ser.). 102p. (J). Date not set. 7.99 (1-888220-09-0) Reality Living.

Miller, Steve & Bowden, Charmel. Over 88 Tips & Ideas to Supercharge Your Exhibit Sales. 100p. (Orig.). 1996. pap. 11.95 (0-9655412-0-7) Hikelly Prod.

*Miller, Steve & Cordell, Bruce. Die Vecna Die! A D&D Adventure. (Dungeons & Dragons Ser.). (Illus.). 160p. (YA). 2000. pap. 24.95 (0-7869-1662-1) TSR Inc.

Miller, Steve & Miller, Becky. Amazing Mazes for Kids: Take Me Through the Bible. (Take Me Through the Bible Ser.). 160p. (J). 1998. pap. 5.99 (1-56507-846-2) Harvest Hse.

*Miller, Steve & Miller, Becky. Bible Trivia for Kids: Take Me Through the Bible. LC 99-20314. 160p. 1999. pap. 5.99 (0-7369-0120-5) Harvest Hse.

Miller, Steve & Miller, Becky. A Child's Garden of Prayer: Turning Little Hearts Toward God. LC 99-12819. (Illus.). 64p. 1999. 16.99 (0-7369-0117-5) Harvest Hse.

An Asterisk (*) at the beginning of an entry indicates that the title is appearing for the first time.

An Asterisk (*) at the beginning of an entry indicates that the title is appearing for the first time.

Miller, Teresa & Pellowski, Anne. Joining In: An Anthology of Audience Participation Stories & How to Tell Them. Livo, Norma J., ed. 136p. (Orig.). (J). 1988. pap. text 14.95 (*0-938756-21-4*) Yellow Moon.

Miller, Terry, jt. auth. see Nguyen, Phong.

Miller, Terry E. Traditional Music of the Lao: Kaen Playing & Mawlum Singing in Northeast Thailand, 13. LC 84-22538. (Contributions in Intercultural & Comparative Studies: No. 13). 333p. 1985. 75.00 (*0-313-24765-X*, MKP/, Greenwood Pr) Greenwood.

Miller, Terry E. & Chonpairot, Jarernchai. A History of Siamese Music Reconstructed from Western Documents, 1505-1932. (Crossroads Ser.: Ser. 8.2). (Illus.). 267p. 1994. pap. 17.95 (*1-877979-97-X*) SE Asia.

Miller, Terry E. & Williams, Sean, eds. Southeast Asia: The Garland Encyclopedia of World Music. LC 97-9671. (Encyclopedia of World Music Ser.: Vol. 4). (Illus.). 1024p. 1998. text 165.00 incl. cd-rom (*0-8240-6040-7*, H1172) Garland.

Miller, Thelma R., jt. auth. see Klein, Roz.

Miller, Theodore. Musculoskeletal Imaging. (Illus.). 546p. 1999. write for info. (*0-07-043257-0*) McGraw-Hill HPD.

Miller, Theodore K. CAS - The Book of Professional Standards for Higher Education. 2nd ed. LC 98-202426. Orig. Title: Standards & Guidelines for Student Services/Development Programs. 260p. 1997. pap. text 22.00 (*0-9659337-0-9*) CASHE.

Miller, Theodore K. & Prince, Judith S. The Future of Student Affairs: A Guide to Student Development for Tomorrow's Higher Education. LC 76-19496. 238p. reprint ed. pap. 73.80 (*0-7837-6521-5*, 204563300007) Bks Demand.

Miller, Theodore R. Graphic History of the Americas. LC 72-88215. 72p. (C). 1972. reprint ed. text 27.50 (*0-88275-103-4*) Krieger.

Miller, Theresa D., jt. auth. see Foord, Eden.

Miller, Thomas. Konstruktion und Begruendung. (Studien und Materialien Zur Geschichte der Philosophie Ser.: Bd. 33). (GER.). iv, 368p. 1991. write for info. (*3-487-09514-9*) G Olms Pubs.

Miller, Thomas A. Modern Surgical Care: Physiologic Foundations & Clinical Applications. 2nd ed. LC 97-50113. 1454p. 1998. 145.00 (*1-57626-060-7*) Quality Med Pub.

Miller, Thomas C. & Maxwell, Hu. West Virginia & Its People. (Illus.). 1997. reprint ed. lib. bdg. 169.50 (*0-8328-6939-2*) Higginson Bk Co.

***Miller, Thomas E. & Miller, Rachel E.** Construction Defects & Your Home. 104p. 2000. pap. 9.95 (*0-929765-83-4*) Seven Locks Pr.

***Miller, Thomas E. & Miller, Rachel M.** Handling Construction Defect Claims: Western States. 3rd ed. LC 99-45862. 1032p. 1999. boxed set 160.00 (*0-7355-1126-8*) Panel Pubs.

Miller, Thomas F. Minnesota Legal Forms: Creditors' Remedies. 190p. 1994. ring bd., wbk. ed. 69.95 incl. disk (*0-614-05901-1*, MICHIE) LEXIS Pub.

— Minnesota Legal Forms: Creditors' Remedies, 1981-1993. (Minnesota Legal Forms Ser.). 200p. 1994. ring bd., suppl. ed. 39.00 (*0-685-74347-0*, MICHIE) LEXIS Pub.

Miller, Thomas G., Jr. The Cactus Air Force. LC 69-15320. (Illus.). 242p. 1990. reprint ed. 15.00 (*0-934841-18-7*) Adm Nimitz Foun.

Miller, Thomas I. & Miller, Michelle A. Citizen Surveys: How to Do Them, How to Use Them, What They Mean. (Special Reports). 213p. 1991. pap. 38.00 (*0-87326-920-9*) Intl City-Cnty Mgt.

Miller, Thomas L. Texas Confederate Scrip Grantees. LC 85-71227. 165p. (Orig.). 1985. pap. 15.00 (*0-911317-38-4*) Ericson Bks.

Miller, Thomas P. The Formation of College English: Rhetoric & Belles Lettres in the British Cultural Provinces. LC 96-45879. (Composition, Literacy, & Culture Ser.). 360p. 1997. pap. 22.95 (*0-8229-5623-3*); text 50.00 (*0-8229-3970-3*) U of Pittsburgh Pr.

Miller, Thomas P., ed. The Selected Writings of John Witherspoon. LC 89-29994. 320p. (C). 1990. 31.95 (*0-8093-1469-X*) S Ill U Pr.

Miller, Thomas R. Taking Time Out: Recreation & Play. Steinhorn, Beth, ed. LC 94-47412. (Our Human Family Ser.). (Illus.). 80p. (YA). (gr. 7 up). 1995. lib. bdg. 22.45 (*1-56711-128-9*) Blackbirch.

Miller, Thomas W., ed. Children of Trauma: Stressful Life Events & Their Effects on Children & Adolescents, No. 8. LC 97-15597. (Stress & Health Ser.: Monograph 8). 200p. 1997. 42.50 (*0-8236-0810-7*) Intl Univs Pr.

— Chronic Pain, Vol. I. 400p. 1990. 57.50 (*0-8236-0850-6*) Intl Univs Pr.

— Chronic Pain, Vol. II. 550p. 1990. 77.50 (*0-8236-0851-4*) Intl Univs Pr.

— Clinical Disorders & Stressful Life Events, No. 7. LC 96-39360. (Stress & Health Ser.: Monograph 7). 297p. 1997. 62.50 (*0-8236-0910-3*) Intl Univs Pr.

— Stressful Life Events. (Stress & Health Ser.: No. 4). 838p. 1989. 90.00 (*0-8236-6165-2*, BN#00165) Intl Univs Pr.

— Theory & Assessment of Stressful Life Events, No. 6. LC 95-40591. (Stress & Health Ser.: Monograph 6). 224p. 1996. 55.00 (*0-8236-6521-6*) Intl Univs Pr.

Miller, Thomas W. & Veltkamp, Lane J. Clinical Handbook of Adult Exploitation & Abuse. LC 97-27650. 245p. 1998. 35.00 (*0-8236-0953-7*, 00953) Intl Univs Pr.

Miller, Thomas W., jt. auth. see Veltkamp, Lane J.

***Miller, Thomasina.** Points of Grace. 1999. pap. write for info. (*1-58235-334-4*) Watermrk Pr.

Miller, Tice L. Bohemians & Critics: American Theatre Criticism in the Nineteenth Century. LC 80-24430. x, 190p. 1981. 24.00 (*0-8108-1377-7*) Scarecrow.

Miller, Tice L., jt. ed. see Engle, Ron.

Miller, Tice L., jt. ed. see Wilmeth, Don B.

Miller-Tiedeman, Anna. How Not to Make It-& Succeed: Life on Your Own Terms. LC 84-60644. (Illus.). 1989. pap. 13.95 (*0-9613436-9-9*) Lifecareer Pr.

— Learning, Practicing & Living the New Careering: A 21st Century Approach. LC 98-54392. 275p. 1999. pap. 33.95 (*1-56032-740-5*) Hemisp Pub.

— Lifecareer: How It Can Benefit You. 2nd ed. Sherf, Terry, ed. LC 92-19764. 50p. 1992. pap. 7.95 (*0-9613436-8-0*) Lifecareer Pr.

— Lifecareer: The Quantum Leap into a Process Theory of Career. 1988. pap. 9.95 (*0-9613436-3-X*) Lifecareer Pr.

Miller, Tim. Shirts & Skin. LC 97-26917. xiv, 296 p. 1997. pap. 12.95 (*1-55583-425-6*) Alyson Pubns.

— Switched Reluctance Motors, Inverters & Controls: A Reference Book of Collected Papers since 1988. 500p. 1992. 150.00 (*1-881855-01-5*) Motorsoft.

Miller, Tim, jt. auth. see Sharpton, Beth.

Miller, Tim D. Teens in Drama Ministry. (Drama Topics Ser.). 55p. 1994. 9.99 (*0-8341-9129-6*, MP-514) Lillenas.

Miller, Timothy. Following in His Steps: A Biography of Charles M. Sheldon. LC 87-5871. (Illus.). 304p. 1987. 35.00 (*0-87049-537-2*) U of Tenn Pr.

— The Hippies & American Values. LC 90-48062. (Illus.). 216p. (C). 1991. pap. 18.95 (*0-87049-694-8*) U of Tenn Pr.

Miller, Timothy. How to Want what You Have: Browne,&Kale. abr. ed. 1995. audio 12.00 (*1-55994-855-8*, CPN 10055) HarperAudio.

Miller, Timothy. How to Want What You Have: Discovering the Magic & Grandeur of Everyday Existence. LC 94-12653. 1995. 19.95 (*0-8050-3317-3*) H Holt & Co.

— How to Want What You Have: Discovering the Magic & Grandeur of Ordinary Existence. 288p. 1996. pap. 12.00 (*0-380-72682-3*, Avon Bks) Morrow Avon.

— The Quest for Utopia in Twentieth Century America. LC 97-48903. 254p. 1998. 34.95 (*0-8156-2775-0*) Syracuse U Pr.

***Miller, Timothy.** The 60's Communes: Hippies & Beyond. LC 99-37768. (Illus.). 576p. 1999. 49.95 (*0-8156-2811-0*); pap. text 29.95 (*0-8156-0601-X*) Syracuse U Pr.

Miller, Timothy. Wanting What You Have: A Self-Discovery Workbook. 228p. 1998. pap. 18.95 (*1-57224-153-5*) New Harbinger.

Miller, Timothy, ed. America's Alternative Religions. LC 94-16605. (SUNY Series in Religious Studies). 474p. (C). 1995. text 74.50 (*0-7914-2397-2*); pap. text 24.95 (*0-7914-2398-0*) State U NY Pr.

— When Prophets Die: The Postcharismatic Fate of New Religious Movements. LC 90-44859. (SUNY Series in Religious Studies). 251p. (C). 1991. text 21.50 (*0-7914-0717-9*) State U NY Pr.

Miller, Timothy C., ed. The Critical Response to John Milton's Paradise Lost, 26. LC 96-37041. (Critical Responses in Arts & Letters Ser.: Vol. 26). 360p. 1997. lib. bdg. 69.50 (*0-313-28926-3*, Greenwood Pr) Greenwood.

Miller, Timothy J., ed. Reactive Power Control in Electric Systems. LC 82-10838. 416p. 1982. 185.00 (*0-471-86933-3*, Wiley-Interscience) Wiley.

Miller, Timothy S. The Birth of the Hospital in the Byzantine Empire. LC 84-26111. (Henry E. Sigerist Supplements to the Bulletin of the History of Medicine, New Ser.: No. 13). 304p. reprint ed. pap. 94.30 (*0-8357-6744-2*, 203539900095) Bks Demand.

— The Birth of the Hospital in the Byzantine Empire. LC 97-201618. 288p. 1997. reprint ed. pap. text 16.95 (*0-8018-5657-4*) Johns Hopkins.

Miller, Timothy S. & Nesbitt, John, eds. Peace & War in Byzantium: Essays in Honor of George T. Dennis, S.J. LC 94-19723. 282p. 1995. 49.95 (*0-8132-0805-X*) Cath U Pr.

Miller, Toby. The Avengers. LC 98-129578. (Illus.). 192p. 1998. pap. text 19.95 (*0-85170-558-8*, Pub. by British Film Inst) Ind U Pr.

— Technologies of Truth: Cultural Citizenship & the Popular Media. LC 97-25952. (Visible Evidence Ser.). (Illus.). 320p. 1998. pap. 21.95 (*0-8166-2985-4*); text 54.95 (*0-8166-2984-6*) U of Minn Pr.

— The Well-Tempered Self: Formations of the Cultural Subject. LC 93-13102. (C). 1994. text 45.00 (*0-8018-4603-X*); pap. text 15.95 (*0-8018-4604-8*) Johns Hopkins.

Miller, Toby & Stam, Robert, eds. A Companion to Film Theory. LC 99-20206. 500p. 1999. 99.95 (*0-631-20644-2*) Blackwell Pubs.

— Film & Theory: An Anthology. LC 99-19390. 800p. 1999. 72.95 (*0-631-20625-6*) Blackwell Pubs.

***Miller, Toby & Stam, Robert, eds.** Film & Theory: An Anthology. LC 99-19390. 800p. 1999. pap. 39.95 (*0-631-20626-4*) Blackwell Pubs.

Miller, Toby, jt. auth. see Martin, Randy.

Miller, Todd D., ed. see Campbell, John Quincy Adams, et al.

Miller, Tom. All-Star Showdown. (Illus.). 76p. (Orig.). (J). (gr. 5-8). 1995. pap. 7.50 (*0-931209-63-3*) Mid-Prairie Bks.

— Angler's Guide to Baja California. (Illus.). 1987. pap. 7.95 (*0-914622-04-8*) Baja Source.

— Copeland Killings. (Illus.). 304p. 1993. mass mkt. 4.99 (*1-55817-675-6*, Pinncle Kensgtn) Kensgtn Pub Corp.

— Eating Your Way Through Baja. (Illus.). 1986. pap. 4.95 (*0-914622-07-2*) Baja Source.

— Fourth & Long. (Illus.). 72p. (Orig.). (J). (gr. 4-8). 1997. pap. 6.95 (*0-931209-70-6*) Mid-Prairie Bks.

***Miller, Tom.** Jack Ruby's Kitchen Sink: Offbeat Travels Through America's Southwest. 2000. 24.00 (*0-7922-7959-X*) Natl Geog.

Miller, Tom. Mexico West Book. 1991. pap. 15.95 (*0-914622-09-9*) Baja Source.

— The Panama Hat Trail: A Journey to South America. LC 87-45913. (Departures Ser.). 272p. 1988. pap. 11.00 (*0-394-75774-2*) Vin Bks.

— This Path of Scattered Glass: A Collection of Poems. LC 92-84067. (Illus.). 96p. (Orig.). (YA). (gr. 7 up). 1993. pap. 6.95 (*1-878893-39-4*) Telcraft Bks.

— Trading with the Enemy: A Yankee Travels Through Castro's Cuba. 352p. 1992. text 24.00 (*0-689-12094-X*, Pub. by Ctrl Bur voor Schimmel) Macmillan.

— The Unfair Advantage. 170p. (Orig.). 1986. pap. 17.95 (*0-9613034-1-7*) Unfair Advan Corp.

Miller, Tom & Hoffman, Carol. The Baja Book III. (Illus.). 1989. pap. 11.95 (*0-914622-08-0*) Baja Source.

Miller, Tom, ed. see Conley, Robert J.

Miller, Tom, ed. see Givens, Charles J.

Miller, Tom, ed. see Hare, Robert D.

Miller, Tom, ed. see McNamara, Eileen.

Miller, Tom, ed. see Zuniga, Jose.

***Miller, Tom O.** 'Tis a Delightful Road: Signs of Faith in Life. 2000. pap. text 8.95 (*0-7880-1465-X*) CSS.

***Miller, Tony.** Redesigning HR for Strategic Advantage: How HR Departments Can Deliver Measurable Value. (Management Briefings Ser.). (Illus.). 1999. pap. 87.50 (*0-273-64505-6*, Pub. by F T P-H) Trans-Atl Phila.

Miller, Tony, jt. auth. see Kearns, Paul.

***Miller, Tracie L. & Gorbach, Sherwood L., eds.** Nutrition Aspects Of HIV Infection. (Illus.). 224p. 1999. text 69.50 (*0-340-74195-3*) OUP.

***Miller, Trevor.** Blair Witch. 1999. pap. text 8.95 (*0-89752-007-6*, Pub. by Fotonovel) BookWorld.

Miller, Trish, ed. see Clement, Brian R.

Miller, Trudi C. Public Sector Performance: A Turning Point. LC 83-23895. 288p. 1984. pap. 15.95 (*0-8018-3147-4*) Johns Hopkins.

Miller, Trudy. Where to Find Everything for Practically Nothing in Chicagoland: A Bargain Hunters Guide to Resale & Thrift Shops. LC 87-82215. 170p. 1987. pap. 6.95 (*0-913587-02-8*) Second T Pub.

Miller, Twila J. Daisy Pridemore's Guide to Down Home Cookin' & More... (Daisy Pridemore's Guide to... Ser.). (Illus.). (Orig.). 1995. mass mkt. 7.95 (*0-9635759-4-5*) Printing Pr.

***Miller, Tyrus.** Late Modernism: Politic, Fiction, & the Arts between the World Wars. LC 98-27436. 280p. 1999. pap. 19.95 (*0-520-21648-2*, Pub. by U CA Pr) Cal Prin Full Svc.

Miller, Tyrus. Late Modernism: Politics, Fiction, & the Arts Between the World Wars. LC 98-27436. 280p. 1999. 45.00 (*0-520-21035-2*, Pub. by U CA Pr) Cal Prin Full Svc.

Miller, Ulrike. Persian Cats. 72p. 1990. pap. 6.95 (*0-8120-4405-3*) Barron.

Miller, Valentine R. & Miller, Reese P., trs. Rene Descartes: Principles of Philosophy. (Synthese Library: No. 4). 353p. 1984. pap. text 44.50 (*90-277-1754-0*, D Reidel) Kluwer Academic.

Miller, Valentine R., tr. see Descartes, Rene.

Miller, Vassar. Approaching Nada. Lomax, Joseph J., ed. LC 77-20734. 1977. pap. 50.00 (*0-930324-03-X*) Wings Pr.

— If I Could Sleep Deeply Enough. 48p. 1974. 6.95 (*0-87140-607-1*, Pub. by Liveright) Norton.

— If I Had Wheels or Love: Collected Poems of Vassar Miller. LC 90-52660. 358p. 1991. 28.95 (*0-87074-315-5*) SMU Press.

— If I Had Wheels or Love: Collected Poems of Vassar Miller. LC 90-52660. 358p. 1991. pap. 14.95 (*0-87074-316-3*) SMU Press.

— Small Change. Lomax, Joseph F. & Whitebird, J., eds. LC 77-20728. 1977. pap. 50.00 (*0-930324-00-5*) Wings Pr.

— Struggling to Swim on Concrete. Cassin, Maxine, ed. LC 84-60413. (Journal Press Bks.). (Illus.). 80p. (Orig.). 1984. pap. 12.00 (*0-938498-05-3*) New Orleans Poetry.

Miller, Vassar, ed. Despite This Flesh: The Disabled in Stories & Poems. 166p. 1985. pap. 8.95 (*0-292-71550-1*) U of Tex Pr.

Miller, Vernell K. Meditations for Adoptive Parents. LC 92-18480. (Illus.). 88p. (Orig.). 1992. pap. 8.99 (*0-8361-3606-3*) Herald Pr.

Miller, Vernon. Brethren Patriots Again: A Thirteen Session Study Guide Proposing Nonviolence As the Potential Power for the Continuing American Revolution. fac. ed. LC BX7829.B6. (Heritage Learning Program Ser.). 64p. 1994. pap. 30.00 (*0-7837-7347-1*, 204730000007) Bks Demand.

Miller, Vernon J. Historical Album of Charm, Ohio. 278p. 1995. 32.00 (*0-9642548-3-2*) Carlisle Press.

***Miller, Vernon J.** Japanese Submarine Losses to Allied Submarines in World War II. (World War II Monograph Ser.: Vol. 56). (Illus.). 36p. 1999. 19.95 (*1-57638-181-1*, M56-H); pap. 9.95 (*1-57638-161-7*, M56-S) Merriam Pr.

Miller, Vickie G. Doris Miller: A Silent Medal of Honor. LC 97-32038. (J). 1997. 12.95 (*1-57168-179-5*) Sunbelt Media.

Miller, Vicky, jt. auth. see Raney, Deborah.

Miller, Victor. The Book of Worries: Hundreds of Horrible Things That Can Happen to You. 224p. (Orig.). 1981. mass mkt. 2.50 (*0-446-91248-4*, Pub. by Warner Bks) Little.

Miller, Victor, jt. auth. see Dobson, Terry.

Miller, Victoria A. Defensive Parenting for the 21st Century. 100p. 1998. pap. 14.95 (*1-58244-002-6*) Rutledge Bks.

Miller, Virgil E., jt. auth. see Miller, Diane M.

Miller, Virginia. Be Gentle! LC 96-35901. (Illus.). 32p. (J). (ps-k). 1997. 15.99 (*0-7636-0251-5*) Candlewick Pr.

— Be Gentle! (Illus.). 32p. (J). (ps-k). 1999. pap. 5.99 (*0-7636-0693-6*) Candlewick Pr.

— Eat Your Dinner! LC 91-58728. (Illus.). 32p. (J). (ps up). 1992. 14.95 (*1-56402-121-1*) Candlewick Pr.

— Eat Your Dinner! LC 91-58728. (Illus.). 32p. (J). (ps up). 1994. pap. 5.99 (*1-56402-368-0*) Candlewick Pr.

— Go to Bed! LC 92-54958. (Illus.). 32p. (J). (ps up). 1993. 14.95 (*1-56402-244-7*) Candlewick Pr.

— Go to Bed! LC 92-54958. (Illus.). (J). (ps up). 1995. pap. 5.99 (*1-56402-509-8*) Candlewick Pr.

***Miller, Virginia.** Go to Bed! LC 92-54958. (Illus.). 22p. (J). 2000. 5.99 (*0-7636-1267-7*) Candlewick Pr.

— I Love You Just the Way You Are. (Illus.). 22p. (J). 2001. 5.99 (*0-7636-1288-X*) Candlewick Pr.

Miller, Virginia. I Love You Just the Way You Are. LC 97-46490. (Illus.). 32p. (J). (ps-k). 1998. 15.99 (*0-7636-0664-2*) Candlewick Press.

***Miller, Virginia.** In a Minute! LC 99-58228. (Illus.). (J). 2001. write for info. (*0-7636-1270-7*) Candlewick Pr.

— On Your Potty! LC 98-4895. (Illus.). 32p. (J). (ps-k). 1998. pap. 5.99 (*0-7636-0694-4*) Candlewick Pr.

***Miller, Virginia.** On Your Potty! LC 98-4895. (Illus.). 22p. (J). 2000. 5.99 (*0-7636-1268-5*) Candlewick Pr.

Miller, Virginia E. The Frieze of the Palace of the Stuccoes, Acanceh, Yucatan, Mexico. LC 91-13724. (Studies in Pre-Columbian Art & Archaeology: No. 31). (Illus.). 88p. 1991. 18.00 (*0-88402-195-5*) Dumbarton Oaks.

Miller, Virginia L., et al, eds. Molecular Genetics of Bacterial Pathogenesis: A Tribute to Stanley Falkow. LC 94-19193. (Illus.). 566p. (C). 1994. 79.00 (*1-55581-082-9*) ASM Pr.

Miller, Virginia L. & Lewis, John G. Interior Woodwork of Winchester, Virginia, 1750-1850, with Some History & Tales. 220p. 1994. text 25.00 (*0-9642862-0-3*) Grim-Moore Hse.

***Miller, Vivien M. L.** Crime, Sexual Violence & Clemency: Florida's Pardon Board & Penal System in the Progressive Era. LC 00-34413. 2000. write for info. (*0-8130-1808-0*) U Press Fla.

Miller, V.L., ed. Bacterial Invasiveness, 209. (Current Topics in Microbiology & Immunology Ser.: Vol. 209). (Illus.). 144p. 1996. 128.00 (*3-540-60065-5*) Spr-Verlag.

Miller, W., et al, eds. Die Lumboischialgie. (Fortbildungskurse fuer Rheumatologie Ser.: Vol. 6). (Illus.). xii, 264p. 1982. pap. 62.75 (*3-8055-2207-X*) S Karger.

Miller, W. B. A History of the Greek People, 1821-1921. (Illus.). 1976. 30.00 (*0-89710-28-9*) Obol Intl.

Miller, W. B., Jr. On Lie Algebras & Some Special Functions of Mathematical Physics. LC 52-42839. (Memoirs of the American Mathematical Society Ser.: No. 50). 43p. 1987. reprint ed. pap. 16.00 (*0-8218-1250-5*, MEMO/1/50C) Am Math.

Miller, W. B., Jr. & Huni, M. Second Course in Ordinary Differential Equations for Scientists & Engineers. (Illus.). xi, 441p. 1987. 69.95 (*0-387-96676-5*) Spr-Verlag.

Miller, W. B., Jr., ed. see Friedman, A.

Miller, W. B., Jr., jt. ed. see Friedman, A.

Miller, W. B., tr. see Luther, Martin.

Miller, W. Barry. Little Foxes That Spoil the Vines. LC 96-78091. 104p. (Orig.). 1997. pap. 7.99 (*0-8361-9056-4*) Herald Pr.

***Miller, W. Barry.** Zorras Pequenas Que Echan A Perder las Vinas.Tr. of Little Foxes That Spoil Vines. (SPA.). 96p. 1998. pap. text 7.50 (*0-311-12112-8*) Casa Bautista.

***Miller, W. Clark & Sonewald, Sabra.** Unauthorized Guide to Collecting Sohio. (Illus.). 176p. 2000. pap. 29.95 (*0-7643-1103-4*) Schiffer.

Miller, W. F., Jr., jt. auth. see Lewis, E. E.

Miller, W. H. History & Genealogy of the Family of Miller, Woods, Harris, Wallace, Maupin, Oldham, Kavanaugh & Brown, & Others. (Illus.). 855p. 1989. reprint ed. pap. 128.00 (*0-8328-0873-3*); reprint ed. lib. bdg. 136.00 (*0-8328-0872-5*) Higginson Bk Co.

Miller, W. H., ed. Dynamics of Molecular Collisions, Pt. A. LC 76-12633. (Modern Theoretical Chemistry Ser.: Vol. 1). (Illus.). 318p. 1976. 95.00 (*0-306-33501-8*, Plenum Trade) Perseus Pubng.

— Dynamics of Molecular Collisions, Pt. B. LC 76-12633. (Modern Theoretical Chemistry Ser.: Vol. 2). (Illus.). 380p. 1976. 95.00 (*0-306-33502-6*, Plenum Trade) Perseus Pubng.

Miller, W. J. Dairy Cattle Feeding & Nutrition. LC 78-51234. (Animal Feeding & Nutrition Ser.). 1979. text 94.00 (*0-12-497650-6*) Acad Pr.

— Geological History of New York. 130p. 1993. reprint ed. lib. bdg. 69.00 (*0-7812-5149-4*) Rprt Serv.

Miller, W. R. Estrogen & Breast Cancer. (Medical Intelligence Unit Ser.). 207p. 1996. 99.00 (*1-57059-047-8*) Landes Bioscience.

— The Golf Primer: A Manual for the Adult Beginner & High Handicap Player. Kraska, M. F., ed. (Illus.). 135p. 1991. pap. 29.95 (*0-9628887-0-2*) Pinecrest AL.

Miller, W. R. & Heather, N. H. Treating Addictive Behaviors: Processes of Change. (Applied Clinical Psychology Ser.). 484p. 1986. 75.00 (*0-306-42248-4*, Plenum Trade) Perseus Pubng.

Miller, W. R. & Miller, Marie F. Handbook for College Teaching. LC 96-209262. (Illus.). (C). 1997. pap. 29.95 (*0-9628887-1-0*) Pinecrest AL.

Miller, W. Thomas, III & Sutton, Richard S., eds. Neural Networks for Control. (Neural Network Modeling & Connectionism). 450p. 1991. 65.00 (*0-262-13261-3*) MIT Pr.

Miller, W. Thomas, ed. see Werbos, Paul J.

Miller, W. Watts. Durkheim, Morals & Modernity. 288p. 1996. 55.00 (*0-7735-1444-9*, Pub. by McG-Queens Univ Pr) CUP Services.

Miller, W. Wesley. Dark Secret. Kratoville, Betty Lou, ed. (Meridian Bks.). (Illus.). 64p. (J). (gr. 3-9). 1989. lib. bdg. 4.95 (*0-87879-620-7*) High Noon Bks.

Miller, Walden, jt. auth. see Miller, Eric.

Miller, Wallace T. Introduction to Clinical Radiology. 291p. 1982. 43.95 (*0-07-105300-X*) McGraw.

***Miller, Wallace T. & Miller, Wallace T., Jr.** Field Guide to the Chest X-Ray. LC 99-17626. 184p. 1999. pap. 29.95 (*0-7817-2028-1*) Lppncott W & W.

Miller, Wallace T., Jr., jt. auth. see Miller, Wallace T.

***Miller, Walter.** Canticle for Leibowitz. 1999. 20.25 (*0-8085-2093-8*) Econo-Clad Bks.

— Virginias Old Time Peanut Recipes. (Illus.). 48p. 1997. 4.95 (*0-9638258-7-9*) Bicast.

Miller, Walter, tr. Cyropaedia, Vol. 2, Bks. 5-8. (Loeb Classical Library: No. 51-52). 486p. 1994. 18.95 (*0-674-99058-7*) HUP.

Miller, Walter B. Lower Class Culture As a Generating Milieu of Gang Delinquency. (Reprint Series in Sociology). (C). 1993. reprint ed. pap. text 1.00 (*0-8290-2623-1*, S-197) Irvington.

Miller, Walter B., jt. auth. see Bequaert, Joseph C.

Miller, Walter B., jt. ed. see Vorontsov, Mikhail A.

Miller, Walter H., et al. Lincoln Lived Here: The Lincoln Heritage Trail. 32p. 1994. 4.95 (*0-9638258-2-8*) Bicast.

Miller, Walter J. Arco SAT Verbal Workbook. 3rd ed. 1992. pap. 10.00 (*0-13-951963-7*, Arco) Macmillan Gen Ref.

— Constitutionally Speaking. 182p. 1997. pap. 10.00 (*1-57502-794-1*, PO2194) Morris Pubng.

— Making an Angel. LC 77-4747. 64p. (Orig.). 1977. pap. 3.95 (*0-918524-01-6*) Lintel.

— Monarch Notes: Dashiell Hammett's the Maltese Falcon, the Thin Man & Other Works. 128p. 1988. pap. 4.50 (*0-671-67128-6*, Arco) Macmillan Gen Ref.

— One Thousand & One Ideas for English Papers. 2nd ed. 288p. 1994. 10.00 (*0-671-88766-1*) Prntice Hall Bks.

Miller, Walter J. & Saidla, Leo E., eds. Engineers As Writers. LC 74-128279. (Essay Index Reprint Ser.). 1977. 26.95 (*0-8369-2000-7*) Ayer.

Miller, Walter J., et al. SAT Verbal Workbook. 4th ed. LC 93-3538. 1993. pap. 10.00 (*0-671-86405-X*, Arco) Macmillan Gen Ref.

— SAT Verbal Workbook. 5th ed. LC 93-44287. 224p. 1994. 10.00 (*0-671-88813-7*, Arco) Macmillan Gen Ref.

— SAT Verbal Workbook: Scholastic Aptitude Test. 3rd ed. 400p. 1992. pap. 10.00 (*0-685-51950-3*, Arco) Macmillan Gen Ref.

Miller, Walter J., tr. see Verne, Jules.

Miller, Walter James. Kurt Vonnegut's Slaughter-House Five: A Guide to Understanding the Classics. 1972. 3.95 (*0-671-00920-6*, Arco) Macmillan Gen Ref.

Miller, Walter M., Jr. A Canticle for Leibowitz. 1997. 17.05 (*0-606-02527-8*, Pub. by Turtleback) Demco.

— A Canticle for Leibowitz. LC 97-26925. 368p. 1997. reprint ed. pap. 12.95 (*0-553-37926-7*, Spectra) Bantam.

— A Canticle for Leibowitz. 1993. reprint ed. lib. bdg. 29.95 (*0-89968-353-3*, Lghtyr Pr) Buccaneer Bks.

— Saint Leibowitz & the Wild Horse Woman. LC 97-3181. 448p. 1997. 23.95 (*0-553-10704-6*) Bantam.

***Miller, Walter M., Jr.** Saint Leibowitz & the Wild Horse Woman. 448p. 2000. pap. 14.95 (*0-553-38079-6*) Bantam.

Miller, Walter M., Jr. & Greenberg, Martin H., eds. Beyond Armageddon. LC 85-80625. 387p. 1986. pap. 3.95 (*0-917657-96-9*, Pub. by D I Fine) Penguin Putnam.

***Miller, Walter W., Jr.** Contracts: Problems, Cases & Materials. LC 99-65647. 460p. 1999. boxed set 55.00 (*0-89089-842-1*) Carolina Acad Pr.

Miller, Walter W. Taxation of Health & Welfare Benefits. 1000p. 1995. 150.00 (*0-7913-2085-5*) Warren Gorham & Lamont.

Miller, Wanda J. Teaching U. S. History Through Children's Literature: Post-World War II. LC 98-34575. 260p. 1998. pap. 27.50 (*1-56308-581-X*) Teacher Ideas Pr.

— U. S. History Through Children's Literature: From the Colonial Period to World War II. LC 96-38234. 240p. 1997. pap. text 25.00 (*1-56308-440-6*) Teacher Ideas Pr.

***Miller, Wanda M.** Reading Faster & Understanding More. 4th ed. 44p. (C). 1999. (*0-321-05797-X*) Benjamin-Cummings.

— Reading Faster & Understanding More Book 1. 4th ed. 48p. (C). 1999. write for info. (*0-321-05796-1*) Addison-Wesley.

Miller, Wanda M., ed. Reading Faster & Understanding More, Bk. 2. (C). 1997. text, teacher ed. 11.00 (*0-673-49652-X*) Addison-Wesley.

Miller, Wanda M. & Steeber, Sharon D. READ FAST UNDERSTAND BK1, Bk. 1. 4th ed. (Illus.). 456p. (C). 1997. pap. 44.00 (*0-673-52385-3*) Addson-Wesley Educ.

Miller, Warren. Lurching from One Near Disaster to the Next. (Illus.). 288p. 1998. pap. 14.95 (*0-9636144-2-8*) W Miller Prods.

***Miller, Warren.** Lurching from One near Disaster to the Next. 288p. 1998. 24.95 (*0-9636144-3-6*) W Miller Prods.

Miller, Warren. Warren Miller, on Film in Print. 2nd ed. (Illus.). 271p. 1995. 24.95 (*0-9636144-1-X*) W Miller Prods.

— Warren Miller's Learn to Ski & Snowboard Better. 1996. pap. 13.00 (*0-684-80012-8*) S&S Trade.

— Warren Miller's Ski Fever! (Illus.). 168p. 1995. pap. 20.00 (*0-06-258662-9*, Pub. by Harper SF) HarpC.

Miller, Warren, et al. Policy Representation in Western Democracies. LC 99-25727. 192p. 2000. text 65.00 (*0-19-829570-7*) OUP.

Miller, Warren A. Wine, Women, Warren, & Skis. 1993. pap. 10.95 (*0-9636144-0-1*) W Miller Prods.

Miller, Warren E. Without Consent: Mass-Elite Linkages in Presidential Politics. LC 88-3217. (Blazer Lectures). 200p. 1988. 24.95 (*0-8131-0550-1*) U Pr of Ky.

Miller, Warren E. & Levitin, Teresa E. Leadership & Change: Presidential Elections from 1952 to 1976. (Illus.). 320p. 1984. reprint ed. pap. text 26.00 (*0-8191-3850-9*) U Pr of Amer.

Miller, Warren E. & Shanks, J. Merrill. The New American Voter. LC 96-8079. (Illus.). 640p. 1996. write for info. (*0-674-60840-2*); 45.00 (*0-674-08402-0*); pap. 22.00 (*0-674-60841-0*) HUP.

Miller, Warren E. & Stokes, Donald E. Constituency Influence in Congress. (Reprint Series in Social Sciences). (C). 1993. reprint ed. pap. text 5.00 (*0-8290-3691-1*, PS-404) Irvington.

Miller, Warren E. & Traugott, Santa A. American National Election Studies Data Sourcebook, 1952-1986. LC 89-7546. (Illus.). 400p. 1989. text 51.95 (*0-674-02636-5*) HUP.

Miller, Warren E., et al. American National Election Studies Data Sourcebook, 1952-1986. (Illus.). 388p. 1980. spiral bd. 35.95 (*0-674-02634-9*) HUP.

— American National Election Study, 1972. LC 82-81968. 1982. reprint ed. boxed set. write for info. (*0-89138-928-8*, ICPSR 7010) ICPSR.

— American National Election Study, 1974. LC 83-81218. 1983. reprint ed. write for info. (*0-89138-918-0*) ICPSR.

Miller, Warren E., jt. auth. see Miller, Arthur.

Miller, Warren E., jt. auth. see National Election Studies, Center for Political St.

Miller, Warren E., jt. auth. see National Election Studies Center for Political Stu.

Miller, Warren E., jt. auth. see National Election Studies Staff.

Miller, Wathena K. Meade County, Kentucky Births, 1852-1859, 1861, 1874-1878, 1894, 1900-1901, 1904 & 1906-1909. 167p. 1987. pap. 17.00 (*1-889221-27-9*) Ancestral Trails.

— Meade County, Kentucky Marriages, 1824-1884. 239p. 1988. pap. 22.00 (*1-889221-33-3*) Ancestral Trails.

— Meade County, Kentucky Marriages, 1885-1934. 262p. 1990. pap. 24.00 (*1-889221-34-1*) Ancestral Trails.

Miller, Wathena K. & Newton, Jane M. Meade County, Kentucky, 1870 Census. 204p. 1991. pap. 20.00 (*1-889221-30-9*) Ancestral Trails.

Miller, Wathena K., jt. auth. see Newton, Jane M.

***Miller, Wayne.** Chicago's South Side, 1946-1948. LC 00-22186. (Series in Contemporary Photography). (Illus.). 125p. 2000. 25.00 (*0-520-22316-0*, Pub. by U CA Pr) Cal Prin Full Svc.

Miller, Wayne, et al. Graphing Calculator Activities for Finite Mathematics. 208p. (C). 1992. pap. 26.95 (*0-534-17460-4*) Brooks-Cole.

— Pass the TASP Test. 2nd ed. Hackworth, Robert & Howland, Joseph W., eds. LC 96-75619. (Illus.). 257p. 1996. pap. 9.95 (*0-943202-55-8*) H & H Pub.

Miller, Wayne C. Negotiated Peace. LC 97-20289. 160p. 1997. pap. text 26.00 (*0-205-27411-0*) P-H.

Miller, Wayne H. A. J., Jr. Faces Peer Pressure. Smith, Denise M., ed. (Sandy Dallas Series of Books for Children, Parents, & Teachers). (Illus.). 100p. (Orig.). (YA). (gr. 6-12). 1995. pap. text 4.95 (*0-9634735-6-5*) Hiram Charles.

— Ellie. Smith, Denise M., ed. (Sandy Dallas Series of Books for Children, Parents, & Teachers). (Illus.). 100p. (Orig.). (YA). (gr. 6-12). 1995. pap. text 4.95 (*0-9634735-7-3*) Hiram Charles.

— The Family Budget. Smith, Denise M., ed. (Sandy Dallas Series of Books for Children, Parents, & Teachers). (Illus.). 100p. (Orig.). (YA). (gr. 6-12). 1995. pap. text 4.95 (*0-9634735-2-2*) Hiram Charles.

— Granny "E" Smith, Denise M., ed. (Sandy Dallas Series of Books for Children, Parents, & Teachers). (Illus.). 100p. (Orig.). (YA). (gr. 6-12). 1995. pap. text 4.95 (*0-9634735-3-0*) Hiram Charles.

— Making New Friends: People Who Look Different. Smith, Denise M., ed. (Sandy Dallas Series of Books for Children, Parents, & Teachers). (Illus.). 100p. (Orig.). (YA). (gr. 6-12). 1995. pap. text 4.95 (*0-9634735-8-1*) Hiram Charles.

— Sandy Dallas. Smith, Denise M., ed. (Sandy Dallas Series of Books for Children, Parents, & Teachers). (Illus.). 100p. (Orig.). (YA). (gr. 6-12). 1995. pap. text 4.95 (*0-9634735-4-9*) Hiram Charles.

— Sandy Dallas Visits the Zoo. Smith, Denise M., ed. (Sandy Dallas Series of Books for Children, Parents, & Teachers). (Illus.). 100p. (Orig.). (YA). (gr. 6-12). 1995. pap. text 4.95 (*0-9634735-5-7*) Hiram Charles.

— Subtle Deceivers. Smith, Denise M., ed. 203p. (Orig.). 1993. pap. text 9.95 (*0-9634735-0-6*) Hiram Charles.

— Why Don't I Listen to My Parents? Smith, Denise M., ed. (Sandy Dallas Series of Books for Children, Parents, & Teachers). (Illus.). 100p. (Orig.). (YA). (gr. 6-12). 1995. pap. text 4.95 (*0-9634735-1-4*) Hiram Charles.

Miller, Wayne L., et al. Graphing Calculator Activities for Algebra. 192p. 1992. pap. 21.95 (*0-534-17463-9*) Brooks-Cole.

— Graphing Calculator Activities for Mathematical Analysis. 168p. (C). 1992. pap. 26.95 (*0-534-17461-2*) Brooks-Cole.

Miller, Wendell E. Forgiveness the Power & the Puzzles. LC 94-94384. 261p. 1994. pap. 10.95 (*0-9641441-0-7*); text 15.95 (*0-9641441-1-5*) ClearBrook.

Miller, Wendy. Around the World with God's Friends: Mission Education Activity Book - Elementary Grades. (Illus.). 24p. (Orig.). (J). (gr. 1-5). 1990. pap. text 1.50 (*1-877736-06-6*, Mission Focus) MB Missions.

— Invitation to Presence: A Guide to Spiritual Disciplines. 144p. 1995. pap. text 11.00 (*0-8358-0736-3*) Upper Room Bks.

— Invitation to Presence Leader's Guide: A Guide to Spiritual Disciplines. 40p. 1995. pap., teacher ed. 5.00 (*0-8358-0774-6*) Upper Room Bks.

— Learning to Listen. 1993. 9.95 (*0-687-60633-0*) Abingdon.

— Learning to Listen: A Guide for Spiritual Friends. LC 92-61441. 128p. 1993. pap. 10.00 (*0-8358-0677-4*) Upper Room Bks.

Miller, White Burkett, Center of Public Affairs St & University of Virginia Staff. Report of the Miller Center Commission on Presidential Disability & the Twenty-Fifth Amendment. 44p. (Orig.). (C). 1988. pap. text 8.00 (*0-8191-6893-9*, Pub. by White Miller Center) U Pr of Amer.

Miller, Wick R. Newe Natekwinappeh: Shoshoni Stories & Dictionary. (Utah Anthropological Papers: No. 94). reprint ed. 24.00 (*0-404-60694-6*) AMS Pr.

— Newe Natekwinappeh: Shoshoni Stories & Dictionary. LC 72-612763. (Anthropological Papers: No. 94). 180p. reprint ed. pap. 55.80 (*0-7837-2606-6*, 204277000006) Bks Demand.

Miller, Wick R. & Dakin, Karen, eds. A Compendium of Nahuatl Grammar. Sullivan, Thelma D. & Stiles, Neville, trs. from SPA. LC 88-17082. 352p. 1988. pap. 25.00 (*0-87480-282-2*) U of Utah Pr.

Miller, Wick R., jt. auth. see Silver, Shirley.

Miller, Wilbur R. Cops & Bobbies: Police Authority in New York & London, 1830-1870. 2nd ed. LC 98-42226. (History of Crime & Criminal Justice Ser.). 259p. 1998. reprint ed. pap. text 16.95 (*0-8142-5013-0*, MILC2X) Ohio St U Pr.

— Revenuers & Moonshiners: Enforcing Federal Liquor Law in the Mountain South, 1865-1900. LC 90-49549. (Illus.). xii, 251p. 1991. pap. 18.95 (*0-8078-4330-X*) U of NC Pr.

***Miller, Wilbur R. & Miller, Marie F.** 50 Hints: Survival Skills for Instructors of Vocational Subjects. LC 99-165093. 58p. 1998. pap. text 5.96 (*0-8269-4142-7*) Am Technical.

Miller, Wilbur R. & Miller, Marie F. Instructors & Their Jobs. 2nd ed. LC 97-33517. (Illus.). 250p. 1998. pap. 38.96 (*0-8269-4164-8*) Am Technical.

Miller, Wilbur R., jt. auth. see McKnight Staff.

Miller, Wilford L. Wildlife of the Prairie. (Illus.). 1976. 8.95 (*0-686-18906-X*); pap. 5.95 (*0-686-18907-8*) Assoc Print.

Miller, Wilhelm & Robbins, Allan H. Circuit Analysis: Theory & Practice. LC 94-10022. (Illus.). 1120p. (C). 1995. mass mkt. 99.95 (*0-8273-5414-2*) Delmar.

Miller, Wilhelm C. & Robbins, Allan H. Circuit Analysis Computerized Test Bank: Theory & Practice CTB. (Electronics Technology Ser.). 1995. text 49.95 (*0-8273-7030-X*) Delmar.

Miller, Will. Why We Watch: Killing the Gilligan Within. 1996. pap. 11.00 (*0-684-83106-6*) S&S Trade.

Miller, Willam, Jr. The Great Luxury Liners, 1927-1952: A Photographic Record. (Illus.). 160p. 1981. pap. 13.95 (*0-486-24056-8*) Dover.

Miller, Willard. On Lie Algebras & Some Special Functions of Mathematical Physics. LC 52-42839. (American Mathematical Society Ser.: No. 50). 49p. reprint ed. pap. 30.00 (*0-608-09175-8*, 205267900002) Bks Demand.

Miller, William. The Balkans: Rumania, Bulgaria, Serbia & Montenegro. LC 72-66. (Select Bibliographies Reprint Ser.). 1977. reprint ed. 30.95 (*0-8369-9965-7*) Ayer.

— The Bus Ride. LC 97-6850. (Illus.). 32p. (J). (gr. k-3). 1998. 15.95 (*1-880000-60-1*) Lee & Low Bks.

— The Conjure Woman: Madame Zina. (Illus.). 32p. (J). (gr. k-3). 1996. 15.00 (*0-689-31962-2*) Atheneum Yung Read.

— Essays on the Latin Orient. LC 78-63360. (Crusades & Military Orders Ser.: Second Series). reprint ed. 72.50 (*0-404-17024-2*) AMS Pr.

Miller, William, Jr The First Great Ocean Liners in Photographs: 180 Views, 1897-1927. (Antiques Ser.). (Illus.). 149p. (Orig.). 1984. pap. 13.95 (*0-486-24574-8*) Dover.

Miller, William. Frederick Douglass: The Last Day of Slavery. LC 94-26542. (Illus.). 32p. (J). (gr. 1 up). 1995. 14.95 (*1-880000-17-2*) Lee & Low Bks.

— Frederick Douglass: The Last Day of Slavery. LC 94-26542. 1995. 11.15 (*0-606-09298-6*, Pub. by Turtleback) Demco.

— Frederick Douglass: The Last Day of Slavery. (Illus.). 32p. (YA). (ps up). 1996. reprint ed. pap. 5.95 (*1-880000-42-3*) Lee & Low Bks.

— A History of the Greek People (1821-1921) LC 83-45816. 1983. reprint ed. 27.50 (*0-404-20178-4*) AMS Pr.

— A House by the River. LC 96-24137. (Illus.). 32p. (YA). (ps up). 1997. 15.95 (*1-880000-48-2*, Pub. by Lee & Low Bks) Publishers Group.

— The Latins in the Levant: A History of Frankish Greece. LC 75-41193. reprint ed. 72.50 (*0-404-14689-9*) AMS Pr.

— Night Golf. LC 98-47168. (Illus.). 32p. (J). (ps-3). 1999. 15.95 (*1-880000-79-2*, Pub. by Lee & Low Bks) Publishers Group.

Miller, William, Jr Ocean Liners of the World. 1984. pap. 11.50 (*0-915276-43-7*) Quadrant Pr.

Miller, William. Old Faith: Poems. LC 92-15312. 64p. 1992. pap. 14.95 (*0-7734-0042-7*, Mellen Poetry Pr) E Mellen.

***Miller, William.** The Piano. LC 99-38004. (Illus.). 32p. (J). (ps-7). 2000. 15.95 (*1-880000-98-9*, Pub. by Lee & Low Bks) Publishers Group.

— ProActive Sales Management: How to Manage More Effectively & Stay Ahead of the Game. 256p. 2000. 24.95 (*0-8144-0545-2*) AMACOM.

— Richard Wright & the Library Card. LC 97-6847. (Illus.). 32p. (YA). (gr. k up). 1999. pap. 6.95 (*1-880000-88-1*, Pub. by Lee & Low Bks) Publishers Group.

— Richard Wright & the Library Card, No. 3. LC 97-6847. (Illus.). 32p. (YA). (gr. 1 up). 1997. 15.95 (*1-880000-57-1*) Lee & Low Bks.

— Tituba. LC 99-6332. (Illus.). 32p. (J). (ps-3). 2000. 16.00 (*0-15-201897-2*, Harcourt Child Bks) Harcourt.

Miller, William. Travels & Politics in the Near East. LC 70-135822. (Eastern Europe Collection). 1971. reprint ed. 33.95 (*0-405-02764-8*) Ayer.

— Zora Hurston & the Chinaberry Tree. LC 94-1291. (Illus.). 32p. (YA). (gr. 1 up). 1994. 14.95 (*1-880000-14-8*) Lee & Low Bks.

— Zora Hurston & the Chinaberry Tree. LC 94-1291. (Illus.). 32p. (YA). (ps up). 1996. pap. 6.95 (*1-880000-33-4*) Lee & Low Bks.

— Zora Hurston & the Chinaberry Tree. LC 94-1291. (J). 1994. 11.15 (*0-606-10109-8*, Pub. by Turtleback) Demco.

Miller, William, ed. Men in Business: Essays on the Historical Role of the Entrepreneur. LC 78-21159. 389p. 1979. reprint ed. lib. bdg. 35.00 (*0-313-20867-0*, MIME, Greenwood Pr) Greenwood.

Miller, William & Boyette, Pat. Texas Days of Glory. LC 98-206450. (Illus.). 64p. (YA). (gr. 6 up). 1998. pap. 9.95 (*1-57168-228-7*, Eakin Pr) Sunbelt Media.

Miller, William & Gordon, Stewart. Sunlight & Steel: The Story of the SS Independence & the SS Constitution. (Illus.). 144p. 1998. per. 22.95 (*0-9667165-0-7*) Prow Pr.

Miller, William & McAuley, Rob. The Liners: A Voyage of Discovery. LC 97-49037. (Illus.). 160p. 1997. 29.95 (*0-7603-0465-3*) MBI Pubg.

Miller, William & Rockwood, D. Stephen, eds. College Librarianship. LC 80-25546. 290p. 1981. 35.00 (*0-8108-1383-1*) Scarecrow.

Miller, William, et al. Natural Analogue Studies in the Geological Disposal of Radioactive Wastes. LC 93-45535. (Studies in Environmental Science: Vol. 57). 412p. 1994. 191.50 (*0-444-81755-7*) Elsevier.

Miller, William, jt. auth. see Ballatore, Ron.

Miller, William, jt. auth. see Brush, Jack.

Miller, William A. Conversations. LC 80-54283. 96p. 1980. pap. 5.95 (*0-934104-04-2*) Woodland.

— Make Friends with Your Shadow: How to Accept & Use Positively the Negative Side of Your Personality. LC 80-67793. 144p. (Orig.). 1981. pap. 12.99 (*0-8066-1855-8*, 10-4238, Augsburg) Augsburg Fortress.

Miller, William A., jt. ed. see McLeod, Donald C.

Miller, William B. & Schenk, Vicki L. All I Need to Know about Manufacturing I Learned in Joe's Garage: World Class Manufacturing Made Simple. 4th ed. 104p. (Orig.). 1999. pap. 9.95 (*0-9630439-3-5*) Bayrock.

— The Day I Learned about Quality in Joe's Garage: High Quality Made Simple. 128p. (Orig.). 2000. pap. 9.95 (*0-9630439-7-8*) Bayrock.

— Manufacturing Beyond Joe's Garage: Value Based Manufacturing. 128p. (Orig.). 2000. pap. 9.95 (*0-9630439-9-4*) Bayrock.

Miller, William B., jt. auth. see Humi, Mayer.

Miller, William C. Alvar Aalto: A Bibliography, No. 1190. 1976. 5.00 (*0-686-19684-8*, Sage Prdcls Pr) Sage.

— Creative Edge. 1989. pap. 19.00 (*0-201-52401-5*) Addison-Wesley.

***Miller, William C.** The Flash of Brillance Workbook: The Eight Keys to Discover, Unlock & Fulfill Your Creative Potential at Work. (Illus.). 136p. 1999. pap. text, wbk. ed. 17.50 (*0-7382-0239-8*, Pub. by Perseus Pubng) HarpC.

Miller, William C. Flash of Brilliance: Inspiring Creativity Where You Work. 320p. 1998. text 25.00 (*0-7382-0018-2*) Perseus Pubng.

— Flash of Brilliance: Inspiring Creativity Where You Work. 2nd ed. 1998. pap. write for info. (*0-201-36090-X*) Addison-Wesley.

— Quantum Quality: Quality Improvement Through Innovation, Learning, & Creativity. LC 93-12408. 208p. 1993. pap. 19.95 (*0-527-91719-2*) Productivity Inc.

***Miller, William C., et al.** Innovation Styles: Games to Explore Innovation Styles. (Card & Board Games for Training Ser.). (Illus.). 70p. 2000. pap. 89.00 (*1-930005-05-9*) Workshops.

Miller, William D. Commercial Bank Valuation. LC 95-40054. 288p. 1995. 155.00 (*0-471-12820-1*) Wiley.

— Memphis During the Progressive Era, 1900-1917. LC 58-21437. 258p. reprint ed. 80.00 (*0-608-16585-9*, 202751800055) Bks Demand.

— Pretty Bubbles in the Air: America in 1919. 248p. 1991. text 29.95 (*0-252-01823-0*) U of Ill Pr.

— Tampa Triangle Dead Zone. 2nd rev. ed. LC 96-35590. (Illus.). xii, 196p. 1997. pap. 14.95 (*0-9660911-0-8*) Tampa Triangle.

— Valuing Banks & Thrifts. 1990. pap. 69.95 (*1-55840-434-1*) Exec Ent Pubns.

Miller, William F. A Letter to My Grandchildren. 579p. 1998. write for info. (*1-86106-620-1*, Pub. by Minerva Pr) Unity Dist.

Miller, William G. The Data of Jurisprudence. LC 97-77291. xv, 477p. 1998. reprint ed. 148.00 (*1-56169-366-9*) Gaunt.

— Data of Jurisprudence. xiv, 477p. 1980. reprint ed. 47.50 (*0-8377-0835-4*, Rothman) W S Hein.

— Lectures on the Philosophy of Law: Designed Mainly As an Introduction to the Study of International Law. xv, 432p. 1979. reprint ed. 45.00 (*0-8377-0834-6*, Rothman) W S Hein.

— Managing Environmental Mandates for Multifamily Housing, 1997: A Compendium of Federal Laws & Regulations. LC 96-61395. 148p. 1996. pap. text 299.95 (*0-87420-799-1*, M02) Urban Land.

Miller, William G., ed. Toward a More Civil Society: U. S.-Soviet Relations. 1989. text 26.95 (*0-88730-220-3*, HarpBusn) HarpInfo.

Miller, William H., Jr. The Fabulous Interiors of the Great Ocean Liners in Historic Photographs. (Illus.). 160p. 1985. pap. 12.95 (*0-486-24756-2*) Dover.

— Great Cruise Ships & Ocean Liners from 1954 to 1986: A Photographic Survey. 6th ed. (Illus.). 128p. (Orig.). 1988. pap. 11.95 (*0-486-25540-9*) Dover.

M

Miller, William H. Miller on Managing: "Straight Talk on the Ups & Downs, Do's & Don'ts of Managing a Water Utility. (Illus.). 180p. (C). 1992. 26.00 (*0-89867-619-3*, 10056) Am Water Wks Assn.

— Modern Cruise Ships, 1965-1990: A Photographic Record. (Illus.). 128p. 1992. pap. 13.95 (*0-486-26753-9*) Dover.

Miller, William H., Jr. Pictorial Encyclopedia of Ocean Liners, 1860-1993: 402 Photographs. 93rd ed. (Illus.). 192p. (Orig.). 1995. pap. 16.95 (*0-486-28137-X*) Dover.

— Picture History of the French Line. LC 97-5791. (Illus.). 128p. (Orig.). 1997. pap. text 13.95 (*0-486-29443-9*) Dover.

— Picture History of the Italian Line, 1932-1977. LC 99-33035. (Illus.). 128p. 1999. pap. text 14.95 (*0-486-40489-7*) Dover.

Miller, William H., et al. More Leaves from the Copper Beeches. Starr, H. W. et al, eds. LC 76-244. (Illus.). 222p. 1976. 15.00 (*0-915010-16-X*) Sutter House.

Miller, William H., jt. auth. see Duffy, Francis J.

Miller, William I. The Anatomy of Disgust. LC 96-35420. 320p. 1997. 24.95 (*0-674-03154-7*) HUP.

— The Anatomy of Disgust. 320p. 1998. pap. 15.95 (*0-674-03155-5*) HUP.

— Bloodtaking & Peacemaking: Feud, Law, & Society in Saga Iceland. xii, 407p. 1996. pap. text 17.95 (*0-226-52680-1*) U Ch Pr.

— Bloodtaking & Peacemaking: Feud, Law, & Society in Saga Iceland. LC 89-77971. (Illus.). 420p. 1998. 35.95 (*0-226-52679-8*) U Ch Pr.

— Humiliation: And Other Essays on Honor, Social Discomfort, & Violence. 288p. 1993. text 35.00 (*0-8014-2881-5*) Cornell U Pr.

— Humiliation: And Other Essays on Honor, Social Discomfort, & Violence. 288p. 1995. pap. text 16.95 (*0-8014-8117-1*) Cornell U Pr.

Miller, William I., jt. auth. see Andersson, Theodore M.

***Miller, William Ian.** The Mystery of Courage. LC 00-29559. 384p. 2000. 29.95 (*0-674-00307-1*) HUP.

Miller, William J. The Battles for Richmond, 1862. (Civil War Ser.). (Illus.). 56p. 1996. pap. 4.95 (*0-915992-93-0*) Eastern National.

Miller, William J., Jr. Crossing the Delaware: The Story of the Delaware Memorial Bridge. 114p. 1990. reprint ed. 9.95 (*0-685-33045-1*); reprint ed. pap. 5.95 (*0-911293-06-X*) Guage Corp.

— Crossing the Delaware: The Story of the Delaware Memorial Bridge, the Longest Twin Suspension Bridge in the World. Demerast, Kathy K., ed. LC 83-71879. (Illus.). 114p. 1983. 9.95 (*0-911293-02-7*); pap. 5.95 (*0-911293-01-9*) Guage Corp.

Miller, William J. Mapping for Stonewall: The Civil War Service of Jed Hotchkiss. LC 93-18611. (Illus.). 176p. 1993. 29.95 (*1-880216-11-6*, Elliott Clark) Black Belt Communs.

Miller, William J., ed. The Peninsula Campaign of 1862 Vol. 3: Yorktown to the Seven Days. (Illus.). 228p. (Orig.). 1997. pap. 16.95 (*1-882810-14-7*, 14-7) Savas Pub.

Miller, William J., et al, eds. The Peninsula Campaign of 1862: Yorktown to the Seven Days, 3 vols., Vol. 1. (Illus.). 238p. 1995. pap. 16.95 (*1-882810-75-9*) Savas Pub.

— The Peninsula Campaign of 1862 Vol. 2: Yorktown to the Seven Days, 3 vols. (Campaign Chronicles Ser.). (Illus.). 208p. 1995. pap. 16.95 (*1-882810-76-7*, 106) Savas Pub.

Miller, William J., Jr., jt. auth. see Broeg, Bob.

Miller, William J., jt. auth. see Pilates, Joseph H.

Miller, William L. Arguing about Slavery: John Quincy Adams & the Great Battle in the United States Congress. 1998. pap. 17.00 (*0-679-76844-0*) Vin Bks.

— The Business of May Next: James Madison & the Founding. 312p. (C). 1994. pap. text 14.50 (*0-8139-1490-6*) U Pr of Va.

— The End of British Politics? (Illus.). 1981. 55.00 (*0-19-827422-X*) OUP.

— Irrelevant Elections? The Quality of Local Democracy in Britain. (Illus.). 258p. 1988. text 65.00 (*0-19-827572-2*) OUP.

— Media & Voters: The Audience, Content, & Influence of Press & the Television at the 1987 General Election. (Illus.). 256p. 1991. 58.00 (*0-19-827377-0*) OUP.

***Miller, William L., et al, eds.** A Culture of Corruption: Coping with Government in Post-Communist Europe. 180p. (C). 2000. 46.95 (*963-9116-98-X*); pap. 21.95 (*963-9116-99-8*) Ctrl Europ Univ.

Miller, William L. & Caird, Edward, eds. Alternatives to Freedom: Arguments & Opinions. LC 94-28992. 264p. (C). 1995. pap. text 25.50 (*0-582-25130-3*, 77018, Pub. by Addison-Wesley) Longman.

Miller, William L. & Morris, Langdon. Fourth Generation R&D: Managing Knowledge, Technology, & Innovation. LC 98-12030. 347p. 1999. 59.95 (*0-471-24093-1*) Wiley.

Miller, William L., et al. How Voters Change: The Nineteen Eighty-Seven British Election Campaign in Perspective. (Illus.). 320p. 1990. text 85.00 (*0-19-827342-8*) OUP.

— Political Culture of Contemporary Britain: People & Politicians, Principles & Practice. (Illus.). 540p. 1996. text 95.00 (*0-19-827984-1*) OUP.

— Religion & the Public Good: A Bicentennial Forum. 139p. 1989. 35.00 (*0-86554-326-7*, MUP-H276) Mercer Univ Pr.

Miller, William L., jt. auth. see Crabtree, Benjamin F.

Miller, William L., Jr., jt. auth. see Jacquet, Jay.

Miller, William L., jt. ed. see Crabtree, Benjamin F.

Miller, William L., jt. ed. see Harrop, Martin.

***Miller, William Lockley, et al.** Models of Local Governance: Public Opinion & Political Theory in Britain. LC 00-33293. 2000. write for info. (*0-312-23772-3*) St Martin.

Miller, William M. The Baha'i Faith: Its History & Teachings. LC 74-8745. (Illus.). 444p. 1984. pap. 11.95 (*0-87808-137-2*) William Carey Lib.

— A Christian's Response to Islam. 1976. pap. 4.99 (*0-87552-335-8*) P & R Pubng.

— My Persian Pilgrimage: An Autobiography. rev. ed. LC 89-995. (Illus.). 408p. 1995. pap. 21.95 (*0-87808-243-3*, WCL243-3) William Carey Lib.

Miller, William R. Clinical Research Guide for Therapists Treating Individuals with Alcohol Abuse & Dependence: Motivational Enhancement Therapy Manual, Vol. 2. 137p. 1996. per. 14.00 (*0-16-061514-3*) USGPO.

Miller, William R., ed. Contemporary American Protestant Thought: 1900-1970. LC 77-151612. 1973. pap. 9.65 (*0-672-60140-0*, AHS84, Bobbs) Macmillan.

— Integrating Spirituality into Treatment: Resources for Practitioners. LC 99-12572. 300p. 1999. text 39.95 (*1-55798-581-2*, 431-726A) Am Psychol.

Miller, William R. The Spirits of Ireland. 158p. 1998. write for info. (*0-9617655-4-2*) Foley Pub.

***Miller, William R. & Clunies, Sandra, eds.** Enhancing Motivation for Change in Substance Abuse Treatment. 243p. (C). 2000. pap. text 35.00 (*0-7567-0163-5*) DIANE Pub.

Miller, William R. & Heather, Nick, eds. Treating Addictive Behaviors. 2nd ed. LC 98-27475. (Applied Clinical Psychology Ser.). (Illus.). 372p. (C). 1998. text 54.50 (*0-306-45852-7*, Kluwer Plenum) Kluwer Academic.

Miller, William R. & Jackson, Kathleen A. Practical Psychology for Pastors. 2nd ed. LC 94-34115. 448p. 1994. pap. text 86.00 (*0-13-171829-0*) P-H.

Miller, William R. & Martin, John E., eds. Behavior Therapy & Religion: Integrating Spiritual & Behavioral Approaches to Change. (Focus Editions Ser.: Vol. 98). 200p. (C). 1988. text 59.95 (*0-8039-3203-0*); pap. text 26.00 (*0-8039-3204-9*) Sage.

— Behavior Therapy & Religion: Integrating Spiritual & Behavioral Approaches to Change. LC 87-31954. (Sage Focus Editions Ser.: Vol. 98). 192p. reprint ed. pap. 59.60 (*0-608-09771-3*, 206994500007) Bks Demand.

Miller, William R. & Rollnick, Stephen. Motivational Interviewing: Preparing People to Change Addictive Behavior. LC 91-16597. 348p. 1991. lib. bdg. 39.95 (*0-89862-566-1*) Guilford Pubns.

— Motivational Interviewing: Preparing People to Change Addictive Behavior. LC 91-16597. 348p. 1992. reprint ed. pap. text 23.00 (*0-89862-469-X*) Guilford Pubns.

Miller, William R., et al. Motivational Enhancement Therapy Manual: A Clinical Research Guide for Therapists Treating Individuals with Alcohol Abuse & Dependence. 121p. (Orig.). (C). 1994. pap. text 35.00 (*0-7881-1476-X*) DIANE Pub.

Miller, William R., jt. auth. see McCrady, Barbara S.

Miller, William R., jt. auth. see Murray, William M.

Miller, William R., jt. ed. see Hester, Reid K.

Miller, William S., jt. ed. see Phillips, G. Briggs.

Miller, Wilma B., jt. auth. see Miller, Frank C.

Miller, Wilma H. Alternative Assessment Techniques for Reading & Writing. LC 95-826. 476p. 1995. pap. text 29.95 (*0-87628-141-2*) Ctr Appl Res.

— Complete Reading Disabilities Handbook. 432p. 1993. spiral bd. 29.95 (*0-87628-249-4*) Ctr Appl Res.

— Complete Reading Disabilities Handbook: Ready-to-Use Techniques for Teaching Reading Disabled Students. (Illus.). 432p. 1997. pap. text 29.50 (*0-87628-275-3*) Ctr Appl Res.

— Reading & Writing Remediation Kit: Ready-to-Use Strategies & Activities to Build Content Reading & Writing Skills. LC 96-41482. 448p. 1996. pap. text 29.95 (*0-87628-753-4*) Ctr Appl Res.

— Reading Comprehension Activities Kit. LC 90-43209. 312p. (C). 1990. pap. text 29.95 (*0-87628-789-5*) P-H.

— Reading Diagnosis Kit. 3rd ed. 368p. 1986. pap. text 24.95 (*0-87628-720-8*) Ctr Appl Res.

— Reading Diagnosis Kit. 3rd ed. 376p. 1986. pap. 27.95 (*0-317-66024-1*) P-H.

— Reading Teacher's Complete Diagnosis & Correction Manual. 328p. 1988. pap. text 29.95 (*0-87628-772-0*) Ctr Appl Res.

— Reading Teacher's Complete Diagnosis & Correction Manual. 296p. 1988. pap. 24.95 (*0-318-35308-3*) P-H.

***Miller, Wilma H.** Ready-to-use Activities & Materials for Improving Content Reading Skills. LC 99-19057. (Illus.). 528p. 1999. 29.95 (*0-13-007815-8*) P-H.

— Strategies for Developing Emergent Literacy. LC 99-26257. 2000. write for info. (*0-07-289372-9*) McGrw-H Hghr Educ.

Miller, Wister, ed. see Yates, Michael.

Miller, Wolfgang. Dictionary of Polygraphy: Fachworterbuch Polygrafie. (ENG & GER.). 1020p. 1981. 175.00 (*0-8288-2228-X*, M11292) Fr & Eur.

Miller, Worth R. Oklahoma Populism: A History of the People's Party in the Oklahoma Territory. LC 87-40214. (Illus.). 304p. 1987. 29.95 (*0-8061-2072-X*) U of Okla Pr.

Miller, Y. What's Wrong with Being Happy. 1994. 18.99 (*0-89906-121-4*); pap. 15.99 (*0-89906-122-2*) Mesorah Pubns.

— What's Wrong with Being Human. 1992. 18.99 (*0-89906-544-9*); pap. 15.99 (*0-89906-545-7*) Mesorah Pubns.

Miller, Yisroel. Guardian of Eden: In Search of the Jewish Woman & Letters to a Jewish Feminist, 2 pts. LC 93-34033. 1993. 16.95 (*0-87306-659-6*) Feldheim.

Miller, Yolanda. Ode to Precious, Priceless & Irreplaceable African-American Men: A Collection of Poems. 70p. (Orig.). 1996. pap. 8.95 (*0-9650852-0-1*) Victory WI.

Miller, Yosef, jt. ed. see Berman, Colette.

Miller, Yvette E., ed. The Fertile Rhythms: Contemporary Women Poets of Mexico. Hoeksema, Thomas & Enriquez, Romelia, trs. LC 89-13659. (Discoveries Ser.). (SPA & ENG.). 126p. 1989. pap. 12.95 (*0-935480-44-7*) Lat Am Lit Rev Pr.

— Song of Madness & Other Poems. Aparicio, Frances R., tr. LC 85-11. (ENG & SPA.). 160p. 1985. pap. 12.95 (*0-935480-18-8*) Lat Am Lit Rev Pr.

Miller, Yvette E. & Ross, Kathleen, eds. Scents of Wood & Silence: Short Stories by Latin American Women Writers. LC 91-30002. (Discoveries Ser.). 220p. 1991. pap. 16.95 (*0-935480-55-2*) Lat Am Lit Rev Pr.

Miller, Yvette E. & Tatum, Charles M., eds. Latin American Women Writers: Yesterday & Today. Lima, Robert et al, trs. 202p. 1977. reprint ed. pap. 12.50 (*0-935480-56-0*) Lat Am Lit Rev Pr.

Miller, Yvette E., ed. see Agosin, Marjorie.

Miller, Yvette E., ed. see Aguilar, Eduardo G.

Miller, Yvette E., ed. see Alegria, Fernando.

Miller, Yvette E., ed. see Bianco, Jose.

Miller, Yvette E., ed. see Bullrich, Silvina.

Miller, Yvette E., ed. see Campos, Julieta.

Miller, Yvette E., ed. see Castellanos, Rosario.

Miller, Yvette E., ed. see Collyer, Jaime.

Miller, Yvette E., ed. see De la Cuesta, Barbara.

Miller, Yvette E., ed. see Delgado, Ana M.

Miller, Yvette E., ed. see Diaz Valcarcel, Emilio.

Miller, Yvette E., ed. see Estrada, Ezequiel M.

Miller, Yvette E., ed. see Galeana, Benita.

Miller, Yvette E., ed. see Galindo, Sergio.

Miller, Yvette E., ed. see Gomez de la Serna, Ramon.

Miller, Yvette E., ed. see Guerra, Lucia.

Miller, Yvette E., ed. see Hahn, Oscar.

Miller, Yvette E., ed. see Kanellos, Nicolas.

Miller, Yvette E., ed. see Levinson, Luisa M.

Miller, Yvette E., ed. see Leviq, Enrique J.

Miller, Yvette E., ed. see Lindo, Hugo.

Miller, Yvette E., ed. see Mallea, Eduardo.

Miller, Yvette E., ed. see Martinez, Eliud.

Miller, Yvette E., ed. see Matute, Ana M.

Miller, Yvette E., ed. see Montes De Oca, Marco A.

Miller, Yvette E., ed. see Muniz-Huberman, Angelina.

Miller, Yvette E., ed. see Naranjo, Carmen.

Miller, Yvette E., ed. see Neruda, Pablo.

Miller, Yvette E., ed. see Nunes, Maria L.

Miller, Yvette E., ed. see Ortega, Julio.

Miller, Yvette E., ed. see Piglia, Ricardo.

Miller, Yvette E., ed. see Ponce, Manuel.

Miller, Yvette E., ed. see Samperio, Guillermo.

Miller, Yvette E., ed. see Sanchez, Marta.

Miller, Yvette E., ed. see Sarduy, Severo.

Miller, Yvette E., ed. see Schevill, Rudolph.

Miller, Yvette E., ed. see Valdivieso, Mercedes.

Miller, Yvette E., ed. see Vallejo, Cesar.

Miller, Yvette E., ed. see Zurita, Raul.

Miller, Z. Reed. Building Celestial Families: How to Find Success in Family & Personal Living. 159p. 1996. pap. 12.98 (*0-88290-588-0*) Horizon Utah.

***Miller, Zane L.** Boss Cox's Cincinnati: Urban Politics in the Progressive Era. (Urban Life & Urban Landscape Ser.). (Illus.). 336p. 2000. 65.00 (*0-8142-0861-4*); pap. 19.95 (*0-8142-5064-5*) Ohio St U Pr.

Miller, Zane L. Boss Cox's Cincinnati: Urban Politics in the Progressive Era. LC 79-21545. 1995. reprint ed. pap. text 12.00 (*0-226-52598-8*, P873) U Ch Pr.

Miller, Zane L. & Melvin, Patricia M. The Urbanism of Modern America: A Brief History. 2nd ed. 264p. (C). 1987. pap. text 16.00 (*0-15-593657-3*) Harcourt Coll Pubs.

Miller, Zane L. & Tucker, Bruce. Changing Plans for America's Inner Cities: Cincinnati's Over-the-Rhine & Twentieth-Century Urbanism. LC 97-26206. (Urban Life & Urban Landscape Ser.). 248p. 1997. text 42.50 (*0-8142-0762-6*); pap. text 16.95 (*0-8142-0763-4*) Ohio St U Pr.

Miller, Zane L. & Wade, Richard C. Boss Cox's Cincinnati: Urban Politics in the Progressive Era. LC 81-6346. (Urban Life in America Ser.). 301p. 1981. reprint ed. lib. bdg. 65.00 (*0-313-22760-8*, MIBC, Greenwood Pr) Greenwood.

Miller, Zane L., ed. see Baldwin, Peter C.

Miller, Zane L., jt. ed. see Gillette, Howard, Jr.

Miller, Zane L., ed. see Schlesinger, Arthur Meier, Sr.

Miller, Zane L., ed. & frwd. see Contosta, David R.

Miller, Zell. Corps Values: Everything You Need to Know I learned in the Marines. LC 96-79800. 96p. 1997. 14.95 (*1-56352-387-6*) Longstreet.

— Corps Values: Everything You Need to Know I Learned in the Marines. 112p. 1998. reprint ed. pap. 9.95 (*0-553-37981-X*) Bantam.

— "Listen to This Voice" Selected Speeches of Governor Zell Miller. LC 98-33971. 640p. 1998. text 50.00 (*0-86554-641-X*) Mercer Univ Pr.

— They Heard Georgia Singing. 272p. 1996. 24.95 (*0-86554-504-9*, MUP/H397) Mercer Univ Pr.

Miller, Zell, jt. auth. see Eby-Ebersole, Sarah.

Miller, Zoe. Colorful Knits for You & Your Child. LC 96-61773. (Illus.). 80p. 1997. 22.95 (*1-57076-080-2*, Trafalgar Sq Pub) Trafalgar.

Miller, Zonelle, jt. auth. see Hughes, Robert J.

Miller/Farese/Eickhorts. Understanding Business: A World of Opportunities. 1991. pap., wbk. ed. 20.75 (*0-314-86318-4*) Thomson Learn.

Miller/Jentz & Jentz. Case Printouts Fundamentals of Business Law. 3rd ed. (SWC-Business Law Ser.). 1995. pap. 21.00 (*0-314-07892-4*) Sth-Wstrn College.

Milleret, Margo & Eakin, Marshall C., eds. Homenagem a Alexandrino Severino: Essays on the Portuguese-Speaking World. (ENG & POR.). 276p. (C). 1993. pap. 15.00 (*0-924047-09-7*); text 35.00 (*0-924047-08-9*) Host Pubns.

Milleret, Toni, jt. auth. see Taylor, Terilyn.

Millergren, Al, jt. auth. see Evans, Paul.

Millermaster, Ralph A., ed. Harwood's Control of Electric Motors. 4th ed. LC 87-16598. 512p. 1987. reprint ed. 61.50 (*0-89464-242-1*) Krieger.

Millero, Frank J., ed. Chemical Oceanography. 2nd ed. (Marine Science Ser.). (Illus.). 496p. 1996. boxed set 104.95 (*0-8493-8423-0*) CRC Pr.

Millero, Frank J. & Sohn, Mary L. Chemical Oceanography. 448p. 1991. lib. bdg. 96.95 (*0-8493-8840-6*, GC111) CRC Pr.

Milleron, Jean-Claude, et al. Efficiency, Stability, & Equity: A Strategy for the Evolution of the Economic System of the European Community. (Illus.). 208p. 1988. pap. 17.95 (*0-19-828629-5*) OUP.

Milleron, Jean-Claude, jt. auth. see Champsaur, Paul.

Millerr, George Oxford. Texas Parks & Campgrounds. LC 99-13456. (Lone Star Guides Ser.). (Illus.). 242p. 1999. pap. 15.95 (*0-89123-034-3*, 3034) Gulf Pub.

Millers, Antonia. Latvian Language for the Use of Students: Grammar, Vocabulary & Exercises. LC 79-89077. (ENG & LAV.). 170p. (C). 1979. 20.00 (*0-912852-26-7*) Echo Pubs.

Millers, Del. Dancing with God: How You Can Make Exercise a Playful Adventure of Body & Soul. (Illus.). 124p. 1999. pap. 14.95 (*0-9666704-0-X*) SpiritWind Pubns.

***Millers, Del.** Del's 10 Minute Total Body Workout: When All You've Got Is 10 Minutes to Spare! LC 00-90195. (Illus.). 112p. 2000. pap. 14.95 (*0-9666704-6-9*) SpiritWind Pubns.

Miller's Publication Staff & Marsh, Madeleine. Miller's Collectables Price Guide, 1998-99. annuals (Miller's Antiques Checklist Ser.). 496p. 1998. 29.95 (*1-84000-055-4*, Pub. by Millers Pubns) Antique Collect.

***Miller's Publications Staff.** Miller's Antiques Shops, Fairs & Auctions 2000. (Illus.). 2000. pap. 24.95 (*1-84000-209-3*) Millers Pubns.

— Miller's Ceramics Buyer's Guide. (Illus.). 384p. 2000. 29.95 (*1-84000-267-0*, Pub. by Millers Pubns) Antique Collect.

— Miller's Collectables Price Guide 2000-2001. (Illus.). 496p. 2000. 29.95 (*1-84000-238-7*, Pub. by Millers Pubns) Antique Collect.

Millers-Younger, Sandra, ed. see Schultze, Kymythy R.

Millerson, Gerald. Effective TV Production. 3rd ed. LC 92-37229. (Media Manuals Ser.). (Illus.). 224p. 1993. 26.95 (*0-240-51324-X*, Focal) Buttrwrth-Heinemann.

***Millerson, Gerald.** Lighting for Television & Film. 3rd ed. 448p. 1999. pap. text 47.95 (*0-240-51582-X*, Focal) Buttrwrth-Heinemann.

Millerson, Gerald. Lighting for Video. 3rd ed. (Media Manuals Ser.). 176p. 1991. pap. 27.95 (*0-240-51303-7*, Focal) Buttrwrth-Heinemann.

— The Technique of Lighting for Television & Film. LC 99-943709. (Library of Communication Techniques Ser.). 400p. 1982. pap. 28.95 (*0-240-51192-1*, Focal) Buttrwrth-Heinemann.

— The Technique of Lighting for Television & Film. 3rd ed. (Library of Communication Techniques Ser.). 448p. 1991. 59.95 (*0-240-51299-5*, Focal) Buttrwrth-Heinemann.

— Technique of Television Production. 12th ed. (Illus.). 566p. (Orig.). 1990. pap. 64.95 (*0-240-51289-8*, Focal) Buttrwrth-Heinemann.

— Television Production. 13th ed. LC 98-49389. 566p. 1999. pap. 56.95 (*0-240-51492-0*, Focal) Buttrwrth-Heinemann.

— TV Scenic Desgin Handbook. 2nd ed. LC 97-193342. 256p. 1997. pap. text 46.95 (*0-240-51493-9*) Buttrwrth-Heinemann.

— Video Camera Techniques: A New Media Manual. 2nd rev. ed. LC 94-18429. (Media Manuals Ser.). 160p. 1994. pap. 26.95 (*0-240-51376-2*, Focal) Buttrwrth-Heinemann.

— Video Production Handbook. 2nd ed. LC 92-10611. (Illus.). 256p. 1992. pap. 36.95 (*0-240-51321-5*, Focal) Buttrwrth-Heinemann.

Milles, George. Health Careers & Medical Sciences. LC 74-79837. (Allied Health Ser.). 1975. pap. write for info. (*0-672-61384-0*) Macmillan.

Milles, James. Internet Handbook for Law Librarians. (Law Library Information Reports: Vol. 15). 64p. 1993. pap. 50.00 (*0-87802-093-4*) Glanville.

Milles, Lee. Heat Pumps - Theory & Service: Instructor's Guide. 68p. 1993. pap. 14.95 (*0-8273-4957-2*) Delmar.

Millet, Alison, jt. ed. see Johnson, David C.

Millet, Allan R. & Maslowski, Peter. For the Common Defense: A Military History of the United States of America, Revised & Expanded. enl. rev. ed. LC 94-5199. 1994. reprint ed. pap. 22.95 (*0-02-921597-8*) Free Pr.

Millet, Claude & Millet, Denise. Castles. LC 92-15955. (First Discovery Book). 24p. (J). (ps-3). 1993. 11.95 (*0-590-46377-2*) Scholastic Inc.

Millet, Denise, jt. illus. see Millet, Claude.

Millet, Francis D. Capillary Crime, & Other Stories. LC 72-157793. (Short Story Index Reprint Ser.). 1977. reprint ed. 20.95 (*0-8369-3905-0*) Ayer.

Millet, Gary W. & Rosenberg, Ralph G. Primer for Graphic Arts Profitability: A Money-Making Formula. 96p. (Orig.). 1992. pap. 14.95 (*1-881637-04-2*) Millet Grp.

Millet, George & Bolitho, William, eds. The Parish Registers of Gulval in the County of Cornwall, 1598-1812. LC 95-221019. 182p. (Orig.). 1893. reprint ed. pap. 23.00 (*0-7884-0273-0*) Heritage Bk.

Millet, Ido, jt. auth. see Pinto, Jeffrey K.

Millet, Jean. La Belle Methode Ou l'Art De Bien Chanter. LC 71-126600. (Music Ser.). 76p. 1973. reprint ed. lib. bdg. 21.50 (*0-306-70044-1*) Da Capo.

Millet, John. Poetry Australia. 128p. (C). 1990. 80.00 (*0-909185-38-7*, Pub. by Pascoe Pub) St Mut.

An Asterisk (*) at the beginning of an entry indicates that the title is appearing for the first time.

— Tail Arse Charlie. 24p. 1984. pap. 2.00 (0-317-07609-4) Samisdat.

Millet, Lydia. George Bush, Dark Prince of Love: A Presidential Romance. LC 99-35606. 160p. 2000. per. 10.00 (0-684-86274-3) S&S Trade.

Millet, Marietta S. Light Revealing Architecture. (Architecture Ser.). (Illus.). 272p. 1995. text 59.95 (0-442-01887-8, VNR) Wiley.

Millet, Marietta S. Light Revealing Architecture. (Architecture Ser.). 183p. 1996. 75.00 (0-471-28644-3, VNR) Wiley.

Millet, N. B. Egyptian Hieroglyphs Wall Chart. (Illus.). 1996. write for info. (0-614-96345-1) Royal Ontario.

Millet, Olivier. Dictionnaire des Citations. (FRE.). 409p. 1992. pap. 16.95 (0-7859-7859-3, 2253061409) Fr & Eur.

Millet, Robert L. Alive in Christ: The Miracle of Spiritual Rebirth. LC 97-14600. xii, 211p. 1997. 15.95 (1-57345-263-7) Deseret Bk.

— Between Time & Eternity: An Introduction to the Mormon Church. LC 97-48600. xi, 222p. 1998. 15.95 (1-57345-359-5) Deseret Bk.

— Joseph Smith: Selected Sermons on Writings. (Sources of American Spirituality Ser.). 1989. 24.95 (0-8091-0427-X) Paulist Pr.

— The Power of the Word: Saving Doctrines from the Book of Mormon. LC 93-44307. x, 342p. 1994. 14.95 (0-87579-826-8) Deseret Bk.

— Steadfast & Immovable: Striving for Spiritual Maturity. LC 92-18727. 166p. 1992. 11.95 (0-87579-635-4) Deseret Bk.

— When a Child Wanders. LC 95-51313. xii, 164p. 1996. 13.95 (1-57345-142-8) Deseret Bk.

— Within Reach. LC 95-7681. 132p. 1995. 13.95 (0-87579-968-X) Deseret Bk.

Millet, Robert L., compiled by. Watch & Be Ready: Preparing for the Second Coming of the Lord. LC 94-27762. iv, 230p. 1994. 14.95 (0-87579-911-6) Deseret Bk.

Millet, Robert L., ed. Studies in Scripture: Acts to Revelation, Vol. 6. LC 87-70686. 303p. 1987. 14.95 (0-87579-084-4) Deseret Bk.

***Millet, Robert L. & Deseret Book Company Staff.** The Redeemer. LC 99-46666. 1999. write for info. (1-57345-598-9) Deseret Bk.

Millet, Robert L. & Jackson, Kent P., eds. Studies in Scripture Vol. 1: The Doctrine & Covenants, Vol. 1. 615p. 1989. reprint ed. 19.95 (0-87579-274-X) Deseret Bk.

Millet, Robert L. & Matthews, Robert J., eds. Plain & Precious Truths Restored. LC 95-77056. 1995. 14.95 (0-88494-987-7) Bookcraft Inc.

Millet, Robert L., jt. auth. see McConkie, Joseph F.

Millet, Robert L., jt. compiled by see Jackson, Kent P.

Millet, Robert L., jt. ed. see Jackson, Kent P.

Millett, Allan R. The General: Robert L. Bullard & Officership in the U. S. Army, 1881-1925, 10. LC 75-68. (Contributions in Military History Ser.: No. 10). (Illus.). 499p. 1975. 75.00 (0-8371-7957-2, MIG/, Greenwood Pr) Greenwood.

— Semper Fidelis: The History of the United States Marine Corps. enl. rev. ed. 800p. 1991. pap. 21.95 (0-02-921596-X); text 40.00 (0-02-921595-1) Free Pr.

Millett, Allan R., ed. A Short History of the Vietnam War. LC 77-23623. 191p. reprint ed. pap. 59.30 (0-7837-1758-X, 205729400024) Bks Demand.

Millett, Allan R. & Cooling, B. F. Doctoral Dissertations in Military Affairs. LC 72-186550. (Libraries Bibliography: No. 10). 1973. reprint ed. 7.50 (0-686-20812-9) KSU.

Millett, Allan R. & Murray, Williamson, eds. Military Effectiveness, 3 vols. 1988. write for info. (0-318-62728-0) Routledge.

— Military Effectiveness, 3 vols., Vol. I: The First World War. 320p. 1988. 65.00 (0-04-445053-2) Routledge.

— Military Effectiveness, 3 vols., Vol. II: The Interwar Period. 320p. 1988. 65.00 (0-04-445054-0) Routledge.

— Military Effectiveness Vol. 1: The First World War. (Mershon Center Series on International Security & Foreign Policy). 384p. 1989. pap. text 24.95 (0-04-445578-X) Routledge.

— Military Innovation in the Interwar Period. 442p. 1998. pap. text 19.95 (0-521-63760-0) Cambridge U Pr.

Millett, Allan R., jt. auth. see Murray, Williamson.

Millett, Allan R., jt. ed. see Murray, Williamson.

Millett, Allan R., jt. ed. see Murray, William.

Millett, Bella, compiled by. Ancrene Wisse, the Katherine Group, & the Wooing Group. (Annotated Bibliographies of Old & Middle English Ser.). 273p. 1996. 75.00 (0-85991-429-1) Boydell & Brewer.

Millett, Bella, ed. Hali Meiohad. (OS 284 Ser.). (Illus.). 1982. 18.95 (0-19-722286-2) OUP.

Millett, Benignus. Four Franciscan Martyrs of Ireland. 1989. pap. 22.00 (1-85390-161-X, Pub. by Veritas Pubns) St Mut.

Millett, Benignus & Lynch, Anthony, eds. Dun Mhuire, Killiney, 1945-1995: Leann Agus Seanches. LC 96-121638. 246p. 1995. 49.95 (1-874675-72-4); pap. 31.95 (1-874675-73-2) Dufour.

***Millett, Declan T. & Welbury, Richard.** Orthodontics & Paediatric Dentistry. LC 99-53892. (Colour Guide Ser.). (Illus.). 1999. write for info. (0-443-06287-0) Church.

Millett, Fred B. Contemporary British Literature, 2 vols., Set. xi, 556p. 1985. reprint ed. lib. bdg. 69.00 (0-7812-0641-3) Rprt Serv.

— Reading Drama: A Method of Analysis with Selections for Study. LC 71-111110. (Play Anthology Reprint Ser.). 1977. reprint ed. 20.95 (0-8369-8203-7) Ayer.

Millett, Fred B. & Bentley, Gerald E. Art of the Drama. (Illus.). 1947. 67.50 (0-89197-034-7) Irvington.

Millett, Fred B., ed. see Webster, John.

Millett, J. D. The Works Progress Administration in New York City. LC 77-74950. (American Federalism-the Urban Dimension Ser.). 1978. reprint ed. lib. bdg. 23.95 (0-405-10496-0) Ayer.

Millett, John. Blue Dynamite. 100p. 1986. pap. 5.00 (0-318-23493-9) Samisdat.

— Clothe Yourself in Summer. 72p. (Orig.). (YA). 1996. pap. 10.00 (1-887573-01-1) Salmon Run.

***Millett, John.** The Iceman Cometh. 100p. 2000. pap. 10.00 (1-887573-07-0) Salmon Run.

Millett, John. The Nine Lives of Big Meg O'Shannessy. 64p. (Orig.). 1989. pap. 9.95 (0-934257-30-2) Story Line.

Millett, John, jt. auth. see McGavin, P. A.

Millett, John D. Conflict in Higher Education: State Government Coordination vs. Institutional Independence. LC 83-24806. 307p. reprint ed. pap. 95.20 (0-7837-6517-7, 204562900007) Bks Demand.

— Decision Making & Administration in Higher Education. LC 68-55383. 171p. reprint ed. pap. 53.10 (0-608-17140-9, 202731100055) Bks Demand.

— New Structures of Campus Power. LC 77-82911. (Jossey-Bass Higher Education Ser.). 316p. reprint ed. pap. 98.00 (0-608-17772-5, 205655700072) Bks Demand.

— The Process & Organization of Government Planning. LC 76-38753. (FDR & the Era of the New Deal Ser.). 188p. 1972. reprint ed. lib. bdg. 29.50 (0-306-70444-7) Da Capo.

Millett, John D., jt. auth. see Macmahon, Arthur W.

Millett, K. C. Random Knotting & Linking. (Series on Knots & Everything). 208p. 1994. text 48.00 (981-02-2005-7) World Scientific Pub.

Millett, Kate. Basement. 1991. pap. 12.95 (0-671-72358-8, Touchstone) S&S Trade Pap.

***Millett, Kate.** Flying. 560p. 2000. reprint ed. pap. 18.95 (0-252-06886-6) U of Ill Pr.

— The Loony-Bin Trip. 320p. 2000. reprint ed. pap. 16.95 (0-252-06888-2) U of Ill Pr.

Millett, Kate. The Politics of Cruelty: An Essay on the Literature of Political Imprisonment. 336p. 1995. pap. 13.00 (0-393-31312-3, Norton Paperbks) Norton.

***Millett, Kate.** Sexual Politics. LC 99-86827. 2000. pap. 17.95 (0-252-06889-0) U of Ill Pr.

— Sita. LC 99-88353. 2000. pap. 14.95 (0-252-06887-4) U of Ill Pr.

Millett, Kenneth C. Piecewise Linear Concordances & Isotopies. LC 74-18328. (Memoirs Ser.: No. 1/153). 73p. 1974. pap. 17.00 (0-8218-1853-8, MEMO/1/153) Am Math.

Millett, Larry. Lost Twin Cities. LC 92-10460. (Illus.). 336p. 1992. pap. 29.95 (0-87351-273-1) Minn Hist.

***Millett, Larry.** Sherlock Holmes & the Ice Palace Murders: From the American Chronicles of John H. Watson, M. D. LC 98-22067. 336p. 1999. pap. 5.99 (0-14-028089-8, Penguin Bks) Viking Penguin.

Millett, Larry. Sherlock Holmes & the Ice Palace Murders: From the American Chronicles of John H. Watson, M.D. LC 98-22067. 322p. 1998. 23.95 (0-670-87944-4) Viking Penguin.

***Millett, Larry.** Sherlock Holmes & the Rune Stone Mystery: From the American Chronicles of John H. Watson, M. D. (Sherlock Holmes Mysteries Ser.). 2000. pap. 5.99 (0-14-029645-X) Penguin Putnam.

Millett, Larry. Sherlock Holmes & the Rune Stone Mystery: From the American Chronicles of John H. Watson, M.D. LC 99-29472. 336p. 1999. 23.95 (0-670-88821-4, Viking) Viking Penguin.

— Twin Cities Then & Now. LC 96-5746. (Illus.). x, 203p. 1996. 40.00 (0-87351-326-6); pap. 24.95 (0-87351-327-4) Minn Hist.

Millett, Lawrence. Sherlock Holmes & the Red Demon. 366p. 1997. pap. 9.95 Penguin Putnam.

Millett, Martin. The Romanization of Britain: An Essay in Archaeological Interpretation. (Illus.). 271p. (C). 1992. pap. text 26.95 (0-521-42864-5) Cambridge U Pr.

Millett, Peter & Heathfield, Elizabeth, eds. Encyclopaedia of Forms & Precedents. ring bd. write for info. (0-406-04424-4, EFP5ASET, MICHIE) LEXIS Pub.

Millett, Richard & Gold-Biss, Michael, eds. Beyond Praetorianism: The Latin American Military in Transition. LC 95-41548. 332p. 1996. pap. 26.95 (1-57454-000-9, 540009, Pub. by U Miami N-S Ctr) L Rienner.

Millett, Richard L. & Will, W. Marvin, eds. The Restless Caribbean: Changing Patterns of International Relations. LC 78-19764. 295p. 1979. 55.00 (0-275-90396-6, C0396, Praeger Pubs) Greenwood.

Millett, Richard L., jt. auth. see Falcoff, Mark.

Millett, Robert. Magnifying Priesthood Power. LC 89-85213. 187p. 1980. reprint ed. 14.98 (0-88290-037-4) Horizon Utah.

Millett, Robert W. The Vultures & the Phoenix. LC 81-65877. (Illus.). 168p. 1983. 32.50 (0-87982-039-X) Art Alliance.

***Millett, Stephen M.** The Scottish Settlers of America: The 17th & 18th Centuries. 234p. 1999. reprint ed. pap. 25.00 (0-8063-4761-9, Pub. by Clearfield Co) ACCESS Pubs Network.

Millett, Stephen M. & Honton, Edward J. A Manager's Guide to Technology Forecasting & Strategy Analysis Methods. LC 91-13690. 112p. 1991. pap. 19.95 (0-935470-63-8) Battelle.

***Millette, Beverly.** A New Owner's Guide to Brittanys. 160p. 2000. 12.95 (0-7938-2807-4) TFH Pubns.

Millette, Brenda, et al. The African-American Experience: A Multi-Disciplinary Approach. 242p. (C). 1995. pap. 22.95 (0-9649476-0-9) Lincoln Univ.

Millette, James R., jt. ed. see Basu, Samarendra.

Millette, Robert & Gosine, Mahin. The Grenada Revolution: Why It Failed. 172p. (Orig.). 1985. pap. 10.00 (0-933524-00-5) Africana Res.

Milletti, Mario A. Voices of Experience: Fifteen Hundred Retired People Talk about Retirement. rev. ed. 208p. 1987. pap. 3.00 (0-9613704-0-8) Tchrs Insurance.

Millettiearum, Scala, jt. auth. see Geesink, R.

***Milley, Don.** The E-Marketplace: Successful Strategies in B2B Ecommerce. 350p. 2000. 24.95 (0-07-136123-5) McGraw.

Millgard, Janie, ed. see Macduff, Nancy.

Millgate, Helen D. Mr. Brown's War: Day by Day Through the Second World War. LC 99-202590. 288p. 1999. 35.95 (0-7509-1783-0) Bks Intl VA.

***Millgate, Helen D.** Mr. Brown's War: Day by Day Through the Second World War. (Illus.). 288p. 1999. pap. 18.95 (0-7509-2325-3, Pub. by Sutton Pub Ltd) Bks Intl VA.

Millgate, Irvine H. Power Lab. (Illus.). 262p. (Orig.). 1992. pap. 24.00 (0-938919-14-8) Six Lights.

— Seeking the Meaning of the Management of "Relationships" Weaver, Joel W., ed. 115p. (Orig.). (YA). (gr. 11 up). 1994. pap. 18.00 (0-938919-31-8) Six Lights.

— Teacher-Manager Systems: Think & Learn & Grow While Nurturing the Human Spirit. (Illus.). 412p. 1991. 24.00 (0-938919-05-9) Six Lights.

Millgate, Irvine H. & Millgate, Rachel W., eds. The Common Language of Values & Ethics. rev. ed. (Illus.). 209p. 1987. pap. 18.00 (0-938919-10-5) Six Lights.

Millgate, Irvine H. & Weaver, Joel W. The Human Side of Systems Engineering. 238p. (Orig.). 1991. pap. 24.00 (0-938919-21-0) Six Lights.

— Power Lab: Creditability & Initiative. (Illus.). 86p. (Orig.). 1994. pap. 18.00 (0-938919-20-2) Six Lights.

— Power Lab: For Children to Nurture the Human Spirit Project Think. (Illus.). 324p. (Orig.). 1993. pap. 24.00 (0-938919-19-9) Six Lights.

— Power Lab: Seeking the Meaning of Mindsets. (Illus.). 87p. (Orig.). (YA). (gr. 11 up). 1994. pap. 18.00 (0-938919-28-8) Six Lights.

— Power Lab: Seeking the Meaning of Outward Passage. (Illus.). 109p. (Orig.). (YA). (gr. 9 up). 1994. pap. 18.00 (0-938919-25-3) Six Lights.

— Power Lab: Seeking Understanding. (Illus.). 54p. (Orig.). (J). (gr. 4 up). 1994. pap. 18.00 (0-938919-24-5) Six Lights.

— Power Lab: What Have We Learned about Thinking? (Illus.). 96p. (Orig.). 1994. pap. 18.00 (0-938919-23-7) Six Lights.

Millgate, Jane. Scott's Last Edition: A Study in Publishing History. (Illus.). x, 154p. 1987. 25.00 (0-85224-541-6, Pub. by Edinburgh U Pr) Col U Pr.

— Walter Scott: The Making of the Novelist. 223p. 1984. pap. 14.95 (0-8020-6692-5) U of Toronto Pr.

— Walter Scott: The Making of the Novelist. LC 84-243112. 237p. reprint ed. pap. 73.50 (0-8357-4144-3, 203691700006) Bks Demand.

Millgate, Jane, ed. Editing Nineteenth-Century Fiction: Papers Given at the Thirteenth Annual Conference on Editorial Problems, University of Toronto, 4-5 November, 1977. LC 78-3393. (Conference on Editorial Problems Ser.: No. 13). 1987. 42.50 (0-404-63663-2) AMS Pr.

Millgate, Michael. Faulkner's Place. LC 97-15109. 160p. 1997. 22.95 (0-8203-1937-6) U of Ga Pr.

— Testamentary Acts: Browning, Tennyson, James, Hardy. 284p. 1992. text 65.00 (0-19-811276-9) OUP.

— Testamentary Acts: Browning, Tennyson, James, Hardy. 288p. 1995. reprint ed. pap. 21.00 (0-19-818366-6) OUP.

— Thomas Hardy: His Career As a Novelist. LC 94-9494. 1994. pap. 19.95 (0-312-12233-0) St Martin.

Millgate, Michael, jt. auth. see Mchaney, Thomas.

Millgate, Michael, ed. see Faulkner, William.

Millgate, Michael, ed. see Gosse, Edmund.

Millgate, Michael, ed. see Hardy, Emma & Hardy, Florence E.

Millgate, Michael, ed. see Hardy, Thomas.

Millgate, Michael, ed. see Tennyson, Alfred Lord.

Millgate, Rachel W., jt. ed. see Millgate, Irvine H.

Millgram, Abraham E. Concepts That Distinguish Judaism, Vol. 5. 1985. pap. 12.00 (0-910250-00-6) Bnai Brith Intl.

— A Short History of Jerusalem. LC 98-27683. 1998. 35.00 (0-7657-6006-1) Aronson.

Millgram, Abraham E., ed. Concepts That Distinguish Judaism. (B'nai B'rith History of the Jewish People Ser.: Vol. V). 368p. (C). 1985. 20.00 (0-910250-01-4); pap. 12.00 (0-685-67350-2) Bnai Brith Intl.

— Creators of the Jewish Experience in the Modern World. (History of the Jewish People Ser.: Vol. II). 384p. (C). 1985. pap. 12.00 (0-910250-04-9) Bnai Brith Intl.

Millgram, Elijah. Practical Induction. LC 96-41362. 192p. 1997. 47.50 (0-674-69597-6) HUP.

Millgram, Elijah. Practical Induction. 184p. 1999. pap. 17.95 (0-674-00073-0) HUP.

Millham, Spencer, et al. Access Disputes in Child-Care. (Illus.). 109p. 1989. 57.95 (0-566-05820-0, Pub. by Avebry) Ashgate Pub Co.

— Lost in Care. 275p. 1986. text 66.95 (0-566-00998-6) Ashgate Pub Co.

Millham, Spencer, ed. see Bullock, Roger & Little, Michael.

Millhauser, Steven. The Barnum Museum. LC 97-23679. 240p. 1997. reprint ed. pap. 12.95 (1-56478-179-8) Dalkey Arch.

— Edwin Mullhouse: The Life & Death of an American Writer, 1943-1954. 305p. 1996. pap. 12.00 (0-679-76652-9) Random.

— Enchanted Night. LC 99-25517. 112p. 1999. 17.00 (0-609-60516-X) Crown.

***Millhauser, Steven.** Enchanted Night. (Contemporaries Ser.). 2000. pap. 11.00 (0-375-70696-8) Vin Bks.

Millhauser, Steven. In the Penny Arcade: Stories. LC 97-51427. 176p. 1998. reprint ed. pap. 11.95 (1-56478-182-8) Dalkey Arch.

— The Knife Thrower & Other Stories. LC 97-45796. 256p. 1998. 22.00 (0-609-60070-2) Crown Pub Group.

— The Knife Thrower & Other Stories. 1999. pap. 12.00 (0-679-78163-3) Vin Bks.

— Little Kingdoms. 1993. 21.00 (0-671-86890-X) S&S Trade.

— Little Kingdoms: Three Novellas. LC 97-34396. 1998. pap. 12.00 (0-375-70143-5) Vin Bks.

— Martin Dressler: The Tale of an American Dreamer. 1997. pap. 12.00 (0-679-78127-7) Vin Bks.

Millhiser, Marlys. Death of the Office Witch. LC 93-19365. 1993. 20.00 (1-883402-02-6) S&S Trade.

— Death of the Office Witch. (Charlie Greene Ser.). 304p. 1995. pap. 5.95 (0-14-024340-2, Penguin Bks) Viking Penguin.

***Millhiser, Marlys.** Killer Commute. LC 00-40255. 2000. write for info. (0-312-26610-3) St Martin.

Millhiser, Marlys. The Mirror. (Illus.). 304p. 1997. reprint ed. pap. 14.95 (0-915230-15-1) Rue Morgue.

— Murder in a Hot Flash: A Charlie Greene Mystery. LC 94-27050. 1995. 20.50 (1-883402-29-8) S&S Trade.

— Nobody Dies in a Casino. LC 99-12859. 288p. 1999. text 22.95 (0-312-20344-6) St Martin.

— Willing Hostage. 256p. 1994. mass mkt. 4.95 (0-7867-0110-2) Carroll & Graf.

Millhollin, Bonnie, jt. auth. see Blackett, Ruth.

Millhollin, Bonnie, jt. auth. see Sherves, Kathey L.

Millhollin, Donna, jt. auth. see Spindel, Robert.

Millhollon, Mary. Microsoft Internet Explorer 3.0 Frontrunner for Macintosh. 1996. pap. 29.99 (1-57610-053-7) Coriolis Grp.

***Millhollon, Mary.** Microsoft Word 2000 Mouse Cheat Sheet. 450p. 1999. 19.99 (0-7897-2114-7) Que.

— Word 2000 - Module III: Forms, Merges & Macros. Nigro, Linea & Savage, Stephanie, eds. (Illus.). 175p. (YA). 1999. pap. write for info. (0-7423-0413-2) ComputerPREP.

Millhollon, Mary, ed. see DeFilippo, Kathleen.

***Millhorn, Jim.** Student's Companion to the World Wide Web: Social Sciences & Humanities Resources. LC 99-41057. 112p. 1999. pap. 18.50 (0-8108-3680-7) Scarecrow.

Millhuff, Charles R. Thunder Overhead: How a Little Boy Survived Chicago. 209p. 1998. pap. 13.95 (1-890622-31-1) Leathers Pub.

***Millian, Lenore Fogelson & Millian, Stephen Jerry.** The Second Wives Club: Secrets for Becoming Lovers for Life. LC 99-31565. 208p. 1999. pap. 14.95 (1-58270-014-1, Pub. by Beyond Words Pub) Publishers Group.

Millian, Louise B. Seasons & Its Weather, Variations & Mood Psychology: Index of New Information. 150p. 1994. 47.50 (0-7883-0052-0); pap. 44.50 (0-7883-0053-9) ABBE Pubs Assn.

Millian, Stephen Jerry, jt. auth. see Millian, Lenore Fogelson.

Millican, Edward. One United People: The Federalist & the National Idea. LC 89-48254. 280p. 1990. text 34.95 (0-8131-1678-3) U Pr of Ky.

Millican-Glenn, Cynthia, ed. see Cannata, Benedene.

Millican, Percy, ed. Index of Wills Proved in the Consistory Court of Norwich: 1550-1603. (British Record Society Index Library: Vol. 73-75). 1969. reprint ed. 95.00 (0-8115-1513-3) Periodicals Srv.

Millican, Peter & Clark, Andy, eds. Machines & Thought: The Legacy of Alan Turing. (Illus.). 308p. 1999. pap. text 24.95 (0-19-823876-2) OUP.

— Machines & Thought: The Legacy of Alan Turing, Vol. I. (Mind Association Occasional Ser.). (Illus.). 308p. 1997. text 55.00 (0-19-823593-3) OUP.

Millican, Peter, jt. ed. see Clark, Andy.

Millican, T. David. dBASE Dialect Software Engineering. 1994. text. write for info. (0-442-00510-5, VNR) Wiley.

Millicap, J. Gordon. The Hyperactive Child with Minimal Brain Dysfunction. (Illus.). 1975. 31.00 (0-8151-5911-0) Mosby Inc.

Millicap, J. Gordon, ed. Learning Disabilities & Related Disorders: Facts & Current Issues. LC 77-73607. (Illus.). 189p. reprint ed. pap. 58.60 (0-8357-6186-X, 203426500089) Bks Demand.

Millicer, Jan. When It Rains. LC 92-31136. (Voyages Ser.). (J). 1993. 2.50 (0-383-03667-4) SRA McGraw.

Millich, E., et al. New Technologies for the Exploration & Exploitation of Oil & Gas Resources, 2 vols., Vol. 1. (C). 1900. lib. bdg. 574.00 (1-85333-058-2) Kluwer Academic.

— New Technologies for the Exploration & Exploitation of Oil & Gas Resources, 2 vols., Vol. 2. (C). 1900. lib. bdg. 108.00 (1-85333-059-0) Kluwer Academic.

Millich, Frank. Interfacial Synthesis Vol. 3: Recent Advances. LC 75-27750. (Illus.). 405p. reprint ed. pap. 125.60 (0-7837-4723-3, 204128500003) Bks Demand.

Millich, Frank & Carraher, Charles E., Jr., eds. Interfacial Synthesis Vol. 1: Fundamentals. LC 75-27750. (Illus.). 312p. reprint ed. pap. 89.00 (0-7837-0979-X, 2041285) Bks Demand.

— Interfacial Synthesis Vol. 2: Polymer Applications & Technology, Vol. 2. LC 75-27750. (Illus.). 560p. reprint ed. pap. 173.60 (0-7837-0719-3, 204104500002) Bks Demand.

Millichamp, A. H. Finance for Non-Financial Managers. 352p. 1995. pap. 70.00 (1-85805-123-1, Pub. by DP Publns) St Mut.

— Foundation Accounting. 512p. 1995. pap. 70.00 (1-85805-108-8, Pub. by DP Publns) St Mut.

Millichap, Denzil, jt. auth. see Matthews, Paul.

An Asterisk (*) at the beginning of an entry indicates that the title is appearing for the first time.

*Millichap, J. Gordon. Attention Deficit Hyperactivity & Learning Disorders: Questions & Answers. LC 98-91663. (Illus.). xi, 253 p. 1998. pap. 14.95 (0-9629115-4-2) PNB Pub.

Millichap, J. Gordon. Environmental Poisons in Our Food. LC 92-91280. (Illus.). 271p. 1993. 29.95 (0-9629115-7-7) PNB Pub.

— The Hyperactive Child with Minimal Brain Dysfunction: Questions & Answers. LC 75-17008. (Illus.). 179p. reprint ed. pap. 55.50 (0-8357-6149-5, 203426600089) Bks Demand.

— Is Our Water Safe to Drink? A Guide to Drinking Water Hazards & Health Risks. LC 95-67490. (Illus.). 212p. 1995. 21.95 (0-9629115-5-0) PNB Pub.

— Progress in Pediatric Neurology I. LC 91-90076. 598p. 1991. text 57.95 (0-9629115-0-X) PNB Pub.

— Progress in Pediatric Neurology III. LC 94-1233. 611p. (C). 1997. 64.95 (0-9629115-6-9) PNB Pub.

— Progress in Pediatric Neurology II. LC 94-66683. (Illus.). 550p. 1994. 64.95 (0-9629115-8-5) PNB Pub.

Millichap, Joseph R. George Catlin. LC 77-76200. (Western Writers Ser.: No. 27). (Illus.). 48p. 1977. pap. 4.95 (0-88430-051-X) Boise St U W Writ Ser.

— Robert Penn Warren: A Study of the Short Fiction. LC 92-14380. (Twayne's Studies in Short Fiction: No. 39). 150p. 1992. 23.95 (0-8057-8346-6, Twayne) Mac Lib Ref.

Millichap, Nancy. Foster Care. LC 93-23237. (Changing Family Ser.). (Illus.). 128p. (YA). (gr. 7-12). 1994. lib. bdg. 24.00 (0-531-11081-8) Watts.

Millidge, Edward A. Esperanto-English Dictionary. (ENG & ESP.). 43.95 (0-87557-018-6) Saphrograph.

*Millidge, Judith. Sacred Imagery. 144p. 1998. write for info. (1-57215-252-4) World Pubns.

*Millier. Nuts, Bolts & Magnetrons: A Practical Guide for Industrial Marketers. 320p. 2000. pap. 39.95 (0-471-85325-9) Wiley.

Millier. Strategy & Marketing. LC 99-13345. 248p. 1999. 60.95 (0-471-98621-6) Wiley.

Millier, Brett C. Elizabeth Bishop: Life & the Memory of It. LC 92-8548. 602p. 1993. 45.00 (0-520-07978-7, Pub. by U CA Pr) Cal Prin Full Svc.

— Elizabeth Bishop: Life & the Memory of It. 602p. 1995. pap. 18.95 (0-520-20345-3, Pub. by U CA Pr) Cal Prin Full Svc.

Milligan, jt. auth. see Bowman.

*Milligan, Barbara. Desperate Hope: Experiencing God in the Midst of Breast Cancer. LC 99-34661. 216p. 1999. pap. 11.99 (0-8308-1924-X) InterVarsity.

Milligan, Barbara, ed. see Eberle, Harold R.

Milligan, Barry. Pleasures & Pains: Opium & the Orient in Nineteenth-Century British Culture. 192p. (C). 1995. text 29.50 (0-8139-1571-6) U Pr of Va.

Milligan, Bryce. Lawmen: Stories of Men Who Tamed the West. LC 94-70797. (Disney's American Frontier Ser.: Bk. 14). (Illus.). 80p. (J). (gr. 1-4). 1994. pap. 3.50 (0-7868-4006-4, Pub. by Disney Pr); lib. bdg. 12.89 (0-7868-5005-1, Pub. by Disney Pr) Little.

— Litany Sung at Hell's Gate. (Illus.). x, 36p. (Orig.). 1990. pap. 8.00 (0-913983-08-X) M & A Edns.

— With the Wind, Kevin Dolan. LC 86-70018. (Multicultural Texas Ser.). (Illus.). 194p. (YA). (gr. 7 up). 1992. pap. 7.95 (0-931722-45-4) Corona Pub.

— Working the Stone. deluxe limited ed. (Illus.). 48p. 1993. pap. 15.00 (0-930324-30-7) Wings Pr.

Milligan, Bryce, ed. Corazon del Norte: A Selection of North Texas Latino Writing. (Illus.). viii, 68p. (Orig.). 1996. pap. 10.00 (0-930324-31-5) Wings Pr.

— Linking Roots: Writing by Six Women with Distinct Ethnic Heritages. 56p. 1993. pap. 7.00 (0-913983-07-1) M & A Edns.

*Milligan, Bryce & McDaniels, Preston. The King of Ireland's Son. LC 00-32042. (Illus.). (J). 2001. write for info. (0-8234-1573-2) Holiday.

Milligan, Bryce, et al. Floricanto Si! A Collection of Latina Poetry. LC 97-34445. xxxv, 310p. 1998. pap. 14.95 (0-14-058893-0) Viking Penguin.

Milligan, Bryce, ed. & intro. see Garcia-Galaviz, Victoria, et al.

Milligan, Charles B. Spenser & the Table Round: A Study in the Contemporaneous Background for Spenser's Use of the Arthurian Legend. 1977. lib. bdg. 59.95 (0-8490-2656-3) Gordon Pr.

Milligan, David & Watts-Miller, William, eds. Liberalism, Citizenship, & Autonomy. LC 92-9982. (Avebury Series in Philosophy). 260p. 1992. 82.95 (1-85628-280-5, Pub. by Avebury) Ashgate Pub Co.

Milligan, Debra. Marshmallow Autumn: Fire Safety. (Child Safety Ser.). (Illus.). 48p. 1986. 5.95 (0-513-01830-1) Denison.

Milligan, Don. Sex-Life: A Critical Commentary on the History of Sexuality. LC 92-36245. 169p. (C). 49.95 (0-7453-0611-X, Pub. by Pluto GBR); pap. 15.95 (0-7453-0612-8, Pub. by Pluto GBR) Stylus Pub VA.

Milligan, E. E., jt. auth. see Palmeri, Joseph.

Milligan, Edward H. Quakers & Railways. 1999. pap. 21.00 (1-85072-099-1, Pub. by W Sessions) St Mut.

Milligan, Elaine G. Forever in His Presence. (Illus.). 125p. (Orig.). 1995. pap. 7.00 (0-9646187-0-2) Milligan Pub.

Milligan, G. & Moulton, James H. The Vocabulary of the Greek Testament. 736p. 1997. reprint ed. 39.95 (1-56563-271-0) Hendrickson MA.

— The Vocabulary of the Greek Testament: Illustrated from the Papyri & Other Non-Literary Sources, 2 vols. 1977. lib. bdg. 250.00 (0-8490-2800-0) Gordon Pr.

Milligan, George, ed. Selections from the Greek Papyri. LC 76-103654. (Select Bibliographies Reprint Ser.). 1977. 21.95 (0-8369-5154-9) Ayer.

Milligan, George, et al, eds. G Proteins & Signal Transduction. (Biochemical Society Symposium Ser.: Vol. 56). 172p. (C). 1990. 110.50 (1-85578-001-1, Pub. by Portland Pr Ltd) Ashgate Pub Co.

Milligan, Graeme, ed. Signal Transduction: A Practical Approach. 2nd ed. LC 99-26199. 209. (Illus.). 424p. 1999. text 115.00 (0-19-963721-0); pap. text 60.00 (0-19-963720-2) OUP.

Milligan, Graeme & Wakelam, Michael, eds. G Proteins: Signal Transduction & Disease. (Illus.). 247p. 1992. text 104.00 (0-12-497515-1) Acad Pr.

Milligan, H. V. Stephen Collins Foster. 1977. 250.00 (0-87968-313-9) Gordon Pr.

Milligan, Hugh H., ed. Tech Tips. (Illus.). 176p. (Orig.). 1993. teacher ed. write for info. (0-9635225-0-7) Jensen Intercep.

Milligan, Ira & Milligan, Judy. Understanding the Dreams You Dream. rev. ed. 264p. 1997. pap. 10.99 (1-56043-284-5, Treasure Hse) Destiny Image.

*Milligan, Ira L. Euroclydon: Illustrating the Four Winds. 194p. 1999. pap. write for info. (0-7392-0388-6, PO3608) Morris Pubng.

Milligan, J. E., rev. Brown's Signalling: How to Learn the International Code of Signals. rev. ed. (C). 1987. 80.00 (0-85174-350-1) St Mut.

Milligan, Jacquie. Lazy Day Adventure: Water Safety. (Child Safety Ser.). (Illus.). 48p. 1986. pap. 5.95 (0-513-01832-8) Denison.

— Spring Cleaning: Household Poisons. (Child Safety Ser.). (Illus.). 48p. 1986. 4.95 (0-513-01829-8) Denison.

Milligan, Jennifer E. The Forgotten Generation: French Women Writers of the Inter-War Period. LC 96-43696. (Berg French Studies). (Illus.). 224p. 1997. 55.00 (1-85973-113-9, Pub. by Berg Pubs); pap. 19.50 (1-85973-118-X, Pub. by Berg Pubs) NYU Pr.

Milligan, Joe. Guide to the Colorado Mountains: Interstate-70 Skylines. LC 97-2937. (Peakfinders Ser.: Vol. 2). 1997. pap. text 2.98 (1-56579-191-6, A157) Westcliffe Pubs.

— Roadside Guide to the Colorado Mountains: Interstate 25 Skylines. LC 95-71149. (Peakfinders Ser.: Vol. 1). (Illus.). 112p. (Orig.). 1996. pap. 16.95 (0-9647522-0-4) Westcliffe Pubs.

Milligan, John. The Resilient Pioneers: A History of the Elastic Rail Spike Company. (Illus.). 1977. 24.95 (0-8464-0791-4) Beekman Pubs.

Milligan, John D. Gunboats Down the Mississippi. LC 79-6119. (Navies & Men Ser.). (Illus.). 1980. reprint ed. lib. bdg. 35.95 (0-405-13047-3) Ayer.

Milligan, John E. Celestial Navigation by H. O. 249. LC 74-1464. (Illus.). 111p. 1974. pap. 7.50 (0-87033-191-4) Cornell Maritime.

Milligan, Judy, jt. auth. see Milligan, Ira.

Milligan, Letica, ed. see Brown, Betty A.

Milligan, Lynda S. & Smith, Nancy J. More Sewing Machine Fun. Holmes, Sharon, ed. (I'll Teach Myself Ser.). (Illus.). 72p. (J). (gr. 2-8). 1993. spiral bd. 15.95 (1-880972-05-0) Pssblts Denver.

— P. S. I Love You: Baby Collection. Holmes, Sharon, ed. (Illus.). 80p. (Orig.). 1990. pap. 16.95 (0-9622477-2-3) Pssblts Denver.

Milligan, Lynda S., jt. auth. see Smith, Nancy.

Milligan, Lynda S., jt. auth. see Smith, Nancy J.

Milligan, Martin, jt. auth. see Magee, Bryan.

Milligan, Martin, tr. see Marx, Karl.

Milligan, Martin, tr. see Marx, Karl & Engels, Friedrich.

Milligan, Maureen. Federally Qualified Health Centers: The First "Essential Community Providers" (Working Paper Ser.: No. 82). 38p. 1995. pap. 5.50 (0-89940-558-4) LBJ Sch Pub Aff.

Milligan, Maureen A. Essential Community Provider Issues in Medicaid Managed Care. (Special Project Reports). 139p. 1997. pap. 15.00 (0-89940-904-0) LBJ Sch Pub Aff.

— Hospital-Based Essential Community Providers: Challenges for Public Hospitals, Teaching Hospitals, & Academic Health Science Centers in Medicaid Managed Care. (Working Paper Ser.: Vol. 83). 1995. pap. 5.50 (0-89940-564-9) LBJ Sch Pub Aff.

Milligan, Maureen A., jt. ed. see More, Ellen S.

Milligan, Melba J. Diet - In Life, Food, Old Age & Research: Index of New Information with Authors & Subjects. rev. ed. LC 96-7238. 179p. 1996. 47.50 (0-7883-1034-8); pap. 44.50 (0-7883-1035-6) ABBE Pubs Assn.

— Diet - Investigations, Research & Results: Index of New Information with Authors & Subjects. 180p. 1993. 47.50 (1-55914-844-6); pap. 44.50 (1-55914-845-4) ABBE Pubs Assn.

— Food Mania & Over-Eating: Index of Modern Authors & Subjects with Guide for Rapid Research. LC 90-56314. 160p. 1991. 47.50 (1-55914-416-5); pap. 44.50 (1-55914-417-3) ABBE Pubs Assn.

Milligan, Peter. Engima. (Illus.). 208p. 1995. mass mkt. 19.95 (1-56389-192-1, Pub. by DC Comics) Time Warner.

— Further Adventures of Cyclops & Phoenix. (Illus.). 96p. 1997. pap. text 12.95 (0-7851-0556-5) Marvel Entrprs.

— Skin. 1996. pap. text 8.95 (1-85809-000-8) Kitchen Sink.

Milligan, Peter & Young, A. Tank Girl Movie Adaptation. LC 96-119231. (Illus.). 64p. 1995. pap. 5.95 (1-56389-219-7, Vertigo) DC Comics.

Milligan, Robert A. & Maloney, Thomas R. Human Resource Management for Golf Course Superintendents. 185p. (C). 1996. text 34.95 (1-57504-038-7, Ann Arbor Press) Sleepng Bear.

Milligan, Robert H. Fetish Folk of West Africa. LC 73-116017. reprint ed. 47.50 (0-404-00200-5) AMS Pr.

Milligan, Rosie. Getting Out of Debt Made Simple. 52p. 1991. pap. text 20.00 (1-881524-01-9) Milligan Bks.

— How to Teach the Black Male Child about His Sexuality. 1992. pap. text 14.95 (1-881524-05-1) Milligan Bks.

— Negroes, Colored People, Blacks, & African Americans in America. 103p. 1992. pap. text 13.95 (1-881524-03-5) Milligan Bks.

— Nigger, Please: Bold, Raw, Provocative Truth. LC 97-104348. (Orig.). 1996. pap. 14.95 (1-881524-06-X) Milligan Bks.

— The Other Woman: The Real Truth about Women & Their Secret Relationships. 216p. (Orig.). 1997. pap. 14.95 (1-881524-07-8) Milligan Bks.

— Resource Guide for African-American Speakers & Writers. LC 99-159569. 132p. 1997. pap. 49.95 (1-881524-08-6) Milligan Bks.

— Satisfying the Black Man Sexually Made Simple. LC 95-218410. 1992. pap. text 14.95 (1-881524-04-3) Milligan Bks.

— Satisfying the Black Woman Sexually Made Simple. 185p. 1990. pap. text 14.95 (1-881524-00-0) Milligan Bks.

— Starting a Business Made Simple. 66p. 1991. pap. text 20.00 (1-881524-02-7) Milligan Bks.

— Why Black Men Choose White Women. 150p. 1998. pap. 12.95 (1-881524-19-1) Milligan Bks.

Milligan, S. R., ed. The Oxford Reviews of Reproductive Biology, Vol. 13. (Illus.). 328p. 1991. 89.00 (0-19-857761-3) OUP.

— Oxford Reviews of Reproductive Biology, Vol. 14. (Illus.). 384p. 1992. text 110.00 (0-19-262241-2) OUP.

— Oxford Reviews of Reproductive Biology, Vol. 15. (Illus.). 384p. 1993. 79.00 (0-19-262346-X) OUP.

Milligan, Sean Paul. Quonset Point Naval Air Station. LC 96-217641. (Images of America Ser.). 128p. 1996. pap. 16.99 (0-7524-0274-9) Arcadia Publng.

— Quonset Point Naval Air Station II. (Images of America Ser.). 1998. pap. write for info. (0-7385-0037-2) Arcadia Publng.

Milligan, Sharlene, ed. see Good, John & Pierce, Ken.

Milligan, Sharlene, ed. see Plumb, Sally.

Milligan, Sharlene, ed. see Wile, Darwin & Duffy, Katy.

Milligan, Spike. Bible According to Spike Milligan. 1994. pap. 11.95 (0-14-023970-7, Pub. by Pnguin Bks Ltd) Trafalgar.

Milligan, Spike. Black Beauty According to Spike Milligan. 128p. 1996. 14.95 (1-85227-615-0, Pub. by Virgin Bks) London Brdge.

Milligan, Spike. Hidden Words. 192p. pap. 13.95 (0-14-058788-8, Pub. by Pnguin Bks Ltd) Trafalgar.

— It Ends with Magic. 1992. pap. 11.95 (0-14-013912-5, Pub. by Pnguin Bks Ltd) Trafalgar.

Milligan, Spike. Lady Chatterly According to Spike Milligan. large type ed. 21.95 (1-85695-379-3, Pub. by ISIS Lrg Prnt) Transaction Pubs.

Milligan, Spike. Lady Chatterly's Lover. 1995. pap. 11.95 (0-14-024299-6, Pub. by Pnguin Bks Ltd) Trafalgar.

Milligan, Spike. Mussolini: His Part in My Downfall. large type ed. 21.95 (1-85695-182-0, Pub. by ISIS Lrg Prnt) Transaction Pubs.

Milligan, Spike. Peace Work. 240p. 1992. pap. 12.95 (0-14-014970-8, Pub. by Pnguin Bks Ltd) Trafalgar.

Milligan, Spike. Rommel? large type ed. 21.95 (1-85695-187-1, Pub. by ISIS Lrg Prnt) Transaction Pubs.

Milligan, Stu. The Rainbow Quest: Anuenue in the Race for the Trans Pac Cup. (Illus.). 184p. (Orig.). 1997. pap. 18.95 (0-913611-09-3) W E C Plant.

Milligan, Thomas A., jt. auth. see Diaz, Leo.

Milligan, Thomas B. The Concerto & London's Musical Culture in the Late Eighteenth Century. LC 83-5915. (Studies in Musicology: No. 69). 386p. reprint ed. pap. 119.70 (0-8357-1441-1, 207051200097) Bks Demand.

Milligan, Thomas B. & Graue, Jerald C. Johann Baptist Cramer (1771-1858) A Thematic Catalogue of His Works. LC 92-275. 1994. lib. bdg. 60.00 (0-945193-41-6) Pendragon NY.

Milligan, Timothy S. Van, see Van Milligan, Timothy S.

*Milligan, Tra L. Every Dreamer's Handbook: The Dreamer's Solution to Prickly Problems: or Don't Sit on the Cactus. LC 99-93859. 178p. 1999. pap. write for info. (0-7392-0207-3, PO3218) Morris Pubng.

Milligan, V., ed. see International Conference on Stability in Open Pit.

Milligan, William. The Ascension & Heavenly Priesthood of Our Lord. 416p. 1977. reprint ed. 14.00 (0-87921-034-6) Attic Pr.

Milligen, M. Jane Van, see Gray, Bill & Van Milligen, M. Jane.

Milligen, M. Jane Van, see Van Milligen, M. Jane, ed.

Millligan, Angela. Simple Guide to Australia: Customs & Etiquette. 2000. pap. text 8.95 (1-86034-061-X) Global Bks.

Millikan, Keith W., jt. ed. see Saclarides, Theodore J.

Millikan, Larry E., jt. ed. see Parish, Lawrence C.

Millikan, Marilyn. Puppet Programs, No. 2. 52p. 1980. pap. 6.99 (0-8341-9242-X, MP-610) Lillenas.

Millikan, Max F., ed. National Economic Planning. (Universities-National Bureau Conference Ser.: No. 19). 423p. 1967. 110.00 (0-87014-310-7) Natl Bur Econ Res.

Millikan, Max F. & Rostow, Walt W. A Proposal: Key to an Effective Foreign Policy. LC 76-39842. 170p. 1977. reprint ed. lib. bdg. 49.75 (0-8371-9346-X, MIAPR, Greenwood Pr) Greenwood.

Millikan, Robert Andrews. The Autobiography of Robert A. Millikan. Cohen, I. Bernard, ed. LC 79-7975. (Three Centuries of Science in America Ser.). (Illus.). 1980. reprint ed. lib. bdg. 29.95 (0-405-12558-5) Ayer.

— The Electron: Its Isolation & Measurement & the Determination of Some of Its Properties. DuMond, Jesse W., ed. LC 63-20910. 330p. reprint ed. pap. 102.30 (0-608-30627-4, 201998000015) Bks Demand.

— Science & Life. LC 76-93360. (Essay Index Reprint Ser.). 1977. 17.95 (0-8369-1307-8) Ayer.

— Science & the New Civilization. LC 76-142671. (Essay Index Reprint Ser.). 1977. reprint ed. 20.95 (0-8369-2418-5) Ayer.

Millikan, Ruth G. Language, Thought, & Other Biological Categories: New Foundation for Realism. 368p. 1987. reprint ed. pap. text 22.00 (0-262-63115-6, Bradford Bks) MIT Pr.

— White Queen Psychology & Other Essays for Alice. (Illus.). 400p. 1995. pap. text 22.00 (0-262-63162-8, Bradford Bks) MIT Pr.

*Millikan, Ruth Garrett. On Clear & Confused Ideas: An Essay about Substance Concepts. LC 99-58059. 2000. write for info. (0-521-62386-3); write for info. (0-521-62553-X) Cambridge U Pr.

Milliken, jt. auth. see Toner.

Milliken, Andy. From the Kwai to the Kingdom LC 86-125946. 156 p. 1985. pap. write for info. (0-551-01257-9, Pub. by M Pickering) Harper SF.

Milliken, Bettina S. All about Us: Orang Utans. (Illus.). 56p. 1997. pap., spiral bd. 12.95 (1-880470-46-2) Creative Des.

Milliken, Charles F. History of Ontario County, N.Y., & Its People, 2 vols., Set. (Illus.). 1996. reprint ed. lib. bdg. 110.00 (0-8328-5215-5) Higginson Bk Co.

Milliken, Diane. Capitol Cuisine. 288p. 1996. pap. 15.95 (0-393-31579-7) Norton.

Milliken, Douglas L., jt. auth. see Milliken, William F.

*Milliken, G. A. & Johnson, D. E. Analysis of Messy Data: Non-Replicated Experiments. Vol. 3. 304p. 1999. 69.95 (0-8493-0317-6) CRC Pr.

Milliken, George A., jt. auth. see Johnson, Dallas E.

Milliken, J. G. & Taylor, G. Metropolitan Water Management. (Water Resources Monograph Ser.: Vol. 6). 180p. 1981. 10.00 (0-87590-307-X) Am Geophysical.

Milliken, Jane, jt. auth. see Northcott, Herbert C.

Milliken, Linda. Alphabet Patterns. (Illus.). 64p. (J). (ps-2). 1993. pap. 6.95 (1-56472-008-X) Edupress Inc.

— Alphabet Pocket Fun: Letter Sound & Word Recognition Activities. (Illus.). 64p. 1994. pap., student ed. 6.95 (1-56472-019-5) Edupress Inc.

Milliken, Linda. Canada Photo Fun Activities. Rogers, Kathy, ed. (Social Studies Photo Fun Activities Ser.). (Illus.). 8p. 1997. 6.95 (1-56472-078-0) Edupress Inc.

Milliken, Linda. Category Pictionary: Thematic Skillbuilder. (Illus.). 64p. 1994. pap., wbk. ed. 6.95 (1-56472-020-9) Edupress Inc.

— China Activity Book: Arts, Crafts, Cooking & Historical Aids. Rogers, Kathy, ed. (Illus.). 48p. (J). (gr. 3-6). 1995. pap., teacher ed., wbk. ed. 6.95 (1-56472-069-1) Edupress Inc.

Milliken, Linda. China Photo Fun Activities. Rogers, Kathy, ed. (Social Studies Photo Fun Activities Ser.). (Illus.). 8p. 1995. 6.95 (1-56472-070-5) Edupress Inc.

Milliken, Linda. Civil War Era Activity Book: Arts, Crafts, Cooking & Historical Aids. Rogers, Kathy, ed. (Illus.). 48p. (J). 1996. pap., wbk. ed. 6.95 (1-56472-108-6) Edupress Inc.

— Classroom Kickoff. 304p. 1992. pap. 21.50 (1-56472-001-2) Edupress Inc.

— Colonial American Activity Book: Explore Colonial Times Through Art, Crafts, Cooking & Historical Aids. abr. ed. Rogers, Kathy, ed. (Illus.). 48p. (J). (gr. 2-6). 1992. pap., wbk. ed. 6.95 (1-56472-003-9) Edupress Inc.

— Fingerplays & Action Rhymes. Rogers, Kathy, ed. (Illus.). 144p. (J). 1996. pap., wbk. ed. 14.95 (1-56472-101-9) Edupress Inc.

— Frontier American Activity Book: Art, Crafts, Cooking. (Illus.). 1990. pap. 6.95 (1-56472-017-9) Edupress Inc.

*Milliken, Linda. Fun & Fancy Alphabet Lined Writing Paper. (Illus.). 32p. 1999. teacher ed. 4.95 (1-56472-177-9) Edupress Inc.

— Fun & Fancy Animal Lined Writing Paper. (Illus.). 32p. 1999. teacher ed. Price not set. (1-56472-176-0) Edupress Inc.

— Fun & Fancy School Lined Writing Paper. (Illus.). 32p. 2000. teacher ed. 4.95 (1-56472-178-7) Edupress Inc.

— Fun & Fancy Seasonal Lined Writing Papers. (Illus.). 32p. 1998. teacher ed. 4.95 (1-56472-110-8) Edupress Inc.

Milliken, Linda. Holiday & Seasonal Patterns: Integrate Holiday & Seasonal Patterns with Thematic Activities Across the Curriculum - Grades PS-2. (Illus.). 40p. 1995. pap., wbk. ed. 5.95 (1-56472-058-6) Edupress Inc.

— Ideas at Your Fingertips: Alphabet & Phonics Activities. Crafts. Cookery. Rainy Day & Outdoor Games. Art & Gift Projects. Number Recognition & Math Activities - Grades K-2. Celecia, Deneen & Rogers, Kathy, eds. (Illus.). 304p. 1995. pap., wbk. ed. 24.95 (1-56472-064-0) Edupress Inc.

— Inexpensive Ideas for Classroom Environments. Celecia, Deneen, ed. (Illus.). 48p. 1994. pap., student ed. 6.95 (1-56472-052-7) Edupress Inc.

Milliken, Linda. Landforms Photo Fun Activities. Rogers, Kathy, ed. (Science Photo Fun Activities Ser.). (Illus.). 8p. 1997. 6.95 (1-56472-083-7) Edupress Inc.

Milliken, Linda. Literature Patterns. (Illus.). 128p. 1993. pap. 11.95 (1-56472-007-1) Edupress Inc.

— Low Cost Ways to Brighten Displays. Celecia, Deneen, ed. (Illus.). 48p. 1994. pap., student ed. 6.95 (1-56472-051-9) Edupress Inc.

— Make Your Own Spanish Category Pictionary: Thematic Skillbuilder. (Illus.). 64p. (J). (gr. k-2). 1994. pap., student ed. 6.95 (1-56472 030-6) Edupress Inc.

— Medieval Times Activity Book. Celecia, Deneen, ed. (Illus.). 48p. 1995. pap., student ed. 6.95 (1-56472-049-7) Edupress Inc.

— Medieval Times Photo Fun Activities. Celecia, Deneen, ed. (Illus.). 8p. (J). (gr. 3-6). 1995. pap. 6.95 (1-56472-050-0) Edupress Inc.

— Multicurricular Springboards & Starters. (Illus.). 144p. 1993. pap. 12.95 (1-56472-010-1) Edupress Inc.

An Asterisk (*) at the beginning of an entry indicates that the title is appearing for the first time.

*Milliken, Linda. My Journal: Primary. Rogers, Kathy, ed. (Illus.). 32p. 1998. 1.99 (1-56472-143-4) Edupress Inc.

— My Journal: Upper Grade. Rogers, Kathy, ed. (Illus.). 32p. 1998. 1.99 (1-56472-144-2) Edupress Inc.

Milliken, Linda. My Parts of Speech Dictionary. Rogers, Kathy, ed. (Illus.). 32p. 1999. pap., teacher ed., wbk. ed. 1.99 (1-56472-610-X) Edupress Inc.

*Milliken, Linda. My Story Book: Primary. Rogers, Kathy, ed. (Illus.). 32p. 1998. 1.99 (1-56472-145-0) Edupress Inc.

— My Story Book: Upper Grade. Rogers, Kathy, ed. (Illus.). 32p. 1998. 1.99 (1-56472-146-9) Edupress Inc.

Milliken, Linda. Native American Activity Book: Arts, Crafts, Cooking & Historical Aids. abr. ed. Rogers, Kathy, ed. (Illus.). 48p. 1980. pap., wbk. ed. 6.95 (1-56472-000-4) Edupress Inc.

— Ocean Life Activity Book. Rogers, Kathy, ed. (Hands-On Science Ser.). (Illus.). 48p. 1998. pap., wbk. ed. 6.95 (1-56472-116-7) Edupress Inc.

— Oodles of Writing Activities. 72p. 1992. pap. 7.95 (1-56472-002-0) Edupress Inc.

— Patriotic Symbols Activity Book. Rogers, Kathy, ed. (Hands-On Heritage Activity Bks.). (Illus.). 48p. (J). (gr. 2-6). 1996. pap. 6.95 (1-56472-075-6) Edupress Inc.

Milliken, Linda. Patriotic Symbols Photo Fun Activities. Lorseyedi, Barb & Rogers, Kathy, eds. (Social Studies Photo Fun Activities Ser.). (Illus.). 8p. 1996. 6.95 (1-56472-076-4) Edupress Inc.

— Photo History Activities: Civil Rights Events. Rogers, Kathy, ed. (Illus.). 8p. 1996. 6.95 (1-56472-094-2) Edupress Inc.

— Photo History Activities: Civil Rights Profiles. Rogers, Kathy, ed. (Illus.). 8p. 1996. 6.95 (1-56472-095-0) Edupress Inc.

— Photo History Activities: Civil War Events. (Illus.). 8p. 1996. 6.95 (1-56472-098-5) Edupress Inc.

— Photo History Activities: Civil War Profiles. (Illus.). 8p. 1996. 6.95 (1-56472-099-3) Edupress Inc.

— Photo History Activities: Revolutionary War Events. Rogers, Kathy, ed. (Illus.). 8p. 1996. 6.95 (1-56472-096-9) Edupress Inc.

— Photo History Activities: Revolutionary War Profiles. Rogers, Kathy, ed. (Illus.). 8p. 1996. 6.95 (1-56472-097-7) Edupress Inc.

— Photo History Activities: World War II. (Illus.). 8p. 1996. 6.95 (1-56472-104-3) Edupress Inc.

— Photo History Activities: World War II Events. (Illus.). 8p. 1996. 6.95 (1-56472-100-0) Edupress Inc.

Milliken, Linda. Poem Patterns: Integrate Poems & Pattern Projects with Thematic Activities Across the Curriculum - Grades PS-2. (Illus.). 40p. 1995. pap., wbk. ed. 5.95 (1-56472-059-4) Edupress Inc.

*Milliken, Linda. Printing Practice Plus: Modern. Rogers, Kathy, ed. (Illus.). 32p. 1998. 4.95 (1-56472-114-0) Edupress Inc.

Milliken, Linda. Printing Practice Plus/Traditional. 32p. 1998. wbk. ed. 4.95 (1-56472-113-2) Edupress Inc.

— Puppet Patterns: Integrate Easy-to-Make Puppets with Thematic Activities Across the Curriculum. (Illus.). 40p. 1995. pap., wbk. ed. 5.95 (1-56472-060-8) Edupress Inc.

— Quick Learning Kits: Art & Literature. 96p. 1992. pap., teacher ed. 8.95 (1-56472-004-7) Edupress Inc.

— Quick Learning Kits: Language & Social Studies. 96p. 1992. pap., teacher ed. 8.95 (1-56472-005-5) Edupress Inc.

— Quick Learning Kits: Math & Science. 96p. 1992. pap., teacher ed. 8.95 (1-56472-006-3) Edupress Inc.

*Milliken, Linda. Renaissance Activity Book. Rogers, Kathy, ed. (Illus.). 48p. 2000. pap. 6.95 (1-56472-167-1) Edupress Inc.

— Renaissance Photo Fun Activites. Rogers, Kathy, ed. (Illus.). 8p. 2000. pap. 6.95 (1-56472-168-X) Edupress Inc.

Milliken, Linda. Revolutionary War Era Activity Book: Arts, Crafts, Cooking & Historical Aids. Rogers, Kathy, ed. (Illus.). 48p. (J). 1996. pap., wbk. ed. 6.95 (1-56472-107-8) Edupress Inc.

— Scissor Skill Patterns. (Illus.). 72p. (J). (ps-2). 1993. pap. 7.95 (1-56472-009-8) Edupress Inc.

— Seasonal & Holiday Springboards & Starters. (Illus.). 144p. (J). (gr. k-6). 1993. pap. 12.95 (1-56472-011-X) Edupress Inc.

— Solar System Activity Book. Rogers, Kathy, ed. (Hands-On Science Ser.). (Illus.). 48p. 1998. pap., wbk. ed. 6.95 (1-56472-124-8) Edupress Inc.

Milliken, Linda. Space Exploration Photo Fun Activities. Rogers, Kathy, ed. (Science Photo Fun Activities Ser.). (Illus.). 8p. 1997. 6.95 (1-56472-086-1) Edupress Inc.

Milliken, Linda & Rogers, Kathy. Canada Activity Book: Arts, Crafts, Cooking & Historical Aids. (Hands-On Heritage Activity Bks.). (Illus.). 48p. (Orig.). (J). (gr. 2-6). 1997. pap., wbk. ed. 6.95 (1-56472-077-2) Edupress Inc.

Milliken, Linda, ed. see Brown, Karen & Engel, Holly.

Milliken, Linda, ed. see Celecia, Deneen.

Milliken, Linda, ed. see Engel, Holly & Brown, Karen.

Milliken, Linda, ed. see Hamman, Joyce.

Milliken, Linda, ed. see Loreen, Wendy.

Milliken, Linda, ed. see Shaw, Nancy & Stout, Charlene.

Milliken, Mary E. Understanding Human Behavior: A Guide for Health Care Providers. 4th ed. LC 86-16758. 304p. (C). 1987. pap. 28.95 (0-8273-2797-8); text 28.50 (0-8273-2798-6) Delmar.

— Understanding Human Behavior: A Guide for Health Care Providers. 4th ed. LC 86-16758. 304p. (C). 1987. teacher ed. 12.00 (0-8273-2799-4) Delmar.

— Understanding Human Behavior: A Guide for Health Care Providers. 5th ed. LC 92-14880. 78p. 1993. pap. 29.95 (0-8273-5473-8) Delmar.

— Understanding Human Behavior: A Guide for Health Care Providers. 5th ed. LC 92-14880. 78p. 1993. pap., teacher ed., student ed. 14.00 (0-8273-5475-4) Delmar.

— Understanding Human Behavior: A Guide for Health Care Providers. 6th ed. LC 97-13707. 576p. (C). 1997. mass mkt. 44.95 (0-8273-8221-9) Delmar.

Milliken, Mary S. City Cuisine. 1994. pap. 14.95 (0-688-13177-8, Hearst) Hearst Commns.

Milliken, Mary S., et al. Cooking with Too Hot Tamales: Recipes & Tips from TV Food's Network Spiciest Cooking Duo. LC 96-28599. 240p. 1997. 22.00 (0-688-15121-3, Wm Morrow) Morrow Avon.

— Mesa Mexicana. LC 93-43099. 262p. 1994. 17.95 (0-688-10649-8, Wm Morrow) Morrow Avon.

— Mexican Cooking for Dummies. (For Dummies Ser.). (Illus.). 384p. 1999. pap. 19.99 (0-7645-5169-8, Dummies Trade Pr) IDG Bks.

Milliken, R. & Wiberg, Randy S. Archaeological Investigations of the Mussel Rock Site, CA-SMa-72, San Mateo County, California. (Illus.). 263p. (C). 1986. reprint ed. pap. text 27.50 (1-55567-436-4) Coyote Press.

Milliken, Randall. Ethnogeography & Ethnohistory of the Big Sur District, California State Park System During the 1770-1810 Time Period. (Illus.). 96p. (C). 1990. reprint ed. pap. text 10.94 (1-55567-441-0) Coyote Press.

Milliken, Randall & Blackburn, Thomas C. A Time of Little Choice: The Disintegration of Tribal Culture in the San Francisco Bay Area 1769-1810. (Ballena Press Anthropological Papers: No. 43). 380p. 1995. pap. 24.95 (0-87919-131-7) Ballena Pr.

— A Time of Little Choice: The Disintegration of Tribal Culture in the San Francisco Bay Area 1769-1810. (Anthropological Papers: No. 43). 380p. (C). 1995. 32.95 (0-87919-132-5) Ballena Pr.

Milliken, Randall & Hildebrandt, William. Culture Change along the Eastern Sierra Nevada/Cascade Front Vol. V: Honey Lake Basin. fac. ed. (Far Western Anthropological Research Group, Inc. Ser.). 371p. (C). 1997. reprint ed. pap. text 38.75 (1-55567-721-5) Coyote Press.

*Milliken, Randall, et al. The Moss Landing Hill Site: A Technical Report on Archaeological Studies at CA-MNT-234. 432p. 1999. pap. text 45.00 (1-55567-926-9) Coyote Press.

Milliken, Randall T., jt. auth. see Shoup, Laurence H.

Milliken, Randy. Ethnohistory of the Rumsen. Dietz, Stephen A., ed. (Northern California Anthropological Group Ser.: No. 2). (Illus.). 130p. (C). 1987. reprint ed. pap. text 14.38 (1-55567-477-1) Coyote Press.

Milliken, Robert I. With Hearts on Fire. 142p. 1997. pap. 9.99 (1-84030-012-4) Emerald House Group Inc.

Milliken, Stephen F. Chester Himes: A Critical Appraisal. LC 75-44081. 320p. reprint ed. pap. 99.20 (0-7837-2356-3, AU0042100006) Bks Demand.

Milliken, W. Plants for Malaria, Plants for Fever: Medicinal Species in Latin America - Bibliographic Study. 150p. 1997. 50.00 (1-900347-29-6, Pub. by Royal Botnic Grdns) Balogh.

Milliken, W., et al. Ethnobotany of the Waimiri Atroari Indians of Brazil. (Illus.). ix, 146p. 1992. pap. 30.00 (0-947643-50-8, Pub. by Royal Botnic Grdns) Balogh.

Milliken, Walter, jt. auth. see McCoy, Elizabeth L.

*Milliken, William & Ratter, J. A. Marac A: The Biodiversity & Environment of an Amazonian Rainforest. LC 97-41832. 528p. 1998. 185.00 (0-471-97917-1) Wiley.

Milliken, William F. & Milliken, Douglas L. Race Car Vehicle Dynamics. LC 94-36941. (Illus.). 922p. 1994. 85.00 (1-56091-526-9, R146) Soc Auto Engineers.

Milliken, William F., et al. Race Car Vehicle Dynamics. 1997. 99.00 (0-7680-0121-8); pap., wbk. ed. 29.00 (0-7680-0103-X) Soc Auto Engineers.

Milliken, William M. Born under the Sign of Libra: An Autobiography. (Illus.). 229p. 1977. 17.95 (0-911704-16-7) Western Res.

Millikin, Donald D. Elementary Cryptography & Cryptanalysis. 139p. (Orig.). 1992. pap. 22.80 (0-89412-173-1) Aegean Park Pr.

Millikin, Jimmy A. Christian Doctrine for Everyman: Introduction to Baptist Beliefs. LC 78-10464. (Orig.). 1989. reprint ed. pap. 4.50 (0-9621902-0-9) KRB Bks.

Millikin, Mark R. Jimmie Foxx: The Pride of Sudlersville. LC 98-14707. (American Sports History Ser.: No. 11). (Illus.), 304p. 1998. 39.50 (0-8108-3453-7) Scarecrow.

Milliman, Don. The Vandals' Crown: How Rebel Currency Traders Overthrew the World's Central Banks. 1996. pap. 13.00 (0-02-874122-6) Free Pr.

Milliman, John D., ed. Climatic Change & the Mediterranean. (Climatic Change & the Level of Seas Ser.). 550p. 1991. 120.00 (0-340-55329-4, A6222, Pub. by E A) Routldge.

Milliman, John D. & Haq, Bilil U., eds. Sea-Level Rise & Coastal Subsidence: Causes, Consequences, & Strategies. (Coastal Systems & Continental Margins Ser.: Vol. 2). 384p. (C). 1996. text 199.00 (0-7923-3933-9) Kluwer Academic.

Milliman, John D. & Qingming, J., eds. Sediment Dynamics on the Changjiang Estuary & the Adjacent East China Sea: A Selection of Edited Papers from the International Symposium Held in Hangzhou, People's Republic of China, April 1983. 236p. 1985. pap. 44.00 (0-08-030257-2, Pergamon Pr) Elsevier.

Milliman, John D. & Summerhayes, Colin P., eds. Upper Continental Margin Sedimentation of Brazil. (Contributions to Sedimentology Ser.: No. 4). (Illus.). iv, 175p. 1975. pap. 47.00 (3-510-57004-9, Pub. by E Schweizerbartsche) Balogh.

Milliman, John D. & Wright, W. Redwood, eds. The Marine Environment. 1986. 81.25 (0-86720-066-9) Jones & Bartlett.

*Millin, Kathleen. The Old Man & the Sea. 28p. 1999. 9.95 (1-56137-403-2) Novel Units.

*Millin, Kathleen & Dennis, Mary. 1984. 36p. (YA). 1999. 11.95 (1-56137-414-8) Novel Units.

Millin, Kathleen, jt. auth. see Dennis, Mary L.

Millin, Laura J., ed. James Turrell: 4 Light Installations. deluxe ed. LC 82-50224. 30p. 1982. 100.00 (0-941104-03-6) Real Comet.

Millin, Peggy T. Mary's Way: A Universal Story of Spiritual Growth & Transformation. (Illus.). 144p. 1995. pap. 11.95 (0-89087-644-4) Celestial Arts.

Millinary Institute Staff. The Art & Craft of Ribbon Work. Nager, Sandra, ed. (Illus.). 120p. 1982. reprint ed. pap. 19.95 (0-9617110-0-0) Antiquity Pr.

Milliner, J. E. The Angel & the Eagle. unabridged ed. (Illus.). 270p. 1998. 24.95 (0-9666852-1-0); pap. 19.95 (0-9666852-0-2) J E Milliner.

Milliner, Michael. Contractor's Business Handbook: Accounting, Tax Management, Finance, Cost Control. (Illus.). 300p. 1988. pap. 42.95 (0-87629-105-1, 67255) R S Means.

Milliner, Michael S. & Home Builder Press Staff. Commercial Building: An Introduction for Home Builders. 208p. 1989. pap. 30.00 (0-86718-329-2) Home Builder.

*Milling, Andrew J. Surface Characterization Methods. LC 99-27808. (Surfectant Science Ser.). (Illus.). 412p. 1999. text 165.00 (0-8247-7336-5) Dekker.

Milling, Bryan E. Financial Tools for the Non-Financial Executive. LC 82-70779. 215p. reprint ed. pap. 66.70 (0-608-15473-3, 202939100060) Bks Demand.

— How to Get a Small Business Loan: A Banker Shows You Exactly What to Do to Get a Loan. 2nd rev. ed. LC 98-10381. Orig. Title: How to Get a Loan or Line of Credit for Your Business. 176p. 1998. pap. 12.95 (1-57071-341-3) Sourcebks.

Milling, Judith. In & Around London for Kids. LC 99-206014. 224p. 1998. pap. 15.95 (1-84018-027-7, Pub. by Mainstream Pubng) Trafalgar.

Milling, P. M. & Zahn, E. O., eds. Computer-Based Management of Complex Systems. (Illus.). xiv, 648p. 1989. pap. 109.00 (0-387-51447-3, 3304) Spr-Verlag.

Millingrton, John. Pentominoes. (Illus.). 1993. pap. 7.95 (0-906212-57-X, Pub. by Tarquin Pubns) Parkwest Pubns.

Millington, jt. auth. see Smith, David.

Millington, A. C., ed. Environmental Change in Drylands: Biogeographical & Geomorphological Perspectives. (British Geomorphological Research Group Symposia Ser.). 456p. 1994. text 140.00 (0-471-94267-7) Wiley.

Millington, Andrew C., jt. auth. see Alexander, Roy.

Millington, Barry. Wagner. rev. ed. (Illus.). 352p. 1992. pap. text 16.95 (0-691-02722-6, Pub. by Princeton U Pr) Cal Prin Full Svc.

*Millington, Barry, ed. The New Grove Wagner: The New Grove Composer Biographies. (Illus.). 112p. 2000. pap. 12.95 (0-312-23324-8, St Martin Griffin) St Martin.

Millington, Barry & Spencer, Stewart, eds. Wagner in Performance. (Illus.). 224p. (C). 1992. 35.00 (0-300-05718-0) Yale U Pr.

*Millington, Jenny. Little Puppy Adventures. LC 98-183779. (Illus.). 10p. (J). (ps-1). 1998. 7.98 (0-7651-0693-0) Smithmark.

Millington, John. Tangrams. 1993. pap. 7.95 (0-906212-56-1, Pub. by Tarquin Pubns) Parkwest Pubns.

— Tropical Visions. (Illus.). 144p. 1988. text 49.95 (0-7022-2079-5, Pub. by Univ Queensland Pr) Intl Spec Bk.

Millington, John P. John Dalton. LC 73-14966. (English Men of Letters Ser.: No. 6). reprint ed. 37.50 (0-404-07896-6) AMS Pr.

Millington, Jon. Curve Stitching: The Art of Sewing Beautiful Mathematical Designs. (Illus.). 96p. (Orig.). 1990. pap. 18.95 (0-906212-65-0, Pub. by Tarquin Pubns) Parkwest Pubns.

Millington, Joyce. Liverpool Friends Service Centre, 1942-1949. 1999. pap. 21.00 (1-85072-123-8, Pub. by W Sessions) St Mut.

Millington, Mark I. An Analysis of the Short Stories of Juan Carlos Onetti: Fictions of Desire. LC 93-29918. 220p. 1993. text 89.95 (0-7734-9340-9) E Mellen.

Millington, Mark I., jt. ed. see McGuirk, Bernard.

Millington, Richard H., jt. ed. see Freedman, Jonathan.

Millington, Susan. Nihongo Pera Pera: A User's Guide to Japanese Onomatopoeia. 152p. 1993. pap. 9.95 (0-8048-1890-8) Tuttle Pubng.

Millington, Thomas. Colombia's Military & Brazil's Monarchy: Undermining the Republican Foundations of South American Independence, 7. LC 95-31341. (Contributions in Latin American Studies: No. 7). 256p. 1996. 65.00 (0-313-29806-8, Greenwood Pr) Greenwood.

— Debt Politics after Independence: The Funding Conflict in Bolivia. (University of Florida Social Sciences Monographs: No. 79). (Illus.). 200p. 1992. 49.95 (0-8130-1140-X) U Press Fla.

Million, Arthur B. & Dixon, Thomas W., Jr. Pere Marquette Power. Shaver, Carl W., ed. LC 85-70004. (Illus.). 224p. (Orig.). 1984. pap. 23.95 (0-939487-06-3) Ches & OH Hist.

Million, Charlotte, ed. see Abdulai, David.

Million, Clive & White, Ken. Million & White: Family Proceedings: a Guide for Urgent Business & Emergencies. 1997. write for info. (0-406-99294-0, MWGUB, MICHIE) LEXIS Pub.

—illion Dollar Round Table Center for Productivity Staff. Million Dollar Closing Techniques. LC 99-22889. 262p. 1999. pap. 16.95 (0-471-32551-1) Wiley.

— Million Dollar Prospecting Techniques. LC 99-25931. 262p. 1999. pap. 16.95 (0-471-32550-3) Wiley.

— Million Dollar Selling Techniques. LC 99-25932. 246p. 1999. pap. 16.95 (0-471-32549-X) Wiley.

Million, John W. State Aid to Railways in Missouri. Bruchey, Stuart, ed. LC 80-1331. (Railroads Ser.). (Illus.). 1981. reprint ed. lib. bdg. 27.95 (0-405-13805-9) Ayer.

Million, Leslie. Duke Dunbar: Louisiana Man. LC 95-26795. 192p. 1996. 15.95 (0-944957-58-7) Rivercross Pub.

Million, Marsha. Building a Dogsled. (Alaska Ser.: Vol. 4). 57p. (Orig.). 1974. reprint ed. pap. 5.95 (1-878051-04-0, CP036) Circumpolar Pr.

Million, Marsha, ed. Stories from Toksook Bay. 28p. 1994. pap. 7.95 (1-878051-45-8) Circumpolar Pr.

Million, Robert P. Zapata: The Ideology of a Peasant Revolution. LC 94-31757. 1995. pap. 6.95 (0-7178-0710-X) Intl Pubs Co.

Million, Rodney R., et al, eds. Management of Head & Neck Cancer: A Multidisciplinary Approach. 2nd ed. LC 93-18326. 913p. (C). 1993. text 178.00 (0-397-51208-2) Lppncott W & W.

*Million, Stacey. The American Institute of Architects Guide to Kansas City Architecture & Public Art. Mobley, Jane et al, eds. (Illus.). 252p. 2000. pap. 20.00 (1-888903-06-6) Highwater Edits.

*Millionaire, Tony. Adventures of Tony Millionaire's Sock Monkey. (Illus.). (YA). 2000. pap. 9.95 (1-56971-490-8) Dark Horse Comics.

— Maakies. 2000. pap. 14.95 (1-56097-391-9) Fantagraph Bks.

Millionschikov, M., et al. Scientific & Technological Revolution: A Study of the Soviet Union, Capitalist, & Third World Countries. 279p. 1975. 26.95 (0-8464-0818-X) Beekman Pubs.

Milliron, Kerry. Anakin Skywalker. 10p. (J). (ps-3). 1999. 7.99 (0-375-80012-3) Random.

*Milliron, Kerry. Battles to Color. (Star Wars). (Illus.). 80p. (J). (ps-3). 1999. pap. 2.99 (0-375-80016-6, Pub. by Random Bks Yng Read) Random.

Milliron, Kerry. Godzilla Likes to Roar. LC 97-75900. (Illus.). 24p. (J). (ps-3). 1998. pap. 3.25 (0-679-89125-0) Random.

*Milliron, Kerry. Great Race. (Illus.). (J). 2000. pap. 3.99 (0-375-80284-3) Random.

— Great Race. (Step into Reading Ser.). (Illus.). (J). 2000. 11.99 (0-375-90284-8) Random Bks Yng Read.

Milliron, Kerry. Lightsaber Marker Activity Book, 4. (Star Wars). (Illus.). 32p. (J). (ps-3). 1999. pap. 3.99 (0-375-80017-4) Random.

*Milliron, Kerry. Podracing Book Plus Magnets. 2000. 8.99 (0-375-80522-2, Pub. by Random Bks Yng Read) Random.

Milliron, Kerry. Princess in Peril: Xena, Warrior Princess. LC 96-7299. (Random House Pictureback Ser.). (J). (ps-3). 1996. pap. 3.25 (0-679-88259-6) Random.

— Queen of the Amazons. LC 96-14179. (Picturebacks Ser.). 23p. (ps-3). 1996. pap. 3.25 (0-679-88296-0) Random.

*Milliron, Kerry. Theodore Hugs the Coast. (Illus.). (J). 2000. pap. 3.25 (0-375-80282-7) Random.

— Watch out, Jar Jar! (Illus.). (J). 1999. pap. 3.99 (0-375-80028-X, Pub. by Random Bks Yng Read) Random.

Milliron, Kerry, jt. auth. see Krulik, Nancy E.

Milliron, Kerry, ed. see Pellicani, Luciano.

*Millis, Barbara J. & Cottell, Philip G., Jr. Cooperative Learning for Higher Education Faculty. (Illus.). 296p. (C). 1999. reprint ed. pap. text 39.95 (1-57356-419-2) Oryx Pr.

Millis, Christopher. Impossible Mirrors. 72p. 1994. pap. 10.95 (1-880286-18-1) Singular Speech Pr.

Millis, Christopher, tr. The Dark of the Sun: Selected Poems of Umberto Saba. 126p. (C). 1994. lib. bdg. 37.50 (0-8191-9330-5) U Pr of Amer.

*Millis, Elisabeth A. W. Clinical Contact Lens Practice. (Illus.). 304p. 2000. text 85.00 (0-7506-4327-7) Buttrwrth-Heinemann.

Millis, Harry A. The Japanese Problem in the United States. Daniels, Roger, ed. LC 78-54828. (Asian Experience in North America Ser.). (Illus.). 1979. reprint ed. lib. bdg. 26.95 (0-405-11285-8) Ayer.

— Organized Labor. LC 74-22752. (Labor Movement in Fiction & Non-Fiction Ser.). reprint ed. 57.50 (0-404-58504-3) AMS Pr.

Millis, Harry A., ed. How Collective Bargaining Works: A Survey of Experience in Leading American Industries. LC 74-156436. (American Labor Ser., No. 2). 1978. reprint ed. 65.95 (0-405-02933-0) Ayer.

Millis, R. The Wallabadah Manuscript. deluxe limited ed. 256p. 89.95 (0-86840-304-0, Pub. by New South Wales Univ Pr) Intl Spec Bk.

Millis, R. L. & Franz, O. G., eds. Identification, Optimization, & Production of Optical Telescope Sites. pap. text. write for info. (0-9618288-0-3) Lowell Observ.

Millis, R. M. Atlas of Breast Pathology. (Current Histopathology Ser.). 144p. 1983. text 234.50 (0-85200-329-3) Kluwer Academic.

Millis, Richard M., jt. ed. see Dutta, Sisir K.

Millis, Walter. Arms & Men: A Study of American Military History. LC 84-4711. 365p. (C). 1984. reprint ed. pap. 17.00 (0-8135-0931-9) Rutgers U Pr.

— The Martial Spirit. Kohn, Richard H., ed. LC 78-22389. (American Military Experience Ser.). (Illus.). 1980. reprint ed. lib. bdg. 37.95 (0-405-11866-X) Ayer.

— This Is Pearl: The United States & Japan, 1941. LC 77-138594. (Illus.). 384p. 1971. reprint ed. lib. bdg. 69.50 (0-8371-5795-1, MITP, Greenwood Pr) Greenwood.

Milliss, Roger. Waterloo Creek. 1995. pap. 51.95 (0-86840-326-1, Pub. by New South Wales Univ Pr) Intl Spec Bk.

M

Millmam, Paul, et al. Buy Book, Get Guy: The Sometimes Politically Incorrect, but Always Truthful, Guide to Men, Women & Dating. LC 96-21259. 160p. 1997. pap. 11.00 (*0-399-52266-2*, Perigee Bks) Berkley Pub.

Millman. Microelectronics. 2nd ed. 1987. text, student ed. 27.50 (*0-07-042331-8*) McGraw.

Millman, Andrew, jt. ed. see Lee, Nicholas.

Millman, Anne, jt. auth. see Rokach, Allen.

Millman, Brock. The Ill-Made Alliance: Anglo-Turkish Relations, 1934-1940. 536p. 1998. 65.00 (*0-7735-1603-4*, Pub. by McG-Queens Univ Pr) CUP Services.

***Millman, Brock.** Managing Domestic Dissent in First World War Britain, 1914-1918. LC 00-25434. (British Politics & Society Ser.). 2000. write for info. (*0-7146-5054-4*) F Cass Pubs.

Millman-Brown, Randi. Fun Places to Go with Children in New York. rev. ed. LC 97-35964. 208p. 1998. pap. text 11.95 (*0-8118-1567-6*) Chronicle Bks.

Millman, Dan. L' Athlete Interieur: Pour Aller Aubout de Sonpotentiel. (FRE.). 1997. 22.95 (*2-89466-011-1*) Edns Roseau.

— Body Mind Mastery: Creating Success in Sport & Life. 3rd rev. ed. LC 98-53429. (Illus.). 208p. 1999. pap. 12.95 (*1-57731-094-2*) New Wrld Lib.

— Les Cartes Exercices du Guerrier Pacifique. LC 97-17467. (ENG & FRE.). 1997. 24.95 (*2-89466-008-1*) Edns Roseau.

— Everyday Enlightenment: The Twelve Gateways to Personal Growth. LC 97-38845. (Illus.). 350p. 1999. mass mkt. 14.99 (*0-446-67497-4*, Pub. by Warner Bks) Little.

— Everyday Enlightenment: The Twelve Gateways to Spiritual Growth. LC 97-38845. 384p. 1998. 22.00 (*0-446-52279-1*, Pub. by Warner Bks) Little.

— The Inner Athlete. 1999. pap. write for info. (*0-446-67500-8*) Warner Bks.

— The Laws of Spirit: Simple, Powerful Truths for Making Life Work. Carleton, Nancy, ed. LC 95-19406. 120p. 1995. 14.00 (*0-915811-64-2*) H J Kramer Inc.

***Millman, Dan.** The Life You Were Born to Lead. 464p. 2000. 9.98 (*1-56731-398-1*, MJF Bks) Fine Comms.

Millman, Dan. The Life You Were Born to Live: A Guide to Finding Your Life Purpose. LC 93-77108. 468p. 1995. pap. 14.95 (*0-915811-60-X*) H J Kramer Inc.

***Millman, Dan.** Living on Purpose: Straight Answers to Universal Questions. 140p. 2000. pap. 14.00 (*1-57731-132-9*, Pub. by New Wrld Lib) Publishers Group.

Millman, Dan. Les Lois de l'Esprit.Tr. of Laws of Spirit. (FRE.). 1996. 19.95 (*2-920083-99-6*) Edns Roseau.

— No Ordinary Moments: A Peaceful Warrior's Guide to Daily Life. Carleton, Nancy, ed. LC 92-9545. 324p. 1992. pap. 12.95 (*0-915811-40-5*) H J Kramer Inc.

***Millman, Dan.** The Peaceful Warrior Collection. 464p. 2000. 9.98 (*1-56731-399-X*, MJF Bks) Fine Comms.

Millman-Dan. Practical Wisdom: Making the Most of Every Moment. 1995. 16.00 incl. audio (*0-671-52904-8*) S&S Trade.

— Quest for the Crystal Castle. LC 92-70302. (Illus.). 32p. (J). (ps-5). 1992. 14.95 (*0-915811-41-3*, Starseed) H J Kramer Inc.

— Sacred Journey of the Peaceful Warrior. Carleton, Nancy, ed. LC 91-11234. 252p. 1991. pap. 11.95 (*0-915811-33-2*) H J Kramer Inc.

— Secret of the Peaceful Warrior. San Souci, Robert D., ed. LC 90-52636. (Illus.). 32p. 1991. 14.95 (*0-915811-23-5*, Starseed) H J Kramer Inc.

— Votre Chemin de Vie: Une Methode pour en Decouvrir la But. Ouellet, Denis, tr.Tr. of Life You Were Born to Live. (FRE.). 613p. 1995. pap. 29.95 (*2-920083-88-0*) Edns Roseau.

— Way of the Peaceful Warrior: A Book That Changes Lives. rev. ed. LC 83-83240. 216p. 1984. reprint ed. pap. 11.95 (*0-915811-00-6*) H J Kramer Inc.

***Millman, Dan.** Way of the Peaceful Warrior: A Book That Changes Lives. 20th anniversary ed. 228p. 2000. pap. 12.95 (*0-915811-89-8*, Pub. by H J Kramer Inc) New Wrld Lib.

***Millman, Dan & Childers, Doug.** Divine Interventions: True Stories of Mysteries & Miracles That Change Lives. 320p. 2000. reprint ed. pap. 14.95 (*1-57954-338-3*, Daybrk) Rodale Pr Inc.

— Divine Interventions: True Stories of Mystery & Miracles That Change Lives. LC 99-36496. 308p. 1999. 21.95 (*1-57954-100-3*, Daybrk) Rodale Pr Inc.

Millman, Don. Economics: Making Good Choices. (HB-Economics Ser.). 1995. mass mkt. 43.95 (*0-538-85303-4*) S-W Pub.

— Economics: Making Good Choices. LC 95-12635. 1996. text 27.95 (*0-538-84559-7*) S-W Pub.

Millman, Ernest J., jt. auth. see Srole, Leo.

***Millman, Gregory J.** The Day Traders: The Untold Story of the Extreme Investors & How They Changed Wall Street Forever. LC 99-16466. 254p. 1999. 25.00 (*0-8129-3186-6*, Times Bks) Crown Pub Group.

— The Vandal's Crown: How Rebel Currency Traders Overthrew the World's Central Banks. abr. ed. 1995. 17.00 incl. audio (*0-671-53744-X*) S&S Audio.

Millman, Howard L., et al. Therapies for Adults. LC 82-48064. (Jossey-Bass Social & Behavioral Science Ser.). 544p. reprint ed. pap. 168.70 (*0-7837-0184-5*, 204048000017) Bks Demand.

— Therapies for School Behavior Problems: A Handbook of Practical Interventions. LC 80-8318. (Social & Behavioral Science Ser.). 557p. 1980. text 98.00 (*0-87589-483-6*) Jossey-Bass.

Millman, Howard L., jt. auth. see Schaefer, Charles E.

Millman, Isaac. Moses Goes to a Concert. (Illus.). 40p. (J). (gr. k-3). 1998. 16.00 (*0-374-35067-1*) FS&G.

***Millman, Isaac.** Moses Goes to School. LC 99-40582. 2000. text 16.00 (*0-374-35069-8*) FS&G.

Millman, Jack H., jt. auth. see Holt, Roger W.

Millman, Jacob. Microelectronics. 2nd ed. 992p. (C). 1999. 107.19 (*0-07-042330-X*) McGraw.

Millman, Jason, ed. Grading Teachers, Grading Schools: Is Student Achievement a Valid Evaluation Measure? LC 97-21050. (Illus.). 304p. 1997. 69.95 (*0-8039-6401-3*); pap. 32.95 (*0-8039-6402-1*) Corwin Pr.

Millman, Jason & Darling-Hammond, Linda. The New Handbook of Teacher Evaluation: Assessing Elementary & Secondary School Teachers. 2nd ed. (Illus.). 448p. (C). 1990. pap. 34.95 (*0-8039-4523-X*, 3810) Corwin Pr.

Millman, Jason, et al. Talking with the Caller: Guidelines for Crisisline & Other Volunteer Counselors. LC 98-19716. 88p. 1998. write for info. (*0-7619-1520-6*) Sage.

Millman, Jason, jt. auth. see Ennis, Robert H.

Millman, Joan. The Effigy: Stories. 112p. 1990. 19.95 (*0-8262-0755-3*) U of Mo Pr.

Millman, Joan & Behrmann, Polly. Parents As Playmates: A Games Approach to the Preschool Years. LC 79-4547. 140p. 1979. pap. 18.95 (*0-87705-404-5*, Kluwer Acad Hman Sci) Kluwer Academic.

***Millman, Joel.** Men of Hellship: World War II Last Untold Story 2002. pap. 13.95 (*0-7868-8495-9*, Pub. by Disney Pr) Time Warner.

Millman, Joel. The Other Americans: How Immigrants Renew Our Country, Our Economy, & Our Values. LC 96-49265. 369p. 1998. pap. 13.95 (*0-14-024217-1*) Viking Penguin.

Millman, Ken, ed. Florida Outdoor Guide, 1993. 300p. 1992. pap. 9.95 (*0-9634818-0-0*) Keynoter Pub.

— South Florida Outdoor Guide, 1994. 300p. 1993. pap. 10.95 (*0-9634818-1-9*) Keynoter Pub.

Millman, Ken, ed. see Miami Hearld Staff.

Millman, Laurence. Parliament of Ravens. 32p. 1986. pap. 5.00 (*0-910477-03-5*) LoonBooks.

Millman, Lawrence. An Evening among Headhunters: And Other Reports from Roads Less Taken. LC 97-42463. 227p. (Orig.). 1998. pap. 15.95 (*1-57129-055-9*, Lumen Eds) Brookline Bks.

— Hero Jesse: A Novel. LC 81-14582. 196p. 1994. reprint ed. pap. 14.95 (*0-87451-663-3*) U Pr of New Eng.

***Millman, Lawrence.** Last Places: A Journey in the North. 2000. pap. 13.00 (*0-618-08248-4*, Mariner Bks) HM.

Millman, Lawrence. Last Places: A Journey in the North. 1990. 18.95 (*0-685-45106-2*) HM Soft-Ref Div.

— Last Places: A Journey in the North. 1992. 10.00 (*0-685-59153-0*) McKay.

— Northern Latitudes. 1999. pap. text 16.95 (*0-9666750-2-9*, Pub. by Nocturnum Pr) Consort Bk Sales.

***Millman, Lawrence.** Northern Latitudes: Prose Poems. (Marie Alexander Prose Poetry Ser.: Vol. 3). 96p. 2000. 14.95 (*0-89823-207-4*, Pub. by New Rivers Pr) Consort Bk Sales.

Millman, Lawrence. The Wrong-Handed Man: Stories. LC 87-27200. 112p. (Orig.). 1988. pap. 12.95 (*0-8262-0674-3*) U of Mo Pr.

Millman, Lawrence W. A Kayak Full of Ghosts: Eskimo Tales. LC 87-11729. 208p. (Orig.). 1987. pap. 9.95 (*0-88496-267-9*) Capra Pr.

Millman, M. C. Cheery Bim Band No. 4: Color War! LC 94-70754. 150p. (YA). 1994. 13.95 (*1-56062-260-1*) CIS Comm.

— Cheery Bim Band No. 5: In the Spotlight! LC 94-60672. 141p. (J). (gr. 5-8). 1994. 12.95 (*1-56062-265-2*) CIS Comm.

— Cheery Bim Band No. 6: Trumpet Trouble. LC 94-72546. 176p. (J). (gr. 5-8). 1994. 13.95 (*1-56062-271-7*) CIS Comm.

Millman, M. C. Face the Music. LC 95-67356. (Cheery Bim Band Ser.: Vol. 9). (Illus.). 142p. (J). (gr. 5-6). 13.95 (*1-56062-295-4*) CIS Comm.

Millman, M. C. Mind Your Own Business. LC 94-70753. 200p. (YA). 1994. 15.95 (*1-56062-264-4*) CIS Comm.

Millman, M. C. Party Time. LC 94-73908. (Cheery Bim Band Ser.: Vol. 8). (Illus.). 143p. (J). (gr. 5-6). 13.95 (*1-56062-294-6*) CIS Comm.

— Stage Fright. (Cheery Bim Band Ser.: Vol. 7). (Illus.). 143p. (J). (gr. 5-6). 13.95 (*1-56062-272-5*) CIS Comm.

Millman, Malka. Too Tough to Care. 150p. (J). (gr. 6). 1993. 11.95 (*1-56062-237-7*) CIS Comm.

Millman, Marcia. The Seven Stories of Love. 1924. write for info. (*0-688-17200-8*, Wm Morrow) Morrow Avon.

Millman, Mary & Bohn, Dave. Master of Line: John Winkler, American Etcher. LC 94-5208. (Illus.). 192p. 1994. 58.00 (*0-88496-358-6*) Capra Pr.

Millman, Michael L. Politics & the Expanding Physician Supply. LC 78-73591. (Conservation of Human Resources Ser.: No. 11). (Illus.). 176p. 1980. text 34.50 (*0-916672-84-0*) Rowman.

Millman, Michael L., jt. auth. see Erwin, Richard E.

Millman, Michael L., ed. see Institute of Medicine, Committee on Monitoring Acc.

Millman, Mike, et al. Boat Fishing. (Illus.). 112p. 1992. pap. 24.95 (*1-85223-685-X*, Pub. by Cro1wood) Trafalgar.

Millman, P. N., ed. see Meteorite Research Symposium Staff.

Millman, R. G. Auburn University Walking Tour Guide. LC 90-44978. 128p. 1991. pap. 9.95 (*0-8173-0523-8*) U of Ala Pr.

Millman, R. S. & Parker, George D. Geometry: A Metric Approach with Models. (Undergraduate Texts in Mathematics Ser.). (Illus.). 355p. 1981. 38.00 (*0-387-90610-X*) Spr-Verlag.

— Geometry: A Metric Approach with Models. 2nd ed. (Undergraduate Texts in Mathematics Ser.). (Illus.). xiii, 370p. 1993. write for info. (*3-540-97412-1*) Spr-Verlag.

— Geometry: A Metric Approach with Models. 2nd ed. Ewing, J. H. et al, eds. (Undergraduate Texts in Mathematics Ser.). (Illus.). 352p. 1995. 49.95 (*0-387-97412-1*) Spr-Verlag.

Millman, Richard S., et al, eds. Differential Geometric Control Theory. (Progress in Mathematics Ser.: Vol. 27). 340p. 1982. 56.50 (*0-8176-3091-0*) Birkhauser.

Millman, Richard S. & Parker, George D. Elements of Differential Geometry. LC 76-28497. (Illus.). 1977. text 51.67 (*0-13-264143-7*) P-H.

Millman, S., ed. see Bell Telephone Laboratories Technical Staff.

Millman, Sandy. Seats: 150 Seating Plans to New York Metro Area Theatres, Concert Halls & Sports Stadiums. LC 97-28481. 320p. 1998. pap. 15.95 (*1-55783-301-X*) Applause Theatre Bk Pubs.

***Millman, Selena.** Messages to You: Short Stories & Essays. LC 00-9408. 2000. write for info. (*1-929882-01-7*) Biograph Pub.

— Something to Think About: Inspirational Poems. 77p. 2000. pap. 10.00 (*1-929882-00-9*) Biograph Pub.

Millmoss, A. B., jt. auth. see Duensing, Edward.

Millner, Cork. Beefcake Bazaar. LC 90-52519. (Orig.). 1984. pap. 6.00 (*0-88734-208-6*) Players Pr.

— Portraits: Creative Conversations with Celebrities. (Illus.). 224p. 1994. 25.00 (*1-56474-087-0*) Fithian Pr.

— Vintage Cork. LC 96-31623. 176p. 1997. 15.00 (*1-56474-197-4*) Fithian Pr.

— Write from the Start. rev. ed. LC 94-28722. 236p. 1994. pap. 10.95 (*1-56474-120-6*) Fithian Pr.

Millner, Denene. The Sistahs' Rules: Secrets For Meeting, Getting, And Keeping A Good Black Man Not To Be Confused With The Rules. LC 97-21792. 144p. 1997. pap. 9.95 (*0-688-15689-4*, Quil) HarperTrade.

***Millner, Denene & Chiles, Nick.** What Brothers Think, What Sistahs Know: The Real Deal on Love & Relationships. LC 98-30617. 144p. 1999. pap. 10.00 (*0-688-16498-6*, Quil) HarperTrade.

— What Brothers Think, What Sistahs Know About Sex: The Real Deal On Passion, Loving, And Intimacy. LC 99-36501. 272p. 2000. pap. 10.00 (*0-688-17107-9*, Wm Morrow) Morrow Avon.

Millner, Dianne, ed. see Browne, Leslie M., et al.

Millner, Dianne, ed. see Moskovitz, Myron & Bishop, Catherine M.

Millner, Dianne, ed. see Weller, Louis S. & Drucker, Cecily Ann.

Millner, Fredrick L. The Operas of Johann Adolf Hasse. Buelow, George, ed. LC 79-11832. (Studies in Musicology: No. 2). (Illus.). 428p. 1979. reprint ed. pap. 132.70 (*0-8357-1006-8*, 207019100064) Bks Demand.

Millner, Lynda. The Magic Makeover: Tricks for Looking Thinner, Younger, & More Confident - Instantly! LC 97-3655. (Illus.). 176p. (Orig.). 1997. pap. 14.95 (*1-56474-222-9*) Fithian Pr.

Millner, Nancy. Creative Aging: Discovering the Unexpected Joys of Later Life Through Personality Type. LC 97-33177. 208p. (Orig.). 1997. pap. 16.95 (*0-89106-111-8*, 7780, Davies-Black Pub) Consulting Psychol.

Millner, Nancy, jt. auth. see Corlett, Eleanor.

Millner, Paul, ed. High Resolution Chromatography: A Practical Approach. LC 98-31925. (Practical Approach Ser.: 204). (Illus.). 333p. 1999. text 120.00 (*0-19-963649-4*); pap. text 60.00 (*0-19-963648-6*) OUP.

Millner, Russell & Treasure, Tom, eds. Explaining Cardiac Surgery: Patient Assessment & Care. 250p. (Orig.). 1995. pap. text 32.00 (*0-7279-0853-7*, Pub. by BMJ Pub) Login Brothers Bk Co.

Millner, Sandra. The Dream Lives On: Martin Luther King, Jr. LC 99-28508. (Illus.). 120p. 1999. 19.98 (*1-56799-649-3*, MetroBooks) M Friedman Pub Grp Inc.

***Millner, Sandra.** The Dream Lives On: Martin Luther King, Jr. LC 99-28508. 1999. write for info. (*1-56799-853-4*) M Friedman Pub Grp Inc.

Millns, Susan, jt. ed. see Bridgeman, Jo.

Millodot, Michel. Diccionario de Optometria. (SPA.). 304p. 1990. write for info. (*0-7859-6039-2*, 8440464142) Fr & Eur.

— Dictionary of Optometry & Visual Science. 4th ed. LC 97-26046. (Illus.). 320p. 2000. pap. text 57.50 (*0-7506-3145-7*) Buttrwrth-Heinemann.

***Millodot, Michel.** Dictionary of Optometry & Visual Science. 5th ed. LC 99-44474. 344p. 2000. pap. text 70.00 (*0-7506-4373-0*) Buttrwrth-Heinemann.

Millon, Henry A. Baroque & Rococo Architecture. LC 61-15492. (Great Ages of World Architecture Ser.). (Illus.). 127p. 1965. pap. 10.95 (*0-8076-0333-3*) Braziller.

— Studies in Art History I: Studies in Italian Art & Architecture. (Fifteenth - Eighteenth Centuries Ser.). (Illus.). 344p. 1980. 56.00 (*0-271-00457-6*) Am Acad Rome.

Millon, Henry A. & Munshower, Susan S., eds. An Architectural Progress in the Renaissance & Baroque: Sojourns in & Out of Italy. (Papers in Art History: Vol. VIII). (Illus.). 929p. (Orig.). 1992. pap. 70.00 (*0-915773-07-4*) Penn St Univ Dept Art Hist.

Millon, Henry A. & Nochlin, Linda, eds. Art & Architecture in the Service of Politics. 1978. 70.00 (*0-262-13137-4*) MIT Pr.

Millon, Henry A., jt. auth. see Green.

Millon, Henry A., ed. see di caccia di Stupinigi, Reale Palazzina.

Millon, J. Paradise Lost & Other Poems. 1961. mass mkt. 7.99 (*0-451-62826-8*) NAL.

Millon, Judith. St. Pauls Within-the-Walls: Rome, a History & Guide, 1870-1980. LC 81-8055. 1982. 9.95 (*0-87233-058-3*) Bauhan.

Millon, Kim, jt. auth. see Millon, Marc.

Millon, Marc. Creative Content for the Web. 192p. 1999. 24.95 (*1-871516-97-8*, Pub. by Intellect) Intl Spec Bk.

Millon, Marc & Millon, Kim. Flavours of Korea. (Illus.). 242p. 1991. pap. 17.95 (*0-233-98635-9*, Pub. by Andre Deutsch) Trafalgar.

— The Wine Roads of France. (Illus.). 416p. (Orig.). 1992. pap. 22.00 (*0-246-13749-5*, Pub. by HarpC) HarpC.

— The Wine Roads of Italy. (Illus.). 529p. 1993. 30.00 (*0-246-13736-3*, Pub. by HarpC); 22.00 (*0-246-13737-1*, Pub. by HarpC) HarpC.

Millon, Rene, ed. see Sempowski, Martha L. & Spence, Michael W.

Millon, T., et al. Handbook of Clinical Health Psychology. LC 82-11236. (Illus.). 632p. (C). 1982. 100.00 (*0-306-40932-1*, Plenum Trade) Perseus Pubng.

Millon, Theodore. The Millon Inventories: Clinical & Personality Assessment. LC 97-7702. 553p. 1997. lib. bdg. 60.00 (*1-57230-184-8*, 0184) Guilford Pubns.

— Personality & Psychopathology: Building a Clinical Science: Selected Papers of Theodore Millon. LC 95-10576. 354p. 1995. 90.00 (*0-471-11685-8*, Wiley-Interscience) Wiley.

— Toward a New Personology: An Evolutionary Model. LC 89-35944. (Series on Personality Processes). 200p. 1990. 80.50 (*0-471-51573-6*) Wiley.

Millon, Theodore, et al, eds. Psychopathy: Antisocial, Criminal & Violent Behavior. LC 98-6845. 476p. 1998. lib. bdg. 60.00 (*1-57230-344-1*, C0344) Guilford Pubns.

Millon, Theodore & Blaney, Paul H., eds. Oxford Textbook of Psychopathology. LC 98-49669. (Oxford Textbooks in Clinical Psychology Ser.). (Illus.). 744p. 1999. text 85.00 (*0-19-510307-6*) OUP.

***Millon, Theodore & Davis, Roger D.** Personality Disorders in Modern Life: Character Disorders. LC 99-30334. 581p. 1999. 55.00 (*0-471-32355-1*) Wiley.

Millon, Theodore & Everly, George S., Jr. Personality & Its Disorders: A Biosocial Learning Approach. LC 84-21995. 304p. (C). 1985. pap. 49.95 (*0-471-87816-2*) Wiley.

Millon, Theodore, et al. Disorders of Personality: DSM-IVTM & Beyond. 2nd ed. LC 95-9045. 832p. 1995. 87.50 (*0-471-01186-X*) Wiley.

Millonas, Mark, et al, eds. Fluctuations & Order: The New Synthesis. LC 95-44878. (Institute for Nonlinear Science Ser.). (Illus.). 448p. 1996. 53.95 (*0-387-94602-0*) Spr-Verlag.

Millones, Luis & Pratt, Mary L. Amor Brujo: Images & Culture of Love in the Andes. LC 89-39918. (Foreign & Comparative Studies Program, Latin American Ser.: No. 10). (Illus.). (Orig.). (C). 1990. pap. text 14.00 (*0-915984-33-4*) Syracuse U Foreign Comp.

Millonig, Virginia L. Today & Tomorrow's Woman - Menopause: Before & After (Girls of 16 to Women of 99) LC 95-48849. 300p. (Orig.). 1996. pap. text 10.00 (*1-878028-23-5*) Hlth Lead Assoc.

Millonig, Virginia L. & Baroni, Mary, eds. The Pediatric Nurse Practitioner Certification Review Guide. 3rd ed. LC 98-29338. 600p. (C). 1998. pap. text 52.00 (*1-878028-17-0*) Hlth Lead Assoc.

Millonig, Virginia L. & Miller, Sally, eds. Adult Nurse Practitioner Certification Review Guide. 3rd ed. LC 98-30168. 700p. (C). 1998. pap. text 52.00 (*1-878028-16-2*) Hlth Lead Assoc.

Millonzi, Joel, jt. auth. see Ehrlich, Daniel J.

Millor, W. J., ed. see John of Salisbury.

Millot, Catherine. Horsexe: Essay on Transsexuality. 150p. 1990. pap. 10.00 (*0-936756-20-9*) Autonomedia.

Millot, Marc D., et al. "The Day After..." Study Vol. I: Nuclear Proliferation in the Post Cold War World: Summary Report. LC 93-33243. 1993. pap. text 15.00 (*0-8330-1459-5*, MR-266-AF) Rand Corp.

— "The Day After..." Study Vol. II: Nuclear Proliferation in the Post Cold War: Main Report. LC 93-27731. 1993. pap. text 15.00 (*0-8330-1424-2*, MR-253-AF) Rand Corp.

Millot, Marc D., jt. auth. see Perry, Walter L.

Milloy, Maryann. Working Together Against Gun Violence. LC 94-1021. (Library of Social Activism). (Illus.). 64p. (YA). (gr. 7-12). 1997. lib. bdg. 16.95 (*0-8239-2612-5*) Rosen Group.

Milloy, Nancy R. Breakdown of Speech: Causes & Remediation. (Therapy in Practice Ser.: No. 20). pap. 32.50 (*0-412-31550-5*) Chapman & Hall.

***Milloy, Peter.** Disciples & Other Believers: Our Expensive Trip on the Disciple-Ship. x, 114p. 2000. pap. write for info. (*1-890939-05-6*) Century Creations.

Milloy, Steven & Gough, Michael. Silencing Science. LC 98-48725. 68p. 1999. pap. text 8.00 (*1-882577-72-8*, Pub. by Cato Inst) Natl Bk Netwk.

Milloy, Steven J. Science-Based Risk Assessment: A Piece of the Superfund Puzzle. (Orig.). 1995. pap. 25.00 (*0-9647463-0-1*) Nat Environ Policy.

— Science Without Sense. 68p. 1996. pap. 8.00 (*1-882577-34-5*) Cato Inst.

Millross, Janice & Speht, Alan. Utilization of the Cook-Freeze Catering System for School Meals. 212p. 1974. text 30.00 (*0-87936-007-0*) Scholium Intl.

Millroy, Wendy L. An Ethnographic Study of the Mathematical Ideas of a Group of Carpenters. LC 91-39453. (Journal for Research in Mathematics Education Monograph Ser.: No. 5). (Illus.). 210p. 1992. pap. 11.95 (*0-87353-341-0*) NCTM.

Mills. Action Research. LC 98-55963. (Illus.). 184p. 1999. pap. text 28.00 (*0-13-772047-5*) P-H.

***Mills.** America's Solvable Problems. LC 99-18670. 1999. text 65.00 (*0-312-22276-9*) St Martin.

— The Anatomy of a Vintage Slot Machine. Post, Dan, ed. (Illus.). 45p. 1978. 6.95 (*0-934422-30-3*, BKS-100360) Mead Pub Corp.

Mills. Aventura de Daniel y los Leones.Tr. of Daniel's Adventures with Lions. (SPA.). 12p. (J). 1994. 6.99 (*1-56063-752-8*, 490313) Editorial Unilit.

An Asterisk (*) at the beginning of an entry indicates that the title is appearing for the first time.

— Aventura de David Con el Gigante.Tr. of David's Adventures with the Giant. (SPA.). 12p. (J). 1994. 6.99 (1-56063-751-X, 490312) Editorial Unilit.

— Basic Heat & Mass Transfer. 2nd ed. LC 98-34111. 1000p. 1998. 105.00 (0-13-096247-3) P-H.

Mills. Clinch that Deal. 224p. 1996. pap. 26.95 (0-566-07704-3) Ashgate Pub Co.

Mills. La Estrella de Belen - Start of Bethlehem. (Libros Ventanitas - Windows Bks.). (SPA.). 8p. (J). 1995. write for info. (1-56063-830-3) Editorial Unilit.

— Fuego! Fuego! - Fire! Fire! (Libros Ventanitas - Windows Bks.). (SPA.). 6p. (J). 1995. write for info. (1-56063-831-1) Editorial Unilit.

— La Fuga - Jail Break. (Libros Ventanitas - Windows Bks.). (SPA.). 5p. (J). 1995. write for info. (1-56063-833-8) Editorial Unilit.

— Heat Transfer. 2nd ed. LC 98-33845. 954p. (C). 1998. 105.00 (0-13-947624-5) P-H.

Mills. History of Behavioral Psychology. pap. text 20.00 (0-8147-5612-3) NYU Pr.

Mills, 3rd. Instrumental Data for Drug Analysis, Vol. 2. 792p. 1992. boxed set 168.95 (0-8493-9522-4) CRC Pr.

— Instrumental Data for Drug Analysis, Vol. 3. 2nd ed. 824p. 1992. boxed set 168.95 (0-8493-9523-2) CRC Pr.

— Instrumental Data for Drug Analysis, Vol. 4. 2nd ed. 282p. 1992. boxed set 168.95 (0-8493-9524-0) CRC Pr.

— Instrumental Data for Drug Analysis, Vol. 5. 2nd ed. 628p. 1992. boxed set 166.95 (0-8493-9516-X) CRC Pr.

Mills. Llueve! Llueve! - Rain! Rain! (Libros Ventanitas - Windows Bks.). (SPA.). (J). 1995. write for info. (1-56063-832-X) Editorial Unilit.

— Mi Dia: Figuras Que Aparecen. (Figuras Que Aparecen (A Chunky Pop-up Bk.)).Tr. of My Day: Chunky Pop-Up Book. (SPA.). 5p. (J). 1995. 3.50 (1-56063-631-9, 494604) Editorial Unilit.

***Mills.** Principles & Practice of Phycology. (C). 1999. text 72.00 (0-443-06016-9, Pub. by Harcourt Coll Pubs) Harcourt.

Mills, jt. auth. see Alston.

Mills, jt. auth. see Fechner.

Mills, jt. auth. see Leoung.

Mills, jt. auth. see Mallouk.

Mills, Henry E. Treatise upon the Law of Eminent Domain. lxvii, 404p. 1982. reprint ed. 45.00 (0-8377-0841-9, Rothman) W S Hein.

Mills, A., et al, eds. Health System Decentralization: Concepts, Issues, & Country Experience. (ENG, FRE & SPA.). 151p. 1990. pap. text 23.40 (92-4-156137-8, 1150340) World Health.

Mills, A. & Canter, K. F. Positron Studies of Solids, Surface & Atoms. 352p. 1986. text 68.00 (9971-978-44-X) World Scientific Pub.

Mills, A. D. A Dictionary of English Place Names. LC 92-43070. (Illus.). 412p. (C). 1993. pap. 6.99 (0-19-283131-3) OUP.

— A Dictionary of English Place-Names. 2nd ed. LC 98-214237. (Oxford Paperback Reference Ser.). (Illus.). 448p. (Orig.). 1998. pap. 12.95 (0-19-280074-4) OUP.

— Dorset Place Names. (C). 1989. 45.00 (1-85455-065-9, Pub. by Ensign Pubns & Print) St Mut.

Mills, A. E. The Acquisition of Gender. (Language & Communication Ser.: Vol. 20). (Illus.). 180p. 1986. 85.95 (0-387-16740-4) Spr-Verlag.

Mills, A. J. The Will to Live: The Battle of a Young Boy Against Muscular Dystrophy. 100p. 1992. pap. 7.95 (0-9633921-0-7) Humor Bks.

Mills, A. J. & Churcher, C. S., eds. The Dakhleh Oasis Project: Reports from the Survey of Dakhleh Oasis 1977-1987. (Dakhleh Oasis Project Monographs; Oxbow Monographs in Archaeology: Nos. 2 & 69). 250p. 1995. 35.00 (1-900188-06-6, Pub. by Oxbow Bks) David Brown.

Mills, A. J., jt. ed. see Churcher, C. S.

Mills, Adelbert P. Materials of Construction, Their Manufacture & Properties. LC 55-73681. (Illus.). 662p. reprint ed. pap. 200.00 (0-608-30319-4, 205513200008) Bks Demand.

Mills, Albert J. & Murgatroyd, Stephen J. Organizational Rules: A Framework for Understanding Organizational Action. 240p. 1990. 118.00 (0-335-09908-4); pap. 34.95 (0-335-09907-6) OpUniv Pr.

Mills, Albert J. & Tancred, Peta. Gendering Organizational Analysis. 336p. (C). 1992. text 49.95 (0-8039-4558-2); pap. text 22.95 (0-8039-4559-0) Sage.

***Mills, Alexandra.** Public Sector Corruption: An International Survey of Prevention Measures. 120p. 1999. pap. 31.00 (92-64-17071-5, 42 1999 04 1 P, Pub. by Org for Econ) OECD.

***Mills, Alice.** Seriously Weird: Papers on the Grotesque. LC 98-10692. 288p. 1999. 54.95 (0-8204-4035-3) P Lang Pubng.

Mills, Alice, ed. The Random House Children's Treasury: Fairy Tales, Nursery Rhymes & Nonsense Verse. (Illus.). 446p. (YA). 1998. 19.99 (0-517-16114-1) Random Hse Value.

Mills, Alice S., jt. auth. see Joseph, Lou.

Mills, Allen. Fool for Christ: The Intellectual Politics of J. S. Woodsworth. 352p. 1991. pap. 18.95 (0-8020-6842-1); text 50.00 (0-8020-2787-3) U of Toronto Pr.

Mills, Allen, jt. auth. see Abizadeh, Sorab.

Mills, Ami C. CIA Off Campus: Building the Movement Against Agency Recruitment & Research. 200p. 1991. 25.00 (0-89608-404-3); pap. 10.00 (0-89608-403-5) South End Pr.

Mills, Andrea. Caravan to Tiern. (Illus.). 1989. 8.95 (0-940244-22-5) Flying Buffalo.

Mills, Andrew, jt. auth. see Mills, Mary E.

***Mills, Anita.** Duke's Double. 2000. mass mkt. 3.99 (0-451-19954-5, Sig) NAL.

Mills, Anita. No Sweeter Wine. 1999. mass mkt. 5.99 (0-451-40770-9, Topaz) NAL.

Mills, Anita, et al. Cherished Moments. 1995. mass mkt. 4.99 (0-312-95473-5) St Martin.

— Christmas Rogues: The Christmas Stranger; The Homecoming; Bayberry & Mistletoe, 3 vols. LC 95-22356. 375p. 1995. per. 4.99 (0-373-83297-4) Harlequin Bks.

Mills, Ann, ed. see Dadaji.

Mills, Anne, ed. The Acquisition of German: The Crosslinguistic Study of Language Acquisition, Vol. 1. (Crosslinguistic Study of Language Acquisition Ser.). 136p. 1986. pap. 14.95 (0-89859-841-9) L Erlbaum Assocs.

***Mills, Anne, ed.** Reforming Health Sectors. (Illus.). 350p. 1999. 110.00 (0-7103-0642-3, Pub. by Kegan Paul Intl) Col U Pr.

Mills, Anne & Lee, Kenneth, eds. Health Economics Research in Developing Countries. LC 92-49379. (Oxford Medical Publications). (C). 1993. pap. write for info. (0-19-262320-6) OUP.

Mills, Anne, jt. ed. see Lee, Kenneth.

***Mills, Anne E., et al.** The Challenge of Health Sector Reform: What Must Governments Do? LC 00-41486. 2000. write for info. (0-333-73618-4) St Martin.

***Mills, Anthony.** Collaborative Engineering & the Internet: Linking Product Development Partners via the Web. LC 98-60976. (Illus.). 380p. 1998. 69.95 (0-87263-498-1, 2709) SME.

Mills, Anthony F. Basic Heat & Mass Transfer. LC 94-28226. (Heat Transfer Ser.). 928p. (C). 1994. text 78.95 (0-256-16388-X, Irwn McGrw-H) McGrw-H Hghr Educ.

— Heat & Mass Transfer. LC 94-146. (Irwin Heat Transfer Ser.). 1280p. (C). 1994. text 88.00 (0-256-11443-9, Irwn Prfssnl) McGraw-Hill Prof.

— Heat Transfer. 888p. (C). 1991. text 75.50 (0-256-07642-1, 19-2997-01, Irwn McGrw-H) McGrw-H Hghr Educ.

— Heat Transfer International. (C). 1992. student ed., per. 37.50 (0-256-12817-0, Irwn McGrw-H) McGrw-H Hghr Educ.

Mills, Anthony R. Drake's Bay. 96p. (Orig.). 1996. pap. 9.95 (1-56474-158-3) Fithian Pr.

— Subic Bay: The Last American Colony. LC 98-85820. 344p. 1998. text 27.95 (1-56167-430-3) Noble Hse MD.

Mills, Antonia. Eagle Down Is Our Law: Witsuwit'en Law, Feasts, & Land Claims. 256p. 1994. pap. 25.95 (0-7748-0513-7) U of Wash Pr.

Mills, Antonia & Slobodin, Richard, eds. Amerindian Rebirth: Reincarnation Belief among North American Indians & Inuit. (Illus.). 240p. 1994. text 60.00 (0-8020-2829-2); pap. text 19.95 (0-8020-7703-X) U of Toronto Pr.

Mills, Arlen C. Communicating the Appraisal: Small Residential Income Property Appraisal Report. (Communicating the Appraisal Ser.: No. 4). (Illus.). 150p. 1990. pap. 18.00 (0-922154-01-5) Appraisal Inst.

Mills, Arlen C. & Mills, Dorothy Z. Communicating the Appraisal: The Small Residential Income Property Appraisal Report. 2nd ed. LC 95-35635. 1995. 25.00 (0-922154-24-4) Appraisal Inst.

— Communicating the Appraisal: The Uniform Residential Appraisal Report. 2nd ed. LC 93-48498. 1994. 25.00 (0-922154-15-5) Appraisal Inst.

Mills, Arlen C. & Reynolds, Anthony. The Valuation of Apartment Properties. LC 98-43647. 1999. write for info. (0-922154-54-6) Appraisal Inst.

Mills, Arlen C., jt. auth. see Mills, Dorothy Z.

Mills, Arthur. Management for Technologists. 272p. 1968. pap. 28.00 (0-8464-1425-2) Beekman Pubs.

Mills, Ava E. West Texans Remember the Home Front. LC 97-67130. (Illus.). x, 159p. (Orig.). 1997. pap. 14.95 (0-9658789-0-2) Doss Bks.

Mills, Ava E., ed. A Legacy of Words: Texas Women's Stories, 1850-1920. LC 98-96325. (Illus.). viii, 174p. 1999. pap. 16.95 (0-9658789-2-9, 096587) Doss Bks.

Mills, B. & Redford, A. H. Machinability of Engineering Materials. (Illus.). 200p. 1983. 54.00 (0-85334-183-4) Elsevier.

***Mills, Barbara.** . . . And Justice for All. 544p. 2000. pap. 27.95 (1-56167-591-1) Am Literary Pr.

***Mills, Barbara J.** Alternative Leadership Strategies in the Prehispanic Southwest. LC 99-50694. 320p. 2000. 40.00 (0-8165-2028-3) U of Ariz Pr.

— Ceramic Production in the American Southwest. (Illus.). 2000. pap. text 19.95 (0-8165-2046-1) U of Ariz Pr.

— Living on the Edge of the Rim: Excavations & Analysis of the Silver Creek Archaeological Resea. 1999. pap. 29.95 (1-889747-70-X) Ariz St Mus.

Mills, Barbara J. & Crown, Patricia L., eds. Ceramic Production in the America Southwest. LC 95-8771. (Illus.). 312p. 1995. 46.00 (0-8165-1508-5) U of Ariz Pr.

Mills, Bebe A., intro. Ert Moore: Experiences of a Pioneer Educator. 74p. 1979. lib. bdg. 27.50 (1-56475-181-3); fiche. write for info. (1-56475-182-1) U NV Oral Hist.

Mills, Betty J. Amanda Goes West. LC 83-70168. (Amanda Ser.: Bk. I). (Illus.). 20p. (Orig.). (J). (gr. 5-7). 1983. pap. 5.95 (0-89672-109-4) Tex Tech Univ Pr.

— Amanda's Home on the Range. (Amanda Ser.: Bk. 3). (Illus.). 24p. (J). (gr. 5-7). 1984. pap. 6.95 (0-89672-122-1) Tex Tech Univ Pr.

— Amanda's New Life. (Amanda Ser.: Bk. 2). (Illus.). 20p. (Orig.). 1983. pap. 6.95 (0-89672-112-4) Tex Tech Univ Pr.

— Calico Chronicle: Texas Women & Their Fashions, 1830-1910. LC 84-52249. (Illus.). 192p. 1985. pap. 15.95 (0-89672-128-0) Tex Tech Univ Pr.

— Flashes of Fashion: Eighteen Thirty to Nineteen Seventy-Two. Webber, Gale, ed. (Illus.). 192p. 1973. 10.00 (0-911618-02-3) Mus Texas.

— Language of Lace. Earnshaw, Pat, ed. 35p. 1984. pap. 5.50 (0-911618-09-0) Mus Texas.

— Seven Sisters Follow a Star: A P. E. O. Saga As Told Through Paper Dolls. 1987. pap. 8.95 (0-89672-162-0) Tex Tech Univ Pr.

Mills, Beverly. Desperation Dinners! Home-Cooked Meals for Frantic Families in 20 Minutes Flat. LC 97-28303. (Illus.). 256p. 1997. 22.95 (0-7611-1039-9); pap. 12.95 (0-7611-0481-X) Workman Pub.

Mills, Billy, ed. Letters from Barcelona. (C). 1990. 23.00 (0-948268-71-9, Pub. by Dedalus) St Mut.

Mills, Billy & Sparks, Nicholas. Wokini: A Lakota Journey to Happiness & Self-Understanding. 2nd ed. LC 99-22585. 192p. 1999. reprint ed. pap. 8.95 (1-56170-660-4) Hay House.

Mills, Bob. Time Rides the River. Spelius, Carol & Spelius, Wayne, eds. 75p. 1993. pap. 7.95 (0-941363-27-9) Lake Shore Pub.

Mills, Bradford. The Impact of Gender Discrimination on the Job Search Strategies of Redeployed Public Sector Workers. (Working Papers: No. 51). 29p. (C). 1994. pap. 7.00 (1-56401-151-8) Cornell Food.

Mills, Bradford & Sahn, David E. Is There Life after Public Sector Service? The Fate of Retrenched Workers in Conakry, Guinea. (Working Papers: No. 42). 55p. (C). 1993. pap. 7.00 (1-56401-142-9) Cornell Food.

Mills, Bradford, et al. Public Finance & Public Employment: An Analysis of Public Sector Retrenchment Programs in Ghana & Guinea. (Working Papers: No. 52). 44p. Date not set. pap. 7.00 (1-56401-152-6) Cornell Food.

Mills, Brett D. Mental Training & Performance Enhancement: A Guide for Volleyball Coaches & Players. 107p. (Orig.). (C). 1995. pap. 24.95 (0-945483-49-X) E Bowers Pub.

***Mills, Brian.** A Story to Tell: Evangelism in the Twentieth Century. 203p. 1999. reprint ed. pap. 16.99 (1-85078-333-0, Pub. by O M Pubng) OM Literature.

***Mills, Brian & Mitchell, Roger.** Sins of the Father. 1999. pap. text 14.99 (1-85240-253-9) SOV5.

Mills, Bronwyn. The Mexican War. Bowman, John, ed. (America at War Ser.). (Illus.). 128p. (YA). (gr. 5-12). 1992. lib. bdg. 19.95 (0-8160-2393-X) Facts on File.

Mills, Bruce. Cultural Reformations: Lydia Maria Child & the Literature of Reform. LC 93-33745. 216p. 1994. 30.00 (0-8203-1638-5) U of Ga Pr.

Mills, Bruce, ed. see Child, Lydia M.

***Mills, C.** Gus & Grandpa Christmas. (Illus.). 48p. (gr. 1-3). 2000. pap. 4.95 (0-374-42815-8) FS&G.

— Lizzie at Last. 2000. text. write for info. (0-374-34632-1) FS&G.

Mills, C. Mystery. (Shadow Creek Ranch Ser.). 1994. pap. 5.99 (1-878951-19-X) Review & Herald.

Mills, C. A. Legends of Lost Treasure. 86p. 1987. pap. 5.00 (0-945598-04-1) Apple Cheeks Pr.

— Legends of Pirate Gold. 92p. 1986. pap. 5.00 (0-945598-03-3) Apple Cheeks Pr.

— Treasure Legends of the Civil War. 82p. 1985. pap. 5.00 (0-945598-02-5) Apple Cheeks Pr.

— Treasure Legends of Virginia. 86p. 1984. pap. 5.00 (0-945598-00-9) Apple Cheeks Pr.

Mills, C. A., ed. see Capgrave, John.

Mills, C. F., ed. Zinc in Human Biology. (Illus.). 388p. 1989. 75.00 (3-540-19529-7, 195297) Spr-Verlag.

Mills, C. F., et al. TEMA Five: Trace Elements in Man & Animals. 977p. (C). 1985. text 108.00 (0-85198-533-5) C A B Intl.

Mills, C. P. Industrial Disputes Law in Malaysia. 2nd ed. xl, 392p. 1984. 88.00 (967-962-000-X, MICHIE) LEXIS Pub.

Mills, C. Wright. The Causes of World War Three. LC 75-31436. 172p. 1976. reprint ed. lib. bdg. 55.00 (0-8371-8513-0, MICW, Greenwood Pr) Greenwood.

— The Middle Classes in Middle-Sized Cities: The Stratification & Political Position of Small Business & Whit. (Reprint Series in Social Sciences). (C). 1993. reprint ed. pap. text 5.00 (0-8290-2662-2, S-198) Irvington.

— New Men of Power: America's Labor Leaders. LC 68-56261. 323p. 1971. reprint ed. 45.00 (0-678-00715-2) Kelley.

— Power Elite. 2nd ed. LC 99-16200. (Illus.). 448p. 2000. pap. 17.95 (0-19-513354-4) OUP.

— Situated Actions & Vocabularies of Motive. (Reprint Series in Sociology). (C). 1993. reprint ed. pap. text 1.90 (0-8290-2668-1, S-200) Irvington.

— Sociological Imagination. 242p. 1967. reprint ed. pap. text 11.95 (0-19-500751-4) OUP.

— The Sociological Imagination: 40th Anniversary Edition. anniversary ed. LC 99-16199. 256p. 2000. 13.95 (0-19-513373-0) OUP.

— White Collar: American Middle Classes. 398p. 1956. pap. text 14.95 (0-19-500677-1) OUP.

Mills, C. Wright, et al. Letters & Autobiographical Writings LC 99-29106. 2000. write for info. (0-520-22072-2) U CA Pr.

Mills, C. Wright, tr. see Weber, Max M.

Mills, Cadman A. & Nallari, Raj. Analytical Approaches to Stabilization & Adjustment Programs. (EDI Seminar Ser.: No. 44). 144p. 1992. pap. 22.00 (0-8213-1943-4, 11943) World Bank.

Mills, Carl. American Grammar: Sound, Form, & Meaning. (American University Studies: Linguistics: Ser. XIII, Vol. 13). XII, 475p. (C). 1990. text 67.95 (0-8204-0952-9) P Lang Pubng.

Mills, Carol & Mills, John, eds. Australasian Serials: Current Developments in Bibliography. LC 91-24326. (Australian & New Zealand Journal of Serials Librarianship). (Illus.). 93p. 1991. lib. bdg. 3.95 (1-56024-195-0) Haworth Pr.

Mills, Carol H., jt. auth. see Powell, Tag.

Mills, Catherine M., et al. Magnetic Resonance Imaging: Atlas of the Head, Neck & Spine. LC 87-29344. 305p. reprint ed. pap. 94.60 (0-7837-2728-3, 204310800006) Bks Demand.

Mills, Charlene, ed. see Ruzicka, Joseph.

Mills, Charles. Attack of the Angry Legend. LC 97-120980. (Shadow Creek Ranch Ser.). (J). (gr. 4-7). 1998. pap. 5.99 (0-8280-1267-9) Review & Herald.

— Bible Based Answers to Love & Sex. LC 97-133179. 96p. (Orig.). (J). (gr. 5). 1997. pap. 7.99 (0-8280-1255-5) Review & Herald.

— Cry at Midnight. (Shadow Creek Ranch Ser.: Vol. 9). (YA). 1996. pap. 5.99 (0-8280-1111-7) Review & Herald.

— Danger in the Depths. LC 95-214786. (Shadow Creek Ranch Ser.: Vol. 8). (YA). 1995. pap. 5.99 (0-8280-0982-1) Review & Herald.

***Mills, Charles.** Echoing God's Love A Contemporary Collection of Inspirational Stories. 1999. 19.99 (0-8280-1326-8) Review & Herald.

Mills, Charles. Escape to Shadow Creek Ranch. (Shadow Creek Ser.: Vol. 1). (J). (gr. 4-7). Date not set. pap. 5.99 (0-8280-0830-2) Review & Herald.

— Heart of the Warrior. LC 94-235458. (Shadow Creek Ranch Ser.: Vol. 6). (J). (gr. 4-7). Date not set. pap. 5.99 (0-8280-0861-2) Review & Herald.

— The History of Chivalry. LC 78-63507. reprint ed. 32.00 (0-404-17156-7) AMS Pr.

— The Master's Touch. LC 93-6802. 1993. pap. 8.99 (0-8280-0754-3) Review & Herald.

— Mystery in the Attic. (Shadow Creek Ser.: Vol. 2). (J). (gr. 4-7). 1994. pap. 5.99 (0-8280-0831-0) Review & Herald.

***Mills, Charles.** Planet of Joy. (Shadow Creek Ranch Ser.: Vol. 12). 1999. pap. 5.99 (0-8280-1359-4) Review & Herald.

Mills, Charles. The Racial Contract. LC 97-15840. 192p. 1997. 19.95 (0-8014-3454-8) Cornell U Pr.

— River of Fear. (Shadow Creek Ranch Ser.: Vol. 7). (J). (gr. 4-7). 1995. pap. 5.99 (0-8280-0935-X) Review & Herald.

— The Secret of Squaw Rock. LC 92-1660. (Shadow Creek Ser.: Vol. 3). 1992. pap. 5.99 (0-8280-0700-4) Review & Herald.

— Stranger in the Shadows. LC 97-31395. (Shadow Creek Ranch Ser.: Vol. 11). (Orig.). (J). (gr. 4-8). 1998. pap. 5.99 (0-8280-1316-0) Review & Herald.

— Treasure of the Merrilee. (Shadow Creek Ranch Ser.: Vol. 4). (J). (gr. 4-7). 1993. pap. 5.99 (0-8280-0717-9) Review & Herald.

— The Tree of Mythology, Its Growth & Fruitage. 1976. lib. bdg. 59.95 (0-8490-2765-9) Gordon Pr.

— Voyager. LC 89-32337. 157p. reprint ed. pap. 48.70 (0-7837-6401-4, 204611700010) Bks Demand.

— Voyager, II. 192p. (Orig.). (J). (gr. 5-8). 1991. pap. 7.99 (0-8280-0595-8) Review & Herald.

— Whispers in the Wind. (Shadow Creek Ranch Ser.: Vol. 5). (J). (gr. 4-7). 1994. pap. 5.99 (0-8280-0767-5) Review & Herald.

Mills, Charles & Brand, Ruth. Heroic Stories. LC 97-47386. 128p. (Orig.). (J). (gr. 1-4). 1997. pap. 8.99 (0-8280-0968-6) Review & Herald.

— Love Stories. LC 95-168509. (Professor Appleby & the Maggie B. Tapes Ser.: Vol. 3). 128p. (J). (gr. 4-7). 1995. pap. 8.99 (0-8280-0934-1) Review & Herald.

Mills, Charles & Brands, Ruth. Amazing Stories from the Bible. LC 95-107272. (Professor Appleby & the Maggie B. Tapes Ser.: Vol. 2). 128p. (J). (gr. 4-7). 1994. pap. 8.99 (0-8280-0708-X) Review & Herald.

— Mysterious Stories from the Bible. LC 94-186085. (Professor Appleby & the Maggie B. Tapes Ser.: Vol. 1). 128p. (J). (gr. 4-7). 1993. pap. 8.99 (0-8280-0709-8) Review & Herald.

Mills, Charles, jt. auth. see Brand, Ruth R.

Mills, Charles A. Echoes of Manassas. 98p. 1988. pap. 6.75 (1-886826-01-3) Manassas Mus.

— If Germany Won World War II. 48p. 1997. pap. 5.00 (0-945598-12-2) Apple Cheeks Pr.

— Lost Treasures & Wonders. 55p. 1996. pap. 5.00 (0-945598-10-6) Apple Cheeks Pr.

— Love, Sex & Marriage in the Civil War. 48p. 1994. pap. 6.00 (0-945598-09-2) Apple Cheeks Pr.

— The Sherlock Holmes Book of Wines & Spirits. 48p. 1998. pap. 6.00 (0-945598-13-0) Apple Cheeks Pr.

— The Sherlock Holmes Cookbook. 49p. 1990. pap. 5.00 (0-945598-06-8) Apple Cheeks Pr.

— Treasure Legends of Georgia. 48p. 1992. pap. 5.00 (0-945598-08-4) Apple Cheeks Pr.

— Treasure Legends of North Carolina. 48p. 1992. pap. 5.00 (0-945598-07-6) Apple Cheeks Pr.

— Who Dreams Shall Live: Enchanted Realms. 48p. 1998. pap. 5.00 (0-945598-11-4) Apple Cheeks Pr.

Mills, Charles E. The Quality Control Audit: A Management Evaluation Tool. 309p. 1989. 57.00 (0-07-042428-4) McGraw.

Mills, Charles K. Charles C. DeRudio. 1976. 16.95 (0-8488-0582-8, J M C & Co) Amereon Ltd.

— Roster of the Seventh Cavalry Campaigns. 1976. 26.95 (0-8488-0012-5, J M C & Co) Amereon Ltd.

Mills, Charles K., intro. General Sturgis & Brice's Crossroads: A Short Biography & Service Profile on the 7th Calvalry's Samuel D. Sturgis. (Guidon Monographs). (Illus.). 1985. 9.00 (0-685-10875-9, J M C & Co) Amereon Ltd.

Mills, Charles M. From Dusk to Dawn: Sermons for Lent & Easter: Cycle B Gospel Texts. LC 93-4024. 1993. pap. 9.75 (1-55673-607-X, 9332) CSS OH.

Mills, Charles M. & Buchheim, Durwood L. Homiletic Meditations, Cycle B, Vol. 2: Lent Through Ascension of Our Lord, First Reading & Gospel, Pt. B. LC 93-44100. 1994. pap. 17.25 (1-55673-638-X) CSS OH.

M

Mills, Charles P. Meet Your Zoning Hearing Board: A Zoning Handbook & Guide. LC 75-9523. 1975. spiral bd. 4.00 (*0-686-05762-7*) C P Mills.

Mills, Charles W. Blackness Visible: Essays on Philosophy & Race. LC 97-45768. 288p. 1998. 39.95 (*0-8014-3467-X*) Cornell U Pr.

— Blackness Visible: Essays on Philosophy & Race. LC 97-45768. (Illus.). 288p. 1998. pap. text 16.95 (*0-8014-8471-5*) Cornell U Pr.

Mills, Charlotte, ed. see Barton, Lois.

Mills, Charlotte, ed. see Pullen, Virginia A.

Mills, Cheryl A. William's World. unabridged ed. (Illus.). 32p. (J). (gr. 1-7). 1997. 15.95 (*0-9661180-0-6*) Seven Setters.

Mills, Christina, tr. see Randall, Margaret.

Mills, Christopher, et al. Performance Management: Fact or Fantasy : a Study of Current & Future Practices in Singapore. LC 97-941514. vii, 76p. 1994. write for info. Miscell Pubs.

Mills, Clark, tr. see Mallarme, Stephane.

Mills, Claudia. After Fifth Grade, the World! 128p. (J). (gr. 3-7). 1991. reprint ed. pap. 2.95 (*0-380-70894-9*, Avon Bks) Morrow Avon.

— Cally's Enterprise. 128p. (J). (gr. 5 up). 1989. pap. 2.75 (*0-380-70693-8*, Avon Bks) Morrow Avon.

— Despues del Quinto Ano . . . El Mundo (After the Fifth Grade . . . the World) Villegas, Paloma, tr. (SPA., Illus.). 144p. (J). (gr. 5-6). 1992. reprint ed. pap. 5.99 (*968-16-3663-5*, Pub. by Fondo) Continental Bk.

— Dinah for President. LC 93-44668. 128p. (J). (gr. 3-7). 1994. pap. 3.95 (*0-689-71854-3*) Aladdin.

— Dinah for President. LC 91-34839. 128p. (J). (gr. 3-7). 1992. lib. bdg. 14.00 (*0-02-766999-8*, Mac Bks Young Read) S&S Childrens.

— Dinah Forever. LC 94-42136. 144p. (J). (gr. 4-7). 1995. 14.00 (*0-374-31788-7*) FS&G.

— Dinah Forever. LC 97-42601. 160p. (J). 1998. pap. 4.95 (*0-7868-1275-3*, Pub. by Hyperion) Time Warner.

— Dinah in Love. LC 93-19258. 144p. (J). (gr. 3-7). 1996. per. 3.95 (*0-689-80325-7*) Aladdin.

— Dinah in Love. LC 93-19256. 128p. (J). (gr. 3-7). 1993. lib. bdg. 14.00 (*0-02-766998-X*, Mac Bks Young Read) S&S Childrens.

— Dinah in Love. LC 93-19258. (J). 1996. 9.05 (*0-606-09191-2*, Pub. by Turtleback) Demco.

Mills, Claudia. Gus & Grandpa. LC 95-13859. (Illus.). 48p. (J). (gr. 1-3). 1997. 13.00 (*0-374-32824-2*) FS&G.

— Gus & Grandpa. (Illus.). 48p. (J). (gr. 1-3). 1999. pap. text 4.95 (*0-374-42847-6*) FS&G.

— Gus & Grandpa & Show & Tell. LC 99-21166. (Illus.). (J). 2000. 13.00 (*0-374-32819-6*) FS&G.

Mills, Claudia. Gus & Grandpa & the Christmas Cookies. LC 96-31254. (Gus & Grandpa Ser.). (Illus.). 48p. (J). (gr. 1-3). 1997. 13.00 (*0-374-32823-4*) FS&G.

— Gus & Grandpa & the Two-Wheeled Bike. LC 97-44203. (Illus.). 48p. (J). (gr. 1-3). 1999. pap. text 13.00 (*0-374-32821-8*) FS&G.

***Mills, Claudia.** Gus & Grandpa at Basketball. (J). 2001. text. write for info. (*0-374-32818-8*) FS&G.

Mills, Claudia. Gus & Grandpa at the Hospital. LC 97-20609. (Illus.). 47p. (J). (gr. 1-3). 1998. 13.00 (*0-374-32827-7*) FS&G.

— Gus & Grandpa Ride the Train. LC 97-4988. (Illus.). 47p. (J). (gr. 1-3). 1998. 13.00 (*0-374-32826-9*) FS&G.

***Mills, Claudia.** Gus & Grandpa Ride the Train. (Illus.). 48p. (J). (ps-3). 2000. pap. 4.95 (*0-374-42813-1*, Sunburst Bks) FS&G.

— Gus & Grandpa Ride the Train. (Illus.). (J). 2000. 10.40 (*0-606-18133-4*) Turtleback.

Mills, Claudia. Losers, Inc. LC 96-30922. 150p. (J). (gr. 3-7). 1997. 16.00 (*0-374-34661-5*) FS&G.

— Losers, Inc. LC 98-14221. 96p. (J). (gr. 3-7). 1998. pap. 4.95 (*0-7868-1274-5*, Pub. by Hyperion) Time Warner.

— Losers, Inc. 160p. 1998. pap. 4.95 (*0-7868-1364-4*, Pub. by Hyprn Ppbks) Little.

— One Small Lost Sheep. LC 96-18609. (Illus.). 32p. (J). (ps-3). 1997. 16.00 (*0-374-35649-1*) FS&G.

— Phoebe's Parade. LC 93-21861. (Illus.). 32p. (J). (gr. k-3). 1994. mass mkt. 14.95 (*0-02-767012-0*, Mac Bks Young Read) S&S Childrens.

— Standing up to Mr. O. LC 98-3843. 165p. (J). (gr. 4-7). 1998. 16.00 (*0-374-34721-2*) FS&G.

***Mills, Claudia.** Standing up to Mr. O. LC 99-37281. 176p. (J). (gr. 3-7). 2000. pap. 5.99 (*0-7868-1404-7*, Pub. by Hyprn Child) Time Warner.

Mills, Claudia. Values & Public Policy. 700p. (C). 1991. pap. text 50.00 (*0-15-594711-7*, Pub. by Harcourt Coll Pubs) Harcourt.

— A Visit to Amy-Claire. LC 91-280. (Illus.). 32p. (J). (gr. k-3). 1992. text 14.95 (*0-02-766991-2*, Mac Bks Young Read) S&S Childrens.

— What about Annie? LC 84-20862. 128p. (J). (gr. 5 up). 1985. 9.95 (*0-8027-6573-4*) Walker & Co.

***Mills, Claudia.** You're a Brave Man, Julius Zimmerman. LC 98-50799. 160p. (J). (gr. 3-7). 1999. 16.00 (*0-374-38708-7*) FS&G.

Mills, Claudia, jt. ed. see Fullinwider, Robert K.

Mills, Claudia, jt. ed. see MacLean, Douglas.

Mills, Claudia E., jt. auth. see Wrobel, David.

Mills-Courts, Karen. Poetry As Epitaph: Representation & Poetic Language. LC 89-13533. 352p. 1990. text 50.00 (*0-8071-1568-1*); pap. text 19.95 (*0-8071-1657-2*) La State U Pr.

Mills, Craig. The Bane of Lord Caladon. 224p. (Orig.). 1982. mass mkt. 3.50 (*0-345-28972-2*, Del Rey) Ballantine Pub Grp.

Mills, Craig. Dreamer in Discord. 1988. mass mkt. 3.50 (*0-345-34591-6*) Ballantine Pub Grp.

Mills, Craig. King's Quest No. 1: The Floating Castle. 304p. (Orig.). 1995. mass mkt. 5.99 (*1-57297-009-X*) Blvd Books.

Mills, Criss B. Designing with Models: A Studio Guide to Making & Using Architectural Design Models. LC 99-26957. 208p. 2000. pap. 44.95 (*0-471-34589-X*) Wiley.

Mills, Crystal S., jt. ed. see Untalan, Faye F.

Mills, D. Chinese Goldfish. (Illus.). 200p. 1991. 26.95 (*7-119-00408-5*, 16035) Tetra Pr.

Mills, D. L. Nonlinear Optics: Basic Concepts. (Illus.). viii, 184p. 1991. 39.95 (*0-387-54192-6*) Spr-Verlag.

— Nonlinear Optics: Basic Concepts. 2nd ed. LC 98-6385. (Illus.). 260p. 1998. pap. 42.50 (*3-540-64182-3*) Spr-Verlag.

— Salmon in the Sea & New Enhancement Strategies. 1993. 85.00 (*0-85238-199-9*) Blackwell Sci.

Mills, D. L., et al, eds. Molecular Strategies of Pathogens & Host Plants. (Illus.). 264p. 1991. 79.95 (*0-387-97448-2*) Spr-Verlag.

Mills, D. L., jt. auth. see Vevers, Gwynne.

Mills, D. L., jt. ed. see Agranovich, V. M.

Mills, D. L., jt. ed. see McIntyre, P.

***Mills, D Quinn.** Internet University: Business School Edition. 1999. pap. text 29.95 (*1-55701-272-5*) New Promise Bks.

Mills, D. Quinn. Internet University: Your Guide to Online College Courses. 3rd ed. 400p. 1999. pap. 19.95 (*1-55701-258-X*) Watsn-Guptill.

Mills, D. Quinn & Friesen, G. Bruce. Broken Promises: An Unconventional View of What Went Wrong at IBM. 224p. (C). 1996. 22.95 (*0-87584-654-8*) Harvard Busn.

Mills, Dallice, et al, eds. Molecular Aspects of Pathogenicity & Resistance: Requirement for Signa Transduction. LC 96-83099. (Illus.). 312p. (C). 1996. text 59.00 (*0-89054-215-5*) Am Phytopathol Soc.

Mills, Damon. Return to Hell's Acre. large type ed. (Dales Large Print Ser.). 243p. 1997. pap. 18.99 (*1-85389-708-6*) Ulverscroft.

Mills, Daniel Q. The Gem Principle: Six Steps to Creating a High Performance Organization. 256p. 1994. 18.00 (*0-939246-75-9*) Wiley.

— The GEM Principle: Six Steps to Creating a High Performance Organization. 146p. 1995. 22.95 (*0-471-13364-7*) Wiley.

— Government, Labor & Inflation: Wage Stabilization in the United States. LC 75-9685. viii, 312p. 1994. lib. bdg. 20.00 (*0-226-52951-7*) U Ch Pr.

— Labor-Management Relations. 5th ed. LC 93-21687. (Series in Management). 704p. (C). 1993. 83.75 (*0-07-042512-4*) McGraw.

***Mills, Daniel S. & Nankervis, Kathryn.** Equine Behaviour: Principles & Practice. LC 98-55558. (Illus.). 240p. 1998. pap. 34.95 (*0-632-04878-6*, Pub. by Blckwell Science) Iowa St U Pr.

Mills, David. The Idea of Loyalty in Upper Canada, 1784-1850. (Illus.). 256p. (C). 1988. text 65.00 (*0-7735-0660-8*, Pub. by McG-Queens Univ Pr) CUP Services.

— Physics: For Scientists & Engineers - Test Bank, Vol. 1. 4th ed. 1998. write for info. (*1-57259-517-5*) Worth.

— Physics: For Scientists & Engineers - Test Bank, Vol. 2. 4th ed. 1998. write for info. (*1-57259-518-3*) Worth.

— Pneumatic Conveying Design. 607p. 1990. text 205.00 (*0-408-04707-0*) Buttrwrth-Heinemann.

— Recycling the Cycle: The City of Chester & Its Whitsun Plays. 320p. 1997. text 55.00 (*0-8020-4096-9*) U of Toronto Pr.

Mills, David, ed. The Chester Mystery Cycle: A New Edition with Modernised Spelling. (Medieval Texts & Studies: No. 9). 460p. 1992. pap. text 16.95 (*0-937191-27-2*) Mich St U Pr.

— The Chester Mystery Cycle: A New Edition with Modernised Spelling. (Medieval Texts & Studies: No. 9). 440p. 1992. text 29.95 (*0-937191-29-9*) Mich St U Pr.

— A Dictionary of English Place Names. (Illus.). 424p. 1992. 35.00 (*0-19-869156-4*) OUP.

— The Pilgrim's Guide: C. S. Lewis & the Art of Witness. 315p. 1999. pap. 16.00 (*0-8028-4689-0*) Eerdmans.

Mills, David, jt. auth. see Lumiansky, Robert M.

Mills, David, jt. ed. see Lumiansky, Robert M.

Mills, David E., jt. ed. see Huang, Yung-Sheng.

Mills, David H., jt. auth. see Fretz, Bruce R.

Mills, Dean. Union on the King's Highway. LC 87-72772. (Campbell-Stone Heritage of Unity Ser.). 188p. 1987. 12.99 (*0-89900-286-2*) College Pr Pub.

Mills, Deanie F. The Jigsaw Man. 320p. 1997. mass mkt. 6.50 (*0-515-12019-7*, Jove) Berkley Pub.

— Ordeal. 1997. 22.95 (*0-614-27902-X*) NAL.

***Mills, Deanie F.** Ordeal. 464p. 1998. mass mkt. 6.99 (*0-451-18894-2*, Sig) NAL.

Mills, Deanie F. Tight Rope, 1 vol. 1999. mass mkt. 6.99 (*0-451-18895-0*) NAL.

***Mills, Deanie Francis.** Torch. 1999. mass mkt. 6.99 (*0-451-19830-1*, Sig) NAL.

***Mills, Deborah C.** How to Tell When You're Deliberately Being Poisoned & Live to Tell about It. 1999. pap. 7.95 (*0-533-12900-1*) Vantage.

Mills, Derek. Ecology & Management of Atlantic Salmon. (Illus.). 368p. (C). 1989. 65.00 (*0-412-32140-8*, A3418) Chapman & Hall.

Mills, Derek, jt. auth. see Jeffries, Michael.

Mills, Dian & Vernon, Michael. Endometriosis: Healing Through Nutrition. (Illus.). 272p. 1998. pap. 14.95 (*1-86204-300-0*, Pub. by Element MA) Penguin Putnam.

Mills, Diana. Crazy Hattie. (Illus.). 12p. (J). (gr. 3-7). 1986. pap. 7.95 (*0-9616555-0-X*) Berry Good Child Bks.

Mills, Dick. Aquarium Fish. LC 93-3155. (Eyewitness Handbooks Ser.). (Illus.). 304p. 1993. 29.95 (*1-56458-294-9*); pap. 18.95 (*1-56458-293-0*) DK Pub Inc.

***Mills, Dick.** The Encyclopedia of Aquarium Fish. (Illus.). 144p. 2000. 29.95 (*0-7641-5300-5*) Barron.

Mills, Dick. A Fishkeeper's Guide to Community Fishes. (Illus.). 120p. 1991. 10.95 (*1-56465-133-9*, 16062) Tetra Pr.

— A Fishkeeper's Guide to Marine Fishes. write for info. (*0-318-59670-9*) S&S Trade.

— A Fishkeeper's Guide to the Tropical Aquarium. rev. ed. (Illus.). 117p. 1991. 10.95 (*1-56465-140-1*, 16061) Tetra Pr.

— God's Word for You. 174p. (Orig.). 1997. mass mkt. 5.99 (*0-88368-273-7*) Whitaker Hse.

— He Spoke & I Was Strengthened. rev. ed. 174p. (Orig.). 1973. pap. 6.95 (*0-9629011-0-5*) D Mills Minis.

— Marine Fishes. rev. ed. (Fishkeeper's Guide Ser.). (Illus.). 120p. 1991. 11.95 (*1-56465-129-0*, 16064) Tetra Pr.

— Marriage Bliss. Orig. Title: How to Have a Happy Marriage. 91p. 1996. mass mkt. 5.99 (*0-88368-394-6*) Whitaker Hse.

— Popular Guide to Tropical Aquarium Fishes. 320p. 1993. 22.95 (*1-56465-109-6*, 16016) Tetra Pr.

— The Spirit Filled Believer's Daily Devotional. Orig. Title: Word Daily Devotional. 384p. (Orig.). 1996. pap. 12.99 (*0-89274-844-3*, HH-844) Harrison Hse.

— The Tetra Encyclopedia of the Marine Aquarium. (Illus.). 208p. 31.95 (*1-56465-141-X*, 16059) Tetra Pr.

— You & Your Aquarium. 1986. pap. 17.00 (*0-394-72985-4*) Knopf.

Mills, Dick, compiled by. A Popular Guide to Garden Ponds. 1992. 17.95 (*1-56465-104-5*, 16012) Tetra Pr.

Mills, Dick & Michael, David. The Messiah & His Hebrew Alphabet. (Orig.). 1994. pap. 9.95 (*0-9629011-1-3*) D Mills Minis.

Mills, Dixie L., jt. auth. see Gardner, Mona J.

Mills, Donald, jt. auth. see Moore, Clement Clarke.

Mills, Donald, tr. see Albertini, Bianca & Bagnoli, Alessandra.

Mills, Donna R. Some Southern Balls (And Allied Families) 344p. 1993. lib. bdg. 38.00 (*0-931069-09-2*) Mills Historical.

Mills, Donna R., compiled by. The First Families of Louisiana Index. LC 92-81054. 105p. 1992. lib. bdg. 19.00 (*0-931069-07-6*) Mills Historical.

— Florida's Unfortunates: The Census, Dependent, Defective, & Delinquent Classes, 1880. LC 92-60783. 112p. 1993. lib. bdg. 19.50 (*0-931069-08-4*) Mills Historical.

Mills, Donna R., ed. Biographical & Historical Memoirs of Natchitoches Parish, Louisana, 1714-1890. LC 85-60815. 122p. 1985. reprint ed. pap. 17.00 (*0-931069-05-X*) Mills Historical.

Mills, Donna R., tr. Florida's First Families: Translated Abstracts of Pre-1821 Spanish Census. LC 91-6661. 201p. 1992. 22.00 (*0-931069-06-8*) Mills Historical.

Mills, Dorothy. The Book of the Ancient Greeks: History & Civilization of Greece. 25.00 (*0-8196-2895-6*) Biblo.

Mills, Dorothy. Renaissance & Reformation Times. LC 83-45667. reprint ed. 55.00 (*0-404-19817-1*) AMS Pr.

Mills, Dorothy H. Dictionary for the Mental Health Professional: Psychiatrists, Psychologists. 250p. 1993. 24.95 (*0-8288-1871-1*, S50021) Fr & Eur.

Mills, Dorothy J. The Sceptre. LC 98-88472. 325p. 1998. 25.00 (*0-7388-0159-3*); pap. 15.00 (*0-7388-0160-7*) Xlibris Corp.

Mills, Dorothy Z. & Mills, Arlen C. Communicating the Appraisal: The Individual Condominium Unit Appraisal Report. 2nd ed. LC 95-30133. 1995. 15.00 (*0-922154-22-8*) Appraisal Inst.

Mills, Dorothy Z., jt. auth. see Mills, Arlen C.

Mills, Doug, et al. Foundations of Accounting. 9th ed. 750p. 1996. pap. 49.95 (*0-908237-92-8*, Pub. by New South Wales Univ Pr) Intl Spec Bk.

Mills, E. Andrew, ed. Supervision & Administration: Programs, Positions, Perspectives. (Illus.). 221p. (C). 1991. 22.00 (*0-937652-56-3*, 247) Natl Art Ed.

Mills, E. S. & Nijkamp, Peter, eds. Handbook of Regional & Urban Economics, Vol. 2. 620p. 1987. 110.00 (*0-444-87970-6*) Elsevier.

Mills, E. S., jt. auth. see Cheshire, P. C.

***Mills, Earl.** Dorothy Dandridge: An Intimate Portrait of Hollywood's First Major Black Film Star. (Illus.). 1999. pap. 14.99 (*0-87067-899-X*) Holloway.

***Mills, Earl & Breen, Betty.** Wampanoag Cape Cod Cookbook: Wampanoag Indian Recipes, Images & Lore. 240p. 2000. pap. 14.95 (*1-57416-057-5*) Clear Light.

Mills, Earl, Sr. & Mann, Alicja. Son of Mashpee: Reflections of Chief Flying Eagle, a Wampanoag. unabridged ed. LC 97-114386. (Illus.). 128p. (Orig.). 1996. pap. 24.75 (*0-9654360-0-4*) Word Studio.

Mills, Edward. Building Maintenance & Preservation: A Guide to Design & Management. 2nd ed. 1997. pap. text 56.95 (*0-7506-3398-0*) Buttrwrth-Heinemann.

Mills, Edward, ed. see McCartney, Francesca.

Mills, Edward D. National Exhibition Centre: Shop Window for the World. (Illus.). 120p. 1976. pap. 14.95 (*0-8464-0667-5*) Beekman Pubs.

Mills, Edward L. Biological Invasions in the Hudson River Basin: An Inventory & Historical Analysis LC 97-61576. (Circular Ser.). 51p. 1997. pap. write for info. (*1-55557-207-3*) NYS Museum.

Mills, Edwin S. The Burden of Government. (Publication Ser.: No. 328). 188p. 1986. text 23.95 (*0-8179-8281-7*) Hoover Inst Pr.

— Studies in the Structure of the Urban Economy. LC 71-179873. (Resources for the Future Ser.). (Illus.). 162p. 1972. 15.95 (*0-8018-1367-0*); pap. 9.95 (*0-8018-1595-9*) Johns Hopkins.

— Toward the Next Massachusetts Miracle: Limits of Economic Development Programs. LC 97-37744. (Paper Ser.: Vol. 14). 140p. 1997. pap. 15.00 (*0-929930-15-0*) Pioneer Inst.

Mills, Edwin S., ed. Economic Analysis of Environmental Problems: A Conference of the Universities - National Bureau Committee for Economic Research & Resources for the Future. LC 74-82378. 486p. reprint ed. pap. 150.70 (*0-8357-7570-4*, 205689100096) Bks Demand.

Mills, Edwin S. & Becker, Charles M. Studies in Indian Urban Development. (World Bank Publication). 224p. 1986. text 29.95 (*0-19-520507-3*) OUP.

Mills, Edwin S. & Byung-Nak Song. Urbanization & Urban Problems. (East Asian Monographs: No. 88). (Illus.). 329p. 1979. 17.50 (*0-674-93133-5*) HUP.

Mills, Edwin S. & Graves, Philip E. The Economics of Environmental Quality. 2nd ed. 368p. (C). 1986. text 23.75 (*0-393-95270-3*) Norton.

Mills, Edwin S. & McDonald, John F., eds. Sources of Metropolitan Growth. LC 91-8650. 331p. (C). 1992. 19.95 (*0-88285-135-7*) Ctr Urban Pol Res.

Mills, Edwin S., ed. see Universities-National Bureau Staff.

Mills, Elaine, jt. auth. see Wilkins, Verna.

Mills, Elise. Ashes for Gold: A Tale from Mexico. LC 94-14349. (Mondo Folktales ser.). 24p. (Orig.). (J). (gr. k-4). 1994. lib. bdg. 9.95 (*1-879531-43-7*) Mondo Pubng.

Mills, Elizabeth. In the Suzuki Style. LC 74-20230. (Illus.). 120p. 1974. pap. 7.95 (*0-87297-023-X*) Diablo.

— In the Suzuki Style. LC 74-20230. (Illus.). 120p. 1974. pap. 6.95 (*0-87297-024-8*) Diablo.

— Senoufo Phonology, Discourse to Syllable: A Prosodic Approach. LC 81-51057. (Publications in Linguistics: No. 72). 217p. 1984. pap. 8.75 (*0-88312-102-6*) S I L Intl.

***Mills, Elizabeth & Mills, Eryn, eds.** Genuine Sympathy. iii, 73p. 1999. 8.95 (*1-928878-02-4*) Temporal Mech Pr.

Mills, Elizabeth & Murphy, Therese, eds. The Suzuki Concept: An Introduction to a Successful Method for Early Music Education. (Illus.). 220p. 1973. 9.95 (*0-87297-002-7*) Diablo.

— The Suzuki Concept: An Introduction to a Successful Method for Early Music Education. (Illus.). 220p. 1973. pap. 7.95 (*0-87297-003-5*) Diablo.

Mills, Elizabeth S., ed. Natchitoches Church Marriages, 1818-1850: Translated Abstracts from the Registers of St. Francois des Natchitoches, Louisiana. LC 84-9654. (Cane River Creole Ser.). vii, 216p. (Orig.). 1985. pap. 22.00 (*0-931069-04-1*) Mills Historical.

Mills, Elizabeth S. & Mills, Gary B. Tales of Old Natchitoches. (Cane River Creole Ser.: No. 3). (Illus.). 142p. 1978. reprint ed. 22.00 (*0-931069-02-5*) Mills Historical.

Mills, Elizabeth Shown. Evidence! Citation & Analysis for the Family Historian. LC 97-72909. 124p. 1997. reprint ed. 16.95 (*0-8063-1543-1*) Genealog Pub.

Mills, Enos, jt. auth. see Dannen, Kent.

Mills, Enos A. Adventures of a Nature Guide & Essays in Interpretation. 2nd ed. Kiley, Enda M. & Goc, Michael J., eds. (Illus.). 248p. 1991. reprint ed. pap. 10.95 (*0-938627-12-0*) New Past Pr.

***Mills, Enos A.** Being Good to Bears & Other Animals' "Tails" rev. ed. iii, 84p. 1999. pap. 9.95 (*1-928878-01-6*) Temporal Mech Pr.

Mills, Enos A. The Grizzly. (Illus.). 1976. reprint ed. pap. 4.95 (*0-89174-006-6*) Comstock Edns.

***Mills, Enos A.** Grizzly Our Greatest Wild Animal. 4th rev. ed. (Illus.). vi, 163p. 1999. 11.95 (*1-928878-07-5*) Temporal Mech Pr.

— Romance of Geology. iv, 181p. 2000. pap. 12.95 (*1-928878-08-3*) Temporal Mech Pr.

Mills, Enos A. The Spell of the Rockies. LC 89-33076. (Illus.). 436p. 1989. pap. 135.20 (*0-608-04824-0*, 206548100004) Bks Demand.

***Mills, Enos A.** Stories of Scotch. rev. ed. (Illus.). 32p. 2000. pap. 7.95 (*1-928878-06-7*) Temporal Mech Pr.

Mills, Enos A. The Story of a Thousand Year Pine. i, 32p. 1999. reprint ed. 6.95 (*1-928878-00-8*) Temporal Mech Pr.

***Mills, Enos A.** The Story of Early Estes Park. 13th ed. (Illus.). ix, 103p. 1999. 13.95 (*1-928878-05-9*) Temporal Mech Pr.

— Waiting in the Wilderness. rev. ed. ii, 146p. 2000. pap. 10.95 (*1-928878-10-5*) Temporal Mech Pr.

Mills, Enos A. Wild Life on the Rockies. fac. ed. LC 87-30203. (Illus.). 373p. 1988. reprint ed. pap. 115.70 (*0-7837-8105-9*, 204790800008) Bks Demand.

***Mills, Enos A. & James, Will.** Watched by Wild Animals. rev. ed. (Illus.). 155p. 2000. pap. 11.95 (*1-928878-11-3*) Temporal Mech Pr.

Mills, Enos A., jt. auth. see Mills, Esther Burnell.

Mills, Eric. Chesapeake Rumrunners of the Roaring Twenties. LC 99-48511. (Illus.). 232p. 2000. 25.95 (*0-87033-518-9*, Tidewtr Pubs) Cornell Maritime.

Mills, Eric L. Biological Oceanography: An Early History, Eighteen Seventy to Nineteen Sixty. LC 89-33048. (Comstock Bk.). 368p. 1989. text 55.00 (*0-8014-2340-6*) Cornell U Pr.

— Chesapeake Bay in the Civil War. LC 95-49361. (Illus.). 326p. 1996. 29.95 (*0-87033-479-4*, Tidewtr Pubs) Cornell Maritime.

Mills, Ernestine, ed. see Shields, Frederic.

Mills, Eryn, jt. ed. see Mills, Elizabeth.

***Mills, Esther Burnell & Mills, Enos A.** A Baby's Life in the Rocky Mountains. (Illus.). 1132p. 1999. 14.95 (*1-928878-03-2*) Temporal Mech Pr.

Mills, Esther L. God Loves You & Other Songs. 1997. pap. text 14.95 (*1-883012-78-3*) Remnant Pubns.

Mills, Eugene S. The Story of Elderhostel. LC 92-53864. (Illus.). 216p. 1993. pap. 15.95 (*0-87451-600-5*); text 25.00 (*0-87451-599-8*) U Pr of New Eng.

Mills, F. E., jt. ed. see Cline, D. B.

Mills, F. John, ed. see Harding, Richard M.

An Asterisk (*) at the beginning of an entry indicates that the title is appearing for the first time.

Mills, Fetzer. Grassroots. 1997. pap. 14.00 (*0-517-88630-8*) Random Hse Value.

Mills, Franklin B. Adams. Family Records of the Adams, Mills & Humason Families. 135p. 1997. reprint ed. pap. 13.50 (*0-8328-7215-6*); reprint ed. lib. bdg. 23.50 (*0-8328-7214-8*) Higginson Bk Co.

Mills, Frederick C. The Behavior of Prices. LC 75-19729. (National Bureau of Economic Research Ser.). (Illus.). 1975. reprint ed. 47.95 (*0-405-07607-X*) Ayer.

— The Behavior of Prices. (General Ser.: No. 11). 598p. 1927. reprint ed. 155.50 (*0-87014-010-8*) Natl Bur Econ Res.

— Contemporary Theories of Unemployment & of Unemployment Relief. LC 68-56670. (Columbia University. Studies in the Social Sciences: No. 93). reprint ed. 24.50 (*0-404-51183-X*) AMS Pr.

— Economic Tendencies in the United States: Aspects of Pre-War & Post-War Changes. LC 75-19727. (National Bureau of Economic Research Ser.). (Illus.). 1975. reprint ed. 54.95 (*0-405-07605-3*) Ayer.

— Economic Tendencies in the United States: Aspects of Pre-War & Post-War Changes. (General Ser.: No. 21). 664p. 1932. reprint ed. 160.00 (*0-87014-020-5*) Natl Bur Econ Res.

— Price-Quality Interactions in Business Cycles. LC 75-19728. (National Bureau of Economic Research Ser.). (Illus.). 1975. reprint ed. 19.95 (*0-405-07606-1*) Ayer.

— Price-Quantity Interactions in Business Cycles. (Twenty-Fifth Anniversary Ser.: No. 2). 152p. 1946. reprint ed. 41.10 (*0-87014-114-7*) Natl Bur Econ Res.

— Prices in a War Economy: Some Aspects of the Present Price Structure of the United States. (Occasional Papers: No. 12). 104p. 1943. reprint ed. 27.10 (*0-87014-327-1*) Natl Bur Econ Res.

— Prices in Recession & Recovery: A Survey of Recent Changes. (General Ser.: No. 31). 601p. 1936. reprint ed. 156.30 (*0-87014-030-2*) Natl Bur Econ Res.

— Productivity & Economic Progress. (Occasional Papers: No. 38). 46p. 1952. reprint ed. 20.00 (*0-87014-353-0*) Natl Bur Econ Res.

— The Structure of Postwar Prices. (Occasional Papers: No. 27). 72p. 1948. reprint ed. 20.00 (*0-87014-342-5*) Natl Bur Econ Res.

Mills, Frederick C. & Long, Clarence D. The Statistical Agencies of the Federal Government: A Report to the Commission on Organization of the Executive Branch of the Government. (General Ser.: No. 50). 215p. 1949. reprint ed. 60.40 (*0-87014-049-3*) Natl Bur Econ Res.

Mills, Frederick E., ed. Advanced Accelerator Concepts: Proceedings from the International Symposium on Advanced Accelerator Concepts Held in Madison, Wisconsin, August 1986. (AIP Conference Proceedings Ser.: No. 156). 610p. 1987. 75.00 (*0-685-58860-2*) Am Inst Physics.

Mills, Fredrick. Crossroads of Traditional Philosophy: A User's Guide. LC 97-72738. 336p. (C). 1997. pap., per. 47.95 (*0-7872-3686-1*, 41368601) Kendall-Hunt.

Mills, G. Riley, et al. The Boy Who Knew No Fear. (J). (gr. 3-9). 1997. pap. 4.50 (*1-57514-252-X*) Encore Perform Pub.

Mills, Gareth. On the Waterfront. 130p. 1994. pap. 30.00 (*1-85902-037-2*, Pub. by Gomer Pr) St Mut.

Mills, Gary B. The Forgotten People: Cane River's Creoles of Color. LC 77-452. (Illus.). xxx, 278p. 1977. pap. 15.95 (*0-8071-0287-3*) La State U Pr.

— Southern Loyalists in the Civil War: A Composite Directory of Case Files Created by the U. S. Commissioner of Claims, 1871-1880, Including Those Appealed to the War Claims Committee of the U. S. House of Representatives & the U. S. Court of Claims. LC 94-76034. 684p. 1994. 45.00 (*0-8063-1441-9*, 3847) Genealog Pub.

Mills, Gary B., jt. auth. see Mills, Elizabeth S.

Mills, Gary K. Quiet Moments Kid's Relaxation: A Guide to the Tape Series for Parents & Teachers. 27p. (Orig.). 1986. pap. 6.00 (*0-938669-07-9*) MediaHlth Pubns.

— Quiet Moments Kid's Relaxation: A Guide to the Tape Series for Parents & Teachers, Set. 27p. (Orig.). 1986. audio 20.00 (*0-938669-12-5*) MediaHlth Pubns.

— Quiet Moments Relaxation: A Guide to Deep Relaxation for Adults. LC 86-16464. (Illus.). 72p. (Orig.). 1986. 60.00 incl. audio (*0-938669-11-7*); pap. 10.00 (*0-938669-00-1*) MediaHlth Pubns.

Mills, Geoffery, jt. ed. see Flinders, David J.

Mills, Geoffrey. On the Board. 2nd ed. 256p. 1985. text 24.95 (*0-04-658250-9*) Routledge.

Mills, Geofrey T. & Rockoff, Hugh, eds. The Sinews of War: Essays on the Economic History of World War II. LC 92-26832. (Illus.). 284p. reprint ed. pap. 88.10 (*0-608-09060-3*, 206969400005) Bks Demand.

Mills, George. The House Sails Out of Sight of Home. (Samuel French Morse Poetry Prize Ser.). 64p. 1991. pap. text 11.95 (*1-55553-113-X*) NE U Pr.

Mills, George. One-Armed Bandits & Other Stories of Iowa's Past & Present. 281p. 1997. pap. 14.00 (*0-931209-66-8*) Focus Bks.

Mills, George, jt. auth. see Aitken, John.

Mills, George H. History of the 16th North Carolina Regiment in the Civil War. LC 91-78346. 82p. 1992. reprint ed. pap. 10.95 (*0-9622393-3-X*) Edmonston Publ.

Mills, George S. The Little Man with the Long Shadow: The Life & Times of Frederick M. Hubbell. LC 88-13117. (Iowa Heritage Collection). (Illus.). 272p. 1988. reprint ed. pap. 10.95 (*0-8138-0242-3*) Iowa St U Pr.

Mills, George T. Navaho Art & Culture. LC 83-5636. (Illus.). 273p. (C). 1983. reprint ed. lib. bdg. 59.75 (*0-313-24008-6*, MINA, Greenwood Pr) Greenwood.

Mills, Glen E. Putting a Message Together. 2nd ed. LC 78-179367. Orig. Title: Message Preparation: Analysis & Structure. 1972. pap. 3.95 (*0-672-61299-2*, SC8, Bobbs) Macmillan.

Mills, Glendola Y. Dancing in My Mother's Mother's Body. LC 98-60013. (Sunscholars Ser.). Date not set. pap. 19.95 (*1-889218-13-8*) Sungai Bks.

Mills, Gordon & Walter, John. Technical Writing. 5th ed. 576p. (C). 1986. text 63.50 (*0-03-062019-8*, Pub. by Harcourt Coll Pubs) Harcourt.

Mills, Gordon, jt. auth. see Duckworth, Mark.

Mills, Gordon E. Analysis in Human Resource Training & Organization Development. 1989. 31.25 (*0-201-09224-7*) Addison-Wesley.

Mills, Greg, jt. ed. see Rotberg, Robert I.

Mills, Gretchen, et al. Discussing Death: A Guide to Death Education. LC 75-17885. 1976. 14.95 (*0-88280-026-4*); pap. 14.95 (*0-88280-027-2*) ETC Pubns.

Mills, H. E., et al. College Women & the Social Sciences. LC 74-152165. (Essay Index Reprint Ser.). 1977. reprint ed. 21.95 (*0-8369-2221-2*) Ayer.

Mills, H. Robert. Practical Astronomy: A User-Friendly Handbook for Skywatchers. (Illus.). 240p. 1994. 29.95 (*1-898563-02-0*) Paul & Co Pubs.

Mills, Harlan D. Software Productivity. LC 88-5099. (Illus.). 288p. 1988. reprint ed. pap. 25.95 (*0-932633-10-2*) Dorset Hse Pub Co.

Mills, Harlow B., et al. A Century of Biological Research. Egerton, Frank N., 3rd, ed. LC 77-74240. (History of Ecology Ser.). (Illus.). 1978. reprint ed. lib. bdg. 17.95 (*0-405-10409-X*) Ayer.

Mills, Harriet C. Intermediate Reader in Modern Chinese, Vol. 3. 1967. pap. 25.00 (*0-8014-9827-9*) Cornell U Pr.

***Mills, Harry.** Artful Persuasion: How to Command Attention, Change Minds & Influence People. LC 99-56754. 240p. 2000. pap. 17.95 (*0-8144-7063-7*) AMACOM.

Mills, Harry A. & Jones, J. Benton, Jr. Plant Analysis Handbook II: A Practical Sampling, Preparation, Analysis & Interpretation Guide. (Illus.). 1996. 79.95 (*1-878148-05-2*) Micro-Macro Pub.

Mills, Heidi & Clyde, Jean A., eds. Portraits of Whole Language Classrooms: Learning for All Ages. LC 89-35937. (Illus.). 307p. (Orig.). (C). (ps). 1990. pap. text 25.00 (*0-435-08510-7*, 08510) Heinemann.

***Mills, Heidi & Donnelly, Amy.** Creating a Culture of Inquiry. 2000. pap. write for info. (*0-325-00267-3*) Heinemann.

Mills, Heidi & O'Keefe, Timothy. Mathematics in the Making: Supporting Authors in Primary Classrooms. LC 96-14198. 197p. 1996. pap. text 25.00 (*0-435-07100-9*) Heinemann.

Mills, Heidi, et al. Looking Closely: Exploring the Role of Phonics in One Whole Language Classroom. (Illus.). 69p. (Orig.). 1992. pap. 11.95 (*0-8141-3031-3*) NCTE.

Mills, Helen. Commanding Sentences. 3rd ed. 378p. 1990. reprint ed. pap. text 27.95 (*0-88133-524-X*) Sheffield WI.

Mills, Hilary. Mailer: A Biography LC 83-24852. 477 p. 1984. write for info. (*0-07-042423-3*) McGraw.

Mills, Howard. Working with Shakespeare. LC 93-13139. 224p. (C). 1993. lib. bdg. 49.50 (*0-389-21009-9*) B&N Imports.

Mills, Howard, ed. see Crabbe, George.

***Mills, Hugh L., Jr. & Anderson, Robert.** Low Level Hell: A Scout Pilot in the Big Red One. 336p. 2000. pap. 19.95 (*0-89141-719-2*) Presidio Pr.

Mills, Ian, et al. Quantities, Units, & Symbols in Physical Chemistry. 2nd ed. LC 92-40104. 176p. 1993. pap. 21.00 (*0-632-03583-8*) Blackwell Sci.

Mills, J., ed. The Account Roll of the Priory of the Holy Trinity, Dublin, 1337-1346. 276p. 1996. boxed set 40.00 (*1-85182-238-0*, Pub. by Four Cts Pr) Intl Spec Bk.

Mills, J., et al, eds. Manufacturing Science & Engineering, 1995 Vol. 2-3: Manufacturing Science & Engineering, 2 vols., Set, Vols. 1 & 2. LC 95-81272. (1995 ASME International Mechanical Engineering Congress & Exposition Ser.: MED-Vol. 2/MH-Vol. 3). 1352p. 1995. 360.00 (*0-7918-1738-5*, H01020) ASME.

Mills, J. Eustace. All Truth. 160p. (Orig.). 1997. reprint ed. pap. 9.95 (*1-883228-16-6*) Invictus MI.

Mills, J. J., jt. auth. see Gorman, G.

Mills, J. J., jt. auth. see Gorman, Gary E.

Mills, J. R. Principles & Practice of Orthodontics. 2nd ed. LC 87-10291. (Dental Ser.). (Illus.). 294p. 1987. pap. text 69.00 (*0-443-03608-X*) Church.

Mills, J. Warner. Mill's Constitutional Annotations: A Compendium of the Law Especially Applicable to State Constitutions & Adapted to the Constitution of Colorado & Cross-Reference to the Constitutions of Other States. viii, 444p. 1992. reprint ed. 55.00 (*0-8377-2441-4*, Rothman) W S Hein.

Mills, Jack & Broughton, Vanda, eds. Bliss Bibliographic Classification: Class A-AL: Philosophy & Logic. 2nd rev. ed. 56p. 1992. text 65.00 (*1-85739-025-3*) Bowker-Saur.

— Bliss Bibliographic Classification: Class B: Physics. 1999. 60.00 (*0-408-70824-7*) Bowker-Saur.

— Bliss Bibliographic Classification: Class C: Chemistry & Materials. 2nd ed. 150p. 2000. 60.00 (*0-408-70825-5*) Bowker-Saur.

— Bliss Bibliographic Classification: Class D: Astronomy & Space. 2nd ed. 150p. 2001. 60.00 (*0-408-70826-3*) Bowker-Saur.

— Bliss Bibliographic Classification: Class GR-GZ: Applied Biology & Agriculture. 2nd ed. 1997. 60.00 (*0-408-70835-2*) Bowker-Saur.

— Bliss Bibliographic Classification: Class H: Anthropology, Human Biology & Life Sciences. 2nd ed. 326p. 1981. text 67.00 (*0-408-70828-X*) Bowker-Saur.

— Bliss Bibliographic Classification: Class I: Psychology & Psychiatry. 62p. 1978. text 35.00 (*0-408-70841-7*) Bowker-Saur.

— Bliss Bibliographic Classification: Class K: Society. 2nd ed. 167p. 1984. text 61.00 (*0-408-70830-1*) Bowker-Saur.

— Bliss Bibliographic Classification: Class P: Religion, the Occult, Morals & Ethics. 2nd ed. 43p. 1977. text 31.00 (*0-408-70832-8*) Bowker-Saur.

— Bliss Bibliographic Classification: Class T: Economics, Management of Economic Enterprises. 2nd ed. 36p. 1977. text 95.00 (*0-408-70834-4*) Bowker-Saur.

— Bliss Bibliographic Classification: Class W: Fine Arts & Music. 2nd ed. 1997. 60.00 (*0-408-70838-7*) Bowker-Saur.

— Bliss Bibliographic Classification: Class X-Z: Language & Literature. 2nd ed. 1997. 60.00 (*0-408-70839-5*) Bowker-Saur.

— Bliss Bibliographic Classification: Classes E-GQ: Biology & Botany. 2nd ed. 150p. 2001. 60.00 (*0-408-70827-1*) Bowker-Saur.

— Bliss Bibliographic Classification: Classes GR-GZ: Applied Biology & Agriculture. 2001. 60.00 (*0-408-70831-X*) Bowker-Saur.

— Bliss Bibliographic Classification: Classes U-V: Technology. Date not set. 60.00 (*0-408-70837-9*) Bowker-Saur.

— Bliss Bibliographic Classification: Classes 2-9: Generalia. 2001. 60.00 (*0-408-70822-0*) Bowker-Saur.

— Bliss Bibliographic Classification: Introduction & Auxiliary Schedules. 268p. 1987. 75.00 (*0-408-70865-4*) Bowker-Saur.

— Bliss Biblographic Classification: Social Welfare & Criminology. 2nd ed. 200p. 1994. 50.00 (*1-85739-121-7*) Bowker-Saur.

Mills, Jack, jt. auth. see Samovar, Larry A.

Mills, Jackie. Sirena of Salado. (Illus.). 32p. (J). (gr. 2-7). 1991. 10.95 (*0-9629284-0-2*) Indian Trail.

Mills, James. Haywire. large type ed. 400p. 31.50 (*0-614-28283-7*) Ulverscroft.

— The Hearing. LC 97-32284. 416p. 1998. 25.00 (*0-446-51958-8*, Pub. by Warner Bks) Little.

— The Hearing. 337p. 1999. mass mkt. 7.99 (*0-446-60718-5*, Pub. by Warner Bks) Little.

***Mills, James.** Madness Cannabis & Colonialism: The Native Only Lunatic Asylums. 2000. text 65.00 (*0-312-23359-0*) St Martin.

Mills, James C. Blue Catalinas of World War II. (Illus.). 176p. 1995. pap. 21.95 (*0-89745-190-2*) Sunflower U Pr.

— History of Saginaw County: Historical, Commercial, Biographical, Profusely Illustrated. (Illus.). 801p. 1997. reprint ed. lib. bdg. 82.50 (*0-8328-6784-5*) Higginson Bk Co.

Mills, James D. The Art of Money Making. LC 73-2524. (Big Business; Economic Power in a Free Society Ser.). 1973. reprint ed. 28.95 (*0-405-05103-4*) Ayer.

Mills, James P. The Lhota Nagas. LC 76-44760. reprint ed. 55.00 (*0-404-15869-2*) AMS Pr.

— The Rengma Nagas. LC 76-44761. reprint ed. 59.50 (*0-404-15870-6*) AMS Pr.

Mills, James P. & Thompson, Brian J., eds. Selected Papers on Apodization - Coherent Optical Systems. (SPIE Milestone Ser.: Vol. MS 119). 1996. 100.00 (*0-8194-2150-2*) SPIE.

***Mills, James R.** The Memoirs of Pontius Pilate: A Novel. 176p. (gr. 13 up). 2000. pap. 9.99 (*0-8007-5722-X*) Revell.

— The Memoirs of Pontius Pilate: A Novel. LC PS3563.I42315M46. (Illus.). 224p. 2000. 16.99 (*0-8007-1773-2*) Revell.

Mills, James R. San Diego Where California Began. 5th rev. ed. (Illus.). 84p. 1985. pap. 4.95 (*0-918740-04-5*) San Diego Hist.

Mills, Jane. Womanwords: A Dictionary of Words about Women. 291p. 1992. text 24.95 (*0-02-921495-5*) Free Pr.

Mills, Jane & Smith, Janet. Design Concepts: A Career Primer. LC 84-80102. (Illus.). 113p. 1984. pap. text 38.00 (*0-87005-498-8*) Fairchild.

Mills, Jane J. First Cap'n General of Liberty Tree. LC 79-90388. 324p. 1979. pap. 5.95 (*0-935344-00-4*) Jupiter Bks.

Mills, Jane L. & Johnson, Larry D. Arnie's Surprise. LC 86-60363. (Search & Find Set Ser.: Level 2). (Illus.). 14p. (Orig.). (J). (ps). 1986. pap. 12.00 (*0-938155-05-9*) Read A Bol.

— Build Like Me. LC 86-60362. (Building Set Ser.: Level 2). (Illus.). 13p. (Orig.). (J). (ps). 1986. pap. 4.00 (*0-938155-01-6*) Read A Bol.

— Build Like Me, 3 vols., Set. LC 86-60362. (Building Set Ser.: Level 2). (Illus.). 13p. (Orig.). (J). (ps). 1986. pap. 12.00 (*0-685-13524-1*) Read A Bol.

— Peek-a-Boo. LC 86-60380. (Search & Find Set Ser.: Level 1). (Illus.). 13p. (Orig.). (J). (ps). 1986. pap. 3.50 (*0-938155-04-0*); pap. 12.00 (*0-685-13530-6*) Read A Bol.

Mills, Jane L., jt. auth. see Johnson, Larry D.

Mills, Janet. Free of Dieting Forever. 208p. (Orig.). 1992. mass mkt. 4.99 (*0-446-36275-1*) Warner Bks.

— Free of Dieting Forever: Eight Steps to Achieve & Maintain Your Ideal Weight. 208p. (Orig.). 1991. pap. 9.95 (*1-878424-00-9*) Amber-Allen Pub.

— Purpose, Meaning, & Grace: The Essential Wisdom of Seth. 168p. 1999. pap. 12.95 (*1-878424-32-7*) Amber-Allen Pub.

Mills, Janet, ed. see Epstein, Donald M.

Mills, Janie. Jems: From My Heart. (Illus.). 65p. 1998. pap. 6.50 (*0-914565-49-4*, 49-4) Capstan Pubns.

— Rejoice: Life Is Both Roses & Thorns. (Illus.). 36p. 1998. pap. 5.00 (*0-914565-47-8*) Capstan Pubns.

Mills, Janie, jt. auth. see Saban, Vera.

Mills, Jason & Paradis, Adrian A. Partnership for Excellence, 1969-1994: The History of EHV-Weidmann Industries, Inc. LC 94-39419. (Illus.). 120p. 1995. 30.00 (*0-914659-72-3*) Phoenix Pub.

Mills, Jean. Moments with Jackie. LC 99-13870. (Illus.). 120p. 1999. 19.98 (*1-56799-852-6*) M Friedman Pub Grp Inc.

***Mills, Jean & Mills, Richard W.** Childhood Studies: A Reader in Perspectives of Childhood. LC 99-39732. 232p. 2000. pap. write for info. (*0-415-21415-7*) Routledge.

Mills, Jean & Mills, Richard W., eds. Primary School People: Getting to Know Your Colleagues. LC 94-20730. 1995. write for info. (*0-415-11396-2*) Routledge.

Mills, Jean, jt. auth. see Cabot, Laurie.

Mills, Jean, jt. ed. see Mills, Richard W.

Mills, Jennifer & Willis, Judith. Conveyancing Law & Practice. 2nd ed. (Legal Practice Course Guides Ser.). 254p. 1995. pap. 26.00 (*1-85941-004-9*, Pub. by Cavendish Pubng) Gaunt.

***Mills, Jenny.** I Buried My Dolls in the Garden: The Life & Works of Elizabeth Blair Barber. 276p. 2000. 75.00 (*1-876268-41-7*, Pub. by Univ of West Aust Pr) Intl Spec Bk.

Mills, Jerry & Mitchell, Roy. General Chemistry Experiments. 2nd ed. (Illus.). 208p. (C). 1987. 21.95 (*0-89582-162-1*) Morton Pub.

Mills, Jerry L. & Hampton, Michael D. Microscale & Macroscale Experiments for General Chemistry. 307p. (C). 1991. lab manual ed. 35.94 (*0-07-042442-X*) McGraw.

— Microscale Experiments for General Chemistry. 2nd ed. 208p. (C). 1991. spiral bd. 35.94 (*0-07-042447-0*) McGraw.

Mills, Jerry L., jt. auth. see Chang, Raymond.

Mills, Jerry L., jt. auth. see Rubin, Louis D.

Mills, Jerry L., jt. ed. see Rubin, Louis D.

Mills, Jo A. Command the Morning. 1989. pap. 6.95 (*0-89137-453-1*) Quality Pubns.

— Leaves Only. 1988. pap. 6.95 (*0-89137-447-7*) Quality Pubns.

— Making It. 1986. pap. 6.95 (*0-89137-439-6*) Quality Pubns.

***Mills, Jo Ann.** The Silver Key: A Book about Friendship. unabridged ed. 141p. 1998. pap. 6.95 (*0-89137-472-8*, 74728) Quality Pubns.

Mills, Joe. A Mountain Boyhood. LC 87-30202. (Illus.). lvi, 311p. 1988. pap. 9.95 (*0-8032-8154-4*, Bison Books) U of Nebr Pr.

Mills, John. Basketball Handbook. (Illus.). 65p. 1980. pap. 8.95 (*0-88839-042-4*) Hancock House.

— Guitar Music from the Student Repertoire. pap. 24.95 incl. audio compact disk (*0-7119-2996-3*, mi 10111) Omnibus NY.

— The John Mills Classical Guitar Tutor. 76p. 1997. reprint ed. pap. text 19.95 (*0-86175-170-1*, AM10038) Music Sales.

— Lizard in the Grass. 256p. (C). 1980. pap. text 3.00 (*0-920802-26-5*, Pub. by ECW) Genl Dist Srvs.

***Mills, John.** Managing the World Economy. LC 00-42239. 2000. write for info. (*0-312-23579-8*) St Martin.

Mills, John. Robertson Davies & His Works. (Canadian Author Studies). 58p. (C). 1985. pap. text 9.95 (*0-920802-65-6*, Pub. by ECW) Genl Dist Srvs.

— Thank Your Mother for the Rabbits. 272p. 1993. pap. write for info. (*0-88984-160-8*) Porcup Quill.

— Three Months' Residence at Nablus: And an Account of the Modern Samaritans. LC 77-87610. reprint ed. 37.50 (*0-404-16434-X*) AMS Pr.

— Traction on the Grand. (Illus.). 96p. 10.00 (*0-919130-27-5*, Pub. by Boston Mills) Genl Dist Srvs.

Mills, John, et al, eds. Antiviral Chemotherapy 4: New Directions for Clinical Application & Research. (Advances in Experimental Medicine & Biology Ser.: Vol. 394). (Illus.). 454p. (C). 1996. text 144.00 (*0-306-45294-4*, Kluwer Plenum) Kluwer Academic.

Mills, John, et al. Antiviral Chemotherapy 5: New Directions for Clinical Application & Research. LC 99-10159. (Advances in Experimental Medicine & Biology Ser.). (C). 1999. text. write for info. (*0-306-46107-2*, Kluwer Plenum) Kluwer Academic.

Mills, John, jt. auth. see Branan, Carl.

Mills, John, jt. ed. see Mills, Carol.

Mills, John, tr. see Nouet, Noel.

Mills, John A. Arthritis: Diseases & Treatment, 3 vols., Set. 3rd ed. Incl. Bk. 2. Arthritis. 1977. pap. text 18.50 (*0-89147-050-6*); Bk. 3. Anti-Inflammatory Therapy. (Illus.). 1977. pap. text 16.50 (*0-89147-051-4*); 1977. Set pap. text 48.00 (*0-89147-048-4*) CAS.

— Control: A History of Behavioral Psychology. LC 98-19699. 1999. text 37.50 (*0-8147-5611-5*) NYU Pr.

— Hamlet on Stage: The Great Tradition, 15. LC 84-22461. (Contributions in Drama & Theatre Studies: No. 15). (Illus.). 304p. 1985. 59.95 (*0-313-24660-2*, MIH/, Greenwood Pr) Greenwood.

— Language & Laughter: Comic Diction in the Plays of Bernard Shaw. LC 68-9339. 192p. reprint ed. pap. 59.60 (*0-608-12772-8*, 202431900037) Bks Demand.

Mills, John F. Peacock Festival: Selected Color Woodcuts. LC 64-8130. (Illus.). 80p. 1964. pap. 20.00 (*0-933652-00-3*) Domjan Studio.

Mills, John Fitzmaurice. Art for Our Children: A "Hands-Off" Guide. 112p. 1991. pap. 16.95 (*0-86327-287-8*) Dufour.

Mills, John M. Canadian Coastal & Inland Steam Vessels, 1809-1930. LC 79-91504. 135p. 1979. 28.00 (*0-913423-01-7*) Steamship Hist Soc.

M

An Asterisk (*) at the beginning of an entry indicates that the title is appearing for the first time.

Mills, John S. & White, Raymond. The Organic Chemistry of Museum Objects. 2nd ed. LC 93-32082. (Series in Conservation & Museology). 224p. 1994. 74.95 (*0-7506-1693-8*) Buttrwrth-Heinemann.

***Mills, John S. & White, Raymond.** Organic Chemistry of Museum Objects. 2nd ed. LC 93-32082. (Illus.). 206p. 2000. pap. 42.95 (*0-7506-4693-4*) Buttrwrth-Heinemann.

Mills, Jonathan. Love, Covenant & Meaning. 140p. 1997. pap. 14.95 (*1-57383-091-7*) Regent College.

Mills, Jonathan W., jt. auth. see Conrad, James M.

***Mills, Joseph.** Obsessions. 2000. pap. text 12.95 (*1-873741-31-6*) Millivres Bks.

— Reading Richard Brautigan's Trout Fishing in America. LC 98-70948. (Western Writers Ser.: Vol. 135). 70p. (C). 1998. pap. 5.95 (*0-88430-134-6*) Boise St U W Writ Ser.

Mills, Joseph. Towards the End. 1992. pap. 13.95 (*0-7486-6031-3*, Pub. by Edinburgh U Pr) Col U Pr.

***Mills, Joseph, ed.** Management of Chronic Lower Limb Ischemia. (An Arnold Publication). 224p. 2000. text 89.50 (*0-340-75956-9*, Pub. by E A) OUP.

Mills, Joseph A. Father, I Give This Day to You: A Collection of Meditations & Commentaries. Battle, Stafford L., ed. LC 90-91700. 87p. (Orig.). 1990. pap. text 8.95 (*0-943454-08-5*) Jotarian.

— Goin' Off. 68p. (Orig.). 1982. pap. text 5.25 (*0-943454-01-8*) Jotarian.

— When Love Speaks, Are You Listening? (Illus.). 100p. 1985. pap. 7.95 (*0-943454-02-6*) Jotarian.

Mills, Joy. Between Heaven & Earth - The Soul Purpose: At the Crossroads Alone. 164p. 1998. pap. 14.95 (*0-9671280-0-5*) J Mills & Assocs.

— One Hundred Years of Theosophy: A History of the Theosophical Society in America. 245p. 1987. pap. 9.95 (*0-8356-0235-4*, Quest) Theos Pub Hse.

Mills, Joy, ed. see Blavatsky, Helena P.

Mills, Joyce C. Gentle Willow: A Story for Children about Dying. LC 93-22770. (Illus.). 32p. (J). (ps-3). 1993. 11.95 (*0-945354-54-1*) Am Psychol.

— Little Tree: A Story for Children with Serious Medical Problems. LC 92-19654. (Illus.). 32p. (J). 1992. 16.95 (*0-945354-52-5*) Am Psychol.

— Little Tree: A Story for Children with Serious Medical Problems. LC 92-19654. (Illus.). 32p. (J). (ps-3). 1992. pap. 8.95 (*0-945354-51-7*) Am Psychol.

***Mills, Joyce C.** Reconnecting to the Magic of Life. (Illus.). 256p. 1999. pap. 19.95 (*0-9673280-0-4*) Imaginal Pr.

Mills, Joyce C. Stories of the Dreamwalkers. (Illus.). 48p. 1989. 48.95 (*0-944082-01-7*) Santa Fe Fine Art.

— Stories of the Dreamwalkers: Storyteller Edition. (Illus.). 48p. 1990. reprint ed. 48.00 (*0-944082-02-5*) Santa Fe Fine Art.

Mills, Joyce C. & Crowley, Richard J. Sammy the Elephant & Mr. Camel: A Story to Help Children Overcome Bedwetting While Discovering Self-Appreciation. LC 88-13581. (Illus.). 48p. (J). (ps-3). 1988. 16.95 (*0-945354-09-6*); pap. 8.95 (*0-945354-08-8*) Am Psychol.

— Therapeutic Metaphors for Children & the Child Within. LC 86-9700. 288p. 1986. text 29.95 (*0-87630-429-3*) Brunner-Mazel.

Mills, Joyce H., jt. auth. see Mills, Watson E.

Mills, Joyce J. & Amatruda, Wheeler M. Elements of Style. 3rd ed. (C). 1995. pap. 2.95 (*0-02-615080-8*, Macmillan Coll) P-H.

Mills, Judie. Robert Kennedy. LC 97-9843. (Illus.). 560p. (YA). (gr. 9 up). 1998. lib. bdg. 34.90 (*1-56294-250-6*) Millbrook Pr.

Mills, Judith C., et al. The Stonehook Schooner. (Illus.). 32p. (J). (gr. k-2). 1997. 14.95 (*1-55013-653-4*) Firefly Bks Ltd.

— The Stonehook Schooner. (Illus.). 32p. (J). (gr. k-2). 1997. pap. 4.95 (*1-55013-719-0*, Pub. by Key Porter) Firefly Bks Ltd.

Mills, Judson & Herman-Jones, Eddie, eds. Cognitive Dissonance: Progress on a Pivotal Theory in Social Psychology. LC 98-49316. (Science Conference Ser.). 411p. 1999. Not sold separately (*1-55798-565-0*) Am Psychol.

Mills, Judy & Dombre, Irene. University of Toronto Doctoral Theses, 1897-1967: A Bibliography. LC 75-354611. 197p. reprint ed. pap. 61.10 (*0-608-14728-1*, 205582200038) Bks Demand.

Mills, Juliet. Mind, Body & Soul in Balance. (Illus.). 140p. 1993. pap. 10.00 (*1-879371-45-6*) Pub Mills.

Mills, K., jt. auth. see Joule, J. A.

Mills, K. C. Thermodynamic Data for Inorganic Sulphides, Selenides & Tellurides. LC 74-173939. 855p. reprint ed. pap. 200.00 (*0-608-10054-4*, 205184200009) Bks Demand.

Mills, K. C., jt. auth. see Lancaster, J. F.

***Mills, K. R.** Magnetic Stimulation of the Human Nervous System. LC 99-20411. (Illus.). 336p. 2000. text 59.50 (*0-19-262986-7*) OUP.

Mills, Katherine H., jt. auth. see Kilmann, Peter R.

***Mills, Kathi.** Obsession. 2001. pap. 12.99 (*0-8054-2149-1*) Broadman.

Mills, Kathi, jt. auth. see Galloway, Dale.

Mills, Kathi, ed. see Getz, Gene A. & Getz, Elaine.

Mills, Kathi, ed. see West, Laurel.

Mills, Kathleen, ed. see Brentano, Robyn & Georgia, Olivia.

***Mills, Kathryn.** Just Say Yes! LC 99-38036. 224p. 1999. pap. 10.95 (*1-58063-090-1*) Renaissance.

Mills, Kathy, ed. see Merrill, Russell G.

Mills, Katie R. Goodlock & Allied Families. (Illus.). 250p. 1997. reprint ed. pap. 38.00 (*0-8328-8771-4*); reprint ed. lib. bdg. 48.00 (*0-8328-8770-6*) Higginson Bk Co.

Mills, Kay. From Pocahontas to Power Suits: Everything You Need to Know about Women's History in America. LC 94-34521. 272p. (Orig.). 1995. pap. 11.95 (*0-452-27152-5*, Plume) Dutton Plume.

— A Place in the News: From the Women's Pages to the Front Page. (Illus.). 384p. 1990. pap. text 19.50 (*0-231-07417-4*) Col U Pr.

— Something Better for My Children: The History & People of Head Start. (Illus.). 352p. 1999. pap. 14.95 (*0-452-27847-3*, Plume) Dutton Plume.

— This Little Light of Mine: The Life of Fannie Lou Hamer. (Illus.). 400p. 1994. pap. 14.95 (*0-452-27052-9*, Plume) Dutton Plume.

Mills, Keith. Mountain Biking. 128p. 1989. pap. 18.95 (*0-8117-2315-1*) Stackpole.

Mills, Ken. A New Way to Fly: An Alternative Way to Achieve Freedom from Alcohol & Drugs. LC 87-60845. 184p. (Orig.). 1987. pap. text 6.95 (*0-942267-00-1*) Profile Press.

Mills, Ken & Keith-Smith, Brian, eds. Georg Buchner - Tradition & Innovation: Fourteen Essays. LC 92-8268. (Bristol German Publications: Vol. 1). 276p. 1992. reprint ed. lib. bdg. 89.95 (*0-7734-1334-0*) E Mellen.

Mills, Kenneth. Idolatry & Its Enemies: Colonial Andean Religion & Extirpation, 1640-1750. LC 96-28847. 346p. 1997. text 55.00 (*0-691-02979-2*, Pub. by Princeton U Pr) Cal Prin Full Svc.

Mills, Kenneth & Taylor, William B., eds. Colonial Spanish America: A Documentary History. LC 97-44250. (Illus.). 366p. (C). 1998. 55.00 (*0-8420-2572-3*); pap. 22.95 (*0-8420-2573-1*) Scholarly Res Inc.

Mills, Kenneth, et al. A Color Atlas of Low Back Pain. (Illus.). 92p. 1990. text 39.00 (*0-8036-9858-5*) Davis Co.

— A Colour Atlas of Cardio-Pulmonary Resuscitation Techniques. (Illus.). 96p. 1986. text 28.95 (*0-7234-1029-1*) Wolfe Pub.

Mills, Kenneth G. Anticipations. (Illus.). 141p. 1980. 17.95 (*0-919842-07-0*, KGOB5) Sun-Scape Ent.

— The Beauty Unfoldment. 1977. pap. 10.95 incl. audio (*0-919842-50-X*, KGOM3) Sun-Scape Ent.

— Change Your Standpoint - Change Your World. unabridged ed. MacQueen, Megan, ed. LC 96-931221. (Illus.). 264p. (Orig.). 1996. pap. 21.95 (*0-919842-21-6*, KGOB 13) Sun-Scape Ent.

— Embellishments. (Illus.). 150p. 1986. 17.95 (*0-919842-08-9*, KGOB6) Sun-Scape Ent.

— Freedom Is Found. unabridged ed. 1991. pap. 10.95 incl. audio (*0-919842-12-7*, KGOC30) Sun-Scape Ent.

— Given to Praise! An Array of Provocative Metaphysical-Philosophical Utterances. 1976. lp 13.99 (*0-685-93126-9*, KGOM2) Sun-Scape Ent.

— Given to Praise! An Array of Provocative Metaphysical-Philosophical Utterances. (Illus.). 152p. 1976. 17.95 (*0-919842-00-3*, KGOB1) Sun-Scape Ent.

— The Golden Nail. (Illus.). 432p. (Orig.). 1993. pap. 29.95 (*0-919842-13-5*, KGOB9) Sun-Scape Ent.

— The Key: Identity. Limper, Mary G. & Brodie, Barry, eds. 432p. 1994. pap. 29.95 (*0-919842-16-X*, KGOB10) Sun-Scape Ent.

— The Key: Identity. Limper, Mary G. & Brodie, Barry, eds. (Illus.). 432p. 1994. 39.95 (*0-919842-18-6*, KGOB11) Sun-Scape Ent.

— Near to the Fire. 1979. audio 5.45 (*0-919842-04-6*, KGOC11) Sun-Scape Ent.

— The New Land! Conscious Experience Beyond Horizons. (Illus.). 77p. 1978. pap. 8.95 (*0-919842-01-1*, KGOB2) Sun-Scape Ent.

— The Newness of the Unchanging. pap. 10.95 incl. audio (*0-919842-02-X*, KGOM5) Sun-Scape Ent.

— The Quickening Spirit of Radiance, Set. unabridged ed. 1990. pap. 10.95 incl. audio (*0-919842-10-0*, KGOC29) Sun-Scape Ent.

— The Seal of Approval, Set. 1979. pap. 10.95 incl. audio (*0-919842-03-8*, KGOM9) Sun-Scape Ent.

— Surprises. (Illus.). 135p. 1980. 17.95 (*0-919842-06-2*, KGOB4) Sun-Scape Ent.

— Tyranny of Love. Leaper, Mary J. & MacQueen, Megan, eds. (Illus.). 264p. (Orig.). 1995. pap. 21.95 (*0-919842-17-8*, KGOB12) Sun-Scape Ent.

— Words of Adjustment. (Illus.). 130p. (Orig.). 1992. pap. 13.95 (*0-919842-09-7*, KGOB7) Sun-Scape Ent.

***Mills, Kenneth George.** Food for No Thought: A Book of Aphorisms. Wingfield, Angela, ed. 104p. 1999. pap. 11.95 (*0-919842-26-7*) Sun-Scape Ent.

Mills, Kenneth H., et al. Applied Visual Merchandising. 3rd ed. 256p. 1994. 84.00 (*0-13-041989-3*) P-H.

Mills, Kevin. Justifying Language: Paul & Contemporary Literary Theory. LC 95-24537. (Studies in Literature & Religion). 224p. 1995. text 59.95 (*0-312-12989-0*) St Martin.

***Mills, Kevin & Mills, Nancy.** Chocolate on the Brain: Foolproof Recipes for Unrepentant Chocoholics. (Illus.). 304p. 2000. pap. 17.00 (*0-395-98358-4*) HM.

Mills, Kevin & Mills, Nancy. Help! My Apartment Has a Dining Room Cookbook: How to Have People over for Dinner Without Stressing Out - More Than 100 Foolproof Recipes. LC 99-12464. (Illus.). 272p. 1999. pap. 16.00 (*0-395-89255-4*) HM.

— Help! My Apartment Has a Kitchen Cookbook: 100+ Great Recipes with Follproof Instructions. Martin, Rux, ed. (Illus.). 272p. (Orig.). 1996. pap. 16.00 (*1-881527-63-8*, Chapters Bks) HM.

Mills, Kirk M. Kirk's Directory of California Golf. (Illus.). 1990. 11.95 (*0-9627273-0-X*) Mills & Assocs.

Mills, Kyle. Free Fall. Date not set. pap. 6.99 (*0-06-109802-7*) HarpC.

***Mills, Kyle.** Free Fall. LC 99-43528. 400p. 2000. 25.00 (*0-06-019333-6*) HarpC.

— Free Fall. large type ed. 640p. 2000. pap. 25.00 (*0-06-095575-9*) HarpC.

Mills, Kyle. Rising Phoenix. 528p. 1998. mass mkt. 6.99 (*0-06-101249-1*, Harp PBks) HarpC.

— Storming Heaven. LC PS3563.I42322S86. 528p. 2000. mass mkt. 6.99 (*0-06-101251-3*) HarpC.

Mills, L. H., jt. auth. see Darmesteter, James.

Mills, Larry W. & McDowell, Danny B. Business Game Student Manual. (C). 1985. pap. text 30.00 (*0-673-39026-8*) Addson-Wesley Educ.

Mills, Laura K. American Allegorical Prints: Constructing an Identity. (Illus.). 31p. (Orig.). (C). 1996. pap. 8.00 (*0-89467-074-3*) Yale Art Gallery.

Mills, Laurel. Canada Geese Coming Home. 46p. 1986. pap. 7.00 (*0-9614462-2-6*) Black Hat Pr.

— The Gull Is My Divining Rod. 2nd ed. Olski, Jennifer, ed. 48p. 1993. pap. 7.00 (*0-9614462-7-7*) Black Hat Pr.

— I Sing Back. 48p. (Orig.). 1997. pap. 8.50 (*1-887649-09-3*) Black Hat Pr.

Mills, Lauren. The Dog Prince. LC 95-5302. (Illus.). 32p. (J). 1999. 15.95 (*0-316-57417-1*) Little.

— Ebony. (Illus.). 32p. (J). 1998. write for info. (*0-316-57359-0*) Little.

— The Fairy Doll. 32p. (J). 1997. write for info. (*0-316-57412-0*) Little.

— Fairy Wings. LC 92-37168. (Illus.). 32p. (J). (gr. k-3). 1995. 15.95 (*0-316-57397-3*) Little.

— The Rag Coat. (Illus.). 32p. (J). (gr. k-3). 1991. 16.95 (*0-316-57407-4*) Little.

***Mills, Lauren & Mills, Nolan.** Fairy Wings. (J). 2001. pap. 5.95 (*0-316-59078-9*) Little.

Mills, Lauren A. The Book of Little Folk: Faery Stories & Poems from Around the World. LC 96-22459. (J). 1999. pap. 23.89 (*0-8037-1459-9*, Dial Yng Read) Peng Put Young Read.

***Mills, Laurence-Khanti.** Buddhism Explained. LC 99-232820. 206p. 1999. pap. 12.00 (*974-7100-85-1*, Pub. by Silk Worm Bks) U of Wash Pr.

— Jewels Within the Heart: Verses of the Buddha's Teachings. LC 99-232863. 144p. 1999. pap. 12.00 (*974-7100-73-8*, Pub. by Silk Worm Bks) U of Wash Pr.

Mills, Lawrence H. Avesta Eschatology: Compared with the Books of Daniel & Revelations. LC 74-24644. reprint ed. 29.50 (*0-404-12816-5*) AMS Pr.

— Dictionary of the Gathic Language of the Zend Avesta. LC 74-21253. (GAE.). reprint ed. 72.50 (*0-404-12804-1*) AMS Pr.

— Our Own Religion in Ancient Persia. LC 74-21262. reprint ed. 62.50 (*0-404-12811-4*) AMS Pr.

— Zarathushtra, Philo, the Achaemenids & Israel. LC 74-21261. reprint ed. 49.50 (*0-404-12815-7*) AMS Pr.

Mills, Lawrence H., ed. A Study of the Five Zarathushtrian (Zoroastrian) Gathas, 4 pts. in 1 vol., Pts. I-IV. LC 74-21252. reprint ed. 110.00 (*0-404-12803-3*) AMS Pr.

Mills, Lennox A. Ceylon under British Rule, 1795-1932. 311p. 1964. 30.00 (*0-7146-2019-X*, Pub. by F Cass Pubs) Intl Spec Bk.

— Southeast Asia: Illusion & Reality in Politics & Economics. LC 64-17805. 373p. reprint ed. pap. 115.70 (*0-8357-7030-3*, 203327100085) Bks Demand.

Mills, Linda G. The Heart of Intimate Abuse: New Interventions in Child Welfare, Criminal Justice & Health Setting. LC 98-25575. (Springer Series on Family Violence). (Illus.). 296p. 1998. 41.95 (*0-8261-1216-1*) Springer Pub.

— A Penchant for Prejudice: Unraveling Bias in Judicial Decision-Making. LC 99-6024. 216p. 1999. text 44.50 (*0-472-10950-2*, 10950) U of Mich Pr.

***Mills, Lynda.** Trompe L'oeil with Stencils: A Step-by-Step Guide to Creating Three Dimensional Effects for the Home. 64p. (Orig.). 1999. pap. text 15.95 (*0-85532-871-1*) Srch Pr.

Mills, Lynn, jt. auth. see Gibson, Rebecca.

Mills, M. & Standingford, S. Modern Office Management. 496p. (C). 1986. 130.00 (*0-7855-5684-2*, Pub. by Inst Pur & Supply) St Mut.

Mills, M. G. Kalahari Hyenas: Mammals. 288p. 1989. pap. 21.95 (*0-04-445329-9*); text 75.00 (*0-04-445328-0*) Routledge.

Mills, M. S., jt. auth. see Thurman, E. M.

Mills, Magnus. All Quiet on the Orient Express: A Novel. LC 99-26990. 240p. 1999. 23.95 (*1-55970-495-0*, Pub. by Arcade Pub Inc) Time Warner.

***Mills, Magnus.** All Quiet on the Orient Express: A Novel. 224p. 2000. pap. 12.00 (*0-684-87168-8*, Scribner Pap Fic) S&S Trade Pap.

Mills, Magnus. The Restraint of Beasts. LC 98-73666. 224p. 1998. 22.95 (*1-55970-437-3*, Pub. by Arcade Pub Inc) Time Warner.

— The Restraint of Beasts. LC 99-28808. 224p. 1999. per. 11.00 (*0-684-86511-4*) S&S Trade.

Mills, Maldwyn, ed. Six Middle English Romances: The Sege of Melayne, Emare, Octavian, Sir Isumbras, Sir Gowther, Sir Amadace. 256p. 1993. pap. 9.95 (*0-460-87225-7*, Everyman's Classic Lib) Tuttle Pubng.

Mills, Maldwyn, intro. Yvain & Gawain, Sir Percyvell, The Anturs of Arthur. 256p. 1992. pap. text 10.95 (*0-460-87077-7*, Everyman's Classic Lib) Tuttle Pubng.

Mills, Maldwyn, ed. see Chaucer, Geoffrey.

Mills, Margaret A. Oral Narrative in Afghanistan: The Individual in Tradition. LC 90-2960. (Folklore & Oral Tradition Ser.). 288p. 1990. text 30.00 (*0-8240-2871-6*) Garland.

— Rhetorics & Politics in Afghan Traditional Storytelling. LC 90-22019. (Publications of the American Folklore Society, Bibliographical & Special Ser.). xi, 387p. (C). 1991. text 22.00 (*0-8122-8199-3*) Bibliotheca Persica.

Mills, Margaret A., ed. see Green, Thomas A., et al.

***Mills, Margaret H., ed.** Slavic Gender Linguistics. LC 99-31514. (Pragmatics & Beyond New Ser.: Vol. 61). xviii, 251p. 1999. 69.00 (*1-55619-824-8*) J Benjamins Pubng Co.

Mills, Margaret H., ed. Topics in Colloquial Russian. LC 90-20776. (American University Studies: Slavic Languages & Literature: Ser. XII, Vol. 11). XII, 203p. (C). 1991. text 36.95 (*0-8204-1251-1*) P Lang Pubng.

Mills, Margaret H., jt. auth. see Hesli, Vicki L.

Mills, Marie A. Narrative Identity & Dementia: A Study of Autobiographical Memories & Emotions. LC 98-70989. (CEDR Ser.). (Illus.). 199p. 1998. text 63.95 (*1-84014-175-1*, Pub. by Ashgate Pub) Ashgate Pub Co.

Mills, Mary, jt. auth. see Vardy, Peter.

Mills, Mary B. Thai Women in the Global Labor Force: Consuming Desires, Contested Selves. LC 98-44992. (Illus.). 240p. (C). 1999. text 50.00 (*0-8135-2653-1*); pap. text 20.00 (*0-8135-2654-X*) Rutgers U Pr.

Mills, Mary E. Historical Israel, Biblical Israel: The Text from Joshua to 2 Kings. 124p. 1999. pap. 15.95 (*0-304-70474-1*) Continuum.

— Human Agents of Cosmic Power in Hellenistic Judaism & the Synoptic Tradition. (JSNTS Ser.: Vol. 41). 184p. 1990. 57.50 (*1-85075-235-4*, Pub. by Sheffield Acad) CUP Services.

— Images of God in the Old Testament. LC 98-7582. 1998. 19.95 (*0-8146-5935-7*) Liturgical Pr.

Mills, Mary E. & Mills, Andrew. A New Owner's Guide to Bichons Frises. (Illus.). 160p. 1997. 12.95 (*0-7938-2779-5*, JG130) TFH Pubns.

Mills, Mary E., jt. auth. see Vardy, Peter.

Mills, Mary V. The Pilgrimage Motif in the Works of the Medieval German Author Hartmann von Aue. LC 95-43256. (Studies in Medieval Literature: Vol. 13). 1996. write for info. (*0-7734-8855-3*) E Mellen.

Mills, Melanie. How to Talk to a Naked Man, Make the Most of Your Love Life, & Live Happily Ever After. LC 96-27101. 157p. 1996. per. 4.99 (*0-373-80507-1*, 1-80507-6) Harlequin Bks.

— Rising to the Occasion. 1997. per. 5.99 (*0-373-80511-X*, Harlequin) Harlequin Bks.

Mills, Michael. David, Lion & Lamb. Sherer, Michael L., ed. (Orig.). 1988. pap. 7.25 (*1-55673-029-2*, 8814) CSS OH.

Mills, Michael & Schiff, William. The Active Eye. 1989. pap., student ed. 10.00 (*1-56321-031-2*); disk 99.00 (*1-56321-030-4*) L Erlbaum Assocs.

— The Active Eye, Set. 1989. pap. 750.00 incl. disk (*1-56321-033-9*); pap. 99.00 incl. disk (*1-56321-032-0*) L Erlbaum Assocs.

***Mills, Michael C.** Barbourville & Knox County, Kentucky. (Images of America Ser.). (Illus.). 128p. 2000. pap. 18.99 (*0-7385-0585-4*) Arcadia Publng.

Mills, Michael P. Prevention, Health, & British Politics. 200p. 1993. 61.95 (*1-85628-190-6*, Pub. by Avebry) Ashgate Pub Co.

Mills, Michael T., jt. auth. see Arthur, Linda L.

Mills, Michele, tr. see Nouet, Noel.

Mills, Mike. The Politics of Dietary Change. 160p. 1992. text 77.95 (*1-85521-226-9*, Pub. by Dartmth Pub) Ashgate Pub Co.

Mills, Mike & King, Fraser, eds. The Promise of Liberalism: A Comparative Analysis of Consensus Politics. LC 95-16699. 256p. 1995. 77.95 (*1-85521-481-4*, Pub. by Dartmth Pub) Ashgate Pub Co.

Mills, Miriam, ed. Alternate Dispute Resolution & Public Policy. (Orig.). 1988. pap. 15.00 (*0-944285-01-5*) Pol Studies.

Mills, Miriam, jt. auth. see Nagel, Stuart S.

Mills, Miriam, jt. ed. see Blank, Robert H.

Mills, Miriam K., ed. Conflict: Resolution & Public Policy, 262. LC 90-36780. (Contributions in Political Science Ser.: No. 262). 232p. 1990. 59.95 (*0-313-27519-X*, MRG, Greenwood Pr) Greenwood.

Mills, Miriam K. & Blank, Robert H., eds. Health Insurance & Public Policy: Risk, Allocation, & Equity, 299. LC 91-43370. (Contributions in Political Science Ser.: No. 299). 252p. 1992. 59.95 (*0-313-28465-2*, MHX/, Greenwood Pr) Greenwood.

Mills, Miriam K. & Nagel, Stuart S., eds. Public Administration in China, 323. LC 92-42675. (Contributions in Political Science Ser.: No. 323). 184p. 1993. 55.00 (*0-313-28847-X*, GM8847, Greenwood Pr) Greenwood.

Mills, Miriam K., jt. auth. see Nagel, Stuart S.

Mills, Miriam K., jt. ed. see Blank, Robert H.

Mills, Miriam K., jt. ed. see Nagel, Stuart S.

Mills, Mona. How to Draw Horses & Other Animals. (How to Draw & Paint Ser.). (Illus.). 32p. (Orig.). pap. 6.95 (*0-929261-82-8*, HT 165) W Foster Pub.

Mills, N. J. Plastics: Microstructure Properties & Applications. 2nd ed. LC 93-15986. 377p. 1994. pap. text 64.95 (*0-470-22132-1*) Halsted Pr.

Mills, Nancy, jt. auth. see Mills, Kevin.

Mills, Nancy L. Can the Neighborhood Watch Really Tell Time?, Vol. 1. (Illus.). 32p. (J). (ps-4). 1999. 15.95 (*1-893815-02-1*) Pie Sky.

— The Knight the Moon & the Stars Got Stuck, Vol. 1. (Illus.). 32p. (J). (ps-4). 1999. 15.95 (*1-893815-01-3*) Pie Sky.

Mills, Nicolaus. Against Its Better Self. 1997. 24.95 (*0-614-27998-4*) HM.

— Like a Holy Crusade: Mississippi, 1964 - The Turning of the Civil Rights Movement in America. 228p. 1992. text 22.50 (*0-929587-96-0*) I R Dee.

— Like a Holy Crusade: Mississippi, 1964 - The Turning of the Civil Rights Movement in America. LC 93-11246. 228p. 1993. reprint ed. pap. 9.95 (*1-56663-026-6*, Elephant Paperbacks) I R Dee.

Mills, Nicolaus, ed. Arguing Immigration: The Debate Over the Changing Face of America. 224p. 1994. pap. 12.00 (*0-671-89558-3*, Touchstone) S&S Trade Pap.

— Culture in an Age of Money: The Legacy of the 1980s in America. (Illus.). 256p. 1990. text 22.50 (*0-929587-35-9*) I R Dee.

— Culture in an Age of Money: The Legacy of the 1980s in America. (Illus.). 256p. 1991. reprint ed. pap. text 12.95 (*0-929587-71-5*, Elephant Paperbacks) I R Dee.

— Legacy of Dissent: Forty Years of Writing from Dissent Magazine. 464p. 1994. pap. 16.00 (*0-671-88879-X*, Touchstone) S&S Trade Pap.

An Asterisk (*) at the beginning of an entry indicates that the title is appearing for the first time.

Mills, Nolan, jt. auth. see Mills, Lauren.

Mills Novelty Company Staff. The Anatomy of a Vintage Slot Machine. Post, Dan R., ed. LC 74-26383. 48p. 1978. 12.95 (*0-911160-60-4*) Post Group.

Mills, P. God's World. (Chunky Pop up Book). (J). (ps). 1994. bds. 3.99 (*0-7814-1513-6*) Chariot Victor.

— El Mundo de Dios: Figuras Que Aparecen. (Figuras Que Aparecen (Chunky Pop-up Bk.)).Tr. of God's World: Chunky Pop-Up Book. (SPA.). 72p. (J). 1993. 3.50 (*1-56063-632-7*, 494606) Editorial Unilit.

— My Day. (Chunky Pop up Book). (J). (ps). 1994. bds. 3.99 (*0-7814-1514-4*) Chariot Victor.

Mills, P., jt. auth. see McGrath, Philomena.

Mills, Pamela, jt. auth. see Mathias, Barbara.

Mills, Pat & O'Neill, Kevin. Marshal Law: Blood Sweat & Fears Collection. (Illus.). 168p. 1993. pap. 15.95 (*1-878574-95-7*) Dark Horse Comics.

Mills, Patricia J. Woman, Nature, & Psyche. LC 87-10408. (Illus.). 286p. 1987. reprint ed. pap. 88.70 (*0-608-07834-4*, 205401000010) Bks Demand.

Mills, Patricia J., ed. Feminist Interpretations of G. W. F. Hegel. LC 95-12708. (Re-Reading the Canon Ser.). 352p. 1996. 50.00 (*0-271-01490-3*); pap. 19.95 (*0-271-01491-1*) Pa St U Pr.

Mills, Patrick L., jt. ed. see Dudukovic, Milorad P.

Mills, Patti A., tr. see Del Castillo, Diego.

Mills, Pattie. Curiosity Shop: Amazing Insects. 16p. 1998. text 39.95 (*1-878631-46-2*) S Kovalik.

Mills, Paul. Writing in Action. LC 95-17125. 240p. (C). 1995. pap. 22.99 (*0-415-11989-8*) Routledge.

Mills, Perry, ed. see Shakespeare, William.

Mills, Peter. Daniel's Adventure with the Lions. (Bible Flap Bks.). 24p. (J). 1994. bds. 7.95 (*0-687-10084-4*) Abingdon.

— David's Adventure with the Giant: (Bible Flap Book) (Illus.). 24p. (J). 1994. bds. 7.95 (*0-687-10278-2*) Abingdon.

— Fire! Fire! LC 96-138835. (Window Bks.). (Illus.). 16p. (J). 1995. pap. text 1.99 (*0-88070-792-5*, Gold n Honey) Zondervan.

***Mills, Peter.** Fire! Fire! Window Book. (Illus.). 1999. 2.50 (*1-85608-199-0*) Hunt GBR.

Mills, Peter. Jailbreak. LC 96-138845. (Window Bks.). (Illus.). 16p. (J). 1995. pap. text 1.99 (*0-88070-790-9*, Gold n Honey) Zondervan.

***Mills, Peter.** Jailbreak: Window Book. (Illus.). 1999. pap. 2.50 (*1-85608-189-3*) Hunt GBR.

Mills, Peter. Rain Rain! LC 96-144227. (Window Bks.). (Illus.). 16p. (J). 1995. pap. text 1.99 (*0-88070-791-7*) Zondervan.

***Mills, Peter.** Rain! Rain! Window Book. (Illus.). 1999. 2.50 (*1-85608-194-X*) Hunt GBR.

Mills, Peter. The Star of Bethlehem. LC 96-165384. (Window Bks.). (Illus.). 16p. (J). 1995. pap. text 1.99 (*0-88070-789-5*, Gold n Honey) Zondervan.

***Mills, Peter.** Star of Bethlehem. (Illus.). 1999. pap. 2.50 (*1-85608-184-2*) Hunt GBR.

Mills, Peter M., et al. Neuro-Adaptive Process Control: A Practical Approach. 228p. 1996. pap. text 170.00 incl. disk (*0-471-95997-9*) Wiley.

Mills, Presley. Islamic Finance. LC 99-21092. 1999. text 75.00 (*0-312-22448-6*) St Martin.

Mills-Price, Jamie. Between the Vines, Vol. II. (Illus.). 90p. 1998. pap. 10.50 (*1-56770-419-0*) S Scheewe Pubns.

— Between the Vines, Vol. 3. (Illus.). 100p. 1999. pap. 12.95 (*1-56770-449-2*) S Scheewe Pubns.

***Mills-Price, Jamie.** Between the Vines, Vol. 4. (Illus.). 88p. 2000. pap. 12.95 (*1-56770-474-3*) S Scheewe Pubns.

Mills, Quinn. Staying Afloat in the Construction Industry: Economic & Political Trends for the 1900's.... 1996. pap. text 29.95 (*1-55701-168-0*) BNI Pubns.

Mills, R. L. Propagators for Many-Particle Systems. xiii, 128p. 1969. text 220.00 (*0-677-02040-6*) Gordon & Breach.

Mills, R. P. & Heijl, A., eds. Perimetry Update, 1990-1991. LC 91-14629. (Illus.). 585p. 1991. lib. bdg. 171.50 (*90-6299-075-4*, Pub. by Kugler) Kugler Pubns.

***Mills, Ralph, Jr.** Grasses Standing: Selected Poems. LC 99-48338. 180p. 2000. pap. 14.95 (*1-55921-245-4*, Pub. by Moyer Bell) Publishers Group.

Mills, Ralph. In the Wind's Edge. LC 96-44932. 92p. 1997. pap. 12.95 (*1-55921-187-3*, Asphodel Pr) Moyer Bell.

Mills, Ralph J., Jr. A While. 74p. Date not set. pap. 5.95 (*0-944024-13-0*) Ellis Pr.

— Cry of the Human: Essays on Contemporary American Poetry. LC 74-14507. 295p. reprint ed. pap. 91.50 (*0-8357-9667-1*, 201901300010) Bks Demand.

— Each Branch. 117p. 1987. 11.95 (*0-933180-89-6*) Spoon Riv Poetry.

— For a Day. 36p. 1985. pap. 3.00 (*0-933180-69-1*) Spoon Riv Poetry.

Mills, Ralph J. Living with Distance. (American Poets Continuum Ser.: No. 3). 71p. 1979. pap. 10.00 (*0-918526-18-3*) BOA Edns.

— Richard Eberhart. LC 66-63487. (University of Minnesota Pamphlets on American Writers Ser.: No. 55). 46p. (Orig.). reprint ed. pap. 30.00 (*0-7837-2872-7*, 205758300006) Bks Demand.

Mills, Ralph J., Jr., ed. see Ignatow, David.

Mills, Randell L. The Grand Unified Theory of Classical Quantum Mechanics. LC 94-77780. (Illus.). 551p. 1995. 50.00 (*0-9635171-1-2*, 727425) BlckLight Power.

— The Grand Unified Theory of Classical Quantum Mechanics. (Illus.). 575p. 1996. 50.00 (*0-9635171-2-0*) BlckLight Power.

— The Grand Unified Theory of Classical Quantum Mechanics. (Illus.). 1048p. 1999. text 75.00 (*0-9635171-3-9*) BlckLight Power.

Mills, Randell L. & Good, William R. Unification of Spacetime, the Forces, Matter & Energy. (Illus.). 224p. 1992. 25.00 (*0-9635171-0-4*) BlckLight Power.

Mills, Randy K. Christ Tasted Death for Every Man: The Story of America's Frontier General Baptist. Date not set. write for info. (*0-9642674-2-X*) Stinson Pr.

***Mills, Randy Keith & Mills, Roxanne.** Unexpected Journey: A Marine Corps Reserve Company in the Korean War. LC 00-30487. (Illus.). 272p. 2000. pap. 29.95 (*1-55750-546-2*) Naval Inst Pr.

Mills, Richard & Collins, Dan. Irish Nature in Focus. 1997. pap. 29.95 (*1-898256-15-2*) Dufour.

Mills, Richard M. As Moscow Sees Us: American Politics & Society in the Soviet Mindset. 320p. 1990. text 55.00 (*0-19-506260-4*) OUP.

Mills, Richard P., ed. Perimetry Update, 1992-1993. LC 93-1932. 609p. 1993. 171.50 (*90-6299-094-0*) Kugler Pubns.

Mills, Richard P., jt. auth. see Weinreb, Robert N.

Mills, Richard P., ed. see International Perimetric Society Staff.

Mills, Richard W. Observing Children in the Primary Classroom: All in a Day. rev. ed. Orig. Title: Classroom Observation of Primary School Children. (Illus.). 170p. 1988. pap. text 16.95 (*0-04-445176-8*) Routledge.

Mills, Richard W. & Mills, Jean, eds. Bilingualism in the Primary School: A Handbook for Teachers. LC 92-32058. 144p. 1993. pap. write for info. (*0-415-08861-5*) Routledge.

Mills, Richard W., jt. auth. see Mills, Jean.

Mills, Richard W., jt. ed. see Mills, Jean.

Mills, Rinsey. Essential AC Cobra: The Cars & Their Story 1962-67. (Essential Ser.). (Illus.). 80p. 1997. pap. 15.95 (*1-870979-85-0*, Bay View Bks) MBI Pubg.

— Original AC, Ace & Cobra: The Restorers Guide to AC, Bristol, & Ford Engined Cars. (Full Color Restoration Guides Ser.). (Illus.). 96p. 1990. text 34.95 (*1-870979-14-1*, Bay View Bks) MBI Pubg.

Mills, Robert. Memorial of Robert Mills. Date not set. pap. write for info. (*0-87770-411-2*) Ye Galleon.

— Space, Time, Quantum Physics. 416p. (C). 1994. pap. text 28.95 (*0-7167-2436-7*) W H Freeman.

Mills, Robert, ed. Mills' Atlas of 1825. 1979. reprint ed. 100.00 (*0-87844-021-6*) Sandlapper Pub Co.

Mills, Robert & Pedersen, John. A Flour Mill Sanitation Manual. LC 90-82381. (Illus.). 164p. 1990. pap. 55.00 (*0-9624407-1-X*) Eagan Pr.

Mills, Robert A. & Haines, Olin R., eds. National Outdoor Guides Directory. (Illus.). 434p. (Orig.). 1987. 12.95 (*0-944080-00-6*) Prof Guides Pub.

Mills, Robert E. Real Men: Daily Nuggets to Inspire Your Walk As a Real Man in a World of Males. LC 96-92760. 175p. (Orig.). 1997. pap. 7.99 (*0-9655593-0-0*) R E M Mktg.

Mills, Robert K. Implement & Tractor: Reflections on 100 Years of Farm Equipment. LC 86-81762. (Illus.). 512p. 1994. pap. text 39.95 (*0-87288-566-6*, I&T 100) Intertec Pub.

Mills, Robert L. It Didn't Happen the Way You Think: The Lincoln Assassination: What the Experts Missed. (Orig.). 1995. pap. text 17.00 (*0-7884-0119-X*) Heritage Bk.

***Mills, Robert P.** And God Spoke All These Words: The Ten Commandments for the Third Millennium. (Foundations of the Faith Ser.). 120p. 2000. pap. 7.00 (*0-9652602-7-5*) PLC Publns.

Mills, Robert P. I Believe . . . The Apostles Creed for the Third Millenium. (Foundations of the Faith Ser.). 144p. 1998. pap. 5.00 (*0-9652602-2-4*) PLC Publns.

***Mills, Robert P.** Truly the Son of God: What the Bible Teaches about Jesus. 2000. pap. 7.50 (*0-9652602-6-7*) PLC Publns.

Mills, Robert P. Whom Alone We Worship & Serve: What the Bible Teaches about God. (In the Life of the Church Ser.). 128p. 1998. pap. 4.50 (*0-9652602-1-6*) PLC Publns.

Mills, Robin K. & Schultz, Jon S. South Carolina Legal Research Handbook. LC 75-21933. vi, 115p. 1976. lib. bdg. 35.00 (*0-930342-16-X*, 301040) W S Hein.

Mills, Roger & Tait, Alan, eds. Supporting the Learner in Open & Distance Learning. 238p. (Orig.). 1997. pap. 72.50 (*0-273-62316-8*, Pub. by Pitman Pub) Trans-Atl Phila.

Mills, Roger, jt. auth. see Tait, Alan.

Mills, Roger C. Realizing Mental Health. 207p. (Orig.). (C). 1995. pap. text 14.99 (*0-945819-78-1*) Sulzburger & Graham Pub.

Mills, Roger F., ed. see Wojowasito, Soewojo.

Mills, Roger M., Jr. & Young, James B. Practical Approaches to the Treatment of Heart Failure. LC 97-41999. 352p. 1997. 45.00 (*0-683-18104-1*) Lppncott W & W.

***Mills, Ron.** Kingdom Tales: Five Stories Jesus Told. 48p. (J). (gr. 6-7). 1998. pap. 3.95 (*0-687-08961-1*) Abingdon.

Mills, Ron. A Rock Is My Brother. (Illus.). 48p. 1999. pap. 3.95 (*0-687-08438-5*) Abingdon.

Mills, Ron & Huff, Allen. Style over Substance: A Critical Analysis of an African American Teenage Subculture. 100p. 1999. pap. 10.95 (*0-913543-62-4*) African Am Imag.

Mills, Ronald E. Long-Term Care Investment Strategies: A Guide to Start-Ups, Facility Conversions & Strategic Alliances. 200p. (C). 1995. text 55.00 (*1-55738-622-6*, Irwn Prfssnl) McGraw-Hill Prof.

***Mills, Rosemary S. & Duck, Steve.** The Developmental Psychology of Personal Relationships LC 99-40991. 304p. 2000. pap. 34.00 (*0-471-99880-X*) Wiley.

Mills, Roxanne, jt. auth. see Mills, Randy Keith.

Mills, Roy. The Soul's Remembrance: Earth Is Not Our Home. 160p. 1999. 16.95 (*1-892714-02-7*) Onjinjinkta.

***Mills, Russell H.** A Clinician's Guide to the Expanded Evaluation of Dysphagia in Adults. LC 99-39484. (For Clinicians by Clinicians Ser.). (Illus.). 2000. pap. write for info. (*0-89079-836-2*) PRO-ED.

Mills, S. E., compiled by. Underground Office Humor: Real Memos, Rude Faxes, Tasteless Jokes & Eye-Popping True Stories from the Workplace. LC 94-20043. (Illus.). 128p. 1994. pap. 9.95 (*0-8065-1567-8*, Citadel Pr) Carol Pub Group.

Mills, Sam. The Money Tree. LC 98-83192. 365p. 1999. 25.00 (*0-7388-0355-3*); pap. 15.00 (*0-7388-0356-1*) Xlibris Corp.

Mills, Sara. Discourse. LC 97-10848. 192p. (C). 1997. 50.00 (*0-415-13854-X*); pap. 12.99 (*0-415-11053-X*) Routledge.

— Feminist Stylistics. LC 94-22697. (Interface Ser.). (Illus.). 248p. (C). 1995. pap. 25.99 (*0-415-05028-6*, A7884) Routledge.

Mills, Sara & Pearce, Lynne. Feminist Readings: An Introduction to Feminist Literature. 2nd ed. 304p. 1996. pap. 25.00 (*0-13-375395-6*) P-H.

Mills, Sara, et al. Feminist Readings - Feminists Reading. 304p. (C). 1989. pap. text 15.00 (*0-8139-1243-1*) U Pr of Va.

Mills, Sara, tr. see Shen, Terry C.

***Mills, Scott A.** Big Clay Pot. (Illus.). 144p. 2000. pap. 12.95 (*1-891830-16-3*, Pub. by Top Shelf Prodns) LPC InBook.

Mills, Scott A. Stranded in the Philippines: Missionary Professor Organizes Resistance to the Japanese. (Illus.). 137p. (Orig.). 1994. pap. 12.50 (*971-10-0519-0*, Pub. by New Day Pub) Cellar.

Mills, Scott A., jt. auth. see Mapes, Victor L.

Mills, Selwyn & Weisser, Max. The Odd Couple Syndrome: Resolving the Neat-Sloppy Dilemma. McNally, Catherine, ed. (Illus.). 160p. 1988. 14.95 (*0-944748-00-7*); pap. 10.95 (*0-944748-01-5*) Jameison Pub.

Mills, Shaun. Constitutional & Administrative Law of the EC. 600p. 1996. pap. write for info. (*1-85941-223-8*, Pub. by Cavendish Pubng) Gaunt.

Mills, Sheila. The Outdoor Dutch Oven Cookbook. LC 97-6193. 170p. 1997. pap. 16.95 (*0-07-043023-3*) McGraw.

Mills, Simon Y. The Dictionary of Modern Herbalism: A Comprehensive Guide to Practical Herbal Therapy. 224p. 1997. reprint ed. 7.98 (*1-56731-223-3*, MJF Bks) Fine Comms.

— The Dictionary of Modern Herbalism: The Complete Guide to Herbs & Herbal Therapy. 208p. 1985. pap. 12.95 (*0-89281-238-9*) Inner Tradit.

Mills, Sophie. Theseus, Tragedy, & the Athenian Empire. LC 97-14789. (Oxford Classical Monographs). 304p. 1998. text 87.00 (*0-19-815063-6*) OUP.

Mills, Stacey E., et al. Neoplasma & Related Lesions of the Head & Neck: Based on the Proceedings of the 59th Annual Anatomic Pathology Slide Seminar of the American Society of Clinical Pathologists. LC 94-21116. 126p. 1994. 35.00 (*0-89189-385-7*) Am Soc Clinical.

Mills, Stacey E., jt. auth. see Fechner, Robert E.

Mills, Stacey E., jt. ed. see Sternberg, Stephen S.

Mills, Staphanie. In Service of the Wild: Restoring & Reinhabiting Damaged Land. 256p. 1996. pap. 15.00 (*0-8070-8535-9*) Beacon Pr.

Mills, Stella, ed. The Collected Letters of Colin MacLaurin. 560p. (C). 1982. text 35.00 (*0-906812-08-9*) Birkhauser.

Mills, Stephanie. Turning away from Technology. LC 97-8045. 320p. 1997. pap. 18.00 (*0-87156-953-1*, Pub. by Sierra) Random.

Mills, Stephanie, ed. In Praise of Nature. LC 90-33875. 255p. 1990. text 35.00 (*1-55963-035-3*) Island Pr.

Mills, Stephen, ed. see Ickringill, Steve.

Mills, Stephen F. The American Landscape. 160p. 1998. pap. 22.00 (*1-85331-179-0*, Pub. by Edinburgh U Pr) Col U Pr.

Mills, Stephen Tukel, jt. auth. see Fouts, Roger.

Mills, Steve. Living & Working in America: How to Gain Entry & How to Settle When You Are There. 5th ed. (Living & Working Abroad Ser.). 272p. 2000. pap. 14.95 (*1-85703-577-9*, Pub. by How To Bks) Midpt Trade.

— Living & Working in America: How to Obtain Entry & Settle in Successfully. 4th ed. (Living & Working Abroad Ser.). 238p. 1997. pap. 19.95 (*1-85703-454-6*, Pub. by How To Bks) Trans-Atl Phila.

Mills, Steve, jt. auth. see Riemer, Pierce.

Mills, Steven, jt. auth. see Reimer, Pierce.

Mills, Susan, jt. ed. see Hawkes, Jane.

Mills, Susan W. Eight Hundred Forty-Nine Traditional Patchwork Patterns: A Pictorial Handbook. (Illus.). 160p. 1989. pap. 7.95 (*0-486-26003-8*) Dover.

Mills, T. C. Composite Monetary Indicators for the United Kingdom: Construction & Empirical Analysis. LC HB0141.. (Bank of England. Discussion Papers. Technical Ser.: No. 3). 72p. pap. 30.00 (*0-608-13899-1*, 202042800018) Bks Demand.

Mills, Tedi L., tr. see Baylor, Byrd.

Mills, Tedi L., tr. see Fienberg, Anna.

Mills, Tedi L., tr. see Hautzig, Deborah.

Mills, Terence C. The Econometric Modelling of Financial Time Series. 255p. (C). 1995. pap. text 24.95 (*0-521-42257-4*) Cambridge U Pr.

— The Econometric Modelling of Financial Time Series. 2nd ed. LC 98-53587. (Illus.). 392p. (C). 1999. 80.00 (*0-521-62413-4*); pap. 27.95 (*0-521-62492-4*) Cambridge U Pr.

— Time Series Techniques for Economists. 387p. (C). 1991. pap. text 25.95 (*0-521-40574-2*) Cambridge U Pr.

Mills, Terence C., ed. Economic Forecasting, 2 vols. LC 99-30947. (The International Library of Critical Writings in Economics Ser.). 1192p. (C). 1999. 435.00 (*1-85278-866-6*) E Elgar.

Mills, Terry, III. Instrumental Data for Drug Analysis, 5 vols., 1. 2nd ed. 1992. 120.00 (*0-444-01281-8*) CRC Pr.

— Instrumental Data for Drug Analysis, 5 vols., 2. 2nd ed. 1992. 120.00 (*0-444-01282-6*) CRC Pr.

— Instrumental Data for Drug Analysis, 5 vols., 3. 2nd ed. 1992. 120.00 (*0-444-01283-4*) CRC Pr.

— Instrumental Data for Drug Analysis, 5 vols., 4. 2nd ed. 1992. 120.00 (*0-444-01284-2*) CRC Pr.

— Instrumental Data for Drug Analysis, 5 vols., 5. 2nd ed. 1992. 120.00 (*0-444-01271-0*, RS189) CRC Pr.

Mills, Terry, III & Roberson, J. Conrad. Instrumental Data for Drug Analysis, Vol. 1. 2nd ed. LC 93-13539. (Forensic & Police Science Ser.). 785p. 1992. reprint ed. boxed set 168.95 (*0-8493-9521-6*, RS189) CRC Pr.

Mills, Terry, et al. Instrumental Data for Drug Analysis: Cumulative Indices. 2nd ed. LC 96-31352. (CRC Series on Forensic & Police Science). 464p. 1996. boxed set 119.95 (*0-8493-8115-0*) CRC Pr.

Mills, Thomas S. & Archibald, Janet S. The Pilot's Reference to ATC Procedures & Phraseology. 7th ed. (Illus.). 370p. 1999. pap. 27.95 (*0-935695-24-9*) Reavco Pub.

Mills-Thornton, Serena G. Mentor Wisdom: Requisites for Living. Allen, Sharon, ed. (Illus.). 31p. (Orig.). (YA). 1993. write for info. (*0-9614338-0-9*) Ideas.

Mills, Velma, ed. see Eager, George B.

Mills, Vicki. Fly Free, Stay Cheap? 72p. 1998. pap. 9.95 (*0-9661876-0-1*) Platypus Pubns.

Mills, Virginia M., et al. Neurologic Rehabilitation: A Guide to Diagnosis, Prognosis & Treatment Planning. LC 97-24813. (Illus.). 1995. pap. 49.95 (*0-86542-514-0*) Blackwell Sci.

Mills, W. Jay. Historic Houses of New Jersey. (History of New Jersey Ser.: Vol. 2). 172p. 1997. 11.95 (*1-58057-013-5*, HHNJ001B) Digital Antiq.

Mills, Watson E. Bibliographies for Biblical Research Vol. VIII: 2 Corinthians. LC 93-30864. (New Testament Ser.). 156p. 1998. text 69.95 (*0-7734-2442-3*, Mellen Biblical Pr) E Mellen.

— A Bibliography of the Nature & Role of the Holy Spirit in Twentieth-Century Writings. LC 93-22748. (Mellen Biblical Press Ser.: Vol. 10). 372p. 1993. 79.95 (*0-7734-2366-4*, Mellen Biblical Pr) E Mellen.

— Critical Tools for the Study of the New Testament. LC 95-31314. (Mellen Biblical Press Ser.: Vol. 47). 156p. 1995. text 69.95 (*0-7734-2405-9*, Mellen Biblical Pr) E Mellen.

— Glossolalia: A Bibliography. LC 85-8987. (Studies in the Bible & Early Christianity: Vol. 6). 132p. 1989. lib. bdg. 69.95 (*0-88946-605-X*) E Mellen.

— Index to Periodical Literature on the Apostle Paul, 1960-1992. LC 93-7974. (New Testament Tools & Studies: Vol. 16). xx, 346p. 1993. 118.00 (*90-04-09674-4*) Brill Academic Pubs.

— Mercer Commentary on the Bible: The Prophets, Vol. 4. 1996. pap. text 18.95 (*0-86554-509-X*, MUP/P136) Mercer Univ Pr.

— New Testament Greek: An Introductory Grammar. 2nd ed. LC 85-11540. 1989. lib. bdg. 79.95 (*0-88946-201-1*) E Mellen.

— Periodical Literature on Christ & the Gospels. LC 98-39186. (New Testament Tools & Studies). xxx, 962p. 1998. 243.00 (*90-04-10098-9*) Brill Academic Pubs.

Mills, Watson E., compiled by. Bibliographies for Biblical Research Vol. II: The Gospel of Mark. LC 93-30864. (New Testament Ser.). 552p. 1994. text 169.95 (*0-7734-2398-2*) E Mellen.

— Bibliographies for Biblical Research Vol. III: The Gospel of Luke. LC 93-30864. (New Testament Ser.). 416p. text 169.95 (*0-7734-2402-4*) E Mellen.

— Bibliographies for Biblical Research Vol. III: The Gospel of Luke. LC 93-30864. (New Testament Ser.). 416p. 1995. text 129.95 (*0-7734-2385-0*) E Mellen.

— Bibliographies for Biblical Research Vol. VI: Romans. LC 93-30864. (New Testament Ser.). 228p. 1996. 89.95 (*0-7734-2418-0*) E Mellen.

— Bibliographies for Biblical Research Vol. VII: I Corinthians. (New Testament Ser.). text. write for info. (*0-7734-2419-9*) E Mellen.

***Mills, Watson E., compiled by.** Bibliographies for Biblical Research Vol. 12: Colossians. LC 93-30864. (New Testament Ser.). 101p. 1999. 59.95 (*0-7734-2476-8*) E Mellen.

— Bibliographies for Biblical Research - Philippians. Vol. XI. LC 93-30864. 97p. 2000. text 59.95 (*0-7734-2474-1*) E Mellen.

— Bibliographies on the Life & Teachings of Jesus Vol. 1: The Birth Narratives. LC 99-36087. 88p. 1999. text 39.95 (*0-7734-2446-6*) E Mellen.

Mills, Watson E., ed. Bibliographies for Biblical Research Vol. I: The Gospel of Matthew. LC 93-30864. (New Testament Ser.). 304p. 1993. text 129.95 (*0-7734-2396-6*) E Mellen.

— A Critical Concordance to the Coptic Thomas. (Computer Bible Ser.: Vol. 43). 188p. 1995. pap. 89.95 (*0-7734-4098-4*) E Mellen.

***Mills, Watson E., ed.** Ephesians. LC 93-30864. (Bibliographies for Biblical Research New Testament Ser.: Vol. 10). 99p. 1999. 59.95 (*0-7734-2472-5*) E Mellen.

Mills, Watson E., ed. Bibliographies for Biblical Research: The Acts of the Apostles. LC 93-30864. (New Testament Ser.: Vol. V). 344p. 1996. text 99.95 (*0-7734-2432-6*, Mellen Biblical Pr) E Mellen.

— Bibliographies for Biblical Research: The Gospel of Mark. LC 93-30864. (New Testament Ser.: Vol. II). 552p. 1994. text 129.95 (*0-7734-2349-4*, Mellen Biblical Pr) E Mellen.

— Bibliographies for Biblical Research: The Gospel of Matthew. LC 93-30864. (New Testament Ser.: Vol. I). 304p. 1993. text 169.95 (*0-7734-2347-8*, Mellen Biblical Pr) E Mellen.

— Bibliographies for Biblical Research Vol. IV: The Gospel of John. LC 93-30864. (New Testament Ser.). 436p. 1995. text 129.95 (*0-7734-2357-5*) E Mellen.

Mills, Watson E., et al, eds. Mercer Commentary on the Bible. LC 94-23638. 1994. 50.00 (*0-86554-406-9*, MUP-H329) Mercer Univ Pr.

— Mercer Dictionary of the Bible. LC 89-13857. (Illus.). 1088p. (C). 1998. pap. 35.00 (*0-86554-373-9*, MUP/P86) Mercer Univ Pr.

Mills, Watson E. & Mills, Joyce H. An Index to Novum Testamentum Volumes 1-35 Vols. 1-35, Set. ix, 256p. 1994. 64.00 (*90-04-10082-2*) Brill Academic Pubs.

Mills, Watson E. & Wilson, Richard F., eds. Mercer Commentary on the Bible: The Gospels. 6th ed. 272p. 1996. pap. text 16.95 (*0-86554-511-1*, MUP/P138) Mercer Univ Pr.

— Mercer Commentary on the Bible Vol. 2: The History of Israel Joshua-Esther. 280p. 1998. pap. text 19.95 (*0-86554-507-3*, P134) Mercer Univ Pr.

***Mills, Watson E. & Wilson, Richard F., eds.** Mercer Commentary on the Bible Vol. 3: Wisdom Writings. (Mercer Commentary on the Bible Ser.). 2000. 19.95 (*0-86554-508-1*) Mercer Univ Pr.

Mills, Watson E. & Wilson, Richard F., eds. Mercer Commentary on the Bible Vol. 7: Acts & Pauline Writings. LC 97-167955. 280p. (Orig.). 1997. pap. text 18.95 (*0-86554-512-X*) Mercer Univ Pr.

***Mills, Watson E. & Wilson, Richard F., eds.** Mercer Commentary on the Bible Vol. 8: The General Epistles & Revelation. 240p. 2000. pap. 19.95 (*0-86554-513-8*) Mercer Univ Pr.

Mills, Watson E. & Wilson, Richard R., eds. Mercer Commentary on the Bible Vol. 1: Pentateuch - Torah. LC 98-141144. 324p. 1998. pap. text 19.95 (*0-86554-506-5*, P133) Mercer Univ Pr.

***Mills, Wes.** Drawing the Primary Sense. (Art Profile Ser.). 1998. 39.95 (*1-889097-19-5*, Pub. by Hard Pr MA) Consort Bk Sales.

Mills, William. The Arkansas: An American River. LC 88-10607. (Illus.). 260p. 1989. text 36.00 (*1-55728-043-6*) U of Ark Pr.

— The Arkansas: An American River. LC 88-10607. (Illus.). 260p. 1989. pap. 24.00 (*1-55728-044-4*) U of Ark Pr.

— I Know a Place: Three Stories. (Illus.). 1976. 15.00 (*0-912960-08-6*) Nightowl.

— Stained Glass: Poems. fac. ed. LC 78-11893. 69p. 1979. reprint ed. pap. 30.00 (*0-7837-7808-2*, 204756400007) Bks Demand.

Mills, William, intro. John William Corrington: Southern Man of Letters. LC 93-24290. 240p. 1997. 24.95 (*0-944436-20-X*) Pelican.

Mills, William, intro. Images of Kansas City. (Illus.). 128p. (C). 1996. 24.95 (*0-8262-1070-8*) U of Mo Pr.

Mills, William C. Flint Ridge. (Archaeology, Ohio History, Prehistoric Indians Ser.). (Illus.). 80p. 1993. reprint ed. pap. 6.25 (*1-56651-093-7*) A W McGraw.

Mills, William J. & Speak, P. Keyguide to Information Sources on the Polar & Cold Regions. LC 97-6587. 330p. 1998. 140.00 (*0-7201-2176-0*) Continuum.

Mills, William J., jt. auth. see Seyer, Martin D.

Mills, William R., jt. auth. see West, Gary.

Mills, Wright C. The Causes of World War Three. LC 85-14381. 188p. (gr. 13). 1985. reprint ed. pap. text 42.95 (*0-87332-357-2*) M E Sharpe.

Millsap, Larry & Ferl, Terry E. Descriptive Cataloging for the AACR2R & the Integrated MARC Format: A How-to-Do-It Workbook. 2nd rev. ed. LC 97-24593. (How-to-Do-It Manuals Ser.). 240p. 1997. pap. 49.95 (*1-55570-284-8*) Neal-Schuman.

Millsap, Larry, jt. auth. see Ferl, Terry E.

Millslagle, Duane G. Motor Development & Sport Skills Clinic. LC 97-41227. 172p. 1997. pap. 59.95 (*0-7734-8425-6*) E Mellen.

Millson, Cecilia. Tales of Old Wiltshire. 96p. 1987. 30.00 (*0-905392-12-4*) St Mut.

Millson, Cecillia. The History of Donnington Hospital. 83p. 1987. pap. 30.00 (*0-905392-51-5*) St Mut.

— Tales of Old Oxfordshire. 96p. 1987. pap. 30.00 (*0-905392-20-5*) St Mut.

Millson, Frank. Light & Color. (Illus.). 24p. (Orig.). (J). (gr. 3-7). 1996. pap. 6.95 (*0-8167-4048-8*) Troll Communs.

Millson, John J., jt. auth. see Buchweitz, Ragnar-Olaf.

Millson, Peter. Penguin Critical Studies. pap. 7.95 (*0-14-077019-4*, Pub. by Pnguin Bks Ltd) Trafalgar.

Millspauch, Ben. Z Car: A Legend in Its Own Time. 1993. pap. 16.95 (*0-8306-4339-7*) McGraw-Hill Prof.

Millspaugh, en P. Let's Build Airplanes & Rockets! LC 96-22405. (Illus.). 128p. (J). (gr. 3-6). 1996. pap., teacher ed. 16.95 (*0-07-042952-9*, Lrng Triangle) McGraw-Hill Prof.

Millspaugh, A. C. The American Task in Persia. LC 73-6293. (Middle East Ser.). 1973. reprint ed. 25.95 (*0-405-05350-9*) Ayer.

Millspaugh, A. C., jt. auth. see Bradley, Julia C.

Millspaugh, A. C., jt. auth. see Bradley, Julia Case.

***Millspaugh, Anita.** Introduction to Object-Oriented Programming with C++ LC 98-86371. (Illus.). 272p. 1998. pap. 54.50 (*0-03-023621-5*) Dryden Pr.

Millspaugh, Anita, jt. auth. see Bradley, Julia C.

Millspaugh, Arthur C. Americans in Persia. LC 76-9837. (Politics & Strategy of World War II Ser.). 1976. reprint ed. lib. bdg. 37.50 (*0-306-70764-0*) Da Capo.

— Crime Control by the National Government. LC 70-168678. (American Constitutional & Legal History Ser). 306p. 1972. reprint ed. lib. bdg. 37.50 (*0-306-70418-8*) Da Capo.

Millspaugh, Ben. Aviation & Space Science Projects. (Illus.). 138p. (J). (gr. 9-12). 1991. pap. 9.95 (*0-8306-2156-3*) McGraw-Hill Prof.

Millspaugh, Ben P. Aviation & Space Science Projects. (J). 1991. 16.95 (*0-8306-2157-1*) McGraw-Hill Prof.

— Z Car: A Legend in Its Own Time. (Illus.). 208p. 1990. 24.95 (*0-8306-3536-X*, 3536) McGraw-Hill Prof.

Millspaugh, Charles F. American Medicinal Plants: An Illustrated & Descriptive Guide to Plants Indigenous to & Naturalized in the United States Which Are Used in Medicine. LC 73-91487. (Illus.). 450p. 1974. reprint ed. pap. 18.95 (*0-486-23034-1*) Dover.

— Medicinal Plants: An Illustrated & Descriptive Guide to Plants Indigenous to & Naturalized in the United States Which Are Used in Medicine, 2 vols., Set. 1132p. 1980. lib. bdg. 200.00 (*0-8490-3103-6*) Gordon Pr.

Millspaugh, Francis Corwin, jt. auth. see Huff, Ann Millspaugh.

***Millst, Hazel.** Scottish Quotations. (Scottish Collection Ser.). (Illus.). 64p. 2000. 8.95 (*0-00-472304-X*, Pub. by HarpC) Trafalgar.

Millstein, Barbara Head. Consuelo Kanaga: American Photo. LC 91-35933. (Illus.). 224p. 1992. pap. 35.00 (*0-295-97228-9*) U of Wash Pr.

Millstein, Gilbert. The Late Harvey Grosbeck. LC 73-83658. 285p. 1974. write for info. (*0-385-01133-4*) BDD LT Grp.

Millstein, Ira M. Corporate Governance: Improving Competitiveness & Access to Capital in Global Markets. A Report to the OECD by the Business Sector Advisory Group on Corporate Governance. Ira M. Millstein, Chairman. LC 98-180641. 112p. 1998. pap. 22.00 (*92-64-16056-6*, 92 98 04 1 P, Pub. by Org for Econ) OECD.

Millstein, Jeff. U. S. Marine Corps Aviation Unit: Insignia, 1941-1946. LC 95-60546. 128p. 1995. 39.95 (*1-56311-211-6*) Turner Pub KY.

Millstein, Jeffrey A., jt. auth. see Turchin, Peter.

Millstein, Jeffrey A., ed. see Khibnik, Alexander I.

Millstein, Jeffrey A., ed. see Levitin, Victor.

Millstein, Susan G., et al, eds. Promoting the Health of Adolescents: New Directions for the Twenty-First Century. (Illus.). 424p. 1994. reprint ed. pap. text 40.00 (*0-19-509188-4*) OUP.

Millstone, David. An Elementary Odyssey: Teaching Ancient Civilization Through Story. LC 94-48431. 212p. 1995. pap. text 25.00 (*0-435-08841-6*, 08841) Heinemann.

Millstone, Erik. Lead & Public Health: Dangers for Children. LC 97-22574. 240p. 1997. pap. 24.95 (*1-56032-724-3*); boxed set 75.00 (*1-56032-723-5*) Hemisp Pub.

Milltown Centennial Staff. Milltown. (Images of America Ser.). 1995. pap. 16.99 (*0-7524-0238-2*) Arcadia Publng.

Millu, Liana. Smoke over Birkenau. Schwartz, Lynne Sharon, tr. from ITA. LC 91-22973. 208p. 1991. 19.95 (*0-8276-0398-3*) JPS Phila.

— Smoke over Birkenau. Schwartz, Lynne Sharon, tr. 202p. 1998. pap. 15.95 (*0-8101-1569-7*) Northwestern U Pr.

***Millunchick, J. M., et al, eds.** Morphological & Compositional Evolution of Heteroepitaxial Semiconductor Thin Films: Materials Research Society Symposium Proceedings, Vol. 618. 2000. text 82.00 (*1-55899-526-9*) Materials Res.

Millward. Ak T/a Wkbk Bio English Lang 3e. 3rd ed. (C). 2001. pap. text 44.50 (*0-15-507417-2*) Harcourt Coll Pubs.

Millward, Alan, jt. auth. see Dyson, Alan.

Millward, C. M. A Biography about English Language. 2nd ed. (C). 1996. text 47.50 (*0-15-501645-8*, Pub. by Harcourt Coll Pubs) Harcourt.

— A Biography of the English Language. 432p. (C). 1989. text 51.00 (*0-03-059431-6*, Pub. by Harcourt Coll Pubs) Harcourt.

— A Biography of the English Language. 2nd ed. (C). 1996. wbk. ed. 24.00 (*0-15-501647-4*, Pub. by Harcourt Coll Pubs) Harcourt.

— A Biography of the English Language: Answer Key. 2nd ed. (C). 1996. pap. text, teacher ed. 33.50 (*0-15-501646-6*, Pub. by Harcourt Coll Pubs) Harcourt.

— L' Oeuvre de Pierre Loti et l'Esprit Fin de Siecle. 9.50 (*0-685-34266-2*) Fr & Eur.

Millward, Carl L., jt. auth. see Schwamm, Harry A.

***Millward, D. J.** Geology of the Ambleside District: Memoir for 1:50 000 Geological Sheet 38 (England & Wales) (Illus.). xii, 228p. 2000. 120.00 (*0-11-884547-0*, Pub. by Statnry Office) Balogh.

Millward, James A. Beyond the Pass: Economy, Ethnicity, & Empire in Qing Central Asia, 1759-1864. LC 97-35503. (Illus.). 450p. 1998. 56.00 (*0-8047-2933-6*) Stanford U Pr.

***Millward, Neil, et al, eds.** All Change at Work? British Employee Relations 1980-1998 Portrayed by Workplace. LC 99-89145. (Illus.). 320p. (C). 2000. text 100.00 (*0-415-20634-0*) Routledge.

***Millward, Neil, et al.** All Change at Work? British Employee Relations 1980-1998 Portrayed by Workplace. LC 99-89145. (Industrial Relations Survey Ser.). 2000. pap. write for info. (*0-415-20635-9*) Routledge.

Millward, Pamela. Mother: A Novel of the Revolution. LC 76-78045. (Writing Ser.: No. 26). 64p. (Orig.). 1970. pap. 2.00 (*0-87704-015-X*) Four Seasons Foun.

Millward, Robert E. & Singleton, John, eds. The Political Economy of Nationalisation in Britain, 1920-50. (Illus.). 339p. (C). 1995. text 64.95 (*0-521-45096-9*) Cambridge U Pr.

Millward, Robert E., et al. Public Sector Economics. LC 82-4609. (Surveys in Economics Ser.). 293p. reprint ed. pap. 90.90 (*0-7837-1590-0*, 204188200024) Bks Demand.

Millward, Robert E., jt. auth. see Foreman-Peck, James.

Millward-Sadler, G. H., et al, eds. Wright's Liver & Biliary Disease: Pathophysiology, Diagnosis & Management, 2 vols. 3rd ed. (Illus.). 1667p. 1992. text 335.00 (*0-7020-1392-7*, Pub. by W B Saunders) Saunders.

Millward, Simon. Fast Guide to Cubase VST. 1999. pap. text 29.95 (*1-870775-57-0*) Cimothas Pub.

Millward, William G., jt. ed. see Mazzaoui, Michel M.

Millwater, Harold W. Fox Fire. 246p. 1997. pap. 14.95 (*1-57502-567-1*, PO1645) Morris Pubng.

Millword, Michael T., jt. ed. see Glaeser, Phyllis S.

Milly, ed. see Proust, Marcel.

***Milly, Deborah J.** Poverty, Equality & Growth: The Politics of Economic Need in Postwar Japan. LC 98-45936. (Harvard East Asian Monographs). 1999. 49.50 (*0-674-69475-9*) HUP.

Milly, Walter De, 3rd. In My Father's Arms: A True Story of Incest. LC 99-6275. (Living Out). 144p. 1999. text 19.95 (*0-299-16510-8*) U of Wis Pr.

Millyard, Anne W., jt. auth. see Wilks, Rick J.

Milman. Western Dada Orbit Vol. 7: United States, Italy, Spain, Holland & Belgium. 2000. 85.00 (*0-8161-7386-9*, G K Hall Lrg Type) Mac Lib Ref.

Milman, Barbara. Light in the Shadows. LC 97-14067. 1997. pap. 14.95 (*0-8246-0401-6*) Jonathan David.

Milman, David, ed. Regulating Enterprise: Law & Business Organisation in the U. K. 288p. 1999. 54.00 (*1-901362-56-6*, Pub. by Hart Pub) Intl Spec Bk.

Milman, Donald & Goldman, George, eds. Techniques of Working with Resistance. LC 85-18653. 417p. 1986. 60.00 (*0-87668-616-1*) Aronson.

Milman, Frank L. Labor Management Relations Implications of Reduction in Force & Reengineering. 13p. 1996. pap. 3.75 (*0-16-061092-3*) USGPO.

Milman, Harry A. & Elmore, Eugene, eds. Biomechanical Mechanisms & Regulations of Intercellular Communication. LC 87-61833. (Advances in Modern Environmental Toxicology Ser.: Vol. 14). (Illus.). 304p. 1987. 65.00 (*0-911131-15-9*) Specialist Journals.

Milman, Harry A. & Weisburger, Elizabeth K., eds. Handbook of Carcinogen Testing. 2nd ed. LC 94-15231. (Illus.). 856p. 1994. 145.00 (*0-8155-1356-9*) Noyes.

Milman, Henry H. History of Christianity from the Birth of Christ to the Abolition of Paganism in the Roman Empire, 3 vols. rev. ed. LC 78-172733. reprint ed. 210.00 (*0-404-04350-X*) AMS Pr.

— History of Latin Christianity, 9 vols. LC 71-172734. reprint ed. lib. bdg. 425.00 (*0-404-04360-7*) AMS Pr.

— The History of the Jews. 640p. 1986. 360.00 (*1-85077-133-2*, Pub. by Darf Pubs Ltd) St Mut.

Milman, Henry H., tr. see Euripides, ed.

Milman, Mario. Extrapolation & Optimal Decompositions: With Applications to Analysis. Dold, A. et al, eds. (Lecture Notes in Mathematics Ser.: Vol. 1580). 1994. 36.95 (*0-387-58081-6*) Spr-Verlag.

Milman, Mario & Schonbek, T., eds. Harmonic Analysis & Partial Differential Equations: (Proceedings of a Conference) LC 90-34635. (Contemporary Mathematics Ser.: Vol. 107). 129p. 1990. pap. 40.00 (*0-8218-5113-6*, CONM/107) Am Math.

Milman, Mario, jt. auth. see Caffarelli, Luis A.

Milman, Mario, jt. auth. see Jawerth, Bjorn.

Milman, V. D., jt. ed. see Lindenstrauss, J.

Milman, Vitali, jt. ed. see Ball, Keith.

Milman, Yoseph. Opacity in the Writings of Robbe-Grillet, Pinter, & Zach: A Study in the Poetics of Absurd Literature. LC 91-43258. (Studies in Comparative Literature: Vol. 18). 148p. 1992. lib. bdg. 69.95 (*0-7734-9701-3*) E Mellen.

Milmed, Bella K. Kant & Current Philosophical Issues: Some Modern Developments of His Theory of Knowledge. LC 61-8058. 272p. reprint ed. pap. 84.40 (*0-608-10062-5*, 205021300058) Bks Demand.

Milmine, Georgine, jt. auth. see Cather, Willa.

Milne. Bartok: The Illustrated Lives of the Great Composers. (Illustrated Lives of the Great Composers Ser.). (Illus.). 122p. 1995. pap. 17.95 (*0-7119-0260-7*, OP 42464) Music Sales.

***Milne.** Family Affaire. 1998. pap., student ed. write for info. (*0-582-74358-3*) Addison-Wesley.

— Investigative Interviewing. LC 98-54607. 240p. 1999. pap. 34.00 (*0-471-98729-8*) Wiley.

Milne. Social Therapy. 288p. (C). 1999. 65.95 (*0-471-98726-3*) Wiley.

***Milne.** Social Therapy. 288p. (C). 1999. pap. 37.00 (*0-471-98727-1*) Wiley.

Milne, A. A., jt. auth. see Perry, Ruth.

Milne, A. A., pseud. A. A. Milne: Complete Tales & Poems. (J). 1996. pap. 50.00 (*0-525-45724-0*, Dutton Child) Peng Put Young Read.

— Baby's First Winnie-the-Pooh: A Soft Storybook. (Illus.). 8p. (J). (ps). 1999. pap. 24.99 (*0-525-45898-0*) NAL.

— Christopher Robin Gives Pooh a Party. (Illus.). 32p. (J). 1993. 4.99 (*0-525-45144-7*, Dutton Child) Peng Put Young Read.

— The Classic Pooh Treasury Vol. 3: The House At Pooh Corner, Set. (Illus.). (J). 1997. write for info. incl. audio (*1-57375-465-X*) Audioscope.

— Collected Verse of A. A. Milne: When We Were Young & Now We Are Six. (Illus.). 224p. 1999. pap. 7.95 (*0-452-27762-0*, Plume) Dutton Plume.

— The Complete Tales of Winnie-the-Pooh. (Illus.). 344p. (J). (ps-3). 1996. 35.00 (*0-525-45723-2*) NAL.

***Milne, A. A., pseud.** Complete Tales of Winnie-the-Pooh. 70th ed. (Illus.). (J). 1999. 40.00 (*0-525-45060-2*, Dutton Child) Peng Put Young Read.

— Eeyore. (Pooh Giant Shaped Board Bks.). (Illus.). 10p. (YA). 2000. bds. 7.99 (*0-525-46332-1*, Dutton Child) Peng Put Young Read.

— Eeyore Clip & Read. abr. ed. (Illus.). 24p. (ps-3). 1999. pap. 2.99 (*0-525-46206-6*, Dutton Child) Peng Put Young Read.

Milne, A. A., pseud. Eeyore Has a Birthday. LC 96-166807. (Illus.). 24p. (J). (ps-k). 1996. pap. 3.99 (*0-525-45528-0*, Dutton Child) Peng Put Young Read.

— Eeyore Has a Birthday. (Slide & Peek Ser.). (ps-k). 1999. pap. 5.99 (*0-525-46118-3*) Peng Put Young Read.

***Milne, A. A., pseud.** Eeyore Loses a Tail. (Illus.). 32p. (J). (ps-3). 2000. 9.99 (*0-525-46456-5*, Dutton Child) Peng Put Young Read.

Milne, A. A., pseud. Eeyore's Gloomy Little Instruction Book. (Illus.). (J). 1996. 8.99 (*0-525-45519-1*, Dutton Child) Peng Put Young Read.

***Milne, A. A., pseud.** Hello, Eeyore! (Illus.). 10p. (J). (ps-k). 2000. 8.99 (*0-525-46458-1*, Dutton Child) Peng Put Young Read.

— Hello, Piglet! (Illus.). 10p. (J). (ps-k). 2000. 8.99 (*0-525-46460-3*, Dutton Child) Peng Put Young Read.

Milne, A. A., pseud. Hello, Tigger! With Embroidered Cloth Cover. (Illus.). 10p. (ps-k). 1999. 7.99 (*0-525-45985-5*, Dutton Child) Peng Put Young Read.

***Milne, A. A., pseud.** Here Comes Tigger! A Storybook & Plush Package. (Illus.). 32p. (J). 2000. 35.00 (*0-525-46276-7*, Dutton Child) Peng Put Young Read.

Milne, A. A., pseud. The House at Pooh Corner. 102p. (J). 1966. pap. 5.95 (*0-87129-641-1*, H31) Dramatic Pub.

— The House at Pooh Corner. (Illus.). 192p. (J). 1999. pap. 7.95 (*0-452-27763-9*, Plume) Dutton Plume.

— The House at Pooh Corner. (Illus.). 192p. (J). (ps up). 1988. 10.99 (*0-525-44444-0*, Dutton Child) Peng Put Young Read.

— The House at Pooh Corner. LC 91-29462. (Illus.). 192p. (J). (ps up). 1991. 22.99 (*0-525-44774-1*, Dutton Child) Peng Put Young Read.

— The House at Pooh Corner. (Illus.). 192p. (J). (ps-3). 1992. pap. 4.99 (*0-14-036122-7*, PuffinBks) Peng Put Young Read.

***Milne, A. A., pseud.** House at Pooh Corner. abr. ed. (J). 1998. mass mkt. 14.95 (*1-85998-651-X*) Trafalgar.

— The House at Pooh Corner, Set. (J). write for info. incl. audio (*1-57375-653-9*, 71524) Audioscope.

Milne, A. A., pseud. I Think I Am a Tram - Mne Kazhetsia Chto Ia Tramvai. Greenhill, Rima, ed. Marshak, S. et al, trs. LC 93-44475. (ENG & RUS., Illus.). 176p. (Orig.). (YA). 1994. pap. 9.00 (*1-55779-068-X*) Hermitage Pubs.

Milne, A. A., pseud. In Which a House Is Built at Pooh Corner for Eeyore. unabridged ed. (Classic Pooh Treasury Ser.). (J). write for info. incl. audio (*1-57375-527-3*, 71394) Audioscope.

Milne, A. A., pseud. In Which Christopher Robin Gives Pooh a Party. unabridged ed. (Winnie-the-Pooh Ser.). (Illus.). (J). write for info. incl. audio (*1-57375-046-8*, 70554) Audioscope.

— In Which Eeyore Has a Birthday & Gets Two Presents. unabridged ed. (Winnie-the-Pooh Ser.). (Illus.). (J). write for info. incl. audio (*1-57375-015-8*, 70134) Audioscope.

Milne, A. A., pseud. In Which It Is Shown That Tiggers Don't Climb Trees. unabridged ed. (Classic Pooh Treasury Ser.). (J). write for info. incl. audio (*1-57375-529-X*, 71414) Audioscope.

Milne, A. A., pseud. In Which Piglet Meets a Heffalump. unabridged ed. (Winnie-the-Pooh Ser.). (Illus.). (J). write for info. incl. audio (*1-57375-014-X*, 70124) Audioscope.

— In Which Pooh Goes Visiting & Gets into a Tight Place & in Which Pooh & Piglet Go Hunting & Nearly Catch a Woozle. unabridged ed. (Winnie-the-Pooh Ser.). (Illus.). (J). write for info. incl. audio (*1-57375-001-8*, 70014) Audioscope.

Milne, A. A., pseud. In Which Tigger Is Unbounced. unabridged ed. (Classic Pooh Treasury Ser.). (J). write for info. incl. audio (*1-57375-528-1*, 71404) Audioscope.

Milne, A. A., pseud. In Which We Are Introduced to Winnie-the-Pooh & Some Bees, & the Stories Begin. unabridged ed. (Winnie-the-Pooh Ser.). (Illus.). (J). write for info. incl. audio (*1-57375-000-X*, 70004) Audioscope.

— Kanga & Baby Roo Come to the Forest. (Illus.). (J). 1995. 9.00 incl. digital audio (*1-57375-050-6*) Audioscope.

***Milne, A. A., pseud.** The Magic Hill. LC 99-42773. (Illus.). 32p. (J). 2000. 14.99 (*0-525-46147-7*, Dutton Child) Peng Put Young Read.

Milne, A. A., pseud. Le Meilleur des Ours. (FRE.). (J). (gr. 3-8). 9.95 (*0-685-23403-7*) Fr & Eur.

— Now We Are Six. (Illus.). 112p. (J). (ps up). 1988. 10.99 (*0-525-44446-7*, Dutton Child) Peng Put Young Read.

— Now We Are Six. (Illus.). 112p. (J). (ps-3). 1992. pap. 4.99 (*0-14-036124-3*, PuffinBks) Peng Put Young Read.

— Now We Are Six. deluxe ed. (Illus.). 112p. (J). (ps-6). 1992. 22.50 (*0-525-44960-4*, Dutton Child) Peng Put Young Read.

— Now We Are Six. unabridged ed. (J). 1997. pap. 10.95 incl. audio (*0-14-086680-9*, Png AudioBks) Viking Penguin.

— The Original Pooh Treasury, Vol. 1, Set. unabridged ed. (J). 1996. 17.00 incl. audio (*1-57375-456-0*, 71294) Audioscope.

— The Original Pooh Treasury: Eeyore Has a Birthday, Kanga & Baby Roo Come to the Forest, Christopher Robin Gives a Pooh Party, Vol. 2. (Illus.). (J). 1996. 20.00 incl. digital audio (*1-57375-458-7*) Audioscope.

***Milne, A. A., pseud.** Piglet. (Pooh Giant Shaped Board Bks.). (Illus.). 10p. (YA). 2000. bds. 7.99 (*0-525-46334-8*, Dutton Child) Peng Put Young Read.

— Piglet Clip & Read Book. abr. ed. (Illus.). 24p. (ps-3). 1999. pap. 2.99 (*0-525-46205-8*, Dutton Child) Peng Put Young Read.

Milne, A. A., pseud. Piglet Has a Bath. LC 99-172612. (Winnie-the-Pooh Collection). (J). 1998. pap. 5.99 (*0-525-46092-6*, Dutton Child) Peng Put Young Read.

— Piglet Is Entirely Surrounded by Water. (Illus.). 32p. (J). 1993. 4.99 (*0-525-45143-9*, Dutton Child) Peng Put Young Read.

— Piglet Is Surrounded by Water Puzzle. (Illus.). 14p. 1999. 7.99 (*0-525-46273-2*, Dutt) Dutton Plume.

***Milne, A. A., pseud.** Playing Poohsticks: Die cut Board Book. abr. ed. (Illus.). 12p. (J). (ps-1). 1999. bds. 6.99 (*0-525-46198-1*, Dutton Child) Peng Put Young Read.

M

Milne, A. A., pseud. The Poems & Hums of Winnie-the-Pooh. (Illus.). 10p. (J). (gr. 4-7). 1994. 5.99 (*0-525-45205-2*, Dutton Child) Peng Put Young Read.
— Pooh ABC. 32p. 1999. pap. 4.99 (*0-14-055750-4*) Viking Penguin.
— Pooh & Piglet Go Hunting. (Slide & Peek Ser.). (ps-k). 1999. pap. 5.99 (*0-525-46117-5*) Peng Put Young Read.
— Pooh & Some Bees. (Illus.). 24p. (J). 1996. pap. 3.99 (*0-525-45526-4*, Dutton Child) Peng Put Young Read.
— Pooh & Some Bees. (Winnie-the-Pooh Collection). (J). 1998. pap. 5.99 (*0-525-46093-4*, Dutton Child) Peng Put Young Read.
— The Pooh Bedtime Book. (Illus.). 48p. (ps-3). 1997. pap. 5.99 (*0-14-038793-5*) Viking Penguin.
— Pooh Board Book. (J). 1999. pap. 4.50 (*0-525-45521-3*) NAL.
— Pooh Board Book. 2nd ed. (J). 1999. pap., bds. 4.50 (*0-525-45522-1*) NAL.
— Pooh Board Book. 3rd ed. (J). 1999. pap., bds. 4.50 (*0-525-45524-8*) NAL.
— Pooh Board Book. 4th ed. (J). 1999. pap. 4.50 (*0-525-45525-6*) NAL.
— Pooh Board Book Collection. 1995. text 14.99 (*0-525-45509-4*) NAL.
***Milne, A. A., pseud.** Pooh Clip & Read. abr. ed. (Illus.). 24p. (ps-3). 1999. pap. 2.99 (*0-525-46203-1*, Dutton Child) Peng Put Young Read.
Milne, A. A., pseud. Pooh Friendship Book. 1999. pap. write for info. (*0-14-037596-1*) Viking Penguin.
— Pooh Goes Visiting. (Illus.). 24p. (J). (ps-k). 1996. pap. 3.99 (*0-525-45527-2*, Dutton Child) Peng Put Young Read.
***Milne, A. A., pseud.** Pooh Goes Visiting. (Illus.). 32p. (J). (ps-3). 2000. 9.99 (*0-525-46457-3*, Dutton Child) Peng Put Young Read.
— Pooh Goes Visiting: And Other Stories. (J). 1998. mass mkt. incl. audio (*1-84032-047-8*) HOD2.
Milne, A. A., pseud. Pooh Goes Visiting Puzzle. (Illus.). 14p. 1999. 7.99 (*0-525-46272-4*, Dutt) Dutton Plume.
— Pooh Solves a Mystery: A Slide & Peek Book. LC 99-190546. 12p. (J). 1998. 5.99 (*0-525-45987-1*, Dutton Child) Peng Put Young Read.
Milne, A. A., pseud. Pooh Song Book. unabridged ed. (J). (gr. 4 up). 1984. audio 50.00 (*0-89845-558-8*, SSBC 702) HarperAudio.
Milne, A. A., pseud. The Pooh Story Book. LC 65-19580. (Illus.). 80p. (J). (gr. k-4). 1965. 14.99 (*0-525-37546-5*, Dutton Child) Peng Put Young Read.
— The Pooh Story Book. LC 96-154709. (Illus.). 80p. (J). (ps-3). 1996. pap. 5.99 (*0-14-038168-6*, PuffinBks) Peng Put Young Read.
Milne, A. A., pseud. Pooh Story Book. 1996. 11.19 (*0-606-09761-9*, Pub. by Turtleback) Demco.
Milne, A. A., pseud. Pooh to Grow on. (Illus.). 48p. (ps-3). 1999. 9.99 (*0-525-46163-9*) NAL.
— Pooh to the Rescue. (Illus.). (J). 1997. pap. 14.99 (*0-525-45689-9*) NAL.
— Pooh Touch & Feel. (Illus.). 12p. (J). 1998. 9.99 (*0-525-45830-1*) NAL.
***Milne, A. A., pseud.** Pooh's Busy Bay. (Illus.). 10p. (J). (ps-k). 2000. 5.99 (*0-525-46461-1*, Dutton Child) Peng Put Young Read.
Milne, A. A., pseud. Pooh's First Clock With Other. LC 98-210004. (Illus.). 6p. (J). (ps-3). 1998. pap. 12.99 (*0-525-45983-9*, Dutton Child) Peng Put Young Read.
***Milne, A. A., pseud.** Pooh's Great Big Word Book. (Illus.). 32p. (J). 2000. pap. 11.99 (*0-525-46335-6*, Dutton Child) Peng Put Young Read.
Milne, A. A., pseud. Pooh's Letters from the Hundred Acre Wood. LC 97-38862. (Illus.). 48p. (J). 1998. 16.99 (*0-525-45890-5*) NAL.
— Pooh's Library, 4 bks., Set. (Illus.). (J). (ps up). 1988. pap. 44.00 (*0-525-44451-3*, Dutton Child) Peng Put Young Read.
— Pooh's Library, 4 bks., Set. (Illus.). 48p. (J). (ps-3). 1992. pap. 20.00 (*0-14-095560-7*, PuffinBks) Peng Put Young Read.
***Milne, A. A., pseud.** Pooh's Little Book of Feng Shui. LC 99-89793. (Illus.). 96p. (YA). 2000. 9.99 (*0-525-46331-3*, Dutton Child) Peng Put Young Read.
Milne, A. A., pseud. Pooh's Treehouse. (J). 1999. write for info. (*0-525-45518-3*) NAL.
— Pooh's Xmas Collection. (J). 1999. pap. 9.99 (*0-525-45500-0*) NAL.
Milne, A. A., pseud. Prince Rabbit. 40p. 1983. pap. 3.50 (*0-87129-776-0*, P56) Dramatic Pub.
— Pu Der Bar. 1999. pap. text 12.95 (*3-423-70395-4*) Distribks Inc.
Milne, A. A., pseud. The Red House Mystery. LC 97-32670. (Dover Mystery Classics). 180p. 1998. pap. 2.00 (*0-486-40129-4*) Dover.
— The Red House Mystery. reprint ed. lib. bdg. 20.95 (*0-89190-487-5*, Rivercity Pr) Amereon Ltd.
***Milne, A. A., pseud.** The Red House Mystery, Set. unabridged ed. (C). 1998. 29.95 incl. audio (*1-55685-614-8*) Audio Bk Con.
— Tigger: Giant Shaped Board Book. (Illus.). (YA). (ps up). 1999. bds. 7.99 (*0-525-46233-3*, Dutton Child) Peng Put Young Read.
— Tigger Clip & Read Book. abr. ed. (Illus.). 24p. (ps up). 1999. pap. 2.99 (*0-525-46207-4*, Dutton Child) Peng Put Young Read.
Milne, A. A., pseud. Tigger Comes to the Forest, 1. (Illus.). 32p. (ps-3). 1999. 12.99 (*0-525-46271-6*, Dutt) Dutton Plume.
— Tigger Has Breakfast. (Illus.). 24p. (J). 1996. pap. 3.99 (*0-525-45529-9*, Dutton Child) Peng Put Young Read.
— Tigger Has Breakfast. 12p. (J). 1998. 5.99 (*0-525-45989-8*, Dutton Child) Peng Put Young Read.
***Milne, A. A., pseud.** Tigger's Bouncy Day. (Illus.). 10p. (J). (ps-k). 2000. 5.99 (*0-525-46463-8*, Dutton Child) Peng Put Young Read.
— Tigger's Breakfast. (Illus.). (J). (ps-1). 1999. pap. 6.99 (*0-525-46200-7*, Dutton Child) Peng Put Young Read.
— Tigger's Giant Lift-the-Flap Book. (Illus.). (J). 2000. 9.99 (*0-525-46399-2*, Dutton Child) Peng Put Young Read.
Milne, A. A., pseud. Two People. 370p. 26.95 (*0-89190-234-1*) Amereon Ltd.
***Milne, A. A., pseud.** Vini-der-Puh: A Yiddish Version of Winnie-the-Pooh. (GER & YID., Illus.). 176p. (J). (ps-3). 2000. 18.99 (*0-525-46338-0*, Dutton Child) Peng Put Young Read.
Milne, A. A., pseud. When We Were Very Young. (Illus.). 112p. (J). (ps up). 1988. 10.99 (*0-525-44445-9*, Dutton Child) Peng Put Young Read.
— When We Were Very Young. (Illus.). 112p. (J). (ps-3). 1992. pap. 4.99 (*0-14-036123-5*, PuffinBks) Peng Put Young Read.
— When We Were Very Young. deluxe ed. (Illus.). 112p. (J). (ps-6). 1992. 22.99 (*0-525-44961-2*, Dutton Child) Peng Put Young Read.
— Winnie Ille Pu. Lenard, Alexander, tr. (LAT., Illus.). 160p. 1991. pap. 11.95 (*0-14-015339-X*, Penguin Bks) Viking Penguin.
***Milne, A. A., pseud.** Winnie Ille Pu Semper Ludet. Staples, Brian, tr. (Winnie-the-Pooh Collection). (LAT., Illus.). 160p. (YA). (gr. 7-12). 1998. 16.95 (*0-525-46091-8*, Dutton Child) Peng Put Young Read.
Milne, A. A., pseud. Winnie l'Ourson. (FRE., Illus.). (J). (gr. 3-8). 9.95 (*0-685-23402-9*) Fr & Eur.
— Winnie-the-Pooh. (Illus.). 176p. (J). 1999. pap. 7.95 (*0-452-27764-7*, Plume) Dutton Plume.
— Winnie-the-Pooh. (Illus.). 1961. write for info. (*0-318-51791-4*) NAL.
— Winnie-the-Pooh. (Illus.). 161p. (YA). (gr. 2 up). 1988. 10.99 (*0-525-44443-2*, Dutton Child) Peng Put Young Read.
— Winnie-the-Pooh. (Illus.). 176p. (J). (ps-3). 1992. pap. 4.99 (*0-14-036121-9*, PuffinBks) Peng Put Young Read.
— Winnie-the-Pooh. 1992. 10.09 (*0-606-08938-1*, Pub. by Turtleback) Demco.
— Winnie-the-Pooh. deluxe ed. LC 91-26203. (Illus.). 176p. (J). (ps up). 1991. 22.99 (*0-525-44776-8*, Dutton Child) Peng Put Young Read.
— Winnie-the-Pooh: Boxed Set. abr. ed. (J). 1997. audio 22.00 (*0-553-47866-4*) BDD Bks Young Read.
— Winnie-the-Pooh: (Full Musical) 1964. 5.50 (*0-87129-364-1*, W01) Dramatic Pub.
***Milne, A. A., pseud.** Winnie the Pooh & Some Bees. (Illus.). (ps-3). 2000. 9.99 incl. audio (*0-14-095450-3*, PuffinBks) Peng Put Young Read.
Milne, A. A., pseud. Winnie-the-Pooh & Some Bees, 1. (Illus.). 32p. (ps-3). 1999. 12.99 (*0-525-46270-8*, Dutt) Dutton Plume.
— Winnie the Pooh & Some Bees Storybooks. 128p. (J). (gr. 2 up). 1993. 4.99 (*0-525-45033-5*, Dutton Child) Peng Put Young Read.
Milne, A. A., pseud. Winnie-the-Pooh & When We Were Very Young, Boxed set. 32p. (J). pap. write for info. incl. audio compact disk (*1-57375-583-4*, 71512) Audioscope.
— Winnie-the-Pooh & When We Were Very Young, Set. abr. ed. 32p. (J). pap., boxed set. write for info. incl. audio (*1-57375-652-0*, 71514) Audioscope.
— Winnie-the-Pooh at Pooh Corner & Now We Are Six, Set. (J). 1998. 29.98 incl. audio Audioscope.
Milne, A. A., pseud. Winnie-The-Pooh Read Aloud Collection, Set. (Illus.). 32p. (J). 1998. 21.99 incl. audio (*0-525-46111-6*, Dutton Child) Peng Put Young Read.
***Milne, A. A., pseud.** Winnie-the-Pooh Tells Time. (Winnie-the-Pooh Sticker Story Bks.). (Illus.). 16p. (J). (ps-3). 2000. pap. 5.99 (*0-525-46336-4*, Dutton Child) Peng Put Young Read.
Milne, A. A., pseud. Winnie-The-Pooh's ABC Sticker Storybook, Vol. 1. 1999. pap. 4.99 (*0-525-46275-9*) NAL.
— Winnie-the-Pooh's Baby Book. (Illus.). 32p. (J). (gr. k up). 1994. 15.99 (*0-525-45298-2*, Dutton Child) Peng Put Young Read.
— Winnie-the-Pooh's Book & Toy Box. (Illus.). 32p. (J). (gr. k up). 1994. pap. 29.99 (*0-525-45342-3*, Dutton Child) Peng Put Young Read.
— Winnie-the-Pooh's Colors. LC 95-214146. (Illus.). 32p. (J). (ps up). 1995. 9.99 (*0-525-45428-4*, Dutton Child) Peng Put Young Read.
— Winnie-the-Pooh's Friendship Book. (Illus.). 48p. (J). (gr. 4-7). 1994. 8.99 (*0-525-45204-4*, Dutton Child) Peng Put Young Read.
— Winnie-the-Pooh's Giant Lift-the-Flap Book. (Illus.). 12p. (J). (ps-2). 1997. 9.99 (*0-525-45841-7*) NAL.
— Winnie-the-Pooh's 1-2-3. LC 96-159489. (Illus.). 32p. (J). 1996. 9.99 (*0-525-45534-5*) NAL.
***Milne, A. A., pseud.** Winnie-the-Pooh's Shapes & Colors. (Winnie-the-Pooh Sticker Story Bks.). (Illus.). 16p. (J). (ps-k). 2000. pap. 5.99 (*0-525-46337-2*, Dutton Child) Peng Put Young Read.
Milne, A. A., pseud. Winnie-the-Pooh's Teatime Cookbook. LC 92-35650. (Illus.). 64p. (J). 1993. 9.99 (*0-525-45135-8*, Dutton Child) Peng Put Young Read.
— Winnie-the-Pooh's Trivia Quiz Book. LC 93-39969. (Illus.). 48p. (J). (gr. 2 up). 1994. 9.99 (*0-525-45265-6*, Dutton Child) Peng Put Young Read.
— Winnie-The-Pooh's 1-2-3 Sticker Storybook, Vol. 1. 1999. pap. 4.99 (*0-525-46274-0*) NAL.
— Winny de Puh.Tr. of Winnie the Pooh. (SPA., Illus.). 176p. (J). (gr. 4-7). 1999. 11.99 (*0-525-44986-8*, Dutton Child) Peng Put Young Read.
— Winny de Puh.Tr. of Winnie the Pooh. 1995. pap. text 9.95 (*84-372-1885-3*) Santillana.
— Winny de Puh.Tr. of Winnie the Pooh. 1992. 15.05 (*0-606-10537-9*, Pub. by Turtleback) Demco.
— The World of Christopher Robin. (Illus.). 256p. (J). (ps up). 1988. 21.99 (*0-525-44448-3*, Dutton Child) Peng Put Young Read.
— The World of Pooh. (Illus.). (J). (gr. 1-4). 1957. boxed set 29.95 (*0-685-46952-2*, 01258-370, Dutt) Dutton Plume.
— The World of Pooh. (Illus.). 320p. (J). (ps-3). 1988. 21.99 (*0-525-44447-5*, Dutton Child) Peng Put Young Read.
— The World of Winnie-the-Pooh, 2 bks. (Illus.). (J). (ps up). 1988. 45.00 (*0-525-44452-1*, Dutton Child) Peng Put Young Read.
***Milne, A. A., pseud & Burgess, Thornton W.** When We Were Very Young, Set. unabridged ed. (J). (gr. 1-2). 1999. 20.95 incl. audio (*1-55685-564-8*) Audio Bk Con.
Milne, A. A., pseud, et al. Pooh Christmas Songs LC 98-234873. 1998. write for info. (*0-7853-2729-0*) Pubns Intl Ltd.
— Pooh's Bedtime Book. LC 80-65523. (Illus.). 48p. (J). (ps-3). 1980. 13.99 (*0-525-44895-0*, Dutton Child) Peng Put Young Read.
Milne, A. J. Human Rights & Human Diversity: An Essay in the Philosophy of Human Rights. LC 86-5804. 186p. (C). 1986. text 19.50 (*0-88706-366-7*) State U NY Pr.
Milne, A. R. Centenary Guide to RHS. 9.00 (*0-901050-00-8*) David Brown.
***Milne, Aileen.** Teach Yourself Counselling. (Teach Yourself Ser.). 192p. 2000. pap. 12.95 (*0-8442-2680-7*, Teach Yrslf) NTC Contemp Pub Co.
Milne, Alan Alexander, see Milne, A. A., pseud.
Milne, Ann, jt. ed. see Folberg, Jay.
Milne, Antony. Beyond the Warming: The Hazards of Climate Prediction in the Age of Chaos. (Illus.). 154p. (Orig.). (C). 1996. pap. text 14.95 (*1-85327-098-9*, Pub. by Prism Pr) Assoc Pubs Grp.
— Doomsday: The Science of Catastrophe. LC 99-32025. 208p. 2000. 55.00 (*0-275-96747-6*) Greenwood.
— Our Drowning World. 192p. 1988. write for info. (*1-85327-004-0*, Pub. by Prism Pr) Assoc Pubs Grp.
Milne, Bill, jt. auth. see Blake, Kathy.
Milne, Bruce. Know the Truth. LC 82-4711. 288p. (Orig.). 1982. pap. 14.99 (*0-87784-392-9*, 392) InterVarsity.
— Know the Truth: A Handbook of Christian Belief. 2nd rev. ed. LC 99-10869. 352p. 1999. pap. 14.99 (*0-8308-1793-X*, 1793) InterVarsity.
Milne, Bruce G. Angels, Cripples, & Culprits. 72p. 1998. pap. 10.00 (*0-9634277-1-7*) Yellow Print & Pub.
***Milne, C.** Prairie Skies. 1999. pap. 16.95 (*1-895618-25-8*) Fifth Hse Publ.
Milne, Christopher. Beyond the World of Pooh: Selections from the Memoirs of Christopher Milne. LC 98-3292. (Winnie-the-Pooh Collection). (Illus.). 304p. 1998. 22.95 (*0-525-45888-3*, Dutton Child) Peng Put Young Read.
Milne, Christopher M. Ethics in Journalism: Experience Pays in the Field. unabridged ed. 96p. 1999. 39.95 (*0-9631050-5-1*) Safe Harbour.
— Ethics in Journalism: Experience Pays in the Field. unabridged ed. (Illus.). 96p. 1999. pap. 24.95 (*0-9631050-2-7*) Safe Harbour.
— Right Time, Right Place: Res Gestae. unabridged ed. (Illus.). 128p. 1999. 24.95 (*0-9631050-8-6*) Safe Harbour.
Milne, Courtney. The Sacred Earth. (Illus.). 246p. 1993. 49.50 (*0-8109-3831-6*, Pub. by Abrams) Time Warner.
— Sacred Places in North America: A Journey into the Medicine Wheel. LC 94-44794. (Illus.). 128p. 1995. 27.50 (*1-55670-414-3*) Stewart Tabori & Chang.
***Milne, Courtney.** Sacred Places in North America: A Journey into the Medicine Wheel. (Illus.). 128p. 1999. pap. 15.00 (*1-55670-957-9*) Stewart Tabori & Chang.
***Milne, Courtney, photos by.** W. O. Mitchell Country: Portrayed by Courtney Milne. (Illus.). 240p. 2000. 60.00 (*0-7710-6106-4*) McCland & Stewart.
Milne, David. The Canadian Constitution. 374p. mass mkt. 10.95 (*1-55028-341-3*, Pub. by J Lorimer); bds. 19.95 (*1-55028-343-X*, Pub. by J Lorimer) Formac Dist Ltd.
— The Scottish Office & Other Scottish Government Departments. LC 85-24792. (New Whitehall Ser.). 237p. 1986. reprint ed. lib. bdg. 65.00 (*0-313-23655-0*, MISO, Greenwood Pr) Greenwood.
Milne, David, Jr. & Silcox, David P. David B. Milne Vol. 2: A Catalogue Raisonne of the Paintings, 2 vols. LC 99-188878. (Illus.). 1222p. 1998. text 500.00 (*0-8020-4102-7*) U of Toronto Pr.
Milne, David, jt. auth. see Baldacchino, Godfrey.
Milne, David H. Marine Life & the Sea. LC 94-20337. 459p. 1994. 80.95 (*0-534-16314-9*) Wadsworth Pub.
Milne, Deborah E. Reflections from a Broken Mirror: Spiritual Values I Learned as a LDS Child of Divorce. LC 98-25906. ix, 147 p. 1998. 15.95 (*1-57345-395-1*) Deseret Bk.
Milne, DeLane, ed. International Symposium on Microelectronics, 1992: Proceedings. (Illus.). 748p. (Orig.). 1992. pap. text 30.00 (*0-930815-36-X*) Intl Soc Hybrid.
— ISHM Proceedings, 1992. 700p. 1992. write for info. (*0-930815-35-1*) Intl Soc Hybrid.
Milne, Derek, ed. Evaluating Mental Health Practice: Methods & Applications. 288p. 1987. lib. bdg. 69.50 (*0-7099-4626-0*, Pub. by C Helm) Routldge.
Milne, Derek & Noone, Steve. Teaching & Training for Non-Teachers. 192p. 1997. pap. 192.00 (*1-85433-184-1*, BPS Bks) Stylus Pub VA.
Milne, Douglas. 1 & 2 Timothy & Titus. (Focus on the Bible Commentary Ser.). 240p. (Orig.). 1996. pap. 10.99 (*1-85792-169-0*, Pub. by Christian Focus) Spring Arbor Dist.
Milne, Douglas, jt. ed. see Haynes, Raymond.
***Milne, Drew.** Reading Marxist Literary Theory. 2001. 64.95 (*0-631-20146-7*); pap. 29.95 (*0-631-20147-5*) Blackwell Pubs.
Milne, Drew, jt. ed. see Eagelton, Terry.
Milne, Drucilla. The Amish of Harmony. King, Martha & Michel, Paula, eds. (Illus.). 134p. (Orig.). 1993. pap. 10.00 (*0-9638637-0-3*) D Milne.
Milne-Edwards, Henri. Introduction a la Zoologie General (Introduction to General Zoology) Cohen, I. Bernard, ed. LC 80-2137. (Development of Science Ser.). 1981. reprint ed. lib. bdg. 18.95 (*0-405-13892-X*) Ayer.
Milne, Elizabeth, et al. Mongolian People's Republic, 1991: Toward a Market Economy. LC 91-4710. (Occasional Papers: No. 79). viii, 81p. (Orig.). 1991. pap. 10.00 (*1-55775-207-9*) Intl Monetary.
Milne, Eric N., et al. Models & Techniques in Medical Imaging Research. LC 82-13141. 596p. 1983. 115.00 (*0-275-91404-6*, C1404, Praeger Pubs) Greenwood.
Milne, Frank. Finance Theory & Asset Pricing. (Vienna Institute for Advanced Studies Lecture Notes). (Illus.). 134p. 1995. pap. text 16.95 (*0-19-877398-6*) OUP.
Milne, G. & Richards, J. Two Anglo-Saxon Buildings & Associated Finds. (Wharram Ser.: Vol. VII). 114p. 1992. 14.00 (*0-946722-09-9*, Pub. by U York Dept Archaeol) David Brown.
Milne, G. J. & Pierre, L., eds. Correct Hardware Design & Verification Methods: IFIP WG10.2 Advanced Research Working Conference CHARME '93, Arles, France, May 24-26, 1993. (Lecture Notes in Computer Science Ser.: Vol. 683). viii, 269p. 1993. 44.95 (*0-387-56778-X*) Spr-Verlag.
Milne, G. W. Properties of Pesticides: User's Guide. 48p. 1995. 264.95 (*0-8493-2448-3*, 2448) CRC Pr.
Milne, G. W., ed. Handbook of Data on Pesticides. 416p. 1994. boxed set 141.95 (*0-8493-2447-5*, 2447) CRC Pr.
Milne, G. W., jt. auth. see Lide, David R.
Milne, G. W., jt. auth. see Lide, David R., Jr.
Milne, G. W., jt. ed. see Lide, David R.
Milne, G. W., jt. ed. see Lide, David R., Jr.
***Milne, G. W. A.** Ashgate Handbook of Anti-Infective Agents. 340p. 2000. 175.00 (*0-566-08385-X*) Ashgate Pub Co.
— Ashgate Handbook of Autineoplastic Agents. 184p. 2000. 144.95 (*0-566-08382-5*) Ashgate Pub Co.
— Ashgate Handbook of Autonomic Nervous System Agents. 300p. 2000. 165.00 (*0-566-08384-1*) Ashgate Pub Co.
— Ashgate Handbook of Cardiovascular Agents. 440p. 2000. 225.00 (*0-566-08386-8*) Ashgate Pub Co.
— Ashgate Handbook of Central Nervous System Agents. 440p. 2000. 225.00 (*0-566-08387-6*) Ashgate Pub Co.
— Ashgate Handbook of Endocrine Agents & Steroids. 160p. 2000. 165.00 (*0-566-08383-3*) Ashgate Pub Co.
— Ashgate Handbook of Pesticides & Agricultural Chemicals. 224p. 2000. 99.95 (*0-566-08388-4*) Ashgate Pub Co.
***Milne, G. W. A., ed.** Drugs: Synonyms & Properties. LC 99-49084. 350p. 1999. 150.00 (*0-566-08228-4*, Pub. by Ashgate Pub) Ashgate Pub Co.
— Traditional Chinese Medicines: Molecular Structures, Natural Sources & Applications. LC 99-39805. 1040p. 1999. 295.00 (*0-566-08210-1*, Pub. by Ashgate Pub) Ashgate Pub Co.
Milne, George, jt. auth. see McDonald, Mark.
Milne, George, jt. ed. see Iyer, Easwar.
Milne, George, ed. see Johnson, Samuel.
Milne, George M. Connecticut Woodlands: A Century's Story of the Connecticut Forest & Park Association. LC 95-3080. 160p. 1995. 30.00 (*0-9619052-3-9*) CT Forest & Pk Assn.
— Connecticut Woodlands: A Century's Story of the Connecticut Forest & Park Association. LC 95-3080. (Illus.). 160p. 1995. 30.00 (*0-914659-73-1*) Phoenix Pub.
— Lebanon: Three Centuries in a Connecticut Hilltop Town. (Illus.). 287p. 1996. reprint ed. lib. bdg. 39.00 (*0-8328-4984-7*) Higginson Bk Co.
***Milne, George W.** Gardner's Chemical Synonyms & Trade Names. 11th ed. LC 98-51143. 1418p. 1999. 295.00 (*0-566-08190-3*) Ashgate Pub Co.
Milne, Gordon. American Political Novel. 1972. pap. 11.95 (*0-8061-1050-3*) U of Okla Pr.
— Ports of Call: A Study of the American Nautical Novel. (Illus.). 132p. (C). 1987. pap. text 17.00 (*0-8191-5674-4*); lib. bdg. 35.50 (*0-8191-5673-6*) U Pr of Amer.
— The Sense of Society: A History of the American Novel of Manners. 305p. 1977. 35.00 (*0-8386-1927-4*) Fairleigh Dickinson.
Milne, H. F. How to Build a Small Two-Manual Chamber Pipe Organ. (Illus.). 1925. pap. 25.00 (*0-913746-03-7*) Organ Lit.
— The Reed Organ: Its Design & Construction. (Illus.). 168p. 1932. pap. 20.00 (*0-913746-02-9*) Organ Lit.
Milne, Hollie A. Crazy but Pieceable: Eight Charming Patterns to Make & Enjoy. Lowe, Melissa, ed. LC 97-9752. (Illus.). 56p. (Orig.). 1997. pap. 12.95 (*1-56477-190-3*, B304) Martingale & Co.
Milne, Hugh. The Heart of Listening: A Visionary Approach to Craniosacral Work. 2nd ed. LC 98-15722. 500p. 1998. text 80.00 (*1-55643-278-X*) North Atlantic.
— The Heart of Listening: A Visionary Approach to Craniosacral Work, Vol. I. LC 98-15082. (Illus.). 240p. 1998. pap. text 25.00 (*1-55643-279-8*) North Atlantic.
***Milne, Hugh.** The Heart of Listening Vol. 2: Anatomy, Technique, Transcendence, Vol. II. LC 98-15082. (Illus.). 344p. (Orig.). 1998. pap. text 35.00 (*1-55643-280-1*) North Atlantic.
Milne, J. G. Catalog of Alexandrian Coins. (Illus.). 1983. reprint ed. lib. bdg. 55.00 (*0-942666-20-8*) S J Durst.
— Greek & Roman Coins & the Study of History. (Illus.). 128p. 1980. 20.00 (*0-916710-80-7*) Obol Intl.
— A History of Egypt under Roman Rule. 3rd ed. (Illus.). xxiii, 331p. (C). 1994. text 35.00 (*0-89005-510-6*) Ares.

— Inscriptiones Graecae Aegypti, No. 1: Cairo. xivi, 153p. 1976. 30.00 (*0-89005-111-9*) Ares.

— Surgical Instruments in Greek & Roman Times. (Illus.). 201p. 1991. 25.00 (*0-89005-127-5*) Ares.

Milne, J. S. Etale Cohomology. LC 79-84003. (Mathematical Ser.: No. 33). 344p. 1980. text 79.50 (*0-691-08238-3*, Pub. by Princeton U Pr) Cal Prin Full Svc.

Milne, James. London Book Window. LC 68-16957. (Essay Index Reprint Ser.). 1977. reprint ed. 18.95 (*0-8369-0709-4*) Ayer.

— Pages in Waiting. LC 74-93357. (Essay Index Reprint Ser.). 1977. 20.95 (*0-8369-1308-6*) Ayer.

Milne, James S. Arithmetic Duality Theorems. (Perspectives in Mathematics Ser.). 230p. 1986. text 86.00 (*0-12-498040-6*) Acad Pr.

Milne, James S., jt. ed. see Clozel, Laurent.

Milne, Jean. The Story of Diamonds. LC 99-36426. (Illus.). 120p. (J). (gr. 4-9). 2000. 21.50 (*0-208-02476-X*, Linnet Bks) Shoe String.

***Milne, Jenni.** Silk Painting. (Illus.). 96p. 1999. spiral bd. 29.95 (*1-86126-215-9*, Pub. by Cro1wood) Trafalgar.

Milne, John. Alive & Kicking. 288p. 1999. pap. 10.95 (*1-56858-145-9*, Pub. by FWEW) Publishers Group.

Milne, John, jt. auth. see Fraser, Charles.

Milne, Kenneth. The Irish Charter Schools. LC 96-161938. 400p. 1996. boxed set 60.00 (*1-85182-232-1*, Pub. by Four Cts Pr) Intl Spec Bk.

***Milne, Kenneth, ed.** History of Christ Church Cathedral, Dublin. (Illus.). 320p. 2000. 55.00 (*1-85182-487-1*, Pub. by Four Cts Pr) Intl Spec Bk.

M

Milne, Lesley, ed. Bulgakov: The Novelist-Playwright. LC 96-178125. (Russian Theatre Archive Ser.: Vol. 5). 249p. 1996. text 65.00 (*3-7186-5619-1*, ECU83, Harwood Acad Pubs); pap. text 25.00 (*3-7186-5620-5*, ECU32, Harwood Acad Pubs) Gordon & Breach.

Milne, Lorna, jt. ed. see Gaffney, John.

Milne, Lorus J. & Milne, Margery. The Behavior & Learning of Animal Babies. (Illus.). 162p. 1998. pap. text 19.00 (*0-7881-5835-X*) DIANE Pub.

— A World Alive: The Natural Wonders of a New Hampshire River Valley. (Illus.). 156p. 1997. reprint ed. pap. 15.00 (*1-880158-14-0*) J N Townsend.

Milne, Luc. Cocksuck Academy: An Erotic Novel. LC 98-5394. 1998. pap. 14.95 (*0-943595-72-X*) Leyland Pubns.

— The Milk Farm: An Erotic Novel. 160p. 1996. pap. 14.95 (*0-943595-61-4*) Leyland Pubns.

Milne, Margery, jt. auth. see Milne, Lorus J.

Milne, Mary. Sunday Dismissals for RCIA: Candidates & Catechumens. 242p. (Orig.). 1993. pap. 19.95 (*0-8146-2145-7*) Liturgical Pr.

Milne, Mary L. The Home of an Eastern Clan: A Study of the Palaungs of the Shan States. LC 77-87048. reprint ed. 30.75 (*0-404-16845-0*) AMS Pr.

Milne, P. H. Fish & Shellfish Farming in Coastal Waters. 1978. 70.00 (*0-7855-6919-7*) St Mut.

— Underwater Acoustic Positioning Systems. LC 83-80348. (Illus.). 294p. 1983. pap. 91.20 (*0-608-04876-3*, 206555700004) Bks Demand.

Milne, Pamela J. Vladimir Propp & the Study of Structure in Biblical Hebrew Narrative. (Bible & Literature Ser.: No. 13). 325p. 1988. 70.00 (*1-85075-087-4*, Pub. by Sheffield Acad); pap. 16.50 (*1-85075-086-6*, Pub. by Sheffield Acad) CUP Services.

***Milne, Penelope A.** Why Do Kittens Do That? Real Answers to the Curious Things Kittens Do. LC 00-9176. (Illus.). 64p. 2000. pap. 6.95 (*1-889540-59-5*) Bowtie Press.

— Why Do Puppies Do That? Real Answers to the Curious Things Puppies Do. LC 00-9223. (Illus.). 64p. 2000. pap. 6.95 (*1-889540-58-7*) Bowtie Press.

Milne, Peter. Fish in a Barrel: Nick Cave & the Bad Seeds on Tour. (Illus.). 118p. 1994. reprint ed. pap. 22.00 (*1-880985-17-9*) Two Thirteen Sixty-one.

Milne, Peter H. BASIC Programs for Land Surveying. 420p. 1984. pap. 35.00 (*0-419-13010-1*, NO. 9086, E & FN Spon) Routledge.

— Computer Graphics for Surveying. 230p. 1987. text 59.50 (*0-419-14080-8*, E & FN Spon); pap. text 27.50 (*0-419-14070-0*, E & FN Spon) Routledge.

— Presentation Graphics for Engineering, Science & Business. (Illus.). 256p. (Orig.). 1991. 49.95 (*0-412-32050-9*, E & FN Spon); pap. write for info. (*0-412-32060-6*, E & FN Spon) Routledge.

— Presentation Graphics for Engineering, Science & Business. (Illus.). 208p. (Orig.). (C). 1991. pap. 37.99 (*0-419-15840-5*, E & FN Spon) Routledge.

Milne, R. & Bramer, M. A., eds. Applications & Innovations in Expert Systems VI: Proceedings of ES98, the 18th Annual International Conference of the British Computer Society Specialist Group on Expert Systems, Cambridge, December, 1998. LC 98-47152. (Illus.), viii, 289p. 1999. pap. (*1-85233-087-2*) Spr-Verlag.

Milne, R. G. The Plant Viruses Vol. 4: The Filamentous Plant Viruses. LC 88-15221. (Viruses Ser.). (Illus.). 440p. (C). 1988. text 110.00 (*0-306-42845-8*, Kluwer Plenum) Kluwer Academic.

Milne, R. J. Structural Engineering: History & Development. LC 98-171733. (Illus.). 160p. (C). 1998. 65.00 (*0-419-20170-X*, C1099, E & FN Spon) Routledge.

Milne, R. S. Malaysian Politics under Mahathir. (Politics in Asia Ser.). 1999. pap. 24.99 (*0-415-17143-1*) Routledge.

***Milne, R. S. & Mauzy, Diane K.** Malaysian Politics under Mahathir. LC 99-222809. 1999. write for info. (*0-415-17142-3*) Routledge.

Milne, R. S. & Ratnam, K. J. Malaysia: New States in a New Nation. (Studies in Commonwealth Politics & History: No. 2). 512p. 1973. 45.00 (*0-7146-2988-X*, Pub. by F Cass Pubs) Intl Spec Bk.

Milne, R. W., jt. auth. see Bramer, Max A.

Milne, Robert. Opportunities in Travel Careers. (Opportunities in... Ser.). (Illus.). 160p. pap. 11.95 (*0-8442-4640-9*, 46409, Natl Textbk Co) NTC Contemp Pub Co.

— Opportunities in Travel Careers. (Opportunities in... Ser.). (Illus.). 160p. 1996. 14.95 (*0-8442-4639-5*, 46395, Natl Textbk Co) NTC Contemp Pub Co.

Milne, Robert D. Into the Sun. (Illus.). 1980. 15.00 (*0-937986-41-0*) D M Grant.

Milne, Robert D., et al. An Alternative Medicine Definitive Guide to Headaches. unabridged ed. LC 96-46914. (Illus.). 525p. (Orig.). 1997. 23.95 (*1-887299-03-3*) AlternMed Bks.

Milne, Robert S. Opportunities in Travel Careers. LC 75-32612. (Illus.). (gr. 8 up). 1985. 13.95 (*0-8442-6215-3*, VGM Career) NTC Contemp Pub Co.

— Opportunities in Travel Careers. LC 75-32612. (Illus.). (gr. 8 up). 1986. pap. 10.95 (*0-8442-6216-1*, VGM Career) NTC Contemp Pub Co.

— Opportunities in Travel Careers. (Illus.). 160p. 1992. 13.95 (*0-8442-8568-4*, VGM Career) NTC Contemp Pub Co.

— Opportunities in Travel Careers. (Illus.). 160p. 1993. pap. 10.95 (*0-8442-8569-2*, VGM Career) NTC Contemp Pub Co.

Milne, Robert S. Opportunities in Travel Careers LC 75-32612. (VGM Career Ser.). 158 p. 1976. write for info. (*0-89022-209-6*) Voc Guidance.

Milne, Seumas. The Enemy Within: M15, Maxwell & the Seargill Affair. 300p. (C). (gr. 13). 1994. 30.00 (*0-86091-461-5*, B2491, Pub. by Verso) Norton.

***Milne, T. A., et al.** Biomass Gasifier Tars: Their Nature, Formation & Conversion. unabridged ed. 68p. 1999. reprint ed. spiral bd. 25.00 (*1-890607-14-2*) Biomass Energy.

Milne, T. S. Micro-Management Is for Mushrooms' Or The "Wave Maker" LC 98-90248. 153p. 2000. pap. 10.95 (*0-533-12746-7*) Vantage.

Milne, Teddy. Cal Coolidge Doesn't Live Here Anymore: Glimpses of Northampton MA. LC 94-74079. 1994. pap. 12.95 (*0-938875-33-7*) Pittenbruach Pr.

— Choose Love. LC 86-62021. 203p. 1986. pap. 10.95 (*0-938875-00-0*) Pittenbruach Pr.

— Christmas Serenity. 1990. pap. 3.50 (*0-938875-24-8*) Pittenbruach Pr.

— Compassionate Democracy - Next Steps in Self Government: Excerpts from 'Choose Love' 40p. 1987. pap. 3.95 (*0-938875-10-8*) Pittenbruach Pr.

— European Spoken Here. Date not set. write for info. (*0-938875-30-2*) Pittenbruach Pr.

— Flight: Earth from Sky in a Poetry Format. 27p. 1998. pap. 4.50 (*0-938875-40-X*) Pittenbruach Pr.

— The Folly of Power: An Irrational Goal. 37p. 1998. pap. 4.50 (*0-938875-42-6*) Pittenbruach Pr.

— Instant Russian: An Easy Introduction to the Russian Language. LC 89-60249. 56p. 1989. pap. 3.60 (*0-938875-17-5*) Pittenbruach Pr.

— Kids Who Have Made a Difference. 34p. 1989. pap. 3.95 (*0-938875-21-3*) Pittenbruach Pr.

— Money, Power, & Responsibility: Common Sense for Today. LC 90-62776. 101p. 1990. pap. 9.95 (*0-938875-13-2*) Pittenbruach Pr.

— Peace Porridge 3: Where Now? (J). 1995. pap. 10.95 (*0-938875-32-9*) Pittenbruach Pr.

— The Public Sammy: A Cat Friendship. 24p. 1998. pap. 4.50 (*0-938875-41-8*) Pittenbruach Pr.

— Quote Quest: Something Different...for the Puzzle Buff. 43p. 1990. pap. 3.50 (*0-938875-25-6*) Pittenbruach Pr.

— Solo Publishing. LC 90-63045. 100p. 1990. pap. 9.95 (*0-938875-23-X*) Pittenbruach Pr.

— War Is a Dinosaur, & Other Songs of Hope, Love & Weltschmerz. LC 86-64053. 96p. (YA). 1987. pap. 9.95 (*0-938875-04-3*) Pittenbruach Pr.

Milne, Teddy, ed. Circumference of Days: An Anthology of Poetry on Endings & Beginnings. LC 97-66540. 84p. 1997. pap. 11.50 (*0-938875-38-8*) Pittenbruach Pr.

Milne, Thomas A., jt. ed. see Soltes, Ed J.

Milne-Thomson, Louis M. The Calculus of Finite Difference. 2nd ed. LC 80-65906. xxiii, 558p. 1980. text 29.50 (*0-8284-0308-2*) Chelsea Pub.

— Russian-English Mathematical Dictionary: Words & Phrases in Pure & Applied Mathematics with Roots & Accents, Arranged for Easy Reference. LC 62-7217. (Mathematics Research Center, United States Army, University of Wisconsin Publication Ser.: No. 7). 205p. reprint ed. pap. 63.60 (*0-608-13399-X*, 205574200034) Bks Demand.

— Theoretical Aerodynamics. (Illus.). 430p. (C). 1973. reprint ed. pap. text 10.95 (*0-486-61980-X*) Dover.

— Theoretical Hydrodynamics. 5th enl. rev. ed. (Illus.). 768p. 1996. reprint ed. pap. 20.95 (*0-486-68970-0*) Dover.

Milne, Tom & Willemen, Paul. The Overlook Film Encyclopedia: Horror. Hardy, Phil, ed. LC 93-23387. (Illus.). 496p. 1994. 65.00 (*0-87951-518-X*, Pub. by Overlook Pr) Penguin Putnam.

Milne, Tom, ed. see Godard, Jean-Luc.

***Milne-Tyte, Robert.** Armada. 1998. pap. 12.99 (*1-85326-688-4*, Pub. by Wrdsworth Edits) Combined Pub.

Milne, W. S. Practical Bengali Grammar. (BEN & ENG.). 1992. 49.95 (*0-8288-8469-2*) Fr & Eur.

Milne, Wendy H. Making Your Own Jewelry: Creative Designs to Make & Wear. Balmuth, Deborah, ed. LC 94-4909. (Illus.). 96p. 1994. 18.95 (*0-88266-883-8*, Storey Pub) Storey Bks.

Milne, William E. Numerical Calculus: Approximations, Interpolation, Finite Differences, Numerical Integration & Curve Fitting. LC 49-7739. 403p. reprint ed. pap. 125.00 (*0-7837-1421-1*, 204177600023) Bks Demand.

Milner. Contemporary Cultural Theory: An Introduction, Nos. 1-4. 192p. pap. 19.95 (*0-04-442292-X*, Pub. by Allen & Unwin Pty) Paul & Co Pubs.

— Explorations of Consciousness. pap. 16.95 (*0-8464-4503-4*) Beekman Pubs.

— Self Assessment in Pediatrics. 1996. 28.00 (*0-7234-2920-0*) Mosby Inc.

— Self-Assessment Picture Tests in Medicine: Pediatrics. (Illus.). 148p. (C). (gr. 13). 1994. pap. text 15.95 (*0-8151-5916-1*, 23092) Mosby Inc.

Milner, A. C. Kerajaan: Malay Political Culture on the Eve of Colonial Rule. LC 81-24016. (Monographs: No. 40). xxiii, 178p. 1982. 16.00 (*0-8165-0772-4*) Assn Asian Studies.

Milner, A. C. & Wilson, Trevor, eds. Australian Diplomacy: Challenges & Options for the Department of Foreign Affairs. LC 87-155223. (Australian Institute of International Affairs, Occasional Paper Ser.: No. 5). 98p. reprint ed. pap. 30.40 (*0-8357-6827-9*, 203551300095) Bks Demand.

Milner, A. D. Childhood Asthma. 2nd ed. 1994. 49.95 (*1-85317-110-7*, M Dunitz) Scovill Paterson.

Milner, A. David & Goodale, Melvyn A. The Visual Brain in Action. (Oxford Psychology Ser.: No. 27). (Illus.). 266p. 1996. reprint ed. pap. text 35.00 (*0-19-852408-0*) OUP.

Milner, A. M. & Oswood, M. W., eds. Freshwaters of Alaska: Ecological Syntheses. LC 95-37682. (Ecological Studies). (Illus.). 368p. 1996. 99.95 (*0-387-94379-X*) Spr-Verlag.

Milner, A. M. & Wood, James D., Jr., eds. Proceedings of the 2nd Glacier Bay Science Symposium. LC 90-5862. (Illus.). (Orig.). (C). 1990. pap. write for info. (*0-943475-03-1*) Natl Pk AK.

Milner, A. R. & Wood, P. R., eds. Johne's Disease: Current Trends in Research, Diagnosis & Management. 1989. text 50.00 (*0-643-04890-1*, Pub. by CSIRO) Accents Pubns.

Milner, Andrew. Literature, Culture & Society. LC 96-8253. 224p. (C). 1996. text 50.00 (*0-8147-5565-8*); pap. text 19.50 (*0-8147-5564-X*) NYU Pr.

Milner, Andrew, et al, eds. Postmodern Conditions. LC 89-31934. 224p. 1990. 19.50 (*0-85496-591-2*) Berg Pubs.

Milner, Angela, ed. Dinosaurs. LC 95-12938. (Nature Company Discoveries Library). (Illus.). 64p. (YA). (gr. 3 up). 1999. 16.00 (*0-7835-4765-X*) Time-Life.

Milner, Angela, jt. auth. see Gardom, Tim.

Milner, Angela, jt. auth. see Gardom, Tom.

Milner, Anita C. Newspaper Genealogical Column Directory. 6th rev. ed. x, 110p. (Orig.). 1996. pap. 14.00 (*0-7884-0507-1*, M347) Heritage Bk.

— Newspaper Indexes, Vol. I. LC 77-7130. 210p. 1977. 26.50 (*0-8108-1066-2*) Scarecrow.

— Newspaper Indexes, Vol. II. LC 77-7130. 203p. 1979. 28.00 (*0-8108-1244-4*) Scarecrow.

— Newspaper Indexes, Vol. III. LC 77-7130. 192p. 1982. 28.00 (*0-8108-1493-5*) Scarecrow.

***Milner, Annalisa.** Email. (Essential Computers Ser.). 72p. 2000. pap. 6.95 (*0-7894-5533-1*, D K Ink) DK Pub Inc.

— Internet: Browsing the Web. LC 99-54351. (Essential Computers Ser.). 72p. 2000. pap. text 6.95 (*0-7894-5527-7*, D K Ink) DK Pub Inc.

Milner, Anthony. The Invention of Politics in Colonial Malaya: Contesting Nationalism & the Expansion of the Public Sphere. (Illus.). 336p. (C). 1995. text 59.95 (*0-521-46565-6*) Cambridge U Pr.

Milner, Anthony, ed. Australia in Asia: Comparing Cultures. 312p. 1996. pap. text 38.00 (*0-19-553672-X*) OUP.

Milner, Anthony & Quilty, Mary, eds. Australia in Asia: Communities of Thought. 234p. (Orig.). 1998. pap. text 35.00 (*0-19-553671-1*) OUP.

Milner, Anthony, et al. Neonatal Repiratory Disorders. (Illus.). 512p. 1996. text 125.00 (*0-340-55242-5*, Pub. by E A) OUP.

Milner, Anthony, jt. ed. see Herbert, Patricia.

Milner, Anthony D. Hospital Pediatrics. 3rd ed. (Orig.). (C). 1998. pap. text 49.95 (*0-443-05392-8*, W B Saunders Co) Harcrt Hlth Sci Grp.

Milner, C. Tatlin & the Russian Avant-Garde. (C). 1990. pap. 150.00 (*0-7855-4442-9*, Pub. by Collets) St Mut.

Milner, Carol. Auditing ARM Portfolios: A Practical Guide. 50p. (Orig.). 1993. pap. 20.00 (*0-945359-19-5*) Mortgage Bankers.

Milner, Chris, ed. Export Promotion Strategies: Theory & Evidence from Developing Countries. 288p. (C). 1990. text 55.00 (*0-8147-5457-0*) NYU Pr.

Milner, Chris & Greenaway, David. An Introduction to International Economics. LC 78-40512. (Illus.). 272p. reprint ed. pap. 84.40 (*0-608-17290-1*, 203032800068) Bks Demand.

Milner, Chris, jt. auth. see Greenaway, David.

Milner, Chris, jt. auth. see Williamson, John.

Milner, Chris, jt. ed. see Arndt, Sven.

Milner, Chris, jt. ed. see Lloyd, Peter.

Milner, Chris R. & Casson, Mark, eds. Developing & Newly Industrializing Countries, 2 vols., Set. LC 98-24857. (Globalization of the World Economy Ser.: Vol. 4). 944p. 1998. 270.00 (*1-85898-663-X*) E Elgar.

Milner, Cinthia & Sexton, Robin. His Little Instruction Book for Getting Her to Say Yes...More Than Once a Month: An Operational Manual for Men. Bolkey, Lorna et al, eds. LC 95-78547. 128p. (Orig.). 1995. pap. 6.95 (*1-56664-087-3*) WorldComm.

Milner, Clyde A., II. Major Problems in the History of the American West: Documents & Essays. LC 88-80718. (Major Problems in American History Ser.). 681p. (C). 1989. pap. text 29.16 (*0-669-15134-3*) HM Trade Div.

Milner, Clyde A., 2nd. A New Significance: Re-Envisioning the History of the American West. (Illus.). 320p. 1996. pap. 21.00 (*0-19-510048-4*); text 60.00 (*0-19-510047-6*) OUP.

Milner, Clyde A., II. With Good Intentions: Quaker Work among the Pawnees, Otos, & Omahas in the 1870's. LC 81-16238. (Illus.). 262p. 1982. reprint ed. pap. 81.30 (*0-608-03992-6*, 206472400010) Bks Demand.

Milner, Clyde A., et al, eds. The Oxford History of the American West. (Illus.). 904p. 1996. reprint ed. pap. 27.50 (*0-19-511212-1*) OUP.

Milner, Clyde A., II & O'Neil, Floyd A., eds. Churchmen & the Western Indians, 1820-1920. LC 85-40477. (Illus.). 272p. 1985. 28.95 (*0-8061-1950-0*) U of Okla Pr.

Milner, Clyde A., II, et al. Major Problems in the History of the American West. 2nd ed. 550p. (C). 1997. pap. text 23.67 (*0-669-41580-4*) HM Trade Div.

Milner, Dan & Kaplan, Paul. Songs of England, Ireland & Scotland: A Bonnie Bunch of Roses. 1983. pap. 21.95 (*0-8256-0256-4*, 63883, Oak) Music Sales.

Milner, David. Pediatrics. (Self-Assessment Picture Tests in Medicine Ser.). 148p. 1993. text 22.50 (*0-7234-1951-5*, Pub. by Wolfe Pub) Mosby Inc.

Milner, David, ed. Comparative Neuropsychology. LC 97-41989. (Illus.). 316p. 1998. text 52.50 (*0-19-852411-0*) OUP.

Milner, David, jt. auth. see Bender, Ruth.

Milner, E. R. The Lives & Times of Bonnie & Clyde. LC 95-4305. (Illus.). 194p. (C). 1996. 24.95 (*0-8093-1977-2*) S Ill U Pr.

***Milner, Eileen M.** Managing Information & Knowledge in the Public Sector. LC 00-20795. 2000. pap. write for info. (*0-415-20423-2*) Routledge.

Milner, Esther. The Failure of Success: The Middle Class Crisis. LC 67-27951. 238p. 1968. 12.50 (*0-87527-054-9*) Green.

— The Failure of Success: The Middle-Class Crisis. 2nd ed. LC 67-27951. 238p. reprint ed. pap. 73.80 (*0-608-18772-0*, 202979100065) Bks Demand.

Milner, Evgeny C., jt. auth. see Volkov, Vladimir.

Milner, Frank. Monet. (Illus.). 1999. pap. 19.95 (*1-57715-072-4*) Knckerbocker.

Milner, G. Drugs & Driving: A Survey of the Relationship of Adverse Drug Reactions, & Drug-Alcohol Interaction to Driving Safety. Avery, G. S., ed. (Monographs on Drugs: Vol. 1). (Illus.). xi, 124p. 1971. 26.25 (*3-8055-1242-2*) S Karger.

Milner, G. B. Samoan Dictionary: Samoan-English, English-Samoan. 465p. 1993. text 32.00 (*0-908597-12-6*) UH Pr.

Milner, George. The Crime Against Marcella. large type ed. (Linford Mystery Library). 288p. 1988. pap. 16.99 (*0-7089-6622-5*, Linford) Ulverscroft.

— A Leavetaking. large type ed. (Linford Mystery Library). 276p. 1989. pap. 16.99 (*0-7089-6635-7*, Linford) Ulverscroft.

— Your Money & Your Life. large type ed. (Linford Mystery Library). 352p. 1988. pap. 16.99 (*0-7089-6514-8*) Ulverscroft.

Milner, George, jt. auth. see Nodal, John.

Milner, George R. The Cahokia Chiefdom: The Archaeology of a Mississippiana Society. LC 98-14333. (Archaeological Inquiry Ser.). (Illus.). 216p. 1998. text 40.00 (*1-56098-814-2*) Smithsonian.

— Sport Marketing Managing the Exchange Process. 1998. write for info. (*0-7637-0873-9*) Jones & Bartlett.

Milner, George R., jt. auth. see Buikstra, Jane E.

Milner, George R., jt. ed. see Larsen, Clark S.

Milner, George W. The Principles & Applications of Polarography & Other Electroanalytical Processes. LC 57-3248. 757p. reprint ed. pap. 200.00 (*0-608-10815-4*, 200494700048) Bks Demand.

Milner-Gulland, E. J. & Mace, Ruth. Conservation of Biological Resources. LC 97-31751. (Illus.). 1998. pap. 62.95 (*0-86542-738-0*) Blackwell Sci.

Milner-Gulland, R. R., ed. Yevgeny Yevtushenko: Selected Poetry. 1963. 6.70 (*0-08-009808-8*, Pergamon Pr); pap. 5.15 (*0-08-009807-X*, Pergamon Pr) Elsevier.

Milner-Gulland, Robin R. The Russians. LC 96-51542. (Peoples of Europe Ser.). (Illus.). 304p. 1997. 31.95 (*0-631-18805-3*) Blackwell Pubs.

***Milner-Gulland, Robin R.** The Russians. (Peoples of Europe Ser.). (Illus.). 304p. 1999. pap. 26.95 (*0-631-21849-1*) Blackwell Pubs.

Milner-Gulland, Tom. The Birth of Three Sides: A Theory of Dimensionality. (Philosophy Ser.). (Illus.). 196p. 1997. text 64.95 (*1-85972-536-8*, Pub. by Avebry) Ashgate Pub Co.

Milner, Helen V. Interests, Institutions & Information: Domestic Politics & International Relations. LC 96-30099. 328p. 1997. text 47.50 (*0-691-01177-X*, Pub. by Princeton U Pr); pap. text 18.95 (*0-691-01176-1*, Pub. by Princeton U Pr) Cal Prin Full Svc.

— Resisting Protectionism: Global Industries & the Politics of International Trade. LC 88-9945. 343p. 1988. reprint ed. pap. 106.40 (*0-608-02918-1*, 206398200008) Bks Demand.

Milner, Helen V., jt. auth. see Mansfield, Edward D.

Milner, Helen V., jt. ed. see Keohane, Robert O.

Milner, Helen V., ed. see Litfin, Karen.

Milner, Henry. The Long Road to Reform: Restructuring Public Education in Quebec. 192p. (C). 1986. text 60.00 (*0-7735-0563-6*, Pub. by McG-Queens Univ Pr); pap. text 27.95 (*0-7735-0564-4*, Pub. by McG-Queens Univ Pr) CUP Services.

— Sweden: Social Democracy in Practice. 280p. 1990. reprint ed. pap. text 19.95 (*0-19-827856-X*) OUP.

Milner, Henry, ed. Making Every Vote Count: Reassessing Canada's Election System. 200p. 1999. pap. 19.95 (*1-55111-256-6*) Broadview Pr.

Milner, Ian, tr. see Fischerova, Sylva.

An Asterisk (*) at the beginning of an entry indicates that the title is appearing for the first time.

Milner, Ian, tr. see Holub, Miroslav.

Milner, Ian, tr. see Macek, Josef.

Milner, James B. Milner's Cases & Materials on Contracts. 3rd ed. Waddams, S. M., ed. LC 75-151396. 915p. reprint ed. pap. 200.00 (*0-7837-1049-6*, 204136100020) Bks Demand.

Milner, Jarmila, tr. see Fischerova, Sylva.

Milner, Jarmila, tr. see Hanzlik, Josef.

Milner, Jay D. Confessions of a Maddog: A Romp Through the High-Flying Texas Music & Literary Era of the Fifties to the Seventies. LC 98-23419. (Illus.). 248p. 1998. 29.95 (*1-57441-050-4*) UNTX Pr.

Milner, Joanne, jt. auth. see Hale, James.

Milner, Joanne, jt. auth. see Julander, Paula.

Milner, Joel S., ed. Neuropsychology of Aggression. 208p. (C). 1991. text 147.50 (*0-7923-1245-7*) Kluwer Academic.

***Milner, John.** Art, War & Revolution in France, 1870-1871. LC 00-23891. (Illus.). 256p. 2000. 55.00 (*0-300-08407-2*) Yale U Pr.

Milner, John. A Dictionary of Russian & Soviet Artists, 1420-1970. (Illus.). 484p. 1993. 99.50 (*1-85149-182-1*) Antique Collect.

— Kazimir Malevich & the Art of Geometry. LC 95-40662. 1996. 52.00 (*0-300-06417-9*) Yale U Pr.

— Mondrian. rev. ed. LC 95-202711. (Illus.). 240p. (C). 1995. pap. 29.95 (*0-7148-3167-0*, Pub. by Phaidon Press) Phaidon Pr.

— The Studios of Paris: The Capital of Art in the Late Nineteenth Century. 256p. (C). 1990. reprint ed. pap. 30.00 (*0-300-04749-5*) Yale U Pr.

— The Studios of Paris: The Capital of Art in the Nineteenth Century. LC 87-30044. 248p. (C). 1988. 57.00 (*0-300-03990-5*) Yale U Pr.

— Vladimir Tatlin & the Russian Avant-Garde. LC 82-25923. (Illus.). 262p. reprint ed. pap. 81.30 (*0-7837-6219-4*, 208022900004) Bks Demand.

Milner, Joseph Obeirne. Bridging English. 2nd ed. LC 98-25239. 549p. 1998. pap. text 63.00 (*0-13-792946-3*) P-H.

Milner, Judith, jt. auth. see Blyth, Eric.

Milner, Kathleen. Healing Arts Collection, 5 audiocass., 3 videocass. & 2 bks.; set. 1995. 165.00 incl. audio, VHS (*1-886903-99-9*) K Milner.

***Milner, Kathleen.** On the Edge Between Two Worlds: Ireland & the Ways of Healing. (Healing Arts Ser.). 2000. pap. write for info. (*1-886903-21-2*) K Milner.

Milner, Kathleen. Reiki & Other Rays of Touch Healing. 2nd ed. (Healing Art Ser.). (Illus.). 152p. (Orig.). 1995. pap. 15.95 (*1-886903-97-2*) K Milner.

***Milner, Kathleen A.** Tera, My Journey Home: Seichem, Shamanism, Symbology, Herbs & Reincarnation. 2nd rev. ed. 308p. 1999. pap. 21.95 (*1-886903-67-0*) K Milner.

Milner, Kathleen A., illus. see Johnson, Brian A.

Milner, Larry S. Hardness of Heart/Hardness of Life: The Stain of Human Infanticide. LC 98-91381. 390p. 1998. pap. 29.95 (*1-57502-768-2*, P02159) Morris Pubng.

Milner, Larry S., ed. Asociaciones de Negocios Para El Siglo XXI: Plano Para El Futuro. 190p. 1997. pap. 25.00 (*0-9700770-7-6*) Ctr Intl Private Enter.

— Business Associations for the 21st Century: A Blueprint for the Future. 227p. 1997. pap. 25.00 (*0-9700770-6-8*) Ctr Intl Private Enter.

— Business Associations for the 21st Century: A Blueprint for the Future. 129p. 1999. pap. 25.00 (*0-9700770-5-X*) Ctr Intl Private Enter.

Milner, Laurie. Royal Scots in the Gulf: First Battalion Royal Scots on Operation GRANBY 1990-1991. (Illus.). 256p. 1994. 27.95 (*0-85052-273-0*, Pub. by Leo Cooper) Trans-Atl Phila.

Milner, M., jt. ed. see Hultin, H. O.

***Milner, Marc.** Canada's Navy: The First Century. (Illus.) 448p. 1999. text 45.00 (*0-8020-4281-3*) U of Toronto Pr.

Milner, Marc. Canadian Military History. (C). 1993. pap. text 29.95 (*0-7730-5257-7*) Addison-Wesley.

— The U-Boat Hunters: The Royal Canadian Navy & the Offensive Against Germany's Submarines. LC 94-66600. (Illus.). 280p. 1994. 31.95 (*1-55750-854-2*) Naval Inst Pr.

— The U-Boat Hunters: The Royal Canadian Navy & the Offensive Against Germany's Submarines. 1994. text 35.00 (*0-8020-0588-8*) U of Toronto Pr.

Milner, Marc & Macpherson, Ken. Corvettes of the Royal Canadian Navy, 1939-1945. (Illus.). 174p. 1993. write for info. (*0-920277-83-7*, Vanwell Pub) Howell Pr VA.

Milner, Marion. Hands of the Living God: An Account of a Psychoanalytic Treatment. LC 78-85201. (Illus.). 444p. 1969. text 75.00 (*0-8236-2320-3*) Intl Univs Pr.

— On Not Being Able to Paint. rev. ed. (Illus.). 184p. (Orig.). 1990. pap. 24.95 (*0-8236-8202-1*, BN23820) Intl Univs Pr.

— The Suppressed Madness of Sane Men: Forty-Four Years of Exploring Psycho-Analysis. (Illus.). 250p. (C). 1987. pap. 19.95 (*0-422-61690-7*, Pub. by Tavistock); lib. bdg. 49.50 (*0-422-61020-8*, Pub. by Tavistock) Routldge.

Milner, Mordaunt. The Godolphin Arabian. 200p. 1990. 65.00 (*0-85131-476-7*, Pub. by J A Allen) St Mut.

Milner, N. P., tr. Vegetius: Epitome of Military Science. rev. ed. 192p. (Orig.). 1996. pap. text 17.95 (*0-85323-910-X*) U of Pa Pr.

Milner, Neal, jt. ed. see Merry, Sally E.

Milner, Nicki, jt. ed. see Miracle, Preston T.

Milner, Oscar I. Successful Management of the Analytical Laboratory. 176p. 1991. lib. bdg. 75.00 (*0-87371-438-5*, L438) Lewis Pubs.

Milner, Pat & Carolin, Birgit. Time to Listen to Children: A Handbook for Students, Professionals & Parents. LC 98-35444. 12p. 1999. 80.00 (*0-415-17197-0*) Routledge.

— Time to Listen to Children: A Handbook for Students, Professionals & Parents. LC 98-35444. xiii, 237 p. 1999. pap. 25.99 (*0-415-17198-9*) Routledge.

Milner, Patricia & Palmer, Stephen. Integrative Stress Counselling: A Humanistic Problem & Goal Focused Approach. LC 98-221243. (Stress Counselling Ser.). 224p. 1998. 75.00 (*0-304-33491-X*); pap. 24.95 (*0-304-33492-8*) Continuum.

***Milner, Paul & Jonas, Linda.** Genealogist's Guide to Discovering Your English Ancestors. 2000. pap. 18.99 (*1-55870-536-8*, Betrwy Bks) F & W Pubns Inc.

Milner, Peter M. The Autonomous Brain: A Neural Theory of Attention & Learning. LC 99-19772. 168p. 1999. 27.95 (*0-8058-3211-4*) L Erlbaum Assocs.

Milner, R. Retriever Training for the Duck Hunter. (Illus.). 168p. 1993. 21.95 (*0-940143-90-9*) Safari Pr.

Milner, Richard. Charles Darwin: Evolution of a Naturalist. (Makers of Modern Science Ser.). 176p. (YA). (gr. 5 up). 1994. lib. bdg. 19.95 (*0-8160-2557-6*) Facts on File.

— Encyclopedia of Evolution: Humanity's Search for Its Origins. (Illus.). 496p. 1995. pap. 25.00 (*0-8050-2717-3*) H Holt & Co.

— Nuclear Physics: Electronuclear Physics with Internal Targets & the Blast Detector. 1999. 122.00 (*981-02-4004-X*) World Scientific Pub.

***Milner, Robert.** Retriever Training: The Back-to-Basics Approach. (Illus.). 240p. 2000. 27.50 (*1-57223-391-5*) Willow Creek Pr.

Milner, Robin. Communicating & Mobile Systems: The Pi-Calculus. (Illus.). 160p. (C). 1999. text 64.95 (*0-521-64320-1*); pap. text 24.95 (*0-521-65869-1*) Cambridge U Pr.

— Communication & Concurrency. 272p. 1995. pap. 40.00 (*0-13-115007-3*, Macmillan Coll) P-H.

***Milner, Robin.** Proof, Language & Interaction: Essays in Honour of Robin Milner. Plotkin, George et al, eds. LC 99-27800. (Foundations of Computing Ser.). (Illus.). 700p. 2000. 60.00 (*0-262-16188-5*) MIT Pr.

Milner, Robin & Tofte, Mads. Commentary on Standard ML. 160p. 1990. pap. text 21.00 (*0-262-63137-7*) MIT Pr.

Milner, Robin, et al. Commentary on Standard ML. rev. ed. 160p. 1990. 35.00 (*0-262-13271-0*) MIT Pr.

— The Definition of Standard ML. rev. ed. LC 97-59. (Illus.). 126p. 1997. pap. text 25.00 (*0-262-63181-4*) MIT Pr.

Milner, Robin, jt. ed. see Wand, Ian.

Milner, Roger. How's the World Treating You? 1967. pap. 5.25 (*0-8222-0541-6*) Dramatists Play.

Milner, Simon, jt. auth. see Metcalf, David.

Milner, Stephen, ed. see Machiavelli, Niccolo.

Milner, Susan. The Dilemmas of Internationalism: French Syndicalism & the International Labour Movement, 1900-1914. LC 90-374. 268p. 1991. 30.00 (*0-85496-617-X*) Berg Pubs.

Milner, Susan, tr. see Kepel, Gilles.

Milner, Toby. The Dictionary of Work & Study in Developing Countries. 1997. pap. 16.95 (*1-85458-170-8*, Pub. by Vac Wrk Pubns) Petersons.

***Milner, W. W. & Montgomery-Smith, Ann.** Information & Communication Technology for Advanced GNVQ. 2nd ed. (Illus.). 272p. 2000. pap. 42.50 (*0-7487-5315-X*, Pub. by S Thornes Pubs) Trans-Atl Phila.

Milner, W. W. & Montgomery-Smith, Ann. Intermediate Information Technology. 320p. 1997. pap. 39.50 (*0-7487-3029-X*, Pub. by S Thornes Pubs) Trans-Atl Phila.

Milnes, A. & Miner, C. J., eds. Semi-Insulating III-V Materials, Toronto, 1990. (Illus.). 480p. 1991. 146.00 (*0-7503-0066-3*) IOP Pub.

Milnes, A. G. Geology & Radwaste. 1985. text 160.00 (*0-12-498070-8*); pap. text 78.00 (*0-12-498071-6*) Acad Pr.

***Milnes, Ellen.** Disney's Some Moms, Some Dads. 10p. (J). 2001. 4.99 (*0-7364-1046-5*, Pub. by Mouse Works) Time Warner.

Milnes, Ellen. Mickey's Day of the Week. (Illus.). (J). 1999. 2.99 (*0-7364-0049-4*, Pub. by Mouse Works) Time Warner.

***Milnes, Ellen.** Trick or Treat, Pooh! (Learn & Grow Ser.). (Illus.). 14p. (J). (ps up). 2000. 5.99 (*0-7364-0104-0*, Pub. by Mouse Works) Time Warner.

Milnes, Gerald. Granny Will Your Dog Bite & Other Mountain Rhymes. LC 99-34243. (Illus.). 48p. (J). (ps-3). 1999. reprint ed. pap. 9.95 (*0-87483-560-7*) August Hse.

— Play of a Fiddle: Traditional Music, Dance & Folklore in West Virginia. LC 98-40733. 264p. 1999. 35.00 (*0-8131-2080-2*) U Pr of Ky.

Milnes, Irma M. Kaarina & the Sugarbag Vest. (Illus.). 80p. (J). (gr. 3-7). 1996. pap. 5.95 (*1-55037-356-0*, Pub. by Annick) Firefly Bks Ltd.

Milnes, Joseph G. Heartfelt Memories. 1998. pap. write for info. (*1-57553-915-2*) Watermrk Pr.

Milnes, Lynne. In a Victoria Garden. (Illus.). 128p. (Orig.). 1995. pap. 18.95 (*1-55143-031-2*) Orca Bk Pubs.

Milnes, M. Ellen. Spice Girls!--And Then There Were Four. LC 98-29491. 1998. write for info. (*1-56799-837-2*, Friedman-Fairfax) M Friedman Pub Grp Inc.

Milnes, Michele, jt. auth. see Eckols, Steve.

Milnor, Hazel S. As Angels Watch. LC 97-90749. 125p. (Orig.). 1997. pap. 8.95 (*0-533-12159-0*) Vantage.

***Milnor, J. Pervis, III, et al.** It Can Break Your Heart: What You & Your Doctor Should Know about Solving Your Weight Problem. (Illus.). 424p. 2000. pap. 29.95 (*0-940829-31-2*) Eagle Wing Bks.

— SmartLoss 60-Day Health Journal. 80p. 2000. wbk. ed. 10.95 (*0-940829-30-4*) Eagle Wing Bks.

Milnor, John. John Milnor Vol. 1: The Fundamental Group. (Collected Papers Ser.). (Illus.). x, 295p. 1994. text 30.00 (*0-914098-30-6*) Publish or Perish.

— John Milnor Vol. 2: The Fundamental Group. (Collected Papers Ser.). (Illus.). xii, 302p. 1995. text 30.00 (*0-914098-31-4*) Publish or Perish.

— Topology from the Differentiable Viewpoint. LC 97-30986. (Princeton Landmarks in Mathematics & Physics Ser.). 76p. 1997. pap. text 9.95 (*0-691-04833-9*, Pub. by Princeton U Pr) Cal Prin Full Svc.

Milnor, John W. Introduction to Algebraic K-Theory. LC 74-161197. (Annals of Mathematics Studies: No. 72). 198p. 1971. reprint ed. pap. 61.40 (*0-608-06480-7*, 206677700009) Bks Demand.

— Morse Theory. (Annals of Mathematics Studies: No. 51). 160p. (Orig.). 1963. pap. text 37.50 (*0-691-08008-9*, Pub. by Princeton U Pr) Cal Prin Full Svc.

— Singular Points of Complex Hypersurfaces. LC 69-17408. (Annals of Mathematics Studies: No. 61). (Illus.). 132p. reprint ed. pap. 41.00 (*0-608-06486-6*, 2066783) Bks Demand.

— Topology from the Differentiable Viewpoint. LC 65-26874. (Illus.). 76p. 1969. reprint ed. pap. 30.00 (*0-608-03186-0*, 206363900007) Bks Demand.

Milnor, John W. & Stasheff, James D. Characteristic Classes. LC 72-4050. (Annals of Mathematics Studies: No. 76). 250p. 1973. pap. text 49.50 (*0-691-08122-0*, Pub. by Princeton U Pr) Cal Prin Full Svc.

Milnor, William R. Cardiovascular Physiology. (Illus.). 520p. 1990. text 39.95 (*0-19-505884-4*) OUP.

Milns, William & Tomkins, William. Ornamental Penmanship. (Illus.). 75p. 1983. pap. 7.95 (*0-486-24449-0*) Dover.

Milo, Abq. A Double Axe: Cancer & the Mind. (Illus.). 14p. (Orig.). 1996. pap., wbk. ed. 2.00 (*0-9653664-0-5*) Balanced Way.

Milo, Antonia G. Healing from Cancer: A Call to Freedom. LC 98-94872. (Illus.). 132p. 1999. pap. 9.95 (*0-9653664-2-1*, Pub. by Balanced Way) ACCESS Pubs Network.

Milo, George E. Transformation of Human Epithelial Cells. 336p. 1992. lib. bdg. 206.00 (*0-8493-6382-9*, RC280) CRC Pr.

Milo, George E., ed. Transformation of Human Diploid Fibroblasts. 304p. 1990. lib. bdg. 202.00 (*0-8493-4956-7*, RC268) CRC Pr.

Milo, Jack, jt. auth. see Day, Filomena T.

Milo, Mary. Guide to Beauty. LC 72-83736. (Family Circle Bks.). (Illus.). 160p. 1977. 12.95 (*0-405-09841-3*) Ayer.

Milo, Mary, jt. auth. see Family Circle Food Staff.

Milo Pergolizzi, Carl, tr. see Moliere.

Milo, Ronald D. Immorality. LC 84-42564. (Studies in Moral, Political, & Legal Philosophy). 286p. 1984. reprint ed. pap. 88.70 (*0-608-03357-X*, 206406900008) Bks Demand.

Milobedzki. Polish Avant Garde Architecture, Rassegna 65. (Illus.). 110p. 1996. pap. 35.00 (*88-85322-23-9*, Pub. by Birkhauser) Princeton Arch.

Milofsky, Carl. Testers & Testing: The Sociology of School Psychology. LC 88-28293. 304p. (C). 1989. text 40.00 (*0-8135-1407-X*) Rutgers U Pr.

Milofsky, Carl, ed. Community Organizations: Studies in Resource Mobilization & Exchange. (Yale Studies in Nonprofit Organizations). (Illus.). 304p. 1988. text 70.00 (*0-19-504680-3*) OUP.

***Milofsky, David.** Color of Law. 336p. 2000. 24.95 (*0-87081-581-4*) Univ Pr Colo.

Milofsky, David. Eternal People. LC 98-24620. 320p. 1998. 22.50 (*0-87081-502-4*) Univ Pr Colo.

***Milofsky, David.** Playing from Memory. LC 99-11759. 270p. 1999. reprint ed. pap. 14.95 (*0-87081-526-1*) Univ Pr Colo.

Milofsky, David, ed. Colorado Review: A Journal of Contemporary Literature. 200p. 1995. pap. text 9.50 (*0-614-00687-2*) CO St U Ctr Literary.

— New Voices: Essays from Colorado State University. 165p. (Orig.). (C). 1995. pap. text 10.00 (*1-885635-01-X*) CO St U Ctr Literary.

— New Voices: Poetry & Fiction from Colorado State University. 300p. (C). 1994. pap. text 10.00 (*1-885635-00-1*) CO St U Ctr Literary.

Miloh, T., ed. Mathematical Approaches in Hydrodynamics. (Miscellaneous Bks.: No. 24). xxi, 517p. 1991. pap. 79.75 (*0-89871-277-7*) Soc Indus-Appl Math.

Milojevic, Svetlana. Die Poesie des Dilettantismus: Zur Rezeption und Wirkung Leopold von Sacher-Masochs. (German Studies in Canada: Vol. 11). (GER.). 282p. 1998. 48.95 (*3-631-33230-0*) P Lang Pubng.

Milojicic, Dejan S. Mobility: Processes, Computers & Agents. LC 99-10175. 704p. (C). 1999. pap. text 39.95 (*0-201-37928-7*) Addison-Wesley.

Milojkovic-Djuric, Jelena. Panslavism & National Identity in Russia & in the Balkans, 1830-1880: Images of the Self & Others. 177p. 1994. 30.50 (*0-88033-291-3*, 394, Pub. by East Eur Monographs) Col U Pr.

— Tradition & Avante-Garde. 1988. 42.00 (*0-685-42856-7*) East Eur Monographs.

— Tradition & Avante-Garde: Literature & Arts in Serbian Culture, 1900-1918. (East European Monographs: No. 234). 224p. 1988. text 55.50 (*0-88033-131-3*, Pub. by East Eur Monographs) Col U Pr.

— Tradition & Avante-Garde: The Arts in Serbian Culture Between the Two World Wars. 175p. 1984. text 51.00 (*0-88033-052-X*, Pub. by East Eur Monographs) Col U Pr.

Milokjevik, P. S. Nonlinear Functional Analysis. (Lecture Notes in Pure & Applied Mathematics Ser.: Vol. 121). (Illus.). 288p. 1989. pap. text 155.00 (*0-8247-8255-0*) Dekker.

Milon, Ellie. Two Hundred One Ways to Enjoy Your Dog. LC 89-18403. (Illus.). 292p. 1990. pap. 18.95 (*0-931866-33-2*) Alpine Pubns.

Milon, Walter J. Integrating Economic & Ecological Indicators. LC 94-37882. 232p. 1995. 65.00 (*0-275-94983-4*, Praeger Pubs) Greenwood.

Milonas, Rolf. Fantasex: A Book of Erotic Games for the Adult Couple. rev. ed. 96p. (Orig.). 1983. pap. 13.00 (*0-399-50839-2*, Perigee Bks) Berkley Pub.

Milone, E. F. Light Curve Modeling of Eclipsing Binary Stars. LC 92-21532. 1992. 89.95 (*0-387-97946-8*) Spr-Verlag.

Milone, E. F., ed. Infrared Extinction & Standardization. (Lecture Notes in Physics Ser.: Vol. 341). iii, 79p. 1989. 45.95 (*0-387-51610-7*) Spr-Verlag.

Milone, E. F. & Mermilliod, J. C., eds. The Origins, Evolution, & Destinies of Binary Stars in Clusters. (ASP Conference Series Proceedings: Vol. 90). 508p. 1996. 34.00 (*1-886733-11-2*) Astron Soc Pacific.

Milone, E. F., jt. auth. see Kallrath, J.

Milone, Frank & Soto, Odalis, contrib. by. Barbershop Favorites Vol. 12: Barbershop Favorites. 100p. (Orig.). 1994. pap. 12.95 (*0-89898-726-1*, WFM00012) Wrner Bros.

Milone, Michael. Things That Go Together. (Illus.). 48p. (J). (gr. 1-4). 1997. pap., wbk. ed. 2.50 (*1-56762-077-9*) Modern Learn Pr.

***Milone, Michael, ed.** Developing Reading Power, Bk. 3. (Illus.). 64p. (J). (gr. 3-4). 1998. pap., wbk. ed. 2.75 (*1-56762-091-4*) Modern Learn Pr.

— Developing Reading Power, Bk. 4. (Illus.). 64p. (J). (gr. 4-5). 1998. pap., wbk. ed. 2.75 (*1-56762-092-2*) Modern Learn Pr.

M

Milone, Michael & Hymes, Donald L. Beyond Bells & Whistles: How to Use Technology to Improve Student Learning. 160p. 1996. 27.95 (*0-87652-207-X*, 021-0559) Am Assn Sch Admin.

Milone, Michael N., Jr. Handwriting Skills, K-8. 64p. (gr. k-8). 1982. teacher ed. 4.95 (*0-88085-018-3*); student ed. 2.59 (*0-685-06079-9*) Zaner-Bloser.

Milone-Nuzzo, Paula, jt. auth. see Humphrey, Carolyn J.

Milone, Richard P. Hip Hop Astro Rap: A Creative Writing & Coloring Experience. 32p. 1993. pap. 20.00 (*0-9639808-0-7*) Classic Intl.

Milonni, Peter W. The Quantum Vacuum: An Introduction to Quantum Electrodynamics. (Illus.). 522p. 1993. text 88.00 (*0-12-498080-5*) Acad Pr.

Milonni, Peter W., et al. Chaos in Laser-Matter Interactions. 384p. 1987. text 70.00 (*9971-5-0179-1*); pap. text 37.00 (*9971-5-0180-5*) World Scientific Pub.

Milonni, Peter W., jt. auth. see Eberly, Joseph H.

***Milor, John W.** Aliens in the Bible: A Biblical Perspective of Supernatural Entities, Realms of Existence & Phenomenon. LC 99-91459. 342p. 1999. 25.00 (*0-7388-0816-4*); pap. 18.00 (*0-7388-0817-2*) Xlibris Corp.

— Apparition. LC 99-90997. 1999. 25.00 (*0-7388-0562-9*); pap. 18.00 (*0-7388-0563-7*) Xlibris Corp.

Milor, Vedat, ed. Changing Political Economics: Privatization in Post-Communist & Reforming Communist States. LC 93-34548. (Emerging Global Issues Ser.). 238p. 1993. lib. bdg. 45.00 (*1-55587-405-3*) L Rienner.

Miloradov, M., ed. The Pollution of the Mediterranean Sea: Proceedings of An IAWPRC International Regional Conference Held in Split, Yugoslavia, 2-5 October 1985. (Water Science & Technology Ser.: No. 18). (Illus.). 338p. 1987. pap. 52.00 (*0-08-035578-1*, Pergamon Pr) Elsevier.

— Water Pollution Control in the Danube Basin. (Water Science & Technology Ser.: No. 22). (Illus.). 303p. 1990. pap. 120.50 (*0-08-040765-X*, Pergamon Pr) Elsevier.

Miloradovic, Z. English-Serbocroat & Serbocroat-English Grammatical Dictionary. 610p. (C). 1988. 160.00 (*0-89771-928-X*, Pub. by Collets) St Mut.

— English-Serbocroat & Serbocroat-English Grammatical Dictionary. 3rd ed. 610p. (C). 1988. 195.00 (*0-7855-6489-6*, Pub. by Collets) St Mut.

Miloradovic, Zivan. English - Serbocroatian, Serbocroatian - English Dictionary: Englesko-Srpskohrvatshi I Srpskohrvatsko-Engleski Recenicnik sa Primenjen. (ENG & SER.). 658p. 1987. 125.00 (*0-8288-0506-7*, F102240) Fr & Eur.

— French - Serbocroatian, Serbocroatian - French Dictionary: Francusko-Srpskohrvatsko-Francuski Recenicnik sa Primen. (FRE & SER.). 600p. 1987. 95.00 (*0-8288-1046-X*, F97180) Fr & Eur.

— Russian-Serbocroatian, Serbocroatian-Russian Dictionary & Grammatical Primer: Rusko-Srpskohrvatski i Srpskohrvatsko-Ruski Recenicnik sa Primenjenon Gramatik. (RUS & SER.). 611p. 1987. 95.00 (*0-8288-1056-7*, F114894) Fr & Eur.

Miloradovich, Milo. Cooking with Herbs & Spices. 320p. 1989. pap. 7.95 (*0-486-26177-8*) Dover.

— Growing & Using Herbs & Spices. 236p. 1986. reprint ed. pap. 6.95 (*0-486-25058-X*) Dover.

Miloradovitch, Hazelle, ed. see Lidl, Andreas.

***Milord, Catherine.** The Voice of Innocence. LC 99-93536. vi, 156p. 1999. pap. write for info. (*0-9674299-0-0*) Spice Island.

Milord, Lisa, jt. auth. see Goldschmidt, Jona.

Milord, Susan. Adventures in Art: Art & Craft Experiences for 8 to 13 Year Olds. rev. ed. Williamson, Susan, ed. LC 97-19327. (Kids Can Ser.). (Illus.). 160p. (J). (gr. 3-7). 1997. pap. 12.95 (*1-885593-13-9*) Williamson Pub Co.

— Bird Tales from Near & Far. LC 97-39453. (Tales Alive! Ser.: Vol. 3). (Illus.). 96p. (J). (ps-3). 1999. pap. 14.95 (*1-885593-18-X*) Williamson Pub Co.

— Hands Around the World: Three Hundred Sixty-Five Creative Ways to Build Cultural Awareness & Global Respect. LC 92-21753. (Kids Can! Ser.: No. 7). (Illus.). 160p. (Orig.). (J). (gr. k-5). 1992. pap. 12.95 (*0-913589-65-9*) Williamson Pub Co.

— The Kids Nature Book: 365 Indoor/Outdoor Activities &

Experiences. rev. ed. Williamson, Susan, ed. (Kids Can! Ser.). (Illus.). 160p. (J). (ps-5). 1996. pap. 12.95 (*1-885593-07-4*) Williamson Pub Co.
— The Kids Nature Book, 365 Indoor/Outdoor Activities & Experiences. LC 96-31542. 1996. 18.05 (*0-606-10240-X*, Pub. by Turtleback) Demco.
— Mexico! 40 Activities to Experience Mexico Past & Present. LC 98-34153. (Kaleidoscope Kids Ser.). 96p. (J). (gr. 1-7). 1999. pap. 10.95 (*1-885593-22-8*) Williamson Pub Co.
— Tales Alive! Ten Multicultural Folktales, with Activities. LC 94-101. (Tales Alive! Ser.: No. 1). (Illus.). 128p. (Orig.). (J). (ps-12). 1994. pap. 15.95 (*0-913589-79-9*) Williamson Pub Co.
— Tales of the Shimmering Sky: Ten Global Folktales with Activities. Jaspersohn, Bill, ed. LC 95-47229. (Tales Alive! Ser.: Vol. 2). (Illus.). 128p. (Orig.). (J). (ps-12). 1996. pap. 15.95 (*1-885593-01-5*) Williamson Pub Co.
Milos, Jon. Through the Needle's Eye. Walker, B., tr. from RUM. 112p. (Orig.). 1990. pap. 19.95 (*0-948259-61-2*, Pub. by Forest Bks) Dufour.
Milos, Marilyn F., jt. ed. see Denniston, George C.
Milosavljevic, M. & Petrovic, Z., eds. Atomic Collision Processes & Particle & Laser Beam Interactions with Solids. 277p. (C). 1996. lib. bdg. 115.00 (*1-56072-400-5*) Nova Sci Pubs.
— Low Temperature & General Plasmas. 317p. (C). 1996. lib. bdg. 145.00 (*1-56072-399-8*) Nova Sci Pubs.
Milosch, Joseph. On the Wing. Thomas, Erikheath A., ed. (Illus.). 35p. (Orig.). 1995. pap. 5.00 (*0-9638412-1-1*) Drury Ln.
Milosh, Joseph E. The Scale of Perfection & the English Mystical Tradition. LC 66-22857. 226p. reprint ed. pap. 70.10 (*0-608-30261-9*, 201097500072) Bks Demand.
Miloslav, Rechcigl. Handbook of Agricultural Productivity, Vol. II: Animal Productivity. 416p. 1982. 226.00 (*0-8493-3963-4*, S494, CRC Reprint) Franklin.
Miloslavich Tupac, Diana, ed. & anno. see Moyano, Maria Elena.
Miloslavskii, I. G. Concise Practical Russian Grammar. 284p. (C). 1987. 50.00 (*0-7855-2310-3*) St Mut.
— Short Practical Russian Grammar. (ENG & RUS.). 244p. (C). 1988. 45.00 (*0-685-39367-4*) Collets.
Miloslavsky, Yury. Urban Romances. 1995. 22.95 (*0-87501-062-8*) Ardis Pubs.
Milostan, Harry. Enduring Poles. LC 76-42844. 1977. 7.95 (*0-918020-01-8*); pap. 4.95 (*0-918020-02-6*) Masspac Pub.
— The Errant Nun. LC 79-83634. (Illus.). 1979. pap. 9.00 (*0-918020-05-0*) Masspac Pub.
— Folksy Fables. LC 84-61017. (Illus.). 80p. (Orig.). 1984. pap. 4.00 (*0-918020-07-7*) Masspac Pub.
Milostan, Harry, ed. Parisville Poles. LC 77-77917. 1977. lib. bdg. 12.00 (*0-918020-03-4*) Masspac Pub.
Milosz, Czeslaw. Beginning with My Streets: Essays & Recollections. Levine, Madeline G., tr. LC 91-33925. 288p. 1992. text 30.00 (*0-374-11010-7*) FS&G.
***Milosz, Czeslaw.** Bells in Winter. Vallee, Lillian, tr. from POL. LC 78-5617. 1999. 13.00 (*0-912946-56-3*, Ecco Press) HarperTrade.
Milosz, Czeslaw. Bells In Winter. Vallee, Lillian, tr. from POL. 80p. 1998. reprint ed. pap. 13.00 (*0-88001-456-3*) HarpC.
— The Captive Mind. Zielonko, Jane, tr. LC 89-40503. 272p. 1990. pap. 13.00 (*0-679-72856-2*) Vin Bks.
Milosz, Czeslaw. Collected Poems. LC 87-24479. 528p. 1990. pap. 19.00 (*0-88001-174-2*) HarpC.
Milosz, Czeslaw. Emperor of the Earth: Modes of Eccentric Vision. LC 76-20005. 1977. pap. 16.95 (*0-520-04503-3*, Pub. by U CA Pr) Cal Prin Full Svc.
— Exiles. expanded rev. ed. (Illus.). 156p. 1998. 91.00 (*0-89381-754-6*) Aperture.
— Facing The River. Hass, Robert, tr. LC 94-43653. 120p. 1995. 22.00 (*0-88001-404-0*) HarpC.
— Facing The River. Hass, Robert, tr. from POL. 80p. 1996. reprint ed. pap. 13.00 (*0-88001-454-7*) HarpC.
— The History of Polish Literature. rev. ed. LC 82-20227. 570p. (C). 1983. pap. 19.95 (*0-520-04477-0*, Pub. by U CA Pr) Cal Prin Full Svc.
— Hymn o Perle. (Michigan Slavic Materials Ser.: No. 21).Tr. of Hymn to the Pearl. 1982. 10.00 (*0-930042-45-X*) Mich Slavic Pubns.
— The Issa Valley: A Novel. Iribarne, Louis, tr. from POL. 304p. 2000. pap. 14.00 (*0-374-51695-2*) FS&G.
— The Land of Ulro. Iribarne, Louis, tr. 304p. 1984. text 17.95 (*0-374-18323-6*) FS&G.
— The Land of Ulro. Iribame, Louis, tr. LC 84-8157. 304p. 2000. pap. 14.00 (*0-374-51937-4*) FS&G.
Milosz, Czeslaw. Legends of Modernity. text. write for info. (*0-374-18499-2*) FS&G.
— Milosz's ABC's. Levine, Madeline, tr. from POL. 256p. 2001. 24.00 (*0-374-19977-9*) FS&G.
Milosz, Czeslaw. Native Realm: A Search for Self-Definition. Leach, Catherine S., tr. 1981. pap. 16.95 (*0-520-04474-6*, Pub. by U CA Pr) Cal Prin Full Svc.
— O Rus! Studia Litteraria Slavica in Honorem Hugh McLean. Karlinsky, Simon et al, eds. 530p. (Orig.). (C). 1995. pap. 50.00 (*1-57201-008-8*) Berkeley Slavic.
— Postwar Polish Poetry: An Anthology. rev. ed. LC 82-16084. 180p. (C). 1983. pap. 15.95 (*0-520-04476-2*, Pub. by U CA Pr) Cal Prin Full Svc.
— Provinces. Hass, Robert, tr. 1991. 19.95 (*0-88001-317-6*) HarpC.
— Provinces. Hass, Robert, tr. LC 92-44647. 1993. pap. 9.95 (*0-88001-321-4*) HarpC.
— Road-Side Dog. LC 98-14026. 200p. 1998. 22.00 (*0-374-25129-0*) FS&G.
***Milosz, Czeslaw.** Road-Side Dog. Haas, Robert, tr. from POL. 224p. 1999. pap. 13.00 (*0-374-52623-0*) FS&G.
Milosz, Czeslaw. Selected Poems. 128p. 1990. reprint ed. pap. 13.00 (*0-88001-455-5*) HarpC.
— Selected Poems - Milosz. rev. ed. LC 80-21470. 129p. 1981. reprint ed. pap. 8.95 (*0-912946-76-8*, Ecco Press) HarperTrade.
— The Separate Notebooks. Hass, Robert et al, trs. 250p. 1986. pap. 12.50 (*0-88001-116-5*) HarpC.
— The Separate Notebooks. Hass, Robert et al, trs. from POL. 212p. 1998. 17.50 (*0-88001-031-2*) HarpC.
— Unattainable Earth. Hass, Robert, tr. from POL. 140p. 1998. 17.95 (*0-88001-098-3*) HarpC.
— Unattainable Earth, Hass, Robert, tr. 1987. pap. 10.95 (*0-88001-102-5*) HarpC.
— Utwory Poetyckie: Poems. 1976. 25.00 (*0-930042-22-0*) Mich Slavic Pubns.
— Visions from San Francisco Bay. Lourie, Richard, tr. from POL. 226p. 1982. 14.95 (*0-374-28488-1*) FS&G.
— The Witness of Poetry. (Charles Eliot Norton Lectures). 128p. 1984. pap. text 11.50 (*0-674-95383-5*) HUP.
— A Year of the Hunter. Levine, Madeline G., tr. 294p. pap. 12.00 (*0-374-52444-0*) FS&G.
— A Year of the Hunter. Levine, Madeline G., tr. LC 93-49598. 288p. 1994. 27.50 (*0-374-29344-9*) FS&G.
Milosz, Czeslaw, ed. A Book of Luminous Things: An International Anthology of Poetry. 348p. (C). 1998. pap. 15.00 (*0-15-600574-3*) Harcourt.
— Piesn Niepodlegla. (Michigan Slavic Materials Ser.: No. 18).Tr. of Invincible Song. 1981. 10.00 (*0-930042-41-7*) Mich Slavic Pubns.
Milosz, Czeslaw, ed. A Book of Luminous Things: An International Anthology of Poetry. LC 95-38060. 336p. 1996. 26.00 (*0-15-100169-3*) Harcourt.
Milosz, Czeslaw, et al. Testimony to the Invisible: Essays on Swedenborg. Lawrence, James F., ed. 176p. (Orig.). 1995. pap. 11.95 (*0-87785-149-2*) Swedenborg.
Milosz, Czeslaw, jt. auth. see Merton, Thomas.
Milosz, Czeslaw, tr. see Herbert, Zbigniew.
Milosz, Czeslaw, tr. see Swir, Anna.
Milosz, O. V. Amorous Initiation: A Novel of Sacred & Profane Love. LC 93-30584. 256p. 1993. 22.95 (*0-89281-418-7*) Inner Tradit.
Milosz, O. V. De L, see De L. Milosz, O. V.
Milosz, Oscar V. De Lubicz, see De Lubicz Milosz, Oscar V.
Milot, Jean-Rene. Muslims & Christians: Enemies or Brothers? Noble, Mary T., tr. from FRE. LC 96-36972.Tr. of Musulmans & Chretiens: Des Freres Ennemis?. 88p. (Orig.). 1997. mass mkt. 4.95 (*0-8189-0779-7*) Alba.
Milotte, Mike. Banished Babies: The Secret History of Ireland's Baby Export Business. LC 97-162328. 224p. 1998. pap. 14.95 (*1-874597-53-7*, Pub. by New Island Books) Dufour.
Milovanov, E. L. English-Russian Dictionary of Environmental Control. (ENG & RUS.). 338p. 1981. write for info. (*0-8288-1401-5*, M15790) Fr & Eur.
Milovanovic, Dragan. Postmodern Criminology. LC 97-10779. (Current Issues in Criminal Justice Ser.: No. 22). (Illus.). 288p. 1997. text 55.00 (*0-8153-2456-1*) Garland.
— Postmodern Law & Disorder: Psychoanalytic Semiotics, Chaos & Juridic Exegeses. (Legal Semiotics Monographs Ser.: Vol. 3). 280p. 1992. 72.00 (*0-9513793-3-X*) Gaunt.
— A Primer in Sociology of Law. 2nd rev. ed. LC 94-26536. (Illus.). 214p. (C). 1994. pap. text 27.50 (*0-911577-27-0*, Criminal Justice) Willow Tree NY.
Milovanovic, Dragan, ed. Chaos, Criminology, & Social Justice: The New Orderly (Dis) Order. LC 96-37114. 240p. 1997. pap. 25.95 (*0-275-95912-0*, Praeger Pubs) Greenwood.
— Chaos, Criminology & Social Justice: The New Orderly (Dis)Order. LC 96-37114. (Praeger Series in Criminology & Crime Control Policy). 240p. 1997. 65.00 (*0-275-95707-1*, Praeger Pubs) Greenwood.
Milovanovic, Dragan, jt. ed. see Henry, Stuart.
Milovanovic, Dragan, jt. ed. see Janikowski, W. Richard.
Milovanovic, G. V., ed. Recent Progress in Inequalities. LC 97-41582. (Mathematics & Its Applications Ser.). 519p. 1998. lib. bdg. write for info. (*0-7923-4845-1*, D Reidel) Kluwer Academic.
Milovanovic, G. V., et al. Topics in Polynomials: Extremal Problems, Inequalities, Zeros. 300p. 1994. text 146.00 (*981-02-0499-X*) World Scientific Pub.
Milovanovic, R. & Elzer, P. F., eds. Experience with the Management of Software Projects, 1988. LC 89-26462. (IFAC Publication: No. 90). (Illus.). 108p. 1989. 47.00 (*0-08-036928-6*, Pergamon Pr) Elsevier.
Milovic, D. Stresses & Displacements for Shallow Foundations. LC 92-10556. (Developments in Geotechnical Engineering Ser.: Vol. 70). 620p. 1992. 255.00 (*0-444-88349-5*) Elsevier.
Milovidov, Petr F. Physik und Chemie des Zellkerns. (Handbuch der Pflanzenanatomie Encyclopedia of Plant Anatomy - Traite d' Anatomie Vegetale Ser.: Teils 1 & 2). (Illus.). xiv, 529p. 1949. 103.00 (*3-443-39017-X*, Pub. by Gebruder Borntraeger) Balogh.
— Physik und Chemie des Zellkerns. (Handbuch der Pflanzenanatomie Encyclopedia of Plant Anatomy - Traite d' Anatomie Vegetale Ser.: Teils 1 & 2). (Illus.). viii, 479p. 1954. 103.00 (*3-443-39018-8*, Pub. by Gebruder Borntraeger) Balogh.
Milovksy, A. Ancient Russian Cities. (Illus.). 226p. (C). 1986. 60.00 (*0-7855-5208-1*, Pub. by Collets) St Mut.
Milovskii, A. Pure Spring: Craft & Craftsmen of the U. S. S. R. 256p. (C). 1987. text 110.00 (*0-7855-5871-3*, Pub. by Collets) St Mut.
Milrod, Barbara, et al. Manual of Panic-Focused Psychodynamic Psychotherapy. 128p. 1997. text 29.00 (*0-88048-871-9*, 8871) Am Psychiatric.
Milroy, Elizabeth. Guide to the Thomas Eakins Research Collection with a Lifetime Exhibition Record & Bibliography. 56p. Date not set. pap. 8.00 (*0-87633-094-4*) Phila Mus Art.
Milroy, Elizabeth, ed. Role-Play: A Practical Guide. (Illus.). 150p. 1982. text 22.00 (*0-08-025744-5*, R130, Pergamon Pr); pap. text 17.90 (*0-08-025745-3*, R132, Pergamon Pr) Elsevier.
— World Literature On: Prazosin: An Evaluation of Its Clinical Efficacy & Safety in the Treatment of Benign Prostatic Hypertrophy. (Journal: Urologia Internationalis: Vol. 45, Suppl. 1, 1990). (Illus.). iv, 64p. 1990. pap. 29.75 (*3-8055-5181-9*) S Karger.
Milroy, Elizabeth & Owens, Gwendolyn. Painters of a New Century: The Eight & American Art. (Illus.). 256p. 1991. pap. 29.95 (*0-944110-08-8*) Milwauk Art Mus.
Milroy, Elizabeth, jt. auth. see Doezema, Marianne.
Milroy, James & Milroy, Lesley. Authority in Language: Investigating Standard English. 3rd ed. LC 98-21927. 1998. 85.00 (*0-415-17412-0*); pap. 20.99 (*0-415-17413-9*) Routledge.
Milroy, James & Milroy, Lesley, eds. Real English: The Grammar of English Dialects in the British Isles. LC 92-42275. (Real Language Ser.). 1993. pap. text. write for info. (*0-582-08176-9*) Longman.
— Real English: The Grammar of English Dialects in the British Isles. LC 92-42775. (Real Language Ser.). 1993. write for info. (*0-582-08177-7*) Longman.
Milroy, Lesley, jt. auth. see Milroy, James.
Milroy, Lesley, jt. ed. see Milroy, James.
Milroy, M. E. Guide to Lace-Making. 70p. 1985. reprint ed. pap. 6.00 (*1-56659-012-4*) Robin & Russ.
Milroy, Steven J., jt. auth. see Miller, Fred.
Milroy, Wallace. The Malt Whisky Almanac. 6th rev. ed. (Illus.). 160p. 1996. 14.95 (*1-897784-26-0*, Pub. by N Wilson Pubng) Interlink Pub.
— The Original Malt Whisky Almanac: A Taster's Guide. 1998. pap. 15.00 (*1-897784-68-6*, Pub. by N Wilson Pubng) Interlink Pub.
Milsavijevich, Helen. Simple to Sew: Appliques. 1996. 7.98 (*0-7858-0361-0*) Bk Sales Inc.
Mil'Shteyn, Y. I., ed. see Scriabin, Alexander.
Milsom, C. H. Guide to the Merchant Navy. (C). 1987. 36.00 (*0-85174-037-5*) St Mut.
Milsom, J. W., jt. ed. see Michelassi, F.
Milsom, Jeffrey W. & Bohm, Bartholomaus. Laparoscopic Colorectal Surgery. LC 95-16248. (Illus.). 304p. 1995. 129.00 (*0-387-94470-2*) Spr-Verlag.
Milsom, Jeffrey W., et al. Endoscopic & Laparoscopic Ultrasonography for Surgeons: Colon, Rectum & Anus. LC 96-52546. 1997. write for info. (*4-260-14338-7*) Igaku-Shoin.
Milsom, John. Field Geophysics. LC 96-15928. (Geological Society of London Professional Handbook Ser.). 198p. 1996. pap. 44.95 (*0-471-96634-7*) Wiley.
Milsom, S. F. The Legal Framework of English Feudalism. LC 85-82332. (Cambridge Studies in English Legal History). 212p. 1986. reprint ed. 55.00 (*0-912004-58-4*) Gaunt.
— Studies in the History of the Common Law. 368p. 1985. 60.00 (*0-907628-61-3*) Hambledon Press.
Milsom, Stroud. The Legal Framework of English Feudalism: The Maitland Lectures Given in 1972. LC 75-2351. (Cambridge Studies in English Legal History). 212p. reprint ed. pap. 60.50 (*0-608-15754-6*, 2031693) Bks Demand.
Milsome, John. From Slave Boy to Bishop. (Faith & Fame Ser.). (J). 1997. mass mkt. 3.95 (*0-87508-600-4*) Chr Lit.
— Heroine of Newgate: Elizabeth Fry. (J). 1982. pap. 3.95 (*0-87508-633-0*) Chr Lit.
Milsome, John, jt. auth. see Damien of Molokai.
Milson, Fred. An Introduction to Community Work. 168p. 1974. 15.95 (*0-7100-7840-4*, Routledge Thoemms); pap. 15.95 (*0-7100-7841-2*, Routledge Thoemms) Routledge.
Milson, Fred, jt. auth. see Holloway, David.
Milson, Fred, jt. auth. see Lawrence, Mike.
Milson, John, selected by. A Byrd Anthology: 14 Anthems & Motets. 120p. 1996. pap. 12.95 (*0-19-352007-9*) OUP.
Milson, Menahem. A Sufi Rule for Novices: Kiteab Eadeab Al-Mureidein of Abeu Al-Najeib Al-Suhrawardei. abr. ed. LC 74-27750. (Harvard Middle Eastern Studies: No. 17). 104p. reprint ed. pap. 32.30 (*0-7837-4436-6*, 205796500012) Bks Demand.
Milstead, Jeri A. Health Policy & Politics: A Nurse's Guide. LC 98-37498. 300p. 1999. 44.00 (*0-8342-1055-X*, 1055X) Aspen Pub.
Milstead, Jessica L. ASIS Thesaurus of Information Science & Librarianship. 150p. 1994. pap. 34.95 (*0-938734-80-6*) Info Today Inc.
— Subject Access Systems. 1984. text 70.00 (*0-12-498120-8*) Acad Pr.
Milstead, Jessica L. & American Society for Information Science Staff. ASIS Thesaurus of Information Science & Librarianship. 2nd ed. LC 97-48723. (Asis Monographs). 1998. pap. 39.95 (*1-57387-050-1*) Info Today Inc.
Milstead, Jessica L. & Pajer, Beverly A. Index to the Inventory of Records of the American Jewish Committee, 1906-80. LC 94-34400. 1994. write for info. (*0-87495-107-0*) Am Jewish Comm.
Milstead, Jessica L., jt. auth. see Hodge, Gail M.
Milstead, John W., et al, eds. Social Problems Through Science Fiction. LC 73-92058. 384p. (Orig.). (C). 1975. pap. text 9.00 (*0-312-73465-4*) St Martin.
***Milsted, David.** The Bluffer's Guide to Whiskey: Bluff Your Way in Whiskey. (Bluffer's Guides Ser.). 64p. 2000. pap. 5.95 (*1-902825-15-2*) Oval Bks.
— Cassell Dictionary of Regrettable Quotations. 1999. pap. 14.95 (*0-304-35213-6*) Continuum.
Milsted, David, jt. auth. see Miall, Antony.
Milstein, G. N. Numerical Integration of Stochastic Differential Equations. (Mathematics & Its Applications Ser.: Vol. 313). 169p. (C). 1994. text 115.00 (*0-7923-3213-X*) Kluwer Academic.
Milstein, Herbert E. Attorney-Client Privilege & Work-Product Doctrine: Corporate Applications. 2nd ed. (Corporate Practice Ser.: No. 22). 1994. ring bd. 95.00 (*1-55871-303-4*) BNA.
***Milstein, Janet B.** The Ultimate Audition Book for Teens: 111 One-Minute Monologues. LC 00-35864. (Young Actors Ser.). (Illus.). (YA). 2000. pap. write for info. (*1-57525-236-8*) Smith & Kraus.
Milstein, Jeff, jt. auth. see Walker, Lester.
Milstein, Linda B. Living in the Aftermath. Warren, Shirley, ed. 36p. 1995. pap. 5.50 (*1-877801-27-5*) Still Waters.
Milstein, Michael. Badlands, Teddy Roosevelt & Wind Cave National Parks. LC 96-11587. (Wildlife Watchers Guide Ser.). (Illus.). 96p. (Orig.). 1996. pap. 11.95 (*1-55971-575-8*, NorthWord Pr) Creat Pub Intl.
— Wolf: Return to Yellowstone. (Illus.). 96p. (Orig.). 1995. pap. 14.95 (*0-9627618-8-5*) Billings Gazette.
— Yellowstone: Celebrating 125 Years of America's Best Idea. (Illus.). 112p. 1997. 17.95 (*1-56037-110-2*) Am Wrld Geog.
— Yellowstone National Park: 125th Anniversary. Wesnick, Richard, ed. LC 96-78550. (Illus.). 112p. 1996. pap. 19.95 (*0-9627618-9-3*) Billings Gazette.
Milstein, Michael, et al. Internship Programs in Educational Administration: A Guide to Preparing Educational Leaders. 176p. (C). 1991. pap. text 19.95 (*0-8077-3079-3*) Tchrs Coll.
Milstein, Mike M. Changing the Way We Prepare Educational Leaders: The Danforth Experience. LC 93-22350. 264p. 1993. 65.95 (*0-8039-6077-8*); pap. 29.95 (*0-8039-6078-6*) Corwin Pr.
— Restructuring Schools: Doing It Right. Herman, Jerry J. & Herman, Janice L., eds. LC 93-17872. (Road Maps to Success Ser.). 80p. (C). 1993. pap. 14.95 (*0-8039-6072-7*) Corwin Pr.
Milstein, Mike M., ed. Schools, Conflict, & Change. LC 79-20327. 320p. reprint ed. pap. 99.20 (*0-608-15810-0*, 203120500074) Bks Demand.
Milstein, Mike M. & Jennings, Robert E. Educational Policy-Making & the State Legislature: The New York Experience. LC 78-185780. (Special Studies in U. S. Economic, Social & Political Issues). 1973. 42.00 (*0-275-28719-X*) Irvington.
Milstein, Mike M., jt. auth. see Henderson, Nan.
Milstein, N. Three Transcriptions: Violin/Piano Great Performers Edition. 1986. pap. 7.50 (*0-7935-5463-2*, 50333740) H Leonard.
Milstein, Rachel. Miniature Painting in Ottoman Baghdad. (Islamic Art & Architecture Ser.: No. 5). (Illus.). 268p. (C). 1989. text 55.00 (*0-939214-60-1*) Mazda Pubs.
Milstein, Rachel, et al. Stories of the Prophets: Illustrated Manuscripts of Qisas al-Anbiya. LC 98-27204. (Islamic Art & Architecture Ser.: Vol. 8). (Illus.). 256p. 1998. lib. bdg. 69.00 (*1-56859-064-4*) Mazda Pubs.
Milstein, Stanley, tr. from GER. Jacques Joseph's Rhinoplasty & Facial Plastic Surgery with a Supplement on Mammaplasty. limited ed.Tr. of Nasenplastik und Sonstige Gesichtsplastik nebst Mammaplastik. (Illus.). 855p. 1987. 395.00 (*0-9605972-1-2*) Columella Pr.
Milstein, Stanley, tr. see Politzer, Adam.
Milstein, Stuart, ed. The Tenth Muse. 64p. 1973. write for info. (*0-318-64147-X*) Poets Pr.
Milstein, Stuart, jt. auth. see Grim Reaper Books Staff.
Milstein, Uri. History of Israel's War of Independence Vol. 2: The First Month. Sacks, Alan, ed. & tr. by. 384p. 1997. 57.50 (*0-7618-0721-7*) U Pr of Amer.
— History of Israel's War of Independence Vol. III: The First Invasion. Sacks, Alan, ed. & tr. by. from HEB. 420p. (C). 1998. 62.00 (*0-7618-0769-1*) U Pr of Amer.
***Milstein, Uri.** History of Israel's War of Independence Vol. IV: Out of Crisis Came Decision. Sacks, Alan, ed. & tr. by. from HEB. 440p. 1999. 64.00 (*0-7618-1489-2*) U Pr of Amer.
Milstein, Uri. History of the War of Independence Vol. 1: A Nation Girds for War. Sacks, Alan, ed. & tr. by. LC 96-17163. 484p. 1996. lib. bdg. 64.00 (*0-7618-0372-6*) U Pr of Amer.
— The Rabin File: An Unauthorized Expose' LC 98-7093. 472p. 1998. 34.95 (*965-229-196-X*) Gefen Bks.
Milsten, David R. Will Rogers: An Appreciation. 1976. lib. bdg. 59.95 (*0-8490-2826-4*) Gordon Pr.
***Milsten, David Randolph.** Will Rogers: The Cherokee Kid. (Illus.). 182p. 2000. pap. 15.95 (*0-9673131-3-9*) HAWK Pubng Grp.
***Milsten, Richard.** Sexual Male: Problems & Solutions. 2000. pap. 14.95 (*0-393-32127-4*) Norton.
Milsten, Richard & Slowinski, Julian. The Sexual Male: Problems & Solutions. LC 99-17523. 296p. 1999. text 25.95 (*0-393-04740-7*) Norton.
Milt, Harry, jt. auth. see Custer, Robert L.
Miltal, Al. Marilyn Had Hands Full of Eyes. (Orig.). 1989. pap. 5.00 (*0-941720-66-7*) Slough Pr TX.
Miltenberger. Behavior Modification: Principles & Procedures. 2nd ed. (Psychology Ser.). 2000. pap. 48.00 (*0-534-36599-X*) Brooks-Cole.
Miltenberger, Raymond G. Behavior Modification: Principles & Procedures. LC 96-17212. (Psychology Ser.). (Illus.). 600p. (C). 1996. mass mkt. 67.95 (*0-534-21012-0*) Brooks-Cole.
— Behavior Modification: Principles & Procedures. 1996. mass mkt., teacher ed. write for info. (*0-534-34493-3*) Brooks-Cole.
Miltenburg, Hans Van, see Van der Hoek, Peter & Van Miltenburg, Hans, eds.
Miltenburg, John. Manufacturing Strategy: How to Formulate & Implement a Winning Plan. (Illus.). 392p. 1995. 45.00 (*1-56327-071-4*) Productivity Inc.

An Asterisk (*) at the beginning of an entry indicates that the title is appearing for the first time.

Miltenyi, Karoly, et al, eds. Population & Population Policy in Hungary. 231p. (C). 1984. 42.00 (*963-05-3870-9*, Pub. by Akade Kiado) St Mut.

Milter, Matt & Wilson, Sarah. Sleepytime Farm: A Move-along-Bead Book. (Fisher-Price Move-Along Bead Bks.: Vol. 1). (Illus.). 12p. (J). (ps-3). 1999. bds. 6.99 (*1-57584-258-0*, Pub. by Rdrs Digest) Random.

Milter, Richard G., et al. Educational Innovation in Economics & Business III. LC 98-5119. 352p. 1998. 108.00 (*0-7923-5001-4*) Kluwer Academic.

Milthorpe, Frederick L., ed. see Easter School in Agricultural Science (3rd: 1956:.

Miltner, Robert. Against the Simple. LC 94-33223. (Wick Poetry Chapbook Ser.: No. 6). 24p. (Orig.). 1995. pap. 4.75 (*0-87338-521-7*) Kent St U Pr.

— The Seamless Serial Hour. 27p. 1993. pap. 7.95 (*0-944754-17-1*) Pudding Hse Pubns.

Miltner, W., jt. auth. see Fichter, M.

Milton. Linear Statistical Models. 2nd ed. 1998. pap. 53.44 (*0-07-232708-1*) McGraw.

***Milton.** The Process of Professional Financial Planning. 2001. pap. 30.00 (*0-324-02030-9*) Sth-Wstrn College.

— The Process of Professional Financial Planning. 2001. pap. 55.00 (*0-324-02029-5*) Thomson Learn.

Milton, Pat. In the Blink of an Eye: The FBI Investigation of TWA Flight 800. LC 99-25359. 1999. 26.95 (*0-375-50086-3*) Random House.

Milton, A. S., ed. Pyretics & Antipyretics. (Handbook of Experimental Pharmacology Ser.: Vol. 60). 715p. 1982. 392.00 (*0-387-11511-0*) Spr-Verlag.

— Temperature Regulation: Recent Physiological & Pharmacological Advances. LC 93-50550. (Advances in Pharmacological Sciences Ser.). xii, 376p. 1994. 119.50 (*0-8176-2992-0*) Birkhauser.

Milton, Adrian. Lavender Light: Daily Meditations for Gay Men in Recovery. LC 94-32616. 1995. pap. 10.00 (*0-399-51939-4*) Berkley Pub.

***Milton, Andrew K.** The Rational Politician: Exploiting the Media in New Democracies. 212p. 2000. text 61.95 (*0-7546-1170-1*, Pub. by Ashgate Pub) Ashgate Pub Co.

Milton, Ann. Ask Me If I'm a Frog. LC 98-19485. (Curious Little Critters Ser.). (Illus.). 40p. (J). (ps-5). 1998. 16.95 (*0-88045-140-8*, Intl Design); pap. 8.95 (*0-88045-143-2*, Intl Design) Stemmer Hse.

Milton, Anthony. Catholic & Reformed: The Roman & Protestant Churches in English Protestant Thought, 1600-1640. (Cambridge Studies in Early Modern British History). 617p. (C). 1995. text 90.00 (*0-521-40141-0*) Cambridge U Pr.

Milton, Arthur. How Your Life Insurance Policies Rob You. LC 81-4679. 178p. (Orig.). 1990. pap. 8.95 (*0-8065-1176-1*, Citadel Pr) Carol Pub Group.

— Will Inflation Destroy America? 1977. 7.95 (*0-8065-0608-3*, Citadel Pr) Carol Pub Group.

— You Are Worth a Fortune. 1977. 6.95 (*0-8065-0589-3*, Citadel Pr) Carol Pub Group.

Milton, Bev. My Baptism. (Illus.). 24p. 1998. pap. 23.95 (*1-55145-296-0*, Pub. by Wood Lake Bks) Logos Prods.

Milton, Brian, intro. MECH '91 Australia: Engineering in a Competitive World, Conference 4: Energy: Resources, Usage, Conservation & the Environment. (Illus.). 163p. 1991. pap. 48.00 (*0-85825-528-6*, Pub. by Inst Engrs Aust-EA Bks) Accents Pubns.

Milton, Colin. Lawrence & Nietzsche: A Study in Influence. 264p. 1987. text 37.90 (*0-08-035067-4*, Pub. by Aberdeen U Pr) Macmillan.

Milton, Corinne H. Corona: Bullfighter & Artist. LC 87-33677. (Illus.). 64p. (Orig.). 1988. pap. 16.95 (*0-86534-119-2*) Sunstone Pr.

Milton, David. Conspiracy of Mirrors. 1992. mass mkt. 4.99 (*1-55817-564-4*, Pinncle Kensgtn) Kensgtn Pub Corp.

— Hyte Maneuver: What It Is, How to Prevent It, How to Stop It. 1989. mass mkt. 3.95 (*1-55817-178-9*, Pinncle Kensgtn) Kensgtn Pub Corp.

— The Politics of U. S. Labor: From the Great Depression to the New Deal. LC 80-8934. 189p. reprint ed. pap. 58.60 (*0-7837-3915-X*, 204376300010) Bks Demand.

***Milton, David.** Using Quicken Deluxe 99 for Windows. 2nd ed. LC 99-28526. 500p. 1999. pap. 37.95 (*0-324-01712-X*) Sth-Wstrn College.

Milton, David, ed. see Bywater, Murray A.

Milton, Deborah. Angel, Mine. 232p. 1998. pap. 16.95 (*1-892745-00-3*) Petals of Life.

Milton, Doris & Benjamin, Samuel G. Complementary & Alternative Therapies: An Implementation Guide to Integrative Health Care. LC 98-45876. xii, 172p. 1999. 35.00 (*1-55648-252-3*) AHPI.

Milton, Earl R., ed. Recollections of a Fallen Sky: Velikovsky & Cultural Amnesia. 176p. 1992. pap. 12.00 (*0-940268-28-0*) Metron Pubns.

Milton, Earl R., jt. auth. see De Grazia, Alfred.

***Milton-Edwards, Beverly.** Contemporary Politics in the Middle East. LC 99-35259. 256p. 2000. text 59.95 (*0-7456-1471-X*, Pub. by Polity Pr); pap. text 26.95 (*0-7456-1472-8*, Pub. by Polity Pr) Blackwell Pubs.

Milton-Edwards, Beverly. Islamic Politics in Palestine. 256p. 1996. text 65.00 (*1-86064-049-4*, Pub. by I B T) St Martin.

— Islamic Politics in Palestine. 1999. 22.50 (*1-86064-475-9*) IBTS.

Milton, Elizabeth. Sarah: A Friend for the Journey. 160p. 1997. pap. 5.95 (*0-9637311-7-3*) Genesis Comm Inc.

Milton, Erma L. Such Is Life. LC 94-61297. 67p. (Orig.). 1996. pap. text 10.95 (*0-9614788-4-5*, 444A) Tivoli Pub.

— Such Is Life. 56p. (Orig.). 1998. reprint ed. pap. 9.95 (*1-890622-23-0*) Leathers Pub.

Milton, Francis. A Trilogy of Sonnets. 64p. (Orig.). 1993. pap. 2.95 (*0-931888-46-8*) Christendom Pr.

Milton, George F. Age of Hate: Andrew Johnson & the Radicals. (History - United States Ser.). 787p. 1992. reprint ed. lib. bdg. 199.00 (*0-7812-6205-4*) Rprt Serv.

***Milton, Giles.** Big Chief Elizabeth: How England's Adventurers Wooed the Native Tribes of America & Won the New World. (Illus.). 352p. 2000. 24.00 (*0-374-26501-1*) FS&G.

— Nathaniel's Nutmeg: Or, the True & Incredible Adventures of the Spice Trader Who Changed the Course of History. (Illus.). 400p. 2000. pap. 13.95 (*0-14-029260-8*) Penguin Putnam.

Milton, Giles. The Riddle & the Knight: In Search of Sir John Mandeville. 240p. 1998. pap. write for info. (*0-7490-0395-2*) Allison & Busby.

Milton, Gladys. Why Not Me? The Story of Gladys Milton, Midwife. LC 92-38694. (Illus.). 128p. 1993. 9.95 (*0-913990-97-3*) Book Pub Co.

Milton, Graeme, jt. ed. see Kohn, Robert.

Milton, Hal. Going Public: A Practical Guide to Developing Personal Charisma. 150p. (Orig.). 1995. pap. 9.95 (*1-55874-360-X*, 360X) Health Comm.

Milton, Hilary. The Gitaway Box, 1. 1999. pap. text 11.95 (*1-57966-009-6*, Black Belt) Black Belt Communs.

***Milton, Hilary.** Legend of Dornar Caule: A Fable for the Modern Age. 1999. 15.95 (*1-57359-023-1*, Starrhill Press) Black Belt Communs.

Milton, Howard. Packaging Design. (Issues in Design Ser.). (Illus.). 104p. (C). 1991. pap. 29.95 (*0-85072-280-2*, Pub. by Design Council Bks) Ashgate Pub Co.

Milton, Isabel. Reinventing Hospitals: Embracing the Future of Health Care in North America. 257p. 1998. pap. text 18.50 (*0-919292-03-8*, Pub. by McLeod Pub) Genl Dist Srvs.

Milton, J. Dynamical Disease: Mathematical Analysis of Human Illness. 1995. pap. 44.95 (*1-56396-370-1*, AIP Pr) Spr-Verlag.

Milton, J. R. Common Law Crimes Vol. II: South African Criminal Law & Procedure. 3rd ed. lxxvii, 849p. 1997. 129.00 (*0-7021-3773-1*, Pub. by Juta & Co) Gaunt.

— South African Criminal Law & Procedure: Common Law Crimes, Vol. II. 2nd rev. ed. 965p. 1990. write for info. (*0-7021-2378-1*, Pub. by Juta & Co) Gaunt.

Milton, J. R., ed. Locke's Moral, Political & Legal Philosophy. (International Library of Critical Essays in the History of Philosophy). 540p. 1999. text 166.95 (*1-84014-413-0*, Pub. by Ashgate Pub) Ashgate Pub Co.

Milton, J. R. & Burchell, J. M. Cases & Materials on Criminal Law. 752p. 1992. 45.00 (*0-7021-2846-5*, Pub. by Juta & Co) Gaunt.

Milton, J. R. & Cowling, M. South African Criminal Law & Procedure: Statutory Offences, Vol. III. 2nd ed. 1988. ring bd. write for info. (*0-7021-2036-7*, Pub. by Juta & Co) Gaunt.

Milton, J. R., jt. auth. see Burchell, J. M.

Milton, J. Susan. Statistical Methods in the Biological & Health Sciences. 2nd ed. (C). 1991. text 63.74 (*0-07-042506-X*) McGraw.

Milton, J. Susan & Arnold, Jesse C. Introduction to Probability & Statistics: Principles & Applications for Engineering & the Computing Sciences. 3rd ed. LC 94-31189. 736p. (C). 1994. 86.88 (*0-07-042623-6*) McGraw.

Milton, J. Susan, et al. Introduction to Statistics. (C). 1996. pap. text, student ed. 32.19 (*0-07-042529-9*) McGraw.

Milton, J. Susan, jt. auth. see Myers, Raymond H.

***Milton, Jane.** Practical Encyclopedia of Mexican Cooking. (Illus.). 2000. 35.00 (*0-7548-0500-X*, Lorenz Bks) Anness Pub.

Milton, Jeremy D., jt. ed. see Rhodes, Jonathan M.

Milton, John. Areopagitica. Jebb, Richard C., ed. LC 72-170811. reprint ed. 22.50 (*0-404-03556-6*) AMS Pr.

— Areopagitica. 80p. 1972. reprint ed. 15.00 (*0-87556-219-1*) Saifer.

— Areopagitica: Freedom of the Press. rev. ed. Ash, A. S., ed. LC 86-64056. (Humanist Classics Ser.). 48p. 1990. pap. 6.95 (*0-942208-04-8*) Bandanna Bks.

— Areopagitica & of Education. Sabine, George H., ed. (Crofts Classics). 128p. 1951. pap. text 4.95 (*0-88295-057-6*) Harlan Davidson.

— Areopagitica & Other Political Writings of John Milton. LC 97-46853. 1998. 20.00 (*0-86597-196-X*); pap. 12.00 (*0-86597-197-8*) Liberty Fund.

— Complete English Poems. 4th ed. Campbell, Gordon, ed. 412p. 1993. pap. 12.95 (*0-460-87275-3*, Everyman's Classic Lib) Tuttle Pubng.

— The Complete Poems. LC 92-52905. 1992. 20.00 (*0-679-40997-1*) Everymns Lib.

— The Complete Poems. Leonard, John, ed. & pref. by. LC 99-216769. 976p. 1999. pap. 15.95 (*0-14-043363-5*) Penguin Putnam.

— Complete Poems & Major Prose: Milton. Hughes, Merritt Y., ed. 1059p. (C). 1957. 105.00 (*0-02-358290-1*, Macmillan Coll) P-H.

— Complete Poetical Works. Bush, Douglas, ed. LC 65-2686. (Cambridge Editions Ser.). 1965. pap. 8.95 (*0-395-07493-2*) HM.

— The Complete Poetry of John Milton. Shawcross, John T., ed. LC 72-150934. 672p. 1971. reprint ed. pap. 15.95 (*0-385-02351-0*, Anchor NY) Doubleday.

— The Complete Prose Works of John Milton, 8 vols. Fogle, French & Patrick, J. Max, eds. Incl. History of Britain & the Miltonic State Papers., 2 pts. 928p. 1971. 125.00 (*0-300-01288-8*); write for info. (*0-318-56513-7*) Yale U Pr.

— The Complete Prose Works of John Milton, Vol. 7. rev. ed. Wolfe, Don M., ed. LC 52-5371. 563p. reprint ed. pap. 174.60 (*0-608-07835-2*, 205401100007) Bks Demand.

— Dynamics of Small Neural Populations. LC 96-6762. (CRM Monograph Ser.: No. 7). 125p. 1996. text 35.00 (*0-8218-0458-8*, CRMM/7) Am Math.

— John Milton. Orgel, Stephen & Goldberg, Jonathan, eds. (Oxford Authors Ser.). (Illus.). 998p. 1991. pap. text 19.95 (*0-19-281379-X*) OUP.

— John Milton's Complete Poetical Works: Reproduced in Photographic Facsimile. Fletcher, Harris F., ed. LC 44-1984. 461p. reprint ed. pap. 143.00 (*0-608-13930-0*, 202021100016) Bks Demand.

— The Latin Poems of John Milton. (BCL1-PR English Literature Ser.). 382p. 1992. reprint ed. lib. bdg. 89.00 (*0-7812-7377-3*) Rprt Serv.

— Latin Writings: A Selection. Hale, John K., ed. & tr. by. LC 98-52891. (Medieval & Renaissance Texts & Studies: No. 191). (ENG & LAT.). 264p. 1998. 26.00 (*0-86698-233-7*, MR191) MRTS.

— A Maske: The Earlier Versions. Sprott, S. E., ed. LC 72-97784. 236p. reprint ed. pap. 73.20 (*0-608-16710-X*, 202638500049) Bks Demand.

— Milton: Paradise Lost. 2nd ed. Fowler, Alastair, ed. LC 97-51835. (Annotated English Poets Ser.). 704p. (C). 1998. pap. 39.06 (*0-582-21518-8*) Addison-Wesley.

— Milton: Poems. 1996. 12.50 (*0-679-45099-8*) McKay.

— Milton on Education. Ainsworth, Oliver M., ed. & intro. by. LC 75-112640. 22.5p. reprint ed. 49.50 (*0-404-00298-6*) AMS Pr.

— Milton on Education: The Tractate of Education with Supplementary Extracts from Other Writings of Milton. Ainsworth, Oliver M., ed. LC 70-145185. 1971. reprint ed. 18.00 (*0-403-01110-8*) Scholarly.

— Milton on Education: The Tractatte of Education. (BCL1-PR English Literature Ser.). 369p. 1992. reprint ed. lib. bdg. 89.00 (*0-7812-7378-1*) Rprt Serv.

— Milton Poetical Works. (Poetry Library). 496p. 1998. pap. 7.95 (*1-85326-410-5*, 4105WW, Pub. by Wrdsworth Edits) NTC Contemp Pub Co.

— Milton's Dramatic Poems. 6th rev. ed. Bullough, Geoffrey & Bullough, Margaret, eds. LC 85-3986. 224p. (C). 1958. pap. 8.95 (*0-485-61009-4*, Pub. by Athlone Pr) Humanities.

— Odes, Pastorals, Masques. Broadbent, John et al, eds. LC 73-94355. (Milton for Schools & Colleges Ser.). 252p. 1975. pap. text 26.95 (*0-521-20456-9*) Cambridge U Pr.

— Paradise Lost. 1998. pap. text 14.95 (*1-55701-231-8*) BNI Pubns.

***Milton, John.** Paradise Lost, Vol. 1. 1999. pap. 4.95 (*0-7910-4146-8*) Chehalem.

Milton, John. Paradise Lost. Flannagan, Roy, ed. LC 92-5970. (Illus.). 686p. (C). 1992. pap. 39.60 (*0-02-338235-X*, Macmillan Coll) P-H.

***Milton, John.** Paradise Lost. (Penguin Classics Ser.). 375p. 2000. pap. 10.00 (*0-14-042426-1*, Penguin Bks) Viking Penguin.

Milton, John. Paradise Lost. large type ed. 1997. pap. 19.95 (*1-55701-220-2*) BNI Pubns.

— Paradise Lost. 395p. 1983. reprint ed. lib. bdg. 29.95 (*0-89966-457-1*) Buccaneer Bks.

— Paradise Lost. Bentley, Richard, ed. (Anglistica & Americana Ser.: Vol. 175). 415p. 1976. reprint ed. lib. bdg. 115.00 (*3-487-06053-1*) G Olms Pubs.

— Paradise Lost. 2nd ed. Fowler, Alastair, ed. LC 97-51835. (English Poets Ser.). 704p. (C). 1998. 98.25 (*0-582-21519-6*) Longman.

— Paradise Lost, Bks. 1 & 2. Broadbent, John, ed. (Milton for Schools & Colleges Ser.). 160p. (gr. 11-12). 1972. pap. text 16.95 (*0-521-08298-6*) Cambridge U Pr.

— Paradise Lost, Bks. 3 & 4. Potter, L. J. & Broadbent, John, eds. LC 75-36681. (Milton for Schools & Colleges Ser.). 143p. 1976. pap. text 16.95 (*0-521-21150-6*) Cambridge U Pr.

— Paradise Lost, Bks. 5 & 6. Hodge, Robert & MacCaffrey, Isabel G., eds. LC 75-8314. (Milton for Schools & Colleges Ser.). (Illus.). 167p. (C). 1975. pap. text 16.95 (*0-521-20796-7*) Cambridge U Pr.

— Paradise Lost, Bks. 7 & 8. Aers, D. & Radzinowics, Mary Ann, eds. LC 77-181884. (Milton for Schools & Colleges Ser.). 154p. 1974. pap. text 16.95 (*0-521-20457-7*) Cambridge U Pr.

— Paradise Lost, Bks. 9 & 10. Houghton, R. E., ed. 244p. 1970. pap. text 8.95 (*0 19 911001 8*) OUP.

— Paradise Lost, Set. Evans, J. M., ed. LC 72-87438. (Milton for Schools & Colleges Ser.). 208p. (C). 1973. pap. text 16.95 (*0-521-20067-9*) Cambridge U Pr.

— Paradise Lost: A Prose Rendition. Shepherd, Robert, Jr., ed. (Illus.). 160p. 1984. 17.95 (*0-8164-0534-4*); 8.95 (*0-8164-2415-2*) Harper SF.

— Paradise Lost: An Authoritative Text, Backgrounds & Sources, Criticism. 2nd ed. Elledge, Scott, ed. LC 92-9988. (Critical Editions Ser.). 688p. (C). 1993. pap. text 14.00 (*0-393-96293-8*) Norton.

— Paradise Lost: Modern Library College Editions. Madsen, William G., ed. 344p. (C). 1969. pap. 8.44 (*0-07-553668-4*, 30997) McGraw.

— Paradise Lost & Other Poems. 1981. 12.09 (*0-606-03885-X*, Pub. by Turtleback) Demco.

— Paradise Lost & Paradise Regained. Ricks, Christopher B., ed. & intro. by. (Signet Classics Ser.). 399p. 1975. mass mkt. 7.95 (*0-451-52474-8*, Sig Classics) NAL.

— Poems: The 1645 Edition. LC 68-24444. 369p. 1968. reprint ed. 75.00 (*0-87752-075-5*) Gordian.

— Poems in English, 2 vols., Set. LC 27-273. (Illus.). 1968. reprint ed. 79.00 (*0-403-00349-0*) Scholarly.

— Poems in English, with Illustrations by William Blake, 2 vols., Set. (BCL1-PR English Literature Ser.). (Illus.). 1992. reprint ed. lib. bdg. 150.00 (*0-7812-7375-7*) Rprt Serv.

— The Poetical Works Vol. 1: Paradise Lost, Vol. 1. Darbishire, Helen, ed. 364p. 1953. text 75.00 (*0-19-811819-8*) OUP.

— The Poetical Works of John Milton, 6 vols. Brydges, Egerton, ed. LC 75-172735. (Illus.). reprint ed. 435.00 (*0-404-04380-1*) AMS Pr.

— The Poetical Works of John Milton - With Notes of Various Authors, 7 vols. (BCL1-PR English Literature Ser.). 1992. reprint ed. lib. bdg. 525.00 (*0-7812-7376-5*) Rprt Serv.

— Political Writings. Dzelainis, Martin, ed. Gruzelier, Claire, tr. (Cambridge Texts in the History of Political Thought Ser.). 304p. (C). 1991. pap. text 19.95 (*0-521-34866-8*) Cambridge U Pr.

— The Portable Milton. Bush, Douglas, ed. & intro. by. (Portable Library: No. 44). 704p. 1976. pap. 15.95 (*0-14-015044-7*, Penguin Bks) Viking Penguin.

***Milton, John.** The Riverside Milton. Flannagan, Roy, ed. LC 97-72469. 1276p. (C). 1998. text 46.36 (*0-395-80999-1*) HM.

Milton, John. Samson Agonistes. Prince, F. T., ed. 144p. 1970. pap. text 14.95 (*0-19-831910-X*) OUP.

— Samson Agonistes & Shorter Poems. Barker, A. E., ed. (Crofts Classics). 128p. 1950. pap. text 4.95 (*0-88295-058-4*) Harlan Davidson.

— Selected Poems. LC 92-29792. (Thrift Editions Ser.). 128p. 1993. reprint ed. pap. 1.50 (*0-486-27554-X*) Dover.

— Selected Poetry. 352p. 1998. pap. 9.95 (*0-19-283527-0*) OUP.

— Selected Prose. rev. ed. Patrides, C. A., ed. LC 85-1027. 464p. 1986. pap. text 14.95 (*0-8262-0484-8*) U of Mo Pr.

— Three Fantasies for Five Viols. Morey, Rita, ed. i, 27p. (Orig.). 1997. pap. text 15.00 (*1-56571-145-9*) PRB Prods.

Milton, John, jt. auth. see Burchell, Jonathan.

Milton, John, jt. auth. see Dore, Gustav.

Milton, John, tr. see Gadotti, Moacir.

Milton, John R. The Novel of the American West. LC 79-17713. 359p. 1980. reprint ed. pap. 111.30 (*0-608-02679-4*, 206333200004) Bks Demand.

— South Dakota: A History. 1989. pap. 9.95 (*0-393-30571-6*) Norton.

Milton, Joyce. Bats! Creatures of the Night. LC 92-43198. (All Aboard Reading Ser.: Level 2). (Illus.). 48p. (J). (gr. 1-3). 1993. pap. 3.95 (*0-448-40193-2*, G & D) Peng Put Young Read.

— Bats & Other Animals of the Night. (Pictureback Ser.). (Illus.). 32p. (Orig.). (J). (ps-2). 1994. pap. 3.25 (*0-679-86213-7*, Pub. by Random Bks Yng Read) Random.

— Bears Are Curious. LC 97-26757. (Step into Reading Ser.: A Step 1 Book). (Illus.). 32p. (J). (gr. k-3). 1998. pap. 3.99 (*0-679-85301-4*) Random.

— Bears Are Curious. LC 97-26757. (Step into Reading Ser.: A Step 1 Book). (Illus.). 32p. (J). (gr. k-3). 1998. lib. bdg. 11.99 (*0-679-95301-9*) Random.

— Big Cats. LC 94-7361. (All Aboard Reading Ser.: Level 2). (Illus.). 48p. (J). (gr. 1-3). 1994. pap. 3.95 (*0-448-40564-4*, G & D) Peng Put Young Read.

— Dinosaur Days. LC 84-17861. (Step into Reading Ser.: A Step 2 Book). (Illus.). 47p. (J). (gr. 1-3). 1985. pap. 3.99 (*0-394-87023-9*, Pub. by Random Bks Yng Read) Random.

— Dinosaur Days. (Step into Reading Ser.: A Step 2 Book). (J). (gr. 1-3). 1985. 9.19 (*0-606-12255-9*, Pub. by Turtleback) Demco.

— Don Quixote (Miguel de Cervantes) (Barron's Book Notes Ser.). (J). (gr. 9-12). 1985. pap. 3.95 (*0-8120-3512-7*) Barron.

***Milton, Joyce.** The First Partner: Hillary Rodham Clinton. 480p. 2000. pap. 14.00 (*0-688-17772-7*, Perennial) HarperTrade.

— The First Partner--hillary Rodham Clinton: A Biography. LC 99-12610. 448p. 1999. 27.00 (*0-688-15501-4*, Wm Morrow) Morrow Avon.

Milton, Joyce. Gorillas: Gentle Giants of the Forest. LC 94-41839. (Step into Reading Ser.: A Step 2 Book). 32p. (J). (gr. 1-3). 1997. pap. 3.99 (*0-679-87284-1*, Pub. by Random Bks Yng Read) Random.

Milton, Joyce. Gorillas: Gentle Giants of the Forest. LC 94-41839. (Step into Reading Ser.: A Step 2 Book). (J). (gr. 1-3). 1997. 9.19 (*0-606-11411-4*, Pub. by Turtleback) Demco.

Milton, Joyce. Heavy-Duty. LC 99-14349. (Illus.). 48p. (J). (gr. 1-3). 1998. lib. bdg. 11.99 (*0-679-98130-6*, Pub. by Random Bks Yng Read) Random.

— Heavy-Duty Trucks. LC 99-14349. (Step into Reading Ser.: A Step 2 Book). (Illus.). 48p. (J). (gr. k-3). 1998. pap. 3.99 (*0-679-88130-1*, Pub. by Random Bks Yng Read) Random.

***Milton, Joyce.** Heavy Duty Trucks. (Step into Reading Ser.). (Illus.). (J). 2000. 9.44 (*0-606-18496-1*) Turtleback.

— Hieroglyphs. 32p. 2000. pap. 6.99 (*0-448-41976-9*, G & D) Peng Put Young Read.

Milton, Joyce. Marching to Freedom: The Story of Martin Luther King Jr. 96p. (Orig.). (J). (gr. k-6). 1987. pap. 3.99 (*0-440-45433-6*, YB BDD) BDD Bks Young Read.

Milton, Joyce. Marching to Freedom: The Story of Martin Luther King, Jr. (Dell Yearling Biography Ser.). (J). 1987. 8.45 (*0-606-03023-9*, Pub. by Turtleback) Demco.

Milton, Joyce. The Merchant of Venice. (Barron's Book Notes Ser.). (C). 1985. pap. 3.95 (*0-8120-3526-7*) Barron.

— Monster Hunters. (J). 1998. pap. 3.99 (*0-679-88575-7*); lib. bdg. 11.99 (*0-679-98575-1*, Pub. by Random Bks Yng Read) Random.

— Mummies. LC 96-19295. (All Aboard Reading Ser.: Level 2). (Illus.). 48p. (J). (gr. 1-3). 1996. pap. 3.99 (*0-448-41325-6*, G & D); lib. bdg. 13.89 (*0-448-41326-4*, G & D) Peng Put Young Read.

— Mummies. (All Aboard Reading Ser.). (J). 1996. 9.15 (*0-606-11648-6*, Pub. by Turtleback) Demco.

***Milton, Joyce.** Pocahontas: An American Princess. (All Aboard Reading Ser.). (Illus.). 48p. (J). (gr. 2-3). 2000. 13.89 (*0-448-42298-0*, Planet Dexter); pap. 3.99 (*0-448-42181-X*, Planet Dexter) Peng Put Young Read.

An Asterisk (*) at the beginning of an entry indicates that the title is appearing for the first time.

Milton, Joyce. The Story of Paul Revere: Messenger of Liberty. large type ed. (Illus.). 1991. 30.00 (*0-614-09884-X*, L-15920-00) Am Printing Hse.
— To Kill a Mockingbird. (Barron's Book Notes Ser.). (C). 1984. pap. 3.95 (*0-8120-3446-5*) Barron.
— Tramp: The Life of Charlie Chaplin. LC 97-41810. (Illus.). 604p. 1998. reprint ed. pap. 17.95 (*0-306-80831-5*) Da Capo.
— Whales: The Gentle Giants. LC 88-15616. (Step into Reading Ser.: A Step 2 Book). (Illus.). 48p. (J). (gr. 1-3). 1989. pap. 3.99 (*0-394-89809-5*, Pub. by Random Bks Yng Read) Random.
— Whales: The Gentle Giants. (Step into Reading Ser.: A Step 2 Book). (J). (gr. 1-3). 1989. 9.19 (*0-606-12568-X*, Pub. by Turtleback) Demco.
— Whales & Other Creatures of the Sea. LC 92-2409. (Pictureback Ser.). (Illus.). 32p. (J). (ps-4). 1993. pap. 3.25 (*0-679-83899-6*, Pub. by Random Bks Yng Read) Random.
— Wild, Wild Wolves. LC 90-8807. (Step into Reading Ser.: A Step 2 Book). (Illus.). 48p. (J). (ps-3). 1992. pap. 3.99 (*0-679-81052-8*, Pub. by Random Bks Yng Read); lib. bdg. 11.99 (*0-679-91052-2*, Pub. by Random Bks Yng Read) Random.
— Wild, Wild Wolves. (Step into Reading Ser.: A Step 2 Book). (J). (gr. 1-3). 1992. 9.19 (*0-606-01497-7*, Pub. by Turtleback) Demco.
Milton, Joyce, jt. auth. see Bronte, Charlotte.
Milton, Joyce, jt. auth. see Radosh, Ronald.
***Milton, Julian A.** As I've Wandered. 2000. pap. 8.95 (*0-533-13019-0*) Vantage.
Milton, Julie & Wiseman, Richard. Guidelines for Extrasensory Perception Research. (Guidelines for Research into Parapsychology Ser.). 94p. 1997. 24.95 (*0-900458-74-7*, Pub. by Univ of Herfordshire) Bold Strummer Ltd.
Milton, June, ed. see Cope-Robinson, Lyn.
Milton, K. A., et al, eds. Beyond the Standard Model II. 400p. (C). 1991. text 118.00 (*981-02-0569-4*) World Scientific Pub.
Milton, Katherine. The Foraging Strategy of Howler Monkeys: A Study in Economics. LC 79-27380. (Illus.). 1980. text 55.50 (*0-231-04850-5*) Col U Pr.
Milton, Kay. Environmentalism & Cultural Theory: Exploring the Role of Anthropology in Environmental Discourse. LC 95-26822. (Environment & Society Ser.). 288p. (C). 1996. 75.00 (*0-415-11529-9*); pap. 24.99 (*0-415-11530-2*) Routledge.
Milton, Kay, ed. Environmentalism: The View from Anthropology. LC 93-14815. (ASA Monographs Ser.: Vol. 32). (Illus.). 224p. (C). 1993. pap. 25.99 (*0-415-09475-5*) Routledge.
Milton, Kay, ed. see Yearly, Steven.
***Milton, Kimball A.** Quantum Legacy: Seminal Papers of Julian Schwinger. 2000. 99.00 (*981-02-4006-6*) World Scientific Pub.
Milton, Kimbell, jt. auth. see Mehra, Jagdish.
Milton, Kwasi. Hieroglyphics the Genesis of Writing. (Illus.). (Orig.). 1992. pap. 10.95 (*1-56411-018-4*) Untd Bros & Sis.
Milton, Marianne, ed. Malachite & Agate 1: Lesbian Poetry. 106p. (Orig.). 1997. pap. 9.95 (*0-9657478-0-8*) Clove Pr.
Milton, Mary. Cat Lips. (Illus.). 36p. (Orig.). 1994. pap. 5.00 (*1-883348-05-6*) Fresh Ink.
Milton, Ohmer, et al. Making Sense of College Grades. LC 85-45910. (Jossey-Bass Higher Education Ser.). (Illus.). 309p. reprint ed. pap. 95.80 (*0-7837-6519-3*, 204563100007) Bks Demand.
Milton, Peter. The Primacy of Touch: The Drawings of Peter Milton. LC 93-17551. (Illus.). 131p. 1993. 45.00 (*1-55595-075-2*) Hudson Hills.
Milton, Ralph. Angels in Red Suspenders: An Unconventional & Humorous Approach to Spirituality. 288p. 1997. 23.95 (*1-896836-10-0*) NStone Publ.
***Milton, Ralph.** Angels in Red Suspenders: An Unconventional & Humorous Approach to Spirituality. 288p. 1998. pap. 19.95 (*1-896836-21-6*) NStone Publ.
Milton, Ralph. Christianity for Beginners. LC 97-50248. 224p. 1998. pap. 9.95 (*0-687-03469-8*) Abingdon.
— Family Story Bible. LC 97-60737. 1999. 19.00 (*0-664-22108-4*) Westminster John Knox.
— Sermon Seasonings: Collected Stories to Spice up Your Sermons. 192p. Date not set. pap. 11.95 (*1-55145-248-0*, Pub. by Wood Lake Bks) Logos Prods.
Milton, Richard. Alternative Science: Challenging the Myths of the Scientific Establishment. LC 96-4983. 272p. 1996. pap. 14.95 (*0-89281-631-7*, Park St Pr) Inner Tradit.
— Forbidden Science: Exposing the Secrets of Suppressed Research. 272p. 1996. reprint ed. pap. 12.95 (*1-85702-302-1*) Trafalgar.
— Forbidden Science: Suppressed Research That Could Change Our Lives. 264p. 1995. 29.95 (*1-85702-188-6*) Fourth Estate.
Milton, Richard. Shattering the Myths of Darwinism. LC 97-9962. (Illus.). 272p. 1997. 24.95 (*0-89281-732-1*) Inner Tradit.
***Milton, Richard.** Shattering the Myths of Darwinism. (Illus.). 320p. 2000. pap. text 16.95 (*0-89281-884-0*) Inner Tradit.
Milton S. Eisenhower Foundation Staff. Locked in the Poorhouse: Cities, Race & Poverty in the United States. Harris, Fred R. & Curtis, Lynn A., eds. LC 98-29542. (Illus.). 192p. 1999. 24.95 (*0-8476-9135-7*) Rowman.
Milton, Steve. Skate: 100 Years of Figure Skating. (Illus.). 208p. 1996. 29.95 (*1-57076-056-X*, Trafalgar Sq Pub) Trafalgar.
— Skate Talk: Figure Skating in the Words of the Stars. (Illus.). 220p. (YA). 1998. pap. 14.95 (*1-55209-209-7*) Firefly Bks Ltd.
Milton, Susan J. Statistical Methods in the Biological & Health Sciences. 3rd ed. LC 98-18214. 600p. 1998. 81.56 (*0-07-290148-9*) McGraw.
Milton, Susan J., et al. Introduction to Statistics. LC 96-22270. 736p. (C). 1996. 66.88 (*0-07-042528-0*) McGraw.
Milton, Suzanne & Malia, Elizabeth. Index Guide to College Journals. LC 98-31373. 672p. 1998. 65.00 (*0-8108-3569-X*) Scarecrow.
Milton, Sybil. In Fitting Memory: The Art & Politics of Holocaust Memorials. LC 91-19603. (Illus.). 348p. reprint ed. pap. 107.90 (*0-608-10568-6*, 207118800009) Bks Demand.
Milton, Sybil, jt. ed. see Friedlander, Henry.
***Milton, Terry.** And the Devil Makes Three: An Italian Saga. LC 99-91667. 2000. 25.00 (*0-7388-1180-7*); pap. 18.00 (*0-7388-1181-5*) Xlibris Corp.
Milton, Toby H., jt. ed. see Schmidtlein, Frank A.
Milton, Tom, jt. auth. see Celente, Gerald.
Milton Woman's Club Staff. Chronicles of Milton: Village Left Behind by Time. LC 97-70832. (Illus.). 416p. 1997. 25.00 (*0-9657126-0-5*) Milton Womans.
Miltoun, F. The Spell of Algeria & Tunisia. 554p. 1985. 300.00 (*1-85077-060-3*, Pub. by Darf Pubs Ltd) St Mut.
Miltz, Arthur I. Art of Advocacy Vol. 1: Discovery. 1982. ring bd. 160.00 (*0-8205-1044-0*) Bender.
Miluck, Michael & Miluck, Nancy B., eds. The Genoa-Carson Valley Book, 1991-92. 4th ed. (Illus.). 96p. 1992. pap. 4.50 (*0-9606382-1-0*) Dragon Ent.
Miluck, Nancy B. Nevada: This Is Our Land. rev. ed. (Illus.). 200p. (Orig.). (YA). (gr. 7 up). 1994. reprint ed. pap. 15.00 (*0-9606382-7-X*) Dragon Ent.
Miluck, Nancy B., jt. ed. see Miluck, Michael.
Miluck, Nancy C. Nevada History Coloring Books: Nevada's Native Americans. (Illus.). 48p. (J). (gr. k-5). 1992. pap. text 4.00 (*0-9606382-4-5*) Dragon Ent.
— Nevada History Coloring Books: The 1st Settlers. (Illus.). 48p. (J). (gr. k-6). 1993. pap. 4.00 (*0-9606382-5-3*) Dragon Ent.
— Nevada History Coloring Books: The 20th Century. (Illus.). 48p. (Orig.). (J). (gr. k-5). 1992. pap. text 4.75 (*0-9606382-3-7*) Dragon Ent.
***Milunsky.** Genetic Destiny. 2000. pap. 26.00 (*0-7382-0377-7*, Pub. by Perseus Pubng) HarpC.
Milunsky, A. Genetic Disorders & the Fetus: Diagnosis, Prevention & Treatment. 2nd ed. LC 86-20477. (Illus.). 924p. (C). 1986. text 155.00 (*0-306-42301-4*, Kluwer Plenum) Kluwer Academic.
Milunsky, Aubrey. Heredity & Your Family's Health. LC 91-25343. 508p. 1991. reprint ed. pap. 18.95 (*0-8018-4331-6*) Johns Hopkins.
Milunsky, Aubrey, ed. Genetic Disorders & the Fetus: Diagnosis, Prevention, & Treatment. 3rd rev. ed. (Illus.). 992p. 1992. text 125.00 (*0-8018-4413-4*) Johns Hopkins.
— Genetic Disorders & the Fetus: Diagnosis, Prevention, & Treatment. 4th ed. LC 97-41341. 1998. text 150.00 (*0-8018-5801-1*) Johns Hopkins.
Milunsky, Aubrey, et al, eds. Advances in Perinatal Medicine, Vol. 1. LC 80-20701. 456p. 1981. 85.00 (*0-306-40482-6*, Kluwer Plenum) Kluwer Academic.
— Advances in Perinatal Medicine, Vol. 2. LC 80-20701. 400p. (C). 1982. 85.00 (*0-306-40763-9*, Kluwer Plenum) Kluwer Academic.
— Advances in Perinatal Medicine, Vol. 3. LC 80-20701. 272p. 1983. 85.00 (*0-306-41208-X*, Kluwer Plenum) Kluwer Academic.
— Advances in Perinatal Medicine, Vol. 4. LC 80-20701. 350p. 1985. 95.00 (*0-306-41840-1*, Kluwer Plenum) Kluwer Academic.
— Advances in Perinatal Medicine, Vol. 5. LC 80-20701. (Illus.). 298p. (C). 1986. text 114.00 (*0-306-42331-6*, Kluwer Plenum) Kluwer Academic.
Milutinovic, Veljko. Surviving the Design of a 200 RISC Microprocessor: Lessons Learned. LC 95-52094. 200p. 1996. pap. 35.00 (*0-8186-7343-5*, BPO7343) IEEE Comp Soc.
— Surviving the Design of Microprocessor & Multi-Microprocessor Systems: Lessons Learned. LC 99-42185. (Series on Parallel & Distributed Computing: Vol. 11). 384p. 2000. 105.00 (*0-471-35728-6*) Wiley.
Milutinovic, Veljko, jt. auth. see Tomasevic, Milo.
Milutinovic, Veljko, jt. ed. see Tartalja, I.
***Milward, Alan S.** European Rescue of Nation-State. 2nd ed. LC 99-44300. 488p. (C). 2000. text. write for info. (*0-415-21628-1*) Routledge.
— The European Rescue of the Nation-State 2nd ed. LC 99-44300. 1999. pap. write for info. (*0-415-21629-X*) Routledge.
Milward, Alan S. The New Order & the French Economy. (Modern Revivals in Economic & Social History Ser.). (Illus.). 336p. 1993. 77.95 (*0-7512-0146-4*, Pub. by Gregg Revivals) Ashgate Pub Co.
— War, Economy & Society: 1939-1945. LC 76-40823. (History of the World Economy in the Twentieth Century Ser.: Vol. 5). 1977. pap. 17.95 (*0-520-03942-4*, Pub. by U CA Pr) Cal Prin Full Svc.
Milward, Alan S. & Brennan, George. Britain's Place in the World: A Historical Enquiry into Import Controls 1945-60. LC 95-26082. (Explorations in Economic History Ser.). 336p. (C). 1996. 90.00 (*0-415-13937-6*) Routledge.
Milward, Alan S., et al. The European Rescue of the Nation-State. LC 92-11223. (C). 1993. 55.00 (*0-520-08137-4*, Pub. by U CA Pr) Cal Prin Full Svc.
Milward, Alan S., ed. see Aerts, E.
***Milward, Bob.** Marxian Political Economy: Theory History & Contemporary Relevance. 2000. text 69.95 (*0-312-23417-1*) St Martin.
Milward, Burton, Jr. Kentucky Criminal Practice, 1 vol. 2nd ed. 442p. 1984. 70.00 (*0-8322-0044-1*) Banks-Baldwin.
— The Sun Salutation Exercise: Surya Namaskara. (Illus.). 33p. 1997. pap. 7.50 (*0-9659191-0-2*) Total Victory.
Milward, G. R., jt. ed. see Pitt, G. J.
Milward, H. Brinton, jt. ed. see Kettl, Donald F.
Milward, Jane M. Playing God's Melodies: The Psalms in Our Lives. 160p. 1996. pap. 39.95 (*0-85439-465-6*, Pub. by St Paul Pubns) St Mut.
Milward-Oliver, Edward. Len Deighton: An Annotated Bibliography, 1954-1985. 100p. 1988. 85.00 (*0-944166-02-4*) Santa Teresa Pr.
Milward, Peter. Apostles & Martyrs. 146p. 1998. pap. 12.95 (*0-85244-390-0*, Pub. by Gra1cewing) Morehouse Pub.
— Biblical Influences in Shakespeare's Great Tragedies. LC 86-45543. 224p. 1987. 20.00 (*0-253-31198-5*) Ind U Pr.
— The Catholicism of Shakespeare's Plays. 144p. 1997. pap. 13.95 (*1-901157-10-5*) St Austin.
— A Challenge to C. S. Lewis. LC 94-34812. 1995. 29.50 (*0-8386-3568-7*) Fairleigh Dickinson.
— Oddities in Modern Japan: Observations of an Outsider. (Illus.). 187p. 1997. pap. 17.95 (*4-590-00628-6*, Pub. by Hokuseido Pr) Book East.
— The Simplicity of the West. 150p. 1998. pap. 16.95 (*1-901157-95-4*) St Augustines Pr.
Milward, Peter, tr. see Natsume Soseki, pseud.
Milward, Peter S. A Commentary on G. M. Hopkins' "The Wreck of the Deutschland" LC 90-25437. (Studies in British Literature: Vol. 13). 200p. 1992. reprint ed. lib. bdg. 79.95 (*0-88946-584-3*) E Mellen.
— A Commentary on the Sonnets of G. M. Hopkins. 2nd ed. LC 96-38108. 232p. 1997. pap. 16.95 (*0-8294-0936-X*) Loyola Pr.
Milward, Peter S., compiled by. An Encyclopedia of Flora & Fauna in English & American Literature. LC 92-14298. 244p. 1992. lib. bdg. 89.95 (*0-7734-9539-8*) E Mellen.
Milward, Peter S., ed. The Mediaeval Dimension in Shakespeare's Plays. LC 90-31081. (Studies in Renaissance Literature: Vol. 7). 156p. 1990. lib. bdg. 69.95 (*0-88946-116-3*) E Mellen.
Milward, R. S. Japan: The Past in the Present. 128p. 1987. pap. 75.00 (*0-904404-29-3*, Pub. by P Norbury Pubns Ltd) St Mut.
Milwaukee Art Museum Staff. Landfall Press: 25 Years of Printmaking. LC 96-77356. (Illus.). 300p. 1996. pap. 39.95 (*0-944110-68-1*, 620663) Milwauk Art Mus.
Milwaukee Brewers Baseball Club, Publicity Dept. S. Robin Yount: The Legend Lives On. (Illus.). 80p. 19.00 (*0-9634967-0-0*) Milwauk BBC.
Milwaukee Journal Sentinel Staff. Greatest Moments in Green Bay Packers History. (Fan Series of Sports Books). 1997. 99.95 (*1-57028-178-5*, Mstrs Pr); 29.95 (*1-57028-168-8*, Mstrs Pr) NTC Contemp Pub Co.
Milwaukee Public Museum Staff. The Rudolph J. Nunnemacher Collection of Projectile Arms, 2 pts., Vol. 1. Metschl, John, ed. LC 74-111395. (Illus.). 1970. reprint ed. lib. bdg. 75.00 (*0-8371-4627-5*, MPMO, Greenwood Pr) Greenwood.
— The Rudolph J. Nunnemacher Collection of Projectile Arms, 2 pts., Vol. 2. Metschl, John, ed. LC 74-111395. (Illus.). 1970. reprint ed. lib. bdg. 75.00 (*0-8371-4628-3*, MPMP, Greenwood Pr) Greenwood.
— The Rudolph J. Nunnemacher Collection of Projectile Arms, 2 pts., Vol. 9--9. Metschl, John, ed. LC 74-111395. (Illus.). 1970. reprint ed. lib. bdg. 125.00 (*0-8371-4626-7*, MPMN, Greenwood Pr) Greenwood.
Milwaukee Public Museum Staff, jt. auth. see Gromme, Owen J.
Milwaukee Shops Inc. Staff. Hiawatha First of the Speedliners: C. M. St. P. & P. R. R. Equipment Built by: The Milwaukee Shops, 1934-1935. Solheim, Carl W. et al, eds. (Illus.). 134p. 1993. 64.95 (*0-9639029-0-3*) Milwaukee Shops.
Milwee, William I., Jr. Modern Marine Salvage. LC 95-30816. (Illus.). 792p. 1996. text 65.00 (*0-87033-471-9*) Cornell Maritime.
Milwertz, Cecilia N. Accepting Population Control: Urban Chinese Women & the One-Child Family Policy. (NIAS Monographs in Asian Studies: No. 74). 280p. (C). 1996. text 48.00 (*0-7007-0437-X*, Pub. by Curzon Pr Ltd); pap. text 23.95 (*0-7007-0457-4*, Pub. by Curzon Pr Ltd) UH Pr.
Milwid, Beth. Working with Men: Women in the Workplace Talk about Sexuality, Success & Their Male Coworkers. 288p. (Orig.). 1992. mass mkt. 4.99 (*0-425-13482-2*) Berkley Pub.
Milwidsky, Benjamin M. & Gabriel, Delia M. Detergent Analysis: A Handbook for Cost-Effective Quality Control. LC 81-19840. (Illus.). 303p. 1989. reprint ed. 76.50 (*0-9608752-3-9*) Micelle Pr.
Milza, Pierre, jt. auth. see Berstein, Serge.
***Mima, Kunioki, et al, eds.** High-Power Lasers in Energy Engineering. 1999. pap. text 145.00 (*0-8194-3484-1*) SPIE.
Mimep, jt. auth. see Galbiati, E.
Mimep, M., jt. auth. see Galbiati, E.
Mimi. Buy This Or Else, Pig: Everything You Wanted to Know about Me! Me! Me! 128p. 1998. write for info. (*0-7868-6405-2*) Hyperion.
***Mimi.** Jake Is Up! (Jake's World Ser.: Vol. 2). (Illus.). 26p. (J). 1999. bds. 6.95 (*1-892780-01-1*) Giggles Grp.
Mimi. A Pot is Not... LC 99-207952. (Jake's World Ser.). 12p. 1999. 9.95 (*1-892780-00-3*) Giggles Grp.
Mimica, Jadran. Intimations of Infinity: The Cultural Meanings of the Iqwaye Counting System & Number. LC 87-22412. (Explorations in Anthropology Ser.). 195p. 1988. 37.50 (*0-85496-145-3*) Berg Pubs.
— Intimations of Infinity: The Mythopoeia of the Iqwaye Counting System & Number. 196p. 1992. pap. 16.50 (*0-85496-854-7*) Berg Pubs.
Mimick, R., jt. auth. see Kudar.
Mimieux, Yvette, jt. auth. see Atzel-Bethlen, Szabolcs.
Mimms, Agneta, ed. see Technical Association of the Pulp & Paper Industry.
Mimms, Kenneth A. & Ross, Leon T. African American Almanac: Day-by-Day Black History. LC 96-44832. 183p. 1997. lib. bdg. 33.50 (*0-89950-675-5*) McFarland & Co.
Mimnaugh, Heather, ed. see Cavalli-Sforza, Luigi L., et al.
Mimnaugh, Heather, ed. see Holland, John.
Mimnaugh, Heather, ed. see Kane, Gordon.
Mimnaugh, Heather, ed. see Wills, Christopher.
Mimnaugh, Michael. Natural Science 097: An Introduction to a Scientific Inquiry Student Activities. 240p. (C). 1996. ring bd. 35.95 (*0-7872-2440-5*, 41244001) Kendall-Hunt.
Mimno, Peter. Data Warehousing Roadmap. (Illus.). 59p. 1997. pap. write for info. (*1-892815-12-5*) Patricia Seybold.
Mimno, Peter R. Cost Justifying a Data Warehouse. (Illus.). 24p. 1997. pap. 195.00 (*1-892815-24-9*) Patricia Seybold.
Mimoso, Adriana R. Modernism in the Puerto Rican Lyric. (Puerto Rico Ser.). 1979. lib. bdg. 59.95 (*0-8490-2973-2*) Gordon Pr.
Mimouni, Francis, jt. ed. see Tsang, Reginald C.
Mimouni, Rachid. The Ogre's Embrace. Eber, Shirley, tr. 224p. 1993. 19.95 (*0-7043-7043-3*, Pub. by Quartet) Interlink Pub.
Mims. Cultural Connections. 2000. pap. text 30.95 (*0-312-15332-5*) St Martin.
***Mims.** Microbiologia Medica. 2nd ed. (C). 1999. text 60.64 (*84-8174-396-8*) Mosby Inc.
Mims, Barbara C., et al. Critical Care Skills: A Clinical Handbook. Eoyang, Thomas, ed. (Illus.). 637p. 1996. pap. text 34.00 (*0-7216-4519-4*, W B Saunders Co) Harcrt Hlth Sci Grp.
Mims, Cedric. When We Die: The Science, Culture & Rituals of Death. LC 98-49816. (Illus.). 352p. 1999. text 25.95 (*0-312-20050-1*) St Martin.
***Mims, Cedric.** When We Die: The Science, Culture & Rituals of Death. (Illus.). 352p. 2000. pap. 15.95 (*0-312-26411-9*) St Martin.
***Mims, Cedric A.** The War Within Us: Everyman's Guide to Infection & Immunity. 320p. 2000. 39.95 (*0-12-498251-4*) Acad Pr.
Mims, Cedric A., et al, eds. The Pathogenesis of Infectious Disease. 4th ed. (Illus.). 414p. 1995. text 48.00 (*0-12-498262-X*); pap. text 33.00 (*0-12-498263-8*) Acad Pr.
Mims, Edwin. The Advancing South: Stories of Progress & Reaction. (BCL1 - United States Local History Ser.). 319p. 1991. reprint ed. lib. bdg. 89.00 (*0-7812-6290-9*) Rprt Serv.
— Great Writers As Interpreters of Religion. LC 70-134116. (Essay Index Reprint Ser.). 1977. reprint ed. 19.95 (*0-8369-1988-2*) Ayer.
— History of Vanderbilt University. Metzger, Walter P., ed. LC 76-55185. (Academic Profession Ser.). (Illus.). 1977. reprint ed. lib. bdg. 41.95 (*0-405-10012-4*) Ayer.
— Sidney Lanier. 1972. 59.95 (*0-8490-1052-7*) Gordon Pr.
Mims, Ferm & Swenson, Melinda. Sexuality: A Nursing Perspective. 1979. pap. text 25.95 (*0-07-042388-1*) McGraw.
***Mims, Forrest M.** The Forrest Mims Circuit Scrapbook, Vol. I. (Illus.). 160p. 2000. pap. 19.95 (*1-878707-48-5*, Pub. by LLH Tech Pub) IPG Chicago.
— The Forrest Mims Circuit Scrapbook, Vol. II. (Illus.). 264p. 2000. pap. 24.95 (*1-878707-49-3*, Pub. by LLH Tech Pub) IPG Chicago.
Mims, Forrest M., II. The Forrest Mims Engineer's Notebook. (Illus.). 168p. 1992. pap. 19.95 (*1-878707-03-5*) LLH Tech Pub.
Mims, James A. Guide on Wedding Anniversaries. 1998. pap. 5.00 (*0-89754-147-2*) Dan River Pr.
Mims, Julian L., III. Records Management: A Practical Guide for Cities & Counties. LC 97-116790. (Special Reports). 191p. 1996. pap. 45.00 (*0-87326-110-0*) Intl City-Cnty Mgt.
Mims, Rick, et al, eds. The Heritage of Chilton County, Alabama. (Heritage of Alabama Ser.: No. 11). (Illus.). 240p. 1999. 55.00 (*1-891647-27-X*) Herit Pub Consult.
Mims, Sam. No Americans Wanted. (J). 1969. 4.95 (*0-87511-085-1*) Claitors.
Mims, W. B. The Linear Electric Field Effect in Paramagnetic Resonance. (Illus.). 1976. 49.50 (*0-19-851944-3*) OUP.
Mims, W. O. Twenty Sermons on Growing As a Christian. Smith, Marvin L., ed. (Illus.). 88p. 1999. pap. 7.00 (*1-882581-20-2*) Campbell Rd Pr.
Mimura, G., et al, eds. Advances of Diabetes Mellitus in East Asia: Proceedings of the 5th China-Japan Symposium on Diabetes Mellitus, Xian, China, 5-8 September 1996. LC 97-18023. (International Congress Ser.: No. 1141). 300p. 1997. 184.50 (*0-444-82664-5*, Excerpta Medica) Elsevier.
Mimura, M., ed. Homotopy Theory & Related Topics. (Lecture Notes in Mathematics Ser.: Vol. 1418). vi, 241p. 1990. 34.80 (*0-387-52246-8*) Spr-Verlag.
Mimura, M. & Toda, H. Topology of Lie Groups, I & II. LC 91-9459. (Translations of Mathematical Monographs: Vol. 91). 451p. 1991. 49.00 (*0-8218-4541-1*, MMONO/91) Am Math.
Mimura, Mamoru, ed. see Adams, J. F.
Mimura, Masato. Natural Home Gardening: A Practical Guide to Growing Vegetables for Macrobiotic & Natural Foods Cooking. (Illus.). 96p. (Orig.). 1996. pap. 8.95 (*1-882984-15-3*) One Peaceful World.
Min & Foner. Koreans. 133p. 1997. pap. 20.00 (*0-205-27455-2*) P-H.
Min, jt. ed. see Akoh.

An Asterisk (*) at the beginning of an entry indicates that the title is appearing for the first time.

*Min, Anchee. Becoming Madame Mao. LC 99-58520. 352p. 2000. 25.00 (*0-618-00407-6*) HM.

Min, Anchee. Katherine. 1996. mass mkt. 6.99 (*0-425-15291-X*) Berkley Pub.

— Red Azalea. 320p. 1995. mass mkt. 6.99 (*0-425-14776-2*) Berkley Pub.

— Red Azalea. 320p. 1999. pap. text 13.00 (*0-425-16687-2*) Berkley Pub.

Min, Anselm K. Dialectic of Salvation: Issues in Theology of Liberation. LC 88-39150. 207p. (C). 1989. text 21.50 (*0-88706-908-8*) State U NY Pr.

Min Chen. The Strategic Triangle & Regional Conflicts: Lessons from the Indochina Wars. LC 91-20699. 230p. 1992. lib. bdg. 40.00 (*1-55587-287-5*) L Rienner.

Min Chen & Pan, Winston. Understanding the Process of Doing Business in China, Taiwan, & Hong Kong: A Guide for International Executives. LC 93-29328. 260p. 1993. 89.95 (*0-7734-9404-9*) E Mellen.

Min, David B. & Smouse, Thomas H., eds. Flavor Chemistry of Fats & Oils. 309p. 1985. 60.00 (*0-935315-12-8*) Am Oil Chemists.

— Flavor Chemistry of Lipid Foods. 488p. 1989. 85.00 (*0-935315-24-1*) Am Oil Chemists.

Min, David B., jt. ed. see McDonald, Richard E.

Min, Dong-Phil, jt. ed. see Ji, Cheung-Ryong.

Min, Dong-Pil, jt. ed. see Ji, Chueng-Ryong.

*Min, Eungjun. Reading the Homeless: The Media's Image of Homeless Culture. LC 98-35370. 240p. 1999. 65.00 (*0-275-95950-3*, Praeger Pubs) Greenwood.

Min, J. L. & Schrage, J. J. Designing Analog & Digital Control Systems. 275p. 1988. text 57.95 (*0-470-21253-5*) P-H.

Min, K. C., jt. ed. see Bien, Z.

Min Kantrowitz & Associates Staff. Design Evaluation of Six Primary Care Facilities for the Purpose of Informing Future Design Decisions. 102p. 1993. pap. write for info. (*0-9638938-0-7*) Ctr for Hlth.

Min, Kellet I. Modern Informative Nursery Rhymes: American History, Book I. LC 89-91719. (Illus.). 64p. (Orig.). (J). (gr. 2-5). 1992. pap. 10.95 (*0-9623411-2-6*) Rhyme & Reason.

— Modern Informative Nursery Rhymes: General Science, Book I. LC 89-91719. (Illus.). 64p. (Orig.). (J). (gr. 2-5). 1993. pap. 10.95 (*0-9623411-4-2*) Rhyme & Reason.

— Modern Informative Nursery Rhymes: The Rationale. 176p. (Orig.). 1991. pap. 10.95 (*0-9623411-1-8*) Rhyme & Reason.

— Modern Informative Nursery Rhymes: Values. LC 89-91719. (General Science, American History Ser.: Bk. I). (Illus.). 32p. (Orig.). (J). (ps-3). 1989. pap. 7.95 (*0-9623411-3-4*) Rhyme & Reason.

Min, Laura. Las Gallinas de la Senora Sato. Ada, Alma F., tr. (Dejame Leer Ser.).Tr. of Mrs. Sato's Hens. (SPA., Illus.). 8p. (J). (ps). 1995. 2.95 (*0-673-36298-1*, GoodYrBooks) Addson-Wesley Educ.

— Mrs. Sato's Hens. 2nd ed. (Let Me Read Ser.). (Illus.). 8p. (J). (ps). 1994. text 2.95 (*0-673-36193-4*, GoodYrBooks) Addson-Wesley Educ.

Min, Lin, tr. see Xu Xing.

Min, P. & Klapisch, Robert, eds. New Applications of Accelerators & Nuclear Detectors to Medical Diagnosis, Vol. 3, No. 2. (Nuclear Science Applications Ser.: Sec. A, Vol. 3, No. 2). 92p. 1988. text 173.00 (*3-7186-4825-3*) Gordon & Breach.

*Min, Pyong G. & Kim, Rose. Struggle for Ethnic Identity: Narratives by Asian American Professionals. (Critical Perspectives on Asian Pacific Americans Ser.: Vol. 4). 250p. 1998. 62.00 (*0-7619-9066-6*); pap. 24.95 (*0-7619-9067-4*) AltaMira Pr.

Min, Sungky. Asymmetric Information & Shareholders' Wealth. rev. ed. LC 96-36708. (Financial Sector of the American Economy Ser.). (Illus.). 138p. 1996. text 47.00 (*0-8153-2805-2*) Garland.

Min, T., ed. see American Society of Mechanical Engineers Staff.

Min, Willemien. Peter's Patchwork Dream. 32p. (J). (ps-1). 1999. 15.95 (*1-902283-45-7*) Barefoot Bks NY.

Min-You, Qi. General Theory of Partial Differential Equations & Microlocal Analysis. (Pitman Research Notes in Mathematics Ser.). 1996. lib. bdg. 57.95 (*0-582-29212-3*) Longman.

Mina, Denise. Garnethill. 352p. 1999. 24.00 (*0-7867-0612-0*) Carroll & Graf.

Mina, Don F. Del La, see Del La Mina, Don F.

*Mina, Eli. The Complete Handbook of Business Meetings. LC 00-38625. 304p. 2000. 27.95 (*0-8144-0560-6*) AMACOM.

Mina, Gianni. An Encounter with Fidel: Interview with Fidel Castro. Todd, Mary, tr. 273p. 1993. 34.95 (*1-875284-22-2*); pap. 13.95 (*1-875284-21-4*) Ocean Pr NJ.

Mina, Hanna. Sun on a Cloudy Day. unabridged ed. Frangieh, Bassam & Brown, Clementina, trs. from ARA.Tr. of Al-Shams fi Youm Gha'im. 192p. (Orig.). (C). 1997. pap. 14.00 (*1-57889-044-6*) Passeggiata.

Mina, M. V. Microevolution of Fishes: Evolutionary Aspects of Phenetic Diversity. Yablokov, A. V., ed. (Russian Translation Ser.: No. 79). (Illus.). 220p. (C). 1990. text 110.00 (*90-6191-032-3*, Pub. by A A Balkema) Ashgate Pub Co.

Mina, M. V., tr. see Klevezal, Galina A.

Mina, Swaminathan. The First Five Years: A Critical Perspective on Early Childhood Care & Education in India. LC 98-19162. 1998. 39.95 (*0-7619-9275-8*); pap. write for info. (*0-7619-9276-6*) Sage.

Mina, V. K. The Splintered Day. 192p. 1999. pap. 13.99 (*1-85242-452-4*, Pub. by Serpents Tail) Consort Bk Sales.

Minachev, K. M., jt. auth. see Shapiro, E. S.

Minachin, V. V., tr. see Ilin, A. M.

Minachin, V. V., tr. see Sharko, V. V.

Minadeo, Richard. The Thematic Sophocles. viii, 200p. 1994. pap. 60.00 (*90-256-1056-0*, Pub. by AM Hakkert) BookLink Distributors.

Minaeva, Oksana. From Paganism to Christianity: Formation of Medieval Bulgarian Art (681-972) LC 97-2291. (Illus.). 270p. 1996. 82.95 (*3-631-30090-5*) P Lang Pubng.

— From Paganism to Christianity: Formation of Medieval Bulgarian Art (681-972) (Illus.). 270p. 1996. 82.95 (*0-8204-3174-5*) P Lang Pubng.

Minaguchi, Hiroshi, ed. Endometriosis Today Vol. 13: Proceedings of the Vth World Congress, Yokohama, Japan, 21-24 October, 1996. LC 97-15483. (Illus.). 496p. 1997. 132.00 (*1-85070-901-7*) Prthnon Pub.

Minahan, Daniel, jt. auth. see Harron, Mary.

*Minahan, James. Miniature Empires. 360p. 1999. lib. bdg. 80.00 (*1-57958-133-1*) Fitzroy Dearborn.

Minahan, James. Miniature Empires: A Historical Dictionary of the Newly Independent States. LC 98-13979. 360p. 1998. lib. bdg. 75.00 (*0-313-30610-9*, Greenwood Pr) Greenwood.

— Nations Without States: A Historical Dictionary of Contemporary National Movements. LC 95-6626. 720p. 1996. lib. bdg. 99.50 (*0-313-28354-0*, Praeger Pubs) Greenwood.

*Minahan, James. One Europe, Many Nations: A Historical Dictionary of European National Groups. LC 99-46040. 800p. 2000. lib. bdg. 99.50 (*0-313-30984-1*) Greenwood.

Minahan, John. The Great Grave Robbery. 1989. 18.95 (*0-393-02721-X*) Norton.

— The Great Harvard Robbery: A Novel. 1988. 16.95 (*0-393-02605-1*) Norton.

Minahan, John A. Abigail's Drum. LC 95-23460. (Illus.). 64p. (J). (gr. 3-5). 1995. text 14.95 (*0-945912-25-0*) Pippin Pr.

— Teaching Democracy: A Professor's Journal. 220p. 1993. 20.00 (*1-883285-01-1*) Delphinium.

— Word Like a Bell: John Keats, Music & the Romantic Poet. LC 91-29422. 232p. 1992. lib. bdg. 32.00 (*0-87338-453-9*) Kent St U Pr.

Minahan, John C., Jr. Nebraska Legal Forms: Bankruptcy. 230p. 1982. ring bd. 69.95 (*0-86678-029-7*, 81974-10, MICHIE); ring bd. 104.95 incl. disk (*1-56257-787-5*, MICHIE) LEXIS Pub.

— Nebraska Legal Forms: Bankruptcy. 230p. 1993. suppl. ed. 42.50 (*1-56257-808-1*, MICHIE) LEXIS Pub.

Minahan, John C., Jr. & Ruser, Kevin. Nebraska Legal Forms: Bankruptcy. 1982. ring bd. 69.95 (*0-327-00997-7*, 81974-10, MICHIE) LEXIS Pub.

Minahen, Charles D. Sartre Revisited. Fourney, Jean-Francois, ed. LC 96-48925. 224p. 1997. text 39.95 (*0-312-16079-8*) St Martin.

— Vortex-t: The Poetics of Turbulence. 200p. 1992. text 35.00 (*0-271-00774-5*) Pa St U Pr.

Minahen, Charles D., ed. Figuring Things: Char, Ponge, & Poetry in the Twentieth Century. LC 94-70553. (French Forum Monographs: No. 84). 256p. (Orig.). 1994. pap. 24.95 (*0-917058-89-5*) French Forum.

Minai, Asghar T. Aesthetics, Mind, & Nature: A Communication Approach to the Unity of Matter & Consciousness. LC 92-36548. 352p. 1993. 80.00 (*0-275-94296-1*, C4296, Praeger Pubs) Greenwood.

— Design As Aesthetic Communication: Structuring Random-Order. (American University Studies: Fine Arts: Ser. XX, Vol. 9). XXVI, 458p. (C). 1989. text 67.95 (*0-8204-0815-8*) P Lang Pubng.

Minai, Yoshitaka, jt. auth. see Tominaga, Takeshi.

Minakata, H. Festschrift of the Symposium in Honor of Tetsuro Kobayaski. 264p. 1994. text 67.00 (*981-02-1417-0*) World Scientific Pub.

Minakir, Pavel A. & Freeze, Gregory L., eds. The Russian Far East: An Economic Handbook. LC 94-18817. (Illus.). 544p. (C). (gr. 13). 1994. text 212.95 (*1-56324-456-X*) M E Sharpe.

Minakowska, Malgorzata, ed. see Baumgartner, Elzbieta.

Minakuchi, Hiroya. In Search of Whales & Dolphins. (Illus.). 104p. 1995. 27.50 (*0-8050-1771-2*) H Holt & Co.

*Minale, Marcello. How to Design a Successful Petrol Station. (Illus.). 224p. 2000. 55.00 (*1-86154-135-X*, Pub. by Booth-Clibborn) Dist Art Pubs.

Minami, Akira, ed. see Tanaka, Keiji, et al.

Minami, Masahiko & Kennedy, Bruce P., eds. Language Issues in Literacy & Bilingual - Multicultural Education. LC 91-75438. (Reprint Ser.: No. 22). 572p. (C). 1991. pap. 35.95 (*0-916690-24-5*) Harvard Educ Rev.

*Minami, Michael, et al. Using ArcMap: ArcInfo 8. 576p. 2000. pap. 49.95 (*1-879102-69-2*, Pub. by ESR Inst) IPG Chicago.

Minami, N. Multiplicative Homology Operations & Transfer. LC 91-28757. (Memoirs Ser.: No. 457). 74p. 1991. pap. 18.00 (*0-8218-2518-6*, MEMO/94/457) Am Math.

Minami, Ryoshin. The Economic Development of China: A Comparison with the Japanese Experience. Jiang, Wenran et al, trs. from JPN. LC 93-15600.Tr. of Chugoku No Keizai Hatten. 262p. 1993. text 49.95 (*0-312-10021-3*) St Martin.

Minami, Ryoshin, et al. Growth, Distribution & Political Change: Asia & the Wider World. LC 98-53723. (Studies in the Economies of East & Southeast Asia). 1999. text 79.95 (*0-312-22267-X*) St Martin.

Minami, Ryoshin, jt. ed. see Kosobud, Richard F.

Minamisono, T., et al, eds. Non-Nucleonic Degrees of Freedom Detected in the Nucleus: Osaka, Japan, 2-5 September, 1996. 430p. 1997. 68.00 (*981-02-3184-9*) World Scientific Pub.

Minamizawa, Kichisaburo. Moriculture: Science of Mulberry Cultivation. (Illus.). 440p. 1997. text 120.00 (*90-5410-287-X*, Pub. by A A Balkema) Ashgate Pub Co.

Minan, John H., jt. ed. see Folsom, Ralph H.

*Minar, Barbra Goodyear. Walking Into the Wind: Being Healthy with a Chronic Disease. LC 00-190582. 209p. 2000. 25.00 (*0-7388-1699-X*); pap. 18.00 (*0-7388-1700-7*) Xlibris Corp.

Minar, Edwin L., Jr. Early Pythagorean Politics in Practice & Theory. Vlastos, Gregory, ed. LC 78-19373. (Morals & Law in Ancient Greece Ser.). (ENG & GRE.). 1979. reprint ed. lib. bdg. 25.95 (*0-405-11563-6*) Ayer.

Minar, Edwin L., Jr., tr. see Burkert, Walter.

Minard, Emma. Words of Praise. 32p. 1999. lib. bdg. 15.95 (*1-892668-02-5*) Prospect Pr.

Minard, M. Elizabeth. History of Westminster: Vermont Sesquicentennial Souvenir of Westminster, 1791-1941. (Illus.). 174p. 1997. reprint ed. pap. 21.50 (*0-8328-6933-3*); reprint ed. lib. bdg. 29.50 (*0-8328-6932-5*) Higginson Bk Co.

Minard, Rosemary, ed. Womenfolk & Fairy Tales, 001. LC 74-26555. (Illus.). 176p. (J). (gr. 2-5). 1975. 18.00 (*0-395-20276-0*) HM.

Minardi, Henry & Riley, Martin. Communication for Nursing Practice: A Skills Based Approach. LC 96-53895. 224p. 1997. pap. text 34.50 (*0-7506-1579-6*) Buttrwrth-Heinemann.

Minardi, John A. & Minardo, James A. The Do-It-Yourself Home Inspection Book: Making Sure Your New Investment Is Safe & Sound. 225p. 1991. per. 16.95 (*1-55738-260-3*, Irwn Prfssnl) McGraw-Hill Prof.

Minardi, Kay W. Short Bike Rides in Ohio: Rides for the Casual Cyclist. LC 98-9767. (Short Bike Rides Ser.). (Illus.). 160p. 1998. pap. 10.95 (*0-7627-0213-3*) Globe Pequot.

Minardo, James A., jt. auth. see Minardi, John A.

Minarik. The Adventures of Little Bear. (Illus.). (J). 1998. 12.95 (*0-06-028044-1*) HarpC.

Minarik, Else H. Am I Beautiful? LC 91-32562. (Illus.). 24p. (J). (ps-3). 1992. 16.00 (*0-688-09911-4*, Grenwillow Bks) HarpC Child Bks.

— Los Amigos de Osito. 1981. 15.15 (*0-606-10479-8*, Pub. by Turtleback) Demco.

— Un Beso Para Osito.Tr. of Kiss for Little Bear. (J). Date not set. pap. text 9.95 (*84-204-3050-1*) Santillana.

— Un Beso Para Osito.Tr. of Kiss for Little Bear. 1981. 15.15 (*0-606-10521-2*, Pub. by Turtleback) Demco.

— Cat & Dog. LC 60-14998. (I Can Read Bks.). (Illus.). 32p. (J). (gr. k-2). 1960. lib. bdg. 15.89 (*0-06-024221-3*) HarpC Child Bks.

— Father Bear Comes Home. (I Can Read Bks.). (Illus.). 64p. (J). (ps-1). 1959. lib. bdg. 14.89 (*0-06-024231-0*) HarpC Child Bks.

— Father Bear Comes Home. LC 59-5794. (I Can Read Bks.). (Illus.). 64p. (J). (ps-3). 1978. pap. 3.95 (*0-06-444014-1*, HarpTrophy) HarpC Child Bks.

— Father Bear Comes Home. LC 59-5794. (I Can Read Bks.). (Illus.). 64p. (J). (ps-3). 1959. 15.95 (*0-06-024230-2*) HarpC Child Bks.

— Father Bear Comes Home. (I Can Read Bks.). (J). (ps-1). 1959. 8.95 (*0-606-02113-2*, Pub. by Turtleback) Demco.

— Father Bear Comes Home: (Papa Oso Vuele a Casa) (I Can Read Bks.). (SPA.). (J). (ps-1). 9.95 (*84-204-3048-X*) Santillana.

— Father Bear Comes Home Book & Tape. unabridged ed. (I Can Read Bks.). (Illus.). 64p. (J). (ps-1). 1995. 8.95 incl. audio (*0-694-70010-X*) HarperAudio.

— A Kiss for Little Bear. LC 57-9263. (I Can Read Bks.). (Illus.). 32p. (J). (ps-3). 1968. 15.95 (*0-06-024298-1*); lib. bdg. 15.89 (*0-06-024299-X*) HarpC Child Bks.

— A Kiss for Little Bear. LC 68-16820. (I Can Read Bks.). (Illus.). 32p. (J). (ps-2). 1984. pap. 3.95 (*0-06-444050-8*, HarpTrophy) HarpC Child Bks.

Minarik, Else H. A Kiss for Little Bear. (I Can Read Bks.). (J). (ps-1). 1984. 9.60 (*0-606-03383-1*, Pub. by Turtleback) Demco.

Minarik, Else H. Little Bear. LC 57-9263. (I Can Read Bks.). (Illus.). 64p. (J). (ps-3). 1957. 15.95 (*0-06-024240-X*); lib. bdg. 15.89 (*0-06-024241-8*) HarpC Child Bks.

— Little Bear. (I Can Read Bks.). (Illus.). 64p. (J). (ps-1). 1978. pap. 3.95 (*0-06-444004-4*, HarpTrophy) HarpC Child Bks.

— Little Bear. (I Can Read Bks.). (J). (ps-1). 1978. 8.95 (*0-606-01530-2*, Pub. by Turtleback) Demco.

— Little Bear. unabridged ed. LC 57-9263. (I Can Read Bks.). (Illus.). 64p. (J). (gr. k-3). 1990. pap. 8.95 incl. audio (*1-55994-234-7*) HarperAudio.

— Little Bear, 3 bks., Set. (I Can Read Bks.). (Illus.). 160p. (J). (ps-3). 1992. pap. 11.25 (*0-06-444197-0*, HarpTrophy) HarpC Child Bks.

— Little Bear - Osito. (SPA.). (J). 9.95 (*84-204-3044-7*) Santillana.

Minarik, Else H. Little Bear Audio Collection. unabridged ed. (I Can Read Bks.). (J). (ps-3). 1992. pap. 11.95 incl. audio (*1-55994-543-5*) HarperAudio.

Minarik, Else H. Little Bear's Friend. LC 60-6370. (I Can Read Bks.). (Illus.). 64p. (J). (ps-3). 1960. lib. bdg. 15.89 (*0-06-024256-6*) HarpC Child Bks.

— Little Bear's Friend. LC 60-6370. (I Can Read Bks.). (Illus.). 64p. (J). (ps-3). 1984. mass mkt. 3.95 (*0-06-444051-6*, HarpTrophy) HarpC Child Bks.

— Little Bear's Friend. (I Can Read Bks.). (J). (ps-1). 1984. 8.95 (*0-606-03384-X*, Pub. by Turtleback) Demco.

— Little Bear's Friend. unabridged ed. LC 60-6370. (I Can Read Bks.). (Illus.). 64p. (J). (gr. k-3). 1990. pap. 8.95 incl. audio (*1-55994-235-5*) HarperAudio.

— Little Bear's Friends - Los Amigos de Osito. (SPA.). (J). 7.95 (*84-204-3049-8*) Santillana.

— Little Bear's Visit. (I Can Read Bks.). (Illus.). 64p. (J). (ps-1). 1961. lib. bdg. 15.89 (*0-06-024266-3*) HarpC Child Bks.

— Little Bear's Visit. LC 61-11451. (I Can Read Bks.). (Illus.). 64p. (J). (ps-3). 1961. 15.95 (*0-06-024265-5*) HarpC Child Bks.

— Little Bear's Visit. LC 61-11451. (I Can Read Bks.). (Illus.). 64p. (J). (ps-3). 1979. pap. 3.95 (*0-06-444023-0*, HarpTrophy) HarpC Child Bks.

— Little Bear's Visit. (I Can Read Bks.). (Illus.). 64p. (J). (ps-1). 1985. 5.98 incl. audio (*0-694-00032-9*, JC-023, HarpTrophy) HarpC Child Bks.

— Little Bear's Visit. (I Can Read Bks.). (J). (ps-1). 1971. 8.95 (*0-606-02159-0*, Pub. by Turtleback) Demco.

Minarik, Else H. Little Bear's Visit. unabridged ed. LC 61-11451. (I Can Read Bks.). (Illus.). 64p. (J). (ps-3). 1990. pap. 8.95 incl. audio (*1-55994-236-3*) HarperAudio.

— No Fighting, No Biting! (I Can Read Bks.). (Illus.). 64p. (J). (gr. 1-3). 1958. 13.00 (*0-06-024290-6*) HarpC Child Bks.

Minarik, Else H. No Fighting, No Biting! LC 58-5293. (I Can Read Bks.). (Illus.). 64p. (J). (ps-3). 1958. lib. bdg. 15.89 (*0-06-024291-4*) HarpC Child Bks.

— No Fighting, No Biting! (I Can Read Bks.). (Illus.). 64p. (J). (gr. 1-3). 1978. pap. 3.95 (*0-06-444015-X*, HarpTrophy) HarpC Child Bks.

Minarik, Else H. No Fighting, No Biting! (I Can Read Bks.). (J). (gr. 1-3). 1978. 8.95 (*0-606-12454-3*, Pub. by Turtleback) Demco.

Minarik, Else H. Osito. LC 69-14452. (Spanish I Can Read Bk.).Tr. of Little Bear. (SPA., Illus.). 64p. (J). (ps-3). 1969. lib. bdg. 10.89 (*0-06-024244-2*) HarpC Child Bks.

— Osito.Tr. of Little Bear. (J). 1980. 15.15 (*0-606-10488-7*, Pub. by Turtleback) Demco.

— Papa Oso Vuelve a Casa.Tr. of Father Bear Comes Home. 1981. 15.15 (*0-606-10489-5*, Pub. by Turtleback) Demco.

Minarik, Else H. La Visita de Osito. 1982. 14.70 (*0-606-10446-1*, Pub. by Turtleback) Demco.

Minarik, Else H. La Visita de Osito. (SPA., Illus.). (J). (gr. 1-6). pap. 9.50 (*84-204-3051-X*) Santillana.

Minarik, Else H. & Tashlin, Frank. El Oso Que No Lo Era (The Bear That Wasn't) (SPA., Illus.). (J). (gr. 2-4). 1995. pap. 10.95 (*958-24-0002-1*, Pub. by Santillana) T R Bks.

Minarik, Else H., jt. auth. see Sendak, Maurice.

Minarik, John P., ed. Kicking Their Heels with Freedom. LC 80-71014. 80p. 1981. pap. 4.00 (*0-939406-00-4*) Acad Prison Arts.

Minarik, Joseph J. Making America's Budget Policy: From the 1980s to the 1990s. LC 89-27503. 248p. (C). (gr. 13). 1990. 66.95 (*0-87332-573-7*) M E Sharpe.

Minarik, Joseph J. Making America's Budget Policy: From the 1980s to the 1990s. LC 89-27503. 248p. (C). (gr. 13). 1990. pap. 34.95 (*0-87332-621-0*) M E Sharpe.

Minarik, Pamela A., et al. Culture & Nursing Care: A Pocket Guide. 1996. pap. text 18.95 (*0-943671-15-9*) UCSF Schl Nursing.

Minars, David. Partnerships Step-by-Step. LC 97-2594. (Legal-Ease Ser.). 240p. 1997. pap. text 14.95 (*0-7641-0184-6*) Barron.

Minars, David A. Business Start-ups: The Professional's Guide to Tax & Financial Strategies. 300p. 1987. text 49.95 (*0-13-107707-4*) P-H.

— Corporations Step-by-Step. (Legal-Ease Ser.). 320p. 1996. pap. text 14.95 (*0-8120-9635-5*) Barron.

Minars, David A. & Davidoff, Howard. Tax Penalties & Interest Handbook, 1990-1991. 340p. 1990. ring bd. 80.00 (*0-88063-748-X*, MICHIE) LEXIS Pub.

Minars, David A., et al. The Financial Troubleshooter: Spotting & Solving Financial Problems in Your Company. 228p. 1993. pap. 14.95 (*0-07-057604-1*) McGraw.

Minars, David A., jt. auth. see Davidoff, Howard.

Minars, Davis A. Accounting. (Barron's EZ-101 Study Keys Ser.). 144p. (Orig.). (C). 1992. pap. text 6.95 (*0-8120-4738-9*) Barron.

Minarski, M. Testudines. (Encyclopedia of Paleoherpetology Ser.: Pt. 7). (Illus.). 130p. 1976. text 70.00 (*3-437-30236-1*) Lubrecht & Cramer.

Minary, Ruth, jt. auth. see Moorman, Charles.

Minas, Anne. Gender Basics: Feminist Perspectives on Women & Men. 545p. (C). 1992. 36.25 (*0-534-17814-6*) Wadsworth Pub.

Minas, Anne, ed. Gender Basics: Feminist Perspectives on Women & Men. 2nd ed. LC 00-20517. (Philosophy). 557p. 2000. pap. 56.95 (*0-534-52839-2*) Wadsworth Pub.

Minasi. Software Skills. (Business Technology Ser.). 1998. text 24.95 (*0-442-02727-3*, VNR) Wiley.

Minasi, Dom. Musician's Manual for Chord Substitution. Gambino, Thomas, ed. 30p. (Orig.). 1973. pap., student ed. 6.00 (*0-936519-03-7*) Sunrise Artistries.

— Principles of Harmonic Substitution. Gambino, Thomas, ed. 48p. (Orig.). 1979. pap., student ed. 11.95 (*0-936519-02-9*) Sunrise Artistries.

— Stress Points. Gambino, Thomas, ed. (Illus.). (Orig.). 1986. pap. 11.95 (*0-936519-00-2*) Sunrise Artistries.

Minasi, Mark. The Complete PC Upgrade & Maintenance Guide. 1996. pap. text 49.99 incl. cd-rom (*0-7821-2039-3*) Sybex.

*Minasi, Mark. Complete PC Upgrade & Maintenance Guide. 10th ed. LC 99-63820. 1616p. 1999. 49.99 (*0-7821-2606-5*) Sybex.

— The Complete PC Upgrade & Maintenance Guide with CD-ROM. 11th ed. 1648p. 2000. 59.99 incl. cd-rom (*0-7821-2800-9*) Sybex.

— Complete PC Upgrade & Maintenance Seminar-in-a-Box. 10th ed. 2000. pap. 99.99 (*0-7821-2706-1*) Sybex.

— Complete PC Upgrade/A+ Certification Box. 3rd ed. 2768p. 1999. pap. 89.99 (*0-7821-2607-3*) Sybex.

Minasi, Mark. Expert Guide to Windows 98. 2nd ed. LC 98-84009. 976p. 1998. 49.99 (*0-7821-1974-3*) Sybex.

— The Expert Guide to Windows 95. LC 95-72703. (Illus.). 528p. (Orig.). 1996. 34.99 incl. cd-rom (*0-7821-1519-5*) Sybex.

— Expert Guide to Windows NT Workstation X. 560p. 1996. pap. text 34.99 incl. cd-rom (*0-7821-1918-2*) Sybex.
— Inside OS - 2 Warp, Ver. 3. 1200p. 1994. pap. 39.99 incl. disk (*1-56205-378-7*) New Riders Pub.
*__Minasi, Mark.__ Mark Minasi's Windows 2000 Resource Kit. 2448p. 2000. pap. 124.96 (*0-7821-2614-6*) Sybex.
__Minasi, Mark.__ Mastering NT Server 4. 3rd ed. 1996. 49.99 (*0-614-20333-3*, Network Pr) Sybex.
— Mastering NT Server 4. 4th ed. 1997. pap. 54.99 (*0-614-28534-8*, Network Pr) Sybex.
— Mastering Windows NT Server 4. 6th ed. (Mastering Ser.). 1616p. 1999. 59.99 (*0-7821-2445-3*) Sybex.
*__Minasi, Mark.__ Mastering Windows NT Server 4. 7th ed. (Illus.). 1696p. 2000. pap. 69.99 (*0-7821-2693-6*) Sybex.
__Minasi, Mark.__ Mastering Windows NT Workstation 4, Vol. 4. 2nd ed. LC 99-60025. (Mastering Ser.). 1152p. 1999. 49.99 (*0-7821-2491-7*) Sybex.
*__Minasi, Mark.__ Mastering Windows 2000 Professional. 4th ed. (Mastering Ser.). 1008p. 2000. pap. 39.99 (*0-7821-2448-8*) Sybex.
__Minasi, Mark.__ Mastering Windows 2000 Server. (Mastering Ser.). 512p. 1999. pap. 39.99 (*0-7821-2447-X*) Sybex.
*__Minasi, Mark.__ Mastering Windows 2000 Server. 4th ed. (Mastering Ser.). 1344p. 1999. 49.99 (*0-7821-2446-1*) Sybex.
— NT 4 Max Box. 6608p. 1999. boxed set 94.98 (*0-7821-2527-1*) Sybex.
__Minasi, Mark.__ PalmPilot's Amazing Secrets. 1998. pap. text 24.99 (*0-7821-2247-7*) Sybex.
— The Software Conspiracy: Why Software Companies Put Out Faulty Products, How They Can Hurt Your & What You Can Do about It. 269p. 1999. 22.95 (*0-07-134806-9*) McGraw.
— Zero Administration for Windows --Now! 1998. pap. text 39.99 (*0-7821-2386-4*) Sybex.
__Minasi, Mark, et al.__ The Complete Network Upgrade & Maintenance Guide. LC 98-86639. (Illus.). 1600p. 1998. 69.99 incl. cd-rom (*0-7821-2259-0*) Sybex.
— Mastering TCP-IP for NT Server. LC 97-68480. 544p. 1997. pap. text 44.99 (*0-7821-2123-3*) Sybex.
*__Minasi, Mark, et al.__ Mastering Windows 2000 Server. 2nd ed. (Illus.). 1632p. 2000. pap. 49.99 (*0-7821-2774-6*) Sybex.
__Minasian, Stanley M.__ The Whales of Hawaii. 1991. pap. 5.95 (*0-9627803-0-8*) Hamilton West.
__Minasian, Stanley M., et al, contrib. by.__ The Whales of Hawaii: Including All Species of Marine Mammals in Hawaiian & Adjacent Waters. (Illus.). 100p. (Orig.). (YA). (gr. 9 up). 1991. pap. text 7.00 (*0-9617803-0-4*) Marine Mammal Fund.
__Minassian, John.__ Many Hills Yet to Climb. 300p. (Orig.). 1986. pap. write for info. (*0-936941-00-6*) Jim Cook.
__Minassian, Martiros.__ Grammaire d'Armenien Oriental. LC 80-18625. (Anatolian & Caucasian Studies). 384p. 1981. 50.00 (*0-88206-040-6*) Caravan Bks.
__Minati, Gianfranco & Collen, Arne.__ Introduction to Systemics. LC 96-61436. (Illus.). 1997. write for info. (*0-924025-06-9*) Eagleye Bks Intl.
__Minato, Robert, jt. auth. see Pitter, Keiko.__
__Minato, Shin-Ichi.__ Binary Decision Diagrams & Applications for VLSI CAD. (International Series in Engineering & Computer Science, Natural Language Processing & Machine Translation). 160p. (C). 1995. text 95.50 (*0-7923-9652-9*) Kluwer Academic.
*__Minatoya, Lydia.__ The Strangers of Beauty. 384p. 2000. reprint ed. pap. 14.00 (*0-393-32140-1*, Norton Paperbks) Norton.
__Minatoya, Lydia.__ Talking to High Monks in the Snow: An Asian-American Odyssey. LC 91-50450. 288p. 1993. pap. 13.00 (*0-06-092372-5*, Perennial) HarperTrade.
*__Minatoya, Lydia Y.__ The Strangeness of Beauty. LC 98-55250. 384p. 1999. 23.00 (*0-684-85362-0*) Simon & Schuster.
__Minault, Gail.__ The Khilafat Movement: Religious Symbolism & Political Mobilization in India. LC 81-4553. (Studies in Oriental Culture: No. 16). 288p. 1982. text 57.50 (*0-231-05072-0*) Col U Pr.
— Secluded Scholars: Women's Education & Muslim Social Reform in Colonial India. LC 97-914025. (Illus.). 374p. 1998. text 35.00 (*0-19-564190-6*) OUP.
— Secluded Scholars: Women's Education & Muslim Social Reform in Colonial India. (Illus.). 374p. 1999. pap. text 14.95 (*0-19-565022-0*) OUP.
__Minault, Gail, ed.__ The Extended Family: Women in India. (C). 1989. reprint ed. 40.00 (*0-685-33289-6*, Pub. by Chanakya) S Asia.
— Voices of Silent: English Translation of Hali's Majalis Un-Nissa & Chup Di Dad. 1986. 18.50 (*81-7001-018-7*, Pub. by Chanakya) S Asia.
__Minault, Gail, ed. see Douglas, Ian H.__
__Minawer, Sidney J., et al.__ Liberese del Cancer.Tr. of Cancer Free. (SPA.). 1995. per. 11.00 (*0-684-81332-7*, Fireside) S&S Trade Pap.
__Minay, C., ed.__ Implementation - View from an Ivory Tower. (C). 1980. 29.00 (*0-7855-3872-0*, Pub. by Oxford Polytechnic) St Mut.
__Minay, C. & Weston, J.__ The Future of Work Jobs in the Environment. (C). 1987. 40.00 (*0-7855-3825-9*, Pub. by Oxford Polytechnic) St Mut.
__Minbiole, Elizabeth A.__ Accounting Principles I Quick Review. LC 99-174015. (Cliffs Quick Reviews Ser.). (Illus.). 203p. (C). 1998. pap. text, student ed. 9.95 (*0-8220-5309-8*, Cliff) IDG Bks.
*__Minbiole, Mark J.__ Handbook of Financial Analysis, Forecasting & Valuation. (Illus.). xii, 359p. 2000. pap. 125.00 (*0-9660030-2-0*) Vector Pub.
— Introduction to Financial Information: Sources & Interpretation. 2nd ed. (Illus.). viii, 182p. 1999. pap. text 30.00 (*0-9660030-1-2*) Vector Pub.
__Minc, Henryk.__ Nonnegative Matrices. LC 87-27416. (Discrete Mathematics Ser.). 206p. 1988. 160.00 (*0-471-83966-3*) Wiley.
— Permanents. (Encyclopedia of Mathematics & Its Applications Ser.: No. 6). 205p. 1984. text 69.95 (*0-521-30226-9*) Cambridge U Pr.
__Minc, Henryk, jt. auth. see Marcus, Marvin.__
__Minc, Rose S., ed. see Desnoes, et al.__
__Minc, Rose S., ed. see Fuentes, Carlos, et al.__
__Mincberg, Mella.__ WordPerfect 6: The Pocket Reference. 3rd ed. 1993. pap. 9.95 (*0-07-881905-9*) Osborne-McGraw.
— WordPerfect 6 Made Easy. 3rd ed. 1993. pap. 24.95 (*0-07-881895-8*) Osborne-McGraw.
__Mincer.__ Schooling, Experience & Earnings. 1993. 59.95 (*0-7512-0125-1*) Ashgate Pub Co.
__Mincer, Jacob.__ Schooling, Experience, & Earnings. (Studies in Human Behavior & Social Institutions: No. 2). 167p. 1974. 45.50 (*0-87014-265-8*) Natl Bur Econ Res.
— Schooling, Experience & Earnings. LC 73-88508. (Human Behavior & Social Institutions Ser.: Vol. 2). (Illus.). 175p. reprint ed. pap. 54.30 (*0-608-20018-2*, 201596400006) Bks Demand.
— Studies in Human Capital Vol. 1: Collected Essays of Jacob Mincer. (Economists of the Twentieth Century Ser.). 448p. 1993. 120.00 (*1-85278-579-9*) E Elgar.
— Studies in Labor Supply Vol. 2: Collected Essays of Jacob Mincer. (Economists of the Twentieth Century Ser.). 352p. 1993. 110.00 (*1-85278-578-0*) E Elgar.
__Mincer, Jacob, ed.__ Economic Forecasts & Expectations: Analysis of Forecasting Behavior & Performance. (Business Cycles Ser.: No. 19). 269p. 1969. text 70.50 (*0-87014-202-X*) Natl Bur Econ Res.
__Minces, Juliette.__ Veiled: Women in Islam. Berrett, A. M., tr. from FRE. LC 93-28544. 176p. 1994. 25.00 (*0-9628715-5-9*) Blue Crane Bks.
__Minceva-Stefanova, J. M., jt. auth. see Kostov, I. R.__
__Mincey, Melvin.__ God Hates Sin... But Loves the Sinner! Abrims, Ethel, ed. (Illus.). 143p. 1995. reprint ed. pap. 11.95 (*0-9637969-1-7*) Mincey Pub Hse.
— Ward Street. (Illus.). 281p. (Orig.). 1994. pap. text 8.95 (*0-9637969-0-9*) Mincey Pub Hse.
— The Worm That Never Dies. rev. ed. Abrims, Ethel, ed. Orig. Title: Ward Street. (Illus.). 223p. 1995. pap. 8.95 (*0-9637969-2-5*) Mincey Pub Hse.
__Minch, John, et al.__ Roadside Geology & Biology of Baja California. (Illus.). iv, 188p. Date not set. 19.95 (*0-9631090-1-4*) J Minch Assocs.
__Minch, Stephen.__ Ken Krenzel's Ingenuities. (Illus.). 224p. 1997. 37.00 (*0-945296-19-3*) Hermetic Pr.
__Minch, Stephen, jt. auth. see Wonder, Tommy.__
__Minch, Stephen, ed. see Lesley, Ted.__
__Minchella, Giulio, ed. see Hughes, Jack.__
__Minchev, G., ed.__ Molecular Beam Epitaxy. 200p. 1991. text 116.00 (*0-87849-614-9*, Pub. by Trans T Pub) Enfield Pubs NH.
__Minchilli, Elizabeth H.__ Private Rome. LC 98-66951. (Illus.). 216p. 1998. 45.00 (*0-8478-2130-7*, Pub. by Rizzoli Intl) St Martin.
— Private Tuscany. (Illus.). 216p. 1999. 45.00 (*0-8478-2178-1*) Rizzoli Intl.
__Minchin, James.__ No Man Is an Island. 384p. 1987. text 37.95 (*0-86861-906-X*) Routledge.
*__Minchin, Timothy J.__ Hiring of the Black Worker: The Racial Integration of the Southern Textile Industry, 1960-1980. LC 98-30146. (Illus.). 360p. 1999. pap. 19.95 (*0-8078-4771-2*); lib. bdg. 49.95 (*0-8078-2470-4*) U of NC Pr.
__Minchin, Timothy J.__ What Do We Need a Union For? The TWUA in the South, 1945-1955. LC 96-25419. (Fred W. Morrison Series in Southern Studies). 296p. (gr. 13). 1997. pap. 17.95 (*0-8078-4625-2*); lib. bdg. 49.95 (*0-8078-2317-1*) U of NC Pr.
__Minchinton, Jerry A.__ Fifty-Two Things You Can Do to Raise Your Self-Esteem. LC 94-78712. 80p. (Orig.). 1995. pap. 6.50 (*0-9635719-6-6*) Arnford MO.
— Maximum Self-Esteem: The Handbook for Reclaiming Your Sense of Self-Worth. LC 92-76034. 254p. (Orig.). 1993. pap. 14.95 (*0-9635719-4-X*) Arnford MO.
*__Minchinton, Jerry A.__ Wising Up: How to Stop Making Such a Mess of Your Life. LC 99-489854. 240p. 2000. pap. 14.50 (*0-9635719-5-8*, Arnford Hse) Arnford MO.
__Minchinton, Walter, et al, eds.__ Virginia Slave-Trade Statistics, 1698-1775. xvi, 218p. (Orig.). 1984. 45.00 (*0-88490-118-1*) Library of VA.
__Minchinton, Walter E., ed.__ Industrial South Wales 1750-1914: Essays in Welsh Economic History. LC 68-21451. (Illus.). xxxi, 264p. 1969. 32.50 (*0-678-05018-X*) Kelley.
— Industrial South Wales, 1750-1914: Essays in Welsh Economic History. 296p. 1969. 35.00 (*0-7146-1344-4*, Pub. by F Cass Pubs) Intl Spec Bk.
__Minciacchi, Diego, et al, eds.__ Thalamic Networks for Relay & Modulation. LC 93-21166. (Studies in Neuroscience). 462p. 1993. 185.25 (*0-08-042274-8*, Pergamon Pr) Elsevier.
__Minck.__ Construction Waste Management. 300p. 59.95 (*0-471-15599-3*) Wiley.
__Minckler, Don S. & Van Buskirk, Michael.__ Glaucoma. Wright, Kenneth W., ed. LC 91-27594. (Color Atlas of Ophthalmic Surgery Ser.). (Illus.). 324p. reprint ed. pap. 100.50 (*0-608-05771-1*, 205973600007) Bks Demand.
__Minckler, Leon S.__ Woodland Ecology: Environmental Forestry for the Small Owner. 2nd ed. (Illus.). 230p. 1980. pap. 17.95 (*0-8156-0154-9*) Syracuse U Pr.
__Minckley, Barbara B. & Walters, Mary D., eds.__ Building Trust Relationships in Nursing. LC 83-19363. 131p. 1983. pap. 6.00 (*0-942146-04-2*) Midwest Alliance Nursing.
__Minckley, Wendell L. & Deacon, James E., eds.__ Battle Against Extinction: Native Fish Management in the American West. LC 91-6977. (Illus.). 517p. 1991. 57.00 (*0-8165-1221-3*) U of Ariz Pr.
__Mincks, William R.__ Construction Contracts Administration. (Construction & Building Trades Ser.). 1996. teacher ed. 10.00 (*0-8273-7153-5*) Delmar.
__Mincks, William R. & Johnson.__ Construction Jobsite Management. LC 97-21518. (Construction & Building Trades Ser.). 432p. (C). 1997. mass mkt. 72.95 (*0-8273-7152-7*) Delmar.
__Minco, Marga.__ Empty House. LC 89-81668. 160p. 1990. 26.00 (*0-7206-0760-4*, Pub. by P Owen Ltd) Dufour.
— The Fall. Ringold, Jeannette K., tr. LC 90-80801. 112p. 1990. 24.95 (*0-7206-0789-2*, Pub. by P Owen Ltd) Dufour.
— Glass Bridge. Knecht, Stacey, tr. from DUT. 111p. 1988. 24.95 (*0-7206-0719-1*, Pub. by P Owen Ltd) Dufour.
__Minco, Marga, et al.__ The Other Side. Levitt, Ruth et al, trs. from DUT. 118p. 1994. 30.00 (*0-7206-0908-9*, Pub. by P Owen Ltd) Dufour.
__Mincoff, Elizabeth & Marriage, Margaret S.__ Pillow Lace: A Practical Handbook. 1981. 22.95 (*0-903585-10-3*) Robin & Russ.
__Mincoff, Marco.__ Things Supernatural & Causeless: Shakespearean Romance. LC 92-53580. 136p. 1992. 28.50 (*0-87413-456-0*) U Delaware Pr.
__Mincolla, Mark D.__ The Tao of Ch'i: Healing with the Unseen Life Force. (Illus.). 52p. (Orig.). 1995. pap. 14.95 (*0-9632811-1-9*) Pennyroyal Pr.
— The Wu Way: A Path to Natural Healing. 52p. (Orig.). 1992. pap. 10.95 (*0-9632811-0-0*) Pennyroyal Pr.
__Mincolla, Mark Dana.__ Maximum Healing. 1998. pap. 19.95 (*0-9632811-2-7*) Pennyroyal Pr.
__Mincu, Julian.__ Diabetic Macro- & Microangiopathy. LC 73-82434. (C). 1975. 150.00 (*3-11-004533-8*) De Gruyter.
__Mincy, Ronald B., ed.__ Nurturing Young Black Males: Challenges to Agencies, Programs, & Social Policy. 260p. 1994. 24.50 (*0-87766-598-2*) Urban Inst.
__Minczeles, Henri, jt. auth. see Silvain, Gerard.__
__Minczeski, John.__ Gravity. x, 67p. 1991. 16.50 (*0-89672-267-8*); pap. 9.50 (*0-89672-268-6*) Tex Tech Univ Pr.
__Minczeski, John, ed.__ Concert at Chopin's House: A Collection of Polish American Writing. 206p. 1987. pap. 14.95 (*0-89823-098-5*) New Rivers Pr.
— The Midnight Butterfly Sings. (Illus.). 164p. (Orig.). 1988. pap. 7.50 (*0-927663-01-5*) COMPAS.
__Minczeski, John, ed. see Reinhard, John.__
__Minczewski, Jerzy, et al.__ Separation & Preconcentration Methods in Inorganic Trace Analysis. (Analytical Chemistry Ser.). 550p. 1982. text 136.00 (*0-470-27169-8*) P-H.
__Mind-Body Medical Institute Staff, et al.__ The Wellness Book: The Comprehensive Guide to Maintaining Health & Treating Stress-Related Illness. (Illus.). 352p. 1991. 21.95 (*1-55972-092-1*, Birch Ln Pr) Carol Pub Group.
__Mind Q Publications Staff, et al.__ Computers & Information Systems: 1995-1996 Edition. 5th ed. (C). 1996. text, per. 48.20 incl. cd-rom (*0-256-22620-2*, Irwn McGrw-H) McGrw-H Hghr Educ.
__Mind Q. Staff.__ Java Live: An Interactive Learning Tool. 1996. pap. text 49.99 incl. cd-rom (*1-56276-482-9*, Ziff-Davis Pr) Que.
__Mind Works Staff.__ A+ Certification Interactive Workbook. 1998. pap., student ed. 128.95 incl. cd-rom (*0-538-68673-1*) S-W Pub.
__Minda, Gary.__ Boycott in America: How Imagination & Ideology Shape the Legal Mind. LC 98-16474. (Illus.). 271p. 1998. 34.95 (*0-8093-2174-2*) S Ill U Pr.
— Postmodern Legal Movements: Law & Jurisprudence at Century's End. LC 94-24934. 350p. (C). 1995. text 45.00 (*0-8147-5510-0*) NYU Pr.
*__Mindancer.__ Tales of Emoria: Past Echoes. viii, 287p. 2000. pap. 17.99 (*0-9674196-7-0*, 008, Silver Dragon) Renaissance Alliance.
__Minde, Ase, jt. auth. see Jennings, Sue.__
__Minde, Klaus & Minde, Regina.__ Infant Psychiatry: An Introduction Textbook. LC 85-14231. (Developmental Clinical Psychology & Psychiatry Ser.: No. 4). 197p. reprint ed. pap. 61.10 (*0-7837-6717-X*, 204634400011) Bks Demand.
__Minde, Regina, jt. auth. see Minde, Klaus.__
*__Mindel, Adrian.__ Condoms. (Illus.). 230p. 2000. pap. text 34.95 (*0-7279-1267-4*) BMJ Pub.
__Mindel, Adrian, ed.__ Genital Warts: Human Papilloma Virus Infection. 304p. 1995. text 85.00 (*0-340-57924-2*, Pub. by E A) OUP.
__Mindel, Adrian & Miller, Robert, eds.__ AIDS: A Pocket Book of Diagnosis & Management. 2nd ed. (Illus.). 384p. 1996. pap. text 27.95 (*0-340-58609-5*, Pub. by E A) OUP.
__Mindel, Charles H., Jr., et al, eds.__ Ethnic Families in America: Patterns & Variations. 3rd ed. 525p. 1988. pap. 27.75 (*0-444-01319-9*) P-H.
__Mindel, Charles H., et al.__ Ethnic Families in America. 4th ed. LC 97-24844. 518p. 1997. pap. text 45.33 (*0-13-531328-7*) P-H.
__Mindel, Charles S., jt. auth. see Markides, Kyriacos C.__
__Mindel, Eugene D. & Vernon, McCay, eds.__ They Grow in Silence: Understanding Deaf Children & Adults. LC 90-21666. (Illus.). 204p. (C). 1987. reprint ed. pap. text 29.00 (*0-89079-325-5*, 1744) PRO-ED.
__Mindel, Nissan.__ The Call of the Shofar. (Illus.). 64p. (YA). 1971. reprint ed. 11.00 (*0-8266-0345-9*, Merkos LInyonei Chinuch) Kehot Pubn Soc.
— Chanuka. (Complete Story of Ser.). (Illus.). 32p. (Orig.). 1946. reprint ed. pap. 2.00 (*0-8266-0318-1*, Merkos LInyonei Chinuch) Kehot Pubn Soc.
— The Complete Story of Passover. 12th ed. (Complete Story of Ser.). (Illus.). 78p. (Orig.). 1946. reprint ed. pap. 7.00 (*0-8266-0320-3*, Merkos LInyonei Chinuch) Kehot Pubn Soc.
— The Complete Story of Purim. (Complete Story of Ser.). (Illus.). 64p. (Orig.). 1946. reprint ed. pap. 6.00 (*0-8266-0319-X*, Merkos LInyonei Chinuch) Kehot Pubn Soc.
— Complete Story of Shavuot. (Complete Story of Ser.). (Illus.). 108p. Date not set. reprint ed. 10.00 (*0-8266-0322-X*, Merkos LInyonei Chinuch) Kehot Pubn Soc.
— Complete Story of Shavuot. (Complete Story of Ser.). (Illus.). 108p. 1946. reprint ed. pap. 7.00 (*0-8266-0321-1*, Merkos LInyonei Chinuch) Kehot Pubn Soc.
— Complete Story of Tishrei. (Complete Story of Ser.). (Illus.). 240p. 1982. 12.00 (*0-8266-0316-5*, Merkos LInyonei Chinuch) Kehot Pubn Soc.
— Dertzeil Mir A Ma'aseh, Vol. 1. (YID., Illus.). 274p. (YA). (gr. 4-9). 1988. reprint ed. 12.00 (*0-8266-0386-6*, Merkos LInyonei Chinuch) Kehot Pubn Soc.
— Dertzeil Mir A Ma'aseh, Vol. 2. (YID., Illus.). 265p. (YA). (gr. 4-8). 1994. reprint ed. 12.00 (*0-8266-0387-4*, Merkos LInyonei Chinuch) Kehot Pubn Soc.
— The Divine Commandments: The Significance & Function of Mitzvot in Chabad Philosophy. 11th rev. ed. 48p. reprint ed. pap. 6.00 (*0-8266-0301-7*) Kehot Pubn Soc.
— My Prayer: Daily Prayers, Vol. 1. (My Prayer Ser.). 332p. 1972. reprint ed. 14.00 (*0-8266-0310-6*, Merkos LInyonei Chinuch) Kehot Pubn Soc.
— My Prayer: Shabbat Prayers, Vol. 2. (My Prayer Ser.). 208p. 1989. reprint ed. 14.00 (*0-8266-0311-4*, Merkos LInyonei Chinuch) Kehot Pubn Soc.
— The Philosophy of Chabad, Vol. 2. (Philosophy of Chabad Ser.). 256p. 1973. reprint ed. 15.00 (*0-8266-0417-X*) Kehot Pubn Soc.
— Rabbi Schneur Zalman of Liadi. LC 98-42623. 1999. 15.00 (*0-8266-0416-1*) Kehot Pubn Soc.
— The Runaway. 6th ed. (Illus.). 1969. reprint ed. pap. 1.00 (*0-8266-0325-4*) Kehot Pubn Soc.
— The Storyteller, Vol. 1. (Illus.). 318p. (YA). 1981. reprint ed. 14.00 (*0-8266-0314-9*, Merkos LInyonei Chinuch) Kehot Pubn Soc.
— The Storyteller, Vol. 2. (Illus.). 268p. (YA). 1984. reprint ed. 14.00 (*0-8266-0313-0*, Merkos LInyonei Chinuch) Kehot Pubn Soc.
— The Storyteller, Vol. 3. (Illus.). 368p. (YA). 1987. reprint ed. 14.00 (*0-8266-0312-2*, Merkos LInyonei Chinuch) Kehot Pubn Soc.
— The Storyteller, Vol. 4. (Illus.). 346p. (YA). 1991. reprint ed. 14.00 (*0-8266-1312-8*, Merkos LInyonei Chinuch) Kehot Pubn Soc.
— The Storyteller, Vol. 5. LC 86-2383. 328p. (J). (gr. 4-7). 1998. 14.00 (*0-8266-1313-6*, Merkos LInyonei Chinuch) Kehot Pubn Soc.
— Yer-Vos-Vu-Ven: Interesting & Curious Facts from the Bible, Talmud & Midrash. Kranzler, Gershon & Zimmer, Uriel, eds. (YID., Illus.). 78p. 1964. 8.00 (*0-8266-0371-8*) Kehot Pubn Soc.
__Mindel, Nissan, ed.__ The Secret of Success & Other Stories. (Illus.). 64p. (YA). 1973. reprint ed. 11.00 (*0-8266-0346-7*, Merkos LInyonei Chinuch) Kehot Pubn Soc.
__Mindel, Nissan & Dershowitz, Yosef.__ The Storyteller: Selected Short Stories. 2nd ed. LC 86-2383. (J). 1986. write for info. (*0-8266-0315-7*, Merkos LInyonei Chinuch) Kehot Pubn Soc.
__Mindel, Nissan, ed. see Schneerson, Menachem M.__
__Mindel, Nissan, tr. see Lehman, Marcus.__
__Mindel, Nissan, tr. see Schneersohn, Yosef Y.__
__Mindel, Nissan, tr. see Schneerson, Joseph I.__
__Mindel, Nissan, tr. see Sceersohn, Yosef Yitchak.__
__Mindeleff, Victor.__ A Study of Pueblo Architecture: Tusayan & Cibola, No. 8. (Smithsonian Institution, Bureau of Ethnology Ser.). (Illus.). 428p. pap. text 44.38 (*1-55567-818-1*) Coyote Press.
__Mindeleff, Victor.__ A Study of Pueblo Architecture in Tusayan & Cibola. LC 88-43115. (Illus.). 653p. (C). 1989. pap. text 29.95 (*0-87474-619-1*) Smithsonian.
__Mindell.__ Infancy, Childhood & Adolescence. 1991. teacher ed. 18.12 (*0-07-061214-5*) McGraw.
— Safe Eating. 1993. 5.99 (*0-446-77690-4*) Warner Bks.
__Mindell, Amy.__ Coma, a Healing Journey: A Guide for Family, Friends & Helpers. LC 98-88184. (Illus.). 330p. 1998. 21.00 (*1-887078-05-3*) Lao Tse Pr.
— Metaskills: The Spiritual Art of Therapy. LC 94-68554. 192p. (Orig.). 1995. pap. 12.95 (*1-56184-119-6*) New Falcon Pubns.
__Mindell, Arnold.__ Dreambody: The Body's Role in Revealing the Self. 2nd ed. (Illus.). 314p. 1998. pap. text 16.00 (*1-887078-04-5*) Lao Tse Pr.
— Dreambody in Relationships. 1987. pap. 9.95 (*0-7102-1072-8*, Routledge Thoemms) Routledge.
*__Mindell, Arnold.__ Dreaming While Awake: Techniques for 24-Hour Lucid Dreaming. 2000. 22.95 (*1-57174-187-9*) Hampton Roads Pub Co.
— Leader as Martial Artist: Techniques & Strategies for Resolving Conflict & Creating Communit. 2000. pap. text 13.95 (*1-887078-65-7*) Lao Tse Pr.
__Mindell, Arnold.__ The Leader As Martial Artist: Techniques & Strategies for Resolving Conflict & Creating Community. LC 91-55333. (Illus.). 176p. 1993. pap. 12.00 (*0-06-250640-4*, Pub. by Harper SF) HarpC.
*__Mindell, Arnold.__ Quantum Mind: The Edge Between Physics & Psychology. LC 99-66088. (Illus.). 632p. 2000. pap. 26.95 (*1-887078-64-9*) Lao Tse Pr.
__Mindell, Arnold.__ The Shaman's Body: A New Shamanism for Transforming Health, Relationships, & the Community. LC 92-56408. 256p. 1993. pap. 14.00 (*0-06-250655-2*, Pub. by Harper SF) HarpC.

An Asterisk (*) at the beginning of an entry indicates that the title is appearing for the first time.

An Asterisk (*) at the beginning of an entry indicates that the title is appearing for the first time.

Minear, Roger A. & Amy, Gary L., eds. Disinfection By-Products in Water Treatment: The Chemistry of Their Formation & Control. LC 95-35535. 520p. 1995. lib. bdg. 85.00 (*1-56670-136-8*, L1136) Lewis Pubs.
— Water Disinfection & Natural Organic Matter: Characterization & Control. LC 96-36454. (Acs Symposium Ser.: Vol. 649). (Illus.). 408p. 1996. text 115.00 (*0-8412-3464-7*, Pub. by Am Chemical) OUP.

Minear, Tish & Limon, Janet. Discover Native America: Arizona Colorado New Mexico & Utah. (Illus.). 300p. (Orig.). 1995. pap. 16.95 (*0-7818-0327-6*) Hippocrene Bks.

Mineau, Anita C. Adventures in Yooperland: Those Happy Days of Childhood. Hendershot, Nancy, ed. (Illus.). 31p. (J). (gr. 4-6). 1998. pap. 11.95 (*0-9662539-0-6*) Bks By Anita.

Mineau, G. W., et al, eds. Conceptual Graphs for Knowledge Representation: Proceedings of the First International Conference on Conceptual Structures, ICCS 93, Quebec, Canada, August 4-7, 1993. (Lecture Notes in Artificial Intelligence Ser.: Vol. 699). ix, 451p. 1993. 65.95 (*0-387-56979-0*) Spr-Verlag.

Mineau, P. Cholinesterase-Inhibiting Insecticides. (Chemicals in Agriculture Ser.: Vol. 2). 360p. 1991. 176.75 (*0-444-88707-5*) Elsevier.

Mineev, V. P. Topologically Stable Defects & Solitons in Ordered Media. 92p. 1998. pap. text 19.00 (*90-5702-272-9*, Harwood Acad Pubs) Gordon & Breach.

***Mineev, V. P. & Samokhin, K.** Introduction to Unconventional Superconductivity. 200p. 1999. text 68.00 (*90-5699-209-0*) Gordon & Breach.

Mineev, V. P., jt. auth. see Khalatnikov, Isaac M.

Mineev, Vladimir, ed. The First Landau Institute Summer School July 1993: Selected Proceedings. 300p. 1995. text 105.00 (*2-88449-138-4*) Gordon & Breach.

Minehan, Maureen, jt. auth. see Ellig, Bruce R.

Minehart, Tom & Heisig, James W. Remembering the Kanji: Hyperkanji! 114p. 1993. disk 160.00 (*0-87040-971-9*) Japan Pubns USA.

Mineka, Francis E., ed. see Mill, John Stuart.

Minelli, A. Biological Systematics: The State of the Art. LC 93-3578. (Illus.). 408p. 1993. write for info. (*0-412-36440-9*) Chapman & Hall.

Minelli, Alesandro, ed. The Botanical Garden of Padua 1545-1995. 2nd ed. Barker, Gus, tr. from ITA. (Illus.). 312p. 1996. reprint ed. 65.00 (*1-56886-020-X*) Marsilio Pubs.

Minelli, Alessandro, ed. Proceedings of the 7th International Congress of Myriapodology. LC 89-9901. xv, 480p. 1989. 201.00 (*90-04-08972-1*) Brill Academic Pubs.

Minelli, Fiorigio, jt. tr. see Browning, John.

Minelli, Giuseppe. Reptiles. LC 86-32907. (History of Life on Earth Ser.). (Illus.). 64p. 1987. 15.95 (*0-8160-1558-9*) Facts on File.

***Minelli, Laura Laurencich.** Inca World: The Development of Pre-Columbian Peru, A. D. 1000-1534. (Illus.). 480p. 2000. 49.95 (*0-8061-3221-3*) U of Okla Pr.

Minelli, Mark J. Beyond Beer Goggles: Interactive Teaching Methods for Alcohol, Other Drugs & AIDS Prevention. 2nd ed. 185p. (Orig.). (C). 1996. pap. text 15.80 (*0-87563-658-6*) Stipes.

***Minelli, Mark J.** Drug Abuse in Sports: A Student Course Manual. 4th ed. 110p. (C). 1999. pap. text 10.00 (*0-87563-935-6*) Stipes.

Minelli, Tali M. Chanukah Fun. (Illus.). 32p. (J). (gr. 1 up). 1995. mass mkt. 7.95 (*0-688-13560-9*, Wm Morrow) Morrow Avon.

Minely, Ivy. Municipal Land Use. (Illus.). 311p. 1982. pap. 35.00 (*0-685-14650-2*) NJ Inst CLE.

***Mineo, Baldassare.** Rock Garden Plants: A Color Encyclopedia. LC 99-20672. (Illus.). 284p. 1999. 59.95 (*0-88192-432-6*) Timber.

Mineo, Higashi, jt. auth. see Tatsuhiro, Oshiro.

Miner, et al. Familial Alzheimer's Disease: Molecular Genetics & Clinical Perspectives. (Neurological Disease & Therapy Ser.: Vol. 3). 440p. 1989. 195.00 (*0-8247-8068-X*) Dekker.

Miner, Adriana, tr. see Vallaut, Jean-Jacques H.

Miner, Albert, tr. see Vallaut, Jean-Jacques H.

Miner, Allison & Smith, Michael P. Jazz Fest Memories. LC 96-47438. (Illus.). 160p. 1997. pap. 19.95 (*1-56554-157-X*) Pelican.

***Miner, Allyn.** Sitar & Sarod in the 18th & 19th Centuries. Richmond, Farley P., ed. 1998. 30.00 (*81-208-1299-9*) Motilal Bnarsidass.

Miner, Barbara, ed. Classroom Crusades: Responding to the Religious Right's Agenda for Public Schools. (Illus.). 80p. 1998. mass mkt. 5.00 (*0-942961-23-4*) Rethinking Schls.

Miner, Barbara, jt. auth. see Lowe, Robert.

Miner, Barbara, ed. see Bigelow, Bill, et al.

Miner, Bonaventure, ed. see Wurth, Othmar.

Miner, Brad. The Concise Conservative Encyclopedia: 200 of the Most Important Ideas, Individuals, Incitements, & Institutions That Have Shaped the Movement: A Personal View. LC 96-5788. (Paperbacks Ser.). 352p. 1996. per. 15.00 (*0-684-80043-8*) Free Pr.

Miner, Brad, jt. ed. see Sykes, Charles.

Miner, Brigitte, et al. Wild Herbs in Your Backyard: A Pocket Guide for Identifying & Using Common Plants of Exceptional Medicinal & Nutritional Value. (Illus.). 80p. (Orig.). 1996. pap. 6.95 (*0-9632814-1-0*) N Wrld CA.

Miner, C. J., et al, eds. Semi-Insulating III-V Materials, Ixtapa, Mexico, 1992: Proceedings of the 7th Conference on Semi-Insulating III-V Materials, Ixtapa, Mexico, 21-24 April 1992. (Illus.). 360p. 1993. 161.00 (*0-7503-0242-9*) IOP Pub.

Miner, C. J., jt. ed. see Milnes, A.

Miner, C. W., ed. & intro. see Williams, Robert H.

Miner, Chalise. Rain Forest Girl: More Than an Adoption Story. LC 97-43457. (Illus.). 48p. (J). (gr. 3-6). 1998. pap. 12.95 (*1-883845-81-5*); lib. bdg. 16.95 (*1-883845-65-3*) M Lane Pubs.

Miner, Charles. History of Wyoming (Valley, Pennsylvania) in a Series of Letters from Charles Minor to His Son William Penn Miner, Esq. 628p. 1991. reprint ed. pap. 35.00 (*1-55613-455-X*) Heritage Bk.

Miner, Colleen & Estrem, Victoria L. Together in the Kitchen. (Illus.). 366p. 1993. spiral bd. 7.50 (*1-879127-25-3*) Lighten Up Enter.

Miner, Colleen, jt. auth. see Campbell, Karen.

Miner, Craig. The Corporation & the Indian: Tribal Sovereignty & Industrial Civilization in Indian Territory, 1865-1907. LC 88-40550. (Illus.). 252p. 1989. reprint ed. pap. 12.95 (*0-8061-2205-6*) U of Okla Pr.
— Grede of Milwaukee: Business Career of an Individualist. 300p. 1989. 22.50 (*0-922820-06-6*) Watermark Pr.
— Harvesting the High Plains: John Kriss & the Business of Wheat Farming, 1920-1950. LC 97-23774. 240p. 1998. 29.95 (*0-7006-0874-5*) U Pr of KS.
— So Many Worlds: Leroy Hill Invention, Management, Philosophy & Risk. LC 97-11191. (Illus.). 320p. 1997. 29.95 (*0-89672-380-1*) Tex Tech Univ Pr.
— West of Wichita: Settling the High Plains of Kansas, 1865-1890. LC 85-26013. (Illus.). viii, 304p. 1986. pap. 14.95 (*0-7006-0364-6*) U Pr of KS.
— The Wichita Reader: A Collection of Writing about a Prairie City. (Illus.). 160p. 1992. 19.95 (*1-880652-13-7*) Wichita Eagle.
— Wolf Creek Station: Kansas Gas & Electric Company in the Nuclear Era. LC 93-14241. (Historical Perspectives on Business Enterprise Ser.). 393p. 1993. text 45.00 (*0-8142-0614-X*) Ohio St U Pr.

Miner, Cynthia, et al. 1994 a Year in Review for the Pacific Northwest Research Station (Long Version) (Illus.). 84p. 1997. reprint ed. pap. 9.40 (*0-89904-908-7*, Ecosytems Resrch) Crumb Elbow Pub.

Miner, Dorothy M. Airedale Terriers. LC 98-10543. (Complete Pet Owner's Manual Ser.). (Illus.). 1998. pap. 6.95 (*0-7641-0307-5*) Barron.

Miner, Earl. The Japanese Tradition in British & American Literature. LC 76-3698. 312p. 1976. reprint ed. lib. bdg. 55.00 (*0-8371-8818-0*, MIJT, Greenwood Pr) Greenwood.

Miner, Earl, ed. A History of Japanese Literature Vol. 2: The Early Middle Ages. Gatten, Aileen & Teele, Nicholas, trs. LC 83-43082. 479p. reprint ed. pap. 148.50 (*0-608-06327-4*, 206668800002) Bks Demand.
— The Works of John Dryden Vol. XV: Plays: Albion & Albanius, Don Sebastian, Amphitryon. 1976. 80.00 (*0-520-02129-0*, Pub. by U CA Pr) Cal Prin Full Svc.

Miner, Earl, intro. Poems on the Reign of William the Third. LC 92-22021. (Augustan Reprints Ser.: No. 166). 1974. reprint ed. 14.50 (*0-404-70166-3*, PR565) AMS Pr.

Miner, Earl & Dearing, Vinton A., eds. The Works of John Dryden Vol. III: Poems: 1685-1692. 1969. 80.00 (*0-520-01625-4*, Pub. by U CA Pr) Cal Prin Full Svc.

Miner, Earl, et al. The Princeton Companion to Classical Japanese Literature. LC 83-24475. (Illus.). 560p. 1986. pap. text 24.95 (*0-691-00825-6*, Pub. by Princeton U Pr) Cal Prin Full Svc.

Miner, Earl, jt. auth. see Brower, Robert H.

Miner, Earl, ed. see Brady, Jennifer, et al.

Miner, Earl, ed. see Konishi, Jinichi.

Miner, Earl, tr. see Brower, Robert H.

Miner, Earl R. Naming Properties: Nominal Reference in Travel Writings by Basho & Sora, Johnson & Boswell. LC 96-8830. 344p. (C). 1996. text 49.50 (*0-472-10699-6*, 10699) U of Mich Pr.

Miner, Earl R., ed. Stuart & Georgian Moments: Clark Library Seminar Papers on Seventeenth & Eighteenth Century Literature. LC 78-100020. (Publications of the 17th & 18th Centuries Studies Group, UCLA: No. 3). 325p. reprint ed. pap. 100.80 (*0-608-18500-0*, 203150700075) Bks Demand.

Miner, Ed. Past & Present of Greene County. (Illus.). 645p. 1995. reprint ed. lib. bdg. 67.00 (*0-8328-4680-5*) Higginson Bk Co.
— Past & Present of Greene County, Illinois. (Illus.). 645p. 1997. reprint ed. lib. bdg. 67.50 (*0-8328-5743-2*) Higginson Bk Co.

Miner, Ellis D. Uranus. 1990. pap. write for info. (*0-318-68273-7*) P-H.
— Uranus: The Planets, Rings & Satellites. (Ellis Horwood Series in Astronomy). 1990. text 94.00 (*0-470-21662-X*) P-H.

Miner, Ernest. Living Thoughts. (Book of Inspirational Thoughts). (Illus.). 84p. 1985. 7.95 (*0-935087-00-1*) Wright Pub Co.

Miner, Ethel N. Hanson, Henson, Hinson, Hynson & Allied Families, Vol. 2: Early Records of the Southeast United States, AL, FL, GE, MS. LC 93-156671. 126p. (Orig.). 1993. pap. text 20.00 (*1-55613-828-8*) Heritage Bk.
— Hanson, Henson, Hinson, Hynson & Allied Family Names: Early Records of the Midwest & Southwest United States. LC 93-156671. xi, 129p. 1993. pap. text 22.50 (*1-55613-737-0*) Heritage Bk.
— Hanson, Henson, Hinson, Hynson & Allied Family Names Vol. V: Early Records of the Mid-Atlantic States (DE, D.C., MD, VA-WV) 174p. 1995. pap. 29.50 (*0-7884-0180-7*) Heritage Bk.
— Hanson, Henson, Hinson, Hynson & Allied Family Names, Vol. 3: Early Records of the Carolinas. 124p. (Orig.). 1993. pap. text 23.00 (*1-55613-923-3*) Heritage Bk.

Miner, Gayle F. Lines & Electromagnetic Fields for Engineers. (Illus.). 1008p. 1996. text 92.00 (*0-19-510409-9*) OUP.

Miner, Gayle F. & Comer, David J. Physical Data Acquisition for Digital Processing: Components, Parameter & Specifications. 480p. 1992. text 75.00 (*0-13-209958-6*) P-H.

Miner, George B. Origin of Mattole: Through the Eyes of a Salmon. (Illus.). 192p. (Orig.). 1996. pap. 10.00 (*0-9653673-0-4*, M-0001) G B Miner.

Miner-Gulland, Robin & Dejeuski, Nikolai. Cultural Atlas of Russia & the Former Soviet Union. rev. ed. LC 98-29263. (Cultural Atlas Ser.). (Illus.). 240p. 1998. 50.00 (*0-8160-3815-5*, Checkmark) Facts on File.

Miner, H. Craig. The Rebirth of the Missouri Pacific, 1956-1983. LC 83-45097. (Illus.). 258p. 1984. 29.95 (*0-89096-159-X*) Tex A&M Univ Pr.
— Wichita: The Early Years, 1865-80. LC 81-23138. 215p. 1982. reprint ed. pap. 66.70 (*0-608-01395-1*, 206215800002) Bks Demand.
— Wichita: The Magic City. LC 88-62144. (Illus.). 210p. 1988. 24.95 (*0-9621250-0-8*) Wichita-Sedgwick Hist Mus.

Miner, H. Craig & Unrau, William E. The End of Indian Kansas: A Study of Cultural Revolution, 1854-1871. LC 77-4410. (Illus.). xiv, 182p. 1977. pap. 9.95 (*0-7006-0474-X*) U Pr of KS.

Miner, H. Craig, jt. auth. see Unrau, William E.

Miner, Horace. Body Ritual Among the Nacirema. (Reprint Series in Social Sciences). (C). 1993. reprint ed. pap. text 5.00 (*0-8290-4182-6*, S-185) Irvington.
— St. Denis: A French-Canadian Parish. LC 63-13068. 1994. pap. text 10.00 (*0-226-52993-2*, P108) U Ch Pr.
— St. Denis: A French-Canadian Parish. LC 63-13068. (Illus.). 1995. lib. bdg. 24.00 (*0-226-52992-4*) U Ch Pr.

***Miner, J. Ronald, et al.** Managing Livestock Wastes to Preserve Environmental Quality. LC 00-33440. 2001. write for info. (*0-8138-2635-7*) Iowa St U Pr.

Miner, James H., ed. History of Richland County: With 1986 Index. (Illus.). 748p. 1996. reprint ed. lib. bdg. 77.50 (*0-8328-5150-7*) Higginson Bk Co.

Miner, Jane C. Alcohol & You. LC 96-49943. (Impact Bks). (YA). (gr. 7-12). 1997. 24.00 (*0-531-11351-5*) Watts.
— Malibu Summer. 360p. (gr. 7-9). 1995. mass mkt. 3.99 (*0-590-20354-1*) Scholastic Inc.

Miner, Janis Hoover. Inspirational Poetry. 1998. pap. 12.95 (*0-941037-52-5*, BIBAL Press) D & F Scott.

Miner, John B. The Four Routes to Entrepreneurial Success. LC 96-18523. 224p. (Orig.). 1996. pap. 18.95 (*1-881052-82-6*) Berrett-Koehler.
— The Human Constraint: The Coming Shortage of Managerial Talent. 1974. text 25.00 (*0-87179-215-X*) Organizat Meas.
— Industrial Organizational Psychology. 704p. (C). 1991. 78.13 (*0-07-042440-3*) McGraw.
— Intelligence in the United States: A Survey - with Conclusions for Manpower Utilization in Education & Employment. LC 72-11482. 180p. 1973. reprint ed. lib. bdg. 55.00 (*0-8371-6667-5*, MIIU, Greenwood Pr) Greenwood.
— Motivation to Manage: A Ten Year Update on the "Studies in Management Education" Research. (Illus.). 1977. text 25.00 (*0-917926-00-5*) Organizat Meas.
— People Problems: The Executive's Answer Book. 1985. text 25.00 (*0-394-55002-1*) Organizat Meas.
— A Psychological Typology of Successful Entrepreneurs. LC 97-8854. 304p. 1997. 69.50 (*1-56720-115-6*, Quorum Bks) Greenwood.
— Role Motivation Theories. LC 92-28816. (People & Organizations Ser.). (Illus.). 304p. (C). 1993. text 49.95 (*0-415-08486-5*, B0012) Routledge.
— Role Motivation Theories. (People & Organizations Ser.). (Illus.). 376p. (C). 1994. pap. 27.99 (*0-415-11994-4*, C03985) Routledge.
— Studies in Management Education. LC 65-16849. (Illus.). 1965. text 25.00 (*0-317-99717-3*) Organizat Meas.

Miner, John B., ed. Administrative & Management Theory. (History of Management Thought Ser.). 456p. 1995. 149.95 (*1-85521-475-X*, Pub. by Dartmth Pub) Ashgate Pub Co.

Miner, John B. & Capps, Michael H. How Honesty Testing Works. LC 96-15352. 200p. 1996. 59.95 (*0-89930-980-1*, Quorum Bks) Greenwood.

Miner, John B. & Crane, Donald P. Human Resource Management: The Strategic Perspective. LC 94-33443. (Illus.). 752p. (C). 1997. 98.00 (*0-06-500496-5*) Addson-Wesley Educ.

Miner, John N. The Grammar Schools of Medieval England: A. F. Leach in Historiographical Perspective. 384p. (C). 1990. text 75.00 (*0-7735-0634-9*, Pub. by McG-Queens Univ Pr) CUP Services.

Miner, John W., jt. auth. see Gillis, Frank J.

Miner, Julie. Shepherds Song. 1999. pap. 13.89 (*0-8037-1197-2*, Dial Yng Read) Peng Put Young Read.

Miner, Kathleen, jt. auth. see Alperin, Melissa.

Miner, Kathleen, jt. auth. see Esoffery, Cam.

Miner, Kathleen R. & Thacker, Netha L. Violence: Health Facts. LC 95-3835. 1996. 12.95 (*1-56071-476-X*, H327) ETR Assocs.

Miner, Kathleen R., jt. auth. see Krantzler, Nora J.

Miner, Kathleen R., jt. auth. see Stang, Lucas.

Miner, Kathleen R., jt. auth. see Thacker, Netha L.

Miner, Lenore & Guzman, Carol, eds. The New Mexico Directory of Hispanic Culture. 2nd ed. (Illus.). 171p. 1992. pap. 8.95 (*0-944725-02-3*) Hispanic Culture.

Miner, Lynn E., et al. Proposal Planning & Writing. 2nd ed. LC 98-16683. 184p. 1998. pap. 34.50 (*1-57356-141-X*) Oryx Pr.

Miner, Lynn E., jt. auth. see Griffith, Jerry.

***Miner, M. Jane.** Mental Essentials: Mental Skills for Becoming a Complete Athlete. 40p. 1999. pap. 4.95 (*1-887476-03-2*) Perf Publns.
— Personal Wisdom: Living from the Inside Out. 65p. 2000. pap. 8.95 (*1-887476-02-4*) Perf Publns.

Miner, M. Jane, et al. Moving Toward Your Potential: The Athlete's Guide to Peak Performance. 157p. (Orig.). 1995. pap., student ed. 18.00 (*1-887476-01-6*) Perf Publns.

Miner, Madonne M. Insatiable Appetites: Twentieth-Century American Women's Bestsellers, 48. LC 83-18331. (Contributions in Women's Studies: No. 48). 158p. 1984. 49.95 (*0-313-23951-7*, MIN/, Greenwood Pr) Greenwood.

Miner, Malcolm. Your Touch Can Heal: A Guide to Healing Touch & How to Use It. 143p. 1992. pap. 6.95 (*0-9633796-0-7*) Faith Ridge.

***Miner, Margaret.** New International Dictionary of Quotations. 3rd rev. ed. 2000. mass mkt. 6.99 (*0-451-19963-4*, Sig) NAL.

Miner, Margaret. Resonant Gaps: Between Baudelaire & Wagner. LC 94-28793. 1995. 50.00 (*0-8203-1709-8*) U of Ga Pr.

Miner, Margaret, et al. Allergies: The Complete Guide To Diagnosis, Treatment & Daily Management. LC 98-50350. 352p. 1999. pap. 13.95 (*0-452-27966-6*) NAL.

Miner, Margaret, jt. ed. see Rawson, Hugh N.

Miner, Martha, et al. Reading Keyboard Music, 4 vols. pap. text 36.00 (*1-881986-16-0*) Demibach Eds.
— Reading Keyboard Music, Vol. 1. 44p. 1994. pap. text 10.00 (*1-881986-13-6*) Demibach Eds.
— Reading Keyboard Music, Vol. 2. 45p. 1994. pap. text 10.00 (*1-881986-14-4*) Demibach Eds.
— Reading Keyboard Music, Vol. 3. 45p. 1994. pap. text 10.00 (*1-881986-15-2*) Demibach Eds.
— Subsequent Materials Guide. 7p. 1993. teacher ed. 5.00 (*1-881986-18-7*) Demibach Eds.
— Written Work Papers, Vols. 1-3. 1993. wbk. ed. 8.00 (*1-881986-17-9*) Demibach Eds.

***Miner, Mary Jean.** Unbroken Circles: The Campgrounds of Martha's Vineyard. (Imago Mundi Ser.). (Illus.). 120p. 2000. 40.00 (*1-56792-121-3*) Godine.

Miner, Michael, jt. auth. see Coleman, Eli.

Miner, Myrtilla, jt. auth. see O'Connor, Ellen M.

Miner, Nagel T. The Golden Gate University Story, Vol. I. (Illus.). 320p. 1983. 20.00 (*0-943844-01-0*) Golden Gate Law.

Miner, Nancy Smith, jt. auth. see Sanders, Roger C.

Miner, Nanette J. 101 Media & Marketing Tips for the Sole Proprietor. 100p. 1998. pap. 7.95 (*0-9650666-2-2*) BVC Pubng.

Miner, Nanette J. & Terri, Sandi. This Affair Is Over! 56p. (Orig.). 1996. pap. text 6.95 (*0-9650666-1-4*) BVC Pubng.

Miner, Newton. Continuum. 64p. 1986. 6.95 (*0-317-42525-0*) Harlo Press.

Miner, Robert, ed. see Mother Earth News Editors.

Miner, Robert C. Dynamic Trading: Dynamic Concepts in Time, Price, Pattern & Trading. 540p. 1997. 97.00 (*0-9675131-0-3*) Dynamic Trader.

Miner, Robert G. Early Homes of New England. Whitehead, Russell F. et al, eds. (Architectural Treasures of Early America Ser.). (Illus.). 223p. 1977. 16.95 (*0-405-10068-X*) Arno Press.

Miner, Robert G. & Early American Society Staff. Early Homes of Massachusetts: From Homes of Material Originally Published as the White Pine Series of Architectural Monographs. Whitehead, Russell F. & Brown, Frank C., eds. 1978. 16.95 (*0-405-10064-7*, 10408) Ayer.

Miner, Ruth. Days to Celebrate. (Illus.). 50p. pap. 1.00 (*0-686-30389-X*) WILPF.

Miner, Sharon. The Delmarva Conspiracy. LC 92-72680. 136p. (YA). (gr. 7-9). 1993. 14.95 (*1-880851-06-7*) Greene Bark Pr.

Miner, Steven M. Between Churchill & Stalin: The Soviet Union, Great Britain, & the Origins of the Grand Alliance. LC 88-4828. 331p. 1988. reprint ed. pap. 102.70 (*0-7837-9015-5*, 204976700003) Bks Demand.

Miner, T., jt. auth. see Swartz, Clifford E.

Miner, Valerie. Range of Light. LC 97-45794. 304p. 1998. pap. 14.00 (*0-944072-86-0*) Zoland Bks.
— Rumors from the Cauldron: Selected Essays, Reviews, & Reportage. 296p. (C). 1991. pap. text 15.95 (*0-472-06472-X*, 06472) U of Mich Pr.
— A Walking Fire. LC 93-35569. (SUNY Series, The Margins of Literature). 254p. (C). 1994. text 39.50 (*0-7914-2007-8*); pap. text 19.95 (*0-7914-2008-6*) State U NY Pr.
— Winter's Edge. LC 96-14181. 216p. 1997. reprint ed. pap. 10.95 (*1-55861-150-9*) Feminist Pr.

Miner, Valerie, jt. ed. see Longino, Helen E.

Miner, Valerie, ed. see Yamauchi, Wakako.

Miner, W. Lawrence, Jr. A Journey into the Fourth Dimension: The Lasting Legacy of Derek Saul. 216p. 2000. pap. 12.00 (*1-928992-01-3*) Granite Pub.

Miner, W. N., ed. see World Metallurgical Congress Staff.

Miner, William N., ed. Plutonium Nineteen-Seventy & Other Actinides: Proceedings of the 4th International Conference on Plutonium & Other Actinides, Santa Fe, New Mexico, October 5-9, 1970, Pt. I. LC QD0181.P9. (Nuclear Metallurgy Ser.: Vol. 17). 550p. 1970. reprint ed. pap. 170.50 (*0-608-08310-0*, 200117000066) Bks Demand.
— Plutonium Nineteen-Seventy & Other Actinides: Proceedings of the 4th International Conference on Plutonium & Other Actinides, Santa Fe, New Mexico, October 5-9, 1970, Pt. II. LC QD0181.P9. (Nuclear Metallurgy Ser.: Vol. 17). 532p. 1970. reprint ed. pap. 165.00 (*0-608-08309-7*, 200117000065) Bks Demand.

Mineral Policy Center Staff, et al. Golden Dreams, Poisoned Streams: How Reckless Mining Pollutes America's Waters, & How We Can Stop It. LC 97-35901. (Illus.). (Orig.). 1997. pap. 24.95 (*1-889617-01-6*) Mineral Pol Ctr.

M

Mines, Jeanette. Reckless: A Teenage Love Story. 176p. 1983. pap. 2.95 (0-380-83717-X, Avon Bks) Morrow Avon.
— Risking It. 160p. (YA). 1988. pap. 2.75 (0-380-75401-0, Avon Bks) Morrow Avon.
Mines, Mattison. Public Faces, Private Voices: Community & Individuality in South India. LC 93-35609. 1994. 50.00 (0-520-08478-0, Pub. by U CA Pr); pap. 19.95 (0-520-08479-9, Pub. by U CA Pr) Cal Prin Full Svc.
Mines, Robert A. Adult Cognitive Development: Methods & Models. LC 85-16969. 192p. 1985. 37.50 (0-275-90012-6, C0012, Praeger Pubs) Greenwood.
Mines, Rosette. The Naked Soul: Poems & Art. (Illus.). 48p. 1999. pap. 8.00 (0-8059-4666-7) Dorrance.
Mines, Stephanie. Sexual Abuse - Sacred Wound: Transforming Deep Trauma. 368p. 1995. pap. text 15.95 (1-886449-11-2) Barrytown Ltd.
Minet, Olaf, et al. Selected Papers on Optical Tomography: Fundamentals & Applications in Medicine. LC 98-3470. (Milestone Ser.). 1998. 118.00 (0-8194-2877-9) SPIE.
***Minett, Joanna.** Living & Working in London: All You Need to Know to Enjoy This Capital City. (Living & Working Abroad Ser.). (Illus.). 144p. 2000. pap. 19.95 (1-85703-556-9, Pub. by How To Bks) Midpt Trade.
Minett, John, ed. Local Planning in the Netherlands & England: A Comparison of the Requirements & Procedures of the Two Systems. (C). 1979. 29.00 (0-7855-3875-5, Pub. by Oxford Polytechnic) St Mut.
Minett, Steve. Power, Politics & Participation in the Firm. 236p. 1992. 82.95 (1-85628-331-3, Pub. by Avebry) Ashgate Pub Co.
Minetti, B., ed. see Cherubini, R. & Dalpiaz, P.
Minetti, L., et al, eds. Debates in Nephrology. (Contributions to Nephrology Ser.: Vol. 34). (Illus.). viii, 132p. 1982. pap. 29.75 (3-8055-3535-X) S Karger.
Minetti, Luigi, ed. The Kidney in Plasma Cell Dyscrasias. (Developments in Nephrology Ser.). (C). 1988. text 226.50 (0-89838-385-4) Kluwer Academic.
Minev, Nikolay. Caro-Kann: Fantasy Variation. (Rare Openings & Variations Ser.). 71p. 1996. pap. 9.95 (0-9661889-0-X) Chess Library.
— French Defense 2. (Illus.). 300p. (Orig.). 1996. pap. 24.95 (0-938650-92-0) Thinkers Pr.
***Minev, Nikolay.** Mastering Tactical Ideas. (Illus.). 200p. 2000. pap. 19.95 (1-879479-83-4) ICE WA.
Minev, Nikolay. Miguel Najdorf: King of the King's Indian Defense. (Illus.). 112p. 1997. pap. 14.95 (0-9661889-1-8) Chess Library.
***Minev, Nikolay.** Players, Opening & Tactics. 200p. 2000. pap. 19.95 (1-879479-84-2) ICE WA.
Minev, Nikolay. The Sicilian Defense in the Last Decade (1986-95) 250 Good & Bad Ideas. Franett, Michael J., ed. (Illus.). (Orig.). 1995. pap. 14.95 (1-879479-28-1) ICE WA.
Minev, Nikolay, jt. auth. see Donaldson, John.
Minev, Nikolay, jt. auth. see Seirawan, Yasser.
Minford, Adrian & Arumugam, R. Illustrated Signs in Clinical Paediatrics. LC 97-43448. (Illus.). 1997. pap. text 24.95 (0-443-05529-7) Church.
Minford, J. Dean. Handbook of Aluminum Bonding Technology & Data. (Illus.). 808p. 1993. text 275.00 (0-8247-8817-6) Dekker.
Minford, J. Dean, ed. Treatise on Adhesion & Adhesives, Vol. 7. (Illus.). 528p. 1991. text 250.00 (0-8247-8112-0) Dekker.
Minford, John & Lau, Joseph S., eds. Classical Chinese Literature Vol. 1: An Anthology of Translations: From Antiquity to the Tang Dynasty. LC 95-49940. 1996. 65.00 (0-231-09676-3) Col U Pr.
Minford, John, jt. see Chin, Yung.
Minford, John, tr. see Chan, Ts'ao.
Minford, John, jt. tr. see Soong, Stephen C.
Minford, Patrick. Rational Expectations Macroeconomics: An Introductory Handbook. 2nd ed. (Illus.). 240p. (C). 1992. pap. 29.95 (0-631-17788-4) Blackwell Pubs.
— The Supply Side Revolution in Britain. 272p. 1991. pap. 30.00 (1-85278-428-8) E Elgar.
— The Supply Side Revolution in Britain. 272p. 1991. 95.00 (1-85278-426-1) E Elgar.
Ming, Alex. Essentials of Geriatric Medicine. (Illus.). 440p. 1997. write for info. (962-356-015-X) Lppncott W & W.
Ming, C. L., jt. ed. see Sien, Chia L.
Ming-Chang Kang, ed. Algebra & Geometry: National Taiwan University, Dec. 26-30, 1995. (Algebra & Geometry Ser.: Vol. 2). 9p. (C). 1998. lib. bdg. 42.00 (1-57146-058-6, KangA&G) Intl Pr Boston.
Ming-Dao, Deng. Chronicles of Tao: The Secret Life of a Taoist Master. LC 92-56409. 496p. 1993. pap. 19.00 (0-06-250219-0, Pub. by Harper SF) HarpC.
— Everyday Tao: Living with Balance & Harmony. LC 96-4404. 272p. 1996. pap. 15.00 (0-06-251395-8, Pub. by Harper SF) HarpC.
Ming Dao Deng. Scholar Warrior: An Introduction to the Tao in Everyday Life. LC 89-46453. (Illus.). 368p. (Orig.). 1990. pap. 23.00 (0-06-250232-8, Pub. by Harper SF) HarpC.
Ming-Dao, Deng. 365 Tao: Daily Meditations. LC 91-55332. (Illus.). 400p. 1992. pap. 16.00 (0-06-250223-9, Pub. by Harper SF) HarpC.
Ming-Dao, Deng, et al. Zen: The Art of Modern Eastern Cooking. LC 98-34104. (Illus.). 176p. 1998. 27.00 (1-57959-004-7, SOMA) BB&T Inc.
Ming-han Ye & Tao Huang. Charm Physics. xii, 562p. 1988. text 190.00 (2-88124-233-2) Gordon & Breach.
Ming-Ju Sun. Japanese Textile Designs. (International Design Library). (Illus.). 48p. 1986. pap. 5.95 (0-88045-085-1) Stemmer Hse.
Ming, Julian L., jt. ed. see Postiglione, Gerard A.
Ming-Kang Liu, Max. Principles & Applications of Optical Communications. LC 95-25240. 1004p. (C). 1996. text 71.50 (0-256-16415-0, TK5103, Irwn McGrw-H) McGrw-H Hghr Educ.
Ming, Lau C. & Jianfa, Shen, eds. China Review 2000. (Illus.). 500p. (C). text 63.50 (962-201-945-5, Pub. by Chinese Univ) U of Mich Pr.
Ming, Li, ed. Transformation of Science & Technology into Productive Power, 2 vols., Set. 2119p. 1991. 620.00 (0-7484-0004-4, Pub. by Tay Francis Ltd) Taylor & Francis.
Ming Li. Pegasus, the Flying Horse. LC 97-39365. (YA). (gr. 2 up). 1998. 16.99 (0-525-65244-2) NAL.
Ming Li & Vitanyi, Paul M. An Introduction to Kolmogorov Complexity & Its Applications. LC 93-10430. (Texts & Monographs in Computer Science). (Illus.). 546p. 1994. 64.95 (0-387-94053-7) Spr-Verlag.
Ming-liang, Hsieh. Catalogue of the Special Exhibition of Ting Ware White Porcelain. 2nd ed. (Collections of the National Palace Museum, Taipei). 231p. 1987. reprint ed. boxed set 65.00 (957-562-123-9) Heian Intl.
Ming, Lillie V. A Joy to Read. (Illus.). (Orig.). 1987. pap. 9.95 (0-318-22520-4) Health Is Wealth.
Ming, Ou, ed. Chinese-English Dictionary of Traditional Chinese Medicine. 640p. 1988. 24.95 (962-04-0207-3, Pub. by Joint Pub) Cheng & Tsui.
Ming, Ruan. Hu Yao Bang on Turning Point of History. 134p. 1994. pap. text 7.00 (0-9625118-9-7) World Scientific Pub.
Ming, Si-Chun, ed. Precursors of Gastric Cancer. LC 83-27025. 334p. 1984. 85.00 (0-275-91444-5, C1444, Praeger Pubs) Greenwood.
Ming, Si-Chun & Goldman, Harvey. Pathology of the Gastrointestinal Tract. 2nd ed. LC 97-22939. 904p. 1997. write for info. (0-683-18007-X) Lppncott W & W.
Ming, Si-Chun & Goldman, Harvey, eds. Pathology of the Gastro-Intestinal Tract. (Illus.). 975p. 1991. text 250.00 (0-7216-6398-2, W B Saunders Co) Harcrt Hlth Sci Grp.
***Ming-Sun, Yen, et al.** Buddhist Healing Touch: A Self-Care Program for Pain Relief & Wellness. (Illus.). 192p. 2001. pap. 19.95 (0-89281-886-7) Inner Tradit.
***Ming Tan, Wooi.** Developing USB PC Peripherals. 2nd ed. (Illus.). 176p. 1999. pap. 29.95 (0-929392-64-7, Pub. by Annabooks) Coriolis Grp.
Ming-Tao Wang, tr. see Yu, James C., ed.
Ming Tat Wong. The Medical Manual for Chinese Family. (CHI.). 200p. pap. 18.00 (0-9635700-0-5) J Wong.
Ming, Wu, ed. & tr. see Dan-an, Cheng.
Ming-Yang Kao, jt. ed. see Wen-Lian Hsu.
Ming, Yuan, jt. auth. see Harding, Harry.
Mingana, Alphonse. The Yezidis: The Devil Worshippers of the Middle East; Their Beliefs & Sacred Books. 1995. pap. 5.95 (1-55818-231-4, Sure Fire) Holmes Pub.
Mingat, Alain, jt. auth. see Jee-Peng Tan.
Mingay, G. E. Land & Society in England, 1750-1980. LC 94-1130. (Themes in British Social History Ser.). 288p. (C). 1994. pap. text 27.50 (0-582-49132-0, 76879, Pub. by Addison-Wesley) Longman.
Mingay, G. E. Parliamentary Enclosure in England: An Introduction to Its Causes, Incidence, & Impact, 1750-1850. LC 97-25200. 176p. (C). 1997. pap. 33.53 (0-582-25725-5) Longman.
Mingay, G. E. Rural Life in Victorian England. (History Paperback Ser.). (Illus.). 240p. 1998. pap. 21.95 (0-7509-1612-5, Pub. by Sutton Pub Ltd) Intl Pubs Mktg.
— The Transformation of Britain, 1830-1939. (Making of Britain Ser.). (Illus.). 233p. (C). 1986. 49.95 (0-7100-9762-X, Routledge Thoemms) Routledge.
Mingay, G. E., ed. The Agrarian History of England & Wales, Vol. 6: 1750-1850. 1248p. 1989. text 195.00 (0-521-22726-7) Cambridge U Pr.
— The Victorian Countryside, 2 vols. (Illus.). 1986. pap. 45.00 (0-685-43559-8, 88888); write for info. (0-7102-0884-7); write for info. (0-7102-0886-3) Routledge.
Mingay, G. E., jt. auth. see Bagwell, Philip S.
Mingay, Helen, jt. auth. see Klier, John.
Mingay, J. M., ed. see Aristotle.
Mingay, John. Internal Exile: Selected Shorter Poems 1988-95. LC 97-171841. 1996. pap. 14.95 (3-7052-0055-0, Pub. by Poetry Salzburg) Intl Spec Bk.
Minge, M. Ronald, et al. Mating. 352p. 1982. pap. 9.95 (0-940162-01-6) Red Lion.
***Minger, Elda.** Baby by Chance. 2000. mass mkt. 4.50 (0-373-82226-X, 1-82226-1) Harlequin Bks.
Minger, Elda. Baby by Chance: (New Arrival) LC 95-8358. (American Romance Ser.). 251p. 1995. per. 3.50 (0-373-16584-6, 1-16584-4) Harlequin Bks.
— Christmas with Eve. 1996. per. 3.50 (0-373-25714-7, 1-25714-6) Harlequin Bks.
— Coup de Foudre a Malibu. (FRE.). 1998. mass mkt. 3.50 (0-373-37479-8, 1-37479-2) Harlequin Bks.
— Daddy's Little Dividend. (American Romance Ser.). 1993. per. 3.50 (0-373-16489-0, 1-16489-6) Harlequin Bks.
— La Douce Surprise de L'Amour. (Rouge Passion Ser.: No. 497). (FRE.). 1999. mass mkt. 3.50 (0-373-37497-6, 1-37497-4) Harlequin Bks.
— Embrace the Night. 352p. (Orig.). 1994. mass mkt. 5.99 (0-515-11373-5, Jove) Berkley Pub.
— The Last Seduction. (Temptation Ser.). 1996. per. 3.50 (0-373-25690-6, 1-25690-8) Harlequin Bks.
— Night Rhythms. 1997. per. 3.50 (0-373-25749-X, 1-25749-2) Harlequin Bks.
— Une Nuit Avec Eve. (Rouge Passion Ser.: Bk. 489). 1999. mass mkt. 3.50 (0-373-37489-5, 1-37489-1) Harlequin Bks.
— She's the One! (Temptation Ser.: No. 665). 1998. per. 3.50 (0-373-25765-1, 1-25765-8) Harlequin Bks.
— Teddy Bear Heir. (American Romance Ser.). 1994. per. 3.50 (0-373-16531-5, 1-6531-5) Harlequin Bks.
— Wed Again. (American Romance Ser.). 1993. mass mkt. 3.50 (0-373-16510-2, 1-16510-9) Harlequin Bks.
Minger, Elda, jt. auth. see Foster, Lori F.
Minger, Miriam. Captive Rose. 384p. 1991. pap. 3.95 (0-380-76311-7, Avon Bks) Morrow Avon.
— Defiant Impostor. 384p. (Orig.). 1992. mass mkt. 4.50 (0-380-76312-5, Avon Bks) Morrow Avon.
— A Hint of Rapture. 400p. 1990. pap. 3.95 (0-380-75863-6, Avon Bks) Morrow Avon.
— My Runaway Heart. 400p. (Orig.). 1995. mass mkt. 5.50 (0-380-78301-0, Avon Bks) Morrow Avon.
— Stolen Splendor. 384p. (Orig.). 1989. pap. 3.95 (0-380-75862-8, Avon Bks) Morrow Avon.
Minger, Mirian. Secrets of Midnight. 352p. (Orig.). 1995. pap. 5.50 (0-515-11726-9, Jove) Berkley Pub.
Minger, Ralph E. William Howard Taft & United States Foreign Policy: The Apprenticeship Years, 1900-1908. LC 75-6691. 253p. reprint ed. pap. 78.50 (0-608-13909-2, 202022800016) Bks Demand.
Mingers, J. Self-Producing Systems: Implications & Applications of Autopoiesis. LC 94-43375. (Contemporary Systems Thinking Ser.). (Illus.). 264p. (C). 1994. text 54.50 (0-306-44797-5, Kluwer Plenum) Kluwer Academic.
Mingers, John & Gill, Anthony. Multimethodology: The Theory & Practice of Integrating Management Science Methodologies. LC 97-9288. 458p. 1997. 82.95 (0-471-97490-0) Wiley.
Minges, B., et al. Kerygma - The Bible in Depth: Leader's Guide. 330p. 1992. pap. 29.00 (1-882236-00-9) Kerygma Prog.
Minghat, Alan & Tan, Jee-Peng. Analytical Tools for Sector Work in Education. LC 87-46373. (Illus.). 202p. 1988. reprint ed. pap. 62.70 (0-608-06717-2, 206691400009) Bks Demand.
***Minghella, Anthony.** Getting Away with Murder: The Making of "The Talented Mr. Ripley" 144p. 1999. pap. 15.95 (0-7868-8526-2) Little.
Minghella, Anthony. Interior, Room - Exterior, City. (Methuen New Theatrescripts Ser.). 130p. (Orig.). (C). 1989. pap. write for info. (0-413-61790-4, A0407, Methuen Drama) Methn.
— Living with Dinosaurs: One Act Plays. (C). 1995. pap. write for info. (0-413-64240-2, A0504) Heinemann.
— Minghella: Plays One. 292p. (C). 1992. pap. 14.95 (0-413-66580-1, A0659, Methuen Drama) Methn.
Minghella, Anthony. Plays, No. 2. LC 98-130607. (Contemporary Dramatists Ser.). 1997. pap. 14.95 (0-413-71520-5) Methn.
— The Talented Mr. Ripley. LC 99-49603. 144p. 1999. pap. 10.95 (0-7868-8521-1, Pub. by Disney Pr) Time Warner.
Minghella, Anthony. Truly, Madly, Deeply. (Illus.). 58p. (C). 1991. pap. 8.95 (0-413-64000-0, A0503, Methuen Drama) Methn.
Minghella, Anthony, ed. The Storyteller. 144p. (C). 1990. 60.00 (1-85283-026-3, Pub. by Boxtree) St Mut.
Minghella, Anthony, jt. auth. see Ondaatje, Michael.
***Minghelli, Marina.** Medusa: The Fourth Kingdom. Allen, Beverly, tr. from ITA. LC 99-17610. 190p. 1999. pap. 10.95 (0-87286-353-0) City Lights.
***Minghuan, Li.** We Need Two Worlds: A Study of Chinese Association in a Western Society. LC 00-308632. (Illus.). 360p. (C). 2000. pap. text 37.50 (90-5356-402-0, Pub. by Amsterdam U Pr) U of Mich Pr.
Mingilton, Jesse, jt. auth. see Dowall, David E.
***Mingins, Christine & Bertr Computer Society Press Staff, eds.** Tools 32: Technology of Object-Oriented Languages & Systems Proceedings of the Conference Melbourne, Australia, 1999. LC 99-67341. 350p. 1999. 120.00 (0-7695-0462-0) IEEE Comp Soc.
Mingins, Christine & Meyer, Bertrand, eds. TOOLS 28 - Technology of Object-Oriented Languages: Proceedings. Conference on Technology of Object-Oriented Languages, TOOLS 28 (1998: Melbourne, Australia) LC 98-89186. 313p. 1999. pap. 110.00 (0-7695-0053-6) IEEE Comp Soc.
Mingins, J., ed. see Bee, R. D., et al.
Mingione, Enzo. Urban Poverty & the Underclass: A Reader. (Studies in Urban & Social Change Ser.). (Illus.). 240p. 1996. 60.95 (0-631-20036-3); pap. 26.95 (0-631-20037-1) Blackwell Pubs.
Mingle, Ida. Poems of Truth & Meditations (1924) 160p. 1998. reprint ed. pap. 17.95 (0-7661-0341-2) Kessinger Pub.
— The Science & Art of Regeneration. 65p. 1984. reprint ed. spiral bd. 12.50 (0-7873-0618-5) Hlth Research.
— Science of Love with Key to Immortality, 2 vols., Set. 1996. reprint ed. pap. 55.00 (0-7873-0616-9) Hlth Research.
— Science of Love with Key to Immortality (1926) 590p. 1996. reprint ed. pap. 33.00 (1-56459-716-4) Kessinger Pub.
— Spiritual Significance of the Body. 355p. 1993. reprint ed. spiral bd. 21.00 (0-7873-0619-3) Hlth Research.
— Spiritual Significance of the Body (1936) 355p. 1996. reprint ed. pap. 20.00 (1-56459-796-2) Kessinger Pub.
— The Unfoldment of Man. 45p. 1987. reprint ed. spiral bd. 13.00 (0-7873-0617-7) Hlth Research.
Mingle, James R. & Hauptman, Arthur M. Standard Setting & Financing in Postsecondary Education: Eight Recommendations for Change in Federal & State Policies. 1994. 15.00 (1-881543-04-8) SHEEO.
Mingle, James R. & Rodriguez, Esther M., eds. Building Coalitions for Minority Success. 1990. 7.00 (0-614-13568-0) SHEEO.
Mingle, James R., et al. Challenges of Retrenchment: Strategies in Consolidating Programs, Cutting Costs, & Reallocating Resources. LC 81-47770. (Jossey-Bass Series in Higher Education). 416p. reprint ed. pap. 129.00 (0-8357-4865-0, 203779700009) Bks Demand.
Minglu, Gau, ed. Inside Out: New Chinese Art. LC 98-21532. (Illus.). 204p. 1998. pap. 29.95 (0-520-21748-9, Pub. by U CA Pr) Cal Prin Full Svc.
Minglu, Gau & Bryson, Norman, eds. Inside Out: New Chinese Art. LC 98-21532. (Illus.). 204p. 1998. 50.00 (0-520-21747-0, Pub. by U CA Pr) Cal Prin Full Svc.
Mingo, Jack. Couch Potato Guide to Life. 1985. pap. 3.50 (0-380-75596-3, Avon Bks) Morrow Avon.
— How to Spit Nickels. (Illus.). 144p. 1993. pap. 9.95 (0-8092-3724-5, 372450, Contemporary Bks) NTC Contemp Pub Co.
— The Juicy Parts: Things Your History Teacher Never Told You about the 20th Century's Most Famous People. 288p. 1996. pap. 12.95 (0-399-52218-2, Perigee Bks) Berkley Pub.
— Magic Card Tricks. (Illus.). 96p. 1995. pap. 14.95 (0-8092-3446-7, 344670, Contemporary Bks) NTC Contemp Pub Co.
— Wannabe Guide to Classical Music. (Illus.). 100p. 1999. pap. 9.95 (1-57143-055-5) RDR Bks.
***Mingo, Jack & Barrett, Erin.** Just Curious, Jeeves: What Are the 1,001 Most Intriguing Questions Asked on the Internet? 468p. 2000. pap. 16.95 (1-930108-01-X) Ask Jeeves Inc.
***Mingo, Jack, et al.** Firecrackers: The Art & History. LC 99-89043. 160p. 2000. pap. 19.95 (1-58008-151-7) Ten Speed Pr.
Mingo, James A., jt. auth. see Fillmore, Peter A.
Mingos, D. M. Essential Trends in Inorganic Chemistry. LC 97-35359. (Illus.). 400p. (C). 1998. pap. text 33.95 (0-19-850108-0) OUP.
— Essentials of Inorganic Chemistry, Vol. 2. 66. (Illus.). 92p. (C). 1998. pap. text 12.95 (0-19-855918-6) OUP.
Mingos, D. M. Essentials of Inorganic Chemistry 1. (Oxford Chemistry Primers Ser.: No. 28). (Illus.). 96p. (C). 1995. pap. text 12.95 (0-19-855848-1) OUP.
Mingos, D. M. Structural & Electronic Paradigms in Cluster Chemistry. LC 97-22417. (Structure & Bonding Ser.). 1997. write for info. (3-540-62791-X); write for info. (0-387-62791-X) Spr-Verlag.
***Mingos, D. M., ed.** Bonding & Charge Distribution in Polyoxometalates, a Bond Valence Approach. (Illus.). 200p. 1998. 189.00 (3-540-64934-4) Spr-Verlag.
Mingos, D. M., ed. Liquid Crystals I. LC 99-201840. (Structure & Bonding Ser.: Vol. 94). (Illus.). 222p. 1999. 159.00 (3-540-64936-0) Spr-Verlag.
— Liquid Crystals II. (Structure & Bonding Ser.: Vol. 95). (Illus.). 200p. 1999. 199.00 (3-540-64937-9) Spr-Verlag.
Mingos, D. M., et al, eds. Chemical Hardness. LC 93-16082. (Structure & Bonding Ser.). 1993. write for info. (3-540-56091-2); 183.95 (0-387-56091-2) Spr-Verlag.
Mingos, D. M., et al. Bond & Structure Models. (Structure & Bonding Ser.: Vol. 63). (Illus.). 190p. 1985. 85.95 (0-387-15820-0) Spr-Verlag.
Mingot, T. Galiana, see Galiana Mingot, T.
Mingotti, Antonio. Maria Cebotari, das Leben Einer Sangerin. Farkas, Andrew, ed. LC 76-29955. (Opera Biographies Ser.).Tr. of Maria Cebotari. (GER., Illus.). 1977. reprint ed. lib. bdg. 19.95 (0-405-09696-8) Ayer.
Mingovits, Victor. A Satan Worshiper's Guide to the American Northeast. 79p. (Orig.). 1991. pap. 4.95 (0-9630465-9-4) Watershed.
Mings Prof Turley & Mings, Turley. The Study of Economics: Principles, Concepts & Applications. 5th ed. 576p. (C). 1996. text 41.76 (0-256-23048-X, Irwn McGrw-H) McGrw-H Hghr Educ.
Mings, Turley. Fundamentals of Economics. 5th ed. 300p. (C). 1995. text, wbk. ed. 16.56 (0-697-31724-2) Brown & Benchmark.
— Study of Economics: Principles, Concepts & Applications. 5th ed. (Illus.). 526p. (C). 1995. text 41.76 (1-56134-303-X, Dshkn McG-Hill) McGrw-H Hghr Educ.
— Working with the Study of Economics. 4th ed. 336p. (C). 1991. per. write for info. (0-87967-922-0) Brown & Benchmark.
— Working with the Study of Economics. 5th ed. 344p. (C). 1995. text 13.75 (1-56134-383-8, Dshkn McG-Hill) McGrw-H Hghr Educ.
Mings, Turley, jt. auth. see Mings Prof Turley.
Mingst. Essentials of International Relations. LC 98-16951. 250p. 1998. pap. 33.50 (0-393-97287-9) Norton.
Mingst, Karen. Essentials of International Relions. (C). pap. text. write for info. (0-393-10344-7) Norton.
Mingst, Karen. The Ivory Trade. (Pew Case Studies in International Affairs). 50p. (C). 1993. pap. text 3.50 (1-56927-154-2) Geo U Inst Dplmcy.
Mingst, Karen A. Politics & the African Development Bank. LC 90-30935. 216p. 1990. text 29.95 (0-8131-1754-2) U Pr of Ky.
Mingst, Karen A. & Karns, Margaret P. The United Nations in the Post-Cold War Era. Lopez, George A., ed. LC 95-5657. (Dilemmas in World Politics Ser.). (Illus.). 224p. (C). 1995. pap. 22.00 (0-8133-2261-8, Pub. by Westview) HarpC.
***Mingst, Karen A. & Karns, Margaret P.** The United Nations in the Post-Cold War Era. 2nd ed. LC 99-48946. (Dilemmas in World Politics Ser.). 250p. 1999. pap. 22.00 (0-8133-6847-2) Westview.
Mingst, Karen A., jt. ed. see Karnes, Margaret.
Minguela, Santiago C. & Riband, Herbert F. Spanish Corporation's Law & Limited Liability Companies Law. LC 95-48139. (Series of Legislation in Translation: No. 9). 1996. 131.00 (90-411-0191-8) Kluwer Law Intl.
Minguez, E., jt. ed. see Velarde, G.
Mingus, Charles. Beneath the Underdog. LC 91-50277. 384p. 1991. pap. 14.00 (0-679-73761-8) Vin Bks.
Mingyu, Wu, jt. auth. see Lalkaka, R.
Mingyuan, Jin, ed. The Directory of Chinese Government Organs. Yanrui, Chang, tr. (CHI.). 944p. 1991. 108.00 (962-7167-13-4, Pub. by New China News) Cypress Co.

M

An Asterisk (*) at the beginning of an entry indicates that the title is appearing for the first time.

Mingyuan, Wang, jt. auth. see Daoran, Li.

***Minh, D. L.** Applied Probability Models. LC 00-40353. 2000. write for info. (*0-534-38157-X*) Brooks-Cole.

***Minh Dang, Luong, et al.** A Global Solution for the "OO" of the Y2K. (Illus.). 1p. 1999. pap. 20.00 (*0-9672470-0-4*) P Chan.

***Minh-ha, Trinh T.** Cinema Interval. LC 99-19959. 1999. pap. 24.95 (*0-415-92201-1*) Routledge.

— Cinema-Interval. LC 99-19959. 288p. (C). 1999. text. write for info. (*0-415-92200-3*) Routledge.

Minh-ha, Trinh T. When the Moon Waxes Red: Representation, Gender & Cultural Politics. (Illus.). 240p. (gr. 13). 1991. pap. 21.99 (*0-415-90431-5*, A5631) Routledge.

— When the Moon Waxes Red: Representation, Gender & Cultural Politics. (Illus.). 240p. (C). (gr. 13). 1991. 75.00 (*0-415-90430-7*, A5627) Routledge.

— Woman, Native, Other: Writing Postcoloniality & Feminism. LC 88-45455. (Illus.). 184p. 1989. 39.95 (*0-253-36603-8*); pap. 15.95 (*0-253-20503-4*, MB-503) Ind U Pr.

Minh-ha, Trinh T., jt. auth. see Bourdier, Jean-Paul.

Minh, Nguyen Q. & Takahashi, Takehiko. Science & Technology of Ceramic Fuel Cells. LC 95-21137. 378p. 1995. 181.50 (*0-444-89568-X*) Elsevier.

Minh Tang, Eric & Ifkovic, Ed. The Minh Man Rules. (J). (gr. 7-9). 2000. pap. 9.99 (*0-88092-419-5*) Royal Fireworks.

Minhinnett, Ray & Young, Bob. The Story of the Fender Stratocaster: "Curves, Contours & Body Horns" LC 94-33586. (Illus.). 128p. 1995. 24.95 (*0-87930-349-2*) Miller Freeman.

Minhinnick, Jeanne. At Home in Upper Canada. LC 98-234529. (Illus.). 240p. 1996. 28.00 (*1-55046-156-7*, Pub. by Boston Mills) Genl Dist Srvs.

Minhinnick, Robert. Drawing down the Moon: Poems & Stories 96. 96p. 1996. pap. 14.95 (*1-85411-155-8*, Pub. by Seren Bks) Dufour.

— Hey Fatman. 64p. 1994. pap. 14.95 (*1-85411-110-8*, Pub. by Seren Bks) Dufour.

— The Looters. LC 89-82059. 72p. 1990. pap. 14.95 (*1-85411-019-5*, Pub. by Seren Bks) Dufour.

— A Postcard Home. Stephens, Meic, ed. (Changing Wales Ser.). 36p. 1994. pap. 11.95 (*0-8464-4743-6*) Beekman Pubs.

— Watching the Fire-Eater. 139p. 1993. pap. 15.95 (*1-85411-075-6*, Pub. by Seren Bks); pap. 15.95 (*0-685-67834-2*, Pub. by Seren Bks) Dufour.

Mini, Anna M. Deliver Us from Evil. 5th rev. ed. Lee, Geri, ed. 210p. (Orig.). 1997. mass mkt. 9.95 (*0-9656854-0-3*) S & H Pub.

Mini Book Staff. Getting Started: Recorder. 1990. 2.50 (*0-685-32163-0*, G162) Hansen Ed Mus.

— Getting Started: Tooter. 1990. 2.50 (*0-685-32162-2*, G163) Hansen Ed Mus.

Mini, John. Day of Destiny: Where Will You Be August, 13, 1999? (Illus.). 220p. 1998. pap. write for info. (*0-9657825-8-1*) Trans Hyper.

Mini, Piero V. John Maynard Keynes: A Study in the Psychology of Original Work. LC 93-48289. 1994. text 55.00 (*0-312-12137-7*) St Martin.

— Philosophy & Economics: The Origins & Development of Economic Theory. LC 74-7122. 305p. 1974. 49.95 (*0-8130-0381-4*) U Press Fla.

Mini, S. M., et al, eds. Application of Synchrotron Radiation Techniques to Materials Science IV Vol. 524: Proceedings Materials Research Society Symposium. LC 98-26378. 383p. 1998. text 79.00 (*1-55899-430-0*) Materials Res.

Miniature Book Collection Library of Congress Staff, jt. auth. see Troll Communications Staff.

***Miniature Book Collection Staff, contrib. by.** Isaac. LC 99-189476. (Pocket Romeos Ser.). (Illus.). 48p. (YA). (gr. 5 up). 1998. 4.98 (*0-7651-0945-X*) Smithmark.

— Leonardo Dicaprio. LC 99-183227. (Pocket Romeos Ser.). (Illus.). 48p. (gr. 5 up). 1998. 4.98 (*0-7651-0941-7*) Smithmark.

— Matt Damon. LC 99-189488. (Pocket Romeos Ser.). (Illus.). 48p. (gr. 5 up). 1998. 4.98 (*0-7651-0940-9*) Smithmark.

— Zac Hanson. LC 99-189479. (Pocket Romeos Ser.). (Illus.). 48p. (gr. 5 up). 1998. 4.98 (*0-7651-0944-1*) Smithmark.

***Miniature Book Collection Staff & Smithmark Staff, contrib. by.** Prince William. LC 99-189484. (Pocket Romeos Ser.). (Illus.). 48p. (gr. 5 up). 1998. 4.98 (*0-7651-0942-5*) Smithmark.

Miniature Quilts Editors. Favorite Foundation-Pieced Minis. LC 96-29677. (Illus.). 34p. (Orig.). 1997. pap. 14.95 (*1-885588-13-5*) Chitra Pubns.

Minich, Elizabeth, jt. auth. see Porter, Catherine.

Minich, Enrico & Schimke, R. T. Apoptosis, Vol. 5. (Pezcoller Foundation Symposium Ser.: Vol. 5). (Illus.). 283p. (C). 1994. text 95.00 (*0-306-44733-9*, Kluwer Plenum) Kluwer Academic.

Minich, Jan. History of Drowning. 26p. 1990. pap. 7.00 (*0-937669-35-0*) Owl Creek Pr.

***Minichiello, J. Kent & White, Anthony W.** From Blue Ridge to Barrier Islands: An Audubon Naturalist Reader. (Illus.). 436p. 2000. pap. 16.95 (*0-8018-6531-X*) Johns Hopkins.

Minichiello, J. Kent & White, Anthony W., eds. From Blue Ridge to Barrier Islands: An Audubon Naturalist Reader. LC 96-1818. (Illus.). 328p. 1996. 29.95 (*0-8018-5384-2*) Johns Hopkins.

Minichiello, Sharon. Retreat from Reform: Patterns of Political Behavior in Interwar Japan. LC 84-8535. 188p. 1984. reprint ed. pap. 58.30 (*0-608-04391-5*, 206517200001) Bks Demand.

Minichiello, Sharon A., ed. Japan's Competing Modernities: Issues in Culture & Democracy, 1900-1930. LC 98-6077. (Illus.). 424p. 1998. text 54.00 (*0-8248-1931-4*); pap. text 25.95 (*0-8248-2080-0*) UH Pr.

***Minichiello, Tom.** Bodybuilders, Drugs & Sex. (Illus.). 336p. 1999. pap. 24.95 (*0-9674174-0-6*) Mid City Pr.

Minichino, Camille. The Beryllium Murder. 272p. 2000. 24.00 (*0-688-17207-5*, Wm Morrow) Morrow Avon.

— The Helium Murder. LC 98-96072. (Periodic Table Mystery Ser.: Bk. 2). 192p. 1998. 18.95 (*0-8034-9298-7*, Avalon Bks) Bouregy.

— The Hydrogen Murder. LC 97-94274. (Periodic Table Mystery Ser.: Bk. 1). 228p. 1997. 18.95 (*0-8034-9268-5*, Avalon Bks) Bouregy.

— The Lithium Murder: A Gloria Lamerino Mystery. LC 98-47505. 240p. 1999. 24.00 (*0-688-16784-5*, Wm Morrow) Morrow Avon.

Minichino, Camille, jt. auth. see Heckman, Richard A.

Minici, Isabella Z., jt. auth. see De Buzzaccarini, Vittoria.

Minick, Polly. A Rug Hooking Book Of Days: Featuring the Fiber Art of Polly Minick. (Illus.). 64p. 1999. spiral bd. 12.95 (*1-881982-15-7*) Stackpole.

Minick, Scott & Ping, Jiao. Arts & Crafts of China. LC 96-60238. (Illus.). 128p. (Orig.). 1996. pap. 19.95 (*0-500-27896-2*, Pub. by Thames Hudson) Norton.

Minicz. English Connections, Vol. 3. Porter, ed. 1994. pap., teacher ed. 10.55 (*0-8092-3701-6*) NTC Contemp Pub Co.

Minicz & Porter. English Connections, Vol. 3. 32p. 1994. pap., wbk. ed. 2.50 (*0-8092-3704-0*) NTC Contemp Pub Co.

Minicz, Elizabeth. Crossroads Cafe: Partner Guide. (Global ESL/ELT Ser.). (Illus.). 48p. (J). 1997. mass mkt., suppl. ed. 4.95 (*0-8384-6614-1*) Heinle & Heinle.

— Crossroads Cafe B-teachers Res Guide. (Global ESL). (J). 1997. pap., teacher ed. 35.50 (*0-8384-6590-0*) Heinle & Heinle.

***Minieka, Edward & Kurzeja, Zoriana Dyschkant.** Statistics for Business with Computer Appications. LC 99-87663. 1031p. 2001. 89.95 incl. cd-rom (*0-324-04163-2*) Sth-Wstrn College.

Minieka, Edward, ed. see Minier, Edward.

Minier, Edward. Optimization Algorithms for Networks & Graphs. 2nd expanded rev. ed. Evans, James R. & Minieka, Edward, eds. (Illus.). 488p. 1992. text 69.75 (*0-8247-8602-5*) Dekker.

Minier, Elizabeth M. & Field, Dorothy M. This & That: Selected Poems of Two Sisters. 32p. 1990. pap. 5.95 (*1-880404-00-1*) Bkwrights.

Miniet, Jay J. End User's Guide to Innovative Flexible Circuit Packaging. LC 86-13373. (Electrical Engineering & Electronics Ser.: Vol. 33). (Illus.). 167p. reprint ed. pap. 51.80 (*0-608-08965-6*, 206960000005) Bks Demand.

***Minifie, Bernard W.** Chocolate, Cocoa & Confectionery: Science & Technology. 904p. 1998. 130.00 (*0-8342-1301-X*) Aspen Pub.

Minifie, Fred D. Introduction to Communication Sciences & Disorders. 1994. teacher ed. 19.95 (*1-56593-378-8*, 0708) Singular Publishing.

— Introduction to Communication Sciences & Disorders. LC 94-3135. (Illus.). 708p. (C). 1994. pap. text 49.95 (*1-56593-202-1*, 0525) Thomson Learn.

— Introduction to Communication Sciences & Disorders. 2nd ed. 708p. (C). 2000. pap. 55.00 (*1-56593-960-3*, 1900) Thomson Learn.

Minifie, Fred D., et al. Introduction to Communication Sciences & Disorders. (Illus.). 128p. (C). 1994. student ed., wbk. ed. 14.95 (*1-56593-361-3*, 0690) Thomson Learn.

Minihan, Michael A., tr. see Mochulsky, Konstantin.

Minihofer, D. Czech-English Dictionary of Computer Science. (CZE & ENG.). 1990. 49.95 (*0-8288-7199-X*) Fr & Eur.

— English-Czech Dictionary of Computer Science. (CZE & ENG.). 1990. 49.95 (*0-8288-7200-7*) Fr & Eur.

— English-Czech Explanatory Dictionary of Computer Science. (CZE & ENG.). 1990. 49.95 (*0-8288-7201-5*) Fr & Eur.

Minihofer, Oldrich, jt. auth. see Kratochvilova, J.

Minikiewicz, William F., ed. Medic's Pocket Reference. (Illus.). iv, 120p. (Orig.). 1997. pap. 12.95 (*0-9656879-0-2*) Medic Pub SC.

***Mininsymposium on Spectral Invariants Heat Equation Approach Staff, et al.** Geometric Aspects of Partial Differential Equations: Proceedings of a Mininsymposium on Spectral Invariants, Heat Equation Approach, September 18-19, 1998, Roskilde, Denmark LC 99-36671. (Contemporary Mathematics Ser.). 1999. write for info. (*0-8218-2061-3*) Am Math.

Minio-Paluello, L., jt. ed. see Kenyon, F. G.

Minio-Paluello, L. Opuscula. The Latin Aristotle. xii, 590p. 1972. text 95.00 (*0-317-54477-2*, Pub. by AM Hakkert) Coronet Bks.

Minio-Paluello, Lorenzo. Education in Fascist Italy. LC 78-63697. (Studies in Fascism: Ideology & Practice). (Illus.). 256p. reprint ed. 37.50 (*0-404-16958-9*) AMS Pr.

***Minion, Ronald & Davies, Sandi J., eds.** Security Supervision: Theory & Practice of Asset Protection. 2nd ed. LC 99-30933. 375p. 1999. pap. 34.95 (*0-7506-7199-8*) Buttrwrth-Heinemann.

Minion, Ronald R. Security Supervisor Training Manual. Davies, Sandi J. et al, eds. 192p. 1995. pap. 39.95 (*0-7506-9632-X*) Buttrwrth-Heinemann.

Minirth, Frank. Father Book: An Instruction Manual. 1995. pap. 10.99 (*0-7852-8188-6*) Nelson.

Minirth, Frank & Dengler, Sandy. The Headache Book. LC 94-46884. 256p. 1995. mass mkt. 6.50 (*0-7852-7715-3*) Nelson.

Minirth, Frank, et al. Etapas del Matrimonio. (Serie Minirth-Meier).Tr. of Passages of Marriage. (SPA.). 431p. 12.99 (*0-88113-189-X*, B001-189X) Caribe Betania.

— The Father Book. 1996. mass mkt. 5.99 (*0-7852-7361-1*) Nelson.

— Hambre de Amor. (Serie Minirth-Meier).Tr. of Love Hunger. (SPA.). 390p. 1995. 12.99 (*0-88113-187-3*, B001-1873) Caribe Betania.

— The Healthy Christian Life. (Minirth-Meier Clinic Bible Study Ser.). 288p. (Orig.). (gr. 11). 1988. pap. 12.99 (*0-8010-6232-2*) Baker Bks.

— El Libro del Padre. (Serie Minirth-Meier).Tr. of Father Book. (SPA.). 288p. 10.99 (*0-88113-231-4*, B001-2314) Caribe Betania.

— Love Hunger: Recovery from Food Addiction. 1991. pap. 12.00 (*0-449-90613-2*) Fawcett.

— Mastering Your Moods. LC 98-53506. 288p. 1999. 18.99 (*0-7852-7869-9*) Nelson.

— Miracle Drugs: How They Work & What You Should Know about Them. 312p. 1996. pap. 12.99 (*0-7852-7865-6*) Nelson.

— 100 Ways to Overcome Depression. 128p. (gr. 11). 1993. reprint ed. mass mkt. 4.99 (*0-8007-8613-0*, Spire) Revell.

— Sex in the Christian Marriage. 160p. 1997. mass mkt. 5.99 (*0-8007-8644-0*, Spire) Revell.

Minirth, Frank, jt. auth. see Carter, Les.

Minirth, Frank B. & Littleton, Mark. You Can! LC 94-27191. 1994. write for info. (*0-8407-7749-3*) Nelson Comm.

Minirth, Frank B. & Meier, Paul. Happiness Is a Choice: The Symptoms, Causes & Cures of Depression. 2nd ed. LC 94-22163. 256p. (YA). (gr. 10). 1994. pap. 9.99 (*0-8010-6314-0*) Baker Bks.

Minirth, Frank B. & Meier, Paul D. Elige Ser Feliz! Happiness Is a Choice. Velez, Jose S., tr. from ENG. 208p. (Orig.). 1988. pap. 8.99 (*0-311-46113-1*) Casa Bautista.

Minirth, Frank B., et al. How to Beat Burnout. pap. 9.99 (*0-8024-2314-0*, 169) Moody.

Minirth, M. Frank. Beating Burnout: Balanced Living for Busy People, 2 vols. in 1. 352p. 1997. 9.99 (*0-88486-162-7*, Bristol Park Bks) Arrowood Pr.

Minisci, Francesco, ed. Free Radicals in Biology & Environment: Proceedings of the NATO Advanced Research Workshop, Bardolino, Italy, 21-26 June 1996. LC 97-8147. (NATO ASI Series: Partnership Sub-Series 3: No. 27). 516p. 1997. text 264.50 (*0-7923-4502-9*) Kluwer Academic.

— Free Radicals in Synthesis & Biology: Proceedings of the NATO Advanced Research Workshop Held in Bardolino (VR), Italy, May 8-13, 1988. (C). 1988. text 245.00 (*0-7923-0070-X*) Kluwer Academic.

Minister, Edward. The Complete Guide to Practical Cutting (1853) 2nd enl. rev. ed. Shep, R. L., ed. LC 92-50696. (Illus.). 480p. 1993. pap. 31.95 (*0-914046-17-9*) R L Shep.

Minister of Information Staff. Republic of Tea Book of Tea & Herbs: The Appreciating the Varietals & Virtues of Fine Teas & Herbs. LC 93-31073. 160p. 1993. pap. 12.95 (*1-56426-570-6*) Cole Group.

Ministere Economic Finance Staff. Economic Dictionary Budget, Finance of the State: French/English/French. (ENG & FRE.). 311p. 1997. 105.00 (*0-320-00474-0*) Fr & Eur.

Ministerial Association Staff, ed. Comunion con Dios (Communion with God) Guia Devocional para Escuela de Oracion. (SPA.). 123p. 1997. pap. 5.95 (*1-57847-018-8*) Genl Conf Svnth-day.

Ministerial Association Staff, ed. see White, Helen G.

Ministerial Leadership Services of the General Con & Mennonite Board of Congregational Ministries Staff. A Mennonite Polity for Ministerial Leadership: A Statement by the Joint Committee on Ministerial Leadership. LC 96-84443. 148p. 1996. pap. 8.95 (*0-87303-319-1*) Faith & Life.

Ministering Circle Members. Cape Fear - Still Cooking: More Favorite Recipes of the Lower Cape Fear. Orig. Title: Favorite Recipes of the Lower Cape Fear. Date not set. write for info. (*0-9664696-0-7*) Ministering Circle.

Ministre du Travail et de la Main d'Oeuvre Staff, ed. Vocabulaire Francais-Anglais des Relations Professionnelles. (ENG & FRE.). 302p. 1972. pap. 37.50 (*0-686-57279-3*, M-4655) Fr & Eur.

Ministries, Kenneth C., ed. see Murray, Andrew.

Ministry & Nurture Committee Staff. The Wounded Meeting: Dealing with Difficult Behavior in Meeting for Worship. 60p. (Orig.). 1993. pap. text 5.00 (*0-9620912-7-8*) Friends Genl Conf.

Ministry for the Environment Staff. The State of New Zealand's Environment. LC 98-137270. (Illus.). 650p. 1997. pap. 69.95 (*0-478-09000-5*, Pub. by GP Pubns) Accents Pubns.

Ministry of Agriculture, Fisheries & Food Staff, compiled by. Fatty Acids: Supplement to McCance & Widdowson's: The Composition of Foods. 200p. 1999. pap. 65.00 (*0-85404-819-7*, Pub. by Royal Soc Chem) Spr-Verlag.

Ministry of Agriculture, Nature Management & Fishe, jt. auth. see International Society for Horticultural Science St.

Ministry of Chemical Industry, Scientific & Techni, ed. China Chemical Industry: World Chemical Industry Yearbook, 1987. 580p. 1987. lib. bdg. 275.00 (*3-527-26738-7*, Wiley-VCH) Wiley.

***Ministry of Defence (Navy) Staff.** The Navy List, 1999: Corrected to 12th April 1999. xiv, 302p. 1999. 50.00 (*0-11-772912-4*, Pub. by Statnry Office) Balogh.

Ministry of Defence (Navy) Staff. War with Japan Vol. 3: The Campaigns in the Solomons & New Guinea. 350p. 1995. 99.00 (*0-11-772819-5*) Statnry Office.

— War with Japan Vol. 6: The Advance to Japan. 351p. 1995. 93.00 (*0-11-772821-7*) Statnry Office.

— War with Japan Vols. 1 & 2: Background to the War & Defensive Phase. 450p. 1995. 99.00 (*0-11-772818-7*) Statnry Office.

— War with Japan Vols. 4 & 5: The South-East Asia Operations & Central Pacific Advance & the Blockade of Japan. 504p. 1995. 116.00 (*0-11-772820-9*) Statnry Office.

Ministry of Defence, Air Historical Branch Staff. The Royal Air Force Builds for War: A History of Design & Construction in the RAF, 1935-1945. (Illus.). 768p. 1997. 130.00 (*0-11-772469-6*, Pub. by Statnry Office) Balogh.

***Ministry of Defence, Flag Institute Staff.** Flags of All Nations. 119p. 1999. ring bd. 90.00 (*0-11-772904-3*, Pub. by Statnry Office) Balogh.

Ministry of Defence Staff. Admiralty Manual of Seamanship. vii, 900p. 1995. pap. 50.00 (*0-11-772462-9*, Pub. by Statnry Office) Balogh.

— British Air Power Doctrine. 410p. 1999. pap. 30.00 (*0-11-887310-5*, Pub. by Statnry Office) Balogh.

— British Maritime Doctrine: BR 1806. 246p. 1999. pap. 30.00 (*0-11-772910-8*, Pub. by Statnry Office) Balogh.

Ministry of Defence Staff. Dissolution of the Luftwaffe: The Work of the British Air Forces of Occupation Germany (February 1944-December 1946), 2 vols., Set. (Illus.). 384p. 1995. 80.00 (*0-11-772822-5*, HM28225, Pub. by Statnry Office) Balogh.

— Hot Rolled Asphalt & Coated Macadam for Airfield Pavement Works. 90p. 1995. pap. 35.00 (*0-11-772688-5*, HM26885, Pub. by Statnry Office) Balogh.

Ministry of Defense of the Russian Federation Staff. Russia's Arms Catalogs/Encyclopedias Vol. 1: Army. 1997. 495.00 (*0-7855-7350-X*) St Mut.

— Russia's Arms Catalogs/Encyclopedias Vol. 2: Air Force. 1997. 495.00 (*0-7855-7351-8*) St Mut.

— Russia's Arms Catalogs/Encyclopedias Vol. 3: Navy. 1997. 495.00 (*0-7855-7352-6*) St Mut.

— Russia's Arms Catalogs/Encyclopedias Vol. 4: Strategic Missile Forces. 1997. 495.00 (*0-7855-7353-4*) St Mut.

— Russia's Arms Catalogs/Encyclopedias Vol. 5: Air Defense. 1997. 495.00 (*0-7855-7354-2*) St Mut.

— Russia's Arms Catalogs/Encyclopedias Vol. 7: Precision Guided Weapons & Ammunition. 1997. 495.00 (*0-7855-7355-0*) St Mut.

Ministry of Defense Staff. Admiralty Manual of Navigation Vol. 1: BR 45(1) xviii, 697p. 1997. reprint ed. pap. 110.00 (*0-11-772880-2*, HM28802, Pub. by Statnry Office) Balogh.

Ministry of Education, New Zealand Staff. Dancing with the Pen: The Learner As a Writer. 152p. 1992. pap. text 25.00 (*0-478-05560-9*, 501) R Owen Pubs.

Ministry of Education of New Zealand Staff, ed. Assessment: Policy to Practice. (Illus.). 52p. (Orig.). (C). 1994. pap. text 14.95 (*1-878450-95-6*, 512, Pub. by Lrning Media) R Owen Pubs.

— The New Zealand Curriculum Framework. 28p. (Orig.). (C). 1994. pap. text 14.95 (*1-878450-96-4*, 511, Pub. by Lrning Media) R Owen Pubs.

Ministry of Education Staff. Japanese Scientific Terms, English-Japanese-English: Oceanography. (ENG & JPN.). 186p. 1981. 75.00 (*0-8288-0421-4*, M 11209) Fr & Eur.

— Reading for Life: The Learner as a Reader. 160p. 1997. pap. text 25.00 (*0-478-20554-6*, 520) R Owen Pubs.

— Scientific Terms, Aeronautics: Japanese-English, English-Japanese. (ENG & JPN.). 235p. 1973. 39.95 (*0-8288-6328-8*, M-9347) Fr & Eur.

Ministry of Industry Staff. Swedish Industry & Industrial Policy, 1985. (Illus.). 122p. (Orig.). 1985. pap. text 115.00 (*91-38-82144-3*) Coronet Bks.

Ministry of Local Government Staff & Norwegian Petroleum Directorate Staff. Safety & Working Environment in the Offshore Petroleum Industry. 1992. pap. 75.00 (*82-7257-366-0*, Pub. by Oljedirektoratet) St Mut.

Ministry of Natural Resources Staff. Canoe Routes of Ontario: A Comprehensive Guide to More Then 100 Canoe Routes Throughout the Province. rev. ed. (Illus.). 112p. 1992. pap. 19.95 (*0-7710-6068-8*) McCland & Stewart.

Ministry of Power Staff. The Regulations for Utilization of Foreign Capital in China's Power Industry. Songbin Systems international Corporation Staff, tr. from CHI. LC 98-136700. 102p. 1997. pap. 199.00 (*0-9659644-0-X*) Songbin Systs.

Ministry of Science, Technology & the Environ. Sta, jt. auth. see Malaysian Coastal Resources Study Team Staff.

Ministry of Social Affairs & Employment Staff. Social Security in the Netherlands. 192p. 1990. pap. 24.00 (*90-6544-493-9*) Kluwer Law Intl.

Ministry on International Trade & Industry Staff. White Paper on International Trade, 1996. 400p. 1996. pap. 113.00 (*4-8224-0757-8*, Pub. by JETRO) Taylor & Francis.

— White Paper on International Trades, Japan, 1995. 400p. 1995. pap. 143.00 (*4-8224-0711-X*, Pub. by JETRO) Taylor & Francis.

— The World of Who's Who of Women, 1993 Japan: Japan 1993. 12th ed. 1200p. 1994. 195.00 (*0-948875-36-4*, Pub. by Melrose) Taylor & Francis.

Minitab, Inc. Staff. Getting Started. 160p. (C). 1998. pap. text. write for info. (*0-201-39716-1*) Addison-Wesley.

Minitab Inc. Staff. Getting Started Guide: The Student Edition of Minitab for Windows. Guardino, Karen, ed. 32p. (C). 1997. pap. text. write for info. (*0-201-69485-9*) Addison-Wesley.

— MINITAB WIN 3.5 SINGL PK. Berrisford, Julia, ed. 1p. 1994. 66.00 (*0-201-59157-X*) Addison-Wesley.

M

— Stat 101: Software for Statistics Instruction. 200p. (C). 1993. pap. text 30.94 incl. disk (*0-201-59087-5*); pap. text 33.75 incl. disk (*0-201-59088-3*) Addison-Wesley.

Minitab Inc. Staff. The Student Edition of Minitab for Windows Manual: Release 12. 1992. cd-rom 63.75 (*0-201-50650-5*) Addison-Wesley.

Minitab, Inc. Staff, jt. auth. see Daniel, Wayne.

Minitab, Inc. Staff, jt. auth. see Mann, Prem S.

***Miniter, Richard F.** The Things I Want Most: The Extraordinary Story of a Boy's Journey to a Family of His Own. 288p. 2000. reprint ed. pap. 12.95 (*0-553-37976-3*) Bantam.

Minium, Dennis & Short, Keith. Objects for Business. (C). 2001. text 38.00 (*0-13-241043-5*) P-H.

Minium, Edward W. A Statisical Reasoning in Psychology. 3rd ed. 280p. 1993. pap., wbk. ed. 33.95 (*0-471-82473-9*) Wiley.

Minium, Edward W. Statistical Reasoning in Psychology & Education. 3rd ed. LC 92-33570. 608p. (C). 1993. text 84.95 (*0-471-82188-8*) Wiley.

Minium, Edward W. & Clarke, Robert. Elements of Statistical Reasoning. LC 81-21843. 496p. (C). 1982. text 74.95 (*0-471-08041-1*) Wiley.

Minium, Edward W., et al. Elements of Statistical Reasoning. 2nd ed. LC 98-23663. 512p. 1998. pap. 64.95 (*0-471-19277-5*) Wiley.

— Statistical Reasoning in Psychology & Education. 888p. 1993. text 62.00 (*0-471-00817-6*) Wiley.

Minix, Dean & Hawley, Sandra M. International Relations. LC 96-38395. 550p. (C). 1997. 40.95 (*0-314-06767-1*) West Pub.

Minjung's Editorial Staff. Essence English-Korean Dictionary. 7th rev. ed. LC 88-80990. (ENG & KOR.). 3190p. 1997. lib. bdg. 85.50 (*1-56591-127-X*) Hollym Intl.

— Minjung's English - Korean & Korean - English Dictionary. LC 90-86010. (ENG & KOR.). 1689p. 1997. 37.50 (*0-930878-02-7*) Hollym Intl.

Minjung's Editorial Staff, ed. Essence Korean-English Dictionary. 3rd ed. LC 88-80991. 2686p. 1997. lib. bdg. 85.50 (*1-56591-128-8*) Hollym Intl.

Mink, Claudia G. Cahokia: City of the Sun: Prehistoric Urban Center in the American Bottom. LC 92-81951. (Illus.). 80p. 1995. reprint ed. pap. text 9.95 (*1-881563-00-6*) Cahokia MMS.

Mink, George, jt. auth. see Ballew, Julius R.

Mink, Gerd, jt. ed. see Schmitz, Franz-Juergan.

Mink, Gerd, jt. ed. see Schmitz, Franz-Jurgen.

Mink, Gwendolyn. Hostile Environment: The Political Betrayal of Sexually Harassed Women. LC 99-46800. 176p. 1999. 21.95 (*0-8014-3644-3*) Cornell U Pr.

— Old Labor & New Immigrants in American Political Development: Union, Party, & State, 1875-1920. LC 85-30963. 304p. 1986. 42.50 (*0-8014-1863-1*) Cornell U Pr.

— Old Labor & New Immigrants in American Political Development: Union, Party, & State, 1875-1920. LC 85-30963. 304p. 1990. reprint ed. pap. text 17.95 (*0-8014-9680-2*) Cornell U Pr.

— The Wages of Motherhood: Inequality in the Welfare State, 1917-1942. 208p. 1995. text 35.00 (*0-8014-2234-5*) Cornell U Pr.

— The Wages of Motherhood: Inequality in the Welfare State, 1917-1942. 216p. 1996. pap. text 12.95 (*0-8014-9534-2*) Cornell U Pr.

— Welfare's End. LC 97-38838. 192p. 1998. text 21.00 (*0-8014-3347-9*) Cornell U Pr.

— Welfare's End. LC 97-38838. 1998. pap. write for info. (*0-8014-8393-X*) Cornell U Pr.

Mink, Gwendolyn, ed. Whose Welfare? LC 99-37636. 1999. pap. 17.95 (*0-8014-8620-3*) Cornell U Pr.

Mink, Herman. Diccionario Tecnico Tomo 1: Aleman-Espanol. 8th ed. (GER & SPA.). 1908p. 1991. 225.00 (*0-8288-5157-3*, S50190) Fr & Eur.

— Diccionario Tecnico Espanol-Aleman-Espanol. 6th ed. (SPA.). 1560p. 1989. 195.00 (*0-8288-2143-7*, S50189) Fr & Eur.

— Technical Dictionary: Diccionario Tecnico: Suplemento, Vol. 2. deluxe ed. (GER & SPA.). 384p. 1981. 59.95 (*0-8288-4437-2*, S50270) Fr & Eur.

Mink, Hermann. Diccionario Tecnico Tomo 2: Espanol-Aleman. 7th ed. (GER & SPA.). 1560p. 1991. 195.00 (*0-7859-5819-3*) Fr & Eur.

— Diccionario Tecnico Espanol-Frances. (FRE & SPA.). 1356p. 1988. 195.00 (*0-7859-5825-8*, 8425414814) Fr & Eur.

— Diccionario Tecnico Frances-Espanol. 3rd ed.Tr. of French-Spanish Technical Diction. (FRE & SPA.). 1152p. 1989. write for info. (*0-7859-5028-1*) Fr & Eur.

Mink, J., et al, eds. Progress in Fourier Transform Spectroscopy: 10th International Conference, August 27-September 1, 1995, Budapest. (Mikrochimica Acta Ser.: Suppl. 14). (Illus.). 800p. 1997. pap., suppl. ed. 213.00 (*3-211-82931-8*) Spr-Verlag.

Mink, Janis. Duchamp. (SPA.). 1995. pap. 12.99 (*3-8228-8842-7*) Benedikt Taschen.

Mink, Janis. Duchamp. (Basic Ser.). (Illus.). 96p. 1995. pap. 9.99 (*3-8228-8883-4*) Taschen Amer.

— Miro. (Basic Ser.). 1994. pap. 9.99 (*3-8228-9649-7*) Taschen Amer.

— Miro. (SPA.). 1996. pap. 9.99 (*3-8228-0685-4*) Taschen Amer.

Mink, Jerrold H., et al. Magnetic Resonance Imaging of the Knee. LC 86-43229. (Illus.). 192p. reprint ed. pap. 59.60 (*0-7837-7122-3*, 204695100004) Bks Demand.

— MRI of the Knee. 2nd ed. LC 92-17023. 502p. 1992. text 147.00 (*0-88167-936-4*, 2417) Lppncott W & W.

Mink, JoAnna S. & Ward, Janet D., eds. Joinings & Disjoinings: The Significance of Marital Status in Literature. LC 91-70903. 200p. (C). 1991. 39.95 (*0-87972-523-0*); pap. 19.95 (*0-87972-524-9*) Bowling Green Univ Popular Press.

Mink, Joanna S. & Ward, Janet D., eds. The Significance of Sibling Relationships in Literature. LC 92-75707. 174p. (C). 1993. pap. 14.95 (*0-87972-613-X*) Bowling Green Univ Popular Press.

Mink, Joanna S., jt. auth. see Ward, Janet D.

Mink, Lauretta. Managing the Medical Practice: The Physician's Handbook for Successful Practice Administration. Stanley, Kay, ed. (Practice Success Ser.). pap. 44.95 (*0-89970-755-6*, OP701295AFR) AMA.

Mink, Lauretta & Reiboldt, Max. Financial Management of the Medical Practice: The Physician's Handbook for Successful Budgeting, Forecasting & Cost Accounting. Stanley, Kay, ed. (Practice Success Ser.). 44.95 (*0-89970-758-0*, OP701195AFR) AMA.

Mink, Len. Gospel Duck. (Illus.). 20p. (J). (ps-5). 1988. reprint ed. pap. text. write for info. (*0-318-63671-9*) Mink Ministries.

— Gospel Duck Goes to School. (Illus.). 24p. (J). (ps-6). 1988. reprint ed. pap. text. write for info. (*0-318-63672-7*) Mink Ministries.

Mink, Louis O. A Finnegans Wake Gazetteer. LC 77-74443. 585p. reprint ed. pap. 181.40 (*0-608-18849-2*, 205673100081) Bks Demand.

— Historical Understanding. Fay, Brian et al, eds. LC 87-47601. (Illus.). 312p. (C). 1987. text 42.50 (*0-8014-1983-2*) Cornell U Pr.

— Mind, History, & Dialectic: The Philosophy of R. G. Collingwood. LC 87-6143. (Wesleyan Paperback Ser.). 287p. 1987. reprint ed. pap. 89.00 (*0-608-02995-5*, 206306200007) Bks Demand.

Mink, Nelson G. How They Entered In. 1993. pap. 11.99 (*0-88019-307-7*) Schmul Pub Co.

Mink, Oscar G,. Change at Work: A Comprehensive Management Process for Transforming Organizations. (Management Ser.). 159p. 1993. text 36.95 (*1-55542-587-9*) Jossey-Bass.

Mink, Oscar G., et al. Open Organizations: A Model for Effectiveness, Renewal, & Intelligent Change. LC 94-22696. (Management Ser.). 240p. 1994. text. write for info. (*0-7879-0028-1*) Jossey-Bass.

Minke, G. Earth Construction Handbook: The Building Material Earth in Modern Architecture. (Advances in Architecture Ser.). (Illus.). 200p. 2000. 63.00 (*1-85312-805-8*, 8058) Computational Mech MA.

***Minke, Kathleen M. & Bear, George G., eds.** Preventing School Problems - Promoting School Success: Strategies & Programs That Work. 425p. 2000. pap. text, wbk. ed. 65.00 (*0-932955-89-4*, N0016) Natl Assn Schl Psych.

Minkel, Margaret & Schutz, Ruth K. A Lamp in the Night: Domestic Violence from a Feminist Perspective. 100p. 1992. pap. 10.00 (*0-9634517-0-7*) M Minkel.

***Minkel, Walter.** How to Do "The Three Bears" with Two Hands: Performing with Puppets. LC 99-28228. 144p. 1999. pap. 28.00 (*0-8389-0756-3*) ALA.

Minkel, Walter & Feldman, Roxanne H. Delivering Web Reference Services to Young People. LC 98-26112. (Illus.). 128p. 1998. 32.00 (*0-8389-0743-1*) ALA.

Minkema, Douglas D. System 35 Teacher's Guide. 48p. (gr. 9-12). text 110.00 (*0-9610582-7-7*) Apollo Com.

Minkema, Douglas D. & Carter, Gerald L. RPG II Programming. 2nd ed. (RPG II Programming-Advanced Topics Ser.). 1977. pap. text 17.50 (*0-9610582-2-6*) Apollo Com.

— RPG II Programming: Teacher's Guide. 175p. text 55.00 (*0-9610582-5-0*) Apollo Com.

Minkema, Douglas D. & Pasquini, Mark T. RPG II Programming Advanced Topics. (RPG II Programming-Advanced Topics Ser.). 187p. 1977. pap. text 14.50 (*0-9610582-3-4*) Apollo Com.

— RPG II Programming Advanced Topics: Teacher's Guide. 210p. (gr. 9-12). text 55.00 (*0-9610582-6-9*) Apollo Com.

Minkema, Douglas D., jt. auth. see Carter, Gerald L.

Minkema, Kenneth P. A Jonathan Edwards Reader. LC 94-41809. 432p. 1995. pap. 16.00 (*0-300-06204-4*) Yale U Pr.

Minkema, Kenneth P., jt. auth. see Edwards, Jonathan.

Minkema, Kenneth P., ed. see Cooper, James R.

***Minkenberg, Mechthild.** Der Aachener Reichsstrom: Wasserrecht und Wassernutzung in Den Beziehungen Zwischen der Reichsstadt und Dem Marienstift im Hoch- Und Spatmittelalter. (Europaische Hochschulschriften Geschichte und Ihre Hilfswissenschaften Ser.). XXXV, 273p. 1999. 48.95 (*3-631-34771-5*) P Lang Pubng.

Minkenberg, Michael & Dittgen, Herbert, eds. The American Impasse: U. S. Domestic & Foreign after the Cold War. (Pitt Series in Policy & Institutional). 304p. 1996. 49.95 (*0-8229-3945-2*) U of Pittsburgh Pr.

— American Impasse: U. S. Domestic & Foreign Policy after the Cold War. (Pitt Series in Policy & Institutional). 304p. 1996. pap. 22.95 (*0-8229-5612-8*) U of Pittsburgh Pr.

Minker, Jack, ed. Foundations of Deductive Databases & Logic Programming. (Illus.). 746p. (C). 1988. text 48.95 (*0-934613-40-0*) Morgan Kaufmann.

Minker, Jack, jt. ed. see Gallaire, Herve.

Minker, Margaret. Medizinisches Woerterbuch. (GER.). 320p. 1992. 29.95 (*0-7859-8496-8*, 3809400580) Fr & Eur.

— Woerterbuch der Medizin. (GER.). 399p. 1991. 59.95 (*0-7859-8495-X*, 3806845352) Fr & Eur.

***Minker, Wolfgang, et al.** Stochastically-Based Semantic Analysis. LC 99-33652. 221p. 1999. write for info. (*0-7923-8571-3*) Kluwer Academic.

Minkhlin, Solomon G. The Problem of the Minimum of a Quadratic Functional. Feinstein, A., tr. LC 64-24626. (Holden-Day Series in Mathematical Physics). 164p. reprint ed. pap. 50.90 (*0-608-10276-8*, 201629200003) Bks Demand.

Minkin, Barry H. Future in Sight: The 100 Trends, Implications & Predictions That Will Most Impact Businesses & the World Economy into the 21st Century. LC 95-18221. 288p. 1995. 22.95 (*0-02-585055-5*) Macmillan.

***Minkin, Barry H.** Future in Sight: 100 of the Most Important Trends, Implications & Predictions for the New Millennium. 256p. 1999. reprint ed. text 23.00 (*0-7881-6400-7*) DIANE Pub.

Minkin, Bert. Legacies of the St. Louis World's Fair. (Illus.). 100p. 1998. pap. 9.95 (*1-891442-05-8*) VA Pub Corp.

Minkin, Jacob S. The Teachings of Maimonides. LC 87-70737. 448p. 1997. pap. 40.00 (*1-56821-039-6*) Aronson.

Minkin, Lewis. The Contentious Alliance: Trade Unions & the Labour Party. 752p. 1991. text 110.00 (*0-7486-0301-8*, Pub. by Edinburgh U Pr) Col U Pr.

Minkin, Mary J. & Wright, Carol. What Every Woman Needs to Know about Menopause. 1996. 25.00 (*0-614-96804-6*) Yale U Pr.

Minkin, Mary J. & Wright, Carol V. What Every Woman Needs to Know about Menopause: The Years Before, During & After. 312p. 1997. pap. text 16.00 (*0-300-07261-9*) Yale U Pr.

Minkin, Mary J., jt. auth. see Burg, Dale.

Minkin, Mary Jane & Wright, Carol V. What Every Woman Needs to Know about Menopause: The Years Before, During, & After. LC 95-52665. 384p. (C). 1999. 27.00 (*0-300-06573-6*) Yale U Pr.

Minkin, Rita, tr. see Salaz, Ruben D.

Minkin, V. I., et al, eds. Telluranes: Synthesis, Structure & Reactivity, Vol. 8, No. 2. (Sulfur Reports: Vol. 8, Pt. 2). 43p. 1988. pap. text 71.00 (*3-7186-4834-2*) Gordon & Breach.

Minkin, V. I., et al. Molecular Design of Tautomeric Compounds. (C). 1987. text 221.50 (*90-277-2478-4*) Kluwer Academic.

Minkin, V. I., et al. Quantum Chemistry of Organic Compounds: Mechanisms of Reactions. (Illus.). xvi, 270p. 1990. 130.95 (*0-387-52530-0*) Spr-Verlag.

Minkin, Vladimir, et al. Aromaticity & Antiaromaticity: Electronic & Structural Aspects. 336p. 1994. 110.00 (*0-471-59382-6*) Wiley.

Minkin, Vladimir I., et al. Dipole Moments in Organic Chemistry. Vaughan, Worth E., ed. & tr. by. from RUS. Hazzard, B. J., tr. from RUS. LC 69-17901. (Physical Methods in Organic Chemistry Ser.). (Illus.). 300p. 1970. reprint ed. pap. 93.00 (*0-608-05484-4*, 206595300006) Bks Demand.

***Minkinnen, Arno R.** Body Land. LC 99-24743. (Motta Photography Ser.). (Illus.). 48p. 1999. 24.95 (*1-56098-880-0*) Smithsonian.

Minkkinen, Arno. Waterline. (Illus.). 112p. 1995. pap. 44.95 (*0-89381-648-5*) Aperture.

***Minkkinen, Panu.** Thinking Without Desire: A First Philosophy of Law. 256p. 1999. 48.00 (*1-84113-048-6*) Hart Pub.

Minkkinen, Petri & Patomaki, Heikki, eds. The Politics of Economic & Monetary Union. LC 97-38342. 252p. 1997. 121.00 (*0-7923-8041-X*, D Reidel) Kluwer Academic.

Minkler, Gary. Philosophy of Goodness & Mercy. 150p. (Orig.). 1991. 18.50 (*0-9621618-3-7*) Magellan Bk.

Minkler, Gary & Minkler, Jing. Aerospace Coordinate Systems & Transformations. (Illus.). 306p. (C). 1990. 78.00 (*0-9621618-0-2*) Magellan Bk.

— CFAR: The Principles of Automatic Radar Detection in Clutter. 300p. (C). 1988. pap. text 65.00 (*0-685-24050-9*) Magellan Bk.

— CFAR: The Principles of Automatic Radar Detection in Clutter. (Illus.). 374p. (C). 1990. 165.00 (*0-9621618-1-0*) Magellan Bk.

— Theory & Application of Kalman Filtering. (Illus.). 608p. (C). 1990. 120.00 (*0-9621618-2-9*) Magellan Bk.

Minkler, Jing, jt. auth. see Minkler, Gary.

Minkler, Meredith, ed. Community Organizing & Community Building for Health. LC 96-49716. 416p. (C). 1997. text 60.00 (*0-8135-2435-0*); pap. text 24.95 (*0-8135-2436-9*) Rutgers U Pr.

Minkler, Meredith & Estes, Carroll L., eds. Critical Gerontology: Perspectives from Political & Moral Economy. LC 97-37071. (Policy, Politics, Health & Medicine Ser.). 390p. 1999. text 56.00 (*0-89503-184-1*) Baywood Pub.

***Minkler, Meredith & Estes, Carroll L., eds.** Critical Gerontology: Perspectives from Political & Moral Economy. LC 97-37071. (Policy, Politics, Health & Medicine Ser.). 390p. 1999. pap. text 36.00 (*0-89503-185-X*) Baywood Pub.

Minkler, Meredith & Estes, Carroll L., eds. Critical Perspectives on Aging: The Political & Moral Economy of Growing Old. (Policy, Politics, Health & Medicine Ser.). 372p. 1991. text 46.00 (*0-89503-076-4*); pap. text 35.50 (*0-89503-075-6*) Baywood Pub.

— Readings in the Political Economy of Aging. (Policy, Politics, Health & Medicine Ser.: Vol. 6). 278p. 1984. pap. 33.00 (*0-89503-042-X*) Baywood Pub.

Minkler, Meredith & Roe, Kathleen M. Grandmothers As Caregivers: Raising the Children of the Crack Cocaine Epidemic. (Family Caregiver Applications Ser.: Vol. 2). (Illus.). 200p. (C). 1993. text 46.00 (*0-8039-4846-8*); pap. text 24.00 (*0-8039-4847-6*) Sage.

Minkler, Penny. Seeing Through Broccoli. (Illus.). 1993. 5.00 (*0-9619744-8-6*) Blue Light Pr.

Minkler, S. A., jt. auth. see Schacht, R. M.

Minkler, Wanda, ed. & illus. see Spencer, Emmett.

Minkoff. Biology Today. 1999. pap., student ed. 50.00 (*0-07-236620-6*) McGraw.

— Exploring America. (C). 1994. teacher ed. 33.75 (*0-15-501229-0*) Harcourt Coll Pubs.

Minkoff, Debra C. Organizing for Equality: The Evolution of Women's & Racial-Ethnic Organizations in America, 1955-1985. LC 94-46688. (Arnold & Caroline Rose Book Series of the American Sociological Association). 150p. (C). 1995. text 48.00 (*0-8135-2208-0*) Rutgers U Pr.

Minkoff, Eli C. Biology. (Barron's EZ-101 Study Keys Ser.). 144p. 1991. pap. 6.95 (*0-8120-4569-6*) Barron.

— Evolutionary Biology. (Biology Ser.). (Illus.). 640p. (C). 1983. teacher ed. write for info. (*0-201-15891-4*) Addison-Wesley.

Minkoff, Harvey, ed. Approaches to the Bible: A Collection of Articles from "Bible Review" & "Biblical Archaeology Review", 1978-1993, 2 vols., Set. (Illus.). (Orig.). (C). 1995. pap. text 29.95 (*1-880317-21-4*, 7H84S) Biblical Arch Soc.

— Approaches to the Bible: A Multitude of Perspectives: A Collection of Articles from "Bible Review" & "Biblical Archaeology Review", 1978-1993, Vol. II. (Illus.). 352p. (Orig.). (C). 1995. pap. text 18.95 (*1-880317-17-6*, 7H84) Biblical Arch Soc.

— Approaches to the Bible: Composition, Transmission & Language: A Collection of Articles from "Bible Review" & "Biblical Archaeology Review", 1978-1993, Vol. I. (Illus.). 384p. (Orig.). (C). 1994. pap. text 18.95 (*1-880317-16-8*, 7H83) Biblical Arch Soc.

Minkoff, Harvey & Melamed, Evelyn B. Exploring America: Perspectives on Critical Issues. LC 93-80867. (Illus.). 704p. (Orig.). (C). 1994. pap. text 40.00 (*0-15-500981-8*) Harcourt.

— Visions & Revisions: Critical Reading & Writing. 480p. (C). 1989. pap. text 19.60 (*0-13-949884-2*) P-H.

Minkoff, Howard L., et al, eds. HIV Infection in Women. LC 94-26754. 352p. 1994. text 111.00 (*0-7817-0236-4*) Lppncott W & W.

— HIV Infection in Women. LC 94-26754. (Illus.). 344p. reprint ed. pap. 106.70 (*0-608-09714-4*, 206988000007) Bks Demand.

Minkoff, I. Materials Processes: A Short Introduction. (Illus.). 160p. (C). 1992. 82.95 (*0-387-18895-9*) Spr-Verlag.

Minkoff, John R. Signals, Noise & Active Sensors: Radar, Sonar, Laser Radar. LC 91-16515. 264p. 1992. 98.95 (*0-471-54572-4*) Wiley.

Minkoff, Kenneth & Drake, Robert, eds. Dual Diagnosis of Major Mental Illness & Substance Disorder. LC 87-646993. (New Directions for Mental Health Services Ser.: No. MHS 50). 1991. pap. 25.00 (*1-55542-794-4*) Jossey-Bass.

Minkoff, Kenneth & Pollack, David, eds. Managed Mental Health Care in the Public Sector: A Survival Manual. (Chronic Mental Illness Ser.: Vol. 4). 410p. 1997. text 44.00 (*90-5702-536-1*, Harwood Acad Pubs) Gordon & Breach.

— Managed Mental Health Care in the Public Sector: A Survival Manual, Vol. 4. LC 98-168725. 410p. 1997. pap. text 23.00 (*90-5702-537-X*, Harwood Acad Pubs) Gordon & Breach.

Minkoff, Philip. Executive Skills. (Business Management English Ser.). 128p. 1994. text 23.60 (*0-13-017781-4*) P-H.

Minkoff, Randy, jt. auth. see Santo, Ron.

Minkova, Donka. The History of Final Vowels in English: The Sound of Muting. LC 91-28082. (Topics in English Linguistics Ser.: No. 4). xii, 220p. 1991. lib. bdg. 72.35 (*3-11-012763-6*) Mouton.

***Minkova, Milena.** The Personal Names of the Latin Inscriptions in Bulgaria, 118. 346p. 2000. 52.95 (*3-631-35141-0*, Pub. by P Lang) P Lang Pubng.

— The Personal Names of the Latin Inscriptions in Bulgaria, 118. (Studien zur Klassischen Philologie: Vol. 118). x, 345p. 2000. pap. 52.95 (*0-8204-4361-1*) P Lang Pubng.

Minkow, Barry. Clean Sweep: The Inside Story of the ZZZZ Best Scam -- One of Wall Street's Biggest Scams. LC 94-42957. x, 244p. 1995. 18.99 (*0-7852-7916-4*) Nelson.

Minkowich, Avram. Success & Failure in Israeli Elementary Education: An Evaluation Study with Special Emphasis on Disadvantaged Students. LC 80-19873. 539p. 1981. 49.95 (*0-87855-370-3*) Transaction Pubs.

Minkowitz, Donna. Ferocious Romance: What My Encounters with the Right Taught Me about Sex, God & Fury. LC 98-28823. 224p. 1998. 24.00 (*0-684-83322-0*) Free Pr.

Minkowitz, Martin, jt. auth. see De Carlo, Donald T.

Minkowski, A. & Monset-Couchard, M., eds. Physiological & Biochemical Basis for Perinatal Medicine. (Illus.). xiv, 370p. 1981. 135.75 (*3-8055-1283-X*) S Karger.

Minkowski, A., ed. see Artificial Ventilation Symposium Staff.

Minkowski, Alexandre, jt. ed. see Evrard, Philippe.

Minkowski, Alexandre, jt. ed. see Kretchmer, Norman.

Minkowski, Hermann. Diophantische Approximationen. LC 56-13056. 19.95 (*0-8284-0118-7*) Chelsea Pub.

— Gesammelte Abhandlungen, 2 Vols. in 1. LC 66-28570. 75.00 (*0-8284-0208-6*) Chelsea Pub.

Minkowycz, W. J. Numerical Heat Transfer. 2nd ed. text 150.00 (*0-471-34878-3*) Wiley.

Minkowycz, W. J. & Sparrow, E. M., eds. Advances in Numerical Heat Transfer. 422p. 1996. 170.00 (*1-56032-441-4*) Hemisp Pub.

Minkowycz, W. J., et al. Handbook of Numerical Heat Transfer. LC 87-23100. 1040p. 1988. 225.00 (*0-471-83093-3*) Wiley.

Minks, A. K. & Harrewijn, P., eds. Aphids: Their Biology, Natural Enemies & Control. (World Crop Pests Ser.: Vol. 2A). 450p. 1987. 289.00 (*0-444-42630-2*) Elsevier.

An Asterisk (*) at the beginning of an entry indicates that the title is appearing for the first time.

— Aphids: Their Biology, Natural Enemies & Control, Vol. C. (World Crop Pests Ser.). 322p. 1989. 228.00 (*0-444-42799-6*) Elsevier.

Minks, A. K., jt. auth. see Hardie, Jim.

Minks, Benton, jt. auth. see Minks, Louise.

Minks, Leah, jt. illus. see Minks, Louise.

Minks, Louis. Traditional Africa. LC 95-20851. (World History Ser.). (Illus.). 96p. (J). (gr. 6-10). 1996. lib. bdg. 22.45 (*1-56006-239-8*) Lucent Bks.

Minks, Louise & Minks, Benton. The Vietnam War. Bowman, John, ed. (America at War Ser.). (Illus.). 144p. (J). (gr. 5-12). 1992. 19.95 (*0-8160-2508-8*) Facts on File.

Minks, Louise & Minks, Leah. Memorial Hall Coloring Book. 24p. (Orig.). (J). (gr. 1-2). 1989. pap. 2.95 (*0-9612876-7-5*) Pocumtuck Valley Mem.

***Minktls, G. E.** A Short Introduction to Intuitionistic Logic. LC 00-35703. (University Series in Mathematics). 2000. write for info. (*0-306-46394-6*) Plenum.

Minkus, Jerome B. The Branched Cyclic Covering of Two Bridge Knots & Links. LC 81-19099. (Memoirs of the American Mathematical Society Ser.: No. 35/255). 68p. 1982. pap. 16.00 (*0-8218-2255-1*, MEMO/35/255) Am Math.

Minlos, R. Many-Particle Hamiltonians: Spectra & Scattering. (Advances in Soviet Matheamtics Ser.: Vol. 5). 194p. 1991. text 75.00 (*0-8218-4104-1*, ADVSOV/5) Am Math.

Minlos, R., jt. auth. see Gelfand, I.

***Minlos, R. A.** Introduction to Mathematical Statistical Physics. LC 99-49593. (University Lecture Ser.: Vol. 19). 103p. 1999. 24.00 (*0-8218-1337-4*) Am Math.

***Minlos, R. A., et al, eds.** On Dobrushin's Way: From Probability Theory to Statistical Physics. LC 91-640741. (TRANS2 Ser.: Vol. 198). 243p. 2000. 99.00 (*0-8218-2150-4*) Am Math.

Minlos, R. A., jt. auth. see Malyshev, V. A.

Minn, Loretta B. Teach Speech. 64p. (J). (gr. 3-7). 1982. 6.99 (*0-86653-058-4*, GA 418) Good Apple.

— Trek for Trivia. (Illus.). 48p. (J). (gr. 3-8). 1985. student ed. 7.99 (*0-86653-291-9*, GA 646) Good Apple.

Minnaar, Maria. The Emu Farmer's Handbook Vol. 2: Commercial Farming, Methods for Emus, Ostriches & Rheas. (Illus.). 320p. (C). 1998. 48.00 (*0-9643741-4-5*) Nyoni Pubng.

Minnaar, Maria, jt. auth. see Minnaar, Phillip.

Minnaar, Maria, ed. see Minnaar, Phillip.

Minnaar, Phillip. Handledning I Emu-Uppfodning. Bellinetto, Alexandra, tr. (SWE., Illus.). 57p. (C). 1996. 20.00 (*0-9643741-5-3*) Nyoni Pubng.

— A Manual on Emu Farming. (Illus.). 44p. (Orig.). 1989. pap. 18.00 (*0-9643741-0-2*) Nyoni Pubng.

— Manual para la Crianza Del Emu. rev. ed. Minnaar, Maria, ed. Nava, Kathryn, tr. (SPA., Illus.). 58p. (C). 1997. 20.00 (*0-9643741-6-1*) Nyoni Pubng.

Minnaar, Phillip & Minnaar, Maria. L'Elevage de l'Emu. Brisson, Renee & Brisson, Claire, trs. (FRE., Illus.). 182p. 1996. 40.00 (*0-9643741-2-9*) Nyoni Pubng.

— The Emu Farmer's Handbook, Vol. 1. (Illus.). 178p. (C). 1992. 40.00 (*0-9643741-1-0*) Nyoni Pubng.

Minnaert, M. G. Light & Color in the Outdoors. 1994. pap. 24.00 (*0-387-84413-9*) Spr-Verlag.

— Light & Color in the Outdoors. (Illus.). 223p. 1995. 24.95 (*0-387-94413-3*) Spr-Verlag.

— Light & Color in the Outdoors, Vol. XVII. rev. ed. Seymour, L., tr. from DUT. LC 92-33748. (Illus.). 417p. 1995. 65.00 (*0-387-97935-2*) Spr-Verlag.

— Nature of Light & Colour in the Open Air. (Illus.). 362p. 1954. pap. text 9.95 (*0-486-20196-1*) Dover.

Minnaert, M. J. Practical Work in Elementary Astronomy. 247p. 1969. text 88.00 (*90-277-0133-4*) Kluwer Academic.

Minnard, Carla V., jt. auth. see Sher, Malcolm.

Minne, S. C., et al. Bringing Scanning Probe Microscopy Up to Speed. LC 99-10284. (Microsystems Ser.). 1999. write for info. (*0-7923-8466-0*) Kluwer Academic.

***Minne-Seve, Viviane & Kergall, Herve.** Romanesque & Gothic France: Art & Architecture. LC 00-38974. (Illus.). 416p. 2000. 75.00 (*0-8109-4436-7*, Pub. by Abrams) Time Warner.

***Minneapolis Institute of Arts, et al.** Treasures from the Minneapolis Institute of Arts. LC 98-66728. (Illus.). 1998. write for info. (*0-912964-63-4*); write for info. (*0-912964-64-2*) Minneapolis Inst Arts.

Minneapolis Institute of Arts, jt. auth. see Peterson, Christian A.

Minneapolis Institute of Arts Staff. Leger's Le Grand Dejeuner. LC 80-80235. (Illus.). 1980. 8.00 (*0-912964-11-1*) Minneapolis Inst Arts.

Minneci, Jennifer, jt. ed. see Walker, John Q.

Minnella, Thomas A. The Copier Productivity Primer. 83p. 1991. pap. 10.95 (*0-9629936-0-3*) Minnella Ent.

Minnella, Thomas A., ed. see Kasper, Juneann.

Minnella, Thomas A., ed. see McKee Ranger, Laurel A.

Minnelli, Vincente & Arce, Hector. I Remember It Well. LC 90-3330. 391p. 1990. reprint ed. pap. 15.95 (*0-573-60607-2*) S French Trade.

Minneman, Paul G. Large Land Holdings in Ohio & Their Operation. Bruchey, Stuart, ed. LC 78-56664. (Management of Public Lands in the U. S. Ser.). 1979. lib. bdg. 18.95 (*0-405-11344-7*) Ayer.

Minnen, Cornelis A. Van, see Van Minnen, Cornelis A.

Minnen, P. Van, see Hoogendijk, F. A. & Van Minnen, P.

Minner, R., ed. see McCrea, Steve.

Minnerly, W. Lee. Electronic Data Interchange (EDI) & the Appraisal Office: Technical Report. LC 96-1676. 1996. pap. 15.00 (*0-922154-26-0*) Appraisal Inst.

Minnerly, William L., jt. auth. see Heldman, Donald P.

Minnery, John. The CIA Catalog of Clandestine Weapons, Tools, & Gadgets. LC 92-15887. 116p. 1992. pap. 10.00 (*0-942637-69-0*) Barricade Bks.

— CIA Catalog of Clandestine Weapons, Tools & Gadgets. (Illus.). 128p. 1990. pap. 16.00 (*0-87364-576-6*) Paladin Pr.

— Fingertip Firepower: Pen Guns, Knives & Bombs. (Illus.). 120p. 1990. pap. 18.00 (*0-87364-560-X*) Paladin Pr.

— Pick Guns: Lock Picking for Spies, Cops & Locksmiths. (Illus.). 128p. 1989. pap. 18.00 (*0-87364-510-3*) Paladin Pr.

Minnesota & Fats. Minnesota Fats on Pool. 1976. 17.95 (*0-8488-1555-6*) Amereon Ltd.

Minnesota Advocates for Human Rights, Internationa. The U. N. Commission on Human Rights Orientation Manual for Nongovernmental Organizations: An Orientation Manual. 100p. 1993. pap. 7.50 (*0-929293-14-2*) MN Advocates.

Minnesota Advocates for Human Rights Staff. Civilians at Risk: Military & Police Abuses in the Mexican Countryside. 36p. (Orig.). 1993. pap. 5.00 (*0-929293-16-9*) MN Advocates.

— Conquest Continued: Disregard for Human & Indigenous Rights in the Mexican State of Chiapas. 93p. 1992. pap. 10.00 (*0-929293-13-4*) MN Advocates.

— No Double Standards in International Law: Linkage of NAFTA with Hemispheric System of Human Rights Enforcement Is Needed - Canada, Mexico & the United States Must Become Full Partners. 22p. (Orig.). 1992. pap. 5.00 (*0-929293-15-0*) MN Advocates.

Minnesota Bride Magazine, Inc. Staff. Minnesota Bride Magazine Wedding Planner. (Illus.). 120p. 1998. pap. 14.95 (*0-9663558-0-6*) Tiger Oak.

Minnesota Center for Corporate Responsibility Staff, jt. auth. see Bockelman, Wilfred.

Minnesota Council on Foundations Staff. Guide to Minnesota Foundations & Corporate Giving Programs, 1991-92. Bill, Patricia, ed. 220p. 1991. per. 30.00 (*0-9616378-1-1*) MN Coun Found.

***Minnesota Department of Natural Resources Staff.** A Guide to Minnesota's Scientific & Natural Areas. 240p. 1999. spiral bd. write for info. (*0-9647451-4-3*) MN Bkstore.

Minnesota District Judges Association, Committee o. Minnesota Jury Instruction Guides, Criminal (CRIMJIG), Vol. 10. 2nd ed. LC 85-51063. (Minnesota Practice Ser.). 510p. 1985. 59.50 (*0-685-13436-9*) West Pub.

Minnesota Early Learning Design Staff. The Safe, Self-Confident Child: A Quick & Easy Guide. (For Your Information Ser.). (Orig.). 1997. pap. 8.95 (*0-614-28111-3*, Signal Hill) New Readers.

Minnesota Fathering Aliance Staff. Working with Fathers: Methods & Perspectives. 1992. pap. 21.95 (*0-9633084-0-8*) Nu Ink Unltd.

Minnesota Heart Association Staff. Rheumatic Fever: A Symposium Held at the University of Minnesota on November 29, 30, & December 1, 1951. Thomas, Lewis, ed. LC 52-11108. 359p. reprint ed. pap. 111.30 (*0-608-14144-5*, 205592200039) Bks Demand.

Minnesota Historical Society Staff. The Fur Trade in Minnesota: An Introductory Guide to Manuscript Sources. LC 77-25902. (Publications of the Minnesota Historical Society). (Illus.). 69p. 1977. reprint ed. pap. 30.00 (*0-608-06677-X*, 206687400009) Bks Demand.

— Map of Minnesota Territory, 1850. (Borealis Bks.). 16p. 1999. pap. 9.95 (*0-87351-374-6*, Borealis Book) Minn Hist.

Minnesota Historical Society Staff, et al. Manuscripts Collections of the Minnesota Historical Society No. 2: Guide. LC 35-27911. (Publications of the Minnesota Historical Society). 228p. reprint ed. pap. 70.70 (*0-8357-3315-7*, 203953900013) Bks Demand.

Minnesota Humanities Commission Staff, ed. Braided Lives: An Anthology of Multicultural American Writing. 288p. (YA). (gr. 9-12). 1991. pap. text 13.00 (*0-9629298-0-8*) MN Humanities.

Minnesota Lawyers Human Rights Committee Staff. The Homicide of Dr. Victor Manuel Oropeza Contreras: A Case Study of Failed Human Rights Reforms in Mexico. 40p. (Orig.). 1991. pap. 5.00 (*0-929293-11-8*) MN Advocates.

— Trimming the Cat's Claws: The Politics of Impunity in Albania. (Minnesota International Human Rights Committee Ser.). 44p. (Orig.). 1992. pap. text 8.50 (*0-929293-28-2*) MN Advocates.

Minnesota Lawyers International Human Rights Commi. Children's Rights in Haiti. 33p. (Orig.). 1989. pap. 5.00 (*0-929293-04-5*) MN Advocates.

— Hidden from View: Human Rights Conditions in the Krome Detention Center. 81p. (Orig.). 1991. pap. 7.00 (*0-929293-10-X*) MN Advocates.

— Oakdale Detention Center: The First Year of Operation. 55p. 1987. pap. 3.00 (*0-929293-17-7*) MN Advocates.

— Shame in the House of Saud: Contempt for Human Rights in the Kingdom of Saudi Arabia. 170p. (Orig.). 1992. pap. 15.00 (*0-929293-12-6*) MN Advocates.

Minnesota Lawyers International Human Rights Commi, ed. see McGuinnes, Celia & Whelan, Leo.

Minnesota Messenia Expedition Staff. Excavations at Nichoria in Southwest Greece Vol. 1: Site, Environs, & Techniques. Rapp, George R., Jr. et al, eds. LC 78-3198. (Illus.). 403p. 1978. reprint ed. pap. 125.00 (*0-608-00795-1*, 205934400001) Bks Demand.

Minnesota Staff. Minnesota Employment Laws: A Compendium of Minnesota Statutes Relating to Employment, Wages & Benefits, Discrimination, Termination, Workplace, Safety, Etc. LC 96-128548. xxxiii, 763 p. 1996. write for info. (*0-314-08243-3*) West Pub.

Minnesota Staff & Herr, David F. General Rules of Practice Annotated. LC 93-219189. xxxi, 470 p. 1993. write for info. (*0-314-02257-0*) West Pub.

***Minnesota Staff & Winthrop & Weinstine Staff.** An Employer's Guide to Employee Stock Ownership Plans. 2nd ed. LC 98-148538. ii, 88 p. 1998. write for info. (*1-888404-09-4*) MN Dept Trade Econ Dev.

Minnesota State Bar Association Staff & Daly, Joseph L. Student Lawyer:guide Minnesota Legal Sys 4e. 4th ed. (Paralegal). 217p. (C). 1986. reprint ed. mass mkt. 24.75 (*0-314-23039-4*) West Pub.

Minnesota University, Graduate School Staff. Social Sciences at Mid-Century. LC 68-55852. (Essay Index Reprint Ser.). 1977. 17.95 (*0-8369-0710-8*) Ayer.

Minnesota Vikings Staff. Minnesota Vikings. CWC Sports Inc., ed. (NFL Team Yearbooks Ser.). (Illus.). (J). (gr. 1-12). 1998. pap. 9.99 (*1-891613-14-6*) Everett Sports.

Minney, R. J. The Private Papers of Hore-Belisha. (Modern Revivals in Military History Ser.). 320p. 1992. 63.95 (*0-7512-0042-5*, Pub. by Gregg Revivals) Ashgate Pub Co.

Minney, R. J., ed. & adapted by see Bates, Dorothy R.

Minni, C. D. & Ciampolini, Anna Foschi, eds. Writers in Transition. 240p. 1990. pap. 13.00 (*0-920717-26-8*) Guernica Editions.

Minni, Dino. Other Selves. 98p. pap. 8.00 (*0-919349-54-4*) Guernica Editions.

— Ricordi. 198p. pap. 18.00 (*0-919349-99-4*) Guernica Editions.

Minnich, Bernd, jt. auth. see Grafton, Antony.

Minnich, Elizabeth, et al. Reconstructing the Academy: Women's Education & Women's Studies. 320p. 1988. pap. text 16.00 (*0-226-53014-0*) U Ch Pr.

— Reconstructing the Academy: Women's Education & Women's Studies. 320p. 1999. lib. bdg. 33.00 (*0-226-53013-2*) U Ch Pr.

Minnich, Elizabeth K. Transforming Knowledge. 240p. 1990. 49.95 (*0-87722-695-4*) Temple U Pr.

— Transforming Knowledge. 240p. 1991. pap. 22.95 (*0-87722-880-9*) Temple U Pr.

Minnich, Jerry. The Michigan Gardening Guide. LC 97-45271. (Illus.). 328p. 1998. pap. 19.95 (*0-472-08398-8*, 08398) U of Mich Pr.

— The Ohio Gardening Guide. (Illus.). 290p. (Orig.). 1995. pap. 18.95 (*0-8214-1118-7*) Ohio U Pr.

— The Wisconsin Garden Guide. 3rd ed. LC 95-2342. (Illus.). 336p. 1995. pap. 18.95 (*1-879483-24-6*) Prairie Oak Pr.

Minnich, Jerry, ed. The Wisconsin Almanac: Being a Loosely Organized Compendium of Facts, History, Lore, Remembrances, Puzzles, Recipes, & Both Household & Gardening Advice with Which to Offer Elucidation, Assistance, & Occasional Amusement to the Conscientious Reader. 2nd ed. LC 97-47785. (Illus.). 264p. 1998. pap. 10.95 (*1-879483-49-1*) Prairie Oak Pr.

Minnich, Jerry, jt. auth. see Visser, Kristin.

Minnich, Joseph L. Communicating the Appraisal: Fannie Mae Desktop Underwriter Quantitative Analysis Appraisal Report Form 2055 & Fannie Mae Desktop Underwriter Quantitative Analysis Appraisal Report Form 2065. LC 97-19780. (Illus.). 145p. 1997. 27.50 (*0-922154-40-6*) Appraisal Inst.

Minnich, Joseph L., jt. auth. see Coleman, Stephanie C.

Minnich, Nelson, ed. see Reasmus, Desiderius.

Minnich, Nelson H. The Catholic Reformation: Council, Churchmen, Controversies. (Collected Studies: No. CS 403). 413p. 1993. 109.95 (*0-86078-350-2*, Pub. by Variorum) Ashgate Pub Co.

— The Fifth Lateran Council, 1512-1517: Studies on its Membership, Diplomacy & Proposals for Reform. (Collected Studies: No. CS 392). 352p. 1993. 113.95 (*0-86078-349-9*, Pub. by Variorum) Ashgate Pub Co.

Minnich, Richard A. The Biogeography of Fire in the San Bernardino Mountains of California: A Historical Study. LC 88-9997. (University of California Publications in Entomology: No. 28). 170p. 1988. pap. 52.70 (*0-7837-7494-X*, 204921600010) Bks Demand.

***Minnich, Richard A.** California. (AAA Essential Guides Ser.). (Illus.). 2000. pap. 8.95 (*0-658-01101-4*, Passprt Bks) NTC Contemp Pub Co.

Minnich, Richard A. & Vizca Ino Ernesto Franco. Land of Chamise & Pines: Historical Accounts & Current Status of Northern Baja California's Vegetation. LC 98-13127. (Publications in Botany Ser.). 168p. 1998. 32.00 (*0-520-09825-0*, Pub. by U CA Pr) Cal Prin Full Svc.

Minnich, Robert G. The Homemade World of Zagaj. (Bergen Studies in Social Anthropology, University of Bergen, Norway: No. 18). 248p. 1985. pap. text 13.95 (*0-936508-56-6*, Pub. by Bergen Univ Dept Social Anthro) MBIPubg.

Minnick, jt. auth. see Leithold.

Minnick, Ann M. Twelve Step Programs: A Contemporary American Quest for Meaning & Spiritual Renewal. LC 97-9178. 208p. 1997. 49.95 (*0-275-95850-7*, Praeger Pubs) Greenwood.

***Minnick, Craig A.** American Express Tax Guide 2000. 2000. pap. text 16.95 (*0-916103-56-0*) Am Express Food.

Minnick, Dale L. How to Get up in Front Without Getting Down. LC 91-76666. 200p. 1991. reprint ed. pap. 15.00 (*0-9633476-0-8*) Desert Rain.

— Speaking Without Fear. rev. ed. 194p. 1995. pap. 14.95 (*0-9633476-8-3*) Desert Rain.

Minnick, Dan, ed. Mail.dat GCA Standard 130-1995, Version 96-1. 2nd rev. ed. (Illus.). 75p. 1996. pap. 48.00 (*0-933505-32-9*) Graph Comm Assn.

Minnick, Karla. Divorce, Humor Me. 66p. 1993. pap. 6.50 (*1-880365-16-2*) Prof Pr NC.

Minnick, Kathleen. Kwanzaa: How to Celebrate It in Your Home. Taylor, Charles, ed. (Big Book African American (In Home) Celebration). (Illus.). 24p. 1994. lib. bdg. 21.95 (*0-935483-19-5*) Praxis Madison.

Minnick, Molly A. Divorce Illustrated. (Illus.). 50p. (Orig.). (C). 1990. 15.00 (*1-878526-02-2*) Pineapple MI.

— Divorce Illustrated: Workbook. (Illus.). 60p. (Orig.). (J). (gr. 4). 1990. pap. 5.00 (*1-878526-03-0*) Pineapple MI.

— Group Work with Children of Divorce. rev. ed. (Illus.). 80p. (C). 1990. 18.00 (*1-878526-01-4*) Pineapple MI.

— A Time to Decide, a Time to Heal. 4th ed. LC 90-91478. 118p. 1994. 6.95 (*1-878526-39-1*) Pineapple MI.

— Yellow Ribbons, Worried Hearts. (Illus.). 65p. (C). 1991. 20.00 (*1-878526-33-2*) Pineapple MI.

— Yesterday I Dreamed of Dreams. 25p. 1991. 1.00 (*1-878526-10-3*) Pineapple MI.

Minnick, Molly A., jt. auth. see Delp, Kathleen J.

Minnick, Roy, ed. Laws for the California Surveyor. 210p. 1996. pap. 40.00 (*0-910845-10-7*, 708) Landmark Ent.

— Plotters & Patterns of American Land Surveying. 232p. 1986. pap. 30.00 (*0-910845-28-X*, 974) Landmark Ent.

Minnick, Roy, jt. auth. see Cuomo, Paul.

Minnick, Roy, ed. see Government Land Office.

Minnick, Roy, ed. see Schmitz, Michael J.

Minnick, Sylvia S. SamFow: The San Joaquin Chinese Lagacy. LC 87-63495. (Illus.). 320p. (C). 1988. 25.00 (*0-944194-09-5*); pap. 14.95 (*0-944194-10-9*) Heritage West.

Minnick, Thomas L., jt. auth. see Gordon, Virginia N.

Minnick, Wayne. The Butcher Bird. LC 97-68997. 1998. pap. 13.95 (*0-88739-168-0*) Creat Arts Bk.

***Minnick, Wayne.** The Crossbow Murder. LC 99-64933. 208p. 2000. pap. 13.95 (*0-88739-301-2*) Creat Arts Bk.

Minnick, William H. Flux Cored Arc Welding Handbook. LC 98-18883. 1998. 25.28 (*1-56637-482-0*) Goodheart.

***Minnick, William H.** Gas Metal Arc Welding Handbook. LC 99-31206. (Illus.). 164p. 2000. 25.28 (*1-56637-692-0*) Goodheart.

— Gas Tungsten Arc Welding Handbook. LC 99-23841. 272p. 2000. 26.64 (*1-56637-694-7*) Goodheart.

Minnicks, Margaret. The Spiritual Significance of Eating: Tracing the Biblical Motifs. 142p. 1998. pap. 10.00 (*1-57502-789-5*, PO2180) Morris Pubng.

Minnigerode, Meade. Certain Rich Men. LC 71-121489. (Essay Index Reprint Ser.). 1977. 20.95 (*0-8369-1714-6*) Ayer.

— Lives & Times. LC 76-121490. (Essay Index Reprint Ser.). 1977. 20.95 (*0-8369-1765-0*) Ayer.

— Some American Ladies. LC 70-93361. (Essay Index Reprint Ser.). 1977. 23.95 (*0-8369-1362-0*) Ayer.

— Some Personal Letters of Herman Melville & a Bibliography. LC 78-75511. (Select Bibliographies Reprint Ser.). 1977. 18.95 (*0-8369-5013-5*) Ayer.

Minnigh, H. N. A History of Company K: "The Boys Who Fought at Home" (Illus.). 152p. 1998. reprint ed. pap. 8.00 (*1-57747-040-0*) Thomas Publications.

Minnikin, David E., jt. ed. see Goodfellow, Michael.

***Minning, Laura J.** Dear Diary. 2000. pap. 7.95 (*0-533-13516-8*) Vantage.

Minninger, Joan. Perfect Letter. 224p. 1991. pap. 11.00 (*0-385-41998-8*) Doubleday.

— Rapid Memory In Seven Days: The Quick & Easy Guide to Better Remembering. Dugan, Eleanor, ed. LC 94-6937. 208p. (Orig.). 1994. pap. 11.95 (*0-399-52130-5*, Perigee Bks) Berkley Pub.

— Total Recall. 276p. 1991. 7.98 (*1-56731-011-7*, MJF Bks) Fine Comms.

— Total Recall. 1989. mass mkt. 5.99 (*0-671-69134-1*) PB.

Minninger, Joan & Dugan, Eleanor. Make Your Mind Work for You. Peters, Sally, ed. 256p. 1990. reprint ed. mass mkt. 4.95 (*0-671-68474-4*) PB.

Minninger, Joan, jt. auth. see Goulter, Barbara.

Minnis, A. J., et al, eds. Essays on Ricardian Literature: In Honour of J. A. Burrow. LC 98-100000. 378p. (C). 1997. 85.00 (*0-19-818282-1*) OUP.

Minnis, A. J., jt. auth. see Biller, Peter.

Minnis, Alastair J. Chaucer & Pagan Antiquity. (Chaucer Studies: No. VIII). 208p. 1982. 75.00 (*0-85991-098-9*) Boydell & Brewer.

— Medieval Literary Theory & Criticism, 1100-1375: The Commentary-Tradition. 2nd ed. Scott, A. B., ed. 560p. 1992. reprint ed. pap. text 35.00 (*0-19-811274-2*, 8526) OUP.

— The Shorter Poems. (Oxford Guides to Chaucer Ser.: Vol. 3). (Illus.). 592p. 1995. text 85.00 (*0-19-811193-2*) OUP.

Minnis, Alastair J., ed. Late-Medieval Religious Texts & Their Transmission: Essays in Honour of A. I. Doyle. (York Manuscripts Conferences: No. 3). (Illus.). 208p. (C). 1994. 75.00 (*0-85991-386-4*) Boydell & Brewer.

— Latin & Vernacular: Studies in Late-Medieval Texts & Manuscripts. (University of York: Centre for Medieval Studies Manuscripts Conference Proceedings: No. 1). 163p. (C). 1989. 75.00 (*0-85991-286-8*) Boydell & Brewer.

— The Medieval Boethius: Studies in the Vernacular Translation of De Consolatione Philosophiae. 207p. 1988. 75.00 (*0-85991-234-5*) Boydell & Brewer.

Minnis, Alastair J. & Biller, Peter, eds. Medieval Theology & the Natural Body. LC 97-1032. (York Studies in Medieval Theology: No. 1). (Illus.). 256p. 1997. 75.00 (*0-9529734-0-5*) Boydell & Brewer.

Minnis, Alastair J., jt. ed. see Brewer, Charlotte.

Minnis, Alastair J., ed. see Chaucer, Geoffrey.

Minnis, M. Lee. The First Virginia Regiment of Foot, 1775-1783. 463p. 1998. 30.00 (*1-888265-29-9*) Willow Bend.

Minnis, Mary M., jt. auth. see Burks, Bennette D.

***Minnis, Paul E.** Biodiversity & Native America. LC 99-55136. (Illus.). 256p. 2000. 34.95 (*0-8061-3232-9*) U of Okla Pr.

— Ethnobotany. LC 99-47294. (Illus.). 384p. 2000. 18.95 (*0-8061-3180-2*) U of Okla Pr.

Minnis, Paul E. Social Adaptation to Food Stress: A Prehistoric Southwestern Example. LC 84-28103. (Prehistoric Archeology & Ecology Ser.). (Illus.). 250p. 1985. pap. text 10.00 (*0-226-53024-8*) U Ch Pr.

M

An Asterisk (*) at the beginning of an entry indicates that the title is appearing for the first time.

— Social Adaptation to Food Stress: A Prehistoric Southwestern Example. LC 84-28103. (Prehistoric Archeology & Ecology Ser.). (Illus.). 256p. 1994. lib. bdg. 20.00 (*0-226-53022-1*) U Ch Pr.

Minnis, Whitney. How to Get an Athletic Scholarship: A Student-Athlete's Guide to Collegiate Athletics. 104p. (YA). (gr. 6-12). 1995. per. 12.95 (*0-9645153-0-X*) ASI Publ.

Minniti, D. & Rix, H. W., eds. Spiral Galaxies in the Near-IR: Proceedings of the ESO Workshop Held at Garching, Germany, 7-9 June 1995. LC 96-15599. (ESO Astrophysics Symposia Ser.). 350p. 1996. 39.95 (*3-540-60937-7*) Spr-Verlag.

Minno, Marc C. & Emmel, Thomas C. Butterflies of the Florida Keys. (Illus.). 168p. (Orig.). 1993. 31.50 (*0-945417-88-8*); pap. 18.95 (*0-945417-87-X*) Sci Pubs.

Minno, Marc C. & Minno, Maria. Florida Butterfly Gardening: A Complete Guide to Attracting, Identifying & Enjoying Butterflies of the Lower South. LC 99-12040. 1999. 34.95 (*0-8130-1665-7*) U Press Fla.

Minno, Maria, jt. auth. see Minno, Marc C.

Minnoch, James E. Aground. 1987. 12.95 (*0-07-155319-3*) McGraw.

— Aground: Coping with Emergency Groundings. LC 85-71609. (Illus.). 160p. 1985. 12.95 (*0-8286-0098-8*) J De Graff.

Minnow, Nell, jt. auth. see Monks, Robert.

Minns, jt. auth. see Verwey.

Minns, A. W., jt. auth. see Abbott, M. B.

Minns, Amina. Citizens Apart: A Portrait of Palestinians of Israel. 1990. 68.75 (*1-85043-204-X*, Pub. by I B T) St Martin.

Minns, Amina & Hijab, Nadia. Citizens Apart: A Portrait of Palestinians of Israel. 250p. 1990. 34.50 (*0-685-38700-3*, Pub. by I B T) St Martin.

— Citizens Apart: A Portrait of the Palestinians in Israel. 1991. 34.50 (*0-685-48183-2*, Pub. by I B T) St Martin.

Minns, Anthony W. Artificial Neural Networks As Subsymbolic Process Descriptions. (IHE Thesis Ser.: Vol. 12). (Illus.). 124p. (C). 1998. text 40.00 (*90-5410-409-0*, Pub. by A A Balkema) Ashgate Pub Co.

Minns, Ellis H. Scythians & Greeks. LC 65-15248. (Illus.). 1913. 60.00 (*0-8196-0277-9*) Biblo.

Minns, F. John, ed. Wealth Well-Given: The Enterprise & Benevolence of Lord Nuffield. (Illus.). 336p. 1994. 33.95 (*0-7509-0656-1*, Pub. by Sutton Pub Ltd) Intl Pubs Mktg.

Minns, H. Azaleas, Rhododendrons & Camellias. LC 98-86299. 112p. 1999. pap. 12.95 (*0-376-03021-6*) Sunset Books.

— House Plants. LC 98-86302. (Illus.). 112p. 1999. pap. 12.95 (*0-376-03338-X*) Sunset Books.

— Read It to Me: Learning at Home & at School. 2nd ed. LC 96-47865. 1997. 77.00 (*0-335-19762-0*); pap. 25.95 (*0-335-19761-2*) OpUniv Pr.

— Vines & Ground Covers. 112p. 1999. pap. 12.95 (*0-376-03821-7*) Sunset Books.

Minns, Karen M. Bloodsong. LC 97-70611. 224p. (Orig.). 1997. pap. 12.95 (*1-887237-08-9*) Odd Girls Pr.

Minns, Michael L. The Underground Lawyer. Robertson, L. R. & Nail, Gene, eds. (Illus.). 625p. (C). 1989. 29.95 (*0-929801-00-8*) Gopher Pubns.

Minns, Robert A., ed. Problems of Intracranial Pressure in Childhood. (Clinics in Developmental Medicine Ser.: Nos. 113-114). (Illus.). 458p. (C). 1991. text 95.00 (*0-521-41272-2*, Pub. by Mc Keith Pr) Cambridge U Pr.

Mino, M., et al, eds. Vitamin E: Its Usefulness in Health & in Curing Diseases. (Illus.). xiv, 368p. 1993. 215.75 (*3-8055-5753-1*) S Karger.

Mino, Rose S. El Cono Sur: Dinamica y Dimensiones de Su Literatura. 243p. (Orig.). 1985. pap. 12.00 (*0-933559-00-3*) Montclair State.

Mino, Y. Pre-Sung Dynasty Chinese Stonewares in the Royal Ontario Museum. (Illus.). 104p. 25.71 (*0-88854-155-4*) Brill Academic Pubs.

Minocha, Aneeta A. Perceptions & Interactions in a Medical Setting: A Sociological Study of a Woman's Hospital. (C). 1996. 21.00 (*81-7075-043-1*, Pub. by Hindustan) S Asia.

Minocha, Anil. The Gastroenterology Resident Pocket Survival Guide. 100p. (C). 1999. pap. 9.95 (*1-883205-39-5*) Intl Med Pub.

Minocha, Subhash C., jt. auth. see Jain, S. Mohan.

Minocha, Vivek S. The Problem in Punjab: A Plea for Introspection. (C). 1989. pap. 2.50 (*81-202-0240-6*, Pub. by Ajanta) S Asia.

Minock, Daniel. Thistle Journal: And Other Essays on Building a House. LC 97-32550. (First Series). 192p. (Orig.). 1998. pap. 14.00 (*0-922811-34-2*) Mid-List.

Minock, Mary. Love in the Upstairs Flat. LC 95-8692. 92p. 1995. pap. 14.95 (*0-7734-2729-5*, Mellen Poetry Pr) E Mellen.

Minogin, V. G. & Letokhov, V. S. Laser Light Pressure on Atoms. xii, 248p. 1987. text 228.00 (*2-88124-080-1*) Gordon & Breach.

Minogue, Brendan. Bioethics. (Philosophy Ser.). 2001. pap. 24.95 (*0-534-20748-0*) Wadsworth Pub.

— Bioethics: A Committee Approach. (Philosophy Ser.). (C). 1995. 40.95 (*0-534-54256-5*) Wadsworth Pub.

Minogue, Brendan P., et al, eds. Reading Engelhardt: Essays on the Thought of H. Tristram Engelhardt, Jr. LC 97-16317. 330p. 1997. text 120.50 (*0-7923-4572-X*) Kluwer Academic.

Minogue, Colene M., jt. auth. see Quinlan, Michael P.

Minogue, Coll. Impressed & Incised Ceramics. 1996. 17.95 (*0-9650786-2-0*) Gentle Br.

Minogue, Coll. Impressed & Incised Ceramics. (Illus.). 128p. 1996. text. write for info. (*90-5703-061-6*, Harwood Acad Pubs) Gordon & Breach.

***Minogue, Coll & Sanderson, Robert.** Wood-Fired Ceramics: Contemporary Practices LC 99-37602. 2000. 45.00 (*0-8122-3514-2*) U of Pa Pr.

Minogue, Kenneth. Politics. (Very Short Introductions Ser.). 132p. 1995. pap. 8.95 (*0-19-285309-0*) OUP.

Minogue, Kenneth R. The Concept of a University. LC 72-95301. 239p. reprint ed. pap. 74.10 (*0-608-17906-X*, 202905400058) Bks Demand.

***Minogue, Kenneth R.** The Liberal Mind. LC 00-35409. 2000. write for info. (*0-86597-308-3*) Liberty Fund.

***Minogue, Kylie.** Kylie. 1999. 39.95 (*1-86154-137-6*) Booth-Clibborn.

Minogue, Martin, ed. Local Government in Britain. LC 76-43105. (Documents on Contemporary British Government Ser.: No. 2). 482p. reprint ed. pap. 137.40 (*0-608-15755-4*, 2031694) Bks Demand.

***Minogue, Martin, et al, eds.** Beyond the New Public Management: Changing Ideas & Practices in Governance. LC 98-4035. (New Horizons in Public Policy Ser.). 328p. 1999. pap. (*1-84064-244-0*) E Elgar.

Minogue, Martin, et al. Beyond the New Public Management: Changing Ideas & Practices in Governance. LC 98-4035. (New Horizons in Public Policy Ser.). 328p. 1999. 95.00 (*1-85898-913-2*) E Elgar.

Minogue, Thomas L. "Trust Me, I'm a Doctor" Understanding & Surviving Modern Health Care. xiv, 326p. (Orig.). 1996. pap. 16.95 (*0-9654891-0-8*) TLM Cnslting.

***Minogue, Thomas L.** "We Did All We Could, but Your Healthcare Died" The Patient's Vital Role in New Reform. (Illus.). 80p. 2000. pap. text 12.00 (*1-55605-295-2*) Wyndham Hall.

Minogue, William F., ed. Managing in an Academic Health Care Environment. LC 92-74401. 213p. (C). 1993. text 50.00 (*0-924674-18-0*) Am Coll Phys Execs.

Minoia, C. & Caroli, S., eds. Applications of Zeeman Graphite Furnace Atomic Absorption Spectroscopy in the Chemical Laboratory & in Toxicology. LC 92-20198. 702p. 1992. 263.75 (*0-08-041019-7*, Pergamon Pr) Elsevier.

Minois, Georges. History of Old Age: From Antiquity to the Renaissance. Tenison, Sarah H., tr. LC 89-5221. x, 354p. 1990. 35.95 (*0-226-53031-0*) U Ch Pr.

— A History of Suicide: Voluntary Death in Western World. LC 98-4069. 420p. 1998. 35.95 (*0-8018-5919-0*) Johns Hopkins.

Minoli, Dan. Distance Learning Technology & Applications. LC 96-6143. 352p. 1996. 83.00 (*0-89006-739-2*) Artech Hse.

— Video Dialtone Technology: Digital Video Services over ADSL, HFC, FTTC, & ATM. LC 94-49661. 1995. 60.00 (*0-07-042724-0*) McGraw.

Minoli, Daniel. Analyzing Outsourcing: Reengineering Information & Communication Systems. LC 94-22273. 1994. 44.00 (*0-07-042593-0*) McGraw.

— Broadband Network Analysis & Design. LC 93-12353. 275p. 1993. 79.00 (*0-89006-675-2*) Artech Hse.

— Client Server Applications on ATM. LC 96-43993. 300p. 1997. 50.00 (*0-13-735300-6*) P-H.

— Enterprise Networking: Fractional T1 to Sonet - Frame Relay to BISDN. LC 92-18854. (Telecommunications Ser.). 734p. 1992. text 110.00 (*0-89006-621-3*) Artech Hse.

— Internet Engineering: Technologies, Protocols, & Applications. LC 96-42361. (Illus.). 424p. 1996. pap. 39.95 (*0-07-042977-4*) McGraw.

— Planning & Managing ATM Networks. 300p. 1996. 48.00 (*0-13-262189-4*) P-H.

— Practical LAN Interconnection: Featuring FDDI. 1993. text 40.00 (*0-07-042524-8*) McGraw.

— Telecommunications Technology Handbook. (Telecommunications Library). 680p. 1991. write for info. (*0-89006-425-3*, C1425) Artech Hse.

— Web Commerce Engineering. LC 97-19682. (Illus.). 621p. 1997. pap. 44.95 (*0-07-042978-2*) McGraw.

Minoli, Daniel & Alles, Anthony. LAN, ATM & LAN Emulation Technologies. LC 96-46062. 309p. 1996. 89.00 (*0-89006-916-6*) Artech Hse.

Minoli, Daniel & Amos, John J. IP Applications with ATM. LC 98-13201. (Illus.). 304p. 1998. pap. 55.00 (*0-07-042312-1*) McGraw.

Minoli, Daniel & Dobrowski, George. Principles of Signaling for Cell Relay & Frame Relay. LC 94-11381. 305p. 1994. 89.00 (*0-89006-708-2*) Artech Hse.

Minoli, Daniel & Keinath, Robert. Distributed Multimedia Through Broadband Communication Services. LC 93-31143. 311p. 1993. 79.00 (*0-89006-689-2*) Artech Hse.

Minoli, Daniel & Minoli, Emma. Delivering Voice over IP Networks. LC 97-48368. 288p. 1998. 49.99 (*0-471-25482-7*) Wiley.

— Voice over Frame. LC 97-46553. 480p. 1998. 59.99 (*0-471-25481-9*) Wiley.

Minoli, Daniel & Schmidt, Andrew. Internet Architectures. LC 98-41311. 544p. 1999. 49.99 (*0-471-19081-0*) Wiley.

— Multiprotocols over ATM: Building State of the Art ATM Intranets. 325p. (C). 1998. 50.00 (*0-13-889270-9*) P-H.

— Network Layer Switched Services. LC 97-31834. 384p. 1998. 49.99 (*0-471-19080-2*) Wiley.

Minoli, Daniel, jt. auth. see Eldib, Osman.

Minoli, Daniel, jt. auth. see Schmidt, Andrew.

Minoli, Emma, jt. auth. see Minoli, Daniel.

Minomura, S., ed. Solid State Physics under Pressure. 1985. text 248.50 (*90-277-1897-0*) Kluwer Academic.

Minon, Miguel Herrero De, see Herrero de Minon, Miguel.

Minor. Art History's History. 224p. (C). 1999. text 7.50 (*0-13-196650-2*, Pub. by P-H) S&S Trade.

— Patient Care Skills. 4th ed. (C). 1999. 36.95 (*0-8385-8131-5*) Appleton & Lange.

Minor, Barbara B., jt. ed. see Ely, Donald P.

Minor, Charles L. The Real Lincoln. 1993. 20.99 (*0-87377-921-5*) GAM Pubns.

Minor, Clorinda. Meshullam! or, Tidings from Jerusalem: Journal of a Believer Recently Returned from the Holy Land. Davis, Moshe, ed. LC 77-70755. (America & the Holy Land Ser.). 1977. reprint ed. lib. bdg. 19.95 (*0-405-10302-6*) Ayer.

Minor, Eugene E. An Exegetical Summary of 2 Timothy. 151p. 1992. pap. 8.30 (*0-88312-818-7*) S I L Intl.

Minor, Florence F. Art for Written Word: Signed Collection Edition. 1995. 50.00 (*0-15-100210-X*) Harcourt.

Minor, Florence F., jt. ed. see Minor, Wendell.

***Minor, H. E. & Hager, W. H., eds.** Hydraulics of Stepped Spillways: Proceedings of the International Workshop on the Hydraulics of Stepped Spillways, Zurich, Switzerland, 22-24 March 2000. (Illus.). 216p. 2000. text 80.00 (*90-5809-135-X*, Pub. by A A Balkema) Ashgate Pub Co.

Minor, Herman, IV. The Seven Habits of Highly Ineffective People: Low-Effort Lessons in Mismanaging for Success. LC 94-20355. (Illus.). 128p. 1994. pap. 8.95 (*0-8065-1582-1*, Citadel Pr) Carol Pub Group.

Minor, Hinda R. Penny Candy, a Memoir. 300p. 1989. 9.95 (*0-9623699-0-X*) R Minor Graph Arts.

Minor, Hinda R., ed. see Chadwick, James M.

Minor, Hollis Greer. Needlework Masterpieces from Winterthur. LC 99-171086. (Illus.). 144p. 1998. 29.95 (*0-7153-0705-3*, Pub. by D & C Pub) Sterling.

Minor, Jewel, ed. see Wenzel, Dorian B.

Minor, Kevin I., jt. auth. see Carlie, Michael K.

Minor, Leslie & Lamberton, Lowell. Working with Others. 224p. (C). 1996. text 21.50 (*0-256-22033-6*, Irwn McGrw-H) McGrw-H Hghr Educ.

Minor, Lewis J. Always in Good Taste: The L. J. Minor Story. 1996. wbk. ed. write for info. (*0-9650750-1-X*) BHZ Pubng.

— Always in Good Taste: The L. J. Minor Story. Knight, John B., ed. LC 96-84259. (Illus.). 720p. 1997. 24.95 (*0-9650750-0-1*) BHZ Pubng.

Minor, Lucian. The Militant Hackwriter: French Popular Literature, 1800-1848 - Its Influence, Artistic & Political. 1975. 11.95 (*0-87972-105-7*) Bowling Green Univ Popular Press.

Minor, Marianne. Coaching & Counseling: A Practical Guide for Managers & Team Leaders. 2nd rev. ed. Crisp, Michael, ed. LC 95-83501. (Illus.). 79p. 1996. pap. 10.95 (*1-56052-386-7*) Crisp Pubns.

— Coaching for Development: Skills for Managers & Team Leaders. Racine, Robert, ed. LC 95-67041. (Fifty-Minute Ser.). (Illus.). 75p. (Orig.). 1995. pap. 10.95 (*1-56052-319-0*) Crisp Pubns.

— Preventing Workplace Violence: Positive Management Strategies. Henry, Carol, ed. LC 93-73145. (Fifty-Minute Ser.). (Illus.). 85p. (Orig.). 1994. pap. 10.95 (*1-56052-258-5*) Crisp Pubns.

Minor, Mark. Literary-Critical Approaches to the Bible: A Bibliograhical Supplement. LC 96-16495. 310p. (C). 1996. lib. bdg. 40.00 (*0-933951-69-8*) Locust Hill Pr.

Minor, Mary A. & Minor, Scott D. Patient Care Skills. 3rd ed. (Illus.). 448p. (C). 1994. pap. text 39.95 (*0-8385-7709-1*, A7709-7) Appleton & Lange.

— Patient Care Skills. 4th ed. LC 98-25824. (C). 1999. pap. text. write for info. (*0-8385-8157-9*) Appleton & Lange.

Minor, Mary A., et al. Kinesiology Laboratory Manual for Physical Therapy Assistants. (Illus.). 302p. (C). 1997. pap. text 28.95 (*0-8036-0203-0*) Davis Co.

Minor, Mary E., ed. see Perry, Katy.

Minor, Marz & Minor, Nono. The American Indian Craft Book. LC 77-14075. (Illus.). 416p. 1978. pap. 10.95 (*0-8032-5891-7*, Bison Books) U of Nebr Pr.

Minor, Michael & Vrzalik, Larry F. From the President's Pen: An Illustrated Guide to Presidential Autographs. limited ed. LC 90-19634. (Illus.). 176p. 1990. 75.00 (*0-938349-61-9*) State House Pr.

Minor, Michael, jt. auth. see Mowen, John C.

Minor, Michael J., jt. auth. see Burt, Ronald S.

Minor, Mitzi. The Spirituality of Mark: Responding to God. 152p. 1996. pap. 15.00 (*0-664-25679-1*) Westminster John Knox.

Minor, Nancy & Bradley, Patricia. Coping with School-Age Motherhood. rev. ed. (YA). (gr. 7-12). 1988. lib. bdg. 17.95 (*0-8239-0923-9*) Rosen Group.

Minor, Nono, jt. auth. see Minor, Marz.

Minor, Plinius. Plinius: Concordantiae in C. Plinii Caecilii Secundi Opera, 4 vols., Set. Heberlein, Friedrich & Slaby, Wolfgang, eds. (Alpha-Omega, Reihe A Ser.: Bd. CXIV-2). (GER.). 3128p. 1991. write for info. (*3-487-09403-7*) G Olms Pubs.

Minor, Raleigh C. Conflict of Laws: or Private International Law. lii, 575p. 1985. reprint ed. 55.00 (*0-8377-0852-4*, Rothman) W S Hein.

— Notes on the Science of Government & the Relation of the States to the United States, 1913. LC 99-47233. x, 192p. 1995. reprint ed. 40.00 (*1-886363-09-9*, 310570) Lawbk Exchange.

Minor, Rick. The Pit-&-Groove Petroglyph Style in Southern California, No. 15. (San Diego Museum of Man, Ethnic Technology Notes Ser.). (Illus.). '33p. 1975. pap. text 3.75 (*1-55567-816-5*) Coyote Press.

Minor, Rick. Prehistoric Settlement & Subsistence in the Upper South Umpqua River Drainage, Southwestern Oregon. (Illus.). 140p. 1989. write for info. (*0-318-64857-1*) NW Herit Pr.

Minor, Rick, ed. Contributions to the Archaeology of Oregon: 1987-1988. (Association of Oregon Archaeologists Occasional Papers). (Illus.). 221p. (Orig.). (C). 1989. pap. text 14.50 (*0-685-40132-4*) Assn Oregon Arch.

Minor, Rick, et al. The Cape Perpetua Shell Middens: Late Prehistoric Subsistence on the Central Oregon Coast. (Illus.). 115p. 1989. write for info. (*0-318-64856-3*) NW Herit Pr.

Minor, Robert N. Radhakrishnan: A Religious Biography. LC 86-30191. 189p. (C). 1987. pap. text 21.95 (*0-88706-555-4*) State U NY Pr.

— The Religious, the Spiritual, & the Secular: Auroville & Secular India. LC 97-50628. (SUNY Series in Religious Studies). (Illus.). 224p. (C). 1998. text 59.50 (*0-7914-3991-7*); pap. text 19.95 (*0-7914-3992-5*) State U NY Pr.

Minor, Roy. In the Fall. LC 98-60367. 182p. 1999. 19.95 (*1-56315-100-6*, Pub. by SterlingHse) Natl Bk Netwk.

Minor, Sandra L. Mind Joggers, Vol. 3. 83p. 1997. spiral bd. 13.95 (*1-879633-29-9*, P215) Eldersong.

Minor, Sandy. Holiday Mind Joggers. (Illus.). 55p. (Orig.). 1994. pap. 9.50 (*1-879633-19-1*) Eldersong.

— Mind Joggers, Vol. 1. 83p. 1993. spiral bd. 13.95 (*1-879633-13-2*) Eldersong.

— Mind Joggers, Vol. 2. 81p. 1995. spiral bd. 13.95 (*1-879633-21-3*) Eldersong.

Minor, Scott D., jt. auth. see Minor, Mary A.

Minor, Terry. My Dream Slipped Away: Inside Football - Clemson University, NCAA, Other Colleges & the Cleveland Browns. 47p. pap. write for info. (*1-882194-13-6*) TN Valley Pub.

Minor, Theodore E. Management of Church Music Programs. 83p. 1991. spiral bd. 14.95 (*0-9630146-0-9*) T Minor Keybd.

Minor, Vernon H. Art History's History. (Illus.). 224p. 1994. 29.95 (*0-8109-1944-3*, Pub. by Abrams) Time Warner.

— Art History's History. LC 93-28088. 211p. 1993. pap. text 30.40 (*0-13-194606-4*) P-H.

— Baroque & Rococo: Art & Culture LC 99-33288. 400p. 1999. 75.00 (*0-8109-4108-2*, Pub. by Abrams) Time Warner.

***Minor, Vernon H.** Baroque & Rococo: Art & Culture 1600-1750. 400p. 1999. pap. 53.33 (*0-13-085649-5*) P-H.

Minor, Vernon H. Passive Tranquility: The Sculpture of Filippo della Valle. LC 97-22739. (Transactions Ser.: Vol. 87, Pt. 5). (Illus.). 304p. 1998. pap. 22.00 (*0-87169-875-7*, T875-miv) Am Philos.

***Minor, Vernon Hyde.** Art History's History. 2nd ed. LC 00-35986. (Illus.). 277p. 2000. pap. 25.00 (*0-13-085133-7*) P-H.

Minor, Wendell. Grand Canyon: Exploring a Natural Wonder. LC 97-40185. (Illus.). 40p. (J). (gr. 1-4). 1998. 16.95 (*0-590-47968-7*, Pub. by Scholastic Inc) Penguin Putnam.

***Minor, Wendell.** Grand Canyon: Exploring a Natural Wonder. (Illus.). 32p. (J). (ps-3). 2000. pap. 5.99 (*0-439-19278-1*) Scholastic Inc.

— Pumpkin Heads! LC 99-86364. (Illus.). 32p. (J). (ps-2). 2000. 15.95 (*0-590-52105-5*, Blue Sky Press) Scholastic Inc.

Minor, Wendell & Minor, Florence F., eds. Art for the Written Word: Twenty-Five Years of Book Cover Art. (Illus.). 160p. 1995. 50.00 (*0-15-195614-6*); pap. 30.00 (*0-15-600212-4*, Harvest Bks) Harcourt.

Minor, William. Goat Pan. (Illus.). 44p. (Orig.). 1984. pap. 5.95 (*0-9612914-0-0*) Betty's Soup.

— Unzipped Souls: A Jazz Journey Through the Soviet Union. LC 94-37345. (Illus.). 256p. (C). 1995. 29.95 (*1-56639-324-8*) Temple U Pr.

Minor, William & Wishner, Bill. Monterey Jazz Festival: 40 Legendary Years. LC 97-4908. (Illus.). 176p. 1997. 40.00 (*1-883318-40-8*) Angel City Pr.

Minor, William, jt. auth. see Oehler, Paul.

Minor, William H. & Nord, Nancy A. Corporate Lobbying: Federal & State Regulation. (Corporate Practice Ser.: No. 25-2). 1998. 95.00 (*1-55871-393-X*) BNA.

Minor, William S., jt. ed. see Broyer, John A.

***Minor, Woodruff.** Pacific Gateway: An Illustrated History of the Port of Oakland. (Illus.). viii, 192p. (C). 2000. pap. 24.95 (*0-9678617-0-5*) Port of Oakland.

Minore, Don. A Method for Estimating the Preharvest Potential for Seedling Height Growth on Cutover Forest Land in Southwestern Oregon. (Illus.). 16p. 1997. reprint ed. pap. 2.30 (*0-89904-768-8*, Ecosytems Resrch) Crumb Elbow Pub.

Minore, Don & Weatherly, Howard G. Yarding-Method & Slash-Treatment Effects on Compaction, Humus, & Variation in Plantation Soils. 10p. 1998. reprint ed. pap. 2.00 (*0-89904-916-8*, Ecosytems Resrch) Crumb Elbow Pub.

Minority Rights Group Staff. World Directory of Minorities. 427p. 1990. 85.00 (*1-55862-016-8*) St James Pr.

Minority Rights Group Staff, ed. No Longer Invisible: Afro-Latin Americans Today. 336p. pap. 21.95 (*1-873194-85-4*, Pub. by Minority Rts Pubns) Paul & Co Pubs.

— No Longer Invisible: Afro-Latin Americans Today. 336p. 1995. 34.95 (*1-873194-80-3*, Pub. by Minority Rts Pubns) Paul & Co Pubs.

— World Directory of Minorities. 2nd ed. LC 97-210587. (Illus.). 840p. 1997. 145.00 (*1-873194-36-6*, Pub. by Minority Rts Pubns) Paul & Co Pubs.

Minorsky, Nicholas. Non Linear Oscillation. LC 74-8918. 734p. 1974. reprint ed. 72.50 (*0-88275-186-7*) Krieger.

Minorsky, V., tr. from PER. Calligraphers & Painters: A Treatise by Qadi Ahmad, Son of Mir-Munshi. (Occasional Papers: Vol. 3, No. 2). (Illus.). 1959. pap. 6.00 (*0-934686-06-8*) Freer.

Minoru, Yoshioka. Celebration in Darkness. Tadayoshi, Onuma, tr. from JPN. LC 84-23423. (Asian Poetry in Translation Ser: Japan: No. 6). 206p. (Orig.). 1985. pap. 10.95 (*0-295-96360-3*) U of Wash Pr.

***Minosh, Joyce.** Caravan Days. 210p. 1999. pap. write for info. (*0-7392-0491-2*, PO3849) Morris Pubng.

Minoso, Minnie & Fagen, Herb. Just Call Me Minnie: My Six Decades in Baseball. LC 94-65394. (Illus.). 205p. 1994. 19.95 (*0-915611-90-2*) Sports Pub.

Minot, Charles S. The Problem of Age, Growth, & Death. Kastenbaum, Robert J., ed. LC 78-22211. (Aging & Old Age Ser.). (Illus.). 1979. reprint ed. lib. bdg. 25.95 (*0-405-11824-4*) Ayer.

***Minot, Eliza.** The Tiny One. LC 99-18516. 253p. 1999. 22.00 (*0-375-40645-X*) Knopf.

— The Tiny One. (Contemporaries Ser.). 2000. pap. 13.00 (*0-375-70633-X*) Vin Bks.

Minot, George R. History of the Insurrections in Massachusetts in the Year 1786 & the Rebellion Consequent Thereon. 2nd ed. LC 70-107823. (Select Bibliographies Reprint Ser.). 1977. 21.95 (*0-8369-5218-9*) Ayer.

— History of the Insurrections in Massachusetts in 1786. LC 76-148912. (Era of the American Revolution Ser.). 1971. reprint ed. lib. bdg. 27.50 (*0-306-70100-6*) Da Capo.

Minot, George R., jt. auth. see Kornfeld, Myra.

Minot, John. Notes on the Classification of Mushrooms. LC 88-63668. 210p. 1989. 35.00 (*0-88000-145-3*) Quarterman.

Minot, John C. The Best Stories of Heroism I Know. 1977. 20.95 (*0-8369-4231-0*, 6042) Ayer.

***Minot, Marcia.** Potpourri of Poetry. 1999. pap. write for info. (*1-58235-105-8*) Watermrk Pr.

Minot, Marcia Chvat. Ebb-Tide. 1998. pap. write for info. (*1-57553-884-9*) Watermrk Pr.

Minot, Stephen. Bending Time. LC 96-36744. 176p. 1997. pap. 16.00 (*1-877946-96-6*) Permanent Pr.

— Crossings. Stories. LC 74-14915. (Illinois Short Fiction Ser.). 166p. 1975. 11.95 (*0-252-00472-8*) U of Ill Pr.

— Three Genres: The Writing of Poetry, Fiction, & Drama. 6th ed. LC 97-20256. 420p. 1997. pap. text 37.00 (*0-13-491929-7*) P-H.

Minot, Susan. Evening. LC 98-15437. 264p. 1998. 23.00 (*0-375-40037-0*) Knopf.

— Evening. 264p. 1999. pap. 12.00 (*0-375-70026-9*) Knopf.

— Evening. large type ed. LC 99-18686. 1999. pap. text 27.95 (*0-7862-1891-6*) Mac Lib Ref.

— Folly. Rosenman, Jane, ed. 288p. 1994. reprint ed. per. 10.00 (*0-671-74951-X*, WSP) PB.

— Lust & Other Stories. 160p. 1990. per. 10.00 (*0-671-70455-9*, WSP) PB.

***Minot, Susan.** Lust & other Stories. (Contemporaries Ser.). 160p. 2000. pap. text 11.00 (*0-375-70925-8*) Vin Bks.

Minot, Susan. Monkeys. 176p. 1989. pap. 12.00 (*0-671-70361-7*, WSP) PB.

***Minot, Susan.** Monkeys. (Contemporaries Ser.). 176p. 2000. pap. 11.00 (*0-375-70836-7*) Vin Bks.

Minot, Susan. Stealing Beauty: A Screenplay. LC 96-19178. 128p. 1996. pap. 11.00 (*0-8021-3492-0*, Grove) Grove-Atltic.

Minott, Jan. Skirts & Pants Patterns: Minott Method. 4th ed. 183p. 1992. pap. 17.00 (*0-9633880-5-3*) Minott Method.

— Total Pattern Fit Minott Method. (Illus.). 221p. (C). 1991. ring bd. 17.00 (*0-9633880-4-5*) Minott Method.

Minow, Martha. Between Vengeance & Forgiveness: Facing History after Genocide & Mass Violence. LC 98-26846. 224p. 1999. pap. 14.00 (*0-8070-4507-1*) Beacon Pr.

— Making All the Difference: Inclusion, Exclusion & American Law. LC 90-1754. 424p. 1990. 39.95 (*0-8014-2446-1*) Cornell U Pr.

— Making All the Difference: Inclusion, Exclusion & American Law. LC 90-1754. 424p. 1991. reprint ed. pap. text 16.95 (*0-8014-9977-1*) Cornell U Pr.

Minow, Martha. Narrative, Violence & The Law: The Essays of Robert Cover. Ryan, Michael & Sarat, Austin, eds. LC 92-30307. (Illus.). 312p. (C). 1995. pap. text 20.95 (*0-472-06495-9*, 06495) U of Mich Pr.

Minow, Martha. Not Only for Myself: Identity Politics & the Law. LC 96-29578. 1997. 25.00 (*1-56584-374-6*, Pub. by New Press NY) Norton.

— Not Only for Myself: Identity, Politics, & the Law. 1998. pap. 14.95 (*1-56584-513-7*, Pub. by New Press NY) Norton.

Minow, Martha, ed. Family Matters: Readings on Family Lives & the Law. LC 92-53737. 432p. 1993. 40.00 (*1-56584-017-8*, Pub. by New Press NY); pap. 24.95 (*1-56584-042-9*, Pub. by New Press NY) Norton.

Minow, Martha, et al, eds. Narrative, Violence, & the Law: The Essays of Robert Cover. (Law, Meaning, & Violence Ser.). 312p. (C). 1993. text 52.50 (*0-472-09495-5*, 09495) U of Mich Pr.

Minow, Martha, jt. ed. see Bellow, Gary.

Minow, Martin, tr. see Sjoman, Vilgot.

Minow, Nell. The Movie Mom's [tm] Guide to Family Movies. LC 99-14406. 720p. 1999. pap. 15.00 (*0-380-78839-X*, Avon Bks) Morrow Avon.

Minow, Nell, jt. auth. see Monks, Robert.

Minow, Nell, jt. auth. see Monks, Robert A.

Minow, Newton & LaMay, Craig. Abandoned in the Wasteland: Children, Television, & the First Amendment. 242p. 1996. pap. text 11.00 (*0-8090-1589-7*) Hill & Wang.

Minow, Newton N. & Sloan, Clifford M. For Great Debates: A New Plan for Future Presidential TV Debates - A Twentieth Century Fund Paper. 71p. (Orig.). (C). 1987. pap. text 10.00 (*0-87078-212-6*) Century Foundation.

Minow-Pinkney, Makiko. Virginia Woolf & the Problem of the Subject. LC 86-26023. 224p. 1987. reprint ed. pap. 69.50 (*0-608-02329-9*, 206297000004) Bks Demand.

Minowitz, Peter. Profits, Priests, & Princes: Adam Smith's Emancipation of Economics from Politics & Religion. LC 93-18798. 364p. (C). 1993. 47.50 (*0-8047-2166-1*) Stanford U Pr.

Minsberg, David. The Agnostic Mystique: A Guide for the Unperplexed. 160p. 1996. pap. 11.00 (*0-940674-00-9*) Littlebee.

— The Bookmonster. (Illus.). 32p. (J). (ps). 1981. 10.00 (*0-940674-01-7*) Littlebee.

Minshall, Bert. On Board with the Duke: John Wayne & the Wild Goose. LC 92-27938. 168p. 1992. text 39.95 (*0-929765-13-3*) Seven Locks Pr.

Minshall, Britt. Renaissance or Ruin: The Final Saga of a Once Great Church. LC 94-68169. 409p. 1995. pap. 14.95 (*0-9642773-0-1*) Renaissance Inst.

Minshall, Sharlene G. Full-Time RVing: How to Make It Happen. LC 97-93848. (Illus.). 192p. (Orig.). 1997. pap. 12.95 (*0-9643970-2-1*) Gypsy Press.

— RVing Alaska! And Canada. LC 97-93847. (Illus.). 192p. (Orig.). 1997. pap. 14.95 (*0-9643970-1-3*) Gypsy Press.

— RVing North America: Silver, Single, & Solo. LC 94-96691. (Illus.). 288p. (Orig.). 1995. pap. 12.95 (*0-9643970-0-5*) Gypsy Press.

Minsheu, John. Ductor in Linguas: The Guide into Tongues. LC 78-14754. (ENG & SPA.). 776p. 1979. reprint ed. lib. bdg. 150.00 (*0-8201-1321-2*) Schol Facsimiles.

Minshew, Deborah H. & Hooper, Chrisan. The Adoptive Family as a Healing Resource for the Sexually Abused Child: A Training Manual. 1990. pap. 14.95 (*0-87868-360-7*) Child Welfare.

Minshull, Evelyn. Crafted with Love. (Illus.). 64p. 1996. pap. 4.95 (*0-936369-87-6*) Son-Rise Pubns.

Minshull, Evelyn, ed. see Michel, Barbara.

Minshull, Evelyn W. Abingdon's Christmas Pageants & Plays: 12 Complete Pageants. 64p. 1990. pap. 5.95 (*0-687-00425-X*) Abingdon.

Minshull, Evelyn W., compiled by. Abingdon's Easter Recitations. 1986. pap. text 5.95 (*0-687-00427-6*) Abingdon.

Minshull, G. N. The New Europe into the 1990s. 4th rev. ed. (Illus.). 348p. 1990. pap. text 27.50 (*0-340-50512-5*, Pub. by Hodder & Stought Ltd) Lubrecht & Cramer.

Minshull, Roger. The American City & Its Citizens: The Dream on the Move. 270p. 1996. 42.50 (*1-85776-101-4*, Pub. by Book Guild Ltd) Trans-Atl Phila.

Minsk, L. David. Snow & Ice Control Manual for Transportation Facilities. (Construction Ser.). (Illus.). 302p. 1998. 59.00 (*0-07-042809-3*) McGraw-Hill Prof.

Minsker, K. S., et al. Degradation & Stabilization of Vinylchloride Based Polymers. LC 87-36029. 520p. 1988. 232.00 (*0-08-034857-2*, Pub. by Pergamon Repr) Franklin.

Minsker, Karl S. Chemistry of Chlorine-Containing Polymers: Syntheses, Degradation, Stabilization. Zaikov, Gennadifi Efremovich, ed. LC 99-54399. 125.00 (*1-56072-757-8*) Nova Sci Pubs.

Minsker, Karl S. & Berlin, Alexandre A. Fast Polymerization Processes. (Polymer Science & Engineering Monographs). 110p. 1995. text 73.00 (*2-88449-149-X*) Gordon & Breach.

Minsker, Karl S., jt. auth. see Berlin, Alexandre A.

Minskoff, Alan. Blue Ink Runs Out on a Partly Cloudy Day. 36p. (Orig.). 1994. pap. 12.00 (*0-931659-16-7*) Limberlost Pr.

***Minsky, Bonnie.** Nutrition in a Nutshell: Build Health & Slow Down the Aging Process. 164p. 2000. 12.95 (*1-890612-17-0*) Vital Health.

***Minsky, Alan.** A Game for All Races: A History of the Negro Leagues. LC 99-29245. (Illus.). 144p. 1999. text 17.98 (*1-56799-419-9*) M Friedman Pub Grp Inc.

Minsky, Alan. Home Run Kings. LC 94-27731. (Illus.). 80p. 1995. 11.98 (*1-56799-142-4*, MetroBooks) M Friedman Pub Grp Inc.

— Kings of Court: Superstars of the NBA. 144p. 1995. text 16.98 (*1-56799-177-7*, MetroBooks) M Friedman Pub Grp Inc.

— March to the Finals: The History of College Basketball's Illustrious Finale. LC 96-39799. 96p. 1997. 12.98 (*1-56799-387-7*, MetroBooks) M Friedman Pub Grp Inc.

— March to the Finals: The History of College Basketball's Illustrious Finales. rev. ed. LC 99-228231. 1999. 15.98 (*1-56799-705-8*, MetroBooks) M Friedman Pub Grp Inc.

Minsky, Hyman P. Can "IT" Happen Again? Essays on Instability & Finance. LC 82-10789. 320p. (gr. 13). 1982. pap. text 39.95 (*0-87332-305-X*) M E Sharpe.

Minsky, Larry. A Jazzy Yule: 7 Jazzy Holiday Songs. 5.95 (*0-7692-9094-9*) Wrner Bros.

Minsky, Laurence, jt. auth. see Calvo, Emily Thornton.

Minsky, Lawrence, jt. auth. see Calvo, Emily.

Minsky, Marvin. Computers & Artificial Intelligence: A Science Masters Series Book. 176p. Date not set. pap. write for info. (*0-465-01351-1*) Basic.

— The Society of Mind. 336p. 1988. pap. 14.95 (*0-671-65713-5*, Touchstone) S&S Trade Pap.

— Three Roads to Quantum Gravity. 176p. 2000. 25.00 (*0-465-01350-3*, Pub. by Basic) HarpC.

Minsky, Marvin, jt. auth. see Harrison, Harry.

Minsky, Marvin L., ed. Semantic Information Processing. LC 68-18239. 440p. 1969. 52.50 (*0-262-13044-0*) MIT Pr.

Minsky, Marvin L. & Papert, Seymour A. Perceptrons: An Introduction to Computational Geometry. expanded ed. 275p. 1987. pap. text 30.00 (*0-262-63111-3*) MIT Pr.

Minsky, Rosalind. Psychoanalysis & Culture: Contemporary States of Mind. LC 98-23538. (C). 1998. text 50.00 (*0-8135-2585-3*); pap. text 20.00 (*0-8135-2586-1*) Rutgers U Pr.

— Psychoanalysis & Gender: An Introductory Reader. LC 95-16457. (Critical Readers in Theory & Practice Ser.). 336p. (C). 1996. 90.00 (*0-415-09220-5*); pap. 25.99 (*0-415-09221-3*) Routledge.

Minson, A. C., et al, eds. Viruses & Cancer: Fifty-First Symposium for the Society for General Microbiology, Held at the University of Cambridge, March 1994. LC 93-46636. (Society for General Microbiology Symposium Ser.: No. 51). (Illus.). 321p. (C). 1994. text 115.00 (*0-521-45472-7*) Cambridge U Pr.

Minson, Jeffrey B. Questions of Conduct: Sexual Harassment, Citizenship, Government. LC 92-30625. 254p. 1993. text 39.95 (*0-312-09121-4*) St Martin.

Minson, Maxine. Angel in the Park. 1983. pap. 1.75 (*0-686-38379-6*) Eldridge Pub.

Minstrel Books. I Lost My Grandfather's Brain. 1999. per. 3.99 (*0-671-02652-6*) PB.

Minstrel Books Staff. Dudley Do-Right. 1999. per. 4.99 (*0-671-03934-2*, Minstrel Bks) PB.

Minstrel of Reims. A Thirteenth-Century Minstrel's Chronicle (Recits d'un Menestrel de Reims) A Translation & Introduction. Levine, Robert, tr. from FRE. (Studies in French Civilization: Vol. 4). 256p. 1990. lib. bdg. 89.95 (*0-88946-623-8*) E Mellen.

Minta, Stephen. Aguirre. 88p. 1995. pap. 11.95 (*0-8050-3104-9*) H Holt & Co.

— Aguirre: The Re-Creation of a Sixteenth-Century Journey Across South America. LC 93-11679. 208p. 1995. write for info. (*0-8050-3103-0*) H Holt & Co.

— Love Poetry in Sixteenth-century France: A Study in Themes & Traditions LC 78-313941. vi, 173 p. 1977. write for info. (*0-7190-0676-7*) Manchester Univ Pr.

— On a Voiceless Shore. LC 97-11474. 1998. text 25.00 (*0-8050-3778-0*) St Martin.

Minta, Steven C., jt. auth. see Clark, Tim W.

Minteer, Gladys C. The Purple Pen. 18p. (Orig.). 1995. pap. 5.00 (*1-884226-04-3*) Dark River.

Mintel, Judith K. Insurance Rate Litigation: A Survey of Judicial Treatment of Insurance Ratemaking & Insurance Rate Regulation. (S. S. Huebner International Ser.). 1983. lib. bdg. 82.00 (*0-89838-139-8*) Huebner Foun Insur.

Minter, ed. see Tirso De Molina.

Minter, Brian. Brian Minter's New Gardening Guide. (Illus.). 240p. 1998. pap. 16.95 (*1-55110-624-8*) Whitecap Bks.

— Brian Minter's New Gardening Guide: Fresh Approaches for American Gardeners. 1998. pap. text. write for info. (*1-55110-822-4*) Whitecap Bks.

Minter, D. W., jt. auth. see Da Silva, M.

Minter, D. W., jt. auth. see Hall, G. S.

Minter, D. W., jt. ed. see Cannon, P. F.

Minter, David. A Cultural History of the American Novel: Henry James to William Faulkner. 292p. (C). 1994. text 64.95 (*0-521-45285-6*) Cambridge U Pr.

— A Cultural History of the American Novel: Henry James to William Faulkner. 292p. 1996. pap. text 19.95 (*0-521-46749-7*) Cambridge U Pr.

— William Faulkner: His Life & Work. LC 80-13089. 344p. 1997. pap. text 15.95 (*0-8018-5747-3*) Johns Hopkins.

Minter, David, ed. see Faulkner, William.

Minter, G., ed. Galdos: Tristana. (Bristol Spanish Texts Ser.). (SPA.). 112p. 1996. pap. 18.95 (*1-85399-386-7*, Pub. by Brist Class Pr) Focus Pub-R Pullins.

Minter, James F. Big Book of Pencil Pastimes: The Best Word Games, Quizzes & Brain Ticklers. 256p. 1991. pap. 7.95 (*0-88486-039-6*) Arrowood Pr.

— Second Big Book of Pencil Pastimes. 248p. 1993. pap. 6.95 (*0-88486-075-2*, Bristol Park Bks) Arrowood Pr.

Minter, Jim. Some Things I Wish We Wouldn't Forget: And Others I Wish We Could. Minter, Rick & Jordan, Bruce L., eds. LC 98-68354. (Illus.). 304p. 1998. 24.95 (*0-9660768-2-6*) Midtown Pubng.

Minter, John, ed. Financial Statistics & Ratios: Private Universities Awarding the Doctoral's As the Highest Degree. (Institutional Research Reports). 70p. 1987. lib. bdg. write for info. (*0-937767-17-4*) Nat Data Service.

Minter, John, ed. Enrollment Management Ratios: American Four-Year Colleges & Universities, No. 1. (Financial Management Ratios Ser.). 1052p. 1986. lib. bdg. 139.50 (*0-937767-02-6*) Nat Data Service.

— Enrollment Statistics & Ratios: Private Colleges & Universities Awarding the Master's As the Highest Degree. (Institutional Research Reports). 70p. 1986. lib. bdg. write for info. (*0-937767-12-3*) Nat Data Service.

— Enrollment Statistics & Ratios: Private Colleges Awarding the Bachelor's As the Highest Degree. (Institutional Research Reports). 79p. 1986. lib. bdg. write for info. (*0-937767-06-9*) Nat Data Service.

— Enrollment Statistics & Ratios: Private Universities Awarding the Doctoral's As the Highest Degree. (Institutional Research Reports). 50p. 1987. lib. bdg. write for info. (*0-937767-18-2*) Nat Data Service.

— Enrollment Statistics & Ratios: Public Colleges Awarding the Bachelor's As the Highest Degree. (Institutional Research Reports). 50p. 1986. lib. bdg. write for info. (*0-937767-39-5*) Nat Data Service.

— Enrollment Statistics & Ratios: Public Colleges Awarding the Comprehensive As the Highest Degree. (Institutional Research Reports). 95p. 1986. lib. bdg. write for info. (*0-937767-45-X*) Nat Data Service.

— Enrollment Statistics & Ratios: Public Universities Awarding the Doctoral's As the Highest Degree. (Institutional Research Reports). 55p. 1987. lib. bdg. write for info. (*0-937767-48-4*) Nat Data Service.

— Faculty Compensation Index, 1985-1986: Private Colleges & Universities Awarding the Comprehensive As the Highest Degree. (Institutional Research Reports). 85p. 1987. lib. bdg. write for info. (*0-937767-32-8*) Nat Data Service.

— Faculty Compensation Index, 1985-1986: Private Colleges Awarding the Bachelor's As the Highest Degree. (Institutional Research Reports). 344p. 1986. lib. bdg. write for info. (*0-937767-07-7*) Nat Data Service.

— Faculty Compensation Index, 1985-1986: Private Universities Awarding the Doctoral's As the Highest Degree. (Institutional Research Reports). 60p. 1987. lib. bdg. write for info. (*0-937767-34-4*) Nat Data Service.

— Faculty Compensation Index, 1985-1986: Public Colleges & Universities Awarding the Master's As the Highest Degree. (Institutional Research Reports). 171p. 1986. lib. bdg. write for info. (*0-937767-13-1*) Nat Data Service.

— Faculty Compensation Index, 1985-1986: Public Colleges Awarding the Bachelor's As the Highest Degree. (Institutional Research Reports). 65p. 1986. lib. bdg. write for info. (*0-937767-40-9*) Nat Data Service.

— Financial Statistics & Ratios: Private Colleges Awarding the Bachelor's As the Highest Degree. (Institutional Research Reports). 50p. 1986. lib. bdg. write for info. (*0-937767-05-0*) Nat Data Service.

— Financial Statistics & Ratios: Public Colleges & Universities Awarding the Comprehensive As the Highest Degree. (Institutional Research Reports). 165p. 1986. lib. bdg. write for info. (*0-937767-44-1*) Nat Data Service.

— Financial Statistics & Ratios: Public Colleges Awarding the Bachelor's As the Highest Degree. (Institutional Research Reports). 95p. 1986. lib. bdg. write for info. (*0-937767-38-7*) Nat Data Service.

— Financial Statistics & Ratios: Public Universities Awarding the Doctoral's As the Highest Degree. (Institutional Research Reports). 100p. 1987. lib. bdg. write for info. (*0-937767-36-0*) Nat Data Service.

— Freshman Class Statistics & Ratios: Private Universities Awarding the Doctoral's As the Highest Degree. (Institutional Research Reports). 50p. 1987. lib. bdg. write for info. (*0-937767-20-4*) Nat Data Service.

— Freshman Class Statistics & Ratios: Public Colleges & Universities Awarding the Comprehensive As the Highest Degree. (Institutional Research Reports). 50p. 1986. lib. bdg. write for info. (*0-937767-46-8*) Nat Data Service.

— Freshman Class Statistics & Ratios: Public Colleges Awarding the Bachelor's As the Highest Degree. (Institutional Research Reports). 25p. 1987. lib. bdg. write for info. (*0-937767-41-7*) Nat Data Service.

— Fund Raising Management Ratios One. (Financial Management Ratios Ser.: No. 1). 450p. 1987. lib. bdg. 95.00 (*0-937767-28-X*) Nat Data Service.

— Fund Raising Statistics & Ratios: Private Colleges & Universities Awarding the Master's As the Highest Degree. (Institutional Research Reports). 50p. 1986. lib. bdg. write for info. (*0-937767-10-7*) Nat Data Service.

— Fund Raising Statistics & Ratios: Private Colleges Awarding the Bachelor's As the Highest Degree. (Institutional Research Reports). 50p. 1986. lib. bdg. write for info. (*0-937767-04-2*) Nat Data Service.

— Fund Raising Statistics & Ratios: Public Colleges & Universities Awarding the Comprehensive As the Highest Degree. (Institutional Research Reports). 50p. 1987. lib. bdg. write for info. (*0-937767-43-3*) Nat Data Service.

— Fund Raising Statistics & Ratios: Public Colleges Awarding the Bachelor's As the Highest Degree. (Institutional Research Reports). 50p. lib. bdg. 85.00 (*0-937767-37-9*) Nat Data Service.

— Fund Raising Statistics & Ratios: Public or Private Universities Awarding the Doctoral's As the Highest Degree. 50p. 1987. lib. bdg. write for info. (*0-937767-16-6*) Nat Data Service.

— Fund Raising Statistics & Ratios: Public Universities Awarding the Doctoral's As the Highest Degree. (Institutional Research Reports). 50p. 1987. lib. bdg. write for info. (*0-937767-33-6*) Nat Data Service.

— Management Ratios for Colleges & Universities. (Financial Management Ratios Ser.: No. 2). 500p. 1986. lib. bdg. write for info. (*0-937767-03-4*) Nat Data Service.

— Management Ratios for Colleges & Universities. (Financial Management Ratios Ser.: No. 3). 550p. (C). 1987. lib. bdg. 125.00 (*0-937767-30-1*) Nat Data Service.

— Tuition-Fees, Financial Aid Statistics: Public Colleges & Universities Awarding the Comprehensive As the Highest Degree. (Institutional Research Reports). 50p. 1987. lib. bdg. write for info. (*0-937767-47-6*) Nat Data Service.

— Tuition-Fees, Financial Aid Statistics: Public Colleges Awarding the Bachelor's As the Highest Degree. (Institutional Research Reports). 50p. 1987. lib. bdg. write for info. (*0-937767-42-5*) Nat Data Service.

— Undergraduate Tuition & Fees: Trends 1977 to 1986. 250p. 1987. lib. bdg. 95.00 (*0-937767-31-X*) Nat Data Service.

Minter, John, intro. Financial Statistics & Ratios: Private Colleges & Universities Awarding the Master's As the Highest Degree. (Institutional Research Reports). 120p. 1986. lib. bdg. write for info. (*0-937767-11-5*) Nat Data Service.

— Freshman Class Statistics & Ratios: Private Colleges Awarding the Bachelor's As the Highest Degree. (Institutional Research Reports). 50p. 1986. lib. bdg. write for info. (*0-937767-08-5*) Nat Data Service.

— Tuition-Fees, Financial Aid Statistics: Private Colleges & Universities Awarding the Master's As the Highest Degree. (Institutional Research Reports). 50p. 1986. lib. bdg. write for info. (*0-937767-15-8*) Nat Data Service.

— Tuition-Fees, Financial Aid Statistics: Private Colleges Awarding the Bachelor's As the Highest Degree. (Institutional Research Reports). 50p. 1986. lib. bdg. write for info. (*0-937767-09-3*) Nat Data Service.

— Tuition-Fees, Financial Aid Statistics: Private Universities Awarding the Doctoral's As the Highest Degree. (Institutional Research Reports). 50p. 1987. lib. bdg. write for info. (*0-937767-21-2*) Nat Data Service.

***Minter, Judy.** Thriving with Arthritis. Joyce, Peggy, ed. 256p. 2000. pap. 14.97 (*1-891985-03-5*) Live Oak LA.

***Minter, Peter.** Empty Texas. 80p. 1999. pap. text 15.95 (*90-5704-036-0*) Gordon & Breach.

M

Minter, Rick, ed. see Minter, Jim.

Minter, Roy. The White Pass: Gateway to the Klondike. (Illus.). 394p. 1987. 24.95 (0-912006-26-9) U of Alaska Pr.

Minter, Scott & Moore-Humphrey, Sheri. Business & the Legal System: Mastering Your Small Business. 1996. pap. 22.95 (1-57410-037-8, 61009701) Dearborn.

Minter, Sue. Greatest Glasshouse: The Rainforests Recreated. (Illus.). 228p. 1990. 29.95 (0-11-250035-8, Pub. by Statnry Office) Balogh.

— The Healing Garden: Flowers & Plants to Nurture the Body, Senses & Spirit. LC 95-40668. (Illus.). 160p. 1996. reprint ed. pap. 19.95 (0-8048-3083-5) Tuttle Pubng.

Minter, Tinch, tr. see Karge, Manfred.

Minter, William. Apartheid's Contras: An Inquiry into the Roots of War in Angola & Mozambique. LC 94-41587. 320p. (C). 1994. text 29.95 (1-85649-266-4, Pub. by Zed Books) St Martin.

— Operation Timber: Pages from the Savimbi Dossier. LC 88-71419. 200p. (C). 1988. 19.95 (0-86543-103-5); pap. 6.95 (0-86543-104-3) Africa World.

— Portuguese Africa & the West. LC 73-8054. 204p. reprint ed. pap. 63.30 (0-608-15883-6, 203076300070) Bks Demand.

Minter, William, ed. Africa's Problems...African Initiatives. 50p. 1992. pap. 7.50 (0-9634238-0-0) Africa Policy Info.

— U. S. Foreign Policy: An African Agenda. 28p. (Orig.). 1994. pap. 6.50 (0-9634238-1-9) Africa Policy Info.

Minter, William, ed. see Austin, Kathi.

Minterne, Don, jt. auth. see Cull, Brian.

Minters, Frances. Chicken for a Day. (Step into Reading Ser.: A Step 2 Book). 48p. (J). (gr. 1-3). 2000. lib. bdg. 11.99 (0-679-99133-6, Pub. by Random Bks Yng Read) Random.

— Chicken for a Day. LC 98-10188. (Step into Reading Ser.). (Illus.). 48p. (J). (gr. k-3). 2000. pap. 3.99 (0-679-89133-1, Pub. by Random Bks Yng Read) Random.

***Minters, Frances.** Chicken for a Day. (Illus.). (J). 2000. 9.44 (0-606-18489-9) Turtleback.

Minters, Frances. Cinder-Elly. LC 93-14533. (Illus.). 32p. (J). (ps-3). 1994. 15.99 (0-670-84417-9, Viking Child) Peng Put Young Read.

— Cinder-Elly. (Illus.). (J). (ps up). 1997. pap. 4.99 (0-614-28895-9, PuffinBks) Peng Put Young Read.

— Cinderelly. (J). 1997. pap. 5.99 (0-14-056126-9) Viking Penguin.

***Minters, Frances.** Sleepless Beauty. (Illus.). 32p. (J). (ps-3). 1999. pap. 5.99 (0-14-056619-8, PuffinBks) Peng Put Young Read.

Minters, Frances. Sleepless Beauty. (Illus.). 32p. (J). (ps-3). 1996. 14.99 (0-670-87033-1) Viking Penguin.

— Too Big Too Small Just Right. LC 98-41010. (J). 2000. 13.00 (0-15-202157-4) Harcourt.

Minthorn, P. Y., intro. Sapatq'ayn: Twentieth Century Nez Perce Artists. (Orig.). 1991. pap. text 12.95 (0-914019-27-9) NW Interpretive.

Minthorn, Philip Y. Vigil of the Wounded. Kenny, Maurice & Gosciak, Josh, eds. (Illus.). 60p. (Orig.). (C). 1987. pap. 5.95 (0-936556-15-3) Contact Two.

***Mintle, Linda.** Before Good Love Goes Bad: How to Avoid the Toxic Attitudes That Can Poison Your Marriage. 224p. 2000. pap. 12.99 (0-88419-732-8) Creation House.

— Getting Unstuck: Escape Three Traps Women Face Today, Vol. 1. 1999. pap. 12.99 (0-88419-652-6) Creation House.

— Kids Killing Kids. LC 99-74172. 216p. 1999. pap. 12.99 (0-88419-669-0) Creation House.

Minto, Barbara. The Minto Pyramid Principle: Logic in Writing, Thinking, & Problem Solving. LC 95-94799. (Illus.). 275p. 1996. 80.00 (0-9601910-3-8); pap. 60.00 (0-9601910-4-6) Minto Intl Inc.

— The Pyramid Principle: The Logic in Writing & Thinking. rev. ed. 250p. 1995. write for info. (0-273-61710-9) F T P H.

Minto, John. Rhymes of Early Life in Oregon & Historical & Biographical Facts. 82p. 1912. reprint ed. pap. 10.00 (0-8466-0185-0, S-185) Shoreys Bkstore.

Minto, M., ed. Platonov: The River Potudan (Reka Potudan) (Bristol Russian Texts Ser.). (RUS.). 1995. pap. 18.95 (1-85399-377-8, Pub. by Brist Class Pr) Focus Pub-R Pullins.

Minto, M., tr. Russian Tales of the Fantastic. 214p. 1994. pap. 20.95 (1-85399-225-9, Pub. by Brist Class Pr) Focus Pub-R Pullins.

Minto, W., ed. see Scott, William B.

Minto, Wally. The Results Book. 174p. 1976. 8.95 (0-89036-112-6) Coleman Pub.

Minto, William. Daniel Defoe. Morley, John, ed. LC 68-58386. (English Men of Letters Ser.). reprint ed. lib. bdg. 27.50 (0-404-51718-8) AMS Pr.

— Logic, Inductive & Deductive. 1977. 19.95 (0-8369-6997-9, 7814) Ayer.

Minton. Journal of Artificial Intelligence Research. (C). 1998. pap. text 70.00 (1-55860-531-2) Morgan Kaufmann.

— Manufacturing. (Techknowledge Reference Ser.). (J). (gr. k-12). 1998. pap. 18.95 (0-538-66140-2) S-W Pub.

Minton, Arthur J. & Shipka, Thomas A., eds. Philosophy: Paradox & Discovery. 4th ed. LC 95-36201. 528p. (C). 1995. pap. 40.63 (0-07-042525-6) McGraw.

Minton, Beverly, jt. auth. see Minton, Gene.

Minton, Bruce & Stuart, John. Men Who Lead Labor. LC 73-93362. (Essay Index Reprint Ser.). 1977. 21.95 (0-8369-1309-4) Ayer.

Minton, David. Triumph: Return of the Legend. 96p. 1995. 12.98 (0-7858-0309-2) Bk Sales Inc.

***Minton, David.** The Triumph Story: Racing & Production Models from 1932 to the Present Day. (Illus.). 176p. 2000. 39.95 (1-85960-413-7, 129530AE, Pub. by J H Haynes & Co) Motorbooks Intl.

Minton, Debbie. Cute Cats & Teddy Bears: 25 Delightful Cross-Stitch Pictures to Sew. (Illus.). 128p. 1998. pap. 24.95 (1-85585-492-9, Pub. by Collins & Br) Trafalgar.

— Oriental Cross Stitch: 25 Exquisite Designs Inspired by the Far East. (Illus.). 128p. 1999. 24.95 (1-85585-675-1, Pub. by Collins & Br) Sterling.

***Minton, Debbie.** Yesteryear in Cross-Stitch: 25 Nostalgic Designs to Make & Cherish. (Illus.). 2000. 24.95 (1-85585-718-9) Collins & Br.

Minton, Gabriel, jt. auth. see Levine, David.

Minton, Gene & Minton, Beverly. Teaching Technology to Children. (Illus.). 470p. (C). 1987. pap. 28.95 (0-87192-189-8) Thomson Learn.

Minton, Helena. The Canal Bed. LC 84-72463. 1985. 6.95 (0-914086-52-9); pap. 9.95 (0-914086-53-7) Alice James Bks.

Minton, Henry. Claiming Subjective Voice. 1997. pap. text 16.95 (0-226-53044-2); lib. bdg. 43.00 (0-226-53043-4) U Ch Pr.

Minton, Henry L. Lewis M. Terman: Pioneer in Educational Testing. (American Social Experience Ser.: No. 12). (Illus.). 254p. (C). 1990. pap. text 20.00 (0-8147-5452-X) NYU Pr.

Minton, Henry L., ed. Gay & Lesbian Studies. LC 92-23738. (Journal of Homosexuality Ser.: Vol. 24, Nos. 1-2). (Illus.). 205p. 1993. pap. 14.95 (1-56023-021-5, Harrington Park); lib. bdg. 39.95 (1-56024-307-4) Haworth Pr.

***Minton, Joe.** Majesty: Prima's Official Strategy Guide. LC 99-69667. (Official Strategy Guides Ser.). (Illus.). 268p. (YA). 2000. pap. 19.99 (0-7615-2772-9) Prima Pub.

Minton, Jonathan. Lost Languages. 30p. 1999. pap. 6.00 (0-9670994-2-0) Longleaf Meth Coll.

Minton, Larry, jt. auth. see Peterson, Michael T.

***Minton, Linda.** Tales Told under a Toadstool. LC 97-90654. (Illus.). 64p. 2000. 15.95 (1-56002-769-X) Serend Prodns.

Minton, M. A., jt. auth. see Whitesell, J. A.

Minton, Mary. Breathless Summer. 320p. 1996. 24.00 (0-7278-4965-4) Severn Hse.

— The Breathless Summer. large type ed. (Magna Large Print Ser.). 400p. 1998. 29.99 (0-7505-1163-X, Pub. by Mgna Lrg Print) Ulverscroft.

— Dark Waters. 320p. 1995. 24.00 (0-7278-4851-8) Severn Hse.

— Dark Waters. large type ed. (General Ser.). 1998. pap. 21.95 (0-7862-1274-8) Thorndike Pr.

— Flamenco Love Song. large type ed. 299p. 1994. pap. 18.99 (1-85389-438-9) Ulverscroft.

— Fortune's Daughter. 256p. 24.00 (0-7278-5215-9) Severn Hse.

— Fortune's Daughter. large type ed. 352p. 1998. 29.99 (0-7505-1248-2) Mgna Lrg Print.

— House of Destiny. large type ed. 647p. 1994. 27.99 (0-7505-0677-6) Ulverscroft.

— The Long Road. large type ed. (Magna Large Print Ser.). 469p. 1997. 27.99 (0-7505-0894-9) Ulverscroft.

Minton, Mary. The Marriage Bowl. large type ed. 512p. 31.99 (0-7505-1242-3, Pub. by Mgna Lrg Print) Ulverscroft.

Minton, Mary. Sea of Love. 256p. 1999. 25.00 (0-7278-5406-2, Pub. by Severn Hse) Chivers N Amer.

***Minton, Mary.** Spinners End. large type ed. 2000. 31.99 (0-7505-1428-0, Pub. by Mgna Lrg Print) Ulverscroft.

Minton, Mary. The Strident Whisper. 288p. 1996. 22.00 (0-7278-4933-6) Severn Hse.

— A Tracing of Angels. large type ed. 1995. 11.50 (0-7505-0806-X, Pub. by Mgna Lrg Print) Ulverscroft.

***Minton, Mary.** Yesterday's Road. large type ed. 512p. 1998. 29.99 (0-7505-1241-5) Mgna Lrg Print.

Minton, N. P. & Clarke, D. J. Clostridia. (Biotechnology Handbooks Ser.: Vol. 3). (Illus.). 318p. (C). 1989. text 85.00 (0-306-43261-7, Kluwer Plenum) Kluwer Academic.

Minton, Paul E. Handbook of Evaporation Technology. LC 86-17978. (Illus.). 390p. 1987. 109.00 (0-8155-1097-7) Noyes.

Minton, Phillip D. & Tennenhouse, Dan J. Delayed Diagnosis of Cancer. iv, 109p. 1995. pap. 54.00 (1-930548-01-X) Tennenhouse Prof Pubns.

***Minton, Roland B.** Calculus: Solutions Manual. 480p. (C). 1999. student ed. 19.38 (0-07-230476-6) McGrw-H Hghr Educ.

Minton, Roland B., jt. auth. see Smith, Robert T.

Minton, Sandra. Choreography: A Basic Approach to Using Improvisation. 2nd rev. ed. LC 96-48348. (Illus.). 136p. 1997. pap. text 19.95 (0-88011-529-7, BMIN0529) Human Kinetics.

Minton, Sandra C. Body & Self: Partners in Movement. LC 88-30383. (Illus.). 196p. 1989. reprint ed. pap. 60.80 (0-608-07068-8, 206727400009) Bks Demand.

Minton, Sherman A. Amphibians & Reptiles of Indiana. LC 97-39713. (Illus.). 400p. 1999. 37.50 (1-883362-10-5) IN Acad Sci.

Minton, Steve. Journal of Artificial Intelligence Research, Vol. 1. (C). 1998. pap. text 75.00 (1-55860-347-6) Morgan Kaufmann.

Minton, Steven. Journal of Artificial Intelligence Research, Vol. 2. (C). 1996. pap. text 79.00 (1-55860-386-7) Morgan Kaufmann.

***Minton, Steven.** Journal of Artificial Intelligence Reserch, 8 Vols., Vols.1-8. Wellman, Michael P., ed. 263p. 1998. pap. 75.00 (1-55860-586-X) Morgan Kaufmann.

Minton, Steven. Journal of Artificial Intelligence Research, Vol. 4. (C). 1996. pap. text 79.00 (1-55860-449-9) Morgan Kaufmann.

— Journal of Artificial Intelligence Research, Vol. 6. (C). 1997. pap. text 79.00 (1-55860-524-X) Morgan Kaufmann.

— Learning Search Control Knowledge: An Explanation-Based Approach. (C). 1988. text 100.50 (0-89838-294-7) Kluwer Academic.

Minton, Steven, ed. Journal of Artificial Intelligence Research, Vol. 3. 600p. (C). 1996. pap. text 79.00 (1-55860-398-0) Morgan Kaufmann.

— Journal of Artificial Intelligence Research, Vol. 5. 350p. (C). 1997. pap. text 75.00 (1-55860-484-7) Morgan Kaufmann.

— Machine Learning Methods for Planning. LC 92-19279. (Series in Machine Learning). 550p. 1993. text 48.95 (1-55860-248-8) Morgan Kaufmann.

Minton, Susanna L. Postcards: An Advanced Listening & Notetaking Workbook. LC 98-168408. (Illus.). 200p. (C). 1998. pap. text 18.95 (0-472-08493-3, 08493) U of Mich Pr.

***Mintrom, Michael.** Policy Entrepreneurs & School Choice. LC 99-36842. (American Governance & Public Policy Ser.). 336p. 2000. pap. text 24.95 (0-87840-771-5) Georgetown U Pr.

— Policy Entrepreneurs & School Choice. LC 99-36842. (American Governance & Public Policy Ser.). (Illus.). 336p. 2000. text 65.00 (0-87840-770-7) Georgetown U Pr.

Mints, G. E. Selected Papers in Proof Theory. (Studies in Proof Theory: Vol. 3). 294p. 1992. 143.50 (0-444-89619-8, North Holland) Elsevier.

Mints, G. E., jt. auth. see Kreinovich, Vladik.

Mints, Grigori. A Short Introduction to Modal Logic. LC 92-2924. (Center for the Study of Language & Information-Lecture Notes Ser.: No. 30). 112p. (C). 1992. 44.95 (0-937073-76-8); pap. 15.95 (0-937073-75-X) CSLI.

Mints, Lloyd W. A History of Banking Theory in Great Britain & the United States. LC 45-4815. 319p. reprint ed. pap. 98.90 (0-8357-8906-3, 205677900085) Bks Demand.

***Mints, Paula.** Legacy of Courage: A Brave Woman's Search for Her Mother's Killer & Her Own Identity - A True Story. LC 99-70157. 324p. 2000. 24.95 (0-88282-186-5,) New Horizon NJ.

Mintu-Wimsatt, Alma T. & Lozada, Hector R., eds. Green Marketing in a Unified Europe. LC 96-27827. (Journal of Euromarketing: Vol. 5, No. 3). 106p. (C). 1996. 39.95 (1-56024-829-7, Intl Busn Pr) Haworth Pr.

Mintu-Wimsatt, Alma T., jt. ed. see Polonsky, Michael J.

Minturn, Leigh & Kapor, Swaran. Sita's Daughters: The Rajput Women of Khalapur Revisited. LC 92-22147. (Illus.). 392p. (C). 1993. pap. text 29.95 (0-19-508035-1) OUP.

— Sita's Daughters Coming : Out of Purdah: The Rajput Women of Khalapur Revisited. LC 92-22147. (Illus.). 392p. (C). 1993. text 61.95 (0-19-507823-3) OUP.

Minturn, Neil. The Music of Sergei Prokofiev. LC 96-27064. (Composers of the Twentieth Century Ser.). 352p. 1997. 35.00 (0-300-06366-0) Yale U Pr.

Minturn, Penny Defoe, ed. see Hall, Susan, et al.

Minty, Gordon. Production Planning & Controlling: A Problem-Based Approach. LC 97-39024. (Illus.). 370p. (YA). (gr. 9-12). 1999. pap. text 37.28 (1-56637-449-9) Goodheart.

Minty, Judith. Dancing the Fault. (University of Central Florida Contemporary Poetry Ser.). 86p. 1991. 19.95 (0-8130-1079-9); pap. 10.95 (0-8130-1080-2) U Press Fla.

— Letters to My Daughters. 24p. (Orig.). 1981. pap. 5.00 (0-932412-03-3) Mayapple Pr.

— The Mad Painter Poems. Bixby, Robert, ed. 36p. (Orig.). 1996. pap. 6.00 (1-882983-25-4) March Street Pr.

***Minty, Judith.** Walking with the Bear: New & Selected Poems. 224p. 2000. pap. 22.95 (0-87013-547-3) Mich St U Pr.

Minty, Judith. Yellow Dog Journal. 75p. 1991. pap. 8.00 (0-938077-85-6) Parallax Pr.

Minty, Leonard L. Constitutional Laws of the British Empire. LC 97-74171. xvii, 258p. 1997. reprint ed. 84.00 (1-56169-324-3, 14640) Gaunt.

Minty, Nancy T. In the Eye of the Beholder: Northern Baroque Paintings from the Collection of Henry H. Weldon. LC 97-68986. (Illus.). 190p. 1997. pap. 29.95 (0-89494-059-7) New Orleans Mus Art.

Minty, William H., 3rd, et al. Win & Walk. 1998. pap. 19.95 (1-887750-85-1) Rutledge Bks.

Mintz, ed. Transfusion Therapy: Clinical Principles & Practice. LC 98-42095. 1998. write for info. (1-56395-099-5) Am Assn Blood.

Mintz, Alan. George Eliot & the Novel of Vocation. LC 77-15510. 224p. 1978. 29.00 (0-674-34873-7) HUP.

— Hurban: Responses to Catastrophe in Hebrew Literature. LC 83-23979. 288p. 1984. text 57.50 (0-231-05634-6) Col U Pr.

— Hurban: Responses to Catastrophe in Hebrew Literature. LC 96-33079. (Judaic Traditions in Literature, Music, & Art Ser.). 283p. 1996. reprint ed. pap. 17.95 (0-8156-0424-6, MIHHP) Syracuse U Pr.

Mintz, Alan, ed. The Boom in Contemporary Israeli Fiction. LC 97-3013. (Tauber Institute Ser.: No. 24). 202p. 1997. pap. 19.95 (0-87451-830-X); text 40.00 (0-87451-820-2) U Pr of New Eng.

— Hebrew in America: Perspectives & Prospects. LC 92-13602. (American Jewish Civilization Ser.). 338p. (C). 1992. 29.95 (0-8143-2351-0) Wayne St U Pr.

Mintz, Alan, ed. see Agnon, Shmuel Yoseph.

Mintz, Alex, jt. auth. see Geva, Nehemia.

Mintz, Alex, jt. ed. see Chan, Steve.

Mintz, Alex, jt. ed. see Doron, Gideon.

Mintz, Ann. Communicating Controversy: Science Museums & Issues Education. (Orig.). 1995. pap. 15.00 (0-944040-40-3) AST Ctrs.

Mintz, Ann, jt. ed. see Thomas, Selma.

Mintz, Barbara, jt. auth. see Katan, Norma J.

Mintz, Benjamin W. OSHA: History, Law & Policy. LC 84-11333. 800p. reprint ed. pap. 200.00 (0-7837-4593-1, 204431200002) Bks Demand.

Mintz, Beth & Rothblum, Esther D., eds. Lesbians in Academia: Degrees of Freedom. LC 97-16999. 304p. (C). 1997. 75.00 (0-415-91701-8); pap. 21.99 (0-415-91702-6) Routledge.

Mintz, Beth & Schwartz, Michael. The Power Structure of American Business. LC 84-8841. (Illus.). 348p. 1985. 33.00 (0-226-53108-2) U Ch Pr.

— The Power Structure of American Business. LC 84-8841. (Illus.). 352p. 1987. pap. text 17.00 (0-226-53109-0) U Ch Pr.

Mintz, Ethan & Yun, John, eds. The Complex World of Teaching: Perspectives from Theory & Practice. LC 98-75466. (Harvard Educational Review Reprint Ser.: Vol. 31). 415p. 1999. pap. 22.95 (0-916690-34-2) Harvard Educ Rev.

Mintz, F. J. Safety Engineering & Risk Analysis: Proceedings, ASME International Mechanical Engineering Congress & Exposition, Atlanta, GA, 1996. LC 96-78680. (SERA Ser.: Vol. 6). 147p. 1996. pap. 72.00 (0-7918-1538-2, T55) ASME.

Mintz, F. J., ed. Safety Engineering & Risk Analysis, 1997: Proceedings, ASME International Mechanical Engineering Congress & Exposition, Dallas, TX, 1997. LC 98-190298. (SERA Ser.: Vol. 7). 71p. 1997. pap. 90.00 (0-7918-1820-9, T55) ASME Pr.

Mintz, Frank P. The Liberty Lobby & the American Right: Race, Conspiracy & Culture, 121. LC 84-10761. (Contributions in Political Science Ser.: No. 121). 251p. 1985. 65.00 (0-313-24393-X, MIL/, Greenwood Pr) Greenwood.

Mintz, Ilse. American Exports During Business Cycles, 1879-1958. (Occasional Papers: No. 76). 106p. 1961. reprint ed. 27.60 (0-87014-390-5) Natl Bur Econ Res.

— Dating Postwar Business Cycles: Methods & Their Application to Western Germany, 1950-67. (Occasional Papers: No. 107). 125p. 1970. reprint ed. 32.50 (0-87014-212-7) Natl Bur Econ Res.

— Deterioration in the Quality of Foreign Bonds Issued in the United States, 1920-1930. Wilkins, Mira, ed. LC 78-3939. (International Finance Ser.). (Illus.). 1979. reprint ed. lib. bdg. 17.95 (0-405-11240-8) Ayer.

— Deterioration in the Quality of Foreign Bonds Issued in the United States, 1920-1930. (General Ser.: No. 52). 112p. 1951. reprint ed. 29.20 (0-87014-051-5) Natl Bur Econ Res.

— Trade Balances During Business Cycles: U. S. & Britain since 1880. (Occasional Papers: No. 67). 111p. 1959. reprint ed. 28.90 (0-87014-381-6) Natl Bur Econ Res.

Mintz, Ira L., jt. ed. see Wilson, C. Philip.

Mintz, Jack M. & Tsiopoulos, Thomas. Corporate Income Taxation & Foreign Direct Investment in Central & Eastern Europe. LC 92-37602. (FIAS Occasional Paper Ser.: No. 4). 28p. 1992. pap. 22.00 (0-8213-2301-6, 12301) World Bank.

Mintz, James W. Jesse. LC 84-80352. (Illus.). 329p. 1984. 14.95 (0-932807-00-3) Overmountain Pr.

Mintz, James W., ed. see Ball, Bonnie.

Mintz, James W., ed. see Lonon, James L.

Mintz, Jerome R. The Anarchists of Casa Viejas. LC 81-19696. 264p. (C). 1992. lib. bdg. 20.00 (0-226-53106-6) U Ch Pr.

— Anarchists of Casa Viejas. LC 81-19696. xvi, 336p. 1984. pap. 10.95 (0-226-53107-4) U Ch Pr.

— The Anarchists of Casas Viejas. LC 93-2425. (Illus.). 368p. reprint ed. pap. 114.10 (0-608-09352-1, 205409800002) Bks Demand.

— Carnival Song & Society. LC 96-46239. 1997. 55.00 (1-85973-183-X, Pub. by Berg Pubs); pap. 19.50 (1-85973-188-0, Pub. by Berg Pubs) NYU Pr.

— Hasidic People: A Place in the New World. 480p. 1992. 50.00 (0-674-38115-7) HUP.

— Hasidic People: A Place in the New World. 448p. 1994. pap. text 17.95 (0-674-38116-5, MINHAX) HUP.

— Legends of the Hasidim: An Introduction to Hasidic Culture & Oral Tradition in the New World. LC 95-6046. 494p. 1996. pap. 40.00 (1-56821-530-4) Aronson.

— Legends of the Hasidim: An Introduction to Hasidic Culture & Oral Tradition in the New World. LC 68-16707. 504p. 1993. reprint ed. pap. text 14.95 (0-226-53103-1, P612) U Ch Pr.

Mintz, Jerome R., jt. ed. see Ben-Amos, Dan.

Mintz, Jerry. Almanac of Education Choices. 1995. 20.00 (0-02-864501-4) Macmillan.

Mintz, Joel A. Enforcement at the EPA: High Stakes & Hard Choices. LC 95-13922. 208p. 1995. 24.95 (0-292-75187-7) U of Tex Pr.

— State & Local Government Environmental Liability. (Liability Prevention Ser.). 1994. write for info. (0-614-32081-X) West Group.

Mintz, Joshua, jt. auth. see Pierson, Jane.

Mintz, Lannon. Wise Hombre Quizzes for Westerners: Western Yarns. LC 88-29437. (Illus.). 48p. 1989. pap. 3.95 (0-86534-128-1) Sunstone Pr.

Mintz, Lawrence E., ed. Humor in America: A Research Guide to Genres & Topics. LC 87-17600. 251p. 1988. lib. bdg. 59.95 (0-313-24551-7, MZH/, Greenwood Pr) Greenwood.

Mintz, Malcolm W. Bikol Dictionary. LC 72-152466. (Hawaii University, Honolulu, Pacific & Asian Linguistics Institute Ser.). 1022p. reprint ed. pap. 200.00 (0-8357-3602-4, 200797900068) Bks Demand.

— Bikol Grammar Notes. LC 76-152467. (Hawaii

An Asterisk (*) at the beginning of an entry indicates that the title is appearing for the first time.

University, Honolulu, Pacific & Asian Linguistics Institute Ser.). 287p. reprint ed. pap. 89.00 (0-8357-7208-X, 200798000068) Bks Demand.
— Bikol Text. LC 73-148650. (Hawaii University, Honolulu, Pacific & Asian Linguistics Institute Ser.). 762p. reprint ed. pap. 200.00 (0-8357-7209-8, 201611400098) Bks Demand.
Mintz, Malcolm W. & Britanico, Jose D. Bikol-English Dictionary.Tr. of Diksionaryong Bikol-Ingles. viii, 555p. (Orig.). 1985. pap. 30.00 (971-10-0212-4, Pub. by New Day Pub) Cellar.
Mintz, Max M. The Generals of Saratoga: John Burgoyne & Horatio Gates. (Illus.). 296p. (C). 1992. reprint ed. pap. 18.00 (0-300-05261-8) Yale U Pr.
— Seeds of Empire: The American Revolutionary Conquest of the Iroquois. LC 99-6006. 264p. 1999. 28.95 (0-8147-5622-0) NYU Pr.
Mintz, Norman, jt. auth. see Gratz, Roberta B.
*__Mintz, Ouida Blatt.__ My Friend Lenny: A Memoir. viii, 357p. 2000. pap. 14.95 (0-615-11879-8) Bravura Bks.
*__Mintz, P. D., ed.__ Transfusion Therapy. (Illus.). xviii, 482p. 1999. write for info. (3-8055-6900-9) S Karger.
Mintz, Patty. Guide to Beaches, Parks & Natural Sites Nova Scotia. 112p. 1999. pap. text 10.95 (1-55109-248-4) Nimbus Publ.
— Rediscover the Evangeline Trail: A Guide to Nova Scotia from Yarmouth to Windsor. (Illus.). 156p. (Orig.). 1996. pap. 10.95 (1-55109-158-5) Nimbus Publ.
Mintz, Penny. The Complete Cholesterol Counter. (Heart Care Titles Ser.). 256p. 1990. mass mkt. 5.99 (0-345-36321-3) Ballantine Pub Grp.
*__Mintz, Robert J. & Doft, Peter S.__ Privacy Plan: How to Keep What You Own Secret from High-Tech Snoops, Lawyers & Con Men, 1 Vol. (Illus.). 268p. 1999. 34.95 (0-9639971-1-4) F OBrien & Sons.
Mintz, Robert J. & Rubens, James J. Lawsuit Proof: Protecting Your Assets from Lawsuits & Claims. LC 94-79491. (Illus.). (Orig.). 1994. pap. text 19.95 (0-915905-37-X) Lawtech Pub.
Mintz, S., et al. On Marxian Perspectives in Anthropology: Essays in Honor of H. Hoijer, 1981. Maquet, Jaques P. & Daniels, N. C., eds. LC 84-52206. (Other Realities Ser.: Vol. 5). vi, 98p. 1985. 26.00 (0-89003-178-9); pap. 16.00 (0-89003-179-7) Undena Pubns.
Mintz, S. L., jt. auth. see Neff, John B.
Mintz, Samuel I. The Hunting of Leviathan: Seventeenth-Century Reactions to the Materialism & Moral Philosophy of Thomas Hobbes. (Key Texts Ser.). 200p. 1996. 75.00 (1-85506-480-4); pap. 20.00 (1-85506-481-2) Bks Intl VA.
— The Hunting of Leviathan: Seventeenth-Century Reactions to the Materialism & Moral Philosophy of Thomas Hobbes. 199p. reprint ed. pap. 56.80 (0-608-15756-2, 2031695) Bks Demand.
Mintz, Samuel I., et al, eds. From Smollett to James: Studies in the Novel & Other Essays Presented to Edgar Johnson. LC 79-25865. 317p. reprint ed. pap. 98.30 (0-608-16732-0, 202706800053) Bks Demand.
Mintz, Sharon L., jt. auth. see Felsenstein, Frank.
Mintz, Sidney W. Caribbean Transformations. 384p. 1989. text 73.50 (0-231-07114-0); pap. text 21.00 (0-231-07115-9) Col U Pr.
— Caribbean Transformations. LC 83-19997. 367p. reprint ed. pap. 113.80 (0-8357-8057-0, 203411300088) Bks Demand.
— Sweetness & Power: The Place of Sugar in Modern History. 1986. pap. 13.95 (0-14-009233-1, Penguin Bks) Viking Penguin.
— Taso: Trabajador de la Cana. LC 88-82494. 321p. 1988. pap. 12.25 (0-940238-73-X) Ediciones Huracan.
— Tasting Food, Tasting Freedom: Excursions into Eating, Culture, & the Past. LC 95-47569. 176p. 1997. pap. 13.00 (0-8070-4629-9) Beacon Pr.
— Worker in the Cane: A Puerto Rican Life History. (Illus.). 320p. 1974. reprint ed. pap. 13.95 (0-393-00731-6) Norton.
Mintz, Sidney W., compiled by. Papers in Caribbean Anthropology. LC 74-123185. (Yale University Publications in Anthropology Reprints Ser.: Nos. 57-64). 252p. 1970. pap. 20.00 (0-87536-524-8) HRAFP.
Mintz, Sidney W. & Price, Richard. The Birth of African-American Culture: An Anthropological Perspective. LC 91-41020. 144p. 1992. pap. 12.50 (0-8070-0917-2) Beacon Pr.
Mintz, Steven. Beyond Wall Street. 1999. pap. 12.95 (0-452-27926-7) NAL.
— Moralists & Modernizers: America's Pre-Civil War Reformers. LC 94-43690. (American Moment Ser.). 208p. 1995. text 38.95 (0-8018-5080-0); pap. text 14.95 (0-8018-5081-9) Johns Hopkins.
— A Prison of Expectations: The Family in Victorian Culture. 232p. (C). 1983. pap. text 17.50 (0-8147-5391-4) NYU Pr.
Mintz, Steven, ed. African American Voices: The Life Cycle of Slavery. rev. ed. (Illus.). 224p. 1996. pap. text 16.50 (1-881089-88-6) Brandywine Press.
*__Mintz, Steven, ed.__ African American Voices: The Life Cycle of Slavery. 2nd ed. (Illus.). 224p. (C). 1999. pap. text 16.50 (1-881089-46-0) Brandywine Press.
— Mexican American Voices. 272p. (C). 2000. pap. text 14.50 (1-881089-44-4) Brandywine Press.
Mintz, Steven, ed. Native American Voices: A History & Anthology. (Illus.). 240p. (C). 1995. pap. text 22.92 (1-881089-25-8) Brandywine Press.
*__Mintz, Steven, ed.__ Native American Voices: A History & Anthology. rev. ed. (Illus.). 240p. (C). 1998. pap. text 18.50 (1-881089-38-X) Brandywine Press.
— Native American Voices: A History & Anthology. 2nd ed. 256p. (C). 2000. pap. text 18.50 (1-881089-59-2) Brandywine Press.
Mintz, Steven & Kellogg, Susan M. Domestic Revolutions: A Social History of American Family Life. 316p. 1989. pap. 13.95 (0-02-921291-X) Free Pr.
Mintz, Steven & Roberts, Randy, eds. Hollywood's America: United States History Through Its Films. 2nd ed. (Illus.). 384p. (C). 1993. pap. text 19.50 (1-881089-48-7) Brandywine Press.
Mintz, Steven, jt. ed. see Davis, David Brion.
Mintz, Steven, jt. ed. see Davis, David B.
Mintz, Steven L. Beyond Wall Street: The Art of Investing. LC 97-45081. 240p. 1998. 24.95 (0-471-24737-5) Wiley.
*__Mintz, Steven L.__ Beyond Wall Street: The Art of Investing. 226p. 1999. pap. 16.95 (0-471-35845-2) Wiley.
Mintz, Steven L. Five Eminent Contrarians: Careers, Perspectives, & Investment Tactics. LC 94-72582. 129p. (Orig.). 1994. pap. 14.00 (0-87034-115-4) Fraser Pub Co.
Mintz, Steven M. Cases in Accounting Ethics & Professionalism. 3rd ed. LC 96-22830. 160p. (C). 1996. pap. 26.88 (0-07-042834-4) McGraw.
Mintz, Susan L. Safe Sex Never Tasted So Good. 5th ed. LC 90-188642. (Illus.). 144p. 1990. reprint ed. lib. bdg. 12.95 (0-9636037-0-1) Boner Pubns.
*__Mintzberg.__ Strategy Safari: A Guided Tour Through the Wilds of Strategic Management. 1998. pap., student ed. write for info. (0-684-85677-8) S&S Trade.
Mintzberg, Henry. Mintzberg on Management: Inside Our Strange World of Organizations. 256p. 1989. 40.00 (0-02-921371-1) Free Pr.
— The Nature of Managerial Work. (Illus.). 298p. (C). 1997. pap. 62.67 (0-06-044556-4) Addson-Wesley Educ.
— The Rise & Fall of Strategic Planning. 288p. 1994. 32.95 (0-02-921605-2) Free Pr.
— The Rise & Fall of Strategic Planning. LC 93-39492. 1993. pap. write for info. (0-13-781824-6) Prntice Hall Bks.
— Structure in Fives: Designing Effective Organizations. 2nd ed. 312p. 1992. pap. text 49.00 (0-13-855479-X) P-H.
— Structuring of Organizations. (Theory of Management Policy Ser.). (Illus.). 512p. 1978. 72.00 (0-13-855270-3) P-H.
Mintzberg, Henry & Quinn, James B. Readings in the Strategy Process. 3rd ed. LC 97-43049. 429p. 1998. pap. text 52.00 (0-13-494964-1) P-H.
— The Strategy Process: Concepts, Contexts & Cases. 3rd ed. LC 95-32626. 990p. (C). 1995. 105.00 (0-13-234030-5) P-H.
Mintzberg, Henry, et al. The Strategy Process. 3rd rev. ed. 1036p. 1998. pap. text 76.00 (0-13-675984-X) P-H.
— The Strategy Process: The Collegiate Edition. LC 94-19998. 595p. 1994. text, student ed. 91.00 (0-13-556557-X) P-H.
— Strategy Safari: A Guided Tour Through the Wilds of Strategic Management. LC 98-9694. (Illus.). 432p. 1998. 26.50 (0-684-84743-4) Free Pr.
Mintzer, Bob. 14 Blues & Funk Etudes. Clark, Larry, ed. (C Instruments Ser.). 60p. 1996. wbk. ed. 26.95 (1-57623-576-9, EL9604CD); wbk. ed. 26.95 (1-57623-579-3, EL9605CD); wbk. ed. 26.95 (1-57623-577-7, EL9606CD); wbk. ed. 26.95 (1-57623-578-5, EL9607CD); wbk. ed. 26.95 (1-57623-575-0, EL9608CD) Wrner Bros.
Mintzer, Irving M. Confronting Climate Change: Risks, Implications & Responses. (Illus.). 396p. (C). 1992. text 110.00 (0-521-42091-1); pap. text 39.95 (0-521-42109-8) Cambridge U Pr.
— Implementing the Framework Convention on Climate Change: Incremental Costs & the Role of the GEF. (Global Environmental Facility Working Papers: No. 4). 44p. 1993. pap. 22.00 (1-884122-03-5, 72035) World Bank.
Mintzer, Kathi, jt. auth. see Mintzer, Rich.
Mintzer, Oscar A. In Defense of the Survivors: The Letters & Documents of Oscar A. Mintzer, AUDC Legal Advisors, Germany, 1945-46. 426p. 1999. pap. 24.95 (0-943376-66-1) Magnes Mus.
*__Mintzer, Rich.__ Everything Guide to New York City. LC 99-55412. (Illus.). 304p. 2000. pap. 12.95 (1-58062-314-X) Adams Media.
Mintzer, Rich. The Everything Investing Book. LC 99-15775. 304p. 1999. pap. 12.95 (1-58062-149-X) Adams Media.
*__Mintzer, Rich.__ The Everything Kids' Online Book: E-mail, Pen Pals, Live Chats, Home Pages, Family Trees, Homework & Much More! (Illus.). 144p. (J). (gr. 2-7). 2000. pap. 9.95 (1-58062-394-8) Adams Media.
— The Everything Mutual Funds Book: How to Pick, Buy & Sell Mutual Funds & Watch Your Money Grow! (Illus.). 304p. 2000. pap. 12.95 (1-58062-419-7) Adams Media.
— FastRead Investing: Understand Stocks, Bonds, Mutual Funds & More! 128p. 2000. pap. 5.95 (1-58062-393-X) Adams Media.
— The Pocket Idiot's Guide to Golf Accessories. (Pocket Idiot's Guides Ser.). 192p. 1999. pap. 9.95 (0-02-863376-8, Pub. by Macmillan Gen Ref) S&S Trade.
Mintzer, Rich & Grossman, Peter. Everything Golf Book. LC 97-28415. (Illus.). 352p. 1997. pap. 12.95 (1-55850-814-7) Adams Media.
*__Mintzer, Rich & Mintzer, Kathi.__ The Everything Money Book: Learn How to Manage, Budget, Save, & Invest Your Money So There's Plenty Left Over. (Illus.). 304p. 1999. pap. 12.95 (1-58062-145-7) Adams Media.
Mintzer, Richard. The Longest Aisle: An Offbeat Guide to Wedding Planning. LC 94-20506. (Illus.). 144p. 1994. pap. 9.95 (0-8065-1575-9) Carol Pub Group.
— Volunteering in New York City: Your Guide to Working Small Miracles in the Big Apple. LC 95-43161. 176p. (Orig.). 1996. pap. 10.95 (0-8027-7481-4) Walker & Co.
Mintzes, Joel J., et al, eds. Teaching Science for Understanding: A Human Constructivist View. LC 97-80819. (Educational Psychology Ser.). (Illus.). 360p. 1998. text 59.95 (0-12-498360-X) Morgan Kaufmann.
*__Mintzes, Joel J., et al.__ Assessing Science Understanding: A Human Constructivist View. 320p. 1999. 69.95 (0-12-498365-0) Acad Pr.
Minucci, Frank. Brother Frank. 256p. 1999. mass mkt. 5.99 (0-7860-0611-0) Kensgtn Pub Corp.
Minucci, Frank & Hoffman, William. Brother Frank. LC 97-72054. 272p. 1996. 22.95 (1-57566-080-6, Knsington) Kensgtn Pub Corp.
Minucci, Mary B. The World Around Me: Exploring Home, Friends, Family, Transportation, & Community. Hayes, Martha A., ed. (Creative Concept Ser.). (Illus.). 48p. 1990. pap. 6.95 (1-878727-04-4) First Teacher.
Minucci, Mary B., ed. see Pfeffer, Wendy.
Minuchin. Family Healing: Strategies for Hope & Understanding. 1998. pap. 12.00 (0-684-85573-9) S&S Trade.
Minuchin, Patricia, et al. Working with Families of the Poor. (Family Therapy Ser.). 248p. 1998. lib. bdg. 39.95 (1-57230-406-5) Guilford Pubns.
— Working with Families of the Poor. LC 98-3805. 248p. 1999. lib. bdg. 21.00 (1-57230-373-5) Guilford Pubns.
Minuchin, Salvador. Families & Family Therapy. LC 73-89710. 268p. 1974. 32.00 (0-674-29236-7) HUP.
— Family Kaleidoscope. 248p. 1984. 22.00 (0-674-29230-8) HUP.
— Family Kaleidoscope: Images of Violence & Healing. 248p. 1984. pap. text 17.50 (0-674-29231-6) HUP.
Minuchin, Salvador & Fishman, H. Charles. Family Therapy Techniques. LC 80-25392. (Illus.). 303p. 1990. 33.50 (0-674-29410-6) HUP.
Minuchin, Salvador & Nichols, Michael P. Family Healing: Tales of Hope & Renewal from Family Therapy. 287p. (C). 1998. text 23.00 (0-7881-5599-7) DIANE Pub.
— Family Healing: Tales of Hope & Renewal from Family Therapy. LC 92-23854. 1992. 27.95 (0-02-921295-2) Free Pr.
— Family Healing: Tales of Hope & Renewal from Family Therapy. 304p. 1994. pap. 12.00 (0-671-88099-3, Touchstone) S&S Trade Pap.
Minuchin, Salvador, et al. Mastering Family Therapy: Journeys of Growth & Transformation. LC 96-22887. 272p. 1996. 59.95 (0-471-15558-6) Wiley.
— Psychosomatic Families: Anorexia Nervosa in Context. 351p. 1978. 38.50 (0-674-72220-5) HUP.
Minuck & Borchers. Colorado Juvenile Law: Cases & Materials. 2nd ed. LC 97-209709. 214p. (C). 1997. spiral bd. 44.95 (0-7872-4368-X, 41436801) Kendall-Hunt.
Minugh, Carol J., ed. see Morris, Glen T. & Ryser, Rudolph C.
Minus, Paul M., ed. The Ethics of Business in a Global Economy. LC 93-7110. (Issues in Business Ethics Ser.: Vol. 4). 160p. 1993. text 106.00 (0-7923-9334-1) Kluwer Academic.
Minutaglio, Bill, jt. auth. see Newton, Nick.
Minutaglio, Bill. First Son: George W. Bush & the Bush Family Dynasty. LC 99-16462. (Illus.). 320p. 1999. 25.00 (0-8129-3139-4, Times Bks) Crown Pub Group.
Minutoli, Armando. Medjugorje, a Pilgrims Journey. 224p. (Orig.). 1991. pap. 9.95 (0-9630544-0-6) Mrng Star NY.
Minutolo, Audrey S. A Pocket Guide to Biking on Mt. Desert Island. LC 96-83694. (Illus.). 64p. (Orig.). 1996. pap. 7.95 (0-89272-367-X) Down East.
Minyard, Applewhite, et al. Decades of Science Fiction. LC 97-348. (Illus.). 480p. Date not set. 29.94 (0-8442-5994-2, 59942) NTC Contemp Pub Co.
Minzer, Marilyn K., et al. Damages in Tort Actions, 10 vols., Set. Updates. 1982. ring bd. 1350.00 (0-8205-1309-1) Bender.
Minzhu, Han, ed. Cries for Democracy: Writings & Speeches from the 1989 Chinese Democracy Movement. (Illus.). 300p. 1990. text 65.00 (0-691-03146-0, Pub. by Princeton U Pr) Cal Prin Full Svc.
Minzner, Pamela B., jt. auth. see Laurence, Robert, pseud.
Minzter, Beth. Manual of Practical Pain Management. (Illus.). 600p. (C). 1999. pap. 54.95 (0-8385-8116-1) McGraw.
Mio, Jeffery S., et al, eds. Key Words in Multicultural Interventions: A Dictionary. LC 99-14839. 320p. 1999. lib. bdg. 89.50 (0-313-29547-6, Greenwood Pr) Greenwood.
Mio, Jeffrey S. & Katz, Albert N., eds. Metaphor: Implications & Applications. 350p. 1996. 59.95 (0-8058-1650-X) L Erlbaum Assocs.
Miodunka, W. Czesc, Jak Sie Masz? (POL.). 229p. 1996. pap. 35.00 (83-7052-985-2, Pub. by Universitas) IBD Ltd.
Mioduski, T. & Salomon, M., eds. Scandium, Yttrium, Lanthanum & Lanthanide Halides in Nonaqueous Solvents. (Illus.). 418p. 1985. 142.00 (0-08-030709-4, Pub. by PPL) Elsevier.
Miola, A. & Temperini, M., eds. Advances in the Design of Symbolic Computation Systems. LC 97-8929. (Texts & Mongraphs in Symbolic Computation). 250p. 1997. pap. 79.95 (3-211-82844-3) Spr-Verlag.
Miola, Alfonso, ed. Design & Implementation of Symbolic Computation Systems: International Symposium, DISCO '93, Gmunden, Austria, September 1993: Proceedings. LC 93-21040. (Lecture Notes in Computer Science Ser.: Vol. 722). 1993. 55.95 (0-387-57235-X) Spr-Verlag.
Miola, Robert S. Shakespeare & Classical Comedy: The Influence of Plautus & Terence. 246p. 1995. text 65.00 (0-19-818269-4) OUP.
— Shakespeare & Classical Tragedy: The Influence of Seneca. 234p. 1992. text 55.00 (0-19-811264-5) OUP.
*__Miola, Robert S.__ Shakespeare's Reading. (Oxford Shakespeare Topics Ser.). (Illus.). 192p. 2000. pap. 19.95 (0-19-871169-7); text 44.00 (0-19-871168-9) OUP.
Miola, Robert S. & Kolin, Philip C., eds. The Comedy of Errors: Critical Essays. LC 97-11299. (Shakespeare Criticism Ser.: Vol. 18). (Illus.). 592p. 1997. text 110.00 (0-8153-1997-5, H1897) Garland.
Mioli, V. A., ed. Virus Hepatitis & Kidney. (Journal: Nephron: Vol. 61, No. 3, 1992). (Illus.). 128p. 1992. pap. 56.75 (3-8055-5621-7) S Karger.
Mionczynski, John. The Pack Goat. LC 92-16298. (Illus.). 147p. 1992. pap. 15.95 (0-87108-828-2) Pruett.
Mione, Antonio. CDE/Motif Quick Primer. LC 97-31838. 500p. (C). 1997. pap. text 65.00 incl. cd-rom (0-13-760828-4) P-H.
*__Mioni, Anthony J., Jr., ed.__ The Popes Against Modern Errors: 16 Famous Papal Documents. LC 98-61396. 365p. 1999. pap. 16.50 (0-89555-643-X, 1588) TAN Bks Pubs.
Miora, Michael. Enterprise Disaster Recovery Planning. (Illus.). 384p. 1997. text 55.00 (0-07-042904-9) McGraw.
Miossec, Pierre, et al. T Cells in Arthritis. LC 98-19065. (PIR - Progress in Inflammation Research Ser.). 1998. 133.00 (0-8176-5853-X) Birkhauser.
Miossec, Pierre P., et al, eds. T Cells in Arthritis. LC 98-19065. (Progress in Inflammation Research Ser.). 250p. 1998. 133.00 (3-7643-5853-X) Spr-Verlag.
Miotto, Enrico. The Universe. LC 94-3839. (Beginnings Origins & Evolution Ser.).Tr. of L'/Universo. (Illus.). 48p. (J). (gr. 3-10). 1994. lib. bdg. 24.26 (0-8114-3334-X) Raintree Steck-V.
Miour, Michael, ed. see Hobbs, Christopher.
Miovic, Michael, ed. see Hobbs, Christopher.
*__Mipham, Jamgon.__ Mo: Tibetan Divination System. rev. ed. 168p. 2000. pap. text. write for info. (1-55939-147-2) Snow Lion Pubns.
Miquel, F. A. Illustration de la Flora de la Archipol Indian. (Illus.). 114p. (C). 1983. 60.00 (0-7855-3242-0, Pub. by Scientific) St Mut.
— Illustration de la Flore de l'Archipel Indian. (C). 1988. text 60.00 (0-7855-6004-1, Pub. by Scientific) St Mut.
Miquel I Verges, Jose Maria. Diccionario de Insurgentes. (SPA.). 29.95 (0-7859-0934-6, S-12335) Fr & Eur.
Miquel, Jaime, et al, eds. Handbook of Free Radicals & Antioxidants in Biomedicine, Vol. I. 352p. 1988. 203.00 (0-8493-3268-0, RB170) CRC Pr.
— Handbook of Free Radicals & Antioxidants in Biomedicine, Vol. II. 384p. 1988. lib. bdg. 229.00 (0-8493-3269-9, RB170) CRC Pr.
— Handbook of Free Radicals & Antioxidants in Biomedicine, Vol. III. 328p. 1988. lib. bdg. 229.00 (0-8493-3270-2, RB170) CRC Pr.
— Handbook of Free Radicals & Antioxidants in Biomedicine, Vols. I-III. 1988. write for info. (0-318-63782-0, RB170) CRC Pr.
Miquel, Jean. Vocabulaire Pratique de la Philosophie: Practical Vocabulary of Philosophy. (FRE.). 260p. 1974. pap. 12.95 (0-8288-6220-6, M-6412) Fr & Eur.
Miquel, Pierre. The Chateaux of the Loire. LC 99-70251. (Illus.). 176p. 1999. 45.00 (0-670-88644-0) Viking Penguin.
— Dictionnaire Symbolique des Animaux. (FRE.). 1991. write for info. (0-7859-8660-X, 286377106X) Fr & Eur.
Miquel, Pierre & Picard, Paula. Dictionnaire des Symboles Mystiques. (FRE.). 637p. 1997. 159.00 (0-320-00454-6) Fr & Eur.
Miquelon, Dale. Dugard of Rouen: French Trade to Canada & the West Indies, 1729-1770. LC 79-345926. (Illus.). 294p. reprint ed. pap. 91.20 (0-7837-1150-6, 204167900022) Bks Demand.
Mir, Afzal, et al. An Aid to the MRCP VIVA. (Illus.). 332p. (Orig.). 1992. pap. text 35.00 (0-443-04659-X) Church.
Mir, Ahmad A. The Qur'an. Mir Ahmed Ali, S. V., tr. 520p. 1991. pap. 5.95 (0-9630687-0-9) Quran Soc.
Mir Ahmed Ali, S. V., tr. see Mir, Ahmad A.
*__Mir-Hosseini, Ziba.__ Islam & Gender: The Religious Debate in Contemporary Iran. LC 99-22786. 304p. 1999. 55.00 (0-691-05815-6, Pub. by Princeton U Pr) Cal Prin Full Svc.
— Islam & Gender: The Religious Debate in Contemporary Iran. LC 99-22786. (Studies in Muslim Politics). 304p. 1999. pap. 18.95 (0-691-01004-8, Pub. by Princeton U Pr) Cal Prin Full Svc.
Mir-Hosseini, Ziba. Marriage on Trial. 256p. 1997. text 24.50 (1-86064-182-2, Pub. by I B T) St Martin.
— Marriage on Trial: Islamic Family Law in Iran & Morocco. (Society & Culture in the Modern Middle East Ser.). 288p. 1993. text 65.00 (1-85043-685-1, Pub. by I B T) St Martin.
Mir, M. Life from Persia to the U. S. A. (Illus.). 140p. 1996. 20.00 (0-9656415-0-3) M Mir.
Mir, M. A. Atlas of Clinical Diagnosis. 1995. text 45.00 (0-7020-1846-5, W B Saunders Co) Harcrt Hlth Sci Grp.
— Atlas of Clinical Skills. 1997. text 39.95 (0-7020-1816-3, W B Saunders Co) Harcrt Hlth Sci Grp.
Mir, Muhammad Taqi. Zikr-i-Mir: The Eighteenth-century Autobiography of the Mughal Poet 'Mir' LC 99-939179. (Illus.). 228p. 2000. text 23.95 (0-19-564588-X) OUP.
Mir, Mustansir. Coherence in the Qur'an. American Trust Publications, ed. 125p. 1987. pap. 7.00 (0-89259-065-3) Am Trust Pubns.
— Coherence in the Quran. 130p. 1996. pap. 10.50 (0-614-21049-6, 139) Kazi Pubns.
— Verbal Idioms of the Qur'an. (Michigan Series on the Middle East: No. 1). 378p. (Orig.). 1989. pap. 21.95 (0-932098-21-5) UM Ctr MENAS.
Mir, Mustansir & Fossum, Jarl E., eds. Literary Heritage of Classical Islam: Arabic & Islamic Studies in Honor of James A. Bellamy. LC 93-785. (Illus.). 356p. 1993. 35.00 (0-87850-099-5) Darwin Pr.

M

An Asterisk (*) at the beginning of an entry indicates that the title is appearing for the first time.

Mir, Mustsir. Verbal Idioms of the Qur'an. 1989. 21.95 (*0-86685-471-1*) Intl Bk Ctr.

Mir, Pedro. Countersong to Walt Whitman & Other Poems. Walsh, Donald D., tr. from SPA. LC 92-74943. 164p. (Orig.). 1993. pap. 12.95 (*0-9632363-3-4*) Azul Edits.

MIR Publishers Staff, ed. Lenin & Gorky: Letters, Reminiscences, Articles. (Illus.). 429p. 1973. 26.95 (*0-8464-0555-5*) Beekman Pubs.

Mir Publishers Staff, tr. see Agronomov, A., et al.

Mir Publishers Staff, tr. see Kireev, V.

Mir Publishers Staff, tr. see Molchanov, V., et al.

Mir Publishers Staff, tr. see Pavlov, Boris & Terentyev, Alexander.

Mir Publishers Staff, tr. see Petrovsky, Boris, et al.

Mir Publishers Staff, tr. see Reutov, O. A.

Mira, C. Chaotic Dynamics: From the One-Dimensional Endomorphism to the Two-Dimensional Diffeomorphism. 472p. (C). 1987. text 87.00 (*9971-5-0324-7*) World Scientific Pub.

Mira, C., et al, eds. Iteration Theory. 400p. (C). 1991. text 118.00 (*981-02-0611-9*) World Scientific Pub.

Mira, C., jt. auth. see Gardini, L.

Mira, C., jt. auth. see Gumowski, Igor.

Mira de Amescua, Antonio. The Devil's Slave. McGaha, Michael D., tr. 114p. 1985. reprint ed. pap. 8.00 (*0-919473-46-6*, DH55, Pub. by Dovehouse) Sterling.

Mira, Eduard, jt. ed. see Bekemans, Leonce.

***Mira, J., et al, eds.** Engineering Applications of Bio-Inspired Artificial Neural Networks: Proceedings of the International Work-Conference on Artificial & Natural Neural Networks, IWANN'99, Alicante, Spain, June 2-4, 1999. LC 99-34573. (Lecture Notes in Computer Science Ser.: Vol. 1607). xxiii, 907p. 1999. pap. 95.00 (*3-540-66068-2*) Spr-Verlag.

— Foundations & Tools for Neural Modeling: Proceedings of the International Work-Conference on Artificial & Natural Neural Networks, IWANN'99, Alicante, Spain, June 2-4, 1999. (Lecture Notes in Computer Science Ser.: Vol. 1606). xxiii, 865p. 1999. pap. 93.00 (*3-540-66069-0*) Spr-Verlag.

Mira, J. Ional, et al, eds. Biological & Artificial Computation from Neuroscience to Neurotechnology: International Work-Conference on Artificial Neural Networks, IWANN'97, Lanzarote, Canary Islands, Spain, June 4-6, 1997, Proceedings. LC 97-20864. (Lecture Notes in Computer Science Ser.: No. 1240). xxi, 1401p. 1997. pap. 154.00 (*3-540-63047-3*) Spr-Verlag.

Mira, Jose & Sandoval, Francisco, eds. From Natural to Artificial Neural Computation: International Workshop on Artificial Neural Networks, Malaga-Torremolinos, Spain, June 7-9, 1995: Proceedings. (Lecture Notes in Computer Science Ser.: Vol. 930). 1995. write for info. (*0-387-59497-3*) Spr-Verlag.

— From Natural to Artificial Neural Computation: International Workshop on Artificial Neural Networks, Malaga-Torremolinos, Spain, June 7-9, 1995: Proceedings. (Lecture Notes in Computer Science Ser.: Vol. 930). 1150p. 1995. 158.00 (*3-540-59497-3*) Spr-Verlag.

Mira, K. K. Police Administration in Ancient India. (C). 1987. 20.00 (*81-7099-005-X*, Pub. by Mittal Pubs Dist) S Asia.

Mira, Mary P., et al. Traumatic Brain Injury in Children & Adolescents: A Sourcebook for Teachers & Other School Personnel. LC 92-3454. 152p. (Orig.). 1992. pap. text 21.00 (*0-89079-531-2*, 4037) PRO-ED.

Mira, Mary P., jt. auth. see Tyler, Janet S.

Mira, Thomas. Speak Smart. 1997. pap. 10.00 (*0-679-77868-3*) Random.

Mirabal, Robert. Skeleton of a Bridge. 116p. (Orig.). 1994. pap. 10.00 (*1-883968-02-X*) Blinking Yellow.

Mirabeau, Honore G. Discours. (FRE.). 1973. pap. 10.95 (*0-7859-4005-7*) Fr & Eur.

— Oeuvres de Mirabeau, 8 vols. LC 79-172736. reprint ed. 160.00 (*0-404-07360-3*) AMS Pr.

Mirabeau, Octave. Journal d'une Femme de Chambre. unabridged ed. (FRE.). pap. 7.95 (*2-87714-167-5*, Pub. by Bookking Intl) Distribks Inc.

Mirabeau, Roch L. Lunging at Life's Problems. LC 97-90796. 61p. 1998. pap. 8.95 (*0-533-12476-X*) Vantage.

Mirabella, Francis M. Internal Reflection Spectroscopy: Methods & Techniques. LC 92-26050. (Practical Spectroscopy Ser.: Vol. 15). (Illus.). 384p. 1992. text 199.00 (*0-8247-8730-7*) Dekker.

— Modern Techniques in Applied Molecular Spectroscopy. LC 97-13437. (Techniques in Analytical Chemistry Ser.). 409p. 1998. 79.95 (*0-471-12359-5*, Wiley-Interscience) Wiley.

Mirabella, Grace. Tiffany. (Illus.). 80p. 1997. 18.95 (*0-7893-0119-9*, Pub. by Universe) St Martin.

Mirabella, M. Bella, jt. ed. see Davis, Lennard J.

Mirabelli, Cesare, et al. Winfried Schulz In Memoriam: Schriften Aus Kanonistik Und Staatskirchenrecht. (Illus.). XLIV, 816p. 1998. 113.95 (*3-631-33073-1*) P Lang Pubng.

Mirabelli, Eugene. The Language Nobody Speaks. LC 99-60139. 144p. 1999. 20.00 (*0-935891-02-1*) Spring Harbor.

— The Language Nobody Speaks: A Novel. LC 99-60139. 139p. 1999. pap. 13.00 (*0-935891-03-X*) Spring Harbor.

— The World at Noon. LC 95-182060. 386p. 1994. pap. 13.00 (*1-55071-000-1*) Guernica Editions.

Mirabello, Mark L. The Odin Brotherhood: A Non-Fiction Account of Contact with an Ancient Brotherhood. 1992. pap. text 9.95 (*1-55818-198-9*, Sure Fire) Holmes Pub.

Mirabile, Lisa, ed. International Directory of Company Histories, Vol. 2. 784p. 1990. 161.00 (*1-55862-012-5*) St James Pr.

Mirabile, M. Analytical & Experimental Fracture Mechanics. Sih, G. C., ed. 970p. (C). 1981. text 278.00 (*90-286-0890-7*) Kluwer Academic.

Mirabito, Michael M. & Morgenstern, Barbara L. The New Communications Technologies. 3rd ed. LC 97-8134. 304p. 1997. pap. text 34.95 (*0-240-80258-6*, Focal) Buttrwrth-Heinemann.

***Mirabito, Michael M. A. & Morgenstern, Barbara L.** New Communications Technologies. 4th ed. (Illus.). 304p. 2000. pap. 32.95 (*0-240-80429-5*, Focal) Buttrwrth-Heinemann.

Mirable, Lisa. The Berlin Wall. (Turning Points in World History Ser.). (Illus.). 64p. (YA). (gr. 7 up). 1991. pap. 7.95 (*0-382-24140-1*); lib. bdg. 14.95 (*0-382-24133-9*) Silver Burdett Pr.

Mirachandani, G. G. Massive Mandate for Rajiv Gandhi. 1985. 24.95 (*0-318-36588-X*) Asia Bk Corp.

Miracle, Andrew W., Jr. & Rees, C. Roger. Lessons of the Locker Room: The Myth of School Sports. LC 93-48666. 243p. (C). 1994. 26.95 (*0-87975-879-1*) Prometheus Bks.

Miracle, Andrew W., jt. auth. see Suggs, David N.

Miracle, Andrew W., jt. ed. see Reese, C. Roger.

Miracle, Berniece B. & Miracle, Mona R. My Sister Marilyn: A Memoir of Marilyn Monroe. LC 94-8652. 232p. 1994. 19.95 (*1-56512-070-1*) Algonquin Bks.

— My Sister Marilyn: A Memoir of Marilyn Monroe. (Illus.). 256p. 1995. pap. 12.00 (*1-57297-026-X*) Blvd Books.

Miracle, D., et al, eds. Intermetallic Matrix Composites II. (Materials Research Society Symposium Proceedings Ser.: Vol. 273). 450p. 1992. text 30.00 (*1-55899-168-9*) Materials Res.

Miracle Distribution Center Staff. An Introduction to "A Course in Miracles" 53p. (Orig.). 1987. pap. 2.95 (*0-9618309-0-5*) Miracle Dist.

***Miracle, Louise & Miracle, Rick.** Trolleys & Squibs: A Golfer's Guide to Irish Links. LC 00-28291. (Illus.). 272p. 2000. pap. 24.95 (*0-7649-1336-0*) Pomegranate Calif.

Miracle, Marvin P. Maize in Tropical Africa. LC 66-11805. (Illus.). 348p. 1966. reprint ed. pap. 107.90 (*0-7837-9789-3*, 206051800005) Bks Demand.

Miracle, Mona R., jt. auth. see Miracle, Berniece B.

Miracle, Preston T. & Milner, Nicki, eds. Consuming Passions & Patterns of Consumption. 271p. 1999. 72.00 (*0-9519420-8-5*, Pub. by McDonald Inst) David Brown.

Miracle, Rick, jt. auth. see Miracle, Louise.

Miracle, Vickie A., jt. auth. see Basham, Kimberley A.

Miraglia, Francisco, jt. auth. see Dickmann, M. A.

Miraglia, Luigi. Comparative Legal Philosophies Applied to Legal Institutions. 1977. lib. bdg. 59.95 (*0-8490-1653-3*) Gordon Pr.

— Comparative Legal Philosophy: Applied to Legal Institutions. (Modern Legal Philosophy Ser.: Vol. 3). xl, 793p. 1998. reprint ed. 208.00 (*1-56169-382-0*) Gaunt.

— Comparative Legal Philosophy: Applied to Legal Institutions. Lisle, John, tr. from ITA. (Modern Legal Philosophy Ser.: Vol. 3). xl, 793p. 1969. reprint ed. 42.50 (*0-8377-2427-9*, Rothman) W S Hein.

Miraglia, M., et al, eds. Mycotoxins & Phycotoxins: Developments in Chemistry, Toxicology & Food Safety. LC 98-70629. 620p. 1998. 175.00 (*1-880293-09-9*) Alaken.

Mirajanian, Laurie. Greater Philadelphia Orphans Court Rules. (Orig.). 1997. write for info. (*1-57786-081-0*) Legal Communs.

Mirak, M. L., jt. auth. see Calasso, M. G.

Mirak, Robert. Torn Between Two Lands: Armenians in America, 1890 to World War I. (Armenian Texts & Studies: No. 7). (Illus.). 370p. 1984. reprint ed. pap. 12.95 (*0-674-89541-X*) HUP.

Mirakhor, Abbas, jt. auth. see Iqbal, Zubair.

Mirakhor, Abbas, jt. ed. see Khan, Muhsin S.

Mirakove, Carole, ed. see Torres, Edwin.

Miraldi, Paul W. Uniforms & Equipment of U. S. Army Infantry, LRRPS & Rangers in Vietnam, 1965-1971. (Illus.). 208p. 1999. 59.95 (*0-7643-0958-7*) Schiffer.

***Miraldi, Paul W.** Uniforms & Equipment of US Military Advisors in Vietnam. (Illus.). 256p. 2000. 59.95 (*0-7643-1183-2*) Schiffer.

Miraldi, Robert. Muckraking & Objectivity: Journalism's Colliding Traditions, 18. LC 89-26010. (Contributions to the Study of Mass Media & Communications Ser.: No. 18). 184p. 1990. 52.95 (*0-313-27298-0*, MMQ/, Greenwood Pr) Greenwood.

***Miraldi, Robert, ed.** The Muckrakers: Evangelical Crusaders. LC 00-25129. 208p. 2000. 63.00 (*0-275-96915-0*, C6915, Praeger Pubs) Greenwood.

Miralejos, Carlos. Rabid Beasts. LC 93-61697. 216p. (Orig.). 1994. pap. 14.95 (*0-9625266-3-0*) Outer Space Pr.

— Texas, 2077: A Futuristic Novel. LC 98-65817. 220p. 1998. 20.95 (*0-9625266-4-9*, 97F002) Outer Space Pr.

Miralles, Enric. Enric Miralles: 1975-1995. LC 96-34503. (Illus.). 272p. 1996. pap. 40.00 (*1-885254-43-1*, Pub. by Monacelli Pr) Penguin Putnam.

Miralles, Francesc. Llorens Artigas: Catalogo de Obra. (Grandes Monografias). (ENG & SPA., Illus.). 432p. 1993. 600.00 (*84-343-0701-4*) Elliots Bks.

Miralles, Francesc & Alzueta, Miquel. Alvar. (ENG, FRE & JPN., Illus.). 359p. 1993. 200.00 (*0-9636243-0-X*) E Newman.

Miralles, Francesc, jt. auth. see Fontbona, Francesc.

Miralles, Maria A. A Matter of Life & Death: Health-Seeking Behavior of Guatemalan Refugees in South Florida. LC 88-36497. (Immigrant Communities & Ethnic Minorities in the U. S. & Canada Ser.: No. 52). 1989. 42.50 (*0-404-19462-1*) AMS Pr.

Mirambel, Andre. Petit Dictionnaire Francais-Grec Moderne et Grec Moderne-Francais: Small Modern Greek - French, French - Modern Greek Dictionary. (FRE & GRE.). 486p. 1969. 49.95 (*0-8288-6610-4*, M-6413) Fr & Eur.

Mirambell, Lorena, ed. Homenaje a Jose Luis Lorenzo. 379p. 1989. pap. 14.00 (*968-6068-61-9*, IN027) UPLAAP.

Miramontes, David J. How to Deal with Sexual Harassment. LC 85-117560. 110p. (Orig.). 1982. pap. text 19.95 (*0-934913-00-5*) Network CA Comm.

Miramontes, Ofelia, et al, eds. Restructuring Schools for Linguistic Diversity: Linking Decision Making to Effective Programs. LC 96-40396. (Language & Literacy Ser.). 320p. (C). 1997. text 52.00 (*0-8077-3604-X*); pap. text 23.95 (*0-8077-3603-1*) Tchrs Coll.

Miramontes, Ofelia, jt. auth. see Howe, Kenneth R.

Mirams, Mike & McElherton, Paul. Gaining & Maintaining New International Quality Standards. (Financial Times Management Ser.). 224p. 1995. pap. 82.50 (*0-273-61777-X*, Pub. by Pitman Pub) Trans-Atl Phila.

Miran-Khan, Karim, jt. ed. see Brukner, Peter.

Mirand, Edwin A. Legacy & History of Roswell Park Cancer Institute, 1898-1998. LC 98-18365. 216p. 1998. 35.00 (*1-57864-036-9*) Donning Co.

***Miranda.** Composing Music with Computers. (Music Technology Ser.). 240p. 2000. pap. 69.95 (*0-240-51567-6*, Focal) Buttrwrth-Heinemann.

Miranda, Altina. Love on an Animal Farm: A Story for Children. (Illus.). 32p. (Orig.). (J). 1993. pap. 8.95 (*0-86534-202-4*) Sunstone Pr.

Miranda, Anne. Baby-Sit, Vol. 1. (J). (ps). 1990. 9.95 (*0-316-57454-6*, Joy St Bks) Little.

***Miranda, Anne.** Beep! Beep! (Illus.). 32p. (YA). (ps up). 2000. pap. 7.95 (*1-890515-20-5*, Pub. by Turtle Bks) Publishers Group.

Miranda, Anne. Beep! Beep! A Vehicle Imagination Book. (Illus.). 32p. (J). (ps up). 1999. 15.95 (*1-890515-14-0*, Pub. by Turtle Bks) Publishers Group.

— The Elephant at the Waldorf. LC 93-33804. (Illus.). 32p. (J). (gr. k-3). 1997. 14.95 (*0-8167-3452-6*) BrdgeWater.

— The Elephant at the Waldorf. LC 93-33804. (Illus.). 32p. (J). (gr. k-3). 1996. pap. 5.95 (*0-8167-3453-4*, Troll Medallion) Troll Communs.

— Glad Monster, Sad Monster: A Book about Feelings. LC 96-45413. (Illus.). 32p. (J). (gr. k-3). 1997. 14.95 (*0-316-57395-7*) Little.

***Miranda, Anne.** Monster Math. LC 98-12933. 32p. (J). (ps-3). 1999. 16.00 (*0-15-201835-2*, Harcourt Child Bks) Harcourt.

Miranda, Anne. Night Songs. LC 92-251. (Illus.). 32p. (J). (ps-1). 1993. lib. bdg. 13.95 (*0-02-767250-6*, Bradbury S&S) S&S Childrens.

— Pignic Vol. 1: An Alphabet Book in Rhyme. LC 95-78075. (Illus.). 32p. (J). (gr. k-3). 1996. 14.95 (*1-56397-558-0*) Boyds Mills Pr.

— To Market, to Market. LC 95-26326. (J). (ps-3). 1997. 16.00 (*0-15-201904-9*) Harcourt.

— To Market, to Market. LC 95-26326. (Illus.). 36p. (J). (ps-3). 1997. 16.00 (*0-15-200035-6*) Harcourt.

***Miranda, Anne.** Vroom, Chugga, Vroom-Vroom. (Illus.). 40p. (YA). (ps up). 2000. pap. 7.95 (*1-890515-19-1*, Pub. by Turtle Bks) Publishers Group.

Miranda, Anne. Vroom, Chugga, Vroom-Vroom: A Number Identification Book. LC 97-41714. (Illus.). 40p. (YA). (ps up). 1998. 15.95 (*1-890515-07-8*, Pub. by Turtle Bks) Publishers Group.

Miranda, Anne M. Does a Mouse Have a House? LC 93-20587. (Illus.). 32p. (J). (ps-1). 1994. mass mkt. 14.95 (*0-02-767251-4*, Mac Bks Young Read) S&S Childrens.

Miranda, C. Partial Differential Equations of Elliptic Type. 2nd rev. ed. LC 71-75930. (Ergebnisse der Mathematik und Ihrer Grenzgebiete Ser.: Vol. 2). 1970. 75.95 (*0-387-04804-9*) Spr-Verlag.

Miranda, Carmen, tr. see Gilmer, Chris & Milam, June M.

Miranda, Carmen, tr. see Milam, June M.

Miranda, Carmen, tr. see Milan, June M., et al.

Miranda, D. R. & Langrehr, D., eds. The ICU -- A Cost Benefit Analysis. 236p. 1987. 148.25 (*0-444-80823-X*, Excerpta Medica) Elsevier.

Miranda, D. Reis. Organisation & Management of Intensive Care: A Prospective Study in 12 European Countries. Vincent, J. L. et al, eds. LC 97-13204. (Update in Intensive Care & Emergency Medicine Ser.: Vol. 29). (Illus.). 220p. 1998. 105.00 (*3-540-62581-X*) Spr-Verlag.

Miranda, D. Reis, et al, eds. Management of Intensive Care. (Developments in Critical Care, Medicine, & Anesthesiology Ser.). (C). 1990. text 171.00 (*0-7923-0754-2*) Kluwer Academic.

Miranda, David, jt. auth. see Hoff, Pablo.

Miranda, Deborah A. Indian Cartogarphy. 1998. pap. text 12.95 (*0-912678-99-2*) Greenfld Rev Lit.

Miranda, Eduardo. Computer Sound Synthesis for the Electronic Musician. LC 98-23416. (Illus.). 240p. 1998. pap. text 49.95 (*0-240-51517-X*, Newnes) Buttrwrth-Heinemann.

***Miranda, Eduardo Reck, ed.** Readings in Music & Artificial Intelligence. (Contemporary Music Studies Ser.: Vol. 20). (Illus.). 278p. 1999. text 51.00 (*90-5755-094-6*, Harwood Acad Pubs) Gordon & Breach.

Miranda, Elizabeth, jt. ed. see Brothers, Theresa.

Miranda, Eve. Fragrant Flowers of the South. LC 91-19270. (Illus.). 126p. 1991. 19.95 (*1-56164-000-X*); pap. 14.95 (*1-56164-002-6*) Pineapple Pr.

Miranda, Evelina O. & Magsino, Romula, eds. Teaching, Schools & Society. 444p. 1990. pap. 39.95 (*1-85000-688-1*, Falmer Pr) Taylor & Francis.

Miranda, Fausto C. & Lacy, John C. Mining Law & Regulations of Mexico, 1992-1993. 263p. 1993. pap., student ed. 125.00 incl. disk (*0-929047-37-0*, MEX2) Rocky Mtn Mineral Law Found.

Miranda, Felipe B., ed. Democratization: Philippine Perspectives. LC 97-946613. 372p. (C). 1999. pap. text 30.00 (*971-542-138-5*, Pub. by U of Philippines Pr) UH Pr.

Miranda, Francisco De, see De Miranda, Francisco.

Miranda, Francisco De Sa De, see De Sa De Miranda, Francisco.

***Miranda, Frank H.** Arcangel, Nathaniel the Fourth. large type ed. 351p. (gr. 8 up). 1999. 29.00i (*0-9673649-0-6*, PBMGP-01) PBM Global.

— Arcangel, Nathaniel the Fourth. large type ed. LC 99-66280. 351p. (YA). 1999. pap. 15.00i (*0-9673649-1-4*, PBMGP-01) PBM Global.

Miranda, Gary. Following a River: Portland's Congregation Neveh Shalom 1869-1989. (Illus.). 170p. 1989. 15.00 (*0-685-29868-X*) Congregation Neveh Shalom.

***Miranda, Gary & Read, Rick.** Splendid Audacity: The Story of Pacific University. LC 99-53530. 143p. 2000. write for info. (*0-935503-30-7*) Document Bk.

Miranda, Gary, tr. see Rilke, Rainer Maria.

Miranda, Guillermo Cobos. Hipnosis, Curso de Hipnologia. (SPA.). 1997. pap. text 9.98 (*968-409-213-X*) Edamex.

Miranda, J. & Mercado, P. A Night in Terror Tower. (Goosebumps Ser.). (Illus.). 144p. 1996. 6.98 incl. audio (*0-7643-0086-5*) Schiffer.

Miranda, James. Wasting My Life. Crowder, R., ed. LC 93-72729. (Illus.). 132p. (C). 1993. 21.95 (*0-935763-02-3*); pap. 9.95 (*0-935763-03-1*) Chester Hse Pubs.

Miranda, Jesse. Liderazgo y Amistad. (SPA.). 1998. pap. 6.99 (*0-8297-0373-X*) Vida Pubs.

Miranda, Jose P. Being & the Messiah: The Message of St. John. LC 77-5388. Orig. Title: El Ser y el Mesias. 255p. (Orig.). reprint ed. pap. 79.10 (*0-8357-8816-4*, 203346700086) Bks Demand.

— Communism in the Bible. Barr, Robert R., tr. from SPA. LC 81-16936. Orig. Title: Comunismo En la Biblia. 95p. (Orig.). reprint ed. pap. 30.00 (*0-7837-5500-7*, 204527000005) Bks Demand.

— Marx Against the Marxists: The Christian Humanism of Karl Marx. Drury, John, tr. from SPA. LC 80-14415. Orig. Title: El Christianism de Marx. 332p. (Orig.). reprint ed. pap. 103.00 (*0-7837-5517-1*, 204528700005) Bks Demand.

— Marx & the Bible: A Critique of the Philosophy of Oppression. Eagleson, John, tr. LC 73-89053. Orig. Title: Marx y la Biblia: Critica a la filosofia de la oppresion. 360p. (Orig.). 1974. reprint ed. pap. 111.60 (*0-7837-9817-2*, 206054600005) Bks Demand.

Miranda, Julia & Lopez, Maria J. Entrelazos. LC 91-73978. (Coleccion Caniqui). (SPA.). 220p. (Orig.). 1992. pap. 19.95 (*0-89729-616-8*) Ediciones.

Miranda, L. E., ed. Multidimensional Approaches to Reservoir Fisheries Management. LC 96-78695. (Symposium Ser.: Vol. 16). 463p. 1996. 92.00 (*0-913235-92-X*, 540.16) Am Fisheries Soc.

Miranda, M., et al, eds. Calculus of Variations & Partial Differential Equations. (Lecture Notes in Mathematics Ser.: Vol. 1340). x, 301p. 1988. pap. 28.60 (*0-685-21872-4*) Spr-Verlag.

Miranda, Maio, tr. see Kaplan, Stuart R.

Miranda, Malvin. A History of Hispanics in Southern Nevada. LC 97-22015. (History & Humanities Ser.). (Illus.). 240p. 1997. 29.95 (*0-87417-291-8*) U of Nev Pr.

Miranda, Manuel R. Forgotten Portuguese. LC 97-92675. 1997. 29.95 (*0-9658927-0-0*) Portuguese-American.

Miranda, Manuel R., jt. ed. see Markides, Kyriakos S.

***Miranda, Marta, et al.** All That Glitters Is Not Gold: Balancing Conservation & Development in Venezuela's Frontier Forests. LC 98-84647. 60p. 1998. pap. 20.00 (*1-56973-251-5*) World Resources Inst.

— All That Glitters Is Not Gold: Balancing Conservation & Development in Venezuela's Frontier Forests. Watson, Burton, tr. (SPA.). 60p. 1998. pap. 20.00 (*1-56973-252-3*) World Resources Inst.

Miranda, Prashant. Avatar & Incarnation: A Comparative Analysis. 1990. 19.50 (*81-85151-42-3*, Pub. by Harman Pub Hse) S Asia.

Miranda, Rafael C. Puerto Rico: Independence Is a Necessity. 3.00 (*0-87348-896-2*) Pathfinder NY.

Miranda, Rick. Algebraic Curves & Riemann Surfaces. LC 95-1947. (Graduate Studies in Mathematics: Vol. 5). 390p. 1995. text 44.00 (*0-8218-0268-2*, GSM/5) Am Math.

***Miranda, Roberto Fernandez.** Mis Relaciones con el General Batista. LC 99-68366. (Coleccion Cuba y sus Jueces). (SPA., Illus.). 223p. 1999. pap. 19.95 (*0-89729-910-8*) Ediciones.

Miranda, Robin. Magic Drum: Stories from Africa's Savannah, Sea, & Skies. LC 95-981891. 1995. 12.95 (*9966-884-05-X*) Nocturnal Sun.

Miranda, Roger, jt. auth. see Ratliff, William E.

Miranda, Roland, jt. auth. see Salas, Marilyn C.

Miranda, Rosalind, ed. The Book of Cruising: Cruising Around the World West to East, Vol. 2. (Illus.). 464p. (Orig.). 1993. pap. text 29.95 (*1-880465-03-5*) Chiodi Advert.

— The Book of Cruising: Introduction to Cruising, Vol. 1. (Illus.). 148p. (Orig.). 1991. pap. text 12.95 (*1-880465-02-7*) Chiodi Advert.

Miranda, Tom, jt. auth. see Barringer, Bernie.

M

Miranda, Veronica. Esa Antigua Constancia: That Ancient Devotion. McEwan, Angela, tr. LC 93-78776. (Coleccion Luz Bilingue Ser.). (ENG & SPA., Illus.). 80p. 1993. pap. 12.50 (*0-9634009-1-6*) Luz Bilingual.
— Estudio Erotico: Erotic Study. McEwan, Angela, tr. LC 95-80207. (Coleccion Luz Bilingue Ser.). (Illus.). 70p. (Orig.). 1996. pap. 10.50 (*0-9634009-3-2*) Luz Bilingual.
Miranda, Veronica, ed. & tr. see Bemitez, Luis.
Miranda, Victoria & Fenini, Camilo. Al Filo de un Cansancio Apatrida: Poemas; On the Edge of a Countryless Weariness: Poems. Fogel, Daniel et al, trs. LC 86-21022. (ENG & SPA.). 56p. (Orig.). 1986. pap. 5.00 (*0-910383-24-3*) Ism Pr.
Mirande, Alfredo. The Chicano Experience: An Alternative Perspective. LC 84-40292. 281p. (C). 1985. pap. text 14.00 (*0-268-00749-7*) U of Notre Dame Pr.
— Gringo Justice. LC 86-40580. 272p. 1987. text 34.50 (*0-268-01012-9*) U of Notre Dame Pr.
— Gringo Justice. LC 86-40580. 261p. (C). 1990. pap. text 16.50 (*0-268-01023-4*) U of Notre Dame Pr.
— Hombres Y Machos: Masculinity & Latino Culture. 208p. (C). 1997. 69.00 (*0-8133-3196-X*, Pub. by Westview) HarpC.
— Hombres y Machos: Masculinity & Latino Culture. 208p. (C). 1997. pap. text 22.00 (*0-8133-3197-8*, Pub. by Westview) HarpC.
Mirande, Alfredo & Enriquez, Evangelina. La Chicana: The Mexican-American Woman. LC 79-13536. (Illus.). x, 284p. (C). 1981. reprint ed. pap. text 13.95 (*0-226-53160-0*) U Ch Pr.
Mirandola, Pico D. Kabbalistic Conclusions. 1993. pap. 4.95 (*1-55818-232-2*) Holmes Pub.
Mirandola, Pico D. & Francesco, Giovanni. Here Is Coteyned the Lyfe of Joan Picus Erle of Myrandula. More, Thomas, tr. LC 77-7421. (English Experience Ser.: No. 884). 1977. reprint ed. lib. bdg. 35.00 (*90-221-0884-8*) Walter J Johnson.
Mirandola, Pico Della, see Della Mirandola, Pico.
Miranker, Daniel. Treat: A New & Efficient Match Algorithm for AI Production Systems. (Research Notes in Artificial Intelligence Ser.). 140p. 1990. pap. text 34.95 (*0-934613-71-0*) Morgan Kaufmann.
Miranker, Willard L. Numerical Methods for Stiff Equations & Singular Perturbation Problems. (Mathematics & Its Applications Ser.: No. 5). 216p. 1980. text 104.50 (*90-277-1107-0*) Kluwer Academic.
Miranker, Willard L., jt. ed. see Toupin, R. A.
***Miranne, Kristine B. & Young, Alma H., eds.** Gendering the City: Women, Boundaries & Visions of Urban Life. LC 99-47148. 256p. 2000. 65.00 (*0-8476-9450-X*) Rowman.
— Gendering the City: Women, Boundaries & Visions of Urban Life. LC 99-47148. 256p. 2000. pap. 24.95 (*0-8476-9451-8*) Rowman.
Miransky, V. A. Dynamical Symmetry Breaking in Quantum Field Theories. 500p. 1994. text 99.00 (*981-02-1558-4*) World Scientific Pub.
Mirante, Edith T. Burmese Looking Glass: A Human Rights Adventure & a Jungle Revolution. 352p. 1994. pap. 12.00 (*0-87113-570-1*, Atlntc Mnthly) Grove-Atltic.
Miranti, Judith G., jt. auth. see Burke, Mary T.
Miranti, Paul J. Accountancy Comes of Age: The Development of an American Profession, 1886-1940. LC 89-27925. 287p. 1990. pap. 89.00 (*0-608-05207-8*, 206574400001) Bks Demand.
Miranti, Paul J., Jr., ed. Commerce, Accounts, & Finance, 2 vols., Set. LC 10-682929. (New Works in Accounting History). 1106p. 1993. reprint ed. text 30.00 (*0-8153-1214-8*) Garland.
Miranti, Paul J., Jr., jt. auth. see Baskin, Jonathan.
Miranville, Alain, jt. auth. see Temam, Roger.
Miras, Domingo. Las Brujas de Barahona. Serrano, Virtudes, ed. (Nueva Austral Ser.: Vol. 273). (SPA.). 1993. pap. text 24.95 (*84-239-7273-9*) Elliots Bks.
Miras-Portugal, M. T., jt. auth. see Municio, A. M.
Mirasdar, Mangala. The Political Ideas in the Pancamahakavyas. LC 95-910681. xix, 348p. 1995. 29.00 (*81-86339-10-8*, Pub. by Eastern Bk Linkers) Nataraj Bks.
Mirassou, Jean B., et al. The Power of Jude. 64p. (Orig.). 1993. pap. 5.95 (*0-9637572-0-2*) Deux Goudez.
Mirat-Ul-Istalah. Encyclopaedic Dictionary of Medieval India. Ahmad, Tasneem, tr. (C). 1993. 62.00 (*81-85067-86-4*, Pub. by Sundeep Prak) S Asia.
Mirau, Peter, jt. auth. see Bovey, Frank A.
Mirault, Don. Dancing ... for a Living. LC 93-85551. 190p. 1994. pap. 15.95 (*0-9637864-4-X*) Rafter Pub.
— Dancing... For a Living Too: Where Are the Jobs? 200p. 1998. pap. 19.95 (*0-9637864-6-6*) Rafter Pub.
Mirault, Don, ed. see Boling, Bobby.
Mirault, Hugues. La Syntaxe des Proposition Relatives. (Publications Universitaires Europeennes: Vol. 226). 268p. 1997. 49.00 (*3-631-32602-5*) P Lang Pubng.
Miravalle, Mark I. Dogma & the Triumph. 176p. 1998. pap. 6.95 (*1-57918-067-1*, 2013) Queenship Pub.
— Heart of the Message of Medugorje. (Illus.). 144p. 1988. pap. 6.95 (*0-940535-08-4*, UP108) Franciscan U Pr.
— Introduction to Mary: The Heart of Marian Doctrine & Devotion. LC 93-83229. 208p. 1993. pap. 6.95 (*1-882972-06-6*, 3101) Queenship Pub.
— Mary: Coredemptrix Mediatrix Advocate. Pavisich-Ryan, Olga, tr. LC 93-84470. (SPA.). 96p. 1993. pap. 1.00 (*1-882972-12-0*, 2000S) Queenship Pub.
— Mary: Coredemptrix Mediatrix Advocate. Rota, Maria, tr. LC 93-87016. (ITA.). 77p. 1993. pap. 1.00 (*1-882972-16-3*, 20001) Queenship Pub.
— Mary: Coredemptrix Mediatrix Advocate. Hamadi, Salwa, tr. LC 93-87014. (FRE.). 79p. 1993. pap. 1.00 (*1-882972-18-X*, 2000F) Queenship Pub.
— Mary: Coredemptrix Mediatrix Advocate. Hatzel, Garte, tr. LC 93-87013. (GER.). 88p. 1993. pap. 1.00 (*1-882972-19-8*, 2000G) Queenship Pub.
— Mary: Coredemptrix Mediatrix Advocate. Hooker, Bridget, tr. LC 93-87015. (POL.). 79p. 1994. pap. 1.00 (*1-882972-17-1*, 2000P) Queenship Pub.
— Mary, Coredemptrix, Mediatrix Advocate. Hooker, Bridget, tr. LC 94-67388. (RUS.). 80p. 1994. pap. 1.00 (*1-882972-38-4*, 2000R) Queenship Pub.
— Mary, Coredemptrix, Mediatrix, Advocate Theological Foundation Vol. II: Papal, Pneumatological, Ecumenical. 1996. pap. text 19.95 (*1-882972-92-9*) Queenship Pub.
— Medjugorje & the Family: Helping Families to Live the Message. 174p. 1990. pap. 6.95 (*0-940535-33-5*, UP133) Franciscan U Pr.
— The Message of Medjugorje: The Marian Message to the Modern World. LC 86-1588. 168p. 1986. pap. 19.50 (*0-8191-5289-7*) U Pr of Amer.
Miravalle, Mark I., ed. Mary; Coredemptrix, Mediatrix, Advocate Theological Foundations: Towards a Papal Definition? LC 95-68326. 327p. 1995. text 25.00 (*1-882972-58-9*); pap. text 12.00 (*1-882972-57-0*) Queenship Pub.
Miravalle, Mark I., ed. see O'Carroll, Michael, et al.
***Miravete, A.** 3-D Textile Reinforcements in Composite Materials LC 99-28542. 1999. 139.95 (*0-8493-1795-9*) CRC Pr.
— Three-Dimensional Textile Reinforcement for Composite Materials. 200p. 1999. boxed set 153.00 (*1-85573-376-5*) Am Educ Systs.
Miravete, Antonio. Optimization of Composite Structures Design. 256p. 1996. 531.00 incl. disk (*1-85573-208-4*, Pub. by Woodhead Pubng) Am Educ Systs.
Miravete, Antonio, jt. auth. see Reddy, J. N.
Mirbach. Starting Your Own Software Company. 1991. pap. 49.95 (*0-13-845504-X*) P-H.
***Mirbach, T.** Entwurfe Fur eine Soziale Stadt. (Europaische Urbanitat-Politik der Stadte Ser.: Vol. 5).Tr. of Scenarios for a Social City. (GER.). 320p. 1998. text 49.00 (*90-5708-033-8*); pap. text 29.00 (*90-5708-034-6*) Gordon & Breach.
Mirbagheri, Farid. Cyprus & International Peacemaking, 1964-1986. LC 98-168923. 224p. (C). 1998. 60.00 (*0-415-91975-4*) Routledge.
Mirbeau, Octave. Abbe Jules. Simborowski, Nicoletta, tr. from FRE. (Empire of the Senses Ser.). 232p. 1997. pap. 13.99 (*1-873982-37-2*, Pub. by Dedalus) Hippocrene Bks.
— Le Calvaire. Donougher, Christine, tr. from FRE. LC 94-145532. (Dedalus European Classics Ser.). (FRE.). 256p. 1996. pap. 16.95 (*0-7818-0106-0*) Hippocrene Bks.
— Le Calvaire. 2nd ed. Murdoch, Adrian, ed. Donougher, Christine, tr. from FRE. (Decadence Ser.). 223p. 1999. reprint ed. pap. 13.99 (*0-946626-99-5*, Pub. by Dedalus) Hippocrene Bks.
— The Diary of a Chambermaid. 2nd ed. Jarman, Douglas, tr. from FRE. 320p. 1997. reprint ed. pap. 11.99 (*0-946626-82-0*, Pub. by Dedalus) Subterranean Co.
— Pierre Bonnard: Sketches of a Journey. (Illus.). 176p. 1989. 35.00 (*0-85667-364-1*) Sothebys Pubns.
— Sebastien Roch. Costa, Margaret J., ed. Simborowski, Nicoletta, tr. from FRE. (Empire of the Senses Ser.). 322p. 2000. pap. 13.99 (*1-873982-43-7*) Dedalus.
— The Torture Garden. 120p. 2000. pap. 12.99 (*0-9651042-6-5*) Juno Bks.
— The Torture Garden. rev. ed. Stableford, Brian, ed. Richardson, Michael, tr. from FRE. (Empire of the Senses Ser.). 208p. 1997. pap. 11.99 (*1-873982-53-4*, Pub. by Dedalus) Subterranean Co.
Mirbt, C. R. The Study of the Stars: An Introduction. Mitchell, David, ed. (Illus.). 33p. 1997. pap. 7.00 (*0-9623978-5-7*) Assn Waldorf Schls.
Mircevska, Suncica, jt. auth. see Hill, Peter M.
Mirchandani, Dilip. One Way up Wall Street: The Fred Alger Story. LC 99-490605. (Illus.). 496p. 1999. 29.95 (*0-9670128-0-5*) J Charlton.
Mirchandani, G. G. Subverting the Constitution, India. 1977. 12.50 (*0-8364-0030-5*) S Asia.
Mirchandani, Jyoti, jt. auth. see Vaswani, J. P.
Mirchandani, Pitu B. & Francis, Richard L., eds. Discrete Location Theory. 9th ed. LC 89-34350. 576p. 1990. 189.95 (*0-471-89233-5*) Wiley.
Mirchandani, Sonu & Khanna, Raman. Fiber Distributed Data Interface (FDDI) Technology & Applications. LC 92-16778. 384p. 1992. 64.99 (*0-471-55896-6*) Wiley.
Mircos, Gus & DeSantis, Gennaro. Gus's Cabin Kitchen: Healthy Cooking Inspired by Colorado's Great Outdoors. (Illus.). 168p. (Orig.). 1997. pap. 15.95 (*0-86541-038-0*) Filter.
Mircovich, Rhonda. Palatable Pantries & Lavish Larders. LC 92-30475. (Illus.). 208p. 1993. pap. 14.95 (*0-942963-33-4*) Distinctive Pub.
Mire, Betty. T-Pierre Frog & T-Felix Frog Go to School. LC 93-74275. (Illus.). 32p. (Orig.). (J). (gr. 1-3). 1994. lib. bdg. 6.95 (*0-9639378-0-4*) Cajun Bay Pr.
— Take God's Hand. 64p. 1990. per. write for info. (*0-8187-0128-5*) Harlo Press.
Mire-Sluis, Anthony & Thorpe, Robin, eds. Cytokines. (Handbook of Immunopharmacology Ser.). (Illus.). 544p. (C). 1998. boxed set 99.95 (*0-12-498340-5*) Acad Pr.
Mire-SLuis, T., jt. ed. see Brown, F.
Mirecki, Paul, jt. auth. see Hedrick, Charles W.
Mirecki, Paul A. Understanding the Bible: Workbook. 144p. (C). 1993. spiral bd. 27.95 (*0-8403-9247-8*) Kendall-Hunt.
Mirecki, Paul A., jt. auth. see BeDuhn, Jason.
Mirecki, Paul A., jt. ed. see Meyer, Marvin.
Mirel, Elizabeth P. Plum Crazy, a Book about Beach Plums. (Illus.). 160p. 1986. reprint ed. pap. 6.95 (*0-940160-34-X*) Parnassus Imprints.
Mirel, James L. & Werth, Karen Bonnell. Stepping Stones to Jewish Spiritual Living: Walking the Path Morning, Noon & Night. LC 98-10939. 240p. 1998. 21.95 (*1-58023-003-2*) Jewish Lights.
Mirel, James L., jt. auth. see Bonnell Werth, Karen.
Mirel, Jeffery, jt. auth. see Angus, David.
***Mirel, Jeffrey.** Rise & Fall of an Urban School System: Detroit, 1907-1981. 2nd ed. LC 99-31492. (Ann Arbor Paperbacks Ser.). 520p. 1999. pap. text 24.95 (*0-472-08649-9*, 08649) U of Mich Pr.
Mirel, Jeffrey, jt. auth. see Angus, David L.
Mirelli, V., jt. ed. see Baras, J. S.
Mirelman, Victor A. Jewish Buenos Aires, 1890-1930: In Search of an Identity. LC 89-16739. (Illus.). 308p. reprint ed. pap. 95.50 (*0-608-10519-8*, 205443000009) Bks Demand.
Mirels, Herbert, jt. ed. see Weary, Gifford.
Mirenda, Pat, jt. auth. see Beukelman, David R.
Mirengoff, William, et al. Ceta: Accomplishments, Problems, Solutions. LC 82-2856. 321p. 1982. pap. 7.00 (*0-911558-96-9*) W E Upjohn.
Mirenkov, Nikolay. Parallel Computing Technologies. 450p. (C). 1991. text 118.00 (*981-02-0698-4*) World Scientific Pub.
Mirer, Thad W. Economic Statistics & Econometrics. 3rd ed. (Illus.). 464p. 1994. 67.60 (*0-02-381831-X*, Macmillan Coll) P-H.
Mirfeld, John. Sinonoma Bartholomei. Mowat, J. L., ed. (Anecdota Oxoniensia Ser.: No. 1). 1988. reprint ed. 37.50 (*0-404-63951-8*) AMS Pr.
Mirfield, Peter. Silence, Confessions & Improperly Obtained Evidence. LC 97-28130. (Oxford Monographs on Criminal Law & Justice). 420p. 1998. text 85.00 (*0-19-826269-8*) OUP.
Mirgon, Barbara B., jt. auth. see Avillion, Adrianne E.
Mirgon, John, et al. Ornamental Water Gardening: How & What to Grow. Weinstein, Gayle, ed. (Illus.). 33p. (Orig.). 1991. pap. 7.95 (*0-9629743-0-7*) Shereth Grp.
Mirhady, David C., jt. ed. see Fortenbaugh, William W.
Mirhady, David C., tr. see Isocrates Staff.
Mirho, Charles A. & Terrisse, Andre. Communications Programming for Windows 95: The Developer's Guide to TAPI & MAPI in Windows 95. (Programming Ser.). 320p. 1996. 39.95 incl. disk (*1-55615-668-5*) Microsoft.
Miriam. Love Is Enough. 1962. 6.50 (*0-8159-6112-X*) Devin.
Miriam-Goldberg, Caryn. Sandra Cisneros: Latina Writer & Activist. LC 98-20828. (Hispanic Biographies Ser.). (Illus.). 112p. (YA). (gr. 6 up). 1998. lib. bdg. 20.95 (*0-7660-1045-7*) Enslow Pubs.
Miriani, Patricia, ed. see Nakajima, Caroline.
Miriani, Patricia, ed. see Shepherd, Michael.
Miriani, Patricia, ed. see Williams, Diane.
Miriani, Patricia L., ed. see Thomas, Jennifer.
Mirical, Martin J. Seventeen Little Miricals: Fun & Success in a Family with 17 Children! LC 91-67483. (Illus.). 228p. (Orig.). 1992. pap. 9.95 (*0-9631593-6-4*) Wydaily Pub.
Mirich, George. Car Leasing from the Inside Out. 1998. pap. text 12.00 (*0-9658059-0-5*) Open Door Pr CO.
Mirick, Benjamin L. & Whittier, John Greenleaf. History of Haverhill, Massachusetts. 228p. Date not set. reprint ed. text 20.00 (*1-878651-10-2*) HPL Pr.
— The History of Haverhill, Massachusetts. 239p. 1991. reprint ed. pap. 23.00 (*1-55613-497-5*) Heritage Bk.
Mirick, Benjamin L., jt. auth. see Saltonstall, Leverett.
Mirikitani, Janice. Shedding Silence. 176p. 1995. pap. 9.95 (*0-89087-493-X*) Celestial Arts.
— We the Dangerous. 176p. 1995. pap. 12.95 (*0-89087-767-X*) Celestial Arts.
Mirikitani, Janice, et al, intros. Watch Out! We're Talking: Speaking Out about Incest & Abuse. 206p. (Orig.). 1993. pap. 12.95 (*0-9622574-2-7*) Glide Word.
Mirikitani, Janice, jt. ed. see Williams, Cecil.
Mirikitani, Leatrice T. Speaking Kapampangan. McKaughan, Howard P., ed. LC 70-152468. (PALI Language Texts Philippines Ser.). 1011p. (C). reprint ed. 200.00 (*0-8357-9827-5*, 201721900004) Bks Demand.
Mirilyubov, Hope B. Tribunal of the Heart. LC 95-91042. 1996. 19.95 (*0-533-11829-8*) Vantage.
Mirimanov, R. G. Multilingual Electronics Dictionary. (DUT, ENG, FRE, GER & RUS.). 544p. 1986. 150.00 (*0-8288-0313-7*, F1927) Fr & Eur.
Mirimanov, R. G., et al, eds. Dictionary of Electronics: English, German, French, Dutch, Russian. (DUT, ENG, FRE, GER & RUS.). 1985. text 160.00 (*90-201-1788-2*) Kluwer Academic.
Mirin, Steven M., ed. Substance Abuse & Psychopathology. LC 84-6291. (Clinical Insights Ser.). 167p. reprint ed. pap. 51.80 (*0-8357-7819-3*, 203619100002) Bks Demand.
Mirin, Steven M., jt. auth. see Weiss, Roger D.
Miringoff, Lee M. & Carvalho, Barbara L. The Cuomo Factor: Assessing the Political Appeal of New York's Governor. LC 86-62229. 126p. (Orig.). 1987. pap. 12.95 (*0-939319-00-4*) Marist Inst.
Miringoff, Marc L. & Miringoff, Marque-Luisa. The Social Health of the Nation: How America Is Really Doing. (Illus.). 272p. (C). 1999. pap. text 19.95 (*0-19-513349-8*) OUP.
Miringoff, Marc L., et al. The Social Health of the Nation: How America Is Really Doing. LC 99-230995. (Illus.). 245p. 1999. 25.00 (*0-19-513348-X*) OUP.
Miringoff, Marque-Luisa. The Social Costs of Genetic Welfare. 200p. (C). 1991. text 35.00 (*0-8135-1706-0*); pap. text 15.00 (*0-8135-1707-9*) Rutgers U Pr.
Miringoff, Marque-Luisa, jt. auth. see Miringoff, Marc L.
Miriszlai, E. Hearing Impairment & the Labyrinthine Perilymphatic System. 134p. (C). 1983. 30.00 (*963-05-3153-4*) St Mut.
Mirka, Harold, ed. see Hayes, L. Raymond & Goethals, Gilbert H.
Mirkhah, Patricia A. Christmas in Holland. (J). 1998. 6.95 (*0-533-12589-8*) Vantage.
Mirkin, B. G., et al. Mathematical Hierarchies & Biology: DIMACS Workshop, November 13-15, 1996. LC 97-26706. (DIMACS Series in Discrete Mathematics & Theoretical Computer Science). 388p. 1997. text 79.00 (*0-8218-0762-5*) Am Math.
Mirkin, B. G., tr. see Rodin, S. N.
Mirkin, Boris G. Mathematical Classification & Clustering. LC 96-28669. (Nonconvex Optimization & Its Applications Ser.). 448p. (C). 1996. text 228.00 (*0-7923-4159-7*) Kluwer Academic.
Mirkin, Gabe. Consultation with Your Sports Doctor. (Orig.). 1985. pap. 6.95 (*0-671-50491-6*) PB.
— Fat Free, Flavor Full: Dr. Gabe Mirkin's Guide to Losing Weight & Gaining Life. 336p. 1995. 21.95 (*0-316-57440-6*) Little.
— The 20 Gram Diet: Fat Counter. LC 94-77443. 96p. (Orig.). 1994. pap. text 4.99 (*0-9642386-0-8*) Linx Corp.
— Twenty Gram Diet Seven-Day Jump Start. 1996. pap. text 6.99 (*0-9642386-4-0*) Linx Corp.
***Mirkin, Gabe.** 20/30 Fat & Fiber Diet Plan. 1999. audio 12.00 (*0-694-52102-7*) HarperAudio.
— The 20/30 Fat & Fiber Diet Plan: The Weight-Reducing, Health-Promoting Nutrition System for Life, 304p. 2000. pap. 14.00 (*0-06-273650-7*) HarpC.
Mirkin, Gabe & Hoffman, Marshall. The Sportsmedicine Book. LC 78-14908. 1978. 24.95 (*0-316-57434-1*, Little Brwn Med Div) Lppncott W & W.
Mirkin, Gabe, jt. ed. see Shangold, Mona M.
Mirkin, Marsha Pravder, ed. Women in Context: Toward a Feminist Reconstruction of Psychotherapy. LC 94-5534. 502p. 1994. lib. bdg. 52.00 (*0-89862-095-3*, C2095) Guilford Pubns.
Mirkin, Stanford M. When Did It Happen? A Noted Research's Almanac of Yesterdays. LC 99-23932. 1999. 38.00 (*0-7808-0317-5*) Omnigraphics Inc.
Mirko, Vincent W. Grandpa Says. 300p. (Orig.). (YA). (gr. 10). 1989. pap. 25.00 (*0-9623257-0-8*) Millsmont Pub.
***Mirkov Publication Staff.** Abandoned: A Jewish Wife's True Story. 1999. pap. text 9.95 (*0-9648508-3-4*) Mirkov Pubns.
Mirkovic, Miroslava C. The Later Roman Colonate & Freedom. LC 97-907. (Transactions Ser.: Vol. 87, Pt.2). 1997. pap. 18.00 (*0-87169-872-2*) Am Philos.
Mirkovich, Thomas R. & Cowgill, Allison A. Casino Gaming in the United States: A Research Guide. LC 96-3186. 432p. 1996. 48.00 (*0-8108-3230-5*) Scarecrow.
Mirkowicz, Tomasz, tr. see Hlasko, Marek.
Mirkowska, C. & Salwicki, Andrzej. Algorithmic Logic. 1987. text 206.50 (*90-277-1928-4*) Kluwer Academic.
Mirkowska, G., jt. ed. see Kreczmar, A.
Mirman, Jacob I. What the Hell Is Homeopathy? 2nd rev. ed. (Illus.). 65p. (Orig.). (YA). 1996. wbk. ed. 4.95 (*0-9651950-0-7*) New Hope Pubs.
Mirman, R. Group Theoretical Foundations of Quantum Mechanics. LC 95-24605. 1996. 79.00 (*1-56072-248-7*) Nova Sci Pubs.
— Group Theory: An Intuitive Approach. 500p. 1995. text 54.00 (*981-02-2183-5*) World Scientific Pub.
— Massless Representations of the Poincare Group. 1995. 75.00 (*1-56072-259-2*) Nova Sci Pubs.
***Mirman, R.** Point Groups, Space Groups, Crystals & Molecules. 1999. 68.00 (*981-02-3732-4*) World Scientific Pub.
Miro, Ferrer G. Nuestro Padre San Daniel. 1989. pap. text 14.95 (*84-85866-18-5*) Ediciones Torre.
Miro, Gabriel. Nuestro Padre San Daniel: El Obispo Leproso. Lozano Marcos, Miguel A., ed. (Nueva Austral Ser.: Vol. 224). (SPA.). 1991. pap. text 34.95 (*84-239-7224-0*) Elliots Bks.
Miro, Joan. Els Tres Joans. deluxe limited aut. ed. Brossa, Joan, ed. (Ediciones Especiales y de Bibliofilo Ser.). (CAT., Illus.). 104p. 1993. 17500.00 (*84-343-0272-1*) Elliots Bks.
— Joan Miro: Selected Writings & Interviews. Auster, Paul & Mathews, Patricia, trs. from CAT. (Illus.). 364p. 1992. reprint ed. pap. 14.95 (*0-306-80485-9*) Da Capo.
— Joan Miro, Litografo, 6 vols. Leiris, Michel et al, eds. (SPA., Illus.). 1410p. 1993. 3300.00 (*0-614-00252-4*) Elliots Bks.
— Joan Miro, Litografo, Vol. I. Leiris, Michel, ed. (SPA., Illus.). 240p. 1993. 750.00 (*84-343-0886-X*) Elliots Bks.
— Joan Miro, Litografo, 1976-1981, Vol. VI. Cramer, Patrick, ed. (SPA., Illus.). 292p. 1993. 275.00 (*2-86941-189-8*) Elliots Bks.
— Joan Miro, Litografo, 1972-1975, Vol. V. Cramer, Patrick, ed. (SPA., Illus.). 192p. 1993. 275.00 (*2-86941-188-X*) Elliots Bks.
— Joan Miro, Litografo, 1964-1970, Vol. III. Teixidor, Joan, ed. (SPA., Illus.). 220p. 1993. 650.00 (*84-343-0263-2*) Elliots Bks.
— Joan Miro, Litografo, 1969-1972, Vol. IV. Calas, Nicolas & Calas, Elena, eds. (SPA., Illus.). 212p. 1993. 650.00 (*84-343-0349-3*) Elliots Bks.
— Joan Miro, Litografo, 1953-1963, Vol. II. Queneau, Joan, ed. (SPA., Illus.). 254p. 1993. 750.00 (*84-343-0221-7*) Elliots Bks.
— Miro Lithographs. (Art Library). (Illus.). 48p. (Orig.). 1983. pap. 4.95 (*0-486-24437-7*) Dover.
Miro, Joan. Miro, les Essencies de la Terra. (CAT.). 1993. 7500.00 (*0-614-00037-8*) Elliots Bks.
— Miro, les Essencies de la Terra. limited ed. (CAT.). 1993. 7500.00 (*0-614-00143-9*) Elliots Bks.
Miro, Ramon, jt. ed. see Merrill, Tim L.
Mirocha, Paul, jt. illus. see Batten, Mary.

An Asterisk (*) at the beginning of an entry indicates that the title is appearing for the first time.

***Mirochnik, Elijah.** Teaching in the First Person: Understanding Voice & Vocabulary in Learning Relationships. LC 98-25590. (Counterpoints Ser.: No. 99). 160p. 2000. pap. text 22.95 (*0-8204-4157-0*) P Lang Pubng.

Mirodan, Vladimir. The Balkan Cookbook. LC 89-35639. 208p. 1989. reprint ed. 14.95 (*0-88289-738-1*) Pelican.

Miroff. Debating Democracy: A Reader in American Politics. 2nd ed. LC 98-72064. 1998. pap. text 19.77 (*0-395-90616-4*) HM.

— Democratic Debate, 2 vols. 2nd ed. LC 97-72980. (C). 1997. pap. text 39.96 (*0-395-87542-0*) HM.

Miroff, Bruce. The Democratic Debate. LC 94-76528. (C). 1994. pap. text 37.56 (*0-395-56086-1*) HM.

Miroff, Bruce. Icons of Democracy: American Leaders as Heroes, Aristocrats, Dissenters & Democrats. 422p. 1999. text 25.00 (*0-7881-6070-2*) DIANE Pub.

***Miroff, Bruce.** Icons of Democracy: American Leaders as Heroes, Aristocrats, Dissenters & Democrats. 440p. 2000. pap. text 17.95 (*0-7006-1018-9*) U Pr of KS.

Miroff, Bruce, et al. The Democratic Debate: An Introduction to American Politics. (C). 1995. text, teacher ed. 11.96 (*0-395-72561-5*) HM.

Miroglio, Abel & Miroglio, Yvonne-Delphie. L' Europe et Ses Populations. 1978. lib. bdg. 387.00 (*90-247-2082-6*) Kluwer Academic.

Miroglio, Yvonne-Delphie, jt. auth. see Miroglio, Abel.

Miroiu, Mihai. Romanian Conversation Guide. (Language Bks.). 200p. (C). 1989. pap. 9.95 (*0-87052-803-3*) Hippocrene Bks.

— Romanian-English - English-Romanian Standard Dictionary. 800p. (Orig.). 1996. pap. 17.95 (*0-7818-0444-2*) Hippocrene Bks.

Mirollo, James V. & Herman, Peter C. Opening the Borders: Inclusivity in Early Modern Studies: Essays in Honor of James V. Mirollo. LC 98-56055. (Illus.). 360p. 1999. 52.50 (*0-87413-675-X*) U Delaware Pr.

***Miron, Dan.** The Image of the Shtetl & Other Studies of Modern Jewish Literary Imagination. LC 99-40005. (Judaic Traditions in Literature, Music & Art Ser.). 2000. pap. 19.95 (*0-8156-2858-7*) Syracuse U Pr.

Miron, Dan. A Traveler Disguised: The Rise of Modern Yiddish Fiction in the Nineteenth Century. 373p. 1995. pap. 19.95 (*0-8156-0330-4*) Syracuse U Pr.

Miron, Dan, jt. intro. see Hadari, Atar.

Miron, Eli. Axes & Adzes from Canaan , 2 vols. LC 93-159560. (Prhahistorische Bronzefunde Ser.). viii, 114 p. 1992. write for info. (*3-515-05789-7*) F Steiner Ver.

Miron, Gaston. Counterpanes, Vol. 1. Egan, Dennis, tr. from FRE. (Essential Poets Ser.: No. 50). 73p. 1994. pap. 8.00 (*0-920717-60-8*) Guernica Editions.

— Embers & Earth: Selected Poems. Jones, D. G. & Plourde, Marc, trs. from FRE. (Essential Poets Ser.: Vol. 18).Tr. of Homme Repaile. 122p. pap. 8.00 (*0-919349-35-8*) Guernica Editions.

Miron, Issachar. Eighteen Gates of Jewish Holidays & Festivals. LC 92-41081. (Illus.). 280p. 1993. 50.00 (*0-87668-563-7*) Aronson.

Miron, J. Iglesia o Secta.Tr. of Church or Cult. 4.99 (*0-7899-0491-8*, 496629) Editorial Unilit.

Miron, Jaime. La Amargura: El Pecado Mas Contagioso. (Serie Cruzada - Crusade Ser.).Tr. of Bitterness: The Most Contagious Sin. (SPA.). 31p. 1993. pap. 1.99 (*1-56063-539-8*, 498026) Editorial Unilit.

— Mi Esposo No Es Cristiano. (Serie Cruzada - Crusade Ser.).Tr. of My Husband Is Not a Christian. (SPA.). 1991. pap. 1.99 (*1-56063-044-2*, 498010) Editorial Unilit.

Miron, Jeffrey A. The Economics of Seasonal Cycles. (Illus.). 288p. (C). 1996. 35.00 (*0-262-13323-7*) MIT Pr.

Miron, John R. Housing in Postwar Canada: Demographic Change, Household Formation, & Housing Demand. 416p. 1988. 65.00 (*0-7735-0614-4*, Pub. by McG-Queens Univ Pr) CUP Services.

Miron, John R., ed. House, Home & Community: Progress in Housing Canadians, 1945-1986. 464p. 1993. 65.00 (*0-7735-0995-X*, Pub. by McG-Queens Univ Pr) CUP Services.

Miron, Louis. The Social Construction of Urban Schooling: Situating the Crisis. Pink, William T. & Noblit, George W., eds. LC 96-21375. (Understanding Education & Policy Ser.). 272p. (C). 1996. text 55.00 (*1-57273-074-9*); pap. text 24.95 (*1-57273-075-7*) Hampton Pr NJ.

Miron, Louis F. Resisting Discrimination: Affirmative Strategies for Principals & Teachers. LC 96-28059. 152p. 1996. pap. 21.95 (*0-8039-6423-4*) Corwin Pr.

— Resisting Discrimination: Affirmative Strategies for Principals & Teachers. LC 96-28059. 152p. 1997. 49.95 (*0-8039-6422-6*) Corwin Pr.

Miron, Murray S. Hostage. (C). 1979. 49.95 (*0-205-14420-9*, H4420); pap. 19.95 (*0-205-14421-7*, H4421) Allyn.

Miron, Murray S. & Goldstein, Arnold P. Hostage. rev. ed. LC 77-16554. (General Psychology Ser.: No. 79). 170p. 1979. text 49.50 (*0-08-023875-0*, Pergamon Pr) Elsevier.

Miron, Nathan B. Winning the Games People Play: How to Master the Art of Changing People's Behavior. LC 76-52149. (Illus.). 1977. 12.95 (*0-918418-01-1*); pap. 7.95 (*0-918418-02-X*) Mission Pr CA.

Miron, Paul & Swannell, Philip. Pricing & Hedging Swaps. 240p. 1991. 245.00 (*1-85564-052-X*, Pub. by Euromoney) Am Educ Systs.

Miron, Radu. The Geometry of Higher-Order Finsler Spaces. 222p. (C). 1998. pap. text 65.00 (*1-57485-033-4*) Hadronic Pr Inc.

— The Geometry of Higher-Order Lagrange Spaces: Applications to Mechanics & Physics. LC 96-52591. (Fundamental Theories of Physics Ser.). 352p. (C). 1997. text 180.50 (*0-7923-4393-X*) Kluwer Academic.

— The Geometry of Lagrange Spaces: Theory & Applications. (Fundamental Theories of Physics Ser.). 304p. (C). 1993. text 196.50 (*0-7923-2591-5*) Kluwer Academic.

Miron, Radu, jt. auth. see Branzei, D.

Miron, Salvador D. Antologia (Anthology) (SPA.). 204p. 1979. pap. 7.99 (*968-16-0290-0*, Pub. by Fondo) Continental Bk.

Miron, Simon. A Petroleum Panorama. 2000. write for info. (*1-57524-096-3*) Krieger.

***Miron, Simon.** A Petroleum Panorama. 2000. pap. write for info. (*1-57524-102-1*) Krieger.

Miron, Thomas. The How-to Book for SAS/GRAPH Software. 336p. (C). 1995. pap. 32.95 (*1-55544-233-1*, BR55203) SAS Publ.

— SAS Software Solutions. 240p. (C). 1993. pap. 28.95 (*1-55544-536-5*, BR56196) SAS Publ.

Mironenko, Sergei, jt. auth. see Maylunas, Andrei.

Mironov, A. A. & Surkov, Vladimir I. Minimax under Transportation Constrains. LC 99-11149. (Applied Optimization Ser.). 1999. write for info. (*0-7923-5609-8*) Kluwer Academic.

***Mironov, Boris N.** A Social History of Imperial Russia, 1700-1917. 612p. 1999. 150.00 (*0-8133-3684-8*) Westview.

Mironov, Boris N. A Social History of Imperial Russia, 1700-1917. (C). 2000. pap. 14.95 (*0-8133-8599-7*) Westview.

***Mironov, Boris N. & Eklof, Ben.** A Social History of Imperial Russia, 1700-1917. LC 99-19884. 300p. 2000. pap. 75.00 (*0-8133-8598-9*) Westview.

Mironov, Boris N. & Eklof, Ben. A Social History of Imperial Russia, 1700-1917, Vol. 2. LC 99-19884. 398p. 1999. 75.00 (*0-8133-3665-1*, Pub. by Westview) HarpC.

Mironov, V. F. Chemistry Reviews: Synthetic Studies in the Field of Organic Germanium Compounds, Vol. 12. Vol'pin, M. E., ed. (Soviet Scientific Reviews Ser.: Vol. 12, Pt. 6). ii, 78p. 1989. pap. text 75.00 (*3-7186-4855-5*) Gordon & Breach.

Mironuck, Jeff. Angling in the Shadows of the Rockies. 176p. 1999. pap. 19.95 (*0-9683955-1-1*) F Amato Pubns.

Miropolsky, Z. L. & Soziev, R. I. Fluid Dynamics & Heat Transfer in Superconducting Equipment. 290p. 1990. 245.00 (*0-89116-852-4*) Hemisp Pub.

Mirosevich, Toni. The Rooms We Make Our Own. LC 96-34564. 112p. (Orig.). 1996. pap. 9.95 (*1-56341-080-X*); lib. bdg. 20.95 (*1-56341-081-8*) Firebrand Bks.

Mirosevich, Toni, et al. Trio: Toni Mirosevich, Charlotte Muse, Edward Smallfield. LC 94-12045. 76p. (Orig.). 1995. pap. 10.00 (*0-9645026-0-7*) Specter Pr.

Miroshnichenko, V. K., ed. see Favorov, P. A.

Miroshnik, Victoria, jt. auth. see Basu.

Miroshnik, Victoria, jt. auth. see Basu, Dipak R.

***Mirouze, Laurant.** World War I Infantry. (Europa Militaria Ser.: No. 3). (Illus.). 66p. 1999. pap. 23.95 (*1-86126-288-4*, Pub. by Cro1wood) Motorbooks Intl.

— World War 2 Infantry. (Europa Militaria Ser.: No. 2). (Illus.). 64p. 1999. pap. 23.95 (*1-86126-287-6*, Pub. by Cro1wood) Motorbooks Intl.

Mirov, S. B., jt. auth. see Basiev, T. T.

Miroviktlskakila, N. S., jt. auth. see Ascher, William.

Mirovitskaya, Natalia, jt. auth. see Ascher, William.

Mirow. Traditional African Designs. LC 96-29852. (Illus.). 48p. pap. 5.95 (*0-486-29622-9*) Dover.

Mirow, Gregory. African Designs Stained Glass Coloring Book. 1999. pap. text 4.50 (*0-486-40571-0*) Dover.

— Ancient Mexican Designs. LC 98-51780. (Illus.). 48p. 1999. pap. 5.95 (*0-486-40468-4*) Dover.

— Celtic Designs Giftwrap Paper. 1993. pap. 3.95 (*0-486-27502-7*) Dover.

— Medieval Designs. LC 97-23626. (Dover Design Library). 1997. pap. 5.95 (*0-486-29791-8*) Dover.

— Paisley Designs: 44 Original Plates. (Illus.). 48p. 1989. pap. 4.50 (*0-486-25987-0*) Dover.

***Mirow, Gregory.** Polynesian & Oceanian Designs. LC 00-31462. (Pictorial Archive Ser.). 2000. pap. write for info. (*0-486-41227-X*) Dover.

Mirow, Gregory. A Treasury of Designs for Artists & Craftsmen. LC 69-18877. (Pictorial Archive Ser.). 125p. 1969. reprint ed. pap. 8.95 (*0-486-22002-8*) Dover.

Mirowicz & Stypula, R. Wielki Slownik Polsko-Rosyjski, 2 vols., Set. (POL & RUS.). 1331p. 1980. 150.00 (*0-8288-1037-0*, M9131) Fr & Eur.

Mirowitz, Scott A. Pitfalls, Variants & Artifacts in Body MR Imaging. (Illus.). 536p. (C). (gr. 13). 1996. text 155.00 (*0-8016-7670-3*, 07670) Mosby Inc.

Mirowski, Philip. Against Mechanism: Protecting Economics from Science. 264p. 1988. pap. 21.95 (*0-8476-7695-1*) Rowman.

— Against Mechanism: Why Economics Needs Protection from Science. 264p. (C). 1988. 62.50 (*0-8476-7436-3*) Rowman.

— More Heat Than Light: Economics as Social Physics, Physics as Nature's Economics. (Historical Perspectives on Modern Economics Ser.). (Illus.). 462p. (C). 1991. pap. text 25.95 (*0-521-42689-8*) Cambridge U Pr.

— Natural Images in Economic Thought: Markets Read in Tooth & Claw. 634p. 1994. pap. text 34.95 (*0-521-47884-7*) Cambridge U Pr.

Mirowski, Philip, ed. Natural Images in Economic Thought: Markets Read in Tooth & Claw. (Historical Perspectives on Modern Economics Ser.). (Illus.). 624p. (C). 1994. pap. 29.95 (*0-521-47877-4*); text 95.00 (*0-521-44321-0*) Cambridge U Pr.

— The Reconstruction of Economic Theory. 1986. lib. bdg. 98.50 (*0-89838-211-4*) Kluwer Academic.

***Mirowski, Philip & Tradewell, Steven.** The Economic Writings of William Thornton, 5 vols. LC 99-28820. 1920p. 1999. 740.00 (*1-85196-388-X*, Pub. by Pickering & Chatto) Ashgate Pub Co.

Mirowski, Philip J. Uncertain Wavering. 0.00 (*0-691-04267-5*) Princeton U Pr.

— Uncertian Waverin. pap. 0.00 (*0-691-00380-7*) Princeton U Pr.

Mirowski, Philip J., ed. Edgeworth's Writings on Chance, Economic Hazard, & Statistics. (Worldly Philosophy Series: Studies at the Intersection of Philosophy & Economics). 470p. (C). 1994. lib. bdg. 49.50 (*0-8476-7751-6*) Rowman.

Mirowsky, John & Ross, Catherine E. Social Causes of Psychological Distress. (Social Institutions & Social Change Ser.). 224p. (C). 1989. pap. text 25.95 (*0-202-30355-1*) Aldine de Gruyter.

Mirr, Michaelene, jt. ed. see Snyder, Mariah.

Mirra, Gerald B. The Fancy Shawl Dancer. large type ed. Bernardo, Karen, ed. LC 98-183078. (Illus.). 32p. (J). (gr. 3-4). 1997. 6.95 (*0-9655486-1-9*) Signature Pub.

***Mirra, Gerald B.** Little Brother of War. large type ed. Bernardo, Karen, ed. (Illus.). 32p. (J). (gr. 3-6). 1999. pap. 6.95 (*0-9655486-2-7*, 103) Signature Pub.

Mirra, Gerald B. Panuel & the Carousel. large type ed. Bernardo, Karen, ed. (Illus.). 32p. (J). (gr. 2-3). 1996. 6.95 (*0-9655486-0-0*) Signature Pub.

Mirra, Joseph M., et al, eds. Bone Tumors: Clinical, Radiologic & Pathologic Correlations, 2 vols., Vol. 1 & 2. LC 88-3019. (Illus.). 1857p. 1989. 295.00 (*0-8121-1156-7*) Lppncott W & W.

Mirren, Ena & Compassionate Friends Staff, eds. Our Children: Coming to Terms with the Loss of a Child: Parents' Own Stories. 204p. 1996. pap. 14.95 (*0-340-62863-4*, Pub. by Hodder & Stought Ltd) Trafalgar.

Mirrer, Louise. Upon My Husband's Death: Widows in the Literature & Histories of Medieval Europe. (Illus.). 368p. (C). 1992. text 52.50 (*0-472-10257-5*, 10257) U of Mich Pr.

— Women, Jews, & Muslims in the Texts of Reconquest Castile. LC 96-10301. (Studies in Medieval & Early Modern Civilization). 208p. (C). 1996. text 44.50 (*0-472-10723-2*, 10723) U of Mich Pr.

Mirrer-Singer, Louise. The Language of Evaluation: A Sociolinguistic Approach to the Story of Pedro el Cruel in Ballad & Chronicle. LC 86-9620. (Purdue University Monographs in Romance Languages: No. 20). xi, 130p. (Orig.). 1986. pap. 35.00 (*0-915027-69-0*) J Benjamins Pubng Co.

***Mirriam-Goldberg, Caryn.** Lot's Wife. Low, Denise, ed. & intro. by. 80p. 2000. pap. 8.00 (*0-939391-27-9*) B Woodley Pr.

Mirriam-Goldberg, Caryn. Write Where You Are: How to Use Writing to Make Sense of Your Life: A Guide for Teens. LC 98-54292. 155p. (YA). (gr. 9 up). 1999. pap. text 14.95 (*1-57542-060-0*) Free Spirit Pub.

Mirrielees, Edith R. Story Writing. LC 72-6277. 1988. pap. 10.00 (*0-87116-137-0*) Writer.

Mirrione, Jim. The Divider. 48p. 1996. pap. 3.00 (*0-87129-472-9*, D61) Dramatic Pub.

Mirrlees, Hope. Lud-in-the-Mist. 315p. 1998. reprint ed. lib. bdg. 24.00 (*1-58287-006-3*) North Bks.

***Mirrlees, James.** Welfare, Incentives & Taxation. 304p. 2000. text 45.00 (*0-19-829521-9*) OUP.

Mirro, Joseph, jt. ed. see Steen, Grant.

Mirschhorn, Robert B., jt. auth. see Bennett, Cathy E.

***Mirsepassi, Ali.** Intellectual Discourse & the Politics of Modernization: Negotiating Modernity in Iran. (Cambridge Cultural Social Studies). (Illus.). 256p. (C). 2000. pap. text Price not set. (*0-521-65997-3*) Cambridge U Pr.

— Intellectual Discourses & the Politics of Modernization: Negotiating Modernity in Iran. LC 99-49057. (Cambridge Cultural Social Studies). (Illus.). 256p. (C). 2000. text. write for info. (*0-521-65000-3*) Cambridge U Pr.

Mirsky. Sir Aurel Stein. 1998. pap. 20.00 (*0-226-53177-5*) U Ch Pr.

Mirsky, D. S. A History of Russian Literature: From Its Beginnings to 1900. Whitfield, Francis J., ed. LC 99-16430. 416p. 1999. pap. 19.95 (*0-8101-1679-0*) Northwestern U Pr.

Mirsky, David. The Life & Work of Ephraim Luzzatto. 1987. 25.00 (*0-88125-139-9*) Ktav.

Mirsky, Dimitry S. Modern Russian Literature. LC 74-6485. (Studies in Russian Literature & Life: No. 100). 1974. lib. bdg. 75.00 (*0-8383-1941-6*) M S G Haskell Hse.

— Pushkin. LC 74-34587. (Studies in Russian Literature & Life: No. 100). 1974. lib. bdg. 75.00 (*0-8383-1998-X*) M S G Haskell Hse.

— Russia: A Social History. Seligman, C. G., ed. LC 83-26517. (Illus.). 312p. 1984. lib. bdg. 75.00 (*0-313-24296-8*, MRUS, Greenwood Pr) Greenwood.

— Stikhotvoreniia; Stat'i o Russkoi Poezii. Smith, G. S. & Perkins, Gareth K., eds. (RUS.). 299p. (Orig.). (C). 1997. pap. 20.00 (*1-57201-005-3*) Berkeley Slavic.

— Uncollected Writings on Russian Literature. (Modern Russian Literature & Culture, Studies & Texts: Vol. 13). (ENG & RUS., Illus.). 406p. (Orig.). (C). 1989. pap. 24.00 (*0-933884-68-0*) Berkeley Slavic.

Mirsky, Dimitry S., tr. see Vladimirtsov, Boris.

Mirsky, Georgiy I. On Ruins of Empire: Ethnicity & Nationalism in the Former Soviet Union, 375. LC 96-5789. (Contributions in Political Science Ser.: No. 375). 192p. 1997. 57.95 (*0-313-30044-5*, Greenwood Pr) Greenwood.

Mirsky, Jeannette. Sir Aurel Stein: A Biography. LC 76-17703. 1992. 25.00 (*0-226-53176-7*) U Ch Pr.

— To the Arctic: The Story of Northern Exploration from Earliest Times to the Present. LC 72-121386. 334p. 1970. pap. 16.95 (*0-226-53179-1*, P376) U Ch Pr.

***Mirsky, Joseph.** Consumer Guide to Diamonds. rev. ed. (Illus.). 47p. 2000. pap. 7.95 (*0-9700074-0-X*) Josephs Jewel.

Mirsky, Judith & Radlett, Marty, eds. Private Decisions, Public Debate: Women, Reproduction & Population. (Illus.). 185p. 1995. pap. 14.95 (*1-870670-34-5*, Pub. by Panos Bks) Paul & Co Pubs.

Mirsky, Laura, jt. auth. see Rotenberg, Mark.

Mirsky, Lawrence. Introduction to Linear Algebra. 440p. 1990. pap. 12.95 (*0-486-66434-1*) Dover.

Mirsky, Lawrence & Tropea, Silvana, eds. The News Aesthetic. LC 97-215283. (Illus.). 64p. (Orig.). 1995. pap. 19.95 (*1-56898-051-5*) Princeton Arch.

Mirsky, Mark. The Red Adam. (New American Fiction Ser.: No. 19). (Illus.). 165p. (Orig.). 1990. pap. 10.95 (*0-940650-92-4*) Sun & Moon CA.

— The Secret Table. LC 74-24914. 167p. 1975. 15.95 (*0-914590-10-3*); pap. 6.95 (*0-914590-11-1*) Fiction Coll.

Mirsky, Mark, ed. see Musil, Robert.

Mirsky, Mark J. The Absent Shakespeare. LC 92-55118. (Illus.). (C). 1995. 32.50 (*0-8386-3511-3*) Fairleigh Dickinson.

Mirsky, Mark J., jt. ed. see Stern, David.

Mirsky, Norman B. Unorthodox Judaism. LC 78-8683. 227p. 1978. reprint ed. pap. 70.40 (*0-608-00917-2*, 206171100011) Bks Demand.

Mirsky, Peter H. Lactose-Free Foods: A Shoppers Guide. LC 95-152873. (Illus.). 70p. 1995. write for info. (*0-9644787-0-6*) Bullseye Info Servs.

Mirsky, Stanley, jt. auth. see Heilman, Joan Rattner.

mirsky, stuart w. The King of Vinland's Saga. LC 98-88295. 325p. 1998. 25.00 (*0-7388-0151-8*); pap. 15.00 (*0-7388-0152-6*) Xlibris Corp.

Mirsky, Yehudah & Ahrens, Matt, eds. Democracy in the Middle East: Defining the Challenges. LC 93-28820. 138p. 1993. pap. 14.95 (*0-944029-53-1*) Wash Inst NEP.

Mirta, Sanjit K. & Kaiser, James F., eds. The Handbook for Digital Signal Processing. LC 92-35700. 1312p. 1993. 180.00 (*0-471-61995-7*) Wiley.

Mirtle, Jack. Billy May Discography, 79. LC 98-37786. (Discographies Ser.: Vol. 79). 568p. 1998. lib. bdg. 79.50 (*0-313-30739-3*, Greenwood Pr) Greenwood.

Mirtle, Jack, compiled by. Thank You Music Lovers: A Bio-Discography of Spike Jones & His City Slickers, 1941-1965, 20. LC 85-27128. (Discographies Ser.: No. 20). 448p. 1986. lib. bdg. 75.00 (*0-313-24814-1*, MSN/, Greenwood Pr) Greenwood.

Mirtschin, Peter & Davis, Richard. Snakes of Australia: Dangerous & Harmless. (Illus.). 216p. 1994. pap. 19.95 (*0-85572-209-6*, Pub. by Hill Content Pubng) Seven Hills Bk.

Mirtskhulava, T. E. Reliability of Hydro-Reclamation Installations. Kothekar, V. S., tr. from RUS. 308p. (C). 1987. text 116.00 (*90-6191-491-4*, Pub. by A A Balkema) Ashgate Pub Co.

— Reliability of Hydro-Reclamation Installations. (C). 1987. 33.00 (*81-204-0196-4*, Pub. by Oxford IBH) S Asia.

Mirvis, David M., ed. Body Surface Electrocardiographic Mapping. (Developments in Cardiovascular Medicine Ser.). (C). 1988. text 150.00 (*0-89838-983-6*) Kluwer Academic.

Mirvis, Philip H. Managing the Merger: Making It Work. 400p. (C). 1991. text 26.00 (*0-13-544636-8*, Busn) P-H.

Mirvis, Philip H., jt. auth. see Kanter, Donald L.

Mirvis, Philip H., jt. auth. see Marks, Mitchell L.

Mirvis, Stuart E. & Young, Jeremy W. Imaging in Trauma & Critical Care. (Illus.). 592p. 1992. 140.00 (*0-683-06075-9*) Lppncott W & W.

Mirvis, Stuart E., jt. auth. see Harris, John H., Jr.

***Mirvis, Tova.** The Ladies Auxiliary. 336p. 2000. pap. 14.00 (*0-345-44126-5*, Ballantine) Ballantine Pub Grp.

Mirvis, Tova. The Ladies' Auxiliary: A Novel. LC 99-30720. 352p. 1999. text 23.95 (*0-393-04814-4*) Norton.

Mirviss, Joan B. & Carpenter, John T. The Frank Lloyd Wright Collection of Surimono. LC 94-41903. (Illus.). 336p. 1995. 70.00 (*0-8348-0327-5*) Weatherhill.

Mirviss, Suzanne, jt. auth. see Nathan, Ann A.

Mirwis, Allan N. Subject Encyclopedias: User Guide, Review Citations & Keyword Index, 2 vols. 752p. 1999. boxed set 135.00 (*1-57356-199-1*) Oryx Pr.

Miryam. The Happy Man & His Dump Truck. LC 98-84181. (Family Storytime Ser.: No. 2). (Illus.). 32p. (J). (ps-k). 1998. 9.95 (*0-307-10218-1*, 10218, Goldn Books) Gldn Bks Pub Co.

Mirza. Double Discrimination. 78.95 (*1-85521-763-5*) Ashgate Pub Co.

Mirza, Hafiz, ed. Global Competitive Strategies in the New World Economy: Multilateralism, Regionalization & the Transnational Firm. LC 97-45219. (New Horizons in International Business Ser.). 360p. 1999. 95.00 (*1-85898-136-0*) E Elgar.

***Mirza, Hafiz & Wee, Kee H., eds.** Transnational Corporate Strategies in the Asean Region. 208p. 2000. 80.00 (*1-84064-164-9*) E Elgar.

Mirza, Heidi S. Black British Feminism: A Reader. LC 96-43946. 320p. (C). 1997. 85.00 (*0-415-15288-7*); pap. 25.99 (*0-415-15289-5*) Routledge.

— Young, Female & Black. LC 91-30180. 256p. (Orig.). (C). (gr. 13). 1992. 85.00 (*0-415-06704-9*, A6788) Routledge.

***Mirza, Humayun.** From Plassey to Pakistan: The Family History of Iskander Mirza, the First President of Pakistan. LC 99-44514. (Illus.). 448p. 1999. 44.50 (*0-7618-1509-0*) U Pr of Amer.

Mirza, Iraj. Iraj Mirza's Poetry. LC 92-70487. (PER.). 328p. (Orig.). 1992. pap. 8.95 (*0-936347-25-2*) IBEX.

Mirza, Jerome. Illinois Tort Law & Practice. 2nd ed. LC 88-82172. 1991. 125.00 (*0-318-43158-0*) West Group.

— Illinois Tort Law & Practice, Suppl. 1993. 2nd ed. LC 88-82172. 1991. 55.00 (*0-317-01748-9*) West Group.

— Winning Litigation the Mirza Way. LC 91-77445. 1992. 135.00 (*0-685-59886-1*) West Group.

An Asterisk (*) at the beginning of an entry indicates that the title is appearing for the first time.

Mirza, Jill & Harris, Nick. Mix Your Own Acrylics. (Artist's Library Ser.). 64p. (Orig.). 1997. pap. 7.95 (*1-56010-224-1*, AL28) W Foster Pub.

***Mirza, K.** Chemical Brothers: Done & Dusted, (Illus.). 47p. 1998. pap. text 14.95 (*0-7119-6803-9*) Omnibus NY.

Mirza, Nasseh A. Syrian Ismailism: The Ever Living Line of Imamate A.D. 1100-1260. 220p. 1996. 70.00 (*0-7007-0506-6*, Pub. by Curzon Pr Ltd); pap. 25.00 (*0-7007-0507-4*, Pub. by Curzon Pr Ltd) Paul & Co Pubs.

— Syrian Ismailism: The Ever Living Line of the Imamate, A. D. 1100-1260. LC 97-181067. xii, 150p. 1997. write for info. (*0-7007-0505-8*) Curzon Pr Ltd.

Mirza, Rocky. Explorations in Macroeconomics 1st Canada. 610p. 1992. pap. text 49.59 (*1-56226-097-9*) CAT Pub.

— Explorations in Macroeconomics Study Guide 1st Canada. 136p. 1992. pap. text, student ed. 24.18 (*1-56226-120-7*) CAT Pub.

Mirza, Rocky, et al. Explorations in Microeconomics, First Canadian. 134p. (C). 1991. pap. text, student ed. 24.18 (*1-56226-058-8*) CAT Pub.

Mirza, Sarah & Strobel, Margaret, eds. Three Swahili Women: Life Histories from Mombasa, Kenya. LC 88-45093. (Illus.). 176p. 1989. pap. 10.95 (*0-253-28854-1*) Ind U Pr.

Mirza, Sarah M., jt. auth. see Hinnebusch, Thomas J.

Mirza, Sarah M., jt. ed. see Strobel, Margaret.

Mirza, William & Lemmons, Thom. Passport. 300p. 1995. pap. 9.99 (*1-56476-390-0*, 6-3390, Victor Bks) Chariot Victor.

Mirza, Youel B. When I Was a Boy in Persia. LC 77-87650. (Illus.). reprint ed. 37.50 (*0-404-16419-6*) AMS Pr.

Mirza, Zaynab. The Mehndi Kit. (Illus.). 80p. 1998. pap. 24.95 (*0-8092-2801-7*, 280170, Contemporary Bks) NTC Contemp Pub Co.

Mirzabeigi, Edwin, jt. auth. see Jordan, Christopher.

Mirzabekian, Z. M. Russian-Persian Polytechnical Dictionary. 2nd ed. 720p. (C). 1983. 140.00 (*0-7855-6492-6*, Pub. by Collets) St Mut.

— Russian-Persian Polytechnical Dictionary. 2nd ed. (PER & RUS.). 720p. 1983. 95.00 (*0-8288-2160-7*, M8890) Fr & Eur.

Mirzadahgi, Shukuh. That Stranger Within Me: A Foreign Woman Caught in the Iranian Revolution. Nooriala, Esmail, tr. from PER. LC 97-46022. (Modern Persian Writers Ser.). 1998. write for info. (*0-936347-83-X*) IBEX.

Mirzai, A. R. Artificial Intelligence: Concepts & Applications. (C). 1990. mass mkt. 71.50 (*0-412-37900-7*) Chapman & Hall.

Mirzai, A. R., ed. Artificial Intelligence: Concepts & Applications. (Artificial Intelligence Ser.). 320p. 1990. 42.00 (*0-262-13256-7*) MIT Pr.

Mirzoeff, Nicholas. Bodyscape: Art, Modernity & the Ideal Figure. LC 95-6735. (Visual Cultures Ser.). (Illus.). 224p. (C). 1995. pap. 20.99 (*0-415-09801-7*) Routledge.

— Diaspora & Visual Culture: Representing Africians & Jews. LC 99-25364. 1999. pap. 24.99 (*0-415-16670-5*) Routledge.

— Introduction to Visual Culture. 1999. 70.00 (*0-415-15875-3*); pap. 19.95 (*0-415-15876-1*) Routledge.

***Mirzoeff, Nicholas, ed.** Diaspora & Visual Culture: Representing Africans & Jews. LC 99-25364. 272p. (C). 1999. text. write for info. (*0-415-16669-1*) Routledge.

Mirzoeff, Nicholas, ed. Virtual States: Globalisation Inequality & the Internet. LC 99-20772. 208p. (C). 1999. pap. 25.99 (*0-415-17214-4*) Routledge.

Mirzoeff, Nick, ed. Visual Culture Reader. LC 99-188035. (Illus.). 544p. (C). 1998. 85.00 (*0-415-14133-8*) Routledge.

Mirzoyan, L. V., et al, eds. Flare Stars in Star Clusters, Associations & the Solar Vicinity. (C). 1990. pap. text 69.00 (*0-7923-0771-2*); lib. bdg. 167.00 (*0-7923-0770-4*) Kluwer Academic.

MIS Press Staff. Concepts in Computer Art. (Welcome to...Ser.). (Illus.). 1993. pap. 19.95 (*1-55828-240-8*, MIS Pr) IDG Bks.

— Islam on the Net. Date not set. write for info. (*1-55828-517-2*, MIS Pr) IDG Bks.

— Teach Yourself Harvard Graphics. 2nd ed. 1995. pap. 21.95 (*1-55828-310-2*, MIS Pr) IDG Bks.

Misa, Thomas J. A Nation of Steel: The Making of Modern America. LC 94-38681. (Studies in the History of Technology). (Illus.). 392p. 1995. text 49.95 (*0-8018-4967-5*) Johns Hopkins.

— Nation of Steel: The Making of Modern America, 1865-1925. (Johns Hopkins Studies in the History of Technology). (Illus.). 400p. 1998. pap. text 22.50 (*0-8018-6052-0*) Johns Hopkins.

***Misaelides, P.** Natural Microporous Materials in Environmental Technology. LC 99-38161. (NATO Science Ser.). 1999. write for info. (*0-7923-5888-0*, Kluwer Plenum) Kluwer Academic.

Misaelides, P., ed. Application of Particle & Laser Beams in Materials Technology. LC 94-46545. (NATO ASI Ser.: Series E, Applied Sciences: Vol. 283). 1995. text 313.00 (*0-7923-3324-1*) Kluwer Academic.

Misaghi, I. J. Physiology & Biochemistry of Plant-Pathogen Interactions. LC 82-18594. 304p. (C). 1982. 65.00 (*0-306-41059-1*, Plenum Trade) Perseus Pubng.

Misak, C. J. Truth & the End of Inquiry: A Peircean Account of Truth. (Oxford Philosophical Monographs). 198p. 1991. text 68.00 (*0-19-824231-X*) OUP.

— Truth, Politics Morality: Pragmatism & Deliberation. LC 99-16328. 208p. 1999. pap. 24.99 (*0-415-14036-6*) Routledge.

Misak, C. J. Verificationism: Its History & Prospects. LC 95-7728. (Philosophical Issues in Science Ser.). 272p. (C). 1995. pap. 24.99 (*0-415-12598-7*) Routledge.

***Misak, Cheryl J.** Truth, Politics, Morality: Pragmatism & Deliberation. LC 99-16328. 208p. (C). 1999. text 65.00 (*0-415-14035-8*) Routledge.

Misaki, Eri. New York Dance Schools - Studios Guide. 6th ed. Belton, Elizabeth, ed. (ENG & JPN., Illus.). 84p. 1998. pap. 15.00 (*1-888275-03-0*) Dance Project.

***Misaki, Eri.** New York Dance School/Studio Guide. 7th rev. ed. Kocich, Julia, ed. (Illus.). 80p. 1999. pap. 12.00 (*1-888275-04-9*) Dance Project.

Misamore, Gary W., jt. ed. see Hawkins, Richard J.

Misanchuk, Earl R. Preparing Instructional Text: Document Design Using Desktop Publishing. LC 91-32872. (Illus.). 327p. (Orig.). 1992. pap. 39.95 (*0-87778-241-5*) Educ Tech Pubns.

Misanchuk, Earl R., jt. auth. see Schwier, Richard A.

Misawa, E. A., ed. Advances in Robust & Nonlinear Control Systems. LC 93-73654. 131p. pap. 45.00 (*0-7918-1259-6*) ASME.

— Advances in Robust & Nonlinear Control Systems. (DSC Ser.: Vol. 43). 96p. 1992. 30.00 (*0-7918-1114-X*, G00758) ASME.

Misawa, Masanaru. Plant Tissue Culture: An Alternative for Production of Useful Metabolites. (Agricultural Services Bulletin Ser.: 108). 93p. 1994. pap. 11.00 (*92-5-103391-9*, F33919, Pub. by FAO) Bernan Associates.

Misawa, Masanaru, ed. see Dicosmo, Frank.

Misbah, Muhammad T. World View: Its Importance & Problems. Saadat, Shahyar, tr. from PER. 24p. (Orig.). 1989. pap. text 1.70 (*1-871031-21-4*) Abjad Bk.

Misbin, Robert, et al, eds. Health Care Crisis: The Search for Answers. 245p. (Orig.). 1995. pap. 25.00 (*1-55572-025-0*) Univ Pub Group.

Misbin, Robert I., ed. Euthanasia: The Good of the Patient, the Good of Society. 245p. 1992. 35.00 (*1-55572-017-X*) Univ Pub Group.

Miscall, Peter D. Isaiah. (Readings Ser.). 200p. 1993. 57.50 (*1-85075-435-7*, Pub. by Sheffield Acad); pap. 19.50 (*1-85075-436-5*, Pub. by Sheffield Acad) CUP Services.

Miscall, Peter D. Isaiah 34 - 35: A Nightmare - A Dream. LC 99-179491. (J. S. O. T. S. Ser.: Vol. 281). 147p. 1999. 52.50 (*1-85075-987-1*, Pub. by Sheffield Acad) CUP Services.

— One Samuel: A Literary Reading. LC 85-42948. (Indiana Studies in Biblical Literature). 224p. (C). 1986. 19.95 (*0-253-34247-3*); pap. 10.95 (*0-253-20365-1*, MB-365) Ind U Pr.

Miscamble, Wilson D. George F. Kennan & the Making of American Foreign Policy, 1947-1950. (Studies in International History & Politics). (Illus.). 436p. 1992. pap. text 22.95 (*0-691-02483-9*, Pub. by Princeton U Pr) Cal Prin Full Svc.

***Miscamble, Wilson D.** Keeping the Faith, Making a Difference. LC 99-48595. 144p. (C). 2000. pap. 9.95 (*0-87793-933-0*) Ave Maria.

Miscamble, Wilson D. & Marszalek, John F., eds. American Political History: Essays on the State of the Discipline. LC 96-28969. 200p. (C). 1997. pap. text 15.00 (*0-268-00652-0*) U of Notre Dame Pr.

Miscevic, Dusanka, jt. auth. see Kwong, Peter.

Miscevic, Nenad. Rationality & Cognition: Against Relativism - Pragmatism. (Toronto Studies in Philosophy). 344p. 1998. text 75.00 (*0-8020-4166-3*); pap. text 24.95 (*0-8020-8028-6*) U of Toronto Pr.

***Miscevic, Nenad, ed.** Nationalism & Ethnic Conflict: Philosophical Perspectives. LC 00-29856. 300p. 2000. 39.95 (*0-8126-9415-5*) Open Court.

Miscevic, Nikola. Necropolis & Songs of Hope: Bilingual Poetry. 128p. 1996. pap. 12.95 (*0-88962-433-X*) Mosaic.

Misch, Carl E. Contemporary Implant Dentistry. 2nd ed. LC 98-27520. (Illus.). 702p. (C). (gr. 13). 1998. text 125.00 (*0-8151-7059-9*, 27496) Mosby Inc.

Misch, Carl E., jt. auth. see Scortecci, Gerard M.

Misch, Georg. A History of Autobiography in Antiquity, 2 vols., Set. LC 73-13406. 1974. reprint ed. lib. bdg. 65.00 (*0-8371-7053-2*, MIAA) Greenwood.

— A History of Autobiography in Antiquity, 2 vols., Vol. 1. LC 73-13406. 1974. reprint ed. lib. bdg. 45.00 (*0-8371-7178-4*, MIAB) Greenwood.

— A History of Autobiography in Antiquity, 2 vols., Vol. 2. LC 73-13406. 1974. reprint ed. lib. bdg. 45.00 (*0-8371-7179-2*, MIAC) Greenwood.

Mischakoff, Anne. Khandoshkin & the Beginning of Russian String Music. LC 83-17847. (Russian Music Studies: No. 9). 217p. reprint ed. pap. 67.30 (*0-8357-1428-4*, 207051300097) Bks Demand.

Mischakoff, Anne, ed. see American String Teachers Association Staff.

Mische, Michael. Reengineering: Systems Integration Success 1999. LC 96-217358. xi, 459 p. 1996. write for info. (*0-7913-2854-6*) Warren Gorham & Lamont.

— Step-by-Step Reengineering: The Comprehensive Guide. LC 96-67531. 288p. 1996. ring bd. 475.00 (*0-88390-476-4*) Jossey-Bass.

***Mische, Michael.** Strategic Renewal: Becoming a High-Performance Organization. LC 99-58142. 300p. 2000. pap. 33.33 (*0-13-021919-3*) P-H.

Mische, Michael, jt. auth. see Bennis, Warren.

Mische, Michael A. Reengineering: Systems Integration Success 1999. 99th ed. LC 99-176673. 456p. 1998. boxed set 95.00 (*0-8493-9968-8*) CRC Pr.

Mische, Michael A., ed. Reengineering: Systems Integration Success, 1998. 98th ed. 336p. (C). 1997. boxed set 155.00 (*0-8493-9952-1*, HD30) CRC Pr.

Mische, Patricia M. Ecological Security & the United Nations System: Past, Present, & Future. (Global Issues Ser.). 98p. 1997. pap. 10.00 (*0-9661131-0-1*) Global Ed Assocs.

— Star Wars & the State of Our Souls: Deciding the Future of Planet Earth. 122p. (Orig.). 1985. 4.95 (*0-86683-450-8*) Harper SF.

Mischel, Jim. The Developer's Guide to WinHelp.Exe: Harnessing the Windows Help Engine. 1995. pap. text. write for info. (*0-471-30327-5*) Wiley.

Mischel, Jim. Macro Magic with Turbo Assembler. Duntemann, Jeff, ed. 368p. 1992. pap. 39.95 incl. disk (*0-471-57815-0*) Wiley.

Mischel, Walter. Introduction to Personality. 5th ed. (C). 1993. pap. text, teacher ed., suppl. ed. 35.00 (*0-03-033707-0*) Harcourt Coll Pubs.

— Introduction to Personality. 6th ed. (C). 1998. text 90.00 (*0-15-505169-5*) Harcourt.

— Personality & Assessment. 376p. 1996. pap. 36.00 (*0-8058-2330-1*) L Erlbaum Assocs.

***Mischitelli, Vincent.** Your New Restaurant: All the Necessary Ingredients for Success. 2nd ed. LC 99-55189. 256p. 2000. pap. 12.95 (*1-58062-193-7*) Adams Media.

Mischka, Joseph. The Percheron Horse in America. (Illus.). 179p. 1991. 19.95 (*0-9622663-5-3*) Heart Prairie Pr.

Mischka, Robert A. Draft Horse Images. (Illus.). 160p. 1995. pap. 24.00 (*1-882199-03-0*) Heart Prairie Pr.

— Draft Horses Today: Work Horses & Mules Find Their Way into the 21st Century. (Illus.). 176p. 1992. 29.50 (*0-9622663-6-1*) Heart Prairie Pr.

— It's Showtime: A Beginner's Guide to Showing Draft Horses. (Illus.). 121p. 1998. 18.00 (*1-882199-04-9*) Heart Prairie Pr.

Mischke. Mechanical Engineering Design. 6th ed. 2000. 85.00 (*0-07-365939-8*) McGraw.

Mischke, C., et al. Labour Dispute Resolution. LC 97-197870. 1997. pap. 32.50 (*0-7021-4156-9*, Pub. by Juta & Co) Gaunt.

Mischke, Carl & Garbers, Christoph. Safety at Work. LC 95-116449. 170p. 1994. pap. 24.00 (*0-7021-3230-6*, Pub. by Juta & Co) Gaunt.

Mischke, Charles R. Mathematical Model Building: An Introduction to Engineering. 2nd rev. ed. LC 79-25436. (Illus.). 408p. 1980. reprint ed. pap. 126.50 (*0-608-00076-0*, 206083900006) Bks Demand.

Mischke, Charles R., jt. auth. see Shigley, Joseph E.

Mischke, Richard E. Intersections Between Particle & Nuclear Physics (Steamboat Springs, 1984), No. 123. LC 84-72790. (AIP Conference Proceedings Ser.). 1162p. 1984. lib. bdg. 65.00 (*0-88318-322-6*) Am Inst Physics.

Misciagno, Patricia S. Rethinking Feminist Identification: The Case for De Facto Feminism. LC 97-19209. 160p. 1997. 49.95 (*0-275-95825-6*, Praeger Pubs) Greenwood.

Miscimarra, Philip A. Government Protection of Employees Involved in Mergers & Acquisitions, 1989-97 Suppl. 1: The NLRB, Successorship, Collective Bargaining Agreements, & WARN. rev. ed. (Labor Relations & Public Policy Ser.: Vol. 34). 220p. 1997. pap. 25.00 (*1-891496-00-X*) J M Olin.

— The NLRB & Managerial Discretion: Plant Closings, Relocations, Subcontracting, & Automation. LC 83-81557. (Labor Relations & Public Policy Ser.: No. 24). (Illus.). 368p. (Orig.). 1983. pap. 25.00 (*0-89546-038-6*) U PA Ctr Hum Res.

Miscimarra, Philip A., jt. auth. see Berkowitz, Alan D.

Miscisin, Jean M. Mas de 1000 Palabras (More Than 1000 Words) (SPA.). 154p. (C). 1995. pap. text. write for info. (*0-9648585-0-9*) Pocasse Pr.

***Misczynski, Dean J.** Proposition 218 after Two Years. 16p. 1998. pap. write for info. (*1-58703-095-0*, CRB-98-016) CA St Libry.

— State General Obligation Bonds for the 1992 Ballots. 9p. 1991. pap. write for info. (*1-58703-000-4*, CRB-91-001) CA St Libry.

— State General Obligation Bonds for the 1992 Ballots. 11p. 1992. pap. write for info. (*1-58703-001-2*) CA St Libry.

Misczynski, Dean J., jt. ed. see Hagman, Donald G.

Mise, Raymond W. The Gothic Heroine & the Nature of the Gothic Novel. Varma, Devendra P., ed. LC 79-8465. (Gothic Studies & Dissertations). 1980. lib. bdg. 31.95 (*0-405-12675-1*) Ayer.

Misel, Lory. Happy & Alive. 96p. (Orig.). 1986. pap. 6.95 (*0-9615902-1-1*) Paragon Group.

— Heavensong. 81p. (Orig.). 1985. pap. 7.00 (*0-9615902-0-3*) Paragon Group.

Misener, Stephen & Krawetz, Stephen A., eds. Bioinformatics Methods & Protocols. LC 99-17054. (Methods in Molecular Biology Ser.: Vol. 132). 512p. 1999. 89.50 (*0-89603-732-0*) Humana.

Misenheimer, David. We, the Church: Eight Small Group Studies. 1993. pap. 12.95 (*0-933173-61-X*) Chging Church Forum.

Misenhimer, Deborah. The Pilgrim Soul. 215p. 1993. pap. 12.00 (*0-9636313-0-6*) D Misenhimer.

***Misenti, Nicholas C.** Safe Harbors: The Asset Protection Guide for Small Business Owners. (Business Owner's Toolkit Ser.). 250p. 2000. pap. 19.95 (*0-8080-0412-3*) CCH INC.

***Miseph, Bryon.** Seekers. 274p. 1999. pap. 16.95 (*0-7414-0225-4*) Buy Books.

***Miser, Brad.** The Complete Idiot's Guide to I-Book. (Complete Idiot's Guides (Computers) Ser.). 380p. 2000. pap. 19.99 (*0-7897-2284-4*) Que.

— The Complete Idiot's Guide to Imac. 380p. 2000. 19.99 (*0-7897-2195-3*) Que.

Miser, Brad. Get on the Internet in 5 Minutes. 2nd ed. 1996. 9.99 (*1-56830-254-1*) Hayden.

***Miser, Brad.** MAC OS 9 Guide. 450p. 2000. pap. 29.99 (*0-7897-2312-3*) Que.

Miser, Hugh J. & Quade, Edward S., eds. Handbook of Systems Analysis Vol. 3: Cases. Vol. 3, Cases. 384p. 1996. 229.95 (*0-471-95357-1*) Wiley.

Miserda, Marko. Subjektivitat Im Glauben: Eine Theologisch-Methodologische Untersuchung zur Diskussion Uber Den "Glaubens-Sinn" in der Katholischen Theologie des 19. Jahrhunderts. (Europaische Hochschulschriften Ser.: Reihe 23, Bd. 569). (GER.). 575p. 1996. 88.95 (*3-631-49200-6*) P Lang Pubng.

Miserendino, Annette, ed. Catholic Telephone Guide. 296p. 1986. 22.00 (*0-910635-54-4*) Cath News Pub Co.

— Catholic Telephone Guide. 304p. 1987. 25.00 (*0-910635-60-9*) Cath News Pub Co.

Miserendino, Leo J. & Pick, Robert M., eds. Lasers in Dentistry. LC 94-41152. (Illus.). 341p. 1995. text 98.00 (*0-86715-282-6*) Quint Pub Co.

Miserez, D., ed. Refugees: The Trauma of Exile. (C). 1989. lib. bdg. 124.50 (*0-7923-0112-9*) Kluwer Academic.

Miserez, M. Characteristics in Contractile Dysfunction in Human Heart Failure. No. 104. 131p. (Orig.). 1994. pap. 52.50 (*90-6186-660-X*, Pub. by Leuven Univ) Coronet Bks.

Mises, Margit Von, see Von Mises, Margit.

Misfeldt, Willard E. The Albums of James Tissot. (Illus.). 134p. 1982. 25.95 (*0-87972-209-6*); pap. 13.95 (*0-87972-210-X*) Bowling Green Univ Popular Press.

Misgeld, Dieter & Nicholson, Graeme, eds. Hans-Georg Gadamer on Education, Poetry, & History: Applied Hermeneutics. Reuss, Monica & Schmidt, Lawrence, trs. from GER. LC 91-15119. (SUNY Series in Contemporary Continental Philosophy). 238p. (C). 1992. text 19.50 (*0-7914-0919-8*) State U NY Pr.

Misgeld, Klaus, et al, eds. Creating Social Democracy: A Century of the Social Democratic Labor Party in Sweden. (Illus.). 520p. (C). 1993. 70.00 (*0-271-00868-7*); pap. 18.95 (*0-271-00931-4*) Pa St U Pr.

Misgeld, Ulrich, jt. auth. see Frotscher, Michael.

Misguich, J., et al, eds. Statistical Description of Transport in Plasma, Astro & Nuclear Physics. (Houches Ser.). (Illus.). 437p. (C). 1993. lib. bdg. 195.00 (*1-56072-152-9*) Nova Sci Pubs.

Misgur, Livio. The Cooking of Piedmont. LC 97-44175. 256p. 1998. text 25.00 (*0-88001-596-9*) HarpC.

Mish, Charles C. English Prose Fiction, Sixteen Hundred to Seventeen Hundred: A Chronological Checklist. LC 68-9322. 110p. reprint ed. pap. 34.10 (*0-608-11518-5*, 200718800062) Bks Demand.

Mish, Charles C., ed. Restoration Prose Fiction, 1666-1700: An Anthology of Representative Pieces. LC 76-98095. 305p. reprint ed. pap. 94.60 (*0-608-16534-4*, 202733800055) Bks Demand.

— Short Fiction of the Seventeenth Century. (Seventeenth Century Ser.). Orig. Title: Anchor Anthology of Short Fiction of the Seventeenth Century. (C). 1968. reprint ed. pap. 2.95 (*0-393-00437-6*) Norton.

Mish, Frederick C., ed. see Merriam-Webster Editors.

Misha. Ke-Qua-Hawk-As. (Illus.). 88p. 1994. pap. 9.95 (*1-877655-13-9*) Wordcraft Oregon.

***Misha.** Red Spider White Web. 236p. 1999. pap. 12.00 (*1-877655-29-5*, Pub. by Wordcraft Oregon) SPD-Small Pr Dist.

Mishal, Shaul. The PLO under Arafat: Between Gun & Olive Branch. LC 86-9140. 206p. reprint ed. pap. 63.90 (*0-7837-4541-9*, 208031000005) Bks Demand.

— Speaking Stones: Communiques from the Intifada Underground. (Contemporary Issues in the Middle East Ser.). 272p. 1993. pap. text 19.95 (*0-8156-2607-X*) Syracuse U Pr.

— Speaking Stones: Communiques from the Intifada Underground. (Contemporary Issues in the Middle East Ser.). 272p. 1994. text 45.00 (*0-8156-2606-1*) Syracuse U Pr.

***Mishal, Shaul & Sela, Avraham.** The Palestinian Hamas: Vision, Violence & Coexistence. LC DS119.76.M57 2000. 2000. 49.50 (*0-231-11674-8*); pap. 17.50 (*0-231-11675-6*) Col U Pr.

Mishan, E. J. Cost Benefit Analysis. 4th ed. 384p. 1988. pap. text 24.95 (*0-04-445092-3*) Routledge.

— The Costs of Economic Growth. 2nd rev. ed. LC 93-19231. 320p. 1993. 62.95 (*0-275-94703-3*, Praeger Pubs) Greenwood.

Mishara, Brian L., ed. The Impact of Suicide. LC 95-7293. (Springer Series on Death & Suicide). (Illus.). 240p. 1995. 41.95 (*0-8261-8870-2*) Springer Pub.

Mishark, John W. Road to Revolution, German Marxism & World War 1. 15.00 (*0-685-16805-0*) Moira.

Mishchenko, A. S., et al. Topology of Lagrangian Manifolds. (Illus.). 320p. 1990. 136.95 (*0-387-13613-4*) Spr-Verlag.

Mishchenko, A. S., ed. see Arveson, William.

Mishchenko, Aleksandra S., jt. auth. see Luke, G. L.

Mishchenko, E. F., ed. Topology, Ordinary Differential Equations, Dynamical Systems: A Collection of Survey Articles. LC 87-959. (Proceedings of the Steklov Institute of Mathematics Ser.: Vol. 169). 260p. 1987. pap. 129.00 (*0-8218-3100-3*, STEKLO/169) Am Math.

***Mishchenko, Michael I., et al, eds.** Light Scattering by Nonspherical Particles. LC 99-61962. 690p. 1999. 115.00 (*0-12-498660-9*) Acad Pr.

Mishchke, Charles R., jt. auth. see Shigley, Joseph E.

Mishel, Kristi L. & Thomas, John J. Profitable Personnel Services: Start & Run a Money-Making Business. 1995. pap. text 18.95 (*0-07-042369-5*) McGraw-Hill Prof.

Mishel, Lawrence & Bernstein, Jared. The State of Working America, 1992-93. LC 91-641696. (Economic Policy Institute Ser.). 520p. (C). (gr. 13). 1993. pap. text 35.95 (*1-56324-212-5*) M E Sharpe.

— The State of Working America, 1994-1995. (Economic Policy Institute Ser.). (Illus.). 410p. (C). (gr. 13). 1994. 77.95 (*1-56324-532-9*) M E Sharpe.

Mishel, Lawrence & Frankel, David M. The State of Working America , 1990-1991. (Economic Policy Institute Ser.). 550p. (C). (gr. 13). 1991. pap. 35.95 (*0-87332-813-2*) M E Sharpe.

M

An Asterisk (*) at the beginning of an entry indicates that the title is appearing for the first time.

Mishel, Lawrence & Voos, Paula B., eds. Unions & Economic Competitiveness. LC 91-21335. (Economic Policy Institutie Ser.). 368p. (gr. 13). 1991. pap. text 34.95 (*0-87332-828-0*) M E Sharpe.

Mishel, Lawrence, et al. The State of Working America, 1996-97. (Economic Policy Institute Ser.). 480p. (C). (gr. 13). 1996. 74.95 (*0-7656-0023-4*); pap. 34.95 (*0-7656-0024-2*) M E Sharpe.

— The State of Working America, 1998-99. LC 98-43250. (Illus.). 480p. 1999. 59.95 (*0-8014-3613-3*, ILR Press) Cornell U Pr.

— The State of Working America, 1994-1995. (Economic Policy Institute Ser.). (Illus.). 410p. (C). (gr. 13). 1994. pap. 35.95 (*1-56324-533-7*) M E Sharpe.

— The State of Working America, 1998-1999. LC 98-43250. 1999. pap. 24.95 (*0-8014-8582-7*) Cornell U Pr.

***Mishel, Lawrence, et al.** The State of Working America, 2000-2001. 2001. 59.95 (*0-8014-3823-3*, ILR Press); pap. 24.95 (*0-8014-8680-7*, ILR Press) Cornell U Pr.

Mishel, Lawrence R. Better Jobs or Working Longer for Less. (Working Papers: No. 101). 1990. 10.00 (*0-944826-25-3*) Economic Policy Inst.

— Manufacturing Numbers: How Inaccurate Statistics Conceal U. S. Industrial Decline. LC 88-81375. 103p. (Orig.). 1988. pap., per. 12.00 (*0-944826-03-2*) Economic Policy Inst.

Mishel, Lawrence R. & Bernstein, Jared. The State of Working America: 1992-93. LC 91-641696. (Economic Policy Institute Ser.). 520p. (C). (gr. 13). 1993. text 77.95 (*1-56324-211-7*) M E Sharpe.

Mishel, Lawrence R. & Frankel, David M. The State of Working America: 1990-91 Edition. Voos, Paula, ed. (Economic Policy Institute Ser.). 550p. (C). (gr. 13). 1991. 77.95 (*0-87332-812-4*) M E Sharpe.

Mishel, Lawrence R. & Simon, Jacqueline. The State of Working America. LC 88-82263. 53p. 1988. 12.00 (*0-944826-04-0*) Economic Policy Inst.

Mishel, Lawrence R. & Teixeira, Ruy A. The Myth of the Coming Labor Shortage: Jobs, Skills, & Incomes of America's Workforce 2000. 1991. 12.00 (*0-944826-33-4*) Economic Policy Inst.

Mishel, Lawrence R. & Voos, Paula, eds. Unions & Economic Competitiveness. LC 91-21335. (Economic Policy Institute). 368p. (C). (gr. 13). 1991. text 70.95 (*0-87332-827-2*) M E Sharpe.

Mishel, Lawrence R., et al. Employee Rights in a Changing Economy: The Issue of Replacement Workers. (Seminar Ser.). 1991. 12.00 (*0-944826-40-7*) Economic Policy Inst.

Mishell. Obstetrics & Gynecology Two Thousand. 2000. 79.00 (*0-8151-2200-4*, 31734) Mosby Inc.

— Obstetrics & Gynecology Two Thousand & Two. 2002. 79.00 (*0-8151-2207-1*, 31736) Mosby Inc.

— Two Thousand & One Year Book of Obstetrics & Gynecology. 2001. 79.00 (*0-8151-2206-3*, 31735) Mosby Inc.

Mishell, Daniel R. Atlas of Reproductive Endocrinology. LC 98-9640. (Atlas of Clinical Gynecology Ser.). 250p. (C). 1998. 125.00 (*0-8385-0319-5*, Apple Lange Med) McGraw.

— 1998 Year Book Obstetrics & Gynecology. 2nd ed. (Illus.). 600p. (C). (gr. 13). 1998. text 79.00 (*0-8151-9704-7*, 24991) Mosby Inc.

Mishell, Daniel R., Jr, ed. Long Acting Steroid Contraception. LC 83-43027. (Advances in Human Fertility & Reproductive Endocrinology Ser.: No. 2). (Illus.). 216p. 1983. reprint ed. pap. 67.00 (*0-7837-9558-0*, 206030700005) Bks Demand.

Mishell, Daniel R., Jr. & Brenner, Paul F., eds. Management of Common Problems in Obstetrics & Gynecology. 3rd ed. LC 93-28312. (Illus.). 912p. 1994. 99.95 (*0-86542-269-9*) Blackwell Sci.

Mishell, Daniel R., jt. auth. see Stenchever, Morton A.

Mishell, Daniel R., jt. ed. see Sitruk-Ware, Regine.

Mishell, Judith & Srebrenick, S. Beyond Your Ego. 420p. (C). 1993. 29.95 (*1-56062-083-8*) CIS Comm.

Mishell, William W. Kaddish for Kovno: Life & Death in a Lithuanian Ghetto, 1941-1945. 408p. 1999. reprint ed. pap. 18.95 (*1-55652-340-8*, Pub. by Chicago Review) IPG Chicago.

Mishetski, Dmitry. The Wheat of Christ. (Orig.). 1988. pap. 3.00 (*0-913026-68-9*) St Nectarios.

Mishev, D. P., jt. auth. see Bainov, D. D.

Mishew, D. Bulgarians in the Past: Pages from the Bulgarian Cultural History. LC 74-135823. (Eastern Europe Collection). 1971. reprint ed. 29.95 (*0-405-02766-4*) Ayer.

***Mishica, Claire.** Is Your Pail Full? (Illus.). 12p. (J). (gr. k-2). 2000. pap. 3.75 (*1-58323-000-9*) Seedling Pubns.

Mishica, Clare. Bible Pals Things to Know. (My Bible Pals Ser.). 24p. (J). (ps-3). 1997. 9.99 (*0-7847-0594-1*, 03824) Standard Pub.

— Billions of Bugs. rev. ed. Caldwell, Lise, ed. LC 97-44170. (Illus.). 24p. (J). (ps-1). 1998. pap. 1.99 (*0-7847-0798-7*, 24-04256) Standard Pub.

— Billions of Bugs: Preschool Activity & Coloring Fun. (Coloring Fun & Activity Bks.). (Illus.). 16p. (J). (ps). 1994. pap. 1.69 (*0-7847-0228-4*, 02248) Standard Pub.

***Mishica, Clare.** Cody's New Friends. Ring, Laura, ed. (Illus.). 24p. (J). (ps-2). 2000. pap. 1.99 (*0-7847-1103-8*, 04308) Standard Pub.

Mishica, Clare. A Friend for Fraidy Cat. rev. ed. Caldwell, Lise, ed. (Illus.). 24p. (J). 1998. pap. 1.99 (*0-7847-0831-2*, 24-04261) Standard Pub.

***Mishica, Clare.** Joey's Christmas Gift. Ring, Laura, ed. LC 99-70911. (Illus.). 24p. (J). (ps-1). 1999. pap. 1.99 (*0-7847-1086-4*, 04282, Bean Sprouts) Standard Pub.

— Lost in the Store. Ring, Laura, ed. (Illus.). 24p. (J). (ps-2). 2000. pap. 1.99 (*0-7847-1102-X*, 04307) Standard Pub.

— Tina Marie's Best Christmas. Ring, Laura, ed. (Illus.). 24p. (J). (ps-1). 1999. pap. 1.99 (*0-7847-1046-5*, 04276, Bean Sprouts) Standard Pub.

Mishica, Clare & Keefer, Mikal. Surprising Stories: Three Read Aloud Stories with a Message. LC 98-61460. (Illus.). 24p. (J). (ps-3). 1999. 5.99 (*0-7847-0969-6*, 03730) Standard Pub.

Mishica, Clare, jt. auth. see Hird, Nancy E.

Mishima, Akio. Bitter Sea: The Human Cost of Minamata Disease. 248p. 1992. pap. 12.95 (*4-333-01479-4*, Pub. by Kosei Pub Co) Tuttle Pubng.

Mishima, S., ed. Diseases of the Retina & Uvea. (Journal: Ophthalmologica: Vol. 185, No. 3). (Illus.). 72p. 1982. pap. 41.75 (*3-8055-3563-5*) S Karger.

Mishima, Sumio. The Broader Way: A Woman's Life in the New Japan. LC 74-138596. 247p. 1970. reprint ed. lib. bdg. 35.00 (*0-8371-5797-8*, MIBW, Greenwood Pr) Greenwood.

Mishima, Yasua. The Mitsubishi: Its Challenge & Strategy. LC 89-15451. (Industrial Development & the Social Fabric Ser.: Vol. 11). 350p. 1990. 73.25 (*1-55938-031-4*) Jai Pr.

Mishima, Yukio, pseud. Acts of Worship: Seven Stories. Bester, John, tr. from JPN. & intro. by. 224p. 1990. reprint ed. pap. 11.95 (*0-87011-824-2*) Kodansha.

— After the Banquet. 271p. 1999. pap. 13.00 (*0-375-70515-5*) Knopf.

— Apres le Banquet. (FRE.). 1979. pap. 10.95 (*0-7859-4117-7*) Fr & Eur.

— Chevaux Echappes (La Mer de la Fertilite II) (FRE.). 499p. 1981. pap. 15.95 (*0-7859-4351-X*, 2070383318) Fr & Eur.

— Confession d'un Masque. (FRE.). 1983. pap. 11.95 (*0-7859-4183-5*) Fr & Eur.

— Confessions of a Mask. Weatherby, Meredith, tr. LC 58-12637. 1968. reprint ed. pap. 10.95 (*0-8112-0118-X*, NDP253, Pub. by New Directions) Norton.

— Death in Midsummer & Other Stories. LC 66-17819. (Orig.). 1966. pap. 9.95 (*0-8112-0117-1*, NDP215, Pub. by New Directions) Norton.

— The Decay of the Angel. Seidensticker, Edward G., tr. from JPN. LC 89-40554. (Vintage International Ser.). 256p. 1990. pap. 13.00 (*0-679-72243-2*) Vin Bks.

— Five Modern No Plays. Keene, Donald, tr. from JPN.Tr. of Kindai Nogakushu. (Illus.). 206p. 1957. pap. 12.95 (*0-8048-1380-9*) Tuttle Pubng.

— Forbidden Colors. Marks, Alfred H., tr. from JPN. LC 98-41723. 403p. 1999. pap. 14.00 (*0-375-70516-3*) Knopf.

— Le Marin Rejete par la Mer. (FRE.). 1979. pap. 10.95 (*0-7859-4122-3*) Fr & Eur.

— Patriotism. Sargent, Geoffrey W., tr. from JPN. LC 95-36529. (New Directions Bibelot Ser.). 64p. 1995. reprint ed. pap. 6.00 (*0-8112-1312-9*, NDP814, Pub. by New Directions) Norton.

— Le Pavillion D'Or. (FRE.). 1975. pap. 11.95 (*0-7859-4039-1*) Fr & Eur.

***Mishima, Yukio, pseud.** The Peacocks. (Short Stories Ser.). 22p. 2000. pap. 3.95 (*1-86092-029-2*, Pub. by Travelman Pub) IPG Chicago.

Mishima, Yukio, pseud. Runaway Horses. Gallagher, Michael, tr. from JPN. LC 89-40560. (Vintage International Ser.). 421p. 1990. pap. 14.00 (*0-679-72240-8*) Vin Bks.

— The Sailor Who Fell from Grace with the Sea. Nathan, John, tr. from JPN. 1994. pap. 12.00 (*0-679-75015-0*) Vin Bks.

— Silk & Insight: A Novel. Gibney, Frank, ed. Sato, Hiroaki, tr. from JPN. & intro. by. LC 98-11263. Orig. Title: Kinu to Meisatsu. 240p. (C). (gr. 13). 1998. text 44.95 (*0-7656-0299-7*) M E Sharpe.

— Silk & Insight (Kinu to Meisatsu) A Novel. Gibney, Frank, ed. Sato, Hiroaki, tr. from JPN. & intro. by. LC 98-11263. 240p. (C). (gr. 13). 1998. pap. text 19.95 (*0-7656-0300-4*) M E Sharpe.

— The Sound of Waves. Weatherby, Meredith, tr. from JPN. 192p. 1994. pap. 11.00 (*0-679-75268-4*) Knopf.

— Spring Snow. Gallagher, Michael, tr. from JPN. LC 89-40565. (Vintage International Ser.: Vol. 1). 400p. 1990. pap. 13.00 (*0-679-72241-6*) Vin Bks.

— Sun & Steel. Bester, John, tr. LC 76-100628. 108p. 1990. pap. 9.00 (*0-87011-425-5*) Kodansha.

— The Temple of Dawn. Saunders, E. Dale & Seigle, Cecilia S., trs. LC 89-40557. Vol. 3. 1990. pap. 14.00 (*0-679-72242-4*) Vin Bks.

— The Temple of the Golden Pavilion. Morris, Ivan, tr. from JPN. 272p. 1994. pap. 13.00 (*0-679-75270-6*) Random.

— The Temple of the Golden Pavilion. Morris, Ivan, tr. LC 94-6237. 1995. 17.00 (*0-679-43315-5*) Random.

— Thirst for Love. Marks, Alfred H., tr. from JPN. 200p. 1999. pap. 12.00 (*0-375-70507-4*) Vin Bks.

— Le Tumulte des Flots. (FRE.). 1978. pap. 10.95 (*0-7859-4095-2*) Fr & Eur.

Mishima, Yukio, pseud & Bownas, Geoffrey, eds. New Writing in Japan. 256p. 1998. reprint ed. pap. text 25.00 (*1-873410-79-4*, Pub. by Curzon Pr Ltd) UH Pr.

Mishima, Yutaka, ed. Cancer Neutron Capture Therapy: Proceedings of the Sixth International Symposium Held in Kobe, Japan, October 31-November 4, 1994. (Illus.). 947p. 1996. 210.00 (*0-306-45307-X*, Kluwer Plenum) Kluwer Academic.

Mishin, Y., et al, eds. Diffusion Mechanisms in Crystalline Materials Vol. 527: Proceedings Materials Research Society Symposium. LC 98-29723. 549p. 1998. text 88.00 (*1-55899-433-5*) Materials Res.

Mishina, Hitoshi, jt. auth. see Okuyama, Shinichi.

Mishk, O. L. Treasure Island & Kidnapped Notes. (Cliffs Notes Ser.). 80p. (Orig.). (C). 1974. pap. text 4.95 (*0-8220-1306-1*, Cliff) IDG Bks.

Mishkin. Dos software. 1997. teacher ed. 11.00 (*0-673-97018-3*, GoodYrBooks) Addson-Wesley Educ.

Mishkin. Mishkin's Economics of Money & Banking. 5th ed. (C). 1998. text. write for info. (*0-321-02844-9*) Addison-Wesley.

— Overhead Transparencies:Economics Of Money, Banking, & Financial Markets. 5th ed. 1p. 1997. pap. text 266.67 (*0-321-01755-2*) Addison-Wesley.

Mishkin, Bernard. Rank & Warfare among the Plains Indians. LC 84-45510. (American Ethnological Society Monographs: No. 3). 1988. reprint ed. 20.00 (*0-404-62903-2*) AMS Pr.

— Rank & Warfare among the Plains Indians. LC 92-15035. xix, 65p. 1992. reprint ed. pap. 6.95 (*0-8032-8185-4*, Bison Books) U of Nebr Pr.

Mishkin, David J. The American Colonial Wine Industry: An Economic Interpretation, 2 vols., Set. (Dissertations in American Economic History Ser.). (Illus.). 1975. 87.95 (*0-405-07208-2*) Ayer.

— The American Colonial Wine Industry: An Economic Interpretation, 2 vols., Vol. 1. (Dissertations in American Economic History Ser.). (Illus.). 1975. 26.95 (*0-405-07209-0*) Ayer.

— The American Colonial Wine Industry: An Economic Interpretation, 2 vols., Vol. 2. (Dissertations in American Economic History Ser.). (Illus.). 1975. 60.95 (*0-405-07210-4*) Ayer.

***Mishkin, Frederic S.** Conversion Guide to a Financial Markets & Institutions. 3rd ed. (C). 2000. pap. text 30.00 (*0-321-06077-6*) Addson-Wesley Educ.

Mishkin, Frederic S. Economic Money Bank & Reader. (C). 1992. text 70.00 (*0-673-52172-9*) Addson-Wesley Educ.

— Economic Policy Review. 112p. (C). 1997. pap. text. write for info. (*0-321-03132-6*) Addison-Wesley.

— The Economics of Money & Banking. 5th ed. 304p. (C). 1997. pap. text, student ed. 24.38 (*0-321-01751-X*) Addson-Wesley Educ.

— The Economics of Money, Banking & Financial Markets. (C). 1986. teacher ed. write for info. (*0-318-60360-8*); student ed. write for info. (*0-316-57477-5*) Little.

— The Economics of Money, Banking & Financial Markets. 5th ed. (C). 1997. pap. text 75.00 (*0-321-03133-4*) Addson-Wesley Educ.

— The Economics of Money, Banking, & Financial Markets. 5th ed. LC 97-19567. 1997. write for info. (*0-673-52550-3*) Addison-Wesley.

— Financial Markets & Institutions. 3rd ed. 352p. (C). 1999. pap. text 22.35 (*0-321-06074-1*) Addison-Wesley.

— Financial Markets & Institutions. 3rd ed. LC 99-28715. 752p. (C). 1999. 96.33 (*0-321-05064-9*) Addson-Wesley Educ.

— Financial Markets, Institutions & Money. LC 94-25039. (C). 1994. 45.00 (*0-673-46997-2*) HarpC.

— Money, Interest Rates & Inflation. LC 93-2700. (Economists of the Twentieth Century Ser.). 352p. 1993. 95.00 (*1-85278-850-X*) E Elgar.

— A Rational Expectations Approach to Macroeconomics: Testing Policy Ineffectiveness & Efficient-Markets Models. LC 82-20049. (National Bureau of Economic Research Monographs). 184p. (C). 1984. pap. text 10.95 (*0-226-53187-2*) U Ch Pr.

— A Rational Expectations Approach to Macroeconomics: Testing Policy Ineffectiveness & Efficient-Markets Models. LC 82-20049. (National Bureau of Economic Research Monographs). 192p. (C). 1993. lib. bdg. 20.00 (*0-226-53186-4*) U Ch Pr.

Mishkin, Frederic S., ed. The Economics of Money, Banking & Financial Markets. 5th ed. 732p. (C). 1999. 98.00 (*0-321-01440-5*) Addson-Wesley Educ.

— Financial Markets, Institutions & Money. 2nd ed. (C). 1998. text. write for info. (*0-321-01283-6*) Addson-Wesley Educ.

— Financial Markets Institutions & Money. 2nd ed. (C). 1998. text 79.69 (*0-321-01465-0*) Addson-Wesley Educ.

Mishkin, Frederic S., jt. auth. see Easton.

Mishkin, Frederic S., jt. auth. see Eaton.

Mishkin, Frederic S., jt. auth. see Morris.

Mishkin, Julia. Cruel Duet, Vol. 7, No. 2. (QRL Poetry Bks.: Vol. XXVI). 1986. 20.00 (*0-614-06416-3*) Quarterly Rev.

Mishkin, M., jt. ed. see Iwai, E.

Mishkin, Tracy. The Harlem & Irish Renaissances: Language, Identity, & Representation. LC 98-27017. 160p. 1998. 49.95 (*0-8130-1611-8*) U Press Fla.

Mishkin, Tracy, ed. Literary Influence & African-American Writers. LC 95-19543. (Wellesley Studies in Critical Theory, Literary History & Culture: Vol. 10). (Illus.). 400p. 1995. text 80.00 (*0-8153-1724-7*, H1849) Garland.

Mishler, Clayton. Sampan Sailor: A Navy Man's Adventures in WWII China. (World War II Commemorative Ser.). 240p. 1994. 23.95 (*0-02-881073-2*) Brasseys.

Mishler, Clifford, jt. auth. see Krause, Chester L.

Mishler, Craig. The Crooked Stovepipe: Athapaskan Fiddle Music & Square Dancing in Northeast Alaska & Northwest Canada. LC 92-36827. (Music in American Life Ser.). (Illus.). 248p. 1993. text 29.95 (*0-252-01996-2*) U of Ill Pr.

Mishler, Craig, ed. Neerihiinjik: We Traveled from Place to Place: Johnny Sarah Haa Googwandak: The Gwich'in Stories of Johnny & Sarah Frank. (Illus.). xxx, 690p. 1996. pap. 29.00 (*1-55500-054-1*) Alaska Native.

***Mishler, Donna.** Historical People for Young Learners. large type ed. (Illus.). 32p. (J). (gr. k-5). 1999. pap. text, student ed. 5.95 (*1-893709-03-5*) Suthernsky.

— Lighthouses of the Mid-Atlantic States. large type ed. (Illus.). 32p. (J). (gr. k-5). 1999. pap. text, student ed. 5.95 (*1-893709-02-7*) Suthernsky.

— Travel Through Virginia, Bk. I. large type ed. (Illus.). 40p. (J). (gr. k-5). 1999. pap. text, student ed. 6.95 (*1-893709-00-0*) Suthernsky.

— Travel Through Virginia, Bk. II. large type ed. (Illus.). 40p. (J). (gr. k-5). 1999. pap. text, student ed. 5.95 (*1-893709-01-9*) Suthernsky.

Mishler, Elliot G. The Discourse of Medicine. Wallat, Cynthia & Green, Judith, eds. LC 84-16832. (Language & Learning for Human Service Professions Ser.: Vol. 3). 224p. 1985. pap. 39.50 (*0-89391-277-8*); text 73.25 (*0-89391-276-X*) Ablx Pub.

— Research Interviewing: Context & Narrative. 208p. 1991. pap. 18.00 (*0-674-76461-7*, MISREX) HUP.

— Storylines: Crafts Artist' Naratives of Identity. LC 99-38230. 256p. 2000. 29.95 (*0-674-83973-0*) HUP.

Mishler, Elliot G. & Waxler, Nancy E., eds. Family Processes & Schizophrenia. LC 84-45085. 336p. 1983. 50.00 (*0-87668-711-7*) Aronson.

Mishler, Lon, jt. auth. see Cole, Robert H.

Mishler, Lon L., jt. auth. see Cole, Robert H.

Mishler, Paul C. Raising Reds: The Young Pioneers, Radical Summer Camps, & Communist Political Culture in the United States. LC 98-39593. 172p. 1999. 45.00 (*0-231-11044-8*); pap. 17.50 (*0-231-11045-6*) Col U Pr.

Mishler, William, tr. see Haugen, Paal-Helge.

***Mishlove, Jeffrey.** PK Man: A True Story of Mind-Over-Matter. (Illus.). 2000. pap. 14.95 (*1-57174-183-6*) N D Walsch.

Mishlove, Jeffrey. The Roots of Consciousness. (Illus.). 416p. 1997. pap. text 22.95 (*1-56924-747-1*) Marlowe & Co.

***Mishlove, Jeffrey.** The Roots of Consciousness: The Classic Encyclopedia of Consciousness Studies. (Illus.). 478p. 1999. pap. text 23.00 (*0-7881-6780-4*) DIANE Pub.

Mishlove, Jeffrey. Thinking Allowed: Conversations on the Leading Edge of Knowledge & Discovery. LC 91-77972. 372p. 1995. pap. 16.95 (*0-933031-64-5*) Coun Oak Bks.

Mishnaevsky, Leon L., Jr. Damage & Fracture in Heterogeneous Materials: Modelling & Application to the Improvement of Drilling Tool. LC 99-496424. (Illus.). 230p. 1998. 64.00 (*90-5410-699-9*) Ashgate Pub Co.

Mishne, Judith M. Clinical Work with Adolescents. 320p. 1986. 32.95 (*0-02-921260-X*) Free Pr.

— Clinical Work with Children. 1983. 32.95 (*0-02-921630-3*) Free Pr.

— The Evolution & Application of Clinical Theory: Perspective from Four Psychologies. LC 92-39586. 1993. 40.00 (*0-02-921635-4*) Free Pr.

— The Learning Curve: Elevating Children's Academic & Social Competence. LC 95-16867. 256p. 1996. 40.00 (*1-56821-568-1*) Aronson.

Mishne, Judith M., jt. ed. see Buchholz, Ester S.

Mishoe, S. & Kelsey, Neal. Ventilator Concepts. 2nd ed. 497p. (C). 1987. pap. text 35.95 (*0-933195-15-X*) CA College Health Sci.

***Mishoe, Shelley C. & Welch, Melvin A., Jr.** Critical Thinking in Respiratory Care: A Problem Based Learning Approach. (Illus.). 528p. 2000. Price not set. (*0-07-134474-8*) McGraw.

Mishr, R. P. Hinduism: The Faith of the Future. 131p. 1981. 16.95 (*0-940500-17-5*) Asia Bk Corp.

Mishra. Archaeology of Mayurbhanj. (C). 1997. 42.00 (*81-246-0084-8*, Pub. by DK Pubs Ind) S Asia.

Mishra, jt. auth. see Bhattachan.

Mishra, jt. auth. see Robertson.

Mishra, A. K., jt. auth. see Patnaik, U. C.

Mishra, Anil Kant. Rural Tension in India. LC 98-905497. 143p. 1998. 25.00 (*81-7141-416-8*, Pub. by Discovery Pub Hse) Nataraj Bks.

Mishra, B., ed. EPD Congress, 1998: Proceedings, Extraction & Processing Division, TMS Annual Meeting, San Antonio, Texas, 1998. (Illus.). 1000p. 1998. 94.00 (*0-87339-388-0*, TP156) Minerals Metals.

***Mishra, B., ed.** EPD Congress, 1999. (Illus.). 22p. 1999. 120.00 (*0-87339-422-4*, 4224) Minerals Metals.

Mishra, B., ed. EPD Congress, 1997. (Illus.). 493p. 1997. 92.00 (*0-87339-367-8*, 3678) Minerals Metals.

Mishra, B. & Kipouros, G. J., eds. Titanium Extraction & Processing. LC 97-73308. (Illus.). 283p. 1997. 68.00 (*0-87339-380-5*, 3805) Minerals Metals.

Mishra, B., jt. ed. see Reddy, R. G.

Mishra, B. K. Breast Feeding & Child Development. viii, 178p. 1993. 20.00 (*81-7024-567-2*, Pub. by Ashish Pub Hse) Nataraj Bks.

Mishra, B. N. Ecology of Poverty in India. 1990. 39.50 (*0-8364-2595-2*, Pub. by Chugh Pubns) S Asia.

Mishra, Baba. Medieval Orissa & Cult of Jagannatha. LC 95-902322. (C). 1995. 29.00 (*81-7013-128-6*, Pub. by Navarang) S Asia.

Mishra, Bhagabat. The Economics of Public Distribution in Foodgrains (India) 1985. 32.00 (*0-8364-1467-5*, Pub. by Ashish Pub Hse) S Asia.

Mishra, Bhubaneswar. Algorithmic Algebra. LC 93-14094. (Texts & Monographs in Computer Science). (Illus.). 416p. 1993. 59.95 (*0-387-94090-1*) Spr-Verlag.

— Algorithmic Algebra. (Texts & Monographs in Computer Science). (Illus.). xiv, 425p. 1993. write for info. (*3-540-94090-1*) Spr-Verlag.

***Mishra, Bibhuti B.** Religious Movements in Orissa: In Nineteenth Century LC 99-931135. xii, 200p. 1998. write for info. (*81-86782-33-8*, Pub. by Publicat Schem) S Asia.

Mishra, Brajendra, jt. ed. see Bautista, Rehato G.

Mishra, D. K. Public Debt & Economic Development in India. 552p. (C). 1984. 225.00 (*81-85009-07-4*, Pub. by Print Hse) St Mut.

Mishra, D. N. RSS: Myth & Reality. 218p. 1980. 19.95 (*0-7069-1020-6*) Asia Bk Corp.

Mishra, Dinesh Kumar, see Singh, Rajendra & Kumar Mishra, Dinesh.

Mishra, G. P. & Joshi, A., eds. Regional Structure of Development & Growth in India, 2 vols., 1. 1985. 38.00 (*0-8364-1446-2*, Pub. by Ashish Pub Hse) S Asia.

An Asterisk (*) at the beginning of an entry indicates that the title is appearing for the first time.

Mishra, G. P. & Pande, P. N. Child Labour in Carpet Industry. (Illus.). vi, 114p. 1996. 14.00 (*81-7024-750-0*, Pub. by Ashish Pub Hse) Nataraj Bks.
— Child Labour in Glass Industry. (Illus.). vi, 122p. 1996. 14.00 (*81-7024-751-9*, Pub. by Ashish Pub Hse) Nataraj Bks.
Mishra, Ganeswar & Satapathy, Sarat C., eds. Selections from Nehru. 1997. reprint ed. pap. 3.50 (*81-250-0319-3*, Pub. by Orient Longman Ltd) S Asia.
Mishra, Girish, ed. Economic Effects of Militarism. 108p. 1984. 12.95 (*0-318-37234-7*) Asia Bk Corp.
Mishra, H. K. Famines & Poverty in India. (C). 1990. 59.00 (*81-7024-374-2*, Pub. by Ashish Pub Hse) S Asia.
Mishra, Hemanta R. & Jefferies, Margaret. The Royal Chitwan National Park: Wildlife Sanctuary of Nepal. (Illus.). 192p. 1991. pap. 18.95 (*0-89886-266-3*) Mountaineers.
Mishra, Jayashri. Social & Economic Conditions under the Imperial Rashtrakutas. (C). 1992. 28.50 (*81-7169-171-4*, Pub. by Commonwealth) S Asia.
Mishra, Kiran. Women in a Tribal Community: A Study of Arunachal Pradesh. 1991. text 12.50 (*0-7069-5836-5*, Pub. by Vikas) S Asia.
Mishra, L. Anguish of the Deprived. (C). 1994. 28.50 (*81-241-0188-4*, Pub. by Har-Anand Pubns) S Asia.
Mishra, Lakshmidhar. Burden of Bondage: An Enquiry into the Affairs of the Bonded Quarry Mine Workers of Faridabad. LC 97-901629. xviii, 478p. 1997. 46.00 (*81-86562-11-7*, Pub. by Manak Pubns Pvt Ltd) Nataraj Bks.
***Mishra, Lakshmidhar.** Child Labour in India. 384p. 2000. text 29.95 (*0-19-565087-5*) OUP.
Mishra, Madhusudan. Critical Study of Amrtacandra's Purusarthasiddhupayah. 1992. 14.00 (*81-85094-55-1*, Pub. by Punthi Pus) S Asia.
— A Critical Study of the Varttikas of Katyayana. LC 96-901541. xii, 208p. 1996. 18.00 (*81-86339-29-9*, Pub. by Eastern Bk Linkers) Nataraj Bks.
— Householders' Discipline in Jainism: A Study of Amrtacandra's Purusarthasiddhyupayah with Edited Text in Devanagari Script. (SAN.). 1996. pap. 14.00 (*81-86339-23-X*, Pub. by Eastern Bk Linkers) S Asia.
Mishra, Manjusree. Freedom of Trade & Commerce & Taxation in India. LC 99-932056. 318 p. 1999. write for info. (*81-7099-713-5*) S Asia.
Mishra, Munmaya K., ed. Macromolecular Design: Concept & Practice: Macromonomers, Macroinitiator, Macroiniferter, Macroinifer - Macroiniter. LC 92-85448. (Advanced Polymers Via Macromolecular Engineering Ser.). 500p. 1994. 125.00 (*0-9639138-0-8*) Polymer Frontiers.
Mishra, Munmaya K., et al, eds. Macromolecular Engineering: Recent Advances: International Conference on Advanced Polymers Via Macromolecular Engineering (1995: Poughkeepsie, New York) LC 95-32590. (Illus.). 342p. (C). 1995. text 115.00 (*0-306-45112-3*, Kluwer Plenum) Kluwer Academic.
***Mishra, Munmaya K. & Kobayashi, Shiro.** Star & Hyperbranched Polymers LC 99-26160. (Plastics Engineering Ser.). (Illus.). 360p. 1999. text 175.00 (*0-8247-1986-7*) Dekker.
Mishra, Munmaya K. & Yagci, Yusuf. Handbook of Vinyl Polymerization. LC 98-16707. (Illus.). 424p. 1998. text 175.00 (*0-8247-9464-8*) Dekker.
Mishra, Nawin C. Molecular Biology of Nucleases. 296p. 1995. boxed set 224.95 (*0-8493-7658-0*, 7658) CRC Pr.
Mishra, Nawin C. & Mehlman, Myron A. Mammalian Cell Transformation by Chemical Carcinogens. LC 82-51185. (Advances in Modern Environmental Toxicology Ser.: Vol. 1). (Illus.). 504p. 1981. text 58.00 (*0-911131-01-9*) Specialist Journals.
Mishra, Neelam. The Socialist Orientation of Jawaharlal Nehru. 200p. 1989. 13.00 (*81-212-0285-X*, Pub. by Gian Publng Hse) S Asia.
Mishra, P. C. Fundamentals of Air & Water Pollution. 1990. 22.00 (*81-7024-306-8*, Pub. by Ashish Pub Hse) S Asia.
— Soil Pollution & Soil Organisms. (C). 1989. 39.00 (*81-7024-258-4*, Pub. by Ashish Pub Hse) S Asia.
Mishra, P. C., et al, eds. Advances in Ecology & Environmental Sciences. (Illus.). xxiii, 651p. 1995. 79.00 (*81-7024-676-8*, Pub. by Ashish Pub Hse) Nataraj Bks.
Mishra, P. K. South Asia: Conflicts & Cooperation. 1997. pap. 96.00 (*0-7855-7491-3*, Pub. by Ratna Pustak Bhandar) St Mut.
— South Asia in International Politics. 498p. 1986. 24.95 (*81-85044-01-5*) Asia Bk Corp.
Mishra, P. K., ed. The Bhagavata Purana: An Illustrated Oriya Palmleaf Manuscript. (Illus.). 60p. 1987. 32.50 (*81-7017-219-5*, Pub. by Abhinav) S Asia.
***Mishra, P. K., ed.** Studies in Hindu & Buddhist Art. LC 99-932710. 413 p. 1999. 58.00 (*81-7017-368-X*, Pub. by Abhinav Pubns) S Asia.
***Mishra, Pankaj.** The Romantics. LC 99-15799. 272p. 2000. 23.95 (*0-375-50274-2*) Random.
— The Romantics. 2001. reprint ed. pap. 13.00 (*0-385-72080-7*, Anchor NY) Doubleday.
***Mishra, Phanikanta.** Researches in Archaeology & Conservation. LC 99-933663. 198p. 1999. write for info. (*81-7574-083-3*, Pub. by Sundeep Prak) S Asia.
Mishra, Phanikanta, ed. Researches in Indian Archaeology, Art, Architecture, Culture & Religion, 2 vols., Set. (C). 1995. 200.00 (*81-85067-82-1*, Pub. by Sundeep Prak) S Asia.
Mishra, Pramod K. Dhaka Summit an SAARC. (C). 1986. 9.50 (*81-7074-000-2*, Pub. by KP Bagchi) S Asia.
Mishra, Pramrod K. Agricultural Risk, Insurance & Income: A Study of the Impact & Design of India's Comprehensive Crop Insurance Scheme. LC 96-86401. 346p. 1997. text 87.95 (*1-85972-060-9*, Pub. by Avebry) Ashgate Pub Co.
Mishra, Pramrod K., jt. auth. see Sullerey, S. K.
Mishra, Prashant, jt. auth. see Singh, Ajay.
Mishra, R., et al, eds. Progress in Ecology Vol. I: Progress of Plant Ecology in India. (Illus.). 162p. 1973. 20.00 (*0-88065-160-1*) Scholarly Pubns.
Mishra, R. B. Caste & Caste Conflict in Rural Society. 1989. 31.00 (*81-7169-013-0*, Pub. by Commonwealth) S Asia.
Mishra, R. K., ed. Living State II. 712p. 1985. 121.00 (*9971-978-26-1*) World Scientific Pub.
— Molecular & Biological Physics of Living Systems. (C). 1990. text 166.50 (*0-7923-0470-5*) Kluwer Academic.
Mishra, R. K., et al. On Self-Organization: An Interdisciplinary Search for a Unifying Principle. LC 93-38258. 1994. 73.95 (*0-387-56485-3*) Spr-Verlag.
Mishra, R. K., tr. see Rossinski, K. I., ed.
Mishra, R. K., tr. see Sokolenko, E. A., ed.
Mishra, R. R., ed. Current Trends in Environmental Biology. (C). 1990. 18.00 (*81-224-0184-8*) S Asia.
Mishra, Rajendra N. Search for Belief in the Poetry of Robert Frost. (C). 1992. 18.00 (*81-7017-291-8*, Pub. by Abhinav) S Asia.
Mishra, Rajiv S., et al, eds. Ultrafine Grained Materials. (Illus.). 444p. 107.00 (*0-87339-472-0*) Minerals Metals.
***Mishra, Rajiv S. & Mukherjee, A. K., eds.** Creep Behavior of Advanced Materials for the 21st Century. LC 98-68634. (Illus.). 20p. 1999. 170.00 (*0-87339-420-8*, 4208) Minerals Metals.
***Mishra, Rajnish Kumar.** Buddhist Theory of Meaning & Literary Analysis. LC 98-917246. xx, 292p. 1999. 25.00 (*81-246-0118-6*, Pub. by D K Printwrld) Nataraj Bks.
Mishra, Ram K., et al, eds. G Protein Methods & Protocols: Role of G Proteins in Psychiatric & Neurological Disorders. (Neuromethods Ser.: Vol. 31). (Illus.). 448p. 1997. 99.50 (*0-89603-490-9*) Humana.
***Mishra, Ramesh.** Globalization & the Welfare State. LC 99-21912. 152p. 1999. 80.00 (*1-85898-221-9*) E Elgar.
— Globalization & the Welfare State. LC 99-21912. 176p. 1999. 25.00 (*1-84064-173-8*) E Elgar.
Mishra, Ramesh. The Welfare State in Capitalist Society: Policies of Retrenchment & Maintenance in Europe, North America, & Australia. 208p. 1990. text 60.00 (*0-8020-5895-7*) U of Toronto Pr.
— The Welfare State in Capitalist Society: Policies of Retrenchment & Maintenance in Europe, North America & Australia. 208p. 1990. pap. text 19.95 (*0-8020-6829-4*) U of Toronto Pr.
Mishra, Ramesh C., et al. Ecology, Acculturation, & Psychological Adaptation: A Study of Adivasis in Bihar. 272p. (C). 1996. 32.00 (*0-8039-9284-X*) Sage.
Mishra, Rammurti S. Fundamentals of Yoga: A Handbook of Theory, Practice & Application. 19th ed. (Illus.). 256p. 1987. pap. 13.95 (*0-517-56422-X*) Harmony Bks.
Mishra, Ramprasad. Bodhipathapradipa of Depankara Srijnana. 1998. 32.00 (*81-86218-09-2*) Kant Pubns.
— Sahajayana: A Study of Tantric Buddhism. (C). 1991. 45.00 (*81-85094-45-4*, Pub. by Punthi Pus) S Asia.
Mishra, Rashmi & Mohanty, Samarendra. Police & Social Change in India. xiv, 229p. 1992. 22.95 (*1-881338-32-0*) Nataraj Bks.
Mishra, Ratan L. The Mortuary Monuments in Ancient & Medieval India. 1991. 18.00 (*81-7018-622-6*, Pub. by BR Pub) S Asia.
Mishra, S. Voice of Truth: The Challenges & Struggles of a Nepalese Woman. 1994. pap. 130.00 (*0-7855-0490-7*, Pub. by Ratna Pustak Bhandar) St Mut.
Mishra, S. G. Legal History of India, 1600-1990. (C). 1992. 22.00 (*81-85565-21-X*, Pub. by Uppal Pub Hse) S Asia.
Mishra, S. K. Sustainable Growth of Agriculture in India. 135p. 1993. pap. 100.00 (*81-85880-30-1*, Pub. by Print Hse) St Mut.
Mishra, Satya N., jt. auth. see Dudewicz, Edward J.
Mishra, Shanti. Fundamental Rights & the Supreme Court Reasonableness of Restrictions. 2nd ed. (C). 1989. 125.00 (*0-7855-4804-1*) St Mut.
— Voice of Truth: Challenges & Struggles of a Nepalese Woman. (C). 1994. 44.00 (*81-7303-022-7*, Pub. by Book Faith) S Asia.
Mishra, Shyam M. Yasavarman of Kanauj: Study of Political History, Society & Cultural Life of Northern India. 1978. 15.00 (*0-8364-0105-0*) S Asia.
Mishra, Srikanta. Ancient Hindu Marriage Law & Practice. LC 94-900506. (C). 1994. 26.50 (*81-7100-582-9*, Pub. by Deep & Deep Pubns) S Asia.
Mishra, Surendra K. & Klimpel, Richard R., eds. Fine Coal Processing. LC 86-3338. (Illus.). 452p. 1987. 48.00 (*0-8155-1123-X*) Noyes.
Mishra, Sweta. Democratic Decentralisation in India: Study in Retrospect & Prospect. (C). 1994. 16.00 (*81-7099-533-7*, Pub. by Mittal Pubs Dist) S Asia.
***Mishra, T. N.** Buddhist Tantra & Buddhist Art. (Illus.). xi, 132p. 2000. 25.00 (*81-246-0141-0*, Pub. by D K Printwrld) Nataraj Bks.
Mishra, T. N. Impact of Tantra on Religion & Art. (Illus.). 184p. (C). 1997. 27.00 (*81-246-0073-2*, Pub. by D K Printwrld) Nataraj Bks.
Mishra, Umesh, jt. ed. see Goronkin, Herb.
Mishra, Umesh, jt. ed. see Shah, Jagdeep.
Mishra, V. D. Youth Culture: A Comparative Study in the Indon Context. (C). 1993. 18.00 (*81-210-0311-3*, Pub. by Inter-India Pubns) S Asia.
Mishra, Vic, jt. ed. see Singh, Indu B.
Mishra, Vidya B. Refunds under Central Excise & Customs. (C). 1990. 100.00 (*0-89771-225-0*) St Mut.
— Supreme Court on Equal Pay for Equal Work. (C). 1989. 125.00 (*0-7855-4768-1*) St Mut.
Mishra, Vijay. Devotional Poetics & the Indian Sublime. LC 98-22842. (SUNY Series on the Sublime). 292p. (C). 1998. text 65.50 (*0-7914-3871-6*); pap. text 21.95 (*0-7914-3872-4*) State U NY Pr.
Mishra, Vijay, jt. auth. see Hodge, Bob.
Mishra, Vinod S. Environment Disasters & the Law. (Illus.). xvi, 146p. 1994. 15.00 (*81-7024-629-6*, Pub. by Ashish Pub Hse) Nataraj Bks.
Mishra, Yogendra, ed. Dimensions of Indian History & Culture. LC 97-905452. 1997. 88.00 (*81-7169-419-5*, Pub. by Commonwealth) S Asia.
Mishriky, Salwa E. Le Misanthrope Ou la Philanthropie de l'Honnete Homme Classique. (Currents in Comparative Romance Languages & Literatures Ser.). (FRE.). XVIII, 237p. (C). 1995. text 49.95 (*0-8204-2398-X*) P Lang Pubng.
Misiek, Jozef, ed. The Problem of Rationality in Science & Its Philosophy: On Popper vs. Polanyi, the Polish Conferences 1988-89. LC 94-17897. (Boston Studies in Philosophy of Science: Vol. 160). 280p. (C). 1995. lib. bdg. 148.50 (*0-7923-2925-2*, Pub. by Kluwer Academic) Kluwer Academic.
Misiewicz, J. J. & Harris, A. W. Helicobacter Pylori. (Illus.). 66p. (Orig.). 1996. pap. text 29.95 (*0-86542-639-2*) Blackwell Sci.
Misiewicz, J. J. & Pounder, R. E., eds. Diseases of the Gut & Pancreas. 2nd ed. (Illus.). 1176p. 1994. 225.00 (*0-632-02783-5*, Pub. by Blckwll Scitfc UK) Blackwell Sci.
Misiewicz, J. J., et al. Atlas of Clinical Gastroenterology. LC 87-176795. 294p. pap. 91.20 (*0-7837-2729-1*, 204310900006) Bks Demand.
Misina, A. P. & Skornjakov, L. A. Abelian Groups & Modules. LC 76-22560. (Translations Ser.: No. 2, Vol. 107). 160p. 1976. text 50.00 (*0-8218-3057-0*, TRANS2/107) Am Math.
Misins, Juris, jt. auth. see Smith, Graig W.
***Misir, Prem, ed.** Ethnic Cleavage & Closure: Interactions of Race, Ethnicity & Class. 300p. 2000. pap. write for info. (*1-928790-00-3*) Carbbn Diaspra U Pr.
***Misiroglu, Gina.** Handy Politics Answer Book. 2000. pap. 19.95 (*1-57859-128-7*) Visible Ink Pr.
Misiroglu, Gina, ed. Girls Like Us: 40 Extraordinary Women Celebrate Girlhood in Story, Poetry, & Song. LC 98-53428. (Illus.). 224p. 1999. 14.95 (*1-57731-084-5*) New Wrld Lib.
***Misiroglu, Gina, ed.** Imagine: The Spirit of 20th Century American Heroes. LC 99-30713. (Illus.). 132p. 1999. text 29.95 (*1-57731-086-1*, Pub. by New Wrld Lib) Publishers Group.
Misiroglu, Gina & Florence, Mari. The Enterprising Woman. LC 97-8649. 336p. (Orig.). 1997. mass mkt. 14.99 (*0-446-67275-0*, Pub. by Warner Bks) Little.
Misiroglu, Gina, jt. auth. see Carney, Charles.
Misiroglu, Gina, ed. see Chapman, Joyce.
Misiroglu, Gina, ed. see Lawrence, Shirley B.
Misiroglu, Gina, ed. see Robinson, Rita.
Misita, Michael. How to Believe in Nothing & Set Yourself Free. 156p. 1994. pap. 9.98 (*0-87554-572-6*, B936) Valley Sun.
Misiunas, Romuald J. & Taagepera, Rein. The Baltic States, Years of Dependence, 1940-1992. LC 92-39806. (C). 1993. pap. 19.95 (*0-520-08228-1*, Pub. by U CA Pr) Cal Prin Full Svc.
Misiurewicz, Michael & Nitecki, Zbigniew. Combinatorial Patterns for Maps of the Interval. LC 91-27263. (Memoirs Ser.). 112p. 1991. pap. 21.00 (*0-8218-2513-5*, MEMO/94/456) Am Math.
Misiwicz, jt. auth. see Marshall.
Miska, John. Ethnic & Native Canadian Literature: A Bibliography. 464p. 1990. text 135.00 (*0-8020-5852-3*) U of Toronto Pr.
Miska, Stefan, ed. see Lubinski, Arthur.
Miskal, James F. Buying Trouble? National Security & Reliance on Foreign Industry. LC 92-42182. 1993. 54.50 (*0-8191-9012-8*); pap. 26.50 (*0-8191-9013-6*) U Pr of Amer.
Miskawah, Ibn. Moral Healing. 234p. 1996. pap. 19.95 (*0-614-21555-2*, 1465) Kazi Pubns.
Miskawayh, Ali. Refinement of Character. Zurayk, Constantine, tr. 1977. pap. 14.00 (*0-8156-6051-0*, Pub. by Am U Beirut) Syracuse U Pr.
Miskawayh, Ibn, et al. The Eclipse of the Abbasid Caliphate, 7 vols. Amedroz, H. F. & Margoliouth, David S., trs. from ARA. (C). reprint ed. lib. bdg. 500.00 (*0-89241-219-4*) Caratzas.
Miskel, Cecil G., jt. auth. see Hoy, Wayne K.
Miskell, J. E., jt. auth. see Ash, J. S.
Miskell, Jane R. & Miskell, Vincent. Motivation at Work. LC 93-18112. 96p. 1993. pap. 10.95 (*1-55623-868-1*, Irwn Prfssnl) McGraw-Hill Prof.
Miskell, Jane R., jt. auth. see Miskell, Vincent.
Miskell, John, jt. auth. see Ash, John.
Miskell, Terri. Protecting the Seeds. (Illus.). 40p. 1997. pap. 8.00 (*0-8059-3965-2*) Dorrance.
Miskell, Vincent & Miskell, Jane R. Overcoming Anxiety at Work. LC 93-12077. 128p. 1993. pap. 10.95 (*1-55623-869-X*, Irwn Prfssnl) McGraw-Hill Prof.
Miskell, Vincent, jt. auth. see Miskell, Jane R.
Miskiel, Lynn W., jt. auth. see Vergara, Kathleen C.
Miskiewicz, Sophia M. & Trehub, Aaron. Social & Economic Rights in the Soviet Union & East Europe. 256p. 1988. 44.95 (*0-88738-186-3*) Transaction Pubs.
Miskimin, Harry A. Cash, Credit & Crisis in Europe, 1300-1600. (Collected Studies: No. CS289). 289p. (C). 1989. lib. bdg. 109.95 (*0-86078-237-9*, Pub. by Variorum) Ashgate Pub Co.
— Money & Power in Fifteenth-Century France. LC 83-21754. (Economic History Ser.). 320p. 1984. 45.00 (*0-300-03132-7*) Yale U Pr.
— Money, Prices, & Foreign Exchange in Fourteenth Century France. LC 63-7942. 1981. reprint ed. 15.00 (*0-08-022307-9*, Pergamon Pr) Elsevier.
Miskimin, Harry A., et al, eds. The Medieval City. LC 77-76302. 355p. reprint ed. pap. 110.10 (*0-8357-8218-2*, 203382800087) Bks Demand.
Miskimins, R. W., jt. auth. see Bonser, Carol.
Miskimins, Ray W. Guide to Floating Whitewater Rivers. (Illus.). 188p. (Orig.). 1987. pap. 8.95 (*0-936608-49-8*) F Amato Pubns.
— Lake Tahoe's Twenty Best Pavement & Dirt Rides. Hemingway-Douglass, Reanne, ed. (Illus.). 48p. (Orig.). 1995. pap. 5.95 (*0-938665-36-7*) Fine Edge Prods.
***Miskimins, Ray W.** Mountain Biking the Reno/Carson Area's Best Trails. (Illus.). 160p. 2000. 14.95 (*0-938665-66-9*) Fine Edge Prods.
Miskin, Alan S. Full Circle - My Plan for Stimulating a Paradigm Shift in the Structure of Education in America for the 21st Century...with Recommendations for the Future. LC 92-81651. 53p. 1992. pap. text 20.00 (*0-9633223-1-1*) ASM Intl.
Miskin, Richard. The Cross & the Ring. 125p. (J). 1987. pap. 3.95 (*0-310-55362-8*, 19038P) Zondervan.
Miskin, Val D., jt. auth. see Gmelch, Walter H.
Misko, James A. How to Finance Any Real Estate Any Place Any Time. LC 94-92042. 212p. 1994. pap. 19.95 (*0-9640826-0-8*) NW Ventures.
Miskov, Kathy. Little Annie Fountainhead. 1998. 14.95 (*0-9654436-3-9*) Honey Creek WI.
Miskovitz, Paul F. & Betancourt, Marian. What to Do If You Get Colon Cancer: A Specialist Helps You Take Charge & Make Informed Choices. LC 97-10074. 240p. 1997. pap. 15.95 (*0-471-15984-0*) Wiley.
Miskovitz, Paul F. & Rochwarger, Arnold. Valva & Treatment of the Patient with Diarrhea. (Illus.). 179p. 1992. text 77.00 (*1-56372-059-0*) Buttrwrth-Heinemann.
Miskowiec, Jay A., et al. Yolteotl: Eight Latino/Chicano/Hispanic Artists. (Illus.). 16p. (Orig.). 1993. pap. 10.00 (*1-889523-07-0*) Tweed Mus.
Miskowiec, Jay A., tr. see Aguilar, Eduardo G.
Miskowksi, Nick. Hiking Guide to Delaware Water Gap National Recreation Area. rev. ed. Chazin, Daniel D., ed. LC 94-21406. 1994. pap. 7.95 (*1-880775-01-8*) NY-NJ Trail Confer.
Miskowski, Mike. Applianoidal Grphcus Birthday Elaps 4-89. (Illus.). 44p. (YA). 1989. pap. text 4.00 (*0-944215-04-1*) Ninth St Lab.
— Suburbreal Drive: A Scattering. (Illus.). 36p. (Orig.). 1987. pap. 3.00 (*0-944215-00-9*) Ninth St Lab.
MisKowski, Mike & Foley, Jack. Artifact Collective - Texts, No. 1. Berry, Jake, ed. 20p. (Orig.). (YA). (gr. 7 up). 1988. pap. 3.00 (*0-944215-02-5*) Ninth St Lab.
Miskulin, M. Sunrunners: Silent Death Forces Book. (Silent Death - The Next Millennium Ser.). (Illus.). 80p. 1996. pap. 12.00 (*1-55806-237-8*, 7211) Iron Crown Ent Inc.
Miskuly, Jason. Thomas Murner & the Eucharist. 200p. 1990. pap. 10.00 (*1-57659-115-8*) Franciscan Inst.
Miskuly, Jason, tr. see Will, Liane, et al.
Misla, Victor M. Little Anabo from Boriken. (Illus.). 28p. (Orig.). (YA). (gr. 6-7). 1987. pap. 5.00 (*0-9626870-0-6*) NW Monarch Pr.
— The Treasure of Camuy's Cave. (Illus.). 30p. (Orig.). (YA). (gr. 6-7). 1987. pap. 5.00 (*0-9626870-1-4*) NW Monarch Pr.
Misler, jt. auth. see Bowlt.
Misler, Nicoletta. Aesthetic Writing Pavel. 0.00 (*0-691-06879-8*) Princeton U Pr.
Mislevy, Robert & Bock, R. Darrell. Bilog 3: Item Analysis & Test Scoring with Binary Logistic Models. 2nd ed. 1990. ring bd. 30.00 (*0-89498-026-2*) Sci Ware.
Mislin, Guido, ed. The Hilton Symposium 1993. LC 94-16852. (CRM Proceedings & Lecture Notes Ser.: Vol. 6). 198p. 1994. pap. 49.00 (*0-8218-0273-9*, CRMP/6) Am Math.
Mislin, Gwynyth L. Just Paint It Red & Forget about It. unabridged ed. 84p. (Orig.). 1996. pap. 9.95 (*0-9650451-1-0*) Glriana Pr.
Mislin, H., jt. ed. see Bachofen, R.
Mislin, Hans & Ravera, O. Cadmium in the Environment. (Experientia Supplementa Ser.: Vol. 50). 148p. 1986. 70.00 (*0-8176-1760-4*, Pub. by Birkhauser) Princeton Arch.
Mislinski, Phil, et al. Trail Runner's Guide to Colorado: 50 Great Trail Runs. LC 98-53615. (Illus.). 208p. 1999. pap. 16.95 (*1-55591-409-8*) Fulcrum Pub.
Mislove, Michael W., jt. ed. see Hofman, Karl H.
Misnad, Sheikha. Development of Modern Education in the Gulf. 386p. 1985. 40.00 (*0-685-14920-X*) Evergreen Dist.
Misner, Charles. Spreadsheet Physics. (C). 1998. pap. text. write for info. (*0-201-83437-5*) Addison-Wesley.
Misner, Charles W., et al. Gravitation. LC 78-156043. (Physics Ser.). (Illus.). 1279p. (C). 1973. pap. text 73.95 (*0-7167-0344-0*) W H Freeman.
Misner, Frank M. Extra Costs & Incidental Costs in the Erection of School Buildings. LC 71-177075. (Columbia University. Teachers College. Contributions to Education Ser.). reprint ed. 37.50 (*0-404-55624-8*) AMS Pr.
Misner, Ivan & Davis, Robert. Business by Referral: A Sure-Fire Way to Generate New Business. LC 97-41046. 1998. 25.95 (*1-885167-28-8*); pap. 15.95 (*1-885167-27-X*) Bard Press.
***Misner, Ivan R.** Masters of Networking: Building Relationships for Your Pocketbook & Soul. 2000. pap. 18.95 (*1-885167-48-2*) Bard Press.
Misner, Ivan R. Seven Second Marketing: How to Use Memory Hooks to Make You Instantly Stand Out in a Crowd. 160p. 1996. 22.95 (*1-885167-21-0*); pap. text 12.95 (*1-885167-15-6*) Bard Press.
Misner, Ivan R. & Devine, Virginia. Worlds Best Known Marketing Secrets: Building Your Business with Word-of-Mouth Marketing. 2nd ed. LC 99-24405. 256p. 1999. pap. 15.95 (*1-885167-37-7*, Pub. by Bard Press) Natl Bk Netwk.
Misner, Peter L., jt. auth. see Glusker, David L.
***Misra, ed.** Psychological Perspectives on Stress & Health. 1999. 32.00 (*81-7022-785-2*, Pub. by Concept) S Asia.

M

Misra, Amaresh. Lucknow, Fire of Grace: The Story of Its Revolution, Renaissance & the Aftermath. LC 98-908915. xix, 369p. 1998. write for info. (*81-7223-338-8*) CE25.

Misra, A. P., ed. see Agnihotri, V. P.

Misra, A. S. Commentaries on U. P. Public Services (Tribunals) (C). 1991. 95.00 (*0-7855-5425-4*) St Mut.

— Commentaries on U. P. Public Services (Tribunals) Act, 1976. 277p. 1980. 100.00 (*0-7855-1369-8*) St Mut.

— Law & Practice of Character & Integrity Rolls. 348p. 1979. 120.00 (*0-7855-1368-X*) St Mut.

Misra, A. S. Law of Bias & Malafides. 298p. 1985. 129.00 (*0-7855-7581-2*) St Mut.

Misra, A. S. Law of Bias & Malafides. 3rd rev. ed. (C). 1986. 75.00 (*0-7855-5640-0*) St Mut.

— Law of Speaking Orders. 1985. 95.00 (*0-7855-1473-2*) St Mut.

— Officer's Companion (In Administration & Law) (C). 1988. 225.00 (*0-89771-783-X*, Pub. by Eastern Book) St Mut.

Misra, A. S., ed. Commentaries on U. P. Public Services (Tribunals) Act, 1980. 2nd rev. ed. (C). 1991. reprint ed. 95.00 (*0-7855-5394-0*) St Mut.

Misra, Anil, ed. Recent Advances in Mechanics of Geomaterials. (Illus.). 80p. (C). 1997. pap. text 25.00 (*1-890643-00-9*) UMA KS.

Misra, Anil & Chang, Ching S., eds. Mechanics of Materils with Discontinuities & Heterogeneities Vol. 201: Mechanics of Materials with Discontinuities & Heterogeneities. LC 95-77286. (1995 Joint ASME Applied Mechanics & Materials Summer Meeting Ser.: Vol. 201). 188p. 1995. 100.00 (*0-7918-1316-9*, H00948) ASME.

Misra, Arun, ed. Virus Taxonomy. 211p. 1985. 25.00 (*1-55528-058-7*) Scholarly Pubns.

Misra, Arun, et al. Plant Tumors. (Illus.). xxl, 222p. (C). 1985. lib. bdg. 25.00 (*1-55528-000-5*) Scholarly Pubns.

— Plant Tumors. (Illus.). xviii, 222p. 1985. 25.00 (*1-55528-045-5*, Pub. by Today Tomorrow) Scholarly Pubns.

Misra, Arun K., et al, eds. AAS/AIAA Astrodynamics Conference, Aug. 16-19, 1993, Victoria, British Columbia, Canada. LC 57-43769. (Advances in the Astronautical Sciences Ser.: Vol. 85). (Illus.). 2750p. 1994. 390.00 (*0-87703-380-3*, Am Astronaut Soc) Univelt Inc.

Misra, Ashok, jt. auth. see David, D. J.

Misra, B. Capitalism, Socialism & Planning. (C). 1988. 11.00 (*81-204-0306-1*, Pub. by Oxford IBH) S Asia.

Misra, B., jt. auth. see Karanam, U. M. Rao.

Misra, B. B. The Administrative History of India, 1834-1947: General Administration. 1971. 19.25 (*0-19-635267-3*) OUP.

Misra, B. B. The Bureaucracy in India: An Historical Analysis of Development to 1947. 1977. text 14.50 (*0-19-560748-1*) OUP.

— District Administration & Rural Development in India: Policy Objectives & Administrative Change in Historical Perspective. 1984. 36.00 (*0-19-561596-4*) OUP.

Misra, B. B. Government & Bureaucracy in India, 1947-1976. 416p. 1986. 29.95 (*0-19-561597-2*) OUP.

Misra, B. B. The Indian Political Parties: An Historical Analysis of Political Behavior up to 1947. 1977. 22.00 (*0-19-560598-5*) OUP.

— The Unification & Division of India. 456p. 1991. text 32.00 (*0-19-562615-X*) OUP.

Misra, B. D. Forts & Fortresses of Gwalior & Its Hinterland. (C). 1993. 30.00 (*81-7304-047-8*, Pub. by Manohar Bk Srv) S Asia.

Misra, B. D., et al. Organization for Change: A Systems Analysis of Family Planning in Rural India. (Michigan Papers on South & Southeast Asia: No. 21). xxiv, 444p. (C). 1982. 5.00 (*0-89148-019-6*) Ctr S&SE Asian.

Misra, Baidyanath. Economic Profile of India. (Illus.). ix, 221p. 1997. 28.00 (*81-7024-818-3*, Pub. by APH Pubng) Nataraj Bks.

Misra, Bal G., jt. auth. see Fairbanks, Gordon H.

Misra, Banarsi. Monitoring of Industrial Sickness. (C). 1990. text 30.00 (*81-7100-266-8*, Pub. by Deep & Deep Pubns) S Asia.

Misra, Bani P. Socioeconomic Adjustments of Tribals: A Case Study of Tripura Jhumias (India) LC 76-903504. 1976. 6.50 (*0-88386-700-1*) S Asia.

Misra, Bhabagrahi & Preston, James, eds. Community, Self, & Identity. (World Anthropology Ser.). xii, 316p. 1978. 50.80 (*90-279-7650-3*) Mouton.

Misra, Bidhanesh, ed. Geographic Information System & Economic Development: Conceptual Applications. (Illus.). x, 186p. 1997. 27.00 (*81-7099-668-6*, Pub. by Mittal Pubs Dist) Nataraj Bks.

Misra, Chitranjan. Harold Pinter: The Dramatist. 1993. 25.00 (*81-85231-12-5*, Pub. by Creative Pubs) Advent Bks Div.

Misra, G. S. Development of Buddhist Ethics. 1984. text 22.00 (*0-685-13698-1*) Coronet Bks.

Misra, Ganeswar. Language, Reality & Analysis: Essays on Indian Philosophy. Mohanty, J. N., ed. LC 90-42506. (Indian Thought & Culture Ser.: Vol. 1). iv, 101p. 1990. 56.00 (*90-04-09305-2*) Brill Academic Pubs.

Misra, Girishwar, ed. Applied Social Psychology in India. 320p. (C). 1990. 27.50 (*0-8039-9645-4*) Sage.

Misra, H. N. Bhutan: Problems & Policies. 1988. 27.00 (*0-8364-2311-9*) S Asia.

— Contributions to Indian Geography: Rural Geography, Vol. 9. 462p. (C). 1987. 54.00 (*0-8364-2100-0*, Pub. by Heritage IA) S Asia.

— Urban System of a Developing Economy. 1988. 32.00 (*0-8364-2312-7*) S Asia.

Misra, Itishree, jt. auth. see Veeraraghavan, Vimala.

***Misra, J. K. & Lichtwardt, Robert W.** Illustrated Genera of Trichomycetes: Fungal Symbionts of Insects & Other Arthropods. (Illus.). 165p. 2000. text 29.95 (*1-57808-080-0*) Science Pubs.

Misra, J. K., ed. see Veer Mehta, Dharm.

Misra, Jayadev. Applied Theory of Concurrency & Composition. 1997. 39.95 (*0-387-94882-1*) Spr-Verlag.

Misra, K. B., ed. Clean Production: Environmental & Economic Perspectives. (Illus.). 854p. 1995. 163.95 (*3-540-60189-9*) Spr-Verlag.

Misra, K. C., ed. Volcanogenic Sulfide & Precious Metal Mineralization in the Southern Appalachians. (Studies in Geology). (Illus.). ii, 236p. 1986. pap. 10.00 (*0-910249-15-6*) U of Tenn Geo.

Misra, K. K. Tribal Elites & Social Transformation. LC 94-900837. (C). 1994. 18.00 (*81-210-0319-9*, Pub. by Inter-India Pubns) S Asia.

Misra, K. N. Women Education & the Upanishadic System of Education. (C). 1993. 30.00 (*81-85613-76-1*, Pub. by Chugh Pubns) S Asia.

Misra, K. P. Quest for an International Order in the Indian Ocean. 159p. 1977. 14.95 (*0-318-37255-X*) Asia Bk Corp.

Misra, K. P. & Gangal, S. C., eds. Gandhi & the Contemporary World: Studies in Peace & War. 1982. 15.00 (*0-8364-0849-7*, Pub. by Chanakya) S Asia.

Misra, K. S. Modern Tragedies & Aristotle's Theory. LC 84-672343. 252 p. 1983. write for info. (*0-391-02692-5*) Humanities.

Misra, Kailash C., jt. ed. see Jing, Naihuan.

Misra, Kalpana. From Post-Maoism to Post-Marxism: The Erosion of Official Ideology in Deng's China. LC 97-45758. 224p. (C). 1998. pap. 21.99 (*0-415-92033-7*) Routledge.

— From Post-Maoism to Post-Marxism: The Erosion of Official Ideology in Deng's China. LC 97-45758. (Illus.). 224p. (C). 1998. 75.00 (*0-415-92032-9*) Routledge.

Misra, Kashi P. Nonaligned Movement: India's Chairmanship. vii, 248p. (C). 1987. 26.00 (*81-7095-001-5*, Pub. by Lancer India) S Asia.

Misra, Krishna B. Reliability Analysis & Prediction: A Methodology Oriented Treatment. LC 92-13149. (Fundamental Studies in Engineering: No. 15). 890p. 1992. 409.25 (*0-444-89606-6*) Elsevier.

Misra, Krishna B., ed. New Trends in System Reliability Evaluation. LC 93-38228. (Fundamental Studies in Engineering: Vol. 16). 732p. 1993. 289.00 (*0-444-81660-7*) Elsevier.

Misra, Kula C. Laboratory Exercises in Physical Geology. 3rd rev. ed. (Illus.). 282p. 1999. pap. text 32.95 (*0-88725-239-7*) Hunter Textbks.

— Mineral & Energy Resources: Current Status & Future Trends. (Studies in Geology). (Illus.). 276p. (Orig.). (C). 1986. pap. text 15.00 (*0-910249-13-X*) U of Tenn Geo.

Misra, Lakshmi. Womens' Issues: An Indian Perspective. (C). 1992. 22.00 (*81-7211-017-0*, Pub. by Northern Bk Ctr) S Asia.

Misra, M. S., jt. ed. see Rath, B. B.

Misra, Manoranjan, ed. Separation Processes - Heavy Metals, Ions & Minerals: Proceedings of the Symposium on Separation Processes. TMS Annual Meeting (1995: Las Vegas, Nevada) (Illus.). 290p. 1995. 10.00 (*0-87339-279-5*, 2795) Minerals Metals.

Misra, Manoranjan, jt. ed. see Smith, Ross W.

***Misra, Maria.** Business, Race & Politics in British, 1850-1960. (Oxford Historical Monographs Ser.). (Illus.). 264p. 1999. text 72.00 (*0-19-820711-5*) OUP.

Misra, Mathura P. A Trilingual Dictionary: Being a Comprehensive Lexicon in English, Urdu & Hindi Exhibiting the Syllabication, Pronunciation, & Etymology of English Words with Their Explanation in English & in Urdu & Hindi in the Roman Character. LC 99-932499. (ENG & HIN.). 94p. 1990. write for info. (*81-206-0342-7*, Pub. by Asian Educ Servs) S Asia.

— Trilingual Dictionary Being a Comprehensive Lexicon in English. (C). reprint ed. 49.00 (*0-8364-2639-8*, Pub. by Asian Educ Servs) S Asia.

Misra, Neeru. Succession & Imperial Leadership among the Mughals, 1526-1707. (C). 1993. 16.00 (*81-220-0337-0*, Pub. by Konark Pubs) S Asia.

Misra, O. P. Economic Thought of Gandhi & Nehru: A Comparative Analysis. 180p. 1995. pap. 115.00 (*0-7855-2730-3*, Pub. by Print Hse) St Mut.

— Economic Thought of Gandhi & Nehru: A Comparative Analysis. 180p. 1995. pap. 120.00 (*81-85880-71-9*, Pub. by Print Hse) St Mut.

Misra, P. R. & Rajagopalan, M., eds. Tennessee Topology Conference: Tennessee State University 10-11 June, 1996. 300p. 1997. 68.00 (*981-02-3291-8*) World Scientific Pub.

Misra, Patitpaban & Swain, B. B. Textbook of Physics: Written Strictly According to the Syllabi of Plus Two, Pre-University, Higher Secondary & Intermediate Classes. 1997. 34.00 (*0-7069-9630-5*, Pub. by Vikas) S Asia.

Misra, Porwal. Inflation Accounting in a Developing Economy. 1985. 12.00 (*0-8364-1503-5*, Pub. by Allied Pubs) S Asia.

Misra, R. D. Manual on Irrigation Agronomy. 422p. (C). 1987. 18.00 (*81-204-0184-0*, Pub. by Oxford IBH) S Asia.

Misra, R. P. Gandhian Model of Development & World Peace. 1990. 32.00 (*81-7022-227-3*, Pub. by Concept) S Asia.

— Multi-Level Planning & Integrated Rural Development in India. 1980. 15.00 (*0-8364-0576-5*, Pub. by Heritage IA) S Asia.

Misra, R. P., ed. Contributions to Indian Geography: Vol. 1, Concepts & Approaches. 1983. 34.00 (*0-8364-0947-7*, Pub. by Heritage IA) S Asia.

— District Planning: A Handbook. 1990. 47.50 (*81-7022-313-X*, Pub. by Concept) S Asia.

Misra, R. P. & Bhooshan, B. S. Human Settlements in Asia: Public Policies & Programs. 1979. 17.50 (*0-8364-0541-2*) S Asia.

Misra, R. P. & Ramesh, A. Fundamentals of Cartography. 2nd rev. ed. (C). 1989. 50.00 (*81-7022-222-2*, Pub. by Concept) S Asia.

Misra, R. P. & Raza, Moonis, eds. Contributions to Indian Geography Vol. 10: Regional Development. (C). 1988. 76.00 (*81-7026-143-0*, Pub. by Heritage IA) S Asia.

Misra, R. P., jt. auth. see Subrahmanyam, V. P.

Misra, R. P., jt. ed. see Singh, Tej V.

Misra, Rajendra K., et al. Rorschach Test: Theory & Practice. LC 96-28316. 295p. 1996. 32.00 (*0-8039-9328-5*) Sage.

***Misra, Ram Shankar.** The Integral Advaitism of Sri Aurobindo. LC 98-908847. xviii, 437 p. 1998. pap. 250.00 (*81-208-1329-4*, Pub. by Motilal Bnarsidass) St Mut.

Misra, Ramesh C., jt. auth. see Ramakant, Ditors.

Misra, Renuka, jt. auth. see Dev, Sukh.

Misra, Renuka, jt. ed. see Dev, Sukh.

Misra, S. G. Metallic Pollution. (C). 1992. 20.00 (*81-7024-473-0*, Pub. by Ashish Pub Hse) S Asia.

Misra, S. G. & Mani, Dinesh. Soil Pollution. (C). 1991. text 22.00 (*81-7024-431-5*, Pub. by Ashish Pub Hse) S Asia.

Misra, S. G. & Mani, Dinesh, eds. Agricultural Pollution, 2 vols. (Illus.). 1994. 25.00 (*0-685-72742-4*, Pub. by Ashish Pub Hse) Nataraj Bks.

— Agricultural Pollution, Vol. 1. (Illus.). iv, 98p. 1994. write for info. (*81-7024-574-5*, Pub. by Ashish Pub Hse) Nataraj Bks.

— Agricultural Pollution, Vol. 2. (Illus.). vi, 188p. 1994. write for info. (*81-7024-601-6*, Pub. by Ashish Pub Hse) Nataraj Bks.

Misra, S. N. India: The Cold War Years. (C). 1994. 22.50 (*81-7003-154-0*, Pub. by S Asia Pubs) S Asia.

Misra, S. P. Introduction to Supersymmetry & Supergravity. 239p. 1992. text 98.00 (*0-470-21862-2*) Halsted Pr.

Misra, Sanjiv. India's Textile Sector: A Policy Analysis. LC 92-46158. (Illus.). 278p. 1993. 36.00 (*0-8039-9474-5*) Sage.

Misra, Satya S. Aryan Problem: A Linguistic Approach. (C). 1992. 14.00 (*81-215-0537-2*, Pub. by M Manoharial) Coronet Bks.

— Ethnic Conflict & Security Crisis in Sri Lanka. iv, 176p. 1995. 29.00 (*81-85163-66-9*, Pub. by Kalinga) Nataraj Bks.

Misra, Shridhar, jt. auth. see Singh, Baljit.

Misra, Sibranjan. Fisheries in India. (C). 1987. 13.50 (*81-7024-099-9*, Pub. by Ashish Pub Hse) S Asia.

Misra, Sibranjan R. Tea Industry in India. 1986. 24.00 (*81-7024-015-8*, Pub. by Ashish Pub Hse) S Asia.

Misra, Suchitra K. Taste of Goa: Illustrated Guide to Goan Cooking. (C). 1992. pap. 14.00 (*81-7023-208-2*, Pub. by Allied Pubs) S Asia.

***Misra, Sunil.** Voluntary Action in Health & Population: The Dynamics of Social Transition. LC 99-46953. 1999. pap. write for info. (*0-7619-9406-8*) Sage.

Misra, Suresh. Politico-Peasantry Conflict in India: Dynamics of Agrarian Change. (C). 1991. 15.00 (*81-7099-306-7*, Pub. by Mittal Pubs Dist) S Asia.

Misra, Surya N. Party Politics & Electoral Choice in an Indian State. (C). 1989. 34.00 (*81-202-0247-3*, Pub. by Ajanta) S Asia.

***Misra, Surya N., et al.** Constitution & Constitutionalism in India. LC 98-917812. 413 p. 1999. write for info. (*81-7648-028-2*, Pub. by Ashish Pub Hse) S Asia.

Misra, Umesh C. Tribal Paintings & Sculptures. (C). 1989. 25.00 (*81-7018-543-2*, Pub. by BR Pub) S Asia.

Misra, V. B. Evolution of the Constitutional History of India. 1987. 32.00 (*81-7099-010-6*, Pub. by Mittal Pubs Dist) S Asia.

Misra, Vidya N. The Descriptive Technique of Panini: An Introduction. (Janua Linguarum, Series Practica: No. 18). 1966. pap. text 58.50 (*90-279-0637-8*) Mouton.

Misra, Vidya N., ed. Modern Hindi Poetry: An Anthology. (C). 1991. 17.00 (*81-7023-299-6*, Pub. by Allied Pubs) S Asia.

Misrach, Myriam W., jt. auth. see Misrach, Richard.

Misrach, Richard. Violent Legacies: Three Cantos. (Illus.). 128p. 1992. 76.00 (*0-89381-519-5*) Aperture.

— Violent Legacies: Three Cantos. 1994. pap. 44.95 (*0-89381-569-1*) Aperture.

***Misrach, Richard, photos by.** Richard Misrach: The Sky Book. (Illus.). 144p. 2000. 65.00 (*1-892041-28-6*) Arena Editions.

Misrach, Richard & Misrach, Myriam W. Bravo Twenty: The Bombing of the American West. LC 90-34150. (Creating the North American Landscape Ser.). (Illus.). 160p. 1990. 49.95 (*0-8018-4064-3*); pap. 29.95 (*0-8018-4065-1*) Johns Hopkins.

Misrack, Robert, jt. auth. see Richards, Tana M.

Misrahi, Mary M., tr. see Nocent, Adrien.

Misrahi, Mary M., tr. see Prevost, Jean-Pierre.

Misrahi, Mary M., tr. see Puglisi, James F.

Misraki, Paul, jt. auth. see Vercors, Jean.

Misri, Al-Ahmad I. Reliance of the Traveller. Keller, Noah H., tr. 1270p. 1996. 65.00 (*0-614-21207-3*, 1067) Kazi Pubns.

Misri, M. L. & Bhat, M. S. Poverty, Planning & Economic Change in Jammu & Kashmir. 1994. 34.00 (*0-7069-7776-9*, Pub. by Vikas) S Asia.

Misri, Shaila. Shouldn't I Be Happy? Emotional Problems of Pregnant & Postpartum Women. 300p. 1995. 22.50 (*0-02-921405-X*) Free Pr.

***Misri, Shaila.** Shouldn't I Be Happy? Emotional Problems of Pregnant & Postpartum Women. 340p. 2000. reprint ed. text 23.00 (*0-7881-6879-7*) DIANE Pub.

Miss Naomi. Forbidden Art: The World of Erotica. (Illus.). 176p. 1998. 49.95 (*0-7643-0607-3*) Schiffer.

Missac, Pierre. Walter Benjamin's Passages. Nicholsen, Shierry W., tr. (Studies in Contemporary German Social Thought). (Illus.). 256p. 1995. 33.00 (*0-262-13305-9*) MIT Pr.

— Walter Benjamin's Passages. (Studies in Contemporary German Social Thought). (Illus.). 256p. 1996. pap. text 16.50 (*0-262-63175-X*) MIT Pr.

Missair, Alfredo R. & Meyer, Bruce F. The Larue D. Carter Memorial Hospital Case-Study: A Behaviorial Approach to Environmental Normalization in Mental Health Settings. (Illus.). 16p. 1983. pap. 8.00 (*0-912431-03-2*) Ctr Env Des Res.

***Missale, Alessandro.** Public Debt Management: Theory & History. LC 99-17544. 320p. 2000. text 70.00 (*0-19-829085-3*) OUP.

Missaoui, R., jt. auth. see Alagar, V. S.

Missar, Charles D., ed. Management of Federally Sponsored Libraries: Case Studies & Analysis. LC 94-48730. (Illus.). 112p. 1995. lib. bdg. 39.95 (*1-56024-395-3*) Haworth Pr.

***Missbach, Michael & Hoffman, Uwe M.** Sap Hardware Solutions: Servers, Storage, & Networks. 2000. pap. 44.99 (*0-13-028084-4*) P-H.

Misselbeck, Reinhold. Geraldo de Barros: Fotoformas. 1999. 49.95 (*3-7913-2189-7*) Prestel.

Misselden, Edward. The Circle of Commerce: Or the Ballance of Trade, in Defense of Free Trade. LC 66-21686. (Reprints of Economic Classics Ser.). 145p. 1971. reprint ed. 29.50 (*0-678-00304-1*) Kelley.

— The Circle of Commerce; or The Balance of Trade, in Defence of Free Trade. LC 72-25886. (English Experience Ser.: No. 166). 1969. reprint ed. 35.00 (*90-221-0166-5*) Walter J Johnson.

— Free Trade: Or the Meanes to Make Trade Florish. LC 67-26245. (Reprints of Economic Classics Ser.). 134p. 1971. reprint ed. 29.50 (*0-678-00305-X*) Kelley.

— Free Trade, or, the Means to Make Trade Flourish. LC 70-25644. (English Experience Ser.: No. 267). 136p. 1970. reprint ed. 25.00 (*90-221-0267-X*) Walter J Johnson.

Missen, Ronald W. Reaction Engineering. 1999. 0.95 (*0-471-33305-0*) Wiley.

Missen, Ronald W., et al. Introduction to Chemical Reaction Engineering & Kinetics. LC 98-27267. 700p. 1998. 106.95 incl. cd-rom (*0-471-16339-2*) Wiley.

Missig, James R. & Vance, Robert W., eds. Applications of Cryogenic Technology, Vol. 7. LC 68-57815. (Cryogenic Society of America Applications of Cryogenic Technology Ser.). (Illus.). 1978. text 35.00 (*0-87936-009-7*) Scholium Intl.

Missildine, W. Hugh. Your Inner Child of the Past. 1991. mass mkt. 5.99 (*0-671-74703-7*) S&S Trade.

Missimer, Connie A. Good Arguments: An Introduction to Critical Thinking. 3rd ed. LC 94-29315. 256p. 1994. pap. text 32.80 (*0-13-311804-5*) P-H.

Missimer, Thomas M. A Leader's Guide to Environmental Liability Management. LC 95-53806. 240p. 1996. lib. bdg. 59.95 (*0-87371-994-8*, L994) Lewis Pubs.

— Water Supply Development & Concentrate Disposal for Membr. 272p. 1994. lib. bdg. 95.00 (*0-87371-954-9*, L954) Lewis Pubs.

***Mission City Press Inc., Staff.** Elsie's Christmas Party: How to Plan, Prepare & Host an Old-Fashioned Christmas Party. (Elsie Dinsmore Ser.). 112p. (YA). (gr. 5-9). 2000. 14.99 (*1-928749-52-6*) Mission City Pr.

— Elsie's Daily Diary. (Elsie Dinsmore Ser.). 192p. (YA). (gr. 5-9). 2001. 12.99 (*1-928749-50-X*) Mission City Pr.

— Elsie's Etiquette Book. (Elsie Dinsmore Ser.). 224p. (YA). (gr. 5-9). 2001. 12.99 (*1-928749-53-4*) Mission City Pr.

— Elsie's Life Lessons Vol. 1: A Study Guide on the Fruit of the Spirit. (Elsie Dinsmore Ser.). 160p. (YA). (gr. 5-9). 2001. pap. 9.99 (*1-928749-51-8*) Mission City Pr.

Mission, Mahayogi Y. Yoga Asanas. LC 98-65538. (Illus.). xiii, 62p. 1998. pap. 15.00 (*0-9663555-0-4*) Mahayogi Yoga.

***Mission, Mahayogi Yoga.** The Gospel of Yoga: The Teachings of Sadgurn Sri Mahayogi Paramahamsa. 220p. 2000. pap. 20.00 (*0-9663555-1-2*) Mahayogi Yoga.

Missionary Research Library Staff. Dictionary Catalog of the Missionary Research Library. 1983. 2120.00 (*0-8161-1378-5*, G K Hall & Co) Mac Lib Ref.

***Missios, Christine.** Jotting. 2000. pap. write for info. (*1-58235-373-5*) Watermrk Pr.

Missiou, Anna. The Subversive Oratory of Andokides: Politics, Ideology & Decision-Making in Democratic Athens, 410-390 B.C. (Cambridge Classical Studies). (Illus.). 228p. (C). 1992. text 59.95 (*0-521-36009-9*) Cambridge U Pr.

Missirlis, Y. F. & Lemm, W., eds. Modern Aspects of Protein Adsorption on Biomaterials. (C). 1991. text 148.50 (*0-7923-0973-1*) Kluwer Academic.

Missirlis, Y. F. & Wautier, J. L., eds. The Role of Platelets in Blood-Biomaterial Interactions. LC 93-2728. 1993. text 148.50 (*0-7923-2162-6*) Kluwer Academic.

Missiroli, Mario. What Italy Owes to Mussolini. 1976. lib. bdg. 250.00 (*0-8490-2817-5*) Gordon Pr.

Mississippi College Staff. With Special Distinction. 1993. 19.95 (*0-9636101-0-4*) MS Coll Ckbk.

Mississippi Cooperative Extension Service, Home Ec, ed. The Mississippi Cookbook. LC 74-185345. 476p. 1972. pap. 17.95 (*0-87805-381-6*) U Pr of Miss.

Mississippi Department of Archives and History Sta. Mississippi Provincial Archives: French Dominion, 3 vols. Rowland, Dunbar & Sanders, A. G., eds. LC 72-172737. reprint ed. 315.00 (*0-404-07370-0*) AMS Pr.

Missler, Chuck. Cosmic Codes: Hidden Messages from the Edge of Eternity. 506p. 1998. 24.95 (*1-57821-093-3*) Koinonia Hse.

***Missler, Chuck.** Revelation Commentary. 2000. 34.95 incl. cd-rom (*1-57821-096-8*) Koinonia Hse.

An Asterisk (*) at the beginning of an entry indicates that the title is appearing for the first time.

Missler, Chuck & Eastman, Mark. Alien Encounters: The Secret Behind UFO Phenomenon. LC 97-12551. 375p. 1997. pap. 14.95 (*1-56507-723-7*) Harvest Hse.
— Alien Encounters: The Secret Behind UFO Phenomenon. 375p. 1997. pap. 14.95 (*1-57821-061-5*) Koinonia Hse.
Missler, Chuck, jt. auth. see Eastman, Mark.
Missler, Chuck, jt. auth. see Young, Woody.
Missler, Nancy. Agape Days Calendar. 1997. pap. 7.95 Koinonia Hse.
Missler, Nancy. Be Ye Transformed: Leader's Guide. 1996. ring bd. 19.95 (*1-57821-003-8*) Koinonia Hse.
— Be Ye Transformed: Understanding God's Truth. (King's High Way Ser.). 109p. 1994. pap., wbk. ed. 5.95 (*1-880532-57-3*) Koinonia Hse.
— Be Ye Transformed Workbook: Understanding Gods Truth. 1996. pap., wbk. ed. 5.95 (*1-57821-002-X*) Koinonia Hse.
***Missler, Nancy.** Faith in the Night Seasons Leaders Guide, Vol. 2. 93p. 2000. teacher ed., ring bd. 19.95 (*1-57821-102-6*) Koinonia Hse.
— Faith in the Night Seasons Workbook. 112p. 2000. wbk. ed. 5.95 (*1-57821-101-8*) Koinonia Hse.
— Kings Highway Gift Set, 3 bks. Incl. Be Ye Transformed: Understanding Gods Truth. Missler, Chuck. (Illus.). 384p. 1996. pap. 12.95 (*1-880532-42-5*); Faith in the Night Seasons. 1999. pap. 12.95 (*1-57821-068-2*); Way of Agape: Understanding God's Love. Missler, Chuck. (Illus.). 384p. 1996. reprint ed. pap. 12.95 (*1-880532-56-5*); 1999. Set pap. 34.95 (*1-57821-080-1*) Koinonia Hse.
Missler, Nancy. Rekindle the Fire, Set. 124p. 1998. pap. 19.95 incl. audio (*1-57821-036-4*) Koinonia Hse.
— The Way of Agape Leadership Manual. 1996. ring bd. 19.95 (*1-880532-46-8*) Koinonia Hse.
— Why Should I Be the First to Change? rev. ed. (King's High Way Ser.). 124p. 1994. reprint ed. pap. text 4.95 (*1-880532-70-0*) Koinonia Hse.
Missner. On Hobbes. (Philosophy Ser.). 1999. pap. text 13.95 (*0-534-57592-7*) Brooks-Cole.
M.I.S.S.O.C. Staff. Social Protection in the Member States of the European Union: Situation on 1 July 1994 & Evolution. 453p. 1995. pap. text 16.00 (*92-826-9973-0*, CE-83-94-555-EN, Pub. by Comm Europ Commun) Bernan Associates.
Misson, Gary, jt. auth. see Harry, John.
Misson, Ray, jt. auth. see Christie, Frances.
Missotten, I. Immunology of the Cornea. 74p. (Orig.). 1994. pap. 29.50 (*90-6186-632-4*, Pub. by Leuven Univ) Coronet Bks.
Missotten, L., ed. European Association for Vision & Eye Research (EVER) Joint European Research Meeting in Ophthalmology & Vision, Palma de Mallorca, October 1998: Abstracts. (Opthalmologica Ser.: Vol. 30, Suppl. 1). 200p. 1999. pap. 61.00 (*3-8055-6794-4*) S Karger.
***Missotten, L., ed.** Ever European Association for Vision & Eye Research: Joint European Research Meeting in Ophthalmology & Vision, Palma de Mallorca, October 1999: Abstracts. (Opthalmologica Ser.: Vol. 31, Suppl. 1). (Illus.). 176p. 1999. pap. 45.25 (*3-8055-6981-5*) S Karger.
Missotten, L., jt. ed. see Maudgal, P. C.
Missouri Association for Criminal Justice Staff. Missouri Crime Survey. LC 68-55778. (Criminology, Law Enforcement, & Social Problems Ser.: No. 10). 1968. reprint ed. 30.00 (*0-87585-010-3*) Patterson Smith.
Missouri Bar Staff. Missouri Juvenile Law. write for info. (*0-318-61044-2*) MO Bar.
Missouri Botanical Garden Staff. Annual Gardening. (American Garden Guides Ser.). (Illus.). 224p. 1995. pap. 25.00 (*0-679-75831-3*) Pantheon.
Missouri Botanical Garden Staff & Science Press of Beijing, contrib. by. Flora of China Vol. 15: Myrsinaceae Through Loganiaceae. 387p. 1996. 85.00 (*0-915279-37-1*, CH-15) Miss Botan.
Missouri Botanical Garden Staff & Science Press of Beijing Staff, contrib. by. Flora of China Vol. 16: Gentianaceae Through Boraginaceae. 479p. 1995. 85.00 (*0-915279-33-9*, CH-16) Miss Botan.
Missouri Editing Group Staff, ed. see Anderson, Kelly.
Missouri Editing Group Staff, ed. see Broeg, Bob.
Missouri Editing Group Staff, ed. see Hendel, John & Carr, Jim.
Missouri Editing Group Staff, ed. see McKenzie, Mike.
Missouri General Assembly, Joint Committee of The. Report of the Joint Committee of the General Assembly Appointed to Investigate the Police Department of the City of St. Louis. LC 70-154587. (Police in America Ser.). 1971. reprint ed. 24.95 (*0-405-03384-2*) Ayer.
***Missouri Group, Group.** Brief News Reporting & Writing. 2000. pap. text. write for info. (*0-312-25055-X*) St Martin.
***Missouri Group Staff.** Brief News Reporting & Writing Exercise Booklet. 2000. pap. text. write for info. (*0-312-25821-6*) St Martin.
Missouri Group Staff. News Reporting & Writing. 5th ed. 1995. pap. text, teacher ed. 10.00 (*0-312-13800-8*) St Martin.
— News Reporting & Writing. 5th ed. 160p. 1996. pap. text, wbk. ed. 24.95 (*0-312-11716-7*) St Martin.
— News Reporting & Writing. 6th ed. LC 98-84337. 1999. pap. 55.95 (*0-312-18019-5*); pap. text, wbk. ed. 24.95 (*0-312-18018-7*) St Martin.
— News Reporting & Writing. 6th ed. 2000. pap. text, teacher ed. 10.00 (*0-312-18020-9*) St Martin.
Missouri Group Staff, contrib. by. News Reporting & Writing. 1995. pap. text 48.00 (*0-312-14502-0*) McGraw.
Missouri Historical Society Staff. Thomas Jefferson Changing West: From Conquest to Conservation. Ronda, James P., ed. LC 96-25330. 224p. 1997. 16.95 (*0-8263-1775-8*) U of NM Pr.
Missouri Historical Society Staff, tr. see Wislizenus, Frederick A.
Missouri Hospice Staff. Sacred Stories: Inspirational Stories from Clients & Members of the Missouri Hospice Organization. pap. 9.95 (*0-9650541-2-8*, Pub. by Offspring Bks) Booksource.
Missouri River Heritage Association Staff. Heritage of Buchanan County, Missouri, Vol. II. (Illus.). 401p. 1986. 50.00 (*0-88107-061-0*) Curtis Media.
Missouri River Heritage Association Staff, ed. Heritage of Buchanan County, MO, Vol. I. (Illus.). 401p. 1986. 55.00 (*0-88107-014-9*) Curtis Media.
Missri, Jose C. Clinical Doppler Echocardiography. 316p. 1989. text 85.00 (*0-07-042436-5*) McGraw-Hill HPD.
Missri, Jose C., ed. Transesophageal Echocardiography: Clinical & Intraoperative Applications. LC 92-23799. (Illus.). 248p. 1992. text 147.00 (*0-443-08852-7*) Church.
Mistakidis, E. S. & Stavroulakis, G. E. Nonconvex Optimization in Mechanics: Algorithms, Heuristics & Engineering Applications by the F. E. M. LC 97-39880. (Nonconvex Optimization & Its Applications Ser.). 285p. 1998. lib. bdg. write for info. (*0-7923-4812-5*) Kluwer Academic.
***Misteil, Sean.** The Communicator's Pocketbook. 112p. 1999. pap. 8.95 (*1-870471-41-5*, Pub. by Mngmnt Pocketbks) Stylus Pub VA.
Mistele, Karl H. The End of a Community: The Destruction of the Jews of Bamberg, Germany, 1938-1942. LC 95-30361. 1995. 29.50 (*0-88125-551-3*) Ktav.
Mister Rogers. Mister Rogers - You Are Special. (MusicTivity Ser.). (Illus.). 32p. (Orig.). (J). 1994. pap. 9.95 incl. audio (*0-7935-2925-5*, 00815025) H Leonard.
Mister Smithster & His Sister Staff. But Mom, There's an Alligator in the Elevator! (Johnny Joe & the Magical Elevator Ser.). (Illus.). 36p. (Orig.). (J). (ps-4). 1996. 16.95 (*1-889637-01-7*); pap. 12.95 (*1-889637-00-9*) Butterfly Las Vegas.
Mister Tom. Fuzzy Buzzard. (Illus.). 32p. (J). (gr. 2-4). 1978. write for info. (*0-318-57345-8*) Oddo.
— Gilly the Goose. (Illus.). 32p. (J). (gr. 2-4). 1978. write for info. (*0-318-57343-1*) Oddo.
— The Little Computer. (Illus.). 32p. (J). (gr. 2-4). 1978. write for info. (*0-318-57344-X*) Oddo.
— Queen Fussy. (Illus.). 48p. (J). (gr. 2-4). 1973. audio. write for info. (*0-318-57347-4*) Oddo.
***Misterka, Adam.** My Soul & I. 1999. pap. write for info. (*1-58235-246-1*) Watermrk Pr.
Mistovich. EMT Basic Self Assessment. 2000. pap. text 19.00 (*0-8359-5134-0*) Globe Fearon.
— Instructor's Manual for Advanced Medical Life. 1999. pap. text, teacher ed. 39.00 (*0-8359-5280-0*) P-H.
Mistovich & Benner. Advance Cardiac Life. 1p. (C). 1997. pap., teacher ed. 295.00 (*0-8359-5145-6*) P-H.
Mistovich & Hafen. Prehospital Emergency Care. 6th ed. 1999. pap. 54.00 (*0-8359-5705-5*) Pearson Custom.
Mistovich, Joseph J. EMT-Intermediate Self Assessment Examination Review Manual. (C). 1999. pap. 22.67 (*0-8359-5019-0*) P-H.
Mistovich, Joseph J., et al. Advanced Cardiac Life Support Manual for Course Preparation & Review. LC 97-8217. 448p. (C). 1997. pap. text 36.40 (*0-8359-5050-6*) P-H.
Mistral, Frederic. The Memoirs of Frederic Mistral. LC 86-8768.Tr. of Moun Espelido. 352p. 1986. pap. 10.95 (*0-8112-1009-X*, NDP632, Pub. by New Directions) Norton.
— The Memoirs of Frederic Mistral. LC 86-8768.Tr. of Moun Espelido. 352p. 1986. 22.95 (*0-8112-0992-X*, Pub. by New Directions) Norton.
— Le Tresor de Felibridge: Dictionnaire Provencal-Francais, 2 vols. (FRE.). 2375p. 250.00 (*0-686-56736-6*, M-6414) Fr & Eur.
Mistral, Gabriela, pseud. Desolacion. (SPA.). 230p. 1972. 10.50 (*0-8288-7130-2*, S8274) Fr & Eur.
— A Gabriela Mistral Reader: A Reader. Jacketti, Maria, tr. 227p. 1997. reprint ed. pap. 15.00 (*1-877727-18-0*) White Pine.
— Invitacion a Gabriela Mistral (Invitation to Gabriela Mistral) (1889-1989) Valdes, Gladys R., ed. (SPA.). 264p. 1990. pap. 12.99 (*968-16-3493-4*, Pub. by Fondo) Continental Bk.
— Poemas de las Madres (The Mothers' Poems) Kyle, Christiane J., tr. (Illus.). 39p. 1996. pap. 25.00 (*0-910055-29-7*) East Wash Univ.
Mistree, Farrokh, jt. ed. see Belegundu, Ashok D.
Mistretta, Charles. Digital Subtraction Arteriography: An Application of Computerized Fluoroscopy. LC 81-14721. (Illus.). 175p. reprint ed. pap. 54.30 (*0-8357-7623-9*, 205694600096) Bks Demand.
Mistretta, Gaetano, jt. auth. see Palmerini, Luca.
Mistretta, Tony, ed. see Keene, Robert D.
Mistrik. Moderna Slovencina. (SLO.). 294p. 1996. write for info. (*80-08-01042-8*, Pub. by Slov Pegagog Naklad) IBD Ltd.
— Zaklady Estetiky a Etikety. (SLO.). 96p. 1996. write for info. (*80-08-01214-5*, Pub. by Slov Pegagog Naklad) IBD Ltd.
Mistrik, J. Stylistika (Stylistics) (SLO.). 584p. 1997. write for info. (*80-08-02529-8*, Pub. by Slov Pegagog Naklad) IBD Ltd.
Mistrik, J., et al. Prakticka Slovencina (Practical Slovak) (SLO.). 290p. 1997. pap. write for info. (*80-08-02402-X*, Pub. by Slov Pegagog Naklad) IBD Ltd.
Mistron, Deborah. Understanding Jamaica Kincaid's Annie John: A Student Casebook to Issues, Sources & Historical Documents. LC 98-12158. 232p. 1999. 39.95 (*0-313-30254-5*, Greenwood Pr) Greenwood.
Mistry, Freny. Nietzsche & Buddhism. (Monographien und Texte zur Nietzsche-Forschung Ser.: Vol. 6). 211p. 1981. 83.10 (*3-11-008305-1*) De Gruyter.
Mistry, Jim. Letters from the Mandali of Avatar Meher Baba, Vol. II. LC 83-142831. 176p. (Orig.). 1983. pap. 7.95 (*0-913078-46-8*) Sheriar Pr.
Mistry, Jim, compiled by. Letters from the Mandali of Avatar Meher Baba, Vol. I. LC 83-142831. 152p. (Orig.). 1981. pap. 7.95 (*0-913078-42-5*) Sheriar Pr.
Mistry, Nilesh. The Illustrated Book of Fairy Tales. LC 97-15492. 160p. (J). (gr. 3-6). 1998. 19.95 (*0-7894-2794-X*) DK Pub Inc.
— The Illustrated Book of Myths: Tales & Legends of the World. LC 95-2156. 192p. (YA). (gr. 5 up). 1995. 19.95 (*0-7894-0202-5*, 5-70615) DK Pub Inc.
Mistry, Nilesh, jt. auth. see Kerven, Rosalind.
Mistry, Pauline. Rationalizing Acute Care Services. LC 96-33576. 1996. write for info. (*1-85775-125-6*, Radcliffe Med Pr) Scovill Paterson.
Mistry, Rohinton. A Fine Balance: A Novel. LC 95-49317. 624p. 1997. pap. 15.00 (*0-679-77645-1*) Knopf.
Mistry, Rohinton. Such a Long Journey. 424p. 1997. mass mkt. 8.95 (*0-7710-9897-9*) McCland & Stewart.
Mistry, Rohinton. Such a Long Journey. LC 91-58052. 339p. 1992. pap. 14.00 (*0-679-73871-1*) Vin Bks.
— Swimming Lessons: And Other Stories from Firozsha Baag. LC 96-31214. 1997. pap. 12.00 (*0-679-77632-X*) Random.
Mistry, S. I., jt. ed. see Nair, S. S.
***Mistry, Sanjay I. & McLain, Timothy, eds.** Fluid Power Systems & Technology, 1999. (FPST Ser.: Vol. 6). 155p. 1999. 90.00 (*0-7918-1647-8*) ASME Pr.
Mistry, Shiavax. Direct Taxes Ready Referencer. (C). 1990. 140.00 (*0-89771-261-7*) St Mut.
Mistry, Tara & Brown, Allan, eds. Race & Groupwork. LC 98-129957. 300p. 1997. 65.00 (*1-86177-011-1*, Pub. by Whiting & Birch); pap. 29.95 (*1-86177-010-3*, Pub. by Whiting & Birch) Paul & Co Pubs.
Mistry, Vikram V. Cheese & Fermented Milk Foods, 2 vols. 3rd ed. Incl. Vol. 2: Procedures & Analysis. 3rd enl. rev. ed. Kosikowski, Frank V. LC 97-92960. (Illus.). x, 330p. 1997. 45.00 (*0-9656456-2-2*); Vol. 1: Origins & Principles. 3rd expanded rev. ed. Kosikowski, Frank Y. LC 97-92960. (Illus.). 728p. 1997. 65.00 (*0-9656456-1-4*); LC 97-92960. 120.00 (*0-9656456-0-6*) F V K LLC.
***Mistycah, Laura Lee.** Kryahgenetics: The Simple Secrets of Human Alchemy. (Illus.). 152p. 1999. pap. 35.00 (*0-9660668-6-3*, Pub. by Mistyc Hse) Greenleaf Tenn.
Misugi, T. & Shibatomi, A. Compound & Josephson High-Speed Devices. (Microdevices: Physics & Fabrication Technologies Ser.). (Illus.). 318p. (C). 1993. text 85.00 (*0-306-44384-8*, Kluwer Plenum) Kluwer Academic.
Misulis, Karl E. Disorders of Mental Status: Dementia, Encephalopathy, Coma, Syncope. LC 97-50382. 303p. 1998. pap. text 40.00 (*0-7506-9988-4*) Buttrwrth-Heinemann.
— Essentials of Clinical Neurophysiology. 2nd ed. LC 96-50458. 378p. 1997. pap. text 47.50 (*0-7506-9887-X*) Buttrwrth-Heinemann.
— Neurologic Localization & Diagnosis. 217p. 1996. pap. text 33.50 (*0-7506-9636-2*) Buttrwrth-Heinemann.
***Misulis, Karl E. & Edwards-Lee, Terri.** Confusion. LC 99-28978. (Most Common Complaints Ser.). 296p. 1999. pap. text 27.95 (*0-7506-7191-2*) Buttrwrth-Heinemann.
Misulis, Karl E. & Spehlmann, R. Spehlmann's Evoked Potential Primer: Visual, Auditory, & Somatosensory Evoked Potentials in Clinical Diagnosis. 2nd rev. ed. LC 94-6178. 243p. 1994. pap. text 57.50 (*0-7506-9512-9*) Buttrwrth-Heinemann.
***Misulis, Karl E., et al.** Review Manual for Neurology in Clinical Practice. 3rd ed. 370p. 2000. pap. text 75.00 (*0-7506-7192-0*) Buttrwrth-Heinemann.
Misulis, Karl E., jt. auth. see Guthkelch, A. Norman.
Misumi, Jyuji. Nuclear Safety: A Human Factors Perspective. LC 99-179121. 350p. 1999. 110.00 (*0-7484-0818-5*) Taylor & Francis.
Misund, Ole A. Distribution & Behaviour Mechanics of Pelagic Fish. 1997. 75.00 (*0-85238-241-3*) Blackwell Sci.
Misuraca, Karen. City Smart: San Francisco. (City Smart Ser.). (Illus.). 272p. 1999. pap. 15.95 (*1-56261-439-8*, City Smart) Avalon Travel.
— Fun with the Family in Northern California. 2nd ed. LC 98-8444. (Fun with the Family Ser.). (Illus.). 288p. 1998. pap. 12.95 (*0-7627-0175-7*) Globe Pequot.
***Misuraca, Karen.** Fun with the Family in Northern California: Hundreds of Ideas for Day Trips with the Kids. 3rd ed. (Fun with the Family Ser.). (Illus.). 2000. pap. 13.95 (*0-7627-0813-1*) Globe Pequot.
Misuraca, Karen. Quick Escapes from San Francisco: 30 Weekend Trips from the Bay Area. 3rd ed. LC 98-41608. (Quick Escapes Ser.). (Illus.). 352p. 1999. pap. 14.95 (*0-7627-0294-X*) Globe Pequot.
***Misuraca, Karen.** Quick Escapes San Francisco: 26 Weekend Getaways from the Bay Area. 4th ed. (Quick Escapes Ser.). (Illus.). 2001. pap. 15.95 (*0-7627-0835-2*) Globe Pequot.
Misuraca, Karen, ed. see Paulson, Lynda R. & Watson, Tom.
Misurella, Fred. Short Time. LC 96-46780. (VIA Folios Ser.: Vol. 8). (Illus.). 49p. (C). 1996. pap. 7.00 (*1-884419-07-0*) Bordighera.
— Understanding Milan Kundera: Public Events, Private Affairs. LC 92-27444. (Understanding Modern European & Latin American Literature Ser.). 231p. (C). 1993. text 29.95 (*0-87249-853-0*) U of SC Pr.
Misyn, R., jt. auth. see Harvey, Ralph.
***Misztal, Barbara A.** Informality: Social Theory & Contemporary Practice. LC 99-16271. (International Library of Sociology Ser.). 1999. pap. 0.00 (*0-415-15674-2*) Routledge.
— Informality: Social Theory & Contemporary Practice. LC 99-16271. (International Library of Sociology Ser.). 256p. (C). 1999. text. write for info. (*0-415-15673-4*) Routledge.
Misztal, Barbara A. Trust in Modern Societies: The Search for the Bases of Social Order. LC 95-47706. 292p. (C). 1995. text 57.95 (*0-7456-1248-2*, Pub. by Polity Pr) Blackwell Pubs.
— Trust in Modern Societies: The Search for the Bases of Social Order. LC 95-47706. 292p. (C). 1996. pap. text 27.95 (*0-7456-1634-8*, Pub. by Polity Pr) Blackwell Pubs.
Misztal, Barbara A. & Moss, David, eds. Action on AIDS: National Policies in Comparative Perspective, 28. LC 89-26034. (Contributions in Medical Studies: No. 28). 280p. 1990. 59.95 (*0-313-26369-8*, MZA/, Greenwood Pr) Greenwood.
Misztal, Bronislaw, ed. Poland after Solidarity: Social Movements versus the State. 1985. 34.95 (*0-88738-049-2*) Transaction Pubs.
Misztal, Bronislaw & Shupe, Anson, eds. Religion & Politics in Comparative Perspective: Revival of Religious Fundamentalism in East & West. LC 92-12120. 240p. 1992. 59.95 (*0-275-94218-X*, C4218, Praeger Pubs) Greenwood.
Misztal, Bronislaw, jt. ed. see Shupe, Anson.
Misztal, Goslaw S. Poslanie.Tr. of Message. (POL.). 160p. (Orig.). 1987. pap. 10.00 (*0-930401-15-8*) Artex Pub.
Misztal, M. Testy Z Anglictiny (Tests in English) (ENG & SLO.). 352p. 1997. pap. write for info. (*80-08-02594-8*, Pub. by Slov Pegagog Naklad) IBD Ltd.
MIT List Visual Arts Center Staff, jt. auth. see Reynolds, Jill.
MIT LNG Research Center Staff. Flameless Vapor Explosions. 62p. 1977. pap. 3.50 (*0-318-12616-8*, M20177) Am Gas Assn.
MIT Staff & Stanford University Staff. Bibliographic Guide to Computer Science, 1989. 250p. 1990. 160.00 (*0-8161-7130-0*, Hall Reference) Macmillan.
M.I.T. Symposium Staff. Women & the Scientific Professions: Proceedings of the M.I.T. Symposium on American Women in Science & Engineering, 1964. Mattfeld, Jacquelyn & Van Aken, Carol, eds. LC 76-2516. 250p. 1976. reprint ed. lib. bdg. 59.50 (*0-8371-8759-1*, MAWSP) Greenwood.
Mita, Munesuke. Social Psychology of Modern Japan. (Japanese Studies). 535p. 1993. 59.95 (*0-7103-0451-X*, A9864) Routledge.
Mita, Randy. ABC Hawaii: A Reference Guide - Everything to Know about the Islands. 208p. 1994. pap. 14.95 (*0-935180-84-2*) Mutual Pub HI.
Mitakidou, Christodoula, jt. auth. see Manna, Anthony L.
Mital. New Law of Arbitration, ADR & Contract in India. LC 97-8441. 1997. 163.00 (*90-411-0358-9*) Kluwer Law Intl.
Mital, A., et al, eds. Advances in Occupational Ergonomics & Safety I. Vol. 1 & 2. (Illus.). 1018p. (Orig.). 1996. pap. 80.00 (*0-9652558-0-8*) Int Soc Occupational.
***Mital, A., et al, eds.** Ergonomics Guidelines & Problem Solving. 530p. 1999. 104.00 (*0-08-043643-9*) Elsevier.
Mital, A., et al. A Guide to Manual Materials Handling. 2nd ed. LC 97-196919. 152p. 1997. pap. 23.95 (*0-7484-0728-6*, Pub. by Tay Francis Ltd) Taylor & Francis.
Mital, Anil. Human Strength. (General Engineering Ser.). 1991. text. write for info. (*0-442-00602-0*, VNR) Wiley.
Mital, Anil & Karwowski, Waldemar. Workspace, Equipment & Tool Design. (Advances in Human Factors-Ergonomics Ser.: Vol. 15). 370p. 1991. 173.50 (*0-444-87441-0*) Elsevier.
Mital, Anil, et al. A Guide to Manual Materials Handling. 120p. 1993. pap. 25.00 (*0-85066-801-8*, Pub. by Tay Francis Ltd) Taylor & Francis.
Mital, Anil, jt. auth. see Ayoub, M. M.
Mital, Anil, jt. ed. see Chen, Jen-Gwo.
Mital, Anil, jt. ed. see Karwowski, Waldemar.
Mital, Anil, jt. ed. see Kumar, Shrawan.
Mital, H. C., ed. see Ramalingam, Vimala, et al.
Mital, K. M. Social Responsibilities of Business: Concepts, Areas & Progress. (C). 1988. 32.00 (*81-7001-035-7*, Pub. by Chanakya) S Asia.
Mital, V. Advanced Information Systems for Lawyers. (C). 1992. mass mkt. 89.50 (*0-412-43290-0*) Chapman & Hall.
Mital, V., ed. Advanced Litigation Support & Document Imaging. LC 95-34234. (Computer/Law Ser.: No. 15). 212p. 1997. pap. 106.00 (*90-411-0113-6*) Kluwer Law Intl.
Mital, V. & Johnson, L. Advanced Information Systems for Lawyers. 304p. 1992. 54.95 (*0-442-31591-0*) Chapman & Hall.
Mitamura, Joyce Y., jt. auth. see Mitamura, Yasuko K.
Mitamura, Taisuke. Chinese Eunuchs: The Structure of Intimate Politics.Tr. of Kangan: Sokkin Seigi no Kozo. 1992. 14.95 (*0-8048-1881-9*) Tuttle Pubng.
Mitamura, Yasuko K. Let's Learn Hiragana. LC 84-82275. 72p. (Orig.). 1985. pap. 13.00 (*0-87011-709-2*) Kodansha.
— Let's Learn Katakana. LC 85-40059. (Illus.). 88p. (Orig.). 1986. pap. 13.00 (*0-87011-719-X*) Kodansha.
— Let's Learn More Kanji: Family Groups, Learning Strategies, & 300 Complex Kanji. 1998. pap. text 30.00 (*4-7700-2069-4*, Pub. by Kodansha Intl) Kodansha.
Mitamura, Yasuko K. & Mitamura, Joyce Y. Let's Learn Kanji: An Introduction to Radicals, Components, & 250 Very Basic Kanji. Hulbert, Paul, ed. LC 97-36398. (JPN., Illus.). 256p. 1998. pap. 22.00 (*4-7700-2068-6*) Kodansha.
Mitch. Handbook of Nutrition & the Kidney. 3rd ed. LC 97-51461. 392p. 1998. 39.95 (*0-7817-1534-2*) Lppncott W & W.

M

— The Public Library of New South Wales Dictionary Catalog of Printed Books. 1982. 4710.00 (0-8161-1362-9, G K Hall & Co) Mac Lib Ref.

— The Public Library of New South Wales Dictionary Catalog of Printed Books, Supplement 1. 1981. suppl. ed. 180.00 (0-8161-1323-8, G K Hall & Co) Mac Lib Ref.

Mitch, Stacy. Courageous Love: A Bible Study on Holiness for Women. LC 99-90086. 136p. 1999. pap. 8.95 (0-9663223-3-9) Emmaus Road.

Mitch, William E. The Progressive Nature of Renal Disease. 2nd ed. (Contemporary Issues in Nephrology Ser.: Vol. 26). 288p. 1992. text 89.00 (0-443-08819-5) Church.

Mitcham, Allison. Grey Owl's Favorite Wilderness. 80p. 1981. 6.95 (0-920806-17-1, Pub. by Penumbra Pr) U of Toronto Pr.

— The Northern Imagination. 103p. 1983. 17.95 (0-920806-46-5, Pub. by Penumbra Pr); pap. 7.95 (0-920806-47-3, Pub. by Penumbra Pr) U of Toronto Pr.

Mitcham, Carl. Thinking Through Technology: The Path Between Engineering & Philosophy. LC 93-44581. 410p. 1994. pap. text 20.00 (0-226-53198-8) U Ch Pr.

Mitcham, Carl, ed. Philosophy of Technology in Spanish Speaking Countries. LC 93-39783. (Philosophy & Technology Ser.). 354p. (C). 1993. lib. bdg. 209.50 (0-7923-2567-2, Pub. by Kluwer Academic) Kluwer Academic.

Mitcham, Carl, et al, eds. Ethics & Technology. (Research in Philosophy & Technology Ser.: Vol. 9). 306p. 1989. 78.50 (0-89232-793-6) Jai Pr.

— Research in Philosophy & Technology, Vol. 1. 390p. 1978. 78.50 (0-89232-022-2) Jai Pr.

— Research in Philosophy & Technology, Vol. 2. 403p. 1979. 78.50 (0-89232-101-6) Jai Pr.

— Research in Philosophy & Technology, Vol. 3. 412p. 1981. 78.50 (0-89232-102-4) Jai Pr.

— Research in Philosophy & Technology, Vol. 4. 305p. 1982. 78.50 (0-89232-181-4) Jai Pr.

— Research in Philosophy & Technology, Vol. 5. 339p. 1983. 78.50 (0-89232-322-1) Jai Pr.

— Research in Philosophy & Technology, Vol. 6. 282p. 1984. 78.50 (0-89232-352-3) Jai Pr.

— Research in Philosophy & Technology, Vol. 8. 280p. 1985. 78.50 (0-89232-593-3) Jai Pr.

— Research in Philosophy & Technology, Vol. 10. 376p. 1990. 78.50 (1-55938-062-4) Jai Pr.

— Research in Philosophy & Technology Vol. 11: Technology & Politics. 422p. 1991. 78.50 (1-55938-212-0) Jai Pr.

— Research in Philosophy & Technology Vol. 12: Technology & the Environment. 364p. 1992. 78.50 (1-55938-456-5) Jai Pr.

— Research in Philosophy & Technology Vol. 14: Technology & Everyday Life. 351p. 1994. 78.50 (1-55938-712-2) Jai Pr.

— Research in Philosophy & Technology Vol. 15: Social & Philosophical Constructions of Technology. LC 96-162569. 423p. 1995. 82.50 (1-55938-886-2) Jai Pr.

Mitcham, Carl & Duval, R. Shannon. Toolkit: Professional Ethics for Engineers. LC 99-47035. 131p. (C). 2000. pap. text 21.33 (0-8053-6436-6, Prentice Hall) P-H.

Mitcham, Carl & Huning, Alois, eds. Philosophy & Technology II. 374p. 1986. text 175.00 (90-277-1975-6, D Reidel) Kluwer Academic.

Mitcham, Carl & Mackey, Robert. Bibliography of the Philosophy of Technology. LC 74-168204. 288p. reprint ed. pap. 89.30 (0-8357-7201-2, 200727700063) Bks Demand.

Mitcham, Carl & Mackey, Robert, eds. Philosophy & Technology: Readings in the Philosophical Problems of Technology. LC 82-19818. 416p. (C). 1983. reprint ed. pap. 18.95 (0-02-921430-0) Free Pr.

Mitcham, Carl & Waks, Leonard J., eds. Research in Philosophy & Technology Vol. 16: Technology & Social Action, Vol. 16. 1997. 78.50 (0-7623-0109-0) Jai Pr.

Mitcham, Carl, jt. ed. see Cutliffe, Stephen H.

Mitcham, Carl, ed. see Durbin, Paul T.

Mitcham, Carl, ed. see Waks, Leonard J.

Mitcham, Howard. Clams, Mussels, Oysters, Scallops & Snails: A Cookbook & a Memoir. (Illus.). 224p. 1990. pap. 12.50 (0-940160-47-1) Parnassus Imprints.

— Creole Gumbo & All That Jazz: A New Orleans Seafood Cookbook. LC 78-8291. (Illus.). 1978. pap. 12.45 (0-201-05585-6) Addison-Wesley.

— Creole Gumbo & All that Jazz: A New Orleans Seafood Cookbook. LC 91-26188. (Illus.). 288p. 1992. reprint ed. pap. 15.95 (0-88289-870-1) Pelican.

— Provincetown Seafood Cookbook. 288p. 1986. reprint ed. pap. 12.50 (0-940160-33-1) Parnassus Imprints.

Mitcham, Judson. Somewhere in Ecclesiastes: Poems. 64p. (Orig.). (C). 1991. text 18.95 (0-8262-0802-9) U of Mo Pr.

***Mitcham, Judson.** The Sweet Everlasting. LC 95-24474. 208p. 2000. reprint ed. pap. 11.00 (0-380-80755-6, Avon Bks) Morrow Avon.

Mitcham, Judson. The Sweet Everlasting: A Novel. LC 95-24474. 200p. 1996. 22.95 (0-8203-1807-8) U of Ga Pr.

— Sweet Everlasting: A Novel. 1997. mass mkt. 6.99 (0-380-73027-8, Avon Bks) Morrow Avon.

Mitcham, Samuel W., Jr. The Desert Fox in Normandy: Rommel's Defense of Fortress Europe. LC 96-49808. 256p. 1997. 26.95 (0-275-95484-6, Praeger Pubs) Greenwood.

— Hitler's Field Marshals. 1993. pap. 17.95 (0-8128-8542-2, Scrbrough Hse) Madison Bks UPA.

***Mitcham, Samuel W., Jr.** The Panzer Legions: A Guide to the German Army Tank Divisions of World War II & Their Commanders. 2000. lib. bdg. write for info. (0-313-31640-6, Greenwood Pr) Greenwood.

— Retreat to the Reich: The German Defeat in France, 1944. LC 99-86096. 352p. 2000. 27.50 (0-275-96857-X, C6857, Praeger Trade) Greenwood.

***Mitcham, Samuel W.** Triumphant Fox: Erwin Rommel & the Rise of the Afrika Korps. 2000. pap. 17.95 (0-8154-1055-7, Pub. by Cooper Sq) Natl Bk Netwk.

Mitcham, Samuel W., Jr. Why Hitler? The Genesis of the Nazi Reich. LC 96-16246. 232p. 1996. 24.95 (0-275-95485-4, Praeger Pubs) Greenwood.

Mitcham, Samuel W., Jr. & Mueller, Gene. Hitler's Commanders. (Illus.). 384p. 1992. 23.95 (0-8128-4014-3, Scrbrough Hse) Madison Bks UPA.

Mitchamore, Pat. Jack Daniel's Hometown Celebration Cookbook, Vol. II. Tolley, Lynne, ed. LC 90-8964. (Illus.). 192p. 1990. 19.95 (1-55853-085-1) Rutledge Hill Pr.

— Miss Mary Bobo's Boarding House Cookbook. LC 94-23511. (Illus.). 256p. 1994. 17.95 (1-55853-314-1) Rutledge Hill Pr.

Mitchamore, Pat, jt. auth. see Tolley, Lynne.

***Mitchard, Jacquelyn.** Aussi Profond Que L'ocean.Tr. of Deep End of the Ocean. 1999. pap. 13.95 (2-266-07864-X) Distribks Inc.

Mitchard, Jacquelyn. The Deep End of the Ocean. 448p. 1999. mass mkt. 7.99 (0-451-19774-7, Sig) NAL.

***Mitchard, Jacquelyn.** The Deep End of the Ocean. 448p. 1999. pap. 12.95 (0-14-028627-6, Penguin Bks) Viking Penguin.

Mitchard, Jacquelyn. The Deep End of the Ocean. large type ed. (Niagara Large Print Ser.). 608p. 1996. 29.50 (0-7089-5848-6) Ulverscroft.

— The Most Wanted. large type ed. LC 98-22083. (Compass Press Large Print Book Ser.). 407p. 1998. 34.99 (1-56895-605-3, Compass) Wheeler Pub.

— The Most Wanted. 392p. 1999. reprint ed. mass mkt. 7.99 (0-451-19685-6, Sig) NAL.

— The Rest of Us: Dispatches from the Mother Ship. 272p. 1999. pap. 12.95 (0-14-027497-9) Viking Penguin.

***Mitchard, Jacquelyn.** Untitled Jacquelyn Mitchard. 2001. 24.95 (0-670-88385-9) Viking Penguin.

Mitchard, Mervyn, ed. Electronic Communication Technologies: Techniques & Technologies for the 21st Century. LC 98-21351. 500p. 1998. 239.00 (1-57491-069-8) Interpharm.

Mitchel, Claire. The Third Third: Seeing the World Through Rose-Colored Bifocals. LC 90-19246. 256p. 1991. 16.95 (0-910155-17-8) Bartleby Pr.

Mitchel, Dale. A Ghost in the Closet - Is There an Alcoholic Hiding? An Honest Look at Alcoholism. LC 98-50581. 250p. 1999. 16.95 (1-56838-328-2, 1372) Hazelden.

Mitchel, Doug. Fantasies in Chrome: The Art of the Custom Motorcycle. (Illus.). 98p. 1996. 24.95 (0-914824-95-3) P Oxman.

— Memorable Japanese Motorcycles, 1959-1996. LC 97-65625. (Schiffer Bks.). (Illus.). 152p. 1997. 34.95 (0-7643-0235-3) Schiffer.

***Mitchel, Doug.** T-Birds. LC 99-10844. 1999. text 14.98 (1-56799-753-8) Cruising Guide.

Mitchel, Fordyce, ed. see Brady, Thomas A.

Mitchel, John. Jail Journal, 1876: or Five Years in British Prisons. LC 96-18963. (Hibernia Ser.). 1996. 65.00 (1-85477-218-X) Continuum.

Mitchel, Larry A. Hellenistic & Roman Strata: A Study of the Stratigraphy of Tell Heshban from the 2nd Century B. C. to the 4th Century A. D. LC 92-72496. (Heshbon Excavations Final Reports: Vol. 7). (Illus.). 208p. (C). 1992. text 45.99 (0-943872-20-0) Andrews Univ Pr.

— A Student's Vocabulary for Biblical Hebrew & Aramaic. 128p. 1984. pap. 12.99 (0-310-45461-1, 11607P) Zondervan.

Mitchel, Ormsby M. The Planetary & Stellar Worlds: A Popular Exposition of the Great Discoveries & Theories of Modern Astronomy. Cohen, I. Bernard, ed. LC 79-7976. (Three Centuries of Science in America Ser.). (Illus.). 1980. reprint ed. lib. bdg. 25.95 (0-405-12559-3) Ayer.

Mitchel, Sue A. & Hughes, Barbara A. From the Bridegroom with Love. 144p. (YA). (gr. 8 up). 1992. pap. 6.95 (0-9634469-0-8) Chereb Pub.

Mitchelhill, A. Bills of Lading: Law & Practice. 2nd ed. 160p. 1990. pap. 36.95 (0-412-35750-X, A4460) Chapman & Hall.

Mitchell. American Government 4/e. 4th ed. 1998. pap. 16.74 (0-07-233514-9) McGraw.

— Basics for Success. 1996. pap. 17.25 (0-07-217965-1) McGraw.

***Mitchell.** Becoming a Consultant: How to Start & Run a Profitable Consulting Business. (Illus.). 168p. 2000. pap. 14.95 (1-85703-392-2, Pub. by How To Bks) Midpt Trade.

— The Dona. 2000. pap. 14.95 (1-891929-55-0) Four Seasons.

— Mad Men & Medusas: Reclaiming Hysteria. 2000. pap. 18.00 (0-465-04614-2, Pub. by Basic) HarpC.

Mitchell. Math Exercises: Algebra. 1994. pap. 2.50 (0-8092-3653-2) NTC Contemp Pub Co.

— Math Exercises: Decimals. 1993. pap. 2.50 (0-8092-3826-8) NTC Contemp Pub Co.

— Math Exercises: Fractions. 1993. pap. 2.50 (0-8092-3827-6) NTC Contemp Pub Co.

— Math Exercises: Geometry. 1994. pap. 2.50 (0-8092-3652-4) NTC Contemp Pub Co.

— Math Exercises: Percents. 1993. pap. 2.50 (0-8092-4168-4) NTC Contemp Pub Co.

— Math Exercises: Pre Algebra. 1994. pap. 2.50 (0-8092-3654-0) NTC Contemp Pub Co.

— Math Exercises: Problelm Solving & Applications. 1993. pap. 2.50 (0-8092-4171-4) NTC Contemp Pub Co.

— Math Exercises: Whole Numbers & Money. 1993. pap. 2.50 (0-8092-3828-4) NTC Contemp Pub Co.

— Nancy Drew & Hardy Boys. (YA). 1996. 23.95 (0-8057-8822-0, Twyne); pap. 13.95 (0-8057-8823-9, Twyne) Mac Lib Ref.

— Natural Medicine for PMS. LC 98-179226. 240p. 1998. mass mkt. 5.99 (0-440-22526-4) Dell.

— Perspectives & Issues in Health Care. (LPN/LVN Nursing Ser.). 1996. teacher ed. 14.95 (0-8273-6320-6) Delmar.

— Perspectives & Issues in Health Care. (LPN/LVN Nursing Ser.). 1998. pap. 24.95 (0-8273-6319-2) Delmar.

— Research Design Explained. 3rd ed. (C). 1995. pap. text, teacher ed., suppl. ed. 35.00 (0-15-503247-X) Harcourt Coll Pubs.

— Research Design Explained: Test Bank. 3rd ed. (C). 1995. pap. text 26.75 (0-15-503249-6) Harcourt Coll Pubs.

— Resrce & Enviro Managemt. (C). 1997. pap. text 28.13 (0-582-23796-3, Pub. by Addison-Wesley) Longman.

— Roots of Wisdom. 3rd ed. (Philosophy Ser.). 2001. pap. 44.25 (0-534-55299-4) Wadsworth Pub.

***Mitchell.** Roots of World Wisdom: A Multicultural Reader. 3rd ed. (Philosophy Ser.). 2001. 20.50 (0-534-56111-X) Wadsworth Pub.

Mitchell. Taking Sides: Western Civilization, Vol. 1. 2nd ed. 400p. 1999. pap. 19.69 (0-07-303195-X) McGraw.

— Traces: Journey to Lost Frontiers. 1995. 22.95 (0-8050-1981-2) H Holt & Co.

— Trumpet Method, Bk. 1. 1990. 8.95 (0-685-32178-9, M304) Hansen Ed Mus.

— Trumpet Method, Bk. 2. 1990. 9.95 (0-685-32179-7, M305) Hansen Ed Mus.

— Trumpet Method, Bk. 3. 1990. 9.95 (0-685-32180-0, M306) Hansen Ed Mus.

— Trumpet Method, Bk. 4. 1990. 9.95 (0-685-32181-9, M307) Hansen Ed Mus.

***Mitchell.** Wildest Place on Earth. 2000. 24.00 (1-58243-046-2, Pub. by Counterpt DC) HarpC.

Mitchell, et al, compiled by. The Carmel & Hermon Town Register, 1904 (Town Histories & Directories) 120p. 1997. reprint ed. pap. 19.00 (0-8328-5825-0) Higginson Bk Co.

— The Cherryfield Register, 1905 (Town History & Directory) 92p. 1997. reprint ed. pap. 17.50 (0-8328-5826-9) Higginson Bk Co.

— The Gorham & Buxton Town Register, 1905 (Town Histories & Directories) 222p. 1997. reprint ed. pap. 27.00 (0-8328-5846-3) Higginson Bk Co.

— The Gray & New Gloucester Register, 1905: Town Histories & Directories. 110p. 1997. reprint ed. pap. 18.00 (0-8328-5848-X) Higginson Bk Co.

— The Hartland & St. Albans Register, 1904 (Town Histories & Directories) 101p. 1997. reprint ed. pap. 17.00 (0-8328-5856-0) Higginson Bk Co.

— The Linconville, Northport, Belmont, Morrill, Searsmont & Waldo Town Register, 1907 (Town Histories & Directories) 175p. 1997. reprint ed. pap. 27.50 (0-8328-5867-6) Higginson Bk Co.

— Milo & Brownville Town Register, 1905: Town Histories & Directories. (Illus.). 120p. 1997. reprint ed. pap. 15.00 (0-8328-5872-2) Higginson Bk Co.

Mitchell, ed. GED Science. 1988. pap., wbk. ed. 8.46 (0-8092-4598-1) NTC Contemp Pub Co.

Mitchell & Barron. Evidence, 1995. (Seattle University Skills Development Ser.). 120p. 1996. pap. text 15.00 (1-55834-322-9, 12508-10, MICHIE) LEXIS Pub.

Mitchell & Campbell. The Milbridge Register, 1905: Town History & Directory. 88p. 1997. reprint ed. pap. 17.50 (0-8328-5871-4) Higginson Bk Co.

— The North Berwick Register, 1904 (Town History & Directory) 112p. 1997. reprint ed. pap. 19.50 (0-8328-5879-X) Higginson Bk Co.

Mitchell & Campbell, compiled by. The Freeport Register, 1904 (Town History & Directory) 108p. 1997. reprint ed. pap. 18.00 (0-8328-5841-2) Higginson Bk Co.

— The Kennebunk Register, 1904 (Town History & Directory) 112p. 1997. reprint ed. pap. 18.00 (0-8328-5863-3) Higginson Bk Co.

— The Lisbon Town Register, 1905 (Town History & Directory) 117p. 1997. reprint ed. pap. 19.50 (0-8328-5868-4) Higginson Bk Co.

— The Scarboro Register, 1905 (Town History & Directory) 95p. 1997. reprint ed. pap. 18.00 (0-8328-5910-9) Higginson Bk Co.

Mitchell & Cavis, compiled by. The Fairfield Register, 1904 (Town History & Directory) (Illus.). 128p. 1997. reprint ed. pap. 17.00 (0-8328-5834-X) Higginson Bk Co.

Mitchell & Daggett. East Livermore & Livermore Register, 1903-4 (Town Histories & Directories) 148p. 1997. reprint ed. pap. 21.00 (0-8328-5832-3) Higginson Bk Co.

Mitchell & Daggett, compiled by. The Clinton & Benton Register, 1904 (Town Histories & Directories) 131p. 1997. reprint ed. pap. 21.00 (0-8328-5827-7) Higginson Bk Co.

Mitchell & Davis. The Winslow Register, 1904 (Town History & Directory) 103p. 1997. reprint ed. pap. 17.50 (0-8328-5930-3) Higginson Bk Co.

Mitchell & Davis, compiled by. The Canton & Dixfield Register, 1905 (Town Histories & Directories) 115p. 1997. reprint ed. pap. 19.00 (0-8328-5822-6) Higginson Bk Co.

— The Otisfield, Harrison, Naples & Sebago Town Register, 1906 (Town Histories & Directories) 169p. 1997. reprint ed. pap. 24.00 (0-8328-5885-4) Higginson Bk Co.

— The Oxford, Hebron & Minot Register, 1906 (Town Histories & Directories) 142p. 1997. reprint ed. pap. 22.00 (0-8328-5886-2) Higginson Bk Co.

— The Paris Register, 1906 (Town History & Directory) 154p. 1997. reprint ed. pap. 23.50 (0-8328-5887-0) Higginson Bk Co.

— The Town Register of Poland, Raymond & Casco, 1906 (Town Histories & Directories) (Illus.). 141p. 1997. reprint ed. pap. 19.00 (0-8328-5897-8) Higginson Bk Co.

— The Vassalboro Register, 1904 (Town History & Directory) 132p. 1997. reprint ed. pap. 21.50 (0-8328-5920-6) Higginson Bk Co.

— The Woodstock, Sumner & Buckfield Town Register, 1905 (Town Histories & Directories) 222p. 1997. reprint ed. pap. 26.50 (0-8328-5933-8) Higginson Bk Co.

Mitchell & Denning, compiled by. The Richmond Register, 1904 (Town History of Directory) (Illus.). 103p. 1997. reprint ed. pap. 15.00 (0-8328-5903-6) Higginson Bk Co.

Mitchell & Dyer. Winning Women. 1999. pap. write for info. (0-14-008091-0, Penguin Bks) Viking Penguin.

Mitchell & Gastonguay. The Thomaston Register, 1904 (Town History & Directory) 102p. 1997. reprint ed. pap. 17.00 (0-8328-5916-8) Higginson Bk Co.

Mitchell & Hunt. Maine Probate Procedure. 1991. ring bd. 115.00 (0-327-01045-2, 81675-10, MICHIE) LEXIS Pub.

Mitchell & Johnson, compiled by. The Hampden Register, 1904 (Town History & Directory) 127p. 1997. reprint ed. pap. 21.00 (0-8328-5851-X) Higginson Bk Co.

***Mitchell & Lasswell.** Secret Lives of Dragonflies. 2002. pap. text. write for info. (0-7167-4090-7, Pub. by W H Freeman) VHPS.

Mitchell & Pittingill, compiled by. The Presque Isle Register, 1904 (Town History & Directory) 130p. 1997. reprint ed. pap. 21.50 (0-8328-5899-4) Higginson Bk Co.

Mitchell & Randall, compiled by. The Madison Register, 1903 (Town History & Directory) 137p. 1997. reprint ed. pap. 21.00 (0-8328-5870-6) Higginson Bk Co.

Mitchell & Remick. The Wilton Register, 1903-1904 (Town History & Directory) 98p. 1997. reprint ed. pap. 19.00 (0-8328-5927-3) Higginson Bk Co.

— The Winthrop Register, 1903-4 (Town History & Directory) 99p. 1997. reprint ed. pap. 18.00 (0-8328-5931-1) Higginson Bk Co.

— The Yarmouth Register, 1904 (Town History & Directory) 112p. 1997. reprint ed. pap. 19.50 (0-8328-5934-6) Higginson Bk Co.

Mitchell & Remick, compiled by. The Dover & Foxcroft Register, 1904 (Town Histories & Directories) 154p. 1997. reprint ed. pap. 24.00 (0-8328-5831-5) Higginson Bk Co.

Mitchell & Russell, compiled by. The Windham Register, 1904 (Town History & Directory) 110p. 1997. reprint ed. pap. 17.00 (0-8328-5929-X) Higginson Bk Co.

Mitchell & West. News Formula. pap. text, wbk. ed. write for info. (0-312-10242-9) St Martin.

Mitchell, et al. The Bridgton Town Register, 1905 (Town History & Directory) 109p. 1997. reprint ed. pap. 17.50 (0-8328-5816-1) Higginson Bk Co.

— Exeter & Hampton, New Hampshire, Census & Business Directory, 1908. LC 79-1145. 1979. reprint ed. 16.00 (0-917890-15-9) Heritage Bk.

— Field Manual for Water Quality Monitoring: An Environmental. 11th ed. LC 97-228516. 336p. 1997. per. 19.95 (0-7872-3730-2) Kendall-Hunt.

— I Am! I Can! Vol. 1: Keys to Quality Child Care. LC 91-67111. 217p. (C). 1992. pap. 19.95 (0-910287-09-0) TelShare Pub Co.

— The Rockport Register, 1904 (Town History & Directory) 94p. 1997. reprint ed. pap. 17.00 (0-8328-5906-0) Higginson Bk Co.

Mitchell, jt. auth. see Bavor.

Mitchell, jt. auth. see Campbell.

Mitchell, jt. auth. see Giesecke.

Mitchell, jt. auth. see Hadley.

Mitchell, jt. auth. see Halderman, James D.

Mitchell, jt. auth. see Jamil.

Mitchell, jt. auth. see Jolley, Janina M.

Mitchell, jt. auth. see Lewis.

Mitchell, jt. auth. see Little.

Mitchell, jt. auth. see McCarthy.

Mitchell, jt. auth. see Wershler-Henry.

Mitchell, ed. see Cicero, Marcus Tullius.

Mitchell, Elizabeth J., jt. ed. see Harrington, John P.

Mitchell, Martin. The Irish in the West of Scotland, 1797-1848: Trade Unions, Strikes & Political Movements. 250p. 1998. pap. 60.00 (0-85976-480-X, Pub. by J Donald) St Mut.

Mitchell & Gauthier Associates (MGA) Inc., Staff. Advanced Continuous Simulation Language (ACSL) Reference Manual. 10th ed. 384p. 1991. pap. 15.00 (0-925649-00-7) Mitchell & Gauthier.

Mitchell & Gauthier Associates Inc. Staff. ACSL for Windows: Installation & How to Use. 10th ed. 70p. 1991. pap. 10.00 (0-925649-01-5) Mitchell & Gauthier.

Mitchell, A. Collins Field Guide: Trees of Britain & Northern Europe. (Illus.). 288p. 1996. 29.95 (0-00-219213-6, Pub. by HarpC) Trafalgar.

— The Young Naturalist. (Hobby Guides Ser.). (Illus.). 32p. (J). (gr. 5 up). 1982. pap. 6.95 (0-86020-653-X) EDC.

— The Young Naturalist. (Hobby Guides Ser.). (Illus.). 32p. (J). (gr. 5 up). 1999. lib. bdg. 14.95 (0-88110-235-0) EDC.

Mitchell, A. & O'Snodaigh, Padraig. Irish Political Documents, 1869-1916. 192p. 1989. 14.95 (0-7165-2422-8, Pub. by Irish Acad Pr) Intl Spec Bk.

Mitchell, A. & Snodaigh, Padraig O., eds. Irish Political Documents, 1916-49. 202p. 1985. 35.00 (0-7165-0588-6, Pub. by Irish Acad Pr) Intl Spec Bk.

Mitchell, A. & Wilkinson, J. Trees of Britain & Northern Europe. (Illus.). 288p. 1997. pap. 24.95 (0-00-219857-6, Pub. by HarpC) Trafalgar.

Mitchell, A., jt. auth. see Cockburn, J.

Mitchell, A., ed. see American Society for Metals Staff, et al.

***Mitchell, A. Duff.** The Fraunhofer Society: A Unique German Contract Research Organization Comes to America. Yoshida, Phyllis G., ed. (Illus.). 95p. (C). 2000. reprint ed. pap. text 25.00 (*0-7881-8735-X*) DIANE Pub.

Mitchell, A. G. Hindu Gods & Goddesses. 1982. reprint ed. pap. 12.50 (*81-85674-63-9*, Pub. by UBS Pubs) S Asia.

Mitchell, A. G. Lady Meed - The Art of Piers Plowman. LC 72-148891. (Select Bibliographies Reprint Ser.). 1977. 15.95 (*0-8369-5679-6*) Ayer.

— Pediatric Bibliography. (SRCD M Ser.: Vol. 6, No. 1). 1941. 25.00 (*0-527-01517-2*) Periodicals Srv.

Mitchell, A. H. & Leach, T. M. Epithermal Gold in the Philippines: Island Arc Geology & Metallogenesis. (Academic Press Geology Ser.). (Illus.). 457p. 1991. text 163.00 (*0-12-499610-8*) Acad Pr.

Mitchell, A. R. & Watkins, P. E. An Introduction to Veterinary Anatomy & Physiology. (Illus.). 216p. 1993. pap. 19.95 (*0-905214-12-9*, Pub. by BSAVA) Iowa St U Pr.

Mitchell, A. R., jt. auth. see Wait, R.

Mitchell, Adrian. Adrian Mitchell's Greatest Hits: His 40 Golden Greats. 96p. 1991. pap. 14.95 (*1-85224-164-0*, Pub. by Bloodaxe Bks) Dufour.

— Blue Coffee: Poems 1985-1996. LC 96-208927. 160p. 1996. pap. 18.95 (*1-85224-362-7*, Pub. by Bloodaxe Bks) Dufour.

— Heart on the Left: Poems, 1953-1984. 320p. 1998. pap. 22.95 (*1-85224-425-9*, Pub. by Bloodaxe Bks) Dufour.

***Mitchell, Adrian.** Mammoth Sails Tonight! 88p. 2000. pap. 13.95 (*1-84002-134-9*) Theatre Comm.

— Maudie & the Green Children. (Illus.). 32p. (J). (gr. k-4). 1996. pap. 14.95 (*1-896580-06-8*, Pub. by T1rad Bks) Tricycle Pr.

— Nobody Rides the Unicorn. LC 99-27374. (Illus.). 32p. (J). (ps-3). 2000. 16.95 (*0-439-11204-4*, A A Levine) Scholastic Inc.

Mitchell, Adrian. Our Mammoth. (Illus.). (J). (ps-3). 1987. 11.95 (*0-15-258838-8*) Harcourt.

— The Patchwork Girl of Oz - Musical. 1994. pap. 5.95 (*0-87129-335-8*, P09) Dramatic Pub.

— The Pied Piper. (Oberon Bks.). 72p. 1997. pap. 12.95 (*1-870259-09-2*) Theatre Comm.

— Plays with Songs. (Oberon Bks.). 264p. 1997. pap. 18.95 (*1-870259-40-8*) Theatre Comm.

— The Siege. (Oberon Bks.). 136p. 1997. pap. 12.95 (*1-870259-67-X*) Theatre Comm.

— Twice My Size. LC 98-34280. (Illus.). 32p. (J). (ps-1). 1999. lib. bdg. 21.40 (*0-7613-1423-7*, Copper Beech Bks) Millbrook Pr.

— The Ugly Duckling. LC 93-39962. (Illus.). 32p. (J). (ps-3). 1994. 14.95 (*1-56458 557 3*) DK Pub Inc.

Mitchell, Adrian, et al. Peace Plays. Lowe, Stephen, ed. (Methuen Theatrescripts Ser.). 135p. (C). 1988. pap. write for info. (*0-413-56000-7*, A0206, Methuen Drama) Methn.

***Mitchell, Adrian, et al.** The Snow Queen. LC 00-27947. (Young Classics Ser.). (J). 2000. write for info. (*0-7894-6680-5*) DK Pub Inc.

Mitchell, Adrian, ed. see Calderon de la Barca, Pedro.

Mitchell, Adrian, ed. see Thomas, Dylan.

***Mitchell, Alan.** Garden Tree: An Illustrated Guide to Choosing, Planting & Caring for 500 Garden Trees. (Illus.). 1999. pap. 24.95 (*1-84188-007-8*) Seven Dials.

Mitchell, Alan. The Gardener's Book of Trees: Over 500 Trees for All. (Illus.). 216p. 1994. pap. 22.95 (*0-460-86085-2*, Pub. by J M Dent & Sons) Trafalgar.

— Hebrews. (Sacra Pagina Ser.: No. 13). Date not set. write for info. (*0-8146-5815-6*, M Glazier) Liturgical Pr.

— Trees of North America. (Spotter's Guides Ser.). (Illus.). 64p. (YA). (gr. 8-12). 1992. lib. bdg. 12.95 (*0-88110-986-X*, Usborne) EDC.

— The Trees of North America. (Spotter's Guides Ser.). (Illus.). 64p. 1993. pap. 4.95 (*0-7460-1627-1*, Usborne) EDC.

— Die Wald und Parkbaeume Europas. Ein Bestimmungsbuch fur Dendrologen und Naturfreunde (The Forest & Park Trees of Europe. An Identification Book for Dendrologists & Nature Lovers) 2nd ed. Krussmann, Gerd, tr. (Illus.). 419p. 1979. 34.00 (*3-8263-8047-9*, Pub. by Blckwell Wissenschafts) Balogh.

Mitchell, Alan, et al. Pareys Buch der Baeume. Nadel- und Laubbaeume in Europa Noerdlich des Mittelmeeres (Parey's Book of Trees. Conifer & Hardwood Trees in Europe North of the Mediterranean) 3rd rev. ed. Schutt, Peter, tr. (Illus.). 272p. 1997. pap. 25.00 (*3-8263-8462-8*, Pub. by Blckwell Wissenschafts) Balogh.

Mitchell, Alan, jt. auth. see Mouchet, Jean-Paul.

Mitchell, Alan, jt. ed. see Kocka, Jurgen.

Mitchell, Alan C., jt. ed. see Wildes, Kevin W.

***Mitchell, Alan K., ed.** Frontiers of Forest Biology: Proceedings of the 1998 Joint Meeting of the North American Forest Biology Workshop & the Western Forest Genetics Association. LC 00-27916. 385p. 2000. 89.95 (*1-56022-070-8*, Food Products) Haworth Pr.

— Frontiers of Forest Biology: Proceedings of the 1998 Joint Meeting of the North American Forest Biology Workshop & the Western Forest Genetics Association. LC 00-27916. (Illus.). 385p. 2000. pap. text 49.95 (*1-56022-079-1*, Food Products) Haworth Pr.

***Mitchell, Alastair.** A Chronicle of First Musical Performances Broadcast in the United Kingdom, 1923-1996. LC 99-43192. 2000. 78.95 (*1-85928-239-3*, Pub. by Ashgate Pub) Ashgate Pub Co.

Mitchell, Alexander, jt. auth. see Malhi, Gin S.

Mitchell, Alice, et al. A Systematic Introduction to Improvisation on the Pianoforte. Anderson, Gordon T., ed. LC 82-17225. (Longman Music Ser.). 128p. (C). 1983. text 20.00 (*0-582-28329-9*) Macmillan.

Mitchell, Alice M. Children & Movies. LC 70-160240. (Moving Pictures Ser.). xxiv, 181p. 1971. reprint ed. lib. bdg. 24.95 (*0-89198-041-5*) Ozer.

Mitchell, Alice R. Interdisciplinary Instruction in Reading Comprehension & Written Communication: A Guide for an Innovative Curriculum. LC 92-41365. 110p. 1993. pap. 20.95 (*0-398-06293-5*) C C Thomas.

— Interdisciplinary Instruction in Reading Comprehension & Written Communication: A Guide for an Innovative Curriculum. LC 92-41365. 110p. (C). 1993. text 31.95 (*0-398-05846-6*) C C Thomas.

Mitchell, Alison. Talismans: Articles of Faith & Enchantment. 144p. 1996. write for info. (*0-8212-2262-7*) Little.

Mitchell, Alison E. The New Jersey Highlands: Treasures at Risk. (Illus.). (Orig.). 1992. pap. 9.95 (*0-913234-10-9*) NJ Cons Foun.

Mitchell, Allan. The Divided Path: The German Influence on Social Reform in France after 1870. LC 90-23845. xx, 410p. (C). 1991. 59.95 (*0-8078-1964-6*) U of NC Pr.

— The German Influence in France after 1870: The Formation of the French Republic. LC 78-31677. 299p. 1979. reprint ed. pap. 92.70 (*0-7837-9025-2*, 204977600003) Bks Demand.

***Mitchell, Allan.** The Great Train Race: Railways & the Franco-German Rivalry, 1815-1914. LC 00-34266. (Illus.). 2000. write for info. (*1-57181-166-4*) Berghahn Bks.

Mitchell, Allan. The Nazi Revolution: Hitler's Dictatorship & the German Nation. 4th ed. 208p. (C). 1997. pap. text 22.36 (*0-669-41694-0*) HM Trade Div.

Mitchell, Allan, ed. The Nazi Revolution: Hitler's Dictatorship & the German Nation. 3rd ed. LC 89-80515. (Problems in European Civilization Ser.). 188p. (C). 1990. pap. text 22.36 (*0-669-20880-9*) HM Trade Div.

Mitchell, Allan & Deak, Istvan. Everyman in Europe, Vol. I. 3rd ed. 240p. (C). 1989. pap. text 23.80 (*0-13-293515-5*) P-H.

Mitchell, Allan, jt ed. see Kocka, Jurgen.

Mitchell, Allan C. & Zemansky, Mark W. Resonance Radiation & Excited Atoms. LC 62-5588. 352p. reprint ed. pap. 100.40 (*0-608-15757-0*, 2031696) Bks Demand.

Mitchell, Allen. Wadmalaw Island: Leaving Traditional Roots Behind. 120p. (Orig.). 1996. pap. 12.95 (*1-57502-120-X*) Morris Pubng.

Mitchell, Allen, jt. auth. see Mitchell, Linda.

Mitchell, Alva, et al. Technical Drawing. 10th ed. 1999. text 40.00 (*0-13-658536-1*, Macmillan Coll) P-H.

Mitchell, Alva, jt. auth. see Giesecke, Frederick E.

Mitchell, Alvan. Little Tom & Fats. Arrington, Veneta B., ed. LC 83-81560. (Illus.). 272p. 1987. reprint ed. 14.95 (*0-9615098-2-1*) Prairie Imp.

***Mitchell, Anastasia.** Josh B'Gosh at School. 10p. (J). 1998. 6.99 (*1-929174-08-X*) Oshkosh BGosh.

Mitchell, Andrew. The Fragile South Pacific: An Ecological Odyssey. (Corrie Herring Hooks Ser.: No. 16). (Illus.). 272p. 1991. 24.95 (*0-292-72466-7*) U of Tex Pr.

— The Young Naturalist. (Usborne Kid Kits Ser.). (Illus.). (YA). (gr. 5-9). 1998. 18.95 (*1-58086-020-6*, Usborne) EDC.

Mitchell, Andrew, et al. Arid Shrubland Plants of Western Australia. 1993. 55.00 (*1-875560-47-5*, Pub. by Univ of West Aust Pr) Intl Spec Bk.

— Arid Shrubland Plants of Western Australia. LC 95-178384. 1998. pap. 45.00 (*1-875560-22-X*, Pub. by Univ of West Aust Pr) Intl Spec Bk.

Mitchell, Andrew, jt. ed. see Achrol, Ravi.

Mitchell, Andrew A., ed. Advertising Exposure, Memory & Choice. (Advertising & Consumer Psychology Ser.). 352p. 1993. text 79.95 (*0-8058-0685-7*) L Erlbaum Assocs.

— The Effect of Information on Consumer & Market Behavior. LC 77-15505. (American Marketing Association, Proceedings Ser.). 122p. reprint ed. pap. 37.90 (*0-608-11942-3*, 202336300032) Bks Demand.

Mitchell, Andrew A., jt. ed. see Alwitt, Linda F.

Mitchell, Andrew R., et al. Mitchell, Taylor & Talbot on Confiscation & the Proceeds of Crime. 2nd ed. LC 98-230453. (Criminal Law Library). lxi, 778 p. 1997. write for info. (*0-421-56750-3*) Sweet & Maxwell.

Mitchell, Andy. The ESRI Guide to GIS Analysis: Geographic Patterns & Relationships. 186p. 1999. pap. 29.95 (*1-879102-06-4*) ESR Inst.

— Zeroing In: Geographic Information Systems at Work in the Community. 114p. 1998. pap. text 19.95 (*1-879102-50-1*) ESR Inst.

Mitchell, Angela, et al. What the Blues Is All About: Black Women Overcoming Stress & Depression. LC 97-24482. 256p. 1998. pap. 12.95 (*0-399-52376-6*, Perigee Bks) Berkley Pub.

Mitchell, Angela, jt. auth. see Jones, Paul.

Mitchell, Angelina M. Angelina's Favorite Recipes: A Personal Collection of Sicilian Style Italian Recipes. LC 87-91260. (Illus.). 102p. (Orig.). 1988. pap. 8.95 (*0-9619750-0-8*) A Mitchell.

Mitchell, Angelyn, ed. Within the Circle: An Anthology of African American Literary Criticism from the Harlem Renaissance to the Present. LC 94-12711. 544p. 1994. text 54.95 (*0-8223-1536-X*); pap. text 19.95 (*0-8223-1544-0*) Duke.

***Mitchell, Angus.** Spain: Interiors, Gardens, Architecture, Landscape. (Illus.). 1999. pap. text. write for info. (*0-7538-0150-7*) Phoenix Hse.

Mitchell, Anita M., et al, eds. Social Learning & Career Decision Making. LC 78-8930. 1979. 18.50 (*0-910328-21-8*); pap. 14.00 (*0-910328-22-6*) Sulzburger & Graham Pub.

Mitchell, Ann. Children in the Middle: Living Through Divorce. 224p. (Orig.). (C). 1985. pap. text 13.95 (*0-422-79270-5*, 9378, Pub. by Tavistock) Routldge.

— Children in the Middle: Living Through Divorce. 224p. (Orig.). 1985. 32.00 (*0-422-79260-8*, 9377, Pub. by Tavistock) Routldge.

— No More Corncraiks: Lord Moray's Feuars in Edinburgh's New Town. 160p. 1994. pap. 30.00 (*1-84017-017-4*) St Mut.

— The People of Calton Hill. 144p. 1996. pap. 40.00 (*1-873644-18-3*, Pub. by Mercat Pr Bks) St Mut.

— Where the Heart Is. LC 96-931634. (Illus.). 80p. 1997. 24.00 (*1-55046-193-1*, Pub. by Boston Mills) Genl Dist Srvs.

Mitchell, Ann & David, Judy, eds. Explorations with Young Children: A Curriculum Guide from the Bank Street College of Education. 1992. pap. 19.95 (*0-87659-160-8*) Gryphon Hse.

Mitchell, Ann K. Someone to Turn To: Experiences of Help Before Divorce. 136p. 1981. text 22.00 (*0-08-025741-0*, Pergamon Pr) Elsevier.

***Mitchell, Ann L. & House, Syd.** David Douglas: Explorer & Botanist. (Illus.). 1999. text 29.95 (*1-85410-591-4*) London Brdge.

Mitchell, Anne. In the Name of God/Good: A New/Old Philosophy for the 21st Century. 150p. 1993. pap. 7.95 (*0-9636910-0-7*) Liberty Bks.

Mitchell, Anne & King, Eric. Problem Solving with Spreadsheets & Databases. (C). 1993. student ed. 25.00 (*1-881592-44-8*) Hayden-McNeil.

Mitchell, Anne, et al. Child Care Choices, Consumer Education, & Low-Income Families. 64p. (Orig.). 1992. pap. text 5.50 (*0-926582-07-0*) NCCP.

— Early Childhood Programs & the Public Schools: Between Promise & Practice. LC 89-31076. 332p. 1989. 52.95 (*0-86569-193-2*, T193, Auburn Hse); pap. 20.95 (*0-86569-192-4*, R192, Auburn Hse) Greenwood.

— Youth, AIDS, & Sexually Transmitted Diseases. LC 96-11013. (Adolescence & Society Ser.). 192p. (C). 1996. 80.00 (*0-415-10632-X*); pap. 24.99 (*0-415-10633-8*) Routledge.

Mitchell, Annie R. Jim Savage & the Tulareno Indians. (Great West & Indian Ser.: Vol. 8). (Illus.). 1990. 19.95 (*0-87026-075-8*) Westernlore.

Mitchell, Arlene H. & Henderson, Darwin L. This I Know: Poetry Across Black Cultures. LC 96-40409. (J). 1998. write for info. (*0-590-45119-7*); pap. write for info. (*0-590-45120-0*) Scholastic Inc.

Mitchell, Arthur. Gold Metal Glory: The Story of America's 1996 Women's Gymnastics Team. LC 97-118433. (J). 1975. mass mkt. 1.50 (*0-671-00945-1*) PB.

— JFK & His Irish Heritage. (Illus.). 186p. (Orig.). 1993. pap. 17.95 (*1-871305-19-5*, Pub. by Moytura Pr) Irish Bks Media.

— Music for Fun & Profit. large type ed. (For Fun & Profit Ser.). (Illus.). 300p. Date not set. pap. 24.95 (*1-56559-905-5*) HGI-Over Fifty.

— The Past in the Present: What Is Civilisation? LC 77-86453. reprint ed. 28.00 (*0-404-16674-1*) AMS Pr.

Mitchell, Arthur, tr. see Bergson, Henri.

Mitchell, Austin V. The Case for Labour. LC 82-17162. 228p. reprint ed. pap. 65.00 (*0-608-14476-2*, 2025267) Bks Demand.

— The Case for Labour. LC 82-17162. 228p. 1983. reprint ed. pap. 70.70 (*0-608-12143-6*, 202526700043) Bks Demand.

Mitchell, B. J. & Dragoo, M. M. How to See the U. S. on Twelve Dollars a Day: (Per Person, Double Occupancy) LC 82-50779. (Illus.). 112p. (Orig.). 1982. pap. 4.95 (*0-943962-00-5*) Viewpoint Pr.

Mitchell, B. R. British Historical Statistics. 900p. 1988. text 170.00 (*0-521-33008-4*) Cambridge U Pr.

— European Statistics: Seventeen Fifty to Nineteen Seventy-Nine. 550p. 1979. pap. text 35.50 (*90-286-0229-1*) Kluwer Academic.

Mitchell, Barb, ed. see Dennis, Anne.

Mitchell, Barbara. America, I Hear You: A Story about George Gershwin. (Creative Minds Ser.). (Illus.). 64p. (J). (gr. 3-6). 1987. lib. bdg. 19.93 (*0-87614-309-5*, Carolrhoda) Lerner Pub.

— Between Two Worlds: A Story about Pearl Buck. (Creative Minds Biographies Ser.). (Illus.). 56p. (J). (gr. 3-6). 1988. lib. bdg. 19.93 (*0-87614-332-X*, Carolrhoda) Lerner Pub.

— Click! A Story about George Eastman. (Creative Minds Ser.). (Illus.). 64p. (J). (gr. 3-6). 1986. lib. bdg. 19.93 (*0-87614-289-7*, Carolrhoda) Lerner Pub.

— Click! A Story about George Eastman. (Creative Minds Bks.). (Illus.). 56p. (J). (gr. 3-6). 1987. reprint ed. pap. 5.95 (*0-87614-472-5*, Lerner Publctns) Lerner Pub.

— Good Morning Mr. President: A Story about Carl Sandburg. LC 88-7265. (Creative Minds Ser.). (Illus.). 56p. (J). (gr. 3-6). 1988. lib. bdg. 19.93 (*0-87614-329-X*, Carolrhoda) Lerner Pub.

— A Pocketful of Goobers: A Story about George Washington Carver. (Creative Minds Ser.). (Illus.). 64p. (J). (gr. 3-6). 1986. lib. bdg. 19.95 (*0-87614-292-7*, Carolrhoda) Lerner Pub.

— A Pocketful of Goobers: A Story about George Washington Carver. (Creative Minds Bks.). (Illus.). 56p. (J). (gr. 3-6). 1987. reprint ed. pap. 5.95 (*0-87614-474-1*, Lerner Publctns) Lerner Pub.

— The Practical Revolutionaries: A New Interpretation of the French Anarchosyndicalists, 5. LC 86-15028. (Contributions to the Study of World History Ser.: No. 5). 325p. 1987. 65.00 (*0-313-25289-0*, MLE/, Greenwood Pr) Greenwood.

— Raggin' A Story about Scott Joplin. (Creative Minds Ser.). (Illus.). 64p. (J). (gr. 3-6). 1987. lib. bdg. 14.95 (*0-87614-310-9*, Carolrhoda) Lerner Pub.

— Raggin' A Story about Scott Joplin. (Illus.). 56p. (J). (gr. 3-6). 1992. pap. 5.95 (*0-87614-589-6*, Carolrhoda) Lerner Pub.

— Red Bird. LC 95-9664. (Illus.). 32p. (J). (gr. k-4). 1996. 16.00 (*0-688-10859-8*) Lothrop.

— Shoes for Everyone: A Story about Jan Matzeliger. (Creative Minds Ser.). (Illus.). 64p. (J). (gr. 3-6). 1986. lib. bdg. 14.95 (*0-87614-290-0*, Carolrhoda) Lerner Pub.

— Shoes for Everyone: A Story about Jan Matzeliger. (Creative Minds Bks.). (Illus.). 56p. (J). (gr. 3-6). 1987. reprint ed. pap. 5.95 (*0-87614-473-3*, First Ave Edns) Lerner Pub.

— Waterman's Child. LC 94-40734. (Illus.). 32p. (J). (gr. k up). 1997. 16.00 (*0-688-10861-X*) Lothrop.

— We'll Race You, Henry: A Story about Henry Ford. (Creative Minds Ser.). (Illus.). 64p. (J). (gr. 3-6). 1986. lib. bdg. 14.95 (*0-87614-291-9*, Carolrhoda) Lerner Pub.

— We'll Race You, Henry: A Story about Henry Ford. (Creative Minds Bks.). (Illus.). 56p. (J). (gr. 3-6). 1987. reprint ed. pap. 5.95 (*0-87614-471-7*, First Ave Edns) Lerner Pub.

— The Wizard of Sound: A Story about Thomas Edison. (Illus.). 56p. (J). (gr. 3-6). 1991. pap. 5.95 (*0-87614-563-2*, Carolrhoda) Lerner Pub.

— The Wizard of Sound: A Story about Thomas Edison. (Creative Minds Ser.). (Illus.). 64p. (J). (gr. 3-6). 1991. lib. bdg. 14.95 (*0-87614-445-8*, Carolrhoda) Lerner Pub.

***Mitchell, Barbara & Mitchell, Ormond.** W. O. The Life of W. O. Mitchell: Beginnings to Who Has Seen the Wind, 1914-1947. (Illus.). 400p. 2000. 37.50 (*0-7710-6107-2*) McCland & Stewart.

Mitchell, Barbara, ed. see Gosselin, Kim.

Mitchell, Barbara A., jt. ed. see LaGuardia, Cheryl M.

Mitchell, Barbara B. Acupuncture & Oriental Medicine Laws: 1999 Edition. v, 181p. 1999. 27.00 (*0-9670262-0-2*) Natl Acup Fndt.

— Legislative Handbook for the Practice of Acupuncture & Oriental Medicine. 62p. 1995. 18.00 (*0-9670262-4-5*) Natl Acup Fndt.

Mitchell, Barry. The Law Relating to Violent Crime. 380p. 1997. 125.00 (*1-85811-121-8*, Pub. by CLT Prof) Gaunt.

— Separable Algebroids. LC 85-15092. (Memoirs of the American Mathematical Society Ser.: No. 333). 96p. 1985. pap. 18.00 (*0-8218-2334-5*, MEMO/57/333) Am Math.

Mitchell, Barry, jt. ed. see Ashworth, Andrew.

Mitchell, Basil. Faith & Criticism. 178p. 1995. text 32.00 (*0-19-826758-4*) OUP.

Mitchell, Basil, ed. Philosophy of Religion. (Oxford Readings in Philosophy Ser.). 206p. (Orig.). (C). 1971. pap. text 18.95 (*0-19-875018-8*) OUP.

***Mitchell, Bass M.** In Every Blade of Rustling Grass: Meditations on Looking & Listening for God. LC 99-58457. 112p. 2000. pap. 8.00 (*0-687-08429-6*) Dimen for Liv.

Mitchell, Ben. Brad Rude: Original Nature. (Illus.). 36p. 1998. pap. 20.00 (*1-891695-00-2*) Holter Museum.

Mitchell, Ben, ed. see Crocket, Dennis.

Mitchell, Ben, ed. see Ganse, Shirley.

Mitchell, Ben, ed. see Kohl, Stephen W.

Mitchell, Ben, ed. see Sampson, Gary.

Mitchell, Ben, ed. see Takemoto, Akira & Walters, Jonathan S.

Mitchell, Ben, ed. see Walters, Jonathan S.

***Mitchell, Benjamin G.** The Second Coming of Elijah the Prophet--Blueprint for Jew & Gentile Reconciliation. 2000. 14.95 (*0-533-13229-0*) Vantage.

Mitchell, Bettie P. A Need for Understanding: A Handbook of Basic Counseling Information. 190p. (Orig.). 1992. pap. 16.00 (*1-885193-03-3*) Good Samaritan.

— The Power of Conflict & Sacrifice: A Therapy Manual for Christian Marriage. 106p. (Orig.). 1988. pap. 5.00 (*1-885193-01-7*) Good Samaritan.

— Who Is My Neighbor? A Parable. (Illus.). 333p. 1990. pap. 16.00 (*1-885193-00-9*) Good Samaritan.

Mitchell, Bettie P. & Gaunt, Rachel O. The Faith of a Little Child. 1998. pap. 5.00 (*1-885193-06-8*) Good Samaritan.

Mitchell, Betty. Delyte Morris of SIU. (Illus.). 256p. 1988. 21.95 (*0-8093-1448-7*) S Ill U Pr.

— I'm Felicia: A Live Toy Poodle. (Illus.). 32p. (Orig.). (J). (gr. 4-6). 1996. pap. 6.95 (*1-886094-32-2*) Chicago Spectrum.

— Southern Illinois University: A Pictorial History. (Illinois Pictorial History Ser.). (Illus.). 1993. write for info. (*0-943963-32-X*) G Bradley.

Mitchell, Betty J., et al. Cost Analysis of Library Functions: A Total Systems Approach. Stueart, Robert D., ed. LC 77-2110. (Foundations in Library & Information Science: Vol. 6). 192p. 1978. 78.50 (*0-89232-072-9*) Jai Pr.

Mitchell, Betty J., ed. see Hernon, Peter & Purcell, Gary R.

Mitchell, Betty L. Edmund Ruffin, a Biography. LC 80-8381. 318p. reprint ed. pap. 98.60 (*0-608-18468-3*, 205671100081) Bks Demand.

Mitchell, Bill, jt. auth. see Canan, Michael J.

***Mitchell, Bob.** Documentation in Counseling Records. 2nd ed. LC 00-40158. (Legal Ser.). 2000. write for info. (*1-55620-179-6*) Am Coun Assn.

Mitchell, Bob. The Heart Has Its Reasons: Reflections on Sports & Life. LC 94-8844. 65p. 1994. 18.95 (*0-912083-71-9*) Diamond Communications.

— How My Mother Accidentally Tossed Out My Entire Baseball-Card Collection: And Other Sports Stories. LC 98-51189. 150p. 1999. pap. 12.95 (*1-883319-88-9*) Frog Ltd CA.

— The Tao of Sports. LC 96-49859. 100p. 1997. pap. 11.95 (*1-883319-56-0*) Frog Ltd CA.

M

An Asterisk (*) at the beginning of an entry indicates that the title is appearing for the first time.

M

Mitchell, Bonner, ed. 1598: A Year of Pageantry in Late Renaissance Ferrara. (Renaissance Triumphs & Magnificences, Medieval & Renaissance Texts & Studies: Vol. 71). (Illus.). 172p. 1990. 24.00 (*0-86698-080-6*, MR71) MRTS.

Mitchell, Brad & Cunningham, Luvern L., eds. Educational Leadership & Changing Contexts of Families, Communities & Schools. (National Society for the Study of Education Publication Ser.: No. 89, Pt. II). 330p. 1992. 25.95 (*0-226-60153-6*) U Ch Pr.

— Educational Leadership & Changing Contexts of Families, Communities, & Schools. LC 89-63574. (National Society for the Study of Education Publication Ser.). (Illus.). x, 288p. 1991. pap. text 13.95 (*0-226-60156-0*) U Ch Pr.

Mitchell, Breon, ed. see Lenz, Siegfried.

Mitchell, Breon, ed. & tr. see Lenz, Siegfried.

Mitchell, Breon, tr. see Boll, Heinrich.

Mitchell, Breon, tr. see Federspiel, J. F.

Mitchell, Breon, tr. see Grzimek, Martin.

Mitchell, Breon, tr. see Kafka, Franz.

Mitchell, Breon, tr. see Kremer, Rudiger.

Mitchell, Breon, tr. see Nadolny, Sten.

Mitchell, Breon, tr. see Rothmann, Ralf.

Mitchell, Breon, tr. & pref. see Kafka, Franz.

Mitchell, Brett. The Sun Is Alive: The Spirit, Consciousness & Intelligence of Our Solar System. unabridged ed. LC 98-201706. (Illus.). 106p. 1997. per. 16.95 (*1-889280-20-8*) Esoteric Publng.

Mitchell, Brian. A Guide to Irish Parish Records. 151p. 1995. reprint ed. 25.00 (*0-8063-1215-7*, 3852) Genealog Pub.

— International Historical Statistics: Asia & Africa. 800p. (C). 1982. text 275.00 (*0-8147-5385-X*) NYU Pr.

— Irish Emigration Lists, 1833-1839: Lists of Emigrants Extracted from the Ordnance Survey Memoirs for Counties Londonderry & Antrim. 128p. 1989. 20.00 (*0-8063-1233-5*, 3854) Genealog Pub.

***Mitchell, Brian.** Irish Genealogy: A Reference Aid. LC 99-72358. 70p. 1999. per. 15.00 (*1-55856-291-5*, 138) Closson Pr.

Mitchell, Brian. Irish Passenger Lists, 1803-1806: Lists of Passengers Sailing from Ireland to America. LC 94-79986. 154p. 1995. 25.00 (*0-8063-1458-3*) Genealog Pub.

— A New Genealogical Atlas of Ireland. 123p. 1998. reprint ed. pap. 18.95 (*0-8063-1152-5*, 3853) Genealog Pub.

— Parish Maps of Ireland: (Depicting All Townlands in the Four Ulster Counties of Armagh, Donegal, Londonderry & Tyrone) 288p. 1988. pap. text 29.95 (*0-933227-33-7*, 514) Closson Pr.

— Pocket Guide to Irish Genealogy. (Illus.). 63p. 1999. pap. 10.95 (*0-8063-1300-5*, 9240) Clearfield Co.

— Running to Keep Fit. 96p. 1980. pap. 2.95 (*0-679-12428-4*) McKay.

— Women in the Military: Flirting with Disaster. LC 97-43081. 304p. 1998. 24.95 (*0-89526-376-9*) Regnery Pub.

Mitchell, Brian, ed. Three Plays: Dead Man's Hat, Paradise Drive, in the Bleak Midwinter. 208p. 1996. pap. 15.95 (*1-85411-114-0*, Pub. by Seren Bks) Dufour.

— Three Plays: House of America, Flowers of the Dead Red Sea, East from the Gantay. 216p. 1995. pap. 15.95 (*1-85411-113-2*, Pub. by Seren Bks) Dufour.

Mitchell, Brian J. & Romanowicz, Barbara A., eds. Q of the Earth: Global, Regional & Laboratory Studies. LC 99-17774. (Pageoph Topical Volumes Ser.). 500p. 1999. (*3-7643-6049-6*) Birkhauser.

Mitchell, Brian R., ed. International Historical Statistics, 1750-1993, 3 vols. 3150p. (C). 1998. 850.00 (*1-56159-233-1*) Groves Dictionaries.

— International Historical Statistics, 1750-1993 Vol. 1: Africa, Asia & Oceania. 1050p. (C). 1998. 350.00 (*1-56159-234-X*) Groves Dictionaries.

— International Historical Statistics, 1750-1993 Vol. 2: The Americas. 1050p. 1998. 350.00 (*1-56159-235-8*) Groves Dictionaries.

— International Historical Statistics, 1750-1993 Vol. 3: Europe. 1050p. 1998. 350.00 (*1-56159-236-6*) Groves Dictionaries.

Mitchell, Brian S. Pocket Guide to Irish Genealogy. 103p. 1988. pap. text 7.95 (*1-55856-000-9*, 137) Closson Pr.

Mitchell, Briar, ed. Illustration West Annual. 35th ed. (Illus.). 234p. (Orig.). 1998. pap. 40.00 (*1-890466-01-8*) Soc of Illust LA.

Mitchell, Briar, ed. see English, John & Weinman, Brad.

Mitchell, Bridget M., jt. auth. see Vogelsang, Ingo.

Mitchell, Broadus. The Depression Decade: From New Era Through New Deal 1929-1941. LC 89-10693. (Economic History of the United States Ser.). 480p. (gr. 13). 1977. pap. text 34.95 (*0-87332-097-2*) M E Sharpe.

Mitchell, Broadus. Frederick Law Olmsted: A Critic of the Old South. (BCL1 - United States Local History Ser.). 158p. 1991. reprint ed. lib. bdg. 69.00 (*0-7812-6288-7*) Rprt Serv.

— Frederick Law Olmsted, a Critic of the Old South. LC 78-64114. (Johns Hopkins University. Studies in the Social Sciences. Thirtieth Ser. 1912: No. 422). reprint ed. 37.50 (*0-404-61229-6*) AMS Pr.

— The Rise of Cotton Mills in the South. LC 78-63974. (Johns Hopkins University. Studies in the Social Sciences. Thirtieth Ser. 1912: 2). reprint ed. 37.50 (*0-404-61219-9*) AMS Pr.

Mitchell, Broadus, intro. The Rise of Cotton Mills in the South. 2nd ed. LC 68-8128. (American Scene Ser.). 1968. reprint ed. lib. bdg. 37.50 (*0-306-71141-9*) Da Capo.

Mitchell, Broadus & Mitchell, George S. Industrial Revolution in the South. LC 75-100818. reprint ed. 29.50 (*0-404-00201-3*) AMS Pr.

Mitchell, Brooks. Bet on Cowboys, Not Horses: A Technological Breakthrough for Employee Selection. Ross, T. J. & Ross, Mary, eds. LC 93-60890. (Illus.). 181p. 1994. 19.95 (*0-9634940-2-3*) York Pub.

Mitchell, Bruce. Geography & Resource Analysis. 2nd ed. 1989. pap. 55.95 (*0-582-46364-5*, Pub. by Addison-Wesley) Longman.

— An Invitation to Old English & Anglo-Saxon England. (Illus.). 352p. 1994. pap. 31.95 (*0-631-17436-2*) Blackwell Pubs.

— A Man's Kitchen: North Georgia's Favorite Recipes. (Illus.). 392p. (Orig.). 1987. pap. 9.95 (*0-9619975-0-8*) Cooking Angles.

— Old English Syntax: Concord, the Parts of Speech & the Sentence, 2 vols., Vol. 1. 884p. 1985. text 165.00 (*0-19-811935-6*) OUP.

— Old English Syntax: Subordination, Indedpendent Element & Element Order, 2 vols., II. 1,124p. 1985. text 200.00 (*0-19-811944-5*) OUP.

Mitchell, Bruce, ed. Integrated Water Management. 224p. 1992. 41.95 (*1-85293-026-8*, Pub. by P P Pubs) CRC Pr.

— Resource & Environmental Management in Canada: Addressing Conflict & Uncertainty. 2nd ed. (Illus.). 456p. (C). 1995. pap. text 35.00 (*0-19-541059-9*) OUP.

Mitchell, Bruce & Robinson, Fred C. Beowulf. LC 97-47428. (Illus.). 320p. 1998. 69.95 (*0-631-17225-4*); pap. 34.95 (*0-631-17226-2*) Blackwell Pubs.

— A Guide to Old English. LC 83-101023. 283p. reprint ed. pap. 87.80 (*0-8357-3661-X*, 203638800003) Bks Demand.

— A Guide to Old English. rev. ed. 416p. 1991. pap. 31.95 (*0-631-16657-2*) Blackwell Pubs.

***Mitchell, Bruce & University of Waterloo. Dept. of Geography.** Sustainability: A Search for Balance. LC 99-159638. (Illus.). 1998. write for info. (*0-921083-92-0*) U4 of Waterloo Dept of Geo.

Mitchell, Bruce, jt. auth. see Dearden, Philip.

Mitchell, Bruce M. Dynamic Classroom. 5th ed. 268p. (C). 1995. pap. text, per. 35.95 (*0-7872-0587-7*, 41058701) Kendall-Hunt.

Mitchell, Bruce M. & Salsbury, Robert E. Multicultural Education: An International Guide to Research, Policies & Programs. LC 95-37337. 400p. 1996. lib. bdg. 85.00 (*0-313-28985-9*, Greenwood Pr) Greenwood.

— Multicultural Education In the U.S. A Guide to Policies & Programs In the 50 States. LC 99-31579. 296p. 2000. lib. bdg. 75.00 (*0-313-30859-4*) Greenwood.

Mitchell, Bruce M. & Salsbury, Robert E., eds. Encyclopedia of Multicultural Education. LC 98-44222. 320p. 1999. lib. bdg. 65.00 (*0-313-30029-1*) Greenwood.

Mitchell, Bruce M., jt. auth. see Williams, William G.

Mitchell-Burnett, Carolyn. The Sites & Sounds of Texas. LC 97-41687. (J). 2000. 15.95 (*1-57168-198-1*, Eakin Pr) Sunbelt Media.

Mitchell, C. Here Little Child. (J). Date not set. pap. 5.95 (*0-399-21717-7*) Putnam Pub Group.

— Reinventing Ourselves As Teachers. LC 99-167506. 1998. text 72.00 (*0-7507-0625-2*, Falmer Pr) Taylor & Francis.

— Reinventing Ourselvles As Teachers. LC 99-167506. 264p. 1998. pap. text 24.95 (*0-7507-0626-0*, Falmer Pr) Taylor & Francis.

Mitchell, C., ed. Applications of Combinatorial Mathematics. LC 96-52178. (The Institute of Mathematics & Its Applications Conference Series, New Series No., 60). (Illus.). 252p. 1997. text 140.00 (*0-19-851192-2*) OUP.

Mitchell, C. A., jt. ed. see Duggan, T. V.

Mitchell, C. B. Mitchell: The Mitchell Record. (Illus.). 183p. 1992. reprint ed. pap. 27.00 (*0-8328-2288-4*); reprint ed. lib. bdg. 37.00 (*0-8328-2287-6*) Higginson Bk Co.

Mitchell, C. Bradford. Paddlewheel Inboard. LC 83-50816. (Illus.). 66p. 1984. pap. 12.00 (*0-913423-06-8*) Steamship Hist Soc.

Mitchell, C. Bradford, ed. Merchant Steam Vessels of the United States, 1790-1868: The "Lytle-Holdcamper List" LC 75-18930. 322p. 1975. 26.00 (*0-913423-02-5*) Steamship Hist Soc.

Mitchell, C. G. I Quit - I Promise. (Illus.). 176p. (Orig.). 1996. pap. 12.00 (*0-9651203-0-9*) Glenn Payne.

Mitchell, C. G., jt. ed. see Cebon, D.

Mitchell, C. M. The Shakespeare Circle. LC 76-30693. (Studies in Shakespeare: No. 24). 1977. lib. bdg. 55.00 (*0-8383-2166-6*) M S G Haskell Hse.

***Mitchell, C. R.** Gestures of Conciliation: Factors Contributing to Successful Olive Branches. LC 99-49412. (Illus.). 2000. text 65.00 (*0-312-23052-4*) St Martin.

Mitchell, C. R. The Structure of International Conflict. LC 79-25423. 368p. 1989. pap. 18.95 (*0-312-02414-2*) St Martin.

Mitchell, C. R. & Webb, K., eds. New Approaches in International Mediation, 223. LC 88-10252. (Contributions in Political Science Ser.: No. 223). 268p. 1988. 65.00 (*0-313-25974-7*, MNA/, Greenwood Pr) Greenwood.

Mitchell, C. Thomas. New Thinking in Design: Conversations on Theory & Practice. (Illus.). 192p. 1996. pap. 62.95 (*0-442-01733-2*, VNR) Wiley.

Mitchell, C. Thomas. New Thinking in Design: Conversations on Theory & Practices. (Architecture Ser.). 208p. 1996. 69.95 (*0-471-28604-4*, VNR) Wiley.

Mitchell, C. Thomas. Redefining Designing: From Form to Experience. 162p. 1992. 49.95 (*0-471-29081-5*, VNR) Wiley.

Mitchell, C. Thomas & Wu, Jiangmei. Living Design: The Daoist Way of Building. LC 97-39997. (Illus.). 256p. 1998. 49.95 (*0-07-042975-8*) McGraw.

Mitchell, Calen P., jt. auth. see Mitchell, Fred L., Jr.

Mitchell, Cameron & Baumann, James. The Art of the Meal: 1,001 Details. LC 98-41651. (Illus.). 136p. 1998. 24.95 (*1-882203-52-6*) Orange Frazer.

Mitchell, Candace & Weiler, Kathleen, eds. Rewriting Literacy: Culture & the Discourse of the Other. LC 91-15503. (Critical Studies in Education & Culture). 312p. 1991. 65.00 (*0-89789-225-9*, H225, Quorum Bks); pap. 21.95 (*0-89789-228-3*, G228, Quorum Bks) Greenwood.

Mitchell, Candace, jt. ed. see Weiler, Kathleen.

Mitchell, Carl D., et al, eds. Proceedings & Papers of the Thirteenth Swan Society Conference. 183p. 1992. pap. 15.00 (*0-9619936-8-5*) Trumpeter Swan Soc.

Mitchell, Carlton T., et al, eds. Images of Man Vol. I: Luce Program on Religion & the Social Crisis. LC 84-14687. ix, 142p. 1984. text 13.95 (*0-86554-124-8*, MUP-H115) Mercer Univ Pr.

Mitchell, Carlton T., ed. see Moltmann, Jurgen, et al.

Mitchell, Carol A. Machine Transcription: A Comprehensive Approach for Today's Office Professional - Short Course. 3rd ed. 1995. teacher ed. 12.90 (*0-02-802226-2*) Glencoe.

Mitchell, Carol A. Machine Transcription: A Comprehensive Approach for Today's Office Specialist. 176p. (C). 1983. teacher ed. write for info. (*0-672-97987-X*); pap. text. write for info. (*0-672-97986-1*); write for info. (*0-672-97988-8*); audio. write for info. (*0-672-97989-6*) Macmillan.

— Machine Transcription: A Comprehensive Approach for Today's Office Specialist. 3rd ed. LC 94-36538. 1995. write for info. (*0-02-802221-1*) Glencoe.

— Machine Transcription: A Comprehensive Approach for Today's Office Specialist, Short Course, Student Text. 3rd ed. LC 94-24755. 1995. write for info. (*0-02-802220-3*) Glencoe.

Mitchell, Carol E. Paths of Blessings. 48p. 1991. pap. write for info. (*0-9631852-0-9*) Sparrow Hse.

Mitchell, Carolyn & Alden, Richard. College English Fundamentals. rev. ed. 264p. (C). 1990. pap. text 26.91 (*1-56226-006-5*) CAT Pub.

Mitchell, Carolyn B. Songs of America. (Let's Sing & Learn Ser.). 24p. (J). 1997. pap. 7.95 incl. audio (*0-8092-2986-2*, 298620, Contemporary Bks) NTC Contemp Pub Co.

Mitchell, Carolyn B., ed. Gender Equity Through Physical Education & Sport. 36p. 1995. pap. text 19.00 (*0-88314-804-8*, 303-10035) AAHPERD.

Mitchell, Carolyn B., jt. auth. see American Film Institute Staff.

Mitchell, Carolyn B., jt. auth. see Audubon Staff.

Mitchell, Carolyn B., jt. auth. see Barnes Foundation Staff.

Mitchell, Carolyn B., jt. auth. see Baron's Educational Series Staff.

Mitchell, Carolyn B., jt. auth. see Better Homes & Gardens.

Mitchell, Carolyn B., jt. auth. see BipQuiz Staff.

Mitchell, Carolyn B., jt. auth. see Bon Appetit Staff.

Mitchell, Carolyn B., jt. auth. see British Broadcasting Corporation Staff.

Mitchell, Carolyn B., jt. auth. see Citykids Staff.

Mitchell, Carolyn B., jt. auth. see Complete Language Courses Staff.

Mitchell, Carolyn B., jt. auth. see Crocker, Betty.

Mitchell, Carolyn B., jt. auth. see Dearborn Financial Publishing Staff.

Mitchell, Carolyn B., jt. auth. see Dearborn Trade Staff.

Mitchell, Carolyn B., jt. auth. see Discovery Communications Staff.

Mitchell, Carolyn B., jt. auth. see Educational Development Corporation Staff.

Mitchell, Carolyn B., jt. auth. see Everymans Library Staff.

Mitchell, Carolyn B., jt. auth. see Fast N Easy Staff.

Mitchell, Carolyn B., jt. auth. see Football Association Staff.

Mitchell, Carolyn B., jt. auth. see Foundation for Inner Peace Staff.

Mitchell, Carolyn B., jt. auth. see Good Housekeeping Editors.

Mitchell, Carolyn B., jt. auth. see Guideposts Staff.

Mitchell, Carolyn B., jt. auth. see Health Care Resources Staff.

Mitchell, Carolyn B., jt. auth. see Junior African Writers Staff.

Mitchell, Carolyn B., jt. auth. see Law School Admissions Council Staff.

Mitchell, Carolyn B., jt. auth. see Lexus Limited Staff.

Mitchell, Carolyn B., jt. auth. see Martha Stewart Living.

Mitchell, Carolyn B., jt. auth. see Metropolitan Museum of Art Staff.

Mitchell, Carolyn B., jt. auth. see Moosewood Collective Staff.

Mitchell, Carolyn B., jt. auth. see Music Sales Corporation Staff.

Mitchell, Carolyn B., jt. auth. see New Yorker Staff.

Mitchell, Carolyn B., jt. auth. see O'Reilly & Associates Staff.

Mitchell, Carolyn B., jt. auth. see Prevention Magazine Staff.

Mitchell, Carolyn B., jt. auth. see Project Inform Staff.

Mitchell, Carolyn B., jt. auth. see Que Et Staff.

Mitchell, Carolyn B., jt. auth. see R. & R. Newkirk Staff.

Mitchell, Carolyn B., jt. auth. see Scientific American Staff.

Mitchell, Carolyn B., jt. auth. see Snapshot Staff.

Mitchell, Carolyn B., jt. auth. see United States Holocaust Memorial Staff.

Mitchell, Carolyn B., jt. auth. see Women & Geography Study Staff.

Mitchell, Carolyn B., jt. auth. see World Press Photo Foundation Staff.

***Mitchell, Carolyn Lee.** All Our Loving: A Beatle Fan's Memoir. 148p. 1999. pap. 10.95 (*1-86105-251-0*) Robson.

Mitchell, Carveth. Sign in the Subway. 1988. pap. 5.95 (*1-55673-056-X*, 8853) CSS OH.

Mitchell, Catherine C., ed. Margaret Fuller's New York Journalism: A Biographical Essay & Key Writings. LC 94-18710. (Illus.). 240p. (C). 1995. text 32.50 (*0-87049-870-3*) U of Tenn Pr.

Mitchell, Charity. Speech Index: An Index to Collections of World Famous Orations & Speeches for Various Occasions-Supplement, 1966-1980. 4th ed. LC 81-23282. 484p. 1982. 70.00 (*0-8108-1518-4*) Scarecrow.

Mitchell, Charlene. Fight to Free Angela Davis: Its Importance for the Working Class. 12p. 1972. pap. 0.25 (*0-87898-085-7*) New Outlook.

Mitchell, Charles. Hammondsport & Keuka Lake. (Images of America Ser.). (Illus.). 128p. 1998. pap. 16.99 (*0-7524-1226-4*) Arcadia Publng.

— The Law of Subrogation. 212p. 1995. text 95.00 (*0-19-825938-7*) OUP.

— Passport South Africa: Your Pocket Guide to South African Business, Customs & Etiquette. Szerlip, Barbara, ed. LC 97-25259. 96p. 1996. pap. 6.95 (*1-885073-19-4*) Thomson Learn.

— Penn Yan & Keuka Lake. (Images of America Ser.). 1999. pap. 16.99 (*0-7524-0558-6*) Arcadia Publng.

— A Short Course in International Business Culture. LC 99-32547. (Short Course in International Trade Ser.). (Illus.). 192p. (Orig.). 1999. pap. 19.95 (*1-885073-54-2*) Wrld Trade Pr.

***Mitchell, Charles.** Short Course in International Marketing Blunders: Learn from Mistakes of Others. 2000. pap. 19.95 (*1-885073-60-7*) Wrld Trade Pr.

Mitchell, Charles, jt. ed. see Bodnar, Edward W.

***Mitchell, Charles Dee.** Joseph Marioni Painter. Siebcke, Irene, tr. 1999. 15.00 (*0-918881-38-2*) Columbus Mus Art.

Mitchell, Charles E. Individualism & Its Discontents: Appropriations of Emerson, 1880-1950. LC 96-39859. 256p. 1997. text 35.00 (*1-55849-073-6*) U of Mass Pr.

Mitchell, Charles P. A Guide to Charlie Chan Films, 23. LC 99-12472. (Bibliographies & Indexes in the Performing Arts Ser.: Vol. 23). 312p. 1999. lib. bdg. 65.00 (*0-313-30985-X*) Greenwood.

Mitchell, Charles P., jt. auth. see Parla, Paul.

Mitchell, Charles W. & Krueger, William E. Birds of Clinton County. 2nd rev. ed. Thaxton, John G., ed. (Illus.). 139p. 1997. pap. 11.95 (*0-9668819-0-7*) High Peaks.

Mitchell, Charlie R. Math Anxiety: What It Is & What to Do about It. rev. ed. 1987. pap. 8.95 (*0-9610794-3-6*) Action Pr.

Mitchell, Charlie R. & Collins, Lauren F. Job Hunting: A Self-Directed Guide. 1982. pap. 8.95 (*0-9610794-0-1*) Action Pr.

Mitchell, Chase D., jt. auth. see Halderman, James D.

Mitchell, Cheryl C. & Mitchell, F. H., Jr. Developing & Managing an Effective Elder Law Practice. 220p. 1991. pap. text 50.00 (*1-879909-01-4*) Mitchell WA.

— Paying for Long Term In-Home & Nursing Home Care, 1991: Washington State. 120p. 1991. pap. text 25.00 (*1-879909-00-6*) Mitchell WA.

Mitchell, Chris & Banks, Michael. Handbook of Conflict Resolution: The Analytical Problem-Solving Approach. 200p. (C). 1996. text 25.95 (*1-85567-277-4*) Bks Intl VA.

Mitchell, Chris, jt. auth. see Maple, Jack.

Mitchell, Christopher. Changing Perspectives in Latin American Studies: Insights from Six Disciplines. LC 88-12187. 256p. reprint ed. pap. 30.00 (*0-608-08906-0*, 206954100004) Bks Demand.

Mitchell, Christopher, ed. Western Hemisphere Immigration & United States Foreign Policy. 384p. 1992. pap. 18.95 (*0-271-00791-5*); text 50.00 (*0-271-00789-3*) Pa St U Pr.

Mitchell, Christopher, jt. ed. see Druckman, Daniel.

Mitchell, Christopher J. & Stavridou, Victoria, eds. Mathematics of Dependable Systems. (Institute of Mathematics & Its Applications Conference Ser.: No. 55). (Illus.). 312p. 1995. text 95.00 (*0-19-853491-4*) OUP.

***Mitchell, Cindi.** Amazing Math Puzzles & Mazes. (Ready-to-Go Reproducibles Ser.). (Illus.). 48p. (J). (gr. 4-5). 2000. pap. 10.99 (*0-439-04236-4*) Scholastic Inc.

— Amazing Math Puzzles & Mazes. (Ready-to-Go Reproducibles Ser.). (Illus.). 48p. (J). 2000. pap. 7.95 (*0-439-04235-6*) Scholastic Inc.

Mitchell, Cindi. Dazzling Math Line Designs: Dozens of Reproducible Activities That Help Build Addition, Subtraction. (Illus.). 64p. 1998. pap. text 9.95 (*0-590-00086-1*) Scholastic Inc.

— Math Skills Made Fun: Dazzling Math Line Designs, 1 vol. (Illus.). 64p. 1999. pap. text 9.95 (*0-590-00088-8*) Scholastic Inc.

***Mitchell, Cindi.** Math Skills Made Fun Dazzling Math Line Designs; Dozens of Reproducible Activities That Build Skills & Working Fractions, Decimals, Percents, Integers & Prime Numbers. 1999. pap. 9.95 (*0-590-00085-3*) Scholastic Inc.

— Math Skills Made Fun: Great Graph Art Decimals & Fractions. (Illus.). (J). 2000. pap. 10.95 (*0-590-64375-4*) Scholastic Inc.

— Math Skills Made Fun: Great Graph Art Multiplication & Division. (Illus.). 64p. (J). (gr. 3-11). 2000. pap. 15.99 (*0-590-64374-6*) Scholastic Inc.

Mitchell, Cindy. Happy Hands & Feet: Art Projects for Young Children. LC 88-82903. (Illus.). 80p. (J). (ps-3). 1989. pap. text 9.95 (*0-86530-062-3*, IP 166-0) Incentive Pubns.

Mitchell, Clarence. River Hill Soliloquy. large type ed. (Illus.). 379p. 1989. 11.50 (*0-7089-1946-4*) Ulverscroft.

An Asterisk (*) at the beginning of an entry indicates that the title is appearing for the first time.

Mitchell, Claudette C., et al. Accidents. (Visions: African-American Experiences: Vol. 29). (Illus.). 8p. (Orig.). (J). (gr. k-1). 1996. pap. text 3.00 (*1-57518-071-5*) Arborlake.
— Am I Ready Now? (Visions: African-American Experiences: Vol. 2). (Illus.). 8p. (Orig.). (J). (gr. k-1). 1996. pap. text 3.00 (*1-57518-044-8*) Arborlake.
— Animal Sounds. (Visions: African-American Experiences: Vol. 30). (Illus.). 30p. (Orig.). (J). (gr. k-1). 1996. pap. text 3.00 (*1-57518-072-3*) Arborlake.
— Ants Everywhere. (Visions: African-American Experiences: Vol. 31). (Illus.). 8p. (Orig.). (J). (gr. k-1). 1996. pap. text 3.00 (*1-57518-073-1*) Arborlake.
— Basketball. (Visions: African-American Experiences: Vol. 16). (Illus.). 8p. (Orig.). (J). (gr. k-1). 1996. pap. text 3.00 (*1-57518-058-8*) Arborlake.
— Big Enough. (Visions: African-American Experiences: Vol. 3). (Illus.). 8p. (Orig.). (J). (gr. k-1). 1996. pap. text 3.00 (*1-57518-045-6*) Arborlake.
— Braids. (Visions: African-American Experiences: Vol. 17). (Illus.). 8p. (Orig.). (J). (gr. k-1). 1996. pap. text 3.00 (*1-57518-059-6*) Arborlake.
— Clean up Your Room. (Visions: African-American Experiences: Vol. 4). (Illus.). 8p. (Orig.). (J). (gr. k-1). 1996. pap. 3.00 (*1-57518-046-4*) Arborlake.
— Daddy Works Out. (Visions: African-American Experiences: Vol. 5). (Illus.). 8p. (Orig.). (J). (gr. k-1). 1996. pap. text 3.00 (*1-57518-047-2*) Arborlake.
— Family Names. (Visions: African-American Experiences: Vol. 6). (Illus.). 8p. (Orig.). (J). (gr. k-1). 1996. pap. text 3.00 (*1-57518-048-0*) Arborlake.
— Glasses. (Visions: African-American Experiences: Vol. 7). (Illus.). 8p. (Orig.). (J). (gr. k-1). 1996. pap. text 3.00 (*1-57518-049-9*) Arborlake.
— Going Fishing. (Visions: African-American Experiences: Vol. 18). (Illus.). 8p. (Orig.). (J). (gr. k-1). 1996. pap. text 3.00 (*1-57518-060-X*) Arborlake.
— Halloween. (Visions: African-American Experiences: Vol. 19). (Illus.). 8p. (Orig.). (J). (gr. k-1). 1996. pap. text 3.00 (*1-57518-061-8*) Arborlake.
— The Hike at Daycamp. (Visions: African-American Experiences: Vol. 20). (Illus.). 8p. (Orig.). (J). (gr. k-1). 1996. pap. text 3.00 (*1-57518-062-6*) Arborlake.
— Hot Sidewalk. (Visions: African-American Experiences: Vol. 21). (Illus.). 8p. (Orig.). (J). (gr. k-1). 1996. pap. text 3.00 (*1-57518-063-4*) Arborlake.
— How to Make a Sandwich. (Visions: African-American Experiences: Vol. 32). (Illus.). 8p. (Orig.). (J). (gr. k-1). 1996. pap. text 3.00 (*1-57518-074-X*) Arborlake.
— I Do Not Like Peas. (Visions: African-American Experiences: Vol. 8). (Illus.). 8p. (Orig.). (J). (gr. k-1). 1996. pap. text 3.00 (*1-57518-050-2*) Arborlake.
— Is a Dollar Enough? (Visions: African-American Experiences: Vol. 33). (Illus.). 8p. (J). (gr. k-1). 1996. pap. text 3.00 (*1-57518-075-8*) Arborlake.
— Jumprope. (Visions: African-American Experiences: Vol. 22). (Illus.). 8p. (Orig.). (J). (gr. k-1). 1996. pap. text 3.00 (*1-57518-064-2*) Arborlake.
— Listen. (Visions: African-American Experiences: Vol. 34). (Illus.). 8p. (Orig.). (J). (gr. k-1). 1996. pap. text 3.00 (*1-57518-076-6*) Arborlake.
— Mama Goes to School. (Visions: African-American Experiences: Vol. 9). (Illus.). 8p. (Orig.). (J). (gr. k-1). 1996. pap. text 3.00 (*1-57518-051-0*) Arborlake.
— The Marketplace. (Visions: African-American Experiences: Vol. 35). (Illus.). 8p. (Orig.). (J). (gr. k-1). 1996. pap. text 3.00 (*1-57518-077-4*) Arborlake.
— My Brother's Motorcycle. (Visions: African-American Experiences: Vol. 10). (Illus.). 8p. (J). (gr. k-1). 1996. pap. text 3.00 (*1-57518-052-9*) Arborlake.
— My Buddy, My Friend. (Visions: African-American Experiences: Vol. 11). (Illus.). 8p. (Orig.). (J). (gr. k-1). 1996. pap. text 3.00 (*1-57518-053-7*) Arborlake.
— My Dog, Miffy. (Illus.). 8p. (Orig.). (J). (gr. k-1). 1996. pap. text 3.00 (*1-57518-054-5*) Arborlake.
— My Teacher Helps Me. (Visions: African-American Experiences: Vol. 23). (Illus.). 8p. (Orig.). (J). (gr. k-1). 1996. pap. text 3.00 (*1-57518-065-0*) Arborlake.
— My Weekly Chores. (Visions: African-American Experiences: Vol. 36). (Illus.). 8p. (Orig.). (J). (gr. k-1). 1996. pap. text 3.00 (*1-57518-078-2*) Arborlake.
— Pockets. (Illus.). 8p. (Orig.). (J). (gr. k-1). 1996. pap. text 3.00 (*1-57518-055-3*) Arborlake.
— Reading under the Covers. (Visions: African-American Experiences: Vol. 14). (Illus.). 8p. (Orig.). (J). (gr. k-1). 1996. pap. text 3.00 (*1-57518-056-1*) Arborlake.
— Shapes in My World. (Visions: African-American Experiences: Vol. 37). (Illus.). 8p. (Orig.). (J). (gr. k-1). 1996. pap. text 3.00 (*1-57518-079-0*) Arborlake.
— Shopping for School. (Visions: African-American Experiences: Vol. 24). (Illus.). 8p. (Orig.). (J). (gr. k-1). 1996. pap. text 3.00 (*1-57518-066-9*) Arborlake.
— Shut the Door. (Visions: African-American Experiences: Vol. 15). (Illus.). 8p. (Orig.). (J). (gr. k-1). 1996. pap. text 3.00 (*1-57518-057-X*) Arborlake.
— Skating Whiz. (Visions: African-American Experiences: Vol. 25). (Illus.). 8p. (Orig.). (J). (gr. k-1). 1996. pap. text 3.00 (*1-57518-067-7*) Arborlake.
— Snakes. (Visions: African-American Experiences: Vol. 38). (Illus.). 8p. (Orig.). (J). (gr. k-1). 1996. pap. text 3.00 (*1-57518-080-4*) Arborlake.
— The Swimming Pool. (Visions: African-American Experiences: Vol. 26). (Illus.). 8p. (Orig.). (J). (gr. k-1). 1996. pap. text 3.00 (*1-57518-068-5*) Arborlake.
— T-Ball. (Visions: African-American Experiences: Vol. 27). (Illus.). 8p. (Orig.). (J). (gr. k-1). 1996. pap. text 3.00 (*1-57518-069-3*) Arborlake.
— What's It For? (Visions: African-American Experiences: Vol. 39). (Illus.). 8p. (Orig.). (J). (gr. k-1). 1996. pap. text 3.00 (*1-57518-081-2*) Arborlake.
— Where Do I Live? (Visions: African-American Experiences: Vol. 40). (Illus.). 8p. (Orig.). (J). (gr. k-1). 1996. pap. text 3.00 (*1-57518-082-0*) Arborlake.
— Working for Dad. (Visions: African-American Experiences: Vol. 28). (Illus.). 8p. (Orig.). (J). (gr. k-1). 1996. pap. text 3.00 (*1-57518-070-7*) Arborlake.
Mitchell, Claudia, jt. auth. see Weber, Sandra J.
Mitchell, Colin. Case of Creationism. LC 95-138466. 280p. Date not set. pap. text 13.99 (*1-873796-35-8*) Review & Herald.
Mitchell, Colin W. Terrain Evaluation: An Introductory Handbook to the History, Principles & Methods of Practical Terrian Assessment. 2nd ed. 1991. pap. 49.95 (*0-582-30122-X*) Addison-Wesley.
Mitchell, Constantina T. & Cote, Paul R. Shaping the Novel: Textual Interplay in the Fiction of Malraux, Hebert & Modiano. LC 95-36839. 240p. 1996. 59.95 (*1-57181-036-6*) Berghahn Bks.
Mitchell, Constantina T., tr. see Laborit, Emmannuelle.
***Mitchell, Craig.** Shang Han Lun: On Cold Damage, Translation & Commentaries. LC 99-21069. 1999. 79.95 (*0-912111-57-7*, Paradgm Pubns) Redwing Bk Co.
Mitchell, Craig & Espeland, Pamela. Teach to Reach: Over 300 Strategies, Tips, & Helpful Hints for Teachers of All Grades. LC 96-7812. (Free Spirited Classroom Ser.). 208p. (Orig.). 1996. pap. 9.95 (*1-57542-010-4*) Free Spirit Pub.
Mitchell, Curtis, jt. auth. see Bolton, Iris.
Mitchell, Cynthia. Halloweena Hecatee & Other Rhymes to Skip To. LC 78-60175. (Illus.). (J). (gr. k-8). 1979. lib. bdg. 10.89 (*0-690-03926-3*) HarpC Child Bks.
Mitchell, D., jt. auth. see Collins, M. P.
Mitchell, D. C. Steamboats on the Fox River: A Pictorial History of Navigation in Northeastern Wisconsin. (Illus.). 210p. 1986. 29.95 (*0-9640937-1-5*) Steamboat Pr.
Mitchell, D. H. & Johnson, T. E. Invertebrate Models in Aging Research. 208p. 1984. 120.00 (*0-8493-5823-X*, QP86, CRC Reprint) Franklin.
Mitchell, D. M., jt. auth. see Ellis, R.
Mitchell, D. M., ed. see Burroughs, William S., et al.
***Mitchell, Dale.** Managed Care & Developmental Disabilities: Reconciling the Realities of Managed Care with the Individual Needs of Persons with Disabilities. LC 99-62954. 200p. 2000. pap. 19.95 (*1-892696-07-X*, Pub. by High Tide Pr) IPG Chicago.
Mitchell, Dale, jt. auth. see Braddock, David.
Mitchell, Dana, jt. auth. see Granger, Stacey.
Mitchell, Daniel J. Essays on Labor & International Trade. (Monograph & Research Ser.: No. 15). 109p. 1970. 6.00 (*0-89215-016-5*) U Cal LA Indus Rel.
— The Future of Industrial Relations. (Monograph & Research Ser.: No. 47). 181p. 1987. 10.00 (*0-89215-136-6*) U Cal LA Indus Rel.
— Human Resource Management: An Economic Approach. 748p. (C). 1989. text 57.25 (*0-534-91870-0*) S W Pub.
— Labor Issues of American International Trade & Investment. LC 76-7052. (Policy Studies in Employment & Welfare: Vol. 24). 126p. reprint ed. pap. 39.10 (*0-608-08790-4*, 206942900004) Bks Demand.
— Unions, Wages & Inflation. LC 79-3776. 304p. 1980. pap. 16.95 (*0-8157-5751-4*) Brookings.
Mitchell, Daniel J. & Azevedo, Ross E. Wage-Price Controls & Labor Market Distortions. (Monograph & Research Ser.: No. 16). 174p. 1976. 6.00 (*0-89215-056-4*) U Cal LA Indus Rel.
Mitchell, Daniel J. & Wildhorn, Jane, eds. Can California Be Competitive & Caring? LC 89-11126. (Monograph & Research Ser.: No. 49). 389p. 1989. pap. 17.00 (*0-89215-152-8*) U Cal LA Indus Rel.
— The Effective Use of Human Resources: A Symposium on New Research Approaches. (Monograph & Research Ser.: No. 52). 81p. (Orig.). 1990. pap. 9.50 (*0-89215-160-9*) U Cal LA Indus Rel.
***Mitchell, Daniel J., et al.** California Policy Options, 1999. Nomura, Patricia, ed. (Illus.). 123p. 1998. pap. 26.75 (*0-9658871-2-X*) UCLA Sch Pub Policy.
Mitchell, Daniel J., jt. auth. see Lewin, David.
Mitchell, Daniel J., jt. auth. see Way-Smith, Susan.
Mitchell, Daniel J., jt. auth. see Weber, Arnold.
Mitchell, Daniel J., ed. see Kimbell, Larry J., et al.
Mitchell, Daniel J. B. Nonunion Employee Representation: History, Contemporary Practice & Policy. Kaufman, Bruce E. & Taras, Daphne Gottlieb, eds. LC 99-32610. 592p. 2000. text 87.95 (*0-7656-0494-9*) M E Sharpe.
***Mitchell, Daniel J. B.** Pensions, Politics & the Elderly: Historic Social Movements & their Lessons for our Aging Society. LC 99-87497. (Illus.). 224p. 2000. text 64.95 (*0-7656-0518-X*) M E Sharpe.
— Pensions Politics & the Elderly: Historic Social Movements & Their Lessons for Our Aging Society. Date not set. write for info. (*0-7656-0519-8*) M E Sharpe.
Mitchell, Darby. Blue Eye of a Pond. (Illus.). 10p. (J). (ps-5). 1991. 8.00 (*0-9631809-0-8*) Castle MI.
— A Ghostly Tale! - by a Ghastly Ghost! (Illus.). 40p. 1995. 10.00 (*0-614-32374-6*) Castle MI.
— A Ghostly Tale - By a Ghastly Ghost! large type ed. (Illus.). 40p. 1998. pap. 19.95 (*0-9631809-2-4*) Castle MI.
Mitchell, Darlene, ed. see Summers, Marshall V.
Mitchell, Darlene E., ed. see Summers, Marshall V.
Mitchell, Darley. Miranda, Her Litel Booke. (Illus.). 1998. pap. 20.00 (*0-9631809-1-6*) Castle MI.
Mitchell, David. The Art of Administration. (Illus.). 244p. 1996. pap. 15.00 (*0-9623978-4-9*) Assn Waldorf Schls.
***Mitchell, David.** The Bluffer's Guide to Law: Bluff Your Way in Law. (Bluffer's Guides Ser.). 64p. 1999. pap. 5.95 (*1-902825-93-4*) Oval Bks.
— Ghostwritten: A Novel. LC 99-44063. 448p. 2000. 24.95 (*0-679-46304-6*) Random.
Mitchell, David. Mathematical Origami: Geometrical Shapes by Paper Folding. 1997. pap. 12.95 (*1-899618-18-X*, Pub. by Tarquin Pubns) Parkwest Pubns.
— The Overlook Martial Arts Handbook. LC 87-22087. (Illus.). 192p. 1988. 17.95 (*0-87951-285-7*, Pub. by Overlook Pr) Penguin Books.
— The Overlook Martial Arts Handbook. (Illus.). 192p. 1997. pap. 13.95 (*0-87951-759-X*, Pub. by Overlook Pr) Penguin Putnam.
— Resource Guide for Waldorf Teachers: Kindergarden Through Eighth Grade. 65p. 1999. pap. 12.00 (*1-888365-01-3*) Assn Waldorf Schls.
— 25 Plays: Inspired by Waldorf Teachers. (Illus.). 298p. 1997. pap. 16.00 (*1-888365-04-8*) Assn Waldorf Schls.
— Waldorf Education: An Annotated Bibliography. (Illus.). 38p. 1997. pap. 4.00 (*1-888365-06-4*) Assn Waldorf Schls.
— Winning Karate Competition. (Illus.). 128p. 1991. pap. write for info. (*0-7136-3402-2*, Pub. by A & C Blk) Midpt Trade.
— The Young Martial Artist. (Illus.). 128p. (J). 1992. 25.00 (*0-87951-422-1*, Pub. by Overlook Pr) Penguin Putnam.
— The Young Martial Artist. (Illus.). 128p. (J). 1995. pap. 17.95 (*0-87951-582-1*, Pub. by Overlook Pr) Penguin Putnam.
***Mitchell, David.** Young Martial Arts. (Young Enthusiast Ser.). (J). (gr. 3-7). 2000. 9.95 (*0-7894-5431-9*) DK Pub Inc.
Mitchell, David. The Young Martial Arts Enthusiast. LC 96-38171. (Young Enthusiast Ser.). (Illus.). 64p. (J). 1997. 15.95 (*0-7894-1508-9*) DK Pub Inc.
Mitchell, David, ed. Developmental Insights: Discussions Between Doctors & Teachers. (Illus.). 302p. 1997. pap. 18.00 (*1-888365-03-X*) Assn Waldorf Schls.
— Recent Advances in Respiratory Medicine 5. 5th ed. (Illus.). 294p. 1991. text 59.00 (*0-443-04467-8*) Church.
— To Grow & Become. Copple, Rudolf, tr. (Illus.). 96p. 1996. pap. 8.50 (*0-9623978-7-3*) Assn Waldorf Schls.
***Mitchell, David & Alsop, Dave, eds.** Administrative Explorations. 180p. 1999. pap. 15.00 (*1-888365-25-0*) Assn Waldorf Schls.
Mitchell, David & Alsop, David. Economic Explorations. 194p. pap. 15.00 (*1-888365-14-5*) Assn Waldorf Schls.
Mitchell, David & Brown, Roy I., eds. Early Intervention for Young Children with Special Needs. (Rehabilitation Education Ser.: No. 4). 320p. 1990. 59.50 (*0-412-31530-0*, A4418) Chapman & Hall.
Mitchell, David & Chaplin, Gillian. The Elegant Shed: New Zealand Architecture Since 1945. (Illus.). (C). 1985. pap. 28.00 (*0-19-558125-3*) OUP.
***Mitchell, David & Livingston, Patricia H.** Will-Developed Intelligence: The Handwork & Practical Arts Curriculum in Waldorf Schools. Riegel, Anne & Jane, Nancy, eds. (Illus.). 196p. 1999. pap. 25.00 (*1-888365-19-6*) Assn Waldorf Schls.
Mitchell, David, jt. auth. see Smit, Jorgen.
Mitchell, David, ed. see Brull, Dieter.
Mitchell, David, ed. see Buzzell, Keith.
Mitchell, David, jt. ed. see Crowley, David.
Mitchell, David, ed. see Debusscle re, Evelynne B.
Mitchell, David, ed. see Eliot, Jane.
Mitchell, David, ed. see Finser, Torin.
Mitchell, David, ed. see Fransillo, Cynthea.
Mitchell, David, ed. see Grobmann, Gerbert.
Mitchell, David, ed. see Lebret, Elizabeth.
Mitchell, David, ed. see Mirbt, C. R.
Mitchell, David, ed. see Pittis, Arthur.
Mitchell, David, ed. see Schmid, Rudolf.
Mitchell, David, ed. see Sheen, A. Renwick.
Mitchell, David, ed. see Spence, Michael.
Mitchell, David, ed. see Uehli, Ernst.
Mitchell, David, ed. see Ulin, Bengt.
Mitchell, David, ed. see Von Mackinsen, Manfred.
Mitchell, David, ed. see Winter, Dorit.
Mitchell, David, ed. see Wolsin, John.
Mitchell, David, ed. & illus. see Adams, Francine.
Mitchell, David, ed. & illus. see Down, Reg.
Mitchell, David, ed. & illus. see Schwartz, Eugene.
Mitchell, David, ed. & illus. see Stark, Dean.
***Mitchell, David A. & Mitchell, Laura.** Oxford Handbook of Clinical Dentistry. 3rd ed. LC 98-42398. (Illus.). 824p. 1999. pap. 39.95 (*0-19-262963-8*) OUP.
Mitchell, David C. The Message of the Psalter: An Eschatological Programme in the Book of Psalms. LC 97-206293. (JSOT Supplement Ser.: No. 252). 428p. 1997. 85.00 (*1-85075-689-9*, Pub. by Sheffield Acad) CUP Services.
Mitchell, David F., jt. auth. see Goldman, Bert A.
Mitchell, David M. AIDS & the Lung. Woodcock, Ashley A. et al, eds. (Illus.). 110p. 1990. pap. text 26.00 (*0-7279-0289-X*, Pub. by BMJ Pub) Login Brothers Bk Co.
Mitchell, David T. & Snyder, Sharon L., eds. The Body & Physical Difference: Discourses of Disability. LC 97-20579. 320p. (C). 1997. pap. text 18.95 (*0-472-06659-5*, 06659) U of Mich Pr.
— The Body & Physical Difference: Discourses of Disability. LC 97-20579. (Corporealities Ser.). (Illus.). 320p. (C). 1997. text 49.50 (*0-472-09659-1*, 09659) U of Mich Pr.
***Mitchell, David T. & Snyder, Sharon L., eds.** Narrative Prosthesis: Disability & the Dependencies of Discourse. (Corporealities Ser.). (Illus.). 264p. (C). 2000. text 49.50 (*0-472-09748-2*, 09748); pap. text 21.95 (*0-472-06748-6*, 06748) U of Mich Pr.
Mitchell, Dean. God's Will to Heal. 32p. 1999. pap. write for info. (*0-9630508-0-X*) Church of ACTS.
Mitchell, Debbie. Debbie Mitchell Cozy Cubby Collection. (Cherished Classics Ser.). 1996. 11.95 (*0-9647429-3-4*) D Mitchells Pubng.
Mitchell, Debby. From the Abundance of the Heart: Inspirational Poetry. 152p. 1997. pap. 15.00 (*0-9650828-2-2*) All Things.
— Touch Softly: Inspirational Poetry. (Illus.). 60p. 1995. pap. 12.00 (*0-9650828-0-6*) All Things.
Mitchell, Deborah. The Broccoli Sprouts Breakthrough. LC 98-216545. 1998. mass mkt. 4.99 (*0-312-96846-9*) St Martin.
— Diabetes. LC 97-202510. (Natural Medicine Ser.). 288p. 1997. mass mkt. 5.99 (*0-440-22273-7*) Dell.
— Natural Medicine for Superimmunity. LC 98-179245. (Natural Medicine Library). 256p. 1998. mass mkt. 5.99 (*0-440-22525-6*) Dell.
***Mitchell, Deborah.** The Sam-e Solution: The Essential Guide to the Revolutionary Antidepression Supplement. 240p. 1999. mass mkt. 8.99 (*0-446-67637-3*, Pub. by Warner Bks) Little.
— Your Ideal Supplement Plan in 3 Easy Steps: The Essential Guide to Choosing the Herbs, Vitamins & Minerals That Are Right for You. 256p. 2000. mass mkt. 5.99 (*0-440-23554-5*) Dell.
***Mitchell, Deborah & Bock, Steven J.** MSM: The Natural Pain Relief Remedy. 224p. 1999. mass mkt. 5.99 (*0-380-80899-4*, Avon Bks) Morrow Avon.
Mitchell, Deborah, jt. ed. see Goodin, Robert E.
Mitchell, Deborah R. Dictionary of Natural Healing, Vol. 1. LC R733.M585 1998. 272p. 1998. pap. 5.99 (*0-312-96516-8*, Pub. by Tor Bks) St Martin.
***Mitchell, Deborah R.** Nature's Painkillers. 256p. 2000. mass mkt. 5.99 (*0-312-97315-2*) St Martin.
Mitchell, Deborah S. Debbie Mitchell's Cozy Cubby Collection We're Back: Featuring All Those Lil' "Celebearties" 1995. 10.95 (*0-9647429-0-X*) D Mitchells Pubng.
— Keep on Stipplin'! reprint ed. 6.95 (*0-9647429-1-8*) D Mitchells Pubng.
***Mitchell, Deborah Sue.** Debbie Mitchell's Cozy Cubby Collection "Ten Years After" Expanding Our Horizons... Look at Us Now! 1999. 10.95 (*0-9647429-4-2*) D Mitchells Pubng.
Mitchell, Dennis J. Cross & Tory Democracy: A Political Biography of Richard Assheton Cross. LC 91-12409. (Modern European History Ser.). 335p. 1991. text 20.00 (*0-8240-2541-5*) Garland.
***Mitchell, Diana & Christenbury, Leila.** Both Art & Craft: Teaching Ideas That Spark Learning. 224p. 2000. pap. 25.95 (*0-8141-0380-4*, 03804) NCTE.
***Mitchell, Domhnall.** Emily Dickinson: Monarch of Perception. LC 99-33651. 336p. 2000. 40.00 (*1-55849-226-7*) U of Mass Pr.
Mitchell, Don. The Lie of the Land: Migrant Workers & the California Landscape. LC 95-30081. 1996. pap. 21.95 (*0-8166-2693-6*); text 54.95 (*0-8166-2692-8*) U of Minn Pr.
Mitchell, Don, jt. auth. see Grimm, Gary.
Mitchell, Don C. The Process of Reading: A Cognitive Analysis of Fluent Reading & Learning to Read. LC 81-21912. 258p. reprint ed. pap. 80.00 (*0-7837-0126-8*, 204040900016) Bks Demand.
Mitchell, Donald. Britten & Auden in the Thirties: The Year 1936. LC 80-25980. (Illus.). 176p. 1981. 25.00 (*0-295-95814-6*) U of Wash Pr.
***Mitchell, Donald.** Cultural Geography: A Critical Introduction. LC 99-49423. 448p. 1999. 59.95 (*1-55786-891-3*) Blackwell Pubs.
— Cultural Geography: A Critical Introduction. LC 99-49423. 448p. 2000. pap. 26.95 (*1-55786-892-1*) Blackwell Pubs.
Mitchell, Donald. Gustav Mahler: The Early Years. rev. ed. Banks, Paul & Matthews, David, eds. LC 79-9694. 360p. 1995. pap. 19.95 (*0-520-20214-7*, Pub. by U CA Pr) Cal Prin Full Svc.
— Gustav Mahler: The Wonderhorn Years. LC 79-9694. 1980. pap. 19.95 (*0-520-04220-4*, Pub. by U CA Pr) Cal Prin Full Svc.
— The Language of Modern Music. LC 94-6523. 192p. (C). 1994. pap. text 14.95 (*0-8122-1543-5*) U of Pa Pr.
***Mitchell, Donald, ed.** Britten & Auden in the Thirties: The Year 1936. 2nd ed. (Aldeburgh Studies in Music Ser.). (Illus.). 194p. 2000. pap. 19.95 (*0-85115-790-4*) Boydell & Brewer.
***Mitchell, Donald & Coles, Carol.** The Irresistible Growth Enterprise: Breakthrough Gains from Uncontrollable Change. 256p. 2000. 27.50 (*1-57922-026-6*) Stylus Pub VA.
Mitchell, Donald & Nicholson, Andrew, eds. The Mahler Companion. LC 98-45827. (Illus.). 656p. 1999. text 75.00 (*0-19-816376-2*) OUP.
Mitchell, Donald & Reed, Philip, eds. Letters from a Life: Selected Letters & Diaries of Benjamin Britten, 2 vols., Vol. Set. LC 90-42998. (Illus.). 1403p. 1991. 195.00 (*0-520-06520-4*, Pub. by U CA Pr) Cal Prin Full Svc.
Mitchell, Donald & Rubenson, David. Native American Affairs & the Department of Defense. LC 95-52248. 80p. (Orig.). 1996. pap. text 15.00 (*0-8330-2351-9*, MR-630-OSD) Rand Corp.
Mitchell, Donald, et al. The 2,000 Percent Solution: Free Your Organization from "Stalled" Thinking to Achieve Exponential Success. LC 98-40541. xii, 258p. 1999. 35.95 (*0-8144-0476-6*) AMACOM.
Mitchell, Donald, ed. see Dalai Lama XIV.
Mitchell, Donald C. Sold American: The Story of Alaska Natives & Their Land, 1867-1959 - The Army to Statehood. LC 96-41871. (Arctic Visions Ser.). (Illus.). 490p. 1997. pap. 24.95 (*0-87451-748-6*); text 55.00 (*0-87451-800-8*) U Pr of New Eng.
Mitchell, Donald D. Ku Kilakila 'O Kamehameha. (Illus.). 160p. (Orig.). 1993. pap. 29.95 (*0-87336-017-6*) Kamehameha Schools.
Mitchell, Donald G. About Old Story Tellers. (Notable American Authors Ser.). 1999. reprint ed. lib. bdg. 125.00 (*0-7812-4568-0*) Rprt Serv.

M

— American Lands & Letters. (Notable American Authors Ser.). 1999. reprint ed. lib. bdg. 125.00 (*0-7812-4572-9*) Rprt Serv.

— The Battle Summer. (Notable American Authors Ser.). 1999. reprint ed. lib. bdg. 125.00 (*0-7812-4559-1*) Rprt Serv.

— Bound Together. (Notable American Authors Ser.). 1999. reprint ed. lib. bdg. 125.00 (*0-7812-4570-2*) Rprt Serv.

— Daniel Tyler. (Notable American Authors Ser.). 1999. reprint ed. lib. bdg. 125.00 (*0-7812-4569-9*) Rprt Serv.

— Dream Life: A Fable of the Seasons. (Notable American Authors Ser.). 1999. reprint ed. lib. bdg. 125.00 (*0-7812-4562-1*) Rprt Serv.

— English Land, Letters & Kings. (Notable American Authors Ser.). 1999. reprint ed. lib. bdg. 125.00 (*0-7812-4571-0*) Rprt Serv.

— Fresh Gleanings. (Notable American Authors Ser.). 1999. reprint ed. lib. bdg. 125.00 (*0-7812-4558-3*) Rprt Serv.

— Fudge Doings. (Notable American Authors Ser.). 1999. reprint ed. lib. bdg. 125.00 (*0-7812-4563-X*) Rprt Serv.

— The Lorgnette. (Notable American Authors Ser.). 1999. reprint ed. lib. bdg. 125.00 (*0-7812-4560-5*) Rprt Serv.

— MRI Principles: A Guide for the Mathematically Illiterate. Brawlow, Lisette, ed. LC 98-12902. (Illus.). 288p. (C). 1998. text 59.00 (*0-7216-6759-7*, W B Saunders Co) Harcrt Hlth Sci Grp.

M

— My Farm of Edgewood. (Notable American Authors Ser.). 1999. reprint ed. lib. bdg. 125.00 (*0-7812-4564-8*) Rprt Serv.

— Picture of Edgewood. (Notable American Authors Ser.). 1999. reprint ed. lib. bdg. 125.00 (*0-7812-4567-2*) Rprt Serv.

— Reveries of a Bachelor. 1972. 59.95 (*0-8490-0951-0*) Gordon Pr.

— Reveries of a Bachelor or: A Book of the Heart. (Notable American Authors Ser.). 1999. reprint ed. lib. bdg. 125.00 (*0-7812-4561-3*) Rprt Serv.

— Seven Stories. (Notable American Authors Ser.). 1999. reprint ed. lib. bdg. 125.00 (*0-7812-4566-4*) Rprt Serv.

— Seven Stories with Basement & Attic. 1972. reprint ed. pap. text 8.95 (*0-8290-0672-9*); reprint ed. lib. bdg. 32.50 (*0-8422-8096-0*) Irvington.

Mitchell, Donald O., et al. The World Food Outlook. (Trade & Development Ser.). 232p. (C). 1997. text 59.95 (*0-521-58010-2*); pap. text 18.95 (*0-521-58984-3*) Cambridge U Pr.

Mitchell, Donald W. Spirituality & Emptiness: The Dynamics of Spiritual Life in Buddhism & Christianity. 240p. 1991. pap. 16.95 (*0-8091-3266-4*) Paulist Pr.

Mitchell, Donald W., ed. Masao Abe: A Zen Life of Dialogue. LC 98-6073. 320p. 1998. pap. 24.95 (*0-8048-3123-8*) Tuttle Pubng.

Mitchell, Donald W. & Wiseman, James, eds. The Gethsemani Encounter: A Dialogue on the Spiritual Life by Buddhist & Christian Monastics. LC 81-40468. 320p. 1997. 29.95 (*0-8264-1046-4*) Continuum.

— The Gethsemani Encounter: A Dialogue on the Spiritual Life by Buddhist & Christian Monastics. LC 56-11950. 336p. 1999. pap. 19.95 (*0-8264-1165-7*) Continuum.

Mitchell, Douglas, jt. auth. see Goertz, Margaret E.

Mitchell, Douglas, jt. auth. see Kerchner, Charles T.

Mitchell, Douglas E., et al, eds. Work Orientation & Job Performance: The Cultural Basis of Teaching Rewards & Incentives. LC 87-1905. (SUNY Series, Educational Leadership). 245p. (C). 1987. pap. text 21.95 (*0-88706-568-6*) State U NY Pr.

Mitchell, Dugald, ed. The Book of Highland Verse. LC 79-144528. reprint ed. 52.50 (*0-404-08673-X*) AMS Pr.

Mitchell, E. Employer's & Personnel Manager's Handbook of Draft Letters of Employment Law. 1977. reprint ed. pap. 45.00 (*0-8464-0373-0*) Beekman Pubs.

Mitchell, E. Douglas, jt. ed. see Lamb, Sydney M.

Mitchell, Ed. Fly Rodding the Coast. (Illus.). 320p. 1995. 29.95 (*0-8117-0628-1*) Stackpole.

— Gold Rush 2000. (Gold Trilogy Ser.). xi, 400p. 1999. 24.95 (*0-9668447-3-4*) CA Coast Pubg.

Mitchell, Edgar & Williams, Dwight. The Way of the Explorer: An Apollo Astronaut's Journey Through the Material & Mystical Worlds. 224p. 1996. 24.95 (*0-399-14161-8*, G P Putnam) Peng Put Young Read.

Mitchell, Edith A. To Feed Thy Soul. Blakely, Romaine & Whitman, Virginia, eds. LC 85-63084. (Illus.). 50p. (Orig.). 1985. pap. 9.95 (*0-88100-051-5*) Natl Writ Pr.

Mitchell, Edward & Schulte, Rainer, eds. Continental Short Stories. (C). 1969. pap. text 25.00 (*0-393-09797-8*) Norton.

Mitchell, Edward C., jt. auth. see Mithcell, Nahum.

Mitchell, Edward C., ed. see Furst, Gesenius.

Mitchell, Edward J., ed. The Deregulation of Natural Gas. LC 83-9989. (AEI Symposia Ser.: No. 83B). 176p. reprint ed. pap. 54.60 (*0-8357-4463-9*, 203730700008) Bks Demand.

— Question of Offshore Oil. LC 76-16665. 171p. reprint ed. pap. 53.10 (*0-608-14345-6*, 201749200007) Bks Demand.

— Vertical Integration in the Oil Industry. LC 76-20267. (National Energy Study Ser.: No. 11). 220p. reprint ed. pap. 68.20 (*0-8357-4542-2*, 203743800008) Bks Demand.

Mitchell, Edward J., jt. ed. see Horwich, George.

Mitchell, Eleanor & Walters, Sheila. Document Delivery Services: Issues & Answers. 333p. 1995. 42.50 (*1-57387-003-X*) Info Today Inc.

Mitchell, Elisabeth, jt. auth. see Bentson, Marilyn.

***Mitchell, Elizabeth.** W: Revenge of the Bush Dynasty. LC 99-58234. 384p. 2000. 22.95 (*0-7868-6630-6*, Pub. by Hyperion) Time Warner.

Mitchell, Elizabeth Dix, see Mitchell, Joyce Slayton & Mitchell, Elizabeth Dix.

Mitchell, Elizabeth Dix, jt. auth. see Mitchell, Joyce Slayton.

***Mitchell, Elizabeth K., et al.** Death by Hogarth. LC 99-27875. (Illus.). 72p. 1999. pap. 15.00 (*1-891771-08-6*) Harvard Art Mus.

Mitchell, Ella. History of Washington County. (Illus.). 173p. 1997. reprint ed. lib. bdg. 26.00 (*0-8328-9952-6*) Higginson Bk Co.

Mitchell, Ella, jt. auth. see Mitchell, Henry.

Mitchell, Ella P. Women - To Preach or Not to Preach: 21 Outstanding Black Preachers Say Yes! 145p. 1991. pap. 13.00 (*0-8170-1169-2*) Judson.

Mitchell, Ella P., ed. Those Preachin' Women, Vol. 1. 128p. 1985. pap. 12.00 (*0-8170-1073-4*) Judson.

— Those Preachin' Women, Vol. 3. 128p. 1996. pap. 12.00 (*0-8170-1249-4*) Judson.

— Those Preachin' Women: More Sermons by Black Women Preachers, Vol. 2. 112p. 1988. pap. 12.00 (*0-8170-1131-5*) Judson.

Mitchell, Ellinor R. Fighting Drug Abuse with Acupuncture: The Treatment That Works. LC 95-69800. (Illus.). 224p. (Orig.). 1995. pap. 17.95 (*1-881896-12-9*) Pacific View Pr.

— Plain Talk about Acupuncture. (Illus.). 123p. (Orig.). 1987. pap. 10.95 (*0-9617918-0-2*) Whalehall Inc.

Mitchell, Elsie P. The Lion-Dog of Buddhist Asia. LC 91-70174. (Illus.). 192p. 1991. 50.00 (*0-9628495-0-2*); pap. 27.50 (*0-9628495-1-0*) Fugaisha US.

***Mitchell, Emma.** Energy Exercises. (Illus.). 72p. 2000. 12.95 (*0-89087-979-6*) Celestial Arts.

Mitchell, Emma. Energy Now: Simple Ways to Gain Vitality, Overcome Tension, & Achieve Harmony & Balance by Unlocking the Energy Secrets of East & West. LC 98-6835. 160p. 1998. pap. 17.95 (*0-02-862675-3*, Schirmer Books) Mac Lib Ref.

***Mitchell, Eric A.** Power: The Power to Create the Future. LC 89-13824. (New Age Ser.). (Illus.). 192p. 1999. mass mkt. 3.95 (*0-87542-499-6*) Llewellyn Pubns.

Mitchell, Eugene S., compiled by. Library Services for Nonaffiliated Patrons. (CLIP Note Ser.: Vol. 21). 151p. (Orig.). (C). 1995. pap. 33.00 (*0-8389-7781-2*) Assn Coll & Res Libs.

Mitchell, F., ed. Proceedings of the Conference on Low-Level Exposure to Chemicals & Neurobiological Sensitivity. (Toxicology & Industrial Health Ser.: Vol. 10, No. 4/5). (Illus.). 252p. 1994. 65.00 (*0-911131-32-9*) Specialist Journals.

Mitchell, F. & Salafantinos, C. Modern Management Accounting Developments. (Financial Times Management Briefings Ser.). 1997. pap. 94.50 (*0-273-63238-8*, Pub. by F T P-H) Trans-Atl Phila.

Mitchell, F. H., Jr., jt. auth. see Mitchell, Cheryl C.

Mitchell, Faith. Hoodoo Medicine: Gullah Herbal Remedies. rev. ed. LC 98-29389. (Illus.). 110p. 1998. pap. 15.00 (*1-887714-33-2*) Summerhse Pr.

Mitchell, Falconer, jt. auth. see Innes, John.

Mitchell, Falconer, jt. ed. see Lapsley, Irvine.

Mitchell, Falconer, ed. see Walker, Stephen P.

Mitchell, Fannie. A Higher Plane. 1997. pap. write for info. (*1-57553-496-7*) Watermrk Pr.

Mitchell, Fannie M., ed. see Stoops, Martha.

Mitchell, Felicia. Case Hysteries: Poems. LC 96-3097. 68p. 1996. pap. 14.95 (*0-7734-2706-6*, Mellen Poetry Pr) E Mellen.

— Words & Quilts: A Selection of Quilt Poems. LC 94-38673. 96p. 1995. 21.95 (*0-8442-2644-0*, Quilt Dgst Pr) NTC Contemp Pub Co.

***Mitchell, Finis.** Wind River Trails. 1999. pap. 6.95 (*0-87480-626-7*) U of Utah Pr.

Mitchell, Finis. Wind River Trails. Davis, Mel, ed. (Illus.). 144p. 1975. pap. 6.95 (*0-915272-03-2*) Wasatch Pubs.

Mitchell, Flint, ed. The Complete LISFAN. 100p. 1991. pap. 19.95 (*1-880417-05-7*) Star Tech.

Mitchell, Flint & Anchors, William E., Jr. The Lost in Space Twenty-Fifth Anniversary Celebration. 94p. 1991. pap. 11.95 (*1-880417-03-0*) Star Tech.

Mitchell, Frances G., ed. see Careless, Dolores A.

Mitchell, Frances R. Experiencing the Great Depression & World War II: A Look Back to an Unforgettable Period. LC 89-81426. (Illus.). 144p. 1990. 23.00 (*0-9625408-0-3*); pap. 15.00 (*0-9625408-1-1*) Bears Paw Pr.

Mitchell, Francis, ed. see Matthews, E. T.

Mitchell, Francis, ed. see Rajhathy, Judit.

Mitchell, Frank. Reading The Irish Landscape. 3rd ed. (Illus.). 400p. 1997. pap. text 29.95 (*1-86059-055-1*, Pub. by Town Hse) Roberts Rinehart.

— Redruth Parish Church - St. Euny's. (C). 1989. 30.00 (*1-85022-036-0*, Pub. by Dyllansow Truran) St Mut.

— The Way That I Followed: A Naturalist's Journey Around Ireland. (Illus.). 288p. 1995. 35.00 (*0-946172-21-8*, TCH220X, Pub. by Town Hse); pap. 21.95 (*0-946172-20-X*, Pub. by Town Hse) Roberts Rinehart.

— Where Has Ireland Come From? (Illus.). 64p. 1995. pap. 9.95 (*0-946172-43-9*, Pub. by Town Hse) Roberts Rinehart.

Mitchell, Frank L., ed. Multiple Chemical Sensitivity: A Scientific Overview. LC 94-74818. (Illus.). 669p. 1995. text 135.00 (*0-911131-53-1*) Specialist Journals.

Mitchell, Frank N. & Wesley, John. The Writings of John Wesley: A Man for All Ages. LC 96-90608. 1997. 29.95 (*0-533-12102-7*) Vantage.

Mitchell, Franklin D. Harry S. Truman & the News Media: Contentious Relations, Belated Respect. LC 98-6620. 296p. 1998. 34.95 (*0-8262-1180-1*) U of Mo Pr.

Mitchell, Fred. At Break of Day. 1997. pap. 11.99 (*1-85792-230-1*, Pub. by Christian Focus) Spring Arbor Dist.

***Mitchell, Fred L., Jr. & Mitchell, Calen P.** The Muscle Energy Manual Vol. 3: Evaluation & Treatment of the Pelvis & Sacrum, 3 vols. (Illus.). 200p. 2000. pap. text 63.00 (*0-9647250-3-7*) MET Pr.

Mitchell, Fred L., Jr. & Mitchell, P. Kai-Galen. The Muscle Energy Manual Vol. 1: Concepts & Mechanisms the Musculoskeletal Screen Cervical Region Evaluation & Treatment. LC 95-77816. (Illus.). 228p. 1995. pap. text 59.00 (*0-9647250-1-0*) MET Pr.

— The Muscle Energy Manual Vol. 2: Evaluation & Treatment of the Thoracic Spine, Lumbar Spine & Rib Cage, 2 vols. LC 95-77816. (Illus.). 240p. (Orig.). 1998. pap. text 68.00 (*0-9647250-2-9*) MET Pr.

Mitchell, G. A to Z Silent Film Comedy. 1999. pap. text 21.95 (*0-7134-7939-6*) B T B.

— Welcoming the French. 1993. 60.00 (*1-85594-054-X*) St Mut.

Mitchell, G. Duncan, ed. A New Dictionary of the Social Sciences. 244p. 1979. lib. bdg. 49.95 (*0-202-30285-7*) Aldine de Gruyter.

Mitchell, G. F., et al, eds. Structural Performance of Pipes: Proceedings of the Second National Conference on Structural Performance of Pipes, Columbus, Ohio, 14-17 March 1993. (Illus.). 174p. (C). 1993. text 110.00 (*90-5410-308-6*, Pub. by A A Balkema) Ashgate Pub Co.

***Mitchell, Gail.** Bone Songs. 95p. 1999. pap. 10.95 (*0-931552-11-7*) Taurean Horn.

Mitchell, Garry. The Trainer's Handbook: The AMA Guide to Effective Training. LC 86-47819. 361p. reprint ed. pap. 112.00 (*0-7837-4238-X*, 204392700012) Bks Demand.

— The Trainer's Handbook: The AMA Guide to Effective Training. 2nd ed. LC 92-27379. 432p. 1992. 75.00 (*0-8144-5062-8*) AMACOM.

***Mitchell, Gary.** Force of Change. 96p. 2000. pap. 16.95 (*1-85459-472-9*) Theatre Comm.

Mitchell, Gary. Tearing the Loom. 96p. 1999. pap. 13.95 (*1-85459-403-6*) Theatre Comm.

— The Trainer's Handbook: The Ama Guide to Effective Training. 3rd rev. ed. LC 97-33473. 428p. 1997. 75.00 (*0-8144-0341-7*) AMACOM.

***Mitchell, Gary.** Trust. (Nick Hern Bks.). 2000. pap. 14.95 (*1-85459-443-5*) Theatre Comm.

Mitchell, Gayle. All Slots Made Easier: (Winning Strategies for Basic Slots, Progressives & Newest Versions) 60p. 1999. pap. 10.00 (*0-9656118-3-3*) Webster Res-Info Servs.

— Casino Gambling Made Easier: (How a Rank Amateur Casino Gambler Can Learn to Win Using Intelligent Gambling) unabridged ed. (Illus.). 107p. (Orig.). 1997. pap. 19.95 (*0-9656118-1-7*) Webster Res-Info Servs.

***Mitchell, Gayle.** Casino Gambling Tips Booklets, 1. (Casino Gambling Tips Booklets). 1999. 20.00 (*0-9656118-5-X*, Casino Players) Webster Res-Info Servs.

Mitchell, Gayle. More Casino Gambling Made Easier: (More Winning Strategies, Casino Selections & Intelligent Gambling with Worldwide Casino Travelogue) (Illus.). 120p. 1998. pap. 19.95 (*0-9656118-6-8*) Webster Res-Info Servs.

***Mitchell, Gayle.** Video Poker Made Easier: (Winning Strategies for Serious Players) 60p. 1998. pap. 10.00 (*0-9656118-4-1*) Webster Res-Info Servs.

Mitchell, Gayle F., jt. ed. see Sargand, Shad M.

Mitchell, George. Carpentry & Joinery. LC 92-6970. (Illus.). 240p. 1998. pap. 28.00 (*0-304-70427-X*) Continuum.

— Comfy Glasgow: An Expression Of Thanks. 1999. pap. text 7.99 (*1-85792-444-4*) Christian Focus.

— I'm Somebody Important: Young Black Voices from Rural Georgia. LC 72-75489. (Illus.). 256p. reprint ed. pap. 79.40 (*0-8357-6150-9*, 203445300090) Bks Demand.

— In Celebration of a Legacy: The Traditional Arts of the Lower Chattahoochee Valley. 130p. 1981. pap. 10.00 (*1-882650-03-4*) Colmbs Mus GA.

— In Celebration of a Legacy: The Traditional Arts of the Lower Chattahoochee Valley. rev. ed. LC 98-12362. (Illus.). 128p. 1999. pap. 24.95 (*0-945477-12-0*) Hist Chattahoochee.

***Mitchell, George.** Making Peace. LC 99-86633. 220p. 2000. pap. text 16.95 (*0-520-22523-6*, Pub. by U CA Pr) Cal Prin Full Svc.

Mitchell, George. Ponce de Leon: An Intimate Portrait of Atlanta's Most Famous Avenue. (Illus.). 160p. (Orig.). 1983. pap. 12.95 (*0-915063-01-8*) Argonne Bks.

— The Practice of Operational Research. LC 93-7352. 256p. 1993. 115.00 (*0-471-93982-X*) Wiley.

***Mitchell, George & Gollings, John.** New Australian Style. LC 99-45698. (Illus.). 208p. 1999. 40.00 (*0-8118-2544-2*) Chronicle Bks.

***Mitchell, George C.** Matthew B. Ridgway: Soldier, Statesman, Scholar, Citizen. LC 99-41830. (Illus.). 252p. 1999. pap. 15.95 (*1-887969-10-1*) Cathedral PA.

Mitchell, George J. Growing-Up in Mai. 1999. pap. write for info. (*0-14-011621-4*, Viking) Viking Penguin.

— Making Peace. LC 99-61004. (Illus.). 191p. 1999. 24.00 (*0-375-40606-9*) Knopf.

— Not for America Alone: The Triumph of Democracy & the Fall of Communism. LC 96-50332. 320p. 1997. 25.00 (*1-56836-083-5*) Kodansha.

***Mitchell-George, Joanne.** How the New 1999 Social Security Changes Affect You. 24p. 1998. pap. 0.59 (*0-87622-799-X*) Aspen Pub.

— How to Make Sure You Have the Right Tax Withheld: Should You Revise Your W-4? 24p. 1998. pap. 0.59 (*0-7355-1295-7*) Panel Pubs.

Mitchell-George, Joanne, jt. auth. see Risteau, Delores.

Mitchell, George S., jt. auth. see Cayton, Horace R.

Mitchell, George S., jt. auth. see Mitchell, Broadus.

Mitchell, George T. Dr. George: An Account of the Life of a Country Doctor. LC 93-16589. (Illus.). 400p. 1993. pap. 21.95 (*0-8093-1916-0*) S Ill U Pr.

Mitchell, George W. The Female Breast & Its Disorders: Essentials of Diagnosis & Management. (Illus.). 384p. 1990. 75.00 (*0-683-06100-3*) Lppncott W & W.

Mitchell, Gerald & Mitchell, Kath. Akita. (Illus.). 160p. 1993. 24.95 (*0-948955-11-2*, Pub. by Ringpr Bks) Seven Hills Bk.

Mitchell, Gerald E. How to Be a Destination Manager. 240p. (C). 1992. student ed., ring bd. 49.95 (*0-945439-11-3*) G E Mitchell & Assocs.

— How to Be a International Tour Director. 225p. (C). 1992. student ed., ring bd. 49.95 (*0-945439-09-1*) G E Mitchell & Assocs.

— How to Be a Tour Guide. 230p. (C). 1992. student ed., ring bd. 49.95 (*0-945439-10-5*) G E Mitchell & Assocs.

— How to Design & Package Tours. 230p. (C). 1992. student ed., ring bd. 49.95 (*0-945439-12-1*) G E Mitchell & Assocs.

— The Travel Consultant's On-Site Inspection Journal. rev. ed. (Illus.). 192p. 1990. reprint ed. student ed. 30.00 (*0-945439-00-8*) G E Mitchell & Assocs.

— Travel the World Free As an International Tour Director: How to Be an International Tour Director, 5, 1. 300p. 1995. 59.95 (*0-945439-13-X*) G E Mitchell & Assocs.

Mitchell, Geraldine. Deeds Not Words: The Life & Work of Muriel Gahan LC 97-224224. 224 p. 1997. write for info. (*1-86058-907-3*) Prof Eng Pubng.

— Practical Strategies for Individual Behaviour Difficulties. LC 98-149254. 96p. 1997. pap. 24.95 (*1-85346-518-6*, Pub. by David Fulton) Taylor & Francis.

Mitchell, German, tr. see Weise, Carlos S.

Mitchell, Gina, jt. auth. see Heaton, Pat.

Mitchell, Ginger & Tompkins, Patsy. Country Classics II. (Illus.). 160p. 1997. 14.95 (*0-9646160-1-7*) Country Classics.

Mitchell, Ginger, jt. auth. see Richardson, Joseph R.

Mitchell, Ginger, jt. auth. see Tompkins, Patsy.

Mitchell, Gladys. Late, Late in the Evening. large type ed. (Linford Mystery Library). 400p. 1996. pap. 16.99 (*0-7089-7941-6*) Ulverscroft.

***Mitchell, Gladys.** Speedy Death. (Black Dagger Crime Ser.). 1999. 21.95 (*0-7540-8547-3*) Chivers N Amer.

Mitchell, Glenn. The Chaplin Encyclopedia. (Illus.). 256p. 1997. pap. 19.95 (*0-7134-7938-8*) BTB Ent.

— The Marx Brothers Encyclopedia. (Illus.). 256p. 1996. pap. 19.95 (*0-7134-7838-1*) Trafalgar.

Mitchell, Glenn, jt. auth. see Mohr, Stephen F.

Mitchell, Gordon. Together in the Land: A Reading of the Book of Joshua. (Journal for the Study of the Old Testament Supplement Ser.: Vol. 134). 224p. 1993. 65.00 (*1-85075-409-8*, Pub. by Sheffield Acad) CUP Services.

***Mitchell, Gordon R.** Strategic Deception. 288p. 2000. 55.00 (*0-87013-557-0*); pap. 24.95 (*0-87013-558-9*) Mich St U Pr.

Mitchell, Grace. Help! What to Do About... 1994. pap. 9.95 (*0-590-49604-2*) Scholastic Inc.

— A Very Practical Guide to Discipline with Young Children. rev. ed. LC 82-16951. 160p. (Orig.). (C). 1998. pap. 14.95 (*0-910287-12-0*, HQ770.4.M57) TelShare Pub Co.

Mitchell, Grace & Dewsnap, Lois. Common Sense Discipline: Building Self-Esteem in Young Children: Stories from Life. LC 95-11901. (Orig.). 1995. pap. 14.95 (*0-910287-11-2*) TelShare Pub Co.

Mitchell, Grace L. Growing with Grace. LC 98-61629. (Illus.). 281p. 1999. 19.95 (*0-910287-13-9*) TelShare Pub Co.

Mitchell, Graham. Medical Physiology: Objectives & Multiple Choice Questions. 2nd ed. 153p. (C). 1986. pap. text 35.00 (*0-409-10727-1*) Buttrwrth-Heinemann.

***Mitchell, Graham R., ed.** America's New Deficit: The Shortage of Information Technology Workers. (Illus.). 42p. 1999. reprint ed. pap. text 15.00 (*0-7881-7897-0*) DIANE Pub.

Mitchell, Grant E., jt. ed. see Haber, Joel D.

Mitchell, Greg. Going Fishing. LC 92-14449. (Voyages Ser.). (Illus.). (J). 1993. 3.75 (*0-383-03625-9*) SRA McGraw.

***Mitchell, Greg.** Joy in Mudville: A Little League Memoir. LC 99-87423. 272p. 2000. 19.95 (*0-671-03531-2*, PB Hardcover) PB.

Mitchell, Greg. Our Playhouse. LC 92-21451. (Voyages Ser.). (Illus.). (J). 1993. 3.75 (*0-383-03647-X*) SRA McGraw.

— Simply Sam. LC 92-21452. (Voyages Ser.). (Illus.). (J). 1993. 3.75 (*0-383-03652-6*) SRA McGraw.

Mitchell, Greg, jt. auth. see Lifton, Robert J.

***Mitchell, Gwendolyn A.** House of Women. LC 00-37760. 2000. pap. write for info. (*0-88378-223-5*) Third World.

Mitchell, H. B. The Theosophical Society & Theosophy. 1988. pap. 3.00 (*0-936072-18-0*) Soc New Lang Study.

***Mitchell, H. E.** The Jonesport (ME) Register. 2000. pap. 19.50 (*0-7404-0041-X*) Higginson Bk Co.

Mitchell, H. E., compiled by. The Farmington Town Register, 1902-3 (Town History & Directory) 126p. 1997. reprint ed. pap. 21.50 (*0-8328-5838-2*) Higginson Bk Co.

— The Oakland Register, 1903 (Town History & Directory) 115p. 1997. reprint ed. pap. 19.50 (*0-8328-5881-1*) Higginson Bk Co.

— The Redfield Register, 1903 (Town History & Directory) (Illus.). 80p. 1997. reprint ed. pap. 16.00 (*0-8328-5902-8*) Higginson Bk Co.

***Mitchell, H. E., ed.** The Jonesport (ME) Register. 112p. 2000. 29.50 (*0-7404-0040-1*) Higginson Bk Co.

Mitchell, H. G., et al. Haggai, Zechariah, Malachi & Jonah: Critical & Exegetical Commentary. (International Critical Commentary Ser.). 544p. 1912. 39.95 (*0-567-05020-3*, Pub. by T & T Clark) Bks Intl VA.

Mitchell, H. J. 32-Bit Microprocessors. 2nd ed. 1991. 66.00 (*0-8493-7713-7*) CRC Pr.

Mitchell, H. L. Mean Things Happening in This Land: The Life & Times of H. L. Mitchell, Cofounder of the Southern Tenant Farmer's Union. LC 78-65660. 372p. 1979. text 17.50 (*0-916672-25-5*) Rowman.

An Asterisk (*) at the beginning of an entry indicates that the title is appearing for the first time.

— Roll the Union On: A Pictorial History of the Southern Tenant Farmers' Union. (Illus.). 96p. (Orig.). 1987. pap. 12.00 (*0-88286-159-X*) C H Kerr.

Mitchell, Harris T. The First Airborne Battalion: (The Story of) the First Airborne Battalion. LC 96-60229. (Illus.). 96p. (Orig.). 1996. pap. 14.95 (*0-9629170-4-4*) Twinbrook Comms.

Mitchell, Harvey. Individual Choice & the Structures of History: Alexis de Tocqueville As Historian Reappraised. LC 96-33255. 304p. (C). 1996. text 59.95 (*0-521-56091-8*) Cambridge U Pr.

Mitchell-Hatton, Sara L. The Davis Book of Medical Abbreviations. 1028p. 1991. pap. text 38.95 (*0-8036-6268-8*) Davis Co.

***Mitchell, Hayley.** Readings on "Black Boy" LC 99-16774. (Literary Companion Ser.). 224p. (YA). (gr. 9-12). 2000. pap. 17.45 (*0-7377-0242-7*); lib. bdg. 27.95 (*0-7377-0243-5*) Greenhaven.

***Mitchell, Hayley R.** The Death Penalty. LC 00-29405. 2000. pap. write for info. (*0-7377-0458-6*) Greenhaven.

Mitchell, Hayley R. Doll's House. LC 98-49695. (Literary Companion Ser.). 160p. 1998. lib. bdg. 27.45 (*0-7377-0049-1*) Greenhaven.

***Mitchell, Hayley R.** Native Son. (Literary Companion Ser.). 224p. (YA). 2000. 17.45 (*0-7377-0320-2*) Greenhaven.

— Native Son. LC 99-53746. (Literary Companion to American Literature Ser.). 224p. (YA). 2000. pap. 13.96 (*0-7377-0319-9*) Greenhaven.

— Readings on a Doll's House. LC 98-49695. (Literary Companion to World Literature Ser.). 160p. 1999. lib. bdg. 17.45 (*0-7377-0048-3*) Greenhaven.

Mitchell, Hayley R. Teen Alcoholism. LC 97-27500. (Overview Ser.). (Illus.). (YA). (gr. 4-12). 1997. lib. bdg. 22.45 (*1-56006-514-1*) Lucent Bks.

***Mitchell, Hayley R.** Teen Suicide. LC 99-30150. (Overview Ser.). (Illus.). 128p. (YA). (gr. 8-12). 2000. lib. bdg. 23.70 (*1-56006-572-9*) Lucent Bks.

Mitchell, Hayley R., ed. Wuthering Heights. LC 98-28876. (Literary Companion Ser.). 156p. (YA). (gr. 9-12). 1998. pap. 17.45 (*1-56510-832-9*); lib. bdg. 27.45 (*1-56510-833-7*) Greenhaven.

Mitchell, Hayley R., ed. see Kim, Frank H.

Mitchell, Hazel B. Okay Nelwyn . . . 1989. pap. 10.95 (*0-938645-26-9*) In His Steps.

Mitchell, Helen B. Roots of Wisdom. (Philosophy Ser.). 1995. pap., student ed. 15.75 (*0-534-23091-1*) Wadsworth Pub.

Mitchell, Helen B., compiled by. Roots of Wisdom: A Multicultural Reader. 4th ed. LC 96-8978. (Philosophy Ser.). 368p. (C). 1996. pap. 24.95 (*0-534-23089-X*) Wadsworth Pub.

— Roots of Wisdom: Speaking the Language of Philosophy. LC 95-9385. 524p. (C). 1995. pap. 39.25 (*0-534-23088-1*) Wadsworth Pub.

— Roots of Wisdom: Speaking the Language of Philosophy. 2nd ed. LC 98-11859. 1998. pap. 61.95 (*0-534-54342-1*) Wadsworth Pub.

— Roots of World Wisdom: A Multicultural Reader. 2nd ed. LC 98-38297. (Philosophy Ser.). 1998. pap. 28.95 (*0-534-54347-2*) Wadsworth Pub.

Mitchell, Helen B., et al. Clashing Views on Controversial Issues in World Civilizations, Vol. I. (Taking Sides Ser.). (Illus.). 368p. 1998. pap. text 13.00 (*0-697-42299-2*, Dshkn McG-Hill) McGrw-H Hghr Educ.

— Clashing Views on Controversial Issues in World Civilizations, Vol. II. (Taking Sides Ser.). (Illus.). 368p. 1998. pap. text 13.00 (*0-697-42300-X*, Dshkn McG-Hill) McGrw-H Hghr Educ.

Mitchell, Henry. Any Day. LC 97-1356. (Illus.). 272p. 1997. 24.95 (*0-253-33308-3*) Ind U Pr.

— The Essential Earthman: Henry Mitchell on Gardening. 1999. pap. 14.00 (*0-395-95768 0*) HM.

***Mitchell, Henry.** Henry Mitchell Gardening Assortment. 1999. pap. text 13.67 (*5-554-09907-6*) HM.

Mitchell, Henry. Henry Mitchell on Gardening. LC 97-35353. 288p. 1998. 24.00 (*0-395-87821-7*) HM.

— Henry Mitchell on Gardening. 1999. pap. 13.00 (*0-395-95767-2*) HM.

— One Man's Garden. 1999. pap. 14.00 (*0-395-95769-9*) HM.

***Mitchell, Henry & Mitchell, Ella.** Together for Good: Lessons from Fifty-Five Years of Marriage, 1. LC 99-22161. 1999. 19.95 (*0-7407-0039-1*) Andrews & McMeel.

Mitchell, Henry H. Black Preaching: The Recovery of a Powerful Art. LC 90-38642. 1990. pap. 14.95 (*0-687-03614-3*) Abingdon.

— Celebration & Experience in Preaching. LC 90-35024. 1990. pap. 13.95 (*0-687-04744-7*) Abingdon.

Mitchell, Henry H. & Thomas, Emil M. Preaching for Black Self-Esteem. LC 94-12500. 192p. (Orig.). 1994. pap. 15.95 (*0-687-33843-3*) Abingdon.

Mitchell, Herb, jt. auth. see Hunter, Norah T.

Mitchell, Herbert. The Fundamentals of Profitable Visual Presentation. 208p. 1987. 125.00 (*0-944074-00-6*) AFS Education.

Mitchell, Hetty. Minnesota A to Z: Coloring Book. (Illus.). (J). 1992. pap. 3.50 (*0-87351-284-7*) Minn Hist.

Mitchell, Howard W. The Hammered Dulcimer. 3rd ed. 57p. 1971. pap. 4.95 (*0-938702-02-5*, FSI-43) Folk-Legacy.

— The Mountain Dulcimer: How to Make It & Play It - After a Fashion. 50p. 1965. pap. 4.95 (*0-938702-01-7*, FSI-29) Folk-Legacy.

Mitchell, I. A. & Teale, G. R. The Practical House Officer. 3rd ed. (Illus.). 272p. 1992. pap. 24.95 (*0-632-03309-6*) Blackwell Sci.

Mitchell, I. V., et al, eds. Concerted European Action on Magnetics. 928p. 1989. 171.00 (*1-85166-383-5*) Elsevier.

Mitchell, I. V. & Barfoot, K. M. Particle-Induced X-Ray Emission Analysis: Application to Analytical Problems, Vol. 1, No. 2. (Nuclear Science Applications Ser.). 63p. 1981. text 74.00 (*3-7186-0085-4*) Gordon & Breach.

Mitchell, Ian. Follow Your Dream - But Watch Your Back: Memoirs, Commentaries & a Challenge to the Church. 250p. (Orig.). 1996. pap. 14.95 (*0-9647935-0-4*) Omega Pubns IN.

— Mountain Footfalls: A Calendar of the Scottish Hills. 136p. 1996. pap. 36.00 (*1-873644-53-1*, Pub. by Mercat Pr Bks) St Mut.

***Mitchell, Ian.** On the Trail of Queen Victoria in the Highlands. 2000. pap. 14.95 (*0-946487-79-0*) Luath Pr Ltd.

— Scotland's Mountains Before the Mountaineers. (Illus.). 228p. 1999. pap. 16.95 (*0-946487-39-1*, Pub. by Luath Pr Ltd) Midpt Trade.

Mitchell, Ian. Second Man on the Rope. 144p. 1997. pap. 28.00 (*1-873644-01-9*, Pub. by Mercat Pr Bks) St Mut.

Mitchell, Ian, jt. auth. see Brown, Dave.

Mitchell, Ian, tr. see Canetti, Veza.

Mitchell, Imogen & Teale, G. R. The Practical House Officer. 2nd ed. LC 96-31455. (Illus.). 352p. 1997. pap. 34.95 (*0-86542-769-0*) Blackwell Sci.

Mitchell International Inc. Staff. Mitchell Automotive Braking Systems. 208p. 1989. pap. 28.00 (*0-13-585480-6*) P-H.

Mitchell International Staff. Asian EFI Driveability, Mitsubishi, Nissan, Toyota: Diagnosis, Procedures & Adjustments: 1981-89 Imported Cars, Light Trucks & Vans. LC 89-208072. 1989. ring bd. write for info. (*0-8470-0180-6*) Mitchell Manuals Inc.

— Mitchell Guide to Diagnostics: Engine Performance, 1983-94 Cars, Light Trucks & Vans: Toyota/Lexus. LC 95-108937. 1994. write for info. (*0-8470-1442-8*) Mitchell Manuals Inc.

Mitchell, Irene M. Beatrice Cenci. LC 90-22598. (American University Studies: History: Ser. IX, Vol. 104). (Illus.). VIII, 236p. (C). 1991. text 46.95 (*0-8204-1525-1*) P Lang Pubng.

Mitchell, Irene M., ed. & tr. see Morra, Isabella.

Mitchell, J. The Atlas of European Mammals. (Poyser Natural History Ser.). 433p. (C). 1999. 60.00 (*0-85661-130-1*) Poyser.

Mitchell, J. & Mori, Scott A. The Cashew & Its Relatives: Anacardium, Anacardiaceae. LC 87-11292. (Memoirs Ser.: Vol. 42). (Illus.). 76p. 1987. pap. 17.50 (*0-89327-313-9*) NY Botanical.

Mitchell, J., tr. see Costabel, U.

Mitchell, J. A., jt. ed. see Belvisi, M. G.

Mitchell, J. B. & Guberman, S., eds. Dissociative Recombination: Theory, Experiment & Application. 352p. (C). 1989. text 93.00 (*9971-5-0618-1*) World Scientific Pub.

Mitchell, J. B., jt. ed. see Larsson, Mats.

Mitchell, J. Clyde. Cities, Society, & Social Perception: A Central African Perspective. (Illus.). 358p. 1987. text 74.00 (*0-19-823253-5*) OUP.

Mitchell, J. Clyde, jt. ed. see Boissevain, Jeremy.

Mitchell, J. D., et al. Flora of the Guianas, Series A: Anacardiaceae, Fascicle 19. Gorts-Van Rijn, A. R. & Jansen-Jacobs, M. J., eds. (Illus.). 79p. 1997. 28.00 (*1-900347-21-0*, Pub. by Royal Botnic Grdns) Balogh.

Mitchell, J. F., ed. see Gaddum, John.

Mitchell, J. K. The Long Road to Recovery: Community Responses to Industrial Disaster. 313p. 30.00 (*92-808-0926-1*, UNUP-926) UN.

Mitchell, J. Leslie. Stained Radiance. 240p. (Orig.). 1993. pap. 15.95 (*0-7486-6141-7*, Pub. by Polygon) Subterranean Co.

Mitchell, J. M. International Cultural Relations. (Key Concepts in International Relations Ser.: No. 3). 256p. (C). 1986. text 55.00 (*0-04-327082-4*); pap. text 21.95 (*0 04-327083-2*) Routledge.

Mitchell, J. M., jt. ed. see Burland, J. B.

Mitchell, J. Murray, Jr., ed. Causes of Climatic Change: A Collection of Papers Derived from the INQUA-NCAR Symposium on Causes of Climate Change, August 30-31, 1968. (Meteorological Monograph Ser.: Vol. 8, No. 30). (Illus.). 159p. 1968. 25.00 (*0-933876-28-9*) Am Meteorological.

Mitchell, J. Paul, ed. Federal Housing Policy & Programs: Past & Present. LC 85-5737. 413p. 1985. pap. 1.00 (*0-88285-107-1*) Ctr Urban Pol Res.

Mitchell, J. R. & Blanshard, J. M., eds. Food Structure: Creation & Evaluation. 400p. 1987. 252.00 (*1-85573-396-X*) Am Educ Systs.

Mitchell, J. R., jt. auth. see Blanshard, J. M. V.

Mitchell, Jack. The Gun Digest Book of Riflesmithing. LC 82-72293. (Illus.). 256p. 1982. pap. 16.95 (*0-910676-47-X*, RIFL, DBI Bks) Krause Pubns.

— Icons & Idols: A Photographer's Chronicle of the Arts, 1960-1995. LC 98-27322. (Illus.). 160p. 1998. 40.00 (*0-8174-4025-9*) Watsn-Guptill.

Mitchell, Jack, photos by. Alvin Ailey American Dance Theater: Jack Mitchell Photographs. LC 93-13582. (Illus.). 160p. 1993. pap. 29.95 (*0-8362-4509-1*); pap. 19.95 (*0-8362-4508-3*) Andrews & McMeel.

Mitchell, Jack, jt. auth. see Morrissey, Maria.

Mitchell, Jack N. Social Exchange, Dramaturgy & Ethnomethodology: Toward a Paradigmatic Synthesis. LC 78-13198. 187p. 1981. lib. bdg. 35.00 (*0-444-99057-7*, MSX/) Greenwood.

Mitchell, Jacqueline, tr. see Grynberg, Henryk.

Mitchell, James. Bulimia Nervosa. 188p. (C). 1990. 27.95 (*0-8166-1626-4*) U of Minn Pr.

— Conservatives & the Union. 224p. 1990. 60.00 (*0-7486-0123-6*, Pub. by Edinburgh U Pr) Col U Pr.

— Conservatives & the Union: A Study of Conservative Party Attitudes to Scotland. 192p. 1991. pap. text 29.00 (*0-7486-0176-7*, Pub. by Edinburgh U Pr) Col U Pr.

— The Craft of Modular Post & Beam: Building Log & Timber Homes Affordably. rev. ed. LC 96-52327. Orig. Title: The Short Log & Timber Book. (Illus.). 320p. 1997. pap. 24.95 (*0-88179-131-8*) Hartley & Marks.

— Indian Summer. large type ed. (Charnwood Large Print Ser.). 400p. 1997. 27.99 (*0-7089-8944-6*, Charnwood) Ulverscroft.

— KGB Kill. large type ed. 416p. 1988. 11.50 (*0-7089-1883-2*) Ulverscroft.

— So Far from Home. 480p. 1996. mass mkt. 10.95 (*0-7472-4881-8*, Pub. by Headline Bk Pub) Trafalgar.

— So Far from Home. large type ed. (Charnwood Large Print Ser.). 512p. 1997. 27.99 (*0-7089-8896-2*, Charnwood) Ulverscroft.

— Strategies Towards Self-Government. (Determinations Ser.). 1996. pap. 24.00 (*0-7486-6113-1*, Pub. by Polygon) Subterranean Co.

Mitchell, James E. Maine Probate Procedure. 2nd rev. ed. 650p. 1994. spiral bd. 115.00 (*1-56257-303-9*, MICHIE) LEXIS Pub.

***Mitchell, James E.** Points of View: Stories of Psychopathology. 2000. pap. 29.95 (*1-58391-005-0*) Brunner-Mazel.

Mitchell, James E., ed. Anorexia Nervosa & Bulimia: Diagnosis & Treatment. LC 84-26933. (University of Minnesota Continuing Medical Education Ser.: Vol. 3). 223p. 1985. reprint ed. pap. 69.20 (*0-608-00793-5*, 205934200010) Bks Demand.

***Mitchell, James E., et al, eds.** Elements of Clinical Research in Psychiatry. LC 99-48422. 224p. 2000. 34.50 (*0-88048-802-6*) Am Psychiatric.

Mitchell, James E. & Hunt, Philip C. Maine Probate Procedure, Issue 6. LC 91-43264. 30p. 1998. ring bd. write for info. (*0-327-00555-6*, 8167616) LEXIS Pub.

Mitchell, James F. Caribbean Crusade. Bobrow, Jill R., ed. (Illus.). (Orig.). 1989. pap. write for info. (*0-9611712-0-0*) Concepts Pub.

— Guiding Change in the Islands: A Collection of Speeches. LC 96-29448. (Orig.). 1996. pap. 9.95 (*0-9611712-1-9*) Concepts Pub.

Mitchell, James K. Community Response to Coastal Erosion: Individual & Collective Adjustments to Hazard on the Atlantic Shore. LC 73-92652. (University of Chicago, Department of Geography, Research Paper Ser.: No. 156). 223p. 1974. reprint ed. pap. 69.20 (*0-608-02284-5*, 206292500004) Bks Demand.

— Crucibles of Hazard: Mega-cities & Disasters in Transition LC 99-6054. 1999. 34.95 (*92-808-0987-3*) UN Univ Pr.

— Fundamentals of Soil Behavior. 2nd ed. LC 92-21521. (Series in Geotechnical Engineering). 456p. 1993. 120.00 (*0-471-85640-1*) Wiley.

Mitchell, James O. Her Black Sparkles! (Illus.). pap. 7.50 (*0-9646017-1-0*) Thirty-Three Hund Pr.

Mitchell, James R. Gem Trails of Arizona. 3rd ed. Nordhues, Robin, ed. LC 94-74211. (Illus.). 184p. 1995. pap. 9.95 (*0-935182-82-9*) Gem Guides Bk.

— Gem Trails of Colorado. rev. ed. Nordhues, Robin, ed. (Illus.). 144p. (Orig.). 1997. pap. 9.95 (*0-935182-91-8*) Gem Guides Bk.

— Gem Trails of Nevada. Shepherd, Robin, ed. LC 91-77395. (Illus.). 120p. (Orig.). 1991. pap. 6.95 (*0-935182-53-5*) Gem Guides Bk.

— Gem Trails of New Mexico. LC 95-81797. (Illus.). 160p. 1996. pap. 9.95 (*0-935182-84-5*) Gem Guides Bk.

— Gem Trails of Northern California. Nordhues, Robin, ed. LC 94-78603. (Illus.). 160p. (Orig.). 1994. pap. 9.95 (*0-935182-67-5*) Gem Guides Bk.

Mitchell, James r. Gem Trails of Oregon. 2nd rev. ed. (Illus.). 1998. pap. 10.95 (*0-935182-99-3*) Gem Guides Bk.

Mitchell, James R. Gem Trails of Southern California. LC 95-75458. (Illus.). 176p. (Orig.). 1996. pap. 8.95 (*0-935182-83-7*) Gem Guides Bk.

Gem Trails of Texas. LC 87-83524. (Illus.). 104p. 1988. pap. 7.95 (*0-935182-34-9*) Gem Guides Bk.

— Gem Trails of Utah. LC 96-75814. (Illus.). 168p. 1996. pap. 9.95 (*0-935182-87-X*) Gem Guides Bk.

— The Rockhound's Handbook. LC 96-77412. (Illus.). 184p. (Orig.). 1996. pap. 12.95 (*0-935182-90-X*) Gem Guides Bk.

Mitchell, James T., compiled by. The Statutes at Large of Pennsylvania from 1682-1801, 17 vols., Set. LC 74-19615. reprint ed. 875.00 (*0-404-12413-5*) AMS Pr.

Mitchell, James V., Jr., ed. The Ninth Mental Measurements Yearbook. LC 39-3422. xxx, 2002p. 1985. 175.00 (*0-910674-29-9*) Buros Inst Mental.

Mitchell, James W., jt. auth. see Zief, Morris.

Mitchell, Jan. Luchow's German Cookbook. Date not set. lib. bdg. 21.95 (*0-8488-1752-4*) Amereon Ltd.

— Sales & Marketing Checklist. LC 97-16957. 1997. pap. 27.50 (*0-86718-435-3*) Home Builder.

***Mitchell, Jan & National Association of Home Builders Staff.** The Best of Sales & Marketing Ideas. LC 99-48470. (Illus.). 122p. 1999. pap. write for info. (*0-86718-488-4*) Home Builder.

Mitchell, Jan, jt. auth. see Mitchell, Mitch.

Mitchell, Jane. When the Stars Stop Spinning. 160p. 1996. pap. 8.95 (*1-85371-639-1*, Pub. by Poolbeg Pr) Dufour.

Mitchell, Jane T. A Thematic Analysis of Mme. D'Aulnoy's "Contes De Fees" LC 78-6947. (Romance Monographs: No. 30). 1978. 24.00 (*84-399-8448-0*) Romance.

Mitchell, Janet. Arizona, University Of: Bear Down: A Chronicle of Athletics at the University of Arizona. 176p. 1992. 29.95 (*0-89781-428-2*) Am Historical Pr.

— Faith Counts, Vol. 1. (Illus.). 4p. (Orig.). 1995. pap. text 4.50 (*0-9644012-2-3*) Heavenly Express.

— Faith Counts, Vol. 2. (Illus.). 8p. (Orig.). 1995. pap. text 6.00 (*0-9644012-3-1*) Heavenly Express.

— Faith Counts, Vol. 3. (Illus.). 8p. (Orig.). 1995. pap. text 6.00 (*0-9644012-4-X*) Heavenly Express.

Mitchell, Janet L. Out-of-Body Experiences. LC 81-8145. 140p. 1981. lib. bdg. 28.50 (*0-89950-031-5*) McFarland & Co.

Mitchell, Jann. Home Sweeter Home: Creating a Haven of Simplicity & Spirit. LC 96-4161. (Illus.). 256p. (C). 1996. pap. 12.95 (*1-885223-33-1*) Beyond Words Pub.

— Love Sweeter Love: Creating Relationships of Simplicity & Spirit. LC 97-49137. (Sweet Simplicity Ser.). (Illus.). 192p. 1998. pap. 12.95 (*1-885223-73-0*) Beyond Words Pub.

Mitchell, Jeffrey & Resnik, H. L. Emergency Response to Crisis. (Illus.). 256p. (C). 1981. text 24.95 (*0-87619-856-6*) P-H.

Mitchell, Jeffrey T. & Everly, George S., Jr. Critical Incident Stress Debriefing: An Operations Manual for the Prevention of Traumatic Stress among Emergency Services & Disaster Workers. 2nd ed. LC 97-193078. (Illus.). 290p. 1996. pap. text 35.00 (*1-883581-02-8*) Chevron Pub.

— Critical Incident Stress Management: The Basic Course Workbook. (Illus.). 78p. 1995. pap. 7.00 (*0-9646356-0-7*) ICISF.

***Mitchell, Jeffrey T. & Everly, George S., Jr.** Critical Incident Stress Management: The Basic Course Workbook. 2nd ed. 80p. 1998. wbk. ed. 8.50 (*0-9646356-2-3*) ICISF.

Mitchell, Jeffrey T. & Everly, George S. Human Elements Training for Emergency Services, Public Safety & Disaster Personnel: An Instructional Guide to Teaching Debriefing, Crisis Intervention & Stress Management Programs. 235p. 1994. pap. text 35.00 (*1-883581-01-X*) Chevron Pub.

Mitchell, Jeffrey T. & Everly, George S., Jr. A Slide Presentation for the Basic Critical Incident Stress Management Program. (Illus.). 80p. (Orig.). 1996. 295.00 incl. sl. (*1-883581-04-4*) Chevron Pub.

Mitchell, Jeffrey T. & Resnik, H. L. Emergency Response to Crisis. (Illus.). 214p. (C). 1994. pap. text 22.00 (*1-883581-11-7*) Chevron Pub.

Mitchell, Jeffrey T., jt. auth. see Everly, George S., Jr.

Mitchell, Jerome. More Scott Operas: Further Analysis of Operas Based on the Works of Sir Walter Scott. 348p. (C). 1996. lib. bdg. 44.00 (*0-7618-0260-6*) U Pr of Amer.

— Scott, Chaucer, & Medieval Romance: A Study in Sir Walter Scott's Indebtedness to the Literature of the Middle Ages. LC 87-8294. 280p. 1987. 34.95 (*0-8131-1609-0*) U Pr of Ky.

— Thomas Hoccleve: A Study in Early Fifteenth-Century English Poetic. LC 67-21855. (Illus.). 165p. reprint ed. 51.20 (*0-608-16118-7*, 201493800094) Bks Demand.

Mitchell, Jerome, jt. ed. see Helterman, Jeffrey.

Mitchell, Jerry. The American Experiment with Government Corporations. LC 98-17109. (Bureaucracies, Public Administration, & Public Policy Ser.). 224p. (gr. 13). 1999. text 57.95 (*0-7656-0361-6*); pap. text 25.95 (*0-7656-0362-4*) M E Sharpe.

Mitchell, Jerry, ed. Public Authorities & Public Policy. (Orig.). 1990. pap. 15.00 (*0-944285-15-5*) Pol Studies.

— Public Authorities & Public Policy: The Business of Government. LC 91-47088. (Contributions in Political Science Ser.: No. 301). 216p. 1992. pap. 21.95 (*0-275-94321-6*, B4321, Praeger Pubs) Greenwood.

— Public Authorities & Public Policy: The Business of Government, 301. LC 91-47972. (Contributions in Political Science Ser.: No. 301). 216p. 1992. 65.00 (*0-313-28503-9*, MBT, Greenwood Pr) Greenwood.

Mitchell, Jerry, et al. Human Figure Drawing Test, HFDT: An Illustrated Handbook for Clinical Interpretation & Standardized Assessment of Cognitive Impairment. (Illus.). 182p. 1993. pap. 49.50 (*0-87424-286-X*, W-286A) Western Psych.

Mitchell, Jerry T. & Cutter, Susan L. Global Change & Environmental Hazards: Is the World Becoming More Disastrous? (Active Learning Modules on the Human Dimensions of Global Change Ser.). (Illus.). 197p. (C) 1997. pap., teacher ed. 20.00 (*0-89291-245-6*); pap., student ed., wbk. ed. 8.75 (*0-89291-246-4*) Assn Am Geographers.

Mitchell, Jet. Finding Funds for a Free Education. (Illus.). 8p. 1994. pap. 2.50 (*1-884241-43-3*, JET1) Energeia Pub.

Mitchell, Joan. Joan Mitchell: Trees & Other Paintings, 1960-1990. (Illus.). 34p. (Orig.). 1992. pap. 15.00 (*1-881138-01-1*) Tallgrass Pr.

— Writing with a Computer. (C). 1989. pap. text 23.56 (*0-395-50515-1*) HM.

— Writing with a Computer. (C). 1989. pap. text, teacher ed. 4.36 (*0-395-50516-X*) HM.

Mitchell, Joan. Joan Mitchell: Bedford Series. 32p. pap. 10.00 (*0-614-13075-1*) Tyler Graphics Ltd.

Mitchell, Joan S., intro. Summaries DDC 21: Dewey Decimal Classification. 21st ed. 20p. 1996. pap. 3.00 (*0-910608-57-1*) OCLC Forest Pr.

Mitchell, Joan S., jt. ed. see Chan, Lois M.

Mitchell, Joan S., ed. see Dewey, Melvil.

Mitchell, Joann, jt. auth. see LeBaron, Gaye.

Mitchell, Joe. Saturday's Heroes. 128p. (Orig.). 1994. pap. 8.95 (*1-898928-05-3*) AK Pr Dist.

Mitchell, John. Alaska Stories. LC 84-60667. 75p. 1984. 11.50 (*0-917635-00-0*); pap. 6.95 (*0-917635-01-9*) Plover Pr.

— Eccentric Lives & Peculiar Notions. (Illus.). 240p. 1987. pap. 7.95 (*0-8065-1031-5*, Citadel Pr) Carol Pub Group.

— Exile in Alaska. LC 86-30277. 113p. 1987. 13.95 (*0-917635-02-7*); pap. 7.95 (*0-917635-03-5*) Plover Pr.

— On the Seventh Day: Portrait of the Artist As a Creative Writer. LC 96-53995. (Plover Nivola Ser.). 90p. 1997. 15.95 (*0-917635-22-1*); pap. 7.95 (*0-917635-25-6*) Plover Pr.

M

An Asterisk (*) at the beginning of an entry indicates that the title is appearing for the first time.

— On the Window Licks the Night: A Nivola. LC 93-48949. (Plover Nivola Ser.). 104p. 1994. pap. 8.95 (*0-917635-18-3*) Plover Pr.

— Organized Labor: Its Problems, Purposes & Ideals & the Present & Future of American Wage Earners. LC 68-56263. (Library of American Labor History). (Illus.). xii, 436p. 1973. reprint ed. 49.50 (*0-678-00733-0*) Kelley.

— Prehistoric Great Lakes: An Illustrated History for Children. (Illus.). 48p. (J). (gr. 2-7). 1999. 16.95 (*0-9621466-3-3*) Suttons Bay Pubns.

***Mitchell, John.** The Temple at Jerusalem: A Revelation. 80p. 2000. (*1-57863-198-X*) Weiser.

Mitchell, John. What the Hell Is a Groom & What's He Supposed to Do? LC 98-37652. 1999. 12.95 (*0-8362-7869-0*) Andrews & McMeel.

Mitchell, John & Smith, Donald M. Aquametry: A Treatise on Methods for the Determination of Water, Pt. 1. LC 77-518. (Chemical Analysis Ser.: Vol. 5). 646p. reprint ed. pap. 200.00 (*0-7837-2402-0*, 204008700006) Bks Demand.

Mitchell, John, tr. see Huidobro, Matias M.

Mitchell, John, tr. see Molina, Silvia.

Mitchell, John, tr. see Romero, Jose R.

Mitchell, John, tr. see Taibo, Paco I., 2nd.

Mitchell, John A. Drowsy. LC 74-16512. (Science Fiction Ser.). (Illus.). 316p. 1975. reprint ed. 25.95 (*0-405-06306-7*) Ayer.

— The Last American. LC 75-104529. reprint ed. lib. bdg. 22.75 (*0-8398-1262-0*) Irvington.

— The Silent War. LC 68-57541. (Muckrakers Ser.). (Illus.). 222p. 1979. reprint ed. lib. bdg. 27.00 (*0-8398-1263-9*) Irvington.

— The Silent War. (Muckrakers Ser.). (Illus.). 222p. (C). 1986. reprint ed. pap. text 6.95 (*0-8290-2004-7*) Irvington.

— That First Affair: Other Sketches. LC 77-98587. (Short Story Index Reprint Ser.). 1977. 19.95 (*0-8369-3161-0*) Ayer.

Mitchell, John B. Seattle University Skills Development Series: Criminal Procedure, 1995. 1995. text 15.00 (*1-55834-219-2*) Bender.

Mitchell, John C. Foundations for Programming Languages. LC 95-45243. (Foundations of Computing Ser.). (Illus.). 868p. (C). 1996. 71.50 (*0-262-13321-0*) MIT Pr.

— Great Lakes & Great Ships: An Illustrated History for Children. (Illus.). 52p. (J). (gr. 2-7). 1991. 16.95 (*0-9621466-1-7*) Suttons Bay Pubns.

***Mitchell, John C.** Hedwig & the Angry Inch. 2000. 21.95 (*1-58567-034-0*, Pub. by Overlook Pr) Penguin Putnam.

Mitchell, John C. Indians of the Great Lakes: An Illustrated History for Children. (Illus.). 48p. (J). (gr. 3-8). 1995. 16.95 (*0-9621466-2-5*) Suttons Bay Pubns.

— Michigan: An Illustrated History for Children. 2nd ed. (Illus.). 52p. (J). (gr. 1-6). 1987. reprint ed. 16.95 (*0-9621466-0-9*) Suttons Bay Pubns.

Mitchell, John C., jt. ed. see Gunter, Carl A.

Mitchell, John C., jt. ed. see Hagiya, Masami.

Mitchell, John D. The Director-Actor Relationship: Essays & Articles by John D. Mitchell. LC 92-71961. (Illus.). 180p. (Orig.). (C). 1992. pap. 19.95 (*1-882763-03-3*) IASTA.

— Gift of Apollo: The Autobiography of John D. Mitchell. LC 92-75254. (Illus.). 418p. (Orig.). (C). 1992. pap. 19.95 (*1-882763-04-1*) IASTA.

— Lost Mines & Buried Treasures along the Old Frontier. LC 77-121730. (Beautiful Rio Grande Classics Ser.). (Illus.). 260p. 1982. reprint ed. pap. 12.00 (*0-87380-144-X*) Popular E Commerce.

— Lost Mines of the Great Southwest. LC 70-114964. (Beautiful Rio Grande Classics Ser.). (Illus.). 202p. 1984. reprint ed. pap. 10.00 (*0-87380-013-3*) Popular E Commerce.

— Making a Broadway Musical: Making It Run, an Anatomy of Entrepreneurship. (Illus.). 131p. 1989. 25.00 (*0-87359-050-3*) Northwood Univ.

— Phedre on Stage. LC 87-61041. 294p. 1987. 25.00 (*0-87359-047-3*); pap. 17.50 (*0-685-25024-5*) Northwood Univ.

— Staging Chekhov: Cherry Orchard. LC 91-73015. (ENG & RUS., Illus.). 416p. (Orig.). (C). 1991. pap. 19.95 (*1-882763-00-9*) IASTA.

Mitchell, John D. & Sarabhai, Mrinalini. Staging a Sanskrit Drama: Bhasa's Vision of Vasavadatta. LC 92-70319. (ENG & SAN., Illus.). 240p. (Orig.). (C). 1992. pap. 19.95 (*1-882763-02-5*) IASTA.

Mitchell, John D., et al. Staging Japanese Theatre: Noh & Kabuki. (Illus.). 245p. (Orig.). (C). pap. text 24.95 (*1-882763-06-8*) IASTA.

Mitchell, John D., jt. auth. see Ernst, Earle.

Mitchell, John D., jt. auth. see Packard, William.

Mitchell, John D., jt. auth. see Royce, Jack.

Mitchell, John D., ed. see Lobb, Roger.

Mitchell, John E. & Pickens, James B. An Evaluation of Procedures Used to Predict Timber Growth & Harvest in the Range & Multiple Resource Interactions Sections of the 1980 RPA Assessment. (Illus.). 18p. 1997. reprint ed. pap. 2.80 (*0-89904-910-9*, Ecosytems Resrch) Crumb Elbow Pub.

Mitchell, John F. Visions at Work: Decision-Making Strategy for the Business Leader. LC 95-37230. 1995. pap. write for info. (*0-07-709085-3*) McGraw.

Mitchell, John G. Descubriendo la Palabra de Dios. (Serie Discipulado - Discipleship Ser.).Tr. of Discovering God's Word. (SPA.). 29p. 1992. pap. 1.99 (*1-56063-361-1*, 498224) Editorial Unilit.

— Dispatches from the Deep Woods. LC 90-36842. 318p. 1991. reprint ed. pap. 98.60 (*0-7837-8906-8*, 204961700001) Bks Demand.

— The Man Who Would Dam the Amazon & Other Accounts from Afield. LC 89-78517. 382p. 1990. reprint ed. pap. 118.50 (*0-7837-8907-6*, 204961800001) Bks Demand.

Mitchell, John H. Ceremonial Time: Fifteen Thousand Years on One Square Mile. LC 96-40349. 1997. pap. 13.00 (*0-201-14937-0*) Addison-Wesley.

— A Field Guide to Your Own Backyard. LC 98-53173. (Illus.). 288p. 1999. reprint ed. pap. 13.95 (*0-88150-474-2*, Pub. by Countryman) Norton.

— Trespassing. LC 97-45190. 336p. 1998. 25.00 (*0-201-44214-0*) Addison-Wesley.

— Trespassing: An Inquiry into the Private Ownership of Land. 320p. 1999. pap. text 15.00 (*0-7382-0146-4*, Pub. by Perseus Pubng) HarpC.

— Walking Towards Walden. LC 96-51483. 1997. pap. 13.00 (*0-201-15487-0*) Addison-Wesley.

— Writing for Technical & Professional Journals. LC 67-31374. (Wiley Series on Human Communication). (Illus.). 415p. reprint ed. pap. 128.70 (*0-608-11425-1*, 201646900002) Bks Demand.

***Mitchell, John Hanson.** Trespassing: An Inquiry into the Private Ownership of Land. 291p. 2000. text 25.00 (*0-7881-9091-1*) DIANE Pub.

Mitchell, John J. Adolescent Struggle for Selfhood & Identity. 218p. (Orig.). (C). 1992. pap. text 18.95 (*1-55059-050-2*) Temeron Bks.

— Adolescent Vulnerability. 255p. (Orig.). 1995. pap. text write for info. (*1-55059-128-2*) Detselig Ents.

— Human Growth & Development: The Childhood Years. 281p. (Orig.). (C). 1990. pap. text 16.95 (*1-55059-002-2*) Temeron Bks.

— The Natural Limitations of Youth: The Predispositions That Shape the Adolescent Character. LC 97-40928. (Developments in Clinical Psychology Ser.). 1998. 73.25 (*1-56750-372-1*); pap. 39.50 (*1-56750-373-X*) Ablx Pub.

Mitchell, John P. Stanford University, 1916-1941. LC 58-59714. 176p. 1958. reprint ed. pap. 30.00 (*0-608-08335-6*, 202492700039) Bks Demand.

Mitchell, John P., jt. auth. see Smith, William V.

Mitchell, John S. An Introduction to Machinery Analysis & Monitoring. 2nd ed. LC 93-30765. 374p. 1993. 84.95 (*0-87814-401-3*) PennWell Bks.

Mitchell, Johnny. Energy--& How We Lost It. LC 78-62621. 240p. 1979. reprint ed. pap. 74.40 (*0-608-07938-3*, 206791100012) Bks Demand.

***Mitchell, Jolyon.** Visually Speaking: Radio & the Renaissance of Preaching. 304p. 2000. pap. 29.95 (*0-664-22244-7*, Pub. by Westminster John Knox) Presbyterian Pub.

***Mitchell, Jolyon P.** Visually Speaking: Radio & the Renaissance of Preaching. 304p. 1999. pap. 24.95 (*0-567-08701-8*) T&T Clark Pubs.

Mitchell, Joni. Joni Mitchell. LC 97-33397. 317p. 1997. 27.50 (*0-609-60008-7*) Random Hse Value.

— Joni Mitchell: The Complete Poems & Lyrics. 352p. 1998. pap. 15.00 (*0-609-80218-6*, Crown) Crown Pub Group.

— Memoirs. 2004. 27.50 (*0-609-60006-0*) Crown Pub Group.

***Mitchell, Joseph.** Joe Gould's Secret. 208p. 2000. 14.95 (*0-679-60339-5*) Random.

— Joe Gould's Secret. 192p. 1999. pap. 9.95 (*0-375-70804-9*) Vin Bks.

Mitchell, Joseph. Up in the Old Hotel. LC 92-50835. 1993. pap. 16.00 (*0-679-74631-5*) Random.

Mitchell, Joseph B. The Badge of Gallantry: Letters from Civil War Medal of Honor Winners. LC 97-49155. 195p. 1998. 24.95 (*1-57249-093-4*) White Mane Pub.

— Decisive Battles of the Civil War. 1985. mass mkt. 5.99 (*0-449-30031-5*, Q745, Prem) Fawcett.

***Mitchell, Joseph B.** Military Leaders in the Civil War. 252p. 1999. pap. 40.00 (*1-86227-075-9*, Pub. by Spellmnt Pubs) St Mut.

Mitchell, Joseph B. Military Leaders of the Civil War. LC 88-24681. (Illus.). 251p. 1988. reprint ed. pap. 10.95 (*0-939009-13-7*, EPM) Howell Pr VA.

Mitchell, Joseph C. The Reptiles of Virginia. LC 93-42002. (Illus.). 384p. 1994. 40.00 (*1-56098-356-6*) Smithsonian.

— The Reptiles of Virginia. (Illus.). 368p. 1997. pap. 24.95 (*1-56098-754-5*) Smithsonian.

Mitchell, Joseph S. Studies in Radiotherapeutics. LC 60-3368. (Illus.). 281p. 1960. 23.95 (*0-674-84930-2*) HUP.

Mitchell, Joshua. The Fragility of Freedom: Tocqueville on Religion, Democracy & the American Future. LC 94-48763. 288p. 1995. 34.95 (*0-226-53208-9*) U Ch Pr.

— Fragility of Freedom: Tocqueville on Religion, Democracy & the American Future: Tocqueville on Religion, Democracy, & the American Future. 274p. 1999. pap. text 16.00 (*0-226-53209-7*) U Ch Pr.

— Not by Reason Alone: Religion, History, & Identity in Early Modern Political Thought. LC 93-3048. 272p. 1993. 34.95 (*0-226-53221-6*) U Ch Pr.

— Not by Reason Alone: Religion, History, & Identity in Early Modern Political Thought. xii, 252p. 1996. pap. text 16.95 (*0-226-53222-4*) U Ch Pr.

Mitchell, Joshua, jt. ed. see Douglass, R. Bruce.

Mitchell, Joy-Elizabeth. The Pictish Colouring Book. (Illus.). 36p. (J). 1998. pap. 9.95 (*1-900428-26-1*) Dufour.

— The Viking Colouring Book. 36p. 1996. pap. 9.95 (*0-946005-94-X*) Dufour.

Mitchell, Joyce. Other Choices for Becoming a Woman. (YA). (gr. 7 up). 1975. pap. 6.00 (*0-912786-34-5*) Know Inc.

Mitchell, Joyce S. College Board Guide to Jobs & Career Planning. 2nd ed. 328p. (C). 1994. pap. 14.00 (*0-87447-467-1*) College Bd.

— Winning the Chemo Battle. 1991. pap. 11.00 (*0-393-30713-1*) Norton.

Mitchell, Joyce S., ed. see RVer Annie.

***Mitchell, Joyce Slayton.** Tractor-Trailer Trucker: A Powerful Truck Book. LC 99-38509. (Illus.). 40p. (YA). (gr. 2-5). 2000. 14.95 (*1-58246-010-8*) Tricycle Pr.

Mitchell, Joyce Slayton & Mitchell, Elizabeth Dix. A Special Delivery: Mother-Daughter Letters from Afar. 144p. 1999. pap. 12.95 (*0-9667393-5-3*) EquiLib Pr.

Mitchell, Joyce Slayton, see Mitchell, Joyce Slayton.

Mitchell, Judith. The Stone & the Scorpion: The Female Subject of Desire in the Novels of Charlotte Bronte, George Eliot, & Thomas Hardy, 142. LC 93-43751. (Contributions in Women's Studies: Vol. 42). 240p. 1994. 59.95 (*0-313-29043-1*, Greenwood Pr) Greenwood.

Mitchell, Judith A., jt. auth. see Poploff, Michelle.

Mitchell, Judy, ed. Cut & Create! At the Zoo: Easy Step-by-Step Projects That Teach Scissor Skills. (Illus.). 80p. (J). (ps-2). 1994. pap., teacher ed. 8.95 (*1-57310-010-2*) Teachng & Lrning Co.

— Cut & Create! For All Seasons: Easy Step-by-Step Projects That Teach Scissor Skills. (Illus.). 80p. (Orig.). (J). (ps-2). 1995. pap. 8.95 (*1-57310-020-X*) Teachng & Lrning Co.

— Cut & Create! On the Farm: Easy Step-by-Step Projects That Teach Scissor Skills. (Illus.). 80p. (Orig.). (J). (ps-2). 1995. pap. 8.95 (*1-57310-019-6*) Teachng & Lrning Co.

— Shapes to Cut: Animals. (Illus.). 32p. (J). (ps-1). 1998. pap., teacher ed. 4.95 (*1-57310-132-X*) Teachng & Lrning Co.

— Shapes to Cut: Food. (Illus.). 32p. (J). (ps-1). 1998. pap., teacher ed. 4.95 (*1-57310-133-8*) Teachng & Lrning Co.

— Shapes to Cut: Hats & Vehicles. (Illus.). 32p. (J). (ps-1). 1998. pap., teacher ed. 4.95 (*1-57310-134-6*) Teachng & Lrning Co.

— Shapes to Cut: Holidays. (Illus.). 32p. (J). (ps-1). 1998. pap., teacher ed. 4.95 (*1-57310-136-2*) Teachng & Lrning Co.

— Shapes to Cut: Plants & Shapes. (Illus.). 32p. (J). (ps-1). 1998. pap., teacher ed. 4.95 (*1-57310-135-4*) Teachng & Lrning Co.

***Mitchell, Judy, ed.** Things to Count: Animals 6-10. (Illus.). 32p. (J). 2000. pap. 4.95 (*1-57310-224-5*) Teachng & Lrning Co.

— Things to Count: Fun with Numbers. 32p. (J). 2000. pap. 4.95 (*1-57310-227-X*) Teachng & Lrning Co.

— Things to Count: Holidays 16-20. (Illus.). 32p. (J). 2000. pap. 4.95 (*1-57310-226-1*) Teachng & Lrning Co.

— Things to Count: Vehicles 1-5. (Illus.). 32p. (J). (ps-1). 2000. pap. 4.95 (*1-57310-223-7*) Teachng & Lrning Co.

Mitchell, Judy & Borst, Donna, eds. Holidays & Seasonal Celebrations Issues 1-8 Clip Art Collection. (Clip Art Collection: Issues 1-8). (Illus.). 64p. (J). (ps-8). 1998. pap., teacher ed. 8.95 (*1-57310-131-1*) Teachng & Lrning Co.

Mitchell, Judy, ed. see Barden, Cindy.

Mitchell, Judy, jt. ed. see Borst, Donna.

Mitchell, Judy, ed. see Boyko, Carrie J. & Rodgers, Julie B.

Mitchell, Judy, ed. see Campbell, Pam.

Mitchell, Judy, ed. see Carroll, Jeri A.

Mitchell, Judy, ed. see Carroll, Jeri A., et al.

Mitchell, Judy, ed. see Cavalline, Jo Jo & O'Donnell, Jo Anne.

Mitchell, Judy, ed. see Clevenger, Bev.

Mitchell, Judy, ed. see Colen, Kimberly.

Mitchell, Judy, ed. see Daniel, Becky.

Mitchell, Judy, ed. see Eagan, Robynne.

Mitchell, Judy, ed. see Eagan, Robynne & Schofield, Tracey A.

Mitchell, Judy, ed. see Eagan, Robynne & Schofield, Tracey Ann.

Mitchell, Judy, ed. see Feeser, Bonnie J.

Mitchell, Judy, ed. see Finkel, Susan & Seberg, Karen.

Mitchell, Judy, ed. see Fisher, Ann R.

Mitchell, Judy, ed. see Fisher, Ann Richmond.

Mitchell, Judy, ed. see Fisher, Ann R. & Fisher, Betsy.

Mitchell, Judy, ed. see Fisher, Ann R. & Fisher, Bryce A.

Mitchell, Judy, ed. see Gould, Judith S. & Gould, Evan J.

Mitchell, Judy, ed. see Gust, John & McChesney, J. Meghan.

Mitchell, Judy, ed. see Hajek, Ellen.

Mitchell, Judy, ed. see Hargrove, Julia.

Mitchell, Judy, ed. see Hein, Marilyn B.

Mitchell, Judy, ed. see Hierstein, Judy.

Mitchell, Judy, ed. see Julio, Susan.

Mitchell, Judy, ed. see Karges-Bone, Linda.

Mitchell, Judy, ed. see Lippman, Jack C.

Mitchell, Judy, ed. see Lipson, Greta B.

Mitchell, Judy, ed. see Majors-Williams, Michelle L.

Mitchell, Judy, ed. see Marion, Cynthia & Hirsh, Carol.

Mitchell, Judy, ed. see McKenzie, Julie & McKenzie, Thomas.

Mitchell, Judy, ed. see McMillan, Dana.

Mitchell, Judy, ed. see Miescke, Lori.

Mitchell, Judy, ed. see Moen, Christine B.

Mitchell, Judy, ed. see Moen, Christine Boardman.

Mitchell, Judy, ed. see O'Brien, Patricia.

Mitchell, Judy, ed. see Rankin, Kim.

Mitchell, Judy, ed. see Rife, Douglas M.

Mitchell, Judy, ed. see Shevick, Edward.

Mitchell, Judy, ed. see Upson, Greta Barclay.

Mitchell, Judy, ed. see Whitacre, Deborah & Radtke, Becky J.

***Mitchell, Julia H.** Estimation Skills, Mathematics-in-context & Advanced Skills in Mathematics: Results from Three Studies of the National Assessment of Educational Progress 1996 Mathematics Assessment. 284p. 1999. per. 25.00 (*0-16-050209-8*) USGPO.

Mitchell, Julia P. St. Jean de Crevecoeur. LC 71-181959. reprint ed. 37.50 (*0-404-04347-X*) AMS Pr.

— St. Jean de Crevecoeur. (BCL1-PS American Literature Ser.). 362p. 1992. reprint ed. lib. bdg. 89.00 (*0-7812-6660-2*) Rprt Serv.

Mitchell, Julian, jt. auth. see Rudnicki, Stefan.

Mitchell, Juliann Whetsell. The Dynamics of Crisis Intervention: Loss as the Common Denominator. LC 98-34004. 299p. 1999. 59.95 (*0-398-06915-8*); pap. 47.95 (*0-398-06916-6*) C C Thomas.

Mitchell, Julie, ed. see OKeefe, JoAnna.

***Mitchell, Juliet.** Mad Men & Medusas: Reclaiming Hysteria. 352p. 2000. 30.00 (*0-465-04613-4*, Pub. by Basic) HarpC.

— Psychoanalysis & Feminism. 512p. 2000. pap. 18.00 (*0-465-04608-8*, Pub. by Basic) HarpC.

Mitchell, Juliet, ed. The Selected Melanie Klein: The Essential Writings. 256p. (Orig.). 1987. pap. 14.95 (*0-02-921481-5*) Free Pr.

Mitchell, Juliet & Rose, Jacqueline, eds. Feminine Sexuality: Jacques Lacan & the Ecole Freudienne. 1985. pap. 13.95 (*0-393-30211-3*) Norton.

Mitchell, Juliet, ed. see Balint, Enid.

Mitchell, Juliet, jt. ed. see Oakley, Ann.

Mitchell, K. A Taste of Philippines. (Illus.). 40p. 1979. 5.95 (*0-318-36280-5*) Asia Bk Corp.

Mitchell, Karen. All That We Need. LC 98-150497. 95p. 1998. pap. 5.95 (*0-89114-290-8*) Baptist Pub Hse.

***Mitchell, Karen & Hawthorne, David.** Contractor's Guide to Peachtree Complete Accounting. 90p. 1999. 29.99 (*0-926111-10-8*) Peachtree Soft.

Mitchell, Karen, et al. Contractor's Guide to QuickBooks Pro. LC 98-22681. (Illus.). 296p. 1998. pap. 39.75 (*1-57218-069-2*) Craftsman.

— Contractor's Guide to Quickbooks Pro 99. 2nd rev. ed. LC 99-32980. (Illus.). 296p. 1999. pap. 42.00 (*1-57218-078-1*) Craftsman.

***Mitchell, Karen, et al.** Contractor's Guide to QuickBooks Pro 2000. 3rd rev. ed. (Illus.). 296p. 2000. pap. 44.50 (*1-57218-090-0*) Craftsman.

Mitchell, Karen, et al. Quicken for Contractors. LC 97-46798. (Illus.). 240p. 1998. pap. 32.50 (*1-57218-043-9*) Craftsman.

Mitchell, Karen, jt. auth. see Bodilly, Susan.

Mitchell, Karen J., et al. Reforming & Conforming: NASDC Principals Discuss School Accountability Systems. LC 96-43663. 1996. pap. 15.00 (*0-8330-2440-X*, MR-716-NASDC) Rand Corp.

Mitchell, Karen L. The Eating Hill. LC 89-23631. 96p. 1989. pap. 10.95 (*0-933377-04-5*, Pub. by Eighth Mount Pr) Consort Bk Sales.

Mitchell, Karyn. Transformational Reiki: Trans-Reiki. 250p. (Orig.). 1997. pap. 19.96 (*0-9640822-6-8*) Mind Rivers.

Mitchell, Karyn, et al. Reiki Mystery School: Transformational Reiki. (Illus.). 220p. (Orig.). 1997. pap. text 19.95 (*0-9640822-5-X*) Mind Rivers.

Mitchell, Karyn K. Abductions: Stop Them Now. (Illus.). 96p. (Orig.). 1995. pap. text, per. 9.95 (*0-9640822-3-3*) Mind Rivers.

— Reiki: A Torch in Daylight. LC 94-75679. 128p. 1994. pap., student ed. 14.95 (*0-9640822-1-7*) Mind Rivers.

— Reiki: Beyond the Usui System. 256p. (Orig.). 1994. pap., student ed. 19.96 (*0-9640822-2-5*) Mind Rivers.

— Walk-Ins: Soul Exchange. unabridged ed. (Illus.). 200p. (Orig.). 1999. pap. 19.95 (*0-9640822-4-1*) Mind Rivers.

Mitchell, Karyn K., jt. auth. see Mitchell, Steven.

Mitchell, Kath, jt. auth. see Mitchell, Gerald.

Mitchell, Kathleen & Wood, Ian, eds. The World of Gregory of Tours. (Illus.). 408p. 1998. 115.50 (*90-04-11034-8*) Brill Academic Pubs.

Mitchell, Kathleen R. Island Adventure. Gormley, Mary, ed. (Illus.). 48p. (J). (ps-7). 1999. boxed set 18.00 (*0-9669648-0-2*) K R Mitchell.

***Mitchell, Kathleen Riley.** Island Adventure. LC 00-90885. 48p. (J). (ps-7). 2000. boxed set 18.00 (*0-9669648-1-0*) K R Mitchell.

Mitchell, Kathy. Ally McBeal: The Totally Unauthorized Guide. LC 98-86739. 192p. 1998. mass mkt. 12.99 (*0-446-67532-6*, Pub. by Warner Bks) Little.

— Joy of Christmas: Favorite Stories, Poems, & Recipes. 1995. 8.05 (*0-606-07752-9*, Pub. by Turtleback) Demco.

— The Joy of Christmas: Favorites Stories, Poems, & Recipes. LC 95-19113. (Illus.). 96p. (J). (gr. 1 up). 1995. pap. 2.95 (*0-8167-3783-5*, Little Rainbow) Troll Communs.

— Silent Night: A Christmas Book with Lights & Music. (Illus.). 12p. (J). (ps-3). 1989. mass mkt. 11.95 (*0-689-71330-4*) Aladdin.

Mitchell, Kathy. Valentine Thoughts. (Sparkle 'n' Twinkle Bks.). (J). (ps-2). 1997. 4.99 (*0-614-29111-9*) Litle Simon.

Mitchell, Kathy & Publications International, Ltd. Editorial Staff. Classic Fairy Tales. LC 98-220439. (Illus.). 88p. (J). 1998. write for info. (*0-7853-2702-9*) Pubns Intl Ltd.

Mitchell, Kathy, jt. auth. see Baum, L. Frank.

Mitchell, Kathy, jt. auth. see Carroll, Lewis, pseud.

Mitchell, Kathy, jt. auth. see Fehlner, Paul.

Mitchell, Kathy, jt. auth. see Holland, Isabelle.

Mitchell, Kathy, jt. auth. see Kunhardt, Edith.

Mitchell, Kay. In Stony Places. 1993. mass mkt. 3.99 (*0-373-26126-8*, 1-26126-2) Harlequin Bks.

— In Stony Places. large type ed. 336p. 1994. 11.50 (*0-7089-3115-4*) Ulverscroft.

— A Lively Form of Death. large type ed. (General Ser.). 336p. 1993. 27.99 (*0-7089-2864-1*) Ulverscroft.

— A Portion for Foxes. 1997. per. 4.99 (*0-373-26235-3*, 1-26235-1, Wrldwide Lib) Harlequin Bks.

— A Rage of Innocents. 1999. per. 4.99 (*0-373-26318-X*, Wrldwide Lib) Harlequin Bks.

An Asterisk (*) at the beginning of an entry indicates that the title is appearing for the first time.

M

An Asterisk (*) at the beginning of an entry indicates that the title is appearing for the first time.

Mitchell, Mark S. The Curious Kingship of Sir George. LC 99-476020. (The Chronicles of the House of Chax Ser.: Bk. 3). 89p. (J). (gr. 3-6). 1998. pap. 9.99 (*0-88092-355-5*, 3555) Royal Fireworks.

Mitchell Market Reports Staff. Zirconia. 250p. 1993. 1090.25 (*1-85617-181-7*, Pub. by Elsvr Adv Tech) Elsevier.

***Mitchell, Mary.** The Complete Idiot's Guide to Business Etiquette. 400p. 1999. pap. text 16.95 (*0-02-863615-5*) Macmillan.

Mitchell, Mary. Complete Idiot's Guide to Etiquette. (Illus.). 1996. 16.95 (*0-02-861094-6*) Macmillan Gen Ref.

— Dear Ms. Demeanor: The Young Person's Etiquette Guide to Handling Any Social Situation with Confidence & Grace. LC 95-30789. 240p. 1995. pap. 9.95 (*0-8092-3272-3*, 327230, Contemporary Bks) NTC Contemp Pub Co.

Mitchell, Mary & Corr, John. The First Five Minutes: How to Make a Great First Impression in Any Business Situation. LC 97-37395. 224p. 1998. pap. 14.95 (*0-471-18478-0*) Wiley.

Mitchell, Mary, jt. auth. see Crowe, Sylvia.

Mitchell, Mary A. Drawn to the Grave. 320p. (Orig.). 1997. mass mkt. 4.99 (*0-8439-4290-8*, Leisure Bks) Dorchester Pub Co.

***Mitchell, Mary Ann.** Drawn to the Grave. 320p. (Orig.). 1999. reprint ed. mass mkt. 4.99 (*0-8439-4638-5*, Pub. by Dorchester Pub Co) CMG.

— Quenched. 368p. 2000. mass mkt. 5.50 (*0-8439-4717-9*, Leisure Bks) Dorchester Pub Co.

Mitchell, Mary Ann. Sips of Blood. 368p. 1999. mass mkt. 5.50 (*0-8439-4555-9*, Leisure Bks) Dorchester Pub Co.

Mitchell, Mary H. History of New Haven County, Connecticut, 3 vols. (Illus.). 2099p. 1997. reprint ed. lib. bdg. 210.00 (*0-8328-5669-X*) Higginson Bk Co.

— Hollywood Cemetery: The Story of a Southern Shrine. (Illus.). xiv, 194p. 1985. 25.00 (*0-88490-109-2*) Library of VA.

Mitchell, Mary K. Nutrition Across the Lifespan: The Life Cycle. Connor, Maura, ed. 432p. 1997. pap. text 51.00 (*0-7216-3784-1*, W B Saunders Co) Harcrt Hlth Sci Grp.

Mitchell, Mary Kay, ed. Nutrition Across the Life Span: The Life Cycle. (Illus.). 512p. 1997. pap., teacher ed. write for info. (*0-7216-5031-7*, W B Saunders Co) Harcrt Hlth Sci Grp.

***Mitchell, Mary L., et al.** Expressions: An Anthology of Poetry, Short Stories & Stuff Like That. 300p. 2000. pap. 14.95 (*1-893196-04-6*) Brittney Pr.

Mitchell, Marybelle. From Talking Chiefs to a Native Corporate Elite: The Birth of Class & Nationalism among Canadian Inuit. LC 97-160439. (McGill-Queen's Native & Northern Ser.). (Illus.). 568p. 1996. 60.00 (*0-7735-1374-4*) McG-Queens Univ Pr.

Mitchell, Maurice & Bevan, Andy. Culture, Cash & Housing: Community & Tradition in Low-Income Building. (Illus.). 130p. 1992. pap. 17.50 (*1-85339-153-0*, Pub. by Intermed Tech) Stylus Pub VA.

Mitchell, Melanie. Analogy-Making As Perception: A Computer Model. LC 92-38045. (Neural Network Modeling & Connectionism Ser.). 284p. 1993. 47.50 (*0-262-13289-3*, Bradford Bks) MIT Pr.

— An Introduction to Genetic Algorithms. LC 95-24489. (Illus.). 217p. 1996. 40.00 (*0-262-13316-4*, Bradford Bks) MIT Pr.

— An Introduction to Genetic Algorithms. (Complex Adaptive Systems Ser.). (Illus.). 224p. 1998. reprint ed. pap. text 22.00 (*0-262-63185-7*, Bradford Bks) MIT Pr.

Mitchell, Melisa, ed. Best Poems of 1997, Vol. B. 1997. 69.95 (*1-57553-655-2*) Watermrk Pr.

— The Ever Flowing Stream. 1997. 69.95 (*1-57553-571-8*) Watermrk Pr.

— The Lasting Joy. 1998. 69.95 (*1-57553-616-1*) Watermrk Pr.

— The Long & Winding Road. LC 97-228380. 1997. 69.95 (*1-57553-407-X*) Watermrk Pr.

— Passages of Light. 1998. 69.95 (*1-57553-609-9*) Watermrk Pr.

— Priceless Treasures. 1997. 69.95 (*1-57553-576-9*) Watermrk Pr.

— The SOF Parade. 1998. 69.95 (*1-57553-732-X*) Nat Lib Poetry.

— Through the Looking Glass. 1997. 19.95 (*1-57553-401-0*) Nat Lib Poetry.

— A Whispering Silence. 1997. 69.95 (*1-57553-566-1*) Watermrk Pr.

Mitchell, Melissa, ed. Andrews Diet Drugs Litigation Source Book. 216p. 1997. pap. 85.00 (*1-890155-03-9*) Andrews Pubns.

— Lyrical Heritage. 1996. 69.95 (*1-57553-157-7*) Watermrk Pr.

— The Nightfall of Diamonds. 1997. 69.95 (*1-57553-351-0*) Nat Lib Poetry.

— Of Moonlight & Wishes. Date not set. 69.95 (*1-57553-345-6*) Watermrk Pr.

Mitchell, Memory F., ed. Addresses & Public Papers of James Baxter Hunt, Jr., Governor of North Carolina, Vol. One Vol. 1, 1977-1981. (Illus.). xxxii, 881p. 1982. 4.00 (*0-86526-178-4*) NC Archives.

Mitchell, Meredith B. Hero or Victim? 313p. 1995. pap. 19.95 (*0-9639405-0-3*) M B Mitchell.

Mitchell, Merle. Mathematical History: Activities, Puzzles, Stories & Games. LC 78-26206. (Illus.). 74p. 1978. pap. 12.95 (*0-87353-138-8*) NCTM.

Mitchell, Michael. Hemorrhoids: A Cure & Preventative. 4th ed. LC 77-86391. (Illus.). 196p. 1997. reprint ed. 19.95 (*0-930926-25-0*) Calif Fin Pubns.

Mitchell, Michael, tr. see Kalbeck, Florian.

Mitchell, Michael, tr. see Kokoschka, Oskar.

Mitchell, Michael, tr. see Loos, Adolf.

Mitchell, Michael, tr. see Meyrick, Gustav.

Mitchell, Michael, tr. see Meyrink, Gustav.

Mitchell, Michael, tr. see Schwab, Werner & Sanford, Gerlinde U.

Mitchell, Michael, tr. & afterword by see Mander, Matthias.

Mitchell, Michael, tr. & afterword by see Sebestyen, Gyorgy.

Mitchell, Michael, tr. & afterword by see Winkler, Josef.

Mitchell, Michael, tr. & comment see Sebestyen, Gyorgy.

Mitchell, Michael A. Developing Enterprise Apps with Visual J++ LC 97-66. 576p. 1997. 39.99 (*1-57169-085-9*) Sams.

Mitchell, Michael D. The Pill Book Guide to Children's Medications. 2nd rev. ed. 320p. 1990. mass mkt. 6.50 (*0-553-56927-9*) Bantam.

Mitchell, Michael E., jt. ed. see Dewan, Paddy.

***Mitchell, Michele.** New Kind of Party Animal: How the Young Are Redefining "Politics As Usual" 224p. 1999. pap. 13.00 (*0-684-85441-4*, Touchstone) S&S Trade Pap.

Mitchell, Michele. A New Kind of Party Animal: How the Young Are Tearing Up the American Political Landscape. LC 98-10495. 224p. (YA). 1998. 22.00 (*0-684-83697-1*) S&S Trade.

***Mitchell, Mike.** Austria. 2nd rev. ed. Vol. 66. 271p. 1999. lib. bdg. 81.00 (*1-85109-297-8*) ABC-CLIO.

Mitchell, Mike, ed. Dedalus - Ariadne Book of Austrian Fantasy: The Meyrink Years, 1890-1930. 416p. 1993. pap. 17.95 (*0-929497-63-5*) Ariadne CA.

Mitchell, Mike, jt. auth. see Kennoy, Ray.

Mitchell, Mike, ed. see Meyrink, Gustav.

Mitchell, Mike, tr. see Blumenfeld, Erwin.

Mitchell, Mike, tr. see Furness, Ray, ed.

Mitchell, Mike, tr. see Grimmelshausen, Johann J.

Mitchell, Mike, tr. see Krausser, Helmut.

Mitchell, Mike, tr. see Kubin, Alfred.

Mitchell, Mike, tr. see Meyrink, Gustav.

Mitchell, Mike, tr. see Rosendorfer, Herbert.

Mitchell, Mike, tr. & intro. see Meyrink, Gustav.

Mitchell-Miller, Judy. Biryani & Plum Pudding. (Passages to India Ser.). (C). 1989. spiral bd. 20.00 (*1-56709-010-9*) Indep Broadcast.

— Vedas, Ragas & Storytellers. (Passages to India Ser.). (C). 1989. spiral bd. 20.00 (*1-56709-012-5*) Indep Broadcast.

Mitchell, Mitch & Mitchell, Jan. Friends & Lovers Couples Study Guide. 62p. 1996. pap. 4.99 (*1-57782-005-3*) Discipleshp.

Mitchell, Mitch & Platt, John. The Hendrix Experience. LC 97-35984. (Illus.). 176p. 1998. reprint ed. pap. 24.95 (*0-306-80818-8*) Da Capo.

— Jimi Hendrix: Inside the Experience. LC 93-35860. 1993. pap. 14.95 (*0-312-10098-1*) St Martin.

Mitchell, Mozella G. New Africa in America Vol. 5: The Blending of African & American Religious & Social Traditions Among Black People in Meridian, Mississippi & Surrounding Counties. LC 93-42526. (Martin Luther King, Jr., Memorial Studies in Religion, Culture, & Social Development: Vol. 5). XII, 240p. (C). 1995. text 39.95 (*0-8204-2425-0*) P Lang Pubng.

Mitchell, Mozella G., ed. The Human Search: Howard Thurman & the Quest for Freedom: Proceedings of the Second Annual Thurman Convacation. LC 91-13995. 246p. 1992. 47.95 (*0-8204-1466-2*) P Lang Pubng.

Mitchell, Murray D., ed. Eicosanoids in Reproduction. 304p. 1990. lib. bdg. 229.00 (*0-8493-6464-7*, QP251) CRC Pr.

Mitchell, Mychal. Backbone. 1994. 12.95 (*0-533-10852-7*) Vantage.

Mitchell, Myron J. & Nakas, James P., eds. Microfloral & Faunal Interactions in Natural & Agro-Ecosystems. (Developments in Biogeochemistry Ser.). 1985. text 220.00 (*90-247-3246-8*) Kluwer Academic.

Mitchell, Nahum. The History of Bridgewater, Massachusetts. 456p. 1997. reprint ed. pap. 31.50 (*0-7884-0675-2*, M373) Heritage Bk.

Mitchell, Nancy. The Danger of Dreams: German & American Imperialism in Latin America LC 98-49537. (Illus.). 336p. 1999. pap. 19.95 (*0-8078-4775-5*) U of NC Pr.

***Mitchell, Nancy.** Danger of Dreams: German & American Imperialism in Latin America. LC 98-49537. (Illus.). 336p. 1999. 49.95 (*0-8078-2489-5*) U of NC Pr.

Mitchell, Nancy. Earth Rising. LC 98-91703. (Changing Earth Trilogy Ser.: Bk. 1). (Illus.). 192p. (Orig.). (J). (ps-12). 1999. mass mkt. 5.95 (*1-892713-00-4*) Lightstream.

***Mitchell, Nancy.** Global Warning. LC 98-91703. (Changing Earth Trilogy Ser.: Bk. 3). (Illus.). 192p. (Orig.). (J). (ps-12). 1999. mass mkt. 5.95 (*1-892713-02-0*) Lightstream.

Mitchell, Nancy, et al. Raging Skies. LC 98-91703. (Changing Earth Trilogy Ser.: Bk. 2). (Illus.). 192p. (Orig.). (J). (ps-12). 1999. mass mkt. 5.95 (*1-892713-01-2*) Lightstream.

Mitchell, Nancy, ed. see Poelstra, Francine.

Mitchell, Nancy S. Quality Performance: How to Implement: Quality Awareness; Statistical Process Control; Task Teams; & Statistical Quality Control for Continuous Improvement in Your Organization. LC 90-91657. (Illus.). 184p. 1991. 39.95 (*0-9626692-5-3*) QP Pub PA.

Mitchell, Naomi. Corn King & Spring Queen. 1988. reprint ed. lib. bdg. 89.00 (*0-7812-0167-5*) Rprt Serv.

Mitchell, Nathan. A Humorous Guide to Understanding Black Women. LC 98-91615. 100p. 1998. pap. 5.99 (*1-57502-876-X*, P2383) Morris Pubng.

— Liturgy & the Social Sciences. LC 98-34981. (American Essays in Liturgy Ser.). 1999. 10.95 (*0-8146-2511-8*) Liturgical Pr.

— A Practical Guide to Winning the Lottery. 102p. 1998. pap. 8.95 (*1-57502-981-2*, PO2682) Morris Pubng.

— Real Presence: The Work of Eucharist. 160p. 1998. pap. 12.00 (*1-56854-265-8*) Liturgy Tr Pubns.

Mitchell, Nathan D. Cult & Controversy: The Worship of the Eucharist Outside Mass. 460p. 1992. pap. 24.95 (*0-8146-6050-9*, Pueblo Bks) Liturgical Pr.

— Eucharist As Sacrament of Initiation. LC 93-46859. (Forum Essays Ser.: Vol. 2). 154p. (Orig.). 1994. pap. 6.00 (*0-929650-81-6*, EUCHIN) Liturgy Tr Pubns.

Mitchell, Nathan D. & Baldovin, John F., eds. Rule of Prayer, Rule of Faith: Essays in Honor of Aidan Kavanagh, O. S. B. 376p. (Orig.). 1996. pap. 34.95 (*0-8146-6158-0*, Pueblo Bks) Liturgical Pr.

Mitchell, Nathan D. & Leonard, John. The Postures of Assembly During Eucharistic Prayer. LC 94-31581. 120p. 1994. pap. 11.95 (*0-929650-64-6*, POSTUR) Liturgy Tr Pubns.

Mitchell, Nathan S. Hilarious Without Being Racy: Light Reading for the Nostalgic. LC 96-68759. 150p. (Orig.). 1996. pap. 9.95 (*1-57502-203-6*, P0835) Morris Pubng.

Mitchell, Neil J. The Conspicuous Corporation: Business, Public Policy & Representative Democracy. LC 97-4704. 264p. (C). 1997. text 44.50 (*0-472-10818-2*, 10818) U of Mich Pr.

— The Generous Corporation: A Political Analysis of Economic Power. LC 88-14417. (Illus.). 173p. 1989. reprint ed. pap. 53.70 (*0-608-07837-9*, 205401300010) Bks Demand.

Mitchell, Nelson S., jt. ed. see Cruess, Richard L.

***Mitchell, Niki Butler.** New Color of Success. LC 99-49381. (Illus.). 268p. 1999. 22.50 (*0-7615-2065-1*) Prima Pub.

Mitchell, Nora. Deli Trays Around the World with Nora Mitchell. (Illus.). 112p. 1990. 29.95 (*0-9626113-0-1*) N Mitchell.

— The Indian Hill-Station: Kodaikanal. LC 72-78250. (University of Chicago, Department of Geography, Research Paper Ser.: No. 141). 214p. (Orig.). 1972. reprint ed. pap. 66.40 (*0-608-02283-7*, 206292400004) Bks Demand.

— Proofreading the Histories. 72p. (Orig.). 1996. pap. 9.95 (*1-882295-10-2*) Alice James Bks.

— Your Skin Is a Country. LC 88-14632. 72p. (Orig.). (C). 1988. pap. 9.95 (*0-914086-83-9*) Alice James Bks.

Mitchell, Norma T. Francis E. Willard: Yours for Home Protection. 36p. 1976. pap. 1.00 (*1-880927-09-8*) Gen Comm Arch.

Mitchell, Olivia. Living with Defined Contribution Pensions: Remaking Responsibility for Retirement. LC 98-13584. (Pension Research Council Publications). (Illus.). 296p. 1998. 47.50 (*0-8122-3439-1*) U of Pa Pr.

***Mitchell, Olivia S.** Forecasting Retirement Needs & Retirement Wealth. LC 99-41733. 1999. 49.95 (*0-8122-3529-0*) U of Pa Pr.

Mitchell, Olivia S. Prospects for Social Security Reform. LC 98-41908. 1999. 49.95 (*0-8122-3479-0*) U of Pa Pr.

Mitchell, Olivia S., ed. As the Workforce Ages: Costs, Benefits, & Policy Challenges. LC 92-31402. (Frank W. Pierce Memorial Lectureship & Conference Ser.: No. 9). 304p. 1993. text 45.00 (*0-87546-195-6*, ILR Press); pap. text 18.95 (*0-87546-196-4*, ILR Press) Cornell U Pr.

Mitchell, Olivia S., jt. auth. see Fields, Gary S.

Mitchell, Ormond, jt. auth. see Mitchell, Barbara.

Mitchell, P. Concepts Basic to Nursing. 3rd ed. (Illus.). 720p. 1981. text 36.95 (*0-07-042582-5*) McGraw.

— Control Applications of Microcomputers. (Illus.). 160p. (C). 1988. pap. text 19.95 (*0-7131-3583-2*, Pub. by E A) Routldge.

Mitchell, P. Chalmers, tr. see Metchnikoff, Elie.

Mitchell, P. J., ed. Electrochemical Engineering & the Environment 1992. LC 92-14500. (EFCE Publication: No. 89). 1992. 99.95 (*1-56032-256-X*) Hemisp Pub.

Mitchell, P. Kai-Galen, jt. auth. see Mitchell, Fred L., Jr.

Mitchell, P. Lynn. Little One Free Forever. LC 97-90555. 1999. pap. 11.95 (*0-533-12427-1*) Vantage.

Mitchell, P. M. Johann Christoph Gottsched (1700-1766) Harbinger of German Classicism. (GERM Ser.). x, 131p. 1995. 55.00 (*1-57113-063-2*) Camden Hse.

Mitchell, P. M., ed. Johann Christoph Gottsched. Ausgewaehlte Werke Vol. 7: Ausfuehrliche Redekunst; Pt. 3, Anhang und Variantenverzeichnis. (Ausgaben Deutscher Literatur des XV bis XVIII Jahrhunderts Ser.). (C). 1975. 176.95 (*3-11-005926-6*) De Gruyter.

Mitchell, P. M. & Ober, Kenneth H., trs. from DAN. The Royal Guest & Other Classical Danish Narrative. LC 77-78070. 1993. pap. 6.95 (*0-226-53214-3*) U Ch Pr.

— The Royal Guest & Other Classical Danish Narrative. LC 77-78070. 1993. lib. bdg. 15.00 (*0-226-53213-5*) U Ch Pr.

Mitchell, P. M., jt. compiled by see Kalinke, Marianne E.

Mitchell, P. M., ed. see Gottsched, Johann C.

Mitchell, P. M., tr. see Dinesen, Isak.

Mitchell, P. M., tr. see Dinsen, Isak.

Mitchell, P. M., tr. & intro. see Holberg, Ludvig.

Mitchell, Pam. Used & Abused. Publishers Design Works Staff, ed. LC 96-96880. (Illus.). 169p. (Orig.). 1996. pap. 12.95 (*0-9653527-0-6*) Bordertown Pr.

Mitchell, Pamela. Wired to Death. 218p. 1997. 20.95 (*1-885173-36-9*) Write Way.

Mitchell, Pamela H., et al. Differentiating Nursing Practice: Into the Twenty-First Century. 452p. (Orig.). (C). 1991. pap. 25.00 (*1-55810-065-2*, G-182, Am Acad Nursing) Am Nurses Pub.

Mitchell, Patrica, ed. see Broadwater, Robert.

***Mitchell, Patricia.** I Have Called You by Name: The Stories of 16 Saints & Christian Heroes. LC 99-88096. (Illus.). 216p. 2000. pap. 12.95 (*0-932085-37-7*) Word Among Us.

Mitchell, Patricia, ed. Touching the Risen Christ: Wisdom from the Fathers. LC 99-12022. 144p. 1999. pap. 12.00 (*0-932085-22-9*, ID BTRLE9) Word Among Us.

— Walking with the Father: Wisdom from Brother Lawrence. LC 98-50286. 144p. 1999. pap. 12.00 (*0-932085-21-0*, ID BWBLE9) Word Among Us.

***Mitchell, Patricia, ed.** Wisdom from Pope John Paul II: Welcoming the New Millennium. LC 99-40926. 144p. 1999. pap. 12.00 (*0-932085-31-8*) Word Among Us.

Mitchell, Patricia, jt. auth. see Zanchettin, Leo.

***Mitchell, Patricia B.** An Affair of the Heart: America's Romance with Louisiana Food. 1999. pap. 4.00 (*0-925117-98-6*) Mitchells.

Mitchell, Patricia B. Apple Country Cooking. 3rd ed. 1991. pap. 4.00 (*0-925117-47-1*) Mitchells.

— As the Mill Wheel Turns. 1999. pap. 4.00 (*0-925117-97-8*) Mitchells.

— At the Table in Colonial America. 1994. pap. 4.00 (*0-925117-76-5*) Mitchells.

— A Bowl of Soup, a Crust of Bread, & Thou. 1995. pap. 4.00 (*0-925117-78-1*) Mitchells.

— Butter 'em While They're Hot. 3rd ed. 1991. pap. 4.00 (*0-925117-50-1*) Mitchells.

— Civil War Celebrations. LC 98-226377. 1998. pap. 4.00 (*0-925117-88-9*) Mitchells.

— Civil War Plants & Herbs. 1996. pap. 4.00 (*0-925117-82-X*) Mitchells.

— Colonial Christmas Cooking. rev. ed. 1991. pap. 4.00 (*0-925117-43-9*) Mitchells.

— Colonial Spices & Herbs. 1997. pap. 4.00 (*0-925117-86-2*) Mitchells.

— Coming Home for Christmas Cookbook. rev. ed. 1991. pap. 4.00 (*0-925117-49-8*) Mitchells.

— Confederate Camp Cooking. rev. ed. 1991. pap. 4.00 (*0-925117-46-3*) Mitchells.

— Confederate Home Cooking. rev. ed. 1991. pap. 4.00 (*0-925117-45-5*) Mitchells.

— Cooking for the Cause: Confederate Recipes, Documented Quotations, Commemorative Recipes. (Illus.). 38p. 1988. pap. 4.00 (*0-925117-06-4*) Mitchells.

— Cooking in the Young Republic, 1780-1850. 1992. pap. 4.00 (*0-925117-57-9*) Mitchells.

— La Cuisine Francaise des Premieres Annees de l'Amerique du Nord. Black, Mary L., tr. 1992. pap. 4.00 (*0-925117-59-5*) Mitchells.

— Delightful Dreams of Dixie Dinners. rev. ed. 1992. pap. 4.00 (*0-925117-63-3*) Mitchells.

— Dining Cars & Depots. 1992. pap. 4.00 (*0-925117-55-2*) Mitchells.

— Footloose, Fancy & Free: A Victorian Vacation Recipe Book. 1992. pap. 4.00 (*0-925117-67-6*) Mitchells.

— Four Centuries of American Herbs. 1993. pap. 4.00 (*0-925117-68-4*) Mitchells.

— French Cooking in Early America. 1991. pap. 4.00 (*0-925117-35-8*) Mitchells.

— Good Food, Good Folks, Good Times: Just Being Southern. 1998. pap. 4.00 (*0-925117-87-0*) Mitchells.

***Mitchell, Patricia B.** The Good Land: Native American & Early Colonial Food. rev. ed. 1999. pap. 4.00 (*0-925117-93-5*) Mitchells.

Mitchell, Patricia B. The Great American Apple: At the Very Core of Our Culture. 1995. pap. 4.00 (*0-925117-81-1*) Mitchells.

— Grist Mill Quick Loaf Breads. 1991. pap. 4.00 (*0-925117-37-4*) Mitchells.

***Mitchell, Patricia B.** Home Front Regiment 1861-1865: Women Fighting from the Hearth. 1999. pap. 4.00 (*0-925117-95-1*) Mitchells.

Mitchell, Patricia B. Just Naturally Sweet: Honey, Sorghum, & Maple Syrup. rev. ed. 1993. pap. 4.00 (*0-925117-66-8*) Mitchells.

— Loaves of Love. rev. ed. 1991. pap. 4.00 (*0-925117-52-8*) Mitchells.

— Northern Ladies' Civil War Recipes. rev. ed. 1994. pap. text 4.00 (*0-925117-75-7*) Mitchells.

— Pack the Skillet: American Pioneer Cooking. 36p. 1997. pap. 4.00 (*0-925117-84-6*) Mitchells.

***Mitchell, Patricia B.** Pilgrims, Puritans & Cavaliers: From Hunger to Feasting. 1999. pap. 4.00 (*0-925117-96-X*) Mitchells.

Mitchell, Patricia B. Plantation Row Slave Cabin Cooking: The Roots of Soul Food. LC 98-161648. 1998. pap. 4.00 (*0-925117-89-7*) Mitchells.

— Real South Cooking: Authentic, Traditional Southern Food. 1997. pap. 4.00 (*0-925117-85-4*) Mitchells.

— Refreshments Now & Then: Colonial, Victorian, & Contemporary Sweets. 1995. pap. 4.00 (*0-925117-79-X*) Mitchells.

— Revolutionary Recipes. rev. ed. 1991. pap. 4.00 (*0-925117-42-0*) Mitchells.

— Simply Scrumptious Southern Sweets. rev. ed. 1991. pap. 4.00 (*0-925117-39-0*) Mitchells.

— Soul on Rice: African Influences on American Cooking. 1993. pap. 4.00 (*0-925117-69-2*) Mitchells.

— Southern Born & Bread. 4th ed. 1992. pap. 4.00 (*0-925117-54-4*) Mitchells.

***Mitchell, Patricia B.** Specialties from the Southern Garden: Nostalgic Vegetable Dishes. 1999. pap. 4.00 (*0-925117-94-3*) Mitchells.

Mitchell, Patricia B. Suited to a Tea. 1995. pap. 4.00 (*0-925117-80-3*) Mitchells.

— Sweet Memories of Christmas. rev. ed. 1991. pap. 4.00 (*0-925117-48-X*) Mitchells.

— Sweet 'n' Slow. 3rd ed. 1992. pap. 4.00 (*0-925117-62-5*) Mitchells.

— True Grist. 3rd ed. 1992. pap. 4.00 (*0-925117-53-6*) Mitchells.

— Union Army Camp Cooking. rev. ed. 1991. pap. 4.00 (*0-925117-41-2*) Mitchells.

— Victorian Christmas Celebration Cookbook. rev. ed. 1991. pap. 4.00 (*0-925117-44-7*) Mitchells.

— Victorian Parlors & Tea Parties. 1991. pap. 4.00 (*0-925117-36-6*) Mitchells.

— Waking up down South. 1992. pap. 4.00 (*0-925117-65-X*) Mitchells.

An Asterisk (*) at the beginning of an entry indicates that the title is appearing for the first time.

***Mitchell, Robin.** Grave Robbers. 2000. pap. 14.95 (0-946487-72-3) Luath Pr Ltd.

Mitchell, Rodger, et al, eds. Acarology IX Proceedings. LC 96-70956. (Illus.). 718p. 1997. pap. text 65.00 (0-86727-123-X) Ohio Bio Survey.

Mitchell, Roger. Clear Pond: The Reconstruction of a Life. (Illus.). 201p. 1991. 29.95 (0-8156-0257-X) Syracuse U Pr.

— Clear Space on a Cold Day. (CSU Poetry Ser.: No. XIX). 80p. (Orig.). 1986. 12.00 (0-914946-65-X); pap. 6.00 (0-914946-55-2) Cleveland St Univ Poetry Ctr.

— The Word for Everything. LC 96-22242. 64p. (Orig.). 1996. pap. 10.95 (1-886157-06-5) BkMk.

Mitchell, Roger, jt. auth. see Mills, Brian.

Mitchell, Roger H. Kimberelites, Orangeites, & Related Rocks. LC 96-3960. (Illus.). 406p. (C). 1995. 95.00 (0-306-45022-4, Kluwer Plenum) Kluwer Academic.

Mitchell, Roger L. Crop Growth & Culture. fac. ed. LC 72-88006. (Illus.). 357p. 1970. reprint ed. pap. 110.70 (0-608-00953-9, 206179900011) Bks Demand.

Mitchell, Ron. Organic Faith: A Call to Authentic Christianity. LC 97-45634. 175p. 1998. pap. 10.95 (0-940895-40-4) Cornerstone IL.

Mitchell, Ronald B. Intentional Oil Pollution at Sea: Environmental Policies & Treaty Compliance. 379p. 1994. 42.50 (0-262-13303-2) MIT Pr.

Mitchell, Ronald E. America: A Practical Handbook. LC 73-13144. (Foreign Travelers in America, 1810-1935 Ser.). 318p. 1974. reprint ed. 26.95 (0-405-05467-X) Ayer.

— Opera: Dead or Alive; Production, Performance, & Enjoyment of Musical Theatre. LC 73-121772. (Illus.). 350p. 1970. reprint ed. pap. 108.50 (0-608-07006-8, 206721400009) Bks Demand.

Mitchell, Rosamond & Myles, Florence. Theoretical Perspectives on Second Language Learning. LC 98-20001. (An Arnold Publication). (Illus.). 240p. 1998. text 65.00 (0-340-66311-1, Pub. by E A); pap. text 19.95 (0-340-66312-X, Pub. by E A) OUP.

Mitchell, Rosamond, jt. ed. see Blue, George M.

***Mitchell, Rose G. & Frisbie, Charlotte J.** The Life Story of Rose Mitchell: A Navajo Woman, C. 1874-1977. LC 00-9014. 2001. pap. write for info. (0-8263-2203-4) U of NM Pr.

***Mitchell, Rosemary C.** Picturing the Past: English History in Text & Image, 1830-1870. LC 99-89337. (Oxford Historical Monographs). (Illus.). 332p. 2000. text 85.00 (0-19-820844-8) OUP.

Mitchell, Roy, jt. auth. see Mills, Jerry.

Mitchell, Ruby D. Virgin of the Sun. LC 84-52477. 1986. 13.95 (0-87212-189-5) Libra.

Mitchell, Ruth. Arkansas Heritage: Fifth Grade History Textbook. LC 85-63310. (Illus.). 192p. 1986. 18.00 (0-914546-62-7) Rose Pub.

— Paradise Lost (Milton) (Barron's Book Notes Ser.). (C). 1984. pap. 2.50 (0-8120-3435-X) Barron.

— Testing for Learning: How New Approaches to Evaluation Can Improve American Schools. 222p. 1992. 27.95 (0-02-921465-3) Free Pr.

Mitchell, Ruth, ed. Measuring up to the Challenge: What Standards & Assessment Can Do for Arts Education. LC 94-31023. 200p. 1994. pap. 19.95 (1-879903-20-2) Am for the Arts.

Mitchell, Ruth & Berth, Patte. Smart Start: Elementary Education for the Twenty-First Century. LC 92-60659. (Illus.). 224p. 1992. 21.95 (1-55591-908-1) Fulcrum Pub.

Mitchell, Ruth, et al. Learning in Overdrive: Designing Curriculum, Instruction, & Assessment from Standards: A Manual for Teachers. LC 95-40972. (Illus.). 160p. (Orig.). 1995. pap., teacher ed. 17.95 (1-55591-933-2) Fulcrum Pub.

Mitchell, Ruth, jt. ed. see Kane, Michael.

Mitchell, Ruth C. Of Human Kindness. LC 74-22798. (Labor Movement in Fiction & Non-Fiction Ser.). reprint ed. 45.00 (0-404-58454-3) AMS Pr.

Mitchell, S. Jane's Aircraft Upgrades, 1998-99. 1998. text 350.00 (0-7106-1781-X) Janes Info Group.

Mitchell, S. J. D. Perse: A History of the Perse School 1615-1976. (Cambridge Town, Gown & County Ser.: Vol. 7). (Illus.). 1976. 25.00 (0-902675-71-0) Oleander Pr.

Mitchell, S. Weir, et al. Gunshot Wounds & Other Injuries of Nerves. (American Civil War Surgery Ser.: No. 3). 164p. 1989. reprint ed. 75.00 (0-930405-13-7) Norman SF.

Mitchell, S. Wier. In War Time. Weigand, William, ed. (Masterworks of Literature Ser.). 1991. 15.95 (0-8084-0420-2) NCUP.

Mitchell, Sally. Daily Life in Victorian England. LC 96-2539. (Daily Life through History Ser.). 336p. 1996. 45.00 (0-313-29467-4, Greenwood Pr) Greenwood.

— The Dictionary of British Equestrian Artists. (Illus.). 518p. 1985. 89.50 (0-907462-42-1) Antique Collect.

— The Fallen Angel: Chastity, Class & Women's Reading, 1835-1880. LC 79-92711. 1981. 16.95 (0-87972-155-3) Bowling Green Univ Popular Press.

— The New Girl: Girls' Culture in England, 1880-1915. LC 95-10929. (YA). 1995. 64.00 (0-231-10246-1) Col U Pr.

— The New Girl: Girls' Culture in England, 1880-1915. 1995. pap. text 19.50 (0-231-10247-X) Col U Pr.

Mitchell, Sally, ed. Farmer Favorites. (Illus.). 160p. (Orig.). 1996. pap. 12.95 (0-85236-340-0, Pub. by Farming Pr) Diamond Farm Bk.

— Victorian Britain: An Encyclopedia. LC 87-29947. (Illus.). 1010p. 1988. text 65.00 (0-8240-1513-4, SS438) Garland.

Mitchell, Sally, jt. auth. see Broomfield, Andrea.

Mitchell, Sally, jt. ed. see Andrews, Richard.

Mitchell, Sally, jt. ed. see Broomfield, Andrea.

Mitchell, Sally, jt. ed. see Costello, Patrick J.

Mitchell, Sally, ed. see Maitzen, Rohan A.

Mitchell, Sally, ed. see Thaden, Barbara Z.

Mitchell, Sam. Pura Vida - Waterfalls & Hot Springs of Costa Rica. (Illus.). 96p. 1995. pap. 9.95 (0-89732-172-3) Menasha Ridge.

Mitchell, Samuel. Reforming Educators: Teachers, Experts & Advocates. LC 98-23551. 272p. 1998. 59.95 (0-275-96366-7, Praeger Pubs) Greenwood.

— Tidal Waves of School Reform: Types of Reform, Government Controls, & Community Advocates. LC 96-16281. 224p. 1996. 59.95 (0-275-95644-X, Praeger Pubs) Greenwood.

***Mitchell, Sara.** Afro-American Biographies: A Bibliography. 242p. 2000. lib. bdg. 49.00 (1-56072-829-9) Nova Sci Pubs.

Mitchell, Sara. A Deadly Snare. LC 89-81809. 192p. 1990. pap. 6.99 (0-89636-263-9, AC 214, LifeJourney) Chariot Victor.

— In the Midst of Lions. (Shadowcatchers Ser.: No. 2). 32p. 1996. pap. 9.99 (1-55661-498-5) Bethany Hse.

— Montclair. LC 97-4712. (Portraits Ser.). 256p. 1997. pap. 8.99 (1-55661-963-4) Bethany Hse.

— Night Music. (Love Inspired Ser.). 1998. per. 4.50 (0-373-87013-2, 1-87013-8) Harlequin Bks.

***Mitchell, Sara.** Ransomed Heart. LC 99-6421. 320p. 1999. pap. text 9.99 (1-55661-499-3) Bethany Hse.

— Ransomed Heart. LC 99-46760. 2000. 30.00 (0-7862-2229-8) Mac Lib Ref.

Mitchell, Sara. Shelter of His Arms. (Love Inspired Ser.). 1998. per. 4.50 (0-373-87031-0, Steeple Hill) Harlequin Bks.

— A Song in the Night. (Serenade Serenata Ser.: No. 37). 192p. 1986. pap. 1.49 (0-310-47712-3, 15624P) Zondervan.

— Trial of the Innocent. LC 95-468. (Shadowcatchers Ser.: Bk. 1). 336p. 1995. pap. 9.99 (1-55661-497-7) Bethany Hse.

***Mitchell, Sara.** Trial of the Innocent. LC 00-32532. 2000. write for info. (0-7862-2726-5) Thorndike Pr.

Mitchell, Sara, et al. Inspirational Romance Reader Vol. 1: Contemporary Collection. unabridged ed. 500p. 1996. pap. 4.97 (1-55748-795-2) Barbour Pub.

Mitchell, Sara T. Through a Glass Darkly, No. 22. (Serenade Serenata Ser.). 1985. pap. 1.49 (0-310-46722-5, 15531P) Zondervan.

Mitchell, Sarah, ed. see Dugas-Bonds, Pat.

***Mitchell, Scott.** Sams Teach Yourself Active Server Pages 3.0 in 21 Days. (Teach Yourself... in 21 Days Ser.). 700p. 2000. pap. 39.99 (0-672-31863-6) Sams.

Mitchell, Scott. Secret Toronto: The Unique Guidebook to Toronto's Hidden Sites, Sounds & Tastes. (Illus.). 200p. 1998. pap. text 19.95 (1-55022-346-1, Pub. by ECW) LPC InBook.

Mitchell, Sharon. Nothing but the Rent. LC 97-34068. 336p. 1998. 23.95 (0-525-94306-4) NAL.

— Nothing but the Rent. 348p. 1999. mass mkt. 6.99 (0-451-19260-5, Sig) NAL.

***Mitchell, Sharon.** Sheer Necessity. 2000. mass mkt. 6.99 (0-451-19947-2, Sig) NAL.

— Sheer Necessity: A Novel. LC 99-35475. 290p. 1999. 23.95 (0-525-94523-7) NAL.

Mitchell, Shayne, tr. see Fumagalli, Vito.

Mitchell, Sherry. Creating Sanctuary: A New Approach to Gardening in Washington, Virginia, & Maryland. LC 96-5409. (Illus.). 240p. 1996. pap. 19.95 (0-939009-97-8, EPM) Howell Pr VA.

— The Townhouse Gardener: Distinctive Landscape Designs for Small Gardens in the Mid-Atlantic Region. LC 97-49065. 1998. 19.95 (1-889324-09-4, EPM) Howell Pr VA.

Mitchell, Silas W. The Autobiography of a Quack & the Case of George Dedlow. LC 68-57542. (Muckrakers Ser.). (Illus.). reprint ed. lib. bdg. 17.00 (0-8398-1264-7) Irvington.

— Complete Poems. (BCL1-PS American Literature Ser.). 447p. 1992. reprint ed. lib. bdg. 99.00 (0-7812-6799-4) Rprt Serv.

— Doctor & Patient. LC 71-180584. (Medicine & Society in America Ser.). 182p. 1972. reprint ed. 18.95 (0-405-03961-1) Ayer.

— Hephzibah Guinness. LC 74-178448. (Short Story Index Reprint Ser.). 1977. reprint ed. 18.95 (0-8369-4049-0) Ayer.

— Hugh Wynne: Free Quaker, 2 vols., Set. LC 17-490. 1969. reprint ed. 15.00 (0-403-00073-4) Scholarly.

— Hugh Wynne, Free Quaker, 2 vols in 1. LC 67-29274. (Americans in Fiction Ser.). 573p. reprint ed. lib. bdg. 17.00 (0-8398-1265-5) Irvington.

— Hugh Wynne, Free Quaker, 2 vols., Set. (BCL1-PS American Literature Ser.). 1992. reprint ed. lib. bdg. 150.00 (0-7812-6800-1) Rprt Serv.

— Hugh Wynne, Free Quaker, 2 vols., Set. 1993. reprint ed. lib. bdg. 150.00 (0-7812-5491-4) Rprt Serv.

— Little Stories. LC 76-85691. (Short Story Index Reprint Ser.). 1977. 17.95 (0-8369-3034-7) Ayer.

— Wear & Tear: or Hints for the Overworked. 5th ed. LC 73-2407. (Mental Illness & Social Policy; the American Experience Ser.). 1973. reprint ed. 16.95 (0-405-05217-0) Ayer.

Mitchell, Simon. Jane's Aircraft Upgrades, 1997-98: Detailed Information on Worldwide Aircraft Upgrades, Overhauls & Retrofit Programs. 5th ed. (Illus.). 1997. 320.00 (0-7106-1533-7) Janes Info Group.

Mitchell, Smoot C., jt. auth. see Quarterman, John S.

***Mitchell, Stacy.** The Home Town Advantage: How to Defend Your Main Street Against Chain Stores... And Why It Matters. (Illus.). 101p. 2000. pap. 14.00 (0-917582-89-6) Inst Local Self Re.

Mitchell, Stan. Inside the Windows 95 File System. LC 97-188704. (Orig.). 1997. pap. 32.95 (1-56592-200-X) Thomson Learn.

Mitchell, Stanley, tr. see Lukacs, Georg.

Mitchell, Stephen. Anatolia: Land, Men & Gods in Asia Minor, 2 vols. Incl. Vol. 1. Anatolia: Land, Men, & Gods in Asia Minor: The Celts in Anatolia & the Impact of Roman Rule. (Illus.). 284p. 1995. pap. text 42.00 (0-19-815029-6); Vol. 2. Anatolia: Land, Men, & Gods in Asia Minor: The Rise of the Church. (Illus.). 216p. 1995. pap. text 42.00 (0-19-815030-X); write for info. (0-614-32259-6) OUP.

— Bestiary A. 2000. 25.00 (0-06-016918-4) HarperTrade.

***Mitchell, Stephen.** Bhagavad Gita: A New Translation. (Illus.). 224p. 2000. 20.00 (0-609-60550-X) Harmony Bks.

Mitchell, Stephen. A Book of Psalms: Selected & Adapted from the Hebrew. 112p. 1994. reprint ed. pap. 12.00 (0-06-092470-5, Perennial) HarperTrade.

— The Essence of Wisdom. 128p. 1999. pap. 10.00 (0-7679-0306-4) Bantam.

— The Essence of Wisdom: Words from the Masters to Illuminate the Spiritual Path. LC 98-17856. 128p. 1998. 15.00 (0-7679-0305-6) Broadway BDD.

— The Frog Prince: A Parable of Love & Transformation. LC 99-20433. 176p. 1999. 18.00 (0-609-60545-3) Crown.

— Genesis: A New Translation of the Classic Bible Stories. 224p. 1997. pap. 13.00 (0-06-092856-5, Perennial) HarperTrade.

— Genesis: A New Translation of the Classic Biblical Stories. LC 96-15566. 224p. 1996. 20.00 (0-06-017249-5) HarpC.

— Genesis: A New Translation of the Classic Biblical Stories. 1996. audio 18.00 (0-694-51653-8) HarperAudio.

— Gospel According To. LC 90-56390. 320p. 1994. pap. 14.00 (0-06-092321-0, Perennial) HarperTrade.

— Meetings with the Archangel: A Comedy of the Spirit. LC 98-18018. 256p. 1999. pap. 13.00 (0-06-093248-1) HarpC.

— Meetings with the Archangel: A Comedy of the Spirit. LC 98-18018. 256p. 1998. 24.00 (0-06-018245-8, Pub. by Harper SF) HarpC.

***Mitchell, Stephen.** Meetings with the Archangel: A Comedy of the Spirit, Set. 1998. audio 18.00 (0-694-52021-7) HarperAudio.

Mitchell, Stephen. Tao Ching. pap. 8.00 (0-685-51784-5, Perennial) HarperTrade.

— Tao Te Ching: A New English Version. LC 88-45123. 144p. 1994. reprint ed. pap. 12.00 (0-06-091608-7, Perennial) HarperTrade.

— Tao Te Ching Persona. 144p. 1994. pap. 7.00 (0-06-081245-1, Perennial) HarperTrade.

Mitchell, Stephen, ed. Bestiary: An Anthology of Poems about Animals. LC 96-33990. 230p. 1996. 25.00 (1-883319-48-X) Frog Ltd CA.

— The Enlightened Heart. LC 89-45320. 192p. 1994. reprint ed. pap. 13.00 (0-06-092053-X, Perennial) HarperTrade.

— The Enlightened Mind. LC 90-55936. 256p. 1994. pap. 13.00 (0-06-092320-2, Perennial) HarperTrade.

— Poetry Collection. 96p. 1998. pap. 12.00 (0-06-095049-8) HarpC.

— Tao Ching. 1989. boxed set. write for info. (0-318-66674-X) HarperTrade.

Mitchell, Stephen, ed. Dropping Ashes on the Buddha: The Teachings of Zen Master Seung Sahn. LC 75-37236. 256p. (Orig.). 1987. pap. 12.00 (0-8021-3052-6, Grove) Grove-Atltic.

Mitchell, Stephen, tr. Full Woman, Fleshly Apple, Hot Moon: Selected Poems of Pablo Neruda. 288p. 1998. pap. 15.00 (0-06-092877-8) HarpC.

— Tao Te Ching: A New English Version. LC 88-45123. 128p. 1988. 15.95 (0-318-35603-1) HarperTrade.

Mitchell, Stephen, tr. The BOOK OF JOB. LC 92-52637. 1994. pap. 12.00 (0-06-096959-8, Perennial) HarperTrade.

Mitchell, Stephen & Waelkens, Marc. Pisidian Antioch: The Site & Its Monuments. (Illus.). 247p. 1998. 59.50 (0-7156-2860-7, Pub. by Classical Pr) David Brown.

Mitchell, Stephen, et al. Cremna in Pisidia: An Ancient City in Peace & War. (Illus.). 256p. 1995. 59.50 (0-7156-2696-5, Pub. by Classical Pr) David Brown.

Mitchell, Stephen, jt. auth. see Autry, James A.

Mitchell, Stephen, jt. auth. see Hass, Robert.

Mitchell, Stephen, tr. see Amichai, Yehuda.

Mitchell, Stephen, tr. see Pagis, Dan.

Mitchell, Stephen, tr. see Rilke, Rainer Maria.

Mitchell, Stephen, tr. & frwd. see Rilke, Rainer Maria.

Mitchell, Stephen, tr. & intro. see Rilke, Rainer Maria.

Mitchell, Stephen A. Freud & Beyond. 320p. 1996. pap. 16.00 (0-465-01405-4) HarpC.

— Heroic Sagas & Ballads. LC 91-9899. (Myth & Poetics Ser.). 256p. 1991. text 35.00 (0-8014-2587-5) Cornell U Pr.

— Hope & Dread in Psychoanalysis. 304p. 1995. pap. 16.00 (0-465-03062-9, Pub. by Basic) HarpC.

— Influence & Autonomy in Psychoanalysis. LC 97-40014. (Relational Perspectives Book Ser.: No. 9). 280p. 1997. 42.50 (0-88163-240-6) Analytic Pr.

Mitchell, Stephen A. Relational Concepts in Psychoanalysis: An Integration. LC 88-11168. 312p. 1988. 45.50 (0-674-75411-5) HUP.

— Relationality: From Attachment to Intersubjectivity. LC 00-33144. (Relational Perspectives Book Ser.). 2000. write for info. (0-88163-322-4) Analytic Pr.

Mitchell, Stephen A. & Aron, Lewis, eds. Relational Psychoanalysis: The Emergence of a Tradition. LC 99-228505. (Relational Perspectives Book Ser.: Vol. 14). 496p. 1999. pap. 39.95 (0-88163-270-8) Analytic Pr.

Mitchell, Stephen A., jt. auth. see Greenberg, Jay R.

Mitchell, Stephen C., ed. Biological Interactions of Sulfur Compounds. 250p. 1996. 99.95 (0-7484-0244-6); pap. 39.95 (0-7484-0245-4) Taylor & Francis.

Mitchell, Steve. How to Speak Southern. 64p. 1984. mass mkt. 6.50 (0-553-27519-4) Bantam.

— More How to Speak Southern. 64p. (Orig.). 1983. mass mkt. 4.99 (0-553-27392-2) Bantam.

Mitchell, Steve, ed. Dramatherapy: Clinical Studies. LC 95-22207. 259p. 1995. pap. 27.50 (1-85302-304-3) Taylor & Francis.

— The Theatre of Self-Expression: Dramatherapy & Its Application in the Clinical Setting. 180p. 1996. pap. 27.00 (1-85302-283-7) Taylor & Francis.

Mitchell, Steve, ed. see Morgan, Clay.

Mitchell, Steven & Bainbridge, David. Sustainable Agriculture in California: A Guide to Information. 198p. (Orig.). 1991. pap. 2.00 (1-879906-01-5, 3349) ANR Pubns CA.

Mitchell, Steven & Mitchell, Karyn K. Hypnotherapy for Healing the Mind & Body. 200p. (Orig.). 1997. student ed., per. write for info. (0-9640822-0-9) Mind Rivers.

Mitchell, Steven, ed. see Pollock, Rebecca.

Mitchell, Steven D., ed. Space: Countdown to the Future: A Report on Third National Space. 314p. 1987. 50.00 (0-9616962-1-4) US Space Found.

Mitchell, Steven M. Internal Medicine, 1. (Clerkship Ser.). 1998. pap. text 24.95 (1-889325-74-0) Fence Crk Pubng.

— Internal Medicine: Solving Patient Problems-Pattern Recognition Process-Case Studies. 1998. pap. text 24.95 (1-889325-07-4) Fence Crk Pubng.

Mitchell, Steven P. Healing Our Schools: A Parent's Guide for Improving Education. LC 94-44297. 150p. 1995. 11.95 (1-885003-08-0) R D Reed Pubs.

Mitchell, Stewart. The Complete Illustrated Guide to Massage: A Step-by-Step Approach to the Healing Art of Touch. LC 97-27754. (Illustrated Health Bks.). (Illus.). 224p. 1997. pap. 24.95 (1-85230-990-3, Pub. by Element MA) Penguin Putnam.

— HE Massage: A Practical Introduction. (Health Essentials Ser.). 128p. 1997. pap. 9.95 (1-86204-066-4, Pub. by Element MA) Penguin Putnam.

— Horatio Seymour of New York. LC 69-19475. (American Scene Ser.). 1970. reprint ed. lib. bdg. 75.00 (0-306-71252-0) Da Capo.

***Mitchell, Stewart.** Illustrated Encyclopedia of Massage. (Illus.). 2000. pap. 29.95 (1-86204-357-4) Element MA.

— Massage: Introductory Guide to the Healing Power of Touch. (New Perspectives Ser.). 2000. pap. 9.95 (1-86204-626-3, Pub. by Element MA) Penguin Putnam.

Mitchell, Stewart. Naturopathy: Understanding the Healing Power of Nature. LC 98-21514. (Health Essentials Ser.). (Illus.). 128p. 1998. 9.95 (1-86204-303-5, Pub. by Element MA) Penguin Putnam.

Mitchell, Susan. American Attitudes: Who Thinks What about the Issues That Shape Our Lives. 2nd ed. LC 99-217496. 472p. 1998. 89.95 (1-885070-17-9) New Strategist.

***Mitchell, Susan.** American Generations: Who They Are. How They Live. What They Think. 2nd rev. ed. LC 98-168800. 496p. 1998. 79.95 (1-885070-14-4) New Strategist.

— American Generations: Who They Are, How They Live, What They Think. 3rd ed. 2000. 89.95 (1-885070-28-4) New Strategist.

— Erotikon: Poems. LC 99-16853. 96p. 2000. 23.00 (0-06-055353-7) HarpC.

Mitchell, Susan. Generation X: The Young Adult Market. 2nd rev. ed. 360p. 1999. 69.95 (1-885070-21-7) New Strategist.

— I'd Kill for a Cookie. 1998. pap. 12.95 (0-452-27644-6, Plume) Dutton Plume.

— Interactive Physiology: Nervous System. (C). 1996. cd-rom 33.95 (0-8053-4798-4) Benjamin-Cummings.

— Interactive Physiology Nervous System II. (C). 1999. pap. text 33.95 (0-8053-4720-8) Addison-Wesley.

— The Official Guide to American Attitudes: Who Thinks What about the Issues That Shape Our Lives. 415p. 1996. 89.95 (1-885070-02-0) New Strategist.

— Rapture: Poems. LC 91-50517. 96p. 1992. pap. 12.00 (0-06-096906-7, Perennial) HarperTrade.

Mitchell, Susan, jt. auth. see Russell, Cheryl.

Mitchell, Susan, ed. see Junior League of Columbus, Georgia, Inc. Staff.

***Mitchell, Susan E.** Arranging Food Beautifully: Tray & Steam Tablle Art. LC 98-45725. 224p. 1999. 49.95 (0-471-28301-0) Wiley.

Mitchell, Susan E. Creative Mexican Cooking. 176p. 1995. pap. 8.95 (1-55867-109-9, Nitty Gritty Ckbks) Bristol Pub Ent CA.

— 30-Minute Meals. 128p. 1998. pap. 12.95 (1-56426-085-2) Cole Group.

Mitchell, Susan L. The Hewitts of Athens County, Ohio. LC 88-60196. (Illus.). 456p. (C). 1989. 40.00 (0-9620263-0-1) S L Mitchell.

Mitchell, Susan M. Daddy Takes the Train to Work: A Story & Activity Book for Commuters' Children. (Illus.). 32p. (Orig.). (J). (ps-4). 1996. pap. 9.95 (0-9651598-0-9) Busy Buddy.

— Golf Buddies: A Storybook Introduction to the Rules, Etiquette, & Game of Golf. (Illus.). 40p. (J). (ps-5). 1998. pap. 8.95 (0-9651598-1-7) Busy Buddy.

Mitchell, Sydney B. Gardening in California. 1992. reprint ed. lib. bdg. 75.00 (0-7812-5065-X) Rprt Serv.

Mitchell, T. B. Bees of the Eastern United States, 2 vols., Set. 1960. 25.00 (0-910914-05-2) J Johnson.

Mitchell, T. Crichton. Charles Wesley: Man with the Dancing Heart. 280p. (Orig.). 1994. kivar 19.99 (0-8341-1449-6) Beacon Hill.

— The Wesley Century. (Great Holiness Classics Ser.: Vol. 2). 508p. 1984. 34.99 (0-8341-0910-7) Beacon Hill.

Mitchell, T. F. Pronouncing Arabic 1. (Illus.). 180p. 1990. text 55.00 (0-19-815151-9) OUP.

— Pronouncing Arabic 2. (Illus.). 322p. 1993. text 70.00 (0-19-823989-0) OUP.

M

— Writing Arabic: A Practical Introduction to Ruq'ah Script. 170p. 1979. pap. text 26.00 (0-19-815150-0) OUP.

Mitchell, T. N., ed. see Cicero, Marcus Tullius.

Mitchell, Tamara, jt. auth. see Mitchell, Wayne.

***Mitchell, Ted.** Thomas Wolfe: A Writer's Life. rev. ed. (Illus.). xv, 120p. 1999. pap. 10.00 (0-86526-286-1) NC Archives.

Mitchell, Terence, jt. auth. see Forbes, Robert.

Mitchell, Terence F. & El-Hassan, Shahir. Modality, Mood & Aspect in Spoken Arabic: With Special Reference to Egypt & the Levant. 320p. (C). 1994. text 93.50 (0-7103-0405-6, A5603) Routledge.

Mitchell, Teresa, ed. see Sanders, Pamelaia.

Mitchell, Theodore D., jt. auth. see Crowne, Henry R.

Mitchell, Theodore R. Political Education in the Southern Farmers Alliance, 1887-1900. LC 87-40141. 256p. 1987. reprint ed. pap. 79.40 (0-608-01980-1, 206263500003) Bks Demand.

Mitchell, Theodore R., jt. ed. see Torres, Carlos A.

Mitchell, Theresa. Movement: From Person to Actor to Character. LC 97-14861. 1998. 29.95 (0-8108-3328-X) Scarecrow.

— Strensall, Near York, in the Mid-Nineteenth Century. (C). 1988. 80.00 (1-85072-055-X, Pub. by W Sessions) St Mut.

Mitchell, Thomas. The Stepping-Stone to Architecture: Consisting of a Series of Questions & Answers Explaining in Simple Language the Principles & Progress of Architecture from the Earliest Times. 110p. 1995. reprint ed. pap. 12.95 (1-56459-514-5) Kessinger Pub.

Mitchell, Thomas G. The Commercial Lease Guidebook: Learn How to Win the Leasing Game! Jessop, Warren, ed. LC 92-80954. (Illus.). 224p. (Orig.). 1992. pap. 19.95 (0-9632982-0-8) Macore Intl.

***Mitchell, Thomas G.** Native vs. Settler: Ethnic Conflict in Israel/Palestine, Northern Ireland & South Africa, 200. LC 00-21075. (Contributions in Military Studies: Vol. 200). 272p. 2000. 64.00 (0-313-31357-1, GM1357, Greenwood Pr) Greenwood.

Mitchell, Thomas M. Machine Learning. LC 97-7692. (Illus.). 432p. (C). 1997. 83.44 (0-07-042807-7) McGraw.

Mitchell, Thomas N. Cicero, the Senior Statesman. 360p. (C). 1991. 42.50 (0-300-04779-7) Yale U Pr.

Mitchell, Thomas O., jt. ed. see Davis, Keith E.

Mitchell, Thomas R. Hawthorne's Fuller Mystery. LC 98-19290. 336p. 1998. 39.95 (1-55849-170-8) U of Mass Pr.

***Mitchell, Thomas W.** From Reconstruction to Deconstruction: Undermining Black Landownership, Political Independence, & Community Through Partition Sales of Tenancies in Common. (Research Paper Ser.: Vol. 132). iii, 65p. 2000. pap. 7.00 (0-934519-81-1) U of Wis Land.

Mitchell-Thome, Raoul C. Geology of the Middle Atlantic Islands. (Beitraege Zur Regionalen Geologie der Erde. Ser.: Vol. 12). (GER., Illus.). ix, 382p. 1976. 117.00 (3-443-11012-6, Pub. by Gebruder Borntraeger) Balogh.

— Geology of the South Atlantic Islands. (Beitraege Zur Regionalen Geologie der Erde. Ser.: Vol. 10). (GER., Illus.). x, 367p. 1970. 89.00 (3-443-11010-X, Pub. by Gebruder Borntraeger) Balogh.

***Mitchell, Tim.** Jonathan Richman, Modern Lover. 212p. (Orig.). 1999. pap. 22.50 (0-7206-1076-1, Pub. by P Owen Ltd) Dufour.

Mitchell, Timothy. Betrayal of the Innocents: Desire, Power, & the Catholic Church in Spain. LC 98-15214. 208p. 1998. 39.95 (0-8122-3453-7); pap. 16.50 (0-8122-1659-8) U of Pa Pr.

— Colonising Egypt. (Illus.). 230p. 1991. reprint ed. pap. 16.95 (0-520-07568-4, MITCOX, Pub. by U CA Pr) Cal Prin Full Svc.

— Passional Culture: Emotion, Religion, & Society in Southern Spain. LC 89-40398. (Illus.). 206p. (C). 1990. text 27.50 (0-8122-8202-7) U of Pa Pr.

Mitchell, Timothy J. Flamenco Deep Song. LC 94-10659. 238p. 1994. reprint ed. pap. 73.80 (0-608-07836-0, 205401200010) Bks Demand.

Mitchell, Tom. The Audio Designer's Tube Register. (Common Low-Power Triodes Ser.: Vol. 1). (Illus.). 144p. 1993. student ed., spiral bd. 18.00 (0-9628170-1-5) Media Cncpt.

Mitchell, Tom, jt. ed. see Steier, David M.

Mitchell, Tom M., et al, eds. Machine Learning: A Guide to Current Research. 1986. reprint ed. text 140.50 (0-89838-214-9) Kluwer Academic.

— Machine Learning: An Artificial Intelligence Approach, Vol. 1. LC 86-2953. (Illus.). 572p. 1983. reprint ed. text 53.95 (0-934613-09-5) Morgan Kaufmann.

Mitchell, Tom M. & Thrun, Sebastian. Recent Advances in Robot Learning, Vol. 368. Franklin, Judy A., ed. LC 96-18680. (International Series in Engineering & Computer Science, Natural Language Processing & Machine Translation). 224p. (C). 1996. text 114.00 (0-7923-9745-2) Kluwer Academic.

***Mitchell, Tony.** Dario Fo: People's Court Jester. 320p. 2000. pap. 19.95 (0-413-73320-3) Methn.

— Female Form: A Private View. 2000. 18.95 (1-85868-775-6, Pub. by Carlton Bks Ltd) Natl Bk Netwk.

— Fetish: Masterpieces of Erotic Fantasy Photography. (Illus.). 224p. 2000. pap. text 27.50 (1-56025-253-7, Thunders Mouth) Avalon NY.

Mitchell, Tony. Popular Music & Local Identity: Pop, Rock & Rap in Europe & Oceania. (Illus.). 224p. (C). 1996. pap. 19.95 (0-7185-0016-4); text 99.90 (0-7185-0019-9) Bks Intl VA.

Mitchell, Tony & Trussler, Simon, eds. File on Brenton. (Methuen Writer-Files Ser.). 96p. (C). 1988. pap. 9.95 (0-413-14540-9, A0091, Methuen Drama) Methn.

Mitchell, Tracy. What Do Fish Have to Do with Anything? And Other Stories. LC 97-1354. 208p. (J). (gr. 5-10). 1997. 17.99 (0-7636-0329-5); pap. 4.99 (0-7636-0412-7) Candlewick Pr.

Mitchell, Tymme M. Living to 102: Natural Health Methods, Testimonials, Personal Experiences, Documentation of Human Longevity. LC 98-68427. xii, 124 p. 1998. write for info. (1-892681-00-5) TM Mind Body.

Mitchell, V. E. Atlantis Station. (Star Trek Next Generation Starfleet Acad Ser.). 1994. 9.09 (0-606-11904-3, Pub. by Turtleback) Demco.

— Atlantis Station, No. 5. (Star Trek: The Next Generation Starfleet Academy Ser.). 128p. (YA). (gr. 3-6). 1994. per. 3.99 (0-671-88449-2, Minstrel Bks) PB.

— Enemy Unseen. Stern, David, ed. (Star Trek Ser.: No. 51). 288p. (Orig.). 1990. mass mkt. 4.99 (0-671-68403-5) PB.

— Imbalance. Stern, Dave, ed. (Star Trek: The Next Generation Ser.: No. 22). 288p. 1992. mass mkt. 5.50 (0-671-77571-5) PB.

— Pool Party Panic! (Secret World of Alex Mack Ser.: No. 28). (J). (gr. 3-6). 1998. pap. 3.99 (0-671-01428-5) PB.

— The Tale of the Bad Tempered Ghost. (Are You Afraid of the Dark? Ser.: No. 15). (YA). (gr. 5-8). 1997. per. 3.99 (0-671-01429-3) PB.

Mitchell, Vance O. Air Force Officers: Personnel Policy Development, 1944-1974. 510p. 1997. 38.00 (0-16-048862-1) AFH & MP.

***Mitchell, Verner D., ed.** This Waiting for Love: Helene Johnson, Poet of the Harlem Renaissance. 128p. 2000. 24.95 (1-55849-256-9) U of Mass Pr.

Mitchell, Viola, jt. auth. see Meier, Joel F.

Mitchell, Violaine S., ed. see Institute of Medicine Staff.

Mitchell, Vivien. Aluminium Nitride. LC 94-184598. 232p. 1994. 1200.00 (1-85617-193-0, Pub. by Elsvr Adv Tech) Elsevier.

Mitchell, W. It's Not What Happens to You, It's What You Do about It. 128p. 1997. 19.95 (0-9637901-0-2) W Mitchell.

Mitchell, W. C. The Cult of the Big Bang: Was There a Bang? LC 94-78655. 240p. 1995. reprint ed. pap. 11.95 (0-9643188-0-6) Cosmic Sense Bks.

Mitchell, W. H. Biographical & Statistical History of the County of Olmsted: Together with a General View of the State of Minnesota from Its Earliest Settlement to (1866) (Illus.). 132p. 1997. reprint ed. lib. bdg. 24.50 (0-8328-6810-8) Higginson Bk Co.

— Dakota County: Its Past & Present, Geographical, Statistical & Historical, Together with a General View of the State. (Illus.). 174p. 1997. reprint ed. pap. 18.50 (0-8328-6799-3); reprint ed. lib. bdg. 26.50 (0-8328-6798-5) Higginson Bk Co.

— Geographical & Statistical History of Steele County: From Its Earliest Settlement to 1868. (Illus.). 110p. 1997. reprint ed. lib. bdg. 21.00 (0-8328-6816-7) Higginson Bk Co.

Mitchell, W. H. & Sawyer, L. A. The Cape Run. (Illus.). 214p. (C). 1988. 150.00 (0-86138-030-4, Pub. by T Dalton) St Mut.

— Sailing Ship to Supertanker. 264p. 1990. 54.00 (0-86138-055-X, Pub. by T Dalton) St Mut.

Mitchell, W. H., jt. auth. see Sawyer, L. A.

Mitchell, W. J. Blake's Composite Art: A Study of the Illuminated Poetry. LC 77-7116. (Illus.). 310p. 1978. reprint ed. pap. 96.10 (0-608-06488-2, 206678500009) Bks Demand.

— Iconology: Image, Text, Ideology. LC 85-1177. x, 226p. 1986. 20.00 (0-226-53228-3) U Ch Pr.

— Iconology: Image, Text, Ideology. LC 85-1177. x, 226p. (C). 1987. pap. text 9.95 (0-226-53229-1) U Ch Pr.

— Image & Text in Arts. (C). 1996. 34.95 (0-226-53231-3) U Ch Pr.

— The Last Dinosaur Book: The Life & Times of a Cultural Icon. LC 98-16676. 308p. 1998. 35.00 (0-226-53204-6) U Ch Pr.

— On Narrative. LC 80-53137. 280p. (C). 1981. pap. text 14.95 (0-226-53217-8) U Ch Pr.

— Picture Theory: Essays on Verbal & Visual Representation. (Illus.). xvi, 462p. 1995. pap. text 18.00 (0-226-53232-1) U Ch Pr.

Mitchell, W. J., ed. Against Theory: Literary Studies & the New Pragmatism. LC 84-29127. vi, 152p. 1985. pap. text 9.95 (0-226-53227-5) U Ch Pr.

— Art & the Public Sphere. (Illus.). 280p. 1992. pap. 19.95 (0-226-53211-9); lib. bdg. 46.50 (0-226-53210-0) U Ch Pr.

— Landscape & Power. LC 93-4907. 264p. 1994. pap. text 13.95 (0-226-53207-0) U Ch Pr.

— Landscape & Power. LC 93-4907. 248p. 1999. lib. bdg. 42.50 (0-226-53206-2) U Ch Pr.

— The Language of Images. LC 80-5225. 314p. 1980. pap. text 17.95 (0-226-53215-1, P887) U Ch Pr.

— The Politics of Interpretation. rev. ed. LC 83-3581. 1993. pap. text 14.95 (0-226-53220-8) U Ch Pr.

— The Politics of Interpretation. rev. ed. LC 83-3581. 1994. lib. bdg. 25.00 (0-226-53219-4) U Ch Pr.

Mitchell, W. J. & Slaughter, J. C. Biology & Biochemistry for Chemists & Chemical Engineers. (Chemical Engineering Ser.). 1989. text 69.95 (0-470-21573-9) P-H.

Mitchell, W. O. According to Jake & the Kid. 1989. 26.95 (0-7710-6073-4) McCland & Stewart.

— According to Jake & the Kid. 280p. 1995. pap. 9.95 (0-7710-6071-8) McCland & Stewart.

— The Black Bonspiel of Willie MacCrimmon. (Illus.). 144p. 1994. 14.95 (0-7710-6081-5) McCland & Stewart.

— An Evening with W. O. Mitchell. LC 97-185866. (Illus.). 261p. 1997. 24.95 (0-7710-6088-2) McCland & Stewart.

Mitchell, W. O. An Evening with W. O. Mitchell: A Collection of the Author's Best-Loved Performance Pieces - A Fitting Final Book. 262p. 1997. pap. 16.99 (0-7710-6089-0) McCland & Stewart.

— How I Spent My Summer Holidays: A Novel. (Douglas Gibson Bks.). 276p. 2000. pap. 18.95 (0-7710-6110-2) McCland & Stewart.

Mitchell, W. O. Roses Are Difficult Here. 304p. 1991. mass mkt. 7.50 (0-7704-2523-2) Bantam.

***Mitchell, W. O.** Roses Are Difficult Here: A Novel. (Douglas Gibson Bks.). 328p. 2000. pap. 18.95 (0-7710-6109-9) McCland & Stewart.

Mitchell, W. O. The Vanishing Point. 1983. mass mkt. 4.95 (0-7704-2080-X) Bantam.

— Who Has Seen the Wind. (Illus.). 1991. 39.95 (0-7710-6078-5) McCland & Stewart.

Mitchell, Waddie. A Cowboy's Night Before Christmas. (Little Night Before Christmas Ser.). (Illus.). 60p. 1992. 5.95 (0-87905-486-7) Gibbs Smith Pub.

Mitchell, Waldo F. The Uses of Bank Funds. Bruchey, Stuart, ed. LC 80-1162. (Rise of Commercial Banking Ser.). (Illus.). 1981. reprint ed. lib. bdg. 18.95 (0-405-13669-2) Ayer.

Mitchell-Walker, Brenda. Garnets & Blackberries Poetry I: Inspirational Verse. (Illus.). 70p. 1997. pap. 23.50 (1-57502-650-3, PO1838) Morris Pubng.

Mitchell, Walter, tr. see Danielou, Jean.

Mitchell, Wayne & Mitchell, Tamara. Your Other Half. LC 97-77348. (Illus.). 144p. 1998. pap. 20.00 (0-9661220-1-1) Echo Wrk Pubs.

***Mitchell, Wesley C.** The Backward Art of Spending Money. 2nd ed. LC 99-24855. 421p. 1999. pap. 29.95 (0-7658-0611-8) Transaction Pubs.

Mitchell, Wesley C. The Backward Art of Spending Money & Other Essays. vii, 421p. 1964. reprint ed. 45.00 (0-678-00026-3) Kelley.

— Business Cycles: The Problem & Its Setting. LC 75-19730. (National Bureau of Economic Research Ser.). (Illus.). 1975. reprint ed. 41.95 (0-405-07608-8) Ayer.

— Business Cycles: The Problem & Its Setting. (Studies in Business Cycles: No. 1). 519p. 1927. reprint ed. 135.00 (0-87014-084-1) Natl Bur Econ Res.

— Business Cycles & Their Causes. LC 86-8182. (Illus.). xii, 226p. 1989. reprint ed. pap. text 12.95 (0-87991-262-6) Porcupine Pr.

— Economic Essays in Honor of Wesley Clair Mitchell Presented to Him by His Former Students on the Occasion of His Sixtieth Birthday. LC 68-16928. (Essay Index Reprint Ser.). 1977. 23.95 (0-8369-0402-8) Ayer.

— Gold, Prices & Wages under the Greenback Standard. LC 66-21688. (Library of Money & Banking History). xv, 627p. 1966. reprint ed. 57.50 (0-678-00200-2) Kelley.

— The Making & Using of Index Numbers. LC 65-19653. (Reprints of Economic Classics Ser.). 114p. 1965. reprint ed. 29.50 (0-678-00098-0) Kelley.

— Wartime "Prosperity" & the Future. (Occasional Papers: No. 9). 48p. 1943. reprint ed. 20.00 (0-87014-324-7) Natl Bur Econ Res.

— What Happens During Business Cycles? A Progress Report. (Studies in Business Cycles: No. 5). 427p. 1951. reprint ed. 111.10 (0-87014-088-4) Natl Bur Econ Res.

Mitchell, Wesley C. & Dorfman, J., eds. Types of Economic Theory: From Mercantilism to Institutionalism, Vol. 2. LC 67-16418. xii, 875p. 1969. 49.50 (0-678-04027-3) Kelley.

Mitchell, Wesley C., et al. Income in the United States: Its Amount & Distribution 1909-1919, Vol. 1. Incl. Vol. 2. LC 75-19731. 1975. 32.00 (0-405-07610-X); LC 75-19731. (National Bureau of Economic Research Ser.). (Illus.). 1975. reprint ed. 16.95 (0-405-07609-6) Ayer.

Mitchell, Wesley C., jt. auth. see Burns, Arthur F.

Mitchell, Wesley C., ed. see King, Willford I., et al.

***Mitchell, Will David.** Debugging JAVA. 2000. pap. 39.99 (0-07-212562-4) Osborne-McGraw.

Mitchell, Willa. Black American Cookbook, 1. 400p. lib. bdg. 5.95 (0-9603014-0-2) Evang Assn.

— Black American Cookbook, 2. 400p. lib. bdg. 6.95 (0-9603014-1-0) Evang Assn.

— Black Heritage Recipes to Treasure. LC 77-94215. (Black American Cookbook Ser.: Vol. 3). (Illus.). 200p. 1984. lib. bdg. 8.95 (0-9603014-2-9) Evang Assn.

Mitchell, William. Building Strong Families. LC 97-1732. 1997. pap. 12.99 (0-8054-6370-4) Broadman.

***Mitchell, William.** E-Topia. (Illus.). 192p. (C). 2000. reprint ed. pap. 13.95 (0-262-63205-5) MIT Pr.

Mitchell, William. A New & Complete System of Book-Keeping by an Improved Method of Double Entry. Brief, Richard P., ed. LC 77-87279. (Development of Contemporary Accounting Thought Ser.). 1978. reprint ed. lib. bdg. 39.95 (0-405-10907-5) Ayer.

— The Place of Minds in the World. LC 77-27201. (Gifford Lectures: 1924-26). 400p. reprint ed. 45.00 (0-404-60477-3) AMS Pr.

— Winged Defense: The Development & Possibilities of Modern Air Power - Economic & Military. 320p. 1988. pap. 9.95 (0-486-25771-1) Dover.

Mitchell, William & Kapper, Ronald G. Paradigm Intermediate keyboarding & Applications, Sessions 61-120: Instructor's guide. 24.00 (0-7638-0207-7) EMC-Paradigm.

Mitchell, William & Pounds, Jerry. Discover the Winning Edge. LC 97-223181. 126p. 1997. write for info. (0-7673-3178-8) LifeWay Christian.

Mitchell, William, et al. Intermediate Keyboarding with Windows, Sessions 61-120: Text with Word 97 & Supplement. 37.95 (0-7638-0203-4) EMC-Paradigm.

— Paradigm Keyboarding, Sessions 1-30: Instructor's guide. 4th ed. text, teacher ed. 24.00 (0-7638-0125-9) EMC-Paradigm.

— Keyboarding with Word 97: Instructor's guide. 4th ed. text, teacher ed. 24.00 (0-7638-0128-3) EMC-Paradigm.

— Keyboarding with Word 97: Sessions 1-30, Text, Easelback. 168p. text 25.95 (0-7638-0208-5) EMC-Paradigm.

— Keyboarding with Word 7, Sessions 1-60: A Computer Managed Approach Instructor's Guide. 24.00 (0-7638-0005-8) EMC-Paradigm.

— Keyboarding with WordPerfect 5.1 for Dos: A Computer Managed Approach, Short Course, Sessions 1-60, User's Guide. 8.95 (1-56118-674-0) EMC-Paradigm.

Mitchell, William, et al. Paradigm Keyboarding & Applications: A Mastery Approach for Microcomputers & Typewriters. 3rd ed. (C). 1990. pap. text, teacher ed. 14.00 (1-56118-151-X) Paradigm MN.

Mitchell, William, et al. Keyboarding with WordPerfect 6.1 for Windows, Sessions 1-60: A Computer Managed Approach, Textbook & user's guide. 35.95 (1-56118-771-2) EMC-Paradigm.

Mitchell, William, jt. auth. see Canan, Michael.

Mitchell, William, jt. auth. see Mach, K. A.

Mitchell, William A., Jr. Foundations of Natural Therapeutics: Biochemical Apologetics & Nuturopathic Medicine. Diamond, Paula M. & Bier, Ian D., eds. (Illus.). 160p. (C). 1996. pap. text 39.00 (1-889705-01-2) SW College.

Mitchell, William A. Linn County, Kansas: A History. 404p. 1994. reprint ed. lib. bdg. 40.00 (0-8328-4001-7) Higginson Bk Co.

Mitchell, William A., jt. auth. see Kolars, John F.

Mitchell, William B., jt. auth. see Canan, Michael J.

Mitchell, William C. Beyond Politics: Markets, Welfare & the Failure of Bureaucracy. 234p. (C). 1994. pap. 25.00 (0-8133-2208-1, Pub. by Westview) HarpC.

Mitchell, William D. Contractor's Survival Manual. LC 86-16620. 160p. (Orig.). 1986. pap. 22.25 (0-910460-42-6) Craftsman.

— Estate & Retirement Planning Answer Book. annuals LC 96-160091. 504p. 1994. 155.00 (1-56706-135-4, S155) Panel Pubs.

— Estate & Retirement Planning Answer Book. 2nd ed. LC 96-213889. 872p. 1996. boxed set 118.00 (1-56706-321-7) Aspen Pub.

Mitchell, William D., jt. auth. see Canan, Michael J.

Mitchell, William E. The Bamboo Fire: Field Work with the New Guinea Wape. 2nd ed. 256p. (C). 1987. pap. text 12.95 (0-88133-248-8) Waveland Pr.

— Mishpokhe: A Study of New York City Jewish Family Clubs. (New Babylon Studies in the Social Sciences: No. 30). (Illus.). 1978. 41.55 (3-10-800287-2) Mouton.

Mitchell, William E., ed. Clowning As Critical Practice: Performance Humor in the South Pacific. LC 92-50195. (Association for Social Anthropology in Oceania Monographs). 272p. (C). 1993. pap. 19.95 (0-8229-5487-7); text 49.95 (0-8229-3734-4) U of Pittsburgh Pr.

Mitchell, William E., jt. auth. see Leichter, Hope J.

Mitchell, William J. City of Bits: Space, Place & the Infobahn. (Illus.). 232p. 1996. pap. text 13.95 (0-262-63176-8) MIT Pr.

— E-Topia: Urban Life, Jim - But Not as We Know It. LC 99-20670. (Illus.). 192p. 1999. pap. 13.95 (0-262-13355-5) MIT Pr.

— The Logic of Architecture: Design, Computation, & Cognition. (Illus.). 304p. (Orig.). 1990. pap. text 21.95 (0-262-63116-4) MIT Pr.

— The Reconfigured Eye: Visual Truth in the Post-Photographic Era. (Illus.). 283p. 1992. pap. text 24.95 (0-262-63160-1) MIT Pr.

— The 365 Day Menu Planner. ix, 495p. 1996. write for info. (0-9658886-0-6) Mitchell Assocs.

Mitchell, William J. & McCullough, Malcolm. Digital Design Media. 2nd ed. (Architecture Ser.). 512p. 1994. pap. 49.95 (0-471-28666-4, VNR) Wiley.

Mitchell, William J. & Salzer, Felix, eds. The Music Forum, Vol. 6, Pt. I. 256p. 1988. text 61.50 (0-231-05832-2) Col U Pr.

Mitchell, William J. & Steel, John R. Fine Structures & Iteration Trees. LC 94-888. (Lecture Notes in Logic Ser.: Vol. 3). vi, 130p. 1994. 43.95 (0-387-57494-8) Spr-Verlag.

Mitchell, William J., ed. see Bach, Carl P.

Mitchell, William M. Keyboarding with Word 97: Sessions 1-60. LC 97-44135. 1998. 37.95 (0-7638-0127-5) Paradigm MN.

— Keyboarding with Word 7: Sessions 1-60. LC 96-53014. 1997. pap. text 34.95 (0-7638-0004-X) Paradigm MN.

— Paradigm Keyboarding: Sessions 1-30. 4th ed. LC 97-44134. 1998. 32.44 (0-7638-0123-2); pap. 37.44 (0-7638-0146-1) Paradigm MN.

— Paradigm Keyboarding & Applications: Sessions 1-60. 4th ed. LC 97-44133. 1998. write for info. (0-7638-0147-X) Paradigm MN.

— The Rise of the Revolutionary Party in the English House of Commons, 1603-1629. LC 75-31471. 209p. 1976. reprint ed. lib. bdg. 59.50 (0-8371-8535-1, MIRR, Greenwood Pr) Greenwood.

Mitchell, William M., et al. Intermediate Keyboarding with Windows: Sessions 61-120. 1996. pap. text 34.95 (1-56118-923-5) Paradigm MN.

— Intermediate Keyboarding with Windows: Sessions 61-120. 1996. pap. text 14.00 (1-56118-925-1) Paradigm MN.

— Keyboarding with WordPerfect. LC 92-25693. 400p. 1993. pap. text 26.95 (1-56118-569-8) Paradigm MN.

— Keyboarding with WordPerfect: A Computer Managed Approach. LC 93-19772. 440p. 1994. pap. text 29.95 (1-56118-599-X) Paradigm MN.

— Keyboarding with WordPerfect: A Computer Managed Approach. LC 93-19772. 160p. 1994. pap. text, teacher ed. 19.00 (1-56118-572-8) Paradigm MN.

M

— Keyboarding with WordPerfect: A Computer Managed Approach: Intermediate Course. 1994. pap. text, teacher ed. 19.00 (*1-56118-693-7*) Paradigm MN.

— Keyboarding with WordPerfect 6.1 for Windows: 30 Sessions. 1995. pap. text 23.95 (*1-56118-842-5*) Paradigm MN.

— Keyboarding with WordPerfect 6.1 for Windows: 30 Sessions. 1995. pap. text 7.95 (*1-56118-815-8*) Paradigm MN.

— Keyboarding with WordPerfect 6.1 for Windows: 30 Sessions. 1995. pap. text 19.00 (*1-56118-772-0*) Paradigm MN.

— Keyboarding with WordPerfect 6.1 for Windows: 60 Sessions. LC 95-36716. 1995. pap. text 32.95 (*1-56118-770-4*) Paradigm MN.

— Keyboarding with WordPerfect Version 6.0. LC 94-31079. 1994. pap. text 26.95 (*1-56118-664-3*) Paradigm MN.

— Keyboarding with WordPerfect 5.1 for Dos: A Computer Managed Approach: Intermediate Course. 424p. 1994. pap. text 30.95 (*1-56118-509-4*) Paradigm MN.

— Paradigm Keyboarding & Applications: A Mastery Approach for Microcomputers & Typewriters. 3rd ed. (C). 1990. pap. text 31.95 (*1-56118-160-9*) Paradigm MN.

M

— Paradigm Keyboarding & Applications: A Mastery Approach for Microcomputers & Typewriters. 3rd ed. (C). 1990. pap. text 18.00 (*1-56118-156-0*); 10.45 (*1-56118-159-5*) Paradigm MN.

— Paradigm Keyboarding & Applications: A Mastery Approach for Microcomputers & Typewriters, Short Course. (C). 1990. pap. 9.95 (*1-56118-155-2*); 10.45 (*1-56118-158-7*) Paradigm MN.

— Paradigm Keyboarding Skills: A Mastery Approach for Microcomputers & Typewriters. (C). 1990. pap. text 17.95 (*1-56118-150-1*) Paradigm MN.

— Paradigm Keyboarding with WordPerfect: Version 5.1: Sessons 1-30. LC 93-27499. 1994. pap. text 22.95 (*1-56118-508-6*) Paradigm MN.

Mitchell, William M., et al. Keyboarding & Applications, Sessions 1-60: Text. 4th ed. LC 97-44133. text 39.95 (*0-7638-0124-0*) EMC-Paradigm.

Mitchell, William M., jt. auth. see Labarre, James.

Mitchell, William P. & Guillet, David, eds. Irrigation at High Altitudes: The Social Organization of Water Control Systems in the Andes. LC 94-20688. (Society for Latin American Anthropology Publication Ser.: Vol. 12). 1994. write for info. (*0-913167-66-5*) Am Anthro Assn.

***Mitchell, William R., Jr.** An Anniversary Celebration of Seventy Homes. Norman, Amy W. & Williams, Linda D., eds. (Illus.). 176p. 1999. 40.00 (*0-9675293-0-1*) H Norman.

Mitchell, William R., Jr. Classic Atlanta: Landmarks of the Atlanta Spirit. (Illus.). 224p. 1991. 39.95 (*0-932958-12-5*) Golden Coast.

— Classic New Orleans. LC 93-77933. (Golden Coast Book Ser.). (Illus.). 2240p. 1993. 50.00 (*0-8203-1576-1*) Golden Coast.

— Classic Savannah. (Illus.). 144p. 1987. 35.00 (*0-932958-07-9*) Golden Coast.

Mitchell, William R. Continuing Tradition. (Illus.). 136p. 1992. 40.00 (*0-932958-14-1*) Golden Coast.

— Lewis Edmund Crook Jr. Architect, 1898-1967: A Twenthieth-Century Traditionalist in the Deep South. LC 84-6240. (Illus.). 144p. 1984. 45.00 (*0-9614203-0-8*) L C Crossley.

Mitchell, William R., Jr. Neel Reid: Of Hentz, Reid & Adler & the Georgia School of Classicists. (Illus.). 224p. 1997. 50.00 (*0-932958-19-2*) Golden Coast.

— The Residential Architecture of Henry Sprott Long & Associates. (Illus.). 104p. 1992. 40.00 (*0-932958-13-3*) Golden Coast.

Mitchell, William R. Voices of the Advent. 2nd rev. ed. (Illus.). 72p. 1998. 11.95 (*1-883938-49-X*) Dry Bones Pr.

***Mitchell, William R.** Voices of the Advent: And Other Voices. 3rd rev. ed. (Illus.). 130p. 1999. reprint ed. pap. 12.95 (*1-883938-50-3*) Dry Bones Pr.

Mitchelly, Carolyn B., jt. auth. see Fast N Easy Staff.

Mitchels, Barbara. Family Law. (C). 1990. 150.00 (*1-85431-084-4*, Pub. by Blackstone Pr) St Mut.

— Family Law. (C). 1991. text 22.00 (*1-85431-129-8*, Pub. by Blackstone Pr) Gaunt.

Mitchelson, Austin. The Baker Street Irregular: The Unauthorized Biography of Sherlock Holmes. 1994. 35.00 (*0-88734-905-6*, Pub. by Players Pr) Empire Pub Srvs.

Mitchelson, Austin & Utechin, Nicholas. Sherlock Holmes & the Earthquake Machine. 1994. 25.00 (*0-86025-283-3*, Pub. by I Henry Pubns) Empire Pub Srvs.

— Sherlock Holmes & the Hellbirds. LC 95-13261. 1995. 35.00 (*0-86025-284-1*) Players Pr.

***Mitchelson, Keith R. & Cheng, Jing.** Capillary Electrophoresis of Nucleic Acids Vol. I: Capillary Electrophoresis System as an Analytical Tool. (Methods in Molecular Biology Ser.: Vol. 162). 560p. 2000. 125.00 (*0-89603-779-7*) Humana.

— Capillary Electrophoresis of Nucleic Acids Vol. II: Practical Applications of Capillary Electrophoresis. (Methods in Molecular Biology Ser.: Vol. 163). 448p. 2000. 125.00 (*0-89603-765-7*) Humana.

Mitchelson, Mitch. The Most Excellent Book of How to Be a Juggler. LC 97-8012. (Most Excellent Book of Ser.). (Illus.). 32p. (J). (gr. 4-6). 1997. pap. 6.95 (*0-7613-0632-3*, Copper Beech Bks); lib. bdg. 19.90 (*0-7613-0618-8*, Copper Beech Bks) Millbrook Pr.

Mitcheltree, Tom. Dataman. 240p. 1998. 22.95 (*1-885173-52-0*) Write Way.

— Katie's Will. 1999. per. 4.99 (*0-373-26328-7*) S&S Trade.

— Katie's Will. 288p. 1997. 22.95 (*1-885173-20-2*) Write Way.

***Mitchem, Jeffrey M.** The West & Central Florida Expeditions of Clarence Bloomfield Moore: Edited & with an Introduction by Jeffrey M. Mitchem. LC 99-6085. 1999. 39.95 (*0-8173-0951-9*) U of Ala Pr.

Mitchem, Jeffrey M., ed. see Moore, Clarence Bloomfield.

Mitchener, C. H., ed. Tuscarawas & Muskingum Valley, Ohio: History, 1775-1840. 392p. 1975. reprint ed. 20.00 (*1-885463-27-8*) Ohio Genealogy.

Mitchener, Carol, jt. auth. see Mitchener, Harold.

***Mitchener, Harold & Mitchener, Carol.** Bristol. LC 00-102558. (Images of America Ser.). (Illus.). 128p. 2000. pap. 18.99 (*0-7385-0427-0*) Arcadia Publng.

***Mitchener, M.** Oriental Coins & Their Values Vol. I: The World of Islam. (Illus.). 510p. 1998. lib. bdg. 265.00 (*0-904173-15-1*) S J Durst.

Mitchener, Tony, ed. The Hampshire Handbook, 1990: Official H. C. C. C. Yearbook. (C). 1989. 39.00 (*1-85455-059-4*, Pub. by Ensign Pubns & Print) St Mut.

— The Hampshire Handbook, 1991: Official H. C. C. C. Yearbook. (C). 1989. 45.00 (*1-85455-069-1*, Pub. by Ensign Pubns & Print) St Mut.

— The Hampshire Handbook, 1992: Official H. C. C. C. Yearbook. (C). 1989. 39.00 (*0-7855-6613-9*, Pub. by Ensign Pubns & Print) St Mut.

Mitchenson, Joe, jt. auth. see Mander, Raymond.

Mitchenson, K. W. Villiers-Plouich: Arras. (Battleground Europe Ser.). 1999. pap. text 16.95 (*0-85052-658-2*) Leo Cooper.

Mitcheson, A., jt. auth. see Ulukoy, K.

Mitcheu, Judy, ed. see Smith, Marilyn K. & Forbes, Victoria Q.

Mitchie Company Staff, jt. auth. see Harriman, D. P.

Mitchill, Samuel Latham. Letter from Dr. Samuel L. Mitchill of New York to Samuel M. Burnside. (LC History-America-E). 1820. reprint ed. lib. bdg. 99.00 (*0-7812-4391-2*) Rprt Serv.

***Mitchinson, Bill.** Epehy: Hindenburg Line. (Battleground Europe Ser.). 1998. pap. text 16.95 (*0-85052-627-2*, Pub. by Leo Cooper) Trans-Atl Phila.

— Riqueval: Hindenburg Line. (Battleground Europe Ser.). 1998. pap. text 16.95 (*0-85052-622-1*, Pub. by Leo Cooper) Trans-Atl Phila.

Mitchinson, David. Celebrating Moore: Works from the Collection of the Henry Moore Foundation. LC 98-203032. (Illus.). 360p. 1998. 65.00 (*0-520-21670-9*, Pub. by U CA Pr) Cal Prin Full Svc.

Mitchinson, J., jt. auth. see Mander, Raymond.

Mitchinson, Malcolm J., et al, eds. Essentials of Pathology. LC 95-14348. 352p. 1995. pap. 44.95 (*0-632-02944-7*) Blackwell Sci.

Mitchinson, Naomi. Corn King & the Spring Queen. LC 73-145186. 1971. reprint ed. 69.00 (*0-403-01111-6*) Scholarly.

Mitchinson, Rosalind. Why Scottish History Matters. (C). 1989. 39.00 (*0-85411-048-8*, Pub. by Saltire Soc) St Mut.

Mitchinson, Wendy. The Nature of Their Bodies: Women & Their Doctors in Victorian Canada. 512p. 1991. text 60.00 (*0-8020-5901-5*); pap. text 22.95 (*0-8020-6840-5*) U of Toronto Pr.

Mitchinson, Wendy, jt. ed. see Cook, G. Ramsay.

Mitchinson, Wendy, jt. ed. see Iacovetta, Franca.

Mitchison, N. Avrion & Sercarz, Eli E. The Semiotics of Cellular Communication in the Immune System. (NATO ASI Series H: Vol. 23). (Illus.). xiii, 335p. 1988. 133.00 (*0-387-18552-6*) Spr-Verlag.

Mitchison, N. Avrion, jt. ed. see Feldmann, Marc.

Mitchison, Naomi. The Corn King & the Spring Queen. LC 93-17897. (Hera Ser.). 721p. 1994. pap. 17.00 (*0-939149-99-0*) Soho Press.

— Life for Africa: The Story of Bram Fischer. (C). 1973. text 29.95 (*0-85036-170-2*, Pub. by MRLN) Paul & Co Pubs.

— Solution Three. LC 94-32515. 183p. (Orig.). 1995. 32.50 (*1-55861-097-9*); pap. 10.95 (*1-55861-096-0*) Feminist Pr.

***Mitchison, Naomi.** To the Chapel Perilous. 2000. pap. 10.95 (*1-928999-05-0*) Green Knight.

Mitchison, Naomi. You May Well Ask: A Memoir, 1920-1940 LC 80-499459. 240 p. 1979. 6.50 (*0-575-02614-6*) V Gollancz.

Mitchison, Naomi M. Barbarian Stories. LC 77-134970. (Short Story Index Reprint Ser.). 1977. 18.95 (*0-8369-3701-5*) Ayer.

— Delicate Fire: Short Stories & Poems. LC 79-145403. (Short Story Index Reprint Ser.). 1977. reprint ed. 23.95 (*0-8369-3778-3*) Ayer.

— When the Bough Breaks, & Other Stories. LC 71-160944. (Short Story Index Reprint Ser.). 1977. reprint ed. 20.95 (*0-8369-3923-9*) Ayer.

Mitchison, Nicholas A. T Cell Subsets in Infectious & Autoimmune Diseases. (Ciba Foundation Symposium Ser.: Vol. 195). 272p. 1996. 128.00 (*0-471-95720-8*) Wiley.

Mitchison, Rosalind. Coping with Destitution: Poverty & Relief in Western Europe. (Joanne Goodman Lectures). 96p. 1991. pap. 13.95 (*0-8020-6859-6*); text 30.00 (*0-8020-5912-0*) U of Toronto Pr.

— History of Scotland. 2nd ed. (Illus.). 480p. (C). 1995. pap. 25.99 (*0-415-05925-9*) Routledge.

— Lordship to Patronage. 1991. pap. text 20.00 (*0-7486-0233-X*, Pub. by Edinburgh U Pr) Col U Pr.

***Mitchison, Rosalind.** The Old Poor Law in Scotland: The Experience of Poverty, 1574-1845. 352p. 2000. pap. text 28.00 (*0-7486-1344-7*) Col U Pr.

Mitchison, Rosalind. Why Scottish History Matters. LC 97-221579. 1993. pap. 28.00 (*0-85411-070-4*, Pub. by Saltire Soc) St Mut.

Mitchison, Rosalind & Leneman, Leah. Girls in Trouble: Sexuality & Social Control in Rural Scotland, 1660-1780. LC 98-185313. 128p. 1997. pap. 27.00 (*1-898218-89-7*) St Mut.

Mitchison, Rosalind, jt. ed. see Leneman, Leah.

Mitchison, Rosalind, jt. ed. see Phillipson, N. T.

***Mitchler, John D. & Covill, Dave.** Hiking Colorado's Summits. LC 98-32352. (Illus.). 272p. 1999. pap. 15.95 (*1-56044-715-X*) Falcon Pub Inc.

Mitchley, Charles, ed. see Mares, Theun.

Mitchner, Clarice J. Senator John Sherman Cooper: Consummate Statesman. 1981. 38.95 (*0-405-14099-1*) Ayer.

Mitchner, Morton & Kruger, Charles H., Jr. Partially Ionized Gases. (Illus.). 518p. (C). 1973. reprint ed. pap. text 4.95 (*0-9635646-0-9*) C H Kruger.

Mitchner, Morton, ed. see Lockheed Symposium on Magnetohydrodynamics Staff.

Mitchum, Hank. Red Buffalo. large type ed. (Nightingale Series Large Print Bks.). 300p. 1992. pap. 14.95 (*0-8161-5322-1*, G K Hall Lrg Type) Mac Lib Ref.

— Seattle. large type ed. 1990. pap. 5.00 (*0-7451-1290-0*, Pub. by Chivers N Amer) Chivers N Amer.

Mitchum, John. Them Ornery Mitchum Boys: The Adventures of Robert & John Mitchum. Stanley, John, ed. LC 88-92904. (Illus.). 400p. (Orig.). 1989. pap. 11.95 (*0-940064-06-5*) Creatures at Large.

Mitchum, Samuel W., Jr. Rommel's Greatest Victory: The Desert Fox & the Fall of Tobruk, Spring 1942. LC 98-12169. 1998. 27.95 (*0-89141-656-0*) Presidio Pr.

Mitchum, William. Blues for Mr. Baldwin. (Illus.). 134p. (Orig.). 1985. 9.95 (*0-9612120-2-0*); pap. 5.95 (*0-9612120-3-9*) Para-Bk-Pr.

— The Devil's Bestseller. (Illus.). 151p. 1983. 9.95 (*0-9612120-0-4*); pap. 3.50 (*0-9612120-1-2*) Para-Bk-Pr.

— How to Exorcise or Delete Race Riots & Rodney King Beatings. (Illus.). 235p. 19.95 (*0-9612120-6-3*) Para-Bk-Pr.

— O. J. Simpson: The Trial vs. Ol' Man River's Saga of the Raft. (Illus.). 203p. 19.95 (*0-9612120-8-X*) Para-Bk-Pr.

— The Power of Raceless Thinking. (Illus.). 189p. 1988. 9.95 (*0-9612120-4-7*); pap. 5.95 (*0-9612120-5-5*) Para-Bk-Pr.

Mitchusson, Don. Introduction to File Processing. 3rd ed. 140p. 1994. pap. text 32.00 (*0-9631748-2-7*) Mitcon.

***Miteff, Deb & Falk, Cathy.** The Un-Halloween Book: A Complete Fall Festival for Children's Ministry. (Illus.). 248p. 1999. pap. 16.99 (*1-885358-74-1*, Lgacy Pr) Rainbow CA.

Mitelman, Felix. Catalog of Chromosome Aberrations in Cancer, 2 vols. 5th ed. Johansson, Bertil & Mertens, Fredrik, eds. LC 94-30796. 4252p. 1994. 675.00 (*0-471-11183-X*) Wiley.

— Catalogue of Chromosome Aberrations in Cancer. (Journal: Cytogenetics & Cell Genetics: Vol. 36, No. 1-2). (Illus.). 516p. 1983. pap. 115.00 (*3-8055-3813-8*) S Karger.

Mitelman, Felix, ed. An International System for Human Cytogenetic Nomenclature (1995) Recommendations of the International Standing Committee on Human Cytogenetic Nomenclature, Memphis, Tennessee, October 1994. LC 96-131951. (Illus.). 114p. 1995. pap. 35.00 (*3-8055-6226-8*) S Karger.

— ISCN Guidelines for Cancer Cytogenetics, 1991: Supplement to an International System for Human Cytogenetic Nomenclature. vi, 58p. 1992. pap. 38.50 (*3-8055-5567-9*) S Karger.

Mitelman, Felix, jt. auth. see Heim, Sverre.

Mitford, A. B. Tales of Old Japan. LC 66-25436. (Illus.). 430p. 1966. reprint ed. pap. 14.95 (*0-8048-1160-1*) Tuttle Pubng.

Mitford, Jessica. The American Way of Birth. 322p. 1999. reprint ed. text 23.00 (*0-7881-6345-0*) DIANE Pub.

— The American Way of Death. 1993. reprint ed. lib. bdg. 25.95 (*1-56849-159-X*) Buccaneer Bks.

***Mitford, Jessica.** The American Way of Death Revisited. 2000. pap. 14.00 (*0-679-77186-7*) Vin Bks.

Mitford, Jessica. Daughters & Rebels: An Autobiography. LC 81-47450. 304p. 1995. pap. 9.95 (*0-8050-1172-2*, Owl) H Holt & Co.

— Hons & Rebels. large type ed. 356p. 1991. 21.95 (*1-85089-441-8*) ISIS Lrg Prnt.

Mitford, John, ed. see Parnell, Thomas.

Mitford, Mary R. Belford Regis: or Sketches of a Country Town, 3 vols, Vol. 1. LC 72-4457. (Short Story Index Reprint Ser.). 1977. reprint ed. 66.95 (*0-8369-4185-3*) Ayer.

— Country Stories. LC 70-110208. (Short Story Index Reprint Ser.). 1977. 20.95 (*0-8369-3359-1*) Ayer.

— Our Village. large type ed. (Isis Clear Type Classic Ser.). 170p. 1992. 23.95 (*1-85089-489-2*, Pub. by ISIS Lrg Prnt) Transaction Pubs.

— Our Village, 1824. LC 95-41976. (Revolution & Romanticism, 1789-1834 Ser.). 1996. 55.00 (*1-85477-185-X*) Continuum.

— Recollections of a Literary Life. LC 74-178342. reprint ed. 67.50 (*0-404-56789-4*) AMS Pr.

Mitford, Mary R., ed. Lights & Shadows of American Life, 3 vols. 1972. reprint ed. lib. bdg. 99.00 (*0-8422-8098-7*) Irvington.

Mitford, Nancy. The Blessing. 224p. 1998. pap. 10.95 (*0-7867-0521-3*) Carroll & Graf.

— Christmas Pudding. 1987. mass mkt. 4.95 (*0-88184-342-3*) Carroll & Graf.

— Christmas Pudding. 192p. 1998. pap. 10.95 (*0-7867-0576-0*) Carroll & Graf.

— Don't Tell Alfred. 223p. 1990. pap. 9.95 (*0-88184-597-3*) Carroll & Graf.

— Frederick the Great. (Illus.). 224p. 1995. pap. 13.95 (*0-14-003653-9*, Penguin Bks) Viking Penguin.

— Highland Fling. 192p. 1988. mass mkt. 3.95 (*0-88184-390-3*) Carroll & Graf.

— Pigeon Pie. 2nd ed. 192p. 1999. pap. 11.95 (*0-7867-0633-3*) Carroll & Graf.

— The Pursuit of Love & Love in a Cold Climate. 19th ed. LC 93-43632. 672p. 1994. 18.50 (*0-679-60090-6*) Random.

— The Sun King. (Illus.). 312p. 1995. pap. 22.95 (*0-14-023967-7*, Penguin Bks) Viking Penguin.

— Voltaire in Love. 1999. pap. 14.95 (*0-7867-0641-4*) Carroll & Graf.

Mitford, Nancy & Roussin, Andre. The Little Hut: Manuscript Edition. 1957. pap. 13.00 (*0-8222-0678-1*) Dramatists Play.

Mitford, Nancy, tr. & intro. see De Lafayette, Madame.

Mitford, T. B. Inscriptions of Kourion. LC 78-121295. (Memoirs Ser.: Vol. 83). (Illus.). 1971. 30.00 (*0-87169-083-7*, M083-MIT) Am Philos.

***Mitgang, Herbert.** Abraham Lincoln: A Press Portrait. 2000. pap. 19.95 (*0-8232-2062-1*) Fordham.

Mitgang, Herbert. Dangerous Dossiers. 340p. 1996. pap. 14.95 (*1-55611-485-0*, Pub. by D I Fine) Penguin Putnam.

— The Man Who Rode the Tiger: The Life & Times of Judge Sammuel Seabury. 2nd ed. xxiv, 380p. 1996. reprint ed. pap. 17.00 (*0-8232-1722-1*) Fordham.

— The Man Who Rode the Tiger: The Life & Times of Judge Samuel Seabury. 2nd ed. LC 96-24906. xxiv, 380p. 1996. reprint ed. 30.00 (*0-8232-1721-3*) Fordham.

— Mr. Lincoln. 58p. 1982. pap. 5.60 (*0-87129-703-5*, M58) Dramatic Pub.

— Mister Lincoln: A Drama in 2 Acts. LC 81-8895. 67p. 1982. 11.95 (*0-8093-1034-1*) S Ill U Pr.

***Mitgang, Herbert.** Once Upon a Time in New York: Jimmy Walker, Franklin Roosevelt & the Last Great Battle of the Jazz Age. LC 99-16631. (Illus.). 272p. 2000. 25.00 (*0-684-85579-8*) Free Pr.

***Mitgang, Herbert, ed.** Abraham Lincoln: A Press Portrait. 2000. 32.95 (*0-8232-2061-3*) Fordham.

Mitgang, Herbert, ed. Civilians under Arms: The Stars & Stripes, Civil War to Korea. 220p. (C). 1996. pap. 14.95 (*0-8093-2109-2*) S Ill U Pr.

***Mitgang, Lee D.** Big Bird & Beyond: The New Media & the Markle Foundation. xxiv, 292p. 2000. 35.95 (*0-8232-2040-0*) Fordham.

***Mitgang, Lee D. & John & Mary R. Markle Foundation Staff.** Big Bird & Beyond: The New Media & the Markle Foundation. LC 00-27540. (Illus.). xxiv, 292p. (J). 2000. pap. 19.95 (*0-8232-2041-9*) Fordham.

Mitgang, Lee D., jt. auth. see Boyer, Ernest L.

Mitgang, N. R., jt. auth. see Haskins, Jim.

Mitgang, Susan, jt. ed. see Robbins, John.

Mitgutsch. In Foreign Lands. Date not set. pap. write for info. (*0-8050-4175-3*) St Martin.

Mitgutsch, Ali. From Blossom to Honey. (Carolrhoda Start to Finish Bks.).Tr. of Von der Blute Zum Honig. (Illus.). 24p. (J). (ps-3). 1981. lib. bdg. 18.60 (*0-87614-146-7*, Carolrhoda) Lerner Pub.

Mitgutsch, Ali, et al. From Dinosaurs to Fossils. LC 80-28596. (Start to Finish Bks.). Orig. Title: Tiere der Urwelt. (Illus.). 24p. (J). (ps-3). 1981. lib. bdg. 18.60 (*0-87614-152-1*, Carolrhoda) Lerner Pub.

— From Egg to Bird. (Start to Finish Bks.). (Illus.). 24p. (J). (ps-3). 1981. lib. bdg. 18.60 (*0-87614-159-9*, Carolrhoda) Lerner Pub.

— From Gold to Money. LC 84-17488. (Start to Finish Bks.).Tr. of Vom Gold zum Geld. (Illus.). 24p. (J). (ps-3). 1985. lib. bdg. 18.60 (*0-87614-230-7*, Carolrhoda) Lerner Pub.

— From Ice to Rain. (Start to Finish Bks.). Orig. Title: Vom Eis Zum Regen. (Illus.). 24p. (J). (ps-3). 1981. lib. bdg. 18.60 (*0-87614-157-2*, Carolrhoda) Lerner Pub.

— From Idea to Toy. (Start to Finish Bks.). (Illus.). 24p. (J). (ps-3). 1988. lib. bdg. 18.60 (*0-87614-352-4*, Carolrhoda) Lerner Pub.

— From Oil to Gasoline. LC 80-29562. (Start to Finish Bks.). Orig. Title: Vom Erdol Zum Benzin. (Illus.). 24p. (J). (ps-3). 1981. lib. bdg. 18.60 (*0-87614-160-2*, Carolrhoda) Lerner Pub.

— From Rubber Tree to Tire. (Start to Finish Bks.).Tr. of Vom Kautschaft zum Reifen. (Illus.). 24p. (J). (ps-3). 1986. lib. bdg. 18.60 (*0-87614-297-8*, Carolrhoda) Lerner Pub.

— From Sea to Salt. LC 84-17466. (Start to Finish Bks.).Tr. of Vom Meer zum Salz. (Illus.). 24p. (J). (ps-3). 1985. lib. bdg. 18.60 (*0-87614-232-3*, Carolrhoda) Lerner Pub.

— From Swamp to Coal. LC 84-17465. (Start to Finish Bks.).Tr. of Vom Urwald zur Kohle. (Illus.). 24p. (J). (ps-3). 1985. lib. bdg. 18.60 (*0-87614-233-1*, Carolrhoda) Lerner Pub.

— From Tree to Table. LC 81-672. (Start to Finish Bks.). Orig. Title: Vom Baum Zum Tisch. (Illus.). 24p. (J). (ps-3). 1981. lib. bdg. 18.60 (*0-87614-165-3*, Carolrhoda) Lerner Pub.

— From Wood to Paper. Lerner, Mark, tr. from GER. (Start to Finish Bks.).Tr. of Vom Holz zum Papier. (Illus.). 24p. (J). (ps-3). 1986. lib. bdg. 18.60 (*0-87614-296-X*, Carolrhoda) Lerner Pub.

Mitgutsch, Anna. In Foreign Cities. Bangerter, Lowell A., tr. LC 94-6441. (Studies in Austrian Literature, Culture, & Thought). 220p. 1995. pap. 20.50 (*0-929497-90-2*) Ariadne CA.

Mitgutsch, Waltraud A. Jakob. 1991. 22.95 (*0-15-145978-9*) Harcourt.

Mithal, Anant Kartik, jt. auth. see Douglas, Sarah A.

Mithal, C. P. Miracles of Urine Therapy. 82p. 1990. pap. 4.95 (*0-8464-4821-1*) Beekman Pubs.

Mithal, M. Textbook of Forensic Pharmacy. 8th ed. (C). 1988. 80.00 (*0-7855-4676-6*, Pub. by Current Dist) St Mut.

***Mitham, Peter J.** Robert W. Service: A Bibliography. LC 99-51768. (Illus.). 440p. 2000. 65.00 (*1-58456-011-8*) Oak Knoll.

An Asterisk (*) at the beginning of an entry indicates that the title is appearing for the first time.

Mithani, Abbas & Wheeler, Sally. Mithani & Wheeler: The Disqualification of Company Directors. 570p. 1995. write for info. (0-406-04362-0, MICHIE) LEXIS Pub.

Mithaug, Dennis E. Equal Opportunity Theory: Fairness in Liberty for All. 336p. (C). 1996. 52.00 (0-7619-0261-9); pap. 24.95 (0-7619-0262-7) Sage.

— How to Teach Prevocational Skills to Severely Handicapped Persons. (Teaching the Autistic Ser.). 62p. 1981. pap. 8.00 (0-89079-056-6, 1037) PRO-ED.

— Self-Determined Kids: Helping Children Succeed. 228p. 1991. 25.95 (0-669-27140-3) Lxngtn Bks.

— Self-Regulation Theory: How Optimal Adjustment Maximizes Gain. LC 92-17812. 256p. 1993. 59.95 (0-275-94422-0, C4422, Praeger Pubs) Greenwood.

Mithaug, Dennis E., jt. ed. see Vitello, Stanley J.

Mithcell, Nahum & Mitchell, Edward C. History of the Early Settlement of Bridgewater, in Plymouth County, Massachusetts, Including an Extensive Family Register. (Illus.). 424p. 1992. reprint ed. lib. bdg. 44.50 (0-8328-2376-7) Higginson Bk Co.

Mithcell, V. E. Windows on a Lost World. Stern, Dave, ed. (Star Trek Ser.: No. 65). 275p. 1993. mass mkt. 5.99 (0-671-79512-0) PB.

Mithell, Mike, tr. see Furness, Ray, ed.

Mithen, Steve. The Prehistory of the Mind: The Cognitive Origins of Art, Religion & Science. LC 96-60367. (Illus.). 288p. 1999. pap. 17.95 (0-500-28100-9, Pub. by Thames Hudson) Norton.

Mithen, Steven. The Prehistory of the Mind: The Cognitive Origins of Art, Religion, & Science. LC 96-60367. (Illus.). 304p. 1996. 27.50 (0-500-05081-3, Pub. by Thames Hudson) Norton.

***Mithen, Steven, ed.** Hunter-Gatherer Landscape Archaeology: The Southern Hebrides Mesolithic Project, Vol. 1. (Illus.). 700p. (C). 2000. 180.00 (1-902937-07-4) David Brown.

— Hunter-Gatherer Landscape Archaeology: The Southern Hebrides Mesolithic Project 1988-1998, Vol. 2. (Illus.). 700p. (C). 2000. 180.00 (1-902937-11-2) David Brown.

Mithen, Steven J. Creativity in Human Evolution & Prehistory. LC 97-43350. (Illus.). 320p. (C). 1998. 99.99 (0-415-16096-0) Routledge.

Mithers, Carol L. Reasonable Insanity: A True Story of the Seventies. LC 93-30571. 1994. 23.00 (0-201-57071-8) Addison-Wesley.

Mithra, Yameema, jt. auth. see Mumtaz, Khavar.

***Mithun, Marianne.** The Languages of Native North America. LC 98-53576. (Cambridge Language Surveys Ser.). (Illus.). 770p. (C). 1999. 80.00 (0-521-23228-7) Cambridge U Pr.

Mithun, Marianne, ed. see Conference on Montague Grammar, Philosophy, & Linguistics, 1977, State Univ. of NY at Albany, Staff.

Miti, Katabaro, jt. auth. see Chipasula, James C.

Mitias, Michael H., ed. Moral Education & the Liberal Arts, 50. LC 91-22369. (Contributions to the Study of Education Ser.: No. 50). 192p. 1992. 55.00 (0-313-27236-0, MMB, Greenwood Pr) Greenwood.

— Possibility of the Aesthetic Experience. 180p. 1986. lib. bdg. 122.00 (90-247-3278-6, Pub. by M Nijhoff) Kluwer Academic.

Mitic, P., et al, eds. Innovation in Mathematics: Proceedings of the Second International Mathematica Symposium. LC 97-67793. 536p. 1997. 254.00 (1-85312-505-9, 5059) Computational Mech MA.

Mitic, P., jt. ed. see Keranen, V.

Mitiche, A. Computational Analysis of Visual Motion. (Advances in Computer Vision & Machine Intelligence Ser.). (Illus.). 252p. (C). 1994. 75.00 (0-306-44786-X, Plenum Trade) Perseus Pubng.

Mitideri, Dario, et al, photos by. Children of Bombay. (Illus.). 160p. 45.00 (1-899235-00-0) Dist Art Pubs.

Mitidieri, Enzo, jt. auth. see Caristi, Gabriella.

Mitiguy, Nancy. The Rich Get Richer & the Poor Write Proposals. LC 79-624731. (Illus.). (Orig.). (C). 1978. pap. 7.00 (0-934210-02-0) Devlp Commy.

Mitiguy, Nancy, jt. auth. see Dale, Duane.

Mitilieri, Robert, ed. see Schwartz, Karl.

Mitin, Vladimir V., et al. Quantum Heterostructures: Microelectronics & Optoelectronics. LC 98-40658. (Illus.). 664p. (C). 1999. text 120.00 (0-521-63177-7); pap. text 49.95 (0-521-63635-3) Cambridge U Pr.

Mitkas, Pericles A., ed. Proceedings of the 1996 Workshop on Data Encoding for Page-Oriented Optical Memories. (Illus.). (C). 1997. pap. text 40.00 (0-9624477-1-4) CSU Coll Eng.

Mitkas, Pericles A. & Hasan, Zameer, eds. Advanced Optical Memories & Interfaces to Computer Storage, Vol. 3468. 1998. 89.00 (0-8194-2923-6) SPIE.

Mitkov, Ruslan & Nicolov, Nicolas, eds. Recent Advances in Natural Language Processing: Selected Papers from RANLP '95. LC 97-38873. (Current Issues in Linguistic Theory Ser.: Vol. 136). xii, 472p. 1997. lib. bdg. 99.00 (1-55619-591-5) J Benjamins Pubng Co.

Mitkova, M. I., jt. ed. see Thorpe, M. F.

Mitlehner, W., et al, eds. First Lox Workshop Symposium - Rationale & Study Design: Proceedings of the First Lox Workshop on Long Term Portable Oxygen Treatment in Severe Disabled COPD, Germany, Berlin, November 1990. (Journal: Respiration: Vol. 59, Suppl. 2, 1992). (Illus.). vi, 46p. 1992. pap. 22.75 (3-8055-5645-4) S Karger.

Mitler, Louis. Contemporary Turkish Writers: A Critical Bio-Bibliography of Leading Writers in the Turkish Republican Period up to 1980. LC 85-60918. (Uralic & Altaic Ser.: Vol. 146). 325p. 1988. 29.50 (0-933070-14-4) Res Inst Inner Asian Studies.

— Ottoman Turkish Writers: A Biographical Dictionary of Significant Ottoman Literature. (American University Studies: General Literature: Ser. XIX, Vol. 15). XVI, 203p. (C). 1988. text 31.50 (0-8204-0633-3) P Lang Pubng.

Mitler, Louis, tr. see Nesin, Aziz.

Mitler, Merrill M., jt. auth. see Poceta, J. Steven.

Mitlin, Vladimir S. Nonlinear Dynamics of Reservoir Mixtures. 272p. 1993. boxed set 129.95 (0-8493-4416-6, TN871) CRC Pr.

***Mitman, Gregg.** Reel Nature: America's Romance with Wildlife on Film. LC 99-26235. 320p. 1999. 29.95 (0-674-71571-3) HUP.

Mitman, Gregg. State of Nature: Ecology, Community & American Social Thought, 1900-1950. (Science & Its Conceptual Foundations Ser.). (Illus.). 304p. (C). 1992. pap. text 26.50 (0-226-53237-2) U Ch Pr.

— State of Nature: Ecology, Community & American Social Thought, 1900-1950. (Science & Its Conceptual Foundations Ser.). (Illus.). 304p. (C). 1992. lib. bdg. 67.00 (0-226-53236-4) U Ch Pr.

Mitman, John L. Premarital Counseling: A Manual for Clergy & Counselors. 128p. (Orig.). 1984. 8.95 (0-86683-879-1, 7874) Harper SF.

Mitnick, Barbara J. The Changing Image of George Washington. (Illus.). 51p. (Orig.). 1989. pap. 3.00 (0-9616415-7-6) Fraunces Tavern.

— Harry Devlin: A Retrospective. Mitnick, John M., ed. 70p. (C). 1991. 4.50 (0-9613046-4-2) Morris Mus.

Mitnick, Barbara J. & Mitnick, John M. The Realist Vision of Adolf Konrad: A Retrospective. 63p. 1992. 9.00 (0-9613046-7-7) Morris Mus.

Mitnick, Barbara J., ed. see Ayres, William, et al.

Mitnick, Barry M., ed. Corporate Political Activity. (Focus Editions Ser.: Vol. 163). (Illus.). 312p. 1993. 59.95 (0-8039-4348-2); pap. 26.00 (0-8039-4349-0) Sage.

Mitnick, Harold. How to Handle Your Divorce Step by Step. LC 80-80875. 177p. 1981. 21.95 (0-685-03094-6); pap. 14.95 (0-936550-00-7) Lone Oak.

Mitnick, John M., jt. auth. see Mitnick, Barbara J.

Mitnick, John M., ed. see Mitnick, Barbara J.

Mitnick, Leonard L., jt. ed. see Lipsitt, Lewis P.

Mitnik, Mark. Was It a Classical Triangle? (RUS., Illus.). 192p. (Orig.). 1988. pap. 12.00 (0-9622027-0-3) M Mitnik.

Mito, M. & Sawa, M., eds. Hepatocyte Transplantation: Tissue Engineering. LC 97-41357. (Karger Landes Systems Publication Ser.). (Illus.). xiv, 348p. 1998. 139.00 (3-8055-6603-4) S Karger.

Mito, Setsuo. The Honda Book of Management: A Leadership Philosophy for High Industrial Success. LC 89-77751. 224p. (C). 1990. text 45.00 (0-485-11317-1, Pub. by Athlone Pr) Humanities.

Mitofsky, Warren J. & Plissner, Martin. Campaign Seventy Eight: A Comprehensive Political Handbook to the Vote Returns & Candidates. 1980. 51.95 (0-405-12517-8) Ayer.

***Mitola, Joseph, III.** Software Radios: Wireless Architectures for the 21st Century (Alpha Release) (Illus.). 290p. (C). 1999. pap. 105.00 (0-9671233-0-5) Mitolas.

— Software Radios Architecture: Object-Oriented Approaches to Wireless Systems Engineering. 450p. 2000. 89.95 (0-471-38492-5) Wiley.

Miton, Deborah. You Call this Love. 200p. 1998. mass mkt. 6.99 (1-58365-012-1, Timeless Romance) BT Pub.

Mitra. Digital Signal Processing. 1999. 24.50 (0-07-232246-2) McGraw.

— Digital Signal Processing. 2nd ed. 888p. 2000. 91.25 (0-07-232105-9) McGraw.

Mitra, A. The Status of Women: Household & Non-Household Economic Activity. 78p. 1979. 6.95 (0-318-37312-2) Asia Bk Corp.

— The Status of Women: Literacy & Employment. (Illus.). 74p. 1979. 6.95 (0-318-37313-0) Asia Bk Corp.

Mitra, A. K. & Sahoo, Basideb, eds. Agricultural Planning & Technology in Rural Development in Honour of Dr. Bidyadhar Misra: In Honour of Dr. Bidyadhar Misra. 266p. (C). 1994. pap. 175.00 (81-85880-49-2, Pub. by Print Hse) St Mut.

Mitra, A. K., jt. auth. see Ray, H. S.

Mitra, A. P. Ionospheric Effects of Solar Flares. LC 74-76480. (Astrophysics & Space Science Library: No. 46). 200p. 1974. lib. bdg. 129.50 (90-277-0467-8) Kluwer Academic.

Mitra, A. P., ed. see COSPAR, Twenty-Second Plenary Meeting Staff.

Mitra, Amitava. Fundamentals of Quality Control & Improvement. LC 92-41164. 688p. (C). 1993. text 92.00 (0-02-381791-7, Macmillan Coll) P-H.

— Fundamentals of Quality Control & Improvement. 2nd ed. LC 97-22434. 723p. 1998. 99.00 (0-13-645086-5) P-H.

Mitra, Ananda. India Through the Western Lens: Creating National Images in Film. LC 98-25111. 1998. pap. write for info. (0-7619-9269-3) Sage.

— India Through the Western Lens: Creating National Images in Film. LC 98-25111. 1998. 39.95 (0-7619-9268-5) Sage.

***Mitra, Ananda.** India Through the Western Lens: Creating National Images in Film. 1999. 30.00 (81-7036-726-3, Pub. by Sage Pubns IND) S Asia.

Mitra, Ananda. Television & Popular Culture in India: A Study of the Mahabharat. LC 93-27379. 1993. 28.50 (0-8039-9134-7) Sage.

Mitra, Ananda & Lankford, Sam. Research Methods in Park, Recreation, & Leisure Services. LC 98-85938. (Illus.). 344p. (C). 1998. text 44.95 (1-57167-030-0) Sagamore Pub.

Mitra, Annie. Chloe's Rainy Day. (Chloe Weather Board Bks.). (Illus.). 14p. (J). 1998. bds. 5.95 (1-86233-041-7) Sterling.

— Chloe's Snowy Day. (Chloe Weather Board Bks.). (Illus.). 14p. (J). 1998. bds. 5.95 (1-86233-046-8) Sterling.

— Chloe's Sunny Day. (Chloe Weather Board Bks.). (Illus.). 14p. (J). 1998. bds. 5.95 (1-86233-031-X) Sterling.

— Chloe's Windy Day. (Chloe Weather Board Bks.). (Illus.). 14p. (J). 1998. bds. 5.95 (1-86233-036-0) Sterling.

Mitra, Ashim K. Ophthalmic Drug Delivery Systems. (Drugs & the Pharmaceutical Sciences Ser.: Vol. 58). (Illus.). 536p. 1993. text 215.00 (0-8247-8806-0) Dekker.

Mitra, Ashok. Calcutta Diary. 206p. 1977. 42.50 (0-7146-3082-9, Pub. by F Cass Pubs) Intl Spec Bk.

Mitra, Asok. Calcutta on the Eve of Her Tercentenary. 1990. 23.00 (81-7017-270-5, Pub. by Abhinav) S Asia.

— The New India, 1948-1955. (C). 1991. 22.50 (81-7154-691-9, Pub. by Popular Prakashan) S Asia.

Mitra, Asok, ed. Functional Classification of India's Urban Areas by Factor-Cluster Method, 1961-1971. 1981. 38.50 (0-8364-0806-3, Pub. by Abhinav) S Asia.

Mitra, Asok, et al. Shifts in the Functions of Cities & Towns of India, 1961-1971. 1981. 47.50 (0-8364-0719-9, Pub. by Abhinav) S Asia.

Mitra, B. B. Criminal Procedure Code, 2 vols. (C). 1988. 480.00 (0-7855-3537-3) St Mut.

— Guardians & Wards Act, 1890. 13th ed. (C). 1988. 200.00 (0-7855-3686-8) St Mut.

***Mitra, Chandan.** The Corrupt Society: The Criminalization of India from Independence to the 1990s LC 99-931905. xii, 209 p. 1998. write for info. (0-670-87875-8) Viking Penguin.

Mitra, D. K., jt. auth. see Raychaudhuri, S. P.

Mitra, Debala. Bronzes from Achutrajpur Orissa. 1978. 50.00 (0-8364-0136-0) S Asia.

Mitra, Debendra B. Monetary System in the Bengal Presidency. (C). 1991. 20.00 (81-7074-100-9) S Asia.

Mitra, Dutta. Quantum-Based Electronic Devices & Systems. 1999. 41.00 (981-02-3700-6) World Scientific Pub.

Mitra, G., et al, eds. Mathematical Models for Decision Support. LC 88-30718. (NATO Asi Series F: Vol. 48). ix, 756p. 1988. 180.95 (0-387-50084-7) Spr-Verlag.

Mitra, Gautam & Wojtal, Steven, eds. Geometries & Mechanisms of Thrusting, with Special Reference to the Appalachians. LC 88-15085. (Geological Society of America Ser.: Vol. 222). (Illus.). 244p. 1988. reprint ed. pap. 75.70 (0-608-07748-8, 206783600010) Bks Demand.

Mitra, Gautam, jt. auth. see Marshak, Stephen.

Mitra, Gautam, jt. auth. see Mukul, Malay.

Mitra, Jaganmay. HIV Speaks: Autobiography of AIDS Virus. 1995. pap. 7.50 (81-224-0734-X) S Asia.

Mitra, M. Legal & Commercial Dictionary. (C). 1990. 180.00 (0-89771-130-0) St Mut.

Mitra, Manimanjari. Calcutta in the Twentieth Century: An Urban Disaster. 1990. 27.50 (0-8364-2627-4, Pub. by Asiatic Bk Agency) S Asia.

Mitra, Mary A. A Book of Inspirational Verse. (C). 1989. 40.00 (0-7223-2360-3, Pub. by A H S Ltd) St Mut.

***Mitra, Narendraneatha, et al.** Selected Short Stories LC 98-908047. 191p. 1998. write for info. (81-260-0481-9) S Asia.

Mitra, Parimal C. Santhali: The Base of World Languages. (C). 1988. 15.00 (0-8364-2379-8, Pub. by Firma KLM) S Asia.

Mitra, Pradeep K. Adjustment in Oil-Importing Developing Countries: A Comparative Economic Analysis. LC 92-36214. (Illus.). 335p. (C). 1994. text 59.95 (0-521-44316-4) Cambridge U Pr.

Mitra, Pramada D., jt. tr. see Ballantyne, J. R.

Mitra, Premendra. Snake & Other Stories. 1990. 17.50 (81-7046-073-5, Pub. by Seagull Bks) S Asia.

Mitra, Rajendralal L. Antiquities of Orissa, 2 vols., Set. (Illus.). 600p. 1990. reprint ed. 27.50 (1-55528-203-2) Scholarly Pubns.

— Antiquities of Orissa, Vol. 2. 269p. 1984. 27.50 (1-55528-086-2, Pub. by Today Tomorrow) Scholarly Pubns.

— The Lalita-Vistara: Memoirs of the Early Life of Sakya Sinha (CHS.1-15) LC 98-906098. 279 p. 1998. write for info. (81-7030-576-4) Sri Satguru Pubns.

Mitra, S. Applied Mossbauer Spectroscopy: Theory & Practice for Geochemists & Archeologists. (Physics & Chemistry of the Earth Ser.: Vol. 18). 400p. 1993. 500.00 (0-08-042199-7, Pergamon Pr) Elsevier.

— Mercury in the Ecosystem. (Illus.). 270p. 1985. 116.00 (0-87849-529-0, Pub. by Trans T Pub) Enfield Pubs NH.

Mitra, S. K. The Early Rulers of Khajuraho. 2nd rev. ed. 1977. 7.95 (0-8426-0913-X, Pub. by Motilal Bnarsidass) S Asia.

Mitra, S. K., ed. Postharvest Physiology & Storage of Tropical & Subtropical Fruits. LC 97-13568. (Illus.). 452p. (C). 1998. text 120.00 (0-85199-210-2) OUP.

Mitra, S. K., jt. auth. see Bose, T. K.

Mitra, S. M. Position of Women in Indian Life. (C). 1995. pap. 10.00 (81-86142-38-X, Pub. by Low Price) S Asia.

Mitra, S. S., ed. see NATO Advanced Study Institute Staff.

Mitra, Sanjit K. Digital Signal Processing: A Computer Based Approach. (Illus.). 896p. (C). 1997. 99.38 (0-07-042953-7) McGraw.

***Mitra, Sanjit K.** Mandatory Package Digital Signal Processing. (C). 1999. pap., lab manual ed. 33.13 (0-07-232876-2) McGrw-H Hghr Educ.

— Nonlinear Image Processing. 450p. 2000. 89.95 (0-12-500451-6) Acad Pr.

Mitra, Sanjit K., jt. auth. see Bogchi, Sonali.

Mitra, Shankar. Structural Geology of Fold & Thrust Belts. LC 91-44214. (Johns Hopkins Studies in Earth & Space Sciences). (Illus.). 264p. reprint ed. pap. 81.90 (0-608-08791-2, 206943000004) Bks Demand.

Mitra Shastri, Ajay. Ancient Indian Heritage: Varaha Mihira's India. 560p. 1996. pap. 1100.00 (81-7305-083-X, Pub. by Print Hse) St Mut.

Mitra, Sourindra. T. S. Eliot - The Critic: A Study in Critical Ideology & Method. xx, 279p. 1985. 16.00 (0-685-67631-5, Pub. by Mittal Pubs Dist) Nataraj Bks.

Mitra, Subrata K. Culture & Rationality The Politics of Social Change in Post-Colonial India. LC 98-52039. 1999. write for info. (0-7619-9314-2) Sage.

***Mitra, Subrata K. & Singh, V. B.** Democracy & Social Change in India: A Cross-Sectional Analysis of the National Electorate LC 99-26780. 1999. write for info. (0-7619-9344-4) Sage.

Mitra, Sunanda, et al, eds. Neural & Fuzzy Systems: The Emerging Science of Intelligent Computing. LC 94-1640. 1994. 40.00 (0-8194-1566-9, IS12); pap. 40.00 (0-8194-1565-0) SPIE.

Mitra, Sunil K. Law of Apartment Ownership in West Bengal. (C). 1989. 180.00 (0-7855-4745-2) St Mut.

Mitra, Ved. Samuchi Hindi Shiksha, Bk. I. 1997. pap. 50.00 (81-209-0787-6, Pub. by Pitambar Pub) St Mut.

— Samuchi Hindi Shiksha, Bk. II. 1997. pap. 50.00 (81-209-0788-4, Pub. by Pitambar Pub) St Mut.

— Samuchi Hindi Shiksha, Bk. III. 1997. pap. 50.00 (81-209-0789-2, Pub. by Pitambar Pub) St Mut.

— Samuchi Hindi Shiksha, Bk. IV. 1997. pap. 50.00 (81-209-0790-6, Pub. by Pitambar Pub) St Mut.

Mitrakas, Andreas. Open EDI & Law in Europe: A Regulatory Framework. LC 97-36841. (Law & Electronic Commerce Ser.: No. 3). 364p. 1997. 115.00 (90-411-0489-5) Kluwer Academic.

Mitrakos, Alexander S. France in Greece in World War I. 1982. text 55.50 (0-914710-95-8, 101) Col U Pr.

Mitrani, I. Probabilistic Modelling. 2nd ed. LC 97-26099. 233p. 1998. text 64.95 (0-521-58511-2); pap. text 24.95 (0-521-58530-9) Cambridge U Pr.

Mitrani, Jose D. The Critical Path Method: A Self-Study Text. 74p. 1977. pap. 7.00 (0-935715-07-X, 0185) Construct Bkstore.

Mitrani, Judith L. A Framework for the Imaginary: Clinical Explorations in Primitive States of Being. LC 95-35054. 328p. 1996. 45.00 (1-56821-479-0) Aronson.

Mitrani, Judith L., jt. auth. see Mitrani, Theodore.

Mitrani, Theodore & Mitrani, Judith L. Encounters with Autistic States: A Memorial Tribute to Frances Tustin. LC 97-3469. 448p. 1997. 50.00 (0-7657-0066-2) Aronson.

Mitrano, Barbara, et al. A Sociology of Gender Roles Across Races, Classes & Cultures. 81p. 1993. ring bd. 49.95 (1-890662-08-9) Prism Coll.

— A Sociology of Gender Roles Across Races, Classes & Cultures: Scripture-Based Version. 2nd rev. ed. 81p. 1993. ring bd. 49.95 (1-890662-09-7) Prism Coll.

Mitrea, Gary, jt. auth. see Stricklin, Julie A.

Mitrea, Marius. Clifford Wavelets, Singular Integrals, & Hardy Spaces. LC 94-9648. (Lecture Notes in Mathematics Ser.: Vol. 1575). 1995. 26.95 (0-387-57884-6) Spr-Verlag.

Mitrinovic, Dragoslav S. Classical & New Inequalities in Analysis. (Mathematics & Its Applications East European Ser.). 760p. (C). 1992. text 403.00 (0-7923-2064-6) Kluwer Academic.

Mitrinovic, Dragoslav S., et al. Means & Their Inequalities. (C). 1987. text 211.50 (90-277-2629-9) Kluwer Academic.

— Recent Advances in Geometric Inequalities. (C). 1989. text 315.00 (90-277-2565-9) Kluwer Academic.

Mitrinovic, Dragoslav S., jt. auth. see Keckic, Jovan D.

Mitrinovic, Dragoslav S., jt. auth. see Sandor, J.

Mitrione, Dan. Suddenly Gone, Vol. 1. 1996. mass mkt. 6.50 (0-312-96052-2) St Martin.

Mitripolsky, Yu A., et al. Systems of Evolution Equations. 1992. lib. bdg. 153.00 (0-7923-2054-9) Kluwer Academic.

***Mitrjushkin, V. & Schierholz, G.** Lattice Fermions & Structure of the Vacuum. LC 00-42086. (NATO Science Ser.). 2000. write for info. (0-7923-6429-5) Kluwer Academic.

Mitro, A. & Palkovits, M. Morphology of the Rat Brain Ventricles, Ependyma & Periventricular Structures. (Bibliotheca Anatomica Ser.: No. 21). (Illus.). x, 110p. 1981. pap. 85.25 (3-8055-2546-X) S Karger.

Mitrofanis, Effie. Casalguidi Style Linen Embroidery. (Illus.). 128p. 1997. reprint ed. pap. 30.00 (0-916896-91-9) Lacis Pubns.

Mitrofanov, F. P., jt. ed. see Rundqvist, D. V.

Mitroff, Alan I. Business NOT As Usual: Rethinking Our Individual, Corporate, & Industrial Strategies for Global Competition. LC 86-46333. (Management Ser.). 215p. 1987. 32.95 (1-55542-030-3) Jossey-Bass.

Mitroff, Ian. Smart Thinking for Crazy Times: The Art of Solving the Right Problems. LC 97-43556. 200p. 1998. 24.95 (1-57675-020-5) Berrett-Koehler.

Mitroff, Ian I. The Subjective Side of Science. (Systems Inquiry Ser.). 328p. 1983. reprint ed. pap. 15.95 (0-914105-21-3) Intersystems Pubns.

— We're So Big & Powerful That Nothing Bad Can Happen to Us. 1990. 19.95 (1-55972-051-4, Birch Ln Pr) Carol Pub Group.

***Mitroff, Ian I. & Anagos, Gus.** Managing Crises Before They Happen: What Every Executive & Manager Needs to Know about Crisis Management. LC 00-30632. 2000. 24.95 (0-8144-0563-0) AMACOM.

Mitroff, Ian I. & Bennis, Warren G. The Unreality Industry. Richardson, Stewart, ed. 292p. 1989. 17.95 (1-55972-014-X, Birch Ln Pr) Carol Pub Group.

— The Unreality Industry: The Deliberate Manufacturing of Falsehood & What It Is Doing to Our Lives. LC 92-44601. (Illus.). 256p. (C). 1993. pap. text 12.95 (0-19-508398-9) OUP.

M

***Mitroff, Ian I. & Denton, Elizabeth A.** A Spiritual Audit of Corporate America: A Hard Look at Spirituality, Religion, & Values in the Workplace. LC 99-6693. 288p. 1999. 32.00 (*0-7879-4666-4*) Jossey-Bass.

Mitroff, Ian I. & Linstone, Harold A. The Unbounded Mind: Breaking the Chains of Traditional Business Thinking. (Illus.). 192p. 1995. pap. 11.95 (*0-19-510288-6*) OUP.

Mitroff, Ian I., et al. The Essential Guide to Managing Corporate Crises: A Step-by-Step Handbook for Surviving Major Catastrophes. (Illus.). 224p. 1996. 35.00 (*0-19-509744-0*) OUP.

Mitroff, Ian I., jt. auth. see Kilmann, Ralph H.

Mitroff, Ian I., jt. auth. see Linstone, Harold A.

Mitroff, Ian J., et al. Framebreak: The Radical Redesign of American Business. LC 93-42749. (Business-Management Ser.). 180p. 1994. 26.95 (*1-55542-606-9*) Jossey-Bass.

Mitroiescu, Ilie. The Smarandache Class of Paradoxes. Muller, R., ed. (Illus.). 75p. (C). pap. 9.99 (*1-879585-46-4*) Erhus Univ Pr.

Mitrokhin, Sergei, jt. contrib. by see Igrunov, Vyacheslav.

Mitrokhin, Vasili, jt. auth. see Andrew, Christopher.

Mitrokhina, V. I. & Motovilova. Russian for Scientists: General Scientific Terminology. (GER & RUS.). 343p. 1981. 49.95 (*0-8288-1561-5*, M13015) Fr & Eur.

Mitronowa, I. Polish-Russian, Russian-Polish Dictionary. deluxe ed. (POL & RUS.). 575p. 1980. 14.95 (*0-8288-4712-6*, M9102) Fr & Eur.

— Russian-Polish-Russian Pocket Dictionary. 19th ed. (POL & RUS.). 575p. 1980. 9.95 (*0-8288-1632-8*, M9102) Fr & Eur.

Mitropolaky, Yu. A. & Lopatin, A. K. Nonlinear Mechanics, Groups & Symmetry. LC 94-48068. (Mathematics & Its Applications Ser.: Vol. 319). 377p. 1995. text 188.00 (*0-7923-3339-X*) Kluwer Academic.

Mitropol'skii, Aristarkh K. Correlation Equations for Statistical Computations. LC 65-25246. 111p. reprint ed. pap. 34.50 (*0-608-14545-9*, 202471200038) Bks Demand.

Mitropolskii, Yu A. & Nguyen Van Dao. Applied Asymptotic Methods in Nonlinear Oscillations. LC 97-20156. 341p. 1997. text 187.00 (*0-7923-4605-X*) Kluwer Academic.

Mitropolsky, S. Kratkaja Grammatika Tserkovno-Slavjanskago Jazika.Tr. of A/Concise Grammer of the Church-Slavonic Language. 92p. 1980. pap. 5.00 (*0-317-30307-4*) Holy Trinity.

Mitropolsky, Y. A., jt. auth. see Bogoliubov, N. N.

Mitros, David. Gone to Wear the Victor's Crown: Morris County, New Jersey & the Civil War: A Documentary Account. LC 98-91477. ix, 216 p. 1998. write for info. (*0-9664119-0-0*) Morrs Cty Hertge.

Mitros, Joseph F. Religions: A Select, Classified Bibliography. LC 77-183042. (Philosophical Questions Ser.: No. 8). 350p. 1973. 75.00 (*0-912116-08-0*) Learned Pubns.

Mitrou, Paris S., jt. ed. see Bergmann, L.

Mitrovi, Dragi S. & Zubrinic, Darko. Fundamentals of Applied Functional Analysis. LC 96-31178. (Pitman Monographs & Surveys in Pure & Applied Mathematics). 1997. lib. bdg. 123.00 (*0-582-24694-6*) Longman.

Mitrovic, Branko, jt. auth. see Vignola.

***Mitrovich, Gregory.** Undermining the Kremlin: America's Strategy to Subvert the Soviet Bloc, 1947-1959. LC UA23..M58 2000. 2000. 32.50 (*0-8014-3711-3*) Cornell U Pr.

Mitrovich, V. L., jt. auth. see Voskoboinikov, B. S.

Mitrovick, Marta. Collected Poems: From the Personal to the Universal. 80p. (Orig.). 1990. pap. 6.00 (*0-9624205-1-4*) Inevitable Pr.

Mitruka, B. & Bonner, M. Methods of Detection & Identification of Bacteria. LC 76-28809. 1977. 152.00 (*0-8493-5116-2*, CRC Reprint) Franklin.

Mitruka, Brij M. & Rawnsley, Howard M. Clinical Biochemical & Hematological Reference Values in Normal Experimental Animals & Normal Humans. 2nd exp. ed. LC 81-17157. (Illus.). 432p. (gr. 13). 1981. 68.50 (*0-89352-163-9*) Mosby Inc.

Mitrushina, Maura, et al. Handbook of Normative Data for Neuropsychological Assessment. (Illus.). 560p. 1998. text 68.50 (*0-19-505675-2*) OUP.

Mitry, Jean. The Aesthetics & Psychology of the Cinema. King, Christopher, tr. LC 96-54298. (Society for Cinema Studies Translation Ser.). (Illus.). 424p. 1998. lib. bdg. 59.95 (*0-253-33302-4*) Ind U Pr.

***Mitry, Jean.** The Aesthetics & Psychology of the Cinema. King, Christopher, tr. (Illus.). 424p. 2000. pap. 22.95 (*0-253-21377-0*) Ind U Pr.

— Semiotics & the Analysis of Film. King, Christopher, tr. (Illus.). 288p. 2000. 49.95 (*0-253-33733-X*) Ind U Pr.

Mitsch. Ecological Engineering. 2nd ed. 500p. (C). 2000. write for info. (*0-471-33264-X*) Wiley.

Mitsch, Darelyn & Blankinship, Marilyn. "I Am That I Am..." Somebody Famous Said That! LC 97-90764. (Illus.). 52p. (J). 1998. pap. 8.95 (*0-533-12480-8*) Vantage.

Mitsch, Erwin. Egon Schiele. (Illus.). 270p. 1995. pap. 29.95 (*0-7148-2862-9*, Pub. by Phaidon Press) Phaidon Pr.

Mitsch, Raymond R. Grieving the Loss of Someone You Love: Daily Meditations to Help You Through the Grieving Process. 200p. 1993. pap. 9.99 (*0-89283-822-1*, Vine Bks) Servant.

Mitsch, William J. Wetlands. 2nd ed. 1993. text 68.95 (*0-442-00805-8*, VNR) Wiley.

Mitsch, William J., ed. Global Wetlands: Old World & New. LC 94-229171. 992p. 1994. 324.25 (*0-444-81478-7*) Elsevier.

Mitsch, William J. & Gosselink, James G. Wetlands. 2nd ed. 736p. 1993. 75.00 (*0-471-28437-8*, VNR) Wiley.

Mitsch, William J. & Jorgensen, Sven E., eds. Ecological Engineering: An Introduction to Ecotechnology. LC 88-23576. (Environmental Science & Technology Ser.). 496p. 1989. 110.00 (*0-471-62559-0*) Wiley.

Mitsch, William J., jt. ed. see Jorgensen, Sven E.

Mitsch, Wolfgang, et al. Hochschule in der Demokratie: Kritische Beitrage zur Erbschaft und Reform der Deutschen Universitat. Metzger, Walter P., ed. LC 76-55204. (Academic Profession Ser.).Tr. of University in a Democracy: Critical Contribution to the Legacy & Reform of the German University. (GER., Illus.). 1977. reprint ed. lib. bdg. 41.95 (*0-405-10034-5*) Ayer.

Mitschein, Thomas A., jt. ed. see Leihner, Dietrich E.

Mitscher, Lester A. The Chemistry of the Tetracycline Antibiotics. LC 78-12971. (Medicinal Research Ser.: Vol. 9). (Illus.). 350p. reprint ed. pap. 108.50 (*0-608-08966-4*, 206960100005) Bks Demand.

Mitscher, Lester A., et al. The Green Tea Book: China's Fountain of Youth. LC 97-26410. (Illus.). 192p. 1997. pap. 9.95 (*0-89529-807-4*, Avery) Penguin Putnam.

Mitscher, Lester A., jt. auth. see Lednicer, Daniel.

Mitschw. Wetlands. 3rd ed. (General Science Ser.). 750p. 2000. text 80.00 (*0-471-29232-X*, VNR) Wiley.

Mitsios, Helen, ed. New Japanese Voices: The Best Contemporary Fiction from Japan. LC 90-967. 224p. 1992. pap. 10.95 (*0-87113-522-1*, Atlntc Mnthly) Grove-Atltc.

Mitsis, Phillip. Epicurus' Ethical Theory: The Pleasures of Invulnerability. LC 88-47746. (Cornell Studies in Classical Philology). 224p. 1988. text 35.00 (*0-8014-2187-X*) Cornell U Pr.

Mitstifer, Dorothy I. & Miller, Julia R. Agenda for Change: Strategic Leadership of the Professions. 46p. 1999. pap. 12.50 (*1-929083-07-6*) Kappa Omi Nu.

Mitstifer, Dorothy I., et al. Mentoring: The Human Touch. 75p. 1994. ring bd. 35.00 (*1-929083-01-7*) Kappa Omi Nu.

Mitstifer, Dorothy I., jt. ed. see Braun, Bonnie.

Mitsubishi Corporation Staff. Japanese Business Language: An Essential Dictionary. 230p. 1987. 31.00 (*0-7103-0199-5*) Routledge.

— Tatemae & Honne: Good Form & Real Intention in Japanese Business Culture. 225p. 1988. 24.95 (*0-02-921591-9*) Free Pr.

Mitsuhashi, Jun, ed. Invertebrate Cell System Applications, 2 Vols., Vol. I. (Studies in Christian Ethics Journal). 288p. 1989. boxed set 195.00 (*0-8493-4373-9*, QL362) CRC Pr.

— Invertebrate Cell System Applications, 2 Vols., Vol. 2. (Studies in Christian Ethics Journal). 320p. 1989. boxed set 229.95 (*0-8493-4374-7*, QL362) CRC Pr.

Mitsuhashi, Jun, jt. ed. see Maramorosch, Karl.

Mitsuhashi, S., et al, eds. Antibiotic Resistance: Proceedings. (Illus.). 410p. 1981. 71.95 (*0-387-10322-8*) Spr-Verlag.

Mitsuhashi, S. & Franceschi, G., eds. Penem Antibiotics. (Illus.). 180p. 1991. 79.95 (*0-387-53142-4*) Spr-Verlag.

Mitsuhashi, Setsuko. Japanese Commodity Flows. LC 78-8319. (University of Chicago, Department of Geography, Research Paper Ser.: No. 187). 185p. 1978. reprint ed. pap. 57.40 (*0-608-02285-3*, 206292600004) Bks Demand.

Mitsui, James M. From a Three-Cornered World: New & Selected Poems. LC 97-2927. 112p. 1997. pap. 12.95 (*0-295-97598-9*) U of Wash Pr.

Mitsui, T. An Introduction to the Physics of Ferroelectrics, Vol. 1. (Ferroelectricity & Related Phenomena Ser.). xiv, 446p. 1976. text 376.00 (*0-677-30600-8*) Gordon & Breach.

Mitsui, T., et al, eds. Electricity & Biophysics: A Special Issue of the Journal Ferroelectrics. iv, 356p. 1988. pap. text 818.00 (*2-88124-336-3*) Gordon & Breach.

Mitsui, T. & Shinohara, Y. Numerical Analysis of Ordinary Differential Equations & Its Applications. 250p. 1995. text 55.00 (*981-02-2229-7*) World Scientific Pub.

Mitsui, Takeo, ed. New Cosmetic Science. LC 97-19326. 410p. 1997. 234.50 (*0-444-82654-8*) Elsevier.

Mitsui, Toru & Hosokawa, Shuhei. Karaoke Around the World: Global Technology, Local Singing. LC 97-19902. (Research in Cultural & Media Studies). 224p. (C). 1998. 75.00 (*0-415-16371-4*) Routledge.

Mitsui, Y. Strabismus & the Sensorimotor Reflex. 228p. 1986. 100.00 (*4-900392-74-X*) Elsevier.

Mitsui, Yasuo. MMIC - Monolithic Microwave Integrated Circuits, Vol. 1. (Japanese Technology Reviews Ser.: Vol. 2). viii, 130p. 1989. text 104.00 (*2-88124-286-3*) Gordon & Breach.

***Mitsumoto, Hiroshi & Munsat, Theodore L.** Amyotrophic Lateral Sclerosis: A Guide for Patients & Families. 2nd ed. 400p. 2000. pap. 34.95 (*1-888799-28-5*, Pub. by Demos Medical) SCB Distributors.

Mitsumoto, Hiroshi & Norris, Forbes H. Amyotrophic Lateral Sclerosis: A Comprehensive Guide to Management. 360p. 1994. pap. 39.95 (*0-939957-58-2*) Demos Medical.

***Mitsumoto, Hiroshi, et al.** Amyotrophic Lateral Sclerosis. LC 97-194. (Contemporary Neurology Ser.: No. 49). (Illus.). 512p. 1998. text 140.00 (*0-8036-0269-3*) OUP.

Mitsuru, Yoshida. Requiem for Battleship Yamato. LC 98-54794. 1999. pap. 14.95 (*1-55750-544-6*) Naval Inst Pr.

Mitsutani, Margaret, tr. see Oe, Kenzaburo.

Mitsutani, Margaret, tr. see Tawada, Yoko.

Mitsuya, Hiroaki. Inhibitors of Reverse Transciptase & Viral Protease. 112p. 1992. pap. text 194.00 (*3-7186-5267-6*, Harwood Acad Pubs) Gordon & Breach.

Mitsuyasu, H., jt. ed. see Toba, Yoshiaki.

Mittag, M. Building Construction Practice: Pratique de la Construction des Batiments. 11th ed. (FRE.). 352p. 1983. 295.00 (*0-7859-4923-2*) Fr & Eur.

Mittag, Martina. Nationale Identitatsbestrebungen und Antispanische Polemik im Englischen Pamphlet, 1558-1630. (Europaische Hochschulschriften, Reihe 14: No. 261). (Illus.). 261p. 1993. 48.80 (*3-631-45942-4*) P Lang Pubng.

Mittal, A. K., et al, eds. Water/Air Transition in Biology. 306p. 2000. text 89.50 (*1-57808-059-2*) Science Pubs.

***Mittal, Anjali.** Hindustani Music & the Aesthetic Concept of Form. (Illus.). x, 174p. 2000. 32.00 (*81-246-0134-8*, Pub. by D K Printwrld) Nataraj Bks.

Mittal, Anu K. Dairy Industry: Information on Marketing Channels & Prices for Fluid Milk. (Illus.). 64p. (C). 1999. pap. text 20.00 (*0-7881-7789-3*) DIANE Pub.

— Dairy Industry: Information on Prices for Fluid Milk & the Factors That Influence Them. (Illus.). 180p. (C). 1999. pap. text 35.00 (*0-7881-7835-0*) DIANE Pub.

Mittal, Anuradha & Rosset, Peter. America Needs Human Rights. LC 99-43435. 256p. 1999. pap. text 13.95 (*0-935028-72-2*) Inst Food & Develop.

Mittal, Ashok. Cinema Industry in India: Pricing & Taxation. LC 95-900037. (C). 1995. 28.00 (*81-7387-023-3*, Pub. by Indus Pub) S Asia.

Mittal, B. L., ed. Supreme Court on Sales Tax, 1950-1988. (C). 1988. 150.00 (*0-7855-4728-2*) St Mut.

Mittal, Bharat B., et al, eds. Advances in Radiation Therapy. LC 97-24461. (Cancer Treatment & Research Ser.: No. 93). 320p. 1997. 290.00 (*0-7923-9981-1*) Kluwer Academic.

Mittal, D. K. Kala Kalash, Bk. I. 80p. 1997. pap. 40.00 (*81-209-0816-3*, Pub. by Pitambar Pub) St Mut.

— Kala Kalash, Bk. II. 80p. 1997. pap. 40.00 (*81-209-0817-1*, Pub. by Pitambar Pub) St Mut.

— Kala Kalash, Bk. III. 72p. 1997. pap. 40.00 (*81-209-0818-X*, Pub. by Pitambar Pub) St Mut.

Mittal, D. P. Double Taxation Agreements & Taxation of Foreign Investments in India. (C). 1989. 350.00 (*0-7855-3662-0*) St Mut.

Mittal, G. S., ed. Computerized Control Systems in the Food Industry. LC 96-31578. (Food Science & Technology Ser.: Vol. 78). (Illus.). 616p. 1996. text 195.00 (*0-8247-9757-4*) Dekker.

Mittal, Gauri. Food Biotechnology: Techniques & Applications. LC 92-60559. 390p. 1992. text 124.95 (*0-87762-888-2*) Technomic.

Mittal, K. L. Adhesion Measurement of Films & Coatings. 444p. 1994. 125.00 (*90-6764-182-0*, Pub. by VSP) Coronet Bks.

— Materialism in Indian Thought. 336p. 1974. 19.95 (*0-318-37022-0*) Asia Bk Corp.

— Metallized Plastics: Fundamental & Applied Aspects, Vol. 3. (Illus.). 410p. (C). 1993. text 130.00 (*0-306-44341-4*, Kluwer Plenum) Kluwer Academic.

— Metallized Plastics: Fundamentals & Applications. LC 97-38708. (Plastics Engineering Ser.). (Illus.). 352p. 1997. text 175.00 (*0-8247-9925-9*) Dekker.

— Particles in Gases & Liquids 3: Detection, Characterization & Control. LC 93-17795. (Illus.). 300p. (C). 1993. text 95.00 (*0-306-44485-2*, Kluwer Plenum) Kluwer Academic.

— Particles on Surfaces: Detection, Adhesion & Removal. (Illus.). 440p. 1994. text 199.00 (*0-8247-9535-0*) Dekker.

— Particles on Surfaces: Detection, Adhesion & Removal, Vol. 1. LC 88-28841. (Illus.). 394p. (C). 1988. text 120.00 (*0-306-43030-4*, Kluwer Plenum) Kluwer Academic.

— Particles on Surfaces: Detection, Adhesion & Removal, Vol. 2. (Illus.). 336p. (C). 1989. text 110.00 (*0-306-43367-2*, Kluwer Plenum) Kluwer Academic.

— Particles on Surfaces: Detection, Adhesion & Removal, Vol. 3. (Illus.). 336p. (C). 1992. text 110.00 (*0-306-44180-2*, Kluwer Plenum) Kluwer Academic.

— Surface & Colloid Science in Computer Technology. LC 87-12273. (Illus.). 456p. 1987. 110.00 (*0-306-42602-1*, Plenum Trade) Perseus Pubng.

Mittal, K. L., ed. Adhesion Aspects of Polymeric Coatings. LC 82-24870. (Illus.). 670p. (C). 1983. text 186.00 (*0-306-41250-0*, Kluwer Plenum) Kluwer Academic.

— Adsorption at Interface: Papers from a Symposium Honoring Robert D. Vold & Majorie J. Vold. LC 74-32040. (American Chemical Society Symposium Ser.: No. 8). 304p. reprint ed. pap. 94.30 (*0-8357-5118-X*, 201523200093) Bks Demand.

— Colloidal Dispersions & Micellar Behavior: Papers from A Symposium Honoring Robert D. Vold & Marjorie J. Vold. LC 74-34072. (American Chemical Society ACS Symposium Ser.: No. 9). (Illus.). 362p. reprint ed. pap. 112.30 (*0-608-30026-8*, 201523300093) Bks Demand.

— Contact Angle, Wettability & Adhesion: In Honor of Professor Robert J. Good. xxiv, 972p. 1993. 225.00 (*90-6764-157-X*) Coronet Bks.

— Metalized Plastics Vol. 2: Fundamental & Applied Aspects. (Illus.). 488p. (C). 1992. text 162.00 (*0-306-44107-1*, Kluwer Plenum) Kluwer Academic.

— Metallized Plastics: Fundamental & Applied Aspects, Vol. 1. LC 89-28395. (Illus.). 292p. (C). 1989. text 114.00 (*0-306-43389-3*, Kluwer Plenum) Kluwer Academic.

— Particles in Gases & Liquids No. 1: Detection, Characterization & Control. (Illus.). 312p. (C). 1989. text 114.00 (*0-306-43151-3*, Kluwer Plenum) Kluwer Academic.

— Particles in Gases & Liquids No. 2: Detection, Characterization & Control. (Illus.). 416p. (C). 1991. text 132.00 (*0-306-43809-7*, Kluwer Plenum) Kluwer Academic.

***Mittal, K. L., ed.** Particles on Surfaces Vols. 5 & 6: Detection, Adhesion & Removal. 362p. 1999. 130.00 (*90-6764-312-2*, Pub. by VSP) Coronet Bks.

Mittal, K. L., ed. Physicochemical Aspects of Polymer Surfaces, Vol. 1. 610p. 1983. 125.00 (*0-306-41189-X*, Plenum Trade) Perseus Pubng.

— Physicochemical Aspects of Polymer Surfaces, Vol. 2. 652p. 1983. 125.00 (*0-306-41190-3*, Plenum Trade) Perseus Pubng.

— Polyimides: Synthesis, Characterization & Applications, 2 vols., Vol. 1. (Illus.). 650p. (C). 1984. text 174.00 (*0-306-41670-0*, Kluwer Plenum) Kluwer Academic.

— Polyimides: Synthesis, Characterization & Applications, 2 vols., Vol. 2. (Illus.). 600p. (C). 1984. text 174.00 (*0-306-41673-5*, Kluwer Plenum) Kluwer Academic.

— Polymer Surface Modification: Relevance to Adhesion. (Illus.). 552p. 1996. 145.00 (*90-6764-201-0*, Pub. by VSP) Coronet Bks.

— Polymers in Information Storage Technology. (Illus.). 466p. (C). text 156.00 (*0-306-43390-7*, Kluwer Plenum) Kluwer Academic.

— Silanes & Other Coupling Agents. 588p. 1992. 147.50 (*90-6764-142-1*) Coronet Bks.

— Solution Chemistry of Surfactants, 2 vols., Vol. 1. LC 79-15067. 542p. 1979. 115.00 (*0-306-40174-6*, Plenum Trade) Perseus Pubng.

— Solution Chemistry of Surfactants, 2 vols., Vol. 2. LC 79-15067. 460p. 1979. 115.00 (*0-306-40175-4*, Plenum Trade) Perseus Pubng.

— Surfactants in Solution, 3 Vols., Set. LC 83-19170. 712p. 1984. 325.00 (*0-685-07795-0*, Plenum Trade) Perseus Pubng.

Mittal, K. L., ed. Surfactants in Solution, Set, Vols. 7-10. (Illus.). 2107p. 1990. 395.00 (*0-685-51856-6*, Plenum Trade) Perseus Pubng.

Mittal, K. L., ed. Surfactants in Solution, 3 vols., Vol. 1. LC 83-19170. 712p. 1984. 125.00 (*0-306-41483-X*, Plenum Trade) Perseus Pubng.

— Surfactants in Solution, 3 vols., Vol. 2. LC 83-19170. 718p. 1984. 125.00 (*0-306-41484-8*, Plenum Trade) Perseus Pubng.

— Surfactants in Solution, 3 vols., Vol. 3. LC 83-19170. 740p. 1984. 125.00 (*0-306-41485-6*, Plenum Trade) Perseus Pubng.

— Surfactants in Solution, Vol. 7. (Illus.). 535p. (C). 1989. text 174.00 (*0-306-43332-X*, Kluwer Plenum) Kluwer Academic.

— Surfactants in Solution, Vol. 8. LC 83-19170. (Illus.). 476p. (C). 1990. text 174.00 (*0-306-43333-8*, Kluwer Plenum) Kluwer Academic.

— Surfactants in Solution, Vol. 9. (Illus.). 548p. (C). 1989. text 174.00 (*0-306-43334-6*, Kluwer Plenum) Kluwer Academic.

— Surfactants in Solution, Vol. 10. (Illus.). 548p. (C). 1989. text 174.00 (*0-306-43335-4*, Kluwer Plenum) Kluwer Academic.

— Surfactants in Solution, Vol. 4, Vol. 4. 550p. 1987. 135.00 (*0-306-42468-1*, Plenum Trade); 325.00 (*0-685-18004-2*, Plenum Trade) Perseus Pubng.

— Surfactants in Solution, Vol. 5, Vol. 5. 575p. 1987. 135.00 (*0-306-42469-X*, Plenum Trade); 325.00 (*0-685-18005-0*, Plenum Trade) Perseus Pubng.

— Surfactants in Solution, Vol. 6, Vol. 6. 600p. 1987. 135.00 (*0-306-42470-3*, Plenum Trade); 325.00 (*0-685-18006-9*, Plenum Trade) Perseus Pubng.

— Treatise on Clean Surface Technology, Vol. 1. (Illus.). 348p. (C). 1987. text 132.00 (*0-306-42420-7*, Kluwer Plenum) Kluwer Academic.

Mittal, K. L., et al, eds. Solution Behavior of Surfactants: Theoretical & Applied Aspects, 2 vols., Vol. 1. LC 82-10120. 770p. 1982. 135.00 (*0-306-41025-7*, Plenum Trade) Perseus Pubng.

— Solution Behavior of Surfactants: Theoretical & Applied Aspects, 2 vols., Vol. 2. LC 82-10120. 822p. 1982. 135.00 (*0-306-41026-5*, Plenum Trade) Perseus Pubng.

Mittal, K. L. & Anderson, H. R., Jr., eds. Acid-Base Interactions: Relevance to Adhesion Science & Technology. (Illus.). 380p. 1991. 115.00 (*90-6764-135-9*, Pub. by VSP) Coronet Bks.

***Mittal, K. L. & Kumar, P.** Handbook of Microemulsion Science & Technology. LC 99-32812. (Illus.). 864p. 1999. text 225.00 (*0-8247-1979-4*) Dekker.

***Mittal, K. L. & Kumar, Promod.** Emulsions, Foams & Thin Films. LC 00-24052. (Illus.). 2000. write for info. (*0-8247-0366-9*) Dekker.

Mittal, K. L. & Lee, K. W., eds. Polymer Surfaces & Interfaces: Characterization, Modification & Application. (Illus.). 435p. 1997. 127.50 (*90-6764-217-7*, Pub. by VSP) Coronet Bks.

***Mittal, K. L. & Pizzi, A.** Adhesion Promotion Techniques: Technological Applications. LC 98-56655. (Materials Engineering Ser.: Vol. 14). (Illus.). 416p. 1999. text 195.00 (*0-8247-0239-5*) Dekker.

Mittal, K. L. & Shah, D. O. Surfactants in Solution, Vol. 11. (Illus.). 720p. (C). 1992. text 165.00 (*0-306-44186-1*, Kluwer Plenum) Kluwer Academic.

Mittal, K. L., jt. auth. see Chattopadhyay, Arun K.

Mittal, K. L., jt. auth. see Pizzi, Antonio.

Mittal, K. L., jt. ed. see Ghosh, Malay K.

Mittal, Kamala. History of Bhopal State: Development of Constitution, Administration & National Awakening, 1901-1949. 1990. 25.00 (*0-685-37832-2*, Pub. by M Manoharial) S Asia.

— History of Bhopal State: Development of Constitution, Administration & National Awakening, 1901-1949. 232p. 1990. reprint ed. 28.50 (*81-215-0474-0*, Pub. by M Manoharial) Coronet Bks.

Mittal, M. M. Law Relating to Highways. (C). 1968. 45.00 (*0-7855-5543-9*) St Mut.

— Supreme Court on Sales Tax, 1950-1988. (C). 1988. 150.00 (*0-7855-3661-2*) St Mut.

Mittal, M. M., jt. auth. see Gupta, A.

Mittal, Mukta, ed. Women in India: Today & Tomorrow. LC 94-907058. (C). 1995. 40.00 (*81-7488-035-6*, Pub. by Anmol) S Asia.

Mittal, Mukta, jt. ed. see Gupta, Sunit.

Mittal, Pawan K. In-Law of Baghdad. LC 97-91363. 1998. pap. 14.95 (*0-533-12648-7*) Vantage.

Mittal, S. C. India Distorted Vol. 1: A Study of British Historians on India, 3 vols. LC 94-906397. 153p. 1995. pap. 113.00 (*81-85880-64-6*, Pub. by Print Hse) St Mut.

— India Distorted Vol. 2: A Study of British Historians on India. 154p. 1996. pap. 175.00 (*81-7533-018-X*, Pub. by Print Hse) St Mut.

***Mittal, S. C.** India Distorted Vol. 3: A Study of Births Historians on India. 1998. pap. 140.00 (*81-7533-079-1*, Pub. by Print Hse) St Mut.

Mittal, S. C., jt. ed. see Datta, V. N.

Mittal, S. N. Taxation Policies & Financial Decisions. (C). 1988. 200.00 (*0-7855-4727-4*) St Mut.

Mittal, Vibhu O. Generating Natural Language Descriptions with Integrated Text & Examples. LC 98-35087. 280p. 1999. 45.00 (*0-8058-2414-6*); pap. 22.50 (*0-8058-2415-4*) L Erlbaum Assocs.

Mittal, Vibhu O., et al, eds. Assistive Technology & Artificial Intelligence: Applications in Robotics, User Interfaces & Natural Language Processing. LC 98-36066. (Lecture Notes in Artificial Intelligence Ser.: Vol. 1458). x, 273p. 1998. pap. 49.00 (*3-540-64790-2*) Spr-Verlag.

Mittar, Vishwa, jt. auth. see Sharma, B. K.

Mitteis, Ludwig. Reichsrecht und Volksrecht in Den Ostlichen Provinzen des Romiscshen Kaiserreichs. xiv, 562p. 1984. reprint ed. write for info. (*3-487-00502-6*) G Olms Pubs.

Mitteis, Ludwig & Wilcken, Ulrich. Grundzuge und Chrestomathie der Papyruskunde, 4 vols., Set. (GER.). cix, 1744p. 1978. reprint ed. write for info. (*0-318-70787-X*) G Olms Pubs.

***Mittelbach, Frank.** The Latex Design Companion. 400p. (C). 1999. pap. text. write for info. (*0-201-36300-3*) Addison-Wesley.

Mittelbach, Frank. The LATEX 3 Style Guide & Reference Manual. (C). 1998. pap. text. write for info. (*0-201-60024-2*) Addison-Wesley.

Mittelbach, H. R. The Injured Hand: A Handbook for General & Clinical Practice. (Illus.). 1979. 84.00 (*0-387-90365-8*) Spr-Verlag.

Mittelbach, Margaret & Crewdson, Michael. Wild New York: A Guide to the Wildlife, Wild Places, & Natural Phenomena of New York City. LC 98-28221. (Illus.). 208p. 1998. pap. 18.00 (*0-609-80348-4*, Crown) Crown Pub Group.

Mittelberg, et al. Becoming Contagious: Overheads, 80 vols. 275p. 1995. pap. 16.99 (*0-310-50091-5*) Zondervan.

Mittelberg, David. The Israel Connection & American Jews. LC 98-44401. 216p. 1999. 55.00 (*0-275-96421-3*, Praeger Pubs) Greenwood.

— Strangers in Paradise: The Israel Kibbutz Experience. 308p. 1988. 39.95 (*0-88738-183-9*) Transaction Pubs.

Mittelberg, Mark, et al. Becoming a Contagious Christian. 1995. pap., teacher ed. 29.99 (*0-310-50081-8*) Zondervan.

Mittelberg, Mark, jt. auth. see Hybels, Bill.

Mittelberg, Victor. House Flipping for Fun & Profit. LC 97-90155. 135p. (Orig.). 1997. pap. 14.75 (*0-9658003-0-X*) Sabra Pub.

Mittelberger, Ernest, jt. auth. see Lamb, Richard.

Mittelberger, Gottlieb. Journey to Pennsylvania. Handlin, Oscar & Clive, John, eds. LC 60-11555. (John Harvard Library Ser.). 122p. reprint ed. pap. 37.90 (*0-608-14442-8*, 205186600012) Bks Demand.

Mittelbrunn, Juan R., et al, eds. Strings & Superstrings: Proceedings of the XVIII International Gift Seminar on Theoretical Physics. 300p. (C). 1988. pap. 46.00 (*9971-5-0524-X*); text 90.00 (*9971-5-0523-1*) World Scientific Pub.

***Mittelbuscher, Barb Eisenbath.** Forgotten Church: The Presbyterian Meeting House at Eagle-Fork, Missouri. (Missouri Research Roundtable Papers: No. 3). (Illus.). 24p. 1999. pap. 4.00 (*0-931227-51-8*) Mallinckrodt Comm.

Mittelhammer, Ron. Mathematical Statistics for Economics & Business. LC 95-37686. 723p. 1996. 54.95 (*0-387-94587-3*) Spr-Verlag.

***Mittelhammer, Ron C., et al.** Econometric Foundations. LC 99-40040. (Illus.). 864p. (C). 2000. 59.95 (*0-521-62394-4*) Cambridge U Pr.

***Mittelkotter, U.** Antiinfektivatabelle 1999. 10p. 1999. 8.75 (*3-8055-6736-7*) S Karger.

Mittell, P., ed. see Paganini, Nicolo.

Mittelman, James H. Globalization: Critical Reflections. (International Political Economy Yearbook Ser.: Vol. 9). 273p. 1997. pap. 19.95 (*1-55587-752-4*) L Rienner.

Mittelman, James H., ed. Globalization: Critical Reflections. 273p. 1996. lib. bdg. 49.95 (*1-55587-565-3*) L Rienner.

Mittelman, James H. & Pasha, Mustapha K. Out from Underdevelopment Revisited: Changing Global Structures & the Remaking of the Third World. LC 96-28753. (International Political Economy Ser.). 256p. 1997. text 55.00 (*0-312-16466-1*) St Martin.

Mittelman, James H., jt. ed. see Gill, Stephen.

***Mittelman, Karen S. & Moss-Vreeland, Patricia.** Memory-Connections Matter, Art-in-Science, Vol. XIV. (Illus.). 32p. 2000. 5.00 (*0-9678657-0-0*) Moss-Vreeland.

Mittelman, Karen S., et al. Creating American Jews: Historical Conversations about Identity. (Brandeis Series in American Jewish History, Culture, & Life). (Illus.). 120p. 1998. pap. 17.95 (*1-891507-01-X*, Pub. by Koeltz Sci Bks) Lubrecht & Cramer.

Mittelman, Mark & Hamet, Marc R. On-Call Radiology. (Illus.). 225p. 1997. pap. text 39.00 (*0-397-58444-X*) Lppncott W & W.

Mittelstadt, Michael. Thucydidean Psychology & the Tragic Process in 'The History' 27p. 1993. 3.00 (*1-883058-12-0*, SAG&IP) Global Pubns.

Mittelstaedt, Carol A. Abdominal Ultrasound. LC 86-17143. (Illus.). 734p. reprint ed. pap. 200.00 (*0-7837-6264-X*, 204597600010) Bks Demand.

Mittelstaedt, Carol A., ed. General Ultrasound. (Illus.). 1231p. 1992. text 260.00 (*0-443-08735-0*) Church.

Mittelstaedt, John R. Samuel. LC 93-84456. (People's Bible Ser.). 336p. 1994. pap. 12.99 (*0-8100-0491-7*, 15N0499) Northwest Pub.

Mittelstaedt, P. & Lahti, Pekka J., eds. Foundations of Modern Physics: Proceedings of the Symposium on "The Foundations of Modern Physics: 50 Years of the Einstein-Podolsky-Rosen Gedanken Experiment", Joensuu, Finland, 16-20 June 1985. 718p. 1985. 116.00 (*9971-5-0004-3*); pap. 75.00 (*9971-5-0005-1*) World Scientific Pub.

— The Foundations of Modern Physics, 1990: Symposium. 540p. 1990. pap. 55.00 (*981-02-0417-5*) World Scientific Pub.

Mittelstaedt, P., et al. Foundations of Modern Physics: Proceedings of the Symposium. 550p. 1994. text 121.00 (*981-02-1507-X*) World Scientific Pub.

— The Quantum Theory of Measurement. Beiglbock, W. et al, eds. (Lecture Notes in Physics Ser.: Vol. M2). xiii, 165p. 1991. 29.00 (*0-387-54334-1*) Spr-Verlag.

Mittelstaedt, P., ed. see Lahti, Pekka J.

Mittelstaedt, Peter. The Interpretation of Quantum Mechanics & the Measurement Process. LC 96-52450. (Illus.). 150p. (C). 1997. text 47.95 (*0-521-55445-4*) Cambridge U Pr.

— Philosophical Problems of Modern Physics. Cohen, R. S., ed. LC 72-92534. (Boston Studies in the Philosophy of Science: No. 18). 211p. 1975. pap. 17.50 (*0-685-02827-5*); lib. bdg. 78.00 (*90-277-0285-3*, D Reidel) Kluwer Academic.

— Quantum Logic. (Synthese Library: 126). 157p. 1978. text 106.00 (*90-277-0925-4*) Kluwer Academic.

Mittelstrass, Juergen. Zukunft des Alterns und Gesellschaftliche Entwicklung. Baltes, Paul B., ed. (Akademie der Wissenschaften zu Berlin, Forschungsbericht Ser.: No. 5). (GER.). xvi, 814p. (C). 1992. pap. text 113.85 (*3-11-013248-6*) De Gruyter.

Mittelstrass, Juergen & Manfred, Riedel, eds. Vernuenftiges Denken. (C). 1978. 119.25 (*3-11-006956-3*) De Gruyter.

Mittelstrass, Juergen, jt. auth. see Carrier, Martin.

Mittelstrass, Juergen, jt. ed. see Brown, James R.

Mittelstrass, Muriel. Creative Giftwrapping for Busy People. Pickens, Judy, ed. (Illus.). 98p. (Orig.). 1990. pap. text 8.95 (*0-9626345-0-6*) Gem Investment.

Mittemeijer, E. J., ed. First ASM Heat Treatment & Surface Engineering Conference in Europe, Pts. 1 & 2. 791p. 1992. 266.00 (*0-87849-642-4*, 6455) ASM.

Mittemeijer, E. J., jt. auth. see Bell, T.

Mittemeijer, E. J., jt. ed. see Delhez, R.

Mitten, David G., et al. Sardis: Twenty-Seven Years of Discovery. Guralnick, Eleanor, ed. (Illus.). 123p. 1988. pap. 12.00 (*0-9609042-1-2*) Archaeol Chi.

Mitten, David G., jt. auth. see Kozloff, Arielle P.

Mittendorf, Bradley C., jt. ed. see Ayers, Edward L.

Mittendorf, John. Truck Company Operations. LC 98-18369. 1998. 48.75 (*0-912212-64-0*) Fire Eng.

Mittendorf, Stefan-Maria. FarbeBekennen Tizian - Rembrandt - Marees: Versuch uber die Farbe an Munchner Werken zur Bestimmung Ihres Stellenwertes in der Kunst Hans bon Marees' (Europaische Hochschulschriften, Reihe 28: Bd. 303). (GER., Illus.). 181p. 1997. 44.95 (*3-631-31627-5*) P Lang Pubng.

Mittendorfer, Josef. Objektorientierte Programmierung mit Turbo Pascal 6.0. 2nd ed. (GER.). (C). 1991. text. write for info. (*0-201-55956-0*) Addison-Wesley.

Mittendorfer, Rudolf. Robert Schuman - Architekt des Neuen Europa. (GER.). viii, 555p. 1983. write for info. (*3-487-07373-0*) G Olms Pubs.

Mittenthal, Robert. Ready Terms. 32p. 1989. pap. 4.00 (*0-921331-14-2*, Pub. by Tsunami Edits) SPD-Small Pr Dist.

Mittenthal, Suzanne M. The Baltimore Trail Book. rev. ed. Poultney, James W., ed. LC 82-21216. (Illus.). 176p. (Orig.). 1983. pap. 14.95 (*0-8018-2943-7*) Johns Hopkins.

Mitter, H., et al, eds. Recent Aspects of Quantum Fields: Proceedings of the XXX Int. Universitatswochen fur Kernphysik, Schladming, Austria February & March 1991. (Lecture Notes in Physics Ser.: Vol. 396). xiii, 332p. 1992. 55.00 (*0-685-54830-9*) Spr-Verlag.

Mitter, H. & Lang, C. B., eds. Recent Developments in High Energy Physics. (Acta Physica Austriaca Ser.: Suppl. 25). (Illus.). 547p. 1983. 111.95 (*0-387-81771-9*) Spr-Verlag.

Mitter, H. & Latal, Heimo, eds. Concepts & Trends in Particle Physics. (Illus.). 340p. 1987. 59.00 (*0-387-17372-2*) Spr-Verlag.

— Physics for a New Generation: Prospects for High-Energy Physics at New Accelerators; Proceedings of the XXVIII, Internationale Universitatswochen fur Kernphysik, Schladming, Austria, March 1989. (Illus.). 344p. 1990. 71.95 (*0-387-52378-2*) Spr-Verlag.

Mitter, H. & Pittner, Ludwig, eds. Stochastic Methods & Computer Techniques in Quantum Dynamics. (Acta Physica Austriaca Ser.: Supplementum 26). (Illus.). vi, 452p. 1984. 97.95 (*0-387-81835-9*) Spr-Verlag.

Mitter, H. & Plessas, W., eds. Nucleon-Nucleon & Nucleon-Antinucleon Interactions. (Acta Physica Austriaca Ser.: Suppl. 27). (Illus.). 724p. 1986. 136.95 (*0-387-81900-2*) Spr-Verlag.

Mitter, H. & Schweiger, W., eds. Fields & Particles: Proceedings of the XXIX Int. Universitatswochen fur Kernphysik, Schladming, Austria, March 1990. (Illus.). 304p. 1991. 70.95 (*0-387-53178-5*) Spr-Verlag.

Mitter, Kathy, jt. auth. see Bergt, Carolyn.

Mitter, Kathy, jt. illus. see Peters, Stephanie T.

***Mitter, Matt.** A B C. (Talking Pages Deluxe Ser.). (Illus.). (J). 2000. 12.95 (*1-58224-133-3*) Futech Interactive.

— Ballyhoo at the Zoo. (Finger Wiggles Ser.). (Illus.). 7p. (J). (ps-k). Date not set. bds. write for info. (*1-57584-430-3*, Pub. by Rdrs Digest) S&S Trade.

— Billy Blazes, Firefighter. (Fisher-Price Action Tool Bks.). (Illus.). 12p. (J). (gr. k-3). 1999. bds. 5.99 (*1-57584-307-2*, RD Childrens) Rdrs Digest.

— Cosmo Helps Out. (Finger Wiggles Ser.). (Illus.). 7p. (J). (ps-k). Date not set. bds. write for info. (*1-57584-429-X*, Pub. by Rdrs Digest) S&S Trade.

Mitter, Matt. Disney's Love Poems. (Look-Look Bks.). 24p. (J). (ps-3). 1998. pap. text 3.29 (*0-307-12981-0*, 12981) Gldn Bks Pub Co.

— Let's Be Thankful. (Little Golden Bks.). 24p. (J). 1998. 2.29 (*0-307-96022-6*, 96022, Goldn Books) Gldn Bks Pub Co.

***Mitter, Matt.** Once upon a Rhyme. (Talking Pages Deluxe Ser.). 2000. 12.95 (*1-58224-131-7*) Futech Interactive.

— 1 2 3. (Talking Pages Deluxe Ser.). (Illus.). 14p. (J). 2000. 12.95 (*1-58224-134-1*) Futech Interactive.

— Rip to the Rescue. (Fisher-Price Action Tool Bks.). (Illus.). 12p. (J). (gr. k-3). 1999. bds. 5.99 (*1-57584-306-4*, Pub. by Rdrs Digest) S&S Trade.

— Rocky Canyon on the Trail. (Action Tool Books Ser.). (Illus.). 12p. (J). 2000. bds. 5.99 (*1-57584-422-2*) Rdrs Digest.

— Same & Different. (Talking Pages Deluxe Ser.). (Illus.). (J). 2000. 12.95 (*1-58224-132-5*) Futech Interactive.

Mitter, Matt. Up, down, All Around: Learning about Opposites. (Fisher-Price Puzzle Playbks.: Vol. 2). (Illus.). 12p. (J). (ps-k). 1999. bds. 6.99 (*1-57584-273-4*, Pub. by Rdrs Digest) Random.

— A Wedding Is Beautiful. LC 97-77002. (Little Golden Bks.). (Illus.). 24p. (J). 1998. 1.99 (*0-307-98877-5*, 98877, Goldn Books) Gldn Bks Pub Co.

Mitter, Matt, et al. Dudley the Dump Truck. (Squeaky Trucks Ser.: No. 1). (Illus.). 10p. (J). (gr. k-3). 1998. bds. 8.99 (*1-57584-209-2*, Pub. by Rdrs Digest) Random.

— Frankie the Fire Engine. (Squeaky Trucks Ser.: No. 2). (Illus.). 10p. (J). (gr. k-3). 1998. bds. 8.99 (*1-57584-210-6*, Pub. by Rdrs Digest) Random.

Mitter, Matt, jt. auth. see Fisher-Price Staff.

Mitter, Matt, jt. auth. see Singer, Mutt.

Mitter, Matt, jt. auth. see Willson, Sarah.

Mitter, P., jt. ed. see Diekmann, A.

Mitter, Partha. Art & Nationalism in Colonial India: Occidental Orientations. (Illus.). 505p. (C). 1995. text 110.00 (*0-521-44354-7*) Cambridge U Pr.

— Much Maligned Monsters: A History of European Reactions to Indian Art. (Illus.). 376p. 1992. pap. text 21.00 (*0-226-53239-9*) U Ch Pr.

Mitter, Partha & Herwitz, Daniel A. Indian Art Today: Four Artists from the Chester & Davida Herwitz Family Collection. LC 85-32106. (Illus.). 56p. 1986. pap. 10.00 (*0-943044-07-3*) Phillips Coll.

***Mitter, Rana.** The Manchurian Myth: Nationalism, Resistance & Collaboration During the Manchurian Crisis, 1931-33. LC 99-46738. 326p. 2000. 45.00 (*0-520-22111-7*, Pub. by U CA Pr) Cal Prin Full Svc.

Mitter, S., jt. ed. see Martens, M. Hosmer.

Mitter, S. K. & Gill, K. S., eds. Computer-Aided Manufacturing & Women's Employment: The Clothing Industry in Four EC Countries. (Artificial Intelligence & Society Ser.). (Illus.). 192p. 1991. 78.95 (*0-387-19656-0*) Spr-Verlag.

Mitter, S. K., tr. see Lions, J. L.

Mitter, Sara S. Dharma's Daughters: Contemporary Indian Women & Hindu Culture. LC 90-19387. (Illus.). 250p. (C). 1991. pap. 16.00 (*0-8135-1678-1*); text 40.00 (*0-8135-1677-3*) Rutgers U Pr.

Mitter, Shomit. Systems of Rehearsal: Stanislavsky, Brecht, Grotowski & Peter Brook. LC 92-43. (Illus.). 192p. (C). (gr. 13). 1992. pap. 22.99 (*0-415-06784-7*, A7101) Routledge.

Mitter Swasti. Common Fate, Common Bond. (C). pap. 13.95 (*0-7453-0026-X*, Pub. by Pluto GBR) Stylus Pub VA.

Mitter Swasti & Rowbotham, Sheila, eds. Women Encounter Technology: Changing Patterns of Employment in the Third World. LC 95-7345. (UNU/Intech Studies in New Technology & Development: No. 1). 378p. (C). 1995. 100.00 (*0-415-12687-8*) Routledge.

— Women Encounter Technology: Changing Patterns of Employment in the Third World. (UNU/Intech Studies in New Technology & Development). 376p. (C). 1997. pap. 29.99 (*0-415-14118-4*) Routledge.

Mitter, Swasti, jt. ed. see Bastos, Maria-Ines.

Mitter Swasti, jt. ed. see Rowbotham, Sheila.

Mitterand, ed. see Zola, Emile.

Mitterand, Francois. The Fist & the Rose. LC 74-82724. write for info. (*0-89388-183-X*) Okpaku Communications.

Mitterand, Henri. Dictionnaire des Oeuvres du XXeme Siecle. (FRE.). 621p. 1995. 110.00 (*0-7859-9899-3*) Fr & Eur.

— Mots Francais. 128p. 1968. 9.95 (*0-8288-7461-1*) Fr & Eur.

Mitterand, Henri, jt. auth. see DuBois, Jean M.

Mitterand, Henri, ed. see Zola, Emile.

Mitterauer, Michael & Sieder, Reinhard. The European Family: Patriarchy to Partnership from the Middle Ages to the Present. Oosterveen, Karla & Horzinger, Manfred, trs. LC 81-21954. 240p. 1982. lib. bdg. 25.00 (*0-226-53240-2*) U Ch Pr.

— The European Family: Patriarchy to Partnership from the Middle Ages to the Present. Oosterveen, Karla & Horzinger, Reinhard, trs. LC 81-21954. xvi, 252p. (C). 1999. pap. text 17.00 (*0-226-53241-0*) U Ch Pr.

Mitterer. Barcode Mnl- Lecture Active Dync Cncp,ii. 2nd ed. (C). 1996. pap. text 294.50 (*0-15-504022-7*) Harcourt Coll Pubs.

— Dynamic Concepts in Psychology. (C). 1993. pap. text, teacher ed. 35.00 (*0-15-500935-4*) Harcourt Coll Pubs.

— Introductory Psychology Acetates. (C). 1994. 110.50 (*0-15-501456-0*) Harcourt Coll Pubs.

Mitterer, Felix. Siberia & Other Plays. (Studies in Austrian Literature, Culture, & Thought. Translation Ser.). 1994. pap. 33.50 (*0-929497-68-6*) Ariadne CA.

— The Wild Woman & Other Plays. Hanlin, Todd C. & Hutchinson, Heidi L., trs. LC 94-43185. (Studies in Austrian Literature, Culture, & Thought). 1995. pap. 28.00 (*1-57241-002-7*) Ariadne CA.

Mitterer, Franz, ed. see Byrn, Anne.

Mittermann, Harald & Schendl, Herbert, eds. A Concordance to the Novels of John Lyly. (Elizabethan Concordance Ser.: Vol. 2). 904p. 1984. lib. bdg. 245.70 (*3-487-07564-4*) G Olms Pubs.

Mittermann, Lauren. Different Paths: Poems by Lauren Mittermann. 52p. 1994. pap. 6.95 (*0-9638558-0-8*) Maple Grove.

Mittermann, Lauren, jt. auth. see Berns, Jennifer.

***Mittermeier, Russell A., et al.** Hotspots: Earth's Biologically Richest & Most Endangered Terrestrial Ecoregions. (Illus.). 432p. 2000. 65.00 (*968-6397-58-2*, Pub. by Conser Intl) U Ch Pr.

Mittermeijer, E. J., jt. ed. see Delhez, R.

Mittermeir, R., ed. Shifting Paradigms in Software Engineering: Proceedings of the 7th Joint Conference of the Austrian Computer Society (OCG) & the John Von Neumann Society for Computing Sciences (NJSZT) in Klagenfurt, Austria, 1992. (Illus.). x, 252p. 1992. 41.95 (*0-387-82408-1*) Spr-Verlag.

Mittermeyer, Helen. The Veil. 384p. (Orig.). 1996. mass mkt. 5.99 (*0-446-60263-9*, Pub. by Warner Bks) Little.

— White Heat. 1989. mass mkt. 2.95 (*0-553-55036-5*) Bantam.

Mitterrand, Francois. Bibliotheque Nationale De France, 1989-1995: Dominique Perrault, Architect. (Illus.). 232p. 1996. 85.00 (*3-7643-5590-5*, Pub. by Birkhauser) Princeton Arch.

Mitterrand, Francois & Wiesel, Elie. Memoir in Two Voices. Seaver, Richard & Bent, TImothy, trs. 192p. 1996. 21.45 (*1-55970-338-5*, Pub. by Arcade Pub Inc) Time Warner.

Mitterrand, Francois & Wiesel, Elie. Memoir in Two Voices. Seaver, Richard & Bent, Timothy, trs. LC 95-53369. 1997. pap. 11.45 (*1-55970-379-2*, Pub. by Arcade Pub Inc) Time Warner.

***Mittiga, Heidi.** Time Families. Haugen, Janie & Von Dohlen, Happy, eds. 20p. 1998. teacher ed. 124.95 (*1-884074-63-4*, PCI 717) PCI Educ Pubg.

— Time Families Worksheet Program. Haugen, Janie & Von Dohlen, Happy, eds. 100p. 1998. wbk. ed. 39.95 (*1-884074-64-2*, PCI 718) PCI Educ Pubg.

Mittiga, Linda, jt. auth. see Berger, E. Roy.

Mittins, William H. Language Awareness for Teachers. (English, Language & Education Ser.). 160p. 1990. pap. 33.95 (*0-335-09559-3*) OpUniv Pr.

Mittl, John. Astral Projection (Modus Operandi) 8p. 1993. reprint ed. spiral bd. 8.00 (*0-7873-0620-7*) Hlth Research.

***Mittleberg.** Building Contagious Churches. 2000. 18.99 (*0-310-22149-8*) Zondervan.

MITTLEBERG, MARK. Building Contagious Church. pap. 10.99 (*0-310-23200-7*) HarpC.

Mittleberger, Ernest. The Wine Cellar Record. Roux, Henry & Sullivan, Maurice T., eds. (Illus.). 1979. 39.95 (*0-932664-06-7*) Wine Appreciation.

Mittleider, Jacob R. Food for Everyone: The Mittleider Method. 2nd ed. (Illus.). 621p. 1970. mass mkt. 59.95 (*0-9656617-0-9*) Food For Every.

Mittleider, Jacob R. The Garden Doctor, 3 vols. (Illus.). 424p. 1990. mass mkt. 72.95 (*1-878951-03-3*) Food For Every.

— Gardening by the Foot. LC 80-84564. (Illus.). 143p. 1985. pap. 16.95 (*1-929982-00-3*) Food For Every.

— Let's Grow Tomatoes. LC 80-84563. (Illus.). 142p. 1986. mass mkt. 16.95 (*1-929982-01-1*) Food For Every.

— The Mittleider Basics Course. write for info. (*1-929982-04-6*) Food For Every.

— The Mittleider Gardening Course. (Illus.). 268p. 1999. pap. 29.95 (*1-929982-03-8*) Food For Every.

— Mittleider Grow-Box Gardens. LC 78-52953. Orig. Title: More Food from Your Garden. (Illus.). 194p. 1975. reprint ed. mass mkt. 16.95 (*1-929982-02-X*) Food For Every.

Mittleider, Jacob R. 6 Steps to Successful Gardening. Hall, Leo D., ed. (Illus.). 58p. 1995. mass mkt. 12.95 (*0-914107-04-6*) Food For Every.

Mittleman, Alan L. Between Kant & Kabbalah: An Introduction to Isaac Breuer's Philosophy of Judaism. LC 89-34101. (SUNY Series in Judaica). 227p. (C). 1990. pap. text 21.95 (*0-7914-0240-1*) State U NY Pr.

— The Politics of Torah: The Jewish Political Tradition & the Founding of Agudat Israel. LC 95-49366. 200p. (C). 1996. text 59.50 (*0-7914-3077-4*); pap. text 19.95 (*0-7914-3078-2*) State U NY Pr.

***Mittleman, Alan L.** The Scepter Shall Not Depart from Judah: Perspectives on the Persistence of the Political in Judaism. LC 99-53428. 200p. 2000. 70.00 (*0-7391-0096-3*); pap. 20.95 (*0-7391-0097-1*) Lxngtn Bks.

Mittleman, Don. BASIC Computing. 430p. (C). 1982. pap. text 19.00 (*0-15-504910-0*) Harcourt Coll Pubs.

Mittleman, M. H. Introduction to the Theory of Laser-Atom Interactions. 2nd ed. (Illus.). 326p. (C). 1993. text 65.00 (*0-306-44432-1*, Kluwer Plenum) Kluwer Academic.

Mittleman, Stu, jt. auth. see Honig, Daniel T.

M

An Asterisk (*) at the beginning of an entry indicates that the title is appearing for the first time.

Mittleman, Stuart. Endurance for Life. 2000. 13.00 (*0-06-273674-4*) HarpC.

Mittleman, Stuart & Callan, Katherine. Slow Burn: Slow down, Burn Fat & Unlock the Energy Within. LC 99-48467. 336p. 2000. 24.00 (*0-06-271612-3*, HarpRes) HarpInfo.

Mittlemann, Hans D. & Roose, Dirk, eds. Continuation Techniques & Bifurcation Problems. (International Series of Numerical Mathematics: No. 92). 225p. 1990. 76.00 (*0-8176-2397-3*) Birkhauser.

Mittler, Abe. Art in Focus. 3rd ed. 1993. 61.96 (*0-02-662312-9*) Glencoe.

Mittler-Battipaglia, Diana. Franz Mittler: Austro-American Composer, Musician, & Humorous Poet. LC 93-25240. (Austrian Culture Ser.: Vol. 8). 178p. (C). 1994. text 42.95 (*0-8204-2063-8*) P Lang Pubng.

Mittler, Elliott. An Assessment of Floodplain Management in Georgia's Flint River Basin. LC 97-25660. (Program on Environment & Behavior Ser.: Vol. 59). 1997. 20.00 (*1-877943-14-2*) Natural Hazards.

— Natural Hazard Policy Setting: Identifying Supporters & Opponents of Nonstructural Hazard Mitigation. (Program on Environment & Behavior Monograph Ser.: No. 48). 282p. (C). 1989. pap. 20.00 (*0-685-28122-1*) Natural Hazards.

— Natural Hazards Policy Setting: Identifying Supporters & Opponents of Nonstructural Hazard Mitigation. (Program on Environment & Behavior Monograph Ser.: No. 48). 282p. 1989. 20.00 (*0-685-62420-X*) Natural Hazards.

M

Mittler, Gene. Art in Focus. 1994. teacher ed. write for info. (*0-02-662313-7*) Glencoe.

Mittler, Gene. Creating & Understanding Drawings. 1988. 38.37 (*0-02-662273-4*) Glencoe.

***Mittler, Gene & Ragans, Rosalind.** Exploring Art: Teacher's Wraparound Edition. (Illus.). 1999. teacher ed. 49.57 (*0-02-662357-9*) Glencoe.

— Understanding Art: Teacher's Wraparound Edition. (Illus.). 1999. teacher ed. 49.10 (*0-02-662361-7*) Glencoe.

***Mittler, Gene, et al.** Introducing Art: Teacher's Wraparound Edition. (Illus.). 1999. teacher ed. 48.06 (*0-02-662364-1*) Glencoe.

Mittler, Helle. Families Speak Out: International Perspectives on Families' Experiences of Disability. LC 94-38388. 94p. 1994. pap. 10.95 (*1-57129-001-X*) Brookline Bks.

Mittler, Mary L., jt. ed. see Bers, Trudy H.

Mittler, P. J., jt. ed. see Hogg, James.

Mittler, P. J., jt. ed. see Hogg, J.

Mittler, Peter, ed. Psychological Assessment of Mental & Physical Handicaps. 886p. 1974. pap. 33.00 (*0-422-75600-8*, NO. 2819, Pub. by Tavistock) Routldge.

Mittler, Peter & Daunt, Patrick, eds. Teacher Education for Special Needs in Europe. (Cassell Education Ser.). (Illus.). 176p. 1996. 100.00 (*0-304-33405-7*); pap. 33.95 (*0-304-33406-5*) Continuum.

Mittler, Peter & Sinason, Valerie, eds. Changing Policy & Practice for People with Learning Disabilities. (Social Science Ser.). (Illus.). 256p. 1996. 90.00 (*0-304-33398-0*); pap. 39.95 (*0-304-33399-9*) Continuum.

Mittler, Peter, ed. see Hart, S. & Mongon, Denis.

Mittler, Peter, ed. see Montgomery, Diane.

Mittler, Peter, ed. see Robson, B.

Mittler, Thomas E., ed. Annual Review of Entomology, Vol. 40. LC 56-5750. 1995. text 47.00 (*0-8243-0140-4*) Annual Reviews.

— Annual Review of Entomology, Vol. 41. LC 56-5750. 1996. 52.00 (*0-8243-0141-2*) Annual Reviews.

Mittler, Thomas E., et al, eds. Annual Review of Entomology, Vol. 22. LC 56-5750. (Illus.). 1977. 40.00 (*0-8243-0122-6*) Annual Reviews.

— Annual Review of Entomology, Vol. 23. LC 56-5750. (Illus.). 1978. 40.00 (*0-8243-0123-4*) Annual Reviews.

— Annual Review of Entomology, Vol. 24. LC 56-5750. (Illus.). 1979. 40.00 (*0-8243-0124-2*) Annual Reviews.

— Annual Review of Entomology, Vol. 25. LC 56-5750. (Illus.). 1980. 40.00 (*0-8243-0125-0*) Annual Reviews.

— Annual Review of Entomology, Vol. 26. LC 56-5750. (Illus.). 1981. 40.00 (*0-8243-0126-9*) Annual Reviews.

— Annual Review of Entomology, Vol. 27. LC 56-5750. (Illus.). 1982. 40.00 (*0-8243-0127-7*) Annual Reviews.

— Annual Review of Entomology, Vol. 28. LC 56-5750. (Illus.). 1983. text 40.00 (*0-8243-0128-5*) Annual Reviews.

— Annual Review of Entomology, Vol. 29. LC 56-5750. (Illus.). 1984. text 40.00 (*0-8243-0129-3*) Annual Reviews.

— Annual Review of Entomology, Vol. 30. LC 56-5750. (Illus.). 1985. text 40.00 (*0-8243-0130-7*) Annual Reviews.

— Annual Review of Entomology, Vol. 31. LC 56-5750. (Illus.). 1986. 40.00 (*0-8243-0131-5*) Annual Reviews.

— Annual Review of Entomology, Vol. 32. LC 56-5750. (Illus.). 1987. 40.00 (*0-8243-0132-3*) Annual Reviews.

— Annual Review of Entomology, Vol. 33. LC 56-5750. (Illus.). 1988. 40.00 (*0-8243-0133-1*) Annual Reviews.

— Annual Review of Entomology, Vol. 34. LC 56-5750. (Illus.). 1989. text 40.00 (*0-8243-0134-X*) Annual Reviews.

— Annual Review of Entomology, Vol. 35. LC 56-5750. 1990. 40.00 (*0-8243-0135-8*) Annual Reviews.

— Annual Review of Entomology, Vol. 36. LC 56-5750. 1991. 40.00 (*0-8243-0136-6*) Annual Reviews.

— Annual Review of Entomology, Vol. 37. 1992. 44.00 (*0-8243-0137-4*) Annual Reviews.

— Annual Review of Entomology, Vol. 38. LC 56-5750. (Illus.). 1993. text 44.00 (*0-8243-0138-2*) Annual Reviews.

— Annual Review of Entomology, Vol. 39. LC 56-5750. (Illus.). 1994. text 47.00 (*0-8243-0139-0*) Annual Reviews.

— Annual Review of Entomology, Vol. 43. LC 56-5750. 1998. text 60.00 (*0-8243-0143-9*) Annual Reviews.

Mittler, Thomas E., jt. ed. see Smith, Ray F.

Mittlestaedt, P. & Lahti, Pekka J., eds. Foundations of Modern Physics 87: The Copenhagen Interpretation 60 Years after the Como Lecture. 544p. (C). 1988. pap. 47.00 (*9971-5-0460-X*); text 121.00 (*9971-5-0382-4*) World Scientific Pub.

Mittman, Barbara G. Spectators on the Paris Stage in the Seventeenth & Eighteenth Centuries. LC 84-16339. (Theater & Dramatic Studies: No. 25). (Illus.). 170p. 1984. reprint ed. pap. 52.70 (*0-8357-1610-4*, 207048400096) Bks Demand.

***Mittman, Bradley.** Nail the Boards: Internal Medicine Board Review Syllabus for the ABIM Exam. LC 00-132303. (Illus.). 336p. 2000. pap. text 225.00 (*0-9677025-2-6*) Frontrunners.

Mittman, Elizabeth, jt. ed. see Joeres, Ruth-Ellen B.

Mittman, I. S., et al, eds. The National Dialogue on Genetics: Congress, College Park, MD., March 1998. (Community Genetics Ser.: Vol. 1, No. 3 (1998)). (Illus.). 92p. 1999. pap. 34.00 (*3-8055-6836-3*) S Karger.

Mittman, Karin & Ihsan, Zatar, eds. Culture Shock! Pakistan. (Illus.). 223p. 1991. pap. 12.95 (*1-55868-059-4*) Gr Arts Ctr Pub.

***Mittman, Robert & Cain, Mary.** The Future of the Internet in Health Care: Five Year Forcast. unabridged ed. Grosel, Charles, ed. 41p. 1999. pap. write for info. (*1-929008-03-1*) CA HlthCare Fnd.

Mittman, Stephanie. The Courtship. 400p. 1997. mass mkt. 5.99 (*0-440-22181-1*) Dell.

— The Courtship. large type ed. LC 98-6685. 1998. 24.95 (*0-7862-1499-6*) Thorndike Pr.

***Mittman, Stephanie.** Head over Heels. 400p. 1999. mass mkt. 6.50 (*0-440-22555-8*) Dell.

— A Heart Full of Miracles. 384p. 2000. mass mkt. 6.50 (*0-440-22556-6*) Dell.

Mittman, Stephanie. A Kiss to Dream On. 400p. 1998. mass mkt. 5.99 (*0-440-22554-X*) Dell.

— The Marriage Bed. 400p. 1996. mass mkt. 5.99 (*0-440-22182-X*) Dell.

Mittnik, S., ed. System-Theoretic Methods in Economic Modelling, No. II. (International Series in Modern Applied Mathematics & Computer Science: No. 22). 209p. 1989. 39.50 (*0-08-037932-X*, Pergamon Pr) Elsevier.

— System-Theoretic Methods in Economic Modelling I. (International Series in Modern Applied Mathematics & Computer Science). 184p. 1989. 39.50 (*0-08-037228-7*, Pergamon Pr) Elsevier.

Mittnik, Stefan & Rachev, S. Modeling Financial Assets with Alternative Stable Models. (Financial Economics Ser.). 874p. 2000. 95.00 (*0-471-95314-8*) Wiley.

Mitton. Histoire de la Presse Francaise, 2 vols., Set. Incl. Tome I. Des Origines a la Revolution. Tome II. Sous la Revolution, le Consulat, l'Empire. 11.90 (*0-685-34002-3*); write for info. (*0-8288-7903-6*) Fr & Eur.

Mitton, C. Leslie. Ephesians. (New Century Bible Ser.). 235p. 1975. pap. 24.50 (*0-551-00909-8*, Pub. by Sheffield Acad) CUP Services.

Mitton, C. Leslie. Social Sciences & the Churches. 1993. pap. 14.95 (*0-567-22305-1*, Pub. by T & T Clark) Bks Intl VA.

Mitton, David, et al, photos by. James in a Mess & Other Thomas the Tank Engine Stories. LC 92-25654. (Pictureback Ser.). (Illus.). 32p. (J). (ps-3). 1993. pap. 3.25 (*0-679-83895-3*, Pub. by Random Bks Yng Read) Random.

Mitton, David & Permane, Terry, photos by. Edward's Exploit & Other Thomas the Tank Engine Stories. LC 92-23189. (Thomas the Tank Engine Picturebacks Ser.). (Illus.). 32p. (J). (ps-3). 1993. pap. 3.25 (*0-679-83896-1*, Pub. by Random Bks Yng Read) Random.

Mitton, G. E., ed. see Scott, James G.

Mitton, Jacqueline. Aliens. LC 98-7464. (Informania Ser.). 92p. (J). (gr. 4-8). 1999. 15.99 (*0-7636-0492-5*, Pub. by Candlewick Pr) Penguin Putnam.

— Discovering the Planets. LC 90-11020. (Exploring the Universe Ser.). (Illus.). 32p. (J). (gr. 4-6). 1991. pap. 4.95 (*0-8167-2131-9*); lib. bdg. 18.60 (*0-8167-2130-0*) Troll Communs.

— Galileo: Scientist & Stargazer. LC 97-27396. (What's Their Story?). (Illus.). 32p. (J). (gr. 1-4). 1998. lib. bdg. 12.95 (*0-19-521405-6*) OUP.

***Mitton, Jacqueline.** Informania: Aliens. LC 98-7464. (Informania Ser.). (Illus.). 92p. (J). (gr. 4-8). 2000. pap. 7.99 (*0-7636-1042-9*) Candlewick Pr.

Mitton, Jacqueline. Key Definitions in Astronomy. LC 82-183. (Quality Paperback Ser.: No. 375). 174p. (Orig.). (C). 1982. pap. text 13.00 (*0-8226-0375-6*) Littlefield.

— Zoo in the Sky: A Book of Animal Constellations. (Illus.). 32p. (J). (gr. 4-6). 1998. 16.95 (*0-7922-7069-X*, Pub. by Natl Geog) S&S Trade.

Mitton, Jacqueline, ed. A Concise Dictionary of Astronomy. (Illus.). 432p. 1992. 30.00 (*0-19-853967-3*) OUP.

***Mitton, Jacqueline, ed.** Penguin Dictionary of Astronomy. 3rd ed. 420p. 2000. pap. 14.95 (*0-14-051375-2*, Pub. by Pnguin Bks Ltd) Trafalgar.

Mitton, Jacqueline & Maran, Stephen P. Gems of Hubble. (Illus.). 127p. (C). 1996. pap. 13.95 (*0-521-57100-6*) Cambridge U Pr.

Mitton, Jacqueline & Mitton, Simon. Scholastic Encyclopedia of Space. LC 98-22852. (Illus.). 80p. (J). (gr. 3-7). 1999. 14.95 (*0-590-59227-0*, Pub. by Scholastic Inc) Penguin Putnam.

Mitton, Jacqueline, jt. auth. see Mitton, Simon.

Mitton, Jacqueline, jt. auth. see Stern, Alan.

Mitton, Jacqueline, jt. ed. see Spencer, John R.

Mitton, Jeffry B. Selection in Natural Populations. LC 96-49688. (Illus.). 256p. 1997. text 60.00 (*0-19-506352-X*) OUP.

***Mitton, Jeffry B.** Selection in Natural Populations. (Illus.). 256p. 2000. pap. text 29.95 (*0-19-513786-8*) OUP.

Mitton, Jennifer. Fadimatu. LC 92-196414. 261p. 1993. pap. 14.95 (*0-86492-121-7*) Goose Ln Eds.

— Sleeping with the Insane. LC 95-152226. 180p. 1995. pap. 12.95 (*0-86492-157-8*, Pub. by Goose Ln Edits) Genl Dist Srvs.

***Mitton, Lavinia, et al, eds.** Microsimulation Modelling for Policy Analysis: Challenges & Innovations. (Department of Applied Economics Occasional Papers: Vol. 65). (Illus.). 320p. 2000. write for info. (*0-521-79006-9*) Cambridge U Pr.

***Mitton, Maureen.** Interior Design Visual Presentation: A Guide to Graphics, Models & Presentation Techniques. LC 98-29271. 192p. 1999. pap. 39.95 (*0-471-29259-1*) Wiley.

Mitton, Michael. The Soul of Celtic Spirituality: In the Lives of Its Saints. LC 95-60929. 160p. (Orig.). 1996. pap. 9.95 (*0-89622-662-X*) Twenty-Third.

Mitton, Roger. English Spelling & the Computer. LC 95-21920. (Studies in language & Linguistics). 1996. text 42.92 (*0-582-23479-4*) Addison-Wesley.

Mitton, Simon & Mitton, Jacqueline. The Young Oxford Book of Astronomy. 160p. (J). (gr. 5-9). 1996. lib. bdg. 30.00 (*0-19-521168-5*) OUP.

— The Young Oxford Book of Astronomy. (Illus.). 160p. 1998. reprint ed. pap. 16.95 (*0-19-521445-5*) OUP.

Mitton, Simon, jt. auth. see Mitton, Jacqueline.

***Mitton, Tony.** Amazing Machines: Dazzling Diggers. (Illus.). 24p. (J). 2000. pap. 3.95 (*0-7534-5304-5*, Kingfisher) LKC.

— Amazing Machines: Flashing Fire Engines. (Illus.). 24p. (J). 2000. pap. 3.95 (*0-7534-5307-X*, Kingfisher) LKC.

— Amazing Machines: Roaring Rockets. (Illus.). 24p. (J). 2000. pap. 3.95 (*0-7534-5305-3*, Kingfisher) LKC.

— Amazing Machines: Terrific Trains. (Illus.). 24p. (J). 2000. pap. 3.95 (*0-7534-5306-1*, Kingfisher) LKC.

Mitton, Tony. Dazzling Diggers. LC 97-9944. (Illus.). 24p. (J). (ps-k). 1997. 8.95 (*0-7534-5105-0*, Kingfisher) LKC.

— Flashing Fire Engines. LC 97-51126. (Illus.). 24p. (J). (ps-1). 1998. 8.95 (*0-7534-5104-2*, Kingfisher) LKC.

— Roaring Rockets. LC 97-5423. (Illus.). 24p. (J). (ps-k). 1997. 8.95 (*0-7534-5106-9*) LKC.

***Mitton, Tony.** There's No Such Thing: Flip-Flap. LC 98-73054. (Illus.). 32p. (J). 1999. pap. text 3.99 (*0-7636-0703-7*) Candlewick Pr.

Mitton, Tony. Where's My Egg? LC 98-73216. (Illus.). 32p. (J). 1999. pap. text 3.99 (*0-7636-0691-X*, Pub. by Candlewick Pr) Penguin Putnam.

— Where's My Egg? LC 96-68743. (Flip-the-Flap Book Ser.). (Illus.). (J). 1998. write for info. (*0-7636-0102-0*) Candlewick Pr.

Mitton, Tony, jt. auth. see Parker, Ant.

Mittonm. Interior Design Graphics. (Interior Design Ser.). 1998. pap. 39.95 (*0-442-02576-9*, VNR) Wiley.

Mittoo-Walker, Dorothy E. The Magical Fountain of Love. (Illus.). 48p. 1994. 10.00 (*0-912444-33-9*) DARE Bks.

Mittra, Raj, ed. Computer Techniques For Electromagnetics. (Summa Bks.). 403p. 1973. reprint ed. pap. 76.95 (*0-89116-820-6*) Hemisp Pub.

Mittra, Raj, jt. auth. see Werner, Douglas H.

Mittra, Sitansu S. Practicing Financial Planning: A Complete Guide for Professionals. (Illus.). 658p. (C). 1993. pap. 29.95 (*0-9636527-0-2*) Mittra & Assocs.

Mittra, Swapnajit. Principles of Verilog PLI. LC 99-18028. xxviii, 372 p. 1999. write for info. (*0-7923-8477-6*) Kluwer Academic.

Mittring, Karl E., tr. see Ridderbos, N. H.

Mittwede, Steven K. & Stoddard, Edward F., eds. Ultramafic Rocks of the Appalachian Piedmont. LC 88-37183. (Geological Society of America Ser.: Vol. 231). (Illus.). 110p. 1989. reprint ed. pap. 34.10 (*0-608-07756-9*, 206784400010) Bks Demand.

Mittwer, Henry. Zen Flowers: Chabana for the Tea Ceremony. (Illus.). 142p. 1992. 14.95 (*0-8048-1882-7*) Tuttle Pubng.

Mitty, Ethel L. Handbook for Directors of Nursing in Long-Term Care. LC 96-4649. (Professional Reference - Nursing Ser.). 400p. 1997. mass mkt. 30.95 (*0-8273-6777-5*) Delmar.

Mitty, Ethel L., ed. Mechanisms of Quality in Long-Term Care: Education. LC 93-30194. 1993. 13.00 (*0-88737-602-9*) Natl League Nurse.

Mitty, Harold A., et al. Genitourinary Tract Disease (Fourth Series) Test & Syllabus. LC 92-21930. (Professional Self-Evaluation & Continuing Education Program Ser.: Vol. 33). (Illus.). 650p. 1992. 190.00 (*1-55903-033-X*) Am Coll Radiology.

***Mitu, Sorin.** National Identity of Romanians in Transylvania. 450p. (C). 2000. 55.95 (*963-9116-95-5*) Ctrl Europ Univ.

Mitwirkung. A Dictionary of Modern Written Arabic: Arabisches Woerterbuch fuer die Schriftsprache der Gegenwart. 5th ed. (ARA, ENG & GER.). 1984. 295.00 (*0-8288-0193-2*, F57980) Fr & Eur.

***Mityushev, Vladimir V. & Rogosin, Sergei V.** Constructive Methods for Linear & Nonlinear Boundary Value Problems for Analytic Functions: Theory & Applications. LC 99-44959. (Monographs & Surveys in Pure & Applied Mathematics). 283p. 1999. write for info. (*1-58488-057-0*, Chap & Hall CRC) CRC Pr.

Mitzel, David P., ed. Resource Development in the Two-Year College. (C). 1988. text 27.95 (*0-9619545-0-7*); pap. text 17.95 (*0-9619545-1-5*) Natl Coun Res Dev.

Mitzel, John. Sports & the Macho Male. 2nd ed. 1976. pap. 2.50 (*0-915480-06-9*) Fag Rag.

Mitzenmacher, Bobbi, et al. Core Concepts in Human Sexuality: Study Guide. 248p. (C). 1995. pap. text, student ed. 18.95 (*1-55934-619-1*, 1619) Mayfield Pub.

Mitzman, Arthur. The Iron Cage: An Historical Interpretation of Max Weber. 340p. (C). 1984. pap. 19.95 (*0-87855-984-1*) Transaction Pubs.

— Michelet, Historia: Rebirth & Romanticism in Nineteenth-Century France. LC 89-27244. 368p. (C). 1990. 42.50 (*0-300-04551-4*) Yale U Pr.

— Michelet, Historian: Rebirth & Romanticism in Nineteenth-Century France. LC 89-27244. 365p. 1990. reprint ed. pap. 113.20 (*0-608-07838-7*, 205401400010) Bks Demand.

— Sociology & Estrangement: Three Sociologists of Imperial Germany. 370p. (C). 1986. pap. 24.95 (*0-88738-605-9*) Transaction Pubs.

Mitzman, D. Integral Bases for Affine Lie Algebras & Their Universal Enveloping Algebras. LC 85-1374. (Contemporary Mathematics Ser.: Vol. 40). 159p. 1985. pap. 27.00 (*0-8218-5043-1*, CONM/40) Am Math.

Mitzner, Ira R. ERISA Litigation: A Basic Guide. Brennan, Mary E., ed. LC 93-78910. 186p. 1993. pap. 15.00 (*0-89154-466-6*) Intl Found Employ.

Miu, Denny K. Mechatronics: Electromechanics & Contromechanics. Ling, Frederick F., ed. LC 92-1604. (Mechanical Engineering Ser.). (Illus.). 264p. 1993. 69.95 (*0-387-97893-3*) Spr-Verlag.

Miu, Florea, ed. see Smarandache, Florentin.

Miuccio, Raymond V., ed. see Miucco, Barbara A.

Miucco, Barbara A. Seeds of Faith for the Seed in Utero. BonGiovanni, Guy & Miuccio, Raymond V., eds. 91p. 1999. 9.95 (*0-9670050-0-0*) MeMe Pubns.

Miura, Akira. English in Japanese. 203p. (Orig.). (C). 1992. pap. 12.95 (*4-89684-701-6*, Pub. by Yohan Pubns) Weatherhill.

— English in Japanese: A Selection of Useful Loanwords. LC 97-51891. 1998. 9.95 (*0-8348-0421-2*) Weatherhill.

— English Loanwords in Japanese: A Selection. LC 78-65031. (ENG & JPN.). 192p. 1979. 14.95 (*0-8048-1248-9*) Tuttle Pubng.

— Japanese Words & Their Uses. LC 82-51099. (JPN.). 240p. 1983. pap. 12.95 (*0-8048-1639-5*) Tuttle Pubng.

***Miura, Akira.** Japanese Words & Their Uses II. (JPN & ENG., Illus.). 2001. pap. 15.95 (*0-8048-3249-8*) Tuttle Pubng.

Miura, Akira, tr. see Tsuboi, Sakae.

Miura, Ayako. Freezing Point. Shimizu, H. & Terry, J., trs. from JPN. (Illus.). 250p. 1987. pap. 11.95 (*0-933704-29-1*) Dawn Pr.

Miura, Dennis S., jt. auth. see Dangman.

Miura, Einen. The Art of Marbled Paper: Marbled Papers & How to Make Them. (Illus.). 160p. 1991. 45.00 (*4-7700-1548-8*) Kodansha.

Miura, Hirofumi, et al, eds. Robotics Research: The 5th International Symposium. (Artificial Intelligence Ser.). 500p. 1990. 70.00 (*0-262-13253-2*) MIT Pr.

Miura, Hiroshi. The Life & Thought of Kanzo Uchimura, 1861-1930. LC 96-52638. 152p. 1997. pap. 22.00 (*0-8028-4205-4*) Eerdmans.

Miura, Isshu & Sasaki, Ruth F. The Zen Koan. LC 65-19104. (Illus.). 172p. 1966. pap. 11.00 (*0-15-699981-1*, Harvest Bks) Harcourt.

Miura-Mattausch, M., jt. ed. see Treitinger, L.

Miura, N., et al, eds. Lowlands: Development & Management. LC 99-225806. (Illus.). 498p. (C). 1994. text 126.00 (*90-5410-603-4*, Pub. by A A Balkema) Ashgate Pub Co.

— Theory & Practice of Earth Reinforcement: Proceedings of the International Geotechnical Symposium on Theory & Practice of Earth Reinforcement, Fukuoka Kyushu, October 5-7, 1988. (Illus.). xiv, 618p. 1988. text 201.00 (*90-6191-820-0*, Pub. by A A Balkema) Ashgate Pub Co.

Miura, Nobuyasu, jt. auth. see Cousineau, Leslie.

Miura, Robert M., ed. Some Mathematical Questions in Biology: DNA Sequence Analysis. LC 80-646696. (Lectures in Mathematics in the Life Sciences: Vol. 17). 124p. 1986. reprint ed. pap. 37.00 (*0-8218-1167-3*, LLSCI/17) Am Math.

— Some Mathematical Questions in Biology: Muscle Physiology. LC 85-28613. (Lectures in Mathematics in the Life Sciences: Vol. 16). 234p. 1986. pap. 45.00 (*0-8218-1166-5*, LLSCI/16) Am Math.

— Some Mathematical Questions in Biology - Neurobiology. LC 82-18418. (Lectures on Mathematics in the Life Sciences: Vol. 15). 122p. 1982. pap. 30.00 (*0-8218-1165-7*, LLSCI/15) Am Math.

Miura, Robert M., jt. auth. see Gross, L. J.

Miura, T., ed. Seasonal Effects on Reproduction, Infection & Psychoses. (Progress in Biometeorology Ser.: Vol. 5). (Illus.). xii, 223p. 1987. 75.00 (*90-5103-005-3*, Pub. by SPB Acad Pub) Balogh.

— Seasonality of Birth. (Progress in Biometeorology Ser.: Vol. 6). (Illus.). xiii, 231p. 1987. 75.00 (*90-5103-006-1*, Pub. by SPB Acad Pub) Balogh.

***Miura, Toru & Philips, John E., eds.** Slave Elites in the Middle East & Africa. (Islamic Area Studies). 380p. 1999. 110.00 (*0-7103-0660-1*, Pub. by Kegan Paul Intl) Col U Pr.

Miura, Toru, jt. ed. see Haneda, Masashi.

Miura, Yuzuru, selected by. Classic Haiku: A Master's Selection. (Illus.). 120p. (Orig.). 1992. pap. 12.95 (*0-8048-1682-4*) Tuttle Pubng.

Miwa, Kimitada, jt. ed. see Schultz, John.

Miwa, M., et al, eds. ADP-Ribosylation, DNA Repair & Cancer: Proceedings of the 13th International Symposium of the Princess Takamatsu Cancer Research Fund, Japan, 1982. 354p. 1983. lib. bdg. 132.25 (*90-6764-003-4*, Pub. by VSP) Coronet Bks.

— Retroviruses in Human Lymphoma-Leukemia:

An Asterisk (*) at the beginning of an entry indicates that the title is appearing for the first time.

Proceedings of the 15th International Symposium of the Princess Takamatsu Cancer Research Fund, Japan, 1984. 352p. 1985. lib. bdg. 135.00 (*90-6764-057-3*, Pub. by VSP) Coronet Bks.

Miwa, T., et al. Mathematics of Solitons. (Tracts in Mathematics Ser.: No. 135). 120p. (C). 1999. text 39.95 (*0-521-56161-2*) Cambridge U Pr.

Miwa, T., jt. ed. see Kashiwara, M.

Miwa, Tetsuji, jt. auth. see Jimbo, Michio.

Miwa, Tetsuji, jt. ed. see Jimbo, Michio.

Miwa, Tetsuji, ed. see Kashiwara, Masaki.

Miwa, Yoshiro. Firms & Industrial Organization in Japan. LC 95-42222. 322p. (C). 1996. text 47.50 (*0-8147-5551-8*) NYU Pr.

Miwatani, T., jt. auth. see Takeda, Yoshihiko.

Mix, Alan, jt. auth. see Abrantes, Fatima.

Mix, Ann B. Touchstones: Guide to Records for Families of WWII Casualties. 133p. pap. 19.95 (*1-877677-72-8*) Herit Quest.

Mix, Don. Stalking Big Ideas in the Advertising Jungle. LC 85-81845. (Illus.). 144p. (Orig.). 1986. 16.50 (*0-937884-11-1*, Bennington Bks) Hystry Mystry.

Mix, Donald. Platies, Keeping & Breeding Them in Captivity: Keeping & Breeding Them in Captivity. (Illus.). 64p. 1996. pap. 6.95 (*0-7938-0362-4*, RE613) TFH Pubns.

***Mix, Floyd M.** House Wiring Simplified: Tells & Shows You How. rev. ed. LC 98-44895. (Illus.). 192p. 1999. text 24.00 (*1-56637-542-8*) Goodheart.

Mix, Godfrey. The Salon Professional's Guide to Foot Care. LC 97-43097. (Milady - Cosmetology). 256p. (C). 1998. text 31.95 (*1-56253-332-0*) Thomson Learn.

Mix, Hal L. Hal Mix's Pocket Billiard Secrets. 2nd rev. ed. (Illus.). 65p. 1994. text 25.00 (*0-9648693-0-6*) Mix Ent.

Mix, James B., ed. see Sutton, Charles.

Mix, John. Blue Ridge Rhapsody. LC 98-89575. 175p. 1999. 23.50 (*0-88739-217-2*); pap. 13.95 (*0-88739-216-4*) Creat Arts Bk.

Mix, Lisa A., jt. ed. see McCall, Nancy.

Mix, Oberst-Ing. The Development of German Aircraft Armament to 1945. 107p. 1991. reprint ed. pap. text 25.95 (*0-89126-154-0*) MA-AH Pub.

Mix, Paul E. Introduction to Nondestructive Testing: A Training Guide. 432p. 1987. 125.00 (*0-471-83126-3*) Wiley.

— Tom Mix: A Heavily-Illustrated Biography of the Western Star, with a Filmography. LC 94-35404. (Illus.). 336p. 1995. lib. bdg. 38.50 (*0-89950-964-9*) McFarland & Co.

Mixco, Mauricio J. Cochimi & Proto-Yuman: Lexical & Syntactic Evidence for a New Language Family in Lower California. (Anthropological Papers: No. 101). 1979. pap. text 15.00 (*0-87480-150-8*) U of Utah Pr.

— Kiliwa Dictionary. (Anthropological Papers: No. 109). 207p. (Orig.). 1985. pap. 27.50 (*0-87480-168-0*) U of Utah Pr.

— Kiliwa Texts: "When I Have Donned My Crest of Stars". (Anthropological Papers: No. 107). (Illus.). xvi, 307p. (Orig.). 1983. pap. 25.00 (*0-87480-219-9*) U of Utah Pr.

Mixdorf, Marcia, jt. auth. see Reynolds, Ed.

Mixer, Jennifer, jt. auth. see Miller, Regina.

Mixer, Joseph R. Principles of Professional Fundraising: Useful Foundations for Successful Practice. LC 93-14551. (Nonprofit Sector-Public Administration Ser.). 277p. 1993. text 32.95 (*1-55542-590-9*) Jossey-Bass.

Mixner, David. Stranger Among Friends. 384p. 1997. pap. 13.95 (*0-553-37554-7*) Bantam.

***Mixner, David & Bailey, Dennis.** Brave Journeys: Profiles in Gay & Lesbian Courage. 384p. 2000. 24.95 (*0-553-10651-1*, Spectra) Bantam.

Mixon, Amy, ed. Testbank Economics. 4th ed. 1997. pap. text 11.00 (*0-673-54159-2*) P-H.

Mixon, Amy, jt. auth. see Buskist, William.

Mixon, Don. Obedience & Civilization: The Origins of Authorized Crime. 208p. 1989. text 34.95 (*0-7453-0331-5*) Routledge.

Mixon, Franklin G. Intermediate Microeconomics: Price Theory & Applications. (C). 1995. text, teacher ed. 2.66 (*0-669-28916-7*) HM Trade Div.

Mixon, J. Wilson, Jr., ed. Private Means, Public Ends: Voluntarism vs. Coercion. LC 96-83410. 230p. (Orig.). 1996. pap. 9.95 (*1-57246-024-5*) Foun Econ Ed.

Mixon, John. Texas Municipal Zoning Law. 2nd ed. 500p. Date not set. ring bd. 120.00 (*0-409-25656-0*, 82603, MICHIE) LEXIS Pub.

— Texas Municipal Zoning Law. 2nd ed. 500p. 1993. suppl. ed. 55.00 (*0-685-74604-6*, MICHIE) LEXIS Pub.

Mixon, John & Dougherty, James L., Jr. Texas Municipal Zoning Law. 3rd ed. 125.00 (*0-409-25628-5*) LEXIS Pub.

Mixon, Laura J. Proxies. LC 98-19417. 416p. 1998. 24.95 (*0-312-85467-6*, Pub. by Tor Bks) St Martin.

Mixon, Laura J. & Gould, Steven. Greenwar. LC 97-1618. 384p. 1997. 25.95 (*0-312-85261-4*, Pub. by Tor Bks) St Martin.

— Greenwar. 1998. mass mkt. 6.99 (*0-8125-7116-9*, Pub. by Tor Bks) St Martin.

***Mixon, Laura M.** Proxies. 480p. 1999. mass mkt. 6.99 (*0-8125-2387-3*, Pub. by Tor Bks) St Martin.

Mixon, Myrtis. Americana: Historical Sportlights in Story & Song. (Illus.). 98p. 1995. pap. 12.95 (*0-943327-13-X*) JAG Pubns.

— Americana 'Easy Reader' Historical Spotlights in Story & Song. (Illus.). 112p. 1996. pap. 12.95 (*0-943327-21-0*) JAG Pubns.

***Mixon, Nicholas.** The Brown Sisters. (Illus.). 64p. 1999. 29.95 (*0-87070-042-1*) Mus of Modern Art.

Mixon, Roy D. Lovers of Truth. 43p. (Orig.). 1986. pap. 2.25 (*0-934942-64-1*, 3874) White Wing Pub.

Mixon, Shirley R. Handbook of Data Processing Administration, Operations & Procedures. LC 75-38914. 405p. reprint ed. pap. 125.60 (*0-608-12137-1*, 202390100034) Bks Demand.

Mixon, Victoria, jt. auth. see Kehoe, Brendan P.

Mixon, Wayne. The People's Writer: Erskine Caldwell & the South. LC 95-8291. (Minds of the New South Ser.). (Illus.). 256p. (C). 1995. 30.00 (*0-8139-1627-5*) U Pr of Va.

***Mixon, Will & Pace, Richard. Build Your Dream Home from Start to Finish: A Guide for Keeping Your Contractor in Check. 1998. 19.99 (0-9674071-0-9) W P Home.**

As you will learn, it takes many tools to construct a new home & the materials in the is book are organized in such a way that anyone can successfully construct their dream home. This book will assist the most experienced or least experienced homebuilder & increases their knowledge of home construction. Most importantly, this book was written to assist the homebuilder in saving money by completing most of the work himself or by using contractors every step of the way. In addition, the information will assist you in making precise decisions & save valuable time & money. This book contains the most economical methods. The information in this book is helpful to contractors, homebuilders & homeowners. Building Your Dream Home from Start to Finish represents the combined effort of two professional homebuilders with 33 years of experience in the fields of remodeling & new construction. ***Publisher Paid Annotation.***

Mixter, ed. see Bronson, Gary J.

Mixter, ed. see Nagler, Eric P.

Mixter, ed. see Umland, Jean B.

Mixter, ed. see Venit, Stewart M.

Mixter, ed. see Venit, Stewart M. & Schleiffers, Sandra M.

Mixter, ed. see Wen, David Y. & Whipple, Grey G.

Mixter, George W. & Headley, Herrold, eds. Primer of Navigation. 632p. 1995. 35.00 (*0-393-03508-5*) Norton.

Mixter, Keith E. General Bibliography for Music Research. 3rd ed. LC 96-6364. (Detroit Studies in Music Bibliography: No. 75). 200p. 1996. 40.00 (*0-89990-103-4*) Harmonie Park Pr.

***Mixx Entertainment Inc., Staff.** Meet Sailor Jupiter-Thunder. (Sailor Moon Scout Guides Ser.). (Illus.). 96p. (J). (gr. 4-7). 2000. pap. 12.95 (*1-892213-30-3*) Mixx Enter Inc.

— Meet Sailor Mars - Fire. (Sailor Moon Scout Guides Ser.). 2000. pap. 12.95 (*1-892213-28-1*) Mixx Enter Inc.

— Meet Sailor Mercury - Ice. (Sailor Moon Scout Guides Ser.). (Illus.). (J). 2000. pap. 12.95 (*1-892213-31-1*) Mixx Enter Inc.

— Meet Sailor Moon - Crystal. (Sailor Moon Scout Guides Ser.). (Illus.). (J). 2000. pap. 12.95 (*1-892213-32-X*) Mixx Enter Inc.

— Meet Sailor Venus - Love. (Sailor Moon Scout Guides Ser.). (Illus.). (J). 2000. pap. 12.95 (*1-892213-29-X*) Mixx Enter Inc.

Miya, K. Magnetomechanics in Magnetic Fusion Reactor Technology. (Series in Theoretical & Applied Mechanics: Vol. 7). 400p. (C). 1993. text 64.00 (*9971-5-0726-9*) World Scientific Pub.

Miyabe, Miyuki. All She Was Worth. Birnbaum, Alfred, tr. from JPN. LC 99-23115. 296p. 1999. pap. 12.00 (*0-395-96658-2*, Mariner Bks) HM.

Miyadera, Isao. Nonlinear Semigroups. Cho, Choong Y., tr. LC 92-11318. (Translations of Mathematical Monographs: Vol. 109). 230p. 1992. text 99.00 (*0-8218-4565-9*, MMONO/109) Am Math.

Miyagawa, Shigeru & Anderson, Stephen, eds. Syntax & Semantics, Vol. 22: Structure & Case Marking in Japanese. 259p. 1989. pap. text 65.00 (*0-12-606103-3*) Acad Pr.

Miyagawa, Stephen. Journey to Excellence: Development of the Military & VA Blind Rehabilitation Programs in the 20th Century. LC 98-39312. (Illus.). 288p. 1999. 39.95 (*1-880090-76-7*) Galde Pr.

Miyagiwa, Kaz. International Capital Mobility & National Welfare. LC 90-3511. (Foreign Economic Policy of the United States Ser.). 105p. 1990. reprint ed. text 10.00 (*0-8240-7470-X*) Garland.

Miyago, Toshio. Paintings of Japanese Beauties in the Meiji Period. (Arts Collection Ser.: Vol. 39). (Illus.). 256p. 1997. pap. 14.95 (*4-7636-1539-4*, Pub. by Kyoto Shoin) Bks Nippan.

Miyagowa, Masako, tr. see Kobayashi, Kazuo, et al.

Miyahara, T., et al. Vacuum Ultraviolet Radiation Physics. LC 97-114238. 1748p. 1996. text 460.00 (*0-444-82245-3*) Elsevier.

***Miyaji, Chikara & Abbott, Paul.** MathLink Network Programming in Mathematica. 400p. (C). 1999. write for info. (*0-521-64172-1*); pap. 24.95 (*0-521-64598-0*) Cambridge U Pr.

Miyaji, Makoto, ed. Animal Models in Medical Mycology. 176p. 1987. 105.00 (*0-8493-5844-2*, RC117, CRC Reprint) Franklin.

***Miyajima, Hideaki, et al, eds.** Policies for Competitiveness: Comparing Business-Government Relationships in the 'Golden Age of Capitalism' LC 99-21238. (Fuji Conference Ser.). (Illus.). 356p. 1999. text 85.00 (*0-19-829323-2*) OUP.

Miyajima, T., jt. auth. see Marinsky, J. A.

Miyajima, T., jt. auth. see Marinsky, Jacob A.

***Miyajima, Tatsuo.** The Whole Relativity of the Cosmos. 216p. 1999. spiral bd. 28.95 (*4-7713-3407-2*, Pub. by Korinsha) Dist Art Pubs.

Miyakada, Ed. Process Architecture No. 120: EDAW: The Integrated World. 1994. pap. 37.95 (*4-89331-120-4*, Pub. by Process Archit) Bks Nippan.

Miyakawa, Michio & Bolomey, Jean-Charles, eds. Non-Invasive Thermometry of the Human Body. 272p. 1995. boxed set 169.95 (*0-8493-4738-6*, 4738) CRC Pr.

Miyakawa, Tadao. The Science of Public Policy: Essential Readings in Policy Sciences. LC 98-35147. 1999. 5.75 (*0-415-19593-4*) Routledge.

Miyake, A. & Suginami, H., eds. Endocrine Regulation of Early Embryonic Development & Implantation: Tokyo Conference of Reproductive Physiology II, Tokyo, August 1994. (Journal: Hormone Research Ser.: Vol. 44, Suppl. 2, 1995). (Illus.). iv, 50p. 1995. pap. 26.25 (*3-8055-6169-5*) S Karger.

Miyake, A., jt. ed. see Mori, H.

Miyake, Akiko. Ezra Pound & the Mysteries of Love: A Plan for The Cantos. LC 90-47376. 308p. 1991. text 37.95 (*0-8223-1105-4*) Duke.

Miyake, Akiko, et al, eds. A Guide to Ezra Pound & Ernest Fenollosa's Classic Noh Theatre of Japan. (Ezra Pound Scholarship Ser.). 453p. 1994. pap. 25.00 (*0-943373-31-X*) Natl Poet Foun.

— A Guide to Ezra Pound & Ernest Fenollosa's Classic Noh Theatre of Japan. (Ezra Pound Scholarship Ser.). 453p. 1994. 47.50 (*0-943373-30-1*) Natl Poet Foun.

Miyake, Akira & Shah, Priti, eds. Models of Working Memory: Mechanisms of Active Maintenance & Exectuive Control. LC 98-35134. (Illus.). 496p. (C). 1999. text 69.95 (*0-521-58325-X*); pap. text 29.95 (*0-521-58721-2*) Cambridge U Pr.

Miyake, Akira, jt. ed. see Kanzaki, Hideharu.

Miyake, Issey. Issey Miyake: Making Things. Chandes, Herve, ed. (Illus.). 192p. 1999. 49.95 (*3-908247-08-X*, Pub. by Scalo Pubs) Dist Art Pubs.

Miyake, T. Modular Forms. (Illus.). 310p. 1989. 107.95 (*0-387-50268-8*) Spr-Verlag.

Miyake, Yoshi. The Little Drummer Boy. 32p. (J). (ps-3). 1998. pap. 3.50 (*0-8167-4809-8*) Troll Communs.

***Miyama, Shoken M., et al, eds.** Numerical Astrophysics. LC 98-53211. (Astrophysics & Space Science Library). 1999. 225.00 (*0-7923-5566-0*) Kluwer Academic.

Miyamoto, A. S. Silver, Copper & Gold Halates. 266p. 1990. 111.25 (*0-08-029208-9*, Pergamon Pr) Elsevier.

Miyamoto, Akira. Natural Gas in Central Asia: Industries, Markets & Export Options of Kazakstan, Turkmenistan & Uzbekistan. 80p. 1998. pap. 15.95 (*1-86203-012-X*, Pub. by Royal Inst Intl Affairs) Brookings.

Miyamoto, Akito, tr. see Okawa, Naomi.

Miyamoto, H., et al, eds. Alkaline Earth Metal Halates. 352p. 1983. 130.00 (*0-08-029213-5*, Pergamon Pr) Elsevier.

Miyamoto, H. & Salomon, M. Alkaline Earth Metal Halates. LC 83-17224. (Solubility Data Ser.: Vol. 14). 1983. reprint ed. 156.00 (*0-08-029212-7*, Pub. by Pergamon Repr) Franklin.

Miyamoto, Hiroshi, ed. Recent Research on Mechanical Behavior of Solids. LC 80-670073. 435p. 1979. reprint ed. pap. 134.90 (*0-608-01245-9*, 206193300001) Bks Demand.

Miyamoto, J., ed. Pesticide Chemistry: Human Welfare & the Environment, Vol. 2. (IUPAC Symposium Ser.). (Illus.). 1983. 20.00 (*0-08-029227-5*, Pub. by Pergamon Repr) Franklin.

Miyamoto, J. & Kearney, Philip C., eds. Pesticide Chemistry - Human Welfare & the Environment: Mode of Action, Metabolism & Toxicology, Vol. 3. (IUPAC Symposium Ser.). (Illus.). 1983. 20.00 (*0-08-029228-3*, Pub. by Pergamon Repr) Franklin.

— Pesticide Chemistry - Human Welfare & the Environment: Pesticide Residues & Formulation Chemistry, Vol. 4. (IUPAC Symposium Ser.). 1983. 20.00 (*0-08-029229-1*, Pub. by Pergamon Repr) Franklin.

— Pesticide Chemistry - Human Welfare & the Environment: Synthesis & Structure Activity Relationships, Vol. 1. (IUPAC Symposium Ser.). 1983. 20.00 (*0-08-029226-7*, Pub. by Pergamon Repr) Franklin.

Miyamoto, J., jt. auth. see Hutson, D. H.

Miyamoto, J., jt. auth. see Kaneko.

Miyamoto, J., jt. auth. see Kurihara, Norio.

Miyamoto, Kazuo. Hawaii: The End of the Rainbow. LC 63-20213. 509p. 1964. pap. 12.95 (*0-8048-0233-5*) Tuttle Pubng.

— One Man's Journey. LC 81-21572. 120p. (Orig.). 1981. pap. 8.95 (*0-938474-01-4*) Buddhist Study.

Miyamoto, Kenro. Plasma Physics for Nuclear Fusion. rev. ed. 640p. 1989. pap. text 35.00 (*0-262-63117-2*) MIT Pr.

Miyamoto, Masao. The Straitjacket Society: A Rebel Bureaucrat Tells All. Carpenter, Juliet W., tr. 208p. 1995. 22.00 (*4-7700-1848-7*) Kodansha.

Miyamoto, Matao, jt. ed. see Yamazaki, Hiroaki.

Miyamoto, Michael M. & Cracraft, Joel, eds. Phylogenetic Analysis of DNA Sequences. (Illus.). 368p. 1991. text 65.00 (*0-19-506698-7*) OUP.

Miyamoto, Naoki. Test Your Go Strength: Fifty Whole Board Problems. Bozulich, Richard, tr. from JPN. (Illus.). 216p. 1991. reprint ed. pap. 12.95 (*4-87187-018-9*, G18) Ishi Pr Intl.

Miyamoto, Sadaaki, jt. auth. see Liu, Z.-Q.

Miyamoto, Sadaski. Fuzzy Sets in Information Retrieval & Cluster Analysis. (C). 1990. text 182.50 (*0-7923-0721-6*) Kluwer Academic.

***Miyamoto, Tadao.** The Light Verb Construction in Japanese: The Role of the Verbal Noun. LC 99-46742. (Linguistik Aktuell/Linguistics Today Ser.: Vol. 29). (ENG & JPN.). xiv, 232p. 2000. 79.00 (*1-55619-913-9*) J Benjamins Pubng Co.

Miyamoto, Tadao. Papa & Me. LC 94-1563. (J). (ps-3). 1994. lib. bdg. 19.95 (*0-87614-843-7*, Carolrhoda) Lerner Pub.

Miyamoto, Tadao, jt. auth. see Kess, Joseph F.

Miyamoto, Terumasa, ed. see Okuda, Minoru.

Miyamoto, Wayne, jt. auth. see Chesney, Lee.

Miyamoto, Y., et al, eds. Functionally Graded Materials: Design, Processing & Applications. LC 99-40751. (Materials Technology Ser.: No. 5). (Illus.). 352p. 1999. pap. 160.00 (*0-412-60760-3*) Kluwer Academic.

Miyamoto, Y., jt. ed. see Shiota, I.

Miyamura, O., et al, eds. High Energy Nuclear Collisions & Quark Gluon Plasma. 350p. (C). 1991. text 89.00 (*981-02-0806-5*) World Scientific Pub.

Miyanaga, Kuniko. The Creative Edge: Emerging Individualism in Japan. 145p. (C). 1993. pap. 24.95 (*1-56000-701-X*) Transaction Pubs.

Miyanishi, Masayoshi. Algebraic Geometry. LC 94-2018. (Translations of Mathematical Monographs: Vol. 136).Tr. of Daisu Kikagaku. 246p. 1994. 100.00 (*0-8218-4615-9*, MMONO/136) Am Math.

— Lectures on Curves on Rational & Unirational Surfaces. (Tata Institute Lecture Notes Ser.). 1979. 38.95 (*0-387-08943-8*) Spr-Verlag.

Miyano, Leland. Hawaii a Floral Paradise. (Illus.). 64p. 1996. 12.95 (*1-56647-102-8*) Mutual Pub HI.

— Hawaii's Beautiful Trees. (Illus.). 64p. 1997. pap. 9.95 (*1-56647-122-2*) Mutual Pub HI.

— A Pocket Guide to Hawaii's Flowers. (Illus.). 112p. 1997. pap. 8.95 (*1-56647-149-4*) Mutual Pub HI.

Miyao, Takahiro & Kanemoto, Yoshitsugu. Urban Dynamics & Urban Externalities, Vol. 11. (Fundamentals of Pure & Applied Economics Ser.: Volume 11). viii, 108p. 1987. pap. text 52.00 (*3-7186-0333-0*) Gordon & Breach.

Miyaoka, Yoichi & Peternell, T. Geometry of Higher Dimensional Algebraic Varieties. LC 97-4314. (DMV Seminar Ser.). 1997. 34.50 (*3-7643-5490-9*) Birkhauser.

Miyares, Alina. Apuntes: Reflexiones Acerca de las Interrogantes Que Agobian Al Pueblo Latinoamericano. LC 92-62950. (SPA.). 80p. (Orig.). 1993. pap. 8.00 (*1-882573-01-3*, Zinnia Bks) Serena Bay.

Miyares, Ines. The Hmong Refugees Experience in the United States: Crossing the River. LC 98-39541. (Asian Americans). 160p. 1998. 43.00 (*0-8153-3279-3*) Garland.

Miyares, Karen L. Living Love: A Journey of Loving Yourself. 110p. 1998. spiral bd. 13.00 (*0-9668365-0-2*) Living Love.

Miyares, Marcelino. Models of Political Participation of Hispanic-Americans. Cortes, Carlos E., ed. LC 79-6216. (Hispanics in the United States Ser.). (Illus.). 1981. lib. bdg. 21.95 (*0-405-13164-X*) Ayer.

Miyares-Piper, Maria H., jt. auth. see Ficklin, Victoria J.

Miyasaka, Kojiro. Shame Faced: The Road to Recovery. 28p. (Orig.). 1986. pap. 3.00 (*0-89486 358 4*, 5452B) Hazelden.

Miyasaka, Kojiro, tr. see Niwano, Nikkyo.

Miyasaka, Masayuki & Trnka, Zdenek, eds. Differentiation Antigens in Lymphohemopoietic Tissues. LC 87-24543. (Immunology Ser.: No. 38). 559p. 1988. reprint ed. pap. 173.30 (*0-608-01303-X*, 206204800001) Bks Demand.

Miyasaki-Ching, Cara. Chasteen's Essentials of Clinical Dental Assisting. 5th ed. 480p. 1997. teacher ed. write for info. (*0-8151-4489-X*) Mosby Inc.

Miyasaki-Ching, Cara & Tennenhouse, Dan J. Dental Risk Prevention: For Dental Auxiliaries. 143p. 1991. pap. 35.00 (*1-930548-03-6*) Tennenhouse Prof Pubns.

Miyasaki-Ching, Cara M. & Chasteen, Joseph E. Essentials of Clinical Dental Assisting. 5th ed. (Illus.). 480p. (C). (gr. 13). 1996. pap. text 46.00 (*0-8151-6211-1*, 25549) Mosby Inc.

Miyashiro, Akiho. Metamorphic Petrology. (Illus.). 416p. (C). 1994. text 76.95 (*0-19-521026-3*) OUP.

Miyashita, Kunihiko. Contemporary Cephalometric Radiography. (Illus.). 292p. 1996. text 195.00 (*4-87417-517-1*) Quint Pub Co.

Miyashita, M. Imada & Takayama, H., eds. Computational Approaches in Condensed Matter Physics: Proceedings of the 6th Nishinomiya-Yukawa Memorial Symposium, Nishinomiya, Japan, October 24 & 25, 1991. LC 92-28269. (Proceedings in Physics Ser.: Vol. 70). 1992. 97.95 (*0-387-55799-7*) Spr-Verlag.

Miyata, Ken, jt. auth. see Forsyth, Adrian.

Miyata, S. & Sasabe, H., eds. Poled Polymers & Their Applications to SHG & EO Devices. (Advances in Nonlinear Optics Ser.: Vol. 4). 292p. 1997. text 98.00 (*90-5699-025-X*) Gordon & Breach.

Miyata, Seizo & Nalwa, Hari S., eds. Organic Electroluminescent Materials & Devices. 496p. 1997. text 117.00 (*2-919875-10-8*) Gordon & Breach.

Miyata, Seizo, jt. ed. see Nalwa, Hari S.

***Miyata, T., et al, eds.** Long-Span Bridges & Aerodynamics. (Illus.). viii, 304p. 1999. 112.00 (*4-431-70259-8*) Spr-Verlag.

Miyawaki, Akira, et al. Vegetation in Eastern North America: Vegetation System & Dynamics under Human Activity in the Eastern North American Cultural Region in Comparison with Japan. 515p. 1994. 250.00 (*0-86008-494-9*, Pub. by U of Tokyo) Col U Pr.

Miyawaki, N., ed. Problems of Advanced Economics. (Studies in Contemporary Economics: Vol. 10). vi, 319p. 1984. 45.00 (*0-387-13740-8*) Spr-Verlag.

Miyayama, H., et al. A Glossary of Agricultural Terms. (ENG & JPN.). 261p. 1975. 125.00 (*0-8288-5891-8*, M9345) Fr & Eur.

Miyazaki, F., jt. ed. see Yoshikawa, T.

Miyazaki, Hayao. Nausicaa of the Valley of the Wind, Vol. 7. (Illus.). 224p. 1997. pap. text 16.95 (*1-56931-197-8*, Viz Comics) Viz Commns Inc.

M

— Nausicaa of the Valley of Wind, Pt. 2, Bk. 1. Horibuchi, Seiji, ed. Lewis, David & Smith, Toren, trs. from JPN. (Illus.). 56p. 1989. pap. 2.95 (*0-929279-07-7*) Viz Commns Inc.

— Nausicaa of the Valley of Wind, Pt. 2, Bk. 2. Horibuchi, Seiji, ed. Lewis, David & Smith, Toren, trs. from JPN. (Illus.). 56p. 1989. pap. 2.95 (*0-929279-08-5*) Viz Commns Inc.

— Nausicaa of the Valley of Wind, Pt. 2, Bk. 3. Horibuchi, Seiji, ed. Lewis, David & Smith, Toren, trs. from JPN. (Illus.). 56p. 1989. pap. 2.95 (*0-929279-09-3*) Viz Commns Inc.

— Nausicaa of the Valley of Wind, Pt. 2, Bk. 4. Horibuchi, Seiji, ed. Lewis, David & Smith, Toren, trs. from JPN. (Illus.). 56p. 1989. pap. 2.95 (*0-929279-10-7*) Viz Commns Inc.

— Nausicaa of the Valley of Wind, Vol. 1. Horibuchi, Seiji, ed. Lewis, David & Smith, Toren, trs. from JPN. (Illus.). 56p. 1988. pap. 2.50 (*0-929279-00-X*) Viz Commns Inc.

— Nausicaa of the Valley of Wind, Vol. 1. (Illus.). 264p. 1995. pap. 17.95 (*1-56931-096-3*) Viz Commns Inc.

— Nausicaa of the Valley of Wind, Vol. 2. Horibuchi, Seiji, ed. Lewis, David & Smith, Toren, trs. from JPN. (Illus.). 56p. 1988. pap. 2.50 (*0-929279-01-8*) Viz Commns Inc.

— Nausicaa of the Valley of Wind, Vol. 2. (Illus.). 284p. 1995. pap. 17.95 (*1-56931-087-4*) Viz Commns Inc.

— Nausicaa of the Valley of Wind, Vol. 3. Horibuchi, Seiji, ed. Lewis, David & Smith, Toren, trs. from JPN. (Illus.). 56p. 1989. pap. 2.50 (*0-929279-02-6*) Viz Commns Inc.

— Nausicaa of the Valley of Wind, Vol. 3. (Perfect Collection Ser.). (Illus.). 264p. 1996. pap. text 17.95 (*1-56931-111-0*) Viz Commns Inc.

— Nausicaa of the Valley of Wind, Vol. 4. Horibuchi, Seiji, ed. Lewis, David & Smith, Toren, trs. from JPN. (Illus.). 56p. 1989. pap. 2.50 (*0-929279-03-4*) Viz Commns Inc.

— Nausicaa of the Valley of Wind, Vol. 4. Horibuchi, Seiji, ed. Lewis, David & Smith, Toren, trs. from JPN. (Perfect Collection Ser.). (Illus.). 138p. 1990. pap. text 13.95 (*0-929279-61-1*) Viz Commns Inc.

— Nausicaa of the Valley of Wind, Vol. 4. (Perfect Collection Ser.). (Illus.). 272p. 1997. pap. text 17.95 (*1-56931-211-7*, Viz Comics) Viz Commns Inc.

— Nausicaa of the Valley of Wind, Vol. 5. Horibuchi, Seiji, ed. Lewis, David & Smith, Toren, trs. from JPN. (Illus.). 56p. 1989. pap. 2.50 (*0-929279-04-2*) Viz Commns Inc.

— Nausicaa of the Valley of Wind, Vol. 6. Horibuchi, Seiji, ed. Lewis, David & Smith, Toren, trs. from JPN. (Illus.). 56p. 1989. pap. 2.95 (*0-929279-05-0*) Viz Commns Inc.

— Nausicaa of the Valley of Wind, Vol. 6. (Illus.). 160p. 1995. pap. 15.95 (*1-56931-095-5*) Viz Commns Inc.

— Nausicaa of the Valley of Wind, Vol. 7. Horibuchi, Seiji, ed. Lewis, David & Smith, Toren, trs. from JPN. (Illus.). 56p. 1989. pap. 2.95 (*0-929279-06-9*) Viz Commns Inc.

***Miyazaki, Hayao.** Nausicaa of the Valley of Wind, Vols. 1-4. (Perfect Collection Ser.). (Illus.). 2000. pap., boxed set 69.95 (*1-56931-348-2*, Viz Comics) Viz Commns Inc.

Miyazaki, Ichisada. China's Examination Hell: The Civil Service Examinations of Imperial China. Schirokauer, Conrad, tr. from CHI. LC 80-54223. Orig. Title: Kakyo-Chugoku No Shikenjigoku. 142p. 1981. reprint ed. pap. 15.00 (*0-300-02639-0*, Y-398) Yale U Pr.

Miyazaki, J. M. Foundations of Biology: Molecules to Organisms. Wilson, Tazewell, ed. (Illus.). 212p. (C). 1998. pap. text 30.00 (*1-878437-25-9*) Pac Crest Soft.

Miyazaki, S., jt. auth. see Fremond, M.

Miyazaki, Tamotsu, et al, eds. The Mechanism & New Approach on Drug Resistance of Cancer Cells: Proceedings of the International Symposium on the Mechanism & New Approach on Drug Resistance of Cancer Cells, Sapporo, 15-17 October 1992. LC 93-15706. (International Congress Ser.: No. 1026). 348p. 1993. 166.75 (*0-444-81480-9*, Excerpta Medica) Elsevier.

Miyazaki, Tamotsu, jt. ed. see Yagi, Kunio.

Miyazaki, Toten. My Thirty-Three Years' Dream: The Autobiography of Miyazaki Toten. Shinkichi, Eto & Jansen, Marius B., trs. LC 81-47925. (Princeton Library of Asian Translations). (Illus.). 327p. 1982. reprint ed. pap. 101.40 (*0-7837-9444-4*, 206018600004) Bks Demand.

Miyazaki, Tsuyoshi. Water Flow in Soils. (Books in Soils, Plants & the Environment: Vol. 28). (Illus.). 312p. 1993. text 175.00 (*0-8247-8982-2*) Dekker.

Miyazaki, Yamato, jt. auth. see Wesson, R. L.

Miyazaki, Yumiko, tr. Buddhism for World Peace. 1997. pap. 14.00 (*81-207-1977-8*, Pub. by Sterling Pubs) S Asia.

Miyazawa. Crime Prevention. LC 96-101572. 1995. pap. text 75.50 (*90-6544-882-9*) Kluwer Academic.

Miyazawa, Kenji. Milky Way Railroad. Sigrist, Joseph & Stroud, D. M., trs. from JPN. (Illus.). 160p. (J). (gr. 7-12). 1996. pap. 11.95 (*1-880656-26-4*) Stone Bridge Pr.

— Once & Forever. 1998. pap. text 12.00 (*4-7700-2184-4*, Pub. by Kodansha Intl) Kodansha.

— Once & Forever: The Tales of Kenji Miyazawa. Shaw, ed. Bester, John, tr. (Illus.). 304p. 1994. 25.00 (*4-7700-1780-4*) Kodansha.

Miyazawa, Masanori, jt. auth. see Goodman, David G.

Miyazawa, T., jt. auth. see Emsley, Clive.

Miyoko, Goto. I Am Alive: The Tanka Poems of Goto Miyoko, 1898-1978. Fitzsimmons, Thomas, ed. Tsukimura, Reiko, tr. from JPN. (Asian Poetry in Translation Ser.: No. 10). 192p. 1988. pap. 20.00 (*0-942668-19-7*); text 30.00 (*0-942668-18-9*) Katydid Bks.

Miyoshi, Hajime. Match Labels In Japan. (Arts Collection Ser.: Vol. 82). 1998. pap. 14.95 (*4-7636-1582-3*, Pub. by Kyoto Shoin) Bks Nippan.

Miyoshi, K. & Chung, Yip-Wah. Surface Diagnostics in Tribology - Fundamental Principles & Applications. LC 93-36748. (Series on Modern Tribology: Vol. 1). 352p. 1993. text 121.00 (*981-02-1516-9*) World Scientific Pub.

***Miyoshi, Kazuyoshi.** Japan Paradise: Exquisite Hotels & Inns. (Illus.). 2000. 29.95 (*1-56931-499-3*) Viz Commns Inc.

Miyoshi, Kozo. In the Road. (Illus.). 65.00 (*3-923922-67-1*) Nazraeli Pr.

Miyoshi, Masahiro. Considerations of Equity in the Settlement of Territorial & Boundary Disputes. LC 93-22109. (International Law in Japanese Perspectives Ser.: Vol. 2). 296p. (C). 1993. lib. bdg. 117.00 (*0-7923-2217-7*) Kluwer Academic.

Miyoshi, Masao. Accomplices of Silence: The Modern Japanese Novel. LC 96-42106. (Michigan Classics in Japanese Studies). xx, 194p. 1996. pap. 15.95 (*0-939512-76-9*) U MI Japan.

— As We Saw Them: The First Japanese Embassy to the United States (1860) Urda, John, ed. LC 94-21572. (Illus.). 240p. 1994. pap. 13.00 (*1-56836-028-2*) Kodansha.

— As We Saw Them: The First Japanese Embassy to the United States (1860) LC 78-62851. (Illus.). 244p. reprint ed. pap. 75.70 (*0-7837-4841-8*, 204448800003) Bks Demand.

— Off Center: Power & Culture Relations Between Japan & the United States. (Convergences: Inventories of the Present Ser.). 304p. 1994. pap. text 17.50 (*0-674-63176-5*, MIYOFX) HUP.

Miyoshi, Masao & Harootunian, H. D., eds. Japan in the World. LC 93-2399. 368p. 1993. pap. text 19.95 (*0-8223-1368-5*); lib. bdg. 42.50 (*0-8223-1350-2*) Duke.

— Postmodernism & Japan. LC 89-7709. 322p. 1989. text 49.95 (*0-8223-0779-0*); pap. text 17.95 (*0-8223-0896-7*) Duke.

Miyoshi, Masao, jt. auth. see Jameson, Fredric.

Miyuki, Mokusen, jt. auth. see Spiegelman, J. Marvin.

Miyuki Takahashi. Mr. Benihana: The Rocky Aoki Story. 1997. pap. text 12.95 (*0-9634335-7-1*) Mangajin.

Miz M. Life Behind the Potted Plant. (Illus.). 236p. 1999. mass mkt. 14.95 (*0-9622608-6-X*) Gabbard Pubns.

Mizahi, A., et al. Mathematics: For Business, Life Sciences, & Social Sciences. 5th ed. 144p. 1993. pap., suppl. ed. 25.95 (*0-471-59097-5*) Wiley.

Mizan Press Staff, tr. see Qutb, Sayyid.

Mizanoglu, Mehmet. Persona: The Meaning Behind the Mask. LC 98-72913. (Illus.). 102p. 1998. pap. 10.95 (*0-9663047-1-3*) BGB Pr.

Mizdal, Richard. Black & White Photography for 35mm: A Guide to Photography & Darkroom Techniques. 128p. 2000. pap. text 29.95 (*0-936262-99-0*, Pub. by Amherst Media) IPG Chicago.

Mize. Readings in Family & Child Development. (C). 1996. pap. text 36.25 (*0-07-047108-8*) McGraw.

Mize, Barbara F. Creative Encounters. (gr. 4-8). 1988. pap. 6.00 (*0-89824-248-7*) Trillium Pr.

Mize, David W. Algeria. (World Education Ser.). (Illus.). 160p. 1978. 4.00 (*0-910054-52-5*) Am Assn Coll Registrars.

Mize, Jackie. Supernatural Childbirth. 128p. 1993. pap. 7.99 (*0-89274-756-0*, HH-756) Harrison Hse.

***Mize, Jean.** Night of Anguish, Morning of Hope. rev. ed. (Illus.). xi, 200p. 2000. reprint ed. pap. 10.95 (*0-9678287-0-8*, 0001) Quest Pubng AR.

Mize, Jim. The Winter of Our Discount Tent: A Humorous Look at Flora, Fauna, & Foolishness Outdoors. LC 94-18752. (Illus.). 140p. 1995. 18.95 (*1-57003-049-9*) U of SC Pr.

Mize, Joe H., ed. Guide to Systems Integration. 434p. 1991. pap. text 35.00 (*0-89806-111-3*, RESYIN) Eng Mgmt Pr.

Mize, Joe H., et al. Operations Planning & Control. (Illus.). 1971. 46.00 (*0-13-637892-7*) P-H.

Mize, Larry, et al. Focus: The Name of the Game, 1. 1999. 12.99 (*0-8499-5505-X*) Word Pub.

Mize, R. Ranney, et al, eds. Nitric Oxide in Brain Development, Plasticity, & Disease. LC 98-40803. (Progress in Brain Research Ser.: Vol. 118). 302p. 1998. 210.00 (*0-444-82885-0*) Elsevier.

Mize, R. Ranney & Erzurumlu, Reha S. Neural Development & Plasticity. LC 96-41471. (Progress in Brain Research Ser.). 434p. 1996. 247.00 (*0-444-82433-2*) Elsevier.

Mize, Sandra Y. & Portier, William L., eds. American Catholic Traditions: Resources for Renewal, Vol. 199. LC 97-11545. (College Theology Society Ser.: No. 42). 272p. (Orig.). 1997. pap. 20.00 (*1-57075-109-9*) Orbis Bks.

Mize, Terry. More Than Conquerors. pap. 7.99 (*0-89274-930-X*, HH-930) Harrison Hse.

Mizejewski, Gerald J. & Jacobson, Herbert I., eds. Biological Activities of Alpha-Fetoprotein, I. 256p. 1987. 155.00 (*0-8493-5637-7*, QP552, CRC Reprint) Franklin.

— Biological Activities of Alpha-Fetoprotein, II. 256p. 1989. 174.00 (*0-8493-5638-5*, CRC Reprint) Franklin.

— Biological Activities of Alpha-Fetoprotein, Set. 256p. 1989. 110.00 (*0-8493-5636-9*, QP552) CRC Pr.

Mizejewski, Linda. Divine Decadence: Fascism, Female Spectacle, & the Makings of Sally Bowles. LC 92-11858. 272p. (C). 1992. pap. text 17.95 (*0-691-02346-8*, Pub. by Princeton U Pr) Cal Prin Full Svc.

— Ziegfeld Girl: Image & Icon in Culture & Cinema. LC 98-38685. 1999. write for info. (*0-8223-2303-6*); pap. 17.95 (*0-8223-2323-0*) Duke.

Mizel, Mark S. & American Orthopaedic Foot & Ankle Society Staff. Orthopaedic Knowledge Update. 2nd ed. LC 98-38633. 1998. write for info. (*0-89203-178-6*) American Academic Assn for Peace in the Middle East.

Mizel, Mark S., jt. auth. see Pfeffer, Glenn B.

Mizel, Mark S., jt. ed. see Pfeffer, Glen.

Mizel, V., et al, eds. Mechanics & Thermodynamics of Continua: A Collection of Papers Dedicated to B.D. Coleman on His Sixtieth Birthday. (Illus.). xii, 578p. 1991. pap. 110.00 (*0-387-52999-3*) Spr-Verlag.

Mizel, Victor, jt. auth. see Marcus, Moshe.

Mizell, Hubert. 95th U. S. Open. Norwood, Bev, ed. (Illus.). 64p. 1995. 20.00 (*1-878843-13-3*) Intl Merc OH.

— Ninety-Fourth U. S. Open. Norwood, Bev, ed. (Illus.). 64p. 1994. 20.00 (*1-878843-10-9*) Intl Merc OH.

— 96th U. S. Open. Norwood, Bev, ed. (Illus.). 64p. 1996. 20.00 (*1-878843-16-8*) Intl Merc OH.

Mizell, Leslie. Dark Seed II: The Official Strategy Guide. LC 95-71557. 1995. pap. 19.95 (*0-7615-0149-5*) Prima Pub.

Mizell, Leslie, jt. auth. see Brumley, Doug.

Mizell, Linda. Racism. (Think Ser.). 160p. (YA). (gr. 7 up). 1992. pap. 9.95 (*0-8027-7365-6*); lib. bdg. 15.85 (*0-8027-8113-6*) Walker & Co.

Mizell, Louis R., Jr. Invasion of Privacy. LC 98-190484. 256p. 1998. pap. 13.00 (*0-425-16088-2*) Berkley Pub.

Mizell, Louis R. Masters of Deception: The Worldwide White Collar Crime Crisis. LC 96-1921. 253p. 1996. 24.95 (*0-471-13355-8*) Wiley.

Mizell, Louis R., Jr. Street Sense for Parents. 176p. (Orig.). 1995. mass mkt. 4.99 (*0-425-14947-1*) Berkley Pub.

— Street Sense for Seniors. 224p. 1994. mass mkt. 4.99 (*0-425-14364-3*) Berkley Pub.

Mizell, Louis R. Street Sense for Seniors. (J. Hook Ser.). 1994. mass mkt. 4.99 (*0-425-14378-3*) Berkley Pub.

— Street Sense for Students. 161p. 1996. mass mkt. 4.99 (*0-425-14986-2*) Berkley Pub.

Mizell, Louis R., Jr. Street Sense for Students. (J. Hook Ser.). 1996. mass mkt. 4.99 (*0-425-15535-8*) Berkley Pub.

— Street Sense for Women. (Orig.). pap. 4.99 (*0-425-13973-5*) Berkley Pub.

— Street Sense for Women. 160p. (Orig.). 1993. mass mkt. 4.99 (*0-425-13971-9*) Berkley Pub.

— Street Sense Parent. (J. Hook Ser.). 1995. mass mkt. 4.99 (*0-425-14950-1*) Berkley Pub.

Mizell, Louis R. Target U.S.A. The Inside Story of the New Terrorist War. LC 97-49235. 210p. 1998. 19.95 (*0-471-17829-2*) Wiley.

Mizen, Paul. Buffer Stock Models & the Demand for Money. LC 94-20722. 1994. text 59.95 (*0-312-12318-3*) St Martin.

Mizen, Paul & Pentecost, Eric J., eds. The Macroeconomics of International Currencies: Theory, Policy & Evidence. LC 96-5321. (Illus.). 272p. (C). 1996. text 95.00 (*1-85898-077-1*) E Elgar.

Mizener, Arthur. F. Scott Fitzgerald. LC 86-51196. (Literary Lives Ser.). (Illus.). 128p. 1999. reprint ed. pap. 12.95 (*0-500-26024-9*, Pub. by Thames Hudson) Norton.

Mizener, Arthur, ed. Modern Short Stories. 4th ed. 874p. (C). 1979. pap. text 37.00 (*0-393-95025-5*); pap. text, student ed. 3.50 (*0-393-95032-8*) Norton.

Mizer, David A., et al. Food Preparation for the Professional. 3rd ed. LC 99-31227. 576p. 1999. 59.95 (*0-471-25187-9*) Wiley.

Mizer, Hamilton B. Niagara Falls: A Selected Topical History of the City's Formative Years. expanded rev. ed. 210p. 1991. 12.95 (*0-614-13514-1*) Niagara Cnty Hist Soc.

Mizera, E., ed. Defects in Crystals. 512p. (C). 1988. text 125.00 (*9971-5-0629-7*) World Scientific Pub.

— Defects in Crystals: Proceedings of the 7th International School Szczyrk, Poland, May 23-30, 1985. 580p. 1987. text 131.00 (*9971-5-0291-7*, Z0395P-P) World Scientific Pub.

Mizerak, Steve & Cohen, Joel. Steve Mizerak's Pocket Billiards Tips & Trick Shots. (Illus.). 192p. 1982. 15.50 (*0-8092-5780-7*) NTC Contemp Pub Co.

Mizerak, Steve & Panozzo, Michael E. Pocket Billiards Tips & Trick Shots. (Illus.). 176p. 1982. pap. 12.95 (*0-8092-5779-3*, 577930, Contemporary Bks) NTC Contemp Pub Co.

— Steve Mizerak's Complete Book of Pool. (Illus.). 208p. (Orig.). 1990. pap. 14.95 (*0-8092-4255-9*, 425590, Contemporary Bks) NTC Contemp Pub Co.

— Steve Mizerak's Play Better Pool. (Illus.). 144p. 1996. pap. 12.95 (*0-8092-3427-0*, 342700, Contemporary Bks) NTC Contemp Pub Co.

— Steve Mizerak's Winning Pool Tips. (Illus.). 160p. 1995. pap. 8.95 (*0-8092-3428-9*, 342890, Contemporary Bks) NTC Contemp Pub Co.

Mizeres, N. J. Human Anatomy: Synoptic Approach. (Synoptic Approach Ser.). 342p. (C). 1992. pap. text 45.00 (*0-8385-3902-5*, A3902-2, Apple Lange Med) McGraw.

Mizerski, J., et al, eds. Quantum Optics & Spectroscopy. 172p. 1993. text 145.00 (*1-56072-110-3*) Nova Sci Pubs.

Mizerski, J. & Fiutak, J., eds. Quantum Optics: Proceedings of the Summer School on Quantum Optics, Sept. 2-8, 1985, Gdansk, Poland. 410p. 1986. pap. 64.00 (*9971-5-0098-1*); text 159.00 (*9971-5-0097-3*) World Scientific Pub.

Mizerski, Richard, jt. ed. see Forrest, Edward.

Mizes, J. Scott, jt. auth. see Miller, Katherine J.

***Mizgorski, Brenda J.** Prentice Hall Finance & Accounting Internet Guide: A Guided Tour of the Information Superhighway. LC 99-10588. (Illus.). 432p. 1999. pap. 49.95 (*0-13-095285-0*) P-H.

Mizhou Hui, Dr. San Shou King Fu of the Chinese Red Army: Practical Skills & Theory of Unarmed Combat. LC 96-204009. (Illus.). 176p. 1996. pap. 25.00 (*0-87364-884-6*) Paladin Pr.

Mizin, I., jt. ed. see Schwartzel, Heinz.

Mizio, Emelicia & Delaney, Anita J., eds. Training for Service Delivery to Minority Clients. LC 80-23468. 208p. reprint ed. pap. 64.50 (*0-8357-8513-0*, 203481000091) Bks Demand.

Miziolek, Andrzej W. & Tsang, Wing, eds. Halon Replacements: Technology & Science. (ACS Symposium Ser.: No. 611). (Illus.). 400p. 1995. text 110.00 (*0-8412-3327-6*, Pub. by Am Chemical) OUP.

Mizner, Addison. Florida Architecture of Addison Mizner. unabridged ed. LC 92-22830. (Illus.). 240p. 1992. reprint ed. pap. text 16.95 (*0-486-27327-X*) Dover.

Mizobuchi, Hiroshi. Dances of the Seasons in Kyoto. (Arts Collection Ser.: Vol. 142). (Illus.). 240p. 1998. pap. 14.95 (*4-7636-1642-0*, Pub. by Kyoto Shoin) Bks Nippan.

Mizoguchi, Fumio. Prolog & Its Applications. (C). 1990. mass mkt. 67.50 (*0-412-37770-5*) Chapman & Hall.

Mizoguchi, Fumio, ed. AI Technology. x, 187p. (gr. 12). 1990. 80.00 (*90-5199-050-2*, Pub. by IOS Pr) IOS Press.

Mizoguchi, Hidetoshi, tr. from ENG. What's Wrong with the Mental Health System & What Can Be Done About It. (JPN.). 1999. pap. 3.00 (*1-58429-047-1*) Rational Isl.

Mizoguti, H. A Fifteen-Somite Human Embryo. (Advances in Anatomy, Embryology & Cell Biology Ser.: Vol. 116). (Illus.). 95p. 1989. 139.00 (*0-387-50565-2*) Spr-Verlag.

Mizokawa, Donald T. Everyday Computing in Academe: A Guide for Scholars, Researchers, Students, & Other Academic Users of Personal Computers. LC 94-2002. 350p. 1994. 39.95 (*0-87778-276-8*) Educ Tech Pubns.

Mizouni, Hedi, tr. see Avinger, Judith.

Mizra, Jill & Harris, Nick. Mix Your Own Acrylics. 64p. 1995. 6.98 (*0-7858-0266-5*) Bk Sales Inc.

Mizrahi. Finite. 8th ed. Date not set. pap. text. write for info. (*0-471-35510-0*) Wiley.

— Mathematics. 7th ed. Date not set. pap. text. write for info. (*0-471-35547-X*) Wiley.

— SSM Finite. 8th ed. 272p. 1999. pap. 33.95 (*0-471-35508-9*) Wiley.

Mizrahi & St. Andre. S.g. Calculus & Analytic Geometry. (Math). 1982. student ed. 10.50 (*0-534-00979-4*) Brooks-Cole.

Mizrahi & Sullivan. S.g. Calculus & Analytic Geometry. 2nd ed. (Math). 1985. student ed. 15.00 (*0-534-05455-2*) Brooks-Cole.

— Ssm, V1 Calculus & Analytic Geometry. 2nd ed. (Math). 1986. student ed. 12.00 (*0-534-05456-0*) Brooks-Cole.

— Ssm, V2 Calculus & Analytic Geometry. 2nd ed. (Math). 1986. student ed. 10.50 (*0-534-05457-9*) Brooks-Cole.

— Stdt Sol V2 - Calc & Analy Geom. (Math). 1983. student ed. 6.75 (*0-534-02816-0*) Brooks-Cole.

Mizrahi, Abe & Sullivan, Michael. Calculus & Analytic Geometry. 2nd ed. 1083p. (C). 1986. mass mkt. 56.75 (*0-534-05454-4*) PWS Pubs.

— Finite Mathematics: An Applied Approach. 8th ed. LC 99-29009. 728p. 1999. text 100.95 (*0-471-32202-4*) Wiley.

Mizrahi, Abe & Sullivan, Michael. Mathematics: An Applied Approach. 7th ed. LC 99-29010. 1080p. 1999. text 102.95 (*0-471-32203-2*) Wiley.

***Mizrahi, Abe & Sullivan, Michael.** Mathematics: An Applied Approach. 7th ed. 470p. 1999. pap. 33.95 (*0-471-34939-9*) Wiley.

Mizrahi, Avshalom, et al, eds. Potentiating Health & the Crisis of the Immune System: Integrative Approaches to the Prevention & Treatment of Modern Diseases. LC 97-16693. (Illus.). 300p. (C). 1997. text 114.00 (*0-306-45602-8*, Kluwer Plenum) Kluwer Academic.

Mizrahi, Avshalom & Lensky, Yaacov, eds. Bee Products - Properties, Applications & Apitherapy: Proceedings of an International Conference Held in Tel Aviv, Israel, May 26-30, 1996. LC 96-51895. 282p. (C). 1997. text 89.50 (*0-306-45502-1*, Kluwer Plenum) Kluwer Academic.

Mizrahi, Eli. Clinical Guide to Neonatal Seizures. LC 97-28764. 285p. 1997. text 79.00 (*0-7817-0296-8*) Lppncott W & W.

Mizrahi, Haim. There Is No Simple Way to Say Simple Things: A Snack for Your Mind. (Illus.). 72p. 1998. 7.95 (*0-9667731-0-1*) Think Cards.

Mizrahi, Irene & Kaplan, Gregory B., eds. Espanol Para los Negocios: Estudios de Casos. (SPA.). 131p. 49.95 (*1-882528-20-4*) Scripta.

Mizrahi, Isaac. Isaac Mizrahi Presents the Adventures of Sandee the Supermodel. LC 97-22667. 1997. 29.95 (*0-684-83511-8*) S&S Trade.

Mizrahi, Judith. Seven Hundred Three American Sephardim: Diversity Within Cohesiveness. 100p. 1992. 12.50 (*0-9635425-0-8*) Gemini Books.

Mizrahi, Salomon S. & Dodonov, Viktor V. Nonlinear Extensions of the Schrodinger Equation. 250p. 1997. 48.00 (*981-02-3249-7*) World Scientific Pub.

Mizrahi, Taura S., jt. auth. see Marlo, Shelby.

Mizrahi, Terry & Morrison, John, eds. Community Organization & Social Administration: Advances, Trends, & Emerging Principles. LC 92-8960. (Illus.). 254p. 1992. lib. bdg. 49.95 (*1-56024-257-4*) Haworth Pr.

— Community Organization & Social Administration: Advances, Trends, & Emerging Principles. LC 92-47278. (Illus.). 254p. 1993. pap. 19.95 (*1-56024-277-9*) Haworth Pr.

Mizruchi, Ephraim H. Regulating Society: Beguines, Bohemians, & Other Marginals. LC 82-48161. xiv, 208p. 1994. pap. text 10.95 (*0-226-53284-4*) U Ch Pr.

Mizruchi, Mark S. The Structure of Corporate Political Action: Interfirm Relations & Their Consequences. (Illus.). 304p. 1992. 48.95 (*0-674-84377-0*) HUP.

Mizruchi, Mark S. & Schwartz, Michael, eds. Intercorporate Relations: The Structural Analysis of Business. (Structural Analysis in the Social Sciences Ser.: No. 1). (Illus.). 340p. (C). 1992. pap. text 19.95 (*0-521-43794-6*) Cambridge U Pr.

Mizruchi, Susan L. The Power of Historical Knowledge: Narrating the Past in Hawthorne, James & Dreiser. 336p. 1988. text 49.50 (*0-691-06725-2*, Pub. by Princeton U Pr) Cal Prin Full Svc.

— The Science of Sacrifice: American Literature & Modern

An Asterisk (*) at the beginning of an entry indicates that the title is appearing for the first time.

Social Theory. LC 97-44317. 496p. 1998. text 65.00 (*0-691-06892-5*, Pub. by Princeton U Pr); pap. text 19.95 (*0-691-01506-6*, Pub. by Princeton U Pr) Cal Prin Full Svc.

Mizsei, Kalman & Rudka, Andrzej. From Association to Accession: The Impact of the Association Agreements on Central Europe's Trade & Integration with the European Union. (POL.). 1995. write for info. (*83-903493-1-0*) Inst EW Stud.

Mizsei, Kalman & Rudka, Andrzej, eds. From Association to Accession: The Impact of the Association Agreements on Central Europe's Trade & Integration with the European Union. 1995. write for info. (*0-913449-44-X*) Inst EW Stud.

Mizsei, Kalman, jt. auth. see Rudka, Andrzej.

Mizuguchi, Sadako, tr. see Takagi, Akimitsu.

Mizuike, A. Enrichment Techniques for Inorganic Trace Analysis. (Chemical Laboratory Practice Ser.). (Illus.). 144p. 1983. 107.95 (*0-387-12051-3*) Spr-Verlag.

Mizukam, Y. Illustrated Textbook on Sericulture. (Illus.). 157p. 1998. 29.95 (*1-57808-039-8*) Science Pubs.

Mizukami, K., jt. ed. see Malanowski, K.

Mizukami, Masahiro, et al, eds. Hypertensive Intracerebral Hemorrhage. LC 81-40890. (Illus.). 272p. 1983. reprint ed. pap. 84.40 (*0-608-00632-7*, 206122000007) Bks Demand.

Mizumachi, Hiroshi, ed. Adhesion Science & Technology. 960p. 1997. text 150.00 (*90-5699-588-X*) Gordon & Breach.

Mizumura, Kazue. Flower Moon Snow: A Book of Haiku. LC 76-41180. (Illus.). (J). (gr. k-4). 1977. lib. bdg. 12.89 (*0-690-01290-X*) HarpC Child Bks.

Mizuno, jt. auth. see Ogawa.

Mizuno, D., et al. Self-Defense Mechanisms: Role of Macrophage. 344p. 1983. 137.50 (*0-444-80460-9*) Elsevier.

Mizuno, E., jt. auth. see Chen, Wai-Fah.

Mizuno, Kogen. Basic Buddhist Concepts. 176p. (Orig.). 1987. pap. 11.95 (*4-333-01203-1*, Pub. by Kosei Pub Co) Tuttle Pubng.

— The Beginnings of Buddhism. Gage, Richard L., tr. from JPN. Orig. Title: Bukkyo No Genten. (Illus.). 220p. 1980. pap. 12.95 (*4-333-00383-0*, Pub. by Kosei Pub Co) Tuttle Pubng.

— Buddhist Sutras: Origin, Development, Transmission. (Illus.). 220p. 1982. pap. 12.95 (*4-333-01028-4*, Pub. by Kosei Pub Co) Tuttle Pubng.

— Essentials of Buddhism: Basic Terminology & Concepts of Buddhist Philosophy & Practice. (Illus.). 296p. 1997. pap. 29.95 (*4-333-01683-5*, Pub. by Kosei Pub Co) Tuttle Pubng.

Mizuno, M., et al, eds. Role of Prolactin in Human Reproduction. (Illus.). x, 314p. 1988. 225.25 (*3-8055-4786-2*) S Karger.

***Mizuno, Ryo.** Record of Lodoss War: The Grey Witch: A Gathering of Heroes. 2nd ed. Jackson, Laura & Kobayashi, Yoko, trs. from JPN.Tr. of Hairo No Majo. (Illus.). ix, 215p. 2000. reprint ed. pap. 15.95 (*1-56219-919-6*, CMX 06141) Central Pk Media.

Mizuno, Sachi. Shinjuku Nights. (Orig.). 1997. mass mkt. 6.50 (*1-56333-493-3*) Masquerade.

Mizuno, Shigeru. Company-Wide Total Quality Control. 1987. pap. text 26.50 (*92-833-1100-0*) Productivity Inc.

— Company-Wide Total Quality Control. 313p. 1988. text 32.50 (*92-833-1099-3*) Productivity Inc.

Mizuno, Shigeru, ed. Management for Quality Improvement: The Seven New QC Tools. LC 88-42625. (Illus.). 323p. 1988. 65.00 (*0-915299-29-1*) Productivity Inc.

Mizuno, Shigeru & Akao, Yoji, eds. QFD: The Customer-Driven Approach to Quality Planning & Deployment. LC 95-169834. (Illus.). 365p. 1994. text 59.95 (*92-833-1121-3*) Productivity Inc.

Mizuno, Shigeru & Akao, Yoji, eds. QFD: The Customer Driven Approach to Quality Planning & Deployment. (Illus.). 365p. 1994. pap. text 49.95 (*92-833-1122-1*) Productivity Inc.

Mizuno, Tadahiko. Nuclear Transmutation: The Reality of Cold Fusion. Mallove, Eugene, ed. Rothwell, Jed, tr. from JPN. LC 98-88307. (Illus.). 152p. 1998. 29.95 (*1-892925-00-1*) Cold Fusion Tech.

Mizuno, Y., ed. First Sandoz Symposium on the Treatment of Parkinson's Disease, Tokyo, October 1992. (Journal: European Neurology: Vol. 33, Suppl. 1, 1993). (Illus.). vi, 70p. 1993. pap. 33.25 (*3-8055-5829-5*) S Karger.

Mizuno, Y., et al, eds. Advances in Research on Neurodegeneration Vol. II: Etiopathogenesis. (Illus.). xiii, 221p. 1994. 104.50 (*0-8176-3762-1*) Birkhauser.

Mizushima & Amor. Autoimmunity, Rheumatoid Arthritis & Cyclosporin A (Sandimmun) 104p. (C). 1991. 35.00 (*1-85070-305-1*) Prthnon Pub.

Mizushima, Masataka. The Theory of Rotating Diatomic Molecules. LC 74-34080. 543p. 1975. 42.50 (*0-471-61187-5*) Krieger.

***Mizuta, Hiroshi.** Adam Smith: Critical Responses, 6 Vol. Set. LC 99-27698. 1999. text. write for info. (*0-415-15794-3*) Routledge.

— Adam Smith's Library: A Catalogue. 400p. 2000. text 120.00 (*0-19-828590-6*) OUP.

Mizuta, Hiroshi & Tanoue, Tomonori. The Physics & Applications of Resonant Tunnelling Diodes. (Studies in Semiconductor Physics & Microelectronic Engineering: Vol. 2). (Illus.). 253p. (C). 1995. text 64.95 (*0-521-43218-9*) Cambridge U Pr.

Mizuta, Kazuo. The Structures of Everyday Life in Japan in the Last Decade of the Twentieth Century. LC 93-1751. 400p. 1993. text 99.95 (*0-7734-9320-4*) E Mellen.

Mizuta, Noriko, tr. see Taeko, Tomioka.

Mizuta, Noriko, tr. see Tomioka, Taeko.

Mizuta, Tamae, jt. auth. see Roberts, Marie M.

Mizuta, Tamae, jt. ed. see Roberts, Marie M.

Mizutani, N., et al, eds. Electroceramics in Japan I. (Key Engineering Materials Ser.: Vol. 157-158). (Illus.). 324p. (C). 142.00 (*0-87849-813-3*, Pub. by Trans T Pub) Enfield Pubs NH.

***Mizutani, N., et al, eds.** Electroceramics in Japan II: Proceedings of the 18th Electronics Division Meeting of the Ceramic Society of Japan, Held in Kawasaki, Japan, October 29-30, 1998. (Key Engineering Materials Ser.: Vol. 169-170). (Illus.). 300p. (C). 1999. text 156.00 (*0-87849-840-0*, Pub. by Trans T Pub) Enfield Pubs NH.

Mizutani, N., ed. see IUMRS International Conference on Advanced Materia.

Mizutani, Nobuko, jt. auth. see NHK Overseas Broadcasting Department Staff.

Mizutani, S., et al, eds. Placental & Endometrial Proteins: Basic & Clinical Aspects: Proceedings of the International Conference, Japan, 1987. 728p. 1988. 175.00 (*90-6764-115-4*, Pub. by VSP) Coronet Bks.

Mizutani, Shinjiro, jt. ed. see Uemura, Takeshi.

Mizutani, T., et al. Geometric Study of Foliations. 512p. 1994. text 109.00 (*981-02-1898-2*) World Scientific Pub.

Mizutani, T., jt. auth. see Garcilazo, H.

Mizutori, Ivan, tr. see McIntyre, Sally.

Mizwa, Stephen P. Frederic Chopin, 1810-1849: Music Book Index. 108p. 1993. reprint ed. lib. bdg. 69.00 (*0-7812-9590-4*) Rprt Serv.

Mizwa, Stephen P., ed. Frederic Chopin, Eighteen Ten to Eighteen Forty-Nine. LC 83-10836. (Illus.). 108p. 1983. reprint ed. lib. bdg. 49.50 (*0-313-24116-3*, MIFR, Greenwood Pr) Greenwood.

Mizzell, Thurman E., Jr., jt. auth. see Christoffel, Katherine T.

M.J. Studios Staff. Daffy Dinosaurs Sticker Pad. 32p. (Orig.). (J). (gr. k-6). 1993. pap. 2.95 (*1-879424-48-7*) Nickel Pr.

— Dress up Sticker Pad. 32p. (J). (gr. k-6). 1993. reprint ed. pap. 2.95 (*1-879424-17-7*) Nickel Pr.

— Monster Madness Sticker Pad. 32p. (J). (gr. k-6). 1993. pap. 2.95 (*1-879424-56-8*) Nickel Pr.

— Wacky Animals Sticker Pad. 32p. (J). (gr. k-6). 1993. reprint ed. pap. 2.95 (*1-879424-30-4*) Nickel Pr.

Mjagkij, Nina. Light in the Darkness: African Americans & the YMCA. 1852-1946. LC 93-19857. (Illus.). 216p. 1993. 24.95 (*0-8131-1852-2*) U Pr of Ky.

Mjagkij, Nina & Spratt, Margaret. Men & Women Adrift: The YMCA & the YWCA in the City. LC 97-4666. 1997. text 55.00 (*0-8147-5541-0*); pap. text 19.50 (*0-8147-5542-9*) NYU Pr.

MJE Code Staff, et al. Checklist of the Flowering Plants & Gymnosperms of Brunei Darussalam. (Illus.). 476p. 1996. 36.00 (*99917-31-00-8*) Royal Botnic Grdns.

Mjelde, K. M. Methods of the Allocation of Limited Resources. LC 82-16002. 96p. reprint ed. pap. 30.00 (*0-8357-4602-X*, 203753500008) Bks Demand.

Mjelde, Michael J. Clipper Ship Captain: Daniel McLaughlin & the Glory of the Seas. (Pacific Maritime History Ser.: Vol. 3). (Illus.). 288p. 1997. 35.00 (*1-889901-04-0*) Glencannon Pr.

— Glory of the Seas. LC 77-105505. (American Maritime Library: No. 1). 315p. reprint ed. pap. 97.70 (*0-8357-2788-2*, 203991400014) Bks Demand.

***MJF Books Staff.** How to Sound Smart: A Quick & Witty Guide. 240p. 2000. 7.98 (*1-56731-364-7*, MJF Bks) Fine Comms.

MJF Books Staff, ed. see Beattie.

MJF Books Staff, ed. see Shermer, Michael.

Mjhor, Ivar A., jt. auth. see Davidson, C. L.

Mjor, Ivar A. Reaction Patterns in Human Teeth. 248p. 1983. 143.00 (*0-8493-6645-3*, RK280) CRC Pr.

Mjor, Ivar A., ed. Dental Materials: Biological Properties & Clinical Evaluation. 224p. 1985. 128.00 (*0-8493-6644-5*, RK652, CRC Reprint) Franklin.

Mkandawire, Thandika & Soludo, Charles C. Our Continent, Our Future: African Perspectives on Structural Adjustment. LC 98-41439. 224p. 1998. 79.95 (*0-86543-704-1*); pap. 21.95 (*0-86543-705-X*) Africa World.

***Mkandiwire, Thankdika & Soludo, Charles C.** African Voices on Structural Adjustment. 280p. 2000. pap. 25.00 (*0-88936-888-0*, Pub. by IDRC Bks) Stylus Pub VA.

Mkangi, C. C. The Social Cost of Small Families & Land Reform: A Case Study of the Wataita of Kenya. (International Population Ser.: Vol. 2). (Illus.). 180p. 1983. text 83.00 (*0-08-028952-5*, Pub. by Pergamon Repr) Franklin.

M'Kee, John R., tr. see Kirsch, J. P.

Mkhondo, Rich. Reporting South Africa. LC 93-32149. 175p. (C). 1993. pap. 13.95 (*0-435-08089-X*, 08089) Heinemann.

M.Kosslyn, Stephen & Koenig, Olivier. Wet Mind: The New Cognitive Neuroscience. 624p. 1995. pap. 19.95 (*0-02-874085-8*) Free Pr.

Mladen, Davidovic. Beginner's Czech. (Language Ser.). (CZE & ENG.). 167p. (Orig.). 1994. pap. 9.95 (*0-7818-0231-8*) Hippocrene Bks.

— Beginner's Persian. 150p. (Orig.). 1997. pap. 14.95 (*0-7818-0567-8*) Hippocrene Bks.

— Bosnian-English - English-Bosnian. 332p. (Orig.). 1996. pap. 8.95 (*0-7818-0499-X*) Hippocrene Bks.

— Bulgarian-English - English-Bulgarian Compact Dictionary. (Compact Dictionaries Ser.). 323p. 1997. pap. 8.95 (*0-7818-0535-X*) Hippocrene Bks.

— Classic French Love Poems. LC 98-6753. (Illus.). 130p. 1997. 17.50 (*0-7818-0573-2*) Hippocrene Bks.

— Comprehensive Bilingual Dictionary of French Proverbs. 400p. 1997. pap. 24.95 (*0-7818-0594-5*) Hippocrene Bks.

— Concise Sanskrit-English Dictionary. (ENG & SAN.). 366p. 1996. reprint ed. pap. 14.95 (*0-7818-0203-2*) Hippocrene Bks.

— English-Hindi Practical Dictionary. (Language Dictionaries Ser.). (ENG & HIN.). 399p. (Orig.). 1991. pap. 11.95 (*0-87052-978-1*) Hippocrene Bks.

— English-Icelandic Comprehensive Dictionary. (ENG & ICE.). 862p. 1996. 60.00 (*0-7818-0465-5*) Hippocrene Bks.

— English-Swedish Comprehensive Dictionary. (ENG & SWE.). 957p. 1997. pap. 39.50 (*0-7818-0475-2*) Hippocrene Bks.

— English-Turkish - Turkish-English Concise Dictionary. (Concise Dictionaries Ser.). 288p. (Orig.). 1993. pap. 8.95 (*0-7818-0161-3*) Hippocrene Bks.

— French Handy Dictionary. LC 84-203565. (Handy Dictionaries Ser.). 120p. 1992. pap. 8.95 (*0-7818-0010-2*) Hippocrene Bks.

— Greek-English - English-Greek Standard Dictionary. (ENG & GRE.). 686p. 1997. pap. 16.95 (*0-7818-0600-3*) Hippocrene Bks.

— Hindi-English - English-Hindi Standard Dictionary. (ENG & HIN.). 800p. 1996. pap. 27.50 (*0-7818-0470-1*) Hippocrene Bks.

— Icelandic-English Comprehensive Dictionary. (ENG & ICE.). 942p. 1996. 60.00 (*0-7818-0464-7*) Hippocrene Bks.

— Irish-English - English-Irish Dictionary & Phrasebook. (Language Dictionaries Ser.). 160p. (Orig.). 1991. pap. 7.95 (*0-87052-110-1*) Hippocrene Bks.

— Japanese Handy Dictionary. (Handy Dictionaries Ser.). (JPN.). 120p. (Orig.). 1991. pap. 8.95 (*0-87052-962-5*) Hippocrene Bks.

— Korean-English - English-Korean Practical Dictionary. (Language Dictionaries Ser.). 365p. (Orig.). 1991. pap. 14.95 (*0-87052-092-X*) Hippocrene Bks.

— Macedonian-English - English-Macedonian Concise Dictionary. LC 97-21876. (ENG & MAC.). 180p. (Orig.). 1997. pap. 14.95 (*0-7818-0516-3*) Hippocrene Bks.

— Mastering Advanced Italian. (Mastering Languages Ser.). (ITA., Illus.). 357p. (Orig.). 1995. pap. text 14.95 (*0-7818-0333-0*) Hippocrene Bks.

— Navajo-English Dictionary. (ENG & NAV.). 165p. 1994. pap. 9.95 (*0-7818-0247-4*) Hippocrene Bks.

— Old Polish Traditions in the Kitchen & at the Table. 304p. 1997. reprint ed. pap. 11.95 (*0-7818-0488-4*) Hippocrene Bks.

— Polish-English - English-Polish. (ENG & POL.). 240p. (Orig.). 1996. pap. 8.95 (*0-7818-0496-5*) Hippocrene Bks.

— Portuguese Handy Dictionary. (Handy Dictionaries Ser.). 120p. (Orig.). 1991. pap. 8.95 (*0-87052-053-9*) Hippocrene Bks.

— Romanized English-Hebrew - Hebrew-English Compact Dictionary. (ENG & HEB.). 157p. (Orig.). 1997. pap. 7.95 (*0-7818-0568-6*) Hippocrene Bks.

— Russian-English - English-Russian Compact Dictionary. (ENG & RUS.). 536p. 1997. pap. 9.95 (*0-7818-0537-6*) Hippocrene Bks.

— Serbian-English - English-Serbian Concise Dictionary. LC 97-10030. 400p. 1997. pap. 14.95 (*0-7818-0556-2*, 326) Hippocrene Bks.

— Slovak-English - English-Slovak Compact Dictionary. (Hippocrene Compact Dictionaries Ser.). (ENG & SLO.). 360p. (Orig.). 1996. pap. 8.95 (*0-7818-0501-5*) Hippocrene Bks.

— Spanish (Latin American) - English, English - Spanish Compact Dictionary. (ENG & SPA.). 310p. (Orig.). 1996. pap. 8.95 (*0-7818-0497-3*) Hippocrene Bks.

— Spanish Verbs: Ser & Estar. (ENG & SPA.). 225p. 1996. pap. 9.95 (*0-7818-0024-2*) Hippocrene Bks.

— Traditional Food from Scotland: The Edinburgh Book of Plain Cookery Recipes. 336p. 1996. pap. 11.95 (*0-7818-0514-7*) Hippocrene Bks.

— Traditional Recipes from Old England. 128p. 1996. pap. 9.95 (*0-7818-0489-2*) Hippocrene Bks.

— Ukrainian-English - English-Ukrainian. (ENG & UKR.). 448p. (Orig.). 1996. pap. 8.95 (*0-7818-0498-1*) Hippocrene Bks.

— Welsh-English - English-Welsh Standard Dictionary. 612p. 1993. pap. 24.95 (*0-7818-0136-2*) Hippocrene Bks.

***Mladen, Sutej.** The Arctic to the Antarctica: Cigra Circumnauigates the Americas. Hemingway-Douglass, Reanne, ed. LC 99-45359. Orig. Title: Na Rubovima Svijeta: Jedrilicom Hrvatska Cigra od Arktika do Antarktike. (Illus.). 160p. 1999. pap. 19.95 (*0-938665-65-0*) Fine Edge Prods.

Mladenka, K. Financial Accounting. 1995. student ed. write for info. (*0-07-041884-5*) McGraw.

Mladenka, Kenneth R. The Unfinished Republic: American Government in the Twenty-First Century. LC 96-32393. 388p. 1996. pap. text 33.33 (*0-13-124496-5*) P-H.

Mladenka, Kenneth R., jt. auth. see Hill, Kim Q.

Mladenoff, David J. & Baker, William L., eds. Spatial Modeling of Forest Landscape Change: Approaches & Applications. LC 98-50552. (Illus.). 320p. 1999. 95.00 (*0-521-63122-X*) Cambridge U Pr.

Mladenov, D. Distributed Intelligence Systems: Methods & Applications. (IFAC Symposia Ser.: Vol. 8904). 372p. 1989. 180.00 (*0-08-035741-5*, Pergamon Pr) Elsevier.

Mladenova, Margarita, ed. Acta Palaeoslavica. (Illus.). 250p. 1998. 89.95 (*954-580-037-2*, Pub. by Heron Pr) Intl Scholars.

Mladenovic, Jeanette. Primary Care Secrets. 2nd rev. ed. LC 98 42098. (Secrets Ser.). (Illus.). 500p. 1998. text 38.00 (*1-56053-305-6*) Hanley & Belfus.

Mladenovic, Nenad, et al. Computerized Numerical Analysis: For Scientists & Engineers, Incl. 3.5 disk pkg. (Programming Tools for Scientists & Engineers Ser.). 600p. 1993. text 60.00 incl. disk (*0-07-911441-5*) McGraw.

Mladenovic, Petr. John Hus at the Council of Constance. Spinka, Matthew, tr. from CZE. & intro. by. LC 65-11019. (Records of Civilization: Sources & Studies: No. 73). 341p. reprint ed. pap. 105.80 (*0-608-18787-9*, 202983200065) Bks Demand.

Mladjenovic, M. A History of Low Energy Nuclear Physics, 1932-1960s. LC 98-23132. (Illus.). 436p. 1998. 150.00 (*0-7503-0472-3*) IOP Pub.

Mladjenovic, Milorad. History of Early Nuclear Physics: Radioactivity & Its Radiations, 1896-1931, Vol. 1. LC 92-32997. 260p. (C). 1992. text 61.00 (*981-02-0807-3*) World Scientific Pub.

***Mladjenovic, Paul.** Unofficial Guide to Picking Stocks. 2000. pap. 16.99 (*0-7645-6202-9*) IDG Bks.

Mladjenovic, Paul, ed. Zero-Cost Marketing. 85p. 1996. pap. 30.00 (*0-915344-58-0*) Todd Pubns.

Mlak, W. Hilbert Space & Operator Theory. (C). text 229.00 (*0-7923-1042-X*) Kluwer Academic.

Mlama, Penina M. Culture & Development: The Popular Theatre Approach. 219p. 1991. write for info. (*91-7106-317-X*, Pub. by Nordic Africa) Transaction Pubs.

Mlawer, Teresa, tr. see Adler, David.

Mlawer, Teresa, tr. see Adler, David A.

Mlawer, Teresa, tr. see Aliki.

Mlawer, Teresa, tr. see Benjamin, A. H.

Mlawer, Teresa, tr. see Bridwell, Norman.

Mlawer, Teresa, tr. see Brown, Marcia.

Mlawer, Teresa, tr. see Brown, Margaret Wise.

Mlawer, Teresa, tr. see De Paola, Tomie.

Mlawer, Teresa, tr. see Eastman, P. D.

Mlawer, Teresa, tr. see Estes, Eleanor.

Mlawer, Teresa, tr. see Ets, Marie H.

Mlawer, Teresa, tr. see Grunsell, Angela.

Mlawer, Teresa, tr. see Havill, Juanita.

Mlawer, Teresa, tr. see Hest, Amy.

Mlawer, Teresa, tr. see Hill, Eric.

Mlawer, Teresa, tr. see Hoff, Syd.

Mlawer, Teresa, tr. see Johnson, Crockett.

Mlawer, Teresa, tr. see Jonas, Ann.

Mlawer, Teresa, tr. see Kraus, Robert.

Mlawer, Teresa, tr. see Levy, Janice.

Mlawer, Teresa, tr. see McCunn, Ruthanne L.

Mlawer, Teresa, tr. see McGrath, Barbara B.

Mlawer, Teresa, tr. see Monjo, F. N.

Mlawer, Teresa, tr. see Most, Bernard.

Mlawer, Teresa, tr. see Nodar, Carmen S.

Mlawer, Teresa, tr. see Numeroff, Laura.

Mlawer, Teresa, tr. see Numeroff, Laura J.

Mlawer, Teresa, tr. see Sendak, Maurice.

Mlawer, Teresa, tr. see Simmons, Steven J.

Mlawer, Teresa, tr. see Slobodkina, Esphry.

Mlawer, Teresa, tr. see Slobodkina, Esphyr.

Mlawer, Teresa, tr. see Steig, William.

Mlay, Wilfred, jt. auth. see Ahmad, Abdel G.

MLB Staff. The Baseball Encyclopedia: The Complete & Definitive Record of Major League Baseball. 9th ed. 2857p. 1993. 55.00 (*0-02-579041-2*) Macmillan.

Mlejnek, H. P., jt. ed. see Argyris, J. H.

***Mleynek, Sherryll.** Knowledge & Mortality: Anagnorisis in Genesis & Narrative Fiction. (American University Studies III: Vol. 56). ix, 140p. (C). 1999. text 36.95 (*0-8204-2772-1*) P Lang Pubng.

M'Liadi, Schneur Z. Likkutei Amarim Tanya. LC 82-81577. (HEB.). 1010p. 1984. reprint ed. 10.00 (*0-8266-1000-5*) Kehot Pubn Soc.

— Likkutei Amarim Tanya: First Versions. LC 81-86392. (HEB.). 896p. 1981. 20.00 (*0-8266-5555-6*) Kehot Pubn Soc.

M'Liadi, Schneur Z. & Lavut, Avraham D. Siddur Torah Ohr Im Perush Shaar Hakollel. LC 86-149. (HEB.). 778p. 1987. reprint ed. 20.00 (*0-8266-5340-5*) Kehot Pubn Soc.

M'Liadi, Schneur Z., jt. auth. see Gansfried, Solomon.

Mlicki, Marek K., jt. ed. see Gasparski, Wojciech W.

MLIHRC Delegate Staff & Gerdtz, Daniel. Paper Protection - Human Rights Violation & the Mexican Criminal Justice System: A Report of the MLIHRC. 65p. (Orig.). (C). 1990. pap. 7.00 (*0-929293-07-X*) MN Advocates.

MLIHRC Delegate Staff, et al. Justice Suspended: The Failure of the Habeas Corpus System in Guatemala. 131p. (Orig.). (C). 1990. pap. 7.00 (*0-929293-08-8*) MN Advocates.

— Restavek - Child Domestic Labor in Haiti: A Report by the MLIHRC. 51p. (Orig.). 1990. pap. 7.00 (*0-929293-06-1*) MN Advocates.

Mlikoff, Irne. Hadji Bektach: Un Mythe et Ses Avatars Gense et Volution du Soufisme Populaire en Turquie. LC 97-35874. (Islamic History & Civilization Ser.: No. 20). 368p. 1998. 109.50 (*90-04-10954-4*) Brill Academic Pubs.

Mlikotin, Anthony M. Diary of a Troubled Mind. (Series in Avant-Garde Thoughts & the Arts). 165p. 18.00 (*0-9629448-2-3*) New Dimens Pr.

— Journey of a Soul: A Solitary Search for Meaning. (Series in Avant Garde Thoughts & the Arts). 213p. (Orig.). 1996. pap. 18.00 (*0-9629448-1-5*) New Dimens Pr.

— Nietzsche: The Mind's Greatest Storyteller. (Series in Avant-Garde Thoughts & the Arts). 303p. 1991. pap. write for info. (*0-9629448-0-7*) New Dimens Pr.

Mlinar, Angelika. Frauenrechte Als Menschenrechte. 254p. 1997. 51.95 (*3-631-31434-5*) P Lang Pubng.

Mlinar, Zdravko, ed. Globalization & Territorial Identities. 140p. 1992. 75.95 (*1-85628-426-3*, Pub. by Avebry) Ashgate Pub Co.

Mlinar, Zdravko, jt. auth. see Teune, Henry.

***Mlinko, Ange.** Matinees. LC 98-54199. 128p. 1999. pap. 13.00 (*1-58195-005-5*, Pub. by Zoland Bks) Consort Bk Sales.

M

MLJ. General Index & Table of Cases Reported, 1932-1988. 1991. 100.00 (*0-409-99595-9*, MICHIE) LEXIS Pub.

Mlodinow, Steven G. America's 100 Most Wanted Birds. LC 96-9547. (Illus.). 512p. 1996. pap. 24.95 (*1-56044-492-4*) Falcon Pub Inc.

Mlodozeniec, Juventyn M. I Knew St. Maximilian. 115p. 1982. pap. 2.95 (*0-911988-48-3*, 42139) AMI Pr.

Mlotek, Eleanor & Mlotek, Joseph. Songs of Generations: New Pearls of Yiddish Song. 301p. 1997. pap. 24.95 (*1-877909-65-3*) Jwsh Bk Ctr Wrkmns Cir.

Mlotek, Eleanor G. Mir Trogn A Gezang Yiddish Songbook: Favorite Yiddish Songs. 239p. 1977. pap. 19.95 (*0-685-05910-3*) Jwsh Bk Ctr Wrkmns Cir.

Mlotek, Eleanor G. & Mlotek, Joseph. Pearls of Yiddish Song: Favorite Folk, Art & Theatre Songs. 286p. (Orig.). 1988. 17.95 (*1-877909-64-5*) Jwsh Bk Ctr Wrkmns Cir.

Mlotek, Joseph. Yiddishe Kinder Alef. 3rd ed. (Illus.). 128p. 1985. 10.00 (*0-318-22116-0*) Jwsh Bk Ctr Wrkmns Cir.

Mlotek, Joseph & Olitsky, Matis. Yiddishe Kinder Beyz. (Illus.). 120p. 1975. pap. 10.00 (*0-318-22117-9*) Jwsh Bk Ctr Wrkmns Cir.

Mlotek, Joseph, jt. auth. see Mlotek, Eleanor.

Mlotek, Joseph, jt. auth. see Mlotek, Eleanor G.

Mlyn, Eric. The State, Society, & Limited Nuclear War. LC 94-10966. (SUNY Series in the Making of Foreign Policy). 241p. (C). 1995. text 59.50 (*0-7914-2347-6*); pap. text 19.95 (*0-7914-2348-4*) State U NY Pr.

Mlynarczyk. In Our Own Words. 1990. pap. text, teacher ed. 0.22 (*0-312-05719-9*) St Martin.

Mlynarczyk, Rebecca. Conversations of the Mind: The Uses of Journal Writing for Second Language Learners. LC 97-30927. 192p. 1998. write for info. (*0-8058-2317-4*); pap. write for info. (*0-8058-2318-2*) L Erlbaum Assocs.

Mlynarczyk, Rebecca & Haber, Steven. In Our Own Words: A Guide with Readings for Student Writers. 2nd ed. 325p. (C). 1996. pap. text 24.95 (*0-521-65764-4*) Cambridge U Pr.

— In Our Own Words: A Guide with Readings for Student Writers: Instructor's Manual. 2nd ed. 29p. (C). 1996. pap., teacher ed. 6.00 (*0-521-65763-6*) Cambridge U Pr.

Mlynarek, J., jt. ed. see Wolski, W.

Mlynek, D. M., jt. ed. see Patyra, M. J.

Mmagu, Ndubueze F. Universalisierung des Friedens Durch Entwicklung und Evangelisierung: Zur Kairologischen Bedeutung der Papstlichen Soziallehre Seit Leo XIII. (Europaische Hochschulschriften Ser.: Reihe 23, Bd. 578). (GER., Illus.). xx, 335p. 1996. 61.95 (*3-631-50003-3*) P Lang Pubng.

M'Mahon, Bernard. The American Gardener's Calendar: Adapted to the Climates & Seasons of the United States. 1977. reprint ed. 25.00 (*0-913728-25-X*) Theophrastus.

Mmari, Geoffrey, jt. ed. see Legum, Colin.

M.M.D.L.T. Staff. History of Hyder Shah, Alias Huder Ali Khan Bahadur: or New Memoirs. (C). 1996. 14.00 (*81-86142-92-4*, Pub. by Low Price) S Asia.

MN Advocates for Human Rights Staf. Domestic Violence in Nepal. 33p. 1998. pap. 5.00 (*0-929293-41-X*) MN Advocates.

MN. Advocates for Human Rights Staff. Another Violence Against Women: The Lack of Accountability in Haiti. 24p. (Orig.). 1995. pap. 5.00 (*0-929293-31-2*) MN Advocates.

— Codificando Represion: El Codige Penal Para el Estado de Chiapas. (SPA.). 10p. (Orig.). 1994. pap. 3.00 (*0-929293-24-X*) MN Advocates.

— Derechos Humanos y Poder Judicial en Mexico. (SPA.). 34p. 1995. pap. 5.00 (*0-614-16437-0*) MN Advocates.

— Domestic Violence in Macedonia. 34p. 1998. pap. 5.00 (*0-929293-40-1*) MN Advocates.

— Harassment of Human Rights Defenders in Mexico. 12p. (Orig.). 1994. pap. 3.00 (*0-929293-20-7*) MN Advocates.

— Massacre in Mexico: Killings & Cover-Up in the State of Guerrero. 33p. (Orig.). 1995. pap. 5.00 (*0-929293-30-4*) MN Advocates.

— The Mexican Coordination of National Public Security: A Discussion of Legal & Human Rights Issues. 9p. (Orig.). 1994. pap. 3.00 (*0-929293-22-3*) MN Advocates.

— The Minnesota Plan: Recommendations for Preventing Gross Human Rights Violations in Kosovo. 8p. (Orig.). 1993. pap. 5.00 (*0-614-16435-4*) MN Advocates.

— No One Can Hear Us: Somali Refugees in Kenya. 57p. (Orig.). 1992. pap. 5.00 (*0-614-16436-2*) MN Advocates.

— Press Restrictions in Albania. 23p. (Orig.). 1995. pap. 7.50 (*0-929293-29-0*) MN Advocates.

— Stifling Human Rights Advocacy in Mexico: The Censure of Brigadier General Jose Francisco Gallardo Rodriguez. 11p. (Orig.). 1994. pap. 3.00 (*0-929293-19-3*) MN Advocates.

— Tunisia: Human Rights Crisis of 1987. (MLIHRC Report Ser.). 70p. (Orig.). (C). 1988. pap. 7.00 (*0-929293-02-9*) MN Advocates.

MN State Catholic Daughters of the Americas Member. Potluck, 1923-1998. (Illus.). 518p. 1996. spiral bd. 15.00 (*0-9653975-0-5*) MN Catholic Dghtrs.

Mnarchuk, G. I. Mathematical Models in Immunology. (Illus.). xxv, 351p. 1983. pap. 89.00 (*0-387-90901-X*) Spr-Verlag.

***Mnaya, Nina.** Sincerely, Silia. 2000. pap. 14.95 (*0-9675685-0-1*) Black Eye.

Mncwabe, Mandla P. Post-Apartheid Education: Towards Non-Racial, Unitary & Democratic Socialisation in the New South Africa. 276p. (C). 1993. lib. bdg. 54.00 (*0-8191-8969-3*) U Pr of Amer.

Mnemozina. Sobranie Socinenij v Stichach i Proze, 4 bde. in 1. (GER.). 782p. 1986. reprint ed. write for info. (*3-487-07675-6*) G Olms Pubs.

Mnookin, Robert H. Child, Family & State: Cases & Materials on Children & the Law. 857p. 1978. 32.00 (*0-316-57650-6*, Aspen Law & Bus) Aspen Pub.

— Children & the Law. 2nd ed. 1989. 48.00 (*0-316-57651-4*, Aspen Law & Bus) Aspen Pub.

— Children & the Law. 3rd ed. 1280p. 1995. 55.00 (*0-316-57649-2*, Aspen Law & Bus) Aspen Pub.

— In the Interest of Children: Advocacy, Law Reform & Public Policy. LC 84-24635. 572p. 1985. pap. text 20.00 (*0-7167-1627-5*) W H Freeman.

— In the Interests of Children: Advocacy, Law Reform, & Public Policy. 2nd ed. 572p. (C). 1996. reprint ed. pap. 20.00 (*0-614-16419-2*) Prog Negot HLS.

Mnookin, Robert H. & Burt, Robert A. In the Interest of Children: Advocacy, Law Reform & Public Policy. LC 96-19837. 1996. pap. write for info. (*1-880711-07-9*, Pon Bks) Prog Negot HLS.

***Mnookin, Robert H. & Weisberg, D. Kelly.** Child, Family & State: Problems & Materials on Children & the Law. 4th ed. LC 99-56741. 2000. boxed set 64.00 (*0-7355-1228-0*) Panel Pubs.

***Mnookin, Robert H., et al.** Beyond Winning: Negotiating to Create Value in Deals & Disputes. LC 00-39787. (Illus.). 368p. 2000. pap. 28.00 (*0-674-00335-7*) HUP.

Mnookin, Robert H., jt. auth. see Maccoby, Eleanor E.

Mnookin, Wendy. Guenever Speaks. 50p. 1991. pap. 10.00 (*0-9630918-0-8*) Round Table.

— To Get Here. (American Poets Continuum Ser.: No. 54). 81p. 1999. pap. 12.50 (*1-880238-73-X*, Pub. by BOA Edns) Consort Bk Sales.

Mnrtin, ed. Scholia in Aratum. (GRE.). 1974. 175.00 (*3-519-01047-X*, T1047, Pub. by B G Teubner) U of Mich Pr.

MNummedal, Dag, ed. Cretaceous Shelf Sandstones & Shelf Depositional Sequences, Western Interior Basin, Utah & New Mexico, No. T119. (IGC Field Trip Guidebooks Ser.). 96p. 1989. 21.00 (*0-87590-629-X*) Am Geophysical.

Mnyampala, Mathias E. The Gogo: History, Customs, & Traditions. Maddox, Gregory H., ed. & tr. by. from SWA. LC 94-33630. (Sources & Studies in World History). (Illus.). 163p. (C). (gr. 13). 1995. 58.95 (*1-56324-405-5*) M E Sharpe.

— The Gogo: History, Customs, & Traditions. Mddox, Gregory H., ed. & tr. by. from SWA. LC 94-33630. (Sources & Studies in World History). (Illus.). 163p. (C). (gr. 13). 1995. pap. 30.95 (*1-56324-406-3*) M E Sharpe.

Mo, B. X., jt. ed. see Wang, X. Y.

Mo, J. S. Butterworth's Student Companions - International Commercial Law. 100p. 1995. pap. write for info. (*0-409-31071-9*, MICHIE) LEXIS Pub.

Mo, John, jt. auth. see Wang, Kuei-kuo.

Mo, Jongryn. Let's Wait for Korea to Decide: An Essay on the Hoover Conference "A New Economic Relationship: the United States & Korea" LC 96-4419. (Essays in Public Policy Ser.: No. 66). 15p. (Orig.). 1996. pap. 5.00 (*0-8179-5712-X*) Hoover Inst Pr.

Mo, Jongryn & Myers, Ramon H., eds. Shaping a New Economic Relationship: The Republic of Korea & the United States. LC 93-24019. (Publication Ser.: No. 417). 202p. 1993. pap. 19.95 (*0-8179-9252-9*); text 32.95 (*0-8179-9251-0*) Hoover Inst Pr.

Mo, Jongryn, jt. auth. see Bueno de Mesquita, Bruce.

Mo, Jongryn, jt. ed. see Henriksen, Thomas H.

Mo, Jongryn, jt. ed. see Moon, Chung-In.

***Mo, Joseph S.** Tales from the Old Kingdom. (Illus.). 196p. 1999. 23.95 (*1-898942-18-8*) Weatherhill.

Mo Tzu. Mo Tzu: Basic Writings. Watson, Burton, tr. LC 63-20339. (Translations from the Oriental Classics Ser.). 140p. (Orig.). 1963. pap. text 17.00 (*0-231-08608-3*) Col U Pr.

Mo, Y. L. Dynamic Behavior of Concrete Structures. LC 94-17073. (Developments in Civil Engineering Ser.: Vol. 44). 424p. 1994. 191.50 (*0-444-81885-5*) Elsevier.

Mo Yen, pseud. Story about Cat. (CHI.). 60p. pap. 9.95 (*7-80005-256-7*, Pub. by China Intl Bk) Distribks Inc.

Moab, Ranne, ed. see Grossman, Leonid P.

Moacanin, Radmila. Jung's Psychology & Tibetan Buddhism: Western & Eastern Paths to the Heart. LC 88-51647. (East-West Book - Grey Ser.). 144p. 1994. pap. 12.95 (*0-86171-042-8*) Wisdom MA.

Moad, Graeme & Solomon, David H. The Chemistry of Free Radical Polymerization. 380p. 1995. write for info. (*0-08-042078-8*, Pergamon Pr); pap. write for info. (*0-08-042079-6*, Pergamon Pr) Elsevier.

Moaddel, Mansoor. Class, Politics, & Ideology in the Iranian Revolution. 300p. 1992. text 46.00 (*0-231-07866-8*) Col U Pr.

Moag, Rodney F. Malayalam: A University Course & Reference Grammar. 3rd rev. ed. 625p. 1994. pap. text 33.60 (*0-89148-046-3*) Ctr S&SE Asian.

Moak, Allen. A Big City ABC. 32p. (J). (ps up). 1989. pap. 6.95 (*0-88776-238-7*) Tundra Bks.

Moak, D. Michael, jt. auth. see Spear, Robert K.

Moak, Jefferson M., jt. ed. see Lloyd, Mark F.

Moak, Lennox L. Municipal Bonds: Planning, Sale, & Administration. (Debt Administration Ser.). (Illus.). 400p. 37.00 (*0-686-84287-1*) Municipal.

Moak, Lennox L. & Cowan, Frank, Jr. Manual of Suggested Practice for Administration of Local Sales & Use Taxes. LC 61-18038. (Illus.). 311p. 1961. 8.00 (*0-317-34948-1*) Municipal.

Moak, Lennox L. & Killian, Kathryn W. Operating Budget Manual. LC 64-12365. (Illus.). 347p. 1963. 12.00 (*0-686-84284-7*) Municipal.

Moak, Sheila, jt. auth. see Fulcher, Norman.

***Moakley, Maureen & Cornwell, Elmer.** Rhode Island Politics & Government. (Politics & Governments of the American States Ser.). (Illus.). 2001. text 70.00 (*0-8032-3218-7*); pap. text 29.95 (*0-8032-8270-2*, Bison Books) U of Nebr Pr.

Moal, Le, see Le Moal.

Moalic, Joseph. Avec Fanon. (FRE.). 320p. 1995. pap. 59.95 (*2-86808-090-1*) Intl Scholars.

Moallem, Minoo, jt. auth. see Krooth, Richard.

Moan. Structural Dynamics: Eurodyn 93, Vol. 1. 650p. 1993. 129.00 (*90-5410-337-X*) Ashgate Pub Co.

— Structural Dynamics: Eurodyn 93, Vol. 2. 650p. 1993. 129.00 (*90-5410-338-8*) Ashgate Pub Co.

Moan. 13th International Ship & Offshore Structures Congress (ISEC 97) 1997. 280.00 (*0-08-042829-0*, Pergamon Pr) Elsevier.

***Moan, Gerry D. & Sabol, George P., eds.** Zirconium in the Nuclear Industry: 12th International Symposium. (Illus.). 2000. text 345.00 (*0-8031-2499-6*, STP1354) ASTM.

Moanfeldt, Peter. Introduction to Autolisp. LC 96-30974. 205p. 1996. pap. text 48.00 (*0-13-206624-6*) P-H.

Moar, Moshe & Lane, Jan-Erik, eds. Comparative Public Administration Vols. I & II: Analytical Frameworks & Critique, Comparative Research. LC 98-34350. (International Library of Politics & Comparative Government Ser.). 1050p. 1999. text 333.95 (*1-84014-072-0*) Ashgate Pub Co.

Moar, N. T. Pollen Grains of New Zealand Dicotyledonous Plants. 1993. 60.00 (*0-478-04500-X*, Pub. by Manaaki Whenua) Balogh.

Moat, Albert G. & Foster, John W. Microbial Physiology. LC 95-15648. 608p. 1995. pap. 86.50 (*0-471-01452-4*) Wiley.

— Microbial Physiology. 3rd ed. LC 95-15648. 608p. 1995. 219.95 (*0-471-01295-5*) Wiley.

Moat, John. Firewater & the Miraculous Mandarin. 1990. pap. 14.95 (*1-870612-70-1*, Pub. by Enitha Pr) Dufour.

— Skeleton Key. 68p. 1997. 45.00 (*0-930126-53-X*) Typographeum.

— Three Stories: Snow, Smoke, The Missing Piece. (Illus.). 60p. 1995. 40.00 (*0-930126-47-5*) Typographeum.

Moates, Marianne M. Truman Capote's Southern Years: Stories from a Monroeville Cousin. LC 95-23384. (Illus.). 256p. (C). 1996. reprint ed. pap. 19.95 (*0-8173-0815-6*) U of Ala Pr.

Moats, Lillian. The Gate of Dreams. 100p. (J). 1996. 21.95 (*0-9636492-0-5*, Cranbrook Pr); pap. 9.95 (*963-649-213-1*, Cranbrook Pr) Cranbrook Educ.

Moats, Lillian. The Gate of Dreams. 2nd ed. (Illus.). 100p. 1996. pap. 9.95 (*0-9636492-1-3*) Three Arts. The Gate of Dreams, second edition, by Lillian Somersaulter Moats, trade paperback, 100 pages, 80 illustrations, $9.95. ISBN: 0963649213 Cranbrook Press c/o Three Arts Press "...an excellent collection for family read-alouds, for classroom use...(Denise Perry Donavin, Editor, American Library Association Best of the Best for Children, Random House). The Gate of Dreams, illustrated profusely in silhouette, is reminiscent of classic fairy tale editions. Yet, the three stories, which appeal to adults as well as children, are entirely new. Indeed, it was the revered fairy tale scholar Bruno Bettelheim who first suggested the publication of the fairy stories of Lillian Somersaulter Moats. "Lillian Somersaulter Moats has created a family keepsake volume by combining stark silhouettes with a lyrical text & unforgettable characters. Moats' writing has an old-fashioned touch to it, & in these tales, good invariably triumphs over evil. But it doesn't happen automatically & readers will revel in the struggle of the heroes & heroines to find their way in a world that often seems overwhelmed by darkness." (Scripps-Howard News Service: 12/08/93). "The stories have a pleasing old-fashioned mood, which is accented by the exquisite illustrations." (School Library Journal: 12/93). South Carolina Children's Book Awards list, 1995. Ingram, Baker & Taylor or Bookmaster's Distribution Services, 800-247-6553. Fax: 419-281-6883. e-mail: order@bookmaster.com.
Publisher Paid Annotation.

Moats, Lillian. Legacy of Shadows. LC 98-96937. (Illus.). 173p. 1999. 18.00 (*0-9669576-0-1*) Three Arts. Legacy of Shadows, Lillian Moats, 192 pages. Hardcover. $18.00. ISBN: 0966957601 Robert Coles: "This book will hold its readers close & tight, will teach them its remarkable, affecting & important lesson: that experiences live & last over a family's generations as memories that shape hearts & minds." Booklist: "Moats...has written a poetic, fictionalized memoir that recounts the most bewildering & frightening of experiences, the onslaught of mental illness....Moats' sequencing of scenes & gift for metaphor & distillation render her psychologically acute narrative as supple as film without sacrificing the beauty unique to language." The Bloomsbury Review: " This is a beautiful, brief book in which the reader is not told about the lives or complexes that 'funneled' into her own, but rather is shown, subtly, how grief, guilt & unassuageable fear can find & wind their way, unintentionally, through the psyches & emotions of three generations....Its genre, a novel written as if a journal. Its pace, compelling. Its images & descriptions, haunting. Its story human.....Lillian Moats is...a brave & generous woman." Kathleen McCrone, PhD., University of Windsor: Legacy of Shadows is a beautiful & profoundly moving tapestry of crisis & connection, forgiveness & healing....likely to be of immense benefit to more readers that (Moats) would ever have imagined. Ingram, Baker & Taylor or Bookmasters Distribution Services: Phone: (800) 247-6553 Fax: (419) 281-6883 E-mail: order@bookmaster.com
Publisher Paid Annotation.

Moats, Louisa C. Spelling: Development, Disabilities & Instruction. LC 95-44438. (Orig.). 1995. pap. 21.50 (*0-912752-40-8*) York Pr.

Moats, Louisa C., jt. auth. see Bailet, Laura L.

Moats, Louisa C., jt. auth. see Greene, Jane F.

Moats, Louisa C., jt. auth. see Hall, Susan L.

Moats, Tamara, ed. Breaking Down the Boundaries: Artists & Museums. LC 89-24501. (Illus.). 32p. 1989. pap. 6.95 (*0-935558-24-1*) Henry Art.

Moats, William A., ed. Agricultural Uses of Antibiotics. LC 86-20614. (ACS Symposium Ser.: No. 320). (Illus.). ix, 200p. 1986. 43.95 (*0-8412-0996-0*) Am Chemical.

— Agricultural Uses of Antibiotics. LC 86-20614. (ACS Symposium Ser.: Vol. 320). 200p. 1986. reprint ed. pap. 62.00 (*0-608-03524-6*, 206424300008) Bks Demand.

Moats, William A. & Medina, Marjorie B., eds. Veterinary Drug Residues: Food Safety, Vol. 636. LC 96-26216. (Symposium Ser.: No. 636). (Illus.). 200p. 1996. text 79.95 (*0-8412-3419-1*, Pub. by Am Chemical) OUP.

Moatti, Claude. The Search for Ancient Rome. Zielonka, Anthony, tr. (Discoveries Ser.). (Illus.). 208p. 1993. pap. 12.95 (*0-8109-2839-6*, Pub. by Abrams) Time Warner.

Moatti, Claude, jt. auth. see Bombarde, Odile.

***Moatti, J. P.** Aids in Europe. LC 99-48728. (Social Aspects of Aids Ser.). 2000. pap. write for info. (*1-85728-508-5*) Taylor & Francis.

Moaveni. Finite Element Analysis. LC 98-31163. 512p. 1999. 100.00 (*0-13-785098-0*, Pub. by P-H) S&S Trade.

Moavenzadeh, Fred. The Global Construction & the Environment & the Construction Industry: Strategies & Opportunities. 293p. 1994. 90.00 (*0-471-01289-0*) Wiley.

Moavenzadeh, Fred, ed. Concise Encyclopedia of Building & Construction Materials. (Advances in Materials Science & Engineering Ser.: No. 4). (Illus.). 698p. 1990. 215.00 (*0-08-034728-2*, Pergamon Pr) Elsevier.

— Concise Encyclopedia of Building & Construction Materials. (Advances in Materials Science & Engineering Ser.). 698p. 1990. 225.00 (*0-262-13248-6*) MIT Pr.

Moawad, Bob. Whatever It Takes: A Journey into the Heart of Human Achievement Thoughts to Inspire & Celebrate Your Commitment to Excellence. (Gift of Inspiration Ser.). 128p. 1996. 12.95 (*0-9640178-3-0*) Compendium Inc.

Moawad, Karen & Costain, Lynne R. New Manual for Managing Dental Office Personnel: A Management Tool for Structuring & Administering Personnel Policies in the Dental Practice. 368p. 1992. 79.95 (*0-87814-372-6*, D4293) PennWell Bks.

Moawad, Karen & Hummingbird Associates Staff. Essence of Nectar, Vol. 1. 1995. pap. write for info. (*0-9647903-0-0*) Hummingbrd Assocs.

Moawad, Karen, et al. The Business of Orthodontics: Management & Administration of Your Orthodontic Practice. 550p. 1991. pap. write for info. (*0-9631446-0-X*) Hummingbrd WA.

Moawad, Karen, jt. auth. see Costain, Lynne R.

Moayyad, Heshmat, intro. Once a Dewdrop: Essays on the Poetry of Parvin E'Tesami. LC 94-13077. (Bibliotheca Iranica Ser.: No. 2). (Illus.). 282p. 1994. lib. bdg. 19.95 (*1-56859-016-4*) Mazda Pubs.

Moayyad, Heshmat, et al. A Nightingale's Lament: Selections from the Poems & Fables of Parvin Etesami (1907-41) LC 84-60071. (Iran-e NO Literary Collection Ser.). 289p. 1985. pap. 11.95 (*0-939214-20-2*) Mazda Pubs.

Moayyad, Heshmat, ed. see Alavi, Bozorg, et al.

Moayyad, Heshmat, tr. see Jamalzada, Mohammad A.

Moazzami, Bakhtiar, jt. auth. see Gupta, Kanhaya L.

Mobarak, Hamed, jt. auth. see Guigale, Marcelo M.

Mobarg, Mats. English "Standard" Pronounciations: A Study of Attitudes. (Gothenburg Studies in English: No. 62). 380p. (Orig.). 1989. pap. 79.50 (*91-7346-214-4*) Coronet Bks.

Mobashery, S., ed. Resolving the Antibiotic Paradox: Progress in Understanding Drug Resistance & Development of New Antibiotics. LC 98-46308. (Advances in Experimental Medicine & Biology Ser.: 456). (Illus.). 294p. (C). 1999. text 97.50 (*0-306-46039-4*, Kluwer Plenum) Kluwer Academic.

Mobasser, Nilou, tr. see Naraghi, Ehsan.

Mobberley, David G. Basic Bible Commentary Vol. 10: Psalms. Deming, Lynne M., ed. LC 94-10965. 160p. (Orig.). 1994. pap. 5.95 (*0-687-02629-6*) Abingdon.

Mobberly, Martin. Astronomical Equipment for Amateurs, 1. Moore, P., ed. LC 98-7025. (Practical Astronomy Ser.). xiii, 256p. 1998. pap. 39.95 (*1-85233-019-8*) Spr-Verlag.

Mobbs, A. J. The Complete Book of Australian Finches. 256p. 2000. 23.95 (*0-7938-0295-4*, TS240) TFH Pubns.

Mobbs, Charles V. & Hof, Patrick R., eds. Functional Endocrinology of Aging, No. 29. LC 98-38917. (Interdisciplinary Topics in Gerontology Ser.: Vol. 29 (1998)). (Illus.). viii, 246p. 1998. 149.75 (*3-8055-6726-X*) S Karger.

An Asterisk (*) at the beginning of an entry indicates that the title is appearing for the first time.

Mobbs, Frank. Beyond Its Authority: The Magisterium & Matters of Natural Law. 357p. 1997. pap. 19.95 (*0-85574-406-5*, Pub. by E J Dwyer) Morehouse Pub.

Mobbs, Michael. Sustainable House: Living for Our Future. (Illus.). 188p. 1999. pap. 45.00 (*1-877133-62-0*) Univ Otago Pr.

Mobbs, S. D. & King, J. C., eds. Waves & Turbulence in Stably Stratified Flows. LC 92-32076. (Institute of Mathematics & Its Applications Conference Series, New Ser.: New Series 40). (Illus.). 480p. (C). 1993. text 130.00 (*0-19-853661-5*, Clarendon Pr) OUP.

Moberg. A. C. & D. C. Motor Control. 1991. pap. text. write for info. (*0-7730-5190-2*) Addison-Wes.

Moberg, Carol L., ed. see Abraham, Edward P., et al.

Moberg, David O. Wholistic Christianity. fac. ed. LC 84-29216. 243p. 1985. pap. 75.40 (*0-7837-7348-X*, 204730100007) Bks Demand.

Moberg, David O., jt. auth. see Greer, Joanne.

Moberg, David O., jt. ed. see Lynn, Monty L.

***Moberg, G. & Mench, J. A., eds.** The Biology of Animal Stress: Basic Principles & Implications for Animal Welfare. LC 99-58357. (CABI Publishing Ser.). 320p. 1999. text 90.00 (*0-85199-359-1*) OUP.

Moberg, Gary P., ed. Animal Stress. (American Physiological Society Book). (Illus.). 332p. 1988. text 42.50 (*0-19-520696-7*) OUP.

Moberg, Gerald A. AC & DC Motor Control. LC 86-11074. 448p. 1987. text 42.50 (*0-471-83700-8*) P-H.

Moberg, Goran G. Writing in Groups: New Techniques for Good Writing Without Drills. 4th ed. 200p. 1994. spiral bd. 21.95 (*0-8403-9342-3*) Kendall-Hunt.

— Writing on Computers in English Composition. 2nd ed. 160p. (Orig.). 1990. spiral bd. 21.95 (*0-8403-5753-2*) Kendall-Hunt.

Moberg, John, jt. auth. see Lee, Kaiman.

Moberg, Kent Davis. The Magic of Our Universe: Beyond the Facts. 359p. 1999. pap. 14.95 (*0-9663797-2-1*) Camelot Prodns.

Moberg, L. Ernest, et al. The History of Trinity Episcopal Church, Folsom, California 1856-1994. 2nd rev. ed. Davidson, Diane, ed. LC 97-191286. (Illus.). 136p. (Orig.). 1996. pap. 12.50 (*0-9650595-0-2*) Trnty Epscpl CA.

Moberg, Mark. Citrus, Strategy, & Class: The Politics of Development in Southern Belize. LC 91-45123. (Illus.). 228p. 1992. text 29.95 (*0-87745-367-5*) U of Iowa Pr.

— Myths of Ethnicity & Nation: Immigration, Work, & Identity in the Belize Banana Industry. LC 96-51261. (Illus.). 256p. 1997. 38.00 (*0-87049-970-X*) U of Tenn Pr.

Moberg, Randy. TNT Teaching: Over 200 Dynamite Ways to Make Your Classroom Come Alive. Espeland, Pamela, ed. LC 93-37991. (Free Spirited Classroom Ser.). (Illus.). 160p. (Orig.). 1994. pap. 19.95 (*0-915793-64-4*) Free Spirit Pub.

Moberg, Roland, jt. ed. see Lundqvist, Nils.

Moberg, Ulf T., ed. Gunnar Ekelof: Dadaist-Constructivist. (Illus.). 60p. 1987. pap. 42.50 (*0-317-65671-6*) Coronet Bks.

Moberg, V. When I Was a Child. 1976. 26.95 (*0-8488-0302-7*) Amereon Ltd.

Moberg, Vilhelm. Emigrants. 1984. mass mkt. 3.62 (*0-446-38115-2*, Pub. by Warner Bks) Little.

— The Emigrants. LC 95-15848. (Emigrant Novels Ser.: Bk. 1). xxxiii, 366p. 1995. reprint ed. pap. 15.95 (*0-87351-319-3*, Borealis Book) Minn Hist.

— Emigrants. 1999. reprint ed. lib. bdg. 37.95 (*1-56849-312-6*) Buccaneer Bks.

— Last Letter. 1984. mass mkt. 3.63 (*0-446-38118-7*, Pub. by Warner Bks) Little.

— The Last Letter Home. LC 95-15845. (Emigrant Novels Ser.: Bk. 4). xxxii, 230p. 1995. reprint ed. pap. 15.95 (*0-87351-322-3*, Borealis Book) Minn Hist.

— The Settlers. 1984. mass mkt. 3.63 (*0-446-38117-9*, Pub. by Warner Bks) Little.

— The Settlers. LC 95-15948. (Emigrant Novels Ser.: Bk. 3). xxix, 399p. 1995. reprint ed. pap. 15.95 (*0-87351-321-5*, Borealis Book) Minn Hist.

— A Time on Earth. 1994. reprint ed. lib. bdg. 29.95 (*1-56849-314-2*) Buccaneer Bks.

— Unto a Good Land. 1984. mass mkt. 3.62 (*0-446-38116-0*, Pub. by Warner Bks) Little.

— Unto a Good Land. 1994. reprint ed. lib. bdg. 29.95 (*1-56849-313-4*) Buccaneer Bks.

— Unto a Good Land. LC 95-15847. (Emigrant Novels Ser.: Bk. 2). xxvii, 372p. 1995. reprint ed. pap. 15.95 (*0-87351-320-7*, Borealis Book) Minn Hist.

Moberly, Elizabeth R. Homosexuality: A New Christian Ethic. (Illus.). 1997. pap. text 9.95 (*0-227-67850-8*, J Clarke-Parkwest) Parkwest Pubns.

— Psychogenesis: The Early Development of Gender Identity. 120p. 1983. 29.95 (*0-7100-9271-7*, Routledge Thoemms) Routledge.

— The Psychology of Self & Other. 112p. 1985. 18.95 (*0-422-79740-5*, 9417, Pub. by Tavistock) Routldge.

Moberly, F. J. Campaign in Mesopotamia, 1914-1918, Vol. I. (Great War Ser.: Vol. 59). (Illus.). 412p. 1997. reprint ed. 49.95 (*0-89839-268-3*) Battery Pr.

— Military Operations, Togoland & the Cameroons, 1918, Vol. III. (Great War Ser.: No. 44). (Illus.). 584p. 1995. reprint ed. 69.95 (*0-89839-235-7*) Battery Pr.

Moberly, Jonathan. Athens. LC 99-231079. (Architecture Guides Ser.). (Illus.). 320p. 1998. pap. 5.95 (*3-8290-0470-2*, 520548) Konemann.

— Hong Kong. (Architecture Guides Ser.). (Illus.). 320p. 1998. pap. 5.95 (*3-8290-0471-0*, 520207) Konemann.

— Milan. (Architecture Guides Ser.). (Illus.). 320p. 1998. pap. 5.95 (*3-8290-0472-9*, 520550) Konemann.

— Moscow. (Architecture Guides Ser.). (Illus.). 320p. 1998. pap. 5.95 (*3-8290-0474-5*, 520211) Konemann.

— South Africa. (Architecture Guides Ser.). (Illus.). 320p. 1998. pap. 5.95 (*3-8290-0476-1*, 520551) Konemann.

***Moberly, Margaret.** Firebirde. LC 98-45967. 1999. pap. text 12.99 (*0-88419-589-9*) Creation House.

Moberly, R. W. Genesis, 12-50. (Old Testament Guides Ser.: Vol. 2). 112p. 1992. pap. 12.50 (*1-85075-371-7*, Pub. by Sheffield Acad) CUP Services.

Moberly, R. W. L. At the Mountain of God: Story & Theology in Exodus 32-34. (JSOT Supplement Ser.: Vol. 22). 258p. 1983. 75.00 (*0-905774-44-2*, Pub. by Sheffield Acad); pap. 23.95 (*0-905774-45-0*, Pub. by Sheffield Acad) CUP Services.

***Moberly, R. W. L.** The Bible, Theology & Faith: A Study of Abraham & Jesus. LC 99-56885. (Cambridge Studies in Christian Doctrine: Vol. 5). 272p. 2000. pap. write for info. (*0-521-78646-0*) Cambridge U Pr.

— The Bible, Theology & Faith: A Study of Abraham & Jesus. LC 99-56885. (Cambridge Studies in Christian Doctrine: Vol. 5). 272p. (C). 2000. write for info. (*0-521-77222-2*) Cambridge U Pr.

Moberly, William. Partnership Management. 250p. (C). 1983. 110.00 (*0-906322-28-6*, Pub. by Blackstone Pr) St Mut.

Mobery, Marilyne V., et al. The Volcanic Eruptions of El Malpais: Volcanic History & Formations of El Malpais National Monument. LC 98-51880. 1999. pap. 11.95 (*1-58096-007-3*) Ancient City Pr.

Mobi. Mianping Introduction to Salin. LC 97-207860. 1997. text 234.00 (*0-7923-4098-1*) Kluwer Academic.

Mobil Oil Corporation Staff. Mobil Highway Atlas 1994. 1993. pap. 4.95 (*0-671-86427-0*, P-H Travel) Prntice Hall Bks.

— Mobil Pocket Atlas, 1994. 1993. pap. 2.50 (*0-671-79987-8*, P-H Travel) Prntice Hall Bks.

— Mobil Road Atlas Trip Planning Guide 1994. 1993. pap. 7.95 (*0-671-79986-X*, P-H Travel) Prntice Hall Bks.

***Mobil Travel Guides Staff.** California & the West 2000. (Mobil Travel Guides Ser.). 2000. pap. 16.95 (*0-7853-4157-9*) Pubns Intl Ltd.

— Great Lakes 2000. (Mobil Travel Guides Ser.). 2000. pap. 16.95 (*0-7853-4158-7*) Pubns Intl Ltd.

— Mid-Atlantic 2000. (Mobil Travel Guides Ser.). 2000. pap. 16.95 (*0-7853-4156-0*) Pubns Intl Ltd.

— Northeast 2000. (Mobil Travel Guides Ser.). 2000. pap. 16.95 (*0-7853-4155-2*) Pubns Intl Ltd.

— Northwest & Great Plains. (Mobil Travel Guides Ser.). 2000. pap. 16.95 (*0-7853-4154-4*) Pubns Intl Ltd.

— Southeast. (Mobil Travel Guides Ser.). 2000. pap. 16.95 (*0-7853-4153-6*) Pubns Intl Ltd.

— Southwest & South Central. (Mobil Travel Guides Ser.). 2000. pap. 16.95 (*0-7853-4152-8*) Pubns Intl Ltd.

***Mobile Botanical Gardens South Alabama Botanical & Horticultural Society Staff.** A Collection of Recipes for Home & Garden. (Illus.). 376p. 1999. spiral bd. 18.00 (*1-56383-097-3*) G & R Pub.

Mobile Junior League Publications Staff. Bay Tables: A Collection of Recipes from the Junior League of Mobile. (Illus.). 255p. 1998. 24.95 (*0-9603054-3-2*) Mobile Jr League Pubns.

Mobile Museum of Art Staff & Huntsville Museum of Art Staff. Alabama Impact: Contemporary Artists with Alabama Ties. (Illus.). 84p. (Orig.). (YA). (gr. 9 up). 1995. pap. text 20.00 (*1-885820-01-1*) Huntsville.

Mobile Source Division Staff, compiled by. California Air Resources Board Technical Staff Reports: 1994 Low-Emission Vehicle & Zero-Emission Vehicle Program Review & Zero-Emission Vehicle Update Technical Support Document. (Electric Vehicle Information Ser.: Vol. 3, Pts. A & B). 215p. 1996. pap. 105.00 (*0-89934-243-4*, BT029); lib. bdg. 155.00 (*0-89934-244-2*, BT929) Bus Tech Bks.

***Mobilia, Wendy & Gordon, Rick.** Education by Design Coaching Kit, Level 1. (Illus.). 173p. 1998. pap. 30.00 (*1-881245-08-X*) Antioch New Eng.

— Education by Design Coaching Kit, Level 2. (Illus.). 143p. 1997. pap. 30.00 (*1-881245-10-1*) Antioch New Eng.

Mobilia, Wendy & Gordon, Rick. Tools. (Illus.). 85p. 1998. 20.00 (*1-881245-09-8*) Antioch New Eng.

Mobilia, Wendy, et al. Education by Design K-3 Coaching Kit: Support for Educators of the Primary Grades. (Illus.). 59p. 1999. pap. 20.00 (*1-881245-11-X*) Antioch New Eng.

Mobilio, Albert. The Geographics. (House of Outside Ser.: Vol. 2). 83p. 1995. pap. 10.00 (*0-9638433-2-X*) Hard Pr MA.

Mobility International U. S. A. Staff. Rights & Responsibilities: A Guide to the Americans with Disabilities Act (ADA) for Exchange Organizations & Participants. Cheshire, Julie A., ed. 1999. pap. write for info. (*1-880034-46-8*) Mobility Intl.

Mobility International U. S. A. Staff & Natl Clearinghouse on Disability & Exch. Staff. Building Bridges: Including People with Disabilities in International Programs. Cheshire, Julie A., ed. 1998. pap. 20.00 (*1-880034-36-0*) Mobility Intl.

***Mobini-Kesheh, Natalie.** The Hadrami Awakening: Community & Identity in the Netherlands East Indies. (Studies on Southeast Asia: Vol. 28). (Illus.). 174p. 1999. pap. 15.00 (*0-87727-727-3*) Cornell SE Asia.

Mobium Corporation Staff, jt. auth. see National Park Service Staff.

Mobium Corporation Staff, ed. see McCausland, Clare.

Mobius, August F. Der Barycentrische Calcul, ein Neues Hulfsmittel Zur Analytischen Behandlung der Geometrie. (GER.). 1997. reprint ed. 118.00 (*3-487-06002-7*) G Olms Pubs.

Mobius, D. & Miller, Reinhard. Drops & Bubbles in Interfacial Research. LC 97-48539. (Studies in Interface Science). 1997. 339.50 (*0-444-82894-X*) Elsevier.

— Proteins at Liquid Interfaces. LC 98-3512. (Studies in Interface Science). 1998. 258.50 (*0-444-82944-X*) Elsevier.

Mobius, Mark. The Investor's Guide to Emerging Markets: Financial Times Series. 192p. 1994. text 45.00 (*0-7863-0320-4*, Irwn Prfssnl) McGraw-Hill Prof.

— Mobius on Emerging Markets. 2nd ed. 256p. 1996. 35.00 (*0-273-62284-6*) F T P-H.

***Mobius, Mark, frwd.** Alternative Investment. 150p. 1999. pap. 145.00 (*962-7762-58-X*) ISI Publications.

***Mobius, Mark & Fenichell, Stephen.** Passport to Profits: Why the Next Investment Windfalls Will Be Found Abroad - And How to Grab Your Share. 2000. pap. 16.95 (*0-446-67605-5*) Warner Bks.

Mobius, Mark & Fenichell, Steve. Passport to Profits: Why the Next Investment Windfalls Will Be Found Abroad - And How to Grab Your Share. LC 98-38868. 416p. 1999. 25.00 (*0-446-52251-1*, Pub. by Warner Bks) Little.

***Mobklin, Robert M.** The Interstitial Cystitis Survival Guide. 200p. 2000. pap. 13.95 (*1-57224-210-8*, Pub. by New Harbinger) Publishers Group.

Moble, Thomas F. & Head, Thomas, eds. Soldiers of Christ: Saints & Saint's Lives from Late Antiquity & the Early Middle Ages. LC 94-6757. 416p. 1995. 50.00 (*0-271-01344-3*); pap. 18.95 (*0-271-01345-1*) Pa St U Pr.

Mobley. Hematology. (Medical Lab Technician Ser.). 1995. pap., lab manual ed. 32.95 (*0-8273-5950-0*) Delmar.

— Urinalysis & Body Fluids. (Medical Lab Technician Ser.). 1996. pap., lab manual ed. 32.95 (*0-8273-5951-9*) Delmar.

Mobley & Cato. Computer Managed Maintenance Systems. LC 98-42550. 166p. 1998. 69.00 (*0-88415-137-9*, 5137) Gulf Pub.

Mobley, Andrea, jt. auth. see Mobley, Chuck.

***Mobley, C. A.** Code of Conflict, 1 vol. 1999. mass mkt. 6.99 (*0-425-17108-6*) Berkley Pub.

Mobley, C. A. Rites of War. 1998. mass mkt. 6.99 (*0-515-12225-4*, Jove) Berkley Pub.

— Rules of Command: A Novel of Crisis & Combat at Sea. 352p. 1998. mass mkt. 6.99 (*0-425-16746-1*) Berkley Pub.

Mobley, Charles D. Light & Water: Radiative Transfer in Natural Waters. (Illus.). 592p. 1994. text 89.00 (*0-12-502750-8*) Acad Pr.

Mobley, Charles M. The Campus Site: A Prehistoric Site at Fairbanks, Alaska. LC 90-29894. (Illus.). xx, 104p. 1991. 30.00 (*0-912006-48-X*); pap. 20.00 (*0-912006-52-8*) U of Alaska Pr.

Mobley, Christine & Deutsch, Sheryl, eds. Medical Staff Management Forms, Policies, & Procedures for Health Care Providers. LC 94-49233. ring bd. 189.00 (*0-8342-0539-4*) Aspen Pub.

Mobley, Christine S. & Deutsch, Sheryl K. The Credentialing Handbook. LC 98-55685. 400p. 1999. 59.00 (*0-8342-0933-0*, 09330) Aspen Pub.

Mobley, Chuck & Mobley, Andrea. Navajo Rugs & Blankets Coloring Book. Mahan, Nancie S., ed. (Illus.). 32p. (Orig.). (J). (ps up). 1994. pap. 3.50 (*0-918080-76-2*) Treas Chest Bks.

Mobley, David F., jt. auth. see Wilson, Steven K.

Mobley, David P. Plastics from Microbes: Microbial Synthesis of Polymers & Polymer Precursors. 280p. (C). 1994. 98.00 (*1-56990-128-7*) Hanser-Gardner.

Mobley, Harry L. & Warren, John W., eds. Urinary Tract Infections: Molecular Pathogenesis & Clinical Management. LC 95-24719. 1995. 89.95 (*1-55581-093-4*) ASM Pr.

Mobley, Harry L. T., jt. ed. see Clayton, Christopher L.

Mobley, Jack, jt. auth. see Morton, C. W.

Mobley, Jane, ed. see Million, Stacey.

Mobley, Jane, ed. see Yu, Po-Lung.

Mobley, Jeff, jt. auth. see Robinson, Jack W., Sr.

Mobley, Jeffrey, jt. auth. see Robinson, Jack W., Sr.

Mobley, Joe A. James City: A Black Community in North Carolina, 1863-1900. (Illus.). xiv, 113p. 1994. reprint ed. pap. 6.00 (*0-86526-190-3*) NC Archives.

— Pamlico County: A Brief History. (Illus.). xiv, 144p. (Orig.). 1991. pap. 10.00 (*0-86526-252-7*) NC Archives.

— Ship Ashore! The U. S. Lifesavers of Coastal North Carolina. (Illus.). 197p. 1996. reprint ed. pap. 12.00 (*0-86526-260-8*) NC Archives.

— USS North Carolina: Symbol of a Vanished Age. (Illus.). 16p. 1996. reprint ed. pap. 3.00 (*0-86526-219-5*) NC Archives.

Mobley, Joe A., ed. The Papers of Zebulon Baird Vance, 1863 Vol. 2. LC 63-24722. (Papers of Zebulon Baird Vance). (Illus.). xxxix, 436p. (C). 1995. 35.00 (*0-86526-262-4*) NC Archives.

Mobley, Jonnie P. NTC's Dictionary of Theatre & Drama Terms. (Illus.). 176p. 1993. 19.95 (*0-8442-5345-6*, 53456, Natl Textbk Co) NTC Contemp Pub Co.

— NTC's Dictionary of Theatre & Drama Terms. LC 98-13124. (Illus.). 176p. 1994. pap. 14.95 (*0-8442-5333-2*, 53332, Natl Textbk Co) NTC Contemp Pub Co.

***Mobley, Keith.** Fluid Power Dynamics. LC 99-35357. 360p. 1999. 59.95 (*0-7506-7174-2*) Buttrwrth-Heinemann.

— Plant Engineers Handbook. (Illus.). 2000p. 2000. 125.00 (*0-7506-7328-1*) Buttrwrth-Heinemann.

Mobley, Lou & McKeown, Kate. Beyond IBM: Leadership, Marketing & Finance for the 1990s. (Illus.). 253p. 1989. reprint ed. 18.95 (*0-9622957-0-1*) Teleonet.

Mobley, Marilyn S. Folk Roots & Mythic Wings in Sarah Orne Jewett & Toni Morrison: The Cultural Function of Narrative. LC 91-15031. (Illus.). 193p. 1994. pap. 11.95 (*0-8071-1964-4*) La State U Pr.

Mobley, Mona. Joyful Hospitality. 1983. pap. 6.95 (*0-89137-431-0*) Quality Pubns.

Mobley, R. Keith. Introduction to Predictive Maintenance. 1990. text 51.95 (*0-442-31828-6*, VNR) Wiley.

***Mobley, R. Keith.** Maintenance Fundamentals. LC 98-53101. 360p. 1999. 59.95 (*0-7506-7151-3*) Buttrwrth-Heinemann.

Mobley, R. Keith. Root Cause Failure Analysis. LC 98-32097. 308p. 1999. 59.95 (*0-7506-7158-0*) Buttrwrth-Heinemann.

— Total Plant Performance Management. LC 98-30907. 286p. 1998. 69.00 (*0-88415-877-2*) Gulf Pub.

— Vibration Fundamentals. LC 98-32098. (Plant Engineering Maintenance Ser.). 295p. 1999. 59.95 (*0-7506-7150-5*) Buttrwrth-Heinemann.

Mobley, William H. Employee Turnover: Causes, Consequences & Control. LC 81-20485. (Managing Human Resources: Wanous Ser.). 224p. (C). 1982. pap. text. write for info. (*0-201-04673-3*) Addison-Wesley.

Mocanu, Constantin. Hertzian Relativistic Electrodynamics & Its Associated Mechanics, 2 vols., Set. (Monographs in Physics: No. V). 439p. 1990. pap. text 100.00 (*0-911767-50-9*) Hadronic Pr Inc.

Mocanu, P. T., jt. auth. see Miller, Sanford.

Mocarski, Stanley, ed. see National Powder Metallurgy Conference Staff.

Mocatta, Moses, tr. see Troki, Isaac.

Moccero, Joyce, jt. auth. see Sanfacon, Cheryl.

Moccheti, Ettore, jt. auth. see Cologni, Franco.

Moccia, Patricia, jt. ed. see Styles, Margretta M.

Mocciola, Michael & Karantzas, Constantinos P. Mastery Approach to Paradox 4.0. 416p. 1993. teacher ed. 8.00 (*1-56118-675-9*); text 26.95 incl. 5.25 hd (*1-56118-606-6*) Paradigm MN.

— Mastery Approach to Paradox 4.0. 5th ed. 416p. 1993. text 26.95 incl. 3.5 hd (*1-56118-609-0*) Paradigm MN.

Moceanu, Dominique. Dominique Moceanu: An American Champion. 1997. 10.09 (*0-606-12679-1*, Pub. by Turtleback) Demco.

Mocete, Melissa, jt. ed. see Macy, Harry, Jr.

Moch, Cheryl, ed. Feels Like Home: Fond Remembrances in Words & Pictures. LC 95-3194. (Illus.). 144p. 1995. 19.95 (*1-56512-082-5*) Algonquin Bks.

Moch, Joseph W. Winning Motor Vehicle Accident Cases. 1986. text 75.00 (*0-934547-01-7*, 5080) CRI-Comm Res.

Moch, Joseph W. & Belli, Melvin M. Winning ATV Cases, 2 vols. 1986. ring bd. 149.00 (*0-934547-03-3*) CRI-Comm Res.

Moch, Joseph W. & Borja, Arthur. Litigating Child Restraint Cases. (Illus.). 576p. 1993. 45.00 (*0-88450-094-2*, 0942-N) Lawyers & Judges.

Moch, Joseph William, jt. auth. see O'Donnell, James T.

Moch, Leslie P. Moving Europeans: Migration in Western Europe since 1650. LC 92-6678. (Interdisciplinary Studies in History). 320p. 1992. 19.95 (*0-253-33859-X*) Ind U Pr.

— Moving Europeans: Migration in Western Europe Since 1650. LC 92-6678. (Interdisciplinary Studies in History). 269p. Date not set. reprint ed. pap. 83.40 (*0-608-20563-X*, 205447700002) Bks Demand.

— Paths to the City: Regional Migration in 19th Century France. LC 83-2955. (New Approaches to Social Science History Ser.: No. 2). (Illus.). 261p. reprint ed. pap. 81.00 (*0-8357-8498-3*, 203477400091) Bks Demand.

Moch, Leslie P. & Stark, Gary D., eds. Essays on the Family & Historical Change. LC 82-45900. (Walter Prescott Webb Memorial Lectures: No. 17). 160p. 1983. 18.95 (*0-89096-151-4*) Tex A&M Univ Pr.

Moch, Leslie P., jt. ed. see Hoerder, Dirk.

Moch, Leslie Page, jt. ed. see Daniels, Christine.

***Moch, Susan D. & Gates, Marie F.** The Researcher Experience in Qualitative Research LC 99-6666. 1999. write for info. (*0-7619-1342-4*) Sage.

Moch, Susan D. & Graubard, Allan. Breast Cancer: Twenty Women's Stories. 160p. (Orig.). 1995. pap. 12.95 (*0-88737-654-1*) Natl League Nurse.

— Breast Cancer: Twenty Women's Stories: Becoming More Alive Through the Experience. 1995. 12.95 (*0-88737-669-X*) Natl League Nurse.

Mocha, Frank. American "Polonia" & Poland, a Sequel to Poles in America: Bicentennial Essays. LC 98-74344. 500p. 1998. 70.00 (*0-88033-393-6*, 496, Pub. by East Eur Monographs) Col U Pr.

Mochan, W. L., jt. ed. see Barrera, R. G.

Moche, Dinah L. Astronomy: A Self Teaching Guide. 4th ed. LC 92-18618. (Illus.). 368p. 1993. pap. 18.95 (*0-471-53001-8*) Wiley.

***Moche, Dinah L.** Astronomy: A Self Teaching Guide. 5th ed. (Illus.). 368p. 2000. pap. 18.95 (*0-471-38353-8*) Wiley.

Moche, Dinah L. Astronomy Today: Planets, Stars, Space Exploration. LC 98-34988. (Library of Knowledge). (Illus.). 96p. (J). (gr. 5 up). 1998. pap. 12.99 (*0-394-84423-8*, Pub. by Random Bks Yng Read) Random.

Moche, Dinah L., jt. auth. see Zeilik, Michael.

Mochel, Frederick A. Reflections on Moments in Time. (Orig.). 1997. pap. write for info. (*1-57553-549-1*) Watermrk Pr.

Mochel, Gerhard. Russian-German Economics Dictionaries: Grosses Oekonomisches Woerterbuch Russisch-Deutsch. 3rd ed. (GER & RUS.). 576p. 1983. 95.00 (*0-8288-0821-X*, M7575) Fr & Eur.

Mochel, Myron G. Fortran Programming, Programs, & Schematic Storage Maps. LC 75-140256. ix, 192p. 1970. write for info. (*0-07-042635-X*) McGraw.

Mochizuki, Ken. Baseball Saved Us. LC 92-73215. (Illus.). 32p. (YA). (ps up). 1993. 15.95 (*1-880000-01-6*) Lee & Low Bks.

— Baseball Saved Us. (Illus.). 32p. (YA). (gr. 2 up). 1995. pap. 6.95 (*1-880000-19-9*) Lee & Low Bks.

— Baseball Saved Us. 1993. 12.15 (*0-606-08914-4*, Pub. by Turtleback) Demco.

M

— El Beisbol Nos Salvo. Gonzalez, Tomas, tr. from ENG. LC 94-32517. (SPA., Illus.). 32p. (J). (gr. 4 up). 1993. pap. 6.95 (*1-880000-22-9*) Lee & Low Bks.
— El Beisbol Nos Salvo. Gonzalez, Tomas, tr. from ENG. LC 94-32517. (SPA., Illus.). 32p. (YA). (gr. 4 up). 1995. 15.95 (*1-880000-21-0*) Lee & Low Bks.
Mochizuki, Ken. El Beisbol Nos Salvo. 1995. 11.15 (*0-606-08917-9*, Pub. by Turtleback) Demco.
Mochizuki, Ken. Heroes. LC 94-26541. (Illus.). 32p. (J). (ps up). 1995. 15.95 (*1-880000-16-4*) Lee & Low Bks.
— Heroes. LC 94-26541. (Illus.). 32p. (YA). (ps up). 1997. pap. 6.95 (*1-880000-50-4*) Lee & Low Bks.
— Heroes. 1997. 12.15 (*0-606-12725-9*, Pub. by Turtleback) Demco.
— Pasaje a la Libertad. LC 98-47514. (Illus.). 32p. (YA). (gr. 1-4). 1999. 15.95 (*1-880000-81-4*, Pub. by Lee & Low Bks) Publishers Group.
— Pasaje a la Libertad: La Historia de Chiune Sugihara. LC 98-47514. (SPA., Illus.). 32p. (YA). (gr. 2 up). 1997. pap. 6.95 (*1-880000-82-2*, Pub. by Lee & Low Bks) Publishers Group.
*__Mochizuki, Ken.__ Passage to Freedom: The Sugihara Story. LC 96-35359. (Illus.). 32p. (YA). (gr. 1 up). 1999. 15.95 (*1-880000-49-0*) Lee & Low Bks.
Mochizuki, Kiichi. The New Silk Road & the Global Counterculture. Mueller, Katherine, ed. 176p. 1999. 39.00 (*1-883223-14-8*) Pacific NY.
*__Mochizuki, Kiichi & Mueller, Kate, eds.__ The World Financial Transformation & It's Political Implications. 128p. 2000. pap. 39.00 (*1-883223-15-6*) Pacific NY.
Mochizuki, Kiichi, jt. ed. see Galvis, Carlos.
Mochizuki, M., et al, eds. Oxygen Transport to Tissue, No. X. LC 87-32879. (Advances in Experimental Medicine & Biology Ser.: Vol. 222). (Illus.). 784p. 1988. 145.00 (*0-306-42795-8*, Plenum Trade) Perseus Pubng.
Mochizuki, Mike. Japan: Domestic Change & Foreign Policy. 120p. 1995. pap. text 15.00 (*0-8330-2308-X*, MR-616-OSD) Rand Corp.
Mochizuki, Mike, et al. Japan & the United States: Troubled Partners in a Changing World. (Institute for Foreign Policy Anaylsis Ser.). 156p. (C). 1991. pap. 11.95 (*0-08-041074-X*) Brasseys.
Mochizuki, Mike, jt. auth. see Green, Michael J.
Mochizuki, Mike M. Japan Reorients: The Quest for Wealth & Security in East Asia. 230p. 1998. 28.95 (*0-8157-5802-2*) Brookings.
Mochizuki, Mike M., ed. Toward a True Alliance: Restructuring U. S. - Japan Security Relations. LC 97-21062. 216p. 1997. 39.95 (*0-8157-5800-6*); pap. 16.95 (*0-8157-5801-4*) Brookings.
*__Mochizuki, Ronald T.__ Taking Charge: The Trade Secrets of Law Enforcement Promotional Oral Boards. (Illus.). 188p. 1999. spiral bd. 24.95 (*0-9676319-0-4*) C & K Pubns.
Mochizuki, Seibu. The Ischemic Heart. Takeda, Nobuakira et al, eds. LC 97-42813. (Progress in Experimental Cardiology Ser.). 624p. 1998. lib. bdg. 205.00 (*0-7923-8105-X*) Kluwer Academic.
Mochizuki, Selbu, ed. Flow Visualization & Image Processing 1997. (Illus.). 372p. 1997. write for info. (*0-9652469-1-4*) Pac Ctr Thermal.
— Flow Visualization & Image Processing 1997, Vol. 2. (Illus.). 346p. 1997. write for info. (*0-9652469-2-2*) Pac Ctr Thermal.
Mochizuki, Selbu, jt. ed. see Yazaki, Yoshio.
Mochizuki, Shinichi. Foundations of P-ADIC Teichmhuller Theory LC 99-26586. (AMS/IP Studies in Advanced Mathematics). 1999. write for info. (*0-8218-1190-8*) Am Math.
*__Mochizuki, Shogo.__ Ko Bi Do Ancient Way of Beauty: The Art of Japanese Facial Massage. (Illus.). 1999. 19.95 (*1-57615-053-4*) Kotobuki Pubns.
— Zoku Shin Do the Art of East Asian Foot Reflexology Vol. 1: Japanese Foot Massage. (Illus.). 1999. pap. 19.95 (*1-57615-056-9*) Kotobuki Pubns.
Mochizuki, Tara K., jt. auth. see Coustan, Donald R.
Mochmann, Ekkehard & Muller, Paul J. Data Protection & Social Science Research. 229p. (C). 1982. text 42.50 (*3-593-32604-3*) Irvington.
Mochmann, Ekkehard, jt. auth. see De Guchteneire, P. F.
Mochnick, Beth R. Angel Voices. 1992. pap. 34.95 (*0-88284-842-9*) Alfred Pub.
— New Holiday Songs for Children: A Creative Approach. Davis, Barbara, ed. (Illus.). iv, 44p. (J). 1988. pap. text 15.95 (*0-916656-25-X*, MFBK 25) Mark Foster Mus.
Mocho, Jill. Murder & Justice Frontier New Mexico. LC 96-10007. (Illus.). 259p. (C). 1997. pap. 19.95 (*0-8263-1800-2*) U of NM Pr.
Mocho, Jill, et al. Murder & Justice Frontier New Mexico. LC 96-10007. (Illus.). 259p. (C). 1997. 50.00 (*0-8263-1765-0*) U of NM Pr.
Mochon, Anne, jt. auth. see Barter, Judith A.
Mochulsky, Konstantin. Aleksandr Blok. Johnson, Doris V., tr. LC 82-20212. 453p. reprint ed. pap. 140.50 (*0-7837-3633-9*, 204350000009) Bks Demand.
— Dostoevsky: His Life & Work. Minihan, Michael A., tr. 712p. 1967. pap. text 29.95 (*0-691-01299-7*, Pub. by Princeton U Pr) Cal Prin Full Svc.
Mock. USP Reference Standards. write for info. (*0-614-06361-2*) US Pharmacopeia.
Mock & Holloman. Oklahoma Corporate Forms, 2 vols., Issue 9. 301p. 1998. ring bd. write for info. (*0-327-00526-2*, 8222914) LEXIS Pub.
Mock, Alfred R., jt. auth. see Gregoire, Christopher P.
Mock, D. W., jt. ed. see Gowaty, P. A.
Mock, David B. History & Public Policy. 228p. (C). 1991. 24.50 (*0-89464-288-X*) Krieger.
Mock, David B., ed. LEGACY WEST: READING VL2, Vol. 2. LC 94-26316. 288p. (C). 1997. pap. text 48.00 (*0-673-99000-1*) Addson-Wesley Educ.
— LEGACY WEST VOL1, Vol. 1. LC 94-26316. 288p. (C). 1997. pap. text 49.00 (*0-673-46999-9*) Addson-Wesley Educ.
Mock, Douglas W. & Parker, Geoffrey A. The Evolution of Sibling Rivalry. LC 97-35790. (Oxford Series in Ecology & Evolution). (Illus.). 478p. 1998. text 120.00 (*0-19-857743-5*); pap. text 59.00 (*0-19-857744-3*) OUP.
Mock, Edward J., jt. auth. see Schuckett, Donald H.
Mock, Eliazbeth B., et al, eds. Built in the U. S. A. 1932-1944. LC 68-57299. (Museum of Modern Art Publications in Reprint). 260p. 1969. reprint ed. 24.95 (*0-405-01526-7*) Ayer.
Mock, Elizabeth B. The Architecture of Bridges. LC 70-169309. (Museum of Modern Art Publications in Reprint). (Illus.). 128p. 1972. reprint ed. 24.95 (*0-405-01568-2*) Ayer.
Mock, Esther G. Roots in Concrete. LC 90-84996. 1992. 15.95 (*0-8158-0466-0*) Chris Mass.
Mock, Gary N., jt. ed. see Grady, Perry L.
Mock, Gloria & Martinez, Wilfred. Sexualidad: Sus Conceptos Basicos. 274p. 1995. pap. text. write for info. (*1-56758-053-X*) Edit Cultl.
Mock, J. Dennis. Accounts Receivable Management for the Medical Practice. 184p. (Orig.). 1995. pap. text 44.95 (*1-57066-082-4*) Practice Mgmt Info.
Mock, James P. Basic Latent Print Development. 3rd ed. LC 93-79307. (Illus.). (C). 1993. pap. 4.95 (*0-9622305-0-2*) Lightning Powder.
Mock, James R. Censorship Nineteen Seventeen. LC 74-37864. (Civil Liberties in American History Ser.). 250p. 1972. reprint ed. lib. bdg. 29.50 (*0-306-70436-6*) Da Capo.
Mock, James R. & Larson, Cedric. Words That Won the War: The Mobilization of Mass Hatred. 1985. lib. bdg. 79.95 (*0-87700-652-0*) Revisionist Pr.
Mock, Jeff. You Can Write Poetry. LC 98-12073. (You Can Write It! Ser.). 128p. 1998. pap. 12.99 (*0-89879-825-6*, Wrtrs Digest Bks) F & W Pubns Inc.
Mock, Jeffery I. IBM Preview 2 Package. 1987. disk 11.95 (*0-8053-2334-1*) Benjamin-Cummings.
— Preview II: An Introduction to Applications Software. 1987. write for info. (*0-8053-2335-X*) Benjamin-Cummings.
— Preview 2 Apple Lab Manuel. 1987. pap. text 11.95 (*0-8053-2407-0*) Benjamin-Cummings.
— Preview 2 Lab Manuel (Without Disk) 1987. pap. text 11.95 (*0-8053-2405-4*) Benjamin-Cummings.
Mock, Jeffrey I., jt. auth. see Weiers, Ronald M.
Mock, Jerrie. First Woman to Fly Solo Around the World: To Finish What Amelia Began. rev. ed. (Illus.). 300p. 1985. pap. write for info. (*0-931515-04-1*) Triumph Pr.
Mock, Jess, ed. The Engineer's Responsibility to Society. LC 78-102888. 76p. reprint ed. pap. 30.00 (*0-608-30609-6*, 201682300005) Bks Demand.
Mock, John. Culture, Community & Change in a Sapporo Neighborhood, 1925-1988: Hanayama. LC 99-23114. (Japanese Studies: Vol. 8). 248p. 1999. 89.95 (*0-7734-7974-0*) E Mellen.
Mock, John. An Early American Christmas for Guitar. 24p. 1996. pap. 20.95 incl. audio compact disk (*0-7866-2668-2*, 96518CDP); pap. 5.95 (*0-7866-2667-4*, 96518) Mel Bay.
— Early American Christmas for Recorder: Beginning Level. 24p. 1996. pap. 6.95 (*0-7866-2642-9*, 96500); pap. 21.95 incl. audio compact disk (*0-7866-2643-7*, 96500CDP) Mel Bay.
Mock, John & O'Neil, Kimberly. Lonely Planet Trekking in the Karakoram & Hindukush. LC 97-126119. (Illus.). 304p. 1996. pap. 16.95 (*0-86442-360-8*) Lonely Planet.
Mock, Nancy. Play-Likes for Preschoolers: Around the World Costume Patterns. Gross, Karen, ed. (Illus.). 08p. (Orig.). (J). (ps-k). 1991. pap. text 5.95 (*1-56309-009-0*, N918101, New Hope) Womans Mission Union.
Mock, Patricia, jt. auth. see Luder, Ian.
Mock, Randall D. Oklahoma Corporate Forms. 1120p. 1993. spiral bd. 250.00 (*0-87189-975-2*, 82225-10, MICHIE) LEXIS Pub.
*__Mock, Randall D. & Holloman, James H., Jr.__ Oklahoma Corporate Forms, Issue 10. 200p. 1999. ring bd. write for info. (*0-327-01582-9*, 8222915) LEXIS Pub.
*__Mock, Roberta.__ Performing Processes. 128p. 2000. pap. 24.95 (*1-84150-010-0*, Pub. by Intellect) Intl Spec Bk.
Mock, Shirley B. The Sowing & the Dawning: Termination, Dedication, & Transformation in Archaeological & Ethnographic Record of Mesoamerica. LC 98-23116. 1998. 60.00 (*0-8263-1983-1*) U of NM Pr.
Mock, Theodore J. Measurement & Accounting Information Criteria. (Studies in Accounting Research: Vol. 13). 116p. 1976. 12.00 (*0-86539-025-8*) Am Accounting.
Mock, Theodore J. & Grove, Hugh D. Measurement, Accounting, & Organizational Information. LC 78-10536. (Wiley Series in Accounting & Information Systems). (Illus.). 256p. reprint ed. pap. 79.40 (*0-7837-3458-1*, 205778400008) Bks Demand.
*__Mock, Theodore J. & Turner, Jerry L.__ Internal Accounting Control Evaluation & Audit Judgment: An Anthology. LC 99-36251. 1999. write for info. (*0-8153-3443-5*) Garland.
Mock, Theodore J., jt. auth. see Turner, Jerry L.
Mock, Valerie E. A.S.M.D. Multi-Graded Arithmetic Practice & Drill Sheets. (Makemaster Bk.). (J). (gr. 1-6). 1977. pap. 16.99 (*0-8224-0462-1*) Fearon Teacher Aids.
Mockaitis, Thomas R. Applied English Skills. 2nd ed. LC 96-5871. 332p. 1996. pap. text, student ed. 19.95 (*1-56118-909-X*) Paradigm MN.
— Applied English Skills. 2nd ed. 78p. (C). 1997. pap. text, teacher ed. 8.00 (*1-56118-910-3*) Paradigm MN.
— Easy Business English. 7p. (C). 1991. teacher ed. 8.00 (*1-56118-015-7*); pap. text 15.95 (*1-56118-016-5*) Paradigm MN.
*__Mockaitis, Thomas R.__ Peace Operations & Intrastate Conflict: The Sword or the Olive Branch? LC 98-50237. (Illus.). 184p. 1999. 55.00 (*0-275-96173-7*, C6173, Praeger Pubs) Greenwood.
Mockel, Birgit. George Grosz in Amerika 1932, 1959. 1997. 73.95 (*3-631-32307-7*) P Lang Pubng.
Mockel, Klaus, jt. auth. see Roesky, Herbert W.
Mocker, Donald W. & Spear, George E., eds. Urban Education: A Guide to Information Sources. LC 78-13627. (Urban Studies Information Guide Ser.: Vol. 3). 216p. 1978. 68.00 (*0-8103-1431-2*) Gale.
Mockerie, Parmenas G. An African Speaks for His People. LC 74-15068. reprint ed. 27.50 (*0-404-12110-1*) AMS Pr.
Mocket, Richard. Doctrina et Politia Ecclesiae Anglicanae: An Anglican Summa : Facsimile with Variants of the Text of 1617. Screech, M. A., ed. & intro. by. LC 94-40063. (Studies in the History of Christian Thought: Vol. 62). 1994. text 155.50 (*90-04-10040-7*) Brill Academic Pubs.
*__Mockford, Caroline.__ What's This? 32p. (J). (ps-1). 2000. 15.95 (*1-84148-018-5*) Barefoot Bks NY.
Mockford, Edward L. North American Psocoptera (Insecta) Arnett, Ross H., Jr., ed. (Flora & Fauna Handbook Ser.: No. 10). (Illus.). xii, 455p. 1993. lib. bdg. 99.95 (*1-877743-12-7*) Sandhill Crane.
Mockford, Hervey, ed. see Flavel, John.
Mockford, Hervey, ed. see Owen, John.
*__Mockler.__ Multinational Strategic Alliance. LC 98-37306. 266p. (C). 1999. 49.95 (*0-471-98775-1*) Wiley.
Mockler, Esther. Eighty Miles from a Doctor. Rosin, Laurie, ed. LC 97-60611. (Illus.). 160p. (Orig.). 1997. pap. 12.95 (*0-965741l-0-9*) Wind Riv Pr.
Mockler, Robert J., ed. Strategic Management: Cases. 1993. 30.00 (*0-536-58303-X*) Pearson Custom.
Mockler, Robert J. & Dologite, D. G. Knowledge-Based Systems for Strategic Corporate Planning. 1987. 29.95 (*0-912841-24-9*) Planning Forum.
— Multinational Cross-Cultural Management: An Integrative Context-Specific Process. LC 96-26270. 336p. 1997. 69.50 (*1-56720-010-9*, Quorum Bks) Greenwood.
Mockler, Robert J., jt. auth. see Dologite, Dorothy G.
Mocko, George P. Lord, Empower Us! Sherer, Michael L., ed. (Orig.). 1987. pap. 3.50 (*0-89536-851-X*, 7810) CSS OH.
Mockor, Jiri. Groups of Divisibility. 1983. text 137.50 (*90-277-1539-4*) Kluwer Academic.
Mockor, Jiri, jt. auth. see Alajbegovic, Jusuf H.
Mockridge, Patricia & Mockridge, Philip. Weathervanes. (Album Ser.: No. 291). (Illus.). 32p. 1989. pap. 5.25 (*0-7478-0191-6*, Pub. by Shire Pubns) Parkwest Pubns.
Mockridge, Philip, jt. auth. see Mockridge, Patricia.
Mockrin, Ida. The Big Parade. (Illus.). 16p. (J). (ps-1). 1983. pap. 2.00 (*0-9612244-0-1*) Honeycomb Pr.
Mockrin, Stephen C., ed. Molecular Genetics & Gene Therapy of Cardiovascular Diseases. LC 95-25992. (Fundamental & Clinical Cardiology Ser.: Vol. 26). (Illus.). 616p. 1996. text 215.00 (*0-8247-9408-7*) Dekker.
Mockus, Jonas. Bayesian Heuristic Approach to Discrete & Global Optimization: Algorithms, Visualization, Software, & Applications. LC 96-48826. (Nonconvex Optimization & Its Applications Ser.). 416p. (C). 1997. text 217.50 (*0-7923-4327-1*) Kluwer Academic.
*__Mockus, Jonas.__ A Set of Examples of Global & Discrete Optimization: Applications of Bayesian Heuristic Approach. LC 00-30652. (Applied Optimization Ser.). 2000. write for info. (*0-7923-6359-0*) Kluwer Academic.
Mocny, Felicitas. Die Begrundbarkeit des Prinzips der Freiheit Als Ontologisches Letztprinzip. (Europaische Hochschulschriften Ser.: Bd. 542). (GER.). 145p. 1997. 35.95 (*3-631-32303-4*) P Lang Pubng.
Mocsy, Istvan I. The Uprooted. 1983. text 55.50 (*0-88033-039-2*, 147, Pub. by East Eur Monographs) Col U Pr.
Moctezuma, Eduardo M. The Great Temple of the Aztecs: Treasures of Tenochtitlan. LC 87-50201. (Illus.). 360p. 1994. pap. 19.95 (*0-500-27752-4*, Pub. by Thames Hudson) Norton.
— Life & Death in the Templo Mayor. Ortiz De Montellano, Bernard R. & Ortiz De Montellano, Thelma, trs. (Illus.). 160p. 1995. pap. 17.50 (*0-87081-400-1*) Univ Pr Colo.
— Muerte a Filo de Obsidiana (Death by the Edge of Obsidian Stone) (SPA.). 158p. 1996. pap. 9.99 (*968-16-4991-5*, Pub. by Fondo) Continental Bk.
— Treasures of the Great Temple. (Illus.). 180p. 1990. 39.95 (*0-9625399-6-1*) ALTI Pub.
*__Moctezuma, Eduardo M.__ Vida y Muerte en el Templo Mayor. 3rd ed. 140p. 1999. pap. 6.99 (*968-16-5712-8*) Fondo CA.
Moctezuma, Eduardo M., contrib. by. Museo del Templo Mayor: Diez Anos. (SPA., Illus.). 157p. 1997. pap. 40.00 (*970-18-0671-9*, IN92, Pub. by Dir Gen Pubicaiones) UPLAAP.
Moctezuma, Eduardo M., jt. auth. see Carrasco, David.
Moczala, H., et al. Small Electric Motors. (Power Ser.: No. 26). 307p. 1998. 110.00 (*0-85296-921-X*, PO026) INSPEC Inc.
Moczar. The Western World, Vol. 1. 208p. 1993. pap. text, student ed. 21.80 (*0-13-946724-6*) P-H.
— The Western World, Vol. 2. 272p. 1994. pap. text, student ed. 21.80 (*0-13-946740-8*) P-H.
— The World since 1500. 7th ed. 1995. pap. text, student ed. 21.80 (*0-13-251175-4*) P-H.
— The World to 1500. 6th ed. 1995. pap. text, student ed. 21.33 (*0-13-251126-6*) P-H.
Moczar, L., jt. auth. see Gordh, Gordon.
Moczydlowski, Pawel. The Hidden Life of Polish Prisons. LC 91-47660. 206p. reprint ed. pap. 63.90 (*0-608-09353-X*, 205409900002) Bks Demand.
Moczygema-McKinsey, Susan B., jt. auth. see Stuart, David E.
*__Modahl, Mary.__ Now or Never: How Companies Must Change to Win the Battle for Internet Consumers, Set. unabridged ed. 2000. audio 25.95 (*0-694-52311-9*) HarperAudio.
— Now or Never: How Companies Must Change Today to Win the Battle for Internet Consumers. LC 99-49437. (Illus.). 272p. 2000. 27.00 (*0-06-662012-0*) HarpC.
*__Modahl, Mary.__ Now or Never: How Companies Must Change Today to Win the Battle for Internet Consumers. 2001. write for info. (*0-06-662013-9*) HarpC.
Modak, B. R. The Ancillary Literature of the Atharva-Veda: A Study with Special Reference to the Parisistas. 570p. 1993. 53.50 (*81-215-0607-7*, Pub. by M Manoharial) Coronet Bks.
Modak, Prasad & Biswas, Asit K. Conducting Environmental Impact Assessment in Developing Countries. LC 99-6139. 364p. 1999. pap. 34.95 (*92-808-0965-2*) UN Univ Pr.
Modan, Shula. Why Jonathan Doesn't Cry. (Illus.). (J). (ps-2). 1988. 7.95 (*1-55774-022-4*) Lambda Pubs.
Modarres, et al. Reliability Engineering & Risk Analysis. LC 99-26668. (Illus.). 542p. 1999. text 165.00 (*0-8247-2000-8*) Dekker.
Modarres, Mohammad, jt. auth. see Ramsey, Charles B.
Modarres, Mohammed. WEESKA Reliability & Risk Analysis. LC 92-32998. (What Every Engineer Should Know Ser.: Vol. 30). (Illus.). 360p. 1992. text 65.00 (*0-8247-8958-X*) Dekker.
Modarres-Sadeqi, Jafar. The Marsh (Gavkhuni) Darbandi, Afkham, tr. from PER. LC 96-44379. (Bibliotheca Iranica Ser.: No. 3).Tr. of Gavkhuni. 110p. (Orig.). 1996. pap. 8.95 (*1-56859-044-X*) Mazda Pubs.
Modarressi, Hossein. Crisis & Consolidation in the Formative Period of Shi'ite Islam: Abu Ja'far ibn Qiba al-Razi & His Contribution to Imamite Shi'ite Thought. LC 92-41266. 280p. 1993. 35.00 (*0-87850-095-2*) Darwin Pr.
Modarressi, Mitra. Monster Stew. LC 97-39418. 48p. (J). (gr. 3-6). 1998. 15.95 (*0-7894-2517-3*) DK Pub Inc.
*__Modarressi, Mitra.__ Yard Sale! LC 99-27592. 32p. (J). 2000. 15.95 (*0-7894-2651-X*, D K Ink) DK Pub Inc.
Moday, Jane. God Loves Little Lamb: A Bend n' Snuggle Book. 18p. (J). (ps). 1999. 9.99 (*0-7847-0972-6*, 03542) Standard Pub.
— Little Bunny's Easter Day: Bend n' Snuggle Book. 18p. (J). (ps). 1999. 9.99 (*0-7847-0971-8*, 03541) Standard Pub.
Moddel, Cantor P. Max Helfman: A Biographical Sketch. 1974. 10.00 (*0-943376-04-1*) Magnes Mus.
Moddelmog, Debra, jt. compiled by see Secor, Robert.
Moddelmog, Debra A. Readers & Mythic Signs: The Oedipus Myth in Twentieth-Century Fiction. LC 92-34304. (Illus.). 208p. (C). 1993. 26.95 (*0-8093-1846-6*) S Ill U Pr.
Moddelmog, Debra A. Reading Desire: In Pursuit of Ernest Hemingway. LC 99-30772. 1999. 45.00 (*0-8014-3604-4*) Cornell U Pr.
*__Moddelmog, Debra A.__ Reading Desire: In Pursuit of Ernest Hemingway. LC 99-30772. 1999. pap. 17.95 (*0-8014-8635-1*) Cornell U Pr.
*__Moddelmog, William E.__ Reconstituting Authority: American Fiction in the Province of the Law, 1880-1920. 272p. 2001. text 32.95 (*0-87745-736-0*) U of Iowa Pr.
Modder, U., jt. auth. see Beyer, D.
Modderno, Francine, jt. auth. see Cantrell, Will.
Moddie, A. D., ed. The Concept of Work in Indian Society. 1990. 29.00 (*81-85425-16-7*, Pub. by Manohar) S Asia.
Moddie, A. D., jt. ed. see Lall, J. S.
Moddy, Frank, jt. auth. see Schoenfield, Leslie J.
Mode, Becky. Fully Committed. Date not set. pap. 5.95 (*0-8222-1768-6*) Dramatists Play.
Mode, C. J. Stochastic Processes in Demography & Their Computer Implementation. (Biomathematics Ser.: Vol. 14). (Illus.). 430p. 1985. 121.95 (*0-387-13622-3*) Spr-Verlag.
*__Mode, Charles T. & Sleeman, Candace K.__ Stochastic Processes in Epidemiology. 600p. 1999. 96.00 (*981-02-4097-X*) World Scientific Pub.
Mode, P. G. The Frontier Spirit in American Christianity. 1977. lib. bdg. 59.95 (*0-8490-1870-6*) Gordon Pr.
Mode, Paul J., jt. auth. see Johnson, David R.
*__Model Airplane Editors, ed.__ Radio Control Airplane Finishing & Detailing. (Master Modeler Ser.). (Illus.). 148p. 2000. pap. 19.95 (*0-911295-51-8*, 130295AP, Pub. by Air Age) Motorbooks Intl.
Model Airplane News Editors, contrib. by. The R/C Pilot's Handbook. (Illus.). 191p. 1995. pap. text 19.95 (*0-911295-38-0*) Air Age.
Model Airplane News Staff. Radio Control Airplane How-To's, Vol. 2. Masi, Frank R., ed. (Illus.). 96p. (Orig.). 1995. pap. 14.95 (*0-911295-33-X*) Air Age.
— Scale Aircraft Drawings: World War One. (Illus.). 154p. 1986. pap. 17.95 (*0-911295-02-X*, Pub. by Air Age) Motorbooks Intl.
Model, Fritz. Geophysikalische Bibliographie von Nordund Ostsee. (GER.). 1966. 29.00 (*3-443-39036-6*, Pub. by Gebruder Borntraeger) Balogh.
Model Jury Instructions Committee. Manual of Model Civil Jury Instructions for the Ninth Circuit. 303p. (C). 1993. pap. text. write for info. (*0-314-02583-9*) West Pub.
*__Model Jury Instructions Committee.__ Virginia Model Jury Instructions, Vols. 1 & 2. LC 98-87419. 500p. 1999. ring bd. write for info. (*0-327-01587-X*, 6799214) LEXIS Pub.

An Asterisk (*) at the beginning of an entry indicates that the title is appearing for the first time.

Model Jury Instructions Committee. Virginia Model Jury Instructions - Civil, 1993 Edition, 2 vols., Set. 1993. spiral bd. 190.00 (*1-55834-145-5*, 67950-10, MICHIE) LEXIS Pub.
— Virginia Model Jury Instructions - Criminal, 1989 Replacement Edition with 1991 Supplements, 2 vols. rev. ed. 1989. 180.00 (*0-87473-482-7*, MICHIE) LEXIS Pub.
— Virginia Model Jury Instructions - Criminal, 1993 Edition, 2 vols., Set. 1993. spiral bd. 190.00 (*1-55834-137-4*, MICHIE) LEXIS Pub.
Model Jury Instructions Committee Staff. Virginia Model Jury Instructions - Civil, 1998 Replacement, 2 vols. LC 98-88800. 1500p. 1998. ring bd. 210.00 (*0-327-00750-8*, 6795011) LEXIS Pub.
— Virginia Model Jury Instructions - Civil, 1998 Replacement, Vol. I. LC 98-88800. 1500p. 1998. ring bd. write for info. (*0-327-00751-6*, 6795011) LEXIS Pub.
— Virginia Model Jury Instructions - Civil, 1998 Replacement, Vol. II. LC 98-88800. 1500p. 1998. ring bd. write for info. (*0-327-00752-4*, 6795011) LEXIS Pub.
***Model, Lisette, photos by.** Lisette Model. 360p. 2000. 85.00 (*0-944092-77-2*) Twin Palms Pub.
Model Procedures Committee, jt. auth. see National Fire Service Incident Management System Committee.
Model Railroad Magazine Staff, jt. auth. see Drury, George.
Model Railroader Magazine Staff. 48 Top-Notch Track Plans from Model Railroader. LC 93-30051. (Model Railroad Handbook Ser.: \). 1993. per. 16.95 (*0-89024-190-2*, 12132) Kalmbach.
— Model Railroad Bridges & Trestles. Emmerich, Michael, ed. (Illus.). 152p. (Orig.). 1992. per. 19.95 (*0-89024-128-7*, 12101) Kalmbach.
— Scenery Tips & Techniques from Model Railroader Magazine. Emmerich, Michael, ed. (Illus.). 116p. 1989. per. 16.95 (*0-89024-095-7*, 12084) Kalmbach.
— 6 HO Railroads You Can Build. LC 93-28560. (Model Railroad Handbook Ser.: No. 38). (Illus.). 144p. 1993. per. 18.95 (*0-89024-189-9*, 12131) Kalmbach.
— Small Railroads You Can Build. 2nd ed. (Illus.). 64p. 1996. pap. 12.95 (*0-89024-225-9*, 12146) Kalmbach.
Modell, Arnold H. Object Love & Reality: An Introduction to a Psychoanalytic Theory of Object Relations. LC 68-24219. 181p. 1968. 30.00 (*0-8236-3720-4*) Intl Univs Pr.
— Other Times, Other Realities: Toward A Theory of Psychoanalytic Treatment. 192p. 1996. pap. text 17.95 (*0-674-64499-9*) HUP.
— Other Times, Other Realities: Toward a Theory of Psychoanalytic Treatment. 208p. 1990. text 27.50 (*0-685-32245-9*) HUP.
— Other Times, Other Realities: Toward a Theory of Psychoanalytic Treatment. 208p. (C). 1990. 40.50 (*0-674-64498-0*) HUP.
— The Private Self. LC 93-14974. 288p. 1993. 36.50 (*0-674-70752-4*) HUP.
— The Private Self. 264p. 1996. pap. text 18.00 (*0-674-70753-2*) HUP.
— Psychoanalysis in a New Context. LC 84-12965. xii, 294p. 1985. 45.00 (*0-8236-5212-2*, 05212) Intl Univs Pr.
Modell, B., et al. Community Genetics Services in Europe: Report on a Survey. (WHO Regional Publications: No. 38). (ENG, FRE & GER.). x, 137p. 1991. pap. text 24.00 (*92-890-1301-X*, 1310038) World Health.
Modell, Bernadette & Modell, Michael. Towards a Healthy Baby: Congenital Disorders & the New Genetics in Primary Health Care. (Illus.). 432p. 1992. 95.00 (*0-19-262234-X*); pap. 49.95 (*0-19-261486-X*) OUP.
Modell, Frank. One Zillion Valentines. LC 81-2215. 40p. (J). (ps-3). 1987. reprint ed. mass mkt. 4.95 (*0-688-07329-8*, Wm Morrow) Morrow Avon.
Modell, Jerome D. Health Foods: Index of New Information with Authors, Subjects, Research Categories & References. 150p. 1996. 47.50 (*0-7883-1218-9*); pap. 44.50 (*0-7883-1219-7*) ABBE Pubs Assn.
Modell, John. The Economics & Politics of Racial Accommodation: The Japanese of Los Angeles, 1900-1942. LC 77-6749. (Illus.). 214p. 1977. text 24.95 (*0-252-00622-4*) U of Ill Pr.
— Into One's Own: From Youth to Adulthood in the United States, 1920-1975. (Illus.). 428p. 1991. reprint ed. pap. 16.95 (*0-520-07641-9*, Pub. by U CA Pr) Cal Prin Full Svc.
Modell, John, jt. ed. see Karsten, Peter.
Modell, John, ed. see Kikuchi, Charles.
Modell, Joseph D., et al. Transmitter Hunting: Radio Direction Finding Simplified. (Illus.). 336p. (Orig.). 1987. pap. 19.95 (*0-8306-2701-4*) McGraw-Hill Prof.
Modell, Judith. Kinship with Strangers: Adoption & Interpretations of Kinship in American Culture. LC 92-37617. 230p. 1994. 42.50 (*0-520-08118-8*, Pub. by U CA Pr) Cal Prin Full Svc.
— A Sealed & Secret Kinship: Policies & Practices in American Adoption. 1999. write for info. (*1-57181-077-3*); pap. write for info. (*1-57181-078-1*) Berghahn Bks.
Modell, Judith S. A Town Without Steel: Envisioning Homestead. LC 98-9030. (Illus.). 284p. 1998. pap. 24.95 (*0-8229-5676-4*); text 45.00 (*0-8229-4071-X*) U of Pittsburgh Pr.
Modell, Martin E. A Professional's Guide to Systems Analysis. 2nd ed. (Illus.). 458p. 1996. 55.00 (*0-07-042948-0*) McGraw.
Modell, Michael & Tester, Jefferson. Thermodynamics & Its Applications. 3rd ed. LC 96-3173. 960p. (C). 1996. 105.00 (*0-13-915356-X*) P-H.
Modell, Michael, et al. Paediatric Problems in General Practice. 3rd ed. (Oxford General Practice Ser.: No. 36). (Illus.). 352p. 1996. pap. text 49.95 (*0-19-262512-8*) OUP.
Modell, Michael, jt. auth. see Modell, Bernadette.
Modelski, Andrew M. Railroad Maps of North America: The First Hundred Years. LC 82-675134. 186p. 1984. 28.00 (*0-8444-0396-2*, 030-004-00021-3) Lib Congress.
Modelski, G. Long Cycles World Politics. LC 86-15731. 256p. 1986. pap. 30.00 (*0-295-96430-8*) U of Wash Pr.
Modelski, George & Thompson, William R. Leading Sectors & World Powers: The Coevolution of Global Economics & Politics. Kegley, Charles W. & Puchala, Donald J., eds. LC 95-4372. (Studies in International Relations). (Illus.). 300p. 1996. text 49.95 (*1-57003-054-5*) U of SC Pr.
***Modelski, Sylvia.** Port Said Revisited. LC 99-96961. (Illus.). 212p. 2000. pap. 14.95 (*0-9676230-0-6*, Pharos Bk) FAROS.
Modelski, Sylvia, tr. see Levi-Strauss, Claude.
Modemann, Martin. Die Taufe in Den Predigten des Hl. Maximus V. Turin. (Europaische Hochschulschriften Ser.: Reihe 23, Bd. 537). (GER.). 220p. 1995. 42.95 (*3-631-49181-6*) P Lang Pubng.
Moden, Karl-Markus. Tax Incentives of Corporate Mergers & Foreign Direct Investments. (IUI Dissertation Ser.: No. 7). 195p. (Orig.). 1993. pap. 52.50 (*91-7204-442-X*) Coronet Bks.
***Modena, Leone & Podet, Allen Howard.** A Translation of the Magen Wa-Hereb by Leon Modena, 1571-1648. LC 99-49899. (Jewish Studies: Vol. 20). 348p. 2000. 99.95 (*0-7734-7821-3*) E Mellen.
Moder, Joseph J., et al. Project Management with CPM, Pert & Precedence Diagramming. 3rd ed. (Illus.). 389p. (C). 1995. pap. text 40.00 (*0-9606344-8-7*) Blitz Pub Co.
Moder, Lee. America Now. 2nd ed. 1997. pap. text 1.15 (*0-312-15256-6*) St Martin.
Modera, Mark P. & Persily, Andrew K., eds. Airflow Performance of Building Envelopes, Components, & Systems, Vol. 1255. LC 95-23430. (STP, Special Technical Publication Ser.: No. 1255). (Illus.). 307p. 1995. text 99.00 (*0-8031-2023-0*, STP1255) ASTM.
Modera, Mark P. & Shankle, Diana, eds. Proceedings: 1996 ACEEE Summer Study on Energy Efficiency in Buildings, 10 vols. 2032p. (Orig.). (C). 1996. pap., per. 200.00 (*0-918249-26-0*) Am Coun Energy.
Modern Curriculum Press Staff. Phonics Practice Readers. pap. text 18.95 (*0-8136-0605-5*) Modern Curr.
Modern Drummer Publications Staff & Van Horn, Rick. The Working Drummer. 144p. 1996. per. 14.95 (*0-7935-7358-0*) H Leonard.
Modern Engineering Practice Staff. Pattern Making for Metal Castings. 138p. 1991. reprint ed. pap. text 12.00 (*1-877767-46-8*) Univ Publng Hse.
Modern Jury Instructions Staff. Virginia Model Jury Instructions--Criminal, 1998 Replacement Edition, Vol. I. LC 98-87419. 1250p. 1998. ring bd., suppl. ed. write for info. (*0-327-00335-9*, 67986-12) LEXIS Pub.
— Virginia Model Jury Instructions--Criminal, 1998 Replacement Edition, Vol. II. LC 98-87419. 1250p. 1998. ring bd., suppl. ed. write for info. (*0-327-00336-7*, 67987-12) LEXIS Pub.
Modern Language Association of America, Center for. Statement of Editorial Principles & Procedures: A Working Manual for Editing Nineteenth Century American Texts. rev. ed. LC PN0162.M6. 35p. 1972. pap. 30.00 (*0-608-05576-X*, 206603600006) Bks Demand.
Modern Language Association of America Staff. Directory of Master's Programs in Foreign Languages, Foreign Literatures, & Linguistics. LC 87-11254. 183p. 1987. pap. 56.80 (*0-608-05586-7*, 206604600006) Bks Demand.
— Directory of Undergraduate Internships in the Humanities. fac. ed. LC 84-25486. 154p. 1984. reprint ed. pap. 47.80 (*0-7837-8037-0*, 204779300008) Bks Demand.
— Proceedings of the Neo-Classicism Conferences, 1967-1968. Korshin, Paul J., ed. (Studies in the Eighteenth Century: No. 1). reprint ed. 34.50 (*0-404-07949-0*) AMS Pr.
— Profession '80: Selected Articles from the Bulletins of the Association of Departments of English & the Association of Foreign Languages. fac. ed. LC LB2365.L4P7. (Illus.). 50p. 1980. reprint ed. pap. 30.00 (*0-7837-8023-0*, 204777900008) Bks Demand.
— Profession '88. fac. ed. Zuses, Carol & FRanklin, Phyllis, eds. LC LB2365.L4P7. 83p. 1988. reprint ed. pap. 30.00 (*0-7837-8029-X*, 204778500008) Bks Demand.
— Profession '81: Selected Articles from the Bulletins of the Association of Departments of English & the Association of Departments of Foreign Languages. fac. ed. LC LB2365.L4P7. (Illus.). 49p. 1981. reprint ed. pap. 30.00 (*0-7837-8024-9*, 204778000008) Bks Demand.
— Profession '82: Selected Articles from the Bulletins of the Association of Departments of English & the Association of Departments of Foreign Languages. fac. ed. LC LB2365.L4P7. 56p. 1982. reprint ed. pap. 30.00 (*0-7837-8025-7*, 204778100008) Bks Demand.
— Profession '79: Selected Articles from the Bulletins of the Association of Departments of English & the Association of Departments of Foreign Languages. fac. ed. Neel, Jasper P. & Brod, Richard I., eds. LC LB2365.L4P7. 65p. 1979. reprint ed. pap. 30.00 (*0-7837-8022-2*, 204777800008) Bks Demand.
— Research Opportunities in Renaissance Drama: The Reports of the Modern Language Association Conferences, 20 nos. in 8 vols., Set. Incl. Vol. 1, No. 1. Chicago Conference, 1955. Vol. 1, No. 2. Washington Conference, 1956. Vol. 1, No. 3. Madison Conference, 1957. Vol. 2, No. 4. New York Conference, 1958. Vol. 2, No. 5. Chicago, 1959 & Philadelphia, 1960, Conferences. Vol. 2, No. 6. Chicago, 1961 & Washington, 1962, Conferences. reprint ed. 335.00 (*0-404-08063-4*) AMS Pr.
— Sexual & Gender Harassment in the Academy: A Guide for Faculty, Students, & Administrators. fac. ed. LC 81-14059. 79p. 1981. reprint ed. pap. 30.00 (*0-7837-8030-3*, 204778600008) Bks Demand.
Modern Language Association of America Staff, jt. auth. see Gibaldi, Joseph.
Modern Language Association Staff. The Little Magazine & Contemporary Literature: A Symposium Held at the Library of Congress, 2 & 3 April, 1965. LC 72-3239. 127p. 1966. pap. 39.40 (*0-608-05587-5*, 206604700006) Bks Demand.
Modern Library. Mother's Day Classics from Modern Library. LC 98-14562. 208p. 1998. pap. 12.00 (*0-375-75153-X*) Modern Lib NY.
Modern Library Staff. America: Classics That Help Define the Nation. LC 99-11787. (Orig.). 1999. pap. 12.95 (*0-375-75381-8*) Modern Lib NY.
— Christmas Classics from the Modern Library. LC 97-24012. 1997. pap. 12.00 (*0-679-60282-8*) Modern Lib NY.
— Love: Classics from Modern Library. LC 98-34560. 224p. 1999. pap. 12.95 (*0-375-75309-5*) Modern Lib NY.
***Modern Library Staff.** Modern Library Christmas Assortment. 1999. write for info. (*0-676-79984-1*) Random House.
Modern Library Staff. Modern Library 100 Best of Non Fiction, Bk. C. 1999. pap. text 12.95 (*0-676-59147-7*) Hse Collectbls.
— Modern Library 100 Best of Non Fiction, Bk. D. 1999. pap. text 9.95 (*0-676-59148-5*) Hse Collectbls.
— Modern Library 100 Best of Non Fiction, Bk. A. 1999. pap. text 12.95 (*0-676-59145-0*) Hse Collectbls.
— Modern Library 100 Best of Non Fiction, Bk. B. 1999. pap. text 11.95 (*0-676-59146-9*) Hse Collectbls.
Modern Library Staff. 100 Best Nonfiction Books. pap. 14.95 (*0-375-75504-7*) Random.
Modern Library Staff & Dickinson, Emily. Selected Poems of Emily Dickinson. 1996. 14.50 (*0-679-60201-1*) Random.
Modern Library Staff, ed. see Poe, Edgar Allan.
Modern Liturgy Editors. The Usher's Book of the Mass. LC 96-4891. 31p. (Orig.). 1996. pap. 5.95 (*0-89390-364-7*) Resource Pubns.
Modern Liturgy Editors, ed. The Triduum Book. LC 96-44051. Orig. Title: Holy Week Book. (Illus.). 176p. 1997. pap. 29.95 (*0-89390-394-9*) Resource Pubns.
Modern Machine Shop Staff. Electrical Discharge Machining Conference Proceedings, 1991. 221p. (C). 1991. pap. 45.00 (*1-56990-066-3*) Hanser-Gardner.
— Electrical Discharge Machining Conference Proceedings, 1993. 250p. (C). 1993. pap. 65.00 (*1-56990-124-4*) Hanser-Gardner.
***Modern Plastics Magazine Staff.** Modern Plastics Handbook. LC 99-56522. 1298p. 2000. 125.00 (*0-07-026714-6*) McGraw.
Modern, R. E. Historia de la Literatura Alemana. (Breviarios Ser.). (SPA.). pap. 9.99 (*968-16-0177-7*, Pub. by Fondo) Continental Bk.
Modern Women Writers Staff. Albatross & Other Stories. 1988. pap. text. write for info. (*0-582-01728-9*, Pub. by Addison-Wesley) Longman.
Moderow, Karen. The Parting: Celebrate a Life by Planning a Meaningful, Creative Funeral. LC 95-60950. 104p. (Orig.). 1996. pap. 8.99 (*0-9643189-0-3*) K Moderow.
Modersohn-Becker, Paula. The Letters & Journals: Paula Modersohn-Becker. Busch, Gunter & Von Reinken, Liselotte, eds. LC 98-155373. (Illus.). 576p. 1998. pap. text 24.95 (*0-8101-1644-8*) Northwestern U Pr.
— The Letters & Journals of Paula Modersohn-Becker. LC 80-18993. 370p. 1980. 29.50 (*0-8108-1344-0*) Scarecrow.
Modert, Jo, ed. see Austen, Jane.
Moderwell, Hiram K. Theatre of To-Day. LC 72-7078. (Select Bibliographies Reprint Ser.). 1977. reprint ed. 40.95 (*0-8369-6950-2*) Ayer.
Modery, Wolfgang. Internationale Wahrungspolitische Arrangements auf dem Prufstand Okonomischer Effizienz. (GER., Illus.). 304p. 1996. 57.95 (*3-631-49953-1*) P Lang Pubng.
Modesco, Jamie A. Miraculous Heart: With Ikan, the Angel of the Rainbow. (Illus.). 49p. (Orig.). (J). (gr. 4 up). 1995. pap. 12.95 (*0-9638758-4-1*) Brockton Pubng.
Modesitt, Jeanne. It's Hanukkah! LC 98-46704. (Illus.). 32p. (J). (gr. k-3). 1999. 15.95 (*0-8234-1451-5*) Holiday.
***Modesitt, Jeanne.** Little Bunny's Easter Surprise. LC 98-28841. (Illus.). 32p. (J). (ps-1). 1999. 12.95 (*0-689-82491-2*) S&S Bks Yung.
Modesitt, Jeanne. Lunch with Milly. LC 93-33808. (Illus.). 32p. (J). (ps-2). 1997. 13.95 (*0-8167-3388-0*) BrdgeWater.
— Lunch with Milly. LC 93-33808. (Illus.). 32p. (J). (gr. k-2). 1996. pap. 4.95 (*0-8167-3389-9*, Troll Medallion) Troll Communs.
— Lunch with Milly. LC 93-33808. 1995. 10.15 (*0-606-09581-0*, Pub. by Turtleback) Demco.
— Mama, If You Had a Wish. LC 91-31354. (Illus.). 40p. (J). (ps-1). 1993. pap. 15.00 (*0-671-75437-8*, Green Tiger S&S) S&S Childrens.
— Mama If You Had a Wish. LC 91-31354. 40p. (J). 1999. per. 5.99 (*0-689-82412-2*) Aladdin.
— Sometimes I Feel Like a Mouse. LC 91-17281. (Illus.). 32p. (J). (ps-2). 1996. pap. 3.95 (*0-590-44836-6*) Scholastic Inc.
— Sometimes I Feel Like a Mouse: A Book about Feelings. 1992. 10.19 (*0-606-09873-9*, Pub. by Turtleback) Demco.
— The Story of Z. LC 89-3923. (Illus.). 28p. (J). (ps up). 1991. pap. 14.95 (*0-88708-105-3*, Picture Book Studio) S&S Childrens.
Modesitt, L. E., Jr. Adiamante, Vol. 1. 1998. mass mkt. 6.99 (*0-8125-4558-3*, Pub. by Tor Bks) St Martin.
— The Chaos Balance. LC 97-16431. 448p. (gr. 5 up). 1997. text 25.95 (*0-312-86389-6*) St Martin.
— The Chaos Balance. (Saga of Recluce Ser.). 596p. 1998. mass mkt. 6.99 (*0-8125-7130-4*, Pub. by Tor Bks) St Martin.
— Colors of Chaos. LC 98-43971. 720p. 1999. 27.95 (*0-312-86767-0*, Pub. by Tor Bks) St Martin.
***Modesitt, L. E., Jr.** Colors of Chaos. 816p. 2000. mass mkt. 7.99 (*0-8125-7093-6*, Pub. by Tor Bks) St Martin.
— Darksong Rising. (Spellsong Cycle Ser.: Bk. 3). 512p. 2000. 27.95 (*0-312-86822-7*, Pub. by Tor Bks) St Martin.
— Darksong Rising. (Spellsong Cycle Ser.: Bk. 3). 2001. mass mkt. 6.99 (*0-8125-6668-8*) Tor Bks.
Modesitt, L. E., Jr. The Death of Chaos. 480p. 1995. 24.95 (*0-312-85721-7*) Tor Bks.
— The Death of Chaos, Vol. 1. LC 95-22690. (Saga of Recluce Ser.). 629p. 1996. mass mkt. 6.99 (*0-8125-4824-8*, Pub. by Tor Bks) St Martin.
— The Ecolitan Enigma. LC 97-2169. 384p. 1997. text 23.95 (*0-312-86339-X*) St Martin.
— The Ecolitan Enigma. 1998. mass mkt. 6.99 (*0-8125-7117-7*, Pub. by Tor Bks) St Martin.
— Fall of Angels. 608p. 1997. mass mkt. 6.99 (*0-8125-3895-1*, Pub. by Tor Bks) St Martin.
— The Forever Hero. 2nd ed. 1999. pap. 17.95 (*0-312-86838-3*, Pub. by Tor Bks) St Martin.
— The Ghost of the Revelator. 320p. 1999. mass mkt. 6.99 (*0-8125-4536-2*, Pub. by Tor Bks) St Martin.
— The Ghost of the Revelator. LC 98-24111. 304p. 2000. 23.95 (*0-312-86426-4*, Pub. by Tor Bks) St Martin.
***Modesitt, L. E., Jr.** Gravity Dreams. 2000. mass mkt. 6.99 (*0-8125-6661-0*) Tor Bks.
Modesitt, L. E., Jr. Gravity Dreams. 2nd ed. LC 99-22966. 1999. 24.95 (*0-312-86826-X*, Pub. by Tor Bks) St Martin.
— Hammer of Darkness. 1996. mass mkt. 4.99 (*0-8125-3692-4*, Pub. by Tor Bks); mass mkt. 4.99 (*0-8125-6322-0*, Pub. by Tor Bks) St Martin.
— The Magic Engineer. (Saga of Recluce Ser.). 617p. 1995. mass mkt. 5.99 (*0-8125-3405-0*, Pub. by Tor Bks) St Martin.
— The Magic of Recluce. (Saga of Recluce Ser.). 501p. 1992. mass mkt. 5.99 (*0-8125-0518-2*, Pub. by Tor Bks) St Martin.
***Modesitt, L. E., Jr.** Magi'i of Cyador. LC 99-55274. 544p. 2000. 25.95 (*0-312-87226-7*, Pub. by Tor Bks) St Martin.
— The Octagonal Raven. 2001. write for info. (*0-312-87720-X*) Tor Bks.
Modesitt, L. E., Jr. Of Tangible Ghosts. 381p. 1995. mass mkt. 5.99 (*0-8125-4822-1*, Pub. by Tor Bks) St Martin.
— The Order War. 480p. 1995. 23.95 (*0-312-85569-9*) Tor Bks.
— The Order War. 480p. 1996. pap., student ed. 4.99 (*0-614-05524-5*); mass mkt. 4.99 (*0-8125-3404-2*, Pub. by Tor Bks) St Martin.
— The Parafaith War. 1997. mass mkt. 6.99 (*0-8125-3894-3*, Pub. by Forge NYC) St Martin.
***Modesitt, L. E., Jr.** Scion of Cyador. 640p. 2000. text 27.95 (*0-312-87379-4*) Tor Bks.
Modesitt, L. E., Jr. The Soprano Sorceress. LC 96-30645. (Spellsong Cycle Ser.: Vol. 2). 512p. 1997. 25.95 (*0-312-86022-6*, Pub. by Tor Bks) St Martin.
— The Soprano Sorceress. (Spellsong Cycle Ser.: 1). 1997. 24.95 (*0-614-20658-8*) Tor Bks.
— The Soprano Sorceress. (Spellsong Cycle Ser.: Bk. 1). 1998. mass mkt. 6.99 (*0-8125-4559-1*, Pub. by Tor Bks) St Martin.
— The Spellsong War. LC 97-29837. (Spellsong Cycle Ser.: 2). 1997. text 25.95 (*0-312-86492-2*) St Martin.
— The Spellsong War. (Spellsong Cycle Ser.: 2). 657p. 1999. mass mkt. 6.99 (*0-8125-4002-6*, Pub. by Tor Bks) St Martin.
***Modesitt, L. E., Jr.** Timegods' World. 544p. 2000. pap. 14.95 (*0-312-87495-2*, Pub. by Tor Bks) St Martin.
Modesitt, L. E., Jr. The Towers of the Sunset. 368p. 1992. 21.95 (*0-312-85297-5*, Pub. by Tor Bks) St Martin.
— The Towers of the Sunset. (Saga of Recluce Ser.). 536p. 1993. mass mkt. 5.99 (*0-8125-1967-1*, Pub. by Tor Bks) St Martin.
— The White Order. 1999. mass mkt. 6.99 (*0-8125-4171-5*, Pub. by Tor Bks) St Martin.
Modesitt, L. E., Jr. & Levinson, Bruce S. The Green Progression, No. 3. 320p. 1995. 4.99 (*0-8125-1641-9*) Tor Bks.
Modest. Radiative Heat Transfer. 1993. text, student ed. 34.68 (*0-07-042676-7*) McGraw.
Modest, Michael F. Radiative Heat Transfer. LC 92-24671. (Mechanical Engineering Ser.). 525p. (C). 1993. 98.75 (*0-07-042675-9*) McGraw.
Modest, Michael F., et al, eds. General Papers in Heat Transfer: Natural & Forced Convection. (HTD Ser.: Vol. 237). 124p. 1993. 37.50 (*0-7918-1150-6*, G00794) ASME.
— General Papers in Radiative Heat Transfer. LC 93-73715. 61p. 1993. pap. 30.00 (*0-7918-1002-X*) ASME.
Modest, Michael F., et al. General Papers on Convection. LC 93-73714. 71p. 1993. pap. 35.00 (*0-7918-1001-1*) ASME.
Modeste, Naomi N. A Dictionary of Public Health Promotion & Education: Terms & Concepts. LC 95-35417. 194p. 1995. 46.00 (*0-7619-0002-0*); pap. 19.95 (*0-7619-0003-9*) Sage.
Modesto, Robert, ed. see Ponce, Mario.

M

Modesto, Ruby & Mount, Guy. Not for Innocent Ears: Spiritual Traditions of a Desert Cahuilla Medicine Woman. rev. ed. (Illus.). 128p. 1986. per. 9.95 (0-9604462-0-6) Sweetlight.

Modgil, Celia, jt. auth. see Modgil, Sohan.

Modgil, Celia, jt. ed. see Modgil, Sohan.

Modgil, Sohan, ed. B. F. Skinner: Consensus & Controversy. LC 86-13518. (International Master Minds Challenged Ser.). 400p. 1987. 138.00 (1-85000-026-3, Falmer Pr) Taylor & Francis.

— Lawrence Kholberg: Consensus & Controversy. LC 86-6361. (International Master Minds Challenged Ser.). 550p. 1986. 138.00 (1-85000-025-5, Falmer Pr) Taylor & Francis.

Modgil, Sohan & Modgil, Celia. Jean Piaget: Consensus & Controversy. LC 81-84205. 446p. 1982. 55.00 (0-275-90862-3, C0862, Praeger Pubs) Greenwood.

Modgil, Sohan & Modgil, Celia, eds. Arthur Jensen: Consensus & Controversy. (International Master Minds Challenged Ser.). 410p. 1987. 138.00 (1-85000-093-X, Falmer Pr) Taylor & Francis.

— Hans Eysenck: Consensus & Controversy. LC 86-11473. (International Master Minds Challenged Ser.: Vol. 2). 400p. 1986. 138.00 (1-85000-021-2, Falmer Pr) Taylor & Francis.

Modglin, Terrence, jt. auth. see O'Neil, Jean.

Modglin, Terry, jt. auth. see Cotton, Michelle.

***Modha, Sanjay.** How to Succeed in Intermediate Level Business GNVQ's. 160p. 1998. pap. 19.95 (0-7494-2215-7, Kogan Pg Educ) Stylus Pub VA.

Modha, Sanjay, jt. auth. see Byron, Mike.

***Modhubuti, Haki R.** Taking Notes: Letters to Young Black Men. 100p. 2000. pap. 10.00 (0-88378-220-0) Third World.

Modi, Gauri, tr. see Kripalvananda, Svami.

Modi, Ishwar, ed. Emerging Trends in Indian Sociology, 3 vols., 1. 320p. 1986. 40.00 (0-8364-1883-2, Pub. by Rawat Pubns) S Asia.

— Emerging Trends in Indian Sociology, 3 vols., 2. 320p. 1986. 40.00 (0-8364-1884-0, Pub. by Rawat Pubns) S Asia.

— Emerging Trends in Indian Sociology, 3 vols., 3. 320p. 1986. 40.00 (0-8364-1885-9, Pub. by Rawat Pubns) S Asia.

Modi, Jagdish J. Parallel Algorithms & Matrix Computation. (Oxford Applied Mathematics & Computing Science Ser.). (Illus.). 272p. 1989. pap. text 39.95 (0-19-859670-7) OUP.

***Modi, Shakuntala.** Memories of God & Creation: Remembering from the Subconscious Mind. 2000. pap. 15.95 (1-57174-196-8) Hampton Roads Pub Co.

Modi, Shakuntala. Remarkable Healings: A Psychiatrist Discovers Unsuspected Roots of Mental & Physical Illness. LC 98-72108. 632p. 1997. pap. text 18.95 (1-57174-079-1) Hampton Roads Pub Co.

Modiano, Marko. Domestic Disharmony & Industrialization in D.H. Lawrence's Early Fiction. (Studia Anglistica Upsaliensia Ser.: No. 62). 124p. (Orig.). 1987. pap. 34.00 (91-554-2084-2, Pub. by Uppsala Univ Acta Univ Uppsaliensis) Coronet Bks.

Modiano, Patrick. Les Boulevards de Ceintures. (FRE.). 1978. pap. 10.95 (0-7859-3390-5) Fr & Eur.

— Les Boulevards de Ceintures. (Folio Ser.: No. 1033). (FRE.). pap. 8.95 (2-07-037033-X) Schoenhof.

— Catherine Certitude. Rodarmor, William, tr. from FRE. (Illus.). 64p. (J). (gr. 4-9). 2000. reprint ed. 17.95 (0-87923-959-X) Godine.

— De Si Brave Garcons. (FRE.). 1987. pap. 8.95 (0-7859-3393-X, 207037811X) Fr & Eur.

— De Si Braves Garcons. (Folio Ser.: No. 1811). (FRE.). pap. 6.95 (2-07-037811-X) Schoenhof.

— Dimanches d'Aout. (FRE.). 1989. pap. 10.95 (0-7859-2918-5) Fr & Eur.

— Dimanches d'Aout. (Folio Ser.: No. 2042). (FRE.). 1989. pap. 8.95 (2-07-038130-7) Schoenhof.

***Modiano, Patrick.** Du Plus Loin D'oubli, Vol. 1. 3rd ed. (FRE.). 1998. pap. 16.95 (2-07-040299-1) CFR Pubns.

Modiano, Patrick. Fleurs de Ruine. (FRE.). 1992. pap. 10.95 (0-7859-2731-X, 2020177161) Fr & Eur.

— Honeymoon. Wright, Barbara, tr. from FRE. (Verba Mundi Ser.). 128p. 1995. 19.95 (0-87923-947-6) Godine.

— Honeymoon. 1999. 12.95 (0-9666750-5-3, Pub. by Nocturnum Pr) Consort Bk Sales.

— Une Jeunesse. (FRE.). 1985. pap. 10.95 (0-7859-3391-3) Fr & Eur.

— Une Jeunesse. (Folio Ser.: No. 1629). (FRE.). pap. 8.95 (2-07-037629-X) Schoenhof.

— Livret de Famille. (FRE.). 1981. pap. 10.95 (0-7859-2897-9) Fr & Eur.

— Livret de Famille. (Folio Ser.: No. 1293). (FRE.). 1981. pap. 8.95 (2-07-037293-6) Schoenhof.

— Memory Lane. 1983. pap. 10.95 (0-7859-2692-5) Fr & Eur.

— Out of the Dark. Stump, Jordan, tr. from FRE. LC 98-13100. Orig. Title: Du Plus Loin de L'Oubli. 139p. 1998. text 45.00 (0-8032-3196-2) U of Nebr Pr.

— Le Place de l'Etoile. (Folio Ser.: No. 698). (FRE.). pap. 8.95 (2-07-036698-7) Schoenhof.

— La Place de l'Etoile. (FRE.). 1975. pap. 10.95 (0-7859-2882-0) Fr & Eur.

— Poupee Blonde. (FRE.). 1992. pap. 14.95 (0-7859-2723-9) Fr & Eur.

— Quartier Perdu. (FRE.). 1988. pap. 10.95 (0-7859-2916-9) Fr & Eur.

— Quartier Perdu. (Folio Ser.: No. 1942). (FRE.). pap. 8.95 (2-07-037942-6) Schoenhof.

— Remise de Peine. (FRE.). 1989. pap. 10.95 (0-7859-2712-3) Fr & Eur.

— La Ronde de Nuit. (FRE.). 1976. pap. 8.95 (0-7859-2887-1) Fr & Eur.

— La Ronde de Nuit. (Folio Ser.: No. 835). (FRE.). 152p. 1976. pap. 6.95 (2-07-036835-1) Schoenhof.

— Rue des Boutiques Obscures. (FRE.). 1982. pap. 10.95 (0-7859-2899-5) Fr & Eur.

— Rue des Boutiques Obscures. (Folio Ser.: No. 1358). (FRE.). 250p. 1982. pap. 8.95 (2-07-037358-4) Schoenhof.

— Vestiaire de l'Enfance. (FRE.). 1991. pap. 10.95 (0-7859-2925-8) Fr & Eur.

— Vestiaire de l'Enfance. (Folio Ser.: No. 2253). (FRE.). pap. 8.95 (2-07-038364-4) Schoenhof.

— Villa Triste. (FRE.). 1977. pap. 10.95 (0-7859-2890-1) Fr & Eur.

— Villa Triste. (Folio Ser.: No. 953). (FRE.). pap. 8.95 (2-07-036953-6) Schoenhof.

— Voyage de Noces. (Folio Ser.: No. 2330). (FRE.). pap. 8.95 (2-07-038454-3) Schoenhof.

Modiano, Patrick & Polizzotti, Mark. Dora Bruder. LC 98-33890. 123p. 1999. 19.95 (0-520-21426-9, Pub. by U CA Pr) Cal Prin Full Svc.

Modiano, Patrick & Sempe, Jean-Jacques. Catherine Certitude. (Folio - Junior Ser.: No. 600). (FRE.). 95p. (J). (gr. 5-10). 1988. pap. 9.95 (2-07-033600-X) Schoenhof.

Modiano, Raimonda. Coleridge & the Concept of Nature. LC 84-8043. xiv, 270p. 1985. 49.95 (0-8130-0808-5) U Press Fla.

***Modic, Jefferey & Stockton, Bayard.** Nothing to Fear. vii, 224p. 1999. 16.00 (0-9672508-0-3) Tres Pinos.

Modica, Andrea. Treadwell: Photographs. LC 95-34059. (Illus.). 85p. 1996. 40.00 (0-8118-1118-2) Chronicle Bks.

***Modica, Joseph B., ed.** The Gospel with Extra Salt: Friends of Tony Campolo Celebrate His Passions for Ministry. 160p. (YA). 2000. pap. 14.00 (0-8170-1313-X) Judson.

Modica, Terry A. Overcoming the Power of the Occult. LC 96-61570. 1997. pap. 9.50 (1-880033-24-0) Queenship Pub.

***Modica, Terry Ann.** Daily Prayers with the Saints for the New Millennium. 192p. 1999. pap. 7.95 (1-877678-52-X) Queenship Pub.

Modigh, Kjell, et al, eds. Anticonvulsants in Psychiatry. LC 94-28069. 176p. 1994. 49.00 (1-871816-25-4, Pub. by Wrightson Biomed) Taylor & Francis.

Modigliani. Drawings of Modigliani. Longstreet, Stephen, ed. (Master Draughtsman Ser.). 1972. pap. 4.95 (0-87505-177-4) Borden.

***Modigliani, Franco.** Adventures of an Economist. 2000. 27.95 (1-58799-007-5) Texere.

Modigliani, Franco. Collected Papers of Franco Modigliani, 3 vols., Vol. 1: Essays in Macroeconomics. Abel, Andrew, ed. 1980. 55.00 (0-262-13150-1) MIT Pr.

— The Collected Papers of Franco Modigliani Vol. 4: Monetary Theory & Stabilization Policies. Johnson, Simon, ed. 350p. 1989. 50.00 (0-262-13244-3) MIT Pr.

— The Collected Papers of Franco Modigliani Vol. 5: Saving, Deficits, Inflation, & Financial Theory. Johnson, Simon, ed. 450p. 1989. 55.00 (0-262-13245-1) MIT Pr.

Modigliani, Franco, jt. auth. see Fabozzi, Frank J.

Modigliani, Franco, jt. ed. see Baldassarri, Mario.

Modigliani, Kathy, et al. Opening Your Door to Children: How to Start a Family Day Care Program. LC 87-60747. 69p. 1987. pap. 3.50 (0-935989-06-4, NAEYC #203) Natl Assn Child Ed.

Modigliani, Kathy, jt. auth. see Dombro, Amy L.

Modin, Yuri. My Five Cambridge Friends. 1995. 23.00 (0-374-21698-3) FS&G.

***Modin, Yuri.** My Five Cambridge Friends: Burgess, Maclean, Philby, Blunt, & Cairncross. Roberts, Anthony, tr. (Illus.). 282p. 2000. reprint ed. pap. 17.00 (0-7881-9413-5) DIANE Pub.

Modin, Yuri. My 5 Cambridge Friends: Burgess, Maclean, Philby, Blunt, & Cairncross by Their KGB Controller. Roberts, Anthony, tr. (Illus.). 282p. 1998. text 23.00 (0-7881-5594-6) DIANE Pub.

Modinos, A. Field, Thermionic, & Secondary Electron Emission Spectroscopy. LC 83-21311. 384p. 1984. 110.00 (0-306-41321-3, Plenum Trade) Perseus Pubng.

— Quantum Theory of Matter: A Novel Introduction. LC 95-49410. 368p. 1996. 155.00 (0-471-96363-1); pap. 64.95 (0-471-96364-X) Wiley.

***Modis.** Conquering Uncertainty. 1999. write for info. (0-07-134889-1) McGraw.

Modis, Lazslo. Organization - The Extracellular Matrix: A Polarz Microsc. Appr. 296p. 1990. lib. bdg. 239.00 (0-8493-5786-1, QM563) CRC Pr.

Modis, Theodore. Conquering Uncertainty: Understanding Corporate Cycles & Positioning Your Company to Survive the Changing Environment. LC 97-49364. 224p. 1998. 19.95 (0-07-043405-0, BusinessWeek Bks) McGraw.

— Predictions: Society's Telltale Signature Reveals the Past & Forecasts the Future. 288p. 1992. 21.00 (0-671-75917-5) S&S Trade.

— An S-Shaped Trail to Wall Street. 204p. 1999. mass mkt. 49.00 (2-9700216-0-9, Pub. by Growth Dynamics) N Nikas.

Modisett, Bill. T. Evetts Haley: A True Texas Legend. LC 95-72439. 232p. 1996. write for info. (0-9650623-0-9); pap. write for info. (0-9650623-1-7) Stked Plains TX.

Modisett, Noah F. & Luter, James G., Jr. Speaking Clearly: The Basics of Voice & Articulation. 4th rev. ed. (Illus.). 304p. 1996. pap. text 28.00 (0-8087-3295-1) Pearson Custom.

Modisett, William E., Jr. Historic Midland: An Illustrated History. (Illus.). 128p. 1998. 29.95 (0-9654999-3-6) Hist Pub Network.

Modjeska, Abigail C., jt. auth. see Modjeska, Lee.

Modjeska, Drusilla. The Orchard. 268p. 1998. pap. 15.95 (0-7043-4514-5, Pub. by Womens Press) Trafalgar.

***Modjeska, Drusilla.** Stravinsky's Lunch. (Illus.). 384p. 2000. 30.00 (0-374-27089-9) FS&G.

Modjeska, Helena O. Memories & Impressions: An Autobiography. (American Biography Ser.). 571p. 1991. reprint ed. lib. bdg. 99.00 (0-7812-8286-1) Rprt Serv.

— Memories & Impressions of Helena Modjeska: An Autobiography. LC 75-81212. (Illus.). 580p. 1972. reprint ed. 24.95 (0-405-08791-8, Pub. by Blom Pubns) Ayer.

Modjeska, Lee. Administrative Law: Practice & Procedure. LC 82-80575. 1982. 112.50 (0-686-35770-1) West Group.

— Administrative Law: Practice & Procedure. LC 82-80575. 1994. suppl. ed. 60.00 (0-317-03153-8) West Group.

Modjeska, Lee & Modjeska, Abigail C. Federal Labor Law: NLRB Practice. rev. ed. LC 94-48176. 1994. write for info. (0-614-32194-8) West Group.

Modler, H. W., jt. ed. see Nakai, Shuryo.

Modler, H. Wayne, jt. ed. see Nakai, Shuryo.

Modler, Peter. Das Phanomen des "Ekels Vor Dem Leben" Bei Pierre Teilhard de Chardin. (Europaische Hochschulschriften Ser.: Reihe 23, Bd. 394). (GER.). 185p. 1990. 43.80 (3-631-42907-X) P Lang Pubng.

Modleski, T. The Women Who Knew Too Much. 176p. (C). 1988. pap. 18.99 (0-415-90176-8) Routledge.

Modleski, Tania. Feminism Without Women: Culture & Criticism in a "Postfeminist" Age. 416p. (C). (gr. 13). 1991. pap. 19.99 (0-415-90417-X, A5342) Routledge.

— Loving with a Vengeance: Mass-Produced Fantasies for Women. 140p. (C). 1984. pap. 18.99 (0-415-90136-7, NO. 9176) Routledge.

— Loving with a Vengeance: Mass-Produced Fantasies for Women. LC 82-8687. 141p. (C). 1982. lib. bdg. 29.50 (0-208-01945-6, Archon Bks) Shoe String.

— Old Wives' Tales: And Other Women's Stories. (Illus.). 264p. 1998. pap. 17.95 (0-8147-5594-1) NYU Pr.

— The Women Who Knew Too Much. 200p. 1987. 35.00 (0-416-01701-0, A0412); pap. 10.95 (0-416-01711-8) Routledge.

Modleski, Tania, ed. Studies in Entertainment: Critical Approaches to Mass Culture. LC 85-45980. (Theories of Contemporary Culture Ser.). (Illus.). 228p. 1986. pap. 10.95 (0-253-20395-3, MB-395) Ind U Pr.

Modlesli, Tania. Old Wives' Tales: And Other Women's Stories. LC 98-25366. (Illus.). 264p. 1998. text 55.00 (0-8147-5593-3) NYU Pr.

Modley, Rudolf & Myers, William R. Handbook of Pictorial Symbols. 143p. 1976. pap. 9.95 (0-486-23357-X) Dover.

— Handbook of Pictorial Symbols: 3,250 Examples from International Sources. 1990. 24.00 (0-8446-5516-3) Peter Smith.

Modlin, Betsy B., et al, eds. Washington County, N. C. A Tapestry. LC 98-73084. (Illus.). 697p. 1998. 50.00 (0-9663776-0-5) Wash Cty NC.

Modlin, Charles E. & Norton, W. W., eds. Winesburg, Ohio: An Authoritative Text, Backgrounds & Contexts, Criticism. LC 95-10378. (Critical Editions Ser.). 224p. (C). 1995. pap. text 9.75 (0-393-96795-6) Norton.

Modlin, Charles E., ed. see Anderson, Sherwood.

Modlin, Charles E., ed. & intro. see Anderson, Sherwood.

Modlin, Dan & Martin, Harry. Farming Talk. LC 85-71902. 221p. 1985. pap. 7.95 (0-9611416-1-1) RRN Bks.

Modlin, Irvin M., jt. ed. see Scarpignato, C.

Modlin, Marian L. Gunter: A Guide Dog. LC 96-86794. 1996. pap. text, mass mkt. 14.95 (1-889131-07-5) CasAnanda.

Modlin, Marilyn J., jt. auth. see Fitzpatrick, Gary L.

Modlin, Rick, ed. see Frolick, Jeanne C.

Modly, Doris M. Home Care Nursing Services: International Lessons. LC 96-53472. 1997. 47.95 (0-8261-9600-4) Springer Pub.

Modly, Doris M., et al, eds. Advancing Nursing Education Worldwide. LC 94-35282. (Illus.). 200p. 1995. 35.95 (0-8261-8650-5) Springer Pub.

Modoc Press Editors. Guide to Schools & Departments of Religion & Seminaries in the U. S. & Canada. 736p. 1987. 100.00 (0-02-921650-8) Free Pr.

Modood, Tariq & Werbner, Pnina. The Politics of Multiculturalism in the New Europe: Racism, Identity, & Community. LC 97-13316. (Postcolonial Encounters Ser.). 1997. pap. 22.50 (1-85649-422-5) Humanities.

— The Politics of Multiculturalism in the New Europe: Racism, Identity, & Community. LC 97-13316. (Postcolonial Encounters Ser.). 1997. text 62.50 (1-85649-421-7) Humanities.

Modood, Tariq, et al. The Position of Ethnic Minorities: The 4th National Survey of Ethnic Minorities in Britain. LC 97-135979. 320p. (C). 1995. pap. 24.95 (0-85374-671-0) Brookings.

Modood, Tariq, jt. ed. see Werbner, Pnina.

Modotti, Tina. Tina Modotti. LC 98-86910. (Aperture Masters of Photography Ser.). (Illus.). 96p. 1998. 18.95 (0-89381-823-2) Aperture.

Modra, Ron C., photos by. Reflections of the Game: Lives in Baseball. LC 98-24520. (Illus.). 160p. 1998. 29.50 (1-57223-180-7) Willow Creek Pr.

Modra, Ronald C. & Roberts, M. B. Garish Gardens, Outlandish Lawns: A Celebration of Eccentric American Landscaping. LC 98-10115. (Illus.). 128p. 1998. 15.95 (1-57223-140-8, 1408) Willow Creek Pr.

Modrak, Deborah K. Aristotle: The Power of Perception. LC 86-19208. x, 260p. (C). 1989. pap. text 17.00 (0-226-53339-5) U Ch Pr.

— Aristotle: The Power of Perception. LC 86-19208. x, 250p. (C). 1995. 35.95 (0-226-53338-7) U Ch Pr.

***Modrak, Deborah K. W.** Aristotle's Theory of Language & Meaning. LC 99-56850. (Illus.). 320p. 2000. 59.95 (0-521-77266-4) Cambridge U Pr.

Modrak, Nancy C., ed. see Benson, Carolyn V.

Modras, Ronald. Jesus of Nazareth: A Life Worth Living. (Nazareth Bks). 128p. 1984. 1.95 (0-86683-713-2) Harper SF.

— Paul Tillich's Theology of the Church: A Catholic Appraisal. LC 76-6082. 314p. reprint ed. pap. 97.40 (0-7837-3605-3, 204347000009) Bks Demand.

Modrezejewsci, Joseph M. Droit Imperial et Traditions Locales dans l'Egypte Romaine. (Collected Studies: No. 321). 336p. 1990. text 119.95 (0-86078-270-0, Pub. by Variorum) Ashgate Pub Co.

Modrezhinskaya, Yelena. Leninism & the Battle of Ideas. 1972. pap. 24.95 (0-8464-4448-8) Beekman Pubs.

Modrick, I. C. Nobody's Warriors. LC 96-69085. 167p. (Orig.). 1997. pap. 14.95 (1-57197-034-7) Pentland Pr.

Modritzer, Helmut. Stigma und Charisma im Neuen Testament und Seiner Umwelt: Zur Soziologie des Urchristentums. (Novum Testamentum et Orbis Antiquus Ser.: Vol. 28). (GER.). 344p. 1994. text 67.25 (3-7278-0938-8, Pub. by Presses Univ Fribourg) Eisenbrauns.

Modrow, John. How to Become a Schizophrenic: The Case Against Biological Psychiatry. 2nd rev. ed. Klumpar, Caroline, ed. LC 92-71410. 295p. (Orig.). 1996. pap. 14.95 (0-9632626-7-X) Apollyon Pr.

Modrzejewski, Joseph M. Jews of Egypt: From Rameses II to Emperor Hadrian. Cornman, Robert, tr. LC 97-33449. 301p. 1997. pap. text 18.95 (0-691-01575-9, Pub. by Princeton U Pr) Cal Prin Full Svc.

— Jews of Egypt, from Rameses II to Emperor Hadrian. 1995. 29.95 (0-8276-0522-6) JPS Phila.

Modrzhinskaya, Y. D., et al. Future of Society: A Soviet View. 375p. 1973. 22.00 (0-8464-0442-7) Beekman Pubs.

Modrzyk, Stanley J. Celebrating Times of Change: A Wiccan Book of Shadows for Family & Coven Growth. LC 95-3719. (Illus.). 160p. (Orig.). 1995. pap. 11.00 (0-87728-820-8) Weiser.

Modrzyk, Stanley J. Turning of the Wheel: A Wiccan Book of Shadows for Moons & Festivals. LC 92-45558. (Illus.). 280p. (Orig.). 1993. pap. 12.95 (0-87728-767-8) Weiser.

Modrzyk, Stanley J. Wedding Videographer's Handbook. 82p. (Orig.). 1986. pap. 4.50 (0-939751-00-3) Seeing Is Believing Video.

Modrzynski, Mike. Hiking Michigan. LC 96-1004. (Illus.). 176p. (Orig.). 1996. pap. 12.95 (1-56044-226-3) Falcon Pub Inc.

Modu, Anaezi & Walker, Andrea. All the Man I Need: Black Women's Loving Expressions on the Men They Desire. LC 98-96211. 1998. pap. 15.95 (1-887646-04-3) Gateway Pubs.

Modu, Emmanuel. The Lemonade Stand: A Guide to Encouraging the Entrepreneur in Your Child. rev. ed. Walker, Andrea, ed. LC 95-78201. 352p. 1996. pap. 19.95 (1-887646-03-5) Gateway Pubs.

***Modu, Emmanuel & Walker, Andrea.** Teenvestor.Com: The Practical Investment Guide for Teens & Their Parents. 2000. pap. text 13.95 (1-887646-05-1) Gateway Pubs.

Modugno, Carolyn & McDermott, Rosalie. EnviroLearn Five. (Illus.). 96p. (Orig.). 1996. pap., teacher ed. 12.95 (1-57022-043-5) ECS Lrn Systs.

— EnviroLearn Four. (Illus.). 80p. 1996. pap., teacher ed. 12.95 (1-57022-042-5) ECS Lrn Systs.

— EnviroLearn K-1. (Illus.). 96p. (Orig.). 1996. pap., teacher ed. 12.95 (1-57022-039-5) ECS Lrn Systs.

— EnviroLearn Three. (Illus.). 96p. (Orig.). 1996. pap., teacher ed. 12.95 (1-57022-041-7) ECS Lrn Systs.

— EnviroLearn Two. (Illus.). 96p. (Orig.). 1996. pap., teacher ed. 12.95 (1-57022-040-9) ECS Lrn Systs.

Modupe' Bode'-Thomas, tr. see Mariama Ba.

Modupe, Talibah F. The Grapevine Still Alive & Workin'! Harris, T. Munirah, ed. (Illus.). 104p. (Orig.). 1995. pap. 11.00 (1-887442-02-2) Modupe Pr.

— Let's Be Frank, Okay! Harris, T. Munirah, ed. (Illus.). 94p. (Orig.). 1994. pap. 7.95 (1-887442-01-4) Modupe Pr.

— Talibah, Can We Talk? Harris, T. Munirah, ed. (Illus.). 111p. (Orig.). 1994. pap. 7.95 (1-887442-00-6) Modupe Pr.

— Transformed. Harris, T. Munirah, ed. (Illus.). 123p. (Orig.). 1995. pap. 13.95 (1-887442-04-9) Modupe Pr.

Modupe, Talibah F., et al. When You Should Really Know - It's Over! 100+ Ways to Let You Know Your Relationship Is Headed Toward Destruction. 34p. (Orig.). 1995. pap. 3.00 (1-887442-03-0) Modupe Pr.

Mody, Ashoka, ed. Infrastructure Delivery: Private Initiative & the Public Good. (EDI Development Studies). 268p. 1996. pap. 22.00 (0-8213-3520-0, 13520) World Bank.

— Infrastructure Strategies in East Asia: The Untold Story. LC 97-34324. (EDI Learning Resources Ser.). 176p. 1997. pap. 22.00 (0-8213-4027-1, 14027) World Bank.

Mody, Bella. Designing Messages for Development Communication: An Audience Participation-Based Approach. 216p. (C). 1992. 52.00 (0-8039-9105-3); pap. 24.95 (0-8039-9106-1) Sage.

Mody, Bella, et al, eds. Telecommunications Politics: Ownership & Control of the Information Highway in Developing Countries. (LEA's Telecommunications Ser.). 360p. 1995. 79.95 (0-8058-1752-2); pap. 39.95 (0-8058-1753-0) L Erlbaum Assocs.

Mody, Istvan, jt. ed. see Gutnick, Michael J.

Mody, Monica. Barney's Book of Airplanes. (Barney's Transportation Ser.). (Illus.). 24p. (J). (ps-k). 1998. pap. 3.25 (1-57064-236-2, Barney Publ) Lyrick Pub.

— Barney's Book of Boats. LC 97-70879. (Barney's Transportation Ser.). (Illus.). 24p. (J). (ps-k). 1997. pap. text 3.25 (1-57064-129-3, Barney Publ) Lyrick Pub.

***Mody, Monica.** Barney's Book of Trains. (Barney's Transportation Ser.). (Illus.). 24p. (J). (ps-k). 1998. pap. 3.25 (1-57064-237-0) Lyrick Pub.

Mody, Monica. Barney's Book of Trucks. LC 97-70880. (Barney's Transportation Ser.). (Illus.). 24p. (J). (ps-k). 1997. pap. 3.25 (*1-57064-128-5*) Lyrick Pub.

***Mody, Monica.** Barney's Easter Party! LC 99-6256. (Barney Ser.). (Illus.). 22p. (J). (ps-k). 2000. 5.95 (*1-57064-714-3*) Lyrick Pub.

— Zoomba in Toyland. Larsen, Margie, ed. LC 95-75422. (Barney Ser.). (Illus.). 24p. (J). (ps-k). 1996. pap. 6.95 incl. audio (*1-57064-095-5*, 99645) Lyrick Pub.

Mody, Monica, jt. auth. see Barney Publishing Staff.

Mody, Nawaz. Indonesia under Suharto: A Study in the Concentration of Power. LC 87-70631. 325p. 1987. text 40.00 (*0-86590-792-7*) Apt Bks.

Mody, Nawaz B. The Parsis in Western India, 1818 to 1920. LC 99-934072. xxxii, 288p. 1998. 0.00 (*81-7023-894-3*) Allied Pubs.

Mody, V. & Jakhete, R. Dust Control Handbook. LC 88-19061. (Pollution Technology Review Ser.: Vol.). (Illus.). 203p. 1989. 79.00 (*0-8155-1182-5*) Noyes.

Modzelewski, Jozef. Der Besuch, "The Visit" Custom Pub. (C). 1994. pap. text 39.50 (*0-07-046860-5*) McGraw.

— Das Pandamonium der Achtziger Jahre: Kurzprosa des Jahres, 1983. LC 90-33820. (Studies in Modern German Literature: Vol. 37). (GER.). XIV, 313p. (C). 1990. text 66.95 (*0-8204-1226-0*) P Lang Pubng.

Modzelewski, Michael. Angeles Crest: A Memoir. LC 99-63270. (Illus.). 261p. 2000. 24.00 (*0-9660625-9-0*, Pub. by Advent Unltd) Partners-West.

— Inside Passage: Living with Killer Whales, Bald Eagles & Kwakiutl Indians. 2nd ed. 186p. 1997. reprint ed. 22.95 (*0-9660625-0-7*) Advent Unltd.

Moe. Teaching Reading in Elementary School. 1996. pap. text 47.00 (*0-205-14198-6*) S&S Childrens.

Moe, Albert W. Nevada's Golden Age of Gambling. LC 96-92834. (Illus.). 120p. (Orig.). 1996. pap. 14.95 (*0-9655215-0-8*) Nevada Collectables.

Moe, Alden J., jt. auth. see Woods, Mary L.

Moe, Atle & Thyrre, Kristina. The Complete Guide to Clubs & Flags. (Illus.). 272p. 1998. pap. 24.95 (*0-9651781-4-5*) Three Stars Co.

***Moe, Atle & Thyrre, Kristina.** The Complete Guide to Clubs & Flags. 4th ed. 275p. 1999. 24.95 (*0-9651781-6-1*) Three Stars Co.

Moe, Atle & Thyrre, Kristina. Flag Usage in Yachting. (Illus.). 20p. 1997. pap. 5.00 (*0-9651781-2-9*) Three Stars Co.

— Flag Usage in Yachting. (Illus.). 20p. 1999. pap. 5.00 (*0-9651781-5-3*) Three Stars Co.

— Stars Register of Yachts Clubs & Flags, 1998. (Illus.). 1040p. 1998. 89.50 (*0-9651781-3-7*) Three Stars Co.

Moe, Atle & Thyrre, Kristina, eds. Stars Register of Yachts, 1996. (Illus.). 1000p. 1996. 100.00 (*0-9651781-0-2*) Three Stars Co.

Moe, Atle, jt. auth. see Marsh, Sarah.

Moe, Barbara. Coping When You Are the Survivor of a Violent Crime. LC 94-14117. (YA). (gr. 7-12). 1995. lib. bdg. 17.95 (*0-8239-1882-3*) Rosen Group.

— Coping with Bias Incidents. LC 93-6895. (Coping Ser.). 192p. (YA). (gr. 7-12). 1993. lib. bdg. 17.95 (*0-8239-1606-5*) Rosen Group.

— Coping with Chronic Illness. Rosen, Ruth C., ed. LC 92-15377. (Coping Ser.). (YA). (gr. 7-12). 1992. lib. bdg. 17.95 (*0-8239-1464-X*) Rosen Group.

— Coping with Eating Disorders. rev. ed. (Coping Ser.). (YA). (gr. 7-12). 1995. lib. bdg. 17.95 (*0-8239-2133-6*) Rosen Group.

***Moe, Barbara.** Everything You Need to Know about Migraines & Other Headaches. LC 00-26927. (Need to Know Library). 2000. write for info. (*0-8239-3291-5*) Rosen Group.

Moe, Barbara. Everything You Need to Know about PMS. LC 94-25640. (Need to Know Library). (Illus.). 64p. (YA). (gr. 7-12). 1995. lib. bdg. 17.95 (*0-8239-1877-7*) Rosen Group.

— Everything You Need to Know about Sexual Abstinence. rev. ed. (Need to Know Library). (Illus.). 64p. (gr. 7-12). 1998. lib. bdg. 17.95 (*0-8239-2747-4*) Rosen Group.

— Inside Eating Disorders Support Groups. LC 98-29942. (Teen Health Library of Eating Disorder Prevention). (Illus.). 64p. (YA). (gr. 7-12). 1998. lib. bdg. 17.95 (*0-8239-2769-5*, EDSUGR) Rosen Group.

***Moe, Barbara.** Teen Smoking & Tobacco Use: A Hot Issue. LC 99-50268. (Hot Issues Ser.). (Illus.). 64p. (YA). (gr. 6 up). 2000. lib. bdg. 19.95 (*0-7660-1359-6*) Enslow Pubs.

— Understanding the Causes of a Negative Body Image 1999. pap. text 6.95 (*1-56838-262-6*) Hazelden.

Moe, Barbara, jt. auth. see Moe, Martin.

Moe, Barbara A. Adoption: A Reference Handbook. LC 98-14254. (Contemporary World Issues Ser.). 303p. 1998. lib. bdg. 45.00 (*0-87436-898-7*) ABC-CLIO.

Moe, Christian H. & Eugene, R. Jackson, eds. Eight Plays for Youth: Varied Theatrical Experiences for Stage & Study. LC 91-18425. (American University Studies: Theatre Arts: Ser. XXVI, Vol. 8). (Illus.). XXVI, 369p. 1991. 59.95 (*0-8204-1554-5*) P Lang Pubng.

Moe, Christian H., ed. see Lash, James.

Moe, Daniel. Problems in Conducting. rev. ed. 20p. 1968. pap. 6.50 (*0-8066-0834-X*, 11-9369, Augsburg) Augsburg Fortress.

Moe, David. Songs from Alaska. 1997. pap. write for info. (*1-57553-590-4*) Watermrk Pr.

Moe, David E. The Making of a Winner. (Illus.). 110p. (Orig.). 1987. pap. 6.95 (*0-9615797-1-4*); lib. bdg. 12.95 (*0-9615797-2-2*) Moe-Tavation.

— Opening Hearts & Minds: The Joy of Teaching. (Illus.). (Orig.). 1985. pap. 6.95 (*0-9615797-0-6*) Moe-Tavation.

Moe, Dean L. Christian Symbols Handbook: Commentary & Patterns for Traditional & Contemporary Symbols. 96p. (Orig.). 1985. pap. 15.99 (*0-8066-2153-2*, 10-1180, Augsburg) Augsburg Fortress.

Moe, Doug. Madison: Meeting the 21st Century. 1990. 29.95 (*0-89781-313-8*) Am Historical Pr.

— The World of Mike Royko. LC 99-6586. (Illus.). 128p. 1999. text 29.95 (*0-299-16540-X*) U of Wis Pr.

Moe, Erik. Couches from the Underworld: Cartoons & Stories from Moe's Notebook. 128p. 1994. pap. 9.95 (*0-9644905-0-1*) E Moe.

Moe, Harold. Make Your Paycheck Last. 4th rev. ed. (Illus.). 128p. 1997. pap. 11.95 (*0-9612310-7-6*) Harsand Pr.

Moe, Harold R. Make Your Paycheck Last: The Complete Step by Step Guide to Financial Success. expanded rev. ed. Choutka, Jeanne, ed. (Illus.). 116p. 1994. student ed. 14.95 (*0-9612310-5-X*) Harsand Pr.

— Make Your Paycheck Last: The Complete Step by Step Guide to Financial Success. 2nd rev. ed. Choutka, Jeanne, ed. (Illus.). 120p. 1994. pap. 7.95 (*0-9612310-2-5*) Harsand Pr.

Moe, J. E., jt. auth. see Asbjornsen, Peter C.

Moe, Jerry & Ways, Peter. Conducting Support Groups for Elementary Children K-6: A Guide for Educators & Other Professionnals. 160p. 1991. pap. 16.50 (*1-56246-018-8*, 3202, HazeldenJohnson Inst) Hazelden.

Moe, Jorgen, jt. auth. see Asbjornsen, Peter C.

Moe, Julie K., jt. ed. see Yancer, Deborah A.

Moe, Kathleen K., jt. auth. see More, Owen A.

Moe, Kenneth A. The Pastor's Survival Manual: 10 Perils in Parish Ministry & How to Handle Them. LC 95-78603. 130p. 1995. pap. 14.95 (*1-56699-157-9*, AL166) Alban Inst.

Moe, Lawrence H., jt. ed. see Wallmann, James L.

Moe, Louisa, ed. Female Artists, Past & Present: International Women's Year 1975 Supplement. 1975. pap. 4.00 (*0-685-70574-9*) Women's Hist.

Moe, Marilynn M. Creative Chords. 88p. 1994. student ed. 15.50 (*1-884816-00-2*) M M Moe.

— Creative Chords Answer Key. 88p. 1994. pap. text 7.95 (*1-884816-01-0*) M M Moe.

— Lydia. 69p. (Orig.). 1995. pap. 5.95 (*1-884816-04-5*) M M Moe.

— Patterns & Pathways. 88p. 1994. 11.95 (*1-884816-02-9*) M M Moe.

— Tastes That Teach: And Other Devotional Object Lessons. (Illus.). 49p. (YA). (gr. 6 up). 1997. 14.95 (*1-884816-03-7*) M M Moe.

***Moe, Martin & Moe, Barbara.** The Marine Aquarists' Quiz Book. 224p. 2000. pap. 15.95 (*0-939960-10-9*) Green Turtle Pubns.

Moe, Martin A., Jr. Breeding the Orchid Dottyback (Pseudochromis Fridmani) An Aquarist's Journal. LC 97-28339. (Illus.). 288p. 1997. pap. 19.95 (*0-939960-09-5*) Green Turtle Pubns.

— Lobsters: Florida, Bahamas, & the Caribbean. LC 91-23948. (Illus.). 512p. (Orig.). 1991. pap. 22.95 (*0-939960-06-0*) Green Turtle Pubns.

— The Marine Aquarium Handbook: Beginner to Breeder. 2nd ed. LC 92-4908. (Illus.). 320p. (Orig.). 1992. pap. 16.95 (*0-939960-07-9*) Green Turtle Pubns.

Moe, Mary, ed. see Sullivan, Mick.

Moe, Michelle. Sprinkles of Love: A Parent's Guide to Infant Message. Woung, Phyllis, ed. (Illus.). 24p. Date not set. pap. 14.95 (*0-9659509-0-5*) Kisses from Heaven.

Moe, Nelson, tr. & intro. see Rella, Franco.

Moe, Richard. The Last Full Measure: The Life & Death of the First Minnesota Volunteers. LC 92-32687. (Illus.). 368p. 1995. 29.95 (*0-8050-2309-7*) H Holt & Co.

— The Last Full Measure: The Life & Death of the First Minnesota Volunteers. 376p. 1994. reprint ed. pap. 15.00 (*0-380-72322-0*, Avon Bks) Morrow Avon.

***Moe, Richard, et al, eds.** With Heritage So Rich. 2nd rev. ed. (Illus.). 243p. 1999. pap. 25.00 (*0-89133-396-7*) Wiley.

Moe, Richard & Wilkie, Carter. Changing Places: Rebuilding Community in the Age of Sprawl. 288p. 1999. pap. 13.95 (*0-8050-6184-3*, Pub. by H Holt & Co) VHPS.

Moe, Terry, jt. ed. see Evers, Williamson.

Moe, Terry M. The Organization of Interests: Incentives & the Internal Dynamics of Political Interests Groups. LC 79-13238. 1980. lib. bdg. 14.95 (*0-226-53351-4*) U Ch Pr.

— The Organization of Interests: Incentives & the Internal Dynamics of Political Interests Groups. 292p. 1988. pap. text 19.95 (*0-226-53353-0*, Midway Reprint) U Ch Pr.

***Moe, Terry M.** Schools, Vouchers, & the American Public. 2000. 29.95 (*0-8157-5808-1*) Brookings.

Moe, Terry M., jt. auth. see Chubb, John E.

Moe, Thomas. Pastoral Care in Pregnancy Loss: A Ministry Long Needed. LC 96-9343. 162p. (C). 1996. pap. 19.95 (*0-7890-0196-9*, Haworth Pastrl) Haworth Pr.

— Pastoral Care in Pregnancy Loss: A Ministry Long Needed. LC 96-9343. 162p. (C). 1997. 39.95 (*0-7890-0124-1*, Haworth Pastrl) Haworth Pr.

Moe, Thorvald. Demographic Developments & Economic Growth in Norway, 1740-1940: An Econometric Study. Bruchey, Stuart, ed. LC 77-77190. (Dissertations in European Economic History Ser.). 1978. lib. bdg. 29.95 (*0-405-10802-8*) Ayer.

Moebius & Jodorowsky. Angel Claw.Tr. of Griffe D'Ange. (Illus.). 72p. 1996. 19.95 (*1-56163-153-1*, Eurotica) NBM.

Moebius, Jean. The Man from the Ciguri. unabridged ed. (Illus.). 80p. (Orig.). (YA). (gr. 11 up). 1996. pap. 7.95 (*1-56971-135-6*) Dark Horse Comics.

Moebius, Jean (G). Arzach. unabridged ed. (FRE., Illus.). 80p. (Orig.). (gr. 11 up). 1996. pap. 6.95 (*1-56971-132-1*) Dark Horse Comics.

Moebs, jt. auth. see Sanny.

Moebs, Betty R. Gilchrist Revisited: For Hers Is the Kingdom. LC 89-91672. 200p. (Orig.). 1989. pap. 8.95 (*0-9623016-0-4*) B R Moebs.

Moebs, William & Sanny, Jeff. University Physics. 350p. 1995. pap. text, student ed. write for info. (*0-697-05886-7*, WCB McGr Hill) McGrw-H Hghr Educ.

— University Physics. 224p. (C). 1995. text, student ed. 27.50 (*0-697-23258-1*, WCB McGr Hill) McGrw-H Hghr Educ.

— University Physics. 1072p. (C). 1995. text. write for info. (*0-697-05884-0*, WCB McGr Hill) McGrw-H Hghr Educ.

Moebs, William, jt. auth. see Sanny, Jeff.

Moechars, Dieder. A Transgenic Mouse Model for Alzheimer's Disease. (Acta Biomedica Lovaniensia Ser.: No. 122). (Illus.). 113p. (Orig.). 1996. pap. 43.50 (*90-6186-727-4*, Pub. by Leuven Univ) Coronet Bks.

***Moeck, Pat.** Medical Assisting Program. 1999. pap. text 15.77 (*1-56870-366-X*) RonJon Pub.

Moeckel, R., ed. Aktuelle Geomorphodynamik und Angewandte Geomorphologie (Present-Day Geomorphodynamics & Applied Geomorphology) Vol. 16: Tagung des Deutschen Arbeitskreises fuer Geomorphologie, Freiburg. (Zeitschrift fuer Geomorphologie - Annals of Geomorphology Ser.: Supplementband 89). (GER., Illus.). iii, 155p. 1991. pap. 64.00 (*3-443-21089-9*, Pub. by Gebruder Borntraeger) Balogh.

Moeckli, Peter. Residual Stresses in CBN & Corundum Ground Gear Tooth Flanks As the Determining Factor in Abrasive Wheel Selections. (Nineteen Eighty-Six Fall Technical Meeting Ser.: Vol. 86FTM11). (Illus.). 14p. 1986. pap., pap. text 30.00 incl. audio compact disk (*1-55589-475-5*, 86FTM11) AGMA.

Moed, Berton R. & Watson, Tracy, eds. Fracture Non-Unions. (Illus.). 256p. 1999. 85.00 (*0-7506-2231-8*) Buttrwrth-Heinemann.

***Moeen.** Elysium Phantasy. Uddin, Moein, ed. 117p. 2000. pap. 12.48 (*0-9661601-9-3*) Globe CA.

Moeglin, C. & Waldspurger, J. L. Decomposition Spectrale et Series d'Eisenstein: Une Paraphase de L'Ecriture. (Progress in Mathematics Ser.: Vol. 113). 1994. 98.00 (*0-8176-2938-6*) Birkhauser.

— A Paraphrase of the Scriptures. (Spectral Decomposition & Eisenstein Ser.: No. 113). (Illus.). 366p. (C). 1995. text 90.00 (*0-521-41893-3*) Cambridge U Pr.

Moeglin, C., et al. Correspondances de Howe sur un Corps P-adique. (Lecture Notes in Mathematics Ser.: Vol. 1291). vii, 163p. 1987. 35.30 (*0-387-18699-9*) Spr-Verlag.

Moehing, Walter G., IV & Stallings, Ronald D. Georgia Corporate Forms, 2 vols. 1994. ring bd., suppl. ed. 89.00 (*0-685-75310-7*, MICHIE) LEXIS Pub.

Moehle, Natalia R. From Myth to Philosophy: Philosophical Implications of the Mythic Understanding of Transtemporal Identity. LC 87-8212. (Illus.). 156p. (Orig.). (C). 1987. lib. bdg. 43.50 (*0-8191-6356-2*) U Pr of Amer.

Moehle-Vieregge, Linda, et al. Surf's Up! A Website Workbook for Basic French. (FRE., Illus.). 268p. 1997. spiral bd. 16.95 (*0-88432-934-8*, B29348) Audio-Forum.

— Surf's Up! A Website Workbook for Basic German. (GER., Illus.). (Orig.). 1996. spiral bd., wbk. ed. 16.95 (*0-88432-922-4*, B29224) Audio-Forum.

— Surf's Up! A Website Workbook for Basic Spanish. (SPA., Illus.). 248p. 1997. spiral bd. 16.95 (*0-88432-953-4*, B29534) Audio-Forum.

Moehlenpah, Arlo & Moehlenpah, Jane. Teaching with Variety. LC 90-43007. (Illus.). 184p. (Orig.). 1990. pap. 8.99 (*0-932581-67-6*) Word Aflame.

***Moehlenpah, Arlo E.** Creation vs. Evolution: Scientific & Religious Consideration. unabridged ed. v, 161p. 1998. pap. 11.95 (*0-9667054-0-8*) Doing Good.

— Master Your Money or It Will Master You. unabridged ed. (Illus.). 158p. 1999. pap. 11.95 (*0-9667054-1-6*) Doing Good.

Moehlenpah, Jane, jt. auth. see Moehlenpah, Arlo.

Moehling, Vohny, jt. auth. see Wilmes, Liz.

Moehlman, Arthur B. Public Education in Detroit. LC 73-11930. (Metropolitan America Ser.). (Illus.). 268p. 1974. reprint ed. 23.95 (*0-405-05404-1*) Ayer.

Moehlman, Arthur B. & Van Zwoll, James A. School Public Relations: Communicating to the Community. LC 83-4371. 1983. write for info. (*0-8290-1331-8*) Irvington.

Moehlmann, Gustaaf R., ed. Nonlinear Optical Properties of Organic Materials IX, Vol. 2852. 304p. 1996. 76.00 (*0-8194-2240-1*) SPIE.

Moehn, Edwin. System und Phylogenie der Lebewesen Vol. 1: Physikalische, Chemische und Biologische Evolution. (Illus.). 884p. 1984. lib. bdg. 198.00 (*3-510-65117-0*, Pub. by E Schweizerbartsche) Balogh.

***Moehn, Heather.** World Holidays: A Watts Guide for Children. LC 99-14673. 1999. 32.00 (*0-531-11714-6*) Watts.

— World Holidays: A Watts Guide for Children. (Reference Ser.). (Illus.). (YA). 2000. pap. 19.95 (*0-531-16490-X*) Watts.

Moehring, Eugene P. Public Works & the Patterns of Urban Real Estate Growth in Manhattan, 1835-1849. 28.00 (*0-317-19169-1*, 19819) Ayer.

— Public Works & the Patterns of Urban Real Estate Growth in Manhattan, 1835-1894. xi, 452p. 1981. 30.95 (*0-405-13948-9*) Arno Press.

— Public Works & Urban Real Estate Growth. 1981. write for info. (*0-318-50874-5*) Ayer.

— Resort City in the Sunbelt: Las Vegas, 1930-1970. LC 89-9130. (Illus.). 344p. 1989. 29.95 (*0-87417-147-4*) U of Nev Pr.

***Moehring, Eugene P.** Resort City in the Sunbelt: Las Vegas, 1930-2000. 2nd ed. LC 00-8308. (History & Humanities Ser.). (Illus.). 360p. 2000. pap. 19.95 (*0-87417-356-6*) U of Nev Pr.

Moehring, Eugene P. Urban America & the Foreign Traveler, 1815-1855. LC 73-13465. (Foreign Travelers in America, 1810-1935 Ser.). 334p. 1974. reprint ed. 25.95 (*0-405-05468-8*) Ayer.

Moehring, Eugene P., ed. see New York Times Staff & Charleston Mercury Staff.

Moehring, Eugene P., jt. ed. see Schlesinger, Arthur Meier, Jr.

***Moehring, H. David & Greenspan, Adam.** Current Diagnosis & Treatment of Fractures LC 99-29747. 1999. write for info. (*1-57340-133-1*) Current Med.

***Moehring, H. David & Greenspan, Adam, eds.** Fractures: Diagnosis & Treatment. (Hazelden Chronic Illness Ser.). 248p. 1999. text. write for info. (*0-07-135902-8*) McGraw-Hill Prof.

Moekstra, Gerald R., ed. see Pevernage, Andre.

Moeleker, P. J. Linear Temporal Stability Analysis. (Series 01 - Aerodynamics: No. 07). (Illus.). 70p. 1998. pap. 14.95 (*90-407-1570-X*, Pub. by Delft U Pr) Coronet Bks.

Moell, Carl J., ed. & intro. see John Paul, II, pseud.

Moell, Joseph D., jt. auth. see Curlee, Thomas N.

Moellendorff, U., jt. auth. see Wilamowitz.

Moeller. Pocket Atlas of Cross-Sectional Anatomy Vol. 1: Head, Neck, Spine & Joints. 2nd ed. 1998. pap. 28.50 (*0-86577-813-2*) Thieme Med Pubs.

***Moeller, Achim & Naumann, Francis M.** Marcel Duchamp: The Art of Making Art in the Age of Mechanical Reproduction - An Exhibition Catalogue. (Illus.). 48p. 1999. pap. 35.00 (*0-9646052-4-4*) A Moeller Fine Art.

Moeller, Adeidine K. The Women As Survivor: The Evolution of the Female Figure in the Works of Heinrich Boll. LC 91-17714. (American University Studies: Germanic Languages & Literature: Ser. I, Vol. 85). 171p. (C). 1992. text 35.95 (*0-8204-1131-0*) P Lang Pubng.

Moeller, Alice M., see Anna, Rose, pseud.

Moeller, Beverly B. Phil Swing & Boulder Dam. LC 71-633550. (Illus.). 217p. reprint ed. pap. 67.30 (*0-608-18501-9*, 203150800075) Bks Demand.

Moeller, Bill. Complete Guide to Full Time RVing. 3rd rev. ed. (Illus.). 512p. 1998. pap. text 29.95 (*0-934798-53-2*) TL Enterprises.

***Moeller, Bill & Moeller, Jan.** Crazy Horse: A Photographic Biography. (Illus.). 112p. 2000. pap. 20.00 (*0-87842-424-5*) Mountain Pr.

Moeller, Bill & Moeller, Jan. Lewis & Clark: A Photographic Journey. LC 99-34862. (Illus.). 116p. 1999. pap. 18.00 (*0-87842-405-9*) Mountain Pr.

— RV Electrical Systems: Basic Troubleshooting, Repair & Improvement. LC 94-30072. (Illus.). 288p. 1994. pap. text 19.95 (*0-07-042778-X*, Ragged Mntain) McGraw-Hill Prof.

— RVing Basics. (Illus.). 224p. 1995. pap. text 14.95 (*0-07-042779-8*, Ragged Mntain) McGraw-Hill Prof.

Moeller, Bill, jt. auth. see Moeller, Jan.

Moeller, Carol, jt. auth. see Otero, George G., Jr.

Moeller, Cheryl, jt. auth. see Moeller, Robert.

Moeller, Dade W. Environmental Health. (Illus.). 332p. (C). 1992. 49.95 (*0-674-25858-4*) HUP.

— Environmental Health. LC 96-43287. (Illus.). 512p. 1997. 52.00 (*0-674-25859-2*) HUP.

Moeller, Dade W., ed. Radioactive & Mixed Waste - Risk As a Basis for Waste Classification. LC 95-22246. (Symposium Proceedings Ser.: No. 2). 201p. (Orig.). 1995. pap. text 30.00 (*0-929600-43-6*) NCRP Pubns.

Moeller, Dietmar P., jt. ed. see Zobel, Richard.

Moeller, Doris. Dear God, When Is It My Turn? 1991. pap. 9.95 (*0-9629058-0-1*) Scandia Pr.

***Moeller, Felix.** The Film Minister: Goebbels & the Cinema in the Third Reich. (Illus.). 192p. 2000. 42.00 (*3-932565-10-X*) Edition A Menges.

Moeller, Henry H. Shattering an American Myth. 1976. 29.95 (*0-8488-1551-5*) Amereon Ltd.

Moeller, Henry W. Shattering an American Myth: Unfurling the History of the Stars & Stripes. Date not set. lib. bdg. 14.95 (*0-8488-1531-9*) Amereon Ltd.

Moeller, Jack, et al. Deutsch Heute: Grundstufe. 6th ed. (GER.). (C). 1998. pap. text, wbk. ed., lab manual ed. 30.36 (*0-395-76687-7*) HM.

— Handbuch zur Deutschen Grammatik: Wiederholen und Anwenden. 2nd ed. LC 96-76971. (GER.). 512p. (C). 1997. text 50.76 (*0-669-39902-7*) HM Trade Div.

— Kaleidoskop: Kultur, Literatur und Grammatik. 5th annot. ed. (GER.). (C). 1998. pap., teacher ed. 51.16 (*0-395-87057-7*) HM.

Moeller, Jack R. Blickpunkt Deutschland, 001. 2nd ed. (C). 1982. pap., teacher ed. 20.80 (*0-395-32894-2*) HM.

— Blickpunkt Deutschland, 001. 2nd ed. (C). 1982. text 66.12 (*0-395-32689-3*) HM.

Moeller, Jack R. Concise German Review, 2 vols. (C). 1994. pap. 31.96 (*0-395-68876-0*) HM.

— Concise German Review, 2 vols., Vol. 2. 2nd ed. LC 94-76529. (C). 1994. pap. text 30.76 (*0-395-68875-2*) HM.

— Deutsch Heute, 5 vols. (C). 1992. pap., teacher ed., suppl. ed. 5.56 (*0-395-59203-8*) HM.

— Deutsch Heute, 5 vols. 5th ed. (C). 1992. pap. text, wbk. ed. 30.36 (*0-395-59142-2*) HM.

Moeller, Jack R. German Today, 001. (C). 1982. pap., wbk. ed. 18.16 (*0-395-30407-5*) HM.

Moeller, Jack R. German Today, 4 vols. (C). 1988. pap., teacher ed. 12.12 (*0-395-47130-3*); pap., teacher ed., suppl. ed. 10.60 (*0-395-47127-3*); pap., wbk. ed. 15.12 (*0-395-47125-7*); pap., lab manual ed. 14.64 (*0-395-47124-9*) HM.

— German Today, 4 vols. (C). 1988. pap., teacher ed. 88.68 (*0-395-48825-7*) HM.

— German Today, 4 vols. (C). 1988. pap. 47.12

M

(0-395-47140-0); pap., teacher ed. 109.72 (0-395-47123-0); pap., wbk. ed. 15.12 (0-395-47139-7); pap., wbk. ed. 14.64 (0-395-47138-9) HM.
— German Today, 4 vols. (C). 1988. pap., teacher ed. 88.68 (0-395-48826-5) HM.
Moeller, Jack R. German Today, 001, Bk. 2. (C). 1982. pap., wbk. ed. 19.08 (0-395-30409-1) HM.
— German Today, 001, Vol. 1. (C). 1985. text 66.40 (0-395-38358-7) HM.
Moeller, Jack R. German Today 1, 4 vols. (C). 1988. text, teacher ed. 58.60 (0-395-47146-X) HM.
— German Today 1, 4 vols. 4th ed. (C). 1988. text 52.12 (0-395-47122-2) HM.
— German Today 1: Test, 4 vols. 4th ed. (C). 1988. pap. text 47.12 (0-395-47126-5) HM.
— German Today 2, 4 vols. 4th ed. (C). 1988. text 55.60 (0-395-47135-4); text, teacher ed. 62.12 (0-395-47136-2) HM.
— Kaleidoscope, 3 vols. 3rd ed. (C). 1991. pap. text, wbk. ed. 37.56 (0-395-57261-4) HM.
— Kaleidoscope, 3 vols. 3rd ed. (C). 1991. pap. text, teacher ed., suppl. ed. 3.16 (0-395-57263-0) HM.
— Kaleidoskop, 4 vols. (C). 1994. pap. 51.16 (0-395-68539-7) HM.
— Kaleidoskop, 4 vols. (C). 1994. pap., teacher ed. 4.76 (0-395-68541-9) HM.
— Kaleidoskop, 4 vols. 4th ed. LC 93-78673. (C). 1994. pap. text 49.96 (0-395-66719-4) HM.
— Kaleidoskop, 4 vols. 4th ed. (C). 1994. pap. text, wbk. ed. 37.56 (0-395-68540-0) HM.
— Kaleidoskope, 3 vols. 3rd ed. (C). 1991. text 51.16 (0-395-57260-6) HM.
Moeller, Jack R. & Liedloff, Helmut. Deutsch Heute. 3rd ed. LC 83-81521. (GER.). 480p. 1984. audio 2.75 (0-685-08252-0) HM.
Moeller, Jack R., et al. Deutsch Heute, 5 vols. 5th ed. (C). 1992. text 61.16 (0-395-47299-7) HM.
— Kaleidoskop: Kultur, Literatur und Grammatik, 2 vols. 2nd ed. LC 86-81691. 384p. (C). 1987. pap. text, student ed. 37.56 (0-395-42418-6) HM.
— Kaleidoskop: Kultur, Literatur und Grammatik, 2 vols. 2nd ed. LC 86-81691. 384p. (C). 1987. reel tape 135.16 (0-395-42433-X) HM.
— Kaleidoskop: Kultur, Literatur und Grammatik, 2 vols. 2nd ed. LC 86-81691. 384p. (C). 1990. pap. 4.76 (0-395-42432-1) HM.
— Kaleidoskop: Kultur, Literatur und Grammatik, 2 vols., Pt. 1. 2nd ed. LC 86-81691. 384p. (C). 1987. audio 29.16 (0-395-42434-8) HM.
— Kaleidoskop: Kultur, Literatur und Grammatik, 2 vols., Pt. 2. 2nd ed. LC 86-81691. 384p. (C). 1987. audio 29.16 (0-395-42435-6) HM.
Moeller, Jan & Moeller, Bill. The Intracoastal Waterway: Norfolk to Miami, a Cockpit Cruising Handbook. 4th ed. (Illus.). 152p. 1996. spiral bd. 19.95 (0-07-042986-3) McGraw.
Moeller, Jan, jt. auth. see Moeller, Bill.
Moeller, Jeff, jt. auth. see Clayton, Skip.
Moeller, Jim, ed. see Bangjiu, Peter Z.
Moeller, Jim, ed. see Zhou, Peter.
Moeller, Karl, ed. see Moeller, Mary.
Moeller, Kathleen H. Gecko's Story. (Books for Young Learners). (Illus.). 12p. (Orig.). (J). (gr. k-2). 1997. pap. text 5.00 (1-57274-079-5, A2460) R Owen Pubs.
— La Historia de Geco. Romo, Alberto, tr. (Books for Young Learners).Tr. of Gecko's Story. (SPA., Illus.). 12p. (J). (gr. k-2). 1999. pap. text 5.00 (1-57274-293-3) R Owen Pubs.
— Hoketichee & the Manatee. (Books for Young Learners). (Illus.). 16p. (J). (gr. k-2). 1998. pap. text 5.00 (1-57274-117-1, A2745) R Owen Pubs.
— Hoketichee y el Manati. Romo, Alberto, tr. (Books for Young Learners).Tr. of Hoketichee & the Manatee. (SPA., Illus.). 16p. (J). (gr. k-2). 1999. pap. text 5.00 (1-57274-292-5) R Owen Pubs.
*Moeller, Marc & Moeller, Victor. Middle School English Teacher's Guide to Active Learning. 200p. 2000. pap. text, teacher ed. 29.95 (1-883001-87-0) Eye On Educ.
Moeller, Marc, jt. auth. see Moeller, Victor.
Moeller, Mary. Fibromyalgia Cookbook: A Daily Guide to Becoming Healthy Again. Moeller, Karl, ed. (Illus.). 163p. 1998. reprint ed. pap. 14.95 (0-9660190-8-3) Fibromyalgia Solns.
Moeller, Mary P. & Schick, Brenda. Sign with Me Vol. 2: Building Concepts Workbook-ASL. 1994. pap. text 8.95 (0-938510-63-0, 76-003) Boys Town Pr.
— Sign with Me Vol. 3: Positive Parenting (ASL) (Orig.). 1997. pap., wbk. ed. 8.95 (1-889322-03-2, 76-005(ASL)) Boys Town Pr.
— Sign with Me Workbook Vol. 3: Positive Parenting (MCE) 1996. pap., wbk. ed. 8.95 (0-938510-84-3, 76-006(MCE)) Boys Town Pr.
Moeller, Mary P. & Schink, Brenda. Sign with Me Vol. I: Building Conversations Workbook-ASL. 1994. pap. text 8.95 (0-938510-62-2, 76-001) Boys Town Pr.
Moeller, Misse. Charted Decorative Initials. (Embroidery, Needlepoint, Charted Designs Ser.). 32p. 1984. pap. 2.95 (0-486-24646-9) Dover.
Moeller, Pamela A. Calvin's Doxology: Worship in the 1559 Institutes, with a View to Contemporary Worship Renewal. LC 97-39259. (Princeton Theological Monographs). 194p. 1998. pap. 25.00 (1-55635-035-X) Pickwick.
*Moeller, Pamela A. Exploring Worship Anew: Dreams & Visions. LC 98-47292. 176p. 1999. pap. 18.99 (0-8272-0813-8) Chalice Pr.
Moeller, Peter, ed. Magnesite: Geology, Mineralogy, Geochemistry, Formation of Mg-Carbonates. (Monograph Series on Mineral Deposits: No. 28). (Illus.). viii, 300p. 1989. 52.00 (3-443-12028-8, Pub. by Gebruder Borntraeger) Balogh.
*Moeller, R. A. Distributed Data Warehousing Using Web Technology: How to Build a More Cost-Effective & Flexible Warehouse. LC 00-38984. (Illus.). 2000. pap. 45.00 (0-8144-0588-6) AMACOM.
Moeller, Robert. Stirring. 324p. 1996. mass mkt. 6.50 (0-7852-7261-5) Nelson.
— To Have & to Hold: Achieving Lifelong Sexual Intimacy & Satisfaction. 224p. 1995. pap. 9.99 (0-88070-679-1) Multnomah Pubs.
Moeller, Robert & Moeller, Cheryl. Marriage Minutes: Inspirational Readings to Share with Your Spouse. LC 98-204278. 284p. 1998. 16.99 (0-8024-2146-6) Moody.
Moeller, Robert G. German Peasants & Agrarian Politics, 1914-1924: The Rhineland & Westphalia. LC 85-14120. xv, 286p. (C). 1986. 49.95 (0-8078-1676-0) U of NC Pr.
— Protecting Motherhood: Women & the Family in the Politics of Postwar West Germany. (C). 1992. 50.00 (0-520-07903-5, Pub. by U CA Pr) Cal Prin Full Svc.
— Protecting Motherhood: Women & the Family in the Politics of Postwar West Germany. LC 92-6622. 346p. (C). 1996. pap. 15.95 (0-520-20516-2, Pub. by U CA Pr) Cal Prin Full Svc.
Moeller, Robert G., ed. Peasants & Lords in Modern Germany: Recent Studies in Agricultural History. LC 85-6113. 256p. 1986. text 60.00 (0-04-943037-8) Routledge.
Moeller, Robert R., et al. Brink's Modern Internal Auditing. 5th ed. LC 98-20229. 1200p. 1999. 130.00 (0-471-52132-9) Wiley.
Moeller, Roger, ed. see Davis, Henry K.
Moeller, Roger W. Practicing Environmental Archaeology: Methods & Interpretations. LC 82-73087. (Occasional Papers: No. 3). (Illus.). 112p. 1982. pap. text 10.00 (0-936322-00-4) Inst Amer Indian.
— Six LF 21: A Paleo-Indian Site in Western Connecticut. LC 80-65186. (Occasional Papers: No. 2). (Illus.). 160p. 1980. pap. 12.50 (0-89488-010-1) Inst Amer Indian.
Moeller, Roger W., ed. Archaeological Bibliography for Eastern North America. 198p. 1977. pap. 7.00 (0-936322-03-9) Inst Amer Indian.
— Experiments & Observations on the Terminal Archaic of the Middle Atlantic Region. (Illus.). iv, 130p. (Orig.). 1990. pap. text 15.00 (0-9622320-1-7) Archaeol Servs.
Moeller, Roger W., jt. ed. see Kinsey, W. Fred, III.
Moeller, Roy. Succeed & Be Happy. (Illus.). 100p. (Orig.). 1996. pap. 12.95 (0-9651952-0-1) O M A Pub.
Moeller-Sally, Stephen, jt. auth. see Greenleaf, Monika.
Moeller, Steve. Effort-Less Marketing for Financial Advisors: Five Steps to a Super-Profitable Business & a Wonderful Life. Frazee, Valerie et al, eds. (Illus.). 250p. 1999. 39.95 (0-9672059-0-5) Am Busn Visions.
Moeller, Susan D. Compassion Fatigue: How the Media Sells Disease, Famine, War & Death. LC 98-14075. (Illus.). 402p. 1998. 27.50 (0-415-92097-3) Routledge.
*Moeller, Susan D. Compassion Fatigue: How the Media Sells Disease, Famine, War & Death. 400p. 1999. pap. 18.95 (0-415-92098-1) Routledge.
Moeller, Susan E., jt. auth. see Ramaswami, Murali.
Moeller, Therald B. Inorganic Syntheses, 5. 280p. 1978. 35.00 (0-88275-869-1) Krieger.
Moeller, Therald B., et al. Chemistry with Inorganic Qualitative Analysis. 3rd ed. 263p. (C). 1989. pap. text, teacher ed. 28.00 (0-15-506457-6) Harcourt Coll Pubs.
Moeller, Therald B., jt. auth. see Reif, Emil.
Moeller, Toreten B., jt. auth. see Reif, Emil.
*Moeller, Torsten B. Normal Findings in CT & MRI. (Illus.). 250p. 1999. pap. 32.00 (0-86577-864-7) Thieme Med Pubs.
Moeller, Torsten B. & Reif, Emil. Pocket Atlas of Cross-Sectional Anatomy: Computer Tomography & Magnetic Resonance Imaging Thorax, Abdomen & Pelvis, Vol. 2. LC 93-43883. 246p. 1994. pap. 28.50 (0-86577-511-7) Thieme Med Pubs.
*Moeller, Torsten B. & Reif, Emil. Pocket Atlas of Sectional Anatomy Vol. 2: Computed Tomography & Magnetic Resonance Imaging. 2nd ed. (Illus.). 264p. 2000. pap. 32.00 (0-86577-872-8) Thieme Med Pubs.
Moeller, Torsten B., et al. Pocket Atlas of Radiographic Anatomy. Reif, Emil, ed. Robertson, Michael, tr. LC 92-49310. 356p. 1993. pap. 28.50 (0-86577-459-5) Thieme Med Pubs.
Moeller, Uwe, tr. see Von Sacher-Masoch, Leopold.
Moeller Van Den Bruck, Arthur. Germany's Third Empire. 1972. 45.00 (0-86527-085-6) Fertig.
*Moeller, Victor & Moeller, Marc. High School Enclish Teacher's Guide to Active Learning. 200p. 2000. pap. text, teacher ed. 29.95 (1-883001-88-9) Eye On Educ.
Moeller, Victor, jt. auth. see Moeller, Marc.
Moellering, H. Spatial Database Transfer Standards 2: Characteristitcs for Assessing Standards & Full Descriptions of the National & International Standards in the World. LC 96-42334. (International Cartographic Association Ser.). 350p. 1997. 182.00 (0-08-042433-3, Pergamon Pr) Elsevier.
Moellering, H., ed. Spatial Database Transfer Standards: Current International Status. 248p. 1991. 107.50 (1-85166-677-X) Elsevier.
Moellering, Robert C., Jr., ed. Oral Cepahlosporins. (Antibiotics & Chemotherapy Ser.: Vol. 47). (Illus.). x, 190p. 1995. 188.00 (3-8055-6163-6) S Karger.
Moellerke, George. Concise Electronics Dictionary, Vol. 1. 5th ed. (ENG & GER.). 174p. 1989. pap. 29.95 (0-8288-4407-0, M15120) Fr & Eur.
— Concise Electronics Dictionary Vol. 2: German-English. 2nd ed. (ENG & GER.). 160p. 1985. pap. 29.95 (0-8288-0291-2, M15119) Fr & Eur.
— Engineering Reader. (ENG & GER.). 101p. 1980. 55.00 (0-8288-1545-3, M15072) Fr & Eur.
Moellman, Carol. Effective State Councils on Vocational Education: A Guide for Staff. 1987. 11.50 (0-317-03878-8, SN55) Ctr Educ Trng Employ.
Moeloek, F. A., et al, eds. Advances in Human Reproduction: Proceedings of the 8th World Congress on Human Reproduction Jointly with the 4th World Conference on Fallopian Tube in Health & Disease, Bali, Indonesia, April 1993. LC 94-21471. (International Congress, Symposium, & Seminar Ser.). 554p. 1995. 88.00 (1-85070-521-6) Prthnon Pub.
Moelwyn-Hughes, E. A. Physical Chemistry. 2nd rev. ed. 1961. text 587.00 (0-08-010846-6, Pub. by Pergamon Repr) Franklin.
*Moemeka, Andrew A. Development Communication in Action: Building Understanding & Creating Participation. LC 99-51517. 336p. 2000. 57.00 (0-7618-1571-6) Rowman.
— Development Communication in Action: Building Understanding & Creating Participation. LC 99-51517. 336p. 2000. pap. 37.50 (0-7618-1572-4) U Pr of Amer.
Moemeka, Andrew A., ed. Communicating for Development: A New Pan-Disciplinary Perspective. LC 93-3456. (SUNY Series, Human Communication Processes). 280p. (C). 1994. pap. text 21.95 (0-7914-1834-0) State U NY Pr.
— Communicating for Development: A New Pan-Disciplinary Perspective. LC 93-3456. (SUNY Series, Human Communication Processes). 280p. (C). 1994. text 64.50 (0-7914-1833-2) State U NY Pr.
Moen. Contemporary Congress. (Political Science Ser.). (C). 1998. pap. 43.95 (0-314-12804-2) Wadsworth Pub.
Moen, Bruce. Voyage Beyond Doubt Vol. 2: Exploring the Afterlife. LC 98-71583. (Exploring the Afterlife Ser.: Vol. 2). 296p. 1998. pap. 13.95 (1-57174-101-1) Hampton Roads Pub Co.
*Moen, Bruce. Voyages into the Afterlife: Charting Unknown Territory. LC 99-71615. (Exploring the Afterlife Ser.: Bk. 3). 320p. 1999. pap. 13.95 (1-57174-139-9) Hampton Roads Pub Co.
Moen, Bruce. Voyages into the Unknown: Exploring the Afterlife, Vol. 1. LC 97-225931. 256p. 1997. pap. 12.95 (1-57174-068-6) Hampton Roads Pub Co.
Moen, Christine B. 25 Reproducible Literature Circle Role Sheets for Fiction & Nonfiction Books. Mitchell, Judy, ed. (Illus.). 64p. (J). (gr. 4-6). 1998. pap., teacher ed. 8.95 (1-57310-141-9) Teachng & Lrning Co.
*Moen, Christine Boardman. Group Project Student Role Sheets: Everything You Need for Successful Group Research Projects - Start to Finish! Mitchell, Judy, ed. 128p. (J). (gr. 4-8). 1999. 12.95 (1-57310-199-0) Teachng & Lrning Co.
— 20 Reproducible Literature Circle Role Sheets for Grades 1-3. Mitchell, Judy, ed. (Illus.). 64p. (J). (gr. 1-3). 2000. pap. 8.95 (1-57310-219-9) Teachng & Lrning Co.
Moen, Daryl R. Newspaper Layout & Design. (Illus.). 274p. (C). 1989. wbk. ed. 21.95 (0-8138-1228-3) Iowa St U Pr.
— Newspaper Layout & Design: A Team Approach. 3rd ed. LC 94-15567. (Illus.). 248p. 1995. pap. text 34.95 (0-8138-1225-9) Iowa St U Pr.
*Moen, Daryl R. Newspaper Layout & Design: A Team Approach. 4th rev. ed. 280p. 2000. pap. 39.95 (0-8138-0729-8) Iowa St U Pr.
*Moen, Elizabeth B. Decline of the Pulp & Paper Industry in Norway, 1950, 1980: A Study of a Closed System in an Open Economy. (Acta Humaniora). 344p. 1998. pap. 43.00 (82-00-12959-4) Scandnvan Univ Pr.
Moen, Elizabeth B., tr. see Borgen, Johan.
Moen, Larry. Meditations for Awakening. 2nd rev. ed. LC 93-37569. 247p. 1994. pap. 11.95 (1-880698-77-3, Pub. by US Pub FL) ACCESS Pubs Network.
— Meditations for Healing. 2nd ed. 247p. 1999. reprint ed. pap. 13.95 (0-9627209-2-5) New Leaf Dist.
— Meditations for Transformation. 2nd rev. ed. LC 93-34925. 247p. 1994. pap. 11.95 (1-880698-33-1, Pub. by US Pub FL) ACCESS Pubs Network.
Moen, Larry & Smith, Patty. Meditations for Healing. rev. ed. LC 93-34926. (Illus.). 264p. 1994. reprint ed. pap. 11.95 (1-880698-69-2) US Pub FL.
Moen, Lynn & Laik, Judy. Around the Circle Gently: A Book of Birth, Families, & Life. 160p. 1995. pap. 11.95 (0-89087-766-1) Celestial Arts.
*Moen, Marcia & Heinen, Margo. Reflections of Courage on D-Day & the Days That Followed: A Personal Account of Ranger "Ace" Parker. Groth, Shane, ed. LC 99-75428. 240p. 1999. pap. 15.95 (0-9649922-6-4) Deforest Pr.
Moen, Marcia, jt. ed. see Den Ouden, Bernard.
Moen, Mary K., jt. auth. see Huyler, Linda.
Moen, Matthew C. The Christian Right & Congress. LC 88-34010. 245p. reprint ed. pap. 76.00 (0-608-09584-2, 205438600006) Bks Demand.
— The Transformation of the Christian Right. LC 91-31447. 223p. reprint ed. pap. 69.20 (0-608-09232-0, 205273600005) Bks Demand.
Moen, Matthew C. & Gustafson, Lowell S., eds. The Religious Challenge to the State. (C). 1991. 59.95 (0-87722-856-6) Temple U Pr.
Moen, Ole O. & Lervik, Leif Magne, eds. Frontiers & Visions: A Casebook in American Civilization Studies. 307p. (C). 1996. pap. 33.00 (82-00-22759-6, Pub. by Scand Univ Pr) IBD Ltd.
Moen, Patricia & Brace, Tom. Report of the Minnesota Attorney General's Arson Task Force. (Illus.). 56p. 1998. pap. text 20.00 (0-7881-7386-3) DIANE Pub.
Moen, Phyllis. Women's Two Roles: A Contemporary Dilemma. LC 91-36728. 192p. 1992. 59.95 (0-86569-198-3, T198, Auburn Hse); pap. 16.95 (0-86569-199-1, R199, Auburn Hse) Greenwood.
— Working Parents: Transformations in Gender Roles & Public Policies in Sweden. LC 88-40439. (Life Course Studies). 192p. (Orig.). (C). 1989. pap. text 16.95 (0-299-12104-6) U of Wis Pr.
Moen, Phyllis, et al, eds. Examining Lives in Context: Perspectives on the Ecology of Human Development. LC 95-5704. (Science Ser.). 708p. 1995. text 24.95 (1-55798-293-7, 431-8380) Am Psychol.
— A Nation Divided: Diversity, Inequality, & Community in American Society. LC 99-15783. 1999. 49.95 (0-8014-3719-9) Cornell U Pr.
— A Nation Divided: Diversity, Inequality & Community in American Society. LC 99-15783. 1999. pap. 18.95 (0-8014-8588-6) Cornell U Pr.
Moen, Robert C., jt. ed. see Breener, Malcolm K.
Moen, Ronald D., et al. Improving Quality Through Planned Experimentation. 416p. (C). 1991. 80.00 (0-07-042673-2) McGraw.
— Quality Improvement Through Planned Experimentation. 2nd ed. (Illus.). 480p. 1998. 64.95 (0-07-043952-4) McGraw.
— Quality Improvement Through Planned Experimentation. 2nd ed. LC 98-8290. 464p. 1998. 69.95 (0-07-913781-4) McGraw.
Moen, Ronald S., ed. Accreditation Handbook for Ambulatory Health Care: 1989-90 Edition. rev. ed. 73p. 1989. pap. 30.00 (0-685-18876-0) Accredit Assn Ambulatory.
Moen, Ruth, ed. see Borrello, Joe.
Moen, Ruth R. Deadly Deceptions. (Kathleen O'Shaughnessy Ser.). 183p. (Orig.). 1994. pap. 7.95 (0-9635653-1-1) Flying Swan.
— Hayseeds in My Hair. 150p. (Orig.). 1992. pap. 12.95 (0-9635653-0-3) R R Moen.
— Only One Way Out. (Kathleen O'Shaughnessy Ser.). (Orig.). (C). 1995. pap. 7.95 (0-9635653-2-X) Flying Swan.
— Return to the Kill. (Kathleen O'Shaughnessy Mystery Ser.: Bk. 3). 228p. (Orig.). 1996. pap. 6.95 (0-9635653-5-4) Flying Swan.
— Self-Publishing Can Be Profitable & Immensely Rewarding. Cocke, Paul, ed. (Kathleen O'Shaghnessy Mystery Ser.). 138p. (Orig.). (C). 1995. pap. 17.49 (0-9635653-4-6) Flying Swan.
Moen, William E. & McClure, Charles R. An Evaluation of the Federal Government's Implementation of the Government Information Locator Service. 451p. 1997. 41.00 (0-16-049186-X) USGPO.
Moench, ed. Northern Appalachian Transect: Southeastern Quebec, Canada, Through Western Maine, U. S. A. (IGC Field Trip Guidebooks Ser.). 56p. 1989. 28.00 (0-87590-559-5, T358) Am Geophysical.
Moench, Cynthia. Binding up the Brokenhearted. 132p. (Orig.). 1991. pap. text 6.99 (0-89900-399-0) College Pr Pub.
Moench, D. Batman: Bloodstorm. O'Neil, Dennis, ed. (Illus.). 96p. 1995. pap. 12.95 (1-56389-185-9, Pub. by DC Comics) Time Warner.
Moench, D., et al. Batman - Spawn: War Devil. O'Neil, Dennis, ed. (Illus.). 48p. 1994. pap. 4.95 (1-56389-144-1) DC Comics.
Moench, Doug. Batman: Crimson Mist. (Illus.). 96p. 1998. 24.95 (1-56389-477-7, Pub. by DC Comics) Time Warner.
Moench, Doug. Batman - Dracula: Red Rain. O'Neil, Dennis, ed. (Illus.). 96p. 1997. pap. 9.95 (1-56389-036-4, Pub. by DC Comics) Time Warner.
Moench, Doug. The Big Book of Conspiracies: Allegedly True Tales of Treachery from the Information Underground! LC 96-116313. (Factoid Books Big Book Ser.: Vol. 4). (Illus.). 224p. 1995. mass mkt. 14.95 (1-56389-186-7, Pub. by DC Comics) Time Warner.
— The Big Book of the Unexplained: Allegedly True Tales of Paranormal Phenomena! Helfer, Andrew, ed. LC 97-170090. (Factoid Books Big Book Ser.). (Illus.). 192p. 1997. mass mkt. 14.95 (1-56389-254-5, Pub. by DC Comics) Time Warner.
— James Bond 007 Bk. 1: Serpent's Tooth. (Illus.). 160p. 1995. pap. 15.95 (1-878574-78-7) Dark Horse Comics.
— Wolverine: Doombringer. (Illus.). 48p. (YA). (gr. 5-12). 1998. pap. 5.95 (0-7851-0583-2) Marvel Entrprs.
Moench, Doug, et al. Batman: Prey. 136p. 1993. mass mkt. 12.99 (0-446-39521-8, Pub. by Warner Bks) Little.
Moench, Doug, et al. Batman: Prodigal. LC 98-167570. (Illus.). 288p. 1998. pap. text 14.95 (1-56389-334-7, Pub. by DC Comics) Time Warner.
Moench, Doug, et al. Batman & Dracula: Red Rain. 96p. 1992. mass mkt. 9.99 (0-446-39465-3, Pub. by Warner Bks) Little.
Moench, Doug, et al. Batman vs. Predator II: Bloodmatch. (Illus.). 144p. 1995. pap. 7.95 (1-56389-221-9, Pub. by DC Comics) Time Warner.
Moench, John O. Taking Command. (Illus.). 495p. 1996. 34.95 (1-877597-05-8) Malia Enterprises.
Moench, John O., ed. The Martin B-26 Marauder: A Bibliography & Guide to Research Sources. 200p. 1992. pap. text 7.95 (1-877597-03-1) Malia Enterprises.
Moench, John O. & Oyster, Esther M. The Martin B-26 Marauder: A Bibliography, 1990. 43p. (Orig.). 1990. pap. 6.50 (1-877597-02-3) Malia Enterprises.
*Moench, Mel. Encyclopedia for Self-Sufficient Homes. (Illus.). 603p. 2000. text 125.00 (0-9673711-1-2) Osprey.
— Planet Earth Home. LC 94-68754. (Illus.). lxxv, 481p. 1999. 65.00 (0-967371l-0-4) Osprey.
Moene, Karl O., jt. ed. see Andersen, Torben M.
Moene, R. Application of Chemical Vapour Deposition in Catalyst Design: Development of High Surface Area Silicon Carbide As Catalyst. 208p. 1995. pap. 97.50 (90-407-1109-7, Pub. by Delft U Pr) Coronet Bks.
Moeng, Sao T. Shan-English Dictionary. LC 94-67927. 458p. 1995. 79.00 (0-931745-92-6) Dunwoody Pr.
Moeng, Sao T., contrib. by. Shan Phonological Drills with Workbook. 1987. audio 24.00 (0-931745-45-4) Dunwoody Pr.
Moeng, Sao T., jt. auth. see Scott, Eileen M.

An Asterisk (*) at the beginning of an entry indicates that the title is appearing for the first time.

Moeng, Sao Tern, jt. auth. see Glick, Irving.

Moeng, Sophearith, ed. The Vital Guide to Military Aircraft. (Illus.). 128p. 1996. 14.95 (1-85310-537-6) Specialty Pr.

Moenich, David. Lizards. (Illus.). 128p. 1990. 9.95 (0-86622-823-3, KW196) TFH Pubns.

Moenke-Blankenburg, Lieselotte. Laser Microanalysis. LC 88-34686. (Chemical Analysis: A Series of Monographs on Analytical Chemistry & Its Applications). 304p. 1989. 175.00 (0-471-63707-6) Wiley.

Moenkemeyer, Heinz. Francois Hemsterhuis. LC 74-13651. (Twayne's World Authors Ser.). 206p. (C). 1975. lib. bdg. 20.95 (0-8057-2419-2) Irvington.

***Moenks, Roger.** Class of Click: Your School Was Never Like This. 1999. 29.95 (3-908161-99-1) Abbeville Pr.

Moenne-Loccoz, Pierre & Reumaux, Patrick. Cortinaires Recents, Nouveaux ou Fantomes. (Fungorum Rariorum Icones Coloratae Ser.: Pars XVIII). (FRE., Illus.). 59p. 1989. 29.00 (3-443-69004-1, Pub. by Gebruder Borntraeger) Balogh.

Moenne-Loccoz, Pierre, et al. Inocybes Criticables et Critiques. (Fungorum Rariorum Icones Coloratae Ser.: Pars XIX). (FRE., Illus.). 55p. 1990. 35.00 (3-443-69005-X, Pub. by Gebruder Borntraeger) Balogh.

Moens, G. Aspects of the Epidemiology & Prevention of Suicide. No. 28. 141p. (Orig.). 1990. pap. 42.50 (90-6186-409-7, Pub. by Leuven Univ) Coronet Bks.

Moens, G. A., jt. auth. see Ratnapala, S.

***Moens, Gabriel, ed.** Constitutional & International Law Perspectives: Achievements & Challenges. 280p. 2000. pap. 29.95 (0-7022-3160-6, Pub. by Univ Queensland Pr) Intl Spec Bk.

Moens, Gabriel & Gillies, Peter. International Trade & Business: Law, Policy & Ethics. LC 98-212555. lv, 819p. 1998. pap. 63.00 (1-876213-25-6, Pub. by Cavendish Pubng) Gaunt.

Moens, Herman, tr. see Brun, Friederike.

***Moens, Marie-Francine.** Automatic Indexing & Abstracting of Document Texts. 288p. 2000. 110.00 (0-7923-7793-1) Kluwer Academic.

Moens, W. J. Register of the Baptisms in the Dutch Church at Colchester from 1645 to 1728: Edited for the Huguenot Society of London. 177p. 1994. pap. text 30.00 (1-55613-998-5) Heritage Bk.

Moenssens, Andre A., et al. Cases & Comments on Criminal Law. 6th ed. LC 98-16315. (University Casebook Ser.). 1044p. (C). 1998. text 41.25 (1-56662-609-9) Foundation Pr.

— Criminal Law, Instructor's Manual for Cases & Comments. 5th ed. (University Casebook Ser.). 201p. 1992. pap. text. write for info. (0-88277-989-3) Foundation Pr.

— Scientific Evidence in Civil & Criminal Cases. 4th ed. 1230p. 1994. text 48.95 (1-56662-233-6) Foundation Pr.

— Scientific Evidence in Criminal Cases. 3rd ed. (University Textbook Ser.). 805p. 1986. 38.95 (0-88277-281-3) Foundation Pr.

Moeran, Brian. Far Valley: Four Years in Japanese Village. 1998. pap. text 17.00 (4-7700-2301-4, Pub. by Kodansha Intl) Kodansha.

— Folk Art Potters of Japan: Beyond an Anthropology of Aesthetics. LC 97-24090. (Anthropology of Asia Ser.). (Illus.). 288p. 1997. text 45.00 (0-8248-2022-3) UH Pr.

— A Japanese Advertising Agency: An Anthropology of Media & Markets. LC 96-20701. (ConsumAsiaN Ser.). (Illus.). 352p. 1996. text 42.00 (0-8248-1872-5); pap. text 19.95 (0-8248-1873-3) UH Pr.

— Okubo Diary: Portrait of a Japanese Valley. 272p. 1985. pap. 12.95 (0-8047-1521-1) Stanford U Pr.

Moeran, Brian, jt. auth. see Kalland, Arne.

Moeran, Brian, jt. ed. see Skov, Lise.

Moerbeek, Kees. Am I a Frog? Kees Moerbeek. LC 96-136127. (Illus.). 8p. (J). (ps-k). 1996. bds. 5.99 (1-56293-861-4, McClanahan Book) Learn Horizon.

— Am I a Tiger? Kees Moerbeek. LC 96-136141. (Illus.). 8p. (J). (ps-k). 1996. bds. 5.99 (1-56293-862-2, McClanahan Book) Learn Horizon.

— Boo Whoo? Mix & Match Pop-Up Book. (Mix-&-Match Pop-Up Book Ser.). (Illus.). 5p. (J). (ps up). 1993. 9.99 (1-888443-61-8) Intervisual Bks.

— Fancy That! LC 91-39451. 9p. (J). 1992. 5.99 (0-85953-543-6) Childs Play.

— Let's Go. LC 91-38117. 9p. (J). 1992. 5.99 (0-85953-542-8) Childs Play.

— Look What I Can Do! (Little Spinners Ser.). (Illus.). 10p. (J). (ps-k). 1998. 7.95 (0-7613-0391-X, Copper Beech Bks) Millbrook Pr.

— My Playful Pets. (Little Spinners Ser.). 10p. (J). (ps-k). 1998. 7.95 (0-7613-0392-8, Copper Beech Bks) Millbrook Pr.

— Night Before Christmas. (Triangle Pop-up Ser.). 12p. (J). (ps up). 1992. pap. 10.99 (0-8431-3445-3, Price Stern) Peng Put Young Read.

— Penguins Slide. LC 91-42040. 9p. (J). 1992. 5.99 (0-85953-544-4) Childs Play.

— Undersea. LC 96-70348. (Open Sesame Bks.). (Illus.). 12p. (J). 1997. pap. 10.95 (0-8431-7897-3, Price Stern) Peng Put Young Read.

***Moerbeek, Kees.** Untitled Moerbeek Pop Up. (Illus.). (J). 2000. 14.95 (0-689-83414-4) Litle Simon.

— Way Home. 1999. 4.99 (0-85953-725-0) Childs Play.

— What's for Dinner? 1999. 4.99 (0-85953-726-9) Childs Play.

Moerbeek, Kees & McClanahan Book Co., Inc. Staff. Crabs Grab! Kees Moerbeek Pop-Up Book. (Illus.). 8p. (J). 1996. bds. 5.99 (1-56293-859-2, McClanahan Book) Learn Horizon.

— Owls Fly! Kees Moerbeek Pop-Up Book. LC 96-136731. (Illus.). 8p. (J). (ps-k). 1996. bds. 5.99 (1-56293-860-6, McClanahan Book) Learn Horizon.

Moerbeek, Kees, jt. auth. see Dijs, Carla.

Moerdijk, Izak. Classifying Spaces & Classifying Topoi, Vol. VII. LC 95-37122. (Lecture Notes in Mathematics Ser.: Vol. 1616). 94p. 1995. 29.95 (3-540-60319-0) Spr-Verlag.

Moerdijk, Izak, jt. auth. see Joyal, A.

Moerdijk, Izak, jt. auth. see Mac Lane, S.

Moerdijk, Izak, jt. auth. see Reyes, G. E.

Moerdyk, Meta, tr. see Elshout, Arie.

Moerenhout, J. A. Travels to the Islands of the Pacific Ocean. Borden, Arthur R., Jr., tr. LC 92-26842.Tr. of Voyages aux Iles de Grand Ocean. 564p. (Orig.). (C). lib. bdg. 68.00 (0-8191-8898-0) U Pr of Amer.

— Travels to the Islands of the Pacific Ocean. Borden, Arthur R., Jr., tr. LC 92-26842.Tr. of Voyages aux Iles de Grand Ocean. 564p. (Orig.). (C). 1993. pap. text 39.50 (0-8191-8899-9) U Pr of Amer.

Moeri, Louise. Forty-Third War. 208p. (YA). 1993. pap. 6.95 (0-395-66955-3) HM.

— Forty-Third War. (J). 1989. 11.05 (0-606-05833-8, Pub. by Turtleback) Demco.

— Save Queen of Sheba. 112p. (J). 1982. pap. 2.95 (0-380-58529-4, Avon Bks) Morrow Avon.

— Save Queen of Sheba. 112p. (J). 1990. pap. 3.50 (0-380-71154-0, Avon Bks) Morrow Avon.

— Save Queen of Sheba. 128p. (J). (gr. 3-7). 1994. pap. 4.99 (0-14-037148-6, PuffinBks) Peng Put Young Read.

— Save the Queen of Sheba. 1994. 9.09 (0-606-07077-X, Pub. by Turtleback) Demco.

— Star Mother's Youngest Child, 001. (Illus.). 48p. (J). (ps-2). 1975. 14.95 (0-395-21406-8, Sandpiper) HM.

— Star Mother's Youngest Child, 001. LC 75-9743. (Illus.). 48p. (J). (gr. 4-7). 1980. pap. 5.95 (0-395-29929-2, Sandpiper) HM.

Moerings, Martin, jt. auth. see Thomas, Philip A.

***Moerk, Ernst L.** The Guided Acquisition of First Language Skills. LC 99-39681. (Advances in Applied Developmental Psychology Ser.). 1999. pap. 73.25 (1-56750-469-8) Ablx Pub.

Moerk, Ernst L. Mother of Eve - As a First Language Teacher. Lipsitt, Lewis P., ed. LC 82-16358. (Monographs on Infancy: Vol. 3). 160p. 1984. text 73.25 (0-89391-162-3) Ablx Pub.

Moerman, Daniel E. Geraniums for the Iroquois: A Field Guide to American Indian Medicinal Plants. Irvine, Keith, ed. LC 81-52514. (Illus.). 1982. 29.00 (0-917256-15-8) Ref Pubns.

— Native American Ethnobotany. LC 97-32877. (Illus.). 928p. 1998. 79.95 (0-88192-453-9) Timber.

Moerman, Daniel R. & Romanucci-Ross, Lola E. The Anthropology of Medicine: From Culture to Method. (Illus.). 416p. (C). 1985. text 44.95 (0-03-062192-5, Bergin & Garvey) Greenwood.

Moerman, Daniel R., jt. ed. see Romanucci-Ross, Lola E.

Moerman, Michael. Talking Culture: Ethnography & Conversational Analysis. LC 87-14973. (Conduct & Communication Ser.). 212p. (C). 1987. pap. text 19.95 (0-8122-1246-0) U of Pa Pr.

Moerman, P. Hidden Worlds: Fresh Clues to the Past : Did Columbus, Magellan & Piri Reis Know the Glareanus Maps? LC 74-194621. 221p. 1974. write for info. (0-285-62130-0) Souvenir Pr Ltd.

Moermond, Curtis. Following in His Footsteps: A Journey to the Holy Land. 64p. 1997. pap. 3.99 (0-570-09670-7, 20-2498) Concordia.

Moermond, Kim I. & Snyder, Jack. The Second Berlin Crisis, 1958-1959. (Pew Case Studies in International Affairs). 50p. (C). 1988. pap. text 3.50 (1-56927-441-X) Geo U Inst Dplmcy.

Moerner, W. E., ed. Persistent Spectral Hole-Burning: Science & Applications. (Topics in Current Physics Ser.: Vol. 44). (Illus.). 325p. 1988. 70.95 (0-387-18607-7) Spr-Verlag.

Moers, Ellen. Harriet Beecher Stowe & American Literature. LC 78-4149. (Illus.). 1978. pap. text 5.00 (0-917482-15-8) Stowe-Day.

Moers, Herman. Katie & the Big, Brave Bear. Martens, Marianne, tr. from GER. LC 94-45208.Tr. of Holpeltolpel Starker Freund. (Illus.). 32p. (J). (gr. k-3). 1995. lib. bdg. 14.88 (1-55858-398-X, Pub. by North-South Bks NYC) Chronicle Bks.

Moersbacher, Lynda. Marketing Magic: A Program for Major & Planned Gifts. 1999. pap. 40.00 (1-56625-135-4) Bonus Books.

Moersch, Martha M., jt. ed. see Schafer, D. Sue.

Moersch, Martha S., jt. ed. see D'Eugenio, Diane B.

Moerschbaecher, Lynda S. Start at Square One: Starting & Managing the Planned Gift Program. LC 97-26588. 230p. 1998. 40.00 (1-56625-089-7) Bonus Books.

Moerschel, Jane R., jt. auth. see Drakesmith, Mary M.

Moertono, Soemarsaid. State & Statecraft in Old Java: A Study of the Later Mataram Period, 16th to 19th Century, Vol. 43. 2nd rev. ed. (Modern Indonesia Project Ser.). 180p. 1981. pap. 9.00 (0-87763-017-8) Cornell Mod Indo.

Moes, Garry J. Applications of Grammar Bk. 1: Basics for Communicating Effectively. rev. ed. (Illus.). 262p. (YA). (gr. 7-8). 1996. pap. text 9.00 (1-930367-19-8, CLP49615) Christian Liberty.

— Applications of Grammar Bk. 1: Basics for Communicating Effectively - Answer Key. rev. ed. 1996. 7.00 (1-930367-20-1) Christian Liberty.

— Applications of Grammar Bk. 1: Basics for Communicating Effectively - Test Packet. rev. ed. 1996. 4.00 (1-930367-21-X) Christian Liberty.

— Applications of Grammar Bk. 2: Structure for Communicating Effectively. rev. ed. (Illus.). 256p. (YA). (gr. 8-9). 1996. pap. text 9.00 (1-930367-22-8, CLP49625) Christian Liberty.

— Applications of Grammar Bk. 2: Structure for Communicating Effectively - Answer Key. rev. ed. 1996. 7.00 (1-930367-23-6) Christian Liberty.

— Applications of Grammar Bk. 2: Structure for Communicating Effectively - Test Packet. rev. ed. 1996. 4.00 (1-930367-24-4) Christian Liberty.

— Applications of Grammar Bk. 3: Analysis of Effective Communication. rev. ed. (Illus.). 318p. (YA). (gr. 9-10). 1998. pap. text 9.00 (1-930367-25-2, CLP49630) Christian Liberty.

— Applications of Grammar Bk. 3: Analysis of Effective Communication - Answer Key. rev. ed. 1998. 7.00 (1-930367-26-0) Christian Liberty.

— Applications of Grammar Bk. 3: Analysis of Effective Communication - Test Packet. rev. ed. 1998. 4.00 (1-930367-27-9) Christian Liberty.

— Building Spelling Skills, Bk. 1. (Illus.). 136p. (J). (gr. 1-2). 1992. pap. text 8.00 (1-930367-04-X, CLP39610) Christian Liberty.

— Building Spelling Skills, Bk. 2. (Illus.). 134p. (J). (gr. 2-3). 1992. pap. text 8.00 (1-930367-05-8, CLP39620) Christian Liberty.

— Building Spelling Skills, Bk. 3. (Illus.). 136p. (J). (gr. 3-4). 1992. pap. text 8.00 (1-930367-07-4, CLP39630) Christian Liberty.

— Building Spelling Skills, Bk. 4. (Illus.). 128p. (J). (gr. 4-5). 1992. pap. text 8.00 (1-930367-09-0, CLP39640) Christian Liberty.

— Building Spelling Skills, Bk. 5. (Illus.). 132p. (J). (gr. 5-6). 1993. pap. text 8.00 (1-930367-11-2, CLP39650) Christian Liberty.

— Building Spelling Skills, Bk. 6. (Illus.). 128p. (YA). (gr. 6-7). 1993. pap. text 8.00 (1-930367-13-9, CLP39660) Christian Liberty.

— Building Spelling Skills, Bk. 7. (Illus.). 136p. (YA). (gr. 7-8). 1993. pap. text 8.00 (1-930367-15-5, CLP39670) Christian Liberty.

— Building Spelling Skills, Bk. 8. (Illus.). 128p. (YA). (gr. 9-10). 1994. pap. text 8.00 (1-930367-17-1, CLP39680) Christian Liberty.

— Building Spelling Skills: Answer Key, Bk. 2. 1992. 3.00 (1-930367-06-6) Christian Liberty.

— Building Spelling Skills: Answer Key, Bk. 3. 1992. 3.00 (1-930367-08-2) Christian Liberty.

— Building Spelling Skills: Answer Key, Bk. 4. 1992. 3.00 (1-930367-10-4) Christian Liberty.

— Building Spelling Skills: Answer Key, Bk. 5. 1993. 3.00 (1-930367-12-0) Christian Liberty.

— Building Spelling Skills: Answer Key, Bk. 6. 1993. 3.00 (1-930367-14-7) Christian Liberty.

— Building Spelling Skills: Answer Key, Bk. 7. 1993. 3.00 (1-930367-16-3) Christian Liberty.

— Building Spelling Skills: Answer Key, Bk. 8. 1994. 3.00 (1-930367-18-X) Christian Liberty.

— Streams of Civilization, Vol. 2. McHugh, Michael J., ed. (Streams of Civilization Ser.). (Illus.). 438p. (YA). (gr. 9-12). 1999. text 19.95 (1-930367-46-5, CLP79560) Christian Liberty.

— Streams of Civilization: Answer Key, Vol. 2. McHugh, Michael J., ed. (Streams of Civilization Ser.: Vol. 2). (YA). (gr. 9-12). 1999. 4.95 (1-930367-47-3, CLP79560) Christian Liberty.

Moes, Garry J., ed. see Sloan, Annie Lee.

***Moes, Mark.** Plato's Dialogue Form & the Care of the Soul. LC 98-50412. (New Perspectives in Philosophical Scholarship Ser.: Vol. 13). 240p. 2000. text 50.95 (0-8204-4459-6) P Lang Pubng.

Moes, Robert. Korean Art. (Illus.). 200p. 1987. pap. 4.95 (0-87663-516-8) Bklyn Mus.

Moes, Robert J. Southeast Asian Ceramics. (Illus.). 16p. 1975. pap. 1.00 (0-87273-051-4) Bklyn Mus.

Moeschberger, Melvin L., jt. auth. see David, H. A.

Moeschberger, Melvin L., jt. auth. see Klein, John P.

Moeschberger, Melvin L., jt. auth. see Madsen, Richard W.

***Moesche, Carl R.** Day-by-Day in Baseball History. 371p. 2000. per. 29.95 (0-7864-0886-3) McFarland & Co.

Moeschl, Richard. Exploring the Sky: Projects for Beginning Astronomers. rev. ed. LC 92-18863. (Ziggurat Bks.). (Illus.). 432p. (YA). (gr. 9-12). 1992. pap. 16.95 (1-55652-160-X) Chicago Review.

***Moeschler, Jacques & Beguelin, Marie-Josee, texts.** Reference Temporelle et Nominale. (Sciences pour la Communication Ser.: Vol. 57). 300p. 1999. 47.95 (3-906761-99-1, Pub. by P Lang) P Lang Pubng.

Moeschlin, O., et al. Experimental Stochastics. Johns, R., tr. from GER. (Illus.). 200p. 1997. pap. 79.95 incl. cd-rom (3-540-14619-9) Spr-Verlag.

Moeschlin, O., jt. ed. see Hehn, R.

Moeser, John V. & Dennis, Rutledge M. The Politics of Annexation: Oligarchic Power in a Southern City. 232p. 1982. 22.95 (0-87073-501-2); pap. 15.95 (0-87073-502-0) Schenkman Bks Inc.

Moeser, John V., jt. auth. see Silver, Christopher.

Moeser, June. Four Sentinels: The Story of San Diego's Lighthouses. LC 91-66002. (Illus.). 70p. (Orig.). 1991. pap. 7.95 (0-938711-10-5) Tecolote Pubns.

Moeshart, Herman, jt. ed. see Lowe, Peter.

Moeskops, J., jt. auth. see Leeuwen, M.

Moesli, Annitta. Know Austria by Cooking: A Cook Book with a Difference. 171p. (C). 1988. 100.00 (0-947621-01-6, Pub. by Stuart Titles Ltd) St Mut.

Moesly, Sue. Circumnavigation - Sail the Trade Winds Vol. I: Ft. Lauderdale to Fiji. Wilensky, Julius M., ed. LC 95-61656. 304p. 1995. pap. 19.95 (0-918752-19-1) Wescott Cove.

— Circumnavigation - Sail the Trade Winds Vol. II: Vanuatu to Florida. Wilensky, Julius M., ed. LC 95-61656. (Illus.). 288p. 1995. pap. 17.95 (0-918752-20-5) Wescott Cove.

***Moessinger, Pierre.** The Paradox of Social Order: Linking Psychology & Sociology. Worrall, Francesca & Scher, Stephan, trs. (Sociological Imagination & Structural Change Ser.). 256p. 1999. pap. text 24.95 (0-202-30576-7) Aldine de Gruyter.

— The Paradox of Social Order: Linking Psychology & Sociology. Worrall, Francesca & Scher, Stephen K., trs. (Sociological Imagination & Structural Change Ser.). 256p. 1999. lib. bdg. 49.95 (0-202-30575-9) Aldine de Gruyter.

***Moessner, David P.** Lord of the Banquet: The Literary & Theological Significance of the Lukan Travel Narrative. LC 98-3559. 384p. 1998. pap. 22.00 (1-56338-242-3) TPI PA.

Moessner, David P., ed. Jesus & the Heritage of Israel: Luke's Narrative Claim upon Israel's Legacy. LC 99-40251. 368p. 2000. pap. 40.00 (1-56338-293-8) TPI PA.

Moessner, Jeanne S., ed. Through the Eyes of Women: Insights for Pastoral Care the Handbook of Womencare. 352p. 1996. pap. 25.00 (0-8006-2928-0, 1-2928, Fortress Pr) Augsburg Fortress.

Moessner, Jeanne S., jt. ed. see Glaz, Maxine.

***Moessner, Jeanne Stevenson.** In Her Own Time: Women & Developmental Issues in Pastoral Care. LC 00-20194. 288p. 2000. pap. 21.00 (0-8006-3137-4, Fortress Pr) Augsburg Fortress.

Moessner, Victoria J., ed. see Robins, Elizabeth, et al.

Moessner, Victoria J., tr. see Black, J. L. & Buse, D. K.

Moessner, Victoria J., tr. see Von Langsdorff, Georg H.

Moesta, Rebecca. Anakin's Quest. (Star Wars: No. 4). (Illus.). (J). (gr. 3-5). 1997. pap. 4.50 (0-425-16824-7) Berkley Pub.

Moesta, Rebecca. Anakin's Quest. (Star Wars: No. 4). 128p. (J). (gr. 3-5). 1997. mass mkt. 4.50 (1-57297-136-3) Blvd Books.

— Delusions of Grandeur. (Star Wars: No. 9). (J). (gr. 3-5). 1997. write for info. (0-614-29188-7) Blvd Books.

— Kenobi's Blade. (Star Wars: No. 6). 118p. (J). (gr. 8-12). 1999. pap. text 4.50 (0-425-17315-1) Berkley Pub.

— Kenobi's Blade. (Star Wars: No. 6). 128p. (J). (gr. 3-5). 1997. mass mkt. 4.50 (1-57297-208-4) Blvd Books.

— Vader's Fortress. (Star Wars: No. 5). (J). (gr. 3-5). 1999. mass mkt. 4.50 (0-425-16956-1) Berkley Pub.

— Vader's Fortress. (Star Wars: No. 5). 128p. (J). (gr. 3-5). 1997. mass mkt. 4.50 (1-57297-173-8) Blvd Books.

Moesta, Rebecca, jt. auth. see Anderson, Kevin.

Moesta, Rebecca, jt. auth. see Anderson, Kevin J.

Moestrup, Jorn. The Structural Patterns of Pirandello's Work. (Etudes Romanes Ser.: No. 2). 294p. (Orig.). 1972. pap. 32.50 (87-7492-056-1, Pub. by Odense Universitets Forlag) Coronet Bks.

Moet, Abdelsamie, jt. auth. see Baer, Eric.

Moet Chandon. International Wine Directory in 6 Languages: English - French - German - Italian - Japanese - Spanish. (ENG, FRE, GER, ITA & JPN.). 850p. 1996. 175.00 (0-7859-9306-1) Fr & Eur.

***Moeveni.** Concepts Every Engineer Should Know: Intro to Engineering. 2001. pap. 50.00 (0-534-38116-2) Brooks-Cole.

Moevs, Christian, tr. see Mazzoleni, Mario.

Moewes, David. Modern Economics. 1996. pap. text, student ed. 29.60 (0-13-150590-4) P-H.

Moeyaert, Bart. Bare Hands. Colmer, David, tr. LC 98-13287. 112p. (J). (gr. 4-6). 1998. 14.95 (1-886910-32-4) Front Str.

***Moeyaert, Bart.** Hornet's Nest. 144p. (YA). (gr. 7 up). 2000. 15.95 (1-886910-48-0, Pub. by Front Str) Publishers Group.

Moeyes, Paul. Siegfreid Sassoon. LC 96-46418. (Illus.). 307p. 1997. text 35.00 (0-312-17277-X) St Martin.

Moffa, Peter E., ed. The Control & Treatment of Combined Sewer Overflows. 2nd ed. (Mechanical Engineering Ser.). 292p. 1997. 90.00 (0-471-29210-9, VNR) Wiley.

— The Control & Treatment of Combined Sewer Overflows. 2nd ed. LC 97-23696. (Mechanical Engineering Ser.). (Illus.). 384p. 1997. 64.95 (0-442-02405-3, VNR) Wiley.

— The Control & Treatment of Industrial & Municipal Stormwater. LC 95-218784. (Environmental Engineering Ser.). 310p. 1995. text 76.95 (0-442-01893-2, VNR) Wiley.

Moffa, Peter E., ed. The Control & Treatment of Industrial & Municipal Stormwater. (Environmental Engineering Ser.). 310p. 1995. 89.95 (0-471-28648-6, VNR) Wiley.

Moffa-Trotter, Michelle, jt. auth. see Anemaet, Wendy.

***Moffat.** Cavalier King Charles Spaniel: An Owner's Guide to a Happy, Healthy Pet. 160p. 2000. 12.95 (1-58245-125-7) Howell Bks.

Moffat. Clarke's Isolation & Identification of Drugs. 2nd ed. 1992. 220.00 (0-85369-166-5, Pub. by Pharmaceutical Pr) Rittenhouse.

Moffat & Neave. Looking at Buildings East Riding. 36p. text 11.95 (0-14-071064-7, Pub. by Pnguin Bks Ltd) Trafalgar.

Moffat, Alexander & Francis, Mark, eds. Johnston, Alan. 1978. pap. 20.00 (0-905836-08-1, Pub. by Museum Modern Art) St Mut.

Moffat, Alfred A. Irish Tunes for Piano. 84p. 17.95 (0-946005-26-5, OS 10698, Pub. by Ossian) Music Sales.

— Scottish Tunes for Piano. 88p. 17.95 (0-946005-27-3, OS 10690, Pub. by Ossian) Music Sales.

Moffat, Alistair. Remembering Charles Rennie Mackintosh: An Illustrated Biography. rev. ed. (Illus.). 160p. 1998. pap. 19.95 (1-900455-45-5, Pub. by Colin Baxter Ltd) Voyageur Pr.

Moffat, Almet S., compiled by. Orange County: A Narrative History. 87p. 1997. reprint ed. pap. 16.00 (0-8328-6193-6) Higginson Bk Co.

M

Moffat, Anne, ed. Multinational Coordinated Arabidopsis Thaliana Genome Research Project: Progress Report: Year Four. (Illus.). 44p. (C). 1998. pap. text 20.00 (*0-7881-7044-9*) DIANE Pub.

Moffat, Anthony F., ed. Instability & Variability of Hot-Star Winds: Proceedings: International Workshop on Instability & Variability of Hot-Star Winds (1993: Quebec Province, Canada) LC 94-45298. 501p. 1995. text 144.00 (*0-7923-3331-4*) Kluwer Academic.

Moffat, Betty C. SoulWork: Clearing the Mind, Opening the Heart, Replenishing the Spirit. LC 94-15339. 200p. (Orig.). 1994. pap. 12.95 (*1-885171-01-3*) Wldcat Canyon.

***Moffat, Bobbie Wells.** "Inherited Genes" Including Families: Wells, Price, Sharpe, Alexander, McKnight. 367p. 2000. 64.00 (*0-7404-1282-5*) Higginson Bk Co.

Moffat, Bobby. The Basic Soccer Guide. LC 75-16004. (Illus.). 144p. (Orig.). 1978. pap. 4.95 (*0-89037-060-5*) Anderson World.

— Intermediate Soccer Guide. (Illus.). 170p. (Orig.). 1982. pap. 12.95 (*0-89037-181-4*) Anderson World.

Moffat, Bruce G. The "L" The Development of Chicago's Rapid Transit System, 1888-1932. LC 94-92465. (Central Electric Railfans' Association Bulletin Ser.: No. 131). (Illus.). 306p. 1995. 55.00 (*0-915348-30-6*) Central Electric.

M

Moffat, Charles & Moffat, Norma. Moffat: Family Histories of Moffat, Crangle, Pierson, Angel, Lichtenw. (Illus.). 168p. 1996. reprint ed. lib. bdg. 37.00 (*0-8328-5309-7*) Higginson Bk Co.

— Moffat. Family Histories of Moffat, Crangle, Pierson, Angel, Lichtenwalter, McNeelan. (Illus.). 168p. 1996. reprint ed. pap. 27.00 (*0-8328-5310-0*) Higginson Bk Co.

— Waggoner, Charles C. Waggoner, Auglaize Co., Ohio, 1805-1879, & Allied Families of Layton, Bitler, Heidrick, Brakney, Hague, Bayliff. (Illus.). 86p. 1996. reprint ed. pap. 18.00 (*0-8328-5312-7*); reprint ed. lib. bdg. 28.00 (*0-8328-5311-9*) Higginson Bk Co.

Moffat, Charles H. A History of the Cabell County Medical Society in West Virginia 1890-1985. 336p. 1986. 76.00 (*0-9616839-0-2*) Cabell Cty Med Soc.

Moffat, Colin & Whittle, Kevin J., eds. Environmental Contaminants in Food Vol. 4: Sheffield Food Technology. (Sheffield Food Technology Ser.: Vol. 4). 592p. 1999. write for info. (*1-85075-921-9*, Pub. by Sheffield Acad) CUP Services.

Moffat, D. B. & Mottram, R. F. Anatomy & Physiology for Physiotherapists. 2nd ed. (Illus.). 680p. 1987. pap. 47.95 (*0-632-01464-4*) Blackwell Sci.

Moffat, David V. UCSD Pascal Examples & Exercises. (Illus.). 224p. 1986. pap. text 16.00 (*0-13-935396-8*) P-H.

Moffat, Donald. Handbook of Indoor Air Quality Management. 412p. (C). 1997. text 69.95 (*0-13-235300-8*) P-H.

Moffat, Donald W. Economics Dictionary. 331p. 1985. 85.00 (*0-7859-0581-2*, M7905) Fr & Eur.

— Economics Dictionary. 2nd ed. 331p. 1984. 43.50 (*0-444-00798-9*) P-H.

— Elementary Statistics for IBM PC's. 192p. 1987. 27.95 (*0-13-260050-1*) P-H.

— Elementary Statistics for the IBM PC's. (Illus.). 160p. 1988. pap. 23.95 (*0-317-62510-1*) P-H.

— The Plant Manager's Daily Planner, 1988. 448p. 1988. text 32.50 (*0-13-680257-5*, Busn) P-H.

Moffat, Donald W. & Poage, Greg A. The Plant Manager's Practical Guide to Accounting & Finance. LC 93-8923. (C). 1993. text 59.95 (*0-13-676966-7*) Prntice Hall Bks.

Moffat, Dorothy H. Too Many Apples. LC 95-17836. 1995. pap. 9.95 (*0-87233-141-5*) Bauhan.

Moffat, Douglas, ed. The Soul's Address to the Body: The Worcester Fragments. LC 86-72187. (Medieval Texts & Studies: No. 1). 133p. 1987. 29.95 (*0-937191-01-9*) Mich St U Pr.

Moffat, Douglas, ed. The Old English "Soul & Body" (Illus.). 111p. (C). 1990. 75.00 (*0-85991-232-9*) Boydell & Brewer.

Moffat, Douglas, jt. ed. see Frantzen, Allen J.

Moffat, Douglas, jt. ed. see McCarren, Vincent.

Moffat, E. L. Holton. Ancestry of Ezra Holton of Northfield, Massachusetts & Sorperton, Ontario, 1785-1824. Gilbert, G., ed. 158p. 1997. reprint ed. pap. 25.00 (*0-8328-9202-5*); reprint ed. lib. bdg. 35.00 (*0-8328-9201-7*) Higginson Bk Co.

Moffat, E. L., jt. auth. see Gilbert, G.

Moffat, Geoffrey, jt. auth. see Hotaling, Robert B.

Moffat, Graham, jt. auth. see James, Stuart C.

Moffat, Gwen. The Corpse Road. large type ed. (Mystery Ser.). 400p. 1993. 27.99 (*0-7089-2990-7*) Ulverscroft.

— Cue the Battered Wife. large type ed. 480p. 1996. 27.99 (*0-7089-3471-4*) Ulverscroft.

— Deviant Death. large type ed. 1995. 27.99 (*0-7089-3436-6*) Ulverscroft.

— Die Like a Dog. large type ed. (Linford Mystery Library). 304p. 1988. pap. 16.99 (*0-7089-6627-6*, Linford) Ulverscroft.

— Grizzly Trail. large type ed. (Linford Mystery Library). 336p. 1987. pap. 16.99 (*0-7089-6357-9*, Linford) Ulverscroft.

— Hard Road West. large type ed. 448p. 1983. 27.99 (*0-7089-0908-6*) Ulverscroft.

— Lady with a Cool Eye. large type ed. (Linford Mystery Large Print Ser.). 384p. 1998. pap. 17.99 (*0-7089-5290-9*, Linford) Ulverscroft.

***Moffat, Gwen.** The Lost Girls. large type ed. 360p. 2000. 31.99 (*0-7089-4172-9*) Ulverscroft.

Moffat, Gwen. Miss Pink at the Edge of the World. 208p. 1995. 19.50 (*0-7451-8667-X*, Black Dagger) Chivers N Amer.

— Miss Pink at the Edge of the World. large type ed. 368p. 1995. 27.99 (*0-7089-3379-3*) Ulverscroft.

— Pit Bull. large type ed. (Ulverscroft Large Print Ser.). 432p. 1997. 27.99 (*0-7089-3780-2*) Ulverscroft.

— The Raptor Zone. large type ed. (General Ser.). 416p. 1993. 11.50 (*0-7089-2881-1*) Ulverscroft.

***Moffat, Gwen.** Running Dogs. 192p. 1999. 25.00 (*0-7278-5456-9*, Pub. by Severn Hse) Chivers N Amer.

Moffat, Gwen. A Short Time to Live. large type ed. 368p. 1995. 27.99 (*0-7089-3336-X*) Ulverscroft.

— Snare. large type ed. 1990. 27.99 (*0-7089-2128-0*) Ulverscroft.

***Moffat, Gwen.** The Storm Seekers. large type ed. 360p. 1999. 31.99 (*0-7089-9118-1*) Ulverscroft.

— A Wreath of Dead Moths. large type ed. 336p. 2000. 31.99 (*0-7505-1518-X*, Pub. by Mgna Lrg Print) Ulverscroft.

Moffat, Hugh. East Anglia's First Railways. 1994. 48.00 (*0-86138-038-X*, Pub. by T Dalton) St Mut.

Moffat, J. B., jt. ed. see Sequeira, C. A.

Moffat, Jeffrey C., jt. auth. see Wigder, Herbert N.

Moffat, Marilyn, jt. auth. see Rusnak-Smith, Sandra.

Moffat, Mary J. The Times of Our Lives: A Guide to Writing Autobiography & Memoir. 3rd ed. LC 95-43411. 64p. (Orig.). 1996. pap. 8.95 (*1-880284-18-9*) J Daniel.

Moffat, Mary J., ed. In the Midst of Winter: Selections from the Literature of Mourning. 1992. pap. 13.00 (*0-679-73827-4*) Vin Bks.

Moffat, Mary J. & Painter, Charlotte, eds. Revelations: Diaries of Women. 1975. pap. 11.00 (*0-394-71151-3*) Vin Bks.

Moffat, Norma, jt. auth. see Moffat, Charles.

Moffat, Pelham. Twenty-One Plays for Children. 224p. 1990. 29.50 (*0-86315-094-2*, 1287, Pub. by Floris Bks) Anthroposophic.

Moffat, R. Burnham. The Barclays of New York: Who They Are & Who They Are Not, & Some Other Barclays. 481p. 1988. reprint ed. pap. 75.00 (*0-8328-0185-2*); reprint ed. lib. bdg. 85.00 (*0-8328-0184-4*) Higginson Bk Co.

Moffat, R. J., jt. ed. see Schmidt, F. W.

Moffat, Riley. Population Statistics & History of Western U. S. Cities. LC 95-14583. 355p. 1996. 45.00 (*0-8108-3033-7*) Scarecrow.

Moffat, Riley, jt. auth. see Fitzpatrick, Gary L.

Moffat, Riley M. Map Index to Topographic Quadrangles of the United States, 1882-1940. LC 84-21984. (Occasional Papers: No. 10). (Illus.). 238p. (Orig.). 1986. 32.50 (*0-939112-12-4*) Western Assn Map.

— Printed Maps of Utah to 1900: An Annotated Cartobibliography. LC 81-659. (Occasional Papers: No. 8). (Illus.). 193p. (Orig.). 1981. pap. 10.00 (*0-939112-09-4*) Western Assn Map.

Moffat, Riley M., jt. auth. see Fitzpatrick, Gary L.

Moffat, Robert. Adventures of a Missionary: Or, Rivers of Water in a Dry Place. LC 70-89387. (Black Heritage Library Collection). 1977. 17.95 (*0-8369-8635-0*) Ayer.

Moffat, Robert C., et al, eds. Perspectives on the Family. LC 90-6472. (Studies in Social & Political Theory: Vol. 8). 400p. 1990. lib. bdg. 109.95 (*0-88946-685-8*) E Mellen.

Moffat, Robert C., ed. see International Association for Philosophy of Law &.

Moffat, Susan D. Kids Explore Boston: The Very Best Kids' Activities Within an Easy Drive of Boston. (J). (gr. 4 up). 1994. pap. 10.95 (*1-55850-392-7*) Adams Media.

Moffatt. How to Get a Teaching Job. LC 99-42480. 174p. 1999. pap. text 21.99 (*0-205-29924-5*, Longwood Div) Allyn.

Moffatt, Betty C. Passwords to English Grammar, Bk. 2. 1997. pap., student ed. 11.72 (*0-8114-2226-7*) Raintree Steck-V.

— Passwords to English Grammar, Bk. 3. 1997. pap., student ed. 11.72 (*0-8114-2227-5*) Raintree Steck-V.

***Moffatt, BettyClare.** An Authentic Woman: Soulwork for the Wisdom Years. LC 98-49912. 208p. 1999. per. 12.00 (*0-684-84444-3*) S&S Trade.

Moffatt, BettyClare. An Authentic Woman: Soulwork for the Wisdom Years. large type ed. LC 99-33106. 1999. pap. 25.95 (*0-7862-2061-9*) Mac Lib Ref.

***Moffatt, BettyClare.** By Divine Design. 144p. 2000. 12.00 (*1-57566-539-5*, Knsington) Kensgtn Pub Corp.

Moffatt, Bettyclare. The Caregiver's Companion: Words to Comfort & Inspire. LC 97-152724. 288p. (Orig.). 1997. pap. 12.00 (*0-425-15617-6*) Berkley Pub.

— Journey Toward Forgiveness: Finding Your Way Home. 176p. 1995. pap. 11.95 (*1-57101-050-5*) MasterMedia Pub.

Moffatt, BettyClare. A Soulworker's Companion: A Year of Spiritual Discovery. LC 96-3275. 240p. (Orig.). 1996. pap. 12.95 (*1-885171-11-0*) Wldcat Canyon.

Moffatt, Bettyclare, jt. auth. see Moffatt, Judith.

Moffatt, Charles C., ed. see American Society of Mechanical Engineers Staff.

Moffatt, Christine J. & Harper, Peter. Leg Ulcers. LC 97-22896. (Access to Clinical Education Ser.). 1997. pap. text 42.00 (*0-443-05533-5*) Church.

Moffatt, David. Exploration in the Ordinary: A Backyard Naturalist's View of Minnesota. (Illus.). 144p. (Orig.). 1996. pap. 9.95 (*0-87839-099-5*) North Star.

Moffatt, Dorothy H. Time for Remembrance: Poems. LC 94-15047. 1994. pap. 8.95 (*0-87233-115-6*) Bauhan.

Moffatt, Edward A., ed. see American Society of Mechanical Engineers Staff.

Moffatt, Emma L. The Primordial Lure. 20p. (Orig.). 1994. pap. write for info. (*1-885206-06-2*, Iliad Pr) Cader Pubng.

— The Silent One & Other Poems. 16p. (Orig.). 1995. pap. write for info. (*1-885206-10-0*, Iliad Pr) Cader Pubng.

— Worthwhile. 14p. (Orig.). 1995. pap. write for info. (*1-885206-24-0*, Iliad Pr) Cader Pubng.

Moffatt, Eva L. Forbes: Ancestry of William Forbes of Barre, Massachusetts & Montreal, Quebec, 1778-1833. Gilbert, G., ed. 103p. 1997. reprint ed. pap. 18.50 (*0-8328-8596-7*); reprint ed. lib. bdg. 28.50 (*0-8328-8595-9*) Higginson Bk Co.

Moffatt, Frank. Grandma Ollie. (Jam Roll Picture Bks.). (Illus.). 32p. (J). 1995. pap. 12.95 (*0-7022-2850-8*, Pub. by Univ Queensland Pr) Intl Spec Bk.

Moffatt, Frederick C. Errant Bronzes: George Grey Barnard's Statues of Abraham Lincoln. LC 97-33147. (Illus.). 240p. 1998. 59.50 (*0-87413-628-8*) U Delaware Pr.

Moffatt, Graham & Chesterman, Michael. Trusts Law: Text & Materials. (Law in Context Ser.). xlii, 746p. 1988. 75.00 (*0-297-79402-7*) W S Hein.

***Moffatt, Gregory K.** Blind-Sided: Homicide Where It Is Least Expected. LC 00-25464. 264p. 2000. 40.00 (*0-275-96929-0*, C6929, Praeger Pubs) Greenwood.

Moffatt, H. K., ed. Topological Aspects of the Dynamics of Fluids & Plasmas. (NATO Advanced Science Institutes Series C: Mathematical & Physical Sciences), 624p. (C). 1992. text 302.00 (*0-7923-1900-1*) Kluwer Academic.

Moffatt, H. K. & Tsinober, A., eds. Topical Fluid Mechanics: Proceedings of the IUTAM Symposium. 823p. (C). 1990. text 145.00 (*0-521-38145-2*) Cambridge U Pr.

***Moffatt, Hazal & Woollard, Vicky, eds.** Museum Gallery Education: A Manual of Good Practice. 246p. 2000. pap. 42.95 (*0-7425-0408-5*) AltaMira Pr.

***Moffatt, I. & Hanley, N.** Measuring & Modelling Sustainable Development: Principles, Analysis & Policies. (Illus.). 300p. 2001. pap. write for info. (*1-84214-008-6*) Prthnon Pub.

Moffatt, Ian. Sustainable Development: Principles, Analysis & Policies. LC 96-13441. 222p. 1996. 65.00 (*1-85070-731-6*) Prthnon Pub.

Moffatt, James. The Approach to the New Testament. LC 77-27150. (Hibbert Lectures: 1921). reprint ed. 35.00 (*0-404-60420-X*) AMS Pr.

— Hebrews: Critical & Exegetical Commentary. Driver, Samuel R. et al, eds. LC 24-21703. (International Critical Commentary Ser.). 336p. 1924. 39.95 (*0-567-05034-3*, Pub. by T & T Clark) Bks Intl VA.

Moffatt, James, tr. The Bible: James Moffatt Translation. 1536p. 1994. 49.99 (*0-8254-3264-2*) Kregel.

Moffatt, James, ed. see Von Harnack, Adolf.

Moffatt, James, tr. see Von Harnack, Adolf.

***Moffatt, Judith.** Bugs. LC 99-28967. (Hello Reader! Ser.). (J). 2000. pap. 3.99 (*0-439-09859-9*) Scholastic Inc.

— Christmas Lights. (Night Glow Board Book Ser.). 12p. (J). (gr. k-3). 1999. pap. 4.99 (*0-689-82269-3*) Litle Simon.

— City Lights: A Night-Light Board Book. (Illus.). 10p. (J). (ps-k). 1997. 4.99 (*0-689-81273-6*) S&S Childrens.

Moffatt, Judith. Halloween Frights. (Night Glow Board Book Ser.). (Illus.). 12p. (J). (gr. k-3). 1999. bds. 4.99 (*0-689-82270-7*) Litle Simon.

— The Pumpkin Man. LC 98-21324. (Hello Reader! Ser.). (Illus.). 32p. (J). (gr. k-2). 1998. 3.99 (*0-590-63865-3*) Scholastic Inc.

***Moffatt, Judith.** Snow Shapes: A Read & Do Book. LC 99-29208. (Hello Reader! Ser.). (Illus.). 32p. (J). (gr. k-2). 2000. 3.99 (*0-439-09858-0*) Scholastic Inc.

— Trick-or-Treat Faces: A Glowing Book You Can Read in the Dark! LC 00-21424. (Illus.). 12p. (J). (ps-k). 2000. pap. 6.95 (*0-439-18299-9*) Scholastic Inc.

Moffatt, Judith. Valentines: A Read-&-Do Book. LC 98-24748. (Hello Reader! Ser.). (J). 1999. write for info. (*0-439-04020-5*) Scholastic Inc.

— Who Stole the Cookies? LC 95-20847. (All Aboard Reading Ser.: Level 1). (Illus.). 32p. (J). (ps-1). 1996. pap. 3.99 (*0-448-41127-X*, G & D) Peng Put Young Read.

Moffatt, Judith. Hide-&-Seek Bunnies. LC 95-77545. (Lift & Look Board Bks.). 12p. (J). (ps). 1996. bds. 4.99 (*0-448-41283-7*, G & D) Peng Put Young Read.

Moffatt, Judith & Moffatt, Bettyclare. Country Lights: A Night-Light Board Book. (Illus.). 10p. (J). (ps-k). 1997. 4.99 (*0-689-81272-8*) S&S Childrens.

Moffatt, Michael. Coming of Age in New Jersey: College & American Culture. 345p. 1989. pap. 15.95 (*0-8135-1359-6*) Rutgers U Pr.

— The Rutgers Picture Book: An Illustrated History of Student Life in the Changing College & University. (Illus.). 250p. 1985. text 12.50 (*0-8135-1091-0*) Rutgers U Pr.

— An Untouchable Community in South India: Structure & Consensus. LC 78-51183. 368p. 1979. reprint ed. pap. 114.10 (*0-7837-9392-8*, 206013700004) Bks Demand.

Moffatt, Michael, ed. & tr. see Dumont, Louis.

***Moffatt, Peter.** Nabokov's Gloves & Iona Rain. 192p. 2000. pap. text 10.95 (*0-413-77180-6*) Methn.

Moffatt, Tracey. Fever Pitch. LC 96-216498. 1996. 35.00 (*0-9587984-5-1*) Dist Art Pubs.

— Tracey Moffatt. 1998. pap. text 29.95 (*3-89322-423-8*) Dr Cantz sche Druckerei GmbH.

***Moffatt, Tracey.** Tracey Moffatt: Laudanum. 80p. 2000. 24.95 (*3-7757-0874-X*) Gerd Hatje.

Moffatt, William D. Your Traffic Ticket Adventure. 270p. 1992. pap. text 23.95 (*0-9634069-0-6*) W D Moffatt.

Moffatt, William G. Handbook of Binary Phase Diagrams, 5 vols. (Illus.). 1500p. 1981. 335.00 (*0-931690-00-5*) Genium Pub.

Moffeit, Tony. Luminous Animal. 56p. (Orig.). 1989. pap. 6.00 (*0-916156-86-9*) Cherry Valley.

— Midnight Knocking at the Door. (Illus.). 46p. 1998. 5.00 (*1-889289-50-7*) Ye Olde Font Shoppe.

— Neon Peppers. LC 92-36466. 64p. (Orig.). 1992. pap. 7.00 (*0-916156-90-7*) Cherry Valley.

— Poetry Is Dangerous: The Poet Is an Outlaw. (Illus.). 104p. (Orig.). 1995. 10.00 (*0-912449-44-6*) Floating Island.

Moffeit, Tony, jt. auth. see Laws, Kyle.

Moffet. Advanced Otolaryngology. 1995. text 85.00 (*0-443-04767-7*) Harcourt.

Moffet, Alice, et al, eds. Pikes Peak Region: A Pictorial Guidebook. (Illus.). 32p. 1998. pap. 6.00 (*1-892717-02-6*, MISB101) Sanborn Ltd.

Moffet, Alice, jt. auth. see Frayne, Colin.

Moffet, Alice, ed. see Hanley, Lucy.

Moffet, Charles H. Ken Hechler. (Maverick Public Ser.). 372p. 1987. 10.00 (*0-941092-18-6*) Mtn St Pr.

Moffet, Hugh L. Pediatric Infectious Diseases: A Problem Oriented Approach. 3rd ed. LC 65-10986. (Illus.). 640p. 1989. text 56.00 (*0-397-50933-2*, Lippnctt) Lppncott W & W.

Moffet, Jim. American Corn Huskers: A Patent History. LC 94-74980. 1994. pap. 7.00 (*0-9641243-1-9*) Thornton Hse.

Moffet, Promise K., jt. auth. see Kloss, Jethro.

Moffet, Ruth. Du'A, on Wings of Prayer. rev. ed. Brown, Keven, ed. LC 84-3486. 96p. 1984. pap. 6.95 (*0-87961-143-X*) Naturegraph.

Moffet, Stanley N. & Ritzman, Marlene. Homeplace: A True Saga of the Midwest. LC 85-128222. (Illus.). 257p. (Orig.). 1984. pap. 22.50 (*0-9614613-8-1*) SNM Pub.

Moffett. Human Physiology. 2nd ed. 1993. 28.75 (*0-697-40357-2*, WCB McGr Hill) McGrw-H Hghr Educ.

Moffett, Berdell, ed. see Chaney, Casey.

Moffett, Blair A., tr. see Girard, Raphael.

Moffett, C. New Painting: Impress, 1874-86. (Illus.). 510p. (Orig.). 1989. pap. 29.95 (*0-295-96883-4*) U of Wash Pr.

Moffett, Carol G. & Strydesky, Rebecca. The Receiving-Checking-Marking-Stocking Clerk. 2nd ed. (Illus.). 160p. (YA). (gr. 10-12). 1980. text 13.32 (*0-07-042667-8*) McGraw.

Moffett, Cerylle A., jt. auth. see Brown, John L.

Moffett, Charles S. The New Painting: Impressionism 1874-1886. (Orig.). 1986. 60.00 (*0-295-96367-0*) U of Wash Pr.

Moffett, Charles S., et al. Impressionists in Winter: Effets de Neige. LC 98-8265. (Illus.). 240p. 1998. pap. 25.00 (*0-943044-23-5*) Antique Collect.

— Impressionists in Winter: Effets de Neige. LC 98-8265. (Illus.). 240p. 1998. 39.95 (*0-85667-495-8*, Pub. by P Wilson) Antique Collect.

Moffett, Cleveland. Through the Wall. 1909th ed. LC 75-32768. (Literature of Mystery & Detection Ser.). (Illus.). 1976. reprint ed. 34.95 (*0-405-07887-0*) Ayer.

Moffett, Eileen. Korean Ways. (Illus.). 56p. (J). (gr. k up). 1986. 12.95 (*0-8048-7013-6*, Pub. by Seoul Intl Tourist) Tuttle Pubng.

Moffett, Emma. Morning Walk. 52p. 1998. pap. 9.95 (*1-885206-62-3*) Cader Pubng.

Moffett, George D., III. Global Population Growth: Twenty-First Century Challenges. Hoepli, Nancy L., ed. LC 94-71669. (Headline Ser.: No. 302). (Illus.). 72p. (Orig.). 1994. pap. 5.95 (*0-87124-158-7*) Foreign Policy.

— The Limits of Victory: The Ratification of the Panama Canal Treaties. LC 84-14920. 263p. reprint ed. pap. 81.60 (*0-608-20924-4*, 207202300003) Bks Demand.

Moffett, Glendon L. Uptown - Downtown: Horsecars - Trolley Cars: Urban Transportation in Kingston, New York, 1866-1930. LC 97-31881. (Illus.). 152p. 1997. pap. 12.50 (*0-935796-91-6*) Purple Mnt Pr.

Moffett-Hall, Deborah J. Easy Seasonal Wall Quilts: 24 Rotary-Cut Pictorial Projects with Quiltcharts. White, Janet, ed. LC 97-27635. (Illus.). 32p. (Orig.). 1997. pap. 12.95 (*1-56477-205-5*, B317) Martingale & Co.

Moffett, Heather. Enlightened Equitation: Riding in True Harmony with Your Horse. (Illus.). 160p. 1999. 27.95 (*0-7153-0810-6*, Pub. by D & C Pub) Sterling.

Moffett, James. Active Voice: A Writing Program Across the Curriculum. 2nd ed. LC 91-46812. 203p. (Orig.). (C). 1992. pap. text 22.00 (*0-86709-289-0*, 0289, Pub. by Boynton Cook Pubs) Heinemann.

— Detecting Growth in Language. LC 92-18851. 88p. (C). 1992. pap. text 16.00 (*0-86709-311-0*, 0311, Pub. by Boynton Cook Pubs) Heinemann.

— Harmonic Learning: Keynoting School Reform. LC 92-23576. 136p. (C). 1992. pap. text 22.00 (*0-86709-312-9*, 0312, Pub. by Boynton Cook Pubs) Heinemann.

— Points of View: An Anthology of Short Stories. 1995. 11.09 (*0-606-00840-3*, Pub. by Turtleback) Demco.

— A Storm in the Mountains: A Case Study of Censorship, Conflict, & Consciousness. LC 87-20614. 280p. (C). 1989. pap. 15.95 (*0-8093-1584-X*) S Ill U Pr.

— Teaching the Universe of Discourse. LC 87-27816. 215p. (C). 1982. pap. text 21.50 (*0-86709-181-9*, 0181, Pub. by Boynton Cook Pubs) Heinemann.

— The Universal Schoolhouse: Spiritual Awakening Through Education. LC 98-15939. 400p. 1998. pap. 19.50 (*0-9663233-2-7*, 323327) Calendar Islands.

— The Universal Schoolhouse: Spiritual Awakening Through Education. LC 93-40694. (Education-Higher Education Ser.). 391p. 1994. pap. 32.00 (*1-55542-607-7*) Jossey-Bass.

Moffett, James & McElheny, Kenneth R., eds. Points of View. rev. ed. 608p. 1995. mass mkt. 7.99 (*0-451-62872-1*, Sig) NAL.

Moffett, James & Tashlik, Phyllis. Active Voices II: A Writer's Reader. 9th ed. LC 86-23305. 317p. (YA). (gr. 7-9). 1987. pap. text 20.00 (*0-86709-111-8*, 0111, Pub. by Boynton Cook Pubs) Heinemann.

Moffett, James & Wagner, Betty J. Student-Centered Language Arts, K-12. 4th ed. LC 91-29010. 437p. (C). 1991. pap. text 32.50 (*0-86709-292-0*, 0292, Pub. by Boynton Cook Pubs) Heinemann.

An Asterisk (*) at the beginning of an entry indicates that the title is appearing for the first time.

Moffett, James, et al. Active Voices I: A Writer's Reader. 6th ed. LC 87-11600. 265p. (J). (gr. 4-6). 1987. text 20.00 (*0-86709-091-X*, 0091, Pub. by Boynton Cook Pubs) Heinemann.

— Active Voices III: A Writer's Reader. LC 86-23300. 414p. (YA). (gr. 10-12). 1987. pap. text 22.00 (*0-86709-113-4*, 0113, Pub. by Boynton Cook Pubs) Heinemann.

— Active Voices IV: A Writer's Reader. LC 85-27996. 344p. (Orig.). (C). 1985. pap. text 22.00 (*0-86709-115-0*, 0115, Pub. by Boynton Cook Pubs) Heinemann.

Moffett, Jerry E. The Computer Buyer Survival Kit: How to Select & Buy a Personal Computer. LC 94-96308. (Illus.). 115p. (Orig.). 1995. pap. 9.95 (*0-9642508-0-2*) Jerett Pubng.

— Self-Publishing: The Art of Turning Words into Cash. LC 94-96309. 150p. (Orig.). pap. 19.95 (*0-9642508-1-0*) Jerett Pubng.

Moffett, Joyce L., ed. Mid-Michigan First: A Capital Choice for Future Growth. (Illus.). 184p. 1993. 29.95 (*0-9616743-4-2*) NTC Contemp Pub Co.

Moffett, Judith. Homestead Year. 320p. 1995. 22.95 (*1-55821-352-X*) Lyons Pr.

— James Merrill: An Introduction to the Poetry. LC 83-15022. (Introduction to Twentieth Century American Poetry Ser.). 247p. 1984. text 43.50 (*0-231-05210-3*) Col U Pr.

— Keeping Time: Poems. fac. ed. LC 76-28256. 87p. 1976. reprint ed. pap. 30.00 (*0-7837-7809-0*, 204756500007) Bks Demand.

***Moffett, Julie.** A Double-Edged Blade. 400p. (Orig.). 2000. pap. 5.50 (*0-505-52369-8*, Love Spell) Dorchester Pub Co.

Moffett, Kathleen. Dreamin' On. Stained Glass Images Inc. Staff, ed. (Illus.). 52p. 1991. pap. 12.95 (*0-936459-15-8*) Stained Glass.

Moffett, Kenworth W. Larry Poons: Paintings, 1971-1981. (Illus.). 32p. (Orig.). 1981. pap. 5.95 (*0-87846-206-6*) Mus Fine Arts Boston.

— Morris Louis in the Museum of Fine Arts, Boston. LC 79-6360. (Illus.). 40p. 1979. pap. 4.95 (*0-87846-135-3*) Mus Fine Arts Boston.

Moffett, Lee. The Diary of Court House Square: Warrenton, Virginia, U. S. A.: From Early Times Through 1986, with 1987-1995 Reflections. rev. ed. LC 97-131385. (Illus.). viii, 364p. (Orig.). 1996. pap. 23.00 (*0-7884-0544-6*, M522) Heritage Bk.

***Moffett, Lee.** Those Who Were: Annotated Inscriptions of Two Thousand People in Warrenton, Virginia Cemetery, 1811-1998. 129p. 1999. pap. 16.00 (*0-7884-1399-6*, M523) Heritage Bk.

Moffett, Lorraine J. Sex Life of Slugs. (All Life Speaks Out Ser.). 10p. 1992. pap. write for info. (*0-9633997-0-5*) Rolaine Pub.

Moffett, Marian & Wodehouse, Lawrence. East Tennessee Cantilever Barns. LC 92-42651. (Illus.). 160p. (C). 1993. text 29.95 (*0-87049-798-7*) U of Tenn Pr.

Moffett, Marian, jt. auth. see Wodehouse, Lawrence.

Moffett, Mark W. High Frontier: Exploring the Tropical Rainforest Canopy. 192p. (C). 1994. text 39.95 (*0-674-39038-5*); pap. text 24.95 (*0-674-39039-3*) HUP.

Moffett, Michael H., jt. ed. see Stonehil, Arthur I.

Moffett, M'Ledge. The Social Background & Activities of Teachers College Students. LC 79-177077. (Columbia University. Teachers College. Contributions to Education Ser.: No. 375). reprint ed. 37.50 (*0-404-55375-3*) AMS Pr.

Moffett, Noel. The Best of British Architecture, 1980-2000. LC 92-40841. (Illus.). 208p. (C). 1993. 90.00 (*0-419-17240-8*, E & FN Spon) Routledge.

Moffett, Ross. Art in Narrow Streets. LC 89-62403. (Provincetown Classics in History, Literature, & Art Ser.: No. 3). (Illus.). 110p. 1989. reprint ed. pap. 6.95 (*0-945135-02-5*) Cape Cod Pilgrim.

Moffett, Ross, jt. auth. see Del Deo, Josephine C.

Moffett, Russell E. Macro-Economic Primer. 240p. (C). 1993. pap. text, per. 24.95 (*0-8403-8526-9*) Kendall-Hunt.

Moffett, S. B. Nervous Systems Regeneration in the Invertebrates: Invertebrate Neural Regeneration. (Zoophysiology Ser.: Vol. 34). (Illus.). 196p. 1996. 158.00 (*3-540-59454-X*) Spr-Verlag.

Moffett, Samuel H. A History of Christianity in Asia Vol. 1: Beginnings to 1500. 2nd ed. LC 97-49236. 560p. (Orig.). 1998. pap. 25.00 (*1-57075-162-5*) Orbis Bks.

— History of Christianity in Asia Vol. II: 1500 to Present, Vol. 2. 1999. 45.00 (*0-06-065880-0*) Harper SF.

Moffett, Toby. Nobody's Business: The Political Intruder's Guide to Everyone's State Legislature. LC 73-83355. (Illus.). 196p. 1973. 9.50 (*0-85699-080-9*); pap. 3.95 (*0-85699-081-7*) Chatham Pr.

Moffi, Larry. Citizen's Handbook. LC 89-8626. 48p. (Orig.). 1989. pap. 6.95 (*0-914061-10-0*) Orchises Pr.

— This Side of Cooperstown: An Oral History of Major League Baseball in the 1950s. LC 95-23761. (Illus.). 282p. 1996. 24.95 (*0-87745-521-X*) U of Iowa Pr.

Moffi, Larry & Kronstadt, Jonathan. Crossing the Line: Black Major Leaguers, 1947-1959. LC 94-9056. 251p. 1994. lib. bdg. 35.00 (*0-89950-930-4*) McFarland & Co.

— Crossing the Line: Black Major Leaguers, 1947-1959. LC 94-9056. 254p. 1996. pap. 12.95 (*0-87745-529-5*) U of Iowa Pr.

Moffic, H. Steven. The Ethical Way: Challenges & Solutions for Managed Behavioral Healthcare. LC 96-53565. (Jossey-Bass Managed Behavioral Healthcare Library). 1997. 36.95 (*0-7879-0841-X*) Jossey-Bass.

Moffic, H. Steven, et al. Mental Health Care for Allied Health & Nursing Professionals. 240p. 1989. pap. 27.50 (*0-87527-344-0*) Green.

Moffill, G. E. & Scholer, M., eds. Physical Processes in Interstellar Clouds. (C). 1987. text 256.00 (*90-277-2563-2*) Kluwer Academic.

Moffit, Gisela. Bonds & Bondage: Daughter-Father Relationships in the Father Memoirs of German-Speaking Women Writers of the 1970s. LC 92-35430. (Studies in Modern German Literature: Vol. 53). VIII, 284p. 1993. 56.95 (*0-8204-2014-X*) P Lang Pubng.

Moffit, L. W. England on Eve of Industrial Revolution. 312p. 1963. reprint ed. 32.00 (*0-7146-1345-2*, BHA-01345, Pub. by F Cass Pubs) Intl Spec Bk.

Moffit, Linda L. The Magic Mirror. LC 89-50125. (Illus.). 80p. (Orig.). (J). (gr. k-7). 1989. pap. 9.95 (*0-87516-615-6*) DeVorss.

Moffit, Robert E., jt. ed. see Meese, Edwin, 3rd.

Moffitt, Alan, et al, eds. The Functions of Dreaming. LC 91-47539. (SUNY Series in Dream Studies). 610p. (C). 1993. pap. text 24.95 (*0-7914-1298-9*) State U NY Pr.

— The Functions of Dreaming. LC 91-47539. (SUNY Series in Dream Studies). 610p. (C). 1993. text 74.50 (*0-7914-1297-0*) State U NY Pr.

Moffitt, Athol, et al. Drug Precipice: Illicit Drugs; Worsening Problems; Organized Crime & Fallacies of Legalization Solutions. LC 98-60219. 1997. pap. 29.95 (*0-86840-552-3*, Pub. by New South Wales Univ Pr) Intl Spec Bk.

Moffitt, Boyd E. Some Good Some Bad Some Indifferent. 176p. (Orig.). 1996. pap. 12.95 (*0-9652895-0-8*) Railrd Earth.

Moffitt, Dale, ed. see Brook, Peter.

Moffitt, Donald. Advest: Celebrating a Century of Service to Investors, 1898-1998. LC 97-77060. (Illus.). 64p. 1997. write for info. (*0-944641-25-3*) Greenwich Pub Group.

Moffitt, Donald, ed. The Wall Street Journal Views America Tomorrow. LC 76-52501. 190p. reprint ed. pap. 58.90 (*0-608-12974-7*, 202393100034) Bks Demand.

Moffitt, Francis H. & Bossler, John D. Surveying. 10th ed. LC 96-53010. 870p. (C). 1997. 100.00 (*0-673-99752-9*, Prentice Hall) P-H.

Moffitt, James, jt. auth. see Orr, Robert T.

Moffitt, John F. Art Forgery: The Case of the Lady of Elche. LC 94-29181. (Illus.). 354p. 1995. 39.95 (*0-8130-1330-5*) U Press Fla.

— The Arts of Spain: From Prehistory to Postmodernism. LC 98-60192. (World of Art Ser.). (Illus.). 240p. 1999. pap. 14.95 (*0-500-20315-6*, Pub. by Thames Hudson) Norton.

— Occultism in Avant-Garde Art: The Case of Joseph Beuys. Foster, Stephen, ed. LC 88-5774. (Studies in the Fine Arts: The Avant-Garde: No. 63). 238p. reprint ed. 73.80 (*0-8357-1881-6*, 207067400016) Bks Demand.

Moffitt, John F. & Sebastian, Santiago. O Brave New People: The European Image of Native Americans. LC 94-48680. (Illus.). 413p. 1996. 55.00 (*0-8263-1639-5*) U of NM Pr.

— O Brave New People: The European Invention of the American Indian. (Illus.). 399p. 1998. pap. 24.95 (*0-8263-1989-0*) U of NM Pr.

Moffitt, Johnny. Delivered: From the Hands of His Enemy. 196p. (Orig.). 1997. pap. 9.99 (*1-884369-33-2*, EBED Pubns) McDougal Pubng.

Moffitt, Kirk, jt. auth. see Melzer, James E.

Moffitt, Leonard C. Connected Community: Subtle Force in a Systemic Web. 263p. 75.00 (*1-56072-373-4*) Nova Sci Pubs.

Moffitt, Leonard C. Connected Community: Subtle Force in a Systemic Web. (Illus.). 189p. Date not set. 24.95 (*1-56072-324-6*) Nova Sci Pubs.

— Global Positioning for the Twenty-First Century: Rethinking Strategic Planning. LC 89-42581. 230p. (C). 1990. text 24.95 (*0-87013-272-5*) Mich St U Pr.

— Religiosity: A Propensity of the Human Phenotype. 1997. 65.00 (*1-56072-521-4*) Nova Sci Pubs.

— Strategic Management: Public Planning at the Local Level. LC 84-47775. (Contemporary Studies in Economic & Financial Analysis: Vol. 45). 160p. 1984. 78.50 (*0-89232-428-7*) Jai Pr.

Moffitt, Mary Anne. Campaign Strategies & Message Design: A Practitioner's Guide from Start to Finish. LC 98-33613. 224p. 1999. 59.95 (*0-275-95592-3*, Praeger Pubns); pap. 22.95 (*0-275-96470-1*, Praeger Pubs) Greenwood.

Moffitt, Merra L. Guide to Knowledgebase Systems: Tools & Products for Support Centers. (Illus.). 240p. (Orig.). 1995. pap. 145.00 (*1-888969-00-8*) Knowldge Netwrks.

Moffitt, Merra L. & Rose, Bill. Automating Your Support Center: A Practical Guide to Assessing Service Automation Tools. 3rd rev. ed. (Illus.). 310p. 1995. pap. 195.00 (*1-888969-01-6*) Knowldge Netwrks.

***Moffitt, Miriam.** The Church of Ireland Community of Killala & Achonry (1870-1940) Thinly Scattered. LC 99-30887. (Maynooth Studies in Local History). 64p. 1999. pap. 10.95 (*0-7165-2682-4*, Pub. by Irish Acad Pr) Intl Spec Bk.

Moffitt, Peggy. Gernreich, Rudi. (Architecture & Design Ser.). (Illus.). 240p. 1999. 29.99 (*3-8228-7197-4*) Taschen Amer.

Moffitt, Phillip & Smolan, Rick. Worth a Thousand Words: Scanning to Communicate. 80p. 1991. pap. 7.95 (*0-9630008-0-2*) Light Source.

Moffitt, Robert A., ed. see National Research Council Staff.

Moffitt, Terrie E. & Mednick, Sarnoff A., eds. Biological Contributions to Crime Causation. 1988. lib. bdg. 191.00 (*90-247-3655-2*) Kluwer Academic.

Mofford, Juliet H. The Beat Generation. (Perspectives on History Ser.: Pt. III). 1998. pap. 6.95 (*1-57960-031-X*) Disc Enter Ltd.

Mofford, Juliet H., ed. Child Labor in America. LC 97-67313. (Perspectives on History Ser.: Pt. II). (Illus.). 64p. 1997. pap. 6.95 (*1-878668-98-6*) Disc Enter Ltd.

— Greater Lawrence: A Bibliography. LC 78-71920. 1978. 10.00 (*0-937474-01-0*) Am Textile Hist.

Mofford, Juliet H., intro. Cry "Witch" - Salem 1692. LC 95-68765. (Perspectives on History Ser.). (Illus.). 68p. (YA). (gr. 5-12). 1995. pap. text 6.95 (*1-878668-52-8*) Disc Enter Ltd.

***Moffot, E.** Custodial Reflection. 24p. 1999. 6.95 (*1-885206-74-7*) Cader Pubng.

Mofid, Bijan. The Butterfly. (J). 1974. 6.00 (*0-87602-111-9*) Anchorage.

***Mofina, Rick.** If Angels Fall. 2000. mass mkt. 6.99 (*0-7860-1061-4*, Pinncle Kensgtn) Kensgtn Pub Corp.

Mofolo, Thomas. Chaka. Kunene, Daniel, tr. (African Writers Ser.). 168p. (Orig.). (C). 1981. pap. 9.95 (*0-435-90229-6*) Heinemann.

Moftah, Ragheb. Coptic Orthodox Liturgy of St. Basil. 2p. 1997. 100.00 (*977-424-437-0*, Pub. by Am Univ Cairo Pr) Col U Pr.

Mofty, Soraya. Kurdish, Easy Way To, 2 cass. unabridged ed. (KUR., Illus.). 60p. 1997. pap. 34.50 incl. audio (*0-88432-940-2*, AFKU10) Audio-Forum.

Mog, Carol F. What Would I Do? Questions & Insights for Personal Reflection. LC 99-72722. 1999. pap. 9.99 (*0-88270-768-X*) Bridge-Logos.

***Mog, Dennis, ed.** Mousetale.com: A Collection of Humorous Stories from the Internet. (Illus.). 1999. pap. 6.99 (*0-88270-792-2*) Bridge-Logos.

***Mog, Dennis D., ed.** Mousetale.com: A Collection of Humorous Stories from the Internet - Includes Mouse Pad. LC 99-64054. 120p. 1999. pap. 10.99 (*0-88270-774-4*, Bridge) Bridge-Logos.

Mog, Dennis D., ed. Touched by an E-Mail: A Collection of Heart-Warming Stories from the Internet. LC 99-64059. 140p. 1999. pap. 9.99 (*0-88270-773-6*, Bridge) Bridge-Logos.

***Mog, Denny, ed.** Touched by an E-Mail: Class of 2000. (Touched by an E-Mail Ser.). (Illus.). 2000. pap. 7.99 (*0-88270-795-7*) Bridge-Logos.

— Touched by an E-Mail for Grandparents. (Touched by an E-Mail Ser.). (Illus.). 2000. pap. 7.99 (*0-88270-798-1*) Bridge-Logos.

— Touched by an E-Mail for Mothers. (Touched by an E-Mail Ser.). (Illus.). 2000. pap. 7.99 (*0-88270-794-9*) Bridge-Logos.

Mog, Hubertine. Wolf Spring Place: Growing up There. LC 96-72551. (Illus.). 240p. (Orig.). 1997. pap. 14.95 (*1-889902-02-0*) Prtnrshp Bk Servs.

Mog, Paul & Althaus, Hans J., eds. Die Deutschen in Ihrer Welt. 264p. 1992. 29.00 (*3-468-49443-2*) Langenscheidt.

Moga, Thomas T. Patent Practice & Policy in the Pacific Rim, 2 vols. 1995. ring bd. 350.00 (*0-379-01263-4*) Oceana.

Mogab, C. J., jt. ed. see Frieser, R. G.

Mogabgab, John. Weavings Reader. 1993. 19.95 (*0-687-61302-7*) Abingdon.

Mogabgab, John, ed. Communion, Community, Commonwealth: Spiritual Readings for Leadership. LC 95-60919. 176p. 1995. 15.00 (*0-8358-0737-1*) Upper Room Bks.

Mogalakwe, Monageng. State & Organized Labour in Botswana, 1966-1990: "Liberal Democracy" in Emergent Capitalism. LC 97-70891. (Making of Modern Africa Ser.). (Illus.). 168p. 1997. text 64.95 (*1-85972-344-6*, Pub. by Ashgate Pub) Ashgate Pub Co.

Mogan, Jewel. Beyond Telling. LC 94-39166. 173p. 1995. 19.95 (*0-86538-082-1*) Ontario Rev NJ.

Mogan, Peter J. & Nemeth, Gerry. Family Trusts for Tax & Estate Planning: How to Set up Your Own in Canada to Save Money & Protect Your Estate. 120p. (Orig.). 1996. reprint ed. pap. 14.95 (*0-88908-848-9*) Self-Counsel Pr.

Mogano, Mike C. How to Make Bigger Profit. 1991. pap. text 22.50 (*1-85333-562-2*) Kluwer Academic.

— How to Make Bigger Profits. (C). 1991. lib. bdg. 41.50 (*1-85333-603-3*, Pub. by Graham & Trotman) Kluwer Academic.

— How to Start & Run Your Own Busines. 1985. lib. bdg. 28.00 (*0-86010-559-8*) Kluwer Academic.

— How to Start & Run Your Own Business. 160p. 1985. pap. text 17.50 (*0-86010-577-6*) G & T Inc.

— How to Start & Run Your Own Business. 160p. 1989. pap. text 18.50 (*1-85333-288-7*) G & T Inc.

— How to Start & Run Your Own Business. (C). 1988. pap. text 17.50 (*1-85333-093-0*, Pub. by Graham & Trotman) Kluwer Academic.

— How to Start & Run Your Own Business. 7th ed. 1989. pap. text 16.00 (*1-85333-191-0*, Pub. by Graham & Trotman); lib. bdg. 33.50 (*1-85333-190-2*, Pub. by Graham & Trotman) Kluwer Academic.

— How to Win a Promotion. 1991. lib. bdg. write for info. (*1-85333-380-8*) Kluwer Academic.

— How to Win Promotion. (Better Business Ser.). 128p. 1990. pap. text 19.00 (*1-85333-381-6*, Pub. by Graham & Trotman) Kluwer Academic.

Mogard, Sue & McDonnell, Ginny. Gobble up Math. (Primary Math Ser.). (Illus.). 136p. (J). (ps-3). 1994. pap. 10.95 (*0-88160-262-0*, LW105) Learning Wks.

Mogard, Sue, jt. auth. see McDonnell, Ginny.

Mogavero, Louis N. & Shane. WEESKA Technology Transfer & Innovation. (What Every Engineer Should Know Ser.: Vol. 8). (Illus.). 168p. 1982. text 59.75 (*0-8247-1863-1*) Dekker.

Mogee, Mary E. Technology Policy & Critical Technologies: A Summary of Recent Reports. 47p. (Orig.). (C). 1993. pap. text 20.00 (*0-7881-0031-9*) DIANE Pub.

Mogel, John, jt. ed. see Bahadur, Shyam.

Mogel, Leonard. Creating Your Career in Communications & Entertainment. (Illus.). 312p. 1998. pap. text 45.00 (*0-88362-208-4*, 1550) GATFPress.

— Kaplan Careers in Communication & Entertainment. 384p. 2000. pap. 20.00 (*0-684-87017-7*) S&S Trade.

— The Magazine: Everthing You Need to Know to Make It in the Magazine Business. 4th rev. ed. LC 98-70934. (Illus.). 224p. 1998. pap. text 40.00 (*0-88362-223-8*, 15404) GATFPress.

— Making It. 76p. 1999. pap. text 12.00 (*0-536-02265-8*) P-H.

— Making It in Advertising: An Inside's Guide to Career Opportunities. LC 92-32051. 193p. 1993. pap. 10.00 (*0-02-034552-6*) Macmillan.

— Making It in Book Publishing. LC 95-34430. 256p. 1996. pap. 16.95 (*0-02-860593-4*) Macmillan Info.

— Making It in Publishing: An Insider's Guide to Career Opportunities. LC 93-9012. 1994. write for info. (*0-02-034533-X*) Macmillan.

***Mogel, Leonard.** The Newspaper: Everything You Need to Know to Make It in the Newspaper Business. (Illus.). 264p. (C). 2000. pap. 40.00 (*0-88362-235-1*) GATFPress.

***Mogel, Wendy.** Blessing of a Skinned Knee. 2001. 24.00 (*0-684-86297-2*) Scribner.

Mogel, William A., jt. auth. see Mulchow, David.

Mogelever, Diane, ed. see Family Circle Editors.

Mogelon, Alex & Laliberte, Norman. Art in Boxes. LC 74-5947. (Illus.). 240p. reprint ed. pap. 74.40 (*0-8357-5759-5*, 200581000054) Bks Demand.

Mogelon, Ronna. Famous People's Cats. 1995. mass mkt. 6.99 (*0-312-95619-3*, Pub. by Tor Bks) St Martin.

Mogelonsky, Marcia. Everybody Eats: Supermarket Consumers in the 1990s. 229p. (C). 1995. 42.50 (*0-936889-31-4*); pap. 29.95 (*0-936889-32-2*) American Demo.

— Who's Buying Food & Drink? 292p. 1996. 69.95 (*1-885070-04-7*) New Strategist.

Mogen, David. Wilderness Visions: The Western Theme in Science Fiction Literature. 2nd ed. LC 92-46389. (I. O. Evans Studies in the Philosophy & Criticism of Literature: No. 1). 128p. 1993. pap. 19.00 (*0-89370-400-8*) Millefleurs.

Mogen, David, et al, eds. The Frontier Experience & the American Dream: Essays on American Literature. LC 88-35474. 288p. 1989. 31.95 (*0-89096-398-3*) Tex A&M Univ Pr.

Mogendovich, Eugene. Hydropulse Systems & Technology in the U. S. S. R. Jones, Steven, ed. 105p. (Orig.). 1985. pap. text 75.00 (*1-55831-030-4*) Delphic Associates.

Mogenet, Joseph, et al. Nicephore Gregoras: Calcul de l'Eclipse de Soleil du 16 Juillet, 1330. (Corpus des Astronomes Byzantins Ser.: Vol. I). (FRE.). 222p. (C). 1983. pap. 54.00 (*90-70265-34-6*, Pub. by Gieben) J Benjamins Pubng Co.

Mogens, Jul. The Quality of Frozen Food. 1984. text 94.00 (*0-12-391980-0*) Acad Pr.

Mogensen. Pattern Animal Book. 1995. pap. 8.95 (*0-201-48037-9*) Addison-Wesley.

Mogensen, Allan H. & Rausa, Rosario. Mogy - An Autobiography: Father of Work Simplification. 2nd ed. Denyes, Jim, ed. 204p. 1990. pap. text 9.95 (*0-9623050-0-6*) Idea Assocs VA.

Mogensen, C. E. & Standl, E., eds. Concepts for the Ideal Diabetes Clinic. LC 92-49365. xiv, 402p. (C). 1993. pap. text 113.85 (*3-11-013231-1*) De Gruyter.

— Pharmacology of Diabetes: Present Practice & Future Perspectives. (Illus.). xii, 374p. (C). 1991. pap. text 98.50 (*3-11-012636-2*) De Gruyter.

— Prevention & Treatment of Diabetic Late Complications. x, 226p. (C). 1989. pap. 69.25 (*3-11-012297-9*) De Gruyter.

— Research Methodologies in Human Diabetes. LC 93-50659. 470p. 1994. 129.25 (*3-11-014248-1*) De Gruyter.

Mogensen, C. E., jt. ed. see Belfiore, F.

Mogensen, Carl E. The Kidney & Hypertension in Diabetes Mellitus. 4th ed. LC 98-8769. 1998. 180.00 (*0-7923-8209-9*) Kluwer Academic.

Mogensen, Carl E., ed. The Kidney & Hypertension in Diabetes Mellitus. (Topics in Renal Medicine Ser.). (C). 1988. text 235.00 (*0-89838-958-5*) Kluwer Academic.

— The Kidney & Hypertension in Diabetes Mellitus. 2nd ed. 576p. 1994. text 233.00 (*0-7923-2829-9*) Kluwer Academic.

— The Kidney & Hypertension in Diabetes Mellitus. 3rd ed. LC 96-48296. 608p. (C). 1996. text 157.50 (*0-7923-4353-0*) Kluwer Academic.

Mogensen, Gunnar V. Danes & Their Politicians: A Summary of the Findings of a Research Project on Political Credibility in Denmark. (Voters in Scandinavia Ser.: Vol. 2). (Illus.). 88p. (Orig.). (C). 1993. pap. 12.95 (*87-7288-451-7*, Pub. by Aarhus Univ Pr) David Brown.

Mogensen, Gunnar V., ed. Work Incentives in the Danish Welfare State: New Empirical Evidence. LC 96-177001. (Illus.). 280p. (Orig.). (C). 1995. pap. 19.95 (*87-7288-480-0*, Pub. by Aarhus Univ Pr) David Brown.

Mogensen, Jan. The Land of the Big. LC 92-18302. (Illus.). 32p. (J). (ps-3). 1993. 14.95 (*1-56656-111-6*, Crocodile Bks) Interlink Pub.

— The Tiger's Breakfast. LC 91-3606. (Illus.). 32p. (J). (ps-3). 1991. 14.95 (*0-940793-83-0*, Crocodile Bks) Interlink Pub.

Mogensen, Sandra & Magarian-Gold, Judi. Exploring with Color Tiles. 96p. 1995. pap. text 9.95 (*0-938587-17-X*) Cuisenaire.

Mogensen, Sandra & Magarian-Gold, Judy. Pattern Animals Book. (Illus.). 48p. 1986. pap. text 8.95 (*0-914040-46-4*) Cuisenaire.

Mogensen, Vernon L. Office Politics: Computers & the Flight for Safety & Health in the Information Age. LC 95-46829. 325p. (C). 1996. text 48.00 (*0-8135-2286-2*); pap. text 17.95 (*0-8135-2287-0*) Rutgers U Pr.

Mogenson, Greg. God Is a Trauma: Vicarious Religion & Soul-Making. LC 89-5998. 168p. (Orig.). 1989. pap. 15.00 (*0-88214-339-5*) Spring Pubns.

M

— Greeting the Angels: An Imaginal View of the Mourning Process. (Death, Value & Meaning Ser.). 171p. 1992. text 27.95 (*0-89503-097-7*) Baywood Pub.

Moger, Allen W. Virginia: Bourbonism to Byrd, 1870-1925. LC 68-8538. (Illus.). 414p. reprint ed. pap. 128.40 (*0-7837-4349-1*, 204405900012) Bks Demand.

Moger, Art. The Complete Pun Book. 256p. 1981. pap. 9.95 (*0-8065-0776-4*, Citadel Pr) Carol Pub Group.

Moger, Byron J. How to Buy a House. LC 69-10635. 1969. 4.95 (*0-8184-0040-4*) Carol Pub Group.

Moger, Susan. Celebrate the Millennium Activity: A Multitude of Creative Activities to Ring in the Year 2000! (Illus.). 64p. 1999. pap. 11.95 (*0-590-00487-5*) Scholastic Inc.

— Pilgrims. (J). 1995. pap. 9.95 (*0-590-49787-1*) Scholastic Inc.

— Teaching the Diary of Anne Frank: An In-Depth Resource for Learning about the Holocaust Through, 1 vol. LC 99-196882. 1999. pap. text 12.95 (*0-590-67482-X*) Scholastic Inc.

Moger, Susan, jt. auth. see Rickards, Tudor.

Mogey, John H., ed. Aiding & Aging: The Coming Crisis in Support for the Elderly by Kin & State, 17. LC 89-25670. (Contributions to the Study of Aging Ser.: No. 17). 304p. 1990. 65.00 (*0-313-27315-4*, MOD/, Greenwood Pr) Greenwood.

M

Mogey, John H., ed. see Howard, Ronald L.

Mogey, John M. Rural Life in Northern Ireland: Five Regional Studies Made for the Northern Ireland Council of Social Service, Inc. LC 77-87692. reprint ed. 38.00 (*0-404-16488-9*) AMS Pr.

Mogford-Bevan, Kay & Sadler, Jane, eds. Child Language Disability Vol. 2: Semantic & Pragmatic Difficulties. 114p. 1991. 59.00 (*1-85359-128-9*, Pub. by Multilingual Matters); pap. 19.50 (*1-85359-127-0*, Pub. by Multilingual Matters) Taylor & Francis.

— Child Language Disability Vol. 3: Hearing Impairment. 120p. 1992. 59.00 (*1-85359-169-6*, Pub. by Multilingual Matters); pap. 19.50 (*1-85359-168-8*, Pub. by Multilingual Matters) Taylor & Francis.

Mogford-Bevan, Kay, jt. ed. see Bishop, Dorothy.

Mogford-Bevan, Kay, jt. ed. see Sadler, Jane.

***Mogg, Ken, et al.** The Alfred Hitchcock Story. LC 99-35294. 211p. 1999. 29.95 (*0-87833-163-8*) Taylor Pub.

Mogg, Rees, jt. auth. see Davidson, James D.

***Moggach, Deborah.** Tulip Fever. LC 99-42048. 288p. 2000. 21.95 (*0-385-33489-3*) Delacorte.

— Tulip Fever. large type ed. LC 99-48479. (General Ser.). 2000. pap. 22.95 (*0-7862-2300-6*) Thorndike Pr.

Moggi, Eugenio, et al, eds. Category Theory & Computer Science: 7th International Conference, CTCS'97, S. Margheria Ligure, Italy, September 4-6, 1997, Proceedings, Vol. 129. LC 97-30987. (Lecture Notes in Computer Science Ser.: Vol. 1290). vii, 313p. 1997. pap. 55.00 (*3-540-63455-X*) Spr-Verlag.

Moggi, Guido, et al. Simon & Schuster's Guide to Garden Flowers. Schuler, Stanley, ed. (Illus.). 512p. 1983. pap. 15.00 (*0-671-46678-X*) S&S Trade.

Moggridge, D. E. British Monetary Policy, 1924-1931: The Norman Conquest of Four Dollars & Eighty-Six Cents. (Modern Revivals in Economic & Social History Ser.). 301p. 1992. 63.95 (*0-7512-0092-1*, Pub. by Gregg Revivals) Ashgate Pub Co.

Keynes. 3rd ed. 200p. 1993. text 45.00 (*0-8020-0515-2*); pap. text 19.95 (*0-8020-6951-7*) U of Toronto Pr.

Moggridge, D. E., ed. Editing Modern Economists: Papers Given at the Twenty-Second Annual Conference on Editorial Problems, University of Toronto, 7-8 November, 1986. LC 87-45817. (Conference on Editorial Problems Ser.: No. 22). 1988. 42.50 (*0-404-63672-1*) AMS Pr.

Moggridge, D. E., jt. ed. see Howson, Susan.

Moggridge, Don. Maynard Keynes: An Economists' Biography. (Illus.). 968p. 1995. pap. 19.95 (*0-415-12676-2*, C0539) Routledge.

— Maynard Keynes: An Economists' Biography. (Illus.). 976p. (C). 1995. pap. 32.99 (*0-415-12711-4*) Routledge.

Moggridge, Donald, ed. see Keynes, John Maynard.

Moggridge, Donald E. John Maynard Keynes: An Economist's Biography. 992p. (C). (gr. 13). 1992. 85.00 (*0-415-05141-X*, A5993) Routledge.

Moggridge, Donald E., ed. Perspectives on the History of Economic Thought: Classicals, Marzians & Neo-Classicals. (Perspectives on the History of Economic Thought Ser.: Vol. 3). 216p. 1990. text 95.00 (*1-85278-293-5*) E Elgar.

— Perspectives on the History of Economic Thought Vol. IV: Keynes, Macroeconomics & Method. (Perspectives on the History of Economic Thought Ser.: Vol. 4). (Illus.). 232p. 1990. text 95.00 (*1-85278-294-3*) E Elgar.

Mogha, V. Indian Conveyancer. (C). 1987. 100.00 (*0-7855-3553-5*) St Mut.

— Law of Pleadings. (C). 1987. 100.00 (*0-7855-3552-7*) St Mut.

Moghadam. Contemporary Social Problems. 1998. 14.74 (*0-07-230432-4*) McGraw.

Moghadam, A. A. The North-South Science & Technology Gap. LC 91-18135. (Developing Economies of the Third World Ser.). 342p. 1991. text 10.00 (*0-8153-0634-2*) Garland.

Moghadam, Fatemeh E. From Land Reform to Revolution: The Politicak Economy of Agrarian Relations in Iran. LC 95-61535. 288p. 1995. 59.50 (*1-86064-006-0*, Pub. by I B T) St Martin.

Moghadam, H. Understanding & Management of Health Problems in Schools: A Resource Manual for School Personnel. 152p. (Orig.). 1995. pap. text. write for info. (*1-55059-121-5*) Detselig Ents.

Moghadam, H. & Fagan, Joel. Attention Deficit Disorder: A Concise Source of Information for Parents & Teachers. 2nd rev. ed. (Illus.). 112p. 1994. pap. 12.95 (*1-55059-082-0*) Temeron Bks.

Moghadam, Valentine M. Modernizing Women: Gender & Social Change in the Middle East. LC 92-37454. (Women & Change in the Developing World Ser.). 312p. 1993. pap. text 19.95 (*1-55587-354-5*) L Rienner.

— Privatization & Democratization in Central & Eastern Europe & the Soviet Union: The Gender Dimension LC 92-245960. (Wider Research for Action Ser.). 73p. 1992. write for info. (*952-9520-09-3*) UN.

— Women, Work, & Economic Reform in the Middle East & North Africa. LC 97-26798. 260p. 1997. lib. bdg. 55.00 (*1-55587-785-0*) L Rienner.

Moghadam, Valentine M., ed. Democratic Reform & the Position of Women in Transitional Economies. (WIDER Studies in Development Economics). (Illus.). 376p. 1994. text 75.00 (*0-19-828820-4*) OUP.

— Gender & National Identity: Women & Politics in Muslim Society. LC 94-10887. 192p. (C). 1994. text 62.50 (*1-85649-245-1*, Pub. by Zed Books); text 22.50 (*1-85649-246-X*, Pub. by Zed Books) St Martin.

— Patriarchy & Economic Development: Women's Position at the End of the Twentieth Century. (Illus.). 382p. (C). 1996. text 89.00 (*0-19-829023-3*) OUP.

Moghaddam. Exploring Universals. 1998. student ed. 61.00 (*0-7167-3478-8*) W H Freeman.

Moghaddam, Fathali. Social Psychology & Culture. 1998. pap. text, student ed. 20.95 (*0-7167-3232-7*) St Martin.

— Social Psychology & Culture. 1998. teacher ed. 24.00 (*0-7167-3231-9*); pap. write for info. (*0-7167-3233-5*) W H Freeman.

Moghaddam, Fathali M. Social Psychology: Exploring Universals Across Cultures. LC 97-25255. 650p. 1997. text 66.95 (*0-7167-2849-4*) W H Freeman.

— The Specialized Society: The Plight of the Individual in an Age of Individualism. LC 96-33186. 200p. 1997. 59.95 (*0-275-95670-9*, Praeger Pubs) Greenwood.

Moghaddam, Fathali M. & Studer, Charles. Illusions of Control: Striving for Control in Our Personal & Professional Lives. LC 97-43944. 192p. 1998. 59.95 (*0-275-96025-0*, Praeger Pubs) Greenwood.

Moghaddam, Fathali M., et al. Social Psychology in Cross-Cultural Perspective. LC 92-23851. 197p. (C). 1992. pap. 20.95 (*0-7167-2355-7*) W H Freeman.

Moghaddam, Fathali M., jt. auth. see Taylor, Donald M.

Moghdam, Dineh. Computers in Newspaper Publishing: User-Oriented Systems. LC 77-17887. (Books in Library & Information Science: No. 22). (Illus.). 221p. reprint ed. pap. 68.60 (*0-7837-3387-9*, 204334500008) Bks Demand.

Moghdam, Dineh, jt. auth. see Borgman, Christine L.

Moghe, S. G. Sraddha-Sagara of Kullukabhatta: With a Critical Exposition & Introduction. 1994. 29.00 (*81-246-0016-3*, Pub. by DK Pubs Ind) S Asia.

***Moghe, S. G.** Studies in Applied Purva-Mimamsa. LC 97-913686. 1998. write for info. (*81-202-0353-4*, Pub. by Ajanta Pubns) S Asia.

Moghe, S. G., ed. Professor Kane's Contribution to Charmasastra Literature. xii, 380p. 1997. 35.00 (*81-246-0075-9*, Pub. by D K Printwrld) Nataraj Bks.

Moghimi, Sasha, ed. see Kian, Fereydoun.

Moghimirad, Giti. Dream Songs. 1997. pap. 5.00 (*0-9627031-8-4*) Stone & Scott Pubs.

Moghissi, A. Alan, ed. Oil Spills. 80p. 1980. pap. 15.50 (*0-08-026237-6*, Pergamon Pr) Elsevier.

***Moghissi, Haideh.** Feminism & Islamic Fundamentalism LC 99-22771. 1999. pap. 19.95 (*1-85649-590-6*) St Martin.

Moghissi, Haideh. Populism & Feminism in Iran: Women's Strugggle in a Male-Defined Revolutionary Movement. 232p. 1997. pap. 19.95 (*0-312-16469-6*) St Martin.

— Populism & Feminism in Iran: Women's Struggle in a Male-Defined Revolutionary Movement. LC 93-47024. 1994. text 69.95 (*0-312-12068-0*) St Martin.

***Moghissi, Hiadeh.** Feminism & Islamic Fundamentalism. LC 99-22771. 1999. text 55.00 (*1-85649-589-2*) St Martin.

Moghissi, Kamran S., ed. Controversies in Contraception. LC 78-15812. 249p. reprint ed. pap. 77.20 (*0-608-15171-8*, 205607000045) Bks Demand.

Moghissi, Kamran S., jt. ed. see Blandau, Richard J.

Moghissi, Kamran S., ed. see Harold C. Mack Symposium on the Physiology & Patho.

Moghtader, M. R. The Persian Garden: Echoes of Paradise. LC 96-44429. (Illus.). 176p. 1998. 75.00 (*0-934211-46-9*) Mage Pubs Inc.

Moghton, John. Scientific Americans. LC 90-175652. 96p. 1997. pap. text 10.95 (*0-88754-488-6*) Theatre Comm.

Mogi, Goro, et al, eds. Immunobiology in Otorhinolaryngology: Progress of a Decade. LC 94-23510. (Illus.). xliv, 674p. 1994. text 188.50 (*90-6299-114-9*) Kugler Pubns.

— Recent Advances in Otitis Media. LC 93-41768. (Illus.). xxxvi, 875p. 1994. text 243.00 (*90-6299-101-7*, Pub. by Kugler) Kugler Pubns.

Mogielski, Nora. The Storytelling Cottage. (Illus.). 32p. 1997. pap. 10.00 (*1-886094-55-1*) Chicago Spectrum.

Mogil, H. Michael, contrib. by. Weather: An Explore Your World Handbook. LC 99-31020. (Illus.). 192p. 1999. pap. 13.95 (*1-56331-802-4*) Discovery.

Mogil, H. Michael & Hirsch, Sol. The Cloud Chart One, Two, Three. (NWA Publication Ser.: No. 1-88). (Illus.). 3p. 1988. pap. text 9.50 (*1-883563-05-4*) Natl Weather.

Mogil, H. Michael & Levine, Barbara G. Anytime Weather Everywhere. (Illus.). 100p. (Orig.). (J). (gr. k-3). 1995. pap. 15.95 (*1-887013-49-0*) How the Weatherworks.

Mogil, Holly, ed. Packaging Sourcebook, 1998: North American Edition. 1328p. 1998. pap. 375.00 (*1-888576-21-9*) North Am Pub Co.

— Printing Industry Goldbook, 1998. 1024p. 1998. pap. 425.00 (*1-888576-22-7*) North Am Pub Co.

Mogill, L. Advanced Scales & Double Tops for the Viola. 32p. 1988. pap. 9.50 (*0-7935-5629-5*, 50331740) H Leonard.

— Scale Studies for Viola: Based on Hrimaly Scale Studies for the Violin. 40p. 1987. pap. 9.95 (*0-7935-5446-2*, 50262330) H Leonard.

Mogilner, A. I. Few-Particle Schrodinger Operators on a Lattice: Applications in Condensed Matter Physics. 300p. (C). 1997. text 40.00 (*981-02-0735-2*) World Scientific Pub.

Mogilner, Alijandra. The Children's Writer's Word Book. 352p. 1992. 19.99 (*0-89879-511-7*, Wrtrs Digest Bks) F & W Pubns Inc.

— The Children's Writer's Word Book. 352p. 1999. pap. 16.99 (*0-89879-951-1*, 10649, Wrtrs Digest Bks) F & W Pubns Inc.

Mogilni, Nikolaj P., jt. auth. see Kowalew, Wjatscheslaw M.

Mogk, Lylas & Mogk, Marja. Macular Degeneration: The Complete Guide to Saving & Maximizing Your Sight. LC 98-46041. (Illus.). 416p. 1999. pap. 13.95 (*0-345-42598-7*) Ballantine Pub Grp.

Mogk, Lylas G. Muscular Degeneration. mass mkt. write for info. (*0-345-42599-5*, Ballantine) Ballantine Pub Grp.

Mogk, Marja, jt. auth. see Mogk, Lylas.

Moglen, Helene. Charlotte Bronte: The Self Conceived. LC 76-16010. 256p. 1984. reprint ed. pap. 14.95 (*0-299-10144-4*); reprint ed. text 16.95 (*0-299-10140-1*) U of Wis Pr.

— The Philosophical Irony of Laurence Sterne. LC 75-4574. 172p. 1975. 49.95 (*0-8130-0363-6*) U Press Fla.

Moglia, Tony. Partners in Performance: Successful Performance Management. LC 96-72502. (Fifty-Minute Ser.). (Illus.). 120p. (Orig.). 1997. pap. 10.95 (*1-56052-446-4*) Crisp Pubns.

— Supervising for Success: A Guide for Supervisors. (Fifty Minute Ser.). (Illus.). 120p. (Orig.). 1997. pap. 10.95 (*1-56052-460-X*) Crisp Pubns.

Mogonagle, Noel. Irish Grammar: A Basic Handbook. 100p. 1998. reprint ed. pap. 9.95 (*0-7818-0667-4*) Hippocrene Bks.

Mogotsi, Isaac. The Alexandra Tales. 172p. (Orig.). 1994. pap. text 14.95 (*0-86975-446-7*, Pub. by Ravan Pr) Ohio U Pr.

Mogstad, T. E., ed. see International Congress of Psychotherapy Staff.

Moguel, Margarita Robleda. 623 Adivinanzas Populares y Un Pilon. 1988. 13.15 (*0-606-10374-0*, Pub. by Turtleback) Demco.

— Trabalenguas, Colmos, Tantanes, Refranes, y Un Pilon. 1989. 13.15 (*0-606-10517-4*, Pub. by Turtleback) Demco.

Moguet, Pamela J., jt. auth. see Belchez, Chito.

Mogul, Kathleen M. & Dickstein, Leah J., eds. Career Planning for Psychiatrists. LC 95-1384. (Issues in Psychiatry Ser.). 288p. 1995. pap. text 19.95 (*0-88048-197-8*, 8197) Am Psychiatric.

Mogutin, Yaroslav, intro. The Art of Yuri Gorbachev. LC 98-7653. (Illus.). 160p. 1998. 45.00 (*0-8478-2143-9*, Pub. by Rizzoli Intl) St Martin.

Mogwe, Gaele. The Magic Pool. (Junior African Writers Ser.). (Illus.). 80p. (J). (gr. 3 up). 1992. pap. 3.88 (*0-7910-2910-7*) Chelsea Hse.

Mogyorodi, J., ed. Statistics & Probability. 1984. lib. bdg. 192.00 (*90-277-1675-7*) Kluwer Academic.

Moh, T. T. Algebra. (Series on University Mathematics). 360p. 1992. text 78.00 (*981-02-1195-3*); pap. text 37.00 (*981-02-1196-1*) World Scientific Pub.

Mohabat-Avin, jt. auth. see Clarke, Robert L.

***Mohaddes, Abbas & ITE Traffic Engineering Council Staff.** Innovative Traffic Control Equipment Procurement Methods: An Informational Report. LC 00-26102. (Illus.). 25p. 2000. pap. 15.00 (*0-935403-46-9*) Inst Trans Eng.

Mohaddessin, Mohammad. Islamic Fundamentalism: The New Global Threat. LC 92-43002. 224p. 1993. pap. 14.95 (*0-929765-22-2*) Seven Locks Pr.

— Islamic Fundamentalism: The New Global Threat. LC 92-43002. 224p. 1993. 18.95 (*0-929765-32-X*) Seven Locks Pr.

Mohafez, Siawosh, jt. auth. see Reyre, Dominique.

Mohaghegh, Mehdi, tr. see Sabzavari, Hadi I.

Mohai, Paul, ed. Change in the United States Department of Agriculture Forest Service & Its Consequences for National Forest Policy, Vol. 23:2. 133p. 1995. pap. 15.00 (*0-944285-45-7*) Pol Studies.

Mohamad, Mahathir & Ishihara, Shintaro. The Voice of Asia: Two Leaders Discuss the Coming Century. Baldwin, Frank, tr. (International Ser.). 160p. 1996. 25.00 (*4-7700-2043-0*) Kodansha.

Mohamad, Mahathir B. Excerpts from the Speeches of Mahathir Mohamad on the Multimedia Super Corridor. LC 98-944139. 104p. 1998. write for info. (*967-978-632-3*, Pub. by Pelanduk) Weatherhill.

Mohamed, A. Beginners' Choice Workbook. 1993. pap. write for info. (*0-582-07103-8*) Addison-Wesley.

Mohamed, Abbas A. White Nile Arabs: Political Leadership & Economic Change. (London School of Economics Monographs on Social Anthropology: No. 53). (Illus.). 193p. (C). 1980. text 42.50 (*0-485-19553-4*, Pub. by Athlone Pr) Humanities.

Mohamed Abdel Magid, Isam, see Rowe, Donald R. & Mohamed Abdel Magid, Isam.

Mohamed Abdel Magid, Isam, jt. auth. see Rowe, Donald R.

Mohamed, Duse. In the Land of Pharoahs: A Short History of Egypt from the Fall of Ismail to the Assassination of Boutrous Pasha. (Illus.). 380p. 1968. reprint ed. 35.00 (*0-7146-1762-8*, Pub. by F Cass Pubs) Intl Spec Bk.

Mohamed, F. A., jt. ed. see Earthman, J. C.

Mohamed, Haji & Robinson, Harold. A Taxonomic Revision of the Moss Families Hookeriaceae & Hypopterygiaceae in Malaya. LC 91-4223. (Smithsonian Contributions to Botany Ser.: No. 80). (Illus.). 48p. reprint ed. pap. 30.00 (*0-7837-1890-X*, 204209400001) Bks Demand.

Mohamed, Hawa, tr. see Hosken, Fran P.

***Mohamed, Jeff.** Teaching English Overseas: A Job Guide for Americans & Canadians. 224p. 2000. 19.95 (*0-9677062-0-3*) English Intl Inc.

Mohamed, M. H. Handbook of Weaving. 1998. text. write for info. (*0-8247-9462-1*) Dekker.

Mohamed, M. H., jt. auth. see Lord, P. R.

Mohamed, Mamdouh N. Hajj & Umrah: From A to Z, Vol. 1. LC 95-42988.Tr. of Pilgrimage. (Illus.). 96p. (Orig.). 1996. pap. 12.50 (*0-915957-54-X*) Amana Corp.

— Pilgrimage: Hajj & Umrah from A to Z. (Illus.). 96p. 1996. pap. 12.95 (*0-9652877-0-X*) M N Mohamed.

Mohamed, O., ed. Formulating a National Policy for Library & Information Services: The Malaysian Experience. 144p. 1988. text 100.00 (*0-7201-1951-0*) Continuum.

***Mohamed, Paloma.** Song: Poems. LC 00-38674. 2000. pap. write for info. (*0-912469-38-2*) Majority Pr.

Mohamed Salih, M. A. Ecology & Politics: Environmental Stress & Security in Africa. Af Ornas, Anders, ed. 255p. 1989. pap. text 20.95 (*91-7106-295-5*) Transaction Pubs.

Mohamed, Tarek & Sakr, Refaat. Early Twentieth-Century Islamic Architecture in Cairo. (Illus.). 256p. (C). 1993. 35.00 (*977-424-300-5*, Pub. by Am Univ Cairo Pr) Col U Pr.

Mohamed, Yasien & Haron, Muhammad. First Steps in Arabic Grammar. unabridged ed. Abdullah, Fadel & Ghaffar, Nadi A., eds. LC 97-73903. (ARA.). 173p. (J). (gr. 6-8). 1997. pap. text 8.00 (*1-56316-016-1*) Iqra Intl Ed Fdtn.

Mohamedou, Mohammad-Mahmoud. Iraq & the Second Gulf War: State Building & Regime Security. LC 97-33151. 206p. 1997. 74.95 (*1-57292-097-1*); pap. 55.00 (*1-57292-096-3*) Austin & Winfield.

Mohammad, Amin A., jt. ed. see Petersen, John R.

Mohammad-Djafari, Ali, ed. Maximum Entropy & Bayesian Methods in Paris, France, 1992: Proceedings of the 12th International Workshop on Maximum Entropy & Bayesian Methods. LC 93-2024. (Fundamental Theories of Physics Ser.). 452p. (C). 1993. text 264.50 (*0-7923-2280-0*) Kluwer Academic.

***Mohammad, Mohammad A.** Word Order, Agreement & Pronominalization in Standard & Palestinian Arabic. LC 99-33595. (Current Issues in Linguistic Theory Ser.: Vol. 181). xvi, 189p. 2000. 69.00 (*1-55619-958-9*) J Benjamins Pubng Co.

Mohammad, Noor. Caste & Primary Occupations: A Geographical Analysis. 1988. 32.00 (*81-7022-038-6*, Pub. by Concept) S Asia.

Mohammad, Noor & Matin, Abdul, eds. Indian Youth: Problems & Prospects. LC 95-901193. (Illus.). xiv, 229p. 1995. 32.00 (*81-7024-649-0*, Pub. by Ashish Pub Hse) Nataraj Bks.

Mohammad Yusuf Khan. Generation Gap: Its Causes & Consequences. (Orig.). 1985. pap. 3.00 (*1-56744-278-1*) Kazi Pubns.

***Mohammadi, Ali.** Iran & Eurasia. 252p. 2000. 62.00 (*0-86372-271-7*, Pub. by Garnet-Ithaca) LPC InBook.

— Questioning Globalization: The Culture of Capital. 2000. pap. 22.50 (*0-7453-1520-8*) Pluto GBR.

Mohammadi, Ali, ed. International Communication & Globalization. 256p. 1997. 79.95 (*0-7619-5553-4*); pap. 29.95 (*0-7619-5554-2*) Sage.

Mohammadi, Ali, jt. auth. see Sreberny-Mohammadi, Annabelle.

Mohammadi, Jamshid, jt. ed. see Ghosh, S. K.

Mohammadi, Kamin, jt. auth. see Evans, David.

***Mohammadian, M., ed.** Advances in Intelligent Systems: Theory & Applications. (Frontiers in Artificial Intelligence & Applications Ser.: Vol. 59). 400p. 2000. 92.00 (*1-58603-043-4*) IOS Press.

Mohammadioun, Mina, jt. ed. see McDonald, Stephen L.

Mohammdi, Annabelle S., jt. ed. see Braman, Sandra.

Mohammed-Ali, Abbas, jt. ed. see Marks, Anthony E.

Mohammed, Azizali F., jt. auth. see Andrus, J. Russell.

Mohammed, Imam W. Al-Islam: Unity & Leadership. LC 91-61449. (Illus.). 176p. (Orig.). 1992. pap. 7.95 (*1-879698-00-5*) Sense Maker.

— Islam's Climate for Business Success. (Illus.). 200p. 1992. pap. 7.95 (*1-879698-01-3*) Sense Maker.

Mohammed, J. L. & Walsh, J., eds. Numerical Algorithms. (Illus.). 368p. 1987. text 60.00 (*0-19-853364-0*) OUP.

Mohammed Khalid Ma'aroof. United Nations & Afghanistan Crisis. 1990. 40.00 (*81-7169-044-0*, Commonwealth) S Asia.

Mohammed, Ovey N. Muslim-Christian Relations: Past, Present, Future. LC 98-47530. 196p. 1999. pap. 16.00 (*1-57075-257-5*) Orbis Bks.

Mohammed, Patricia, ed. Rethinking Caribbean 'Difference' Feminist Review Issue 59. (Feminist Review Ser.: Issue 59). 216p. (C). (gr. 13). 1998. pap. 14.00 (*0-415-18420-7*, D5245) Routledge.

Mohammed Second. The Turkes Secretarie, Conteining His Sundrie Letters to Divers Emperours. LC 72-217. (English Experience Ser.: No. 263). 34p. 1970. reprint ed. 20.00 (*90-221-0263-7*) Walter J Johnson.

Mohammeds Group Staff. Evolution of a Community. 56p. 1995. pap. text 6.95 (*0-9649341-0-8*) WDM Pubns.

Mohan. Amazing Stories Anthology, Vols. 2. 1997. mass mkt. write for info. (*0-8125-5156-7*) Tor Bks.

— Pakistan Under Musharraf. 2000. 34.00 (*81-7341-138-7*, Pub. by Chanakya) S Asia.

Mohan, Anand, jt. ed. see SarDesai, D. R.

An Asterisk (*) at the beginning of an entry indicates that the title is appearing for the first time.

Mohan, Anil & Kripavikshu. Miracles Still Happen in Brindavan. (Illus.). vi, 240p. 1991. 21.00 (*81-85318-55-7*, Pub. by H K Pubs & Dist) Nataraj Bks.

Mohan, B. M., jt. auth. see Datta, K. B.

***Mohan, Bernard A., et al.** English as a Second Language in the Mainstream: Teaching, Learning & Identity. LC 00-32740. (Applied Linguistics & Language Studies). 2000. write for info. (*0-582-23484-0*) Longman.

Mohan, Brij. Democracies of Unfreedom: The United States & India. LC 96-916. 192p. 1996. 52.95 (*0-275-94994-X*, Praeger Pubs) Greenwood.

— Eclipse of Freedom: The World of Oppression. LC 92-37529. 200p. 1993. 57.95 (*0-275-94373-9*, C4373, Praeger Pubs) Greenwood.

— Global Development: Post-Material Values & Social Praxis. LC 91-32923. 152p. 1992. 47.95 (*0-275-93946-4*, C3946, Praeger Pubs) Greenwood.

— Unification of Social Work. LC 99-22110. 176p. 1999. 57.95 (*0-275-96114-1*, C6114, Praeger Pubs) Greenwood.

Mohan, Brij, ed. New Horizons of Social Welfare & Policy. (Illus.). 140p. (Orig.). 1985. 18.95 (*0-87073-158-0*); pap. 13.95 (*0-87073-159-9*) Schenkman Bks Inc.

— Toward Comparative Social Welfare. (Illus.). 192p. (Orig.). (C). 1986. 18.95 (*0-87047-025-6*); pap. 14.95 (*0-87047-026-4*) Schenkman Bks Inc.

Mohan, C. Raja, et al. Indian Ocean & U.S.-Soviet Detente. 1991. 22.50 (*81-7050-131-8*, Pub. by Patriot Pubs) S Asia.

***Mohan, Chilukuri K.** Frontiers of Expert Systems: Reasoning with Limited Knowledge. LC 00-28579. (International Engineering & Computer Science Ser.). 2000. write for info. (*0-7923-7815-6*) Kluwer Academic.

Mohan, Claire J. Give Me Jesus: A Collection of Thoughts, Prayers & Stories. (Illus.). 1997. pap. 7.95 (*0-9621500-4-5*) Young Sparrow Pr.

— Kaze's True Home: The Young Life of a Modern Day Saint, Mother Maria Kaupas. LC 91-66722. (Christian Hero Ser.). (Illus.). 64p. (J). (gr. 4-9). 1992. 14.95 (*0-9621500-5-3*) Young Sparrow Pr.

— St. Maximilian Kolbe: The Story of the Two Crowns. (Christian Hero Ser.). (Illus.). 72p. 1999. pap. 8.95 (*0-9621500-3-7*) Young Sparrow Pr.

— The Young Life of Mother Teresa of Calcutta. (Illus.). 64p. (J). (gr. 3-8). 1996. pap. 7.95 (*0-943135-25-7*); text 14.95 (*0-943135-26-5*) Young Sparrow Pr.

— The Young Life of Pope John Paul II. (Illus.). 64p. (Orig.). (J). (gr. 3-8). 1995. pap. 7.95 (*0-943135-12-5*); text 14.95 (*0-943135-11-7*) Young Sparrow Pr.

***Mohan, Claire J.** The Young Life of St. Maria Faustina. LaChance, Stephen, ed. (Young Life Ser.). (Illus.). 114p. (YA). (gr. 5-8). 1999. pap. text 7.95 (*0-944203-36-1*) Marian Pr.

Mohan, Cynthia, jt. auth. see Peters, Gloria.

Mohan, Dinesh. Pile Foundations. 178p. (C). 1988. text 60.00 (*90-6191-918-5*, Pub. by A A Balkema) Ashgate Pub Co.

Mohan, Dinesh, jt. ed. see Berger, Lawrence R.

Mohan, Gaudens E. Initia Operum Franciscalium. ix, 498p. 1975. pap. 23.00 (*1-57659-108-5*) Franciscan Inst.

***Mohan, Giles.** Structural Adjustment: Theory Practice & Impacts. LC 99-48397. 240p. 2000. pap. 29.99 (*0-415-12522-7*) Routledge.

***Mohan, Giles, et al.** Structural Adjustment: Theory, Practice & Impacts. LC 99-48397. 240p. (C). 2000. text. write for info. (*0-415-12521-9*) Routledge.

Mohan, I. Environment & Habitat. (C). 1989. 44.00 (*81-7024-240-1*, Pub. by Ashish Pub Hse) S Asia.

— Environmental Awareness & Urban Development: A Global Study of Environmental Constraints, Pollution, City Planning, Wasteland Development, Social Forestry. (C). 1988. 36.00 (*81-7024-194-4*, Pub. by Ashish Pub Hse) S Asia.

— Environmental Issues & Urban Development of Walled Cities. (C). 1992. text 22.00 (*81-7099-319-9*, Pub. by Mittal Pubs Dist) S Asia.

— Environmental Pollution & Management. (C). 1989. 50.00 (*81-7024-242-8*, Pub. by Ashish Pub Hse) S Asia.

— The Fragile Environment. (C). 1990. 48.00 (*81-7024-365-3*, Pub. by Ashish Pub Hse) S Asia.

Mohan, I., ed. Environmental Issues & Programmes. (New World Environment Ser.). 1989. 48.50 (*81-7024-256-8*, Pub. by Ashish Pub Hse) S Asia.

Mohan, Jean. Doll Furniture Identification & Price Guide, 1950 - 1980. LC 97-208175. (Illus.). 144p. 1997. pap. 24.95 (*0-87588-478-4*, 5299) Hobby Hse.

Mohan, John. A National Health Service? The Restructuring of Health Care in Britain since 1979. LC 94-22962. 1995. text 59.95 (*0-312-12410-4*) St Martin.

***Mohan, John.** A United Kingdom? Economic, Social & Political Geographies. (An Arnold Publication). (Illus.). 272p. 2000. pap. text 29.95 (*0-340-67752-X*) OUP.

Mohan, Kamlesh. Militant Nationalism in the Punjab, 1919-1935. 447p. 1986. 40.00 (*0-8364-1956-1*, Pub. by Manohar) S Asia.

Mohan, Kim, ed. Amazing Stories: The Anthology. 320p. 1995. pap. 13.95 (*0-312-89048-6*, Pub. by Tor Bks) St Martin.

— Amazing Stories: The Anthology, No. 2. LC 97-29861. 320p. 1998. pap. 24.95 (*0-312-86473-6*) St Martin.

***Mohan, Kim, ed.** More Amazing Stories. 2000. pap. 14.95 (*0-312-87437-5*) St Martin.

Mohan, Madan & Hull, Ronald E., eds. Teaching Effectiveness: Its Meaning, Assessment & Improvement. LC 75-14090. 326p. 1975. 39.95 (*0-87778-084-6*) Educ Tech Pubns.

Mohan, Mary L. Organizational Communication & Cultural Vision: Approaches for Analysis. LC 92-30247. (SUNY Series, Human Communication Processes). 202p. (C). 1993. text 64.50 (*0-7914-1537-6*); pap. text 21.95 (*0-7914-1538-4*) State U NY Pr.

Mohan, N. Shantha. Returns from Education to Employed Women in India. (C). 1989. 30.00 (*81-85024-63-4*, Pub. by Uppal Pub Hse) S Asia.

***Mohan, Ned.** Electric Drives: An Integrative Approach. (Illus.). 400p. (C). 2000. write for info. (*0-9663530-1-3*) Univ of MN Print.

Mohan, Ned, et al. Power Electronics: Converters, Applications & Design. 2nd ed. 824p. 1995. text 99.95 (*0-471-58408-8*) Wiley.

Mohan, P. C., ed. Bibliography of Publications: Africa Region, 1990-97. LC 97-38491. (Technical Paper Ser.: No. 393). 76p. 1998. pap. 22.00 (*0-8213-4089-1*, 14089) World Bank.

— Bibliography of Publications: Africa Region, 1993-98. LC 99-10214. (Technical Paper Ser.: Vol. 425). 59p. 1999. pap. 22.00 (*0-8213-4424-2*, 14424) World Bank.

— Bibliography of Publications: Technical Department, Africa Region, July 1987 to April 1996. (World Bank Technical Papers: No. 329). 64p. 1996. pap. 22.00 (*0-8213-3696-7*, 13696) World Bank.

Mohan, P. E. Scheduled Castes: History of Elevation, Tamil Nadu, 1900-1955. 1993. 19.00 (*0-8364-2875-7*, Pub. by New Era Pub) S Asia.

Mohan, P. V. Ananda, jt. auth. see Swamy, M. N.

Mohan, Piare, jt. auth. see Adamson, J. C.

Mohan, Prem, ed. Anti-AIDS Drug Development: Challenges, Strategies & Prospects. 304p. 1995. text 94.00 (*3-7186-5698-1*, Harwood Acad Pubs) Gordon & Breach.

Mohan, R. Vasundhara. Identity Crises of Muslims in Sri Lanks. 163p. 1987. 15.00 (*0-8364-2077-2*, Pub. by Mittal Pubs Dist) S Asia.

Mohan, Raj P., ed. Management & Complex Organizations in Comparative Perspective, 36. LC 78-22133. (Contributions in Sociology Ser.: No. 36). (Illus.). 273p. 1979. 69.50 (*0-313-20752-6*, MMA/, Greenwood Pr) Greenwood.

— The Mythmakers: Intellectuals & the Intelligentsia in Perspective, 63. LC 86-29597. (Contributions in Sociology Ser.: No. 63). 159p. 1987. 49.95 (*0-313-25836-8*, MMY/, Greenwood Pr) Greenwood.

Mohan, Raj P. & Martindale, Don, eds. Handbook of Contemporary Developments in World Sociology, 17. LC 75-70. (Contributions in Sociology Ser.: No. 17). 493p. 1975. 125.00 (*0-8371-7961-0*, MWS/, Greenwood Pr) Greenwood.

Mohan, Raj P. & Wilkie, Arthur S., eds. International Handbook of Contemporary Developments in Sociology. LC 93-37504. 856p. 1994. lib. bdg. 155.00 (*0-313-26719-7*, Greenwood Pr) Greenwood.

Mohan, Raj P., jt. see Kinloch, Graham Charles.

Mohan, Rakesh. Understanding the Developing Metropolis: Lessons from the City Study of Bogota & Cali, Colombia. (World Bank Publication). 344p. 1994. text 35.00 (*0-19-520882-X*) OUP.

— Work, Wages & Welfare in a Developing Metropolis: Consequences of Growth in Bogota, Colombia. (World Bank Publications). 416p. 1987. text 35.00 (*0-19-520540-5*) OUP.

Mohan, Robert, tr. see Scupoli, Dom L.

Mohan, S. Krishna, jt. ed. see Schwartz, Howard F.

Mohan, Satish & Maher, Mary L., eds. Expert Systems for Civil Engineers: Education. 135p. 1989. 26.00 (*0-87262-741-1*) Am Soc Civil Eng.

Mohan, Seshadri, jt. auth. see Anderson, John B.

Mohan, Surendra. Awadh Under the Nawabs: Politics, Culture, & Communal Relations, 1722-1856. LC 97-914055. 242 p. 1997. write for info. (*81-7304-203-9*) Manohar.

Mohan Upadhyay, Chandr. Human Rights in Pre-Trial Detention. 1998. 36.00 (*81-7024-998-8*) Ashish Pub Hse.

Mohan, Vasundhara R. Identity Crisis of Sri Lankan Muslims. xv, 183p. (C). 1987. 14.00 (*0-8364-2168-X*, Pub. by Mittal Pubs Dist) S Asia.

Mohanan, K. P. The Theory of Lexical Phonology. 1986. pap. text 57.00 (*90-277-2124-6*, Pub. by Kluwer Academic) Kluwer Academic.

— The Theory of Lexical Phonology. 1986. lib. bdg. 118.50 (*90-277-2226-9*, Pub. by Kluwer Academic) Kluwer Academic.

— The Theory of Lexical Phonology. 1987. pap. text 23.00 (*0-317-56507-9*) Kluwer Academic.

Mohanan, K. P., ed. Experiencer Subjects in South Asian Languages. LC 90-84176. 365p. 1991. 54.95 (*0-937073-60-1*) CSLI.

— Experiencing Subjects in South Asian Languages. LC 90-84176. 365p. 1991. pap. 19.95 (*0-937073-61-X*) CSLI.

Mohanan, Tara. Argument Structure in Hindi. LC 94-12973. (Dissertations in Linguistics Ser.). 300p. 1995. 49.95 (*1-881526-44-5*); pap. 22.95 (*1-881526-43-7*) CSLI.

Mohanan, Tara & Wee, Lionel, eds. Grammatical Semantics: Evidence for Structure in Meaning. LC 99-19329. 296p. (C). 1999. 64.95 (*1-57586-201-8*, Pub. by CSLI); pap. 24.95 (*1-57586-202-6*, Pub. by CSLI) Cambridge U Pr.

Mohanan, V. K. Crime, Community & Police. 1987. 27.50 (*81-212-0107-1*, Pub. by Gian Publng Hse) S Asia.

— Crime, Community & Police. (C). 1990. 120.00 (*0-89771-159-9*) St Mut.

Mohandas, Narla, jt. ed. see Shohet, Stephen B.

***Mohania, M. & Tjoa, A. M., eds.** Data Warehousing & Knowledge Discovery: First International Conference, DaWaK'99, Florence, Italy, August 30 - September 1, 1999, Proceedings. LC QA76.9.D37D396 1999. (Lecture Notes In Computer Science: Vol. 1676). xii, 400p. 1999. pap. 69.00 (*3-540-66458-0*) Spr-Verlag.

Mohanna, Tim, ed. see Medley, Wes.

Mohanraj, Mary A. Torn Shapes of Desire: Internet Erotica. Larson, Dale L., ed. (Illus.). 128p. (Orig.). 1997. pap. 9.95 (*1-885876-03-3*) Intangible Assets.

***Mohanraj, Mary Anne, ed.** Aqua Erotica: 22 Stories for a Steamy Bath. 176p. 2000. pap. 14.95 (*0-609-80656-4*, FIC005000, Three Riv Pr) Crown Pub Group.

Mohanram, Radhika. Black Body: Women, Colonialism, & Space. LC 99-26268. (Public Worlds Ser.: Vol. 6). 242p. 1999. lib. bdg. 44.95 (*0-8166-3542-0*, Pub. by U of Minn Pr) Chicago Distribution Ctr.

— Black Body: Women, Colonialism, & Space. LC 99-26268. (Public Worlds Ser.: Vol. 6). (Illus.). 250p. 1999. pap. 17.95 (*0-8166-3543-9*, Pub. by U of Minn Pr) Chicago Distribution Ctr.

Mohanram, Radhika & Rajan, Gita, eds. English Postcoloniality: Literatures from Around the World, 66. LC 95-33071. (Contribution to the Study of World Literature Ser.: No. 66). 232p. 1996. 65.00 (*0-313-28854-2*, Greenwood Pr) Greenwood.

Mohanram, Radhika, jt. ed. see Rajan, Gita.

Mohanti, K. K. Social Mobility & Caste Dynamics. (C). 1993. 18.00 (*81-7033-211-7*, Pub. by Rawat Pubns) S Asia.

Mohanti, Prafulla. Through Brown Eyes. 160p. 1985. 24.95 (*0-19-211784-X*) OUP.

Mohanty, Amarendra. Indian Prison System. 1990. 30.00 (*81-7024-308-4*, Pub. by Ashish Pub Hse) S Asia.

Mohanty, B. Pata-Paintings of Orissa. 52p. 1984. 49.95 (*0-318-36346-1*) Asia Bk Corp.

— Rock Fragmentation by Blasting: Proceedings of the 5th International Symposium, FRAGBLAST-5, Montreal, 26-29 August 1996. 472p. 1996. 155.00 (*90-5410-824-X*, Pub. by A A Balkema) Ashgate Pub Co.

Mohanty, Bedabati. Economics of Small Scale Industry, India. 218p. 1986. 28.00 (*81-7024-049-2*, Pub. by Ashish Pub Hse) S Asia.

— Employment Perspectives in Rural India. LC 96-914289. (Illus.). xxii, 303p. 1997. 35.00 (*81-7024-829-9*, Pub. by APH Pubng) Nataraj Bks.

Mohanty, Bijoyini. Municipal System in India: Citizens' Involvement. (Illus.). vi, 245p. 1993. 20.00 (*81-7024-530-3*, Pub. by Ashish Pub Hse) Nataraj Bks.

Mohanty, Chandra, ed. see Nijeholt, Geertje A. & Wieringa, Saskia.

Mohanty, Chandra T., et al, eds. Third World Women & the Politics of Feminism. LC 90-43510. (Illus.). 352p. 1991. 39.95 (*0-253-33873-5*); pap. 15.95 (*0-253-20632-4*, MB-632) Ind U Pr.

Mohanty, Chandra T., jt. ed. see Alexander, M. Jacqui.

***Mohanty, J. N.** Explorations in Indian Philosophy. Gupta, Bina, ed. 224p. 2000. text 19.95 (*0-19-565083-2*) OUP.

— Explorations in Western Philosophy. Gupta, Bina, ed. 256p. 2000. text 19.95 (*0-19-565086-7*) OUP.

Mohanty, J. N. J. N. Mohanty: Essays on Indian Philosophy, Traditional & Modern. Bilimoria, Purusottama, ed. 386p. 1994. text 48.00 (*0-19-563142-0*) OUP.

***Mohanty, J. N.** Self & Other: Philosophical Essays. 204p. 2000. text 19.95 (*0-19-564576-6*) OUP.

Mohanty, J. N., jt. ed. see Bilimoria, Purusottama.

Mohanty, J. N., jt. ed. see Gupta, Bina.

Mohanty, J. N., ed. see Misra, Ganeswar.

Mohanty, Jagganath. Indian Education in the Emerging Society. 205p. 1982. 24.95 (*0-940500-52-3*, Pub. by Sterling) Asia Bk Corp.

Mohanty, Jitendra N. The Concept of Intentionality. LC 70-176186. (Illus.). 224p. 1971. 12.50 (*0-87527-115-4*) Green.

— Edmund Husserl's Theory of Meaning. 3rd enl. ed. (Phaenomenologica Ser.: No. 14). 159p. 1976. lib. bdg. 67.00 (*90-247-0247-X*, Pub. by M Nijhoff) Kluwer Academic.

— Phenomenologie & Ontology. (Phaenomenologica Ser.: No. 37). 228p. 1970. lib. bdg. 81.00 (*90-247-5053-9*, Pub. by M Nijhoff) Kluwer Academic.

— The Possibility of Transcendental Philosophy. (Phaenomenologica Ser.: Vol. 98). 282p. 1985. pap. text 49.00 (*90-247-3146-1*, Pub. by M Nijhoff); lib. bdg. 132.00 (*90-247-2991-2*, Pub. by M Nijhoff) Kluwer Academic.

— Reason & Tradition in Indian Thought: An Essay on the Nature of Indian Philosophical Thinking. 316p. 1993. text 65.00 (*0-19-823960-2*) OUP.

Mohanty, Jitendra N., ed. Readings on Edmund Husserl's Logical Investigations. 219p. 1977. pap. text 92.50 (*90-247-1928-3*, Pub. by M Nijhoff) Kluwer Academic.

Mohanty, Jitendra N. & Gupta, Bina. Classical Indian Philosophy: An Introductory Text. LC 99-36603. 176p. 1999. 62.95 (*0-8476-8932-8*); pap. 17.95 (*0-8476-8933-6*) Rowman.

Mohanty, Jitendranath. Gangesa's Theory of Truth Containing the Text of Gangesa's Pramanya Vada. (C). 1989. 26.00 (*81-208-0618-2*, Pub. by Motilal Bnarsidass) S Asia.

— Husserl & Frege. LC 81-48554. (Studies in Phenomenology & Existential Philosophy). 157p. 1982. reprint ed. pap. 48.70 (*0-608-00004-3*, 205929500006) Bks Demand.

***Mohanty, Jitendranath.** Logic, Truth & the Modalities: From a Phenomenological Perspective LC 98-33160. (Synthese Library). 1999. write for info. (*0-7923-5550-4*) Kluwer Academic.

Mohanty, Jitendranath. Phenomenology: Between Essentialism & Transcendental Philosophy. LC 97-6392. (Studies in Phenomenology & Existential Philosophy). 1997. 59.95 (*0-8101-1401-1*); pap. 19.95 (*0-8101-1402-X*) Northwestern U Pr.

Mohanty, Jyotsnamoyee. Glimpses of Indian Women in Freedom Struggle. (C). 1996. 34.00 (*81-7141-324-2*, Pub. by Discovery Pub Hse) S Asia.

Mohanty, Manoranjan, et al. People's Rights: Social Movements & the State in the Third World. LC 97-31054. 1997. write for info. (*0-7619-9212-X*) Sage.

Mohanty, Niranjan. White Whispers: Selected Poems of Salabega LC 98-908715. 109p. 1998. write for info. (*81-260-0483-5*, Pub. by Rabindra Bhawn) S Asia.

Mohanty, Nirode C. Random Signals Estimation & Identification: Analysis & Applications. 640p. 1986. text 89.95 (*0-442-26396-1*, VNR) Wiley.

— Space Communication & Nuclear Scintillation. 1991. text 84.95 (*0-442-23696-4*, VNR) Wiley.

Mohanty, Nivedita. Oriya Nationalism: Quest for a United Orissa. 1983. 21.00 (*0-8364-0954-X*, Pub. by Manohar) S Asia.

Mohanty, O. N. & Sivaramakrishnan, C. S., eds. Rapid Solidification Processing & Technology. 436p. 1990. text 163.00 (*0-87849-599-1*, Pub. by Trans T Pub) Enfield Pubs NH.

Mohanty, O. N., ed. see Indo-U. S. Workshop LCFA Staff.

Mohanty, P. K. Collective Bargaining in Steel Industry in India. (C). 1988. 44.00 (*81-7141-028-6*) S Asia.

Mohanty, Padma C. Mass Media & Education. (C). 1992. 22.00 (*81-7024-439-0*, Pub. by Ashish Pub Hse) S Asia.

Mohanty, Prafulla K. Stories from Sarala's Mahabharat. 205p. 1990. text 27.50 (*0-7069-4589-1*, Pub. by Vikas) S Asia.

Mohanty, Pragati. Hotel Industry & Tourism in India. (Illus.). xiv, 262p. 1992. 25.00 (*81-7024-507-9*, Pub. by Ashish Pub Hse) Nataraj Bks.

Mohanty, Sachidananda. In Search of Wonder: Understanding Cultural Exchange: Fulbright Program in India LC 98-902570. 240 p. 1997. write for info. (*81-7094-292-6*) S Asia.

Mohanty, Samarendra. Crimes & Criminals: A Socio-Economic Survey. 1990. 24.00 (*81-7024-326-2*, Pub. by Ashish Pub Hse) S Asia.

Mohanty, Samarendra, jt. auth. see Mishra, Rashmi.

Mohanty, Saroj K. Concept of Action: An Analytical Study. (C). 1992. 18.00 (*81-85182-67-1*, Pub. by Indus Pub) S Asia.

Mohanty, Sashi B. & Dutta, Sukanta K. Veterinary Virology. LC 80-26157. 382p. 1981. reprint ed. pap. 118.50 (*0-7837-2849-2*, 205762300006) Bks Demand.

Mohanty, Satya P. Literary Theory & the Claims of History: Postmodernism, Objectivity, Multicultural Politics. LC 97-3820. 304p. 1996. text 39.95 (*0-8014-2902-1*); pap. text 15.95 (*0-8014-8135-X*) Cornell U Pr.

Mohanty, Susama. Political Development & Ethnic Identity in Africa: A Study of Angola since 1960. vii, 246p. (C). 1992. text 27.95 (*0-685-55354-X*, Pub. by Radiant Pubs) S Asia.

Mohapatra, A. R. Philosophy of Religion. 1985. 16.95 (*0-318-37030-1*) Asia Bk Corp.

Mohapatra, Amulya. Hinduism: Analytical Study. (C). 1993. 15.00 (*81-7099-388-1*, Pub. by Mittal Pubs Dist) S Asia.

Mohapatra, Bimal C. Buddhism & Socio-Economic Life of Eastern India: With Special Reference to Bengal & Orissa, 8th-12th Centuries AD. (Illus.). 200p. (C). 1995. 32.00 (*81-246-0055-4*, Pub. by D K Printwrld) Nataraj Bks.

***Mohapatra, P. K., ed.** Social Justice: Philosophical Perspectives. LC 98-915720. (Studies in Philosophy). viii, 251 p. 1999. 25.00 (*81-246-0119-4*, Pub. by D K Printwrld) S Asia.

Mohapatra, R. N. Unification & Supersymmetry. (Contemporary Physics Ser.). (Illus.). xiv, 328p. 1986. 44.00 (*0-387-96285-9*) Spr-Verlag.

— Unification & Supersymmetry: The Frontiers of Quark-Lepton Physics. 2nd ed. (Graduate Texts in Contemporary Physics Ser.). (Illus.). 424p. 1996. 49.95 (*0-387-97646-9*) Spr-Verlag.

Mohapatra, R. N. & Lai, C. H., eds. Gauge Theories of Fundamental Interactions. 702p. 1981. text 70.00 (*9971-83-013-2*); pap. text 41.00 (*9971-83-014-0*) World Scientific Pub.

Mohapatra, R. N. & Pal, Palash B. Massive Neutrinos in Physics & Astrophysics. 336p. 1991. text 78.00 (*981-02-0434-5*); pap. text 41.00 (*981-02-0435-3*) World Scientific Pub.

Mohapatra, R. N., jt. ed. see Gates, S. James, Jr.

Mohapatra, R. P. Fashion Styles of Ancient India: A Study of Kalinga from Earliest Times to Sixteenth Century AD. (C). 1992. 88.00 (*81-7018-723-0*, Pub. by BR Pub) S Asia.

Mohapatra, Rabindra N. & Pal, Palash B. Massive Neutrinos in Physics & Astrophysics. 380p. 1998. 48.00 (*981-02-3373-6*) World Scientific Pub.

Mohapatra, Ramesh Prasad. Ornaments of Orissa. Donaldson, Thomas, ed. LC 98-908308. 1998. 148.00 (*81-7646-031-1*, Pub. by BR Pub) S Asia.

Mohapatra, S., jt. auth. see Das, Hari H.

Mohar, Ronald E. & Cupples, Vince. A Glossary of Wireless (MMDS/ITFS) Terms. large type rev. ed. (Illus.). 47p. 1995. pap. 9.95 (*1-888552-01-8*, B-011) Elect Pr.

Mohar, Ronald E., ed. see Garner, Robert, et al.

Moharaj, Saraswati J., jt. auth. see Swami Guru Devanand.

***Moharir, P. S.** Nonuniqueness in Geoscientific Inference. LC 99-89544. (Uncertainty Theory in Artificial Intelligence Ser.). 2000. 95.00 (*0-86380-217-6*) Research Studies Pr Ltd.

Mohassess, Ardeshir. Closed Circuit History. LC 89-34243. (Illus.). 232p. 1989. 50.00 (*0-934211-18-3*) Mage Pubs Inc.

— Life in Iran: The Library of Congress Drawings. LC 93-40224. (Illus.). 48p. 1993. pap. 20.00 (*0-934211-39-6*) Mage Pubs Inc.

***Mohatt, Gerald & Eagle Elk, Joseph.** The Price of a Gift: A Lakota Healer's Story. LC 99-47755. (Illus.). 2000. text 29.95 (*0-8032-3204-7*) U of Nebr Pr.

M

Mohatt, Gerald, jt. auth. see Lipka, Jerry.

Mohawk Hudson Region Juried Exhibition, et al. 1997 Artists of the Mohawk Hudson Region Juried Exhibition: June 17 Through July 31, 1997, University Art Museum, University at Albany, State University of New York. LC 97-60955. (Illus.). 1997. write for info. (*0-910763-16-X*) U Albany Art Mus.

Mohawk, John. Utopian Legacies: A History of Conquest & Oppression in the Western World. LC 99-38701. (Illus.). 256p. 1999. 24.95 (*1-57416-034-6*); pap. 14.95 (*1-57416-040-0*) Clear Light.

Mohay, A. Modern Greek-Hungarian Concise Dictionary. 773p. (C). 1988. 45.00 (*963-05-4387-7*, Pub. by Akade Kiado) St Mut.

Mohay, George, jt. auth. see Gough, John.

Mohbat, Joseph, ed. see Wiener, Daniel P., et al.

Mohd, Wani Gull, see Gull Mohd, Wani.

Mohdx, Nilavu, et al. New Place, Old Ways: Essays on Indian Society & Culture in Modern Singapore. Walker, Anthony E., ed. (C). 1994. 36.00 (*81-7075-027-X*, Pub. by Hindustan) S Asia.

Mohebi, Mohsen. The International Law Character of the Iran-United States Claims Tribunal. LC 98-30406. (Developments in International Law Ser.). 1998. 138.00 (*90-411-1067-4*) Kluwer Law Intl.

Mohele, A. T., jt. auth. see Boesen, Jannik.

Mohen, Jean-Pierre. Megaliths: Stones of Memory. LC 98-50716. (Discoveries Ser.). (Illus.). 176p. 1999. 12.95 (*0-8109-2861-2*, Pub. by Abrams) Time Warner.

— The World of Megaliths. LC 89-16972. (Illus.). 318p. reprint ed. pap. 98.60 (*0-7837-6689-0*, 204630500011) Bks Demand.

***Mohen, Jean-Pierre & Eluere, Christiane.** The Bronze Age in Europe. (Discoveries Ser.). (Illus.). 160p. 2000. 12.95 (*0-8109-2882-5*, Pub. by Abrams) Time Warner.

Moheno, Phillip B. Educating Our 21st Century Adventurers. 114p. (Orig.). (C). 1996. pap. text 29.50 (*0-7618-0276-2*) U Pr of Amer.

Mohiaddin, R. H. & Longmore, D. B. Atlas of Whole Body MRI. (Series in Radiology). (C). 1992. text 191.50 (*0-7923-8974-3*) Kluwer Academic.

***Mohican Nation Youth.** Stories of Our Elders. (Illus.). 21p. (YA). (gr. 4). 1999. pap. 10.00 (*0-935790-06-3*, Pub. by Muh-He-Con-Neew) A E Miller.

Mohide, Thomas. International Silver Trade. (International Trade Ser.). (Illus.). 192p. 1992. 170.00 (*1-85573-067-7*, Pub. by Woodhead Pubng) Am Educ Systs.

Mohieldin, Mahmoud, jt. ed. see El Evian, Mohamed.

Mohilio, Albert. Bendable Siege Poems. 14p. 1991. 3.00 (*0-87376-068-9*) Red Dust.

Mohin, Andrea & Robertiello, Jack. New York Dogs. LC 96-35980. (Illus.). 1997. 14.95 (*0-8118-1658-3*) Chronicle Bks.

Mohin, Ann. The Farm She Was: A Novel. LC 97-42255. 245p. 1998. 22.95 (*1-882593-21-9*) Bridge Wrks.

***Mohin, Ann.** The Farm She Was: A Novel. LC 97-42255. 245p. 2000. pap. 13.95 (*1-882593-34-0*) Bridge Wrks.

Mohin, Lilian, ed. An Intimacy of Equals: Lesbian Feminist Ethics. 180p. 1996. pap. text 19.95 (*1-56023-881-X*) Haworth Pr.

Mohindroo, K. K. Basic Principles of Physics, Vol. 1. 804p. 1997. pap. 125.00 (*81-209-0199-1*, Pub. by Pitambar Pub) St Mut.

— Basic Principles of Physics, Vol. 2. 1014p. 1997. pap. 160.00 (*81-209-0200-9*, Pub. by Pitambar Pub) St Mut.

— Microcomputers: Programming & Utilization. 200p. 1997. pap. 60.00 (*81-209-0015-4*, Pub. by Pitambar Pub) St Mut.

Mohindroo, K. K., jt. auth. see Verma, Virendra.

Mohite, Dilip H. Indo-U. S. Relations: Issues in Conflict & Cooperation. LC 95-901195. (C). 1995. 20.00 (*81-7003-178-8*, Pub. by S Asia Pubs) S Asia.

***Mohitpour, Mo, et al.** Pipeline Design & Construction: A Practical Approach / LC 00-40625. 2000. write for info. (*0-7918-0156-X*) ASME Pr.

Mohl. A Textbook of Occlusion. Zarb, George A. et al, eds. (Illus.). 413p. 1988. text 56.00 (*0-86715-167-6*, 1676) Quint Pub Co.

Mohl, F. George. Introduction a la Chronologie du Latin Vulgaire. xii, 339p. 1974. reprint ed. write for info. (*3-487-05222-9*) G Olms Pubs.

Mohl, Perle. Village Voices: Co-existence & Communication in a Rural Community in Central France. 200p. 1996. pap. 45.00 (*87-7289-344-3*, Pub. by Mus Tusculanum) Paul & Co Pubs.

Mohl, Raymond A. The New City: Urban America in the Industrial Age, 1860-1920. Eisenstadt, A. S. & Franklin, John H., eds. LC 84-214170. (American History Ser.). 256p. (C). 1985. pap. text 13.95 (*0-88295-830-5*) Harlan Davidson.

Mohl, Raymond A., ed. The Making of Urban America. 2nd rev. ed. LC 97-2493. 368p. (C). 1997. 50.00 (*0-8420-2637-1*, SR Bks); pap. 21.95 (*0-8420-2639-8*, SR Bks) Scholarly Res Inc.

— Searching for the Sunbelt: Historical Perspectives on a Region. LC 89-77169. 264p. 1990. pap. 81.90 (*0-608-05197-7*, 206573400001) Bks Demand.

— Searching for the Sunbelt: Historical Perspectives on a Region. LC 89-77169. 272p. 1993. reprint ed. pap. 18.00 (*0-8203-1579-6*) U of Ga Pr.

Mohl, Raymond A. & Betten, Neil. Steel City: Urban & Ethnic Patterns in Gary, Indiana, 1906-1950. LC 85-963. (Illus.). 227p. 1986. 34.95 (*0-8419-1010-3*); pap. 23.50 (*0-8419-1077-4*) Holmes & Meier.

Mohl, Raymond A., jt. ed. see Goings, Kenneth W.

Mohl, Raymond A., jt. ed. see Hirsch, Arnold R.

Mohle, Helmut, jt. auth. see Meinck, Fritz.

Mohle, K., jt. auth. see Meinck, Fritz.

Mohle, R. Henry, jt. auth. see Murthy, A. S.

Mohle, Robert. Adventure Kayaking Vol. 2: Trips from Big Sur to San Diego. LC 98-17885. (Illus.). 176p. 1998. pap. 15.95 (*0-89997-224-1*) Wilderness Pr.

Mohlenbrock, Robert H. Ferns. LC 99-17308. 1999. 39.95 (*0-8093-2255-2*) S Ill U Pr.

— Flowering Plants: Basswoods to Spurges. LC 81-8585. (Illustrated Flora of Illinois Ser.). (Illus.). 256p. 1982. 31.95 (*0-8093-1025-2*) S Ill U Pr.

— Flowering Plants: Flowering Rush to Rushes. LC 69-16117. (Illustrated Flora of Illinois Ser.). (Illus.). 286p. 1970. 31.95 (*0-8093-0407-4*) S Ill U Pr.

— Flowering Plants: Lilies to Orchids. LC 69-16118. (Illustrated Flora of Illinois Ser.). (Illus.). 304p. 1970. 31.95 (*0-8093-0408-2*) S Ill U Pr.

— Flowering Plants: Magnolias to Pitcher Plants. LC 80-18529. (Illustrated Flora of Illinois Ser.). (Illus.). 276p. 1981. 31.95 (*0-8093-0920-3*) S Ill U Pr.

— Flowering Plants: Willows to Mustards. LC 79-10981. (Illustrated Flora of Illinois Ser.). (Illus.). 302p. 1980. 31.95 (*0-8093-0922-X*) S Ill U Pr.

— The Illustrated Flora of Illinois: Flowering Plants: Nightshades to Mistletoe. LC 89-8353. (Illus.). 256p. (C). 1990. text 41.95 (*0-8093-1567-X*) S Ill U Pr.

— Macmillan Field Guide to Trees & Shrubs. 1987. pap. 12.95 (*0-02-063430-7*) Macmillan.

— Sedges: Carex. (Illustrated Flora of Illinois Ser.). (Illus.). 448p. 1998. 59.95 (*0-8093-2074-6*) S Ill U Pr.

— You Can Grow Tropical Fruit Trees. (Illus.). 80p. 1979. pap. 6.95 (*0-8200-0409-X*) Great Outdoors.

Mohlenbrock, Robert H. & Ladd, Douglas M. Distribution of Illinois Vascular Plants. LC 77-15987. (Illus.). 289p. (Orig.). 1978. pap. 14.95 (*0-8093-0848-7*) S Ill U Pr.

Mohlenbrock, Robert H. & Thomson, Paul M., Jr. The Illustrated Flora of Illinois: Flowering Plants: Smartweeds to Hazelnuts. LC 86-6698. (Illus.). 256p. 1986. text 41.95 (*0-8093-1104-6*) S Ill U Pr.

Mohlenbrock, Robert H. & Voigt, John W. Flora of Southern Illinois. LC 73-12984. (Arcturus Books Paperbacks). 399p. 1974. pap. 8.95 (*0-8093-0662-X*) S Ill U Pr.

Mohlenbrock, Robert H., jt. auth. see Voigt, John W.

Mohlenbrink, Tim. Kirche und Bodenreform In der Sowjetischen Besatzungszone Deutschlands (SBZ), 1945-1949: Eine Untersuchung Uber das Verhalten der Evangelischen Landeskirchen und der Katholischen Kirche Wahrend der "Demokratischen Bodenreform" in der SBZ Unter Berucksichtigung der Auswirkungen der Bodenreform Auf das Kirchliche Vermogen. (Europaische Hochschulschriften Ser.: Reihe 2, Bd. 2206). (GER., Illus.). 391p. 1997. 76.95 (*3-631-32149-X*) P Lang Pubng.

Mohler, Diana, jt. auth. see Turner, Deborah.

Mohler, Dorothy A., jt. ed. see Dunn, Catherine.

Mohler, J. Electroplating & Related Processes. 1969. 65.00 (*0-8206-0037-7*) Chem Pub.

Mohler, James & Duff, John. Advanced Graphics & Web Page Design. 1997. 49.99 (*1-57521-317-6*) Sams.

Mohler, James, jt. auth. see Duff, Jon.

Mohler, James A. Dimensions of Faith: Yesterday & Today. LC 69-13120. 229p. reprint ed. pap. 71.00 (*0-8357-8569-6*, 203493500001) Bks Demand.

— Heresy of Monasticism. LC 76-148683. 1971. 5.95 (*0-8189-0183-7*) Alba.

— Love, Marriage & the Family: Yesterday & Today. LC 82-8699. 224p. (Orig.). 1982. pap. 7.95 (*0-8189-0434-8*) Alba.

— School of Jesus. LC 72-11835. 280p. 1973. 5.95 (*0-8189-0262-0*) Alba.

Mohler, Johann A. Symbolism: Exposition of the Doctorinal Differences Between Catholics & Protestants As Evidenced by Their Symbolical Writings. Robertson, James Burton, tr. from GER. LC 96-51962. 552p. 1997. pap. 29.95 (*0-8245-1665-6*) Crossroad NY.

— Unity in the Church or the Principles of Catholicism: Presented in the Spirit of the Church Fathers of the First Three Centuries. Erb, Peter C., tr. from GER. LC 95-7264.Tr. of Einheit in der Kirche. 487p. 1996. 49.95 (*0-8132-0621-9*) Cath U Pr.

Mohler, Lisa, jt. auth. see Career Press Editors.

Mohler, M. Teresa. COTA Examination Review Manual: A Practical Guide to Receiving Professional Certification. 2nd ed. LC 97-8104. 1997. pap. 24.00 (*1-55642-346-2*) SLACK Inc.

***Mohler, Marie.** Homosexual Rites of Passage: A Road to Visibility & Validation. LC 99-29260. 108p. 1999. pap. 18.95 (*1-56023-978-6*, Harrington Park); lib. bdg. 39.95 (*1-56023-977-8*, Harrington Park) Haworth Pr.

Mohler, Mary & Glennon, Lorraine. Those Who Can... Teach! Celebrating Teachers Who Make a Difference. LC 99-39353. 225p. 1999. pap. 12.95 (*1-885171-35-8*) Wldcat Canyon.

Mohler, Peter, jt. ed. see Borg, Ingwer.

Mohler, R. Albert, Jr. & Hart, D. G., eds. Theological Education in the Evangelical Tradition. LC 96-35212. 320p. 1996. pap. 24.99 (*0-8010-2061-1*) Baker Bks.

Mohler, Ronald R. Nonlinear Systems Vol. 1: Dynamics & Control, Vol. 1. 288p. 1990. text 63.00 (*0-13-623489-5*) P-H.

Mohler, Rudy. Practical Welding Technology. LC 83-23298. (Illus.). 220p. (C). 1983. 30.95 (*0-8311-1143-7*) Indus Pr.

Mohler, Sarah, jt. ed. see Ruiz, Karen.

Mohlgassner, Dietlinde, tr. see Lichtenberger, Elisabeth.

Mohlie, Steven, jt. ed. see Bloomberg, Mark.

Mohline, Dick & Mohline, Jane. Emotional Wholeness. LC 97-157015. 216p. 1997. pap. 12.99 (*1-56043-290-X*, Treasure Hse) Destiny Image.

Mohline, Jane, jt. auth. see Mohline, Dick.

Mohline, William, ed. Zugmann/Schindler. (Illus.). 1996. 25.00 (*1-889629-00-6*) Form Zero.

Mohlmann, D., ed. Laboratory Planetology: Proceedings of the B2 Symposium of COSPAR Scientific Commissioin B Which Was Held During the 30th COSPAR Scientific Assembly, Hamburg, Germany, 11-21 July, 1994. (Advances in Space Research Ser.: Vol. 15). 87p. 1995. pap. 97.75 (*0-08-042618-2*, Pergamon Pr) Elsevier.

Mohn, Caroline & Bays, Kathryn, eds. Dual Diagnosis Bibliography: 1995 Edition. 101p. (C). 1995. pap. 18.00 (*1-884442-13-7*) Vida Pubng.

Mohn, J. F., ed. see International Convocation on Immunology Staff.

Mohn, Jerry, ed. & tr. see Mukomla, Supron.

Mohn, Martin F. Family Fare 2: A Guide to Fun in & Around Michigan. 144p. 1993. pap. 9.95 (*0-937247-56-1*) Detroit Pr.

Mohn, Paul O., jt. auth. see Cooper, Donald H.

Mohn, Paul O., jt. auth. see Garoyan, Leon.

***Mohn, Reinhard.** Humanity Wins: A Strategy for Progress & Leadership in Times of Change. 192p. 2000. 20.00 (*0-609-60806-1*, Crown) Crown Pub Group.

Mohn, Reinhard. Success Through Partnership: An Entrepreneurial Strategy. 2nd ed. LC 96-7860. 288p. 1996. reprint ed. 19.95 (*0-385-48593-X*) Doubleday.

Mohn, Ronald D. Shortcuts in Gun Dog Training. (Illus.). 112p. (Orig.). 1991. pap. 11.95 (*0-9629840-9-4*) RDM Enter.

Mohnach, Mary Beth E. & Ryan, Kathryn. Deskbook for Lawyers & Planners: Land Use Law & Practice in New York. Nolon, John R., ed. 120p. 1998. pap. 24.95 (*0-9668221-1-0*) Pace Univ Land Use.

Mohnarke, B. Steven. Prescription for Mayhem: Drug Legalization. LC 97-210213. 220p. 1997. 28.95 (*0-9639422-3-9*) Striking Impress.

***Mohne, Kimberly, ed.** Great Monologues in Dialect for Young Actors. 192p. (YA). 2000. pap. 14.95 (*1-57525-250-3*) Smith & Kraus.

— Great Scenes in Dialect for Young Actors. 224p. (YA). 2000. pap. 14.95 (*1-57525-251-1*) Smith & Kraus.

Mohney, David & Easterling, Keller. Seaside: Making a Town in America. (Illus.). 272p. (Orig.). 1991. pap. 29.95 (*0-910413-26-6*) Princeton Arch.

***Mohney, David & Jenkins, Stover.** The Houses of Philip Johnson. (Illus.). 2001. 75.00 (*0-7892-0114-3*) Abbeville Pr.

Mohney, Kirk F. Beautiful in All Its Details: The Architecture of Maine's Public Library Buildings, 1878-1942. 120p. (C). 1997. pap. 25.00 (*0-935447-12-1*) ME Hist Preserv.

Mohney, Nell W. Don't Put a Period Where God Put a Comma: Self-Esteem for Christians. LC 93-359. 104p. 1993. pap. 12.00 (*0-687-11061-0*) Dimen for Liv.

***Mohney, Nell W.** Get a Faith Lift! Reshape Your Outlook with Guidance from God. large type ed. LC 99-54020. 144p. 2000. pap. 12.00 (*0-687-09016-4*) Dimen for Liv.

Mohney, Nell W. How to Be up on down Days. LC 96-47759. 144p. 1997. pap. 12.00 (*0-687-01781-5*) Dimen for Liv.

— Keep on Kicking as Long as You're Ticking. LC 98-43829. 144p. 1999. pap. 12.00 (*0-687-08171-8*) Dimen for Liv.

Mohney, Ralph W., jt. auth. see Harding, Joe A.

***Mohnike, Charles.** Sams Teach Yourself Coldfusion in 21 Days with CD-ROM. 2nd ed. (Teach Yourself... in 21 Days Ser.). (Illus.). 800p. 2000. pap. 39.99 (*0-672-31796-6*) Sams.

Mohnot, S. M., jt. auth. see Roonwal, Mithan L.

Mohnot, S. R., ed. Cier's Industrial Databook, 1998. 1079p. 1998. 105.00 (*0-7619-9245-6*, T59) Sage.

Mohns, Judith, jt. auth. see Deschamps, Francois.

Mohnsen, Bonnie. Using Technology in Physical Education. 2nd ed. LC GV364, M64. (Illus.). 183p. (C). 1998. reprint ed. pap. text 25.00 (*1-893166-26-0*, A34) Bonnies Fitware.

Mohnsen, Bonnie S. Teaching Middle School Physical Education. LC 96-39066. (Illus.). 360p. (Orig.). 1997. pap. text 29.00 (*0-88011-513-0*, BMOH0513) Human Kinetics.

Mohnsen, Bonnie S. & National Association for Sport & Physical Education Staff. Concepts of Physical Education: What Every Student Needs to Know. LC 98-163516. 249 p. 1998. write for info. (*0-88314-705-X*) Natl Assn Sport.

Moholy-Nagy, Laszlo. Book of New Artists. (GER, FRE & ENG., Illus.). 92p. 1996. pap. 30.00 (*1-56898-068-X*) Princeton Arch.

— In Focus - Laszlo Moholy-Nagy: Photographs from the J. Paul Getty Museum. LC 94-42443. (In Focus Ser.). (Illus.). 128p. (Orig.). 1995. pap. 16.95 (*0-89236-324-X*, Pub. by J P Getty Trust) OUP.

— The Street Markets of London. LC 72-84542. (Illus.). 1972. reprint ed. 19.95 (*0-405-08792-6*, Pub. by Blom Pubns) Ayer.

Moholy-Nagy, Laszlo, et al. Moholy-Nagy: An Anthology. (Quality Paperbacks Ser.). (Illus.). 238p. 1991. reprint ed. pap. 15.95 (*0-306-80455-7*) Da Capo.

Mohon, Michelle R., jt. auth. see Mohon, Monty D.

Mohon, Monty D. & Mohon, Michelle R. Gillespie County, a View of Its Past. LC 95-53791. 1996. write for info. (*0-89865-964-7*) Donning Co.

Mohor, Arthur B., Jr. Basic Budget Guide for Small Cities & Counties. rev. ed. 49p. 1985. pap. 6.00 (*0-89854-112-3*) U of GA Inst Govt.

Mohowski, Robert. New York, Ontario & Western in the Diesel Age. (Illus.). 96p. (Orig.). 1994. pap. 29.95 (*0-944119-15-8*) Andover Junction.

Mohowski, Robert E. The New York, Ontario & West Railway & the Industry of Central New York State: Milk Cans, Mixed Trains & Motor Cars. LC 95-17349. (Illus.). x, 350p. 1996. 62.50 (*0-9620844-6-8*) Garrigues Hse.

Mohr. Language of International Trade in English. 128p. 1987. pap. text 15.40 (*0-13-523317-8*) P-H.

— UNIX Web Server Administrator Interactive Workbook. LC 99-215578. (C). 1998. wbk. ed. 34.99 (*0-13-020065-4*) S&S Trade.

Mohr, C. Plant Life of Alabama. (Illus.). 1969. reprint ed. 64.00 (*3-7682-0622-X*) Lubrecht & Cramer.

Mohr, Carole, jt. auth. see Goodman, Donald J.

Mohr, Carole, jt. auth. see Nist, Sherrie L.

Mohr, Carole, jt. auth. see Smith, R. Kent.

Mohr, Carolyn, et al. Books That Heal: A Whole Language Approach. xiv, 283p. 1991. pap. text 23.50 (*0-87287-829-5*) Teacher Ideas Pr.

***Mohr, Clarence L. & Gordon, Joseph E.** Tulane: The Emergence of a Modern University, 1945-1980. (Illus.). 456p. 2000. 39.95 (*0-8071-2553-9*) La State U Pr.

Mohr, D. V., et al, eds. Advances in Controlled Clinical Inhalation Studies. (ILSI Monographs). (Illus.). 384p. 1993. 211.00 (*0-387-54958-7*) Spr-Verlag.

Mohr, David & Schwartz, Faye. From Birth to Death. 1983. 3.50 (*0-89536-599-5*, 0604) CSS OH.

Mohr, David H. Liquid Rocket Propulsion Design Principles. Date not set. write for info. (*0-89464-064-X*) Krieger.

Mohr, Donald D., jt. auth. see Allen, Elizabeth L.

Mohr, E. & Brouwers, P., eds. Handbook of Clinical Trials: The Neurobehavioral Approach. 388p. 1991. 67.00 (*90-265-1028-4*) Swets.

***Mohr, Ernst, ed.** The Transfer of Economic Knowledge. LC 98-53415. 256p. 1999. 80.00 (*1-85898-855-1*) E Elgar.

Mohr, Eugene V. The Nuyorican Experience: Literature of the Puerto Rican Minority, 62. LC 82-9282. (Contributions in American Studies; No. 62). 137p. 1982. 45.00 (*0-313-23334-9*, MNE/, Greenwood Pr) Greenwood.

Mohr, Franz. My Life with the Great Pianists. Life Publishers International Staff, tr. (RUS., Illus.). 400p. (C). 1999. pap. write for info. (*0-7361-0081-4*) Life Pubs Intl.

Mohr, Franz & Schaeffer, Edith. My Life with the Great Pianists. 2nd ed. LC 96-216092. 200p. (YA). (gr. 10). 1996. pap. 14.99 (*0-8010-5710-8*, Ravens Ridge) Baker Bks.

Mohr, G. A. Finite Elements for Solids. 624p. 1992. 125.00 (*0-19-856369-8*); pap. 55.00 (*0-19-856368-X*) OUP.

Mohr, Hans. Photomorphogenesis. Shropshire, Walter, Jr., ed. (Encyclopedia of Plant Physiology Ser.: Vol. 16, Pts. A & B). (Illus.). 900p. 1983. 398.95 (*0-387-12143-9*) Spr-Verlag.

Mohr, Hans. Plant Physiology. Orig. Title: Lehrbuch der Pflanzenphysiologie. 1995. 64.95 (*3-540-58016-6*) Spr-Verlag.

Mohr, Hans & Schopfer, Peter. Plant Physiology. Lawlor, Gudron & Lawlor, David W., trs. from GER. LC 94-21765. Orig. Title: Lehrbuch der Pflanzenphysiologie. (Illus.). 640p. 1995. 59.95 (*0-387-58016-6*) Spr-Verlag.

Mohr, Harriet. What the Soul Teaches. 170p. 1994. pap. 6.95 (*0-9629467-1-0*) New Focus Pr.

Mohr, Harriet, jt. auth. see Mohr, William L.

Mohr, Howard. How to Talk Minnesotan. 224p. 1987. pap. 12.95 (*0-14-009284-6*, Penguin Bks) Viking Penguin.

Mohr, J. P. Manual of Clinical Problems in Neurology: With Annotated Key References. (Spiral Manual Ser.). 1984. spiral bd. 21.00 (*0-316-57747-2*, Little Brwn Med Div) Lppncott W & W.

— Manual of Neurology. 2nd ed. 1989. 32.95 (*0-316-57748-0*, Little Brwn Med Div) Lppncott W & W.

— Manual of Neurology ISE. 2nd ed. 1989. 15.95 (*0-316-57749-9*, Little Brwn Med Div) Lppncott W & W.

Mohr, J. P. & Gautier, J. C., eds. Guide to Clinical Neurology. LC 95-8195. (Illus.). 1995. text 115.00 (*0-443-08927-2*) Church.

Mohr, James. Linux User's Resource: Developer's Resource. LC 97-22733. (Developer's Resource Ser.). 848p. (C). 1997. pap. 49.95 incl. cd-rom (*0-13-842378-4*) P-H.

— SCO Companion. 208p. (C). 1997. pap. text 79.95 incl. cd-rom, disk (*0-13-679291-X*) P-H.

— SCO Companion: The Essential Guide for Users & System Administrators. LC 96-18098. 816p. (C). 1996. pap. text 49.99 (*0-13-451683-4*) P-H.

— SCO Users Companion. 1996. 34.95 (*0-614-14494-9*) P-H.

— Supporting Windows NT & 2000 Workstation & Server. 770p. (C). 1999. pap. 49.99 (*0-13-083068-2*) P-H.

Mohr, James C. Abortion in America: The Origins & Evolution of National Policy, 1800-1900. (Illus.). 331p. 1979. reprint ed. pap. text 11.95 (*0-19-502616-0*) OUP.

— Doctors & the Law: Medical Jurisprudence in Nineteenth-Century America. LC 95-48061. (Illus.). 330p. (C). 1996. pap. text 15.95 (*0-8018-5398-2*) Johns Hopkins.

Mohr, James C., ed. Radical Republicans in the North: State Politics During Reconstruction. LC 75-36939. 219p. reprint ed. pap. 67.90 (*0-7837-3389-5*, 204334700008) Bks Demand.

Mohr, James C. & Winslow, Richard E., 3rd, eds. The Cormany Diaries: A Northern Family in the Civil War. LC 81-16345. 623p. 1982. pap. 193.20 (*0-7837-8550-X*, 204936500011) Bks Demand.

***Mohr, Jean.** At the Edge of the World. 1999. pap. 24.95 (*1-86189-048-6*, Pub. by RBL) Consort Bk Sales.

Mohr, Jeanne M. All That Glitters. Roper, Sandi, ed. vi, 186p. 1997. pap. 12.95 (*0-9660383-2-0*) Living Praise.

— And the Beat Goes On. 163p. 1991. pap. 8.95 (*0-9660383-1-2*) Living Praise.

— Battle Plan: A Walk in Deliverance & Warfare. (Illus.). v, 136p. 1983. pap. 9.95 (*0-9660383-0-4*) Living Praise.

An Asterisk (*) at the beginning of an entry indicates that the title is appearing for the first time.

Mohr, Joseph. Silent Night. LC 84-8113. (J). 1988. pap. 4.95 (*0-685-57131-9*, Dutton Child) Peng Put Young Read.

***Mohr, Joseph.** Silent Night, Holy Night: A Christmas Carol. LC 99-21121. (Illus.). 32p. (J). 1999. 15.95 (*0-7358-1152-0*, Pub. by North-South Bks NYC); lib. bdg. 15.88 (*0-7358-1153-9*, Pub. by North-South Bks NYC) Chronicle Bks.

Mohr, Julie, jt. auth. see Nelson, Ray.

Mohr, K. Geologie und Minerallagerstaetten des Harzes. viii, 496p. 1993. pap. 51.00 (*3-510-65154-5*, Pub. by E Schweizerbartsche) Balogh.

— Harz- Westlicher Teil. 5th ed. (Sammlung Geologischer Fuehrer Ser.: Band 58). (GER.). 1998. write for info. (*3-443-15071-3*, Pub. by Gebruder Borntraeger) Balogh.

— Montangeologisches Woerterbuch Fuer den Westharz: Mit Stichwoertern aus der Geologie, Palaeontologie, Petrographie, Mineralogie, Lagerstaettenkunde und dem Bergbau von A-Z. iii, 182p. 1989. 23.00 (*3-510-65142-1*, Pub. by E Schweizerbartsche) Balogh.

Mohr, Konrad. German Insider & Stock Exchange Law. 352p. 1994. 120.00 (*3-7819-2842-X*, Pub. by Woodhead Pubng) Am Educ Systs.

Mohr, Kurt. Harzvorland - Westlicher Teil. (Sammlung Geologischer Fuehrer Ser.: Band 70). (GER.). viii, 155p. 1982. spiral bd. 23.00 (*3-443-15029-2*, Pub. by Gebruder Borntraeger) Balogh.

Mohr, Lawrence B. The Causes of Human Behavior: Implications for Theory & Method in the Social Sciences. LC 95-52492. 193p. (C). 1996. text 39.50 (*0-472-10665-1*, 10665) U of Mich Pr.

— Explaining Organizational Behavior. LC 81-20747. (Jossey-Bass Social & Behavioral Science Ser.). 280p. reprint ed. pap. 86.80 (*0-8357-4999-1*, 203793200009) Bks Demand.

— Impact Analysis for Program Evaluation. 1992. pap. 21.95 (*0-8039-4981-2*) Sage.

— Impact Analysis for Program Evaluation. 314p. 1995. 56.00 (*0-8039-5935-4*); pap. 26.00 (*0-8039-5936-2*) Sage.

— Understanding Significance Testing. (Quantitative Applications in the Social Sciences Ser.: Vol. 73). (Illus.). 96p. (C). 1990. pap. text 10.95 (*0-8039-3568-4*) Sage.

Mohr, Lawrence C., et al, eds. International Case Studies in Risk Assessment & Risk Management. (Illus.). vii, 112p. (Orig.). 1997. pap. text. write for info. (*0-9657650-0-8*) Learned Pr.

***Mohr, Marian M. & MacLean, Marion S.** Teacher-Reseachers at Work. LC 99-51530. (Illus.). 290p. 1999. pap. 15.00 (*1-883920-14-0*) Nat Writing Proj.

Mohr, Marie H. St. Philomena: Powerful with God. LC 88-50160. 136p. 1993. reprint ed. pap. 8.00 (*0-89555-332-5*) TAN Bks Pubs.

Mohr, Marilyn. Satchel. Barkan, Stanley H., ed. (Review Jewish Writers Chapbook Ser.: No. 8). 48p. 1992. 15.00 (*0-89304-312-5*); pap. 5.00 (*0-89304-313-3*) Cross-Cultrl NY.

— Satchel: Mini. Barkan, Stanley H., ed. (Review Jewish Writers Chapbook Ser.: No. 8). 48p. 1992. 15.00 (*0-89304-314-1*); pap. 5.00 (*0-89304-315-X*) Cross-Cultrl NY.

Mohr, Matthias. Negotiating the Boundary: The Response of Kwa Mashu Zionists to a Volatile Political Climate. 288p. 1997. pap. text 38.95 (*3-8258-3015-2*) Transaction Pubs.

Mohr, Merilyn, jt. auth. see Moores, Ted.

Mohr, Merilyn S. Art of Soapmaking. (Illus.). 126p. 1989. pap. 9.95 (*0-920656-03-X*) Firefly Bks Ltd.

Mohr, Merilyn S., ed. see Buckingham, Sandra.

***Mohr, Merilyn Simonds.** The Games Treasury: More Than 300 Indoor & Outdoor Favorites with Strategies, Rules, & Traditions. (Illus.). 351p. 1999. reprint ed. pap. text 20.00 (*0-7881-6721-9*) DIANE Pub.

Mohr, Nancy L. The Lady Blows a Horn. 2nd ed. (Illus.). 116p. 1997. 36.00 (*0-9660282-0-1*, HCP-97002) Horse Cntry Pr.

Mohr, Nicholasa. All for the Better: A Story of el Barrio. LC 92-23639. (Stories of America Ser.). (Illus.). 56p. (J). (gr. 2-5). 1992. lib. bdg. 24.26 (*0-8114-7220-5*) Raintree Steck-V.

— El Bronx Remembered. LC 75-6306. (Trophy Keypoint Bk.). (Illus.). 272p. (YA). (gr. 7-12). 1993. pap. 4.95 (*0-06-447100-4*, HarpTrophy) HarpC Child Bks.

— El Bronx Remembered. (J). 1994. 18.50 (*0-8446-6779-X*) Peter Smith.

— El Bronx Remembered: A Novella & Stories. (J). 1975. 10.05 (*0-606-05255-0*, Pub. by Turtleback) Demco.

— Felita. 112p. (J). 1995. pap. 4.50 (*0-440-41295-1*) BDD Bks Young Read.

— Felita. (J). 1990. 9.09 (*0-606-03280-0*, Pub. by Turtleback) Demco.

***Mohr, Nicholasa.** Felita Reissue Edition, Vol. 1. 1999. pap. 4.99 (*0-14-130643-2*, PuffinBks) Peng Put Young Read.

Mohr, Nicholasa. Going Home. (J). 1996. pap. 4.99 (*0-553-54249-4*) BDD Bks Young Read.

***Mohr, Nicholasa.** Going Home. (J). (gr. 4-7). 1999. pap. 4.99 (*0-14-130644-0*, PuffinBks) Peng Put Young Read.

Mohr, Nicholasa. The Magic Shell. LC 93-30403. (Illus.). 64p. (J). (gr. 2-5). 1995. 13.95 (*0-590-47110-4*, Scholastic Hardcover) Scholastic Inc.

— A Matter of Pride & Other Stories. LC 96-39826. 164p. 1997. 19.95 (*1-55885-163-1*); pap. 11.95 (*1-55885-177-1*) Arte Publico.

— Nilda. 2nd ed. LC 87-70274. 292p. (YA). (ps up). 1986. pap. 11.95 (*0-934770-61-1*) Arte Publico.

— El Regalo Magico (The Magic Shell)Tr. of Magic Shell. (SPA., Illus.). 96p. (J). (gr. 2-5). 1996. pap. 2.99 (*0-590-50210-7*) Scholastic Inc.

— Rituals of Survival: A Woman's Portfolio. LC 84-72300. 158p. (Orig.). (C). 1985. pap. 11.95 (*0-934770-39-5*) Arte Publico.

— The Song of el Coqui & Other Tales of Puerto Rico. (Illus.). 1995. 16.99 (*0-670-86296-7*, Viking) Viking Penguin.

— La Vieja Letivia y el Monte de los Pesares. Orig. Title: Old Letivia & the Mountain of Sorrows. (SPA., Illus.). 32p. (J). (ps-3). 1996. 15.99 (*0-670-86324-6*, Viking Child) Peng Put Young Read.

Mohr, Peter & Pomerening, Klaus. Affinity Chromatography: Practical & Theoretical Aspects. (Chromatographic Science Ser.: Vol. 33). (Illus.). 320p. 1985. text 175.00 (*0-8247-7468-X*) Dekker.

Mohr, Peter, et al. Immunosorption Techniques: Fundamentals & Applications. 173p. 1992. 75.00 (*3-05-501350-6*, Pub. by Akademie Verlag) Wiley.

Mohr, Peter J. & Wiese, Wolfgang L., eds. Atomic & Molecular Data & Their Applications: First International Conference. LC 98-71563. (AIP Conference Proceedings Ser.: Vol. 434). (Illus.). 406p. 1998. 110.00 (*1-56396-751-0*) Am Inst Physics.

Mohr, R., et al. Structural Pattern Analysis. (Series in Computer Science: Vol. 19). 268p. (C). 1990. pap. 18.00 (*981-02-0147-8*); text 74.00 (*981-02-0097-8*) World Scientific Pub.

Mohr, Renate M., jt. ed. see Roberts, Julian V.

Mohr, Rephael & Goor, Daniel A. Management of Bleeding after Open Heart Surgery. LC 97-13740. (Medical Intelligence Unit Ser.). 219p. 1997. text 99.00 (*1-57059-056-7*) Landes Bioscience.

Mohr, Richard D. Gay Ideas: Outing & Other Controversies. (Illus.). 336p. 1994. pap. 15.00 (*0-8070-7921-9*) Beacon Pr.

— Gays - Justice: A Study of Ethics, Society & Law. 357p. 1989. pap. text 19.00 (*0-231-06735-6*) Col U Pr.

— A More Perfect Union: Why Straight America Must Stand up for Gay Rights. 144p. 1995. pap. 9.00 (*0-8070-7933-2*) Beacon Pr.

Mohr, Sabine. Einfluss Von Kern und Zytoplasma Auf die Organisation und Expression Mitochondrialer Gene Bei Triticum, Tricale und Secale. (Dissertationes Botanicae Ser.: Band 180). (GER., Illus.). viii, 124p. 1991. pap. 48.00 (*3-443-64092-3*, Pub. by Gebruder Borntraeger) Balogh.

Mohr, Stephen F. Designing Distributed Applications with ASP, MSMQ, XML IE5 & LDAP. 400p. 1999. pap. 49.99 (*1-86100-227-0*) Wrox Pr Inc.

***Mohr, Stephen F.** Professional XML Schema Design. 800p. 2000. pap. 49.99 (*1-86100-356-0*) Wrox Pr Inc.

Mohr, Stephen F. & Mitchell, Glenn. Functionality of Trade Dress: A Review & Analysis of U. S. Case Law. 107p. 1994. pap. 50.00 (*0-939190-15-X*) Intl Trademark.

Mohr, Stephen F., et al. U. S. Trade Dress Law. LC 98-146050. 1996. pap. 83.95 (*0-939190-22-2*) Intl Trademark.

Mohr, Stephen F., jt. auth. see Wrox Press Inc., Staff.

Mohr-Stephens, Judy. Fence Me In...with Understanding, Vol. 28, Bk. 7. Riegert, Evelyn, ed. (Please Understand Us Ser.). (Illus.). 1990. write for info. (*0-935323-28-7*) Barrington Hse.

— Fence Me In...with Understanding, Vol. 29. Riegert, Evelyn, ed. (Please Understand Us Ser.). (Illus.). 1990. teacher ed. write for info. (*0-935323-29-5*) Barrington Hse.

— Fence Me In...with Understanding, Vol. 30, Bk. 7. Riegert, Evelyn, ed. (Please Understand Us Ser.). (Illus.). 1990. write for info. (*0-935323-30-9*) Barrington Hse.

— Fence Me In...with Understanding, Vol. 31, Bk. 8. Riegert, Evelyn, ed. (Please Understand Us Ser.). (Illus.). 1990. write for info. (*0-935323-31-7*) Barrington Hse.

— Fence Me In...with Understanding, Vol. 32, Bk. 8. Riegert, Evelyn, ed. (Please Understand Us Ser.). (Illus.). 1990. teacher ed. write for info. (*0-935323-32-5*) Barrington Hse.

— Fence Me In...with Understanding, Vol. 33, Bk. 8. Riegert, Evelyn, ed. (Please Understand Us Ser.). (Illus.). 1990. write for info. (*0-935323-33-3*) Barrington Hse.

— Is the World As I See It? Riegert, Evelyn, ed. (Please Understand Us Ser.). (Illus.). 1990. write for info. (*0-935323-01-5*, VOL. 1, BK. 1, STUDENT BK.); write for info. (*0-935323-02-3*); write for info. (*0-935323-16-3*); write for info. (*0-935323-17-1*); write for info. (*0-935323-18-X*); write for info. (*0-935323-19-8*); write for info. (*0-935323-20-1*); write for info. (*0-935323-21-X*) Barrington Hse.

— Is the World As I See It?, Vol. 3, Bk. 1. Riegert, Evelyn, ed. (Please Understand Us Ser.). (Illus.). 1990. write for info. incl. audio (*0-935323-03-1*) Barrington Hse.

— My Little World Book, Vol. 4. Riegert, Evelyn, ed. (Please Understand Us Ser.). (Illus.). 500p. 1990. student ed. write for info. (*0-935323-04-X*) Barrington Hse.

— My Little World Book, Vol. 5. Riegert, Evelyn, ed. (Please Understand Us Ser.). (Illus.). 500p. 1990. teacher ed. write for info. (*0-935323-05-8*) Barrington Hse.

— My Little World Book, Vol. 6. Riegert, Evelyn, ed. (Please Understand Us Ser.). (Illus.). 500p. 1990. write for info. incl. audio (*0-935323-06-6*) Barrington Hse.

— My Little World Book, Vol. 7. Riegert, Evelyn, ed. (Please Understand Us Ser.). (Illus.). 500p. 1990. teacher ed. write for info. (*0-935323-07-4*) Barrington Hse.

— My Little World Book, Vol. 8. rev. ed. Riegert, Evelyn, ed. (Please Understand Us Ser.). (Illus.). 500p. 1990. teacher ed. write for info. (*0-935323-08-2*) Barrington Hse.

— My Little World Book, Vol. 9. rev. ed. Riegert, Evelyn, ed. (Please Understand Us Ser.). (Illus.). 500p. 1990. student ed. write for info. (*0-935323-09-0*) Barrington Hse.

— My Little World Book, Vol. 10, Bk. 1: Text. Riegert, Evelyn, ed. (Please Understand Us Ser.). (Illus.). 1990. write for info. (*0-935323-10-4*) Barrington Hse.

— My Little World Book, Vol. 11: Teacher's Tips. Riegert, Evelyn, ed. (Please Understand Us Ser.). (Illus.). 1990. write for info. (*0-935323-11-2*) Barrington Hse.

— My Little World Book, Vol. 12: Teacher's Tips. Riegert, Evelyn, ed. (Please Understand Us Ser.). (Illus.). 1990. write for info. (*0-935323-12-0*) Barrington Hse.

— My Little World Book, Vol. 13, Bk. 2: Text. Riegert, Evelyn, ed. (Please Understand Us Ser.). (Illus.). 1990. write for info. (*0-935323-13-9*) Barrington Hse.

— My Little World Book, Vol. 14, Bk. 2: Teacher's Tips. Riegert, Evelyn, ed. (Please Understand Us Ser.). (Illus.). 1990. write for info. (*0-935323-14-7*) Barrington Hse.

— My Little World Book, Vol. 15, Bk. 2: Role Plays. Riegert, Evelyn, ed. (Please Understand Us Ser.). (Illus.). 1990. write for info. (*0-935323-15-5*) Barrington Hse.

— Open Minded Kids!, Vol. 22, Bk. 5. Riegert, Evelyn, ed. (Please Understand Us Ser.). (Illus.). 1990. write for info. (*0-935323-22-8*) Barrington Hse.

— Open Minded Kids!, Vol. 23, Bk. 5. Riegert, Evelyn, ed. (Please Understand Us Ser.). (Illus.). 1990. write for info. (*0-935323-23-6*) Barrington Hse.

— Open Minded Kids!, Vol. 24, Bk. 5. Riegert, Evelyn, ed. (Please Understand Us Ser.). (Illus.). 1990. write for info. (*0-935323-24-4*) Barrington Hse.

— Open Minded Kids!, Vol. 25, Bk. 6. Riegert, Evelyn, ed. (Please Understand Us Ser.). (Illus.). 1990. write for info. (*0-935323-25-2*) Barrington Hse.

— Open Minded Kids!, Vol. 26, Bk. 6. Riegert, Evelyn, ed. (Please Understand Us Ser.). (Illus.). 1990. write for info. (*0-935323-26-0*) Barrington Hse.

— Open Minded Kids!, Vol. 27, Bk. 6. Riegert, Evelyn, ed. (Please Understand Us Ser.). (Illus.). 1990. write for info. (*0-935323-27-9*) Barrington Hse.

— Please Understand Us! Is the World As I See It?; My Little World Book; Open Minded Kids!; Fence Me In...with Understanding, 33 vols., Set. Riegert, Evelyn, ed. (Illus.). 500p. (J). (gr. k-8). 1990. 139.95 (*0-935323-00-7*) Barrington Hse.

Mohr, Thomas. A Christian Day School for Anyone: A New Look at Christian Day Schools. LC 98-92435. (Illus.). ix, 196p. (C). 1998. pap. 19.95 (*0-9663098-0-4*) ACTS Multi-Ministries.

Mohr, Ulrich, ed. International Classification of Rodent Tumours Pt. I: The Rat, 10 fascicles. Incl. Female Genital System. (Illus.). 94p. 1997. pap. text 29.50 (*92-832-0129-9*, Pub. by IARC); Fascicle No. 1. Respiratory System. Capen, C. C. LC 93-178961. (Illus.). 68p. 1993. pap. text 30.00 (*92-832-0121-3*, Pub. by IARC); Fascicle No. 2. Soft Tissue & Muscoskeletal System. LC 93-178961. (Illus.). 72p. 1992. pap. text 30.00 (*92-832-0122-1*, Pub. by IARC); Fascicle No. 3. Urinary System. Capen, C. C. (Illus.). 56p. 1993. pap. text 30.00 (*92-832-0123-X*, Pub. by IARC); Fascicle No. 4. Haematopoietic System. Capen, C. C. LC 93-178961. (Illus.). 38p. 1993. pap. text 30.00 (*92-832-0124-8*, Pub. by IARC); Fascicle No. 5. Integumentary System. Capen, C. C. (Illus.). 56p. 1993. pap. text 30.00 (*92-832-0125-6*, Pub. by IARC); Fascicle No. 6. Endocrine System. (Illus.). 88p. 1994. pap. text 30.00 (*92-832-0126-4*, Pub. by IARC); Fascicle No. 7. Central Nervous System; Heart; Eye; Mesothelium. (Illus.). 92p. 1994. pap. text 30.00 (*92-832-0127-2*, Pub. by IARC); Fascicle No. 8. Male Genital System. (Illus.). 52p. 1997. pap. text 29.95 (*92-832-0128-0*, Pub. by IARC); Fascicle No. 10. Digestive System. (Illus.). 124p. 1997. pap. text 29.50 (*92-832-0130-2*, Pub. by IARC); (Scientific Publication Ser.: No. 122). 80p. write for info. (*92-832-2122-2*, Pub. by IARC) OUP.

Mohr, Ulrich, et al, eds. Correlations Between In Vitro & In Vivo Investigations in Inhalation Toxicology. (Illus.). 600p. 1996. pap. 85.00 (*0-944398-47-2*) ILSI.

— Toxic & Carcinogenic Effects of Solid Particles in the Respiratory Tract. LC 94-75676. (Illus.). 652p. 1994. 95.00 (*0-944398-14-6*) ILSI.

Mohr, Ulrich, ed. see Hanover International Carcinogenesis Meeting Staff.

Mohr, Ulrich, ed. see International Agency for Research on Cancer Staff.

Mohr, Ulrich, jt. ed. see Turusov, V. S..

Mohr, V. & Lewkowski, J. P. The Effect of Diet on Tumor Development in Animals. LC 88-10680. 144p. 1988. 100.00 (*0-89573-453-2*, Wiley-VCH) Wiley.

Mohr, Walter H. Federal Indian Relations, Seventeen Seventy-Four - Seventeen Eighty-Eight. LC 76-158854. reprint ed. 37.50 (*0-404-07147-3*) AMS Pr.

Mohr, Werner, jt. ed. see Kohlschmidt, Werner.

Mohr, William L. & Mohr, Harriet. Quality Circles: Changing Images of People at Work. LC 83-5970. (Illus.). 256p. 1983. write for info. (*0-201-05207-5*) Addison-Wesley.

Mohraz, Judy J. The Separate Problem: Case Studies of Black Education in the North, 1900-1930, 42. LC 78-4026. (Contributions in Afro-American & African Studies: No. 42). 165p. 1979. 52.95 (*0-313-20411-X*, MSP/, Greenwood Pr) Greenwood.

Mohrbacher, Nancy & Stock, Julie. The Breastfeeding Answer Book. 2nd expanded rev. ed. Torgus, Judy, ed. LC 96-78580. (Illus.). 608p. 1997. spiral bd. 55.00 (*0-912500-48-4*, 480a) La Leche.

Mohrbacher, Nancy, jt. ed. see Halonen, Virginia S.

Mohrbacher, Paul. The Chancellor's Tale. (Orig.). 1992. pap. 5.95 (*0-87129-168-1*, C85) Dramatic Pub.

Mohren, G. M., et al, eds. Impacts of Global Change of Tree Physiology & Forest Eco System. LC 97-49848. 372p. 1998. lib. bdg. 169.00 (*0-7923-4921-0*) Kluwer Academic.

Mohren, Paul, jt. auth. see Menges, Georg.

Mohrenschildt, Dimitri Von, see Von Mohrenschildt, Dimitri.

Mohrer, Fruma, ed. see YIVO Institutue for Jewish Research Staff.

Mohrhardt, David. Encyclopedia of Bird Reference Drawings: More Than 215 Varieties of Birds Accurately Portrayed. 2nd ed. (Illus.). 80p. 1985. pap. 14.95 (*1-56523-009-4*) Fox Chapel Pub.

— How to Paint Dabbling Ducks. LC 90-38135. (How to Paint Ser.). (Illus.). 128p. (Orig.). 1991. pap. 24.95 (*0-8117-3010-7*) Stackpole.

Mohrhardt, David & Schinkel, Richard E. Suburban Nature Guide: How to Discover & Identify the Wildlife in Your Backyard. LC 90-10237. (Illus.). 192p. (Orig.). 1991. pap. 16.95 (*0-8117-3080-8*) Stackpole.

Mohrhardt, David, ed. see Mainone, Robert F.

Mohri, Hideo. New Horizons in Sperm Cell Research. xx, 516p. 1987. text 361.00 (*2-88124-254-5*) Gordon & Breach.

Mohri, Hideo, et al, eds. Biology of the Germ Line: In Animals & Man. (Illus.). x, 304p. 1993. 170.50 (*3-8055-5773-6*) S Karger.

***Mohriak, Webster & Talwani, Manik, eds.** Atlantic Rifts & Continental Margins. LC 99-55016. (Geophysical Monograph Ser.: Vol. 115). 354p. 2000. 75.00 (*0-87590-098-4*) Am Geophysical.

Mohrig. Experimental Organic Chemistry. 1998. text. write for info. (*0-7167-3329-3*) W H Freeman.

Mohrig, Jerry R. Experimental Organic Chemistry: A Balanced Approach, Macroscale & Microscale. LC 97-9409. 800p. 1997. pap. text 74.95 (*0-7167-2818-4*) W H Freeman.

— Experimental Organic Chemistry: A Balanced Approach, Macroscale & Microscale. LC 98-7687. 1998. pap. text 74.95 (*0-7167-3330-7*) W H Freeman.

Mohrig, Jerry R. & Child. Chemistry in Perspective. 560p. 1987. teacher ed. write for info. (*0-318-61504-5*, H05648) P-H.

Mohrig, Wolfgang, ed. Dramatische Szenen. (Literatur der Romantik Ser.: Vol. 1.1). (GER.). 1994. write for info. (*3-487-09913-6*) G Olms Pubs.

— Werke: Samtliche Romane und Novellenbucher, 19 vols. (Literatur der Romantik Ser.: Vol. 1). (GER.). 1994. reprint ed. write for info. (*3-487-09158-5*) G Olms Pubs.

— Zwei Schauspiele, die Zwerge, Vol. 1.2. (Literatur der Romantik Ser.). (GER.). 1994. write for info. (*3-487-09914-4*) G Olms Pubs.

Mohring, Herbert, ed. The Economics of Transport, 2 vols., Set. LC 93-32024. (International Library of Critical Writings in Economics: Vol. 34). 1096p. 1994. 430.00 (*1-85278-186-6*) E Elgar.

Mohring, R. H., ed. Graph-Theoretic Concepts in Computer Science. (Lecture Notes in Computer Science Ser.). ix, 360p. 1991. 39.95 (*0-387-53832-1*) Spr-Verlag.

— Graph-Theoretic Concepts in Computer Science: Proceedings, 23rd International Workshop, WG'97, Berlin, Germany, June 18-20, 1997. (Lecture Notes in Computer Science Ser.: Vol. 1335). x, 373p. 1997. pap. 59.00 (*3-540-63757-5*) Spr-Verlag.

Mohrlant, Keith, ed. Digitest User's Guide: The Standard PostScript Digital Device Test. 36p. (Orig.). 1993. pap. 278.00 (*0-933505-29-9*) Graph Comm Assn.

Mohrman, Allan M., Jr., et al. Designing Performance Appraisal Systems: Aligning Appraisals & Organizational Realities. LC 88-32894. (Management Ser.). 256p. 1989. text 35.45 (*1-55542-149-0*) Jossey-Bass.

— Large-Scale Organizational Change. LC 89-45602. (Management Ser.). 336p. 1989. text 36.95 (*1-55542-164-4*) Jossey-Bass.

Mohrman, Allan M., jt. auth. see Mohrman, Susan A.

Mohrman, David E. & Heller, Lois J. Cardiovascular Physiology. 3rd ed. 224p. 1991. text 27.00 (*0-07-027999-3*) McGraw-Hill HPD.

— Cardiovascular Physiology. 4th ed. (Illus.). 240p. 1996. text 27.00 (*0-07-028025-8*) McGraw-Hill HPD.

Mohrman, Kathryn. Adult Students & the Humanities. 48p. 1983. 2.00 (*0-911696-17-2*) Assn Am Coll.

Mohrman, Kathryn & Verman, Shelley. Adult Students & the Humanities: An Analysis of New Data. LC LC5219.M6. 60p. 1981. reprint ed. pap. 30.00 (*0-608-01795-7*, 206244800003) Bks Demand.

Mohrman, Margaret E. Medicine As Ministry: Reflections on Ethics, Suffering & Hope. LC 95-18069. 120p. (Orig.). 1995. pap. 12.95 (*0-8298-1073-0*) Pilgrim OH.

Mohrman, Susan A. & Mohrman, Allan M. Designing & Leading Team-Based Organizations: A Workbook for Organizational Self-Design. LC 96-48676. (The Jossey-Bass Business & Management Ser.). 1997. pap. 25.95 (*0-7879-0864-9*) Jossey-Bass.

Mohrman, Susan A. & Wohlstetter, Priscilla. School-Based Management: Organizing for High Performance. LC 94-17756. (Education Ser.). 330p. 1994. text 38.45 (*0-7879-0035-4*) Jossey-Bass.

Mohrman, Susan A., et al. Designing Team-Based Organizations: New Forms for Knowledge Work. (Management Ser.). 419p. 1995. text 34.95 (*0-7879-0080-X*) Jossey-Bass.

Mohrman, Susan A., jt. ed. see Von Glinow, Mary A.

Mohrman, Susan Albers, see Albers Mohrman, Susan.

Mohrmann, Gerald, ed. see Stewart, Charles I.

Mohrmann, Margaret E. & Hanson, Mark J., eds. Pain Seeking Understanding: Suffering, Medicine & Faith. LC 99-34494. 224p. 1999. pap. 19.95 (*0-8298-1354-3*) Pilgrim OH.

Mohrmann, Renate, ed. see Riecke, Christiane.

Mohrt, Francoise. The Givenchy Style. LC 98-20096. 208p. 1998. text 65.00 (*0-86565-999-0*) Vendome.

Mohrt, Michel. Le Campagne d'Italie. (FRE.). 1973. pap. 10.95 (*0-7859-4015-4*) Fr & Eur.

— Deux Indiennes a Paris. (FRE.). 1978. pap. 10.95 (*0-7859-4090-1*) Fr & Eur.

M

— Les Moyens du Bord. (FRE.). 1982. pap. 11.95 (*0-7859-4164-9*) Fr & Eur.

— La Prison Maritime. (FRE.). 1973. pap. 10.95 (*0-7859-4009-X*, 2070364089) Fr & Eur.

Mohs, Bruce B. The Amazing Mr. Mohs. (Illus.). 256p. (Orig.). (C). 1984. pap. 14.95 (*0-931279-00-3*) Mohs Seaplane Co.

— Free Enterprise: A Wisconsin Constitutional Amendment. (Illus.). (Orig.). 1985. reprint ed. pap. 3.50 (*0-317-13759-X*) Mohs Seaplane Co.

Mohsen, J. P., ed. see Technical Council on Computer Practice, Committee.

Mohsen, Johann C. Geschichte der Wissenschaften in der Mark Brandenburg, Besonders der Arzneiwissenschaft. (GER.). 1997. reprint ed. 138.00 (*3-487-05831-6*) G Olms Pubs.

Mohsen, Shahbazzadeh. Role of Multinational Companies in Nation's Economy: A Case Study of Iran. (C). 1994. 42.00 (*81-7018-747-8*, Pub. by BR Pub) S Asia.

Mohseni. Java Beans Developer's Guide. 1997. 39.95 (*0-8055-1573-9*, M&T Bks) IDG Bks.

Mohseni, Mahmoud, tr. see Shariati, Ali.

Mohseni, Piroz. The Waite Group's NC Guide. LC 97-19460. 338p. 1997. 29.99 (*1-57169-106-5*) Sams.

Mohsenifar, Zab & Shah, P. K. Practical Critical Care in Cardiology. LC 97-45024. (Fundamental & Clinical Cardiology Ser.). (Illus.). 472p. 1997. text 165.00 (*0-8247-0097-X*) Dekker.

M

Mohsenin, Nuri N. Electromagnetic Radiation Properties of Foods & Agricultural Products. xiv, 676p. 1984. text 312.00 (*0-677-06190-0*) Gordon & Breach.

— Physical Properties of Food & Agricultural Materials: A Teaching Manual. x, 147p. (C). 1989. text 102.00 (*0-677-05630-3*) Gordon & Breach.

— Physical Properties of Plant & Animal Materials. 758p. 1970. 150.00 (*0-677-02300-6*) Gordon & Breach.

— Physical Properties of Plant & Animal Materials. 2nd ed. xviii, 892p. 1986. text 283.00 (*0-677-21370-0*) Gordon & Breach.

— Thermal Properties of Food & Agricultural Materials. x, 408p. 1980. text 316.00 (*0-677-05450-5*) Gordon & Breach.

Mohsin, Nadeem. Lull after the Storm: Poverty & Integrated Rural Development. 1989. 28.50 (*81-7169-035-1*, Pub. by Commonwealth) S Asia.

Mohta, Viraf D. Netscape Communicator 4 for Dummies. LC 96-77276. (Quick Reference Ser.). (Illus.). 224p. 1997. spiral bd. 12.99 (*0-7645-0041-4*) IDG Bks.

Mohta, Viraf D. Netscape Communicator 4.5 for Dummies Quick Reference. LC TK5105.883.N49M642. (For Dummies). (Illus.). 224p. 1999. spiral bd. 12.99 (*0-7645-0325-1*) IDG Bks.

Mohts, Susan B. When God's People Pray: Pastorial Prayers for the Congregation First United Methodist Church, Dallas. Hale, Margaret, ed. 96p. (Orig.). 1989. pap. 4.95 (*0-685-26559-5*) First United Meth Ch.

***Mohun, Arwen.** Steam Laundries: Gender, Technology & Work in the United States & Great Britain, 1880-1940. LC 98-38245. (Studies in the History of Technology). 1999. 48.00 (*0-8018-6002-4*) Johns Hopkins.

Mohun, Arwen, jt. ed. see Horowitz, Roger.

Mohun, Simon, ed. Debates in Value Theory. LC 93-44298. 1994. text 65.00 (*0-312-12098-2*, Pub. by Macmillan) St Martin.

Mohyla, Lolita V., et al. Construction in Australia: Law & Project Delivery. 280p. 1996. pap. 50.00 (*0-455-21379-8*, Pub. by Cavendish Pubng) Gaunt.

Mohyla, O., jt. auth. see Ludvik, M.

Moi. In the Kitchen with Miss Piggy: Fabulous Recipes from My Famous Celebrity Friends. LC 95-52383. (Illus.). 127p. (J). (gr. 11). 1996. 17.95 (*0-7835-4781-1*) Time-Life.

Moi, Toril. Sexual-Textual Politics. (New Accents Ser.). xv, 206p. 1995. pap. 18.99 (*0-415-02974-0*, 9451) Routledge.

— Simone de Beauvoir: The Making of an Intellectual Woman. 352p. 1994. pap. 28.95 (*0-631-19181-X*) Blackwell Pubs.

***Moi, Toril.** What Is a Woman? And Other Essays. LC 99-16111. (Illus.). 544p. 2000. 35.00 (*0-19-812242-X*) OUP.

Moi, Toril & Radway, Janice, eds. Materialist Feminism. 200p. 1994. pap. 10.00 (*0-8223-6421-2*) Duke.

Moi, Toril, ed. see Kristeva, Julia.

Moidel, Steve. Speed Reading. 2nd ed. LC 98-2996. (Barron's Business Success Ser.). 96p. 1998. pap. 6.95 (*0-7641-0401-2*, 835937Q) Barron.

Moignan, Luke Le, see Le Moignan, Luke.

Moignard, Elizabeth. Corpus Vasorum Antiquorum: Great Britian, Fasciucule 16: The National Museums of Scotland, Edinburgh. (British Academy Ser.). (Illus.). 128p. 1990. text 130.00 (*0-19-726077-2*) OUP.

— Corpus Vasorum Antiquorum: The Glasgow Collections. LC 97-216960. (Corpus Vasorum Antiquorum British Academy Ser.). (Illus.). 122p. 1997. text 110.00 (*0-19-726168-X*) OUP.

Moigno, Yves. Dictionnaire Pratique de Sexualite. (FRE.). 1991. write for info. (*0-7859-7889-5*, 2-501-01407-3) Fr & Eur.

Moignot, Daniel, jt. auth. see Gallimard Jeunesse Publishing Staff.

Moiin, A., et al, eds. Dermatology in Pigmented Skin. (Illus.). 320p. 1998. write for info. (*0-443-05467-3*) Church.

Moikobu, Josephine M. Blood & Flesh: Black American & African Identifications, 59. LC 80-1706. (Contributions in Afro-American & African Studies: No. 59). (Illus.). 226p. 1981. 55.00 (*0-313-22549-4*, MBF/, Greenwood Pr) Greenwood.

Moilanen, Markku & Tiittula, Liisa, eds. Ueberredung in der Presse: Texte, Strategien, Analysen. (Sprache, Politik, Oeffentlichkeit Ser.: Bd. 3). (GER.). 249p. (C). 1994. lib. bdg. 103.10 (*3-11-014346-1*) De Gruyter.

Moiles, Steven. Summer of My First Pediddle. 190p. (YA). (gr. 9-12). 1995. pap. 9.99 (*0-88092-122-6*) Royal Fireworks.

Moiliili Community Members, ed. The Tastes & Tales of Moiliili. 230p. 1997. reprint ed. pap. 14.95 (*0-9676548-0-7*, Pub. by Moiliili) Booklines Hawaii.

Moille, T. G. La, see La Moille, T. G., compiled by.

***Moin, Baqer.** Khomeini: Life of the Ayatollah. (Illus.). 2000. 27.95 (*0-312-26490-9*, Thomas Dunne) St Martin.

Mo'in, Mohammad. Mo'in's: Intermediate Persion Dictionary, 6 vols., Set. (PER., Illus.). 8058p. 1994. lib. bdg. 195.00 (*1-56859-031-8*) Mazda Pubs.

Moin, Parichehr, tr. see Ravanipur, Moniru.

Moine, Donald J. & Lloyd, Kenneth. Unlimited Selling Power: How to Master Hypnotic Skills. 288p. (C). 1990. pap. text 14.95 (*0-13-689126-8*) P-H.

Moine, Donald J. & McCord, William J. Better Than Gold: An Investors Guide to Swiss Annuities. LC 97-14648. 272p. 1998. 34.95 (*0-89526-415-3*) Regnery Pub.

Moine, Donald J., jt. auth. see Gschwandtner, Gerhard.

Moine, Marie-Pierre. French Vegetarian Cooking: A Step-by-Step Guide. (In a Nutshell Ser.). (Illus.). 64p. 1999. 7.95 (*1-86204-382-5*, Pub. by Element MA) Penguin Putnam.

Moine, Marie-Pierre, jt. auth. see Bremness, Lesley.

Moine, Roger Le, see Le Moine, Roger.

Moingeon, Bertrand & Edmondson, Amy, eds. Organizational Learning & Competitive Advantage. 224p. 1996. 75.00 (*0-7619-5166-0*); pap. 26.95 (*0-7619-5167-9*) Sage.

***Moini, Alireza.** Vision Chips. LC 99-46027. (International Series in Engineering & Computer Science). 1999. write for info. (*0-7923-8664-7*) Kluwer Academic.

Moini, Mohsen, tr. see Krishnamurti.

***Moinot, Pierre.** As Night Follows Day. 2000. 24.95 (*1-56649-154-1*) Welcome Rain.

Moinot, Pierre. La Chasse Royale. (FRE.). 1981. pap. 10.95 (*0-7859-4146-0*) Fr & Eur.

— Le Guetteur d'Ombre. (FRE.). 1984. pap. 15.95 (*0-7859-4204-1*) Fr & Eur.

— Le Sable Vif. (FRE.). 1979. pap. 10.95 (*0-7859-4120-7*) Fr & Eur.

***Moio, Dominick.** Be-Bop Phrasing for Drums. 24p. 1998. pap. 17.95 incl. audio compact disk (*0-7866-2869-3*, 96681BCD) Mel Bay.

— Latin Percussion in Perspective. 64p. 1997. pap. 19.95 incl. audio compact disk (*0-7866-2870-7*, 96682BCD) Mel Bay.

Moioli, G. Dictionnaire de Dietique. (FRE.). 364p. 1993. pap. 59.95 (*0-7859-5640-9*, 2732817066) Fr & Eur.

Moir, Alfred. Caravaggio. (Masters of Art Ser.). (Illus.). 128p. 1989. 24.95 (*0-8109-3150-8*, Pub. by Abrams) Time Warner.

— Drawings by Seventeenth-Century Italian Masters from the Collection of Janos. (Illus.). 150p. 1973. pap. 7.00 (*0-942006-40-2*) U of CA Art.

— European Drawings in the Collection of the Santa Barbara Museum of Art. LC 76-4685. (Illus.). 298p. (Orig.). 1976. pap. 12.00 (*0-89951-021-3*) Santa Barb Mus Art.

— The Italian Followers of Caravaggio, 1. LC 66-10315. 359p. reprint ed. pap. 111.30 (*0-608-11338-7*, 200601700054) Bks Demand.

— The Italian Followers of Caravaggio, 2. LC 66-10315. 345p. reprint ed. pap. 107.00 (*0-608-11339-5*, 200601700055) Bks Demand.

— Regional Styles of Drawing in Italy. (Illus.). 123p. 1977. pap. 12.00 (*0-942006-52-6*) U of CA Art.

Moir, Alfred, text. Anthony Van Dyck. LC 94-8419. (Illus.). 128p. 1994. 24.95 (*0-8109-3917-7*, Pub. by Abrams) Time Warner.

Moir, Alfred, jt. auth. see Berns, Marla C.

***Moir, Allison & Gibbons, David.** Partners in Peace & Prosperity: A Premier & a Governor in Bermuda. LC 99-91943. 2000. 25.00 (*0-7388-1406-7*); pap. 18.00 (*0-7388-1407-5*) Xlibris Corp.

Moir, Anne. Brain Sex: The Real Difference Between Men & Women. 1991. 17.95 (*0-8184-0543-0*, Delta Trade) Dell.

— Why Men Don't Iron: The Science of Gender Studies. LC 99-38599. 320p. 1999. 22.50 (*1-55972-521-4*) Carol Pub Group.

Moir, Anne & Jessel, David. Brain Sex: The Real Difference Between Men & Women. 256p. 1992. pap. 13.95 (*0-385-31183-4*, Delta Trade) Dell.

Moir, C. B. & Dawson, J. Distribution. Maunder, W. F. & Fleming, M. C., eds. 296p. (C). (gr. 13). 1992. ring bd. 204.95 (*0-412-35670-8*, A5653, Chap & Hall CRC) CRC Pr.

Moir, Donald D. Pain Relief in Labour. 5th ed. LC 85-11702. (Illus.). 196p. 1985. pap. text. write for info. (*0-443-03389-7*) Church.

Moir, Frederick L. After Livingstone: An African Trade Romance. 1977. 17.95 (*0-8369-9212-1*, 9068) Ayer.

Moir, Guthrie. Beyond Hatred. LC 74-119326. 183p. reprint ed. pap. 56.80 (*0-8357-7157-1*, 202696300053) Bks Demand.

Moir, Ian, jt. auth. see Elliott, Keith.

***Moir, Lance.** Managing Corporate Liquidity. 196p. 1999. 65.00 (*1-888998-64-4*) Glenlake Pub.

Moir, Lance. Managing Corporate Liquidity. 2nd ed. LC 00-551136. 250p. 1999. 60.00 (*0-8144-0508-8*) AMACOM.

— Managing Liquidity. 2nd ed. (Association of Corporate Treasurers Ser.). 192p. 1997. pap. 45.00 (*1-85573-335-8*, Pub. by Woodhead Pubng) Am Educ Systs.

***Moir, Lance, ed.** Managing Corporate Liquidity. 250p. 1999. 65.00 (*1-57958-185-4*) Fitzroy Dearborn.

Moir, Lindsay, jt. auth. see Dempsey, Hugh Aylmer.

Moir, Lyn, tr. see Simenon, Georges.

Moir, Martin I., et al, eds. J. S. Mill's Encounter with India. 328p. 1998. text 60.00 (*0-8020-0713-9*) U of Toronto Pr.

Moir, May A. The Garden Watcher. rev. ed. LC 82-24782. (Illus.). 136p. 1989. pap. text 15.00 (*0-8248-1224-7*) UH Pr.

Moir, Peter W. Efficient Past Imaging: Cim & Its Applications for Today's Industry. 1989. text 54.95 (*0-470-21352-3*) P-H.

— Profit by Quality. (Industry & Applied Technology Ser.). 108p. 1988. text 36.95 (*0-470-21143-1*) P-H.

Moir, Phyllis L., ed. see Toal, Susan B.

***Moir, Rita.** Buffalo Jump: A Woman's Travels. 168p. 1999. pap. 10.95 (*1-55050-144-5*, Pub. by Coteau) Genl Dist Srvs.

Moir, S. D. Monitoring Elder Compliance & Response: A Self Learning Programme for Community Nurses. 125p. 1996. spiral bd. write for info. (*0-443-05525-4*) Church.

Moir, Sheila, jt. auth. see Smith, LeCain W.

Moir, T. Dictionnaire des Images, Symboles du Reve. (FRE.). 247p. 1997. 55.00 (*0-320-00480-5*) Fr & Eur.

Moir, William H. Forests of Mount Rainier. (Illus.). 111p. (Orig.). 1989. pap. text 8.95 (*0-914019-24-4*) NW Interpretive.

Moir, William J., ed. Past & Present of Hardin County. (Illus.). 1051p. 1997. reprint ed. lib. bdg. 105.00 (*0-8328-6682-2*) Higginson Bk Co.

Moir, Zawahir, jt. auth. see Shackle, Christopher.

Moir, Zawahir, jt. auth. see Shakle, Shristopher.

***Moira, Stephan.** Teach Yourself Excel 2000. (Teach Yourself Ser.). 192p. 2000. pap. 10.95 (*0-658-00245-7*, 002457, Teach Yrslf) NTC Contemp Pub Co.

— Teach Yourself Word 2000. (Teach Yourself Ser.). 192p. 2000. pap. 10.95 (*0-658-00246-5*, 002465, Teach Yrslf) NTC Contemp Pub Co.

Moirand. Dictionnaire Technologique, (Ebenisterie-Menuiserie-Scierie-Technologie), Vol. 6. (FRE.). 356p. 1986. pap. 150.00 (*0-7859-3910-5*, 2856080219) Fr & Eur.

Moirand, Sophie, et al, eds. Parcours Linguistiques de Discours Specialises: Actes du Colloque en Sorbonne (Paris, Septembre 1992) 2nd ed. (Sciences pour la Communication Ser.: Vol. 41). (FRE.). 404p. 1995. 60.95 (*3-906751-28-7*, Pub. by P Lang) P Lang Pubng.

Moirant, R., jt. auth. see Cassart, C.

Moirant, T. Technical Dictionary of Woodworking: French Definitions Plus Index with Appendix of Technical Terms in French-German-English-Spanish-Dutch-Italian-Swedish. 350p. 1986. pap. 75.00 (*2-85608-021-9*) IBD Ltd.

Moisa, Ralph. Great Eagle & Small One. Thies, Susan C., ed. LC 98-205842. (Illus.). 56p. (J). (gr. 2-4). 1997. 13.55 (*0-7807-6685-7*); pap. 8.35 (*0-7891-2000-3*) Perfection Learn.

— Little Fish. Thies, Susan C., ed. LC 98-207752. (Illus.). 56p. (J). (gr. 2-4). 1997. 13.55 (*0-7807-6691-1*); pap. 8.35 (*0-7891-2003-8*) Perfection Learn.

***Moisala, Pirkko & Diamond, Beverley.** Music & Gender LC 99-6791. 2000. write for info. (*0-252-06865-3*) U of Ill Pr.

Moisan, Ed, ed. see Theberge, Remy.

Moisan, M., jt. auth. see Ferreira, C. M.

Moisan, Michel & Pelletier, Jacques, eds. Microwave Excited Plasmas. LC 92-30694. (Plasma Technology Ser.: Vol. 4). 520p. 1992. 214.25 (*0-444-88815-2*) Elsevier.

Moisan, R., ed. see Theberge, J. Remy.

Moisan, R., ed. see Theberge, Remy.

Moise, E. Warren. Impeachment Evidence: Attacking & Supporting the Credibility of Witnesses in South Carolina. LC 96-232978. 222p. (Orig.). 1996. pap. 30.00 (*0-943856-72-8*, 640) SC Bar CLE.

Moise, Edwin E. Elementary Geometry from a Advanced Standpoint. 3rd ed. 512p. (C). 1990. text 85.00 (*0-201-50867-2*) Addison-Wesley.

— Elementary Geometry from an Advanced Standpoint. 2nd ed. LC 73-2347. (C). 1974. text 37.56 (*0-201-04793-4*) Addison-Wesley.

— Introductory Problem Courses in Analysis & Topology. (Universitext Ser.). 94p. 1982. 31.95 (*0-387-90701-7*) Spr-Verlag.

— Land Reform in China & North Vietnam: Consolidating the Revolution at the Village Level. LC 82-15900. 319p. 1983. reprint ed. pap. 98.90 (*0-608-03564-5*, 205964800009) Bks Demand.

— Modern China: A History. (Illus.). 256p. (C). 1989. pap. text 30.80 (*0-582-49077-4*, 73474) Longman.

— Modern China: A History. 2nd ed. LC 93-47289. (Present & Past Ser.). (C). 1995. pap. text 35.00 (*0-582-07480-0*, 76772) Addison-Wesley.

— Modern China: A History (Present & the Past) (Illus.). 256p. (C). 1986. boxed set 26.95 (*0-582-49076-6*, 73474) Longman.

— Tonkin Gulf & the Escalation of the Vietnam War. 304p. 1999. 40.00 (*0-7881-5989-5*) DIANE Pub.

— Tonkin Gulf & the Escalation of the Vietnam War. LC 96-12159. 400p. (C). 1996. 39.95 (*0-8078-2300-7*) U of NC Pr.

Moise, Elaine, jt. auth. see Schwartz, Rebecca.

Moise, Kenneth J., jt. ed. see Fisk, Nicholas M.

Moise, Linda, tr. see Kamava, Connie H.

Moise, Lotte. Barbara & Fred: Grownups Now, Living Fully with Developmental Disabilities. LC 97-74323. Orig. Title: As We Grew up with Barbara. (Illus.). 224p. 1997. pap. 16.95 (*1-882897-08-0*) Lost Coast.

Moiseev, N. N. Politics & Science in the U. S. S. R. & Russia: Biographical Memoir. LC 99-15145. (Russian Documents, Bibliography, & Memoirs Ser.: Vol. 1). (RUS.). 540p. 1999. 119.95 (*0-7734-3244-2*) E Mellen.

***Moiseev, S. S.** Non-Linear Instabilities in Plasmas & Hydrodynamics. LC 99-49916. (Plasma Physics Ser.). 176p. 1999. 80.00 (*0-7503-0483-9*) IOP Pub.

Moiseev, Yu V. & Zaikov, G. E. Chemical Resistance of Polymers in Aggressive Media. Mosley, R. J., tr. from RUS. LC 87-9075. (Illus.). 384p. (C). 1987. text 144.00 (*0-306-10997-2*, Kluwer Plenum) Kluwer Academic.

Moiseiwitsch, Benjamin L. Variational Principles. LC 66-17233. (Interscience Monographs & Texts in Physics & Astronomy: Vol. 20). 320p. reprint ed. pap. 99.20 (*0-608-11644-0*, 201614800098) Bks Demand.

Moiser, C. H. & Philips, V. A. Practice & Procedure in Magistrates Courts. 3rd ed. 268p. 1992. 75.00 (*1-85190-163-9*, Pub. by Tolley Pubng) St Mut.

Moiser, Jeremy. Silent Pilgrimage to God: The Spirituality of Charles de Foucauld. LC 74-32516. 100p. reprint ed. pap. 31.00 (*0-8357-4072-2*, 203676200005) Bks Demand.

Moises, Carlos Felipe, ed. see Machado de Assis, Joaquim Maria.

Moises, Rosalio, et al. A Yaqui Life: The Personal Chronicle of a Yaqui Indian. LC 76-56789. Orig. Title: The Tall Candle: the Personal Chronicle of a Yaqui Indian. (Illus.). lxviii, 261p. 1977. reprint ed. pap. 14.95 (*0-8032-8175-7*, Bison Books) U of Nebr Pr.

Moiseyev, Ivan V. A Russian Martyr. 1974. 1.95 (*0-89985-107-X*) Christ for the Nations.

Moisil, G. & Sneddon, Ian N. Algebraic Theory of Switching Circuits. LC 63-10024. (International Series of Monographs on Pure & Applied Mathematics: Vol. 41). 1969. 314.00 (*0-08-010148-8*, Pub. by Pergamon Repr) Franklin.

Moisio. Guide to Health Insurance Billing. (Allied Health Ser.). 2000. pap. 36.00 (*0-7668-1207-3*) Thomson Learn.

***Moisio, Elmer W. & Moisio, Marie A.** Med Terminology: Student-Centered Appr/Flashcards. (C). 2001. 8.00 (*0-7668-1527-7*) Thomson Learn.

Moisio, Elmer W., jt. auth. see Moisio, Marie A.

Moisio, Marie A. & Moisio, Elmer W. Understanding Laboratory & Diagnostic Tests. LC 97-13352. (Health Information Management Ser.). 416p. (C). 1997. mass mkt. 45.95 (*0-8273-7854-8*) Delmar.

Moisio, Marie A., jt. auth. see Moisio, Elmer W.

Moisio, Marie A., jt. auth. see Sormunen, Carolee.

***Moisl, Hermann.** Lordship & Tradition in Barbarian Europe. LC 99-13603. 1999. write for info. (*0-88946-684-X*) E Mellen.

— Lordship & Tradition in Barbarian Europe. LC 99-13603. (Studies in Classics: Vol. 10). 224p. 1999. text 89.95 (*0-7734-8151-6*) E Mellen.

Moissac, Jeanne M. De, see De Moissac, Jeanne M.

Moitessier, Bernard. The Long Way. 1996. pap. text 14.95 (*0-07-042958-8*) McGraw.

— The Long Way. (Illus.). 252p. 1995. pap. 14.95 (*0-924486-84-8*) Sheridan.

— A Sea Vagabond's World. Rodarmor, William, tr. from ENG. LC 98-12995. (Illus.). 216p. (Orig.). 1998. pap. 19.95 (*1-57409-021-6*) Sheridan.

— Tamata & the Alliance. Rodarmor, William, tr. (Illus.). 400p. 1995. 35.00 (*0-924486-77-5*) Sheridan.

Moitoza, Joe. The Kibitzer. (Illus.). 96p. 1984. 9.95 (*0-915509-04-0*); pap. 4.95 (*0-915509-03-2*) Argos Pub Co.

Moitra, Shefali, jt. ed. see Banerjee, S. P.

Moivre, Abraham De, see De Moivre, Abraham.

Moix, Ana M. Dangerous Virtues. Jones, Margaret E., tr. LC 96-31317. (European Women Writers Ser.). Orig. Title: Dangerous Virtues. vii, 153p. 1997. pap. 10.00 (*0-8032-8237-0*); text 40.00 (*0-8032-3189-X*) U of Nebr Pr.

***Moix, Terenci.** Mujercismas. 1998. pap. text 9.95 (*84-08-02013-7*) Planeta Edit.

Moizer, Barbara, jt. auth. see Moizer, Stan.

Moizer, Stan & Moizer, Barbara. Pet Owner's Guide to Budgerigars. (Pet Owner's Guide Ser.). (Illus.). 80p. 1997. 8.00 (*1-86054-038-4*, Pub. by Ringpr Bks) Seven Hills Bk.

Mojab, Cynthia A., et al. Innovative Materials Development & Testing, Vol. 5: Partial Depth Spall Repair. 197p. (C). 1993. pap. text 15.00 (*0-309-05613-6*, SHRP-H-356) SHRP.

Mojaiev. English-Russian Dictionary of Forestry & Forest Industries. (ENG & RUS.). 670p. 1983. 49.95 (*0-8288-0331-5*, M14046) Fr & Eur.

Mojares, Resil B., jt. ed. see Kerkvliet, Benedict J.

Mojasevic, Miljan. English for Economists: Serbian/English/Serbian. (ENG & SER.). 345p. 1997. 75.00 (*0-320-00052-4*) Fr & Eur.

Mojay, Gabriel. Aromatherapy for Healing the Spirit: A Guide to Restoring Emotional & Mental Balance Through Essential Oils. (Illus.). 191p. 1998. pap. text 19.00 (*0-7881-5814-7*) DIANE Pub.

***Mojay, Gabriel.** Aromatherapy for Healing the Spirit: Restoring Emotional & Mental Balance with Essential Oils. LC 99-40650. (Illus.). 192p. 2000. pap. 19.95 (*0-89281-887-5*) Inner Tradit.

Moje. Kids Chemistry. LC 99-26152. 96p. (J). (gr. 4-6). 1999. pap. 14.95 (*0-8069-6349-2*) Sterling.

— 100 Simple Science Experiments in Paper. LC 98-34948. (Illus.). 128p. 1999. pap. 14.95 (*0-8069-6391-3*) Sterling.

***Moje, Elizabeth B.** All the Stories That We Have: Adolescents' Insights about Literacy & Learning in Secondary Schools. (Kids InSight Ser.). 2000. pap., teacher ed. 19.95 (*0-87207-264-9*, 264) Intl Reading.

***Moje, Elizabeth B. & O'Brien, David G.** Constructions of Literacy: Studies of Teaching & Learning in & Out of Secondary Schools. LC 99-89996. 2000. pap. write for info. (*0-8058-2949-0*) L Erlbaum Assocs.

***Moje, Steven W.** 100 Science Experiments with Paper. (J). 1999. pap. text 5.95 (*0-8069-6353-0*) Sterling.

An Asterisk (*) at the beginning of an entry indicates that the title is appearing for the first time.

Moje, Steven W. Paper Clip Science: Simple & Fun Experiments. LC 96-10993. (Illus.). 96p. (J). (gr. 3). 1996. 14.95 (*0-8069-4385-8*) Sterling.
— Paper Clip Science: Simple & Fun Experiments. (Illus.). 96p. (J). 1997. pap. 4.95 (*0-8069-4386-6*) Sterling.
Mojetta, Angelo. Sharks: History & Biology of the Lords of the Seas. LC 98-48583. (Illus.). 168p. 1999. pap. 17.98 (*1-57145-178-1*, Thunder Bay) Advantage Pubs.
— Simon & Schuster's Guide to Saltwater Fish & Fishing. (Illus.). 256p. (Orig.). 1992. per. 14.00 (*0-671-77947-8*) S&S Trade Pap.
Moji, Clifton C., jt. auth. see Baratloo, Balch.
Mojica, Monique. Princess Pocahontas & the Blue Spots. 86p. pap. 9.95 (*0-88961-165-3*, Pub. by Womens Pr) LPC InBook.
Mojica-Sandoz, Luis. Aguedo Mojica: La Luminosa Entrega. LC 83-82447. 336p. 1983. pap. 13.50 (*0-940238-70-5*) Ediciones Huracan.
— La Meditacion Segun la Mas Antigua Tradicion Budista. (UPREX, Manuales Ser.: No. 54). (SPA., Illus.). 92p. 1979. pap. text 1.50 (*0-8477-0054-2*) U of PR Pr.
Mojica, Yvonne, tr. see Royo, Luis.
Mojkowski, Charles, et al. Developing Leaders for Restructuring Schools: New Habits of Mind & Heart. 72p. 1991. 4.75 (*0-87652-168-5*, 021-0348) Am Assn Sch Admin.
Mojsisch, Burkhard. Sprachphilosophie in Antike und Mittelalter: Bochumer Kolloquim, 2-4, June 1982. (Bochum Studies in Philosophy: No. 3). (GER.). viii, 448p. 1986. 59.00 (*90-6032-233-9*, Pub. by B R Gruner) Humanities.
***Mojsisch, Burkhard, et al, eds.** Bochumer Philosophisches Jahrbuch fur Antike & Mittelalter, Band 3. (Bochumer Philosophisches Jahrbuch: Vol. 3). vi, 288p. 1999. pap. 88.00 (*90-6032-446-3*) J Benjamins Pubng Co.
— Bochumer Philosophisches Jahrbuch fur Antike und Mittelalter, Band 2. vi, 340p. 1998. pap. 88.00 (*90-6032-445-5*, Pub. by B R Gruner) J Benjamins Pubng Co.
Mojsisch, Burkhard, et al, eds. Bochumer Philosophisches Jahrbuch fur Antike und Mittelalter, Band 1. (ENG, FRE, GER & ITA.). 284p. 1997. 88.00 (*90-6032-444-7*) J Benjamins Pubng Co.
***Mojsisch, Burkhard, et al, eds.** Bochumer Philosophisches Jahrbuch fur Antike und Mittelalter, Band 4. (GER.). v, 306p. 2000. pap. 98.00 (*90-6032-447-1*, Pub. by B R Gruner) J Benjamins Pubng Co.
Mojsisch, Burkhard & Pluta, Olaf, eds. Historia Philosophiae Medii Aevi: Studien zur Geschichte der Philosophie des Mittelalters, Festschrift fur Kurt Flasch zu Seinem 60, Geburtstag, 2 vols., Set. LC 91-47183. (GER.). xxxv, 1164p. 1992. 177.00 (*90-6032-090-5*, Pub. by B R Gruner) Humanities.
— Historia Philosophiae Medii Aevi: Studien zur Geschichte der Philosophie des Mittelalters, zu Seinem 60, Geburtstag, Band I & II, 2 vols., 1. LC 91-47183. (GER.). 1992. write for info. (*90-6032-333-5*) B R Gruner.
— Historia Philosophiae Medii Aevi: Studien zur Geschichte der Philosophie des Mittelalters, zu Seinem 60, Geburtstag, Band I & II, 2 vols., 2. LC 91-47183. (GER.). Date not set. write for info. (*90-6032-343-2*) B R Gruner.
Mojtabai, A. G. Blessed Assurance: At Home with the Bomb in Amarillo, Texas. LC 97-25167. xvi, 255p. 1997. pap. 17.95 (*0-8156-0508-0*) Syracuse U Pr.
— Soon: Tales from Hospice. LC 98-29015. 224p. 1998. 22.00 (*0-944072-91-7*) Zoland Bks.
Mojtahed-Zadeh, Pirouz. Security & Territoriality in the Persian Gulf. 288p. 1998. 75.00 (*0-7007-1098-1*, Pub. by Curzon Pr Ltd) Paul & Co Pubs.
Mojumdar, Kanchanmoy. Anglo-Nepalese Relations in the Nineteenth Century. LC 73-906205. vi, 195p. 1973. 9.00 (*0-88386-214-X*) S Asia.
Mojumder, Atindra, tr. from BEN. The Caryapadas: Tantric Poems of the Eighty-Four Mahasiddhas (Siddhacaryas) 2nd rev. ed. 225p. 1980. text 13.95 (*0-935548-03-3*) Codex Pr.
Mojzes, Paul. Religion & the War in Bosnia. LC 97-49123. (AAR the Religions Ser.). 300p. 1998. pap. 19.95 (*0-7885-0428-2*, 01 12 03) OUP.
Mojzes, Paul, compiled by. Church & State in Postwar Eastern Europe: A Bibliographical Survey, 11. LC 87-8358. (Bibliographies & Indexes in Religious Studies: No. 11). 120p. 1987. lib. bdg. 59.95 (*0-313-24002-7*, MOJ/, Greenwood Pr) Greenwood.
Mojzes, Paul, ed. Religious Liberty in Eastern Europe & the U. S. S. R. Before & after the Great Transformation. 400p. 1992. text 85.50 (*0-88033-234-4*, 337, Pub. by East Eur Monographs) Col U Pr.
— Varieties of Christian-Marxist Dialogue. 210p. (Orig.). 1978. pap. 3.00 (*0-931214-02-5*) Ecumenical Phila.
Mojzes, Paul & Swidler, Leonard, eds. Christian Mission & Interreligious Dialogue. LC 91-2010. (Religions in Dialogue Ser.: Vol. 4). 288p. 1991. lib. bdg. 89.95 (*0-88946-520-7*) E Mellen.
Mojzes, Paul, jt. auth. see Swidler, Leonard.
Mojzes, Paul, jt. ed. see Foster, Durwood.
Mojzes, Paul, jt. ed. see Swidler, Leonard.
***Mok, Clement.** Designing Business 2.0: E-Business Success Strategies. 264p. 2000. pap. 49.99 (*0-201-70283-5*) Adobe Pr.
Mok, Clement. Kiier Web Design: Net Objects Fusion. LC 96-78596. 240p. 1997. 49.99 (*1-56830-340-8*) Hayden.
Mok, David W. S. Cytokini vs. Chemistry Activity & Function. 352p. 1994. lib. bdg. 195.00 (*0-8493-6252-0*) CRC Pr.
Mok, Esther. Sumo, the Wrestling Elephant. LC 92-82936. (Illus.). 24p. (J). (gr. 2-5). 1994. pap. 4.95 (*0-943864-68-2*) Davenport.
***Mok, G. C.** Scans (Shipping Cask Analysis System), Microcomputer- Based Analysis System for Shipping Cask Design Review: User's Manual Version 3a. 212p. 1998. per. 18.00 (*0-16-062905-5*) USGPO.
Mok, G. C., et al, eds. Seismic, Shock & Vibration Isolation. LC 95-78459. (Proceedings of the 1995 ASME/JSME Pressure Vessels & Piping Conference Ser.: PVP-Vol. 319). 332p. 1995. 130.00 (*0-7918-1325-8*, H00957) ASME.
Mok, Jacqueline & Newell, Marie-Louise, eds. HIV Infection in Children: A Guide to Practical Management. (Illus.). 327p. (C). 1995. text 85.00 (*0-521-45421-2*) Cambridge U Pr.
***Mok, Ka-Ho.** Gdr Society & Social Institutions: Facts & Figures. LC 99-16306. 232p. 2000. text 65.00 (*0-312-22488-5*) St Martin.
Mok, Leo. International Handbook on Pensions Law & Similar Employee Benefits. 352p. 1989. lib. bdg. 221.00 (*0-86010-994-1*) Kluwer Academic.
Mok, N., ed. Metric Rigidity Theorems on Hermitian Locally Symmetric Manifolds. (Series in Pure Mathematics: Vol. 6). 292p. (C). 1989. text 61.00 (*9971-5-0800-1*); pap. text 32.00 (*9971-5-0802-8*) World Scientific Pub.
Mok, Olivia, tr. see Jin Yong.
Mokabe, Paul, jt. auth. see Zorc, R. David.
***Mokae, Gomolemo.** The Secret in My Bosom. 86p. 1998. 29.95 (*0-86543-686-X*) Africa World.
— The Secret in My Bosom. 86p. 1999. pap. 12.95 (*0-86543-687-8*) Africa World.
— Short, Not Tall Stories. 120p. 1998. 29.95 (*0-86543-684-3*) Africa World.
— Short, Not Tall Stories. 120p. 1999. pap. 12.95 (*0-86543-685-1*) Africa World.
Mokaila, Dingaan M., jt. auth. see Cole, Desmond T.
Mokashi, D. B. Palkhi: An Indian Pilgrimage. Engblom, Philip C. & Zelliot, Eleanor, trs. LC 86-30001. 291p. (C). 1987. pap. text 23.95 (*0-88706-462-0*) State U NY Pr.
Mokashi-Punekar, S., jt. auth. see Naik, M. K.
Mokbel, K. M. MCQs in Applied Basic Sciences for the Primary FRCS. (C). 1992. pap. text 22.50 (*0-7923-8994-8*) Kluwer Academic.
Moke, Susan & Shermis, Michael. The Active Learner: Help Your Child Learn by Doing. Smith, Carl B., ed. (Successful Learner Ser.). (Illus.). 136p. 1996. pap. 12.95 (*0-9628556-9-3*) Grayson Bernard Pubs.
Moked, Gabriel. Particles & Ideas: Bishop Berkeley's Corpuscularian Philosophy. 256p. 1988. text 59.00 (*0-19-824990-X*) OUP.
Mokeddem, Malika. The Forbidden Woman (L'Interdite) Marcus, K. Melissa, tr. from ENG. LC 97-22024. (European Women Writers Ser.). xv, 156p. 1998. pap. 15.00 (*0-8032-8240-0*); text 40.00 (*0-8032-3193-8*) U of Nebr Pr.
***Mokeddem, Malika.** Of Dreams & Assassins. LC 99-43291. (Caraf Bks.). 2000. pap. 16.95 (*0-8139-1994-0*) U Pr of Va.
— Of Dreams & Assassins. Marcus, K. Melissa, tr. from FRE. LC 99-43291. (Caraf Bks.). 128p. 2000. 45.00 (*0-8139-1933-9*) U Pr of Va.
Mokeme, Oscar O. The Igbos & the Masks of Africa. 55p. 1996. pap. write for info. (*0-9644596-3-9*) Ekumeku Commun.
Mokgoro, Job, jt. auth. see Cloete, Fanie.
***Mokhemar, Mary Ann.** The Central Auditory Processing Book, Bk. 1. 180p. (J). (gr. 1-8). 1999. spiral bd. 41.95 (*0-7606-0304-9*) LinguiSystems.
— The Central Auditory Processing Book, Bk. 2. 180p. (J). (gr. 1-8). 1999. spiral bd. 41.95 (*0-7606-0305-7*) LinguiSystems.
— The Central Auditory Processing Book, Bk. 3. 180p. (J). (gr. 1-8). 1999. spiral bd. 41.95 (*0-7606-0306-5*) LinguiSystems.
Mokhesi-Parker, Joyce, jt. auth. see Parker, Peter.
Mokhiber, Russell. Corporate Crime & Violence: Big Business Power & the Abuse of the Public Trust. LC 87-4730. 384p. 1989. pap. 16.00 (*0-87156-608-7*, Pub. by Sierra) Random.
Mokhiber, Russell & Weissman, Robert. Corporate Predators: The Hunt for Mega-Profits & the Attack on Democracy. LC 99-17255. 192p. 1999. pap. 11.21 (*1-56751-158-9*); lib. bdg. 29.95 (*1-56751-159-7*) Common Courage.
Mokhlis, Hassan. Theorie du Tasrif et Traitement du Lexique Chez les Grammairiens Arabes. (Publications Universitaires Europeennes, Serie 28: Vol. 185). (Illus.). 297p. 1997. 57.95 (*3-631-31273-3*) P Lang Pubng.
Mokhtar, G. General History of Africa Vol. II: Ancient Africa. abr. ed. 1990. pap. 16.95 (*0-520-06697-9*, Pub. by U CA Pr) Cal Prin Full Svc.
Mokhtar, G., ed. see UNESCO Staff.
***Mokhtari, Mohand & Marie, Michel.** Engineering Applications of Matlab 5 & Simulink 3. LC 99-89481. 540p. 2000. 59.95 (*1-85233-214-X*) Spr-Verlag.
Mokken, Robert J. A Theory & Procedure of Scale Analysis with Applications in Political Research. (Methods & Models in the Social Sciences Ser.). 353p. 1971. text 50.80 (*90-279-6882-9*) Mouton.
Mokken, Robert J. & Roschar, Frans M. Dutch Parliamentary Election Study, 1971. LC 75-32254. 1975. write for info. (*0-89138-118-X*) ICPSR.
Mokobodzki, G., jt. ed. see Hirsch, F.
Mokoena, A. D. Sesotho Made Easy: A Step-by-Step Guide to Learning & Mastering Sesotho. LC 98-172974. xi, 243p. 1998. write for info. (*0-627-02301-0*) J L Van Schaik.
Mokoena, Kenneth, ed. South Africa & the United States: The Declassified History. 344p. 1994. 35.00 (*1-56584-081-X*, Pub. by New Press NY) Norton.
Mokoena, Kenneth, ed. see National Security Archive Staff & Chadwyck-Healey Staff.
Mokoli, Mondonga M. State Against Development: The Experience of Post-1965 Zaire, 150. LC 91-47973. (Contributions in Afro-American & African Studies: No. 150). 168p. 1992. 49.95 (*0-313-28213-7*, MKD, Greenwood Pr) Greenwood.
— The Transition Towards Democracy in Post-1990 Zaire: Contradictions & Dilemmas. LC 96-53469. 200p. 1997. 69.95 (*1-57309-144-8*, U Pr W Africa); pap. 49.95 (*1-57309-143-X*, U Pr W Africa) Intl Scholars.
Mokonyane, Dan. The Big Sell Out: Recent Developments in South Africa & the Eclipse of the Revolutionary Perspective. 140p. (Orig.). 1995. pap. 11.00 (*0-614-09360-0*, Pub. by Nakong Ya Rena) AK Pr Dist.
— Lessons of Azikwelwa: The Bus Boycott in South Africa. 2nd ed. 119p. (Orig.). 1995. pap. 11.00 (*0-614-09359-7*, Pub. by Nakong Ya Rena) AK Pr Dist.
Mokotoff, Gary. How to Document Victims & Locate Survivors of the Holocaust. LC 95-16574. (Illus.). 208p. (Orig.). 1995. pap. 25.95 (*0-9626373-8-6*) Avotaynu.
Mokotoff, Gary, compiled by. WOWW Companion: A Guide to the Communities Surrounding Central & Eastern European Towns. LC 95-1210. (Monographs). 208p. (Orig.). 1995. text 25.95 (*0-9626373-6-X*) Avotaynu.
***Mokotoff, Gary & Blatt, Warren.** Getting Started in Jewish Genealogy. LC 99-52151. (Illus.). 72p. 1999. pap. text 9.95 (*1-886223-10-6*) Avotaynu.
Mokri, M. Kurdish-Arabic Dictionary: Al-Hadiyati 'l-Hamidiyah. (ARA.). 1975. 29.95 (*0-86685-126-7*) Intl Bk Ctr.
— Lexique Encyclopedique Thematique de L'Iran: Nom Vallee Topoymes. (FRE.). 1998. 69.95 (*0-320-00152-0*) Fr & Eur.
Mokrinskaia, Nina. Moia Zhizn' (My Life) Detstvo v Sibiri, Junost' v Shankkhaie. Valk, Gabriel, ed. LC 90-85815. (RUS., Illus.). 224p. (Orig.). (J). 1991. pap. 16.00 (*0-911971-61-0*) Effect Pub.
Mokros, Hartmut B., ed. Interaction & Identity. (Information & Behavior Ser.: Vol. 5). vii, 452 p. (C). 1995. 49.95 (*1-56000-191-7*) Transaction Pubs.
Mokros, Jan & TERC Staff. Beyond Facts & Flashcards: Exploring Math with Your Kids. LC 95-36594. (Illus.). 133p. (Orig.). 1996. pap. 16.95 (*0-435-08375-9*, 08375) Heinemann.
Mokros, Jan, et al. Beyond Arithmetic: Changing Mathematics in the Elementary Classroom. Cory, Beverly, ed. (Investigations in Number, Data, & Space Ser.). (Illus.). 137p. (Orig.). 1995. pap., teacher ed. 13.95 (*0-86651-846-0*, DS21259) Seymour Pubns.
Mokros, Jan, jt. auth. see Rubin, Andee.
Mokros, Jan, jt. auth. see Russell, Susan J.
Mokry, Benjamin W. Entrepreneurship & Public Policy: Can Government Stimulate Business Start-Ups? LC 87-24934. 169p. 1988. 52.95 (*0-89930-239-4*, MSV/, Quorum Bks) Greenwood.
Mokrzycki, Edmund, jt. ed. see Bryant, Christopher G.
Moktefi, Mokhtar. The Arabs: In the Golden Age. LaRose, Mary K., tr. LC 92-4989. (Peoples of the Past Ser.). (Illus.). 64p. (J). (gr. 4-6). 1992. lib. bdg. 22.40 (*1-56294-201-8*) Millbrook Pr.
— The Arabs: In the Golden Age. LaRose, Mary K., tr. (Peoples of the Past Ser.). (Illus.). 64p. (J). (gr. 4-6). 1996. pap. 7.95 (*0-7613-0098-8*) Millbrook Pr.
— Arabs in the Golden Age. LC 92-4989. (Peoples of the Past Ser.). 1992. 13.15 (*0-606-09010-X*, Pub. by Turtleback) Demco.
Mokuau, Noreen, ed. Handbook of Social Services for Asian & Pacific Islanders. LC 91-11339. 272p. 1991. lib. bdg. 62.95 (*0-313-26116-4*, MKH/, Greenwood Pr) Greenwood.
Mokujiki. Mokujiki: Thirteen Tanka. Pendell, Dale & Tanahaski, Kazuaki, trs. from JPN. 20p. 1988. 6.00 (*1-882623-07-X*) Exiled-Am Pr.
Mokwa, Michael P. & Permut, Steven E., eds. Government Marketing: Theory & Practice. LC 81-308. (Public & Nonprofit Sector Marketing Ser.). 384p. 1981. 65.00 (*0-275-90685-X*, C0685, Praeger Pubs) Greenwood.
Mokwa, Michael P., et al. Marketing the Arts: Praeger Series in Public & Nonprofit Sector Marketing. Permut, Steven E., ed. LC 79-26603. (Praeger Special Studies). 286p. 1980. 59.95 (*0-275-90526-8*, C0526, Praeger Pubs) Greenwood.
Mokwunye, A. Uzo, ed. Alleviating Soil Fertility Constraints to Increase Crop Production in West Africa. (Developments in Plant & Soil Sciences Ser.). 264p. (C). 1991. text 194.00 (*0-7923-1221-X*) Kluwer Academic.
Mokwunye, A. Uzo, jt. ed. see Gerner, Henry.
Mokwunye, Uzo M. & Vlek, Paul L., eds. Management of Nitrogen & Phosphorus Fertilizers in Sub-Saharan Africa. (Developments in Plant & Soil Sciences Ser.). 1986. text 248.00 (*90-247-3312-X*) Kluwer Academic.
Mokyr, J. Twenty-Five Centuries of Technological Change: An Historical Survey, Vol. 35. Lesourne, Jacques & Sonnenschein, Hugo, eds. (Fundamentals of Pure & Applied Economics Ser.: 35). viii, 148p. 1990. pap. text 83.00 (*3-7186-4936-5*) Gordon & Breach.
***Mokyr, Joel.** The British Industrial Revolution: An Economic Assessment. 2nd ed. 368p. (C). 1998. pap. 30.00 (*0-8133-3389-X*, Pub. by Westview) HarpC.
Mokyr, Joel. The Lever of Riches: Technological Creativity & Economic Progress. (Illus.). 368p. 1992. pap. text 16.95 (*0-19-507477-7*) OUP.
— Why Ireland Starved: A Quantitative & Analytical History of the Irish Economy, 1800-1850. (Illus.). 344p. 1985. pap. text 24.95 (*0-04-941014-8*) Routledge.
Mokyr, Joel, ed. The Economics of the Industrial Revolution. LC 84-17757. 250p. (C). 1985. text 56.00 (*0-86598-148-5*) Rowman.
Mol, Annemarie, jt. auth. see Berg, Marc.
Mol, Annemarie, jt. ed. see Berg, Marc.
Mol, Arthur P. The Refinement of Production: Ecological Modernization Theory & the Chemical Industry. 452p. (Orig.). 1996. pap. 49.00 (*90-6224-979-5*, Pub. by Uitgeverij Arkel) LPC InBook.
***Mol, Arthur P. J., et al, eds.** The Voluntary Approach to Environmental Policy: Joint Environmental Approach to Environmental Policy. 280p. 2000. text 60.00 (*0-19-924116-3*) OUP.
***Mol, Arthur P. J. & Sonnenfeld, David, eds.** Ecological Modernisation Around the World: Perspectives & Critical Debates. 250p. 2000. 57.50 (*0-7146-5064-1*, Pub. by F Cass Pubs); pap. 24.50 (*0-7146-8113-X*, Pub. by F Cass Pubs) Intl Spec Bk.
Mol, B. D., jt. ed. see Vincent, C.
Mol, Dick, et al. Mammoths. 1993. pap. 5.95 (*0-9624750-2-5*) L Agenbroad.
Mol, Hans, ed. Western Religion: A Country by Country Sociological Inquiry. (Religion & Reason Ser.: No. 2). (Illus.). 642p. 1972. text 86.15 (*90-279-7004-1*) Mouton.
Mol, Hendrick. Fundamentals of Phonetics Vol. 2: Acoustical Models Generating the Formants of the Vowel Phonemes. LC 70-110954. (Janua Linguarum, Ser. Minor: No. 26). (Illus.). (Orig.). 1970. pap. text 25.40 (*90-279-0715-3*) Mouton.
Mol, J. C., jt. auth. see Ivin, K. J.
***Mol, Jan A. & Clegg, Roger A.** Biology of the Mammary Gland. LC 00-33102. (Advances in Experimental Medicine & Biology Ser.). 2000. write for info. (*0-306-46414-4*) Kluwer Academic.
Mol, Joseph N. & Van der Krol, Alexander R., eds. Antisense Nucleic Acids & Proteins: Fundamentals & Applications. (Illus.). 248p. 1991. text 150.00 (*0-8247-8516-9*) Dekker.
Mol, Pieter L. Grand Promptness. Bloemheuvel, Marente, ed. 324p. 1996. 50.00 (*90-75380-03-8*, Pub. by Artimo Fnd) Dist Art Pubs.
Mola, Dolores Loret De, see Piedra, Joaquin E.
***Molaa, Luca.** The Silk Industry of Renaissance Venice LC 99-43542. 2000. 48.00 (*0-8018-6189-6*) Johns Hopkins.
***Molad, Clarissa Behar.** Women Weaving Webs: Will Women Rule the Internet? King, Judy, ed. 138p. 2000. pap. 14.95 (*0-9675835-0-0*) C B M Pr.
Molaire, Mike F. African-American Who Was Who, Greater Rochester Area: The NeWMillenium Edition. Jones, Marsha, ed. (Illus.). 140p. 1998. pap. 14.95 (*0-9649390-5-3*) Norex Publns.
— African-American Who's Who: Greater Rochester Area. 144p. 1994. 24.95 (*0-9649390-1-0*); pap. 14.95 (*0-9649390-0-2*) Norex Publns.
— African-American Who's Who: Greater Rochester Area. (Illus.). 1994. pap. 24.95 (*1-57087-027-6*) Prof Pr NC.
— African-American Who's Who, Past & Present, Greater Rochester Area. Jones, Marsha, ed. (Illus.). 240p. 1998. pap. 24.95 (*0-9649390-4-5*) Norex Publns.
— African-American Who's Who, Past & Present Greater Rochester Area, the NeWMillenium Edition. Jones, Marsha, ed. (Illus.). 310p. 1998. 54.95 (*0-9649390-3-7*) Norex Publns.
— Shadow of Dreams. 50p. 1996. pap. 7.50 (*0-9649390-2-9*) Norex Publns.
Molak, Vlaska. Fundamentals of Risk Analysis & Risk Management. LC 96-19681. 512p. 1996. lib. bdg. 85.00 (*1-56670-130-9*) Lewis Pubs.
Molan, Christine. Heroic Stories. LC 93-45413. (Story Library). 260p. (J). (gr. 1 up). 1994. pap. 7.95 (*1-85697-983-0*) LKC.
Molan, Michael T. Administrative Law. 18th ed. 368p. 1996. pap. 95.00 (*0-7510-0698-X*, Pub. by HLT Pubns) St Mut.
— Constitutional Law. 344p. 1996. pap. 95.00 (*0-7510-0686-6*, Pub. by HLT Pubns) St Mut.
— Criminal Law. 230p. (C). 1991. 65.00 (*1-85352-697-5*, Pub. by HLT Pubns) St Mut.
— Criminal Law. 460p. 1996. pap. 95.00 (*0-7510-0684-X*, Pub. by HLT Pubns) St Mut.
Molan, Michael T., ed. Administrative Law Cases. 382p. 1996. pap. 95.00 (*0-7510-0664-5*, Pub. by HLT Pubns) St Mut.
— Constitutional & Administrative Law. 235p. (C). 1991. 60.00 (*1-85352-693-2*, Pub. by HLT Pubns); 60.00 (*1-85352-352-6*, Pub. by HLT Pubns); pap. 70.00 (*1-85352-822-6*, Pub. by HLT Pubns) St Mut.
— Constitutional Law Cases. 192p. 1996. pap. 95.00 (*0-7510-0654-8*, Pub. by HLT Pubns) St Mut.
— Criminal Law. 230p. (C). 1991. pap. 65.00 (*1-85352-833-1*, Pub. by HLT Pubns) St Mut.
— Criminal Law Cases. 458p. 1996. pap. 95.00 (*0-7510-0651-3*, Pub. by HLT Pubns) St Mut.
Molana Shah Maghsoud Sadegh Angha. Psalm of the Gods. LC 97-68912. 1997. write for info. (*0-910735-78-6*) MTO Printing & Pubn Ctr.
Moland, Louis, ed. see Voltaire.
Molander, Cecilia. Kvinni i Vietnam. (Kvinna i U-Land Ser.). 144p. 1978. write for info. (*91-7106-132-0*, Pub. by Nordic Africa) Transaction Pubs.
Molander, Christopher, ed. Human Resources at Work. 591p. 1996. 40.00 (*87-16-13441-9*, Pub. by Copenhagen Busn Schl) Bks Intl VA.
Molander, Christopher, jt. ed. see Winterton, Jonathan.
Molander, D. W., ed. Diseases of the Lymphatic System: Diagnosis & Therapy. (Illus.). 500p. 1983. 224.00 (*0-387-90850-1*) Spr-Verlag.
Molander, Per. Society in War: Planning Perspectives. 141p. (Orig.). 1994. pap. text 30.00 (*0-7881-1227-9*) DIANE Pub.
Molander, Roger, et al. Strategic Information Warfare Rising. LC 98-23428. (Illus.). 97p. 1998. pap. text 15.00 (*0-8330-2622-4*, MR-964-OSD) Rand Corp.
Molander, Roger C. & Nichols, Robbie. Who Will Stop the Bomb? A Primer on Nuclear Proliferation. LC 85-10362. 160p. reprint ed. pap. 49.60 (*0-7837-5341-1*, 204508300005) Bks Demand.

Molander, Roger C., et al. Cyberpayments & Money Laundering: Problems & Promise. (Illus.). 125p. 1998. pap. text 15.00 (*0-8330-2616-X*, MR-965-OSTP) Rand Corp.

— Strategic Futures: Evolving Missions for Traditional Strategic Delivery Vehicles. LC 94-16172. (Illus.). xxv, 100p. (Orig.). 1995. pap. text 15.00 (*0-8330-1617-2*, MR-375-DAG) Rand Corp.

— Strategic Information Warfare: A New Face of War. LC 95-53673. 105p. (Orig.). 1996. pap. 15.00 (*0-8330-2352-7*, MR-661) Rand Corp.

Molander, Roger C., jt. auth. see Wilson, Peter A.

Molano, Walter T. The Logic of Privatization: The Case of Telecommunications in the Southern Cone of Latin America, 182. LC 96-18230. (Contributions in Economics & Economic History Ser.). 152p. 1997. 57.95 (*0-313-30055-0*) Greenwood.

Molarsky, Osmond. A Sky Full of Kites. LC 95-41082. (Illus.). 32p. (J). (gr. k-2). 1996. 12.95 (*1-883672-26-0*) Tricycle Pr.

Molas-Gallart, Jordi. Military Production & Innovation in Spain, Vol. 2, Issue 2. LC 92-30353. 212p. 1992. text 101.00 (*3-7186-5280-3*) Gordon & Breach.

Molas Ribalta, Pere. Manual de Historia de Espana Vol. 3: Edad Moderna (1474-1808) 582p. 1989. 125.00 (*84-239-5093-X*) Elliots Bks.

***Molasky, Michael & Rabson, Steve, eds.** Southern Exposure: Modern Japanese Literature from Okinawa. 352p. 2000. text 54.00 (*0-8248-2169-6*); pap. text 27.95 (*0-8248-2300-1*) UH Pr.

***Molasky, Michael S.** The American Occupation of Japan & Okinawa: Literature & Memory LC 99-21088. (Asia's Transformations Ser.). 1999. write for info. (*0-415-19194-7*) Routledge.

***Molasso, Eeva.** The Chocolate Set. (Illus.). 128p. 1999. pap. 12.95 (*1-889668-15-X*) S & D.

Molatore, Gary. Learn by Doing: A Step-by-Step How-To Guide about Multi-Level Marketing. (Illus.). 233p. 1998. pap., wbk. ed. 30.00 (*0-9664144-1-1*) Garys Ideas.

Molau, U. Flora of Ecuador Nos. 127-128 & 130-131: Bixaceae, Cochlospermaceae, Elatinaceae, Caricaceae. (Opera Botanica Series B). 48p. 1983. pap. 15.00 (*91-86344-09-9*, Pub. by Coun Nordic Pubs) Balogh.

Molau, U., jt. auth. see Holmgren, N. H.

Molau, Ulf. Scrophulariaceae Pt. I: Calceolarieae. (Flora Neotropica Monographs: No. 47). 326p. 1988. pap. 59.00 (*0-89327-327-9*) NY Botanical.

Molau, Ulf, jt. ed. see Ollgaard, Benjamin.

Molay, Mollie. Daddy by Christmas. (American Romance Ser.: No. 799). 1999. per. 3.99 (*0-373-16799-7*, 1-16799-8) Harlequin Bks.

— Father in Training: New Arrivals. (American Romance Ser.: No. 776). 1999. per. 3.99 (*0-373-16776-8*, 1-16776-6) Harlequin Bks.

***Molay, Mollie.** The Groom Came C. O. D. (American Romance Ser.). 2000. mass mkt. 4.25 (*0-373-16839-X*, 1-16839-2) Harlequin Bks.

Molay, Mollie. Her Two Husbands: Husband for Hire. (Harlequin American Romance Ser.: No. 597). 1995. per. 3.50 (*0-373-16597-8*) Harlequin Bks.

— Like Father, Like Son. (Harlequin American Romance Ser.: No. 638). 1996. per. 3.75 (*0-373-16638-9*, 1-16638-8) Harlequin Bks.

— Marriage by Mistake. LC 96-2789. (American Romance Ser.). 248p. 1996. per. 3.50 (*0-373-16616-8*, 1-16616-4) Harlequin Bks.

***Molay, Mollie.** Married by Midnight. (American Romance Ser.: Vol. 815). 2000. mass mkt. 4.25 (*0-373-16815-2*) Harlequin Bks.

Molay, Mollie. Nanny & the Bodyguard. (American Romance Ser.: No. 682). 1997. per. 3.75 (*0-373-16682-6*, 1-16682-6) Harlequin Bks.

— Overnight Wife. 1997. per. 3.75 (*0-373-16703-2*, 1-16703-0) Harlequin Bks.

— Wanted: Daddy. (American Romance Ser.). 1998. per. 3.99 (*0-373-16729-6*, 1-16729-5) Harlequin Bks.

Molay, Robert Paul, jt. ed. see Fabozzi, Frank J.

Molcan, Poorman W. Good Thinking: Test-Taking, Problem Solving & Study Skills for Nursing Students. (Illus.). 300p. (C). 1994. pap. text 27.00 (*0-9640556-0-0*) Stat Nursing.

Molchan, Deborah S. Our Secret Feelings: Activities for Children of Alcoholics in Support Groups. 58p. (Orig.). 1989. pap. 10.95 (*1-55691-020-7*, 207) Learning Pubns.

Molchan, James J., jt. auth. see Jewel, Matthew J.

Molchan, Peter, jt. auth. see McNally, Clayton L.

Molchan, Peter, jt. auth. see Sayles, Jonathan S.

Molchanov, A. & Zanadvorov, P. Electrical & Radio Engineering for Physicists. (Illus.). 480p. 1975. 30.00 (*0-8464-0360-9*) Beekman Pubs.

Molchanov, Boris. The Antichrist. (Illus.). 28p. (Orig.). 1987. pap. 2.50 (*0-912927-24-0*, X025) St John Kronstadt.

Molchanov, Ilya S. Limit Theorems for Unions of Random Closed Sets. (Lecture Notes in Mathematics Ser.: Vol. 1561). 1993. 35.95 (*0-387-57393-3*) Spr-Verlag.

Molchanov, S. A. & Woyczynski, Wojbor A., eds. Stochastic Models in Geosystems. LC 96-38280. (IMA Volumes in Mathematics & Its Applications). 460p. 1996. 76.95 (*0-387-94873-2*) Spr-Verlag.

Molchanov, S. A., jt. auth. see Carmona, Rene A.

Molchanov, V., et al. Propedeutics of Children's Diseases. Mir Publishers Staff, tr. from RUS. (Illus.). 392p. (C). 1975. 29.00 (*0-8464-0768-X*) Beekman Pubs.

Molchanov, V. Y., jt. auth. see Magdich, L. N.

Molchanova, I. V., jt. auth. see Kulikov, N. V.

Moldan, Bedrich & Cerny, Jiri, eds. Biogeochemistry of Small Catchments: A Tool for Environmental Research. LC 93-5685. 448p. 1994. 255.00 (*0-471-93723-1*) Wiley.

Moldan, Bedrich & Klarer, Jurg. The Environmental Challenge for Central European Economies in Transition. LC 96-43361. 304p. 1997. 105.00 (*0-471-96609-6*) Wiley.

Moldave, Divie, jt. ed. see Cohn, Waldo E.

Moldave, Kivi, ed. Progress in Nucleic Acid Research & Molecular Biology, Vol. 60. (Illus.). 353p. (C). 1998. text 89.95 (*0-12-540060-8*) Acad Pr.

***Moldave, Kivie.** Progress in Nucleic Acid Research & Molecular Biology. (Progress in Nucleic Acid Research & Molecular Biology Ser.: Vol. 65). 375p. 2000. 99.95 (*0-12-540065-9*) Acad Pr.

— Progress in Nucleic Acid Research & Molecular Biology, Vol. 64, Vol. 64. 392p. 2000. 99.95 (*0-12-540064-0*) Acad Pr.

Moldave, Kivie, ed. Progress in Nucleic Acid Research & Molecular Biology, Vol. 5. (Illus.). 404p. (C). 1997. text 89.95 (*0-12-540058-6*) Morgan Kaufmann.

— Progress in Nucleic Acid Research & Molecular Biology, Vol. 57. (Illus.). 348p. (C). 1997. text 89.00 (*0-12-540057-8*) Morgan Kaufmann.

— Progress in Nucleic Acid Research & Molecular Biology, Vol. 59. (Illus.). 373p. (C). 1997. text 89.95 (*0-12-540059-4*) Morgan Kaufmann.

— Progress in Nucleic Acid Research & Molecular Biology, Vol. 61. (Illus.). 431p. (C). 1998. text 89.95 (*0-12-540061-6*) Acad Pr.

— Progress in Nucleic Acid Research & Molecular Biology, Vol. 62. (Illus.). 407p. 1998. text 89.95 (*0-12-540062-4*) Acad Pr.

***Moldave, Kivie, ed.** Progress in Nucleic Acid Research & Molecular Biology Vol. 63. 350p. 1999. 99.95 (*0-12-540063-2*) Acad Pr.

Moldave, Kivie, jt. ed. see Cohn, Waldo E.

Moldave, Kivie, jt. ed. see Wu, Ray.

Moldaw, Carol. Chalkmarks on Stone. LC 97-78137. 96p. 1998. pap. 12.00 (*1-888809-07-8*) La Alameda Pr.

— Taken from the River: Poems. LC 92-74649. (Series of Poetry & Verse Translation). 48p. (Orig.). 1993. pap. 10.00 (*1-882509-00-5*) Alef Bks.

Molde, B. Danish-Swedish Dictionary: Dansk-Svensk Ordbok. 3rd ed. (DAN & SWE.). 722p. 1980. 125.00 (*0-8288-1675-1*, M4577) Fr & Eur.

Moldea, Dan. A Washington Tragedy: How the Death of Vincent Foster Ignited A Political Firestorm. LC 98-14634. 304p. 1998. 24.95 (*0-89526-382-3*) Regnery Pub.

Moldea, Dan E. The Killing of Robert F. Kennedy: An Investigation of Motive, Means, & Opportunity. 342p. 1997. pap. 14.00 (*0-393-31534-7*) Norton.

Molden, David. Managing with the Power of NLP: Neuro-Linguistic Programming for Competitive Advantage. (Illus.). 225p. (Orig.). 1996. pap. 17.95 (*0-273-62063-0*) F T P-H.

***Molden, David & Symes, Jon.** Realigning for Change: 8 Principles for Successful Change Management in Your Organization. (Illus.). 287p. 1999. pap. 47.50 (*0-273-63381-3*, Pub. by Pitman Pbg) Trans-Atl Phila.

Moldenhauer, Esther R. From Grandma's Corner: Do You Really See & Hear the Outdoors? LC 95-67296. (Illus.). (J). (gr. k-2). 1995. pap. 6.95 (*0-9643937-4-3*) Rutledge Bks.

— From Grandma's Corner: Gardening Your Life. (Illus.). (Orig.). (J). (gr. k-3). 1997. pap. 6.95 (*1-887750-51-7*) Rutledge Bks.

Moldenhauer, Hans & Irvine, Demar B., compiled by. Anton Von Webern: Perspectives. LC 77-9523. (Music Reprint Ser.: 1978). (Illus.). 1978. reprint ed. lib. bdg. 32.50 (*0-306-77518-2*) Da Capo.

Moldenhauer, Janice. Developing Dictionary Skills. 64p. (J). (gr. 3-8). 1979. 8.99 (*0-916456-48-X*, GA120) Good Apple.

Moldenhauer, Joseph J., ed. see Thoreau, Henry David.

Moldenhauer, Kermit, ed. Christian Worship. LC 93-84935. 1993. student ed. 29.99 (*0-8100-0501-8*) Northwest Pub.

— Christian Worship: A Lutheran Hymnal. 960p. 1993. 18.50 (*0-8100-0422-4*, 03N3000) Northwest Pub.

Moldenhauer, William C., pref. Soil Conservation Policies: An Assessment. LC 80-406. 154p. (Orig.). 1980. pap. 7.50 (*0-935734-04-X*) Soil & Water Conserv.

Moldenhauer, William C., jt. ed. see Hudson, N. W.

Moldenhawer, Julius. Voice of Books. LC 70-121491. (Essay Index Reprint Ser.). 1977. 19.95 (*0-8369-1766-9*) Ayer.

Moldenke, Alma L., jt. auth. see Moldenke, Harold N.

Moldenke, Charles E. The Tale of Two Brothers. 60p. 1988. pap. 6.95 (*0-933121-16-4*) Black Classic.

Moldenke, Harold N. A Fifth Summary of the Verbenaceae, Avicenniaceae, Stilbaceae, Dicrastylidaceae, Simphoremaceae, Nyctanthaceae, & Eriocaulaceae of the World As to Valid Taxa, Geographic Distribution & Synonymy, 2 vols. (Illus.). 974p. 1971. pap. text 25.00 (*0-934454-65-5*) Lubrecht & Cramer.

Moldenke, Harold N. & Moldenke, Alma L. Plants of the Bible. 384p. 1986. reprint ed. pap. 11.95 (*0-486-25069-5*) Dover.

Molderings, G. J., jt. ed. see Gothert, M.

Moldeven, Meyer. Military-Civilian Teamwork in Suicide Prevention: Armed Forces Strategies, Procedures & Responsibilities to Implement Their Policy That Suicide Prevention Is Everybody's Business. LC 88-90534. 272p. 1994. pap. 10.95 (*0-9615092-7-9*) M Moldeven.

Moldi-Ravenna, Cristiana, et al. Secret Gardens in Venice. (Illus.). 168p. 1996. 50.00 (*88-7743-169-5*, Pub. by Arsenale Editrice) Antique Collect.

Moldovan, Dan I. Parallel Processing from Applications to Systems. LC 92-44256. 567p. 1993. text 69.95 (*1-55860-254-2*) Morgan Kaufmann.

Moldovan, Russell. Martin Luther King, Jr. A History of His Religious Witness & of His Life. LC 99-27995. 284p. 1999. 74.95 (*1-57309-346-7*); pap. 54.95 (*1-57309-345-9*) Intl Scholars.

Moldoveanu, Serban C. Analytical Pyrolysis of Natural Organic Polymers. LC 98-46335. (Techniques & Instrumentation in Analytical Chemistry Ser.: Vol. 20). 496p. 1998. 284.50 (*0-444-82203-8*) Elsevier.

Moldow, D. Gay & Martinson, Ida M. Home Care for Seriously Ill Children: A Manual for Parents. 2nd ed. 92p. 1991. reprint ed. pap. 7.95 (*0-932321-00-3*) Child Hospice VA.

Moldow, Gloria. Women Doctors in Gilded-Age Washington: Race, Gender, & Professionalization. LC 86-19251. (Women in American History Ser.). (Illus.). 262p. 1987. text 27.50 (*0-252-01379-4*) U of Ill Pr.

Moldowan, J. Michael, jt. auth. see Yen, T. F.

***Moldrem, Leverne J.** So, Ya Wanna Be a Cowboy. LC 00-91067. (Illus.). 2000. pap. 8.00 (*0-9649498-4-9*) Flying M Pr.

— Tiger Tales: An Anecdotal History of the Flying Tiger Line. LC 00-131193. 2000. 35.00 (*0-9649498-7-3*) Flying M Pr.

Moldstad, John A., Jr. Predestination: Bible Study - PBT. 1998. 37.99 (*0-8100-0798-3*, 22N0906) Northwest Pub.

— Predestination: Chosen in Christ. LC 97-66994. (People's Bible Teachings Ser.). 125 p. 1997. 8.99 (*0-8100-0752-5*) Northwest Pub.

Moldstad, Joslyn W. At Home with Jesus. LC 92-80392. 216p. (Orig.). (J). (ps-9). 1992. pap. 10.99 (*0-8100-0428-3*, 06N0693) Northwest Pub.

Moldvay, Albert & Fabian, Erika. The Travel Photographer's Handbook: Professional Techniques - The National Geographic Way. (Illus.). 104p. (Orig.). 1995. pap., spiral bd. 14.95 (*0-9638417-2-6*) Eriako Assocs.

Moldvay, Albert, jt. auth. see Fabian, Erika.

Moldvay, Tom. Chateau D'Amervilles. 1981. 5.50 (*0-394-51838-1*) Random.

— Star Frontiers Reference Scroll. 1983. 5.50 (*0-394-53156-6*) Random.

Moldvay, Tom, jt. auth. see Acres, M.

Mole, Dale M., jt. auth. see Mole, Robert L.

Mole, David, ed. Managing the New Hong Kong Economy. (Illus.). 162p. 1997. pap. text 32.00 (*0-19-590042-1*) OUP.

Mole, Elsie H. A Christmas Tree from Puddin' Stone Hill. (Illus.). 36p. (J). (ps-8). 1985. 6.95 (*0-920806-74-0*, Pub. by Penumbra Pr) U of Toronto Pr.

Mole, Gary D. Levinas, Blanchot, Jabes: Figures of Estrangement. LC 97-12250. (CrossCurrents). 240p. 1997. 49.95 (*0-8130-1505-7*) U Press Fla.

Mole, Gary D., tr. see Levinas, Emmanuel.

***Mole, Graham.** Managing Management Development. LC 99-88205. (Managing Work & Organizations Ser.). 2000. pap. write for info. (*0-335-20134-2*) Taylor & Francis.

Mole, J. Hot Air. 1996. mass mkt. 7.95 (*0-340-65701-4*, Pub. by Hodder & Stought Ltd) Trafalgar.

Mole, John. Copycat. LC 96-44224. (Illus.). 32p. (J). (ps-k). 1997. 15.95 (*0-7534-5008-9*) LKC.

— Mind Your Manners: Managing Business Cultures in Europe. 236p. 1996. reprint ed. pap. 17.95 (*1-85788-085-4*) Nicholas Brealey.

— The Wrongful Dismissal Handbook. 216p. 1990. pap. 37.00 (*0-409-88842-7*, MICHIE) LEXIS Pub.

***Mole, Kenneth.** Easy PC: How to Use Your First Computer. (Illus.). 128p. 2001. pap. 6.95 (*0-7160-2130-7*, Pub. by Elliot RW Bks) Midpt Trade.

Mole, Peter. HE Acupuncture: Energy Balancing for Body, Mind & Spirit. (Health Essentials Ser.). (Illus.). 128p. 1997. pap. 9.95 (*1-86204-043-5*, Pub. by Element MA) Penguin Putnam.

— HE Acupuncture: For Health, Vitality & First Aid. (Health Essentials Ser.). 1993. pap. 9.95 (*1-85230-319-0*, Pub. by Element MA) Penguin Putnam.

Mole, Robert L. & Mole, Dale M. For God & Country. LC 98-66442. 200p. 1998. per. 10.00 (*1-57258-138-7*) Teach Servs.

Mole, S., jt. auth. see Waterman, P.

Mole, Veronica & Elliot, Dave. Enterprising Innovation: Technology for People. 220p. 1992. 47.50 (*0-86187-577-X*, Pub. by P P Pubs) Cassell & Continuum.

***Molea, Joseph.** Duck Blood Soup. LC 99-69765. 192p. 2001. pap. 13.95 (*0-88739-332-2*) Creat Arts Bk.

Moleah, Alfred T. Namibia: The Struggle for Liberation. 341p. (Orig.). 1983. 22.95 (*0-913255-00-9*); pap. 12.95 (*0-913255-01-7*) Disa Press Inc.

— South Africa: Colonialism, Apartheid & African Dispossession. 550p. (Orig.). 1993. 45.00 (*0-913255-02-5*); pap. 35.00 (*0-913255-03-3*); text 45.00 (*0-685-67439-8*); pap. text 35.00 (*0-685-67441-X*); lib. bdg. 45.00 (*0-685-67438-X*) Disa Press Inc.

Moleas, Wendy. The Development of the Greek Language. (Studies in Modern Greek). 118p. (Orig.). (C). 1989. pap. text 16.00 (*0-89241-486-3*); lib. bdg. 25.00 (*0-89241-485-5*) Caratzas.

***Molefi Kete Asante.** The Egyptian Philosophers: Ancient African Voices from Imhotep to Akhenaten. 1999. pap. 14.95 (*0-913543-66-7*) African Am Imag.

Molen, Art. Take Two & Hit to Right. 1976. 21.95 (*0-8488-1575-0*) Amereon Ltd.

Molen, Lise Van der, see Van der Molen, Lise, compiled by.

***Molen, Rami der.** A Hieroglyphic Dictionary of Egyptian Coffin Texts. LC 99-87059. (Problem der Hagyptologie Ser.). 900p. 2000. 245.00 (*90-04-11654-0*) Brill Academic Pubs.

Molen, Ron. My New Life. LC 96-14254. 240p. (Orig.). 1996. pap. 14.95 (*1-56085-073-6*) Signature Bks.

Molenaar, A. A., jt. ed. see Francken, L.

Molenaar, Cor. Interactive Marketing. Knegt, John, tr. from DUT. 238p. 1995. 83.95 (*0-566-07713-2*, Pub. by Gower) Ashgate Pub Co.

Molenaar, Dee. The Challenge of Rainier. LC 79-14923. (Illus.). 384p. 1979. pap. 18.95 (*0-916890-70-8*) Mountaineers.

Molenaar, Erik J. Coastal State Jurisdiction over Vessel-source Pollution. LC 98-49924. (International Environmental Law And Policy Ser.). xx, 632p. 1998. 187.00 (*90-411-1127-1*) Kluwer Law Intl.

Molenaar, Ivo W., jt. ed. see Fischer, Gerhard H.

Molenaar, Martien. Introduction to the Theory of Spatial Object Modelling for GIS. LC 99-206899. 1998. 95.00 (*0-7484-0775-8*); pap. 44.95 (*0-7484-0774-X*) Taylor & Francis.

Molenaar, Peter C., jt. ed. see Newell, Karl M.

Molenberghs, G., jt. auth. see Verbeke, G.

Molenberghs, Geert, jt. auth. see Verbeke, Geert.

Molenda, Michael. What's That Sound? The Audible Audio Dictionary. 1997. pap. 14.95 incl. audio compact disk (*0-7935-6853-6*) H Leonard.

***Molenda, Sandee.** Parrotlet: An Owner's Guide to a Happy Healthy Pet. (Illus.). 2000. 12.99 (*0-7645-6171-5*) IDG Bks.

Molendijk, Arie L. & Pels, Peter. Religion in the Making. LC 98-34510. (Studies in the History of Religions). 1998. 109.00 (*90-04-11239-1*) Brill Academic Pubs.

Molendijk, Arie L., jt. auth. see Platvoet, Jan.

Moler, Cleve B., jt. auth. see Forsythe, George E.

Moler, Cleve B., ed. see Hill, David R.

Moler, Jeffrey L., jt. ed. see Dorko, Ernest A.

Moler, Kenneth L. Jane Austen's Art of Allusion. LC 68-12704. 240p. reprint ed. pap. 74.40 (*0-7837-1470-X*, 205716500017) Bks Demand.

— Pride & Prejudice: A Study in Artistic Economy. (Twayne's Masterwork Studies: No. 21). 144p. 1988. 25.95 (*0-8057-7983-3*, Twyne); pap. 18.00 (*0-8057-8032-7*, Twyne) Mac Lib Ref.

Moler, Lee. Bone Music. LC 98-46826. 320p. 1999. 23.00 (*0-684-84355-2*) Scribner.

Moler, Paul E. & Ashton, Ray E., Jr., eds. Rare & Endangered Biota of Florida Vol. 3: Amphibians & Reptiles. (Illus.). 272p. 1992. 49.95 (*0-8130-1141-8*) U Press Fla.

— Rare & Endangered Biota of Florida Vol. 3: Amphibians & Reptiles, Vol. 3. (Illus.). 272p. 1992. pap. 29.95 (*0-8130-1142-6*) U Press Fla.

***Moler, Robert E.** If I Were a Halloween Monster. (Illus.). 16p. (J). (gr. 2-5). 2000. 13.95 (*0-316-57778-2*) Little.

Molera, Antonio M. Diccionario Anadaluz, 4 vols. (SPA.). 2000p. 1980. 175.00 (*0-7859-3708-0*, 8430027696) Fr & Eur.

— Diccionario Anadaluz, Vol. 1. (SPA.). 500p. 1980. 45.00 (*0-7859-6460-6*) Fr & Eur.

— Diccionario Andaluz, Vol. 2. (SPA.). 500p. 1980. 45.00 (*0-7859-5880-0*, 8430027718) Fr & Eur.

— Diccionario Andaluz, Vol. 3. (SPA.). 500p. 1980. 45.00 (*0-7859-5881-9*, 8430027726) Fr & Eur.

— Diccionario Andaluz, Vol. 4. (SPA.). 500p. 1980. 45.00 (*0-7859-5882-7*, 8430027734) Fr & Eur.

Molera, E. J., jt. auth. see Eldridge, Zoeth S.

Molero, Jose, ed. Technological Innovations, Multinational Corporations & the New International Competitiveness: The Case of Intermediate Countries, Vol. 2. 336p. 1996. text 35.00 (*3-7186-5685-X*, Harwood Acad Pubs) Gordon & Breach.

Moles, Alistair. Nietzsche's Philosophy of Nature & Cosmology. (American University Studies: Philosophy: Ser. V, Vol. 80). XVII, 435p. (C). 1990. text 35.95 (*0-8204-0970-7*) P Lang Pubng.

Moles, E. & Peacock, N. A. The Seventeenth Century: Directions Old & New. 144p. 1993. 49.00 (*0-85261-344-X*, Pub. by Univ of Glasgow) St Mut.

Moles, J. L., ed. see Plutarch.

Moles, Marci. Loving Joseph Smith Out of Hell. LC 94-96578. 188p. 1994. pap. write for info. (*1-886389-02-0*) Inside Job.

Moles, Oliver C. Reaching All Families: Creating Family-Friendly Schools. 59p. 1996. pap. 4.50 (*0-16-063583-7*) USGPO.

Moles, Oliver C., ed. Reaching All Families: Creating Family-Friendly Schools. (Illus.). 53p. 1997. pap. text 20.00 (*0-7881-4702-1*) DIANE Pub.

Moles, Oliver C., ed. see Funkhouser, Janie E. & Gonzales, Miriam R.

Moles, Peter & Terry, Nicholas. The Handbook of International Financial Terms. LC 96-31008. (Illus.). 684p. 1997. text 110.00 (*0-19-828885-9*) OUP.

— The Handbook of International Financial Terms. LC 99-21235. (Illus.). 685p. 1999. pap. 45.00 (*0-19-829481-6*) OUP.

Moles, Randall C. Ending Head & Neck Pain: The TMJ Connection. (Illus.). 200p. (Orig.). 1989. pap. 12.95 (*0-925004-02-2*) Randall Moles.

Moleski, Joanne E. Mirrors of Fate: A Journey into Past Lives. (Illus.). 158p. (Orig.). 1988. pap. 9.95 (*1-882053-00-1*) Tamaris Pub Hse.

***Moleski, Martin X.** Personal Catholicism. LC 99-41885. 2000. 64.95 (*0-8132-0964-1*) Cath U Pr.

Molesworth, Candy T., jt. auth. see Molesworth, J. T.

***Molesworth, Carl.** P-40 Warhawk Aces of the CBI. (Aircraft of the Aces Ser.: Vol. 35). (Illus.). 96p. 2000. pap. 17.95 (*1-84176-079-X*, 130585AE, Pub. by Osprey) Motorbooks Intl.

— Sharks over China: The 23rd Fighter Group in World War II. 1999. pap. 17.95 (*1-57488-225-2*) Brasseys.

Molesworth, Carol, jt. auth. see Suisman, Charles.

Molesworth, Charles. Donald Barthelme's Fiction: The Ironist Saved from Drowning. LC 81-69833. (Literary Frontiers Editions Ser.). 96p. 1982. pap. 12.95 (*0-8262-0338-8*) U of Mo Pr.

— Marianne Moore: A Literary Life. 472p. 1991. reprint ed. pap. text 20.00 (1-55553-115-6) NE U Pr.

Molesworth, J. T. English-Marathi Dictionary. (ENG & MAR.). 864p. 1981. 75.00 (0-8288-1152-0, M14469) Fr & Eur.

— English-Marathi Dictionary. 2nd ed. (ENG & MAR.). 1990. 45.00 (0-7859-8958-7) Fr & Eur.

— Marathi English Dictionary. 952p. 1989. 95.00 (0-8288-8470-6, F27270) Fr & Eur.

Molesworth, J. T. & Molesworth, Candy T. Marathi English Dictionary. 1986. reprint ed. 50.00 (0-8364-1702-X, Pub. by Popular Prakashan) S Asia.

Molesworth, Melanie. Junk Style. LC 97-31725. 144p. 1998. 27.50 (1-55670-653-7) Stewart Tabori & Chang.

Molesworth, Ralph. Introduction to Assembly Language for the TI Home Computer. Davis, Steve, ed. 140p. 16.95 (0-317-13069-2) P-H.

Molesworth, W., ed. see Hobbes, Thomas.

Moleta, Vincent. From Francis to Giotto. 120p. 1983. 20.00 (0-8199-0853-3, Frncscn Herld) Franciscan Pr.

Molett, William E. Robert Peary & Matthew Henson at the North Pole. (Illus.). xiii, 123p. 1996. 19.95 (0-9651653-0-2) Ky Color Pub.

Molette, Barbara, jt. auth. see Molette, Carlton.

Molette, Barbara J., jt. auth. see Molette, Carlton W.

Molette, Carlton & Molette, Barbara. Rosalee Pritchett. 1972. pap. 3.25 (0-8222-0968-3) Dramatists Play.

Molette, Carlton W. & Molette, Barbara J. Black Theatre: Premise & Presentation. rev. ed. LC 86-50584. 266p. (C). 1992. pap. text 20.00 (0-932269-94-X) Wyndham Hall.

— Black Theatre: Premise & Presentation. 2nd rev. ed. LC 86-50584. 266p. (C). 1992. text 32.00 (1-55605-212-X) Wyndham Hall.

Moley, J. F. Molecular Genetics in Surgical Oncology. (Medical Intelligence Unit Ser.). 115p. 1994. 99.00 (1-879702-18-5) Landes Bioscience.

Moley, Raymond. After Seven Years. LC 71-168390. (FDR & the Era of the New Deal Ser.). 446p. 1972. reprint ed. lib. bdg. 55.00 (0-306-70327-0) Da Capo.

— Daniel O'Connell: Nationalism Without Violence. LC 73-93142. xxi, 246p. 1974. 30.00 (0-8232-0977-6) Fordham.

— The Hays Office. LC 73-160241. (Moving Pictures Ser.). 266p. 1971. reprint ed. lib. bdg. 31.95 (0-89198-042-3) Ozer.

— Our Criminal Courts. LC 74-3835. (Criminal Justice in America Ser.). 1974. reprint ed. 25.95 (0-405-06181-1) Ayer.

— Our Criminal Courts. xxiii, 271p. 1997. reprint ed. 88.50 (1-56169-341-3) Gaunt.

— Politics & Criminal Prosecution. LC 73-19161. (Politics & People Ser.). 256p. 1974. reprint ed. 20.95 (0-405-05883-7) Ayer.

— Twenty-Seven Masters of Politics, in a Personal Perspective. (History - United States Ser.). 276p. 1993. reprint ed. lib. bdg. 79.00 (0-7812-4812-4) Rprt Serv.

***Molfese, Dennis L.** Temperament & Personality Development Across the Life Span. LC 00-28821. 2000. write for info. (0-8058-3338-2) L Erlbaum Assocs.

Molfese, Dennis L. & Segalowitz, Sidney J., eds. Brain Lateralization in Children: Developmental Implications. LC 88-11269. 612p. 1988. lib. bdg. 80.00 (0-89862-719-2) Guilford Pubns.

***Molfino, Alessandra M.** Poldi Pezzoli Museum in Milan. 1999. pap. text 30.00 (88-422-0827-2) Allemandi.

Molgaard. Veterinarian's Anatomy & Physiology. (Agriculture Ser.). 1998. teacher ed. 12.00 (0-8273-7872-6); teacher ed., lab manual ed. 12.00 (0-8273-7874-2) Delmar.

— Veterinarian's Anatomy & Physiology Lab Manual. (Agriculture Ser.). 1998. lab manual ed. 21.00 (0-8273-7873-4) Delmar.

Molgaard, Craig, ed. Neuroepidemiology: Theory & Method. (Illus.). 381p. 1993. text 27.00 (0-12-504220-5) Acad Pr.

Molgard, Bette. Best Baptism Ever: Jake's Story. 1993. pap. 4.95 (0-88494-880-3) Bookcraft Inc.

— The Best Baptism Ever: Jenny's Story. 1993. pap. 4.95 (0-88494-868-4) Bookcraft Inc.

Molgard, Bette, jt. auth. see Molgard, Max.

Molgard, Max & Molgard, Bette. The Lord Looketh on the Heart. 1998. 13.95 (1-57008-438-6) Bookcraft Inc.

Molgard, Max H., jt. auth. see Burgess, Allan K.

Molhan, Suzanne P. & Kavanagh, Jack. A Mother's Mission: The Sue Molhan Story. (Illus.). 195p. 1996. 22.95 (0-912083-86-7) Diamond Communications.

Molho, Anthony. Florentine Public Finances in the Early Renaissance, 1400-1433. LC 70-168431. (Historical Monographs: No. 65). (Illus.). 244p. 1971. 20.00 (0-674-30665-1) HUP.

— Marriage Alliance in Late Medieval Florence. LC 93-8470. (Harvard Historical Studies: No. 117). (Illus.). 472p. 1994. text 59.00 (0-674-55070-6) HUP.

Molho, Anthony & Wood, Gordon S. Imagined Histories: American Historians Interpret the Past. LC 98-10246. 512p. 1998. text 65.00 (0-691-05810-5, Pub. by Princeton U Pr); pap. text 24.95 (0-691-05811-3, Pub. by Princeton U Pr) Cal Prin Full Svc.

Molho, Emanuel. The Dictionary Catalogue. LC 80-67876. 250p. 1988. 14.95 (0-8288-0150-9) Fr & Eur.

Molho, Ian. The Economics of Information: Lying & Cheating in Markets & Organizations. LC 97-2335. 220p. 1997. pap. text 36.95 (0-631-20666-3) Blackwell Pubs.

Molho, M., ed. see Molho, Maurice.

Molho, Maurice. Romans Picaresques Espagnols. Molho, M., ed. (FRE.). 1120p. 1968. lib. bdg. 95.00 (0-7859-3786-2, 2070104842) Fr & Eur.

— Semantique et Poetique. (Coll. Ducros, Ser.). 9.95 (0-685-36656-1) Fr & Eur.

Molholm, Kurt, et al, eds. Government Information & Policy: Changing Roles in a New Administration. (1994 NFAIS Report). 125p. (Orig.). 1994. pap. 75.00 (0-942308-44-1) NFAIS.

Molholt, Pat, jt. ed. see Petersen, Toni.

Molian, David & Leleux, Benoit. European Casebook Entrepreneurship & New Ventures. 256p. 1996. pap. 46.00 (0-13-310681-0) P-H.

Molian, S. Mechanism Design: The Practical Kinematics & Dynamics of Machinery. 2nd ed. LC 97-17649. 248p. 1997. 89.00 (0-08-042264-0, Pergamon Pr) Elsevier.

Moliere. L' Amour Medecin. (FRE.). 128p. 1992. reprint ed. pap. 8.95 (0-685-73252-5) Fr & Eur.

— Amphitryon. Wilbur, Richard, tr. from FRE. 1995. pap. 5.25 (0-8222-1439-3) Dramatists Play.

— Amphitryon. (FRE.). 1973. 7.95 (0-8288-9933-9, F39870) Fr & Eur.

— Amphitryon. Wilbur, Richard, tr. & afterword by by. 160p. 1995. 20.00 (0-15-100156-1); pap. 12.00 (0-15-600211-6) Harcourt.

— Amphitryon: George Dandin. L'Avare. (Folio Ser.: No. 333). (FRE.). 1973. pap. 9.95 (2-07-036333-3) Schoenhof.

— Amphitryon: George Dandin; L'Avare. (FRE.). 1973. pap. 12.95 (0-7859-2873-1) Fr & Eur.

— Amphytrion. Mandel, Oscar, tr. from FRE. LC 76-41934. (Illus.). 1977. 7.50 (0-914502-03-4) Spectrum Prods.

— L' Avare. 1966. pap. 2.95 (0-685-11020-6) Fr & Eur.

— L' Avare. 210p. 1969. write for info. (0-7859-5278-0) Fr & Eur.

— L' Avare. (FRE.). 1986. pap. 10.95 (0-7859-3130-9) Fr & Eur.

— L' Avare. (FRE.). (C). 1985. pap. 7.95 (0-8442-1988-6, VF1988-6) NTC Contemp Pub Co.

— L' Avare, le Misanthrope, le Bourgeois... unabridged ed. (FRE.). pap. 5.95 (2-87714-137-3, Pub. by Bookking Intl) Distribks Inc.

— Le Bourgeois Gentilhomme. Thoraval, Jean, ed. (FRE.). 64p. 1975. 7.95 (0-7859-0050-0, FC1413) Fr & Eur.

— Le Bourgeois Gentilhomme. (FRE.). (C). 1963. pap. 9.95 (0-8442-1989-4, VF1989-4) NTC Contemp Pub Co.

— Le Bourgeois Gentilhomme. Les Femmes Savantes. Le Malade Imaginaire. (FRE.). 1973. pap. 12.95 (0-7859-2874-X, 2070363341) Fr & Eur.

— Le Bourgeois Gentilhomme. Les Femmes Savantes. Le Malade Imaginaire. (Folio Ser.: No. 334). (FRE.). 448p. 1973. pap. 10.95 (2-07-036334-1) Schoenhof.

— The Bourgeois Gentleman. Cohen, Robert, tr. from FRE. (Classics Ser.). 52p. 1996. pap. 4.50 (1-57514-170-1, 1154) Encore Perform Pub.

***Moliere.** The Bourgeois Gentleman. Sahlins, Bernard, tr. & adapted by by. LC 00-20882. (Plays for Performance Ser.). (Illus.). 96p. 2000. 15.95 (1-56663-303-6, Pub. by I R Dee); pap. 7.95 (1-56663-304-4, Pub. by I R Dee) Natl Bk Netwk.

Moliere. La Critique de l'Ecole des Femmes. (FRE.). 1985. pap. 8.95 (0-7859-4648-9) Fr & Eur.

— The Doctor in Spite of Himself. 51p. 1981. pap. 5.50 (0-87129-742-6, D36) Dramatic Pub.

— The Doctor in Spite of Himself. Landes, William-Alan, ed. Landes, S. H., tr. LC 97-49023. 55p. 1998. pap. 7.00 (0-88734-812-2) Players Pr.

— Doctor in Spite of Himself: One-Act Translation. Clark, I. E., tr. (Illus.). 41p. 1969. pap. 3.25 (0-88680-040-4) I E Clark.

— Doctor in Spite of Himself: One-Act Translation - Director's Script. Clark, I. E., tr. (Illus.). 41p. 1969. pap. 10.00 (0-88680-041-2) I E Clark.

— The Doctor in Spite of Himself & the Bourgeois Gentleman. Bermel, Albert, tr. (Actor's Moliere Ser.: Vol. 2). 128p. 1987. pap. 6.95 (0-936839-77-5) Applause Theatre Bk Pubs.

— Dom Juan. (Class. Ill. Hachette Ser.). (FRE.). pap. 7.95 (0-8288-9936-3, F39936) Fr & Eur.

Dom Juan, ou, Le Festin de Pierre. Howarth, W. D., ed. (Bristol French Texts Ser.). (FRE.). 144p. 1992. reprint ed. 16.95 (0-631-00580-3) Blackwell Pubs.

— Don Juan. McLeish, Kenneth, tr. (Nick Hern Books, Drama Classics). 96p. 1997. pap. 6.95 (1-85459-356-0, Pub. by N Hern Bks) Theatre Comm.

— Don Juan: And Other Plays. Maclean, Ian, ed. & tr. by. Graveley, George, tr. 416p. 1998. pap. 8.95 (0-19-283551-3) OUP.

— Don Juan/El Tartufo. 1998. pap. 8.95 (84-320-4883-6) Planeta.

— Ecole des Femmes. (Coll. Class. du Theatre). (FRE.). 1964. pap. 7.95 (0-8288-9937-1, F39942) Fr & Eur.

— L' Ecole des Femmes. (FRE.). 1986. pap. 10.95 (0-7859-3131-7) Fr & Eur.

— L' Ecole des Femmes. (FRE.). (C). 1970. pap. 7.95 (0-8442-1943-6, VF1943-6) NTC Contemp Pub Co.

— L' Ecole des Femmes: La Critique de l'Ecole des Femmes. (FRE.). 1985. pap. 16.95 (0-7859-2911-8) Fr & Eur.

— L' Ecole des Maris. L'Ecole des Femmes. La Critique de l'Ecole des Femmes. L'Impromptu de Versailles. (Folio Ser.: No. 1688). (FRE.). 1985. pap. 12.95 (2-07-037688-5) Schoenhof.

— Eight Plays by Moliere. 27.95 (0-88411-448-1) Amereon Ltd.

— Les Facheux. (Coll. Le Theatre et les Peintres). 595.00 (0-685-34235-2) Fr & Eur.

— Les Femmes Savantes. (ENG & FRE.). pap. 7.95 (0-8288-9938-X, F39956) Fr & Eur.

— Les Femmes Savantes, les Precieuses... unabridged ed. (FRE.). pap. 5.95 (2-87714-148-9, Pub. by Bookking Intl) Distribks Inc.

— Les Fourberies de Scapin. (FRE., Illus.). 1965. pap. 7.95 (0-8288-9939-8, F39974) Fr & Eur.

— Les Fourberies de Scapin: L'Amour Medicin: Le Medicin Malgre Lui. (FRE.). 1978. pap. 12.95 (0-7859-3389-1) Fr & Eur.

— Les Fourberies de Scapin/Le Malade Imaginaire/Le Medecin Malgre Lui. unabridged ed. (FRE.). Date not set. reprint ed. pap. 7.95 (2-87714-342-2, Pub. by Bookking Intl) Distribks Inc.

— George Dandin. (Coll. Petits Class. Bordas). (FRE.). pap. 7.95 (0-8288-9940-1, F39980) Fr & Eur.

— George Dandin: Amphitryon. 1987. pap. 10.95 (0-7859-3140-6, 2253042862) Fr & Eur.

— The Hypochondriac. Sorrell, Martin, tr. 128p. 1994. pap. 6.00 (1-85459-197-5, Pub. by N Hern Bks) Theatre Comm.

— The Imaginary Cuckold. Wilbur, Richard, tr. 1993. pap. 5.25 (0-8222-1331-1) Dramatists Play.

— Les Incompatibles: Montpellier, Sixteen Fifty-Five. (FRE.). 32p. 1969. pap. 19.95 (0-7859-5386-8) Fr & Eur.

— La Jalousie du Barbouille. 5.95 (0-686-54770-5) Fr & Eur.

— La Jalousie du Barbouille et G. Dandin. Peacock, N. A., ed. (Exeter French Texts Ser.: Vol. 55). (FRE.). 128p. Date not set. pap. text 19.95 (0-85989-211-5, Pub. by Univ Exeter Pr) Northwestern U Pr.

— Joguenet Ou les Viellards Dupes: Geneve, 1868. 150p. 1968. 24.00 (0-686-54771-3) Fr & Eur.

— The Kiltartan Moliere. Gregory, Augusta, tr. LC 70-175879. 231p. 1972. reprint ed. 25.95 (0-405-08793-4, Pub. by Blom Pubns) Ayer.

— The Learned Ladies. Wilbur, Richard, tr. from FRE. 1977. pap. 5.25 (0-8222-0648-X) Dramatists Play.

— The Learned Ladies. Waller, A. R., tr. (Drama Classics Ser.). 80p. 1996. pap. 6.95 (1-85459-375-7, Pub. by N Hern Bks) Theatre Comm.

— Le Malade Imaginaire. (Coll. Class. du Theatre). (FRE., Illus.). 1964. pap. 7.95 (0-8288-9941-X, F39998) Fr & Eur.

— Le Medecin Malgre Lui. (Univers des Lettres Bordas Ser.). (FRE.). 1964. pap. 7.95 (0-8288-9942-8, F10008) Fr & Eur.

Moliere. The Misanthrope. Date not set. lib. bdg. 14.95 (0-8488-1655-2) Amereon Ltd.

Moliere. The Misanthrope. Wilbur, Richard, tr. from FRE. 1965. pap. 5.25 (0-8222-1389-3) Dramatists Play.

— The Misanthrope. LC 96-172587. 98p. 1996. pap. 10.95 (0-571-17909-6) Faber & Faber.

— The Misanthrope. Wall, Charles H., tr. from FRE. LC 93-16948. 1993. pap. 7.00 (0-88734-267-1) Players Pr.

— Le Misanthrope. 49.95 incl. audio (0-685-21217-3); pap. 7.95 (0-685-34239-5) Fr & Eur.

— Le Misanthrope. (Coll. Class. du Theatre). (FRE., Illus.). 1965. pap. 7.95 (0-8288-9943-6, F40016) Fr & Eur.

— Le Misanthrope. (Absolute Classics Ser.). 92p. 1998. pap. 12.95 (1-84002-032-6, Pub. by Oberon Bks Ltd) Theatre Comm.

— The Misanthrope. (Thrift Editions Ser.). 64p. 1992. reprint ed. pap. 1.00 (0-486-27065-3) Dover.

— The Misanthrope & Other Plays. Frame, Donald M., tr. (Orig.). 1968. mass mkt. 6.95 (0-451-52415-2, CE1721, Sig Classics) NAL.

***Moliere.** Misanthrope & Other Plays: A New Selection. (Penguin Classics Ser.). 320p. 2000. pap. 8.95 (0-14-044730-X, Penguin Bks) Viking Penguin.

— The Miser. 1942. 5.50 (0-87129-454-0, M28) Dramatic Pub.

Moliere. The Miser. 1993. pap. 5.25 (0-8222-1341-9) Dramatists Play.

— The Miser & George Dandin: Two Plays. Bermel, Albert, tr. (Actor's Moliere Ser.: Vol. 1). 176p. 1987. pap. 6.95 (0-936839-75-9) Applause Theatre Bk Pubs.

— The Miser & Other Plays. Wood, John, tr. Incl. Don Juan. 1953. Love's the Best Doctor. 1953. That Scoundrel Scapin. 1953. Would-Be Gentleman. 1953. (Classics Ser.). 288p. (Orig.). (YA). (gr. 9 up). 1953. Set pap. 8.95 (0-14-044036-4, Penguin Classics) Viking Penguin.

***Moliere.** Miser & Other Plays: A New Selection. (Penguin Classics Ser.). 336p. 2000. pap. 8.95 (0-14-044728-8, Penguin Bks) Viking Penguin.

— Moliere - Four Plays: The Bourgeois Gentleman, the Doctor in Spite of Himself, the Miser, the Affected Damsels. Caso, Adolph, ed. Milo Pergolizzi, Carl, tr. from FRE. LC 99-18379. 368p. 1999. pap. 19.95 (0-8283-2038-1) Branden Bks.

Moliere. Monologues from Moliere. Dotterer, Dick, ed. & tr. by. from FRE. 80p. (Orig.). 1991. pap. 9.95 (0-940669-11-0, D-22) Dramaline Pubns.

— Oeuvres Completes, 11 tomes, Set. Meyer, ed. (Illus.). 850.00 (0-685-34234-4) Fr & Eur.

— Oeuvres Completes, Vol. 1. deluxe ed. Couton, Georges, ed. (FRE.). 1488p. 1972. 115.00 (0-7859-3765-X, 2070103609) Fr & Eur.

— Oeuvres Completes, Vol. 2. Couton, Georges, ed. (FRE.). 1584p. 1988. lib. bdg. 110.00 (0-7859-3766-8, 2070103617) Fr & Eur.

— Oeuvres Completes, 2 tomes, Vol. 2. deluxe ed. Courton, ed. (Pleiade Ser.). (FRE.). 1933. 72.95 (2-07-010361-7) Schoenhof.

— One-Act Comedies of Moliere: Seven Plays, Vol. 4. Bermel, Albert, tr. from FRE. & intro. by. 192p. 1991. reprint ed. pap. 9.95 (1-55783-109-2) Applause Theatre Bk Pubs.

— Precieuses Ridicules. (FRE.). 1965. pap. 7.95 (0-8288-9944-4, F40042) Fr & Eur.

Scapin & Don Juan. Bermel, Albert, tr. (Actor's Moliere Ser.: Vol. 3). 1987. pap. 6.95 (0-936839-80-5) Applause Theatre Bk Pubs.

— The School for Husbands. Wilbur, Richard, tr. 1991. pap. 5.25 (0-8222-0998-5) Dramatists Play.

— The School for Husbands. Wilbur, Richard, tr. 1992. 18.95 (0-15-179577-0) Harcourt.

— The School for Husbands: Director's Script. (Illus.). 43p. 1966. pap. 10.00 (0-88680-170-2) I E Clark.

— The School for Husbands: One-Act Adaptation. (Illus.). 43p. 1966. pap. 3.25 (0-88680-169-9) I E Clark.

— The School for Husbands & Sganarelle: or The Imaginary Cuckold. Wilbur, Richard, tr. & intro. by. 136p. 1994. pap. 12.95 (0-15-679500-0) Harcourt.

— The School for Wives. Wilbur, Richard, tr. 1991. pap. 5.25 (0-8222-0999-3) Dramatists Play.

— The School for Wives. Landes, William-Alan, ed. Landes, S. H., tr. LC 97-51850. 55p. 1998. pap. 7.00 (0-88734-780-0) Players Pr.

— The School for Wives. Wilbur, Richard, ed. LC 70-153693. 1972. reprint ed. pap. 6.95 (0-15-679501-9, HB228, Harvest Bks) Harcourt.

— The School for Wives & the Learned Ladies. Wilbur, Richard, tr. 324p. 1991. pap. 10.95 (0-15-679502-7, Harvest Bks) Harcourt.

— Le Tartuffe. (ENG & FRE.). 1992. pap. 10.95 (0-7859-3240-2, 2266043218) Fr & Eur.

***Moliere.** Tartuffe. LC 99-44074. 2000. pap. 1.50 (0-486-41117-6) Dover.

Moliere. Tartuffe. Wilbur, Richard, tr. 1988. pap. 5.25 (0-8222-1111-4) Dramatists Play.

— Tartuffe. Wilbur, Richard, tr. (ENG & FRE.). 1997. 25.00 (0-614-29407-X) Harcourt.

— Tartuffe. (FRE.). (C). pap. 7.95 (0-8442-1991-6, VF1991-6) NTC Contemp Pub Co.

— Tartuffe. Wilbur, Richard, tr. LC 63-17778. 182p. 1968. reprint ed. pap. 5.95 (0-15-688180-2, Harvest Bks) Harcourt.

— Tartuffe: A Comedy in Five Acts, 1669. Wilbur, Richard, tr. LC 96-47083. (FRE & ENG.). 240p. 1997. 25.00 (0-15-100281-9) Harcourt.

— Tartuffe: Acting Edition. Hartle, Robert W., tr. 1965. pap. 4.95 (0-672-60275-X, LLA87, Bobbs) Macmillan.

— Le Tartuffe: Don Juan; Le Misanthrope. (FRE.). 1973. pap. 11.95 (0-7859-2872-3) Fr & Eur.

— Tartuffe - Dom Juan. unabridged ed. (FRE.). pap. 5.95 (2-87714-197-7, Pub. by Bookking Intl) Distribks Inc.

— Tartuffe & Other Plays. (Signet Classics Ser.). 1960. mass mkt. 6.95 (0-451-52454-3, Sig Classics) NAL.

— Tartuffe & The Bourgeois Gentleman: A Dual-Language Book. Appelbaum, Stanley, ed. & tr. by. LC 98-26498. Orig. Title: Le Tartuffe et Le Bourgeois Gentilhomme. (FRE & ENG.). 368p. 1998. pap. 9.95 (0-486-40438-2) Dover.

— Tartuffe. Don Juan. Le Misanthrope. (Folio Ser.: No. 332). (FRE.). pap. 9.95 (2-07-036332-5) Schoenhof.

— Le Tartuffe ou L'Imposteur. Martin, Daniel R., ed. (Illus.). 141p. 1989. 10.95 (1-878417-21-5) Hestia Pr.

— The Trickeries of Scapin. Yalman, Tunc, tr. 1989. pap. 5.25 (0-8222-1173-4) Dramatists Play.

Moliere & Burleson, Noyce. Tartuffe. 1994. 3.95 (0-87129-422-2, T61) Dramatic Pub.

Moliere & Charpentier, Marc-Antoine. Marc-Antoine Charpentier: Music for Moliere's Comedies. Powell, John S., ed. (Recent Researches in the Music of the Baroque Era Ser.: No. RRB63). (Illus.). 93, xliiip. 1990. pap. 45.00 (0-89579-239-7) A-R Eds.

Moliere & Dear, Nick. Le Bourgeois Gentilhomme: A New Version. 80p. 1992. pap. 12.95 (0-948230-53-3, Pub. by Absolute Classics) Theatre Comm.

Moliere & Nelson, R. Don Juan. 1989. 6.95 (0-88145-078-2) Broadway Play.

Moliere, jt. auth. see Caywood, Paul.

Moliere, jt. auth. see Caywood, Pual.

Molin, Donald H. Actor's Encyclopedia of Dialects. 2nd rev. ed. (Illus.). 256p. 1991. pap. 16.95 (0-9628545-0-6) Bragi Pr.

Molin, Paulette, jt. auth. see Hirschfelder, Arlene B.

Molin, Paulette Fairbanks, jt. auth. see Hirschberger, Arlene B.

Molin, Sven E., jt. auth. see Goodefellowe, R.

Molina, jt. auth. see Cullen.

Molina, jt. auth. see Ghosh.

Molina, A. & Senovilla, J. M. Inhomogeneous Cosmological Models. 260p. 1995. text 74.00 (981-02-2341-2) World Scientific Pub.

***Molina, A., et al.** Handbook of Life Cycle Engineering: Concepts, Models & Technologies LC 99-189060. xiv, 618p. 1998. write for info. (0-412-81250-9) Kluwer Academic.

Molina, Alfonso H. The Social Basis of the Microelectronics Revolution. 1990. pap. text 28.00 (0-85224-605-6, Pub. by Edinburgh U Pr) Col U Pr.

Molina, Alicia. El Agujero Negro (The Black Hole) (SPA., Illus.). 48p. (J). (gr. 3-4). 1992. reprint ed. pap. 5.99 (968-16-3676-7, Pub. by Fondo) Continental Bk.

— El Zurcidor del Tiempo (Time Weaver) (SPA., Illus.). (YA). 1995. pap. 5.99 (968-16-4863-3, Pub. by Fondo) Continental Bk.

Molina Aranda, Fernando. Diccionario Tecnico Hostelero. (SPA.). 245p. 1972. pap. 19.95 (0-8288-6365-2, S-50021) Fr & Eur.

Molina, Armando. El Amanecer de los Tontos. Solaris Staff, ed. Borja, Lalo, tr. (SPA.). 220p. 1989. 11.95 (1-877870-21-8) Ed Solaris.

Molina, Armando & Galindo, Martivon. Imponiendo Presencias: Breve Antologia de Otros Narradores Expatriados Latinamericanos. (SPA.). 128p. 1995. pap. 10.00 (1-877870-44-7) Ed Solaris.

Molina, Bruce. Alaska's Glaciers. LC 72-92087. (Alaska Geographic Ser.: Vol. 9, No. 1). (Illus.). 144p. 1993. lib. bdg. 24.95 (1-56661-017-6) Alaska Geog Soc.

Molina, Carlos W. & Aguirre-Molina, Marilyn, eds. Latino Health in the U. S. A Growing Challenge. LC 96-147979. 513p. 1994. pap. 42.50 (0-87553-215-2) Am Pub Health.

Molina, Cesar A., tr. see Dieste, Rafael.

Molina, David. Graphing Power High School Activities for the TI-81 & TI-82. Aguirre, Alma, ed. (Illus.). 208p. 1994. pap. 19.95 (0-86651-827-4) Seymour Pubns.

M

An Asterisk (*) at the beginning of an entry indicates that the title is appearing for the first time.

Molina, David J. & Giermanski, James R. Linking or Isolating Economies? A Look at Trucking along the Texas-Mexico Border. (U. S. - Mexican Policy Reports: No. 6). 100p. 1994. pap. 15.00 (0-89940-322-0) LBJ Sch Pub Aff.

Molina, E. C. Poisson's Exponential Binomial Limit. 56p. 1973. reprint ed. pap. 10.50 (0-88275-107-7) Krieger.

Molina, Felipe S., ed. Coyote Songs - Wo'i Bwikam: Songs from the Yaqui Bow Leaders' Society. Miller, Cynthia, tr. & illus. by. LC 89-680. 44p. (Orig.). (C). 1989. 200.00 (0-925904-01-5) Chax Pr.

Molina, Felipe S., ed. Coyote Songs - Wo'i Bwikam: Songs from the Yaqui Bow Leaders' Society. Evers, Larry, tr. & intro. by. LC 89-680. (Illus.). 44p. (Orig.). (C). 1989. pap. 8.00 (0-925904-02-3) Chax Pr.

Molina, Felipe S., jt. auth. see Evers, Larry.

Molina, Gonzalo Argote De, see Argote De Molina, Gonzalo.

Molina, Huberto, et al. Empowering the Second-Language Classroom: Putting the Parts Together. LC 97-14647. 88p. (C). 1997. pap. text 19.95 (1-880192-23-3) Caddo Gap Pr.

Molina Iturrondo, Angeles. Ninos y Ninas Que Exploran y Construyen: Curriculo para el Desarrollo Integral. (SPA.). 384p. 1994. pap. 19.95 (0-8477-0213-8) U of PR Pr.

Molina, Janet. Helping Our Peers Effectively: A Skills Development Manual. 220p. 1992. pap. text 19.95 (0-9634612-0-6) Metamorphic.

Molina, Jose L. Malo de, see Malo de Molina, Jose L.

***Molina, Juan Antonio, contrib. by.** Flavio Garciandia: Recent Works. 2000. pap. 19.95 (89013-378-6) Museum NM Pr.

Molina, Juan I. Geographical, Natural & Civil History of Chili, 2 vols. LC 76-172738. reprint ed. 115.00 (0-404-04354-2) AMS Pr.

Molina, Louis & DeBenedictis, Michel. Picture Yourself: A Casebook for Reading & Writing. 222p. (C). 1994. pap. text, per. 34.95 (0-8403-9613-9) Kendall-Hunt.

Molina, Louis, et al. Multimedia Sound & Video. LC 96-70684. (Illus.). 192p. 1997. 58.00 (1-57576-647-7) Sams.

Molina, Miguel De, see De Molina, Miguel.

Molina, Miguel E. Inscriptiones Corinthi - Index Erborum in Inscriptiones Corinthi et Coloniarum. (Alpha-Omega, Reihe A Ser.: Bd. CXVII). (GER.). xii, 173p. 1990. write for info. (3-487-09364-2) G Olms Pubs.

— Inscriptiones Megarae: Index Verborum in Inscriptiones Megarae et Coloniarum. (Alpha-Omega, Reihe A Ser.: Bd. CXXI). (GER.). xiii, 398p. 1991. write for info. (3-487-09401-0) G Olms Pubs.

Molina-Negro, P., ed. Vestibular Neurotology. (Advances in OtoRhinoLaryngology Ser.: Vol. 28). (Illus.). viii, 148p. 1982. 100.00 (3-8055-3490-6) S Karger.

Molina, Nestor. El Caballero de Paris: Romance de un Principe Habanero. Space Classics Staff, ed. (SPA., Illus.). 180p. Date not set. 15.00 (1-891766-00-7); pap. 13.00 (1-891766-01-5) Space Clsscs.

Molina, Randy, et al. Biology, Ecology, & Social Aspects of Wild Edible Mushrooms in the Forests of the Pacific Northwest: A Preface to Managing Commercial Harvesr. (Illus.). 50p. 1998. reprint ed. pap. 10.00 (0-89904-778-5, Cascade Geog Soc) Crumb Elbow Pub.

— Biology, Ecology & Social Aspects of Wild Edible Mushrooms in the Forests of the Pacific Northwest: A Preface to Managing Commercial Harvest. (Illus.). 50p. 1998. reprint ed. 15.00 (0-89904-777-7, Cascade Geog Soc) Crumb Elbow Pub.

Molina, Randy, jt. ed. see Pilz, David.

Molina, Sara P., tr. see Edge, Findley B.

Molina, Silvia. El Amor Que Me Juraste. 170p. 1998. pap. text 19.95 (968-27-0724-2) E Joaqn Mortiz.

— Gray Skies Tomorrow: A Novel. Mitchell, John & de Aguilar, Ruth M., trs. from SPA. LC 92-42497. 104p. 1993. 17.95 (0-917635-14-0); pap. 8.95 (0-917635-15-9) Plover Pr.

***Molina, Silvia.** The Love You Promised Me. Unger, David, tr. from SPA. LC 99-27587. 152p. 1999. pap. 14.95 (1-880684-62-4, Pub. by Curbstone) SPD-Small Pr Dist.

Molina, Tarea. Your Life Depends on It! Four Easy Steps to Food Storage, Vol. 1. Lamb, Toni, ed. (Illus.). 33p. (Orig.). 1993. pap., student ed. 9.99 (0-9642779-6-4) T Molina Ent.

— Your Life Depends on It! Vol. II: A Complete Emergency Workbook. Lamb, Toni, ed. (Illus.). 70p. 1994. pap. 14.99 (0-9642779-1-3) T Molina Ent.

Molina, Tarea, ed. & intro. see Longfellow, Henry Wadsworth.

Molina, Tirso de. El Burlador de Sevilla. Arellano, Ignacio, ed. (Nueva Austral Ser.: Vol. 86). (SPA.). pap. 10.95 (84-239-1886-6) Elliots Bks.

— El Condenado Por Desconfiado. Fernandez, Angel R., ed. (Nueva Austral Ser.: Vol. 139). (SPA.). 1991. pap. text 24.95 (84-239-1939-0) Elliots Bks.

Molina, Tirso De. El Vergonzoso en Palacio: El Condenado por Desconfiado, el Burlador de Sevilla. (SPA.). pap. 9.95 (968-432-602-5, Pub. by Porrua) Continental Bk.

Molina, Vincent G. Communicating with a Former Spouse: Thoughts & Experiences for Greater Relationships & a Happier Life. unabridged ed. LC 97-91900. (Orig.). 1998. pap. 12.95 (0-9657536-0-3) Creat Alternat.

Molina, Wendy W. Modern Commercial Correspondence in English & Spanish. (ENG & SPA.). 172p. 1991. pap. 49.95 (0-7859-9599-4) Fr & Eur.

Molina y Vedia, Caroline, ed. see Brecht, Bertolt.

Molina y Vedia, Caroline, ed. see Nietzsche, Friedrich Wilhelm.

Molinar, G., jt. auth. see Pavese, F.

Molinard. Counterman's Guide to Parts & Service Management. (Automotive Technology Ser.). 1989. pap., teacher ed. 13.50 (0-8273-3630-6) Delmar.

Molinard, Gary A. Counterman's Guide to Parts & Service Management. (Automotive Technology Ser.). 1989. mass mkt. 38.50 (0-8273-3629-2) Delmar.

Molinard, Ursule. Fat Skeletons. 144p. 1998. pap. 11.95 (1-897959-02-8, Pub. by Serif) IPG Chicago.

Molinari, A., et al, eds. The Many Facets of Nuclear Physics. 288p. (C). 1989. text 86.00 (9971-5-0630-0) World Scientific Pub.

***Molinari, Andrea Lorenzo.** The Acts of Peter & the Twelve Apostles (NHC 6.1) Allegory, Ascent, & Ministry in the Wake of the Decian Persecution. (Dissertation Ser.: Vol. 174). xxv, 264p. 2000. 45.00 (0-88414-017-2) Soc Biblical Lit.

Molinari, Carol. Americans, Wake Up! 258p. (Orig.). 1995. pap. 12.95 (0-929686-05-5) Temple Golden Pubns.

Molinari, Gustavo De, see De Molinari, Gustavo.

Molinari, John A. & Terezhalmy, Geza. Cottone's Practical Infection Control in Dentistry. 3rd ed. 350p. 39.95 (0-683-30728-2) Lppncott W & W.

Molinari, Joseph, jt. auth. see Langman, Larry.

***Molinari, Luca.** Santiago Calatrava. (Illus.). 224p. 1999. 25.00 (88-8118-525-3, Pub. by Skira IT) Abbeville Pr.

Molinari, Paolo. Julian of Norwich: The Teaching of A 14th Century English Mystic LC 77-11976. x, 214p. 1977. write for info. (0-8492-1823-3) R Westerman.

Molinari, Susan, ed. Current Amtrak Financial Condition: Hearing Before the Committee on Transportation & Infrastructure, U. S. House of Representatives. 189p. (C). 1998. pap. text 30.00 (0-7881-7286-7) DIANE Pub.

Molinari, Victor, ed. Professional Psychology of Long-Term Care. LC 99-37326. (CE Book Ser.). 214p. 1999. pap. 39.95 (1-57826-035-3, Pub. by Hatherleigh) Norton.

Molinaro, Julius A. Matteo Maria Boiardo: A Bibliography of Works & Criticism from 1487-1980. (CFH-FCEH Ser.: No. 5). (Illus.). 100p. (Orig.). (C). 1984. pap. 10.00 (0-920050-94-8, Pub. by Can Fed Human) Speedimpex.

Molinaro, Julius A., ed. Petrarch to Pirandello: Studies in Italian Literature in Honour of Beatrice Corrigan. LC 72-185276. 276p. reprint ed. pap. 85.60 (0-608-13763-4, 202050900018) Bks Demand.

Molinaro, Julius A., jt. ed. see Chandler, Stanley B.

Molinaro, Julius A., tr. see Alfieri, Vittorio.

Molinaro, Larry. Exceeding Expectations: Proceedings from the Wildlife Habitat Council's 1997 Wildlands Conference. (Illus.). 20p. (Orig.). 1997. pap. 12.95 (1-889685-01-1) Wildlife Habitat.

— A Roadmap to Resolution. 20p. 1995. pap. text. write for info. (0-9646852-6-4) Wildlife Habitat.

Molinaro, Larry, et al. Agenda for Action. 24p. 1994. pap. text. write for info. (0-9646852-0-5) Wildlife Habitat.

Molinaro, Nina. Foucault, Feminism & Power: Reading Esther Tusquets. LC 90-55653. 128p. 1991. 27.50 (0-8387-5200-4) Bucknell U Pr.

Molinaro, Paolo, ed. see American Society of Civil Engineers Staff.

Molinaro, Ursule. Analects of Self-Contempt: Sweet Cheat of Freedom. 24p. (Orig.). 1983. pap. 3.00 (0-917061-16-0) Top Stories.

— The Autobiography of Cassandra, Princess & Prophetess of Troy. 2nd ed. LC 92-17468. 112p. 1992. pap. 9.00 (0-929701-24-0) McPherson & Co.

— Bastards: Footnotes to History. deluxe ed. (Treacle Story Ser.: No. 7). (Illus.). 48p. 1979. 12.50 (0-914232-27-4) McPherson & Co.

***Molinaro, Ursule.** Demons & Divas: Three Novels. deluxe ed. LC 99-48888. 240p. 2000. 25.00 (0-929701-59-3) McPherson & Co.

Molinaro, Ursule. Encores for a Dilettante. LC 77-81003. 1977. 10.95 (0-914590-44-8); pap. 6.95 (0-914590-45-6) Fiction Coll.

— A Full Moon of Women: Twenty-Nine Word Portraits of Notable Women from Different Times & Places Plus One Void of Course. LC 90-30077. 149p. 1993. reprint ed. pap. 10.00 (0-929701-32-1) McPherson & Co.

— Needlepoint: A Dialogue. LC 87-42543. 24p. 1987. pap. 3.00 (0-87376-055-7) Red Dust.

— The New Moon with the Old Moon in Her Arms. 119p. (Orig.). 1993. 22.00 (0-7043-5057-2); pap. 10.00 (0-929701-29-1) McPherson & Co.

— Positions with White Roses. LC 82-24916. 104p. 1983. 12.95 (0-914232-58-4); 25.00 (0-914232-59-2) McPherson & Co.

— Positions with White Roses. LC 82-24916. 104p. 1989. reprint ed. pap. 8.00 (0-929701-00-3) McPherson & Co.

— Power Dreamers: The Jocasta Complex. 128p. 1994. 16.00 (0-929701-44-5) McPherson & Co.

— Thirteen. LC 89-31186. 128p. 1989. 16.00 (0-929701-02-X); pap. 9.00 (0-929701-01-1) McPherson & Co.

Molinaro, Ursule, jt. auth. see Evans, John.

Molinaro, Ursule, tr. see Hesse, Hermann.

Molinaro, Ursule, tr. see Ollier, Claude.

Molinaro, Ursule, tr. see Sollers, Philippe.

Molinary, Paul & Hennessy, Anne. The Vocation & Mission of Joseph & Mary. 60p. 1992. 5.95 (1-85390-149-0) Ignatius Pr.

Molinatti, Gian M., et al, eds. Androgenization in Women: Pathophysiology & Clinical Aspects. fac. ed. LC 81-48338. (Illus.). 216p. pap. 67.00 (0-7837-7216-5, 204708200005) Bks Demand.

Moline, Johanna C. The Server's Art I: A Guide for the Serving Professional. rev. ed. (Illus.). 50p. (Orig.). (C). 1996. pap. text 9.95 (0-9644063-0-6) Anvilcross.

— The Server's Art II: A Short Course for the Serving Professional. abr. ed. (Illus.). 16p. (C). 1995. pap. text 4.25 (0-9644063-1-4) Anvilcross.

Moline, Jon. Plato's Theory of Understanding. LC 81-50826. 272p. 1981. reprint ed. pap. 84.40 (0-7837-9790-7, 206051900005) Bks Demand.

Moline, Judi. Virtual Environments for Health Care. (Illus.). 53p. (C). 1997. reprint ed. pap. text 20.00 (0-7881-4280-1) DIANE Pub.

***Moline, Judi & Otto, Steve.** Electronic Access: Blueprint for the National Archives & Records Administration. (Illus.). 51p. (C). 2000. reprint ed. pap. text 20.00 (0-7881-8611-6) DIANE Pub.

Moline, Judi & Otto, Steve. A User Study: Informational Needs of Remote National Archives & Records Administration Customers. (Illus.). 118p. (C). 1996. reprint ed. pap. text 25.00 (0-7881-3065-X) DIANE Pub.

Moline, Karen. Belladonna. 1999. mass mkt. 7.50 (0-446-60739-8, Pub. by Warner Bks) Little.

— Lunch. 336p. 1996. mass mkt. 6.50 (0-380-72306-9, Avon Bks) Morrow Avon.

Moline, Margaret L., jt. auth. see Severino, Sally K.

Moline, Mary. Anne: A Norman Rockwell Character Story. LC 82-60730. 1982. 20.00 (0-913444-08-1) M Moline.

— Best of Ford: An Anthology. LC 73-86527. (Illus.). 352p. 1973. 20.00 (0-913444-01-4, A 490 710) M Moline.

— The Eagle & the Butterfly: Spiritual Growth. (Illus.). 57p. (Orig.). 1986. pap. 8.00 (0-913444-10-3) M Moline.

— Love Shadows: An Unbelievable Tryst with the Holy Ghost. 380p. 1999. pap. 10.00 (0-913444-13-8) M Moline.

— Model A Miseries & Cures. 230p. 1999. pap. 22.00 (0-913444-00-6, A 384 267) M Moline.

Moline, Mary E., et al. Documenting Psychotherapy: Essentials for Mental Health Practitioners. LC 97-4884. 176p. 1997. 39.95 (0-8039-4691-0); pap. 19.95 (0-8039-4692-9) Sage.

Moline, Norman T. Mobility & the Small Town, 1900 to 1930. LC 79-133029. (Research Papers: No. 132). (Illus.). 1971. pap. text 14.50 (0-89065-039-X, 132) U Ch Pr.

Moline, Steve. I See What You Mean: Children at Work with Visual Information. LC 95-39708. (Illus.). iii, 152p. (C). 1995. pap. text 21.00 (1-57110-031-8) Stenhse Pubs.

Molineaux, David, tr. see Gebara, Ivone.

Molineaux, Jane. Big Family Games. 12p. (J). 1995. bds. write for info. (1-85479-708-5, Pub. by M OMara) Assoc Pubs Grp.

Molineaux, Othello. Beginning Steel Drum. Cavalier, Debbie, ed. (Illus.). 48p. (Orig.). (YA). 1995. pap. text 14.95 (0-89724-979-3, EL03959CD) Wrner Bros.

Molinelli, Lambert. Eureka & Its Resources: A Complete History. LC 82-4948. (Vintage Nevada Ser.). (Illus.). 144p. 1998. reprint ed. pap. 10.95 (0-87417-069-9) U of Nev Pr.

Molinelli, Paul & Grisham, Dana. Cooperative Learning. (Professional's Guide Ser.). 80p. 1995. pap., teacher ed. 9.95 (1-55734-842-1) Tchr Create Mat.

Moliner, Maria D. Diccionario de Uso del Espagnol, 2 vols., Set. (SPA.). 1991. 180.00 (84-249-1344-2) IBD Ltd.

— Diccionario de Uso del Espanol. (SPA.). 1996. 195.00 incl. cd-rom (0-7859-9353-3) Fr & Eur.

— Diccionario de Uso del Espanol, 2 vols. 4th ed. (SPA.). 3088p. 1993. 239.50 (0-685-75413-8) Elliots Bks.

— Diccionario de Uso del Espanol, 1. (SPA.). 1991. write for info. (0-7859-5791-X) Fr & Eur.

— Diccionario de Uso del Espanol, 2. (SPA.). 1991. 150.00 (0-7859-5792-8) Fr & Eur.

— Diccionario de Uso del Espanol, Set. (SPA.). 1991. 295.00 (0-7859-5790-1) Fr & Eur.

Moliner, Maria D., tr. I Can Read Spanish: My First English-Spanish Word Book. LC 94-25774. (Illus.). 96p. (J). (gr. 2-4). 1994. pap. 9.95 (1-56294-755-9); lib. bdg. 19.90 (1-56294-547-5) Millbrook Pr.

Molinero, Clayton, jt. auth. see Mathews, Craig.

Molinero, Leticia, tr. see Zuckerman, Martin M.

Molinet, F., jt. auth. see Bouche, Daniel.

Molineux, G., jt. ed. see Testa, N. G.

Molineux, Marie A. A Phrase Book from the Poetic & Dramatic Works of Robert Browning. 1972. 59.95 (0-8490-0831-X) Gordon Pr.

Molini, Cindy & Garlock, Diane, eds. Faith Moments: A Reproducible Book of Weekly Reflections on Christian Spirituality. 104p. (Orig.). 1990. pap. 69.95 (1-55612-301-9) Sheed & Ward WI.

Molinie, Georges. Dictionnaire de Rhetorique. (FRE.). 352p. 1992. pap. 22.95 (0-7859-8635-9, 225306257x) Fr & Eur.

Molino, Anthony. The Couch & the Tree: Dialogues in Psychoanalysis & Buddhism. LC 98-27577. 400p. 1998. 30.00 (0-86547-520-2) N Point Pr.

***Molino, Anthony, ed.** The Couch & the Tree: Dialogues in Psychoanalysis & Buddhism. 384p. 1999. pap. 15.00 (0-86547-574-1) N Point Pr.

Molino, Anthony, ed. Elaborate Selves: Reflections & Reveries of Christopher Bollas, Michael Eigen, Polly Young-Eisendrath, Samuel & Evelyn Laeuchli, & Marie Coleman Nelson. LC 96-38178. 225p. 1996. 34.95 (0-7890-0011-3) Haworth Pr.

Molino, Anthony, ed. Freely Associated: Encounters in Psychoanalysis with Christopher Bollas, Joyce McDougall, Michael Eigen, Adam Phillips, & Nina Coltart. 213p. 1998. 50.00 (1-85343-384-5, Pub. by Free Assoc Bks); pap. 19.50 (1-85343-386-1, Pub. by Free Assoc Bks) NYU Pr.

Molino, Anthony, tr. see De Filippo, Eduardo.

Molino, Anthony, tr. see Porta, Antonio.

***Molino, Cornelia Rosales de.** Cuisines of the World: Spain. LC 00-21947. (Illus.). 2000. 14.98 (1-57145-259-1, Thunder Bay) Advantage Pubs.

Molino, Francesco. Book of Preludes. Stang, Aaron, ed. 24p. (Orig.). (C). 1985. pap. text 6.00 (0-7692-1331-6, K04179) Wrner Bros.

Molino, Michael R. Questioning Tradition, Language, & Myth: The Poetry of Seamus Heaney. LC 93-42712. 215p. 1994. pap. 19.95 (0-8132-0797-5) Cath U Pr.

Molino, Pierre. Riemannian Foliations. (Progress in Mathematics Ser.: No. 73). 360p. 1987. 60.50 (0-8176-3370-7) Birkhauser.

Molino, Pierre, et al. Integrable Systems & Foliations. LC 96-48688. (Progress in Mathematics Ser.: Vol. 145).Tr. of Feuilletages et Systemes Integrables. (FRE.). 375p. 1997. 69.50 (0-8176-3894-6) Birkhauser.

— Integrable Systems & Foliations: Feuilletages et Syst Emes Int Egrables. LC 96-48688. (Progress in Mathematics Ser.). (FRE.). 1996. write for info. (3-7643-3894-6) Birkhauser.

Molino, Tony, tr. see Magrelli, Valerio.

Molino, Virginia & Nadeau, Lyn. Not More Writing?! (Activity Book Ser.). (Illus.). 144p. (Orig.). 1996. pap. 17.95 (1-57022-048-4) ECS Lrn Systs.

Molinos, Manuel, jt. auth. see Ruiz, Arturo.

Molinos, Michael. The Spiritual Guide. Edwards, Gene, ed. 110p. 1982. pap. 8.95 (0-940232-08-1) Seedsowers.

Molins, Ricardo A., ed. Phosphates in Food. 272p. 1990. lib. bdg. 225.00 (0-8493-4588-X, TX553) CRC Pr.

Molins, Victoria. Henry de Osso: Priest & Teacher. 108p. 1993. pap. 6.95 (0-9638041-0-3) Soc St Teresa.

***Molinski, Michael & Anderson, Constance.** Investing in Latin America: Best Stocks - Best Funds. LC 99-17934. 304p. 1999. 24.95 (1-57660-065-3, Pub. by Bloomberg NJ) Norton.

Molinsky. Classmate Level 1-4. 1997. pap. text, teacher ed. write for info. (0-13-505645-4) P-H.

— Classmates, Level 4. 2001. pap. text. write for info. (0-13-565946-9) P-H.

— Crossroads, Vol. 1A. 1999. pap. text 5.33 (0-13-194689-7) P-H.

— Crossroads, Vol. 1B. 1999. pap. text 10.67 (0-13-194697-8) P-H.

— Expressway Access. 2nd ed. 1997. pap. text, suppl. ed. 9.33 (0-13-385261-X) P-H.

— Expressway Access. 2nd ed. 160p. 1999. pap. text, wbk. ed. 10.00 (0-13-384645-8) P-H.

— Expressway Access, Bk. 4. 2nd ed. 1997. pap. text. write for info. (0-13-385907-X) P-H.

— Expressway Standard Course Guide Book, Vol. 1. 2nd ed. 1996. pap. text 32.10 (0-13-385311-X) P-H.

Molinsky. Expressways: Achievement Test, Vol. 1A. 40p. 1992. pap. text 16.60 (0-13-298787-2) P-H.

— Expressways Bk. 1: Placement Test. 52p. 1992. pap. text 16.60 (0-13-298795-3) P-H.

Molinsky. Expressways Composition Workbook B. 1988. pap. text 7.00 (0-13-297789-3) P-H.

— Expressways Composition 3B. 1987. pap. text 10.00 (0-13-298357-5) P-H.

— Fast Score, Bk. 1. 2nd ed. 1998. pap. text 22.60 (0-13-010891-X) P-H.

— Line by Line Beginning Typing. 2nd ed. 1990. text. write for info. (0-13-536897-9) P-H.

— SBS TV Video Workbook. 2nd ed. 1995. pap. text 14.20 (0-13-816570-X) P-H.

— Side by Side: English Grammar Through Guided Conversation 2A, Vol. 2A. 1983. pap. text, teacher ed. 23.40 (0-13-809608-2) P-H.

— Side by Side Bk. 4: Secondary School Edition. 176p. 1996. pap. text 16.60 (0-13-440157-3) P-H.

— Side by Side Secondary School, 3 vols. 160p. 1996. pap. text 16.60 (0-13-440140-9) P-H.

— Teachers Guide Level 3 Classmates Level 3, Level 3. 2001. pap. text. write for info. (0-13-568916-3) P-H.

— Wall Charts Foundations. 2nd ed. 1997. pap. 41.93 (0-13-906405-2) P-H.

— Word By Word Basic Literacy. (C). 1999. pap., wbk. ed. 14.40 (0-13-278524-2, Macmillan Coll) P-H.

— Word by Word Picture Dictionary: Haitian. 324p. 1997. pap. text 14.33 (0-13-278615-X) P-H.

Molinsky, ed. Transform Foundations Inorganic. 2nd ed. 1997. pap. 23.73 (0-13-906397-8) P-H.

Molinsky & Bli. Navigator, Vol. 1. 2001. pap. text, teacher ed. write for info. (0-13-359605-2) P-H.

— Navigator, Vol. 3. 2001. pap. text. write for info. (0-13-359589-7) P-H.

— Navigator, Vol. 4. 2001. pap. text. write for info. (0-13-359597-8) P-H.

— Navigator Basic, Vol. 1. 2001. pap. text 9.27 (0-13-359555-2) P-H.

— Word Picture Basic Spanish Bilingual. LC 97-127726. 192p. 1996. pap. text 14.33 (0-13-278573-0) P-H.

Molinsky & Bliss. Foundations. 2nd ed. 1996. pap. text, teacher ed. 22.00 (0-13-384869-8) P-H.

— Side By Side. 1983. teacher ed. 23.40 (0-13-809491-8) P-H.

— Side By Side, Bk. 2. 2nd ed. 1989. pap. text, teacher ed. 25.40 (0-13-811282-7) P-H.

Molinsky, jt. auth. see Bliss.

Molinsky, S. J. Word by Word Basic Mono Dictionary Japan. 192p. 1996. pap. text 14.33 (0-13-462581-1) P-H.

Molinsky, Steven. Side by Side. 160p. (YA). (gr. 6-8). 1995. pap. text 16.60 (0-13-440132-8) Prentice ESL.

Molinsky, Steven & Bliss, Bill. Full Set Wall Charts. (C). 1994. pap. text 315.00 (0-13-121120-X) P-H.

— Set Three Wall Charts. (C). 1994. pap. text 115.00 (0-13-121112-9) P-H.

— Word by Word Picture Dictionary: English /Chinese Edition. LC 96-211643. (CHI & ENG.). 160p. 1996. pap. text 14.93 (0-13-125824-9) P-H.

— Word by Word Picture Dictionary: Korean-English Edition. LC 97-121277. (ENG & KOR.). 160p. 1996. pap. text 14.93 (0-13-125840-0) P-H.

— Word by Word Picture Dictionary: Russian-English Edition. (ENG & RUS.). 160p. 1996. pap. text 14.93 (0-13-125857-5) P-H.

— Word by Word Picture Dictionary: Spanish-English Edition. (ENG & SPA.). 160p. 1995. pap. text 14.93 (0-13-125865-6) P-H.

An Asterisk (*) at the beginning of an entry indicates that the title is appearing for the first time.

— Word by Word Picture Dictionary: Vocabulary Game Cards, Set 2. 1994. 10.80 (*0-13-121146-3*) P-H.

— Word by Word Picture Dictionary: Vocabulary Game Cards, Set 3. 1994. 10.80 (*0-13-121153-6*) P-H.

— Word by Word Picture Dictionary Portuguese/English Dictionary. LC 96-146327. (ENG & POR.). 160p. 1996. pap. text 14.93 (*0-13-128018-X*) P-H.

Molinsky, Steven, jt. auth. see Bliss, Bill.

Molinsky, Steven H. & Bliss, Bill. Communicator II: The Comprehensive Course in Functional English. LC 94-23686. (Illus.). 192p. 1995. pap. text 18.20 (*0-13-340688-1*) P-H.

Molinsky, Steven J. Beginning Word by Word. 160p. 1994. pap. text, wbk. ed. 10.80 (*0-13-278269-3*) P-H.

— Communicator 1. (C). 1995. pap. text, teacher ed. 22.00 (*0-13-310913-5*) P-H.

— Communicator 2. (C). 1995. pap. text, teacher ed. 22.00 (*0-13-340696-2*) P-H.

— Expressways, Bk. 1. 2nd ed. 1996. pap. text, wbk. ed. 10.53 (*0-13-570870-2*) P-H.

— Expressways Book1, Bk. 1. 2nd ed. (e). 224p. 1995. pap. text 15.80 (*0-13-385295-4*) P-H.

— Intermediate Word by Word. 160p. 1994. pap. text, wbk. ed. 10.80 (*0-13-278458-0*) P-H.

— Literacy Workbook. (C). 1998. pap. 13.33 (*0-13-150939-X*) P-H.

— Patterns of Ellipsis in Russian Compound Noun Formations. LC 72-94527. (Slavistic Printings & Reprintings Ser.: No. 278). 1973. text 90.80 (*90-279-2474-0*) Mouton.

— A Russian Course: Teacher's Manual. (Illus.). 222p. (Orig.). 1981. pap. 12.95 (*0-89357-083-4*) Slavica.

— Side By Side. 1996. pap., wbk. ed. 14.20 incl. VHS (*0-13-158163-5*) P-H.

— Side By Side, Bk. 3. 2nd ed. 140p. 1989. pap. text 15.53 (*0-13-811761-6*) P-H.

— Side by Side, Bk. 4. 2nd ed. 140p. 1989. pap. text 15.53 (*0-13-811811-6*) P-H.

— Side by Side Bk. 2: Global Village Edition. (C). 1995. pap. text 13.60 (*0-13-467334-4*) P-H.

— Side by Side Bk. 3: Global Village Edition. (C). 1995. pap. text 13.60 (*0-13-467812-5*) P-H.

— Side by Side Bk. 4: Global Village Edition. (C). 1995. pap. text 13.60 (*0-13-467821-4*) P-H.

Molinsky, Steven J. Side by Side Vol. 1: Activity Workbook. 2nd ed. 1989. pap. text, wbk. ed. 11.13 (*0-13-811696-2*) P-H.

— Side by Side Vol. 2: Activity Workbook. 2nd ed. 1989. pap. text, wbk. ed. 11.13 (*0-13-811746-2*) P-H.

— Side by Side Vol. 3: Activity Workbook. 2nd ed. 1989. pap. text, wbk. ed. 11.13 (*0-13-811795-0*) P-H.

— Side by Side Vol. 4: Activity Workbook. 2nd ed. 1989. pap. text, wbk. ed. 11.13 (*0-13-811845-0*) P-H.

Molinsky, Steven J. Side by Side Student Text 1: Global Village Edition. (C). 1995. pap. text 13.60 (*0-13-467292-5*) P-H.

Molinsky, Steven J. Word By Word 1997. pap. text, wbk. ed. 11.33 (*0-13-278516-1*) P-H.

Molinsky, Steven J. Word by Word Picture Dictionary: English Vietnamese Edition. LC 96-205486. (ENG & VIE.). 160p. 1996. pap. text 14.93 (*0-13-278607-9*) P-H.

— Word by Word Picture Dictionary: English/Haitian Kreyol Edition. LC 97-100813. 160p. 1995. pap. text 14.93 (*0-13-278581-1*) P-H.

***Molinsky, Steven J.** Word by Word Primary Picture Dictionary. LC 99-15215. 1999. 21.00 (*0-13-022206-2*, P-H Gardening) Prntice Hall Bks.

Molinsky, Steven J. & Blass, Bill. Expressways Student Course, Bk. 2. 2nd ed. 208p. 1995. pap. text 15.80 (*0-13-385337-3*) P-H.

— Side by Side: English Grammar Through Guided Conversations Bk. II. 224p. (C). 1981. pap. text 24.00 (*0-13-809855-7*) P-H.

— Word by Word: Teachers Resource Book & Activity Masters. LC 94-231. 608p. (C). 1994. pap. text 37.80 (*0-13-124264-4*) P-H.

Molinsky, Steven J. & Bliss. Access: Fundamentals of Literacy & Communication. 1991. pap. text, teacher ed. 23.00 (*0-13-005992-7*) P-H.

Molinsky, Steven J. & Bliss, Bill. Access: Fundamentals of Literacy & Communication. 128p. (C). 1990. pap. text 16.80 (*0-13-004235-8*) P-H.

— Act Workbook Side by Side 1B: English Grammar through Guided Conversation 1B. 128p. (C). 1983. pap. text, student ed., wbk. ed. 10.00 (*0-13-809582-5*) P-H.

— Act Workbook Side by Side 2A: English Grammar Through Guided Conversation 2A. 128p. (C). 1983. pap. text 7.60 (*0-13-809640-6*) P-H.

— Act Workbook Side by Side 2B: English Grammar Through Guided Conversation 2B. 128p. (C). 1983. pap. text, student ed., wbk. ed. 10.00 (*0-13-809699-6*) P-H.

— Classmates, Level 1. 144p. 1995. pap. text 9.67 (*0-13-350000-4*) P-H.

— Core Conversation Course: Beginning Text. 2nd ed. 208p. (C). 1989. pap. text 26.60 (*0-13-811860-4*) P-H.

— Day by Day: English for Employment Communication. LC 93-44412. 1994. pap. text 15.00 (*0-13-328238-4*) P-H Intl.

— Express Ways-Book II (Advanced) 240p. (C). 1986. pap. text 25.80 (*0-13-298274-9*) P-H.

— Express Ways-Book IIB (Advanced) 112p. (C). 1987. pap. text 10.00 (*0-13-298316-8*) P-H.

— Expressways, Bk. 2. 2nd ed. 128p. 1996. pap. text, wbk. ed. 10.53 (*0-13-570888-5*) P-H.

— Expressways, Bk. 3. 2nd ed. 112p. 1997. pap. text, wbk. ed. 10.53 (*0-13-570896-6*) P-H.

— ExpressWays, Bk. 3. 2nd ed. 208p. 1996. pap. text, student ed. 15.80 (*0-13-385535-X*) P-H.

— Expressways, Bk. 4. 2nd ed. 1997. pap. text, wbk. ed. 10.53 (*0-13-570904-0*) P-H.

— Expressways, Bk. IB. 112p. (C). 1988. pap. text 10.00 (*0-13-298449-0*) P-H.

Molinsky, Steven J. & Bliss, Bill. Expressways: English for Communication, Bk. I. (Illus.). 224p. (C). 1988. pap. text 19.40 (*0-13-298423-7*) P-H.

Molinsky, Steven J. & Bliss, Bill. Expressways: English for Communication Foundations, 3 pts., Pt. B. (Illus.). 112p. (C). 1988. pap. text. write for info. (*0-318-62294-7*) P-H.

— Expressways: English for Communication Foundations, 3 pts., Set. (Illus.). 224p. (C). 1988. pap. text. write for info. (*0-318-62295-5*) P-H.

— Expressways Bk. 2: Student Course Book 2nd ed. (C). 1996. text 49.33 incl. audio (*0-13-385386-1*, Macmillan Coll) P-H.

— Expressways Bk. 2A: English for Communication. (Illus.). 120p. (C). 1987. pap. text 10.00 (*0-13-298373-7*) P-H.

— Expressways Bk. 2A: English for Communication, Bk. 2. (Illus.). 122p. (C). 1987. pap. text 19.40 (*0-13-298365-6*) P-H.

— Expressways Bk. 2A: English for Communication, Bk. 2B. (Illus.). 112p. (C). 1987. pap. text 10.00 (*0-13-298381-8*) P-H.

— Expressways Bk. 2A: English for Communication, Bk. 3A. 224p. (C). 1987. pap. text, student ed. 24.20 (*0-13-298399-0*) P-H.

— Expressways Bk. 2A: English for Communication, Bk. 3B. 224p. (C). 1987. pap. text, student ed. 24.20 (*0-13-298407-5*) P-H.

— Expressways Bk. 2A: English for Communication, 2 bks., Bk. IA. (Illus.). 112p. (C). 1987. pap. text 13.20 (*0-13-298431-8*) P-H.

— Expressways Bk. 2A: English for Communication, 2 bks., Bk. IB. (Illus.). 112p. (C). 1988. pap. text. write for info. (*0-318-62137-1*) P-H.

— ExpressWays-Book 3A. 112p. (C). 1987. pap. text 10.00 (*0-13-298282-X*) P-H.

— Foundations. 2nd ed. LC 95-38865. 240p. (C). 1995. pap. text 16.13 (*0-13-384604-0*) P-H.

— Line By Line: Beginning Text. 2nd ed. 128p. (C). 1989. pap. text 20.40 (*0-13-536871-5*, Macmillan Coll) P-H.

— Line by Line: English Through Grammar Stories, Bk. 1A. (Illus.). 128p. (C). 1983. pap. text 10.00 (*0-13-537092-2*) P-H.

— Line by Line: English Through Grammar Stories, Bk. 2A. (Illus.). 128p. (C). 1983. pap. text 10.00 (*0-13-537241-0*) P-H.

— Line by Line: English Through Grammar Stories, Bk. 2B. (Illus.). 28p. (C). 1983. pap. text 7.60 (*0-13-537258-5*) P-H.

— Line by Line: English Through Grammar Stories, Bk.1B. (Illus.). 112p. (C). 1983. pap. text 10.00 (*0-13-537175-9*) P-H.

— Line by Line: Intermediate Text. 2nd ed. 112p. (C). 1991. pap. text 20.40 (*0-13-536889-8*) P-H.

— Navigator 2. 160p. 1997. pap. text 9.73 (*0-13-359571-4*) P-H.

— Placement Test. (C). 1989. text. write for info. (*0-318-65462-8*) P-H.

— Side by Side, Bk. 1. LC 95-23474. 176p. 1995. pap. text 16.60 (*0-13-440124-7*, Pub. by P-H) S&S Trade.

— Side by Side, Bk. 1. LC 95-23474. 1995. text, boxed set 24.20 (*0-13-456187-2*) P-H.

— Side by Side, Bk. 1. 2nd ed. 160p. 1988. pap. text 15.53 (*0-13-811076-X*) P-H.

— Side by Side, Bk. 2. (C). 1995. text 24.20 (*0-13-456195-3*) P-H.

— Side by Side: English Grammar Through Guided Conversation 1A. 128p. (C). 1982. pap. text, wbk. ed. 7.60 (*0-13-809525-6*) P-H.

— Side by Side: English Grammar Through Guided Conversation 1A. 128p. (C). 1983. pap. text 13.00 (*0-13-809715-1*) P-H.

— Side by Side: English Grammar Through Guided Conversation 2A. 128p. (C). 1983. pap. text 9.80 (*0-13-809772-0*) P-H.

— Side by Side: English Grammar Through Guided Conversation 2B. 128p. (C). 1983. pap. text 13.00 (*0-13-809798-4*) P-H.

— Side by Side: English Grammar Through Guided Conversations, Bk. I. 224p. (C). 1980. pap. text 24.00 (*0-13-809848-4*) P-H.

— Side by Side Bk. 1B: English Grammar through Guided Conversation, Bk 1B. 128p. (C). 1983. pap. text 9.80 (*0-13-809723-2*) P-H.

— Side by Side Core Conversation, Intermediate Text. 2nd ed. 208p. (C). 1991. pap. text 26.60 (*0-13-811878-7*) P-H.

— Word by Word Basic Monoling Picture Dictionary. LC 95-717. 192p. 1995. pap. text 14.33 (*0-13-278565-X*) P-H.

— Word by Word Basic Teacher's Resource Book: Teacher's Resource Book & Activity Masters. LC 95-47374. (C). 1996. pap. text 37.80 (*0-13-278466-1*) P-H.

— Word by Word Picture Dictionary: A Talking Picture Dictionary English. LC 93-21129. 144p. 1993. pap. text 14.93 (*0-13-278235-9*) P-H.

— Word by Word Picture Dictionary: A Talking Picture Dictionary English. LC 93-21129. 1993. text 21.40 (*0-13-278319-3*) P-H.

— Word by Word Picture Dictionary: Beginner's Workbook. (C). 1995. wbk. ed. 53.00 incl. audio (*0-13-434515-0*, Macmillan Coll) P-H.

Molinsky, Steven J., et al. Expressways, Bk. 4. 2nd ed. LC 96-20553. 224p. 1996. pap. text 15.80 (*0-13-385759-X*) P-H.

Molinsky, Steven J., jt. auth. see Bliss.

Molinsky, Steven J., jt. auth. see Bliss, Bill.

Molinuevo, Jose L. Die Zweideutigkeit des Ursprunglichen Bei Martin Heidegger: Aus Dem Spanischen Ubersetzt von Dieter Wiggert. (GER.). 211p. 1996. 42.95 (*3-631-30197-9*) P Lang Pubng.

Molis, Petra, et al. Lithuanian Scouting. 2nd rev. ed. Vitas, Robertas, ed. (Illus.). 40p. 1983. reprint ed. pap. write for info. (*0-9611488-0-2*) Lith Scouts.

***Molisch, Andreas F.** Wideband Wireless Digital Communication. (Illus.). 500p. 2000. 70.00 (*0-13-022333-6*) P-H.

Molisch, Andreas F. & Oehry, Bernhard P. Radiation Trapping in Atomic Vapours. LC 98-47477. (Illus.). 536p. 1999. text 165.00 (*0-19-853866-9*) OUP.

Moliterno, Arlene, jt. auth. see Schmalz, Kathleen.

Moliterno, Frank. The Dialectics of Sense & Spirit in Pater & Joyce. LC 97-60606. (British Authors 1880-1920 Ser.: Vol. 12). 192p. (C). 1998. 30.00 (*0-944318-11-8*) ELT Pr.

Moliterno, Gino, ed. Encyclopedia of Contemporary Italian Culture. LC 99-38356. (Encyclopedias of Contemporary Culture Ser.). 744p. 1999. 140.00 (*0-415-14584-8*) Routledge.

Moliterno, James E. Cases & Materials on the Law Governing Lawyers. LC 99-15996. (C). 1999. 51.95 (*0-87084-425-3*) Anderson Pub Co.

***Moliterno, James E.** Cases & Materials on the Law Governing Lawyers: Rules Handbook. 1999. pap. text 15.95 (*0-87084-426-1*) Anderson Pub Co.

Moliterno, James E. Ethics of Lawyer's Work. Levy, John M., ed. (American Casebook Ser.). 320p. (C). 1993. pap. text. write for info. (*0-314-02414-X*) West Pub.

***Moliterno, James E.** Professional Responsibility. LC 99-39533. (Roadmap Ser.). 384p. 1999. pap. text 20.95 (*1-56706-536-8*) Panel Pubs.

Moliterno, James E. & Lederer, Frederic. An Introduction to Law, Law Study & the Lawyer's Role. LC 91-70489. 206p. 1991. 24.95 (*0-89089-453-1*); pap. 17.50 (*0-89089-452-3*) Carolina Acad Pr.

Moliterno, James E. & Levy, John M. Ethics of Lawyer's Work. (American Casebook Ser.). 305p. (C). 1993. pap. 25.50 (*0-314-02395-X*) West Pub.

Moliterno, Steven, ed. see American Institue of Certified Public Accountants.

Molitor, Brian D. The Power of Agreement. LC 98-48100. 256p. 1999. 14.99 (*0-8054-1836-9*) Broadman.

Molitor, Christian. Lohnflexibilitat auf Regionalen Arbeitsmarkten in Deutschland und Europa: Aur Curchfuhrbarkeit der Tarifpolitischen Strategie Regionaler Lohnflexibilitat unter Besonderer Berucksichtigung Neuerer Ansatze der Lohntheorie und Politokonomischer Aspekte. (Europaische Hochschulschriften: Reihe 5: Bd. 2031). (GER., Illus.). 341p. 1996. pap. 51.95 (*3-631-31141-9*) P Lang Pubng.

Molitor, David. Open Spaces: Country Poems. (Illus.). 80p. (Orig.). 1996. pap. 10.95 (*0-918292-19-0*) Griggs Print.

Molitor, Devora L. Fun at Forty Power: Microscope Projects for Beginners. 2nd ed. (Illus.). 43p. (YA). (gr. 5 up). 1984. pap. 3.00 (*0-9629834-0-3*) Lab Bench.

Molitor, Michael R., ed. International Environmental Law. 580p. 1991. 85.00 (*90-6544-527-7*) Kluwer Law Intl.

Molitoris, Jamie, ed. see Thompson, Roger.

Molitoris, Milo, intro. The International Concordance of Inspired Writings: 1989 Edition. 676p. (Orig.). 1989. pap. 20.00 (*0-9624058-0-9*); disk 20.00 (*0-9624058-1-7*) Milo Molitoris.

Molk, Jules, jt. auth. see Tannery, Jules.

***Molk, Laurel.** Good Job, Oliver. 32p. (J). 2001. pap. 6.99 (*0-440-41737-6*) BDD Bks Young Read.

Molk, Laurel. Good Job, Oliver. LC 97-21265. 40p. (J). 1999. 14.00 (*0-517-70975-9*, Pub. by Crown Bks Yng Read) Random.

— Good Job, Oliver! LC 97-21265. (J). 1999. lib. bdg. 15.99 (*0-517-70976-7*) Crown Pub Group.

Molk, Ulrich, ed. see Spanke, Hans.

Molkenthin, A. Influence Surfaces of Two-Span Continuous Plates with Free Longitudinal Edges: Bilingual Edition. (ENG & GER., Illus.). 220p. 1971. 103.95 (*0-387-05212-7*) Spr-Verlag.

Moll. Eponyms in Orthopaedics & Rheumatology. (Illus.). (C). (gr. 13). 1995. 22.00 (*0-412-27200-8*) Chapman & Hall.

— Rheumatology. 2nd ed. 1998. pap. text 16.95 (*0-443-05887-3*, W B Saunders Co) Harcrt Hlth Sci Grp.

Moll, Albert. Hypnotism. (Hypnosis & Altered States of Consciousness Ser.). 626p. 1982. reprint ed. lib. bdg. 49.50 (*0-306-76079-7*) Da Capo.

— Libido Sexualis: Studies in the Psychosexual Laws of Love Verified by Clinical Sexual Case Histories. Berger, David, tr. from GER. LC 72-11288. reprint ed. 36.00 (*0-404-57481-5*) AMS Pr.

— Perversions of the Sex Instinct. LC 72-11289.Tr. of Die/Contraere Sexualempfindung. (ENG.). reprint ed. 38.50 (*0-404-57482-3*) AMS Pr.

— The Sexual Life of the Child. Paul, Eden, tr. from GER. LC 72-11290. reprint ed. 39.00 (*0-404-57483-1*) AMS Pr.

Moll, Aristides A. Aesculapius in Latin America. LC 76-101589. (Illus.). 1969. reprint ed. 25.00 (*0-87266-022-2*) Argosy.

Moll, Ernest G. The View from a Ninetieth Birthday: Lyrical Poems of Old Age. Iddings, Kathleen, ed. LC 91-77893. (Illus.). 71p. (Orig.). 1992. per. 10.00 (*0-931721-12-1*) La Jolla Poets.

Moll, Gary & Young, Stanley. Growing Greener Cities: A Tree-Planting Handbook. Berland, Dinah, ed. LC 91-78089. (Illus.). 126p. (Orig.). 1992. pap. 7.95 (*1-879326-13-2*) Living Planet Pr.

Moll, H. A. The Economics of Oil Palm. (C). 1991. text 395.00 (*0-89771-598-5*, Pub. by Intl Bk Distr) St Mut.

Moll, H. David, jt. auth. see Wolfe, Dwight F.

Moll, H. J. Van, see Van Moll, H. J.

Moll, Harold W., ed. see Baierlain, E. R.

Moll, J. M. Rheumatology. 2nd ed. LC 96-39719. (Colour Guide Ser.). 1997. write for info. (*0-443-05805-9*) Harcrt Hlth Sci Grp.

Moll, Joy K., jt. auth. see Flood, Barbara J.

Moll, Kevin N. Counterpoint & Compositional Process in the Time of Dufay: Perspectives from German Musicology. Owens, Jessie A., ed. LC 97-25691. (Criticism & Analysis of Early Music Ser.: Vol. 2). 411p. 1997. reprint ed. text 79.00 (*0-8153-2346-8*, H1982) Garland.

Moll, Linda J. A Poison Tree: A Children's Fairy Tale. (Illus.). 40p. (J). (gr. 1). 1994. 12.95 (*0-9641641-1-6*) Punking Pr.

Moll, Louise. Literary Cryptograms. LC 97-43672. 128p. 1998. 5.95 (*0-8069-9616-1*) Sterling.

Moll, Louise B. Clever Cryptograms. LC 94-17397. (Illus.). 128p. 1994. pap. 5.95 (*0-8069-0756-8*) Sterling.

— Cryptogram-a-Day Book. LC 96-28210. 128p. 1996. pap. 5.95 (*0-8069-8110-5*) Sterling.

— Great Book of Cryptograms. LC 92-39447. (Illus.). 128p. (YA). (gr. 10-12). 1993. pap. 5.95 (*0-8069-8784-7*) Sterling.

***Moll, Lucy.** Energy Eating: The Vegetarian Way. LC 98-56394. (Illus.). 376p. 1999. pap. 13.95 (*0-399-52512-2*, Perigee Bks) Berkley Pub.

Moll, Lucy, jt. auth. see Vegetarian Times Editors.

Moll, Luis C., ed. Vygotsky & Education: Instructional Implications & Applications of Socio-Historical Psychology. (Illus.). 451p. (C). 1992. pap. text 25.95 (*0-521-38579-2*) Cambridge U Pr.

Moll, Manfred. Beers & Coolers. 155.00 (*1-898298-09-2*) Spr-Verlag.

Moll, Patricia B. Children & Books I: African American Story Books & Activities for All Children. (Children &... Ser.). (Illus.). 250p. 1994. spiral bd. 14.95 (*0-9616511-5-6*) Hampton Mae.

— Children & Books I: African American Story Books & Activities for All Children. 2nd ed. (Children &... Ser.). (Illus.). 250p. 1994. pap. 14.95 (*0-9616511-4-8*) Hampton Mae.

Moll, R. N., et al. An Introduction to Formal Language Theory. (Texts & Monographs in Computer Science). (Illus.). 232p. 1988. 54.00 (*0-387-96698-6*) Spr-Verlag.

Moll, Richard W. Playing the Selective College Admissions Game. 2nd ed. 256p. (Orig.). 1994. pap. 11.95 (*0-14-051303-5*, Penguin Bks) Viking Penguin.

Moll, Robert & Zaiter, Raafat M. How to Jump Start Your Quest for Financial Freedom. (Illus.). 112p. 1996. 19.95 (*0-9650611-0-8*) Zaiter-Moll.

Moll, Verna P. St. Kitts-Nevis. LC 95-194311. (World Bibliographical Ser.: Vol. 174). 212p. 1995. lib. bdg. 62.00 (*1-85109-222-6*) ABC-CLIO.

— Virgin Islands. LC 92-146826. (World Bibliographical Ser.). 242p. 1992. lib. bdg. 78.00 (*1-85109-165-3*) ABC-CLIO.

Moll, Victor, jt. auth. see McKean, Henry.

Moll, Walter L., tr. see Ehrlich, Eugen.

Molla, Juan. Teatro Espanol e Iberoamericano en Madrid (1962-1991) LC 92-64365. (SPA.). 204p. 1993. pap. 40.00 (*0-89295-070-6*) Society Sp & Sp-Am.

Molla, Rafiqul K. Electronic Color Separation. (Illus.). 288p. (C). 1988. 59.95 (*0-9620453-0-6*) RK Printing & Pub.

Mollaghasemi, Mansooreh & Pet-Edwards, J. Multiple Objective Decision Making. LC 96-45233. 100p. 1996. pap. 15.00 (*0-8186-7407-5*) IEEE Comp Soc.

***Mollan, John B.** Seattle Snapshot, 1952: A Five-Year-Old's-View. LC 99-90570. (Illus.). 104p. 1999. pap. 9.95 (*1-929211-00-7*, EPO Bks) Ed Passport Optns.

— Thirty Years by the Chalkboard: Some Irreverent Observations on Education. LC 99-90762. 170p. 1999. pap. 9.95 (*1-929211-10-4*) Ed Passport Optns.

Mollan-Masters, Renee. You Are Smarter Than You Think! A Practical Guide to Academic Success Using Your Personal Learning Style. (Orig.). (C). 1992. audio 10.00 (*0-9608622-2-6*); VHS 30.00 (*0-9608622-3-4*) Reality Prods.

— You Are Smarter Than You Think! Learning Made Easier in Three Simple Steps. 2nd rev. ed. LC 96-95469. (Illus.). 177p. 1997. pap. text 19.95 (*0-9608622-4-2*) Reality Prods.

Molland, Einar. Church Life in Norway: 1800-1950. Harris, Kaasa, tr. LC 78-2711. 120p. 1978. reprint ed. lib. bdg. 49.50 (*0-313-20342-3*, MOCL, Greenwood Pr) Greenwood.

Molland, George. Mathematics & the Medieval Ancestry of Physics. (Collected Studies: Vol. CS481). 352p. 1995. 113.95 (*0-86078-470-3*, Pub. by Variorum) Ashgate Pub Co.

Mollanen, Tuula & Martin, Christopher. Financial Evaluation of Environmental Investments. 200p. 1996. 60.00 (*0-88415-293-6*, 5293) Gulf Pub.

Mollard, F. R., jt. ed. see Murty, Y. V.

Mollard, Patrice, jt. ed. see Nichols, Robert A.

Mollat, G., ed. see Bernardus Guidonis.

Mollat, Michel. The Poor in the Middle Ages: An Essay in Social History. Goldhammer, Arthur, tr. from FRE. LC 86-1686. 336p. 1986. 47.50 (*0-300-02789-3*) Yale U Pr.

— The Poor in the Middle Ages: An Essay in Social History. (FRE.). 1990. pap. 20.00 (*0-300-04605-7*) Yale U Pr.

Mollay, Mollie. Un Reveillon Pas Comme les Autres. (Horizon Ser.: Bk. 491). 1999. mass mkt. 3.50 (*0-373-39491-8*, 1-39491-5) Harlequin Bks.

Molldrem, Mark J. The Victory of Faith: New Testament Sermons for Lent & Easter. LC 96-37185. 88p. (Orig.). 1997. pap. 10.75 (*0-7880-1005-0*) CSS OH.

Molle-Matthews, Elizabeth, jt. auth. see Hosley, Julie B.

Molle, Philippe. Classic Cooking with Pork: Over 100 Luscious Ways to Prepare Today's Lean & Healthy Pork. (Illus.). 240p. (Orig.). 1997. pap. 19.95 (*1-55013-876-6*) Firefly Bks Ltd.

M

An Asterisk (*) at the beginning of an entry indicates that the title is appearing for the first time.

Molle, Willem. The Economics of European Integration: Theory, Practice, Policy. 3rd ed. LC 97-21667. (Illus.). 584p. 1997. pap. 44.95 (*1-84014-035-6*, Pub. by Ashgate Pub); text 91.95 (*1-84014-030-5*, Pub. by Ashgate Pub) Ashgate Pub Co.

Molle, Willem & Cappellin, Riccardo. Regional Impact of Community Policies in Europe. 210p. 1988. text 87.95 (*0-566-05587-2*, Pub. by Avebry) Ashgate Pub Co.

Molle, Willem & Van Mourik, Aad. Wage Differentials in the European Community: Convergence or Divergence? (Illus.). 203p. 1989. text 87.95 (*0-566-07098-7*, Pub. by Avebry) Ashgate Pub Co.

Mollel, Tololwa. Dume's Roar. unabridged ed. LC 98-120282. (Illus.). 32p. (J). (ps-3). 1998. 14.95 (*0-7737-3003-6*) STDK.

— The Flying Tortoise: An Igboo Tale. unabridged ed. (Illus.). 32p. (J). (ps-4). 1998. 14.95 (*0-19-540990-6*) STDK.

Mollel, Tololwa M. Big Boy. (Illus.). (J). 1995. write for info. (*0-318-72305-0*, Clarion Bks) HM.

— Big Boy. (Illus.). 32p. (J). (ps-2). 1997. pap. 5.95 (*0-395-84515-7*, Clarion Bks) HM.

— Big Boy. (J). 1997. 11.15 (*0-606-11122-0*, Pub. by Turtleback) Demco.

— Big Boy. (Illus.). 32p. (J). 1994. 14.95 (*0-395-67403-4*, Clarion Bks) HM.

— The King & the Tortoise. LC 92-12485. (Illus.). 32p. (J). (gr. k-3). 1993. 14.95 (*0-395-64480-1*, Clarion Bks) HM.

— Kitoto the Mighty. LC 96-932304. (Illus.). 32p. (J). (gr. k-3). 1998. 14.95 (*0-7737-3019-2*) STDK.

— My Rows & Piles of Coins. LC 98-21586. (Illus.). 32p. (J). (gr. k-3). 1999. 15.00 (*0-395-75186-1*, Clarion Bks) HM.

— The Orphan Boy. (Illus.). (J). 1991. 14.95 (*0-685-53587-8*, Clarion Bks) HM.

— The Orphan Boy. (Illus.). 32p. (J). (gr. k-3). 1991. 16.00 (*0-89919-985-2*) HM.

— The Orphan Boy. LC 90-2358. (J). (ps-3). 1995. pap. 5.95 (*0-395-72079-6*, Clarion Bks) HM.

— The Orphan Boy: A Maasai Story. (J). 1990. 11.40 (*0-606-07977-7*) Turtleback.

— Rhinos for Lunch & Elephants for Supper! (Illus.). 32p. (J). (ps-3). 1992. 16.00 (*0-395-60734-5*, Clarion Bks) HM.

***Mollel, Tololwa M.** Rhinos for Lunch & Elephants for Supper! A Maasai Tale. (Illus.). 32p. (J). (ps-3). 2000. pap. 6.95 (*0-618-05156-2*, Clarion Bks) HM.

Mollel, Tololwa M. Shadow Dance. LC 96-47332. (Illus.). 32p. (J). (gr. k-3). 1998. 15.00 (*0-395-82909-7*) HM.

— Song Bird. LC 98-22690. (Illus.). 32p. (J). (gr. k-3). 1999. 15.00 (*0-395-82908-9*, Clarion Bks) HM.

— Subira Subira. LC 98-22564. (Illus.). 32p. (J). (gr. k-4). 2000. 15.00 (*0-395-91809-X*, Clarion Bks) HM.

***Mollel, Tololwa M.** To Dinner, for Dinner. LC 00-24329. (Illus.). 32p. (ps-3). 2000. 16.95 (*0-8234-1527-9*) Holiday.

Mollel, Tolowa. Se Kele's Secret. (Illus.). (J). 1997. pap. 14.99 (*0-525-67559-0*, Dutton Child) Peng Put Young Read.

Mollema, K. Y. Audit of Information Processing. 116p. 1990. 82.25 (*0-946395-67-5*, Pub. by Elsvr Adv Tech) Elsevier.

Mollenauer, L. F. & White, J. C., eds. Tunable Lasers. (Topics in Applied Physics Ser.: Vol. 59). (Illus.). 425p. 1987. 97.00 (*0-387-16921-0*) Spr-Verlag.

Mollenauer, Robert. Introduction to Modernity: A Symposium on Eighteenth Century Thought. LC 65-16473. 181p. reprint ed. pap. 56.20 (*0-608-10114-1*, 200469400045) Bks Demand.

Mollendorff, U. V., ed. Emerging Nuclear Energy System: Proceedings of the 5th International Conference. 356p. (C). 1989. text 151.00 (*981-02-0010-2*) World Scientific Pub.

Mollenhauer, Hans-Joachim, tr. see Strecker, Georg.

Mollenhauer, Peter. Friedrich Nicolais Satiren: Ein Beitrag Zur Kulturgeschichte Des 18. Jahrhunderts. (German Language & Literature Monographs: No. 2). viii, 267p. 1977. 59.00 (*90-272-4006-X*) J Benjamins Pubng Co.

Mollenhauer, Peter, ed. see Steiner, Rudolf.

Mollenhauer, Peter, ed. & tr. see Steiner, Rudolf.

Mollenhauer, Peter, tr. see Steiner, Rudolf.

Mollenhoff, Clark R. Ballad to an Iowa Farmer & Other Reflections by Clark Mollenhoff. LC 91-11279. (Illus.). 116p. 1991. 26.95 (*0-8138-1458-8*) Iowa St U Pr.

Mollenhoff, David V. Frank Lloyd Wright's Monona Terrace: The Enduring Power of A Civic Vision. LC 98-29148. 323p. 1999. 55.00 (*0-299-15500-5*) U of Wis Pr.

Mollenkamp, Robert A. Introduction to Automatic Process Control: Student Text. LC 84-170349. (Instructional Resource Package Ser.). 177p. 1984. reprint ed. pap. 54.90 (*0-7837-5133-8*, 204486100004) Bks Demand.

***Mollenkopf, Jim.** The Great Black Swamp: Historical Tales of 19th-Century Northwest Ohio. LC 99-73706. (Illus.). 128p. 1999. pap. 11.95 (*0-9665910-1-1*) Lake Cat.

Mollenkopf, Jim. Lake Erie Sojourn: An Autumn Tour of the Parks, Public Places & History of the Lake Erie Shore. LC 98-67389. (Illus.). 128p. 1998. pap. 10.95 (*0-9665910-0-3*) Lake Cat.

Mollenkopf, John H. A Phoenix in the Ashes: The Rise & Fall of Koch Coalition in New York City Politics. (Illus.). 280p. 1992. text 47.50 (*0-691-07854-8*, Pub. by Princeton U Pr) Cal Prin Full Svc.

— A Phoenix in the Ashes: The Rise & Fall of the Coalition in New York City Politics. 280p. (C). 1992. pap. text 15.95 (*0-691-03673-X*, Pub. by Princeton U Pr) Cal Prin Full Svc.

Mollenkopf, John H., ed. Power, Culture & Place: Essays on New York City. LC 88-39077. 320p. 1989. 40.00 (*0-87154-603-5*) Russell Sage.

Mollenkopf, John H. & Castells, Manuel. Dual City: The Restructuring of New York. LC 90-45448. 256p. 1991. 45.00 (*0-87154-606-X*) Russell Sage.

Mollenkopf, John H. & Castells, Manuel, eds. Dual City: The Restructuring of New York. (Illus.). 496p. 1992. pap. 16.95 (*0-87154-608-6*) Russell Sage.

Mollenkott, Virginia R. The Divine Feminine: The Biblical Imagery of God As Female. 128p. 1984. pap. 10.95 (*0-8245-0669-3*) Crossroad NY.

— Sensuous Spirituality: Out from Fundamentalism. 192p. 1992. pap. 12.95 (*0-8245-1168-9*) Crossroad NY.

Mollenkott, Virginia R., jt. auth. see Scanzoni, Letha D.

***Moller.** Gee up Gordon Bennet. 2000. pap. 7.50 (*0-85131-609-3*, Pub. by J A Allen) Trafalgar.

Moller. Pediatric Cardiovascular Medicine. 1999. text 115.00 (*0-443-07677-4*, W B Saunders Co) Harcrt Hlth Sci Grp.

Moller & Horton. Connecticut Practice Book Annotated - Supreme Court & Appellate Court Rules & Forms. 336p. 1985. pap. 28.50 (*0-317-52100-4*) West Pub.

Moller, A. P., jt. auth. see Birkhead, Tim R.

***Moller, Aage R.** Hearing: Its Physiology & Pathophysiology. (Illus.). 416p. 2000. 59.95 (*0-12-504255-8*) Acad Pr.

Moller, Aage R. Intraoperative Neurophysiologic Monitoring. 300p. 1995. pap. text 42.00 (*3-7186-0593-7*, Harwood Acad Pubs) Gordon & Breach.

— Intraoperative Neurophysiologic Monitoring. 346p. 1995. text 83.00 (*3-7186-0592-9*, Harwood Acad Pubs) Gordon & Breach.

Moller, Aage R., jt. ed. see Schramm, J.

Moller, Aage R., jt. ed. see Vernon, Jack A.

Moller, Anders P. Sexual Selection & the Barn Swallow. LC 93-37324. (Series in Ecology & Evolution). (Illus.). 376p. (C). 1994. 65.00 (*0-19-854029-9*); pap. text 35.00 (*0-19-854028-0*) OUP.

Moller, Anders P., et al, eds. Advances in the Study of Behavior Vol. 27: Stress & Behavior, Vol. 27. (Illus.). 552p. (C). 1998. text 99.95 (*0-12-004527-3*) Morgan Kaufmann.

Moller, Anders P. & Swaddle, John P. Asymmetry, Developmental Stability & Evolution. (Oxford Series in Ecology & Evolution). (Illus.). 302p. 1998. pap. text 39.95 (*0-19-854894-X*) OUP.

Moller, Anders P., jt. ed. see Birkhead, Tim R.

***Moller, Astrid.** Naukratis: Trade in Archaic Greece. LC 99-86587. (Oxford Monographs on Classical Archaeology). (Illus.). 320p. 2000. text 85.00 (*0-19-815284-1*) OUP.

Moller, Barbel, jt. auth. see Damskis, Horst.

Moller, Bernard. Constructing Programs from Specifications. x, 516p. 1991. 167.50 (*0-444-89184-6*, North Holland) Elsevier.

Moller, Bernard & Meinke, Karl. Higher-Order Algebra, Logic, & Term Rewriting: Selected Papers of the Second International Workshop, Hoa '95, Paderborn, Germany, September 21-22, 1995. LC 96-18318. (Lecture Notes in Computer Science Ser.: Vol. 107). 287p. 1996. pap. 49.00 (*3-540-61254-8*) Spr-Verlag.

Moller, Bernhard, et al, eds. Mathematics of Program Construction: 3rd International Conference, MPC '95, Kloster Irsee, Germany, July 17-21, 1995, Proceedings, Vol. VIII. LC 97-51958. (Lecture Notes in Computer Science Ser.: Vol. 947). 472p. 1995. 75.00 (*3-540-60117-1*) Spr-Verlag.

Moller, Bernhard & Schuman, Steve. Formal Program Development: IFIP TC 2-WG 2.1 State of the Art Report. LC 93-41255. 1993. 55.95 (*0-387-57499-9*) Spr-Verlag.

Moller, Bernhard & Tucker, J. V., eds. Prospects for Hardware Foundations: ESPRIT Working Group 8533: NADA - New Hardware Design Methods, Survey Chapters. LC 98-52459. x, 468p. 1998. pap. 69.00 (*3-540-65461-5*) Spr-Verlag.

Moller, Bill. The Gift of Hand That Heal: After the Tragic Loss of His Teenage Son, a Man Discovers His Ability to Heal Others Through Spirit Guidance. viii, 204p. 1999. 19.95 (*0-9669262-0-X*) She-I.

Moller, Bjorn. Common Security & Nonoffensive Defense: A Neorealist Perspective. LC 91-28864. 285p. 1992. lib. bdg. 45.00 (*1-55587-259-X*) L Rienner.

— The Dictionary of Alternative Defense. LC 92-27347. 540p. 1995. lib. bdg. 79.95 (*1-55587-386-3*) L Rienner.

— Resolving the Security Dilemma in Europe: The German Debate on Non-Offensive Defense. 339p. 1991. 56.00 (*0-08-041315-3*, Pub. by Brasseys) Brasseys.

Moller, Bjorn, ed. Security, Arms Control & Defence Restructuring in East Asia. LC 98-6525. 286p. 1998. text 72.95 (*1-84014-006-2*, Pub. by Ashgate Pub) Ashgate Pub Co.

Moller, Bjorn & Cawthra, Gavin, eds. Defensive Restructuring of the Armed Forces in Southern Africa. LC 97-2977. 192p. 1997. text 72.95 (*1-85521-951-4*, Pub. by Ashgate Pub) Ashgate Pub Co.

Moller, C. Theory of Relativity. 2nd ed. (International Series of Monographs on Physics). (Illus.). 572p. 1976. pap. text 21.50 (*0-19-560539-X*) OUP.

Moller, Chris. Evolution, Civilisation & the Horse! 128p. 1990. pap. 30.00 (*0-85131-564-X*, Pub. by J A Allen) Trafalgar.

Moller, Claus, jt. auth. see Barlow, Janelle.

***Moller, D., ed.** Atmospheric Environmental Research: Critical Decisions Between Technological Progress & Preservation of Nature. LC 99-38999. (Illus.). xiv, 208p. 1999. 62.00 (*3-540-63559-9*) Spr-Verlag.

Moller, David, ed. Insulin Resistance. LC 93-18929. 440p. 1993. 290.00 (*0-471-93977-3*) Wiley.

Moller, David W. Death & Dying: Values, Institutions, & Human Mortality. (Illus.). 320p. (C). 1996. pap. text 23.95 (*0-19-504296-4*) OUP.

— On Death Without Dignity: The Human Impact of Technological Dying. (Perspectives on Death & Dying Ser.). 134p. 1990. text 45.95 (*0-89503-067-5*) Baywood Pub.

***Moller, David Wendell.** Life's End: Technocratic Dying in an Age of Spiritual Yearning. LC 99-33740. 195p. 1999. 36.00 (*0-89503-202-3*) Baywood Pub.

Moller, Deanna. Line upon Line: Challenging Crossword Classics for Latter-Day Saints. 56p. 1993. 8.98 (*0-88290-480-9*, 2061) Horizon Utah.

Moller, Elfriede. Shibori: The Art of Fabric Folding, Pleating & Dyeing. (Illus.). 64p. 1999. pap. 17.95 (*0-85532-895-9*, 8959, Pub. by Srch Pr) A Schwartz & Co.

Moller, Erik. Trends in Civil Jury Verdicts since, 1985. LC 96-19851. xxi, 84p. (Orig.). 1996. pap. 15.00 (*0-8330-2360-8*, MR-694-ICJ) Rand Corp.

Moller, Erik, et al. Punitive Damages in Financial Injury Jury Verdicts. LC 97-196864. (Illus.). 84p. 1997. pap. 9.00 (*0-8330-2536-8*, MR-888-ICJ) Rand Corp.

— Punitive Damages in Financial Injury Jury Verdicts: An Executive Summary. LC 97-196893. (Illus.). 41p. 1997. pap. 9.00 (*0-8330-2534-1*, MR-889-ICJ) Rand Corp.

Moller, Erik, jt. auth. see Rolph, Elizabeth S.

Moller, Faron & Birtwistle, Graham. Logics for Concurrency: Structure vs. Automata. LC 96-5558. (Lecture Notes in Computer Science Ser.: Vol. 1043). xi, 266p. 1996. pap. 49.00 (*3-540-60915-6*) Spr-Verlag.

Moller, Garth I., ed. see Knierim, Rolf P., et al.

Moller, Gayle, jt. auth. see Katzenmeyer, Marilyn.

Moller, George D. Massachusetts Military Shoulder Arms, 1784-1877. LC 88-60020. (Illus.). 124p. 1988. 24.00 (*0-917218-34-5*) A Mowbray.

Moller, H., et al, eds. Quantitive Estimation & Prediction of Human Cancer Risks. (IARC Scientific Publications Ser.: No. 131). 440p. 1999. pap. text 69.00 (*92-832-2131-1*) OUP.

Moller, H. & Oeser. Drug Master Files: Global Harmonization of Quality Standards. 1992. 66.00 (*3-8047-1207-X*) CRC Pr.

Moller, H. J., et al. Polycrystalline Semiconductors Grain Boundaries & Interfaces. (Proceedings in Physics Ser.: Vol. 35). (Illus.). 380p. 1989. 85.95 (*0-387-50887-2*) Spr-Verlag.

Moller, Hans J. Semiconductors for Solar Cells. LC 92-40718. (Optoelectronics Library). 275p. 1993. text 29.00 (*0-89006-574-8*) Artech Hse.

Moller, I. M., et al, eds. Plant Mitochondria: From Gene to Function. (Illus.). 618p. 1998. 174.50 (*90-5782-009-9*) Backhuys Pubs.

Moller, I. M., jt. ed. see Larsson, C.

Moller, Ingrid K. S., jt. auth. see Sherlock, Basil J.

Moller, Iver H., jt. ed. see Lind, Jens.

Moller, J. Orstrom. The End of Internationalism: Or World Governance? LC 99-22109. 224p. 2000. 59.95 (*0-275-96701-8*) Greenwood.

— The Future European Model: Economic Internationalization & Cultural Decentralization. LC 94-21688. (Praeger Studies on the 21st Century). 152p. 1995. 65.00 (*0-275-95012-3*, Praeger Pubs); pap. 19.95 (*0-275-95187-1*) Greenwood.

Moller, James H., ed. Surgery of Congenital Heart Disease: The Pediatric Cardiac Care Consortium 1984-1995. (Perspectives in Pediatric Cardiology Ser.: No. 6). (Illus.). 412p. 1997. pap. 97.00 (*0-87993-678-9*) Futura Pub.

Moller, James H. & Neal, William A. Fetal, Neonatal & Infant Cardiac Disease. (Illus.). 1061p. (C). 1992. pap. text 210.00 (*0-8385-2575-X*, A2575-7, Apple Lange Med) McGraw.

Moller, Jarub. Theme of Identity in the Essays of James Baldwin. 196p. (Orig.). 1975. pap. text 47.50 (*91-7346-008-7*) Coronet Bks.

Moller, Jens T., et al, eds. Archaeology & Geophysical Prospections. (Working Papers: No. 14). (Illus.). 215p. (Orig.). (C). 1984. pap. 21.00 (*87-480-0574-6*, Pub. by Aarhus Univ Pr) David Brown.

Moller, Jesper. Lectures on Random Voronoi Tesselations. LC 94-248. (Lecture Notes in Statistics Ser.: Vol. 87). (Illus.). 144p. 1994. 39.95 (*0-387-94264-5*) Spr-Verlag.

Moller, Jonathan R. Los Beneficios del Protocob. (SPA.). 1994. pap. 110.00 (*1-884045-01-4*) Protocol Res.

— The Protocol Advantage. LC 93-93668. (Illus.). 408p. (Orig.). 1993. pap. 110.00 (*1-884045-00-6*) Protocol Res.

— The Protocol Advantage: A Comprehensive Guide to Modern Protocol, Etiquette & Dignitary Management Techniques. rev. ed. (Illus.). 400p. 1997. 60.00 (*1-884045-02-2*) Protocol Res.

— Software Metrics: A Practical Guide. (C). 1992. pap. 41.95 (*0-412-45900-0*) Chapman & Hall.

Moller, Karlind T. & Starr, Clark D., eds. Cleft Palate: Interdisciplinary Issues & Treatment. LC 92-12022. (For Clinicians by Clinicians Ser.). 409p. 1993. pap. text 36.00 (*0-89079-567-3*, 4046) PRO-ED.

Moller, Kristian & Wilson, David T., eds. Business Marketing: An Interaction & Network Perspective. LC 94-29887. 656p. (C). 1995. lib. bdg. 151.50 (*0-7923-9504-2*) Kluwer Academic.

Moller, Lis. The Freudian Reading: Analytical & Fictional Constructions. LC 91-22539. 184p. (Orig.). (C). 1991. text 32.50 (*0-8122-3126-0*); pap. text 14.95 (*0-8122-1381-5*) U of Pa Pr.

***Moller, Lis & Svane, Marie-Louise, eds.** Romanticism in Theory. (Illus.). 240p. 2000. pap. 29.95 (*87-7288-786-9*, Pub. by Aarhus Univ Pr) David Brown.

Moller, Lisa, ed. see Billstein, Richard, et al.

Moller, Lisa, ed. see Nagle, R. Kent.

Moller, Lisa, ed. see Triola, Mario F.

Moller, Mary E. Thoreau in the Human Community. LC 79-22549. 224p. 1980. lib. bdg. 30.00 (*0-87023-293-2*) U of Mass Pr.

Moller, Michael F. Die Ersten Freigelassenen der Schopfung: Das Menschenbild Johann Gottfried Herders Im Kontext Von Theologie Und Philosophie der Aufklarung Herausgegeben Von Ulrich Kuhn. 158p. 1998. 31.95 (*3-631-33568-7*) P Lang Pubng.

Moller, Paulette, tr. see Gaarder, Jostein.

Moller, Peter & Lueders, Volker, eds. Formation of Hydrothermal Vein Deposits - Case Study of the Pb-Zn, Barite & Fluorite Deposits of the Harz Mountains. (Monograph Series on Mineral Deposits: No. 30). (Illus.). viii, 291p. 1993. pap. 88.00 (*3-443-12030-X*, Pub. by Gebruder Borntraeger) Balogh.

Moller, Peter, jt. auth. see LeCroy, Dori.

Moller, Poul B., jt. ed. see Dybbroe, Susanne.

Moller, Richard. Marijuana: Your Legal Rights. LC 81-621. 1981. pap. 9.95 (*0-201-04777-2*) Addison-Wesley.

Moller, Rolf, jt. ed. see Marti, Othmar.

Moller, Ros Maria. Effects of the North American Free Trade Agreement (NAFTA) on State Policies. 64p. 1995. pap. write for info. (*1-58703-039-X*, CRB-95-005) CA St Libry.

Moller, Rosa Maria. Brief Overview of Recent Patterns of California Exports. 8p. 1995. pap. write for info. (*1-58703-040-3*) CA St Libry.

— Hong Kong's Reversion to the People's Republic of China: Implications for California. 27p. 1997. pap. write for info. (*1-58703-071-3*, CRB-97-010) CA St Libry.

— Other States' Incentives to Attract or Encourage Aerospace Manufacturing. 47p. 1999. pap. write for info. (*1-58703-109-4*, CRB-99-010) CA St Libry.

— Profile of California Computer & Internet Users. 21p. 2000. pap. write for info. (*1-58703-123-X*, CRB-00-002) CA St Libry.

— Report on Small Business Credit Availability. 72p. 1996. pap. write for info. (*1-58703-045-4*, CRB-96-001) CA St Libry.

— Securities Regulations & Their Effects on Small Businesses. 85p. 2000. pap. write for info. (*1-58703-124-8*, CRB-00-005) CA St Libry.

Moller, Rosa Maria, jt. auth. see Koehler, Gus.

Moller, S., jt. auth. see McPherson, M. J.

***Moller, Sharon Chickering.** Library Service to Spanish Speaking Patrons: A Practical Guide. 200p. 2000. 28.00 (*1-56308-719-7*) Libs Unl.

Moller, Susann. I Dance in Your Light That Is Also My Own. LC 93-32605. 64p. 1993. pap. 14.95 (*0-7734-2793-7*, Mellen Poetry Pr) E Mellen.

Moller, Tomas & Haines, Eric. Real-Time Rendering. LC 99-29006. (Illus.). 512p. (C). 1999. text 49.95 (*1-56881-101-2*) AK Peters.

***Moller, Torsten B.** Normal Findings in Radiology. LC 99-40799. (Illus.). 280p. 1999. pap. 32.00 (*0-86577-871-X*) Thieme Med Pubs.

Moller, Torsten B. & Reif, Emil. MRI Atlas of the Musculoskeletal System. LC 93-2493.Tr. of MR-Atlas des Muskuloskelettalen Systems. 308p. 1993. 250.00 (*0-86542-291-5*) Blackwell Sci.

***Moller, Torsten B. & Reif, Emil.** Normal Findings in CT & MRI. LC 99-33663. 1999. write for info. (*3-13-116521-9*) Thieme Med Pubs.

Moller, Valerie, ed. Quality of Life in South Africa. LC 97-225175. 300p. 1997. 130.50 (*0-7923-4797-8*) Kluwer Academic.

Mollerke, G., jt. auth. see Flack, H. K.

Mollerup, Per. Marks of Excellence: The History & Taxonomy of Trademarks. (Illus.). 240p. 1997. 75.00 (*0-7148-3448-3*, Pub. by Phaidon Press) Phaidon Pr.

— Marks of Excellence: The History & Taxonomy of Trademarks. 1999. pap. text 29.95 (*0-7148-3838-1*) Phaidon Press.

Molles. Ecology. 2nd ed. 2001. 53.25 (*0-07-029416-X*) McGraw.

***Molles.** Evolution Chapter 21 Ecology. 1999. pap. text 2.00 (*0-07-235942-0*) McGraw.

Molles, Manuel C. Ecology: Concepts & Applications. LC 98-4525. 1998. 67.38 (*0-07-042716-X*) McGraw.

Molleson, Diane. How Ducklings Grow. (Read with Me Paperback Ser.). (Illus.). 32p. (J). (ps-2). 1993. pap. 2.50 (*0-590-45201-0*) Scholastic Inc.

Mollett, J. A., ed. Migrants in Agricultural Development. 260p. (C). 1991. text 80.00 (*0-8147-5459-7*) NYU Pr.

Mollett, Ken, jt. auth. see Jenkins, Robert.

Mollhausen, Balduin. Ausgewahlte Werke Band 2.1: Daraus: Abteilung I: Erzahlungen. (GER.). 688p. 1998. reprint ed. 110.00 (*3-487-10167-X*, Pub. by G Olms Verlag) Lubrecht & Cramer.

— Ausgewahlte Werke Band 2.2: Daraus: Abteilung I: Erzahlungen. (GER.). 688p. 1998. reprint ed. 110.00 (*3-487-10168-8*, Pub. by G Olms Verlag) Lubrecht & Cramer.

Mollhausen, Baldwin. Diary of a Journey from the Mississippi to the Coasts of the Pacific: With a United States Government Expedition, 2 vols., Set. (American Biography Ser.). 1991. reprint ed. lib. bdg. 148.00 (*0-7812-8287-X*) Rprt Serv.

Molli, Jeanne, jt. auth. see Gabriel, Vernice.

Mollica, Anthony S. Gar Wood Boats - Power Classics of a Golden Era: Classics from the Golden Era. LC 99-12437. (Illus.). 128p. 1999. 24.95 (*0-7603-0607-9*, 128073AP) Motorbooks Intl.

Mollica, Anthony S. & Northup, Bill. Those Wonderful Chris-Craft Speedboats. (Coloring the Classics Ser.). (Illus.). 28p. (J). 1992. student ed. 3.95 (*1-883029-02-3*) CHP NY.

Mollica, Peter. Stained Glass Primer, Vol. 1. 1971. pap. 6.95 (*0-9601306-1-6*) Mollica Stained Glass.

M

An Asterisk (*) at the beginning of an entry indicates that the title is appearing for the first time.

M

— Otto's Box of Bad Feelings. (Kid Safe Ser.). (Illus.). (Orig.). (J). (ps-3). 1995. pap. 5.00 (*0-9644142-1-X*) Open Book Pubng.

— Some Touch Is Good, Some Touch Is Bad. (Kid Safe Ser.). (Illus.). 16p. (Orig.). (J). (ps-1). 1994. pap. 5.00 (*0-9644142-0-1*) Open Book Pubng.

— Some Touch Is Good, Some Touch Is Bad - The Coloring Book. (Illus.). 8p. (Orig.). (J). (ps-k). 1995. pap. 1.25 (*0-9644142-4-4*) Open Book Pubng.

Molnar, Jane. Logic Mysteries. 1999. pap. text 12.95 (*0-7690-0001-0*) Seymour Pubns.

Molnar, John. Facilities Management Handbook. 256p. (gr. 13). 1983. text 70.95 (*0-442-26347-3*) Chapman & Hall.

***Molnar, Judy.** You Don't Have to Be Thin to Win: The Official Chub Club Coach's Workout Program. LC 99-48598. 2000. 19.95 (*0-375-50414-1*) Villard Books.

Molnar, Julie A. Out from under the Artist's Brush: A Lacanian Approach to Painting & Naturalism. LC 91-3967. (American University Studies, II, Romance Language & Literature: Vol. 176). XV, 173p. (C). 1994. text 43.95 (*0-8204-1642-8*) P Lang Pubng.

Molnar, Lawrence A., et al. Sustaining Economic Growth: The Positive Impact of the Michigan Incubator Industry 1985-1995. 1996. pap. 29.95 (*1-887183-37-X*) NBIA.

Molnar, M., tr. see Shvarts, Elena.

Molnar, Michael R. The Star of Bethlehem: The Legacy of the Magi. LC 98-55376. (Illus.). 208p. 1999. 25.00 (*0-8135-2701-5*) Rutgers U Pr.

Molnar, Miklos. Egy Vereseg Diadala. Kis, Janos, ed. (Adalekok az Ujabbikori Magyar Tortenelemhe Ser.). (HUN., Illus.). 221p. (Orig.). 1988. reprint ed. pap. 16.00 (*0-929322-00-2*) Atl Rsch & Pubns.

— From Bela Kun to Janos Kadar: Seventy Years of Hungarian Communism. Pomerans, Arnold J., tr. LC 89-28943.Tr. of De Bela Kun a Janos Kadar: Soixante-dix ans de Communisme. 305p. 1990. 19.50 (*0-85496-599-8*) Berg Pubs.

Molnar, Miklos & Nagy, Laszlo. In Defense of the Hungarian People.Tr. of Nagy Imre a Magyar nep Vedelmeben. (HUN.). 250p. (Orig.). 1984. pap. 13.00 (*0-930888-23-5*) Brooklyn Coll Pr.

Molnar, Niklos & Nagy, Laszlo. Reformer Vagy Forradalmar Volt-e Nagy Imre? LC 83-61981. (HUN.). 160p. 1983. pap. 10.00 (*0-930888-22-7*) Brooklyn Coll Pr.

Molnar, P., jt. auth. see Burtman, V. S.

Molnar, P., jt. ed. see Lissak, K.

Molnar, Paul D. Karl Barth & the Theology of the Lord's Supper Vol. 1: A Systematic Investigation. (Issues in Systematic Theology Ser.). XI, 333p. (C). 1996. pap. text 39.95 (*0-8204-2825-6*) P Lang Pubng.

Molnar, Peter, jt. ed. see Segerstrale, Ullica.

Molnar, Ralph E., jt. auth. see Farlow, James O.

Molnar, Stephen. Human Variation: Races, Types, & Ethnic Groups. 4th ed. LC 97-1104. 396p. 1997. pap. text 46.00 (*0-13-269523-5*) P-H.

Molnar, Thomas. Archetypes of Thought. 160p. (C). 1995. pap. text 21.95 (*1-56000-848-2*) Transaction Pubs.

— Authority & Its Enemies. rev. ed. LC 94-21409. 162p. (C). 1994. pap. 21.95 (*1-56000-777-X*) Transaction Pubs.

— Bernanos: His Political Thought & Prophecy. LC 96-17937. 215p. (Orig.). 1996. pap. text 21.95 (*1-56000-932-2*) Transaction Pubs.

— Christian Humanism, a Critique of the Secular City & Its Ideology. 172p. 1978. 7.95 (*0-8199-0694-8*, Frncsen Herld) Franciscan Pr.

— The Decline of the Intellectual. rev. ed. LC 94-14112. 380p. (C). 1994. pap. 24.95 (*1-56000-743-5*) Transaction Pubs.

— Dialogues & Ideologues. 169p. 1977. reprint ed. 4.95 (*0-8199-0679-4*, Frncscn Herld) Franciscan Pr.

— The Emerging Atlantic Culture. LC 93-11170. 120p. (C). 1993. text 34.95 (*1-56000-124-0*) Transaction Pubs.

— God & the Knowledge of Reality. LC 92-32934. 263p. (C). 1993. pap. text 24.95 (*1-56000-665-X*) Transaction Pubs.

— Philosophical Grounds. LC 91-10918. (American University Studies: Philosophy: Ser. V, Vol. 114). 162p. (C). 1991. text 32.95 (*0-8204-1485-9*) P Lang Pubng.

— Return to Philosophy. 113p. 1996. text 24.95 (*1-56000-251-4*) Transaction Pubs.

— Theist & Atheist: A Typology of Non-Belief. 1979. text 60.80 (*90-279-7788-7*) Mouton.

— Utopia, the Perennial Heresy. rev. ed. 260p. (C). 1990. reprint ed. text 43.00 (*0-8191-7667-2*); reprint ed. pap. text 24.00 (*0-8191-7668-0*) U Pr of Amer.

Molnar, Thomas S. The Church, Pilgrim of Centuries. fac. ed. LC 90-41597. 192p. 1990. reprint ed. pap. 59.60 (*0-7837-7965-8*, 204772100008) Bks Demand.

— The Pagan Temptation. LC 87-8898. 205p. (Orig.). reprint ed. pap. 63.60 (*0-7837-0519-0*, 204084300018) Bks Demand.

— Twin Powers: Politics & the Sacred. LC 88-10204. 157p. reprint ed. pap. 48.70 (*0-7837-0520-4*, 204084400018) Bks Demand.

Molnar, Zoltan. Development of Thalamocortical Connections. LC 97-36608. (Neuroscience Intelligence Unit Ser.). 249p. 1998. 169.00 (*3-540-64225-0*) Spr-Verlag.

Molnarfi, Laszlo. Kasus und Passivierung: Ein Beitrag zur Kasustheorie. (Europaische Hochschulschriften Ser.: Reihe 21, Bd. 189). (Illus.). 304p. 1997. 57.95 (*3-631-31965-7*) P Lang Pubng.

Molnia, Bruce F. Alaska's Glaciers. LC 72-92087. (Alaska Geographic Ser.: Vol. 9, No. 1). (Illus.). 144p. 1993. pap. 19.95 (*1-56661-016-8*) Alaska Geog Soc.

Molnia, Bruce F., ed. Glacial-Marine Sedimentation. LC 83-19104. 854p. 1984. 145.00 (*0-306-41497-X*, Plenum Trade) Perseus Pubng.

Molnia, Bruce F., jt. ed. see Anderson, J. B.

Molnos, Angela. Our Responses to a Deadly Virus: The Group-Analytic Approach. 220p. 1990. pap. text 15.00 (*0-946439-80-X*, Pub. by H Karnac Bks Ltd) Other Pr LLC.

— A Question of Time: Essentials of Brief Dynamic Therapy. 152p. 1995. pap. text 25.00 (*1-85575-107-0*, Pub. by H Karnac Bks Ltd) Other Pr LLC.

Molo, Graham. Paper Chain. 380p. mass mkt. 4.99 (*1-896329-81-0*) Picasso Publ.

***Molock, Brother.** Voodoo Magick Course: Powers of Voodoo, 8, Set. Templar, Thor, ed. (Illus.). 400p. 2000. 120.00 (*1-57179-077-2*) Intern Guild ASRS.

Molod, Alan H. Pennsylvania Limited Liability Company Forms & Practice Manual. LC 96-22275. 644p. 1996. ring bd. 219.90 (*1-57400-003-9*) Data Trace Pubng.

Molodenskii, M. S. Methods for Study of the External Gravitational Field & Figure of the Earth. LC 62-61244. 254p. reprint ed. pap. 78.80 (*0-608-30227-9*, 200233200012) Bks Demand.

***Molodowsky, Kadia.** Paper Bridges: Selected Poems of Kadya Molodowsky. 1999. 49.95 (*0-8143-2846-6*) Wayne St U Pr.

Molodowsky, Kadia & Hellerstein, Kathryn. Paper Bridges: Selected Poems of Kadya Molodowsky. LC 98-15479. 1999. pap. 29.95 (*0-8143-2718-4*) Wayne St U Pr.

Moloff, Ronald L. & Stein, Stephen D. Realities of Dental Therapy: A Detailed Review of Periodontal Prosthetic Treatment. (Illus.). 471p. 1982. text 110.00 (*0-931386-42-X*) Quint Pub Co.

***Molohan, Cathy.** Germany & Ireland, 1945-1955: Two Nations' Friendship. LC 99-13449. (Illus.). 136p. 1999. 52.50 (*0-7165-2631-X*, Pub. by Irish Acad Pr); pap. 24.50 (*0-7165-2708-1*, Pub. by Irish Acad Pr) Intl Spec Bk.

Molokhovets, Elena. Classic Russian Cooking: Elena Molokhovets' A Gift to Young Housewives. Toomre, Joyce, tr. & anno. by. LC 91-46254. (Indiana-Michigan Series in Russian & East European Studies). (Illus.). 704p. 1992. 44.95 (*0-253-36026-9*) Ind U Pr.

Molokhovets, Elena. Classic Russian Cooking: Elena Molokhovets' A Gift to Young Housewives. Toomre, Joyce, tr. & anno. by. LC 91-46254. (Indiana-Michigan Series in Russian & East European Studies). (Illus.). 704p. 1998. pap. 35.00 (*0-253-21210-3*) Ind U Pr.

Molon, Dominic, et al. Mariko Mori. LC 98-8268. (Illus.). 80p. 1998. pap. 20.00 (*0-933856-57-1*) Mus Art Chicago.

Moloney, Brian, intro. Novelle del Novecento. (Italian Texts Ser.). (ITA.). 150p. (Orig.). 1988. reprint ed. text 16.95 (*0-7190-0200-1*, Pub. by Manchester Univ Pr) St Martin.

Moloney, Ed & Pollak, Andy. Paisley. (Illus.). 464p. 1986. pap. 13.95 (*0-905169-75-1*, Pub. by Poolbeg Pr) Dufour.

Moloney, Francis J. Belief in the Word: Reading John 1-4. LC 92-21757. 248p. 1993. pap. 25.00 (*0-8006-2584-6*, 1-2584) Augsburg Fortress.

— A Body Broken for a Broken People: Eucharist in the New Testament. 152p. 1991. reprint ed. 12.95 (*0-85924-892-5*) Harper SF.

— A Body Broken for a Broken People: Eucharist in the New Testament. rev. ed. LC 96-43159. 212p. 1997. pap. 14.95 (*1-56563-258-3*) Hendrickson MA.

— Glory Not Dishonor: Reading John 13-21. LC 98-42251. 208p. 1998. 25.00 (*0-8006-3140-4*, 1-3140) Augsburg Fortress.

— The Gospel of the Lord: Reflections on the Gospel Readings, Cycle B. 232p. (Orig.). 1996. pap. 12.95 (*0-8146-2269-0*, Litурg Pr Bks) Liturgical Pr.

— Gospel of the Lord: Reflections on the Gospel Readings, Cycle C. LC 94-6110. 208p. 1994. pap. 11.95 (*0-8146-2270-4*) Liturgical Pr.

— Signs & Shadows: Reading John 5-12. LC 96-11618. 224p. 1996. pap. 22.00 (*0-8006-2936-1*, Fortress Pr) Augsburg Fortress.

Moloney, G. E. A Doctor in Saudi Arabia. (Arabia Past & Present Ser.: Vol. 23). (Illus.). 356p. 1982. 32.50 (*0-906672-81-3*) Oleander Pr.

Moloney-Harmon, Patricia A. Managing Pediatric Emergencies. (Cardiopulmonary Arrest Ser.). (Illus.). 104p. (Orig.). 1984. pap. text 9.50 (*0-932491-03-0*) Res Appl Inc.

Moloney-Harmon, Patricia A., jt. auth. see Czerwinski, Sandra.

Moloney, J. V., ed. Nonlinear Optical Materials. (IMA Volumes in Mathematics & Its Applications Ser.). (Illus.). 267p. 1997. 69.95 (*0-387-98581-6*) Spr-Verlag.

Moloney, James. Angela. LC 99-222863. (YA). 1998. 22.95 (*0-7022-3082-0*, Pub. by Univ Queensland Pr) Intl Spec Bk.

— Buzzard Breath & Brains. LC 99-210789. (Storybridge Ser.). 96p. (J). 1998. pap. 10.95 (*0-7022-2956-3*, Pub. by Univ Queensland Pr) Intl Spec Bk.

— Crossfire. 144p. (YA). 1998. reprint ed. pap. 12.95 (*0-7022-2384-0*, Pub. by Univ Queensland Pr) Intl Spec Bk.

— Dougy. (YA). 1993. pap. 11.95 (*0-7022-2499-5*, Pub. by Univ Queensland Pr) Intl Spec Bk.

— Gracey. (J). 1998. pap. 12.95 (*0-7022-2610-6*, Pub. by Univ Queensland Pr) Intl Spec Bk.

— The House on River Terrace. (YA). 1995. pap. 11.95 (*0-7022-2742-0*, Pub. by Univ Queensland Pr) Intl Spec Bk.

— Swashbuckler. (Storybridge Ser.). 96p. (J). (gr. 4-7). 1995. pap. 9.95 (*0-7022-2825-7*, Pub. by Univ Queensland Pr) Intl Spec Bk.

***Moloney, James.** Touch Me. 2000. pap. 14.95 (*0-7022-3151-7*, Pub. by Univ Queensland Pr) Intl Spec Bk.

Moloney, James H. Bowties of the Fifties. (Illus.). 248p. 1996. 34.95 (*0-8376-0955-0*) Bentley Pubs.

— Early Ford V8s 1932-1942 Photo Album. LC 98-75274. (Illus.). 112p. 1999. pap. 19.95 (*1-882256-97-2*, 128232AE) Iconografix.

— Studebaker Cars. (Crestline Ser.). (Illus.). 392p. 1994. 44.95 (*0-87938-884-6*, Crestline Pub) MBI Pubg.

Moloney, Jerome V. & Newell, Alan C. Nonlinear Optics. (ATIMS Ser.). 320p. (C). 1992. 46.95 (*0-201-51014-6*) Addison-Wesley.

Moloney, John. A Soul Came into Ireland: Thomas Davis, 1814-1845. LC 95-231112. (Illus.). 385p. 1995. pap. 39.95 (*0-906602-65-3*, Pub. by Geography Pubns) Irish Bks Media.

Moloney, Kevin. Lobbyists for Hire. LC 96-1352. (Illus.). 200p. 1996. 77.95 (*1-85521-794-5*, Pub. by Dartmth Pub) Ashgate Pub Co.

***Moloney, Kevin.** Rethinking Public Relations: The Spin & the Substance. LC 99-86064. 2000. write for info. (*0-415-21759-8*) Routledge.

Moloney, Laurie, ed. see Ashton, Tia, et al.

***Moloney, Mark G.** Reaction Mechanisms at a Glance. LC 99-28232. (Illus.). 1999. pap. 24.95 (*0-632-05002-0*) Blackwell Sci.

***Moloney, Mick.** Farewell to the Groves of Shiloh. 2001. 29.95 (*0-609-60720-0*, Pub. by Crown Pub Group) Random House.

Moloney, Niamh, ed. Conflict of Laws. 320p. 1996. pap. 95.00 (*0-7510-0702-1*, Pub. by HLT Pubns) St Mut.

— Conflict of Laws Cases. 340p. 1996. pap. 95.00 (*0-7510-0667-X*, Pub. by HLT Pubns) St Mut.

Moloney, Norah. The Young Oxford Book of Archaeology. LC 97-16096. (Illus.). 160p. (YA). (gr. 5 up). 1997. 25.00 (*0-19-910067-5*) OUP.

***Moloney, Norah.** The Young Oxford Book of Archaeology. (Illus.). 160p. 2000. pap. 16.95 (*0-19-910100-0*) OUP.

Moloney, Raymond. Eucharist. (Problems in Theology Ser.). 290p. 1995. pap. 19.95 (*0-8146-5853-9*) Liturgical Pr.

***Moloney, Raymond.** Knowledge of Christ. 224p. 2000. pap. 24.95 (*0-304-70577-2*) Continuum.

Moloney, Rodger T., ed. see Easterling, David M.

Moloney, Susie. Bastion Falls. 336p. 1999. mass mkt. 6.99 (*0-440-22344-X*) Dell.

— A Dry Spell. 400p. 1997. pap. 29.95 (*0-385-25663-9*) Bantam.

— A Dry Spell. 448p. 1998. mass mkt. 6.99 (*0-440-22345-8*) Doubleday.

Moloney, Thomas. Westminster, Whitehall, & the Vatican: The Role of Cardinal Hinsley, 1935-43. 264p. 1994. 36.00 (*0-86012-138-0*, Pub. by Srch Pr) St Mut.

Molony & Waszynski. Gerontological Nursing: A Primary Care Clinical Guide. LC 98-45637. (Illus.). 639p. 1999. pap. text 44.95 (*0-8385-3131-8*, Medical Exam) Appleton & Lange.

Molony, Barbara. Technology & Investment: The Pre-War Japanese Chemical Industry. LC 89-48815. (East Asian Monographs: No. 145). 350p. 1990. 35.00 (*0-674-87260-6*) HUP.

Molony, David. American Association of Oriental Medicine's Complete Guide to Chinese Herbal Medicine. LC 98-150436. 288p. 1998. pap. 13.00 (*0-425-15705-9*) Berkley Pub.

Molony, John C. Ireland's Tragic Comedians. LC 73-134117. (Essay Index Reprint Ser.). 1977. 21.95 (*0-8369-1933-5*) Ayer.

Molot, Maureen A., jt. auth. see Laux, Jeanne K.

Molot, Maureen Appel, jt. ed. see Hampson, Fen Osler.

Molotch, Harvery, jt. auth. see Warner, Kee.

Molotch, Harvey L., jt. ed. see Logan, John R.

***Molotkov, A.** Not from Around Now: Poetry for a Small Choir. (Illus.). 115p. (C). 2000. pap. 16.00 (*0-9678919-2-2*) Discord.

***Molotkov, A., et al.** The Gospel According to the Christ Brothers - The Texture of the Sky. 300p. (C). 2000. write for info. (*0-9678919-0-6*) Discord.

— Long Distance Whisper - Artificial Words. 200p. (C). 2000. write for info. (*0-9678919-1-4*) Discord.

Molotov, V. M. Molotov Remembers: Inside Kremlin Politics: Conversations with Felix Chuev. Chuev, Felix & Resis, Albert, eds. LC 93-11253.Tr. of Sto Sorok Besed s Molotovym. 464p. 1993. text 29.95 (*1-56663-027-4*) I R Dee.

Molotskii, M. I. Chemistry Reviews: Electronic Excitation During the Plastic Deformation & Fracture of Crystals, Vol. 13. Vol'pin, M. E., ed. (Soviet Scientific Reviews Ser.: Vol. 13, Pt. 3). ii, 94p. 1989. pap. text 71.00 (*3-7186-4949-7*) Gordon & Breach.

Moloy, Peter & Nicolson, Garth L., eds. Cellular Oncology: New Approaches in Biology, Diagnosis & Treatment, 1. LC 83-11222. (Cancer Research Monographs). 305p. 1983. 69.50 (*0-275-91405-4*, C1405, Praeger Pubs) Greenwood.

— Occult Nodal Metastasis in Solid Carcinomata: Second International Symposium on Celluar Oncology, 5. LC 87-15764. 267p. 1987. 75.00 (*0-275-92665-6*, C2665, Praeger Pubs) Greenwood.

***Mols, Stephan T. A. M.** Wooden Furniture in Herculaneum: Form, Technique & Function. (Circumvesuvia: Vol. 2). 332p. 1999. 92.00 (*90-5063-317-X*) J Benjamins Pubng Co.

Molseed, Elwood. The Genus Tigridia (Iridaceae) of Mexico & Central America. LC 70-626142. (University of California Publications in Social Welfare: Vol. 54). (Illus.). 139p. reprint ed. pap. 43.10 (*0-608-17959-0*, 201469900093) Bks Demand.

***Molsky, Bruce.** Bruce Molsky - Lost Boy. 88p. 1999. pap. 14.95 (*0-7866-3526-6*, 97120) Mel Bay.

Molson, K. M. & Shortt, A. J. The Curtiss HS Flying Boats. (Illus.). 156p. 1995. pap. 35.00 (*1-55750-142-4*) Naval Inst Pr.

***Molstad, Stephen.** The Patriot. 304p. 2000. mass mkt. 6.99 (*0-06-102076-1*) HarpC.

Molt, Cynthia M. Vivien Leigh: A Bio-Bibliography, 35. LC 92-23785. (Bio-Bibliographies in the Performing Arts Ser.: No. 35). 352p. 1992. lib. bdg. 55.00 (*0-313-27578-5*, MVL, Greenwood Pr) Greenwood.

Molt, Mary K. Food for Fifty. 10th ed. LC 96-8658. 693p. (C). 1996. 80.00 (*0-13-382839-5*) P-H.

***Molt, Mary K.** Food for Fifty. 11th ed. LC 00-34022. (Illus.). 2001. write for info. (*0-13-020535-4*) P-H.

***Molter, Carey.** Sh. LC 00-33207. (Blends Ser.). (Illus.). (J). 2000. write for info. (*1-57765-412-9*) ABDO Pub Co.

— Tr. LC 00-33203. (Blends Ser.). (Illus.). (J). 2000. write for info. (*1-57765-411-0*) ABDO Pub Co.

— Wh. LC 00-33205. (Blends Ser.). (Illus.). (J). 2000. write for info. (*1-57765-410-2*) ABDO Pub Co.

Molthop, Susan. Hitting 50. 185p. 1998. mass mkt. 5.99 (*1-58365-002-4*, Timeless Romance) BT Pub.

Moltke-Hansen, David, jt. ed. see O'Brien, Michael.

Moltke, Helmuth J. Von, see Von Moltke, Helmuth J.

Moltmann, Johann F., jt. ed. see Rombke, Jorg.

Moltmann, Jurgen. The Church in the Power of the Spirit: A Contribution to Messianic Ecclesiology. Kohl, Margaret, tr. from GER. LC 93-29951. (Works of Jurgen Moltmann). 407p. 1993. pap. 22.00 (*0-8006-2821-7*, 1-2821, Fortress Pr) Augsburg Fortress.

— The Coming of God: A Christian Eschatology. Kohl, Margaret, tr. LC 96-209711. 368p. 1996. 30.00 (*0-8006-2958-2*, 1-2958, Fortress Pr) Augsburg Fortress.

— The Crucified God: The Cross of Christ as the Foundation & Criticism of Christian Theology. Wilson, R. A. & Bowden, John, trs. from GER. LC 93-29953. (Works of Jurgen Moltmann Ser.). 346p. 1993. pap. 22.00 (*0-8006-2822-5*, 1-2822, Fortress Pr) Augsburg Fortress.

***Moltmann, Jurgen.** God for a Secular Society: The Public Relevance of Theology. LC 99-19747. 1999. pap. text 20.00 (*0-8006-3184-6*, Fortress Pr) Augsburg Fortress.

Moltmann, Jurgen. God in Creation: A New Theology of Creation & the Spirit of God. LC 93-26365. (Works of Jurgen Moltmann). 384p. 1993. pap. 22.00 (*0-8006-2823-3*, 1-2823, Fortress Pr) Augsburg Fortress.

— Jesus Christ for Today's World. Kohl, Margaret, tr. LC 94-13407. (Works of Jurgen Moltmann). 140p. 1994. pap. 13.00 (*0-8006-2817-9*, 1-2817, Fortress Pr) Augsburg Fortress.

— Man: Christian Anthropology in the Conflicts of the Present. LC 73-88350. 136p. (Orig.). reprint ed. pap. 42.20 (*0-608-16308-2*, 202687200053) Bks Demand.

— The Source of Life: The Holy Spirit & the Theology of Life. Kohl, Margaret, tr. LC 97-25134. 160p. 1997. pap. text 16.00 (*0-8006-3099-8*, 1-3099, Fortress Pr) Augsburg Fortress.

— The Spirit of Life: A Universal Affirmation. Kohl, Margaret, tr. LC 92-18513. (Works of Jurgen Moltmann). 380p. 1992. 30.00 (*0-8006-2737-7*, 1-2737, Fortress Pr) Augsburg Fortress.

— Theology of Hope: On the Ground & the Implications of a Christian Eschatology. Leitch, James W., tr. LC 93-29966. (Works of Jurgen Moltmann). 352p. 1993. pap. 22.00 (*0-8006-2824-1*, 1-2824, Fortress Pr) Augsburg Fortress.

— The Trinity & the Kingdom: The Doctrine of God. Kohl, Margaret, tr. from GER. LC 93-29952. (Works of Jurgen Moltmann). (ENG.). 272p. 1993. reprint ed. pap. 20.00 (*0-8006-2825-X*, 1-2825, Fortress Pr) Augsburg Fortress.

— The Way of Jesus Christ: Christology in Messianic Dimensions. Kohl, Margaret, tr. from GER. LC 93-29961. (Works of Jurgen Moltmann). 416p. 1993. pap. 23.00 (*0-8006-2826-8*, 1-2826, Fortress Pr) Augsburg Fortress.

Moltmann, Jurgen, ed. How I Have Changed: Reflections on Thirty Years of Theology. LC 97-39107. 160p. 1998. pap. 15.00 (*1-56338-241-5*) TPI PA.

Moltmann, Jurgen & Dabney, D. Lyle. Is There Life after Death?, Vol. 199. LC 98-9062. (Lecture in Theology Ser.). 1998. 15.00 (*0-87462-578-5*) Marquette.

Moltmann, Jurgen, et al. Communities of Faith & Radical Discipleship: Luce Program on Religion & the Social Crisis. Mitchell, Carlton T. & Bryan, McLeod G., eds. LC 86-16452. x, 130p. 1986. text 16.95 (*0-86554-216-3*, H195) Mercer Univ Pr.

Moltmann, Jurgen, jt. auth. see Lapide, Phinn E.

Moltmann, Jurgen, jt. ed. see Kung, Hans.

Moltmann-Wendel, Elisabeth. Autobiography. 1997. pap. 27.00 (*0-334-02708-X*) TPI PA.

Moltmann-Wendel, Elisabeth. I Am My Body: A Theology of Embodiment. Bowden, John, tr. LC 94-37801. 128p. (C). 1995. pap. 11.95 (*0-8264-0786-2*) Continuum.

Moltmann-Wendel, Elizabeth. Liberty, Equality, Sisterhood: On the Emancipation of Women in Church & Society. Gritsch, Ruth, tr. LC 77-15240. 95p. reprint ed. pap. 30.00 (*0-608-16780-0*, 202691900053) Bks Demand.

Molton, Warren L. Friends, Partners & Lovers: Marks of Vital Marriage. rev. ed. LC 93-16196. 192p. 1993. pap. 16.00 (*0-8170-1187-0*) Judson.

Moltrecht, K. H. Machine Shop Practice, Vol. 1. 2nd ed. LC 79-91236. (Illus.). 496p. (C). 1981. 20.95 (*0-8311-1126-7*) Indus Pr.

— Machine Shop Practice, Vol. 2. 2nd ed. LC 79-91236. (Illus.). 517p. (C). 1981. 20.95 (*0-8311-1132-1*) Indus Pr.

Moltz, Howard. Symbiosis in Parent-Offspring Interactions. Rosenblum, Leonard A., ed. 300p. 1983. 65.00 (*0-306-41410-4*, Plenum Trade) Perseus Pubng.

***Moltz, James & Mansourov, Alexandre, eds.** North Korean Nuclear Program: Security Strategy & New Perspectives from Russia. LC 99-20510. 288p. (C). 1999. text. write for info. (*0-415-92369-7*) Routledge.

Moltz, James C. & Mansourov, Alexandre. The North Korean Nuclear Program: Security, Strategy & New Perspectives from Russia. LC 99-20510. 1999. pap. 24.99 (*0-415-92370-0*) Routledge.

An Asterisk (*) at the beginning of an entry indicates that the title is appearing for the first time.

Momma, H. The Composition of Old English Poetry. (Cambridge Studies in Anglo-Saxon England: Vol. 20). 218p. (C). 1997. text 59.95 (0-521-55481-0) Cambridge U Pr.

Mommaas, H., et al, eds. Leisure Research in Europe: Methods & Traditions. LC 97-144800. (CAB International Publication Ser.). (Illus.). 304p. 1997. text 70.00 (0-85198-773-7) OUP.

Mommaers, P. & Tournoy, G., eds. Jan van Ruusbroec: The Sources, Content & Sequels of His Mysticism. No. 12. 207p. (Orig.). 1984. pap. 49.50 (90-6186-141-1, Pub. by Leuven Univ) Coronet Bks.

Mommaers, Paul & Van Bragt, Jan. Mysticism: Buddhist & Christian: Encounters with Jan van Ruusbroec. LC 94-31692. (Nanzan Studies in Religion & Culture). 272p. 1995. 29.95 (0-8245-1455-6) Crossroad NY.

Mommen, Andre. The Belgian Economy in the Twentieth Century. LC 93-34914. (Contemporary Economic History of Europe Ser.). 256p. (C). (gr. 13). 1994. 90.00 (0-415-01936-2, B3913) Routledge.

Mommen, Andre, jt. auth. see Fern Andez Jilberto, A. E.

Mommer, Peter & Thiel, Winfried, eds. Altes Testament - Forschung und Wirkung: Festschrift Fur Henning Grav Reventlow. (GER., Illus.). XII, 407p. 1994. 55.95 (3-631-46609-9) P Lang Pubng.

Mommsen, A. Athenae Christianae. (Illus.). 177p. 1977. pap. 25.00 (0-89005-216-6) Ares.

Mommsen, H. Diccionario Medico Labor para la Familia. (SPA.). 1979. write for info. (0-8288-4775-4, S50063) Fr & Eur.

— Diccionario Medico Labor para la Familia. 6th ed. (SPA.). 880p. 1982. 150.00 (0-7859-5093-1) Fr & Eur.

Mommsen, Hans. From Weimar to Auschwitz. O'Connor, Philip, tr. LC 91-23617. 379p. 1991. reprint ed. pap. 117.50 (0-608-07633-3, 205994900010) Bks Demand.

***Mommsen, Hans, ed.** The Third Reich Between Vision & Reality: New Perspectives on German History, 1918-1945. (German Historical Perspectives Ser.). 256p. 2000. 65.00 (1-85973-254-2, Pub. by Berg Pubs) NYU Pr.

Mommsen, Katharina, ed. Goethe, Johann Wolfgang von: Who Is Goethe? Willson, Jeanne & Willson, Leslie, trs. LC 82-10674. (Illus.). 127p. (Orig.). 1983. 15.00 (3-518-03054-X, Pub. by Suhr Verlag) Intl Bk Import.

Mommsen, Katharina, ed. see Bernhardt, Eva D.

Mommsen, Katharina, ed. see Bruggemann, Diethelm.

Mommsen, Katharina, ed. see Goethe, Johann Wolfgang Von.

Mommsen, Katharina, ed. see Guthke, Karl S.

Mommsen, Katharina, ed. see Mommsen, Momme.

***Mommsen, Momme.** Lebendige Uberlieferung: George - Holderlin - Goethe. Mommsen, Katharina, ed. (Germanic Studies in America: Bd. 69). x, 406 p. 1999. 56.95 (3-906760-67-7, Pub. by P Lang) P Lang Pubng.

Mommsen, T. P., jt. auth. see Hochachka, Peter W.

Mommsen, T. P., jt. ed. see Hochachka, Peter W.

Mommsen, Theodor. Abriss Des Romischen Staatsrechts. Mayer, J. P., ed. LC 78-67369. (European Political Thought Ser.). (GER.). 1980. reprint ed. lib. bdg. 30.95 (0-405-11721-3) Ayer.

— Gesammelt Schriften Bd. IV: Historische Schriften. viii, 566p. 1965. write for info. (3-296-14644-X) G Olms Pubs.

— Gesammelt Schriften, Bd. I: Juristische Schriften. viii, 479p. 1965. write for info. (3-296-14641-5) G Olms Pubs.

— Gesammelt Schriften, Bd. II: Juristische Schriften. viii, 459p. 1965. write for info. (3-296-14642-3) G Olms Pubs.

— Gesammelt Schriften, Bd. III: Juristische Schriften. xii, 632p. 1965. write for info. (3-296-14643-1) G Olms Pubs.

— Gesammelt Schriften, Bd. V: Historische Schriften. vi, 617p. 1965. write for info. (3-296-14645-8) G Olms Pubs.

— Gesammelt Schriften, Bd. VI: Historische Schriften. viii, 695p. 1965. write for info. (3-296-14646-6) G Olms Pubs.

— Gesammelt Schriften, Bd. VII: Philologische Schriften. xi, 825p. 1965. write for info. (3-296-14647-4) G Olms Pubs.

— Gesammelt Schriften, Bd. VIII: Epigraphische und Numismatische Schriften. x, 626p. 1965. write for info. (3-296-14648-2) G Olms Pubs.

— A History of Rome under the Emperors. Wiedemann, Thomas, ed. Krojzl, Clare, tr. (Illus.). 656p. (C). 1996. 65.00 (0-415-10113-1) Routledge.

— History of Rome under the Emperors. 656p. 1999. pap. 30.00 (0-415-20647-2) Routledge.

— Inscriptiones Regni Neapolitani Latinae. xxiv, 526p. reprint ed. write for info. (0-318-72105-8) G Olms Pubs.

— Provinces of the Roman Empire: The European Provinces. Broughton, T. Robert, ed. LC 68-16707. (Classic European Historians Ser.). (Illus.). 1968. pap. text 4.50 (0-226-53395-6, P305) U Ch Pr.

— Reden und Aufsatze. vi, 479p. 1976. reprint ed. write for info. (3-487-06043-4) G Olms Pubs.

— Roemische Geschichte, 4. (GER.). 121p. 1966. pap. text 13.95 (3-487-10124-6) G Olms Pubs.

— Romische Forschungen, 2 vols. viii, 952p. 1962. reprint ed. write for info. (0-318-71178-8) G Olms Pubs.

— Die Unteritalischen Dialekte. (Illus.). viii, 368p. reprint ed. write for info. (0-318-71603-8) G Olms Pubs.

Mommsen, Theodor & Meyer, Paul M., eds. Codex Theodosianus, Vol. I, Pars 1. 1970. write for info. incl. 3.5 hd (3-296-11701-6) G Olms Pubs.

— Codex Theodosianus, Vol. I, Pars 2. iv, 932p. 1971. write for info. incl. 3.5 hd (3-296-11702-4) G Olms Pubs.

— Codex Theodosianus Vol. II: Novellae. cx, 220p. 1971. write for info. incl. 3.5 hd (3-296-11703-2) G Olms Pubs.

Mommsen, Theodor & Rice, Eugene F., Jr. Medieval & Renaissance Studies. LC 82-2855. (Illus.). 353p. 1982. reprint ed. lib. bdg. 59.75 (0-313-23482-5, MOMM, Greenwood Pr) Greenwood.

Mommsen, Theodor & Von Wilamowitz-Moellendorff, Ulrich. Briefwechsel. (GER.). 1996. write for info. (3-615-00178-8) G Olms Pubs.

Mommsen, Theodor, jt. ed. see Kruger, Paul.

Mommsen, Theodor, ed. see Solinus.

Mommsen, Theodorus, ed. see Augustus, Justinianus.

Mommsen, W. J., ed. The Emergence of the Welfare State in Britain & Germany, 1850-1950. 443p. 1981. 37.50 (0-7099-1710-4, Pub. by C Helm) Routldge.

Mommsen, W. J. & De Moor, J. A., eds. European Expansion & Law: The Encounter of European & Indigenous Law in 19th- & 20th-Century Africa & Asia. 352p. 1992. 47.50 (0-85496-762-1) Berg Pubs.

Mommsen, Wolfgang, ed. The Long Way to Europe: Historical Observations from a Contemporary View. LC 93-36819. 254p. 1994. 24.95 (0-86715-270-2) Edition Q.

Mommsen, Wolfgang J. Imperial Germany, 1867-1918: Politics, Culture, & Society in an Authoritarian State. Deveson, Richard, tr. LC 95-31744. (An Arnold Publication). 320p. 1995. pap. text 19.95 (0-340-59360-1) OUP.

Mommsen, Wolfgang J. Max Weber & German Politics, 1890-1920. Steinberg, Michael S., tr. LC 84-16274. xxii, 528p. 1990. pap. text 24.00 (0-226-53399-9) U Ch Pr.

— Max Weber & German Politics, 1890-1920. Steinberg, Michael S., tr. LC 84-16274. 520p. 1997. lib. bdg. 60.00 (0-226-53397-2) U Ch Pr.

— The Political & Social Theory of Max Weber: Collected Essays. LC 88-36950. 240p. 1989. 47.95 (0-226-53398-0) U Ch Pr.

— The Political & Social Theory of Max Weber: Collected Essays. LC 88-36950. xiv, 240p. 1992. pap. text 15.50 (0-226-53400-6) U Ch Pr.

— Theories of Imperialism. Falla, P. S., tr. LC 81-16091. 192p. (C). 1982. reprint ed. pap. text 13.00 (0-226-53396-4) U Ch Pr.

Mommsen, Wolfgang J., jt. ed. see Huebinger, Gangolf.

Momo, Taro. Adorable Mini Dolls. (Illus.). 96p. (Orig.). 1988. pap. 12.95 (0-87040-761-9) Japan Pubns USA.

***Momoh, James A. & El-Hawary, Mohamed E.** Electric Systems, Dynamics & Stability with Artificial Intelligence Applications. LC 99-51465. (Power Engineering Ser.: Vol. 8). (Illus.). 356p. 1999. text 150.00 (0-8247-0233-6) Dekker.

Momorsky, Jeffrey D., ed. Health Care Guide. LC 94-186078. 1995. 297.00 (0-7913-1968-7) Warren Gorham & Lamont.

Momotani, Yoshihide. Flying Bird Origami. (Illus.). 70p. (Orig.). 1993. pap. 15.00 (0-87040-908-5) Japan Pubns USA.

— Origami Dinosaurs. Noma, Chikako & Einzig, Barbara, eds. (Illus.). 68p. 1993. pap. 12.00 (1-56836-008-8) Kodansha.

— Trick Origami. (Illus.). 69p. 1994. pap. 15.00 (0-87040-929-8) Japan Pubns USA.

Mompou, F. Canciones & Danzas, Nos. 5-8. 16p. 1984. pap. 3.95 (0-7935-3340-6, 00009287) H Leonard.

Mompremier, Roosevelt. Cruisin' With Vengeance. LC 98-68228. 200p. 1998. pap. 14.95 (0-9666426-0-0) Cruisin Pr.

Momrow, Edward G. Creative Partnership: A Guide for Couples in Serious Relationships. 119p. (Orig.). 1992. pap. text 9.95 (0-9641321-0-9) E G Momrow.

Momsen, Janet. Women & Development in the Third World. LC 90-43653. (Introductions to Development Ser.). (Illus.). 128p. (C). 1991. pap. 15.99 (0-415-01695-9, A5479) Routledge.

Momsen, Janet H. Gender, Migration & Domestic Service. LC 99-11633. 320p. 1999. 90.00 (0-415-19067-3) Routledge.

— St. Lucia, Vol. 185. LC 96-191957. (World Bibliographical Ser.). 214p. 1996. lib. bdg. 62.00 (1-85109-136-X) ABC-CLIO.

Momsen, Janet H., ed. Women & Change in the Caribbean. LC 93-422. 320p. 1993. 35.00 (0-253-33897-2); pap. 9.95 (0-253-33896-4) Ind U Pr.

Momsen, Janet H. & Kinnaird, Vivian, eds. Different Places, Different Voices: Gender & Develpment in Africa, Asia, & Latin America. LC 92-18427. (International Studies of Women & Places). (Illus.). 304p. (C). 1993. pap. 25.99 (0-415-07563-7, A9891) Routledge.

Momsen, John. Ultra-Reliable Seasonal Trades. 185p. 1999. 65.00 (0-930233-69-7, Pub. by Windsor) Natl Bk Netwk.

Momson, Ann M., et al, eds. Breaking the Glass Ceiling: Can Women Reach the Top of America's Largest Corporations? 2nd ed. 256p. 1994. pap. 13.00 (0-201-62702-7) Addison-Wesley.

Momyer, William W. Airpower in Three Wars. Gilbert, James B., ed. LC 79-7287. (Flight: Its First Seventy-Five Years Ser.). (Illus.). 1980. lib. bdg. 27.95 (0-405-12196-2) Ayer.

Mon, K. K., et al, eds. Computer Simulation in Condensed-Matter Physics Vol. XVI: 9th Annual Workshop, University of Georgia, 4-9 March 1996. LC 96-46773. (Springer Proceedings in Physics Ser.: Vol. 82). (Illus.). 190p. 1997. 119.00 (3-540-61876-7) Spr-Verlag.

Mon, K. K., jt. ed. see Landau, D. P.

Mon, Susan, jt. auth. see McCullough, Bonnie Runyan.

***Mona, Erik.** Living Greyhawk Gazetteer. 2000. pap. text 26.95 (0-7869-1743-1) Wizards Coast.

Monacco, A. P., ed. Transplantation Therapeutics. (Journal: Nephron: Vol. 46, Suppl. 1, 1987). (Illus.). iv, 60p. 1987. pap. 20.00 (3-8055-4642-4) S Karger.

Monacelli, Linda. Lacing the Moon. (Cleveland Poets Ser.: No. 17). 40p. 1978. pap. 2.50 (0-914946-11-0) Cleveland St Univ Poetry Ctr.

Monachesi, Elio D., jt. auth. see Hathaway, Starke R.

Monachesi, Paola. A Lexical Approach to Italian Cliticization. (Lecture Notes Ser.: No. 84). 200p. 1999. text 64.95 (1-57586-109-7); pap. text 24.95 (1-57586-108-9) CSLI.

Monaco, A. P., ed. Pulsed Field Gel Electrophoresis: A Practical Approach. (The Practical Approach Ser.: No. 158). (Illus.). 216p. 1995. text 95.00 (0-19-963536-6); pap. text 45.00 (0-19-963535-8) OUP.

Monaco, Carol. At Last. 257p. (Orig.). 1994. pap. text 10.00 (0-9645158-0-6) Designs Extraord.

Monaco, Chris, ed. see Levy, Moses E.

Monaco, David. Analysis of Total Nonresponse in the 1993-94 Schools & Staffing Survey (SASS) LC 98-108948. 286p. 1997. pap. 19.00 (0-16-049300-5) USGPO.

Monaco, Fabrizio. Thyroid Diseases: Clinical Fundamentals & Therapy. 688p. 1993. lib. bdg. 265.00 (0-8493-4821-8, RC655) CRC Pr.

Monaco, Fabrizio, et al, eds. Thyroid Diseases: Clinical Fundamentals & Therapy. 1993. 249.95 (0-8439-4821-3, RC655) CRC Pr.

Monaco, Frank. They Dwell in Monasteries. (Illus.). 80p. (Orig.). 1984. 7.95 (0-8164-2409-8) Harper SF.

Monaco, Fred. Essential Mathematics for Electronics. (C). 1990. pap. text, student ed. 18.00 (0-675-21173-5, Merrill Coll) P-H.

— Introduction to Microwave Technology. 208p. (C). 1990. pap. text, lab manual ed. 24.40 (0-675-21031-3, Merrill Coll) P-H.

— Preparing for the FCC General Radiotelephone Operator Exam. 336p. (C). 1991. pap. text 38.20 (0-675-21313-4, Merrill Coll) P-H.

***Monaco, James.** Dictionary of New Media: The New Digital World: Video, Audio, Print. 1999. pap. 19.95 (0-9669744-0-9) Harbor Electronic.

Monaco, James. The French Revolutionary Perpetual Calendar. (Illus.). 32p. 1982. pap. 4.95 (0-918432-43-X) Baseline Bks.

— How to Read a Film: Movies, Media, Multimedia. 3rd ed. LC 97-1832. (Illus.). 672p. 2000. pap. 24.95 (0-19-503869-X) OUP.

— How to Read a Film: The Art, Technology, Language, History, & Theory of Film & Media. rev. ed. (Illus.). 576p. 1981. text 40.00 (0-19-502802-3) OUP.

***Monaco, James.** How to Read a Film: The World of Movies, Media, Multimedia: Language, History & Theory. 3rd ed. LC 97-1832. (Illus.). 672p. 2000. 40.00 (0-19-513981-X) OUP.

Monaco, James. Who's Who in American Film Now. (Illus.). 600p. 1984. 39.95 (0-918432-63-4); pap. 19.95 (0-918432-62-6) Baseline Bks.

Monaco, James & Baseline Editors. The Movie Guide. 1152p. (Orig.). 1995. pap. 25.00 (0-399-51914-9, Perigee Bks) Berkley Pub.

Monaco, James & Monaco, Jeannette. Fee Mining Adventures & Rock Hunting Expeditions in the U. S. Nordhues, Robin, ed. (Illus.). 134p. (Orig.). 1997. pap. 11.95 (0-935182-92-6) Gem Guides Bk.

Monaco, James, jt. auth. see Baseline Editors.

Monaco, Jeannette, jt. auth. see Monaco, James.

Monaco, John E., jt. auth. see Mazel, Judy.

Monaco, Lawrence. The Actors Master Log Book. 131p. 1987. student ed. 10.95 (0-9618647-0-2) Shoreham Dr Pub.

Monaco, Nora & Hubbs, Juliet. Universal Cards - Angelically Inspired. 3rd expanded rev. ed. (Illus.). 128p. 1997. 28.50 (0-9631714-1-0) AngelStar.

Monaco, Nora & Hubbs, Juliet J. Angel Reflections: A Personal Journal of Awareness. (Illus.). 112p. 1995. pap. write for info. (0-9631714-3-7) AngelStar.

— Angel Whispers: A Personal Journal of Reflection. (Universal Angels Ser.). (Illus.). 112p. 1994. pap. 9.95 (0-9631714-2-9) AngelStar.

Monaco, Paul. Cinema & Society: France & Germany During the Twenties. LC 75-40650. 194p. 1981. lib. bdg. 35.00 (0-444-99019-4, MOC/) Greenwood.

— Ribbons in Time: Movies & Society since 1945. LC 86-42996. (Interdisciplinary Studies in History). 170p. reprint ed. pap. 52.70 (0-7837-3719-X, 205789700009) Bks Demand.

***Monaco, Paul.** Understanding Society, Culture, & Television. LC 97-43945. 152p. 1998. 55.00 (0-275-96057-9, Praeger Pubs) Greenwood.

— Understanding Society, Culture, & Television. 2000. pap. write for info. (0-275-97095-7, Praeger Trade) Greenwood.

Monaco, Paul, et al. Art Around the Bay: A Guide to Galleries & Art Museums in the San Francisco Bay Area. (Illus.). (Orig.). 1990. pap. 12.95 (0-9627649-1-4) Trumpetvine.

Monaco, R., ed. Discrete Kinetic Theory, Lattice Gas Dynamics & Foundations of Hydrodynamics. 432p. (C). 1989. text 108.00 (9971-5-0815-X) World Scientific Pub.

Monaco, R. & Preziosi, L. Fluid Dynamic Applications of the Discrete Boltzmann Equation Vol. 3: Advances in Mathematics for Applied Science. 250p. 1991. text 44.00 (981-02-0466-3) World Scientific Pub.

Monaco, Rachel. Reflections of the Heart: A Collection of Beautiful Poems. Singh, Kavi, ed. (Illus.). 200p. 1997. 39.95 (0-9657840-0-2) Poets Intl.

Monaco, Richard & Bascom, Lionel. Rubouts: Mob Murders in America. 200p. (Orig.). 1991. mass mkt. 4.50 (0-380-75938-1, Avon Bks) Morrow Avon.

Monaco, Richard & Burt, Bill. The Dracula Syndrome. 184p. (Orig.). 1993. mass mkt. 4.99 (0-380-77062-8, Avon Bks) Morrow Avon.

Monaco, Richard, jt. auth. see Briggs, John.

Monaco, Robert, jt. auth. see Malloy, Terry.

Monaco, Steve, jt. auth. see Fruzzetti, Mike.

Monaco, Theresa. Biographical Dictionary of Gifted Education. 1988. pap. 15.00 (0-89824-183-9) Trillium Pr.

***Monaco, Theresa.** Gifted Program Evaluation: Ensuring Equity & Excellence. 90p. 1999. pap. 15.00 (0-88092-240-0, 2400) Royal Fireworks.

Monaco, Thomas J., jt. auth. see Ashton, Floyd M.

Monadjemi. Macroassembler. 2nd ed. (C). 1990. text. write for info. (0-201-55908-0) Addison-Wesley.

— Quick Assembler. (C). 1990. text. write for info. (0-201-56207-3) Addison-Wesley.

Monadjemi, P. Macro und Quickassembler. 2nd ed. (GER.). (C). 1990. text. write for info. (0-201-55938-2) Addison-Wesley.

Monadjemi, Peter. Professionelles Programmieren mit Microsoft Basic PDS. (GER.). (C). 1991. text. write for info. (0-201-55940-4) Addison-Wesley.

— Das Programmer's Workbench Buch Zu Microsoft Basic Pds. (GER.). (C). 1991. text. write for info. (0-201-55939-0) Addison-Wesley.

— Turbo Debugger. 2nd ed. (C). 1990. text. write for info. (0-201-55936-6) Addison-Wesley.

Monafo, Jaent, jt. selected by see Pratt, Constance Flavell.

Monafo, Janet, jt. auth. see Pratt, Constance.

Monafo, William W. & Pappalardo, Carlos. The Treatment of Burns: Principles & Practice. LC 71-138827. (Illus.). 286p. 1971. 22.50 (0-87527-055-7) Green.

Monagan, John S. The Grand Panjandrum: Mellow Years of Justice Holmes. LC 87-34628. (Illus.). 170p. (Orig.). (C). 1988. lib. bdg. 43.00 (0-8191-6853-X) U Pr of Amer.

— Horace: Priest of the Poor. LC 85-10042. (Illus.). 240p. reprint ed. pap. 74.40 (0-7837-6702-1, 204633400011) Bks Demand.

Monagan, Robert T. The Disappearance of Representative Government: A California Solution. (Illus.). 184p. (Orig.). 1990. pap. 10.95 (0-933994-10-9) Comstock Bon.

***Monagham, John & Just, Peter.** Social & Cultural Anthropology: A Very Short Introduction. LC 99-59055. (Very Short Introductions Ser.). (Illus.). 144p. 2000. pap. 8.95 (0-19-285346-5) OUP.

Monaghan, jt. auth. see Russell.

Monaghan, Andrew. God's People? One Hundred & Ten Characters in the Story of Scottish Religion. 288p. (C). 1992. pap. 59.00 (0-7855-6837-9, Pub. by St Andrew) St Mut.

— God's People? One Hundred & Ten Characters in the Story of Scottish Religion. 288p. 1993. pap. 30.00 (0-7152-0656-7, Pub. by St Andrew) St Mut.

Monaghan, Charles. The Murrays of Murray Hill. (Illus.). x, 166p. 1998. 25.00 (0-9662430-0-5) Urban History.

Monaghan, Claire, jt. auth. see Midwinter, Arthur.

Monaghan, Daniel & Wenthold, Robert, eds. The Ionotropic Glutamate Receptors. (Receptors Ser.). (Illus.). 392p. 1996. 135.00 (0-89603-456-9) Humana.

Monaghan, Earl A. Whiskey Dan & Me. LC 95-92281. 162p. (Orig.). (YA). (gr. 8-12). 1995. pap. text 7.50 (0-9622840-1-7) NEB Pr.

Monaghan, Earl A., ed. Anthology Seven. LC 89-91096. 128p. (Orig.). 1989. pap. text 7.50 (0-9622840-0-9) NEB Pr.

Monaghan, Floyd V., jt. auth. see Corcos, Alain F.

Monaghan, Frank. John Jay. LC 74-153339. reprint ed. 45.00 (0-404-04647-9) AMS Pr.

— John Jay, Defender of Liberty Against Kings & Peoples. (History - United States Ser.). 497p. 1993. reprint ed. lib. bdg. 99.00 (0-7812-4879-5) Rprt Serv.

Monaghan, Frank & Lowenthal, Marvin. This Was New York: The Nation's Capital in 1789. LC 70-117884. (Select Bibliographies Reprint Ser.). 1977. reprint ed. 29.95 (0-8369-5337-1) Ayer.

Monaghan, Gail. Perfect Picnics for All Seasons. (Illus.). 96p. 1994. 15.95 (1-55859-802-2) Abbeville Pr.

Monaghan, Gail, jt. auth. see Key, Sarah.

Monaghan, James. The Man Who Elected Lincoln. LC 73-7310. (Illus.). 334p. 1973. reprint ed. lib. bdg. 35.00 (0-8371-6920-8, MOMW, Greenwood Pr) Greenwood.

— Overland Trail. LC 73-107726. (Essay Index Reprint Ser.). 1977. 30.95 (0-8369-1999-8) Ayer.

Monaghan, James, ed. Grammar in the Construction of Texts. (Open Linguistics Ser.). 224p. 1992. 49.00 (0-86187-627-X) St Martin.

Monaghan, James, jt. auth. see Cheepen, Christine.

Monaghan, Jay. Abraham Lincoln Deals with Foreign Affairs: A Diplomat in Carpet Slippers. LC 96-49210. (Illus.). xx, 510p. 1997. pap. 22.00 (0-8032-8231-1, Bison Books) U of Nebr Pr.

— Australians & the Gold Rush: California & Down Under, 1849-1854. LC 66-23182. 345p. reprint ed. pap. 107.00 (0-8357-5895-8, 203144000074) Bks Demand.

— Civil War on the Western Border, 1854-1865. LC 84-11856. viii, 454p. 1984. reprint ed. pap. 15.00 (0-8032-8126-9, Bison Books) U of Nebr Pr.

— Custer: The Life of General George Armstrong Custer. LC 59-5937. (Illus.). xii, 479p. 1971. reprint ed. pap. 17.95 (0-8032-5732-5, Bison Books) U of Nebr Pr.

— Diplomat in Carpet Slippers: Abraham Lincoln Deals with Foreign Affairs. LC 79-39200. (Select Bibliographies Reprint Ser.). 1977. reprint ed. 34.95 (0-8369-6802-6) Ayer.

— Tom Horn: Last of the Bad Men. LC 97-1508. (Illus.). xix, 290p. 1997. pap. 14.95 (0-8032-8234-6, Bison Books) U of Nebr Pr.

Monaghan, Joe & Huffaker, Julie S. Espresso! Starting & Running Your Own Specialty Coffee Business. LC 95-17895. 224p. 1995. pap. 14.95 (0-471-12138-X) Wiley.

An Asterisk (*) at the beginning of an entry indicates that the title is appearing for the first time.

Monaghan, John. The Covenants with Earth & Rain: Exchange, Sacrifice & Revelation in Mixtec Sociality. LC 95-2527. 1995. 42.95 (*0-8061-2762-7*) U of Okla Pr.
*__Monaghan, John.__ The Covenants with Earth & Rain: Exchange, Sacrifice & Revelation in Mixtec Society. (Illus.). 416p. 1999. pap. 16.95 (*0-8061-3192-6*) U of Okla Pr.
Monaghan, John, jt. auth. see Hill, Robert M., II.
Monaghan, John M., jt. auth. see Singer, Albert.
Monaghan, Kelly. Air Courier Bargains: How to Travel World-Wide for Next to Nothing. 7th rev. ed. LC 98-72668. 232p. 1998. pap. 14.95 (*1-887140-08-5*, Pub. by Intrepid Trvlr) Natl Bk Netwk.
— Air Travel's Bargain Basement: The International Directory of Consolidators, Bucket Shops & Other Sources of Discount Travel. LC 99-71538. 128p. 1999. pap. 9.95 (*1-887140-13-1*) Intrepid Trvlr.
*__Monaghan, Kelly.__ Fly Cheap! How to Beat the Airlines at Their Own Game & Save Up to 50- or More - Every Time You Fly. 2nd ed. 2000. pap. 14.95 (*1-887140-16-6*) Intrepid Trvlr.
Monaghan, Kelly. Fly Cheap: How to Save 5to 50- Or More - Every Time You Fly. LC 98-75041. 256p. 1999. pap. 14.95 (*1-887140-11-5*) Intrepid Trvlr.
— Home-Based Travel Agent: How to Cash in on the Exciting New World of Travel Marketing. 3rd ed. LC 98-75042. 400p. 1999. pap. 29.95 (*1-887140-10-7*, Pub. by Intrepid Trvlr) Natl Bk Netwk.
— Orlando's Other Theme Parks: What to Do When You've Done Disney. 2nd rev. ed. LC 98-72666. (Illus.). 480p. 1998. pap. 16.95 (*1-887140-09-3*, Pub. by Intrepid Trvlr) Natl Bk Netwk.
— A Shopper's Guide to Independent Agent Opportunities. 2nd rev. ed. LC 97-70115. 79p. 1997. pap. 39.95 (*1-887140-01-8*) Intrepid Trvlr.
*__Monaghan, Kelly.__ A Shopper's Guide to Independent Agent Opportunities. 3rd ed. 96p. 1999. pap. 49.95 (*1-887140-15-8*, Pub. by Intrepid Trvlr) Natl Bk Netwk.
Monaghan, Kelly. Universal Studios Escape: The Ultimate Guide to the Ultimate Theme Park Adventure. LC 98-75641. (Illus.). 244p. 2000. pap. 14.95 (*1-887140-12-3*) Intrepid Trvlr.
Monaghan, Kelly, jt. auth. see Scanlon, Sally.
Monaghan, M. J., jt. ed. see Chambers, John.
Monaghan, Margaret. Index to Accounting & Auditing Technical Pronouncements, As of October 1, 1989. Wolfteich, Lois, ed. LC 78-648377. 838p. reprint ed. pap. 200.00 (*0-7837-1060-7*, 204155400021) Bks Demand.
Monaghan, Margaret, ed. see American Institute of Certified Public Accountants.
Monaghan, Mark J. Practical Echocardiography & Doppler. 154p. 1990. 284.95 (*0-471-92069-X*) Wiley.
*__Monaghan, Nancy.__ The Druid Stone: Celtic Mysteries. LC 99-91961. 155p. 2000. 25.00 (*0-7388-1418-0*); pap. 18.00 (*0-7388-1419-9*) Xlibris Corp.
*__Monaghan, Patricia.__ The Goddess Companion: Daily Meditations on the Feminine Spirit. LC 99-37890. (Illus.). 408p. 1999. pap. 17.95 (*1-56718-463-4*) Llewellyn Pubns.
Monaghan, Patricia. The Goddess Path: Myths, Invocations & Rituals. LC 99-11387. (Illus.). 288p. (Orig.). 1999. pap. 14.95 (*1-56718-467-7*) Llewellyn Pubns.
— Magical Gardens: Myth, Mulch, & Marigolds. LC 97-27784. (Illus.). 192p. (Orig.). 1997. pap. 17.95 (*1-56718-466-9*, K466-9) Llewellyn Pubns.
— The New Book of Goddesses & Heroines. LC 97-17471. (Illus.). 384p. 1999. pap. 19.95 (*1-56718-465-0*) Llewellyn Pubns.
— The Office Oracle: Wisdom at Work. LC 98-53170. Orig. Title: Working Wisdom. (Illus.). 224p. 1999. 7.95 (*1-56718-464-2*) Llewellyn Pubns.
— Seasons of the Witch. (Illus.). 234p. (Orig.). 1992. pap. 11.95 (*1-878980-09-2*) Delphi IL.
Winterburning. (New Alaskan Poets Ser.). 78p. (Orig.). 1991. pap. 7.95 (*0-914221-10-8*) Fireweed Pr AK.
Monaghan, Patricia, ed. The Next Parish Over: A Collection of Irish American Writing. LC 93-83973. (Many Minnesotas Project Ser.). 367p. (Orig.). 1993. pap. 17.95 (*0-89823-150-7*) New Rivers Pr.
Monaghan, Patricia & Viereck, Eleanor G. Meditation: The Complete Guide. LC 99-34298. 384p. 1999. pap. 16.95 (*1-57731-088-8*) New World Lib.
Monaghan, Patrick C. Writing Letters That Sell: You, Your Ideas, Products & Services. LC 68-19911. 205p. reprint ed. pap. 63.60 (*0-608-15516-0*, 202974300064) Bks Demand.

Monaghan, Patrick Erin. Because They Never Do. LC 00-102973. (Illus.). xii, 464p. 2000. pap. 19.95 (0-9700558-0-3, TBS-55803) Blackthorn Scribe. In the mid-nineteenth century, famine hits Ireland, threatening an entire population & jeopardizing the future of two young lovers. The people fear they will be cleared from the land, losing their homes & all that they own. Word arrives that the landlord will load them onto ships, sending all to America. Lovers Mary & Michael are separated & Mary is packed into the steerage of the aging freighter Virginius. Michael promises he will send for her when the famine ends. But within months, news is sent that the Virginius has gone down & all aboard her lost. The people riot & threaten revenge, spurring brutal punitive punishment. The landlord is murdered & the story spread that the lover of a girl on the Virginius had killed him. Michael flees Ireland for America, where he falls prey to the sharps on the waterfront, left with little hope. He takes up with the unsavory wharf rats. Then one night, he stumbles upon the Virginius. Mary does survive the crossing to Grosse Ile, the quarantine station in the St. Lawrence. She, like thousands of others would eventually attempt the walk from Montreal to New York City. Michael, seeing the Virginius afloat, would turn towards Quebec. Neither would make their destinations yet fate would bring them together. The Blackthorn Scribe - Publishers, P.O. Box 31, Whitewater, WI 53190 (262) 473-1172, Email: mail@blackthornscribe.com *Publisher Paid Annotation.

Monagle, John F. Risky Business: Risk Management from the Trenches. 350p. Date not set. 49.00 (*0-8342-0599-8*, 20599) Aspen Pub.
Monagle, John F. & Thomasma, David C. Health Care Ethics: Critical Issues for the 21st Century. 2nd ed. LC 97-23734. 672p. 1997. 65.00 (*0-8342-0911-X*, 20911) Aspen Pub.
Monagle, John F. & Thomasma, David C., eds. Medical Ethics: Policies, Protocols, Guidelines & Programs. LC 92-21893. ring bd. 230.00 (*0-8342-0349-9*) Aspen Pub.
Monaham, Kevin M. & Society of Photo-Optical Instrumentation Engineers, eds. Integrated Circuit Metrology & Process Control: Proceedings of a Conference Held 27-29 September 1993, California, Monterey. LC 94-27970. (Critical Reviews of Optical Science & Technology Ser.: Vol. CR52). 1994. 40.00 (*0-8194-1363-1*) SPIE.
Monahan. Media an English Approach. 1989. pap. text. write for info. (*0-582-87426-2*, Pub. by Addison-Wesley) Longman.
— Multivoice Magic. 1991. pap. text. write for info. (*0-582-86849-1*, Pub. by Addison-Wesley) Longman.
— A Pocket Companion for Medical-Surgical Nursing: Foundations for Clinical Practice. 2nd ed. 1997. pap. 17.95 (*0-7216-7334-1*, W B Saunders Co) Harcrt Hlth Sci Grp.
— Reading Skills. LC 99-47229. 465p. 2000. pap. text 40.00 (*0-205-28329-2*) Allyn.
Monahan & Walker. Social Science in Law. 4th ed. LC 98-121132. 1998. 42.95 (*1-56662-578-5*) Foundation Pr.
Monahan, Arthur, tr. see Aegidius.
Monahan, Arthur P. Consent, Coercion & Limit: The Medieval Origins of Parliamentary Democracy. 368p. 1987. 65.00 (*0-7735-1012-5*, Pub. by McG-Queens Univ Pr) CUP Services.
— From Personal Duties Towards Personal Rights: Late Medieval & Early Modern Political Thought, 1300-1600. (McGill-Queen's Studies in the History of Religion Ser.). 472p. 1994. 65.00 (*0-7735-1017-6*, Pub. by McG-Queens Univ Pr) CUP Services.
Monahan, B. The Problem of the Medical Profession: A Political Primer for Patients & Doctors. 1991. lib. bdg. 69.00 (*0-8490-4404-9*) Gordon Pr.
Monahan, Barbara. A Dictionary of Russian Gesture. LC 83-26413. (Illus.). 188p. (C). 1984. pap. text 10.50 (*0-938920-38-3*) Hermitage Pubs.
*__Monahan, Brent.__ The Bell Witch: An American Haunting. 208p. 2000. pap. 10.95 (*0-312-26292-2*) St Martin.
Monahan, Brent. Blood of the Covenant. 1997. mass mkt. 5.99 (*0-312-96214-2*) St Martin.
*__Monahan, Brent.__ The Jekyl Island Club. LC 00-24415. 288p. 2000. 23.95 (*0-312-26183-7*, Minotaur) St Martin.
Monahan, C. C. Early Fatigue Crack Growth at Welds. LC 95-67469. (Topics in Engineering Ser.: No. 26). 208p. 1995. 139.00 (*1-56252-288-4*, 3641) Computational Mech MA.
Monahan, David M. All You Need to Know about Copyrights & Trademarks. 105p. 1994. pap. 14.95 (*1-57002-010-8*) Univ Publng Hse.
Monahan-Earley, Rita A., jt. auth. see Dvorak, Ann M.
Monahan-Earley, Rita A., jt. ed. see Dvorak, Ann M.
Monahan, Edward C. & Niocaill, Gearoid M., eds. Oceanic Whitecaps & Their Role in Air-Sea Exchange Processes. 1986. text 169.50 (*90-277-2251-X*) Kluwer Academic.
Monahan, Edward C. & Van Patten, Margaret A., eds. Climate & Health Implications of Bubble-Mediated Sea-Air Exchange. (Illus.). (Orig.). (C). 1989. pap. 12.50 (*0-685-29355-6*) CT Sea Grant.
Monahan, Edward J. Construction of Fills. 2nd ed. LC 93-29806. (Series of Practical Construction Guides). 265p. 1993. 99.00 (*0-471-58523-8*) Wiley.
*__Monahan, Eric.__ Disjecta Membra. (FRE., Illus.). 250p. 2000. 34.00 (*1-55246-228-5*) Battered Silicon.
*__Monahan, Evelyn M. & Neidel-Greenlee, Rosemary.__ All This Hell: U. S. Nurses Imprisoned by the Japanese. (Illus.). 264p. 2000. 22.50 (*0-8131-2148-5*) U Pr of Ky.
Monahan, Frances D. Medical-Surgical Nursing. 2nd ed. (C). 1998. pap. text 75.00 (*0-7216-8137-9*, W B Saunders Co) Harcrt Hlth Sci Grp.
Monahan, Frances D., et al, eds. Nursing Care of Adults. (Illus.). 1994. teacher ed. write for info. (*0-7216-4926-2*, W B Saunders Co) Harcrt Hlth Sci Grp.
— Nursing Care of Adults, Test Manual. (Illus.). 1994. write for info. (*0-7216-3504-0*, W B Saunders Co) Harcrt Hlth Sci Grp.
Monahan, Frances D. & Neighbors, Marianne. Medical-Surgical Nursing: Foundations for Clinical Practice. 2nd ed. Cullen, Barbara N., ed. LC 96-51069. (Illus.). 2000p. 1998. text 72.95 (*0-7216-7006-7*, W B Saunders Co) Harcrt Hlth Sci Grp.
Monahan, Frances D. & Neighbors, Marianne, eds. Medical-Surgical Nursing: Foundations for Clinical Practice. 2nd ed. (Illus.). 2175p. 1998. teacher ed. write for info. (*0-7216-7007-5*, W B Saunders Co); pap. write for info. (*0-7216-7553-0*, W B Saunders Co) Harcrt Hlth Sci Grp.
Monahan, Frank J., jt. auth. see Coons, John E.
*__Monahan, George E.__ Management Decision Making: Spreadsheet Modeling, Analysis & Application. LC 99-57330. (Illus.). 600p. 2000. write for info. (*0-521-78118-3*) Cambridge U Pr.
Monahan, J. & Steadman, H. J. Mentally Disordered Offenders: Perspectives from Law & Social Science. LC 83-2329. (Perspectives in Law & Psychology Ser.: Vol. 6). (Illus.). 318p. (C). 1983. 62.50 (*0-306-41151-2*, Plenum Trade) Perseus Pubng.
Monahan, James H. Method of Law: An Essay on the Statement & Arrangement of the Legal Standard of Conduct. viii, 204p. 1996. reprint ed. 35.00 (*0-8377-2480-5*, Rothman) W S Hein.
Monahan, Jean. Believe It or Not. LC 98-17119. 90 p. 1999. pap. 12.95 (*0-914061-77-1*) Orchises Pr.
Monahan, Joan. Time, a Collection of Fragile Moments. LC 98-17873. (Illumination Bks.). (Illus.). 64p. 1998. pap. 5.95 (*0-8091-3793-3*, 3793-3) Paulist Pr.
Monahan, John. The Clinical Prediction of Violent Behavior. LC 95-42845. 152p. 1995. pap. 30.00 (*1-56821-489-8*) Aronson.
— Food Poisoning. rev. ed. 125p. 1987. pap. 11.95 (*0-317-67410-2*) Med-Info Bks.
— Predicting Violent Behavior: An Assessment of Clinical Techniques. LC 81-851. (Sage Library of Social Research: No. 114). 183p. reprint ed. pap. 56.80 (*0-8357-8499-1*, 203477500091) Bks Demand.
— Social Science Law. 3rd ed. Date not set. pap. text, teacher ed. write for info. (*1-56662-143-7*) Foundation Pr.
Monahan, John & Steadman, Henry J. Violence & Mental Disorder: Developments in Risk Assessment. (John D. & Catherine T. MacArthur Foundation Series on Mental Health & Development). (Illus.). 324p. 1996. reprint ed. pap. text 17.00 (*0-226-53406-5*) U Ch Pr.
Monahan, John & Steadman, Henry J., eds. Violence & Mental Disorder: Developments in Risk Assessment. LC 93-1670. (John D. & Catherine T. MacArthur Foundation Series on Mental Health & Development). (Illus.). 344p. 1996. 38.50 (*0-226-53405-7*) U Ch Pr.
Monahan, John & Walker, Laurens. Social Science in Law: Cases & Materials. 3rd ed. LC 93-32890. (University Casebook Ser.). 609p. 1993. text. write for info. (*1-56662-121-6*) Foundation Pr.
— Social Science in Law: Cases & Materials, Revised Teachers Manual To. 2nd ed. 52p. (C). 1992. text. write for info. (*0-318-69339-9*) Foundation Pr.
Monahan, John, jt ed. see Bonnie, Richard J.
Monahan, John, jt. ed. see Dennis, Deborah L.
*__Monahan, John F.__ Numerical Methods of Statistics. (Cambridge Series in Statistical & Probabilistic Mathematics: Vol. 7). (Illus.). 450p. 2001. write for info. (*0-521-79168-5*) Cambridge U Pr.
Monahan, John P. Food Poisoning. LC 83-63604. 125p. 1984. pap. 11.95 (*0-916093-00-X*) Med-Info Bks.
*__Monahan, Joseph M.__ Global Finance: A Market Approach - Spot, Swap, Futures, Forwards & Options. 2nd rev. ed. Good, Cynthia B., ed. (Illus.). 200p. (C). 1999. text 65.00 (*0-9654592-3-3*) Monohan Assocs.
Monahan, Joseph M. Global Financial Engineering: Case Studies & Methodology. Goode, Cynthia B., ed. 300p. (C). 1999. text 45.00 (*0-9654592-2-5*) Monohan Assocs.
— Global Financial Trading Simulation. Goode, Cynthia B., ed. 1998. text 100.00 (*0-9654592-5-X*, 9801) Monohan Assocs.
*__Monahan, K. L.__ Kidnapped. 1999. pap. 14.95 (*1-58630-011-3*) Word Wrangler.
*__Monahan, Kathleen N. & Nolan, James S., eds.__ Technology in American Literature. 296p. 2000. 47.50 (*0-7618-1709-3*) U Pr of Amer.
*__Monahan, Kevin & Douglass, Don.__ GPS Instant Navigation: A Practical Guide from Basics to Advanced Techniques. 2nd rev. ed. LC 00-35333. (Illus.). 2000. 29.95 (*0-938665-76-6*) Fine Edge Prods.
Monahan, Kevin, jt. auth. see Douglass, Don.
Monahan, Laila, jt. ed. see Loescher, Gilburt D.
Monahan, Lynda. A Slow Dance in the Flames. 88p. 1999. pap. 7.95 (*1-55050-139-9*) Genl Dist Srvs.
Monahan, Marta. Strength of Character & Grace: Develop the Courage to be Brilliant. Andrus, Jeff, ed. (Illus.). 178p. 2000. 24.00 (*1-892409-13-5*) Vittorio Media.
*__Monahan, Marta.__ Your Bouquet of Beautiful Things: Giving the Gift of You. 172p. 2001. pap. 12.95 (*1-892409-00-3*, Pub. by Vittorio Media) Midpt Trade.
Monahan, Michael. Attic Dreamer. LC 68-20321. (Essay Index Reprint Ser.). 1977. 20.95 (*0-8369-0711-6*) Ayer.
— Nemesis. LC 68-54362. (Essay Index Reprint Ser.). 1977. 20.95 (*0-8369-0712-4*) Ayer.
— New Adventures. LC 77-93363. (Essay Index Reprint Ser.). 1977. 26.95 (*0-8369-1310-8*) Ayer.
— Nova Hibernia, Irish Poets & Dramatists of Today & Yesterday. LC 67-23249. (Essay Index Reprint Ser.). 1977. 21.95 (*0-8369-0713-2*) Ayer.
Monahan, Noel. Snowfire. 61-p. 1996. pap. 12.95 (*1-897648-41-3*, Pub. by Poolbeg Pr) Dufour.
*__Monahan, Patricia.__ Art School: A Complete Painters Course. (Illus.). 2000. pap. 24.95 (*0-600-60146-3*) P HM.
— Figure Drawing: A Complete Step-by-Step Guide to Techniques & Materials. (Illus.). 2000. pap. text 15.95 (*1-85974-163-0*) New5 Holland.
Monahan, Patricia. Landscape Drawing & Painting. LC 97-38972. (Illus.). 144p. 1998. 24.95 (*0-7621-0031-1*, Pub. by RD Assn) Penguin Putnam.
*__Monahan, Patricia.__ Landscape Painting. 1999. 14.99 (*0-7858-1145-1*) Book Sales.
Monahan, Patricia. Light in Watercolor. (Illus.). 96p. 1996. 19.95 (*0-289-80123-0*, Pub. by SVista Bks) Sterling.
*__Monahan, Patricia.__ Painting Birds & Animal. 1999. 14.99 (*0-7858-1144-3*) Book Sales.
Monahan, Patricia. Step by Step Art School: Watercolor. 1987. 12.98 (*0-671-08907-2*) S&S Trade.
*__Monahan, Patricia.__ Watercolor. (Step by Step Art School Ser.). (Illus.). 160p. 1999. pap. 16.95 (*0-600-59954-X*, Pub. by Hamlyn Publishing Group Ltd) Sterling.
*__Monahan, Patricia & Clouse, Wendy.__ Acrylics. (Step by Step Art School Ser.). (Illus.). 160p. 1999. pap. 16.95 (*0-600-59952-3*, Pub. by Hamlyn Publishing Group Ltd) Sterling.
Monahan, Patricia & Rodwell, Jenny. The Oil Painter's Handbook. (Illus.). 256p. 1996. 29.95 (*0-289-80137-0*, Pub. by SVista Bks) Sterling.
*__Monahan, Patricia & Seligman, Patricia.__ Oils. (Step by Step Art School Ser.). (Illus.). 160p. 1999. pap. 16.95 (*0-600-59953-1*, Pub. by Hamlyn Publishing Group Ltd) Sterling.
*__Monahan, Patricia & Wiseman, Albany.__ The Beginner's Guide Figure Drawing: A Complete Step-By-Step Guide to Techniques & Materials. 2000. pap. 15.95 (*1-85974-164-9*) New5 Holland.
Monahan, Patrick J. Constitutional Law. (Essentials of Canadian Law Ser.). xxvii, 492p. 1997. pap. 31.95 (*1-55221-019-7*, Pub. by Irwin Law) Gaunt.
Monahan, Patrick J. Meech Lake: The Inside Story. 336p. 1991. text 50.00 (*0-8020-5969-4*); pap. text 19.95 (*0-8020-6896-0*) U of Toronto Pr.
Monahan, Patrick J., jt. ed. see McRoberts, Kenneth.
Monahan, Ray E. Engineering Documentation Control: Practices & Procedures. LC 94-24923. (Mechanical Engineering Ser.: Vol. 94). (Illus.). 208p. 1995. text 99.75 (*0-8247-9574-1*) Dekker.
Monahan, Sherry. Taste of Tombstone No. 1: A Hearty Helping of History. Simmons, Jennifer & Henson, Gwen, eds. (Illus.). 230p. 1998. pap. 16.95 (*1-889473-97-9*) Royal Spectrum.
*__Monahan, Susanne C., et al.__ Sociology of Religion: A Reader. LC 00-39198. 512p. 2000. pap. 32.00 (*0-13-025380-4*) P-H.
Monahan, Thomas J., jt. auth. see Margolis, Alan M.
Monahan, W. Gregory. Year of Sorrows: The Great Famine of 1709 in Lyon. LC 92-45193. (Illus.). 256p. reprint ed. pap. 79.40 (*0-608-09859-0*, 206982400006) Bks Demand.
*__Monahan, William G.__ Light House. LC 99-86047. 208p. 2000. 21.95 (*1-57322-158-9*, Riverhead Books) Putnam Pub Group.
Monahan, William G. & Smith, Edwin R. Leading People: What School Leaders Can Learn from Military Leadership Development. 2nd ed. LC 94-34930. (Illus.). 216p. 1995. 24.95 (*0-590-49749-9*) Scholastic Inc.
Monahon, Cynthia. Children & Trauma: A Parent's Guide to Helping Children Heal. LC 97-15328. 240p. 1997. pap. 17.95 (*0-7879-1071-6*) Jossey-Bass.
Monakhov, V. N. Boundary-Value Problems with Free Boundaries for Elliptic Systems of Equations. McFaden, H. H., tr. LC 83-2754. (Translations of Mathematical Monographs: Vol. 57). 522p. 1983. text 149.00 (*0-8218-4510-1*, MMONO/57) Am Math.
Monakov, Mikhail, jt. auth. see Rohwer, Jurgen.
Monaldo, Jonathan, ed. see Merton, Thomas.
*__Monamy, Vaughan.__ Animal Experimentation: A Guide for Students. 144p. (C). 2000. 42.95 (*0-521-66093-9*); pap. 15.95 (*0-521-66786-0*) Cambridge U Pr.
Monan, Jim. Australia's Trade: Green & Just? : Books from Community Aid Abroad. (Books from Community Aid Abroad). 86p. (C). 1994. pap. 15.95 (*0-646-17615-3*, Pub. by Oxfam Pub) Stylus Pub VA.
— Bangladesh: The Strength to Succeed. (Country Profiles Ser.). 64p. (C). 1990. pap. 9.95 (*0-85598-127-X*, Pub. by Oxfam Pub) Stylus Pub VA.
— Bangladesh: The Strength to Succeed. 2nd ed. (Oxfam Country Profiles Ser.). (Illus.). 64p. (C). 1995. pap. 9.95 (*0-85598-328-0*, Pub. by Oxfam Pub) Stylus Pub VA.
— Landmines & Underdevelopment. (C). 1995. pap. 4.50 (*962-664-001-4*) Humanities.
Monane, Tazuko A. Japanese Made Easy. LC 79-6482. (JPN.). 202p. (Orig.). 1979. pap. 12.95 (*0-8048-1219-5*) Tuttle Pubng.
Monappa, Arun & Engineer, Mahrukh. Liberalisation & Human Resource Management: Challenges for the Corporations of Tomorrow. LC 98-20680. 1998. 38.00 (*0-7619-9273-1*); pap. 38.00 (*0-7619-9274-X*) Sage.
Monarch. Quick Course Classic American Literature. 384p. 1995. pap. 14.95 (*0-02-860016-9*) Macmillan.
— Quick Course Shakespeare. 384p. 1995. pap. 14.95 (*0-02-860015-0*) Macmillan.
Monarch Books Staff. Monarch's Preparation SAT. pap. 8.95 (*0-317-56747-0*) PB.
Monarch Notes Staff & Beckett, Samuel. Waiting for Godot & Other Works. 1969. 3.95 (*0-671-00756-4*, Arco) Macmillan Gen Ref.
Monarch Notes Staff & Eliot, T. S. T.S. Eliot's The Wasteland: A Guide to Understanding the Classics. (C). 1971. 3.95 (*0-671-00903-6*, Arco) Macmillan Gen Ref.
Monarch Notes Staff & Ellison, Ralph. Invisible Man. (C). 1971. 3.95 (*0-671-00901 X*, Arco) Macmillan Gen Ref.
Monarch Notes Staff & Golding, William. Monarch Notes on Golding's Lord of the Flies & Other Works. (C). 3.95 (*0-671-00616-9*, Arco) Macmillan Gen Ref.
Monarch Notes Staff & Hardy, Thomas. Monarch Notes on Hardy's Mayor of Casterbridge. (C). 3.95 (*0-671-00617-7*, Arco) Macmillan Gen Ref.
Monarch Notes Staff & Lewis, Sinclair. Monarch Notes on Babbitt. (C). 3.95 (*0-671-00683-5*, Arco) Macmillan Gen Ref.

M

An Asterisk (*) at the beginning of an entry indicates that the title is appearing for the first time.

Monarch Notes Staff & London, Jack. Call of the Wild. 1989. 3.95 (*0-671-00685-1*, Arco) Macmillan Gen Ref.

Monarch Staff. Greek & Roman Classics. 1997. 2.25 (*0-671-00500-6*) S&S Trade.

Monarch Staff, ed. Monarch Notes on Marxist & Utopian Socialists. (J). (gr. 7-12). 3.95 (*0-671-00544-8*, Arco) Macmillan Gen Ref.

— Monarch Notes on Mythology. (C). 3.95 (*0-671-00523-5*, Arco) Macmillan Gen Ref.

Monarch Staff & Hugo, Victor. Les Miserables. (C). 3.95 (*0-671-00844-7*, Arco) Macmillan Gen Ref.

Monardes, Nicolas. Joyfull Newes Out of the Newe Founde Worlde, 2 vols. Frampton, John, tr. LC 25-20529. (Tudor Translations, Second Ser.: Nos. 9, 10). reprint ed. 115.00 (*0-404-51990-3*) AMS Pr.

— Joyfull Newes Out of the Newe Founde Worlde. Frampton, J., tr. LC 74-25786. (English Experience Ser.: No. 251). 110p. 1970. reprint ed. 30.00 (*90-221-0251-3*) Walter J Johnson.

Monardo, Anna. The Courtyard of Dreams. large type ed. LC 93-40853. 415p. 1994. lib. bdg. 17.95 (*0-7862-0126-6*) Thorndike Pr.

Monas, Sidney, tr. see Kaganov, G. Z.

Monas, Sidney, tr. & afterword by see Dostoyevsky, Fyodor.

Monasa, Frank F., ed. see Structures Congress Staff.

Monash, John. Australian Victories in France in 1918. (Great War Ser.: No. 24). (Illus.). 424p. reprint ed. 39.95 (*0-89839-181-4*) Battery Pr.

Monassebian, Jeff. A Survival Guide to Computer Contracts: How to Select & Negotiate for Business Computer Systems. Gordon, Marcy J., ed. LC 95-83000. (Illus.). 312p. 1996. pap. 24.95 (*0-9650971-7-X*) Applicat Pubng.

Monasterio, J., et al, eds. Antiphospholipid Antibodies. (Journal: Haemostasis: Vol. 24, No. 3, 1994). (Illus.). iv, 56p. 1994. pap. 20.00 (*3-8055-6027-3*) S Karger.

— International Congress on Thrombosis: Plenary Lectures, 13th Congress, Bilbao, 1994. (Journal: Haemostasis: Vol. 24, No. 2, 1994). (Illus.). 94p. 1994. pap. 20.00 (*3-8055-6019-2*) S Karger.

Monasterio, J. & Samama, M. M., eds. Low-Molecular-Weight Heparins: A New Therapeutic Approach to Thrombosis Proceedings. (Journal Ser.: Vol. 26, No. 2, 1996). (Illus.). iv, 66p. 1996. pap., suppl. ed. 21.75 (*3-8055-6277-2*) S Karger.

Monasterio, Maximina, jt. ed. see Vuilleumier, Francois.

Monasterio, Pablo O. The Last City. LC 96-188506. 112p. 1995. 45.00 (*0-944092-32-2*) Twin Palms Pub.

Monastersky, Glenn M. & Robi, James M., eds. Strategies in Transgenic Animal Science. LC 95-2396. 1995. 65.00 (*1-55581-096-9*) ASM Pr.

Monastery of Arkashea Staff, jt. auth. see Nier, Susan.

Monastier, Antoine. A History of the Vaudois Church from Its Origin & of the Vaudois of Piedmont to the Present Day. LC 80-24096. (Heresies of the Early Christian & Medieval Era Ser.: Second Ser.). reprint ed. 57.50 (*0-404-16554-0*) AMS Pr.

Monastyrskii, Mikhaililich. Riemann, Topology, & Physics. 2nd ed. Cooke, Roger, tr. from ENG. LC 98-7034. 1999. write for info. (*3-7643-3789-3*) Birkhauser.

Monastyrsky, M. Topology of Gauge Fields & Condensed Matter. LC 92-43571. (Illus.). 372p. (C). 1993. text 110.00 (*0-306-44336-8*, Kluwer Plenum) Kluwer Academic.

Monastyrsky, M., jt. ed. see Arnold, V. I.

Monastyrsky, M., jt. ed. see Arnold, V.

Monastyrsky, Michael. Modern Mathematics in the Light of the Fields Medal. 2nd ed. LC 96-22137. 176p. (C). 1998. reprint ed. pap. 19.95 (*1-56881-083-0*) AK Peters.

— Riemann, Topology & Physics. 1986. 39.50 (*0-8176-3262-X*) Birkhauser.

— Riemann, Topology & Physics. 2nd ed. Cooke, Roger, tr. LC 98-7034. 210p. 1997. 34.50 (*0-8176-3789-3*) Birkhauser.

Monat, Alan & Lazarus, Richard S. Stress & Coping. 3rd ed. 1991. pap. text 39.00 (*0-231-07457-3*) Col U Pr.

Monat, Hugh R. Otterhound: AKC Rank #142. (Rare Breed Ser.). (Illus.). 96p. 1998. 19.95 (*0-7938-0775-1*, RX-125) TFH Pubns.

Monat, Jacques & Sarfati, Hedva, eds. Workers' Participation: A Voice in Decisions, 1981-1985. 284p. 1986. pap. 27.00 (*92-2-105232-X*) Intl Labour Office.

Monat, Macques, jt. ed. see Markey, Raymond.

Monath, Norman. How to Play Popular Guitar in 10 Easy Lessons. 128p. 1994. pap. 14.95 (*0-8092-3765-2*, 376520, Contemporary Bks) NTC Contemp Pub Co.

— How to Play Popular Piano in 10 Easy Lessons. (Illus.). 141p. (Orig.). 1984. pap. 10.95 (*0-671-53067-4*, Fireside) S&S Trade Pap.

Monath, Thomas P., ed. Arboviruses: Epidemiology & Ecology, 5 vols. 1988. write for info. (*0-318-63026-5*, QR201) CRC Pr.

— Arboviruses: Epidemiology & Ecology, 5 vols. 256p. 1988. 145.00 (*0-8493-4388-7*, QR201, CRC Reprint) Franklin.

— Arboviruses: Epidemiology & Ecology, 5 vols., Vol. I: General Principles. LC 87-29992. 336p. 1988. 191.00 (*0-8493-4385-2*, QR201, CRC Reprint) Franklin.

— Arboviruses: Epidemiology & Ecology, 5 vols., Vol. II: African Horse Sickness to Dengue. LC 87-29992. 288p. 1988. 161.00 (*0-8493-4386-0*, QR201, CRC Reprint) Franklin.

— Arboviruses: Epidemiology & Ecology, 5 vols., Vol. III: Oropouche Fever to Venezuelan Equine Enc. 256p. 1988. 140.00 (*0-8493-4387-9*, QR201, CRC Reprint) Franklin.

— Arboviruses: Epidemiology & Ecology, 5 vols., Vol. V: Wesselsbron Virus Disease to Vesicular Sto. LC 87-29992. 256p. 1988. 144.00 (*0-8493-4389-5*, QR201, CRC Reprint) Franklin.

***Monbaron, Simon.** Subud the Coming New Age of Reality Vol. 1: The Most Complete Book on Subud. LC 99-90925. 600p. 1999. pap. 34.95 (*0-9672753-1-8*) Simar Enterp.

Monbeck, Michael E. The Meaning of Blindness: Attitudes Toward Blindness & Blind People. LC 73-77853. 224p. reprint ed. pap. 69.50 (*0-8357-9225-0*, 201763000007) Bks Demand.

Monberg, Torben. Bellona Island Beliefs & Rituals. LC 90-20224. (Pacific Islands Monographs: No. 9). (Illus.). 480p. 1991. text 42.00 (*0-8248-1147-X*) UH Pr.

Monbleau, Marcia, jt. auth. see Bragdon, Allen D.

Monbleau, Wayne F. Arise & Eat. 20p. (Orig.). 1991. pap. 2.00 (*0-944648-08-8*) Loving Grace Pubns.

— Friendship with God. 159p. (Orig.). 1982. pap. 7.00 (*0-944648-02-9*) Loving Grace Pubns.

— Grace: The Essence of God. 205p. (Orig.). 1989. reprint ed. pap. 7.00 (*0-944648-05-3*) Loving Grace Pubns.

— Living in Love: Real Values for a Relevant Faith. 158p. (Orig.). 1987. pap. 7.00 (*0-944648-00-2*) Loving Grace Pubns.

— Love One Another: In Defense of Our Catholic Brothers & Sisters. 47p. (Orig.). 1983. pap. 4.00 (*0-944648-03-7*) Loving Grace Pubns.

Monbleau, Wayne F., intro. The Odes of Solomon: An Authentic 1st Century Book of Christian Psalms. 89p. 1989. pap. 7.00 (*0-944648-04-5*) Loving Grace Pubns.

Monboddo, James B. Of the Origin & Progress of Language, 6 vols. LC 76-147982. reprint ed. 895.00 (*0-404-08260-2*) AMS Pr.

Monbrun, Estelle. Murder Chez Proust. Martyn, David, tr. LC 94-39260. (ENG & FRE.). 240p. 1995. 19.45 (*1-55970-283-4*, Pub. by Arcade Pub Inc) Time Warner.

— Murder Chez Proust. 240p. 1996. pap. 10.45 (*1-55970-341-5*, Pub. by Arcade Pub Inc) Time Warner.

Moncada, Rogelio. Contrast Media Biological Effects & Clinical Application, Vol. 2. LC 86-11697. 200p. 1987. 113.00 (*0-8493-4502-2*, RC78) Franklin.

Moncada, Rogelio, jt. auth. see Parvez, Z.

Moncada, S., et al, eds. The Biology of Nitric Oxide, Pt. 6. (Portland Press Proceedings Ser.: Vol. 15). 350p. (C). Date not set. text 170.00 (*1-85578-127-1*, Pub. by Portland Pr Ltd) Ashgate Pub Co.

— Biology of Nitric Oxide Pt. 1: Physiological & Clinical Aspects. (Portland Press Proceedings Ser.: Vol. 1). 420p. (C). 1992. text 148.75 (*1-85578-012-7*, Pub. by Portland Pr Ltd) Ashgate Pub Co.

— Biology of Nitric Oxide Pt. 2: Enzymology, Biochemistry & Immunology. (Portland Press Proceedings Ser.: Vol. 1). 230p. (C). 1993. text 97.75 (*1-85578-013-5*, Pub. by Portland Pr Ltd) Ashgate Pub Co.

— Biology of Nitric Oxide Pt. 3: Physiological & Clinical Aspects. (Portland Press Proceedings Ser.: Vol. 8). 450p. (C). 1995. text 224.40 (*1-85578-063-1*, Pub. by Portland Pr Ltd) Ashgate Pub Co.

— Biology of Nitric Oxide Pt. 4: Enzymology, Biothemistry & Immunology. (Portland Press Proceedings Ser.: Vol. 8). 500p. (C). 1995. text 190.40 (*1-85578-068-2*, Pub. by Portland Pr Ltd) Ashgate Pub Co.

— Nitric Oxide: Brain & Immune System. (Proceedings Ser.: Vol. 5). 384p. (C). 1994. text 132.60 (*1-85578-046-1*, Pub. by Portland Pr Ltd) Ashgate Pub Co.

— Nitric Oxide & the Cell: Proliferation, Differentiation & Death. (Portland Press Proceedings Ser.: Vol. 13). 280p. 1998. 136.00 (*1-85578-120-4*, Pub. by Portland Pr Ltd) Ashgate Pub Co.

Moncada, S., et al. The Biology of Nitric Oxide Pt. 5: Proceedings of the Fourth International Meeting on the Biology of Nitric Oxide Held at Amelia Island, Florida on September 17-21, 1995. (Proceedings Ser.: Vol. 10). 394p. 1996. 170.00 (*1-85578-102-6*, Pub. by Portland Pr Ltd) Ashgate Pub Co.

***Moncada, Salvador, et al.** Nitric Oxide & the Cell: Proliferation, Differentiation & Death: Proceedings of the Symposium Held in Calabria, Italy, in September 1996, under the Auspices of the British & Italian Pharmacological Societies. LC 98-44445. 1998. 99.50 (*0-691-00716-0*, Pub. by Princeton U Pr) Cal Prin Full Svc.

Moncarz, Raul. International Trade & the New Economic Order. LC 95-2526. (Series in International Business & Economics). 350p. 1995. text 63.75 (*0-08-042574-7*, Pergamon Pr) Elsevier.

Moncayo, Helga E., jt. ed. see Moncayo, Roy.

Moncayo, Roy & Moncayo, Helga E., eds. Ovarian Autoimmunity: Clinical & Experimental Data. LC 94-42131. (Neuroscience Intelligence Unit Ser.). 120p. 1995. text 69.00 (*1-57059-219-5*) Landes Bioscience.

Monceau, Pierre. Electronic Properties of Inorganic Quasi-One-Dimensional Compounds, Pt. I, Theoretical. 1985. lib. bdg. 138.00 (*90-277-1789-3*) Kluwer Academic.

— Electronic Properties of Inorganic Quasi-One-Dimensional Compounds, Pt. I Experimental. 1987. lib. bdg. 100.50 (*90-277-1801-6*) Kluwer Academic.

— Electronic Properties of Inorganic Quasi-One-Dimensional Compounds, Pt. II Experimental. 1985. lib. bdg. 168.50 (*90-277-1800-8*) Kluwer Academic.

Monceaux, Morgan. Jazz. LC 93-38177. (Illus.). (J). 1994. 18.00 (*0-679-86518-7*) Knopf Bks Yng Read.

Monceaux, Morgan & Katcher, Ruth. My Heroes, My People: African Americans & Native Americans in the West. LC 98-45400. (Illus.). 64p. (YA). (gr. 5-9). 1999. 18.00 (*0-374-30770-9*, Frances Foster) FS&G.

Moncel, Corinne, jt. auth. see Negroni, Francois de.

Moncel, Theodore A. Du, see Du Moncel, Theodore A.

Monch, Winfried. Semiconductor Surfaces & Interfaces. LC 93-9523. (Surface Sciences Ser.: Vol. 26). 1993. 79.00 (*0-387-54423-2*) Spr-Verlag.

— Semiconductor Surfaces & Interfaces. 2nd ed. LC 95-1412. (Series in Surface Sciences: Vol. 26). 1995. write for info. (*0-358-67533-2*) Spr-Verlag.

— Semiconductor Surfaces & Interfaces. 2nd ed. (Surface Sciences Ser.: Vol. 26). (Illus.). 432p. 1995. 49.95 (*3-540-58625-3*) Spr-Verlag.

Monch, Winfried, ed. Electronic Structure of Metal-Semiconductor Contacts. (C). 1990. text 248.50 (*0-7923-0854-9*) Kluwer Academic.

Monchak, Ronald W. The Last White Christmas. LC 94-12611. (Illus.). 193p. 1994. 16.95 (*1-879094-17-7*, Avnstoke Pr) Momentum Bks.

Monckton, Charles A. Last Days in New Guinea. LC 75-35142. reprint ed. 25.00 (*0-404-14158-7*) AMS Pr.

— Taming New Guinea. LC 75-35143. (Illus.). reprint ed. 28.50 (*0-404-14159-5*) AMS Pr.

Monckton, E. The White Canoe & Other Legends of the Ojibways. 1977. lib. bdg. 59.95 (*0-8490-2819-1*) Gordon Pr.

Monckton, P. L. Construction Technology for Civil Engineering Technicians. LC 82-32466. (Longman Technician Series, Construction & Civil Engineering). (Illus.). 323p. reprint ed. pap. 100.20 (*0-8357-6075-8*, 203447500090) Bks Demand.

Monckton, Shirley. Arranging Flowers. (Illus.). 144p. 1990. pap. write for info. (*1-85391-152-6*, Pub. by Merehurst Ltd) Sterling.

— The Complete Book of Wedding Flowers: Stunning Flower Arranging Inspiration for Everyone & Every Location. (Illus.). 96p. 1995. pap. 16.95 (*0-304-34565-2*, Pub. by Cassell) Sterling.

Moncla, Susie M., jt. auth. see Campbell, Collier A.

Monclova, Lidio C. Baldorioty De Castro. (Puerto Rico Ser.). 1979. lib. bdg. 59.95 (*0-8490-2870-1*) Gordon Pr.

Monclts, Antonio. Educacion de Adultos. (SPA.). pap. 10.99 (*968-16-5196-0*, Pub. by Fondo) Continental Bk.

Moncomble, Gerard. Octave & His Flute. (Finding Out about Music Ser.). (Illus.). 275p. (Orig.). (J). (gr. 1-5). 1994. pap. 19.95 (*0-572-01965-3*, Pub. by W Foulsham) Trans-Atl Phila.

— Octave & His Piano. (Finding Out about Instruments Ser.). (Illus.). 275p. (J). (gr. 1-5). 1993. pap. 19.95 (*0-572-01966-1*, Pub. by W Foulsham) Trans-Atl Phila.

— Octave & His Violin. (Finding Out about Instruments Ser.). (Illus.). (Orig.). (J). (gr. 1-5). 1994. pap. 19.95 (*0-572-01967-X*, Pub. by W Foulsham) Trans-Atl Phila.

Moncreif, William A. & National Rural Electric Cooperative Association St. Single-Phase to Three-Phase Electric Power Converters: A Concise Application Guide. LC 96-8666. 1996. write for info. (*0-917599-18-7*) Natl Rural.

Moncrief, David J. Got a Drop of Oil? An Introduction & Price Guide to Small Oilers. (Illus.). 160p. 1998. pap. 19.95 (*0-89538-097-8*) L-W Inc.

Moncrief, Gary & Thompson, Joel. Campaign Finance in State Legislative Elections. LC 97-42272. 250p. (C). (gr. 11). 1997. text 52.95 (*1-56802-148-8*); pap. text 29.95 (*1-56802-149-6*) Congr Quarterly.

Moncrief, Gary G. & Thompson, Joel A., eds. Changing Patterns in State Legislative Careers. LC 92-26575. (Illus.). 248p. (C). 1992. text 47.50 (*0-472-10344-X*, 10344) U of Mich Pr.

***Moncrief, Nancy D.** Fun with Mammals. (Illus.). 36p. (J). (gr. 1-3). 1999. pap. 4.95 (*1-884549-13-6*) VA Mus Natl Hist.

Moncrief, Nancy D., et al, eds. Proceedings of the 2nd Symposium on Southeastern Fox Squirrels. 90p. 1993. pap. 15.00 (*0-9625801-6-3*) VA Mus Natl Hist.

Moncrief, Troy, ed. The Turba Philosophorum: or The Assembly of the Sages: An Ancient Alchemical Treatise. Waite, A. E., tr. from LAT. (Illus.). 1997. pap. 11.95 (*1-55818-389-2*, Alchemical) Holmes Pub.

Moncrief, William C. & Shipp, Shannon. Sales Management. LC 96-24657. 774p. (C). 1997. 98.00 (*0-673-46903-4*) Addson-Wesley Educ.

Moncrief, William C., jt. auth. see Shipp, Shannon.

Moncrieff, A. D. Pre-Shave Gear Cutting Tools. (Technical Papers: Vol. P129.07). (Illus.). 31p. 1949. pap. text 30.00 (*1-55589-155-1*) AGMA.

Moncrieff, A. R. Romance & Legend of Chivalry: Myths & Legends. (Illus.). 439p. 1998. pap. text 15.00 (*0-7881-5227-0*) DIANE Pub.

Moncrieff, Anthony, jt. auth. see Charlton, Michael.

Moncrieff, Elspeth. Farm Animal Portraits in Britain, 1780-1900. LC 97-121246. (Illus.). 288p. 1996. 69.50 (*1-85149-239-9*) Antique Collect.

Moncrieff, J., jt. auth. see Grace, J.

Moncrieff, K. Scott, tr. see De Moncrif, Paradis.

Moncrieff, K. Scott, tr. & intro. see De Moncrif, Francois A.

Moncrieff, Mollie. The British Monarchy & the Divine Right of Kings. 150p. 1995. write for info. (*1-888477-01-6*) Saunders & Rakauskas.

— Memoirs of Esotericist. 250p. 1995. write for info. (*1-888477-00-8*) Saunders & Rakauskas.

— Prisoners of Time: A Simplified Cosmo-Conception. 100p. 1995. write for info. (*1-888477-02-4*) Saunders & Rakauskas.

Moncrif, Francois A. De, see De Moncrif, Francois A.

Moncrif, Paradis De, see De Moncrif, Paradis.

***Moncur, Michael.** CNA/CNE 5 Study Guide: Administration & Design. LC 98-83174. (Certification NetWare 5 Ser.). 816p. 1999. 44.99 (*0-7821-2387-2*) Sybex.

— MCSE: The Core Exams in a Nutshell. 2nd ed. O'Reilly, Tim, ed. (Illus.). 450p. 2000. pap. 24.95 (*1-56592-721-4*) OReilly & Assocs.

Moncur, Michael. MCSE: The Electives in a Nutshell. (Illus.). 372p. 1998. pap. 19.95 (*1-56592-482-7*) OReilly & Assocs.

— Networking Essentials Flashcards. O'Reilly, Tim, ed. 1999. pap. 29.95 (*1-56592-568-8*) OReilly & Assocs.

— Sams Teach Yourself JavaScript 1.3 in 24 Hours. LC 98-86224. (Teach Yourself Ser.). (Illus.). 364p. 1999. pap. 19.99 (*0-672-31407-X*) Sams.

***Moncur, Michael.** TCP/IP Windows NT 4.0 Flashcards: MCSE Elective Exam 70-059. O'Reilly, Tim, ed. 140p. 1999. pap. 29.95 (*1-56592-583-1*) OReilly & Assocs.

Moncur, Michael & Chellis, James. CNA Study Guide for Intranetware. 2nd ed. LC 97-67411. 784p. 1997. 54.99 incl. cd-rom (*0-7821-2098-9*) Sybex.

Moncur, Michael, et al. CNE Study Guide for IntranetWare. 2nd ed. LC 97-65905. (Illus.). 1520p. 1997. pap. text, student ed. 89.99 (*0-7821-2090-3*) Sybex.

Moncur, Michael G. NetWare 5 CNE. LC 99-60004. (Certification NetWare 5 Ser.). 704p. 1999. 44.99 (*0-7821-2389-9*); 39.99 (*0-7821-2390-2*) Sybex.

— The Network Press Administration's Handbook to NetWare 4.11. LC 96-69288. 576p. 1996. pap. text 34.99 (*0-7821-1949-2*) Sybex.

Moncur, Peter, jt. auth. see Heatley, R. V.

Moncur, Susan. They Still Shoot Models My Age. 114p. 1993. pap. 12.99 (*1-85242-230-0*) Serpents Tail.

Moncure, James, ed. Research Guide to European Historical Biography, Vols. 1-4. (Illus.). 2240p. 1992. lib. bdg. 325.00 (*0-933833-28-8*) Beacham Pub Corp.

— Research Guide to European Historical Biography, Vols. 5-8. 2995p. 1993. lib. bdg. 325.00 (*0-933833-30-X*) Beacham Pub Corp.

Moncure, Jane Belk. Apes Find Shapes. LC 87-11747. (Magic Castle Readers Ser.). (Illus.). 32p. (J). (ps-2). 1988. lib. bdg. 21.36 (*0-89565-364-8*) Childs World.

— The Bears Upstairs. LC 87-11715. (Magic Castle Readers Ser.). (Illus.). 32p. (J). (ps-2). 1988. lib. bdg. 21.36 (*0-89565-373-7*) Childs World.

— Caring for My Things. (Growing Responsible Bks.). (Illus.). 32p. (J). (ps-2). 1990. lib. bdg. 18.50 (*0-89565-670-1*) Childs World.

— The Child's World of Caring. rev. ed. (Child's World of Values Ser.). (Illus.). 24p. (J). (gr. k-2). 1996. lib. bdg. 18.50 (*1-56766-297-8*) Childs World.

— The Child's World of Courage. rev. ed. (Child's World of Values Ser.). (Illus.). 24p. (J). (ps-2). 1996. lib. bdg. 18.50 (*1-56766-296-X*) Childs World.

— The Child's World of Joy. rev. ed. (Child's World of Values Ser.). (Illus.). 24p. (J). (ps-2). 1996. lib. bdg. 18.50 (*1-56766-299-4*) Childs World.

— The Child's World of Kindness. rev. ed. (Child's World of Values Ser.). (Illus.). 24p. (J). (ps-2). 1996. lib. bdg. 18.50 (*1-56766-293-5*) Childs World.

— The Child's World of Responsibility. LC 96-39559. (Child's World of Values Ser.). (Illus.). 24p. (J). (ps-2). 1997. lib. bdg. 18.50 (*1-56766-392-3*) Childs World.

— A Color Clown Comes to Town. LC 87-11605. (Magic Castle Readers Ser.). (Illus.). 32p. (J). (ps-2). 1988. lib. bdg. 21.36 (*0-89565-369-9*) Childs World.

— Courage. rev. ed. LC 80-39515. (Values to Live By Ser.). (Illus.). 32p. (J). (ps-2). 1980. lib. bdg. 21.36 (*0-89565-1024-1*) Childs World.

— Un Dinosaurio de Deseos (A Wish-For Dinosaur) LC 88-20302. (Castillo Magico Ser.). (SPA., Illus.). 32p. (J). (ps-2). 1989. lib. bdg. 21.36 (*0-89565-908-5*) Childs World.

— Happy Birthday, Word Bird. LC 83-15256. (Word Bird Library). (Illus.). 32p. (J). (ps-2). 1983. lib. bdg. 21.36 (*0-89565-256-0*) Childs World.

— Hear. rev. ed. LC 97-6269. (My 5 Senses Ser.). (Illus.). 24p. (J). (ps-3). 1997. lib. bdg. 19.93 (*1-56766-285-4*) Childs World.

— Here We Go 'Round the Year. LC 87-13257. (Magic Castle Readers Ser.). (Illus.). 32p. (J). (ps-2). 1988. lib. bdg. 21.36 (*0-89565-402-4*) Childs World.

— Hi, Word Bird! LC 80-15919. (Word Bird Library). (Illus.). 32p. (J). (ps-2). 1981. lib. bdg. 21.36 (*0-89565-159-9*) Childs World.

— Hide-&-Seek Word Bird. LC 81-18068. (Word Bird Library). (Illus.). 32p. (J). (ps-2). 1982. lib. bdg. 21.36 (*0-89565-218-8*) Childs World.

— Honesty. rev. ed. (Child's World of Values Ser.). (Illus.). 24p. (J). (ps-3). 1996. lib. bdg. 18.50 (*1-56766-300-1*) Childs World.

— Ice-Cream Cows & Mitten Sheep. LC 87-14603. (Magic Castle Readers Ser.). (Illus.). 32p. (J). (ps-2). 1988. lib. bdg. 21.36 (*0-89565-403-2*) Childs World.

— Little Too-Tall. LC 87-11632. (Magic Castle Readers Ser.). (Illus.). 32p. (J). (ps-2). 1988. lib. bdg. 21.36 (*0-89565-374-5*) Childs World.

— Love. rev. ed. (Child's World of Values Ser.). (Illus.). 24p. (J). (ps-3). 1996. lib. bdg. 18.50 (*1-56766-298-6*) Childs World.

— The Magic Moon Machine. LC 87-30959. (Magic Castle Readers Ser.). (Illus.). 32p. (J). (ps-2). 1988. lib. bdg. 21.36 (*0-89565-410-5*) Childs World.

— Mr. Doodle Had a Poodle. LC 87-15808. (Magic Castle Readers Ser.). (Illus.). 32p. (J). (ps-2). 1988. lib. bdg. 21.36 (*0-89565-409-1*) Childs World.

— El Monito Travieso Por Encima de Todo (One Tricky Monkey up on Top) LC 87-11612. (Castillo Magico Ser.). (SPA., Illus.). 32p. (J). (ps-2). 1989. lib. bdg. 21.36 (*0-89565-921-2*) Childs World.

— My "a" Sound Box. LC 84-17024. (Sound Box Library). (Illus.). 32p. (J). (ps-2). 1984. lib. bdg. 21.36 (*0-89565-296-X*) Childs World.

— My "b" Sound Box. LC 77-23588. (Sound Box Library). (Illus.). 32p. (J). (ps-2). 1977. lib. bdg. 21.36 (*0-913778-92-3*) Childs World.

— My "c" Sound Box. LC 78-23638. (Sound Box Library). (Illus.). 32p. (J). (ps-2). 1979. lib. bdg. 21.36 (*0-89565-052-5*) Childs World.

— My "d" Sound Box. LC 78-8450. (Sound Box Library). (Illus.). 32p. (J). (ps-2). 1978. lib. bdg. 21.36 (*0-89565-044-4*) Childs World.

An Asterisk (*) at the beginning of an entry indicates that the title is appearing for the first time.

— My "e" Sound Box. LC 84-17021. (Sound Box Library). (Illus.). 32p. (J). (ps-2). 1984. lib. bdg. 21.36 (*0-89565-297-8*) Childs World.
— My Eight Book. LC 85-30962. (My Number Bks.). (Illus.). 32p. (J). (ps-2). 1986. lib. bdg. 21.36 (*0-89565-319-2*) Childs World.
— My "f" Sound Box. LC 77-9377. (Sound Box Library). (Illus.). 32p. (J). (ps-2). 1977. lib. bdg. 21.36 (*0-913778-93-1*) Childs World.
— My First Book. LC 84-17455. (Sound Box Library). (Illus.). 32p. (J). (ps-2). 1984. lib. bdg. 21.36 (*0-89565-271-4*) Childs World.
— My Five Book. LC 85-9699. (My Number Bks.). (Illus.). 32p. (J). (ps-2). 1985. lib. bdg. 21.36 (*0-89565-316-8*) Childs World.
— My Four Book. LC 85-9700. (My Number Bks.). (Illus.). 32p. (J). (ps-2). 1985. lib. bdg. 21.36 (*0-89565-315-X*) Childs World.
— My "g" Sound Box. LC 78-22037. (Sound Box Library). (Illus.). 32p. (J). (ps-2). 1979. lib. bdg. 21.36 (*0-89565-053-3*) Childs World.
— My "H" Sound Box. LC 77-8977. (Sound Box Library). (Illus.). 32p. (J). (ps-2). 1977. lib. bdg. 21.36 (*0-913778-94-X*) Childs World.
***Moncure, Jane Belk.** My "H" Sound Box. LC 99-56560. (Illus.). (J). 2000. lib. bdg. write for info. (*1-56766-774-0*) Childs World.
Moncure, Jane Belk. My "i" Sound Box. LC 84-17022. (Sound Box Library). (Illus.). 32p. (J). (ps-2). 1984. lib. bdg. 21.36 (*0-89565-298-6*) Childs World.
— My "j" Sound Box. LC 78-23178. (Sound Box Library). (Illus.). 32p. (J). (ps-2). 1979. lib. bdg. 21.36 (*0-89565-049-5*) Childs World.
— My "k" Sound Box. LC 78-22034. (Sound Box Library). (Illus.). 32p. (J). (ps-2). 1979. lib. bdg. 21.36 (*0-89565-050-9*) Childs World.
— My "l" Sound Box. LC 78-8373. (Sound Box Library). (Illus.). 32p. (J). (ps-2). 1978. lib. bdg. 21.36 (*0-89565-045-2*) Childs World.
— My "m" Sound Box. LC 78-24458. (Sound Box Library). (Illus.). 32p. (J). (ps-2). 1979. lib. bdg. 21.36 (*0-89565-051-7*) Childs World.
— My "n" Sound Box. LC 78-22053. (Sound Box Library). (Illus.). 32p. (J). (ps-2). 1979. lib. bdg. 21.36 (*0-89565-054-1*) Childs World.
— My Nine Book. LC 85-30959. (My Number Bks.). (Illus.). 32p. (J). (ps-2). 1986. lib. bdg. 21.36 (*0-89565-320-6*) Childs World.
— My "o" Sound Box. LC 84-17023. (Sound Box Library). (Illus.). 32p. (J). (ps-2). 1984. lib. bdg. 21.36 (*0-89565-299-4*) Childs World.
— My One Book. LC 85-5897. (My Number Bks.). (Illus.). 32p. (J). (ps-2). 1985. lib. bdg. 21.36 (*0-89565-312-5*) Childs World.
— My "p" Sound Box. LC 78-7841. (Sound Box Library). (Illus.). 32p. (J). (ps-2). 1978. lib. bdg. 21.36 (*0-89565-047-9*) Childs World.
— My "q" Sound Box. LC 79-13085. (Sound Box Library). (Illus.). 32p. (J). (ps-2). 1979. lib. bdg. 21.36 (*0-89565-100-9*) Childs World.
— My "r" Sound Box. LC 78-7842. (Sound Box Library). (Illus.). 32p. (J). (ps-2). 1978. lib. bdg. 21.36 (*0-89565-048-7*) Childs World.
— My "s" Sound Box. LC 77-8970. (Sound Box Library). (Illus.). 32p. (J). (ps-2). 1977. lib. bdg. 21.36 (*0-913778-95-8*) Childs World.
— My Seven Book. LC 86-2594. (My Number Bks.). (Illus.). 32p. (J). (ps-2). 1986. lib. bdg. 21.36 (*0-89565-318-4*) Childs World.
— My Six Book. LC 85-30961. (My Number Bks.). (Illus.). 32p. (J). (ps-2). 1985. lib. bdg. 21.36 (*0-89565-317-6*) Childs World.
— My Sound Parade. LC 79-15930. (Sound Box Library). (Illus.). 32p. (J). (ps-2). 1979. lib. bdg. 21.36 (*0-89565-103-3*) Childs World.
— My "t" Sound Box. LC 77-23587. (Sound Box Library). (Illus.). 32p. (J). (ps-2). 1977. lib. bdg. 21.36 (*0-913778-96-6*) Childs World.
— My Ten Book. LC 86-2293. (My Number Bks.). (Illus.). 32p. (J). (ps-2). 1986. lib. bdg. 21.36 (*0-89565-321-4*) Childs World.
— My Three Book. LC 85-5898. (My Number Bks.). (Illus.). 32p. (J). (ps-2). 1985. lib. bdg. 21.36 (*0-89565-314-1*) Childs World.
— My Two Book. LC 85-7885. (My Number Bks.). (Illus.). 32p. (J). (ps-2). 1985. lib. bdg. 21.36 (*0-89565-313-3*) Childs World.
— My "u" Sound Box. LC 84-17012. (Sound Box Library). (Illus.). 32p. (J). (ps-2). 1984. lib. bdg. 21.36 (*0-89565-300-1*) Childs World.
— My "v" Sound Box. LC 79-13084. (Sound Box Library). (Illus.). 32p. (J). (ps-2). 1979. lib. bdg. 21.36 (*0-89565-101-7*) Childs World.
— My "w" Sound Box. LC 78-8614. (Sound Box Library). (Illus.). 32p. (J). (ps-2). 1978. lib. bdg. 21.36 (*0-89565-046-0*) Childs World.
— My "x, y, z" Sound Box. LC 79-13086. (Sound Box Library). (Illus.). 32p. (J). (ps-2). 1979. lib. bdg. 21.36 (*0-89565-102-5*) Childs World.
— No! No! Word Bird. LC 80-29491. (Word House Words Ser.). (Illus.). 32p. (J). (ps-2). 1981. lib. bdg. 21.36 (*0-89565-161-0*) Childs World.
— One Tricky Monkey up on Top. LC 87-11612. (Magic Castle Readers Ser.). (Illus.). 32p. (J). (ps-2). 1988. lib. bdg. 21.36 (*0-89565-365-6*) Childs World.
— Play with A & T. LC 89-774. (Sound Box Library). (Illus.). 32p. (J). (ps-2). 1989. lib. bdg. 21.36 (*0-89565-505-5*) Childs World.
— Play with E & D. LC 73-4743. (Sound Box Library). (Illus.). 32p. (J). (ps-2). 1989. lib. bdg. 21.36 (*0-89565-508-X*) Childs World.
— Play with I & G. LC 73-4739. (Sound Box Library). (Illus.). 32p. (J). (ps-1). 1989. lib. bdg. 21.36 (*0-89565-507-1*) Childs World.
— Play with O & G. LC 73-4742. (Sound Box Library). (Illus.). 32p. (J). (ps-2). 1989. lib. bdg. 21.36 (*0-89565-506-3*) Childs World.
— Play with U & G. LC 73-4741. (Sound Box Library). (Illus.). 32p. (J). (ps-2). 1989. lib. bdg. 21.36 (*0-89565-509-8*) Childs World.
— A Pocketful of Pets. LC 87-11748. (Magic Castle Readers Ser.). (Illus.). 32p. (J). (ps-2). 1988. lib. bdg. 21.36 (*0-89565-370-2*) Childs World.
— Polka-Dot Puppy. LC 87-15813. (Magic Castle Readers Ser.). (Illus.). 32p. (J). (ps-2). 1988. lib. bdg. 21.36 (*0-89565-407-5*) Childs World.
— A Que Jugamos Hoy? (What Can We Play Today?) LC 87-32565. (Castillo Magico Ser.). (SPA., Illus.). 32p. (J). (ps-2). 1989. lib. bdg. 21.36 (*0-89565-923-9*) Childs World.
— Que Puedes Decir Cuando un Monito Actua Asi? (What Do You Say When a Monkey Acts This Way?) LC 87-11736. (Castillo Magico Ser.). (SPA., Illus.). 32p. (J). (ps-2). 1989. lib. bdg. 21.36 (*0-89565-925-5*) Childs World.
— Rabbits' Habits. LC 87-12841. (Magic Castle Readers Ser.). (Illus.). 32p. (J). (ps-2). 1988. lib. bdg. 21.36 (*0-89565-406-7*) Childs World.
— See. rev. ed. LC 97-808. (My 5 Senses Ser.). (Illus.). 24p. (J). (ps-3). 1997. lib. bdg. 19.93 (*1-56766-281-1*) Childs World.
— Short "a" & Long "a" Play a Game. LC 79-10300. (Sound Box Library). (Illus.). 32p. (J). (ps-2). 1979. lib. bdg. 21.36 (*0-89565-089-4*) Childs World.
Moncure, Jane Belk. Short "e" & Long "e" Play a Game. LC 79-10305. (Sound Box Library). (Illus.). 32p. (J). (ps-2). 1979. lib. bdg. 21.36 (*0-89565-090-8*) Childs World.
Moncure, Jane Belk. Short "i" & Long "i" Play a Game. LC 79-10303. (Sound Box Library). (Illus.). 32p. (J). (ps-2). 1979. lib. bdg. 21.36 (*0-89565-091-6*) Childs World.
— Short "o" & Long "o" Play a Game. LC 79-10304. (Sound Box Library). (Illus.). 32p. (J). (ps-2). 1979. lib. bdg. 21.36 (*0-89565-092-4*) Childs World.
— Short "u" & Long "u" Play a Game. LC 79-10306. (Sound Box Library). (Illus.). 32p. (J). (ps-2). 1979. lib. bdg. 21.36 (*0-89565-093-2*) Childs World.
— Smell. rev. ed. LC 97-6268. (My 5 Senses Ser.). (Illus.). 24p. (J). (ps-3). 1997. lib. bdg. 19.93 (*1-56766-282-X*) Childs World.
— Smile, Says Little Crocodile. LC 87-13833. (Magic Castle Readers Ser.). (Illus.). 32p. (J). (ps-2). 1989. lib. bdg. 18.50 (*0-89565-401-6*) Childs World.
— Step into Fall: A New Season. LC 90-30637. (Discovery World Ser.). (Illus.). 32p. (J). (ps-2). 1989. lib. bdg. 21.36 (*0-89565-573-X*) Childs World.
— Step into Spring: A New Season. LC 90-30375. (Discovery World Ser.). (Illus.). 32p. (J). (ps-2). 1989. lib. bdg. 21.36 (*0-89565-571-3*) Childs World.
— Step into Winter: A New Season. LC 90-30636. (Discovery World Ser.). (Illus.). 32p. (J). (ps-2). 1989. lib. bdg. 21.36 (*0-89565-574-8*) Childs World.
— Stop! Go! Word Bird. LC 80-16273. (Word Bird Library). (Illus.). 32p. (J). (ps-2). 1980. lib. bdg. 21.36 (*0-89565-160-2*) Childs World.
— Taste. rev. ed. LC 97-6267. (My 5 Senses Ser.). (Illus.). 24p. (J). (ps-3). 1997. lib. bdg. 19.93 (*1-56766-283-8*) Childs World.
— Touch. rev. ed. LC 97-815. (My 5 Senses Ser.). (Illus.). 24p. (J). (ps-3). 1997. lib. bdg. 19.93 (*1-56766-284-6*) Childs World.
— Watch Out! Word Bird. (Word Bird Library). (Illus.). 32p. (J). (ps-2). 1982. lib. bdg. 21.36 (*0-89565-219-6*) Childs World.
— What Can We Play Today? LC 87-32565. (Magic Castle Readers Ser.). (Illus.). 32p. (J). (ps-2). 1988. lib. bdg. 21.36 (*0-89565-412-1*) Childs World.
— What Do You Say When a Monkey Acts This Way? LC 87-11736. (Magic Castle Readers Ser.). (Illus.). 32p. (J). (ps-2). 1988. lib. bdg. 21.36 (*0-89565-368-0*) Childs World.
— What Does Word Bird See? LC 81-21594. (Word Bird Library). (Illus.). 32p. (J). (ps-2). 1982. lib. bdg. 21.36 (*0-89565-220-X*) Childs World.
— Where Is Baby Bear? LC 87-12840. (Magic Castle Readers Ser.). (Illus.). 32p. (J). (ps-2). 1988. lib. bdg. 21.36 (*0-89565-405-9*) Childs World.
— Word Bird Asks What? What? What? LC 83-15258. (Word Bird Library). (Illus.). 32p. (J). (ps-2). 1983. lib. bdg. 21.36 (*0-89565-258-7*) Childs World.
— Word Bird Builds a City. LC 83-15275. (Word Bird Library). (Illus.). 32p. (J). (ps-2). 1983. lib. bdg. 21.36 (*0-89565-257-9*) Childs World.
— Word Bird Makes Words with Cat: A Short "a" Adventure. LC 83-23948. (Word Bird Library). (Illus.). 32p. (J). (ps-2). 1984. lib. bdg. 21.36 (*0-89565-259-5*) Childs World.
— Word Bird Makes Words with Dog: A Short "o" Adventure. LC 83-23946. (Word Bird Library). (Illus.). 32p. (J). (ps-2). 1984. lib. bdg. 21.36 (*0-89565-263-3*) Childs World.
— Word Bird Makes Words with Duck: A Short "u" Adventure. LC 83-23943. (Word Bird Library). (Illus.). 32p. (J). (ps-2). 1984. lib. bdg. 21.36 (*0-89565-261-7*) Childs World.
— Word Bird Makes Words with Hen: A Short "e" Adventure. LC 83-23944. (Word Bird Library). (Illus.). 32p. (J). (ps-2). 1984. lib. bdg. 21.36 (*0-89565-260-9*) Childs World.
— Word Bird Makes Words with Pig: A Short "i" Adventure. LC 83-23945. (Word Bird Library). (Illus.). 32p. (J). (ps-2). 1984. lib. bdg. 21.36 (*0-89565-262-5*) Childs World.
***Moncure, Jane Belk.** Word Bird's Christmas Words. (Word Bird Library). (Illus.). 32p. (ps-2). 1999. lib. bdg. 21.36 (*1-56766-625-6*) Childs World.
Moncure, Jane Belk. Word Bird's Circus Surprise. LC 80-29528. (Word Bird Library). (Illus.). 32p. (J). (ps-2). 1981. lib. bdg. 21.36 (*0-89565-162-9*) Childs World.
— Word Bird's Dinosaur Day. (Word Bird Library). (Illus.). 32p. (J). (ps-2). 1991. lib. bdg. 21.36 (*0-89565-617-5*) Childs World.
***Moncure, Jane Belk.** Word Bird's Easter Words. (Word Bird Library). (Illus.). 32p. (ps-2). 1999. lib. bdg. 21.36 (*1-56766-626-4*) Childs World.
Moncure, Jane Belk. Word Bird's Fall Words. LC 85-5935. (Word Bird Library). (Illus.). 32p. (J). (ps-2). 1985. lib. bdg. 21.36 (*0-89565-308-7*) Childs World.
— Word Bird's Halloween Words. LC 86-31024. (Word Bird Library). (Illus.). 32p. (J). (ps-2). 1987. lib. bdg. 21.36 (*0-89565-359-1*) Childs World.
***Moncure, Jane Belk.** Word Bird's Halloween Words. (Word Bird Library). (Illus.). 32p. (ps-2). 1999. lib. bdg. 21.36 (*1-56766-627-2*) Childs World.
Moncure, Jane Belk. Word Bird's Hats. LC 81-18065. (Word Bird Library). (Illus.). 32p. (J). (ps-2). 1982. lib. bdg. 21.36 (*0-89565-221-8*) Childs World.
— Word Bird's Magic Wand. LC 90-1645. (Word Bird Library). (Illus.). 32p. (J). (ps-2). 1990. lib. bdg. 21.36 (*0-89565-580-2*) Childs World.
— Word Bird's New Friend. LC 90-37002. (Word Bird Library). (Illus.). 32p. (J). (ps-2). 1991. lib. bdg. 21.36 (*0-89565-616-7*) Childs World.
— Word Bird's Rainy-Day Dance. LC 90-31693. (Word Bird Library). (Illus.). 32p. (J). (ps-2). 1990. lib. bdg. 21.36 (*0-89565-579-9*) Childs World.
— Word Bird's School Words. LC 89-7179. (Word Bird Library). (Illus.). 32p. (J). (ps-2). 1989. lib. bdg. 21.36 (*0-89565-510-1*) Childs World.
— Word Bird's Shapes. LC 83-15255. (Word Bird Library). (Illus.). 32p. (J). (ps-2). 1983. lib. bdg. 21.36 (*0-89565-255-2*) Childs World.
— Word Bird's Spring Words. LC 85-5902. (Word Bird Library). (Illus.). 32p. (J). (ps-2). 1985. lib. bdg. 21.36 (*0-89565-310-9*) Childs World.
— Word Bird's Summer Words. LC 85-5930. (Word Bird Library). (Illus.). 32p. (J). (ps-2). 1985. lib. bdg. 21.36 (*0-89565-311-7*) Childs World.
— Word Bird's Thanksgiving Words. LC 86-32639. (Word Bird Library). (Illus.). 32p. (J). (ps-2). 1987. lib. bdg. 21.36 (*0-89565-360-5*) Childs World.
***Moncure, Jane Belk.** Word Bird's Thanksgiving Words. (Word Bird Library). (Illus.). 32p. (ps-2). 1999. lib. bdg. 21.36 (*1-56766-628-0*) Childs World.
Moncure, Jane Belk. Word Bird's Valentine Day Words. (Word Bird Library). (Illus.). 32p. (J). (ps-2). 1987. lib. bdg. 21.36 (*0-89565-362-1*) Childs World.
***Moncure, Jane Belk.** Word Bird's Valentine's Day Words. (Word Bird Library). (Illus.). 32p. (ps-2). 1999. lib. bdg. 21.36 (*1-56766-629-9*) Childs World.
Moncure, Jane Belk. Word Bird's Winter Words. LC 85-5942. (Word Bird Library). (Illus.). 32p. (J). (ps-2). 1985. lib. bdg. 21.36 (*0-89565-309-5*) Childs World.
Moncure, John. Forging the King's Sword: Military Education Between Tradition & Modernization: the Case of the Royal Prussian Cadet Corps, 1871- 1918. LC 92-18515. (American University Studies: History: Ser. IX, Vol. 132). (Illus.). VIII, 323p. 1993. 58.95 (*0-8204-1960-5*) P Lang Pubng.
Moncure-Sime, A. H. Shakespeare: His Music & Song. LC 70-177518. 196p. 1972. reprint ed. 26.95 (*0-405-08795-0*, Pub. by Blom Pubns) Ayer.
Moncuse, Steve. Fish Police. 1987. mass mkt. 8.95 (*0-446-38739-8*, Pub. by Warner Bks) Little.
Moncy, Agnes, tr. see Blanco-Aguinaga, Carlos.
***Monczka, Robert M.** New Product Development. LC 99-47759. 2000. write for info. (*0-87389-468-5*) ASQ Qual Pr.
Monczka, Robert M. & Trent, Robert J. Cross-Functional Sourcing Team Effectiveness. Ketchum, Carol L., ed. LC 93-73254. 72p. (Orig.). (C). 1993. pap. text 20.00 (*0-945968-15-9*) Ctr Advanced Purchasing.
— Purchasing & Sourcing Strategy: Trends & Implications. LC 94-68975. 77p. (C). 1995. pap. text 20.00 (*0-945968-19-1*) Ctr Advanced Purchasing.
Monczka, Robert M., et al. Purchasing & Supply Chain Management. 2nd ed. (SWC-General Business Ser.). 2000. pap. 60.75 (*0-324-02315-4*) Thomson Learn.
Monczka, Robert M., jt. auth. see Carter, William K.
Mond, D., jt. ed. see Bruce, J.W.
Mond, D., jt. ed. see Montaldi, J. A.
Mond, James J., et al, eds. Cell Activation: Genetic Approaches. LC 91-20473. (Advances in Regulation of Cell Growth Ser.: Vol. 2). 350p. 1991. reprint ed. pap. 108.50 (*0-608-03432-0*, 206413300008) Bks Demand.
— Regulation of Cell Growth & Activation. LC 89-10328. (Advances in Regulation of Cell Growth Ser.). 304p. 1989. reprint ed. pap. 94.30 (*0-608-04666-3*, 206538700004) Bks Demand.
Mond, Robert W. What Christians & Muslims Should Know about Themselves. 1994. write for info. (*0-9625301-4-X*) Forum Islamic.
***Monda, Lorena.** The Practice of Wholeness: Spiritual Transformation in Everyday Life. (Illus.). xxvi, 286p. 2000. pap. 16.95 (*0-9678137-0-0*) Golden Flower.
Monda, Robin L. & Tango, Jenny, contrib. by. Bloody Wymmin, No. 3. (Illus.). 40p. 1998. pap. 3.95 (*0-9663427-0-4*) Bldy Wymmin.
Mondadori. English-Italian Business Dictionary. (ENG & ITA.). 306p. 1986. 49.95 (*0-8288-7350-X*, 8804289775) Fr & Eur.
— Italian English - English Italian Dictionary. (ITA & ENG.). 1990. per. 5.99 (*0-671-72721-4*) S&S Trade.
Mondain, M. Cochlear Implants in Children. (Advances in OtoRhinoLaryngology Ser.: Vol. 50). (Illus.). x, 210p. 1995. 173.25 (*3-8055-6095-8*) S Karger.
Mondaito, Meha. Sex & Reality: The Time Has Come! LC 95-74971. (Illus.). 192p. (Orig.). 1996. pap. 14.95 (*1-56184-082-3*) New Falcon Pubns.
Mondak, Jeffrey J. Nothing to Read: Newspapers & Elections in a Social Experiment. LC 95-16976. 200p. 1995. text 44.50 (*0-472-09599-4*, 09599); pap. text 19.95 (*0-472-06599-8*, 06599) U of Mich Pr.
Mondal, M. S. Pollen Morphology & Systematic Relationships of Families Sabiaceae & Connaraceae. (Advances in Pollen Spore Research Ser.: Vol. 12). (Illus.). 152p. 1990. 65.00 (*1-55528-222-9*, Pub. by Today Tomorrow) Scholarly Pubns.
Mondal, Sekh R. Dynamics of Muslim Society. LC 94-900458. (C). 1993. 28.50 (*81-210-0322-9*, Pub. by Inter-India Pubns) S Asia.
Mondal, Sekh R., jt. ed. see Bhadra, R. K.
Mondale, Clarence, jt. auth. see Steiner, Michael.
Mondale, Joan. Letters from Japan. (Illus.). iv, 148p. 1997. pap. 24.95 (*0-9662220-0-8*) J Mondale.
Mondano, Mark R. Divers Guide to Shipwrecks: Cape Canaveral to Jupiter Light. (Illus.). 150p. (Orig.). 1992. pap. 19.00 (*0-9631346-1-2*) Sandman Prods.
Mondavi, Robert. America's Rising Star Chefs: At the Robert Mondavi Great Chefs Cooking School in Napa Valley. (Illus.). 128p. 1994. pap. 19.95 (*0-9641403-0-6*) Santa Fe Ventures.
— Harvests of Joy: How the Good Life Became Great Business. 376p. 1999. pap. 14.00 (*0-15-601056-9*, Harvest Bks) Harcourt.
***Mondavi, Robert & Chutkow, Paul.** Harvests of Joy: My Life, My Way: How Great Taste Became Great Business. LC 98-19170. (Illus.). 368p. (C). 1998. 27.00 (*0-15-100346-7*) Harcourt.
Mondavi, Robert, et al. Seasons of the Vineyard: A Year of Celebration & Recipes from the Robert Mondavi Winery. (Illus.). 224p. 1996. 40.00 (*0-684-80758-0*) Simon & Schuster.
***Monday, D. Charone & Dobolek, Roberta, eds.** Arizona Wildlife Views: Special Edition. (Illus.). 155p. 1999. pap. 12.95 (*0-917563-99-9*) AZ Game & Fish.
***Monday, Glenn.** Know Your Swing: For Golfers Who Want the Edge. Scarr, Michael, ed. (Illus.). 245p. 1999. pap. text 40.00 (*0-9673841-0-9*) Glenn Monday.
Monday, Jane C. & Colley, Betty B. Voices from the Wild Horse Desert: The Vaquero Families of the King & Kenedy Ranches. LC 96-45639. (Illus.). 288p. 1997. pap. 15.95 (*0-292-75205-9*) U of Tex Pr.
— Voices from Wild Horse Desert: The Vaquero Families of the King & Kennedy Ranches. (Illus.). 288p. 1997. 35.00 (*0-292-75204-0*) U of Tex Pr.
Monday, Jane C., jt. auth. see Prather, Patricia S.
Monday, John C. & Shugart, Timothy, eds. Coating & Lining Work for Power Plant Cooling Water Systems Manual: Sponsored by ASTM Committee D-33 on Protective Coating & Lining Work for Power Generation Facilities; Prepared by ASTM Sub-Committee D33-12 on Service & Circulating Cooling Water Systems. LC 95-43136. (MNL, Manual Ser.: No. 28). (Illus.). 1995. text 35.00 (*0-8031-2070-2*, MNL28) ASTM.
Monday, Mark & Stubblefield, Gary. Killing Zone: A Professional's Guide to Preparing or Preventing Ambushes. 264p. 1994. pap. 25.00 (*0-87364-786-6*) Paladin Pr.
Monday Morning Staff, ed. see Svid, Murray.
***Monday, Paul.** San Francisco Component Frameworks: An Introduction. LC 99-43462. (Illus.). 400p. 1999. pap. text 44.95 (*0-201-61587-8*) Addisn-Wesley Iberoamer.
Monday, Stella, ed. see Frank, Cynthia.
Mondejar, Publio L., jt. intro. see Ramey, Edward.
Mondelli, Alfred A., jt. ed. see Bisognano, Joseph J.
Mondello. Multidimensional Chromatography: Techniques & Applications. text. write for info. (*0-471-98869-3*) Wiley.
Mondello, C. Credits & Collections: Techniques to Improve Your Cash Flow. Brett, Elaine, ed. LC 90-84234. (Fifty-Minute Ser.). (Illus.). 79p. (Orig.). 1991. pap. 10.95 (*1-56052-080-9*) Crisp Pubns.
Mondello, Giulio. The Secret of Costa Brava. 120p. pap. 9.95 (*0-9630779-0-2*) PPC Bks.
***Mondello, Lisa.** The Marriage Contract. 148p. 2000. pap. 12.95 (*1-58345-471-3*) Domhan Bks.
Mondello, Salvatore A. The Italian Immigrant in Urban America, 1880-1920, As Reported in the Contemporary Periodical Press. Cordasco, Francesco, ed. LC 80-880. (American Ethnic Groups Ser.). 1981. lib. bdg. 30.95 (*0-405-13441-X*) Ayer.
— The Private Papers of John Vanderlyn (1775-1852), American Portrait Painter. LC 89-9380. (Studies in American History: Vol. 3). (Illus.). 250p. 1990. lib. bdg. 89.95 (*0-88946-096-5*) E Mellen.
Monden, Yasuhiro. Cost Management in the New Manufacturing Age: Innovations in the Japanese Automotive Industry. Vitek, Stephen, tr. from JPN. (Illus.). 198p. 1992. 30.00 (*0-915299-90-9*) Productivity Inc.
— Cost Reduction Systems: Target Costing & Kaizen Costing. (JPN., Illus.). 400p. 1995. text 50.00 (*1-56327-068-4*) Productivity Inc.
— Japanese Cost Management. (Series on Technology Management). 430p. 1999. 68.00 (*1-86094-185-0*) World Scientific Pub.
Monden, Yasuhiro. Japanese Management Accounting: A World Class Approach to Profit Management. 1997. pap. text 30.00 (*1-56327-187-7*) Productivity Inc.

M

An Asterisk (*) at the beginning of an entry indicates that the title is appearing for the first time.

Monden, Yasuhiro. The Toyota Management System: Linking the Seven Key Functional Areas. LC 92-27133. 245p. 1996. pap. 30.00 (*1-56327-139-7*) Productivity Inc.

— Toyota Production System: An Integrated Approach to Just-in-Time. 3rd ed. LC 97-46509.Tr. of Shin Toyota Shisutemu. 502p. 1998. 57.95 (*0-89806-180-6*, NWTYPS) Eng Mgmt Pr.

Monden, Yasuhiro & Sakurai, Michiharu. Metodos Japoneses de Contabilidad: La Contabilidad en el Entorno de Nuevas Tecnologias. (SPA., Illus.). 336p. (Orig.). 1992. pap. 60.00 (*84-87022-76-6*) Productivity Inc.

Monden, Yasuhiro, et al. Estilo Japones de Direccion de Empresas. (SPA.). 219p. (Orig.). 1989. pap. 40.00 (*84-87022-56-1*) Productivity Inc.

Mondenard, J. P. Dictionary of Doping Substances & Procedures in Sports. (FRE.). 288p. 1991. 125.00 (*0-8288-6959-6*, 2225822905) Fr & Eur.

Monder, Eric. George Sidney: A Bio-Bibliography, 56. LC 94-10853. (Bio-Bibliographies in the Performing Arts Ser.: No. 56). 360p. 1994. lib. bdg. 69.50 (*0-313-28457-1*, Greenwood Pr) Greenwood.

***Mondesir-Itiaba, Juliana & Itiaba, Kibe.** Diabetes: Everybody's Business. 2nd ed. LC 98-90879. 1999. pap. 8.95 (*0-533-12964-8*) Vantage.

Mondey, David. Concise Guide to American Aircraft of World War II. 1994. 10.98 (*0-7858-0147-2*) Bk Sales Inc.

— Concise Guide to British Aircraft of Worle War II. 1994. 10.98 (*0-7858-0146-4*) Bk Sales Inc.

Mondfeld, Wolfram Z. Historic Ship Models. LC 89-11380. (Illus.). 352p. 1989. pap. 21.95 (*0-8069-5733-6*) Sterling.

Mondimore, Francis M. Depression: The Mood Disease. rev. ed. LC 92-40513. 248p. 1993. 24.95 (*0-8018-4592-0*) Johns Hopkins.

— Depression, the Mood Disease. (Health Bks.). 248p. 1995. reprint ed. pap. 15.95 (*0-8018-5184-X*) Johns Hopkins.

— A Natural History of Homosexuality. LC 96-16191. (Illus.). 275p. 1996. pap. 15.95 (*0-8018-5440-7*); text 35.00 (*0-8018-5349-4*) Johns Hopkins.

Mondimore, Francis Mark. Bipolar Disorder: A Guide for Patients & Families. LC 98-41913. (Johns Hopkins Press Health Bks.). 1999. 39.95 (*0-8018-6117-9*) Johns Hopkins.

— Bipolar Disorder: A Guide for Patients & Families. LC 98-41913. (Johns Hopkins Press Health Bks.). (Illus.). 277p. 1999. pap. 16.95 (*0-8018-6118-7*) Johns Hopkins.

Mondino, Jean-Baptiste, photos by. Deja Vu. (Illus.). 320p. 1999. 100.00 (*3-8238-9963-5*) te Neues.

Mondl, Michael J. Grasp: A Spiritually Uplifting Adventure. 124p. 1998. pap. text 8.95 (*1-886389-13-6*) Inside Job.

Mondlin, Marvin. Appraisals, a Guide for Bookmen. LC 97-210958. 64p. (Orig.). 1997. pap. 20.00 (*0-9656798-0-2*) Amer Sunbeam.

Mondon, Kathryn T., jt. auth. see Wennergren, Kenneth H.

Mondor, ed. see Mallarme, Stephane.

Mondor, Todd, jt. auth. see Freidlitz, Mikael.

Mondorf Seminar Staff, et al. The Future of European Social Statistics: Use of Administrative Registers & Dissemination Strategies : Proceedings of the Mondorf Seminar, Third Session, 25 & 26 January 1996. LC 98-224619. (ENG & FRE.). 227 p. 1996. write for info. (*92-827-9171-8*, Pub. by Comm Europ Commun) Bernan Associates.

***Mondot, Jean & Larrere, Catherine.** Lumieres et commerce: L'exemple bordelais, 28. 201p. 2000. 33.95 (*3-906764-35-4*, Pub. by P Lang) P Lang Pubng.

Mondovi, Bruno, ed. Structure & Functions of Amine Oxidases. 304p. 1986. 167.00 (*0-8493-5869-8*, QP603, CRC Reprint) Franklin.

Mondradon, J. Sanchez & Wolf, K. B., eds. Lie Methods in Optics. (Lecture Notes in Physics Ser.: Vol. 250). xiv, 249p. 1986. 39.00 (*0-387-16471-5*) Spr-Verlag.

Mondragon, Delfi. Religious Values of the Terminally Ill: A Handbook for Health Professionals. LC 97-16793. 1997. write for info. (*0-940866-64-1*) U Scranton Pr.

Mondragon, J. R., jt. auth. see Abas, J.

Mondragon, Joniva M., ed. see McKinney, Larry J.

Mondragon, Juan P., et al. Oranges in Eastern Mexico: An Economic Analysis of Production & Marketing Channels. LC 97-43526. (Illus.). 129p. 1998. pap. 30.00 (*0-944961-04-5*) FL Sci Source.

Mondre, Michael. Verwertungspflichten Im Abfall-Immissionsschutz- und Atomrecht. (Europaische Hochschulschriften Ser.: Reihe 2, Vol. 2355). 241p. 1998. pap. 45.95 (*3-631-33156-8*) P Lang Pubng.

Mondrian, Piet. Natural Reality & Abstract Reality: An Essay in Trialogue Form (1919-1920) James, Martin, tr. from DUT. LC 94-38785. 144p. 1995. pap. 14.95 (*0-8076-1372-X*, Pub. by Braziller) Norton.

— The New Art - The New Life: The Collected Writings of Piet Mondrian. Holtzman, Harry & James, Martin S., eds. & trs. by. from DUT. (Illus.). 440p. 1992. reprint ed. pap. 24.95 (*0-306-80508-1*) Da Capo.

Mondrone, Domenico. Mama! Why Did You Kill Us? LC 67-62523. 49p. 1998. pap. 2.00 (*0-89555-616-2*, 1541) TAN Bks Pubs.

Mondros, Jacqueline B. & Wilson, Scott M. Organizing for Power & Empowerment. LC 93-31676. (Empowering the Powerless Ser.). 279p. 1994. 61.50 (*0-231-06718-6*); pap. 26.50 (*0-231-06719-4*) Col U Pr.

Monds, F. C. The Business of Electronic Product Development. Montgomerie, G. A., ed. (Management Ser.: No. 2). 152p. 1984. reprint ed. pap. 54.00 (*0-86341-012-X*, MT002) INSPEC Inc.

***Mondschein, Marsha.** Measurit: Achieving Profitable Training. 280p. 1999. pap. 39.95 (*1-58597-006-9*) Leathers Pub.

***MONDSHINE, MARION.** Chihuahuas 1998. 98th ed. LC 99-205933. (New Owner's Guide to Ser.). 1999. 12.95 (*0-7938-2801-5*) TFH Pubns.

***Mondt, James Robert.** Cleaner Cars: The History & Technology of Emission Control since the 1960s. LC 99-57250. 280p. 2000. 29.00 (*0-7680-0222-2*, R-226) Soc Auto Engineers.

Mondy. Human Resource Management. 7th ed. 1998. pap. text, student ed. 16.00 (*0-13-010480-9*) P-H.

Mondy & Premeaux. Supervision. 3rd ed. LC 97-67116. 1998. 62.95 (*0-87393-637-X*) Dame Pubns.

Mondy, et al. Personal Selling: Function, Theory, & Practice. 4th ed. LC 97-67107. 1997. 69.95 (*0-87393-638-8*) Dame Pubns.

Mondy, Nell I. You Never Fail until You Stop Trying: The Story of a Pioneer Woman Chemist. (Illus.). 232p. 1999. 19.00 (*0-8059-4628-4*) Dorrance.

***Mondy, Premeaux.** Management: Concepts, Practices & Skills. 8th ed. (SWC-General Business Ser.). 1999. 39.95 (*0-324-03309-5*) Sth-Wstrn College.

Mondy, R. Wayne & Noe, Robert M., III. Human Resource Management. 4th ed. 650p. 1989. text 52.00 (*0-205-12121-7*, H21215) Allyn.

— Human Resource Management. 4th ed. 650p. 1989. teacher ed. write for info. (*0-318-66375-9*, H21223); student ed. 18.00 (*0-685-29836-1*, H20787); write for info. (*0-318-66376-7*, H21223); trans. write for info. (*0-318-66377-5*, H21249) P-H.

Mondy, R. Wayne, et al. Human Resource Management. 7th ed. LC 98-12218. 688p. 1998. 96.00 (*0-13-922782-2*) P-H.

— Management & Organizational Behavior. 720p. 1989. student ed. 18.00 (*0-685-29837-X*, H20621) Allyn.

— Management & Organizational Behavior. 720p. 1989. teacher ed. write for info. (*0-318-66379-1*, H20571); write for info. (*0-318-66380-5*, H20597); write for info. (*0-318-66382-1*, H23948); trans. write for info. (*0-318-66381-3*, H20605); VHS. write for info. (*0-318-66383-X*, H26131) P-H.

— Management, Concepts, Practices & Skills. 5th ed. (Illus.). 768p. 1990. text 51.00 (*0-205-12614-6*, H26149) Allyn.

— Personal Selling: Function, Theory, & Practice. 3rd ed. 480p. 1988. teacher ed. write for info. (*0-318-63843-6*, H19185) P-H.

— Supervision. 2nd ed. 520p. 1990. teacher ed. write for info. (*0-318-66378-3*, H25067) P-H.

Mondy, Robert W. Pioneers & Preachers: Stories of the Old Frontier. LC 79-16906. (Illus.). 272p. 1980. text 46.95 (*0-88229-619-1*) Burnham Inc.

Mondzak, Susan, jt. auth. see Cosentino, Joe.

Mone, Edward M. & London, Manuel. HR to the Rescue. LC 98-20775. (Improving Human Performance Ser.). 232p. 1998. 37.95 (*0-88415-397-5*, 5397) Gulf Pub.

Mone, Edward M., jt. ed. see London, Manuel.

Mone, Franz J. Geschichte des Heidenthums im Nordlichen Europa, 2 vols., Set. xl, 1085p. 1990. reprint ed. write for info. (*0-318-70732-2*) G Olms Pubs.

Monea, Michael J. St. Anthony's Guide to Radiology Managed Care & Capitation: Radiology, Diagnostic Imaging, Radiation Therapy. Lechtman, Jay & Persinos, John F., eds. 200p. (C). Date not set. 349.00 (*1-56329-312-9*) St Anthony Pub.

Moneger, Lionel. Knopf City Guide: Paris. 1998. pap. 14.95 (*0-375-70253-9*) Knopf.

Monek, Francis H. Canes Through the Ages: With Value Guide. LC 95-31567. (Illus.). 320p. 1995. 79.95 (*0-88740-862-1*) Schiffer.

Monell, Charles. Grace & Peace. (Illus.). 148p. 1995. 40.00 (*0-944996-13-2*) Carlsons.

Monell, Gary E., jt. auth. see Nasatir, Abraham P.

Monelle, Raymond. Linguistics & Semiotics in Music. (Contemporary Music Studies). 350p. 1992. text 52.00 (*3-7186-5208-0*, Harwood Acad Pubs); pap. text 25.00 (*3-7186-5209-9*, Harwood Acad Pubs) Gordon & Breach.

***Monelle, Raymond.** The Sense of Music: Semiotic Essays. LC 00-32659. (Illus.). 336p. 2000. 26.95 (*0-691-05716-8*) Princeton U Pr.

— Sense of Music: Semiotic Essays. (Illus.). 336p. 2000. 65.00 (*0-691-05715-X*) Princeton U Pr.

Monelle, Raymond, ed. Musica Significans Pt. 1, Vol. 2. 4th ed. 88p. 1998. pap. text 14.00 (*90-5755-013-X*, Harwood Acad Pubs) Gordon & Breach.

— Musica Significans Pt. 3, Vol. 3. 71p. 1998. pap. text 22.00 (*90-5755-015-6*, Harwood Acad Pubs) Gordon & Breach.

— Musica Significans Pt. 4, Vol. 4. 101p. 1998. pap. text 22.00 (*90-5755-017-2*, Harwood Acad Pubs) Gordon & Breach.

— Musica Significans Pt. 5, Vol. 5. 94p. 1998. pap. text 22.00 (*90-5755-019-9*, Harwood Acad Pubs) Gordon & Breach.

— Musica Significans Pt.1, Vol. 1. 78p. 1998. pap. text 22.00 (*90-5755-012-1*, Harwood Acad Pubs) Gordon & Breach.

Monemuastis, George. Olive Oil: Source of Life. (ENG & FRE.). 144p. 1998. 17.95 (*960-7436-44-X*) Grco Crd GR.

***Moneo, Rafael & Wettstein, Hannes.** Grand Hyatt Berlin. (Illus.). 112p. 1999. pap. 38.00 (*3-7643-6104-2*) Birkhauser.

Moner, Fray F. Obras Castellanas Tomo I: Poemas Menores, 2. Cocozeella, Peter, ed. LC 91-20691. (Hispanic Literature Ser.: Vols. 2 & 3).Tr. of SPA. 1991. 99.95 (*0-88946-388-3*) E Mellen.

— Obras Castellanas Tomo I: Poemas Menores, Vol. 3. Cocozeella, Peter, ed. LC 91-20691. (Hispanic Literature Ser.: Vols. 2 & 3).Tr. of SPA. 1991. 99.95 (*0-88946-389-1*) E Mellen.

Mones, Isidre. It's Time to Wash! Snow White & the Seven Dwarfs. LC 94-71695. (Surprise Lift-the-Flap Bk.). 18p. (J). (ps-k). 1995. 9.95 (*0-7868-3030-1*, Pub. by Disney Pr) Little.

— Pocahontas: Looking for Meeko. LC 95-83655. (Follow the Tracks Bk.). 16p. (J). (ps-k). 1996. 12.95 (*0-7868-3094-8*, Pub. by Disney Pr) Little.

Mones, Nicole. Lost in Translation. LC PS3563.O519L67 1998. 384p. 1998. 23.95 (*0-385-31934-7*) Delacorte.

— Lost in Translation. 366p. 1999. pap. 12.95 (*0-385-31944-4*, Delta Trade) Dell.

Mones, Paul. Stalking Justice: The Dramatic True Story of the Detective Who First Used DNA Testing to Catch a Serial Killer. Zion, Claire, ed. 320p. 1995. 23.00 (*0-671-70348-X*) PB.

— Stalking Justice: The Dramatic True Story of the Detective Who First Used DNA Testing to Catch a Serial Killer. 1996. mass mkt. 6.99 (*0-671-00201-5*) PB.

— When a Child Kills. Zion, Claire, ed. 416p. 1992. reprint ed. pap. 6.99 (*0-671-67421-8*) PB.

Monesson, Harry S. Up a Cranberry Tree II: Piney Poems. (Illus.). 94p. (Orig.). 1997. reprint ed. pap. 5.00 (*0-9633735-1-X*) H S Monesson.

— The World's Biggest Tummy. LC 92-96830. (Illus.). 40p. (Orig.). (J). (gr. k-3). 1992. pap. 4.95 (*0-9633735-0-1*) H S Monesson.

Monet, Anny, jt. auth. see Girard, Marie-Helene.

Monet, Claude. Art Mini-Monet. (Illus.). 96p. 2000. pap. text 4.95 (*3-8290-2936-5*) Konemann.

— The Bridge at Argenteuil. (Fine Art Jigsaw Puzzles Ser.). 1989. 9.95 (*0-934967-50-4*) Battle Rd Pr.

— Monet: A Postcard Book. (Postcard Bks.). (Illus.). 64p. (Orig.). 1989. pap. text 8.95 (*0-89471-683-2*) Running Pr.

Monet, Jacques. The Last Cannon Shot: A Study of French-Canadian Nationalism, 1837-1850. LC 70-455781. 432p. reprint ed. pap. 134.00 (*0-608-16319-8*, 202653700050) Bks Demand.

Monet, Jean. The Cassock & the Crown: Canada's Most Controversial Murder Trial. LC 97-114899. (Illus.). 160p. 1996. 49.95 (*0-7735-1399-X*, Pub. by McG-Queens Univ Pr); pap. 19.95 (*0-7735-1449-X*, Pub. by McG-Queens Univ Pr) CUP Services.

Monet, Rubye, tr. see Paudras, Francis.

Moneta, Daniela P., ed. Chas. F. Lummis: The Centennial Exhibition Commemorating His Tramp Across the Continent. LC 84-27589. (Illus.). 80p. (Orig.). 1985. pap. 14.95 (*0-916561-01-1*) Southwest Mus.

***Moneta, Elisabetta Mazza.** Deutsche und Italiener: Der Einflub von Stereotypen auf interkulturelle Kommunikation Deutsche und italienische Selbst und Fremdbilder und ihre Wirkung auf die Wahrnehmung von Italienern in Deutschland. 2000. 45.95 (*3-631-34960-2*) P Lang Pubng.

Moneta, Giuseppina. On Identity: A Study in Genetic Phenomenology. (Phaenomenologica Ser.: No. 71). 108p. 1977. pap. text 71.50 (*90-247-1860-0*, Pub. by M Nijhoff) Kluwer Academic.

Moneta, Giuseppina, et al, eds. The Collegium Phaenomenologicum: The First Ten Years. 352p. (C). 1988. text 201.00 (*90-247-3709-5*) Kluwer Academic.

Monetary International Fund, ed. Financial Sector Development in Sub-Saharan African Countries. 1998. write for info. (*1-55775-758-5*) Intl Monetary.

Moneti, Annamaria, jt. auth. see Lazzarino, Graziana.

Monett, Clarence. Keweenaw Central Railroad & the Crestview Resort. LC 97-149041. (Copper Country Local History Ser.: Vol. 52). (Illus.). 128p. 1997. 5.00 (*0-942363-51-5*) C J Monette.

Monetta, Dominic J., jt. auth. see Carlisle, Rodney P.

Monette, Clarence J. Delaware, Michigan, Its History. (Copper Country Local History Ser.: Vol. 28). (Illus.). 120p. (Orig.). 1987. pap. 3.00 (*0-942363-27-2*) C J Monette.

— The Gay, Michigan, Story. (Copper Country Local History Ser.: No. 31). (Illus.). 128p. (Orig.). 1988. pap. 5.00 (*0-942363-30-2*) C J Monette.

— Lac La Belle. (Copper Country Local History Ser.: Vol. 28). (Illus.). 128p. 1990. 5.00 (*0-942363-37-X*) C J Monette.

— Lake Linden's Living History - 1985. (Copper Country Local History Ser.: Vol. 29). (Illus.). 112p. (Orig.). 1987. pap. 2.50 (*0-942363-28-0*) C J Monette.

— Some of the Best from C & H News & Views, Vol. II. (Copper Country Local History Ser.: No. 30). (Illus.). 120p. (Orig.). 1987. pap. 2.50 (*0-942363-29-9*) C J Monette.

Monette, Duane R. Applied Social Research. 3rd ed. (C). 1993. pap. text, teacher ed. 33.75 (*0-03-092546-0*) Harcourt Coll Pubs.

— Applied Social Research. 3rd ed. (C). 1994. text 64.00 (*0-03-092545-2*, Pub. by Harcourt Coll Pubs) Harcourt.

— Applied Social Research. 4th ed. LC 97-75356. (C). 1997. text 76.50 (*0-03-019444-X*) Harcourt.

— Applied Social Research. 4th ed. (C). 1997. pap. text, teacher ed. 28.00 (*0-03-019447-4*) Harcourt Coll Pubs.

Monette, John W. History of the Discovery & Settlement of the Valley of the Mississippi by the Three Great European Powers Spain, France, & Great Britain, & the Subsequent Occupation Settlement & Extension of Civil Government by the United States Until the Year 1846, 2 vols. LC 78-146408. (First American Frontier Ser.). (Illus.). 1971. reprint ed. 74.95 (*0-405-02868-7*) Ayer.

Monette, Louis G. Index to l'Art du Facteur d'Orgues. 62p. 1992. pap. 9.00 (*0-913746-34-7*) Organ Lit.

***Monette, Madeline.** Double Suspect: A Novel. Von Flotow, Luise, tr. 250p. 2000. pap. 15.00 (*1-55071-113-X*, Pub. by Guernica Editions) Paul & Co Pubs.

***Monette, Marlyn W.** So Good . . .Make You Slap Your Mama! xviii, 167p. 1999. pap. 14.95 (*0-9673339-0-3*) M W Monette.

Monette, Maurice L. Kindred Spirits: Bonding of Religious & Laity. LC 87-61530. 100p. (Orig.). 1987. pap. 6.95 (*1-55612-070-2*) Sheed & Ward WI.

Monette, Maurice L., ed. Partners in Ministry: Priests in Collaboration with Parish Life Coordinators. LC 88-62579. 72p. (Orig.). (C). 1988. pap. 4.95 (*1-55612-243-8*) Sheed & Ward WI.

Monette, Maurice L., jt. ed. see Institute for Pastoral Life Staff.

Monette, Paul. Becoming a Man: Half a Life Story. LC 92-54661. 288p. 1993. reprint ed. pap. 14.00 (*0-06-250724-9*, Pub. by Harper SF) HarpC.

— Borrowed Time: An AIDS Memoir. 400p. 1988. 22.00 (*0-15-113598-3*) Harcourt.

— Borrowed Time: An AIDS Memoir. LC 98-219384. 352p. 1998. pap. 13.00 (*0-15-600581-6*) Harcourt.

— Borrowed Time: An AIDS Memoir. 1990. pap. 12.50 (*0-380-70779-9*, Avon Bks) Morrow Avon.

— The Gold Diggers. LC 99-178819. 373p. 1999. reprint ed. pap. 10.00 (*1-55583-458-2*) Alyson Pubns.

— Halfway Home. 272p. 1992. pap. 11.00 (*0-380-71797-2*, Avon Bks) Morrow Avon.

— Last Watch of the Night: Essays Too Personal & Otherwise. LC 93-47655. 1994. 21.95 (*0-15-100071-9*) Harcourt.

— Last Watch of the Night: Essays Too Personal & Otherwise. 320p. 1995. pap. 12.00 (*0-15-600202-7*) Harcourt.

— The Long Shot. 328p. 1988. reprint ed. pap. 14.95 (*0-8216-2004-5*) Carol Pub Group.

— Love Alone: Eighteen Elegies for Rog. (Stonewall Inn Editions Ser.). 80p. 1988. pap. 8.95 (*0-312-02602-1*) St Martin.

— The Politics of Silence. LC 93-33721. (National Book Week Lectures Ser.). 21p. 1994. write for info. (*0-8444-0808-5*) Lib Congress.

— Sanctuary: A Tale of Life in the Woods. LC 96-30551. 1997. 16.50 (*0-684-83286-0*, Scribner Pap Fic) S&S Trade Pap.

— Sanctuary: A Tale of Life in the Woods. 96p. (YA). 1999. reprint ed. pap. 9.95 (*1-55583-531-7*, Pub. by Alyson Pubns) Consort Bk Sales.

— Selected from Borrowed Time: An AIDS Memoir. abr. ed. Literacy Volunteers of New York City Staff & Fogarty, Patricia, eds. (Writers' Voices Ser.). 64p. (Orig.). 1992. pap. text 3.95 (*0-929631-56-0*, Signal Hill) New Readers.

— Taking Care of Mrs. Carroll. (Stonewall Inn Editions Ser.). 288p. 1988. pap. 12.95 (*0-312-01515-1*) St Martin.

Monette, S. Nouveau Dictionnaire des Aliments. 2nd ed. (FRE.). 638p. 1997. 95.00 (*0-320-00483-X*) Fr & Eur.

Monette, Solange. Dictionnaire Encyclopedique des Aliments. (FRE.). 1991. write for info. (*0-7859-8203-5*, 2-89037-475-0) Fr & Eur.

Monetti-Souple, Marta. A Year-Round Recruitment & Retention Plan. (How to Development Ser.). 53p. (Orig.). 1990. pap. 8.00 (*1-55833-047-X*) Natl Cath Educ.

Money, A. H., jt. auth. see Gonin, R.

Money, Arthur, et al. Effective Measurement & Management of It Costs & Benefits: Key Issues. 2nd ed. 160p. 2000. pap. text 54.95 (*0-7506-4420-6*) Buttrwrth-Heinemann.

Money, Bill & Hodgson, Geoff. Manual of Contract Documents for Highway Works: A User's Guide & Commentary, 1993-1994 Amendments. 284p. 1996. 48.00 (*0-7277-2088-0*) Am Soc Civil Eng.

Money, D. K. The English Horace: Anthony Alsop & the Tradition of British Latin Verse. LC 99-199821. (British Academy Postdoctoral Fellowship Monographs). (Illus.). 416p. 1999. text 65.00 (*0-19-726184-1*) OUP.

Money, Jeannette. Fences & Neighbors: Immigration Issues in the 1990s. (CIR Working PaperS: No. 6). 1994. pap. 15.00 (*0-86682-097-3*) Ctr Intl Relations.

— Fences & Neighbors: The Political Geography of Immigration Control. LC 98-46766. 1999. 39.95 (*0-8014-3570-6*) Cornell U Pr.

Money, Jeannette, jt. auth. see Tsebelis, George.

Money, John. The Adam Principle: Genes, Genitals, Hormones & Gender - Selected Readings in Sexology. LC 93-1384. (New Concepts in Human Sexuality Ser.). 364p. (C). 1993. 43.95 (*0-87975-804-X*) Prometheus Bks.

— The Destroying Angel: Fitness, & Food in the Legacy of Degeneracy Theory, Graham Crackers, Kellogg's Corn Flakes, & American Health History. LC 84-43104. 213p. 1985. 32.95 (*0-87975-277-7*) Prometheus Bks.

— Gay, Straight & In-Between: The Sexology of Erotic Orientation. (Illus.). 304p. 1988. text 29.95 (*0-19-505407-5*) OUP.

— Gay, Straight & In-Between: The Sexology of Erotic Orientation. (Illus.). 286p. 1990. reprint ed. pap. 11.95 (*0-19-506331-7*) OUP.

— The Kaspar Hauser Syndrome of Psychosocial Dwarfism: Deficient Statural, Intellectual, & Social Growth Induced by Child Abuse. LC 92-11008. 290p. (C). 1992. 31.95 (*0-87975-754-X*) Prometheus Bks.

***Money, John.** The Lovemap Guidebook. LC 99-28248. 300p. 1999. 39.50 (*0-8264-1203-3*) Continuum.

Money, John. Lovemaps: Clinical Concepts of Sexual-Erotic Health & Pathology, Paraphilia & Gender Transposition in Childhood, Adolescence & Maturity. LC 85-24153. (Illus.). 350p. (C). 1986. 34.50 (*0-8290-1589-2*) Irvington.

— Lovemaps: Clinical Concepts of Sexual-Erotic Health & Pathology, Paraphilia & Gender Transposition in Childhood, Adolescence & Maturity. LC 85-24153. 351p. 1986. pap. 19.95 (*0-87975-456-7*) Prometheus Bks.

— Lovemaps: Clinical Concepts of Sexual-Erotic Health &

An Asterisk (*) at the beginning of an entry indicates that the title is appearing for the first time.

Pathology, Paraphilia & Gender Transposition in Childhood, Adolescence & Maturity. LC 85-24153. (Illus.). 350p. (C). 1989. reprint ed. pap. 18.95 (*0-8290-1892-1*) Irvington.

— Principles of Developmental Sexology. LC 56-7503. 324p. (C). 1997. 59.50 (*0-8264-1026-X*) Continuum.

— Sex Errors of the Body: Dilemmas, Education, Counseling. LC 68-15447. (Illus.). 160p. reprint ed. pap. 49.60 (*0-7837-3393-3*, 204335100008) Bks Demand.

— Sin, Science & the Sex Police: Essays on Sexology & Sexosophy. LC 98-37663. 393p. 1999. 32.95 (*1-57392-253-6*) Prometheus Bks.

— Unspeakable Monsters in All Our Lives. LC 99-23002. (Illus.). 250p. 1999. pap. 18.95 (*1-57392-707-4*) Prometheus Bks.

— Venuses Penuses. LC 85-46047. 681p. 1986. 43.95 (*0-87975-327-7*) Prometheus Bks.

Money, John, ed. The Disabled Reader: Education of the Dyslexic Child. LC 66-20713. 441p. reprint ed. pap. 136.80 (*0-8357-9266-8*, 201190000080) Bks Demand.

Money, John & Ehrhardt, Anke A. Man & Woman, Boy & Girl: Differentiation & Dimorphism of Gender Identity from Conception to Maturity. LC 72-4012. (Illus.). 327p. (Orig.). reprint ed. pap. 101.40 (*0-7837-3394-1*, 204335200008) Bks Demand.

Money, John & Lamacz, Margaret. Vandalized Lovemaps: Paraphilic Outcome of Seven Cases in Pediatric Sexology. LC 89-4037. 224p. 1989. 32.95 (*0-87975-513-X*) Prometheus Bks.

Money, John, et al. The Breathless Orgasm: A Lovemap Biography of Asphyxiophilia. LC 90-26691. 178p. (C). 1991. 27.95 (*0-87975-664-0*) Prometheus Bks.

Money, John, jt. auth. see Keyes, Ronald W.

Money, John, ed. see American Psychopathological Assn. Staff.

Money, John, jt. ed. see Green, Richard.

Money, John, ed. see Johns Hopkins Conference on Research Needs & Prosp.

Money, John, jt. ed. see Krivacska, James J.

Money, John, jt. ed. see Paddison, Ronan.

Money, John, jt. ed. see Wolman, Benjamin B.

***Money, Kimberly K. & Money, R. Bruce.** Creating a Functional Family in a Dysfunctional World. LC 99-32896. 1999. pap. 12.95 (*0-87833-238-3*) Taylor Pub.

Money-Kyrle, R. E. Psychoanalysis & Politics: A Contribution to the Psychology of Politics & Morals. LC 72-12143. 182p. 1973. reprint ed. lib. bdg. 75.00 (*0-8371-6714-0*, MOPS, Greenwood Pr) Greenwood.

Money, Lloyd J. Transportation Energy & the Future. (Illus.). 144p. (C). 1984. text 38.00 (*0-13-930230-1*) P-H.

Money Magazine Editors. Money Magazine: A Guide to Your Home. 1999. write for info. (*0-316-57835-5*) Little.

***Money Magazine Editors, ed.** Money Adviser 2000. (Illus.). 2000. 24.95 (*1-883013-89-5*, People Bks) Tme Inc.

Money Magazine Editors, jt. auth. see Sprouse, Mary L.

Money Magazine Staff. The 1999 Money Adviser: Investing Moves for Today. 225p. 1999. write for info. (*1-883013-59-3*, People Bks) Tme Inc.

Money, N. Geografia Historica Mundo Biblica.Tr. of Historical Bible Geography. (SPA.). 288p. 1969. pap. 6.99 (*0-8297-0558-9*) Vida Pubs.

***Money, Peter.** Finding It: Selected Poems. 48p. 2000. pap. 8.00 (*1-890887-15-3*) Mille Grazie.

Money, Peter. These Are My Shoes. 96p. (Orig.). 1991. pap. 6.95 (*0-9623193-8-4*) Boz Pub.

Money, R. Bruce, jt. auth. see Money, Kimberly K.

Money, Royce. Ministering to Families. LC 86-72162. 300p. 1987. pap. 10.95 (*0-915547-92-9*) Abilene Christ U.

Money, S. A. Practical Microprocessor Interfacing. LC 87-23204. 247p. 1987. 125.00 (*0-471-63788-2*) Wiley.

Money, Steve. Newnes Microprocessor Pocket Book. 1990. 22.00 (*0-8493-7146-5*) CRC Pr.

— Newnes Radio Amateur & Listener's Pocket Book. 1988. 27.00 (*0-434-91259-X*) CRC Pr.

— Radio Amateur & Listener's Data Handbook. (Illus.). 240p. 1995. pap. text 34.95 (*0-7506-2094-3*) Buttrwrth-Heinemann.

Money, Steve A. Newnes Microprocessor Pocket Book. LC 89-45982. (Illus.). 260p. 1989. pap. 80.60 (*0-608-04989-1*, 206560700004) Bks Demand.

Moneyhon, Carl & Roberts, Bobby. Portraits of Conflict: A Photographic History of Texas in the Civil War. LC 98-8827. (Illus.). 344p. 1998. 75.00 (*1-55728-533-0*) U of Ark Pr.

Moneyhon, Carl H. Arkansas & the New South, 1874-1929. LC 97-26932. (Histories of Arkansas Ser.). 176p. 1997. pap. 16.00 (*1-55728-490-3*) U of Ark Pr.

— Arkansas & the New South, 1874-1929. LC 97-26932. (Histories of Arkansas Ser.). 1997. 28.00 (*1-55728-489-X*) U of Ark Pr.

— Impact of the Civil War & Reconstruction on Arkansas: Persistence in the Midst of Ruin. LC 93-26080. (Illus.). 336p. (C). 1993. text 47.50 (*0-8071-1840-0*) La State U Pr.

Moneyhon, Carl H., jt. auth. see Hanson, Gerald.

Moneyhon, Carl H., jt. auth. see Roberts, Bobby.

Moneyhon, Jack N. Buying Actuals: An Investor's Manual for Evaluating Gold & Silver. (Illus.). 80p. (Orig.). 1984. pap. 16.95 (*0-930907-00-0*) Great & Sm Pubs.

Monfardini, S., et al, eds. Manual of Adult & Paediatric Medical Oncology. (Illus.). 420p. 1987. 58.95 (*0-387-15347-0*) Spr-Verlag.

Monfardini, S. & Veronesi, U., eds. The Management of Non-Hodgkin's Lymphomas in Europe. (ESO Intercity Reports). viii, 92p. 1990. 68.95 (*0-387-52297-2*) Spr-Verlag.

Monfardini, Silvio, jt. ed. see Fentiman, Ian S.

Monfasani, J. George of Trebizond: A Biography & a Study of his Rhetoric & Logic. 1976. 43.00 (*90-04-04370-5*, CSCT, 1) Brill Academic Pubs.

Monfasani, John. Byzantine Scholars in Renaissance Italy: Cardinal Bessarion & Other Emigres. (Collected Studies: No. CS485). 368p. 1995. 115.95 (*0-86078-477-0*, Pub. by Variorum) Ashgate Pub Co.

— Fernando of Cordova: A Biographical & Intellectual Profile. LC 92-72642. (Transactions Ser.: Vol. 82, Pt. 6). 125p. (C). 1992. pap. 18.00 (*0-87169-826-9*, T826-MOJ) Am Philos.

— Language & Learning in Renaissance Italy: Selected Articles. (Collected Studies: NO. CS460). (Illus.). 352p. 1994. 115.95 (*0-86078-403-7*, Pub. by Variorum) Ashgate Pub Co.

Monfasani, John, ed. Collectanea Trapezuntiana: Texts, Documents, & Bibliographies . . . of George of Trebizond. LC 83-19366. (Medieval & Renaissance Texts & Studies: Vol. 25). 888p. 1984. 60.00 (*0-86698-060-1*, MR25) MRTS.

Monfasani, John, et al, eds. Supplementum Festivum: Studies in Honor of Paul Oskar Kristeller. LC 87-18422. (Medieval & Renaissance Texts & Studies: Vol. 49). (Illus.). 672p. 1987. 60.00 (*0-86698-033-4*, MR49) MRTS.

Monfasani, John & Musto, Ronald G., eds. Renaissance Society & Culture: Essays in Honor of Eugene F. Rice, Jr. LC 90-55872. (Illus.). 334p. 1995. pap. 25.00 (*0-934977-34-8*) Italica Pr.

Monfasoni, John, ed. Collectanea Trapezuntiana: Texts, Documents, & Bibliographies of George of Trebizond. (Renaissance Text Ser.: No. 8). xxii, 866p. 1984. 60.00 (*0-685-11970-X*) Renaiss Society Am.

Monford, B. LaMont, Sr. From Valleys to Victories. LC 95-95189. 68p. 1995. pap. write for info. (*0-7880-0647-9*, Fairway Pr) CSS OH.

Monfort, Alain, jt. auth. see Gourieroux, Christian.

Monfort, Franklin, jt. auth. see Orfield, Gary.

Monfort, J. C., et al. Guide Pratique de Psycho-Geriatrie, Vol. 1. (FRE.). 174p. pap. 54.00 (*2-906077-32-1*) Elsevier.

— Guide Pratique de Psycho-Geriatrie, Vol. 2. (FRE.). 176p. pap. 58.00 (*2-906077-49-6*) Elsevier.

Monfort, Platt. Geodesic Airolite Boats: An Inexpensive Low Tech System Utilizing Exotic Materials. 1996. pap. text 5.95 (*0-07-042856-5*) McGraw.

Monforte, J. M., jt. auth. see Casciaro, J. M.

Monforte, Joseph R., ed. Analytical Toxicology of Cannabinoids. 176p. (Orig.). 1994. pap. 40.00 (*0-912474-17-3*) Preston Pubns.

— Analytical Toxicology of Cocaine. 288p. (Orig.). 1994. pap. 50.00 (*0-912474-19-X*) Preston Pubns.

Monfredo, Miriam G. Blackwater Spirits. 368p. 1996. reprint ed. mass mkt. 5.99 (*0-425-15266-9*) Berkley Pub.

— Must the Maiden Die? LC 99-29295. (Seneca Falls Historical Mystery Ser.: No. 6). 1999. 21.95 (*0-425-16699-6*, Prime Crime) Berkley Pub.

***Monfredo, Miriam G.** Must the Maiden Die? (Seneca Falls Historical Mysteries Ser.). 2000. mass mkt. 6.99 (*0-425-17610-X*) Berkley Pub.

Monfredo, Miriam G. Seneca Falls Inheritance. 304p. 1994. mass mkt. 5.99 (*0-425-14465-8*, Prime Crime) Berkley Pub.

***Monfredo, Miriam G.** Sisters of Cain: A Seneca Falls Civil War Mystery. LC 99-89770. 2000. 21.95 (*0-425-17672-X*) Berkley Pub.

Monfredo, Miriam G. The Stalking Horse. LC 97-21547. 352p. 1997. pap. 21.95 (*0-425-15783-0*, Prime Crime) Berkley Pub.

— The Stalking Horse. (Historical Mystery Ser.: Vol. 5). 352p. 1999. reprint ed. pap. 5.99 (*0-425-16695-3*, Prime Crime) Berkley Pub.

— Through a Gold Eagle: A Glynis Tryon Mystery. 384p. 1997. mass mkt. 5.99 (*0-425-15898-5*, Prime Crime) Berkley Pub.

Monfredo, Miriam G. & Newman, Sharan, eds. Crime Through Time: New & Original Tales of Historical Mystery. LC 97-197215. 384p. 1997. mass mkt. 6.99 (*0-425-15761-X*, Prime Crime) Berkley Pub.

— Crime Through Time II. 352p. 1998. mass mkt. 6.99 (*0-425-16410-1*) Berkley Pub.

***Monfried, Lucia.** Jokes about School, Vol. 1. (Mr. Potato Head's Ser.). 1999. pap. 2.99 (*0-525-46279-1*, Dutton Child) Peng Put Young Read.

— Jokes about Sports, Vol. 1. (Mr. Potato Head's Ser.). 1999. pap. 2.99 (*0-525-46280-5*, Dutton Child) Peng Put Young Read.

— Keep on Smilin: A Bendy Legs Book, Vol. 1. (Illus.). 5p. (YA). 1999. bds. 6.99 (*0-525-46258-9*, Dutton Child) Peng Put Young Read.

— Mr. Potato Head: Giddyap, Cowspud! (Illus.). (J). 2000. pap. 4.99 (*0-525-46339-9*, Dutton Child) Peng Put Young Read.

— Mr. Potato Head & Cinderspud. (Illus.). (J). 2000. pap. 3.49 (*0-525-46341-0*, Dutton Child) Peng Put Young Read.

— Mr. Potato Head Leads the Parade. (Illus.). (J). 2000. pap. 3.49 (*0-525-46342-9*, Dutton Child) Peng Put Young Read.

— Mr. Potato Head's Wonderful Wedding. (Illus.). (J). 2000. pap. 4.99 (*0-525-46340-2*, Dutton Child) Peng Put Young Read.

— Mr. Potato Head's Big Night Out, Vol. 1. (Mr. Potato Head's Ser.). 1999. pap. 3.49 (*0-525-46277-5*, Dutton Child) Peng Put Young Read.

— Official Easy-Bake Cookbook, Vol. 1. (Illus.). 48p. 1999. pap. 7.99 (*0-525-46256-2*, Dutton Child) Peng Put Young Read.

— Santa's Little Helper. (Mr. Potato Head's Ser.). 1999. pap. 3.49 (*0-525-46278-3*, Dutton Child) Peng Put Young Read.

Monfries, Marcelle. Gardening in the Shade. (Illus.). 76p. (Orig.). 1995. pap. 11.95 (*0-86417-623-6*) Seven Hills Bk.

Mong, Lee S. Understanding Jade: A Layman's Guide. 2nd ed. 104p. 1992. reprint ed. 11.95 (*981-204-388-8*) Heian Intl.

Mong, RoseMary. Barefoot Forever. (Illus.). 96p. 1986. 12.95 (*0-941974-07-3*) Baranski Pub Co.

Monga, Celestin. The Anthropology of Anger: Civil Society & Democracy in Africa. 219p. 1996. 48.00 (*1-55587-644-7*) L Rienner.

***Monga, Celestin.** The Anthropology of Anger: Civil Society & Democracy in Africa. 219p. 1998. reprint ed. pap. 19.95 (*1-55587-841-5*) L Rienner.

Monga, G. S., jt. auth. see Sanctis, V. J.

Monga, Luigi. In the Very Heart of Man: The Life & Poetry of Carlo Porta. LC 86-11092. (ENG & ITA.). 51p. (Orig.). 1986. reprint ed. pap. 46.90 (*0-608-04475-X*, 206522000001) Bks Demand.

Monga, Pradeep, ed. Energy, Environment & Sustainable Development in the Himalayas. (C). 1992. 32.00 (*81-85182-76-0*, Pub. by Indus Pub) S Asia.

Monga, Pradeep & Lakhanpal, T. N. Rural Energy Alternatives in the Hilly Areas: (Social Forestry & Biogas Systems) (International Bioscience Monographs: Vol. XX). (Illus.). 225p. 1988. 39.00 (*1-55528-155-9*) Scholarly Pubns.

Mongait, A. L., jt. auth. see Tretiakov, P. N.

Mongan, Agnes. David to Corot: French Drawings in the Fogg Art Museum. Stewart, Miriam, ed. (Illus.). 448p. 1993. 135.00 (*0-674-19320-2*) HUP.

Mongan, Agnes, ed. Edward Waldo Forbes: Yankee Visionary. (Illus.). 172p. 1971. pap. 4.95 (*0-916724-17-4*) Harvard Art Mus.

— Harvard Honors Lafayette. (Illus.). 160p. 1976. pap. 4.95 (*0-916724-03-4*) Harvard Art Mus.

— One Hundred Master Drawings. LC 75-95129. (Illus.). 208p. 1971. reprint ed. lib. bdg. 59.50 (*0-8371-3989-9*, MOMD, Greenwood Pr) Greenwood.

***Mongan, John & Suojanen, Noah.** Programming Interviews Exposed: Secrets to Landing Your Next Job. LC 00-28304. 272p. 2000. pap. 24.99 (*0-471-38356-2*) Wiley.

Mongar, Richard. Original Marxism. (C). 1996. pap. text 21.50 (*0-7453-0592-X*) Westview.

Mongar, Thomas. Original Marxism. (C). 1996. text 57.95 (*0-7453-0426-5*) Westview.

Mongar, Thomas M. The Death of Communism & the Rebirth of Original Marxism. LC 94-12459. 400p. 1994. text 99.95 (*0-7734-9074-4*) E Mellen.

— Only with Marx & Jesus. LC 97-8605. 1997. write for info. (*0-7618-0775-6*) U Pr of Amer.

Mongault, Henri, jt. auth. see Merimee, Prosper.

Monge, Jose T. El Choque de Dos Culturas Juridicas en Puerto Rico: El Caso de la Respons Civil Extracontrac. 470p. 1991. 60.00 (*0-409-25574-2*, MICHIE) LEXIS Pub.

— Historia Constitucional de Puerto Rico, Vol. IV. LC 79-55193. 487p. 1983. 15.00 (*0-8477-0871-3*) U of PR Pr.

— Sociedad, Derecho y Justicia. LC 84-25862. (SPA.). 538p. 1986. lib. bdg. 25.00 (*0-8477-3020-4*) U of PR Pr.

Monge-Rafuls, Pedro R., ed. & intro. see Barquet, Jesus J., et al.

Monge-Rafuls, Pedro R., ed. & intro. see Cairo, Gabriel J., et al.

Monge Rivera, Jaime. San Juan de Puerto Rico: Guia Historica (1508-1993) (SPA.). 152p. 1995. pap. write for info. (*0-929441-72-9*) Pubns Puertorriquenas.

Mongeon, Joanne. Water & Spirit: Be Born Again Level 1, Teacher's Edition. 1999. pap. write for info. (*0-02-655922-6*, Benzger Pub) Glencoe.

Mongeon, John E., jt. ed. see Ziebold, Thomas O.

Monger, Christopher. The Englishman Who Went up a Hill but Came down a Mountain. LC 95-170001. 256p. 1995. pap. 9.70 (*0-7868-8140-2*, Pub. by Hyperion) Time Warner.

Monger, Christopher. The Englishman Who Went up a Hill but Came down a Mountain. large type ed. 1996. 23.95 (*1-56895-321-6*, Compass) Wheeler Pub.

Monger, J. W. & Francheteau, J., eds. Circum-Pacific Orogenic Belts & Evolution of the Pacific Ocean Basin. (Geodynamics Ser.: Vol. 18). (Illus.). 176p. 1987. 22.00 (*0-87590-519-6*) Am Geophysical.

Monger, Joyce, jt. auth. see Coleman, Diane.

Monger, Rod F. Managerial Decision Making with Technology. (Studies in Productivity: No. 45). 69p. 1986. pap. text 55.00 (*0-08-029517-7*) Work in Amer.

Monger, Sam. Testing & Balancing HVAC Air & Water Systems. 2nd ed. LC 95-17282. 277p. 1995. 74.00 (*0-88173-210-9*) Fairmont Pr.

***Monger, Sam.** Testing & Balancing HVAC Air & Water Systems. 3rd ed. LC 00-37526. (Illus.). 2000. pap. write for info. (*0-88173-342-3*) Fairmont Pr.

Monger, Samuel C. HVAC Optimization Handbook. LC 92-10683. 496p. (C). 1992. text 69.95 (*0-13-446493-1*) P-H.

— Testing & Balancing HVAC Air & Water Systems. LC 88-45792. 300p. 1989. text 67.00 (*0-88173-075-0*) Fairmont Pr.

— Testing & Balancing HVAC Air & Water Systems. 2nd ed. LC 88-45792. 290p. (C). 1995. 69.00 (*0-13-462276-6*) P-H.

Mongerson, Paul. The Power Press: Its Impact on America & What You Can Do about It. LC 97-26223. 224p. (Orig.). 1997. pap. 22.95 (*1-55591-347-4*) Fulcrum Pub.

Monges, Henry B., tr. see Steiner, Rudolf.

Monges, Lisa D., tr. see Steiner, Rudolf.

Monges, Maud B., tr. see Steiner, Rudolf.

Monges, Miriam M. Kush, the Jewel of Nubia: Reconnecting the Root System of African Civilization. LC 96-43315. 150p. 1996. 79.95 (*0-86543-528-6*); pap. 21.95 (*0-86543-529-4*) Africa World.

Mongia, J. N. Banking Around the World: A Treatise on Comparative Banking. 583p. 1982. 35.00 (*0-318-37331-9*) Asia Bk Corp.

Mongia, J. N., ed. India's Economic Development Strategies: 1951-2000 A.D. 1986. lib. bdg. 248.00 (*90-277-2200-5*) Kluwer Academic.

— India's Economic Policies. 1985. 42.00 (*0-8364-1444-6*, Pub. by Allied Pubs) S Asia.

Mongia, Padmini, ed. Contemporary Postcolonial Theory: A Reader. LC 96-16143. 416p. 1996. pap. text 19.95 (*0-340-65288-8*, Pub. by E A) OUP.

Mongia, Rajesh, et al. Coupled Lines & Circuits for RF & Microwave Applications. LC 99-21677. 17p. 1999. 99.00 (*0-89006-830-5*) Artech Hse.

Mongiardino, Renzo. Roomscapes: The Decorative Architecture of Renzo Mongiardino. LC 93-10435. (Illus.). 208p. 1993. 60.00 (*0-8478-1553-6*, Pub. by Rizzoli Intl) St Martin.

Mongiardo, M., jt. auth. see Rozzi, T.

Mongiello, Joseph. Engineering Resins - High Performance, Traditional & Alloys - Blends: A Realistic Appraisal of Their Competitive Environment. 183p. 1998. 3250.00 (*1-56965-277-5*, P-164) BCC.

***Mongillo, John & Booth, Bibi, eds.** Environmental Activists. 269p. 2001. 50.00 (*0-313-30884-5*, GR0884, Greenwood Pr) Greenwood.

Mongillo, John & Zierdt-Warshaw, Linda. Encyclopedia of Environmental Science. (Illus.). 504p. 2000. boxed set 95.00 (*1-57356-147-9*) Oryx Pr.

Mongin, Jean Marie, jt. auth. see Jouineau, Andre.

Mongini, Franco. Headache & Facial Pain. LC 99-25746. 1999. write for info. (*0-86577-852-3*) Thieme Med Pubs.

Mongiovi, Gary & Petri, Fabio. Utilitarianism: Key Nineteenth-Century Journal Sources, 4 vols. fac. ed. Pyle, Andrew, ed. & intro. by. (Wellesley Ser.). 2000p. (C). (gr. 13). 1998. 655.00 (*0-415-17944-0*, D6365) Routledge.

Mongiovi, Gary & Ruhl, Christof, eds. Macroeconomic Theory: Diversity & Convergence. 272p. 1993. 95.00 (*1-85278-368-0*) E Elgar.

Mongis, H. Heidegger et la Critique de la Notion de Valeur. (Phaenomenologica Ser.: No. 74). 234p. 1977. lib. bdg. 141.50 (*90-247-1904-6*, Pub. by M Nijhoff) Kluwer Academic.

Mongkolsuk, S., et al. Biotechnology & Environmental Science: Molecular Approaches. (Illus.). 240p. (C). 1993. text 85.00 (*0-306-44352-X*, Kluwer Plenum) Kluwer Academic.

Mongle, Thomas. Dr. Simplespread: Or, How I Learned to Quit Losing & Started Taking Money out of Wall Street. 171p. 1986. pap. 21.95 (*0-938063-05-7*) Ivers St Lloyd.

Mongolia Society Staff. Bulletin, Vols. 4-6 In 1 Vol. 1966. pap. 5.00 (*0-910980-02-0*) Mongolia.

— Newsletter, Vols. 1-3. 1964. pap. 5.00 (*0-910980-01-2*) Mongolia.

Mongolian People's Republic Academy of Sciences St, tr. & compiled by see Pergamon Press Staff, ed.

***Mongomery, Benard Law.** Concise History of Warfare. (Illus.). 2000. pap. 12.99 (*1-84022-223-9*, Pub. by Wrdsworth Edits) Combined Pub.

Mongon, Denis, et al. Improving Classroom Behaviour: New Directions for Teachers & Pupils. 256p. (C). 1989. pap. text 18.95 (*0-8077-2995-7*) Tchrs Coll.

Mongon, Denis, jt. auth. see Hart, S.

***Mongoven, Anne Marie.** Prophetic Spirit of Catechesis: How We Share the Fire in Our Hearts. LC 99-49017. 320p. 2000. pap. 22.95 (*0-8091-3922-7*) Paulist Pr.

Mongredien, Georges & Robert, Jean. Dictionnaire Biographique des Comediens Francais du 17e Siecle. 3rd ed. (FRE.). 330p. 1981. 75.00 (*0-7859-4842-2*) Fr & Eur.

Mongredien, Jean. French Music from the Enlightenment to Romanticism: 1789-1830. Fremaux, Sylvain, tr. from FRE. (Illus.). 394p. 1996. 39.95 (*1-57467-011-5*, Amadeus Pr) Timber.

Mongredien, Jean, ed. see Le Sueur, Jean-Francois & Dercy, Palat dit.

Mongredien, Sue. New Place, New Face. 144p. (J). 1997. pap. 6.95 (*0-09-926319-X*, Pub. by Random) Trafalgar.

***Monguzzi, Bruno.** A Designer's Perspective: Issues in Cultural Theory 2. (Illus.). 200p. 1999. pap. 19.95 (*1-890761-01-X*, 910641, Pub. by Univ MD Fine Arts) Dist Art Pubs.

Monheit, Alan C. Informing American Health Care Policy: The Dynamics of Medical Expenditure & Insurance Policy. LC 99-6870. 256p. 1999. 44.95 (*0-7879-4599-4*) Jossey-Bass.

Monheit, Herbert. Beyond Belief: A Guide to Spirituality. 120p. (Orig.). 1995. pap. 9.95 (*0-9646841-0-1*) Plum Street.

Monhemius, A. J., ed. Iron Control in Hydrometallurgy. 700p. 1986. text 184.00 (*0-470-20721-3*) P-H.

Monhollen, Christine. Razor Moon. 72p. 1993. pap. 7.95 (*1-884118-00-3*) Doorjamb Pr.

Monhollen, Christine, ed. see Harris, Bill, et al.

Monhollen, Christine, ed. see Harryman, Carla, et al.

Monhollen, Christine, ed. see Mikolowski, Ken & Vranich, Mick.

Monhollon, Lake P. God Flows Within You. 1998. pap. 5.95 (*0-9657561-4-9*) Reflection TX.

— What Does Dying Mean? LC 97-91836. (Illus.). 38p. (J). (ps-5). 1998. 14.95 (*0-9657561-1-4*) Reflection TX.

Monhollon, Michael L. Divine Invasion. LC 97-91837. 340p. 1998. 21.95 (*0-9657561-0-6*) Reflection TX.

Monica, Elaine L. La, see La Monica, Elaine L.

M

Monicard, Robert P. Properties of Reservoir Rocks: Core Analysis. (Illus.). 184p. 1980. 330.00 (*2-7108-0387-9*, Pub. by Edits Technip) Enfield Pubs NH.

Monich, Timothy, jt. auth. see Skinner, Edith.

Monich, Timothy, ed. see Skinner, Edith.

Monick, Eugene A. Castration & Male Rage: The Phallic Wound. 144p. 1995. pap. 16.00 (*0-919123-51-1*, Pub. by Inner City Bks) BookWorld.

— Evil, Sexuality & Disease in Grunewald's Body of Christ. LC 92-46068. (Illus.). 190p. (Orig.). 1993. pap. 18.50 (*0-88214-356-5*) Spring Pubns.

— Phallos. (Illus.). 144p. 1995. pap. 16.00 (*0-919123-26-0*, Pub. by Inner City Bks) BookWorld.

Monick, S. Douglas Tale of the Peninsular & Waterloo. 1997. 35.00 (*0-85052-565-9*, Pub. by Leo Cooper) Combined Pub.

Monico, Michael D. & Spevack, Barry A. Seventh Circuit Criminal Handbook. pap. 90.00 (*0-327-10935-1*) LEXIS Pub.

Monico, Michael D., jt. auth. see Spevack, Barry.

Monie, Karin, et al. The Library of the Eighties: Swedish Public Library Buildings, 1980-89. (Illus.). 78p. (Orig.). 1990. pap. 65.00 (*0-685-41471-X*) Coronet Bks.

Monien, B., et al, eds. Automata, Languages & Programming: 23rd International Colloquium, ICALP '96, Paderborn, Germany July 8-12 1996 Proceedings, Vol. 1099. (Lecture Notes in Computer Science Ser.). xii, 681p. 1996. pap. 100.00 (*3-540-61440-0*) Spr-Verlag.

— Data Structures & Efficient Algorithms: Final Report on the DFG Special Joint Initiative. LC 92-10725. (Lecture Notes in Computer Science Ser.: Vol. 594). vii, 389p. 1992. write for info. (*3-540-55488-2*); 62.00 (*0-387-55488-2*) Spr-Verlag.

Monien, B. & Cori, R., eds. STACS, '89. (Lecture Notes in Computer Science Ser.: Vol. 349). 544p. 1989. 54.00 (*0-387-50840-6*) Spr-Verlag.

Monien, B. & Vidal-Naquet, G., eds. STACS, '86. (Lecture Notes in Computer Science Ser.: Vol. 210). ix, 368p. 1986. pap. 42.00 (*0-387-16078-7*) Spr-Verlag.

***Monier, Charles J.** Electric Circuit Analysis. LC 00-27423. 944p. 2000. 86.67 (*0-13-014410-X*) P-H.

Monier, Stephen R., jt. auth. see Ahlgren, Greg.

Monier-Williams, M. English-Sanskrit Dictionary. (ENG & SAN.). 880p. 1995. 62.50 (*81-215-0283-7*, Pub. by M Manoharial) Coronet Bks.

— A Practical Grammar of Sanskrit Language. 2000. reprint ed. 34.50 (*81-215-0939-4*, Pub. by M Manoharial) Coronet Bks.

Monier-Williams, Monier. Buddhism, in Its Connection with Brahmanism & Hinduism & in Contrast with Christianity. 2nd ed. LC 78-70101. reprint ed. 57.50 (*0-404-17349-7*) AMS Pr.

— A Dictionary English & Sanskrit. (ENG & SAN.). 1979. 65.00 (*0-89744-966-5*) Auromere.

— English-Sanskrit Dictionary. 4th ed. 871p. 1986. 95.00 (*0-8288-1783-9*, M14103) Fr & Eur.

— Hinduism: Non-Christian Religious Systems. 1972. lib. bdg. 79.95 (*0-87968-546-8*) Krishna Pr.

— Indian Epic Poetry: An Analysis of Ramayana. 1972. lib. bdg. 79.95 (*0-87968-547-6*) Krishna Pr.

— Kalidasa-Sakoontala: or The Lost Ring. 238p. 1979. 16.95 (*0-318-36909-5*) Asia Bk Corp.

— Sanskrit-English Dictionary. (ENG & SAN.). 1372p. 95.00 (*0-7859-9821-7*) Fr & Eur.

— Sanskrit-English Dictionary. 4th ed. 1333p. 1986. 125.00 (*0-8288-4403-8*, M14103) Fr & Eur.

Monier-Williams, Monier, et al. Sanskrit-English Dictionary. 2nd rev. ed. (ENG & SAN.). 1,370p. 1920. text 155.00 (*0-19-864308-X*) OUP.

Monif, Gilles R. Antibiotic Selection in Obstetrics & Gynecology. 140p. 1997. pap. 11.95 (*1-880906-07-4*) IDI Pub.

— Interpretation of Wet Mount Preparation. (Illus.). 39p. 1995. 9.95 (*1-880906-44-9*) IDI Pub.

— A Physician's Guide for the Collection of Bacteriological & Viral Specimens. 55p. 7.95 (*1-880906-73-2*) IDI Pub.

— Torch Syndrome: Infections of the Human Fetus. (Illus.). 171p. 1993. text 14.95 (*1-880906-02-3*) IDI Pub.

Monif, Gilles R. & Baker, David. Infectious Diseases in Obstetrics & Gynecology. 4th ed. (Illus.). 912p. 1998. text 179.95 (*1-880906-57-0*) IDI Pub.

Monif, Gilles R. G. Understanding Genital Herpes: To Conquer a Dragon. 2nd ed. (Women's Health Care Ser.). (Illus.). 74p. 1994. pap. 6.95 (*1-880906-38-4*) IDI Pub.

Monif, Gilles R. G., jt. auth. see Cavalleri, Stephen J.

Monighan-Nourot, Patricia M., et al. Looking at Children's Play: The Bridge from Theory to Practice. (Early Childhood Education Ser.). 176p. (C). 1987. pap. text 16.95 (*0-8077-2872-1*) Tchrs Coll.

Monigle, Martha. Mother, Love Me: Playscript. LC 87-61308. (Orig.). 1986. pap. 5.00 (*0-88734-313-9*) Players Pr.

Monin, A. S. Fundamentals of Geophysical Fluid Dynamics. (C). 1990. text 299.50 (*0-7923-0426-8*) Kluwer Academic.

— An Introduction to the Theory of Climate. 1986. text 192.00 (*90-277-1935-7*) Kluwer Academic.

Monin, A. S. & Ozmidov, R. V. Turbulence in the Ocean. 1985. text 147.00 (*90-277-1735-4*) Kluwer Academic.

Monin, A. S., et al. Synoptic Eddies in the Ocean. 1986. text 234.00 (*90-277-1925-X*) Kluwer Academic.

Monin, Hippolyte. L' Etat de Paris En 1789: Etudes et Documents Sur L'ancien Regime a Paris. LC 70-172739. reprint ed. 135.00 (*0-404-52556-3*) AMS Pr.

Monin, J. P., et al. Initiation to the Mathematics of the Processes of Diffusion, Contagion & Propagation. Brandon, M., tr. (Methods & Models in the Social Sciences Ser.: No. 4). 1976. pap. text 19.25 (*90-279-7611-2*) Mouton.

Moning. Veterinary Helmenthology & Entomology. 1987. 460.00 (*81-7089-041-1*, Pub. by Intl Bk Distr) St Mut.

Moning, Karen. Beyond the Highland Mist. 384p. 1999. mass mkt. 5.99 (*0-440-23480-8*) Dell.

***Moning, Karen M.** To Tame a Highland Warrior. 384p. 1999. mass mkt. 5.99 (*0-440-23481-6*) Dell.

***Moning, Karen Marie.** The Highlander's Touch. 2000. mass mkt. 5.99 (*0-440-23652-5*) Dell.

Monington, Carol. Learning Center Activities/Brain Teasers. 80p. (J). (gr. k-2). 1997. pap. 9.95 (*1-57690-073-8*) Tchr Create Mat.

Moniot, Janet. Clay Whistles...the Voice of Clay. LC 89-51777. (Illus.). 56p. (Orig.). (J). (gr. 5 up). 1990. 24.95 incl. VHS (*0-9624893-1-X*) Whistle Pr.

— Clay Whistles...the Voice of Clay. LC 89-51777. (Illus.). 56p. (Orig.). (YA). (gr. 5 up). 1990. pap., spiral bd. 11.95 (*0-9624893-0-1*) Whistle Pr.

Monir, M. Law of Evidence. (C). 1990. 175.00 (*0-89771-177-7*) St Mut.

— Law of Evidence & Field's Medico Legal Guide. (C). 1988. 175.00 (*0-7855-3535-7*) St Mut.

— Law of Evidence with Medico-Legal Guide. (C). 1988. 275.00 (*0-7855-3682-5*) St Mut.

— Principles & Digest of Law of Evidence. (C). 1988. 550.00 (*0-7855-3683-3*) St Mut.

— Principles & Digest of the Law of Evidence, 2 vols., Set. Nandan, Deoki, ed. (C). 1990. 325.00 (*0-89771-178-5*) St Mut.

Monismith, Carl L. Asphalt Concrete: An Extraordinary Material for Engineering Applications. (Illus.). 79p. (C). 1998. reprint ed. pap. text 25.00 (*0-7881-7148-8*) DIANE Pub.

— TRB Distinguished Lecture, 1992. LC 92-29494. 100p. 1992. 21.00 (*0-309-05218-1*, R1354) Transport Res Bd.

Monismith, Carl L., et al. Asphalt Paving Technology. (Illus.). 480p. 1997. text 64.95 (*0-07-042983-9*) McGraw.

Monismith, Carl L., jt. auth. see Creegan, Patrick J.

Monismith, Samuel W., jt. auth. see Olsen, Larry K.

Monissen, Hans G., ed. see Fisher, Irving.

Monit, P. L. Diccionario Enciclopedica Informatica. (SPA.). 275p. 1989. 39.95 (*0-7859-6257-3*, 8476761166) Fr & Eur.

Monition, Lucien, et al. Micro Hydroelectric Power Stations. fac. ed. McMullan, Joan, tr. LC 84-7454. 187p. pap. 58.00 (*0-7837-7377-3*, 204718700005) Bks Demand.

Monito, Lisa. Access for Windows Quick Reference. (Quick Reference Guides Ser.). (Illus.). 184p. (Orig.). 1993. 9.99 (*1-56529-233-2*) Que.

Monitor. Enciclopedia Salvat para Todos, 13 vols., Set. (SPA.). 6760p. 1965. 995.00 (*0-8288-6752-6*, S-12311) Fr & Eur.

***Moniz.** Adobe Indesign 1.5. (C). 2000. pap. 21.95 (*0-619-01751-1*) Course Tech.

Moniz, B. J. Metallurgy. 2nd ed. LC 92-17869. (Illus.). 538p. 1994. 46.96 (*0-8269-3509-5*) Am Technical.

Moniz, B. J. Metallurgy. 2nd ed. (Illus.). 538p. 1996. wbk. ed. 13.96 (*0-8269-3510-9*) Am Technical.

Moniz, B. J. & Pollock, Walter I., eds. Process Industries Corrosion: The Theory & Practice. LC 86-62318. (Illus.). 858p. 1986. 58.00 (*0-915567-46-6*) NACE Intl.

Moniz, E., jt. ed. see Brodsky, S.

Moniz, Joseph. Enterprise Application Architecture with VB, ASP, MTS. 500p. 1999. pap. 59.99 (*1-86100-258-0*) Wrox Pr Inc.

Moniz, Joseph, jt. auth. see Lhotka, Rockford.

Moniz, Karletta. Cozy Book of Breakfast & Brunches. (Illus.). 144p. 1996. boxed set 13.00 (*0-7615-0453-2*) Prima Pub.

***Moniz, Miguel D.** Azores. 312p. 1999. lib. bdg. 72.00 (*1-85109-283-8*) ABC-CLIO.

Moniz, Steve. Photoshop Studio Skills. 4th ed. LC 96-80340. 338p. 1997. 35.00 (*1-56830-356-4*) Hayden.

***Moniz, Steve.** Short Order Macromedia Dreamweaver 2.0. 304p. 2000. pap. text 19.99 (*0-7897-2150-3*) Que.

Monjaras-Ruiz, Jesus, jt. ed. see Brambila, Rosa.

Monjardino, J. Molecular Biology of Human Hepatitis Viruses. LC 98-214266. 150p. 1997. text 24.00 (*1-86094-048-X*) World Scientific Pub.

Monji, Michael A. Does It Pay to Die? Living Trust Workbook. 4th large type rev. ed. LC 90-92203. 160p. 2000. per., wbk. ed. 24.99 (*0-9627839-1-9*) M Monji Assocs.

Monjo, Ann, ed. see Kristof, Nicholas D. & WuDunn, Sheryl.

Monjo, F. N. The Drinking Gourd: A Story of the Underground Railroad. (I Can Read Bks.). (Illus.). 64p. (J). (gr. 2-4). 1970. lib. bdg. 15.89 (*0-06-024330-9*) HarpC Child Bks.

— The Drinking Gourd: A Story of the Underground Railroad. LC 92-10823. (I Can Read Bks.). (Illus.). 64p. (J). (ps-3). 1970. 14.95 (*0-06-024329-5*) HarpC Child Bks.

— The Drinking Gourd: A Story of the Underground Railroad. LC 92-10823. (I Can Read Bks.). (Illus.). 64p. (J). (gr. 2-4). 1983. pap. 3.95 (*0-06-444042-7*, HarpTrophy) HarpC Child Bks.

Monjo, F. N. The Drinking Gourd: A Story of the Underground Railroad. (I Can Read Bks.). (Illus.). (J). (gr. 2-4). 1983. 8.95 (*0-606-03214-2*, Pub. by Turtleback) Demco.

— The Drinking Gourd: A Story of the Underground Railroad. unabridged ed. LC 92-10823. (I Can Read Bks.). (Illus.). 64p. (J). (gr. 2-4). 1991. audio 8.95 (*1-55994-355-6*, TBC 3556) HarperAudio.

Monjo, F. N. La Osa Menor: Una Historia del Ferrocarril Subterraneo. Mlawer, Teresa, tr. LC 95-26309. (Ya Se Leer Ser.).Tr. of Drinking Gourd. (SPA., Illus.). 64p. (J). (gr. k-3). 1997. pap. 4.95 (*0-06-444217-9*, HpArco Iris) HarpC Child Bks.

— La Osa Menor: Una Historia del Ferrocarril Subterraneo.Tr. of Drinking Gourd. 1997. 10.15 (*0-606-10860-2*, Pub. by Turtleback) Demco.

Monk. Cpsq Intro Bus Infosys:acct160. 1998. pap. text 9.00 (*0-07-233518-1*) McGraw.

Monk. Electroanalytical Chemistry. text. write for info. (*0-471-88036-1*); pap. text. write for info. (*0-471-88140-6*) Wiley.

— Hospital Builders. text. write for info. (*0-471-48964-6*) Wiley.

Monk. Thermoset Materials. 1996. write for info. (*0-582-04071-X*, Pub. by Addison-Wesley) Longman.

Monk. Understanding Physical Chemistry. text. write for info. (*0-471-49180-2*); pap. text. write for info. (*0-471-49181-0*) Wiley.

— Viologens. LC 98-36747. 332p. (C). 1998. 215.00 (*0-471-98603-8*) Wiley.

***Monk & Brady.** Concepts in Enterprise Resource Management. (Miscellaneous/Catalogs Ser.). (C). 2000. pap. 35.00 (*0-619-01593-4*) Course Tech.

Monk & Hanighe. Round Midnight Sextet. 1995. pap. text 20.00 (*0-7935-4819-5*, 00000690) H Leonard.

Monk, Abraham, ed. The Age of Aging: A Reader in Social Gerontology. LC 79-2727. 367p. (C). 1979. pap. 16.95 (*0-87975-114-2*) Prometheus Bks.

— The Columbia Retirement Handbook. LC 92-35740. 605p. 1994. 76.00 (*0-231-07626-6*) Col U Pr.

— Handbook of Gerontological Services. 2nd ed. 656p. 1990. text 76.00 (*0-231-06902-2*) Col U Pr.

— Health Care of the Aged: Needs, Policies & Services. LC 90-4941. (Journal of Gerontological Social Work: Vol. 15, Nos. 3-4). 185p. 1990. text 39.95 (*1-56024-065-2*) Haworth Pr.

Monk, Abraham & Cox, Carole. Home Care for the Elderly: An International Perspective. LC 90-1280. 184p. 1991. 49.95 (*0-86569-005-7*, T005, Auburn Hse) Greenwood.

Monk, Abraham, et al. Resolving Grievances in the Nursing Home: A Study of the Ombudsman Program. (Social Work & Social Issues Ser.). 1984. text 57.50 (*0-231-05702-4*) Col U Pr.

Monk, Abraham, jt. ed. see Kaye, Lenard W.

Monk, Abraham, ed. see Moody, Harry R.

Monk, Abraham, ed. see Streib, Gordon.

Monk, Andrew F., jt. ed. see Ahrweiler, Petra.

***Monk, Anthony.** The Art & Architecture of Paul Rudolph. 128p. 1999. pap. 45.00 (*0-471-99778-1*) Wiley.

Monk, Arlene & Cooper, Nancy. Convenience Food Facts: A Quick Guide for Choosing Healthy Brand-Name Foods in Every Aisle of the Supermarket. 4th ed. LC 96-49307. 472p. 1997. 12.95 (*1-885115-36-9*) IDC Pub.

Monk, Arlene, et al. Managing Type Two Diabetes: Your Invitation to a Healthier Lifestyle. 2nd rev. ed. LC 87-20218. 192p. 1996. 11.95 (*1-885115-26-1*) Wiley.

Monk, Connie. The Apple Orchards. large type ed. 720p. 1995. 27.99 (*0-7089-3395-5*) Ulverscroft.

— Beyond Downing Wood. large type ed. (Large Print Ser.). 656p. 1996. 27.99 (*0-7089-3556-7*) Ulverscroft.

— Family Reunions. large type ed. (Ulverscroft Large Print Ser.). 656p. 1997. 27.99 (*0-7089-3725-X*) Ulverscroft.

— Jessica. large type ed. 528p. 1988. 15.95 (*0-7089-1803-4*) Ulverscroft.

— On the Wings of the Storm. large type ed. (Charnwood Large Print Ser.). 512p. 1998. 29.99 (*0-7089-8997-7*, Charnwood) Ulverscroft.

— Rachel's Way. large type ed. 1991. 27.99 (*0-7089-2521-9*) Ulverscroft.

— The Running Tide. large type ed. (Large Print Ser.). 624p. 1996. 27.99 (*0-7089-3594-X*) Ulverscroft.

Monk, David & Underwood, Julie, eds. Micro-Level School Finance: Issues & Implications for Policy. 344p. 1988. text 35.00 (*0-88730-291-2*, HarpBusn) HarpInfo.

Monk, David H. & Brent, Brian O. Raising Money for Education: A Guide to the Property Tax. LC 97-4885. (Illus.). 168p. 1997. 51.95 (*0-8039-6406-4*); pap. 22.95 (*0-8039-6407-2*) Corwin Pr.

Monk, Dennis, ed. see Asplmary, Franz.

Monk, Donny, jt. auth. see Hernandez, Betsy.

Monk, Edwin. How to Build Wooden Boats: With Sixteen Small-Boat Designs. unabridged ed. LC 92-20138. Orig. Title: Small Boat Building. (Illus.). 96p. 1993. reprint ed. pap. text 7.95 (*0-486-27313-X*) Dover.

Monk, Eric. Keys - Their History & Collection. 64p. 1989. pap. 25.00 (*0-85263-254-1*, Pub. by Shire Pubns) St Mut.

Monk, Gerald, et al, eds. Narrative Therapy in Practice. LC 96-16258. (Psychology Ser.). 320p. 1996. 36.95 (*0-7879-0313-2*) Jossey-Bass.

***Monk, Gerald & Winslade, John.** Narrative Mediation: A New Approach to Conflict Resolution. LC 99-48273. 256p. 2000. 34.95 (*0-7879-4192-1*) Jossey-Bass.

Monk, Gerald, jt. auth. see Winslade, John.

Monk, Geraldine. Interregnum. unabridged ed. 128p. 1993. pap. 12.95 (*1-871592-16-X*) Creation Books.

Monk, Harold L., Jr., et al. Guide to Preparing Nonprofit Financial Statements, 2 vols. Incl. Vol. 1. Guide to Preparing Nonprofit Financial Statements. 1997. ring bd. 177.00 (*0-7646-0238-1*); Vol. 2. 1997. ring bd. 177.00 (*0-7646-0239-X*); 150.00 (*0-7646-0237-3*) Prctnrs Pub Co.

— Guide to Preparing Nonprofit Financial Statements, 2 vols., Set. 1995. ring bd. 150.00 (*1-56433-693-X*) Prctnrs Pub Co.

— Guide to Preparing Nonprofit Financial Statements, Vol. 1. 1995. ring bd. write for info. (*1-56433-694-8*) Prctnrs Pub Co.

— Guide to Preparing Nonprofit Financial Statements, Vol. 2. 1995. ring bd. write for info. (*1-56433-695-6*) Prctnrs Pub Co.

Monk, Henry C. Pose of Life. 1998. pap. write for info. (*1-57553-759-1*) Watermrk Pr.

Monk, Ian, tr. see Pennac, Daniel.

***Monk, Isabell.** Family. LC 00-9398. (Illus.). (J). 2001. lib. bdg. write for info. (*1-57505-485-X*, Carolrhoda) Lerner Pub.

Monk, Isabell. Hope. LC 98-16339. (Illus.). (J). 1998. 15.95 (*1-57505-230-X*, Carolrhoda) Lerner Pub.

Monk, J. D. Cardinal Functions on Boolean Algebras. (Lectures in Mathematics ETH Zurich). 164p. 1990. 29.50 (*0-8176-2495-3*) Birkhauser.

— Cardinal Invariants on Boolean Algebras. LC 96-14892. (Progress in Mathematics Ser.: Vol. 142). 312p. 1996. 64.95 (*0-8176-5402-X*); 64.95 (*3-7643-5402-X*) Birkhauser.

— Handbook of Boolean Algebras, Vol. 3. 1989. 275.50 (*0-444-87153-5*, North Holland) Elsevier.

Monk, J. D., ed. Handbook of Boolean Algebras, 3 vols., 1. 344p. 1989. 116.50 (*0-444-70261-X*) Elsevier.

Monk, Janice. Geography: Discipline Analysis, Vol. 7I. (Women in the Curriculum Ser.). 22p. (Orig.). 1997. pap. 7.00 (*1-885303-25-4*) Towson St Univ.

Monk, Janice & Dolors, Maria, eds. Women of the European Union: The Politics of Work & Daily Life. LC 95-44459. (International Studies of Women & Places). 304p. (C). 1996. 85.00 (*0-415-11879-4*); pap. 25.99 (*0-415-11880-8*) Routledge.

Monk, Janice, jt. auth. see Norwood, Vera.

Monk, Janice, jt. ed. see Katz, Cindi.

Monk, John S., jt. auth. see Keefe, James W.

Monk, Karyn. Once a Warrior. 384p. 1997. mass mkt. 5.99 (*0-553-57422-1*, Fanfare) Bantam.

***Monk, Karyn.** The Rose & the Warrior. 352p. 2000. mass mkt. 5.99 (*0-553-57761-1*) Bantam Dell.

Monk, Karyn. Surrender to a Stranger. 496p. 1994. mass mkt. 5.99 (*0-553-56909-0*) Bantam.

— The Witch & the Warrior. 352p. 1998. mass mkt. 5.99 (*0-553-57760-3*) Bantam.

Monk, Karyn. The Witch & the Warrior. 384p. 1998. mass mkt. 5.99 (*0-553-55760-2*) Bantam.

Monk, Katherine A., et al. The Ecology of Nusa Tenggara & Maluka, Vol. 5. (Ecology of Indonesia Ser.). (Illus.). 1016p. Date not set. 49.95 (*962-593-076-0*, Periplus Eds) Tuttle Pubng.

Monk, Lee H., jt. auth. see Dick, Joab J.

Monk, Leland. Standard Deviations: Change & the Modern British Novel. LC 92-38358. 216p. (C). 1993. 35.00 (*0-8047-2174-2*) Stanford U Pr.

***Monk, Linda R.** The Bill of Rights: A User's Guide. 3rd rev. ed. Sass, Charles, ed. LC 99-55459. 250p. 2000. pap. 15.45 (*0-932765-86-6*) Close Up Fnd.

Monk, Linda R. The First Amendment: America's Blueprint for Tolerance. LC 94-35273. 56p. (YA). (gr. 7-12). 1994. pap. 7.95 (*0-932765-54-8*) Close Up Fnd.

Monk, Linda R. & Sass, Charles, eds. Ordinary Americans. 190p. 1994. teacher ed., ring bd. 14.95 (*0-614-14108-7*) Close Up Fnd.

— Ordinary Americans: U. S. History Through the Eyes of Everyday People. LC 93-33401. 296p. 1994. pap. 15.95 (*0-932765-47-5*, 1304-94) Close Up Fnd.

Monk, Maria & Grob, Gerald N. Awful Disclosures by Marcia Monk of the Hotel Dieu Nunnery of Montreal. LC 76-46089. (Anti-Movements in America Ser.). 1977. lib. bdg. 35.95 (*0-405-09962-2*) Ayer.

Monk, Marion, jt. auth. see Soltes, Ori Z.

Monk, Martin & Dillon, Justin, eds. Learning to Teach Science: Activities for Student Teachers & Mentors. LC 94-39748. 224p. 1995. 89.95 (*0-7507-0385-7*, Falmer Pr); pap. 29.95 (*0-7507-0386-5*, Falmer Pr) Taylor & Francis.

Monk, Martin, jt. auth. see Osborne, Jonathan.

Monk, Michael A., jt. auth. see Sheehan, John.

Monk, Noel E. & Guterman, Jimmy. 12 Days on the Road. LC 92-11416. 1992. pap. 10.00 (*0-688-11274-9*, Quil) HarperTrade.

***Monk of New Skete Staff.** Hymns of Repentance: Hymns for Great Lent Used at New Skete. deluxe large type ed. Mancuso, Laurence, ed. & tr. by. from GRE. 232p. 2000. lib. bdg. 150.00 (*0-935129-42-1*) Monks of New Skete.

Monk of Prophet Elias Skete. Elder Basil of Poiana Marului: Spiritual Father of St. Paisy Velichkovsky & Progenitor of the Optina Tradition. 192p. 1997. 15.00 (*0-912927-69-0*, X048) St John Kronstadt.

Monk of the Eastern Church Staff. The Jesus Prayer. Kallistos Ware, ed. LC 86-33916. 124p. 1987. pap. 9.95 (*0-88141-013-6*) St Vladimirs.

— Orthodox Spirituality: An Outline of the Orthodox Ascetical & Mystical Tradition. LC 96-26144. 111p. 1978. pap. 8.95 (*0-913836-51-6*) St Vladimirs.

— Serve the Lord with Gladness. Breck, John, tr. from FRE. LC 90-20916. 112p. (Orig.). 1990. pap. 7.95 (*0-88141-085-3*) St Vladimirs.

Monk of the Skete of the Propher Elias Staff, ed. Legal Memorandum Before the Council of State: Concerning the Skete of the Prophet Elias. 65p. 1995. pap. 10.00 (*0-912927-64-X*, D031) St John Kronstadt.

Monk, Patricia. The Gilded Beaver: An Introduction to the Life & Work of James De Mille. 293p. (C). 1991. pap. 26.00 (*1-55022-106-X*, Pub. by ECW) Genl Dist Srvs.

Monk, Patricia. Mud & Magic Shows: Robertson Davies' Fifth Business. (Canadian Fiction Studies: No. 13). 88p. (C). 1992. pap. text 14.95 (*1-55022-128-0*, Pub. by ECW) Genl Dist Srvs.

Monk, Paul M., et al. Electrochromism: Fundamentals & Applications. LC 95-202047. 216p. 1995. 145.00 (*3-527-29063-X*, Wiley-VCH) Wiley.

Monk, Peter. Technological Change in the Information Economy. 256p. 1992. 54.00 (*0-86187-713-6*, Pub. by P P Pubs) Cassell & Continuum.

Monk, Ray. Bertrand Russell: Great Philosophers. LC 99-22642. (Great Philosophers Ser. : Vol. 7). 64p. 1999. pap. 6.00 (*0-415-92386-7*) Routledge.

An Asterisk (*) at the beginning of an entry indicates that the title is appearing for the first time.

— Bertrand Russell: The Spirit of Solitude, 1872-1921. 695p. 1996. 34.50 (*0-684-82802-2*) Free Pr.

— Electrolytic Dissociation Applications. 1961. text 55.00 (*0-12-504550-6*) Acad Pr.

— Fundamentals of Human-Computer Interaction. 1984. text 86.00 (*0-12-504580-8*) Acad Pr.

— A Life of Bertrand Russell. 1996. 35.00 (*0-02-921672-9*) Free Pr.

— Ludwig Wittgenstein: The Duty of Genius. (Illus.). 654p. 1990. 40.00 (*0-02-921670-2*) Free Pr.

— Ludwig Wittgenstein: The Duty of Genius. (Illus.). 672p. 1991. reprint ed. pap. 19.95 (*0-14-015995-9*, Penguin Bks) Viking Penguin.

*__Monk, Ray, ed.__ Great Philosophers. 416p. 2000. 35.00 (*0-415-92817-6*) Routledge.

Monk, Ray & Palmer, Anthony, eds. Bertrand Russell & The Origins of Analytical Philosophy. 360p. 1996. pap. 30.00 (*1-85506-476-6*) Bks Intl VA.

Monk, Raymond, ed. Edward Elgar: Music & Literature. 300p. 1993. 79.95 (*0-85967-937-3*, Pub. by Scolar Pr) Ashgate Pub Co.

— Elgar Studies. (Illus.). 320p. 1990. text 91.95 (*0-85967-810-5*, Pub. by Scolar Pr) Ashgate Pub Co.

Monk, Rich, ed. Wisdom: One Hundred One of the Wisest Human Perceptions of All Time. 20p. 1992. 1.99 (*1-882342-00-3*) Panther IL.

Monk, Richard. Digital Electronics: A Practical Approach with Easy PC & Pulsar. LC 98-229345. (Illus.). 256p. 1998. pap. text 34.95 incl. disk (*0-7506-3099-X*, Newnes) Buttrwrth-Heinemann.

— The MG Collection: The Post War Models. (Illus.). 192p. 1995. 29.95 (*1-85260-516-2*, Pub. by J H Haynes & Co) Motorbooks Intl.

— The MG Collection Vol. 1: Pre-War Models, Vol. 1. (Illus.). 192p. 1994. 39.95 (*1-85260-496-4*, Pub. by J H Haynes & Co) Motorbooks Intl.

Monk, Richard C. Clashing Views on Controversial Issues in Crime & Criminology. 4th ed. (Taking Sides Ser.). (C). 1995. per. write for info. (*1-56134-446-X*, Dshkn McG-Hill) McGrw-H Hghr Educ.

— Clashing Views on Controversial Issues in Crime & Criminology. 5th ed. (Taking Sides Ser.). (Illus.). 384p. 1998. pap. text 13.00 (*0-697-39109-4*, Dshkn McG-Hill) McGrw-H Hghr Educ.

— Taking Sides: Clashing Views on Controversial Issues. 4th ed. (C). 1997. text. write for info. (*0-697-39263-5*, WCB McGr Hill) McGrw-H Hghr Educ.

— Taking Sides: Clashing Views on Controversial Issues in Race & Ethnicity. 2nd ed. LC 95-83858. 384p. (C). 1996. text. write for info. (*0-697-31294-1*) Brown & Benchmark.

Monk, Richard C., ed. Taking Sides: Clashing Views on Controversial Issues in Race & Ethnicity. LC 93-35780. (Illus.). 324p. (C). 1993. text 13.95 (*1-56134-127-4*, Dshkn McG-Hill) McGrw-H Hghr Educ.

Monk, Richard C., jt. auth. see Henderson, Joel H.

Monk, Robert, ed. see Als, Hilton.

Monk, Robert, ed. see Rosenblum, Robert & Powers, Kimiko.

Monk, Robert C. John Wesley: His Puritan Heritage. 2nd ed. LC 99-13626. (Pietist & Wesleyan Studies: No. 11). 296p. 1999. 65.00 (*0-8108-3637-8*) Scarecrow.

Monk, Robert C. & Hofheinz, Walter C. Exploring Religious Meaning. 5th ed. LC 97-45935. 340p. (C). 1998. pap. text 41.00 (*0-13-778358-2*) P-H.

Monk, Robert C. & Stamey, Joseph D. Exploring Christianity: An Introduction. 2nd ed. 256p. (C). 1989. pap. text 28.60 (*0-13-296153-9*) P-H.

Monk, Samuel A., ed. The Works of John Dryden Vol. XVII: Prose: 1668-1691, An Essay of Dramatic Poesie & Shorter Works. 1972. 80.00 (*0-520-01814-1*, Pub. by U CA Pr) Cal Prin Full Svc.

Monk, Samuel H., jt. auth. see Latt, David J.

Monk, Silas L. Songs of Zion. 416p. 1999. write for info. (*1-887399-03-8*) Colbert Hse.

Monk, T. COMPSEC '92. 494p. 1992. 222.25 (*1-85617-168-X*, Pub. by Elsvr Adv Tech) Elsevier.

— The PC Security Guide, 1993-94. viii, 213p. 1992. 325.00 (*1-85617-127-2*, Pub. by Elsvr Adv Tech) Elsevier.

— Think of One Sextet. 1995. pap. text 20.00 (*0-7935-4820-9*, 00000700) H Leonard.

Monk, Timothy H. How to Make Shift Work Safe & Effective. 58p. 1988. 23.00 (*0-939874-84-9*) ASSE.

Monk, Timothy H. & Folkard, Simon. Making Shiftwork Tolerable. 101p. 1992. pap. 25.00 (*0-85066-822-0*, Pub. by Tay Francis Ltd) Taylor & Francis.

Monk, Timothy H., jt. auth. see Alward, Ruth R.

Monk, Timothy H., jt. ed. see Folkard, Simon.

Monk-Turner, Elizabeth. Community College Education & Its Impact on Socioeconomic Status Attainment. LC 98-44215. (Studies in Education: Vol. 41). 136p. 1998. text 69.95 (*0-7734-8253-9*) E Mellen.

Monk, Val. Abuse. Schulz, William, ed. (Guidance for Grades 1). 112p. (Orig.). (gr. 1-8). 1989. pap., teacher ed. 8.00 (*0-920541-63-1*) Peguis Pubs Ltd.

Monk, William E. Theodore & Alice - A Love Story: The Life & Death of Alice Lee Roosevelt. 80p. 1994. lib. bdg. 20.00 (*1-55787-117-5*, NY71061, Empire State Bks) Hrt of the Lakes.

Monkcom, Stephen, jt. ed. see Smith, Colin.

Monke, Eric & Pearson, Scott R. Policy Analysis Matrix for Agricultural Development. LC 88-47938. 312p. 1989. text 47.50 (*0-8014-1953-0*); pap. text 18.95 (*0-8014-9551-2*) Cornell U Pr.

Monke, Eric, et al. Agricultural Policy in Kenya: Applications of the Policy Analysis Matrix. (Food Systems & Agrarian Change Ser.). (Illus.). 328p. 1996. text 47.50 (*0-8014-3085-2*) Cornell U Pr.

— Structural Change & Small-Farm Agriculture in Northwest Portugal. LC 92-54973. (Food Systems & Agrarian Change Ser.). 240p. (C). 1993. text 42.50 (*0-8014-2640-5*) Cornell U Pr.

Monke, Eric A., et al, eds. Small Farm Agriculture in Southern Europe: CAP Reform & Structural Change. LC 98-70984. (Illus.). 160p. 1998. text 55.95 (*1-84014-162-X*, Pub. by Ashgate Pub) Ashgate Pub Co.

Monke, Ingrid. Boston. LC 88-20202. (Downtown America Ser.). (Illus.). 60p. (J). (gr. 3 up). 1988. lib. bdg. 13.95 (*0-87518-382-4*, Dillon Silver Burdett) Silver Burdett Pr.

Monke, Lowell, jt. auth. see Burniske, R. W.

Monkerud, Don. Twister Country: A Novel. 232p. (Orig.). 1996. pap. 11.95 (*1-886312-03-6*) Buying Best.

Monkewitz, P. A., jt. auth. see Machiels, L.

Monkhouse & Small. Dictionary of Geography. 381p. 1983. 22.00 (*0-86685-753-2*) Intl Bk Ctr.

Monkhouse, jt. ed. see Rhodes.

Monkhouse, Allan. Books & Plays. LC 72-292. (Essay Index Reprint Ser.). 1977. reprint ed. 19.95 (*0-8369-2807-5*) Ayer.

— Mary Broome: A Comedy in Four Acts. LC 83-45818. reprint ed. 16.00 (*0-404-20181-4*) AMS Pr.

— Moscow, 1911-1933. LC 76-115566. (Russia Observed Ser., No. 1). 1970. reprint ed. 23.95 (*0-405-03051-7*) Ayer.

Monkhouse, Christopher P. American Furniture in Pendleton House. (Illus.). 228p. (C). 1986. pap. 25.00 (*0-911517-44-8*) Mus of Art RI.

Monkhouse, F. J. Diccionario de Terminos Geograficos: Dictionary of Geographical Terms. (SPA.). 560p. 1978. 150.00 (*0-8288-4894-7*, S50017) Fr & Eur.

Monkhouse, Francis John. Dictionary of the Natural Environment: English-Arabic. pap. 14.95 (*0-7131-5958-8*) E Arnld Pubs.

Monkhouse, Francis John. The Material Resources of Britain: An Economic Geography of the United Kingdom. LC 72-185556. xi, 241 p. 1971. write for info. (*0-582-52633-7*) Longman.

*__Monkhouse, Richard & Cox, John.__ 3-D Atlas of the Stars & Galaxies. LC 99-26690. (Illus.). v, 91p. 2000. 42.00 (*1-85233-189-5*, Pub. by Spr-Verlag) Spr-Verlag.

Monkkonen, Eric H. America Becomes Urban: The Development of U. S. Cities & Towns, 1780-1980. 336p. (C). 1995. pap. 16.95 (*0-520-06972-2*, Pub. by U CA Pr) Cal Prin Full Svc.

— The Local State: Public Money & American Cities. LC 95-1074. (Stanford Studies in the New Political History). 214p. 1995. 39.50 (*0-8047-2412-1*) Stanford U Pr.

*__Monkkonen, Eric H.__ Murder in New York City. (Illus.). 225p. 2000. 29.95 (*0-520-22188-5*, Pub. by U CA Pr) Cal Prin Full Svc.

Monkkonen, Eric H., ed. Crime & Justice in American History, 11 vols., Set. Incl. Vol. 1, Pt. 1. Colonies & Early Republic. 450p. 1991. 240.00 (*3-598-41408-0*); Vol. 1, Pt. 2. Colonies & Early Republic. 450p. 1991. 240.00 (*3-598-41409-9*); Vol. 2. Courts & the Criminal Procedure. 560p. 1991. 120.00 (*3-598-41410-2*); Vol. 3. Delinquency & Disorderly Behavior. 325p. 1991. 120.00 (*3-598-41411-0*); Vol. 4, Pt. 1. Frontier. 450p. 1991. 120.00 (*3-598-41412-9*); Vol. 5, Pts. 1, 2 & 3. Policing & Crime Control. 550p. 1992. 365.00 (*3-598-41413-7*); Vol. 6, Pts. 1 & 2. Prison & Jails. 360p. 1992. 240.00 (*3-598-41415-3*); Vol. 7, Pts. 1 & 2. South. 336p. 1992. 240.00 (*3-598-41417-X*); Vol. 8, Pts. 1 & 2. Prostitution, Drugs, Gambling & Organized Crime. 360p. 1992. 240.00 (*3-598-41418-8*); Vol. 10. Reform. 425p. 1992. 120.00 (*3-598-41422-6*); Vol. 11, Pts. 1 & 2. Theory & Methods in Criminal Justice History. 550p. 1992. 240.00 (*3-598-41423-4*); Vols. 9, Pts. 1, 2 & 3. Violence & Theft. 525p. 1992. 365.00 (*3-598-41420-X*); 2175.00 (*3-598-41407-2*) K G Saur Verlag.

— Engaging the Past: The Uses of History across the Social Sciences. LC 93-37086. 208p. 1994. text 49.95 (*0-8223-1431-2*); pap. text 17.95 (*0-8223-1440-1*) Duke.

— Walking to Work: Tramps in America, 1790-1935. LC 83-21807. 259p. reprint ed. pap. 80.30 (*0-7837-1844-6*, 204204400001) Bks Demand.

Monkkonen, Eric H., jt. ed. see Johnson, Eric A.

*__Monkman, Betty C.__ The White House: Its Historic Furnishings & First Families. LC 00-27085. (Illus.). 2000. 60.00 (*0-7892-0624-2*) Abbeville Pr.

*__Monkman, Jerry.__ Discover Acadia National Park: A Guide to Hiking, Biking & Paddling. LC 99-87916. (Illus.). 2000. pap. 16.95 (*1-878239-92-9*) AMC Books.

Monkman, Karen, jt. auth. see Stromquist, Nelly P.

Monkman, Leslie. A Native Heritage: Images of the Indian in English-Canadian Literature. 208p. 1981. text 35.00 (*0-8020-5537-0*) U of Toronto Pr.

Monkman, Roberta, jt. ed. see Kupfersmid, Joel.

Monkres, Peter R. & Ostermiller, R. Kenneth. The Rite of Confirmation: Moments When Faith Is Strengthened. LC 94-39954. 92p. (Orig.). 1995. pap. 9.95 (*0-8298-1020-X*) Pilgrim OH.

Monks, Alfred L. The Soviet Intervention in Afghanistan. LC 81-2003. (Studies in Defense Policy: Vol. 314). 64p. reprint ed. 30.00 (*0-608-16776-2*, 202755400055) Bks Demand.

Monks, Dave. San Francisco Movie Map. 1997. pap. text 6.95 (*0-9649431-0-7*) Reel Map Co.

Monks, Franz J., et al, eds. Education of the Gifted in Europe: Theoretical & Research Issues Report of the Educational Research Workshop Held in Nijmegen, The Netherlands, July 23-26, 1991. LC 92-5639. (European Meetings on Educational Research Ser.: Vol. 28, Pt. A). 252p. 1992. 76.00 (*90-265-1262-7*) Swets.

Monks, John, Jr. Ribbon & a Star: The Third Marines at Bougainville. LC 79-19749. (Illus.). 1980. reprint ed. 26.95 (*0-89201-077-0*) Zenger Pub.

Monks, Joseph G. Operations Management. 3rd ed. (Management Ser.). 800p. (C). 1987. pap. text 69.25 (*0-07-042727-5*) McGraw.

— Schaum's Outline of Operations Management. 2nd ed. (Schaum's Outline Ser.). 352p. (C). 1995. pap. 15.95 (*0-07-042764-X*) McGraw.

— Schaum's Outline of Theory & Problems of Operations Management. 38p. (C). 1985. pap. text 13.95 (*0-07-042726-7*) McGraw.

Monks, Joseph G., jt. auth. see Ingram, John A.

*__Monks, Karen E.__ Pocket Companion to Home Health Nursing. LC 99-44468. 475p. 2000. pap. text. write for info. (*0-7216-8558-7*, W B Saunders Co) Harcrt Hlth Sci Grp.

Monks, Karen E. Surgical Decision Making. 4th ed. (Illus.). 380p. 1999. text 79.00 (*0-7216-7985-4*, W B Saunders Co) Harcrt Hlth Sci Grp.

Monks, Lydia. The Cat Barked? Goyette, Cecile, ed. LC 98-10134. (Illus.). 32p. (J). (ps-2). 1999. 13.99 (*0-8037-2338-5*, Dial Yng Read) Peng Put Young Read.

Monks, Merri M. & Pistolis, Donna R. Hit List: Frequently Challenged Books for Young Adults. LC 96-14418. 150p. 1996. 22.00 (*0-8389-3459-5*) American Library Association National Library.

*__Monks of Ampleforth Abbey.__ The Life & Teaching of Pachomius. (Wellsprings of Life Ser.). 136p. 1999. pap. 6.95 (*0-85244-416-8*, 6115, Pub. by Gracewing) Morehouse Pub.

— A New Beginning: Tertullian, Cyril & Augustine on Baptism. 128p. 1999. pap. 6.95 (*0-85244-430-3*, 6117, Pub. by Gracewing) Morehouse Pub.

— Seeds of Life: Early Christian Martyrs. 120p. 1999. pap. 6.95 (*0-85244-431-1*, 6116, Pub. by Gracewing) Morehouse Pub.

Monks of New Skete. Annunciation of the Theotokos: Choral Chants. Mancuso, Laurence, tr. from GRE. (Liturgical Music Series I: Vol. 12). 35p. Date not set. pap. 15.00 (*0-935129-33-2*) Monks of New Skete.

Monks of New Skete. Art of Raising a Puppy. 274p. (gr. 8). 1991. 23.95 (*0-316-57839-8*) Little.

— Ascension of Christ: Choral Chants. Mancuso, Laurence, tr. from GRE. (Liturgical Music Series I: Great Feasts: Vol. 11). 26p. 1999. pap. text 15.00 (*0-935129-41-3*) Monks of New Skete.

— Birth of the Theotokos: Choral Chants. Mancuso, Laurence, tr. from GRE. (Liturgical Music Series I: Great Feasts: Vol. 3). 25p. 1986. pap. 10.00 (*0-935129-04-9*) Monks of New Skete.

— A Book of Prayers: Horologion, Casoslov. Mancuso, Laurence, tr. from GRE. 628p. 1988. 69.00 (*0-935129-12-X*) Monks of New Skete.

— The Christmas Season: Choral Chants. Mancuso, Laurence, tr. from CHU. (Liturgical Music Series I: Great Feasts: Vol. 7). viii, 221p. 1990. pap. text 50.00 (*0-935129-16-2*) Monks of New Skete.

Monks of New Skete. The Divine Liturgy: Choral Chants. Mancuso, Laurence, tr. from GRE. (Liturgical Music Series II: No. 3). 112p. 1995. pap. text 40.00 (*0-935129-22-7*) Monks of New Skete.

Monks of New Skete. The Divine Liturgy: Four Orthodox Catholic Liturgies. Mancuso, Laurence, tr. from CHU. 306p. 1988. 50.00 (*0-935129-11-1*) Monks of New Skete.

— The Divine Liturgy of St. John Chrysostom: The Traditional Text. Mancuso, Laurence, tr. from CHU. 190p. 1994. pap. text 25.00 (*0-935129-24-3*) Monks of New Skete.

— Dormition of the Theotokos: Choral Chants. Mancuso, Laurence, tr. (Liturgical Music Series I: Great Feasts: Vol. 2). 40p. 1986. pap. text 12.00 (*0-935129-03-0*) Monks of New Skete.

Monks of New Skete. Encounter of Christ: Choral Chants. Mancuso, Laurence, tr. from GRE. (Liturgical Music Series I: Vol. 10). 45p. 1995. pap. 15.00 (*0-935129-32-4*) Monks of New Skete.

Monks of New Skete. Entry of the Theotokos: Choral Chants. Mancuso, Laurence, tr. from GRE. (Liturgical Music Series I: Great Feasts: Vol. 5). 40p. 1986. pap. text 12.00 (*0-935129-06-5*) Monks of New Skete.

— Exaltation of the Holy Cross: Choral Chants. Mancuso, Laurence, tr. from GRE. (Liturgical Music Series I: Great Feasts: Vol. 4). 60p. 1986. pap. text 15.00 (*0-935129-05-7*) Monks of New Skete.

— Great & Holy Pascha: Choral Chants. Mancuso, Laurence, tr. from GRE. (Liturgical Music Series I: Great Feasts: Vol. 6). 60p. 1986. pap. text 15.00 (*0-935129-07-3*) Monks of New Skete.

— How to Be Your Dog's Best Friend: A Training Manual for Dog Owners. LC 78-8553. (Illus.). 202p. (gr. 8). 1978. 22.95 (*0-316-60491-7*) Little.

— Hymns of Entreaty: Selections from the Octoechos or Book of Eight Tones. Mancuso, Laurence, ed. (Monastic Offices at New Skete Ser.). 450p. 1987. text 49.50 (*0-935129-09-X*) Monks of New Skete.

— In the Spirit of Happiness. LC 99-22489. 352p. (gr. 8). 1999. 22.95 (*0-316-57851-7*) Little.

— Monastic Typicon: Rule of Life. 2nd rev. ed. viii, 59p. 1988. reprint ed. pap. 10.00 (*0-935129-13-8*) Monks of New Skete.

— New Skete Communities: An Introduction. 32p. 1985. pap. 2.00 (*0-9607924-9-X*) Monks of New Skete.

— Pannychis: The Office of Christian Burial. Mancuso, Laurence, tr. from GRE. (Liturgical Music Series II: Divine Services: Vol. 1). 40p. 1987. pap. text 15.00 (*0-935129-08-1*) Monks of New Skete.

— Passion & Resurrection: Lazarus Saturday, Entry into Jerusalem, Holy & Great Week, the Pasch of the Lord. Mancuso, Laurence, ed. 332p. 1995. 65.00 (*0-935129-25-1*) Monks of New Skete.

Monks of New Skete. St. Francis of Assisi: Choral Chants. (Liturgical Music Series I: No. 9). 40p. 1996. pap. 20.00 (*0-935129-34-0*) Monks of New Skete.

— Theophany of Christ: Choral Chants. Mancuso, Laurence, tr. from GRE. (Liturgical Music Series I: Vol. 8). 96p. 1995. pap. 25.00 (*0-935129-17-0*) Monks of New Skete.

Monks of New Skete. Transfiguration of Christ: Choral Chants. Mancuso, Laurence, tr. (Liturgical Music Series I: Great Feasts: Vol. 1). 40p. 1986. pap. text 12.00 (*0-935129-02-2*) Monks of New Skete.

— Vespers & Matins: Choral Chants. Mancuso, Laurence, tr. from GRE. (Liturgical Music Series II: Divine Services: Vol. 2). 220p. 1988. pap. 45.00 (*0-935129-10-3*) Monks of New Skete.

— Vespers & Matins: New Skete Usage. abr. large type ed. Mancuso, Laurence, ed. & tr. by. from GRE. 166p. 1993. pap. 20.00 (*0-935129-23-5*) Monks of New Skete.

Monks of New Skete, tr. The Psalter: 150 Psalms & 9 Canticles. 286p. 1984. 39.50 (*0-9607924-5-7*) Monks of New Skete.

Monks of New Skete Staff. December Feasts: Choral Chants. Mancuso, Laurence, ed. & tr. by. 1997. pap. text 45.00 (*0-935129-35-9*) Monks of New Skete.

Monks of New Skete Staff. The Divine Liturgy of Our Father among the Saints - St. James of Jerusalem. Mancuso, Laurence, ed. & tr. by. from GRE. 78p. (Orig.). 1996. pap. text 18.00 (*0-935129-37-5*) Monks of New Skete.

Monks of New Skete Staff. The Divine Liturgy of St. James of Jerusalem: Choral Chants. Mancuso, Laurence, tr. from GRE. (Liturgical Music Series II: Vol. 4). 30p. 1996. pap. 20.00 (*0-935129-38-3*) Monks of New Skete.

— In the Spirit of Happiness: A Book of Spiritual Wisdom. 352p. 2001. pap. 14.95 (*0-316-60694-4*, Back Bay) Little.

— Pentecost: Choral Chants. Mancuso, Laurence, ed. & tr. by. (Liturgical Music Series I: Vol. 13). 44p. 2000. pap. text 25.00 (*0-935129-43-X*) Monks of New Skete.

Monks of New Skete Staff. The Prayerbook: Book of Hours. Mancuso, Laurence, tr. from GRE. (Illus.). 752p. 1976. 35.00 (*0-9607924-3-0*) Monks of New Skete.

Monks of New Skete Staff. Sighs of the Spirit: Prayers for Major Feasts & Seasons of the Church Year. deluxe ed. Mancuso, Laurence, ed. & tr. by. 424p. 1997. lib. bdg. 95.00 (*0-935129-28-6*) Monks of New Skete.

Monks of Solesmes. Eastertide. audio compact disk 15.95 (*1-55725-108-8*, 930-071, Pub. by Paraclete MA) BookWorld.

Monks of the Abbey of St. Peter of Solesmes Staff. Benedictiones Mensae. (LAT.). 16p. pap. 4.95 (*2-85274-058-3*, 3018, Pub. by Abbey St Peter Solesmes) Paraclete MA.

Monks of the Ramakrishna Order Staff. Meditation. Bhavyananda, Swami, ed. 161p. 1977. pap. 16.00 (*0-7025-0073-9*) Vedanta Pr.

Monks, Peter R. The Brussels Horloge de Sapience: Iconography & Text of Brussels, Bibliotheque Royale, MS. IV 111. LC 90-2215. (Litterae Textuales Ser.). (ENG & FRE., Illus.). viii, 224p. 1990. pap. 67.50 (*90-04-09088-6*) Brill Academic Pubs.

Monks, Peter R. & Owen, D. D., eds. Medieval Codicology, Iconography, Literature, & Translation: Studies for Death Val Sinclair. LC 94-2818. (Litterae Textuales Ser.). 1994. 155.50 (*90-04-09958-1*) Brill Academic Pubs.

Monks, Pieta, tr. see Baranskaya, Natalya.

Monks, Robert & Minnow, Nell. Watching the Watchers: Corporate Governance for the 21st Century. 320p. 1996. text 28.95 (*1-55786-866-2*) Blackwell Pubs.

Monks, Robert & Minow, Nell. Corporate Governance. (Illus.). 400p. 1994. pap. 47.95 (*1-55786-490-X*) Blackwell Pubs.

Monks, Robert A. The Emperor's Nightingale: Restoring the Integrity of the Corporation in the Age of Shareholder Activism. 320p. 1999. pap. text 16.00 (*0-7382-0133-2*, Pub. by Perseus Pubng) HarpC.

Monks, Robert A. & Minow, Nell. Power & Accountability: Restoring the Balance of Power Between Corporations, Owners, & Society. 224p. 1991. 22.95 (*0-88730-512-1*, HarpBusn) HarpInfo.

— Power & Accountability: Restoring the Balance of Power Between Corporations, Owners, & Society. LC 91-58519. 304p. 1992. reprint ed. pap. 12.00 (*0-88730-534-2*, HarpBusn) HarpInfo.

Monkshood, G., tr. see De Goncourt, Edmond L.

Monleon, Jose B. A Specter Is Haunting Europe: A Sociohistorical Approach to the Fantastic. 199p. (C). 1990. text 32.50 (*0-691-06862-3*, Pub. by Princeton U Pr) Cal Prin Full Svc.

Monleon, Jose B., jt. ed. see Geist, Anthony L.

Monloubou, Louis. Diccionario Biblico Compendiado. (SPA.). 300p. 1991. pap. 39.95 (*0-7859-6086-4*, 8470502689) Fr & Eur.

— Dictionnaire Biblique Abrege. (FRE.). 1989. 59.95 (*0-7859-7959-X*, 2-7189-0399-6) Fr & Eur.

— Universal Bible Dictionary: Dictionnaire Biblique Universel. (FRE.). 772p. 1985. 150.00 (*0-8288-1203-9*, F10644) Fr & Eur.

Monluc. Commentaires. (FRE.). 1964. lib. bdg. 99.50 (*0-8288-3567-5*, F30400) Fr & Eur.

— Vine & Branches: Chronique des Guerres de Religion, Vol. 2. 1640p. 42.95 (*0-686-56543-6*) Fr & Eur.

Monmarche, Carole & Salesians of Don Bosco Staff. Saint John Bosco: The Friend of Children & Young People. (Along the Paths of the Gospel Ser.). (Illus.). 72p. (J). (gr. 2-5). 1998. 9.95 (*0-8198-7003-X*) Pauline Bks.

Monmonier, Mark. Air Apparent. 1996. pap. 14.95 (*0-226-53423-5*) U Ch Pr.

Monmonier, Mark. Air Apparent: How Meteorologists Learned to Map, Predict, & Dramatize Weather. LC 98-25797. (Illus.). 344p. 1999. 27.50 (*0-226-53422-7*) U Ch Pr.

Monmonier, Mark. Bullwinkles & Bushmanders. 1997. 25.00 (*0-226-53424-3*) U Ch Pr.

— Cartographies of Surveillance. 1999. 25.00 (*0-226-53427-8*) U Ch Pr.

Monmonier, Mark. Drawing the Line: Tales of Maps & Cartocontroversy. LC 94-16945. 1995. 27.50 (*0-8050-2581-2*) H Holt & Co.

M

An Asterisk (*) at the beginning of an entry indicates that the title is appearing for the first time.

— Drawing the Line: Tales of Maps & Cartocontroversy. (Illus.). 88p. 1995. pap. 14.95 (*0-8050-4699-2*, Owl) H Holt & Co.

— How to Lie with Maps. LC 90-40687. (Illus.). 168p. 1992. lib. bdg. 27.50 (*0-226-53414-6*) U Ch Pr.

— How to Lie with Maps. LC 90-40687. (Illus.). 184p. 1999. pap. 14.95 (*0-226-53415-4*) U Ch Pr.

— How to Lie with Maps. 2nd ed. LC 95-32199. 212p. 1996. lib. bdg. 36.00 (*0-226-53420-0*) U Ch Pr.

— How to Lie with Maps. 2nd expanded rev. ed. LC 95-32199. (Illus.). xiv, 208p. 1996. pap. 15.00 (*0-226-53421-9*) U Ch Pr.

— Mapping It Out: Expository Cartography for the Humanities & Social Sciences. LC 92-39894. (Chicago Guides to Writing, Editing & Publishing Ser.). (Illus.). 316p. (C). 1993. pap. 15.95 (*0-226-53417-0*); lib. bdg. 41.00 (*0-226-53416-2*) U Ch Pr.

— Maps with the News: The Development of American Journalistic Cartography. LC 88-23829. (Illus.). 346p. 1989. 29.95 (*0-226-53411-1*) U Ch Pr.

— Maps with the News: The Development of American Journalistic Cartography. 1999. pap. 16.00 (*0-226-53413-8*) U Ch Pr.

Monmonier, Mark & MacEachren, Alan M., eds. Geographic Visualization. (Cartography & Geographic Information Systems Journal Ser.: Vol. 19, No. 4). 76p. 1992. 20.00 (*0-614-06093-1*, AC194) Am Congrs Survey.

Monmonier, Mark S. Cartographies of Danger: Mapping Hazards in America. LC 96-35082. 364p. 1997. 25.00 (*0-226-53418-9*) U Ch Pr.

— Cartographies of Danger: Mapping Hazards in America. LC 96-35082. (Illus.). 364p. 1998. pap. 15.00 (*0-226-53419-7*) U Ch Pr.

— Technological Transistion in Cartography. LC 84-40499. (Illus.). 304p. 1985. text 25.00 (*0-299-10070-7*) U of Wis Pr.

— Technological Transition in Cartography. LC 84-40499. (Illus.). 303p. reprint ed. pap. 94.00 (*0-608-20455-2*, 207170800002) Bks Demand.

*__Monn, David E.__ 365 Ways to Prepare for Christmas. (Illus.). 288p. 2000. 8.99 (*0-517-16181-8*) Random Hse Value.

Monna, G. L. Design of Low-Voltage Integrated Filter-Mixer Systems. x, 122p. (Orig.). 1996. pap. 47.50 (*90-407-1374-X*, Pub. by Delft U Pr) Coronet Bks.

Monnas, L. & Granger-Taylor, H. Ancient & Medieval Textiles. 1990. pap. 33.00 (*0-903859-15-7*, Pub. by Textile Inst) St Mut.

Monne, Miguel A. & Giesbert, Edmund F. Checklist of the Cerambycidae & Disteniidae (Coleoptera) of the Western Hemisphere. (C). 1994. lib. bdg. 74.60 (*1-885850-00-X*) Wolfsgarden.

— Checklist of the Cerambycidae & Disteniidae (Coleoptera) of the Western Hemisphere: 1995 Edition. (C). 1995. 74.60 (*1-885850-01-8*) Wolfsgarden.

Monner, Fred M. & Monner, Linda A. Florida: Be Aware (Or Beware)!! large type ed. (Illus.). vi, 80p. 1997. spiral bd. 12.50 (*0-9661529-0-5*) Moncom Co.

Monner, Linda A., jt. auth. see Monner, Fred M.

Monneret. Renoir. 1990. 19.99 (*0-7126-3738-9*) Random Hse Value.

Monneret, Sophie. David & Neo-Classicism. Miller, Chris & Snowdon, Peter, trs. (Illus.). 207p. 1999. pap. 27.50 (*2-87939-217-9*, Pub. by Pierre Terrail) Rizzoli Intl.

— L' Impressionisme et son Epoque Dictionnaire International Vol. 1: Noms Propres A-T. (FRE.). 1040p. 1987. pap. 49.95 (*0-7859-7804-6*, 2221054121) Fr & Eur.

— L' Impressionisme et son Epoque Dictionnaire International Vol. 2: Noms Propres U-Z, Noms Communs A-Z. (FRE.). 1200p. 1987. pap. 49.95 (*0-7859-8632-4*, 222105413x) Fr & Eur.

— Renoir. (Illus.). 160p. 1995. 29.95 (*0-8050-1359-8*) H Holt & Co.

Monnerie, Annie. Bienvenue en France, No. 1. (FRE., Illus.). 159p. 1989. pap. text 18.95 (*2-278-01869-8*, Pub. by Edns Didier) Hatier Pub.

— Bienvenue en France, No. 1. (FRE., Illus.). 1991. VHS 217.95 (*2-278-02555-4*, Pub. by Edns Didier) Hatier Pub.

— Bienvenue en France, No. 2. (FRE., Illus.). 191p. 1989. pap. text 19.95 (*2-278-01870-1*, Pub. by Edns Didier) Hatier Pub.

— Bienvenue en France, No. 2. (FRE., Illus.). 1991. VHS 217.95 (*2-278-02556-2*, Pub. by Edns Didier) Hatier Pub.

— La France aux Cent Visages: Livre de L'Etudiant. (FRE., Illus.). 223p. 1996. pap. text 26.95 (*2-278-04377-3*) Hatier Pub.

Monnerie, Annie, ed. Le Nouvel Observateur: Arts, Idees, Spectacles. (FRE.). 109p. 1994. pap. 17.25 (*0-8442-1786-7*, Natl Textbk Co) NTC Contemp Pub Co.

Monnerie, L. & Suter, U. W., eds. Advances in Polymer Science: Atomitic Modeling Physical Properties of Polymers, Vol. 116. 398p. 1994. 227.95 (*0-387-57827-7*) Spr-Verlag.

Monnerot, Jules. Sociology of Communism. Degras, Jane & Rees, Richard, trs. LC 76-46469. 1977. reprint ed. lib. bdg. 65.00 (*0-8371-9309-5*, MOSO, Greenwood Pr) Greenwood.

Monnett, H. N., jt. auth. see Vanderslice, H.

Monnett, Howard N. Action Before Westport, 1864. 3rd ed. (Illus.). 296p. (Orig.). 1995. pap. 22.50 (*0-87081-413-3*) Univ Pr Colo.

Monnett, John H. The Battle of Beecher Island & the Indian War of 1867-1869. (Illus.). 248p. 1993. pap. 22.50 (*0-87081-347-1*) Univ Pr Colo.

*__Monnett, John H.__ Massacre at Cheyenne Hole: Lieutenant Austin Henely & the Sappa Creek Controversy. LC 99-10853. (Illus.). 128p. 1999. 24.95 (*0-87081-527-X*) Univ Pr Colo.

— A Rocky Mountain Christmas: Yuletide Stories of the West. 3rd ed. LC 99-39281. 172p. 1999. pap. 14.95 (*0-87108-906-8*) Pruett.

Monnett, John H. & McCarthy, Michael. Colorado Profiles: Men & Women Who Shaped the Centennial State. (Illus.). 344p. 1996. pap. 24.95 (*0-87081-439-7*) Univ Pr Colo.

Monnette, Barbara, jt. auth. see Steen, Charlene.

Monney, Neil T., ed. Ocean Energy Resources: Presented at the Energy Technology Conference, Houston, Texas, Sept. 18-23, 1977. LC 77-82206. Vol. 4. (Illus.). 110p. reprint ed. pap. 31.40 (*0-317-09776-8*, 2016806) Bks Demand.

Money, Paul-Andre, jt. auth. see Kohlas, Jurg.

Monnich, Michael G. Footprints in the Snow. 1995. 24.95 (*0-533-10958-2*) Vantage.

Monnich, Uwe, ed. Aspects of Philosophical Logic. 296p. 1981. text 148.50 (*90-277-1201-8*, D Reidel) Kluwer Academic.

Monnier, Adrienne. The Very Rich Hours of Adrienne Monnier. McDougall, Richard, tr. & intro. by. LC 96-29079. (Illus.). xiv, 536p. 1996. pap. 23.00 (*0-8032-8227-3*, Bison Books) U of Nebr Pr.

Monnier, Cynthia L., ed. Business in Indianapolis. 904p. (Orig.). 1995. pap. 39.95 (*0-9649160-0-2*) I B J.

Monnier, Eric, et al, eds. Consumer Behavior & Energy Policy: An International Perspective. LC 86-9295. 357p. 1986. 65.00 (*0-275-92179-4*, C2179, Praeger Pubs) Greenwood.

Monnier, G. & Goss, M. J., eds. Soil Compaction & Regeneration: Proceedings of the Workshop on "Soil Compaction: Consequences, Structural Regeneration Processes", Avignon, 17-18 September 1985. 160p. (C). 1987. text 91.00 (*90-6191-780-8*, Pub. by A A Balkema) Ashgate Pub Co.

Monnier, Richard. Richard Monnier. (Illus.). 108p. (Orig.). 1993. pap. 25.00 (*2-908257-07-6*, Pub. by F R A C) Dist Art Pubs.

*__Monnier, Virginie.__ Balthus: Catalogue Raisonne of the Complete Works. Clair, Jean, ed. 576p. 1999. 225.00 (*0-8109-6394-9*, Pub. by Abrams) Time Warner.

Monnig, Eckhard, ed. Der Macrocephalen Oolith von Hildesheim. (GER.). xx, 77p. 1995. 25.00 (*3-487-10060-6*) G Olms Pubs.

Monnig, Judith, jt. auth. see Carter, Sharon.

Monniger & Taigen, Theodore. The Nature of Life. (C). 1992. pap. text, teacher ed. 20.31 (*0-07-003150-9*) McGraw.

Monninger, Frieder. The Eiffel Programming Handbook. (C). 1998. pap. text. write for info. (*0-201-18390-0*) Addison-Wesley.

Monninger, Joe. Razor's Song. 256p. 1993. mass mkt. 4.99 (*0-380-71874-X*, Avon Bks) Morrow Avon.

*__Monninger, Joseph.__ Home Waters. LC 00-24600. 192p. 2000. pap. 12.00 (*0-7679-0515-6*) Broadway BDD.

— Home Waters: Fishing with an Old Friend. LC 98-39431. 192p. 1999. 22.95 (*0-8118-2284-2*) Chronicle Bks.

— Home Waters: Fishing with an Old Friend. LC 99-89115. (Americana Series). 2000. 27.95 (*0-7862-2458-4*) Thorndike Pr.

Monninger, Michael, jt. auth. see Dietz, Matthias.

Monniot, Cl., et al. Coral Reef Ascidians of New Caledonia. (Faune Tropicale Ser.: Vol. XXX). (Illus.). 248p. 1991. pap. 66.00 (*2-7099-1050-0*, Pub. by LInstitut Francais) Balogh.

Monnot, Michel. From Rage to Courage: The Road to Dignity Walk. (Illus.). 350p. (Orig.). 1988. pap. 10.00 (*0-9621309-0-7*) St Denis Pr.

Monobe, David. The Snow Woman. 165p. 1984. 7.95 (*0-89697-167-8*) Intl Univ Pr.

Monod, Adolphe. A Dying Man's Regrets. rev. ed. 32p. 1992. pap. 2.95 (*1-879737-07-8*) Calvary Press.

Monod, David. Store Wars: Shopkeepers & the Culture of Mass Marketing, 1890-1939. (Illus.). 464p. 1996. text 55.00 (*0-8020-0650-7*); pap. text 22.95 (*0-8020-7604-1*) U of Toronto Pr.

Monod-Fontaine, Isabelle, jt. ed. see Tabart, Marielle.

Monod, Lucien. Aide-Memoire de l'Amateur et du Professionnel. 1972. 370.00 (*0-8115-0045-4*) Periodicals Srv.

Monod, Maurice, ed. see Conrad, Joseph.

Monod, Paul K. The Power of Kings: Monarchy & Religion in Europe, 1589-1715. LC 99-17815. (Illus.). 384p. 1999. 35.00 (*0-300-07810-2*) Yale U Pr.

Monod, Sylvere, ed. see Dickens, Charles.

*__Monod, Theodore.__ Sahara: The Forbidding Sands. LC 00-38084. (Illus.). 162p. 2000. 49.50 (*0-8109-4187-2*, Pub. by Abrams) Time Warner.

Monoghon, John, ed. see Smith, Mary E.

Monohan. Life & Laughter. 1990. pap. text. write for info. (*0-582-86839-4*, Pub. by Addison-Wesley) Longman.

Mononen, Iikka. Aspartylglycosaminuria: Lysosomal Disease & Inborn Errors of Metabolism. Aronson, Nathan N., Jr., ed. (Medical Intelligence Unit Ser.). 178p. 1997. 99.00 (*1-57059-443-0*) Landes Bioscience.

Monory, Jacques, jt. auth. see Lyotard, Jean Francois.

Monos, Dimitris. The Greek Americans. Stotsky, Sandra, ed. LC 95-716. (Immigrant Experience Ser.). 120p. (YA). (gr. 5 up). 1995. lib. bdg. 19.95 (*0-7910-3356-2*) Chelsea Hse.

*__Monoson, S. Sara.__ Plato's Democratic Entanglements: Athenian Politics & the Practice of Philosophy. LC 99-54924. 256p. 2000. 39.50 (*0-691-04366-3*, Pub. by Princeton U Pr) Cal Prin Full Svc.

Monosson, Sonny, ed. MIT Class of 1948: Fiftieth Reunion Book. (Illus.). 450p. 1998. pap. 40.00 (*0-9660524-9-8*) Monosson Technologies.

Monostory, Denes, jt. ed. see Ryan, Thomas E.

Monreal, David. A Season's Harvest. LC 87-63154. 168p. 1997. pap. 14.95 (*0-944870-11-2*) Pacific Writers Pr.

Monreal, David N. Cinco de Mayo: An Epic Novel. 180p. 1990. 25.00 (*0-685-38354-7*) Floricanto Pr.

— The New Neighbor & Other Stories. 2nd ed. LC 87-63154. 173p. 1987. pap. 14.95 (*0-944870-09-0*) Pacific Writers Pr.

Monreal, M., jt. ed. see Latorre, J.

Monreal-Wickert, Irene. Die Sprachforschung der Aufklaerung Im Spiegel der Grossen Franzoesischen Enzyklopaedie. (GER.). 210p. 1977. 59.95 (*0-8288-5518-8*, M7054) Fr & Eur.

Monreal y Tejada, Luis. Castles of Spain. (Illus.). 312p. 1999. 19.95 (*3-8290-2221-2*, 521008) Konemann.

Monreal y Tejada, Luis & Haggar, R. G. Diccionario de Terminos de Arte. (SPA.). 426p. 1992. pap. 40.00 (*84-261-2701-0*) IBD Ltd.

Monro. Implementing NT Server. 2001. pap. text 38.64 (*0-13-185307-4*) P-H.

Monro, C. H., ed. Digest IX. 2. Lex Aquilia: Lex Aquilia. LC 93-79700. 106p. 1994. reprint ed. 40.00 (*1-56169-058-9*) Gaunt.

Monro, Cecil, ed. Letters of Queen Margaret of Anjou & Bishop Beckington & Others. LC 17-1255. (Camden Society, London. Publications, First Ser.: No. 86). reprint ed. 45.00 (*0-404-50186-9*) AMS Pr.

Monro, Charles H., tr. The Digest of Justinian, 2 vols. 1998. reprint ed. 270.00 (*1-56169-412-6*, 15594) Gaunt.

Monro, David B. A Grammar of the Homeric Dialect. 2nd enl. rev. ed. 436p. 1993. 25.00 (*0-9637069-0-X*) W H Allen Bksell.

— A Grammar of the Homeric Dialect. 2nd ed. xxiv, 436p. 1986. reprint ed. 76.70 (*3-487-05307-1*) G Olms Pubs.

Monro, David H. Empiricism & Ethics. LC 67-12143. 244p. reprint ed. pap. 69.60 (*0-608-13579-8*, 2022462) Bks Demand.

Monro, Harold. The Collected Poems of Harold Monro. 217p. 1933. reprint ed. 39.00 (*0-403-08943-3*) Somerset Pub.

— Collected Poems of Harold Monro. 1988. reprint ed. lib. bdg. 59.00 (*0-7812-0007-5*) Rprt Serv.

— Collected Poems of Harold Monro. 1971. reprint ed. 49.00 (*0-403-03562-7*) Scholarly.

Monro, Harold, ed. Twentieth Century Poetry: An Anthology. reprint ed. 29.00 (*0-403-03062-5*) Somerset Pub.

Monro, Hector. The Ambivalence of Bernard Mandeville. 1975. 45.00 (*0-19-812061-3*) OUP.

Monro, Isabel S., jt. ed. see Cook, Dorothy E.

Monro, Margaret T. Book of Unlikely Saints. LC 77-107727. (Essay Index Reprint Ser.). 1977. 21.95 (*0-8369-1528-3*) Ayer.

Monro, R., et al. Mind-Body Therapies: A Select Bibliography of Books in English. 176p. 1987. text 90.00 (*0-7201-1811-5*) Continuum.

Monro, Rolland, jt. ed. see Hetherington, Kevin.

Monrobey, Hank. Bear Fruit in Plenty: Economic Lessons of the Supreme Economist. (Illus.). 200p. (Orig.). 1990. write for info. (*0-9623564-4-1*); pap. text. write for info. (*0-9623564-3-3*) H Monrobey & Assocs.

— Financial Economic Freedom on the Electronic Super Highway. (Illus.). 74p. (Orig.). 1994. 15.00 (*0-9623564-5-X*) H Monrobey & Assocs.

— Good Bye Recessions: Removing Economic Pollution. LC 90-92304. (Illus.). 250p. (Orig.). 1990. pap. text. write for info. (*0-9623564-1-7*) H Monrobey & Assocs.

— The Monrobey Report: An Economic Detective Story Solving the Mysteries of Inflations & Recessions. LC 89-174366. (Illus.). 362p. 1989. 42.50 (*0-9623564-2-5*); pap. 29.90 (*0-9623564-0-9*) H Monrobey & Assocs.

Monroe. Changing Earth: Exploring Geology & Evolutions with Infotrac. 2nd ed. (Earth Science Ser.). 1997. 51.25 incl. cd-rom (*0-534-54098-8*) Wadsworth Pub.

Monroe & Wicander. Changing Earth: Current Issues in Geology, 1997. 2nd ed. 1997. write for info. (*0-314-21074-1*) Thomson Learn.

Monroe, jt. auth. see Dutch.

Monroe, jt. auth. see Wicander.

Monroe, jt. ed. see Johnson.

Monroe, jt. ed. see Roberts.

Monroe, Alan D. Essentials of Political Research. (Essentials of Political Science Ser.). 250p. 1999. pap. 49.95 (*0-8133-6865-0*); pap. 49.95 (*0-8133-6866-9*) Westview.

*__Monroe, Ann.__ The Word: Imagining the Gospel in Modern America. 208p. 2000. 21.95 (*0-664-22141-6*) Westminster John Knox.

Monroe, Ann F., jt. auth. see Nelson, Harry.

Monroe, Anne S. Happy Valley. LC 90-7167. (Northwest Reprints Ser.). 392p. 1991. reprint ed. pap. 13.95 (*0-87071-507-0*); reprint ed. text 24.95 (*0-87071-506-2*) Oreg St U Pr.

Monroe, Arthur E. Early Economic Thought. 1975. 300.00 (*0-87968-251-5*) Gordon Pr.

Monroe, Barbara. Out of Death Came Life. 15.95 (*0-9700876-0-8*) J&M Pubng NC.

Monroe, Barbara & Callier, Billue, eds. Parent's Guide to Houston Private Schools. 4th ed. (Illus.). iv, 102p. 1998. reprint ed. pap. 24.95 (*0-9665964-0-4*) Schls & Such.

Monroe, Barbara, ed. see Oliviere, David.

Monroe, Betsy. My Visit to My Doctor: A Coloring Book for Kids. (Medical Ser.: No. 4). (Illus.). 24p. (Orig.). (J). (gr. k-4). 1989. pap. write for info. (*1-878083-01-5*) Color Me Well.

— My Visit to the Emergency Room: A Coloring Book for Kids. (Medical Ser.: No. 1). (SPA., Illus.). 32p. (J). (gr. k-4). 1990. reprint ed. pap. write for info. (*1-878083-03-1*) Color Me Well.

— My Visit to the Hospital: A Coloring Book for Kids. (Medical Ser.: No. 2). (Illus.). 32p. (Orig.). (J). (gr. k-4). 1986. pap. write for info. (*1-878083-02-3*) Color Me Well.

— My Visit to the Outpatient Department: A Coloring Book for Kids. (Medical Ser.: No. 3). (Illus.). 24p. (J). (gr. k-4). 1986. pap. write for info. (*1-878083-04-X*) Color Me Well.

— Sibling Scrapbook: An Activity Book for the New Big Brother & Big Sister. (Medical Ser.: No. 5). (Illus.). 24p. (Orig.). (J). (gr. k-4). 1989. pap. write for info. (*1-878083-00-7*) Color Me Well.

Monroe, Betty. Huntsville Heritage Cookbook. LC 67-30090. 387p. 1986. reprint ed. 12.95 (*0-9618113-0-7*) J L Huntsville.

Monroe, Burt L., Jr. The Birds of Kentucky. LC 93-44364. (Illus.). 166p. (C). 1994. 49.95 (*0-253-33892-1*) Ind U Pr.

Monroe, Burt L., Jr. & Sibley, Charles G. A World Checklist of Birds. LC 93-60341. 400p. 1993. 50.00 (*0-300-05547-1*) Yale U Pr.

— A World Checklist of Birds. 416p. 1997. pap. 20.00 (*0-300-07083-7*) Yale U Pr.

Monroe, Burt L., Jr., jt. auth. see Sibley, Charles G.

Monroe, Bury L., Jr., jt. auth. see Sibley, Charles G.

Monroe, Carolyn. Help Wanted: Daddy Fabulous Father. (Romance Ser.). 1993. per. 2.75 (*0-373-08970-8*, 5-08970-1) Silhouette.

— Kiss of Bliss. (Romance Ser.: No. 847). 1992. per. 2.59 (*0-373-08847-7*, 5-08847-1) Silhouette.

Monroe, Charles B., jt. auth. see McGrew, J. Chapman, Jr.

Monroe, Charles E. World Religions: An Introduction. LC 94-40049. 439p. (C). 1995. pap. 17.95 (*0-87975-942-9*) Prometheus Bks.

Monroe, Charles E., tr. see Brunswig, Heinrich.

Monroe, Charles R. Motoring to Yellowstone in Slim's Model T, 1927. (Illus.). 64p. (Orig.). 1994. pap. 9.95 (*0-9615125-1-2*) Merryleaf.

*__Monroe, Cloteal J.__ Overcoming the Demons. LC 99-93939. 2000. pap. 9.95 (*0-533-13201-0*) Vantage.

*__Monroe County Heritage Museum Staff.__ Monroeville: The Search of Harper Lee's Maycomb. (Images of America Ser.). 128p. 1999. pap. 18.99 (*0-7385-0204-9*) Arcadia Publng.

Monroe, Craig, jt. auth. see Di Salvo, Vincent S.

Monroe, Dan L., et al. Gifts of the Spirit Vol. 132: Works by Nineteenth-Century & Contemporary Native American Artists. LC 97-146739. (Illus.). 240p. 1996. 50.00 (*0-88389-110-7*, Essx Institute) Peabody Essex Mus.

Monroe, Day. Chicago Families: A Study of Unpublished Census Data. LC 70-169395. (Family in America Ser.). 370p. 1972. reprint ed. 20.95 (*0-405-03872-0*) Ayer.

Monroe, Debra. Newfangled: A Novel. LC 97-36281. 320p. 1998. 21.50 (*0-684-81905-8*) S&S Trade.

*__Monroe, Debra.__ Newfangled: A Novel. 304p. 2000. per. 12.00 (*0-684-85197-0*) S&S Trade.

Monroe, Debra. The Source of Trouble. 176p. 1995. pap. 10.00 (*0-671-89716-0*) S&S Trade.

— The Source of Trouble. LC 90-31189. (Flannery O'Connor Award for Short Fiction Ser.). 184p. 1990. 19.95 (*0-8203-1246-0*) U of Ga Pr.

— A Wild, Cold State: Stories. 272p. 1995. 21.00 (*0-671-89717-9*) S&S Trade.

Monroe, Douglas. The Lost Books of Merlyn: Druid Magic from the Age of Arthur. LC 98-20787. (Illus.). 480p. 1998. pap. 14.95 (*1-56718-471-5*) Llewellyn Pubns.

— The 21 Lessons of Merlyn: A Study in Druid Magic & Lore. LC 92-20033. (Illus.). 448p. 1992. pap. 14.95 (*0-87542-496-1*) Llewellyn Pubns.

Monroe, Elizabeth. Philby of Arabia. 1998. pap. 21.95 (*0-86372-239-3*, Pub. by Garnet-Ithaca) LPC InBook.

— Philby of Arabia. 7.95 (*0-7043-3346-5*, Pub. by Quartet) Charles River Bks.

Monroe, Elizabeth B. The Wheeling Bridge Case: Its Significance in American Law & Technology. 256p. 1992. text 50.00 (*1-55553-130-X*) NE U Pr.

*__Monroe, Elizabeth Rae.__ Hindsight. 2000. pap. text. write for info. (*1-928781-44-6*) Hollis Bks.

Monroe, Elvira. A Guide to Places of Worship in & Around San Francisco. 186p. (Orig.). 1984. pap. 6.95 (*0-933174-24-1*) Wide World-Tetra.

— Say Cheesecake & Smile. 2nd rev. ed. LC 80-54453. (Illus.). 176p. 1983. pap. 6.95 (*0-933174-17-9*) Wide World-Tetra.

— Walk Don't Run. LC 79-63351. 1979. pap. 3.95 (*0-933174-04-7*) Wide World-Tetra.

Monroe, Elvira & Margah, Irish. Hawaii Cooking with Aloha. 6th ed. LC 87-51516. (Illus.). 220p. 1990. pap. 9.95 (*0-933174-95-0*) Wide World-Tetra.

Monroe, Elvira & Monroe, Mia, eds. Hawaii: Island Paradise. LC 86-51426. (Illus.). 150p. 1987. pap. 9.95 (*0-933174-42-X*) Wide World-Tetra.

Monroe, Elvira, jt. auth. see Arnot, Phil.

Monroe, Elvira, jt. auth. see Pappas, Theoni.

Monroe, Eula E. Silver Burdett Mathematics Dictionary for Young People. LC 97-1069. (J). 1998. write for info. (*0-382-39630-8*); pap. write for info. (*0-382-39631-6*) Silver Burdett Pr.

Monroe, Gary. Life in South Beach. (Illus.). 52p. 1989. pap. 18.00 (*0-9618986-3-1*) Forest & Trees.

Monroe, Gary L. Haiti: Photographs by Gary Monroe. (Illus.). 56p. 1992. pap. 15.00 (*0-9618986-2-3*) Forest & Trees.

— A Handbook for the Traveling Free-Lance Physician: A Guide for Free-Lancers, Part-time Physicians, & Moonlighters. Streetman, James, ed. LC 90-92170. (Illus.). 154p. 1990. 75.00 (*0-9628241-0-0*) Magellan Pub.

— Life in South Beach. (Illus.). 52p. 1989. 30.00 (*0-9618986-0-7*) Forest & Trees.

Monroe, Gary L., jt. auth. see Singer, Isaac Bashevis.

Monroe, Gregory. Colorado's Modern Narrow Gauge Circle. (Illus.). 96p. 1994. 37.95 (0-9604122-8-X) Fox Pubns.

— Moffat! Rio Grande - Southern Pacific - Union Pacific West of Dencer, Co. LC 97-60870. (Illus.). 128p. 1997. 41.95 (1-884831-05-2) Fox Pubns.

Monroe, Harriet. The New Poetry: An Anthology. LC 78-64048. (Des Imagistes: Literature of the Imagist Movement Ser.). reprint ed. 49.50 (0-404-17080-3) AMS Pr.

— Poets & Their Art. 322p. 1977. 18.95 (0-8369-0714-0) Ayer.

— Poets & Their Art. (BCL1-PS American Literature Ser.). 300p. 1992. reprint ed. lib. bdg. 79.00 (0-7812-6630-0) Rprt Serv.

— Poet's Life. LC 71-93777. reprint ed. 22.50 (0-404-04349-6) AMS Pr.

— A Poet's Life: 70 Years in a Changing World. (American Biography Ser.). 488p. 1991. reprint ed. lib. bdg. 89.00 (0-7812-8288-8) Rprt Serv.

— A Poet's Life: 70 Years in a Changing World. (BCL1-PS American Literature Ser.). 488p. 1993. reprint ed. lib. bdg. 99.00 (0-7812-6995-4) Rprt Serv.

Monroe, Hary. Time & Time Again: Two Immigrant Groups. (Illus.). 1985. 3.00 (0-614-32308-8) Balch IES Pr.

Monroe, Haskell M., Jr., ed. see Davis, Jefferson.

Monroe Historical Society Staff. The Village of Monroe: The Celebration of a Century. limited ed. (Illus.). 400p. 1994. pap. 20.00 (0-88092-185-4) Royal Fireworks.

— The Village of Monroe: The Celebration of a Century. limited ed. (Illus.). 400p. 1994. 30.00 (0-88092-186-2) Royal Fireworks.

Monroe, Howard & Williams, John. California Open Coast. (California Wildlife Regions Ser.). 126p. (C). 1996. pap. text 14.95 (1-885827-02-4) NatureGraphics.

Monroe, Howard, jt. auth. see Williams, John.

*Monroe, J. P. The Political Party Matrix: The Persistence of Organization. (C). 2001. pap. text 16.95 (0-7914-4918-1) State U NY Pr.

— The Political Party Matrix: The Persistence of Organization. (C). 2001. text 49.50 (0-7914-4917-3) State U NY Pr.

Monroe, James. Writings, 7 vols. Hamilton, Stanislaus M., ed. LC 69-18218. reprint ed. write for info. (0-404-04400-X) AMS Pr.

— The Writings of James Monroe, Including a Collection of His Public & Private Papers & Correspondence, Now for the First Time Printed, 7 vols. (American Biography Ser.). 1991. reprint ed. lib. bdg. 630.00 (0-7812-8289-6) Rprt Serv.

Monroe, James R. Civil Surveying Practice Exam for the California Special Civil Engineer Exam. LC 98-32101. 32p. 1999. pap. 22.95 (1-888577-31-2, CSURV) Prof Pubns CA.

Monroe, James S. Changing Earth. 2nd ed. LC 96-49067. 825p. 1997. 53.25 (0-314-09577-2) West Pub.

— Physical Geology. 3rd ed. 1998. student ed. 17.25 (0-534-53776-6) Brooks-Cole.

— Physical Geology. 4th ed. (Earth Science Ser.). 2000. 49.50 (0-534-57222-7) Wadsworth Pub.

— Physical Geology. 21st ed. (Earth Science Ser.). 1994. write for info. (0-314-05663-7) Wadsworth Pub.

— Physical Geology: Exploring the Earth. 2nd ed. (Earth Science Ser.). 1995. pap., student ed. 18.00 (0-314-05444-8) Wadsworth Pub.

— Physical Geology: Exploring the Earth with InfoTrac. 3rd ed. (Earth Science Ser.). 1997. 49.50 (0-534-53782-0) Wadsworth Pub.

Monroe, James S. & Wicander, Reed. The Changing Earth: Exploring Geology & Evolution. Westby, ed. LC 93-43307. 650p. (C). 1994. pap. text 57.50 (0-314-02833-1) West Pub.

— Physical Geology. 4th ed. (Earth Science Ser.). 2000. student ed. 19.95 (0-534-37520-0) Thomson Learn.

— Physical Geology: Exploring the Earth. Westby, ed. 639p. (C). 1992. text 58.75 (0-314-92195-8) West Pub.

— Physical Geology: Exploring the Earth. 3rd ed. LC 97-30966. (C). 1997. pap. 51.95 (0-534-53775-8) Wadsworth Pub.

*Monroe, James S. & Wicander, Reed. Physical Geology: International Version. 4th ed. 2000. pap. 55.00 (0-534-37788-2) Thomson Learn.

Monroe, James S., jt. auth. see Dutch, Steve I.

Monroe, James S., jt. auth. see Jackson, Bonnie.

Monroe, James S., jt. auth. see Wicander, Reed.

Monroe, James T. The Art of Badi az-Zaman Al Hamadhani: As Picaresque Narrative. 175p. (Orig.). 1984. pap. text 15.00 (0-8156-6070-7, Pub. by Am U Beirut) Syracuse U Pr.

— The Shu'Ubiyya in Al'Andalus: The Risala of Ibn Garcia & Five Refutations. LC 77-627464. (University of California Publications, Near Eastern Studies: No. 13). (Illus.). 113p. reprint ed. pap. 35.10 (0-608-17537-4, 203067900069) Bks Demand.

Monroe, James T., jt. auth. see Liu, Benjamin M.

Monroe, Jean G., jt. auth. see Williamson, Ray A.

Monroe, Jeffrey W. & Bushy, Thomas L. Marine Radionavigation & Communications. LC 98-38876. (Illus.). 336p. 1998. text 40.00 (0-87033-510-3) Cornell Maritime.

Monroe, Joel H. A Century & a Quarter of History: Geneva from 1787 to 1912. (Illus.). 234p. 1997. reprint ed. lib. bdg. 32.00 (0-8328-6146-4) Higginson Bk Co.

— Historical Records of a Hundred & Twenty Years, Auburn, NY. (Illus.). 1913p. 1996. pap. 28.00 (0-7884-0496-2, M558) Heritage Bk.

— Schenectady, Ancient & Modern: A Complete & Connected History of Schenectady from the Granting of the First Patent in 1661 to 1914. (Illus.). 285p. 1997. reprint ed. lib. bdg. 35.00 (0-8328-6227-4) Higginson Bk Co.

Monroe, John D. Chapters in the History of Delaware County. (Illus.). 132p. 1997. reprint ed. pap. 17.50 (0-8328-6130-8) Higginson Bk Co.

Monroe, John G., jt. auth. see McDonnall, Denis L.

Monroe, Jonathan. A Poverty of Objects: The Prose Poem & the Politics of Genre. LC 86-24026. 352p. 1987. 42.50 (0-8014-1967-0) Cornell U Pr.

— A Poverty of Objects: The Prose Poem & the Politics of Genre. LC 86-24026. 351p. reprint ed. pap. 108.90 (0-608-20925-2, 2072024) Bks Demand.

Monroe, Judy. Alcohol. LC 93-28607. (Drug Library Ser.). (Illus.). 128p. (YA). (gr. 6 up). 1994. lib. bdg. 20.95 (0-89490-470-1) Enslow Pubs.

— Antidepressants. LC 96-23354. (Drug Library Ser.). 128p. (YA). (gr. 6 up). 1997. lib. bdg. 20.95 (0-89490-848-0) Enslow Pubs.

*Monroe, Judy. Herbal Drug Dangers. LC 99-38290. (Drug Dangers Ser.). (Illus.). 64p. (YA). (gr. 4-10). 2000. lib. bdg. 19.95 (0-7660-1319-7) Enslow Pubs.

Monroe, Judy. Inhalant Drug Dangers. LC 98-33668. (Drug Dangers Ser.). (Illus.). 64p. (YA). (gr. 4-10). 1999. lib. bdg. 19.95 (0-7660-1153-4) Enslow Pubs.

*Monroe, Judy. Inhalant Drug Dangers. LC 98-33668. (Drug Dangers Ser.). (Illus.). 64p. (YA). (gr. 4-10). 1999. pap. 10.95 (0-7660-1739-7) Enslow Pubs.

— The Lindbergh Baby Kidnapping Trial: A Headline Court Case. LC 99-50666. (Headline Court Cases Ser.). (Illus.). 128p. (gr. 6 up). 2000. lib. bdg. 20.95 (0-7660-1389-8) Enslow Pubs.

Monroe, Judy. LSD, PCP & Hallucinogen Drug Dangers. LC 99-14105. (Drug Dangers Ser.). (Illus.). 64p. (gr. 4-10). 2000. lib. bdg. 19.95 (0-7660-1318-9) Enslow Pubs.

— Nicotine. LC 94-47280. (Drug Library Ser.). (Illus.). 128p. (YA). (gr. 6 up). 1995. lib. bdg. 20.95 (0-89490-505-8) Enslow Pubs.

— The Nineteenth Amendment: Women's Right to Vote. LC 97-23363. (Constitution Ser.). (Illus.). 128p. (YA). (gr. 6 up). 1998. lib. bdg. 20.95 (0-89490-922-3) Enslow Pubs.

— Phobias: Everything You Wanted to Know but Were Afraid to Ask. LC 95-32931. (Issues in Focus Ser.). (Illus.). 112p. (YA). (gr. 6 up). 1996. lib. bdg. 20.95 (0-89490-723-9) Enslow Pubs.

*Monroe, Judy. The Sacco & Vanzetti Controversial Murder Trial: A Headline Court Case. (Headline Court Cases Ser.). (Illus.). 112p. (YA). (gr. 6 up). 2000. lib. bdg. 20.95 (0-7660-1387-1) Enslow Pubs.

Monroe, Judy. Steroid Drug Dangers. LC 98-39942. (Drug Dangers Ser.). (Illus.). 64p. (YA). (gr. 4-10). 1999. lib. bdg. 19.95 (0-7660-1154-2) Enslow Pubs.

*Monroe, Judy. Steroid Drug Dangers. LC 98-39942. (Drug Dangers Ser.). (Illus.). 64p. (YA). (gr. 4-10). 1999. pap. 10.95 (0-7660-1742-7) Enslow Pubs.

— Understanding Weight Loss Programs. 1999. pap. text 6.95 (1-56838-263-4) Hazelden.

Monroe, Judy M. & Harrison, Supenn. Cooking the Thai Way. (Easy Menu Ethnic Cookbooks Ser.). (Illus.). 48p. (J). (gr. 5 up). 1986. lib. bdg. 19.93 (0-8225-0917-2, Lerner Publctns) Lerner Pub.

Monroe, Judy M., jt. auth. see Chung, Okwha.

Monroe, Judy M., jt. auth. see Nguyen, Chi T.

Monroe, Kelly K., ed. Finding God at Harvard: Spiritual Journeys of Thinking Christians. 368p. 1997. pap. 12.99 (0-310-21922-1) Zondervan.

Monroe, Kent B. Pricing: Making Profitable Decisions. 2nd ed. 1990. text 63.50 (0-07-042782-8) McGraw.

Monroe, Kent B., jt. ed. see Hung, Kineta.

Monroe, Kristen R. Contemporary Empirical Political Theory. LC 97-1113. 364p. 1997. 45.00 (0-520-20725-4, Pub. by U CA Pr); pap. 16.95 (0-520-20726-2, Pub. by U CA Pr) Cal Prin Full Svc.

— The Heart of Altruism: Perceptions of a Common Humanity. LC 95-39585. 320p. (C). 1996. text 45.00 (0-691-04355-8, Pub. by Princeton U Pr) Cal Prin Full Svc.

— Heart of Altruism: Perceptions of a Common Humanity. 314p. 1996. pap. text 17.95 (0-691-05847-4, Pub. by Princeton U Pr) Cal Prin Full Svc.

— Presidential Popularity & the Economy. LC 83-13943. 289p. 1984. 55.00 (0-275-91231-0, C1231, Praeger Pubs) Greenwood.

Monroe, Kristen R., ed. The Political Process & Economic Change. LC 83-11866. 250p. 1983. 42.00 (0-87586-063-X); pap. 18.00 (0-87586-062-1) Agathon.

Monroe, Kristen Renwick, ed. Economic Approach to Politics. (C). 1997. 40.06 (0-673-46426-1) Addson-Wesley Educ.

Monroe, Lee S., jt. auth. see Spencer, Francis M.

Monroe, Lewis B., ed. Dialogues & Dramas. LC 78-38602. (Granger Index Reprint Ser.). 1977. reprint ed. 19.95 (0-8369-6334-2) Ayer.

— Humorous Readings. LC 70-121932. (Granger Index Reprint Ser.). 1977. 21.95 (0-8369-6173-0) Ayer.

— Miscellaneous Readings. LC 71-38603. (Granger Index Reprint Ser.). 1977. 23.95 (0-8369-6335-0) Ayer.

*Monroe, Lorraine. Nothing's Impossible: Leadership Lessons from Inside & Outside the Classroom. LC 99-19298. 240p. 1999. pap. 12.00 (1-891620-20-7, Pub. by PublicAffairs NY) HarpC.

Monroe, Lucy. Creepy Cuisine. LC 92-41654. (Illus.). 80p. (J). (gr. 4-7). 1993. pap. 5.99 (0-679-84402-3, Pub. by Random Bks Yng Read) Random.

— Fifty Nifty Ways to Paint Your Face. LC 92-549. (Illus.). 64p. (J). 1992. pap. 3.95 (1-56565-029-8) Lowell Hse.

Monroe, Manus & Abrams, Karl. Experimental Chemistry: A Laboratory Course. 2nd ed. (Illus.). 400p. (C). 1991. text 36.95 (0-89863-151-3) Star Pub CA.

Monroe, Margaret E., ed. Seminar on Bibliotherapy: Proceedings of Sessions on Bibliotherapy Madison, Wisconsin, June 21-23, 1978. 180p. 1978. pap. 6.00 (0-936442-07-7) U Wis Sch Lib.

Monroe, Marilyn. Marilyn. 176p. 1995. pap. 14.95 (0-85965-145-2, Pub. by Plexus) Publishers Group.

Monroe, Marion. Growing into Reading: How Readiness for Reading Develops at Home & at School. LC 70-95130. 274p. 1970. reprint ed. lib. bdg. 65.00 (0-8371-2533-2, MOGR, Greenwood Pr) Greenwood.

Monroe, Mark. An Indian in White America. Reyer, Carolyn, ed. LC 94-2065. (Illus.). 256p. (C). 1994. text 69.95 (1-56639-234-9); pap. text 22.95 (1-56639-235-7) Temple U Pr.

Monroe, Martha C. What Works: A Guide to Environmental Education & Communication Projects for Practitioners & Donors. (Education for Sustainability Ser.). (Illus.). 120p. (C). 1999. pap. 12.95 (0-86571-405-3, Pub. by New Soc Pubs) Consort Bk Sales.

Monroe, Martha C., et al, eds. Environmental Problem Solving: Theory, Practice & Possibilities in Environmental Education. (Monograph Ser.). 150p. (Orig.). 1994. pap. 19.00 (1-884008-13-5) NAAEE.

Monroe, Martha C. & Cappaert, David. Integrating Environmental Education into the School Curriculum. (EEToolbox-Workshop Resource Manual Ser.). (Illus.). 56p. 1994. 8.00 (1-884782-04-3) Natl Consort EET.

Monroe, Martha C., jt. auth. see Braus, Judy A.

Monroe, Martha C., jt. auth. see Disinger, John F.

Monroe, Martha C., jt. auth. see Osborn, Nancy A.

Monroe, Martha C., ed. see Pennock, Margaret T. & Bardwell, Lisa V.

*Monroe, Mary. God Don't Like Ugly. 2000. pap. 15.00 (1-57566-607-3) Kensgtn Pub Corp.

Monroe, Mary Alice. The Book Club. 408p. 1999. per. 5.99 (1-55166-530-1, 1-66530-6, Mira Bks) Harlequin Bks.

*Monroe, Mary Alice. The Four Seasons. 2001. mass mkt. 6.50 (1-55166-789-4, Mira Bks) Harlequin Bks.

Monroe, Mary Alice. Girl in the Mirror. 1998. pap. 5.99 (1-55166-451-8) Harlequin Bks.

Monroe, Melissa. Machine Language. (Series of Poetry & Translation). 48p. (Orig.). 1997. pap. 12.00 (1-882509-05-6) Alef Bks.

Monroe, Mia, jt. ed. see Monroe, Elvira.

Monroe, Michael W. & Diamonstein, Barbaralee. The White House Collection of American Crafts. LC 95-75050. (Illus.). 128p. 1995. 35.00 (0-8109-4035-3, Pub. by Abrams) Time Warner.

Monroe, Paul. The Lost in Space Handbook. 174p. 1991. pap. 19.95 (1-880417-02-2) Star Tech.

— Textbook in the History of Education. LC 77-109914. reprint ed. 49.50 (0-404-04357-7) AMS Pr.

Monroe, Paula A. Left-Brain Finance for Right-Brain People: A Money Guide for the Creatively Inclined. 2nd rev. ed. LC 98-13241. (Illus.). 352p. 1998. pap. 18.95 (1-57071-340-5) Sourcebks.

Monroe, Phil, et al, eds. What to Do in a Pediatric Emergency. 60p. (Orig.). (C). 1996. pap. text 22.00 (0-7279-1032-9, Pub. by BMJ Pub) Login Brothers Bk Co.

Monroe, Robert A. Far Journeys. 304p. 1992. pap. 13.95 (0-385-23182-2) Doubleday.

— Journeys Out of the Body. LC 72-15761. 288p. 1992. reprint ed. pap. 13.95 (0-385-00861-9, Anchor NY) Doubleday.

— Ultimate Journey. 320p. 1996. pap. 13.95 (0-385-47208-0, Anchor NY) Doubleday.

Monroe, Robin P. God Is Awesome. LC 97-215529. 1997. 6.99 (0-570-05022-7, 56-1846) Concordia.

— I Have a New Family Now: Understanding Blended Families. LC 98-162156. (Comforting Little Hearts Ser.). (ps-1). 1998. 6.99 (0-570-05039-1, 56-1863) Concordia.

— When Will I Feel Better? Understanding Chronic Illness. LC 98-162155. (Comforting Little Hearts Ser.). (ps-1). 1998. 6.99 (0-570-05038-3, 56-1862) Concordia.

— Why Don't We Live Together Anymore? Understanding Divorce. LC 98-162157. (Comforting Little Hearts Ser.). (ps-1). 1998. 6.99 (0-570-05037-5, 56-1861) Concordia.

Monroe, Ruseell R. Creative Brainstorms: The Relationship Between Madness & Genius. (Frontiers of Consciousness Ser.). 312p. 1992. 24.95 (0-8290-1769-0) Irvington.

Monroe, Russell R. Episodic Behavioral Disorders: A Psychodynamic & Neurophysiologic Analysis. LC 72-95916. (Illus.). 536p. reprint ed. pap. 166.20 (0-7837-1719-9, 205724800024) Bks Demand.

Monroe, Stephen B., jt. auth. see Rochon, Louis-Philippe.

Monroe-Terrance, Heidi. Don't Read This Book!! Unless You Really Want to Know the Answers to All of Those Questions That You've Had about Death! LC 97-93554. (Illus.). 252p. 1997. pap. 7.95 (0-9646797-3-6) H Monroe-Terrance.

Monroe-Terrance, Heidi R. You've Got to Read This Book!! Answers to Those Questions That Have Been Bothering You for Years! 3rd ed. LC 98-93622. (Illus.). 90p. (Orig.). 1999. pap. 4.95 (0-9646797-2-8) H Monroe-Terrance.

Monroe, Tom. Engine Builder's Handbook: A Complete Guide to Professional Blueprinting & Assembly Techniques. 192p. (Orig.). 1996. pap. 17.95 (1-55788-245-2, HP Books) Berkley Pub.

— How to Rebuild Your Nissan & Datsun OHC Engine. LC 98-230615. (Illus.). 160p. 1998. pap. 19.95 (1-55561-159-1) Fisher Bks.

Monroe, Valerie, jt. auth. see Haven, Susan P.

Monroe, W. S. Turkey & the Turks. 448p. 1985. 280.00 (1-85077-061-1, Pub. by Darf Pubs Ltd) St Mut.

*Monroe Walker, Jesse. The Marilyn Monroe Story. 20p. 1999. pap. write for info. (1-882194-58-6) TN Valley Pub.

Monroe, Wayne & Peters, Mike. Becoming a Christian: Leading Accountable Young People to Salvation. (Illus.). 34p. 1975. pap., teacher ed. 3.00 (0-89225-376-2, 270040) Gospel Advocate.

— Becoming a Christian: Leading Accountable Young People to Salvation. (Illus.). 34p. (YA). (gr. 7-12). 1975. pap., wbk. ed. 2.50 (0-89225-375-4, 270040) Gospel Advocate.

Monroe, Will S. Comenius & the Beginnings of Educational Reform. LC 78-135824. (Eastern Europe Collection). 1971. reprint ed. 16.95 (0-405-02765-6) Ayer.

— History of the Pestalozzian Movement in the United States. LC 70-89206. (American Education: Its Men, Institutions, & Ideas. Series 1). 1971. reprint ed. 21.95 (0-405-01444-9) Ayer.

Monroe, William E., jt. auth. see Leib, Michael S.

Monroe, William F. Power to Hurt: The Virtues of Alienation. LC 97-4639. 256p. 1997. text 36.95 (0-252-02351-X); pap. text 16.95 (0-252-06657-X) U of Ill Pr.

*Monroe/Wicander. Changing Earth. 3rd ed. 2001. pap. 58.50 (0-534-37550-2) Thomson Learn.

— Changing Earth. 3rd ed. 2001. pap. 19.95 (0-534-37553-7) Thomson Learn.

*Monrose, Marilyn. Advanced Word 97 for the Legal User Made Easy. (Illus.). viii, 244p. 1998. 149.99 (0-9669761-1-8) M Monrose.

— Advanced WordPerfect 7 & 8 for the Legal User Made Easy. (Illus.). viii, 297p. 1998. 149.99 (0-9669761-2-6) M Monrose.

— How to Make Up to $25 Per Hour As a Temporary Legal Word Processor in New York City: Working Days, Evenings & Weekends. v, 105p. 1998. 29.99 (0-9669761-0-X) M Monrose.

Monroy, Bert. Adobe Photoshop: A Visual Guide for the MAC. 160p. (C). 1995. pap. text 34.95 (0-201-48993-7) Addison-Wesley.

*Monroy, Bert. Bert Monroy: Photorealistic Techniques with Photoshop & Illustrator. 2000. pap. text 49.99 (0-7357-0969-6) New Riders Pub.

Monroy, C., jt. auth. see Perales, T.

Monroy, Douglas. Rebirth: Mexican Los Angeles from the Great Migration to the Great Depression. LC 98-50013. 321p. 1999. pap. 17.95 (0-520-21333-5, Pub. by U CA Pr) Cal Prin Full Svc.

*Monroy, Douglas. Rebirth: Mexican Los Angeles from the Great Migration to the Great Depression. LC 98-50013. 321p. 1999. 45.00 (0-520-21332-7, Pub. by U CA Pr) Cal Prin Full Svc.

Monroy, Douglas. Thrown among Strangers: The Making of Mexican Culture in Frontier California. LC 89-49035. (Illus.). 288p. 1990. 40.00 (0-520-06914-5, Pub. by U CA Pr) Cal Prin Full Svc.

— Thrown among Strangers: The Making of Mexican Culture in Frontier California. 1993. pap. 17.95 (0-520-08275-3, Pub. by U CA Pr) Cal Prin Full Svc.

Monsanto, J. M., tr. see Zwickel, Jean W.

Monsarrat, John. Angel on the Yardarm: The Beginnings of Fleet Radar Defense & the Kamikaze Threat. LC 85-13850. (Historical Monographs: No. 6). (Illus.). 188p. (C). 1985. pap. 4.25 (0-9637973-7-9) Naval War Coll.

— Angel on the Yardarm: The Beginnings of Fleet Radar Defense & the Kamikaze Threat. (Illus.). 188p. 1994. reprint ed. pap. text 35.00 (0-7881-1453-0) DIANE Pub.

Monsarrat, Nicholas. The Cruel Sea. Sweetman, Jack, ed. LC 88-15126. (Classics of Naval Literature Ser.). (Illus.). 400p. 1988. 32.95 (0-87021-055-6) Naval Inst Pr.

— The Cruel Sea. LC 99-87253. (Classics of War Ser.). 520p. 2000. reprint ed. pap. 18.95 (1-58080-046-7) Burford Bks.

Monsarrat, Nicholas. The Kappillan of Malta. large type ed. 1976. 27.99 (0-85456-564-7) Ulverscroft.

— The Ship That Died of Shame, & Other Stories. LC 70-163044. (Short Story Index Reprint Ser.). 1977. reprint ed. 18.95 (0-8369-3958-1) Ayer.

— Smith & Jones. 20.95 (0-89190-349-6) Amereon Ltd.

Monsaur, Mary Ann & Douanchand Hayes, Margo. Culinary Secrets: Treasures from Margo & Mary Ann's Louisiana Kitchen. 304p. (Orig.). 1998. pap. 17.95 (0-9668152-0-3) Culinary Secrets.

Monse, Keith, jt. auth. see Weissman, Martin.

Monseau. Complete Guide to Young Adult Literature: Over 1000 Critiques & Synopsis from the Alan Review. 1997. text 115.00 (0-86709-425-7, Pub. by Boynton Cook Pubs) Heinemann.

Monseau, Virginia. Presenting Ouida Sebestyen. (Twayne's Young Adult Authors Ser.). 152p. 1994. 28.00 (0-8057-8224-9, Twyne) Mac Lib Ref.

— Responding to Young Adult Literature. LC 96-20. (Young Adult Literature Ser.). 103p. 1996. pap. text 18.50 (0-86709-401-X, 0401, Pub. by Boynton Cook Pubs) Heinemann.

*Monseau, Virginia & Salvner, Gary M. Reading Their World: The Young Adult Novel in the Classroom. 2nd ed. 2000. pap. text 22.00 (0-86709-473-7, Pub. by Boynton Cook Pubs) Heinemann.

Monseau, Virginia R. & Salvner, Gary M., eds. Reading Their World: The Young Adult Novel in the Classroom. LC 92-22108. (Young Adult Literature Ser.). 200p. (YA). (gr. 6 up). 1992. pap. text 21.50 (0-86709-306-4, 0306, Pub. by Boynton Cook Pubs) Heinemann.

Monsees, J. E., jt. ed. see Bowerman, L. D.

Monsees, Laurie S. Building the Temple: A Selection of Herald Articles. 100p. (Orig.). 1992. pap. text 10.00 (0-8309-0607-X) Herald Pub Hse.

The Temple. LC 93-20854. 1994. 25.00 (0-8309-0648-7) Herald Pub Hse.

Monsein, Matt, ed. see Headley, Barbara J.

Monselise, Shaul P. Handbook of Fruit Set & Development. 624p. 1986. 317.00 (0-8493-3260-5, SB357, CRC Reprint) Franklin.

M

An Asterisk (*) at the beginning of an entry indicates that the title is appearing for the first time.

Monsell, Helen A. Robert E. Lee: Young Confederate. LC 86-10736. (Childhood of Famous Americans Ser.). (Illus.). 192p. (J). (gr. 3-7). 1986. reprint ed. mass mkt. 4.95 (0-02-042020-X) Macmillan.

Monsell, Helen A. Robert E. Lee, Young Confederate. (Childhood of Famous Americans Ser.). (J). 1986. 10.05 (0-606-03259-2, Pub. by Turtleback) Demco.

— Susan B. Anthony: Champion of Women's Rights. (Childhood of Famous Americans Ser.). (J). 1986. 10.05 (0-606-03263-0, Pub. by Turtleback) Demco.

Monsell, Helen A. Susan B. Anthony: Champion of Women's Rights. LC 86-10716. (Childhood of Famous Americans Ser.). (Illus.). 192p. (J). (gr. 3-7). 1986. reprint ed. mass mkt. 4.95 (0-02-041800-0) Macmillan.

— Tom Jefferson: The Third President of the United States. LC 89-37841. (Childhood of Famous Americans Ser.). (Illus.). 192p. (J). (gr. 3-7). 1989. reprint ed. mass mkt. 4.95 (0-689-71347-9) Aladdin.

Monsell, Helen Albee. Tom Jefferson; Third President of the United States. (Childhood of Famous Americans Ser.). (J). 1989. 10.05 (0-606-08310-3, Pub. by Turtleback) Demco.

Monsell, Mary E. Mr. Pin: The Chocolate Files. MacDonald, Patricia, ed. (Illus.). 64p. (J). 1992. reprint ed. per. 2.99 (0-671-74085-7, Minstrel Bks) PB.

— The Mysterious Cases of Mr. Pin. MacDonald, Patricia, ed. (Illus.). 64p. (J). 1992. pap. 3.50 (0-671-74084-9, Minstrel Bks) PB.

— The Spy Who Came North from the Pole: Mr. Pin. LC 92-24646. (Mr. Pin Ser.: Vol. 3). (Illus.). 64p. (J). (gr. 1-4). 1993. 12.95 (0-689-31754-9) Atheneum Yung Read.

— The Spy Who Came North from the Pole: Mr. Pin. Childs, Alexandria, ed. (Mr. Rogers' First Experience Bks.: Vol. III). 64p. (J). 1995. pap. 3.50 (0-671-88399-2, Minstrel Bks) PB.

— Toohy & Wood. LC 91-38217. (Illus.). 80p. (J). (gr. 2-5). 1992. 12.95 (0-689-31721-2) Atheneum Yung Read.

— Underwear! Levine, Abby, ed. LC 87-25419. (Illus.). 24p. (J). (ps-2). 1988. lib. bdg. 13.95 (0-8075-8308-1) A Whitman.

— Underwear! (J). (ps-2). 1993. pap. 5.95 (0-8075-8309-X) A Whitman.

*__Monsell, Stephen, ed.__ Control of Cognitive Processes. (Attention & Performance Ser.: Vol. XVIII). (Illus.). 698p. (C). 2000. 90.00 (0-262-13367-9, Bradford Bks) MIT Pr.

Monsell, Thomas. Hamlet. large type ed. 1990. 40.50 (0-614-09882-3, L-38814-00) Am Printing Hse.

— Nixon on Stage & Screen: The Thirty-Seventh President As Depicted in Films, Television, Plays, & Opera. LC 97-44651. 247p. 1998. lib. bdg. 42.50 (0-7864-0163-X) McFarland & Co.

Monsen & Baer Staff. Perfume Bottle Auction Three: May 1, 1993. (Illus.). 80p. 1993. pap. 28.00 (0-9636102-0-1) Monsen & Baer.

*__Monsen, Christine T. & Zenk, Stan.__ Guide Me to Eternity. LC 94-24151. 216p. 1998. pap. 11.95 (1-56236-240-2, Pub. by Aspen Bks) Origin Bk Sales.

Monsen, Elaine R. Research: Successful Approaches. LC 91-31303. 1991. pap. 29.95 (0-88091-092-5, 0180) Am Dietetic Assn.

Monsen, Harry, tr. see Pernkopf, Eduard.

Monsen, Laura. Easy Microsoft Excel 97. 2nd ed. LC 98-85093. 1998. 19.99 (0-7897-1717-4) Que.

— Migrating to Office 95 & Office 97. LC 97-80900. 1998. 16.99 (0-7897-1569-4, Que New Media) MCP SW Interactive.

Monsen, Lauren. Nieto, Vol. 1. limited ed. (Illus.). 80p. 1996. boxed set, lthr. 5000.00 (0-9632328-2-7) Marco Fine Arts.

*__Monsen, Randall B.__ A Century of Perfume: Monsen & Baer Perfume Bottle Auction Ten. (Illus.). 128p. 2000. 45.00 (1-928655-00-9) Monsen & Baer.

Monsen, Randall B. Collectors' Compendium of Roseville Pottery, Vol. 1. (Illus.). 128p. 1995. 35.00 (0-9636102-2-8) Monsen & Baer.

— Collectors' Compendium of Roseville Pottery, Vol. 2. (Illus.). 128p. 1997. 45.00 (0-9636102-6-0) Monsen & Baer.

— For the Love of Perfume: Monsen & Baer Perfume Bottle Auction IX. (Illus.). 128p. 1999. 45.00 (0-9636102-9-5) Monsen & Baer.

— Price Guide - Collectors' Compendium of Roseville Pottery, Vols. 1 & 2. 12p. 1997. pap. 5.00 (0-9636102-7-9) Monsen & Baer.

Monsen, Randall B., ed. Perfume Bottle Auction Five Vol. V: May 6, 1995. (FRE & GER., Illus.). 96p. 1995. pap. 35.00 (0-9636102-3-6) Monsen & Baer.

— Perfume Bottle Auction Four Vol. IV: May 14, 1994. (Illus.). 80p. 1994. pap. 29.00 (0-9636102-1-X) Monsen & Baer.

Monsen, Randall B. & Lefkowith, Christie M. Memories of Perfume: Monsen & Baer Perfume Bottle Auction VIII. Baer, Rodney L., ed. (Illus.). 128p. 1998. 45.00 (0-9636102-8-7) Monsen & Baer.

Monsen, Randall B., et al. The Legacies of Perfume No. 7: Monsen & Baer Perfume Bottle Auction. (Illus.). 128p. 1997. 45.00 (0-9636102-5-2) Monsen & Baer.

Monsen, Stephen B. & Kitchen, Stanley G. Proceedings - Ecology & Management of Annual Rangelands. (Illus.). 428p. 1997. reprint ed. 50.00 (0-89904-602-9, Bear Meadows Resrch Grp); reprint ed. pap. 44.00 (0-89904-603-7, Bear Meadows Resrch Grp) Crumb Elbow Pub.

Monsenfelder, D. Vocabulary for World of Work 1. 1985. pap. text 13.82 (0-87694-229-X) Ed Design Inc.

Monser, George J. Antenna Design: A Practical Design. (Illus.). 163p. 1996. 60.00 (0-07-042843-3) McGraw.

Monserrat, Catherine P., jt. auth. see Barr, Linda.

Monserrat, Ileana G. La Habana, 1995. LC 90-84647. (Coleccion Caniqui). (SPA.). 80p. (Orig.). 1991. pap. 9.95 (0-89729-565-X) Ediciones.

Monserrat Robledo Galvan, Carmen De, see Cuadriello, Jaime.

Monset-Couchard, M., jt. ed. see Minkowski, A.

Monsey, Barbara, jt. auth. see Mattessich, Paul.

Monsey, Barbara R., et al. What Works in Preventing Rural Violence: Strategies, Risk Factors, & Assessment Tools. LC 94-49041. 1995. pap. 17.00 (0-940069-04-0) A H Wilder.

Monsey, Barbara R., jt. auth. see Mattessich, Paul W.

Monshau, Michael. Praying with Dominic. Koch, Carl, ed. (Companions for the Journey Ser.). (Illus.). 120p. (Orig.). 1993. pap. 8.95 (0-88489-288-3) St Marys.

Monshi, Eskandar B. History of Shah'Abbas Vol. III: Index. Savory, Roger M., tr. from PER. (Persian Heritage Ser.: Vol. 28). ix, 355p. 1986. text 29.50 (0-933273-01-0) Bibliotheca Persica.

Monshipouri, Mahmood. Democratization, Liberalization, & Human Rights in the Third World. LC 94-31377. 200p. 1995. pap. text 18.95 (1-55587-550-5) L Rienner.

— Islamism, Secularism & Human Rights in the Middle East. LC 98-9424. 270p. 1998. lib. bdg. 55.00 (1-55587-782-6) L Rienner.

Monsho, K. Anoa, ed. see Bashir, Askia H.

Monsholl, Evelyn, ed. see Michel, Barbara.

Monsi, M. & Saeki, T., eds. Ecophysiology of Photosynthetic Productivity. LC 78-670166. (JIBP Synthesis Ser.: No. 19). 280p. 1978. reprint ed. pap. 86.80 (0-608-01247-5, 206193500001) Bks Demand.

Monsivais, Carlos. Mexican Postcards. Kraniaukas, John, tr. LC 96-52425. (Critical Studies in Latin American Culture). 240p. 1997. pap. 18.00 (0-86091-604-9, B4627, Pub. by Verso) Norton.

Monske, Ken & Moore, Diana. Travelers Guide to the Historic Columbia River Highway. (Illus.). 52p. 1994. pap. 2.95 (1-883606-26-8) Intl Lov Touch.

Monsma, Hester. Devotions for Graduates. 32p. (Orig.). (gr. 11). 1984. mass mkt. 2.99 (0-8010-2939-2) Baker Bks.

— Devotions for Mothers. 32p. (gr. 11). 1984. mass mkt. 2.99 (0-8010-2942-2) Baker Bks.

Monsma, Stephen V. Positive Neutrality: Letting Religious Freedom Ring, 69. LC 92-25738. (Contributions in Legal Studies: No. 69). 304p. 1992. 59.95 (0-313-27963-2, MUY, Greenwood Pr) Greenwood.

— When Sacred & Secular Mix: Religious Nonprofit Organizations & Public Money. (Religious Forces in the Modern Political World Ser.). 252p. (C). 2000. pap. 27.95 (0-8476-8182-3) Rowman.

Monsma, Stephen V. & Soper, J. Christopher. The Challenge of Pluralism: Church & State in Five Democracies. LC 97-9791. (Religious Forces in the Modern Political World Ser.). 228p. 1997. 55.50 (0-8476-8568-3); pap. 23.95 (0-8476-8569-1) Rowman.

Monsma, Stephen V. & Soper, J. Christopher, eds. Equal Treatment of Religion in a Pluralistic Society. LC 97-45848. 216p. 1998. pap. 18.00 (0-8028-4296-8) Eerdmans.

Monsman, Gerald. Confessions of a Prosaic Dreamer: Charles Lamb's Art of Autobiography. LC 84-4021. vii, 165p. 1984. text 38.95 (0-8223-0596-8) Duke.

— Olive Schreiner's Fiction: Landscape & Power. LC 91-9431. 220p. (C). 1991. text 45.00 (0-8135-1724-9) Rutgers U Pr.

— Oxford University's Old Mortality Society: A Study in Victorian Romanticism. LC 98-22818. 140p. 1998. text 69.95 (0-7734-8362-4) E Mellen.

Monsman, Gerald, ed. & intro. see Pater, Walter.

Monsman, Gerald C. Walter Pater. LC 76-58511. (Twayne's English Authors Ser.). 213p. (C). 1977. lib. bdg. 20.95 (0-8057-6676-6) Irvington.

— Walter Pater's Art of Autobiography. LC 80-11941. 184p. reprint ed. pap. 57.10 (0-8357-3753-5, 203647900003) Bks Demand.

Monson, A. M. The Secret of Sanctuary Island. ALC Staff, ed. LC 90-6479. 176p. (J). (gr. 4-7). 1992. mass mkt. 4.95 (0-688-11693-0, Wm Morrow) Morrow Avon.

— The Secret of Sanctuary Island. 1992. 10.05 (0-606-01383-0, Pub. by Turtleback) Demco.

— Wanted: Best Friend. (Illus.). (J). (ps-3). 1997. 14.99 (0-614-28689-1, Dial Yng Read) Peng Put Young Read.

Monson, Angela, jt. auth. see Burke, Bob.

Monson-Burton, Marianne. Girls Know Best: Your World, Your Words, Vol. 3. LC 99-25495. 152p. (YA). (gr. 2-11). 1999. pap. 8.95 (1-58270-016-8) Beyond Words Pub.

Monson, Christine. A Flame Run Wild. 400p. 1988. pap. 3.95 (0-380-89976-0, Avon Bks) Morrow Avon.

— Golden Nights. 352p. 1990. mass mkt. 4.95 (0-446-35586-0, Pub. by Warner Bks) Little.

— Stormfire. 592p. 1984. pap. 3.95 (0-380-87668-X, Avon Bks) Morrow Avon.

— Surrender the Night. 400p. 1987. pap. 3.95 (0-380-89969-8, Avon Bks) Morrow Avon.

— This Fiery Splendor. 1991. mass mkt. 4.95 (0-446-35589-5, Pub. by Warner Bks) Little.

Monson, Craig A. Disembodied Voices: Music & Culture in an Early Modern Italian Convent. LC 94-28823. 394p. 1995. 45.00 (0-520-08875-1, Pub. by U CA Pr) Cal Prin Full Svc.

Monson, Craig A., ed. The Crannied Wall: Women, Religion & the Arts in Early Modern Europe. (Studies in Medieval & Early Modern Civilization). (Illus.). 256p. (C). 1992. text 52.50 (0-472-10271-0, 10271) U of Mich Pr.

Monson, Dale, ed. Adriano in Siria. LC 86-750172. (Giovanni Battista Pergolesi Complete Works: No. 1, Vol. III). (Illus.). 1987. lib. bdg. 187.00 (0-918728-32-0) Pendragon NY.

Monson, Dianne L. & McClenathan, DayAnn K., eds. Developing Active Readers: Ideas for Parents, Teachers, & Librarians. LC 79-9058. 112p. reprint ed. pap. 34.80 (0-8357-4308-X, 203710500007) Bks Demand.

Monson, Dwight E. Shared Beliefs - Honest Differences: Reconciling the Disagreements of Mormons & Other Christians. 224p. 1998. 18.98 (0-88290-633-X, 1091) Horizon Utah.

*__Monson-Fitzjohn, G. J.__ Quaint Signs of Olde Inns. (Illus.). 157p. 2000. reprint ed. pap. text 20.00 (0-7881-9222-1) DIANE Pub.

Monson, Gale & Phillips, Allan R. Annotated Checklist of the Birds of Arizona. 2nd annot. rev. expanded ed. LC 81-11687. (Illus.). 272p. pap. 84.40 (0-608-20015-8, 207129100007) Bks Demand.

Monson, Gale, jt. auth. see Russell, Stephen M.

Monson-Haefel, Richard. Enterprise JavaBeans. Loukides, Mike, ed. (Illus.). 344p. 1999. pap. 34.95 (1-56592-605-6) OReilly & Assocs.

*__Monson-Haefel, Richard.__ Enterprise JavaBeans. 2nd ed. Loukides, Mike, ed. (Illus.). 480p. 2000. pap. 34.95 (1-56592-869-5) OReilly & Assocs.

Monson, Harry, tr. see Pernkopf, Eduard.

Monson, Ingrid. The African Diaspora: A Musical Perspective. LC 99-45341. (Conceptual Issues in Ethnomusicology Ser.). 300p. 2000. text 45.00 (0-8153-2382-4) Garland.

— Saying Something: Jazz Improvisation & Interaction. LC 96-23224. (Chicago Studies in Ethnomusicology). (Illus.). 253p. 1997. pap. text 14.95 (0-226-53478-2); lib. bdg. 39.95 (0-226-53477-4) U Ch Pr.

Monson, J. Bruce. All the Marbles: A Novel. LC 91-11721. 288p. (Orig.). 1991. pap. 10.95 (0-931832-91-8) Fithian Pr.

— Crimson Ice, Sugar & Spice: A Novel of Suspense. LC 93-33522. 224p. (Orig.). 1994. pap. 10.95 (1-56474-083-8) Fithian Pr.

Monson, James E., jt. auth. see Hoagland, Albert S.

Monson, John P. Challenges in Growth Hormone Therapy. LC 99-17635. (Illus.). 1999. 135.00 (0-632-05164-7) Blackwell Sci.

*__Monson, John R., et al.__ Surgical Emergencies. LC 98-17789. (Illus.). 406p. 1999. 99.95 (0-632-05047-0) Blackwell Sci.

Monson, Luetta, jt. auth. see Myers, John.

Monson, Mavis K., jt. auth. see Parker, Lorne A.

Monson, Michele P. & Monson, Robert J. Guided by Performance - Elementary Edition: Building Stronger Bridges Between Learning, Curriculum, & Assessment. 240p. 1997. pap. 49.00 (1-56976-080-2, 1090-F3) Zephyr Pr AZ.

— Guided by Performance - Secondary Edition: Building Stronger Bridges Between Learning, Curriculum, & Assessment. 256p. 1997. pap. 49.00 (1-56976-081-0, 1091-F3) Zephyr Pr AZ.

Monson, Nancy. Smart Guide to Boosting Your Energy. LC 99-14560. 192p. 1999. pap. 10.95 (0-471-31859-0) Wiley.

Monson, Rela G. Jewish Campus Life: A Survey of Student Attitudes Toward Marriage & Family. LC 84-70026. 52p. 1984. pap. 3.00 (0-87495-060-0) Am Jewish Comm.

Monson, Rela G., ed. Jewish Women on the Way Up: The Challenge of Family, Career & Community. LC 87-73347. 36p. (Orig.). 1987. pap. 5.00 (0-87495-097-X) Am Jewish Comm.

Monson, Rela G., jt. auth. see Crawford, Albert G.

Monson, Richard R. Occupational Epidemiology. 232p. 1986. 132.00 (0-8493-5793-4, RC964, CRC Reprint) Franklin.

— Occupational Epidemiology. 2nd ed. 312p. 1990. boxed set 146.95 (0-8493-4927-3, RC964) CRC Pr.

Monson, Robert J., jt. auth. see Monson, Michele P.

Monson, Steven I. Using Autosketch. LC 88-33610. (C). 1990. pap. text 21.95 (0-8273-3242-4) Delmar.

Monson, Suzanne, jt. auth. see Cohn, Rosanne.

Monson, Terri, ed. see Dewazien, Karl.

Monson, Thomas S. Be Your Best Self. LC 79-54782. 209p. 1979. 12.95 (0-87747-787-6) Deseret Bk.

— A Christmas Dress for Ellen LC 99-166683. 14p. (J). 1998. write for info. (1-57345-435-4) Deseret Bk.

— Faith Rewarded: A Personal Account of Prophetic Promises to the East German Saints. LC 96-8147. ix, 182p. 1996. 14.95 (1-57345-186-X) Deseret Bk.

— Inspiring Experiences That Build Faith: From the Life & Ministry of Thomas S. Monson. LC 94-28433. x, 277p. 1994. 14.95 (0-87579-901-9) Deseret Bk.

— Live the Good Life. LC 88-71770. 135p. 1988. 12.95 (0-87579-192-1) Deseret Bk.

— Pathways to Perfection. LC 73-88634. xiv, 302p. 1973. 14.95 (0-87747-511-3) Deseret Bk.

Monson, Thomas S., compiled by. Favorite Quotations from the Collection of Thomas S. Monson. LC 85-16279. viii, 296p. 1985. 14.95 (0-87747-749-3) Deseret Bk.

Monsonego, Joseph & Franco, Eduard. New Developments in Cervical Cancer Screening & Prevention. LC 96-37506. (Illus.). 464p. 1997. 145.00 (0-632-04765-8) Blackwell Sci.

Monsour, Leslie. Gringuita Poems. LC 90-91893. (Illus.). 50p. (Orig.). 1990. pap. text. write for info. (0-9627316-0-9) L Monsour.

Monsour, Margaret, ed. Senior Services Resource Directory. 53p. (Orig.). 1989. spiral bd. write for info. (0-9623088-0-3) Europa Public.

Monsour, Sally & Dorn, Pamela. Sounds of the World: Music of the Middle East (Teacher's Guide) (Sounds of the World Ser.). (Illus.). 5p. 1990. pap., teacher ed. write for info. incl. audio (0-940796-73-2, 3040) MENC.

Monssen, Franz. MicroSim PSpice with Circuit. 2nd ed. LC 96-30084. 548p. (C). 1997. pap. text, student ed. 50.00 (0-02-382010-1) P-H.

Monsted, Mette & Parveen, Walji. A Demographic Analysis of East Africa: A Sociological Interpretation. 212p. (Orig.). 1978. pap. 21.50 (91-7106-126-6, Pub. by Nordisk Afrikainstitutet) Coronet Bks.

Monsted, Mette, jt. auth. see Kongstad, Per.

*__Mont, Daniel, et al.__ Workers' Compensation: Benefits, Coverage & Cost 1996 New Estimates. 20p. 1999. pap. text 15.00 (1-884902-07-3) Natl Acad.

Mont, J. Du, see Tartakower, A. & Du Mont, J.

Mont, Jay. Confessions of a Weight Loss Doctor: The Fen-Phen Program. Heimlich, Patti, ed. LC 97-90379. (Illus.). 180p. (Orig.). 1997. pap. 12.95 (0-9658136-0-6) Weight Manag.

Mont, Johnson D. La, see La Mont Johnson, D.

Mont-Joy, Marc D. The New American Challenge. LC 85-1445. 1988. pap. 13.95 (0-87949-263-5) Ashley Bks.

Mont-Laurier Benedictine Nuns Staff. Goat Cheese Small-Scale Production. 2nd ed. Inksetter, Eveline, tr. from FRE. Orig. Title: Fromages De Chevre Fabrication Artisinale. (Illus.). 96p. 1983. pap. 8.95 (0-9607404-1-4) Cheesemakers Jrnl.

Monta, George. The Prophecy Handbook: A Theologian Looks at Millennial Myths & Scriptural Truths. LC 99-218659. 181p. 1998. pap. 14.95 (1-883179-10-6) Weston Bible.

Monta, Howard A. Cops Who Succeed: The Key to a Long & Successful Career in Law Enforcement. 1999. pap. 30.00 (0-938609-42-4) Graduate Group.

Montabue, Shillaber. Beyond Beyond Beyond: The Morrow of Life. 90p. (Orig.). 1990. pap. 9.95 (0-9623473-1-0) Wide-Awake Bks.

Montacute, Charles M. Administration of Health Service. (C). 1987. pap. 120.00 (0-7855-3756-2) St Mut.

Montada, L. & Lerner, M. J. Current Societal Concerns about Justice. LC 96-43658. (Critical Issues in Social Justice Ser.). (Illus.). 301p. (C). 1996. 59.00 (0-306-45395-9, Kluwer Plenum) Kluwer Academic.

Montada, Leo, et al, eds. Life Crises & Experiences of Loss in Adulthood. 560p. 1992. text 99.95 (0-8058-1001-3) L Erlbaum Assocs.

Montada, Leo & Lerner, Melvin J., eds. Responses to Victimization & Belief in a Just World. LC 98-34332. (Critical Issues in Social Justice Ser.). 278p. 1998. 49.50 (0-306-46030-0, Kluwer Plenum) Kluwer Academic.

Montada, Leo, jt. ed. see Bierhoff, Hans-Werner.

Montag, Carol, jt. ed. see Jervis, Kathe.

Montag, H. J., jt. auth. see Muller-Wohlahrt, H W.

Montag, Horst & Reigber, Christoph, eds. Geodesy & Physics of the Earth: Geodetic Contributions to Geodynamics, 7th International Symposium Geodesy & Physics of the Earth, Potsdam, October 5-10, 1992. LC 93-33122. (International Association of Geodesy Symposia Ser.: No. 112). 1993. 168.95 (0-387-56572-8) Spr-Verlag.

Montag, Leona. Mitchell County, Iowa. (Illus.). 484p. 1989. 55.00 (0-88107-151-X) Curtis Media.

Montag, Paul M. Time - A Conceptual Explaination: The Nature & Concept of Time. Montag, Sandra J., ed. LC 98-91319. (Illus.). 285p. 1998. pap. 29.95 (0-9663756-9-6) New Mill Publ.

Montag, Sandra J., ed. see Montag, Paul M.

Montag, Tom. Ben Zen: The Ox of Paradox. 46p. 1999. pap. 6.00 (1-889460-01-X) CrosspIusRds.

— The Essential Ben Zen. (Chickadee Ser.: No. 6). 1992. pap. 6.00 (1-55780-123-1) Juniper Pr ME.

— Learning to Read Again. 1976. 1.00 (0-916866-01-7) Cats Pajamas.

Montag, Ulrich, ed. Will the Chain Break? Differential Pricing As Part of a New Pricing Structure for Research Literature & Its Consequences for the Future of Scholarly Communication. (IFLA Publications: Vol. 61). 95p. 1992. lib. bdg. 45.00 (3-598-21789-7) K G Saur Verlag.

Montag, Warren. The Unthinkable Swift: Spontaneous Philosophy of a Church of England Man. 152p. (C). 1994. pap. 18.00 (1-85984-000-0, B4691, Pub. by Verso) Norton.

Montag, Warren & Stolze, Ted, eds. The New Spinoza. LC 97-27337. (Theory Out of Bounds Ser.: Vol. 11). 512p. 1997. pap. 24.95 (0-8166-2541-7); text 62.95 (0-8166-2540-9) U of Minn Pr.

Montag, Warren, jt. ed. see Hill, Mike.

Montag, William E. Best Resumes for $75,000 + Executive Jobs. 2nd ed. LC 98-8156. 304p. 1998. pap. 14.95 (0-471-29720-8) Wiley.

Montagana, Francesco. Birkhauser Architectural Guide Japan: 20th Century. LC 97-10104. (Illus.). 288p. 1997. 30.00 (3-7643-5676-6, Pub. by Birkhauser) Princeton Arch.

— Birkhauser Architekturfuhrer Japan: 20. Jahrhundert. (Birkhauser Architectural Guides Ser.). (GER., Illus.). 288p. 1997. 30.00 (3-7643-5675-8, Pub. by Birkhauser) Princeton Arch.

Montage Staff, ed. Montage. (Illus.). 72p. (Orig.). 1989. pap. 5.95 (0-9623452-1-0) Oregon Coast Cmnty Col.

Montagna, F. Joseph. The Herbal Desk Reference. 1280p. 1990. boxed set 86.95 (0-8403-5813-X) Kendall-Hunt.

Montagna, Frank C. Responding to "Routine" Emergencies. LC 99-33297. 245p. 1999. write for info. (0-912212-81-0) Fire Eng.

Montagna, Paul D. Certified Public Accounting: A Sociological View of a Profession in Change. LC 73-90140. 1975. text 30.00 (0-914348-14-0) Scholars Bk.

Montagna, W., et al. Atlas of Normal Human Skin. (Illus.). 384p. 1994. 155.00 (0-387-97769-4) Spr-Verlag.

Montagna, W., jt. ed. see Noback, C. R.

An Asterisk (*) at the beginning of an entry indicates that the title is appearing for the first time.

Montagna, William. Nonhuman Primates in Biomedical Research. LC 76-7881. (Wesley W. Spink Lectures on Comparative Medicine: No. 3). (Illus.). 161p. reprint ed. pap. 50.00 (*0-8357-8972-1*, 203327300085) Bks Demand.

Montagna, William, et al, eds. Black Skin: Structure & Function. LC 93-14784. 158p. 1993. text 58.00 (*0-12-505260-X*) Acad Pr.

Montagne, Jacques. Atlas of Foot Radiology. (C). (gr. 13). 1981. 81.50 (*0-89352-097-7*) Mosby Inc.

Montagne, Mary. Staying Straight: Adolescent Recovery. 32p. (Orig.). 1987. pap. 3.95 (*0-9613416-6-1*) Comm Intervention.

Montagne, Michael, jt. auth. see Basara, Lisa R.

Montagne, Michael, jt. auth. see Bleidt, Barry.

Montagne, Rogelio S., jt. auth. see Casad, Robert C.

Montagnes, Anne. Jade Slash Laverna. LC 97-145446. 288p. 1995. 19.95 (*0-88784-169-4*, Pub. by Hse of Anansi Pr) Genl Dist Srvs.

— Jade Slash Laverna. 288p. 1997. pap. 14.95 (*0-88784-600-9*, Pub. by Hse of Anansi Pr) Genl Dist Srvs.

Montagnes, Ian, jt. ed. see Harman, Eleanor.

Montagnier, Jean-Paul, ed. see Gervais, Charles-Hubert.

***Montagnier, Luc.** Virus: The Co-Discoverer of HIV Tracks Its Rampage & Charts the Future. LC 99-19650. (Illus.). 256p. 1999. 24.95 (*0-393-03923-4*) Norton.

Montagnier, Luc & Gougeon, Marie-Lise. New Concepts in AIDS Pathogenesis. LC 93-4765. (Illus.). 344p. 1993. text 145.00 (*0-8247-9127-4*) Dekker.

Montagnier, Luc & Pasquier, C., eds. Oxidative Stress in Cancer, AIDS & Neurodegenerative Diseases. LC 97-41304. (Oxidative Stress & Disease Ser.). (Illus.). 578p. 1997. text 195.00 (*0-8247-9862-7*) Dekker.

Montagnini, Florencia, jt. auth. see Ashton, Mark S.

Montagnon, Peter, ed. European Competition Policy. (Chatham House Papers). 128p. (Orig.). 1990. pap. 14.95 (*0-87609-090-0*) Coun Foreign.

Montagu, Lord. Jaguar. 7th ed. (Illus.). 276p. 1998. 40.00 (*1-899163-34-4*, Pub. by Quiller Pr) Cimino Pub Grp.

Montagu, Ashley. The Biosocial Nature of Man. LC 72-11331. 123p. 1973. reprint ed. lib. bdg. 49.50 (*0-8371-6658-6*, MOBN, Greenwood Pr) Greenwood.

— Coming into Being among the Australian Aborigines: A study of the procreative beliefs of the native tribes of Australia. LC 75-41195. (Illus.). reprint ed. 55.00 (*0-404-14573-6*) AMS Pr.

— Darwin: Competition & Cooperation. LC 72-11332. 148p. 1973. reprint ed. lib. bdg. 35.00 (*0-8371-6657-8*, MODC, Greenwood Pr) Greenwood.

— Education & Human Relations. LC 72-11333. 191p. 1973. reprint ed. lib. bdg. 55.00 (*0-8371-6659-4*, MOEH, Greenwood Pr) Greenwood.

— The Elephant Man: A Study in Human Dignity. 3rd rev. ed. Angers, Trent, ed. LC 95-79903. (Illus.). 120p. 1995. 14.95 (*0-925417-17-3*) Acadian Hse Pub.

— Growing Young. 2nd ed. LC 88-27610. 303p. 1988. 62.95 (*0-89789-167-8*, Bergin & Garvey); pap. 19.95 (*0-89789-166-X*, Bergin & Garvey) Greenwood.

— Man, His First Two Million Years: A Brief Introduction to Anthropology. LC 80-15749. (Illus.). 262p. 1980. reprint ed. lib. bdg. 35.00 (*0-313-22600-8*, MOMH, Greenwood Pr) Greenwood.

— Man's Most Dangerous Myth: The Fallacy of Race. 6th ed. LC 97-21132. 704p. 1997. 45.00 (*0-8039-4647-3*) AltaMira Pr.

— Man's Most Dangerous Myth: The Fallacy of Race. 6th abr. ed. LC 97-21132. 304p. 1997. pap., student ed. 19.95 (*0-8039-4648-1*) AltaMira Pr.

***Montagu, Ashley.** The Natural Superiority of Women. 5th ed. 300p. 1998. 62.00 (*0-7619-8981-1*); pap. 19.95 (*0-7619-8982-X*) AltaMira Pr.

Montagu, Ashley. On Being Intelligent. LC 72-11742. 236p. 1973. reprint ed. lib. bdg. 59.50 (*0-8371-6704-3*, MOOB, Greenwood Pr) Greenwood.

— Race & IQ. expanded ed. 496p. 1999. 35.00 (*0-19-510220-7*) OUP.

— Race & IQ. expanded ed. 400p. 2000. pap. 14.95 (*0-19-510221-5*) OUP.

— Touching: The Human Significance of the Skin. LC 75-151290. (Illus.). 1971. text 52.50 (*0-231-03488-1*) Col U Pr.

— Touching: The Human Significance of the Skin. 3rd ed. 512p. 1986. pap. 16.00 (*0-06-096028-0*, Perennial) HarperTrade.

Montagu, Ashley, ed. The Concept of Race. LC 80-21682. 270p. 1980. reprint ed. lib. bdg. 35.00 (*0-313-22721-7*, MOCR, Greenwood Pr) Greenwood.

— The Meaning of Love. LC 72-11335. 248p. 1974. reprint ed. lib. bdg. 35.00 (*0-8371-6656-X*, MOML, Greenwood Pr) Greenwood.

— Science & Creationism. LC 82-14173. (Illus.). 320p. 1984. text 35.00 (*0-19-503252-7*) OUP.

— Science & Creationism. LC 82-14173. (Illus.). 434p. 1984. pap. text 27.95 (*0-19-503253-5*) OUP.

— Studies & Essays in the History of Science & Learning. LC 74-26275. (History, Philosophy & Sociology of Science Ser.). (Illus.). 1975. reprint ed. 52.95 (*0-405-06603-1*) Ayer.

— Toynbee & History: Critical Essays & Reviews. (Extending Horizons Ser.). 385p. (C). 1956. 7.00 (*0-87558-026-2*) Porter Sargent.

Montagu, Ashley, jt. auth. see Steen, Edwin B.

***Montagu, Basil.** Opinions of Different Authors upon the Punishment of Death, 1 vol. 2nd ed. viii, 310p. 2000. reprint ed. 96.00 (*1-56169-625-0*) Gaunt.

Montagu, Don. Sensuous Garden. 1998. 32.50 (*0-676-57326-6*) Random.

Montagu, Elizabeth. 18th Century Shakespeare: 1785-1839, Vol. 12. 292p. 1970. reprint ed. 28.50 (*0-7146-2515-9*, Pub. by F Cass Pubs) Intl Spec Bk.

Montagu, Elizabeth R. An Essay on the Writings & Genius of Shakespeare: Compared with the Greek & French Dramatic Poets. LC 73-96372. (Eighteenth Century Shakespeare Ser.: No. 12). 288p. 1970. reprint ed. lib. bdg. 27.50 (*0-678-05139-9*) Kelley.

— Essay on the Writings & Genius of Shakespeare Compared with the Greek & French Dramatic Poets. 6th ed. LC 17-29281. reprint ed. 45.00 (*0-404-04358-5*) AMS Pr.

— The Letters of Mrs. Elizabeth Montagu, with Some of the Letters of Her Correspondents, 4 vols. LC 72-37704. 1813. reprint ed. 295.00 (*0-404-56800-9*) AMS Pr.

Montagu, Gerald & Weston, Mark. Legal Practice Companion, 1998-99. LC 99-199726. 435p. 1998. pap. 58.00 (*1-85431-862-4*) Gaunt.

Montagu, Gerald & Dieckmann, Janna L. Caring for the Chronically Ill: Philadelphia, 1945-1965. rev. ed. LC 98-37265. (Studies on the Elderly in America). 416p. 1999. 84.00 (*0-8153-3251-3*) Garland.

Montagu, Gwen, jt. auth. see Montagu, Jeremy.

Montagu, Henry. Contemplatio Mortis et Immortalitatis. LC 72-218. (English Experience Ser.: No. 337). 148p. 1971. reprint ed. 20.00 (*90-221-0337-4*) Walter J Johnson.

Montagu, Ivor. With Eisenstein in Hollywood. 356p. 1969. pap. 1.95 (*0-7178-0220-5*) Intl Pubs Co.

Montagu, Ivor, tr. see Eisenstein, Sergei M.

Montagu, Jean-Yves. Burma. (Evergreen Ser.). 1998. 19.99 (*3-8228-7644-5*) Taschen Amer.

***Montagu, Jean-Yves.** El Oeste Americano. 1998. 25.99 (*3-8228-8031-0*) Benedikt Taschen.

Montagu, Jean-Yves. Western America. 1998. 19.99 (*3-8228-7755-7*) Taschen Amer.

Montagu, Jennifer. Alessandro Algardi, Vols. 1 & 2. LC 84-52244. (Illus.). 762p. 1985. reprint ed. pap. 200.00 (*0-608-07839-5*, 205401500010) Bks Demand.

— Alessandro Algardi. LC 84-53344. (Illus.). 762p. 1985. 140.00 (*0-300-03173-4*) Yale U Pr.

— The Expression of the Passions: The Origin & the Influence of Charles Le Brun's "Conference Sur l'Expression Generale et Particuliere" LC 94-130. (Illus.). 256p. 1994. 50.00 (*0-300-05891-8*) Yale U Pr.

— Gold, Silver & Bronze: Metal Sculpture of the Roman Baroque. LC 95-15892. 1996. 60.00 (*0-300-06336-9*) Yale U Pr.

— Gold, Silver, & Bronze: Metal Sculpture of the Roman Baroque. (Bollingen Series: Vols. 35 & 39). 280p. 1996. text 59.50 (*0-691-02736-6*, Pub. by Princeton U Pr) Cal Prin Full Svc.

— Roman Baroque Sculpture: The Industry of Art. LC 88-30482. 244p. (C). 1989. 60.00 (*0-300-04392-9*) Yale U Pr.

— Roman Baroque Sculpture: The Industry of Art. (Illus.). 256p. (C). 1993. reprint ed. pap. 30.00 (*0-300-05366-5*) Yale U Pr.

Montagu, Jeremy. The Flute. (Album Ser.: Vol. 252). (Illus.). 32p. 6.25 (*0-7478-0085-5*, Pub. by Shire Pubns) Lubrecht & Cramer.

— The Flute. 1989. pap. 25.00 (*0-7855-7042-X*, Pub. by Shire Pubns) St Mut.

— The French Horn. (Album Ser.: No. 254). (Illus.). 32p. 1989. pap. 6.95 (*0-7478-0086-3*, Pub. by Shire Pubns) Parkwest Pubns.

— The World of Baroque & Classical Musical Instruments. LC 78-65227. (Illus.). 136p. 1979. 39.95 (*0-87951-089-7*, Pub. by Overlook Pr) Penguin Putnam.

— The World of Medieval & Renaissance Musical Instruments. LC 76-5987. (Illus.). 136p. 1976. 39.95 (*0-87951-045-5*, Pub. by Overlook Pr) Penguin Putnam.

— The World of Romantic & Modern Musical Instruments. LC 80-26106. (Illus.). 136p. 1981. 39.95 (*0-87951-126-5*, Pub. by Overlook Pr) Penguin Putnam.

Montagu, Jeremy & Montagu, Gwen. Minstrels & Angels: Carvings of Musicians in Medieval English Churches. LC 97-38360. (Reference Books in Music: Vol. 33). (Illus.). 212p. 1998. 36.00 (*0-914913-40-9*, Fallen Lef Pr); pap. 19.95 (*0-914913-41-7*, Fallen Lef Pr) Scarecrow.

***Montagu, John Drogo.** Battles of the Greek & Roman Worlds: A Chronological Compendium of 667 Battles to 31 BC, from the Historians of the Ancient World. 256p. 2000. 49.95 (*1-85367-389-7*, Pub. by Greenhill Bks) Stackpole.

Montagu, Lady Mary Wortley. Embassy to Constantinople. (Illus.). 224p. (C). 1988. 30.00 (*0-941533-41-7*, NAB) I R Dee.

— Essays & Poems & Simplicity, a Comedy. Halsband, Robert & Grundy, Isobel, eds. (Illus.). 442p. 1993. reprint ed. pap. text 22.00 (*0-19-812288-8*) OUP.

— Letters. LC 92-52913. 592p. 1992. 20.00 (*0-679-41747-8*) Everymns Lib.

— Letters from the Levant: During the Embassy to Constantinople, 1716-18. LC 71-135825. (Eastern Europe Collection). 1971. reprint ed. 32.95 (*0-405-02767-2*) Ayer.

— Letters from the Right Honourable Lady Mary Wortley Montagu, 1709-1762. (BCL1-PR English Literature Ser.). 551p. 1992. reprint ed. lib. bdg. 99.00 (*0-7812-7391-9*) Rprt Serv.

— Nonsense of Common Sense, 1737-1738. Halsband, Robert, ed. LC 71-129373. (Northwestern University. Humanities Ser.: No. 17). reprint ed. 27.50 (*0-404-50717-4*) AMS Pr.

— Romance Writings. Grundy, Isobel, ed. LC 95-25046. 304p. (C). 1996. text 70.00 (*0-19-818319-4*, Clarendon Pr) OUP.

— Turkish Embassy Letters: Lady Mary Wortley Montagu. LC 93-928. 200p. (C). 1993. 35.00 (*0-8203-1580-X*) U of Ga Pr.

Montagu, Lady Mary Wortley & Wharncliffe, Jame A. Letters & Works of Lady Mary Wortley Montagu, 2 vols., Set. Lord Wharncliffe, ed. LC 70-115358. reprint ed. 125.00 (*0-404-04378-X*) AMS Pr.

Montagu, Lord & Burgess-Wise, David. A Daimler Century: The Full History of Britain's Oldest Car Maker. (Illus.). 256p. 1995. 44.95 (*1-85260-494-8*, Pub. by J H Haynes & Co) Motorbooks Intl.

Montagu-Nathan, Montagu. Contemporary Russian Composers. LC 72-109795. 329p. 1970. reprint ed. lib. bdg. 65.00 (*0-8371-4285-7*, MORC, Greenwood Pr) Greenwood.

— Contemporary Russian Composers. 329p. 1990. reprint ed. lib. bdg. 79.00 (*0-7812-9041-4*) Rprt Serv.

— Glinka. LC 74-24156. reprint ed. 29.50 (*0-404-13049-6*) AMS Pr.

— A History of Russian Music. LC 76-82815. 1918. 30.00 (*0-8196-0251-5*) Biblo.

— A History of Russian Music: Being an Account of the Rise & Progress of the Russian School of Composers, with a Survey of Their Lives & a Description of Their Works. 346p. 1990. reprint ed. lib. bdg. 79.00 (*0-7812-9034-1*) Rprt Serv.

— Moussorgsky. LC 74-24157. 100 p. 1976. reprint ed. 29.50 (*0-404-13050-X*) AMS Pr.

— Rimsky-Korsakov. LC 74-24158. reprint ed. 29.50 (*0-404-13051-8*) AMS Pr.

Montagu, Richard. Appello Caesarem: A Just Appeale from Two Unjust Informers. LC 75-38210. (English Experience Ser.: No. 475). 348p. 1972. reprint ed. 75.00 (*90-221-0475-3*) Walter J Johnson.

— A Gagg for the New Gospel? No: A New Gagg for an Old Goose. LC 74-28872. (English Experience Ser.: No. 751). 1975. reprint ed. 26.00 (*90-221-0751-5*) Walter J Johnson.

Montagu, Walter. The Shepherds' Paradise. Poynting, Sarah, ed. LC 99-188044. (Illus.). 146p. 1998. text 45.00 (*0-19-729035-3*) OUP.

Montague. Abstracts & Recursion Theory. (Studies in Logic). write for info. (*0-444-86159-9*, North Holland) Elsevier.

Montague, Alan P. Legal Problems in Emergency Medicine. (Illus.). 176p. 1996. text 54.00 (*0-19-262497-0*) OUP.

Montague, Alan P. & Hopper, Andrew. Legal Problems in Emergency Medicine. (Illus.). 176p. 1996. pap. text 49.95 (*0-19-262496-2*) OUP.

***Montague, Andrew A.** Successful Shotgun Shooting. (Illus.). 200p. 2000. pap. 16.95 (*1-56833-164-9*) Madison Bks UPA.

Montague, Bill. Concord Guidebook: Tourist Information for Concord, Mass. Roof, Christopher, ed. LC 95-67744. (Illus.). 56p. 1995. pap. text 15.95 (*0-9638644-4-0*) Concord MouseTrap.

— Little Mouse: The Mouse Who Lived with Henry David Thoreau at Walden Pond. Roof, Christopher, ed. LC 93-73231. (Illus.). 56p. (Orig.). (J). (gr. 2-4). 1993. pap. text 7.95 (*0-9638644-0-8*) Concord MouseTrap.

Montague-Brown, Anthony, jt. auth. see Howlett, Peter.

Montague, C. J. Sixty Years in Waifdom: The Ragged School Movement in English History. LC 79-5721. (Social History of Education 1st Ser.: No. 7). (Illus.). xv, 459p. 1969. reprint ed. 17.50 (*0-678-08450-5*) Kelley.

— Sixty Years in Waifdom or, the Ragged School Movement in English History. LC 70-108225. (Criminology, Law Enforcement, & Social Problems Ser.: No. 108). 1970. reprint ed. 18.00 (*0-87585-108-8*) Patterson Smith.

Montague, Charles E. Action & Other Stories. LC 70-134971. (Short Story Index Reprint Ser.). 1977. 19.95 (*0-8369-3702-3*) Ayer.

— Dramatic Values. (BCL1-PR English Literature Ser.). 274p. 1992. reprint ed. lib. bdg. 79.00 (*0-7812-7095-2*) Rprt Serv.

— Dramatic Values. reprint ed. 14.00 (*0-403-01112-4*) Scholarly.

— Fiery Particles. LC 79-131781. 1971. 29.00 (*0-403-00668-6*) Scholarly.

— Tales of a Nomad: or Sport & Strife. LC 72-5559. (Black Heritage Library Collection). 1977. reprint ed. 21.95 (*0-8369-9144-3*) Ayer.

Montague, Clifford. Farewell, Goodbye, the End? The Secret History of a Literary Era. 96p. (Orig.). 1993. pap. 8.95 (*1-56474-050-1*) Fithian Pr.

Montague, D. Dictionary of Building & Civil Engineering: English-French - French-English. (ENG & FRE.). 468p. (C). 1996. 75.00 (*0-419-19910-1*) Routledge.

Montague, Dan. Second Chance. LC 98-12908. 368p. 1998. 26.95 (*0-525-94420-6*) NAL.

— Second Chance: A Novel. 384p. 1999. mass mkt. 6.99 (*0-451-19738-0*) NAL.

— White Wings. 1998. mass mkt. 6.99 (*0-451-19565-5*, Sig) NAL.

Montague, Darlana. Inner Pathways. (Illus.). 190p. (Orig.). 1998. pap. 17.95 (*1-889529-04-4*) Two Feathers.

— Messages from Home . . . Gifts from the Pleiades. (Illus.). 107p. 1994. mass mkt. 29.95 (*1-889529-03-6*) Two Feathers.

— Messages from Your Angels, 3 vols., Set. (Illus.). (Orig.). (J). (gr. 1-5). 1998. pap. 22.95 (*1-889529-09-5*) Two Feathers.

— Messages from Your Angels, Vol. I. (Illus.). 24p. (Orig.). (J). (gr. 1-5). 1995. pap. 7.95 (*1-889529-06-0*) Two Feathers.

— Messages from Your Angels, Vol. II. (Illus.). 18p. (Orig.). (J). (gr. 1-5). 1998. pap. 7.95 (*1-889529-07-9*) Two Feathers.

— Messages from Your Angels, Vol. III. (Illus.). 20p. (Orig.). (J). (gr. 1-5). 1998. pap. 7.95 (*1-889529-08-7*) Two Feathers.

— Your Body Speaks: Having 'Pun' with Your Body. (Illus.). 184p. (Orig.). 1998. pap. 11.95 (*1-889529-05-2*) Two Feathers.

Montague, Francis C. Arnold Toynbee. LC 78-63786. (Johns Hopkins University, Studies in the Social Sciences, Thirtieth Ser.: Vol. 1). reprint ed. 11.50 (*0-404-61051-X*) AMS Pr.

— History of England from the Accession of James First to the Restoration, 1603-1660. LC 78-5631. (Political History of England Ser.: No. 7). reprint ed. 45.00 (*0-404-50777-8*) AMS Pr.

Montague, Francis C., ed. see Bentham, Jeremy.

Montague, G. W. History & Genealogy of Peter Montague, of Nansemond & Lancaster County, Virgina & His Descendants, 1621-1894. (Illus.). 494p. 1989. reprint ed. pap. 74.00 (*0-8328-0879-2*); reprint ed. lib. bdg. 82.00 (*0-8328-0878-4*) Higginson Bk Co.

Montague, G. W. & Montague, W. L. History & Genealogy of the Montague Family of America, Descended from Richard Montague of Hadley, Mass., & Peter of Lancaster County, Virginia, with Genealogical Notes of Other Families by the Name of Montague. (Illus.). 785p. 1989. reprint ed. pap. 117.50 (*0-8328-0877-6*); reprint ed. lib. bdg. 125.50 (*0-8328-0876-8*) Higginson Bk Co.

Montague, George T. The Apocalypse & the Third Millennium: Today's Guide to the Book of Revelation. rev. ed. LC 98-28993. Orig. Title: The Apocalypse. 260p. 1998. pap. 10.99 (*1-56955-106-5*) Servant.

— Holy Spirit: Growth of a Biblical Tradition. 374p. 1994. pap. 16.95 (*1-56563-056-4*) Hendrickson MA.

— Mark: Good News for Hard Times - A Popular Commentary on the Earliest Gospel. 197p. 1992. 9.95 (*0-940535-53-X*, UP 153) Franciscan U Pr.

— Our Father, Our Mother: Mary & the Faces of God. 175p. 1990. pap. 3.48 (*0-940535-28-9*, UP128) Franciscan U Pr.

— Understanding the Bible: A Basic Introduction to Biblical Interpretation. LC 97-22381. 272p. (Orig.). 1997. pap. 19.95 (*0-8091-3744-5*, 3744-5) Paulist Pr.

***Montague, George T.** The Vision of the Beloved Disciple: Meeting Jesus in the Gospel of John. LC 99-54875. 96p. 2000. pap. 5.95 (*0-8189-0835-1*) Alba.

Montague, George T., et al. The Living Light Vol. 35, No. 1: Fall, 1998 - Special Feature - Countdown to the Third Millennium - God the Father. Marthaler, Berard L., ed. 104p. 1998. pap. 8.95 (*1-57455-274-0*) US Catholic.

Montague, George T., jt. auth. see McDonnell, Kilian.

Montague, Gilbert H. The Rise & Progress of the Standard Oil Company. LC 73-2525. (Big Business; Economic Power in a Free Society Ser.). 1973. reprint ed. 15.95 (*0-405-05104-2*) Ayer.

Montague, H. Patrick. The Saints & Martyrs of Ireland. (Illus.). 138p. 1981. 18.95 (*0-86140-106-9*, Pub. by Smyth); pap. 7.95 (*0-86140-107-7*, Pub. by Smyth) Dufour.

Montague, Jeanne. Child of the Mist. large type ed. (Magna Large Print Ser.). 562p. 1998. 29.99 (*0-7505-1191-5*, Pub. by Mgna Lrg Print) Ulverscroft.

— Flower of My Heart. large type ed. (Black Satin Romance Ser.). 376p. 1997. 27.99 (*1-86110-047-7*) Ulverscroft.

— Rupert the Devil. large type ed. (Dales Large Print Ser.). 1995. pap. 18.99 (*1-85389-575-X*, Dales) Ulverscroft.

— Touch Me with Fire. large type ed. (Dales Large Print Ser.). 422p. 1995. pap. 18.99 (*1-85389-508-3*, Dales) Ulverscroft.

— Wild Bride. large type ed. (Black Satin Romance Ser.). 487p. 1997. 27.99 (*1-86110-039-6*) Ulverscroft.

Montague, Jeanne F. Cavalier. large type ed. (Dales Large Print Ser.). 379p. 1996. pap. 18.99 (*1-85389-574-1*, Dales) Ulverscroft.

— Courtney's Wench. large type ed. 390p. 1994. pap. 18.99 (*1-85389-485-0*) Ulverscroft.

— The Falcon & the Dove. large type ed. (Dales Large Print Ser.). 373p. 1997. pap. 18.99 (*1-85389-682-9*) Ulverscroft.

— The Lord of Kestle Mount. large type ed. (Dales Large Print Ser.). 389p. 1996. pap. 18.99 (*1-85389-666-7*, Dales) Ulverscroft.

— The Why of Albert Schweitzer. large type ed. 16p. 1967. 27.99 (*0-85456-575-2*) Ulverscroft.

Montague, Joel B., Jr. Class & Nationality: English & American Studies. 1963. pap. 16.95 (*0-8084-0080-0*) NCUP.

Montague, John. About Love: Poems. LC 93-14670. 169p. (Orig.). 1993. pap. 13.95 (*1-878818-23-6*, Pub. by Sheep Meadow) U Pr of New Eng.

— Basic Perspective Drawing. 2nd ed. LC 92-36128. 1993. pap. 32.95 (*0-442-01263-2*, VNR) Wiley.

— Basic Perspective Drawing. 3rd ed. LC 97-44552. (Architecture Ser.). 1998. text 32.95 (*0-442-02510-6*, VNR) Wiley.

— Basic Perspective Drawing: A Visual Approach. 3rd ed. 272p. 1998. pap. 39.95 (*0-471-29231-1*) Wiley.

— Book of Irish Verse: Irish Poetry from the Six Century to the Present. 400p. 12.95 (*0-88486-192-9*, Bristol Park Bks) Arrowood Pr.

— Book of Irish Verse: Irish Poetry from the Sixth Century to the Present. 1995. 10.98 (*0-88365-881-X*) Galahad Bks.

— Born in Brooklyn. 115p. 1991. pap. 10.00 (*1-877727-13-X*) White Pine.

— Collected Poems. LC 95-61011. 376p. (C). 1995. 31.95 (*0-916390-69-1*); pap. 19.95 (*0-916390-68-3*) Wake Forest.

— The Death of a Chieftain: And Other Stories. LC 99-176321. 168p. 1999. pap. 15.95 (*0-86327-673-3*) Irish Amer Bk.

— The Figure in the Cave & Other Essays. LC 89-4635. (Irish Studies). 240p. (Orig.). 1989. pap. 17.95 (*0-8156-0240-5*) Syracuse U Pr.

— The Great Cloak. 63p. 1978. pap. 6.95 (*0-916390-07-1*) Wake Forest.

— Love Present: And Other Stories. 1999. pap. 11.95 (*0-86327-672-5*) Wolfhound Press.

— Mount Eagle. LC 88-40663. 75p. 1989. pap. 6.95 (*0-916390-33-0*) Wake Forest.

— An Occasion of Sin. LC 94-176670. 200p. 1992. pap. 12.00 (*1-877727-21-0*) White Pine.

Montague, John & Butz, William. Building the Weekend Skiff. (Illus.). 180p. 1997. pap. 19.95 (*1-888671-10-6*) Tiller.

Montague, John & Redshaw, Thomas D. The Rough Field. 5th rev. ed. LC 89-40526. (Illus.). 100p. 1989. pap. 7.95 (*0-916390-42-X*) Wake Forest.

Montague, John, tr. see Guillevic.

Montague, Ludwell L. General Walter Bedell Smith As Director of Central Intelligence, October 1950 - February 1953. 500p. 1992. 45.00 (*0-271-00750-8*); pap. 22.50 (*0-271-00751-6*) Pa St U Pr.

Montague, Margaret P. Up Eel River. LC 77-150552. (Short Story Index Reprint Ser.). (Illus.). 1977. reprint ed. 19.95 (*0-8369-3849-6*) Ayer.

Montague, Marjorie. Computers, Cognition, & Writing Instruction. LC 89-27033. (SUNY Series in Computers in Education). (Illus.). 205p. (C). 1990. text 64.50 (*0-7914-0335-1*); pap. text 21.95 (*0-7914-0336-X*) State U NY Pr.

Montague, Mary J. Cruising at 55: A Humorous Guide to RV Life & Travel. LC 95-78633. (Illus.). 120p. (Orig.). 1995. pap. 12.50 (*0-9647787-0-X*) Big Blckft Pubng.

Montague, Masani. Dread Culture: A Rastawoman's Story. LC 95-170572. 190p. 1994. per. write for info. (*0-920813-53-4*) Sister Vis Pr.

***Montague, Michiyo.** Settlement Alternatives Workbook. 2000. pap. 9.95 (*1-883697-01-8*) Hara Pub.

Montague, Owen, jt. ed. see Fraser, George C.

Montague, Phillip. In the Interests of Others: An Essay in Moral Philosophy. LC 92-20029. (Philosophical Studies in Philosophy: Vol. 55). 160p. (C). 1992. lib. bdg. 113.00 (*0-7923-1856-0*, Pub. by Kluwer Academic) Kluwer Academic.

— Punishment As Societal Defense. (Studies in Social & Political Philosophy). 224p. (C). 1995. pap. text 22.95 (*0-8476-8072-X*); lib. bdg. 56.50 (*0-8476-8071-1*) Rowman.

***Montague, Rebecca.** A Wild Sea. LC 99-90869. 174p. 2000. pap. 12.95 (*0-9671203-2-2*) Cape Winds Pr.

Montague, Richard. Formal Philosophy: Selected Papers of Richard Montague. LC 73-77159. 375p. reprint ed. pap. 116.30 (*0-8357-8134-8*, 203382900087) Bks Demand.

Montague, Richard & Goldstein, Joel. Lotus 1-2-3 the Easy Way. (Illus.). 53p. (Orig.). (C). 1990. pap. text 5.95 (*0-936285-09-5*) U New Haven Pr.

Montague, Rosie. Brazilian Three-Dimensional Embroidery: Instructions & 60 Transfer Patterns. (Embroidery, Needlework Designs Ser.). (Illus.). 64p. (Orig.). 1983. pap. 4.95 (*0-486-24384-2*) Dover.

Montague-Smith, Ann. Mathematics in Nursery Education. LC 97-199883. 160p. 1997. pap. 24.95 (*1-85346-472-4*, Pub. by David Fulton) Taylor & Francis.

— Supporting Science & Technology: A Handbook for Those Who Assist in Early Years Settings. LC 98-184565. vi, 106p. 1998. pap. 24.95 (*1-85346-513-5*, Pub. by David Fulton) Taylor & Francis.

Montague, Stephen. Live Electronics. (Contemporary Music Review Ser.). 237p. 1991. text 23.00 (*3-7186-5116-5*, Harwood Acad Pubs) Gordon & Breach.

Montague, Terry. Fireweed. LC 92-72487. 1992. pap. 10.95 (*1-55503-407-1*, 01111078) Covenant Comms.

Montague, Terry B. Mine Angels Round About: Mormon Missionary Evacuation from Western Germany - 1939. 13.50 (*0-685-30414-0*) Roylance Pub.

Montague, W. L., jt. auth. see Montague, G. W.

Montague, William P. Belief Unbound. LC 72-109630. (Select Bibliographies Reprint Ser.). 1977. 18.95 (*0-8369-5239-1*) Ayer.

— The Way of Things: A Philosophy of Knowledge, Nature & Value. LC 75-3283. reprint ed. 49.50 (*0-404-59271-6*) AMS Pr.

Montaigne, Fen. Reeling in Russia: An American Angler in Russia. LC 98-10241. 275p. 1998. text 24.95 (*0-312-18595-2*) St Martin.

— Reeling in Russia: An American Angler in Russia. 288p. 1999. pap. 14.95 (*0-312-20809-X*) St Martin.

Montaigne, Fen & Kalugin, Oleg. The First Directorate: My 32 Years in Intelligence & Espionage Against the West. (Illus.). 375p. 1997. reprint ed. text 24.00 (*0-7881-5111-8*) DIANE Pub.

Montaigne, Michel de. An Apology for Raymond Sebond. Screech, M. A., ed. & tr. by. 240p. 1988. pap. 10.95 (*0-14-044493-9*, Penguin Classics) Viking Penguin.

— The Autobiography of Michel de Montaigne. Lowenthal, Marvin, ed. & tr. by. from FRE. LC 98-36153. (Nonpareil Bks.: Vol. 80). 408p. 1999. pap. 17.95 (*1-56792-098-5*) Godine.

— The Complete Essays. Screech, M. A., ed. & tr. by. 1,344p. 1993. pap. 23.95 (*0-14-044604-4*, Penguin Classics) Viking Penguin.

— The Complete Essays of Montaigne. Frame, Donald M., tr. xxiii, 883p. 1958. 65.00 (*0-8047-0485-6*); pap. 22.50 (*0-8047-0486-4*) Stanford U Pr.

— The Complete Works of Montaigne: Essays, Travel Journal, Letters. Frame, Donald M., tr. xxvi, 1094p. 1957. 85.00 (*0-8047-0484-8*) Stanford U Pr.

— De la Vanite. (FRE.). 141p. 1989. pap. 18.95 (*0-7859-1556-7*, 2869302282) Fr & Eur.

— La Educacion de los Hijos. (Fondo 2000 Ser.). (SPA.). pap. 2.99 (*968-16-5119-7*, Pub. by Fondo) Continental Bk.

— Essais. Chapman, J. Carol & Mouret, Francois J., eds. (Renaissance Library). (FRE.). 202p. (C). 1978. text 18.95 (*0-485-13810-7*, Pub. by Athlone Pr) Humanities.

— Les Essais. (Coll. Prestige). (FRE.). 49.95 (*0-685-34190-9*); pap. 5.95 (*0-685-34191-7*) Fr & Eur.

— Les Essais, 3 vols. (FRE.). 1973. write for info. (*0-318-63469-4*) Fr & Eur.

— Les Essais. fac. ed. Rat, Maurice, ed. (Class. Garnier Ser.). (FRE.). 1225p. 1976. write for info. (*0-7859-5256-X*) Fr & Eur.

— Essais, 3 vols., 1. (Folio Ser.: Nos. 289, 290, & 291). (FRE.). 1973. 10.95 (*2-07-036289-2*) Schoenhof.

— Essais, 3 vols., 2. (Folio Ser.: Nos. 289, 290, & 291). (FRE.). 1973. 10.95 (*2-07-036290-6*) Schoenhof.

— Essais, 3 vols., 3. (Folio Ser.: Nos. 289, 290, & 291). (FRE.). 1973. 10.95 (*2-07-036291-4*) Schoenhof.

— Les Essais, 5 vols. in 3, Set. (FRE.). cxxxviii, 2832p. 1981. reprint ed. write for info. (*3-487-07049-9*) G Olms Pubs.

— Essais, Tome I. (FRE.). 512p. 1973. pap. 13.95 (*0-7859-3729-3*) Fr & Eur.

— Essais, Tome II. (FRE.). 640p. 1973. pap. 13.95 (*0-7859-3730-7*) Fr & Eur.

— Essais, Tome III. (FRE.). 1973. pap. 13.95 (*0-7859-3731-5*) Fr & Eur.

— Essays, 2 vols, Set. Friswell, J. H., ed. 1975. 500.00 (*0-87968-311-2*) Gordon Pr.

— The Essays: A Selection. Screech, M. A., ed. & tr. by. LC 95-105730. 480p. 1994. pap. 12.95 (*0-14-044602-8*, Penguin Classics) Viking Penguin.

— Journal de Voyage. (FRE.). 1983. pap. 19.95 (*0-7859-4185-1*) Fr & Eur.

— Journal de Voyage. (Folio Ser.: No. 1473). (FRE.). 512p. 1983. pap. 15.95 (*2-07-037473-4*) Schoenhof.

— Montaigne: Essays. 1993. pap. 12.95 (*0-14-017897-X*, Penguin Classics) Viking Penguin.

— Montaigne's Essays & Selected Writings. Frame, Donald M., ed. (ENG & FRE.). 496p. (Orig.). 1969. pap. 23.95 (*0-312-54635-1*) St Martin.

— Oeuvres Completes. Thibaudet, Albert, ed. (FRE.). 1824p. 1962. lib. bdg. 125.00 (*0-7859-3767-6*, 2070103633) Fr & Eur.

— Oeuvres Completes. deluxe ed. Thibaudet, Albert & Rat, eds. (Pleiade Ser.). (FRE.). 85.95 (*2-07-010363-3*) Schoenhof.

— Selected Essays. LC 95-49132. (Thrift Editions Ser.). (Illus.). 96p. (Orig.). 1996. pap. text 1.50 (*0-486-29109-X*) Dover.

— Selections from the Essays. Frame, Donald M., ed. & tr. by. (Crofts Classics). 144p. 1943. pap. text 4.95 (*0-88295-105-X*) Harlan Davidson.

Montaigne, Michel de & Boetie, Etienne De La. Discours de la Servitude Volontaire ou le Contr'un. (FRE.). 90p. 1947. 13.95 (*0-8288-9628-3*) Fr & Eur.

Montaigne, Michel de & Dedeyan, Charles. Journal de Voyage en Italie. (FRE.). 520p. 1946. 23.50 (*0-7859-0696-7*) Fr & Eur.

Montaigne, Michel de, et al. Trois Essais de Montaigne. 4th ed. (FRE.). 150p. 1967. 15.00 (*0-686-54778-0*) Fr & Eur.

Montaigne, Michel de, see Montaigne, Michel de.

Montaigue, Erle. Advanced Dim-Mak: The Finer Points of Death-Point Striking. (Illus.). 328p. 1994. pap. 35.00 (*0-87364-779-3*) Paladin Pr.

***Montaigue, Erle.** Baguazhang: Fighting Secrets of the Eight Trigram Palms. 152p. 1999. 39.00 (*1-58160-037-2*) Paladin Pr.

Montaigue, Erle. Dim-Mak: Death-Point Striking. (Illus.). 240p. 1993. pap. 25.00 (*0-87364-718-1*) Paladin Pr.

— The Dim-Mak Encyclopedia: The Main Meridians. (Illus.). 432p. 1997. pap. 50.00 (*0-87364-923-0*) Paladin Pr.

***Montaigue, Erle.** Tai Chi: An Introduction to the Chinese Art of Healing & Self-Defense. (Illus.). 96p. 2000. pap. 18.95 (*1-85868-868-X*, Pub. by Carlton Bks Ltd) Natl Bk Netwk.

Montaigue, Erle. Ultimate Dim-Mak: How to Fight a Grappler & Win. (Illus.). 256p. 1996. pap. 35.00 (*0-87364-878-1*) Paladin Pr.

Montaigue, Erle & Babín, Michael. Power Taiji. (Illus.). 200p. 1995. pap. 25.00 (*0-87364-846-3*) Paladin Pr.

Montaigue, Erle & Simpson, Wally. The Encyclopedia of Dim-Mak: The Extra Meridians, Points, & More. LC 97-169713. (Illus.). 136p. 1997. text 30.00 (*0-87364-928-1*) Paladin Pr.

Montalban, Juan Perez De, see Perez De Montalban, Juan.

Montalban, M. Vasquez. El Premio. 1998. pap. 9.95 (*84-08-02239-3*) Planeta.

— Tres Historias de Amor. 1999. pap. text 9.95 (*84-08-02810-3*) Planeta.

***Montalban, M Vazquez.** Quinteto De Buenos Aires. 1999. pap. text 12.95 (*84-08-02812-X*) Planeta.

Montalban, Manuel V. The Angst-Ridden Executive. Emery, Ed, tr. from SPA. (Mask Noir Ser.). 240p. (Orig.). 1990. pap. 9.95 (*1-85242-159-2*) Serpents Tail.

— Barcelonas. Robinson, Andrew, tr. LC 92-4830. (Illus.). 280p. (gr. 13). 1992. 35.00 (*0-86091-353-8*, A6395, Pub. by Verso) Norton.

— Galindez. Christensen, Carol & Christensen, Thomas, trs. from SPA. 320p. 1992. text 21.00 (*0-689-12121-0*, Pub. by Ctrl Bur voor Schimmel) Macmillan.

— Murder in the Central Committee. 224p. 1997. pap. text 12.99 (*1-85242-131-2*) Serpents Tail.

Montalban, Manuel Vazquez. Quinteto de Buenos Aires. 1997. 27.95 (*84-08-02213-X*) Planeta Edit.

Montalban, Manuel Vazquez, see Vazquez Montalban, Manuel.

***Montalban, Vazquez.** Off Side. 278p. 2000. pap. 13.00 (*1-85242-742-6*) Serpents Tail.

— Olympic Death. (Mask Noir Ser.). 207p. 2000. pap. 11.99 (*1-85242-257-2*) Serpents Tail.

— Southern Seas. LC 99-65166. 214p. 2000. pap. 13.00 (*1-85242-700-0*) Serpents Tail.

Montalbano, Andrew J. Sicilian Sun. LC 97-91452. (Illus.). 815p. 1997. 55.00 (*0-9656710-0-3*) New Writers Ink.

Montalbano, Bill, jt. auth. see Hiaasen, Carl.

***Montalbano, William D.** Basilica. 304p. 1999. 23.95 (*0-399-14418-8*) Putnam Pub Group.

— Basilica. 2000. reprint ed. mass mkt. 6.99 (*0-515-12723-X*, Jove) Berkley Pub.

Montalbetti, Rocio, ed. see Carlson, Daniel J.

Montalbo, Thomas. Public Speaking Made Easy. 1994. pap. 10.00 (*0-87980-434-3*) Wilshire.

Montaldi, J., tr. see Sernesi, Edoardo.

Montaldi, J. A. & Mond, D., eds. Singularity Theory & Its Applications Vol. I: Warwick 1989: Symposium Held at the University of Warwick 1988-1989. (Lecture Notes in Mathematics Ser.: Vol. 1462). viii, 428p. 1991. 62.95 (*0-387-53737-6*) Spr-Verlag.

Montaldi, James, jt. ed. see Kaiser, Robin.

Montaldo, Jonathan, ed. see Merton, Thomas.

Montale, Eugenio. The Bones of Cuttlefish. Mazza, Antonino, tr. Orig. Title: Ossi di Seppia. 1995. pap. 9.95 (*0-88962-197-7*) Mosaic.

— The Butterfly of Dinard. Singh, G., tr. LC 72-160048. 186p. reprint ed. pap. 57.70 (*0-7837-9584-X*, 206033300005) Bks Demand.

— Collected Poems, 1920-1954: Bilingual Edition. Galassi, Jonathan, tr. & anno. by. LC 97-16641. (ENG & ITA.). 624p. 1998. text 40.00 (*0-374-12554-6*) FS&G.

***Montale, Eugenio.** Collected Poems, 1920-1954: Bilingual Edition. Galassi, Jonathan, tr. & anno. by. (ITA & ENG.). 624p. 2000. pap. 18.00 (*0-374-52625-7*) FS&G.

Montale, Eugenio. Cuttlefish Bones. Arrowsmith, William, tr. 1994. pap. 10.95 (*0-393-31171-6*) Norton.

— It Depends: A Poet's Notebook. Singh, G., tr. from ITA. & intro. by. LC 80-16629.Tr. of Quaderno Di Quattro Anni. 192p. 1980. 7.95 (*0-8112-0773-0*, Pub. by New Directions) Norton.

— The Occasions. Arrowsmith, William, tr. from ITA. & pref. by. LC 86-16269.Tr. of Le/Occasion. 169p. 1987. pap. 9.95 (*0-393-30324-1*) Norton.

— Satura. LC 97-32720. 240p. 2000. pap. 13.00 (*0-393-31977-6*) Norton.

— Satura: 1962-1970. Warren, Rosanna, ed. Arrowsmith, William, tr. & notes by. LC 97-32720. 384p. 1998. 29.95 (*0-393-04647-8*) Norton.

Montale, Eugenio. 2nd Life of Art. Galassi, Jonathan, ed. & tr. by. from ITA. LC 81-9861. 350p. 1985. pap. 14.00 (*0-912946-85-7*, Ecco Press) HarperTrade.

Montale, Eugenio. The Second Life of Art: Selected Essays of Eugenio Montale. Galassi, Jonathan, ed. & tr. by. from ITA. LC 81-9861. 375p. 1982. 17.50 (*0-912946-84-9*, Ecco Press) HarperTrade.

— Selected Poems. Camson, Glauco, ed. LC 65-15669. 192p. 1966. pap. 9.95 (*0-8112-0119-8*, NDP193, Pub. by New Directions) Norton.

— The Storm & Other Poems. Wright, Charles, tr. from ITA. (Field Translation Ser.: No. 1). 1978. pap. 8.95 (*0-932440-01-0*) Oberlin Coll Pr.

Montale, Eugenio & Reed, Jeremy. Coast Guard's House. 224p. 1990. pap. 18.95 (*1-85224-100-4*, Pub. by Bloodaxe Bks) Dufour.

Montalembert, Charles, pseud. The Monks of the West from St. Benedict to St. Bernard, 6 vols., Set. LC 03-11386. reprint ed. 410.00 (*0-404-04410-7*) AMS Pr.

Montali, Richard J., ed. Mycobacterial Infections of Zoo Animals. LC 77-60860. (Research Symposia of the National Zoological Park Ser.: No. 1). (Illus.). 276p. 1979. text 30.00 (*0-87474-644-2*, MOMI); pap. text 18.95 (*0-87474-645-0*, MOMIP) Smithsonian.

Montali, Richard J. & Migaki, George, eds. The Comparative Pathology of Zoo Animals. LC 79-24354. (Research Symposia of the National Zoological Park Ser.: No. 6). (Illus.). 684p. 1980. pap. text 29.95 (*0-87474-643-4*, MOCCP) Smithsonian.

Montalto, Karen, ed. Insurance Department Directory. rev. ed. 204p. (C). 1996. ring bd. 45.00 (*0-89382-405-4*) Nat Assn Insurance.

— Insurance Department Directory. rev. ed. 206p. (C). 1998. ring bd. 45.00i (*0-89382-517-4*, INS-OM) Nat Assn Insurance.

— Insurance Department Directory. 7th rev. ed. 207p. (C). 1997. ring bd. 45.00 (*0-89382-470-4*, INS-OM) Nat Assn Insurance.

— Issues 1998. 10th rev. ed. 82p. 1998. pap. 35.00i (*0-89382-544-1*, ISS-ZB98) Nat Assn Insurance.

— Issues 1996. 8th rev. ed. 80p. (Orig.). (C). 1996. pap. 35.00 (*0-89382-399-6*, ISS-ZB) Nat Assn Insurance.

— Proceedings Cumulative Index, 1990-1994. 660p. 1998. 150.00i (*0-89382-577-8*, PCI-ZB90) Nat Assn Insurance.

— Proceedings of the NAIC. 1286p. (Orig.). (C). 1996. pap. 325.00 (*0-89382-423-2*, PRC-2C) Nat Assn Insurance.

— Proceedings of the NAIC. rev. ed. 980p. (Orig.). (C). 1997. 325.00 (*0-89382-439-9*, PRC-ZS) Nat Assn Insurance.

— Proceedings of the NAIC: 1996 Third Quarter. 858p. (C). 1997. 180.00 (*0-89382-490-9*, PRC-ZS) Nat Assn Insurance.

— Proceedings of the NAIC: 1996 Third Quarter, Vol. II. 586p. (C). 1997. 180.00 (*0-89382-491-7*, PRC-ZS) Nat Assn Insurance.

— Proceedings of the NAIC: 1996 2nd Quarter. 1152p. (C). 1997. 325.00 (*0-89382-467-4*, PRC-ZS) Nat Assn Insurance.

— Proceedings of the NAIC, 1994, 4th Quarter. rev. ed. 1350p. (C). 1996. 325.00 (*0-89382-378-3*, PRC-25) Nat Assn Insurance.

— Proceedings of the NAIC, 1995, 2nd Quarter. annuals rev. ed. 920p. (Orig.). (C). 1996. 325.00 (*0-89382-409-7*, PRC-ZS) Nat Assn Insurance.

— Proceedings of the NAIC 1997 First Quarter. rev. ed. 1164p. (C). 1999. 180.00i (*0-89382-578-6*, PRC-ZS97-1) Nat Assn Insurance.

— Proceedings of the National Association of Insurance Commissioners. rev. ed. 950p. (Orig.). 1996. 325.00 (*0-89382-388-0*) Nat Assn Insurance.

— Proceedings of the National Association of Insurance Commissioners: 1995 3rd Quarter. 1130p. (Orig.). (C). 1996. 325.00 (*0-89382-413-5*, PRC-ZS) Nat Assn Insurance.

— Proceedings of the National Association of Insurance Commissioners, 1991, Vol. II. 1343p. (C). 1992. 125.00 (*0-89382-176-4*) Nat Assn Insurance.

Montalto, Nicholas V., ed. The International Institute Movement: A Guide to Records of Immigrant Service Agencies in the United States. (Illus.). xx, 74p. 1978. pap. text 6.95 (*0-932833-01-2*) Immig His Res.

Montalva, Eduardo Frei, see Frei Montalva, Eduardo.

Montalvao e Silva, J. M. & Pina da Silva, F. A., eds. Vibration & Wear in High Speed Rotating Machinery: Proceedings of the NATO Advanced Study Institute on Vibration & Wear Damage in High Speed Rotating Machinery, Troia, Sebutal, April 10-22, 1989. (C). 1990. text 392.50 (*0-7923-0533-7*) Kluwer Academic.

Montalvdao e Silva, J. M., jt. auth. see Maia, Nuno Manuel Mendes.

Montalvo-Barbot, Alfredo. Political Conflict & Constitutional Change in Puerto Rico, 1898-1952. LC 97-33539. 176p. (C). 1997. 37.00 (*0-7618-0901-5*) U Pr of Amer.

Montalvo, Berta. Miniaturas. LC 88-84023. (Coleccion Espejo de Paciencia). (SPA., Illus.). 38p. (Orig.). 1991. pap. 6.00 (*0-89729-522-6*) Ediciones.

— Para Mi Gaveta. LC 88-84022. (Coleccion Espejo de Paciencia). (SPA.). 139p. (Orig.). 1990. pap. 12.00 (*0-89729-523-4*) Ediciones.

Montalvo, Jose A. Ordonez y, see Ordonez y Montalvo, Jose A., ed.

Montalvo, Joseph G., Jr., ed. Cotton Dust: Controlling an Occupational Health Hazard. LC 82-6857. (ACS Symposium Ser.: No. 189). 1982. 49.95 (*0-8412-0716-X*) Am Chemical.

— Cotton Dust: Controlling an Occupational Health Hazard. LC 82-6857. (ACS Symposium Ser.: Vol. 189). 352p. reprint ed. pap. 109.20 (*0-608-03114-3*, 206356700007) Bks Demand.

Montalvo, Juan. Montalvo en Su Epistolario. LC 78-9810. (Illus.). 456p. 1982. pap. 10.00 (*0-8477-0856-X*) U of PR Pr.

Montalvo, Maria, tr. see Esparza, June F.

Montalvo, Soledad De, see De Montalvo, Soledad.

Montan, Denise, ed. see Heydary, Rassol.

Montana. Stepping Our, Starting Over. 1992. pap. text 19.25 (*0-07-042832-8*) McGraw.

— Stepping Out, Starting Over. 2nd ed. LC 99-229195. 1999. pap. 25.94 (*0-07-234773-2*) McGraw.

Montana & NILS Publishing Company. Montana Related Laws to the Insurance Laws. LC 97-75434. 1997. write for info. (*0-89246-488-7*) NILS Pub.

***Montana, Andrew.** The Art Movement in Australia: Design, Taste & Society, 1875-1900. (Illus.). 450p. 2000. 80.00 (*0-522-84879-6*, Pub. by Melbourne Univ Pr) Paul & Co Pubs.

Montana, Bruce, jt. auth. see Ulferts, Stuart.

Montana Council of Teachers of Mathematics, ed. Integrated Mathematics: A Modeling Approach Using Technology. LC 96-222251. 194p. 1996. 13.00 (*0-536-59532-1*) Pearson Custom.

Montana, Denby. Orion's Belt. Mould, Owen, ed. 85p. (Orig.). 1994. pap. 8.00 (*0-9644856-9-9*, Celtic Butterfly) Spellman-Tris.

Montana Fish, Wildlife & Parks Department Staff, et al. A Field Guide to Montana Fishes. 2nd ed. LC 96-17534. (Illus.). 104p. 1996. pap. 12.95 (*1-56044-479-7*) Falcon Pub Inc.

***Montana, Gladiola.** Cowgirl Saddle Pals. (Small Treasures Ser.: Vol. 5). (Illus.). 60p. 2000. 5.95 (*1-58685-001-6*) Gibbs Smith Pub.

Montana, Gladiola. Grit & Gumption: A Cowgirl's Guide. (Illus.). 64p. 1999. 5.95 (*0-87905-916-8*) Gibbs Smith Pub.

— Never Ask a Man the Size of His Spread: A Cowgirl's Guide to Life. LC 92-43920. (Illus.). 144p. 1993. pap. 6.95 (*0-87905-554-5*) Gibbs Smith Pub.

***Montana, Gladiola.** Romance & Barbed Wire: Cowgirls in Love. (Little Western Treasures Ser.: Vol. 3). (Illus.). 60p. 2000. 5.95 (*0-87905-969-9*) Gibbs Smith Pub.

Montana, Gladiola, jt. auth. see Bender, Texas B.

Montana Historical Society Staff. F. Jay Haynes, Photographer. LC 81-6712. 192p. 1981. 14.95 (*0-917298-04-7*) MT Hist Soc.

— Guide to Historic Glendive, \. LC 98-37699. (Montana Mainstreets Ser.: Vol. 2). (Illus.). 88p. 1998. pap. 6.95 (*0-917298-58-6*) MT Hist Soc.

Montana, Joe. Joe Montana's Art & Magic of Quarterbacking. LC 97-30517. (Illus.). 256p. (YA). (gr. 9 up). 1995. 25.00 (*0-8050-4277-6*, Bks Young Read) H Holt & Co.

Montana, Joe & Raissman, Bob. Audibles: My Life in Football. 1990. pap. 3.95 (*0-380-71326-8*, Avon Bks) Morrow Avon.

Montana, Joe & Schaap, Dick. Montana. (Illus.). 144p. 1999. pap. text 25.00 (*0-7881-6009-5*) DIANE Pub.

Montana, Joe & Steinberg, Alan. Cool under Fire: Reflections on the San Francisco 49ers-How We Came of Age in the 1980's. 1989. 17.95 (*0-316-57847-9*) Little.

Montana, Joe & Weiner, Richard. Joe Montana's Art & Magic of Quarterbacking: The Secrets of the Game from One of the All-Time Best. (Illus.). 224p. 1998. pap. 14.95 (*0-8050-4278-4*, Owl) H Holt & Co.

***Montana, Joe & Weiner, Richard.** Joe Montana's Art & Magic of Quarterbacking: The Secrets of the Game from One of the All-Time Best. (Illus.). 212p. 2000. reprint ed. text 25.00 (*0-7881-6866-5*) DIANE Pub.

Montana, John C., jt. auth. see Skupsky, Donald S.

An Asterisk (*) at the beginning of an entry indicates that the title is appearing for the first time.

Montana Land Reliance Staff & Hunter, Christopher J. Better Trout Habitat: A Guide to Stream Restoration & Management. LC 90-47860. 320p. 1990. pap. 30.00 (0-933280-77-7) Island Pr.

Montana Land Reliance Staff & Land Trust Exchange Staff. Private Options: Tools & Concepts for Land Conservation. LC 82-13070. 292p. (Orig.). 1982. pap. text 29.95 (0-933280-15-7) Island Pr.

Montana, LeRoy & Waldron, Linda. The Crystal Oracle. 128p. 1993. pap. 29.95 (1-883783-01-1) Crystal Oracle.

Montana, LeRoy, jt. auth. see Waldron, Linda.

Montana Magazine Staff, compiled by. Weekender: Montana Road Trips. (Illus.). 112p. 1999. pap. 15.95 (1-56037-136-6, Montana Magazine) Am Wrld Geog.

Montana, Montie, Jr. Cowboy Cuisine: The Ultimate Cowboy Cookbook. Dunbar, Arlo, ed. LC 95-96015. (Illus.). 416p. 1995. pap. 19.95 (0-9649626-8-3) Bufflo Bills Wild West.

— Montie Montana: Not Without My Horse! (Illus.). 350p. 1993. pap. 19.95 (1-883472-55-5) Double M CA.

Montana Palaez, Servando, ed. see Canales, Nemesio.

Montana, Pat. Babies Inc. (Bundles of Joy) (Romance Ser.). 1995. per. 2.99 (0-373-19076-X, 1-19076-8) Silhouette.

— Fairy-Tale Family. (Romance Ser.: No. 1369). 1999. per. 3.50 (0-373-19369-6, 1-19369-7) Silhouette.

***Montana, Pat.** Une Famill de Conte de Fees. (Horizon Ser.: No. 538). (FRE.). 2000. mass mkt. 3.99 (0-373-39538-8, 1-39538-3, Harlequin French) Harlequin Bks.

Montana, Pat. One Unbelievable Man. (Romance Ser.). 1994. per. 2.75 (0-373-08993-7, 5-08993-3) Silhouette.

— Storybook Bride. 1996. per. 3.25 (0-373-19190-1, 1-19190-7) Silhouette.

— Storybook Cowboy. 1995. per. 2.99 (0-373-19111-1, 1-19111-3) Silhouette.

Montana, Patrick. Management. (Barron's EZ-101 Study Keys Ser.). 144p. 1991. pap. 5.95 (0-8120-4606-4) Barron.

Montana, Patrick & Charnov, Bruce. Management. 2nd ed. LC 92-27960. (Barron's Business Review Ser.). 492p. 1993. pap. 13.95 (0-8120-1549-5) Barron.

Montana, Patrick J. Managing Public & Nonprofit Organizations: A Results Oriented Approach. 340p. (C). 1994. pap. text 29.50 (0-07-042833-6) McGraw.

Montana, Patrick J., ed. Marketing in Nonprofit Organizations. LC 78-18322. 316p. reprint ed. pap. 98.00 (0-608-12806-6, 202354700033) Bks Demand.

***Montana, Patrick J. & Charnov, Bruce H.** Management. 3rd ed. LC 99-16327. (Business Review Ser.). 2000. 14.95 (0-7641-1276-7) Barron.

Montana, Patrick J. & Roukis, George S., eds. Managing Terrorism: Strategies for the Corporate Executive. LC 82-11224. 182p. 1983. 52.95 (0-89930-013-8, MTE/, Quorum Bks) Greenwood.

Montana, Patrick J., jt. ed. see Roukis, George S.

Montana, Ron. The Cathedral Option. (Orig.). 1978. mass mkt. 2.25 (0-89083-404-0, Zebra Kensgtn) Kensgtn Pub Corp.

***Montana, Ron.** Ride a White Zebra. LC 99-91438. 1999. 25.00 (0-7388-0776-1); pap. 18.00 (0-7388-0777-X) Xlibris Corp.

Montana, Sybil. Doc Holliday's Trails & Alluring Tales . . . 2nd ed. (Illus.). 116p. 1997. pap. 8.00 (1-892035-01-4) Sybil Montana.

— Jesse James Notable Memorabilia. (Illus.). 68p. 1995. pap. 7.00 (1-892035-03-0) Sybil Montana.

— Jesse James Outlawry Days. 2nd rev. ed. (Illus.). 72p. 1995. pap. 7.00 (1-892035-02-2) Sybil Montana.

— Quantrill's Scattered Bones Buried at Last. rev. ed. (Illus.). 72p. 1994. pap. 7.00 (1-892035-04-9) Sybil Montana.

— Sweethearts of the Notorious Outlaws. (Illus.). 92p. 1995. pap. 7.50 (1-892035-05-7) Sybil Montana.

— Wyatt Earp's Missouri Legend. 2nd ed. (Illus.), 96p. 1995. reprint ed. pap. 7.50 (1-892035-00-6) Sybil Montana.

Montanari. The Violet Hour: A Novel of Suspense. 320p. 1999. mass mkt. 6.99 (0-380-79532-9, Avon Bks) Morrow Avon.

Montanari, jt. auth. see Narcisi.

Montanari, Alessandro, et al, eds. Miocene Stratigraphy: An Integrated Approach, Vol. 15. LC 97-19654. (Developments in Palaeontology & Stratigraphy Ser.). 694p. 1997. 247.00 (0-444-82498-7) Elsevier.

***Montanari, Alessandro & Koeberl, Christian.** Impact Stratigraphy: The Italian Record. LC 00-38827. (Lecture Notes in Earth Sciences Ser.). (Illus.). 2000. pap. write for info. (3-540-66368-1) Spr-Verlag.

Montanari, Armando & Williams, Allan M., eds. European Tourism: Regions, Spaces & Restructuring. LC 96-100390. 294p. 1995. 130.00 (0-471-95286-9, GE11) Wiley.

Montanari, D. Dizionario Delle Attivita Sementiere E Vivais Tiche. (DUT, ENG, FRE, GER & ITA.). 270p. 1981. 35.00 (0-8288-0038-3, M15642) Fr & Eur.

Montanari, Ellen O., ed. Get Well Care: Guidelines for Programs Serving Mildly Ill Children. 30p. 1989. reprint ed. pap. 10.95 (1-882149-40-8) CPG Pub.

Montanari, F. & Casella, L., eds. Metalloporphyrins Catalyzed Oxidations. LC 93-43396. (Catalysis by Metal Complexes Ser.: Vol. 17). 368p. (C). 1994. text 204.50 (0-7923-2657-1) Kluwer Academic.

Montanari, Franco. I Frammenti Dei Grammatici Agathokles, Hellanikos, Ptolemaios Epithetes: In Appendice I Grammatici Theophilos, Anaxagoras, Xenon. (Sammlun Griechischer und Lateinisher Grammatik Ser.: Vol. 7). vi, 265p. (C). 1988. lib. bdg. 173.10 (3-11-010721-X) De Gruyter.

Montanari, Massimo. The Culture of Food. Le Goff, Jacques, ed. (The Making of Europe Ser.). 232p. 1996. pap. 21.95 (0-631-20283-8) Blackwell Pubs.

Montanari, Massimo, jt. ed. see Flandrin, Jean-Louis.

Montanari, Massimo, jt. ed. see Flandrin, John-Louis.

Montanari, R., jt. auth. see Boyd, B.

Montanari, Richard. Deviant Way. 1997. per. 6.50 (0-671-51109-2) PB.

***Montanari, Richard.** The Midnight Room. 2001. write for info. (0-380-97593-9, Wm Morrow) Morrow Avon.

Montanari, Richard. The Violet Hour: A Novel of Suspense. LC 97-32290. 368p. 1998. 15.95 (0-380-97592-0, Avon Bks) Morrow Avon.

Montanari, Sally. Look Again! Clues to Modern Paintings. (Illus.). 68p. (Orig.). 1989. pap. 8.95 (0-913515-36-1, Starrhill Press) Black Belt Communs.

Montanari, Ugo, et al, eds. Principles & Practice of Constraint Programming - CP '95: First International Conference, Cassis, France, September 19-22, 1995, Proceedings, Vol. XIII. (Lecture Notes in Computer Science Ser.: Vol. 976). 651p. 1995. 100.00 (3-540-60299-2) Spr-Verlag.

MOntanari, Ugo, jt. ed. see Habermann, A. Nico.

Montanaro, Ann R. Pop-Up & Movable Books: A Bibliography. (Illus.). 588p. 1993. 62.50 (0-8108-2650-X) Scarecrow.

***Montanaro, Ann R.** Pop-Up & Movable Books Supplement 1: A Bibliography: 1991-1997. 960p. 2000. 95.00 (0-8108-3728-5) Scarecrow.

Montanaro, Anthony, jt. ed. see Bardana, Emil J.

Montanaro, Bruno. Guitar Hispanio - Americano: Spanish American Guitars. Date not set. write for info. (0-614-13889-2, T050) Bold Strummer Ltd.

Montanaro, Caroline Vincenti. Palazzi & Villas of Rome. 191p. 1999. pap. 9.95 (88-7743-202-0) Arsenale Editrice.

Montanaro, John S. Complex & Simplified Forms of Chinese Characters with Conversion Tables. rev. ed. (Mirror Ser.: No. C-16). (CHI.). 88p. 1985. 6.95 (0-88710-142-9) Yale Far Eastern Pubns.

— Getting by in Chinese. 2nd ed. LC 96-3254. 1997. pap. 18.95 incl. audio (0-8120-8450-0) Barron.

Montanaro, John S., ed. Chinese Vocabulary Cards. rev. ed. (CHI & ENG.). 1987. 17.95 (0-88710-126-7) Yale Far Eastern Pubns.

Montanaro, Silvana Q. Understanding the Human Being: The Importance of the First Three Years of Life. (Illus.). 166p. (Orig.). (C). 1991. pap. text 14.95 (1-879341-00-X) N Montessori.

Montand, Y. Alexander Men: A Man for Our Times. Bigham, Steven, tr. 231p. 1995. per. 14.95 (1-879038-12-9) Oakwood Pubns.

Montandon, Denys, et al. Plastic & Reconstructive Surgery of the Orbitopalpebral Region. (Illus.). 360p. 1990. text 98.00 (0-443-04486-4) Church.

Montandon, Mario Bottinelli. Mario Bottinelli Montandon. (Illus.). 128p. 1999. pap. 35.00 (88-8158-218-X, Pub. by Charta) Dist Art Pubs.

***Montandon, Pat.** Celebrities & Their Angels. 120p. 1999. 16.95 (1-58063-106-1) Renaissance.

Montane, Diana, jt. auth. see Martinez, Ana Margarita.

Montanelli, Dale S. & Stenstrom, Patricia. People Come First: User-Centered Academic Library Service. LC 98-43719. (ACRL Publications in Librarianship : No. 53). 202p. 1999. 31.00 (0-8389-7999-8) Assn Coll & Res Libs.

Montaner, Carlos. The Witches' Poker Game & Other Stories. Robinson, Robert, tr. from SPA. LC 73-84203. 171p. 1973. pap. 1.95 (0-913480-18-5) Inter Am U Pr.

Montaner, Carlos A. Cuba: Claves para una Conciensa en Crisis. 154p. 1982. pap. text 21.95 (84-359-0286-2) Transaction Pubs.

— Cuba Hoy: (La Lenta Muerte del Castrismo) LC 96-83380. (Coleccion Cuba y sus Jueces). (SPA.). 193p. (Orig.). 1996. pap. 19.00 (0-89729-794-6) Ediciones.

— Fidel Castro: Y la Revolucion Cubana. 255p. 1983. pap. text 32.95 (84-359-0344-3) Transaction Pubs.

— Fidel Castro & the Cuban Revolution: Age, Position, Character, Destiny, Personality, & Ambition. 244p. 1989. 39.95 (0-88738-235-5) Transaction Pubs.

— Two Hundred Years of Gringos. Fernandez de la Torriente, Gaston & Horton, James F., trs. 142p. (Orig.). (C). 1983. pap. text 19.50 (0-8191-3375-2); lib. bdg. 45.00 (0-8191-3374-4) U Pr of Amer.

Montaner, Carlos A., ed. see Muzaurrieta, Jose M.

Montaner, Carlos Alberto. No Perdamos Tambien el Sigl. (SPA.). 1997. pap. text 17.95 (84-01-01077-2, Pub. by Plaza) Lectorum Pubns.

Montaner, J. M. Barcelona. (Big Ser.). (Illus.). 300p. 1997. 24.99 (3-8228-9653-5) Taschen Amer.

Montaner, Josep. Ugalde House. (Illus.). 90p. 1998. pap. 22.00 (84-89698-49-X, Pub. by Actar) Dist Art Pubs.

Montaner, Josep M., text. Antoni De Moragas i Gallissa: Architect. (Illus.). 119p. 1998. pap. 25.00 (84-88258-10-0, 810761, Pub. by Actar) Dist Art Pubs.

Montaner, Joseph M. Mendes Da Rocha. (Current Architecture Catalogues Ser.). (Illus.). 96p. 1997. pap. text 29.95 (84-252-1682-6) Watsn-Guptill.

— New Museums. (Illus.). 188p. 1997. 39.95 (1-85454-600-7) Chronicle Bks.

Montanez, Carmen L. Subversion y Creatividad: El Personaje Femenino en la Cuentistica de Varias Escritoras Puertorriquenas. (Wor(l)ds of Change Ser.: Vol. 33). (SPA.). X, 117p. (C). 1998. text 35.95 (0-8204-3491-4) P Lang Pubng.

Montanez-Cartaxo, Luis E., jt. ed. see Vieitez-Utesa, Luis.

Montanez, Isabel P., et al, eds. Basin-Wide Diagenetic Patterns: Integrated Petrologic, Geochemical & Hydrologic Considerations. (Special Publications: No. 57). (Illus.). 300p. 1997. 101.00 (1-56576-035-2) SEPM.

Montanez, Nivea O., jt. auth. see Izcoa, Carmen R.

Montange, Charles H. Preserving Abandoned Railroad Rights-of-Way for Public Use: A Legal Manual. 178p. (Orig.). (C). 1989. pap. text 42.50 (0-925794-00-7) Rails Trails.

Montangero, Carlo. Software Process Technology: 5th European Workshop, EWSPT '96, Nancy, France, October 8-11, 1996, Proceedings, Vol. 114. LC 96-43203. (Lecture Notes on Computer Science Ser.). ix, 291p. 1996. 49.00 (3-540-61771-X) Spr-Verlag.

Montangero, Jacques. Understanding Changing in Time: The Development of Diachronic Thinking in 7-12 Year Old Children. LC 96-156972. 240p. 1996. 79.95 (0-7484-0470-8); pap. 27.95 (0-7484-0471-6) Taylor & Francis.

Montangero, Jacques & Maurice-Naville, Danielle. Piaget or the Advance of Knowledge: An Overview & Glossary. LC 97-12995. 192p. 1997. pap. 22.50 (0-8058-2568-1) L Erlbaum Assocs.

— Piaget or the Advance of Knowledge: An Overview & Glossary. LC 97-12995. 192p. 1997. 45.00 (0-8058-2567-3) L Erlbaum Assocs.

Montani. Physiology. 1997. pap. text. write for info. (0-7216-5058-9, W B Saunders Co) Harcrt Hlth Sci Grp.

Montanino, Anna, ed. see Harris, Raina Wissing.

Montano, Judith B. The Art of Silk Ribbon Embroidery. Townsend, Louise O., ed. LC 92-53801. (Illus.). 120p. 1993. pap. 21.95 (0-914881-55-8, 10072) C & T Pub.

— The Crazy Quilt Handbook. LC 86-71560. (Illus.). 80p. (Orig.). 1986. pap. 18.95 (0-914881-05-1, 10007) C & T Pub.

— Crazy Quilt Odyssey: Adventures in Victorian Needlework. Frankel, Candie, ed. LC 90-86060. (Illus.). 144p. (Orig.). 1991. pap. 21.95 (0-914881-41-8, 10048) C & T Pub.

— Elegant Stitches: An Illustrated Stitch Guide & Source Book of Inspiration. Konzak-Kuhn, Barbara, ed. (Illus.). 176p. 1995. ring bd. 24.95 (0-914881-85-X, 10106) C & T Pub.

— Judith Baker Montano: Art & Inspirations. Kuhn, Barbara & Roberts, Diana, eds. LC 97-14715. (Art & Inspirations Ser.: No. 2). (Illus.). 144p. 1997. 35.95 (1-57120-038-X, 1061); pap. 29.95 (1-57120-037-1, 10162) C & T Pub.

— Recollections. Nadel, Harold, ed. LC 92-44544. (Illus.). 128p. 1993. 16.95 (0-914881-59-0, 10071) C & T Pub.

***Montano, Judith Baker.** Floral Stitches: An Illustrated Guide. (Illus.). 2000. spiral bd. 26.95 (1-57120-107-6, Pub. by C & T Pub) Watsn-Guptill.

Montano, Linda. Art in Everyday Life. LC 81-65318. (Illus.). 152p. (Orig.). 1981. pap. 10.00 (0-937122-05-X) Astro Artz Eighteenth St.

***Montano, Linda M.** Performance Artists: Talking in the Eighties. (Illus.). 420p. 2000. 60.00 (0-520-21021-2, Pub. by U CA Pr); pap. 24.95 (0-520-21022-0, Pub. by U CA Pr) Cal Prin Full Svc.

Montano, Macrina C., ed. see Zollars, Jean A.

Montano, Mary. Loving Mozart: A Past Life Memory of the Composer's Final Years. 239p. 1995. pap. 21.00 (0-9642577-0-X) Cantus Verus.

Montano, Richard & Simms, Eduard T. Adobe Kingdom No. 1: New Mexico 1598-1958 As Experienced by the Families Lucero De Godoy y Baca. (Illus.). 282p. (Orig.). 1995. pap. text 21.95 (0-9628974-3-4) El Escrito.

Montano, Rocco. Shakespeare's Concept of Tragedy: The Bard As Anti-Elizabethan. LC 85-4536. 288p. 1986. pap. 12.00 (0-89526-810-8) Regnery Pub.

Montano, Severino. Selected Plays of Severino Montano, Vol. 1. (Illus.). 234p. (Orig.). 1982. pap. 12.50 (0-686-37565-3, Pub. by New Day Pub) Cellar.

— Selected Plays of Severino Montano, Vol. 2. (Illus.). 319p. (Orig.). 1982. pap. 15.00 (0-686-37566-1, Pub. by New Day Pub) Cellar.

— Selected Plays of Severino Montano, Vol. 3. (Illus.). 64p. (Orig.). 1983. pap. 7.50 (971-10-0046-6, Pub. by New Day Pub) Cellar.

Montanus, Charlotte, et al. Micro Skills Lab: Beginning WordPerfect Works for DOS. 244p. 1994. pap. 21.95 (0-534-24108-5) Course Tech.

Montapert, Alfred A. Distilled Wisdom. 10th ed. LC 64-8181. 1977. 14.00 (0-9603174-0-6, 21618) Bks of Value.

— Laws of Life: Nature's Laws to Successful Living. 1992. per. 10.00 (0-614-04219-4); pap. 14.00 (0-614-24517-6) Bks of Value.

— Personal Planning Manual. LC 67-12652. 1967. 14.00 (0-9603174-1-4, 85920) Bks of Value.

— Personal Planning Manual. 1977. pap. 6.95 (0-87505-364-5) Borden.

— Pray to Win! A Blueprint for Success. LC 86-73037. 235p. 1986. per. 10.00 (0-9603174-4-9) Bks of Value.

— The Supreme Philosophy of Man. 7th ed. LC 70-119515. 1977. 10.00 (0-9603174-2-2) Bks of Value.

— The Supreme Philosophy of Man: The Laws of Life. 1977. pap. 4.95 (0-87505-368-8) Borden.

— The Way to Happiness. LC 77-13678. 1978. pap. 10.00 (0-9603174-3-0) Bks of Value.

— The Way to Happiness. (Eternal Quest of Mankind Ser.). 1978. pap. 10.00 (0-13-946228-7) Borden.

— Words of Wisdom to Live By: An Encyclopedia of Wisdom in Condensed Form. LC 86-73036. 280p. 1986. per. 10.00 (0-9603174-5-7) Bks of Value.

Montaperto, Ronald N., jt. auth. see Zhang, Ming.

Montar, Karel, et al, eds. Naval Leadership: Voices of Experience. 2nd ed. LC 98-2550. (Illus.). 536p. 1998. 35.00 (1-55750-596-9) Naval Inst Pr.

Montaser, Abkar, ed. Inductively Coupled Plasma Mass Spectrometry: From A to Z. 350p. 1996. 100.00 (1-56081-902-2, Wiley-VCH) Wiley.

Montaser, Abkar & Golightly, D. W., eds. Inductively Coupled Plasmas in Analytical Atomic Spectrometry. 2nd rev. ed. 1017p. 1992. 200.00 (0-471-18811-5) Wiley.

***Montaser, Akbar.** Inductively Coupled Plasma Mass Spectrometry. LC 97-34234. 1000p. 1998. 165.00 (0-471-18620-1, Wiley-VCH) Wiley.

Montaser, Akbar & Golightly, D. W., eds. Inductively Coupled Plasmas in Analytical Atomic Spectrometry. 2nd ed. LC 92-25254. 1017p. 1992. 195.00 (1-56081-514-0, Wiley-VCH) Wiley.

Montasser, Thomas. Lexikon der Rechtsbegriffe. (GER.). 512p. 1991. 29.95 (0-7859-8566-2, 3927117692) Fr & Eur.

Montaudo, Giorgio & Lattimer, Robert P. Mass Spectrometry of Polymers. 1999. 99.95 (0-8493-3127-7) CRC Pr.

***Montauk.** How to Get into the Top Colleges. 2000. pap. 20.00 (0-13-030962-1) P-H.

Montauk, Richard. How to Get into the Top MBA Programs. LC 96-9041. 352p. 1996. pap. 19.95 (0-13-246323-7) P-H.

— How to Get into the Top MBA Programs. 1996. 19.95 (0-614-20413-5) P-H.

***Montauk, Richard J.** How to Get into the Top Law Schools. (Illus.). 352p. 2000. pap. 20.00 (0-7352-0101-3) PH Pr.

Montauk, Susan L. Guide to the Family Medicine Clerkship. pap. text. write for info. (0-7817-2349-3) Lppncott W & W.

Montauk, Susan L. & Grasha, Anthony. Adult HIV Outpatient Care: A Handbook for Clinical Teaching. 754p. (C). 1993. write for info. (0-9639194-0-7) U Cinn CMFM.

Montauredes, Rita, jt. auth. see Marks, Edith.

Montavon, Jay. A History Mystery: The Curse of King Tut's Tomb. 96p. (Orig.). (J). 1991. pap. 3.50 (0-380-76220-X, Avon Bks) Morrow Avon.

***Montavon, Jay R.** Case of the Killer Bugs. (Digital Detective Mysteries Ser.). 2000. pap. 4.95 (0-7624-0905-3) Running Pr.

— When Nightmares Come True. (Digital Detective Mysteries Ser.). 2000. pap. 4.95 (0-7624-0906-1) Running Pr.

Montcalm, Henriette, jt. auth. see Caya, Rene.

Montchamp, Joseph, jt. auth. see Alplin, Richard.

Montclair Art Museum, jt. auth. see Wheeler, Steve.

Montclair Art Museum Staff, jt. auth. see Docherty, Linda J.

Montclair Captain NJSAR. Story of Montclair: Its People in Peace & War Times. (Illus.). 202p. 1997. reprint ed. lib. bdg. 29.00 (0-8328-6878-7) Higginson Bk Co.

Montclos, Jean-Marie P. De, see De Montclos, Jean-Marie P.

Monte, Alfredo Del, see Del Monte, Alfredo, ed.

Monte, Christopher F. Beneath the Mask. 5th ed. (C). 1994. pap. text, teacher ed., suppl. ed. 49.75 (0-15-501856-6) Harcourt Coll Pubs.

— Beneath the Mask. 6th ed. (C). 1998. pap. text 31.50 (0-15-505204-7) Harcourt.

— Beneath the Mask. 6th ed. (C). 1998. text 90.50 (0-15-505199-7) Harcourt.

— Beneath the Mask: An Introduction to the Theories of Personality. 5th ed. LC 94-30056. (C). 1994. text 86.00 (0-15-501541-9) Harcourt Coll Pubs.

— Merlin: The Sorcerer's Guide to Survival in College. 130p. (C). 1990. 12.00 (0-534-13482-3) Wadsworth Pub.

— Still Life: Clinical Portraits in Psychopathology. LC 92-49802. 240p. 1992. pap. text 17.40 (0-13-137217-3) P-H.

Monte, Emily C. The Lost Sword of the Confederate Ghost: A Mystery in Two Centuries. LC 98-20332. (J). 1999. 5.99 (1-57249-132-9) White Mane Pub.

Monte, Esther & Whiting, Louise T. An Artist's Portrayal of Madonna & Child: With Stories of Mothers, Grandmothers & Children. (Illus.). 1998. pap. 19.95 (1-58147-024-X) Pac Ocean.

Monte, J. Fred Astaire Dance Book. (Ballroom Dance Ser.). 1986. lib. bdg. 250.00 (0-8490-3363-2) Gordon Pr.

— Fred Astaire Dance Book. (Ballroom Dance Ser.). 1985. lib. bdg. 250.00 (0-87700-701-2) Revisionist Pr.

Monte, John De, see De Monte, John, ed.

Monte, Kiki Bel. Blood Speak. 25p. Date not set. write for info. (0-88100-114-7) Natl Writ Pr.

***Monte, Peter & Cerbone, John.** Complete Idiot's Guide to Stock Car Racing. (Complete Idiot's Guides Ser.). 400p. 2000. pap. 16.95 (0-02-863181-1, Alpha Ref) Macmillan Gen Ref.

Monte, Providencia C., ed. Learning Modules for the Basic Course in English, Vol. 1. LC 79-22332. 304p. 1980. pap. 7.00 (0-8477-3324-6) U of PR Pr.

***Monte, Steven.** Invisible Fences: Prose Poetry as a Genre in French & American Literature. LC 00-37426. 352p. 2000. text 50.00 (0-8032-3211-X) U of Nebr Pr.

Monte, Tom. The Complete Guide to Natural Healing. 1997. pap. 16.95 (0-614-27364-1, Perigee Bks) Berkley Pub.

***Monte, Tom.** The Complete Guide to Natural Healing. 613p. 2000. reprint ed. text 35.00 (0-7881-9121-7) DIANE Pub.

Monte, Tom. Staying Young. 1996. mass mkt. 6.99 (0-425-15483-1) Berkley Pub.

— Staying Young: How to Prevent, Slow or Reverse More Than 60 Signs of Aging. Grimm, Christine, tr. 400p. 1996. reprint ed. mass mkt. 6.99 (0-425-15251-0) Berkley Pub.

— The Way of Hope: Michio Kushi's Anti-AIDS Program. 1990. mass mkt. 12.95 (0-446-39174-3, Pub. by Warner Bks) Little.

Monte, Tom, jt. auth. see Burmeister, Alice.

Monte, Tom, jt. auth. see Cowens, Deborah.

Monte, Tom, jt. auth. see Decoz, Hans.

Monte, Tom, jt. auth. see EastWest Natural Health Editors.

Monte, Tom, jt. auth. see Kantor, David.

Monte, Tom, jt. auth. see Kushi, Aveline.

Monte, Tom, jt. auth. see Lawson, Margaret.

Monte, Tom, jt. auth. see Levy, Elinor.

Monte, Tom, jt. auth. see McClellan, Sam.

Monte, Tom, jt. auth. see Ohashi, Watari.

Monte, Tom, jt. auth. see Robertson, Joel C.

Monte, Tom, jt. auth. see Sattilaro, Anthony J.

Monte-White, Anta, jt. ed. see Dibble, Harold L.

Monteagudo, Ana & Timor-Tritsch, Ilan E. Ultrasound & Multifetal Pregnancy. LC 97-39909. (Progress in Obstetric & Gynecological Sonography Ser.). 1997. 78.00 (*1-85070-986-6*) Prthnon Pub.

Monteath, Colin. Antarctica: Beyond the Southern Oceans. LC 97-1248. (Illus.). 160p. 1997. 29.95 (*0-7641-5040-5*) Barron.

— Hall & Ball: Kiwi Mountaineers: From Mount Cook to Everest. (Illus.). 160p. 1997. 35.00 (*0-938567-42-X*) Mountaineers.

Monteath, Doug. Do Nows: Math Concept Review & Test Practice. 1997. text 11.95 (*0-86651-464-3*) Seymour Pubns.

Monteath, Peter. The Spanish Civil War in Literature, Film & Art: An International Bibliography of Secondary Literature, 43. LC 94-16070. (Bibliographies & Indexes in World Literature Ser.: No. 43). 160p. 1994. lib. bdg. 59.95 (*0-313-29262-0*, Greenwood Pr) Greenwood.

— Writing the Good Fight: Political Commitment in the International Literature of the Spanish Civil, 52. LC 93-21130. (Contributions to the Study of World Literature Ser.: No. 52). 240p. 1994. 59.95 (*0-313-28766-X*, Greenwood Pr) Greenwood.

Monteath, Peter, jt. ed. see Alter, Reinhard.

Monteau, P. Building Dictionary, French-English/English-French. (ENG & FRE.). 301p. 1994. pap. 95.00 (*0-7859-9640-0*) Fr & Eur.

Montebello, Anthony R. Work Teams That Work: Skills for Managing Across the Organization. 1994. 24.95 (*0-9636268-1-7*) Best Sell Pub.

Montebello, Philippe De, see Barbier, Jean P.

Montebello, Philippe De, see De Montebello, Philippe, selected by.

Montebello, Philippe De, see Barbier, Jean P.

Montecel, Maria Robledo, et al. Hispanic Families As Valued Partners: An Educator's Guide. (Illus.). 90p. 1993. pap. 19.95 (*1-878550-47-0*) Inter Dev Res Assn.

— The State of Literacy in San Antonio in the 1990s. (Illus.). 24p. 1994. pap. text 6.00 (*1-878550-50-0*) Inter Dev Res Assn.

Montecino, Marcel. Big Time. Rubenstein, Julie, ed. 544p. 1991. reprint ed. per. 6.99 (*0-671-70971-2*, Pocket Star Bks) PB.

— Crosskiller. 1989. mass mkt. 6.99 (*0-671-67894-9*) PB.

— Sacred Heart. LC 97-34572. 375p. 1997. 23.00 (*0-671-01539-7*, PB Hardcover) PB.

— Sacred Heart. 1998. mass mkt. 6.99 (*0-671-01540-0*) PB.

Montecucco, C., ed. Clostridial Neurotoxins: The Molecular Pathogenesis of Tetanus & Botulism. (Current Topics in Microbiology & Immunology Ser.: Vol. 195). (Illus.). 320p. 1995. 165.95 (*3-540-58452-8*) Spr-Verlag.

Montecucco, Cesare, jt. ed. see Rappuoli, Rino.

Montedison S.P.A. Staff, jt. auth. see Moore, Edward P.

Montefiore, Alan, ed. Philosophy in France Today. LC 82-9730. 223p. 1983. pap. text 22.95 (*0-521-29673-0*) Cambridge U Pr.

Montefiore, Alan & Vines, David. Integrity in the Public & Private Domains. LC 98-9406. 336p. (C). 1999. 90.00 (*0-415-18031-7*) Routledge.

Montefiore, C. G. The Old Testament & After. 601p. 1977. 26.95 (*0-8369-6862-X*) Ayer.

Montefiore, Claude G. Judaism & St. Paul. LC 73-2222. (Jewish People; History, Religion, Literature Ser.). 1978. reprint ed. 25.95 (*0-405-05284-7*) Ayer.

— Some Elements of the Religious Teaching of Jesus According to the Synoptic Gospels. LC 73-2223. (Jewish People; History, Religion, Literature Ser.). 1973. reprint ed. 19.95 (*0-405-05285-5*) Ayer.

Montefiore, Claude J. Lectures on the Origin & Growth of Religion As Illustrated by the Religion of the Ancient Hebrews. 3rd ed. LC 77-27162. (Hibbert Lectures: 1892). reprint ed. 59.50 (*0-404-60410-2*) AMS Pr.

Montefiore, Hugh. Communicating the Gospel in a Scientific Age. 76p. (C). 1988. pap. text 30.00 (*0-7152-0631-1*) St Mut.

Montefiore, Hugh, ed. Communicating the Gospel in a Scientific Age. 76p. (C). 1989. pap. 20.00 (*0-7855-6823-9*, Pub. by St Andrew) St Mut.

Montefiore, Hugh, jt. ed. see Franklin, F. William.

Montefiore, Jan. Feminism & Poetry: Language, Experience & Identity in Women's Writing. 300p. 1994. pap. text 13.00 (*0-04-440893-5*) NYU Pr.

***Montefiore, Jan.** Feminism & Poetry: Language, Experience & Identity in Women's Writing. 304p. 2000. pap. text 15.00 (*0-86358-419-5*) Pandora.

Montefiore, Janet. Men & Women Writers of the 1930s: Gender, Agency & History. LC 96-1885. 280p. (C). 1996. 90.00 (*0-415-06892-4*); pap. 27.99 (*0-415-06893-2*) Routledge.

Monteflores, Carmen De, see De Monteflores, Carmen.

Montegna, Donna. Prisoner of Innocence. LC 89-12775. 120p. (Orig.). 1989. pap. 8.95 (*0-9613205-7-5*) Launch Pr.

Monteil, Charles. Les Khassonke: Monographie d'Une Peuplade du Soudan Francais. (B. E. Ser.: No. 137). (FRE.). 1915. 45.00 (*0-8115-3060-4*) Periodicals Srv.

— Soudan Francais: Contes Soudanaises. (B. E. Ser.: No. 119). (FRE.). 1905. 25.00 (*0-8115-3048-5*) Periodicals Srv.

Monteil, Jean-Marc. Social Context & Cognitive Performance: Towards a Social Psychology of Cognition. (European Monographs in Social Psychology Ser.). 1999. 37.50 (*0-86377-784-8*) L Erlbaum Assocs.

Monteil, Peter J., jt. ed. see Hinkle, Lawrence E.

Monteilhet, Hubert. Sophie Ou les Glanteries Exemplaires. (FRE.). 1978. pap. 10.95 (*0-7859-4097-9*) Fr & Eur.

Monteiro, Barry E. Airline Career Opportunities. 52p. 1994. pap. 12.95 (*0-9639973-0-0*) Airline Career.

Monteiro, Estela & Veloso, F. Tavarela, eds. Inflammatory Bowel Diseases: New Insights into Mechanisms of Inflammation & Challenges in Diagnosis & Treatment. LC 95-20104. 1995. text 129.00 (*0-7923-8884-4*) Kluwer Academic.

Monteiro, George. Conversations with Elizabeth Bishop. LC 95-39349. (Literary Conversations Ser.). 224p. 1996. pap. 16.95 (*0-87805-872-9*) U Pr of Miss.

— Critical Essays on Ernest Hemingway's A Farewell to Arms. LC 94-19102. (Critical Essays on American Literature Ser.). 208p. 1994. 48.00 (*0-7838-0011-8*, Twyne) Mac Lib Ref.

***Monteiro, George.** Fernando Pessoa & Nineteenth-Century Anglo-American Literature. (Studies in Romance Languages: Vol. 46). 240p. (C). 2000. 24.95 (*0-8131-2182-5*) U Pr of Ky.

Monteiro, George. Henry James & John Hay: The Record of a Friendship. LC 65-24094. 219p. reprint ed. 67.90 (*0-608-16590-5*, 202751900055) Bks Demand.

— The Presence of Camoes: Influences on the Literature of England, America, & Southern Africa. LC 95-46725. (Studies in Romance Languages: No. 40). (Illus.). 200p. (C). 1996. text 24.95 (*0-8131-1952-9*) U Pr of Ky.

— The Presence of Pessoa: English, American, & Southern African Literary Responses. LC 97-40435. (Studies in Romance Languages). (Illus.). 164p. (C). 1998. 24.95 (*0-8131-2053-5*) U Pr of Ky.

— Robert Frost & the New England Renaissance. LC 88-5479. 192p. 1988. 24.95 (*0-8131-1649-X*) U Pr of Ky.

Monteiro, George, ed. Conversations with Elizabeth Bishop. LC 95-39349. (Literary Conversations Ser.). 1996. 39.50 (*0-87805-871-0*) U Pr of Miss.

Monteiro, George, tr. from POR. Fernando Pessoa: Self-Analysis & Thirty Other Poems. LC 88-82009. 89p. 1988. 10.00 (*0-943722-14-4*) Gavea-Brown.

Monteiro, George & Murphy, Brenda, eds. John Hay-Howells Letters: The Correspondence of John Hay & William Dean Howells 1861 - 1905. (American Literary Manuscripts Ser.). 1980. 21.50 (*0-8057-9652-5*, Twyne) Mac Lib Ref.

Monteiro, George, ed. see James, Henry & Adams, Henry (Brooks).

Monteiro, George, tr. see Almeida, Onesimo T., ed.

Monteiro, George, tr. & intro. see Migueis, Jose Rodrigues.

***Monteiro, George E.** Stephen Crane's Blue Badge of Courage. (Illus.). 280p. 2000. 65.00 (*0-8071-2578-4*); pap. 24.95 (*0-8071-2650-0*) La State U Pr.

Monteiro, J. J. Angola & the River Congo, 2 vols., Set. 1968. reprint ed. 85.00 (*0-7146-1838-1*, BHA-01838, Pub. by F Cass Pubs) Intl Spec Bk.

Monteiro, José. Computer-Aided Design Techniques for Low Power Sequential Logic Circuits. LC 96-45081. (Kluwer International Series in Engineering & Computer Science). 200p. (C). 1996. text 106.50 (*0-7923-9829-7*) Kluwer Academic.

Monteiro, Juanita, ed. see Shaw, Christie V.

Monteiro, Kenneth. Pak: Ethnicity & Psychology. 96p. (C). 1995. pap., student ed., per. write for info. (*0-7872-0470-6*); pap., per. write for info. (*0-7872-0425-0*) Kendall-Hunt.

Monteiro, Mariana. Legends & Popular Tales of the Basque People. LC 72-173115. 274p. 1972. reprint ed. 18.95 (*0-405-08796-9*, Pub. by Blom Pubns) Ayer.

Monteiro Marques, Manuel D. Differential Inclusions in Nonsmooth Mechanical Problems: Shocks & Dry Friction. LC 93-17931. (Progress in Nonlinear Differential Equations & Their Applications Ser.: Vol. 9). 179p. 1993. 81.50 (*0-8176-2900-9*) Birkhauser.

Monteiro, Palmyra V. A Catalogue of Latin American Flat Maps, 1926-1964 Vols. 1 & 2, 1. LC 67-64686. (Guides & Bibliographies Ser.: No. 2). 411p. reprint ed. pap. 127.50 (*0-608-17218-9*, 202732500001) Bks Demand.

— A Catalogue of Latin American Flat Maps, 1926-1964 Vols. 1 & 2, 2. LC 67-64686. (Guides & Bibliographies Ser.: No. 2). 442p. reprint ed. pap. 137.10 (*0-608-18708-9*, 202732500002) Bks Demand.

Monteiro, Sylvio, Jr., tr. see Baratieri, Luiz N., et al.

Monteith, Ann. Business of Wedding Photography: A Professional's Guide to Marketing & Managing a... (Illus.). 192p. 1996. 35.00 (*0-8174-3617-0*, Amphoto) Watsn-Guptill.

— The Professional Photographers Management Handbook. LC 99-19351. (Illus.). 144p. 1999. pap. text. write for info. (*0-9658571-3-1*) Marathon NE.

Monteith, J. L., et al, eds. Resource Capture by Crops. 496p. 1999. 200.00 (*1-897676-21-2*, Pub. by Nottingham Univ Pr) St Mut.

Monteith, J. L. & Unsworth, M. H. Principles of Environmental Physics. 2nd ed. (Illus.). 228p. 1990. pap. text 39.95 (*0-7131-2931-X*, Pub. by E A) Routldge.

Monteith, J. L., ed. see Easter School of Agricultural Science (20th: 1973:.

Monteith, Jay. ABCs African Art Coloring Book. (Illus.). 32p. (J). (ps-3). 1992. pap. text 6.95 (*0-9627366-3-5*) Arts & Comns NY.

— African Art: Activity Workbook. (Illus.). 24p. (Orig.). (J). 1993. pap. text, wbk. ed. 8.75 (*0-9627366-4-3*) Arts & Comns NY.

— A Multicultural Activity Workbook: Africa, Asia & the Americas. (Illus.). 72p. (Orig.). (J). (gr. 1 up). 1991. pap. text 7.95 (*0-9627366-1-9*) Arts & Comns NY.

Monteith, John & Webb, Colin. Soil-Water & Nitrogen: In Mediterranean-Type Environments. 1981. text 184.00 (*90-247-2406-6*) Kluwer Academic.

Monteith, Marcy, ed. Taste California: A Sampling of the Golden State. (Illus.). 150p. (Orig.). 1993. pap. text 11.95 (*0-9638619-0-5*) CA Dietetic.

Monteith, Moira. Computers & Language. 160p. (Orig.). 1993. pap. text 22.95 (*1-871516-27-7*, Pub. by Intellect) Cromland.

— It for Learning Enhancement. LC 98-6283. 1998. 69.00 (*90-265-1524-3*) Swets.

***Monteith, Moira, ed.** It for Learning Enhancement. 192p. 2000. pap. 24.95 (*1-84150-036-4*, Pub. by Intellect) Intl Spec Bk.

Monteith, Moira & Miles, Robert, eds. Teaching Creative Writing: Theory & Practice. 192p. 1992. 123.00 (*0-335-15685-1*) OpUniv Pr.

***Monteith, Sharon.** Advancing Sisterhood? Interracial Friendships in Contemporary Southern Fiction. LC 00-41800. 2001. write for info. (*0-8203-2249-0*) U of Ga Pr.

Monteith, Sharon, jt. auth. see Ling, Peter J.

Monteith, Stanley. AIDS, the Unnecessary Epidemic: America under Seige. 392p. 1995. reprint ed. pap. 14.95 (*0-925591-17-3*) Covenant Hse Bks.

***Monteith, Stanley.** Brotherhood of Darkness. 2000. pap. 12.95 (*1-57558-063-2*) Hearthstone OK.

Monteith, W. Graham. Disability: Faith & Acceptance. 126p. (C). 1988. pap. text 35.00 (*0-7152-0614-1*) St Mut.

Montejano, David. Anglos & Mexicans in the Making of Texas, 1836-1986. (Illus.). 397p. 1987. pap. 14.95 (*0-292-77596-2*) U of Tex Pr.

Montejano, David, ed. Chicano Politics & Society in the Late Twentieth Century. LC 98-15617. (Illus.). 304p. 1999. 35.00 (*0-292-75214-8*); pap. 15.95 (*0-292-75215-6*) U of Tex Pr.

Montejano, Luis, et al. Beta-Homotopy Equivalences Have Alpha Cross Sections. LC 82-20616. (Memoirs Ser.: No. 41/274). 37p. 1982. pap. 16.00 (*0-8218-2274-8*, MEMO 41/274) Am Math.

Montejo, Ruperto. Cuentos de San Pedro Soloma: Ik'ti' yet Tz'uluma' (MYN & SPA., Illus.). 96p. (Orig.). 1996. pap. 6.95 (*1-886502-12-9*, Ediciones Yax Te) Yax Te Found.

Montejo, Victor. The Bird Who Cleans the World: And Other Mayan Fables. Kaufman, Wallace, tr. from SPA. LC 90-52757. (Illus.). 126p. (Orig.). (J). 1991. 22.95 (*0-915306-93-X*) Curbstone.

— The Bird Who Cleans the World: And Other Mayan Fables. Kaufman, Wallace, tr. from SPA. LC 90-52757. (Illus.). 120p. (Orig.). (J). 1992. pap. 13.95 (*1-880684-03-9*) Curbstone.

— Sculpted Stones (Piedas Labradas) Perera, Victor, tr. from SPA. 107p. 1995. pap. 11.95 (*1-880684-14-4*) Curbstone.

— Testimony: Death of a Guatemalan Village. Perera, Victor, tr. LC 86-71063. 113p. 1987. pap. 12.95 (*0-915306-65-4*) Curbstone.

***Montejo, Victor.** Voices from Exile: Violence & Survival in Modern Maya History. LC 99-27677. 304p. 1999. 25.95 (*0-8061-3171-3*) U of Okla Pr.

***Montejo, Victor, et al.** El Q'anil, Man of Lightning: A Legend of Jacaltenango, Guatemala, in English, Spanish & Popb'al Ti' LC 00-9431. (Sun Tracks Ser.). (ENG & SPA.). 2001. write for info. (*0-8165-2082-8*) U of Ariz Pr.

Montejo, Victor, tr. see La Farge, Oliver & Byers, Douglas.

Montejo, Victor D. Las Adventuras de Mister Puttison Entre los Mayas. (SPA.). 193p. 1998. pap. 12.95 (*1-886502-18-8*) Yax Te Found.

— El Kanil: Man of Lightning. (ENG & SPA.). 61p. 1984. pap. 6.95 (*0-930095-01-4*) Signal Bks.

***Montejo, Victor D.** El Pajaro Que Limpia el Mundo. (MYN & SPA.). 169p. 2000. pap. 12.95 (*1-886502-29-3*) Yax Te Found.

Montejo, Victor D. Q'anil: El Hombre Rayo. (MYN & SPA.). 165p. 1998. pap. 12.95 (*1-886502-22-6*) Yax Te Found.

Montel, Paul. Familles Normales. LC 73-14649. xiii, 301p. 1974. text 19.95 (*0-8284-0271-X*) Chelsea Pub.

Montel, Pierre. Enciclopedia de la Fotografria. (SPA.). 464p. 1975. 49.95 (*0-8288-5864-0*, S50554) Fr & Eur.

Monteleone, James A. Child Maltreatment: A Clinical Guide & Reference & a Comprehensive Photo Atlas, 2 vols. 2nd rev. ed. Incl. Vol. 1. Child Maltreatment: A Clinical Guide & Reference. 2nd rev. ed. LC 97-41395. (Illus.). 658p. 2000. boxed set 100.00 (*1-878060-22-8*, 30958); Vol. 2. Child Maltreatment: A Comprehensive Photographic Reference Identifying Potential Child Abuse. 2nd rev. ed. LC 97-41395. (Illus.). 337p. 2000. boxed set 115.00 (*1-878060-23-6*, 30959); LC 97-41395. 2000. 189.00 (*1-878060-26-0*) GW Medical.

— A Parent's & Teacher's Handbook on Identifying & Preventing Child Abuse: Warning Signs, Choosing a Day Care Center & Babysitters, Keeping Children Safe on the Internet. LC 98-22804. (Illus.). 200p. 2000. pap. 18.95 (*1-878060-27-9*, 31141) GW Medical.

Monteleone, James A., ed. Child Abuse: Quick Reference for Healthcare Professionals, Social Services & Law Enforcement. LC 97-40035. (Illus.). 317p. (Orig.). 2000. pap. 39.95 (*1-878060-28-7*, 31142) GW Medical.

— Child Maltreatment: Identifying, Interpreting, & Reporting Child Abuse. (Illus.). 500p. (C). 2000. pap. 95.00 (*1-878060-25-2*, 30962) GW Medical.

Monteleone, John & Crisfield, Deborah. The Louisville Slugger Complete Book of Women's Fast-Pitch Softball. LC 98-55221. (Illus.). 240p. 1999. pap. 19.95 (*0-8050-5809-5*, Pub. by H Holt & Co) VHPS.

Monteleone, John J., ed. Branch Rickey's Little Blue Book: Wit & Strategy from Baseball's Last Wise Man. LC 95-4146. (Illus.). 160p. 1995. 14.95 (*0-02-860400-8*) Macmillan.

Monteleone, John J. & Gola, Mark. The Louisville Slugger Ultimate Book of Hitting. LC 96-46283. 1995. pap. 16.95 (*0-8050-4413-2*) H Holt & Co.

Monteleone, Susan. Proceedings of the United States Nuclear Regulatory Commission: Twenty-Fourth Water Reactor Safety Information Meeting, Plenary Session, High Burnup Fuel, Containment & Structural Aging, Vol. 1. 372p. 1997. per. 33.00 (*0-16-063014-2*) USGPO.

— Twenty-Fifth Water Reactor Safety Information Meeting: Bethesda Marriott Hotel, Bethesda, Maryland, October 20- 22, 1997. 144p. 1997. per. 15.00 (*0-16-063021-5*) USGPO.

— Twenty Seventh Water Reactor Safety Information Meeting: Held at Bethesda Marriott Hotel, Bethesda, Maryland, October 25- 27, 1999. 604p. 2000. per. 52.00 (*0-16-059195-3*) USGPO.

— Twenty-Sixth Water Reactor Safety Information Meeting: Bethesda Mariott Hotel, Bethesda, Maryland, October 26- 28, 1998. 146p. 1998. per. 13.00 (*0-16-063030-4*) USGPO.

— United States Nuclear Regulatory Commission: Twenty Fourth Water Reactor Safety Information Meeting, Vol. 2. 443p. 1997. per. 40.00 (*0-16-063016-9*) USGPO.

— United States Nuclear Regulatory Commission: Twenty-Fourth Water Reactor Safety Information Meeting, Vol. 3. 178p. 1997. per. 17.00 (*0-16-063017-7*) USGPO.

— United States Nuclear Regulatory Commission Twenty-fifth Water Reactor Safety Information Meeting: Bethesda Marriott Hotel, Bethesda, Maryland, October 20-22, 1997, Vol. 1. 376p. 1998. per. 30.00 (*0-16-063023-1*) USGPO.

— United States Nuclear Regulatory Commission Twenty-Fifth Water Reactor Safety Information Meeting: Held at Bethesda Marriott Hotel, Bethesda, Maryland, October 20-22, 1997, Vol. 2. 236p. 1998. per. 19.00 (*0-16-063022-3*) USGPO.

— United States Nuclear Regulatory Commission Twenty-Fifth Water Reactor Safety Information Meeting, Held At Bethesda Marriott Hotel, Bethesda, Maryland, October 20-22, 1997, Vol. 3. 365p. 1998. per. 29.00 (*0-16-063024-X*) USGPO.

***Monteleone, Thomas.** Vengeance. 2000. mass mkt. 6.99 (*0-8125-7524-5*) Tor Bks.

Monteleone, Thomas F. Blood of the Lamb. 448p. 1993. mass mkt. 5.99 (*0-8125-2222-2*, Pub. by Tor Bks) St Martin.

— Borderlands. 1990. pap. 3.95 (*0-380-75924-1*, Avon Bks) Morrow Avon.

— Night of Broken Souls. 448p. 1998. mass mkt. 6.50 (*0-446-60577-8*, Pub. by Warner Bks) Little.

***Monteleone, Thomas F.** The Reckoning. LC 99-52232. 416p. 1999. 27.95 (*0-312-86931-2*, Pub. by Forge NYC) St Martin.

Monteleone, Thomas F. The Resurrectionist. 416p. 1997. mass mkt. 6.50 (*0-446-60399-6*, Pub. by Warner Bks) Little.

Monteleone, Thomas F., ed. Borderlands 4, Vol. 4. 1995. pap. 5.99 (*1-56504-110-0*, 11805, Borealis) White Wolf.

— Borderlands Two. 304p. (Orig.). 1991. mass mkt. 4.99 (*0-380-76517-9*, Avon Bks) Morrow Avon.

Monteleone, Thomas F., ed. see Ellison, Harlan, et al.

Monteleone, Thomas F., ed. see Vachss, Andrew H., et al.

Monteleone, Thomas F., ed. see Wilson, F. Paul, et al.

Montelius, Johan. Exploiting Fine-Grain Parallelism in Concurrent Constraint Languages. LC 99-165301. (Theses in Computing Science Ser.). 206 p. 1997. write for info. (*91-506-1215-8*) Coronet Bks.

Montelius, Oscar. Civilization of Sweden in Heathen Times. LC 68-25251. (World History Ser.: No. 48). (Illus.). 1969. reprint ed. lib. bdg. 75.00 (*0-8383-0216-5*) M S G Haskell Hse.

— Dating in the Bronze Age with Special Reference to Scandinavia. 148p. (Orig.). 1986. pap. 37.50 (*91-7402-182-6*) Coronet Bks.

Montell, Lynwood, ed. see Ancelet, Barry J., et al.

Montell, William L. Don't Go up Kettle Creek: Verbal Legacy of the Upper Cumberland. LC 82-8566. (Illus.). 264p. reprint ed. pap. 81.90 (*0-608-00934-2*, 206172800011) Bks Demand.

— Ghosts along the Cumberland: Deathlore in the Kentucky Foothills. LC 74-32241. (Illus.). 272p. 1975. pap. 16.95 (*0-87049-535-6*) U of Tenn Pr.

— Kentucky Ghosts. LC 93-37211. (New Books for New Readers). 64p. 1993. pap. 5.95 (*0-8131-0909-4*) U Pr of Ky.

— Killings: Folk Justice in the Upper South. 216p. 1986. pap. 18.00 (*0-8131-0824-1*) U Pr of Ky.

— Saga of Coe Ridge: A Study in Oral History. LC 74-77846. (Illus.). 256p. 1970. pap. 17.00 (*0-87049-315-9*) U of Tenn Pr.

— Singing the Glory Down: Amateur Gospel Music in South Central Kentucky, 1900-1991. LC 91-8688. (Illus.). 264p. 1991. text 29.95 (*0-8131-1757-7*) U Pr of Ky.

— Upper Cumberland. LC 93-6972. (Folklife in the South Ser.). (Illus.). 256p. 1993. pap. 16.95 (*0-87805-631-9*); text 37.50 (*0-87805-630-0*) U Pr of Miss.

Montell, William L. & Morse, Michael L. Kentucky Folk Architecture. LC 95-31103. (Illus.). 120p. 1995. pap. 12.50 (*0-8131-0843-8*) U Pr of Ky.

Montell, William L., jt. auth. see Kohn, Rita T.

***Montell, William Lynwood.** Ghosts Across Kentucky. LC 00-32058. 2000. write for info. (*0-8131-2176-0*) U Pr of Ky.

— Ghosts Across Kentucky. (Illus.). 208p. 2000. pap. 17.00 (*0-8131-9007-X*) U Pr of Ky.

Montella, Ralph. Plastics in Architecture: A Guide to Acrylic & Polycarbonate. LC 85-1645. (Plastics Engineering Ser.: No. 10). (Illus.). 231p. reprint ed. pap. 71.70 (*0-7837-0868-8*, 204117600019) Bks Demand.

Montellano, Bernard R. Ortiz De, see Ortiz De Montellano, Bernard R.

Montellano, Marisol. Mammalian Fauna of the Judith River Formation, Late Cretaceous, Judithian, Northcentral Montana. (Publications in Geological Sciences: Vol. 136). (C). 1992. pap. 18.95 (*0-520-09768-8*, Pub. by U CA Pr) Cal Prin Full Svc.

Montemayer, Raymond, et al, eds. Personal Relationships During Adolescence. (Advances in Adolescent Development Ser.: Vol. 6). (C). 1994. text 58.00 (*0-8039-5680-0*); pap. text 26.00 (*0-8039-5681-9*) Sage.

Montemayor, Aurelio M. WOW: Workshop on Workshops. rev. ed. (Illus.). 134p. 1994. pap. text 25.00 (*1-878550-52-7*) Inter Dev Res Assn.

Montemayor, Carlos. Blood Relations. Carter, Dale & Gonzalez, Alfonso, trs. from SPA. LC 95-1265. (Contemporary Latin-American Classics in English Translation Ser.).Tr. of Mal de Piedra. 111p. 1995. 17.95 (*0-917635-16-7*) Plover Pr.

— Gambusino. Copeland, John, tr. from SPA. LC 96-53996. Orig. Title: Minas del Retorno. 120p. 1997. 17.95 (*0-917635-21-3*); pap. 8.95 (*0-917635-24-8*) Plover Pr.

Montemayor, Jorge De, see De Montemayor, Jorge.

Montemayor, Raymond, et al, eds. From Childhood to Adolescence: A Transitional Period? LC 89-28707. (Advances in Adolescent Development Ser.: No. 2). 312p. 1990. pap. 96.80 (*0-608-05071-7*, 206562600005) Bks Demand.

— From Childhood to Adolescence: A Transitional Period? (Advances in Adolescent Development Ser.: Vol. 2). (Illus.). 300p. (C). 1990. 58.00 (*0-8039-3725-3*); pap. 26.00 (*0-8039-3726-1*) Sage.

***Montemayor, Raymond, et al.** Adolescent Diversity in Ethnic, Economic & Cultural Contexts. LC 99-50651. (Advances in Adolescent Development Ser.). (Illus.). (C). 1999. write for info. (*0-7619-2127-3*) Sage.

Montemurro, Donald G. & Bruni, J. Edward. The Human Brain in Dissection. 2nd ed. (Illus.). 208p. 1988. pap. text 29.95 (*0-19-504926-8*) OUP.

Montenari, F. W., et al, eds. Resource Mobilization for Drinking Water & Sanitation in Developing Nations. 768p. 1987. 90.00 (*0-87262-629-6*) Am Soc Civil Eng.

Montenat, C. & Plateaux, L. How to Read the World: Creation & Evolution. (Adult Christian Formation Program Ser.). (Illus.). 144p. 1985. pap. 10.95 (*0-8245-0721-5*) Crossroad NY.

Montenbruck, O. Astronomy on the Personal Computer. 2nd ed. LC 94-28233. (Illus.). 312p. 1994. 59.95 incl. disk (*0-387-57700-9*) Spr-Verlag.

Montenbruck, O. & Pfleger, T. Astronomy on the Personal Computer. Dunlop, S., tr. from GER. (Illus.). 272p. 1991. 51.00 incl. disk (*0-387-52754-0*) Spr-Verlag.

***Montenbruck, O. & Pfleger, T.** Astronomy on the Personal Computer. 4th rev. ed. Dunlop, S., tr. (Illus.). xv, 310p. 2000. 54.95 incl. cd-rom (*3-540-67221-4*) Spr-Verlag.

***Montenbruck, Oliver & Gill, E.** Satellite Orbits: Models, Methods & Applications. LC 00-38815. (Illus.). xi, 372p. 2000. 65.00 incl. cd-rom (*3-540-67280-X*) Spr-Verlag.

Montenbruck, Oliver & Pfleger, T. Astronomy on the Personal Computer. 3rd ed. Dunlop, S. & Dunlop, Storm, trs. LC 97-43252. (Illus.). xiii, 312p. (C). 1998. 59.95 incl. disk (*3-540-63521-1*) Spr-Verlag.

Montenegro, Carlos. Magical Herbal Baths of Santeria. 1997. pap. 5.95 (*0-942272-45-5*) Original Pubns.

— Palo Mayombe: Spirits, Rituals, Spells. (Illus.). 154p. 1997. pap. 9.95 (*0-942272-42-0*) Original Pubns.

— Powerful Amulets of Santeria. 90p. 1997. pap. 9.95 (*0-942272-46-3*) Original Pubns.

Montenegro, Carlos H., jt. ed. see Caicedo, Xavier.

Montenegro, Carolos. Santeria Candles Oils Incense. 1998. pap. 14.95 (*0-942272-52-8*) Original Pubns.

Montenegro Duque, Angel, et al. Historia de Espana Vol. 1, No. 2: La Conquista y la Explotacion Economica. 762p. 1992. 189.50 (*84-239-4983-4*) Elliots Bks.

Montenegro, M. Irene, et al, eds. Microelectrodes: Theory & Applications. (C). 1991. text 237.50 (*0-7923-1229-5*) Kluwer Academic.

Montenegro, Omar L. El Desierto que Canta: Poesia Underground Cubana. (SPA.). 85p. (C). 1993. pap. 8.00 (*1-884619-01-0*) Endowment CAS.

Montenegro, Riccardo, jt. auth. see Martegani, Paolo.

Montenegro, W. Introduccion a las Doctrinas Politico-Economicas. (Breviarios Ser.). (SPA.). pap. 9.99 (*968-16-0609-4*, Pub. by Fondo) Continental Bk.

Montenegro, Xenia. Women & Racial Minority Representation in School Administration, 1993. 20p. 1993. pap. 11.00 (*0-87652-203-7*, 21-00417) Am Assn Sch Admin.

Montengon, Pedro. Pedro Montengon's Frioleras Eruditas y Curiosas para la Publica Instruccion. Ramos-Garcia, Luis A., ed. LC 97-48899. (Hispanic Literature Ser.: Vol. 38). 324p. 1998. text 99.95 (*0-7734-8492-2*) E Mellen.

Monteon, Michael. Chile & the Great Depression: The Politics of Underdevelopment, 1927-1948. LC 98-18509. (Illus.). 408p. (Orig.). (C). 1998. pap. 38.95 (*0-87918-090-0*) ASU Lat Am St.

Monter, E. William. Judging the French Reformation: Heresy Trials by Sixteenth-Century Parlements. LC 99-19419. (Illus.). 324p. 1999. 35.00 (*0-674-48860-1*) HUP.

Monter, William. Enforcing Morality in Early Modern Europe. 1987. 109.95 (*0-86078-214-X*) Ashgate Pub Co.

Monterde, Francisco, ed. see Raluy, Poudevila A.

Monterey Bay Aquarium Staff. A Field Guide to the Monterey Bay Aquarium. LC 98-36560. 1999. spiral bd. 14.95 (*1-878244-21-3*) Monterey Bay Aquarium.

Monterey Bay Aquarium Staff, jt. auth. see Slager, Christina Joie.

Montero de Pedro, Jose. The Spanish in New Orleans & Louisiana. Chandler, Richard E., tr. from SPA. LC 99-52154. (Illus.). 320p. 2000. 24.95 (*1-56554-685-7*) Pelican.

Montero, F. Puyol, see Puyol Montero, F.

Montero, Gloria. The Summer the Whales Sang. 159p. (YA). (gr. 5 up). 1995. mass mkt. 6.95 (*0-88862-903-6*); bds. 16.95 (*0-88862-904-4*) Formac Dist Ltd.

— The Villa Marini. 320p. 1998. pap. 15.00 (*0-88001-609-4*) HarpC.

— The Villa Marini: A Family Saga. LC 97-15463. 309p. 1997. 23.00 (*0-88001-577-2*) HarpC.

Montero, Gloria. We Stood Together: First Hand Accounts of Dramatic Events in Canada's Labour Past. 261p. 1979. 24.95 (*0-88862-268-6*, Pub. by J Lorimer) Formac Dist Ltd.

Montero, Jane B. Tree. (Illus.). 16p. (Orig.). (J). (ps-6). 1995. pap. 5.00 (*0-9650829-0-3*) J B Montero.

Montero, Jose P. El Pintor de Trenes. (SPA.). 1996. 11.95 (*84-241-3342-0*) Lectorum Pubns.

Montero, Julio, ed. see Blanc, Iris & Hildebrandt, Elinore J.

Montero, Lidia D., tr. see Goetz, Joan.

Montero, Luis A. & Smeyers, Yves G. Trends in Applied Theoretical Chemistry. LC 92-12289. (Topics in Molecular Organization & Engineering Ser.: Vol. 9). 224p. (C). 1992. text 166.50 (*0-7923-1745-9*) Kluwer Academic.

Montero, Mayra. In the Palm of Darkness: A Novel. 192p. 1998. pap. 12.00 (*0-06-092906-5*) HarpC.

***Montero, Mayra.** The Last Night I Spent with You: A Novel. Grossman, Edith, tr. LC 99-86223. 128p. 2000. 19.95 (*0-06-095290-3*) HarpC.

— The Messenger: A Novel. Grossman, Edith, tr. from SPA. LC 98-41176. 224p. 1999. 23.00 (*0-06-019223-2*, HarperFlamingo) HarpC.

— The Messenger: A Novel. Grossman, Edith, tr. 224p. 2000. pap. 13.00 (*0-06-092961-8*, Perennial) HarperTrade.

Montero, Miguel, tr. see Ronnholm, Ursula O.

Montero, Oscar. The Name Game: Writing/Fading Writer in de Donde Son los Cantantes. LC 88-14376. (North Carolina Studies in the Romance Languages & Literatures: No. 231). 152p. reprint ed. pap. 47.20 (*0-608-20071-9*, 207134300011) Bks Demand.

Montero, Oscar, tr. see Molloy, Sylvia.

Montero, Patricia Espinosa De Los, see Espinosa De Los Montero, Patricia.

Montero, Rosa. Absent Love: A Chronicle. De la Torre, Cristina & Glad, Diana, trs. LC 90-28657. (European Women Writers Ser.). 214p. 1991. pap. 66.40 (*0-608-05115-2*, 206567400005) Bks Demand.

— The Delta Function. Easton, Kari A. & Gavilan, Yolanda M., trs. from SPA. LC 91-16576. (European Women Writers Ser.). viii, 267p. 1992. text 45.00 (*0-8032-3152-0*) U of Nebr Pr.

— The Delta Function. Easton, Kari A. & Gavilan, Yolanda M., trs. from SPA. LC 91-16576. (European Women Writers Ser.). viii, 267p. 1992. pap. 14.95 (*0-8032-8183-8*, Bison Books) U of Nebr Pr.

— La Hija del Canibal. (SPA.). 1998. pap. 14.95 (*84-239-9656-5*, Pub. by Espasa Calpe) Continental Bk.

Montero, Rose. Te Tratare Como Una Reina (I'll Treat You Like a Queen) 1997. pap. 9.95 (*84-322-1501-5*, Pub. by E Seix Barral) Continental Bk.

Montero-Sieburth, Martha & Villarruel, Francisco, eds. Making Invisible Latino Adolescents Visible: A Critical Approach for Building Upon Latino Diversity. LC 99-35516. (MSU Series on Children, Youth & Families). 350p. 1999. 60.00 (*0-8153-2344-1*, SS1103) Garland.

Montero-Sieburth, Martha, jt. ed. see Anderson, Gary L.

Monteros, Maria. Flamenco. 80p. 1999. pap. 8.00 (*0-8059-4740-X*) Dorrance.

— Stars over Tangier. 88p. 1998. pap. 9.00 (*0-8059-4322-6*) Dorrance.

Monterrey, Manuel, ed. see Olmos, Edward James.

Monterrosa, Augusto. Triptico (Triptic) (SPA.). 410p. 1995. pap. 16.99 (*968-16-4613-4*, Pub. by Fondo) Continental Bk.

Monterrosa, Ricardo, tr. see Quain, Bill.

Monterroso, Augusto. Antologia del Cuento Triste. (SPA.). 1998. pap. text 24.95 (*968-19-0342-0*) Santillana.

— Los Buscadores de Oro: The Gold Searchers. 136p. 1995. pap. 12.50 (*0-679-76098-9*) Villard Books.

— Complete Works & Other Stories. Grossman, Edith, tr. from SPA. LC 95-14550. (Pan American Ser.). 176p. 1996. pap. 12.95 (*0-292-75184-2*) U of Tex Pr.

Montes. Using Microsoft Works 4 for Macintosh. 1994. 27.99 (*1-56529-920-5*) Que.

Montes, Al. Robots & Gardens: Science Fantasy Poems. 48p. 1985. 4.00 (*0-918476-14-3*) Cornerstone Pr.

Montes, Carmel. Computer Shorthand: Dictionary. 151p. (C). 1987. pap. 13.99 (*0-9618340-0-5*) Prof Educ Dist.

Montes, Carmen Gil de, see Laita, Luis M. & Gil de Montes, Carmen.

Montes de Oca, Elena. Nadie Espera Que Escriba. Zapata, Sergio, ed. (SPA., Illus.). 50p. (Orig.). 1996. pap. write for info. (*0-9654846-3-7*) E M de Oca.

Montes De Oca, Marco A. Twenty-One Poems. Miller, Yvette E., ed. Villasenor, Laura, tr. LC 82-20833. (Discoveries Ser.). (ENG & SPA.). 73p. 1982. pap. 9.00 (*0-935480-09-7*) Lat Am Lit Rev Pr.

Montes, Elizabeth & Hart, Corinne. Baby's Baptism: Sacrament of Welcome. (Illus.). 32p. 1990. reprint ed. pap. text 3.60 (*1-55904-119-8*, 9444) Franciscan Comns.

Montes, Elizabeth, jt. auth. see Aisenberg, Gino.

Montes, F., jt. ed. see Maten, J. M.

Montes, Fernando. Enciclopedia de la Sexualidad.Tr. of Span.. 944p. 1975. 44.95 (*0-8288-5865-9*, S32223) Fr & Eur.

Montes Garces, Elizabeth. El Cuestionamiento de los Mecanismos de Representacion en la Novelistica de Fanny Buitrago. (Wor(l)ds of Change: No. 25). (SPA.). XII, 195p. (C). 1997. text 44.95 (*0-8204-3308-X*) P Lang Pubng.

Montes, Graciela. Federico y el Mar. (Illus.). 1995. 15.75 (*950-07-0849-3*) T R Bks.

— La Venganza de la Trenza (Revenge of the Ponytail) (SPA., Illus.). 28p. (J). (gr. 2). 1997. pap. 5.99 (*968-16-5437-4*, Pub. by Fondo) Continental Bk.

Montes-Huidobro, Matias. El Laud del Desterrado. 182p. 1995. pap. 10.95 (*1-55885-082-1*) Arte Publico.

— Ojos para No Ver. LC 79-52160. (Coleccion Teatro). (SPA., Illus.). 59p. 1980. pap. 6.00 (*0-89729-229-4*) Ediciones.

— Persona: Vida y Mascara en el Teatro Puertorriqueno. LC 84-19721. (SPA., Illus.). 560p. (C). 1984. pap. 15.00 (*0-913480-61-4*) Inter Am U Pr.

Montes, Manuel V. Public Policy for Developing Market Economies. 119p. 1969. pap. 2.50 (*0-8477-2425-5*) U of PR Pr.

***Montes, Marisa.** Egg-napped ! LC 99-87295. (Illus.). 32p. (J). (ps-2). 2020. 15.95 (*0-06-028950-3*) HarpC.

— Egg-Napped ! LC 99-87295. (Illus.). 32p. (J). (ps-2). 5.95 (*0-06-443676-4*) HarpC.

— Egg-Napped ! LC 99-87295. (Illus.). 32p. (J). (ps-2). 2020. 15.89 (*0-06-028951-1*) HarpC.

— Juan Bobo Goes to Work. LC 99-52381. (Illus.). 32p. (J). (ps-4). 2000. 15.95 (*0-688-16233-9*, Wm Morrow); lib. bdg. 15.89 (*0-688-16234-7*, Wm Morrow) Morrow Avon.

— Something Wicked's in Those Woods. 224p. (YA). (gr. 8-12). 2000. 17.00 (*0-15-202391-7*, Harcourt Child Bks) Harcourt.

Montes, Sergio. Hydraulics of Open Channel Flow. LC 98-20532. 712p. 1998. 99.00 (*0-7844-0357-0*) Am Soc Civil Eng.

Montesano, R., et al, eds. Long-Term & Short-Term Assays for Carcinogens: A Critical Appraisal. (IARC Scientific Publications: No. 83). (Illus.). 580p. 1987. pap. 70.00 (*92-832-1183-9*) OUP.

— Molecular & Cellular Aspects of Carcinogen Screening Tests. (IARC Scientific Publications: No. 27). (Illus.). 372p. 1986. 43.00 (*0-19-723027-X*) OUP.

Montesano, R., ed. see International Agency for Research on Cancer Staff.

***Montesano, Ronald.** 3active AutoCAD 2000 in 48 Hours: Step by Step Instruction for AutoCAD 2000. (Illus.). 130p. 1999. pap. 29.95 (*0-9665063-6-7*) Threeactive Pr.

— 3active AutoCAD 2000 in 48 Hours: Step by Step Instruction for AutoCAD 2000 & LT. 3rd large type ed. 250p. 2000. pap. 39.99 (*0-9665063-7-5*) Threeactive Pr.

Monteschi, A. Dictionnaire des Reves. (FRE.). 445p. 1997. 69.95 (*0-320-00482-1*) Fr & Eur.

Montesi, Albert J. Historical Survey of the Southern Review, 1935-1942: Radical Conservatism. Weeks, Dennis L., ed. LC 99-20023. (Studies in American Literature: Vol. 30). 313p. 1999. text 99.95 (*0-7734-8036-6*) E Mellen.

***Montesi, Albert J.** Lafayette Square. (Images of America Ser.). 1999. pap. 18.99 (*0-7385-0022-4*) Arcadia Publng.

Montesi, Albert J. Peter Bently: The Super Sleuth Cat. 60p. 1987. pap. 5.00 (*0-918476-15-1*) Cornerstone Pr.

— Windows & Mirrors. LC 77 89821. 1977. 3.95 (*0-918476-00-3*) Cornerstone Pr.

Montesinos, Jose M. Classical Tesselations & Three Manifolds. (Universitext Ser.). (Illus.). xvii, 230p. 1987. 61.95 (*0-387-15291-1*) Spr-Verlag.

Montesquieu. Considerations on the Greatness of the Romans & Their Decline. Lowenthal, David, tr. from FRE. LC 99-28814. 248p. (C). 1999. reprint ed. pap. text 12.95 (*0-87220-496-0*); reprint ed. lib. bdg. 36.95 (*0-87220-497-9*) Hackett Pub.

— Lettres Persanes. (Folio Ser.: No. 475). (FRE.). pap. 9.95 (*2-07-036475-5*) Schoenhof.

— Lettres Persanes. unabridged ed. (FRE.). pap. 7.95 (*2-87714-141-1*, Pub. by Bookking Intl) Distribks Inc.

— Selected Political Writings. rev. ed. Richter, Melvin, tr. from FRE. & intro. by. LC 89-29578. 299p. (C). 1990. reprint ed. pap. text 12.95 (*0-87220-090-6*) Hackett Pub.

Montesquieu, Charles de Secondat. The Persian Letters. Healy, George R., tr. from FRE. LC 62-21265. 1964. 29.50 (*0-672 51053 7*) Irvington.

— Selected Political Writings. rev. ed. Richter, Melvin, tr. from FRE. & intro. by. LC 89-29578. 299p. (C). 1990. reprint ed. lib. bdg. 34.95 (*0-87220-091-4*) Hackett Pub.

Montesquieu, Charles-Louis De, see De Montesquieu, Charles-Louis.

Montesquiou-Fezensac, Raymond. The Russian Campaign, 1812. LC 70-90563. 159p. reprint ed. pap. 49.30 (*0-608-15806-2*, 203109100073) Bks Demand.

***Montessi, Anna L. & Montessi, Peter M.** Everybody Wants Your Money: A Guidebook to Keeping It. Rothman, Judith L., ed. (Illus.). 216p. 2000. pap. 29.99 (*0-9678614-0-3*) Jordan AZ.

Montessi, Peter M., jt. auth. see Montessi, Anna L.

Montessori, Maria. The Absorbent Mind. LC 95-18404. 1995. pap. 14.95 (*0-8050-4156-7*, Owl) H Holt & Co.

— The Absorbent Mind. 1993. reprint ed. lib. bdg. 29.95 (*1-56849-212-X*) Buccaneer Bks.

— The Discovery of the Child. 242p. 1986. mass mkt. 6.99 (*0-345-33656-9*) Ballantine Pub Grp.

— Discovery of the Child. 1976. 26.95 (*0-8488-0583-6*) Amereon Ltd.

— Dr. Montessori's Own Handbook. LC 65-14827. (Illus.). 192p. (C). 1988. pap. 11.00 (*0-8052-0921-2*) Schocken.

— The Mass Explained to Children. 116p. (J). (gr. 3-9). 1998. reprint ed. 14.95 (*0-912141-61-1*) Roman Cath Bks.

— The Montessori Method. LC 64-24014. 416p. (C). 1988. pap. 14.00 (*0-8052-0922-0*) Schocken.

— Montessori Method. 1976. 26.95 (*0-8488-0303-5*) Amereon Ltd.

— Pedagogie Scientifique, 3 tomes, Set. 99.95 (*0-685-33998-X*) Fr & Eur.

— The Secret of Childhood. 416p. 1982. mass mkt. 5.99 (*0-345-30583-3*) Ballantine Pub Grp.

— The Secret of Childhood: A Book for All Parents & Teachers. Carter, Barbara B., tr. from ITA. viii, 239p. (C). 1983. text 14.95 (*0-86131-375-5*, Pub. by Kalakshetra Pubns) N Montessori.

Montet, Pierre. Everyday Life in Egypt in the Days of Ramesses the Great. LC 80-26390. 400p. 1980. pap. 21.95 (*0-8122-1113-8*) U of Pa Pr.

— Everyday Life in Egypt in the Days of Ramesses the Great. Maxwell-Hyslop, A. R. & Drower, Margaret S., trs. LC 74-3625. (Illus.). 365p. 1974. reprint ed. lib. bdg. 69.50 (*0-8371-7446-5*, MOLE, Greenwood Pr) Greenwood.

Monteton, Otto V. Uber die Reitkunst, 2 bde. in 1. 726p. 1995. write for info. (*3-487-08346-9*) G Olms Pubs.

Montevecchi, William A. & Tuck, Leslie M. Newfoundland Birds: Exploitation, Study, Conservation. (Publications of the Nuttall Ornithological Club: No. 21). (Illus.). 273p. 1987. 10.50 (*1-877973-31-9*) Nuttall Ornith.

Monteverde, Alonso A. Pan-Americanism from Monroe to the Present: A View from the Other Side. rev. ed. Zatz, Asa, tr. LC 68-13659. 192p. reprint ed. pap. 59.60 (*0-7837-3914-1*, 204376200010) Bks Demand.

Monteverdi, Claudio. Madrigals, Bk. 8. 384p. 1991. pap. 19.95 (*0-486-26739-3*) Dover.

— Madrigals, Bks. 4-5. 256p. 1986. pap. 12.95 (*0-486-25102-0*) Dover.

— Ten Madrigals. Stevens, Denis, ed. 106p. 1979. pap. 16.95 (*0-19-343676-0*) OUP.

***Monteverdi, Claudio.** The Third Book of Madrigals: Apt for Voices, Viols & Recorders. Charteris, Richard, ed. Newbegin, Nerida, tr. (Viol Consort Ser.: Vol. 34).Tr. of Terzo Libro de Madrigali. (Illus.). xviii, 110p. 2000. pap. 86.00 (*1-56571-153-X*, VC034) PRB Prods.

Montey, Sharon. Looking Out for Ollie. (Storybridge Ser.). 80p. (J). (gr. 3-7). 1995. pap. 9.95 (*0-7022-2734-X*, Pub. by Univ Queensland Pr) Intl Spec Bk.

Montez, Lola. Timeless Beauty: Advice to Ladies & Gentlemen from Lola Montez. Leisch, Juanita, ed. (Illus.). 184p. 1998. pap. 12.00 (*1-57747-043-5*) Thomas Publications.

Montez, Susan. Radio-Free Queens. LC 93-39304. 80p. 1994. pap. 10.95 (*0-8076-1345-2*) Braziller.

Montfaucon, Bernard De, see De Montfaucon, Bernard.

Montfaucon De Villars, Abbe N. De, see De Montfaucon De Villars, Abbe N.

Montfiro, H., tr. see Consigleri, Pederoso.

Montfleury. Le Mary Sans Femme. Forman, ed. (Exeter French Texts Ser.: Vol. 59). (FRE.). 154p. Date not set. pap. text 19.95 (*0-85989-212-3*, Pub. by Univ Exeter Pr) Northwestern U Pr.

Montford, Heather. Contraceptive Care: Meeting Individual Needs. 256p. 1993. pap. 47.75 (*1-56593-213-7*, 0554) Singular Publishing.

Montford, John T., et al. A Guide to Texas Workers' Compensation Reform, 2 vols., Set. 1000p. 1991. ring bd. 250.00 (*0-409-25480-0*, MICHIE) LEXIS Pub.

Montfort, Catherine R., ed. Literary Women & the French Revolution of 1789. LC 94 69023. (Illus.). 318p. 1995. lib. bdg. 45.95 (*1-883479-07-X*) Summa Pubns.

Montfort, Matthew C. Ancient Traditions-Future Possibilities: Rhythmic Training Through the Traditions of Africa, Bali & India. Delma, Adriana, ed. LC 86-60024. 141p. (C). 1987. pap. text 29.95 (*0-937879-00-2*) Ancient Future Music.

***Montfort, Sue & Brick, Peggy.** Unequal Partners: Teaching about Power & Consent in Adult-Teen Relationships. 156p. (gr. 5-12). 1999. 25.00 (*0-9609366-4-5*) Plan Parenthood.

Montfort, Sue, et al. Healthy Foundations: Developing Positive Policies & Programs Regarding Young Children. 22p. 1993. 5.00 (*0-9609366-8-8*) Plan Parenthood.

Montgelas, Maximilian. Versaille Verdic. Vesey, Constance, ed. LC 74-12765. Orig. Title: Lertfaden Zur Kriegsschuldfrage. 255p. 1975. reprint ed. lib. bdg. 65.00 (*0-8371-7741-3*, MOVV, Greenwood Pr) Greenwood.

Montgolfier, Bernard De, see De Montgolfier, Bernard.

Montgomerie, Deborah, jt. ed. see Daley, Caroline.

Montgomerie, G. A., ed. see Monds, F. C.

Montgomery. Building Object-Oriented Software. Date not set. 65.00 (*0-07-043196-5*) McGraw.

— Collaboration Between General & Special Education. 2002. pap. text. write for info. (*1-56593-086-X*) Thomson Learn.

— Design Analysis Experiments. 4th ed. 1997. pap. text 25.00 (*0-471-17188-3*) Wiley.

— Double Entry Cornerstone. 1996. pap. text. write for info. (*0-205-26278-3*) Allyn.

— Earth Science. 2000. pap. text 39.00 (*0-697-29300-9*) McGraw.

— Earth Then & Now. 3rd ed. 1996. 14.06 (*0-697-33996-3*, WCB McGr Hill) McGrw-H Hghr Educ.

— Fundamentals of Geology. 2nd ed. 1992. teacher ed. 13.12 (*0-697-09807-9*, WCB McGr Hill) McGrw-H Hghr Educ.

— Introduction to Linear Regression Analysis. 544p. 1994. pap. 84.95 (*0-471-00772-2*) Wiley.

— Physical Geology. 3rd ed. 1992. teacher ed. 13.43 (*0-697-12329-4*) McGraw.

— Small Business Accounting. 1997. pap. text, student ed. 16.80 (*0-13-647992-8*) P-H.

— Yellow Eyes. 1940. pap. 1.75 (*0-590-02429-9*) Scholastic Inc.

Montgomery, ed. American History. (C). 2001. text. write for info. (*0-673-99816-9*) Addison-Wesley.

— American History, Vol. 1. (C). 2002. text. write for info. (*0-673-99817-7*) Addison-Wesley.

— American History, Vol. 2. (C). 2002. text. write for info. (*0-673-99818-5*); pap. text, student ed. write for info. (*0-673-99820-7*) Addison-Wesley.

M

— American History, Volume 1. (C). 2002. pap. text, student ed. write for info. (*0-673-99819-3*) Addison-Wesley.

Montgomery & Dathe. Earth: Then & Now. 2nd ed. 1994. pap. text, teacher ed. 14.06 (*0-697-13623-X*) McGraw.

Montgomery, et al. Cornerstone. 2nd ed. 386p. 1999. pap. 30.80 (*0-205-29069-8*, Longwood Div) Allyn.

— Reduction, Symmetry & Phases in Mechanics. LC 90-1143. (Memoirs Ser.: Vol. 88/436). 110p. 1990. pap. 20.00 (*0-8218-2498-8*, MEMO/88/436) Am Math.

— What Made Them Great Series, 5 bks., Set. (Illus.). 832p. (J). (gr. 5-8). 1990. pap. 29.75 (*0-382-09984-2*); lib. bdg. 90.65 (*0-382-09983-4*) Silver Burdett Pr.

Montgomery, jt. auth. see Borgatta, Edgar J.

Montgomery, jt. auth. see Mandelker, Daniel R.

***Montgomery, Donna Lagorio.** Aged Wine. Montgomery, Donald E., ed. (Illus.). 200p. 2000. 14.95 (*0-938577-19-0*, Pub. by St Johns Pub) Indpndnt Pubs.

Montgomery, Alan C. Acronyms & Abbreviations in Library & Information Work: A Reference Handbook of British Usage. 4th ed. LC 90-44886. 254p. 1990. reprint ed. pap. 78.80 (*0-608-08872-2*, 206951100004) Bks Demand.

Montgomery, Albert A. Washington Municipal Expenditures, 1941-1957: An Economic Analysis. LC 63-63374. (Illus.). 179p. reprint ed. pap. 55.50 (*0-8357-8370-7*, 203410400088) Bks Demand.

Montgomery, Alesia. Educational Reforms & Students at Risk: Review of the Current State of the Art. 170p. 1997. pap. 12.00 (*0-16-063595-0*) USGPO.

Montgomery, Alexander. The Cherrie & the Slaye. Composed in Scottis Meeter. LC 72-219. (English Experience Ser.: No. 338). 32p. 1971. reprint ed. 20.00 (*90-221-0338-2*) Walter J Johnson.

Montgomery, Anne, ed. Having Children: The Best Resources to Help You Prepare. 2nd ed. 301p. 1999. pap. text 24.95 (*1-892148-06-4*) Res Pathways.

Montgomery, Anne, jt. ed. see Laffin, Arthur J.

Montgomery, Anne, ed. & photos by see Ingram, Gwen.

Montgomery, Anson. Cyberhacker. (Choose Your Own Adventure Ser.: No. 183). (Illus.). 112p. (J). (gr. 3-7). 1998. pap. 3.50 (*0-553-56747-0*) Bantam.

— Moon Quest. (Choose Your Own Adventure Ser.: No. 167). (Illus.). 128p. (J). (gr. 4-7). 1995. pap. 3.50 (*0-553-56621-0*, Choose) BDD Bks Young Read.

— Moon Quest. (Choose Your Own Adventure Ser.: No. 167). (J). (gr. 4-8). 1996. 8.60 (*0-606-08572-6*, Pub. by Turtleback) Demco.

— Snowboard Racer. (Choose Your Own Adventure Ser.: No. 165). (J). (gr. 4-8). 1995. 8.60 (*0-606-08608-0*, Pub. by Turtleback) Demco.

Montgomery, Barbara M. & Baxter, Leslie A., eds. Dialectical Approaches to Studying Personal Relationships. LC 97-37789. 250p. 1998. write for info. (*0-8058-2112-0*); pap. write for info. (*0-8058-2113-9*) L Erlbaum Assocs.

Montgomery, Barbara M. & Duck, Steve, eds. Studying Interpersonal Interaction. LC 90-20933. (Communication Ser.). 346p. 1991. lib. bdg. 42.00 (*0-89862-312-X*) Guilford Pubns.

— Studying Interpersonal Interaction. LC 90-20933. (Communication Ser.). 46p. 1993. pap. text 25.00 (*0-89862-290-5*) Guilford Pubns.

Montgomery, Barbara M., jt. auth. see Baxter, Leslie A.

***Montgomery, Becky.** Girls & Boys Getting Along: Teaching Sexual Harassement Prevention in the Elementary Classroom. (Illus.). 150p. 1999. reprint ed. pap. text 25.00 (*0-7881-8199-8*) DIANE Pub.

Montgomery, Becky, jt. auth. see Grimm, Carol.

Montgomery, Becky, ed. see Oxley, Robert R.

Montgomery, Bernard. Approach to Sanity: A Study of East-West Relations. LC 74-156696. (Essay Index Reprint Ser.). 1977. reprint ed. 17.95 (*0-8369-2779-6*) Ayer.

Montgomery, Bertha V. & Nabwire, Constance. Cooking the African Way. (Easy Menu Ethnic Cookbooks Ser.). (Illus.). 48p. (J). (gr. 5 up). 1988. lib. bdg. 19.93 (*0-8225-0919-9*, Lerner Publctns) Lerner Pub.

***Montgomery, Bill.** Kurtis Kraft Midget: A Genealogy of Speed. (Illus.). 224p. 1999. 39.95 (*1-891390-02-3*) Witness Prods.

Montgomery, Bob. An Irish Roadside Camera: Ireland's Earliest Motorists & Their Automobiles 1896-1906. LC 98-120548. (Illus.). 120p. 1998. 29.95 (*1-86023-058-X*, Pub. by Martello Bks) Irish Amer Bk.

Montgomery, Bob & Hill, Willie. Learning to Sight Read Jazz, Rock, Latin, & Classical Styles. (Illus.). 202p. (C). 1994. pap. text 29.95 (*1-880157-16-0*) Ardsley.

***Montgomery, Bob & Morris, Laurel.** Surviving: Coping with a Life Crisis. LC 99-54870. 240p. 2000. pap. 14.00 (*1-55561-239-3*) Fisher Bks.

Montgomery, Bucky. The Stonebearer. (Orig.). (YA). (gr. 6 up). 1995. pap. 9.99 (*0-88092-258-3*) Royal Fireworks.

Montgomery, C. Barry & Allen, Richard B., eds. Defense Counsel Training Manual: Essays by Experienced Defense Lawyers. 2nd enl. rev. ed. LC 95-75258. 360p. 1995. pap. 93.00 (*0-9621989-5-1*) IADC IL.

Montgomery, C. G., et al, eds. Principles of Microwave Circuits. (Electromagnetic Waves Ser.: No. 25). 502p. 1987. 99.00 (*0-86341-100-2*, EW025) INSPEC Inc.

Montgomery, Cam J. Last Seen in Vermont with a Big, White Dog. 192p. (Orig.). 1996. pap. write for info. (*1-57502-207-9*, P0844) Morris Pubng.

***Montgomery, Carl H.** Why Worry When God: Scriptural Therapy for Anxiety. LC 00-91448. 126p. 2000. pap. 15.00 (*0-9678976-0-2*) Charis Hse.

Montgomery, Carla W. Earth: Then & Now. 4th ed. 2000. 58.25 (*0-07-303635-8*); pap., student ed. 21.50 (*0-07-303636-6*) McGraw.

— Environmental Geology. 4th ed. 1994. 155.00 (*0-697-15820-9*, WCB McGr Hill) McGrw-H Hghr Educ.

— Environmental Geology. 4th ed. 512p. (C). 1994. per. 45.00 (*0-697-15811-X*, WCB McGr Hill) McGrw-H Hghr Educ.

— Environmental Geology. 4th ed. 1994. teacher ed. 13.75 (*0-697-15812-8*, WCB McGr Hill) McGrw-H Hghr Educ.

— Environmental Geology. 4th ed. 1994. 16.50 (*0-697-27083-1*, WCB McGr Hill) McGrw-H Hghr Educ.

— Environmental Geology. 5th ed. 176p. 1997. pap. 25.94 (*0-697-34282-4*) McGraw.

— Environmental Geology. 5th ed. LC 97-11486. 512p. (C). 1997. text. write for info. (*0-697-34278-6*, WCB McGr Hill) McGrw-H Hghr Educ.

***Montgomery, Carla W.** Environmental Geology. 5th ed. LC 99-14628. 1999. write for info. (*0-07-230140-6*) McGrw-H Hghr Educ.

Montgomery, Carla W. Fundamentals of Geology. 2nd ed. 352p. (C). 1992. text. write for info. (*0-697-09806-0*, WCB McGr Hill) McGrw-H Hghr Educ.

— Fundamentals of Geology. 3rd ed. LC 96-83509. 400p. (C). 1996. text. write for info. (*0-697-32986-0*, WCB McGr Hill) McGrw-H Hghr Educ.

— Fundamentals of Geology. 3rd ed. 432p. (C). 1997. per. write for info. (*0-07-114587-7*, WCB McGr Hill) McGrw-H Hghr Educ.

— Student Study Guide to Accompany Environmental Geology. 4th ed. 160p. (C). 1994. text 23.12 (*0-697-15813-6*, WCB McGr Hill) McGrw-H Hghr Educ.

Montgomery, Carla W. & Dathe, David. Earth: Then & Now. 2nd ed. 592p. (C). 1993. text. write for info. (*0-697-13622-1*, WCB McGr Hill) McGrw-H Hghr Educ.

— Earth: Then & Now. 2nd ed. 592p. (C). 1993. text, student ed. 23.75 (*0-697-17232-5*, WCB McGr Hill) McGrw-H Hghr Educ.

— The Earth: Then & Now. 3rd ed. LC 96-83506. 608p. (C). 1996. text. write for info. (*0-697-28281-3*, WCB McGr Hill) McGrw-H Hghr Educ.

Montgomery, Carla W. & Griffin, Kenneth F. The Earth: Then & Now. 3rd ed. 208p. (C). 1996. text 23.75 (*0-697-28283-X*, WCB McGr Hill) McGrw-H Hghr Educ.

— Fundamentals of Geology. 3rd ed. 160p. (C). 1996. text, student ed. 23.75 (*0-697-35906-9*, WCB McGr Hill) McGrw-H Hghr Educ.

— Physical Geology. 3rd ed. 192p. (C). 1992. text, student ed. 23.75 (*0-697-12330-8*, WCB McGr Hill) McGrw-H Hghr Educ.

Montgomery, Carol. Outlines. (Illus.). 32p. 1990. 35.00 (*0-934714-21-5*); pap. 3.00 (*0-934714-20-7*) Swamp Pr.

— Starting Something. LC 91-73630. 90p. (Orig.). 1992. pap. 6.95 (*1-879603-01-2*) Los Hombres.

Montgomery, Carol L. Healing Through Communication: The Practice of Caring. (Illus.). 180p. (C). 1993. text 42.00 (*0-8039-5120-5*); pap. text 18.50 (*0-8039-5121-3*) Sage.

Montgomery, Charles. The Choir Director's Handbook. Montgomery, Jane, ed. (Illus.). 44p. (Orig.). 1984. pap. 3.95 (*0-916043-01-0*) Light Hearted Pub Co.

Montgomery, Charles, ed. see Miller, Sarah W. & Madaris, Don L.

Montgomery, Charles, ed. see Montgomery, Jane.

Montgomery, Charlotte B. Como Darle una Mano a los Perros y los Gatos: (How to Be a Helping Hand for Dogs & Cats) (ENG & SPA., Illus.). 32p. (Orig.). (J). (gr. k). 1992. pap., student ed. 3.00 (*0-941246-07-8*) NAHEE.

Montgomery, Claire, contrib. by. Flying Colors. 40p. (J). 1998. pap. 4.00 (*0-87440-069-4*) Bakers Plays.

Montgomery Co. Vocational Education Planning Dist,. Tuning into My Future: A Middle School Career Guidance Program. 36p. (YA). (gr. 7-10). 1992. pap., student ed. write for info. (*1-57515-038-7*) PPI Pubng.

Montgomery County Chapter, O. G. S. Staff. Montgomery County, Ohio Vol. II: 5-Generation Pedigree Charts. LC 95-78197. 235p. 1995. pap. 15.00 (*1-887665-09-9*) MCC OGS.

Montgomery County Chapter of the Ohio Genealogical. Harrison Township Vol. IV: Book a Union (Old Beardshear) Cemetery, Willowview Cemetery, Kerr-Drill (Kerr or Florence) Cemetery. LC 82-222963. (Montgomery County, Ohio Cemetery Inscriptions Ser.). 379p. 1995. pap. 25.00 (*1-887665-04-8*) MCC OGS.

— Harrison Township Vol. IV: Book B Shiloh Park Cemetery, Westmont Cemetery. LC 82-222963. (Montgomery County, Ohio Cemetery Inscriptions Ser.). 248p. 1995. pap. 20.00 (*1-887665-05-6*) MCC OGS.

Montgomery County Chapter OGS Staff, ed. see Duhart, Karen J.

Montgomery County Historical Society, Genealogy Se. Family Histories, Montgomery County, Indiana. LC 89-51787. 416p. 1989. 55.00 (*0-938021-74-5*) Turner Pub KY.

Montgomery, Cynthia A. Resource-Based & Evolutionary Theories of the Firm: Towards a Synthesis. LC 95-3537. 288p. (C). 1995. lib. bdg. 106.00 (*0-7923-9562-X*) Kluwer Academic.

Montgomery, Cynthia A. & Porter, Michael E., eds. Strategy: Seeking & Securing Competitive Advantage. (Harvard Business Review Book Ser.). 512p. 1991. 35.00 (*0-87584-243-7*) Harvard Busn.

Montgomery, Cynthia A., jt. auth. see Collis, David J.

Montgomery, D. B. Montgomery: A Genealogy History of the Montgomerys & Their Descendants. (Illus.). 436p. 1991. reprint ed. pap. 67.50 (*0-8328-1712-0*); reprint ed. lib. bdg. 77.50 (*0-8328-1711-2*) Higginson Bk Co.

Montgomery, D. H., ed. Heroic Ballads. LC 68-58820. (Granger Index Reprint Ser.). 1977. 20.95 (*0-8369-6031-9*) Ayer.

Montgomery, D. H., jt. auth. see McHugh, Michael J.

Montgomery, Dan. Beauty in the Stone. LC 95-51452. 256p. 1996. 18.99 (*0-7852-7745-5*) Nelson.

— Finding Your Way: A Christian Guide to Transforming Your Personality & Relationships. LC 99-29516. 208p. 1999. pap. 14.99 (*0-8066-3870-2*, Augsburg) Augsburg Fortress.

— God & Your Personality. LC 95-3256. 176p. 1995. reprint ed. pap. 9.95 (*0-8198-3075-5*) Pauline Bks.

— The Mystery of Half Moon Cove: A Kimmy O'Keefe Mystery. LC 96-5207. (Kimmy O'Keefe Mystery Ser.: Vol. 2). 204p. (Orig.). (YA). (gr. 8-11). 1996. pap. 6.95 (*0-8198-4785-2*) Pauline Bks.

— The Mystery of the Aspen Bandits: A Kimmy O'Keefe Mystery. LC 96-5209. (Kimmy O'Keefe Mystery Ser.: Vol. 1). 204p. (YA). (gr. 8-11). 1996. pap. 6.95 (*0-8198-4788-7*) Pauline Bks.

— Practical Counseling Tools for Pastoral Workers. LC 96-1949. 144p. (Orig.). 1996. pap. 10.95 (*0-8198-5899-4*) Pauline Bks.

Montgomery, Dan & Montgomery, Katie. Heroes of God. LC 98-21256. (Family Read-Aloud Collection). (Illus.). 128p. (J). (gr. k-7). 1998. 15.99 (*0-8066-3607-6*, 9-3607) Augsburg Fortress.

Montgomery, Dan, ed. see Bernal, Dick.

Montgomery, Daniel B. Fire in the Lotus: The Dynamic Buddhism of Nichiren. 1991. pap. 16.00 (*1-85274-091-4*, Pub. by Mandala) IBD Ltd.

Montgomery, Daniel J., jt. auth. see Murphy, Jamie.

Montgomery, David. American Left. (C). (gr. 13). 1999. write for info. (*0-415-90673-3*); pap. write for info. (*0-415-90674-1*) Routledge.

— Beyond Equality: Labor & the Radical Republicans, 1862-1872. LC 80-24434. 552p. 1981. reprint ed. pap. text 15.95 (*0-252-00869-3*) U of Ill Pr.

— Citizen Worker: The Experience of Workers in the United States with Democracy & the Free Market During the Nineteenth Century. 201p. (C). 1994. text 34.95 (*0-521-42057-1*) Cambridge U Pr.

— Citizen Worker: The Experience of Workers in the United States with Democracy & the Free Market During the Nineteenth Century. 201p. 1995. pap. text 15.95 (*0-521-48380-8*) Cambridge U Pr.

— The Fall of the House of Labor: The Workplace, the State & American Labor Activism, 1865-1925. (Illus.). 508p. 1987. text 54.95 (*0-521-22579-5*) Cambridge U Pr.

— The Fall of the House of Labor: The Workplace, the State & American Labor Activism, 1865-1925. (Illus.). 512p. 1989. pap. text 19.95 (*0-521-37982-2*) Cambridge U Pr.

— Mountain Man Crafts & Skills: An Illustrated Guide to Clothing, Shelter, Equipment & Wilderness Living. LC 80-82706. (Illus.). 1981. 17.98 (*0-88290-156-7*, 4024) Horizon Utah.

***Montgomery, David.** Native American Crafts & Skills. (Illus.). 2000. pap. 14.95 (*1-58574-070-5*) Lyons Pr.

Montgomery, David. Workers' Control in America: Studies in the History of Work, Technology, & Labor Struggles. 208p. 1980. pap. text 17.95 (*0-521-28006-0*) Cambridge U Pr.

Montgomery, David & Van Der Linden, Marcel, eds. August Sartorius von Waltershausen: The Workers' Movement in the United States, 1879-1885. LC 97-47495. (Illus.). 275p. (C). 1998. 49.95 (*0-521-63021-5*) Cambridge U Pr.

Montgomery, David, et al. Carbon Charges As a Response to Global Warming: The Effects of Taxing Fossil Fuels. (Illus.). 69p. 1999. reprint ed. pap. text 20.00 (*0-7881-7664-1*) DIANE Pub.

Montgomery, David C. Mongolian Newspaper Reader. LC 78-627747. (Uralic & Altaic Ser.: Vol. 102). 203p. (Orig.). 1969. pap. text 13.00 (*0-87750-083-5*) Res Inst Inner Asian Studies.

— Theory of the Unmagnetized Plasma. (Illus.). 412p. 1971. 169.00 (*0-677-03350-8*) Gordon & Breach.

Montgomery, David R. Indian Crafts & Skills: An Illustrated Guide for Making Authentic Indian Clothing, Shelters & Ornaments. LC 85-60510. 224p. 1985. 17.98 (*0-88290-300-4*) Horizon Utah.

***Montgomery, David R.** Mountainman Crafts & Skills: A Fully Illustrated Guide to Wilderness Living & Survival. LC 00-21623. (Illus.). 2000. pap. 14.95 (*1-58574-066-7*) Lyons Pr.

Montgomery, David R., jt. see Gurnell, A. M.

Montgomery, Dennis. A Link among the Days: The Life & Times of the Reverend Doctor William Archer Rutherfoord Goodwin. (Illus.). 344p. 1998. 25.95 (*0-87517-100-1*); pap. 19.95 (*0-87517-094-3*) Dietz.

Montgomery, Diana. Children with Learning Difficulties. 224p. 1990. pap. 29.95 (*0-89397-351-3*) Nichols Pub.

***Montgomery, Diana L.** Book of Love - Beautiful, Meaningful, Song Lyric Poems. (Illus.). 72p. 2000. pap. 12.00 (*1-929448-25-2*) Etrnl Prsprty.

— 365 Daily Positive Thoughts for Happiness Comfort & Encouragement. 2nd rev. ed. 204p. 1999. pap. 20.00 (*1-929448-17-1*, 17-1) Etrnl Prsprty.

Montgomery, Diane. Children with Learning Difficulties. Mittler, Peter, ed. (Special Needs in Ordinary Schools Ser.). 304p. 1990. pap. text 35.95 (*0-304-31472-2*) Continuum.

— Positive Teacher Appraisal Through Classroom Observation. 1999. pap. text 29.95 (*1-85346-607-7*) David Fulton.

— Spelling: Remedial Strategies. (Special Needs in Ordinary Schools Ser.). (Illus.). 160p. 1996. pap. 35.00 (*0-304-32974-6*); text 89.50 (*0-304-32972-X*) Continuum.

***Montgomery, Don.** Rapture: Post Tribulation & Pre-Wrath. 2000. pap. 11.95 (*1-57921-227-1*, Pub. by WinePress Pub) BookWorld.

Montgomery, Don. Those Wild Fuel Altereds: Drag Racing in the 60s. LC 97-177458. (Illus.). 192p. 1997. 33.95 (*0-9626454-5-1*) D Montgomery.

Montgomery, Donald E., ed. see Montgomery, Donna Lagorio.

Montgomery, Donald E., ed. see Montgomery, Donna L.

Montgomery, Donald E., ed. see Uarlamoff, Susan.

Montgomery, Donald R. Authentic Hot Rods: The Real "Good Old Days" (Illus.). 208p. 1994. 32.95 (*0-9626454-4-3*) D Montgomery.

— Hot Rod Memories: Relived Again. LC 91-194605. (Illus.). 176p. 1991. 32.95 (*0-9626454-2-7*) D Montgomery.

— Hot Rods As They Were: Another Blast from the Past. LC 90-164762. (Illus.). 160p. 1989. 32.95 (*0-9626454-1-9*) D Montgomery.

— Supercharged Gas Coupes: Remembering the "Sixties" (Illus.). 192p. 1992. 32.95 (*0-9626454-3-5*) D Montgomery.

Montgomery, Donna L. Bread & Wine. Montgomery, Donald E., ed. (Illus.). 208p. 1997. 14.95 (*0-938577-17-4*) St Johns Pub.

***Montgomery, Donna L.** Business Briefs. 194p. 1999. pap. 8.95 (*0-938577-18-2*) St Johns Pub.

Montgomery, Donna L. Coffee Talk. (Illus.). 201p. (Orig.). 1995. 14.95 (*0-938577-09-3*) St Johns Pub.

— Kids + Modeling = Money: How to Help Your Children Succeed in Modeling. 178p. 1984. 9.95 (*0-13-515172-4*) St Johns Pub.

— Love, Life & Chocolate Chip Cookies. 120p. (Orig.). 1995. pap. 6.95 (*0-938577-10-7*) St Johns Pub.

— Parenting a Business. LC 88-63423. (Illus.). (Orig.). 1989. pap. 14.95 (*0-938577-04-2*) St Johns Pub.

— Surviving Motherhood. (Illus.). 200p. (Orig.). 1986. pap. 6.95 (*0-938577-00-X*) St Johns Pub.

Montgomery, Donna L., ed. see Tamler, Julie.

Montgomery, Dorothy B. Angling for Words: The Teacher's Line. 1975. pap., student ed. 14.00 (*0-87879-105-1*) Acad Therapy.

Montgomery, Dorothy B. & Gipson, Linda M. Basic Angling. (Angling for Words Ser.). 48p. 1980. teacher ed. 8.00 (*0-87879-519-7*); student ed. 12.00 (*0-87879-518-9*) Acad Therapy.

Montgomery, Douglas C. Design & Analysis of Experiments. 2nd ed. 287p. (C). 1984. pap. text 25.00 (*0-471-86799-3*) Wiley.

— Design & Analysis of Experiments. 4th ed. LC 96-18037. 720p. 1996. text 112.95 (*0-471-15746-5*) Wiley.

***Montgomery, Douglas C.** Design & Analysis of Experiments. 5th ed. LC 99-57472. 672p. 2000. text. write for info. (*0-471-31649-0*) Wiley.

— Design & Analysis of Experiments & Educational Version of Design Expert. 4th ed. 1997. text 136.90 (*0-471-26008-8*) Wiley.

Montgomery, Douglas C. Introduction to Statistical Quality Control. 3rd ed. LC 95-51507. 752p. 1996. text 105.95 (*0-471-30353-4*) Wiley.

***Montgomery, Douglas C.** Introduction to Statistical Quality Control. 4th ed. 816p. (C). 2000. write for info. (*0-471-31648-2*) Wiley.

Montgomery, Douglas C. Introduction to Statistical Quality Control. 20th ed. 240p. 1991. pap. text, suppl. ed. 20.00 (*0-471-53523-0*) Wiley.

Montgomery, Douglas C. & Peck, Elizabeth A. Introduction to Linear Regression Analysis. 2nd ed. LC 91-21553. (Probability & Mathematical Statistics: Applied Probability & Statistics Section Ser.: No. 1346). 544p. 1992. 89.95 (*0-471-53387-4*) Wiley.

Montgomery, Douglas C. & Runger, George C. Applied Statistics & Probability for Engineers. 2nd ed. LC 98-34994. 944p. 1998. text 108.95 (*0-471-17027-5*) Wiley.

Montgomery, Douglas C. & Runger, George C. Engineering Statistics. LC 97-39795. 528p. 1997. text 103.95 (*0-471-17026-7*) Wiley.

***Montgomery, Douglas C., et al.** Engineering Statistics. 2nd ed. 512p. (C). 2000. write for info. (*0-471-38879-3*) Wiley.

Montgomery, Douglas C., et al. Process Redesign & Management: Beyond Reengineering. LC 96-60496. (Illus.). x, 262p. 1996. write for info. (*0-9652178-0-9*) Windham Brannon.

Montgomery, Douglas C., jt. auth. see Hines, William W.

Montgomery, Douglas C., jt. auth. see Johnson, Lynwood A.

Montgomery, Douglas C., jt. auth. see Keats, J. Bert.

Montgomery, Douglas C., jt. auth. see Myers, Raymond H.

Montgomery, Douglas C., jt. ed. see Keats, J. Bert.

***Montgomery, Ed.** Breaking the Spirit of Poverty. LC 98-73618. (Orig.). 1999. pap. text 10.99 (*0-88419-549-X*) Creation House.

Montgomery, Ed. Heaven in Your Heart. 1999. pap. text 10.99 (*0-88419-560-0*) Creation House.

— What to Do When It Hurts So Bad. 240p. 1993. pap. 12.99 (*1-56043-124-5*) Destiny Image.

Montgomery, Elizabeth. The Builder Also Grows. Ashton, Sylvia, ed. LC 77-82653. 1979. 19.95 (*0-87949-099-3*) Ashley Bks.

Montgomery, Elizabeth M. Best of MGM. 1993. 15.98 (*1-55521-953-5*) Bk Sales Inc.

***Montgomery, Elizabeth M.** Best of MGM. rev. ed. (Illus.). 192p. 2000. 25.00 (*0-7881-9261-2*) DIANE Pub.

Montgomery-Fate, Tom. Beyond the White Noise: Mission in a Multicultural World. LC 97-6390. 136p. (Orig.). 1997. pap. 14.99 (*0-8272-0223-7*) Chalice Pr.

Montgomery, Fiona & Collette, Christine, eds. Into the Melting Pot: Teaching Women's Studies into the New Millennium. LC 97-73410. 192p. 1997. text 59.95 (*1-85972-557-0*, Pub. by Ashgate Pub) Ashgate Pub Co.

Montgomery, Frances T. Billy Whiskers: Autobiography of a Goat. (Illus.). 259p. (J). (gr. 2 up). 1969. reprint ed. pap. 4.95 (*0-486-22345-0*) Dover.

An Asterisk (*) at the beginning of an entry indicates that the title is appearing for the first time.

Montgomery, G. Gene, ed. The Evolution & Ecology of Armadillos, Sloths & Vermilinguas. LC 84-600292. (Illus.). 462p. (Orig.). 1986. pap. text 51.00 (*0-87474-649-3*, MOESP) Smithsonian.

Montgomery, Gayle B., et al. One Step from the White House: The Rise & Fall of Senator William F. Knowland. LC 97-50545. 400p. 1998. 29.95 (*0-520-21194-4*, Pub. by U CA Pr) Cal Prin Full Svc.

Montgomery, George, ed. see Montgomery, William R.

Montgomery, George A. The Eye of the Eagle: A Historical Novel of the First Major American Gold Rush. LC 96-72194. 220p. 1996. pap. 8.99 (*1-881636-88-7*) Windsor Hse Pub Grp.

— Pillow of Gold. 256p. 1985. mass mkt. 3.95 (*0-939332-13-2*) J Pohl Assocs.

Montgomery, George R., tr. see Leibniz, Gottfried Wilhelm.

Montgomery, Glenn E. & Schuch, Harold C. GIS Data Conversion Handbook. (Illus.). 292p. (Orig.). (C). 1993. text 27.95 (*0-9625063-4-6*) GIS World Bks.

***Montgomery, Glenn E. & Schuch, Harold C.** GIS Data Conversion Handbook. 320p. (Orig.). (C). 1998. 90.00 (*0-471-32983-5*) Wiley.

Montgomery, H. Mongoose Magoo. LC 68-56822. (Illus.). 64p. (J). (gr. 2-5). 1968. lib. bdg. 10.95 (*0-87783-026-6*) Oddo.

— Mongoose Magoo. deluxe ed. LC 68-56822. (Illus.). 64p. (J). (gr. 2-5). 1968. pap. 3.94 (*0-87783-100-9*) Oddo.

Montgomery, H. R. Memoirs of Sir Richard Steele, 2 vols., Set. LC 76-128570. (English Biography Ser.: No. 31). 1970. reprint ed. lib. bdg. 150.00 (*0-8383-0903-8*) M S G Haskell Hse.

Montgomery, Harry H., Jr. Personal Affairs: Family & Estate Records Organizer. LC 94-90049. (Illus.). 139p. 1994. ring bd. 34.95 (*0-9640265-0-3*) Windmark Pubns.

Montgomery, Henry & Svenson, Ola, eds. Process & Structure in Human Decision Making. LC 88-33788. 335p. 1989. reprint ed. pap. 103.90 (*0-608-04603-5*, 206537300003) Bks Demand.

Montgomery, Henry, jt. ed. see Justin, Peter.

Montgomery, Herb. Beyond Sorrow: Reflections on Death & Grief. 1977. pap. text 5.95 (*0-03-022961-8*) H Holt & Co.

Montgomery, Herb & Montgomery, Mary. Beyond Sorrow: Christian Reflections on Death & Grief. 32p. 1991. reprint ed. pap. 4.95 (*1-879779-03-X*) Montgomery Pr.

— Beyond Sorrow: Reflections on Death & Grief. LC 77-78260. (Books to Encourage & Inspire). 32p. 1984. 6.95 (*0-86683-622-5*, AY8649) Harper SF.

— Beyond Sorrow: Reflections on Death & Grief. rev. ed. 32p. 1985. 3.70 (*0-86683-461-3*) Harper SF.

— The Joy of the Psalms. (Illus.). 64p. (Orig.). 1982. 8.95 (*0-86683-631-4*) Harper SF.

Montgomery, Herb, jt. auth. see Maanum, Armand.

Montgomery, Herb, jt. auth. see Montgomery, Mary.

Montgomery, Hugh L. Ten Lectures on the Interface Between Analytic Number Theory & Harmonic Analysis. LC 94-26864. (CBMS Regional Conference Mathematics Ser.: No. 84). 220p. 1994. pap. 29.00 (*0-8218-0737-4*, CBMS/84) Am Math.

Montgomery, Ian. London. (C). 1988. 45.00 (*1-85368-028-1*, Pub. by New5 Holland) St Mut.

Montgomery, Ian A. Dead Duck: A Jud Carson Mystery. Spafford, Jacalyn A., ed. 120p. (Orig.). 1993. pap. 9.95 (*1-890538-15-9*) Rhiannon Pubns.

— Laura Dean. Spafford, Jacalyn A., ed. 150p. (Orig.). (YA). (gr. 9 up). 1997. pap. 9.95 (*1-890538-14-0*) Rhiannon Pubns.

— The Legend of the Firedrake, Vol. 2. 2000. pap. write for info. (*1-890538-21-3*) Rhiannon Pubns.

— The Legend of the Firedrake, Vol. 3. 2000. pap. write for info. (*1-890538-22-1*) Rhiannon Pubns.

— The Legend of the Firedrake: To Find a Dragon, Vol. 1. Spafford, Jacalyn A., ed. 143p. (Orig.). 1995. pap. 9.95 (*1-890538-20-5*) Rhiannon Pubns.

— Sin in the Camp. 2000. pap. write for info. (*1-890538-16-7*) Rhiannon Pubns.

Montgomery, J. E. The Vagaries of the Qasidah: The Tradition & Practice of Early Arabic Poetry. (Gibb Literary Studies). 280p. 1997. 59.00 (*0-906094-35-6*) David Brown.

Montgomery, J. P., ed. see Kreis, E. J.

Montgomery, J. W. Cross & Crucible Set, Vols. I & II: Johann Valentin Andreae (1586-1654) Phoenix of Theologians. (International Archives of the History of Ideas Ser.: No. 55). 595p. 1974. lib. bdg. 321.50 (*90-247-5054-7*) Kluwer Academic.

Montgomery, Jacqueline. Physical Therapy for Traumatic Head Injury. 1994. text 69.00 (*0-443-08908-6*) Church.

Montgomery, Jacqueline, jt. auth. see Hislop, Helen J.

Montgomery, James. A Practical Detail of the Cotton Manufacture of the United States of America. LC 68-56266. (Library of Early American Business & Industry: No. 32). (Illus.). 219p. 1969. reprint ed. 39.50 (*0-678-00572-9*) Kelley.

Montgomery, James, et al. Poems on the Abolition of the Slave Trade. LC 79-149871. (Black Heritage Library Collection). 1977. 24.95 (*0-8369-8751-9*) Ayer.

Montgomery, James A. Arabia & the Bible. rev. ed. (Library of Biblical Studies). 1969. 25.00 (*0-87068-090-0*) Ktav.

— Daniel: Critical & Exegetical Commentary. Driver, Samuel R. et al, eds. LC 27-14200. (International Critical Commentary Ser.). 520p. 1926. 39.95 (*0-567-05017-3*, Pub. by T & T Clark) Bks Intl VA.

— Isaiah, Vol. 2. 1967. pap. 2.50 (*0-89315-126-2*) Lambert Bk.

— Kings I & II: Critical & Exegetical Commentary. Driver, Samuel R. et al, eds. LC 52-8522. (International Critical Commentary Ser.). 624p. 1951. 39.95 (*0-567-05006-8*, Pub. by T & T Clark) Bks Intl VA.

Montgomery, James A. & Harris, Zellig S. The Ras Shamra Mythological Texts. LC 36-2726. (American Philosophical Society, Philadelphia. Memoirs Ser.: Vol. 4). 139p. reprint ed. pap. 43.10 (*0-608-10829-4*, 200035400025) Bks Demand.

Montgomery, James D. & Fairbrothers, David E. New Jersey Ferns & Fern-Allies. LC 91-40920. (Illus.). 300p. (C). 1992. text 45.00 (*0-8135-1817-2*) Rutgers U Pr.

Montgomery, James H. Dawn Two Thousand: Seven Million Churches to Go. LC 89-61042. 200p. (C). 1989. pap. 8.95 (*0-87808-220-4*) William Carey Lib.

Montgomery, James H. & McGavran, Donald A. The Discipling of a Nation. LC 80-17255. 1980. 4.80 (*0-318-17874-5*) Overseas Crusade.

Montgomery, James M. Water Treatment Principles & Design. LC 85-5344. 712p. 1985. 160.00 (*0-471-04384-2*, Wiley-Interscience) Wiley.

Montgomery, James R., et al. To Foster Knowledge: A History of the University of Tennessee, 1794-1970. LC 83-1050. (Illus.). 506p. 1983. text 40.00 (*0-87049-391-4*) U of Tenn Pr.

Montgomery, James W. Liberated Woman: A Life of May Arkwright Hutton. LC 85-8401. (Illus.). 407p. 1985. reprint ed. 21.95 (*0-87770-353-1*); reprint ed. pap. 16.95 (*0-87770-354-X*) Ye Galleon.

Montgomery, Jane. The Handbook for the Ultimate Church Musician. Montgomery, Charles, ed. 1985. pap. 3.95 (*0-916043-04-5*) Light Hearted Pub Co.

— Old Songs, Fellowships & a Few Skits for Younger Senior Adults. Montgomery, Charles, ed. 1985. write for info. (*0-916043-03-7*) Light Hearted Pub Co.

Montgomery, Jane, ed. see Montgomery, Charles.

Montgomery, Jane F., jt. auth. see Shantharam, S.

Montgomery, Jaye L. Sell Your Short Stories & Poetry to the Right Markets! 88p. 1988. pap. 15.95 (*0-86617-038-3*) Multi Media TX.

Montgomery, Jill D. & Greif, Ann C., eds. Masochism: The Treatment of Self-Inflicted Suffering. 1989. 42.50 (*0-8236-3145-1*, BN#03145) Intl Univs Pr.

Montgomery, Jim. Then the End Will Come: Great News about the Great Commission. LC 96-49863. 216p. (Orig.). 1997. pap. 7.95 (*0-87808-272-7*) William Carey Lib.

Montgomery, John. Brighton Past & Present. 96p. 1987. 30.00 (*0-905392-70-1*) St Mut.

— Fifties. 368p. 1965. 69.50 (*0-614-00066-1*); 69.50 (*0-614-00277-X*) Elliots Bks.

— Great Pretender. 2000. pap. 17.95 (*1-58501-009-X*) CeShore Pubg.

***Montgomery, John.** Groundwater Chemicals Desk Reference. 3rd ed. (Illus.). 1384p. 2000. boxed set 159.95 (*1-56670-498-7*) Lewis Pubs.

Montgomery, John. Troubleshooting Your Multimedia PC. LC 95-1577. 304p. (C). 1995. pap. 19.95 (*0-201-48347-5*) Addison-Wesley.

Montgomery, John, compiled by. Kerouac at the "Wild Boar" & Other Skirmishes. LC 86-81178. 159p. 1986. 30.00 (*0-685-19183-4*); 48.00 (*0-918704-07-3*); pap. 16.95 (*0-918704-06-5*) Fels & Firn.

Montgomery, John, ed. The Kerouac We Knew: Unposed Portraits, Action Shots. rev. ed. LC 87-80922. 48p. 1987. kivar 5.25 (*0-918704-04-9*) Fels & Firn.

Montgomery, John, jt. auth. see Chen, Vincent.

Montgomery, John, jt. auth. see Thornley, Andy.

Montgomery, John, tr. see Muston, Alexis.

Montgomery, John D. Bureaucrats & People: Grassroots Participation in Third World Development. LC 87-15344. (Johns Hopkins Studies in Development). 158p. reprint ed. pap. 49.00 (*0-608-08789-0*, 206942800004) Bks Demand.

Montgomery, John D., et al, eds. Great Policies: Strategic Innovations in Asia & the Pacific Basin. LC 95-13915. 264p. 1995. 65.00 (*0-275-95050-6*, Praeger Pubs) Greenwood.

— Patterns of Policy: Comparative & Longitudinal Studies of Population Events. LC 77-94305. 300p. 1979. 44.95 (*0-87855-269-3*) Transaction Pubs.

Montgomery, John D. & Carroll, Thomas F. Human Rights: Positive Policies in Asia & the Pacific Rim. LC 98-43209. 1998. 29.95 (*1-884186-09-2*) Hollis Pub.

Montgomery, John D. & Rondinelli, Dennis A. Great Policies: Strategic Innovations in Asia & the Pacific Basin. LC 95-13915. 272p. 1995. pap. 25.95 (*0-275-95398-X*, Praeger Pubs) Greenwood.

Montgomery, John D. & Sullivan, William, frwds. Aftermath: Tarnished Outcomes of American Foreign Policy. LC 85-11176. 217p. (C). 1985. 49.95 (*0-86569-126-6*, Auburn Hse) Greenwood.

Montgomery, John D., jt. ed. see Carroll, Thomas F.

Montgomery, John D., ed. see Pacific Basin Research Center Staff & Heffron, John M.

Montgomery, John F. History of Old Stone Presbyterian Church. 1983. write for info. (*0-9611706-0-3*) Old Stone Pres Church.

Montgomery, John F., jt. auth. see Krieger, Gary R.

Montgomery, John F., jt. ed. see Kreiger, Gary R.

Montgomery, John H. Agrochemicals Desk Reference. 672p. 1993. lib. bdg. 110.00 (*0-87371-738-4*, L738) Lewis Pubs.

— Agrochemicals Desk Reference. 2nd ed. LC 97-77. 696p. 1997. boxed set 114.95 (*1-56670-167-8*) CRC Pr.

— Groundwater Chemicals Desk Reference. 320p. 1991. lib. bdg. 69.95 (*0-87371-554-3*, L554) Lewis Pubs.

— Groundwater Chemicals Desk Reference. 2nd ed. LC 95-45365. 1392p. 1995. lib. bdg. 120.00 (*1-56670-165-1*, L1165) Lewis Pubs.

Montgomery, John H. & Welkom, Linda M. Ground Water Chemicals Desk Reference. Vol. I. (Illus.). 672p. 1989. lib. bdg. 99.95 (*0-87371-286-2*, L286) Lewis Pubs.

***Montgomery, John W.** Defending the Gospel Through the Centuries: A History of Christian Apologetics. 95p. 1999. pap. text 10.00 (*1-896363-10-5*) CN Inst for Law.

Montgomery, John W. Demon Possession. LC 75-19313. 384p. 1976. pap. 14.99 (*0-87123-102-6*) Bethany Hse.

— Faith Founded on Fact: Essays in Evidential Apologetics. 240p. (C). 1994. pap. text 12.95 (*1-885914-01-6*) Trinity Bible Coll.

— History & Christianity. LC 83-47517. 112p. 1986. reprint ed. pap. 7.99 (*0-87123-890-X*) Bethany Hse.

— Human Rights & Human Dignity. LC 96-1697. (Illus.). 319p. 1995. reprint ed. pap. 17.50 (*1-896363-01-6*) CN Inst for Law.

— Human Rights & Human Dignity: An Apologetic for the Transcendent Perspective. 192p. 1986. pap. 14.95 (*0-310-28571-2*, 18392P) Zondervan.

— Law & Gospel: A Study in Integrating Faith & Practice. 52p. 1994. reprint ed. pap. 7.50 (*1-896363-00-8*) CN Inst for Law.

Montgomery, John W., ed. Christianity for the Tough Minded: Essays in Support of an Intellectually Defensible Religious Commitment. 296p. (C). 1994. pap. text 14.95 (*1-885914-00-8*) Trinity Bible Coll.

— Demon Possession: A Medical, Historical, Anthropological & Theological Symposium. 384p. (C). 1994. pap. text 14.95 (*1-885914-05-9*) Trinity Bible Coll.

— Evidence for Faith: Deciding the God Question. LC 91-8917. 366p. (Orig.). (C). 1991. pap. 14.99 (*0-945241-15-1*) Probe Bks.

— God's Inerrant Word: A International Symposium on the Trustworthiness of Scripture. (C). 1994. pap. text 14.95 (*1-885914-02-4*) Trinity Bible Coll.

***Montgomery, John W., ed.** Myth, Allegory & Gospel: An Interpretation of J. R. R. Tolkien, C. S. Lewis, G. K. Chesterton, Charles Williams. 2nd ed. 159p. 2000. reprint ed. pap. 12.50 (*1-896363-11-3*) CN Inst for Law.

Montgomery, John W. & Gudel, Joseph P. Defending the Biblical Gospel: Study Guide. (Illus.). 96p. 1997. pap., student ed. 10.00 (*1-896363-06-7*) CN Inst for Law.

Montgomery, John W., jt. auth. see Fletcher, Joseph.

Montgomery, John W., ed. see Fuller, Edmund, et al.

Montgomery, Jonathan. Health Care Law. LC 96-36931. 532p. 1997. text 95.00 (*0-19-876260-7*); pap. text 42.00 (*0-19-876259-3*) OUP.

Montgomery, Joseph C. & Levine, Lawrence O., eds. The Transition to Agile Manufacturing: Staying Flexible for Competitive Advantage. 306p. 1996. 37.00 (*0-87389-347-6*, H0898) ASQ Qual Pr.

***Montgomery, Judith H.** Passion. 50p. 1999. pap. 6.00 (*0-9673495-0-8*) Defined Prov.

Montgomery, Julie. Listening to the Engine. 118p. 1995. 19.95 (*1-886701-03-2*) Lifescapes.

Montgomery, June. Fundamental Musicianship Skills Elementry Level C: For Piano & Keyboard. 32p. 1994. pap. 6.50 (*0-7390-0495-6*, 6692) Alfred Pub.

— I'm Not Afraid. 4p. 1990. pap. 1.95 (*0-7390-0876-5*, 3665) Alfred Pub.

— Mist on the Lake. 4p. Date not set. pap. 2.50 (*0-7390-0719-X*, 19701) Alfred Pub.

— Piano Camp, Bk. 3. 48p. 1999. pap. 6.95 (*0-7390-0593-6*, 14595) Alfred Pub.

— Piano Camp Primer. Date not set. write for info. (*0-7390-0649-5*, 14655) Alfred Pub.

Montgomery, June & Hinson, Maurice. Meet the Great Composers Repertoire Book, Bk. 2. 44p. 1998. pap. 7.50 (*0-88284-944-1*, 18117) Alfred Pub.

Montgomery, June & Hison, Maurice. Meet the Great Composers, Bk. 1. 1995. pap. 19.90 incl. audio compact disk (*0-88284-855-0*) Alfred Pub.

Montgomery, June & Mier, Martha. Musical Concepts Level 2. (Alfred's Basic Piano Library Ser.). 1996. pap. 7.50 (*0-7390-0003-9*, 14521) Alfred Pub.

Montgomery, June C. Theory Through the Year, Level 1A. (Basic Piano Library). 24p. 1995. pap. 6.50 (*0-7390-0736-X*, 5759) Alfred Pub.

Montgomery, K. C., jt. auth. see Holmes, Frank, Jr.

Montgomery, K. Leon. Document Retrieval Systems: Factors Affecting Search Time. LC 75-18692. (Books in Library & Information Science: No. 14). 156p. reprint ed. pap. 48.40 (*0-7837-0928-5*, 204123300019) Bks Demand.

Montgomery, Kate. Carpal Tunnel Syndrome: Prevention & Treatment. Gage, Diane, ed. (Illus.). 80p. (Orig.). 1992. student ed. 14.95 (*1-878069-03-9*) Sports Touch.

— Carpal Tunnel Syndrome: Prevention & Treatment. 3rd rev. ed. Gage, Diane, ed. LC 95-161098. (Illus.). 41p. (Orig.). 1994. pap. 16.95 (*1-878069-35-7*) Sports Touch.

— Carpal Tunnel Syndrome: Prevention & Treatment. 4th ed. Gage, Diane, ed. (Illus.). 117p. (Orig.). 1996. pap., wbk. ed. 19.95 (*1-878069-05-5*) Sports Touch.

Montgomery, Kate. Carpal Tunnel Syndrome: The Invisible Threat. 140p. 10.95 incl. audio (*1-880688-03-4*) New Life Opt.

Montgomery, Kate. End Your Carpal Tunnel Pain Without Surgery: A Daily Program to Prevent & Treat Carpal Tunnel. LC 98-9366. (Illus.). 192p. 1998. pap. 14.95 (*1-55853-591-8*) Rutledge Hill Pr.

— Sports Touch: The Athletic Ritual. Trainer, Beverly, ed. (Illus.). 162p. (Orig.). 1990. student ed. 24.95 (*1-878069-00-4*) Sports Touch.

***Montgomery, Kathleen.** 100 Meditations: Selections from Unitarian Universalist Meditation Manuals. LC 00-28536. 2000. write for info. (*1-55896-403-7*, Skinner Hse Bks) Unitarian Univ.

Montgomery, Kathleen. Practical Guide of Authentic Assessment for Elementary Teachers. 128p. (C). 2000. pap. 29.33 (*0-321-03782-0*) Addison-Wesley.

Montgomery, Kathryn C. Target: Prime Time: Advocacy Groups & the Struggle over Entertainment Television. (Communication & Society Ser.). (Illus.). 288p. 1990. reprint ed. pap. 9.95 (*0-19-506320-1*) OUP.

Montgomery, Katie, jt. auth. see Montgomery, Dan.

Montgomery, Katie, ed. see Bernal, Dick.

Montgomery, Kristen S., jt. ed. see Fitzpatrick, Joyce J.

Montgomery, L. June. Young Adults: A Call to Dialogue. LC 79-92088. 1980. 12.00 (*0-87212-112-7*) Libra.

Montgomery, L. M. Across the Miles: Tales of Correspondence. 1997. 10.09 (*0-606-11024-0*, Pub. by Turtleback) Demco.

— After Many Days: Tales of Time Passed. 320p. (YA). 1992. mass mkt. 4.99 (*0-553-29184-X*) Bantam.

Montgomery, L. M. Akin to Anne. 22.95 (*0-8488-2656-6*) Amereon Ltd.

Montgomery, L. M. Akin to Anne: Tales of Other Orphans. 224p. (YA). 1990. mass mkt. 4.99 (*0-553-28387-1*) Bantam.

Montgomery, L. M. Along the Shore: Tales by the Sea. 22.95 (*0-8488-2655-8*) Amereon Ltd.

Montgomery, L. M. Along the Shore: Tales by the Sea. 288p. (YA). 1990. mass mkt. 4.99 (*0-553-28589-0*) Bantam.

— Among the Shadows. 1976. 23.95 (*0-8488-1433-9*) Amereon Ltd.

— Anne d'Avonlea. (Avonlea Ser.: No. 2).Tr. of Anne of Avonlea. (FRE.). 88p. (YA). (gr. 5-8). 1988. 10.95 (*0-920304-88-5*, Pub. by Gynergy-Ragweed) U of Toronto Pr.

— Anne, la Maison aux Pignons Verts. (Avonlea Ser.: No. 1).Tr. of Anne of Green Gables. (FRE.). 87p. (YA). (gr. 5-8). 1987. 10.95 (*0-920304-50-8*, Pub. by Gynergy-Ragweed) U of Toronto Pr.

— Anne of Avonlea. (Avonlea Ser.: No. 2). 376p. (YA). 1976. 22.95 (*0-89190-155-8*) Amereon Ltd.

— Anne of Avonlea. (Avonlea Ser.: No. 2). 288p. (YA). (gr. 5-8). 1984. mass mkt. 3.95 (*0-7704-2206-3*) Bantam.

— Anne of Avonlea. (Avonlea Ser.: No. 2). (YA). (gr. 5-8). 1997. pap. 5.50 (*0-87129-791-4*, A72) Dramatic Pub.

— Anne of Avonlea. (Avonlea Ser.: No. 2). 336p. (YA). (gr. 5-8). 1991. pap. 3.25 (*0-590-44556-1*, Apple Classics) Scholastic Inc.

— Anne of Avonlea. (Avonlea Ser.: No. 2). 304p. (YA). (gr. 7-8). 1995. 2.99 (*0-8125-5196-6*, Pub. by Tor Bks) St Martin.

— Anne of Avonlea. (Avonlea Ser.: No. 2). (YA). (gr. 5-8). 1997. pap. 2.95 (*0-8167-0466-X*) Troll Communs.

— Anne of Avonlea. (Avonlea Ser.: No. 2). (YA). (gr. 5-8). 1976. 9.09 (*0-606-00791-1*, Pub. by Turtleback) Demco.

— Anne of Avonlea. (Avonlea Ser.: No. 2). (Illus.). 336p. (YA). (gr. 5-8). 1997. pap. 4.99 (*0-14-036798-5*) Viking Penguin.

— Anne of Avonlea. large type ed. (Avonlea Ser.: No. 2). 401p. (YA). (gr. 5-8). 1998. lib. bdg. 35.95 (*1-58118-039-X*, 22507) LRS.

— Anne of Avonlea. large type ed. LC 93-22574. (Avonlea Ser.: No. 2). 425p. (YA). (gr. 5-8). 1993. lib. bdg. 17.95 (*1-56054-780-4*) Thorndike Pr.

— Anne of Avonlea. large type ed. (Avonlea Ser.: No. 2). 435p. (YA). (gr. 5-8). 1993. reprint ed. lib. bdg. 24.00 (*0-939495-26-0*) North Bks.

— Anne of Avonlea. (Avonlea Ser.: No. 2). 270p. (YA). (gr. 5-8). 1998. reprint ed. lib. bdg. 24.00 (*1-58287-013-6*) North Bks.

— Anne of Avonlea, No. 2. (Avonlea Ser.: No. 2). 304p. (J). (gr. 4-7). 1984. mass mkt. 3.99 (*0-553-21314-8*) Bantam.

— Anne of Green Gables. (Avonlea Ser.: No. 1). 244p. (YA). (gr. 5-8). 1976. 23.95 (*0-8488-0584-4*) Amereon Ltd.

— Anne of Green Gables. (Avonlea Ser.: No. 1). (YA). (gr. 5-8). 1995. pap. 6.50 (*0-87602-335-9*) Anchorage.

— Anne of Green Gables. LC 96-35040. (Avonlea Ser.: No. 1). 112p. (YA). (gr. 5-8). 1998. 12.95 (*0-385-32333-6*, Delacorte Pr Bks) BDD Bks Young Read.

— Anne of Green Gables. (Avonlea Ser.: No. 1). 112p. (YA). (gr. 5-8). 1999. pap. 3.99 (*0-440-41356-7*) BDD Bks Young Read.

— Anne of Green Gables. LC 83 47616. (Avonlea Ser.: No 1). 336p. (J). (gr. 4-7). 1982. mass mkt. 4.50 (*0-553-21313-X*, Bantam Classics) Bantam.

— Anne of Green Gables. (Avonlea Ser.: No. 1). 320p. (YA). (gr. 5-8). 1983. mass mkt. 3.95 (*0-7704-2205-5*) Bantam.

Montgomery, L. M. Anne of Green Gables. (Avonlea Ser.: No. 1). (YA). (gr. 5-8). 1997. pap. 12.48 (*0-553-33306-2*); mass mkt. 11.97 (*0-553-33307-0*) Bantam.

— Anne of Green Gables. (Avonlea Ser.: No. 1). 280p. (YA). (gr. 5-8). 2000. pap. text 15.00 (*0-7881-9155-1*) DIANE Pub.

Montgomery, L. M. Anne of Green Gables. LC 94-34985. (Avonlea Ser.: No. 1). (Illus.). iv, 91p. (YA). (gr. 5-8). 1995. pap. text 1.00 (*0-486-28366-6*) Dover.

***Montgomery, L. M.** Anne of Green Gables. LC 99-88555. 320p. 2000. pap. 2.50 (*0-486-41025-0*) Dover.

Montgomery, L. M. Anne of Green Gables. (Avonlea Ser.: No. 1). (YA). (gr. 5-8). 1989. pap. 5.50 (*0-87129-242-4*, A41) Dramatic Pub.

***Montgomery, L. M.** Anne of Green Gables. LC 97-51658. (Great Stories Ser.). 282p. (J). (gr. 4-7). 1999. 15.99 (*1-56179-625-5*) Focus Family.

Montgomery, L. M. Anne of Green Gables. LC 94-76339. (Avonlea Ser.: No. 1). (FRE., Illus.). xx, 486p. (YA). (gr. 5-8). 1995. 15.95 (*0-8050-3126-X*) H Holt & Co.

— Anne of Green Gables. (Avonlea Ser.: No. 1). (Illus.). 256p. (YA). (gr. 5-8). 1994. 25.00 (*0-88363-994-7*) H L Levin.

***Montgomery, L. M.** Anne of Green Gables. LC 98-27873. (Avonlea Ser.: No. 1). 80p. (YA). (gr. 5-8). 1999. 2.99 (*0-694-01284-X*, HarpFestival) HarpC Child Bks.

Montgomery, L. M. Anne of Green Gables. (Avonlea Ser.: No. 1). (YA). (gr. 5-8). 2000. write for info. (*0-06-028227-4*) HarpC Child Bks.

M

An Asterisk (*) at the beginning of an entry indicates that the title is appearing for the first time.

— Anne of Green Gables. LC 95-15327. (Avonlea Ser.: No. 1). (Illus.). 396p. (YA). (gr. 4-7). 1995. 14.95 (*0-679-44475-0*, Evrymans Lib Childs) Knopf.

— Anne of Green Gables. MQ Publications Staff, ed. (Little Brown Notebooks Ser.). 1998. 9.99 (*1-84072-063-8*, Pub. by M Q Pubns) Watsn-Guptill.

— Anne of Green Gables. (Avonlea Ser.: No. 1). (YA). (gr. 5-8). 1999. 23.95 (*0-8057-8090-4*, Twyne) Mac Lib Ref.

— Anne of Green Gables. (Avonlea Ser.: No. 1). 320p. (YA). (gr. 5-8). 1987. mass mkt. 4.95 (*0-451-52112-9*, Sig Classics) NAL.

***Montgomery, L. M.** Anne of Green Gables. (Avonlea Ser.: No. 1). 44p. (YA). (gr. 5-8). 1999. 9.95 (*1-56137-341-9*) Novel Units.

Montgomery, L. M. Anne of Green Gables. Bassett, Jennifer, ed. (Avonlea Ser.: No. 1). (Illus.). 48p. (YA). (gr. 5-8). 1995. pap. text 5.95 (*0-19-422725-1*) OUP.

— Anne of Green Gables. LC 83-47616. (Avonlea Ser.: No. 1). (Illus.). 382p. (YA). (gr. 4-7). 1983. 15.99 (*0-448-06030-2*, G & D) Peng Put Young Read.

— Anne of Green Gables. Hanft, Joshua, ed. (Great Illustrated Classics Ser.: Vol. 42). (Illus.). 240p. (J). (gr. 3-6). 1995. 9.95 (*0-86611-993-0*) Playmore Inc.

— Anne of Green Gables. LC 93-36331. (Step into Classics Ser.). 107p. (J). (gr. 2-6). 1994. pap. 3.99 (*0-679-85467-3*, Pub. by Random Bks Yng Read) Random.

— Anne of Green Gables. (Avonlea Ser.: No. 1). 256p. (YA). (gr. 5-8). 1998. 5.99 (*0-517-18968-2*) Random Hse Value.

— Anne of Green Gables. LC 88-46103. (Avonlea Ser.: No. 1). 384p. (J). (gr. 4-7). 1989. pap. 4.50 (*0-590-42243-X*, Apple Classics) Scholastic Inc.

— Anne of Green Gables. (Avonlea Ser.: No. 1). 320p. (YA). (gr. 4-7). 1995. 2.99 (*0-8125-5152-4*, Pub. by Tor Bks) St Martin.

— Anne of Green Gables. LC 92-12703. (Avonlea Ser.: No. 1). (Illus.). 47p. (YA). (gr. 5-8). 1992. pap. 5.95 (*0-8167-2867-4*) Troll Communs.

— Anne of Green Gables. (Avonlea Ser.: No. 1). (YA). (gr. 5-8). 1997. pap. 2.95 (*0-8167-0465-1*) Troll Communs.

***Montgomery, L. M.** Anne of Green Gables. (Illus.). 352p. (YA). (gr. 4 up). 2000. 24.95 (*0-88776-515-7*) Tundra Bks.

Montgomery, L. M. Anne of Green Gables. (Avonlea Ser.: No. 1). (YA). (gr. 5-8). 1987. 8.60 (*0-606-00282-0*, Pub. by Turtleback) Demco.

Montgomery, L. M. Anne of Green Gables. Morgan, Sally, ed. LC 93-36331. (Avonlea Ser.: No. 1). (YA). (gr. 5-8). 1994. 9.09 (*0-606-09006-1*, Pub. by Turtleback) Demco.

Montgomery, L. M. Anne of Green Gables. abr. ed. (Avonlea Ser.: No. 1). (YA). (gr. 5-8). 1986. pap. 12.95 incl. audio (*1-882071-07-7*, 009) B&B Audio.

— Anne of Green Gables. large type ed. (Avonlea Ser.: No. 1). 472p. (YA). (gr. 5-8). 1998. lib. bdg. 35.95 (*1-58118-035-7*, 22019) LRS.

— Anne of Green Gables. large type ed. (Avonlea Ser.: No. 1). 494p. (YA). (gr. 5-8). 1993. reprint ed. lib. bdg. 24.00 (*0-939495-25-2*) North Bks.

— Anne of Green Gables. large type ed. LC 92-43772. (Avonlea Ser.: No. 1). 487p. (YA). (gr. 5-8). 1993. reprint ed. pap. 15.95 (*1-56054-643-3*) Thorndike Pr.

— Anne of Green Gables. (Avonlea Ser.: No. 1). 429p. (YA). (gr. 5-7). 1977. reprint ed. lib. bdg. 27.95 (*0-89966-262-5*) Buccaneer Bks.

— Anne of Green Gables. (Avonlea Ser.: No. 1). 352p. (YA). (gr. 5-8). 1992. reprint ed. 16.95 (*1-55109-013-9*) Nimbus Publ.

— Anne of Green Gables. (Avonlea Ser.: No. 1). 310p. (YA). (gr. 5-8). 1998. reprint ed. lib. bdg. 24.00 (*1-58287-014-4*) North Bks.

— Anne of Green Gables, Vol. 1. LC 83-47616. Vol. 1. 320p. (YA). (gr. 5-9). 1984. pap. 4.50 (*0-553-15327-7*) Bantam.

— Anne of Green Gables, Vol. 1. (Avonlea Ser.: No. 1). (Illus.). 384p. (YA). (gr. 5-8). 1996. pap. 4.99 (*0-14-036741-1*, PuffinBks) Peng Put Young Read.

Montgomery, L. M. Anne of Green Gables: Press Out Model House. 1994. pap. 12.95 (*0-7704-2590-9*) Bantam.

Montgomery, L. M. Anne of Green Gables Birthday Book. (Illus.). 128p. (J). 1990. 8.95 (*0-7704-2362-0*) Bantam.

— Anne of Green Gables Book & Charm. LC 98-35542. (Charming Classic Bks.). 400p. (J). (gr. 3-7). 1999. pap. 5.95 (*0-694-01251-3*, HarpFestival) HarpC Child Bks.

— Anne of Green Gables Boxed Set, 3 vols., Set. LC 85-30606. (Avonlea Ser.). (Illus.). xvi, 634p. (YA). (gr. 5-8). 1988. 11.99 (*0-517-60517-1*) Random Hse Value.

— Anne of Green Gables Coloring Book. 1995. pap. text 2.95 (*0-486-28589-8*) Dover.

Montgomery, L. M. Anne of Green Gables Cookbook. 22.95 (*0-8488-2657-4*) Amereon Ltd.

— Anne of Green Gables Diary. 22.95 (*0-8488-2654-X*) Amereon Ltd.

Montgomery, L. M. Anne of Ingleside. (Avonlea Ser.: No. 10). (YA). (gr. 5-8). 23.95 (*0-8488-0890-8*) Amereon Ltd.

— Anne of Ingleside. (Avonlea Ser.: No. 10). 286p. (YA). (gr. 5-8). 1976. 23.95 (*0-8488-1101-1*) Amereon Ltd.

— Anne of Ingleside. (Avonlea Ser.: No. 10). (Illus.). 341p. (YA). (gr. 5-8). 6.98 (*0-7710-6180-3*) McClelland & Stewart.

— Anne of Ingleside. (Avonlea Ser.: No. 10). 320p. (YA). (gr. 5-8). 1999. mass mkt. 3.95 (*0-451-52643-0*, Sig Classics) NAL.

— Anne of Ingleside. (Avonlea Ser.: No. 10). (YA). (gr. 5-8). 1967. 9.09 (*0-606-00375-4*, Pub. by Turtleback) Demco.

— Anne of Ingleside. 6th ed. (Avonlea Ser.: No. 10). 288p. (YA). (gr. 5-8). 1984. pap. 3.95 (*0-7704-2207-1*) Bantam.

— Anne of Ingleside, No. 6. (Avonlea Ser.: No. 10). 304p. (YA). (gr. 5-8). 1984. mass mkt. 3.99 (*0-553-21315-6*, Bantam Classics) Bantam.

— Anne of the Island. (Avonlea Ser.: No. 4). 252p. (YA). (gr. 5-8). 1976. 22.95 (*0-8488-0585-2*) Amereon Ltd.

— Anne of the Island. 256p. (YA). (gr. 5-8). 1983. mass mkt. 3.95 (*0-7704-2204-7*) Bantam.

— Anne of the Island. (Avonlea Ser.: No. 4). 272p. (YA). (gr. 5-8). 1983. mass mkt. 3.99 (*0-553-21317-2*, Bantam Classics) Bantam.

— Anne of the Island. 256p. (YA). (gr. 5-8). 1992. pap. 4.50 (*0-553-48066-9*) Bantam.

— Anne of the Island. 320p. (YA). (gr. 5-8). 1993. pap. 3.25 (*0-590-46163-X*, Apple Classics) Scholastic Inc.

— Anne of the Island. (Avonlea Ser.: No. 4). (YA). (gr. 5-8). pap. 4.95 (*0-8167-2899-2*) Troll Communs.

— Anne of the Island. (Avonlea Ser.: No. 4). (YA). (gr. 5-8). 1976. 8.05 (*0-606-00792-X*, Pub. by Turtleback) Demco.

— Anne of the Island. (Avonlea Ser.: No. 4). 304p. (YA). (gr. 5-8). 1998. pap. 4.99 (*0-14-036777-2*) Viking Penguin.

— Anne of the Island. large type ed. (Avonlea Ser.: No. 4). 376p. (YA). (gr. 5-8). 1998. lib. bdg. 34.95 (*1-58118-036-5*, 22020) LRS.

***Montgomery, L. M.** Anne of the Island, Set. unabridged ed. (Avonlea Ser.: No. 4). (YA). (gr. 5-8). 1999. 35.95 incl. audio (*1-55685-580-X*) Audio Bk Con.

Montgomery, L. M. Anne of Windy Poplars. (Avonlea Ser.: No. 9). 268p. (YA). (gr. 5-8). 1976. 22.95 (*0-8488-0586-0*) Amereon Ltd.

— Anne of Windy Poplars. (Avonlea Ser.: No. 9). 288p. (YA). (gr. 5-8). 1983. mass mkt. 3.99 (*0-553-21316-4*, Bantam Classics) Bantam.

— Anne of Windy Poplars. (Avonlea Ser.: No. 9). 288p. (YA). (gr. 5-8). 1992. pap. 3.99 (*0-553-48065-0*) Bantam.

Montgomery, L. M. Anne of Windy Poplars. (Avonlea Ser.). (J). 1987. 9.09 (*0-606-02371-2*, Pub. by Turtleback) Demco.

Montgomery, L. M. Anne of Windy Poplars. 4th ed. (Avonlea Ser.: No. 9). 272p. (YA). (gr. 5-8). 1983. mass mkt. 3.95 (*0-7704-2167-9*) Bantam.

— Anne's House of Dreams. (Avonlea Ser.: No. 5). 192p. (YA). (gr. 5-8). 1976. 20.95 (*0-8488-0587-9*) Amereon Ltd.

— Anne's House of Dreams. (Avonlea Ser.: No. 5). 256p. (YA). (gr. 5-8). 1983. mass mkt. 3.99 (*0-553-21318-0*, Bantam Classics) Bantam.

— Anne's House of Dreams. (Avonlea Ser.: No. 5). (YA). (gr. 5-8). 1972. 8.60 (*0-606-00376-2*, Pub. by Turtleback) Demco.

— Anne's House of Dreams. large type ed. (Avonlea Ser.: No. 5). 364p. (YA). (gr. 5-8). 1999. lib. bdg. 34.95 (*1-58118-048-9*, 22517) LRS.

— Anne's House of Dreams. 5th ed. (Avonlea Ser.: No. 5). 240p. (YA). (gr. 5-8). 1983. mass mkt. 3.95 (*0-7704-2210-1*) Bantam.

***Montgomery, L. M.** Anne's House of Dreams, Set. unabridged ed. (Avonlea Ser.: No. 5). (YA). (gr. 5-8). 1999. 35.95 incl. audio (*1-55685-586-9*) Audio Bk Con.

Montgomery, L. M. The Annotated Anne of Green Gables. annot. ed. Jones, Mary E. Doody et al, eds. LC 96-45018. (Illus.). 504p. (J). 1997. 35.00 (*0-19-510428-5*) OUP.

— At the Altar: Matrimonial Tales. 240p. (YA). 1995. mass mkt. 5.50 (*0-553-56748-9*) Bantam.

— Aunt Maud's Recipe Book: From the Kitchen of L. M. Montgomery. Crawford, Kelly & Crawford, Elaine, eds. LC 98-221661. (Illus.). xi, 140p. 1997. 20.95 (*1-896867-01-4*) Moulin Publ.

***Montgomery, L. M.** Avonlea Boxed Set: Anne of Green Gables; Anne of Avonlea. (Avonlea Ser.: No. 1-2). 536p. (YA). (gr. 5-8). 2000. 8.98 (*0-7624-0560-0*, Courage) Running Pr.

— Avonlea Boxed Set: Anne of the Island; Anne's House of Dreams. (Avonlea Ser.: No. 4-5). 464p. (YA). (gr. 5-8). 1999. reprint ed. 8.98 (*0-7624-0561-9*) Running Pr.

Montgomery, L. M. The Blue Castle. Date not set. 22.95 (*0-8488-2370-2*) Amereon Ltd.

— The Blue Castle. 224p. (YA). (gr. 7 up). 1989. mass mkt. 4.99 (*0-553-28051-1*, Starfire BDD) BDD Bks Young Read.

— The Blue Castle. 224p. (J). 1988. mass mkt. 4.50 (*0-7704-2315-9*) Bantam.

— The Blue Castle. (Illus.). 260p. (J). pap. 4.98 (*0-7710-6166-8*) McClelland & Stewart.

— Christmas with Anne: And Other Holiday Stories. Wilmshurst, Rea, ed. LC 96-11657. 224p. (YA). 1996. pap. 16.95 (*0-385-32288-7*) Delacorte.

— Chronicles of Avonlea. (Avonlea Ser.: No. 3). 318p. (YA). (gr. 5-7). 1976. 24.95 (*0-8488-0719-7*) Amereon Ltd.

— Chronicles of Avonlea. (Avonlea Ser.: No. 3). 192p. (YA). (gr. 5-8). 1987. mass mkt. 3.99 (*0-7704-2161-X*) Bantam.

— Chronicles of Avonlea. (Avonlea Ser.: No. 2). 192p. (YA). (gr. 5-8). 1988. mass mkt. 3.99 (*0-553-21378-4*, Bantam Classics) Bantam.

Montgomery, L. M. Chronicles of Avonlea. (Avonlea Ser.: No. 3). (YA). (gr. 5-8). 1988. 9.09 (*0-606-03755-1*, Pub. by Turtleback) Demco.

— The Complete Anne of Green Gables: The Life & Adventures of the Most Beloved & Timeless Heroine in All of Fiction. (J). (gr. 4-7). 1990. mass mkt. 32.43 (*0-553-60941-6*) Bantam.

— The Doctor's Sweetheart. 22.95 (*0-8488-1708-7*) Amereon Ltd.

Montgomery, L. M. The Doctor's Sweetheart. 192p. (J). 1993. mass mkt. 4.50 (*0-553-56330-0*) Bantam.

— The Doctor's Sweetheart & Other Stories. lib. bdg. 18.95 (*0-8488-1749-4*) Amereon Ltd.

— The Doctor's Sweetheart & Other Stories. 192p. 1993. mass mkt. 4.99 (*0-7704-2583-6*) Bantam.

— Emily, 3 vols., Set. (YA). (gr. 9-12). 1990. boxed set 10.50 (*0-553-33308-9*) Bantam.

— Emily Climbs. 336p. (YA). 1976. 25.95 (*0-8488-0588-7*) Amereon Ltd.

— Emily Climbs. 336p. (YA). 1983. mass mkt. 4.99 (*0-553-26214-9*, Starfire BDD) BDD Bks Young Read.

— Emily Climbs. 336p. (J). 1984. mass mkt. 4.99 (*0-7704-2032-X*) Bantam.

— Emily Climbs. 336p. (J). pap. 4.95 (*0-7710-9980-0*) McClelland & Stewart.

— Emily of New Moon. 360p. (J). 1976. 25.95 (*0-8488-0589-5*) Amereon Ltd.

— Emily of New Moon. LC 97-4255. 144p. (J). 1998. 12.95 (*0-385-32506-1*, Delacorte Pr Bks) BDD Bks Young Read.

— Emily of New Moon. 144p. (J). 1999. pap. 3.99 (*0-440-41613-2*) BDD Bks Young Read.

— Emily of New Moon. 352p. (YA). 1983. mass mkt. 4.99 (*0-553-23370-X*) Bantam.

— Emily of New Moon. 352p. (J). 1983. mass mkt. 4.99 (*0-7704-1798-1*) Bantam.

— Emily of New Moon. 336p. (J). pap. 4.95 (*0-7710-9979-7*) McClelland & Stewart.

— Emily's Quest. 236p. (J). 1976. 21.95 (*0-8488-0590-9*) Amereon Ltd.

— Emily's Quest. 240p. (YA). 1983. mass mkt. 4.99 (*0-553-26493-1*) Bantam.

— Emily's Quest. 240p. (J). 1985. mass mkt. 4.99 (*0-7704-2060-5*) Bantam.

— Emily's Quest. 248p. (J). pap. 4.95 (*0-7710-9981-9*) McClelland & Stewart.

— Further Chronicles of Avonlea. (Avonlea Ser.: No. 7). 208p. (YA). (gr. 5-8). 1989. mass mkt. 3.50 (*0-553-21381-4*, Starfire BDD) BDD Bks Young Read.

— Further Chronicles of Avonlea. (Avonlea Ser.: No. 7). 208p. (YA). (gr. 5-8). 1987. mass mkt. 3.95 (*0-7704-2162-8*) Bantam.

— The Golden Road. 382p. (J). 1976. 23.95 (*0-8488-0720-0*) Amereon Ltd.

— The Golden Road. 224p. (J). 1987. mass mkt. 3.95 (*0-7704-2182-2*) Bantam.

— The Golden Road. 224p. (J). 1989. mass mkt. 3.99 (*0-553-21367-9*, Bantam Classics) Bantam.

— Jane of Lantern Hill. (J). 1976. 21.95 (*0-8488-1434-7*) Amereon Ltd.

— Jane of Lantern Hill. 224p. (J). 1989. mass mkt. 3.99 (*0-7704-2314-0*) Bantam.

— Kilmeny of the Orchard. 264p. (J). 1976. 22.95 (*0-8488-0721-9*) Amereon Ltd.

— Kilmeny of the Orchard. 144p. (J). 1987. mass mkt. 3.95 (*0-7704-2181-4*) Bantam.

— Kilmeny of the Orchard. 144p. (YA). 1989. mass mkt. 3.99 (*0-553-21377-6*) Bantam.

— Magic for Marigold. 284p. (J). 1976. 23.95 (*0-8488-1102-X*) Amereon Ltd.

— Magic for Marigold. 288p. (J). 1988. mass mkt. 3.99 (*0-7704-2233-0*) Bantam.

— Magic for Marigold. 288p. (YA). 1989. mass mkt. 4.50 (*0-553-28046-5*) Bantam.

— Mistress Pat. (J). 1976. 23.95 (*0-8488-1103-8*) Amereon Ltd.

— Mistress Pat. 288p. (YA). 1997. mass mkt. 3.99 (*0-7704-2246-2*) Bantam.

— Pat of Silver Bush. Date not set. 22.95 (*0-8488-2371-0*) Amereon Ltd.

— Pat of Silver Bush. 288p. (YA). 1988. mass mkt. 4.50 (*0-7704-2247-0*) Bantam.

— Pat of Silver Bush. (Illus.). 380p. (J). pap. 4.98 (*0-7710-6167-6*) McClelland & Stewart.

— The Poetry of Lucy Maud Montgomery. 1999. pap. text 9.95 (*1-55041-402-X*) Fitzhenry & W Ltd.

— Rainbow Valley. (Avonlea Ser.: No. 7). 234p. (YA). (gr. 5-8). 1976. 21.95 (*0-8488-0591-7*) Amereon Ltd.

— Rainbow Valley. (Avonlea Ser.: No. 7). 256p. (J). (gr. 4-7). 1985. mass mkt. 3.99 (*0-553-26921-6*) Bantam.

— Rainbow Valley. (Avonlea Ser.: No. 6). 240p. (YA). (gr. 5-8). 1987. mass mkt. 4.99 (*0-7704-2268-3*) Bantam.

— Rainbow Valley. (Avonlea Ser.: No. 6). (YA). (gr. 5-8). 1985. 9.09 (*0-606-02613-4*, Pub. by Turtleback) Demco.

— Rebecca of Sunnybrook Farm. Hanft, Joshua, ed. (Great Illustrated Classics Ser.: Vol. 48). (Illus.). 240p. (J). (gr. 3-6). 1995. 9.95 (*0-86611-999-X*) Playmore Inc.

— Rilla of Ingleside. (Avonlea Ser.: No. 8). 286p. (YA). (gr. 5-8). 1976. 23.95 (*0-8488-0592-5*) Amereon Ltd.

— Rilla of Ingleside. (Avonlea Ser.: No. 8). 304p. (YA). (gr. 5-8). 1985. mass mkt. 3.99 (*0-553-26922-4*) Bantam.

— Rilla of Ingleside. (Avonlea Ser.: No. 8). 288p. (J). (gr. 5-8). 1987. mass mkt. 3.95 (*0-7704-2185-7*) Bantam.

— Rilla of Ingleside. LC 96-48093. (Avonlea Ser.: No. 8). (Illus.). (YA). (gr. 5-8). 1997. 7.99 (*0-517-18083-9*) Random Hse Value.

— Rilla of Ingleside. (Avonlea Ser.: No. 8). (YA). (gr. 5-8). 1985. 9.60 (*0-606-00747-4*, Pub. by Turtleback) Demco.

— The Road to Yesterday. 416p. (YA). 1993. mass mkt. 4.99 (*0-553-56068-9*) Bantam.

— The Rock to Yesterday. 416p. (J). 1993. mass mkt. 4.50 (*0-7704-2551-8*) Bantam.

— The Selected Journals of L. M. Montgomery Vol. 1: 1889-1910. Rubio, Mary et al, eds. (Illus.). 448p. 1986. 35.00 (*0-19-540503-X*) OUP.

— The Selected Journals of L. M. Montgomery Vol. 2: 1910-1921. Waterston, Elizabeth & Rubio, Mary, eds. (Illus.). 464p. 1988. 35.00 (*0-19-540586-2*) OUP.

— The Selected Journals of L. M. Montgomery Vol. 3: 1921-1929. Rubio, Mary & Waterston, Elizabeth, eds. (Illus.). 464p. 1993. 35.00 (*0-19-540936-1*) OUP.

— The Selected Journals of L. M. Montgomery Vol. IV: 1929-1935. (Illus.). 464p. 1999. 35.00 (*0-19-541381-4*) OUP.

— The Story Girl. Date not set. 22.95 (*0-8488-2372-9*) Amereon Ltd.

— The Story Girl. 272p. (J). 1987. mass mkt. 4.99 (*0-7704-2285-3*) Bantam.

— A Tangled Web. 264p. 1976. 22.95 (*0-8488-0722-7*) Amereon Ltd.

— A Tangled Web. 288p. (YA). 1989. pap. 5.99 (*0-7704-2245-4*, Seals Bks) Doubleday.

Montgomery, L. M., et al. Spirit of Place: Lucy Maud Montgomery & Prince Edward Island. Bolger, Francis William Pius, ed. & selected by by. LC 83-175927. (Illus.). 86p. 1983. 14.95 (*0-19-540389-4*) OUP.

Montgomery, L. M., jt. auth. see Center for Learning Network Staff.

Montgomery, Laurie. Tea Party. LC 96-233635. 198p. 1996. 14.95 (*0-938577-11-5*) St Johns Pub.

Montgomery, Lee, ed. see Krusoe, Jim.

***Montgomery, Les.** Idaho Anthem. (Illus.). xxi, 340p. 2000. pap. 18.95 (*0-9662621-2-3*) W Shore Pr.

Montgomery, Linda Boudreaux. Abbeville - Someplace Special on the Bayou. (Illus.). 20p. (J). (gr. 1-6). 1996. pap. text 4.95 (*1-890113-02-6*) LB Collection.

— A Coloring Guide to the Historic Conrad Rice Mill: Americas Oldest Rice Mill & Home to Konriko. (Illus.). 20p. (J). (gr. k-4). 1995. text 4.95 (*1-890113-13-1*) LB Collection.

— How Texas Laws Are Made - A Children's Guide. LC 97-93379. (Illus.). 20p. (J). (gr. 1-6). 1997. pap. text 4.95 (*1-890113-05-0*) LB Collection.

— Miss Ellen's Zoo Critters Scribble Art. (Illus.). 20p. (J). (gr. 1-6). 1996. pap. text 4.95 (*1-890113-11-5*) LB Collection.

— A Visit to Louisiana's Jean Lafitte National Historical Park & Preserve. (Illus.). 20p. (J). (gr. 1-6). 1996. pap. text 4.95 (*1-890113-00-X*) LB Collection.

— A Visit to the Alabama Capitol - Montgomery, Alabama. LC 97-94385. (Illus.). 20p. (J). (gr. 1-6). 1997. pap. text 4.95 (*1-890113-07-7*) LB Collection.

— A Visit to the Arizona Capitol - Phoenix, Arizona. (Illus.). 20p. (J). (gr. 1-6). 1997. pap. text 4.95 (*1-890113-08-5*) LB Collection.

— A Visit to the International UFO Museum & Research Center-Roswell New Mexico. LC 97-92798. (Illus.). 20p. (J). (gr. 1-6). 1997. pap. text 4.95 (*1-890113-09-3*) LB Collection.

— A Visit to the Texas Capitol. LC 96-95443. (Illus.). 20p. (J). (gr. 1-6). 1997. pap. text 4.95 (*1-890113-04-2*) LB Collection.

— A Visit to the University of Texas at Austin McDonald Observatory & the W. L. Moody, Jr. Visitor's Information Center, Fort Davis, Texas. LC 96-95249. (Illus.). 20p. (J). (gr. 1-6). 1996. pap. text 4.95 (*1-890113-03-4*) LB Collection.

— Una Visita a Capitolio de Tejas - Austin, Tejas. (SPA., Illus.). 20p. (J). (gr. 1-6). 1997. pap. text 4.95 (*1-890113-06-9*) LB Collection.

Montgomery, Linda J. Silent Strength. Alicino, Nick & Zopf, Jane, eds. LC 89-81213. (Illus.). 48p. (Orig.). 1989. pap. 16.95 (*0-9624768-0-3*) Divine Designs.

Montgomery, Lizzie W. Sketches of Old Warrenton, North Carolina: Traditions & Reminiscences of the Town & People Who Made It. LC 83-23120. (Illus.). 488p. 1999. reprint ed. 45.00 (*0-87152-393-0*, 83-23120) Reprint.

***Montgomery, Lola.** Southern Bound: Literary Landmarks in the South. LC 99-52738. (Illus.). 160p. 2000. pap. 12.50 (*1-892514-21-4*, Hill St Guides) Hill St Pr.

Montgomery, Louise. Mrs. Mahoney of the Tenement. LC 74-128741. (Short Story Index Reprint Ser.). (Illus.). 1977. 17.95 (*0-8369-3632-9*) Ayer.

Montgomery, Lynn. Health & Safety Guidelines for the Laboratory. LC 94-8501. 1995. 20.00 (*0-89189-382-2*) Am Soc Clinical.

Montgomery, M. L. History of Berks County, Pennsylvania. (Illus.). 1204p. 1989. reprint ed. lib. bdg. 129.50 (*0-8328-1431-8*) Higginson Bk Co.

Montgomery, M. R. A Field Guide to Airplanes of North America. LC 83-26438. (Illus.). 1984. ring bd. 12.95 (*0-685-09372-7*) HM.

— Jefferson & the Gun-Men: How the West Was Almost Lost. LC 99-46547. (Illus.). 352p. 2000. 25.95 (*0-517-70212-6*, HIS036040, Crown) Crown Pub Group.

— Many Rivers to Cross: Good Running Water, Trout & Remains of Wilderness. (Illus.). 256p. 1996. per. 12.00 (*0-684-81829-9*, Touchstone) S&S Trade Pap.

— Many Rivers to Cross: Of Good Running Water, Native Trout & the Remains of Wilderness. 254p. 1999. reprint ed. text 22.00 (*0-7881-6428-7*) DIANE Pub.

— The Way of the Trout: Anglers, Wild Fish & Running Water. 288p. 1993. reprint ed. pap. 11.00 (*0-380-71884-7*, Avon Bks) Morrow Avon.

Montgomery, M. R. & Foster, Gerald L. A Field Guide to Airplanes. rev. ed. (Illus.). 256p. 1992. pap. 17.00 (*0-395-62888-1*) HM.

Montgomery, Mabel G. & Pettem, Silvia. A Story of Gold Hill Colorado: Seventy-Odd Years in the Heart of the Rockies. rev. ed. (Illus.). 37p. 1987. reprint ed. pap. 5.95 (*0-9617799-1-8*) Book Lode.

Montgomery, Maria G., jt. auth. see Montgomery, Richard J., Sr.

Montgomery, Maria K., jt. auth. see Helewitz, Jeffrey A.

Montgomery, Marian A., ed. see Hunt, Conover.

Montgomery, Marian A., ed. see Trask, Richard B.

Montgomery, Marilyn J. Building Bridges with Parents: Tools & Techniques for Counselors. LC 98-40273. (Practical Skills for Counselors (PSFC) Ser.). (Illus.). 96p. 1999. 39.95 (*0-8039-6708-X*); pap. 16.95 (*0-8039-6709-8*) Corwin Pr.

Montgomery, Marion. Concerning Intellectual Philandering: Poets & Philosophers, Priests & Politicians. LC 98-7792. 240p. 1998. 53.00 (*0-8476-9200-0*) Rowman.

An Asterisk (*) at the beginning of an entry indicates that the title is appearing for the first time.

Montgomery, Marion. Eliot's Reflective Journey to the Garden. LC 78-57220. x, 170p. 1979. 36.00 (*0-87875-142-4*) Whitston Pub.

Montgomery, Marion. Liberal Arts & Community: The Feeding of the Larger Body. LC 89-12792. 184p. 1990. text 30.00 (*0-8071-1558-4*) La State U Pr.

— Making: The Proper Habit of Our Being. LC 99-19017. 344p. 1999. 37.50 (*1-890318-39-6*) St Augustines Pr.

— The Men I Have Chosen for Fathers: Literary & Philosophical Passages. LC 90-10854. 264p. 1990. text 32.50 (*0-8262-0740-5*) U of Mo Pr.

— Romantic Confusions of the Good: Beauty As Truth, Truth Beauty. LC 96-36051. 288p. 1996. 66.00 (*0-8476-8393-1*) Rowman.

Montgomery, Marion. Romantic Confusions of the Good: Beauty As Truth, Truth Beauty. LC 96-36051. 288p. 1996. pap. 25.95 (*0-8476-8394-X*) Rowman.

Montgomery, Marion. The Truth of Things: Liberal Arts & the Recovery of Reality. LC 98-49943. 305p. 1999. 24.95 (*0-9653208-7-1*) Spence Pub.

— Virtue & Modern Shadows of Turning: Preliminary Agitations. 186p. (C). 1989. pap. text 22.50 (*0-8191-7656-7*); lib. bdg. 45.00 (*0-8191-7655-9*) U Pr of Amer.

— Why Flannery O'Connor Stayed Home. (Prophetic Poet & the Spirit of the Age Ser.: Vol. I). 486p. 1981. pap. 14.95 (*0-89385-033-0*) Sugden.

— Why Hawthorne Was Melancholy. (Prophetic Poet & the Spirit of the Age Ser.: Vol. III). 576p. 1984. 26.95 (*0-89385-027-6*) Sugden.

— Why Poe Drank Liquor. (Prophetic Poet & the Spirit of the Age Ser.: Vol. II). 442p. 1982. pap. 14.95 (*0-89385-036-5*) Sugden.

Montgomery, Marion, et al. Steps Toward Restoration: The Consequences of Richard Weaver's Ideas. Smith, Ted, ed. LC 98-73009. 170p. 1998. 24.95 (*1-882926-26-9*) ISI Books.

Montgomery, Mark, et al. La Relation Entre le Nombre des Enfants et de la Scolarisation: Le Cas de la Cote d'Ivoire et du Ghana. (LSMS Working Papers: No. 112-F).Tr. of Tradeoff Between Number of Children & Child Schooling: Evidence from Cote D'Ivoire & Ghana. (FRE.). 108p. 1995. pap. 22.00 (*0-8213-3374-7*, 13374) World Bank.

— The Tradeoff Between Number of Children & Child Schooling: Evidence from Cote d'Ivoire & Ghana. LC 94-23764. (LSMS Working Papers: Vol. 112). 108p. 1995. pap. 22.00 (*0-8213-3123-X*, 13123) World Bank.

Montgomery, Mark A. Politics & Sustainable Development: Guinea-Bissau & Hazardous Waste Imports. (Pew Case Studies in International Affairs). 50p. (C). 1996. pap. text 3.50 (*1-56927-214-X*, GU Schl Foreign) Geo U Inst Dplmcy.

Montgomery, Mark R., ed. see Committee on Population, National Research Council.

Montgomery, Martin. An Introduction to Language & Society. 220p. 1986. text 25.00 (*0-416-34620-0*, 9789); pap. text 10.95 (*0-416-34630-8*, 9803) Routledge.

Montgomery, Martin & Coulthard, Malcolm, eds. Studies in Discourse Analysis. 1981. pap. 15.95 (*0-7100-0510-5*, Routledge Thoemms) Routledge.

Montgomery, Martin, et al. Ways of Reading: Advanced Reading Skills for Students of English Literature. LC 91-39237. 272p. (C). (gr. 13). 1992. pap. 24.99 (*0-415-05320-X*, A7142) Routledge.

***Montgomery, Martin, et al.** Ways of Reading: Advanced Reading Skills for Students of English Literature. 2nd ed. LC 99-48287. 304p. (C). 2000. pap. 24.99 (*0-415-22206-0*) Routledge.

Montgomery, Marvin. Practice Makes Perfect: The Professional's Guide to Sales Success. LC 95-24239. 144p. 1995. pap. 12.95 (*1-886939-02-0*, Pub. by OakHill Pr VA) ACCESS Pubs Network.

Montgomery, Mary & Baraldi, Severino. Marie Curie. (What Made Them Great Ser.). (Illus.). 104p. (J). (gr. 5-8). 1990. lib. bdg. 12.95 (*0-382-09981-8*) Silver Burdett Pr.

Montgomery, Mary & Clawson, Marion. History of Legislation & Policy Formation of the Central Valley Project. Bruchey, Stuart, ed. LC 78-53558. (Development of Public Land Law in the U. S. Ser.). 1979. reprint ed. lib. bdg. 23.95 (*0-405-11381-1*) Ayer.

Montgomery, Mary & Montgomery, Herb. Easter Is Coming: Lenten Celebrations for the Family. (Illus.). 120p. (Orig.). 1985. 7.95 (*0-86683-609-8*) Harper SF.

— A Final Act of Caring: Ending the Life of an Animal Friend. 32p. 1993. pap. 4.95 (*1-879779-02-1*) Montgomery Pr.

— Good-Bye My Friend: Grieving the Loss of a Pet. 32p. 1991. pap. 4.95 (*1-879779-00-5*) Montgomery Pr.

— Your Aging Pet: Making the Senior Years Healthy & Rewarding. 32p. 1997. pap. 4.95 (*1-879779-04-8*) Montgomery Pr.

Montgomery, Mary, jt. auth. see Montgomery, Herb.

Montgomery-Massingberd, Hugh. Great Houses of England & Wales. LC 94-6987. (Illus.). 424p. 1994. 85.00 (*0-8478-1824-1*, Pub. by Rizzoli Intl) St Martin.

— Great Houses of Scotland. LC 97-66472. (Illus.). 272p. 1997. 85.00 (*0-8478-2038-6*, Pub. by Rizzoli Intl) St Martin.

Montgomery-Massingberd, Hugh & Sykes, Christopher S. Great Houses of Ireland. LC 99-70299. (Illus.). 272p. 1999. 85.00 (*0-8478-2206-0*, Pub. by Rizzoli Intl) St Martin.

Montgomery, Maureen. Gilded Prostitution. 332p. 1989. 37.50 (*0-415-00626-0*) Routledge.

Montgomery, Maureen E. Displaying Women: Spectacles of Leisure in Edith Wharton's New York. LC 97-31983. (Illus.). 272p. (C). 1998. pap. 18.99 (*0-415-90566-4*) Routledge.

— Displaying Women: Spectacles of Leisure in Edith Wharton's New York. LC 97-31983. 272p. (C). 1998. 75.00 (*0-415-90565-6*) Routledge.

Montgomery, Maxine L. The Apocalypse in African-American Fiction. LC 95-36850. 136p. (C). 1996. 39.95 (*0-8130-1389-5*) U Press Fla.

Montgomery, Melissa, ed. Annual Statement Diskette Filing Specifications - Fraternal. 9th rev. ed. 362p. (C). 1997. ring bd. 125.00 (*0-89382-475-5*, ASD-FM) Nat Assn Insurance.

— Annual Statement Diskette Filing Specifications - Health Maintenance Organizations. 6th rev. ed. 134p. (C). 1997. ring bd. 125.00 (*0-89382-476-3*, ASD-HM) Nat Assn Insurance.

— Annual Statement Diskette Filing Specifications - Hospital, Medical, Dental & Indemnity Service Corporation. 5th rev. ed. 282p. (C). 1997. ring bd. 125.00 (*0-89382-478-X*, ASD-MM) Nat Assn Insurance.

— Annual Statement Diskette Filing Specifications - Life. 10th rev. ed. 488p. (C). 1997. ring bd. 125.00 (*0-89382-477-1*, ASD-LM) Nat Assn Insurance.

— Annual Statement Diskette Filing Specifications - Property/Casualty. 10th rev. ed. 438p. (C). 1997. ring bd. 125.00 (*0-89382-479-8*, ASD-PM) Nat Assn Insurance.

— Annual Statement Diskette Filing Specifications - Title. 3rd rev. ed. 306p. (C). 1997. ring bd. 125.00 (*0-89382-480-1*, ASD-TM) Nat Assn Insurance.

Montgomery, Melvin A. Small Business Accounting. LC 97-11601. 380p. 1997. pap. text 50.00 (*0-13-628793-X*) P-H.

Montgomery, Michael. Fifth Men. 256p. 1995. 24.95 (*1-85158-678-4*, Pub. by Mainstream Pubng) Trafalgar.

— An Introduction to Language & Society. 2nd rev. ed. LC 95-7513. (Studies in Culture & Communication). (Illus.). 304p. (C). 1995. pap. 19.99 (*0-415-07238-7*) Routledge.

Montgomery, Michael, ed. Crucible of Carolina: Essays on the Development of Gullah Language & Culture. LC 93-32145. (Illus.). 256p. 1994. 50.00 (*0-8203-1623-7*) U of Ga Pr.

Montgomery, Michael, jt. auth. see Demuth, Patricia.

Montgomery, Michael B. & Bailey, Guy, eds. Language Variety in the South: Perspectives in Black & White. LC 84-16396. (Illus.). 441p. reprint ed. pap. 136.80 (*0-608-09233-9*, 205273700005) Bks Demand.

Montgomery, Michael B. & Little, Greta D., eds. Centennial Usage Studies. LC 94-31291. (Publications of American Dialect Society: No. 78). 1994. pap. text 16.00 (*0-8173-0739-7*) U of Ala Pr.

Montgomery, Michael B., jt. auth. see McMillan, James B.

Montgomery, Michael B., ed. see Andrews, Scottie D.

Montgomery, Michael B., ed. see Kingsmore, Rona K.

Montgomery, Michael S. Telling the Beads. 80p. 1994. write for info. (*0-932616-50-X*) Brick Hse Bks.

Montgomery, Michael S., compiled by. American Puritan Studies: An Annotated Bibliography of Dissertations, 1882-1981. 1. LC 84-6553. (Bibliographies & Indexes in American History Ser.: No. 1). 419p. 1984. lib. bdg. 99.50 (*0-313-24237-2*, MON/) Greenwood.

Montgomery, Michael T., jt. ed. see Redding, Spencer W.

Montgomery, Michael V. Carnivals & Commonplaces: Bakhtin's Chronotope, Cultural Studies & Film. LC 93-8772. (American University Studies, IV: English Language & Literature: Vol. 173). 142p. (C). 1994. text 43.95 (*0-8204-2194-4*) P Lang Pubng.

***Montgomery, Monty.** Dodge Power Wagon Photo History. LC 99-76054. (Illus.). 120p. 2000. pap. 24.95 (*1-58388-019-4*, 130084AE, Pub. by Iconografix) Motorbooks Intl.

Montgomery, Monty. The One & Only Original Sanibel-Captiva Alphabet Coloring Book. (Illus.). 32p. (Orig.). (YA). (gr. 7 up). 1988. pap. 6.95 (*0-945026-00-5*) S-ME Pr.

Montgomery, Morton L. History of Berks County in the Revolution, from 1774 to 1783: Book I, Revolution; Book II, Biographical Sketches. (Illus.). 295p. 1997. reprint ed. lib. bdg. 37.50 (*0 8328 6389 0*) Higginson Bk Co.

Montgomery Museum of Fine Arts Staff. Art Inc: American Paintings from Corporate Collections. Kahan, Mitchell D., ed. LC 78-65838. (Illus.). (J). (ps-12). 1979. 15.00 (*0-89616-008-4*) Montgomery Mus.

— Art of the Eighties: Selections from the Permanent Collection of the Whitney Museum of American Art. Ausfeld, Margaret L., ed. LC 90-13475. (Illus.). 42p. 1990. pap. text 9.00 (*0-89280-026-7*) Montgomery Mus.

— The Blount Collection of American Art. LC 93-20408. (Illus.). 52p. 1993. pap. 18.00 (*0-89280-031-3*) Montgomery Mus.

— The Grand Tour: The Tradition of Patronage in Southern Art Museums. LC 88-19929. (Illus.). 80p. (J). (ps-12). 1988. pap. 12.00 (*0-89280-025-9*) Montgomery Mus.

— Italian Master Prints of the 18th Century: Selections from the Collection of Mr. & Mrs. Adolf Weil Jr. LC 84-18876. (Illus.). 50p. 1984. pap. 8.00 (*0-89280-022-4*) Montgomery Mus.

— Lively Times & Exciting Events: The Drawings of Bill Traylor. LC 93-29034. (Illus.). 40p. 1993. pap. 12.50 (*0-89280-032-1*) Montgomery Mus.

— Master Printmakers of 3 Centuries: Durer, Rembrandt, & Beyond: From the Collection of Adolph Weil, Jr. Ausfeld, Margaret L., ed. LC 94-11868. (Illus.). 1994. pap. 10.00 (*0-89280-033-X*) Montgomery Mus.

— 1992 Montgomery Biennial: In-Outsiders from the American South. LC 92-25883. (Illus.). 68p. 1992. pap. 15.00 (*0-89280-030-5*) Montgomery Mus.

— A Symphony of Color: The World of Kelly Fitzpatrick. Ausfeld, Margaret L., ed. LC 90-25173. (Illus.). 72p. (J). (ps-12). 1991. pap. 18.00 (*0-89280-028-3*) Montgomery Mus.

Montgomery Museum of Fine Arts Staff & Gustafson, Elaine D. Visual Splendors. LC 97-34217. 1997. pap. 14.00 (*0-89280-036-4*) Montgomery Mus.

Montgomery Museum of Fine Arts Staff, jt. auth. see Rembrandt Harmenszoon van Rijn Staff.

Montgomery, Myles. Best Choices in Ohio. LC 88-83473. 700p. 1989. pap. 14.95 (*1-877912-06-9*) Monongahela PA.

Montgomery, N. L., jt. auth. see Montgomery, W. H.

Montgomery, Nancy L. & Olson, Scott S. International Environmental Management Systems Handbook. LC 99-13383. 500p. 1999. 89.95 incl. cd-rom (*1-56670-270-4*, L1270) CRC Pr.

Montgomery, P. Nancy, jt. auth. see Locke, Marie.

Montgomery, Pam. Partner Earth: A Spiritual Ecology. LC 97-27281. (Illus.). 176p. 1997. pap. 12.95 (*0-89281-741-0*) Inner Tradit.

Montgomery, Patricia. Mythmaking: Heal Your Past, Claim Your Future. LC 95-167758. 224p. 1994. pap. 14.95 (*0-9638327-3-5*) Sibyl Pubns.

Montgomery, Patricia C. & Connolly, Barbara, eds. Motor Control & Physical Therapy: Theoretical Framework & Practical Applications. (Illus.). 240p. (Orig.). (C). 1991. pap. text 34.95 (*1-879971-00-3*) Chattanga Grp.

— Therapeutic Exercise in Developmental Disabilities. 2nd ed. (Illus.). 244p. (Orig.). (C). 1993. pap. text 34.95 (*1-879971-01-1*) Chattanga Grp.

Montgomery, Patricia C., jt. auth. see Richter, Eileen W.

Montgomery, Paul. Monarch Notes on Goethe's Faust. (Orig.). (C). 1989. 3.95 (*0-671-00521-9*, Arco) Macmillan Gen Ref.

Montgomery, Paul J. Demographic Profile of African Americans by States. 145p. (Orig.). 1995. pap. 19.95 (*0-9621865-4-6*) Prod Info Analysis.

— Demographic Profile of Spanish/Hispanic Americans by State. 145p. (Orig.). 1997. pap. 19.95 (*0-9621865-5-4*) Prod Info Analysis.

— Nutritional Cereal Counter. (Illus.). 102p. (Orig.). (YA). (gr. 9 up). 1998. pap. 3.50 (*0-9621865-1-1*) Prod Info Analysis.

Montgomery, Paula K. Approaches to Literature Through Literary Form. LC 95-23876. (Reading Motivation Ser.). 168p. 1995. pap. 29.95 (*0-89774-775-5*) Oryx Pr.

— Approaches to Literature Through Subject. LC 93-967. (Reading Motivation Ser.). 256p. 1993. pap. 29.95 (*0-89774-774-7*) Oryx Pr.

Montgomery, Paula K. How to Believe When You Hurt. 96p. 1991. pap. 0.99 (*0-8163-1024-6*) Pacific Pr Pub Assn.

Montgomery, Paula K., jt. auth. see Leonard, Phyllis B.

Montgomery, Peter C., jt. ed. see McQuillan, Lawrence J.

Montgomery, R. A. On Tour: Passport 3. (YA). 1992. mass mkt. 3.95 (*0-553-54090-4*) BDD Bks Young Read.

Montgomery, R. G., et al. Franciscan Awatovi: The Excavation & Conjectural Reconstruction of a Seventeenth Century Spanish Mission. (Harvard University Peabody Museum of Archaeology & Ethnology Papers: Vol. 36). 1949. 30.00 (*0-527-01292-0*) Periodicals Srv.

Montgomery, Ramsey. Outlaw Gulch. (Choose Your Own Adventure Ser.: No. 125). (J). (gr. 4-8). 1992. 8.60 (*0-606-00596-X*, Pub. by Turtleback) Demco.

— U. N. Adventure. (Choose Your Own Adventure Ser.: No. 157). (J). (gr. 4-8). 1995. 8.60 (*0-606-08331-6*, Pub. by Turtleback) Demco.

Montgomery, Raymond A. Castle of Darkness. (Choose Your Own Nightmare Ser.: No. 4). 96p. (J). (gr. 4-7). 1995. pap. 3.50 (*0-553-48232-7*) Bantam.

— Castle of Darkness. (Choose Your Own Nightmare Ser.: No. 4). (J). (gr. 4-8). 1996. 8.60 (*0-606-09140-8*, Pub. by Turtleback) Demco.

— Death in the Dorm. (Choose Your Own Adventure Ser.: No. 171). (J). (gr. 4-8). 1996. 8.60 (*0-606-09189-0*, Pub. by Turtleback) Demco.

— The Haunted House. (Choose Your Own Adventure Ser. (For Younger Readers): No. 2). (J). (gr. 2-4). 1981. 8.70 (*0-606-02400-X*, Pub. by Turtleback) Demco.

— Killer Virus. (Choose Your Own Adventure Ser.: No. 177). (Illus.). 112p. (J). (gr. 4-8). 1997. pap. 3.50 (*0-553-56753-5*) Bantam.

— Last Run. (Choose Your Own Adventure Ser.: No. 153). (J). (gr. 4-8). 1994. 8.60 (*0-606-07021-4*, Pub. by Turtleback) Demco.

— Motocross Mania. (Choose Your Own Adventure Ser.: No. 139). (J). (gr. 4-8). 1993. 8.60 (*0-606-05478-2*, Pub. by Turtleback) Demco.

— Possessed! (Choose Your Own Adventure Ser.: No. 161). (J). (gr. 4-8). 1995. 8.60 (*0-606-08034-1*) Turtleback.

— Project UFO. (Choose Your Own Adventure Ser.: No. 143). (J). (gr. 4-8). 1994. 9.09 (*0-606-05981-4*, Pub. by Turtleback) Demco.

— Space & Beyond. (Choose Your Own Adventure Ser.: No. 4). (J). (gr. 4-8). 1989. 8.60 (*0-606-01824-7*, Pub. by Turtleback) Demco.

— Tattoo of Death. (Choose Your Own Adventure Ser.: No. 159). (J). (gr. 4-8). 1995. 8.60 (*0-606-08270-0*, Pub. by Turtleback) Demco.

Montgomery, Raymond A. & Hubbard-Brown, Janet. It Happened at Camp Pine Tree. (Choose Your Own Nightmare Ser.: No. 10). (J). (gr. 4-8). 1996. 8.60 (*0-606-09139-4*, Pub. by Turtleback) Demco.

***Montgomery, Rebekah.** A Harvest of Faithfulness. 224p. 2000. pap. 8.99 (*1-57748-842-3*, Promise Pr) Barbour Pub.

— A Harvest of Joy. 224p. 2000. pap. 8.99 (*1-57748-845-8*, Promise Pr) Barbour Pub.

— A Harvest of Love. 224p. 2000. pap. 8.99 (*1-57748-843-1*) Barbour Pub.

— A Harvest of Peace. 224p. 2000. pap. 8.99 (*1-57748-844-X*, Promise Pr) Barbour Pub.

— Ordinary Miracles: True Stories of an Extraordinary God Who Works in Our Everyday Lives. 2000. 12.99 (*1-57748-744-3*) Barbour Pub.

Montgomery, Reid H. & Crews, Gordon A. A History of Correctional Violence: An Examination of Reported Causes of Prison Riots & Disturbances. LC 98-13879. (Illus.). 171p. 1998. pap. 34.95 (*1-56991-078-2*) Am Correctional.

Montgomery, Rex & Chappell. Biochemistry: A Case-Oriented Approach. 6th ed. (Illus.). 704p. (C). (gr. 13). 1996. pap. text 57.00 (*0-8151-6483-1*, 26342) Mosby Inc.

Montgomery, Rhonda & Moody, Dan. Cornerstone. 400p. 1996. pap. text 29.33 (*0-205-18578-9*) Allyn.

Montgomery, Rhonda J., ed. Family Seminars for Caregiving: Helping Families Help (Facilitator's Manual) 223p. 1985. 135.00 incl. audio, sl. (*0-295-72509-5*); student ed. 45.00 (*0-295-96316-6*); ring bd. 50.00 (*0-295-96286-0*) U of Wash Pr.

***Montgomery, Rhonda J. & Moody, Patricia G.** Cornerstone Building on Your Best: Concise Edition. 2nd ed. 336p. 2000. pap. 24.00 (*0-13-089254-8*) P-H.

Montgomery, Rhonda J. & Strick, Sandra K. Meetings, Conventions, & Expositions: An Introduction to the Industry. (Hospitality, Travel & Tourism Ser.). 336p. 1994. 59.95 (*0-471-28439-4*, VNR) Wiley.

Montgomery, Rhonda J., et al. Cornerstone: Building on Your Best. LC 98-13854. 294p. 1998. pap. text 24.00 (*0-205-28268-7*) Allyn.

Montgomery, Richard G. The White-Headed Eagle: John McLoughlin, Builder of an Empire. LC 76-164616. (Select Bibliographies Reprint Ser.). 1977. reprint ed. 26.95 (*0-8369-5900-0*) Ayer.

Montgomery, Richard J., Sr. The Basics of Drawing. (Illus.). 14p. 1997. pap. 14.95 (*0-9660715-1-4*) Mtn Art Pub.

Montgomery, Richard J. & Elliot, William D. Investigations in Biology. 2nd ed. (C). 1994. text, teacher ed. 2.66 (*0-669-34085-5*) HM Trade Div.

Montgomery, Richard J. & Elliott, William D. Investigations in Biology. 2nd ed. 405p. (C). 1994. pap. text 34.76 (*0-669-34084-7*) HM Trade Div.

Montgomery, Richard J., Sr. & Montgomery, Maria G. The Book of Learning, Vol. 1. (Illus.). 85p. (J). (gr. k-2). 1997. pap. text 19.95 (*0-9660715-6-5*) Mtn Art Pub.

Montgomery, Rick & Kasper, Shirl. Kansas City: An American Story. Dodd, Monroe, ed. (Illus.). ix, 388p. 1999. 49.95 (*0-9604884-0-5*) Kansas Cty Star.

***Montgomery, Robert, ed.** Your Guide to the ISO Commercial Lines Policies. 8th rev. ed. 360p. 1999. pap. 76.50 (*0-923240-29-2*) Stndrd Publishing.

Montgomery, Robert, jt. auth. see Montgomery, Robert L.

Montgomery, Robert, jt. auth. see Shackleford, Lee E.

Montgomery, Robert, ed. see Brown, Douglas R.

Montgomery, Robert E. The Visionary D. H. Lawrence: Beyond Philosophy & Art. 256p. (C). 1994. text 64.95 (*0-521-45213-9*) Cambridge U Pr.

Montgomery, Robert H. Auditing Theory & Practice. LC 75-18477. (History of Accounting Ser.). (Illus.). 1979. reprint ed. 53.95 (*0-405-07559-6*) Ayer.

— Fifty Years of Accountancy. Brief, Richard P., ed. LC 77-87280. (Development of Contemporary Accounting Thought Ser.). 1978. reprint ed. lib. bdg. 58.95 (*0-405-10908-3*) Ayer.

Montgomery, Robert H., ed. see Dicksee, Lawrence R.

Montgomery, Robert L. The Diffusion of Religions: A Sociological Perspective. LC 96-15351. 242p. 1996. pap. text 32.00 (*0-7618-0345-9*); lib. bdg. 52.00 (*0-7618-0344-0*) U Pr of Amer.

Montgomery, Robert L. A Great Memory. unabridged ed. (Smart Tapes Ser.). 36p. 1994. pap., pap. text 19.95 incl. audio (*1-55678-051-6*, 3220) Learn Inc.

— Introduction to the Sociology of Missions. LC 99-16057. 208p. 1999. 57.95 (*0-275-96691-7*) Greenwood.

Montgomery, Robert L. Memory Made Easy: The Complete Book of Memory Training. LC 79-10889. 122p. reprint ed. pap. 37.90 (*0-608-10679-8*, 202262300028); reprint ed. pap. 34.80 (*0-608-30647-9*, 2022623) Bks Demand.

— A Quick & Easy Way to Top Selling. unabridged ed. 51p. 1985. pap. text 39.95 incl. audio (*1-55678-023-0*, 1598) Learn Inc.

— Terms of Response: Language & the Audience in Seventeenth- & Eighteenth-Century Theory. 208p. 1991. 35.00 (*0-271-00764-8*) Pa St U Pr.

Montgomery, Robert L. & Giffen, Debra. Memory Made Easy. 32p. 1994. pap. 59.95 incl. audio (*1-55678-048-6*) Learn Inc.

Montgomery, Robert L. & Montgomery, Robert. Listen Up. unabridged ed. (Smart Tapes Ser.). 28p. 1994. pap., pap. text 19.95 incl. audio (*1-55678-053-2*, 3225) Learn Inc.

— Speak for Yourself. unabridged ed. (Smart Tapes Ser.). 36p. 1994. pap., pap. text 19.95 incl. audio (*1-55678-052-4*, 3235) Learn Inc.

Montgomery, Robert L., tr. & pref. see Mazzoni, Jacopo & Mazzoni, Giacopo.

Montgomery, Robert R. The Collected Poems of Robert Rice Montgomery Vol. VIII: 1997. viii, 64p. 1997. pap. 7.50 (*0-9662136-0-2*) Huntfield Pubs.

Montgomery, Roger & Marshall, Dale R., eds. Housing Policy for the Eighties. (C). 1979. pap. 15.00 (*0-918592-36-4*) Pol Studies.

Montgomery, Roger, jt. auth. see Pouratzal, Haleh.

Montgomery, Roger, jt. auth. see Woodbridge, Sally B.

Montgomery, Royal E. Industrial Relations in the Chicago Building Trades. LC 77-156434. (American Labor Ser., No. 2). 1971. reprint ed. 23.95 (*0-405-02934-9*) Ayer.

Montgomery, Royce L., et al. Appleton & Lange's Review of Anatomy USMLE, Step 1. 5th ed. LC 94-31509. 331p. (C). 1996. pap. text 34.95 (*0-8385-0246-6*, A0246-7, Apple Lange Med) McGraw.

Montgomery, Ruth. Aliens among Us. 1986. mass mkt. 5.99 (*0-449-20809-5*, Crest) Fawcett.

M

An Asterisk (*) at the beginning of an entry indicates that the title is appearing for the first time.

M

— Born to Heal. 1986. mass mkt. 5.99 (*0-449-21111-8*) Fawcett.
— Here & Hereafter. 176p. 1985. mass mkt. 5.99 (*0-449-20830-3*, Crest) Fawcett.
— A Search for the Truth. 256p. (Orig.). 1985. mass mkt. 5.99 (*0-449-21085-5*, Crest) Fawcett.
— Threshold to Tomorrow. 1985. mass mkt. 5.99 (*0-449-20847-8*) Fawcett.
— The World Before. 1985. mass mkt. 5.95 (*0-449-20923-7*, Crest) Fawcett.
— World Beyond. 1985. mass mkt. 5.99 (*0-449-20832-X*) Fawcett.
— The World to Come: The Guides' Long-Awaited Predictions for the Dawning Age. LC 99-13083. 160p. 1999. 18.95 (*0-609-60479-1*, Harmony) CPG.
***Montgomery, Ruth.** The World to Come: The Guides' Long-Awaited Predictions for the Dawning Age. 160p. 2000. reprint ed. pap. 9.95 (*0-609-80537-1*, Three Riv Pr) Crown Pub Group.
Montgomery, Rutherford, ed. Western Writers of America: A Saddlebag of Tales. (Illus.). 1977. 18.95 (*0-8369-4140-3*) Ayer.
Montgomery, Rutherford G. The Capture of the Golden Stallion. 22.95 (*0-8488-0132-6*) Amereon Ltd.
— The Golden Stallion's Victory. 20.95 (*0-8488-0133-4*) Amereon Ltd.
— Kildee House. (Newbery Honor Roll Ser.). (J). 1993. 13.05 (*0-606-05899-0*, Pub. by Turtleback) Demco.
— Kildee House. (Newbery Honor Roll Ser.). (Illus.). 224p. (J). (gr. 3-7). 1993. reprint ed. pap. 7.95 (*0-8027-7388-5*) Walker & Co.
— A Kinkajou on the Town. 1976. 18.95 (*0-8488-0835-5*) Amereon Ltd.
Montgomery, S., ed. Group Actions on Rings. LC 85-11242. (Contemporary Mathematics Ser.: Vol. 43). 277p. 1985. reprint ed. pap. 38.00 (*0-8218-5046-6*, CONM/43) Am Math.
Montgomery, S., et al, eds. Noncommutative Rings. (Mathematical Sciences Research Institute Publications: Vol. 24). 200p. 1991. 53.95 (*0-387-97704-X*) Spr-Verlag.
Montgomery, S. A. & Den-Boer, Johan A. Series in Depression & Anxiety. LC 98-3702. (Perspectives in Psychiatry Ser.). 202p. 1998. 100.50 (*0-471-97877-9*) Wiley.
Montgomery, S. A. & Rouillon, F. Long-term Treatment of Depression, Vol. 3. LC 91-40088. (Perspectives in Psychiatry Ser.: No. 1951). 286p. 1992. 235.95 (*0-471-92892-5*, Wiley-Liss) Wiley.
Montgomery, Sarah, jt. auth. see Oster, Gerald D.
Montgomery, Scott. Rights of Passage. 1997. pap. text 19.95 (*0-226-53481-2*) U Ch Pr.
Montgomery, Scott L. Minds for the Making: The Role of Science in American Education, 1750-1990. LC 93-38389. 316p. 1994. pap. text 18.95 (*0-89862-188-7*); lib. bdg. 42.00 (*0-89862-189-5*) Guilford Pubns.
— The Moon & the Western Imagination LC 99-6090. 1999. pap. write for info. (*0-8165-1989-7*) U of Ariz Pr.
— The Moon & the Western Imagination. LC 99-6090. (Illus.). 264p. 1999. 35.00 (*0-8165-1711-8*) U of Ariz Pr.
Montgomery, Scott L. Science in Translation: Movements of Knowledge Through Cultures & Time. LC 99-53389. (Illus.). 296p. 1997. 28.00 (*0-226-53480-4*) U Ch Pr.
Montgomery, Scott L. The Scientific Voice. LC 95-43660. (Conduct of Science Ser.). 460p. 1995. pap. text 19.95 (*1-57230-019-1*, 0019); lib. bdg. 44.50 (*1-57230-016-7*, 0016) Guilford Pubns.
Montgomery, Scott M. A Theology for Youth: God 101. 128p. (YA). (gr. 9-12). 1994. pap. 7.95 (*0-9641817-0-3*) S M Montgomery.
Montgomery-Smith, Ann, jt. auth. see Milner, W. W.
Montgomery, Stephen, ed. see Keirsey, David West.
Montgomery, Stephen E. The Pygmalion Project Vol. I: The Artisans. 178p. (Orig.). 1989. pap. 9.95 (*0-9606954-2-7*) Prometheus Nemesis.
— The Pygmalion Project Vol. II: The Guardian. (Love & Coercion among the Types Ser.). 255p. (Orig.). (C). 1990. pap. 9.95 (*0-9606954-5-1*) Prometheus Nemesis.
— The Pygmalion Project Vol. III: The Idealist, Vol. 3. 297p. (Orig.). (C). 1993. pap. 9.95 (*0-9606954-9-4*) Prometheus Nemesis.
Montgomery, Stephen E., ed. see Keirsey, David West.
Montgomery, Stephen E., ed. see Keirsey, David West & Choiniere, Ray.
Montgomery, Stephen J. Build Your Own Intelligent, Mobile, Space Robot. (Illus.). 352p. 1997. text 49.95 (*0-07-912034-2*); pap. text 29.95 (*0-07-912035-0*) McGraw.
Montgomery, Stuart, jt. ed. see Freeman, Isobel.
Montgomery, Stuart A., ed. Psychopharmacology of Panic. LC 92-16486. (British Association for Psychopharmacology Monographs: No. 12). (Illus.). 160p. 1993. text 47.50 (*0-19-262087-8*) OUP.
Montgomery, Stuart A. & Corn, Tim H., eds. The Psychopharmacology of Depression. LC 93-44896. (British Association for Psychopharmacology Monographs: No. 13). 272p. (C). 1994. 98.50 (*0-19-262278-1*) OUP.
Montgomery, Stuart A., jt. ed. see Halbreich, Uriel.
Montgomery, Susan. Hopf Algebras & Their Actions on Rings. LC 93-25786. (CBMS Regional Conference Mathematics Ser.: Vol. 82). 238p. 1993. pap. 25.00 (*0-8218-0738-2*, CBMS/82) Am Math.
Montgomery, Susan, jt. ed. see Bergen, Jeffrey.
Montgomery, Susan B., ed. see United States Trademark Association Staff.
Montgomery, Susan J. The Ceramics of William H. Grueby: The Spirit of New Idea in Artistic Handicraft. Rago, David & Schoen, Michelle S., eds. (Illus.). 165p. 1993. 55.00 (*0-9637896-0-0*); pap. 40.00 (*0-9637896-3-5*) Arts & Crafts.
Montgomery, Susan J., et al. Healthy Living in Wisconsin. (Orig.). 1988. pap. 12.95 (*0-929807-00-6*) Montgomery Media.
Montgomery, Susan J., jt. auth. see Reeds, Roger C.
***Montgomery, Sy.** The Curious Naturalist. 256p. 2000. pap. 16.95 (*0-89272-510-9*) Down East.
Montgomery, Sy. Journey of the Pink Dolphins: An Amazon Quest. LC 99-45840. (Illus.). 320p. 2000. 26.00 (*0-684-84558-X*) S&S Trade.
Montgomery, Sy. Nature's Everyday Mysteries: A Field Guide to the World in Your Backyard. LC 92-36189. (Curious Naturalist Ser.). (Illus.). 152p. (Orig.). 1993. pap. 9.95 (*0-9631591-9-4*, Chapters Bks) HM.
Montgomery, Sy. The Snake Scientist. LC 98-6124. (The Scientists in the Field Ser.). (Illus.). 48p. (J). (gr. 2-7). 1999. 16.00 (*0-395-87169-7*) HM.
— Walking with the Great Apes: Jane Goodall, Dian Fossey, Birute Galdikas. 304p. 1998. pap. 15.00 (*0-395-61156-3*) HM.
Montgomery, Tama, ed. see Frank, Marjorie & Forte, Imogene.
Montgomery, Tama, ed. see Frank, Marjorie & Poulos, Charlotte.
Montgomery, Tama, ed. see Frank, Marjorie & Preskenis, Sheri.
Montgomery, Tama, ed. see Graham, Leland & McCoy, Isabelle.
Montgomery, Theron, ed. see Musgrove, David.
Montgomery, Thomas. La Ley Moral de Dios: Un Estudio de los Diez Mandamientos. Negrete, Omar Ibanez, tr. (SPA.). 142p. Date not set. pap. 3.10 (*1-928980-01-5*) Pub Faro.
Montgomery, Thomas. Medieval Spanish Epic: Mythic Roots & Ritual Language. LC 97-13077. (Penn State Studies in Romance Literatures). 1998. 42.50 (*0-271-01738-4*) Pa St U Pr.
***Montgomery, Thomas, ed.** La Fe Biblica e Historica del Evangelio: Las Doctrinas de la Gracia. Negrete, Omar Ibanez, tr. (SPA., Illus.). 104p. 1999. pap. 2.10 (*1-928980-06-6*) Pub Faro.
Montgomery, Thomas, tr. see Brooks, Thomas.
Montgomery, Thomas, tr. see Burroughs, Jeremiah.
Montgomery, Thomas, tr. see Flavel, John.
Montgomery, Thomas, tr. see Owen, John.
Montgomery, Thomas, tr. see Pink, A. W.
Montgomery, Thomas, tr. see Ryle, J. C.
Montgomery, Tim, ed. see Smith, Paul.
Montgomery, Tommie Sue, ed. Peacemaking & Democratization in the Western Hemisphere: Multilateral Missions. 360p. 2000. pap. 26.95 (*1-57454-045-9*, Pub. by U Miami N-S Ctr) L Rienner.
Montgomery, Vickie. The Smart Woman's Guide to Starting a Business. (Smart Woman's Guides Ser.). 271p. (Orig.). 1996. lib. bdg. 19.95 (*0-7910-4487-4*) Chelsea Hse.
— Woman Managers Troubleshooter. LC 96-38662. 352p. (C). 1996. text 39.95 (*0-13-460080-0*) P-H.
Montgomery, Vickie L. The Smart Woman's Guide to Starting a Business. 2nd ed. LC 98-30416. (Smart Woman's Guides Ser.). 288 p. 1998. pap. 15.99 (*1-56414-368-6*) Career Pr Inc.
Montgomery, W. St. Augustine: Aspects of His Life & Thought. 1977. lib. bdg. 34.95 (*0-8490-2556-7*) Gordon Pr.
Montgomery, W., jt. auth. see Troeltsch, Ernst.
Montgomery, W. David, jt. auth. see Bohi, Douglas R.
Montgomery, W. H. & Montgomery, N. L. Dare Family History. (Illus.). 340p. 1991. reprint ed. pap. 54.00 (*0-8328-1810-0*); reprint ed. lib. bdg. 64.00 (*0-8328-1809-7*) Higginson Bk Co.
Montgomery, W. V., Jr. Senior Citizen Alert! Enjoy Your Financial Future Without Fear! 2nd rev. ed. 229p. 1995. pap. 19.95 (*0-9630975-1-2*) Mont Assocs.
— Senior Citizen Alert! Enjoy Your Financial Future Without Fear! 3rd rev. ed. 229p. 1997. pap. 19.95 (*0-9630975-2-0*) Mont Assocs.
— The Truth about Long-Term Care Insurance. 52p. 1997. pap. 4.50 (*0-9630975-4-7*) Mont Assocs.
Montgomery, Walter S., jt. auth. see Foster, Vernon.
Montgomery Ward & Co. Staff. Catalogue & Buyers Guide Summer & Spring 1895: No. 57. (Illus.). 624p. 1969. reprint ed. pap. 22.95 (*0-486-22377-9*) Dover.
Montgomery, Wes. Wes Montgomery - Jazz Guitar Artistry. Saood, Zafar, tr. 144p. 1995. pap. 17.95 (*0-7866-0283-X*, 95314) Mel Bay.
Montgomery, William. Formative Years of Islamic Thought. 1998. pap. 23.95 (*1-85168-152-3*, Pub. by Onewrld Pubns) Penguin Putnam.
***Montgomery, William.** Power-Up Teams & Tools: For Process Improvement & Problem Solving. 2nd rev. ed. (Illus.). 280p. 1999. pap. text 39.95 (*0-9641124-2-6*) Montgomery.
Montgomery, William A., jt. auth. see Hannay, William M.
Montgomery, William E. Under Their Own Vine & Fig Tree: The African-American Church in the South, 1865-1900. LC 92-21041. 358p. (C). 1994. pap. 14.95 (*0-8071-1965-2*) La State U Pr.
Montgomery, William H. & Atkins. Decision Making in Emergency Cardiology. 1991. 40.00 (*0-8016-3486-5*) Mosby Inc.
Montgomery, William L. Power-Up Teams & Tools: For Process Improvement & Problem Solving. LC 94-96139. 305p. 1995. pap. 39.95 (*0-9641124-0-X*) Montgomery.
Montgomery, William R. Georgia Sharpshooter: The Civil War Diary & Letters of William Rhadamanthus Montgomery. Montgomery, George, ed. LC 97-21316. (Illus.). (Orig.). 1997. pap. 16.00 (*0-86554-572-3*, MUP/P168) Mercer Univ Pr.
Montgomery, William V., Jr. Baby Boomer Alert! Plan for Fifty More! 250p. (Orig.). 1997. pap. 19.95 (*0-9630975-5-5*) Mont Assocs.
— Christians & Their Money. 284p. (Orig.). 1996. pap. 15.95 (*0-9630975-3-9*) Mont Assocs.
Montgomery, William W. Surgery of the Upper Respiratory System, Vol. 1. 3rd ed. LC 96-5668. (Illus.). 704p. 1997. 129.00 (*0-683-06121-6*) Lppncott W & W.
— Surgery of the Upper Respiratory System, Vol. 2. 2nd ed. LC 78-9004. (Illus.). 760p. 1988. text 110.00 (*0-8121-1142-7*) Lppncott W & W.
Montgomery, Yvonne. Obstacle Course. 192p. (Orig.). 1990. pap. 3.50 (*0-380-75992-6*, Avon Bks) Morrow Avon.
— Scavengers. 256p. 1990. pap. 3.50 (*0-380-71002-1*, Avon Bks) Morrow Avon.
Montgomery, Zach. Poison Drops in the Federal Senate: The School Question from a Parental & Non-Sectarian Standpoint. 138p. 1983. reprint ed. pap. 4.95 (*0-685-04742-3*) St Thomas.
Montgomery, Zach, ed. Poison Drops in the Federal Senate. LC 72-172221. (Right Wing Individualist Tradition in America Ser.). iv, 138 p. 1972. reprint ed. 19.95 (*0-405-00430-3*) Ayer.
Month, M. Frontiers of Accelerator Technology: 1994 International Accelerator. 850p. 1999. 120.00 (*981-02-3838-X*) World Scientific Pub.
Month, M. & Herrera, J. C., eds. Nonlinear Dynamics & the Beam-Beam Interaction. LC 79-57341. (AIP Conference Proceedings Ser.: No. 57). (Illus.). 340p. lib. bdg. 20.50 (*0-88318-156-8*) Am Inst Physics.
Month, M. & Turner, S., eds. Frontiers of Particle Beams. (Lecture Notes in Physics Ser.: Vol. 296). xii, 700p. 1988. 96.95 (*0-387-19022-8*) Spr-Verlag.
— Frontiers of Particle Beams, Observation, Diagnosis & Correction. (Lecture Notes in Physics Ser.: Vol. 343). ix, 509p. 1989. 74.95 (*0-387-51616-6*) Spr-Verlag.
Month, M., ed. see American Institute of Physics Staff.
Month, Melvin. Physics of High Energy Particle Accelerators: SLAC Summer School, 1982. LC 83-72986. (AIP Conference Proceedings Ser.: No. 105). 1102p. 1983. lib. bdg. 55.50 (*0-88318-304-8*) Am Inst Physics.
Month, Melvin, et al, eds. Physics of High Energy Particle Accelerators: BNL-SUNY Summer School. LC 85-70057. (AIP Conference Proceedings Ser.: No. 127). 970p. 1985. lib. bdg. 65.00 (*0-88318-326-9*) Am Inst Physics.
— The Physics of Particle Accelerators Vols. 1 & 2: AIP Conference Proceedings, 2 vols. LC 92-52843. (AIP Conference Proceedings Ser.). (Illus.). 220p. (C). 1992. 245.00 (*0-88318-789-2*) Am Inst Physics.
— The State of High Energy Physics, No. 134. LC 85-73170. 382p. 1985. lib. bdg. 46.00 (*0-88318-333-1*) Am Inst Physics.
— The State of Particle Accelerators & High Energy Physics (Fermilab Summer School, 1981) LC 82-73861. (AIP Conference Proceedings Ser.: No. 92). 337p. 1982. lib. bdg. 33.75 (*0-88318-191-6*) Am Inst Physics.
Month, Melvin & Dienes, Margaret. Physics of Particle Accelerators, 2 vols. LC 87-70103. (AIP Conference Proceedings Ser.: No. 153). 1748p. 1987. lib. bdg. 175.00 (*0-88318-353-6*) Am Inst Physics.
Month, Melvin & Dienes, Margaret, eds. Physics of Particle Accelerators. LC 89-83575. (AIP Conference Proceedings Ser.: No. 184). 2376p. 1990. lib. bdg. 199.00 (*0-88318-384-6*) Am Inst Physics.
Monthan, Doris, ed. see Harmsen, Dorothy.
Monthei, Dean L. Package Electrical Modeling, Thermal Modeling & Processing for GAAS Wireless Applications. LC 98-46068. (Electronic Packaging & Interconnects Ser.). xi, 234 p. 1999. write for info. (*0-7923-8364-8*) Kluwer Academic.
Monthei, Sharon L., jt. auth. see Willoughby, Doris M.
Monthule, Pierre. Relais et Chateaux, 1994. (ENG, FRE & GER.). 1994. pap. 9.95 (*0-7859-7428-8*) Fr & Eur.
— Silencehotels: Relais du Silence. (ENG, FRE & GER.). 192p. 1994. pap. 9.95 (*0-7859-7426-1*) Fr & Eur.
Monti-Belkaoui, Janice & Riahi-Belkaoui, Ahmed. Fairness in Accounting. LC 95-38764. 192p. 1996. 65.00 (*1-56720-018-4*, Quorum Bks) Greenwood.
— The Nature, Estimation & Management of Political Risk. LC 98-5287. 176p. 1998. 55.00 (*1-56720-196-2*, Quorum Bks) Greenwood.
— Qaddafi: The Man & His Policies. 107p. 1996. text 61.95 (*1-85972-385-3*, Pub. by Avebry) Ashgate Pub Co.
Monti-Belkaoui, Janice, jt. auth. see Riahi-Belkaoui, Ahmed.
Monti, Daniel J., Jr. The American City: A Social & Cultural History. LC 99-22427. 384p. (C). 1999. text 62.95 (*1-55786-917-0*); pap. text 26.95 (*1-55786-918-9*) Blackwell Pubs.
Monti, Daniel J. Race, Redevelopment, & the New Company Town. LC 89-21829. (SUNY Series in Urban Public Policy). 250p. (C). 1990. text 21.50 (*0-7914-0325-4*) State U NY Pr.
— Wannabe. LC 94-7851. Orig. Title: America's Suburban Gangs. 240p. (Orig.). 1994. pap. 22.95 (*1-55786-615-5*) Blackwell Pubs.
Monti, Daniel J., jt. ed. see Cummings, Scott.
Monti, Enrico. Global Positioning System Coordinates: Sanibel Island to Lower Keys Fla. (Illus.). 50p. (Orig.). 1996. pap. text, spiral bd. 25.00 (*1-890322-00-8*) Monti & Assocs.
— The Inshore Guide to Fishing & Diving Waypoints: Loran-C & Global Positioning Systems Coordinates. (Illus.). 19p. (Orig.). 1997. pap. text, spiral bd. 25.00 (*1-890322-02-4*) Monti & Assocs.
— The Midway Guide to Fishing & Diving Waypoints: Loran C & Global Positioning System Coordinates. (Illus.). 29p. 1997. pap. text 25.00 (*1-890322-03-2*) Monti & Assocs.
— The Offshore Guide to Forty-Eight Fishing Waypoints: Loran C & Global Positioning System Coordinates. (Illus.). 9p. (Orig.). 1996. pap. text, spiral bd. 25.00 (*1-890322-01-6*) Monti & Assocs.
Monti, Harry & Monti, Trudy. Stars of Magic Cookbook. (Illus.). 256p. Date not set. pap. 24.95 (*0-9649321-6-4*) Tiger Press.
Monti, Harry, jt. auth. see Monti, Trudy.
Monti, James. Kings Good Servant but God's First. LC 96-78015. 1997. pap. text 19.95 (*0-89870-625-4*) Ignatius Pr.
— The Week of Salvation: History & Traditions of Holy Week. LC 93-83256. 448p. (Orig.). 1993. 21.95 (*0-87973-532-5*, 532) Our Sunday Visitor.
Monti, James, jt. auth. see Groeschel, Benedict.
Monti, Joseph. Arguing about Sex: The Rhetoric of Christian Sexual Morality. LC 94-26956. 365p. (C). 1995. text 59.50 (*0-7914-2479-0*); pap. text 19.95 (*0-7914-2480-4*) State U NY Pr.
Monti, Laura V., jt. ed. see Bigelow, Gordon E.
Monti, Lisa, jt. auth. see Higginbotham, Sylvia.
Monti, Mario. Single Market & Tomorrow's Europe: The Monti Report. 1996. pap. text 19.95 (*0-7494-2266-1*) Kogan Page Ltd.
Monti, Mario, ed. Fiscal Policy, Economic Adjustment, & Financial Markets. x, 283p. 1989. pap. 16.00 (*1-55775-118-8*) Intl Monetary.
— Fiscal Policy, Economic Adjustment & Financial Markets. LC 89-19934. 294p. reprint ed. pap. 91.20 (*0-7837-1260-X*, 204139700020) Bks Demand.
Monti, Peter M., et al. Treating Alcohol Dependence: A Coping Skills Training Guide. LC 88-36838. (Treatment Manuals for Practitioners Ser.). 240p. 1989. pap. text 23.00 (*0-89862-215-8*) Guilford Pubns.
Monti, Peter M., jt. ed. see Curran, James P.
Monti, Peter M., ed. see Goddard, Perilou.
Monti, R. George & Barile, Andrew. A Practical Guide to Finite Risk Insurance & Reinsurance. LC 95-20443. 341p. 1995. 220.00 (*0-471-12818-X*) Wiley.
Monti, Ralph. Bet on Your Golf Game! An Indispensable Guide for Betting on the Golf Course. LC 93-74488. (Illus.). 160p. 1994. pap. 7.95 (*1-884490-20-4*) Fortune Media.
— Career Opportunities in Magazine Publishing: The Ultimate Guide to Succeeding in the Business. (Illus.). 200p. (Orig.). (C). 1999. pap. 22.95 (*1-884490-16-6*) Fortune Media.
— I Remember Brooklyn: Memories of Favorite Sons & Daughters. (Illus.). 224p. 1991. 22.95 (*1-55972-093-X*, Birch Ln Pr) Carol Pub Group.
Monti, Richard C. Terence Andria. (Latin Commentaries Ser.). 153p. (Orig.). (C). 1986. pap. text 8.00 (*0-929524-58-6*) Bryn Mawr Commentaries.
Monti, Trudy & Monti, Harry. The Magic of Fat-Free Cooking. 176p. (Orig.). 1996. pap. 12.95 (*0-9649321-5-6*) Tiger Press.
Monti, Trudy, jt. auth. see Monti, Harry.
Montias, John M. Artists & Artisans in Delft: A Socio-Economic Study of the Seventeenth Century. LC 81-11953. (Illus.). 445p. reprint ed. pap. 138.00 (*0-8357-2920-6*, 203916000011) Bks Demand.
— Central Planning in Poland, 13--13. LC 74-6785. (Yale Studies in Economics: No. 13). (Illus.). 410p. 1974. reprint ed. lib. bdg. 79.50 (*0-8371-7560-7*, MOCP, Greenwood Pr) Greenwood.
— The Structure of Economic Systems. LC 75-43327. 336p. reprint ed. pap. 104.20 (*0-8357-8335-9*, 203383000087) Bks Demand.
— Vermeer & His Milieu: A Web of Social History. (Illus.). 427p. 1989. pap. text 24.95 (*0-691-00289-4*, Pub. by Princeton U Pr) Cal Prin Full Svc.
Montias, John M., et al. Comparative Economics, Vol. 57. LC 93-38882. 181p. 1994. pap. text 39.00 (*3-7186-5451-2*) Gordon & Breach.
Montias, John M., jt. ed. see Marer, Paul.
Monticelli, A. State Estimation in Electric Power Systems: A Generalized Approach LC 99-20753. (International Series In Engineering & Computer Science). 1999. write for info. (*0-7923-8519-5*) Kluwer Academic.
Monticelli, Barbara S. Fun Sculpting: A Humorous Approach to the Three-Dimensional Cartooning in Clay. LC 84-51804. (Illus.). 52p. (Orig.). 1984. pap. text 2.98 (*0-916809-11-0*) Scott Pubns MI.
Monticelli, Carlo & Papi, Luca. European Integration, Monetary Co-Ordination, & the Demand for Money. LC 95-43817. (Illus.). 240p. (C). 1996. text 55.00 (*0-19-829011-X*, Clarendon Pr) OUP.
Monticelli, Daniel. How to Increase Personal Power & Influence Others. (Illus.). 96p. (Orig.). 1997. pap. 11.95 (*1-890420-11-5*) Genesis NM.
Monticone, Diane K. Montesquieu & His Reader: A Study of the Esprit des Lois. LC 89-38370. (Illus.). 168p. (C). 1989. lib. bdg. 41.00 (*0-8191-7596-X*) U Pr of Amer.
Monticone, Ronald C. The Catholic Church in Communist Poland, 1945-1985: Forty Years of Church-State Relations. (East European Monographs: No. 205). 227p. 1986. text 48.50 (*0-88033-102-X*, Pub. by East Eur Monographs) Col U Pr.
Montie, T. C., ed. Pseudomonas. (Biotechnology Handbooks Ser.: Vol. 10). (Illus.). 352p. (C). 1998. text 110.00 (*0-306-45849-7*, Kluwer Plenum) Kluwer Academic.
Montiel, Francisco-Felix. El Tercer Ejercito de la U. R. S. S. LC 88-81600. (SPA.). 116p. (Orig.). 1989. pap. 12.00 (*0-89729-497-1*) Ediciones.
Montiel, Miguel, jt. auth. see Padilla, Raymond V.
Montiel, Peter J., jt. auth. see Agbenor, Pierre Richard.
Montiel, Peter J., jt. auth. see Agenor, Pierre-Richard.
Montiero, Aristides. War Reminiscences. 1976. 22.95 (*0-8488-1104-6*) Amereon Ltd.
***Montiglio, Silvia.** Silence in the Land of Logos LC 99-36892. 2000. 45.00 (*0-691-00472-2*, Pub. by Princeton U Pr) Cal Prin Full Svc.
Montignac, Michel. Dine Out & Lose Weight. 1991. pap. 19.95 (*2-906236-17-9*, Pub. by Editions Artulen) Montignac USA.

An Asterisk (*) at the beginning of an entry indicates that the title is appearing for the first time.

— Eat Yourself Slim. LC 99-61527. 288p. 1999. pap. 19.95 (*1-893162-05-2*) Erica Hse.

***Montignac, Michel.** Eat Yourself Slim Cookbook. LC 99-64663. (Illus.). 260p. 1999. pap. 24.95 (*1-893162-10-9*, Pub. by Erica Hse) Bookazine Co Inc.

Montignac, Michel. Je Mange Donc je Maigris.Tr. of Eat & Lose Weight. (FRE.). boxed set 14.95 incl. audio (*2-921997-55-X*, Pub. by Coffragants) Penton Overseas.

***Montignac, Michel.** More Montignac Menus. 32p. 1999. pap. 4.95 (*1-893162-07-9*) Erica Hse.

— Les 7 Habitudes des Gens Efficaces. (French Audiobooks Ser.).Tr. of 7 Habits of Highly Effective People. (FRE.). 1999. pap., boxed set 14.95 incl. audio (*2-921997-90-8*, Pub. by Coffragants) Penton Overseas.

Montignac, Michel & Robert, Hervbe. Eat Yourself Slim or the Secrets of Nutrition. 5th ed. LC 98-221288. 267 p. 1996. write for info. (*2-906236-41-1*) Editions Artulen.

Montigny, Edgar-Andre. Foisted upon the Government? State Responsibilities, Family Obligations, & Care of the Dependent Aged in Late 19th-Century Ont. LC 99-173167. 232p. 1993. 44.95 (*0-7735-1616-6*, Pub. by McG-Queens Univ Pr) CUP Services.

Montigny, Gerald A. De, see De Montigny, Gerald A.

Montijo, Yolanda, jt. auth. see Margolin, Malcolm.

Montilla, M. Robert, jt. auth. see Ramelet, A. A.

Montin, Karin, tr. see Irigaray, Luce.

***Montin, Leif R.** Get Out in Town! Montreal! 52 Fun Things to Do Right Here in Montreal. (Illus.). 144p. 1998. pap. text 10.95 (*0-9681732-2-5*) No Fixed Add.

Montin, Leif R. Get Outta Town! Montreal: 52 Fun Things to Do Within Easy Reach of Montreal. 1998. pap. text 10.95 (*0-9681732-0-9*) No Fixed Add.

Montinari, Mazzino. Friedrich Neitzsche: Eine Einfuhrung. (GER., Illus.). xv, 146p. (C). 1991. pap. text 24.65 (*3-11-012213-8*) De Gruyter.

Montinari, Mazzino, jt. ed. see Colli, C.

Montinari, Mazzino, jt. ed. see Colli, G.

Montinari, Mazzino, ed. see Nietzsche, Friedrich Wilhelm.

Montinho, Luiz. Future Trends in Marketing. (C). 1998. text. write for info. (*0-201-40388-9*) Addison-Wesley.

Montini, Giovanni Battista, see Paul, VI, pseud.

Montinola, Lourdes R. Breaking the Silence. 138p. 1998. pap. text 18.00 (*971-542-128-8*) UH Pr.

Montironi, R. & Schulman, C. C., eds. Precursors of Prostatic Adenocarcinoma: Recent Findings & New Concepts. (Journal: European Urology: Vol. 30, No. 2, 1996). (Illus.). iv, 148p. 1996. reprint ed. 77.50 (*3-8055-6367-1*) S Karger.

Montiwalla, Luvai. A Primer on EXSYS for DOS. LC 94-145. 128p. (C). 1995. per. 25.95 (*0-256-16336-7*, Irwn Prfssnl) McGraw-Hill Prof.

Montizambert, Dave. Creative Lighting Techniques for Studio Photographers. 120p. 1999. pap. text 29.95 (*1-58428-003-4*, Pub. by Amherst Media) IPG Chicago.

Montjoy, Robert S. Innovations in Election Administration: Mail Voter Registration Programs. (Illus.). 55p. (Orig.). (C). 1994. pap. text 25.00 (*0-7881-1254-6*) DIANE Pub.

Montjoy, Robert S., jt. auth. see O'Toole, Laurence J.

Montler, Timothy. Saanich, North Straits Salish: Classified Word List, Vol. 119. (Mercury Ser.: CES No. 119). 184p. 1991. pap. 17.95 (*0-660-12908-6*, Pub. by CN Mus Civilization) U of Wash Pr.

Montler, Timothy, jt. ed. see Mattina, Anthony.

Montlick, Terry. Distributed Smalltalk Survival Guide: Advice for Effectively Managing Large-Scale Smalltalk Projects. (Advances in Object Technology Ser.: No. 19). 240p. (C). 1999. pap. 34.95 (*0-521-64552-2*) Cambridge U Pr.

Montmarquet. African-American Philosophy. (Philosophy). 1999. pap. 52.95 (*0-534-57393-2*) Wadsworth Pub.

Montmarquet, James. Conversations on Moral Issues. 144p. (C). 1997. spiral bd. 14.95 (*0-7872-4379-5*) Kendall-Hunt.

Montney, Charles B. Senior Citizen Services, 4 Vols., Vol. 4. 1992. 100.00 (*0-8103-8319-5*) Gale.

— Senior Citizen Services: Midwest, Vol. 3. 1992. 40.00 (*0-8103-8322-5*) Gale.

— Senior Citizen Services: Northeast, Vol. 1. 1992. 40.00 (*0-8103-8320-9*) Gale.

— Senior Citizen Services: Southeast, Vol. 2. 1992. 40.00 (*0-8103-8321-7*) Gale.

— Senior Citizen Services: West, Vol. 4. 1992. 40.00 (*0-8103-8323-3*) Gale.

Monto, Alexander. The Roots of Mexican Labor Migration. LC 93-25058. 272p. 1994. 65.00 (*0-275-94630-4*, C4630, Praeger Pubs) Greenwood.

Montoff, Alexei. Guide to Owning Siberian Huskies: AKC Rank #17. (Guide to Owning Ser.). (Illus.). 64p. 1995. pap. 6.95 (*0-7938-1860-5*, RE-310) TFH Pubns.

Monton, Dennis, jt. auth. see Maris, Michael.

Montonati, Angelo. A Journalist Looks at the Parables. 144p. (C). 1996. pap. 39.95 (*0-85439-385-4*, Pub. by St Paul Pubns) St Mut.

Montone, Deborah. Power Building in Documentation. Williams, Adrianne, ed. LC 97-34986. 320p. (C). 1998. pap. text 18.95 (*0-7216-6933-6*, W B Saunders Co) Harcrt Hlth Sci Grp.

— Power Building in Scheduling. Biblis, Margaret, ed. 256p. 1997. pap. text 18.95 (*0-7216-6932-8*, W B Saunders Co) Harcrt Hlth Sci Grp.

— Power Building in the Money Trail. Williams, Adrianne, ed. LC 98-25996. (Illus.). 430p. (C). 1998. pap. text 24.95 (*0-7216-6931-X*, W B Saunders Co) Harcrt Hlth Sci Grp.

— Power Building Medical Coding. LC 98-4061. (C). 1998. pap. text 19.95 (*0-7216-6930-1*) Harcourt.

Montone, Wayne V., jt. auth. see Miller, Richard K.

Montonen, C., jt. auth. see Laurikainen, K. V.

Montonen, M., jt. auth. see Partanen, J.

Montoni. Physiology Review Book. Date not set. pap. text. write for info. (*0-7216-5177-1*, W B Saunders Co) Harcrt Hlth Sci Grp.

Montor, Karel. Naval Leadership: Voices of Experience. LC 87-10986. (Illus.). 504p. (C). 1987. text 27.95 (*0-87021-325-3*) Naval Inst Pr.

Montor, Karel, compiled by. Ethics for the Junior Officer: Selected Cases from Current Military Experience. LC 93-42085. 301p. 1994. 26.95 (*1-55750-591-8*) Naval Inst Pr.

Montorsi, A., ed. The Hubbard Model. 300p. (C). 1992. reprint ed. text 86.00 (*981-02-0585-6*); reprint ed. pap. text 40.00 (*981-02-0586-4*) World Scientific Pub.

Montorsi, A. & Rasetti, M. G., eds. Integrable Systems in Statistical Mechanics. (Series on Advances in Statistical Mechanics: Vol. 1). 178p. 1985. text 47.00 (*9971-978-11-3*); pap. text 30.00 (*9971-978-14-8*) World Scientific Pub.

Montouri, Alfonso A. Evolutionary Competence: Creating the Future. x, 378p. 1990. pap. 40.00 (*90-5063-047-2*, Pub. by Gieben) J Benjamins Pubng Co.

Montouri, Don, jt. ed. see Ortman, John.

Montovani, Roberto. Everest: The History of the Himalayan Giant. Fortney, William, tr. from ITA. LC 97-223517. (Illus.). 144p. 1997. 35.00 (*0-89886-534-4*) Mountaineers.

Montoya-Aguilar, C., jt. auth. see Roemer, M.

Montoya, Alex D. Hispanic Ministry in North America. 160p. (Orig.). 1987. pap. 9.95 (*0-310-37741-2*, 12058P) Zondervan.

***Montoya, Alex D.** Preaching with Passion. 2000. pap. 10.99 (*0-8254-3346-0*) Kregel.

Montoya, Ana M., tr. see Pena, Betty W.

Montoya, Andres. The Iceworker Sings & Other Poems. LC 99-12111. 79p. 2000. pap. 9.00 (*0-927534-86-X*, Pub. by Biling Rev-Pr) SPD-Small Pr Dist.

Montoya, Candace G. & Roxberg, Joan M. Thinking & Writing Persuasivly. LC 94-34638. 496p. (C). 1994. pap. 37.00 (*0-02-382431-X*, Macmillan Coll) P-H.

Montoya, Candace Glass, see Glass Montoya, Candace.

Montoya, Jose. In Formation: 20 Years of Joda. 254p. 1992. pap. 17.95 (*0-9624536-1-7*) Chusma Hse.

— El Sol y los de Abajo. (ENG & SPA., Illus.). 13p. 1992. 175.00 (*0-9614597-8-6*) Ninja Pr.

Montoya-Ramirez, Maria I., ed. Texto y Concordancias de la Defenssa de Virtuossas Mugeres de Mosen Diego de Valera, MS. 1341 de la Biblioteca Nacional. (Spanish Ser.: No. 72). 8p. 1992. 10.00 incl. fiche (*0-940639-73-4*) Hispanic Seminary.

Montoya Ramirez, Maria Isabel, ed. see Keller, John E.

Montoya, Thomas C. & Kelsey, David H. New Mexico Domestic Relations Law & Forms. LC 95-79155. 1995. spiral bd. 105.00 (*0-250-47252-X*, 63825, MICHIE) LEXIS Pub.

***Montoya, Tracy.** Isabela's Dreams. (Encanto Ser.). 2000. mass mkt. 3.99 (*0-7860-1154-8*, Pinncle Kensgtn); mass mkt. 3.99 (*0-7860-1158-0*, Pinncle Kensgtn) Kensgtn Pub Corp.

Montoya-Welsh, Sharon & Speare-Yerxa, Marjorie. Oyster Cookery. 2nd ed. (Illus.). 168p. 1984. reprint ed. pap. 9.95 (*0-9613895-0-8*) Shoalwater Kitch.

Montparker, Carol. The Anatomy of the New York Debut Recital: A Chronicle. (Illus.). 94p. 1984. reprint ed. 14.95 (*0-912483-48-2*, T055) Bold Strummer Ltd.

— A Pianist's Landscape. LC 97-49643. (Illus.). 297p. 1998. 24.95 (*1-57467-039-5*, Amadeus Pr) Timber.

***Montpensier, Anne-Marie-Louise d'Orleans & Pitts, Vincent J.** La Grande Mademoiselle at the Court of France, 1627-1693. LC 00-8266. 2000. 42.00 (*0-8018-6466-6*) Johns Hopkins.

Montpetit, Charles, jt. auth. see Rathjen, Heidi.

Montplaisir, Jacques & Godbout, Roger, eds. Sleep & Biological Rhythms: Basic Mechanisms & Applications to Psychiatry. (Illus.). 256p. 1990. text 49.95 (*0-19-505825-9*) OUP.

Montreal--Rochester--Syracuse--Toronto Meeting (McGill University). Toward the Theory of Everything: MRST '98. Cline, James M. et al, eds. LC 98-88416. (AIP Conference Proceedings Ser.: Vol. 452). 288p. 1999. 98.00 (*1-56396-845-2*) Am Inst Physics.

Montreal Museum of Arts Staff, jt. ed. see Eidelbeger, Martin.

Montresor, Beni. Bedtime. LC 77-25639. (Illus.). (J). (ps-3). 1978. 11.95 (*0-06-024353-8*) HarpC Child Bks.

Montresor, Jaye B., ed. The Critical Response to Ann Beattie, 4. LC 92-46531. (Critical Responses in Arts & Letters Ser.: No. 4). 296p. 1993. lib. bdg. 59.95 (*0-313-28358-3*, MTW, Greenwood Pr) Greenwood.

Montresor, M., jt. auth. see Marino, D.

Montreuil, Gerbert De, see Lowe, L. F.

Montreuil, Gerbert De, see Lowe, L. F. & De Montreuil, Gerbert.

Montreuil, Jean, et al, eds. Glycoproteins: Part 1. (New Comprehensive Biochemistry Ser.: Vol. 29A). 672p. 1995. 275.50 (*0-444-81260-1*); pap. 113.75 (*0-444-82075-2*) Elsevier.

— Glycoproteins II. LC 97-40500. (New Comprehensive Biochemistry Ser.: Vol. 29B). 664p. 1997. 290.75 (*0-444-82393-X*) Elsevier.

Montreuil, Jean, et al. Glycoproteins & Disease. LC 96-33252. (New Comprehensive Biochemistry Ser.). 512p. 1996. 222.25 (*0-444-82396-4*) Elsevier.

Montreuil, Margaret. Love's Face. 163p. 1997. mass mkt. 11.00 (*0-9659320-2-8*) Lvg Waters.

Montreville, Doris De, see De Montreville, Doris, ed.

Montreynaud, F. Robert Dictionnaire des Citations du Monde Entier. (FRE.). 506p. 1997. 69.95 (*0-320-00491-0*) Fr & Eur.

— Robert Dictionnaire des Proverbes et Dictons. (FRE.). 491p. 1997. 59.95 (*0-320-00437-6*) Fr & Eur.

Montreynaud, Florence. Diccionario de Citas Literarias. (SPA.). 640p. 1990. 59.95 (*0-7859-5771-5*) Fr & Eur.

— Dictionaire de Proverbes et Dictions. (FRE.). 750p. 1989. 45.00 (*0-7859-9193-X*) Fr & Eur.

— Dictionnaire de Citations du Monde Entier. (FRE.). 869p. 1990. 34.95 (*0-7859-9216-2*) Fr & Eur.

— Dictionnaire de Citations du Monde Entier. (FRE.). 520p. 1993. 110.00 (*0-7859-9210-3*) Fr & Eur.

— Dictionnaire de Proverbes & Dictons. (FRE.). 520p. 1993. 110.00 (*0-7859-9185-9*) Fr & Eur.

— Love: A Century of Love & Passion. (Illus.). 400p. 1998. 39.99 (*3-8228-7645-3*) Taschen Amer.

— Robert Dictionnaire de Proverbs et Dictions. (FRE.). 750p. 1989. pap. 28.95 (*0-7859-8059-8*, 2850361046) Fr & Eur.

Montreynaud, Florence & Matignon, Jeanne. Robert Dictionnaire de Citations du Monde Entier. (FRE.). 794p. 1989. 75.00 (*0-8288-9466-3*) Fr & Eur.

Montreynuad, Florence. Dictionnaire des Citations Francaises et Etrangeres. (FRE.). 544p. 1985. 69.95 (*0-7859-7727-9*, 2092910612) Fr & Eur.

Montroll. Easy Origami. LC 92-16933. (Illus.). 64p. pap. 3.50 (*0-486-27298-2*) Dover.

Montroll. Origami for the Enthusiast: Step-by-Step Instructions in over 700 Diagrams. (Illus.). 80p. pap. 7.95 (*0-486-23799-0*) Dover.

Montroll, Andrew, ed. see Montroll, John.

Montroll, Andrew, ed. see Montroll, John & Lang, Robert.

Montroll, E. W. & Lebowitz, Joel L., eds. Fluctuation Phenomena. (North-Holland Personal Library). viii, 390p. 1992. reprint ed. pap. 68.75 (*0-444-87038-5*, North Holland) Elsevier.

Montroll, John. African Animals in Origami. LC 91-76400. (Illus.). 160p. (Orig.). (YA). 1993. pap. 9.95 (*1-877656-09-7*) Antroll Pub.

— African Animals in Origami. (Illus.). 160p. (Orig.). 1991. pap. 9.95 (*0-486-26977-9*) Dover.

— Animal Origami for the Enthusiast: Step-by-Step Instructions in over 900 Diagrams. 56th ed. 128p. 1985. pap. 9.95 (*0-486-24792-9*) Dover.

— Birds in Origami. LC 94-40618. (Illus.). 48p. 1995. pap. 3.50 (*0-486-28341-0*) Dover.

***Montroll, John.** Bringing Origami to Life. (Illus.). 120p. 1999. pap. text 10.95 (*1-877656-13-5*) Antroll Pub.

Montroll, John. Bringing Origami to Life. LC 99-41234. 128p. 1999. pap. text 10.95 (*0-486-40714-4*) Dover.

***Montroll, John.** Dollar Bill Animals in Origami. (Illus.). 120p. 2000. pap. text 10.95 (*1-877656-14-3*) Antroll Pub.

— Dollar Bill Animals in Origami. (Illus.). 2000. pap. 10.95 (*0-486-41157-5*) Dover.

Montroll, John. Favorite Animals in Origami. (Illus.). 48p. 1996. pap. 3.50 (*0-486-29136-7*) Dover.

— Mythological Creatures & the Chinese Zodiac in Origami. LC 95-83963. (Illus.). 120p. 1996. pap. 9.95 (*1-877656-11-9*) Antroll Pub.

— Mythological Creatures & the Chinese Zodiac in Origami. (Illus.). 128p. 1996. pap. 10.95 (*0-486-28971-0*) Dover.

— North American Animals in Origami. LC 94-96743. (Illus.). 120p. (Orig.). 1995. pap. text 9.95 (*1-877656-10-0*) Antroll Pub.

— North American Animals in Origami. LC 94-49013. 128p. (Orig.). 1995. pap. 9.95 (*0-486-28667-3*) Dover.

— Origami American Style. (Illus.). 32p. (J). (gr. 2 up). 1990. pap. 6.00 (*0-9627254-0-4*) Zenagraf.

— Origami Inside-Out. LC 95-90214. (Illus.). 120p. (YA). 1993. pap. 9.95 (*1-877656-08-9*) Antroll Pub.

— Origami Inside-Out. LC 93-4147. 1993. reprint ed. pap. 9.95 (*0-486-27674-0*) Dover.

— Origami Sculptures. 2nd ed. Montroll, Andrew, ed. LC 89-81888. (Illus.). 120p. (Orig.). (YA). 1990. pap. text 9.95 (*1-877656-02-X*) Antroll Pub.

— Origami Sculptures. 2nd ed. 144p. (Orig.). 1990. pap. 9.95 (*0-486-26587-0*) Dover.

— Origami Sea Life. 256p. 1991. pap. 10.95 (*0-486-26765-2*) Dover.

— Prehistoric Origami: Dinosaurs & Other Creatures. LC 88-84160. (Illus.). 120p. (Orig.). 1989. pap. text 9.95 (*1-877656-01-1*) Antroll Pub.

Montroll, John. Prehistoric Origami Dinosaurs & Other Creatures. 143p. 1990. pap. 9.95 (*0-486-26588-9*) Dover.

Montroll, John. Teach Yourself Origami. LC 97-95291. (Illus.). 120p. 1998. pap. text 9.95 (*1-877656-12-7*) Antroll Pub.

— Teach Yourself Origami. LC 98-2563. 1998. pap. 9.95 (*0-486-40141-3*) Dover.

Montroll, John & Lang, Robert. Origami Sea Life. 2nd ed. Montroll, Andrew, ed. LC 90-80778. (Illus.). 192p. 1991. pap. text 10.95 (*1-877656-05-4*) Antroll Pub.

Montrond, Julia L., tr. see Seely, Contee & Romijn, Elizabeth.

Montrose, Catherine. The Wendigo Border. 288p. (Orig.). 1995. mass mkt. 4.99 (*0-8125-2432-2*, Pub. by Tor Bks) St Martin.

Montrose, Donald W. Guerra Espiritual: El Ocultismo Tiene Influencia Demoniaca. 30p. 1991. 1.00 (*1-56036-016-X*, 48350) AMI Pr.

— Spiritual Warfare: The Occult Has Demonic Influence. 28p. 1991. 0.50 (*1-56036-014-3*, 36492) AMI Pr.

Montrose, Jim. Improvising Cooking: The Complete Guide to Cooking Gourmet Vegetarian Meals. 2nd rev. ed. LC 97-60259. (Illus.). 112p. 1997. pap. 11.95 (*0-9656319-0-7*) Enliven Bks & Tapes.

Montrose, Ken & Dulcy, Dennis. Celebrating Small Victories: A Primer of Approaches & Attitudes for Helping Clients with Dual Disorders. LC 95-18958. 177p. 1995. 19.95 (*1-56838-092-5*) Hazelden.

Montrose, Louis A. The Purpose of Playing: Shakespeare & the Cultural Politics of the Elizabethan Theatre. 248p. 1996. pap. text 16.00 (*0-226-53483-9*) U Ch Pr.

— The Purpose of Playing: Shakespeare & the Cultural Politics of the Elizabethan Theatre. 248p. 1998. lib. bdg. 45.00 (*0-226-53482-0*) U Ch Pr.

***Montrose, Mark I.** PCB Design Techniques for EMC Compliance. 2nd ed. (Series on Electronics Technology). 336p. 2000. 79.95 (*0-7803-5376-5*) Inst Electrical.

Montrose, Mark I. & IEEE Electromagnetic Compatibility Society Staff. EMC & the PCB: Design, Theory & Layout Made Simple. LC 98-35408. (Electronics Technology Ser.). 1998. 69.99 (*0-7803-4703-X*) IEEE Comp Soc.

Montrose, Mark I., jt. auth. see IEEE, Electromagnetic Compatibility Society Staff.

Montross, C. & Canzona. U. S. Marine Operations in Korea Vol. I: The Pusan Perimeter. (Illus.). 271p. (C). 1992. reprint ed. lib. bdg. 25.00 (*0-944495-01-X*) R J Speights.

— U. S. Marine Operations in Korea Vol. II: The Inchon-Seoul Operation. (Illus.). 361p. (C). 1992. reprint ed. lib. bdg. 25.00 (*0-944495-02-8*) R J Speights.

— U. S. Marine Operations in Korea Vol. III: The Chosin Reservoir Campaign. (Illus.). 432p. (C). 1992. reprint ed. lib. bdg. 25.00 (*0-944495-03-6*) R J Speights.

Montross, C. & Kuokku, Hicks. U. S. Marine Operations in Korea Vol. IV: The East Central Front. (Illus.). 342p. (C). 1992. reprint ed. lib. bdg. 25.00 (*0-944495-04-4*) R J Speights.

Montross, Ca, jt. auth. see Montross, Lynn.

Montross, Constance M. & Levine, Esther. Vistas: Voces del Mundo Hispanico. 2nd ed. (Illus.). 224p. (C). 1994. pap. text 35.80 (*0-13-181686-1*) P-H.

Montross, David H. & Shinkman, Christopher J., eds. Career Development: Theory & Practice. (Illus.). 442p. 1992. pap. 49.95 (*0-398-06294-3*) C C Thomas.

— Career Development: Theory & Practice. (Illus.). 442p. (C). 1992. text 71.95 (*0-398-05764-8*) C C Thomas.

Montross, David H., et al. Real People, Real Jobs: Reflecting Your Interests in the World of Work: 40 People Tell Their Stories. LC 95-8818. 272p. (Orig.). 1995. pap. 15.95 (*0-89106-077-4*, 7115, Davies-Black Pub) Consulting Psychol.

Montross, Lois S. Among Those Present. LC 77-132121. (Short Story Index Reprint Ser.). 1977. 19.95 (*0-8369-3678-7*) Ayer.

Montross, Lois S., jt. auth. see Montross, Lynn.

Montross, Lynn. War Through the Ages. (C). 1996. pap. text 68.50 (*0-8133-7108-2*) Westview.

Montross, Lynn & Canzona, Nicholas A. The Chosin Reservoir Campaign. 7th ed. (Elite Unit Ser.). 432p. 1986. reprint ed. 35.00 (*0-89839-098-2*) Battery Pr.

— U. S. Marine Operations in Korea, 1950-53, 4 vols. 1971. reprint ed. 250.00 (*0-403-00030-0*) Scholarly.

— U. S. Marine Operations in Korea, 1950-53, 4 vols., Ea. 1971. reprint ed. 50.00 (*0-318-68145-5*) Scholarly.

Montross, Lynn & Montross, Ca. U. S. Marine Operations in Korea, 1950-53, 4 vols. 1988. reprint ed. lib. bdg. 295.00 (*0-7812-0421-6*) Rprt Serv.

Montross, Lynn & Montross, Lois S. Town & Gown. LC 70-132122. (Short Story Index Reprint Ser.). 1977. 19.95 (*0-8369-3679-5*) Ayer.

***Montroy, Kevin.** How to Organize & Arrange for Simpler Funeral Services. (Illus.). 1999. pap. 29.00 incl. VHS (*0-9684839-0-9*) Siml Times.

***Montroy, Pierette.** Gratitudes: Works from a Life in Progress. 64p. 1998. pap. 12.95 (*0-9667436-9-5*) Post Meridian Pr.

***Montroy, S. E.** Finding Aloha: Face to Face with the Breath of Life. LC 99-91458. 1999. 25.00 (*0-7388-0814-8*); pap. 18.00 (*0-7388-0815-6*) Xlibris Corp.

***Montrucchio, Alessandra.** Cardiofitness. 192p. 1999. 27.95 (*1-902881-03-6*, Pub. by Toby Pr Ltd) Toby Pr.

— Cardiofitness. 192p. 2000. pap. 12.95 (*1-902881-19-2*, Pub. by Toby Pr Ltd) Toby Pr.

Montrucchio, Sally & Shaw, Ron. Bright Eyes. (Illus.). 32p. (Orig.). (J). (ps-3). 1997. pap. 12.95 (*0-9656539-0-0*) S Montrucchio.

Montseny, E. & Frau, J., eds. Specialized Processors for Real-Time Image Analysis: Workshop Proceedings. (ESPRIT Basic Research Ser.). xi, 220p. 1994. 63.95 (*0-387-57016-0*) Spr-Verlag.

Montserrat, Del Amo. Mao Tiang Pelos Tiesos. pap. text 8.50 (*84-216-3153-5*) Bruno Edit.

Montserrat, Dominic. Changing Bodies, Changing Meanings: Studies on the Human Body in Antiquity. LC 97-2928. (Illus.). 256p. (C). 1997. 75.00 (*0-415-13584-2*) Routledge.

— Sex & Society in Graeco-Roman Egypt. (Illus.). 280p. 1996. 110.00 (*0-7103-0530-3*, Pub. by Kegan Paul Intl) Col U Pr.

Montserrat, Dominic, jt. auth. see Lieu, Samuel N.

Montserrat, Dominic, jt. ed. see Lieu, Samuel.

Montserrat, Joseph M. Diccionari Manual de la Llengua Catalana. (CAT.). 1401p. 1975. 65.00 (*0-8288-5800-4*, S31550) Fr & Eur.

Montt, Luis, jt. auth. see Mayorga, Roberto.

Montufar, Aurora. Estudios Palinoecologicos en Baja California Sur y Su Posible Relacion Con los Grupos Cazadores-Recolectores de la Region. 68p. 1994. pap. 5.00 (*968-29-5116-X*, IN058) UPLAAP.

Montuori, Alfonso, ed. Unusual Associates: A Festschrift for Frank Barron. LC 96-6381. 480p. 1996. 89.50 (*1-881303-57-8*); pap. 34.50 (*1-881303-58-6*) Hampton Pr NJ.

Montuori, Alfonso & Purser, Ronald, eds. Social Creativity, Vol. 1. (Perspectives on Creativity Ser.). 388p. (C). 1998. text 72.50 (*1-57273-128-1*); pap. text 27.50 (*1-57273-129-X*) Hampton Pr NJ.

Montuori, Alfonso, ed. see Laszlo, Ervin.

Montuori, Alfonso, jt. ed. see Purser, Ronald.

Montuori, Alfonso, tr. see Bocchi, Gianluca & Ceruti, Mauro.

M

Montuori, Mario. De Socrate Iuste Damnato: The Rise of the Socratic Problem in the Eighteenth Century. (London Studies in Classical Philology: Vol. 7). 153p. (C). 1981. pap. 30.00 (90-70265-73-7, Pub. by Gieben) J Benjamins Pubng Co.
— John Locke: On Toleration & the Unity of God. 285p. (C). 1983. 64.00 (90-70265-25-7, Pub. by Gieben) J Benjamins Pubng Co.
— Socrates - An Approach. (Philosphica Ser.: Vol. 2). 241p. (C). 1988. 60.00 (90-70265-89-3, Pub. by Gieben) J Benjamins Pubng Co.
— Socrates Physiology of a Myth. (London Studies in Classical Philology: Vol. 6). viii, 246p. (C). 1981. pap. 47.00 (90-70265-23-0, Pub. by Gieben) J Benjamins Pubng Co.
— The Socratic Problem: The History - Solutions, From the Eighteenth Century to the Present Time. (Philosophica Ser.: Vol. IV). 485p. 1992. 107.00 (90-5063-048-0, Pub. by Gieben) J Benjamins Pubng Co.
Monture, Joel. Cloudwalker: Contemporary Native American Stories. LC 95-42815. (Fulcrum Kids Ser.). (Illus.). 64p. (J). (gr. 4-7). 1996. 15.95 (1-55591-225-7) Fulcrum Pub.
— The Native American Guide to Traditional Beadwork. LC 93-12101. (Illus.). 112p. 1993. pap. 14.00 (0-02-066430-3) Macmillan.
— Turtle Belly: A Novel. LC 97-38309. (American Indian Literature & Critical Studies Ser.: No. 25). 304p. 1998. 24.95 (0-8061-3010-5) U of Okla Pr.
Montville, Thomas J. Food Microbiology, 2 vols., Set. LC 86-24461. 480p. 1987. 221.00 (0-8493-6474-4, QR115, CRC Reprint) Franklin.
— Food Microbiology Vol. 1: Concepts in Physiology & Metabolism. LC 86-24461. 1987. 102.00 (0-8493-6478-7, CRC Reprint) Franklin.
— Food Microbiology Vol. 2: New & Emerging Technologies. LC 86-24461. 1987. 120.00 (0-8493-6479-5, CRC Reprint) Franklin.
Montville, Vicki, ed. see Houde, Mary J.
Montwieler, Nancy H. The Immigration Reform Law of 1986: Analysis, Text, & Legislative History. LC 87-15784. 571p. reprint ed. pap. 177.10 (0-7837-6418-9, 204639800012) Bks Demand.
Montwill, Michael A., et al. Public Awareness of the Nebraska Regional Poison Control Center. 14p. (Orig.). 1979. pap. 1.50 (1-55719-023-2) U NE CPAR.
Monty, C. L., et al, eds. Carbonate Mud-Mounds: Their Origins & Evolution. LC 94-41305. (Special Publications of the International Association of Sedimentologists: No. 23). 1995. pap. 95.00 (0-86542-933-2) Blackwell Sci.
Monty, Claude, jt. ed. see Bertrand-Sarfati, Janine.
***Monty, Jeanne R.** The Descendants of Jean Monty, 1639(?)-1755: Monty/Monte/Montee/Montie Families. 796p. 1999. pap. 57.00 (0-7884-1294-9, M553) Heritage Bk.
Monty, Lise, jt. auth. see Biggs, Michael.
Monty, Margaret. Cumulative Index of First Days Magazine, Incl. Yearly Updates. 350p. 1992. pap. text 14.95 (1-879390-11-6) AFDCS.
Monty Python. The Life of Brian. 124p. (C). 1992. pap. 19.95 (0-7493-0997-0, A0665) Heinemann.
Montz, Burrell E., jt. auth. see Tobin, Graham A.
Montz, G., jt. auth. see Brown, C.
***Montz, Larry & Smoller, Daena.** The Ghosts of New Orleans. (Illus.). 160p. 2000. pap. 14.95 (0-7643-1184-0) Schiffer.
Montzka, Arthur & Timmerman, Craig. Suzuki Images. LC 88-62934. 64p. (Orig.). 1988. pap. text 19.95 (0-9621416-0-7) Shar Prods.
***Monush, Barry.** The Biographical Encyclopedia of Hollywood: Film Actors. (Illus.). 1024p. 2000. 85.00 (1-55783-449-0) Applause Theatre Bk Pubs.
Monush, Barry. International Motion Picture Almanac, Vol. 62. 760p. 1991. 77.00 (0-900610-44-1) Quigley Pub Co.
— International Television & Video Almanac, 1991, Vol. 36. 752p. 1991. 77.00 (0-900610-45-X) Quigley Pub.Co.
Monush, Barry, ed. International Motion Picture Almanac. 66th ed. 800p. 1995. 91.00 (0-900610-52-2) Quigley Pub Co.
— International Motion Picture Almanac, 1993. 1993. 85.00 (0-900610-48-4) Quigley Pub Co.
— International Motion Picture Almanac, 1994. 800p. 1994. 88.50 (0-900610-50-6) Quigley Pub Co.
— International Television & Video Almanac. 40th ed. 800p. 1995. 91.00 (0-900610-53-0) Quigley Pub Co.
— International Television & Video Almanac, 1993. 1993. 85.00 (0-900610-49-2) Quigley Pub Co.
— International Television & Video Almanac, 1994. 800p. 1994. 88.50 (0-900610-51-4) Quigley Pub Co.
Monush, Barry, jt. auth. see Willis, John.
Monush, Barry, jt. ed. see Quigley, Martin.
Monush, Barry, jt. ed. see Willis, John.
Monvay, Istvan & Munster, Gernot. Quantum Fields on a Lattice. 505p. 1997. pap. text 47.95 (0-521-59917-2) Cambridge U Pr.
Monvel, Anne B. De, see De Monvel, Anne B.
Monvel, L. Boutet De, see Boutet De Monvel, L.
Monvel, Roger B. De, see De Monvel, Roger B.
Monville-Burston, Monique, jt. auth. see Jakobson, Roman.
Monville-Burston, Monique, ed. see Jakobson, Roman.
Monye, Ambrose A. Proverbs in African Orature: The Aniocha-Igbo Experience. LC 95-51095. 224p. (C). 1996. lib. bdg. 44.00 (0-7618-0244-4) U Pr of Amer.
Monye, Sylvester. Handbook of International Marketing Communications. LC 99-32754. 350p. 1999. 69.95 (0-631-20913-1); pap. 39.95 (0-631-20091-6) Blackwell Pubs.
Monye, Sylvester O. The International Business Blueprint. (Business Blueprints Ser.). (Illus.). 240p. (Orig.). (C). 1997. pap. text 36.95 (0-631-19665-X) Blackwell Pubs.
Monypenny, Julian & Pence, Roger. Ready-to-Run RPG/400 Techniques. LC 98-58129. 203p. 1999. pap. 69.95 incl. cd-rom (1-58304-046-3) News Four-Hund.
Monz, John, ed. see Fisher, Franklin M.
Monzert. Practical Distiller. 1987. reprint ed. pap. 8.95 (0-917914-58-9) Lindsay Pubns.
Monzingo, Robert. Thomas Starr King. (Illus.). 1991. pap. 12.50 (0-940168-20-0) Boxwood.
Monzon, F. M. Alto Mayo: La Reconstruction. pap. 30.00 (1-85339-280-4, Pub. by Intermed Tech) Stylus Pub VA.
Moo, Barbara E., jt. auth. see Koenig, Andrew.
Moo, D. J. The Old Testament in the Gospel Passion Narratives. (Almond Press Individual Titles Ser.). 464p. 1975. pap. 18.95 (0-907459-29-3, Pub. by Sheffield Acad) CUP Services.
Moo, Douglas. The Epistle to the Romans: The New International Commentary on the New Testament. LC 96-26077. (New International Commentary on the New Testament Ser.). 1037p. 1996. 50.00 (0-8028-2317-3) Eerdmans.
— The Gospel & Contemporary Perspective: Viewpoints from the Trinity Journal. LC 96-36837. 208p. 1996. pap. 11.99 (0-8254-3349-5) Kregel.
— James. Tasker, Randolph V., ed. (Tyndale New Testament Commentaries Ser.). 176p. (Orig.). 1986. pap. 12.00 (0-8028-0079-3) Eerdmans.
Moo, Douglas, ed. Biblical Authority & Conservative Perspectives: Viewpoints from the Trinity Journal. LC 96-40920. 224p. 1996. pap. 11.99 (0-8254-3348-7) Kregel.
***Moo, Douglas J.** Letters of James. 2000. 28.00 (0-8028-3730-1) Eerdmans.
Moo, Douglas J. 2 Peter/Jude. LC 96-35833. (NIV Application Commentary Ser.). 256p. 1996. 22.99 (0-310-20104-7) Zondervan.
Moo, G. Gregory. Power Grab: How the National Education Association Is Betraying our Kids. LC 99-28645. 308p. 1999. 24.95 (0-89526-315-7) Regnery Pub.
Moo-Sook, Hahn. Encounter: A Novel of Nineteenth-Century Korea. Chang, Ok Y., tr. (Voices from Asia Ser.: No. 5). (C). 1992. pap. 18.95 (0-520-07381-9, Pub. by U CA Pr) Cal Prin Full Svc.
Moo-Young, M., ed. Comprehensive Biotechnology: The Practice of Biotechnology: Current Comodity Products, Vol. 3. LC 85-6509. (Illus.). 1136p. 1985. 576.00 (0-08-032511-4, Pergamon Pr); 995.00 (0-317-63020-2, Pergamon Pr) Elsevier.
— Comprehensive Biotechnology: The Principles, Applications & Regulations of Biotechnology in Industry, Agriculture & Medicine, 4 vols. (Illus.). 3764p. 1985. 1844.00 (0-08-026204-X, Pergamon Pr); 321.75 (0-08-032510-6, Pergamon Pr) Elsevier.
— Comprehensive Biotechnology: The Principles of Biotechnology: Scientific Fundamentals, Vol. 1. LC 85-6509. (Illus.). 688p. 1985. 346.50 (0-08-032509-2, Pergamon Pr); 995.00 (0-317-63019-9, Pergamon Pr) Elsevier.
Moo-Young, M. & Chakrabarty, Ananda M., eds. Environmental Biotechnology - Principles & Technology: Proceedings of the International Symposium Held at the University of Waterloo, Waterloo, Ontario, Canada, July 4-8, 1994. LC 95-47779. 768p. (C). 1996. text 257.50 (0-7923-3877-4) Kluwer Academic.
Moo-Young, M. & Robinson, C. W., eds. Comprehensive Biotechnology: The Practice of Biotechnology: Specialty Products & Service Activities, Vol. 4. LC 85-6509. (Illus.). 1308p. 1985. 650.75 (0-08-032512-2, Pergamon Pr); 995.00 (0-317-63021-0, Pergamon Pr) Elsevier.
Moo-Young, M., jt. auth. see United Nations Environment Programme Staff.
Mooar, G. The Cummings Memorial: A Genealogical History of the Descendants of Isaac Cummings, an Early Settler of Topsfield, Mass. 535p. 1989. reprint ed. pap. 67.50 (0-8328-0443-6); reprint ed. lib. bdg. 77.50 (0-8328-0442-8) Higginson Bk Co.
Mooar, Pekka A., jt. auth. see Gates, Sharon J.
Mooberry, F. M. & Scott, Jane H. Grow Native Shrubs in Your Garden. LC 80-69807. 1980. 4.95 (0-940540-01-0) Brandywine Conserv.
Moock, Joyce L. Diversity, Farmer Knowledge & Sustainability. Rhoades, Robert E., ed. LC 92-52768. (Food Systems & Agrarian Change Ser.). 293p. reprint ed. pap. 90.90 (0-608-20926-0, 207202500003) Bks Demand.
Moock, Joyce L. & Rhoades, Robert E., eds. Diversity, Farmer Knowledge, & Sustainability. LC 92-52768. (Food Systems & Agrarian Change Ser.). (Illus.). 296p. 1992. 49.95 (0-8014-2682-0); pap. 19.95 (0-8014-9968-2) Cornell U Pr.
Moock, R. Theodore, Jr. Get That Interview! The Indispensable Guide for College Grads. LC 95-40585. (Barron's Educational Ser.). 160p. 1996. pap. 8.95 (0-8120-9561-8) Barron.
Mood. Sports Recreation. 10th ed. 1990. 13.75 (0-697-40339-4, WCB McGr Hill) McGrw-H Hghr Educ.
— Sports Recreational Activities. 12th ed. 672p. 1998. pap. 43.13 (0-07-092111-3) McGraw.
Mood, A. M. Introduction to Policy Analysis. 302p. 1982. 49.75 (0-444-00671-0, North Holland) Elsevier.
Mood, Alexander M., et al. Introduction to the Theory of Statistics. 3rd ed. (Illus.). 480p. (C). 1974. 97.50 (0-07-042864-6) McGraw.
Mood, Eric W., ed. Housing & Health: APHA-CDC Recommended Minimum Housing Standards. LC 86-10884. 1986. 8.50 (0-87553-138-5) Am Pub Health.
— Public Swimming Pools: Recommended Regulations for Design & Construction, Operation & Maintenance. LC 81-68843. 72p. 1981. 6.00 (0-87553-096-6, 055) Am Pub Health.
Mood, John J. Rilke on Love & Other Difficulties: Translations & Considerations of Rainer Maria Rilke. 120p. 1994. pap. 10.95 (0-393-31098-1) Norton.
Mood, Terry A. Distance Education: An Annotated Bibliography. xi, 191p. 1995. pap. text 27.50 (1-56308-160-1) Libs Unl.
Moodie, C. L., jt. ed. see Nof, Shimon Y.
Moodie, Colin, et al, eds. Manufacturing Cells: A Systems Engineering View. LC 96-133476. 398p. 1995. 59.95 (0-7484-0327-2, Pub. by Tay Francis Ltd) Taylor & Francis.
Moodie, Craig. Our Perfect Youth. LC 99-208336. 184p. 1998. pap. write for info. (0-9665640-0-6) Water Front Pr.
— A Sailor's Valentine: Stories. 1999. pap. text 14.95 (0-940160-80-3) Parnassus Imprints.
Moodie, D. C. History of the Battles & Adventures of the British, the Boers & the Zulus, Etc. in Southern Africa, 2 vols., Set. (Illus.). 1968. reprint ed. 95.00 (0-7146-1776-8, Pub. by F Cass Pubs) Intl Spec Bk.
Moodie, Fiona. Nabulela. LC 96-27938. (Illus.). 32p. (J). (ps-3). 1997. 15.00 (0-374-35486-3) FS&G.
— The Sugar Prince. (Illus.). (J). (ps-3). 1987. 12.95 (1-55774-005-4) Lambda Pubs.
Moodie, John. Hath the Lion Prevailed. (Illus.). (Orig.). pap. 6.95 (1-56411-060-5) Untd Bros & Sis.
Moodie-Kublalsingh, Sylvia. The Payols of Trinidad: A Vanishing Culture. 272p. 1994. text 65.00 (1-85043-660-6) I B T.
Moodie, Michael. The Dreadful Fury: Advanced Military Technology & the Atlantic Alliance, 136. LC 88-38059. (CSIS Washington Papers). 155p. 1989. 49.95 (0-275-93236-2, Praeger Pubs); pap. 14.95 (0-275-93237-0, Praeger Pubs) Greenwood.
Moodie, Michael, jt. auth. see Bray, Frank T.
Moodie, Roy L. The Antiquity of Disease. LC 75-23743. reprint ed. 29.50 (0-404-13298-7) AMS Pr.
— Paleopathology: An Introduction to the Study of Ancient Evidences of Disease. LC 75-23744. reprint ed. 74.50 (0-404-13350-9) AMS Pr.
Moodie, Roy L., ed. see Ruffer, Marc A.
Moodie, S., et al, eds. Viva. Incl. 1991. 7.67 (0-582-05391-9); 1991. VHS 22.61 (0-582-06300-0); 1991. 7.67 (0-582-05390-0); 1991. audio 22.61 (0-582-08689-2); 1991, 18.60 (0-582-07755-9); 1991. 7.67 (0-582-05392-7); 1991. audio 22.61 (0-582-09829-7); 1991. write for info. (0-318-70411-0) Longman.
Moodie, Susanna. Life in the Clearings Versus the Bush. 344p. 1996. pap. text 6.95 (0-7710-9976-2) McCland & Stewart.
— Roughing It in the Bush. 544p. 1996. pap. text 8.95 (0-7710-9975-4) McCland & Stewart.
Moodie, T. Dunbar & Ndatshe, Vivienne. Going for Gold: Men, Mines & Migration. LC 93-28187. 1994. 50.00 (0-520-08130-7, Pub. by U CA Pr); pap. 17.95 (0-520-08644-9, Pub. by U CA Pr) Cal Prin Full Svc.
Moodie, William. Hypnosis in Treatment. 1960. 16.95 (0-87523-121-7) Emerson.
Moodley, Kogila A., ed. Beyond Multicultural Education: International Perspectives. 318p. (Orig.). (C). 1992. pap. text 18.95 (1-55059-029-4) Temeron Bks.
Moodley, Kogila A., jt. auth. see Adam, Heribert.
Moodley, Parimala, et al. Patient Management Problems in Psychiatry: For the Mrcpsych Oral Examination. (Illus.). 144p. (Orig.). 1991. pap. text 27.95 (0-443-04374-4) Church.
Moody. Believer's Life System. (Believer's Lifesystem Ser.). 1996. pap. 54.99 (0-8024-2757-X); lthr. 54.99 (0-8024-2755-3) Moody.
***Moody.** Believer's Life System: Putting God at the Center of All You Do. 1999. 24.99 (0-8024-4936-0) Moody.
Moody. Believer's Life System Premier Edition: Leather Binder, Green Zipper Closure. (Believer's Lifesystem Ser.). 1998. 99.99 (0-8024-2751-0) Moody.
— Computer Experiments for Calculus 91. 248p. (C). 1997. pap. 33.00 (0-06-044578-5) Addison-Wesley.
— Lifekeeper, Monthly/Weekly Wire-Bound. 1998. 10.99 (0-8024-8456-5); 10.99 (0-8024-8457-3); 10.99 (0-8024-8458-1) Moody.
— Technology Machine: How Manufacturing Will Work in the Year 2020. LC 99-26716. 336p. 1999. pap. 27.50 (0-684-83709-9) S&S Trade.
Moody, et al. Hablaron de la Gracia. Austin, Bobby, ed. Arancibia, Rene, tr. (SPA.). 192p. 1994. pap. text. write for info. (0-9639640-2-X) Grace Vision.
Moody, jt. auth. see Ingalls.
Moody, A. Believer's Life System. 1998. pap. text 62.99 (0-8024-2752-9) Moody.
— Lifekeeper. 1998. 5.99 (0-8024-8470-0) Moody.
— Lifekeeper: Large Monthly. 1998. 8.99 (0-8024-8465-4) Moody.
— Lifekeeper: Monthly/Weekly Wirebound. 1998. 10.99 (0-8024-8459-X) Moody.
— Lifekeeper Pocket Monthly. 1998. 3.99 (0-8024-8477-8) Moody.
— Lifekeeper: Small Monthly. 1998. 5.49 (0-8024-8468-9); 5.49 (0-8024-8481-6) Moody.
— Lifekeeper: Small Pocket. 1998. 5.99 (0-8024-8472-7) Moody.
— Lifekeeper: Weekly Wirebound. 1998. 8.99 (0-8024-8460-3); 8.99 (0-8024-8461-1); 8.99 (0-8024-8462-X); 8.99 (0-8024-8463-8) Moody.
Moody, A. David. Thomas Stearns Eliot: Poet. 2nd ed. 420p. (C). 1995. pap. text 20.95 (0-521-46750-0) Cambridge U Pr.
— Tracing T. S. Eliot's Spirit: Essays on His Poetry & Thought. LC 95-47586. 216p. (C). 1996. text 49.95 (0-521-48060-4) Cambridge U Pr.
Moody, A. David, ed. The Cambridge Companion to T. S. Eliot. LC 93-43558. (Cambridge Companions to Literature Ser.). 279p. (C). 1995. pap. text 18.95 (0-521-42127-6) Cambridge U Pr.
Moody-Adams, Michele M. Fieldwork in Familiar Places: Morality, Culture, & Philosophy. LC 97-12694. 288p. 1997. 35.00 (0-674-29953-1) HUP.
Moody, Ann B. U & I. 200p. 1994. pap. 9.95 (0-9639366-0-3) A B Moody.
Moody, Anne. Coming of Age in Mississippi. 384p. 1992. mass mkt. 6.99 (0-440-31488-7, LE) Dell.
Moody, Barron, jt. auth. see Shrader, Terry.
***Moody, Betty G.** Magical Wish. LC 98-174991. (Illus.). (J). 1998. 15.95 (0-9663522-1-1) Character Lines.
Moody Bible Institute Staff. First Steps for the New Christian. (Christian Life Application Ser.). 1995. pap. 6.99 (1-56570-024-4) Meridian MI.
***Moody, Bill.** Bird Lives! An Evan Horne Mystery. (WWL Mystery Ser.: Bk. 350). 2000. per. 5.99 (0-373-26350-3, 1-26350-8, Wrldwide Lib) Harlequin Bks.
Moody, Bill. Bird Lives! An Evan Horne Mystery. LC 98-54789. 256p. 1999. 22.95 (0-8027-3327-1) Walker & Co.
— Death of A Tenor Man: An Evan Horne Mystery. LC 95-13048. 240p. 1995. 21.95 (0-8027-3269-0) Walker & Co.
— The Jazz Exiles: American Musicians Abroad. LC 92-26936. (Illus.). 168p. 1993. 21.95 (0-87417-214-4) U of Nev Pr.
— Solo Hand. 1994. 19.95 (0-8027-3248-8) Walker & Co.
— The Sound of the Trumpet: An Evan Horne Mystery. LC 96-42149. (Evan Horne Mystery Ser.). 240p. 1997. 21.95 (0-8027-3291-7) Walker & Co.
Moody Blues, jt. auth. see Murley, Mark.
Moody, Charles S. Backwoods Surgery & Medicine. (Shorey Lost Arts Ser.). 1974. reprint ed. pap. 10.00 (0-8466-6034-2, U 34) Shoreys Bkstore.
Moody, Chip. Moments: The Life & Career of a Texas Newsman. LC 95-35286. (Illus.). 216p. 1995. 19.95 (0-87833-895-0) Taylor Pub.
Moody, Chris, ed. Advances in Nitrogen Heterocycles, Vol. 2. 1996. 109.50 (0-7623-0056-6) Jai Pr.
Moody, Chris & Fowler, Frank W., eds. Advances in Nitrogen Heterocycles, Vol. 1. 1995. 109.50 (0-89232-864-9) Jai Pr.
Moody, Christopher. Advances in Nitrogen Heterocycles, Vol. 3. 1998. 109.50 (0-7623-0209-7) Jai Pr.
Moody, Christopher J. & Whitham, Gordon H. Reactive Intermediates. (Oxford Chemistry Primers Ser.: No. 8). (Illus.). 96p. (C). 1992. pap. text 12.95 (0-19-855672-1) OUP.
Moody, Christopher L. The Wit & Wisdom of Idi Amin. LC 77-88611. (Illus.). 1977. pap. 2.75 (0-930830-01-6) Great Basin.
***Moody, Clifford J.** Cast down the Waters: A Bosnia in Flames. LC 99-95527. 300p. 2000. 24.95 (0-9666721-1-9, Pub. by GoldenIsle Pubs) Baker & Taylor.
Moody, Dale. Apostasy: A Study in the Epistle to the Hebrews & in Baptist History. LC 97-171195. 84p. 1993. pap. text 8.00 (0-9628455-3-1) Smyth & Helwys.
— The Word of Truth: A Summary of Christian Doctrine Based on Biblical Revelation. fac. ed. LC 80-19103. 640p. 1990. reprint ed. pap. 198.40 (0-7837-7966-6, 204772200008) Bks Demand.
Moody, Dan, jt. auth. see Ingalls, Anna.
Moody, Dan, jt. auth. see Montgomery, Rhonda.
Moody, David. Scottish Local History. 178p. 1994. reprint ed. pap. 18.95 (0-8063-1269-6, 3861) Genealog Pub.
Moody, David E., ed. Peroxisome Proliferators: Unique Inducers of Drug-Metabolizing Enzymes. 208p. 1994. lib. bdg. 199.00 (0-8493-8305-6, 8305) CRC Pr.
Moody, Debby, jt. auth. see Rettig, Tom.
Moody, Denman, ed. see Criswell, Ann.
Moody, Don. America's Worst Train Disaster: The 1910 Wellington Tragedy. LC 98-87426. (Illus.). 184p. 1999. 24.95 (1-892298-12-0) Abique.
Moody, Douglas C., ed. Patterson's American Education. rev. ed. 900p. 1996. 81.00 (0-910536-67-8) Ed Direct.
— Patterson's Elementary Education. rev. ed. LC 89-646629. 900p. 1996. 81.00 (0-910536-68-6) Ed Direct.
Moody, Dwight A. Free & Faithful: Christian Discipleship in the 21st Century. LC 98-65355. 64p. 1998. pap. 10.95 (1-57736-097-4) Providence Hse.
Moody, Dwight Lyman. El Camino Hacia Dios.Tr. of Way to God. (SPA.). 144p. 1983. mass mkt. 4.99 (0-8254-1490-3, Edit Portavoz) Kregel.
— Commending the Faith: The Preaching of D. L. Moody. Rosell, Garth M., ed. LC 99-28573. 308p. 1999. pap. 16.95 (1-56563-113-7) Hendrickson MA.
— Doscientas Anecdotas e Ilustraciones.Tr. of Two Hundred Anecdotes & Illustrations. (SPA.). 128p. 1982. mass mkt. 4.99 (0-8254-1491-1, Edit Portavoz) Kregel.
— 1100 Illustrations from the Writings of D. L. Moody: For Teachers, Preachers, & Writers. LC 96-20563. 384p. (YA). (gr. 10). 1996. pap. 19.99 (0-8010-9022-9) Baker Bks.
— God's Abundant Grace. LC 98-231767. (Moody Classics Ser.). (Orig.). 1998. mass mkt. 4.99 (0-8024-5432-1) Moody.
— Heaven. LC 95-196461. (Classics Ser.). mass mkt. 4.99 (0-8024-5446-1, 388) Moody.
— The Joy of Answered Prayer. 168p. 1997. mass mkt. 5.99 (0-88368-303-2) Whitaker Hse.
— Men God Challenged. LC 98-195260. (Moddy Classics Ser.). 1998. mass mkt. 4.99 (0-8024-5433-X) Moody.
— Moody's Child Stories. LC 94-70941. (Illus.). 237p. 1994. reprint ed. 19.95 (1-880045-12-5) Back Home Indust.

An Asterisk (*) at the beginning of an entry indicates that the title is appearing for the first time.

An Asterisk (*) at the beginning of an entry indicates that the title is appearing for the first time.

Moody, Peter R., Jr. Tradition & Modernization in China & Japan. LC 94-16413. 360p. (C). 1994. pap. text 34.00 (0-534-24546-3) Harcourt.

Moody, Peter R., Jr., ed. China Documents Annual, 1989-1990-1991-1992. 1992. 77.00 (0-87569-160-9) Academic Intl.

Moody Press Editors. Bind Us Together: An Illustrated Treasury for Couples. 1999. 9.99 (0-8024-4627-2) Moody.

— Joy of Christmas. (Illus.). 96p. (J). 1999. 12.99 (0-8024-4625-6) Moody.

***Moody Press Editors.** Life Essentials: A Guide for Spiritual Growth. 1999. 29.99 (0-8024-4978-6); 29.99 (0-8024-4979-4) Moody.

Moody Press Editors. Memorize God's Word: Advanced 2. 1998. pap. text 9.99 (0-8024-6793-8) Moody.

— Memorize God's Word: Basic. 1998. pap. text 9.99 (0-8024-6791-1) Moody.

— Peace Be on Your Home: An Illustrated Treasury. 1999. 9.99 (0-8024-4626-4) Moody.

— What Christians Believe. mass mkt. 4.99 (0-8024-9378-5, 318) Moody.

Moody Press Staff, prod. What Ever Happened to the American Dream?, Set. 1993. audio 14.99 (0-8024-7176-5) Moody.

Moody, Ralph. The Dry Divide. LC 94-14522. (Illus.). 230p. 1994. pap. 10.95 (0-8032-8216-8, Bison Books) U of Nebr Pr.

— The Fields of Home. LC 92-37788. (Illus.). 335p. (C). 1993. pap. 12.95 (0-8032-8194-3, Bison Books) U of Nebr Pr.

— The Fields of Home. 340p. 1991. reprint ed. lib. bdg. 29.95 (0-89966-831-3) Buccaneer Bks.

— The Home Ranch. LC 93-39762. (Illus.). 279p. 1994. pap. 11.95 (0-8032-8210-9, Bison Books) U of Nebr Pr.

— Horse of a Different Color. (J). 1976. 23.95 (0-8488-1106-2) Amereon Ltd.

— A Horse of a Different Color: Reminiscences of a Kansas Drover. LC 94-14523. 272p. 1994. pap. 10.95 (0-8032-8217-6, Bison Books) U of Nebr Pr.

— Little Britches. (J). 1976. 23.95 (0-8488-1105-4) Amereon Ltd.

— Little Britches. 262p. 1986. reprint ed. lib. bdg. 29.95 (0-89966-563-2) Buccaneer Bks.

— Little Britches: Father & I Were Ranchers. LC 91-4139. (Illus.). 260p. 1991. reprint ed. pap. 10.95 (0-8032-8178-1, Bison Books) U of Nebr Pr.

— Man of the Family. (J). 1976. 26.95 (0-8488-1436-3) Amereon Ltd.

— Man of the Family. LC 92-37787. (Illus.). 272p. (C). 1993. pap. 10.95 (0-8032-8195-1, Bison Books) U of Nebr Pr.

— Man of the Family. 1986. reprint ed. lib. bdg. 29.95 (0-89966-564-0) Buccaneer Bks.

— Mary Emma. (J). 1976. 23.95 (0-8488-1107-0) Amereon Ltd.

— Mary Emma & Company. (J). 1976. 26.95 (0-8488-1513-0) Amereon Ltd.

— Mary Emma & Company. LC 93-43936. (Illus.). 235p. (J). 1994. pap. 9.95 (0-8032-8211-7, Bison Books) U of Nebr Pr.

— Shaking the Nickel Bush. (J). 1976. 22.95 (0-8488-1108-9) Amereon Ltd.

— Shaking the Nickel Bush. LC 94-14503. (Illus.). 236p. 1994. reprint ed. pap. 10.95 (0-8032-8218-4, Bison Books) U of Nebr Pr.

— Stagecoach West. LC 98-23270. (Illus.). xvi, 342p. 1998. pap. 15.00 (0-8032-8245-1, Bison Books) U of Nebr Pr.

Moody, Randy. Living in the Real Church: A Fresh Look at How Christians Treat One Another. LC 97-47608. 1998. pap. 12.99 (0-89900-801-1) College Pr Pub.

Moody, Raymond. Reunions. 1997. pap. 12.00 (0-449-00119-9) Fawcett.

Moody, Raymond & Perry, Paul. Reunions: Visionary Encounters with Departed Loved Ones. 1994. mass mkt. 5.99 (0-8041-1235-5) Ivy Books.

Moody, Raymond, jt. ed. see Moore, Cornelia N.

Moody, Raymond A., Jr. The Last Laugh: A New Philosophy of Near-Death Experiences, Apparitions & the Paranormal. LC 98-71589. 196p. 1999. reprint ed. pap. 12.95 (1-57174-106-2) Hampton Roads Pub Co.

— Life after Life. 208p. 1979. mass mkt. 6.99 (0-553-27484-8) Bantam.

— Life after Life. 176p. 1981. 14.95 (0-89176-037-7, Mckingbird) R Bemis Pub.

Moody, Raymond A. Life after Life: The Investigation of a Phenomenon, Survival of Bodily Death. large type ed. 240p. 1988. pap. 9.95 (0-8027-2599-6) Walker & Co.

Moody, Raymond A., Jr. The Light Beyond. 224p. 1989. mass mkt. 6.50 (0-553-27813-4) Bantam.

Moody, Raymond A. Scrying: The Art of Female Divination. 175p. 1996. pap. 9.95 (0-89176-999-4) R Bemis Pub.

Moody, Raymond A., jt. auth. see Weiss, Brian L.

Moody, Raymond A., tr. see Page, Earle C.

Moody, Regina B. Coming to Terms: Subject Search Strategies in the School Library Media Center. LC 94-37893. 250p. (Orig.). 1995. pap. 32.95 (1-55570-225-2) Neal-Schuman.

Moody, Richard. A Book about Ned Harrigan & Tony Hart. 1999. write for info. (0-316-57920-3) Little.

— Fossils. (Illus.). 128p. 1979. 8.95 (0-600-36313-9) Transatl Arts.

— Fossils: How to Find & Identify over 300 Genera. (Field Guide Ser.). (Illus.). 192p. 1986. pap. 11.95 (0-02-063370-X) Macmillan.

— Over Sixty-Five Million Years Ago: Before the Dinosaurs Died. LC 91-44774. (History Detectives Ser.). (Illus.). 32p. (YA). (gr. 6 up). 1992. lib. bdg. 20.00 (0-02-767270-0, Mac Bks Young Read) S&S Childrens.

Moody, Rick. The Black Veil. 1999. write for info. (0-316-57899-1) Little.

***Moody, Rick.** Demonology: Stories. 288p. 2001. 24.95 (0-316-58874-1) Little.

Moody, Rick. Garden State: A Novel. LC 96-80326. 224p. 1997. pap. 12.95 (0-316-55763-3) Little.

— Garden State: A Novel. 1998. pap. 12.95 (0-316-19007-1, Back Bay) Little.

— Garden State: A Novel. 1992. 18.50 (0-916366-73-1, Pub. by Pushcart Pr) Norton.

— Garden State: A Novel. 1993. pap. 11.50 (0-916366-85-5, Pub. by Pushcart Pr) Norton.

— The Ice Storm. 288p. 1995. reprint ed. mass mkt. 10.99 (0-446-67148-7, Pub. by Warner Bks) Little.

— Joyful Noise: The New Testament Revisited. Steinke, Darcey, ed. 1998. mass mkt. 13.00 (0-316-19139-6, Back Bay) Little.

— Purple America. 1998. pap. 13.95 (0-316-19006-3, Back Bay) Little.

— Purple America: A Novel. LC 96-48781. 304p. (gr. 8). 1997. 23.95 (0-316-57925-4) Little.

— Purple America: A Novel. 304p. 1998. pap. 13.95 (0-316-55977-6) Little.

— The Ring of Brightest Angels Around Heaven. 256p. 1996. reprint ed. mass mkt. 13.95 (0-446-67240-8, Pub. by Warner Bks) Little.

***Moody, Rick.** Surplus Value Books: Catalog Number 13. (Illus.). 30p. 2000. pap. 20.00 (0-9677410-4-1) Danger Bks.

— Surplus Value Books: Catalog Number 13. deluxe ed. (Illus.). 30p. 2000. pap. 40.00 (0-9677410-3-3) Danger Bks.

Moody, Rick & Steinke, Darcey, eds. Joyful Noise: The New Testament Revisited. 256p. 1999. pap. 13.00 (0-316-57995-5) Little.

Moody, Rick, jt. auth. see Elkin, Stanley.

Moody, Robert E., ed. Papers of Leverett Saltonstall, 1816-1845, Vol. 1. LC 78-70086. (Collections of the Massachusetts Historical Society: Vol. 82). (Illus.). 1978. 50.00 (0-934909-21-0, Pub. by Mass Hist Soc) NE U Pr.

— Papers of Leverett Saltonstall, 1816-1845, Vol. 2. LC 78-70086. (Collections of the Massachusetts Historical Society: Vol. 83). (Illus.). 1981. 50.00 (0-934909-22-9, Pub. by Mass Hist Soc) NE U Pr.

— Papers of Leverett Saltonstall, 1816-1845, Vol. 3. LC 78-70086. (Collections of the Massachusetts Historical Society: Vol. 84). (Illus.). 1984. 50.00 (0-934909-23-7, Pub. by Mass Hist Soc) NE U Pr.

— Papers of Leverett Saltonstall, 1816-1845, Vol. 4. LC 78-70086. (Collections of the Massachusetts Historical Society: Vol. 85). (Illus.). 1991. 50.00 (0-934909-37-7, Pub. by Mass Hist Soc) NE U Pr.

— Papers of Leverett Saltonstall, 1816-1845, Vol. 5. (Collections of the Massachusetts Historical Society: Vol. 86). (Illus.). 1992. 50.00 (0-934909-53-9, Pub. by Mass Hist Soc) NE U Pr.

— The Saltonstall Papers, 1607-1815, Vol. 1. (Collections of the Massachusetts Historical Society Ser.: Vol. 80). (Illus.). 1972. 50.00 (0-934909-24-5, Pub. by Mass Hist Soc) NE U Pr.

— The Saltonstall Papers, 1607-1815, Vol. 2. (Collections of the Massachusetts Historical Society Ser.: Vol. 81). (Illus.). 574p. 1978. 50.00 (0-934909-25-3, Pub. by Mass Hist Soc) NE U Pr.

— The Saltonstalls of New England: 350 Years in Public Life. LC 78-106214. (Picture Bks.). 1978. pap. 4.00 (0-934909-14-8) Mass Hist Soc.

Moody, Robert E. & Simmons, Richard C., eds. The Glorious Revolution in Massachusetts: Selected Documents, 1689-1692. (Publication: Vol. 65). (Illus.). 760p. (C). 1989. 30.00 (0-9620737-0-9) Colonial MA.

Moody, Robert V. & Pianzola, Arturo. Lie Algebra with Triangular Decompositions. LC 92-46890. (Canadian Mathematical Society Ser. & Advanced Texts). 712p. 1995. text 118.00 (0-471-63304-6, Pub. by Interscience) Wiley.

Moody, Rodger. Unbending Intent. 26p. 1997. 5.00 (0-614-30125-4) Skydog OR.

Moody, Rodger, ed. see Caine, Shulamith W.

Moody, Rodger, ed. see Goldman, Judy.

Moody, Rodger, ed. see Humes, Harry.

Moody, Rodger, ed. see Turco, Lewis.

Moody, Roger. Mining & the Politics of Risk: Political Risk Insurance in the Mining Industry. 200p. (Orig.). 1997. pap. 24.95 (90-5727-006-4, Pub. by Uitgeverij Arkel) LPC InBook.

Moody, Ron. The Amazon Box. (Illus.). 278p. (Orig.). (J). (gr. 4-7). 1998. 25.95 (1-86105-049-6, Pub. by Robson Bks) Parkwest Pubns.

Moody, Sally A., ed. Cell Lineage & Fate Determination. LC 98-88229. (Illus.). 644p. (C). 1998. boxed set 149.95 (0-12-505255-3) Acad Pr.

Moody, Shirley. Charmers. LC 87-61416. 65p. (Orig.). 1991. pap. 9.95 (0-932662-69-2) St Andrews NC.

Moody, Skye K. Blue Poppy. (WWL Mystery Ser.: No. 293). 1998. per. 4.99 (0-373-26293-0, 0-26293-1, Wrldwide Lib) Harlequin Bks.

— Rain Dance. (WWL Mystery Ser.). 1998. per. 4.99 (0-373-26278-7, 1-26278-1, Wrldwide Lib) Harlequin Bks.

Moody, Skye K., ed. Southern Lights: PEN-South Literary Journal. (PEN-South Literary Ser.). 128p. (Orig.). 1995. pap. 10.00 (0-9638061-1-4) M DeLeon Bksmith.

Moody, Skye Kathleen. Habitat. LC 99-16993. 288p. 1999. text 24.95 (0-312-20390-X) St Martin.

— Wildcrafters. Vol. 332. 272p. 2000. per. 4.99 (0-373-26332-5) Harlequin Bks.

— Wildcrafters. LC 98-25170. 320p. 1998. text 23.95 (0-312-19364-5) St Martin.

Moody, Spurgeon, Whitefield, MacKay Staff. They Spoke of Grace. Austin, Bobby W., ed. & intro. by. 190p. (Orig.). 1994. pap. write for info. (0-9639640-1-1) Grace Vision.

Moody Staff. Believers Life System: Simulated Leather Binder Black Zipper Closure, Premier Edtion. (Believer's Lifesystem Ser.). 1998. 49.99 (0-8024-6964-7) Moody.

Moody, Sue, jt. ed. see Dingwall, Gavin.

Moody, Susan. Death Takes a Hand. 240p. 1995. mass mkt. 4.99 (0-425-14639-1, Prime Crime) Berkley Pub.

— Death Takes a Hand. 288p. 1994. 20.00 (1-883402-00-X) S&S Trade.

— Death Takes a Hand. large type ed. LC 94-19360. 397p. 1994. pap. 17.95 (0-7862-0278-5) Thorndike Pr.

— Doubled in Spades. LC 96-44457. 1997. 21.50 (0-684-80259-7) S&S Trade.

— Doubled in Spades. large type ed. LC 97-30880. 1997. 22.95 (1-56895-494-8) Wheeler Pub.

***Moody, Susan.** Dummy Hand. large type ed. 368p. 1999. 31.99 (0-7089-4088-9) Ulverscroft.

Moody, Susan. Grand Slam. 272p. 1996. mass mkt. 5.99 (0-425-15229-4, Prime Crime) Berkley Pub.

— Grand Slam. LC 94-29364. 1995. 20.50 (1-883402-32-8) S&S Trade.

— King of Hearts: A Cassandra Swann Bridge Mystery. LC 95-19993. 320p. 1996. 21.00 (0-684-80258-9) S&S Trade.

— King of Hearts: A Cassandra Swann Bridge Mystery. 304p. 1997. reprint ed. mass mkt. 5.99 (0-425-15725-3, Prime Crime) Berkley Pub.

— Misselthwaite. large type ed. (Charnwood Large Print Ser.). 624p. 1996. 27.99 (0-7089-8914-4) Ulverscroft.

— Penny Black. (Missing Mysteries Ser.: Vol. 1). 1997. mass mkt. 7.95 (1-890208-01-9) Poisoned Pen.

— Penny Pinching. large type ed. 1991. 27.99 (0-7089-2374-7) Ulverscroft.

— Penny Saving. large type ed. (Mystery Ser.). 464p. 1993. 27.99 (0-7089-2938-9) Ulverscroft.

— Return to the Secret Garden. 352p. 1998. mass mkt. 5.99 (0-451-19228-1, Sig) NAL.

— Return to the Secret Garden. 1998. 11.09 (0-606-13738-6, Pub. by Turtleback) Demco.

— Return to the Secret Garden. large type ed. LC 98-23614. 1998. 27.95 (0-7838-0279-X, G K Hall & Co) Mac Lib Ref.

Moody, T. W. Growth Factors, Peptides & Receptors. LC 93-18563. (GWUMC Department of Biochemistry Annual Spring Symposium Ser.). (Illus.). 478p. (C). 1993. text 135.00 (0-306-44484-4, Kluwer Plenum) Kluwer Academic.

Moody, T. W., et al, eds. A Chronology to Irish History to Nineteen Seventy-Six: A Companion to Irish History, Part 1. (New History of Ireland Ser.: No. 8). (Illus.). 602p. 1983. text 145.00 (0-19-821744-7) OUP.

Moody, T. W. & Hawkins, R. A., eds. Florence Arnold-Forster's Irish Journal. 624p. 1988. pap. 105.00 (0-19-822405-2) OUP.

Moody, T. W. & Martin, F. X., eds. The Course of Irish History. rev. ed. (Illus.). 504p. (C). 1995. pap. 16.95 (1-57098-015-2) Roberts Rinehart.

Moody, T. W., et al. Maps, Genealogies, & Lists: A Companion to Irish History, Pt. II. (New History of Ireland Ser.: No. 9). (Illus.). 688p. 1984. text 198.00 (0-19-821745-5) OUP.

Moody, T. W., ed. see Tone, Theobald Wolfe.

Moody, Terry W., ed. Neural & Endocrine Peptides & Receptors. LC 86-20462. (GWUMC Department of Biochemistry Annual Spring Symposium Ser.). (Illus.). 734p. (C). 1986. text 192.00 (0-306-42300-6, Kluwer Plenum) Kluwer Academic.

Moody, Thomas E., jt. ed. see Schmitt, Richard.

Moody, Todd C. Does God Exist? A Dialogue. LC 96-25398. 112p. (Orig.). (C). 1996. pap. text 5.95 (0-87220-343-3); lib. bdg. 24.95 (0-87220-344-1) Hackett Pub.

Moody, Ula, jt. auth. see Irwin, Ann M.

Moody, Vernie A. Slavery on Louisiana Sugar Plantations. LC 74-22753. (Labor Movement in Fiction & Non-Fiction Ser.). reprint ed. 29.50 (0-404-58505-1) AMS Pr.

Moody, Virgil B., jt. auth. see Moody, Mary C.

Moody, Walton S. Building a Strategic Air Force. (Illus.). 515p. 1996. pap. 33.00 (0-16-049267-X) AFH & MP.

Moody, William. Langue des Signes Vol. 3: Dictionnaire Billingue Elementaire. (FRE.). 224p. 1990. pap. 105.00 (0-7859-8227-2, 2904461025) Fr & Eur.

Moody, William B. And the Greatest of These. 112p. 10.00 (0-9616499-1-7) Good Soldier.

— The Good Soldiers. (Illus.). 129p. 1986. 9.95 (0-9616499-0-9) Good Soldier.

Moody, William E., jt. auth. see Skimin, Robert.

Moody, William J., ed. Artistic Intelligences: Implications for Education. 240p. (C). 1990. text 21.00 (0-8077-3050-5) Tchrs Coll.

Moody, William Vaughn. Poems & Plays, 2 vols. LC 70-80719. reprint ed. 97.50 (0-404-04388-7) AMS Pr.

— Poems & Plays, 2 vols., Set. (BCL1-PS American Literature Ser.). 1992. reprint ed. lib. bdg. 150.00 (0-7812-6801-X) Rprt Serv.

— Some Letters of William Vaughn Moody. Mason, D. G., ed. LC 76-94471. reprint ed. 31.50 (0-404-04359-3) AMS Pr.

— Some Letters of William Vaughn Moody. (American Biography Ser.). 170p. 1991. reprint ed. lib. bdg. 59.00 (0-7812-8290-X) Rprt Serv.

— Some Letters of William Vaughn Moody. (BCL1-PS American Literature Ser.). 170p. 1992. reprint ed. lib. bdg. 69.00 (0-7812-6802-8) Rprt Serv.

Moody, Winfield S. Pickwick Ladle, & Other Collector's Stories. LC 70-37556. (Short Story Index Reprint Ser.). 1977. reprint ed. 21.95 (0-8369-4115-2) Ayer.

Moodys Investor Service Staff. Moody's Handbook of Dividend Achievers, 1994. 1994. pap. 19.95 (1-56429-007-7) F I S.

Moody's Investors Service Staff. Moody's Handbook of Dividend Achievers, 1992. 400p. 1992. pap. 19.95 (1-56429-003-4) F I S.

Moody's Staff. Handbook of Common Stocks. 1991. pap. 80.00 (1-56429-002-6) F I S.

— Handbook of NASDAQ Stocks. 1991. pap. 25.00 (1-56429-001-8) F I S.

Mooers, Bob. Winter Hikes in Puget Sound & the Olympic Foothills: Mostly Snow-Free Trails from Lowland Forests to Summit Views. LC 98-28097. (Illus.). 208p. 1998. pap. 15.95 (1-57061-149-1) Sasquatch Bks.

Mooers, C., ed. Baroclinic Processes on Continental Shelves. (Coastal & Estuarine Sciences Ser.: Vol. 3). (Illus.). 144p. 1986. 25.00 (0-87590-252-9) Am Geophysical.

Mooers, C. N., ed. Coastal Ocean Prediction. LC 98-51611. (Coastal & Estuarine Studies: Vol. 56). 523p. 1999. 65.00 (0-87590-270-7) Am Geophysical.

Mooers, Colin. The Making of Bourgeois Europe. 192p. (C). 1991. pap. 19.00 (0-86091-507-7, A4510, Pub. by Verso) Norton.

Mooers, Vernon. Gypsy Hymns. 64p. 1993. pap. 7.15 (1-895387-23-X) Creative Bk Pub.

Moog, Bob, ed. see Cahill, Kent & Cahill, Kathleen.

Moog, Bob, ed. see Soza, Jan & Soza, Harry.

Moog, Bob, ed. see Stewart, Patricia A. & Maples, Edna H.

Moog, Helmut, jt. ed. see Pratt, Rosalie R.

***Moog, Richard S.** Chemistry: A Guided Inquiry. 344p. 1998. pap. text 33.95 (0-471-33050-7) Wiley.

Moog, Richard S. & Farrell, John J. Chemistry: A Guided Inquiry. 319p. 1996. pap. 28.95 (0-471-16923-4) Wiley.

Moog, Robert S. Whose Interests Are Supreme? Organizational Politics in the Civil Courts in India. LC 96-36657. (Monograph & Occasional Papers: No. 54). 1996. 33.00 (0-924304-30-8) Assn Asian Studies.

***Moogk, Peter.** Small Planets: Saul Bellow & the Art of Short Fiction. Bach, Gerhard & Cronin, Gloria L., eds. LC 99-23854. 425p. 2000. pap. 25.95 (0-87013-529-5) Mich St U Pr.

***Moogk, Peter M.** La Nouvelle France: The Making of French Canada - A Cultural History. (Illus.). 320p. 2000. pap. 25.95 (0-87013-528-7) Mich St U Pr.

Moohan, Elaine, ed. see Martini, Johannes.

Mooi, Richard & Telford, Malcolm, eds. Echinoderms: San Francisco: Proceedings of the 9th International Echinoderm Conference, San Francisco, August, 1996. LC 99-496423. (Illus.). 923p. (C). 1998. text 122.00 (90-5410-929-7, Pub. by A A Balkema) Ashgate Pub Co.

Mooi, W. J. & Krausz, T. Biopsy Pathology of Melanocytic Disorders. (Biopsy Pathology Ser.: No. 17). (Illus.). 433p. 1992. text 95.00 (0-412-32350-8, Pub. by E A) OUP.

Mooij, A. Psychoanalysis & the Concept of a Rule: An Essay in the Philosophy of Psychoanalysis. Firth, S. & Scheffer, J. H., trs. from DUT. 100p. 1991. 31.95 (0-387-53573-X) Spr-Verlag.

Mooij, Brian A., jt. auth. see Tanford, J. Alexander.

Mooij, E. Linear Quadratic Regulator Design for an Unpowered, Winged Re-Entry Vehicle. (Series 08 - Astrodynamics & Satellite Systems 03). (Illus.). 150p. 1998. pap. 32.50 (90-407-1597-1, Pub. by Delft U Pr) Coronet Bks.

Mooij, J. J. A. Fictional Realities: The Uses of Literary Imagination. LC 93-1452. (Utrecht Publications in General & Comparative Literature: No. 30). xii, 290p. 1993. 67.00 (1-55619-429-3) J Benjamins Pubng Co.

Mooij, Jos. Food Policy & the Indian State: The Public Distribution System in South India. LC 99-933481. 308p. 1999. 35.00 (0-19-564566-9) OUP.

Mooij, Ruud A. De, see De Mooij, Ruud A.

Mooij, T. Interactional Multi-Level Investigation into Pupil Behaviour, Achievement, Competence & Orientation in Educational Situations. (Selecta Reeks Ser.: Vol. 68). viii, 234p. 1987. 32.00 (90-6472-112-2) Taylor & Francis.

***Mooijaart, Ab, et al.** Longitudinal Data Analysis: Designs, Models & Methods. Bijleveld, Catrien C. J. H. & Der Kamp, Leo Van, eds. LC 98-61162. 432p. 1998. 94.00 (0-7619-5537-2) Sage.

Mook, Bertha. The Dutch Family in the 17th & 18th Centuries: An Explorative-Descriptive Study. LC 81-459372. 123p. 1977. reprint ed. pap. 38.20 (0-608-02185-7, 206285400003) Bks Demand.

Mook, Byron T. The World of the Indian Field Administrator. 272p. 1983. text 25.00 (0-7069-1960-2, Pub. by Vikas) S Asia.

***Mook, David & Mook, Sarah.** Each Leaf. (Illus.). 70p. 2000. pap. 11.95 (0-9652733-7-7) Freewheeling.

— Each Leaf: Poems. (Illus.). 72p. 1999. 25.00 (0-9652733-6-9) Freewheeling.

Mook, Dean T., jt. auth. see Nayfeh, Ali H.

Mook, Delo E. & Vargish, Thomas. Inside Relativity. (Illus.). 320p. 1988. pap. text 17.95 (0-691-02520-7, Pub. by Princeton U Pr) Cal Prin Full Svc.

Mook, Douglas. Psychological Research. (C). text. write for info. (0-393-97620-3) Norton.

Mook, Douglas G. Motivation: The Organization of Action. 2nd ed. LC 95-32839. (C). 1995. text 75.00 (0-393-96717-4) Norton.

Mook, Hurbertus J. Van, see Van Mook, Hurbertus J.

Mook, Jennifer, ed. see Vernet, Harry.

Mook, Johnaton R., ed. see Ogletree, Frank, et al.

Mook, Jonathan R., ed. see Ogletree, Deakins, Nash, Smoak & Stewart Staff.

Mook, Sarah, jt. auth. see Mook, David.

Mookerjee, Ajay S. Global Electronic Wholesale Banking. (C). 1990. lib. bdg. 89.00 (1-85333-415-4, Pub. by Graham & Trotman) Kluwer Academic.

Mookerjee, Ajit. 5000 Designs & Motifs from India. LC 96-11366. (Illus.). 208p. 1996. pap. 11.95 (0-486-29061-1) Dover.

An Asterisk (*) at the beginning of an entry indicates that the title is appearing for the first time.

— Kali: The Feminine Force. 112p. 1988. pap. 14.95 (*0-89281-212-5*, Destiny Bks) Inner Tradit.

— Kundalini: The Arousal of the Inner Energy. (Illus.). 112p. (Orig.). 1983. pap. 14.95 (*0-89281-020-3*, Destiny Bks) Inner Tradit.

— Ritual Art of India. LC 98-3994. (Illus.). 176p. 1998. pap. 29.95 (*0-89281-721-6*) Inner Tradit.

— Tantra Art: Its Philosophy & Physics. LC 95-905182. 154p. 1998. pap. 300.00 (*81-7167-258-2*, Pub. by Print Hse) St Mut.

Mookerjee, Ajit & Khanna, Madhu. The Tantric Way: Art-Science-Ritual. LC 88-51353. (Illus.). 350p. (Orig.). 1989. pap. 16.95 (*0-500-27088-0*, Pub. by Thames Hudson) Norton.

Mookerjee, Amalendu P. Social & Political Ideas of Bipin Chandra Pal. LC 75-901635. 1974. 11.00 (*0-88386-473-8*) S Asia.

Mookerjee, Anjali. Environment - Nursery of Life. 103p. 1985. 9.95 (*0-318-36790-4*) Asia Bk Corp.

Mookerjee, Asutosh. Juvenile Justice: An In-Depth Study on Matters Relating to Children. (C). 1990. 100.00 (*0-89771-174-2*) St Mut.

Mookerjee, Nanda, ed. see Max Mueller, F.

Mookerjee, Sameer C. Role of Comptroller & Auditor General in Indian Democracy. (C). 1989. 64.00 (*81-7024-224-X*, Pub. by Ashish Pub Hse) S Asia.

Mookerjee, Satkari. The Jaina Philosophy of Non-Absolutism. 289p. 1978. 24.95 (*0-89684-021-2*) Asia Bk Corp.

Mookerjee, Stakari. The Jaina Philosophy of Non-Absolutism: Critical Study of Anekantaveda. (C). 1978. reprint ed. 27.50 (*0-614-96746-5*, Pub. by Motilal Bnarsidass) S Asia.

Mookerjee, Syama P. Leaves from a Diary. (Illus.). 260p. 1993. text 26.00 (*0-19-563119-6*) OUP.

Mookerji, R. K. Asoka. 289p. 1986. reprint ed. pap. 19.95 (*81-208-0086-9*, Pub. by Motilal Bnarsidass) S Asia.

— Chandragupta Maurya & His Times. (C). 1988. reprint ed. 18.00 (*81-208-0405-8*, Pub. by Motilal Bnarsidass) S Asia.

— Gupta Empire. (C). 1989. reprint ed. text 27.00 (*81-208-0089-3*, Pub. by Motilal Bnarsidass) S Asia.

— Local Government in Ancient India. 1989. reprint ed. 11.50 (*81-85395-01-2*, Pub. by Low Price) S Asia.

— Men & Thought in Ancient India. 1996. reprint ed. 10.00 (*81-208-1171-2*, Pub. by Motilal Bnarsidass) S Asia.

Mookerji, R. K., ed. Asoka. (C). 1995. reprint ed. 19.00 (*81-208-0582-8*, Pub. by Motilal Bnarsidass) S Asia.

Mookerji, Radha K. Gupta Empire. 1997. pap. 17.50 (*81-208-0440-6*) Motilal Bnarsidass.

***Mookerji, Radha Kumud.** Indian Shipping: A History of the Sea-Borne Trade & Maritime Activity of the Indians from the Earliest Times. (Illus.). 310p. 1999. 37.50 (*81-215-0916-5*, Pub. by M Manoharial) S Asia.

Mookherjee, A. & Bhattacharjee, S. B., eds. Aspects of Radiation Biophysics. 120p. (C). 1984. 80.00 (*81-85017-16-6*, Pub. by Interprint) St Mut.

Mookherjee, Dilip, ed. Indian Industry: Policies & Performance. (Oxford in India Readings Ser.; Themes in Economics). (Illus.). 386p. 1995. text 29.95 (*0-19-563666-X*) OUP.

— Indian Industry: Policies & Performance. (Oxford in India Readings Ser.). (Illus.). 386p. 1997. reprint ed. pap. text 14.95 (*0-19-564163-9*) OUP.

Mookherjee, Dilip & Ray, Debraj. Economic Theory & Practice: Essays in Honour of Dipak Baherjee. Dutta, Bahskar et al, eds. (Illus.). 320p. 1991. 19.95 (*0-19-562545-5*) OUP.

Mookherjee, Dilip, jt. auth. see Das-Gupta, Arindam.

Mookherjee, G. C. Text Book of Medicine. (C). 1989. 150.00 (*0-89771-371-0*, Pub. by Current Dist) St Mut.

Mookini, Esther T., ed. O Na Holoholona Wawae Eha O Ka Lama Hawaii: The Four-Footed Animals of Ka Lama Hawaii. Richards, William, tr. LC 84-72886. (Illus.). 129p. (Orig.). 1985. pap. 8.00 (*0-910043-09-4*) Bamboo Ridge Pr.

Mookini, Esther T. & Nakoa, Sarah, trs. from HAW. The Wind Gourd of La' Amaomao. LC 89-64411. 144p. (Orig.). 1990. pap. text 7.95 (*0-9623102-0-4*) Kalamaku Pr.

Mookini, Esther T., ed. & illus. see Gutmanis, June.

Moolenburgh, H. C. Handbook of Angels. 185p. 1984. pap. 13.95 (*0-85207-169-8*, Pub. by C W Daniel) Natl Bk Netwk.

— A Handbook of Angels. (Illus.). 256p. (Orig.). pap. 20.95 (*0-8464-4223-X*) Beekman Pubs.

— Meetings with Angels. 256p. (Orig.). pap. 19.95 (*0-8464-4253-1*) Beekman Pubs.

— Meetings with Angels: A Hundred & One Real-Life Encounters. 187p. 1993. pap. 19.95 (*0-85207-260-0*, Pub. by C W Daniel) Natl Bk Netwk.

Moolenburgh, Hans C. As Chance Would Have It: A Study in Coincidences. (Illus.). 192p. 1998. pap. 23.95 (*0-85207-317-8*, Pub. by C W Daniel) Natl Bk Netwk.

Moolgavkar, Suresh H. Scientific Issues in Quantitative Cancer Risk Assessment. 320p. 1990. 64.00 (*0-8176-3501-7*) Birkhauser.

— Stochastic Models of Cancer. (Monographs on Statistics & Applied Probability). 1996. 54.95 (*0-412-99481-X*, Chap & Hall NY) Chapman & Hall.

Moolgavkar, Suresh H. & Prentice, Ross L., eds. Modern Statistical Methods in Chronic Disease Epidemiology: Proceedings of a Conference Sponsored by SIAM Institute for Mathematics & Society & Supported by the Department of Energy. LC 86-1597. 282p. 1986. 145.00 (*0-471-83904-3*, Wiley-Interscience) Wiley.

Moolten, David N. Plums & Ashes. LC 94-29229. (Samuel French Morse Poetry Prize Ser.). 64p. 1994. pap. text 11.95 (*1-55553-208-X*) NE U Pr.

Moom, S. C. & Keda, H. I. Database Systems for Advanced. (Advanced Database Research & Development Ser.). 468p. 1993. text 121.00 (*981-02-1380-8*) World Scientific Pub.

Moom, Theresa M. How Do You Know What They Know What They Know? A Handbook of Helps for Grading & Evaluating Student Progress. (Illus.). 200p. 1997. pap. 14.95 (*0-929320-11-5*) Grove Pub.

Moomaw, Sally. More Than Singing: Discovering Music in Preschool & Kindergarten. LC 97-19869. (Illus.). xii, 257 p. (Orig.). 1997. pap. 29.95 incl. audio (*1-884834-34-5*, 3050) Redleaf Pr.

Moomaw, Sally & Hieronymus, Brenda. More Than Counting: Whole Math Activities for Preschool & Kindergarten. LC 95-13460. (Illus.). 244p. (Orig.). 1995. pap. 24.95 (*1-884834-03-5*, 3019) Redleaf Pr.

— More Than Magnets: Exploring the Wonders of Science in Preschool & Kindergarten. LC 97-23247. (Illus.). (Orig.). 1997. pap. 24.95 (*1-884834-33-7*, 4024) Redleaf Pr.

***Moomaw, Sally & Hieronymus, Brenda.** More Than Painting: Exploring the Wonders of Art for Preschool & Kindergarten. LC 99-35321. (More Than... Ser.). (Illus.). 320p. 1999. pap. 24.95 (*1-884834-67-1*, 406401, Pub. by Redleaf Pr) Gryphon Hse.

— Much More Than Counting: More Math Activities for Preschool & Kindergarten. LC 99-31622. (More Than... Ser.). (Illus.). 320p. 1999. pap. 24.95 (*1-884834-66-3*, 406501, Pub. by Redleaf Pr) Gryphon Hse.

Moomaw, W. Hugh. Virginia's Belt Line Railroad: The Norfolk & Portsmouth, 1898-1997. LC 98-21335. 1998. write for info. (*0-9653759-2-7*) Hallmark Publng.

Moomaw, William, jt. auth. see Baudot, Barbara S.

Moomaw, William, jt. ed. see Susskind, Lawrence E.

Moomaw, William R., et al, eds. Papers on International Environmental Negotiation, Vol. V. 220p. (Orig.). (C). 1995. pap. 20.00 (*1-880711-06-0*, Pon Bks) Prog Negot HLS.

Moomaw, William R., et al. Near-Term Electric Vehicle Costs, Oct., 1994. (Electric Vehicle Information Ser.: Vol. 14). (Illus.). 126p. 1996. pap. 85.00 (*0-89934-267-1*, BT041); lib. bdg. 135.00 (*0-89934-268-X*, BT941) Bus Tech Bks.

Moomey, Diane. While on the Way Home. LC 87-72319. (Illus.). 64p. 1988. 18.00 (*0-9619714-0-1*) Dayseye Pr.

Moon. Cpsm Intro Probablty Stat 3e. 3rd ed. 1998. pap. text 23.50 (*0-07-229129-X*) McGraw.

***Moon.** Grim & Savage Game. 352p. 2000. pap. 17.00 (*0-306-80956-7*, Pub. by Da Capo) HarpC.

Moon. Intro Probability & Statistics. 4th ed. 1998. 47.00 (*0-07-233558-0*) McGraw.

— Introduction to Probability & Statistics. 1997. 18.25 (*0-07-292583-3*) McGraw.

— Opinion Polls. 1999. pap. 24.95 (*0-7190-4224-0*) St Martin.

***Moon.** Russian Peasantry, 1600-1930. LC 98-51943. 416p. (C). 1999. pap. 34.60 (*0-582-09507-7*) Addison-Wesley.

Moon & McCaig. Barking Man. (J). 1997. mass mkt. 8.95 (*0-340-68618-9*, Pub. by Hodder & Stought Ltd) Trafalgar.

Moon, David. The Russian Peasantry: The World the Peasants Made. LC 98-51943. 1999. text 78.95 (*0-582-09508-5*) Longman.

Moon, A., jt. auth. see Williams, T.

Moon, Ailee & Song, Young-In. Korean American Women Living in Two Cultures. LC 96-79728. 320p. (Orig.). (C). 1997. pap. 25.00 (*0-9657616-0-6*) Academia Koreana.

Moon, Ailee, jt. ed. see Song, YoungI.

Moon, Angelina. The Christmas of the Witch. (Tales from NoWay Ser.: Vol. I). (Illus.). (J). (gr. 2-6). 1999. pap. 10.95 (*1-892247-00-3*) Family Time.

— Havoc at Holiday House. (Tales from NoWay Ser.: Vol. III). (Illus.). (J). (gr. 2-6). 1999. pap. write for info. (*1-892247-02-X*) Family Time.

— The Witchmaker: The Birth of Carmella. (Tales from NoWay Ser.: Vol. II). (Illus.). (J). (gr. 2-6). 1999. pap. write for info. (*1-892247-01-1*) Family Time.

Moon, April. Flying Biscuit Cafe Cookbook: Breakfast & Beyond. LC 97-76259. 144p. 1998. pap. text 14.95 (*1-56352-465-1*) Longstreet.

Moon, B. P., jt. ed. see Dardis, G. F.

Moon, Beverly, ed. An Encyclopedia of Archetypal Symbolism Vol. 1: The Archive for Research in Archetypal Symbolism, Vol. 1. 520p. 1997. 125.00 (*1-57062-250-7*, Pub. by Shambhala Pubns) Random.

***Moon, Beverly Ann & Benard, Elisabeth Anne, eds.** Goddesses Who Rule. LC 99-47723. 288p. 2000. 49.95 (*0-19-512130-9*); 19.95 (*0-19-512131-7*) OUP.

***Moon, Bob.** The Cleveland Browns, the Great Tradition. 3rd rev. ed. (Illus.). 368p. 1999. pap. 36.95 (*0-9667660-1-6*) SporTradition Pubns.

Moon, Bob. A Guide to the National Curriculum: Bob Moon. 2nd ed. LC 93-46428. 1994. write for info. (*0-19-288000-4*) OUP.

Moon, Bob, ed. Modular Curriculum. 192p. (C). 1988. 50.00 (*1-85396-008-X*, Pub. by P Chapman) St Mut.

Moon, Bob, jt. ed. see Galton, Maurice.

Moon, Brenda E., compiled by. Periodicals for South-East Asian Studies: A Union Catalogue of Holdings in British & Selected European Libraries. 630p. 1979. 170.00 (*0-7201-0730-X*) Continuum.

***Moon, Brian.** Literary Terms: A Practical Glossary. LC 99-46413. (Chalkface Ser.). (Illus.). 192p. 1999. pap. 21.95 (*0-8141-3008-9*, 30089) NCTE.

— Studying Literature: New Approaches to Poetry & Fiction. (Chalkface Ser.). 75p. 2000. pap. write for info. (*0-8141-4871-9*) NCTE.

Moon, Bruce E. Dilemmas of International Trade. LC 95-46998. (Dilemmas in World Politics Ser.). 1996. pap. write for info. (*0-614-11088-2*) Westview.

— Dilemmas of International Trade. (Dilemmas in World Politics Ser.). 224p. (C). 1996. pap. 22.00 (*0-8133-1845-9*, Pub. by Westview) HarpC.

***Moon, Bruce E.** Dilemmas of International Trade. 2nd ed. (Dilemmas in World Politics Ser.). 204p. 2000. pap. 20.00 (*0-8133-6768-9*) Westview.

Moon, Bruce E. The Political Economy of Basic Human Needs. LC 91-14912. 336p. 1991. 49.95 (*0-8014-2448-8*); pap. text 17.95 (*0-8014-9982-8*) Cornell U Pr.

Moon, Bruce L. Art & Soul: Reflections on an Artistic Psychology. LC 96-32928. (Illus.). 156p. 1996. text 36.95 (*0-398-06676-0*); pap. text 25.95 (*0-398-06677-9*) C C Thomas.

— The Dynamics of Art As Therapy with Adolescents. LC 98-37400. (Illus.). 260p. 1999. text 52.95 (*0-398-06923-9*) C C Thomas.

— The Dynamics of Art as Therapy with Adolescents. LC 98-37400. (Illus.). xxii, 237p. 1998. pap. text 39.95 (*0-398-06924-7*) C C Thomas.

— Essentials of Art Therapy Training & Practice. (Illus.). 188p. 1992. pap. 28.95 (*0-398-06295-1*) C C Thomas.

— Essentials of Art Therapy Training & Practice. (Illus.). 188p. (C). 1992. text 39.95 (*0-398-05794-X*) C C Thomas.

***Moon, Bruce L.** Ethical Issues in Art Therapy. LC 00-32542. (Illus.). 2000. pap. write for info. (*0-398-07101-2*) C C Thomas.

Moon, Bruce L. Existential Art Therapy: The Canvas Mirror. 2nd ed. LC 95-3655. (Illus.). 230p. (C). 1995. text 52.95 (*0-398-05999-3*); pap. text 35.95 (*0-398-06514-4*) C C Thomas.

— Introduction to Art Therapy: Faith in the Product. (Illus.). 222p. 1994. pap. 31.95 (*0-398-06297-8*) C C Thomas.

— Introduction to Art Therapy: Faith in the Product. LC 93-36346. (Illus.). 222p. (C). 1994. text 50.95 (*0-398-05893-8*) C C Thomas.

Moon, Bucklin. High Cost of Prejudice. LC 70-111584. 168p. 1970. reprint ed. lib. bdg. 59.50 (*0-8371-4608-9*, MCP&) Greenwood.

Moon, C., jt. auth. see Moon, G.

Moon, C. Jean & Schulman, Linda. Finding the Connections: Linking Assessment, Instruction, & Curriculum in Elementary Mathematics. LC 94-46724. 151p. 1995. pap. text 22.00 (*0-435-08370-8*, 08370) Heinemann.

Moon, Chung-In & Mo, Jongryn, eds. Democracy & the Korean Economy. LC 98-10420. (Publication Ser.: No. 447). 192p. 1998. pap. 17.95 (*0-8179-9552-8*) Hoover Inst Pr.

Moon, Chung-In, jt. auth. see Crawford, Natalie W.

Moon, Chung-In, jt. ed. see Kil, Soong Hoom.

Moon, Cliff & Raban, Bridie. A Question of Reading: National Curriculum Edition. 3rd ed. 240p. 1992. pap. 32.50 (*1-85346-146-6*, Pub. by David Fulton) Taylor & Francis.

***Moon, Constance & Chase, JoAnne.** You Can Change Your Life Through Psychic Power. 2000. pap. 34.95 (*0-671-77651-7*, 77651, Pocket Books) PB.

Moon, Craig O. Golfing in the Dark. LC 95-9235. 1995. pap. 11.95 (*0-89876-221-9*) Gardner Pr.

Moon, Cyris H. A Korean Minjung Theology: An Old Testament Perspective. LC BR1320.M66. 93p. (Orig.). reprint ed. pap. 30.00 (*0-8357-4064-1*, 203675400005) Bks Demand.

Moon, Dolly M. My First Book of Marches. 48p. 1998. pap. 3.95 (*0-486-26338-X*) Dover.

— My Very First Piano Book of Cowboy Songs: Twenty-Two Favorite Songs Easy in Piano Arrangement. (Illus.). 46p. (J). (gr. 2 up). 1998. pap. 3.50 (*0-486-24311-7*) Dover.

Moon, Don & Moon, Ruth. Collection of Poetry. LC 85-63483. (Illus.). 64p. 7.95 (*0-9615098-0-5*) Prairie Imp.

Moon, Elaine L. Untold Tales, Unsung Heroes: An Oral History of Detroit's African American Community, 1918-1967. LC 93-26073. (African American Life Ser.). (Illus.). 410p. (C). 1994. pap. 19.95 (*0-8143-2465-7*) Wayne St U Pr.

***Moon, Elizabeth.** Change of Command. LC 99-26627. 320p. 1999. 21.00 (*0-671-57840-5*) Baen Bks.

Moon, Elizabeth. The Deed of Paksenarrion. 1040p. 1992. reprint ed. per. 15.00 (*0-671-72104-6*) PB.

— Divided Allegiance, Bk. II. (Deed of Paksenarrion Ser.: Bk. 2). 528p. (Orig.). 1988. mass mkt. 6.99 (*0-671-69786-2*) Baen Bks.

— Hunting Party. 384p. 1993. per. 6.99 (*0-671-72176-3*) Baen Bks.

— The Legacy of Gird. 864p. 1996. per. 15.00 (*0-671-87747-X*) Baen Bks.

— Liar's Oath. 480p. (Orig.). 1992. mass mkt. 5.99 (*0-671-72117-8*) Baen Bks.

— Oath of Gold. (Deed of Paksenarrion Ser.: Bk. III). 512p. 1989. mass mkt. 5.99 (*0-671-69798-6*) Baen Bks.

— Once a Hero. LC 96-48176. 416p. 1997. 21.00 (*0-671-87769-0*) Baen Bks.

— Once a Hero. 1998. per. 6.99 (*0-671-87871-9*) Baen Bks.

***Moon, Elizabeth.** Once a Hero. 1999. per. 1.99 (*0-671-57842-1*) S&S Trade.

Moon, Elizabeth. Phases. 1997. per. 5.99 (*0-671-87855-7*) Baen Bks.

— Remnant Population. 352p. 1996. 22.00 (*0-671-87718-6*) Baen Bks.

— Remnant Population. 352p. 1997. pap. 5.99 (*0-671-87770-4*) Baen Bks.

— Rules of Engagement. LC 98-39189. 368p. 1998. 22.00 (*0-671-57777-8*) Baen Bks.

***Moon, Elizabeth.** Rules of Engagement. 1999. per. 7.99 (*0-671-57841-3*) S&S Trade.

Moon, Elizabeth. Sheepfarmer's Daughter, Bk. I. (Deed of Paksenarrion Ser.: Bk. 1). 512p. (Orig.). 1988. mass mkt. 5.99 (*0-671-65416-0*) Baen Bks.

— Winning Colors. 416p. 1995. per. 6.99 (*0-671-87677-5*) Baen Bks.

Moon, Elizabeth, jt. auth. see McCaffrey, Anne.

Moon, Eric. A Desire to Learn: Selected Writings. LC 93-15146. (Illus.). 458p. 1993. 50.00 (*0-8108-2686-0*) Scarecrow.

Moon, F. C. & International Union of Theoretical & Applied Mechanics Staff. IUTAM Symposium on New Applications of Nonlinear & Chaotic Dynamics in Mechanics: Proceedings of the IUTAM Symposium Held in Ithaca, New York, U. S. A., 27 July-1 August, 1997. LC 98-36912. (Solid Mechanics & Its Applications Ser.). 11p. 1998. 268.00 (*0-7923-5276-9*) Kluwer Academic.

Moon, Francis C. Applied Dynamics: With Applications to Multibody & Mechatronic System. LC 97-20250. 504p. (C). 1998. 94.95 (*0-471-13828-2*) Wiley.

— Chaotic & Fractal Dynamics: An Introduction for Applied Scientists & Engineers. 2nd ed. LC 92-25350. 528p. 1992. 89.95 (*0-471-54571-6*) Wiley.

— Dynamics & Chaos in Manufacturing Processes. LC 96-29975. (Wiley Series in Nonlinear Science). 316p. 1997. 89.95 (*0-471-15293-5*) Wiley.

— Magneto-Solid Mechanics. LC 83-23372. (Wiley-Interscience Publications). 448p. reprint ed. pap. 138.90 (*0-7837-2403-9*, 204008800006) Bks Demand.

Moon, Francis C., ed. see American Society of Mechanical Engineers Staff.

Moon, Francis M. Superconducting Levitation: Applications to Bearings & Magnetic Transportation. 295p. 1994. 99.95 (*0-471-55925-3*) Wiley.

Moon, G. & Moon, C. Lost Indian Magic: A Mystery Story of the Red Man As He Lived Before the White Man Came. 1977. lib. bdg. 39.95 (*0-8490-2185-5*) Gordon Pr.

Moon, Gary. The Bible Ride Vol. 3: Still More Adventures That Bring the Gospel to Life, Bk. 3. LC 99-21312. 240p. 1999. pap. 12.99 (*1-56955-049-2*, Vine Bks) Servant.

Moon, Gary W. The Bible Ride Bk. 2: More Adventures That Bring the Gospel to Life. LC 97-7782. (Bible Ride Ser.). 300p. 1997. pap. 12.99 (*0-89283-981-3*, Vine Bks) Servant.

— Homesick for Eden: Confessions about the Journey of a Soul. LC 96-178538. 268p. 1996. pap. 11.95 (*0-911866-28-0*) LifeSprings Res.

Moon, Geoff. Field Guide to New Zealand Birds. 1999. 25.00 (*0-8117-1399-7*) Stackpole.

Moon, Gillian. Free Trade: What's in It for Women. 56p. (C). 1995. pap. 11.95 (*1-875870-14-8*, Pub. by Oxfam Pub) Stylus Pub VA.

Moon, Gillian, ed. Making Her Rights a Reality: Women's Human Rights & Development. LC 97-123679. 120p. 1997. pap. 15.95 (*1-875870-24-5*, Pub. by Oxfam Pub) Stylus Pub VA.

Moon, Graham & Jones, Kelvyn. Health, Disease & Society: An Introduction to Medical Geography. (Illus.). 256p. 1988. pap. text 19.95 (*0-7102-1219-4*, Routledge Thoemms) Routledge.

Moon, Graham, jt. auth. see Atkinson, Rob.

***Moon, Gwang Hun.** Schreiben als Anders Lesen: Avantgardismus, Politik und Kultursemantik in Peter Weiss' Roman Die Asthetik des Widerstands. 1999. 48.95 (*3-631-35397-9*) P Lang Pubng.

Moon, Gypsy. Done & Been: Steel Rail Chronicles of American Hobos. LC 95-18796. 216p. 1996. pap. 12.95 (*0-253-21035-6*) Ind U Pr.

Moon, H. Office Procedures & Management. 5th ed. (KU - Office Procedures Ser.). 1986. pap. 32.75 (*0-87350-290-6*) Course Tech.

— Office Procedures & Management. 5th ed. (KU - Office Procedures Ser.). 1986. 43.95 (*0-471-85029-2*) S-W Pub.

Moon, Harry R. English for Office Professionals. 240p. 1987. text 17.50 (*0-471-85536-7*) P-H.

— English for Office Professionals. (Business Communications Ser.). 1987. pap. text 16.00 (*0-471-85537-5*) Thomson Learn.

— Office Procedures & Technology. 1990p. 2.25 (*0-87350-339-2*) Milady Pub.

— Office Procedures & Technology. 2nd ed. 1990p. 1984. teacher ed. 19.95 (*0-87350-337-6*) Milady Pub.

— Office Procedures & Technology. 2nd ed. 1990p. 1988. 35.00 (*0-87350-289-2*) Milady Pub.

— Typing from Rough Drafts. 1977. pap. 11.50 (*0-87350-306-6*) Thomson Learn.

Moon, Harry R., ed. see Elia, Lewis M. & Fall, Joseph A.

Moon, Henry. The Interstate Highway System. Cromley, Robert & Cromley, Ellen, eds. (Resource Publications in Geography). 1995. 15.00 (*0-89291-215-4*) Assn Am Geographers.

Moon, Henry L. Balance of Power: The Negro Vote. LC 77-4915. 256p. 1977. reprint ed. lib. bdg. 65.00 (*0-8371-9619-1*, MOBA, Greenwood Pr) Greenwood.

Moon, High. Picturecology: A Picture Book for "Living Lightly on the Earth" 3rd ed. Hurley-Basu, Maura & Hill, Anne, trs. from JPN. (Illus.). 96p. 1998. pap. text 25.00 (*0-7881-7377-4*) DIANE Pub.

Moon, J. Donald. Constructing Community: Moral Pluralism & Tragic Conflicts. 248p. 1993. pap. text 17.95 (*0-691-02550-9*, Pub. by Princeton U Pr) Cal Prin Full Svc.

— Constructing Community: Moral Pluralism & Tragic Conflicts. LC 93-12930. 256p. 1993. text 45.00 (*0-691-08642-7*, Pub. by Princeton U Pr) Cal Prin Full Svc.

Moon, J. E., jt. auth. see Gillett, W. B.

Moon Ja Yoon. Korean Cooking for You. LC 87-81793. (Illus.). 111p. 1987. 17.50 (*0-942091-02-7*) Golden Pond Pr.

M

Moon, Jaekyun & Carley, L. Richard. Sequence Detection for High-Density Storage Channels. LC 92-2346. (International Series in Engineering & Computer Science, VLSI, Computer Architecture, & Digital Screen Processing: SECS 63). 176p. (C). 1992. text 98.00 (*0-7923-9264-7*) Kluwer Academic.

Moon, Janell. Lesbian Speaker's Bureau. Harriss, Clarinda, ed. (Illus.). 28p. (Orig.). 1996. pap. 8.00 (*0-932616-53-4*, 932616) Brick Hse Bks.

— The Mouth of Home: Poems. LC 98-74910. 63p. 1999. pap. 12.00 (*0-9657015-2-2*) Arctos Pr.

Moon, Jean. Developing Judgment: Assessing Children's Work in Mathematics. LC 97-1577. 173p. 1997. pap. text 22.00 (*0-435-07140-8*) Heinemann.

Moon, Jean O. What Is an Angel? 1997. pap. 6.95 (*0-7880-0915-X*, Fairway Pr) CSS OH.

***Moon, Jenny A.** Learning Journals: A Handbook for Teachers, Lecturers & Journal Writers. 160p. 2000. pap. 25.00 (*0-7494-3045-1*, Pub. by Kogan Page Ltd) Stylus Pub VA.

Moon, Jeremy. European Integration in British Politics, 1950-1963: A Study of Issue Change. 278p. 1985. text 79.95 (*0-566-00786-X*, Pub. by Dartmth Pub) Ashgate Pub Co.

— Innovative Leadership in Democracy: Policy Change under Thatcher. 170p. 1993. 72.95 (*1-85521-420-2*, Pub. by Dartmth Pub) Ashgate Pub Co.

Moon, Jeremy, jt. auth. see Richardson, J.

Moon, Jerry A. W. C. White & Ellen G. White: The Relationship Between the Prophet & Her Son. (Andrews University Seminary Doctoral Dissertation Ser.: Vol. 19). 497p. 1993. pap. 19.99 (*1-883925-01-0*) Andrews Univ Pr.

Moon, John C. An Instructor for the Drum. LC 80-29134. (Musick of the Fifes & Drums Ser.: Vol. 4). (Illus.). 50p. (Orig.). 1981. pap. 4.95 (*0-87935-059-8*) Colonial Williamsburg.

— Quick Marches. LC 75-19259. (Musick of the Fifes & Drums Ser.: Vol. 1). 24p. 1976. pap. 7.95 (*0-87935-031-8*) Colonial Williamsburg.

Moon, John C., ed. Slow Marches. LC 75-19259. (Musick of the Fifes & Drums Ser.: Vol. 2). 24p. 1977. pap. 7.95 (*0-87935-046-6*) Colonial Williamsburg.

Moon, John C., et al. Medleys. LC 75-19259. (Musick of the Fifes & Drums Ser.: Vol. 3). 23p. 1980. pap. 2.99 (*0-87935-050-4*) Colonial Williamsburg.

Moon, Karen. George Walton: Designer & Architect. (Illus.). 200p. 55.00 (*1-873487-01-0*, Pub. by White Cockade) Paul & Co Pubs.

Moon, Katherine H. Sex among Allies: Military Prostitution in U. S.-Korea Relations. LC 97-2641. (Illus.). 304p. 1997. pap. 17.50 (*0-231-10643-2*); lib. bdg. 50.00 (*0-231-10642-4*) Col U Pr.

Moon, Lawrence D. WinterGames/SummerGames. 600p. (Orig.). 1996. pap. 13.95 (*0-9651996-0-6*) Edit von Rapp.

Moon, Lynelle. Waiting for Elective Surgery in Australian Public Hospitals, 1995. LC 97-144170. viii, 55 p. 1996. write for info. (*0-642-24701-3*) Aust Inst Criminology.

Moon, M. Sherril, ed. Making School & Community Recreation Fun for Everyone: Places & Ways to Integrate. LC 94-28438. 256p. 1994. pap. 32.00 (*1-55766-155-3*) P H Brookes.

Moon, Margaret & Maurine. Wedge: The Extraordinary Communications of an Earthbound Spirit. (Illus.). 136p. 1975. pap. 3.95 (*0-87542-497-X*) Llewellyn Pubns.

Moon, Margaret & Moon, Maurine. The Jupiter Experiment. LC 76-3897. (Illus.). 230p. 1976. pap. 1.95 (*0-87542-498-8*) Llewellyn Pubns.

Moon, Marianne, jt. auth. see Joyce, Jerry.

Moon, Marilyn. Medicare Now & in the Future. 285p. 1996. 61.00 (*0-87766-652-0*) Urban Inst.

— Medicare Now & in the Future. 2nd ed. LC 98-159087. 1996. pap. text 26.50 (*0-87766-653-9*) Urban Inst.

Moon, Marilyn & Mulvey, Janemarie. Entitlements & the Elderly: Protecting Promises, Recognizing Realities. 194p. 1995. 21.00 (*0-87766-636-9*) Urban Inst.

Moon, Marjorie. Benjamin Tabart's Juvenile Library: A Bibliography of Books for Children, Published, Written, Edited, & Sold by Mr. Tabart 1801-1820. (Illus.). 197p. 1990. 36.00 (*0-906795-89-3*) Oak Knoll.

— The Children's Books of Mary (Belson) Elliott: Blending Sound Christian Principles with Cheerful Cultivation - A Bibliography. 171p. 1987. 28.00 (*0-906795-44-3*) Oak Knoll.

Moon, Marjorie N. A Is for Art: An Alphabetical Tour of the Milwaukee Art Museum. 1988. pap. 10.95 (*0-9620834-0-2*) M Moon.

Moon, Marjorie N., ed. A Is for Art. (Illus.). (Orig.). (J). (ps-2). 1988. pap. 10.95 (*0-317-91187-2*) M Moon.

Moon, Marylin, ed. Economic Transfers in the United States. LC 84-52. (National Bureau of Economic Research Studies in Income & Wealth: Vol. 49). (Illus.). 400p. 1984. lib. bdg. 54.00 (*0-226-53505-3*) U Ch Pr.

Moon, Maurine, jt. auth. see Moon, Margaret.

Moon, Maxine L., jt. auth. see Clark, Laura A.

Moon, Michael. Disseminating Whitman: Revision & Corporeality in Leaves of Grass. LC 90-35138. 264p. 1991. 40.00 (*0-674-21276-2*, MOODIS) HUP.

— Disseminating Whitman: Revision & Corporeality in Leaves of Grass. 264p. (C). 1993. pap. 22.50 (*0-674-21245-2*) HUP.

***Moon, Michael.** Firebrands! Building Brand Loyalty in the Internet Age. 2000. pap. 29.99 (*0-07-212449-0*) Osborne-McGraw.

Moon, Michael. A Small Boy & Others: Imitation & Initiation in American Culture from Henry James to Andy Warhol. LC 97-37858. (Series Q). 208p. 1998. pap. 16.95 (*0-8223-2173-4*) Duke.

— A Small Boy & Others: Imitation & Initiation in American Culture from Henry James to Andy Warhol. LC 97-37858. (Series Q). (Illus.). 208p. 1998. 49.95 (*0-8223-2161-0*) Duke.

Moon, Michael & Davidson, Cathy N., eds. Subjects & Citizens: Nation, Race, & Gender from Oroonoko to Anita Hill. LC 95-10297. 496p. 1995. text 54.95 (*0-8223-1529-7*); pap. text 18.95 (*0-8223-1539-4*) Duke.

Moon, Modean. Los Colores de la Noche: Forgotten Vows. (Deseo Ser.). (SPA.). 1996. per. 3.50 (*0-373-35165-8*, 1-35165-9) Harlequin Bks.

***Moon, Modean.** La Esposa Perdida (The Lost Wife) Lost & Found Bride. (Deseo Ser.: No. 196). (SPA.). 2000. per. 3.50 (*0-373-35326-X*, 1-35326-7) Silhouette.

Moon, Modean. Evermore. (Illus.). 352p. 1993. mass mkt. 4.99 (*0-446-36213-1*) Warner Bks.

— Forgotten Vows (The Wedding Night) (Desire Ser.). 1996. per. 3.50 (*0-373-05995-7*, 1-05995-5) Silhouette.

— From This Day Forward. (Intimate Moments Ser.). 1996. per. 3.99 (*0-373-07739-4*, 1-07739-5) Silhouette.

— The Giving. (Desire Ser.). 1994. per. 2.99 (*0-373-05868-3*, 1-05868-4) Silhouette.

— La Heredera Perdida: (The Lost Heiress) (Deseo Ser.: Bk. 148). (SPA.). 156p. 1999. per. 3.50 (*0-373-35278-6*, 1-35278-0) Harlequin Bks.

— Interrupted Honeymoon. (Desire Ser.). 1995. per. 2.99 (*0-373-05904-3*, 1-05904-7) Silhouette.

— Lost & Found Bride. (Desire Ser.: No. 1235). 1999. per. 3.75 (*0-373-76235-6*, 1-76235-5) Silhouette.

— Overnight Heiress. 1998. per. 3.75 (*0-373-76150-3*, 1-76150-1) Silhouette.

Moon, Myra B., ed. see Smith, Duane.

***Moon, Nicola.** Happy Birthday, Amelia. (Illus.). 32p. (J). 1999. 17.95 (*1-86205-208-5*, Pub. by Pavilion Bks Ltd) Trafalgar.

— I Am Reading: Alligator Tales. (Illus.). 48p. (YA). 2000. pap. 3.95 (*0-7534-5121-2*, Kingfisher) LKC.

— J. J. Rabbit & the Monster. (I Am Reading Ser.). (Illus.). 48p. (J). 2000. pap. 3.95 (*0-7534-5288-X*, Kingfisher) LKC.

Moon, Nicola. Penguins in the Fridge. (Illus.). 32p. (J). (gr. 1-3). 1997. pap. 9.95 (*1-85793-793-7*, Pub. by Pavilion Bks Ltd) Trafalgar.

— Something Special. LC 96-24127. (Illus.). (J). 1997. 14.95 (*1-56145-137-1*) Peachtree Pubs.

Moon, Norman F. Terror in the Medical Office. 29.50 (*1-57529-066-9*) Kabel Pubs.

Moon, P. & Spencer, D. E. Field Theory Handbook: Including Coordinate Systems, Differential Equations & Their Solutions. 2nd ed. LC 77-178288. (Illus.). viii, 236p. 1971. 59.40 (*0-387-02732-7*) Spr-Verlag.

Moon, Parry & Spencer, Domina E. Theory of Holors: A Generalization of Tensors. (Illus.). 416p. 1986. text 100.00 (*0-521-24585-0*) Cambridge U Pr.

Moon, Pat. The Spying Game. LC 98-13069. (J). (gr. 5 up). 1999. 16.99 (*0-399-23354-7*) Putnam Pub Group.

Moon, Penderel. The British Conquest & Dominion of India. LC 89-2003. 1248p. 1989. 49.95 (*0-253-33836-0*) Ind U Pr.

— Divide & Quit: An Eyewitness Account of the Partition of India. (Oxford India Paperbacks Ser.). (Illus.). 348p. 1998. pap. text 17.50 (*0-19-564422-0*) OUP.

Moon, Penderel, ed. see Wavell, Archibald.

Moon, Peter. The Black Sun: Montauk's Nazi-Tibetan Connection. (Illus.). 300p. 1997. pap. 19.95 (*0-9631889-4-1*) Sky Bks NY.

Moon, Peter, jt. auth. see Nichols, Preston B.

Moon, Peter, ed. see Bruce, Alexandra.

Moon, Peter, ed. see Swerdlow, Stewart.

Moon, R. Encyclopedia of High Fiber Cooking. 224p. 1996. 19.98 (*0-7858-0623-7*) Bk Sales Inc.

Moon, Ralph, ed. see Tulku, Tarthang.

Moon, Robert A. & Davis, Robert D. Elementary Algebra. 528p. (C). 1980. suppl. ed. write for info. (*0-318-54301-X*, Merrill Pub Co) Macmillan.

Moon, Robert G., Jr., et al. Basic Arithmetic. 3rd ed. 528p. (C). 1990. pap. text 42.00 (*0-675-20136-5*, Merrill Coll) P-H.

Moon, Robert O. Hippocrates & His Successors in Relation to the Philosophy of Their Time. LC 75-23745. reprint ed. 37.50 (*0-404-13351-7*) AMS Pr.

Moon, Rosamund. Fixed Expressions & Idioms in English: A Corpus-Based Approach. LC 97-46861. (Oxford Studies in Lexicography & Lexicology). (Illus.). 352p. 1998. text 85.00 (*0-19-823614-X*) OUP.

Moon, Rosemary. American Harvest Cookbook: Cooking with Pumpkins & Squash. 1998. 12.99 (*0-7858-0898-1*) Bk Sales Inc.

— American Harvest Cookbook: Cooking with Pumpkins & Squash. 1998. 12.99 (*0-7858-0896-5*) Bk Sales Inc.

***Moon, Rosemary.** High Fiber, High Flavor: More Than 180 Recipes for Good Health. (Illus.). 224p. 2000. pap. 19.95 (*1-55209-518-5*) Firefly Bks Ltd.

Moon, Rosemary. The Ice-Cream Machine Recipe Book. 128p. 1997. 12.98 (*0-7858-0875-2*) Bk Sales Inc.

***Moon, Rosemary.** Onions, Onions, Onions: Globe, Spanish, Vidalia, Walla Walla, Shallot & More - In a Wave of Flavor & Aroma. LC 99-931650. (Illus.). 144p. 2000. pap. 19.95 (*1-55209-364-6*) Firefly Bks Ltd.

Moon, Rosemary. Rosemary Moon's Aga Cookbook. LC 99-170940. (Illus.). 160p. 1998. 27.95 (*0-7153-0649-9*) Sterling.

***Moon, Russell G.** The End of the Concept of "Time"! 146p. 2000. pap. 12.95 (*0-9679298-0-6*) Gordons Pubns.

Moon, Ruth, jt. auth. see Moon, Don.

Moon, S., jt. auth. see Friedman, L.

Moon, Samuel. Tall Sheep: Harry Goulding, Monument Valley Trader. LC 91-50866. (Illus.). 268p. 1992. 27.95 (*0-8061-2415-6*) U of Okla Pr.

Moon, Samuel, ed. One Act - Eleven Short Plays of the Modern Theatre: Miss Julie, August Strindberg; Purgatory, William Butler Yeats; The Man with the Flower in His Mouth, Luigi Pirandello; Pullman Car Hiawatha, Thornton Wilder; Hello Out There, William Saroyan. 384p. 1961. reprint ed. pap. 14.00 (*0-8021-3053-4*, Grove) Grove-Atltic.

Moon, Samuel D. & Sauter, Steven L., eds. Beyond Biomechanics; Psychosocial Aspects of Musculoskeletal Disorders in Office Work. 320p. 1995. 85.00 (*0-7484-0321-3*, Pub. by Tay Francis Ltd); pap. 39.95 (*0-7484-0322-1*, Pub. by Tay Francis Ltd) Taylor & Francis.

Moon, Sheila. Changing Woman & Her Sisters. LC 84-27901. 233p. (Orig.). 1985. 14.00 (*0-917479-02-5*); pap. 11.50 (*0-917479-03-3*) Guild Psy.

— Deepest Roots. LC 86-19578. (Illus.). 240p. (J). (gr. 8-12). 1986. pap. 8.95 (*0-917479-10-6*) Guild Psy.

— Dreams of a Woman: An Analyst's Inner Journey. LC 83-10826. (Illus.). 207p. 1983. 27.50 (*0-938434-17-9*); pap. 13.95 (*0-938434-14-4*) Sigo Pr.

— Hunt down the Prize. LC 86-19576. (Illus.). 245p. (J). (gr. 8-12). 1986. reprint ed. pap. 8.95 (*0-917479-09-2*) Guild Psy.

— Knee-Deep in Thunder. LC 86-19534. (Illus.). 307p. (J). (gr. 8-12). 1986. reprint ed. pap. 8.95 (*0-917479-08-4*) Guild Psy.

— A Magic Dwells: A Poetic & Psychological Study of the Navaho Emergence Myth. LC 85-12620. 206p. 1985. pap. 7.95 (*0-917479-06-8*) Guild Psy.

Moon, Sheila, ed. see Pelgrin, Mark.

Moon, Sidney M., jt. ed. see Sprenkle, Douglas H.

Moon, Simon Y. Korean & American Monastic Practices: A Comparative Case Study. LC 97-36802. 256p. 1998. text 89.95 (*0-7734-2251-X*) E Mellen.

Moon, Spencer. Reel Black Talk: A Sourcebook of 50 American Filmmakers. LC 96-47539. 416p. 1997. lib. bdg. 79.50 (*0-313-29830-0*, Greenwood Pr) Greenwood.

Moon, Sun Myung. The Divine Principle. 2nd rev. ed. 536p. 1973. 10.95 (*0-910621-05-5*); pap. 7.95 (*0-685-42755-2*) HSA Pubns.

— The Divine Principle. 2nd rev. ed. 536p. (C). 1973. pap. 7.95 (*0-910621-04-7*) HSA Pubns.

— The Divine Principle. 5th rev. ed. 536p. (C). 1977. pap. 5.95 (*0-910621-03-9*) HSA Pubns.

— Home Church. LC 82-88432. (Illus.). 474p. 1983. 14.95 (*0-318-03061-6*); pap. 11.95 (*0-910621-21-7*) HSA Pubns.

— A Life of Prayer. 142p. 14.95 (*0-910621-59-4*); pap. 9.95 (*0-910621-60-8*) HSA Pubns.

— New Hope: 12 Talks. 2nd ed. 1982. 4.95 (*0-910621-02-0*) HSA Pubns.

— Science & Absolute Value: Twenty Addresses. LC 97-22323. 1997. 14.95 (*0-89226-201-X*) ICF Pr.

— True Love. 266p. 15.95 (*0-910621-53-5*); pap. 11.95 (*0-685-61698-3*) HSA Pubns.

— The Way of God's Will. 418p. (Orig.). reprint ed. pap. 6.95 (*0-910621-31-4*) HSA Pubns.

— The Way of Tradition, Vol. 1. 326p. reprint ed. pap. 6.95 (*0-910621-22-5*) HSA Pubns.

— The Way of Tradition, Vol. 2. 295p. reprint ed. pap. 6.95 (*0-910621-23-3*) HSA Pubns.

— The Way of Tradition IV. 462p. 1980. pap. 8.00 (*0-910621-35-7*) HSA Pubns.

— The Way of Tradition III. 541p. reprint ed. pap. 6.95 (*0-910621-24-1*) HSA Pubns.

Moon, Sun Myung & Hak Ja Han Moon. Textbook for World Peace. 64p. 1992. pap. text 4.95 (*0-910621-64-0*) HSA Pubns.

Moon, Susan. Aunt Marty & Uncle Charlie Go to Giza. (Illus.). 18p. (Orig.). 1987. pap. 5.95 (*0-931416-05-1*) Open Books.

***Moon, Susan.** The Telling Signs. limited ed. (Working Signs Ser.). 48p. 2000. 15.00 (*0-911287-41-8*) Blue Begonia.

Moon, Susan, jt. auth. see Cabasso, Jackie.

Moon, Susan, jt. auth. see Green, Neville.

Moon, Susan, jt. auth. see Hayes, Alice.

Moon, Sylvia & Stang, David J. Network Security Secrets. (Illus.). 1200p. 1993. pap. 49.95 (*1-56884-021-7*) IDG Bks.

Moon, Teresa S., jt. auth. see Davis, Nancy M.

Moon, Terry & Brokmeyer, Ron. Then & Now: On the One Hundreth Anniversary of the First General Strike in the U. S. (Illus.). 50p. 1977. pap. 1.00 (*0-914441-17-5*) News & Letters.

Moon, Thomas E. & Micozzi, Marc S. Nutrition & Cancer Prevention. (Illus.). 608p. 1988. text 225.00 (*0-8247-7993-2*) Dekker.

Moon, Thomas E., jt. auth. see Micozzi, Marc S.

***Moon, Todd K.** Mathematical Methods & Algorithms for Signal Processing. LC 99-31038. 937p. (C). 1999. text 105.00 incl. cd-rom, audio compact disk (*0-201-36186-8*, Prentice Hall) P-H.

Moon, Tom. The Lemon County Chronicles. 180p. 1992. pap. 7.95 (*0-9632808-0-5*) Lemon Seed Pr.

***Moon Travel Handbooks Editors.** Moon Handbooks: Australia. 2nd ed. Vol. 2. (Illus.). 940p. 2000. 21.95 (*1-56691-158-3*, Moon Handbks) Avalon Travel.

***Moon, Vasant.** Growing Up Untouchable in India: A Dalit Autobiography. Omvedt, Gail, tr. 224p. 2000. 65.00 (*0-7425-0880-3*) Rowman.

— Growing up Untouchable in India: A Dalit Autobiography. Omvedt, Gail, tr. 224p. 2000. pap. 19.95 (*0-7425-0881-1*) Rowman.

Moon, Vicky. The Official Middleburg Life Cookbook. (Illus.). (Orig.). 1989. 10.00 (*0-9617683-0-4*) Pink Sheet.

Moon, Warren G., ed. Ancient Greek Art & Iconography. LC 83-47765. (Wisconsin Studies in Classics). (Illus.). 365p. 1983. reprint ed. pap. 113.20 (*0-608-07477-2*, 206769900009) Bks Demand.

— Polykleitos, the Doryphoros, & Tradition. LC 94-30288. (Wisconsin Studies in Classics). (Illus.). 1995. 50.00 (*0-299-14310-4*) U of Wis Pr.

***Moon, Y. M.** Assessment of RELAP5/MOD 3.2 for Reflux Condensation Experiment. 103p. 2000. per. 9.00 (*0-16-059227-5*) USGPO.

Moonan, Lawrence. Divine Power: The Medieval Power Distinction up to Its Adoption by Albert, Bonaventure, & Aquinas. LC 93-30542. 408p. 1994. text 65.00 (*0-19-826755-X*, Clarendon Pr) OUP.

Moonan, Shastri. Technology Transfer: Rejuvenating Matured Industries. LC 97-38585. (Garland Studies on Industrial Productivity). (Illus.). 305p. 1997. text 75.00 (*0-8153-2997-0*) Garland.

Moonbeam, Kathy M. Why? The Road from There to Here Was Tough, but Now I'm on the Highway. LC 91-76844. (Illus.). 192p. (Orig.). 1992. pap. 9.95 (*1-880601-07-9*) Danon Pub.

Moondance, Wolf. Bone Medicine. LC 99-12226. (Illus.). 160p. 1999. pap. 12.95 (*0-8069-9797-4*) Sterling.

— Rainbow Medicine: A Visionary Guide to Native American Shamanism. LC 93-39600. (Illus.). 192p. 1994. pap. 12.95 (*0-8069-0364-3*) Sterling.

— Rainbow Spirit Journeys: Native American Meditations & Dreams. LC 99-44619. 144p. 2000. pap. 14.95 (*0-8069-0563-8*) Sterling.

— Spirit Medicine: Native American Teachings to Awaken the Spirit. LC 95-20796. (Illus.). 160p. 1995. pap. 12.95 (*0-8069-1368-1*) Sterling.

— Star Medicine: Native American Path to Emotional Healing. LC 97-1003. (Illus.). 192p. 1997. pap. 12.95 (*0-8069-9547-5*) Sterling.

Moone, Colin. Obeah. 1997. pap. 9.95 (*1-874509-18-2*, Pub. by X Pr) LPC InBook.

Moone, Eric, jt. auth. see Gale, D.

***Moonen, C. T. & Bandettini, P. A., eds.** Functional MRI. (Medical Radiolgoy Ser.). (Illus.). xii, 578p. 2000. pap. 75.00 (*3-540-67215-X*) Spr-Verlag.

Moonen, J. & Plomp, T., eds. Eurit 86: Developments in Educational Software & Courseware. 762p. 1987. 326.00 (*0-08-032693-5*, Pub. by Pergamon Repr); 45.00 (*0-08-035833-0*, Pub. by Pergamon Repr) Franklin.

Moonen, Joep, et al. Surinaamse Slangeninkleur: Surinam Snakes in Color. (Illus.). 119p. 1979. pap. 29.95 (*0-88359-016-6*) R Curtis Pubng.

Moonen, Marc & Catthoor, Francky, eds. Algorithms & Parallel VLSI Architectures III: Proceedings of The International Workshop, Algorithms & Parallel VLSI Architectures III, Leuven, Belgium, August 29-31, 1994. LC 94-44668. 424p. 1995. 204.50 (*0-444-82106-6*) Elsevier.

Moonen, Marc & De Moor, Bart, eds. SVD & Signaling Processing III: Algorithms, Architectures, & Applications. LC 95-3193. 498p. 1995. 210.50 (*0-444-82107-4*) Elsevier.

Moonen, Marc S., ed. Linear Algebra for Large-Scale & Real-Time Applications: Proceedings of the NATO Advanced Study Institute, Leuven, Belgium, August 3-14, 1992. (NATO ASI Series E, Applied Sciences). 436p. (C). 1993. text 241.50 (*0-7923-2151-0*) Kluwer Academic.

***Mooners, Vernon.** Briefly a Candle. large type ed. 236p. 1999. pap. 14.25 (*0-9684792-0-0*, Pub. by Funldy Prodn) Genl Dist Srvs.

Mooney. Social Problems. 1996. pap., student ed. 15.25 (*0-314-06719-1*) West Pub.

Mooney & Knox. Understanding Social Problems. 2nd ed. LC 99-33087. (Sociology - Introductory Level Ser.). 1999. pap. 51.95 (*0-534-56511-5*); pap., student ed. 14.75 (*0-534-56512-3*) Wadsworth Pub.

Mooney & Pratzel. Missouri Civil Procedure Forms, Issue 8. 1995. ring bd. 159.00 (*0-327-03927-2*, 81899-10, MICHIE) LEXIS Pub.

— Missouri Civil Procedure Forms, No. 9. 100p. 1998. ring bd. write for info. (*0-327-00321-9*, 81902-14) LEXIS Pub.

Mooney, Jonathan M., jt. ed. see Descour, Michael R.

Mooney, Alfred J., et al. The Recovery Book. LC 92-50284. (Illus.). 597p. 1992. pap. 14.95 (*1-56305-084-6*, 3084) Workman Pub.

Mooney, Ann & Munton, Tony. Choosing Childcare: A Guide for Parents & Providers. LC 97-209198. 100p. 1997. pap. text 17.95 (*1-85742-361-5*, Pub. by Arena) Ashgate Pub Co.

Mooney, Ann J. Sock Monkey's Family Reunion. LC 98-92028. (Sock Animals Ser.: Vol. 3). (Illus.). 34p. (J). (ps-2). 1998. pap. 7.95 (*0-9631035-5-5*) Jamondas Pr.

— Tiger's New Friends. LC 91-76359. (Sock Animals Ser.: Vol. 1). (Illus.). 32p. (Orig.). (J). (ps-2). 1992. pap. 7.95 (*0-9631035-0-4*) Jamondas Pr.

— Tiger's Vacation. (Sock Animals Ser.: Vol. 2). 1994. pap. text 7.95 (*0-9631035-2-0*) Jamondas Pr.

Mooney, Barbara J., et al. Feeling Good about Me. (Illus.). 17p. (J). (gr. 3-8). 1993. pap. 6.00 (*1-57402-302-0*); pap., teacher ed., student ed. 6.00 (*1-57402-304-7*) Athena Info Mgt.

— Feelings: Having Them - Sharing Them. (Illus.). 21p. (J). (gr. 3-8). 1993. pap., teacher ed., student ed. 6.00 (*1-57402-303-9*); pap., student ed. 6.00 (*1-57402-301-2*) Athena Info Mgt.

Mooney, Bel. Perspectives for Living: Conversations on Bereavement & Love. (Illus.). 208p. 1993. pap. 18.95 (*0-7195-5125-0*, Pub. by John Murray) Trafalgar.

— Voices of Silence. 192p. (YA). (gr. 5 up). 1998. mass mkt. 4.99 (*0-440-22758-5*, LLL BDD) BDD Bks Young Read.

— Voices of Silence. 1998. 9.60 (*0-606-13887-0*, Pub. by Turtleback) Demco.

An Asterisk (*) at the beginning of an entry indicates that the title is appearing for the first time.

Mooney, Bill & Holt, David. Storyteller's Guide: Storytellers Discuss Experiences in Classrooms, Boardrooms, Showrooms... LC 96-9500. 224p. 1996. pap. text 23.95 (*0-87483-482-1*) August Hse.

Mooney, Bill, jt. auth. see Holt, David.

Mooney, Bill, jt. ed. see Holt, David.

Mooney, Blake. Altitude-Rated Places: A Medical Atlas, Vol. 1. 2nd rev. ed. Landry, Juliette, ed. (Illus.). 225p. (Orig.). 1994. pap. 16.95 (*0-9638226-0-8*) Med-Travel Bks.

Mooney, Brad. Submersibles & Marine Technologies in Russia's Far East & Siberia. unabridged ed. (WTEC Panel Reports). (Illus.). 139p. (Orig.). 1996. pap. write for info. (*1-883712-41-6*) Intl Tech Res.

Mooney, Brian. Introduction to Biology. LC 96-40251. (Test Yourself Ser.). 192p. (C). 1996. pap. 14.95 (*0-8442-2364-6*) NTC Contemp Pub Co.

Mooney, Carmel, jt. ed. see Torrance, Andrew.

Mooney, Carol A., jt. auth. see Shaffer, Thomas L.

Mooney, Carol G. Reflections on Parenting. xii, 167p. (Orig.). 1996. pap. 14.95 (*0-9609466-2-4*) NEAEYC.

***Mooney, Carol Garhart.** Theories of Childhood: An introduction to Erikson, Piaget, Vygotsky, Montessori, & Dewwy. 188p. 2000. pap. 19.95 (*1-884834-85-X*, 155601, Pub. by Redleaf Pr) Gryphon Hse.

Mooney, Catherine, ed. Eat, Drink & Sleep Smoke-Free. (Illus.). 258p. (Orig.). 1995. pap. 14.95 (*1-899583-00-9*, Pub. by JARR UK) Seven Hills Bk.

— The Good Vegetarian Travel Guide. (Illus.). 162p. (Orig.). 1995. pap. 14.95 (*1-899583-01-7*, Pub. by JARR UK) Seven Hills Bk.

***Mooney, Catherine M.** Gendered Voices: Medieval Saints & Their Interpreters. LC 98-54774. (Middle Ages Ser.). 1999. 19.95 (*0-8122-1687-3*) U of Pa Pr.

***Mooney, Catherine M., ed.** Gendered Voices. LC 98-54774. (Middle Ages Ser.). 248p. 1999. 39.95 (*0-8122-3485-5*) U of Pa Pr.

Mooney, Charles W. Doctor in Belle Starr Country. LC 74-30947. (Illus.). 291p. 1975. write for info. (*0-685-53674-2*) Century Pr.

Mooney, Charles W., Jr., ed. see Honnold, John O. & Harris, Steven L.

Mooney, Chase. William H. Crawford, 1772 to 1834. LC 70-190534. 386p. reprint ed. pap. 119.70 (*0-608-12708-6*, 202436100037) Bks Demand.

***Mooney, Chris.** Deviant Ways. 384p. 2000. 24.95 (*0-671-04059-6*) PB.

Mooney, Christopher F. Cybernation, Responsibility & Providential Design. (Teilhard Studies: No. 24). 1991. pap. 3.50 (*0-89012-063-3*) Am Teilhard.

— Theology & Scientific Knowledge: Changing Models of God's Presence in the World. LC 95-16517. 288p. (C). 1996. pap. text 15.00 (*0-268-04200-4*) U of Notre Dame Pr.

— Theology & Scientific Knowledge: Changing Models of God's Presence in the World. 256p. 1996. text 34.95 (*0-268-01892-8*) U of Notre Dame Pr.

Mooney, Christopher F., ed. The Presence & Absence of God. LC 68-8748. (Cardinal Bea Lectures). 190p. reprint ed. pap. 58.90 (*0-7837-0458-5*, 204078100018) Bks Demand.

Mooney, Christopher Z. Monte Carlo Simulation. LC 96-45873. (Quantitative Applications in the Social Sciences Ser.: Vol. 116). 96p. 1997. pap. 10.95 (*0-8039-5943-5*) Sage.

Mooney, Christopher Z., ed. The Public Clash of Private Values: The Politics of Morality Policy. LC 99-50743. (Illus.). 312p. 2000. pap. text 29.95 (*1-889119-40-7*, Chatham House Pub) Seven Bridges.

Mooney, Christopher Z. & Duval, Robert D. Bootstrapping: A Nonparamentric Approach to Statistical Inference. (Quantitative Applications in the Social Sciences Ser.: Vol. 95). (Illus.). 96p. (C). 1993. pap. text 10.95 (*0-8039-5381-X*) Sage.

Mooney, Chuck, III, jt. auth. see Jones, Mike.

Mooney, D., et al, eds. Biomaterials Regulating Cell Function & Tissue Development Vol. 530: Proceedings Materials Research Society Symposium. 119p. 1998. text 79.00 (*1-55899-436-X*) Materials Res.

Mooney, Dale. Western Glass Auctions: Auction Catalog, 3 vols., 1. (Illus.). 1991. 16.00 (*1-883192-00-5*) Wstrn Glass.

— Western Glass Auctions: Auction Catalog, 3 vols., 2. (Illus.). 1992. 18.00 (*1-883192-01-3*) Wstrn Glass.

— Western Glass Auctions: Auction Catalog, 3 vols., 3. (Illus.). 1992. 20.00 (*1-883192-02-1*) Wstrn Glass.

Mooney, Douglas & Swift, Randall. A Course in Mathematical Modeling. LC 98-85688. (Classroom Resource Materials Ser.). 450p. 1999. pap. text 41.95 (*0-88385-712-X*) Math Assn.

Mooney, E. F., ed. Annual Reports on NMR Spectroscopy, Vol. 6a. 1975. 85.00 (*0-12-505306-1*) Acad Pr.

Mooney, E. F. & Webb, Graham A. Annual Reports on NMR Spectroscopy, Vol. 15. 1984. text 237.00 (*0-12-505315-0*) Acad Pr.

Mooney, E. F. & Webb, Graham A., eds. Annual Reports on NMR Spectroscopy, 13 vols., Vol. 2. 1983. text 259.00 (*0-12-505313-4*); text 167.00 (*0-12-505314-2*) Acad Pr.

— Annual Reports on NMR Spectroscopy, Vol. 10A. 1980. text 237.00 (*0-12-505310-X*) Acad Pr.

— Annual Reports on NMR Spectroscopy, Vol. 10B. 1980. text 246.00 (*0-12-505348-7*) Acad Pr.

— Annual Reports on NMR Spectroscopy, Vol. 11A. 1981. text 237.00 (*0-12-505311-8*) Acad Pr.

— Annual Reports on NMR Spectroscopy, Vol. 12. 1982. text 237.00 (*0-12-505312-6*) Acad Pr.

***Mooney, E. S.** Blossoming Out. (Powerpuff Girls Ser.). (Illus.). (J). 2000. pap. 3.99 (*0-439-16022-7*) Scholastic Inc.

— Cartoon Crazy. (Powerpuff Girls Ser.). (Illus.). (J). 2000. pap. 3.99 (*0-439-16021-9*) Scholastic Inc.

Mooney, Edward. Selves in Discord & Resolve: Essays in Kierkegaard's Moralreligious Psychology from Either/Or to Sickness unto Death. 224p. (C). 1996. 75.00 (*0-415-91369-1*); pap. 18.99 (*0-415-91370-5*) Routledge.

Mooney, Edward F. Knights of Faith & Resignation: Reading Kierkegaard's "Fear & Trembling" LC 90-36515. (SUNY Series in Philosophy). 205p. (C). 1991. text 19.50 (*0-7914-0572-9*) State U NY Pr.

— Wilderness & the Heart: Henry Bugbee's Philosophy of Place, Presence, & Memory. LC 98-26779. (Orig.). 1999. 45.00 (*0-8203-2070-6*) U of Ga Pr.

Mooney, Edward F., ed. Wilderness & the Heart: Henry Bugbee's Philosophy of Place, Presence, & Memory. LC 98-26779. (Orig.). 1999. pap. 19.95 (*0-8203-2098-6*) U of Ga Pr.

***Mooney-Eichacker, Joanne.** Varieties of Irish Republican Womanhood. (Women in Irish History Ser.). (Illus.). 144p. 2000. 39.50 (*0-7165-2688-3*, Pub. by Irish Acad Pr); pap. 22.50 (*0-7165-2719-7*, Pub. by Irish Acad Pr) Intl Spec Bk.

Mooney, Frances, jt. auth. see Walker, Bob.

***Mooney, Gavin & Scotton, Richard, eds.** Economics & Australian Health Policy. 320p. 1999. pap. 35.00 (*1-86448-749-6*, Pub. by Allen & Unwin Pty) Paul & Co Pubs.

Mooney, Gavin A., jt. auth. see Lawford, R. G.

Mooney, Gavin H. Economics, Medicine & Health Care. 2nd ed. 170p. (C). 1992. text 63.50 (*0-389-20991-0*) Rowman.

— International Perspectives in Health Economics: Selected Papers from the World Congress in Health Economics, Leiden, the Netherlands, September 1980. (Journal of Social Science & Medicine Ser.: No. 15). 72p. 1981. pap. 18.00 (*0-08-028131-1*, Pergamon Pr) Elsevier.

Mooney, Gavin H. & Jensen, Uffe J., eds. Changing Values in Medical & Healthcare Decision-Making. LC 89-70700. 206p. 1990. 239.95 (*0-471-92634-5*) Wiley.

Mooney, George W., ed. see Suetonius.

Mooney, Gerry, jt. auth. see Lavalette, Michael.

Mooney, Gerry, jt. ed. see Lavalette, Michael.

Mooney, Harold A. Supplement to the Botany of Bihar & Orissa. 294p. 1986. reprint ed. 140.00 (*0-7855-3110-6*, Pub. by Intl Bk Distr) St Mut.

Mooney, Harold A., et al, eds. Ecosystem Experiments: Scope Forty-Five. LC 91-7558. (Scientific Committee on Problems of the Environment Ser.: No. 1409). 296p. 1991. 330.00 (*0-471-92926-3*) Wiley.

— Functional Roles of Biodiversity: A Global Perspective. LC 96-12983. (SCOPE Ser.: Vol. 55). 518p. 1996. 190.00 (*0-471-95601-5*) Wiley.

— Response of Plants to Multiple Stresses. (Physiological Ecology Ser.). (Illus.). 422p. 1991. text 89.00 (*0-12-505355-X*) Acad Pr.

Mooney, Harold A. & Bernardi, G., eds. Introduction of Genetically-Modified Organisms into the Environment. LC 90-35076. (Scientific Committee on Problems of the Environment Ser.: No. 44). 224p. 1990. 325.00 (*0-471-92677-9*) Wiley.

Mooney, Harold A. & Drake, J. A., eds. The Ecology of Biological Invasions of North America & Hawaii. (Ecological Studies, Analysis & Synthesis: Vol. 58). (Illus.). 330p. 1986. 87.00 (*0-387-96289-1*) Spr-Verlag.

***Mooney, Harold A. & Hobbs, Richard J., eds.** Invasive Species in a Changing World. 375p. 2000. pap. 30.00 (*1-55963-782-X*) Island Pr.

— Invasive Species in a Changing World. 375p. 2000. 55.00 (*1-55963-781-1*) Island Pr.

Mooney, Harold A., jt. auth. see Lange, O. L.

Mooney, Harold A., jt. auth. see Luo, Yiqi.

Mooney, Harold A., jt. ed. see Hobbs, R. J.

Mooney, Harold A., jt. ed. see Huenneke, L. F.

Mooney, Harold A., jt. ed. see Koch, George W.

Mooney, Harold A., jt. ed. see Margaris, N. S.

Mooney, Harold A., jt. ed. see Schulze, Ernst-Detlef.

Mooney, Harry J. & Staley, Thomas F., eds. The Shapeless God: Essays on Modern Fiction. LC 68-21630. 232p. reprint ed. pap. 72.00 (*0-608-16762-2*, 202631400049) Bks Demand.

Mooney, J. M. & Renfro, Sheila T., eds. Heavener (LeFlore County) Oklahoma: Heavener, Indian Territory. (Illus.). 500p. 1996. 54.95 (*0-938041-68-1*) Arc Pr AR.

Mooney, J. Michael. Just Add Sunshine Vol. 1: Solar Electricity Will Set You Free. LC 96-80182. (Illus.). 116p. 1997. pap. 24.95 (*0-938041-27-4*) Arc Pr AR.

Mooney, Jack. Printers in Appalachia: The International Printing Pressmen & Assistants' Union of North America, 1907-1967. LC 93-70235. 193p. (C). 1993. 39.95 (*0-87972-576-1*) Bowling Green Univ Popular Press.

Mooney, Jack, ed. A History of Tennessee Newspapers. (Illus.). vi, 192p. 1996. pap. 25.00 (*0-9655550-0-3*) Tennessee Pr.

Mooney, James. The District of Columbia Fire Fighters' Project: A Case Study in Occupational Folklife. LC 84-600291. (Illus.). 244p. (Orig.). 1975. pap. text 5.95 (*0-87474-653-1*, MCDFP) Smithsonian.

— Ghost-Dance Religion & the Sioux OutbreaK of 1890. Wallace, Anthony F., ed. LC 64-24971. (Orig.). 1965. pap. text 14.00 (*0-226-53517-7*, P176) U Ch Pr.

— The Ghost-Dance Religion & the Sioux Outbreak of 1890. LC 91-24546. (Illus.). xxx, 531p. 1991. reprint ed. pap. 35.00 (*0-8032-8177-3*, Bison Books); reprint ed. text 80.00 (*0-8032-3155-5*) U of Nebr Pr.

— Ghost-Dance, Religion & Wounded Knee. (Illus.). 544p. 1991. pap. 12.95 (*0-486-26759-8*) Dover.

— The Ghost Danced. 498p. 1996. write for info. (*1-57215-201-X*) World Pubns.

— James Mooney's History, Myths & Sacred Formulas of the Cherokees. LC 91-42830. (Illus.). 768p. 1992. pap. 17.95 (*0-914875-19-1*, Historical Images) Bright Mtn Bks.

— Myths of the Cherokee. LC 70-108513. (American Indian History Ser.). 1970. reprint ed. 89.00 (*0-403-00221-4*) Scholarly.

— Myths of the Cherokee. unabridged ed. LC 95-22350. (Illus.). 608p. 1996. reprint ed. pap. text 14.95 (*0-486-28907-9*) Dover.

— Myths of the Cherokee & Sacred Formulas of the Cherokees. LC 72-188151. (Illus.). 1982. reprint ed. 29.95 (*0-918450-22-5*); reprint ed. pap. 16.95 (*0-918450-05-5*) C Elder.

— The Siouan Tribes of the East. (Bureau of American Ethnology Bulletins Ser.). 101p. 1995. lib. bdg. 79.00 (*0-7812-4022-0*) Rprt Serv.

— The Siouan Tribes of the East. LC 73-108504. (American Indian History Ser.). (Illus.). 1970. reprint ed. 39.00 (*0-403-00348-2*) Scholarly.

— Swimmer Manuscript: Cherokee Sacred Formulas & Medicinal Prescriptions. (Bureau of American Ethnology Bulletins Ser.). 319p. 1995. lib. bdg. 99.00 (*0-7812-4099-9*) Rprt Serv.

Mooney, James, jt. auth. see Forman, Maury.

Mooney, James E., compiled by. Maps, Globes, Atlases & Geographies Through the Year 1800: The Eleanor Houston & Lawrence M. C. Smith Cartographic Collection. (Illus.). 168p. (C). 1988. 75.00 (*0-939561-03-4*) Univ South ME.

Mooney, James E., jt. auth. see Shipton, Clifford K.

Mooney, James W. & West, Thomas R., eds. Vietnam: A History & Anthology. 341p. (C). 1994. pap. text 16.50 (*1-881089-28-2*) Brandywine Press.

Mooney, James W., jt. ed. see West, Thomas R.

***Mooney, Jayne.** Gender Violence & the Social Order. LC 99-88131. 2000. text 59.95 (*0-312-23157-1*) St Martin.

Mooney, Jean F., jt. ed. see Tourse, Robbie W. C.

Mooney, Jennifer, ed. Sink or Float? Theme Pack. (Early Science Ser.). (Illus.). (J). (ps-2). 1997. pap. text 49.95 (*1-56784-395-6*) Newbridge Educ.

Mooney, Jennifer, ed. see Nayer, Judy.

Mooney, Jennifer, ed. see Parkes, Brenda.

Mooney, Jennifer, ed. see Trumbauer, Lisa.

Mooney, Joan C. Country Adventures in Maryland, Virginia & West Virginia. 164p. 1995. pap. 10.95 (*0-915168-25-1*) Wash Bk Trad.

Mooney, John D. Vatican Observatory & the Arts: The Sculpture of John David Mooney at Castel Gandolfo. (From the Vatican Observatory Foundation Ser.). 112p. 2000. pap. 39.95 (*0-268-04350-7*, Pub. by U of Notre Dame Pr) Chicago Distribution Ctr.

Mooney, Jon W. Inventor's Guide to Identifying Profitable Ideas. Janning, John L., ed. LC 96-92512. (Illus.). x, 86p. (Orig.). 1996. pap. 17.95 (*0-9653592-0-4*) Rapid Product.

***Mooney, Jonathan & Cole, David.** Learning Outside the Lines: Two Ivy League Students with ADHD & Learning Disabilities Show You How to Gain the Academic Edge. (Illus.). 256p. 2000. pap. 13.00 (*0-684-86598-X*, Fireside) S&S Trade Pap.

***Mooney, Julie.** The World of Ripley's Believe It or Not! A Global Retrospective of Amazing Achievements, Bizarre Behavior & Extraordinary Events. Ripley Entertainment Editors, ed. LC 99-38964. (Illus.). 160p. 1999. 24.98 (*1-57912-088-1*) Blck Dog & Leventhal.

Mooney, Linne R. The Index of Middle English Prose Handlist XI: Manuscripts in the Library of Trinity College, Cambridge. 290p. (C). 1995. 75.00 (*0-85991-457-7*, DS Brewer) Boydell & Brewer.

Mooney, Linne R., jt. auth. see Somer, John.

Mooney, Loren. A Kid's Guide to NASCAR. Gramling, Scott & Holder, Sherie, eds. (Illus.). 32p. (J). (gr. 1-9). 1999. pap. 3.99 (*1-886749-51-5*) SI For Kids.

Mooney, Louise. Newsmakers, 1994 Subscription. 94th ed. 1994. 129.00 (*0-8103-8560-0*, 001820) Gale.

Mooney, Margaret. Developing Life-Long Readers. 30p. (C). 1988. reprint ed. pap. text 7.95 (*0-478-02701-X*, 23) R Owen Pubs.

— A Matter of Balance. LC 93-26222. (Illus.). (J). 1994. 4.25 (*0-383-03759-X*) SRA McGraw.

— Outwitting the Tiger: A Chinese Legend. LC 93-26261. (Illus.). (J). 1994. 4.25 (*0-383-03776-X*) SRA McGraw.

Mooney, Margaret E. Reading to, with, & by Children. LC 90-30678. 104p. (Orig.). (C). 1990. pap. text 12.95 (*0-913461-18-0*, 8) R Owen Pubs.

Mooney, Margaret L., jt. auth. see Peabody, Kathleen L.

Mooney, Margaret M. & Pratzel, Alan D. Missouri Civil Procedure Forms. 500p. 1994. spiral bd. 209.00 (*0-87189-066-6*, MICHIE); ring bd., suppl. ed. 87.00 (*0-685-74598-8*, MICHIE) LEXIS Pub.

***Mooney, Margaret M. & Pratzel, Alana D.** Missouri Civil Procedure Forms, Issue 10. 100p. 1999. ring bd. write for info. (*0-327-01693-0*, 8190215) LEXIS Pub.

Mooney, Martin. Brett Favre. LC 97-14960. (Football Legends Ser.). (Illus.). 64p. (J). (gr. 3 up). 1997. lib. bdg. 15.95 (*0-7910-4396-7*) Chelsea Hse.

— Grub. 85p. 1994. pap. 11.95 (*0-85640-500-0*, Pub. by Blackstaff Pr) Dufour.

— John Daly. LC 97-46464. (Golf Legends Ser.). (Illus.). 64p. (YA). (gr. 3 up). 1999. 15.95 (*0-7910-4581-1*) Chelsea Hse.

Mooney, Martin J. Comanche Indians. (Junior Library of American Indians). 1993. 13.15 (*0-606-07383-3*, Pub. by Turtleback) Demco.

Mooney, Martin N. The Math Playbook: A Math Skill Development System. (Illus.). 176p. (Orig.). (YA). 1997. per. 24.95 (*0-9656857-0-5*) Alexandrian Schl.

Mooney, Mary F., tr. see Baudouin-Croix, Marie.

***Mooney, Matthew L.** Kentucky Administrative Procedures Act: KRS 13B Annotated. 148p. 2000. pap. 42.00 (*1-58757-032-7*, PM037) Univ of KY.

Mooney, Michael. Ancient Voices & Other Stories. (Orig.). 1987. pap. 8.95 (*0-935399-04-6*) Main St Pub.

— Names. deluxe ed. (Treacle Story Ser.: No. 10). 64p. 1979. 12.50 (*0-914232-33-9*) McPherson & Co.

— Shakespeare's Dramatic Transactions. LC 90-2770. 243p. (C). 1990. text 39.95 (*0-8223-1039-2*) Duke.

— Vico in the Tradition of Rhetoric. (Illus.). 318p. (C). 1994. pap. 19.95 (*1-880393-24-7*, Hermagoras) L Erlbaum Assocs.

— Vico in the Tradition of Rhetoric. LC 84-42569. 343p. reprint ed. pap. 106.40 (*0-8357-2930-3*, 203916900011) Bks Demand.

Mooney, Michael, jt. auth. see Vergel, Nelson R.

Mooney, Michael, ed. see Kristeller, Paul O.

***Mooney, Michael E.** Hamlet: An Annotated Bibliography of Shakespeare Studies, 1604-1998. LC 99-49463. (Shakespeare Bibliographies Ser.). 130p. 2000. pap. 9.95 (*1-889818-21-6*) Pegasus Pr.

***Mooney, Nan.** Day at the Races. 2000. 25.00 (*0-06-019853-2*); pap. 13.00 (*0-06-095808-1*) HarpC.

***Mooney, Pamela J. & Ostler, Elliott.** The "Who Cares" Book of Math Activities. 72p. 1999. pap. 15.95 (*0-7414-0058-8*) Buy Books.

Mooney, Pat, jt. auth. see Fowler, Cary.

Mooney, Patrick H. American Farm & Farmworkers Movement. 1994. 26.95 (*0-8057-4517-3*, Twyne) Mac Lib Ref.

Mooney, Patrick H,. American Farm & Farmworkers Movement. 1994. pap. 14.95 (*0-8057-4518-1*, Twyne) Mac Lib Ref.

Mooney, Patrick H. & Majka, Theo J. Farmers' & Farm Workers' Movements. LC 94-18178. (Twayne's Social Movements Past & Present Ser.). 288p. 1994. pap. 20.00 (*0-8057-3870-3*, Twyne) Mac Lib Ref.

— Farmers' & Farm Workers' Movements. LC 94-18178. (Twayne's Social Movements Past & Present Ser.). 288p. 1994. 26.95 (*0-8057-3869-X*, Twyne) Mac Lib Ref.

M

Mooney, Paula Y. Payroll Accounting. 94th ed. LC 93-35659. 290p. 1993. pap. text 65.00 (*0-13-091308-1*) P-H.

Mooney, Philip. Images of Personal Value. LC 94-19425. 192p. (Orig.). 1994. pap. 10.95 (*1-55612-705-7*) Sheed & Ward WI.

Mooney, Raymond, jt. ed. see Porter, Bruce.

Mooney, Raymond J. A General Explanation-Based Learning Mechanism & Its Applications to Narrative Understanding. (Research Notes in Artificial Intelligence Ser.). (C). 1989. pap. text 36.95 (*1-55860-091-4*) Morgan Kaufmann.

Mooney, Richard E. Gods of Air & Darkness: The Possibility of a Nuclear War in the Past LC 75-331192. 203p. 1975. write for info. (*0-285-62176-9*) Souvenir Pr Ltd.

Mooney, Rick. Double Stops for Cello. 40p. 1995. pap. text 7.95 (*0-87487-761-X*) Summy-Birchard.

— Ensembles for Cello, Vol. 3. 40p. 1991. pap. text 6.50 (*0-87487-299-5*) Summy-Birchard.

— Position Pieces for Cello. 64p. 1997. pap. text 8.95 (*0-87487-762-8*) Summy-Birchard.

— Thumb Position for Cello, Bk. 1. 72p. 1998. pap. text 9.95 (*0-87487-763-6*) Summy-Birchard.

***Mooney, Rick.** Thumb Position for Cello, Bk. 2. 80p. 1999. pap. text 9.95 (*0-87487-764-4*) Summy-Birchard.

Mooney, Rick, des. Ensembles for Cello, Vol. 2. 24p. 1991. pap. text 6.50 (*0-87487-298-7*) Summy-Birchard.

Mooney, Rick, ed. Ensembles for Cello, Vol. I. 87p. 1987. 6.95 (*0-87487-296-0*) Summy-Birchard.

Mooney, Robert F. The Advent of Douglass. 48p. pap. 6.95 (*0-924771-36-4*, Covered Brdge Pr) Douglas Charles Ltd.

— Tales of Nantucket: Chronicles & Characters of America's Favorite Island. (Illus.). 184p. (Orig.). 1990. pap. 12.95 (*0-9627851-0-5*) Wesco Pub MA.

Mooney, Robert F., text. Portrait of Nantucket, 1659-1890: Paintings by Rodney Charman. 45p. text 50.00 (*0-9638910-3-0*); pap. text 20.00 (*0-9638910-4-9*) Mill Hill Pr.

Mooney, Robert F., jt. auth. see Miller, Richard F.

Mooney, Samantha. A Snowflake in My Hand. large type ed. LC 95-17990. (Large Print Bks.). 1995. pap. 19.95 (*1-56895-227-9*) Wheeler Pub.

Mooney, Sean F. Insuring Your Business: What You Need to Know to Get the Best Insurance Coverage for Your Business. LC 91-29128. 306p. 1992. 22.50 (*0-932387-29-2*) Insur Info.

Mooney, Shane. Bass Masters Classic Tournament Edition: Prima's Official Strategy Guide. LC 98-67558. (Games Ser.). 240p. 1998. per. 19.99 (*0-7615-1892-4*) Prima Pub.

— Cyberstorm 2: Corporate Wars: Prima's Official Strategy Guide. LC 98-65452. 240p. 1998. per. 19.99 (*0-7615-1574-7*) Prima Pub.

***Mooney, Shane.** Useless Sexual Trivia: Tastefully Prurient Facts about Everyone's Favorite Subject. LC 99-41157. 224p. 2000. pap. 12.00 (*0-684-85927-0*) S&S Trade.

Mooney, Sheila. A Strange Kind of Loving. 192p. 1990. pap. 11.95 (*1-85371-076-8*, Pub. by Poolbeg Pr) Dufour.

Mooney, Sheila A., jt. auth. see Ramsay, Caroline C.

Mooney, Sheilia A., ed. see Ramsay, Caroline C.

Mooney, Stephen. News from the South: Poems. 2nd ed. LC 66-14773. 78p. reprint ed. pap. 30.00 (*0-608-14399-5*, 202178100023) Bks Demand.

Mooney, Ted. Easy Travel to Other Planets. LC 91-58057. 1992. pap. 12.00 (*0-679-73883-5*) Vin Bks.

— Singing into the Piano. LC 97-49467. 357p. 1998. 25.00 (*0-679-41692-7*) Knopf.

— Singing into the Piano. 1999. pap. 14.00 (*0-679-74306-5*) Knopf.

— Traffic & Laughter. 1992. pap. 12.00 (*0-679-73884-3*) Vin Bks.

Mooney, Terrance L., ed. The Challenge of Development Within Conflict Zones. LC 96-148045. 46p. (Orig.). 1995. pap. 8.00 (92-64-14640-7, Pub. by Org for Econ) OECD.

Mooney, Thomas O., et al. Sexual Options for Paraplegics & Quadriplegics. (Illus.). 150p. 1975. pap. 29.95 (0-316-57937-8, Little Brwn Med Div) Lppncott W & W.

Mooney, Tom. The Amoralists. 1985. pap. 3.00 (0-317-28509-2) T Mooney.

— Black Tuesday: A Story of Nuclear War. 1982. pap. 3.00 (0-317-28511-4) T Mooney.

— The Boom & Bust Cycle. 1985. pap. 3.00 (0-317-28512-2) T Mooney.

— The Early History of a Purpose Machine. 1976. 5.95 (0-9601240-1-2); pap. 2.95 (0-9601240-2-0) T Mooney.

— Notes on the Nature of Man. 1985. pap. 3.00 (0-317-28508-4) T Mooney.

— Wally Wooluf & Other Stories: A Young Person's Guide to Humor. 1985. pap. 3.00 (0-317-28510-6) T Mooney.

— War: Toward a Solution. 1985. pap. 2.00 (0-317-28513-0) T Mooney.

Mooney, W. D., jt. ed. see Pakiser, L. C.

Moonie, Neil, et al, eds. Human Behavior in the Caring Context. 200p. (Orig.). 1999. pap. 27.50 (0-7487-1769-2, Pub. by S Thornes Pubs) Trans-Atl Phila.

M

Moonis, Ali, ed. Industrial & Engineering Applications of Artificial Intelligence & Expert Systems. 1192p. 1988. pap. text 118.00 (0-89791-271-3, Harwood Acad Pubs) Gordon & Breach.

Moonitz, Maurice. The Entity Theory of Consolidated Statements. Brief, Richard P., ed. LC 77-87282. (Development of Contemporary Accounting Thought Ser.). 1978. reprint ed. lib. bdg. 19.95 (0-405-10910-5) Ayer.

— Obtaining Agreement on Standards in the Accounting Profession. (Studies in Accounting Research: Vol. 8). 93p. 1974. 12.00 (0-86539-020-7) Am Accounting.

Moonitz, Maurice & Brief, Richard P., eds. Three Contributions to the Development of Accounting Thought. LC 77-87315. (Development of Contemporary Accounting Thought Ser.). 1978. lib. bdg. 37.95 (0-405-10928-8) Ayer.

Moonitz, Maurice, jt. ed. see Zeff, Stephen A.

Moonlight, Rabbi. The Brand New Testament. LC 85-60482. (Illus.). 128p. 1985. pap. 4.95 (0-913483-04-4) Joydeism Pr.

Moonlitz, Maurice. Selected Writings of Maurice Moonlitz, 2 vols., Set. (Accounting History & Thought Ser.). 540p. 1990. reprint ed. text 35.00 (0-8240-3322-1) Garland.

Moonman, Eric. British Computers & Industrial Innovation: Implications of the Parliamentary Select Committee. 1971. pap. 22.00 (0-8464-0210-6) Beekman Pubs.

Moonman, Eric, ed. Violent Society. 168p. 1987. 35.00 (0-7146-3309-7, Pub. by F Cass Pubs); pap. 12.50 (0-7146-4055-7, Pub. by F Cass Pubs) Intl Spec Bk.

Moons, Anselm, jt. auth. see Walsh, Flavian.

Moor, Andrea M. The Boss's Boss. LC 95-39093. 244p. (Orig.). 1996. pap. 16.95 (0-945456-23-9) PT Pubns.

Moor, Andrew. Architectural Glass Art. LC 97-68145. (Illus.). 160p. 1998. 50.00 (0-8478-2073-4, Pub. by Rizzoli Intl) St Martin.

— Contemporary Stained Glass. 1996. 29.50 (1-85732-437-4, Pub. by Reed Illust Books) Antique Collect.

Moor, Bart de, see Moonen, Marc & De Moor, Bart, eds.

Moor, C. Fletcher Case: Account of the Descent & Relationships of the Late Christopher Fletcher F. Netherwasdale, Yeoman, & of His Will. (Illus.). 86p. 1997. reprint ed. pap. 16.50 (0-8328-8580-0); reprint ed. lib. bdg. 26.50 (0-8328-8579-7) Higginson Bk Co.

Moor, Christine H. From School to Work: Effective Counselling & Guidance. LC 74-31569. (Sage Studies in Social & Educational Change: Vol. 3). 192p. reprint ed. pap. 59.60 (0-608-11840-0, 202193400026) Bks Demand.

Moor, Douglas V., ed. see Leinfelder, Karl F. & Taylor, Duane F.

Moor, Ed de, see de Moor, Ed.

Moor, Edward. Hindu Pantheon. 29.95 (0-89314-409-6) Philos Res.

Moor, Fred B., et al. Manual of Hydrotherapy & Massage. LC 64-23214. 169p. 1964. 12.99 (0-8163-0023-2, 13160-7) Pacific Pr Pub Assn.

Moor, Gilbert. Rage. (Illus.). 304p. 1993. pap. 10.95 (0-88184-973-1) Carroll & Graf.

Moor, J. A. De, see Mommsen, W. J. & De Moor, J. A., eds.

Moor, J. A. De, see De Moor, J. A., ed.

Moor, J. C. De, see De Moor, J. C., ed.

Moor, J. H. Notices of the Indian Archipelago & Adjacent Countries. 398p. 1968. reprint ed. 85.00 (0-7146-2020-3, Pub. by F Cass Pubs) Intl Spec Bk.

Moor, James. An Essay on Historical Composition: Read, February, 6, 1752 (from Essays Read to a Literary Society) LC 92-25503. (Augustan Reprints Ser.: No. 187). 1978. reprint ed. 14.50 (0-404-70187-6, D13.M66) AMS Pr.

Moor, James, jt. ed. see Bynum, Terrell W.

Moor-Jankowski, J., ed. see Conference on Experimental Medicine & Surgery in P.

Moor-Jankowski, J., ed. see Conference on Marmosets in Experimental Medicine,.

Moor, Jo Ellen. Animals with Backbones: Grades 1-3. Evans, Marilyn, ed. (Science Works for Kids Ser.: Vol. 2). (Illus.). 80p. 1998. pap., teacher ed. 9.95 (1-55799-683-0, 854) Evan-Moor Edu Pubs.

— Animals Without Backbones: Grades 1-3. Evans, Marilyn, ed. (Science Works for Kids Ser.: Vol. 3). (Illus.). 80p. 1998. pap., teacher ed. 9.95 (1-55799-684-9, 855) Evan-Moor Edu Pubs.

— Energy: Heat, Light & Sound. Evans, Marilyn, ed. (Science Works for Kids Ser.: Vol. 9). (Illus.). 80p. 1998. pap., teacher ed. 9.95 (1-55799-690-3, 861) Evan-Moor Edu Pubs.

— Geology: Grades 1-3. Evans, Marilyn, ed. (Science Works for Kids Ser.: Vol. 5). (Illus.). 80p. 1998. pap., teacher ed. 9.95 (1-55799-686-5, 857) Evan-Moor Edu Pubs.

— Giant Science Resource Book: Grades 1-6. Evans, Marilyn, ed. (Illus.). 304p. 1998. pap., teacher ed. 24.95 (1-55799-696-2, 398) Evan-Moor Edu Pubs.

— Habitats: Grades 1-3. Evans, Marilyn, ed. (Science Works for Kids Ser.: Vol. 7). (Illus.). 80p. 1998. pap., teacher ed. 9.95 (1-55799-688-1, 859) Evan-Moor Edu Pubs.

— How Your Body Works: Grades 1-3. Evans, Marilyn, ed. (Science Works for Kids Ser.: Vol. 4). (Illus.). 80p. 1998. pap., teacher ed. 9.95 (1-55799-685-7, 856) Evan-Moor Edu Pubs.

— The Human Body: Grades 1-3. Evans, Marilyn, ed. (Science Picture Cards Ser.: Vol. 1). (Illus.). 24p. 1998. pap., teacher ed. 12.95 (1-55799-692-X, 863) Evan-Moor Edu Pubs.

— Life in the Ocean: Grades 1-3. Evans, Marilyn, ed. (Science Picture Cards Ser.: Vol. 3). (Illus.). 24p. 1998. pap., teacher ed. 12.95 (1-55799-694-6, 865) Evan-Moor Edu Pubs.

— Plants: Grades 1-3. Evans, Marilyn, ed. (Science Picture Cards Ser.: Vol. 2). (Illus.). 24p. 1998. pap., teacher ed. 12.95 (1-55799-693-8, 864) Evan-Moor Edu Pubs.

— Plants: Grades 1-3. Evans, Marilyn, ed. (Science Works for Kids Ser.: Vol. 6). (Illus.). 80p. 1998. pap., teacher ed. 9.95 (1-55799-687-3, 858) Evan-Moor Edu Pubs.

— Simple Machines: Grades 1-3. Evans, Marilyn, ed. (Science Works for Kids Ser.: Vol. 8). (Illus.). 80p. 1998. pap., teacher ed. 9.95 (1-55799-689-X, 860) Evan-Moor Edu Pubs.

— Water: Grades 1-3. Evans, Marilyn, ed. (Science Works for Kids Ser.: Vol. 10). (Illus.). 80p. (J). 1998. pap., teacher ed. 9.95 (1-55799-691-1, 862) Evan-Moor Edu Pubs.

Moor, Johannes C., jt. auth. see Korpel, Marjo C.

Moor, John, jt. ed. see Smith, Larry.

Moor, Keith. Crims in Grass Castles: The Trimbole Affair. 224p. (C). 1990. 45.00 (0-947087-17-6, Pub. by Pascoe Pub) St Mut.

Moor, Lise. Glossary of Psychiatry: Glossaire de Psychiatrie. (FRE.). 196p. 1986. 75.00 (0-8288-1819-3, M6417) Fr & Eur.

— Lexicon of Usual Terms in Psychiatry, Neuropsychiatry & Psychopathology. 3rd ed. (ENG, FRE & GER.). 236p. 1980. 49.95 (0-8288-0584-9, M 15383) Fr & Eur.

Moor, Margriet De, see De Moor, Margriet.

Moor, Paul, ed. see Morgenthaler, Fritz.

Moor, Robert De, see De Moor, Robert.

Moor, S. Fiddlesticks & Firestones. (Illus.). (J). 1996. mass mkt. 8.95 (0-340-66099-6, Pub. by Hodder & Stought Ltd) Trafalgar.

Mooradian, A., et al, eds. Tunable Lasers & Applications. (Optical Sciences Ser: Vol. 3). 1976. 46.95 (0-387-07968-8) Spr-Verlag.

Mooraj, Anwer, jt. ed. see Khuhro, Hamida.

Moorby, Edward. How to Succeed in Employee Development: Moving from Vision to Results. 2nd ed. LC 96-12284. (Training Ser.). 1996. pap. write for info. (0-07-709151-5) McGraw.

Moorby, Jeffrey. Transport Systems in Plants. LC 80-41374. (Integrated Themes in Biology Ser.). (Illus.). 175p. reprint ed. pap. 54.30 (0-8357-3573-7, 203450300090) Bks Demand.

Moorby, Philip R., jt. auth. see Thomas, D. E.

Moorby, Philip R., jt. auth. see Thomas, Donald E.

Moorcock, Michael. The Bane of the Black Sword. (Elric Saga). 160p. 1987. mass mkt. 4.99 (0-441-04885-4) Ace Bks.

— Behold the Man. (Illus.). 96p. 1996. 12.95 (1-885418-05-1) MOJO Pr.

— Blood: A Southern Fantasy. 1996. pap. 12.00 (0-614-20746-0, Avon Bks) Morrow Avon.

***Moorcock, Michael.** Blood: Souther Novl. 2000. 22.00 (0-380-97259-X) Morrow Avon.

Moorcock, Michael. Breakfast in the Ruins. 176p. 1980. pap. 3.50 (0-380-49148-6, Avon Bks) Morrow Avon.

— Breakfast in the Ruins. 1991. reprint ed. lib. bdg. 21.95 (1-56849-086-0) Buccaneer Bks.

— The Cornelius Chronicles, Vol. 1. 992p. 1977. mass mkt. 4.95 (0-380-00878-5, Avon Bks) Morrow Avon.

— The Cornelius Chronicles, Vol. II. 352p. 1986. pap. 3.50 (0-380-75003-1, Avon Bks) Morrow Avon.

— The Cornelius Chronicles, Vol. III. 352p. 1987. pap. 3.50 (0-380-70255-X, Avon Bks) Morrow Avon.

***Moorcock, Michael.** Corum: The Coming of Chaos. (Eternal Champion Ser.: Vol. 7). (Illus.). 400p. 1999. pap. 16.99 (1-56504-196-8, 12522) White Wolf.

Moorcock, Michael. Corum - The Coming of Chaos: The Eternal Champion, 3 bks. in 1. Vol. 7. (Illus.). 1997. 21.99 (1-56504-182-8, 12508, Borealis) White Wolf.

***Moorcock, Michael.** Count Brass. 2000. 24.99 (1-56504-987-X) White Wolf.

Moorcock, Michael. Crystal & the Amulet. (Illus.). 100p. (Orig.). 1981. pap. 12.95 (0-86130-044-0, Pub. by Savoy Bks) AK Pr Dist.

— The Dancers at the End of Time, Vol. 10. (Eternal Champion Ser.). 1998. reprint ed. 22.99 (1-56504-186-0, 12512, Borealis) White Wolf.

***Moorcock, Michael.** The Dreamthief's Daughter. 2001. write for info. (0-446-52618-5, Aspect) Warner Bks.

— Earl Aubec. (Eternal Champion Ser.). (Illus.). 1999. 24.99 (1-56504-986-1, 12498, Borealis) White Wolf.

Moorcock, Michael. Elric: Song of the Black Sword. (Eternal Champion Ser.: Vol. 5). (Illus.). 504p. 1995. 19.99 (1-56504-180-1, 12506, Borealis) White Wolf.

— Elric: Song of the Black Sword. (Eternal Champion Ser.: Vol. 6). 1997. reprint ed. pap. 14.99 (1-56504-195-X, 12521, Borealis) White Wolf.

— Elric: The Stealer of Souls. (Eternal Champion Ser.: Vol. 11). 1998. 22.99 (1-56504-187-9, 12513, Borealis) White Wolf.

— Elric at the End of Time. (Elric of Melnibone Ser.: Vol. 7). 224p. 1985. pap. 4.50 (0-88677-228-1, Pub. by DAW Bks) Penguin Putnam.

— Elric of Melnibone. (Elric Saga: Bk. 1). 1987. mass mkt. 5.50 (0-441-20398-1) Ace Bks.

— Elric of Melnibone: Weird of the White Wolf, No. 31. deluxe limited ed. Fitch, Laurel & Friederich, Michael, eds. (Illus.). 140p. 1991. 39.95 (0-936211-29-6) Graphitti Designs.

— The Eternal Champion. (Eternal Champion Ser.: Vol. 1). (Illus.). 1996. pap. text 14.99 (1-56504-191-7, Borealis) White Wolf.

***Moorcock, Michael.** The Eternal Champion: Legends from the End of Time. (Eternal Champion Ser.: No. 13). (Illus.). 1999. 24.99 (1-56504-189-5, 12515) White Wolf.

— The Eternal Champion: Prince with the Silver Hand. (Eternal Champion Ser.: No. 8). (Illus.). 1999. reprint ed. 24.99 (1-56504-188-7, 12514, Borealis) White Wolf.

Moorcock, Michael. Fabulous Harbors. 1997. 24.00 (0-614-20651-0, Avon Bks) Morrow Avon.

— Hawkmoon: The Eternal Champion, Vol. 3. 1996. pap. text 14.99 (1-56504-193-3, Borealis) White Wolf.

***Moorcock, Michael.** Kane of Old Mars. (Eternal Champion Ser.). 2000. pap. 16.99 (1-56504-988-8) White Wolf.

— Kane of Old Mars: The Eternal Champion, Vol. 9. 1998. 22.99 (1-56504-184-4, Borealis) White Wolf.

Moorcock, Michael. The Land Leviathan. 19.95 (0-89190-153-1) Amereon Ltd.

— Lunching with the AntiChrist: A Family History. 1994. 25.00 (0-929480-46-5) Mark Ziesing.

— Lunching with the AntiChrist: A Family History. limited ed. 1994. 60.00 (0-929480-47-3) Mark Ziesing.

— Michael Moorcock's Multiverse. (Illus.). 288p. 1999. pap. text 19.95 (1-56389-516-1, Pub. by DC Comics) Time Warner.

— A Nomad of the Time Streams Vol. 4: The Eternal Champion, 3 bks. in 1. Vol. 4. (Illus.). 1997. pap. 14.99 (1-56504-194-1, 12520, Borealis) White Wolf.

— The Revenge of the Rose. 256p. 1994. mass mkt. 5.99 (0-441-00106-8) Ace Bks.

— The Roads Between the Worlds: The Eternal Champion, Vol. 6. (Illus.). 1996. 21.99 (1-56504-181-X, 12507, Borealis) White Wolf.

— The Roads Between Worlds. (Eternal Champion Ser.: Vol. 6). 1998. reprint ed. pap. 14.99 (1-56504-197-6, 12543, Borealis) White Wolf.

— Sailing to Utopia. (The Eternal Champion: Vol. 8). (Illus.). 1997. 21.99 (1-56504-183-6, 12509, Borealis) White Wolf.

— The Sailor on the Seas of Fate. (Elric Saga: Bk. 2). 1987. mass mkt. 5.50 (0-441-74863-5) Ace Bks.

— Sojan. 160p. (Orig.). 1980. pap. 11.95 (0-86130-000-9, Pub. by Savoy Bks) AK Pr Dist.

— Stormbringer. 1987. pap. 4.99 (0-441-78754-1) Ace Bks.

— Tales from the Texas Woods. 170p. 1997. 20.95 (1-885418-17-5) MOJO Pr.

— The Vanishing Tower. 176p. 1987. mass mkt. 5.99 (0-441-86039-7) Ace Bks.

— Von Bek Vol. 2: The Eternal Champion, 15 vols., Set. (Eternal Champion Ser.). (Illus.). 600p. 1996. reprint ed. pap. 14.99 (1-56504-192-5, 12518, Borealis) White Wolf.

— The War Against the Angels. 304p. 1998. pap. 12.50 (0-380-78079-8, Avon Bks) Morrow Avon.

— The War Amongst the Angels: An Autobiographical Story. LC 97-28609. 304p. 1997. mass mkt. 24.00 (0-380-97597-1, Avon Bks) Morrow Avon.

— The War Hound & the World's Pain: A Fable. LC 81-9030. 239p. 1981. 25.00 (0-671-43708-9) Ultramarine Pub.

— The Weird of the White Wolf. (Elric Saga: Bk. 3). 1988. mass mkt. 5.50 (0-441-88805-4) Ace Bks.

Moorcock, Michael, ed. England Invaded: A Collection of Fantasy Fiction. LC 78-300443. 245 p. (J). 1977. 4.95 (0-491-02191-7) Virgin Bks.

Moorcock, Michael, jt. auth. see Cawthorne, James.

Moorcock, Michael, jt. auth. see Thomas, Roy.

Moorcock, Michael, ed. see Wells, H. G.

Moorcraft, Paul L. African Nemesis: War & Revolution in Southern Africa, 1945-2010. (Illus.). 549p. 1994. pap. 25.00 (1-85753-140-X, Pub. by Brasseys) Brasseys.

Moorcroft, Christine. The Taj Mahal. LC 97-15619. (Great Buildings Ser.). 48p. (J). (gr. 5 up). 1998. 25.69 (0-8172-4920-6) Raintree Steck-V.

Moorcroft, Sheila M., ed. Visions for the Twenty-First Century. LC 92-35824. (Praeger Studies on the 21st Century). 1993. 59.95 (0-275-94571-5, C4571, Praeger Pubs) Greenwood.

— Visions for the Twenty-First Century. LC 92-35824. (Praeger Studies on the 21st Century). 1993. pap. 17.95 (0-275-94572-3, B4572, Praeger Pubs) Greenwood.

***Moorcroft, Walter.** Walter Moorcroft Memories of Life & Living. 1999. 45.00 (0-903685-71-X) R Dennis.

Moorcroft, William H. Sleep, Dreaming, & Sleep Disorders: An Introduction. 2nd ed. 508p. (Orig.). (C). 1993. pap. text 39.50 (0-8191-9251-1); lib. bdg. 64.50 (0-8191-9250-3) U Pr of Amer.

Moore. Ancestor's Footsteps. (Indian Culture Ser.). (Illus.). 40p. (J). (gr. 6-9). 1978. pap. 4.95 (0-89992-073-X) Coun India Ed.

— Animal Life Cycles: Mammals & . . . (Illus.). 16p. (J). (gr. 1-3). 1987. pap., teacher ed. 5.95 (1-55799-103-0, 813) Evan-Moor Edu Pubs.

— Animals Head to Toe. (Illus.). 64p. (J). (gr. k-2). 1997. pap., teacher ed. 11.95 (1-55799-635-0, 646) Evan-Moor Edu Pubs.

***Moore.** Basic Practice of Statistics. 2nd ed. 1999. pap. text, student ed. 22.95 (0-7167-3617-9) W H Freeman.

— Basic Practice of Statistics. 2nd ed. 1999. pap. text, student ed. 19.95 (0-7167-3610-1) W H Freeman.

— Basic Practice of Statistics: Excel. 2nd ed. 1999. pap. text 19.95 (0-7167-3611-X) W H Freeman.

— Basic Practice of Statistics: Minitab Manual. 2nd ed. 1999. pap. text 25.95 (0-7167-3613-6) W H Freeman.

— Basic Practice of Statistics: Telecourse. 2nd ed. 1999. pap. text, student ed. 18.95 (0-7167-3819-8) W H Freeman.

— Basic Practice of Statistics: TI-83 Guide. 2nd ed. 1999. pap. text, student ed. 19.95 (0-7167-3614-4) W H Freeman.

Moore. Basic Practice of Statitics. 1997. 68.00 (0-7167-3368-4) W H Freeman.

— Beginning Map Skills. (Illus.). 32p. (J). (gr. k-1). 1996. pap., teacher ed. 2.95 (1-55799-528-1, 4130) Evan-Moor Edu Pubs.

— Biology. Date not set. 55.74 (0-697-29253-3) McGraw.

— Botany. 2nd ed. 144p. 1997. student ed., spiral bd. 25.31 (0-697-28631-2) McGraw.

— Botany Sampler. 1997. 12.00 (0-697-42291-7, WCB McGr Hill) McGrw-H Hghr Educ.

***Moore.** Brian Moore - Autobiography. 2000. 29.95 (1-85225-234-0, Pub. by Transworld Publishers Ltd) Trafalgar.

— Brian Moore Autobiography. 2000. pap. 12.95 (0-552-14484-3, Pub. by Transworld Publishers Ltd) Trafalgar.

Moore. Build Spelling Skills. (Illus.). 160p. (J). (gr. 1-2). 1998. pap., teacher ed. 16.95 (1-55799-652-0, 725) Evan-Moor Edu Pubs.

— Build Spelling Skills. (Illus.). 160p. (J). (gr. 3-4). 1998. pap., teacher ed. 16.95 (1-55799-653-9, 726) Evan-Moor Edu Pubs.

— Build Spelling Skills. (Illus.). 160p. (J). (gr. 5-6). 1998. pap., teacher ed. 16.95 (1-55799-654-7, 727) Evan-Moor Edu Pubs.

***Moore.** Building Scientific Apparatus. 3rd ed. 2000. pap. 25.00 (0-7382-0335-1, Pub. by Perseus Pubng) HarpC.

Moore. Changes in Nature. (Illus.). 64p. (J). (gr. k-2). 1997. pap., teacher ed. 11.95 (1-55799-631-8, 642) Evan-Moor Edu Pubs.

— The Chemical World. 2nd ed. (C). 1997. 441.50 (0-03-024381-5) Harcourt.

— The Chemical World. 2nd ed. (C). 1996. pap. text, teacher ed. 28.00 (0-03-024378-5) Harcourt Coll Pubs.

— The Chemical World. 2nd ed. (C). 1997. pap. text 10.50 (0-03-024376-9); pap. text 14.75 (0-03-024377-7) Harcourt Coll Pubs.

— The Chemical World. 2nd ed. (C). 1997. pap. text 31.00 (0-03-024379-3, Pub. by Harcourt Coll Pubs) Harcourt.

— The Chemical World. 2nd ed. LC 97-205592. (Illus.). 906p. (C). 1997. text 100.00 (0-03-019094-0, Pub. by SCP) Harcourt.

— The Chemical World. 2nd ed. 160p. (C). 1997. pap. text, student ed. 34.00 (0-03-024374-2, Pub. by SCP) Harcourt.

— Classic & Modern Readings. (C). 1995. pap. text 23.50 (0-03-097108-X, Pub. by Harcourt Coll Pubs) Harcourt.

— Clinical Educator Role. 1996. pap. text 60.00 (0-443-05300-6, W B Saunders Co) Harcrt Hlth Sci Grp.

— Coal Mining Women. 1996. 15.95 (0-8057-9239-2, Hall Reference) Macmillan.

***Moore.** Conservative Laws: Unit C. LC 98-196493. 240p. 1998. pap. 17.50 (0-07-043049-7) McGrw-H Hghr Educ.

Moore. Daily Language Review 5. (Illus.). 112p. (J). (gr. 5-6). 1998. pap., teacher ed. 14.95 (1-55799-659-8, 583) Evan-Moor Edu Pubs.

— Daily Language Review 2. (Illus.). 112p. (J). (gr. 2-3). 1998. pap., teacher ed. 14.95 (1-55799-656-3, 580) Evan-Moor Edu Pubs.

— Data Disk for Basic Practice of Statistics. (C). 1994. pap. text 16.00 (0-7167-2732-3) W H Freeman.

— Data Sets for Moore/BPS & Greenberg/Minitab Guide for BPS. (C). 1995. 16.00 (0-7167-2924-5) W H Freeman.

***Moore.** Dependent Gene: How All Traits Develop Through Gene Environment. 2000. pap. text. write for info. (0-7167-4024-9) W H Freeman.

Moore. The Developing Human: Clinical. 6th ed. (C). 1998. text. write for info. (0-8089-2101-0, Grune & Strat) Harcrt Hlth Sci Grp.

— The Developing Human: International Edition. 6th ed. (C). 1998. pap. text 33.00 (0-8089-2064-2, Grune & Strat) Harcrt Hlth Sci Grp.

— Discovering Universe. 4th ed. (C). 2000. pap. text, teacher ed. 16.00 (0-7167-2755-2) W H Freeman.

— The Discovery Process. (C). 1998. text 28.95 (0-8273-8088-7); pap. text, teacher ed. 12.95 (0-8273-8089-5) Delmar.

— Electromagnetic Fields: Unit E. 1998. 13.50 (0-07-043054-3) McGraw.

— Environmental Control Systems. 1993. teacher ed. 21.25 (0-07-042890-5) McGraw.

— Grammar & Punctuation. (Illus.). 88p. (J). (gr. 3-4). 1997. pap., teacher ed. 14.95 (1-55799-599-0, 480) Evan-Moor Edu Pubs.

— Grammar & Punctuation. (Illus.). 88p. (J). (gr. 5-6). 1997. pap., teacher ed. 14.95 (1-55799-600-8, 481) Evan-Moor Edu Pubs.

— Holiday Art Projects. (Illus.). 80p. (J). (gr. 1-6). 1997. pap., teacher ed. 7.95 (1-55799-622-9, 722) Evan-Moor Edu Pubs.

— IBM Basic Statistics. 1995. 48.00 (0-7167-2678-5) W H Freeman.

***Moore.** Industrial Explosion Protection Systems. 2000. 125.00 (0-7506-1179-0) Buttrwrth-Heinemann.

An Asterisk (*) at the beginning of an entry indicates that the title is appearing for the first time.

Moore. International Light, Shape & Sound Signals. 2nd ed. 140p. 1982. 52.95 (*0-7506-1699-7*) Buttrwrth-Heinemann.
— Introduction & Practice of Statstic. 3rd ed. 1998. 80.00 incl. cd-rom (*0-7167-3407-9*) W H Freeman.
— Introduction to Basic Statistics. 1997. pap. text, teacher ed. 24.00 (*0-7167-2676-9*) W H Freeman.
— Introduction to Practice Statistic. 3rd ed. 1998. 71.00 incl. audio compact disk (*0-7167-3458-3*) W H Freeman.
***Moore.** Introduction to the Practice of Statistics. 2000. pap. text. write for info. (*0-7167-3913-5*) W H Freeman.
Moore. IPS & Data Sets. 2nd ed. (C). 1993. text 64.00 (*0-7167-2493-6*) W H Freeman.
— Irreversal Process: Unit T. 1998. 13.50 (*0-07-043056-X*) McGraw.
Moore. Lads in Action. 192p. 1994. pap. 24.95 (*1-85742-204-X*) Ashgate Pub Co.
Moore. Laws, Physics & the Universe: Unit N. 1998. 13.50 (*0-07-043055-1*) McGraw.
— Lethal Medicine: The Story of America's Worst Drug Disaster. 1995. 23.00 (*0-671-87016-5*) S&S Trade.
— Live With It. LC 94-163018. 641p. 1994. pap. 10.95 (*0-921368-39-9*) Blizzard Publ.
— Mac Basic Statistics. 1995. 48.00 (*0-7167-2679-3*) W H Freeman.
— Mass Communication Law & Ethics. Bryant, Jennings & Zillmann, Dolf, eds. (Communication Ser.). 64p. 1994. teacher ed. write for info. (*0-8058-1460-4*) L Erlbaum Assocs.
— The Night Before Christmas. LC 98-15890. 32p. (J). 1999. 16.00 (*0-15-201713-5*, Harcourt Child Bks) Harcourt.
— The Night Before Christmas. LC 97-40335. (Illus.). 32p. (J). (ps-k). 1998. lib. bdg. 13.49 (*0-7868-2252-X*, Pub. by Hyperion) Time Warner.
— Nutrion Care. 4th ed. 2000. write for info. (*0-323-00843-7*) Mosby Inc.
— Oceanography: Ocean Environment. (C). 1997. pap. text, teacher ed. 12.00 (*0-03-097379-1*) Harcourt Coll Pubs.
— Oceanography: Ocean Environment. (C). 1999. text 61.50 (*0-03-097346-5*) Harcourt Coll Pubs.
— Oht-oceanography:ocean Environments&proc. (C). 1997. pap. text 201.00 (*0-03-097380-5*) Harcourt.
— Options in Corporate Finance. 2nd ed. 1998. 23.00 (*0-07-232707-3*) McGraw.
— Paper Crafts. (Illus.). 80p. (J). (gr. 1-6). 1997. pap., teacher ed. 7.95 (*1-55799-623-7*, 723) Evan-Moor Edu Pubs.
— Patterns of Inductive Reasoning: Developing Critical Thinking Skills. 4th ed. 302p. 1997. per. 22.95 (*0-7872-4408-2*) Kendall-Hunt.
— PDQ Embryology. 1986. 27.95 (*0-8016-3533-0*) Mosby Inc.
— Planetary Adventures. Sellers, Jance, ed. 1999. per. 15.00 (*0-671-04007-3*, Pocket Books) PB.
— The Planets. (Illus.). 16p. (J). (gr. 1-3). 1987. pap., teacher ed. 5.95 (*1-55799-102-2*, 812) Evan-Moor Edu Pubs.
***Moore.** Practice of Clinical Neuropsychiatry & Behavioural Neurology. (Illus.). 450p. 2001. 100.00 (*0-7506-4940-2*) Buttrwrth-Heinemann.
Moore. Printed Test Bank Basic Statistics. 1995. pap. text 24.00 (*0-7167-2677-7*) W H Freeman.
— Read & Understand Stories & Activities. (Illus.). 144p. (J). (gr. 2-3). 1997. pap., teacher ed. 12.95 (*1-55799-628-8*, 639) Evan-Moor Edu Pubs.
— Read & Understand Stories & Activities. (Illus.). 144p. (J). (gr. 3-4). 1997. pap., teacher ed. 12.95 (*1-55799-629-6*, 640) Evan-Moor Edu Pubs.
— Reviewing 3rd Grade (Math) (Illus.). 32p. (J). (gr. 3-4). 1997. pap., teacher ed. 2.95 (*1-55799-485-4*, 4087) Evan-Moor Edu Pubs.
— Science Stories, Vol. 3. (Illus.). 64p. (J). (gr. k-2). 1997. pap., teacher ed. 11.95 (*1-55799-630-X*, 641) Evan-Moor Edu Pubs.
— Secondary Instructional Met. 1993. teacher ed. 10.93 (*0-697-20982-2*, WCB McGr Hill) McGrw-H Hghr Educ.
— Separation & Divorce. 1984. pap. 2.00 (*0-86683-844-9*) Harper SF.
— Sequencing. (Illus.). 112p. (J). (ps-1). 1998. pap., teacher ed. 14.95 (*1-55799-662-8*, 737) Evan-Moor Edu Pubs.
Moore. Shooting Stars. (*0-393-02463-6*) Norton.
Moore. Six Ideas in Physics. 1997. text 76.50 (*0-07-561355-7*) McGraw.
— Six Ideas That Shaped Physics. 2nd ed. 2001. 76.50 (*0-07-229152-4*) McGraw.
— Sport Activity: Golf. 2nd ed. 2001. pap. 10.30 (*0-07-235402-X*) McGraw.
— Star Trek: The Next Generation Role Playing Game. 1998. 35.00 (*0-671-04000-6*) S&S Trade.
Moore. Steelmaking 2nd Edition. 1991. 32.00 (*0-901462-70-5*) Institute of Management Consultants.
Moore. Telephone Communications. (General Business & Business Education Ser.). 1995. teacher ed. 10.00 (*0-8273-6359-1*); pap. 18.60 (*0-8273-6358-3*) Delmar.
— Texas Instruments Graphing Calculator. (C). pap., suppl. ed. 18.95 (*0-7167-2923-7*) W H Freeman.
Moore. Trying for a Baby. 1996. pap. 12.95 (*0-7459-3421-8*, Pub. by Lion Pubng) Trafalgar.
Moore. Underground. 1995. 24.95 (*0-8057-9113-2*, Twyne) Mac Lib Ref.
***Moore.** While You Were Chasing a Hat. LC 99-60913. 24p. (J). (ps up). 2001. 9.95 (*0-694-01342-0*) HarpC Child Bks.
Moore. Writing about Biology. (C). 1992. pap. text, teacher ed. 34.00 (*0-03-093237-8*) Harcourt Coll Pubs.
— Writing to Learn Science. 2nd ed. (C). 1995. pap. text, teacher ed. 6.75 (*0-03-097927-7*) Harcourt Coll Pubs.
Moore, ed. Carbonate Rock Sequences from the Cretaceous of Texas, No. T376. (IGC Field Trip Guidebooks Ser.). 56p. 1989. 13.00 (*0-87590-656-7*) Am Geophysical.
Moore & Alder. Family & Medical Leave: Federal & State Regulations. 1995. ring bd. 80.00 (*0-327-03971-X*, 60443-10, MICHIE) LEXIS Pub.
Moore & Arntson. PageMaker 4 for MAC Concepts & Applications Desktop. (DF - Computer Applications Ser.). (C). mass mkt. 34.95 (*0-538-70609-0*) S-W Pub.
Moore & Behnke. Athletic Training. 2nd ed. 1999. pap. text 30.00 (*0-697-29499-4*) McGraw.
Moore & Davis. All about Plants. (Illus.). 32p. (J). (ps-1). 1996. pap., teacher ed. 2.95 (*1-55799-490-0*, 4092) Evan-Moor Edu Pubs.
— Homes Near & Far. (Illus.). 48p. (J). (gr. 1-3). 1996. pap., teacher ed. 9.95 (*1-55799-564-8*, 550) Evan-Moor Edu Pubs.
Moore & Evans. Animal Life Cycles: Birds . . . (Illus.). 16p. (J). (gr. 1-3). 1994. pap., teacher ed. 5.95 (*1-55799-093-X*, 803) Evan-Moor Edu Pubs.
— Be a Backyard Scientist. (Illus.). 32p. (J). (ps-1). 1996. pap., teacher ed. 2.95 (*1-55799-496-X*, 4098) Evan-Moor Edu Pubs.
— My Five Senses. (Illus.). 16p. (J). (gr. 1-3). 1994. pap., teacher ed. 5.95 (*1-55799-094-8*, 804) Evan-Moor Edu Pubs.
— Plants. (Illus.). 16p. (J). (gr. 1-3). 1986. pap., teacher ed. 5.95 (*1-55799-091-3*, 801) Evan-Moor Edu Pubs.
— Reptiles & Amphibians. (Illus.). 32p. (J). (gr. 2-3). 1996. pap., teacher ed. 2.95 (*1-55799-503-6*, 4105) Evan-Moor Edu Pubs.
— Water. (Illus.). 16p. (J). (gr. 1-3). 1994. pap., teacher ed. 5.95 (*1-55799-095-6*, 805) Evan-Moor Edu Pubs.
***Moore & Hungr.** Engineering Geology & the Environment, Vol. 1. 1998. 90.00 (*90-5410-991-2*) Ashgate Pub Co.
— Engineering Geology & the Environment, Vol. 2. 1998. 90.00 (*90-5410-992-0*) Ashgate Pub Co.
— Engineering Geology & the Environment, Vol. 3. 1998. 90.00 (*90-5410-993-9*) Ashgate Pub Co.
— Engineering Geology & the Environment, Vol. 4. 1998. 90.00 (*90-5410-994-7*) Ashgate Pub Co.
— Engineering Geology & the Environment, Vol. 5. 1998. 90.00 (*90-5410-995-5*) Ashgate Pub Co.
— Engineering Geology & the Environment, Vol. 6. 90.00 (*90-5410-996-3*) Ashgate Pub Co.
Moore & Jepson. Birds. (Illus.). 32p. (J). (gr. 2-3). 1996. pap., teacher ed. 2.95 (*1-55799-504-4*, 4106) Evan-Moor Edu Pubs.
— Dinosaurs. (Illus.). 32p. (J). (gr. 2-3). 1996. pap., teacher ed. 2.95 (*1-55799-500-1*, 4102) Evan-Moor Edu Pubs.
— Fish & Other Water Animals. (Illus.). 32p. (J). (gr. 2-3). 1996. pap., teacher ed. 2.95 (*1-55799-505-2*, 4107) Evan-Moor Edu Pubs.
— Mammals. (Illus.). 32p. (J). (gr. 2-3). 1996. pap., teacher ed. 2.95 (*1-55799-506-0*, 4108) Evan-Moor Edu Pubs.
— Our Solar System. (Illus.). 32p. (J). (gr. 2-3). 1996. pap., teacher ed. 2.95 (*1-55799-510-9*, 4112) Evan-Moor Edu Pubs.
***Moore & McCabe.** Introduction to the Practice of Statistics. 1998. pap. text, teacher ed. 19.95 (*0-7167-3402-8*, Pub. by W H Freeman) VHPS.
Moore & McCabe. Introduction to the Practice of Statistics. 2nd ed. 896p. (C). 1993. 56.00 (*0-7167-2505-3*) W H Freeman.
***Moore & McCabe.** Introduction to the Practice of Statistics. 3rd ed. 1999. pap. text, student ed. 19.95 (*0-7167-3657-8*, Pub. by W H Freeman) VHPS.
— Introduction to the Practice of Statistics. 3rd ed. 2000. pap. text 19.95 (*0-7167-4003-6*) W H Freeman.
— Introduction to the Practice of Statistics Minitab Guide. 2nd ed. 1992. pap. text 22.95 (*0-7167-2483-9*, Pub. by W H Freeman) VHPS.
— Introduction to the Practice of Statistics Spss Guide. 3rd ed. 1998. pap. text 19.95 (*0-7167-3399-4*, Pub. by W H Freeman) VHPS.
Moore & McCabe. Statistics. (C). 1992. text 8.80 (*0-7167-2450-2*) W H Freeman.
Moore & McMahon. All about Animals. (Illus.). 32p. (J). (ps-1). 1996. pap., teacher ed. 2.95 (*1-55799-491-9*, 4093) Evan-Moor Edu Pubs.
— Animal Homes. (Illus.). 32p. (J). (ps-1). 1996. pap., teacher ed. 2.95 (*1-55799-492-7*, 4094) Evan-Moor Edu Pubs.
— Animals Without Backbones. (Illus.). 32p. (J). (gr. 2-3). 1996. pap., teacher ed. 2.95 (*1-55799-507-9*, 4109) Evan-Moor Edu Pubs.
— Kitchen Chemistry. (Illus.). 32p. (J). (gr. 2-3). 1996. pap., teacher ed. 2.95 (*1-55799-511-7*, 4113) Evan-Moor Edu Pubs.
— Science Experiments at Home. (Illus.). 32p. (J). (ps-1). 1996. pap., teacher ed. 2.95 (*1-55799-495-1*, 4097) Evan-Moor Edu Pubs.
Moore & Morgan. Jumbo Fun with the Alphabet. 2nd ed. (Illus.). 304p. (J). (ps-1). 1997. pap., teacher ed. 24.95 (*1-55799-603-2*, 774) Evan-Moor Edu Pubs.
Moore & Norris. Real Math for Young Learners. (Illus.). 112p. (J). (ps-1). 1998. pap., teacher ed. 14.95 (*1-55799-669-5*, 744) Evan-Moor Edu Pubs.
Moore & Robison. Animal Life Cycles. (Illus.). 32p. (J). (gr. 2-3). 1996. pap., teacher ed. 2.95 (*1-55799-501-X*, 4103) Evan-Moor Edu Pubs.
— Habitats. (Illus.). 32p. (J). (gr. 2-3). 1996. pap., teacher ed. 2.95 (*1-55799-508-7*, 4110) Evan-Moor Edu Pubs.
— The World of Plants. (Illus.). 32p. (J). (gr. 2-3). 1996. pap., teacher ed. 2.95 (*1-55799-502-8*, 4104) Evan-Moor Edu Pubs.
Moore & Shipman. Bats. (Illus.). 48p. (J). (gr. 1-3). 1995. pap., teacher ed. 9.95 (*1-55799-385-8*, 535) Evan-Moor Edu Pubs.
— Bread Around the World. (Illus.). 48p. (J). (gr. 1-3). 1995. pap., teacher ed. 9.95 (*1-55799-388-2*, 539) Evan-Moor Edu Pubs.
— How to Write Simple Science Reports. (Illus.). 128p. (J). (gr. 1-4). 1995. pap., teacher ed. 12.95 (*1-55799-379-3*, 395) Evan-Moor Edu Pubs.
Moore & Supancich. All about My Body. (Illus.). 32p. (J). (ps-1). 1996. pap., teacher ed. 2.95 (*1-55799-489-7*, 4091) Evan-Moor Edu Pubs.
— Beginning Maps & Globes. (Illus.). 32p. (J). (gr. 1-3). 1996. pap., teacher ed. 2.95 (*1-55799-532-X*, 4134) Evan-Moor Edu Pubs.
— How Your Body Works. (Illus.). 32p. (J). (gr. 2-3). Date not set. pap., teacher ed. 2.95 (*1-55799-499-4*, 4101) Evan-Moor Edu Pubs.
— Science Fun. (Illus.). 32p. (J). (gr. 2-3). 1997. pap., teacher ed. 2.95 (*1-55799-515-X*, 4117) Evan-Moor Edu Pubs.
Moore & Tryon. Sun, Moon & Stars. (Illus.). 16p. (J). (gr. 1-3). 1986. pap., teacher ed. 5.95 (*1-55799-096-4*, 806) Evan-Moor Edu Pubs.
Moore & Vodopich, Darrell S. General Biology. 424p. 1991. spiral bd., lab manual ed. 21.95 (*0-8016-4486-0*) Mosby Inc.
Moore & Winters. Ghost Watchers. (Illus.). (J). 1997. mass mkt. 7.95 (*0-340-68980-3*, Pub. by Hodder & Stought Ltd) Trafalgar.
Moore & Yaqub, Adil M. Linear Algebra: A Student's Solution Manual. (C). 1992. pap. text 18.00 (*0-673-46288-9*) Addson-Wesley Educ.
Moore, et al. Botany. 1995. teacher ed. 38.75 (*0-697-12162-3*) McGraw.
— Botany. 1995. lab manual ed. 11.25 (*0-697-26069-0*) McGraw.
— Giant Write Every Day. (Illus.). 176p. (J). (gr. 1-6). 1997. pap., teacher ed. 14.95 (*1-55799-604-0*, 775) Evan-Moor Edu Pubs.
— Labman - Botany. 2nd ed. 1997. pap., lab manual ed. 15.31 (*0-697-28629-0*) McGraw.
— Pockets & Pouches. (Illus.). 48p. (J). (ps-1). 1995. pap., teacher ed. 9.95 (*1-55799-391-2*, 543) Evan-Moor Edu Pubs.
***Moore, et al.** Practice of Business Statistics. 2001. pap. text. write for info. (*0-7167-4111-3*, Pub. by W H Freeman) VHPS.
Moore, et al. Researching Disability Issues. (Disability, Human Rights, & Society Ser.). 192p. 1997. 85.00 (*0-335-19804-X*); pap. 26.95 (*0-335-19803-1*) OpUniv Pr.
— Simple Science Experiments. (Illus.). 32p. (J). (gr. 2-3). 1996. pap., teacher ed. 2.95 (*1-55799-514-1*, 4116) Evan-Moor Edu Pubs.
— What Happens Next? (Science) (Illus.). 32p. (J). (ps-1). 1996. pap., teacher ed. 2.95 (*1-55799-497-8*, 4099) Evan-Moor Edu Pubs.
Moore, jt. auth. see Alder.
Moore, jt. auth. see Brown.
Moore, jt. auth. see Center.
Moore, jt. auth. see Coveney.
Moore, jt. auth. see Davidson.
Moore, jt. auth. see Jolly, Peggy B.
Moore, jt. auth. see Mankin, Ian.
Moore, jt. auth. see Mattox.
Moore, jt. auth. see Morgan.
Moore, jt. auth. see Mosley.
Moore, jt. auth. see Seidman.
Moore, jt. auth. see Sparkes.
Moore, jt. auth. see Vodopich, Darrell S.
***Moore, Karen A.** Babies of the Bible. LC 99-38650. 1999. pap. 6.99 (*0-7814-3351-7*, Chariot Bks) Chariot Victor.
Moore, A. Questions & Answers on Ballroom Dancing. (Ballroom Dance Ser.). 1984. lib. bdg. 79.95 (*0-87700-511-7*) Revisionist Pr.
Moore, A., jt. auth. see Ball, J.
Moore, A. L. Moore Family History, 1599-1962. 42p. 1994. reprint ed. pap. 8.50 (*0-8328-4127-7*) Higginson Bk Co.
Moore, A. Leroy. Adventism in Conflict. LC 95-30879. 1995. pap. 10.99 (*0-8280-1033-1*) Review & Herald.
Moore, A. M. T., et al. Village on the Euphrates: The Excavation of Abu Hureyra. (Illus.). 512p. 2000. pap. 35.00 (*0-19-510807-8*); text 60.00 (*0-19-510806-X*) OUP.
Moore, A. Tuell & Gibson, H. M. ADF: Automatic Direction Finding Computer Instruction Manual. (ENG & SPA.). 1984. teacher ed. 3.50 (*0-317-91368-9*) MAG Mfg.
— ADF: Automatic Direction Finding Computer Instruction Manual. rev. ed. (ENG & SPA.). 1984. reprint ed. 5.85 (*0-317-91367-0*); reprint ed. 3.95 (*0-317-91369-7*) MAG Mfg.
Moore, A. W. A History of the Isle of Man, 2 vols. 1977. 75.00 (*0-89979-020-8*) British Am Bks.
— The Infinite. (Problems of Philosophy Series: Their Past & Present). 288p. (C). 1991. pap. 24.99 (*0-415-07048-1*, A6254) Routledge.
Moore, A. W. Points of View. LC 97-200685. (Illus.). 328p. (C). 1997. text 35.00 (*0-19-823692-1*) OUP.
***Moore, A. W.** Points of View. 2000. pap. 19.95 (*0-19-825062-2*) OUP.
Moore, A. W., ed. Meaning & Reference. LC 92-27073. (Oxford Readings in Philosophy Ser.). (Illus.). 308p. 1993. pap. text 22.00 (*0-19-875125-7*) OUP.
Moore, Aaron. Carpentry Toolmaking: An Instructor's Guide. 208p. 1993. pap., teacher ed. 29.50 (*1-85339-196-4*, Pub. by Intermed Tech) Stylus Pub VA.
***Moore, Aaron & Sithole, Musaemura.** How to Make Carpentry Tools: An Illustrated Manual. 2nd ed. (Illus.). 240p. 1998. pap. 27.00 (*1-85339-406-8*, Pub. by Intermed Tech) Stylus Pub VA.
Moore, Adam. Broken Arrow Boy. Thatch, Nancy R., ed. LC 90-5933. (Books for Students by Students). (Illus.). 26p. (J). (gr. 3-8). 1990. lib. bdg. 15.95 (*0-933849-24-9*) Landmark Edns.
Moore, Adam C. Song from the Starting Tree. 48p. 1986. 20.00 (*0-7223-2034-5*, Pub. by A H S Ltd) St Mut.
Moore, Adam D., ed. Intellectual Property: Moral, Legal, & International Dilemmas. LC 96-46626. (Philosophy & the Global Context Ser.: No. 106). 352p. 1997. 71.00 (*0-8476-8426-1*); pap. 26.95 (*0-8476-8427-X*) Rowman.
Moore, Addison W. The Functional Versus the Representational Theories of Knowledge in Locke's Essay. LC 75-3629. reprint ed. 24.50 (*0-404-59002-0*) AMS Pr.
Moore, Adrian, ed. Infinity. (International Research Library of Philosophy). 480p. 1993. 163.95 (*1-85521-260-9*, Pub. by Dartmth Pub) Ashgate Pub Co.
Moore, Adrian D., jt. auth. see Ball, John.
***Moore, Adrian T., ed.** Privatization '98: 12th Annual Report on Privatization. (Illus.). 61p. (C). 1999. pap. text 20.00 (*0-7881-7882-2*) DIANE Pub.
Moore, Alan. Batman: The Killing Joke. O'Neil, Dennis, ed. 48p. 1995. mass mkt. 4.95 (*0-930289-45-5*, Pub. by Warner Bks) Little.
— Brief Biology (combined Majors) 1998. 59.00 (*0-07-027497-5*) McGraw.
— Butterworths Ireland Vat Acts, 1993-94. 1993. pap. text 99.00 (*1-85475-636-2*, IE, MICHIE) LEXIS Pub.
— From Hell, Vol. 1. Amara, Philip, ed. (Illus.). 64p. 1994. reprint ed. pap. 4.95 (*0-87816-286-0*) Kitchen Sink.
— From Hell, Vol. 2. Amara, Philip, ed. (Illus.). 64p. 1994. pap. 4.95 (*0-87816-287-9*) Kitchen Sink.
— From Hell, Vol. 3. (Illus.). 80p. 1993. reprint ed. pap. 4.95 (*0-87816-252-6*) Kitchen Sink.
— From Hell: Being a Melodrama in Sixteen Parts, Vol. 6. Amara, Philip, ed. (Illus.). 64p. 1994. pap. 4.95 (*0-87816-308-5*) Kitchen Sink.
— From Hell Vol. 7: Being a Melodrama in Sixteen Parts. Amara, Philip, ed. (Illus.). 48p. (YA). 1995. pap. 4.95 (*0-87816-338-7*) Kitchen Sink.
— Opia. 84p. 1986. pap. 15.95 (*0-85646-161-X*, Pub. by Anvil Press) Dufour.
***Moore, Alan.** Promethea. (Illus.). 160p. (J). 2000. 24.95 (*1-56389-655-9*, Pub. by DC Comics) Time Warner.
Moore, Alan. The Saga of Swamp Thing. 184p. (Orig.). 1987. mass mkt. 10.95 (*0-446-38690-1*, Pub. by Warner Bks) Little.
— Saga of the Swamp Thing. Marx, Barry, ed. (Illus.). 88p. 1998. mass mkt. 12.95 (*0-930289-22-6*, Pub. by Warner Bks) Little.
— A Small Killing. (Illus.). 96p. (Orig.). 1993. pap. 11.95 (*1-878574-45-0*) Dark Horse Comics.
— Swamp Thing Love & Death. 1990. mass mkt. 17.95 (*0-446-39192-1*, Pub. by Warner Bks) Little.
***Moore, Alan.** Tom Strong. (Illus.). 160p. (J). 2000. 24.95 (*1-56389-654-0*, Pub. by DC Comics) Time Warner.
— Tomes of Delphi: WIN32 Multimedia API. (Illus.). 2000. pap. text 59.95 (*1-55622-666-7*) Wordware Pub.
Moore, Alan. V for Vendetta. Carlson, KC, ed. (Illus.). 288p. 1995. mass mkt. 19.95 (*0-930289-52-8*, Pub. by Warner Bks) Little.
— Voodoo: Dancing in the Dark. (Illus.). 104p. 1999. pap. text 9.95 (*1-56389-533-1*, Pub. by DC Comics) Time Warner.
— Watchmen. (Illus.). 416p. 1995. mass mkt. 19.95 (*0-930289-23-4*, Pub. by Warner Bks) Little.
Moore, Alan. WildC. A. T. S. Gang War. 176p. pap. 16.95 (*1-56389-560-9*, Pub. by DC Comics) Time Warner.
Moore, Alan. WildC. A. T. S. Gang War. (Illus.). 176p. 1998. pap. 16.95 (*1-58240-037-7*) Image Comics.
***Moore, Alan.** WildC.A.T.S. Homecoming. (Wild C.A.T.s Ser.). (Illus.). 206p. (YA). 2000. pap. 19.95 (*1-56389-582-X*, Pub. by DC Comics) Time Warner.
— Worm: The Longest Comic Strip in the World. (Illus.). (J). 2000. pap. 19.95 (*1-899866-37-X*) Slab-O-Concrete Pubns.
Moore, Alan & Gibbons, Dave. Watchmen. 384p. 1987. mass mkt. 14.95 (*0-446-38689-8*, Pub. by Warner Bks) Little.
Moore, Alan & Gosciak, Josh, eds. Day in the Life: Tales from the Lower East. (Illus.). 192p. (Orig.). (C). 1990. pap. 7.95 (*0-936556-22-6*) Autonomedia.
Moore, Alan & Lloyd, David. V for Vendetta. 288p. 1990. pap. 14.95 (*0-446-39190-5*, Pub. by Warner Bks) Little.
Moore, Alan & Redmond-Pyle, David. Graphical User Interface Design & Evaluation: A Practical Process. 188p. 1995. pap. 46.00 (*0-13-315193-X*) P-H.
Moore, Alan, et al. Butterworths Ireland Capital Tax Acts, 1993-94. 1993. pap. text 99.00 (*0-614-05555-5*, IE, MICHIE) LEXIS Pub.
— Butterworths Ireland Tax Acts, 1993-94. 1993. pap. text 126.00 (*1-85475-631-1*, IE, MICHIE) LEXIS Pub.
— Superman: Whatever Happened to the Man of Tomorrow? LC 97-177240. 64p. (J). 1997. pap. text 5.95 (*1-56389-315-0*, Pub. by DC Comics) Time Warner.
Moore, Alan, ed. see Huncke, Herbert, et al.
***Moore, Alasdair.** Manual of Advanced Veterinary Nursing. (Illus.). 250p. 2000. pap. text 99.95 (*0-905214-51-X*, Pub. by BSAVA) Iowa St U Pr.
Moore, Albert. Gabriel's Odyssey. 210p. (Orig.). (YA). (gr. 12). 1990. pap. 15.95 (*1-85371-081-4*, Pub. by Poolbeg Pr) Dufour.
Moore, Albert B. Conscription & Conflict in the Confederacy. Sproat, John S., ed. LC 96-26451. (Southern Classics Ser.). 380p. 1996. pap. 18.95 (*1-57003-152-5*) U of SC Pr.
Moore, Albert C. Arts in Religions of the Pacific: Symbols of Life. LC 95-6217. (Arts & Religion Ser.). (Illus.). 256p. 1997. 110.00 (*0-86187-186-3*) Bks Intl VA.
Moore, Albert C. Arts in Religions of the Pacific: Symbols of Life. LC 97-36168. (Arts & Religion Ser.). (Illus.). 256p. 1997. reprint ed. pap. 35.00 (*0-304-70058-4*) Bks Intl VA.

M

Moore, Albert J., et al. Trial Advocacy: Inferences, Arguments & Techniques, Teacher's Manual to Accompany. 318p. 1995. teacher ed. write for info. (*0-314-07879-7*) West Pub.

— Trial Advocacy: Inferences, Arguments & Trial Techniques. LC 95-37257. (American Casebook Ser.). 330p. (C). 1995. 31.50 (*0-314-06530-X*) West Pub.

Moore, Albert M. How Much Price Competition? The Prerequisites of an Effective Canadian Competition Policy. LC 71-135415. 231p. reprint ed. pap. 71.70 (*0-7837-6930-X*, 204675900003) Bks Demand.

Moore, Alec, jt. auth. see Hearnden, Keith.

Moore, Alex. Ballroom Dancing. (Ballroom Dance Ser.). 1984. lib. bdg. 250.00 (*0-87700-499-4*) Revisionist Pr.

— Instructions to Young Dancers. (Ballroom Dance Ser.). 1985. lib. bdg. 75.00 (*0-87700-664-4*) Revisionist Pr.

— Popular Variations in Ballroom Dancing. (Ballroom Dance Ser.). 1984. lib. bdg. 79.95 (*0-87700-508-7*) Revisionist Pr.

— Revised Technique of Ballroom Dancing. (Ballroom Dance Ser.). 1984. lib. bdg. 79.95 (*0-87700-498-6*) Revisionist Pr.

— Teaching Multicultured Students. LC 99-28143. (Studies in Inclusive Education Ser.). 176p. 1999. 77.00 (*0-7507-0826-3*, Pub. by Falmer Pr UK); pap. 23.95 (*0-7507-0825-5*, Pub. by Falmer Pr UK) Taylor & Francis.

M

Moore, Alex & Quickmire, Carolyn, eds. Biographical Directory of the South Carolina House of Representatives, 1816-1828, Vol. V. 384p. 1992. 15.00 (*1-880067-07-2*) SC Dept of Arch & Hist.

Moore, Alexander. Cultural Anthropology: The Field Study of Human Beings. 2nd ed. LC 97-78022. (Illus.). 540p. (C). 1998. pap. text 42.75 (*0-939693-48-8*) Collegiate Pr.

Moore, Alexander, jt. auth. see Smith, Henry A.

Moore, Alexis, jt. auth. see Hayre, Ruth W.

Moore, Alick. A Field Guide to the Warblers of Britain & Europe. (Illus.). 1984. 24.95 (*0-19-217710-9*) OUP.

Moore, Alick, jt. auth. see Howard, Richard.

Moore, Alison. Small Spaces Between Emergencies. LC 91-30614. 184p. 1992. 18.95 (*1-56279-022-6*) Mercury Hse Inc.

— Synonym for Love. LC 94-40442. 256p. 1995. text 19.95 (*1-56279-074-9*) Mercury Hse Inc.

Moore, Allan D., jt. auth. see Martin, David G.

Moore, Allan F. The Beatles: Sgt. Pepper's Lonely Hearts Club Band. LC 96-6714. (Cambridge Music Handbks.). 112p. (C). 1997. text 39.95 (*0-521-57381-5*); pap. text 12.95 (*0-521-57484-6*) Cambridge U Pr.

Moore, Allen B. & Brooks, Rusty. Transforming Your Community: Empowering for Change. LC 96-14555. (Professional Practices in Adult Education & Human Resource Development Ser.). (Illus.). 202p. (C). 1996. 26.50 (*0-89464-899-3*) Krieger.

Moore, Allen B. & Feldt, James A. Facilitating Community & Decision-Making Groups. 168p. (C). 1993. 20.50 (*0-89464-650-8*) Krieger.

Moore, Allen J., ed. Religious Education As Social Transformation. LC 88-36413. 258p. (Orig.). 1989. pap. 24.95 (*0-89135-069-1*) Religious Educ.

Moore, Alvin, Jr., ed. see Coomaraswamy, Ananda K.

Moore, Alvin, Jr., tr. see Guenon, Rene.

Moore, Alvin E. Border Patrol: A Novel. LC 87-16004. 128p. (Orig.). 1988. pap. 10.95 (*0-86534-113-3*) Sunstone Pr.

— Red Jewel of the East. 300p. 1989. per. 11.95 (*0-89697-310-7*) Intl Univ Pr.

— The Secret UFO Diary of CIA Operative: Exposing the Existence of the Alien Skymen. 260p. 16.95 (*0-938294-25-3*) Inner Light.

Moore, Amanda L., jt. auth. see Finch, Edward R., Jr.

Moore, Amy G., ed. see Martin, Thomas M.

Moore, Andrea A. Culinary Artists: Tidewater's Regional Chefs. Wilbur, Leah & Laux, Don, eds. LC 96-96208. (Illus.). 128p. (Orig.). 1996. pap. 18.95 (*0-9652142-0-6*) Culinary Art Tidewtr.

Moore, Andrew. The Right Road: A History of Right Wing Politics in Australia. (Australian Retropective Ser.). 176p. 1995. pap. text 24.95 (*0-19-553512-X*) OUP.

— The Secret Army & the Premier: Conservative Paramilitary Organizations in NSW 1930-32. 312p. 1990. pap. 24.95 (*0-86840-283-4*, Pub. by New South Wales Univ Pr) Intl Spec Bk.

Moore, Andrew, jt. auth. see McNair, James.

Moore, Andrew, jt. auth. see McQuay, Henry.

Moore, Andy. Moore's Imaging Dictionary. 2nd ed. 19.95 (*0-936648-74-0*) Telecom Bks.

Moore, Andy & Moore, Susan. The Penny Bank Book: Collecting Still Banks. (Schiffer Book for Collectors Ser.). (Illus.). 192p. 1997. 49.95 (*0-7643-0377-5*) Schiffer.

***Moore, Andy & Moore, Susan.** The Pennybank Book. 3rd ed. (Illus.). 192p. 2000. 49.95 (*0-7643-1082-8*) Schiffer.

Moore, Angela. Building a Successful Network Marketing Company: The System, the Products & Know-How. LC 98-9245. 320p. 1998. boxed set 30.00 (*0-7615-1273-X*) Prima Pub.

***Moore, Angela L. & Stringfellow, Lisa H.** The Very Best Opportunity for Women. 2000. 16.00 (*0-7615-2831-8*) Prima Pub.

Moore, Anita G. God's Amazing Grace. 48p. 1998. 16.95 (*1-892668-00-9*) Prospect Pr.

Moore, Ann. The Bible Made Easy: Hebrews: God's Last Will & Testament. (Illus.). 544p. (Orig.). 1995. pap. 24.00 (*1-888041-03-X*) Frnds of God.

— Prayer Planner: A Daily Journal. (Illus.). 384p. 1995. spiral bd. 36.00 (*1-888041-00-5*, Prayer Planner) Frnds of God.

Moore, Ann P., jt. auth. see Petty, Nicola J.

Moore, Anne. Passion's Glory. 1983. mass mkt. 3.50 (*0-685-07868-X*, Zebra Kensgtn) Kensgtn Pub Corp.

Moore, Annette C. The Game Finder: A Leader's Guide to Great Activities. LC 92-61287. (Illus.). 200p. (C). 1992. pap. text 18.95 (*0-910251-57-6*) Venture Pub PA.

Moore, Anthony, ed. see Klemp, Harold.

***Moore, Anthony T.** Father, Son & Healing Ghosts. LC 00-23243. 2000. write for info. (*0-935652-52-3*) Ctr Applications Psych.

Moore, Antony S., jt. auth. see Ogilvie, Gregory K.

Moore, April. The Earth & You: Eating for Two. Stark, Elizabeth, ed. (Illus.). 165p. (Orig.). (YA). (gr. 8-12). 1993. 6.95 (*0-938443-05-4*) Potomac Val Pr.

Moore, Archimandrite L. St. Seraphim of Sarov: A Spiritual Biography. 504p. 1994. pap. write for info. (*1-880364-13-1*) New Sarov.

***Moore, Arden.** 50 Simple Ways to Pamper Your Cat. (Illus.). 144p. 2000. pap. 9.95 (*1-58017-311-X*, 67311) Storey Bks.

— 50 Simple Ways to Pamper Your Dog. (Illus.). 144p. 2000. pap. 9.95 (*1-58017-310-1*, 67310) Storey Bks.

Moore, Arden, et al. Faster, Better Healing: How to Combine the World's Most Powerful Cures to Remedy Common Ailments As Quickly As Possible. LC 98-31951. (Prevention's New Approaches to Health Ser.). 1999. write for info. (*1-57954-059-7*) Rodale Pr Inc.

***Moore, Arden, et al.** Herbs That Heal: Natural Medicine at its Best LC 99-28951. (Women's Edge Health Enhancement Ser.). 1999. write for info. (*1-57954-119-4*) Rodale Pr Inc.

Moore, Arden, jt. auth. see Stengler, Mark.

Moore, Arthur. River of Fortune: The Passion. (Orig.). 1979. mass mkt. 2.50 (*0-89083-561-6*, Zebra Kensgtn) Kensgtn Pub Corp.

— The Tempest. (Orig.). 1979. mass mkt. 2.50 (*0-89083-521-7*, Zebra Kensgtn) Kensgtn Pub Corp.

— The Triumph. (Orig.). 1979. mass mkt. 2.50 (*0-89083-522-5*, Zebra Kensgtn) Kensgtn Pub Corp.

Moore, Arthur A. An Introduction to Galliculus. (Wissenschaftliche Abhandlungen-Musicological Studies: Vol. 18). 100p. 1970. lib. bdg. 32.00 (*0-912024-79-8*) Inst Mediaeval Mus.

Moore, Arthur A., ed. Galliculus, Gesamtausgabe. (Gesamtausgaben - Collected Works: Vol. Viii, Pt. 1). (ENG & GER.). 120p. 1976. lib. bdg. 4.00 (*0-912024-69-0*) Inst Mediaeval Mus.

— Galliculus, Gesamtausgabe: The Magnificats. (Gesamtausgaben - Collected Works: Vol. VIII, Pt. 2). 120p. 1988. 80.00 (*0-931902-59-2*) Inst Mediaeval Mus.

— Galliculus, Gesamtausgabe: The Motets. (Gesamtausgaben - Collected Works: Vol. VIII, Pt. 3). 214p. 1988. 86.00 (*0-931902-66-5*) Inst Mediaeval Mus.

Moore, Arthur C. The Powers of Preservation: New Life for Historic Structures. LC 98-2784. (Illus.). 256p. 1998. 59.95 (*0-07-043394-1*) McGraw.

Moore, Arthur H. & Elonka, Stephen M. Electrical Systems & Equipment for Industry. LC 77-5640. (Illus.). 368p. 1977. reprint ed. lib. bdg. 34.50 (*0-88275-561-7*) Krieger.

Moore, Arthur K. The Frontier Mind: A Cultural Analysis of the Kentucky Frontiersman. LC 57-11379. 276p. reprint ed. 85.60 (*0-8357-9785-6*, 201609800098) Bks Demand.

— Secular Lyric in Middle English. LC 71-100170. 255p. 1970. reprint ed. lib. bdg. 35.00 (*0-8371-2973-7*, MOME, Greenwood Pr) Greenwood.

Moore, Arthur W., ed. Manx Ballads & Music. LC 78-72642. (Celtic Language & Literature Ser.: Goidelic & Brythonic). reprint ed. 32.50 (*0-404-17575-9*) AMS Pr.

Moore, Arva, jt. auth. see Pincus, Laura.

Moore, Audria V., et al. Treasure Coast Black Heritage: A Pictorial History. LC 96-40908. 1996. write for info. (*0-89865-983-3*) Donning Co.

Moore, B. J. Poetry: Telling It Like It Is. 80p. 1996. 10.00 (*0-533-11375-X*) Vantage.

***Moore, B. J.** Poetry: Telling It Like It Is - II. 87p. 2000. 11.95 (*0-533-12771-8*) Vantage.

Moore, B. Keith, jt. auth. see Phillips, Ralph W.

Moore, Barbara. Farewell to the Body. LC 90-71210. 76p. 1990. 10.00 (*0-915380-27-7*) Word Works.

***Moore, Barbara.** 1999 U. S. Master Payroll Guide. 400p. 1999. pap. 75.00 (*0-8080-0305-4*) CCH INC.

***Moore, Barbara, et al.** U. S. Master Payroll Guide, 2000. 600p. 2000. pap. 75.00 (*0-8080-0390-9*) CCH INC.

Moore, Barbara, ed. see Archibald, Allene, et al.

Moore, Barbara, ed. see Foote, Horton.

Moore, Barbara C., jt. auth. see Hewitt, Lonnie B.

Moore, Barbara Coffin, jt. auth. see Hewitt, Lonnie Burstein.

Moore, Barbara Griffin, see Griffin Moore, Barbara.

Moore, Barbara H., ed. The Entrepreneur in Local Government. LC 83-10806. (Practical Management Ser.). (Illus.). 214p. (Orig.). (C). 1983. pap. 23.95 (*0-87326-039-2*) Intl City-Cnty Mgt.

Moore, Barbara W. & Weesner, Gail. Back Bay: A Living Portrait. LC 95-67827. (Illus.). 144p. 1995. 35.00 (*0-9632077-2-5*); pap. 25.00 (*0-9632077-3-3*) Centry Hill Pr.

— Beacon Hill: A Living Portrait. 120p. 1992. 33.00 (*0-9632077-0-9*); pap. 22.00 (*0-9632077-1-7*) Centry Hill Pr.

Moore, Barbara W. & Weesner, Gail, eds. Hidden Gardens of Beacon Hill. 4th ed. 88p. 1999. 25.00 (*0-9628658-3-4*); pap. 15.00 (*0-9628658-2-6*) Beacon MA.

Moore, Barbara W., ed. see Lee, Henry, et al.

Moore, Barrington, Jr. Authority & Inequality under Capitalism & Socialism: U. S. A., U. S. S. R., & China. 160p. 1987. text 39.95 (*0-19-828540-X*) OUP.

— Injustice: The Social Bases of Obedience & Revolt. LC 77-98162. 560p. (gr. 13). 1978. text 103.95 (*0-87332-114-6*) M E Sharpe.

Moore, Barrington, Jr. Injustice: The Social Bases of Obedience & Revolt. LC 77-98162. 560p. (gr. 13). 1978. pap. text 43.95 (*0-87332-145-6*) M E Sharpe.

Moore, Barrington, Jr. Moral Aspects of Economic Growth, & Other Essays. LC 97-45210. (Wilder House Series in Politics, History, & Culture). 240p. 1998. 29.95 (*0-8014-3376-2*) Cornell U Pr.

***Moore, Barrington, Jr.** Moral Purity & Persecution in History. LC BJ1533.P97M66 2000. 149p. 2000. 24.95 (*0-691-04920-3*, Pub. by Princeton U Pr) Cal Prin Full Svc.

Moore, Barrington. Privacy: Studies in Social & Cultural History. LC 83-23524. 342p. reprint ed. pap. 106.10 (*0-7837-0041-5*, 204010600014) Bks Demand.

Moore, Barrington, Jr. Social Origins of Dictatorship & Democracy: Lord & Peasant in the Making of the Modern World. LC 93-17802. 592p. 1993. pap. 23.00 (*0-8070-5073-3*) Beacon Pr.

Moore, Barrington, Jr. Soviet Politics - The Dilemma of Power: The Role of Ideas in Social Change. LC 76-19137. 518p. (gr. 13). 1976. reprint ed. pap. text 65.95 (*0-87332-088-3*) M E Sharpe.

Moore, Barrington, Jr. Terror & Progress U. S. S. R. Some Sources of Change & Stability in the Soviet Dictatorship. LC 54-5995. (Russian Research Center Studies: No. 12). 278p. 1954. 29.00 (*0-674-87450-1*) HUP.

Moore, Barry. Credit Institutions & Banking, Vol. II-3. (Single Market Review Ser.). 1998. 95.00 (*0-7494-2315-3*) Kogan Page Ltd.

***Moore, Barry S.** Human Inclusion. 2000. pap. 12.99 (*0-9679919-0-0*) Rockbusters Pub.

Moore, Barry W. Aesthetic Aspects of Recent Experimental Film. Jowett, Garth S., ed. LC 79-6680. (Dissertations on Film, 1980 Ser.). 1980. lib. bdg. 15.95 (*0-405-12913-0*) Ayer.

Moore, Basil, ed. Basil Moore's Lincoln. LC 91-60340. (Illus.). 90p. 1991. 19.95 (*1-878044-02-8*) Mayhaven Pub.

Moore, Basil J. Horizontalists & Verticalists: The Macroeconomics of Credit Money. (Illus.). 440p. 1988. text 95.00 (*0-521-35079-4*) Cambridge U Pr.

— An Introduction to Modern Economic Theory. LC 77-96708. (C). 1973. 24.95 (*0-02-921960-4*) Free Pr.

Moore, Beier. Penguin Book of Modern African Poetry. 4th ed. 384p. 1999. pap. 15.95 (*0-14-118100-1*) Penguin Putnam.

Moore, Bert S. & Isen, Alice M. Affect & Social Behavior. (Studies in Emotion & Social Interaction). (Illus.). 287p. (C). 1990. text 64.95 (*0-521-32768-7*) Cambridge U Pr.

Moore, Beta. Jesus, the One & Only: A Study of Christ Through the Ages. unabridged ed. (Orig.). 1997. pap. text. write for info. (*0-9656362-1-6*) Living Proof.

***Moore, Beth.** Breaking Free: Making Liberty in Christ a Reality in Life. 224p. 2000. 18.99 (*0-8054-2294-3*) Broadman.

— Breaking Free: Making Liberty in Christ a Reality in Life. 224p. 1999. pap. text 12.95 (*0-7673-9112-8*, LifeWy Press) LifeWay Christian.

Moore, Beth. Filled & Free: Exploring the Fruit of the Spirit. unabridged ed. (Orig.). 1997. pap. text. write for info. (*0-9656362-0-8*) Living Proof.

— A Heart Like His: Intimate Reflections on the Life of David. LC 99-24850. 224p. 1999. 16.99 (*0-8054-2035-5*) Broadman.

Moore, Beth. A Heart Like His: Seeking the Heart of God Through a Study of David. 240p. 1996. pap. text 12.95 (*0-7673-2596-6*, LifeWy Press) LifeWay Christian.

— Living Beyond Yourself: Exploring the Fruit of the Spirit. 224p. 1998. pap. text 12.95 (*0-7673-9275-2*, LifeWy Press) LifeWay Christian.

— Praying God's Word: Breaking Free from Spiritual Strongholds. LC 99-55801. 256p. 2000. 16.99 (*0-8054-2351-6*) Broadman.

Moore, Beth. Things Pondered... From the Heart of a Lesser Woman: From the Heart of a Lesser Woman. LC 97-17520. (Illus.). 128p. 1997. pap. text 14.99 (*0-8054-0166-0*, LifeWy Press) LifeWay Christian.

Moore, Beth. To Live Is Christ: The Life & Ministry of Paul. 224p. 1997. pap. text 12.95 (*0-7673-3412-4*, LifeWy Press) LifeWay Christian.

— Whispers of Hope. 264p. 1998. pap. text 14.95 (*0-7673-9278-7*, LifeWy Press) LifeWay Christian.

— A Woman's Heart: God's Dwelling Place. 240p. 1995. pap. text 12.95 (*0-8054-9836-2*, LifeWy Press) LifeWay Christian.

Moore, Bette D. Redeemed! Readers Theatre for Building the Body. LC 95-190691. 1995. 15.99 (*0-8341-9271-3*, MP-756) Lillenas.

Moore, Betty, jt. auth. see Moore, Rudy.

Moore-Betty, Maurice, jt. auth. see Travers, Pamela L.

Moore, Beverly. Echo's Song. (Illus.). 40p. (J). (gr. k-3). 1993. lib. bdg. 13.95 (*0-9637288-7-3*) River Walker Bks.

Moore, Bill. Two on the Square. LC 86-20781. (Illus.). 208p. 1986. 14.95 (*0-914875-13-2*) Bright Mtn Bks.

Moore, Blaine F. Supreme Court & Unconstitutional Legislation. LC 68-56672. (Columbia University. Studies in the Social Sciences: No. 133). reprint ed. 31.50 (*0-404-51133-3*) AMS Pr.

Moore, Blaine R., jt. ed. see Mankad, Vipul N.

Moore, Bloomfield. Keely & His Discoveries. 373p. 1996. reprint ed. spiral bd. 27.50 (*0-7873-0621-5*) Hlth Research.

Moore-Blunt, ed. Platonis. (GRE.). 1985. 27.95 (*3-322-00423-6*, T1588, Pub. by B G Teubner) U of Mich Pr.

Moore-Blunt, J. J. A Commentary on Ovid Metamorphoses Vol. II. LC 95-117515. viii, 192p. 1977. pap. 56.00 (*90-256-0638-5*, Pub. by AM Hakkert) BookLink Distributors.

— A Commentary on Ovid Metamorphoses II. 192p. 1977. pap. text 44.00 (*0-685-43581-4*, Pub. by AM Hakkert) Coronet Bks.

Moore, Bob. A Bridge with a View: Poems. LC 97-93758. 63 p. 1997. write for info. (*0-9658091-0-2*) Little Rabbit.

***Moore, Bob.** This Our Joy & This Our Feast. 1999. 15.95 (*5-550-71732-8*); 16.00 (*5-550-71857-X*); pap. 10.95 (*5-550-71735-2*) Nairi.

Moore, Bob. Victims & Survivors, 1940-1944: The Nazi Persecution of the Jews in the Netherlands 1940-1945. LC 97-4209. (Illus.). 352p. 1997. pap. text 19.95 (*0-340-69157-3*) OUP.

***Moore, Bob, ed.** Resistance in Western Europe. (Illus.). 256p. 2000. 65.00 (*1-85973-274-7*, Pub. by Berg Pubs); pap. 19.50 (*1-85973-279-8*, Pub. by Berg Pubs) NYU Pr.

Moore, Bob & Fedorowich, Kent, eds. Prisoners-of-War & Their Captors in World War II. (Illus.). 352p. 1996. 65.00 (*1-85973-157-0*, Pub. by Berg Pubs); pap. 22.50 (*1-85973-152-X*, Pub. by Berg Pubs) NYU Pr.

Moore, Bob & Grauwels, Patrick. Route 66 - A Guidebook to the Mother Road. 2nd ed. LC 98-128325. (Illus.). 140p. 1997. spiral bd. 19.95 (*0-9641457-0-7*) Inovative Pubng.

Moore, Bob & Moore, Maxine. Up from the Roots: Growing a Vocabulary. (Illus.). 320p. 1993. 13.95 (*0-942257-20-0*) New Chapter Pr.

Moore, Bob & Moore, Maxine, eds. NTC's Dictionary of Latin & Greek Origins. LC 96-25819. (Illus.). 400p. 1996. 19.95 (*0-8442-8320-7*, 83207, Natl Textbk Co) NTC Contemp Pub Co.

Moore, Bob & Reynolds, R. J., intros. Nascar Yearbook & Press Guide. (Illus.). 110p. (Orig.). 1992. pap. 6.95 (*0-318-17137-6*) Nat Assn Stock.

Moore, Bob, et al. NTC's Dictionary of Latin & Greek Origins. LC 96-25819. (LAT, GRE & ENG., Illus.). 400p. 1996. pap. 15.95 (*0-8442-8321-5*, 83215, Natl Textbk Co) NTC Contemp Pub Co.

Moore, Bob, jt. auth. see Center, Bill.

Moore, Bradley S., jt. auth. see Moore, Franklin.

Moore, Bradley S., jt. ed. see Moore, Franklin L.

Moore, Brenda L. To Serve My Country . . . Race. 1998. pap. text 18.00 (*0-8147-5587-9*) NYU Pr.

— To Serve My Country, to Serve My Race: The Story of the Only African-American WACs Stationed Overseas During World War II. (Illus.). 272p. (C). 1996. text 45.00 (*0-8147-5522-4*) NYU Pr.

Moore, Brenda M. Together on the Mountain. LC 98-5434. (Illus.). 32p. (J). (ps-3). 1998. 14.95 (*1-890326-14-3*) First Story Pr.

Moore, Brian. Black Robe. 256p. 1997. pap. 12.95 (*0-452-27865-1*, Plume) Dutton Plume.

— Cold Heaven: A Novel. LC 97-12747. 272p. 1997. reprint ed. pap. 12.95 (*0-452-27867-8*, Plume) Dutton Plume.

— The Color of Blood. 1988. mass mkt. 4.95 (*0-7710-6422-5*) McCland & Stewart.

— Devotions to the Holy Spirit. 72p. 1989. pap. 1.95 (*0-8198-1859-3*) Pauline Bks.

— The Gospel Day by Day Through Easter: Gospel Reflections for the Easter Season. 94p. (Orig.). 1991. pap. 6.95 (*0-8146-2003-5*) Liturgical Pr.

— Lies of Silence. Date not set. pap. write for info. (*0-582-08170-X*, Pub. by Addison-Wesley) Longman.

— Lies of Silence. 208p. 1991. pap. 9.00 (*0-380-71547-3*, Avon Bks) Morrow Avon.

— Lies of Silence. large type ed. 1991. 27.99 (*0-7089-8611-0*, Charnwood) Ulverscroft.

— The Lonely Passion of Judith Hearne. 223p. 1988. pap. 11.95 (*0-316-57966-1*) Little.

***Moore, Brian.** The Lonely Passion of Judith Hearne. 1999. pap. write for info. (*0-316-57981-5*) Little.

— The Lonely Passion of Judith Hearne. 248p. 1997. pap. text. write for info. (*0-7710-9992-4*) NCanadian Lib.

Moore, Brian. The Magician's Wife. LC 97-34064. 240p. 1999. pap. 12.95 (*0-452-27959-3*, Plume) Dutton Plume.

Moore, Brian. The Magician's Wife. LC 97-931173. 300p. (J). 1997. 28.01 (*0-676-97090-7*) Random.

— The Magician's Wife LC 97-50372. 358 p. 1998. write for info. (*0-7540-1142-9*) Chivers N Amer.

Moore, Brian. The Magician's Wife. large type ed. LC 97-50372. (Basic Ser.). 1998. 27.95 (*0-7862-1388-4*) Thorndike Pr.

— No Other Life. LC 97-14797. 224p. 1997. pap. 11.95 (*0-452-27878-3*, Plume) Dutton Plume.

— No Other Life. large type ed. LC 93-33308. 277p. 1993. lib. bdg. 22.95 (*0-8161-5897-5*, G K Hall Lrg Type) Mac Lib Ref.

— The Statement. 1997. pap. 11.95 (*0-452-27632-2*, Plume); pap. 11.95 (*0-614-27293-9*, Plume) Dutton Plume.

— Two Stories. limited ed. (Santa Susana Press Ser.). 1979. 35.00 (*0-937048-22-4*); 60.00 (*0-937048-29-1*) Santa Susana.

Moore, Brian C. An Introduction to the Psychology of Hearing. 4th ed. LC 96-36717. (Illus.). 384p. 1997. pap. text 49.95 (*0-12-505627-3*) Morgan Kaufmann.

— Perceptual Consequences of Cochlear Damage. (Illus.). 246p. 1995. text 90.00 (*0-19-852330-0*) OUP.

Moore, Brian C., ed. Hearing. 2nd ed. (Handbook of Perception & Cognition Ser.). (Illus.). 468p. 1995. text 65.00 (*0-12-505626-5*) Acad Pr.

Moore, Brian C. & Patterson, Roy D., eds. Auditory Frequency Selectivity. LC 86-22700. (NATO ASI Series A, Life Sciences: Vol. 119). 466p. 1986. 105.00 (*0-306-42462-2*, Plenum Trade) Perseus Pubng.

Moore, Brian C. J. Cochlear Hearing Loss. 1998. pap. text 44.95 (*1-86156-091-5*) Whurr Pub.

An Asterisk (*) at the beginning of an entry indicates that the title is appearing for the first time.

Moore, Brian F. Sharing the Gains of Productivity. (Studies in Productivity: No. 24). 57p. 1982. pap. 55.00 (*0-08-029505-3*) Work in Amer.

Moore, Brian L. Cultural Power, Resistance & Pluralism: Colonial Guyana, 1838-1900. (Illus.). 500p. 1995. 65.00 (*0-7735-1354-X*) McG-Queens Univ Pr.

— Race, Power & Social Segmentation in Colonial Society. 320p. 1987. 48.00 (*2-88124-203-0*) Gordon & Breach.

— Race, Power & Social Segmentation in Colonial Society: Plantation Guyana after Slavery, 1838-1891. (Caribbean Studies: Vol. 4). xiv, 310p. 1987. text 68.00 (*0-677-21980-6*) Gordon & Breach.

Moore, Brooke N. & Bruder, Kenneth. Philosophy: The Power of Ideas, Brief. 2nd abr. ed. LC 94-37688. 422p. 1995. pap. text 42.95 (*1-55934-435-0*, 1435) Mayfield Pub.

Moore, Brooke N. & Parker, Richard. Critical Thinking: CT Review for Windows. 1998. disk 9.95 (*0-7674-0158-1*) Mayfield Pub.

— Critical Thinking: Evaluating Claims & Arguments in Everyday Life. 5th ed. LC 97-20527. xiii, 578p. 1997. pap. text 45.95 (*1-55934-836-4*, 1836) Mayfield Pub.

— Critical Thinking Instructor's Manual: The Logical Accessory. 5th rev. ed. 364p. (C). 1997. pap. text, teacher ed. write for info. (*1-55934-837-2*, 1837) Mayfield Pub.

Moore, Brooke N. & Stewart, Robert M. Moral Philosophy: A Comprehensive Introduction. LC 93-11106. xii, 660p. (C). 1993. 57.95 (*1-55934-037-1*, 1037) Mayfield Pub.

Moore, Brooke N., et al. Critical Thinking Study Guide. 5th ed. 213p. (C). 1997. pap. text, teacher ed. 19.95 (*1-55934-966-2*, 1966) Mayfield Pub.

Moore, Brooke Noel. Making Your Case: Critical Thinking & the Argumentative Essay. LC 94-38160. x, 246p. (C). 1995. pap. text 25.95 (*1-55934-331-1*, 1331) Mayfield Pub.

Moore, Brooke Noel & Bruder, Kenneth. Philosophy: The Power of Ideas. 4th rev. ed. LC 98-10285. xxii, 586p. 1998. text 53.95 (*1-55934-988-3*, 988-3) Mayfield Pub.

***Moore, Brooke Noel & Parker, Richard.** Critical Thinking. 6th ed. LC 99-86473. 2000. write for info. (*0-7674-1067-X*) Mayfield Pub.

***Moore, Bruce.** The Australian Concise Oxford Dictionary of Current English. 3rd ed. (Illus.). 1,632p. 2000. 45.00 (*0-19-550617-0*) OUP.

Moore, Bruce D. Eye Care for Infants & Young Children. LC 97-2666. 474p. 1997. pap. text 65.00 (*0-7506-9646-X*) Buttrwrth-Heinemann.

Moore, Bruce D., jt. auth. see Press, Leonard J.

Moore, Bryony. Risk Assessment: A Practitioner's Guide to Predicting Harmful Behaviour. 250p. 1996. 65.00 (*1-871177-83-9*, Pub. by Whiting & Birch); pap. 25.00 (*1-871177-84-7*, Pub. by Whiting & Birch) Paul & Co Pubs.

Moore, Bud. The Lochsa Story: Land Ethics in the Bitterroot Mountains. LC 96-27228. (Illus.). 476p. 1996. pap. 20.00 (*0-87842-333-8*) Mountain Pr.

— The Lochsa Story: Land Ethics in the Bitterroot Mountains. LC 96-27228. (Illus.). 450p. 1996. 36.00 (*0-87842-341-9*) Mountain Pr.

***Moore, Burness E.** Psychoanalysis: The Major Concepts. (Illus.). 608p. 1999. 27.50 (*0-300-08078-6*) Yale U Pr.

Moore, Burness E. & Fine, Bernard D., eds. Psychoanalysis: The Major Concepts. LC 95-173. 562p. 1995. 60.00 (*0-300-06329-6*) Yale U Pr.

— Psychoanalytic Terms & Concepts. LC 89-36223. 225p. (C). 1990. pap. 18.00 (*0-300-04701-0*) Yale U Pr.

***Moore, Burton M.** Love & Riot in Los Angeles: The Biography of Oscar Zeta Acosta. Cabello, Andrea, ed. (Nuestra Historia Ser.: Vol. 4). 160p. 2000. pap. 24.95 (*0-915745-29-1*) Floricanto Pr.

Moore, Burton M., jt. auth. see Moore, Joan W.

Moore, Byron. The First Five Million Miles. Gilbert, James B., ed. LC 79-7289. (Flight: Its First Seventy-Five Years Ser.). (Illus.). 1980. reprint ed. lib. bdg. 28.95 (*0-405-12197-0*) Ayer.

Moore, C. Night Before Christmas: Full-Color Sturdy Book. LC 98-20335. (Illus.). 12p. (J). 1998. pap. 1.00 (*0-486-40256-8*) Dover.

Moore, C., jt. auth. see English, P. T.

Moore, C., jt. auth. see Frye, D.

***Moore, C. Bryan.** Pray Tell: The Containment of the Prince of Darkness. 1998. pap. 11.95 (*0-9665299-2-8*) Coomansingh.

Moore, C. Bryan. Pray Tell Vol. 2: The Shining Light, 2 vols. 79p. (YA). (gr. 11 up). 1999. pap. 11.95 (*0-9665299-3-6*) Coomansingh.

Moore, C. C., ed. Group Representations, Ergodic Theory, Operator Algebras, & Mathematical Physics: Proceedings of a Conference in Honor of George W. Mackey. (Mathematical Sciences Research Institute Publications: Vol. 6). (Illus.). 290p. 1986. 59.95 (*0-387-96471-1*) Spr-Verlag.

Moore, C. C., jt. auth. see Auslander, Louis.

Moore, C. E. Amanda: The Untold Story. (Orig.). 1995. mass mkt. 5.99 (*1-57297-056-1*) Blvd Books.

— Melrose Place: Sister Dearest: The Sydney & Jane Story. 304p. (Orig.). (YA). (gr. 7 up). 1996. mass mkt. 5.99 (*1-57297-087-1*) Blvd Books.

Moore, C. Eugene. Interior Solutions from Armstrong, the 1960s. LC 98-46031. (Illus.). 176p. (Orig.). 1999. pap. 29.95 (*0-7643-0700-2*) Schiffer.

Moore, C. H. Carbonate Diagenesis & Porosity. (Developments in Sedimentology Ser.: Vol. 46). 338p. 1989. 158.75 (*0-444-87415-1*) Elsevier.

Moore, C. J. Peter William Butterblow. (J). pap. 14.95 (*0-86315-125-6*, 1459, Pub. by Floris Bks) Anthroposophic.

***Moore, C. Kenneth.** Colt Single Action Army Revolvers: U. S. Alterations. LC 98-68169. (Illus.). 112p. 1999. 35.00 (*0-917218-85-X*) A Mowbray.

Moore, C. Kenneth. Colt Single Action Army Revolvers & the London Agency. LC 90-60405. (Illus.). 144p. 1990. 35.00 (*0-917218-43-4*) A Mowbray.

Moore, C. L. The Best of C. L. Moore. (Orig.). 1993. reprint ed. lib. bdg. 18.95 (*0-89968-354-1*, Lghtyr Pr) Buccaneer Bks.

— Jirel of Joiry. 224p. 1982. mass mkt. 2.75 (*0-441-38570-2*) Ace Bks.

Moore, C. N., jt. auth. see Banuelos, R.

Moore, C. Raymond & Laudon, Lowell R. Evolution & Classification of Paleozoic Crinoids: Geological Society of America Special Papers, Vol. 46. Gould, Stephen Jay, ed. LC 79-8352. (History of Paleontology Ser.). (Illus.). 1980. reprint ed. lib. bdg. 17.95 (*0-405-12721-9*) Ayer.

Moore, Cairl E. Concrete Form Construction. 1977. mass mkt. 43.95 (*0-8273-1094-3*) Delmar.

Moore, Calvin C., jt. auth. see Auslander, Louis.

Moore, Calvin C., ed. see Pure Mathematics Symposium Staff.

Moore Campbell, Gini, ed. see Burke, Bob.

Moore Campbell, Gini, ed. see Burke, Bob & Creel, Von R.

Moore, Carey & Moore, Pamela Rosewell. What Happens When Husbands & Wives Pray Together? 205p. (C). (gr. 13). 1999. pap. 5.99 (*0-8007-8659-9*, Spire) Revell.

Moore, Carey A. Daniel, Esther, & Jeremiah: The Additions. LC 76-42376. (Anchor Bible Ser.: Vol. 44). (Illus.). 1977. 34.00 (*0-385-04702-9*, Anchor NY) Doubleday.

— Judith. LC 83-11694. (Anchor Bible Ser.: Vol. 40). (Illus.). 312p. 1985. 14.00 (*0-385-14424-5*) Doubleday.

— Studies in the Book of Esther. 1982. 79.50 (*0-87068-718-2*) Ktav.

— Tobit: A New Translation with Introduction & Commentary. (Anchor Bible Ser.: Vol. 40A). (Illus.). 368p. 1996. 34.95 (*0-385-18913-3*) Doubleday.

Moore, Carey A., ed. Esther. LC 75-140615. (Anchor Bible Ser.: Vol. 7B). 192p. 1971. 29.00 (*0-385-00472-9*, Anchor NY) Doubleday.

Moore, Carl H. The Federal Reserve System: A History of the First 75 Years. LC 89-43660. (Illus.). 280p. 1990. lib. bdg. 42.50 (*0-89950-503-1*) McFarland & Co.

Moore, Carl M. Group Processes for Idea Building. 2nd ed. (Applied Social Research Methods Ser.: Vol. 9). 160p. (C). 1994. text 42.00 (*0-8039-5642-8*); pap. text 18.95 (*0-8039-5643-6*) Sage.

Moore, Carlos. Castro, the Blacks, & Africa. (Afro-American Culture & Society Monographs: Vol. 8). (Illus.). 472p. 1988. pap. 23.50 (*0-934934-33-9*) CAAS Pubns.

— Fela, Fela. (Illus.). 287p. 1992. pap. write for info. (*0-8052-8221-1*) Schocken.

Moore, Carlos, ed. African Presence in the Americas. 532p. 1995. pap. 18.95 (*0-86543-233-3*) Africa World.

Moore, Carlos, et al, eds. African Presence in the Americas. 532p. 1996. 59.95 (*0-86543-232-5*) Africa World.

Moore, Carman, jt. auth. see Beethoven, Jane.

Moore, Carol. The Davidian Massacre: Disturbing Questions about Waco Which Must Be Answered. LC 96-214366. (Illus.). 494p. 1995. pap. 7.00 (*1-880692-22-8*) Legacy Comms.

Moore, Carol, jt. auth. see Bonars, Stephen G.

Moore, Carol, ed. see Rivers-Moore, Judith.

Moore, Carol J. Carol's Kitchen. LC 93-91479. (Illus.). 421p. (Orig.). 1997. reprint ed. ring bd. 27.00 (*0-9645003-0-2*) C J Moore.

Moore, Carol-Lynne & Yamamoto, Kaoru. Beyond Words: Movement Observation & Analysis. xvi, 306p. (C). 1988. text 37.00 (*2-88124-250-2*); pap. text 20.00 (*2-88124-251-0*); pap. text, teacher ed. 16.00 (*2-88124-252-9*); VHS 161.00 (*2-88124-313-4*); VHS 167.00 (*2-88124-315-0*) Gordon & Breach.

Moore, Carolyn, ed. see Calandro, Ed.

Moore, Carolyn E., intro. Quick Check Food Facts. LC 98-25679. (Barron's Educational Ser.). 240p. 1999. pap. 4.95 (*0-7641-0874-3*) Barron.

Moore, Carolyn E., et al. Keys to Children's Nutrition. (Parenting Keys Ser.). 160p. 1991. pap. 5.95 (*0-8120-4675-7*) Barron.

Moore, Carolynne, jt. auth. see Miles, John.

Moore, Casey & Alessi, Bob. The Complete Fantasy Sports Handbook: Comprehensive Rules & Guidelines for Playing Fantasy Versions of All Four Major Sports. 106p. (Orig.). 1994. pap. write for info. (*0-9641982-0-7*) FSF.

Moore, Cassandra C. Haunted Housing: How Toxic Scare Stories Are Spooking the Public Out of House & Home. LC 97-485. 283p. 1997. 21.95 (*1-882577-41-8*); pap. 11.95 (*1-882577-42-6*) Cato Inst.

Moore, Catherine. Water under the Bridge. 400p. 1999. 24.00 (*0-8059-4440-0*) Dorrance.

***Moore, Cathy & Bernstein, Robin F.** Journal for Healing: Writing Through Pain & Illness. 337p. 1999. reprint ed. text 19.00 (*0-7881-6617-4*) DIANE Pub.

Moore, Cathy, jt. auth. see Bernstein, Robin F.

Moore, Catriona. Indecent Exposures: Shifts in Feminist Photography 1970-90. (Illus.). 220p. (Orig.). 1994. pap. text 19.95 (*1-86373-162-8*, Pub. by Allen & Unwin Pty) Paul & Co Pubs.

Moore, Catriona, ed. Dissonance: Feminism & the Arts 1970-90. LC 93-206053. (Illus.). 240p. 1994. pap. 18.95 (*1-86373-325-6*, Pub. by Allen & Unwin Pty) Paul & Co Pubs.

Moore, Celia L., jt. auth. see Michel, George F.

Moore, Charles. The Exercise of Church Leadership. 1976. pap. 2.75 (*0-88027-032-2*) Firm Foun Pub.

— A Full Inquiry into the Subject of Suicide: To Which Are Added Two Treatises on Duelling & Gaming, 2 vols. 874p. 1998. 295.00 (*1-85506-590-8*) Thoemmes Pr.

— Functioning Leadership in the Church. 1973. pap. 2.75 (*0-88027-034-9*) Firm Foun Pub.

— Moore about Revelation. 184p. 1997. 12.00 (*0-8059-4205-X*) Dorrance.

— North West under Three Flags, 1635-1796. (C). 1996. reprint ed. 62.00 (*81-206-1153-5*, Pub. by Asian Educ Servs) S Asia.

Moore, Charles, photos by. The Mother Lode: A Celebration of California's Gold Country. rev. ed. LC 98-47519. (Illus.). 132p. 1999. pap. 18.95 (*0-8118-2357-1*) Chronicle Bks.

Moore, Charles & Moore, Lisa. Dominique: Quick Shots. (Illus.). 128p. (Orig.). 1996. pap. 12.95 (*0-941613-83-6*, Caliber Comics) Stabur Pr.

Moore, Charles, et al. The City Observed: Los Angeles: A Guide to Its Architecture & Landscapes. LC 98-25056. (California Architecture & Architects Ser.: Vol. 16). (Illus.). 413p. 1998. reprint ed. pap. 22.50 (*0-940512-14-9*) Hennessey.

— A Place of Houses. LC 70-182776. (Illus.). 288p. 1995. pap. 19.95 (*0-8050-1044-0*, Owl) H Holt & Co.

Moore, Charles, ed. see Burnham, Daniel H. & Bennett, Edward H.

Moore, Charles, tr. see Papadopoulos, George.

Moore, Charles A., ed. The Chinese Mind: Essentials of Chinese Philosophy & Culture. LC 66-24011. 411p. 1967. pap. text 18.00 (*0-8248-0075-3*) UH Pr.

— The Japanese Mind: Essentials of Japanese Philosophy & Culture. LC 67-16704. 367p. 1982. pap. text 15.00 (*0-8248-0077-X*) UH Pr.

— Philosophy: East & West. LC 72-119008. (Essay Index Reprint Ser.). 1977. 26.95 (*0-8369-1677-8*) Ayer.

Moore, Charles A., ed. see East-West Philosophers Conference (4th: 1964, Univ.

Moore, Charles A., jt. ed. see Radhakrishnan, Sarvepalli.

Moore, Charles A., ed. see Takakusu, J.

Moore, Charles A., ed. see Takakusu, Junjiro.

Moore, Charles C. Behind the Bars. 2nd ed. 259p. 1990. pap. 9.00 (*0-910309-65-5*, 5332) Am Atheist.

— Dog Fennel in the Orient. (Illus.). 323p. 1984. reprint ed. pap. 9.00 (*0-910309-16-7*, 5336) Am Atheist.

***Moore, Charles E.** The Good, the Bad & the Homely: Essays from An Old-Fashioned, Country, Plastic Surgeon LC 99-35545. 1999. write for info. (*1-893357-03-1*) Ardor Scrib.

Moore, Charles E., ed. see Kierkegaard, Soren.

Moore, Charles H. Development & Character of Gothic Architecture. 1977. lib. bdg. 139.95 (*0-8490-1713-0*) Gordon Pr.

— The Mediaeval Church Architecture of England. LC 74-37900. (Select Bibliographies Reprint Ser.). 1977. reprint ed. 21.95 (*0-8369-6738-0*) Ayer.

Moore, Charles N., jt. auth. see Badnuelos, Rodrigo.

Moore, Charles W. The New Masonic Trestle-Board: Adapted to the Work & Lectures As Practiced in the Lodges, Chapters, Councils, & Encampments of Knight Templars in the U. S. A. (Illus.). 207p. 1994. reprint ed. pap. 16.95 (*1-56459-462-9*) Kessinger Pub.

***Moore, Charles W.** You Have to Pay for the Public Life: Selected Essays of Charles W. Moore. Keim, Kevin P., ed. (Illus.). 400p. 2000. 45.00 (*0-262-13373-3*) MIT Pr.

Moore, Charles W. & Attoe, Wayne, eds. Ah, Mediterranean: Twentieth Century Classicism in America, Vol. 2. (Illus.). 128p. 1986. pap. 22.00 (*0-8478-5414-0*) Ctr for Amer Archit.

Moore, Charles W., et al. The Poetics of Gardens. (Illus.). 288p. 1988. 50.00 (*0-262-13231-1*) MIT Pr.

— The Poetics of Gardens. (Illus.). 272p. 1993. pap. text 26.95 (*0-262-63153-9*) MIT Pr.

Moore, Charles W., jt. auth. see Bloomer, Kent C.

Moore, Charles W., jt. auth. see Lyndon, Donlyn.

***Moore, Charles Willard, et al.** The Place of Houses. LC 99-43787. (Illus.). 288p. 2000. 22.50 (*0-520-22357-8*, Pub. by U CA Pr) Cal Prin Full Svc.

Moore, Charlotte. Belated Bride. (Romance Ser.). 1995. per. 2.99 (*0-373-19088-3*, 1-19088-3) Silhouette.

— Martha's Ark. 272p. 1998. pap. 10.95 (*0-09-955351-1*, Pub. by Arrow Bks) Trafalgar.

— The Maverick Takes a Wife. (Romance Ser.). 1996. per. 2.99 (*0-373-19129-4*, 1-19129-5) Silhouette.

— Not the Marrying Kind. (Romance Ser.). 1993. per. 2.75 (*0-373-08975-9*, 5-08975-0) Silhouette.

— Trust Me. LC 96-2451. (Shadows Ser.). 248p. 1996. per. 3.50 (*0-373-27062-3*, 1-27062-8) Silhouette.

Moore, Chauncey O., jt. auth. see Moore, Ethel.

Moore, Cherie. Guide to Nutrition. 152p. (C). 1998. per. 25.95 (*0-7872-5415-0*, 41541501) Kendall-Hunt.

***Moore, Cherie.** Sports & Fitness Nutrition. 140p. (C). 2000. per. 41.95 (*0-7872-7217-5*) Kendall-Hunt.

Moore, Chinelu. Dark Storm Rising. 1998. mass mkt. 4.99 (*0-345-42220-1*) Ballantine Pub Grp.

— Dark Storm Rising. LC 94-77079. 190p. 1994. pap. 10.95 (*1-885478-05-4*, Pub. by Genesis Press) BookWorld.

***Moore, Chip, ed.** Maritime Trade & Transportation. (Illus.). 128p. (C). 2000. pap. text 30.00 (*0-7567-0030-2*) DIANE Pub.

Moore, Chris. The Arches of Arches National Park, Vol. 4, Supplement 3. (Illus.). 120p. 2001. spiral bd. 12.95 (*1-891858-09-2*, 0605) Arch Hunter Bks.

— A Guide Book to the Natural Arches of Canyonlands National Park. (Illus.). 120p. 2002. pap. 9.95 (*1-891858-13-0*, 4016) Arch Hunter Bks.

— A Guide Book to the Natural Arches of Capitol Reef National Park. (Illus.). 90p. 2001. pap. 8.95 (*1-891858-06-8*, 4000) Arch Hunter Bks.

— A Guide Book to the Natural Arches of the Moab Utah Area (North) (Illus.). 56p. 1998. pap. 6.95 (*1-891858-03-3*, 4003) Arch Hunter Bks.

— A Guide Book to the Natural Arches of the Moab Utah Area (South) (Illus.). 56p. 1998. pap. 6.95 (*1-891858-04-1*, 4005) Arch Hunter Bks.

— A Guide Book to the Natural Arches of the San Rafael Swell of Southern Utah. (Illus.). 120p. 2000. pap. 8.95 (*1-891858-05-X*, 4001) Arch Hunter Bks.

— The Natural Arches of Rattlesnake Canyon. (Illus.). 32p. 2000. pap. 1.95 (*1-891858-12-2*, 4015) Arch Hunter Bks.

— The Natural Arches of the Moab Area. (Illus.). 125p. 2001. mass mkt. 12.95 (*1-891858-15-7*, 4052) Arch Hunter Bks.

Moore, Chris. The Oceans & the Jungles. (J). 1988. write for info. (*0-318-62377-3*, PuffinBks) Peng Put Young Read.

Moore, Chris. A Recreation Guide to the Book Cliffs. (Illus.). 90p. 2001. pap. 7.95 (*1-891858-10-6*, 4013) Arch Hunter Bks.

Moore, Chris & Booth, Simon A. Managing Competition: Meso-Corporatism, Pluralism, & the Negotiated Order in Scotland. (Illus.). 184p. 1989. text 49.95 (*0-19-827578-1*) OUP.

Moore, Chris & Dunham, Philip, eds. Joint Attention: Its Origin & Role in Development. LC 94-40160. 296p. 1995. text 59.95 (*0-8058-1437-X*) L Erlbaum Assocs.

Moore, Chris & Remakel, John. A Guide Book to the Natural Arches of Arches National Park. Wunder, Dick, ed. (Illus.). 54p. 1998. pap. 6.95 (*1-891858-01-7*, 4009) Arch Hunter Bks.

Moore, Chris, et al. The Arches of Arches National Park Vol. 3: Supplement Two. (Illus.). 112p. 1998. spiral bd. 12.95 (*1-891858-00-9*, 0604) Arch Hunter Bks.

Moore, Chris, jt. auth. see Lever, William.

Moore, Chris, ed. see Allen, Virginia.

***Moore, Christian.** Cardassian Union. 1999. 35.00 (*0-671-04013-8*) S&S Childrens.

— Star Trek: Deep Space Nine Players Guide. 160p. 2000. 26.00 (*0-671-03514-2*) PB.

***Moore, Christian & Hite, Ken.** The Andorians. 128p. 2000. per. 22.00 (*0-671-04017-0*) PB.

— Final Frontiers. 160p. 2000. 26.00 (*0-671-03511-8*) PB.

— The Star Trek Guide to Parallel Planets. 128p. 2000. 20.00 (*0-671-03520-7*) PB.

***Moore, Christian & Isaacs, Ross.** The Klingon Empire. 128p. 2000. mass mkt. 35.00 (*0-671-04011-1*) PB.

— The Romulan Companion. 160p. 2000. 26.00 (*0-671-03518-5*) PB.

— The Starfleet Security Handbook. 128p. 2000. 20.00 (*0-671-03517-7*) PB.

***Moore, Christian & Long, Steve.** The Bajorans. 128p. 2000. mass mkt. 22.00 (*0-671-04012-X*) PB.

— Core Rules Book. (Star Trek Deep Space Nine Ser.). (Illus.). 296p. 2000. mass mkt. 35.00 (*0-671-03500-2*) PB.

— Dominion War. 128p. 20.00 (*0-671-03515-0*) PB.

— Raiders, Renegades & Rogues. (Star Trek Deep Space Nine Ser.). (Illus.). 128p. 2000. per. 20.00 (*0-671-03504-5*) PB.

— RPG Narrator's Toolkit. (Star Trek Deep Space Nine Ser.). (Illus.). 64p. 2000. mass mkt. 16.00 (*0-671-03501-0*) PB.

— The Starfleet Starship Construction Manual. 128p. 2000. mass mkt. 20.00 (*0-671-04019-7*) PB.

Moore, Christian S. & Seyler, Owen M. ARIA Roleplaying. (ARIA Ser.). (Illus.). 528p. 1994. pap. 29.95 (*0-9645903-0-1*) Last Unicorn Games.

— ARIA Worlds. (ARIA Ser.). (Illus.). 336p. 1994. pap. 25.95 (*0-9645903-1-X*) Last Unicorn Games.

Moore, Christine, jt. auth. see English, Philip T.

***Moore, Christopher.** Bloodsucking Fiends: A Love Story. 304p. 2000. pap. 12.50 (*0-380-72813-3*, Avon Bks) Morrow Avon.

Moore, Christopher. Coyote Blue. 1994. 21.00 (*0-671-88188-4*) S&S Trade.

***Moore, Christopher.** Coyote Blue. 304p. 2000. reprint ed. pap. 12.00 (*0-380-72523-1*, Avon Bks) Morrow Avon.

Moore, Christopher. 1867, Vol.1. 1999. pap. 16.95 (*0-7710-6096-3*) McCland & Stewart.

— 1867: How the Fathers Made a Deal. LC 98-160134. 256p. 1998. 23.95 (*0-7710-6094-7*) McCland & Stewart.

— His Lordship's Arsenal. 232p. 1985. 15.95 (*0-88191-033-3*) Freundlich.

— Island of the Sequined Love Nun. LC 96-54696. 1997. mass mkt. 23.00 (*0-380-97505-X*, Avon Bks) Morrow Avon.

— Island of the Sequined Love Nun. 416p. 1998. mass mkt. 6.99 (*0-380-79273-7*, Avon Bks) Morrow Avon.

***Moore, Christopher.** Island of the Sequined Love Nun. 336p. 2000. pap. 13.00 (*0-380-81654-7*, Avon Bks) Morrow Avon.

Moore, Christopher. The Law Society of Upper Canada & Ontario's Lawyers, 1797-1997. LC 97-127666. (Illus.). 395p. 1997. text 45.00 (*0-8020-4127-2*) U of Toronto Pr.

— Loyalists: Revolution, Exile, Settlement. 280p. 1994. pap. 16.95 (*0-7710-6093-9*) McCland & Stewart.

— The Lust Lizard of Melancholy Cove. LC 98-46850. 320p. 1999. 23.00 (*0-380-97506-8*, Avon Bks) Morrow Avon.

***Moore, Christopher.** The Lust Lizard of Melancholy Cove. 320p. 2000. pap. 13.00 (*0-380-79274-5*, Avon Bks) Morrow Avon.

Moore, Christopher. Practical Demonkeeping. 320p. 1999. mass mkt. 6.99 (*0-380-73037-5*, Avon Bks) Morrow Avon.

***Moore, Christopher.** Practical Demonkeeping. 256p. 2000. pap. 13.00 (*0-380-81655-5*, Avon Bks) Morrow Avon.

Moore, Christopher & Johnson, Pamela. Santa & Pete: A Novel of Christmas Present & Past. LC 98-27776. (Illus.). 176p. 1998. 14.95 (*0-684-85495-3*) Simon & Schuster.

Moore, Christopher, jt. auth. see Kingwell, Mark.

Moore, Christopher, jt. auth. see Stuart, Ralph B., III.

Moore, Christopher C. Opening the Clergy Parachute: Soft Landings for Church Leaders Who Are Seeking Change. 160p. (Orig.). 1995. pap. 14.95 (*0-687-08659-0*) Abingdon.

M

An Asterisk (*) at the beginning of an entry indicates that the title is appearing for the first time.

Moore, Christopher W. The Mediation Process: Practical Strategies for Resolving Conflict. 2nd rev. ed. (Conflict Resolution Ser.). 400p. 1996. 36.95 (0-7879-0248-9) Jossey-Bass.

Moore, Cindy & Windom, Tricia. Planning a Wedding When Your Parents Are Divorced. 2nd rev. ed. (Illus.). 208p. 1997. pap. 12.95 (0-942407-35-0) Father & Son.

Moore, Clancy & Chafin, M. B. Tennis Everyone. 5th ed. 238p. 1994. pap. text 15.95 (0-88725-205-2) Hunter Textbks.

Moore, Clarence Bloomfield. The East Florida Expeditions of Clarence Bloomfield Moore. Mitchem, Jeffrey M., ed. LC 98-58053. (Classics in Southeastern Archaeology Ser.). 1999. 39.95 (0-8173-0950-0) U of Ala Pr.

— Lower Mississippi Valley Expeditions of Clarence Bloomfield Moore. LC 98-19292. (Classics in Southeastern Archaeology Ser.). 472p. 1998. pap. text 39.95 (0-8173-0949-7) U of Ala Pr.

***Moore, Clarence Bloomfield.** The Southern & Central Alabama Expeditions of Clarence Bloomfield Moore. LC 99-50751. (Classics in Southeastern Archaeology Ser.). 240p. 2000. pap. 39.95 (0-8173-1019-3) U of Ala Pr.

Moore, Clarence Bloomfield & Larson, Lewis H. The Georgia & South Carolina Expeditions of Clarence Bloomfield Moore. LC 98-19728. (Classics in Southeastern Archaeology Ser.). 312p. 1998. pap. text 34.95 (0-8173-0941-1) U of Ala Pr.

***Moore, Clarence Bloomfield & Polhemus, Richard R.** The Tennessee, Green & Lower Ohio Rivers Expeditions of Clarence Bloomfield Moore. LC 99-6649. (Classics in Southeastern Archaeology Ser.). 2000. pap. write for info. (0-8173-1018-5) U of Ala Pr.

Moore, Clayton & Thompson, Frank. I Was That Masked Man. 304p. 1996. 22.95 (0-87833-939-6) Taylor Pub.

— I Was That Masked Man. (Illus.). 280p. 1998. pap. 10.95 (0-87833-216-2) Taylor Pub.

Moore, Clement Clarke. Disney Babies: The Night Before Christmas. LC 91-58969. (Disney Babies Ser.). (Illus.). (J). 1992. 11.95 (1-56282-244-6, Pub. by Disney Pr) Little.

— The Night Before Christmas. (Children's Classics Ser.). (Illus.). 32p. (J). 1991. 6.95 (0-8362-4917-8) Andrews & McMeel.

— The Night Before Christmas. (Illus.). 16p. 1992. 4.95 (0-8362-3027-2) Andrews & McMeel.

***Moore, Clement Clarke.** The Night Before Christmas. (Illus.). (J). 2000. pap. 1.00 (0-486-41031-5) Dover.

Moore, Clement Clarke. The Night Before Christmas. pap. 6.95 (0-8378-8504-3) Gibson.

— The Night Before Christmas. (Super Shape Bks.). (Illus.). 24p. (J). (ps-k). 1991. 3.29 (0-307-10038-3, 10038) Gldn Bks Pub Co.

— The Night Before Christmas. (Look-Look Bks.). (J). 1996. pap. text 3.29 (0-307-13080-0, 13080, Goldn Books) Gldn Bks Pub Co.

— The Night Before Christmas. (Little Golden Storybks.). (J). 1997. 3.99 (0-307-16178-1, 16178, Goldn Books) Gldn Bks Pub Co.

— The Night Before Christmas. (Illus.). 24p. (J). (ps-2). 1984. pap. 2.95 (0-89542-498-3, Ideals Child) Hambleton-Hill.

— The Night Before Christmas. (Illus.). 16p. (J). (ps-1). 1994. pap. 7.95 (1-57102-011-X, Ideals Child) Hambleton-Hill.

— The Night Before Christmas. LC 97-34352. (Illus.). 40p. (J). 1999. 16.95 (0-06-026608-2) HarpC.

— The Night Before Christmas. LC 90-22388. (Merry Christmas Bk.). (Illus.). 24p. (J). (ps up). 1991. 2.95 (0-694-00365-4) HarpC Child Bks.

— The Night Before Christmas. LC 97-34352. (Illus.). 40p. (J). (ps-3). 1999. lib. bdg. 16.89 (0-06-028380-7) HarpC Child Bks.

— The Night Before Christmas. (Chubby Board Bks.). (Illus.). 16p. (J). (ps up). 1984. pap. 3.95 (0-671-50952-7) Litle Simon.

— The Night Before Christmas. (Illus.). 32p. (J). (ps-1). 1986. pap. 5.95 (0-671-62209-9) Litle Simon.

— The Night Before Christmas. LC 96-28153. (Illus.). 32p. (J). (gr. k-3). 1997. 13.95 (0-316-57963-7) Little.

— The Night Before Christmas. LC 98-21623. (Illus.). 32p. (J). (gr. k-3). 1999. 14.95 (0-316-85579-0) Little.

— The Night Before Christmas. LC 96-48760. (Illus.). 64p. (J). 1997. per. 18.00 (0-689-81375-9) McElderry Bks.

— The Night Before Christmas. (Illus.). 10p. (J). (ps-7). 1989. pap. 3.95 (0-922589-06-2) More Than a Card.

— The Night Before Christmas. LC 95-1775. (Illus.). 32p. (J). (ps-2). 1995. lib. bdg. 16.88 (1-55858-466-8, Pub. by North-South Bks NYC) Chronicle Bks.

— The Night Before Christmas. LC 92-27138. (All Aboard Bks.). (Illus.). 32p. (J). (ps-3). 1993. pap. 2.95 (0-448-40482-6, G & D) Peng Put Young Read.

***Moore, Clement Clarke.** The Night Before Christmas. (Jellybean Bks.). (Illus.). 24p. (J). (ps-k). 1999. lib. bdg. 7.99 (0-375-90147-7, Pub. by Random Bks Yng Read) Random.

Moore, Clement Clarke. The Night Before Christmas. LC 98-67793. (Jellybean Bks.). (Illus.). 24p. (J). (ps-3). 1999. 1.99 (0-375-80147-2, Pub. by Random Bks Yng Read) Random.

— The Night Before Christmas. (Illus.). 40p. (J). (ps up). 1996. 10.95 incl. audio (0-689-80793-7) S&S Bks Yung.

***Moore, Clement Clarke.** The Night Before Christmas. (Illus.). 60p. (J). (ps-1). 1999. pap. 12.98 (1-58048-065-9) Sandvik Pub.

Moore, Clement Clarke. The Night Before Christmas. 1987. pap. 1.75 (0-8167-1223-9) Troll Communs.

— The Night Before Christmas. LC 87-15343. (Illus.). 48p. (J). (gr. k-3). 1988. lib. bdg. 19.95 (0-8167-1209-3) Troll Communs.

— The Night Before Christmas. (Blue Ribbon Bks.). (J). 1985. 10.15 (0-606-01915-4, Pub. by Turtleback) Demco.

— The Night Before Christmas. (Illus.). 32p. (J). (ps up). 1994. mass mkt. 16.00 (0-02-767646-3, Mac Bks Young Read) S&S Childrens.

— The Night Before Christmas. abr. ed. (Classic Christmas Sticker Storybook Ser.). (Illus.). 18p. (J). (ps-3). 1996. 3.50 (0-689-80256-0) Aladdin.

— The Night Before Christmas. abr. ed. LC 95-20326. (Wee Books for Wee Folks). (Illus.). 64p. (ps-3). 1995. 6.95 (1-55709-410-1) Applewood.

— The Night Before Christmas. abr. ed. LC 80-84842. (Illus.). 12p. (J). (ps-3). 1995. 12.95 (0-8050-0900-0, Bks Young Read) H Holt & Co.

— The Night Before Christmas. abr. ed. (Illus.). 32p. (J). (ps-3). 1993. pap. 5.95 (0-395-66508-6, Clarion Bks) HM.

— The Night Before Christmas. abr. ed. LC 98-16589. (Illus.). 24p. (J). (ps-2). 1998. 6.95 (1-57102-135-3, Ideals Child) Hambleton-Hill.

— The Night Before Christmas. abr. ed. LC 80-11758. (Illus.). 32p. (J). (ps-3). 1980. pap. 6.95 (0-8234-0417-X); lib. bdg. 16.95 (0-8234-0414-5) Holiday.

— The Night Before Christmas. abr. ed. LC 92-22712. (Illus.). 40p. (J). (ps-3). 1992. 14.95 (0-88708-261-0, Rabbit Ears) Litle Simon.

— The Night Before Christmas. abr. ed. LC 95-1775. (Illus.). 32p. (J). (ps-3). 1995. 16.95 (1-55858-465-X, Pub. by North-South Bks NYC) Chronicle Bks.

— The Night Before Christmas. abr. ed. LC 75-7511. (Illus.). 32p. (J). (ps-3). 1975. pap. 3.25 (0-394-83019-9, Pub. by Random Bks Yng Read) Random.

— The Night Before Christmas. abr. ed. LC 88-35019. (Illus.). 40p. (J). (ps-3). 1990. 8.99 (0-394-82698-1, Pub. by Random Bks Yng Read) Random.

— The Night Before Christmas. abr. ed. LC 88-35019. (Illus.). 32p. (J). (ps-3). 1989. pap. 3.25 (0-671-68408-6) S&S Trade.

— The Night Before Christmas. abr. ed. LC 89-22386. (Illus.). 32p. (J). (ps-3). 1989. pap. 2.99 (0-590-42758-X) Scholastic Inc.

— The Night Before Christmas. abr. ed. LC 87-15343. (Illus.). 48p. (J). (ps-3). 1989. pap. 5.95 (0-8167-1210-7) Troll Communs.

— The Night Before Christmas. abr. ed. (Illus.). 32p. (J). (gr. 1-4). 1996. pap. 2.95 (0-8167-4058-5, Whistlstop) Troll Communs.

— The Night Before Christmas. abr. ed. LC 87-15343. (Illus.). 48p. (J). (ps up). 1997. pap. 2.95 (0-8167-1890-3) Troll Communs.

— The Night Before Christmas. LC 95-67986. (Illus.). 32p. (J). (ps-3). 1997. reprint ed. pap. 3.99 (0-7636-0351-1) Candlewick Pr.

— The Night Before Christmas. (Illus.). 40p. 1971. reprint ed. pap. 2.95 (0-486-22797-9) Dover.

— The Night Before Christmas. LC 98-66375. (Illus.). 26p. (J). 1998. reprint ed. 14.95 (1-56352-533-X) Longstreet.

— The Night Before Christmas. LC 89-34789. (Illus.). 32p. (J). 1990. reprint ed. 14.95 (0-88289-755-1) Pelican.

— The Night Before Christmas. rev. ed. (Illus.). 24p. (J). (ps-1). 1995. 6.95 (1-57102-082-9, Ideals Child); pap. 2.49 (1-57102-076-4, Ideals Child) Hambleton-Hill.

— The Night Before Christmas. unabridged ed. (Illus.). (J). (gr. k-3). 1984. 24.95 incl. audio (0-941078-39-6); pap. 15.95 incl. audio (0-941078-37-X) Live Oak Media.

— The Night Before Christmas, Mini Edition. (Illus.). 32p. (J). 1996. 4.99 (0-679-87930-7) Knopf.

— The Night Before Christmas, 4 bks., Set. LC 87-15343. (Illus.). (J). (gr. k-3). 1984. pap., teacher ed. 37.95 incl. audio (0-941078-38-8) Live Oak Media.

— The Night Before Christmas: A Reproduction of an Antique Christmas Classic. LC 88-19600. (Illus.). 32p. (J). 1989. 17.95 (0-399-21614-6, Philomel) Peng Put Young Read.

***Moore, Clement Clarke.** Night Before Christmas: A Trim-a-tree Story. 1999. 6.99 (1-57866-076-9) Galahad Bks.

— Night Before Christmas: A Victorian Vision of the Christmas Classic. (Illus.). 32p. (J). (ps-3). 2000. pap. 6.99 (0-375-81047-1) Random.

— The Night Before Christmas: The Classic Edition. abr. ed. LC 95-67238. (Children's Illustrated Classics Ser.). (Illus.). 48p. (J). (ps-3). 1995. 9.98 (1-56138-476-3, Courage) Running Pr.

Moore, Clement Clarke. The Night Before Christmas: The Classic Poem. LC 97-11482. (Illus.). 32p. (J). (gr. k-2). 1997. 11.95 (0-8249-4084-9, Candy Cane Pr); bds. 6.95 (0-8249-4089-X, Candy Cane Pr) Ideals.

— The Night Before Christmas: Told in Signed English. (Awareness & Caring Ser.). (Illus.). 64p. (J). (gr. k-6). 1995. lib. bdg. 17.95 (1-56674-109-2) Forest Hse.

— The Night Before Christmas: Told in Signed English. LC 94-11477. (Illus.). 64p. 1994. 14.95 (1-56368-020-3, Pub. by K Green Pubns) Gallaudet Univ Pr.

— The Night Before Christmas Board Book. abr. ed. LC 91-46766. (Illus.). 26p. (J). (ps up). 1992. 6.95 (0-694-00424-3) HarpC Child Bks.

— The Night Before Christmas Coloring Book. (J). 1986. pap. 2.95 (0-671-62959-X) Litle Simon.

— Night Before Christmas Gift Set. 1999. 17.98 (0-7624-0644-5) Running Pr.

— The Night Before Christmas in Hawaii. (Illus.). 32p. (J). 1991. text 8.98 (0-9627294-2-6) Hawaiian Resources.

***Moore, Clement Clarke.** The Night Before Christmas Mini Book. (Illus.). 32p. (J). 1999. 7.95 (0-7358-1226-8, Pub. by North-South Bks NYC) Chronicle Bks.

— Teddy Bears' Night Before Christmas. (ps-3). 1999. 103.60 (0-439-11752-6) Scholastic Inc.

Moore, Clement Clarke. The Teddy Bears' Night Before Christmas. LC 98-61147. (Illus.). 40p. (J). (ps-2). 1999. 12.95 (0-590-03243-7, Pub. by Scholastic Inc) Penguin Putnam.

— The Three-D Night Before Christmas. LC 94-60904. 32p. (J). 1994. pap. text 7.95 (0-9641811-5-0) Three-D Revel.

— 'Twas the Night Before Christmas. (Christmas Fun-to-Read Fairy Tales Ser.). (Illus.). 24p. (J). (gr. k-3). 1992. pap. 2.50 (1-56144-163-5, Honey Bear Bks) Modern Pub NYC.

— 'Twas the Night Before Christmas. anniversary ed. LC 93-40243. (Illus.). 48p. (J). 1992. pap. 4.95 (0-395-64374-0) HM.

— 'Twas the Night Before Christmas: A Visit from St. Nicholas, 001. (Illus.). 32p. (J). (ps-2). 1912. 15.00 (0-395-06952-1) HM.

— A Visit from St. Nicholas. LC 93-33703. (Little Activity Bks.). (Illus.). 32p. (J). (gr. 2 up). 1994. pap. 1.00 (0-486-27978-2) Dover.

— A Visit from St. Nicholas. (Illus.). 32p. (J). (ps-3). 1998. 14.95 (1-55209-286-0) Firefly Bks Ltd.

— A Visit from St. Nicholas. Hodson, Sue, ed. LC 97-40730. (Illus.). 32p. (J). (ps-k). 1997. 14.95 (0-87328-171-3) Huntington Lib.

***Moore, Clement Clarke.** A Visit from St. Nicholas. (Illus.). 32p. (J). 1999. reprint ed. pap. 5.99 (1-55209-429-4) Firefly Bks Ltd.

***Moore, Clement Clarke & Mills, Donald.** The Night Before Christmas. LC 00-20434. 2000. write for info. (0-8249-4186-1, Candy Cane Pr) Ideals.

Moore, Clement Clarke & Pomaska, Anna. The Night Before Christmas Sticker Storybook. (Illus.). 16p. (Orig.). (J). 1996. pap. text 1.00 (0-486-29197-9) Dover.

Moore, Clement Clarke & Williams, Jenny. The Night Before Christmas. (Glitter Glow Board Bks.). (Illus.). 12p. (J). (ps-2). 1997. 4.99 (0-689-81692-8) Simon & Schuster.

Moore, Clement Clarke, et al. The Night Before Christmas: A Classic Illustrated Edition. LC 97-4101. (Illus.). (J). (ps up). 1998. 16.95 (0-8118-1712-1) Chronicle Bks.

Moore, Clifton A., jt. auth. see Ashford, Norman J.

Moore, Clyde B. Civic Education, Its Objectives & Methods for a Specific Case Group: A Study in Educational Sociology. LC 70-177080. (Columbia University. Teachers College. Contributions to Education Ser.: No. 151). reprint ed. 37.50 (0-404-55151-3) AMS Pr.

***Moore, Coleen.** The Newbies' Money Guide: For Rookies & Late Starters; Simple Steps to Wealth & Security. 309p. 2000. pap. 14.95 (0-9676954-1-4, Pub. by Pnt of View) ACCESS Pubs Network.

Moore, Coleman, jt. auth. see Carney, Glandion.

Moore, Colleen G. Pud's in Practice. LC 85-51488. 94p. 1985. pap. 36.95 (0-87420-644-8, P36) Urban Land.

Moore College of Arts & Design Staff. Terry Fox: Articulations. (Labyrinth - Text Works). (Illus.). 46p. 1992. pap. 15.00 (0-685-67186-0) Feldman Fine Arts.

Moore-Colyer, Richard J. Man's Proper Study. 182p. (C). 1982. 30.00 (0-85088-944-8, Pub. by Gomer Pr) St Mut.

Moore-Colyer, Richard J., ed. A Land of Pure Delight: Selections from the Letters of Thomas Johnes of Hafod 1748 - 1816. 314p. (C). 1992. 50.00 (0-86383-751-4, Pub. by Gomer Pr) St Mut.

Moore, Connie. Snow Globes: The Collector's Guide to Selecting, Displaying, & Restoring Snow Globes. 1999. pap. text 12.95 (1-57715-077-5) Knckerbocker.

***Moore, Connie & Rinker, Harry.** Snow Globes: The Collector's Guide to Selecting, Displaying & Restoring Snow Globes. (Illus.). 80p. 2000. 17.00 (0-7881-9401-1) DIANE Pub.

Moore, Connie, jt. auth. see Grainger, Janette.

Moore, Cornelia N. & Moody, Raymond, eds. Comparative Literature East & West: Traditions & Trends. (Literary Studies: East & West: Vol. 1). 304p. 1989. pap. text 18.00 (0-8248-1247-6) UH Pr.

Moore, Cornelia N., ed. see East-West Center Staff, et al.

Moore, Cornelia N., jt. ed. see Rauch, Irmengard.

Moore, Cornelia N., jt. ed. see Wayne, Valerie.

Moore Cornwell, David John, see Le Carre, John, pseud.

Moore, Craig. Sports Law & Litigation. 196p. 1997. pap. 62.00 (1-85811-161-7, Pub. by CLT Prof) Gaunt.

Moore, Craig, jt. auth. see Stevens, Benjamin H.

Moore, Craig L., et al. The Impact of Banking on the Regional Income Multiplier. (Discussion Papers: No. 112). 1979. pap. 10.00 (1-55869-053-0) Regional Sci Res Inst.

Moore, Cristopher, jt. auth. see Griffeath, David.

Moore, Curtis & Miller, Alan. Green Gold: Japan, Germany, the United States, & the Race for Environmental Technology. 288p. (C). 1996. pap. 14.95 (0-8070-8531-6) Beacon Pr.

Moore, Cyd. A Frog Inside My Hat: A First Book of Poems. LC 93-22200. 64p. (J). (ps-3). 1997. pap. 5.95 (0-8167-3130-6, Troll Medallion) Troll Communs.

— Goldilocks & the Three Bears: Big Book. large type ed. (Little Books & Big Bks.). 8p. (J). (ps-1). 1998. pap. text 19.89 (0-8215-0861-X) Sadlier.

***Moore, Cyd & Gary, Amy, eds.** Picturebook 2K: The Directory of Children's Illustration. (Illus.). 328p. 2000. pap. 29.95 (1-882077-92-X) WaterMark Inc.

Moore, Cyd, jt. ed. see Gary, Amy.

Moore, Cynthia. Paraprofessionals in Village-Level Development in Sri Lanka: The Sarvodaya Shramadana Movement. (Special Series on Paraprofessionals: No. 4). 64p. (Orig.). (C). 1981. pap. 6.85 (0-86731-047-2) Cornell CIS RDC.

Moore, D. Zen Gardening Kit. (Illus.). 96p. 1992. 30.00 (1-56138-148-9) Running Pr.

Moore, D. & Hungr, O., eds. Engineering Geology & the Environment: Proceedings of the 8th International Congress of the IAEG, Vancouver, 21-25 September, 1998, 6 vols. 5000p. (C). 1998. text 449.00 (90-5410-990-4, Pub. by A A Balkema) Ashgate Pub Co.

Moore, D. Elizabeth. The Librarian's Genealogy Notebook: A Guide to Resources. LC 98-19110. x, 142 p. 1998. 32.00 (0-8389-0744-X) ALA.

Moore, D. F. Elastomer Friction Lubrication. 305p. (C). 1975. text 137.00 (0-08-016749-7, Pub. by Pergamon Repr) Franklin.

— Principles & Applications of Tribology. (C). 1975. 181.00 (0-08-017902-9, Pub. by Pergamon Repr) Franklin.

Moore, D. J. A Metaphysics of the Computer: The Reality Machine & a New Science for the Holistic Age. LC 92-10574. 392p. 1992. lib. bdg. 99.95 (0-7734-2302-8) E Mellen.

Moore, D. M. The Vascular Flora of the Falkland Islands. (British Antarctic Survey Report Ser.: No. 60). (Illus.). 214p. 1968. 36.00 (0-85665-032-3, Pub. by Brit Antarctic Surv) Balogh.

Moore, D. M., tr. see Martin, Marie-Louise.

Moore, D. R., jt. auth. see Turner, S.

Moore, Dahlia. Labor Market Segmentation & Its Implications: Inequality, Deprivation & Entitlement. LC 91-23810. (Library of Sociology: Vol. 21). 356p. 1992. text 25.00 (0-8240-6994-3, 665) Garland.

Moore, Dalian. Madman on Lakeshore Drive. LC 94-71400. 32p. 1994. pap. text 9.95 (1-885206-00-3, Iliad Pr) Cader Pubng.

***Moore, Dan Ray.** The Decendants of John Moore of Somerset County, Maryland. LC 99-489842. (Illus.). 679p. 1999. 60.00 (1-890307-25-4) Boyd Pub Co.

Moore, Dana T. Quicksilver & Quills. LC 94-60196. 272p. 1994. pap. 12.95 (1-884570-06-2) Research Triangle.

Moore, Daniel. Ramadan Sonnets. (Orig.). 1996. pap. 10.95 (0-9652031-0-7) City Lights.

Moore, Daniel C. Regional Block: A Handbook for Use in the Clinical Practice of Medicine & Surgery. 4th ed. (Illus.). 532p. 1981. 53.95 (0-398-01337-3) C C Thomas.

Moore, Daniel G. Enter Without Knocking. LC 68-22333. (Illus.). 271p. reprint ed. pap. 84.10 (0-7837-5171-0, 204490100004) Bks Demand.

Moore, Daniel J. Electronic Design Laboratory Manual. 88p. (C). 1996. text, lab manual ed. 16.00 (0-256-21150-7, Irwn McGrw-H) McGrw-H Hghr Educ.

Moore, Danny M. When a Ship Misses a Harbor, It's Rarely the Harbor's Fault: A Collection of 300 Power Phrases. LC 97-72780. 124p. 1997. pap. 6.95 (1-890622-01-X) Leathers Pub.

***Moore, Daphna.** Certified Nurse Assistant's Exam Questions for Long Term Care Certification. 3rd rev. ed. (Illus.). 210p. (C). 2000. pap. 49.95 (1-892693-60-7) Hughes Henshaw Pubs.

Moore, Daphna. The Rabbi's Tarot: Spiritual Secrets of the Tarot. LC 89-2489. (New Age Tarot Ser.). (Illus.). 408p. (Orig.). 1999. pap. 12.95 (0-87542-572-0) Llewellyn Pubns.

***Moore, Daphna R.** Don't Camp Out in the Garden of Eden. 160p. 1999. pap. 14.95 (1-892693-10-0) Hughes Henshaw Pubs.

— Massage National Exam Questions & Answers. 3rd rev. ed. (Illus.). 202p. 2000. pap. 49.95 (1-892693-08-9) Hughes Henshaw Pubs.

Moore, Daphna R. Self-Publishing for Greater Profits. 2nd rev. ed. LC 99-12417. Orig. Title: How to Publish, Market & Distribute Your Own Books. 101p. 1999. pap. 12.95 (1-892693-03-8) Hughes Henshaw Pubs.

Moore, Daphna R. & Perrusquia, Gina. Massage Therapy Exam Questions. 2nd rev. ed. LC 99-12414. Orig. Title: How to Pass Your Massage Therapy Exams. 141p. 1999. pap. text 38.00 (1-892693-02-X) Hughes Henshaw Pubs.

Moore, Darrick. Mark of a Shadow. (Illus.). 72p. 1998. pap. 10.00 (0-9667048-0-0) SilkWorks.

Moore, David. Age of Progress, or, a Panorama of Time: In Four Visions. LC 76-154453. (Utopian Literature Ser.). (Illus.). 1976. reprint ed. 26.95 (0-405-03535-7) Ayer.

***Moore, David.** Dynamic Duos. (Fast Breaks Ser.). (J). (gr. 2-4). 1998. pap. text 4.99 (0-590-12079-4) Scholastic Inc.

— Dynamic Duos, 3. (Fast Breaks Ser.). 1998. 8.60 (0-606-13376-3, Pub. by Turtleback) Demco.

Moore, David. Fast Breaks No. 2. LC 97-140288. (J). (gr. 5-7). 1997. mass mkt. 3.50 (0-590-13772-7) Scholastic Inc.

— Fungal Morphogenesis. LC 97-43011. (Developmental & Cell Biology Ser.: No. 35). (Illus.). 480p. (C). 1998. 80.00 (0-521-55295-8) Cambridge U Pr.

— The Lads in Action: Ethnicity, Identity & Social Process Amongst Australian Skinheads. (Popular Cultural Studies). 192p. 1994. 59.95 (1-85742-203-1, Pub. by Arena) Ashgate Pub Co.

— Reinventing NASA. (Illus.). 41p. (Orig.). (C). 1994. pap. text 25.00 (0-7881-1403-4) DIANE Pub.

Moore, David. Spiritual Prescriptions: Rx for Health, Happiness & Abundance. 3rd ed. 96p. 1981. pap. 5.00 (0-8315-0011-5) Speller.

Moore, David, et al, eds. Biological & Medical Research in Space: An Overview of Life Sciences Research in Microgravity. LC 95-49025. (Illus.). 232p. 1996. 148.00 (3-540-60636-X) Spr-Verlag.

Moore, David & Hoaglin, David, eds. Perspectives on Contemporary Statistics. LC 91-62170. (MAA Notes Ser.: Vol. 21). 192p. 1991. pap. text 18.00 (0-88385-075-3, NTE-21) Math Assn.

Moore, David, ed. see Buscaino, Dale & Daniel, Scott.

Moore, David, jt. ed. see Chiu, Siu W.

Moore, David, ed. see Moreno, Richard.

Moore, David, ed. see Thomas, R. Dale & Allen, Charles M.

An Asterisk (*) at the beginning of an entry indicates that the title is appearing for the first time.

Moore, David, tr. see Alfieri, Dino.

Moore, David, tr. see Malaparte, Curzio.

Moore, David B. & Schmitz, Gerald J., eds. Debating Development Discourse: Institutional & Popular Perspectives. (International Political Economy Ser.). 288p. 1995. text 75.00 (*0-312-12886-X*) St Martin.

Moore, David C. Government Contract Negotiations: A Practical Guide for Small Business. LC 95-39205. 288p. 1996. 105.00 (*0-471-13451-1*) Wiley.

— Politics of Deference: A Study of the Mid-Ninteenth Century English Political System. (Modern Revivals in History Ser.). 576p. 1994. 96.95 (*0-7512-0236-3*, Pub. by Gregg Revivals) Ashgate Pub Co.

Moore, David D. Choosing a Path. 39p. 1990. pap. 5.95 (*0-913543-17-9*) African Am Imag.

Moore, David G. The Battles for Hell: A Survey & Evaluation of Evangelicals' Growing Attraction to the Doctrine of Annihilationism. LC 95-10744. 118p. (C). 1995. lib. bdg. 34.00 (*0-8191-9955-9*) U Pr of Amer.

— False Idols. (Orig.). pap. 15.95 (*0-9639494-0-3*) Jupiter NY.

***Moore, David G. & Hesse, Gary.** Ephemeral Beings. (Illus.). 76p. 2000. pap. 13.95 (*0-9639494-1-1*) Jupiter NY.

Moore, David G., ed. see Worthy, James C.

Moore, David L. Dark Sky, Dark Land: Stories of the Hmong Boy Scouts, Troop 100. LC 89-51103. (Illus.). 191p. (Orig.). 1989. pap. 14.95 (*0-9623029-0-2*) St Johns Pub.

Moore, David M. Flora of Tierra del Fuego. (Illus.). 396p. 1983. lib. bdg. 75.00 (*0-904614-05-0*) Lubrecht & Cramer.

Moore, David M. & Dwyer, Francis M., eds. Visual Literacy: A Spectrum of Visual Learning. LC 93-2437. 450p. 1994. 49.95 (*0-87778-264-4*) Educ Tech Pubns.

***Moore, David P.** The Little Black Book of Psychiatry. LC 99-24497. (Little Black Book Ser.). 1999. pap. 32.95 (*0-86542-562-0*) Blackwell Sci.

Moore, David P. Partial Seizures & Interictal Disorders: The Neuropsychiatric Elements. LC 97-4329. 234p. 1997. text 70.00 (*0-7506-9931-0*) Buttrwrth-Heinemann.

Moore, David P. & Jefferson, James W. Handbook of Medical Psychiatry. LC 96-15602. (Illus.). 560p. (C). (gr. 13). 1996. text 49.95 (*0-8151-6484-X*, 26343) Mosby Inc.

***Moore, David R.** The Address Directory of Celebrities in Entertainment, Sports, Business & Politics. 170p. 1999. pap. 39.95 (*0-9667961-2-8*) Americana Grp.

Moore, David R. Arts & Crafts of Torres Strait. (Ethnography Ser.: Nol 10). (Illus.). 64p. 1989. pap. 10.50 (*0-7478-0007-3*, Pub. by Shire Pubns) Parkwest Pubns.

Moore, David S. The Active Practice of Statistics: A Text for Multimedia Learning. (Illus.). 411p. 1997. text 69.95 incl. cd-rom (*0-7167-3141-X*) W H Freeman.

— The Active Practice of Statistics: A Textbook for Multimedia Learning. LC 97-21730. 411p. 1997. pap. 51.95 (*0-7167-3140-1*) W H Freeman.

— The Basic Practice of Statistics. LC 94-40756. 704p. (C). 1995. pap. text 68.95 (*0-7167-2628-9*) W H Freeman.

— The Basic Practice of Statistics. (C). 2000. 54.00 (*0-7167-2925-3*) W H Freeman.

***Moore, David S.** The Basic Practice of Statistics. 2nd ed. (Illus.). 619p. 1999. 58.50 (*0-7167-3627-6*) W H Freeman.

Moore, David S. The Basic Practice of Statistics/Student Minitab Guide. (C). 2000. student ed. write for info. (*0-7167-2927-X*) W H Freeman.

— Basic Statistics. 1995. pap. text, student ed. 22.95 (*0-7167-2682-3*) W H Freeman.

— Basic Statistics. (C). 1995. pap., student ed. 22.95 (*0-7167-2680-7*) W H Freeman.

— Introduction to the Practice of Statistics. 1998. 87.50 (*0-7167-3502-4*) W H Freeman.

— Statistics, Concepts & Controversies. 4th ed. LC 96-44489. 464p. 1996. pap. text 41.95 (*0-7167-2863-X*) W H Freeman.

Moore, David S. & McCabe, George P. Introduction to the Practice of Statistics. 2nd ed. LC 92-22880. (C). 1992. text 70.95 (*0-7167-2250-X*) W H Freeman.

— Introduction to the Practice of Statistics. 3rd ed. LC 97-45727. 1999. pap. 99.00 (*0-7167-3286-6*) W H Freeman.

***Moore, David S. & McCabe, George P.** Introduction to the Practice of Statistics 3rd ed. LC 97-45727. 1999. write for info. incl. disk (*0-7167-3409-5*) W H Freeman.

Moore, David S. & Nestor, Darryl. Statistics - Concepts & Controversies: Instructor's Manual. 4th ed. 1997. teacher ed. 12.80 (*0-7167-2769-2*) W H Freeman.

Moore, David T. Five Lies of the Century: How Many Do You Believe? LC 95-33097. 240p. 1995. pap. 12.99 (*0-8423-1869-0*) Tyndale Hse.

Moore, David W. The Superpollsters: How They Measure & Manipulate Public Opinion in America. LC 91-30396. 426p. 1992. 21.95 (*0-941423-74-3*) FWEW.

— The Superpollsters: How They Measure & Manipulate Public Opinion in America. 2nd ed. 426p. 1995. pap. 15.95 (*1-56858-023-1*) FWEW.

***Moore, David W., et al, eds.** Struggling Adolescent Readers: A Collection of Teaching Strategies. 2000. pap., teacher ed. 29.95 (*0-87207-272-X*, 272) Intl Reading.

Moore, David W., ed. see Moore, Sharon A., et al.

Moore Davis, Mollie E. The Wire Cutters. LC 97-33380. 396p. 1997. pap. 16.95 (*0-89096-796-2*) Tex A&M Univ Pr.

Moore, Dean M. Composition of U. S. Merchandise Trade 1991-95: A Chartbook. (Illus.). 132p. (Orig.). (C). 1997. pap. text 30.00 (*0-7881-4489-8*) DIANE Pub.

Moore, Deborah D. At Home in America: Second Generation New York Jews. LC 80-18777. (Columbia History of Urban Life Ser.). (Illus.). 280p. 1983. pap. text 23.00 (*0-231-05063-1*) Col U Pr.

— B'nai B'rith & the Challenge of Ethnic Leadership. LC 81-906. (SUNY Series in Modern Jewish History). 288p. (C). 1981. text 19.50 (*0-87395-480-7*) State U NY Pr.

— To the Golden Cities: Pursuing the American Jewish Dream in Miami & L. A. 300p. 1994. 24.95 (*0-02-922111-0*) Free Pr.

— To the Golden Cities: Pursuing the American Jewish Dream in Miami & L. A. (Illus.). 384p. 1996. pap. 15.95 (*0-674-89305-0*) HUP.

Moore, Deborah D., ed. Yivo. annuals 536p. 1996. text 69.95 (*0-8101-0933-6*) Northwestern U Pr.

— YIVO Annual, Vol. 22. 300p. 1994. 49.95 (*0-8101-1196-9*) Northwestern U Pr.

Moore, Deborah D., jt. ed. see Hyman, Paula.

Moore, Deborah D., jt. ed. see Kugelmass, Jack.

Moore, Deborah D., jt. ed. see Seckler, David.

Moore, Debra, jt. auth. see Crutsinger, Carla.

Moore, Debra K. Set Free from the Prison of Unforgiveness. 1991. pap. write for info. (*1-56588-000-5*) Moore Educ.

Moore, Debra K. & Kutter, Jackie A. Parties for Children: Ideas & Instructions for Invitations, Decorations, Refreshments, Favors, Crafts & Games for 19 Theme Parties. LC 95-2594. (Illus.). 182p. 1995. pap. 26.50 (*0-7864-0104-4*) McFarland & Co.

Moore, Della H. Hot Springs of North Carolina. (Illus.). 140p. (Orig.). 1994. write for info. (*0-9642625-0-9*) D H Moore.

— Yesteryears of Hot Springs, North Carolina. (Illus.). 150p. (Orig.). 1995. lib. bdg. write for info. (*0-9642625-1-7*) D H Moore.

Moore, Denese, jt. auth. see Stuttard, Marie.

Moore, Denise, ed. see McNeil, Edna.

Moore, Dennis. Big-Block Chevy Marine Performance. LC 98-24477. (Illus.). 176p. 1998. pap. 16.95 (*1-55788-297-5*, HP Books) Berkley Pub.

— Children of Light: A Perspective about the Signs Preceding Jesus Christ's Second Coming. 1997. text 19.95 (*0-9660630-0-7*, COL00001) Moore Cnslting.

***Moore, Dennis.** Small-Block Chevy Marine Performance. LC 99-47390. (Illus.). 208p. 2000. pap. 17.95 (*1-55788-317-3*, HP Books) Berkley Pub.

— Substance Use Disorder Treatment for People with Physical & Cognitive Disabilities: Treatment Improvement Protocol. 156p. 2000. reprint ed. pap. text 30.00 (*0-7881-8588-8*) DIANE Pub.

Moore, Dennis D., ed. see De Crevecoeur, J. Hector.

Moore, Dennis W., jt. auth. see Stommel, Henry.

Moore, Denton, ed. see Blackstone, Elizabeth.

Moore, Denton R. Alaska's Lost Frontier: Life in the Days of Homesteads, Dog Teams, & Sailboat Fisheries. LC 94-67836. (Illus.). 448p. 1995. 21.95 (*0-9628828-9-5*); pap. 19.95 (*0-9628828-8-7*) Prospector Pr.

— Gentlemen Never Sail to Weather: The Story of an Accidental Odyssey. 2nd ed. LC 93-83834. (Illus.). 512p. 1993. pap. 19.95 (*0-9628828-3-6*) Prospector Pr.

Moore, Derry. Evening Ragas: A Photographer in India. (Illus.). 128p. 1998. 35.00 (*0-7195-5809-3*, Pub. by John Murray) Trafalgar.

Moore, Derry, jt. auth. see Lee-Milne, Avide.

Moore, Derry, jt. auth. see Plumptre, George.

Moore, Desmond F. Thermodynamic Principles of Energy Degrading. (Illus.). 155p. (C). 1981. 40.00 (*0-333-29504-8*); pap. 26.50 (*0-333-29506-4*) Scholium Intl.

Moore, Dessie. Let's Pretend Board Book. LC 95-128173. (Jump at the Sun Board Bks.). (Illus.). 16p. (J). (ps up). 1994. 5.95 (*0-694-00591-6*) HarpC Child Bks.

Moore, Dewey J. Preventing Misbehavior in Children. 2nd ed. LC 96-8763. 158p. 1996. text 36.95 (*0-398-06671-X*); pap. text 23.95 (*0-398-06672-8*) C C Thomas.

Moore, Diana, jt. auth. see Monske, Ken.

Moore, Diane M. Iran: In a Persian Market. LC 79-93424. 118p. (Orig.). 1980. pap. 5.00 (*0-686-61402-X*) D M Moore.

— Martin's Quest. (Illus.). 96p. (Orig.). (J). (gr. 5-12). 1995. pap. 8.00 (*1-884725-05-8*) Blue Heron LA.

— Martin's Quest. (Illus.). (Orig.). (J). (gr. 5-12). 1995. 10.00 (*1-884725-12-0*) Blue Heron LA.

Moore, Dianne J. Emotional Child Abuse: Breaking the Cycle. 20p. (Orig.). 1992. pap. 4.00 (*1-880670-02-X*) Write On Servs.

— How Can I Help When Someone Dies: What Do I Say after, I'm Sorry? 17p. 1992. pap. 4.00 (*1-880670-00-3*) Write On Servs.

— It's Not Fair: And Other Parenting Pressures. 38p. 1993. pap. 5.00 (*1-880670-03-8*) Write On Servs.

Moore, Dianne J. A Maze of Grace: Claiming Your Twelve Powers. 220p. Date not set. pap. write for info. (*1-880670-05-4*) Write On Servs.

Moore, Dianne J. Shortcuts to Business Success. 27p. 1992. pap. 4.00 (*1-880670-01-1*) Write On Servs.

Moore, Dick. Acting Careers. LC 98-18390. (Opportunities in... Ser.). 160p. 1998. 14.95 (*0-8442-6419-9*, 64199); pap. 11.95 (*0-8442-6420-2*, 64202) NTC Contemp Pub Co.

— Opportunities in Acting Careers. rev. ed. LC 74-25904. (Illus.). (C). 1989. 13.95 (*0-8442-6229-3*, VGM Career) NTC Contemp Pub Co.

Moore, Dinty. The Accidental Buddhist. 224p. 1999. pap. 12.00 (*0-385-49267-7*) Doubleday.

— The Emperor's Virtual Clothes: The Naked Truth about Internet Culture. LC 95-21180. 240p. 1995. 17.95 (*1-56512-096-5*, 72096) Algonquin Bks.

Moore, Dinty W. The Accidental Buddhist: Mindfulness, Enlightenment & Sitting Still, y ~ _. LC 97-19918. 228p. 1997. 19.95 (*1-56512-142-2*, 72142) Algonquin Bks.

— Toothpick Men. LC 98-87192. 154p. (Orig.). 1998. pap. 15.00 (*0-9666028-0-3*, Mammoth Bks) Mammoth Press.

Moore, Dolores L. Penny: Half Coyote, or Half Wolf - & All Heart. Nielson, Helen, ed. (Illus.). 156p. (Orig.). 1996. pap. 10.00 (*1-888844-00-0*) Lghthse Publns.

***Moore, Don.** Low & Slow: A Personal History of a Liaison Pilot in World War II. LC 99-70896. 234 p. 1999. write for info. (*0-9670334-0-3*) SA Hts Pub Co.

Moore, Don. Webster: The Critical Heritage. (Critical Heritage Ser.). 172p. 1981. 69.50 (*0-7100-0773-6*, Routledge Thoemms) Routledge.

Moore, Don, jt. auth. see Fane, Francis D.

Moore, Don, jt. auth. see Kasal, Mark.

Moore, Donald. All about Crosswords: Choirs. Busch, Brian, ed. (A.A.C. Ser.). (Illus.). 40p. (Orig.). (YA). 1994. pap. text 24.95 (*0-89898-716-4*, SVB00108) Wrner Bros.

— All about Crosswords: Composers. Busch, Brian, ed. (A.A.C. Ser.). (Illus.). 40p. (Orig.). (YA). 1994. pap. text 24.95 (*0-89898-756-3*, SVB00109) Wrner Bros.

— All about Crosswords: Instruments. Busch, Brian, ed. (A.A.C. Ser.). (Illus.). 40p. (Orig.). (YA). 1994. pap. text 24.95 (*0-89898-715-6*, SVB00107) Wrner Bros.

— All about Crosswords: Rock & Pop. Busch, Brian, ed. (A.A.C. Ser.). (Illus.). 40p. (Orig.). (YA). 1994. pap. text 24.95 (*0-89898-714-8*, SVB00106) Wrner Bros.

— Cavalrymen. (Illus.). 48p. 1983. 20.00 (*0-88014-060-7*) Mosaic Pr OH.

— A Daily Guide to a Better Marriage. 32p. 1984. pap. 0.75 (*0-88144-021-3*) Christian Pub.

— Daily Guide to a Better Marriage. (Mini-Bks.). 32p. 1988. pap. 1.00 (*0-89274-554-1*, HH-554) Harrison Hse.

— Financial Aid Officers: What They Do - To You & for You. 10th ed. 32p. 1998. pap. 5.00 (*1-57509-035-X*) Octameron Assocs.

— Improving Your Christian Personality. 61p. 1984. pap. 2.25 (*0-88144-037-X*) Christian Pub.

Moore, Donald G. Buddha's Eyes. Date not set. pap. 13.95 (*1-57532-233-1*) Press-Tige Pub.

Moore, Donald J. The Human & the Holy: The Spirituality of Abraham Joshua Heschel. LC 89-80461. viii, 215p. 1989. pap. 17.00 (*0-8232-1236-X*) Fordham.

Moore, Donald J. Martin Buber: Prophet of Religious Secularism. 2nd rev. ed. LC 95-46078. xxxiii, 298p. 1996. 32.50 (*0-8232-1639-X*); pap. 18.00 (*0-8232-1640-3*) Fordham.

Moore, Donald K., jt. ed. see Erdman, David V.

Moore, Donna, ed. see Campbell, Stu.

Moore, Donna J. Take Charge of Your Own Career. 2nd ed. LC 79-88808. (Illus.). 184p. (Orig.). 1981. 10.00 (*0-9605466-0-X*) D J Moore.

— Up Close & Personal: Experiential Exercises for Building a Spiritual Community. (Illus.). 80p. (Orig.). 1997. pap. text 15.00 (*0-614-26981-4*) D J Moore.

Moore, Doris L. The Technique of the Love Affair. Epstein, Norrie, ed. LC 98-34354. (Illus.). 222p. 1999. 19.95 (*0-679-44402-5*) Pantheon.

Moore, Dorothy, jt. auth. see Stonebraker, Michael.

Moore, Dorothy D. Mischievous Molly. LC 95-60902. (Illus.). 48p. (J). (gr. 1-5). 1995. pap. 9.95 (*1-883650-25-9*) Windswept Hse.

Moore, Dorothy L. Guide for the Development & Management of Nursing Libraries & Information Resources. LC 97-14566. 1997. 19.95 (*0-88737-729-7*) Natl League Nurse.

Moore, Dorothy N., jt. auth. see Moore, Raymond S.

Moore, Dorothy N., jt. auth. see Moore, Ryamond S.

Moore, Dorothy P. & Buttner, E. Holly. Women Entrepreneurs: Moving Beyond the Glass Ceiling. LC 97-4854. 276p. 1997. text 46.00 (*0-7619-0463-8*); pap. text 19.95 (*0-7619-0464-6*) Sage.

Moore, Dorothy P., jt. auth. see Moore, Jamie W.

***Moore, Dorothy Perrin.** CareerBlazers: Lessons from Leading Women Entrepreneurs on Building a Career Without Boundaries. LC 00-22628. 198p. 2000. 28.95 (*0-89106-144-4*, Davies-Black Pub) Consulting Psychol.

Moore, Douglas. Entertainment: Movies Basic Terms. (All about Language Ser.). (Illus.). 50p. (J). (gr. 7 up). 1986. audio 22.00 (*0-939990-48-2*) Intl Linguistics.

— Guide to Musical Styles: From Madrigal to Modern Music. (Illus.). 1963. pap. 13.95 (*0-393-00200-4*) Norton.

— Post Office: Basic Terms. (All about Language Ser.). (Illus.). 1987. pap. text 22.00 incl. audio (*0-939990-52-0*) Intl Linguistics.

Moore, Douglas & Winitz, Harris. Dictionary for Spontaneous Descriptions. (Illus.). 120p. 1985. pap. text 20.00 (*0-939990-43-1*) Intl Linguistics.

— Transportation: Basic Terms. (All about Language Ser.). (Illus.). 35p. (Orig.). 1987. pap. text 22.00 incl. audio (*0-939990-51-2*) Intl Linguistics.

Moore, Douglas, jt. auth. see Lennon, Patricia.

Moore, Douglas, jt. auth. see Winitz, Harris.

Moore, Douglas B., ed. see Foote, Arthur.

Moore, Douglas W., jt. auth. see Wuerthner, George.

Moore, Duane M. & Reynolds, Robert C., Jr. X-Ray Diffraction & the Identification & Analysis of Clay Minerals. 2nd ed. (Illus.). 400p. 1997. pap. text 47.95 (*0-19-508713-5*) OUP.

Moore, Dulce D. A Place in Mind. LC 92-70845. 265p. 1992. 18.00 (*0-9627509-9-9*) Baskerville.

— A Place in Mind: A Novel. large type ed. LC 92-33395. 430p. 1993. reprint ed. lib. bdg. 16.95 (*1-56054-587-9*) Thorndike Pr.

Moore, Duncan & Walker, Henry. Yield Simulation for Integrated Circuits. (C). 1987. text 84.00 (*0-89838-244-0*) Kluwer Academic.

Moore, Duncan T., ed. Selected Papers on Gradient-Index Optics. LC 92-34884. (Milestone Ser.: Vol. MS 67). 1992. pap. 35.00 (*0-8194-1058-6*) SPIE.

— Selected Papers on Gradient-Index Optics. LC 92-34884. (Milestone Ser.: Vol. MS 67/HC). 1992. 45.00 (*0-8194-1059-4*) SPIE.

— Tutorials in Optics. LC 92-80124. 151p. (Orig.). 1992. pap. 61.00 (*1-55752-038-0*) Optical Soc.

Moore, Dwayne R., jt. ed. see Warren-Hicks, William J.

Moore, E. Dante & His Early Biographers. LC 70-122459. (Studies in Dante: No. 9). (C). 1970. reprint ed. lib. bdg. 75.00 (*0-8383-1002-8*) M S G Haskell Hse.

— Studies in Dante, First Series. LC 68-24955. (Studies in Dante: No. 9). 1969. reprint ed. lib. bdg. 75.00 (*0-8383-0217-3*) M S G Haskell Hse.

— Studies in Dante, Second Series. LC 68-24956. (Studies in Dante: No. 9). 1969. reprint ed. lib. bdg. 75.00 (*0-8383-0218-1*) M S G Haskell Hse.

— Studies in Dante, Third Series. LC 68-24957. (Studies in Dante: No. 9). (Illus.). 1969. reprint ed. lib. bdg. 75.00 (*0-8383-0219-X*) M S G Haskell Hse.

— Studies in Dante Fourth Series: A Textual Criticism of the Convivo & Miscellaneous Essays. LC 68-29737. (Studies in Dante: No. 9). 1968. reprint ed. lib. bdg. 75.00 (*0-8383-0220-3*) M S G Haskell Hse.

Moore, E. Hamilton. English Miracle Plays & Moralities. LC 77-100517. reprint ed. 17.25 (*0-404-00598-5*) AMS Pr.

— English Miracle Plays & Moralities. (BCL1-PR English Literature Ser.). 199p. 1992. reprint ed. lib. bdg. 69.00 (*0-7812-7100-2*) Rprt Serv.

Moore, E. Manvel. The Skip Tracer's Black Book. 1998. pap. 24.95 (*0-9660883-4-4*) Intell Info Srvs.

Moore, E. Neil, jt. auth. see Morganroth, Joel.

Moore, E. Neil, jt. ed. see Morganroth, Joel.

Moore, Earl F. Silent Arrows. 3rd ed. LC 23-939860. 1977. 12.95 (*0-939860-03-1*) Tremaine Graph & Pub.

— Western Echoes. LC 23-939860. (Illus.). 198p. (J). (gr. 4-12). 1980. 12.95 (*0-939860-00-7*) Tremaine Graph & Pub.

Moore, Earl V. & Heger, Theodore E. The Symphony & the Symphonic Poem. 6th rev. ed. LC 57-63375. (C). 1974. text 15.95 (*0-914004-01-8*) Ulrich.

Moore Easter, Mary. Walking from Origins, Vol. 1. (Northfield Women Poets Chapbook Ser.). 20p. 1993. 4.00 (*0-9614314-9-0*) Heywood Pr.

Moore, Ed. Apocalypse When? (Illus.). 284p. (Orig.). (C). 1990. pap. 10.00 (*0-9624843-0-X*) Christchurch Pubns.

***Moore-Ede, Martin C.** Practical Guide to Managment 24 Hours Operations. 131p. 1998. pap. 69.95 (*0-9648893-1-5*) Circadian Info.

Moore-Ede, Martin C. Working Nights Guia de Salud y Seguridad. 2nd rev. ed. Orig. Title: Shiftwork & Your Health. (SPA., Illus.). 36p. 1997. pap. 17.95 (*0-9648893-3-1*, BK22) Circadian Info.

— Working Nights Health & Safety Guide. 2nd rev. ed. Orig. Title: Shiftwork & Your Health. (Illus.). 36p. 1997. pap. 17.95 (*0-9648893-2-3*, BK21) Circadian Info.

Moore-Ede, Martin C. & Czeisler, Charles A., eds. Mathematical Models of the Circadian Sleep-Wake Cycle. LC 83-19054. (Illus.). 224p. 1984. reprint ed. pap. 69.50 (*0-608-00639-4*, 206122700007) Bks Demand.

Moore-Ede, Martin C. & LeVert, Suzanne. The Complete Idiot's Guide to Getting a Good Night's Sleep. 352p. 1998. pap. text 16.95 (*0-02-862394-0*) Macmillan Gen Ref.

— The Pocket Idiot's Guide to Getting a Good Night's Sleep. (Pocket Idiot's Guides Ser.). (Illus.). 215p. 1999. pap. 9.95 (*0-02-863380-6*, Pub. by Macmillan Gen Ref) S&S Trade.

Moore-Ede, Martin C., et al. The Clocks That Time Us: Physiology of the Circadian Timing System. LC 81-6780. (Commonwealth Fund Publications). (Illus.). 464p. 1984. pap. 18.95 (*0-674-13581-4*) HUP.

Moore Educational Publishers Staff. CPNez. (Illus.). 1996. lab manual ed. 15.95 (*1-56588-001-3*) Moore Educ.

— Read Me First. Palmer, Nina et al, eds. (Illus.). (Orig.). (C). 1996. pap. text. write for info. (*1-56588-002-1*) Moore Educ.

Moore, Edward. The Foundling & the Gamester. Amberg, Anthony, ed. & intro. by. LC 94-41277. (Illus.). 448p. 1996. 59.50 (*0-87413-530-3*) U Delaware Pr.

— Studies in Dante Second Series: Miscellaneous Essays. LC 68-57628. (Illus.). 386p. 1970. reprint ed. lib. bdg. 69.50 (*0-8371-0908-6*, MOSD, Greenwood Pr) Greenwood.

Moore, Edward A. Story of a Cannoneer under Stonewall Jackson. LC 77-146866. (Select Bibliographies Reprint Ser.). 1977. reprint ed. 24.95 (*0-8369-5633-8*) Ayer.

Moore, Edward C. American Pragmatism: Peirce, James & Dewey. LC 84-25291. 285p. 1985. reprint ed. lib. bdg. 52.50 (*0-313-24740-4*, MOOA, Greenwood Pr) Greenwood.

— Forty Years of Opera in Chicago. Farkas, Andrew, ed. LC 76-29956. (Opera Biographies Ser.). (Illus.). 1977. reprint ed. lib. bdg. 44.95 (*0-405-09697-6*) Ayer.

Moore, Edward C., ed. Charles S. Peirce: The Essential Writings. (Great Books in Philosophy). 330p. 1998. pap. 10.95 (*1-57392-256-0*) Prometheus Bks.

— Charles S. Peirce & the Philosophy of Science: Papers from the Harvard Sesquicentennial Congress. LC 92-28877. 512p. (C). 1993. text 49.95 (*0-8173-0665-X*) U of Ala Pr.

Moore, Edward C. & Robin, Richard S., eds. From Time & Chance to Consciousness: Studies in the Metaphysics of Charles Peirce - Papers from the Sesquicentennial Harvard Congress. LC 93-18010. 224p. 1994. 49.50 (*0-85496-379-0*) Berg Pubs.

Moore, Edward C., ed. see Peirce, Charles Sanders.

M

Moore, Edward P. Polypropylene Handbook: Polymerization, Characterization, Properties, Processing, Applications. 419p. 1996. 140.00 (*1-56990-208-9*) Hanser-Gardner.

Moore, Edward P. & Montedison S.P.A. Staff. The Rebirth of Polypropylene: Supported Catalysts: How the People of the Montedison Laboratories Revolutionized the PP Industry. LC 98-33641. 1998. 58.00 (*1-56990-254-2*) Hanser-Gardner.

Moore, Elaine. Beware of the Haunted Toilet. 144p. (J). (gr. 3-7). 1998. pap. 3.95 (*0-8167-4812-8*) Troll Communs.

— Chocolate Daze. (Digests Ser.). (J). (gr. 3-7). 1997. pap. 3.95 (*0-8167-4323-1*) Troll Communs.

— Get That Girl Out of the Boys' Locker Room! (Digests Ser.). 160p. (J). (gr. 3-7). 1997. pap. 3.95 (*0-8167-4341-X*) Troll Communs.

— Grandma's Garden. LC 90-6052. (J). (ps-3). 1994. 15.00 (*0-688-08693-4*) Lothrop.

— Grandma's Smile. LC 94-23679. (Illus.). 32p. (J). (ps up). 1995. 16.00 (*0-688-11075-4*) Lothrop.

— The Peanut Butter Trap. (Illus.). 64p. (Orig.). (J). (gr. 1-4). 1996. pap. 3.95 (*0-8167-3624-3*, Little Rainbow) Troll Communs.

— The Peanut Butter Trap. (Orig.). (J). 1996. 9.15 (*0-606-09732-5*, Pub. by Turtleback) Demco.

— Roly-Poly Puppies: A Counting Book. LC 95-30067. (Story Corner Ser.). (Illus.). 32p. (J). (ps-3). 1996. 6.95 (*0-590-46665-8*, Cartwheel) Scholastic Inc.

— The Substitute Teacher from Mars. LC 93-37527. (Illus.). 96p. (J). (gr. 2-6). 1993. pap. text 2.95 (*0-8167-3283-3*) Troll Communs.

— There's a Mastodon in My Living Room. 144p. (Orig.). (J). (gr. 3-7). 1996. pap. 3.95 (*0-8167-4015-1*) Troll Communs.

— The Trouble with Valentines. (J). 1998. pap. text 3.50 (*0-590-37234-3*, Little Apple) Scholastic Inc.

— The Trouble with Valentines. (J). 1998. 8.60 (*0-606-13871-4*, Pub. by Turtleback) Demco.

— Who Let Girls in the Boys' Locker Room? LC 94-820. (Illus.). 144p. (J). (gr. 3-6). 1996. pap. 3.95 (*0-8167-3439-9*) Troll Communs.

***Moore, Elaine, et al.** 121 North: A Collection of Short Stories by North Texas Professional Writers Association. Hushour, C. Kaye, ed. 199p. 2000. pap. 14.95 (*1-928704-76-X*, Fusion Pr) Authorlink.

Moore, Elaine, jt. auth. see Smart, Lesley.

Moore, Elizabeth. Dreams of Revenge. (Dark Moon Ser.). 1995. 9.09 (*0-606-07452-X*, Pub. by Turtleback) Demco.

— Dreams of Revenge: Dark Moon, Bk. II. 176p. (gr. 7-9). 1995. mass mkt. 3.99 (*0-590-25510-X*) Scholastic Inc.

— Kiss of Death. (Dark Moon Ser.). 1995. 9.09 (*0-606-07763-4*, Pub. by Turtleback) Demco.

— Kiss of Death: Dark Moon, Bk. I. 176p. (gr. 7-9). 1995. mass mkt. 3.99 (*0-590-25509-6*) Scholastic Inc.

Moore, Elizabeth, et al. Ancient Capitals of Thailand. (Illus.). 352p. 1996. 80.00 (*1-872727-77-8*, Pub. by River Books) Weatherhill.

— Myanmar Style. 220p. 1998. 45.00 (*962-593-397-2*, Periplus Eds) Tuttle Pubng.

— Shwedagon: Golden Pagoda of Myanmar. LC 98-19282. (Illus.). 192p. 1999. 40.00 (*0-500-97483-7*, Pub. by Thames Hudson) Norton.

Moore, Elizabeth, jt. auth. see Couvillon, Alice.

Moore, Elizabeth, jt. auth. see Couvillon, Alice W.

Moore, Elizabeth, jt. auth. see Siribhadra, Smitthi.

Moore, Ella M., jt. auth. see Moore, Fred H.

Moore, Ellen. Lead Me to the Exit. LC 77-9949. 1977. 6.95 (*0-918056-01-2*) Ariadne Pr.

Moore, Ellen, jt. auth. see Wiberg, Randy S.

Moore, Ellen J. Fossil Mollusks of Coastal Oregon. LC 71-634653. (Oregon State Monographs. Studies in Geology: No. 10). 64p. reprint ed. pap. 30.00 (*0-7837-3943-5*, 204369800011) Bks Demand.

***Moore, Ellen J.** Fossil Shells from Western Oregon: A Guide to Identification. LC 00-102253. (Illus.). 131p. 2000. pap. 12.00 (*0-9640066-1-8*) Chintimini Pr.

Moore, Ellen W. The Fairs of Medieval England: An Introductory Study. (Illus.). xii, 401p. pap. text 44.57 (*0-88844-072-3*) Brill Academic Pubs.

Moore, Elsie G., jt. auth. see Bock, R. Darrell.

***Moore, Elvet.** The Year of the Tiger. LC 97-75509. 1998. 25.95 (*1-57197-091-6*) Pentland Pr.

Moore, Elwood S. American Influence in Canadian Mining. Bruchey, Stuart, ed. LC 80-561. (Multinational Corporations Ser.). (Illus.). 1981. reprint ed. lib. bdg. 19.95 (*0-405-13358-8*) Ayer.

Moore, Emily. Just My Luck. 1991. 9.09 (*0-606-04952-5*, Pub. by Turtleback) Demco.

— My Story. 10p. 1998. pap. 2.50 (*1-891972-01-4*) Beastkraft Pubg.

— Whose Side Are You On? LC 87-46392. 128p. (J). (gr. 4-7). 1988. 14.00 (*0-374-38409-6*) FS&G.

— Whose Side Are You On? 128p. (J). (gr. 4-7). 1990. pap. 4.95 (*0-374-48373-6*) FS&G.

Moore, Emily B. Phineas F. Bresee: Mr. Nazarene. 72p. 1973. kivar 6.99 (*0-8341-0157-2*) Nazarene.

***Moore, Emmett B.** The Environmental Impact Statement Process & Environmental Law. 2nd ed. LC 00-26083. 162p. 2000. pap. 19.95 (*1-57477-092-6*) Battelle.

***Moore, Emmett Burris, contrib. by.** An Introduction to the Management & Regulation of Hazardous Waste. LC 99-57216. 150p. 2000. pap. 19.95 (*1-57477-088-8*) Battelle.

Moore, Ercelle. Going for the Butter. 32p. 1988. pap. 3.00 (*1-880649-21-7*) Writ Ctr Pr.

Moore, Eric. Following the Pillar of God. 1998. pap. 14.95 (*0-9660883-7-9*) Benjamin Pub.

— Gardening in the Middle East. 1986. 39.95 (*0-86685-548-3*) Intl Bk Ctr.

— Gardening in the Middle East. (Illus.). 144p. 1986. boxed set 39.95 (*0-905743-49-0*, Pub. by Stacey Intl) Intl Bk Ctr.

— How to Find Friends, Lost Family, & Missing Persons, Vol. 1. 217p. 1997. pap. 24.95 (*0-9660883-0-1*) Intell Info Srvs.

— Subliminal Selling Skills: How to Develop Your Subliminal Selling Skills to Get What You Want. 1998. pap. 19.95 (*0-9660883-5-2*) Intell Info Srvs.

— Super Subconscious Language Learning: Using the Powers of Your Mind to Learn a Language. 1998. pap. 24.95 (*0-9660883-8-7*) Intell Info Srvs.

— Super Subconscious Learning for Your Mind: Learn How to Develop the Brain of an Einstein. 1998. pap. 24.95 (*0-9660883-9-5*) Intell Info Srvs.

Moore, Eric G., jt. ed. see Clark, William A.

Moore, Eric M. How to Develop Supernatural Faith. 1998. pap. 24.95 (*0-9660883-2-8*) Benjamin Pub.

— Is the Bible Full of Contradictions? An Explanation of Biblical Verses. 1998. pap. 24.95 (*0-9660883-1-X*) Benjamin Pub.

— Voice of the Soul. 1998. pap. 14.95 (*0-9660883-3-6*) Benjamin Pub.

Moore, Eric S. The $51 Fantasy: Legal Prostitution for American Man. 16.00 (*1-55950-202-9*) Loompanics.

Moore, Erin. Gender, Law, & Resistance in India. LC 98-8961. 190p. 1998. 32.95 (*0-8165-1803-3*) U of Ariz Pr.

Moore, Ernest. Trauma Handbook. (C). 1999. pap. text 35.00 (*0-8385-9011-X*) Appleton & Lange.

Moore, Ernest E., et al. Trauma. 3rd ed. (Illus.). (C). 1998. pap. text 165.00 (*0-8385-9010-1*, A9010-8, Apple Lange Med) McGraw.

Moore, Ernest E., jt. ed. see Harken, Alden H.

Moore, Ethel, ed. Letters from Thirty-One Artists. (Gallery Notes Ser.). (Illus.). (Orig.). 1970. pap. 1.50 (*0-914782-97-5*, C214) Buffalo Fine-Albrght-Knox.

Moore, Ethel & Moore, Chauncey O. Ballads & Folksongs of the Southwest: More than 600 Titles, Melodies, & Texts Collected in Oklahoma. LC M 1627.M6. 432p. reprint ed. pap. 134.00 (*0-8357-5951-2*, 200726100063) Bks Demand.

Moore, Eugene C. Inspiring Interiors from Armstrong 1950s. LC 97-42009. 160p. 1998. pap. 29.95 (*0-7643-0458-5*) Schiffer.

Moore, Eugenia. Climb the Waterfall & the Days of Rye. Derman, Elizabeth, ed. LC 86-28061. (Illus.). 216p. 1987. 14.95 (*0-9617284-1-8*); pap. 9.95 (*0-9617284-0-X*) Sand & Silk.

— Dark Moon Rising. Leiper, Esther M., ed. 32p. (Orig.). 1989. pap. 3.95 (*0-9617284-7-7*) Sand & Silk.

— Home Cooking from the Hollow. 32p. 1987. pap. 3.95 (*0-9617284-3-4*) Sand & Silk.

— In a Minute! Leiper, Esther M., ed. 32p. (Orig.). (YA). (gr. 9 up). 1988. pap. 3.95 (*0-9617284-9-3*) Sand & Silk.

— Kidnapped by an Angel. Leiper, Esther M., ed. (Illus.). 32p. (Orig.). (J). (gr. 3-4). 1988. pap. 3.95 (*0-9617284-4-2*) Sand & Silk.

— The Sweet Water River. LC 90-92340. (Illus.). 72p. 1991. pap. 7.95 (*1-878116-05-3*) JVC Bks.

Moore, Eugenia, ed. see Leiper, Esther M.

Moore, Eugenia, ed. see Lindow, Sandra.

***Moore, Eunice R.** Lofty Dreams. (Illus.). 200p. (J). (gr. 3-8). 2000. pap. 7.99 (*1-57532-295-1*, Pub. by Press-Tige Pub) Barnes & Noble Inc.

Moore, Eva. Buddy, the First Seeing Eye Dog. LC 95-6725. (Hello Reader! Ser.). (Illus.). 32-48p. (J). (gr. 2-4). 1996. pap. 3.99 (*0-590-26585-7*, Cartwheel) Scholastic Inc.

Moore, Eva. Buddy, the First Seeing Eye Dog. (Hello, Reader! Ser.). 1996. 9.19 (*0-606-09114-9*, Pub. by Turtleback) Demco.

Moore, Eva. The Day of the Bad Haircut. LC 95-30062. (Hello Reader! Ser.: Level 2). (Illus.). (J). 1997. 3.50 (*0-590-69770-6*) Scholastic Inc.

Moore, Eva. The Day of the Bad Haircut. (Hello, Reader! Ser.). 1997. 8.70 (*0-606-11240-5*, Pub. by Turtleback) Demco.

— Franklin & the Baby. (Franklin TV Storybook Ser.). (Illus.). 32p. (J). (ps-3). 1999. pap. 10.95 (*1-55074-706-1*) Kids Can Pr.

— Franklin & the Baby. (Franklin TV Storybook Ser.). (Illus.). 32p. (J). (ps-2). 1999. pap. text 4.50 (*0-439-08365-6*) Scholastic Inc.

Moore, Eva. Johnny Appleseed. (J). (ps-3). 1987. pap. 4.99 (*0-590-40297-8*) Scholastic Inc.

***Moore, Eva.** The Search for the Missing Bones. (Magic School Bus:: No. 2). (Illus.). 80p. (J). (gr. 1-4). 2000. pap. 4.99 (*0-439-10799-7*) Scholastic Inc.

— Space Explorers. (Illus.). (J). 2000. pap. 3.99 (*0-439-11493-4*) Scholastic Inc.

Moore, Eva. Story of George Washington Carver. 96p. (J). (gr. 4-7). 1990. pap. 3.99 (*0-590-42660-5*) Scholastic Inc.

***Moore, Eva.** The Truth about Bats. (Magic School Bus:: No. 1). (Illus.). 80p. (J). (gr. 1-4). 2000. pap. 4.99 (*0-439-10798-9*) Scholastic Inc.

— The Wild Whale Watch. (Magic School Bus:: No. 3). (Illus.). 80p. (J). (ps-3). 2000. pap. 3.99 (*0-439-10990-6*) Scholastic Inc.

Moore, Eva, et al, eds. Sing a Song of Popcorn: Every Child's Book of Poems. (Illus.). 160p. (J). (ps up). 1988. 18.95 (*0-590-43974-X*, Scholastic Hardcover) Scholastic Inc.

***Moore, Eva & Nelvana (Firm) Staff.** Franklin & the Baby. (Franklin TV Storybook Ser.). (Illus.). 32p. (J). (ps-3). 1999. 4.95 (*1-55074-708-8*) Kids Can Pr.

Moore, Evan. Perfect Woman. 304p. 1999. mass mkt. 4.99 (*0-7860-0205-0*) Kensgtn Pub Corp.

Moore, Evelyn, ed. see Gums, Bonnie L.

Moore, Evelyn, ed. see Jelks, Edward B., et al.

Moore, Evelyn, ed. see Skele, Mikels.

Moore, Evelyn, ed. see Walthall, John A. & Benchley, Elizabeth D.

Moore, Evelyn C. Math for Merchandising: A Step-by-Step Approach. LC 97-25438. 308p. 1997. pap. text 54.00 (*0-13-268723-2*) P-H.

***Moore, Evelyn C.** Math for Merchandising: A Step-by-step Approach. 2nd ed. 352p. 2000. pap. 40.00 (*0-13-018202-8*) P-H.

Moore, Evelyn C., jt. auth. see Johnson, Maurice J.

Moore, Evelyn C., jt. auth. see Johnson, Mauriece J.

Moore, Evelyn K. The Passions of Rhetoric: Lessing's Theory of Argument & the German Enlightenment. LC 93-13187. (Library of Rhetorics: Vol. 3). 144p. (C). 1993. text 124.50 (*0-7923-2308-4*) Kluwer Academic.

***Moore, Evelyn Lee, et al.** Behind the Old Brick Wall: A Cemetery Story. 2nd ed. LC 98-75081. xiii, 307 p. 1998. write for info. (*1-890306-15-0*) Warwick Hse.

Moore, F. Descriptions of New Indian Lepidoperous Insects from the Collection of Late Mr. W. S. Atkinson, M.A., F.L.S., Pts. 1-2. 1987. 750.00 (*0-7855-3109-2*, Pub. by Intl Bk Distr) St Mut.

— Descriptions of New Indian Lepidoterous Insects from the Collection of Late Mr. W. S. Atkinson, Pts. 1-2. 1987. 375.00 (*81-7089-889-7*, Pub. by Intl Bk Distr) St Mut.

— Descsriptions of New Indian Lepidoterous Insects from the Collection of Late Mr. W. S. Atkinson, Pts. 1-2. (C). 1987. text 400.00 (*0-7855-6588-4*, Pub. by Intl Bk Distr) St Mut.

Moore, F., ed. Descriptions of New Indian Lepidoterous Insects from the Collection of Late Mr. W. S. Atkinson, Pts. 1-2. (C). 1987. 600.00 (*0-7855-6880-8*, Pub. by Intl Bk Distr) St Mut.

— Descriptions of New Indian Lepidoterous Insects from the Collection of Late Mr. W. S. Atkinson, Pts. 1 & 2. 1987. 200.00 (*0-7855-6544-2*, Pub. by Intl Bk Distr) St Mut.

Moore, F. C. Bergson: Thinking Backwards. (Modern European Philosophy Ser.). (Illus.). 174p. (C). 1996. text 59.95 (*0-521-41340-0*); pap. text 18.95 (*0-521-42402-X*) Cambridge U Pr.

Moore, F. Michael. Drag! Male & Female Impersonators on Stage, Screen & Television: An Illustrated World History. LC 94-10984. (Illus.). 311p. 1994. lib. bdg. 48.50 (*0-89950-996-7*) McFarland & Co.

Moore, F. Richard. Elements of Computer Music. (C). 1990. pap. text 48.00 (*0-13-252552-6*) P-H.

Moore, Farrar, jt. auth. see Cook, Sheryl.

Moore, Fauzya. Beyond Development Cooperation: Toward a New Era of Global & Human Security. 78p. 1994. pap. write for info. (*0-88936-714-0*) IDRC Bks.

Moore, Felicity. Vasilieff & His Art. (Illus.). 1983. 58.00 (*0-19-554324-6*) OUP.

Moore, Francis. Old Moore's Almanack, 1994. 79p. 1993. pap. 1.95 (*0-572-01879-7*, Pub. by Foulsham UK) Assoc Pubs Grp.

Moore, Francis A. Silly Saguaros. 3rd rev. ed. (Illus.). 64p. 1998. pap. 2.95 (*0-935810-67-6*) R H Pub.

Moore, Francis D. A Miracle & a Privilege: Recounting a Half-Century of Surgical Advance. (Illus.). 488p. (Orig.). (C). 1995. 29.95 (*0-309-05188-6*, Joseph Henry Pr) Natl Acad Pr.

Moore, Francis J., compiled by. Prayers for All Occasions. large type ed. 96p. 1987. pap. 2.50 (*0-88028-100-6*, 883) Forward Movement.

Moore, Frank. American Eloquence: A Collection of Speeches & Address. (Notable American Authors Ser.). 1999. reprint ed. lib. bdg. 125.00 (*0-7812-4574-5*) Rprt Serv.

— The Civil War in Song & Story, 2 vols., Set. 1980. lib. bdg. 195.75 (*0-8490-3130-3*) Gordon Pr.

— Coffee Shop Theology: Translating Doctrinal Jargon into Everyday Life. LC 97-45883. 152p. 1998. pap. 13.99 (*0-8341-1732-0*) Beacon Hill.

— Diary of the American Revolution from Newspaper & Original. (Notable American Authors Ser.). 1999. reprint ed. lib. bdg. 125.00 (*0-7812-4575-3*) Rprt Serv.

— Dismantling the Myths. LC 97-16703. 220p. (Orig.). 1997. pap. 16.99 (*0-8341-1679-0*) Beacon Hill.

— Heros & Martyrs. (Notable American Authors Ser.). 1999. reprint ed. lib. bdg. 125.00 (*0-7812-4577-X*) Rprt Serv.

— Lyrics of Loyalty. (Notable American Authors Ser.). 1999. reprint ed. lib. bdg. 125.00 (*0-7812-4579-6*) Rprt Serv.

— The Magic Moving Alphabet. (Illus.). 32p. 1978. pap. 3.95 (*0-486-23593-9*) Dover.

— Materials for History. (Notable American Authors Ser.). 1999. reprint ed. lib. bdg. 125.00 (*0-7812-4576-1*) Rprt Serv.

— More Coffee Shop Theology. LC 98-25705. 1998. 13.99 (*0-8341-1746-0*) Nazarene.

— Personal & Political Ballads of the War. (Notable American Authors Ser.). 1999. reprint ed. lib. bdg. 125.00 (*0-7812-4580-X*) Rprt Serv.

— Rebel Rhymes & Rhapsodies. (Notable American Authors Ser.). 1999. reprint ed. lib. bdg. 125.00 (*0-7812-4581-8*) Rprt Serv.

— Rebellion Record: A Diary of American Events. 1980. 27.95 (*0-405-10877-X*) Ayer.

— Record of the Year. (Notable American Authors Ser.). 1999. reprint ed. lib. bdg. 125.00 (*0-7812-4584-2*) Rprt Serv.

— Songs & Ballads of American Revolution. (Notable American Authors Ser.). 1999. reprint ed. lib. bdg. 125.00 (*0-7812-4573-7*) Rprt Serv.

— Songs & Ballads of the American Revolution. (BCL1 - U. S. History Ser.). 288p. 1991. reprint ed. lib. bdg. 79.00 (*0-7812-6106-6*) Rprt Serv.

— Songs & Ballads of the Southern People. (Notable American Authors Ser.). 1999. reprint ed. lib. bdg. 125.00 (*0-7812-4585-0*) Rprt Serv.

— Songs of the Soldiers. (Notable American Authors Ser.). 1999. reprint ed. lib. bdg. 125.00 (*0-7812-4578-8*) Rprt Serv.

— Speeches of Andrew Johnson. (Notable American Authors Ser.). 1999. reprint ed. lib. bdg. 125.00 (*0-7812-4582-6*) Rprt Serv.

— Women of the War. (Notable American Authors Ser.). 1999. reprint ed. lib. bdg. 125.00 (*0-7812-4583-4*) Rprt Serv.

— Women of the War: Heroines of the War Between the States. LC 97-43477. (Illus.). 304p. 1997. reprint ed. pap. 16.95 (*1-888295-00-7*, Blue Grey Bks) Elephant Books.

— Women of the War: Their Heroism & Self-Sacrifice. xvi, 596p. reprint ed. 69.00 (*0-932051-34-0*) Rprt Serv.

Moore, Frank, ed. Rebel Rhymes & Rhapsodies. 1976. lib. bdg. 59.95 (*0-8490-2503-6*) Gordon Pr.

— Rebellion Record: A Diary of American Events, 12 vols., Set. (Illus.). 1976. reprint ed. pap. 300.00 (*0-405-09846-4*) Ayer.

Moore, Frank & Decker, Peter, eds. Diary of the American Revolution: From Newspapers & Original Documents, 2 vols., Set. LC 72-76563. (Eyewitness Accounts of the American Revolution Ser.). (Illus.). 1969. reprint ed. 46.95 (*0-405-01165-2*) Ayer.

— Diary of the American Revolution: From Newspapers & Original Documents, 2 vols., Vol. 1. LC 72-76563. (Eyewitness Accounts of the American Revolution Ser.). (Illus.). 1969. reprint ed. 23.95 (*0-405-01166-0*) Ayer.

— Diary of the American Revolution: From Newspapers & Original Documents, 2 vols., Vol. 2. LC 72-76563. (Eyewitness Accounts of the American Revolution Ser.). (Illus.). 1969. reprint ed. 23.95 (*0-405-01167-9*) Ayer.

— Songs & Ballads of the American Revolution. LC 79-76562. (Eyewitness Accounts of the American Revolution Ser.). (Illus.). 1976. reprint ed. 25.95 (*0-405-01164-4*) Ayer.

Moore, Frank & Hynam, John. The Horses Knew the Way: Memories of a Lincolnshire Life. 160p. 1991. pap. 22.95 (*0-86299-989-8*, Pub. by Sutton Pub Ltd) Intl Pubs Mktg.

Moore, Frank G. The Roman's World. LC 65-23486. (Illus.). 502p. (J). (gr. 7 up). 1936. 30.00 (*0-8196-0155-1*) Biblo.

Moore, Frank G., tr. see Von Pufendorf, Samuel.

Moore, Frank J. The Incredible Moving Picture Book. 32p. (J). (gr. 1 up). 1987. pap. 3.95 (*0-486-25374-0*) Dover.

Moore, Frank J., et al. Thailand: Its People, Its Society, Its Culture. LC 74-79218. (Survey of World Cultures Ser.: No. 15). 629p. reprint ed. pap. 195.00 (*0-608-11736-6*, 201045400068) Bks Demand.

Moore, Frank L. Crowell's Handbook of World Opera. LC 73-3025. (Illus.). 683p. 1974. reprint ed. lib. bdg. 43.00 (*0-8371-6822-8*, MOCH, Greenwood Pr) Greenwood.

***Moore, Frank L. & Varcher, Mary.** Dictionary of the Performing Arts. 2nd ed. LC 98-49884. 576p. 2000. pap. 24.95 (*0-8092-3010-0*, 301000, Contemporary Bks) NTC Contemp Pub Co.

***Moore, Frank Ledlie & Varchaver, Mary.** Dictionary of the Performing Arts. 2nd ed. LC 98-49884. (Illus.). 592p. 2000. 50.00 (*0-8092-3009-7*, 300970, Contemporary Bks) NTC Contemp Pub Co.

Moore, Frank W., ed. Readings in Cross-Cultural Methodology. LC 66-28127. (Comparative Studies). 350p. 1966. reprint ed. 15.00 (*0-87536-101-3*); reprint ed. pap. 10.00 (*0-87536-102-1*) HRAFP.

Moore, Franklin. Agents Bonding Guide. 24th rev. ed. Kowatch, Diana, ed. 180p. 1998. pap. text 44.95 (*1-56461-242-2*, 26080) Rough Notes.

Moore, Franklin & Moore, Bradley S. Property & Casualty Insurance: Core Book. 600p. (Orig.). 1996. pap. 50.00 (*1-56461-155-8*) Rough Notes.

Moore, Franklin L. Property & Casualty Insurance: Study Guide. 1991. student ed. 50.00 (*0-942326-25-3*, 26629) Rough Notes.

Moore, Franklin L. & Moore, Bradley S., eds. Property & Casualty State Law Study Guide: Pennsylvania. 50p. 1996. student ed. write for info. (*1-56461-172-8*) Rough Notes.

Moore, Franklin L., et al. A Study Guide for Life, Accident & Health Insurance LC 98-207885. viii, 274p. 1997. write for info. (*1-56461-229-5*) Rough Notes.

Moore, Fred, compiled by. Iraq Speaks: Documents on the Gulf Crisis. 92p. (Orig.). (C). 1993. pap. text 30.00 (*0-7881-0029-7*) DIANE Pub.

Moore, Fred H. & Moore, Ella M. The Texas State Capitol: Selected Essays from the Southwestern Historical Quaterly. LC 95-16736. (Fred H. & Ella Mae Moore Texas History Reprint Ser.: Vol. 14). (Illus.). 170p. 1995. pap. 13.95 (*0-87611-150-9*) Tex St Hist Assn.

Moore, Frederick W. Balkan Trial. LC 75-134826. (Eastern Europe Collection). 1971. reprint ed. 26.95 (*0-405-02768-0*) Ayer.

Moore, Frederick W., tr. see Gumplowicz, Ludwig.

Moore, Fuller. Concepts of Architectural Structures. 304p. 1998. pap. 74.69 (*0-07-043253-8*) McGraw.

— Environmental Control Systems: Heating, Cooling, Lighting. (C). 1992. 58.75 (*0-07-042889-1*) McGraw.

Moore, G. Practice of Social Inquiry. 136p. 1984. text 23.00 (*0-08-030369-2*, Pergamon Pr); pap. text 14.50 (*0-08-030370-6*, Pergamon Pr) Elsevier.

Moore, G. & Wood, C. Social Work & Criminal Law in Scotland. 2nd ed. 336p. 1989. pap. 60.00 (*1-873644-07-8*, Pub. by Mercat Pr Bks) St Mut.

Moore, G., jt. auth. see Haye, S.

Moore, G. Alexander. Life Cycles in Atchalan: The Diverse Careers of Certain Guatemalans. LC 72-93732. 232p. reprint ed. pap. 72.00 (*0-608-12762-0*, 202432900037) Bks Demand.

Moore, G. E. The Elements of Ethics. (C). 1991. 69.95 (*0-87722-770-5*) Temple U Pr.

— G. E. Moore: Selected Writings. Baldwin, Thomas, ed. LC 93-16366. (International Library of Philosophy). 232p. (C). 1993. pap. 25.99 (*0-415-09854-8*, B2419) Routledge.

An Asterisk (*) at the beginning of an entry indicates that the title is appearing for the first time.

— Principia Ethica. LC 88-61329. (Great Books in Philosophy). 253p. (C). 1988. pap. 8.95 (*0-87975-498-2*) Prometheus Bks.

— Principia Ethica: With the Preface to the Second Edition & Other Papers. rev. ed. Baldwin, Thomas, ed. LC 93-6493. 351p. (C). 1993. text 59.95 (*0-521-44378-4*); pap. text 21.95 (*0-521-44848-4*) Cambridge U Pr.

Moore, G. E., jt. auth. see Bennett, P. R.

Moore, G. F. & BICC Cables Ltd. Staff. Electric Cables Handbook. 3rd ed. LC 97-24044. 1098p. 1997. text 175.00 (*0-632-04075-0*) Blackwell Sci.

Moore, G. L., ed. Introduction to Inductively Coupled Plasma Atomic Emission Spectroscopy. (Analytical Spectroscopy Library: No. 3). 340p. 1989. 171.00 (*0-444-43029-6*) Elsevier.

Moore, G. R. & Pettigrew, G. W. Cytochromes C: Evolutionary, Structural & Physicochemical Aspects. Rich, A., ed. (Molecular Biology Ser.). (Illus.). xvi, 478p. 1990. 153.95 (*0-387-50852-X*) Spr-Verlag.

Moore, G. R., jt. auth. see Pettigrew, G. W.

Moore, G. T., jt. ed. see Zube, Ervin H.

Moore, Gareth. Believing in God. 300p. 1996. pap. 29.95 (*0-567-08535-X*, Pub. by T & T Clark) Bks Intl VA.

— Believing in God: A Philosophical Essay. 300p. 1989. 39.95 (*0-567-09498-7*, Pub. by T & T Clark) Bks Intl VA.

Moore, Gary. Golf, Gambling & Gamesmanship. 1986. pap. 7.95 (*0-89746-054-5*) Gambling Times.

— A March of Centuries: Lawyers & the Law in Jacksonville 1564 to 1997. LC 97-73764. (Illus.). 113p. 1997. 30.00 (*0-9659460-0-2*) Jacksnvl Bar Assn.

— Ten Golden Rules for Financial Success: Riches I've Gathered from Legendary Mutual Fund Manager Sir John M. Templeton. 224p. 1997. pap. 12.99 (*0-310-21933-7*) Zondervan.

Moore, Gary, jt. auth. see Richardson, William B.

Moore, Gary D. End Times Money Management: Protecting Your Resources from Financial Chaos. LC 98-46641. 1999. pap. 10.99 (*0-310-22360-1*) Zondervan.

— Spiritual Investments: Wall Street Wisdom from Sir John Templeton. LC 98-38607. 112p. 1998. 12.95 (*1-890151-18-1*) Templeton Fnd.

Moore, Gary S. Living with the Earth: Concepts in Environmental Health S Cience : A Web-enhanced Book. LC 99-10845. 672p. 1999. boxed set 79.95 (*1-56670-357-3*) Lewis Pubs.

Moore, Gary T. Early Childhood Physical Environment Observation Schedules & Rating Scales: Preliminary Scales for the Measurement of the Physical Environment of Child Care Centers & Related Environments. vi, 74p. (C). 1995. per. 12.00 (*0-938744-83-6*, R94-2) U of Wis Ctr Arch-Urban.

Moore, Gary T., compiled by. Comprehensive Bibliography on Child Care & Preschool Design. v, 49p. (C). 1995. per. 11.00 (*0-938744-84-4*, R94-3) U of Wis Ctr Arch-Urban.

Moore, Gary T., ed. Genesis II: Advanced Lunar Outpost. (Publications in Architecture & Urban Planning: No. R91-2). (Illus.). xvi, 70p. 1991. 10.00 (*0-938744-74-7*) U of Wis Ctr Arch-Urban.

Moore, Gary T. & Lackney, Jeffrey A. Educational Facilities for the Twenty-First Century: Research Analysis & Design Patterns. (Publications in Architecture & Urban Planning: No. R94-1). (Illus.). 90p. 1994. per. 22.00 (*0-938744-80-1*) U of Wis Ctr Arch-Urban.

Moore, Gary T. & Marans, Robert W., eds. Advances in Environment, Behavior, & Design Vol. 4: Toward the Integration of Theory, Methods, Research & Utilization, Vol. 4. (Illus.). 396p. (C). 1997. 79.50 (*0-306-45343-6*, Plenum Trade) Perseus Pubng.

Moore, Gary T., et al. Environmental Design: Research Directions. LC 84-15975. 222p. 1984. 55.00 (*0-275-91232-9*, C1232, Praeger Pubs) Greenwood.

— Recommendations for Child Care Centers. rev. ed. (Publications in Architecture & Urban Planning: No. R79-2). (Illus.). viii, 450p. 1994. per. 29.50 (*0-938744-06-2*) U of Wis Ctr Arch-Urban.

Moore, Gary T., jt. auth. see University of Wisconsin Ph.D Faculty Staff.

Moore, Gary T., ed. see Baschiera, Dino, et al.

Moore, Gary T., ed. see Burg, Cynthia M., et al.

Moore, Gary T., ed. see Gartz, William F., et al.

Moore, Gary T., ed. see Huebner-Moths, Janis, et al.

Moore, Gary T., ed. see Schnarsky, Anthony J., et al.

Moore, Gary T., jt. ed. see Zube, Ervin H.

Moore, Gay M. Seaport in Virginia: George Washington's Alexandria. LC 73-188711. 288p. reprint ed. 89.30 (*0-8357-9817-8*, 201920300011) Bks Demand.

Moore, Gene E. Bucco. (Illus.). 64p. 1992. pap. 6.95 (*0-9633267-0-8*) Greenhawk Bks.

— Gossamer: The Green Giraffe. 44p. reprint ed. pap. 4.00 (*0-9633267-1-6*) Greenhawk Bks.

Moore, Gene M., ed. Conrad on Film. LC 97-390. (Illus.). 278p. (C). 1998. text 59.95 (*0-521-55448-9*) Cambridge U Pr.

Moore, Gene M., jt. ed. see Knowles, Owen.

Moore, Gene M., tr. see Amsterdamski, Stefan.

Moore, Geoff, jt. auth. see Higginson, Richard.

Moore, Geoff, jt. ed. see Long, David.

***Moore, Geoffrey.** Inside the Tornado: Marketing strategies from Silicon Valley's Cutting Edge. abr. ed. 1998. audio 18.00 (*0-694-51937-5*, CPN2728) HarperAudio.

Moore, Geoffrey. Living on the Fault Line. Date not set. pap. 15.00 (*0-88730-971-2*, HarpBusn) HarpInfo.

***Moore, Geoffrey, et al.** The Gorilla Game: Picking Winners in High Technology. rev. ed. LC 99-35046. (Illus.). 384p. 1999. 27.00 (*0-88730-957-7*) HarpC.

Moore, Geoffrey, et al. Romantic Poets: Byron, Keats, Shelley, Wordsworth. Porter, Peter, ed. LC 97-112123. (Illus.). 224p. 1996. 14.95 (*1-85410-232-X*, Pub. by Aurum Pr) London Brdge.

Moore, Geoffrey, jt. auth. see Klein, Philip A.

Moore, Geoffrey, ed. & intro. see James, Henry.

Moore, Geoffrey A. Crossing the Chasm: Marketing & Selling High-Tech Products to Mainstream Customers. LC 98-55078. 256p. 1999. pap. 16.00 (*0-06-662002-3*) HarpC.

— Crossing the Chasm: Marketing & Selling High-Tech Products to Mainstream Customers. 256p. 1995. pap. 16.00 (*0-88730-717-5*, HarpBusn) HarpInfo.

***Moore, Geoffrey A.** The Gorilla Game: An Investor's Guide to Picking Winners in High Technology. abr. ed. 1998. audio 18.00 (*0-694-51928-6*, CPN2717) HarperAudio.

Moore, Geoffrey A. Inside the Tornado: Marketing Strategies from Silicon Valley's Cutting Edge. 272p. 1995. 26.00 (*0-88730-765-5*, HarpBusn) HarpInfo.

— Inside the Tornado: Marketing Strategies from Silicon Valley's Cutting Edge. 256p. 1999. pap. 16.00 (*0-88730-824-4*, HarpBusn) HarpInfo.

***Moore, Geoffrey A.** Living on the Fault Line: Managing for Shareholder Value in the Age of the Internet. LC 00-26312. 288p. 2000. 27.00 (*0-88730-888-0*, Hrpr Busn) HarpCollins.

Moore, Geoffrey A., et al. The Gorilla Game: An Investor's Guide to Picking Winners in High Technology. LC 97-50099. (Illus.). 321p. 1998. 26.00 (*0-88730-887-2*, HarpBusn) HarpInfo.

Moore, Geoffrey H. Business Cycles: Inflation & Forecasting. 2nd ed. LC 83-3829. (National Bureau of Economic Research, Studies in Business Cycles: No. 24). 499p. reprint ed. pap. 154.70 (*0-8357-6986-0*, 205706900009) Bks Demand.

— Measuring Recessions. (Occasional Papers: No. 61). 64p. 1958. reprint ed. 20.00 (*0-87014-375-1*) Natl Bur Econ Res.

— Production of Industrial Materials in World Wars I & II. (Occasional Papers: No. 18). 84p. 1944. reprint ed. 21.90 (*0-87014-333-6*) Natl Bur Econ Res.

— Statistical Indicators of Cyclical Revivals & Recessions. (Occasional Papers: No. 31). 104p. 1950. reprint ed. 27.10 (*0-87014-346-8*) Natl Bur Econ Res.

Moore, Geoffrey H., ed. Business Cycle Indicators, 1. LC 60-14062. (National Bureau of Economic Research Ser.: Vol. 10). 793p. reprint ed. pap. 200.00 (*0-8357-7486-4*, 200591700055) Bks Demand.

— Business Cycle Indicators, 2. LC 60-14062. (National Bureau of Economic Research Ser.: Vol. 10). 197p. reprint ed. pap. 61.10 (*0-8357-7487-2*, 201964400013) Bks Demand.

Moore, Geoffrey H. & Klein, Philip A. The Quality of Consumer Instalment Credit. (Financial Research Program II: Studies in Consumer Installment Financing: No. 13). 282p. 1967. reprint ed. 73.40 (*0-87014-484-7*) Natl Bur Econ Res.

Moore, Geoffrey H. & Moore, Melita H. International Economic Indicators: A Sourcebook. LC 84-19194. (Illus.). 373p. 1985. lib. bdg. 75.00 (*0-313-21989-3*, MII/, Greenwood Pr) Greenwood.

Moore, Geoffrey H. & Shiskin, Julius. Indicators of Business Expansions & Contractions. (Occasional Papers: No. 103). 141p. 1967. reprint ed. 36.70 (*0-87014-444-8*) Natl Bur Econ Res.

Moore, Geoffrey H., jt. auth. see Cagan, Phillip.

Moore, Geoffrey H., jt. auth. see Wallis, W. Allen.

Moore, Geoffrey H., jt. ed. see Lahiri, Kajal.

Moore, George. A Communication to My Friends. LC 74-8663. (English Literature Ser.: No. 33). 1974. lib. bdg. 75.00 (*0-8383-1910-6*) M S G Haskell Hse.

— Confessions of a Young Man. (BCL1-PR English Literature Ser.). 301p. 1992. reprint ed. lib. bdg. 89.00 (*0-7812-7601-2*) Rprt Serv.

— Confessions of a Young Man. LC 70 145188. (Literature Ser.). (Illus.). 314p. 1972. reprint ed. 29.00 (*0-403-01113-2*) Scholarly.

— Conversations with George Moore. LC 73-21564. (English Literature Ser.: No. 33). 1974. lib. bdg. 75.00 (*0-8383-1811-8*) M S G Haskell Hse.

— A Drama in Muslin. 330p. 1981. 32.00 (*0-86140-055-0*, Pub. by Smyth); pap. 15.95 (*0-86140-056-9*, Pub. by Smyth) Dufour.

— Esther Waters. Skilton, David, ed. (Oxford World's Classics Ser.). 432p. 2000. pap. 9.95 (*0-19-283712-5*) OUP.

— Esther Waters. large type ed. (Large Print Ser.). 440p. 1993. reprint ed. lib. bdg. 24.00 (*0-939495-29-5*) North Bks.

— Esther Waters. 400p. 1998. reprint ed. lib. bdg. 24.00 (*1-58287-026-8*) North Bks.

— Flowers of Passion. Fletcher, Ian & Stokes, John, eds. LC 76-20138. (Decadent Consciousness Ser.). 1978. lib. bdg. 46.00 (*0-8240-2778-7*) Garland.

— George Moore in Transition: Letters to T. Fisher Unwin & Lena Milman, 1894-1910. Gerber, Helmut E., ed. LC 67-23323. 343p. reprint ed. pap. 106.40 (*0-608-16489-5*, 202763500055) Bks Demand.

— Grasville Abbey: A Romance, 3 vols., Set. LC 73-22769. (Gothic Novels II Ser.). 792p. 1979. reprint ed. 94.95 (*0-405-06019-X*) Ayer.

— Hail & Farewell. Crave, R., ed. (Illus.). 774p. 1976. 60.00 (*0-900675-64-0*, Pub. by Smyth) Dufour.

— Hail & Farewell. Crave, R., ed. 774p. 1985. pap. 19.95 (*0-86140-198-0*, Pub. by Smyth) Dufour.

— Hail & Farewell: Ave, Salve, Vale. Cave, Richard A., ed. LC 85-465. (Illus.). 774p. reprint ed. pap. 200.00 (*0-7837-4633-4*, 204435700002) Bks Demand.

— Impressions & Opinions. LC 72-80501. 346p. 1972. reprint ed. 26.95 (*0-405-08797-7*, Pub. by Blom Pubns) Ayer.

— In Minor Keys: The Uncollected Short Stories of George Moore. Eakin, David B. & Gerber, Helmut E., eds. (Irish Studies). (Illus.). 180p. 1985. text 44.95 (*0-8156-2338-0*) Syracuse U Pr.

— In Single Strictness. LC 73-37557. (Short Story Index Reprint Ser.). 1977. reprint ed. 23.95 (*0-8369-4116-0*) Ayer.

— The Lake. 286p. 1980. 30.00 (*0-900675-75-6*, Pub. by Smyth); pap. 14.95 (*0-901072-82-6*, Pub. by Smyth) Dufour.

— Ppm For Automotive Technicians 4e. 4th ed. (Business Math). (C). 1991. mass mkt. 14.75 (*0-8273-4622-0*) Delmar.

— Practical Problems in Mathematics for Auto Technologies. 5th ed. LC 97-11280. 256p. (C). 1997. pap. 19.95 (*0-8273-7944-7*) Delmar.

— Practical Problems in Mathematics for Auto Technologies. 5th ed. (C). 1998. pap. text, teacher ed. 12.00 (*0-8273-7945-5*) Delmar.

— Practical Problems in Mathematics for Automotive Technicians Instructors Guide. 4th ed. 1991. teacher ed. 13.00 (*0-8273-4623-9*) Delmar.

— A Story-Teller's Holiday, 2 vols., Set. (BCL1-PR English Literature Ser.). 1992. reprint ed. lib. bdg. 150.00 (*0-7812-7602-0*) Rprt Serv.

— The Untilled Field. LC 70-125233. (Short Story Index Reprint Ser.). 1977. 30.95 (*0-8369-3600-0*) Ayer.

— The Use of the Body in Relation to the Mind. LC 78-72812. reprint ed. 32.50 (*0-404-60882-5*) AMS Pr.

Moore, George, ed. An Anthology of Pure Poetry. 1973. pap. 2.75 (*0-87140-276-9*, Pub. by Liveright) Norton.

Moore, George & Lamie, Judith. Translate or Communicate: English As a Foreign Language in Japanese Schools. 198p. (C). 1997. lib. bdg. 75.00 (*1-56072-418-8*) Nova Sci Pubs.

Moore, George & Wood, Chris. Social Work & Criminal Law in Scotland. 220p. 1982. text 22.00 (*0-08-025731-3*, Pergamon Pr) Elsevier.

— Social Work & Criminal Law in Scotland. 2nd ed. (Aberdeen University Press Bks.). 250p. 1991. text 25.50 (*0-08-041221-1*, Pub. by Aberdeen U Pr) Macmillan.

— Social Work & Criminal Law in Scotland: An Update. (Aberdeen University Press Bks.). 32p. 1987. pap. text 8.00 (*0-08-035069-0*, Pub. by Aberdeen U Pr) Macmillan.

Moore, George, tr. see Longus.

Moore, George B. Gertrude Stein's The Making of Americans: Repetition & the Emergence of Modernism. LC 95-21813. (American Univ. Studies, XXIV, Am. Lit.: No. 61). 267p. 1998. 45.95 (*0-8204-2680-6*) P Lang Pubng.

— The Petroglyphs at Wedding Rocks & Other Poems. LC 96-45642. 72p. 1997. pap. 14.95 (*0-7734-2699-X*, Mellen Poetry Pr) E Mellen.

Moore, George Edward. Commonplace Book 1919-53: 1962 Edition. (Key Texts Ser.). 426p. 1996. reprint ed. pap. 29.95 (*1-85506-231-3*) Bks Intl VA.

— Esther Waters. Laurie, Hilary, ed. 384p. 1993. pap. 9.95 (*0-460-87326-1*, Everyman's Classic Lib) Tuttle Pubng.

Moore, George F. History of Religions, 2 vols., Vol. 1. 654p. 1914. 49.95 (*0-567-07202-9*, Pub. by T & T Clark) Bks Intl VA.

— History of Religions, 2 vols., Vol. 2. 568p. 1920. 49.95 (*0-567-07203-7*, Pub. by T & T Clark) Bks Intl VA.

— Judaism in the First Centuries of the Christian Era: The Age of the Tannaim, 3 vols. in 2. 1258p. 1997. reprint ed. 59.95 (*1-56563-286-9*) Hendrickson MA.

— Judges: Critical Exegetical Commentary. Driver, Samuel R. et al, eds. LC 25-19368. (International Critical Commentary Ser.). 528p. 1995. 39.95 (*0-567-05004-1*, Pub. by T & T Clark) Bks Intl VA.

Moore, George T., jt. auth. see Barron, Eric J.

Moore, George T., jt. auth. see Stanley, Daniel J.

Moore, George W. Moore: Genealogy of the Moore Family of Londonderry, N.H. & Peterborough, N.H. 1648-1924. (Illus.). 109p. 1995. reprint ed. pap. 18.00 (*0-8328-4928-6*); reprint ed. lib. bdg. 28.00 (*0-8328-4927-8*) Higginson Bk Co.

Moore, George W. & Sullivan, Nicholas. Speleology: Caves & the Cave Environment. 3rd ed. LC 77-18176. (Illus.). 1997. 21.95 (*0-939748-46-0*) Cave Bks MO.

— Speleology: Caves & the Cave Environment. 3rd ed. LC 77-18176. (Illus.). xiii, 176p. 1997. reprint ed. pap. 15.95 (*0-939748-45-2*) Cave Bks MO.

Moore, Gerald. Am I too Loud, a Musical Autobiography. 288p. reprint ed. lib. bdg. 59.00 (*0-7812-0570-0*) Rprt Serv.

— The Chosen Tongue: English Writing in the Tropical World. LC 76-479762. 222 p. 1969. write for info. (*0-582-11011-4*) Addison-Wesley.

— Singer & Accompanist: The Performance of Fifty Songs. LC 73-11859. (Illus.). 232p. 1974. reprint ed. lib. bdg. 49.75 (*0-8371-7090-7*, MOSC, Greenwood Pr) Greenwood.

— Tsuen-Wan Township: Study Group Report on Its Development. LC DS0796.H76T7. 47p. reprint ed. pap. 30.00 (*0-608-11788-9*, 201771900007) Bks Demand.

Moore, Gerald, et al. Things Fall Apart--Chinua Achebe. LC 75-321426. (Books in focus Ser). 10 p. 1974. write for info. (*0-435-28091-0*) Heinemann.

Moore, Gerald, tr. see Lopes, Henri.

Moore, Gerald, tr. see Pressburger, Giorgio & Pressburger, Nicola.

Moore, Gerald T. & Scully, Marian O., eds. Frontiers of Nonequilibrium Statistical Physics. LC 85-31171. (NATO ASI Series B, Physics: Vol. 135). 510p. 1986. 125.00 (*0-306-42233-6*, Plenum Trade) Perseus Pubng.

Moore, Gerard. Vatican II & the Collects for Ordinary Time: A Study in the Roman Missal. LC 98-20607. 840p. 1998. 74.95 (*1-57309-217-7*) Intl Scholars.

— Vatican II & the Collects for Ordinary Time: A Study in the Roman Missal (1975) LC 98-20607. 840p. 1997. pap. 54.95 (*1-57309-216-9*) Intl Scholars.

Moore, Gilbert. Lorraine As in a Chagall Painting: Lorraine Comme Dans une Toile de Chagall. Livingstone, Harrison E., ed. (ENG & FRE.). 96p. 1990. pap. text 8.95 (*0-941401-03-0*) Conservatory.

Moore-Gilbert, B. J., et al. Postcolonial Criticism. LC 97-255. (Critical Readers Ser.). 312p. (C). 1997. pap. 29.06 (*0-582-23798-X*) Addison-Wesley.

— Postcolonial Criticism. LC 97-255. (Critical Readers Ser.). (C). 1998. text 68.44 (*0-582-23797-1*) Longman.

Moore-Gilbert, Bart. Postcolonial Theory: Contexts, Practices, Politics. LC 97-16324. 1997. pap. 20.00 (*1-85984-034-5*, Pub. by Verso) Norton.

Moore-Gilbert, Bart, ed. The Arts in the 1970s: Cultural Closure? LC 93-3712. 320p. (C). 1994. pap. 27.99 (*0-415-09906-4*) Routledge.

— The Arts in the 1970s: Cultural Closure? LC 93-3712. 320p. (C). (gr. 13). 1994. text 69.95 (*0-415-09905-6*) Routledge.

— Writing India, 1757-1990: The Literature of British India. LC 95-31538. 256p. 1996. text 79.95 (*0-7190-4265-8*, Pub. by Manchester Univ Pr); text 27.95 (*0-7190-4266-6*, Pub. by Manchester Univ Pr) St Martin.

Moore, Gilbert W., jt. auth. see Irons, Edward D.

Moore, Gina. Cushions & Covers: A Step-by-Step Guide to Creative Pillow Covers, Tablecloths & Seat Coverings. LC 97-22201. (Practical Home Decorating Ser.). 1997. 24.95 (*0-89577-980-3*, Pub. by RD Assn) Penguin Putnam.

Moore, Giselle. Women & Cancer: Gynecology Oncology Nursing. (Nursing Ser.). (C). 1996. 64.95 (*0-86720-714-0*) Jones & Bartlett.

— Women & Cancer Clinical Pocket Guide. (Nursing Ser.). 224p. 1997. pap. 32.50 (*0-7637-0548-9*) Jones & Bartlett.

***Moore, Glenice.** Bitterroot Backroads, Vol. 4. (Illus.). 40p. 2000. pap. 10.50 (*1-56770-478-6*) S Scheewe Pubns.

Moore, Glenice, jt. auth. see Nickel, Glenice M.

Moore, Glenn. Plan to Win: Success Guide for Young Athletes. LC 93-72102. (Illus.). 176p. (Orig.). 1993. pap. 12.95 (*0-9637345-0-4*) Champ Spts Pr.

Moore, Gloria, jt. auth. see Moore, Ronald.

Moore Glover, Judith. Family Treasures. (Illus.). 190p. 1997. pap. 10.95 (*1-878149-38-5*) Counterpoint Pub.

Moore, Gordon E., ed. see National Academy of Sciences, Committee on Linking.

Moore, Gordon P., jt. ed. see Rosenberg, Martin.

Moore, Grace. You're Only Human Once. Farkas, Andrew, ed. LC 76-29958. (Opera Biographies Ser.). (Illus.). 1977. reprint ed. lib. bdg. 25.95 (*0-405-09698-4*) Ayer.

Moore, Graham. Nonwood Fibre Applications in Papermaking: A Literature Review. 110p. 1996. pap. 110.00 (*1-85802-106-5*) Pira Internatl.

— Wet & Chemistry Strategies: A Literature Review. 101p. 1996. pap. 95.00 (*1-85802-006-9*, Pub. by Pira Internatl) Bks Intl VA.

Moore, Graham, jt. auth. see Attwood, Brian.

Moore, Graham, jt. ed. see Sasaki, Takuji.

Moore, Grant H., et al, trs. Khibaru Fan'yi Mikhie Be: The New Testament in the Soso Language. 1988. spiral bd. write for info. (*0-318-66962-5*) Open Bible.

Moore, Granville M. Poisonous Snakes of the World: Manual for Use by the United States Amphibious Forces. (Illus.). 220p. 1979. reprint ed. boxed set 31.00 (*0-16-002014-X*, S/N 008-045-00009-7) USGPO.

Moore Gray, Libba. Is There Room on the Feather Bed? LC 96-42387. (Illus.). 32p. (J). (ps-1). 1997. 16.95 (*0-531-30013-7*); lib. bdg. 17.99 (*0-531-33013-3*) Orchard Bks Watts.

Moore, Greg. Impact of Airline Marketing Practices on Corporate Travel Costs & Earnings: Frequent Flyer Programs & Their Role in Airline Anti-Competitive Practices. Cripe, Helen, ed. (Illus.). 101p. 1999. pap. 249.00 (*0-9643916-7-8*) Integ Tech Res.

— Rock & Roll Collectibles. LC 93-91812. (Illus.). 112p. 1993. pap. 22.95 (*0-9639495-0-0*) G Moore Pubng.

— Seduced by a Mile. Cripe, Helen, ed. LC 99-166168. 258p. 1998. pap. 24.95 (*0-9643916-5-1*) Integ Tech Res.

— Travel Services Commercial Agreements: Survey of Practices & Contracts in Use. Cripe, Helen, ed. (Illus.). 40p. 1997. pap., spiral bd. 249.00 (*0-9643916-4-3*) Integ Tech Res.

Moore, Greg & Hilton, Joe. Rock-n-Roll Treasures Identification & Value Guide. 256p. 1999. pap. text 19.95 (*1-57432-122-6*) Collector Bks.

Moore, Greg & McClaran, Don. Idaho Whitewater: The Complete River Guide. Hesselbarth, Woody, ed. LC 89-90989. (Illus.). 224p. (Orig.). 1989. pap. text 19.95 (*0-9623828-0-9*) Class Six.

Moore, Greg & Pizzo, Joe. Bubble Bath Containers: Identification & Values. LC 99-192283. 160p. 1998. pap. 19.95 (*1-57432-074-2*) Collector Bks.

Moore, Gregory H., ed. see Russell, Bertrand.

Moore, Gregory J. MSC - Nastran Design Sensitivity & Optimization. rev. ed. (Illus.). 350p. 1994. pap. text 65.00 (*1-58524-005-2*) MacNeal-Schwendler.

Moore, Gregory R., jt. auth. see Guerrieri, James P.

Moore, Gwen, et al, eds. Deindustrialization & the Restructuring of American Industry, Vol. 3. (Research in Politics & Society Ser.). 294p. 1988. 73.25 (*0-89232-714-6*) Jai Pr.

Moore, Gwen & Whitt, J. Allen, eds. The Political Consequence of Social Networks, Vol. 4. (Research in Politics & Society Ser.). 360p. 1993. 73.25 (*0-89232-994-7*) Jai Pr.

— Research in Politics & Society, Vol. 5. 294p. 1995. 73.25 (*1-55938-117-5*) Jai Pr.

— Research in Politics & Society, Vol. 6. Date not set. 73.25 (*0-7623-0043-4*) Jai Pr.

— Studies & the Structure of National Elite Groups. (Research in Politics & Society Ser.: Vol. 1). 283p. 1985. 73.25 (0-89232-335-3) Jai Pr.

— Women & Politics: Activism, Attitudes & Office-Holding, Vol. 2. (Research in Politics & Society Ser.). 304p. 1986. 73.25 (0-89232-556-9) Jai Pr.

Moore, Gwen B. & Serby, Todd. Becoming Whole Through Games. 288p. 1991. pap. 16.95 (0-915190-70-2, JP9072-2) Jalmar Pr.

Moore, Gwendolyn, tr. see Paris, Ginette.

Moore, Gwendolyn B., et al. Prescription for the Future: How the Technology Revolution Is Changing the Pulse of Global Health. 200p. 1996. 24.95 (1-888232-10-2) Knowldge Exchange.

Moore, H. F. Shot Peening & the Fatigue of Metals. (Technical Papers: Vol. P100). (Illus.). 23p. 1944. pap. text 30.00 (1-55589-221-3) AGMA.

Moore, H. Miles. Early History of Leavenworth City & County (Kansas) (Illus.). 339p. 1993. reprint ed. lib. bdg. 36.00 (0-8328-2957-9) Higginson Bk Co.

Moore, H. P. Moor: The Descendants of Ensign John Moor of Canterbury, N.H., born 1696 - died 1786. (Illus.). 370p. 1992. reprint ed. pap. 57.00 (0-8328-2691-X); reprint ed. lib. bdg. 67.00 (0-8328-2690-1) Higginson Bk Co.

Moore, H. S., et al, eds. Biotechnology & the Conservation of Genetic Diversity. (Symposia of the Zoological Society of London Ser.: No. 64). (Illus.). 256p. 1992. 110.00 (0-19-854030-2) OUP.

Moore, Hagan. Fair by Eleven. (Illus.). 87p. (Orig.). 1987. pap. 6.95 (0-916930-15-7) Gardner Oregon.

Moore, Hal G. & Yaqub, Adil. A First Course in Linear Algebra with Applications. 3rd ed. LC 97-46320. (Illus.). 632p. 1998. text 69.95 (0-12-505760-7) Acad Pr.

Moore, Hannah. Religion of the Heart. Helms, Hal M., ed. LC 93-84600. (Living Library). 226p. 1993. 8.95 (1-55725-063-4) Paraclete MA.

Moore, Hannah H. Wedgwood & His Imitators. 2nd rev. ed. LC 76-2888. (Illus.). 1978. 29.95 (0-89344-005-1) Ars Ceramica.

***Moore-Harell, Alice.** Gordon & the Sudan: Prologue to the Mahdiyya, 1877-1880. LC 00-34575. 2001. write for info. (0-7146-5081-1, Pub. by F Cass Pubs) Intl Spec Bk.

Moore, Harlan D., Jr., ed. Parables of the Good Shepherd: A Compilation of Parables Spoken by Jesus. LC 95-75970. (Illus.). 120p. (Orig.). 1996. pap. 8.95 (1-887076-17-4) Journey Bkshelf.

Moore, Harold G. & Galloway, Joseph. We Were Soldiers Once..and Young: Galloway,&Joseph L. abr. ed. 1993. audio 18.00 (1-55994-867-1, CPN 2410) HarperAudio.

— We Were Soldiers Once...And Young: Ia Drang - The Battle That Changed The War in Vietnam. LC 93-15836. (Illus.). 528p. 1993. reprint ed. pap. 16.00 (0-06-097576-8, Perennial) HarperTrade.

Moore, Harriet L. Soviet Far Eastern Policy, 1931-1945. 1982. 40.00 (0-86527-187-9) Fertig.

Moore, Harris W. Chip Carving. LC 75-19755. (Illus.). 32p. 1976. reprint ed. pap. 3.50 (0-486-23256-5) Dover.

Moore, Harry D., ed. Materials & Processes for NDT Technology. (Illus.). 204p. 1984. reprint ed. 44.50 (0-931403-06-5, 2250) Am Soc Nondestructive.

Moore, Harry H., ed. Survival or Suicide. LC 77-134118. (Essay Index Reprint Ser.). 1977. 20.95 (0-8369-2001-5) Ayer.

Moore, Harry L. A Geologic Trip Across Tennessee by Interstate 40. LC 93-43322. (Outdoor Tennessee Ser.). (Illus.). 384p. (C). 1994. pap. 19.95 (0-87049-832-0) U of Tenn Pr.

— A Roadside Guide to the Geology of the Great Smoky Mountains National Park. LC 87-18796. (Illus.). 192p. 1988. pap. 14.95 (0-87049-558-5) U of Tenn Pr.

Moore, Harry N. Silver Wings in Pacific Skies Australia's First Trans-Pacific Airline: British Commonwealth Pacific Airlines. 166p. 1995. 65.00 (0-7855-2774-5, Pub. by Boolarong Pubns) St Mut.

Moore, Harry T. Henry James. 2nd ed. LC 98-61522. (Literary Lives Ser.). (Illus.). 128p. 1999. reprint ed. pap. 12.95 (0-500-26032-X, Pub. by Thames Hudson) Norton.

Moore, Harry T., ed. see Paolucci, Anne.

Moore, Harry T., jt. ed. see Partlow, Robert B., Jr.

Moore, Harvey A. Drug Users & Emergent Organizations. LC 77-9901. (University of Florida Monographs: Social Sciences: No. 60). 144p. reprint ed. pap. 44.70 (0-7837-5065-X, 204476000004) Bks Demand.

Moore, Heather. Cooking for One: 100 Easy & Quick Recipes. (Illus.). 100p. (C). 1998. pap. 34.95 (1-57555-171-3) Cedar Bay Pr.

Moore, Helen A., jt. auth. see Ollenberger, Jane C.

Moore, Helen H. Beavers. LC 95-50295. (Illus.). 32p. (J). (gr. 2-6). 1996. pap. 4.95 (1-57255-111-9) Mondo Pubng.

— Los Castores. Gonzalez-Prats, Martha, tr. (SPA., Illus.). 32p. (J). (ps-3). 1998. pap. 4.95 (1-57255-508-4) Mondo Pubng.

— 100 Best Brain-Boosters: Puzzles & Games to Stimulate Students' Thinking. (Illus.). 1994. pap. text 9.95 (0-590-49795-2) Scholastic Inc.

— Pyramids to Pueblos: 15 Pop-Up Models for Students to Make. 1996. pap. text 9.95 (0-590-67481-1) Scholastic Inc.

— 25 Bilingual Mini-Books. (ENG & SPA.). (J). 1994. pap. text 9.95 (0-590-49802-9) Scholastic Inc.

— 25 Mother Goose Peak-a-Books: Reproducible, Easy-to-Make, Easy-to-Read. (Illus.). 1993. pap. text 9.95 (0-590-49729-4) Scholastic Inc.

Moore, Helen H., jt. auth. see Sorvillo, Carmen R.

Moore, Henrietta. Feminism & Anthropology. LC 88-22032. (Feminist Perspectives Ser.). ix, 246p. (Orig.). 1989. pap. 17.95 (0-8166-1750-3) U of Minn Pr.

Moore, Henrietta, ed. The Future of Anthropological Knowledge. LC 95-31964. (Uses of Knowledge Ser.). 192p. (C). 1996. pap. 25.99 (0-415-10787-3) Routledge.

Moore, Henrietta, jt. auth. see Vaughan, Megan.

Moore, Henrietta L. Anthropological Theory Today. LC 99-26798. 1999. pap. 26.95 (0-7456-2023-X, Pub. by Polity Pr); text 59.95 (0-7456-2022-1, Pub. by Polity Pr) Blackwell Pubs.

— A Passion for Difference: Essays in Anthropology & Gender. LC 94-31477. 186p. 1995. 39.95 (0-253-33858-1); pap. 14.95 (0-253-20951-X) Ind U Pr.

— Space, Text & Gender: An Anthropological Study of the Marakwet of Kenya. LC 95-46816. (Mappings). (Illus.). 234p. 1995. pap. text 17.95 (0-89862-825-3, 2825) Guilford Pubns.

***Moore, Henrietta L., et al, eds.** Those Who Play with Fire: Gender, Fertility & Transformation in East & Southern Africa. LC 99-12208. (London School of Economics Monographs on Social Anthropology: Vol. 69). 240p. 1999. 90.00 (0-485-19569-0, Pub. by Athlone Pr) Transaction Pubs.

Moore, Henry. Drawings of Henry Moore. (Master Draughtsman Ser.). (Illus.). 1970. pap. 4.95 (0-87505-178-2) Borden.

— Instructions for Preparing Abstracts of Titles: After the Most Improved System of Eminent Conveyancers: To Which Is Added a Collection of Precedents, Shewing the Method Not Only of Abstracting Every Species of Deeds, but of So Connecting Them Together, by Collateral Documents, As to Form a Complete Title. LC 98-5525. 107p. 1998. reprint ed. 35.00 (0-8377-2484-8, Rothman) W S Hein.

Moore, Henry. The Life of Mrs. Mary Fletcher, Consort & Relict of the Rev. John Fletcher. 295p. 1997. pap. 13.99 (0-88019-371-9) Schmul Pub Co.

Moore, Henry & Clark, Kenneth. Henry Moore's Sheep Sketchbook. LC 80-50325. (Illus.). 112p. 1998. pap. 19.95 (0-500-28072-X, Pub. by Thames Hudson) Norton.

Moore, Henry & Hedgecoe, John. Henry Moore: My Ideas, Inspiration & Life as an Artist. (Illus.). 208p. 1999. pap. 24.95 (1-85585-735-9, Pub. by Collins & Br) Sterling.

Moore, Henry & Scott, Deborah E. Henry Moore: Maquettes & Working Models. Leveton, Deborah, ed. (Illus.). 24p. (Orig.). 1987. pap. 3.00 (0-942614-11-9) Nelson-Atkins.

Moore, Henry, jt. auth. see Hedgecoe, John.

Moore, Henry, jt. auth. see Kaufman, Shirley.

Moore, Henry L. Economic Cycles: Their Law & Cause. LC 67-16342. (Reprints of Economic Classics Ser.). (Illus.). viii, 149p. 1967. reprint ed. 29.50 (0-678-00229-0) Kelley.

— Forecasting the Yield & Price of Cotton. LC 67-16343. (Reprints of Economic Classics Ser.). (Illus.). vi, 173p. 1967. reprint ed. 35.00 (0-678-00230-4) Kelley.

— Generating Economic Cycles. LC 65-26370. (Reprints of Economic Classics Ser.). (Illus.). xi, 141p. 1967. reprint ed. 29.50 (0-678-00231-2) Kelley.

— Law of Wages: An Essay in Statistical Economics. LC 65-26371. (Reprints of Economic Classics Ser.). (Illus.). 196p. 1967. reprint ed. 35.00 (0-678-00232-0) Kelley.

— Synthetic Economics. LC 67-18571. (Reprints of Economic Classics Ser.). vii, 186p. 1967. reprint ed. 35.00 (0-678-00233-9) Kelley.

Moore, Herb. Axis Correlation: A Modern Guide to Tonal Colors. rev. ed. Moore, Sharon, ed. 72p. 1993. pap. text 15.00 (0-9635896-0-7) Moores Music.

Moore, Herbert L., Jr. Rows of Corn: A True Account of a Parris Island Recruit. LC 83-3229. (Illus.). 232p. 1983. 4.95 (0-87844-048-8) Sandlapper Pub Co.

Moore, Herbert P. Seeds of Thought. (Illus.). 32p. 1999. pap. write for info. (0-9671890-1-2) L B Strawn.

Moore, Hillary. Sunburst Guide to Cross Stitch. 1994. 4.98 (0-7858-0008-5) Bk Sales Inc.

— Sunburst Guide to Patchwork. 1994. 4.98 (0-7858-0009-3) Bk Sales Inc.

— Sunburst Guide to Sewing. 1994. 4.98 (0-7858-0011-5) Bk Sales Inc.

Moore, Hilmar. Rudolf Steiner's Contribution to the History & Practice of Agricultural Education. 1992. pap. 12.95 (0-938250-33-7, 420) Bio-Dynamic Farm.

Moore, Hilmar, jt. auth. see Querido, Rene.

Moore, Honor. Memoir. LC 88-25647. 79p. (Orig.). 1988. pap. 11.95 (0-961911-1-5) Chicory Blue.

Moore, Howard E. Protecting Residences from Wildfires: A Guide for Homeowners, Lawmakers, & Planners. 44p. (Orig.). (C). 1993. pap. text 20.00 (1-56806-971-5) DIANE Pub.

Moore, Howard W. Plowing My Own Furrow. LC 93-7918. (Studies on Peace & Conflict Resolution). 224p. 1993. reprint ed. pap. 19.95 (0-8156-0276-6) Syracuse U Pr.

Moore, Hubert. Left-Handers. 72p. 1996. pap. 15.95 (1-870612-42-6, Pub. by Enitha Pr) Dufour.

— Rolling Stock. 56p. (Orig.). 1991. pap. 14.95 (1-870612-51-5, Pub. by Enitha Pr) Dufour.

Moore-Humphrey, Sheri, jt. auth. see Minter, Scott.

Moore, I. D., jt. ed. see Bevin, Keith J.

Moore, Ian & Legner, E. F. An Illustrated Guide to the Genera of the Staphylinidae of America North of Mexico. LC 78-75027. (Illus.). 344p. 1979. pap. 10.00 (0-931876-31-1, 4093) ANR Pubns CA.

Moore, Inga. The Adventures of Mr. Toad: From the Wind in the Willows. LC 98-23599. (Illus.). 86p. (YA). (gr. k up). 1998. 21.99 (0-7636-0581-6) Candlewick Pr.

— A Big Day for Little Jack. LC 93-6272. (Illus.). 32p. (J). (ps-1). 1997. reprint ed. pap. 5.99 (0-7636-0155-1) Candlewick Pr.

— Oh, Little Jack. LC 91-71827. (Illus.). 32p. (J). (ps up). 1992. 14.95 (1-56402-028-2) Candlewick Pr.

— Six Dinner Sid. LC 90-42749. (Illus.). 32p. (J). (ps-3). 1991. mass mkt. 15.00 (0-671-73199-8) S&S Bks Yung.

— Six Dinner Sid. LC 90-42749. (Illus.). 32p. (J). (ps-3). 1993. mass mkt. 5.95 (0-671-79613-5) S&S Bks Yung.

— Six Dinner Sid. (J). 1991. 11.15 (0-606-05606-8, Pub. by Turtleback) Demco.

— The Truffle Hunter. (Illus.). 32p. (J). (gr. k-3). 1999. pap. 7.95 (0-916291-92-8) Kane-Miller Bk.

— The Truffle Hunter. (Illus.). 32p. (J). (ps-3). 1999. 10.95 (0-916291-09-X) Kane-Miller Bk.

Moore, Inga, ed. & illus. see Grahame, Kenneth.

Moore, Iola, jt. auth. see Moore, Lonnie W.

Moore, Ira T. History of the Town of Livermore, Androscoggin County: From Its Inception in 1735 & Its Grant of Land in 1772, to Its Organization & Incorporation in 1795 up to 1928. (Illus.). 275p. 1997. reprint ed. lib. bdg. 34.00 (0-8328-6743-8) Higginson Bk Co.

Moore, Ishbel. Branch of the Talking Teeth. 96p. (J). (gr. 5-9). 1995. pap. 5.95 (1-896184-06-5) Roussan Pubs.

***Moore, Ishbel.** Daughter. 216p. (YA). (gr. 6-8). 1999. 16.95 (1-55074-535-2) Kids Can Pr.

Moore, Ishbel. Dolina May. (Illus.). 136p. (YA). (gr. 7 up). 1997. pap. 6.95 (1-896184-20-0) Roussan Pubs.

— Dolina's Grad. 136p. (YA). (gr. 8-12). 1998. pap. 7.95 (1-896184-42-1) Roussan Pubs.

— The Medal. 126p. (J). (gr. 5-9). 1994. pap. 5.95 (1-896184-02-2) Roussan Pubs.

— The Summer of the Hand. 136p. (J). (gr. 3-7). 1994. pap. 5.95 (2-921212-37-4) Roussan Pubs.

— Xanthe's Pyramid. 118p. (YA). (gr. 9 up). 1998. pap. 6.95 (1-896184-34-0) Roussan Pubs.

***Moore, Ishbel L.** Daughter. (J). 1999. 6.95 (1-55074-537-9) Kids Can Pr.

Moore, J. & Jennings, D. Reading Business Park: A Bronze Age Landscape. (Kennet Valley Ser.: Vol. 1). (Illus.). 130p. 1992. pap. 28.00 (0-947816-81-X, Pub. by Oxford Univ Comm Arch) David Brown.

Moore, J. Bernard. Skagway in Days Primeval: Writings of J. Bernard Moore, 1886-1904. rev. ed. (Illus.). 208p. 1997. pap. 14.95 (0-945284-06-3) Lynn Canal Pub.

***Moore, J. C.** Mathematical Methods for Economic Theory 1. Aliprantis, C. D. & Yannelis, N. C., eds. LC 99-46807. (Studies in Economic Theory: Vol. 9). (Illus.). xii, 414p. 1999. 64.95 (3-540-66235-9) Spr-Verlag.

Moore, J. C., jt. auth. see Eilenberg, S.

Moore, J. C., jt. auth. see Eilenberg, Samuel.

Moore, J. Casey, ed. Structural Fabric in Deep Sea Drilling Project Cores from Forearcs. LC 86-22864. (Geological Society of America Ser.: Vol. 166). (Illus.). 180p. reprint ed. pap. 55.80 (0-608-07716-X, 206780400010) Bks Demand.

Moore, J. Elton, et al, eds. Foundations of Rehabilitation Counseling with Persons Who Are Blind or Visually Impaired. LC 97-4409. 464p. (C). 1997. text 59.95 (0-89128-945-3) Am Foun Blind.

Moore, J. F., jt. auth. see Chaykin, Howard.

Moore, J. F. A. Monitoring Building Structures. 150p. (C). (gr. 13). 1992. mass mkt. 102.95 (0-442-31333-0) Chapman & Hall.

Moore, J. Floyd. Friends in the Carolinas. 47p. 1997. pap. 4.50 (0-942727-30-4) NC Yrly Pubns Bd.

Moore, J. G., jt. auth. see Ballard, Robert Duane.

Moore, J. George, jt. auth. see Hacker, Neville F.

Moore, J. H., jt. ed. see Dorey, A. P.

Moore, J. I. Pharmacology. 3rd ed. (Oklahoma Notes Ser.). (Illus.). 280p. 1992. 17.95 (0-387-97779-1) Spr-Verlag.

Moore, J. I., ed. Pharmacology. (Oklahoma Notes Ser.). xi, 247p. (C). 1988. pap. 14.95 (0-387-96332-4) Spr-Verlag.

— Pharmacology. (Oklahoma Notes Ser.). xi, 251p. 1991. pap. 15.95 (0-387-97194-7) Spr-Verlag.

Moore, J. J. Continuous Casting Vol. III: The Application of Electromagnetic Stirring (EMS) in the Continuous Casting of Steel, Vol. III. LC 83-81654. 129p. 1984. 70.00 (0-89520-159-3) Iron & Steel.

Moore, J. J., jt. ed. see Srivatsan, T. S.

Moore, J. Kenneth, ed. see Phillips, Harry R.

Moore, J. M. & Brunt, P. A., eds. Res Gestae Divi Augusti. 96p. 1969. pap. text 15.95 (0-19-831772-7) OUP.

Moore, J. M. & Evans, J. J. Variorum: A Greek Translation Book. 158p. 1991. pap. 16.95 (1-85399-190-2, Pub. by Brist Class Pr) Focus Pub-R Pullins.

Moore, J. M., jt. ed. see Hollier, R.

Moore, J. M., tr. & intro. see Aristotle, et al.

Moore, J. Michael. Shang Han Lun & Other Traditional Formulas: A Clinical Reference. LC 93-35804. 1993. write for info. (0-941942-42-2) Orient Heal Arts.

Moore, J. Percy, jt. auth. see Harding, W. A.

Moore, J. Staunton. The Annals & History of Henrico Parish, Diocese of Virginia & St. John's P.E. Church. LC 78-72949. (Illus.). 578p. 1996. reprint ed. pap. 45.00 (0-8063-0829-X) Clearfield Co.

Moore, J. Strother. Piton: A Mechanically Verified Assembly-Level Language. LC 95-48177. (Automated Reasoning Ser.: Vol. 3). 328p. (C). 1996. text 169.00 (0-7923-3920-7) Kluwer Academic.

Moore, J. Strother, jt. auth. see Boyer, Robert S.

Moore, J. Stuart. Chiropractic in America: The History of a Medical Alternative. LC 92-48232. (Illus.). 240p. (C). 1993. text 39.95 (0-8018-4539-4) Johns Hopkins.

Moore, J. T. Introduction to Abstract Algebra. 1975. text 73.00 (0-12-505750-4) Acad Pr.

Moore, J. T., jt. auth. see Kruglak, Haym.

Moore, J. Thomas. Night after Christmas. (J). (gr. k up). 1990. pap. 5.95 (0-925928-07-0) Tiny Thought.

Moore, J. W. Anasazi. LC 79-56134. (Illus.). 88p. (Orig.). 1980. pap. 8.95 (0-935800-00-X) Sunrise Pr IL.

— Balancing the Needs of Water Use. (Environmental Management Ser.). (Illus.). 310p. 1988. 161.00 (0-387-96709-5) Spr-Verlag.

— The Changing Environment. (Environmental Management Ser.). (Illus.). x, 240p. 1986. 79.00 (0-387-96314-6) Spr-Verlag.

— Inorganic Contaminants of Surface Water: Research & Monitoring Priorities. DeSanto, R. S., ed. (Environmental Management Ser.). (Illus.). 392p. 1990. 130.00 (0-387-97281-1) Spr-Verlag.

— Moore's Federal Rules Pamphlet, 3 vols. 1961. ring bd. write for info. (0-8205-2800-5) Bender.

— Rev. John Moore of Newtown, of Newtown, Long Island, & Some of His Descendants. (Illus.). 541p. 1989. reprint ed. pap. 81.00 (0-8328-0881-4); reprint ed. lib. bdg. 89.00 (0-8328-0880-6) Higginson Bk Co.

Moore, J. W. & Ramamoorthy, S. Heavy Metals in Natural Waters. (Environmental Management Ser.). (Illus.). 255p. 1983. 117.00 (0-387-90885-4) Spr-Verlag.

— Organic Chemicals in Natural Water: Applied Monitoring & Impact Assessment. (Environmental Management Ser.). (Illus.). 290p. 1984. 117.00 (0-387-96034-1) Spr-Verlag.

Moore, Jack. Complete Book of Sports Betting: A New, Nonsense Approach to Sports Gambling. (Illus.). 208p. 1996. pap. 14.95 (0-8184-0579-1, L Stuart) Carol Pub Group.

— 97 Ways to Make a Baby Laugh. 1997. pap. 83.40 (0-7611-0860-2) Workman Pub.

— 97 Ways to Make a Baby Laugh. LC 97-6437. (Illus.). 112p. 1997. pap. text 6.95 (0-7611-0736-3, 10736) Workman Pub.

— Skinheads Shaved for Battle: A Cultural History of American Skinheads. LC 93-70440. (Illus.). 200p. 1993. 37.95 (0-87972-582-6); pap. 14.95 (0-87972-583-4) Bowling Green Univ Popular Press.

— Taming Ancient Rivers of Greece. 337p. 1981. 75.00 (0-9507476-0-2) St Mut.

Moore, Jack, jt. auth. see Mammone, Lisa E.

Moore, Jack, ed. & illus. see Ross, Bob.

Moore, Jack B. Joe DiMaggio: Baseball's Yankee Clipper. LC 85-14665. (Popular Culture Bio-Bibliographies Ser.). (Illus.). 263p. 1986. lib. bdg. 45.00 (0-313-23917-7, MJD/, Greenwood Pr) Greenwood.

— Joe DiMaggio: Baseball's Yankee Clipper. LC 87-2369. 263p. 1987. pap. 12.95 (0-275-92712-1, B2712, Praeger Pubs) Greenwood.

Moore, Jack B., jt. auth. see Snyder, Robert E.

***Moore, Jack O. My Outdoor Buddy. 208p. 2000. pap. 19.95 (0-87012-608-3) McClain.**
MY OUTDOOR Buddy is the ultimate book for hikers, backpackers & campers. For unforgettable campfire memories keep records of all your outings in your outdoor diary. It will help you prepare for a more enjoyable & safer outing. Includes basic first aid. Loads of trivia for question games; scary tale starters & even bible time. This book will become your OUTDOOR Buddy. *Publisher Paid Annotation.*

Moore, Jack S. The Official Redneck Handbook. Chichester, A. Lee, ed. (Illus.). 146p. (Orig.). Date not set. pap. 14.95 (0-89896-076-2) Larksdale.

Moore, Jackie. Venture Through Life. 1997. pap. write for info. (1-57553-709-5) Watermrk Pr.

Moore, Jacob B. Annals of the Town of Concord, in the County of Merrimack, from Its First Settlement in the Year 1726 to the Year 1823, with Several Biographical Sketches. (Illus.). 112p. 1995. reprint ed. pap. 21.00 (0-8328-4705-4) Higginson Bk Co.

Moore, Jacob B., jt. auth. see Farmer, John.

Moore, Jacqueline M. Leading the Race: The Transformation of the Black Elite in the Nation's Capital, 1880-1920. LC 99-31004. (Illus.). 1999. 37.50 (0-8139-1903-7) U Pr of Va.

Moore, Jacqueline S. Moments of My Life. Hunter, Ann A., ed. 1999. 18.50 (1-893846-75-X) Loft Pr.

***Moore, James.** Ananasi. 2000. pap. text 17.95 (1-56504-359-6) White Wolf.

Moore, James. Christmas Gifts That Always Fit. 1996. 9.80 (0-614-20414-3, 061482) Abingdon.

— Gurdjieff: The Anatomy of a Myth. 1991. pap. 27.95 (1-85230-114-7, GURDJC, Pub. by Element MA) Penguin Putnam.

— Gurdjieff: The Anatomy of a Myth-a Biography. (Illus.). 425p. 1993. pap. 19.95 (1-85230-450-2, Pub. by Element MA) Penguin Putnam.

— Gurdjieff: The Anatomy of a Myth-a Biography. 416p. 1999. pap. 16.95 (1-86204-606-9, Pub. by Element MA) Penguin Putnam.

— World of Darkness Outcasts: A Players Guide to Pariahs. (Werewolf Ser.). 128p. 1999. 15.00 (1-56504-312-X, 3065) White Wolf.

Moore, James, contrib. by. Robert M. Ellis - A Painter's Space: Paintings & Works on Paper, 1951-1990. (Illus.). 29p. (Orig.). 1990. pap. 10.50 (0-944282-10-5) UNM Art Mus.

Moore, James & Micolean, Tyler. Football Techniques Illustrated. LC 62-17402. 96p. reprint ed. pap. 30.00 (0-608-13662-X, 205517600011) Bks Demand.

Moore, James, et al. 365 Meditations for Men. LC 98-28159. 352p. 1998. pap. 14.00 (0-687-07680-3) Dimen for Liv.

Moore, James, jt. auth. see Skemp, Ethan.

Moore, James, jt. ed. see Baylor, Robert.

***Moore, James A.** Under the Over Tree. 440p. 2000. 16.00 (1-892065-19-3) Meisha Merlin.

Moore, James A. Werewolf Storytellers Screen. 2nd ed. 1994. 10.00 (1-56504-113-5, 3601) White Wolf.

— Wild West Companion. (Werewolf Ser.). (Illus.). 1998. pap. 18.00 (1-56504-344-8, 3704) White Wolf.

Moore, James A. & Pearcy, Derek. Book of Legions. 1998. pap. 18.00 (1-56504-652-8) White Wolf.

Moore, James A., ed. see NATO Advanced Study Institute Staff.

***Moore, James C.** Mathematical Methods for Economic Theory 2. Aliprantis, C. D. & Yannelis, N. C., eds. LC 99-46807. (Studies in Economic Theory: Vol. 10). (Illus.). x, 339p. 1999. 64.95 (3-540-66242-1) Spr-Verlag.

Moore, James C., et al. Trade, Theory & Econometrics: Essays in Honour of John S. Chipman. LC 98-3068. (Illus.). 352p. (C). 1999. 115.00 (0-415-14831-6) Routledge.

***Moore, James E.** The Bahamas. 3rd ed. Hester, Elliott Neal, ed. (Pelican Guide Ser.). (Illus.). 336p. 1999. pap. text 17.95 incl. audio compact disk (1-56554-328-9) Pelican.

Moore, James E., et al. Back Pain Helpbook: A Proven Self-Care Program for Managing Chronic or Recurrent Back Pain. LC 99-60037. 240p. 1999. pap. text 15.00 (0-7382-0112-X, Pub. by Perseus Pubng) HarpC.

Moore, James F. Christian Theology After the Shoah: A Re-Interpretation of the Passion Narratives. LC 93-2806. (Studies in the Shoah: Vol. VII). 204p. (C). 1993. lib. bdg. 47.50 (0-8191-9074-8) U Pr of Amer.

— The Death of Competition: Leadership & Strategy in the Age of Business Ecosystems. (Illus.). 297p. 1998. text 25.00 (0-7881-5800-7) DIANE Pub.

— Death of Competition: Leadership & Strategy in the Age of Business Ecosystems. 320p. 1997. pap. 14.00 (0-88730-850-3, HarpBusn) HarpInfo.

— Death of Competition: Leadership & Strategy in the Age of Business Ecosystems. 1999. text 40.95 (0-471-96810-2) Wiley.

***Moore, James G.** Exploring the Highest Sierra. LC 99-16229. 448p. 2000. pap. 17.95 (0-8047-3703-7) Stanford U Pr.

Moore, James N. & Allen, Douglas. A Guide to Equine Acute Laminitis. 40p. 1994. pap. text 21.00 (1-884254-17-9) Vet Lrn Syst.

Moore, James N. & Janick, Jules, eds. Methods in Fruit Breeding. LC 81-80945. (Illus.). 464p. 1983. 49.95 (0-911198-63-6) Purdue U Pr.

Moore, James N., jt. auth. see White, Nathaniel A.

Moore, James N., jt. ed. see Janick, Jules.

Moore, James R., ed. History, Humanity & Evolution: Essays for John C. Greene. (Illus.). 441p. (C). 1990. text 74.95 (0-521-33511-6) Cambridge U Pr.

Moore, James R., Jr., jt. auth. see Moore, Madeleine H.

Moore, James T. Two Paths to the New South: The Virginia Debt Controversy, 1870-1883. LC 73-86404. 181p. reprint ed. pap. 56.20 (0-8357-4296-2, 203709500007) Bks Demand.

Moore, James T. & Chaston, Peter R. Jokes & Puns for Groan-Ups. unabridged ed. LC 96-71116. (Illus.). 74p. (Orig.). 1996. per. 15.00 (0-9645172-3-X) Chaston Scient.

Moore, James W. Attitude Is Your Paintbrush: It Colors Every Situation. LC 98-2666. 160p. 1998. pap. 12.00 (0-687-07670-6) Dimen for Liv.

— Can You Remember to Forget: And 32 Other Questions for Tomorrow's Leaders. 1991. 8.95 (0-687-04628-9) Abingdon.

— Christmas Gifts That Always Fit. LC 96-19532. 144p. 1996. 14.00 (0-687-06148-2) Dimen for Liv.

— The Cross Walk: A Lenten Study for Adults. LC 99-31063. 1999. 4.00 (0-687-03281-4) Abingdon.

— Healing Where It Hurts. LC 92-45706. 144p. (Orig.). 1993. pap. 10.00 (0-687-16743-4) Dimen for Liv.

Moore, James W. Is There Life after Stress? Includes Study Guide. pap. 12.00 (0-687-07481-9) Dimen for Liv.

Moore, James W. Moore's Federal Practice, 26 vols. 3rd ed. LC 97-137086. 1948. ring bd. 3820.00 (0-8205-1410-1) Bender.

— Moore's Manual: Federal Practice & Procedure, 3 vols. 1962. ring bd. 780.00 (0-8205-1411-X) Bender.

— Seizing the Moments. 1992. pap. 9.95 (0-687-37151-1) Abingdon.

— Software Engineering Standards: A User's Road Map. LC 97-29227. 304p. 1997. pap. 40.00 (0-8186-8008-3, BP08008) IEEE Comp Soc.

— Software Engineering Standards: A User's Road Map. LC 97-19179. 1997. write for info. (1-55937-925-1) IEEE Standards.

— Some Folks Feel the Rain... Others Just Get Wet: Includes Study Guide. LC 99-32837. 1999. pap. 12.00 (0-687-07754-0) Dimen for Liv.

— Some Things Are Too Good Not to Be True. LC 93-44091. 144p. (Orig.). 1994. pap. 10.00 (0-687-00237-0) Dimen for Liv.

— Standing on the Promises, or Sitting on the Premises. LC 95-8274. 144p. (Orig.). 1995. pap. 11.00 (0-687-00807-7) Dimen for Liv.

***Moore, James W.** Top Ten List for Christians: Includes Study Guide. LC 99-11348. 1999. pap. 12.00 (0-687-97570-0) Dimen for Liv.

Moore, James W. The Top Ten List for Graduates: Priorities for Faithful Living. LC 96-50331. (Illus.). 112p. 1997. pap. 8.00 (0-687-00700-3) Dimen for Liv.

— When All Else Fails... Read the Instructions: Includes Study Guide. LC 92-24122. 144p. 1993. pap. 12.00 (0-687-44918-9) Dimen for Liv.

— When Grief Breaks Your Heart. LC 94-19609. 80p. (Orig.). 1995. pap. 4.95 (0-687-00791-7) Abingdon.

— When You're a Christian, the Whole World Is from Missouri: Living the Life of Faith in a "Show Me" World. LC 97-33163. 144p. 1997. pap. 10.00 (0-687-00786-0) Abingdon.

Moore, James W. When You're a Christian... The Whole World is from Missouri: Living the Life of Faith in a "Show Me" World: Includes Study Guide. pap. 12.00 (0-687-08924-7) Dimen for Liv.

Moore, James W. Yes, Lord, I Have Sinned but I Have Several Excellent Excuses: Includes Study Guide. LC 90-40832. 1991. pap. 12.00 (0-687-05383-8) Dimen for Liv.

Moore, James W. & Frumer, Louis R. Moore's Manual: Federal Practice Forms, 7 vols. 1965. ring bd. 1100.00 (0-8205-1413-6) Bender.

Moore, Jamie W. & Moore, Dorothy P. The Army Corps of Engineers & the Evolution of Federal Flood Plain Management Policy. Dane, Sylvia, ed. (Environment & Behavior Program, Special Publication Ser.: No. 20). 200p. (Orig.). (C). 1989. pap. 20.00 (1-877943-00-2) Natural Hazards.

Moore, Jan, et al. The Asparagus Festival Cookbook: Recipes from the Stockton Asparagus Festival. LC 96-42091. (Illus.). 96p. 1997. pap. 5.95 (0-89087-829-3) Celestial Arts.

Moore, Jane. Cityward Migration: Swedish Data. 1938. 69.50 (0-686-51354-1) Elliots Bks.

***Moore, Jane.** Mary Wollstonecraft. (Writers & Their Works Ser.). 112p. 1999. pap. text 19.00 (0-7463-0747-0, Pub. by Northcote House) U Pr of Miss.

Moore, Janet B. Pendulum Plus Kit. (Illus.). 32p. 1992. pap. 29.95 (0-9635665-1-2) Pendulum Plus.

***Moore, Janet Matthews.** Pathway to the Light of Inner Peace: A Synopsis of Life's Experiences in Poetry. 93p. 2000. pap. 10.95 (0-7414-0370-6) Buy Books.

***Moore, Janet W.** Massachusetts Basic Practice Manual: Drafting Simple Will & Trust Clauses. (Massachusetts Basic Practice Ser.). 150p. 1999. pap. write for info. (1-57589-161-1) Mass CLE.

Moore, Janice, jt. ed. see Clayton, Dale H.

Moore, Janice T., jt. ed. see Farley, Blanche F.

Moore, Jared S. The Foundations of Psychology. 1977. text 18.95 (0-8369-8189-8, 8327) Ayer.

Moore, Jean. Wheaton: A Pictorial History. 2nd ed. (Illinois Pictorial History Ser.). (Illus.). 1997. reprint ed. write for info. (0-943963-36-2) G Bradley.

Moore, Jean & Crabb, Richard. Young People's Story of DuPage County. (Illus.). 120p. 1981. 15.00 (0-916445-03-8) Crossroads Comm.

Moore, Jean, jt. auth. see Burzon, Nancy.

Moore, Jean A. ABC of Child Protection Work. 2nd ed. 120p. 1992. pap. 24.95 (1-85742-027-6, Pub. by Arena) Ashgate Pub Co.

Moore, Jeanne, et al. The Faces of Homelessness in London. LC 94-42385. (Illus.). 368p. 1995. text 61.95 (1-85521-252-8, Pub. by Dartmth Pub) Ashgate Pub Co.

Moore, Jeff & Carlton, Geoff. The Book of Slugs: A Guide to Slug Fun in the Garden & the Home. (Illus.). 140p. 1982. pap. 4.95 (0-9606752-1-3) Sauvie Island.

***Moore, Jennifer.** Reading Bridge: 4th Grade. Willie, Kirsten et al, eds. (Illus.). 96p. (J). (gr. 4). 1999. pap., wbk. ed. 9.95 (1-887923-11-X, Pub. by Rainbow UT) Midpt Trade.

— Reading Bridge: 5th Grade. Willie, Kirsten et al, eds. (Illus.). 96p. (J). (gr. 5). 1999. pap., wbk. ed. 9.95 (1-887923-12-8, Pub. by Rainbow UT) Midpt Trade.

***Moore, Jennifer, et al.** Math Bridge: 4th Grade. Willie, Kirsten et al, eds. (Illus.). 96p. (J). (gr. 4). 1999. pap., wbk. ed. 9.95 (1-887923-16-0, Pub. by Rainbow UT) Midpt Trade.

Moore, Jennifer, et al. Math Bridge: 5th Grade. Willie, Kirsten et al, eds. (Illus.). 96p. (J). (gr. 5). 1999. pap., wbk. ed. 9.95 (1-887923-17-9, Pub. by Rainbow UT) Midpt Trade.

Moore, Jenny & Scott, Eleanor. Invisible People & Processes: Writing Gender & Childhood into European Archaeology. (Illus.). 19.95p. 1997. pap. 26.50 (0-7185-0024-5); text 59.95 (0-7185-0023-7) Bks Intl VA.

Moore, Jeremy, tr. see Louys, Pierre.

Moore, Jeri, jt. ed. see Thorson, Esther.

Moore, Jerrold Northrop. The Confederate Commissary General: Lucius Bellinger Northrop & the Subsistence Bureau of the Southern Army. LC 95-53036. (Illus.). 340p. 1996. 24.95 (0-942597-75-3) White Mane Pub.

— Edward Elgar: A Creative Life. (Illus.). 858p. 1999. pap. text 45.00 (0-19-816366-5) OUP.

***Moore, Jerrold Northrop.** Sound Revolutions: A Biography of Fred Gaisberg, Founding Father of Commercial Sound Recording. 1999. pap. text 19.95 (1-86074-235-1) Sanctuary Pr.

Moore, Jerrold Northrop, ed. Elgar & His Publishers: Letters of a Creative Life, 2 vols., Set. (Illus.). 958p. 1987. text 120.00 (0-19-315446-3) OUP.

Moore, Jerry & Imwalle, Michael. Archaeological Investigations at CA-SBA-1809, a Protohistoric Settlement, Goleta, Santa Barbara County, California. (Archives of California Prehistory Ser.: Vol. 19). (Illus.). 76p. (Orig.). (C). 1988. pap. text 8.75 (1-55567-053-9) Coyote Press.

Moore, Jerry, jt. ed. see Moore, Tim.

Moore, Jerry D. Architecture & Power in the Ancient Andes: The Archeology of Public Buildings. (New Studies in Archaeology). (Illus.). 269p. (C). 1996. text 64.95 (0-521-55363-6) Cambridge U Pr.

— Visions of Culture: An Introduction to Anthropological Theories & Theorists. LC 96-25386. 290p. 1996. 65.00 (0-8039-7096-X); pap. 24.95 (0-8039-7097-8) AltaMira Pr.

Moore, Jesse T., Jr. A Search for Equality: The National Urban League, 1910-1961. LC 80-24302. (Illus.). 264p. 1981. 30.00 (0-271-00302-2) Pa St U Pr.

Moore, Jessica C. The Words Don't Fit in My Mouth. 125p. (Orig.). 1997. pap. 15.00 (0-9658308-0-2) Moore Black.

Moore, Jessica C., ed. see Williams, Saul Stacey.

Moore, Jim. Acts & Contrition. 72p. 1997. pap. 5.00 (0-87440-053-8) Bakers Plays.

***Moore, Jim.** Assisted Living, 2000: Practical Strategies for the Next Millennium. 325p. 1998. pap. 40.00 (1-893405-00-1) Westridge Pub.

— Blood Magic: Secrets of Thaumaturgy. (Vampire Ser.). 144p. 1999. pap. text 19.95 (1-56504-246-8) White Wolf.

Moore, Jim. By Way of the Wind. (Illus.). 224p. 1996. pap. 14.95 (1-57409-003-8) Sheridan.

— Clinton: Young Man in a Hurry. (Illus.). 290p. 1992. 22.95 (1-56530-006-8) Summit TX.

— Conspiracy of One: The Definite Book on the Kennedy Assassination. 1991. pap. 11.95 (0-9626219-6-X) Summit TX.

— The Freedom of History: Poems. LC 88-42975. (Illus.). 104p. (Orig.). 1988. pap. 10.95 (0-915943-32-8) Milkweed Ed.

— The Long Experience of Love. LC 94-32531. 104p. (Orig.). 1995. pap. 12.95 (1-57131-401-6) Milkweed Ed.

— Official Secrets. 214p. 1996. pap. 19.95 (0-945980-58-2) Nrth Country Pr.

— Official Secrets. LC 96-70108. 224p. 1997. 24.95 (0-945980-64-7) Nrth Country Pr.

— Swan: The Second Voyage. (Illus.). 224p. 1998. pap. 16.50 (1-57409-049-6) Sheridan.

***Moore, Jim.** Tales from the Small Time: A Loving Look at Small College Athletics. 208p. 2000. 14.95 (0-929765-77-X, Chapman Univ) Seven Locks Pr.

Moore, Jim. Tales from the Trails: Mexico. 1999. pap. text 14.95 (1-56504-345-6) White Wolf.

— Under the Overtree. 456p. 2000. pap. 16.00 (1-892065-15-0) Meisha Merlin.

— UNIX: A Minimal Manual. LC 88-29943. 238p. (C). 1988. pap. text 30.95 (0-7167-8195-6) W H Freeman.

— World of Darkness: Demon Hunter X. (Vampire Ser.). (Illus.). 1998. pap. 15.00 (1-56504-202-6, 2227) White Wolf.

Moore, Jim, as told by. How I Got Out of Jail & Ran for Governor of Indiana: The Jim Moore Story. LC 95-5818. 190p. (Orig.). (YA). 1995. pap. 10.00 (0-916147-66-5) Regent Pr.

Moore, Jim & Bridges, Bill. Rage Across the World: Rage Across New York/Rage Across the Amazon. (Warewolf Ser.: No. 3). (Illus.). 224p. 1999. pap. 18.00 (1-56504-324-3, 3071) White Wolf.

Moore, Jim & Vermilyea, Natalie. Ernest Thayer's "Casey at the Bat" Background & Characters of Baseball's Most Famous Poem. LC 94-18911. (Illus.). 376p. 1994. lib. bdg. 37.50 (0-89950-997-5) McFarland & Co.

Moore, Jim & Waterman, Cary, eds. Minnesota Writes: Poetry. LC 87-200754. 240p. (Orig.). 1987. pap. 11.95 (0-915943-21-2) Milkweed Ed.

***Moore, Jim, et al.** Aberrant: Year One. (Aberrant Ser.). (Illus.). 96p. 1999. pap. 14.95 (1-56504-629-3, 8502) White Wolf.

Moore, Jim, et al. In - Sights: Moore Photographs. Leabhart, Thomas, ed. (Mime Journal Ser.). (Illus.). 232p. (Orig.). 1988. pap. text 12.00 (0-9611066-3-8) Mime Jour.

Moore, Jim, jt. auth. see Clinton, Roger.

Moore, Jim, jt. auth. see McKinney, Deena.

Moore, Jo E. Addition with Carrying (Math) (Mathematics Ser.). (Illus.). 32p. (J). (gr. 3-5). 1996. pap., teacher ed. 2.95 (1-55799-462-5, 4064) Evan-Moor Edu Pubs.

— Advanced Division (Math) (Mathematics Ser.). (Illus.). 32p. (J). (gr. 4-6). 1996. pap., teacher ed. 2.95 (1-55799-471-4, 4073) Evan-Moor Edu Pubs.

— Beginning Addition (Math) (Mathematics Ser.). (Illus.). 32p. (J). (gr. 1-2). 1996. pap., teacher ed. 2.95 (1-55799-446-3, 4048) Evan-Moor Edu Pubs.

— Beginning Counting with Mother Goose (Math) (Mathematics Ser.). (Illus.). 32p. (J). (ps-k). 1996. pap., teacher ed. 2.95 (1-55799-439-0, 4041) Evan-Moor Edu Pubs.

— Beginning Geography Vol. 2: Landforms & Bodies of Water. (Illus.). 16p. (J). (gr. k-2). 1993. pap. text 5.95 (1-55799-253-3, EMC 272) Evan-Moor Edu Pubs.

— Beginning Geography Vol. 3: Continents & Oceans. (Illus.). 16p. (J). (gr. k-2). 1993. pap. text 5.95 (1-55799-254-1, EMC 273) Evan-Moor Edu Pubs.

— Beginning Sounds. (Reading & Writing Ser.). (Illus.). 32p. (J). (gr. k-2). 1997. pap., teacher ed. 2.95 (1-55799-404-8, 4006) Evan-Moor Edu Pubs.

— Big Book of Science Stories, Vol. 2. (Illus.). 64p. (J). (gr. k-2). 1994. pap. text 11.95 (1-55799-265-7, EMC 381) Evan-Moor Edu Pubs.

— Categories. (Reading & Writing Ser.). (Illus.). 32p. (J). (gr. 2-3). 1997. pap., teacher ed. 2.95 (1-55799-411-0, 4013) Evan-Moor Edu Pubs.

— Colors & Shapes. (Reading & Writing Ser.). (Illus.). 32p. (J). (ps-k). 1997. pap., teacher ed. 2.95 (1-55799-398-X, 4000) Evan-Moor Edu Pubs.

— Cursive Handwriting (Language) (Reading & Writing Ser.). (Illus.). 32p. (J). (gr. 2-6). 1996. pap., teacher ed. 2.95 (1-55799-425-0, 4027) Evan-Moor Edu Pubs.

— Dinosaurs & Other Prehistoric Animals. (Illus.). 48p. (J). (gr. 1-3). 1992. pap. 9.95 (1-55799-213-4, EMC 253) Evan-Moor Edu Pubs.

— Dragons. (Illus.). 48p. (J). (gr. 3-6). 1990. pap. 5.95 (1-55799-161-8, EMC 236) Evan-Moor Edu Pubs.

— Draw & Talk. (Reading & Writing Ser.). (Illus.). 32p. (J). (ps-k). 1997. pap., teacher ed. 2.95 (1-55799-401-3, 4003) Evan-Moor Edu Pubs.

— Endangered Species. (Illus.). 48p. (J). (gr. 3-6). 1992. pap. 5.95 (1-55799-217-7, EMC 257) Evan-Moor Edu Pubs.

— Everyday Reading Skills. (Real-Life Reading Activities Ser.). (Illus.). 64p. (J). (gr. 2-3). 1996. pap., teacher ed. 7.95 (1-55799-591-5, 568) Evan-Moor Edu Pubs.

— Families Around the World. (Illus.). 48p. (J). (ps-1). 1992. pap. 9.95 (1-55799-214-2, EMC 254) Evan-Moor Edu Pubs.

— Forms for Report Writing. (Writing Ser.). (Illus.). 64p. (J). (gr. 3-6). 1994. pap. text 7.95 (1-55799-286-X, EMC 288) Evan-Moor Edu Pubs.

— Fun with Math. (Mathematics Ser.). (Illus.). (J). (gr. k-1). 1997. pap., teacher ed. 2.95 (1-55799-441-2, 4043) Evan-Moor Edu Pubs.

— Geometric Shapes & Beginner Fractions. (Mathematics Ser.). (Illus.). 32p. (J). (gr. 1-2). 1997. pap., teacher ed. 2.95 (1-55799-449-8, 4051) Evan-Moor Edu Pubs.

— Getting Ready for Math. (Basic Mathematic Skills Ser.). (Illus.). 32p. (J). (ps-k). 1997. pap., teacher ed. 2.95 (1-55799-437-4, 4039) Evan-Moor Edu Pubs.

— Grammar & Punctuation 1-2 (Language) (Reading & Writing Ser.). (Illus.). 32p. 1996. pap., teacher ed. 2.95 (1-55799-421-8, 4023) Evan-Moor Edu Pubs.

— How to Write a Report (Language) (Reading & Writing Ser.). (Illus.). 32p. (YA). (gr. 6 up). 1996. pap., teacher ed. 2.95 (1-55799-429-3, 4031) Evan-Moor Edu Pubs.

— How to Write a Story. (Writing Ser.). (Illus.). 48p. (J). (gr. 3-6). 1994. pap. text 5.95 (1-55799-284-3, EMC286) Evan-Moor Edu Pubs.

— How to Write Nonfiction. (Writing Ser.). (Illus.). 48p. (J). (gr. 3-6). 1994. pap. text 5.95 (1-55799-285-1, EMC287) Evan-Moor Edu Pubs.

— Language Fundamentals. (Illus.). 240p. (J). (gr. 1-3). 1995. pap., teacher ed. 19.95 (1-55799-378-5, 394) Evan-Moor Edu Pubs.

— Learning about Money. (Mathematics Ser.). (Illus.). 32p. (J). (gr. 1-2). 1997. pap., teacher ed. 2.95 (1-55799-450-1, 4052) Evan-Moor Edu Pubs.

— Learning about the Earth. (Learning About Science Series for PreK-1: Vol. 2). (Illus.). 48p. 1994. pap. text 5.95 (1-55799-306-8, EMC845) Evan-Moor Edu Pubs.

— Learning about Weather. (Learning About Science Series for PreK-1: Vol. 1). (Illus.). 48p. (J). (ps-1). 1994. pap. text 5.95 (1-55799-305-X, EMC844) Evan-Moor Edu Pubs.

— Long Vowels (Language) (Reading & Writing Ser.). (Illus.). 32p. (J). (gr. 1-2). 1996. pap., teacher ed. 2.95 (1-55799-406-4, 4008) Evan-Moor Edu Pubs.

— Manip. Math - Multiplication & Division. (Mathematics Ser.). (Illus.). 32p. (J). (gr. 2-3). 1997. pap., teacher ed. 2.95 (1-55799-459-5, 4061) Evan-Moor Edu Pubs.

— Manipulative Math - Addition & Subtraction. (Mathematics Ser.). (Illus.). 32p. (J). (gr. 1-2). 1996. pap., teacher ed. 2.95 (1-55799-444-7, 4046) Evan-Moor Edu Pubs.

— Manuscript Handwriting. (Reading & Writing Ser.). (Illus.). 32p. (J). (gr. k-2). 1996. pap., teacher ed. 2.95 (1-55799-420-X, 4022) Evan-Moor Edu Pubs.

— Math & Classroom Pets. (Math Is Everywhere Ser.). (Illus.). 48p. (J). (gr. k-1). 1994. pap. text, teacher ed. 6.45 (1-55799-322-X, EMC 094) Evan-Moor Edu Pubs.

— Math at Playtime. (Math Is Everywhere Ser.). (Illus.). 48p. (J). (gr. k-1). 1994. pap. text, teacher ed. 6.45 (1-55799-323-8, EMC 095) Evan-Moor Edu Pubs.

— Math for Autumn 2-3. (Daily Problem Solving Ser.). (Illus.). 44p. (J). (gr. 2-3). 1996. pap., teacher ed. 14.95 (1-55799-584-2, 478) Evan-Moor Edu Pubs.

— Math for Spring 2-3. (Daily Problem Solving Ser.). (Illus.). 44p. (J). (gr. 2-3). 1996. pap., teacher ed. 14.95 (1-55799-582-6, 476) Evan-Moor Edu Pubs.

— Math for Summer 2-3. (Daily Problem Solving Ser.). (Illus.). 44p. (J). (gr. 2-3). 1996. pap., teacher ed. 14.95 (1-55799-583-4, 477) Evan-Moor Edu Pubs.

— Math for Winter 2-3. (Daily Problem Solving Ser.). (Illus.). 44p. (J). (gr. 2-3). 1996. pap., teacher ed. 14.95 (1-55799-581-8, 475) Evan-Moor Edu Pubs.

— Math Mysteries (Math) (Mathematics Ser.). (Illus.). 32p. (J). (gr. 3-5). 1996. pap., teacher ed. 2.95 (1-55799-466-8, 4068) Evan-Moor Edu Pubs.

— Math Riddles. (Mathematics Ser.). (Illus.). 32p. (J). (gr. 2-3). 1996. pap., teacher ed. 2.95 (1-55799-454-4, 4056) Evan-Moor Edu Pubs.

— Money. (Mathematics Ser.). (Illus.). 32p. (J). (gr. 2-3). 1997. pap., teacher ed. 2.95 (1-55799-456-0, 4058) Evan-Moor Edu Pubs.

— My Pets. (Illus.). 48p. (J). (ps-1). 1988. pap. 9.95 (1-55799-131-6, EMC 185) Evan-Moor Edu Pubs.

— Reading Around the School. (Real-Life Reading Activities Ser.). (Illus.). 64p. (J). (gr. k-1). 1996. pap., teacher ed. 7.95 (1-55799-585-0, 562) Evan-Moor Edu Pubs.

— Reading for Information. (Real-Life Reading Activities Ser.). (Illus.). 64p. (J). (gr. 2-3). 1996. pap., teacher ed. 7.95 (1-55799-589-3, 566) Evan-Moor Edu Pubs.

— Reading Sight Words. (Reading & Writing Ser.). (Illus.). 32p. (J). (gr. 1-2). 1997. pap., teacher ed. 2.95 (1-55799-408-0, 4010) Evan-Moor Edu Pubs.

— Reading to Follow Instructions. (Real-Life Reading Activities Ser.). (Illus.). 64p. (J). (gr. 2-3). 1996. pap., teacher ed. 7.95 (1-55799-590-7, 567) Evan-Moor Edu Pubs.

— Reference Skills. (Reading & Writing Ser.). (Illus.). 32p. (J). (gr. 4-6). 1997. pap., teacher ed. 2.95 (1-55799-418-8, 4020) Evan-Moor Edu Pubs.

— Review First Grade (Language) (Reading & Writing Ser.). (Illus.). 32p. (J). (gr. 1). 1996. pap., teacher ed. 2.95 (1-55799-431-5, 4033) Evan-Moor Edu Pubs.

— Review Kindergarten (Language) (Reading & Writing Ser.). (Illus.). 32p. 1996. pap., teacher ed. 2.95 (1-55799-430-7, 4032) Evan-Moor Edu Pubs.

— Review Second Grade (Language) (Reading & Writing Ser.). (Illus.). 32p. 1996. pap., teacher ed. 2.95 (1-55799-432-3, 4034) Evan-Moor Edu Pubs.

— Reviewing Kindergarten (Math) (Mathematics Ser.). (Illus.). 32p. 1997. pap., teacher ed. 2.95 (1-55799-482-X, 4084) Evan-Moor Edu Pubs.

— Reviewing 1st Grade (Math) (Mathematics Ser.). (Illus.). 32p. 1997. pap., teacher ed. 2.95 (1-55799-483-8, 4085) Evan-Moor Edu Pubs.

M

— Reviewing 2nd Grade (Math) (Mathematics Ser.). (Illus.). 32p. 1997. pap., teacher ed. 2.95 (*1-55799-484-6*, 4086) Evan-Moor Edu Pubs.
— Rhyming Words. (Reading & Writing Ser.). (Illus.). 32p. (J). (gr. 1-2). 1997. pap., teacher ed. 2.95 (*1-55799-410-2*, 4012) Evan-Moor Edu Pubs.
— Sequencing. (Reading & Writing Ser.). (Illus.). 32p. (J). (ps-k). 1997. pap., teacher ed. 2.95 (*1-55799-403-X*, 4005) Evan-Moor Edu Pubs.
— Sequencing Simple Stories (Language) (Reading & Writing Ser.). (Illus.). 32p. (J). (gr. 1-2). 1996. pap., teacher ed. 2.95 (*1-55799-407-2*, 4009) Evan-Moor Edu Pubs.
— Sharks. (Illus.). 48p. (J). (gr. 3-6). 1992. pap. 5.95 (*1-55799-215-0*, EMC 255) Evan-Moor Edu Pubs.
— Shoe Box Centers Writing Activities: Shoe Box Centers. (Illus.). 64p. (J). (gr. 1-3). 1992. pap. 7.95 (*1-55799-224-X*, EMC 261) Evan-Moor Edu Pubs.
— Shoebox Center: Math Activities. (Illus.). 64p. (J). (gr. 1-3). 1993. pap. text 7.95 (*1-55799-252-5*, EMC 108) Evan-Moor Edu Pubs.
— Short Vowels. (Reading & Writing Ser.). (Illus.). 32p. (J). (gr. 1-2). 1996. pap., teacher ed. 2.95 (*1-55799-405-6*, 4007) Evan-Moor Edu Pubs.
— Solving Word Problems (Math) (Mathematics Ser.). (Illus.). 32p. (J). (gr. 3-5). 1996. pap., teacher ed. 2.95 (*1-55799-461-7*, 4063) Evan-Moor Edu Pubs.
— Stories about Children from Many Lands. (Illus.). 64p. (J). (gr. k-2). 1993. pap., teacher ed. 11.95 (*1-55799-248-7*, EMC 310) Evan-Moor Edu Pubs.
— Subtract with Borrowing. (Mathematics Ser.). (Illus.). 32p. (J). (gr. 3-5). 1996. pap., teacher ed. 2.95 (*1-55799-463-3*, 4065) Evan-Moor Edu Pubs.
— Subtract W/O Borrowing. (Mathematics Ser.). (Illus.). 32p. (J). (gr. 2-3). 1996. pap., teacher ed. 2.95 (*1-55799-452-8*, 4054) Evan-Moor Edu Pubs.
— Telling Time. (Mathematics Ser.). (Illus.). 32p. (J). (gr. 2-3). 1997. pap., teacher ed. 2.95 (*1-55799-455-2*, 4057) Evan-Moor Edu Pubs.
— Think & Do. (Reading & Writing Ser.). (Illus.). 32p. (J). (ps-k). 1997. pap., teacher ed. 2.95 (*1-55799-399-8*, 4001) Evan-Moor Edu Pubs.
— Trace & Write. (Reading & Writing Ser.). (Illus.). 32p. (J). (ps-k). 1996. pap., teacher ed. 2.95 (*1-55799-400-5*, 4002) Evan-Moor Edu Pubs.
— Understand Numbers 1-100. (Mathematics Ser.). (Illus.). 32p. (J). (gr. 1-2). 1996. pap., teacher ed. 2.95 (*1-55799-445-5*, 4047) Evan-Moor Edu Pubs.
— Understand Numbers 1-1000. (Mathematics Ser.). (Illus.). 32p. (J). (gr. 2-3). 1996. pap., teacher ed. 2.95 (*1-55799-458-7*, 4060) Evan-Moor Edu Pubs.
— Understanding Fractions. (Mathematics Ser.). (Illus.). 32p. (J). (gr. 3-5). 1997. pap., teacher ed. 2.95 (*1-55799-467-6*, 4069) Evan-Moor Edu Pubs.
— Understanding Numbers 1-20. (Mathematics Ser.). (Illus.). 32p. (J). (gr. k-1). 1997. pap., teacher ed. 2.95 (*1-55799-440-4*, 4042) Evan-Moor Edu Pubs.
— What Time Is It? (Mathematics Ser.). (Illus.). 32p. (J). (gr. k-1). 1997. pap., teacher ed. 2.95 (*1-55799-443-9*, 4045) Evan-Moor Edu Pubs.
— Who Discovered America? (Illus.). 48p. (J). (gr. 3-6). 1992. pap. 5.95 (*1-55799-218-5*, EMC 258) Evan-Moor Edu Pubs.
— Word Families. (Reading & Writing Ser.). (Illus.). 32p. (J). (gr. 2-3). 1996. pap., teacher ed. 2.95 (*1-55799-409-9*, 4011) Evan-Moor Edu Pubs.
— Word Problems. (Mathematics Ser.). (Illus.). 32p. (J). (gr. 1-2). 1996. pap., teacher ed. 2.95 (*1-55799-448-X*, 4050) Evan-Moor Edu Pubs.
— Writing Paragraphs. (Reading & Writing Ser.). (Illus.). 32p. (J). (gr. 2-4). 1996. pap., teacher ed. 2.95 (*1-55799-424-2*, 4026) Evan-Moor Edu Pubs.

Moore, Jo E. & Evans, Joy. Basic Math Skills, Grade 1. (Illus.). 192p. 1994. pap. text, teacher ed. 19.45 (*1-55799-333-5*, EMC 089) Evan-Moor Edu Pubs.
— Basic Math Skills, Grade 2. (Illus.). 192p. 1994. pap. text, teacher ed. 19.45 (*1-55799-334-3*, EMC 090) Evan-Moor Edu Pubs.
— Basic Math Skills, Grade 3. (Illus.). 192p. 1994. pap. text, teacher ed. 19.45 (*1-55799-335-1*, EMC 091) Evan-Moor Edu Pubs.
— Beginning Geography Vol. 1: How to Use a Map. (Geography Mini-Unit Ser.). (Illus.). 16p. (J). (gr. k-2). 1992. pap. text 5.95 (*1-55799-219-3*, EMC 259) Evan-Moor Edu Pubs.
— Categorias. Wolfe, Liz & Ficklin, Dora, trs. from ENG. (SPA., Illus.). 32p. (J). (gr. 1-2). 1990. pap. text 5.95 (*1-55799-180-4*, EMC 022) Evan-Moor Edu Pubs.
— Creative Writing Ideas. (Creative Writing Ser.). (Illus.). 96p. (J). (gr. 1-6). 1997. pap. 9.95 (*1-55799-060-3*, EMC206) Evan-Moor Edu Pubs.
— My Skeleton & Muscles. (Illus.). 16p. (J). (gr. 1-3). 1987. pap., teacher ed. 5.95 (*1-55799-101-4*, 811) Evan-Moor Edu Pubs.
— Wolves. (Illus.). 48p. (J). (gr. 3-6). 1990. pap. 5.95 (*1-55799-163-4*, EMC 238) Evan-Moor Edu Pubs.
— Write a SUPER Sentence. 2nd ed. (Illus.). 32p. (J). (gr. 1-3). 1997. pap. text 6.95 (*1-55799-606-7*, EMC205) Evan-Moor Edu Pubs.

Moore, Jo E. & Tryon, Leslie. Animal Life Cycles Science Sequencing Cards. (Science Picture Card Ser.: No. 4). (Illus.). 24p. (J). (ps-1). 1988. pap. 12.95 (*1-55799-695-4*, EMC816) Evan-Moor Edu Pubs.
— Bears Bears Bears. (Illus.). 48p. (J). (ps-1). 1988. pap. 9.95 (*1-55799-130-8*, EMC 184) Evan-Moor Edu Pubs.
— The Big Book of Science Rhymes & Chants. (Illus.). 64p. (J). (gr. k-2). 1991. pap. 11.95 (*1-55799-211-8*, EMC306) Evan-Moor Edu Pubs.
— The Big Book of Science Stories, Vol. 1. (Illus.). 64p. (J). (gr. k-2). 1991. pap. 11.95 (*1-55799-210-X*, EMC 305) Evan-Moor Edu Pubs.

Moore, Jo E. & Tyron, Leslie. Paragraph Writing. 2nd ed. (Illus.). 80p. (J). (gr. 2-4). 1997. pap. 7.95 (*1-55799-608-3*, EMC246) Evan-Moor Edu Pubs.

Moore, Jo E., et al. A Happy, Healthy Me. (Thematic Resource Unit Ser.). (Illus.). 48p. (J). (ps-1). 1990. pap. text 9.95 (*1-55799-170-7*, EMC 199) Evan-Moor Edu Pubs.
— How to Do Plays with Children. (Illus.). 288p. (J). (gr. k-6). 1994. pap. text, teacher ed. 28.80 (*1-55799-332-7*, EMC 110) Evan-Moor Edu Pubs.
— Making Seasonal Big Books with Children. (Illus.). 64p. (J). (gr. k-2). 1990. pap. 11.95 (*1-55799-194-4*, EMC304) Evan-Moor Edu Pubs.
— Whales. (Illus.). 48p. (J). (gr. 3-6). 1990. pap. 5.95 (*1-55799-164-2*, EMC 239) Evan-Moor Edu Pubs.

Moore, Jo E., jt. auth. see DeWeese, Robert.

Moore, Jo E., jt. auth. see Evans, Jo.

Moore, Jo E., jt. auth. see Evans, Joy.

Moore, Jo E., jt. auth. see Shiran, Gary.

***Moore, Jo Ellen.** Addition & Subtraction - Grades 1-2: Great Practice for Standardized Tests. Evans, Marilyn, ed. (Learn on the Go Practice Bks.). (Illus.). 64p. (J). (gr. 1-2). 1998. pap., wbk. ed. 2.25 (*1-58610-013-0*, Learn on the Go) Learn Horizon.
— Addition with Carrying: Basic Mathematic Skills. (Illus.). 30p. (J). (gr. 3-5). 1995. pap., wbk. ed. 2.50 (*1-58610-083-1*, Learn on the Go) Learn Horizon.
— Advanced Division: Basic Mathematics Skills. (Illus.). 30p. (J). (gr. 4-6). 1995. pap., wbk. ed. 2.50 (*1-58610-092-0*, Learn on the Go) Learn Horizon.
— Advanced Multiplication & Division - Grades 4-6: Great Practice for Standardized Tests. Evans, Marilyn, ed. (Learn on the Go Practice Bks.). (Illus.). 64p. (J). (gr. 4-6). 1998. pap., wbk. ed. 2.25 (*1-58610-015-7*, Learn on the Go) Learn Horizon.
— Africa. Evans, Marilyn, ed. (Geography Units Ser.: Vol. 7). (Illus.). 80p. (J). (gr. 3-6). 1999. pap. 12.95 (*1-55799-716-0*, 769) Evan-Moor Edu Pubs.
— All about Animals. Evans, Joy, ed. (Science Ser.). (Illus.). 31p. (J). (ps-1). Date not set. pap., wbk. ed. 2.50 (*1-58610-111-0*) Learn Horizon.
— All about Me: Reading & Writing Skills. (Illus.). 32p. (J). (gr. 1-3). 1995. pap., wbk. ed. 2.50 (*1-58610-057-2*, Learn on the Go) Learn Horizon.
— All about My Body. (Science Ser.). (Illus.). 32p. (J). (ps-1). Date not set. pap., wbk. ed. 2.50 (*1-58610-110-2*) Learn Horizon.
— Alphabet Sounds: Fun Early Learning Activities. Evans, Marilyn, ed. (Learn on the Go Practice Bks.). (Illus.). 64p. (J). (ps-k). 1998. pap., wbk. ed. 2.25 (*1-58610-006-8*, Learn on the Go) Learn Horizon.
— Antarctica. Evans, Marilyn, ed. (Geography Units Ser.: Vol. 6). (Illus.). 80p. (J). (gr. 3-6). 1999. pap. 12.95 (*1-55799-715-2*, 768) Evan-Moor Edu Pubs.
— Asia. Evans, Marilyn, ed. (Geography Units Ser.: Vol. 4). (Illus.). 80p. (J). (gr. 3-6). 1999. pap. 12.95 (*1-55799-713-6*, 766) Evan-Moor Edu Pubs.
— Australia. Evans, Marilyn, ed. (Geography Units Ser.: Vol. 3). (Illus.). 80p. (J). (gr. 3-6). 1999. pap. 12.95 (*1-55799-712-8*, 765) Evan-Moor Edu Pubs.
— Basic Math Skills. Evans, Marilyn, ed. (Partners in Learning). (Illus.). 192p. (J). (gr. 1-3). Date not set. pap., wbk. ed. 19.95 (*1-58610-136-6*) Learn Horizon.
— Beginning Addition: Basic Mathematics Skills. (Illus.). 30p. (J). (gr. 1-2). 1995. pap., wbk. ed. 2.50 (*1-58610-068-8*, Learn on the Go) Learn Horizon.
— Beginning Counting with Mother Goose: Readiness for Mathematics. (Illus.). 30p. (ps-k). 1995. pap., wbk. ed. 2.50 (*1-58610-060-2*, Learn on the Go) Learn Horizon.
— Beginning Map Skills. Evans, Joy, ed. (People & Places Ser.). (Illus.). 31p. (J). (gr. k-1). Date not set. pap., wbk. ed. 2.50 (*1-58610-128-5*) Learn Horizon.
— Beginning Maps & Globes. Evans, Joy, ed. (People & Places Ser.). (Illus.). 31p. (J). (gr. 1-3). Date not set. pap., wbk. ed. 3.50 (*1-58610-129-3*) Learn Horizon.
— Beginning Math - Grade PK-K: Fun Early Learning Activities. Evans, Marilyn, ed. (Learn on the Go Practice Bks.). (Illus.). 64p. (J). (ps-k). 1998. pap., wbk. ed. 2.25 (*1-58610-012-2*, Learn on the Go) Learn Horizon.
— Beginning Multiplication & Division - Grade 3: Great Practice for Standardized Tests. Evans, Marilyn, ed. (Learn on the Go Practice Bks.). (Illus.). 64p. (J). (gr. 3). 1998. pap., wbk. ed. 2.25 (*1-58610-014-9*, Learn on the Go) Learn Horizon.
— Beginning Reading: Fun Early Learning Activities. Evans, Marilyn, ed. (Learn on the Go Practice Bks.). (Illus.). 64p. (J). (ps-k). 1998. wbk. ed. 2.25 (*1-58610-007-6*) Learn Horizon.
— Beginning Sounds: Reading & Writing Skills. (Illus.). 32p. (J). (gr. k-2). 1995. pap., wbk. ed. 2.50 (*1-58610-025-4*, Learn on the Go) Learn Horizon.
— Beginning Writers: Grade K-2. Evans, Marilyn, ed. (How to Make Books with Children Ser.). (Illus.). 160p. 1999. pap., teacher ed. 16.95 (*1-55799-730-6*, 776) Evan-Moor Edu Pubs.
— Blank Map Forms the World. Evans, Marilyn, ed. (Partners in Learning). (Illus.). 48p. (J). (gr. 3-6). Date not set. pap., wbk. ed. 6.45 (*1-58610-147-1*) Learn Horizon.
— Blends & Diagraphs Word Machines: Grade 1-3. Evans, Marilyn, ed. (Word Machines Ser.). (Illus.). 28p. 2000. pap., teacher ed. 12.95 (*1-55799-759-4*, 782) Evan-Moor Edu Pubs.
— Capital & Lowercase Letters: Fun Early Learning Activities. Evans, Marilyn, ed. (Learn on the Go Practice Bks.). (Illus.). 64p. (J). (ps-k). 1998. pap., wbk. ed. 2.25 (*1-58610-005-X*, Learn on the Go) Learn Horizon.
— Colors & Shapes: Preparing to Read & Write. (Illus.). 32p. (J). (ps-k). 1995. pap., wbk. ed. 2.50 (*1-58610-019-X*, Learn on the Go) Learn Horizon.
— Cursive Handwriting: Reading & Writing Skills. (Illus.). 32p. (J). (gr. 2-6). 1995. pap., wbk. ed. 2.50 (*1-58610-045-9*, Learn on the Go) Learn Horizon.
— Daily Math Practice, Grade 3. Evans, Marilyn, ed. (Daily Math Practice Ser.: Vol. 3). 112p. 1999. pap., teacher ed. 14.95 (*1-55799-743-8*, 752) Evan-Moor Edu Pubs.
— Daily Math Practice, Grade 2. Evans, Marilyn, ed. (Daily Math Practice Ser.: Vol. 2). 112p. 1999. pap., teacher ed. 14.95 (*1-55799-742-X*, 751) Evan-Moor Edu Pubs.
— Daily Summer Activities, Moving from First to Second Grade. Evans, Marilyn, ed. (Daily Summer Activities Ser.). (Illus.). 160p. 2000. pap. 14.95 (*1-55799-766-7*, 1028) Evan-Moor Edu Pubs.
— Daily Summer Activities, Moving from Kindergarten to First Grade. Evans, Marilyn, ed. (Daily Summer Activities Ser.). (Illus.). 160p. 2000. pap. 14.95 (*1-55799-765-9*, 1027) Evan-Moor Edu Pubs.
— Daily Summer Activities, Moving from Second to Third Grade. Evans, Marilyn, ed. (Daily Summer Activities Ser.). (Illus.). 160p. 2000. pap. 14.95 (*1-55799-767-5*, 1029) Evan-Moor Edu Pubs.
— Dinosaurs. Evans, Marilyn, ed. (Science Ser.). (Illus.). 33p. (J). (gr. 2-3). Date not set. pap., wbk. ed. 3.50 (*1-58610-117-X*) Learn Horizon.
— Draw & Talk: Preparing to Read & Write. (Illus.). 32p. (J). (ps-k). 1995. pap., wbk. ed. 2.50 (*1-58610-022-X*, Learn on the Go) Learn Horizon.
— Drawing Animals. Evans, Joy, ed. (Partners in Learning). (Illus.). 64p. (J). (gr. 1-6). Date not set. pap., wbk. ed. 6.95 (*1-58610-146-3*) Learn Horizon.
— Europe. Evans, Marilyn, ed. (Geography Units Ser.: Vol. 5). (Illus.). 80p. (J). (gr. 3-6). 1999. pap. 12.95 (*1-55799-714-4*, 767) Evan-Moor Edu Pubs.

Moore, Jo Ellen. Exploring Space: Grades 1-3. Evans, Marilyn, ed. (Science Works for Kids Ser.: Vol. 1). (Illus.). 80p. 1998. pap., teacher ed. 9.95 (*1-55799-682-2*, 853) Evan-Moor Edu Pubs.

Moore, Jo Ellen. First Grade Language: Reading & Writing Skills. Evans, Marilyn, ed. (Illus.). 30p. (J). (gr. 1). 1995. pap., wbk. ed. 2.50 (*1-58610-051-3*, Learn on the Go) Learn Horizon.
— First Grade Math: Basic Mathematics Skills. Evans, Joy, ed. (Illus.). 30p. (J). (gr. 1). 1995. pap., wbk. ed. 2.50 (*1-58610-104-8*, Learn on the Go) Learn Horizon.
— Folktales & Fables: Read & Understand: Grade 2-3. Evans, Marilyn, ed. (Read & Understand Ser.). (Illus.). 144p. 2000. pap., teacher ed. 12.95 (*1-55799-750-0*, 757) Evan-Moor Edu Pubs.
— Fun with Math: Basic Mathematics Skills. (Illus.). 30p. (J). (gr. k-1). 1995. pap., wbk. ed. 2.50 (*1-58610-062-9*, Learn on the Go) Learn Horizon.
— Fun with Measurement: Basic Mathematics Skills. DeWeese, Bob, ed. (Illus.). 31p. (J). (gr. 2-3). 1995. pap., wbk. ed. 2.50 (*1-58610-079-3*, Learn on the Go) Learn Horizon.
— Fun with the Alphabet. Evans, Marilyn, ed. (Partners in Learning). (Illus.). 159p. (J). (gr. k-1). Date not set. pap., wbk. ed. 6.95 (*1-58610-139-0*) Learn Horizon.
— Games & Puzzles - Grade 1: Learning That's Extra Fun. Evans, Marilyn, ed. (Learn on the Go Practice Bks.). (Illus.). 64p. (J). (gr. 1). 1998. pap., wbk. ed. 2.25 (*1-58610-016-5*, Learn on the Go) Learn Horizon.
— Games & Puzzles - Grade 3: Learning That's Extra Fun. Evans, Marilyn, ed. (Illus.). 64p. (J). (gr. 3). 1998. pap., wbk. ed. 2.25 (*1-58610-018-1*, Learn on the Go) Learn Horizon.
— Games & Puzzles - Grade 2: Learning That's Extra Fun. Evans, Marilyn, ed. (Illus.). 64p. (J). (gr. 2). 1998. pap., wbk. ed. 2.25 (*1-58610-017-3*, Learn on the Go) Learn Horizon.
— Geometric Shapes & Beginning Fractions: Basic Mathematics Skills. (Illus.). 30p. (J). (gr. 1-2). 1995. pap., wbk. ed. 2.50 (*1-58610-071-8*, Learn on the Go) Learn Horizon.
— Getting Ready for Math: Basic Mathematics Skills. (Illus.). 30p. (J). (ps-k). 1995. pap., wbk. ed. 2.50 (*1-58610-058-0*, Learn on the Go) Learn Horizon.
— Grammar & Punctuation: Reading & Writing Skills. (Illus.). 32p. (J). (gr. 1-2). 1995. pap., wbk. ed. 2.50 (*1-58610-042-4*, Learn on the Go) Learn Horizon.
— Habitats. (Science Ser.). (Illus.). 32p. (J). (gr. 2-3). Date not set. pap., wbk. ed. 3.50 (*1-58610-118-8*) Learn Horizon.
— Hands-On Math Multiplication & Division: Basic Mathematics Skills. (Illus.). 30p. (J). (gr. 2-3). 1995. pap., wbk. ed. 2.50 (*1-58610-081-5*, Learn on the Go) Learn Horizon.
— How Big Is It? Basic Mathematics Skills. Evans, Joy, ed. (Illus.). 30p. (J). (gr. k-1). 1995. pap., wbk. ed. 2.50 (*1-58610-063-7*, Learn on the Go) Learn Horizon.
— How to Write a Report: Reading & Writing Skills. (Illus.). 32p. (J). (gr. 6 up). 1995. pap., wbk. ed. 2.50 (*1-58610-049-1*, Learn on the Go) Learn Horizon.
— How Your Body Works. (Science Ser.). (Illus.). 29p. (J). (gr. 2-3). Date not set. pap., wbk. ed. 3.50 (*1-58610-116-1*) Learn Horizon.
— Kindergarten Language: Reading & Writing Skills. Evans, Marilyn, ed. (Illus.). 31p. (J). (gr. k). 1995. pap., wbk. ed. 2.50 (*1-58610-050-5*, Learn on the Go) Learn Horizon.
— Kindergarten Math: Basic Mathematics Skills. Evans, Joy, ed. (Illus.). 30p. (J). (gr. k). 1995. pap., wbk. ed. 2.50 (*1-58610-103-X*, Learn on the Go) Learn Horizon.
— Kitchen Chemistry. Evans, Joy, ed. (Science Ser.). (Illus.). 32p. (J). (gr. 2-3). Date not set. pap., wbk. ed. 2.50 (*1-58610-120-X*) Learn Horizon.
— Language Fundamentals. Evans, Marilyn, ed. (Partners in Learning). (Illus.). 192p. (J). (gr. 1-3). Date not set. pap., wbk. ed. 19.95 (*1-58610-140-4*) Learn Horizon.
— Learning about Money: Basic Mathematics Skills. (Illus.). 32p. (J). (gr. 1-2). 1995. pap., wbk. ed. 2.50 (*1-58610-065-3*, Learn on the Go) Learn Horizon.
— Locating Information Fast: Reading & Writing Skills. Evans, Joy, ed. (Illus.). 32p. (J). (gr. 4-6). 1995. pap., wbk. ed. 2.50 (*1-58610-039-4*, Learn on the Go) Learn Horizon.
— Long Vowel Word Machines: Grade 1-3. Evans, Marilyn, ed. (Word Machines Ser.). (Illus.). 28p. 2000. pap., teacher ed. 12.95 (*1-55799-758-6*, 781) Evan-Moor Edu Pubs.
— Long Vowels: Reading & Writing Skills. (Illus.). 32p. (J). (gr. k-2). 1995. pap., wbk. ed. 2.50 (*1-58610-027-0*, Learn on the Go) Learn Horizon.
— Manipulative Math - Addition & Subtraction. (Illus.). 29p. (J). (gr. 1-2). 1995. pap., wbk. ed. 2.50 (*1-58610-066-1*, Learn on the Go) Learn Horizon.
— Manuscript Writing: Reading & Writing Skills. (Illus.). 32p. (J). (gr. k-2). 1995. pap., wbk. ed. 2.50 (*1-58610-041-6*, Learn on the Go) Learn Horizon.
— Math Around the House: Basic Mathematics Skills. (Illus.). 31p. (J). (ps-k). 1995. pap., wbk. ed. 2.50 (*1-58610-059-9*, Learn on the Go) Learn Horizon.
— Math Mysteries: Basic Mathematics Skills. (Illus.). 30p. (J). (gr. 3-5). 1995. pap., wbk. ed. 2.50 (*1-58610-087-4*, Learn on the Go) Learn Horizon.
— Math Puzzles, Riddles & Dot-to-Dots: Basic Mathematics Skills. (Illus.). 30p. (J). (gr. 2-3). 1995. pap., wbk. ed. 2.50 (*1-58610-074-2*, Learn on the Go) Learn Horizon.
— Math Riddles: Basic Mathematics Skills. Evans, Joy, ed. (Illus.). 30p. (J). (gr. 2-3). 1995. pap., wbk. ed. 2.50 (*1-58610-075-0*, Learn on the Go) Learn Horizon.
— Math Skills for Trips: Basic Mathematics Skills. DeWeese, Bob, ed. (Illus.). 30p. (J). (gr. 4-6). 1995. pap., wbk. ed. 2.50 (*1-58610-099-8*, Learn on the Go) Learn Horizon.
— Math with Charts & Graphs: Basic Mathematics Skills. Evans, Joy, ed. (Illus.). 32p. (J). (gr. 2-3). 1995. pap., wbk. ed. 2.50 (*1-58610-076-9*, Learn on the Go) Learn Horizon.
— Money: Basic Mathematics Skills. (Illus.). 32p. (J). (gr. 2-3). 1995. pap., wbk. ed. 2.50 (*1-58610-078-5*, Learn on the Go) Learn Horizon.
— More Read & Understand Stories & Activities, Grade 2. Evans, Marilyn, ed. (Read & Understand Ser.: Vol. 6). (Illus.). 144p. 1999. pap., teacher ed. 12.95 (*1-55799-736-5*, 746) Evan-Moor Edu Pubs.
— More Read & Understand Stories & Activities, Grade 3. Evans, Marilyn, ed. (Read & Understand Ser.: Vol. 7). (Illus.). 144p. 1999. pap., teacher ed. 12.95 (*1-55799-738-1*, 747) Evan-Moor Edu Pubs.
— Motor Skills - Grades PK-K: Preparing to Read & Write. (Illus.). 32p. (J). (ps-k). 1995. pap., wbk. ed. 2.50 (*1-58610-023-8*, Learn on the Go) Learn Horizon.
— North America. Evans, Marilyn, ed. (Geography Units Ser.: Vol. 1). (Illus.). 80p. (J). (gr. 3-6). 1999. pap. 12.95 (*1-55799-710-1*, 763) Evan-Moor Edu Pubs.
— Our Solar System. Evans, Marilyn, ed. (Science Ser.). (Illus.). 33p. (J). (gr. 2-3). Date not set. pap., wbk. ed. 3.50 (*1-58610-119-6*) Learn Horizon.
— Preschool & Kindergarten Skills: Fun Early Learning Activities. Evans, Marilyn, ed. (Learn on the Go Practice Bks.). (Illus.). 64p. (J). (ps-k). 1998. pap., wbk. ed. 2.25 (*1-58610-004-1*, Learn on the Go) Learn Horizon.
— Reading Comprehension - Grade 1: Great Practice for Standardized Tests. Evans, Jarilyn, ed. (Learn on the Go Practice Bks.). (Illus.). 64p. (J). (gr. 1). 1998. pap., wbk. ed. 2.25 (*1-58610-008-4*, Learn on the Go) Learn Horizon.
— Reading Comprehension - Grade 3: Great Practice for Standardized Tests. Evans, Marilyn, ed. (Learn on the Go Practice Bks.). (Illus.). 64p. (J). (gr. 3). 1998. pap., wbk. ed. 2.25 (*1-58610-010-6*, Learn on the Go) Learn Horizon.
— Reading Comprehension - Grade 2: Great Practice for Standardized Tests. Evans, Marilyn, ed. (Learn on the Go Practice Bks.). (Illus.). 64p. (J). (gr. 2). 1998. pap., wbk. ed. 2.25 (*1-58610-009-2*, Learn on the Go) Learn Horizon.
— Reading Sight Words: Reading & Writing Skills. (Illus.). 32p. (J). (gr. 1-2). 1995. pap., wbk. ed. 2.50 (*1-58610-029-7*, Learn on the Go) Learn Horizon.
— Rhyming Words: Reading & Writing Skills. DeWeese, Bob, ed. (Illus.). 32p. (J). (gr. 1-2). 1995. pap., wbk. ed. 2.50 (*1-58610-031-9*, Learn on the Go) Learn Horizon.
— Science Experiments at Home. Evans, Joy, ed. (Science Ser.). (Illus.). 33p. (J). (ps-1). Date not set. pap., wbk. ed. 2.50 (*1-58610-113-7*) Learn Horizon.
— Science Fun. Evans, Marilyn, ed. (Science Ser.). (Illus.). 30p. (J). (gr. 2-3). Date not set. pap., wbk. ed. 2.50 (*1-58610-122-6*) Learn Horizon.
— Science Puzzles. Evans, Joy, ed. (Science Ser.). (Illus.). 28p. (J). (gr. 4-6). Date not set. pap., wbk. ed. 2.50 (*1-58610-126-9*) Learn Horizon.
— Seasonal Activities. Evans, Marilyn, ed. (Partners in Learning). (Illus.). 192p. (J). (gr. 1-6). Date not set. pap., wbk. ed. 14.95 (*1-58610-144-7*) Learn Horizon.
— Second Grade Language: Reading & Writing Skills. Evans, Marilyn, ed. (Illus.). 30p. (J). (gr. 2). 1995. pap., wbk. ed. 2.50 (*1-58610-052-1*, Learn on the Go) Learn Horizon.
— Second Grade Math: Basic Mathematics Skills. Evans, Joy, ed. (Illus.). 30p. (J). (gr. 2). 1995. pap., wbk. ed. 2.50 (*1-58610-105-6*, Learn on the Go) Learn Horizon.
— Sequencing Simple Stories: Reading & Writing Skills. (Illus.). 32p. (J). (gr. 1-2). 1995. pap., wbk. ed. 2.50 (*1-58610-028-9*, Learn on the Go) Learn Horizon.
— Short Vowel Word Machines: Grade 1-3. Evans, Marilyn, ed. (Word Machines Ser.). (Illus.). 28p. 2000. pap., teacher ed. 12.95 (*1-55799-757-8*, 780) Evan-Moor Edu Pubs.

An Asterisk (*) at the beginning of an entry indicates that the title is appearing for the first time.

— Short Vowels: Reading & Writing Skills. (Illus.). 32p. (J). (gr. k-2). 1995. pap., wbk. ed. 2.50 (*1-58610-026-2*, Learn on the Go) Learn Horizon.
— Sight Words Word Machines: Grade 1-3. Evans, Marilyn, ed. (Word Machines Ser.). (Illus.). 28p. 2000. pap., teacher ed. 12.95 (*1-55799-760-8*, 783) Evan-Moor Edu Pubs.
— Solving Math Word Problems. Evans, Joy, ed. (Partners in Learning). (Illus.). 176p. (J). (gr. 2-3). Date not set. pap., wbk. ed. 19.95 (*1-58610-142-0*) Learn Horizon.
— Solving Word Problems: Basic Mathematics Skills. Evans, Marilyn, ed. (Illus.). 30p. (J). (gr. 3-5). 1995. pap., wbk. ed. 2.50 (*1-58610-082-3*, Learn on the Go) Learn Horizon.
— South America. Evans, Marilyn, ed. (Geography Units Ser.: Vol. 2). (Illus.). 80p. (J). (gr. 3-6). 1999. 12.95 (*1-55799-711-X*, 764) Evan-Moor Edu Pubs.
— Subtraction with Borrowing: Basic Mathematics Skills. (Illus.). 30p. (J). (gr. 3-5). 1995. pap., wbk. ed. 2.50 (*1-58610-084-X*, Learn on the Go) Learn Horizon.
— Subtraction Without Borrowing: Basic Mathematics Skills. (Illus.). 30p. (J). (gr. 2-3). 1995. pap., wbk. ed. 2.50 (*1-58610-073-4*, Learn on the Go) Learn Horizon.
— Synonyms, Antonyms & Homophones: Reading & Writing Skills. Evans, Joy, ed. (Illus.). 32p. (J). (gr. 4-6). 1995. pap., wbk. ed. 2.50 (*1-58610-040-8*, Learn on the Go) Learn Horizon.
— Tangram Puzzles: Basic Mathematics Skills. DeWeese, Bob, ed. (Illus.). 33p. (J). (gr. 4-6). 1995. pap., wbk. ed. 2.50 (*1-58610-090-4*, Learn on the Go) Learn Horizon.
— Telling Time: Basic Mathematics Skills. (Illus.). 32p. (J). (gr. 2-3). 1995. pap., wbk. ed. 2.50 (*1-58610-077-7*, Learn on the Go) Learn Horizon.
— Think & Do: Preparing to Read & Write. (Illus.). 32p. (J). (ps-k). 1995. pap., wbk. ed. 2.50 (*1-58610-020-3*, Learn on the Go) Learn Horizon.
— Trace & Write: Preparing to Read & Write. (Illus.). 32p. (J). (ps-k). 1995. pap., wbk. ed. 2.50 (*1-58610-021-1*, Learn on the Go) Learn Horizon.
— Understanding Fractions: Basic Mathematics Skills. (Illus.). 30p. (J). (gr. 3-5). 1995. pap., wbk. ed. 2.50 (*1-58610-088-2*, Learn on the Go) Learn Horizon.
— Understanding Numbers 1-100: Basic Mathematics Skills. (Illus.). 29p. (J). (gr. 1-2). 1995. pap., wbk. ed. 2.50 (*1-58610-067-X*, Learn on the Go) Learn Horizon.
— Understanding Numbers 1-1000: Basic Mathematics Skills. (Illus.). 30p. (J). (gr. 2-3). 1995. pap., wbk. ed. 2.50 (*1-58610-080-7*, Learn on the Go) Learn Horizon.
— Understanding Numbers 1-20: Basic Mathematics Skills. (Illus.). 30p. (J). (gr. k-1). 1995. pap., wbk. ed. 2.50 (*1-58610-061-0*, Learn on the Go) Learn Horizon.
— What Comes Next? Preparing to Read & Write. (Illus.). 32p. (J). (ps-k). 1995. pap., wbk. ed. 2.50 (*1-58610-024-6*, Learn on the Go) Learn Horizon.
— What Goes Together? Reading & Writing Skills. (Illus.). 32p. (J). (gr. 2-3). 1995. pap., wbk. ed. 2.50 (*1-58610-032-7*, Learn on the Go) Learn Horizon.
— What Happens Next? The Science Series. Evans, Joy, ed. (Illus.). 29p. 1995. pap., wbk. ed. 2.50 (*1-58610-114-5*) Learn Horizon.
— What Time Is It? Basic Mathematics Skills. (Illus.). 32p. (J). (gr. k-1). 1995. pap., wbk. ed. 2.50 (*1-58610-064-5*, Learn on the Go) Learn Horizon.
— Word Families: Reading & Writing Skills. (Illus.). 32p. (J). (gr. 2-3). 1995. pap., wbk. ed. 2.50 (*1-58610-030-0*, Learn on the Go) Learn Horizon.
— Word Problems: Basic Mathematics Skills. (Illus.). 30p. (J). (gr. 1-2). 1995. pap., wbk. ed. 2.50 (*1-58610-070-X*, Learn on the Go) Learn Horizon.
— Writing Forms--Tops & Bottoms: Grade K-3. Evans, Marilyn, ed. (Illus.). 160p. 1999. pap., teacher ed. 16.95 (*1-55799-735-7*, 596) Evan-Moor Edu Pubs.
— Writing Paragraphs: Reading & Writing Skills. (Illus.). 32p. (J). (gr. 2-4). 1995. pap., wbk. ed. 2.50 (*1-58610-044-0*, Learn on the Go) Learn Horizon.
— Writing Poetry with Children: Grade 1-6. Evans, Marilyn, ed. (Illus.). 96p. 1999. pap., teacher ed. 10.95 (*1-55799-734-9*, 734) Evan-Moor Edu Pubs.
— Writing Stories: Reading & Writing Skills. Evans, Joy, ed. (Illus.). 32p. (J). (gr. 3-6). 1995. pap., wbk. ed. 2.50 (*1-58610-047-5*, Learn on the Go) Learn Horizon.
Moore, Jo Ellen & De Weese, Bob. Phonics Fundamentals. Evans, Marilyn, ed. (Partners in Learning). (Illus.). 192p. (J). (gr. 1-3). Date not set. pap., wbk. ed. 19.95 (*1-58610-143-9*) Learn Horizon.
***Moore, Jo Ellen & Evans, Joy.** Draw... Then Write: Grade 1-3. Evans, Marilyn, ed. (Illus.). 96p. 1999. pap., teacher ed. 10.95 (*1-55799-731-4*, 731) Evan-Moor Edu Pubs.
Moore, Jo Ellen & Tryon, Leslie. Maps of the U. S. A. Evans, Marilyn, ed. (Partners in Learning). (Illus.). 63p. (J). (gr. 3-6). Date not set. pap., wbk. ed. 6.95 (*1-58610-141-2*) Learn Horizon.
Moore, Jo Ellen, et al. Write Every Day. (Partners in Learning). (Illus.). 64p. (J). (gr. 2-6). Date not set. pap., wbk. ed. 6.45 (*1-58610-148-X*) Learn Horizon.
Moore, Jo Ellen, jt. auth. see Evans, Joy.
Moore, Jo Ellen, jt. auth. see Omdorf, Eleanor.
Moore, Jo Ellen, ed. see DeWeese, Bob.
Moore, Jo Ellen, ed. see Edwards, Phyllis.
Moore, Jo Ellen, ed. see Evans, Joy.
Moore, Jo Ellen, ed. see Evans, Marilyn.
Moore, Jo Ellen, ed. see Norris, Jill & Evans, Marilyn.
Moore, Joan. Cat Lover's Companion. 1997. pap. 9.99 (*1-85833-722-4*, Pub. by CLib Bks) Whitecap Bks.
— The Cat Lovers Companion: A Book of Cat Days & Cat Ways. (Illus.). 180p. 1999. text 25.00 (*0-7881-6136-9*) DIANE Pub.
Moore, Joan & Pinderhughes, Raquel, eds. In the Barrios: Latinos & the Underclass Debate. 352p. 1993. 49.95 (*0-87154-612-4*); pap. 16.95 (*0-87154-613-2*) Russell Sage.
Moore, Joan, jt. ed. see Glick, Ronald.
Moore, Joan A. Camp Country Recipes: Now You Can Really Eat Well in the Wild! LC 99-158830. 248p. 1998. pap. 14.50 (*0-9664309-0-5*) Mntain Bay.
Moore, Joan Trustly. On the Cross Road: A Daily Devotional for Lent. LC 98-50657. 1999. pap. 12.00 (*0-8170-1316-4*) Judson.
Moore, Joan W. Going down to the Barrio: Homeboys & Homegirls in Change. (C). 1991. 59.99 (*0-87722-854-X*); pap. 22.95 (*0-87722-855-8*) Temple U Pr.
Moore, Joan W. & Moore, Burton M. Social Problems. (Illus.). 464p. (C). 1982. text 46.90 (*0-13-817387-7*) P-H.
Moore, Joan W. & Pachon, Harry. Hispanics in the United States. (Illus.). 208p. (C). 1985. pap. text 28.00 (*0-13-388984-X*) P-H.
Moore, Joanna D. Participating in Explanatory Dialogues: Interpreting & Responding to Questions in Context. (ACL-MIT Series in Natural Language Processing). (Illus.). 366p. 1994. 55.00 (*0-262-13301-6*, Bradford Bks) MIT Pr.
Moore, JoAnne, jt. auth. see Garrett, Linda J.
Moore, JoAnne, jt. auth. see Roach, Catharyn.
Moore, Joanne I. Immigrants in Courts. LC 98-45387. (Illus.). 264p. 1999. pap. text 19.95 (*0-295-97780-9*) U of Wash Pr.
Moore, Joanne I., ed. Pharmacology. 4th ed. LC 94-43678. (Oklahoma Notes Ser.). 235p. 1995. 17.95 (*0-387-94394-3*) Spr-Verlag.
Moore, Joanne Madeline. Love & Sex Signs: Venus, Mars & Astrology. 1998. pap. text 14.95 (*0-7318-0667-0*) Simon & Schuster.
Moore, Jodi, jt. auth. see Moore, Larry.
Moore, Joe. Japanese Workers & the Struggle for Power, 1945-1947. LC 82-70552. 327p. reprint ed. pap. 101.40 (*0-608-20456-0*, 207170900002) Bks Demand.
Moore, Joe, ed. The Other Japan: Conflict, Compromise, & Resistance since 1945. rev. ed. LC 96-35872. (Japan in the Modern World Ser.). 422p. (C). (gr. 13-13). 1996. text 85.95 (*1-56324-867-0*, East Gate Bk) M E Sharpe.
— The Other Japan: Conflict, Compromise, & Resistance since 1945. rev. ed. LC 96-35872. (Japan in the Modern World Ser.). (Illus.). 424p. (gr. 13). 1996. pap. text 24.95 (*1-56324-868-9*, East Gate Bk) M E Sharpe.
Moore, Joe B. Japanese Workers & the Struggle for Power, 1945-1947. LC 82-70552. (Illus.). 272p. 1983. 24.95 (*0-299-09320-4*) U of Wis Pr.
Moore, Joellen. Getting Ready to Read Vol. 1: Readiness Fundamentals. (Illus.). 240p. (J). (ps-1). 1995. pap. text, teacher ed. 19.95 (*1-55799-371-8*, EMC 389) Evan-Moor Edu Pubs.
Moore, Joellen, jt. auth. see Evans, Joy.
Moore, Johanna & Walker, Marilyn, eds. Empirical Methods in Discourse: Interpretation & Generation: Papers from the 1995 Spring Symposium. (Technical Reports). (Illus.). 188p. 1995. spiral bd. 25.00 (*0-929280-89-X*) AAAI Pr.
Moore, Johanna D., ed. see Cognitive Science Society Staff.
Moore, John. Amazing Book of the Tarot. 128p. 1996. 14.98 (*0-7858-0567-2*) Bk Sales Inc.
— The Blue Field. large type ed. (Reminiscence Ser.). 1998. 25.95 (*0-7531-5434-X*, Pub. by ISIS Lrg Prnt) Transaction Pubs.
— Brensham Village. large type ed. 1997. 25.95 (*0-7531-5433-1*, Pub. by ISIS Lrg Prnt) Transaction Pubs.
— Colloquial Thai. 336p. 1994. pap., pap. text 39.99 incl. audio (*0-415-09576-X*) Routledge.
— Colloquial Thai: Complete Language Course. (Colloquials Ser.). 1997. audio compact disk 39.99 (*0-415-15535-5*) Routledge.
— Colloquial Thai: Complete Language Course. (Colloquials Ser.). (C). 1997. audio compact disk 27.99 (*0-415-15534-7*) Routledge.
— Colloquial Vietnamese. 320p. (C). (gr. 13). 1994. pap. 34.95 incl. audio (*0-415-09207-8*, Pub. by Tavistock) Routldge.
— Feel Safe Anywhere: You Can Be Your Own Bodyguard. Ancona, Joe, ed. LC 92-61239. 101p. (Orig.). 1992. pap. 10.00 (*0-9633458-0-X*) Tiger Ent.
— The First Fleet Marines: Seventeen Eighty-Six to Seventeen Ninety-Two. LC 86-30904. (Illus.). 345p. 1988. text 39.95 (*0-7022-2065-5*, Pub. by Univ Queensland Pr) Intl Spec Bk.
Moore, John. Interpreting Young Adult Literature: Literary Theory in the Secondary Classroom. LC 97-5045. (Young Adult Literature Ser.). (Orig.). (C). 1997. pap. text 27.50 (*0-86709-414-1*, 0414, Pub. by Boynton Cook Pubs) Heinemann.
Moore, John. Portrait of Elmbury. large type ed. (Isis Large Print Ser.). 1997. 25.95 (*0-7531-5432-3*) T T Beeler.
— Ramon de la Cruz. LC 70-153997. (Twayne's World Authors Ser.). 181p. (C). 1972. lib. bdg. 20.95 (*0-8290-1746-1*) Irvington.
— Readings in Ethics. 175p. 1989. 20.00 (*0-614-13741-1*) Haven Pubns.
***Moore, John.** Slay & Rescue. LC 99-91672. 208p. 2000. 25.00 (*0-7388-1188-2*); pap. 18.00 (*0-7388-1189-0*) Xlibris Corp.
Moore, John. Superman: The Dark Side. (Illus.). 160p. 1999. pap. text 12.95 (*1-56389-526-9*, Pub. by DC Comics) Time Warner.
— Tille Hoyuk Vol. 1: The Medieval Period. (Illus.). 205p. 1993. 80.00 (*1-898249-00-8*, Pub. by Brit Inst Arch) David Brown.
— The Wrong Stuff. (Illus.). 216p. 1997. 19.95 (*1-883809-10-X*) Specialty Pr.
Moore, John, ed. MIT Marine-Related Research Directory, 1993-1994. write for info. (*1-56172-008-9*) MIT Sea Grant.
***Moore, John, ed.** Pope Innocent III & His World. LC 99-20427. 408p. 1999. text 87.95 (*1-84014-646-X*, Pub. by Ashgate Pub) Ashgate Pub Co.
Moore, John & Moore, Patricia. Enjoy Arithmetic: Addition. (C). 1988. text 30.00 (*1-871044-15-4*, Pub. by Hawthorns Pubns) St Mut.
— Enjoy Arithmetic: Answers. (C). 1988. text 30.00 (*1-871044-30-8*, Pub. by Hawthorns Pubns) St Mut.
— Enjoy Arithmetic: Division. (C). 1988. text 30.00 (*1-871044-10-3*, Pub. by Hawthorns Pubns) St Mut.
— Enjoy Arithmetic: Multiplication. (C). 1988. text 21.00 (*1-871044-05-7*, Pub. by Hawthorns Pubns) St Mut.
— Enjoy Arithmetic: Revision. (C). 1988. text 21.00 (*1-871044-25-1*, Pub. by Hawthorns Pubns) St Mut.
— Enjoy Arithmetic: Subtraction. (C). 1988. text 21.00 (*1-871044-20-0*, Pub. by Hawthorns Pubns) St Mut.
Moore, John & Morrison, Neil. Someone Else's Problem? Teacher Development to Meet Special Educational Needs. 180p. 1988. 65.00 (*1-85000-373-4*, Falmer Pr); pap. 34.95 (*1-85000-374-2*, Falmer Pr) Taylor & Francis.
Moore, John & Rodchue, Soawalak. Colloquial Thai: A Complete Language Course. LC 94-11582. 19p. (C). (gr. 13). 1994. audio 27.99 (*0-415-09575-1*) Routledge.
— Colloquial Thai: A Complete Language Course. LC 94-11582. (Illus.). 336p. (gr. 13). 1994. pap. 20.99 (*0-415-09574-3*) Routledge.
Moore, John & Vuong, Tuan D. Colloquial Vietnamese. LC 93-33737. (C). (gr. 13). 1994. audio 27.99 (*0-415-09206-X*) Routledge.
— Colloquial Vietnamese. LC 93-33737. (Illus.). 320p. (gr. 13). 1994. pap. 19.99 (*0-415-09205-1*) Routledge.
— Colloquial Vietnamese: Complete Language Course. (Colloquials Ser.). (C). 1997. audio compact disk 27.99 (*0-415-15536-3*) Routledge.
— Colloquial Vietnamese: Complete Language Course. (Colloquials Ser.). 1997. audio compact disk 39.99 (*0-415-15537-1*) Routledge.
Moore, John, et al. Voices of the People: The Politics & Life of "La Sociale" at the End of the Second Empire. (History Workshop Ser.). 376p. 1988. text 65.00 (*0-7102-1308-5*, Routledge Thoemms) Routledge.
Moore, John, jt. auth. see Corlett, William.
Moore, John, jt. auth. see Gabriel, Michael.
Moore, John, jt. auth. see Sayer, Karen.
Moore, John, tr. see Agasso, Domenica.
Moore, John, tr. see Lefebvre, Henri.
Moore, John A. Anabaptist Portraits. LC 84-12769. 256p. (Orig.). 1984. pap. 12.99 (*0-8361-3361-7*) Herald Pr.
— Baptist Mission Portraits. 184p. 1994. pap. 14.00 (*1-880837-79-X*) Smyth & Helwys.
— The Cheyenne. (Peoples of America Ser.). (Illus.). 320p. 1996. 29.95 (*1-55786-484-5*) Blackwell Pubs.
— Digital Control Devices: Equipment & Applications. LC 86-10542. (Illus.). 219p. 1986. reprint ed. pap. 67.90 (*0-7837-8773-1*, 204951800012) Bks Demand.
Moore, John A., Jr. The Pursuit of Happiness: Government & Politics in America. 5th ed. 448p. (C). 1991. pap. text 67.00 (*0-02-383190-1*, Macmillan Coll) P-H.
Moore, John A. Science As a Way of Knowing: The Foundations of Modern Biology. (Illus.). 544p. (C). 1993. text 37.50 (*0-674-79480-X*) HUP.
— Science as a Way of Knowing: The Foundations of Modern Biology. (Illus.). 528p. 1993. text 37.50 (*0-674-79481-8*) HUP.
— Science as a Way of Knowing: The Foundations of Modern Biology. (Illus.). 530p. 1999. pap. 18.95 (*0-674-79482-6*) HUP.
— Write for the Religion Market. LC 80-25607. 128p. 1981. 17.95 (*0-88280-084-1*) ETC Pubns.
Moore, John A., Jr. & Murphy, John E., eds. A Grand Experiment: The Constitution at 200. LC 87-16754. 192p. 1987. 45.00 (*0-8420-2289-9*) Scholarly Res Inc.
***Moore, John A., Jr. & Pubantz, Jerry.** To Create a New World? American Presidents & the United Nations. LC E840.M586 1999. XI, 378p. (C). 1999. pap. 33.00 (*0-8204-3935-5*) P Lang Pubng.
Moore, John A., Jr., jt. ed. see Englehart, Stephen F.
Moore, John B. Digest of International Law, 8 vols. LC 77-101908. reprint ed. write for info. (*0-404-04420-4*) AMS Pr.
— Four Phases of American Development: Federalism, Democracy, Imperialism, Expansion. LC 72-109551. (Law, Politics & History Ser.). 1970. reprint ed. lib. bdg. 32.50 (*0-306-71905-3*) Da Capo.
— History & Digest of the International Arbitrations to Which the United States Has Been a Party, 6 vols., Set. LC 74-19729. reprint ed. 1800.00 (*0-404-12270-1*) AMS Pr.
— History & Digest of the International Arbitrations to Which the United States Has Been a Party, 6 vols., Set. LC 94-79747. 5400p. 1995. reprint ed. ring bd. 495.00 incl. fiche (*0-89941-915-1*, 308580) W S Hein.
— International Law & Some Current Illusions: And Other Essays. xviii, 381p. 1987. reprint ed. 45.00 (*0-8377-2435-X*, Rothman) W S Hein.
— Treatise on Extradition & Interstate Rendition: With Appendices Containing the Treaties & Statutes Relating to Extradition; the Treaties Relating to the Desertion of Seamen; & the Statutes, Rules of Practice, & Forms, in Force in the Several States & Territories, Relating to Interstate Rendition, 2 vols., Set. LC 96-42915. 1624p. 1996. reprint ed. 165.00 (*0-8377-2482-1*, Rothman) W S Hein.
Moore, John B., ed. International Adjudications Ancient & Modern History & Documents Together with Mediatorial Reports, Advisory Opinions, & the Decisions of Domestic Commissions,..., Vols. 1-7. LC 96-75389. 1996. reprint ed. 650.00 (*1-57588-095-4*, 310480) W S Hein.
Moore, John B., jt. auth. see Kelmke, Uwe.
Moore, John B., Jr., jt. auth. see Magill, Jane M.
Moore, John B., ed. see Buchanan, James.
Moore, John C. Country Men. LC 69-17585. (Essay Index Reprint Ser.). 1977. 20.95 (*0-8369-0088-X*) Ayer.
Moore, John C., et al. Reduced Constructions in Spanish. rev. ed. Hankamer, Jorge, ed. LC 96-36742. (Outstanding Dissertations in Linguistics Ser.). 283p. 1996. text 79.00 (*0-8153-2579-7*) Garland.
Moore, John C., jt. ed. see Sheringham, Hugh.
Moore, John D. I Must Fly! LC 97-68741. (Illus.). 383p. (Orig.). 1997. pap. 17.95 (*0-9658720-5-X*) Sugarpine.
— Lecture Notes on Seiberg-Witten Invariants, Vol. 162. LC 96-36335. (Lecture Notes in Mathematics Ser.). 105p. 1996. pap. 29.00 (*3-540-61455-9*) Spr-Verlag.
Moore, John E. Practical Tax: Individual & Estate Taxation for the Non-Tax Lawyer. 313p. 1998. pap. 185.00 incl. audio (*0-943380-98-7*) PEG MN.
Moore, John E. Winning Numbers: Accounting & Finance for Lawyers. 188p. 1994. pap. 185.00 (*0-943380-36-7*) PEG MN.
Moore, John E., ed. Jane's Fighting Ships, 1975-76. LC 75-15172. 1975. 79.50 (*0-531-03251-5*) Key Bk Serv.
— Jane's Fighting Ships, 1976-77. LC 75-15172. 1976. 79.50 (*0-934636-03-6*) Key Bk Serv.
Moore, John E., et al, eds. Groundwater: A Primer. (AGI Environmental Awareness Ser.: Vol. 1). (Illus.). 53p. (Orig.). (YA). (gr. 9 up). Date not set. pap. 7.50 (*0-922152-28-4*) Am Geol.
Moore, John E. & Jackson, Julia A., eds. Geology, Hydrology & History of the Washington DC Area. LC 89-83680. (Illus.). 114p. (Orig.). 1989. pap. text 18.75 (*0-922152-00-4*) Am Geol.
Moore, John E. & Wilson, William E., eds. Glossary of Hydrology. LC 98-4291. 250p. 1998. pap. 40.00 (*0-922152-35-7*) Am Geol.
Moore, John E., jt. auth. see Wilson, William E.
Moore, John F. Tales of the Age of Apocalypse: Sinister Bloodlines. (Illus.). 48p. (YA). (gr. 5-12). 1998. pap. 5.95 (*0-7851-0584-0*) Marvel Entrprs.
Moore, John Francis. The Ultimate Factor X. (Illus.). 96p. 1995. pap. 8.95 (*0-7851-0128-4*) Marvel Entrprs.
Moore, John G. & Rothenberg, Ellen. The Molecular Biology of B-Cell & T-Cell Development. LC 98-12613. (Contemporary Immunology Ser.). (Illus.). 608p. 1998. 175.00 (*0-89603-536-0*) Humana.
Moore, John H. Building Scientific Apparatus. 3rd ed. 1999. write for info. (*0-201-36087-X*) Addison-Wesley.
***Moore, John H.** The Cheyenne. (Peoples of America Ser.). (Illus.). 320p. 1999. pap. 24.95 (*0-631-21862-9*) Blackwell Pubs.
Moore, John H. The Cheyenne Nation: A Social & Demographic History. LC 87-5856. 416p. 1987. reprint ed. pap. 129.00 (*0-608-02377-9*, 206301900004) Bks Demand.
— Columbia & Richland County: A South Carolina Community, 1740-1990. LC 92-18919. (Illus.). 534p. 1992. 24.95 (*0-87249-827-1*) U of SC Pr.
— The Emergence of the Cotton Kingdom in the Old Southwest: Mississippi, 1770-1860. LC 87-2803. (Illus.). 352p. 1988. pap. text 19.95 (*0-8071-1404-9*) La State U Pr.
— The Emergence of the Cotton Kingdom in the Old Southwest: Mississippi, 1770-1860. LC 87-2803. (Illus.). 352p. 1988. text 47.50 (*0-8071-1382-4*) La State U Pr.
— The Federal Role in University Research: The Coming Years. Pejovich, Steve & Dethloff, Henry, eds. (Series on Public Issues: No. 20). 9p. 1985. pap. 2.00 (*0-86599-056-5*) PERC.
— The Political Economy of North American Indians. LC 92-50719. 320p. 1993. 29.95 (*0-8061-2505-5*) U of Okla Pr.
— South Carolina in the 1880s: A Gazetteer. LC 89-6377. 342p. 1989. 9.95 (*0-87844-069-0*) Sandlapper Pub Co.
— Southern Homefront, 1861-1865. (Illus.). 250p. 1998. 24.95 (*1-887714-30-8*) Summerhse Pr.
Moore, John H., ed. The Confederate Housewife: Receipts & Remedies Together with Sundry Suggestions for Garden, Farm & Plantation. LC 97-3226. 160p. 1997. pap. text 14.95 (*1-887714-09-X*) Summerhse Pr.
— Legacies of the Collapse of Marxism. 276p. (C). 1994. 62.50 (*0-913969-71-0*); pap. 26.50 (*0-913969-72-9*) Univ Pub Assocs.
— A Plantation Mistress on the Eve of the Civil War: The Diary of Keziah Goodwyn Hopkins Brevard, 1860-1861. LC 92-23308. (Illus.). 148p. 1996. pap. 12.95 (*1-57003-125-8*) U of SC Pr.
— To Promote Prosperity: U. S. Domestic Policy in the Mid-1980's. (Publication Ser.: No. 295). 464p. 1984. 7.98 (*0-8179-7951-4*) Hoover Inst Pr.
Moore, John H., et al. Building Scientific Apparatus. 1983. text 39.95 (*0-201-05532-5*) Addison-Wesley.
— Building Scientific Apparatus. 2nd ed. (Illus.). 576p. (C). 1989. 52.95 (*0-201-13187-0*); pap. 50.00 (*0-201-13189-7*) Addison-Wesley.
Moore, John H., ed. see Vignoles, Charles B.
Moore, John H., ed. see Zaleski, Eugene.
***Moore, John L.** The Breaking of Ezra Riley, 3 bks. in 1. rev. ed. LC 99-55395. 784p. 2000. pap. 14.99 (*0-8054-2331-1*) Broadman.
Moore, John L. The Land of Empty Houses. LC 98-3838. 272p. 1998. pap. 12.99 (*0-8054-1648-X*) Broadman.
— Loosening the Reins: Stories of a Father & His Son. 224p. 1992. pap. 9.99 (*0-310-57721-7*) Zondervan.

M

An Asterisk (*) at the beginning of an entry indicates that the title is appearing for the first time.

— Speaking of Washington: Facts, Firsts, Folklore. LC 93-30363. 288p. (C). 1993. pap. text 19.95 (*0-87187-741-4*) Congr Quarterly.
— Take the Reins. rev. ed. LC 96-50947. 224p. 1997. 12.99 (*0-7852-7226-7*) Nelson.
Moore, John L., jt. ed. see Diller, Daniel C.
Moore, John M. Aristotle & Xenophon on Democracy & Oligarchy. LC 74-16713. 1975. pap. 17.95 (*0-520-02909-7*, Pub. by U CA Pr) Cal Prin Full Svc.
— The South Today. LC 75-152996. (Select Bibliographies Reprint Ser.). 1977. reprint ed. 25.95 (*0-8369-5748-2*) Ayer.
— Three Aspects of the Late Alfred Lord Tennyson. LC 79-185968. (Studies in Tennyson: No. 27). vi, 144p. 1972. reprint ed. lib. bdg. 75.00 (*0-8383-1387-6*) M S G Haskell Hse.
Moore, John M., ed. Friends in the Delaware Valley: Philadelphia Yearly Meeting, 1681-1981. 273p. 1981. 5.00 (*0-9609122-0-7*); pap. 3.00 (*0-9609122-1-5*) Friends Hist Assn.
Moore, John M., jt. ed. see Frost, J. William.
Moore, John N. Crisis in the Gulf: Enforcing the Rule of Law. (Terrorism, Documents of International & Local Control, Second Ser.: Vol. 1). 677p. 1992. text 60.00 (*0-379-20166-6*) Oceana.
— Law & the Indo-China War. LC 73-166383. 830p. 1972. reprint ed. pap. 200.00 (*0-608-03326-X*, 206403800008) Bks Demand.
— The Secret War in Central America: Sandinista Assault on World Order. LC 86-28092. 204p. 1987. lib. bdg. 47.95 (*0-313-27041-4*, U7041, Greenwood Pr) Greenwood.
Moore, John N., ed. The Arab-Israeli Conflict, Vol. IV: The Difficult Search for Peace, 1975-1988, 2 pts. (American Society of International Law Ser.). 1104p. 1992. text 99.50 (*0-691-05672-2*, Pub. by Princeton U Pr) Cal Prin Full Svc.
— The Arab-Israeli Conflict, Vol. IV: The Difficult Search for Peace, 1975-1988, 2 pts., Pt. 2. (American Society of International Law Ser.). 1990p. 1992. text 99.50 (*0-691-05678-1*, Pub. by Princeton U Pr) Cal Prin Full Svc.
— Deception & Deterrence: In "Wars of National Liberation," State-Sponsored Terrorism, & Other Forms of Secret Warfare. LC 95-68696. 274p. (C). 1997. 39.95 (*0-89089-858-8*) Carolina Acad Pr.
— International & United States Documents on Oceans Law & Policy, 5 vols., Set. LC 86-83006. 4550p. 1986. lib. bdg. 265.00 (*0-89941-529-6*, 304640) W S Hein.
— Law & Civil War in the Modern World. LC 73-19338. 672p. 1974. reprint ed. pap. 200.00 (*0-608-04013-4*, 206474900011) Bks Demand.
— The Vietnam Debate: A Fresh Look at the Arguments. LC 89-30902. 330p. (Orig.). (C). 1990. pap. text 24.50 (*0-8191-7417-3*) U Pr of Amer.
Moore, John N. & Turner, Robert F. International Law & the Brezhnev Doctrine. 144p. (Orig.). (C). 1987. pap. text 17.00 (*0-8191-5795-3*); lib. bdg. 40.50 (*0-8191-5794-5*) U Pr of Amer.
Moore, John N., et al. National Security Law Documents. LC 94-72699. 994p. (C). 1995. lib. bdg. 75.00 (*0-89089-854-5*) Carolina Acad Pr.
Moore, John N., jt. auth. see Nordquist, Myron H.
Moore, John N., jt. ed. see Nordquist, Myron H.
Moore, John N., ed. see Turner, Robert F., et al.
***Moore, John Norton & Morrison, Alex, eds.** Strengthening the United Nations & Enhancing War Prevention. LC 99-68891. 304p. 2000. 30.00 (*0-89089-838-3*) Carolina Acad Pr.
Moore, John R. Daniel Defoe: Citizen of the Modern World. LC 58-11950. 1958. lib. bdg. 20.00 (*0-226-53577-0*) U Ch Pr.
— Daniel Defoe, Citizen of the Modern World. LC 58-11950. (Illus.). 425p. reprint ed. pap. 131.80 (*0-608-09024-7*, 206965900005) Bks Demand.
— Defoe's Sources for Robert Drury's Journal. LC 72-6862. (English Literature Ser.: No. 33). 1972. reprint ed. lib. bdg. 75.00 (*0-8383-1656-5*) M S G Haskell Hse.
— The Impact of Foreign Direct Investment on an Underdeveloped Economy: The Venezuelan Case. Bruchey, Stuart & Bruchey, Eleanor, eds. LC 76-5018. (American Business Abroad Ser.). 1976. lib. bdg. 31.95 (*0-405-09285-7*) Ayer.
— Senator Josiah William Bailey of North Carolina: A Political Biography. LC 68-24639. 271p. reprint ed. 84.10 (*0-8357-9118-1*, 201791400010) Bks Demand.
Moore, John R., ed. The Economic Impact of TVA. LC 67-12217. 179p. reprint ed. pap. 55.50 (*0-608-14036-8*, 202222000025) Bks Demand.
— Representative Essays: English & American. LC 72-284. (Essay Index Reprint Ser.). 1977. reprint ed. 23.95 (*0-8369-2808-3*) Ayer.
Moore, John T. The Bishop of Cottontown: A Story of the Southern Cotton Mills. LC 72-4610. (Black Heritage Library Collection). (Illus.). 1977. reprint ed. 35.95 (*0-8369-9113-3*) Ayer.
— Pepito's Journey. 25p. pap. 3.95 (*92-1-100308-3*, E.87.I.4) UN.
— Pepito's World. 1988. 4.95 (*92-1-100399-7*, E.88.I.14) UN.
— Songs & Stories from Tennessee. LC 70-94739. (Short Story Index Reprint Ser.). 1977. 23.95 (*0-8369-3119-X*) Ayer.
Moore, John T., et al, eds. Tennessee Civil War Questionnaires, 5 vols., 1. 1985. 30.00 (*0-89308-216-3*) Southern Hist Pr.
— Tennessee Civil War Questionnaires, 5 vols., 2. 1985. 30.00 (*0-89308-217-1*) Southern Hist Pr.
— Tennessee Civil War Questionnaires, 5 vols., 3. 1985. 30.00 (*0-89308-218-X*) Southern Hist Pr.
— Tennessee Civil War Questionnaires, 5 vols., 4. 1985. 30.00 (*0-89308-219-8*) Southern Hist Pr.
— Tennessee Civil War Questionnaires, 5 vols., 5. 1985. 30.00 (*0-89308-220-1*) Southern Hist Pr.
— Tennessee Civil War Questionnaires, 5 vols., Set. 1985. 150.00 (*0-89308-221-X*) Southern Hist Pr.
Moore, John T., jt. ed. see Elliott, Colleen M.
Moore, John Travers. Poems: On Writing Poetry. LC 79-181366. 1971. 5.00 (*0-87212-025-2*) Libra.
Moore, John V., Jr. Gwinnett County, Georgia: Eighteen-Sixty Census. 242p. 1986. 20.00 (*0-914923-03-X*) Gwinnett Hist.
— Gwinnett County, Georgia: Eighteen-Twenty, Eighteen-Thirty, Eighteen-Forty Census. 356p. 1992. 20.00 (*0-914923-11-0*) Gwinnett Hist.
Moore, John W. Chemical World. 2nd ed. LC 96-71994. 568p. (C). 1997. pap. text 61.50 (*0-03-024586-9*) SCP.
— The Chemical World, Vol. 2. 2nd ed. 592p. (C). 1997. pap. text 35.00 (*0-03-024587-7*) SCP.
— Chemical World: Concepts & Applications. 2nd ed. (C). 1998. text 143.00 incl. cd-rom (*0-03-020799-1*) Harcourt.
— Complete Encyclopedia of Music. LC 72-1713. reprint ed. 79.50 (*0-404-09916-5*) AMS Pr.
— A Dictionary of Musical Information. LC 72-1714. reprint ed. 32.50 (*0-404-09915-7*) AMS Pr.
— Labor Union Elections & Corporate Financial Performance. rev. ed. LC 94-45049. (Studies on Industrial Productivity). 173p. 1995. text 15.00 (*0-8153-1973-8*) Garland.
— New & Critical Plants from Raiatea. (BMB Ser.: No. 102). 1974. reprint ed. pap. 25.00 (*0-527-02208-X*) Periodicals Srv.
Moore, John W. & Pearson, Ralph G. Kinetics & Mechanism. 3rd ed. LC 81-981. 480p. 1981. 110.00 (*0-471-03558-0*) Wiley.
Moore, Johnnie N., jt. auth. see Fritz, William J.
Moore, Johnny. Family Centennial. LC 98-96576. (Illus.). 400p. 1999. pap. 17.95 (*0-9658720-6-8*) Sugarpine.
Moore, Johnny R. But Still, We Dream. LC 99-72739. (Illus.). 36p. 1999. pap. text 7.95 (*1-58521-006-4*) Bks Black Chldn.
— Howie Has a Stomachache. (Illus.). 12p. (J). (gr. k-1). 1996. pap. 3.75 (*1-880612-52-3*) Seedling Pubns.
***Moore, Johnny R.** Talking Tyrone Said It. LC 99-72738. (Illus.). 60p. 1999. pap. text 6.95 (*1-58521-007-2*) Bks Black Chldn.
***Moore, Johnny Ray.** A Leaf. (Illus.). 8p. 1999. pap. 3.75 (*1-880612-90-9*) Seedling Pubns.
Moore, Jonathan, ed. Campaign for President: The Managers Look at '84. LC 85-20070. 313p. 1986. 55.00 (*0-86569-132-0*, Auburn Hse) Greenwood.
— Moral Search: Humanitarian Intervention in Internal Conflicts. LC 98-19157. 336p. 1998. pap. 24.95 (*0-8476-9031-8*); text 65.00 (*0-8476-9030-X*) Rowman.
Moore, Jonathan, jt. auth. see Marty, Martin E.
Moore, Joseph. Choice: Confirmation Journal. 96p. 1993. pap. text 5.95 (*0-8091-9572-0*) Paulist Pr.
— Choice: Leader's Guide, a Confirmation Process for Emerging Young Adults. 160p. 1993. pap. 11.95 (*0-8091-9573-9*) Paulist Pr.
— Friend for the Journey: A Peer Ministry Training Program for Teens. 150p. 1994. pap., teacher ed. 12.95 (*0-86716-210-4*); pap., student ed. 5.95 (*0-86716-211-2*) St Anthony Mess Pr.
— Monday Morning Jesus. 96p. (Orig.). 1984. pap. 6.95 (*0-8091-2591-9*) Paulist Pr.
— Nurturing Young Catholics: A Guide for Confirmation Sponsors, & Other Caring Adults. LC 95-7826. 64p. (Orig.). 1995. pap. 4.95 (*0-8091-3575-2*) Paulist Pr.
— When a Teenager Chooses You - As Friend, Confidante, Confirmation Sponsor: Practical Advice for Any Adult. rev. ed. 82p. 1989. pap. text 4.95 (*0-86716-139-6*) St Anthony Mess Pr.
***Moore, Joseph.** When a Teenager Chooses You - As Friend, Confidante, Confirmation Sponsor: Practical Advice for Any Adult. 2nd ed. 2000. pap. 7.95 (*0-86716-407-7*) St Anthony Mess Pr.
Moore, Joseph A. Famous Leaders of Industry: Life Stories of Men Who Have Succeeded, Fifth Series. LC 68-8505. (Essay Index Reprints - Famous Leaders Ser). 1977. reprint ed. 28.95 (*0-8369-2326-X*) Ayer.
Moore, Joseph H., ed. First Families of Henry County, Georgia Vol. I, Vol.I. (Illus.). 766p. 1993. 65.00 (*0-9628557-3-1*) Genlgcl Socs Henry & Clayton.
***Moore, Joseph K.** Crossing the Line. LC 98-72203. 128p. 1999. pap. 12.50 (*0-88739-155-9*) Creat Arts Bk.
Moore, Joseph R. H., jt. auth. see Winslow, Hattie L.
Moore, Joseph T. Pride Against Prejudice: The Biography of Larry Doby. LC 87-32874. 206p. 1988. pap. 12.95 (*0-275-92984-1*, B2984, Praeger Pubs) Greenwood.
— Pride Against Prejudice: The Biography of Larry Doby, 113. LC 87-17743. (Contributions in Afro-American & African Studies: No. 113). 206p. 1988. 55.00 (*0-313-25995-X*, MPJ/, Greenwood Pr) Greenwood.
Moore, Josephine C. Brain Atlas & Functional Systems. (Illus.). 58p. (Orig.). (C). 1993. 26.00 (*1-56900-000-X*) Am Occup Therapy.
Moore, Joyce E. Haunt Hunter's Guide to Florida. LC 97-44235. (Illus.). 192p. 1998. pap. 12.95 (*1-56164-150-2*) Pineapple Pr.
Moore, Judith. The Appearance of Truth: The Story of Elizabeth Canning & Eighteenth-Century Narrative. LC 93-46260. 1994. 42.50 (*0-87413-494-3*) U Delaware Pr.
— The Left Coast of Paradise: California & the American Heart. LC 87-20481. 256p. 1987. 17.95 (*0-939149-03-6*) Soho Press.
— Never Eat Your Heart Out. LC 96-36024. 328p. 1997. 23.00 (*0-374-22073-5*) FS&G.
— Never Eat Your Heart Out. 336p. 1998. pap. text 13.00 (*0-86547-518-0*) N Point Pr.
Moore, Judy. Vietnam Guide. (Illus.). 288p. (Orig.). 1996. pap. 14.95 (*1-883323-39-8*) Open Rd Pub.
***Moore, Judy & Hoese, Lauri.** Texas Guide. 2nd ed. 480p. 2000. pap. text 16.95 (*1-892975-24-6*) Open Rd Pub.
Moore, Julia. While You Sleep. 32p. (J). 1999. pap. 5.99 (*0-14-055982-5*) Viking Penguin.
Moore, Julia & Johnson, Barbara. Choosing Losing. 1995. write for info. (*0-87397-998-2*, Strode Pubs) Circle Bk Service.
Moore, Julia, jt. auth. see Blakeley, Ann.
Moore, Julia A. Mortal Refrains: The Complete Collected Poetry, Prose & Songs of Julia A. Moore, the Sweet Singer of Michigan. Riedlinger, Thomas J., ed. LC 98-10566. (Illus.). 256p. 1998. pap. 24.95 (*0-87013-449-3*) Mich St U Pr.
Moore, Julian. Impressionist Paris: The Essential Guide to the City of Light. (Illus.). 208p. 1998. 24.95 (*1-85793-832-1*, Pub. by Pavilion Bks Ltd) Trafalgar.
Moore, June H. The Etiquette Advantage: Rules for the Business Professional. LC 97-52205. (Life@Work Ser.). (Illus.). 240p. 1998. pap. 12.99 (*0-8054-0154-7*) Broadman.
— You Can Raise a Well-Mannered Child. 192p. 1996. pap. 10.99 (*0-8054-6076-4*, 4260-76) Broadman.
Moore, Justin Hartley, jt. auth. see Itivuttaka.
***Moore, K.** Feminine Wiles. 256p. 1998. mass mkt. 9.95 (*0-352-33235-2*) Buccaneer Bks.
***Moore, Karen Ann.** The ABC Bible Storybook. LC 00-39363. (Illus.). (J). 2000. write for info. (*0-7814-3390-8*, Chariot Bks) Chariot Victor.
— Animal Babies' Easter: A Fun for Touch Book! (Illus.). 16p. (J). 2000. bds. 10.99 (*0-7814-3379-7*) Chariot Victor.
Moore, Karen Ann. Baby King. LC 99-38651. 1999. pap. text 9.99 (*0-7814-3253-7*) Chariot Victor.
***Moore, Karen Ann.** Follow Me Little Lamb. (Illus.). 16p. (J). 2000. bds. 7.99 (*0-7814-3393-2*) Chariot Victor.
— Ten Ways to Please God. (Illus.). 20p. 2000. bds. 8.99 (*0-7814-3394-0*) Chariot Victor.
Moore, Karen Ann. You Can Write Greeting Cards. (You Can Write It! Ser.). 128p. 1999. pap. 12.99 (*0-89879-824-8*, 10696, Wrtrs Digest Bks) F & W Pubns Inc.
***Moore, Karen Ann & Kersten, Pete.** How Noah Knew What to Do. LC 00-27300. (Illus.). (J). 2000. write for info. (*0-7814-3440-8*) Chariot Victor.
Moore, Karen B. Book Binding Made Easy. (Illus.). 129p. 1994. pap. 14.95 (*1-57002-009-4*) Univ Publng Hse.
Moore, Karina. Packing Heat. (Black Lace Ser.). 1999. mass mkt. 6.95 (*0-352-33356-1*) Virgin Bks.
***Moore, Karl.** Birth of the Multinational: 2000 Years of Ancient Business History - From Ashur to Augustus. 1999. 48.00 (*87-16-13468-0*) Copenhagen Busn Schl.
***Moore, Karl & Lewis, David.** Foundations of Corporate Empire: A Complete History of the Rise of the Multinational Enterprise. (Illus.). 288p. 2000. 52.50 (*0-273-63964-1*, Pub. by F T P-H) Trans-Atl Phila.
Moore, Karl, jt. auth. see Coveney, Patrick.
Moore, Kate. An Improper Widow. 224p. (Orig.). 1995. mass mkt. 3.99 (*0-380-77542-5*, Avon Bks) Morrow Avon.
— The Mercenary Major. 224p. (Orig.). 1994. mass mkt. 3.99 (*0-380-77541-7*, Avon Bks) Morrow Avon.
— Prince among Men. 384p. 1997. mass mkt. 5.99 (*0-380-78458-0*, Avon Bks) Morrow Avon.
— Sweet Bargain. 224p. (Orig.). 1993. mass mkt. 3.99 (*0-380-77056-3*, Avon Bks) Morrow Avon.
— To Kiss a Thief. (Regency Romance Ser.). 224p. (Orig.). 1992. mass mkt. 3.99 (*0-380-76473-3*, Avon Bks) Morrow Avon.
— Winterburn's Rose. 352p. (Orig.). 1996. mass mkt. 5.50 (*0-380-78457-2*, Avon Bks) Morrow Avon.
Moore, Katherine D., jt. auth. see Van Vactor, David.
Moore, Kathleen D. Holdfast: At Home in the Natural World. LC 98-30763. 176p. 1999. 20.00 (*1-55821-780-0*) Lyons Pr.
— Inductive Arguments: Developing Critical Thinking Skills. 3rd ed. 176p. (C). 1994. per. 20.95 (*0-8403-8475-0*) Kendall-Hunt.
— Pardons: Justice, Mercy, & the Public Interest. 288p. 1997. reprint ed. pap. 18.95 (*0-19-511394-2*) OUP.
— Riverwalking: Reflections on Moving Water. LC 96-11364. 224p. 1996. pap. 12.00 (*0-15-600461-5*, Harvest Bks) Harcourt.
— Riverwalking: Reflections on Moving Water. 176p. 1995. 19.95 (*1-55821-408-9*) Lyons Pr.
Moore, Kathleen M. Al-Mughtaribun: American Law & the Transformation of Muslim Life in the United States. 225p. 1996. pap. 16.95 (*0-614-21469-6*, 1416) Kazi Pubns.
— Al-Mughtaribun: American Law & the Transformation of Muslim Life in the United States. LC 95-16487. (SUNY Series in Middle Eastern Studies). 211p. (C). 1995. text 49.50 (*0-7914-2579-7*); pap. text 16.95 (*0-7914-2580-8*) State U NY Pr.
Moore, Kathleen M. Al-Mughtaribun: American Law & the Transformation of Muslim Life in the United States. LC 95-16487. (C). 1995. pap., ring bd. 16.95 (*0-7914-2580-0*) State U NY Pr.
Moore, Kathryn. Manhole Covers of Ft. Wayne, Indiana. (Illus.). 128p. (Orig.). Date not set. pap. 10.95 (*0-89708-191-9*) And Bks.
Moore, Kathryn C. Our Flight. rev. ed. Hutson, Ronald, ed. Orig. Title: My First Flight. (Illus.). (J). (ps-4). 1991. lib. bdg. 3.95 (*0-9633295-0-2*) K Cs Bks N Stuff.
Moore, Kathryn M. & Amey, Marilyn J. Making Sense of the Dollars: The Costs & Uses of Faculty Compensation. Fife, Jonathan D., ed. & frwd. by. (ASHE-ERIC Higher Education Reports: No. 94-5). 111p. (Orig.). 1994. pap. 24.00 (*1-878380-26-5*) GWU Grad Schl E&HD.
Moore, Kathryn M. & Twombly, Susan B., eds. Administrative Careers & the Marketplace. LC 85-644752. (New Directions for Higher Education Ser.: No. HE 72). 1991. pap. 22.00 (*1-55542-808-8*) Jossey-Bass.
Moore, Kathy. Song of Hope. LC 99-72141. 200p. 1999. pap. 12.20 (*0-9628801-9-1*) Coyote Pub.
Moore, Kay. If You Lived at the Time of the American Revolution. LC 98-114622. (Illus.). 80p. (J). (gr. 2-6). 1998. pap. text 5.99 (*0-590-67444-7*) Scholastic Inc.
— If You Lived at the Time of the American Revolution. 1998. 11.09 (*0-606-13514-6*, Pub. by Turtleback) Demco.
— If You Lived at the Time of the Civil War. LC 94-196976. 64p. (J). (gr. 2-5). 1993. pap. 5.99 (*0-590-45422-6*) Scholastic Inc.
— If You Lived at the Time of the Civil War. (J). 1994. 11.19 (*0-606-05370-0*, Pub. by Turtleback) Demco.
***Moore, Kay.** When the Heart Soars Free. LC 99-90645. 360p. 1999. pap. 12.95 (*0-929292-87-1*) Hannibal Bks.
***Moore, Keith Diaz.** Towards a Language of Assisted Living. (Publications in Architecture & Urban Planning Ser.: Vol. R99-1). 1999. 15.00 (*0-938744-97-6*) U of Wis Ctr Arch-Urban.
Moore, Keith L. Clinically Oriented Anatomy. 3rd ed. (Illus.). 930p. 1992. 53.00 (*0-683-06133-X*) Lppncott W & W.
— Clinically Oriented Anatomy. 4th ed. LC 98-48704. (Illus.). 9p. (C). 1998. write for info. (*0-683-06141-0*) Lppncott W & W.
Moore, Keith L. & Agur, Anne. Essential Clinical Anatomy. 3rd ed. 930p. 1992. 83.00 (*0-683-06136-4*) Lppncott W & W.
Moore, Keith L. & Agur, Anne M. Essential Clinical Anatomy. LC 94-36235. (Illus.). 512p. 1995. pap. 39.00 (*0-683-06128-3*) Lppncott W & W.
Moore, Keith L. & Persaud, T. V. Before We Are Born: Essentials of Embryology & Birth Defects. 5th ed. Schmitt, William, ed. LC 97-50318. (Illus.). 320p. (C). 1998. pap. text 34.95 (*0-7216-7377-5*, W B Saunders Co) Harcrt Hlth Sci Grp.
— The Developing Human. 6th ed. Schmitt, William, ed. LC 97-27844. (Illus.). 432p. (C). 1998. pap. text 39.95 (*0-7216-6974-3*, W B Saunders Co) Harcrt Hlth Sci Grp.
— Study Guide & Review Manual of Human Embryology: Review Manual. 5th ed. Schmitt, William, ed. LC 97-33990. (Illus.). 176p. (C). 1998. pap. text, student ed. 22.95 (*0-7216-7378-3*, W B Saunders Co) Harcrt Hlth Sci Grp.
Moore, Keith L., et al. Color Atlas of Clinical Embryology. LC 93-26435. 1994. text 105.00 (*0-7216-4663-8*, W B Saunders Co) Harcrt Hlth Sci Grp.
***Moore, Keith L., et al.** Color Atlas of Clinical Embryology. 2nd ed. (Illus.). 270p. 2000. text. write for info. (*0-7216-8263-4*, W B Saunders Co) Harcrt Hlth Sci Grp.
Moore, Keith L., et al. Qur'an & Modern Science: Correlation Studies. (Illus.). 62p. (Orig.). (C). 1991. pap. text 5.95 (*0-9627236-0-6*) Islamic Academy Sci Res.
Moore, Keith M. Risk Arbitrage: An Investor's Guide. LC 99-18864. (Frontiers in Finance Ser.). 304p. 1999. 69.95 (*0-471-24884-3*) Wiley.
Moore, Keith W., jt. ed. see Galante, Steven P.
Moore, Kelly. Deadly Medicine. 1989. mass mkt. 3.99 (*0-312-91579-9*) St Martin.
Moore, Ken. Bread Baking: Problems & Their Solutions. 2nd rev. ed. 32p. 1992. 2.25 (*0-9632986-0-7*) Moores Pub.
Moore, Kendall & Thompson, Sally. The Surgical Beauty Racket. LC 78-51044. 1979. 22.95 (*0-87949-126-4*) Ashley Bks.
Moore, Kenneth. Classroom Teaching Skills. 5th ed. 2000. 32.00 (*0-07-232238-1*) McGraw.
Moore, Kenneth, ed. Waymarks: The Notre Dame Inaugural Lectures in Anthropology. LC 86-40339. 160p. 1988. text 22.00 (*0-268-01939-8*); pap. text 11.50 (*0-268-01941-X*) U of Notre Dame Pr.
Moore, Kenneth & Collins, Michael, eds. Forages: CD-ROM Companion, 2 vols. 5th ed. 1997. 64.95 incl. cd-rom (*0-8138-2600-4*) Iowa St U Pr.
Moore, Kenneth D. Classroom Teaching Skills. 3rd ed. LC 94-11081. (C). 1994. pap. text 32.25 (*0-07-042922-7*) McGraw.
— Classroom Teaching Skills. 4th ed. LC 97-9323. 360p. (C). 1997. pap. 41.56 (*0-07-042994-4*) McGraw.
Moore, Kenneth D. & Quinn, Cheri L. Secondary Instructional Methods. 512p. (C). 1993. text. write for info. (*0-697-11792-8*) Brown & Benchmark.
Moore, Kenneth D., jt. auth. see Hopkins, W. Scott.
Moore, Kenneth J. Post-Harvest Physiology & Reservation of Forages. LC 95-6087. (Special Publication Ser.: Vol. 22). 115p. 1995. 28.00 (*0-89118-539-9*) Crop Sci Soc Am.
Moore, Kenny. Best Efforts. LC 80-2057. 199p. 1992. reprint ed. pap. 12.95 (*0-915297-10-8*, BES) Cedarwinds.
Moore, Kevin. A Companion Guide to Homer. LC 96-157828. 203 p. 1995. write for info. (*1-85863-996-4*, Pub. by Minerva Pr) Unity Dist.
***Moore, Kevin.** Museum & Popular Culture. (Contemporary Issues in Museum Cultures Ser.). 2000. pap. text 24.95 (*0-7185-0227-2*) Leicester U Pr.
Moore, Kevin, ed. Managment in Museums. LC 98-30552. 285p. 1999. pap. 33.95 (*0-485-90008-4*, Pub. by Athlone Pr) Transaction Pubs.
— Museum Management. LC 94-9057. (Leicester Readers in Museums Studies Ser.). (Illus.). 256p. (C). 1994. pap. 32.99 (*0-415-11279-6*, B4634) Routledge.
— Museum Management. LC 94-9057. (Leicester Readers in Museums Studies Ser.). (Illus.). 256p. (C). (gr. 13). 1994. 110.00 (*0-415-11278-8*, B4630) Routledge.

M

Moore, Kevin L. Iterative Learning Control for Deterministic Systems. Grimble, Michael J. & Johnson, M., eds. LC 92-15936. (Advances in Industrial Control Ser.). (Illus.). 200p. 1992. 69.95 (*0-387-19707-9*) Spr-Verlag.

***Moore, Kevin N.** The Islands of Assateaque & Chincoteaque: A Photographer's View. (Illus.). 32p. 2000. reprint ed. 5.95 (*0-9678618-2-9*) Marketplace Merch.

***Moore, Kevin N., photos by.** 2001 Delaware Seashore Calendar. 12p. 2000. 11.95 (*0-9678618-0-2*) Marketplace Merch.

— 2001 Islands of Assateaque & Chincoteaque Calendar. (Illus.). 12p. 2000. 11.95 (*0-9678618-1-0*) Marketplace Merch.

— 2001 Ocean City, Maryland Calendar. (Illus.). 12p. 2000. 6.95 (*0-9678618-3-7*) Marketplace Merch.

Moore, Kevin P., jt. auth. see Ramrakha, Punit s.

Moore, Kevin Z. The Descent of the Imagination: Postromantic Culture in the Later Novels of Thomas Hardy. 319p. (C). 1993. pap. text 22.50 (*0-8147-5499-6*) NYU Pr.

Moore, Kirsten, jt. ed. see Zeidenstein, Sondra.

***Moore, Kristin, et al.** A Statistical Portrait of Adolescent Sex, Contraception & Childbearing. 40p. 1998. pap. 15.00 (*1-58671-013-3*) Natl Cpgn Teen Preg.

Moore, Kristin A., contrib. by. Report to Congress on Out-of-Wedlock Childbearing. (Illus.). 265p. (C). 1997. reprint ed. pap. text 40.00 (*0-7881-4713-7*) DIANE Pub.

Moore, Kristin A., et al. Choice & Circumstance: Race Differences in Adolescent Sexuality & Fertility. 179p. 1986. pap. 21.95 (*0-88738-773-X*) Transaction Pubs.

Moore, Kristina M. & Zuckerman, Alan S. Making Sense of Federal Employment & Training Policy for Youth & Adults Vol. II: Expert Recommendations to Create a Comprehensive & Unified System. 54p. 1995. pap. text. write for info. (*1-887031-51-0*) Am Youth Policy.

Moore, L. Baptism As Thirty Celebrations: The Blessing of Baptism in the Orthodox Church. 1990. pap. 3.95 (*0-937032-74-3*) Light&Life Pub Co MN.

Moore, L. B. & Edgar, E. Flora of New Zealand: Indigenous Monocots Except Grasses, Vol. II. 1970. 25.00 (*0-614-07536-X*, Pub. by Manaaki Whenua) Balogh.

Moore, L. David. The Christian Conspiracy: How the Teachings of Christ Have Been Altered by Christians. LC 94-66236. 360p. (Orig.). 1994. pap. 14.95 (*0-9635665-2-0*) Pendulum Plus.

— Christianity & the New Age Religion: A Bridge Toward Mutual Understanding. LC 92-82117. 248p. 1993. pap. 12.95 (*0-9635665-0-4*) Pendulum Plus.

— A Personal Pathway to God: Our Song of Freedom. (Illus.). 288p. (Orig.). 1995. pap. 13.95 (*0-9635665-3-9*) Pendulum Plus.

Moore, L. David, ed. The Joy of Knowing: We Are One: Transformational Channelings from the Masters. LC 96-92577. 270p. (Orig.). 1996. pap. 13.95 (*0-9635665-4-7*) Pendulum Plus.

Moore, L. Frank. The Frymaster Story: An Insider's Look at the First Five Decades & Beyond... (Illus.). 128p. 1999. write for info. (*0-9671376-0-8*) J & F Moore Fndt.

Moore, Lance & Michal, Dan. Firm Foundations: An Architect & a Pastor Guide Your Church Construction. LC 98-45795. (Illus.). 144p. 1999. pap. 24.95 (*0-7880-1345-9*) CSS OH.

Moore-Landecker, Elizabeth. Fundamentals of the Fungi. 4th ed. LC 95-47939. 574p. (C). 1996. 105.33 (*0-13-376864-3*) P-H.

Moore, Lane. The Talisman Technique: A Formula for Making Two Hundred Dollars a Hour. (Illus.). (Orig.). 1988. pap. text 9.95 (*0-945556-00-4*) How-To Pubns.

Moore, Langdon W. His Own Story of His Eventful Life. LC 70-164617. (Select Bibliographies Reprint Ser.). 1977. reprint ed. 44.95 (*0-8369-5901-9*) Ayer.

Moore-Lanning, Linda. Breaking the Myth: The Truth about Texas Women. 240p. 1987. 14.95 (*0-89015-565-8*) Sunbelt Media.

Moore, Larry. Improving Workforce Basic Skills: The Foundation for Quality. 176p. 1992. text 29.95 (*0-527-91662-5*, 916625) Productivity Inc.

Moore, Larry & Moore, Jodi. Think Tank: Gems from the Archives. LC 98-126706. (Illus.). 160p. 1997. 39.95 (*0-9661818-0-8*) L Moore Prodns.

Moore, Larry F. & Jennings, P. Devereaux, eds. Human Resource Management on the Pacific Rim: Institutions, Practices, & Attitudes. (Studies in Organization: No. 60). 400p. (C). 1995. pap. text 29.95 (*3-11-014747-5*) De Gruyter.

Moore, Larry F. & Jennings, P. Deverreaux, eds. Human Resource Management on the Pacific Rim: Institutions, Practices, & Attitudes. LC 94-36058. (Studies in Organization: No. 60). 400p. (C). 1995. lib. bdg. 84.95 (*3-11-014053-5*) De Gruyter.

Moore, Larry F., jt. ed. see Pinder, Craig C.

Moore, Laura & Skinner, Deborah. Simply Whidbey: A Collection of Regional Recipes from Whidbey Island, Washington. LC 90-81675. (Illus.). 224p. (Orig.). 1991. pap. 16.95 (*0-9628766-0-7*) Saratoga Pubs.

Moore, Laura, ed. see Ubbelohde, Shelly.

***Moore, Laurence.** Is Greenland Really Green? A Cornucopia of Surprising Answers to Questions You Never Knew You Had! 229p. 1999. reprint ed. pap. text 11.00 (*0-7881-6461-9*) DIANE Pub.

Moore, Laurence J., jt. auth. see SangLee.

Moore, LaVoone B. Missouri Town, 1855: A Program in Architectural Preservation. (Illus.). 109p. 1987. pap. 14.95 (*0-932845-26-6*) Lowell Pr.

Moore, Lawrence C., jt. auth. see Smith, David A.

Moore, Lazarus. Sacred Tradition in the Orthodox Church: The Orthodox Christian View on Sacred Tradition. 1984. pap. 3.95 (*0-937032-34-4*) Light&Life Pub Co MN.

Moore, Lazarus, ed. from GRE. The Life of Our Holy Mother Mary of Egypt. 3rd ed. (Illus.). 48p. 1995. reprint ed. pap. 3.50 (*0-913026-31-X*) St Nectarios.

Moore, Lazarus, tr. see Brianchaninov, Ignatius.

Moore, Lenard D. Forever Home. 52p. Date not set. pap. 9.95 (*1-879934-05-1*) St Andrews NC.

Moore, Leon R. & Moore, Orene, eds. Ancestors Charts of the Saline County History & Heritage Society Members. 120p. 1993. 17.50 (*0-945183-17-8*) Saline Cnty Hist Heritage Soc.

Moore, Leonard. Enciclopedia Juvenil de la Naturaleza. 2nd ed. (SPA.). 256p. (J). 1982. 59.95 (*0-7859-5097-4*) Fr & Eur.

Moore, Leonard J. Citizen Klansmen: The Ku Klux Klan in Indiana, 1921-1928. LC 91-2602. xvi, 260p. (C). 1991. 49.95 (*0-8078-1981-6*) U of NC Pr.

— Citizen Klansmen: The Ku Klux Klan in Indiana, 1921-1928. LC 91-50257. (Illus.). 276p. (C). 1997. pap. 18.95 (*0-8078-4627-9*) U of NC Pr.

Moore, Les. Letters to Henry. LC 95-206434. 356p. (Orig.). (C). 1995. pap. 15.95 (*0-964711-0-9*) Little Lion.

Moore, Leslie E. Beautiful Sublime: The Making of "Paradise Lost," 1701-1734. 256p. 1990. 35.00 (*0-8047-1632-3*) Stanford U Pr.

Moore, Lewis D. & MacDonald, John D. Meditations on America: John D. MacDonald's Travis McGee Series & Other Fiction. 200p. (C). 1994. 39.95 (*0-87972-663-6*); pap. text 17.95 (*0-87972-664-4*) Bowling Green Univ Popular Press.

Moore, Lilian. Adam Mouse's Book of Poems. LC 91-42223. (Illus.). 48p. (J). (gr. k-5). 1992. text, lib. bdg. 12.95 (*0-689-31765-4*) Atheneum Yung Read.

— Don't Be Afraid, Amanda. LC 91-19661. (Illus.). 80p. (J). (gr. 2-5). 1992. 12.95 (*0-689-31725-5*) Atheneum Yung Read.

— I Never Did That Before: Poems. LC 95-2119. (Illus.). 32p. (J). (ps-k). 1995. 15.00 (*0-689-31889-8*) Atheneum Yung Read.

— I'll Meet You at the Cucumbers. LC 87-15195. (Illus.). 72p. (J). (gr. 2-6). 1988. 14.00 (*0-689-31243-1*) Atheneum Yung Read.

— My First Counting Book. (Little Golden Treasures Ser.). 26p. (J). (ps). 1998. 5.99 (*0-307-20311-5*, 20311, Goldn Books) Gldn Bks Pub Co.

Moore, Lilian, jt. auth. see Charlip, Remy.

Moore, Lillian. Poems Have Roots. (Illus.). 48p. (J). (gr. 3-8). 1997. 15.00 (*0-689-80029-0*) Atheneum Yung Read.

Moore, Lillian C. Images of the Dance: Historical Treasures of the Dance Collection, 1581-1861. LC 65-18552. (Illus.). 86p. 1965. 15.00 (*0-87104-093-X*) NY Pub Lib.

Moore, Lin. High Lakes Rider: Mountain Biking West of Bend. (Illus.). 96p. (Orig.). 1990. pap. 8.95 (*0-9627569-0-3*) Big Juniper Pr.

Moore, Linda. Home of the Heart. LC 95-95228. 192p. 1996. 18.95 (*0-8034-9153-0*, Avalon Bks) Bouregy.

Moore, Linda, jt. auth. see McCloskey, Marsha.

Moore, Linda, jt. des. see Redican, Kerry.

Moore, Lindy. Aberdeen University & the Education of Women, 1860-1920: Bajanellas & Semilinas. (Quincentennial Studies in the History of the University of Aberdeen). (Illus.). 192p. 1991. pap. text 17.90 (*0-08-040918-0*, Pub. by Aberdeen U Pr) Macmillan.

— Bajanellas & Semilinas: Aberdeen University & the Education of Women 1860-1920. (SWSS Ser.). (Illus.). 192p. 1991. pap. text 17.90 (*0-08-041202-5*, Pub. by Aberdeen U Pr) Macmillan.

Moore, Lisa. Degrees of Nakedness. LC 96-111858. 160p. pap. 14.50 (*1-55128-023-X*, Pub. by Mercury Bk) LPC InBook.

— Fifty Algae Stories of Hope, Health & Freedom. Andrecht, Summer, ed. LC 96-72084. (Illus.). 184p. 1997. pap. 12.95 (*0-941903-18-4*) Ransom Hill.

Moore, Lisa, jt. auth. see Moore, Charles.

Moore, Lisa C., ed. Does Your Mama Know? An Anthology of Black Lesbian Coming Out Stories. LC 97-177620. 314p. (Orig.). 1997. pap. 19.95 (*0-9656659-0-9*) RedBone Pr.

Moore, Lisa L. Dangerous Intimacies: Toward a Sapphic History of the British Novel. LC 97-7609. 191p. 1997. pap. text 16.95 (*0-8223-2049-5*); lib. bdg. 49.95 (*0-8223-2036-3*) Duke.

Moore, Lois. Linney's Secret. 200p. 1998. pap. 10.95 (*1-57532-161-0*) Press-Tige Pub.

Moore, Lola & Quinn, Elizabeth. Osceola: Jewel of Tug Hill, 1844-1984. (Illus.). 400p. 1985. pap. 14.95 (*0-685-43033-2*) Moore & Quinn.

Moore, Lonnie W. Gates of Hell: The Wrath of Judge Isaac Parker. LC 98-91752. (Illus.). 105p. (YA). (gr. 3 up). 1998. pap. 12.95 (*0-9661244-1-3*, PO2516) I&L Pubs.

— The Joaquin Murrieta Legacy. (Illus.). 52p. 1997. 12.95 (*0-9661244-0-5*, PO1922) I&L Pubs.

***Moore, Lonnie W. & Moore, Iola.** A Cherokee Spirit: The Saga of Oroville Annie & White Wolf. (Illus.). 45p. 1999. pap. 15.00 (*0-9661244-2-1*) I&L Pubs.

— The Forgotten Legend: Temple Lea Houston. (Illus.). 100p. 2000. pap. 15.00 (*1-930002-05-X*) I&L Pubs.

Moore, Lorraine A. Back Roads & Buggy Trails: A Visitor's Guide to Ohio Amish Country. 4th ed. LC 98-70327. (Illus.). 278p. 1998. pap. 11.95 (*1-881122-03-4*) Bluebrd Ohio.

Moore, Lorraine O. Inclusion: A Practical Guide for Parents: Tools to Enhance Your Child's Success in Learning. LC 96-67057. 146p. 1996. pap. 19.95 (*0-9644271-3-3*) Peytral Pubns.

***Moore, Lorraine O.** Inclusion: A Practical Guide for Parents: Tools to Enhance Your Child's Success in Learning. rev. ed. 192p. 2000. lib. bdg. 19.95 (*1-890455-44-X*, P300) Peytral Pubns.

Moore, Lorraine O. Inclusion: Strategies for Working with Young Children: A Resource Guide for Teachers, Childcare Providers & Parents. LC 97-65272. 188p. 1997. pap. 21.95 (*0-9644271-2-5*) Peytral Pubns.

Moore, Lorrie. Anagrams. LC 97-14788. 240p. 1997. mass mkt. 11.99 (*0-446-67272-6*, Pub. by Warner Bks) Little.

— Birds of America: Stories. LC 98-6144. 291p. 1998. 23.00 (*0-679-44597-8*) Knopf.

***Moore, Lorrie.** Birds of America: Stories. 2nd ed. LC 99-35828. (Illus.). 304p. 1999. pap. 14.00 (*0-312-24122-4*) St Martin.

— The Forgotten Helper: A Christmas Story. LC 00-23146. (Illus.). (J). 2000. 12.95 (*0-385-32791-9*) Delacorte.

Moore, Lorrie. Like Life. 192p. 1991. reprint ed. pap. 11.95 (*0-452-26637-8*, Plume) Dutton Plume.

— Who Will Run the Frog Hospital? LC 94-278. 1994. 20.00 (*0-679-43484-4*) Knopf.

Moore, Lorrie. Who Will Run the Frog Hospital? 160p. 1995. mass mkt. 12.99 (*0-446-67191-6*, Pub. by Warner Bks) Little.

Moore, Lorrie, ed. I Know Some Things: Stories about Childhood by Contemporary Writers. 256p. 2000. pap. 13.00 (*0-571-19802-3*) Faber & Faber.

— Ploughshares Fall, 1998: Fiction Issue Edited by Lorrie Moore, Vol. 24, Nos. 2 & 3. 247p. 1998. pap. 9.95 (*0-933277-23-7*) Ploughshares.

Moore, Louis, jt. auth. see Hillestad, Richard J.

Moore, Louis A., jt. auth. see Adams, Dana.

Moore, Louis C. The Impostors of Monterey: Bouchard & One-Eyed Charley. (Illus.). 232p. 1985. pap. text 11.95 (*0-9616361-0-6*) L C Moore.

Moore, Lucia W., et al. The Story of Eugene. 2nd ed. (Illus.). 344p. 1995. reprint ed. pap. 12.95 (*0-9648434-0-4*) Lane Cnty Hist.

Moore, Lucy. The Thieves' Opera: The Mesmerizing Story of Two Notorious Criminals in Eighteenth-Century London. LC 97-36740. xii, 304p. (C). 1998. 25.00 (*0-15-100364-5*) Harcourt.

***Moore, Lucy.** The Thieves' Opera: The Mesmerizing Story of Two Notorious Criminals in Eighteenth-Century London. 320p. 2000. pap. 14.00 (*0-15-600640-5*, Harvest Bks) Harcourt.

Moore, Lynda. Not As Far As You Think: The Realities of Working Women. LC 85-40109. 224p. (C). 1986. pap. text 14.95 (*0-669-10836-7*) Free Pr.

Moore, Lynden. Britain's Trade & Economic Structure: Impact of the Eu. LC 99-219862. 304p. (C). 1998. 90.00 (*0-415-16920-8*) Routledge.

— Britain's Trade & Economic Structure: Impact of the European Union. LC 99-219862. 400p. (C). (gr. 13). 1998. pap. 29.99 (*0-415-16921-6*) Routledge.

— The Growth & Structure of International Trade since the Second World War. LC 84-11105. (Illus.). 414p. 1985. 58.50 (*0-389-20498-6*, BNB 08061) B&N Imports.

***Moore, Lynn.** Little Boy Jesus. (Baby Blessings Ser.). (Illus.). 12p. (J). 2000. 7.99 (*0-7847-1190-9*, 04330) Standard Pub.

— Sunday Bunny. (Baby Blessings Ser.). (Illus.). 6p. (J). 2000. 7.99 (*0-7847-1188-7*, 04328) Standard Pub.

Moore, Lynn, jt. ed. see Taggart, Judith F.

***Moore, Lynn Mitchell.** Wild-n-Tame Fish-n-Game. rev. ed. (Illus.). x, 212p. 2000. write for info. (*0-9702161-0-6*) Wild Tame Fish Game.

Moore, M. From the Heart of a Gentle Brother. 203p. 1987. pap. 10.95 (*0-9614010-2-8*) High Mesa Pr.

— Planetary Brother. (I Come As a Brother Ser.: Bk. 4). 176p. (Orig.). 1991. pap. 10.95 (*0-9614010-6-0*) High Mesa Pr.

— Quarterly Review of Literature: The 1940s, Special Issue, Vol. IV, No. 2. 1940. pap. 50.00 (*1-888545-19-4*) Quarterly Rev.

— Reflections of an Elder Brother: Awakening from the Dream. 177p. (Orig.). 1989. pap. 10.95 (*0-9614010-5-2*) High Mesa Pr.

Moore, M., ed. Crystallography Reviews, Vol. 3. 74p. 1993. pap. text 117.00 (*2-88124-958-2*) Gordon & Breach.

— Crystallography Reviews, Vol. 4. 76p. 1994. pap. text 116.00 (*2-88124-997-3*) Gordon & Breach.

— Crystallography Reviews: A Special Issue of the Journal Crystallography Reviews, Issue 1. 84p. 1987. pap. text 107.00 (*2-88124-218-9*) Gordon & Breach.

— Crystallography Reviews: A Special Issue of the Journal Crystallography Reviews, Vol. 2. 106p. 1987. pap. text 107.00 (*2-88124-217-0*) Gordon & Breach.

— Crystallography Reviews Issue 1, Vol. 6. 156p. 1997. pap. text 53.00 (*90-5699-048-9*) Gordon & Breach.

— Crystallography Reviews Issue 2, Vol. 4. 134p. 1995. pap. text 351.00 (*2-88449-037-X*) Gordon & Breach.

— Crystallography Reviews Issue 2, Vol. 6. 152p. 1997. pap. text 49.00 (*90-5699-083-7*) Gordon & Breach.

— Crystallography Reviews Issue 3, Vol. 4. 72p. 1995. pap. text 189.00 (*2-88449-055-8*) Gordon & Breach.

Moore, M., jt. auth. see Vell.

Moore, M., ed. see Bartholomew.

Moore, M., ed. see Newnham, Robert E., et al.

Moore, M. H. Sketches of the Pioneers of Methodism in North Carolina & Virginia. 314p. 1977. reprint ed. 12.50 (*0-87921-039-7*) Attic Pr.

Moore, M. H., tr. see Cournot, Antoine A.

Moore, M. J. & Sieverding, C. H., eds. Aerothermodynamics of Low Pressure Steam Turbines & Condensers. (Von Karman Institute Bks.). 290p. 1986. 115.00 (*0-89116-446-4*) Hemisp Pub.

Moore, M. M. Through the Years: Poems by M. M. Moore. 64p. (Orig.). 1990. pap. write for info. (*0-9639290-2-X*) Good Times.

Moore, M. R., et al. Disorders of Porphyrin Metabolism. LC 87-14125. (Topics in Hematology Ser.). (Illus.). 396p. (C). 1987. text 110.00 (*0-306-42625-0*, Kluwer Plenum) Kluwer Academic.

Moore, MacDonald S. Yankee Blues: Musical Culture & American Identity. LC 83-49407. (Illus.). 223p. reprint ed. pap. 69.20 (*0-7837-3720-3*, 205789800009) Bks Demand.

Moore, Madeleine H. & Moore, James R., Jr. Fats in Your Diet, Live a Longer Life: Guide to Lower Saturated Fat, Lower Cholesterol. LC 86-90364. (Orig.). 1986. pap. 8.95 (*0-936833-00-9*) MHM Pub.

Moore, Madeline. As You Desire. LC 93-84275. 180p. (Orig.). 1993. pap. 9.95 (*0-933216-95-5*) Spinsters Ink.

— The Short Season Between Two Silences. (Illus.). 240p. (C). 1984. text 39.95 (*0-04-800022-1*) Routledge.

— The Short Season Between Two Silences: The Mystical & the Political in the Novels of Virginia Woolf. 216p. 1986. pap. text 12.95 (*0-04-800098-1*) Routledge.

Moore, Maggie, jt. auth. see Wade, Barrie.

Moore, Malcolm, jt. auth. see Bassett, Patrick F.

Moore, Malcolm A. Maturation Factors & Cancer. LC 80-5836. (Progress in Cancer Research & Therapy Ser.: Vol. 23). 405p. 1982. reprint ed. pap. 125.60 (*0-608-00323-9*, 206104000007) Bks Demand.

Moore, Malcolm T., jt. auth. see Fox, Edward J., Jr.

Moore, Mallie, et al. Talk Story. (Illus.). 115p. (Orig.). 1987. 7.95 (*0-9618620-0-9*) Bright Design.

Moore, Mamie. Make Way for August. Literacy Volunteers of New York City Staff, ed. (New Writers' Voices Ser.). (Illus.). 64p. (Orig.). 1991. pap. text 3.50 (*0-929631-36-6*, Signal Hill) New Readers.

M

Moore, Manvel. Arabic Slang. Arabic Slang: The Easy Way to Learn Arabic Slang. 1998. pap. 34.95 (*0-9660883-6-0*) Benjamin Pub.

Moore, Marat. Women in the Mines: Portraits of Life & Work, 1914-1994. LC 95-45620. (Oral History Ser.: No. 20). (Illus.). 350p. 1996. 28.95 (*0-8057-7834-9*, Twyne) Mac Lib Ref.

Moore, Mardell & Klein, Charna. Washington Foundation Directory: How to Get Your Slice of the Pie. 3rd ed. 500p. Date not set. pap. 44.92 (*0-614-14931-2*) Consult Serv NW.

— Washington Foundation Directory, 1994: How to Get Your Slice of the Pie. 2nd ed. 456p. 1994. pap. 39.83 (*0-9617216-2-6*) Consult Serv NW.

Moore, Margaret. The Baron's Quest. (Historical Ser.). 1996. per. 4.99 (*0-373-28928-6*, 1-28928-9) Harlequin Bks.

— China Blossom. 1992. per. 3.99 (*0-373-28749-6*, 1-28749-9) Harlequin Bks.

— Complete Charleston: A Guide to the Architecture, History & Gardens of Charleston. LC 97-90985. (Illus.). viii, 216p. 1997. pap. 16.50 (*0-9660144-0-5*) TM Photog.

— The Dark Duke. (Most Unsuitable...Ser.). 1997. per. 4.99 (*0-373-28964-2*, 1-28964-4) Harlequin Bks.

***Moore, Margaret.** The Duke's Desire. (Historical Ser.: Vol. 528). 2000. mass mkt. 4.99 (*0-373-29128-0*, 1-29128-5) Harlequin Bks.

Moore, Margaret. Forests of the Night. large type ed. 1990. 27.99 (*0-7089-2175-2*) Ulverscroft.

— Foundations of Liberalism. LC 92-22186. 232p. 1993. text 48.00 (*0-19-827385-1*, Clarendon Pr) OUP.

***Moore, Margaret.** Manual of Veterinary Nursing. (Illus.). 208p. 2000. pap. text 69.95 (*0-905214-50-1*, Pub. by BSAVA) Iowa St U Pr.

Moore, Margaret. National Self-Determination & Secession. 296p. 1998. text 65.00 (*0-19-829384-4*) OUP.

— The Norman's Heart. (Historical Ser.). 1996. per. 4.50 (*0-373-28911-1*, 1-28911-5) Harlequin Bks.

***Moore, Margaret.** A Rogue's Embrace. 384p. 2000. mass mkt. 5.99 (*0-380-80268-6*, Avon Bks) Morrow Avon.

Moore, Margaret. The Rogue's Return. 1997. per. 4.99 (*0-373-28976-6*, 1-28976-8) Harlequin Bks.

— The Saxon. LC 95-13553. (Historical Ser.). 299p. 1995. per. 4.50 (*0-373-28868-9*, 1-28868-7) Harlequin Bks.

— A Scoundrel's Kiss. 384p. 1999. mass mkt. 5.99 (*0-380-80266-X*, Avon Bks) Morrow Avon.

— A Study of Young High School Graduates. LC 74-177081. (Columbia University. Teachers College. Contributions to Education Ser.: No. 583). reprint ed. 37.50 (*0-404-55583-7*) AMS Pr.

— Understanding British English. rev. ed. LC 97-16018. 240p. 1997. pap. text 12.95 (*0-8065-1939-8*, Citadel Pr) Carol Pub Group.

— The Viking. (Historical Ser.). 1993. mass mkt. 3.99 (*0-373-28800-X*, 1-28800-0) Harlequin Bks.

— Vows: (Weddings, Inc.) (Historical Ser.). 1994. per. 3.99 (*0-373-28848-4*, 1-28848-9) Harlequin Bks.

— A Warrior's Bride. (Warrior Ser.: No. 395). 1998. per. 4.99 (*0-373-28995-2*, 1-28995-8) Harlequin Bks.

— A Warrior's Honor: Warrior Series. (Historical Ser.: Vol. 420). 1998. per. 4.99 (*0-373-29020-9*, 1-29020-4) Harlequin Bks.

***Moore, Margaret.** Warrior's Kiss. (Historical Ser.: Vol. 504). 2000. per. 4.99 (*0-373-29104-3*) Harlequin Bks.

Moore, Margaret. A Warrior's Passion. (Historical Ser.: No. 440). 1998. per. 4.99 (*0-373-29040-3*, 0-29040-3) Harlequin Bks.

— A Warrior's Quest. (Historical Ser.). 1993. mass mkt. 3.99 (*0-373-28775-5*, 1-28775-4) Harlequin Bks.

— A Warrior's Way. 1994. per. 3.99 (*0-373-28824-7*, 1-28824-0) Harlequin Bks.

— The Wastrel. 1996. per. 4.99 (*0-373-28944-8*, 1-28944-6) Harlequin Bks.

— The Welshman's Bride. (Historical Ser.: No. 459). 1999. per. 4.99 (*0-373-29059-4*, 1-29059-2) Harlequin Bks.

— The Welshman's Way. LC 96-3730. 354p. 1995. per. 4.50 (*0-373-28895-6*, 1-28895-0) Harlequin Bks.

***Moore, Margaret & Palmer, Norman.** Calculations for Veterinary Nurses. (Illus.). 208p. 2000. pap. text 21.95 (*0-632-05498-0*, Pub. by Blckwell Science) Iowa St U Pr.

Moore, Margaret A., jt. auth. see Diamond, Barbara J.

An Asterisk (*) at the beginning of an entry indicates that the title is appearing for the first time.

Moore, Margaret B. The Salem World of Nathaniel Hawthorne. LC 97-38150. 296p. 1998. 37.50 (*0-8262-1149-6*) U of Mo Pr.

Moore, Margaret F. & Brown, P. Hume. The Lands of the Scottish Kings in England: The Honour of Huntington, the Liberty of Tyndale, & the Honour of Penrith. LC 70-91997. xii, 141p. 1973. reprint ed. lib. bdg. 35.00 (*0-678-00728-4*) Kelley.

Moore, Mariann, ed. & intro. see Moore, Paul E., Jr.

Moore, Marianne. Complete Poems. 320p. 1994. pap. 13.95 (*0-14-018851-7*, Penguin Classics) Viking Penguin.

— Complete Poems. 1995. reprint ed. lib. bdg. 39.95 (*1-56849-631-1*) Buccaneer Bks.

— Selected Letters of Marianne Moore. 624p. 1998. pap. 15.95 (*0-14-118120-6*) Viking Penguin.

Moore, Marianne, et al. Homage to Henry James (1934) 200p. 1971. 12.00 (*0-911858-17-2*) Appel.

Moore, Marianne, tr. see Stifter, Adalbert.

Moore, Marie A. Mastiffs. (Illus.). 1997. pap. 9.95 (*0-7938-2317-X*, KW-180S) TFH Pubns.

Moore, MariJo. Crow Quotes. 3rd rev. ed. (Illus.). 32p. (Orig.). 1996. pap. 7.00 (*0-9654921-0-9*) Renegade Planets.

Moore, Marijo. Returning to the Homeland: Cherokee Poetry & Short Stories. LC 94-61389. (Illus.). 112p. (Orig.). 1995. pap. 9.95 (*1-56664-073-3*) WorldComm.

— Spirit Voices of Bones. LC 96-72584. 96p. (Orig.). 1997. pap., per. 12.95 (*0-9654921-2-5*) Renegade Planets.

Moore, MariJo. Stars Are Birds: And Other Writings. LC 96-92712. (Illus.). 32p. (Orig.). (J). (gr. 1-12). 1996. pap. 8.95 (*0-9654921-1-7*) Renegade Planets.

— Tree Quotes. (Illus.). 32p. 1998. pap. 7.00 (*0-9654921-4-1*) Renegade Planets.

***Moore, MariJo, ed.** Feeding the Ancient Fires: A Collection of Writings by N. C. American Indians. (Illus.). 80p. 1999. pap. 12.00 (*0-9672180-0-4*, Pub. by Crossrds Pr NC) Renegade Planets.

Moore, MariJo, ed. see Sunalei.

Moore, Marilyn. Bigger Tips for Better Waitressing. 48p. 1998. pap. 4.95 (*0-910653-35-6*, 8118V, Red River Pr) Archival Servs.

— Gone to Missouri: From Whence They Came - to Where & When. 296p. (Orig.). 1991. pap. 19.95 (*1-56524-050-2*) InfoTech Pubns.

— A Guide to Licensing Your Artwork. 2nd rev. ed. x, 160p. 1999. pap. 16.95 (*0-9666327-0-2*) Cullen Grace.

***Moore, Marilyn, et al.** Foghorn Outdoors - Florida Camping. 2nd rev. ed. (Foghorn Outdoors Ser.). (Illus.). 670p. 2001. pap. 19.95 (*1-56691-215-6*, Pub. by Avalon Travel) Publishers Group.

Moore, Marilyn A., ed. see Knight-Ridder Corporation Staff.

Moore, Marilyn M. The Self-Published Cook: How to Write, Publish & Sell Your Own Cookbook. (Illus.). 142p. (Orig.). 1995. pap. 14.95 (*0-9603788-1-2*) Wooden Spoon.

— Wooden Spoon Baking Memoir: Apple-Butter Muffins, Shoofly Pie, & Other Amish-Mennonite Favorites. LC 96-47069. 160p. 1997. 22.00 (*0-87113-700-3*, Atlntc Mnthly) Grove-Atltic.

— Wooden Spoon Book of Home-Style Soups, Stews, Chowders, Chilis & Gumbos. LC 92-4961. 240p. 1993. pap. 14.00 (*0-87113-555-8*, Atlntc Mnthly) Grove-Atltic.

— The Wooden Spoon Book of Old Family Recipes: Meat & Potatoes & Other Comfort Foods. rev. ed. 208p. 1997. reprint ed. pap. 12.00 (*0-87113-694-5*, Atlntc Mnthly) Grove-Atltic.

— The Wooden Spoon Bread Book: The Secrets of Successful Baking. LC 86-32180. 432p. 1992. pap. 15.00 (*0-87113-505-1*, Atlntc Mnthly) Grove-Atltic.

— The Wooden Spoon Cookie Book: Favorite Home-Style Recipes from the Wooden Spoon Kitchen. LC 94-1256. 160p. 1994. 15.00 (*0-87113-601-5*, Atlntc Mnthly) Grove-Atltic.

— The Wooden Spoon Dessert Book: The Best You Ever Ate. LC 95-993. (Illus.). 304p. 1995. pap. 12.00 (*0-87113-607-4*, Atlntc Mnthly) Grove-Atltic.

Moore, Mark. How to Dodge a Dragon. (Small Group Studies). 80p. 1998. pap. 5.99 (*0-89900-828-3*) College Pr Pub.

— The Ministry of Ushering. 64p. 1986. pap. 5.99 (*0-8341-1143-8*) Beacon Hill.

Moore, Mark A. Moore's Historical Guide to the Battle of Bentonville. 2nd ed. (Illus.). 104p. 1997. pap. 14.95 (*1-882810-15-5*, 15-5) Savas Pub.

— Moore's Historical Guide to the Wilmington Campaign & the Battles for Fort Fisher. (Illus.). 240p. (Orig.). 1999. pap. 15.95 (*1-882810-19-8*) Savas Pub.

Moore, Mark H. Creating Public Value: Strategic Management in Government. LC 95-18074. (Illus.). 416p. (C). 1995. text 45.00 (*0-674-17557-3*) HUP.

— Creating Public Value: Strategic Management in Government. (Illus.). 416p. 1997. pap. text 24.95 (*0-674-17558-1*) HUP.

— Creating Public Value: Strategic Management in Government. LC 97-45635. 417p. 1997. reprint ed. lib. bdg. 37.95 (*0-7351-0004-7*) Replica Bks.

— From Children to Citizens. LC 87-9976. 1987. 96.95 (*0-387-96474-6*) Spr-Verlag.

Moore, Mark H., et al, eds. Public Duties: The Moral Obligations of Government Officials. LC 81-6253. 328p. reprint ed. pap. 101.70 (*0-7837-3835-8*, 204365600010) Bks Demand.

Moore, Mark H. & Gates, Margaret J. Inspectors General. LC 86-6728. (Social Science Perspectives Ser.). 112p. 1986. pap. text 9.95 (*0-87154-605-1*) Russell Sage.

Moore, Mark H. & Stephens, Darrel W. Beyond Command & Control: The Strategic Management of Police Departments. LC 91-60999. 145p. (Orig.). 1991. pap. 16.50 (*1-878734-25-3*) Police Exec Res.

Moore, Mark H., et al. Dangerous Offenders: The Elusive Target of Justice. (Illus.). 264p. 1985. 31.50 (*0-674-19065-3*) HUP.

Moore, Mark H., jt. auth. see Tonry, Michael H.

Moore, Mark H., ed. see National Research Council (U. S.), Panel on Altern.

Moore, Marsha L., jt. compiled by see Davis, Lenwood G.

Moore, Martha. Angels on the Roof. 192p. (YA). (gr. 7 up). 1999. reprint ed. mass mkt. 4.99 (*0-440-22806-9*) Dell.

— To Dance down Winter. 80p. 1995. pap. 8.95 (*1-887649-03-4*) Black Hat Pr.

— Under Mermaid Angel. (J). 1995. 20.95 (*0-385-31000-5*) BDD Bks Young Read.

Moore, Martha. Under the Mermaid Angel. LC 95-1991. (J). 1997. 9.09 (*0-606-12027-0*, Pub. by Turtleback) Demco.

Moore, Martha A. Under the Mermaid Angel. LC 95-1991. 192p. (YA). (gr. 7 up). 1995. 14.95 (*0-385-32160-0*, Delacorte Pr Bks) BDD Bks Young Read.

Moore, Martha M., et al, eds. Mammalian Cell Mutagenesis. LC 87-21784. (Banbury Reports: No. 28). (Illus.). 280p. 1988. text 77.00 (*0-87969-228-6*) Cold Spring Harbor.

Moore, Marti & Bostaph, Charles. Crossroads: A Back to School Career Guide for Adults. LC 79-2112. 128p. 1979. pap. 6.95 (*0-910328-29-3*) Sulzburger & Graham Pub.

Moore, Martin. Boston Revival, Eighteen Forty-Two: A Brief History of the Evangelical Churches of Boston, Together with a More Particular Account of the Revival of 1842. (Revival Library). (Illus.). 148p. (C). 1980. reprint ed. lib. bdg. 11.50 (*0-940033-16-X*) R O Roberts.

Moore, Martin L. ISDN Strategies. 312p. 1995. pap. 29.99 (*1-56884-459-X*) IDG Bks.

Moore, Marvelene C., jt. ed. see Anderson, William M.

Moore, Marven E., jt. auth. see De Jong, Nicolas J.

Moore, Marvin. The Antichrist & the New World Order. LC 92-42089. 127p. 1993. pap. 2.99 (*0-8163-1150-1*) Pacific Pr Pub Assn.

***Moore, Marvin.** The Coming Global Crisis: A Spiritual Survival Guide. LC 00-31374. 2000. write for info. (*0-8163-1798-4*) Pacific Pr Pub Assn.

Moore, Marvin. The Coming Great Calamity. LC 96-22749. 1996. pap. 10.99 (*0-8163-1354-7*) Pacific Pr Pub Assn.

— Conquering the Dragon Within: God's Provision for Assurance & Victory in the End Time. LC 94-39860. 1995. 13.99 (*0-8163-1252-4*) Pacific Pr Pub Assn.

— The Crisis of the End Time. LC 91-40487. (Anchor Ser.). 253p. 1992. pap. 11.99 (*0-8163-1085-8*) Pacific Pr Pub Assn.

Moore, Marvin, ed. see Venden, Morris L.

Moore, Marvin L. The Gospel vs. Legalism: How to Deal with Legalism's Insidious Influence. LC 93-45399. 1994. pap. 10.99 (*0-8280-0734-9*) Review & Herald.

Moore, Mary. Book of Snow. 30p. 1998. pap. 6.00 (*1-880834-36-7*) Cleveland St Univ Poetry Ctr.

— Forever Black but Always Proud. 195p. 1988. pap. text 19.95 (*0-9638983-0-2*) Moore-Ferguson.

— I'll Meet You in the Lobby. (American Autobiography Ser.). 250p. 1995. reprint ed. lib. bdg. 79.00 (*0-7812-8596-8*) Rprt Serv.

Moore, Mary A. Hide-&-Seek with God. LC 94-7551. 112p. (J). (ps-3). 1994. pap. 14.00 (*1-55896-277-8*, Skinner Hse Bks) Unitarian Univ.

Moore, Mary B. Attic Red-Figured & White-Ground Pottery. LC 96-52922. (Athenian Agora Ser.: Vol. 30). (Illus.). xxx, 420p. 1997. 160.00 (*0-87661-230-3*) Am Sch Athens.

***Moore, Mary B.** Desiring Voices: Women Sonneteers & Petrarchism. LC 99-36812. (Ad Feminam Ser.). 2000. 44.95 (*0-8093-2307-9*) S Ill U Pr.

Moore, Mary B. & Philippides, Mary Z. Attic Black-Figured Pottery. LC 86-20615. (Athenian Agora Ser.: Vol. 23). (Illus.). xvi, 382p. 1986. 60.00 (*0-87661-223-0*) Am Sch Athens.

Moore, Mary B., ed. see Beazley, John D.

Moore, Mary C. How to Master Change in Your Life: Sixty Seven Ways to Handle Life's Toughest Moments. LC 96-46476. 368p. (Orig.). 1997. pap. 14.00 (*1-57043-123-X*) Eckankar.

— Pocket Guide to Nutrition & Diet Therapy. 3rd ed. LC 96-15024. (Illus.). 496p. (C). (gr. 13). 1996. text 22.95 (*0-8151-7370-9*, 28269) Mosby Inc.

— Twenty-Eight Songs. (Women Composers Ser.). 1988. 27.50 (*0-306-79716-X*) Da Capo.

***Moore, Mary E.** A Crack in the Foundation: Using God's Principles to Strenghten Race Relations. Maahs, Iris, ed. 140p. 1999. pap. 19.95 (*0-9610702-9-3*) Mstrd Seed Pr.

Moore, Mary E. Ministering with the Earth. LC 97-44507. 160p. 1998. pap. 19.99 (*0-8272-2323-4*) Chalice Pr.

***Moore, Mary E.** Teaching from the Heart: Theology & Educational Method. LC 98-35795. 256p. 1998. pap. 17.00 (*1-56338-253-9*) TPI PA.

Moore, Mary E., et al, eds. Learning about Lupus: A User Friendly Guide. rev. ed. LC 97-73837. (Illus.). 224p. 1997. pap. text 7.00 (*0-9659530-0-9*) LFDV Inc.

***Moore, Mary Elizabeth.** Covenant & Call: Mission of the Future Church. LC 98-88818. 2000. pap. 14.95 (*0-88177-272-0*, DR272) Discipleship Res.

Moore, Mary L. & Givens, Susan R. Window of Opportunity: Interviewing by the Perinatal Nurse. Damus, Karla & Freda, Margaret C., eds. LC 94-39542. 1994. write for info. (*0-86525-063-4*) March of Dimes.

Moore, Mary Lou. Realities in Childbearing. 2nd ed. 1160p. 1983. text 79.00 (*0-7216-6498-9*, W B Saunders Co) Harcrt Hlth Sci Grp.

Moore, Mary M., ed. see Bartholomew.

Moore, Mary-Margaret. Reflections of an Elder Brother: Awakening from the Dream. 2nd rev. ed. LC 98-14943. 176p. 1998. pap. 12.95 (*1-56170-387-7*, 867) Hay House.

Moore, Mary R. The Zodiac: Exploring Human Qualities & Characteristics. 2nd rev. ed. LC 84-17977. (Vocabureader Workbook Ser.: No. 1). (Illus.). 112p. (Orig.). 1994. pap. text 10.50 (*0-86647-080-8*) Pro Lingua.

Moore, Mary S. Fireside Tales. (Illus.). 21p. (Orig.). (J). (gr. 5-12). 1990. pap. 7.95 (*0-913678-18-X*) New Day Pr.

— Fireside Tales. unabridged ed. (Illus.). 21p. (Orig.). (J). (gr. 5-12). 1990. pap. 10.00 incl. audio (*0-913678-19-8*) New Day Pr.

— Teen Self-Steam Pocket Coach: Exploring Life's Puzzles & Developing Personal Strength, 2 wkbks., Set. LC 94-92393. (YA). (gr. 6-12). 1994. pap. text 11.95 (*1-885574-01-0*) Courage Press.

— Young Entrepreneur's Guide to Creating What Matters Most: Building Attitudes, Behaviors & an Action Plan for Success in Your Own Business. LC 94-92392. 64p. (YA). (gr. 6-12). 1994. pap. text 9.95 (*1-885574-03-7*) Courage Press.

Moore, Mary T. After All. LC 96-2267. 416p. 1996. mass mkt. 6.50 (*0-440-22303-2*) Dell.

Moore, Mary V. Limited Liability Companies: Legal Research Guide - Pathfinder. LC 94-16191. (Legal Research Guides Ser.: Vol. 17). 96p. 1994. 40.00 (*0-89941-872-4*, 308250) W S Hein.

Moore, MaryAnn, jt. auth. see Kitchen, V. Rose.

Moore, Matthew S. "Dummy" Hoy: The Life & the Legend. 1999. pap. 40.00 (*0-9634016-4-5*, Deaf Life Pr) MSM Prods.

Moore, Matthew S. & Levitan, Linda. For Hearing People Only: Answers to Some of the Most Commonly Asked Questions about the Deaf Community, Its Culture & the "Deaf Reality" 2nd ed. 336p. (Orig.). 1993. pap. 19.95 (*0-9634016-1-0*); lib. bdg. 35.00 (*0-9634016-2-9*) MSM Prods.

Moore, Matthew S. & Panara, Robert. Great Deaf Americans. 2nd ed. LC 96-24582. 1996. pap. 24.95 (*0-9634016-6-1*, Deaf Life Pr) MSM Prods.

Moore, Maureen. Labor & Employment in Louisiana. 2nd rev. ed. LC 98-67065. 501p. 1998. ring bd. 105.00 (*0-327-00205-0*) LEXIS Pub.

Moore, Maureen F. Ada Compliance Manual for Employers. 2nd ed. 95.00 (*0-327-10318-3*) LEXIS Pub.

Moore, Maureen F. ADA Compliance Manual for Employers, Issue 3. 2nd ed. LC 94-65339. 200p. 1999. ring bd. write for info. (*0-327-00983-7*, 8012914) LEXIS Pub.

***Moore, Maureen F.** Employer Forms, Policies & Checklists. 3rd ed. 800p. 1999. ring bd. 110.00 (*0-327-04954-5*, 8232320) LEXIS Pub.

Moore, Maureen F. Personnel Forms & Employment Checklist, Issue 7. 2nd ed. 100p. 1999. ring bd. write for info. (*0-327-01030-4*, 8232417) LEXIS Pub.

— Personnel Forms & Employment Checklists. 440p. 1994. ring bd. 79.50 incl. disk (*0-614-05944-5*, MICHIE) LEXIS Pub.

— Personnel Forms & Employment Checklists. 2nd ed. Date not set. ring bd. 95.00 (*0-327-01026-6*, 82323-11, MICHIE) LEXIS Pub.

Moore, Maureen F. & Alder, Jonathan L. ADA Compliance Manual for Employers, Issue 9. 90p. 1997. ring bd. 95.00 (*0-409-25691-9*, 80125-11, MICHIE) LEXIS Pub.

— Family & Medical Leave: Federal & State Requirements. LC 93-35004. 540p. 1993. spiral bd. 80.00 (*0-250-48602-4*, MICHIE) LEXIS Pub.

Moore, Maureen F., et al. Labor & Employment in Louisiana. LC 93-19122. 370p. Date not set. ring bd. 95.00 (*0-409-25716-8*, 81356, MICHIE) LEXIS Pub.

Moore, Maureen F., jt. auth. see Alder, Jonathan L.

Moore, Maurice E., jt. auth. see Shaw, Clifford R.

Moore, Maurice G. Worlds in Motion. 46p. (Orig.). 1964. pap. text 9.00 (*0-943956-05-6*) Trippensee Pub.

Moore, Mavor. Six Plays by Mavor Moore. 208p. 1989. pap. 14.95 (*0-88922-271-1*, Pub. by Talonbks) Genl Dist Srvs.

Moore, Mavor & Dickens, Charles. A Christmas Carol - Musical. 72p. 1996. pap. 5.95 (*0-87129-609-8*, C07) Dramatic Pub.

Moore, Mavor, tr. see Gelinas, Gratien.

Moore, Maxine, jt. auth. see Moore, Bob.

Moore, Maxine, jt. ed. see Moore, Bob.

Moore, Maxori, et al. Transformation: A Rites of Passage Manual for African American Girls. 2nd ed. (Illus.). 83p. 1987. reprint ed. pap. 15.00 (*0-9621527-0-6*) Stars Pr.

Moore, Megan. Thrift Store Prospecting. (Illus.). 95p. 1994. reprint ed. pap. 29.95 (*1-879878-13-5*) Penultimate Pr.

Moore, Melinda K. & Forst, Martin L., eds. AIDS Education: Reaching Diverse Populations. LC 95-49715. (Illus.). 248p. 1996. 59.95 (*0-275-94904-4*, Praeger Pubs) Greenwood.

Moore, Melissa, ed. see Lafferty, Jerry.

Moore, Melita H., jt. auth. see Moore, Geoffrey H.

Moore, Melodie. The Complete Idiot's Guide to Household Solutions. (Complete Idiot's Guides Ser.). 352p. 1998. pap. 16.95 (*0-02-862706-7*) Macmillan Gen Ref.

— Vim & Vinegar: Moisten Cakes, Eliminate Grease, Remove Stains, Kill Weeds, Cean Pots & Pans, Soften Laundry, Unclog Drains, Control Dandruff, Season Salads. LC 96-45253. 224p. 1997. pap. 11.00 (*0-06-095223-7*, Perennial) HarperTrade.

Moore, Meredith A., jt. ed. see Carlin, Diana P.

Moore, Michael. Adventures in a TV Nation. LC 98-3581. (Illus.). 256p. 1998. pap. 13.00 (*0-06-098809-6*, Perennial) HarperTrade.

— Battalion at War: Singapore 1942. (C). 1989. 59.00 (*0-947893-11-3*) St Mut.

— Chocolate Chips - Contemporary Haiku. 6th ed. Barker, Windy, ed. 100p. (Orig.). 1995. per. 12.95 (*0-9610702-4-2*) Mstrd Seed Pr.

— Downsize This! Random Threats from an Unarmed American. 1997. pap. 66.00 (*0-06-097737-X*) HarpC.

— Downsize This! Random Threats from an Unarmed American. LC 97-26001. (Illus.). 336p. 1997. pap. 12.00 (*0-06-097733-7*, Perennial) HarperTrade.

— Herbs for the Urinary Tract. LC 98-15966. (Good Herb Guides Ser.). 96p. 1998. pap. 4.95 (*0-87983-815-9*, 38159K, Keats Publng) NTC Contemp Pub Co.

— Home Grown in the Haiku Garden. 4th ed. Barker, Windy, ed. 108p. (Orig.). Date not set. per. 12.95 (*0-9610702-5-0*) Mstrd Seed Pr.

— Knowing When . . . Being There. Perez, Barbara, ed. 73p. (Orig.). 1989. pap. 5.00 (*0-9610702-2-6*) Mstrd Seed Pr.

— Medicinal Plants of the Desert & Canyon West. (Illus.). 200p. 1989. pap. text 13.95 (*0-89013-182-1*) Museum NM Pr.

— Medicinal Plants of the Mountain West. 216p. 1979. pap. 13.95 (*0-89013-104-X*) Museum NM Pr.

— Medicinal Plants of the Pacific West. (Illus.). 360p. 1993. pap. 22.50 (*1-878610-31-7*) Red Crane Bks.

— Placing Blame: A Theory of Criminal Law. LC 98-137950. 870p. (C). 1998. text 115.00 (*0-19-825417-2*) OUP.

— Los Remedios: Traditional Herbal Remedies of the Southwest. LC 90-61682. (Illus.). 120p. (Orig.). 1990. pap. 9.95 (*1-878610-06-6*) Red Crane Bks.

Moore, Michael, et al. Contemporary Veiw of Haiku: Vista Contemporanea de Haiku. Galavan, Alicia Z., tr. (ENG & SPA., Illus.). 81p. (Orig.). 1996. pap. 12.95 (*0-9610702-6-9*) Mstrd Seed Pr.

Moore, Michael, jt. auth. see Geyerman, Chris.

Moore, Michael, ed. see Conroy, Teddie B., et al.

Moore, Michael, ed. & intro. see Curtin, L. S.

Moore, Michael, tr. see Ceronetti, Guido.

Moore, Michael C. Archeology of the Mixed Grass Prairie, Phases II & III: Hay & Cyclone Creeks Surveys & Predictive Modeling in the Quartermaster Watershed. (Archeological Resource Survey Report: No. 33). (Illus.). 244p. (C). 1988. pap. text 10.00 (*1-881346-22-6*) Univ OK Archeol.

Moore, Michael C., et al. Archeological Investigations Within the Central Little River Drainage Basin, Cleveland & Pottawatomie Counties, Oklahoma. (Archeological Resource Survey Report: No. 31). (Illus.). 186p. (C). 1988. pap. text 6.00 (*1-881346-20-X*) Univ OK Archeol.

Moore, Michael G. The Unicorn Riders of the Orb. (Illus.). 227p. 1986. pap. 2.95 (*0-9613282-1-5*) MGM Bks.

Moore, Michael G., et al, eds. Contemporary Issues in American Distance Education. 446p. 1990. 99.95 (*0-08-040233-X*, Prgamon Press) Buttrwrth-Heinemann.

— Contemporary Issues in American Distance Education. LC 90-31196. (Illus.). 445p. 1990. reprint ed. pap. 138.00 (*0-608-07431-4*, 206765800009) Bks Demand.

Moore, Michael G., pref. Distance Education for Corporate & Military Training. LC 98-160510. (Readings in Distance Education Ser.: No. 3). 145p. (C). 1992. pap. text 25.00 (*1-877780-08-1*) ACSDE.

Moore, Michael G. & Kearsley, Greg P. Distance Education: A Systems View. (Education Ser.). 1995. pap. 81.95 (*0-534-26496-4*) Wadsworth Pub.

Moore, Michael G. & Koble, Margaret A., eds. K-12 Distance Education: Learning, Instruction, & Teacher Training. LC 98-160565. (Readings in Distance Education Ser.: Vol. 5). 137p. (Orig.). (C). 1997. pap. text 25.00 (*1-877780-20-0*) ACSDE.

— Video-Based Telecommunications in Distance Education. (Readings in Distance Education Ser.: No. 4). 144p. (Orig.). (C). 1995. pap. text 25.00 (*1-877780-12-X*) ACSDE.

Moore, Michael G., jt. auth. see Thompson, Melody M.

Moore, Michael J. & Viscusi, W. Kip. Compensation Mechanisms for the Job Risks: Wages, Workers' Compensation, & Product Liability. LC 89-28882. (Illus.). 198p. reprint ed. pap. 61.40 (*0-608-02564-X*, 206320900004) Bks Demand.

Moore, Michael L. A Review of Search & Reconnaissance Theory Literature. LC 75-131015. 104p. 1970. 22.00 (*0-403-04520-7*) Scholarly.

Moore, Michael L. & Outslay, Edmund. U. S. Tax Aspects of Doing Business Abroad. 4th rev. ed. LC 95-5646. 1995. 66.00 (*0-87051-164-5*) Am Inst CPA.

***Moore, Michael L. & Outslay, Edmund.** U. S. Tax Aspects of Doing Business Abroad. 5th ed. LC 99-89702. 823p. 2000. pap. text 56.25 (*0-87051-291-9*, 061068) Am Inst CPA.

Moore, Michael L. & Outslay, Edmund. Unites State Tax Aspects of Doing Business Abroad. 4th rev. ed. LC 95-5646. 836p. Date not set. reprint ed. pap. 200.00 (*0-608-20768-3*, 207186700003) Bks Demand.

Moore, Michael P., ed. see Franz, Marion J.

***Moore, Michael S.** Educating Oneself in Public: Critical Essays in Jurisprudence. 480p. 2000. text 98.00 (*0-19-826879-3*) OUP.

Moore, Michalea. Next Services. LC 80-5677. (Lucky Heart Bk.). (Illus.). 27p. 1980. reprint ed. pap. 30.00 (*0-7837-9152-6*, 204985200003) Bks Demand.

***Moore, Michele.** The Only Menopause Guide You'll Need. LC 99-54553. (Illus.). 157p. 2000. 42.50 (*0-8018-6407-0*); pap. 13.95 (*0-8018-6408-9*) Johns Hopkins.

Moore, Michele, et al, eds. Children's Reflections on Family Life. 160p. 1996. 79.95 (*0-7507-0573-6*, Falmer Pr); pap. 27.95 (*0-7507-0574-4*, Falmer Pr) Taylor & Francis.

Moore, Michele M. Oklahoma City: A Detailed Account of the Bombing of the Alfred P. Murrah Federal Building, Oklahoma City, OK, April 19, 1995, 3 vols. Incl. Vol. 1. Oklahoma City Day One: A Detailed Account of the Bombing of the Alfred P. Murrah Federal Building,

An Asterisk (*) at the beginning of an entry indicates that the title is appearing for the first time.

Oklahoma City, OK, April 19, 1995. unabridged ed. (Illus.). 640p. 1996. pap. 29.95 (0-9653307-1-0); 75.00 (0-9653307-0-2) Harvest Trust.
Moore, Michelle. Dispatcher's Guide to Policing. 96p. 1995. pap. text, per. 19.95 (0-7872-1387-X) Kendall-Hunt.
Moore, Michelle M. Oklahoma City Day One: A Detailed Account of the Bombing of the Alfred P. Murrah Federal Building, Oklahoma City, OK, April 19, 1995, Vol. 1. limited num. unabridged ed. 640p. 1996. 60.00 (0-9653307-9-6) Harvest Trust.
Moore, Mickela, jt. ed. see Campbell, Dennis.
Moore, Midge. Embosom. LC 96-90452. 293p. (Orig.). 1996. pap. 12.95 (0-9653213-0-4) Upstart Press.
Moore, Mike. Marmosets in Captivity. (C). 1989. 50.00 (0-946873-95-X, Pub. by Basset Pubns) St Mut.
Moore, Mike, jt. auth. see Burgard, Mike.
Moore, Miles D. The Bears of Paris. LC 95-61228. (Capital Collection). 80p. (Orig.). 1996. pap. 10.00 (0-915380-32-3) Word Works.
Moore, Milton. How Much Price Competition. (C). 1970. 27.95 (0-7735-0083-9, Pub. by McG-Queens Univ Pr) CUP Services.
Moore, Miltona, jt. auth. see Pinkston, Patricia T.
Moore, Miriam. The Kwanzaa Contest. LC 95-26631. (Illus.). 64p. (J). (gr. 3-4). 1996. pap. 3.95 (0-7868-1122-6, Pub. by Hyprn Ppbks) Little.
— The Kwanzaa Contest. 1996. 9.40 (0-606-10245-0) Turtleback.
Moore, Miriam & Taylor, Penny. Koi's Python. LC 97-23994. (Illus.). 64p. (J). (gr. 3-4). 1998. lib. bdg. 14.49 (0-7868-2285-6, Pub. by Hyperion) Little.
— Koi's Python. LC 97-23994. (Illus.). 64p. (J). (gr. 3-4). 1998. pap. 3.95 (0-7868-1227-3, Pub. by Hyprn Child) Time Warner.
— The Kwanzaa Contest. (Illus.). 64p. (J). 1997. lib. bdg. 13.89 (0-7868-2336-4, Pub. by Disney Pr) Little.
— The Kwanzaa Contest. LC 95-26631. (Illus.). 64p. (J). (gr. 3-4). 1996. 13.45 (0-7868-0261-8, Pub. by Hyprn Child) Time Warner.
Moore, Miriam A. Last Dance. 256p. (Orig.). 1997. mass mkt. 5.99 (0-380-79118-8, Avon Bks) Morrow Avon.
Moore, Miriam Ann. I Will Survive. LC 99-94815. (Marti Hirsch Mystery Ser.). 304p. 1999. mass mkt. 5.99 (0-380-79120-X, Avon Bks) Morrow Avon.
— Stayin' Alive. (Marti Hirsch Mystery Ser.). 272p. 1998. mass mkt. 5.99 (0-380-79119-6, Avon Bks) Morrow Avon.
***Moore, Missy.** Americans in Bear Country: Living the Russian Way. LC 00-190557. 235p. 2000. 25.00 (0-7388-1822-4); pap. 18.00 (0-7388-1823-2) Xlibris Corp.
Moore, Mordecai, jt. auth. see Petrizzi, Jennifer A.
Moore, Moses. Orishatukeh Faduma: Liberal Theology & Evangelical Pan-Africanism, 1857-1946. LC 95-39630. (ATLA Monographs: No. 40). 320p. 1996. 49.50 (0-8108-3091-4) Scarecrow.
***Moore, Myreah.** Date Like A Man . . . . . To Get the Man You Want, LC 99-51635. 256p. 2000. 19.95 (0-06-019498-7) HarpC.
Moore, N. Pulpit Confessions: Exposing the Black Church. 93p. 1997. 16.00 (0-9658299-2-8, Exodus Bks) AOP Bks.
Moore, N., ed. The Book of the Foundation of St. Bartholomew's Church in London. (Early English Text Society Original Ser.: No. 163). 1996. reprint ed. 27.00 (0-85991-901-3, Pub. by EETS) Boydell & Brewer.
Moore, N., tr. see Windisch, Ernst W.
Moore, N. Anthony. Mosby's USMLE Step 1 Reviews: Anatomy. LC 96-2738. (Ace the Boards Ser.). (Illus.). 480p. (C). (gr. 13). 1996. pap. text 29.95 incl. 3.5 hd (0-8151-6905-1, 27051) Mosby Inc.
Moore, N. Hudson. The Collector's Manual. LC 76-30474. (Paperback Ser.). (Illus.). 1977. reprint ed. pap. 6.95 (0-306-80061-6) Da Capo.
Moore, N. M., Jr. & Darring, Walt. The Crossroader: Memoirs of a Professional Gambler. (Illus.). 177p. (Orig.). 1992. pap. 12.50 (0-9633399-6-6) Regency Pr AL.
Moore, N. W. & International Union for Conservation of Nature & Natural Resources Staff. Dragonflies. LC 98-121785. vx, 28 p. 1997. write for info. (2-8317-0420-0, Pub. by IUCN) Island Pr.
Moore, Nancy. The Olympic Ideal of Persistence Vol. 4: Personal Leadership Through the Olympic Ideals. (U. S. Olympic Committee's Curriculum Guide Ser.). (Illus.). 16p. (YA). 1997. pap., wbk. ed. 3.95 (1-58000-003-7) Griffin CA.
Moore, Nancy, ed. The Five Olympic Ideals Vol. 1: Personal Leadership Through the Olympic Ideals. (U. S. Olympic Committee's Curriculum Guide Ser.). (Illus.). 16p. (YA). 1997. pap., teacher ed. 3.95 (1-58000-000-2) Griffin CA.
— The Olympic Ideal of Commitment Vol. 6: Personal Leadership Through the Olympic Ideals. (U. S. Olympic Committee's Curriculum Guide Ser.). (Illus.). 16p. (YA). 1997. pap., wbk. ed. 3.95 (1-58000-005-3) Griffin CA.
— The Olympic Ideal of Discipline Vol. 5: Personal Leadership Through the Olympic Ideals. (U. S. Olympic Committee's Curriculum Guide Ser.). (Illus.). 16p. (YA). 1997. pap., wbk. ed. 3.95 (1-58000-004-5) Griffin CA.
— The Olympic Ideal of Focus Vol. 3: Personal Leadership Through the Olympic Ideals. (U. S. Olympic Committee's Curriculum Guide Ser.). (Illus.). 16p. (YA). 1997. pap., wbk. ed. 3.95 (1-58000-002-9) Griffin CA.
Moore, Nancy & Komras, Henrietta. Patient-Focused Healing: Integrating Caring & Curing in Health Care. LC 93-4218. (Health-Management Ser.). 226p. 1993. text 39.95 (1-55542-584-4) Jossey-Bass.
Moore, Nancy, ed. see Retton, Mary L.
Moore, Nancy Y. & Arroyo Center Staff. Materiel Distribution: Improving Support to Army Operations in Peace & War. LC 96-9515. 1997. pap. text 9.00 (0-8330-2424-8, MR-642-A) Rand Corp.
Moore, Nancy Y., et al. Assessment of the Economic Impacts of California's Drought on Urban Areas: A Research Agenda. LC 93-42318. 1993. pap. text 13.00 (0-8330-1489-7, MR-251-CUWA) Rand Corp.
— Marine Corps Sourcing Competitions: Historical Performance & Direction for Improvement. (Illus.). 71p. 1999. pap. 6.00 (0-8330-2692-5, DB-250-USMC) Rand Corp.
Moore, Nathan, ed. Mislah Oh! A Tribute to William Barnabas Moore of Charlotteville, Tobago. (Illus.). x, 166p. (Orig.). 1997. pap. 13.95 (0-9657359-0-7) Phoenyx Binding.
Moore, Nathaniel F. Ancient Mineralogy: An Inquiry Respecting Mineral Substances Mentioned by the Ancients. Albritton, Claude C., Jr., ed. LC 77-6532. (History of Geology Ser.). 1978. reprint ed. lib. bdg. 23.95 (0-405-10452-9) Ayer.
***Moore, Neecie.** Bountiful Health, Boundless Energy, Brilliant Youth: The Facts about DHEA. 216p. 1999. pap. 12.95 (0-9660700-2-X, Pub. by Validation Pr) ACCESS Pubs Network.
— A Long & Healthy Life: The Facts about High Level Wellness. 144p. 1999. pap. 12.95 (0-9660700-1-1, Pub. by Validation Pr) ACCESS Pubs Network.
Moore, Neecie. The Missing Link: The Facts about Glyconutrients. LC 99-198149. 288p. 1999. pap. 14.95 (0-9660700-0-3, Pub. by Validation Pr) ACCESS Pubs Network.
Moore, Nelson J. An Annotated Checklist of the Birds of Killdeer Plains Wildlife Area. (Informative Circular Ser.: No. 2). 1996. pap. text 2.00 (0-86727-124-8) Ohio Bio Survey.
Moore, Nelwyn B., jt. auth. see Davidson, J. Kenneth, Sr.
Moore, Nelwyn B., jt. auth. see Davidson, J. Kenneth.
Moore, Newlyn B., jt. ed. see Davidson Sr., Kenneth J.
***Moore, Nick.** How to Do Research: The Complete Guide to Designing & Managing Research Projects. 3rd ed. 173p. 2000. 35.00 (1-85604-358-4, Pub. by Library Association) Bernan Associates.
Moore, Nick, jt. ed. see Hughes, Kirsty.
Moore-Nickel, Glenice. Bitterroot Backroads, Vol. 3. (Illus.). 40p. 1996. pap. 10.50 (1-56770-369-0) S Scheewe Pubns.
***Moore, Nina M.** Governing Race: Policy, Process & the Politics of Race. LC 00-22859. 240p. 2000. 59.00 (0-275-96761-1, C6761, Praeger Pubs) Greenwood.
Moore, Norman. The History of the Study of Medicine in the British Isles. LC 75-23746. reprint ed. 32.50 (0-404-13352-5) AMS Pr.
— NYT Forecasting Budgets: 25 Keys to Successful Planning. LC 99-44631. (Illus.). 104p. 1999. pap. 12.95 (0-86730-776-5) Lebhar Friedman.
Moore, Olive. Collected Writings. LC 91-29755. 424p. 1992. 22.95 (1-56478-000-7) Dalkey Arch.
— Spleen. 2nd rev. ed. LC 96-16131. 136p. 1996. pap. 10.95 (1-56478-148-8) Dalkey Arch.
Moore, Opha. History of Franklin County, Ohio, 3 vols., Set. (Illus.). 1424p. 1993. reprint ed. lib. bdg. 139.00 (0-685-66022-2) Higginson Bk Co.
Moore, Orene, jt. ed. see Moore, Leon R.
***Moore, P.** Astronomy, Vol. 1. 288p. 2000. 40.00 (0-7503-0620-3) IOP Pub.
Moore, P. Lebanon: A New Era. 1997. 170.00 (1-85564-547-5, Pub. by Euromoney) Am Educ Systs.
Moore, P., ed. see Mobberly, Martin.
Moore, P., ed. see Ratledge, David.
Moore, P. B., jt. ed. see Nriagu, Jerome O.
Moore, P. D., et al. Pollen Analysis. 2nd ed. (Illus.). 224p. 1994. pap. 49.95 (0-86542-895-6) Blackwell Sci.
Moore, P. D., jt. auth. see Cox, C. B.
Moore, P. G. Risk in Business Decision. LC 73-179508. (London Business School Ser.). (Illus.). xi, 365p. 1972. write for info. (0-582-45003-9) Longman.
Moore, P. G. & Seed, R., eds. The Ecology of Rocky Coasts: Essays Presented to J. R. Lewis. (Illus.). 467p. (C). 1998. text 40.00 (0-7881-5506-7) DIANE Pub.
Moore, P. G. & Seed, Raymond B. The Ecology of Rock Coasts. 455p. 1986. text 87.00 (0-231-06274-5) Col U Pr.
Moore, P. J., ed. Analysis & Design of Foundations for Vibration. 520p. (C). 1984. 214.00 (90-6191-525-2, Pub. by A A Balkema) Ashgate Pub Co.
Moore, P. K., jt. auth. see Brain, Susan D.
Moore, P. M. & Lahita, Robert G. Neuropsychiatric Manifestations of Systemic Lupus Erythematosus. LC 97-28522. (Annals of the New York Academy of Sciences Ser.: No. 823). 336p. 1997. pap. 110.00 (1-57331-081-6) NY Acad Sci.
Moore, P. W., jt. auth. see Nachtigall, P. E.
Moore, Pamela. VoCab: Comic Mnemonics. LC 97-71731. (Newton Street Educational Ser.: Vol. 1). (Illus.). 106p. 1997. 25.00 (0-9658307-9-9) Headcode.
Moore, Pamela, ed. Building Bodies. LC 96-49717. (Illus.). 224p. (C). 1997. text 48.00 (0-8135-2437-7); pap. text 17.95 (0-8135-2438-5) Rutgers U Pr.
Moore, Pamela, et al. Student Manual for Computers: Inside & Out. 5th ed. Witte, Joan L., ed. (Illus.). 272p. 1996. pap. 12.00 (1-880066-14-9) Pippin Publishing.
Moore, Pamela J., ed. see G'Orge-Walker, Pat.
Moore, Pamela Joy, ed. see Walker, Pat George.
Moore, Pamela Rosewell. Safer Than a Known Way. LC 88-26514. 224p. (gr. 11). 1990. pap. 9.99 (0-8007-9175-4) Chosen Bks.
— Safer Than a Known Way. LC 88-26514. 224p. (YA). (gr. 10). 1996. mass mkt. 5.99 (0-8007-8631-9, Spire) Revell.
***Moore, Pamela Rosewell.** When Spring Comes Late: Finding Your Way Through Depression. 176p. 2000. pap. 11.99 (0-8007-9279-3) Chosen Bks.
Moore, Pamela Rosewell, jt. auth. see Moore, Carey.
Moore, Patricia, jt. auth. see Moore, John.
Moore, Patricia, ed. see Berlit, Peter.
***Moore, Patricia M.** Neuropsychotic Manifestations of Systematic Lupus Erythematosus. 1999. pap. text 22.50 (0-8018-6216-7) Johns Hopkins.
Moore, Patricia M. & Lahita, Robert G., eds. Neuropsychiatric Manifestations of Systemic Lupus Erythemafosus, Vol. 823. LC 97-28522. (Annals of the New York Academy of Sciences Ser.: No. 823), 336p. 1997. 110.00 (1-57331-080-8) NY Acad Sci.
Moore, Patrick. Atlas of the Universe. LC 99-162477. (Illus.). 288p. (C). 1998. 39.95 (0-521-64210-8) Cambridge U Pr.
— Atlas of the Universe. LC 94-22177. 272p. 1994. 29.95 (0-528-83704-4) Rand McNally.
— Comets & Shooting Stars. LC 94-43938. (Starry Sky Ser.). (Illus.). 24p. (J). (gr. k-3). 1993. lib. bdg. 18.90 (1-56294-625-0, Copper Beech Bks) Millbrook Pr.
***Moore, Patrick.** Exploring the Night Sky with Binoculars. (Illus.). 224p. (C). 2000. text Price not set. (0-521-79053-0) Cambridge U Pr.
Moore, Patrick. Exploring the Night Sky with Binoculars. 3rd ed. (Illus.). 221p. (C). 1996. pap. 16.95 (0-521-55538-8); text 32.95 (0-521-55492-6) Cambridge U Pr.
***Moore, Patrick.** Exploring the Night Sky with Binoculars. 4th ed. (Illus.). 224p. (C). 2000. pap. text 18.95 (0-521-79390-4) Cambridge U Pr.
Moore, Patrick. Eyes on the Universe: The Story of the Telescope. LC 97-7324. (Illus.). 128p. 1997. pap. 19.95 (3-540-76164-0) Spr-Verlag.
— The Great Astronomical Revolution: 1534-1687 & the Space Age Epilogue. 256p. pap. 18.95 (1-898563-19-5, Pub. by Horwood Pub) Paul & Co Pubs.
— The Great Astronomical Revolution: 1534-1687 & the Space Age Epilogue. 256p. 1995. 34.95 (1-898563-18-7, Pub. by Horwood Pub) Paul & Co Pubs.
***Moore, Patrick.** Green Spirit: Trees Are the Answer. 2000. 20.00 (0-9686404-0-0, Pub. by GEL1) Genl Dist Srvs.
Moore, Patrick. Iowa. 2nd ed. (Orig.). 1998. reprint ed. mass mkt. 7.95 (1-56333-702-9, Hard Candy) Masquerade.
— Mission to the Planets: The Illustrated Story of Man's Exploration of the Solar System. 1990. 24.95 (0-393-02872-0) Norton.
— Modern Amateur Astronomer. (Practical Astronomy Ser.). (Illus.). 176p. 1995. 24.95 (0-387-19900-4) Spr-Verlag.
— Observational Amateur Astronomer. (Practical Astronomy Ser.). (Illus.). 288p. 1995. 24.95 (0-387-19899-7) Spr-Verlag.
— The Observer's Year. LC 97-42028. (Illus.). 400p. 1997. pap. 29.95 (3-540-76147-0) Spr-Verlag.
— Patrick Moore on Mars. LC 99-218330. (Illus.). 224p. 1999. 29.95 (0-304-35069-9) Continuum.
***Moore, Patrick.** Patrick Moore on Mars. (Illus.). 2000. pap. 19.95 (1-84188-004-3) Seven Dials.
Moore, Patrick. The Planet Neptune. 1989. text 29.95 (0-470-21366-3) P-H.
— The Planets. LC 94-43928. (Starry Sky Ser.). (Illus.). 24p. (J). (gr. k-3). 1996. lib. bdg. 18.90 (1-56294-624-2, Copper Beech Bks) Millbrook Pr.
***Moore, Patrick.** Stargazing: Astronomy Without a Telescope. (Illus.). 210p. 2000. pap. write for info. (0-521-79445-5) Cambridge U Pr.
— Stargazing: Astronomy Without a Telescope. 2nd ed. (Illus.). 210p. 2000. 32.95 (0-521-79052-2) Cambridge U Pr.
Moore, Patrick. The Starry Sky. (Illus.). 96p. (J). (gr. k-3). 1995. 12.95 (1-56294-181-X, Copper Beech Bks) Millbrook Pr.
***Moore, Patrick.** Starry Sky, LC 99-40547. (Illus.). 96p. (J). (gr. k-3). 1999. 12.95 (0-7613-0825-3, Copper Beech Bks) Millbrook Pr.
Moore, Patrick. The Stars. LC 94-43937. (Starry Sky Ser.). (Illus.). 24p. (J). (gr. k-3). lib. bdg. 18.90 (1-56294-623-4, Copper Beech Bks) Millbrook Pr.
— Sun. (Illus.). 1968. 4.95 (0-393-06276-7) Norton.
— The Sun & Moon. (Starry Sky Ser.). (Illus.). 24p. (J). (gr. k-3). 1995. lib. bdg. 18.90 (1-56294-622-6, Copper Beech Bks) Millbrook Pr.
— Suns, Myths & Men. rev. ed. LC 68-27145. (Illus.). 1969. 7.95 (0-393-06364-X) Norton.
— Teach Yourself Astronomy. LC 94-68413. (Illus.). 224p. 1995. pap. 12.95 (0-8442-3903-8, Teach Yrslf) NTC Contemp Pub Co.
Moore, Patrick, ed. The Modern Amateur Astronomer. (Practical Astronomy Ser.). 1995. pap. 24.95 (3-540-19900-4) Spr-Verlag.
— The Observational Amateur Astronomer. (Practical Astronomy Ser.). 1995. pap. 24.95 (3-540-19899-7) Spr-Verlag.
— Small Astronomical Observatories: Amateur & Professional Designs & Constructions. LC 96-13224. (Practical Astronomy Ser.). 240p. 1996. pap. 32.95 (3-540-19913-6) Spr-Verlag.
***Moore, Patrick & Chapman, A.** Patrick Moore's Millennium Yearbook: The View from 1001 AD. LC 99-37448. (Illus.). xii, 100p. 1999. pap. 19.95 (1-85233-619-6, Pub. by Spr-Verlag) Spr-Verlag.
Moore, Patrick & Jackson, Francis. Life on Mars. (Illus.). 1966. 4.50 (0-393-05225-7) Norton.
Moore, Patrick & Tirion, Wil. The Cambridge Guide to Stars & Planets. (Illus.). 256p. (C). 1997. pap. 14.95 (0-521-58582-1) Cambridge U Pr.
Moore, Patrick, jt. auth. see Cattermole, Peter.
Moore, Patrick, jt. auth. see Hunt, Garry E.
Moore, Patrick, jt. auth. see Maunder, Michael.
Moore, Patrick, jt. auth. see Maunder, Michael J. de F.
Moore, Patrick J. & Wheelock, Angela, eds. Wolverine Myths & Visions: Dene Traditions from Northern Alberta. LC 89-29379. (Studies in the Anthropology of North American Indians). (Illus.). xvi, 259p. 1990. text 45.00 (0-8032-8161-7) U of Nebr Pr.
Moore, Patrick O., jt. auth. see Tracy, Noel A.
***Moore, Paul.** Presences: A Bishop's Life in the City. LC 99-33821. (Illus.). 344p. 1999. pap. 16.95 (1-56101-168-1) Cowley Pubns.
Moore, Paul. Presences: A Bishop's Life in the City. (Illus.). 344p. 1997. text 28.00 (0-374-17567-5) FS&G.
Moore, Paul, et al. All about Citrus & Subtropical Fruits. Bond, Richard H., ed. LC 85-70878. (Illus.). 96p. (Orig.). 1985. pap. 9.95 (0-89721-065-4, Ortho Bks) Meredith Bks.
Moore, Paul, jt. auth. see Dye, David.
***Moore, Paul E., Jr.** Results by Action, Not by Thoughts: Become a Superman, Super Woman. Moore, Mariann, ed. & intro. by. (Illus.). 280p. (C). 2000. pap. write for info. (0-9619918-1-X) Discovery Lab.
Moore, Pauline. Journeys of the Heart. LC 99-61586. 48p. 1999. pap. 5.95 (1-56167-439-7, Five Star Spec Ed) Am Literary Pr.
Moore, Peggy. Before I Wake. 160p. 1991. per. 7.95 (0-8187-0136-6) Harlo Press.
Moore, Peggy A. How Not to Abuse Your Child. (Illus.). 60p. 1984. pap. text 5.00 (0-9613078-3-8) Detroit Black.
— Neighbors & Family Coloring Book. (Illus.). 20p. (Orig.). (J). (gr. k up). 1989. pap. 2.50 (0-9613078-4-6) Detroit Black.
Moore, Peggy S. The Case of the Missing Bike & Other Things. 2nd rev. ed. (Illus.). 40p. (Orig.). (J). (gr. 4-6). 1992. pap. 5.95 (0-9613078-1-1) Detroit Black.
— My Very First Book of Poetry & Other Things. (Poetry & Essays Ser.: No. 1). (Illus.). 16p. (J). (gr. 3-5). 1982. pap. 1.98 (0-9613078-0-3) Detroit Black.
Moore, Perry. Evaluating Health Maintenance Organizations: A Guide for Employee Benefits Managers. LC 91-4719. 208p. 1991. 57.95 (0-89930-557-1, MHG/, Quorum Bks) Greenwood.
Moore, Peter. The Destruction of Penn Station. (Illus.). 144p. 1999. 35.00 (1-891024-05-1) Dist Art Pubs.
— Gone Writing: The Poems of Moore on Sunday. LC 99-36021. 120p. 1999. 12.95 (0-8166-3432-7, Pub. by U of Minn Pr) Chicago Distribution Ctr.
Moore, Peter, ed. Can a Bishop Be Wrong? Ten Scholars Challenge John Shelby Spong. LC 97-36015. 176p. 1998. pap. 17.95 (0-8192-1726-3) Morehouse Pub.
— Handbook of Botulinum Toxin Treatment. LC 95-184. 320p. 1995. 110.00 (0-632-03616-8) Blackwell Sci.
Moore, Peter & Hey, Kenneth R. The Caterpillar Doesn't Know: How Personal Change Drives Organizational Change. LC 98-11999. 256p. 1998. 30.00 (0-684-83429-4) S&S Trade.
***Moore, Peter C.** A Church to Believe In. 2nd ed. Wetzel, Cheryl, ed. (Illus.). 2000. 14.00 (1-893051-01-3) Latimer Pr.
Moore, Peter D., et al. Global Environmental Change. LC 96-6168. 1996. pap. 42.95 (0-632-03638-9) Blackwell Sci.
Moore, Peter D., jt. auth. see Cox, C. Barry.
Moore, Peter G. The Business of Risk. LC 82-23594. 256p. 1984. pap. text 19.95 (0-521-28497-X) Cambridge U Pr.
Moore, Phil. Using Computers in English: A Practical Guide. (Teaching Secondary English Ser.). 200p. 1986. pap. 14.95 (0-416-36190-0, 9929) Routledge.
Moore, Philip. Acting Out: Therapy for Groups. 176p. 1997. text 65.95 (1-85742-274-0, Pub. by Arena) Ashgate Pub Co.
— Brazil: The Next Step. 3rd ed. (Euromoney Country Guide Ser.). 1998. 170.00 (1-85564-676-5, Pub. by Euromoney) Am Educ Systs.
— Islamic Finance: A Partnership for Growth. 254p. 1997. 170.00 (1-85564-552-1, Pub. by Euromoney) Am Educ Systs.
— Nightmare of the Apocalypse: The Rabbi Conspiracy. LC 97-91511. (Illus.). 365p. (Orig.). 1997. pap. 15.00 (1-57915-998-2) Rams Head Pr.
Moore, Philip J., jt. ed. see Telfer, Ross A.
Moore, Philip N. The End of Earth: As We Know It. (Illus.). 490p. 1999. pap. 15.00 (1-57915-995-8) Rams Head Pr.
— The End of History Vol. 1: Messiah Conspiracy, 2 Vols. abr. ed. 1050p. 1995. pap. write for info. (0-9648623-3-6) Rams Head Pr.

M

reinterpretation of the Messianic prophecies, to the sorrow of many, then & now. We are the first to examine this conspiracy in such depth! We also present evidence that Columbus was a Jew who believed in Jesus & that Isaac Newton, who believed the 2nd coming would occur in the 21st century, considered his own biblical/apocalyptic writings more important than his works on science. We feature previously unpublished letters written by Albert Einstein, urging that the Newton papers on religion be made public. We cover Christian Zionists who saved Jews from the holocaust. We also give reasons to believe we are within approximately 30 years of the Apocalypse & Second Coming! Also contains the latest information of near-death experiences & the Dead Sea Scrolls, as well as scientific evidence proving creation over evolution. Some say Rabin's assassination was encoded in Hebrew Bible text. We quote the text Gematria. This 1,238-page volume is the result of 12 years of research & is illustrated with 600 photos! To order & for additional information about 4 shorter titles (released in 1997-8) related to this subject, by the same author contact: RamsHead Press International, P.O. Box 12227, Atlanta, GA 30355; 404-233-8023; 1-800-RAMS-HEAD(1-800-726-7432); FAX: 404-816-9994. Also available via Amazon.com & Bookwire.com. (PA) ***Publisher Paid Annotation.***

— The End of History Vol. 2: Messiah Conspiracy, 2 Vols. 1050p. 1995. pap. write for info. (*0-9648623-1-X*) Rams Head Pr.

— The End of History Vols. 1 & 2: Messiah Conspiracy, 2 vols. 1050p. 1995. pap. write for info. (*0-9648623-2-8*) Rams Head Pr.

***Moore, Philip N.** The End of History - Messiah Conspiracy. Seliktar, Ofira, ed. LC 95-92646. 1238p. 1999. reprint ed. pap. (*1-57915-993-1*) Rams Head Pr.

Moore, Philip N. Eternal Security for True Believers: The Rabin Assassination Predicted. LC 97-66134. (Illus.). 64p. (Orig.). 1997. pap. 5.00 (*1-57915-999-0*) Rams Head Pr.

— A Liberal Interpretation on the Prophecy of Israel-Disproved: Nostradamus Biblical Sage or Socerer. LC 97-68229. (Illus.). 50p. (Orig.). 1997. pap. 5.00 (*1-57915-997-4*) Rams Head Pr.

— What If Hitler Won the War: Where Would We Be Today. LC 98-92925. (Illus.). 190p. 1998. pap. 19.95 (*1-57915-996-6*) Rams Head Pr.

***Moore, Phillip.** The Pfandbrief: A European Perspective. 2000. pap. text 225.00 (*1-85564-755-9*, Pub. by Euromoney) Am Educ Systs.

Moore, Phillip, jt. auth. see Fairley, Alan.

Moore, Phyllis B. No Other Gods: An Interpretation of the Biblical Myth for a Transbiblical Age. (Chiron Monographs: Vol. 6). 208p. (Orig.). 1992. pap. 5.95 (*0-933029-46-2*) Chiron Pubns.

Moore, Phyllis B., ed. see Clarson, Laura E.

Moore Picture Trust Staff. Nelson Augustus Moore: Connecticut Landscape Painter. (Illus.). 144p. 1994. text 40.00 (*0-9637491-0-2*) Moore Picture.

Moore, Powell A. Calumet Region, Indiana's Last Frontier. 685p. 1999. pap. 27.95 (*1-885323-16-6*) IN Hist Bureau.

Moore, Prentiss. The Garden in Winter & Other Poems. LC 81-13117. (University of Texas Press Poetry Ser.: Vol. 7). 116p. 1981. reprint ed. pap. 36.00 (*0-7837-8939-4*, 204964900002) Bks Demand.

— Mediterraneans: A Serenade. (Orig.). 1986. pap. text 2.95 (*0-941169-03-0*) Black Chin Pr.

Moore, R. Biology. Date not set. pap. text, lab manual ed. 32.25 (*0-697-29269-X*) McGraw.

— An Introduction to Numerical Functional Analysis. LC 84-25168. (Mathematics & Its Applications Ser.). 156p. 1985. text 44.95 (*0-470-20119-3*) P-H.

Moore, R. & Reppert, S. Suprachiasmatic Nucleus: The Mind's Clock. Klein, Donald F. et al, eds. (Illus.). 488p. 1991. text 88.00 (*0-19-506250-7*) OUP.

Moore, R. E. Methods & Applications of Interval Analysis. LC 79-67191. (Studies in Applied Mathematics: No. 2). xi, 190p. 1979. pap. text 36.00 (*0-89871-161-4*) Soc Indus-Appl Math.

Moore, R. H. 1st & 2nd Stuart Horse Artillery. (Virginia Regimental Histories Ser.). (Illus.). 185p. 1998. 25.00 (*1-56190-108-3*) H E Howard.

Moore, R. I. The Birth of Popular Heresy. LC 95-165459. (Medieval Academy Reprints for Teaching Ser.: MART 33). 176p. (C). 1995. reprint ed. pap. text 14.95 (*0-8020-7659-9*) U of Toronto Pr.

***Moore, R. I.** The First European Revolution. 2000. 62.95 (*0-631-18479-1*); pap. 27.95 (*0-631-22277-4*) Blackwell Pubs.

Moore, R. I. The Formation of a Persecuting Society: Power & Deviance in Western Europe. 192p. 1990. pap. 29.95 (*0-631-17145-2*) Blackwell Pubs.

— The Origins of European Dissent. (MART Thirty Medieval Academy Reprints for Teaching Ser.: No. 30). 322p. 1994. reprint ed. pap. text 17.95 (*0-8020-7566-5*) U of Toronto Pr.

Moore, R. I., jt. ed. see Mayr-Harting, Henry.

Moore, R. J. Churchill, Cripps, & India, 1939-1945. 1979. 49.95 (*0-19-822485-0*) OUP.

— The Crisis of Indian Unity, 1917-1940. 280p. 1974. 36.00 (*0-19-821560-6*) OUP.

Moore, R. J. Endgames of Empire: Studies of Britain's Indian Problem. 240p. 1989. 24.95 (*0-19-562143-3*) OUP.

— Making the New Commonwealth. (Illus.). 224p. 1987. text 59.00 (*0-19-820112-5*) OUP.

Moore, R. Kelvin. The Psalms of Lamentation & the Enigma of Suffering. LC 95-46887. (Biblical Press Ser.: Vol. 50). 144p. 1996. text 69.95 (*0-7734-2416-4*, Mellen Biblical Pr) E Mellen.

Moore, R. Laurence. Religious Outsiders & the Making of Americans. 272p. 1987. pap. text 19.95 (*0-19-505188-2*) OUP.

— Selling God: American Religion in the Marketplace of Culture. 336p. 1995. pap. 14.95 (*0-19-509838-2*) OUP.

Moore, R. T. Measurable, Continuous & Smooth Vectors for Semigroups & Group Representations. LC 52-42839. (Memoirs Ser.: No. 1/78). 80p. 1968. pap. 16.00 (*0-8218-1278-5*, MEMO/1/78) Am Math.

***Moore, Rachel O.** Savage Theory: Cinema as Modern Magic. 256p. 1999. pap. text 17.95 (*0-8223-2388-5*) Duke.

— Savage Theory: Cinema as Modern Magic. LC 99-14159. (Illus.). 256p. 1999. 49.95 (*0-8223-2354-0*) Duke.

Moore, Ralph. Financial Freedom: Learn to Manage Your Personal Money Matters. (Illus.). 177p. (Orig.). 1990. mass mkt. write for info. (*0-9628127-0-6*) Straight St.

Moore, Ralph & Tanner, Dinah. Porcelain & Pottery Tea Tiles. LC 95-126901. (Illus.). 48p. 1994. pap. 6.48 (*1-57080-004-9*, 4071) Antique Pubns.

Moore, Ralph E. Friends: How to Evangelize Gen X. Ching, Darlene O.S., ed. LC 99-204514. 1997. pap. text 13.95 (*0-9628127-6-5*) Straight St.

Moore, Ralph E. & Beach, Dan. Let Go of the Ring: The Hope Chapel Story. 3rd rev. ed. 200p. Date not set. mass mkt. 13.95 (*0-9628127-1-4*) Straight St.

***Moore, Ralph E. & Beach, Dan.** Let Go of the Ring: The Hope Chapel Story. 4th ed. (Illus.). 240p. 2000. pap. text 12.95 (*0-9628127-2-2*) Straight St.

Moore, Ralph L. Basic Instrumentation Lecture Notes & Study Guide, 2 vols., Vol. 1. 3rd ed. LC 82-81083. (Illus.). 187p. (Orig.). reprint ed. pap., student ed. 58.00 (*0-7837-4884-1*, 204487700001) Bks Demand.

— Basic Instrumentation Lecture Notes & Study Guide, 2 vols., Vol. 2. LC 82-81083. (Illus.). 125p. (Orig.). reprint ed. pap., student ed. 38.80 (*0-7837-4885-X*, 204487700002) Bks Demand.

Moore, Ralph L. Control of Centrifugal Compressors. LC 88-35767. 311p. reprint ed. pap. 96.50 (*0-608-20290-8*, 207154900001) Bks Demand.

Moore, Ralph L. Environmental Protection by the Neutralization of Wastewater Using pH Control. LC 95-10626. 1995. 50.00 (*1-55617-526-4*) ISA.

— Neutralization of Waste Water by pH Control. LC 77-94491. (Instrument Society of America Monographs: No. 1). (Illus.). 177p. reprint ed. pap. 54.90 (*0-7837-6058-2*, 205250400007) Bks Demand.

Moore, Ralph L., ed. see Instrument Society of America Staff.

Moore, Ramona C. Little Angel Tiffany & the Boy Who Wants a Toy. (Illus.). 16p. (J). (gr. k-3). 1997. pap. 6.00 (*0-8059-4115-0*) Dorrance.

***Moore, Ramona L.** Lap Talks: Casual Conversations with God. 156p. 1999. pap. 9.95 (*0-7392-0230-8*, PO3267) Morris Pubng.

Moore, Randall C. Writing to Learn Botany. 112p. (C). 1995. text. write for info. (*0-697-17455-7*, WCB McGr Hill) McGrw-H Hghr Educ.

Moore, Randall c. & Lewis, Ricki. Life, 6 pts. 2nd ed. 936p. 1994. boxed set. write for info. (*0-697-15925-6*, WCB McGr Hill) McGrw-H Hghr Educ.

Moore, Randall C. & Vodopich, Darrell S. Biology. 368p. (C). 1995. student ed., spiral bd. write for info. (*0-697-03777-0*, WCB McGr Hill) McGrw-H Hghr Educ.

— Botany. 2nd ed. LC 96-60294. 832p. (C). 1997. text. write for info. (*0-697-28623-1*, WCB McGr Hill) McGrw-H Hghr Educ.

— Botany. 2nd ed. 304p. (C). 1997. text, lab manual ed. write for info. (*0-697-28628-2*, WCB McGr Hill) McGrw-H Hghr Educ.

Moore, Randall C., et al. Botany. LC 94-70837. 928p. (C). 1994. text. write for info. (*0-697-03775-4*, WCB McGr Hill) McGrw-H Hghr Educ.

— Botany. 208p. (C). 1995. text, student ed. 20.00 (*0-697-03776-2*, WCB McGr Hill) McGrw-H Hghr Educ.

— Botany, Vols. 1 & 2. (C). 1995. ring bd. write for info. (*0-697-29398-X*, WCB McGr Hill) McGrw-H Hghr Educ.

Moore, Randall c., et al. Botany: Plant Diversity-Botany, Vol. 2. 384p. (C). 1994. text. write for info. (*0-697-16657-0*, WCB McGr Hill) McGrw-H Hghr Educ.

— Botany: Plant Form & Function, Vol. 1. 592p. (C). 1994. text. write for info. (*0-697-16656-2*, WCB McGr Hill) McGrw-H Hghr Educ.

Moore, Randall c., jt. auth. see Lewis, Ricki.

Moore, Randall S., jt. auth. see Madsen, Clifford K.

Moore, Randy. Writing to Learn Biology. 352p. (C). 1992. pap. text 26.50 (*0-03-074189-0*, Pub. by SCP) Harcourt.

— Writing to Learn Science. LC 96-68672. (C). 1995. pap. text 23.50 (*0-03-096488-1*, Pub. by Harcourt Coll Pubs) Harcourt.

Moore, Randy, ed. Biology Labs That Work: The Best of How-to-Do-Its. 1994. 12.00 (*0-941212-18-1*) Natl Assn Bio Tchrs.

— Vegetative Compatibility Responses in Plants. LC 83-72004. (Illus.). 176p. 1983. pap. 19.50 (*0-918954-40-1*) Baylor Univ Pr.

Moore, Ray A., ed. Culture & Religion in Japanese-American Relations: Essays on Uchimura Kanzo. LC 81-21966. (Michigan Papers in Japanese Studies: No. 5). x, 142p. 1982. pap. 8.95 (*0-939512-10-6*) U MI Japan.

Moore, Rayburn S. Constance Fenimore Woolson. LC 62-19478. (Twayne's United States Authors Ser.). 1963. pap. text 4.95 (*0-8290-0008-9*); lib. bdg. 11.95 (*0-89197-710-4*) Irvington.

— Paul Hamilton Hayne. Bowman, Sylvia E., ed. LC 73-125818. (Twayne's United States Authors Ser.). 184p. (C). 1972. lib. bdg. 20.95 (*0-8290-1711-9*) Irvington.

Moore, Rayburn S., ed. see James, Henry.

Moore, Rayburn S., ed. see Woolson, Constance F.

Moore, Raymond A., jt. auth. see Whicker, Marcia L.

Moore, Raymond C. Treatise on Invertebrate Paleontology Pt. U: Echinodermata 3: Asterozoa-Echinozoa, 2 vols. LC 53-12913. (Illus.). 725p. 1966. reprint ed. 62.00 (*0-8137-3022-8*) Geol Soc.

Moore, Raymond C., ed. Treatise on Invertebrate Paleontology. LC 53-12913. 267p. reprint ed. pap. 82.80 (*0-7837-1257-X*, 204139400020) Bks Demand.

— Treatise on Invertebrate Paleontology Pt. I: Mollusca 1. LC 53-12913. (Illus.). 374p. 1960. 43.75 (*0-8137-3009-0*) Geol Soc.

— Treatise on Invertebrate Paleontology Pt. D: Protista 3 (Chiefly Radiolaria, Tintinnina) LC 53-12913. (Illus.). 207p. 1954. reprint ed. 25.00 (*0-8137-3004-X*) Geol Soc.

— Treatise on Invertebrate Paleontology Pt. F: Coelenterata. LC 53-12913. (Illus.). 508p. 1956. 27.50 (*0-8137-3006-6*) Geol Soc.

— Treatise on Invertebrate Paleontology Pt. H: Brachiopoda, 2 vols. LC 53-12913. (Illus.). 959p. 1965. reprint ed. 65.00 (*0-8137-3008-2*) Geol Soc.

— Treatise on Invertebrate Paleontology Pt. K: Mollusca 3. LC 53-12913. (Illus.). 547p. 1964. 44.00 (*0-8137-3011-2*) Geol Soc.

— Treatise on Invertebrate Paleontology Pt. N: Mollusca 6, Bivalvia, Vols. 1-2. LC 53-12913. (Illus.). 989p. 1969. 44.25 (*0-8137-3014-7*) Geol Soc.

— Treatise on Invertebrate Paleontology Pt. O: Arthropoda 1. LC 53-12913. (Illus.). 579p. 1959. 27.50 (*0-8137-3015-5*) Geol Soc.

— Treatise on Invertebrate Paleontology Pt. P: Arthropoda 2. LC 53-12913. (Illus.). 198p. 1955. 24.50 (*0-8137-3016-3*) Geol Soc.

— Treatise on Invertebrate Paleontology Pt. Q: Arthropoda 3: Crustacea: Ostracoda. LC 53-12913. (Illus.). 465p. 1961. 26.75 (*0-8137-3017-1*) Geol Soc.

— Treatise on Invertebrate Paleontology Pt. S: Echinodermata 1: General Characters Homalozoa-Crinozoa (Except Crinoidea), 2 vols. LC 53-12913. (Illus.). 679p. 1967. 32.00 (*0-8137-3020-1*) Geol Soc.

— Treatise on Invertebrate Paleontology Pt. W: Miscellanea. LC 53-12913. (Illus.). 284p. 1962. 18.00 (*0-8137-3024-4*) Geol Soc.

— Treatise on Invertebrate Paleontology Vol. I, Pt. H: Brachcopoda. rev. ed. (Illus.). 560p. 1997. 100.00 (*0-8137-3108-9*) Geol Soc.

— Treatise on Invertebrate Paleontology Vol. I, Pt. O: Trilobita. rev. ed. (Illus.). 260p. 1997. 100.00 (*0-8137-3115-1*) Geol Soc.

Moore, Raymond C. & Teichert, Curt, eds. Treatise on Invertebrate Paleontology Pt. R: Arthropoda 4: Crustacea (Except Ostracoda): Myriapoda, Vols. 1-2. LC 53-12913. (Illus.). 687p. 1969. 32.00 (*0-8137-3018-X*) Geol Soc.

— Treatise on Invertebrate Paleontology Pt. T: Echinodermata 2: Crinoidea, 3 vols. LC 53-12913. (Illus.). 1978. 61.00 (*0-8137-3021-X*) Geol Soc.

Moore, Raymond C., et al. Invertebrate Fossils. 765p. (C). 1952. 95.31 (*0-07-043020-9*) McGraw.

Moore, Raymond C., ed. see Bulman, O. M.

Moore, Raymond C., ed. see Loeblich, Alfred R., Jr. & Tappan, Helen.

Moore, Raymond C., ed. see Stenzel, Henryk B.

Moore, Raymond S. Communications Receivers: The Vacuum Tube Era, 1932-1981. 4th rev. ed. (Illus.). 136p. 1997. pap. 19.95 (*0-9618882-4-5*) RSM Comns.

— School Can Wait II. LC 78-19198. xii, 281p. 1979. pap. 12.95 (*0-8425-1314-0*) Moore Fnd.

— Transmitters, Exciters & Power Amplifiers: 1930-1980. (Illus.). 144p. 1997. pap. 21.95 (*0-9618882-3-7*) RSM Comns.

Moore, Raymond S. & Moore, Dorothy N. Home Grown Kids: A Practical Handbook for Teaching Your Children at Home. LC 80-53252. 233p. 1981. reprint ed. pap. 9.95 (*0-8499-3007-3*) Moore Fnd.

— Home Made Health: A Family Guide to Nutrition, Exercise, Stress Control, & Preventive Medicine. 5th ed. LC 86-15874. 233p. 1996. reprint ed. pap. 11.95 (*0-8499-3172-X*) Moore Fnd.

— Home Style Teaching: A Handbook for Parents & Teachers. 10th ed. LC 84-5127. 203p. 1991. 9.95 (*0-8499-0397-1*) Moore Fnd.

— Minding Your Own Business: A Common Sense Guide to Home Management & Industry. large type unabridged ed. LC 90-44989. xii, 267p. (Orig.). 1994. pap. 11.95 (*0-7852-7830-3*) Moore Fnd.

— On, No! Miss Dent Is Coming to Dinner: A Story of Manners. 2nd ed. (Illus.). 32p. (J). (gr. 3-5). 1985. 5.95 (*0-8407-6654-8*) Moore Fnd.

— The Successful Homeschool Family Handbook: A Creative & Stress-Free Approach to Homeschooling. 10th large type rev. unabridged ed. LC 93-40688. 300p. 1997. pap. 12.99 (*0-7852-8175-4*) Nelson.

Moore, Raymond S., et al. Better Late Than Early: A New Approach to Your Child's Education. 7th unabridged ed. LC 74-22275. xx, 229p. 1993. reprint ed. pap. 9.95 (*0-88349-049-8*) Moore Fnd.

— Guess Who Took the Battered-Up Bike: A Story of Kindness. 2nd ed. (Illus.). 30p. (J). (gr. 3-5). 1985. 5.95 (*0-8407-6651-3*) Moore Fnd.

— Home Built Discipline: Developing Initiative, Self-Control, & Responsibility in Your Child. 2nd rev. unabridged ed. (Illus.). 257p. 1990. pap. 11.95 (*0-8407-3159-0*) Moore Fnd.

— Quit? Not Me! A Story of Dependability. 2nd ed. (Illus.). 30p. (J). (gr. 3-5). 1985. 5.95 (*0-8407-6652-1*) Moore Fnd.

Moore, Raymond S., ed. see McGuffey, William H.

Moore, Reavis. Native Artists of Europe. LC 94-11128. (Rainbow Warrior Artists Ser.). (Illus.). 48p. (J). (gr. 4-7). 1994. 14.95 (*1-56261-158-5*, J Muir) Avalon Travel.

— Native Artists of Europe. (Illus.). 48p. 1995. pap. text 9.95 (*1-56261-230-1*) Avalon Travel.

— Native Artists of North America. LC 93-16254. (Rainbow Warrior Artists Ser.). (Illus.). 48p. (J). (gr. 4-7). 1993. 14.95 (*1-56261-105-4*) Avalon Travel.

Moore, Rebecca. In Defense of People's Temple. LC 88-8933. (Studies in American Religion: Vol. 32). 150p. 1988. lib. bdg. 69.95 (*0-88946-676-9*) E Mellen.

— The Jonestown Letters: Correspondence of the Moore Family, 1970-1985. LC 86-18192. (Studies in American Religion: Vol. 23). (Illus.). 398p. 1986. lib. bdg. 109.95 (*0-88946-667-X*) E Mellen.

Moore, Rebecca & McGehee, Fielding, III, eds. The Need for a Second Look at Jonestown: Remembering Its People. (Studies in American Religion: Vol. 41). 248p. 1989. write for info. (*0-88946-649-1*) E Mellen.

Moore, Rebecca & McGehee, Fielding M., III, eds. New Religious Movements, Mass Suicide & Peoples Temple: Scholarly Perspectives on a Tragedy. LC 88-34382. (Studies in American Religion). 256p. 1989. lib. bdg. 89.95 (*0-88946-680-7*) E Mellen.

Moore, Renee, tr. see Flynn, Ted & Flynn, Maureen.

Moore, Rhonda, tr. see Day, Marlena & Nature Institute Staff.

Moore, Richard. Bottom Is Back. LC 94-6557. 96p. (Orig.). 1994. pap. 11.95 (*0-914061-43-7*) Orchises Pr.

***Moore, Richard.** The Creation of Reality in Psychoanalysis: A View of the Contributions of Donald Spence, Roy Schafer, Robert Stolorow, Irwin Z. Hoffman & Beyond. LC 98-52181. 200p. 1999. 34.50 (*0-88163-303-8*) Analytic Pr.

Moore, Richard. The High Blood Pressure Solution: Natural Prevention & Cure with the K Factor. LC 92-46210. 256p. (Orig.). 1993. pap. 14.95 (*0-89281-446-2*, Heal Arts VT) Inner Tradit.

— The Investigator. 220p. 1991. 18.95 (*0-934257-77-9*) Story Line.

— The Mouse Whole: An Epic. LC 95-69220. 223p. 1996. pap. 15.95 (*0-942544-50-1*) Negative Capability Pr.

— No More Bottom. LC 90-28176. 80p. (Orig.). 1991. pap. 10.00 (*0-914061-22-4*) Orchises Pr.

— Pygmies & Pyramids. LC 97-41900. 80p. 1998. pap. 12.95 (*0-914061-71-2*) Orchises Pr.

Moore, Richard, photos by. Gardens of Georgia. (Illus.). 1989. 50.00 (*0-934601-76-3*) Peachtree Pubs.

— Gardens of Georgia. limited ed. (Illus.). 1989. 75.00 (*1-56145-009-X*) Peachtree Pubs.

Moore, Richard, jt. auth. see Hoese, H Dickson.

Moore, Richard, tr. see Fedorov, V. B., ed.

Moore, Richard, tr. see Slavitt, David R. & Bovie, Palmer, eds.

Moore, Richard B. The Name "Negro" (African Studies). reprint ed. 18.00 (*0-938818-97-X*) ECA Assoc.

— The Name "Negro" Its Origin Evil Use. 88p. 1994. reprint ed. pap. 7.00 (*1-56411-087-7*, 4BBG0095) Untd Bros & Sis.

— The Name "Negro" - Its Origin & Evil Use. rev. ed. Turner, W. Burghardt & Turner, Joyce M., eds. LC 91-77147. 110p. 1992. reprint ed. 19.95 (*0-933121-36-9*); reprint ed. pap. 8.95 (*0-933121-35-0*) Black Classic.

Moore, Richard C., ed. Carlisle's Guide to Government. LC 93-85942. (Orig.). 1993. pap. 12.95 (*0-9639034-0-3*) Univ Wholesale.

— Carlisle's Guide to Government. 256p. (Orig.). 1994. pap. 12.95 (*0-9639034-4-6*) Univ Wholesale.

Moore, Richard C. & Ettore, Eugene. Anthology of French Horn Music. 160p. 1986. spiral bd. 17.95 (*1-56222-191-4*, 93801) Mel Bay.

Moore, Richard E. & Purcell, Nadine H., eds. Pacific Northwest Americana Supplement, 1949-1974. LC 81-65510. 372p. 1981. pap. 20.00 (*0-8323-0389-5*) Binford Mort.

Moore, Richard H. Theodis Boneright in the Land of Make Believe. (Illus.). 32p. (J). (gr. 2-5). 1995. 12.95 (*0-9648170-0-4*) World Crusade.

Moore, Richard J., jt. auth. see Dietz, Henry A.

Moore, Richard V., ed. Nuclear Power. LC 77-142962. (Institution of Electrical Engineers Monograph Ser.: Vol. 6). (Illus.). 208p. reprint ed. pap. 64.50 (*0-8357-8975-6*, 203345300086) Bks Demand.

Moore, Richter H., Jr., et al. Readings in Criminal Justice. LC 75-38727. 1976. pap. 10.95 (*0-672-61371-9*, Bobbs) Macmillan.

Moore, Richter H., Jr., jt. ed. see Fields, Charles B.

Moore, Rick Dale. God Saves: Lessons from the Elisha Stories. (JSOT Supplement Ser.: No. 95). 169p. 1990. 52.50 (*1-85075-259-1*, Pub. by Sheffield Acad) CUP Services.

Moore, Rickie. Make the Circle Bigger: We Need Each Other. LC 90-4065. (Illus.). 128p. (Orig.). 1990. pap. 19.95 (*0-89334-133-9*) Humanics Ltd.

— Make the Circle Bigger: We Need Each Other. LC 90-4065. (Illus.). 128p. (Orig.). 1990. lib. bdg. 29.95 (*0-89334-193-2*, 193-2) Humanics Ltd.

Moore-Rinvolucri, Mina, tr. see Veyne, Paul.

An Asterisk (*) at the beginning of an entry indicates that the title is appearing for the first time.

Moore, Rob & Ozga, Jenny, eds. Curriculum Policy. 158p. 1990. text 33.50 (*0-08-041022-7*, Pergamon Pr); pap. text 17.50 (*0-08-040818-4*, Pergamon Pr) Elsevier.

Moore, Robert. Logic & Representation. LC 94-40413. (CSLI Lecture Notes Ser.: No. 39). 210p. 1995. 49.95 (*1-881526-16-X*); pap. 20.95 (*1-881526-15-1*) CSLI.

— Positive Action in Action: Equal Opportunities & Declining Opportunities on Merseyside. LC 97-71713. (Research in Ethnic Relations Ser.). (Illus.). 144p. 1997. text 59.95 (*1-84014-108-5*, Pub. by Ashgate Pub) Ashgate Pub Co.

Moore, Robert & Gillette, Douglas. King, Warrior, Magician, Lover: Rediscovering the Archetypes of the Mature Masculine. LC 89-45991. (Illus.). 192p. 1991. reprint ed. pap. 14.00 (*0-06-250606-4*, Pub. by Harper SF) HarpC.

— The King Within: Accessing the King in the Male Psyche. 344p. 1993. pap. 11.00 (*0-380-72068-X*, Avon Bks) Morrow Avon.

— The Lover Within: Accessing the Lover in the Male Psyche. 288p. 1995. pap. 12.50 (*0-380-72071-X*, Avon Bks) Morrow Avon.

— The Magician Within: Accessing the Shaman in the Male Psyche. 304p. 1994. reprint ed. pap. 12.50 (*0-380-72070-1*, Avon Bks) Morrow Avon.

— The Warrior Within: Accessing the Knight in the Male Psyche. 328p. 1993. pap. 11.00 (*0-380-72069-8*, Avon Bks) Morrow Avon.

Moore, Robert, ed. see Rivers-Moore, Judith.

Moore, Robert A. A Life for the Confederacy: As Recorded in the Pocket Diaries of Pvt. Robert A. Moore, Co. G 17th Mississippi Regiment, Confederate Guards, Holly Springs, Mississippi. Silver, James W., ed. (Illus.). 182p. 1992. reprint ed. 25.00 (*0-916107-38-8*) Broadfoot.

Moore, Robert C. The Political Reality of Freedom of the Press in Zambia. 158p. (C). 1992. lib. bdg. 41.00 (*0-8191-8649-X*) U Pr of Amer.

Moore, Robert C., jt. ed. see Pisacane, Vincent L.

Moore, Robert E. Henry Purcell & the Restoration Theatre. LC 73-15057. (Illus.). 223p. (C). 1974. reprint ed. lib. bdg. 59.50 (*0-8371-7155-5*, MOHQ, Greenwood Pr) Greenwood.

Moore, Robert E., jt. auth. see Terrell, Milton J.

Moore, Robert H., II. The Charlottesville, Lee, Lynchburg & Johnson's Bedford Artillery. (Virginia Regimental Histories Ser.). (Illus.). 142p. 1990. 19.95 (*1-56190-008-7*) H E Howard.

Moore, Robert H. Chew's Ashby, Shoemaker's Lynchburg & the Newtown Artillery. (Virginia Regimental Histories Ser.). (Illus.). 126p. 1995. 19.95 (*1-56190-076-1*) H E Howard.

Moore, Robert H., II. The Danville, Eighth Star New Market & Dixie Artillery. (Virginia Regimental Histories Ser.). (Illus.). 110p. 1989. 19.95 (*0-930919-72-6*) H E Howard.

— Graham's Petersburg, Jackson's Kanawha, & Lurty's Roanoke Horse Artillery. (Virginia Regimental Histories Ser.). (Illus.). 140p. 1996. 25.00 (*1-56190-097-4*) H E Howard.

Moore, Robert H. Miscellaneous Light Artillery (1st Virginia, Wise, Middlesex, Hanover, Magruder, Manchester, Campbell Long Island Artillery) (Virginia Regimental Histories Ser.). (Illus.). 141p. 1998. 19.95 (*1-56190-105-9*) H E Howard.

— The Richmond, Fayette, Hampden, Thomas & Blount's Lynchburg Artillery. (Virginia Regimental Histories Ser.). (Illus.). 178p. 1991. 19.95 (*1-56190-018-4*) H E Howard.

Moore, Robert J., Jr. Native Americans: A Portrait: The Art & Travels of Charles Bird King, George Catlin, & Karl Bodmer. LC 97-8563. (Illus.). 280p. 1997. 60.00 (*1-55670-616-2*) Stewart Tabori & Chang.

***Moore, Robert J., Jr.** Natural Wonders of the World. (Illus.). 2000. 59.95 (*0-7892-0667-6*) Abbeville Pr.

***Moore, Robert J. & Accomazzo, Laura.** America from the Air LC 99-38886. 1999. write for info. (*1-57145-218-4*) Advantage Pubs.

Moore, Robert J. & Schwenz, Richard W., eds. Physical Chemistry: Developing a Dynamic Curriculum. LC 92-35619. (Illus.). 488p. 1993. pap. text 55.00 (*0-8412-2503-6*, Pub. by Am Chemical) OUP.

Moore, Robert J., jt. auth. see Morton, Leslie T.

Moore, Robert K., Jr. The Sociology of Work. (C). 2000. 36.00 (*0-205-15899-4*, Macmillan Coll) P-H.

Moore, Robert L. Foundations of Point Set Theory. LC 62-8325. (Colloquium Publications: Vol. 13). 419p. 1932. reprint ed. pap. 83.00 (*0-8218-1013-8*, COLL/13) Am Math.

— John Wesley & Authority: A Psychological Perspective. LC 79-13709. (American Academy of Religion. Dissertation Ser.: No. 29). 255p. reprint ed. pap. 79.10 (*0-7837-5417-5*, 204518100005) Bks Demand.

— Jung & Christianity in Dialogue: Faith, Feminism & Hermeneutics. Meckel, Daniel J., ed. (Jung & Christianity Ser.). 1990. pap. 12.95 (*0-8091-3187-0*) Paulist Pr.

Moore, Robert L., ed. Sources of Vitality in American Church Life. LC 78-71065. (Studies in Ministry & Parish Life). 1978. text 14.95 (*0-913552-14-3*) Exploration Pr.

Moore, Robert L. & Studenmund, A. H. Instructor's Manual to Accompany Introduction to Economics: The Wealth & Poverty of Nations, by Gwartney & Stroup. 180p. (C). 1994. pap. text, teacher ed. 33.75 (*0-03-001836-6*) Dryden Pr.

***Moore, Robert M., III, ed.** The Hidden America: Social Problems in Rural America for the Twenty-First Century. 2001. 48.50 (*1-57591-047-0*) Susquehanna U Pr.

Moore, Robert P. Silent Doomsday. 400p. 1998. mass mkt. 5.99 (*0-8439-4395-5*, Leisure Bks) Dorchester Pub Co.

Moore, Robert S., jt. ed. see Lupinski, John H.

Moore, Robert T., jt. auth. see Jorgensen, Palle E.

Moore, Roberta, et al. College Success. 254p. 1996. pap. text 33.00 (*0-13-527391-9*) P-H.

Moore, Roberta, jt. auth. see Mantus, Roberta.

Moore, Robin. The Bread Sister of Sinking Creek. LC 89-36400. (Illus.). 160p. (J). (gr. 4-7). 1990. 15.00 (*0-397-32418-9*); lib. bdg. 14.89 (*0-397-32419-7*) HarpC Child Bks.

— The Bread Sister of Sinking Creek. LC 89-36400. (Trophy Bk.). 160p. (J). (gr. 4-7). 1992. pap. 4.95 (*0-06-440357-2*, HarpTrophy) HarpC Child Bks.

Moore, Robin. The Bread Sister of Sinking Creek. (J). 1992. 9.05 (*0-606-12200-1*, Pub. by Turtleback) Demco.

Moore, Robin. Creating a Family Storytelling Tradition: Awakening the Hidden Storyteller. LC 99-42776. 160p. 1999. pap. 19.95 (*0-87483-565-8*) August Hse.

— Encounter on the Moon. (Classified Ser.). 96p. (YA). (gr. 5 up). 1996. pap. 5.95 (*0-7534-5006-2*, Kingfisher) LKC.

***Moore, Robin.** The Green Berets. rev. ed. LC 65-15849. (Illus.). 394p. 1999. pap. 14.95 (*1-893135-00-4*) Moore-Hill Pub.

Moore, Robin. Hercules. (Illus.). (J). (gr. 2-5). 1997. 15.00 (*0-614-29061-9*); pap. 3.99 (*0-614-29062-7*) S&S Childrens.

Moore, Robin. Hercules, Hero of the Night Sky. 1997. 9.19 (*0-606-11457-2*, Pub. by Turtleback) Demco.

Moore, Robin. Maggie among the Seneca. rev. ed. LC 89-77110. 112p. (J). (gr. 4-7). 1990. 13.95 (*0-397-32455-3*); lib. bdg. 14.89 (*0-397-32456-1*) HarpC Child Bks.

— The Moscow Connection. 500p. 1994. 20.00 (*1-879915-11-1*) Affil Writers America.

— My Life with the Indians: The Story of Mary Jemison. LC 97-13606. (Incredible Journey Ser.). (Illus.). (J). 1997. 16.95 (*0-382-39922-6*); pap. write for info. (*0-382-39923-4*) Silver Burdett Pr.

— The Sparrowhook Curse. 424p. (Orig.). 1996. pap. 12.95 (*0-924771-70-4*, Covered Brdge Pr) Douglas Charles Ltd.

— The Story of Hercules. LC 96-42477. (Illus.). 64p. (J). 1997. 14.00 (*0-689-81228-0*) S&S Childrens.

— The Story of Hercules. LC 96-42477. (Illus.). 80p. (J). (gr. 2-5). 1997. pap. 3.99 (*0-689-81229-9*) S&S Childrens.

— The White Tribe. 550p. 1991. 24.95 (*1-879915-03-0*) Affil Writers America.

Moore, Robin & Dempsey, Al. Phase of Darkness. LC 73-92799. 1974. 30.00 (*0-89388-136-8*) Okpaku Communications.

Moore, Robin, jt. auth. see Flynn, Raymond.

Moore, Robin C. Plants for Play: A Plant Selection Guide for Children's Outdoor Environments. LC 92-62234. 1993. pap. 16.95 (*0-944661-18-1*) MIG Comns.

Moore, Robin C., et al, eds. Play for All Guidelines: Planning, Design & Management of Outdoor Play Settings for All Children. LC 87-73243. (Illus.). 266p. (Orig.). 1987. pap. text 24.00 (*0-944661-00-9*, L009) AAHPERD.

— Play for All Guidelines: Planning, Design & Management of Outdoor Play Settings for All Children. 2nd ed. LC 92-64424. (Illus.). 300p. (Orig.). 1992. pap. 39.95 (*0-944661-17-3*) MIG Comns.

Moore, Robin C. & Wong, Herbert H. Natural Learning: The Life History of an Environmental Schoolyard. LC 96-39184. (Illus.). (Orig.). 1997. pap. text 29.95 (*0-944661-24-6*) MIG Comns.

Moore, Robin C., et al. Childhood's Domain: Play & Place in Child Development. LC 90-60586. (Illus.). 336p. 1990. pap. 21.95 (*0-944661-01-7*) MIG Comns.

Moore, Robin D. Nationalizing Blackness: Afrourbanismo & Artistic Revolution in Havana, 1920-1940. LC 97-21045. (Illus.). 312p. 1997. pap. 19.95 (*0-8229-5645-4*); text 45.00 (*0-8229-4040-X*) U of Pittsburgh Pr.

Moore, Rod. Monkey. 78p. (Orig.). 1985. pap. 4.95 (*0-933515-04-9*) Exile Pr.

Moore, Rod V. Igloo among Palms. 216p. 1997. pap. 11.00 (*0-9660829-0-7*) Hinterlands.

— Igloo among Palms. LC 94-22499. (Iowa Short Fiction Award Ser.). 145p. 1994. 11.50 (*0-87745-475-2*) U of Iowa Pr.

***Moore, Rogan H.** The Civil War Memoirs of Sergeant George W. Darry, 1861-1865. 185p. 1999. pap. 17.50 (*0-7884-1307-4*, M552) Heritage Bk.

Moore, Rogan H. A History & Genealogy of the Moore Family of Fayette County, Pennsylvania. LC 99-236041. (Illus.). 328p. 1999. pap. 28.00 (*0-7884-1114-4*, M560) Heritage Bk.

Moore, Roger. Broken Ghosts. 69p. 1986. pap. 6.95 (*0-86492-082-2*, Pub. by Goose Ln Edits) Genl Dist Srvs.

Moore, Roger A., jt. ed. see Lake, Carol L.

Moore, Roger E. Dragon Magazine. 90th ed. 1993. pap. text 3.50 (*1-56076-766-9*) TSR Inc.

— Dragon Magazine. 91st ed. (Illus.). 1993. pap. text. write for info. (*1-56076-767-7*) TSR Inc.

— Dragon Magazine. 93rd ed. (Illus.). 1993. pap. text. write for info. (*1-56076-769-3*) TSR Inc.

— Dragon Magazine. 98th ed. 1993. pap. text 3.50 (*1-56076-774-X*) TSR Inc.

— Greyhawk: The Adventure Begins. 1998. pap. 19.95 (*0-7869-1249-9*, Pub. by TSR Inc) Random.

— Return of the Eight. 1998. 13.95 (*0-7869-1247-2*, Pub. by TSR Inc) Random.

Moore, Roger L., et al. Organizing Outdoor Volunteers: A Step-by-Step Program for Grassroots Environmental Action Groups. 2nd ed. LC 92-22621. (Illus.). 128p. 1992. pap. 4.95 (*1-878239-16-3*) AMC Books.

***Moore, Ron.** Making Common Sense Common Practice: Models for Manufacturing Excellence. 1999. write for info. (*0-08-815899-3*) Elsevier.

Moore, Ron. Making Common Sense Common Practice: Models for Manufacturing Excellence. LC 98-54948. 352p. 1999. 29.95 (*0-88415-899-3*, 5899, Cashman Dud) Gulf Pub.

Moore, Ronald, ed. Aesthetics for Young People. 127p. (Orig.). 1995. pap. text 18.00 (*0-937652-73-3*, 253) Natl Art Ed.

Moore, Ronald & Moore, Gloria. Margaret Sanger & the Birth Control Movement: A Bibliography, 1911-1984. LC 86-10119. 230p. 1986. 30.00 (*0-8108-1903-1*) Scarecrow.

Moore, Ronald E. Vehicle Extrication & Rescue. (C). (gr. 13). 1997. teacher ed. 65.00 (*0-8151-2274-8*, 31739) Mosby Inc.

— Vehicle Rescue & Extrication. (Illus.). 336p. (C). (gr. 13). 1990. pap. text 29.95 (*0-8016-3351-6*, 03351) Mosby Inc.

Moore, Ronnie. Tricks That Stick. (Illus.). 124p. (Orig.). 1996. pap. 15.95 (*0-9649694-0-8*) MC Pubng.

Moore, Rosalie. Gutenberg in Strasbourg. (Illus.). 128p. 1995. pap. 12.00 (*0-912449-52-7*) Floating Island.

— Of Singles & Doubles. LC 78-68474. 1979. 7.95 (*0-913506-06-0*) Woolmer-Brotherson.

Moore, Rosalind, ed. The Dell Big Book of Crosswords & Pencil Puzzles, No. 7. 320p. (Orig.). (J). 1989. pap. 11.99 (*0-440-50161-X*) Dell.

— The Dell Book of Logic Problems, No. 1. 176p. (Orig.). 1984. pap. 10.99 (*0-440-51891-1*, Dell Trade Pbks) Dell.

— The Dell Book of Logic Problems, No. 2. 176p. (Orig.). 1986. pap. 11.99 (*0-440-51875-X*, Dell Trade Pbks) Dell.

Moore, Rosalind, jt. ed. see Rafferty, Kathleen.

***Moore, Rosemary A.** The Light in Their Consciences: The Early Quakers in Britain, 1646-1666. LC 99-35185. 2000. pap. 22.50 (*0-271-01989-1*) Pa St U Pr.

— The Light in Their Consciences: The Early Quakers in Britain, 1646-1666. 2000. 65.00 (*0-271-01988-3*) Pa St U Pr.

***Moore, Roslyn.** Meeting Papaji. 256p. 1999. pap. 16.50 (*0-9646999-1-5*) DO Publng.

Moore, Roslyn, jt. auth. see Olney, Dick.

***Moore, Rowan & Lloyd, Sampson.** Panoramas of London. (Illus.). 160p. 2000. pap. 17.95 (*1-85799-954-1*) Phoenix Hse.

***Moore, Rowan, et al.** Buiilding Tate Modern: Herzog & de Meuron with Giles Gilbert Scott. (Illus.). 200p. 2000. 75.00 (*1-85437-331-5*) U of Wash Pr.

Moore, Rowan, ed. see Betsky, Aaron & Sudjic, Deyan.

Moore, Rowan, ed. see Powell, Kenneth.

Moore, Roy & Smith, F. T. Carpet Cleaners Guide to Increased Sales & Profit. Griffin, William R., ed. (Illus.). 42p. 1987. pap. text 25.00 (*0-944352-01-4*) Cleaning Cons.

— Upholstery Cleaning: Onsite. rev. ed. Griffin, W. R., ed. 57p. (C). 1993. pap. text 25.00 (*0-944352-00-6*) Cleaning Cons.

Moore, Roy & Smith, F. W. Fire Restoration & Insurance Work. Griffin, William R., ed. 60p. 1987. pap. 25.00 (*0-9601054-6-8*) Cleaning Cons.

Moore, Roy, et al. Thomas Jefferson's Journey to the South of France. LC 98-32376. (Illus.). 160p. 1999. text 29.95 (*1-55670-892-0*) Stewart Tabori & Chang.

Moore, Roy L. History of Woodford County: Concise History of the Settlement & Growth of Woodford County. (Illus.). 248p. 1997. reprint ed. lib. bdg. 32.50 (*0-8328-5804-8*) Higginson Bk Co.

— Mass Communication Law & Ethics. (Communication Ser.). 616p. (C). 1994. text 45.00 (*0-8058-0240-1*) L Erlbaum Assocs.

— Mass Communication Law & Ethics. 2nd ed. LC 98-36329. (LEA's Communication Ser.). 696p. 1999. 55.00 (*0-8058-2599-1*) L Erlbaum Assocs.

— Mass Communication Law & Ethics: A Casebook. LC 99-17431. (LEA's Communication Ser.). 344p. 1999. pap. 29.95 (*0-8058-3278-5*) L Erlbaum Assocs.

— Mass Communication Law & Ethics: 1996 Update. (LEA's Communication Ser.). 86p. 1995. text Not sold separately (*0-8058-2219-4*) L Erlbaum Assocs.

Moore, Roy L., et al. Advertising & Public Relations Law. LC 96-39933. (LEA's Communication Ser.). 568p. 1997. write for info. (*0-8058-1679-8*) L Erlbaum Assocs.

Moore, Royall T. Deuteromycete Studies: Collected Mycological Papers. (Bibliotheca Mycologica: Vol. 108). (GER., Illus.). iv, 180p. 1987. 53.00 (*3-443-59009-8*, Pub. by Gebruder Borntraeger) Balogh.

Moore, Rudy. Arithmetic Series Two, Quarter Three: Classic Curriculum Workbook. (J). (gr. 2). 1989. pap. 8.99 (*0-88062-238-5*) Mott Media.

— Arithmetic Series Two, Quarter Two: Classic Curriculum Workbook. (J). (gr. 2). 1995. pap. 8.99 (*0-88062-237-7*) Mott Media.

Moore, Rudy & Moore, Betty. Arithmetic Series Four, Quarter Four: Classic Curriculum Workbook. (J). 1994. pap. 8.99 (*0-88062-247-4*) Mott Media.

— Arithmetic Series Four, Quarter One: Classic Curriculum Workbook. (J). (gr. 4). 1991. pap. 8.99 (*0-88062-244-X*) Mott Media.

— Arithmetic Series Four, Quarter Three: Classic Curriculum Workbook. 1994. pap. 8.99 (*0-88062-246-6*) Mott Media.

— Arithmetic Series Four, Quarter Two: Classic Curriculum Workbook. (J). (gr. 4). 1994. pap. 8.99 (*0-88062-245-8*) Mott Media.

— Arithmetic Series One, Quarter Four: Classic Curriculum Workbook. (J). (gr. 1). 1991. pap. 8.99 (*0-88062-235-0*) Mott Media.

— Arithmetic Series One, Quarter One: Classic Curriculum Workbook. (J). (gr. 1). 1988. pap. 8.99 (*0-88062-232-6*) Mott Media.

— Arithmetic Series One, Quarter Three: Classic Curriculum Workbook. (J). (gr. 1). 1995. pap. 8.99 (*0-88062-234-2*) Mott Media.

— Arithmetic Series One, Quarter Two: Classic Curriculum Workbook. (J). (gr. 1). 1995. pap. 8.99 (*0-88062-233-4*) Mott Media.

— Arithmetic Series Three, Quarter Four: Classic Curriculum Workbook. (J). (gr. 3). 1991. pap. 8.99 (*0-88062-243-1*) Mott Media.

— Arithmetic Series Three, Quarter One: Classic Curriculum Workbook. (J). (gr. 3). 1989. pap. 8.99 (*0-88062-240-7*) Mott Media.

— Arithmetic Series Three, Quarter Three: Classic Curriculum Workbook. (J). (gr. 3). 1991. pap. 8.99 (*0-88062-242-3*) Mott Media.

— Arithmetic Series Three, Quarter Two: Classic Curriculum Workbook. (J). (gr. 3). 1989. pap. 8.99 (*0-88062-241-5*) Mott Media.

— Arithmetic Series Two, Quarter Four: Classic Curriculum Workbook. (J). (gr. 2). 1991. pap. 8.99 (*0-88062-239-3*) Mott Media.

— Arithmetic Series Two, Quarter One: Classic Curriculum Workbook. (J). (gr. 2). 1988. pap. 8.99 (*0-88062-236-9*) Mott Media.

— Reading Series 4, Quarter 4: Classic Curriculum Workbook. (J). (gr. 4). 1994. pap. 8.99 (*0-88062-215-6*) Mott Media.

— Reading Series 4, Quarter 1: Classic Curriculum Workbook. (J). (gr. 4). 1988. pap. 8.99 (*0-88062-212-1*) Mott Media.

— Reading Series 4, Quarter 3: Classic Curriculum Workbook. (J). (gr. 4). 1988. pap. 8.99 (*0-88062-214-8*) Mott Media.

— Reading Series 4, Quarter 2: Classic Curriculum Workbook. (J). (gr. 4). 1988. pap. 8.99 (*0-88062-213-X*) Mott Media.

— Reading Series 1, Quarter 4: Classic Curriculum Workbook. (J). (gr. 1). 1991. pap. 8.99 (*0-88062-203-2*) Mott Media.

— Reading Series 1, Quarter 1: Classic Curriculum Workbook. (J). (gr. 1). 1988. pap. 8.99 (*0-88062-200-8*) Mott Media.

— Reading Series 1, Quarter 3: Classic Curriculum Workbook. (J). (gr. 1). 1994. pap. 8.99 (*0-88062-202-4*) Mott Media.

— Reading Series 1, Quarter 2: Classic Curriculum Workbook. (J). (gr. 1). 1995. pap. 8.99 (*0-88062-201-6*) Mott Media.

— Reading Series 3, Quarter 4: Classic Curriculum Workbook. (J). (gr. 3). 1994. pap. 8.99 (*0-88062-211-3*) Mott Media.

— Reading Series 3, Quarter 1: Classic Curriculum Workbook. (J). (gr. 3). 1988. pap. 8.99 (*0-88062-208-3*) Mott Media.

— Reading Series 3, Quarter 3: Classic Curriculum Workbook. (J). (gr. 3). 1989. pap. 8.99 (*0-88062-210-5*) Mott Media.

— Reading Series 3, Quarter 2: Classic Curriculum Workbook. (J). (gr. 3). 1988. pap. 8.99 (*0-88062-209-1*) Mott Media.

— Reading Series 2, Quarter 4: Classic Curriculum Workbook. (J). (gr. 2). 1991. pap. 8.99 (*0-88062-207-5*) Mott Media.

— Reading Series 2, Quarter 1: Classic Curriculum Workbook. (J). (gr. 2). 1988. pap. 8.99 (*0-88062-204-0*) Mott Media.

— Reading Series 2, Quarter 3: Classic Curriculum Workbook. (J). (gr. 2). 1989. pap. 8.99 (*0-88062-206-7*) Mott Media.

— Reading Series 2, Quarter 2: Classic Curriculum Workbook. (J). (gr. 2). 1988. pap. 8.99 (*0-88062-205-9*) Mott Media.

— Writing Series 4, Quarter 4: Classic Curriculum Workbook. (J). (gr. 4). 1994. pap. 8.99 (*0-88062-231-8*) Mott Media.

— Writing Series 4, Quarter 1: Classic Curriculum Workbook. (J). (gr. 4). 1988. pap. 8.99 (*0-88062-228-8*) Mott Media.

— Writing Series 4, Quarter 3: Classic Curriculum Workbook. (J). (gr. 4). 1989. pap. 8.99 (*0-88062-230-X*) Mott Media.

— Writing Series 4, Quarter 2: Classic Curriculum Workbook. (J). (gr. 4). 1988. pap. 8.99 (*0-88062-229-6*) Mott Media.

— Writing Series 1, Quarter 4: Classic Curriculum Workbook. (J). (gr. 1). 1991. pap. 8.99 (*0-88062-219-9*) Mott Media.

— Writing Series 1, Quarter 1: Classic Curriculum Workbook. (J). (gr. 1). 1988. pap. 8.99 (*0-88062-216-4*) Mott Media.

— Writing Series 1, Quarter 3: Classic Curriculum Workbook. (J). (gr. 1). 1989. pap. 8.99 (*0-88062-218-0*) Mott Media.

— Writing Series 1, Quarter 2: Classic Curriculum Workbook. (J). (gr. 1). 1988. pap. 8.99 (*0-88062-217-2*) Mott Media.

— Writing Series 3, Quarter 4: Classic Curriculum Workbook. (J). (gr. 3). 1991. pap. 8.99 (*0-88062-227-X*) Mott Media.

— Writing Series 3, Quarter 1: Classic Curriculum Workbook. (J). (gr. 3). 1988. pap. 8.99 (*0-88062-224-5*) Mott Media.

— Writing Series 3, Quarter 3: Classic Curriculum Workbook. (J). (gr. 3). 1991. pap. 8.99 (*0-88062-226-1*) Mott Media.

— Writing Series 3, Quarter 2: Classic Curriculum Workbook. (J). (gr. 3). 1988. pap. 8.99 (*0-88062-225-3*) Mott Media.

— Writing Series 2, Quarter 4: Classic Curriculum Workbook. (J). (gr. 2). 1991. pap. 8.99 (*0-88062-223-7*) Mott Media.

— Writing Series 2, Quarter 1: Classic Curriculum Workbook. (J). (gr. 2). 1988. pap. 8.99 (*0-88062-220-2*) Mott Media.

M

— Writing Series 2, Quarter 3: Classic Curriculum Workbook. (J). (gr. 2). 1989. pap. 8.99 (0-88062-222-9) Mott Media.

— Writing Series 2, Quarter 2: Classic Curriculum Workbook. (J). (gr. 2). 1988. pap. 8.99 (0-88062-221-0) Mott Media.

Moore, Russell, tr. see Amin, Samir.

Moore, Russell G. The Little Striker. LC 81-80507. (Illus.). 128p. (Orig.). 1981. pap. 5.00 (0-936972-03-3) Lower Cape.

Moore, Russell M. Multinational Corporations & the Regionalization of the Latin American Automotive Industry. Bruchey, Stuart, ed. LC 80-584. (Multinational Corporations Ser.). 1981. lib. bdg. 36.95 (0-405-13376-6) Ayer.

Moore, Russell M., jt. ed. see Lehman, Cheryl R.

Moore, Ruth. Candlemas Bay. 1994. pap. 10.95 (0-942396-70-7) Blackberry ME.

***Moore, Ruth.** In the Potter's Hands. Perry, Charles E., Jr., ed. 84p. 2000. pap. 6.95 (0-9677054-3-6) Nethope Pub.

Moore, Ruth. Speak to the Winds. 1987. pap. 9.95 (0-942396-54-5) Blackberry ME.

— Spoonhandle. 1986. pap. 10.95 (0-942396-49-9) Blackberry ME.

— The Tired Apple Tree. 160p. (Orig.). 1990. pap. 8.50 (0-942396-59-6) Blackberry ME.

— The Walk Down Main Street. 386p. 1988. reprint ed. pap. 10.95 (0-942396-56-1) Blackberry ME.

— The Weir. 1986. pap. 10.95 (0-942396-48-0) Blackberry ME.

Moore, Ruth, ed. see Knox, Mel.

Moore, Ruth N. The Christmas Surprise. LC 89-15213. (Illus.). 160p. (Orig.). (J). (gr. 4-8). 1989. pap. 6.99 (0-8361-3499-0) Herald Pr.

— Distant Thunder: A Sequel to the Christmas Surprise. LC 91-10845. (Illus.). 160p. (Orig.). (J). (gr. 4-8). 1991. pap. 6.99 (0-8361-3557-1) Herald Pr.

— Ghost Town Mystery. LC 87-2874. (Sara & Sam Mysteries Ser.: Vol. 5). (Illus.). 144p. (J). (gr. 4 up). 1987. pap. 6.99 (0-8361-3445-1) Herald Pr.

— Mystery at Captain's Cove. LC 91-40805. (Sara & Sam Mysteries Ser.: Vol. 7). (Illus.). 160p. (Orig.). (J). (gr. 4-7). 1992. pap. 6.99 (0-8361-3581-4) Herald Pr.

— Mystery at the Spanish Castle. LC 89-29290. 112p. (Orig.). (J). (gr. 4-8). 1990. pap. 6.99 (0-8361-3515-6) Herald Pr.

— Mystery of the Secret Code. LC 85-5441. (Sara & Sam Mysteries Ser.: Vol. 2). (Illus.). 128p. (Orig.). (J). (gr. 7-9). 1985. pap. 6.99 (0-8361-3394-3) Herald Pr.

— Where the Eagles Fly. LC 94-630. 104p. (Orig.). (J). (gr. 4-7). 1994. pap. 5.99 (0-8361-3664-0) Herald Pr.

Moore, Ryamond S. & Moore, Dorothy N. Mejor Tarde Que Temprano: Un Nuevo Enfoque a la Educacion de Su Hijo. Mejias, Alicia, tr.Tr. of Better Late Than Early. (SPA., Illus.). 300p. 1997. pap. 7.99 (1-56063-900-8, 498389) Editorial Unilit.

Moore, S. Skin & Bone. mass mkt. 8.95 (0-340-70455-1, Pub. by Hodder & Stought Ltd) Trafalgar.

— Spilling the Magic. (Illus.). (J). 1996. mass mkt. 8.95 (0-340-66098-8) Hodder & Stought Ltd.

— Tooth & Claw. (Illus.). (J). mass mkt. 8.95 (0-340-70454-3, Pub. by Hodder & Stought Ltd) Trafalgar.

Moore, S. & Navaretta, Cynthia, eds. Artists & Their Cats: In Their Own Voices. LC 90-81443. (Illus.). 64p. (Orig.). 1990. pap. text 10.00 (1-877675-02-4) Midmarch Arts.

Moore, S., jt. auth. see Rice, H.

Moore, S. Craig, et al. A Framework for Characterization of Military Unit Training Status. LC 94-49663. (Illus.). 85p. 1995. pap. text 15.00 (0-8330-1625-3, MR-261-OSD) Rand Corp.

Moore, Sabra. Petroglyphs: Ancient Language, Sacred Art. LC 98-11903. (Illus.). 192p. 1998. 19.95 (1-57416-011-7) Clear Light.

***Moore, Sally.** Country Roads of New Mexico: Drives, Day Trips & Weekend Excursions. 2nd ed. (Country Roads of... Ser.). 240p. 1999. pap. 12.95 (1-56626-203-8, 62038, Cntry Rds Pr) NTC Contemp Pub Co.

Moore, Sally. Country Roads of Pennsylvania. LC 93-11611. (Country Roads Ser.). (Illus.). 176p. (Orig.). 1993. pap. 9.95 (1-56626-032-9, Cntry Rds Pr) NTC Contemp Pub Co.

Moore, Sally F. Power & Property in Inca Peru. LC 72-5456. 190p. 1973. lib. bdg. 35.00 (0-8371-6441-9, MOPO, Greenwood Pr) Greenwood.

Moore, Sally F., ed. Moralizing States & the Ethnography of the Present. LC 93-33898. (American Ethnological Society Monograph Ser.: Vol. 5). 1993. write for info. (0-913167-60-6) Am Anthro Assn.

Moore, Sally F. & Puritt, Paul. The Chagga & Meru of Tanzania. LC 78-309993. (Ethnographic Survey of Africa: East Central Africa Ser.: No. 18). 156p. reprint ed. pap. 48.40 (0-8357-6963-1, 203902300009) Bks Demand.

Moore, Sally Falk. Anthropology & Africa: Changing Perspectives on a Changing Scene. LC 93-40047. 205p. (C). 1994. text 35.00 (0-8139-1504-X); pap. text 12.00 (0-8139-1505-8) U Pr of Va.

Moore, Sam. American by Choice: The Remarkable Fulfillment of an Immigrant's Dream. LC 97-48388. (Illus.). 240+16p. 1998. 14.99 (0-7852-7453-7) Nelson.

Moore, Sam H. Passing of the Times Vol. 1, Pt. 1, Bk. 1A: Old Virginia. 1994. write for info. (0-89904-232-5); pap. write for info. (0-89904-233-3) Crumb Elbow Pub.

— Passing of the Times Vol. 2, Pt. 2, Bk. 1B: Old Virginia. 1994. write for info. (0-89904-234-1); pap. write for info. (0-89904-235-X) Crumb Elbow Pub.

— Passing of the Times Vol. 3, Pt. 2, Bk. 2A: Old Virginia. 1994. write for info. (0-89904-236-8); pap. write for info. (0-89904-237-6) Crumb Elbow Pub.

— Passing of the Times Vol. 4, Pt. 2, Bk. 2B: Old Virginia. 1994. write for info. (0-89904-238-4); pap. write for info. (0-89904-239-2) Crumb Elbow Pub.

— Passing of the Times Vol. 5, Pt. 1, Bk. 1A: Trips. 1994. write for info. (0-89904-240-6); pap. write for info. (0-89904-241-4) Crumb Elbow Pub.

— Passing of the Times Vol. 6, Pt. 1, Bk. 1B: Trips. 1994. write for info. (0-89904-242-2); pap. write for info. (0-89904-243-0) Crumb Elbow Pub.

— Passing of the Times Vol. 7, Pt. 2, Bk. 2A: Trips. 1994. write for info. (0-89904-244-9); pap. write for info. (0-89904-245-7) Crumb Elbow Pub.

— Passing of the Times Vol. 8, Pt. 2, Bk. 2B: Trips. 1994. write for info. (0-89904-246-5); pap. write for info. (0-89904-247-3) Crumb Elbow Pub.

— Passing of the Times Vol. 9, Pt. 3, Bk. 3A: Trips. 1994. write for info. (0-89904-248-1); pap. write for info. (0-89904-249-X) Crumb Elbow Pub.

— Passing of the Times Vol. 10, Pt. 3, Bk. 3B: Trips. 1994. write for info. (0-89904-250-3); pap. write for info. (0-89904-251-1) Crumb Elbow Pub.

— Passing of the Times Vol. 11, Pt. 3, Bk. 3C: Trips. 1994. write for info. (0-89904-252-X); pap. write for info. (0-89904-253-8) Crumb Elbow Pub.

— Passing of the Times Vol. 12, Pt. 3, Bk. 4: Trips. 1994. write for info. (0-89904-254-6); pap. write for info. (0-89904-255-4) Crumb Elbow Pub.

— Passing of the Times Vol. 13, Pt. 3, Bk. 4A: Trips. 1994. write for info. (0-89904-256-2); pap. write for info. (0-89904-257-0) Crumb Elbow Pub.

— Passing of the Times Vol. 14: Occupations. 1994. write for info. (0-89904-258-9); pap. write for info. (0-89904-259-7) Crumb Elbow Pub.

— Passing of the Times Vol. 16, Pt. 2, Bk. 2A: 150 Years of the Moore Family. 1994. write for info. (0-89904-262-7); pap. write for info. (0-89904-263-5) Crumb Elbow Pub.

— Passing of the Times Vol. 17, Pt. 2, Bk. 2B: 150 Years of the Moore Family. 1994. write for info. (0-89904-264-3); pap. write for info. (0-89904-265-1) Crumb Elbow Pub.

— Passing of the Times Vol. 18, Pt. 2, Bk. 1A: 150 Years of the Moore Family. 1994. write for info. (0-89904-266-X); pap. write for info. (0-89904-267-8) Crumb Elbow Pub.

— Passing of the Times Vol. 19, Pt. 2, Bk. 1B: 150 Years of the Moore Family. 1994. write for info. (0-89904-268-6); pap. write for info. (0-89904-269-4) Crumb Elbow Pub.

— Passing of the Times Vol. 20, Pt. 1, Bk. 1A: These Stories Are True. 1994. write for info. (0-89904-270-8); pap. write for info. (0-89904-271-6) Crumb Elbow Pub.

— Passing of the Times Vol. 21, Pt. 1, Bk. 1B: These Stories Are True. 1994. write for info. (0-89904-272-4); pap. write for info. (0-89904-273-2) Crumb Elbow Pub.

Moore, Samuel & Knott, Thomas A. Elements of Old English. 1955. pap. 18.00 (0-911586-23-7) Wahr.

Moore, Samuel, jt. auth. see Marckwardt, Albert H.

Moore, Samuel, tr. see Marx, Karl & Engels, Friedrich.

Moore, Samuel P. Confederate States Medical & Surgical Journal. (American Civil War Medical Ser.: No. 12). 272p. 1992. reprint ed. 95.00 (0-930405-40-4) Norman SF.

— Regulations of the C. S. A. Medical Department: IN: Regulations for the Army of the Confederate States. (American Civil War Medical Ser.: No. 8). 420p. 1991. 50.00 (0-930405-36-6) Norman SF.

Moore, Samuel P. & Rutkow, Ira M., intros. A Manual of Military Surgery: Prepared for the Use of the Confederate States Army. LC 88-60874. (American Civil War Surgery Ser.: No. 2). (Illus.). 297p. 1989. reprint ed. 75.00 (0-930405-14-5) Norman SF.

***Moore, Samuel T. & Alexander, James E.** Flight Surgeon: With the 81st Fighter Group in WWII. (Illus.). 240p. 1999. 24.95 (0-939965-14-3) Macedon Prod.

Moore, Samuel T., ed. see Barron, Clarence W.

Moore, Sandra. High Country Cowboy. 1994. per. 3.50 (0-373-09918-5, 1-09918-3) Harlequin Bks.

Moore, Sandra C. Private Woods. 288p. 1988. 18.95 (0-15-174710-5); 18.95 (0-685-22051-6) Harcourt.

***Moore, Sandre.** The Family Fairytale Cookbook: Fun Recipes for Familes to Create & Eat Together. (Illus.). 224p. 2000. pap. 16.95 (1-58182-093-3, Cumberland Hearthside) Cumberland Hse.

Moore, Sara. Peace Without Victory for the Allies, 1918-1932. 352p. 39.50 (1-85973-026-4) Berg Pubs.

Moore, Sarah. Joyce Neimanas. (Illus.). 24p. 1984. pap. 7.95 (0-938262-11-4) Ctr Creat Photog.

Moore, Sarah, et al. Little Christmas Classics: Jolly Old Santa Claus & The Nutcracker, 2 Bks., Set. rev. ed. (Illus.). 24p. (J). (ps-2). 4.99 incl. audio (1-57102-083-7, Ideals Child) Hambleton-Hill.

— Little Christmas Classics: The Night Before Christmas & The Story of Christmas for Children, 2 Bks., Set. rev. ed. (Illus.). 24p. (J). (ps-2). 4.99 incl. audio (1-57102-084-5, Ideals Child) Hambleton-Hill.

***Moore, Sarah.** T. J. Finds a Home. (Illus.). (J). (gr. 1-3). 2000. 10.95 (0-533-13390-4) Vantage.

Moore, Sarah J. & Morfit, Christine A., eds. Language & International Studies: A Richard Lambert Perspective. 386p. (C). 1993. pap. text 12.00 (1-880671-02-6) NFLC Pubns.

Moore, Sarah J., et al. Introducing Chinese into High Schools: The Dodge Initiative. Yates, Mary V., ed. (National Foreign Language Center Monographs). 135p. (Orig.). (C). 1992. pap. text 7.50 (1-880671-01-8) NFLC Pubns.

***Moore, Schuyler M.** The Biz: The Basic Business, Legal & Financial Aspects of the Film Industry. LC 99-89791. 240p. 2000. pap. 26.95 (1-879505-53-3, Pub. by Silman James Pr) SCB Distributors.

Moore, Schuyler M. Taxation of Specialized Industries: The Entertainment Industry. Silva & Cooley, eds. 1995. 520.00 (0-7913-2313-7) Warren Gorham & Lamont.

***Moore, Schuyler M.** Taxation of the Entertainment Industry, 1. 440p. 1999. pap. text 145.00 (0-7355-1076-8) Panel Pubs.

Moore, Schuyler M. Taxation of the Entertainment Industry, 1999. LC 98-37117. 1998. 145.00 (0-7355-0221-8) Aspen Pub.

Moore, Scotty & Dickerson, James. That's Alright, Elvis: The Untold Story of Elvis's First Guitarist & Manager, Scotty Moore. LC 96-6614. (Illus.). 271p. 1997. 25.00 (0-02-864599-5) Mac Lib Ref.

— That's Alright, Elvis: The Untold Story of Elvis's First Guitarist & Manager, Scotty Moore. (Illus.). 271p. 2000. reprint ed. text 25.00 (0-7881-6173-3) DIANE Pub.

***Moore, Sean.** How to Make Money as an Artist: The 7 Winning Strategies of Successful Fine Artists. 160p. 2000. pap. 10.95 (1-55652-413-7, Pub. by Chicago Review) IPG Chicago.

Moore, Sean, ed. Vascular Injury & Atherosclerosis. LC 81-15228. (Biochemistry of Disease Ser.: No. 9). (Illus.). 253p. reprint ed. pap. 78.50 (0-7837-3344-5, 204330200008) Bks Demand.

Moore, Sean, ed. see Steiner, Josef & Steiner, Gerhard.

Moore, Sean A. Conan & the Grim Grey God. 1996. pap. text 9.99 (0-8125-5267-9, Pub. by Tor Bks) St Martin.

— Conan & the Grim Grey God, Vol. 1. 1997. mass mkt. 5.99 (0-8125-9062-7, Pub. by Tor Bks) St Martin.

— Conan & the Shaman's Curse. 1996. mass mkt. 4.99 (0-8125-5265-2, Pub. by Tor Bks) St Martin.

— Conan the Hunter. 256p. 1994. mass mkt. 4.99 (0-8125-3531-6, Pub. by Tor Bks) St Martin.

Moore, Sebastian. The Crucified Jesus Is No Stranger. 1984. 8.95 (0-86683-891-0) Harper SF.

— Let This Mind Be in You: A Quest for Identity Through Oedipus to Christ. 192p. 1985. 13.95 (0-86683-797-3, 8597) Harper SF.

***Moore, Sharon.** Lupus: Alternative Therapies That Work. 256p. 2000. pap. 14.95 (0-89281-889-1) Inner Tradit.

Moore, Sharon. News from Marion: Marion County, OH, 1844-1861. 211p. (Orig.). 1995. pap. 63.50 (0-7884-0343-5) Heritage Bk.

Moore, Sharon, ed. see Moore, Herb.

***Moore, Sharon A.** We Love Harry Potter! We'll Tell You Why. 1999. mass mkt. write for info. (0-312-26481-X) St Martin.

Moore, Sharon A., et al. Developing Readers & Writers in the Content Areas, K-12. 3rd ed. Moore, David W., ed. LC 97-15087. 384p. (J). (gr. k-12). 1997. pap. 56.00 (0-8013-1856-4) Addison-Wesley.

Moore, Sharon C. A Determined Spirit... 224p. 1995. pap. 10.99 (1-56043-261-6, Treasure Hse) Destiny Image.

Moore, Sharon E., jt. auth. see Dhooper, Surjit Singh.

Moore, Sheila. The Little Boy Book: A Guide to the First Eight Years. LC 97-97007. 320p. 1998. pap. 11.00 (0-345-42350-X) Ballantine Pub Grp.

— Samson Svenson's Baby. LC 82-48262. (Illus.). 48p. (J). (gr. 1-4). 1983. 11.95 (0-06-022612-9) HarpC Child Bks.

Moore, Sheila & Frost, Roon. The Little Boy Book: A Guide to the First Eight Years. 320p. 1987. mass mkt. 5.99 (0-345-34466-9) Ballantine Pub Grp.

Moore, Shirley. To Place Our Deeds: The African American Community in Richmond, California, 1910-1963. LC 99-15209. 266p. 1999. 40.00 (0-520-21565-6, Pub. by U CA Pr) Cal Prin Full Svc.

Moore, Shirley, ed. A French-English Music Dictionary. Austin, John & Chalifour, Martin, trs. LC 85-80710. (ENG & FRE.). 99p. (Orig.). (C). 1985. pap. text 9.95 (0-9615337-0-6) Leihall Pubns.

Moore, Shirley T., ed. see Corbett, Julia.

Moore, Shirley T., ed. see Darvill, Fred T., Jr.

Moore, Shirley T., ed. see Driedger, Carolyn L.

Moore, Shirley T., ed. see Farley, Dale.

Moore, Shirley T., ed. see Hartig, Louis F.

Moore, Shirley T., ed. see Laven, Edward E.

Moore, Sidney, ed. see Haldeman, James.

Moore, Silas. Scarlet Arena 30303. Oddo, Genevieve, ed. LC 74-190272. (Illus.). 196p. (J). (gr. 8-12). 1972. lib. bdg. 3.95 (0-87783-063-0) Oddo.

***Moore, Simon.** Blink 182. 48p. 2000. pap. 12.95 (0-8256-1802-9) Music Sales.

Moore, Simon. An Invitation to Public Relations. 128p. 1997. 90.00 (0-304-33810-9); pap. 29.95 (0-304-33811-7) Continuum.

— Multithreaded Processor Design. (Kluwer International Series in Engineering & Computer Science: Vol. 358). 160p. (C). 1996. text 109.00 (0-7923-9718-5) Kluwer Academic.

— Penknives & Other Folding Knives. (Album Ser.: No. 223). (Illus.). 32p. 1989. pap. 25.00 (0-85263-966-X, Pub. by Shire Pubns) Parkwest Pubns.

— Spoons, 1650-1930. (Album Ser.: Vol. 211). 32p. 1989. pap. 4.75 (0-85263-910-4, Pub. by Shire Pubns) Parkwest Pubns.

— Table Knives & Forks. (Album Ser.: No. 320). (Illus.). 32p. 1995. pap. 4.75 (0-7478-0295-5, Pub. by Shire Pubns) Parkwest Pubns.

Moore, Simon, jt. auth. see Seymour, Mike.

Moore-Sines, Fay, jt. auth. see Johnson, Meldra.

Moore-Slater, Carole. Dana Doesn't Like Guns Anymore. (Illus.). (Orig.). (J). 1991. 10.95 (0-377-00246-1) Friendship Pr.

Moore, Sonia. The Stanislavski System: The Professional Training of an Actor: Digested From the Teachings of Konstantin S. Stanislavski. 2nd rev. ed. 144p. 1984. pap. 11.95 (0-14-046660-6, Penguin Bks) Viking Penguin.

— Stanislavsky Revealed: The Actor's Guide to Spontaneity on Stage. (Acting Ser.). 256p. 1991. pap. 9.95 (1-55783-103-3) Applause Theatre Bk Pubs.

Moore, Sophie, jt. auth. see Caviris, George.

Moore, Sparky. What If Cruella De Ville Was Your Lunch Lady? (J). 1996. pap. 4.95 (0-7868-4155-9) Hyprn Child.

Moore, Sparky, et al. Pooh Christmas Days. LC 96-227808. (J). 1996. write for info. (0-7853-1784-8) Pubns Intl Ltd.

Moore, Stanley A. A Wolf Called Motka. LC 96-61463. (Illus.). x, 240p. (Orig.). 1996. pap. 11.95 (0-9655251-0-4) Fayetteville Floral Pub Co.

Moore, Stanley B. Ornamental Horticulture As a Vocation. 2nd ed. (Illus.). (J). 1988. text 11.95 (0-912178-01-9) Mor-Mac.

Moore, Stanley W. Marx vs. Markets. 136p. 1993. 30.00 (0-271-00865-2) Pa St U Pr.

Moore, Stanley W., et al. The Child's Political World: A Longitudinal Perspective. LC 84-15975. 304p. 1985. 67.95 (0-275-90167-X, C0167, Praeger Pubs) Greenwood.

***Moore, Stephanie Perry.** Flame, , Vol. 1. (Natural Luv Ser.: Vol. 1). (Illus.). 180p. 1999. pap. 10.00 (1-929606-00-1) Soul Pubg Inc.

— Seeing Truth, 5 vols., Vol. 1. (Amber "Senses" Ser.: Vol. 1). (Illus.). 100p. (J). (gr. 3-6). 2000. pap. 8.00 (1-929606-25-7) Soul Pubg Inc.

— Storm, , Vol. 2. (Natural Luv Ser.: Vol. 2). 180p. 2000. pap. 10.00 (1-929606-01-X) Soul Pubg Inc.

Moore, Stephen. Do We Need New Taxes? 1990. pap. 5.00 (0-943802-84-9, BG105) Natl Ctr Pol.

— Federal Budget Issue: Do We Need an Energy Tax? (BG127 Ser.). 18p. (Orig.). 1993. pap. 5.00 (1-56808-010-7, BG127) Natl Ctr Pol.

— God's Gym: Divine Male Bodies of the Bible. LC 95-44257. (Illus.). 192p. (C). 1996. 75.00 (0-415-91756-5); pap. 21.99 (0-415-91757-3) Routledge.

— Government - America's No. 1 Growth Industry: How the Relentless Growth of Government Is Impoverishing America. 2nd ed. (Illus.). 114p. 1995. pap. 9.95 (0-9646127-0-4) Instit Policy Innov.

— Immigration & the Rise & Decline of American Cities. LC 97-24973. (Essays in Public Policy Ser.: No. 81). 1997. pap. 5.00 (0-8179-5862-2) Hoover Inst Pr.

***Moore, Stephen.** It's Getting Better All the Time: 101 Greatest Trends of the 20th Century. (Illus.). 2000. pap. 14.95 (1-882577-97-3) Cato Inst.

Moore, Stephen. Power & Corruption: The Rotten Core of Government & Big Business. (Illus.). 202p. 1999. pap. 14.95 (1-883319-83-8) Frog Ltd CA.

— Social Welfare Alive! 2nd ed. (Illus.). 400p. 1998. pap. 44.50 (0-7487-2581-4, Pub. by S Thornes Pubs) Trans-Atl Phila.

— Sociology. LC 94-65938. (Illus.). 400p. 1995. pap., student ed. 13.95 (0-8442-3649-7, Teach Yrslf) NTC Contemp Pub Co.

— Sociology Alive! 2nd ed. 320p. 1996. pap. 34.50 (0-7487-1531-2, Pub. by S Thornes Pubs) Trans-Atl Phila.

— State Governments Turn to New Taxes. 1990. pap. 5.00 (0-943802-85-7, BG106) Natl Ctr Pol.

***Moore, Stephen.** Welfare for the Well-Off: How Business Subsidies Fleece Taxpayers. (Essays in Public Policy Ser.: No. 88). 31p. 1999. pap. 5.00 (0-8179-5932-7) Hoover Inst Pr.

***Moore, Stephen & Simon, Julian L.** It's Getting Better All the Time: 100 Greatest Trends of the 20th Century. (Illus.). 2000. 29.95 (1-882577-96-5) Cato Inst.

Moore, Stephen, jt. auth. see Briggs, Vernon M., Jr.

Moore, Stephen, jt. auth. see Murphy, Donn B.

Moore, Stephen C., jt. auth. see Agran, Martin.

Moore, Stephen D. Mark & Luke in Poststructuralist Perspectives: Jesus Begins to Write. LC 91-30523. 192p. (C). 1992. 30.00 (0-300-05197-2) Yale U Pr.

— Postructuralism & the New Testament: Derrida & Foucault at the Foot of the Cross. LC 94-2954. 144p. 1994. pap. 17.00 (0-8006-2599-4, Fortress Pr) Augsburg Fortress.

Moore, Stephen D., jt. ed. see Anderson, Janice C.

Moore, Stephen D., jt. ed. see Clines, David J. A.

Moore, Stephen D., jt. ed. see Exum, J. Cheryl.

Moore, Stephen E. Church Words: Origins & Meanings. 136p. (Orig.). 1996. pap. 6.95 (0-88028-172-3, 1383) Forward Movement.

Moore, Stephen G., et al. The Buzzard Brigade: Torpedo Squadron Ten at War. LC 95-73264. (Illus.). 324p. 1996. 29.95 (1-57510-011-8) Pictorial Hist.

***Moore, Stephen L.** Taming Texas: Captain William T. Sadler's Lone Star Service. LC 00-36519. (Illus.). 424p. 2000. 34.95 (1-880510-68-5); pap. 24.95 (1-880510-69-3) State House Pr.

— Taming Texas: Captain William T. Sadler's Lone Star Service. limited ed. LC 00-36519. (Illus.). 424p. 2000. 150.00 (1-880510-70-7) State House Pr.

Moore, Stephen W. Griffith's Instructions for Patients. 6th ed. Kersey, Ray, ed. (Illus.). 9624p. 1998. pap. text 55.00 (0-7521-6737-5, W B Saunders Co) Harcrt Hlth Sci Grp.

— Griffith's Instructions for Patients. 6th ed. Kersey, Ray, ed. LC 98-3258. (Illus.). 624p. (C). 1998. pap. text 55.00 (0-7216-7375-9, W B Saunders Co) Harcrt Hlth Sci Grp.

Moore, Steve. Back to the Bleachers. LC 96-201796. 1995. 8.95 (0-02-860850-X) Macmillan.

— Designing with Analog Switches. (Electrical Engineering & Electronics Ser.: Vol. 68). (Illus.). 296p. 1991. text 145.00 (0-8247-8421-9) Dekker.

— Trigrams of Han. 1989. 12.95 (0-85030-808-9, Pub. by Aqrn Pr) Harper SF.

Moore, Steve & Beuthin, Timothy M., eds. The University Through the Eyes of Faith. LC 99-163916. 160p. 1998. pap. 10.99 (0-89367-228-9) Light & Life Comm.

Moore, Steven. A Reader's Guide to William Gaddis's "The Recognitions" LC 81-7572. 349p. 1982. reprint ed. pap. 108.20 (0-7837-4667-9, 204439400002) Bks Demand.

An Asterisk (*) at the beginning of an entry indicates that the title is appearing for the first time.

— Ronald Firbank: An Annotated Bibliography of Secondary Materials, 1905-1995. LC 96-15667. (Bibliography Ser.: No. 3). 160p. (Orig.). 1996. pap. 30.00 (*1-56478-133-X*) Dalkey Arch.
— William Gaddis. (United States Authors Ser.: No. 546). 176p. 1989. 22.95 (*0-8057-7534-X*, TUSAS 546) Macmillan.
Moore, Steven, ed. The Vampire in Verse: An Anthology. 196p. (Orig.). 1985. pap. 7.95 (*0-9611944-2-1*) Dracula Pr.
Moore, Steven, ed. see Dahlberg, Edward.
Moore, Steven, ed. see Firbank, Ronald.
Moore, Steven, jt. ed. see Kuehl, John.
Moore, Steven R., intro. Geriopharmacotherapy in Home Health Care: New Frontiers in Pharmaceutical Care. LC 93-6677. (Journal of Geriatric Drug Therapy: Vol. 7, No. 3). (Illus.). 71p. 1993. lib. bdg. 29.95 (*1-56024-415-1*) Haworth Pr.
Moore, Stuart, ed. see Reiber, John Ney.
Moore, Stuart, ed. see Robertson, Darick, et al.
Moore, Sue. Nursing Math Simplified: Math Magic. 3rd ed. Howland, Tom, ed. & illus. by. 70p. (Orig.). (C). 1992. pap. text 11.95 (*0-943202-58-2*) H & H Pub.
Moore, Sue, jt. auth. see Stephan, Naomi I.
Moore, Sue C. & Stephan, Naomi I. The Fulfill Your Soul's Purpose Workbook: A Guide for Self-Study How to Find Your Life Mission & Live with Intention. 136p. 1997. pap. 14.95 (*0-9631262-8-8*) Life Mission.
Moore, Susan. Chiropractic. (Alternative Health Ser.). 1993. pap. 12.95 (*0-8048-1831-2*) Tuttle Pubng.
— Understanding Pain & Its Relief in Labour. (Illus.). 184p. 1996. pap. write for info. (*0-443-05026-0*) Church.
Moore, Susan, et al. Orientation to Higher Education in California. 176p. (C). 1994. pap. text, per. 11.95 (*0-8403-9689-9*) Kendall-Hunt.
Moore, Susan, jt. auth. see Moore, Andy.
Moore, Susan G. Nursing Math Simplified: Math Magic. Howland, Joseph W. & Savige, Katherine, eds. (Illus.). 60p. (Orig.). (C). 1986. pap. text 7.50 (*0-943202-22-1*) H & H Pubs.
Moore, Susan J., ed. see Roach, Margaret J.
Moore, Susan M. & Rosenthal, Doreen A. Adolescent Sexuality in Social Context. LC 93-9869. (Adolescence & Society Ser.). 272p. (C). 1993. pap. 24.99 (*0-415-07528-9*, B0894) Routledge.
— Adolescent Sexuality in Social Context. LC 93-9869. (Adolescence & Society Ser.). 272p. (C). (gr. 13). 1993. text 62.95 (*0-415-07527-0*, B0890) Routledge.
***Moore, Susanna.** In the Cut: A Novel. LC 99-42898. 1999. pap. 12.95 (*0-452-28129-6*, Plume) Dutton Plume.
Moore, Susanna. In the Cut: A Novel. LC 95-17595. 177p. 1995. 21.00 (*0-679-42258-7*) Knopf.
— In the Cut: A Novel. 1996. mass mkt. 6.99 (*0-614-20516-6*, Onyx) NAL.
— Jennifer Bartlett: Important Works, 1974-1995. (Illus.). 36p. (Orig.). 1996. pap. 20.00 (*1-879173-26-3*) Locks Gallery.
— Sleeping Beauties. 240p. 1994. pap. 12.00 (*0-679-75539-X*) Vin Bks.
— Sleeping Beauties. large type ed. LC 94-2973. 340p. 1994. lib. bdg. 19.95 (*0-7862-0198-3*) Thorndike Pr.
Moore, Susannah. In Cut. 224p. 1996. mass mkt. 6.99 (*0-451-40722-9*, Onyx) NAL.
Moore, Suzanne. Looking for Trouble: Writings on Film, Shopping & Gender. 308p. (Orig.). (C). 1992. pap. 15.99 (*1-85242-242-4*) Serpents Tail.
***Moore, Suzanne & Benseler, David, eds.** The Modern Language Journal Index, 82 vols., Set. 1000p. 1999. 299.95 (*0-631-21827-0*) Blackwell Pubs.
Moore, Suzanne T. Coffee. (Illus.). 144p. 1974. pap. 4.95 (*0-938758-00-4*) MTM Pub Co.
— Coffee Too. 64p. (Orig.). 1975. pap. 3.95 (*0-938758-03-9*) MTM Pub Co.
— Palestina. 1983. 8.95 (*0-938758-13-6*) MTM Pub Co.
Moore, Suzi & Moore, Terrence. Under the Sun: Desert Style & Architecture. (Illus.). 248p. 1999. pap. 29.95 (*0-8212-2587-1*, Pub. by Bulfinch Pr) Little.
Moore, Sylvia. No Bluebonnets, No Yellow Roses: Texas Women in the Arts. LC 87-63478. (Women/Art Ser.). (Illus.). 138p. (Orig.). 1989. pap. 10.95 (*0-9602476-8-8*) Midmarch Arts.
Moore, Sylvia, ed. Yesterday & Tomorrow: California Women Artists. LC 88-63871. (Regional Women Artists Ser.). (Illus.). 378p. (Orig.). 1989. pap. text 15.95 (*0-9602476-9-6*) Midmarch Arts.
Moore, Sylvia, jt. ed. see Faxon, Alicia.
Moore, T. Lalla Rookh. 304p. 1987. 80.00 (*1-85077-148-0*, Pub. by Darf Pubs Ltd) St Mut.
Moore, T., jt. auth. see Woolley, P.
Moore, T. C. Biochemistry & Physiology of Plant Hormones. 2nd ed. (Illus.). xv, 330p. 1989. 102.95 (*0-387-96984-5*, 2731) Spr-Verlag.
— A Man May Fish. (Illus.). 226p. 1985. reprint ed. 35.00 (*0-86140-024-0*, Pub. by Smyth) Dufour.
— Research Experiences in Plant Physiology: A Laboratory Manual. 2nd ed. (Illus.). 348p. 1981. pap. 52.95 (*0-387-90606-1*) Spr-Verlag.
Moore, T. E. & Waite, J. H., eds. Modeling Magnetospheric Plasma. (Geophysical Monograph Ser.: Vol. 44). 344p. 1989. 38.00 (*0-87590-070-4*) Am Geophysical.
Moore, T. G., ed. Anthony & Berryman's Magistrates' Court Guide. 510p. 1994. pap. 59.00 (*0-406-02873-7*, MICHIE) LEXIS Pub.
— Anthony & Berryman's Magistrates' Court Guide. 1997. pap. write for info. (*0-406-89020-X*, ABMC1997, MICHIE) LEXIS Pub.
Moore, T. Harvey, jt. ed. see Lindley, David.
Moore, T. M. Making God's Good News Known. (Orig.). 1985. pap. text 4.95 (*0-934688-18-4*); pap. text, teacher ed. 3.95 (*0-934688-19-2*) Great Comm Pubns.
Moore, T. O. & Hadlock, E. H. Complex Analysis. (Series in Pure Mathematics). 404p. (C). 1991. text 67.00 (*981-02-0246-6*); pap. text 32.00 (*981-02-0247-4*) World Scientific Pub.
Moore, T. Owens. The Science of Melanin: Dispelling the Myths. 140p. 1995. pap. 12.95 (*0-931761-38-7*) Beckham Pubns.
Moore, T. Sturge. Poems of T. Sturge Moore, 4 vols., Set. 1982. reprint ed. lib. bdg. 125.00 (*0-403-01114-0*) Scholarly.
Moore, T. V. Haggai, Zechariah & Malachi. (Geneva Series of Commentaries). 408p. 1993. reprint ed. 23.99 (*0-85151-666-1*) Banner of Truth.
— The Last Days of Jesus. 212p. (Orig.). 1981. pap. 8.99 (*0-85151-321-2*) Banner of Truth.
— A Study in Reaction Time & Movement. (Psychology Monographs General & Applied: Vol. 6). 1974. reprint ed. pap. 55.00 (*0-8115-1405-6*) Periodicals Srv.
Moore, T. W. Philosophy of Education: An Introduction. (International Library of the Philosophy of Education). 100p. (Orig.). 1982. pap. 13.95 (*0-7100-9192-3*, Routledge Thoemms) Routledge.
Moore, Tedde, jt. ed. see Green, Lynda Mason.
Moore, Terence. The Captured Harvest: Creating Exquisite Objects from Nature. (Illus.). 160p. 1995. pap. 19.95 (*1-57076-012-8*, Trafalgar Sq Pub) Trafalgar.
— The New Captured Harvest: Creative Crafts from Nature. (Illus.). 160p. 1995. 29.95 (*1-57076-022-5*, Trafalgar Sq Pub) Trafalgar.
— New Captured Harvest: Creative Crafts From Nature. (Illus.). 160p. Date not set. write for info. (*1-85967-097-0*, Lorenz Bks) Anness Pub.
— New Flower Design. 1999. 19.98 (*1-84038-208-2*) Hermes Hse.
Moore, Terence F. Administrative Warfare. 114p. 1992. pap. 8.00 (*0-9633518-5-0*) Ivory Grp.
— Power: Its Use & Abuse. 94p. (Orig.). 1997. pap. text 8.00 (*0-9633518-6-9*) Ivory Grp.
Moore, Terence F. & Simendinger, Earl A. The Effective Health Care Executive: A Guide to a Winning Management. 240p. 1986. 73.00 (*0-87189-386-X*) Aspen Pub.
Moore, Terence F. & Simendinger, Earl A., eds. Managing the Nursing Shortage: A Guide to Recruitment & Retention. (Health Care Administration Ser.). 284p. 1989. 79.00 (*0-8342-0046-5*) Aspen Pub.
Moore, Teresa E., jt. auth. see Kinsey, L. Christine.
Moore, Terrence, photos by. Under the Sun: Desert Architecture & Style. LC 95-11432. (Illus.). 248p. 1995. 50.00 (*0-8212-2226-0*, Pub. by Bulfinch Pr) Little.
Moore, Terrence, jt. auth. see Moore, Suzi.
Moore, Terrence F., jt. ed. see Simendinger, Earl A.
Moore, Terris. Mt. McKinley: The Pioneer Climbs. LC 81-1002. (Illus.). 224p. 1981. reprint ed. pap. 12.95 (*0 89886-021-0*) Mountaineers.
Moore, Terry. The Collected Strangers in Paradise, Vol. 1. (Illus.). 96p. 1994. reprint ed. pap. 8.95 (*1-892597-00-4*) Abstract Studio.
— The Complete Stranger in Paradise, Vol. 1. (Illus.). 120p. 1998. reprint ed. 29.95 (*1-892597-05-5*) Abstract Studio.
***Moore, Terry.** The Complete Strangers in Paradise. (Strangers in Paradise Ser.: Vol. 2). (Illus.). 296p. 1999. reprint ed. 49.95 (*1-892597-06-3*) Abstract Studio.
Moore, Terry. Strangers in Paradise: Immortal Enemies. (Illus.). 152p. 1998. reprint ed. pap. 14.95 (*1-892597-04-7*) Abstract Studio.
— Strangers in Paradise: It's a Good Life. (Illus.). 88p. 1996. reprint ed. pap. 8.95 (*1-892597-02-0*) Abstract Studio.
— Strangers in Paradise: Love Me Tender. (Illus.). 128p. 1997. reprint ed. pap. 12.95 (*1-892597-03-9*) Abstract Studio.
— Strangers in Paradise Vol. 2: I Dream of You. (Illus.). 208p. 1996. reprint ed. pap. 16.95 (*1-892597-01-2*) Abstract Studio.
— Strangers in Paradise Vol. 3: High School! (Illus.). 80p. 1999. reprint ed. pap. 8.95 (*1-892597-07-1*, SIPTPB6) Abstract Studio.
***Moore, Terry.** Strangers in Paradise Vol. 3: Sanctuary. (Illus.). 176p. 1999. pap. 15.95 (*1-892597-09-8*, TPB7) Abstract Studio.
Moore, Terry. Toothpaste & Peanut Butter. Bryce, Herb, ed. (Illus.). 140p. (Orig.). 1987. pap. 9.95 (*0-88839-207-9*) Hancock House.
Moore, Terry & Rivers, Jerry. The Passions & Howard Hughes. abr. ed. 1996. write for info. incl. audio (*1-882071-74-3*, 636828, Pub. by B&B Audio) Lndmrk Audiobks.
Moore, Terry J. My Subtle Shift from Baptist Fundamentalist to... Sermons of a Newly Liberated Ministry. LC 98-85959. 325p. 1998. 25.00 (*0-7388-0002-3*); pap. 15.00 (*0-7388-0041-4*) Xlibris Corp.
Moore, Terry J. & Hampton, Anita B. Book Bridges: Story-Inspired Activities for Children Three Through Eight. (Illus.). 218p. (Orig.). 1991. pap. text 21.50 (*0-87287-919-4*) Teacher Ideas Pr.
Moore, Thomas. Book of Job. LC 97-45166. (Sacred Text Ser.). 432p. 1998. pap. 11.00 (*1-57322-674-2*, Riverhd Trade) Berkley Pub.
— Care of the Soul: A Guide for Cultivating Depth & Sacredness in Everyday Life. LC 91-50463. 336p. 1994. pap. 14.00 (*0-06-092224-9*, Perennial) HarperTrade.
— Care of the Soul: A Guide for Cultivating Depth & Sacredness in Everyday Life. large type ed. LC 93-13239. 496p. 1993. pap. 16.95 (*0-8027-2674-7*) Walker & Co.
Moore, Thomas. Care of the Soul: A Guide for Cultivating Depth & Sacredness in Everyday Life, Set. abr. ed. 1992. audio 16.00 (*1-55994-603-2*, 394520) HarperAudio.
Moore, Thomas. Dark Eros: The Imagination of Sadism. rev. ed. LC 94-35587. 202p. (Orig.). 1994. pap. 17.50 (*0-88214-365-4*) Spring Pubns.
Moore, Thomas. Education of the Heart: Moore,&Thomas, Set. abr. ed. 1996. audio 18.00 (*0-694-51739-9*, 394231) HarperAudio.
Moore, Thomas. The Education of the Heart: Readings & Sources for "Care of the Soul," "Soul Mates," & "The Re-Enchantment of Everyday Life" large type ed. 368p. 1997. pap. 14.00 (*0-06-092860-3*, Perennial) HarperTrade.
— Fast Track MCSE/MCSD SQL Server 7 Database Design. New Riders Publishing Staff, ed. LC 99-62349. (MCSE Fast Track Ser.). 1999. pap. text 29.99 (*0-7357-0040-0*) New Riders Pub.
***Moore, Thomas.** God's Breath: Sacred Scriptures of the World-Essential Texts of Buddhism, Christianity, Judaism., Vol. 1. Miller, John & Kenedi, Aaron, eds. LC 99-43283. (Illus.). 560p. 1999. 24.95 (*1-56924-623-8*) Marlowe & Co.
Moore, Thomas. Illustrated Care of the Soul: Cultivating Depth & Sacredness in Everyday Life. LC 98-23018. (Illus.). 256p. 1988. 35.00 (*0-06-757511-0*) HarpC.
— The Journal of Thomas Moore, 1843-1847, Vol. 6. Dowden, Wilfred S., ed. LC 79-13541. (Illus.). 408p. 1992. 70.00 (*0-87413-258-4*) U Delaware Pr.
— Lalla Rookh, an Oriental Romance. (BCL1-PR English Literature Ser.). 179p. 1992. reprint ed. lib. bdg. 69.00 (*0-7812-7605-5*) Rprt Serv.
— The Life, Letters & Journals of Lord Byron. 735p. reprint ed. lib. bdg. 99.00 (*0-7812-0248-5*) Rprt Serv.
— Life of the R. Hon. Richard B. Sheridan, 2 vols. 1981. reprint ed. lib. bdg. 59.00 (*0-403-01763-7*) Scholarly.
— Life of the Right Honorable Richard Brinsley Sheridan, 2 vols., Set. 1826. 59.00 (*0-403-00072-6*) Scholarly.
— Meditations. 1996. pap. 13.50 (*0-614-17409-0*) HarpC.
— Meditations: On the Monk Who Dwells in Daily Life. 128p. 1995. pap. 10.00 (*0-06-092700-3*, Harp PBks) HarpC.
— Memoirs, Journal, & Correspondence of Thomas Moore, 8 vols., Set. (BCL1-PR English Literature Ser.). 1992. reprint ed. lib. bdg. 600.00 (*0-7812-7606-3*) Rprt Serv.
— Memoirs of Captain Rock (pseud.) the Celebrated Irish Chieftain: With Some Account of His Ancestors. LC 75-28831. reprint ed. 67.50 (*0-404-13821-7*) AMS Pr.
— Memoirs of the Life of the Right Honorable Richard Brinsley Sheridan, 2 Vols. LC 79-152997. (Select Bibliographies Reprint Ser.). 1977. reprint ed. 44.95 (*0-8369-5749-0*) Ayer.
— Memoirs of the Life of the Right Honorable Richard Brinsley Sheridan, 2 vols. LC 69-14001. 1969. reprint ed. lib. bdg. 75.00 (*0-8371-9944-1*, Greenwood Pr) Greenwood.
— Memoirs of the Life of the Right Honorable Richard Brinsley Sheridan, 2 vols., Set. (BCL1-PR English Literature Ser.). 1992. reprint ed. lib. bdg. 150.00 (*0-7812-7401-X*) Rprt Serv.
— Memoirs of the Life of the Right Honorable Richard Brinsley Sheridan, 2 vols., Vol. 1. LC 69-14001. 1969. reprint ed. lib. bdg. 75.00 (*0-8371-0573-0*, MORA, Greenwood Pr) Greenwood.
— Memoirs of the Life of the Right Honorable Richard Brinsley Sheridan, 2 vols., Vol. 2. LC 69-14001. 1969. reprint ed. lib. bdg. 75.00 (*0-8371-0826-8*, MORB, Greenwood Pr) Greenwood.
— Moore's Irish Melodies with Symphonies & Accompaniments. LC 81-81465. 261p. 1981. 65.00 (*0-89453-259-6*) Scholarly Res Inc.
***Moore, Thomas.** Original Self: Living with Paradox & Originality. LC 99-45049. (Illus.). 160p. 2000. 22.00 (*0-06-019542-8*) HarpC.
Moore, Thomas. The Planets Within: The Astrological Psychology of Marsilio Ficino. 240p. 1993. reprint ed. pap. 16.95 (*0-940262-28-2*, Lindisfarne) Anthroposophic.
— The Poetical Works of Thomas Little. LC 90-31439. (Revolution & Romanticism Ser.). 204p. 1990. reprint ed. 48.00 (*1-85477-050-0*) Continuum.
— The Poetical Works of Thomas Moore. Godley, A. D., ed. LC 75-41197. reprint ed. 42.50 (*0-404-14688-0*) AMS Pr.
— The Poetical Works of Thomas Moore. (BCL1-PR English Literature Ser.). 751p. 1992. reprint ed. lib. bdg. 109.00 (*0-7812-7604-7*) Rprt Serv.
— The Re-Enchantment of Everyday Life. large type ed. LC 96-5877. 384p. 1996. 25.95 (*0-7838-1819-X*, G K Hall Lrg Type) Mac Lib Ref.
— The Re-Enchantment of Everyday Life. large type ed. 656p. 1997. pap. 23.95 (*0-7838-1969-2*, G K Hall Lrg Type) Mac Lib Ref.
— The Re-enchantment of Everyday Life. large type ed. LC 96-6400. 416p. 1997. pap. 14.00 (*0-06-092824-7*, Perennial) HarperTrade.
Moore, Thomas. Reenchantment of Everyday Life: Moore,&Thomas, Set. 1996. audio 18.00 (*0-694-51691-0*, 628149) HarperAudio.
— Soul & Everyday Life. 121p. 1995. pap. 19.95 incl. audio (*1-879323-16-8*) Sound Horizons AV.
Moore, Thomas. Soul Mates: Honoring the Mysteries of Love & Relationship. 288p. 1994. pap. 14.00 (*0-06-092575-2*) HarperTrade.
Moore, Thomas. Soul Mates- Reflections on Love's Mysteries: Moore,&Thomas, Set. abr. ed. 1994. audio 17.00 (*1-55994-941-4*, CPN 2419) HarperAudio.
Moore, Thomas. The Soul of Sex: Cultivating Life As an Act of Love. 336p. 1998. 25.00 (*0-06-018697-6*) HarpC.
— The Soul of Sex: Cultivating Life As an Act of Love. (Illus.). 336p. 1999. pap. 14.00 (*0-06-093095-0*) HarpC.
— Soulmates. 1996. pap. 13.50 (*0-614-17408-2*) HarpC.
— Souls Relight. 1999. pap. 13.00 (*0-06-093019-5*) HarpC.
— The Style of Connectedness: "Gravity's Rainbow" & Thomas Pynchon. LC 86-16093. 320p. 1987. text 37.50 (*0-8262-0625-5*, 83-36331) U of Mo Pr.
— Tom Moore's Diary. Priestley, J. B., ed. LC 76-131783. 1971. reprint ed. 49.00 (*0-403-00670-8*) Scholarly.
— Tom Moore's Diary: A Selection. (BCL1-PR English Literature Ser.). 218p. 1992. reprint ed. lib. bdg. 79.00 (*0-7812-7607-1*) Rprt Serv.
Moore, Thomas, ed. The Education of the Heart. large type ed. LC 97-12438. (Inspirational Ser.). 511p. 1997. lib. bdg. 26.95 (*0-7838-8201-7*, G K Hall Lrg Type) Mac Lib Ref.
***Moore, Thomas, ed.** Teaching Statistics: Resources for Undergraduate Instructors. LC 00-103315. (MAA Notes Ser.: Vol. 52). 260p. (C). 2000. 31.50 (*0-88385-162-8*) Math Assn.
Moore, Thomas, frwd. No Greater Love. LC 96-43158. 224p. 1997. 21.00 (*1-57731-006-3*) New Wrld Lib.
Moore, Thomas, jt. auth. see Hillman, James.
Moore, Thomas, jt. auth. see Schiller, Pam.
Moore, Thomas A. Evidence in Negligence Cases. 463p. 1991. text 135.00 (*0-87224-027-4*, H1-3002) PLI.
— A Traveler's Guide to Spacetime: An Introduction to the Special Theory of Relativity. LC 94-39850. 224p. (C). 1995. pap. 31.25 (*0-07-043027-6*) McGraw.
Moore, Thomas A., jt. auth. see Kramer, Daniel C.
Moore, Thomas C. Neurovasc Immun: Vasoactive Neurotrans & Modul-Cell Immun. 480p. 1992. lib. bdg. 199.00 (*0-8493-6894-4*, QP356) CRC Pr.
Moore, Thomas G. Climate of Fear: Why We Shouldn't Worry about Global Warming. LC 98-3143. 1998. 18.95 (*1-882577-64-7*); pap. 9.95 (*1-882577-65-5*) Cato Inst.
— Environmental Fundamentalism. LC 92-25696. (Essays in Public Policy Ser.: No. 33). 1992. pap. text 5.00 (*0-8179-5382-5*) Hoover Inst Pr.
— Global Warming: A Boon to Humans & Other Animals. LC 95-12011. (Essays in Public Policy Ser.: No. 61). 1995. pap. text 5.00 (*0-8179-5662-X*) Hoover Inst Pr.
Moore, Thomas G., jt. ed. see Holmes, Kim R.
Moore, Thomas G., jt. ed. see Leube, Kurt R.
Moore, Thomas H., ed. see Miller, Henry.
Moore, Thomas J. Deadly Medicine: Why Tens of Thousands of Hearts Died in America's Worst Drug Disaster. 1995. 23.00 (*0-684-80417-4*) S&S Trade.
— Lifespan: New Perspectives on Extending Human Longevity. 320p. 1994. pap. 12.00 (*0-671-88622-3*, Touchstone) S&S Trade Pap.
— Lifespan: What Really Affects Human Longevity. (Illus.). 352p. 1993. 23.00 (*0-671-72966-7*) S&S Trade.
— Prescription for Disaster: The Hidden Dangers in Your Medicine Cabinet. 1999. mass mkt. 5.99 (*0-440-23484-0*) Dell.
— Prescription for Disaster: The Hidden Dangers in Your Medicine Cabinet. LC 97-47081. 272p. 1998. 25.00 (*0-684-82998-3*) S&S Trade.
***Moore, Thomas J.** The Wisdom of Jesus: His Life & Teachings in Calligraphy & Illustration. LC 99-41159. (Illus.). 112p. 2000. pap. 12.95 (*0-8091-3909-X*) Paulist Pr.
Moore, Thomas M. & McKenna, Robert G., eds. Characterization of Integrated Circuit Packaging Materials. LC 93-7685. (Materials Characterization Ser.). 274p. 1993. text 94.95 (*0-7506-9267-7*) Buttrwrth-Heinemann.
Moore, Thomas R. Plantagenet Descent: 31 Generations from William the Conqueror to Today. (Illus.). xviii, 242p. 1995. 49.50 (*0-9644929-0-3*) T R Moore.
— A Thick & Darksome Veil: The Rhetoric of Hawthorne's Sketches, Prefaces, & Essays. 192p. 1994. text 37.50 (*1-55553-184-9*) NE U Pr.
Moore, Thomas R., et al, eds. Gynecology & Obstetrics: A Longitudinal Approach. (Illus.). 984p. 1993. text 121.00 (*0-443-08811-X*) Church.
Moore, Thomas R., jt. auth. see Smith, Elliott Dunlap.
Moore, Thomas S. The Disposable Work Force: Worker Displacement & Employment Instability in America. LC 95-21943. (Social Institutions & Social Change Ser.). 167p. 1996. pap. text 19.95 (*0-202-30520-1*); lib. bdg. 38.95 (*0-202-30519-8*) Aldine de Gruyter.
Moore, Thomas S., Jr. Lipid Metabolism in Plants. 672p. 1993. 218.00 (*0-8493-4907-9*, QK898) CRC Pr.
Moore, Thomas S. Some Soldier Poets. LC 68-16958. (Essay Index Reprint Ser.). 1977. 18.95 (*0-8369-0715-9*) Ayer.
Moore, Thomas V., jt. auth. see Bergman, Robert E.
***Moore, Thurston.** Alabama Wildman. 150p. 2000. 18.95 (*0-934953-70-8*) Water Row Pr.
— Alabama Wildman. (Illus.). 150p. 2000. 65.00 (*0-934953-71-6*) Water Row Pr.
***Moore, Tim.** Frost on My Moustache: The Arctic Exploits of a Lord & a Loafer. LC 99-55860. (Illus.). 288p. 2000. text 23.95 (*0-312-25319-2*, Truman Talley) St Martin.
Moore, Tim & Davis, Carol. On the Move: How to Succeed & Survive As an Entrepreneur. LC 99-191505. (Illus.). 288p. 1997. pap. 16.50 (*0-919292-01-1*, Pub. by McLeod Pub) Genl Dist Srvs.
***Moore, Tim & Moore, Jerry, eds.** Short Stories for Students. 5th ed. 350p. 1999. text 60.00 (*0-7876-2220-6*) Gale.
Moore, Timothy J. The Theater of Plautus: Playing to the Audience. LC 98-13014. (Illus.). 280p. 1999. 35.00 (*0-292-75208 3*) U of Tex Pr.
— The Theatre of Plautus: Playing to the Audience. LC 98-13014. 1998. pap. 17.95 (*0-292-75217-2*) U of Tex Pr.
Moore, Todd. The Man in the Black Chevrolet. LC 76-29870. 1976. pap. 1.50 (*0-916918-04-1*) Duck Down.
***Moore, Todd.** Shotgun Blues. 24p. 1999. pap. 3.95 (*0-9676660-2-3*, Pick Pocket Pr) Phony Lid Pubns.
Moore, Todd. Working on My Duende. (Illus.). 80p. 1998. per. write for info. (*1-888832-08-8*) Kings Estate.

Moore, Tom. Rituals of the Imagination. 2nd ed. 64p. 1999. pap. 12.00 (*0-911005-03-X*) Dallas Inst Pubns.

Moore, Tom I. Social Patterns in Australian Literature. LC 71-133027. 360p. reprint ed. pap. 111.60 (*0-608-15844-5*, 20314100074) Bks Demand.

Moore, Toni. The Exalted One. LC 95-94869. 1995. 17.95 (*0-9648195-0-3*); pap. 9.95 (*0-9648195-1-1*) T Moore.

Moore, Tracy, ed. Lesbiot. 1995. pap. 21.95 (*0-304-33158-9*) LPC InBook.

Moore, Tracy, ed. see Swinford, Betty.

Moore, Tracy, ed. see Taylor, Kenneth.

Moore, Tracy, ed. & illus. see Massey, Craig.

Moore, Tracy, ed. & illus. see Massey, Craig & Massey, Louise.

Moore, Tracy L. Songs in the Night. 44p. (Orig.). 1995. pap. 8.00 (*0-9646927-0-8*) T L Moore.

Moore, Trevor. Scraps. 160p. 1994. pap. 8.95 (*0-9643369-0-1*) Poindexter Pr.

Moore, V. Farm Workshop & Maintenance. 3rd ed. (Book of the Farmers Weekly). (Illus.). 256p. 1992. pap. 39.95 (*0-632-02538-7*) Blackwell Sci.

***Moore, Van Dolan.** Elohiym: The Pillar of Fire. Jenkins, Vivian, ed. (Illus.). 256p. 1999. 18.95 (*0-9676824-0-1*); pap. write for info. (*0-9676824-1-X*) Prophetic Pubng.

***Moore, Vance.** Prophecy Bk. III: Masquerade Cycle. (Magic Ser.: Vol. 3). 320p. 2000. pap. 6.99 (*0-7869-1570-6*) TSR Inc.

Moore, Vic. Farm Workshop & Maintenance: The Book of the Farmers Weekly Series. 3rd ed. (Illus.). 248p. 1988. pap. 34.95 (*0-8464-1299-3*) Beekman Pubs.

Moore, Vickie. Seared Satin. (Scarlet Ser.). 1998. mass mkt. 3.99 (*1-85487-883-2*, Pub. by Scarlet Bks) London Brdge.

— Shadowed Promises. (Scarlet Ser.). 1997. mass mkt. 3.99 (*1-85487-720-8*, Pub. by Scarlet Bks) London Brdge.

— This Time Forever. 400p. (Orig.). 1996. mass mkt. 3.99 (*1-85487-721-6*, Pub. by Scarlet Bks) London Brdge.

Moore, Victor. A Practical Approach to Planning Law. 368p. (C). 1987. 190.00 (*1-85185-070-8*, Pub. by Blackstone Pr) St Mut.

— A Practical Approach to Planning Law. 4th ed. 415p. 1994. pap. 42.00 (*1-85431-355-X*, Pub. by Blackstone Pr) Gaunt.

— A Practical Approach to Planning Law. 5th ed. 562p. 1995. pap. 38.00 (*1-85431-483-1*, Pub. by Blackstone Pr) Gaunt.

— A Practical Approach to Planning Law. 6th ed. LC 98-226958. 576p. 1997. pap. 44.00 (*1-85431-685-0*, Pub. by Blackstone Pr) Gaunt.

Moore, Victor & Hughes, David. Blackstone's Statutes on Planning Law. 444p. (C). 1995. pap. 30.00 (*1-85431-125-5*, Pub. by Blackstone Pr) Gaunt.

— Blackstone's Statutes on Planning Law. 2nd ed. 507p. 1995. pap. 30.00 (*1-85431-490-4*, Pub. by Blackstone Pr) Gaunt.

Moore, Virginia. Life & Eager Death of Emily Bronte. LC 78-173844. (English Biography Ser.: No. 31). 1971. reprint ed. lib. bdg. 75.00 (*0-8383-1345-0*) M S G Haskell Hse.

Moore, Vivian A. Memories, Blessings & Tears. 1998. pap. write for info. (*1-57553-850-4*) Watermrk Pr.

Moore, W. American Negro Slavery & Abolition. LC 73-148362. 1971. 29.95 (*0-89388-000-0*); pap. 14.95 (*0-89388-001-9*) Okpaku Communications.

Moore, W. C. Diccionario de Geografia: Dictionary of Geography. (SPA.). 158p. 1972. 19.95 (*0-8288-6354-7*, S-50246) Fr & Eur.

Moore, W. G. Clothing. (Man & His World Ser.). (Illus.). 112p. 1977. 15.95 (*0-7175-0772-6*) Dufour.

— Homes. (Man & His World Ser.). (Illus.). 144p. 1976. 14.95 (*0-7175-0691-6*) Dufour.

— The Tutorial System & Its Future. LC 67-30293. (C). 1968. 40.00 (*0-08-012659-6*, Pub. by Pergamon Repr) Franklin.

Moore, W. G., ed. Advances in Steam Turbine Technology for the Power Generation Industry: Proceedings of the International Joint Power Generation Conference, Phoenix, AZ, 1994. 330p. 1994. pap. 65.00 (*0-7918-1382-7*) ASME.

Moore, W. H., jt. auth. see Mortimer, C. H.

Moore, W. Harrison. Act of State in English Law. x, 178p. 1987. reprint ed. 35.00 (*0-8377-2433-3*, Rothman) W S Hein.

— Act of State in English Law, No. 1. x, 178p. 1999. reprint ed. 60.00 (*1-56169-461-4*) Gaunt.

Moore, W. J. Diaries & Memoirs of a Sailor. 80p. (C). 1989. pap. 40.00 (*0-7223-1728-X*, Pub. by A H S Ltd) St Mut.

— Physical Chemistry. 1972. pap. 37.95 (*0-582-44234-6*, Pub. by Addison-Wesley) Longman.

Moore, W. J., jt. auth. see Johnson, D. R.

Moore, W. Joan, et al. Homeboys: Gangs, Drugs & Prison in the Barrios of Los Angeles. LC 78-11808. (Illus.). 1980. pap. 19.95 (*0-87722-114-6*) Temple U Pr.

Moore, W. Kent. Ultimate Elvis Quiz Book: What Do You Know about the King of Rock 'n' Roll? LC 99-478499. 160p. 1999. pap. 9.95 (*1-55853-748-1*) Rutledge Hill Pr.

***Moore, W. Kent & Scott.** The Ultimate Elvis Quiz Book. 2000. 6.99 (*0-517-20865-2*) Random.

Moore, W. Kent, jt. auth. see Scott, David L.

Moore, W. R., jt. auth. see Delgado-Frias, J. G.

Moore, W. R., jt. ed. see Delgado-Frias, Jose G.

Moore, W. Tabb & Eastman, Richard C., eds. Diagnostic Endocrinology. 2nd ed. LC 95-35681. (Illus.). 512p. (C). (gr. 13). 1996. text 95.00 (*0-8151-5957-9*, 24090) Mosby Inc.

Moore, Waddy W. Arkansas in the Guilded Age, Eighteen Seventy-four to Nineteen Hundred. (Illus.). 229p. 1976. pap. 14.95 (*0-914546-08-2*) J W Bell.

Moore, Walker. You Wanna Pierce What? Getting a Grip on Today's Family. LC 97-220874. 240p. 1997. pap. 8.99 (*1-57778-025-6*, Pub. by Albury Pub) Appalach Bk Dist.

Moore, Wallace. Wally Moore's Wedding & Banquet Reference. 154p. 1991. spiral bd. write for info. (*0-9631447-0-7*) T C & I.

Moore, Walter. A Life of Erwin Schrodinger. (Canto Book Ser.). (Illus.). 363p. (C). 1994. pap. 12.95 (*0-521-46934-1*) Cambridge U Pr.

— Prospect Spirit of Creative Poetry. 72p. 1999. pap. 8.00 (*0-8059-4444-3*) Dorrance.

— Schrodinger: Life & Thought. (Illus.). 528p. (C). 1989. text 69.95 (*0-521-35434-X*) Cambridge U Pr.

— Schrodinger: Life & Thought. (Illus.). 525p. (C). 1992. pap. 27.95 (*0-521-43767-9*) Cambridge U Pr.

Moore, Walter J. Erwin Schrodinger: Una Vida (A Life of Erwin Schrodinger)Tr. of Erwin Schrodinger: A Life. (SPA., Illus.). 453p. (C). 1996. pap. 19.95 (*0-521-55593-0*) Cambridge U Pr.

— Grundlagen der Physikalischen Chemie. (GER.). xxiv, 819p. (C). 1990. lib. bdg. 67.70 (*3-11-009941-1*) De Gruyter.

— Physikalische Chemie. 3rd ed. (GER.). 1236p. 1983. 75.40 (*3-11-008554-2*) De Gruyter.

Moore, Ward. Bring the Jubilee. 240p. 1997. pap. 11.00 (*0-345-40502-1*) Ballantine Pub Grp.

— Greener Than You Think. 1993. reprint ed. lib. bdg. 18.95 (*0-89968-355-X*, Lghtyr Pr) Buccaneer Bks.

— Lot & Lot's Daughter. 72p. 1996. pap. 10.00 (*0-9648320-1-1*) Tachyon Pubns.

Moore, Ward W., jt. auth. see Byrd, Cecil K.

Moore, Ward W., jt. ed. see Byrd, Cecil K.

Moore, Warren. Mountain Voices. 2nd ed. (Illus.). 288p. 1997. 35.95 (*0-9654911-0-2*); pap. 25.95 (*0-9654911-1-0*) Blair.

Moore, Waylon B. Living God's Word: Practical Lessons for Applying Scripture to Life. 96p. 1997. pap. text 7.95 (*0-7673-2604-0*, LifeWy Press) LifeWay Christian.

Moore, Wayne C. Small Computers in Construction: Proceedings of a Symposium Sponsored by the Construction Division. 89p. 1984. 16.00 (*0-87262-400-5*) Am Soc Civil Eng.

Moore, Wayne C., ed. Applications of Small Computers in Construction: Proceedings of a Session Sponsored by the Construction Division (A Follow-Up of a Symposium on Small Computers in Construction) 62p. 1984. 5.00 (*0-87262-416-1*) Am Soc Civil Eng.

Moore, Wayne C. & Herbison, Mark. Looking Back at Tennessee: A Photographic Retrospective. LC 96-78410. (Illus.). 224p. 1996. 29.95 (*1-57736-014-1*, Hillsboro Pr) Providence Hse.

Moore, Wayne D. Constitutional Rights & Powers of the People. 304p. 1996. pap. text 18.95 (*0-691-00244-4*, Pub. by Princeton U Pr) Cal Prin Full Svc.

— Constitutional Rights & Powers of the People. 304p. 1996. text 39.50 (*0-691-01111-7*, Pub. by Princeton U Pr) Cal Prin Full Svc.

Moore, Wayne D. & Bunker, Merton W., eds. National Fire Alarm Code Handbook. 3rd ed. LC 96-35522. 1997. 88.00 (*0-87765-410-7*) Natl Fire Prot.

Moore, Wayne D., jt. auth. see Bunker, Merton W., Jr.

Moore, Wendell, ed. see National Phonograph Company Staff.

Moore, Wendy. Kathmandu: The Forbidden Valley. 2000. 35.00 (*0-312-04610-3*) Weatherhill.

— Sydney in a Week. 1998. pap. 24.95 (*1-86436-278-2*, Pub. by New5 Holland) Sterling.

— This Is Malaysia. 1998. 39.95 (*1-85368-375-2*, Pub. by New5 Holland) Sterling.

***Moore, Wendy.** This Is Sydney. 2000. pap. 24.95 (*1-86436-597-8*, Pub. by New Holland) BHB Intl.

Moore, Wendy. This Is Sydney. (Illus.). 160p. 1998. 39.95 (*1-86436-214-6*, Pub. by New5 Holland) Sterling.

— West Malaysia & Singapore. (Passport's Regional Guides of Malaysia Ser.). (Illus.). 288p. 1994. pap. 17.95 (*0-8442-9891-3*, 98913, Passprt Bks) NTC Contemp Pub Co.

— West Malaysia & Singapore. 288p. 1993. pap. 19.95 (*0-945971-64-8*) Periplus.

Moore, Wesley S. Vascular Surgery: A Comprehensive Review. 5th ed. Bralow, Lisette, ed. LC 96-35522. (Illus.). 832p. 1997. text 195.00 (*0-7216-6962-X*, W B Saunders Co) Harcrt Hlth Sci Grp.

Moore, Wesley S., ed. Surgery for Cerebrovascular Disease. 2nd ed. (Illus.). 736p. 1996. text 230.00 (*0-7216-3624-1*, W B Saunders Co) Harcrt Hlth Sci Grp.

Moore, Wesley S. & Malone. Lower Extremity Amputation. 352p. 1989. text 105.00 (*0-7216-6485-7*, W B Saunders Co) Harcrt Hlth Sci Grp.

Moore, Wesley S., jt. auth. see Ahn, Samuel S.

Moore, Wilbert E. American Negro Slavery & Abolition: A Sociological Study. Zuckerman, Harriet & Merton, Robert K., eds. LC 79-9015. (Dissertations on Sociology Ser.). 1980. lib. bdg. 19.95 (*0-405-12982-3*) Ayer.

— Economic Demography of Eastern & Southern Europe. LC 72-4283. (World Affairs Ser.: National & International Viewpoints). 304p. 1972. reprint ed. 23.95 (*0-405-04576-X*) Ayer.

— Industrial Relations & the Social Order. rev. ed. Stein, Leon, ed. LC 77-70517. (Illus.). 1977. reprint ed. lib. bdg. 59.95 (*0-405-10186-4*) Ayer.

— The Professions: Roles & Rules. LC 78-104184. 316p. 1970. 39.95 (*0-87154-604-3*) Russell Sage.

Moore, Wilbert E. & Feldman, Arnold S. Labor Commitment & Social Change in Developing Areas. LC 82-6144. 378p. 1982. reprint ed. lib. bdg. 69.50 (*0-313-23572-4*, MOLC, Greenwood Pr) Greenwood.

Moore, Wilbert E., jt. auth. see Davis, Kingsley.

Moore, Wilbert E., jt. auth. see Young, Donald R.

Moore, Wilbert E., jt. ed. see Gurvich, Georgy D.

Moore, Wilbert E., jt. ed. see Sheldon, Eleanor B.

Moore, Wilbur E., jt. auth. see Black, John W.

Moore, Wilford H. The Light of the Living, Set, Vols. 1 & 2. 256p. pap. 10.95 (*0-9644872-0-9*) W H Moore.

Moore, Will, et al, eds. Field-Programmable Logic & Applications: 5th International Workshop, FPL '95, Oxford, United Kingdom, August 29-September 1, 1995, Proceedings, Vol. XII. LC 95-24945. (Lecture Notes in Computer Science Ser.: Vol. 975). 450p. 1995. 75.00 (*3-540-60294-1*) Spr-Verlag.

Moore, Will G., et al, eds. French Mind: Studies in Honour of Gustave Rudler. LC 75-167386. (Essay Index Reprint Ser.). 1977. reprint ed. 22.95 (*0-8369-2464-9*) Ayer.

Moore, Will R., jt. ed. see Delgado-Frias, Jose G.

Moore, Willard. Molokan Oral Tradition: Legends & Memorates of an Ethnic Sect. LC 72-619685. (University of California Publications, Folklore Studies: No. 28). 93p. reprint ed. pap. 30.00 (*0-608-13910-6*, 202120700021) Bks Demand.

Moore, Willard B., et al. Circles of Tradition: Folk Arts in Minnesota. LC 88-37753. (Illus.). xii, 162p. 1989. pap. 18.95 (*0-87351-239-1*) Minn Hist.

Moore, William. Blind Man on a Freeway: The Community College Administrator. LC 72-168858. (Jossey-Bass Higher Education Ser.). 201p. reprint ed. pap. 62.40 (*0-8357-7320-5*, 202566400045) Bks Demand.

— Dogs: A Guide to Popular Breeds, 1. LC 98-47970. 1999. 19.98 (*1-57145-169-2*, Thunder Bay) Advantage Pubs.

— Home Beermaking. 3rd ed. (Illus.). 68p. 1991. pap. 5.95 (*0-9605318-1-5*) Ferment Pr.

— 1996 International Workshop on Human Factors in Offshore Operations Held December 16-18, 1996, New Orleans, Louisiana: Summary of Proceedings & Submitted Papers. unabridged ed. Bea, Robert G. et al, eds. (Illus.). 444p. 1998. pap. 50.00 (*0-943870-00-3*) Am Bur Shipping.

— The Philadelphia Experiment. 1987. mass mkt. 5.99 (*0-449-21471-0*) Fawcett.

— The Sicarii. LC 89-63164. 192p. (Orig.). 1990. pap. 8.95 (*0-945563-01-9*) Penumbra Pub.

***Moore, William.** Thin Yellow Line. 1999. pap. text. write for info. (*1-84022-215-8*, Pub. by Wrdsworth Edits) Combined Pub.

Moore, William & Wagstaff, Lonnie H. Black Educators in White Colleges. LC 73-12066. (Jossey-Bass Series in Higher Education). 240p. reprint ed. pap. 74.40 (*0-8357-4953-3*, 203788500009) Bks Demand.

Moore, William A. History of Itsekiri. 2nd rev. ed. 224p. 1970. 45.00 (*0-7146-1701-6*, Pub. by F Cass Pubs) Intl Spec Bk.

***Moore, William A.** Sacred Grounds. LC 99-91124. 370p. 1999. 25.00 (*0-7388-0630-7*); pap. 18.00 (*0-7388-0631-5*) Xlibris Corp.

Moore, William B., Jr. Letters to Rebecca. (Illus.). 378p. (Orig.). 1995. pap. 27.50 (*0-7884-0304-4*) Heritage Bk.

Moore, William B., jt. auth. see Licht, Lilla M.

Moore, William C. Wall Street: Its Mysteries Revealed, Its Secrets Exposed Together with A Complete Course of Instruction in Speculation & Investment & Rules for Safe Guidance Therein. LC 66-19018. 1969. reprint ed. pap. 12.00 (*0-87034-041-7*) Fraser Pub Co.

Moore, William I., jt. auth. see Berlitz, Charles.

Moore, William L. & Pessemier, Edgar A. Product Planning & Management: Designing & Delivering Value. LC 92-13522. (Marketing Ser.). (C). 1993. text 66.25 (*0-07-043046-2*) McGraw.

Moore, William L., jt. auth. see Berlitz, Charles.

Moore, William L., jt. auth. see Tushman, Michael L.

Moore, William R. & Winston, Anthony. Laboratory Manual for Organic Chemistry: A Microscale Approach. 350p. (C). 1995. pap. 50.31 (*0-07-043052-7*) McGraw.

Moore, William S. The Estate Plan Book & the Taxpayer Relief Act of 1997: Income & Estate Tax Changes That Affect You. (Economic Education Bulletin Ser.: No. 12). (Illus.). 122p. 1997. pap. 10.00 (*0-913610-05-4*) Am Inst Econ Res.

***Moore, William S.** How to Make Tax-Saving Gifts. (Economic Education Bulletin Ser.: Vol. 39, No. 7). 43p. 1999. pap. 3.00 (*0-913610-10-0*) Am Inst Econ Res.

Moore, William V., jt. auth. see Graham, Cole B., Jr.

Moore, William W. William W. Moore. LC 98-37974. (Connections). 1998. 15.00 (*0-943198-63-1*) Earthquake Eng.

Moore, Willis L. The Cosmist: The Religion of Science & Philosophy. 215p. 1998. reprint ed. spiral bd. 16.00 (*1-885395-70-1*) Book Tree.

Moore, Winfred B., Jr., et al, eds. Developing Dixie: Modernization in a Traditional Society, 127. LC 87-24954. (Contributions in American History Ser.: No. 127). 380p. 1988. 67.95 (*0-313-26061-3*, MDX/, Greenwood Pr) Greenwood.

Moore, Winfred B., Jr. & Tripp, Joseph F., eds. Looking South: Chapters in the Story of an American Region, 136. LC 89-1888. (Contributions in American History Ser.: No. 136). 301p. 1989. 65.00 (*0-313-26694-8*, MLU, Greenwood Pr) Greenwood.

Moore, Winfred B., Jr., jt. ed. see Fraser, Walter J., Jr.

Moore, Yvette. The Birth of Christ. (Jubilee Year Bible Stories Ser.). 16p. (J). 1993. pap. 6.00 (*0-9637273-0-3*) Jubilee Yr Bks.

— Freedom Songs. LC 92-20289. 176p. (YA). (gr. 7 up). 1992. pap. 4.99 (*0-14-036017-4*, PuffinBks) Peng Put Young Read.

Moore, Yvette. Freedom Songs. (J). 1992. 10.09 (*0-606-01693-7*, Pub. by Turtleback) Demco.

Moore, Zena, ed. Foreign Language Teacher Education: Multiple Perspectives. LC 96-32902. 352p. 1996. pap. text 34.00 (*0-7618-0467-6*) U Pr of Amer.

Moorefield, Arthur A. An Introduction to Galliculus, Vol. 18. (Wissenschäftliche Abhandlungen - Musicological Studies). 1996. 24.00 (*0-912024-88-7*) Inst Mediaeval Mus.

Moorefield, Arthur A., ed. Galliculus: Gesamtausgabe, Isagoge de Composicione Cantus. (Gesamtausgaben - Collected Works: Vol. VIII, Pt. 4). (LAT.). 37p. 1992. 52.00 (*0-931902-74-6*) Inst Mediaeval Mus.

Moorefield, Arthur A., ed. see Galliculus, Johannes.

Moorehead, Alan. The Blue Nile. 1976. 24.95 (*0-8488-0766-9*) Amereon Ltd.

***Moorehead, Alan.** The Blue Nile. 320p. 2000. pap. 14.00 (*0-06-095640-2*, Perennial) HarperTrade.

Moorehead, Alan. Cooper's Creek. 1976. 21.95 (*0-8488-0593-3*) Amereon Ltd.

***Moorehead, Alan.** Desert War, 1940-1943: The Classic Account of WWII Battles in North Africa. 1999. pap. 18.95 (*0-14-027514-2*) Pnguin Bks Ltd.

Moorehead, Alan. Eclipse: An Eyewitness Account of the Invasion of Europe. LC 98-31947. 300p. 1999. pap. 13.00 (*1-56947-164-9*) Soho Press.

— Gallipoli. (Wordsworth Collection). 336p. 1998. pap. 11.95 (*1-85326-675-2*, Pub. by Wrdsworth Edits) Combined Pub.

— Gallipoli. LC 82-2242. (Great War Stories Ser.). (Illus.). 384p. 1982. reprint ed. 26.95 (*0-933852-28-2*) Nautical & Aviation.

— A Late Education: Episodes in a Life. LC 98-31945. 207p. 1999. pap. 11.00 (*1-56947-163-0*) Soho Press.

— The Russian Revolution. (Illus.). 301p. 1987. pap. 10.95 (*0-88184-331-8*) Carroll & Graf.

— The White Nile. lib. bdg. 27.95 (*0-8488-2006-1*) Amereon Ltd.

***Moorehead, Alan.** The White Nile. 432p. 2000. pap. 14.00 (*0-06-095639-9*, Perennial) HarperTrade.

Moorehead, Alan. The White Nile. rev. ed. LC 95-75324. (Adventure Library: Vol. 4). (Illus.). 424p. 1995. reprint ed. lib. bdg. 35.00 (*1-885283-03-2*) Advent Library.

Moorehead, Albert. Official Rules of Card Games. 1996. pap. 12.95 (*0-449-91158-6*) Fawcett.

Moorehead, Bob. Gentlemen Start Your Engines. 168p. 1995. pap. 8.99 (*0-9639496-3-2*) Overlake Press.

— Give Me One Good Reason to Miss Eternal Life. 148p. 1993. pap. 4.99 (*0-9639496-0-8*) Overlake Press.

— Husband Handbook. 139p. 1989. pap. 8.99 (*0-9639496-2-4*) Overlake Press.

— The Marriage Repair Kit. 115p. 1988. pap. 7.99 (*0-9639496-1-6*) Overlake Press.

— A Passion for Victory: Living Triumphantly Every Day. LC 96-23256. 190p. 1996. 15.99 (*1-878990-64-0*) Howard Pub LA.

— Words Aptly Spoken. 198p. 1995. 14.99 (*0-9639496-6-7*) Overlake Press.

Moorehead, Caroline. Bertrand Russell. 1999. pap. 11.95 (*0-14-023640-6*) Viking Penguin.

Moorehead, Caroline. Biography of Martha Gellhorn. pap. text 30.00 (*0-8050-6553-9*); pap. text 16.00 (*0-8050-6554-7*) St Martin.

— The Collected Letters of Martha Gellhorn. pap. text 27.50 (*0-8050-6555-5*); pap. text 16.00 (*0-8050-6556-3*) St Martin.

Moorehead, Caroline. Dunant's Dream: War, Switzerland & the History of the Red Cross. (Illus.). 816p. 1999. 38.00 (*0-7867-0609-0*) Carroll & Graf.

— Lost & Found. (Illus.). 336p. 1997. pap. 13.95 (*0-14-023950-2*) Penguin Putnam.

— Namibia: Apartheid's Forgotten Children. (C). 1986. pap. text 35.00 (*0-85598-111-3*, Pub. by Oxfam Pubns) St Mut.

Moorehead, Ellen D., et al, eds. Sonoma County... Its Bounty: Recipes from Chefs, Wineries & Food Producers. (Illus.). 224p. 1997. 19.95 (*0-9658701-0-3*) E D Moorehead.

Moorehead, Finola. Remember the Tarantella. pap. 13.95 (*0-7043-4376-2*, Pub. by Womens Press) Trafalgar.

Moorehead, Harold, ed. & photos by see Bodo, Martin.

Moorehead, John, ed. see Singh, Billy Arjan.

***Moorehead, Ruth J.** Waiting for Christmas. (Jellybean Bks.). (Illus.). 24p. (J). (ps-k). 1999. 1.99 (*0-375-80102-2*, Pub. by Random Bks Yng Read) Random.

Moorehead, Warren K. American Indian in the United States, Period 1850-1914. LC 71-75512. (Select Bibliographies Reprint Ser.). 1977. 38.95 (*0-8369-5014-3*) Ayer.

— Archaeology of the Arkansas River Valley. LC 76-43780. reprint ed. write for info. (*0-404-15634-7*) AMS Pr.

***Moorehead, Warren K.** Cahokia Mounds - Ancient Metropolis. LC 99-47252. 2000. pap. write for info. (*0-8173-1010-X*) U of Ala Pr.

— Exploration of the Etowah Site in Georgia. (Southeastern Classics in Archaeology, Anthropology & History). (Illus.). 224p. 2000. pap. 29.95 (*0-8130-1793-9*) U Press Fla.

Moorehead, Warren K. Fort Ancient, the Great Prehistoric Earthwork of Warren County, Ohio. LC 76-43781. (Illus.). reprint ed. 55.00 (*0-404-15637-1*) AMS Pr.

— The Hopewell Mound Group of Ohio. LC 76-43782. (Field Museum of Natural History. Publication Ser.: 211). (Illus.). reprint ed. 74.50 (*0-404-15638-X*) AMS Pr.

— The Hopewell Mound Group of Ohio. LC 23-2204. (Field Museum of Natural History, Publication 211 Ser.: Vol. 6, No. 5). 165p. 1922. reprint ed. pap. 51.20 (*0-608-02112-1*, 206276100004) Bks Demand.

— The Indian Tribes of Ohio: Historically Considered, a Preliminary Paper. LC 76-43783. reprint ed. 31.50 (*0-404-15639-8*) AMS Pr.

— The Indian Tribes of Ohio: Historically Considered 1600-1840. (Historic Indians, Ohio History Ser.). (Illus.). 109p. (C). 1992. reprint ed. pap. 8.30 (*1-56651-080-5*); reprint ed. lib. bdg. 29.80 (*1-56651-059-7*) A W McGraw.

— Primitive Man in Ohio. (Ohio History, Prehistoric Indians, Archaeology Ser.). (Illus.). 276p. (C). 1991. reprint ed. pap. 31.80 (*1-56651-017-1*); reprint ed. lib. bdg. 48.90 (*1-56651-018-X*) A W McGraw.

— Primitive Man in Ohio. LC 76-43787. reprint ed. 41.50 (*0-404-15642-8*) AMS Pr.

— A Report on the Archaeology of Maine: Being a Narrative

of Explorations in That State, 1912-1920, Together with Work at Lake Champlain, 1917. LC 76-43788. (Phillips Academy). reprint ed. 74.50 (*0-404-15643-6*) AMS Pr.

Moorehead, Warren K., et al. Prehistoric Implements. LC 76-43785. (Illus.). reprint ed. 115.00 (*0-404-15641-X*) AMS Pr.

— Stone Ornaments Used by Indians in the U. S. & Canada. LC 76-43790. reprint ed. 55.00 (*0-404-15645-2*) AMS Pr.

Moorehouse. Historia Del Alfabeto. (Breviarios Ser.). (SPA.). pap. 9.99 (*968-16-1158-6*, Pub. by Fondo) Continental Bk.

Mooren, Thomas. Auf der Grenze - Die Andersheit Gottes und die Vielfalt der Religionen: Der Interkulturelle Dialog Aus Anthropologischer Sicht Als Anfrage an eine Theologie der Religionen. (Europaische Hochschulschriften Ser.: Reihe 23, Bd. 434). (GER.). 201p. 1991. 43.80 (*3-631-44213-0*) P Lang Pubng.

— On the Border - The Otherness of God & the Multiplicity of the Religions: The Intercultural Dialogue from an Anthropological Perspective As an Inquiry into the Theology of Religions. Pandimakil, Peter G., tr. from GER. LC 94-145215. (European University Studies: Series 23, Vol. 500). (Illus.). 210p. 1994. pap. 37.95 (*3-631-47000-2*) P Lang Pubng.

Moores, Amanda. Dream Palace. 288p. 1993. 21.00 (*0-671-75919-1*) S&S Trade.

Moores, B. M., et al, eds. Physical Aspects of Medical Imaging: Proceedings of a Meeting Held at the University of Manchester, June 25-27, 1980. LC 82-116267. (Illus.). 354p. reprint ed. pap. 109.80 (*0-8357-8622-6*, 203504500091) Bks Demand.

Moores, B. M., et al. Practical Guide to Quality Assurance in Medical Imaging. LC 86-24529. 139p. reprint ed. pap. 43.10 (*0-7837-6390-5*, 204610300010) Bks Demand.

Moores, Donald F. Educating the Deaf, 4 vols. 4th ed. (C). 1995. text 74.76 (*0-395-74130-0*) HM.

Moores, Donald F. & Meadow-Orlans, Kathryn P., eds. Educational & Developmental Aspects of Deafness. LC 90-14014. (Illus.). 464p. (C). 1990. text 39.95 (*0-930323-52-1*) Gallaudet Univ Pr.

Moores, Eldridge M. & Twiss, Robert J. Tectonics. LC 95-10975. 415p. (C). 1995. pap. text 79.95 (*0-7167-2437-5*) W H Freeman.

***Moores, Eldridge M., et al.** Classic Cordilleran Concepts. LC 99-23409. (Special Paper Ser.). 489p. 1999. write for info. (*0-8137-2338-8*) Geol Soc.

Moores, Eldridge M., jt. auth. see Twiss, Robert J.

Moores, Eldridge M., ed. see Time-Life Books Editors.

Moores, John D. Wrestling with Rationality in Paul: Romans 1-8 in a New Perspective. (Society for New Testament Studies Monographs: No. 82). 226p. (C). 1995. text 59.95 (*0-521-47223-7*) Cambridge U Pr.

Moores, John D., ed. see Davies, Sam.

Moores, Lawrence. Thieves in the Schoolhouse. LC 78-50636. 1979. 22.95 (*0-87949-119-1*) Ashley Bks.

Moores Rowland Staff. Moores Rowland'S Yellow & Orange Tax Guides 1994-95: Orange, 2 pts. Incl. Moores Rowland's Yellow & Orange Tax Guides, 1994-1995. 1995. pap. 31.95 (*0-406-03648-9*, MICHIE); 31.95 (*0-406-03647-0*, MICHIE) LEXIS Pub.

Moores, Shaun. Interpreting Audiences: The Ethnography of Media Consumption. (Media, Culture & Society Ser.). (C). 1994. text 59.95 (*0-8039-8446-4*); pap. text 22.95 (*0-8039-8447-2*) Sage.

***Moores, Shaun.** Media & Everyday Life in Modern Society. 208p. 2000. pap. text 24.00 (*0-7486-1179-7*) Col U Pr.

Moores, Shaun, jt. auth. see Jackson, Stevi.

Moores, Susan, jt. auth. see Israel, Donna.

***Moores, Ted.** Canoecraft: An Illustrated Guide to Fine Woodstrip Construction. 2nd rev. expanded ed. (Illus.). 208p. 2000. pap. 19.95 (*1-55209-342-5*) Firefly Bks Ltd.

Moores, Ted. Kayakcraft: Fine Woodstrip Kayak Construction. LC 99-33080. 176p. 1999. pap. 19.95 (*0-937822-56-6*) WoodenBoat Pubns.

Moores, Ted & Mohr, Merilyn. Canoecraft: A Harrowsmith Illustrated Guide to Fine Woodstrip Construction. (Illus.). 148p. 1988. pap. 16.95 (*0-920656-24-2*) Firefly Bks Ltd.

***Moorewood, M.** Oxford Pocket Latin Set, 2. 1999. 36.80 (*0-19-521505-2*) OUP.

Moorey, James. Living with Anorexia & Bulimia. (Living with Ser.). 176p. (C). 1993. text 17.95 (*0-7190-3369-1*, Pub. by Manchester Univ Pr) St Martin.

— Living with Grief & Mourning. LC 94-40872. (Living With Ser.). 1995. text 17.95 (*0-7190-3945-2*, Pub. by Manchester Univ Pr) St Martin.

Moorey, P. R. Ancient Egypt. (Illus.). 64p. 1995. reprint ed. pap. 12.95 (*0-907849-76-8*, 768, Pub. by Ashmolean Mus) A Schwartz & Co.

***Moorey, P. R.** Ancient Mesopotamian Materials & Industries: The Archeological Evidence. xxiii, 414p. 1999. text 89.50 (*1-57506-042-6*) Eisenbrauns.

Moorey, P. R. Ancient Near East. (Illus.). 58p. 1987. pap. 12.95 (*0-907849-58-X*, 58-X, Pub. by Ashmolean Mus) A Schwartz & Co.

Moorey, P. R., et al. Ancient Glass, Jewellery & Terracottas from the Collection of Mr & Mrs James Bomford: Catalogue of an Exhibition at the Ashmolean Museum, Department of Antiquities, 20th November to 12th December 1971. LC 74-159694. 72p. 1971. write for info. (*0-900090-05-7*, Pub. by Ashmolean Mus) A Schwartz & Co.

Moorey, Peter R., jt. auth. see Buchanan, Briggs.

Moorey, T. Beginners Guide: Ghosts. mass mkt. 11.95 (*0-340-73064-1*, Pub. by Hodder & Stought Ltd) Trafalgar.

Moorey, Teresa. Aquarius. (Reach Your Potential Ser.). (Illus.). 96p. 1998. pap. 9.95 (*0-340-69719-9*, Pub. by Headway) Trafalgar.

— Aries. (Reach Your Potential Ser.). (Illus.). 96p. 1998. pap. 9.95 (*0-340-69709-1*, Pub. by Headway) Trafalgar.

***Moorey, Teresa.** Beginners Guide to Earth Mysteries. (Guides for Beginners Ser.). (Illus.). 96p. 1999. mass mkt. 11.95 (*0-340-74248-8*, Pub. by Headway) Trafalgar.

— Beginners Guide to Paganism. (Guides for Beginners Ser.). (Illus.). 96p. 1999. mass mkt. 11.95 (*0-340-74249-6*, Pub. by Headway) Trafalgar.

Moorey, Teresa. Beginners Guide to Witchcraft. 1999. mass mkt. 11.95 (*0-340-73757-3*) Headway.

— Cancer. (Reach Your Potential Ser.). (Illus.). 96p. 1998. pap. 9.95 (*0-340-69712-1*, Pub. by Headway) Trafalgar.

— Capricorn. (Reach Your Potential Ser.). (Illus.). 96p. 1998. pap. 9.95 (*0-340-69718-0*, Pub. by Headway) Trafalgar.

— Earth Mysteries: A Beginner's Guide. (Illus.). 96p. 1998. pap. 11.95 (*0-340-70516-7*, Pub. by Headway) Trafalgar.

***Moorey, Teresa.** Fairies & Nature Spirits. (Guides for Beginners Ser.). (Illus.). 96p. 1999. mass mkt. 11.95 (*0-340-75359-5*, Pub. by Headway) Trafalgar.

Moorey, Teresa. Gemini. (Reach Your Potential Ser.). (Illus.). 96p. 1998. pap. 9.95 (*0-340-69711-3*, Pub. by Headway) Trafalgar.

***Moorey, Teresa.** Ghosts: A Beginner's Guide. (Headway Guides for Beginners Ser.). (Illus.). 96p. 2000. pap. 11.95 (*0-340-77486-X*, Pub. by Headway) Trafalgar.

Moorey, Teresa. The Goddess: A Beginner's Guide. (Illus.). 96p. 1997. pap. 11.95 (*0-340-68390-2*, Pub. by Headway) Trafalgar.

— Leo. (Reach Your Potential Ser.). 96p. 1998. pap. 9.95 (*0-340-69713-X*, Pub. by Headway) Trafalgar.

— Libra. (Reach Your Potential Ser.). (Illus.). 96p. 1998. pap. 9.95 (*0-340-69715-6*, Pub. by Headway) Trafalgar.

***Moorey, Teresa.** The Magic & Mystery of Trees: A Beginner's Guide. (Headway Guides for Beginners Ser.). (Illus.). 96p. 2000. pap. 11.95 (*0-340-77204-2*, Pub. by Headway) Trafalgar.

Moorey, Teresa. The Magic & Mystery of Trees: A Beginner's Guide. (Beginner's Guide Ser.). (Illus.). 86p. 1998. pap. 11.95 (*0-340-70494-2*, Pub. by Hodder & Stought Ltd) Trafalgar.

— Pisces. (Reach Your Potential Ser.). (Illus.). 96p. 1998. pap. 9.95 (*0-340-69720-2*, Pub. by Headway) Trafalgar.

— Sagittarius. (Reach Your Potential Ser.). (Illus.). 96p. 1998. pap. 9.95 (*0-340-69717-2*, Pub. by Headway) Trafalgar.

— Scorpio. (Reach Your Potential Ser.). (Illus.). 96p. 1998. pap. 9.95 (*0-340-69716-4*, Pub. by Headway) Trafalgar.

— Taurus. (Reach Your Potential Ser.). (Illus.). 96p. 1998. pap. 9.95 (*0-340-69710-5*, Pub. by Headway) Trafalgar.

***Moorey, Teresa.** UFOs. (Guides for Beginners Ser.). (Illus.). 96p. 2000. pap. 11.95 (*0-340-75834-1*, Pub. by Headway) Trafalgar.

Moorey, Teresa. Virgo. (Reach Your Potential Ser.). (Illus.). 96p. 1998. pap. 9.95 (*0-340-69714-8*, Pub. by Headway) Trafalgar.

Moorey, Teresa & Brideson, Jane. Wheel of the Year: Myth & Magic Through the Seasons. (Illus.). 160p. 1997. pap. 17.95 (*0-340-68386-4*, Pub. by Headway) Trafalgar.

Moorgat, Elisabeth, jt. auth. see Beckers, Marion.

Moorhawk, Gilli. Meditations & Positive Thoughts for Pregnancy & Birth. 128p. 1995. text 14.95 (*0-7499-1395-9*, Pub. by Piatkus Bks) London Brdge.

Moorhead. Environmental 2nd ed. pap. text, lab manual ed. write for info. (*0-471-37223-4*) Wiley.

— Organ Behavior, 5 vols. 5th ed. LC 97-72522. (C). 1997. text 72.76 (*0-395-84196-8*) HM.

— Supervision. (C). 1996. pap. text, teacher ed. write for info. (*0-03-033089-0*); pap. text, teacher ed., suppl. ed. write for info. (*0-03-033083-1*); pap. text, student ed. write for info. (*0-03-033087-4*) Harcourt Coll Pubs.

Moorhead, et al. The American Winemaking Society Presents the Complete Handbook of Winemaking. Reichwaye, Randall J., ed. (Illus.). 225p. (Orig.). 1993. pap. 15.95 (*0-9619072-2-3*) G W Kent.

Moorhead, jt. auth. see Spangle.

Moorhead, A. J., et al, eds. Structural Ceramics Joining II. (Ceramic Transactions Ser.: Vol. 35). 334p. 1993. 74.00 (*0-944904-65-3*, CT035) Am Ceramic.

Moorhead, Andrea D. & Moorhead, Robert K. Deerfield, 1797-1997: A Pictorial History of the Academy. LC 96-72637. (Illus.). 228p. 1997. 40.00 (*0-9632800-1-5*) Deerfield Acad.

Moorhead, Bruce B. The Forest Elk: Roosevelt Elk in Olympic National Park. (Illus.). 62p. (Orig.). 1994. pap. text 11.95 (*0-914019-34-1*, 5379) NW Interpretive.

Moorhead, Carol A. Colorado's Backyard Wildlife: A Natural History, Ecology, & Action Guide to Front Range Urban Wildlife. (Illus.). 145p. (Orig.). (J). (gr. 6-8). 1992. pap. 10.95 (*1-879373-08-4*) Roberts Rinehart.

— Wild Horses. (Wonder Ser.). (Illus.). 64p. (Orig.). (J). (gr. 1-6). 1994. pap. 7.95 (*1-879373-51-3*) Roberts Rinehart.

Moorhead, Desiree, jt. auth. see Black, Peter.

Moorhead, E. J. Our Yesterdays: The History of the Actuarial Profession in North America, 1809-1979. LC 89-31624. 1989. text 60.00 (*0-938959-08-5*) Soc Actuaries.

Moorhead, Elizabeth. Pittsburgh Portraits. (Orig.). 1955. pap. 1.95 (*0-910286-25-6*) Boxwood.

Moorhead, Finola. Still Murder. 293p. 1997. pap. 14.95 (*0-7043-4397-5*, Pub. by Womens Press) Trafalgar.

Moorhead, Gregory. Organizational Behavior: Exams, 4 vols. (C). Date not set. text. write for info. (*0-395-71681-0*) HM.

Moorhead, Gregory & Griffin, Ricky W. Organizational Behavior. 2nd ed. LC 88-81348. 1989. teacher ed. 3.16 (*0-318-36899-4*); student ed. write for info. (*0-318-63322-1*); trans. write for info. (*0-318-63323-X*) HM.

— Organizational Behavior: Managing People & Organizations, 4 vols. 4th ed. 736p. (C). 1994. text 72.76 (*0-395-70898-2*) HM.

— Organizational Behavior: Managing People & Organizations, 4 vols. 4th ed. (C). 1995. text, teacher ed. 11.96 (*0-395-71233-5*) HM.

Moorhead, J. K., ed. see Eckermann, Johann P.

Moorhead, Jack, ed. Numerical Control, Vol. 1. LC 80-52723. (Illus.). 250p. 1980. reprint ed. pap. 77.50 (*0-7837-9733-8*, 206046200001) Bks Demand.

— Numerical Control, Vol. 2. LC 80-52723. (Illus.). 270p. 1980. reprint ed. pap. 83.70 (*0-7837-9734-6*, 206046200002) Bks Demand.

Moorhead, James H. American Apocalypse: Yankee Protestants & the Civil War, 1860-1869. LC 77-14360. 293p. reprint ed. pap. 90.90 (*0-8357-8016-3*, 203383200087) Bks Demand.

— World Without End: Mainstream American Protestant Visions of the Last Things, 1880-1925. LC 99-24448. (Religion in North America Ser.). 241p. 1999. 29.95 (*0-253-33580-9*) Ind U Pr.

Moorhead, John. Ambrose: Church & Society in the Late Roman World. LC 99-12447. (The Medieval World Ser.). 248p. 1999. pap. 25.06 (*0-582-25113-3*) Addison-Wesley.

— Ambrose: Church & Society in the Late Roman World. LC 99-12447. 248p. (C). 1999. text 66.95 (*0-582-25112-5*) Addison-Wesley.

— Justinian. LC 93-33762. (Medieval World Ser.). (C). 1994. text 41.50 (*0-582-06304-3*, 76703) Longman.

— Justinian. LC 93-33762. (Medieval World Ser.). 192p. (C). 1995. pap. 31.20 (*0-582-06303-5*, 76715) Longman.

Moorhead, John. Theoderic in Italy. 308p. 1993. text 69.00 (*0-19-814781-3*) OUP.

Moorhead, John, tr. from LAT. Victor of Vita: A History of the Vandal Persecution. (Translated Texts for Historians Ser.). 136p. (Orig.). (C). 1992. pap. text 15.95 (*0-85323-127-3*, Pub. by Liverpool Univ Pr) U of Pa Pr.

Moorhead, John, ed. see European Dialysis & Transplant Association Staff.

Moorhead, John, tr. see Suger, Abbot of St. Denis.

Moorhead, John D., jt. auth. see Combs, Richard E.

Moorhead, Kelly J., jt. auth. see Morgan, Helen C.

Moorhead, Max L. New Mexico's Royal Road: Trade & Travel on the Chihuahua Trail. LC 94-35293. (Illus.). 242p. 1995. 14.95 (*0-8061-2651-5*) U of Okla Pr.

— The Presidio: Bastion of the Spanish Borderlands. LC 74-15908. (Illus.). 304p. 1991. pap. 15.95 (*0-8061-2317-6*) U of Okla Pr.

Moorhead, Max L., ed. see Gregg, Josiah.

Moorhead, Robert K., jt. auth. see Moorhead, Andrea D.

Moorhead, Stephen & Grice, Gordan, eds. Landscape Architecture. (Illus.). 208p. 1998. 44.99 (*1-56496-101-X*) Rockport Pubs.

Moorhead, Sue & Delaney, Connie W. Information Systems Innovations for Nursing: New Visions & Ventures. LC 98-9026. (Series on Nursing Administration). 251p. 1998. 59.00 (*0-7619-1670-9*); pap. 26.95 (*0-7619-1671-7*) Sage.

Moorhead, Sue & Huber, Diane G., eds. Nursing Roles: Evolving or Recycled? LC 96-35619. (Series on Nursing Administration: Vol. 9). 245p. 1997. 39.95 (*0-7619-0149-3*) Sage.

Moorhill, Mollie. A Few Late Leaves. 30p. 1978. 55.00 (*0-9506373-0-0*, Pub. by Yew Tree Bks) St Mut.

Moorho, jt. auth. see Bacon.

Moorhound, Slayton. The Deer Cat, Vol. 300. unabridged ed. Waring, John N., ed. LC 98-67698. 1999. 13.95 (*0-9656507-2-3*, 002-OOMP, Manypaws Pr) J N H Waring.

— The Witches at the Foot of the Mountain. unabridged ed. LC 97-70312. 158p. (Orig.). 1997. pap. 13.95 (*0-9656507-0-7*, 002-00MP, Manypaws Pr) J N H Waring.

Moorhouse. Sydney C. 2000. write for info. (*0-15-100530-3*) Harcourt.

Moorhouse, A. C. The Syntax of Sophocles. xii, 353p. 1982. pap. 59.00 (*90-04-06599-7*, MNS, 75) Brill Academic Pubs.

Moorhouse, Anne, jt. auth. see Yeo, Michael.

Moorhouse, Ashleigh. Art, Sight & Language. (Illus.). 164p. 1989. pap. 21.95 (*0-921254-05-9*, Pub. by Penumbra Pr) U of Toronto Pr.

Moorhouse, Ashleigh, tr. see Schmemann, Alexander.

Moorhouse, Barry, jt. auth. see Bacon, Tony.

Moorhouse, David M., tr. see Debicki, Andrew & Rozo, Teresa.

Moorhouse, E. Hallam. Samuel Pepys. LC 74-30375. (English Biography Ser.: No. 31). 1974. lib. bdg. 75.00 (*0-8383-1908-4*) M S G Haskell Hse.

Moorhouse, Frank. Forty-Seventeen. 175p. 1989. 16.95 (*0-15-132695-9*) Harcourt.

Moorhouse, Frank, ed. see Rudd, Steele.

Moorhouse, Geoffrey. The Boat & the Town. large type ed. 448p. 1983. 27.99 (*0-7089-0949-3*) Ulverscroft.

— Hell's Foundations: A Social History of the Town of Bury in the Aftermath of the Gallipoli Campaign. 272p. 1995. pap. 14.95 (*0-8050-2652-5*) H Holt & Co.

— Imperial City. large type ed. 1989. 27.99 (*0-7089-2093-4*) Ulverscroft.

***Moorhouse, Geoffrey.** India Britannica: A Vivid Introduction to the History of British India. (Illus.). 260p. 1999. pap. 16.95 (*0-89733-482-5*) Academy Chi Pubs.

— Sun Dancing. 35p. 1999. pap. 13.00 (*0-15-600602-2*) Harcourt.

Moorhouse, Geoffrey. Sun Dancing: A Vision of Medieval Ireland. LC 97-8748. 272p. 1997. 27.00 (*0-15-100277-0*) Harcourt.

***Moorhouse, Geoffrey.** Sydney: The Story of a City. LC 99-44110. 296p. 2000. 25.00 (*0-15-100601-6*) Harcourt.

***Moorhouse, John.** Clock Logbook & Good Owner's Guide. (Illus.). 240p. 1999. 22.95 (*0-7198-0280-6*, Pub. by R Hale Ltd) Seven Hills Bk.

Moorhouse, K. Suzanne. Little Dog Lost: In Search of Honey. (Illus.). 122p. 1997. 20.00 (*1-85776-181-2*, Pub. by Book Guild Ltd) Trans-Atl Phila.

Moorhouse, Karin. A Child's Story of Canada. 72p. (J). (ps-8). 1987. pap. 8.95 (*0-920806-50-3*, Pub. by Penumbra Pr) U of Toronto Pr.

Moorhouse, Leigh, ed. see Sutherland, Howard.

Moorhouse, Mary F. & Doenges, Marilynn E. Nurse's Clinical Pocket Manual: Nursing Diagnoses, Care Planning & Documentation. 477p. (C). 1990. spiral bd. 18.95 (*0-8036-6314-5*) Davis Co.

Moorhouse, Mary F., et al. Critical Care Plans: Guidelines for Advanced Medical-Surgical Care. LC 87-6740. 472p. 1987. 29.95 (*0-8036-6311-0*) Davis Co.

Moorhouse, Mary F., jt. auth. see Doenges, Marilynn E.

Moorhouse, Paul. Albert Irvin: Painting in to Life. 1998. 75.00 (*0-85331-719-4*, Pub. by Lund Humphries) Antique Collect.

— Dali. LC 98-49707. (Illus.). 112p. 1998. 15.98 (*0-7924-5326-3*, Thunder Bay) Advantage Pubs.

— Dali. (Illus.). 112p. 1999. pap. 19.95 (*1-57715-098-8*) Knckerbocker.

Moorhouse, Paul, ed. Leon Kossoff. LC 96-60370. (Illus.). 176p. 1996. 45.00 (*0-500-09264-8*, Pub. by Thames Hudson) Norton.

Moorhouse, R. Gordon, jt. auth. see Bransden, B. H.

Moorhus, Donita M., jt. auth. see Grathwol, Robert P.

Mooring, Linwood E., Jr. Releasing Power from Within & the Real You. (Illus.). 230p. (Orig.). pap. write for info. (*0-9646104-0-X*) Mooring Hse Pr.

Moorings, A. Beginners Bible: The Easter Story. LC 95-72060. (Illus.). (J). 1996. pap. 3.25 (*0-679-87534-4*) Random.

Moorings Staff, jt. auth. see Imray Laurie Norie & Wilson, Ltd. Staff.

Mooris, Floyd. 272 Artistic Silhouettes. (Illus.). 96p. 1996. 13.28 (*1-56637-313-1*) Goodheart.

***Moorjani, Angela B.** Beyond Fetishism & Other Excursions in Psychopragmatics. LC 99-27687. 2000. text 45.00 (*0-312-22625-X*) St Martin.

Moorjani, K. & Coey, J. M. Disordered Solids. write for info. (*0-318-56698-2*) Elsevier.

***Moorman, Arlene.** Encore Poetry. 16p. 2000. pap. text 9.00 (*0-615-11619-1*, MP50) A Moorman.

Moorman, Charles. The Pearl-Poet. Bowman, Sylvia E., ed. LC 68-17243. (Twayne's English Authors Ser.). 148p. (C). 1968. lib. bdg. 20.95 (*0-8290-1722-4*) Irvington.

Moorman, Charles, ed. The Works of the Gawain-Poet. LC 76-40190. (Illus.). 464p. reprint ed. pap. 143.90 (*0-8357-4347-0*, 203715000007) Bks Demand.

Moorman, Charles & Minary, Ruth. An Arthurian Dictionary. 117p. 1999. pap. 8.95 (*0-89733-348-9*) Academy Chi Pubs.

Moorman, Charles W. The Celtic Literature of Defeat: An Extraordinary Assortment of Irregularities. LC 93-24624. 176p. 1993. text 79.95 (*0-7734-9332-8*) E Mellen.

— The Statistical Determination of Affiliation in the Landmark Manuscripts of the 'Canterbury Tales' LC 93-413. 224p. 1993. text 89.95 (*0-7734-9276-3*) E Mellen.

Moorman, Chick. Parent Talk: Words That Empower, Words That Wound. (Illus.). 200p. 1998. 24.95 (*0-9616046-4-6*) Prsnl Power Pr.

— Talk Sense to Yourself: Language & Personal Power. 200p. 1985. 12.95 (*0-9616046-0-3*) Prsnl Power Pr.

— Where the Heart Is: Stories of Home & Family. Lewis, Nancy, ed. 323p. (Orig.). 1996. pap. text 14.95 (*0-9616046-3-8*) Prsnl Power Pr.

Moorman, Chick & Dishon, Dee. Our Classroom: We Can Learn Together. rev. ed. (Illus.). 218p. 1986. reprint ed. 19.95 (*0-9616046-1-1*) Prsnl Power Pr.

Moorman, Chick & Moorman-Weber, Nancy. Teacher Talk: What It Really Means. 160p. 1989. pap. 12.95 (*0-9616046-2-X*) Prsnl Power Pr.

Moorman, Donald. Harvest Waiting. LC 93-21088. 222p. 1993. 9.95 (*0-570-09936-6*, 16-3000) Concordia.

Moorman, Frederic W. Interpretation of Nature in English Poetry from Beowulf to Shakespeare. LC 78-172741. reprint ed. 36.00 (*0-404-04398-4*) AMS Pr.

Moorman, Jere. All Things Are Possible: Humorous Interpretations of Scripture. 96p. (Orig.). 1983. pap. 3.00 (*0-915561-00-X*) Ctr Studies Person.

— The Humorous Dictionary of Economics. LC 83-71998. (Illus.). 52p. 1984. pap. 2.95 (*0-915561-01-8*) Ctr Studies Person.

Moorman, Jere & Stillwell, Will. Conflict Is Inevitable - War Is Spiritual. (Illus.). 92p. 1998. pap. 10.00 (*0-915561-02-6*) Ctr Studies Person.

Moorman, Jerry W. Contemporary Entrepreneurship. (GB - Basic Business Ser.). (C). 1995. mass mkt., wbk. ed. 10.00 (*0-538-71262-7*) S-W Pub.

— Contemporary Entrepreneurship. (GB - Basic Business Ser.). (C). 1995. mass mkt. 61.95 (*0-538-71261-9*) S-W Pub.

— Entrepreneurship. 2nd ed. (Basic Business Ser.). Date not set. pap., teacher ed. 34.95 (*0-538-68272-8*) S-W Pub.

— Entrepreneurship Ideas in Action. (Introduction to Business). 1999. text 55.95 (*0-538-68268-X*); text 93.95 (*0-538-68269-8*); mass mkt., student ed., wbk. ed. 12.95 (*0-538-68270-1*) S-W Pub.

Moorman, John. History of the Franciscan Order. 641p. 1988. 25.00 (*0-8199-0921-1*, Frncscn Herld) Franciscan Pr.

M

M

Moorman, John A. Managing Small Library Collections in Businesses & Community Organizations: Advice for Non-Librarians. LC 88-36877. (Illus.). 36p. 1989. reprint ed. pap. 30.00 (0-7837-9683-8, 206041200005) Bks Demand.

Moorman, John R. Anglican Spiritual Tradition. LC 82-29111. 240p. 1985. pap. 14.95 (0-87243-139-8) Templegate.

— Church Life in England in the Thirteenth Century. LC 76-29401. reprint ed. 49.50 (0-404-15352-6) AMS Pr.

— Medieval Franciscan Houses. (History Ser.). xxxii, 710p. 1983. pap. 40.00 (1-57659-079-8) Franciscan Inst.

— St. Francis of Assisi. 118p. 1986. pap. 4.95 (0-8199-0904-1, Frncscn Herld) Franciscan Pr.

Moorman, Kenneth, jt. ed. see Ram, Ashwin.

Moorman, Madison. Journal of Madison Berryman Moorman. (American Autobiography Ser.). 150p. 1995. reprint ed. lib. bdg. 69.00 (0-7812-8597-6) Rprt Serv.

Moorman, Margaret. Light the Lights! A Story about Celebrating Hanukkah & Christmas. (Illus.). 32p. (J). (ps-2). 1994. 12.95 (0-590-47003-5, Cartwheel) Scholastic Inc.

***Moorman, Margaret.** Light the Lights! A Story about Celebrating Hanukkah & Christmas. (Illus.). 32p. (J). (gr. k-2). 1999. mass mkt. 5.99 (0-590-48383-8, Cartwheel) Scholastic Inc.

Moorman, Margaret. Waiting to Forget: A Motherhood Lost & Found. 216p. 1998. pap. 13.00 (0-393-31783-8) Norton.

Moorman, Nancy W. Memorable Meals: A Delicious Blend of Classic & Contemporary Cuisines. LC 97-39867. (Illus.). 256p. 1997. 24.95 (1-57168-210-4, Eakin Pr) Sunbelt Media.

Moorman, Robert. Cultural Anthropology: A Supplement. 100p. (C). 1994. pap. text, per. 16.95 (0-8403-7902-1) Kendall-Hunt.

Moorman, Robert B., jt. auth. see Parcel, John.

Moorman, Ruth & Williams, Lalla. A Salad a Day: Scrumptious Salads for Every Day of the Week. (Gift Cookbook Ser.: No. 3). (Illus.). 80p. 1980. ring bd. 5.95 (0-937552-02-X) Quail Ridge.

— Seven Chocolate Sins: A Devilishly Delicious Collection of Chocolate Recipes. (Gift Cookbook Ser.: No. 2). (Illus.). 80p. 1979. ring bd. 5.95 (0-937552-01-1) Quail Ridge.

— Twelve Days of Christmas Cookbook. (Gift Cookbook Ser.: No. 1). (Illus.). 80p. 1978. ring bd. 5.95 (0-937552-00-3) Quail Ridge.

Moorman, Theo. Weaving As an Art Form. LC 86-61202. (Illus.). 104p. 1986. pap. 12.95 (0-88740-068-X) Schiffer.

Moorman-Weber, Nancy, jt. auth. see Moorman, Chick.

Moormann, Eric M., jt. ed. see Lulof, Patricia S.

Moors, Astra, ed. see Janelsina, Veronika.

Moors, Hein & Palomba, Rossella, eds. Population, Family, & Welfare: A Comparative Survey of European Attitudes, Vol. II. (Illus.). 306p. 1999. text 82.00 (0-19-828842-5) OUP.

Moors, Hein G. Child Spacing & Family Size in the Netherlands. 1974. pap. 18.00 (90-207-0491-5) Kluwer Academic.

Moors, Hein G., et al, eds. Population & Family in the Low Countries, No. 1. (Publications of the Netherlands Inter-University Demographic Institute & the Population & Family Study Centre Ser.). 1976. pap. text 85.50 (90-247-1859-7) Kluwer Academic.

Moors, J. F. Civil War Infantry, History of the 52nd Regiment, Mass. Volunteers. (Illus.). 283p. 1995. reprint ed. lib. bdg. 38.00 (0-8328-4628-7) Higginson Bk Co.

Moors, Joseph. French & Dutch Legal Dictionary: Dictionnaire Juridique. (DUT & FRE.). 1984. 125.00 (0-8288-0975-5, M521) Fr & Eur.

Moors, Kent. An Introduction to the Study of Politics. 180p. (Orig.). (C). 1988. pap. text 19.50 (0-8191-7185-9) U Pr of Amer.

Moors, Marilyn M., jt. ed. see Loucky, James.

Moorsom, Richard, jt. auth. see Eriksen, Tore L.

Moorsteen, Richard & Abramowitz, Morton. Remaking China Policy: U. S.-China Relations & Governmental Decisionmaking. LC 74-164428. (Rand Corporation Research Studies). 174p. 1971. 22.50 (0-674-75981-8) HUP.

Moorsteen, Richard H. & Powell, Raymond P. The Soviet Capital Stock, 1928 to 1962. LC 65-27841. (Economic Growth Center, Yale University Publication Ser.). 695p. reprint ed. pap. 200.00 (0-8357-8328-6, 203383300087) Bks Demand.

Moortgat, Anton. Geschichte Vorderasiens Bis Zum Hellenismus. (GER.). 342p. 1984. reprint ed. write for info. (3-487-07303-X) G Olms Pubs.

Moortgat, Elisabeth, jt. auth. see Beckers, Mirion.

Moortgat, G. K., et al, eds. Low-Temperature Chemistry of the Atmosphere. (Global Environmental Change Ser.). 544p. 1994. 287.95 (0-387-58111-1) Spr-Verlag.

Moortgat, Michael. Categorial Investigations: Logical & Linguistic Aspects of the Lambek Calculus. (Groningen-Amsterdam Studies in Semantics: No. 9). xiv, 278p. 1988. pap. 40.70 (90-6765-387-X) Mouton.

— Perspectives on Functional Grammar. 2nd ed. Van Der Hulst, Harry et al, eds. x, 352p. 1983. reprint ed. pap. 41.45 (90-70176-27-0) Mouton.

Moorthy, Nirmala. Maya. LC 97-904976. 1997. write for info. (0-14-026533-3) Penguin Books.

Moorthy, R. S., et al. Uncompromising Integrity: Motorola's Global Challenge. 250p. 1998. write for info. (1-56946-025-6, MUP-41-001); pap. write for info. (1-56946-026-4, MUP-41-001) Motorola Univ.

Moorthy, Vasantha. Complete Vegetable Cookbook: Guide to Cooking Vegetables in over 300 Ways. (C). 1995. reprint ed. 22.00 (81-7476-009-1, Pub. by UBS Pubs Dist) S Asia.

— The Menu Book: A Comprehensive Guide to Authentic Indian Vegetarian Cuisine. 287p. 1992. 23.95 (0-9634681-0-3) G Moorthy.

— Vegetarian Menu Book: A Comprehensive Guide to Authentic Indian Vegetarian Cuisine. (C). 1993. pap. 14.00 (81-85944-18-0, Pub. by UBS Pubs Dist) S Asia.

Moorton, Richard F., Jr., ed. Eugene O'Neill's Century: Centennial Views on America's Foremost Tragic Dramatist, 36. LC 90-47536. (Contributions in Drama & Theatre Studies: No. 36). 264p. 1991. 55.00 (0-313-26826-6, MEF/, Greenwood Pr) Greenwood.

Moorton, Richard F., jt. auth. see Tichener, Frances B.

Moos, David, text. Sorel Etrog: Human Traces: Paintings, Drawings & Sculpture By Sorel Etrog. (Illus.). 144p. 1995. pap. 24.95 (0-88962-587-5) Mosaic.

***Moos, David, et al.** Jonathan Lasker: Selective Identity: Paintings from the 1990s. LC 99-39167. (Illus.). 1999. write for info. (0-931394-44-9) Birmingham Mus.

Moos, David, jt. auth. see Crone, Rainer.

Moos, David, jt. auth. see DeSalvo, Donna.

Moos, Elayne. The Herb Gardener's Mail Order Source Book. (Illus.). 176p. 1987. pap. 6.95 (0-912661-08-9) Woodsong Graph.

Moos, Malcolm, ed. see Mencken, H. L.

Moos, Malcolm C., ed. see Mencken, H. L.

Moos, Marion Von, see Von Moos, Marion.

Moos, Merry K. & Freda, Margaret C. Preconceptional Health Promotion. Damus, Karla, ed. LC 94-37837. 1994. write for info. (0-86525-061-8) March of Dimes.

Moos, Merry K., jt. auth. see Cefalo, Robert C.

Moos, Merry K., jt. ed. see Miller, C. Arden.

Moos, Michael & Francisco, Patricia W., eds. The Language of Light. (Illus.). 180p. (Orig.). 1983. pap. 5.00 (0-927663-08-2) COMPAS.

Moos, Michael, jt. ed. see Bradford, Gigi.

Moos, Michel A., ed. Media Research: Technology, Art, Communication. (Critical Voices Ser.). 160p. 1997. text 23.00 (90-5701-091-7); pap. text 18.00 (90-5701-081-X) Gordon & Breach.

Moos, N. H. How to Acquire a Million. 1985. pap. 4.95 (0-912576-08-1) R Collier.

Moos, Paul. Die Philosophie der Musik von Kant Bis Eduard von Hartmann. (GER.). 666p. 1992. reprint ed. write for info. (3-487-05605-4) G Olms Pubs.

Moos, Peter Von, see Von Moos, Peter.

Moos, R. H. Coping with Life Crises: An Integrated Approach. LC 85-28149. (Stress & Coping Ser.). (Illus.). 444p. (C). 1986. 75.00 (0-306-42133-X, Plenum Trade) Perseus Pubng.

Moos, Rudolf H. Evaluating Correctional & Community Settings. LC 85-10873. 244p. reprint ed. pap. 75.70 (0-608-08670-3, 206919300003) Bks Demand.

— Evaluating Educational Environments. LC 79-83568. (Jossey-Bass Higher Education & Social & Behavioral Science Ser.). 352p. reprint ed. pap. 109.20 (0-7837-0185-3, 204048100017) Bks Demand.

— Evaluating Treatment Environments: A Social Ecological Approach. LC 73-17450. (Health, Medicine, & Society: A Wiley-Interscience Ser.). 409p. reprint ed. pap. 126.80 (0-608-16164-0, 205575600037) Bks Demand.

— Evaluating Treatment Environments: The Quality of Psychiatric & Substance Abuse Programs. 2nd ed. LC 96-38940. 294p. 1997. text 34.95 (1-56000-294-8) Transaction Pubs.

Moos, Rudolf H., ed. Coping with Life Crises. An Integrated Approach. LC 85-28149. (Stress & Coping Ser.). (Illus.). 444p. (C). 1986. pap. 45.00 (0-306-42144-5, Plenum Trade) Perseus Pubng.

Moos, Rudolf H. & Lemke, Sonne. Evaluating Residential Facilities: The Multiphasic Environmental Assessment Procedure. LC 96-9945. 280p. 1996. 34.95 (0-7619-0242-2) Sage.

— Group Residences for Older Adults: Physical Features, Policies, & Social Climate. LC 93-32701. (Illus.). 304p. 1994. text 65.00 (0-19-506257-4) OUP.

Moos, Rudolf H., et al. Alcoholism Treatment: Context, Process, & Outcome. (Illus.). 304p. 1990. text 49.95 (0-19-504362-6) OUP.

***Moos, W. H. & Pavia, M. R., eds.** Annual Reports in Combinatorial Chemistry & Molecular Diversity, Vol. 2. 170p. 1999. 120.00 (0-7923-5722-1) Kluwer Academic.

Moos, Walter H., et al, eds. Annual Reports in Combinatorial Chemistry & Molecular Diversity. 300p. 1997. lib. bdg. 120.00 (90-72199-23-5, Pub. by Escom Sci Pubs) Kluwer Academic.

Moos, Walter H., jt. auth. see Clark, Colin R.

Moosa, A. R., jt. auth. see Block, George E.

Moosa, Ebrahim, ed. & intro. see Rahman, Fazlur.

***Moosa, Imad A., contrib. by.** Exchange Rate Forecasting: Techniques & Applications. LC 99-42138. (Finance & Capital Market Ser.). 2000. text 150.00 (0-312-22892-9) St Martin.

Moosa, Imad A. & Bhatti, Razzaque H. International Parity Conditions: Theory, Econometric Testing & Empirical Evidence. LC 96-44007. (Illus.). 368p. 1997. text 79.95 (0-312-17262-1) St Martin.

Moosa, Matti. The Early Novels of Naguib Mahfouz: Images of Modern Egypt. (Illus.). 304p. 1994. 49.95 (0-8130-1309-7) U Press Fla.

— Extremist Shiites: The Ghulat Sects. (Contemporary Issues in the Middle East Ser.). 400p. 1987. text 44.95 (0-8156-2411-5) Syracuse U Pr.

— The Maronites in History. LC 86-1919. 400p. 1986. reprint ed. pap. 124.00 (0-608-06966-3, 206717400009) Bks Demand.

— The Origins of Modern Arabic Fiction. 2nd rev. ed. LC 97-21883. 458p. 1997. 59.95 (0-89410-683-X, Three Contnts) L Rienner.

Moosang, Faith, jt. auth. see Meyer, Christine.

Moosavi, Seyyed M., et al. Studies in the Ontology of Mulla Sadra. 1998. pap. 17.00 (1-883058-26-0, Nur) Global Pubns.

Moosbrugger, Patty. Lemon Magic: 200Beauty & Household Uses for Lemons & Lemon Juice. LC 98-28900. 1999. pap. 10.00 (0-609-80340-9) Crown Pub Group.

— Solve It with Salt: 110 Suprising & Ingenious Household Uses for Table Salt. LC 97-32775. 1998. pap. 10.00 (0-609-80234-8) Crown Pub Group.

***Moose.** My Life as a Dog. LC 99-57695. (Illus.). 144p. 2000. 19.95 (0-06-105172-1, HarpEntertain) Morrow Avon.

Moose, Christina J. Budgeting. (Money & Me Ser.). 48p. (J). (gr. 3-8). 1997. lib. bdg. 22.60 (1-57103-609-1) Rourke Pr.

— Budgeting. LC 97-6366. (Money & Me Ser.). (J). 1997. 16.95 (0-86625-609-1) Rourke Pubns.

— Debt. LC 97-10254. (Money & Me Ser.). 48p. (J). (gr. 3-8). 1998. lib. bdg. 22.60 (0-86625-610-5) Rourke Pubns.

***Moose, Christina J.** Indonesia. LC 00-25282. (Dropping in on Ser.). (Illus.). (J). 2000. pap. write for info. (1-55916-281-3) Rourke Bk Co.

— New Zealand. LC 00-29071. (Dropping in on Ser.). (Illus.). 2000. write for info. (1-55916-283-X) Rourke Bk Co.

Moose, Katie. Annapolis: The Guidebook. (Illus.). 168p. 1998. pap. 13.95 (0-9666610-0-1) Conduit Press.

***Moose, Katie.** Chesapeake's Bounty. (Illus.). 240p. 2000. pap. 16.95 (0-9666610-3-6, Pub. by Conduit Press) Wash Bk Distrib.

— Eastern Shore of Maryland: The Guide Book. (Illus.). 188p. 1999. pap. 15.95 (0-9666610-2-8, Pub. by Conduit Press) Wash Bk Distrib.

Moose, Ruth. Smith Grove: Poems. (Illus.). 28p. 1997. pap. 9.00 (1-885912-15-3) Sows Ear Pr.

— The Wreath Ribbon Quilt. 126p. 1988. 14.00 (0-932662-66-8); pap. 10.00 (0-932662-67-6) St Andrews NC.

Moose, Ruth, ed. Twelve North Carolina Christmas Stories: And Twelve Poems, Too. LC 97-69662. (Illus.). 179p. 1997. 17.95 (1-878086-61-8, Pub. by Down Home NC) Blair.

Moose, Ruth & Page, Carolyn, eds. Potato Eyes, Vol. 17. (Illus.). 96p. 1998. pap. 9.95 (1-879205-76-9) Nightshade Pr.

Moose, Werner E. Five Black Preachers in Army Blue, 1884-1901: The Buffalo Soldier Chaplains. LC 98-44211. 260p. 1998. 89.95 (0-7734-2249-8) E Mellen.

Mooser, Stephen. Disaster in Room 101. LC 93-24055. (Illus.). 80p. (J). (gr. 2-4). 1993. pap. text 2.95 (0-8167-3279-5) Troll Communs.

— Into the Unknown: Nine Astounding Stories. Stevenson, Dinah, ed. LC 79-3336. (Illus.). (J). (gr. 5 up). 1980. 11.95 (0-397-31855-3) HarpC Child Bks.

— The Thing Upstairs. LC 93-50676. (Illus.). 144p. (J). (gr. 3-6). 1996. pap. 2.95 (0-8167-3421-6) Troll Communs.

— Young Marian's Adventures in Sherwood Forest. LC 96-53114. (Girls to the Rescue Ser.). (J). 1997. pap. 4.95 (0-88166-277-1) Meadowbrook.

— Young Marian's Adventures in Sherwood Forest. LC 96-53114. 156p. (J). (gr. 3-7). 1997. lib. bdg. 4.50 (0-671-57551-1) S&S Childrens.

Mooser, Stephen & Oliver, Lin. Tad & Dad. LC 87-40340. (Catch the Reading Bug Ser.). (Illus.). (J). (ps-2). 1990. 4.95 (1-55782-023-6) Little.

Moosewad. Assorted Moosewood Rest. 1998. pap. 22.00 (0-676-58494-2) Random.

Moosewood Collective Staff. Low-Fat Favorites: Flavorful Recipes for Healthful Meals. Krauss, Pam, ed. LC 96-49430. (Moosewood Collective Ser.). (Illus.). 466p. 1996. pap. 22.00 (0-517-88494-1) Crown Pub Group.

— Moosewood Restaurant Book of Desserts. LC 97-1234. 416p. 1997. 32.50 (0-517-70209-6); pap. 22.00 (0-517-88493-3) C Potter.

— Moosewood Restaurant Cooks at Home: Fast & Easy Recipes for Any Day. LC 93-39126. (Illus.). 416p. 1994. per. 16.00 (0-671-67992-9, Fireside) S&S Trade Pap.

— The Moosewood Restaurant Cooks for a Crowd: Recipes with a Vegetarian Emphasis for 24 or More. LC 95-41512. 500p. 1996. 34.95 (0-471-12017-0) Wiley.

***Moosewood Collective Staff.** Moosewood Restaurant Daily Special: More Than 275 Recipes for Soups, Stews, Salads & Extras. 384p. 1999. 35.00 (0-609-60166-0) Crown Pub Group.

Moosewood Collective Staff. New Recipes from Moosewood Restaurant. (Illus.). 320p. 1987. pap. 21.95 (0-89815-208-9) Ten Speed Pr.

— New Recipes from Moosewood Restaurant. (Illus.). 302p. 1987. 19.95 (0-89815-209-7) Ten Speed Pr.

***Moosewood Collective Staff.** New Recipes from Moosewood Restaurant. rev. ed. 320p. 2000. pap. 19.95 (1-58008-148-7) Ten Speed Pr.

***Moosewood Collective Staff, ed.** Moosewood Restaurant Daily Special: More Than 275 Recipes for Soups, Stews, Salads & Extras. LC 99-13543. 384p. 1999. pap. 24.00 (0-609-80242-9, Crown) Crown Pub Group.

Moosewood Collective Staff & Mitchell, Carolyn B. Sundays at Moosewood Restaurant: Ethnic & Regional Recipes from the Cooks at the Legendary Restaurant. 736p. 1990. pap. 21.50 (0-671-67990-2) S&S Trade.

Moosewood College Staff. Moosewood Restaurant Big Book. 2001. 40.00 (0-609-60165-2); pap. 27.50 (0-609-80241-0) C Potter.

Moosewood Restaurant Staff. The Moosewood Restaurant Cooks for a Crowd: Recipes with Vegetarian Emphasis for 24 or More. (Illus.). 520p. 1997. pap. 24.95 (0-471-23877-5) Wiley.

Moosleitner, Horst, jt. auth. see Erhardt, Harry.

Moossa, A. R., et al. Comprehensive Textbook of Oncology, 2 vols. 2nd ed. 1918p. 1990. 199.00 (0-683-06147-X) Lppncott W & W.

Moossa, A. R., ed. see Cuschieri, A., et al.

MOOST, NELE. It's All Mine! Or the Little Raven's Mischief. LC 99-35466. 28p. 1999. 14.95 (0-7892-0529-7) Abbeville Pr.

Moosvi, Shireen. The Economy of the Mughal Empire, 1595-1596: A Statistical Study. (Illus.). 454p. 1987. text 35.00 (0-19-561725-8) OUP.

Moote, A. Lloyd. Louis XIII, the Just. 417p. (C). 1989. 55.00 (0-520-06485-2, Pub. by U CA Pr) Cal Prin Full Svc.

— Louis XIII, the Just. (Illus.). 417p. 1991. reprint ed. pap. 17.95 (0-520-07546-3, Pub. by U CA Pr) Cal Prin Full Svc.

Moote, Alanson L. The Revolt of the Judges: The Parlement of Paris & the Fronde, 1643-1652. LC 78-155003. 423p. reprint ed. pap. 131.20 (0-8357-3851-5, 203658400004) Bks Demand.

Moote, Margaret A., jt. auth. see Cortner, Hanna J.

Mooten-Silver, Alice. Climbing the Acropolis. 64p. 1996. pap. 9.95 (1-886094-48-9) Chicago Spectrum.

Moothart, Lorene. Heartbeat for the World: Story of Gustave & Pauline Woerner. (Jaffray Collection). 187p. pap. 9.99 (0-87509-818-5) Chr Pubns.

Moothart, Lorene. Outstandingly His: The Life Story of Paul & Mary Williams (Uncle Paul & Aunt Mary) (Orig.). 1993. pap. 7.95 (1-885729-02-2) Toccoa Falls.

— Sunbursts: True Adventures of Toccoa Falls College Missionaries. (Illus.). 232p. (Orig.). 1992. pap. 7.95 (1-885729-03-0) Toccoa Falls.

Mootoo, Shani. Cereus Blooms at Night. LC 98-20932. 272p. 1998. 23.00 (0-8021-1633-7, Grove) Grove-Atltic.

***Mootoo, Shani.** Cereus Blooms at Night. 272p. 1999. pap. 12.50 (0-380-73199-1, Avon Bks) Morrow Avon.

Mootoo, Shani. Cereus Blooms at Night. LC PR9199.3.M6353C47. 216p. 1996. pap. 15.95 (0-88974-064-X, Pub. by Press Gang Pubs) LPC InBook.

Mootoo, Shani. Cereus Blooms at Night. large type ed. Date not set. 30.00 (0-7862-1734-0, G K Hall Lrg Type) Mac Lib Ref.

Mootoo, Shani. Out on Main Street: And Other Stories. 128p. 1993. pap. 12.95 (0-88974-052-6, Pub. by Press Gang Pubs) LPC InBook.

Mootry, Maria K. Looking for Langston. (Illus.). 45p. 1998. pap. 10.00 (0-9651768-2-7) Hunan Pr.

Mootry, Maria K. & Smith, Gary. A Life Distilled: Gwendolyn Brooks, Her Poetry & Fiction. LC 86-11356. 286 P. ;p. 1987. write for info. (0-252-01367-0) U of Ill Pr.

Mootry, Maria K. & Smith, Gary, eds. A Life Distilled: Gwendolyn Brooks, Her Poetry & Fiction. LC 86-11356. 296p. 1989. reprint ed. pap. text 15.95 (0-252-06065-2) U of Ill Pr.

Mootz, Robert D. & Bowers, Linda J. Chiropractic Care for Special Populations. LC 99-31809. 200p. 1999. pap. 39.00 (0-8342-1374-5) Aspen Pub.

Mootz, Robert D. & Hansen, Daniel T. Chiropractic Technologies. LC 99-31808. 200p. 1999. pap. 39.00 (0-8342-1373-7) Aspen Pub.

***Mootz, Robert D. & McCarthy, Kevin A.** Sports Chiropractic & Rehabilitation. LC 99-31781. 200p. 1999. pap. 39.00 (0-8342-1375-3) Aspen Pub.

***Mootz, Robert D. & Vernon, Howard.** Chiropractic Care for Special Populations. LC 99-29381. 200p. 1999. pap. 39.00 (0-8342-1376-1) Aspen Pub.

Moove, Mary. Down but Not Out. 68p. 1999. pap. write for info. (0-7392-0065-8, P02896) Morris Pubng.

Mooy, John. Sidney: The Story of a Kingfisher. (Illus.). 32p. (J). (gr. k-6). 1991. text 15.00 (1-883960-08-8) Henry Quill.

— The Tale of Boris: (A Fable of the Red-Tailed Hawk) (Illus.). 32p. (J). (gr. k-6). 1991. lib. bdg. 15.00 (1-883960-06-1) Henry Quill.

Mooyoung. Biotechnology Advances, ser. vol. 1. (Biotechnology Advances). 1984. pap. 66.00 (0-08-031708-1, Pergamon Pr) Elsevier.

Mooz, William E., Jr. Introduction to Doing Business in Mexico. LC 94-7487. 1995. 45.00 (1-56425-037-7) Transnatl Pubs.

Mopales, Gladys C. Treasures from the Heart. 11p. 1996. wbk. ed. 5.00 (0-9649937-1-6) P M Pubng.

Mopper, Susan & Strauss, Sharon Y., eds. Genetic Structure in Natural Insect Populations: Effects of Ecology, Life History & Behavior. LC 97-7322. 368p. 1997. write for info. (0-412-08031-1) Kluwer Academic.

Moppett, Samantha A., jt. auth. see Ramy, Herbert N.

Mopsik, Wendy, jt. auth. see Robinson, Doris.

Moqbel, Redwan, ed. Allergy & Immunity to Helminths: Common Mechanisms or Divergent Pathways? LC 92-26365. 1992. 110.00 (0-7484-0022-2) Taylor & Francis.

Moquet, ed. see Rimbaud, Arthur.

Moquette-Magee, Elaine. Eat Well for a Healthy Menopause: The Low-Fat, High-Nutrition Guide. LC 95-41711. 288p. 1996. pap. 15.95 (0-471-12250-5) Wiley.

— Taste vs. Fat: Rating the Low-Fat & Fat-Free Foods: How to Save Money, Time, & Your Taste Buds by Knowing Which Brand-Name Products Rate the Highest on Taste & Nutrition. LC 98-231227. 208p. (Orig.). 1997. pap. 12.95 (1-56561-109-8) Wiley.

— 200 Kid-Tested Ways to Lower the Fat in Your Child's Favorite Foods: How to Make the Brand-Name & Homemade Foods Your Kids Love More Healthful - & Delicious. 297p. 1994. pap. 12.95 (1-56561-034-2, 004231) Wiley.

Moquin, Brian P., jt. auth. see Richter, Stephen B.

Moquin, Brian P., jt. auth. see Richter, Stephen B.

An Asterisk (*) at the beginning of an entry indicates that the title is appearing for the first time.

M

An Asterisk (*) at the beginning of an entry indicates that the title is appearing for the first time.

M

*Moragne, Wendy. New Jersey, 5 vols. , Set. LC 98-43948. (Celebrate the States Ser.). (Illus.). 144p. (J). (gr. 4-7). 2000. lib. bdg. 35.64 (*0-7614-0673-5*, Benchmark NY) Marshall Cavendish.

Morahg, Mordecai, jt. auth. see Morahg, Ruhama.

Morahg, Ruhama & Morahg, Mordecai. Towards Joy Profound. Freifield, Larry, ed. 282p. (Orig.). 1990. pap. 12.95 (*0-9625998-0-8*) M & R Project.

Moraillon, Robert & Legeay, Yves. Dictionnaire Pratique de Therapeutique Canine et Feline. 4th ed. (FRE.). 544p. 1997. 195.00 (*0-320-00431-7*) Fr & Eur.

Moraillon, Robert, et al. Dictionnaire Pratique de Therapeutique Canine et Feline. 3rd rev. ed. (FRE.). 1992. 195.00 (*0-7859-7831-3*, 2-225-82579-3) Fr & Eur.

Morain, Lloyd & Morain, Mary. Humanism as the Next Step. 2nd rev. ed. Poudrier, Almira F., ed. LC 97-74611. 145p. 1998. pap. 10.00 (*0-931779-09-X*, Humanist Press) Am Humanist.

Morain, Mary, ed. Bridging Worlds Through General Semantics. LC 84-82325. 347p. 1984. pap. 21.95 (*0-918970-34-2*) Intl Gen Semantics.

— Enriching Professional Skills Through General Semantics. LC 86-81557. xix, 326p. 1986. 44.95 (*0-918970-35-0*); pap. 21.95 (*0-685-14231-0*) Intl Gen Semantics.

— Teaching General Semantics. 2nd ed. LC 75-108193. 142p. 1977. reprint ed. pap. text 19.95 (*0-918970-04-0*) Intl Gen Semantics.

Morain, Mary, ed. Classroom Exercises in General Semantics. 2nd ed. (Illus.). 192p. (C). 1996. pap. 21.95 (*0-918970-43-1*) Intl Gen Semantics.

Morain, Mary, jt. auth. see Morain, Lloyd.

*Morain, Stan. GIS Solutions in Natural Resource Management: Balancing the Technical Political Equation. LC 97-45605. (C). 1998. pap. text 52.95 (*1-56690-146-4*) Thomson Learn.

Morain, Stan & Baros, Shirley L., eds. Raster Imagery in Geographic Information Systems. 560p. (C). 1996. pap. 68.95 (*1-56690-097-2*, 4110) Thomson Learn.

Morain, Thomas J. Prairie Grass Roots: An Iowa Small Town in the Early Twentieth Century. LC 88-652. (Henry A. Wallace Series on Agricultural History & Rural Studies). (Illus.). 306p. 1988. 27.95 (*0-8138-0068-4*) Iowa St U Pr.

Morain, William D. The Sword of Laban: Joseph Smith, Jr. & the Dissociated Mind. 432p. 1998. 24.95 (*0-88048-864-6*, 8864) Am Psychiatric.

Morain, William D., ed. see Advances in Plastic & Reconstructive Surgery Staff.

Morais. Are We Having Fun yet Activities Inspired by Nickelodeon Magazine. 144p. (J). 1998. mass mkt. 3.99 (*0-671-01682-2*, Pocket Books) PB.

Morais, Herbert, jt. auth. see Boyer, Richard.

Morais, Robert J. Social Relations in a Philippine Town. (Special Reports: No. 19). (Illus.). 151p. (C). 1981. pap. 14.95 (*1-877979-69-4*) SE Asia.

Moraitis. The Relevance of the Use of the Couch in Contemporary Psychoanalysis. (Psychoanalytic Inquiry Ser.: Vol. 15, No. 3). 1995. pap. 20.00 (*0-88163-994-X*) Analytic Pr.

Moraitis, ed. Phobias. (Psychoanalytic Inquiry Ser.: Vol. 11, No. 3). 1995. 20.00 (*0-88163-950-8*) Analytic Pr.

Moraitis, Dimitri, jt. auth. see Martin, Barbara Y.

Moraitis, George & Pollock, George H., eds. Psychoanalytic Studies of Biography. LC 86-27750. (Emotions & Behavior Monographs: No. 4). 1987. 85.00 (*0-8236-4515-0*, BN#04515) Intl Univs Pr.

Moral, Jose Zorrilla y, see De Molina, Tirso & Zorrilla y Moral, Jose.

Moraldo, Sandro M. Wandlungen des Doppelgangers: Shakespeare - E. T. A. Hoffmann - Pirandello - Von der Kwillingskomodie (The Comedy of Errors) zur Identitatsgefahrdung (Prinzessin Brambilla); Il fu Mattia Pascal) (GER.). 236p. 1996. 51.95 (*3-631-49313-4*) P Lang Pubng.

Morales, A., ed. Weak Interactions & Neutrinos: Proceedings of the 8th International Workshop, Javea, Spain, Sept. 5-11. 1982. 820p. 1983. 125.00 (*9971-950-89-8*) World Scientific Pub.

Morales, Adelaida G. The South & Bene. LC 99-17852. (European Women Writers Ser.). 104p. 1999. pap. 12.00 (*0-8032-7080-1*, Bison Books); text 30.00 (*0-8032-2178-9*, Bison Books) U of Nebr Pr.

Morales, Alejandro. Barrio on the Edge/Caras Viejas y Vino Nuevo. rev. ed. Lomeli, Francisco, tr. from SPA. LC 97-27425. (Clasicos Chicanos/Chicano Classics Ser.: Vol. 10). 224p. 1998. pap. 16.00 (*0-927534-72-X*) Biling Rev-Pr.

— The Brick People. 2nd ed. LC 88-10409. 320p. 1992. pap. 11.95 (*0-934770-91-3*) Arte Publico.

— Death of an Anglo. Ginsberg, Judith, tr. from SPA. LC 88-70371.Tr. of La/Verdad Sin Voz. 241p. 1988. 26.00 (*0-916950-82-4*); pap. 16.00 (*0-916950-83-2*) Biling Rev-Pr.

— The Rag Doll Plagues. LC 91-2381. 200p. 1993. pap. 9.50 (*1-55885-104-6*) Arte Publico.

— Reto en el Paraiso. LC 82-73753. (ENG & SPA.). 381p. 1983. pap. 18.00 (*0-916950-34-4*) Biling Rev-Pr.

Morales, Alejandro, ed. see Coleman, George.

Morales, Alessandra, ed. see Depin, Daniel.

Morales, Alfredo J. Cathedral of Seville, 1. 1999. pap. text 25.00 (*1-85759-203-4*) Scala Books.

— Royal Palace of Seville, 1. 1999. pap. text 25.00 (*1-85759-201-8*) Scala Books.

Morales, Amparo & Vaquero, Maria. El Habla culta de San Juan: Materiales para su Estudio. LC 89-32488. 456p. (Orig.). 1990. pap. 12.50 (*0-8477-3641-5*) U of PR Pr.

*Morales, Armando & Sheafor, Bradford W. Social Work: A Professional of Many Faces. 9th ed. LC 00-27635. 672p. 2000. 60.00 (*0-205-31740-5*) Allyn.

Morales, Armando T. & Sheafor, Bradford W. Social Work: A Profession of Many Faces. 5th ed. 740p. 1989. boxed set 44.00 (*0-205-11888-7*, H18880) Allyn.

— Social Work: A Profession of Many Faces: Instructor's Manual & Test Bank. 8th ed. 112p. (C). 1997. text, teacher ed. write for info. (*0-205-27430-7*, T7430-6) Allyn.

Morales, Aurora L. Medicine Stories: History, Culture, & the Politics of Integrity. LC 98-31479. 135p. 1998. 40.00 (*0-89608-582-1*) South End Pr.

— Medicine Stories: History, Culture, & the Politics of Integrity. 135p. 1998. pap. 14.00 (*0-89608-581-3*) South End Pr.

Morales, Aurora L. & Morales, Rosario. Getting Home Alive. LC 86-22769. 216p. (Orig.). 1986. pap. 11.95 (*0-932379-19-2*); lib. bdg. 24.95 (*0-932379-20-6*) Firebrand Bks.

Morales, Aurora Levins. Remedios: Stories of Earth & Iron from the History of Puertoriquenas. LC 98-17498. 235p. 1998. 24.00 (*0-8070-6516-1*) Beacon Pr.

Morales, B. 666: The New Currency: La Nueva Moneda. (SPA.). 4.99 (*0-7899-0512-4*, 550152) Editorial Unilit.

Morales, Brigitte, tr. see Allen, Diane & Frederick, Larry.

Morales, Brigitte, tr. see Black, Susan E.

Morales, Brigitte, tr. see Borglum, Lincoln.

Morales, Brigitte, tr. see Bowman, Lori & Bowman, Carl.

Morales, Brigitte, tr. see Cox, W. Eugene.

Morales, Brigitte, tr. see Davies, Denny.

Morales, Brigitte, tr. see Den Dooven, K. C.

Morales, Brigitte, tr. see Dengler, William.

Morales, Brigitte, tr. see Fiero, G. William.

Morales, Brigitte, tr. see Gilmore, Jackie.

Morales, Brigitte, tr. see Hagood, Allen & West, Linda.

Morales, Brigitte, tr. see Helms, Christopher L.

Morales, Brigitte, tr. see Hilbruner, Roberta.

Morales, Brigitte, tr. see Hunter, Wilson, Jr.

Morales, Brigitte, tr. see Jackson, Victor L.

Morales, Brigitte, tr. see Kimball, Stanley B. & Kimball, Violet T.

Morales, Brigitte, tr. see Ladd, Gary.

Morales, Brigitte, tr. see Mack, James A.

Morales, Brigitte, tr. see Mark, Stephen R.

Morales, Brigitte, tr. see Martin, Linda.

Morales, Brigitte, tr. see Maxon, James C.

Morales, Brigitte, tr. see McKenzie, Leonard.

Morales, Brigitte, tr. see Murphy, Dan.

Morales, Brigitte, tr. see Nielsen, Cindy.

Morales, Brigitte, tr. see Norton, Stephen L.

Morales, Brigitte, tr. see Price, L. Greer.

Morales, Brigitte, tr. see Quiring, James P.

Morales, Brigitte, tr. see Rasp, Richard A.

Morales, Brigitte, tr. see Reed, Allen C.

Morales, Brigitte, tr. see Scharf, Janet.

Morales, Calva. Prosas Para Sonreir, Pensar y Refrescar. (SPA.). 1997. pap. text 7.50 (*968-409-763-8*) Edamex.

Morales, Camilo, jt. ed. see Basch, Miguel.

Morales-Canadas, Esther. Di Verzierungen der Spanischen Musik Im 17. und 18. Jahrhundert. (Europaische Hochschulschriften Ser.: Reihe 36, Vol. 174). (Illus.). 279p. 1998. pap. 48.95 (*3-631-32886-9*) P Lang Pubng.

Morales, Carlos Brassel. El Maestro De la Palabra. 1997. pap. text 10.98 (*968-409-956-8*) Edamex.

Morales, Carmen A. Ay Bendito! (Aqui y Ahora Ser.). 100p. 1997. pap. 6.95 (*0-8477-0291-X*) U of PR Pr.

Morales, Carmen A., jt. auth. see Needham, Christina W.

Morales-Carrion, Arturo. Albores Historicos del Capitalismo en Puerto Rico. 2nd ed. (UPREX, Humanidades Ser.: No. 9). 140p. (C). 1980. pap. 1.50 (*0-8477-0009-7*) U of PR Pr.

Morales Carrion, Arturo. Puerto Rico en la Lucha por la Hegemonia del Caribe: Siglos XVI-XVIII. (SPA.). 272p. 1995. 14.95 (*0-8477-0251-0*) U of PR Pr.

— Puerto Rico y la Lucha por la Hegemonia en el Caribe. (Caribbean Collection). (SPA.). 272p. 1995. pap. 12.95 (*0-8477-0196-4*) U of PR Pr.

Morales-Carrion, Arturo. Testimonios de una Gestion Universitaria. LC 77-11056. (Illus.). 329p. 1978. pap. 3.00 (*0-8477-2740-8*) U of PR Pr.

Morales, Cecilio J., Jr., et al, eds. A Survey of Press Freedom in Latin America, 1985-1986. 64p. (Orig.). 1986. pap. 8.95 (*0-937551-00-7*) Coun Hemispheric Aff.

Morales, Christopher, ed. see Sullivan, Joseph R. & Leafgren, Fred.

Morales, Dan. The Evolving Protection of State Laws & the Environment: NAFTA from a Texas Perspective. (U. S. - Mexican Occasional Paper Ser.: No. 5). 32p. 1994. pap. 10.00 (*0-89940-501-0*) LBJ Sch Pub Aff.

Morales, Dionicio. Dionicio Morales: A Life in Two Cultures. LC 97-22160. 200p. (YA). (gr. 6-12). 1997. pap. text 9.95 (*1-55885-219-0*) Arte Publico.

Morales, Edgar O., tr. see Houk, Margaret.

Morales, Edgar O., tr. see Shelley, Marshall.

Morales, Edmundo. Cocaine: White Gold Rush in Peru. LC 88-30303. 228p. 1990. pap. 17.95 (*0-8165-1159-4*) U of Ariz Pr.

— The Guinea Pig: Healing,Food, & Ritual in the Andes. LC 95-4343. (Illus.). 177p. 1995. 46.00 (*0-8165-1479-8*); pap. 19.95 (*0-8165-1558-1*) U of Ariz Pr.

Morales, Esther, ed. see Sandler, Susan.

Morales, Francisco. Ethnic & Social Background of the Franciscan Friars in Seventeenth Century Mexico. (Monograph Ser.). 1973. 30.00 (*0-88382-060-9*) AAFH.

— Inventario del Fondo Franciscano del Museo de Antropologia e de Mexico. (Bibliographical Ser.). 1978. 35.00 (*0-88382-103-6*) AAFH.

Morales, Francisco, ed. Franciscan Presence in the Americas. (Miscellaneous Ser.). 1984. 35.00 (*0-88382-258-X*) AAFH.

Morales-Front, Alfonso, jt. auth. see Nunez-Cedeno, Rafael A.

Morales, Gladys C. Intercessors Manuel. Thombs, Annie C., ed. 33p. 1995. 10.95 (*0-9649937-0-8*) P M Pubng.

Morales, Gladys Elena, jt. auth. see Green, Michael.

Morales, Goldie L. Eternal Etching. 24p. 1977. pap. 2.50 (*0-910083-00-2*) Heritage Trails.

— Floating Petals. (Illus.). 46p. (C). 1982. pap. 2.50 (*0-910083-09-6*) Heritage Trails.

— Moving Image. 24p. 1978. pap. 2.50 (*0-910083-02-9*) Heritage Trails.

— Poet Philosophers. (Illus.). 48p. (Orig.). 1983. pap. 3.00 (*0-910083-16-9*) Heritage Trails.

*Morales-Gomez, Daniel, ed. Transnational Social Policies: The New Development Challenges of Globalization. 280p. 1999. pap. 19.95 (*0-88936-854-6*) IDRC Bks.

Morales-Gomez, Daniel A. & Torres, Carlos A. The State, Corporatist Politics & Educational Policy Making in Mexico. LC 89-29986. 224p. 1990. 55.00 (*0-275-93484-5*, C3484, Praeger Pubs) Greenwood.

Morales-Gomez, Daniel A., jt. auth. see Torres, A. Mario.

Morales-Gomez, Daniel A., jt. ed. see Torres, Carlos A.

Morales-Gomez, Hildegard, jt. auth. see Gebel, Terri A.

Morales-Gudmundsson, Lourdes E., ed. Women & the Church: The Feminine Perspective. LC 95-77895. 235p. (C). 1995. pap. 11.99 (*1-883925-08-8*) Andrews Univ Pr.

Morales, Harry, tr. see Berne, Stanley, et al.

Morales, Helen, jt. ed. see Sharrock, Alison.

Morales, Humberto L. La Ensenanza del Espanol como Lengua Materna. (SPA.). 274p. 1991. pap. 15.50 (*0-8477-3615-6*) U of PR Pr.

— Espanol Basico I. 12th ed. (SPA.). 160p. (C). 1991. reprint ed. pap. text 7.95 (*1-56328-018-3*) Edit Plaza Mayor.

— Redaccion I. 3rd ed. (SPA.). 144p. 1990. reprint ed. pap. 7.75 (*0-8477-3617-2*) U of PR Pr.

— Redaccion II. 229p. 1990. pap. 9.25 (*0-8477-3624-5*) U of PR Pr.

Morales, J. Onieva. La Gramatica de la Real Academia Espanola. 2nd ed. (SPA.). 316p. 1994. pap. 29.95 (*0-7859-9179-4*) Fr & Eur.

Morales, Jorge L. Alfonso Reyes y la Literatural Espanola. LC 79-19455. (Coleccion Mente y Palabra). (SPA.). 193p. (C). 1980. 5.00 (*0-8477-0558-7*); pap. 4.00 (*0-8477-0559-5*) U of PR Pr.

— Espana en Alfonso Reyes. LC 76-1892. (Coleccion Mente y Palabra). (SPA.). xiii, 181p. (Orig.). 1976. 5.00 (*0-8477-0522-6*); pap. 4.00 (*0-8477-0523-4*) U of PR Pr.

— Nueva Antologia Poetica. 368p. 1975. pap. 5.00 (*0-8477-3217-7*) U of PR Pr.

— Obelisco (Diosa-Madre-Poesia) (Poetry Ser.). 128p. 1990. 50.00 (*0-317-05414-7*); pap. 25.00 (*0-317-05415-5*) Instit Nacional.

— ORBE. (Poetry Ser.). 160p. 1992. 50.00 (*0-317-05418-X*); pap. 40.00 (*0-317-05419-8*) Instit Nacional.

— Ouranos (Cinabrio-Verb-Maria) (Poetry Ser.). 133p. 1991. 50.00 (*0-317-05416-3*); pap. 40.00 (*0-317-05417-1*) Instit Nacional.

— Poesia Afroantillana y Negrista: Puerto Rico, Republica Dominica, Cuba. LC 80-25893. 456p. 1981. pap. 10.00 (*0-8477-3230-4*) U of PR Pr.

— Los Rios Redimidos. (Illus.). 55p. (C). 1969. 1.75 (*0-8477-3209-6*) U of PR Pr.

Morales, Jorge L., jt. ed. see Villa, Eugenia.

Morales, Jose. El Cacao: A Novel on Migrants & Their Problem of Adaptation. 2nd ed. Uceda, Mario A., ed. (SPA.). 114p. reprint ed. pap. 4.95 (*0-938693-01-8*) Maya Pubns.

— Creation Theology. 272p. 1999. pap. 39.50 (*1-85182-264-X*, Pub. by Four Cts Pr) Intl Spec Bk.

— El Morro: Derrota y Muerte de Piratas: De Ingleses, Holandeses y Franceses. (SPA.). 160p. 1998. pap. 6.00 (*0-938693-14-X*) Maya Pubns.

Morales, Jose L., tr. see Arintero, Juan G.

*Morales, Jose Santos. The Telling Task. Lindgren, Joan, tr. (ENG & SPA.). 36p. 2000. pap. 7.00 (*0-932264-27-1*, Pub. by Trask Hse Bks) SPD-Small Pr Dist.

Morales, Juan A. & McMahon, Gary, eds. Economic Policy & the Transition to Democracy: The Latin American Experience. LC 95-2567. (International Political Economy Ser.). 1996. text 59.95 (*0-312-12645-X*) St Martin.

Morales, Juan A., jt. auth. see Sachs, Jeffrey.

Morales, Juan L. Intercomunicacion No. 3: El Proceso de la Redaccion. 5th ed. (SPA.). 256p. (C). 1994. reprint ed. pap. text 14.95 (*1-56328-038-8*) Edit Plaza Mayor.

Morales, Julio, Jr. Puerto Rican Poverty & Migration: We Just Had to Try Elsewhere. LC 85-19439. 271p. 1986. 59.95 (*0-275-92020-8*, C2020, Praeger Pubs) Greenwood.

Morales, Karla & Inlander, Charles B. So You're Going to Be a Mother: Taking Control of Your Pregnancy. LC 95-31205. (Illus.). 160p. 1995. pap. 14.95 (*1-882606-23-X*) Peoples Med Soc.

Morales, Karla, jt. auth. see Brisco, Paula.

Morales, Karla, jt. auth. see Inlander, Charles B.

Morales, Laura, tr. see Smith, M. Sherry & Hanson, Karen.

*Morales, Lazaro E. Expediente de un Emigrante. (SPA.). 350p. 1999. pap. 19.95 (*0-9675859-0-2*) L E Morales.

Morales-Lebron, Mariano. Diccionario-Juridico Segun la Jurisprudencia Del Tribunal Supremo De Puerto Rico: Palabras, Frases y Doctrinas, 2 vols., Set. (SPA.). 925p. 195.00 (*0-685-73078-6*) U Cinn Law.

— Diccionario-Juridico Segun la Jurisprudencia del Tribunal Supremo de Puerto Rico: Palabras, Frases y Doctrinas, 2 vols., Set. (SPA.). 925p. 195.00 (*0-9626291-1-1*) U Cinn Law.

Morales, Lenore Freeman. A Starhopper's Guide to Messier Objects. LC 83-11621. (Illus.). 28p. 1983. pap. 8.95 (*0-913399-57-4*) Every Universe.

Morales, Lopez. Espanol Basico II. (SPA.). 160p. 1995. pap. text 12.95 (*1-56328-042-6*) Edit Plaza Mayor.

Morales, Lucy, ed. see Rader, Mamie.

Morales, M. F., et al, eds. Annual Review of Biophysics & Bioengineering, Vol. 1. LC 79-188446. (Illus.). 1972. text 55.00 (*0-8243-1801-3*) Annual Reviews.

Morales, Manual S. El Homero de Aristoteles. (SPA.). 200p. 1994. pap. 46.00 (*90-256-1064-1*, Pub. by AM Hakkert) BookLink Distributors.

Morales, Manuel D. The Calderonian Stage: Body & Soul. LC 96-18808. (Illus.). 288p. 1996. 43.50 (*0-8387-5331-0*) Bucknell U Pr.

Morales, Maria H. Perfect Equality: John Stuart Mill on Well-Constituted Communities. LC 96-19391. (Studies in Social, Political, & Legal Philosophy). 238p. (C). 1996. pap. text 24.95 (*0-8476-8181-5*); lib. bdg. 60.50 (*0-8476-8180-7*) Rowman.

*Morales, Mario R. Face of the Earth, Heart of the Sky. Hood, Edward W., tr. from SPA. LC 99-47067.Tr. of Senores Bajo los Arboles. 142p. 2000. pap. 11.00 (*0-927534-88-6*, Pub. by Biling Rev-Pr) SPD-Small Pr Dist.

Morales, Max, Jr. The Plano Diet. (Illus.). 87p. (Orig.). 1984. pap. 6.95 (*0-934157-00-6*) Morales Pubns.

Morales, Michael, ed. Aspects of Mesozoic Geology & Paleontology on the Colorado Plateau. (Bulletin Ser.). 192p. 1993. pap. 19.95 (*0-89734-114-7*, BS-59) Mus Northern Ariz.

Morales, Michael, jt. auth. see Colbert, Edwin H.

Morales, Michael, jt. ed. see Beus, Stanley S.

Morales, P. Gott'cha! Rubik's Cube. 1982. pap. 5.95 (*0-937816-17-5*) Tech Data.

Morales Padron, F. Canarias y America. (Gran Enciclopedia de Espana y America Ser.). (SPA., Illus.). 1989. 200.00 (*84-87053-12-2*) Elliots Bks.

— Historia del Descubrimiento y Conquista de America. (SPA.). 720p. 1993. 150.00 (*84-249-1417-1*) Elliots Bks.

Morales, Radames. The Story Teller: A Collection of Short Stories, Bk. 1. LC 94-94610. 148p. (YA). (gr. 6 up). 1994. pap. 6.95 (*0-9642626-0-6*) R Morales.

Morales, Rafael C., tr. see Garmirian, Paul B.

Morales, Rebecca. Flexible Production: Restructuring of the International Automobile Industry. LC 94-6157. 220p. (C). 1994. 47.95 (*0-7456-0752-7*) Blackwell Pubs.

Morales, Rebecca & Bonilla, Frank. Latinos in a Changing U. S. Economy: Comparative Perspectives on Growing Inequality. (Series on Race & Ethnic Relations: Vol. 7). (Illus.). 316p. (C). 1993. text 52.00 (*0-8039-4923-5*); pap. text 24.00 (*0-8039-4924-3*) Sage.

Morales, Richard. The Promotion Point Accelerator: The Consolidated Army Correspondence Course Program. 2nd rev. ed. Hornung, Janine H., ed. LC 97-141123. (Fast Mover Ser.: Vol. 97-1). Orig. Title: The Promotion Point Accelerator: TRADOC Correspondence Courses & Subcourses. (Illus.). 92p. 1997. pap. 19.95 (*0-9654788-0-7*) Non Com Pub.

Morales, Roberto N. Los Desesperados: Tragicomedia Creada y Rimada en Decimas. LC 97-80257. (Coleccion Espejo de Paciencia). (SPA.). 213p. 1997. pap. 15.00 (*0-89729-857-8*) Ediciones.

Morales, Rodney. The Speed of Darkness. LC 88-24246. (Bamboo Ridge Ser.: Nos. 39-40). 177p. 1988. pap. 8.00 (*0-910043-16-7*) Bamboo Ridge Pr.

Morales, Rodney, ed. Ho'i Ho'i Hou, A Tribute to George Helm & Kimo Mitchell. LC 84-70273. (Bamboo Ridge Ser.: No. 22). (Illus.). 114p. (Orig.). 1984. pap. 8.00 (*0-910043-08-6*) Bamboo Ridge Pr.

Morales, Ronald J. Amateur Astronomer's Catalog of Five Hundred Deep-Sky Objects: Astronomy for the Serious Amateur. (Illus.). 128p. 1986. pap. 12.50 (*0-89404-076-6*) Aztex.

Morales, Rosario, jt. auth. see Morales, Aurora L.

*Morales Ruiz, Juan J. Differential Galois Theory & Non-Integrability of Hamilton Systems LC 99-35342. (Progress in Mathematics Ser.). 1999. pap. write for info. (*0-8176-6078-X*) Birkhauser.

— Differential Galois Theory & Non-Integrability of Hamilton Systems. LC 99-35342. (Progress in Mathematics Ser.: Vol. 179). 184p. 1999. 69.95 (*3-7643-6078-X*, Pub. by Birkhauser) Spr-Verlag.

Morales Santos, Francisco. Diccionario Escolar Centroamericano. (SPA.). 600p. 1988. pap. write for info. (*0-7859-6335-9*, 8483772310) Fr & Eur.

Morales, Valdemar. La Biblia Libro por Libro 7: Alumnos Adultos.Tr. of Bible Book by Book 7: Adult Pupils. (SPA.). 224p. 1997. pap. text 5.99 (*0-311-11267-6*) Casa Bautista.

— La Biblia Libro por Libro 7: Alumnos Jovenes.Tr. of Bible Book by Book 7: Youth Pupils. (SPA.). 224p. 1997. pap. text 5.99 (*0-311-11277-3*) Casa Bautista.

Morales, Vivian B. & Braidwood, Robert J. Figurines & Other Clay Objects from Sarab & Cayonu. LC 89-63967. (Communications Ser.: No. 25). (Illus.). xvi, 92p. 1990. pap. text 20.00 (*0-918986-59-1*) Orient Inst.

Morales y Marin, Jose L. Los Toros en el Arte. 2nd ed. 310p. 1989. 295.00 (*84-239-5262-2*) Elliots Bks.

Moramarco, Cindy, ed. see Boshart, Char.

Moramarco, Fred & Zolynas, Al, eds. Men of Our Time: An Anthology of Male Poetry in Contemporary America. LC 91-31462. 472p. 1992. 45.00 (*0-8203-1404-8*); pap. 19.95 (*0-8203-1430-7*) U of Ga Pr.

Moramarco, Fred, et al. Modern American Poetry, 1865-1950. (Critical History of Poetry Ser.). 304p. 1989. 23.95 (*0-8057-8451-9*, Twyne) Mac Lib Ref.

Moramarco, Fred S. & Sullivan, William J. Containing Multitudes Poetry In the United States Since 1950: Contemporary American Poetry. LC 97-36476. 1998. 33.00 (*0-8057-1647-5*) Mac Lib Ref.

MoraMarco, Jacques. The Complete Ginseng Handbook. LC 97-35368. 240p. 1998. pap. 12.95 (*0-8092-2971-4*, 297140, Contemporary Bks) NTC Contemp Pub Co.

An Asterisk (*) at the beginning of an entry indicates that the title is appearing for the first time.

*MoraMarco, Jacques. The Way of Walking: Eastern Strategies for Vitality, Longevity, & Peace of Mind. LC 99-52832. 256p. 2000. pap. 14.95 (0-8092-2586-7, 258670, Contemporary Bks) NTC Contemp Pub Co.

Moramarco, Nick. Missing in Action: A World War II Memoir. LC 98-19973. (Illus.). 128p. (Orig.). 1999. pap. 10.95 (1-56474-269-5) Fithian Pr.

Moran. Basic Concepts in Immunotechnology. 1969. text. write for info. (0-471-89910-0); pap. text. write for info. (0-471-89911-9) Wiley.

Moran. The Changing Display Industry. LC 97-132506. 184p. 1994. 2650.00 (1-56965-220-1, GB-171) BCC.

— Context Design. (HCI Ser.: Vol. 9, No. 1). 1994. 20.00 (0-8058-9970-7) L Erlbaum Assocs.

— Current Perspectives on Participatory Design. (Human-Computer Interaction Ser.: Vol. 11, No. 3). 1997. pap. 20.00 (0-8058-9886-7) L Erlbaum Assocs.

*Moran. Fundamentals Of Engineering Thermodynamics with Problem Set Supplements & with User's Manual Set. 3rd ed. 1000p. 1998. pap. text 72.00 (0-471-29944-8) Wiley.

— Fundamentals of Fluid Mehcanics & Fundamental of Engineering Thermodynamics. 3rd ed. 2036p. 1997. text 114.00 (0-471-29478-0) Wiley.

Moran. International Business Case Studies: Instructor's Guide. (Managing Cultural Differences Ser.). 1994. teacher ed. 24.95 (0-88415-194-8, 5194) Gulf Pub.

— Introduction to Culture. (Teaching Methods Ser.). 2001. pap. 20.95 (0-8384-6676-1) Wadsworth Pub.

— Managing Cultural Differences: European Supplement - Instructor's Manual. 300p. 1996. pap., teacher ed. 20.00 (0-88415-472-6, 5472) Gulf Pub.

— Managing Cultural Differences: Latin American Supplement - Instructor's Manual. 300p. 1996. pap., teacher ed. 20.00 (0-88415-470-X, 5470) Gulf Pub.

— Meteorology. 5th ed. 1997. pap. text, teacher ed. write for info. (0-13-280793-9) Allyn.

*Moran. Scopes Trial: A Brief History with Documents. 2001. pap. text. write for info. (0-312-24919-5) St Martin.

Moran. Solutions Manual to Accompany Fundamentals of Engineering. 1408p. 1996. pap. text 39.90 (0-471-10571-6) Wiley.

*Moran. Thermo Appendices. 4th rev. ed. 1999. text 132.00 (0-471-38142-X) Wiley.

Moran. Thermodynamics 3rd ed. pap. text. write for info. (0-471-37201-3) Wiley.

— Thermodynamics. 4th ed. text 77.00 (0-471-37332-X) Wiley.

Moran. Thermodynamics 4th ed. text 79.00 (0-471-36361-8) Wiley.

Moran & Davis. Precalculus in Context: Concepts & Project for Real World. 2nd ed. (Mathematics Ser.). 2000. pap. 45.00 (0-534-36240-0) Brooks-Cole.

Moran & Horn. Surface Modification Industry Reviews. LC 96 136015. 1995. 1500.00 (1-56965-329-1, DSM94) BCC.

Moran & Mullick. Systemic Pathology of HIV Infections & AIDS in Children. 328p. Date not set. pap. text 62.00 (1-881041-40-9) Am Registry Path.

*Moran, et al. Precalculus: Contexts & Concepts. 2nd ed. (Mathematics Ser.). (C). 2000. text 12.00 (0-534-37822-6) Brooks-Cole.

— Precalculus in Context: Concepts & Project for the Real World. 2nd ed. (Mathematics Ser.). (C). 2000. text 15.00 (0-534-37902-8) Brooks-Cole.

Moran, jt. auth. see Davis.

Moran, jt. auth. see Hinoorani.

Moran, A. P. & O'Morain, C. A., eds. Pathogenesis & Host Response in Helicobacter Pylori Infections. 1997. pap. 30.00 (0-926592-19-X) Normed Verlag.

Moran, Aidan. Managing Your Own Learning at the University. 128p. 1997. pap. 10.95 (1-900621-04-5) Dufour.

Moran, Aidan P., ed. The Psychology of Concentration in Sport Performers: A Cognitive Analysis. 328p. 1996. 49.95 (0-86377-443-1) L Erlbaum Assocs.

Moran, Albert, ed. Film Policy: International, National, & Regional Perspectives. LC 95-48260. (Culture, Policy, & Politics Ser.). (Illus.). 304p. (C). 1996. 80.00 (0-415-09790-8); pap. 24.99 (0-415-09791-6) Routledge.

Moran, Albert & O'Regan, Tom, eds. An Australian Film Reader. (Australian Screen Ser.). 392p. (Orig.). (C). 1985. pap. 24.95 (0-86819-123-X, Pub. by Currency Pr) Accents Pubns.

Moran, Albert & Tulloch, John. A Country Practice: Quality Soap. 301p. (C). 1986. pap. 17.95 (0-86819-142-6, Pub. by Currency Pr) Accents Pubns.

*Moran, Alex. Come Here, Tiger. LC 00-9726. (Green Light Readers Ser.). (Illus.). (J). 2001. write for info. (0-15-216225-9) Harcourt.

Moran, Alex. Popcorn. LC 98-15566. (Green Light Readers Ser.). (Illus.). 20p. (J). 1999. pap. 3.95 (0-15-201998-7) Harcourt.

*Moran, Alex. Popcorn. (Green Light Readers Ser.). (J). 2000. 10.95 (0-15-202375-5) Harcourt.

— Six Silly Foxes. LC 99-6813. (Illus.). 20p. (J). (gr. k-2). 2000. pap. 3.95 (0-15-202566-9, Harcourt Child Bks) Harcourt.

— Six Silly Foxes. (Green Light Readers Ser.). (Illus.). 20p. (J). (gr. k-2). 2000. 10.95 (0-15-202560-X) Harcourt.

Moran, Amanda, ed. see Bianco, David J.

Moran, Anthony, ed. see Paolini, Albert J.

Moran, B., jt. ed. see Brinson, L. C.

Moran, Barbara, intro. Special Species by California Kids. 4th ed. (Anthology Ser.: No. 4). (Illus.). 90p. (J). (gr. k-12). 1994. pap. 14.95 (0-9634474-2-4) Special Species Project.

Moran, Barbara, ed. see San Diego County School Children Staff.

Moran, Barbara B. Academic Libraries: The Changing Knowledge Centers of Colleges & Universities. Fife, Jonathan D., ed. LC 85-61910. (ASHE-ERIC Higher Education Reports: No. 84-8). 97p. 1985. pap. 24.00 (0-913317-17-9) GWU Grad Schl E&HD.

Moran, Barbara B., jt. auth. see Stueart, Robert D.

Moran, Barbara K., jt. ed. see Gornick, Vivian.

Moran, Beth. Intuitive Healing: A Woman's Guide to Finding the Healer Within. LC 98-6451. 224p. 1998. 19.95 (1-86204-376-0, Pub. by Element MA) Penguin Putnam.

Moran, Beth & Schultz, Kkakthy. Finding the Healer Within: Taking Control of Your Health. 234p. (Orig.). 1996. pap. 12.95 (0-88737-681-9) Natl League Nurse.

Moran, Bill. The Mary Wanna Student Activity Book. (Illus.). 23p. (J). (gr. 4-6). 1989. pap. 2.50 (0-942493-10-9) Woodmere Press.

Moran, Bill & Mann, Peggy. The Mary Wanna Student Activity Book: Based Upon: The Sad Story of Mary Wanna Or How Marijuana Harms You. rev. ed. (Illus.). 26p. (J). (gr. 4-6). 1990. pap. text 2.95 (0-942493-11-7) Woodmere Press.

Moran, Brenda & Smith, Bob. Kingdom of Light. 48p. (J). (ps up). 1993. 12.95 (0-9638144-3-5) BrightWay Bks.

Moran, Brendan, jt. auth. see Schmadeka, Reid.

Moran, Brian. Battery Toys. LC 83-51743. (Illus.). 192p. 1984. 29.50 (0-88740-003-5) Schiffer.

— Battery Toys. 2nd rev. ed. (Illus.). 192p. 1999. 29.95 (0-7643-0818-1) Schiffer.

*Moran, Brian, et al. e-Counsel: The Executive's Legal Guide to Electronic Commerce. 2000. pap. 39.95 (0-9700166-0-3) Mountainside Pr.

Moran, Bridget. Judgement at Stoney Creek. 196p. 1998. pap. 12.95 (1-55152-053-2, Pub. by Arsenal Pulp) LPC InBook.

— A Little Rebellion. 164p. 1994. per. 12.95 (0-88978-252-0, Pub. by Arsenal Pulp) LPC InBook.

— Stoney Creek Woman: 10th Anniversary Edition. anniversary ed. LC 98-104229. 160p. 1997. pap. 11.95 (1-55152-047-8, Pub. by Arsenal Pulp) LPC InBook.

Moran, Bruce, jt. ed. see Hildreth, Martha.

Moran, Bruce T. Chemical Pharmacy Enters the University: Johannes Hartman & the Didactic Care of Chymiatria. 90p. (Orig.). 1991. 16.00 (0-931292-24-7) Am Inst Hist Pharm.

— Chemical Pharmacy Enters the University: Johannes Hartmann & the Didactic Care of Chymiatria. 90p. (Orig.). (C). 1991. pap. 8.50 (0-931292-23-9) Am Inst Hist Pharm.

Moran, Bruce T., ed. Patronage & Institutions: Science, Technology & Medicine at the European Court, 1500-1750. (Illus.). 267p. (C). 1991. 75.00 (0-85115-285-6) Boydell & Brewer.

Moran, C. G. The Heralds of the Law. 120p. 1996. reprint ed. 60.00 (1-56169-213-1) Gaunt.

Moran, Carrol, et al. Keys to the Classroom: A Teacher's Guide to the First Month of School. (ENG & SPA.). 200p. 1992. pap. 29.95 (0-8039-6014-X) Corwin Pr.

Moran, Ceri, jt. auth. see Williamson, Alan.

Moran, Charles, jt. ed. see Herrington, Anne.

Moran, Chris, ed. see Lange, Ed & Sohler, Stan.

Moran, Chris, ed. see Langner, Lawrence & Robinson, Julian.

Moran, Chris, ed. see League of Women Voters of Ohio Staff.

Moran, Christine A., ed. Hand Rehabilitation. (Clinics in Physical Therapy Ser.: Vol. 9). (Illus.). 232p. 1986. text 44.95 (0-443-08353-3) Church.

Moran, Colette. Disney's The Lion King. (Look & Find Ser.). (Illus.). 24p. (J). (gr. k-6). 1995. lib. bdg. 14.95 (1-56674-144-0, HTS Bks) Forest Hse.

Moran, Cynthia K., jt. auth. see Inlander, Charles B.

Moran, D. F., et al. Earthquake & Fire. 15p. 1958. pap. 4.00 (0-685-14382-1) Earthquake Eng.

— Peru Earthquake of October, 1974. 85p. 1975. pap. 12.00 (0-318-16327-6) Earthquake Eng.

Moran, Dan. Herbal Kitchen: A Guide to Growing & Using Herbs. (Illus.). 176p. 1996. pap. 14.95 (1-885061-12-9) Adventure Pubns.

Moran, Daniel. The Flame Key. 224p. (Orig.). 1987. pap. 2.95 (0-8125-4600-8, Pub. by Tor Bks) St Martin.

Moran, Daniel & Vesterman, William. Juxtapositions Instructor's Resource Guide: Connections & Contrasts. iv, 156p. (C). 1995. pap. text, teacher ed. write for info. (1-55934-450-4, 1450) Mayfield Pub.

Moran, Daniel, jt. ed. see Paret, Peter.

Moran, Daniel T. Dancing for Victoria: The Poems of Daniel Thomas Moran. LC 91-90156. 80p. 1992. 12.95 (0-9629221-0-2) D T Moran.

— Gone to Innisfree: Poems. Planz, Allen, ed. LC 93-91379. (Orig.). 1993. pap. 12.00 (0-9629221-1-0) D T Moran.

*Moran, Daniel T. In Praise of August: Poems. LC 98-72198. 107p. 1999. pap. 15.00 (1-886435-07-3) Canios Edit.

Moran, Daniel T. Sheltered by Islands: New & Selected Poems, 1985-1995. LC 95-95187. (Orig.). 1995. pap. text 15.00 (0-9629221-2-9) D T Moran.

Moran, David T. Life on the Wing: Adventures with Birds of Prey. LC 96-71286. (Illus.). xvii, 275p. 1997. 75.00 (0-9655519-0-3) Round Table CO.

Moran, David T. & Rowley, J. Carter. Visual Histology. LC 87-3835. 299p. reprint ed. pap. 92.70 (0-7837-2730-5, 204311000006) Bks Demand.

Moran, Denis M. The Allotment Movement in Britain. (American University Studies: Geography: Ser. XXV, Vol. 1). (Illus.). 203p. (C). 1990. text 44.50 (0-8204-0812-3) P Lang Pubng.

Moran, Dennis P. Gabriel Marcel: Existentialist Philosopher, Dramatist, Educator. 140p. (Orig.). (C). 1992. pap. text 19.50 (0-8191-8822-0); lib. bdg. 39.50 (0-8191-8821-2) U Pr of Amer.

Moran, Dennis W., jt. ed. see Hudson, Deal W.

*Moran, Dermot. Introduction to Phenomenology. LC 99-42071. 584p. 1999. pap. 24.99 (0-415-18373-1) Routledge.

— Introduction to Phenomenology. LC 99-42071. 592p. (C). 2000. text 75.00 (0-415-18372-3) Routledge.

Moran, E. C., Jr. Bunker Genealogy, Ancestry & Descendants of Benjamin 3 (James 2, James 1) 232p. 1993. reprint ed. pap. 37.50 (0-8328-3561-7); reprint ed. lib. bdg. 47.50 (0-8328-3560-9) Higginson Bk Co.

— Bunker Genealogy, The Charlestown & Nantucket, Mass., Branches, & Some Unconnected Groups. 302p. 1993. reprint ed. pap. 46.50 (0-8328-3559-5); reprint ed. lib. bdg. 56.50 (0-8328-3558-7) Higginson Bk Co.

Moran, Edward C., Jr. Bunker Genealogy, Dover Branch, Vol. III. 389p. 1993. reprint ed. pap. 59.50 (0-8328-3555-2); reprint ed. lib. bdg. 69.50 (0-8328-3554-4) Higginson Bk Co.

*Moran, Edward G. The Global Ecology. LC 99-39007. (Reference Shelf Ser.). 213p. 1999. 30.00 (0-8242-0965-6) Wilson.

Moran, Eileen G., jt. ed. see Bart, Pauline B.

*Moran, Elaine. Bon Appetit, Baby! The Breastfeeding Kit. Gotsch, Gwen, ed. (Illus.). 272p. 2000. 24.95 (0-9674315-0-6, Pub. by Treas Child Pubns) IPG Chicago.

Moran, Elizabeth. Bradymania! Everything You Always Wanted to Know & a Few Things You Probably Didn't. 25th anniversary ed. LC 94-35376. 238p. 1995. pap. 9.95 (1-55850-418-4) Adams Media.

— Speed Racer: The Official 30th Anniversary Guide. (J). 1997. pap. 91.60 (0-7868-9941-7, Pub. by Hyperion) Little.

— Speed Racer: The Official 30th Anniversary Guide. LC 97-3161. (Illus.). 128p. (J). 1997. pap. 11.45 (0-7868-8246-8, Pub. by Hyperion) Time Warner.

Moran, Elizabeth & Biktashev, Val. The Complete Idiot's Guide to Feng Shui. LC 99-62545. (Illus.). 432p. 1999. pap. 18.95 (0-02-863105-6, Pub. by Macmillan Gen Ref) S&S Trade.

*Moran, Elizabeth & Field, Stephen L. The Complete Idiot's Guide to I-Ching. 2001. pap. 16.95 (0-02-863979-0, Alpha Ref) Macmillan Gen Ref.

Moran, Elizabeth & Krasny, Marianne. Water Wise: Lessons in Water Resources. (Illus.). 87p. (J). (gr. 4-7). 1989. pap. 8.95 (1-57753-253-8, 147WW) Corn Coop Ext.

Moran-Ellis, Jo, jt. auth. see Hutchby, Ian.

Moran, Emilio F. Deforestation in the Brazilian Amazon. Conway, Dennis, ed. (Series on Environment & Development). 36p. (Orig.). 1992. pap. 2.00 (1-881157-10-5) In Ctr Global.

— Developing the Amazon. LC 80-8382. (Illus.). 309p. 1981. pap. 95.80 (0-608-05036-9, 205969700004) Bks Demand.

— Human Adaptability: An Introduction to Ecological Anthropology. (Illus.). 404p. (C). 1982. pap. 36.00 (0-86531-431-4, Pub. by Westview) HarpC.

— Human Adaptability: An Introduction to Ecological Anthropology. 2nd ed. 400p. (C). 2000. pap. text 25.00 (0-8133-1254-X) Westview.

— Through Amazonian Eyes: The Human Ecology of Amazonian Populations. LC 93-1148. (Illus.). 252p. 1993. pap. 12.95 (0-87745-418-3); text 34.95 (0-87745-417-5) U of Iowa Pr.

Moran, Emilio F., ed. The Comparative Analysis of Human Societies: Toward Common Standards for Data Collection & Reporting. LC 94-3601. 202p. 1994. lib. bdg. 45.00 (1-55587-514-9) L Rienner.

— The Ecosystem: Approach in Anthropology. rev. ed. 496p. 1990. pap. text 22.95 (0-472-08102-0, 08102) U of Mich Pr.

— Transforming Societies, Transforming Anthropology. 376p. 1996. text 54.50 (0-472-10574-4, 10574) U of Mich Pr.

Moran, Eric T., jt. auth. see Gabriel, Lester H.

Moran, F., et al, eds. Advances in Artificial Life: Third European Conference on Artificial Life, Granada, Spain, June 4-6, 1995: Proceedings. (Lecture Notes in Computer Science Ser.: Vol. 929). 1995. write for info. (0-387-59496-5) Spr-Verlag.

— Advances in Artificial Life: Third European Conference on Artificial Life, Granada, Spain, June 4-6, 1995: Proceedings. (Lecture Notes in Computer Science Ser.: Vol. 929). 960p. 1995. 129.00 (3-540-59496-5) Spr-Verlag.

Moran, Fawn. Witness the Love: Stories from AIDS Caregivers. (Illus.). 240p. 1996. pap. 14.95 (0-9640878-0-4) Journey Home.

Moran, Frances. Listening: A Pastoral Style. LC 98-194769. 160p. (Orig.). 1997. pap. 11.95 (0-85574-318-2, Pub. by E J Dwyer) Morehouse Pub.

Moran, Frances M. Subject & Agency in Psychoanalysis: Which Is to Be Master? LC 92-48288. (Psychoanalytic Crosscurrents Ser.). 208p. (C). 1993. text 45.00 (0-8147-5482-1) NYU Pr.

Moran, Freddy. Freddy's House: Brilliant Color in Quilts. Kuhn, Barb & Aune, Carolyn, eds. LC 99-6117. (Illus.). 112p. 1999. 24.95 (1-57120-074-6, 10194) C & T Pub.

Moran, Gabrial & Devitt, Patrick M. How Adult Is Are? 336p. 1989. pap. 45.00 (1-85390-123-7, Pub. by Veritas Pubns) St Mut.

Moran, Gabriel. Design for Religion: Towards Ecumenical Education. 168p. 1994. pap. 20.00 (0-85532-277-2, Pub. by Srch Pr) St Mut.

— Religious Education As a Second Language. LC 89-33871. 254p. (Orig.). 1989. pap. 24.95 (0-89135-072-1) Religious Educ.

— Showing How: The Act of Teaching. LC 96-50492. 256p. (Orig.). 1997. pap. 20.00 (1-56338-187-7) TPI PA.

— Theology of Revelation. 1984. 9.95 (0-8164-2567-1) Harper SF.

— Vision & Tactics: Towards an Adult Church. 158p. 1994. pap. 20.00 (0-85532-018-4, Pub. by Srch Pr) St Mut.

Moran, Gabriel, jt. auth. see Harris, Maria.

Moran, Gary, jt. auth. see Pearl, Bill.

Moran, Gary T. & McGlynn, George. Dynamics of Strength Training. 176p. (C). 1989. text. write for info. (0-697-07638-5) Brown & Benchmark.

— Dynamics of Strength Training. 2nd ed. LC 95-83954. 160p. (C). 1996. per. write for info. (0-697-12655-2) Brown & Benchmark.

Moran, Gary T. & McGlynn, George H. Cross-Training for Sports. LC 96-52228. (Illus.). 240p. (Orig.). 1997. pap. 19.95 (0-88011-493-2, PMOR0493) Human Kinetics.

Moran, Gary T., et al. Fit & Able. 224p. (C). 1995. pap. text. write for info. (0-697-11286-1) Brown & Benchmark.

Moran, George. Fresh Eggs. LC 97-74044. (Illus.). 128p. 1997. pap. 5.95 (0-9627403-8-1) Lake Isle Pr.

Moran, George C. & Labine, Paul, eds. Corrosion Monitoring in Industrial Plants Using Nondestructive Testing & Electrochemical Methods: STP 908. LC 86-13994. (Special Technical Publication (STP) Ser.). (Illus.). 514p. 1986. text 64.00 (0-8031-0471-5, STP908) ASTM.

Moran, Gerald F. & Vinovskis, Maris A. Religion, Family & the Life Course: Explorations in the Social History of Early America. 272p. (C). 1992. text 49.50 (0-472-10312-1, 10312) U of Mich Pr.

M

Moran, Gerard. Radical Priest in Mayo: The Rise & Fall of an Irish Nationalist 1825-86. (Illus.). 240p. 1994. 39.50 (1-85182-163-5, Pub. by Four Cts Pr) Intl Spec Bk.

— Radical Priest in Mayo: The Rise & Fall of an Irish Nationalist 1825-86. (Illus.). 240p. 1994. pap. 19.95 (1-85182-173-2, Pub. by Four Cts Pr) Intl Spec Bk.

Moran, Gerard, ed. Radical Irish Priests, 1660-1950. LC 98-192520. 220p. 1998. boxed set 45.00 (1-85182-249-6, Pub. by Four Cts Pr) Intl Spec Bk.

— Ten Radical Priests. 220p. 1996. pap. 25.00 (1-85182-281-X, Pub. by Four Cts Pr) Intl Spec Bk.

Moran, Gerard, jt. ed. see Gillespie, Raymond.

Moran, Gordon. Silencing Scientists & Scholars in Other Fields: Power Paradigm Controls, Peer Review & Scholarly Communication. LC 97-30773. (Contemporary Studies in Information Management, Policy & Services). 1998. 73.25 (1-56750-342-X); pap. 39.50 (1-56750-343-8) Ablx Pub.

Moran, J. B. Moran Family: Two Hundred Years in Detroit. (Illus.). 152p. 1991. reprint ed. pap. 28.00 (0-8328-2036-9); reprint ed. lib. bdg. 38.00 (0-8328-2035-0) Higginson Bk Co.

Moran, J. M. & Hewitt, J. N., eds. Gravitational Lenses. (Lecture Notes in Physics Ser.: Vol. 330). xiv, 238p. 1989. 45.95 (0-387-51061-3) Spr-Verlag.

Moran, J. M., jt. auth. see Ho, P. T.

Moran, J. M., jt. ed. see Reid, M. J.

Moran, James. The Double Crown Club: A History of Fifty Years. (Illus.). 128p. (C). 1989. 400.00 (0-903696-03-7, Pub. by Hurtwood Pr Ltd) St Mut.

— Fit to Be Styled a Typographer: History of the Society of Typographic Designers, 1928-78. 80p. (C). 1989. 110.00 (0-903696-11-8, Pub. by Hurtwood Pr Ltd) St Mut.

Moran, James P., jt. ed. see Simpson, Theresa C.

Moran, Jamesart M. Building Your Kevlar Canoe: A Foolproof Method & Three Foolproof Designs. (Illus.). 224p. 1995. pap. 19.95 (0-07-043036-5, Ragged Mntain) McGraw-Hill Prof.

Moran, Jan. Fabulous Fragrances: How to Select Your Perfume Wardrobe-The Woman's Guide to Prestige Perfumes. Heyes, Eileen & Halper, Jan, eds. 240p. 1994. 29.00 (0-9639065-5-0) Crescent Hse.

*Moran, Jan. Fabulous Fragrances Vol. 2: How to Select Your Perfume Wardrobe. Hayes, Eileen, ed. (Illus.). 256p. 2000. 32.00 (0-9639065-4-2) Crescent Hse.

Moran, Jaya C. Irish Fairy Cards: For Inspiration & Guidance. LC 97-13783. (Illus.). 156p. 1997. pap. 32.95 (1-884695-34-5) Wrds of Wizdom.

*Moran, Jeffrey P. Teaching Sex: The Shaping of Adolescence in the 20th Century. LC 99-54303. 288p. 2000. pap. text 27.95 (0-674-00227-X) HUP.

Moran, Jim. Some Things Never Change: Classic Thoughts That Stand the Test of Time. LC 96-19980. 168p. 1995. pap. 5.95 (1-56245-223-1) Great Quotations.

— Why Men Shouldn't Marry. LC 69-10633. 1969. 3.00 (0-8184-0094-3) Carol Pub Group.

Moran, Jo Ann H. The Growth of English Schooling, 1340-1548: Learning, Literacy, & Laicization in Pre-Reformation York Diocese. LC 84-42570. (Illus.). 347p. 1985. reprint ed. pap. 107.60 (0-608-06474-2, 206677100009) Bks Demand.

*Moran, Joe. Star Authors: Literary Celebrity in America. LC 99-54537. 2000. write for info. (0-7453-1524-0) Pluto GBR.

— Star Authors: Literary Celebrity in America. 192p. 2000. pap. 19.95 (0-7453-1519-4, Pub. by Pluto GBR) Stylus Pub VA.

Moran, Joe, et al, contrib. by. Aqui Estamos...Y No Nos Vamos: Here We Are...& We're Not Leaving. LC 90-32219. (Illus.). 40p. (Orig.). 1990. pap. 10.00 (0-945486-07-3) CSU SBRVFAM.

Moran, John. Taking the High Ground. 255p. 1997. pap. 9.99 (0-934998-69-8) Evangel Indiana.

Moran, John. Toward the World & Wisdom of Wittgenstein's "Tractatus" 1973. pap. text 49.25 (90-279-2394-9) Mouton.

Moran, John, et al. Daily Management: A System for Individual & Organizational Optimization. (Illus.). 100p. (Orig.). 1990. pap. 24.95 (1-879364-07-7) GOAL-QPC.

— Term Paper Study Aids. (J). 1986. pap. 2.25 (0-87738-025-2) Youth Ed.

Moran, John B. Creating a Legend: The Complete Record of Writing About the United States Marine Corps. LC 79-139570. (Illus.). 688p. 1973. lib. bdg. 24.95 (0-912286-00-8) Moran Andrews.

Moran, John C. An F. Marion Crawford Companion. LC 80-1707. (Illus.). 548p. 1981. lib. bdg. 115.00 (0-313-20926-X, MCC/, Greenwood Pr) Greenwood.

— Last Days & Death of Dr. & Gen. William Walker. (Worthies Library: No. 3). (Illus.). 100p. 1988. 10.00 (0-318-20644-7) F M Crawford.

Moran, John C., et al, eds. The Romanist, 1982-84, No. 6-8. 1986. 10.00 (0-318-20642-0) F M Crawford.

— The Romantist, 1985-86, No. 9-10. 1988. 10.00 (0-317-01473-0) F M Crawford.

Moran, John C., ed. see Crawford, Anne & Von Rable, Baroness.

Moran, John C., ed. see Crawford, Francis M.

Moran, John C., ed. see Fraser, Hugh & Stahlmann, J. I.

Moran, John H., tr. see Rousseau, Jean-Jacques & Herder, Johann G.

Moran, John J. A Defense of Edgar Allan Poe. LC 79-171361. reprint ed. 27.50 (0-404-04399-2) AMS Pr.

— Employment Law: New Challenges in the Business Enivornment. LC 96-34105. 594p. 1996. 92.00 (0-13-448250-6) P-H.

— Practical Business Law. 3rd ed. LC 94-25594. 480p. 1994. 62.00 (0-13-138660-3) P-H.

Moran, John J., jt. auth. see Rosenau, Milton D.

Moran, John P. Living Our Life Story: Spiritual Transformation in a Turbulent World. Neary, R. Patrick & St. George, Michele, eds. LC 94-76730. (Illus.). 208p. 1994. pap. 9.95 (0-9640806-9-9) Lightsmith Multimed.

Moran, John W. & Moreau, Nancy A. Experimental Physics. (Illus.). 1989. student ed. 6.95 (0-913811-06-8) Northeast A S.

Moran, John W., jt. auth. see Burton, Terrence T.

Moran, Joseph Declan. You Can Call Me Al: The Colorful Journey of College Basketball's Original Flower Child--Al McGuire. LC 99-18577. (Illus.). 332p. 1999. pap. 16.95 (1-879483-52-1) Prairie Oak Pr.

Moran, Joseph J. Assessing Adult Learning: A Guide for Practitioners. LC 96-17541. (Professional Practices in Adult Education & Human Resource Development Ser.). (Illus.). 188p. (C). 1996. 22.50 (0-89464-938-8) Krieger.

Moran, Joseph M. & Moran, Michael D. Meteorology: The Atmosphere & Science of Weather. 5th ed. LC 96-43449. (Illus.). 530p. (C). 1996. 74.00 (0-13-266701-0) P-H.

Moran, Joseph M. & Morgan, Michael D. Essentials of Weather. LC 94-10979. (Illus.). 368p. (C). 1994. pap. text 69.00 (0-02-383831-0, Macmillan Coll) P-H.

— Meteorology: The Atmosphere & the Science of Weather. 4th ed. LC 93-1035. (Illus.). 550p. (C). 1994. pap. text, student ed. 23.80 (0-02-383345-9, Macmillan Coll) P-H.

Moran, Judith, et al. Precalculus Concepts in Context. LC 95-35595. (Mathematics Ser.). 1997. mass mkt. 93.95 (0-534-19789-2) PWS Pubs.

Moran, Judy, ed. New Langton Arts: The First 15 Years. (Illus.). 96p. (Orig.). 1990. pap. 30.00 (0-9627010-0-9) New Langton Arts.

Moran, Judy Flagg, jt. auth. see Davis, Marsha.

Moran, Julie L. Golf Vacations Even Non-Golfers Will Enjoy: Southeastern United States. LC 96-28706. (Illus.). (Orig.). 1996. pap. 17.95 (0-89587-153-X) Blair.

Moran, Karen. Literature Online: Reading & Internet Activities for Libraries & Schools. LC 99-21415. 94p. 1999. pap. 16.95 (1-57950-032-3, Alleyside) Highsmith Pr.

Moran, Kate. Investment Appraisal for Non-Financial Managers: A Step-by-Step Guide to Profitable Decisions. 2nd ed. (Institute of Management Ser.). 250p. 1997. pap. 48.50 (0-273-62682-5, Pub. by Pitman Pub) Trans-Atl Phila.

***Moran, Kelly L.** Shelley Chintz: Unlocking the Secrets of the Pattern Books. (Illus.). 140p. 2000. 79.95 (0-9676925-0-4) Thaxted Cottage Pubs.

Moran, Ken & Storch, Neil. UMD Comes of Age: The First One Hundred Years. LC 96-18263. 1996. write for info. (0-89865-970-1) Donning Co.

Moran, Kerry. Moon Handbooks: Hong Kong: Including Macau & Guangzhou. 2nd rev. ed. LC 96-648119. (Illus.). 380p. 1998. pap. 16.95 (1-56691-108-7, Moon Handbks) Avalon Travel.

***Moran, Kerry.** Moon Handbooks: Nepal. 3rd rev. ed. (Illus.). 500p. 2000. pap. 18.95 (1-56691-164-8, Moon Handbks) Avalon Travel.

Moran, Kerry, jt. auth. see Johnson, Russell.

***Moran, Kerry.** Nepal: The Mountain Kingdom. (Illus.). 280p. 2000. reprint ed. pap. text 20.00 (0-7881-9106-3) DIANE Pub.

Moran, Leila, jt. ed. see Fusonie, Alan.

Moran, Leslie. The Homosexuality of Law. LC 95-26467. 256p. (C). 1996. 85.00 (0-415-07952-7); pap. 27.99 (0-415-07953-5) Routledge.

Moran, Leslie J., et al. Legal Queeries: Lesbian, Gay & Transgender Legal Studies. LC 97-52265. 1998. 69.95 (0-304-33863-X); pap. 24.95 (0-304-33864-8) Continuum.

***Moran-Lever, Tery.** Official Export Guide: 1999 Edition. 2612p. 1999. 575.00 (1-891131-03-6) Primedia Directories.

Moran-Lever, Tery. U. S. Custom House Guide 1999: 1999 Edition. 2886p. 1998. 575.00 (1-891131-04-4) Primedia Directories.

Moran-Lever, Tery, ed. North American Trade Guide, 1997. (Illus.). 1984p. 1996. pap. text 399.00 (0-9649630-3-5) Primedia Directories.

— Official Export Guide, Supplement II, 1996. 336p. 1996. pap. text 95.00 (0-9649630-0-0) Primedia Directories.

— Official Export Guide: 1997 Edition. (Illus.). 2492p. 1996. text 425.00 (0-9649630-6-X) Primedia Directories.

— Official Export Guide: 1998 Edition. (ISSN Ser.: No. 0278-6389). (Illus.). 2612p. 1997. text 455.00 (0-9649630-9-4) Primedia Directories.

***Moran-Lever, Tery, ed.** Official Export Guide: 2000 Edition. (Illus.). 2648p. 1999. 475.00 (1-891131-06-0) Primedia Directories.

Moran-Lever, Tery, ed. U. S. Custom House Guide: 1996 Edition. (Illus.). 2912p. 1996. text 399.00 (0-9649630-2-7) Primedia Directories.

— U. S. Custom House Guide: 1997 Edition. (Illus.). 2892p. 1997. text 425.00 (0-9649630-5-1) Primedia Directories.

***Moran-Lever, Tery, ed.** U. S. Custom House Guide: 2000 Edition. (Illus.). 3056p. 1999. 475.00 (1-891131-07-9) Primedia Directories.

Moran-Lever, Tery, ed. U. S. Custom House Guide, 1998: 1998 Edition. (ISSN Ser.: No. 1084-8681). (Illus.). 1997. text 455.00 (0-9649630-8-6) Primedia Directories.

Moran-Lever, Tery, jt. ed. see Birnie, Dianna.

Moran, Linda, et al. Keeping Teams on Track: What to Do When the Going Gets Rough. 288p. 1996. text 30.00 (0-7863-0475-8, Irwn Prfssnl) McGraw-Hill Prof.

— Keeping Teams on Track: What to Do When the Going Gets Rough. 1996. 30.00 (0-614-95727-3, Irwn Prfssnl) McGraw-Hill Prof.

Moran, Lois, ed. The Craftsman's Cookbook. LC 72-91347. (Illus.). 192p. 1972. 10.80 (0-88321-000-2) Am Craft.

Moran-Lopez, J. L., ed. Current Problems in Condensed Matter: Proceedings of an International Workshop on Current Problems in Condensed Matter: Theory & Experiment Held in Cocoyoc, Mexico, January 5-9, 1997. LC 98-20242. (Illus.). 370p. (C). 1998. 125.00 (0-306-45915-9, Plenum Trade) Perseus Pubng.

Moran-Lopez, J. L. & Sanchez, J. M. New Trends in Magnetism, Magnetic Materials & Their Applications. LC 94-39745. (Illus.). 486p. (C). 1994. text 135.00 (0-306-44829-7, Kluwer Plenum) Kluwer Academic.

— Theory & Applications of the Cluster Variation & Path Probability Methods: Proceedings of an International Workshop Held in Juan Teotihuacou, Mexico, June 19-23, 1995. LC 96-35752. (Illus.). 435p. (C). 1996. text 155.00 (0-306-45461-0, Kluwer Plenum) Kluwer Academic.

Moran-Lopez, J. L. & Sanchez, Juan M., eds. Advanced Topics in Materials Science & Engineering. LC 93-12843. (Illus.). 366p. (C). 1993. text 110.00 (0-306-44487-9, Kluwer Plenum) Kluwer Academic.

Moran-Lopez, J. L. & Schuller, I. K., eds. Oxygen Disorder Effects in High Tc Superconductors. (Illus.). 228p. 1990. 75.00 (0-306-43409-1, Plenum Trade) Perseus Pubng.

Moran-Lopez, J. L., et al. Structural & Phase Stability of Alloys. LC 92-8513. (Illus.). 280p. (C). 1992. 89.50 (0-306-44211-6, Plenum Trade) Perseus Pubng.

Moran, Louise. A Social History Approach to Research in Distance Education. (C). 1991. pap. 24.00 (0-7300-1350-2, IDE806, Pub. by Deakin Univ) St Mut.

Moran, M. J., jt. ed. see Stecco, S. S.

Moran, Marilyn A. Birth & the Dialogue of Love. LC 81-81200. (Illus.). 233p. (Orig.). (C). 1981. pap. 24.95 (0-940128-01-2) Terra Publng.

— Pleasurable Husband/Wife Childbirth: The Real Consummation of Married Love. (Illus.). 228p. (Orig.). 1997. pap. 22.95 (0-940128-05-5) Terra Publng.

Moran, Marilyn A., ed. Happy Birth Days: Personal Accounts of Birth at Home the Intimate, Husband/Wife Way. (Illus.). 134p. (Orig.). 1986. pap. 12.95 (0-940128-02-0) Terra Publng.

Moran, Mark. The OSHA Answer Book: The Employers Manual That Answers Every Osha Question. 4th rev. large type ed. 320p. 1993. pap. 59.95 (1-890966-52-5) Moran Assocs.

Moran, Mark M. Accident Prevention. (OSHA Written Compliance Programs Ser.: No. 1). (Illus.). 37p. 1992. ring bd. 169.00 (0-9632296-5-6) Moran Assocs.

— Assured Equipment Grounding Conductor Program. (OSHA Written Compliance Programs Ser.: No. 2). (Illus.). 23p. 1992. ring bd. 169.00 (0-9632296-4-8) Moran Assocs.

— Cadmium Compliance Program. (OSHA Written Compliance Programs Ser.: No. 3). (Illus.). 85p. 1992. ring bd. 169.00 (0-9632296-3-X) Moran Assocs.

— Chemical Hygiene Plan. (OSHA Written Compliance Programs Ser.: No. 4). 42p. 1992. ring bd. 169.00 (0-9632296-2-1) Moran Assocs.

— Confined Space Program. (OSHA Written Compliance Programs Ser.: No. 5). (Illus.). 42p. 1992. ring bd. 169.00 (0-9632296-1-3) Moran Assocs.

— Construction Safety Handbook: A Practical Guide to OSHA Compliance & Injury Prevention. 469p. 1996. pap. text 79.00 (0-86587-547-2) Gov Insts.

— Crane & Derrick Safety Manual. (OSHA Written Compliance Programs Ser.: No. 6). (Illus.). 41p. 1992. ring bd. 169.00 (0-9632296-0-5) Moran Assocs.

— Electrical Safety Program. (OSHA Written Compliance Programs Ser.: No. 7). (Illus.). 50p. 1992. ring bd. 169.00 (1-890966-01-0) Moran Assocs.

— Emergency Action Plan. (OSHA Written Compliance Programs Ser.: No. 8). (Illus.). 20p. 1992. ring bd. 169.00 (1-890966-02-9) Moran Assocs.

— Ergonomics Program. (OSHA Written Compliance Programs Ser.: No. 9). (Illus.). 36p. 1992. ring bd. 169.00 (1-890966-03-7) Moran Assocs.

— Exposure Control Plan: A Written Compliance Program. (OSHA Written Compliance Programs Ser.: No. 10). (Illus.). 36p. 1992. ring bd. 169.00 (1-890966-04-5) Moran Assocs.

— Fall Protection Program. (OSHA Written Compliance Programs Ser.: No. 11). (Illus.). 32p. 1992. ring bd. 169.00 (1-890966-05-3) Moran Assocs.

— Fire Prevention Program. (OSHA Written Compliance Programs Ser.: No. 12). (Illus.). 38p. 1992. ring bd. 169.00 (1-890966-06-1) Moran Assocs.

— Hazard Communication Program. (OSHA Written Compliance Programs Ser.: No. 13). (Illus.). 58p. 1992. ring bd. 169.00 (1-890966-07-X) Moran Assocs.

— Hazardous Waste & Emergency Action. (OSHA Written Compliance Programs Ser.: No. 14). (Illus.). 126p. 1992. ring bd. 169.00 (1-890966-08-8) Moran Assocs.

— Hearing Conservation Program. (OSHA Written Compliance Programs Ser.: No. 15). (Illus.). 59p. 1992. ring bd. 169.00 (1-890966-10-X) Moran Assocs.

— Injury/Illness Prevention Program. (OSHA Written Compliance Programs Ser.: No. 16). (Illus.). 37p. 1992. ring bd. 169.00 (1-890966-09-6) Moran Assocs.

— Issues & Answers for Developing Your Hazard Communications Program. (OSHA Issues & Answers Ser.: No. 3). (Illus.). 50p. (Orig.). 1996. pap. 25.00 (1-890966-21-5) Moran Assocs.

— Issues & Answers for Developing Your Workplace Safety Committee. (OSHA Issues & Answers Ser.: No. 2). (Illus.). 23p. (Orig.). 1996. pap. 25.00 (1-890966-20-7) Moran Assocs.

— Issues & Answers for Fall Protection in the Construction Industry. (OSHA Issues & Answers Ser.: No. 6). (Illus.). 35p. (Orig.). 1996. pap. 25.00 (1-890966-23-1) Moran Assocs.

— Issues & Answers for Occupational Exposure to Bloodborne Pathogens. (OSHA Issues & Answers Ser.: No. 4). (Illus.). 37p. (Orig.). 1996. pap. 25.00 (1-890966-22-3) Moran Assocs.

— Issues & Answers for the Hazardous Waste Operations & Emergency Response. (OSHA Issues & Answers Ser.: No. 1). (Illus.). 33p. (Orig.). 1996. pap. 25.00 (1-890966-19-3) Moran Assocs.

— Issues & Answers on How to Prepare & Respond to an OSHA Inspection. (OSHA Issues & Answers Ser.: No. 7). (Illus.). 47p. (Orig.). 1996. pap. 25.00 (1-890966-24-X) Moran Assocs.

— Lead Compliance Program: A Written Compliance Program. (OSHA Written Compliance Programs Ser.: No. 17). (Illus.). 58p. 1992. ring bd. 169.00 (1-890966-11-8) Moran Assocs.

— Lockout - Tagout Program. (OSHA Written Compliance Programs Ser.: No. 18). (Illus.). 34p. 1992. ring bd. 169.00 (1-890966-13-4) Moran Assocs.

— Medical Surveillance Program. (OSHA Written Compliance Programs Ser.: No. 19). (Illus.). 24p. 1992. ring bd. 169.00 (1-890966-12-6) Moran Assocs.

— Motor Vehicle Occupant Protection Program. (OSHA Written Compliance Programs Ser.: No. 20). (Illus.). 20p. 1992. ring bd. 169.00 (1-890966-14-2) Moran Assocs.

— The OSHA Answer Book: The Employers Manual That Answers Every OSHA Question. 4th rev. ed. 316p. 1999. pap. 59.95 (0-9632296-7-2) Moran Assocs.

— OSHA's Electrical Safety & Lockout/Tagout Standards: Proven Written Programs for Compliance. LC 96-193899. 182p. 1996. pap. text 69.00 incl. disk (0-86587-502-2) Gov Insts.

— OSHA's Hazard Communication Standard: A Proven Written Program for Compliance. LC 96-189435. 161p. (Orig.). 1996. pap. 69.00 incl. disk (0-86587-499-9) Gov Insts.

— OSHA's Process Safety Management Standard: A Proven Written Program for Compliance. LC 96-182419. 235p. 1996. pap. text 69.00 incl. disk (0-86587-500-6) Gov Insts.

— Personal Protection Equipment Program. (OSHA Written Compliance Programs Ser.: No. 21). (Illus.). 60p. 1992. ring bd. 169.00 (1-890966-15-0) Moran Assocs.

— Process Safety Management Program. (OSHA Written Compliance Programs Ser.: No. 22). (Illus.). 60p. 1992. ring bd. 169.00 (1-890966-16-9) Moran Assocs.

— Respiratory Protection Program. (OSHA Written Compliance Programs Ser.: No. 23). (Illus.). 50p. 1992. ring bd. 169.00 (1-890966-17-7) Moran Assocs.

— Safety & Health Program. (OSHA Written Compliance Programs Ser.: No. 24). (Illus.). 37p. 1992. ring bd. 169.00 (1-890966-18-5) Moran Assocs.

— The Safety Handbook: A Practical Guide to OSHA Compliance & Injury Prevention for General Industry. 330p. 1998. pap. 59.95 (1-890966-50-9) Moran Assocs.

Moran, Mark M. & Moran, Robert D. The OSHA 500. 2nd rev. ed. (Illus.). 313p. 1995. ring bd. 99.95 (0-9632296-6-4) Moran Assocs.

Moran, Mark M. & Padro, Alexander M. The Internet Answer Book for Human Resource Professionals. LC 97-4399. (Illus.). 266p. 1997. pap. 29.95 (1-890966-00-2) Moran Assocs.

Moran, Mark M., jt. auth. see Moran, Robert D.

***Moran, Martha & Donnellan, John.** Selling & Promoting Products: Closing the Sale: Workbook. Woodbury, Debbie, ed. LC 99-75996. (Retailing Smarts Ser.: Vol. 7). (Illus.). 56p. 1999. pap., wbk. ed. 7.95 (1-56052-572-X) Crisp Pubns.

— Selling & Promoting Products: Completing the Sales Transaction: Workbook. Woodbury, Debbie, ed. LC 99-75997. (Retailing Smarts Ser.: Vol. 8). (Illus.). 64p. 1999. pap., wbk. ed. 7.95 (1-56052-573-8) Crisp Pubns.

Moran, Martha, jt. auth. see Donnellan, John.

Moran, Martin. Alps 4000: 75 Peaks in 52 Days. (Illus.). 240p. 1998. pap. 14.95 (0-7153-0690-1, Pub. by D & C Pub) Sterling.

— Alps 4000: Seventy-Five Peaks in Fifty-Two Days. (Illus.). 288p. 1995. 24.95 (0-7153-0268-X, Pub. by D & C Pub) Sterling.

— Tincture of Time: The Story of 150 Years of Medicine in Atlanta. 140p. 1995. 45.00 (0-9647461-0-7) Med Assn Atlanta.

Moran, Mary. Student Financial Aid & Women: Equity Dilemma? LC 86-72856. (ASHE-ERIC Higher Education Reports: No. 86-5). 153p. (Orig.). 1987. pap. 24.00 (0-913317-32-2) GWU Grad Schl E&HD.

Moran, Mary C., ed. Ordinary & Sacred as Blood: Alabama Women Speak. LC 99-63719. xii, 244p. 1999. pap. 11.95 (0-9672676-0-9) Rivers Edge Pubg Co.

Moran, Mary H. Civilized Women: Gender & Prestige in Southeastern Liberia. LC 89-22398. (Anthropology of Contemporary Issues Ser.). (Illus.). 208p. (Orig.). 1990. 39.95 (0-8014-2293-0); pap. text 14.95 (0-8014-9554-7) Cornell U Pr.

— Margaret Drabble: Existing Within Structures. LC 83-332. 144p. 1983. 21.95 (0-8093-1080-5) S Ill U Pr.

— Penelope Lively. LC 93-7655. (Twayne's English Authors Ser.: Vol. 503). 192p. 1993. 22.95 (0-8057-7028-3, Twyne) Mac Lib Ref.

Moran, Mary Y. & Flanagan, Anne J. Jesus Comes to Us: Activity Book. 80p. (J). (gr. 2). pap. 2.25 (0-8198-3922-1) Pauline Bks.

— Jesus Loves Us: Activity Book. 80p. (J). (gr. 1). pap. 2.25 (0-8198-3919-1) Pauline Bks.

Moran, Mary Y. & Myers, Theresa F. Jesus Teaches Us: Activity Book. 77p. (J). (gr. 3). pap. 2.25 (0-8198-3925-6) Pauline Bks.

Moran-McGlynn & McGlynn. Dynamics Strength (DM) 3rd ed. 1999. 10.25 (0-697-29577-X, WCB McGr Hill) McGrw-H Hghr Educ.

***Moran, Michael.** Governing the Health Care State: A Comparative Study of the United Kingdom, the United States, & Germany. LC 99-43349. 224p. 1999. 69.95 (0-7190-4296-8, Pub. by Manchester Univ Pr) St Martin.

— Governing the Health Care State: A Comparative Study of the United Kingdom, the United States & Germany. LC 99-43349. (Political Analyses Ser.). 1999. pap. 24.95 (0-7190-4297-6, Pub. by Manchester Univ Pr) St Martin.

Moran, Michael. Nothing but Net! An Essay on the Culture of Pickup Basketball. LC 91-76837. 118p. (Orig.). 1991. pap. 7.95 (0-9631597-0-4) Full Ct TX.

— Younger Than That Now: A Peace Corps Volunteer Remembers Morocco. LC 94-96345. 143p. (Orig.). 1994. pap. 12.95 (0-9631597-8-X) Full Ct TX.

Moran, Michael, intro. Rauf Denktash at the United Nations: Speeches on Cyprus. 378p. 1997. 65.00 (0-906719-50-X, Pub. by Eothen); pap. 39.95 (0-906719-55-0, Pub. by Eothen) Paul & Co Pubs.

Moran, Michael & Prosser, Tony, eds. Privatization & Regulatory Change in Europe. LC 93-30284. (Law & Political Change Ser.). 1994. 104.95 (0-335-19073-1); pap. 41.95 (0-335-19072-3) OpUniv Pr.

Moran, Michael & Willen, Rachel. Karma Violation Pad. 64p. 1996. mass mkt. 6.99 (0-446-67233-5, Pub. by Warner Bks) Little.

Moran, Michael, jt. ed. see Hancher, Leigh.

Moran, Michael, jt. ed. see Parry, Geraint.

Moran, Michael C., ed. see Journal of Urban Law Editors.

Moran, Michael D., jt. auth. see Moran, Joseph M.

Moran, Michael G., ed. Eighteenth Century British & American Rhetorics & Rhetoricians: Critical Studies & Sources. LC 93-35838. 328p. 1994. lib. bdg. 89.50 (0-313-27909-8, Greenwood Pr) Greenwood.

***Moran, Michael G. & Ballif, Michelle.** Twentieth-Century Rhetorics & Rhetoricians: Critical Studies & Sources. LC 99-59559. 2000. lib. bdg. write for info. (0-313-30391-6, Greenwood Pr) Greenwood.

Moran, Michael G. & Jacobi, Martin J., eds. Research in Basic Writing: A Bibliographic Sourcebook. LC 89-38229. 268p. 1990. lib. bdg. 72.95 (0-313-25564-4, MRB/, Greenwood Pr) Greenwood.

Moran, Michael G. & Journet, Debra, eds. Research in Technical Communication: A Bibliographic Sourcebook. LC 84-8977. 512p. 1985. lib. bdg. 95.00 (0-313-23431-0, MRT/, Greenwood Pr) Greenwood.

Moran, Michael G. & Lunsford, Ronald F., eds. Research in Composition & Rhetoric: A Bibliographic Sourcebook. LC 83-22568. (Illus.). 506p. 1984. lib. bdg. 89.50 (0-313-23308-X, MOR/, Greenwood Pr) Greenwood.

Moran, Michael G., jt. auth. see Kynell, Teresa C.

Moran, Michael J Thermo Appendices. 4th ed. pap. text 14.00 (0-471-36348-0) Wiley.

Moran, Michael J., ed. Availability Analysis: A Guide to Efficient Energy Use. rev. ed. 260p. 1989. 40.00 (0-7918-0009-1, 800091) ASME Pr.

Moran, Michael J. & Shapiro, Howard N. Fundamentals of Engineering Thermodynamics. 4th ed. LC 99-26489. 936p. (C). 1999. text 105.95 (0-471-31713-6) Wiley.

— Fundamentals of Engineering Thermodynamics: SI Version. 3rd ed. LC 97-29222. 814p. 1998. pap. text 79.95 (0-471-97960-0) Wiley.

— Fundamentals of Engineering Thermodynamics & Appendices Set. 3rd ed. 1020p. 1998. text 191.80 (0-471-16970-6) Wiley.

***Moran, Michael J. & Shapiro, Howard N.** Fundamentals of Engineering Thermodynamics & Interactive Thermodynamics Software & Appendices Set. 3rd ed. 1020p. 1998. text 145.85 (0-471-16971-4) Wiley.

Moran, Michael J. & Zylla-Jones, Elizabeth. Learning about Voice: Vocal Hygiene Activities for Children; A Resource Manual. LC 98-10016. (Illus.). 180p. 1998. pap. 49.95 (1-56593-942-5, 1866) Thomson Learn.

Moran, Michael L., jt. auth. see Brimer, Mark A.

Moran, N. K. Singers in Late Byzantine & Slavonic Painting. (Byzantina Neerlandica Ser.: No. 9). (Illus.). xiv, 173p. 1986. 64.50 (90-04-07809-6) Brill Academic Pubs.

Moran, Neil. Northcountry Gardening. LC 95-79339. (Illus.). 214p. 1995. pap. 16.95 (0-932212-87-5) Avery Color.

Moran, P. Electrochemical Techniques in Corrosion Science & Engineering. (Corrosion Technology Ser.). Date not set. write for info. (0-8247-9917-8) Dekker.

— Electrochemical Techniques in Corrosion Science & Technology. (Corrosion Technology Ser.). Date not set. write for info. (0-8247-9926-7) Dekker.

An Asterisk (*) at the beginning of an entry indicates that the title is appearing for the first time.

Moran, P. A. An Introduction to Probability Theory. 542p. 1984. reprint ed. pap. text 36.00 (*0-19-853242-3*) OUP.

Moran, Pablo & Mur, Frank X., eds. A. Alekhine: Agony of a Chess Genius. LC 89-42737. 328p. 1989. lib. bdg. 45.00 (*0-89950-440-X*) McFarland & Co.

Moran, Pat & Maguire, Jon. German Headgear in World War II Vol. 1: Army/Luftwaffe/Kriegsmarine: A Photographic Study of German Hats & Helmets. LC 96-70420. (Illus.). 312p. 75.00 (*0-7643-0176-4*) Schiffer.

— German Headgear in World War II Vol. II: SS, NSDAP, Police, Civilian, & Misc. - A Photographic Study of German Hats & Helmets. LC 96-70420. (Illus.). 160p. 1997. 75.00 (*0-7643-0245-0*) Schiffer.

***Moran, Patricia.** Oil Painter's Ultimate Flower & Portrait Companion. (Illus.). 2000. pap. 24.99 (*1-929834-03-9*) Intl Artist Pubg.

Moran, Patricia. Word of Mouth: Body Language in Katherine Mansfield & Virginia Woolf. LC 96-19760. (Feminist Issues Ser.). 208p. 1996. text 32.50 (*0-8139-1675-5*) U Pr of Va.

Moran, Patricia, jt. auth. see Bifulco, Antonia.

***Moran, Patricia B.** Perfectly Still: A Journey Through the Heart of Loss to an Inspiring Discovery of Love Without Barriers. 2000. pap. 13.95 (*1-58177-063-4*) Barrytown Ltd.

Moran, Patrick E., tr. from CHI. Three Smaller Wisdom Books: Lao Zi's Dao De Jing, the Great Learning (Da Zue), & the Doctrine of the Mean (Zhong Yong) 310p. (Orig.). (C). 1993. pap. text 28.50 (*0-8191-9215-5*); lib. bdg. 51.50 (*0-8191-9214-7*) U Pr of Amer.

Moran, Patrick R. Lexicarry: An Illustrated Vocabulary-Builder for Second Languages. 2nd rev. ed. LC 84-1007. (Supplementary Materials Handbook Ser.: No. 2). (Illus.). 128p. 1989. reprint ed. pap. text 11.00 (*0-86647-032-8*) Pro Lingua.

— Lexicarry: French Word List. rev. ed. Suquet, Annie, tr. LC 84-18026. (FRE.). 25p. 1991. pap. text 4.00 (*0-86647-045-X*) Pro Lingua.

— Lexicarry: Spanish Word List. rev. ed. DeFantini, Beatriz C., tr. LC 84-17939. (SPA.). 26p. 1991. pap. text 4.00 (*0-86647-046-8*) Pro Lingua.

— Lexicarry Posters: Twenty-Five Wall Charts. (Illus.). 26p. 1990. pap. text 25.00 (*0-86647-034-4*) Pro Lingua.

Moran, Patrick R., ed. Lexicarry: Japanese Word List. rev. ed. Nishizawa, Tetsuo & Kubota, Ryuko, trs. (JPN.). 106p. 1991. pap. text 15.00 (*0-86647-054-9*) Pro Lingua.

Moran, Patrick R., et al. The Grammar Handbook Part One: Elementary-Intermediate ESL. 2nd rev. ed. LC 84-11548. (Interplay ESL Ser.). (Illus.). 176p. 1991. pap. text 12.00 (*0-86647-042-5*) Pro Lingua.

Moran, Patrick R., jt. auth. see Hawkinson, Annie.

Moran, Patti J. Pet Sitting for Profit. (Illus.). 72p. (Orig.). 1987. pap. 9.95 (*0-944165-00-1*) New Beginnings.

— Pet Sitting for Profit. rev. ed. (Illus.). 112p. (Orig.). 1988. pap. 9.95 (*0-944165-11-7*) New Beginnings.

— Pet Sitting for Profit: A Complete Manual for Success. (Illus.). 192p. 1992. pap. 15.95 (*0-87605-770-9*) Howell Bks.

Moran, Peter. Hybrid Microelectric Technology. (Electrocomponent Science Monographs: Vol. 4). viii, 222p. 1984. text 240.00 (*0-677-06560-4*) Gordon & Breach.

Moran, Philip, tr. see Bykhovsky, Bernard.

Moran, Ran, ed. see Lira-Powell, Julianne H.

Moran, Reid. The Flora of Guadalupe Island. (Memoirs of the California Academy of Sciences Ser.: No. 19). (Illus.). 190p. 1996. 40.00 (*0-940228-40-8*) Calif Acad Sci.

Moran, Richard. Earth Winter. 320p. 1996. mass mkt. write for info. (*0-614-05519-9*); mass mkt. 6.99 (*0-8125-3012-8*) Tor Bks.

— The Empire of Ice. 1995. mass mkt. 5.99 (*0-8125-3009-8*, Pub. by Tor Bks) St Martin.

— Fear No Yellow Stickies. LC 98-9750. 160p. 1998. mass mkt. 8.00 (*0-684-85219-5*, Fireside) S&S Trade Pap.

Moran, Richard, jt. auth. see Rickwell, Robert.

Moran, Richard A. Beware Those Who Ask for Feedback. 160p. 1994. pap. 36.00 (*0-88730-715-9*, HarpBusn) HarpInfo.

— Never Confuse a Memo with Reality: And Other Business Lessons too Simple Not to Know. 96p. 1993. pap. 48.00 (*0-88730-679-9*, HarpBusn) HarpInfo.

— Never Confuse a Memo with Reality: And Other Business Lessons Too Simple Not to Know. LC 93-14376. 160p. 1993. pap. 8.00 (*0-88730-669-1*, HarpBusn) HarpInfo.

***Moran, Richard A.** Never Confuse a Memo with Reality: And Other Business Lessons Too Simple Not to Know. 1999. pap. 6.95 (*0-06-662033-3*, HarpBusn) HarpInfo.

Moran, Richard D., jt. auth. see Hornung, Mark.

Moran, Robert. The Changing Display Industry: CRT & Flat Panel. LC 98-120798. 237p. 1997. 2950.00 (*1-56965-249-X*, GB-171R) BCC.

— A Hiking Guide to Acadia National Park & Mount Desert Island. (Illus.). 24p. 1988. reprint ed. pap. 2.50 (*0-934745-07-2*) Acadia Pub Co.

— Major Display Materials: Markets, Technologies. LC 98-124883. 174p. 1997. 3250.00 (*1-56965-456-5*, GB-203) BCC.

Moran, Robert, ed. Thin Film/Diamond Industry Review. 261p. 1996. 1500.00 (*1-56965-342-9*, DTF95) BCC.

Moran, Robert & Grub, Phillip D., eds. Global Business Strategies for the Year 2000, 2 vols., Set. 1200p. 1995. lib. bdg. 110.00 (*0-933833-36-9*) Beacham Pub Corp.

Moran, Robert, jt. auth. see Hogan, Ben.

***Moran, Robert D.** The OSHA Inspection Book: What Every Employer Needs to Know about OSHA Inspections. 250p. 1999. pap. 59.95 (*1-890966-54-1*) Moran Assocs.

Moran, Robert D. & Moran, Mark M. OSHA Made Easy: A Guide to Recordkeeping, Reporting, & Compliance. LC 94-12508. 471p. 1994. text 120.95 (*0-442-01908-4*, VNR) Wiley.

Moran, Robert D. & Moran, Mark M. OSHA Made Easy: A Guide to Recordkeeping, Reporting, & Compliance. (Industrial Health & Safety Ser.). 471p. 1994. 149.00 (*0-471-28653-2*, VNR) Wiley.

Moran, Robert D., jt. auth. see Moran, Mark M.

Moran, Robert F., contrib. by. Considerations in the Simultaneous Measurement of Blood Gases, Electrolytes, & Related Analytes in Whole Blood: Proposed Guideline (1993) 1993. 75.00 (*1-56238-206-3*, C32-P) NCCLS.

Moran, Robert T. Getting Your Yen's Worth: How to Negotiate with Japan, Inc. fac. ed. LC 84-10882. 200p. pap. 62.00 (*0-7837-7428-1*, 204722300006) Bks Demand.

Moran, Robert T. & Abbott, Jeffrey D. NAFTA: Managing the Cultural Differences. LC 94-12482. (Managing Cultural Differences Ser.). 160p. 1994. pap. 14.95 (*0-88415-500-5*, 5500) Gulf Pub.

Moran, Robert T. & Harris, Philip R. Managing Cultural Differences. 4th ed. 300p. 1996. pap., teacher ed. 20.00 (*0-88415-466-1*, 5466) Gulf Pub.

Moran, Robert T. & Reisenberger, John R. The Global Challenge: Building the New Worldwide Enterprise. LC 94-10893. 1994. text 26.95 (*0-07-709022-5*) McGraw.

Moran, Robert T. & Stripp, William G. Dynamics of Successful International Business Negotiations. 250p. 1991. 27.50 (*0-87201-196-8*, 1196) Gulf Pub.

Moran, Robert T., et al. Developing the Global Organization: Strategies for Human Resource Professionals. LC 92-21197. 318p. 1993. 32.50 (*0-88415-071-2*, 5071) Gulf Pub.

— International Business Case Studies for the Multicultural Marketplace. LC 93-45859. (Managing Cultural Differences Ser.). 416p. 1994. pap. 29.95 (*0-88415-193-X*, 5193) Gulf Pub.

Moran, Robert T., jt. auth. see Harris, Philip R.

Moran, Robert T., jt. ed. see Braaten, David O.

Moran, Roberto. Manual of Mental Subnormality. (SPA.). 482p. 1968. 7.00 (*0-8477-2900-1*) U of PR Pr.

— Ninos con Problemas de Conducta y Aprendizaje: Temas Contemporaneos y Estrategias. 381p. 1984. pap. 12.50 (*0-8477-2906-0*) U of PR Pr.

Moran, Ronald. Fish Out of Water, Vol. 67. 1999. pap. 8.50 (*1-55780-181-9*) Juniper Pr ME.

— Getting the Body to Dance Again. 40p. 1995. pap. 7.95 (*0-944754-25-2*) Pudding Hse Pubns.

— So Simply Means the Rain. 1965. pap. 4.95 (*0-87511-086-X*); text 6.95 (*0-87511-087-8*) Claitors.

— Sudden Fictions. 59p. 1994. pap. 6.00 (*1-55780-130-4*) Juniper Pr ME.

Moran, Ronald, jt. auth. see Lensing, George S.

***Moran, Rosslyn.** Please, Mr. Crocodile! Poems about Animals. 40p. (J). (gr. 1-5). 1999. 16.95 (*1-902283-62-7*) Barefoot Bks NY.

Moran, Ruth A., jt. auth. see Baker, Lucia F.

Moran, Sally. A Woman for All Seasons: Reflections on Mary. LC 92-60892. 112p. (Orig.). 1993. pap. 7.95 (*0-89622-531-3*) Twenty-Third.

***Moran, Sarah.** Alien Abductions: Real-life Encounters with Extraterrestrial Beings. 1999. 14.99 (*1-84100-238-0*) Quadrillion Pub.

Moran, Sarah. Alien Art: Extraterrestrial Expressions on Earth. (Illus.). 128p. 1998. 12.99 (*1-85833-859-X*) Quadrillion Pubng.

***Moran, Sarah.** Psychics: The Paranormal Investigators' Files. 1999. 14.99 (*1-84100-295-X*) Quadrillion Pub.

Moran, Sarah. Secret World of Cults: From Ancient Druids to Heaven's Gate. 1999. 14.99 (*1-84100-132-5*) Quadrillion Media.

Moran, Sean F. Patrick Pearse & the Politics of Redemption: The Mind of the Easter Rising, 1916. LC 93-26449. 233p. 1994. 42.95 (*0-8132-0775-4*) Cath U Pr.

— Patrick Pearse & the Politics of Redemption: The Mind of the Easter Rising, 1916. 233p. 1998. pap. text 14.95 (*0-8132-0912-9*) Cath U Pr.

Moran, Sue E., ed. Inside a Terrorist Group: The Red Brigades of Italy. 272p. 1986. pap. text 35.00 (*1-57979-146-8*) DIANE Pub.

Moran, Susan, jt. auth. see Tighe, Karen.

Moran, Susan D. Gathered in the Spirit: Beginnings of the First Church in Cambridge. LC 95-16998. 192p. 1995. 18.95 (*0-8298-1069-2*) Pilgrim OH.

Moran, T. Legal Competence in Environmental Health. 208p. 1997. text. write for info. (*0-412-71580-5*, Chap & Hall NY) Chapman & Hall.

Moran, Ted, jt. auth. see Carlson, Richard.

Moran, Terence. Legal Competence in Environmental Health. LC 98-171432. (Illus.). 352p. (C). (gr. 13). 1998. 75.00 (*0-419-23000-9*, D5809, E & FN Spon) Routledge.

***Moran, Terrence J.** In the Spirit of Saint Alphonsus: 30 Prayer Services for the Church Year. 160p. 2000. pap. 12.95 (*0-7648-0667-X*) Liguori Pubns.

Moran, Theodore H. American Economic Policy & National Security. (Pew Project Ser.). 96p. 1992. pap. 10.95 (*0-87609-137-0*) Coun Foreign.

–Foreign Direct Investment & Development: The New Policy Agenda for Developing Countries & Economies-in-Transition. LC 97-48803. 1998. pap. 20.00 (*0-88132-258-X*) Inst Intl Eco.

Foreign direct investment (FDI) has grown dramatically & is now the largest & most stable source of private capital for developing countries & economies in transition, accounting for nearly 50 percent of all those flows. Meanwhile, the growing role of FDI in host countries has been accompanied by a change of attitude, from critical wariness toward multinational corporations to sometimes uncritical enthusiasm about their role in the development process. What are the most valuable benefits & opportunities that foreign firms have to offer? What risks & dangers do they pose? Beyond improving the micro & macroeconomic "fundamentals" in their own countries & building an investment-friendly environment,do authorities in host countries need a proactive (rather than passive) policy toward foreign investment. In one of those most comprehensive studies on FDI in two decades, Theodore Moran synthesizes evidence drawn from a wealth of case literature to assess policies toward FDI in these countries. His focus is on investment promotion, domestic content mandates, export-performance, requirements, joint-venture requirements & technology-licensing mandates. The study demonstrates that there is indeed a large, energetic & vital role for host authorities to play in designing policies toward FDI but that the needed actions differ substantially from conventional beliefs on the topic. Dr. Moran offers a new & controversial agenda for host governments, aimed at maximizing the benefits they can obtain from FDI while minimizing the dangers & suggests how they might best pursue this agenda. *Publisher Paid Annotation.*

— Managing International Political Risk. LC 98-7600. 300p. 1998. 59.95 (*0-631-20880-1*); pap. 29.95 (*0-631-20881-X*) Blackwell Pubs.

— Multinational Corporations & the Politics of Dependence: Copper in Chile. LC 74-2973. 303p. reprint ed. pap. 94.00 (*0-8357-4289-X*, 203708800007) Bks Demand.

— Oil Prices & the Future of OPEC: The Political Economy of Tension & Stability in the Organization of Petroleum Exporting Countries. LC 78-2983. (Resources for the Future. Research Paper Ser.: No. R-8). 108p. reprint ed. pap. 33.50 (*0-608-18094-7*, 203216000078) Bks Demand.

Moran, Theodore H., et al. Investing in Development: New Roles for Private Capital. 224p. (Orig.). 1986. text 39.95 (*0-88738-074-3*); pap. text 21.95 (*0-88738-644-X*) Transaction Pubs.

Moran, Thomas. The Man in the Box. 272p. 1998. pap. 12.00 (*1-57322-649-1*, Riverhd Trade) Berkley Pub.

— The Man in the Box. LC 96-41042. 272p. 1997. 21.95 (*1-57322-060-4*, Riverhead Books) Putnam Pub Group.

— The Man in the Box. large type ed. LC 97-1888. (Core Ser.). 344p. 1997. 26.95 (*0-7838-8123-1*, G K Hall Lrg Type) Mac Lib Ref.

***Moran, Thomas.** Water, Carry Me. LC 99-41383. 252p. 2000. 24.95 (*1-57322-138-4*, Riverhead Books) Putnam Pub Group.

— Water, Carry Me. large type ed. LC 00-25974. (Basic Ser.). 388p. 2000. 28.95 (*0-7862-2510-6*) Thorndike Pr.

Moran, Thomas. The World I Made for Her. LC 97-46699. 267p. 1998. 23.95 (*1-57322-084-1*, Riverhead Books) Putnam Pub Group.

— The World I Made for Her. 275p. 1999. reprint ed. pap. 12.00 (*1-57322-731-5*, Riverhd Trade) Berkley Pub.

Moran, Thomas, ed. Multimodal Interfaces: A Special Issue of Human Computer Interaction. 230p. 1997. pap. write for info. (*0-8058-9867-0*) L Erlbaum Assocs.

Moran, Thomas. Watercolor Sketches of Thomas Moran: Yellowstone & Grand Teton National Park. 8p. 1991. pap. 9.95 (*0-931895-21-9*) Grand Teton NHA.

Moran, Thomas, jt. ed. see Olson, Gary.

Moran, Thomas F. American Presidents: Their Individualities & Their Contributions to American Progress. (Essay Index Reprint Ser.). 1977. reprint ed. 21.95 (*0-518-10157-6*) Ayer.

Moran, Thomas P. & Carroll, John M., eds. Design Rationale: Concepts, Techniques, & Use. (Computers, Cognition, & Work Ser.). 496p. 1996. pap. 49.95 (*0-8058-1567-8*); text 99.95 (*0-8058-1566-X*) L Erlbaum Assocs.

Moran, Tom. Los Angeles International Airport: From Lindbergh's Landing Strip for World Air Center. LC 93-36904. 1993. 29.95 (*1-884166-01-6*) Am Historical Pr.

— The U. S. Army. (Armed Services Ser.). (Illus.). 88p. (YA). (gr. 5 up). 1990. lib. bdg. 23.93 (*0-8225-1434-6*, Lerner Publctns) Lerner Pub.

Moran, Tom, jt. ed. see Bossi, Richard H.

Moran, Tracey. Sylvester Sly & the Mystery of the Missing Sunglasses. (Illus.). 22p. (J). (gr. 1-6). 1998. pap. 5.00 (*0-9661592-1-7*) Benchmrk Bks.

Moran, Ursula K. Odyssey to Freedom: My Journey Eastern Europe to the Rocky Mountains of Montana. LC 98-90484. 1998. 19.95 (*0-533-12816-1*) Vantage.

Moran, Victoria. Compassion the Ultimate Ethic: An Exploration of Veganism. 4th ed. 128p. 1997. reprint ed. pap. 7.95 (*0-942401-16-6*) Am Vegan Soc.

— Creating a Charmed Life: Sensible, Spiritual Secrets Every Busy Woman Should Know. LC BJ1610.M65 1999. 240p. (Orig.). 1999. pap. 12.00 (*0-06-251580-2*, Pub. by Harper SF) HarpC.

Moran, Victoria. Creating a Charmed Life: Special Market. 240p. pap. 12.00 (*0-06-095508-2*) HarpC.

Moran, Victoria. Love Yourself Thin: The Revolutionary Spiritual Approach to Weight Loss. 352p. 1999. mass mkt. 6.99 (*0-451-19721-6*, Sig) NAL.

— Love Yourself Thin: The Revolutionary Spiritual Approach to Weight Loss. LC 97-15793. (Illus.). 256p. 1997. text 19.95 (*0-87596-461-3*) Rodale Pr Inc.

— Shelter for the Spirit: Create Your Own Haven in a Hectic World. 240p. 1998. pap. 12.00 (*0-06-092922-7*, Perennial) HarperTrade.

Moran, W. Dean. It's about Time: Teacher's Time Teaching Resource Book & Student Work Sheets. 1988. 127.00 (*0-317-93590-9*) Time Teaching.

Moran, W. E. Settlements on the Eastern End of Long Island, Vol. 5, No. 2. 1993. reprint ed. lib. bdg. 89.00 (*0-7812-5325-X*) Rprt Serv.

Moran, W. R., ed. see Maude.

Moran, Wesley, ed. see Forward Arts Foundation Staff.

Moran, William, jt. ed. see Pollington, Andrew.

Moran, William C. Workers' Compensation Law Review, 1974-98, 20 vols., Vol. 18. LC 73-93978. 1998. 995.00 (*0-930342-54-2*, 108550) W S Hein.

Moran, William J., jt. auth. see Panje, William R.

Moran, William L. The Amarna Letters. 464p. 1992. text 68.00 (*0-8018-4251-4*) Johns Hopkins.

Moran, William R., compiled by. Nellie Melba: A Contemporary Review, 5. LC 83-26444. (Contributions to the Study of Music & Dance Ser.: No. 5). (Illus.). 491p. 1985. 69.50 (*0-313-23893-6*, MOM/, Greenwood Pr) Greenwood.

Moran, William R., ed. Herman Klein & the Gramophone. LC 89-36903. (Illus.). 620p. 1990. 54.95 (*0-931340-18-7*, Amadeus Pr) Timber.

Moran, William R., jt. compiled by see Fagan, Ted.

Moran-Zenteno, Dante. The Geology of the Mexican Republic. Wilson, James L. & Sanchez-Barreda, Luis, trs. from SPA. (Studies in Geology: No. 39). (Illus.). vii, 160p. 1994. 44.00 (*0-89181-047-1*, 530) AAPG.

Morana, Veronique, jt. auth. see Morana, Virginie.

Morana, Virginie & Morana, Veronique. The Parisian Woman's Guide to Style. 128p. 1999. pap. 19.95 (*0-7893-0372-8*, Pub. by Universe) St Martin.

Morand, Anne. Thomas Moran: The Field Sketches, 1856-1923, Vol. 4. LC 94-49719. (Illus.). 325p. 1996. 75.00 (*0-8061-2704-X*) U of Okla Pr.

Morand, Anne R. Splendors of the American West: Thomas Moran's Art of the Grand Canyon & Yellowstone: Painting. LC 90-1049. 1991. pap. text 19.95 (*0-931394-29-5*) U of Wash Pr.

Morand, Henri J. & Ohayon, Roger. Fluid-Structure Interaction: Applied Numerical Methods. 220p. 1995. 125.00 (*0-471-94459-9*) Wiley.

Morand, James M., jt. ed. see Cawley, William A.

Morand, Kate. Linguistically & Culturally Diverse Students Populations: African American & Hmong. LC 98-163767. 109p. (Orig.). 1997. pap. text 21.00 (*1-57337-049-5*) WI Dept Pub Instruct.

Morand, Kathleen. Claus Sluter: Artist at the Court of Burgundy. (Illus.). 400p. 1991. text. write for info. (*0-905203-15-1*) Gordon & Breach.

Morand, Kathleen & Finn, David. Claus Sluter: Artist at the Court of Burgundy. (Illus.). 400p. 1991. 75.00 (*0-292-71117-4*) U of Tex Pr.

Morand, Lynn L. Craft Industries at Fort Michilimackinac, 1715-1781. (Archaeological Completion Reports: Vol. 15). (Illus.). 94p. (Orig.). 1994. pap. 10.00 (*0-911872-65-5*) Mackinac St Hist Pks.

Morand, Martin J., jt. ed. see McCoy, Ramelle.

Morand, Paul. Closed All Night. LC 78-130067. (Short Story Index Reprint Ser.). 1977. 16.95 (*0-8369-3648-5*) Ayer.

— Fancy Goods - Open All Night. Pound, Ezra, tr. from FRE. LC 83-23705. 160p. 1984. 16.00 (*0-8112-0888-5*, Pub. by New Directions); pap. 7.50 (*0-8112-0889-3*, NDP567, Pub. by New Directions) Norton.

— Le Flagellant de Seville. (FRE.). 1982. pap. 13.95 (*0-7859-4167-3*) Fr & Eur.

Morand, Paul. Green Shoots. LC 70-150553. (Short Story Index Reprint Ser.). 1977. reprint ed. 16.95 (*0-8369-3850-X*) Ayer.

Morand, Paul. Les Idees Politiques de Louis-Ferdinand Celene. 39.95 (*0-685-37274-X*) Fr & Eur.

— Nouvelles Completes, Vol. 1. Collomb, Michel, ed. (FRE.). 1992. lib. bdg. 160.00 (*0-7859-3900-8*) Fr & Eur.

— Tendres Stocks. (FRE.). 1981. pap. 8.95 (*0-7859-4159-2*) Fr & Eur.

Morand, Sheila. Santa Fe Then & Now: Historic Sites in the Famous New Mexico City. LC 84-2503. (Illus.). 96p. (Orig.). 1984. pap. 16.95 (*0-86534-046-3*) Sunstone Pr.

***Moranda, Ted.** Me 'n Paul & Old Hueneme. (Illus.). vi, 221p. 1999. pap. write for info. (*0-9671590-0-8*) T Moranda.

Morandeira, J. R., et al, eds. European Society for Surgical Research (ESSR) Abstracts, 27th Congress, May 1992, Zaragoza, Spain: Journal: European Surgical Research, Vol. 24, Suppl. 2, 1992. (Illus.). xii, 124p. 1992. pap. 41.75 (*3-8055-5615-2*) S Karger.

Morandi, G. The Role of Topology in Classical & Quantum Physics. Beiglbock, W. et al, eds. (Lecture Notes in Physics, New Series, Monographs: Vol. M7). xiv, 239p. (C). 1992. 61.95 (*0-387-55088-7*) Spr-Verlag.

***Morandi, G., et al, eds.** Field Theories for Low-Dimensional Condensed Matter Systems: Spin Systems & Strongly Correlated Electrons. (Series in Solid-State Sciences: Vol. 131). (Illus.). xii, 274p. 2000. 69.95 (*3-540-67177-3*) Spr-Verlag.

Morandi, Giuseppe. Statistical Mechanics: An Intermediate Course. LC 95-24957. 650p. 1995. text 78.00 (*981-02-2299-8*) World Scientific Pub.

Morandi, Larry. Assessing the State Legislative Response to Global Warming. (State Legislative Reports: Vol. 17, No. 6). 4p. 1992. pap. 15.00 (1-55516-278-9, 7302-1706) Natl Conf State Legis.
— Financing Clean Water: Drinking Water. 13p. 1991. pap. text 5.00 (1-55516-502-8, 4336) Natl Conf State Legis.
— Financing Clean Water: Wetlands. 14p. 1991. pap. text 5.00 (1-55516-503-6, 4335) Natl Conf State Legis.
— Groundwater Protection Legislation: Survey of State Action 1988-1992. LC 97-170646. 65p. 1994. 15.00 (1-55516-504-4, 4340) Natl Conf State Legis.
— Legislative Guidance for Comprehensive State Groundwater Protection Programs. (State Legislative Reports: Vol. 19, No. 3). 10p. 1994. 15.00 (1-55516-405-6, 7302-1903) Natl Conf State Legis.
— Moving Western Water: At Whose Cost? 37p. 1991. pap. 10.00 (1-55516-500-1, 4333) Natl Conf State Legis.
— Rethinking Western Water Policy: Assessing the Limits of Legislation. LC 97-170647. 64p. 1994. pap. text 10.00 (1-55516-404-8, 4339) Natl Conf State Legis.
— Superfund & Economic Development. (State Legislative Reports: Vol. 19, No. 9). 7p. 1994. 15.00 (1-55516-227-4, 7302-1909) Natl Conf State Legis.
— Wastewater Permitting & Finance: New Issues in Water Quality Protection. (State Legislative Reports: Vol. 17, No. 8). 8p. 1992. pap. text 15.00 (1-55516-280-0, 7302-1708) Natl Conf State Legis.

Morandi, Larry & Azodmanesh, Sam. Financing Water Quality Infrastructure: An Update on State Revolving Funds. (State Legislative Reports: Vol. 17, No. 20). 8p. 1992. 15.00 (1-55516-292-4, 7302-1720) Natl Conf State Legis.

Morandi, Larry & Worthley, Justin. Rural Growth in Western States: Economic & Environmental Issues. 40p. 1995. 10.00 (1-55516-402-1, 4341) Natl Conf State Legis.

Morandi, Larry, jt. auth. see Doyle, Paul.

Morandi, Larry, jt. auth. see Runyon, Cheryl C.

Morandi, Larry B. & National Conference of State Legislatures Staff. Water Table: Negotiating the Bay-delta Accord. LC 98-233166. 16 p. 1998. write for info. (1-55516-918-X) Natl Conf State Legis.

Morandi, Patrick. Field & Galois Theory. (Graduate Texts in Mathematics Ser.: Vol. 167). 281p. 1996. 42.50 (0-387-94753-1) Spr-Verlag.

Morandini, Giuliana. The Cafe of Mirrors. Quartermaine, Luisa, tr. & intro. by. 160p. 1997. pap. 16.95 (0-85989-469-X, Pub. by Univ Exeter Pr) Northwestern U Pr.

Morando, Bruno. Mouvement d'un Satellite Artificiel de la Terre. 256p. 1974. pap. text 77.00 (0-677-50755-0) Gordon & Breach.

Morange, Michel. A History of Molecular Biology. Cobb, Matthew, tr. from FRE. LC 97-47158. 384p. 1999. 39.95 (0-674-39855-6) HUP.

***Morange, Michel.** History of Molecular Biology. 2000. 18.95 (0-674-00169-9) HUP.

Morani, ed. Nemesii Emeseni. (GRE.). 1987. 47.50 (3-322-00358-2, T1548, Pub. by B G Teubner) U of Mich Pr.

Morano, Daniel. The American Dream: Whose Dream Is It? 80p. 1999. pap. write for info. (0-7392-0073-9, PO2926) Morris Pubng.

Morano, Donald V., jt. ed. see Casey, Edward S.

Morano, John. A Wing & a Prayer. 150p. 1999. pap. 11.00 (1-883573-09-2) Pride & Imprints.

Morano, Roy W. The Protestant Challenge to Corporate America: Issues of Social Responsibility. LC 84-8514. (Research for Business Decisions Ser.: No. 69). 256p. reprint ed. pap. 79.40 (0-8357-1592-2, 207040800088) Bks Demand.

Morant, Geoffrey M. The Races of Central Europe: A Footnote to History. LC 77-87532. reprint ed. 32.50 (0-404-16598-2) AMS Pr.

Morant, Mack B., jt. auth. see White, Mosezelle.

***Morante, Elsa.** History. 2nd ed. Weaver, William, tr. from ITA. (Steerforth Italia Ser.). (Illus.). 608p. 2000. pap. 18.00 (1-58642-004-6, Pub. by Steerforth Pr) Publishers Group.

Morante, Elsa. L' Lle d'Arturo. (FRE.). 606p. 1979. pap. 15.95 (0-7859-4110-X, 2070370763) Fr & Eur.
— La Storia, Tome I. 1987. pap. 15.95 (0-7859-4132-0) Fr & Eur.
— La Storie, Tome II. 1987. pap. 13.95 (0-7859-4133-9) Fr & Eur.

Morante, Paolo, tr. see Igliori, Paola, ed.

Morantte, P. C. Remembering Carlos Bulosan. 164p. (Orig.). (C). 1984. pap. 16.50 (971-10-0184-5, Pub. by New Day Pub) Cellar.

Morantz, Regina M., et al, eds. In Her Own Words: Oral Histories of Women Physicians, 8. LC 81-13349. (Contributions in Medical History Ser.: No. 8.). (Illus.). 284p. 1982. 62.95 (0-313-22686-5, MHO/, Greenwood Pr) Greenwood.

Morantz, Robert A. & Walsh, John W., eds. Brain Tumors: A Comprehensive Text. (Neurological Disease & Therapy Ser.: Vol. 20). (Illus.). 864p. 1993. text 255.00 (0-8247-8826-5) Dekker.

***Morantz-Sanchez, Regina.** Conduct Unbecoming a Woman. (Illus.). 304p. 2000. pap. 14.95 (0-19-513928-3) OUP.

Morantz-Sanchez, Regina. Conduct Unbecoming a Woman: Medicine on Trial in Turn-of-the-Century Brooklyn. LC 98-29764. (Illus.). 304p. 1999. 30.00 (0-19-512624-6) OUP.

***Morantz-Sanchez, Regina.** Sympathy & Science: Women Physicians in American Medicine. LC 00-27309. 464p. 2000. pap. 14.95 (0-8078-4890-5) U of NC Pr.

Morantz, Toby, jt. auth. see Francis, Daniel.

Moranville, Winifred. Record Player: And Other Stories. LC 98-89719. 2000. pap. 14.95 (0-89823-198-1) New Rivers Pr.

***Moranwali.** Quatrains. 2000. 12.50 (81-202-0542-1, Pub. by Ajanta Pubns) S Asia.

Morari, Manfred & Shogestad, Sigurd. Fundamentals of Distillation Column Dynamics & Control. (C). 2001. 74.67 (0-13-345687-0, Macmillan Coll) P-H.

Morari, Manfred & Zafiriou, Evanghelos. Robust Process Control. 512p. 1988. text 57.00 (0-13-782153-0) P-H.

Morari, Manfred, jt. auth. see Prett, David M.

Moras, Chris. Creativity & Its Contexts. LC 96-100448. 84p. 1995. pap. 12.95 (1-874675-67-8) Dufour.

Moras, Dino, et al, eds. Crystallography in Molecular Biology. LC 87-2509. (NATO ASI Series A, Life Sciences: Vol. 126). 454p. 1987. 125.00 (0-306-42497-5, Plenum Trade) Perseus Pubng.

Moras, E. R. Autology: Study Thyself, Autopathy & Cure Thyself (1893) 278p. 1998. reprint ed. pap. 24.95 (0-7661-0637-3) Kessinger Pub.

Morash. Bridge to Abstract Math. 2nd ed. 1991. teacher ed. 19.06 (0-07-043045-4) McGraw.

Morash, Christopher. The Hungry Voice: The Poetry of the Irish Famine. (Illus.). 300p. (C). 1989. pap. 12.95 (0-7165-2453-8, Pub. by Irish Acad Pr) Intl Spec Bk.
— Writing the Irish Famine. 222p. 1995. text 49.95 (0-19-818279-1) OUP.

Morash, Christopher, jt. ed. see Hayes, Richard.

Morash, Marian. The Victory Garden Cookbook. LC 81-48132. (Illus.). 352p. 1982. pap. 39.95 (0-394-70780-X) Knopf.

Morash, Merry, jt. auth. see Trojanowicz, Robert C.

Morash, Ronald P. Bridge to Abstract Mathematics: Mathematical Proof & Structures. 2nd ed. 480p. (C). 1991. 70.94 (0-07-043043-8) McGraw.

Morasky, Robert L. Behavioral Systems. LC 82-12334. 181p. 1982. 45.00 (0-275-90863-1, C0863, Praeger Pubs) Greenwood.

Morassi, Antonio, jt. tr. see Ratti, Carlo G.

Morasso, P. & Sanguineti, Vittorio. Self-Organization, Computational Maps, & Motor Control, Vol. 119. LC 97-36. (Advances in Psychology Ser.). 654p. 1997. 168.75 (0-444-82323-9) Elsevier.

Morasso, P. G., jt. auth. see Masulli, F.

Morasso, P. G., jt. ed. see Marinaro, M.

Morat, Franz A., jt. ed. see Guse, Ernst-Gerhard.

Morath, Inge. Russian Journal. (Illus.). 128p. 1991. 60.00 (0-89381-473-3) Aperture.

***Morath, Inge.** Saul Steinberg Masquerade. (Illus.). 80p. 2000. 19.95 (0-670-89425-7, Viking) Viking Penguin.

Morath, Julianne M. The Quality Advantage: A Strategic Guide for Health Care Leaders. LC 98-36020. 248p. 1998. 36.00 (1-55648-256-6) Aha Pub.

Morath, Max. Best of Ragtime Piano. pap. text 8.95 (0-89524-749-6, Pub. by Cherry Lane) H Leonard.
— Max Morath - Cripple Creek. pap. text 8.95 (0-89524-748-8) Cherry Lane.

Morath, Max, et al. Max Morath: The Road to Ragtime. LC 99-19509. 1999. write for info. (1-57864-068-7) Donning Co.

Moratin. La Comedia Nueva O El Cafe - El Si De Las Ninas. (SPA.). 143p. 1979. 9.95 (0-8288-7061-6, S9170) Fr & Eur.
— Comedia Nueva O El Cafe - La Derrota de Los Pedantes. (SPA.). 126p. 1973. 7.95 (0-8288-7107-8) Fr & Eur.
— El Si de las Ninas. (SPA.). 130p. 1980. 4.95 (0-8288-7104-3) Fr & Eur.
— El Si de las Ninas. unabridged ed. (SPA.). pap. 5.95 (84-410-0055-7, Pub. by Bookking Intl) Distribks Inc.

***Moratin, L F De.** El Si de las Ninas. (SPA.). 1999. 13.00 (84-481-0950-3, McGrw-H College) McGrw-H Hghr Educ.

Moratin, Leandro F. El Si de las Ninas. (SPA.). pap. 11.25 (84-376-0038-3, Pub. by Ediciones Catedra) Continental Bk.

Moratin, Leandro Fernandez De, see Fernandez de Moratin, Leandro.

Moratto, Michael. Archaeological Investigations of Site 4-Cal-S-414, a Rockshelter in Calaveras County, California. fac. ed. (San Francisco State University, Archaeological Research Lab Ser.). (Illus.). 30p. (C). 1976. reprint ed. pap. text 3.75 (1-55567-677-4) Coyote Press.

Moratto, Michael, compiled by. A Bibliography: Conservation Archaeology. 2nd fac. ed. (San Francisco State University, Archaeological Research Lab Ser.: Papers No. 1). 52p. (C). 1977. reprint ed. pap. text 6.56 (1-55567-685-5) Coyote Press.

Moratto, Michael J. An Archeological Overview of Redwood National Park, No. 8. Bancroft, John, ed. (National Park Service, Western Archaeological & Conservation Center Publications in Anthropology). (Illus.). 119p. 1973. reprint ed. pap. text 13.13 (1-55567-423-2) Coyote Press.
— A Study of Prehistory in the Tuolumne River Valley, California. fac. ed. (San Francisco State College - Treganza Anthropology Museum Papers: No. 9). (Illus.). 186p. 1971. reprint ed. pap. text 20.00 (1-55567-580-8) Coyote Press.

Moratto, Michael J., jt. auth. see King, Thomas.

Moraux, Paul. Aristotelismus bei den Griechen von Andronikos bis Alexander von Aphrodisias, Vol. 1: Die Renaissance des Aristotelismus im 1.Jh.v.Chr. (Peripatoi Ser.: Vol. 5). 520p. (C). 1973. 161.55 (3-11-004361-0) De Gruyter.
— Le Commentaire D'Alexandre D'Aphrodise aux "Seconds Analytiques" D'Aristote. (Peripatoi Ser.). (C). 1979. text 78.50 (3-11-007805-8) De Gruyter.

Moraux, Paul, et al, eds. Aristoteles Graecus. Die Griechischen Manuskripte des Aristoteles untersucht und beschrieben, Vol. 1, Vol. 1. (C). 1976. 315.40 (3-11-006732-5) De Gruyter.
— Zweifelhaftes im Corpus Aristotelicum - Studien zu Einigen Dubia. (GER.). 401p. 1983. 176.95 (3-11-008980-7) De Gruyter.

Morava, Lillian B. Camper's Guide to Oregon Parks, Lakes, Forests, & Beaches. (Camper's Guide Ser.). (Illus.). 192p. 1995. pap. 18.95 (0-87201-212-3, 1212) Gulf Pub.
— Camper's Guide to Washington State Parks, Lakes, Forests, & Beaches. (Camper's Guide Ser.). (Illus.). 176p. 1994. pap. 16.95 (0-87201-210-7, 1210) Gulf Pub.

Morava, Lillian B. & Little, Mickey. Camper's Guide to U. S. National Parks Vol. 1: West of the Rockies. LC 92-43236. (Camper's Guide Ser.). 228p. 1993. pap. 18.95 (0-88415-061-5, 5061) Gulf Pub.

Morava, Lillian B., jt. auth. see Little, Mickey.

Moravanszky, Akos. Competing Visions: Aesthetic Invention & Social Imagination in Central European Architecture, 1867-1918. LC 97-19684. (Illus.). 524p. 1998. 55.00 (0-262-13334-2) MIT Pr.

Moravcik, Ivo, ed. & tr. see Englis, Karel.

Moravcsik, Andrew. The Choice for Europe: Social Purpose & State Power from Messina to Maastricht. LC 98-34333. (Illus.). 420p. 1998. pap. 19.95 (0-8014-8509-6); text 59.95 (0-8014-3509-9) Cornell U Pr.

Moravcsik, Andrew, ed. Centralization or Fragmentation: Europe Before the Challenges & Deepening, Diversity, & Democracy. LC 98-9064. 150p. 1998. pap. 18.95 (0-87609-224-5) Coun Foreign.

Moravcsik, G. Studia Byzantina: Studies in English, French, German, Italian, Russian & Neo-Greek. 438p. (C). 1967. 65.00 (963-05-2222-5, Pub. by Akade Kiado) St Mut.

Moravcsik, Gyula, ed. Constantine Porphyrogenitus, De Administrando Imperio. Jenkins, R. J., tr. LC 85-6950. (Dumbarton Oaks Texts: Vol. 1). (ENG & GRE.). 356p. 1985. reprint ed. 15.00 (0-88402-021-5) Dumbarton Oaks.

Moravcsik, Julius. Meaning, Creativity, & the Partial Inscrutability of the Human Mind. LC 98-13456. (CSLI Lecture Notes Ser.: No. 79). 350p. (C). 1998. pap. 21.95 (1-57586-126-7); text 59.95 (1-57586-127-5) CSLI.

Moravcsik, Julius M. Understanding Language: A Study of Theories of Language in Linguistics & in Philosophy. (Janua Linguarum, Ser. Minor: No. 169). 95p. 1977. pap. text 29.25 (90-279-3111-9) Mouton.

Moravcsik, Julius M., ed. Patterns in Plato's Thought. LC 73-83566. (Synthese Historical Library: No. 6). 220p. 1973. text 126.50 (90-277-0286-1, D Reidel) Kluwer Academic.

Moravec, Frantisek. Parasitic Nematodes of Freshwater Fishes of Europe. LC 93-215. 477p. (C). 1995. text 239.50 (0-7923-2172-3) Kluwer Academic.

Moravec, Hans. Mind Children: The Future of Robot & Human Intelligence. (Illus.). 176p. 1988. pap. text 14.95 (0-674-57618-7) HUP.

Moravec, Hans. Robot: Mere Machine to Transcendent Mind. LC 97-47328. (Illus.). 240p. 1998. 25.00 (0-19-511630-5) OUP.

***Moravec, Hans.** Robot: Mere Machine to Transcendent Mind. (Illus.). 240p. 2000. pap. 15.95 (0-19-513630-6) OUP.

Moravec, Hans P. Robot Rover Visual Navigation. LC 81-7512. (Computer Science: Artificial Intelligence Ser.: No. 3). (Illus.). 169p. 1981. reprint ed. pap. 52.40 (0-608-18764-X, 207002300063) Bks Demand.

Moravec, Ivo. Tightrope Passage: The Memoir of an Emigrant. LC 97-158118. 256p. 1997. 21.95 (0-7710-6500-0) McCland & Stewart.

***Moravec, Kathryn.** Life's Little Lessons: A Guide Book to Get You Through. 200p. 2000. pap. 15.95 (1-887472-73-8) Sunstar Pubng.

Moravec, Marilyn. Facing down Our Fears: Finding Courage When Anxiety Grips the Heart Small Group Leader's Guide. (1995 50-Day Spiritual Adventure Ser.). (Illus.). 56p. (Orig.). 1994. pap. text, student ed. 6.99 (1-879050-51-X) Chapel of Air.
— What to Do When You Don't Know What to Do: Small Group Leader's Guide. Hayes, Brian, ed. (Nineteen Ninety-Six 50-Day Spiritual Adventure Ser.). (Illus.). 64p. (Orig.). 1995. pap., wbk. ed. 7.00 (1-879050-75-7) Chapel of Air.

Moravec, Paul, ed. New Tonality. (Contemporary Music Review Ser.). 126p. 1992. pap. text 15.00 (3-7186-5187-4, Harwood Acad Pubs) Gordon & Breach.

Moravec, Randy. Claude. (Illus.). 1994. pap. 9.95 (0-425-14139-X) Berkley Pub.

Moravek, T. M., jt. auth. see Jenson, Jack E.

Moravia. Sette Racconti. text 8.95 (0-88436-060-1) EMC-Paradigm.

Moravia, Alberto, pseud. L' Amour Conjugal. (FRE.). 1972. pap. 10.95 (0-7859-3988-1) Fr & Eur.
— Boredom. Davidson, Angus, tr. from ITA. LC 99-31900. 292p. 1999. pap. 12.95 (0-940322-28-5, Pub. by NY Rev Bks) Midpt Trade.
— The Conformist. (Film Ink Ser.). 383p. 1999. pap. 12.00 (1-85375-311-0, Pub. by Prion) Trafalgar.
— The Conformist. Calliope, Tami, tr. from ITA. LC 99-47391. (Steerforth Italia). 375p. 1999. pap. 15.00 (1-883642-65-5) Steerforth Pr.
— Contempt. (Film Ink Ser.). 255p. 1999. pap. text 12.00 (1-85375-312-2, Pub. by Prion) Trafalgar.
— Contempt. Davidson, Angus, tr. from ITA. LC 99-31899. 272p. 1999. reprint ed. pap. 12.95 (0-940322-27-7, Pub. by NY Rev Bks) Midpt Trade.
— Le Desobeissance. (FRE.). 1973. pap. 10.95 (0-7859-4022-7) Fr & Eur.
— Gli Indifferenti. 1999. 14.95 (88-452-0647-5) Fabbri.
— Racconti di Alberto Moravia. Traversa, Vincenzo, ed. LC 68-11595. (ITA., Illus.). (Orig.). (C). 1979. reprint ed. pap. text 12.95 (0-89197-368-0) Irvington.

***Moravia, Alberto, pseud.** The Time of Indifference: A Novel. Calliope, Tami, tr. from ITA. (Steerforth Italia Ser.). 400p. 2000. pap. 16.00 (1-58642-005-4, Pub. by Steerforth Pr) Publishers Group.
— The Woman of Rome: A Novel. LC 99-15664. (Steerforth Italia Ser.). 408p. 1999. reprint ed. pap. 16.00 (1-883642-80-9) Steerforth Pr.

***Moravia, Alberto, pseud & Elkann, Alain.** Life of Moravia. Weaver, William, tr. from ITA. (Steerforth Italia Ser.). Orig. Title: Vita di Moravia. (Illus.). 350p. 2000. 27.00 (1-883642-50-7, Pub. by Steerforth Pr) Publishers Group.

Moravia, Sergio. The Enigma of the Mind: The Mind-Body Problem in Contemporary Thought. 335p. (C). 1995. pap. text 21.95 (0-521-40557-2) Cambridge U Pr.
— The Enigma of the Mind: The Mind-Body Problem in Contemporary Thought. 335p. (C). 1995. text 59.95 (0-521-40550-5) Cambridge U Pr.

Moravscik, Julius, ed. see Henry, Philip.

Moravscik, M., ed. On the Road to Worldwide Science. 576p. (C). 1989. text 114.00 (9971-5-0617-3); pap. text 44.00 (9971-5-0620-3) World Scientific Pub.

Morawa, Jozef. Die Communio-Kirche Als Sakrament des Heils in und Fur die Welt: Zum Erneuerten Verstandnis der Sendung der Kirche in der Gegenwart Im Werk Walter Kaspers. (Europaische Hochschulschriften Ser.: Reihe 23, Bd. 588). (GER.). 424p. 1996. 63.95 (3-631-31050-1) P Lang Pubng.

Morawetz, Anita & Walker, Gillian. Brief Therapy with Single-Parent Families. LC 83-21367. 294p. 1985. text 41.95 (0-87630-350-5) Brunner-Mazel.

Morawetz, Cathleen S. Lectures on Nonlinear Waves & Shocks. (Tata Institute Lectures on Mathematics). 137p. 1982. 31.95 (0-387-10830-0) Spr-Verlag.
— Notes on Time Decay & Scattering for Some Hyperbolic Problems. (CBMS-NSF Regional Conference Ser.: No. 19). v, 81p. 1975. pap. text 23.50 (0-89871-016-2) Soc Indus-Appl Math.

Morawetz, David. Twenty-Five Years of Economic Development, 1950 to 1975. LC 77-17243. 139p. reprint ed. pap. 43.10 (0-7837-4257-6, 204394700012) Bks Demand.

Morawetz, Herbert. Macromolecules in Solution. 2nd ed. LC 83-11991. (High Polymer Ser.: Vol. 21). 572p. (C). 1983. reprint ed. text 61.50 (0-89874-659-0) Krieger.
— Polymers: The Origins & Growth of a Science. unabridged ed. LC 95-6700. (Illus.). xiv, 306p. 1995. reprint ed. pap. text 11.95 (0-486-68732-5) Dover.

***Morawetz, Thomas.** Law's Premises & Law's Promise: Jurisprudence after Wittgenstein. LC 99-39396. (Collected Essays in Law Ser.). 300p. 1999. text 96.95 (0-7546-2013-1, Pub. by Ashgate Pub) Ashgate Pub Co.

Morawetz, Thomas, ed. Criminal Law. (International Library of Essays in Law & Legal Theory). 520p. (C). 1991. lib. bdg. 150.00 (0-8147-5464-3) NYU Pr.
— Justice. (International Library of Essays in Law & Legal Theory). 488p. (C). 1991. lib. bdg. 150.00 (0-8147-5465-1) NYU Pr.

***Morawetz, Tom, ed.** Criminal Law. 2nd ed. LC 99-39721. (International Library of Essays in Law & Legal Theory). 540p. 2000. text 175.95 (1-84014-775-X, Pub. by Ashgate Pub) Ashgate Pub Co.
— Law & Language. LC 99-38742. (International Library of Essays in Law & Legal Theory). 380p. 2000. text 175.95 (1-84014-770-9, Pub. by Ashgate Pub) Ashgate Pub Co.

Morawiec, H., jt. ed. see Stroz, D.

Morawiex, H. & Stroz, D. Applied Crystallography. 500p. 1995. text 109.00 (981-02-2153-3) World Scientific Pub.

Morawinska, Agnieszka. Voices of Freedom: Polish Women Artists & the Avant-Garde. LC 91-34492. (Illus.). 56p. 1991. pap. 18.95 (0-940979-19-5) Natl Museum Women.

Morawitz, Christof. Die Lebenswelt Von Landwirten Vor Dem Hintergrund des Moglichen Einsatzes Von Rekombinanten Wachstumshormonen Rbst Und Rpst in der Eigenen Tierhaltung: Eine Empirische Untersuchung in Sudniedersachsen. (Illus.). 374p. 1998. 56.95 (3-631-33444-3) P Lang Pubng.

Morawska, Ewa. Insecure Prosperity: Small-Town Jews in Industrial America, 1890-1940. LC 95-30471. 440p. 1996. text 37.50 (0-691-03735-3, Pub. by Princeton U Pr) Cal Prin Full Svc.

***Morawska, Ewa.** Insecure Prosperity: Small-Town Jews in Industrial America, 1890-1940. 1999. 19.95 (0-691-00537-0, Pub. by Princeton U Pr) Cal Prin Full Svc.

Morawski, Jill G. Practicing Feminisms, Reconstructing Psychology: Notes on a Liminal Science. LC 94-10786. (Critical Perspectives on Women & Gender Ser.). 288p. (C). 1994. text 44.50 (0-472-09481-5, 09481); pap. text 18.95 (0-472-06481-9, 06481) U of Mich Pr.

Morawski, Stefan. Inquiries into the Fundamentals of Aesthetics. 1978. pap. text 16.50 (0-262-63066-4) MIT Pr.
— The Trouble with Postmodernism. LC 95-16085. (Illus.). 160p. (C). 1996. 65.00 (0-415-09386-4) Routledge.

Morawski, Stefan, ed. see Marx, Karl & Engels, Friedrich.

Moray, Helga. Across the Years. large type ed. 320p. 1988. 27.99 (0-7089-1917-0) Ulverscroft.
— Beacon of Gold. large type ed. 483p. 1989. 27.99 (0-7089-1979-0) Ulverscroft.
— Blood on the Wind. large type ed. 400p. 1985. 27.99 (0-7089-1270-2) Ulverscroft.
— Footsteps in the Night. large type ed. 512p. 1988. 27.99 (0-7089-1884-0) Ulverscroft.
— The Harvest Burns. large type ed. 448p. 1984. 27.99 (0-7089-1173-0) Ulverscroft.

An Asterisk (*) at the beginning of an entry indicates that the title is appearing for the first time.

— Quest in the Sun. large type ed. 1991. 27.99 (*0-7089-2396-8*) Ulverscroft.
— The Savage Earth. large type ed. 400p. 1984. 27.99 (*0-7089-1116-1*) Ulverscroft.
— Sunny Days. large type ed. LC 97-12334. 245p. 1997. 22.95 (*0-7862-1110-5*) Thorndike Pr.
— Tender Is the Search. large type ed. 288p. 1989. 27.99 (*0-7089-2030-6*) Ulverscroft.
— That Woman. large type ed. 384p. 1986. 27.99 (*0-7089-1449-7*) Ulverscroft.
— Tisa. large type ed. 496p. 1985. 27.99 (*0-7089-1314-8*) Ulverscroft.
— To Make a Light. large type ed. 393p. 1989. 27.99 (*0-7089-1947-2*) Ulverscroft.
— Trenfell Castle. large type ed. 416p. 1989. 27.99 (*0-7089-2016-0*) Ulverscroft.
— Untamed. large type ed. 512p. 1983. 11.50 (*0-7089-1046-7*) Ulverscroft.

Moray, Jeremy. Timmy & the Otters. (Timmy the Tug Ser.). (Illus.). 46p. (J). 1997. pap. text 12.95 (*1-55017-007-4*) Harbour Pub Co.

Moray, Jeremy. Timmy & the Whales. (Illus.). 46p. 1997. pap. text 12.95 (*1-55017-006-6*) Harbour Pub Co.

Moray, N., jt. ed. see Senders, J.

Moray, Neville, et al, eds. Robotics, Control & Society: Essays in Honor of T. B. Sheridan. 280p. 1991. text 90.00 (*0-85066-850-6*, Pub. by Tay Francis Ltd) Taylor & Francis.

Moraze, Charles. The Logic of History. Clough, Wilson, tr. (New Babylon Ser.: No. 11). 260p. 1976. text 64.65 (*90-279-7781-X*) Mouton.

***Morazzoni, Marta.** The Alphonse Courrier Affair. Rose, Emma, tr. (ITA.). 2000. 15.00 (*1-86046-574-9*, Pub. by Harvill Press) FS&G.

Morbeck, Mary E., et al. The Evolving Female: A Life-History Perspective. LC 96-20402. 344p. 1997. text 60.00 (*0-691-02748-X*, Pub. by Princeton U Pr); pap. text 27.95 (*0-691-02747-1*, Pub. by Princeton U Pr) Cal Prin Full Svc.

Morbidelli, Massimo, jt. auth. see Varma, Arvind.

Morcay, Raoul & Muller, A. Histoire de la Litterature Francais - Renaissance. (FRE.). 487p. 1960. 24.95 (*0-8288-7421-2*) Fr & Eur.

***Morch, Audun J.** Novelistic Approach to the Utopian Question: Platonov's Cevengur in the Light of Dostoevskij's Anti Utopian Legacy. (Acta Humaniora). 216p. 1998. pap. 28.00 (*82-00-12995-0*) Scandnvan Univ Pr.

Morch, Dea T. Evening Star. Tate, Joan, tr. LC 87-30083. (Modern Scandinavian Literature in Translation Ser.). (Illus.). 269p. reprint ed. pap. 83.40 (*0-7837-6173-2*, 204589500009) Bks Demand.
— Winter's Child. Tate, Joan, tr. from DAN. LC 85-24512. (Modern Scandinavian Literature in Translation Ser.).Tr. of Vinterborn. (Illus.). vi, 271p. 1986. reprint ed. pap. 9.95 (*0-8032-8133-1*, Bison Books) U of Nebr Pr.

Morch, Dea T., ed. see Nielson, Palle.

Morch, J., ed. Calcium Ion Antagonists in Cardiovascular Disease: Proceedings of an International Conference, 12-13 October 1979, Toronto, Canada. 200p. 1981. pap. 48.00 (*0-08-027376-9*, Pergamon Pr) Elsevier.

Morchin, William C., Jr. Golden Age of Homespun. (Radar Ser.). 472p. 1993. reprint ed. per. 88.00 (*0-7812-5239-3*) Rprt Serv.

Morchin, William C. Radar Engineer's Sourcebook. LC 92-18686. (Artech House Radar Library). 494p. 1993. reprint ed. pap. 153.20 (*0-608-02081-8*, 206273400003) Bks Demand.

Morcillo, Aurora G. True Catholic Womanhood: Gender Ideology in Franco's Spain. LC 99-22907. 220p. 1999. 36.00 (*0-87580-256-7*, 256-7) N Ill U Pr.

Morcillo, Maria J. Que tal? An Introductory Course, Listening Comprehension Manual. 3rd ed. 1991. pap. text. write for info. (*0-07-017745-7*) McGraw.

Morcira, Marcillo M. The Brazilian Quandary. A Twentieth Century Fund Paper. 87p. (Orig.). (C). 1986. pap. 7.00 (*0-87078-171-5*) Century Foundation.

***Morck, Irene.** Five Pennies: A Prairie Boy's Story. (Illus.). 176p. 1999. pap. 11.95 (*1-894004-32-9*) Fifth Hse Publ.

Morck, Irene. Tyler's New Boots. (Illus.). 40p. (J). 1998. pap. 6.95 (*0-8118-2143-9*) Chronicle Bks.
— Tyler's New Boots. LC 98-16816. (Illus.). 40p. (J). (gr. 2-5). 1998. 14.95 (*0-8118-2248-6*) Chronicle Bks.

***Morck, Randall.** Concentrated Corporate Ownership. LC 99-86549. (National Bureau of Economic Research Conference Report Ser.). 2000. pap. text 62.00 (*0-226-53678-5*) U Ch Pr.

***Morcol, Goktug & Dennard, Linda F., eds.** New Sciences for Public Administration & Policy: Connections & Reflections. LC 99-50556. x, 314p. 2000. pap. 24.95 (*1-57420-070-4*) Chatelaine.

Morcom & Parry. Capital Transfer Tax. 2nd ed. 336p. 1981. 65.00 (*0-85941-055-2*) St Mut.

Morcom, Christopher. Morcom: A Guide to the Trade Marks Act 1994. (Butterworths Annotated Legislation Service Ser.). 1994. pap. write for info. (*0-406-04581-X*, AMGT1994, MICHIE) LEXIS Pub.
— Morcom: The Modern Law of Trade Marks & Service Marks. 1997. ring bd. write for info. (*0-406-06552-7*, MMLTSUB, MICHIE) LEXIS Pub.

Morcom, John. The John Morcom Collection of Western Greek Bronze Coins. Price, Martin, ed. (Sylloge of Coins of the British Isles). (Illus.). 96p. 1995. text 60.00 (*0-19-726152-3*) OUP.

Morcos, Nabil, jt. ed. see Lambrecht, Richard M.

Mordan, C. B. American West Designs. (International Design Library). (Illus.). 48p. (Orig.). 1994. pap. 5.95 (*0-88045-127-0*) Stemmer Hse.

Mordan, C. B., jt. auth. see Ketchum, Liza.

Mordarski, Sheila W., jt. auth. see Bond, Anita W.

***Mordasini, Don.** Wild Child: How You Can Help Your Child with Attention Deficit Disorder (ADD) & Other Behavioral Disorders. 2000. 59.95 (*0-7890-1101-8*) Haworth Pr.
— Wild Child: How You Can Help Your Child with Attention Deficit Disorder & Other Behavioral Disorders. LC 00-40735. 2000. write for info. (*0-7890-1102-6*) Haworth Pr.

Mordden, Ethan. Beautiful Mornin' The Broadway Musical in the 1940s. LC 99-10088. 288p. 1999. 30.00 (*0-19-512851-6*) OUP.
— Broadway Babies: The People Who Made the American Musical. 256p. 1988. pap. 10.95 (*0-19-505425-3*) OUP.
— Buddies. (Stonewall Inn Editions Ser.). 256p. 1987. pap. 9.95 (*0-312-01005-2*) St Martin.
— Coming up Roses: The Broadway Musical in the 1950s. (Broadway Musicals Ser.). 272p. 1998. 30.00 (*0-19-511710-7*) OUP.

***Mordden, Ethan.** Coming up Roses: The Broadway Musical in the 1950s. 272p. 2000. pap. 15.95 (*0-19-514058-3*) OUP.

Mordden, Ethan. Everybody Loves You. (Stonewall Inn Editions Ser.). 1989. pap. 10.95 (*0-312-03334-6*) St Martin.
— A Guide to Orchestral Music: The Handbook for Non-Musicians. (Illus.). 587p. 1986. pap. 15.95 (*0-19-504041-4*) OUP.
— The Hollywood Studios, Set. unabridged ed. 1997. 62.95 incl. audio (*0-7861-1217-4*, 1996) Blckstn Audio.
— How Long Has This Been Going On. 1996. pap. 12.95 (*0-345-37862-8*, Ballantine) Ballantine Pub Grp.
— How Long Has This Been Going On. 604p. 1997. pap. 14.95 (*0-312-16867-5*) St Martin.
— I've a Feeling We're Not in Kansas Anymore. LC 95-45091. Vol. 1. 208p. 1996. pap. 9.95 (*0-312-14112-2*) St Martin.
— Make-Believe: The Broadway Musical in the 1920s. LC 96-40962. 272p. 1997. 30.00 (*0-19-510594-X*) OUP.
— One Last Waltz. (Stonewall Inn Editions Ser.). 1988. pap. 7.95 (*0-312-01801-0*) St Martin.
— Opera Anecdotes. 288p. 1988. pap. 12.95 (*0-19-505661-2*) OUP.
— Rodgers & Hammerstein. (Illus.). 224p. 1992. 45.00 (*0-8109-1567-7*) Abrams.
— Rodgers & Hammerstein. 224p. 1999. 24.95 (*0-8109-2911-2*, Pub. by Abrams) Time Warner.
— Some Men Are Lookers. 352p. 1998. pap. 13.95 (*0-312-19336-X*) St Martin.
— Some Men Are Lookers. LC 96-53928. 352p. 1997. text 23.95 (*0-312-15660-X*) St Martin.
— Venice Adriana. LC 97-39714. 304p. 1998. text 23.95 (*0-312-18202-3*) St Martin.
— Venice Adriana. 324p. 1999. pap. 13.95 (*0-312-20680-1*) St Martin.

Mordecai & Gordon Staff. Sunsong. Date not set. pap. text. write for info. (*0-582-76555-2*, Pub. by Addison-Wesley) Longman.

Mordecai, Carolyn. De Man: A Performance Poem. LC 95-193838. 80p. Date not set. pap. write for info. (*0-920813-23-2*) Sister Vis Pr.

Mordecai, Carolyn. Weddings, Dating & Love Customs of Cultures including Royalty. LC 96-68875. (Illus.). 280p. (YA). (gr. 10-12). 1999. 28.00 (*0-9613823-2-5*) Nittany Pubs.

Mordecai, Diane. How to Find Your True Love Now: No-Nonsense Ways for Busy & Selective Singles. 334p. (Orig.). 1997. pap. 19.95 (*0-9654685-4-2*) Diamondworks.

***Mordecai, Martin & Mordecai, Pamela.** Culture & Customs of Jamaica. LC 00-35340. (Culture & Customs of Latin America & the Caribbean Ser.). 2000. write for info. (*0-313-30534-X*) Greenwood.

Mordecai, Pamela & Wilson, Betty, eds. Her True-True Name: An Anthology of Women's Writing from the Caribbean. (Caribbean Writers Ser.). 202p. (Orig.). (C). 1990. pap. 9.95 (*0-435-98906-5*, 98906) Heinemann.

Mordecai, Pamela, jt. auth. see Mordecai, Martin.

Mordecai, Samuel. Richmond in Be-Gone Days: Being Reminiscences of an Old Citizen. LC 75-1861. (Leisure Class in America Ser.). 1975. reprint ed. 23.95 (*0-405-06927-8*) Ayer.

Mordecai, Siegal, ed. Cornell Book of Cats. LC 89-40195. 1989. 30.00 (*0-394-56787-0*) Random.

Mordecai, Trevor T. Cut the Mustard: Create Your Own Destiny. LC 88-30239. (Illus.). 134p. (Orig.). (C). 1988. 19.95 (*0-9621302-0-6*) Chemam Pub Co.

Mordechai, Tova. Goodnight My Friend Aleph. (Illus.). 32p. (J). (ps-1). 1989. 9.95 (*0-922613-12-5*); pap. 7.95 (*0-922613-13-3*) Hachai Pubng.

Mordell, Albert, ed. Notorious Literary Attacks. LC 69-18932. (Essay Index Reprint Ser.). 1977. 18.95 (*0-8369-0047-2*) Ayer.

Mordell, Albert, ed. see Hearn, Lafcadio.

Mordell, Albert, ed. see James, Henry.

Morden, A. R. Business Strategy & Planning: A Strategic Management Approach. LC 92-40088. 1993. write for info. (*0-07-707718-0*) McGraw.

Morden, Bettie J. Women's Army Corps, 1945-1978. 563p. 1990. per. 25.00 (*0-16-026914-8*) USGPO.

Morden, Tony. Principles of Management. LC 96-23917. 1996. pap. write for info. (*0-07-709123-X*) McGraw.

***Mordeson, J. N. & Nair, P. S.** Fuzzy Graphs & Fuzzy Hypergraphs. (Studies in Fuzziness & Soft Computing). (Illus.). xiv, 248p. 2000. 78.00 (*3-7908-1286-2*, Pub. by Spr-Verlag) Spr-Verlag.

***Mordeson, John N.** Fuzzy Commutative Algebra. LC 98-48515. (Pure Mathematics Ser.). 1999. 90.00 (*981-02-3628-X*) World Scientific Pub.

***Mordeson, John N. & Nair, Premchand S.** Fuzzy Mathematics: An Introduction for Engineers & Scientists. LC 98-29345. (Studies in Fuzziness & Soft Computing: Vol. 20). (Illus.). xiv, 258p. 1998. 78.00 (*3-7908-1121-1*) Spr-Verlag.

Mordfin, Leonard, ed. Mechanical Relaxation of Residual Stresses, STP 993. LC 88-15450. (Special Technical Publication (STP) Ser.). (Illus.). 128p. 1988. pap. text 38.00 (*0-8031-1166-5*, STP993) ASTM.

Mordfin, Leonard, jt. ed. see Berger, Harold.

Mordi, A. Richard. Attitudes Toward Wildlife in Botswana. LC 91-20257. (Environment: Problems & Solutions Ser.). 240p. 1991. text 20.00 (*0-8240-0471-X*) Garland.

***Mordike, B. L., ed.** Eclat: European Conference on Laser Treatment of Materials. 628p. 1999. 195.00 (*3-527-29931-9*) Wiley.

Mordike, B. L., ed. see Kainer, K. U.

Mordinoff, Nicolas & Lipkind, William. Finders Keepers. LC 51-12326. (Illus.). 32p. (J). (gr. k-4). 1989. pap. 7.00 (*0-15-630950-5*, Voyager Bks) Harcourt.

Mordinoff, Nicolas, jt. auth. see Lipkind, William.

Mordock, John. Measuring Outcomes in Children's Services. 1998. 75.00 (*1-884937-47-0*) Manisses Communs.

Mordock, John & Adams, Walter. Pattern Glass Mugs. (Illus.). 160p. 1995. 44.95 (*1-57080-011-1*); pap. 34.95 (*1-57080-010-3*) Antique Pubns.

***Mordock, John B.** Counseling the Defiant Child. 2000. 25.00 (*0-7657-0260-6*) Aronson.

Mordock, John B. Custody Evaluations: A Clinician's Guide to Interviewing & Report Writing. 130p. (Orig.). 1997. pap. 49.95 (*1-884937-43-8*) Manisses Communs.

***Mordock, John B.** Selecting Treatment Interventions: A Casebook for Clinical Practice in Child & Adolescent Managed Mental Health. 2nd ed. 172p. 1999. pap. 79.95 (*1-884937-59-4*) Manisses Communs.

Mordue, J. E. & Ainsworth, G. C., eds. Ustilaginales of the British Isles. (Mycological Papers: No. 154). 96p. (C). 1984. pap. text 27.00 (*0-00-000081-7*) C A B Intl.

Mordukhai-Boltovskoi, D., ed. The River Volga & Its Life. (Monographiae Biologicae: No. 33). 1979. text 211.50 (*90-6193-084-7*) Kluwer Academic.

Mordukhovich, Boris & Sussmann, Hector J., eds. Nonsmooth Analysis & Geometric Methods in Deterministic Optimal Control. LC 96-13083. (IMA Volumes in Mathematics & Its Applications Ser.: Vol. 78). 264p. 1996. 54.95 (*0-387-94764-7*) Spr-Verlag.

Mordune, Ruby Q. Sexology Encyclopedia Vol. 3: Menopause: Index & Reference Books of New Information. Bartone, John C., ed. (Illus.). 154p. 1996. pap. 39.95 (*0-7883-0855-6*) ABBE Pubs Assn.
— Sexology Encyclopedia Vol. 3: Menopause: Index & Reference Books of New Information, 25 vols., Set. Bartone, John C., ed. (Illus.). 154p. 1996. 49.95 (*0-7883-0854-8*) ABBE Pubs Assn.

More. Critical Thinking: Learning to Discern. (C). 2001. 17.25 (*0-7668-1328-2*) Thomson Learn.

More, Alan S., jt. ed. see Rice, Stan.

More, Carey, photos by. Views from a French Farmhouse. (Illus.). 144p. 1992. pap. 13.95 (*0-943955-55-6*, Trafalgar Sq Pub) Trafalgar.

More, Carey & More, Julian. A Taste of Provence. (Illus.). 160p. 1991. pap. 24.95 (*1-85145-528-0*, Pub. by Pavilion Bks Ltd) Trafalgar.

More, Caroline E. & Griffin, Irma M. History of the Town of Roxbury. (Illus.). 281p. 1997. reprint ed. lib. bdg. 35.00 (*0-8328-6215-0*) Higginson Bk Co.

More, Charles. Industrial Age. 449p. (C). 1989. pap. text 28.50 (*0-582-49427-3*, 78243) Longman.
— Industrial Age. 2nd ed. LC 96-46242. 400p. (C). 1997. 82.00 (*0-582-27766-3*) Addison-Wesley.
— The Industrial Age: Economy & Society in Britain, 1750-1995. 2nd ed. LC 96-46242. (Illus.). 456p. (C). 1997. pap. 31.20 (*0-582-27767-1*) Longman.
— The Training of Teachers, 1849-1947: A History of the Church Colleges in Cheltenham. 232p. 1992. 45.00 (*1-85285-077-9*) Hambledon Press.

***More, Charles.** Understanding the Industrial Revolution. LC 00-28065. (Illus.). 2000. pap. write for info. (*0-415-18405-3*) Routledge.

More, Daphne. Discovering Beekeeping. (Handbook Ser.: No. 236). (Illus.). 48p. 1996. pap. 6.25 (*0-7478-0318-8*, Pub. by Shire Pubns) Parkwest Pubns.

More, Daphne. Discovering Country Winemaking. (Handbook Ser.: No. 249). (Illus.). 33p. 1986. pap. 8.50 (*0-85263-480-3*, 3381209, Pub. by Shire Pubns) Parkwest Pubns.

More, David. 101 Ways to Recycle a Hockey Stick: The Definitive Guide. (Illus.). 128p. 1992. pap. 7.95 (*0-88995-089-X*, Pub. by Red Deer) Genl Dist Srvs.

More, David F. More: History of the More Family, & an Account of Their Reunion in 1890, with a Genealogical Record. (Illus.). 409p. 1992. reprint ed. pap. 63.00 (*0-8328-2429-1*); reprint ed. lib. bdg. 73.00 (*0-8328-2428-3*) Higginson Bk Co.

More, E. A. Managing Changes: Exploring State of the Art. LC 98-15098. (Monographs in Organizational Behavior & Industrial Relations: Vol. 22). 1998. 78.50 (*0-7623-0415-4*) Jai Pr.

More, Elizabeth A., jt. auth. see Irwin, Harry.

***More, Ellen S.** Restoring the Balance: Women Physicians & the Profession of Medicine, 1850-1995. LC 99-38185. (Illus.). 320p. 2000. 49.95 (*0-674-76661-X*) HUP.

More, Ellen S. & Milligan, Maureen A., eds. The Empathic Practitioner: Empathy, Gender, & Medicine. LC 94-10061. 265p. (C). 1994. text 45.00 (*0-8135-2118-1*); pap. text 20.00 (*0-8135-2119-X*) Rutgers U Pr.

More, Gillian, jt. ed. see Shaw, Jo.

More, Grace V., ed. More: Chronicles of the More Family. (Illus.). 424p. 1993. reprint ed. pap. 63.50 (*0-8328-3376-2*); reprint ed. lib. bdg. 73.50 (*0-8328-3375-4*) Higginson Bk Co.

More, Hannah. Coelebs in Search of a Wife: Comprehending Observations on Domestic Habits & Manners, Religion & Morals, 2 vols., 1 bk. LC 79-8178. reprint ed. 44.50 (*0-404-62052-3*) AMS Pr.
— Coelebs in Search of a Wife: 1808-9 Edition. Roberts, Marie M., ed. (For Her Own Good Ser.). 288p. 1996. reprint ed. pap. 29.95 (*1-85506-383-2*) Bks Intl VA.
— The Cottage Cook: Or, Mrs. Jones' Cheap Dishes. (Illus.). 16p. 1989. reprint ed. pap. 2.75 (*1-877984-08-6*) Hendricksn Group.
— The Spirit of Prayer: From the Works of Hannah More. 144p. 1986. pap. 6.95 (*0-310-43641-9*, 10272P) Zondervan.
— Strictures on Female Education, 1801. LC 94-35575. (Revolution & Romanticism, 1789-1834 Ser.). 1995. 95.00 (*1-85477-186-8*) Continuum.
— Strictures on the Modern System of Female Education, 1799, 2 vols. Stern, Jeffrey, ed. & intro. by. (Classics in Education Ser.). 648p. 1996. reprint ed. 170.00 (*1-85506-297-6*) Bks Intl VA.
— Tom White, the Post Boy. unabridged ed. (Children's Heritage Ser.). (Illus.). 47p. (J). (gr. 4-6). 1996. pap. 4.25 (*1-58339-121-5*, D21) Triangle Press.
— Two Wealthy Farmers. unabridged ed. (Children's Heritage Ser.). (Illus.). 188p. (J). (gr. 4-6). 1996. pap. 8.75 (*1-58339-128-2*, D28) Triangle Press.
— Village Politics, 1793: With the Shepherd of Salisbury Plain. LC 94-35577. (Revolution & Romanticism Ser.). 1995. 35.00 (*1-85477-187-6*) Continuum.

M

More, Hannah & Burney, Frances. Considerations on Religion & Public Education, with Remarks on the Speech of M. Dupont, Delivered in the National Convention of France: And Brief Reflections Relative to the Emigrant French Clergy. LC 92-23650. (Augustan Reprints Ser.: No. 262). 1990. reprint ed. 14.50 (*0-404-70262-7*, BX1492) AMS Pr.

More, Hannah, et al. The Harvest Home. unabridged ed. (Children's Heritage Ser.). (Illus.). 40p. (J). (gr. 4-6). 1996. pap. 4.20 (*1-58339-102-9*, D2) Triangle Press.

More, Harry W. Police Organization & Management, Instructor's Guide To. 8th ed. (Police Science Ser.). 93p. 1993. pap. text. write for info. (*1-56662-086-4*) Foundation Pr.
— Special Topics in Policing. 2nd ed. LC 98-11109. 331p. (C). 1998. pap. 33.95 (*0-87084-839-9*) Anderson Pub Co.

More, Harry W., Jr. & O'Neill, Michael E. Contemporary Criminal Justice Planning. (Illus.). 214p. (C). 1984. text 42.95 (*0-398-05009-0*) C C Thomas.

More, Harry W. & O'Neill, Michael E. Contemporary Criminal Justice Planning. (Illus.). 214p. 1984. pap. text 27.95 (*0-398-06644-2*) C C Thomas.

More, Harry W. & Unsinger, Peter C. The Police Assessment Center. (Illus.). 232p. 1987. 54.95 (*0-398-05331-6*); pap. 38.95 (*0-398-06299-4*) C C Thomas.

More, Harry W. & Unsinger, Peter C., eds. Managerial Control of the Police: Internal Affairs & Audits. 208p. 1991. pap. 29.95 (*0-398-06298-6*) C C Thomas.
— Managerial Control of the Police: Internal Affairs & Audits. 208p. (C). 1991. text 44.95 (*0-398-05751-6*) C C Thomas.

More, Harry W. & Wegener, W. Fred. Behavioral Police Management. (Illus.). 576p. (C). 1992. teacher ed. write for info. (*0-318-69531-6*) Macmillan.
— Behavioral Police Management. (Illus.). 576p. (C). 1992. text 44.20 (*0-02-383350-5*, Macmillan Coll) P-H.

***More, Harry W., et al.** Effective Police Supervision. 3rd ed. (Criminology Ser.). 1999. pap. 18.95 (*0-87084-423-7*) Anderson Pub Co.

More, Harry W., et al. Effective Police Supervision. 3rd ed. LC 98-43078. 462p. (C). 1999. pap. 40.95 (*0-87084-539-X*) Anderson Pub Co.

More, Harry W., jt. auth. see Kenney, John P.

More, Harry W., jt. auth. see Leonard, V. A.

More, Harry W., jt. ed. see Unsinger, Peter C.

More, Henry. The Complete Poems of Henry More, 2 vols., Set. LC 03-30555. (Chertsey Worthies' Library: Vol. 2). reprint ed. 42.50 (*0-404-50292-X*) AMS Pr.
— Democritus Platonissans: or An Essay upon the Infinity of Worlds Out of Platonick Principles. LC 92-24821. reprint ed. 14.50 (*0-404-70130-2*, PR3605) AMS Pr.
— Enthusiasmus Triumphatus: Or A Brief Discourse of the Nature, Causes, Kinds & Cure of Enthusiasm. LC 92-23647. (Augustan Reprints Ser.: No. 118). 1966. reprint ed. 14.50 (*0-404-70118-3*, BR112) AMS Pr.
— Philosophical Writings of Henry More. MacKinnon, Flora I., ed. LC 78-95151. reprint ed. 42.50 (*0-404-04409-3*) AMS Pr.
— A Platonick Song of the Soul. Jacob, Alexander, ed. & intro. by. LC 97-47288. 688p. 1998. 65.00 (*0-8387-5366-3*) Bucknell U Pr.

More, Hilary. Simple to Sew: Needlepoint. 48p. 1996. 7.98 (*0-7858-0362-9*) Bk Sales Inc.
— Soft Furnishings. (Pleasures of Home Ser.). (Illus.). 128p. 1997. 21.95 (*0-304-34629-2*, Pub. by Cassell) Sterling.
— Soft Furnishings: Pleasures of Home. (Illus.). 128p. 1998. pap. 14.95 (*0-304-35091-5*) Continuum.

More, Ian A. & Brown, Ian L. General Pathology. (Colour Aids Ser.). (Illus.). 130p. (Orig.). 1991. pap. text 19.95 (*0-443-04057-5*) Church.
— General Pathology. LC 93-29877. (Colour Guide Ser.). (Orig.). 1994. pap. text 16.95 (*0-443-04949-1*) Harcrt Hlth Sci Grp.

More, James F. History of Queens County, Nova Scotia. 255p. 1995. reprint ed. lib. bdg. 32.00 (*0-8328-4726-7*) Higginson Bk Co.

More, John W., ed. Trial of A. J. Monson, No. 1. (Notable British Trials Ser.). vii, 472p. 1995. reprint ed. 145.00 (*1-56169-152-6*) Gaunt.

More, Jorge J. & Wright, S. J. Optimization Software Guide. LC 93-33771. (Frontiers in Applied Mathematics Ser.: No. 14). xii, 154p. 1993. pap. 31.00 (*0-89871-322-6*) Soc Indus-Appl Math.

***More, Joseph.** Thoughts in Silence. 64p. 1999. pap. 7.00 (*0-9666115-1-9*, Our Ladys Pr) Eureka Pub.

— Thoughts in Stillness. 64p. 1999. pap. 7.00 (*0-9666115-2-7*, Our Ladys Pr) Eureka Pub.

More, Julian. Impressionist Paris: The Essential Guide to the City of Light. (Illus.). 208p. 1999. reprint ed. pap. 19.95 (*1-86205-210-7*, Pub. by Pavilion Bks Ltd) Trafalgar.

— A Taste of Burgundy. (Illus.). 160p. 1993. 14.98 (*1-55859-464-7*) Abbeville Pr.

More, Julian, jt. auth. see More, Carey.

More, Kate & Whittle, Stephen. Reclaiming Genders: Transsexual Grammars at the Fin de Siecle. LC 98-41804. 224p. 1999. 55.00 (*0-304-33777-3*); pap. 19.95 (*0-304-33776-5*) Continuum.

More, Louise B. Wage Earners' Budgets: A Study of Standards & Cost of Living in New York City. LC 73-137178. (Poverty U. S. A. Historical Record Ser.). 1977. reprint ed. 23.95 (*0-405-03116-5*) Ayer.

More, Mary. A Way to God: A Biography of George More. (C). 1990. text 45.00 (*0-947988-45-9*, Pub. by Wild Goose Pubns) St Mut.

More, Meredith. October Obsession. 192p. 1988. pap. 8.95 (*0-941483-18-5*) Naiad Pr.

More, Owen A. & Moe, Kathleen K. Diagnosing Disease Using Kinetic Enzyme Assays. Stanitski, Conrad L., ed. (Modular Laboratory Program in Chemistry Ser.). 12p. (C). 1996. pap. text 1.50 (*0-87540-483-9*, ANAL 483-9) Chem Educ Res.

More, Paul E. On Being Human. LC 68-57334. (Essay Index Reprint Ser.). 1977. 19.95 (*0-8369-0717-5*) Ayer.

— Selected Shelburne Essays. reprint ed. 39.00 (*0-403-07240-9*) Somerset Pub.

More, Phyllis K. & Mandell, Sandy, eds. Nursing Case Management: An Evolving Practice. LC 96-13465. (Illus.). 304p. 1996. text 24.00 (*0-07-105481-2*) McGraw-Hill HPD.

More, R. M. Laser Interactions with Atoms, Solids, & Plasmas. (NATO ASI Series B, Physics: Vol. 327). (Illus.). 486p. (C). 1994. 145.00 (*0-306-44801-7*, Plenum Trade) Perseus Pubng.

More, Richard. The Carpenter's Rule to Measure Ordinarie Timber. LC 74-26026. (English Experience Ser.: No. 252). 56p. 1970. reprint ed. 15.00 (*90-221-0252-1*) Walter J Johnson.

More, Robert P., jt. auth. see Palmer, Philip M.

More, T. A., jt. auth. see Nayar, N. M.

More, Thomas. The Answer to a Poisoned Book. Foley, Stephen & Miller, Clarence H., eds. LC 63-7949. (Complete Works of St. Thomas More: Vol. II). 434p. 1985. 80.00 (*0-300-03129-7*) Yale U Pr.

— The Apologye of Syr Thomas More, Knyght. Taft, Arthur Irving, ed. & intro. by. (EETS, OS Ser.: No. 180). 1972. reprint ed. 65.00 (*0-527-00177-5*) Periodicals Srv.

— The Apolyge of Syr Thomas More. LC 72-221. (English Experience Ser.: No. 228). 1970. reprint ed. 65.00 (*90-221-0228-9*) Walter J Johnson.

***More, Thomas.** Be Merry in God: 60 Reflections from the Writings of Saint Thomas More. LC 99-19445. 1999. pap. 9.99 (*1-56955-090-5*) Servant.

More, Thomas. A Book for All Seasons. 178p. 1990. pap. 11.95 (*0-87243-184-3*) Templegate.

— Complete Works of St. Thomas More: The Debellation of Salem & Bizance, Vol. 10. Guy, John A. et al, eds. LC 63-7949. Vol. 10. 600p. (C). 1988. 80.00 (*0-300-03376-1*) Yale U Pr.

— A Concordance to the Utopia of St. Thomas More & a Frequency Word List. Bolchazy, Ladislaus J. et al, eds. (Alpha-Omega, Reihe B Ser.: Bd. II). (GER.). vii, 332p. 1978. lib. bdg. 63.70 incl. 3.5 hd (*3-487-06514-2*) G Olms Pubs.

— The Correspondence of Sir Thomas More. Rogers, Elizabeth F., ed. LC 74-119961. (Select Bibliographies Reprint Ser.). 1977. reprint ed. 33.95 (*0-8369-5404-1*) Ayer.

— De Tristitia Christi: Complete Works of St. Thomas More, Vol. 14, Pts. 1 & 2. Miller, Clarence H., ed. LC 63-7949. Vol. 14. 1976. 105.00 (*0-300-01793-6*) Yale U Pr.

— A Dialogue of Comfort Against Tribulation. 320p. 1998. 24.95 (*1-889334-14-6*); pap. 14.95 (*1-889334-13-8*) Scepter Pubs.

— A Dialogue of Comfort Against Tribulation. (Complete Works of St. Thomas More: No. 12). 1976. 95.00 (*0-300-01609-3*) Yale U Pr.

— A Dialogue of Comfort Against Tribulation. Manley, Frank, ed. & intro. by. 331p. 1977. 60.00 (*0-300-02082-1*) Yale U Pr.

— A Dyaloge Wherein be Treatyd Dyvers Maters. LC 74-28873. (English Experience Ser.: No. 752). 1975. reprint ed. 30.00 (*90-221-0752-3*) Walter J Johnson.

— English Prayers of Sir Thomas More: Written While He Was a Prisoner in the Tower of London in 1534. Hallet, Philip E., ed. LC 95-60059. 96p. 1995. pap. 9.95 (*0-87243-214-9*) Templegate.

— His Witness Is True: John & His Interpreters. (American University Studies: Theology & Religion: Ser. VII, Vol. 42). VIII, 242p. (C). 1989. text 43.00 (*0-8204-0626-0*) P Lang Pubng.

— The History of King Richard III. Sylvester, Richard S., ed. (Complete Works of St. Thomas More: No. 2). (ENG & LAT., Illus.). 1963. 75.00 (*0-300-00984-4*) Yale U Pr.

— The History of King Richard III & Selections from the English & Latin Poems. Sylvester, Richard S., ed. (Selected Works of St. Thomas More). (Illus.). 1976. pap. 17.00 (*0-300-01925-4*) Yale U Pr.

— The History of King Richard III & Selections from the English & Latin Poems. Sylvester, Richard S., ed. (Selected Works of St. Thomas More). 1976. 37.50 (*0-300-01840-1*) Yale U Pr.

— In Defense of Humanism: Letter to Martin Dorp, Letter to the University of Oxford, Letter to Edward Lee, Letter to a Monk, with a New Latin Text & Translation of "The History of Richard III" Kinney, Daniel, ed. LC 63-7949. (Complete Works of St. Thomas More: Vol. 15). 662p. 1986. 80.00 (*0-300-03161-0*) Yale U Pr.

— Letter to Bugenhagen: Supplication of Souls' & Letter Against Frith. Manley, Frank, ed. (Yale Edition of the Complete Works of St. Thomas More Ser.: Vol. 7). xxx, 752p. (C). 1990. 90.00 (*0-300-03809-7*) Yale U Pr.

— Responsio Ad Lutherum, 2 vols. Headley, John M., ed. LC 63-7949. (Complete Works of St. Thomas More: No. 5). 1969. 105.00 (*0-300-01123-7*) Yale U Pr.

— The Sadness of Christ. (Yale University Press Translation Ser.). 184p. 1997. pap. 9.95 (*0-933932-66-9*) Scepter Pubs.

— St. Thomas More: Selected Letters. Rogers, Elizabeth F., ed. LC 61-14944. (Yale Edition of the Works of St. Thomas More: Modernized Ser.). 297p. 1961. reprint ed. pap. 92.10 (*0-8357-8331-6*, 203387600087) Bks Demand.

— St. Thomas More Vol. 3, Pt. 2: Latin Poems. Miller, Clarence H. et al, eds. LC 63-7949. (Yale Edition of the Complete Works of St. Thomas More Ser.: Vol. 3). 800p. 1984. 90.00 (*0-300-02591-2*) Yale U Pr.

— Sir Thomas More: Selected Letters. LC 61-14944. (Yale Edition of the Works of St. Thomas More: Modernized Ser.). reprint ed. pap. 74.00 (*0-608-13494-5*, 2022022) Bks Demand.

— The Supplycacyon of Soulys: Agaynst the Supplycacyon of Beggars. LC 72-220. (English Experience Ser.: No. 353). 88p. 1971. reprint ed. 25.00 (*90-221-0353-6*) Walter J Johnson.

— Thomas More's Prayer Book: A Facsimile Reproduction of the Annotated Pages. Martz, Louis L. & Sylvester, Richard S., trs. LC 69-15454. (Elizabethan Club Ser.: No. 4). (ENG & LAT., Illus.). 1969. 47.50 (*0-300-00179-7*) Yale U Pr.

— Treatise on the Passion: Complete Works of St. Thomas More, Vol. 13. Haupt, Garry E., ed. Incl. Instructions & Prayers. LC 63-7949. 1976. Treatise on the Blessed Body. LC 63-7949. 1976. Treatise on the Passion. LC 63-7949. 1976. LC 63-7949. Vol. 13. 1976. 80.00 (*0-300-01794-4*) Yale U Pr.

— Utopia. Date not set. lib. bdg. 18.95 (*0-8488-0836-3*) Amereon Ltd.

— Utopia. Logan, George M. & Adams, Robert M., eds. (Cambridge Texts in the History of Political Thought Ser.). 176p. (C). 1989. text 29.95 (*0-521-34573-1*); pap. text 8.95 (*0-521-34797-1*) Cambridge U Pr.

— Utopia. Wooten, David, tr. from LAT. & intro. by. LC 98-47076. 208p. (C). 1999. pap. 6.95 (*0-87220-376-X*); lib. bdg. 29.95 (*0-87220-377-8*) Hackett Pub.

— Utopia. Ogden, H. V., ed. & tr. by. (Crofts Classics). 96p. 1949. pap. text 4.95 (*0-88295-062-2*) Harlan Davidson.

— Utopia. 1992. 15.00 (*0-679-41076-7*) McKay.

— Utopia. Sacks, David H., ed. LC 98-87540. 208p. 1999. pap. text 12.95 (*0-312-10145-7*) St Martin.

— Utopia. Turner, Paul, tr. & intro. by. (Penguin Classics Ser.). 154p. 1965. pap. 7.95 (*0-14-044165-4*, Penguin Classics) Viking Penguin.

— Utopia. (Classics of World Literature Ser.). 1998. pap. 5.95 (*1-85326-474-1*, 4741WW, Pub. by Wrdsworth Edits) NTC Contemp Pub Co.

— Utopia. Surtz, Edward, ed. (Selected Works of St. Thomas More: No. 2). (Illus.). (C). 1964. pap. 10.00 (*0-300-00238-6*, Y119) Yale U Pr.

— Utopia. large type ed. 206p. 1996. 21.95 (*1-56000-545-9*) Transaction Pubs.

— Utopia. Marshall, P., tr. 150p. 1990. reprint ed. lib. bdg. 18.95 (*0-89966-706-6*) Buccaneer Bks.

— Utopia. LC 97-25114. (Illus.). 96p. 1997. reprint ed. pap. text 1.50 (*0-486-29583-4*, 706420Q) Dover.

— Utopia. unabridged ed. Robynson, Ralph, tr. from LAT. (Illus.). 176p. 1999. pap. 14.95 (*0-87243-241-6*) Templegate.

— Utopia. 2nd ed. Sheehan, John & Donnelly, John, trs. 190p. 1984. reprint ed. pap. 10.00 (*0-87462-448-7*) Marquette.

— Utopia: A Revised Translation, Backgrounds, Criticism. 2nd ed. Adams, Robert M., ed. & tr. by. (Critical Editions Ser.). (C). 1991. pap. text 9.25 (*0-393-96145-1*) Norton.

— Utopia: Latin Text & English Translation. Logan, George M. et al, eds. LC 93-42534. (LAT & ENG., Illus.). 336p. (C). 1995. text 85.00 (*0-521-40318-9*) Cambridge U Pr.

— Utopia & a Dialogue of Comford Against Tribulation. 440p. 1994. pap. 5.95 (*0-460-87431-4*, Everyman's Classic Lib) Tuttle Pubng.

More, Thomas, et al, eds. A Dialogue Concerning Heresies: Complete Works of St. Thomas More, Set, Vol. 6, Pts. 1 & 2. LC 63-7949. Vol. 6. (Illus.). 910p. (C). 1981. 100.00 (*0-300-02211-5*) Yale U Pr.

More, Thomas, et al. Ideal Commonwealths. 2nd ed. (Dedalus European Classics Ser.). 416p. 1997. reprint ed. pap. 14.95 (*0-946626-26-X*, Pub. by Dedalus) Subterranean Co.

— Three Early Modern Utopias: Thomas More: Utopia / Francis Bacon: New Atlantis / Henry Neville: The Isle of Pines. Bruce, Susan, ed. (Oxford World's Classics Ser.). (Illus.). 320p. 2000. pap. 9.95 (*0-19-283885-7*) OUP.

More, Thomas, tr. see Mirandola, Pico D. & Francesco, Giovanni.

More, Tony. Defis et Enjeux de l'Excedent de la Balance des Paiements du Japon: Risques pour le Developpement du Commerce Mondial et le Systeme Financier International. (Publications Universitaires Europeennes Ser.: Series 5, Vol. 1855). (FRE.). viii, 363p. 1996. 54.95 (*3-906754-44-8*, Pub. by P Lang) P Lang Pubng.

— Thanks, Americans . . . Thanks. LC 97-91029. 1998. pap. 12.95 (*0-533-12545-6*) Vantage.

More, Yu. 4-Wheel Drive. 80p. 1997. pap. 19.95 (*0-87040-987-5*) Japan Pubns USA.

Morea, Deborah. Through the Doors of Truth, Find Thyself. 1978. 5.50 (*0-9603022-0-4*) Davida Pubns.

— The Transmutation of Attitudes. 1979. pap. 6.50 (*0-9603022-1-2*) Davida Pubns.

Morea, J. M., jt. ed. see Lansana, Quraysh A.

Morea, Peter. In Search of Personality: Christianity & Modern Psychology. 1997. pap. text 27.00 (*0-334-02682-2*) S C M Pr Ltd.

Moreau & Velkov, eds. Excerpta Valesiana. (LAT.). 1968. 15.95 (*3-322-00863-0*, T1306, Pub. by B G Teubner) U of Mich Pr.

Moreau, A. Scott. Essentials of Spiritual Warfare. LC 97-9817. 208p. 1997. pap. 10.99 (*0-87788-167-7*, H Shaw Pubs) Waterbrook Pr.

***Moreau, A. Scott.** Evangelical Dictionary of World Missions. LC 99-44001. 1168p. 2000. 60.00 (*0-8010-2074-3*) Baker Bks.

Moreau, A. Scott. Spiritual Warfare. (Fisherman Bible Studyguide Ser.). 96p. 1995. pap. text 4.99 (*0-87788-777-2*, H Shaw Pubs) Waterbrook Pr.

Moreau, C. X. Distant Valor. 416p. 1998. mass mkt. 6.99 (*0-8125-5389-6*, Pub. by Forge NYC) St Martin.

***Moreau, C. X.** Distant Valor. 351p. 1999. reprint ed. text 24.00 (*0-7881-6623-9*) DIANE Pub.

— Promise of Glory. 304p. 2000. text 24.95 (*0-312-87272-0*) Forge NYC.

Moreau, Claude. Moulds, Toxins & Food. Moss, Maurice, tr. LC 78-8715. (Illus.). 491p. reprint ed. pap. 152.30 (*0-608-17604-4*, 203045400069) Bks Demand.

***Moreau, Daniel.** Getting Started in Financial Information. LC 99-32352. (Getting Started in Ser.). 241p. 1999. pap. 18.95 (*0-471-32429-9*) Wiley.

Moreau, Daniel. Take Charge of Your Career: Survive & Profit from a Mid-Career Change. 258p. 1996. pap. 15.00 (*0-8129-2829-6*) Kiplinger Bks.

Moreau, David & Springhouse Publishing Company Staff. Handbook of Critical Care Nursing. (Illus.). 736p. 1996. per. 34.95 (*0-87434-774-2*) Springhouse Corp.

Moreau, David, ed. see SPC Staff.

Moreau, Fernand. Botanique. (Methodique Ser.). (FRE.). 1534p. 1965. pap. 125.00 (*0-7859-1589-3*, 207010396X) Fr & Eur.

Moreau, J. F. & Mueller, G. O., trs. from FRE. French Penal Code. (American Series of Foreign Penal Codes: Vol. 1). xviii, 258p. 1960. 15.00 (*0-8377-0021-3*, Rothman) W S Hein.

Moreau, J. J. & Panagiotopoulos, P. D., eds. Nonsmooth Mechanics & Applications. (CISM Courses & Lectures: Vol. 302). (Illus.). v, 462p. 1988. 103.95 (*0-387-82066-3*) Spr-Verlag.

Moreau, J. J., et al. Topics in Nonsmooth Mechanics. 320p. 1988. 267.00 (*0-8176-1907-0*) Birkhauser.

Moreau, Jacques. Die Christenverfolgung im roemischen Reich. 2nd ed. 119p. (C). 1971. 22.30 (*3-11-002456-X*) De Gruyter.

— Inscriptiones Latinae Christianae Veteres: Supplementband. Marrou, Henri-Irenee, ed. viii, 165p. 1985. write for info. (*3-296 13501 9*) G Olms Pubs.

Moreau, Jeffrey. Muni Photographs. LC 91-72515. 64p. 1991. pap. 22.00 (*0-934406-04-9*) Carbarn Press.

Moreau, Jeffrey, jt. auth. see Brueckman, Henry.

Moreau, Jeffrey, jt. auth. see Cushing, Raymond.

Moreau, Joseph. L' Ame du Monde de Platon aux Stoiciens. 200p. 1981. reprint ed. write for info. (*3-487-04094-8*) G Olms Pubs.

— La Construction de l'Idealisme Platonicien. 515p. 1986. reprint ed. write for info. incl. 3.5 hd (*3-487-01830-6*) G Olms Pubs.

— Dictionnaire de Geographie Historique de la Gaule et de la France.Tr. of Historical Dictionary of the Geography of Gaul & France. (FRE.). 426p. 1972. pap. 99.50 (*0-8288-6371-7*, M-6593) Fr & Eur.

— L' Univers Leibnizien. 256p. 1988. reprint ed. write for info. (*3-487-07903-8*) G Olms Pubs.

Moreau, Josephine, jt. auth. see Cotteret.

***Moreau, Linda.** Da Nang to Memphis. (Illus.). 96p. 1999. 15.00 (*0-8059-4794-9*) Dorrance.

Moreau, Louis & Franck, Adolphe. Reflexions sur les Idees de Saint-Martin & la Philosophie Mystique en France a la Fin du Eighteenth Siecle, Vol. VII. Amadou, Robert, ed. (FRE.). 228p. reprint ed. write for info. (*0-318-71418-3*) G Olms Pubs.

Moreau, Lynda, ed. see Sons of Confederate Veterans Organization Staff.

Moreau, M. Underground Storage Systems. (General Engineering Ser.). 1992. text. write for info. (*0-442-00390-0*, VNR) Wiley.

Moreau, M. & Turq, P., eds. Chemical Reactivity in Liquids: Fundamental Aspects. LC 88-17980. (Illus.). 642p. 1988. 135.00 (*0-306-42922-5*, Plenum Trade) Perseus Pubng.

Moreau, Michael, ed. see O'Neil, Leslie S.

Moreau, Nancy A. N & N Science Series-Physics. 3rd ed. Garnsey, Wayne, ed. (Science Ser.). (Illus.). 352p. 1998. pap. text 7.95 (*0-935487-55-7*) N & N Pub Co.

Moreau, Nancy A., jt. auth. see Moran, John W.

Moreau, P., jt. ed. see Poirier, G.

Moreau, Philippe, tr. see Lewis, Lon D., et al.

Moreau, Pierre-Francois, jt. ed. see Curley, Edwin.

Moreau, R. Magnetohydrodynamics. (C). 1990. text 182.50 (*0-7923-0937-5*) Kluwer Academic.

Moreau, R. & Aubert, G. Neural Networks-Les Reseaux de Neurones: Biological Computers or Electronic Brains-Ordinateurs Biologiques Ou Cervceaux Electroniques. (Entretiens de Lyon Ser.). (Illus.). viii, 195p. 1990. 70.95 (*0-387-59540-6*) Spr-Verlag.

Moreau, R., jt. ed. see Lielpeteris, J.

Moreau, Rene. The Computer Comes of Age: The People, the Hardware, & the Software. 225p. 1986. reprint ed. pap. text 13.00 (*0-262-63103-2*) MIT Pr.

***Moreau, Roger.** Dinosaur Mazes. (Illus.). (J). 2000. pap. 5.95 (*0-8069-5929-0*) Sterling.

Moreau, Roger. Giant Book of Mazes: Costco Edition. (J). 1997. 19.95 (*0-8069-5719-0*) Sterling.

— Great Escape Mazes. 1999. pap. text 5.95 (*0-8069-7098-7*) Sterling.

— Great Explorer Mazes. LC 97-378. (Illus.). 64p. 1997. pap. 5.95 (*0-8069-9606-4*) Sterling.

— Jungle Mazes. (Illus.). 64p. (J). 1998. 5.95 (*0-8069-0876-9*) Sterling.

— Lost Treasure Mazes. 1999. pap. text 5.95 (*0-8069-7811-2*) Sterling.

— Maze Madness! Great Explorer Mazes & Mountain Mazes. 1997. pap. text 95.20 (*0-8069-9879-2*) Sterling.

— Mountain Mazes. (Illus.). 64p. 1996. pap. 5.95 (*0-8069-6110-4*) Sterling.

— Natural Disaster Mazes. (Illus.). 64p. (J). (gr. 3-7). Date not set. 5.95 (*0-8069-5727-1*) Sterling.

— Save the Earth Maze Book. 1996. pap. text 59.50 (*0-8069-9625-0*) Sterling.

— Save the Earth Maze Book. (Illus.). 64p. (J). 1996. pap. 5.95 (*0-8069-9456-8*) Sterling.

— Space Mazes. 1997. pap. text 59.50 (*0-8069-1309-6*) Sterling.

— Space Mazes. (Illus.). 64p. 1997. 5.95 (*0-8069-9863-6*) Sterling.

— Space Mazes - Mountain Mazes. 1997. pap. text 95.20 (*0-8069-1311-8*) Sterling.

Moreau-Sipiere, Ermine. The Sloughi: The Arabian Sighthound. (Illus.). 75p. 1996. reprint ed. pap. 20.00 (*0-9664669-2-6*) Alet Publ.

Moreau, W. M. Semiconductor Lithography: Principles, Practices, & Materials. LC 87-29077. (Microdevices: Physics & Fabrication Technologies Ser.). (Illus.). 952p. (C). 1988. 159.50 (*0-306-42185-2*, Plenum Trade) Perseus Pubng.

Moreaux, Michel, jt. ed. see Laffont, Jean-Jacques.

Morecambe, Gary. Wipe Out. 224p. 1999. 25.00 (*0-7278-2242-X*, Pub. by Severn Hse); pap. text 25.00 (*0-7278-2243-8*, Pub. by Severn Hse) Chivers N Amer.

Morecambe, Gary, jt. auth. see Sellers, Michael.

Morecki, A. Biomechanics of Engineering. (CISM International Centre for Mechanical Sciences Ser.: No. 291). (Illus.). vi, 186p. 1987. 41.95 (*0-387-81974-6*) Spr-Verlag.

Morecki, A., ed. Biomechanics of Motion. (CISM Courses & Lectures: Vol. 263). (Illus.). 217p. 1981. 51.95 (*0-387-81611-9*) Spr-Verlag.

— Robotics & Manipulators: Theory & Practice. 36p. 1983. pap. 10.00 (*0-08-030530-X*, 11, Pergamon Pr) Elsevier.

Morecki, A., et al, eds. RoManSy Nine: Proceedings of the Ninth CISM-IFToMM Symposium on Theory & Practice of Robots & Manipulators, Udine, Italy, Sept. 1-4, 1992. (Lecture Notes in Control & Information Sciences: Vol. 187). (Illus.). xxxi, 438p. 1993. 104.95 (*0-387-19834-2*) Spr-Verlag.

***Morecki, A., et al, eds.** ROMANSY 12. Theory & Practice of Robots & Manipulators: Proceedings of the 12th CISM-IFToMM Symposium. (CISM International Centre for Mechanical Sciences Ser.: No. 405). (Illus.). x, 461p. 1999. pap. 93.00 (*3-211-83143-6*) Spr-Verlag.

Morecki, A., et al, eds. RoManSy 11 Theory & Practice of Robots & Manipulators: Proceedings of the Eleventh CISM-IFToMM Symposium. (CISM International Centre for Mechanical Sciences Ser.: No. 381). (Illus.). x, 232p. pap. 95.00 (*3-211-82903-2*) Spr-Verlag.

— Theory & Practice of Robots & Manipulators: Proceedings of RoManSy 10, the Tenth CISM-IFToMM Symposium. (International Centre for Mechanical Sciences Ser.: No.361). 427p. 1995. 110.95 (*3-211-82697-1*) Spr-Verlag.

***Morecki, A. & Knapczyk, J., eds.** Basics of Robotics: Theory & Components of Manipulators & Robots. (CISM International Centre for Mechanical Sciences Ser.: Suppl. 402). (Illus.). x, 580p. 1999. pap. (*3-211-83150-9*) Spr-Verlag.

Morecki, A. & Waldron, K. J., eds. Human & Machine Locomotion. (CISM International Centre for Mechanical Sciences Ser.: No. 375). (Illus.). vii, 315p. 1997. pap. 80.00 (*3-211-82905-9*) Spr-Verlag.

Morecki, A., et al. Cybernetic Systems of Limb Movements in Man, Animals & Robots. LC 82-15717. 250p. 1985. text 95.95 (*0-470-27374-7*) P-H.

Morecroft, John D., ed. Modeling for Learning Organization. LC 94-17395. (System Dynamics Ser.). (Illus.). 400p. 1994. 45.00 (*1-56327-060-9*) Productivity Inc.

Morecroft, Joseph, III. With Liberty & Justice for All: Christian Politics Made Simple. 2nd ed. (C). 1995. pap. 7.95 (*0-925591-37-8*) Covenant Hse Bks.

Moree, Cody. Her Senior Year: A One-Act Play. (Illus.). 17p. (YA). (gr. 9-12). 1998. pap. 3.50 (*0-88680-453-1*, C4531) I E Clark.

Moreell, Ben & Hoover, Herbert C. Our Nation's Water Resources: Policies & Politics. LC 72-2857. (Use & Abuse of America's Natural Resources Ser.). 290p. 1972. reprint ed. 23.95 (*0-405-04521-2*) Ayer.

***Moreen, Vera Basch.** In Queen Esther's Garden: An Anthology of Judeo-Persian Literature. LC 99-44912. (Judaica Ser.). 416p. 2000. 45.00 (*0-300-07905-2*) Yale U Pr.

Moreen, Vera Basch. Miniatures in Judaeo-Persian Manuscripts. (Bibliographica Judaica Ser.: No. 9). 56p. 1985. pap. 15.00 *(0-87820-907-7)* Hebrew Union Coll Pr.

Moreh, S. Studies in Modern Arabic Prose & Poetry. (Illus.). Xi, 179p. 1988. text 53.00 *(90-04-08359-6)* Brill Academic Pubs.

Moreh, S., tr. see Al-Jabarti, Abal R.

Moreh, Shmuel. Jewish Contributions to Nineteenth-Century Arabic Theatre: Plays from Algeria & Syria - a Study & Texts. 456p. 1996. text 65.00 *(0-19-922274-6)* OUP.

Moreh, Shmuel. Live Theatre & Dramatic Literature in the Medieval Arabic World. (Eastern Civilization Ser.). 240p. (C). 1992. text 45.00 *(0-8147-5481-3)* NYU Pr.

Moreh, Shmuel, jt. auth. see Crone, Patricia.

Moreh, Shmuel, jt. comment see Crone, Patricia.

Morehead, Albert H. According to Hoyle. 1976. 23.95 *(0-8488-0348-5)* Amereon Ltd.

— The Complete Book of Solitaire & Patience Games. (Illus.). 192p. 1983. mass mkt. 6.50 *(0-553-26240-8)* Bantam.

— The Complete Guide to Winning Poker. 286p. 1973. pap. 8.95 *(0-671-21646-5*, Fireside) S&S Trade Pap.

— Hoyle's Rules of Games. 1983. pap. 12.95 *(0-452-26416-2*, Plume) Dutton Plume.

Morehead, Albert H. & Morehead, Loy. New American Crossword Puzzle Dictionary. 1986. mass mkt. 6.99 *(0-451-14503-8*, Sig) NAL.

Morehead, Albert H. & Mott-Smith, Geoffrey. Hoyle Up-to-Date: Official Rules for All Important Games. (Illus.). 1970. pap. 12.95 *(0-399-12827-1*, Perigee Bks) Berkley Pub.

Morehead, Albert H. & Mott-Smith, Geoffrey, eds. Hoyle's Rules of Games. 1946. mass mkt. 6.99 *(0-451-16309-5*, Sig) NAL.

Morehead, Albert L. New Complete Hoyle: The Authoritative Guide to the Official Rules of All Popular Games of Skill. 720p. 1991. 27.00 *(0-385-24962-4)* Doubleday.

Morehead, Andrew. Spanish-English Dictionary. (SPA & ENG.). 1290p. 1996. mass mkt. 4.50 *(0-451-18874-8*, Sig) NAL.

Morehead, Andrew & Ramondino, Salvatore. The New World Spanish-English, English-Spanish Dictionary. rev. ed. 1296p. 1996. pap. 29.95 incl. disk *(0-525-94205-X)* Viking Penguin.

Morehead, Andrew T., jt. auth. see Pirrung, Michael C.

Morehead, Ann, jt. auth. see Morehead, Don.

Morehead-Coleman, Dorothy. Child Development in the 1997 Society Reading Development for the Beginner Phonics Particularly the Inner City. 120p. Date not set. pap. text 30.00 *(0-9669926-0-1)* D Morehead Clemn.

Morehead, Debby. A Special Place for Charlee: A Child's Companion Through Pet Loss. LC 96-92552. (Illus.). 36p. (Orig.). (J). (gr. 2-6). 1996. pap. 6.95 *(0-9654049-0-0)* Partners In Pub.

Morehead, Don & Morehead, Ann. A Short Season: Story of a Montana Childhood. LC 97-33357. (Illus.). 190p. 1998. pap. 13.00 *(0-8032-8244-3*, A Bison Orig) U of Nebr Pr.

Morehead, Gary, et al. 1995 CUES Staffing Manual for Credit Unions. 2nd rev. ed. 102p. 1995. pap. 99.00 *(1-889394-34-3)* Credit Union Execs.

Morehead, Gary, jt. auth. see Schmitt, Stephen.

Morehead, George, tr. see Leblanc, Maurice.

Morehead, Jacqueline, jt. auth. see Spangle, Michael.

Morehead, James B. In My Sights: The Memoir of a P-40 Ace. LC 97-33031. (Illus.). 384p. 1997. 24.95 *(0-89141-634-X)* Presidio Pr.

— In My Sights: The Memoir of a P-40 Ace. large type ed. LC 98-10151. 336p. 1998. 22.95 *(0-7838-8451-6*, G K Hall & Co) Mac Lib Ref.

Morehead, Joe. Essays on Public Documents & Government Policies. LC 86-9840. (Technical Services Quarterly Ser.: Vol. 3, Nos. 3-4). 364p. 1986. 10.95 *(0-86656-248-6)* Haworth Pr.

— Introduction to United States Government Information Sources. 5th ed. LC 96-6246. (Library Science Text Ser.). 380p. 1996. pap. text 40.00 *(1-56308-460-0)*; lib. bdg. 55.00 *(1-56308-485-6)* Libs Unl.

***Morehead, Joe.** Introduction to United States Government Information Sources. 6th ed. LC 99-35598. (Library & Information Science Text Ser.). 440p. 1999. 65.00 *(1-56308-734-0)*; pap. 47.50 *(1-56308-735-9)* Libs Unl.

Morehead, Judith & Morehead, Richard. The New Texas Wild Game Cookbook. rev. ed. (Illus.). 104p. 1985. pap. 13.95 *(0-89015-526-7)* Sunbelt Media.

Morehead, Loy, jt. auth. see Morehead, Albert H.

Morehead, Philip D. New American Roget's College Thesaurus. 1985. pap. 13.95 *(0-452-00977-4*, Plume) Dutton Plume.

Morehead, Philip D. The New American Roget's College Thesaurus in Dictionary Form. 1985. 10.09 *(0-606-03348-3*, Pub. by Turtleback) Demco.

Morehead, Philip D. The New American Roget's College Thesaurus in Dictionary Form, Vol. I. enl. rev. ed. 656p. (YA). (gr. 9 up). 1957. mass mkt. 5.99 *(0-451-15167-4*, Sig) NAL.

— The New International Dictionary of Music. 1999. pap. 7.99 *(0-451-17379-1*, Sig) NAL.

Morehead, Philip D., ed. The New American Webster Handy College Dictionary. 3rd ed. 800p. (C). 1995. mass mkt. 5.99 *(0-451-18166-2)* NAL.

Morehead, Phillip. Expanded New World Spanish-English/English-Spanish Dictionary. 1969. mass mkt. 4.50 *(0-451-17941-2*, Sig) NAL.

Morehead, Richard. Fifty Years of Texas Politics. 336p. 1982. 16.95 *(0-89015-342-6)* Sunbelt Media.

Morehead, Richard, jt. auth. see Morehead, Judith.

Morehead, Ruth J. The Christmas Story with Holly Babes. LC 85-32305. (Pictureback Ser.). (Illus.). 32p. (J). (ps-1). 1986. pap. 3.25 *(0-394-88051-X*, Pub. by Random Bks Yng Read) Random.

— Waiting for Christmas. (Jellybean Bks.). (Illus.). 24p. (J). (ps-k). 1999. lib. bdg. 7.99 *(0-375-90102-7*, Pub. by Random Bks Yng Read) Random.

Morehead, Ruth J. A Christmas Countdown with Ruth J. Morehead's Holly Babes. LC 90-61905. (Chunky Shape Bks.). 22p. (J). (ps). 1991. 3.99 *(0-679-81417-5*, Pub. by Random Bks Yng Read) Random.

Morehen, John, ed. English Choral Practice, 1400-1650. (Studies in Performance Practice: No. 5). (Illus.). 260p. (C). 1996. text 69.95 *(0-521-44143-9)* Cambridge U Pr.

Morehouse, Barbara J. A Place Called Grand Canyon: Contested Geographies. (Society, Environment, & Place Ser.). 202p. 1996. 42.00 *(0-8165-1603-0)*; pap. 19.95 *(0-8165-1628-6)* U of Ariz Pr.

Morehouse, Brian. Yastiks: Cushion Covers & Storage Bags of Anatolia. Mendenhall, Bethany, ed. (Illus.). 116p. 1996. 55.00 *(1-889666-01-7*, 01) Phila Eighth ICOC.

Morehouse, Cynthia T., jt. ed. see Culligan, Michael.

Morehouse, David. Psychic Warrior, Vol. 1. 1998. mass mkt. 6.99 *(0-312-96413-7)* St Martin.

— Psychic Warrior: Inside the CIA's Stargate Program: The True Story of a Soldier's Espionage & Awakening. (Illus.). 258p. 1999. reprint ed. text 24.00 *(0-7881-6203-9)* DIANE Pub.

Morehouse, David A. Nonlethal Weapons: War Without Death. LC 96-16271. 160p. 1996. 55.00 *(0-275-95170-7*, Praeger Pubs) Greenwood.

Morehouse, Debra, jt. auth. see Capezio, Peter.

Morehouse, G. L., ed. Maltby-Morehouse Family: A List of Pedigrees with Genealogical Notes. 157p. 1994. reprint ed. pap. 25.00 *(0-8328-4344-X)*; reprint ed. lib. bdg. 35.00 *(0-8328-4343-1)* Higginson Bk Co.

Morehouse Hegne, Barbara. Yonder Hills: Shady Cove, Elk Creek, Persist, Trail, Etna. 128p. (Orig.). 1989. spiral bd. 13.95 *(0-9623847-1-2)* B Hegne.

Morehouse, Jayne. Salonovations' Public Relations for the Salon. (Salon Business Ser.). (Illus.). 192p. 1996. pap. 31.95 *(1-56253-271-5)* Thomson Learn.

Morehouse, Jayne, ed. Std Txtbk Prof Barber Styl-Swb 2E. 2nd rev. ed. (HAIR). 193p. 1993. 20.25 *(1-56253-146-8)* Thomson Learn.

Morehouse, Jayne, ed. see Milady Publishing Company Staff.

Morehouse, Jeffrey M., ed. see International Solar Energy Conference Staff.

***Morehouse, John M., ed.** Navigation Rules - Rules of the Road: For Inland & International Waters. 7th rev. ed. 104p. 2000. pap. 9.95 *(0-939837-40-4*, Pub. by Paradise Cay Pubns) R Hale & Co.

Morehouse, Kathleen M. Rain on the Just: A Novel. LC 79-18762. (Lost American Fiction Ser.). 333p. 1980. reprint ed. 21.95 *(0-8093-0945-9)* S Ill U Pr.

Morehouse, Laurence E. Total Fitness in Thirty Minutes. 1990. pap. 5.99 *(0-671-72993-4)* S&S Trade.

Morehouse, Lawrence G., jt. ed. see Wyllie, Thomas D.

Morehouse, Matt. Navigation Rules: Rules of the Road. 5th rev. ed. 96p. 1999. pap. 8.95 *(0-939837-30-7)* Paradise Cay Pubns.

Morehouse, Matt, ed. see Her Majesty's Nautical Almanac Office, Rutherford Appleton Laboratory Staff & Nautical Almanac Office of the U. S. Naval Observatory Staff.

Morehouse, Matt, ed. see Her Majesty's Nautical Almanac Office Staff & U. S. Naval Observatory Staff.

Morehouse Publishing Staff. The Altar Guild Calendar 1999-2000: 16 Months - September to December. pap. 11.50 *(0-8192-3124-X*, 6179) Morehouse Pub.

— Burial of the Dead. 3.95 *(0-8192-1766-2*, 6208) Morehouse Pub.

— The Christian Planning Calendar, 2000-2001. 2000. pap. 10.95 *(0-8192-3131-2)* Morehouse Pub.

— Christian Planning Calendar, 1999-2000. pap. 10.95 *(0-8192-3123-1*, 6177) Morehouse Pub.

— Christian Pocket Diary, 2000. 1999. pap. 10.95 *(0-8192-3126-6)* Morehouse Pub.

— Christian Pocket Diary, 2001. 2000. 10.95 *(0-8192-3129-0)* Morehouse Pub.

— The Episcopal Church Annual, 2001. 2000. 32.00 *(0-8192-3156-8)* Morehouse Pub.

— The Episcopal Church Lesson Calendar 2000. pap. 12.50 *(0-8192-3127-4*, 6176) Morehouse Pub.

— The Episcopal Church Lesson Calendar, 2001. 2000. pap. 12.50 *(0-8192-3130-4)* Morehouse Pub.

— Hymns Ancient & Modern. 1999. write for info. *(0-907547-38-9)* Canterbury Press Norwich.

— New English Hymnal. 1999. write for info. *(0-907547-51-6)*; 15.95 *(1-85311-097-3)* Canterbury Press Norwich.

— Seasons & Saints Handwork Kit. pap. 2.50 *(0-8192-4051-6*, 1406) Morehouse Pub.

— Seasons & Saints Teachers. 60p. pap. 4.75 *(0-8192-4049-4*, 1408) Morehouse Pub.

— 2000 Year Round Women's Calendar for Taking Time Out. (Illus.). 1999. pap. 12.95 *(0-8192-3128-2*, 6210) Morehouse Pub.

***Morehouse Research Institute Staff & Institute for American Values Staff.** Turning the Corner On: Father Absence in Black America. (Illus.). 32p. 1999. write for info. *(0-9659841-4-1)* Inst for Am Val.

Morehouse, Richard, jt. auth. see Maykut, Pamela.

Morehouse, Sarah M. The Governor As Party Leader: Campaigning & Governing. LC 97-21108. (Illus.). 344p. 1998. text 49.50 *(0-472-10848-4*, 10848) U of Mich Pr.

Morehouse, Thomas A. The Alaska Native Claims Settlement Act, 1991, & Tribal Government. (Occasional Papers: No. 19). (Illus.). 29p. 1988. 2.00 *(0-88353-040-6)* U Alaska Inst Res.

— Alaska's Elections, 1958-1984. (Occasional Papers: No. 17). (Illus.). 37p. 1985. 2.00 *(0-88353-036-8)* U Alaska Inst Res.

— Native Claims & Political Development. (Occasional Papers: No. 18). (Illus.). 28p. 1987. 2.00 *(0-88353-039-2)* U Alaska Inst Res.

Morehouse, Thomas A. & Harrison, Gordon S. An Electoral Profile of Alaska: Interparty Competition Between 1958 & 1972. LC 73-620227. (ISER Reports: No. 37). (Illus.). 100p. 1973. pap. 3.00 *(0-88353-010-4)* U Alaska Inst Res.

Morehouse, Thomas A., et al. Alaska's Urban & Rural Governments. LC 83-25887. (Illus.). 272p. (Orig.). (C). 1984. pap. 25.00 *(0-8191-3771-5)* U Pr of Amer.

Morehouse, Thomas A., jt. auth. see McBeath, Gerald A.

Morehouse, Thomas A., jt. ed. see McBeath, Gerald A.

Morehouse, Tim. Basic Projects & Plantings for the Garden. LC 92-30915. (Illus.). 192p. (Orig.). 1993. pap. 12.95 *(0-8117-3048-4)* Stackpole.

Morehouse, Ward. George M. Cohan, Prince of the American Theater. LC 79-165445. (Illus.). 240p. 1972. reprint ed. lib. bdg. 35.00 *(0-8371-6225-4*, MOGC, Greenwood Pr) Greenwood.

— Separate, Unequal, but More Autonomous. 50p. 1981. pap. text 14.95 *(0-685-54936-4)* Transaction Pubs.

Morehouse, Ward, ed. Science & the Human Condition in India & Pakistan. LC 68-56606. (Illus.). 252p. 1968. 7.50 *(0-87470-010-8)* Rockefeller.

Morehouse, Ward & Subramaniam, Arun. The Bhopal Tragedy: What Really Happened & What It Means for American Workers & Communities at Risk. (Illus.). 190p. 1986. pap. 13.50 *(0-936876-47-6)* LRIS.

Morehouse, Ward, jt. auth. see Dembo, David.

Morehouse, Ward, ed. see Benello, C. George, et al.

Morehouse, Ward, ed. see Carnegie Endowment for International Peace Staff.

Moreillon, Judi. Sing down the Rain. LC 97-70357. (Illus.). 32p. (J). (gr. 2-5). 1997. 14.95 *(1-885772-07-6)* Kiva Pubng.

Morein, B., jt. ed. see Dinter, Z.

Moreira, Ana, ed. see ECOOP '99 Staff.

Moreira, Antonio R. & Wallace, Kimberlee K., eds. Computer & Information Science Applications in Bioprocess Engineering: Proceedings of the NATO Advanced Study Institute on 'Use of Computer & Informatic Systems in Bioprocess Engineering', Ofir, Portugal, May 18-29, 1992. LC 95-47404. (NATO ASI Series E: Applied Sciences: No. 305). 496p. (C). 1996. text 254.00 *(0-7923-3865-0)* Kluwer Academic.

Moreira de Roberts, Rosina E., tr. see Horne, Steven H.

***Moreira, Isabel.** Dreams, Visions & Spiritual Authority in Merovingian Gaul. 2000. 49.95 *(0-8014-3661-3)* Cornell U Pr.

Moreira, Mauricio M. Industrialization, Trade & Market Failures: The Role of Government Intervention in Brazil & South Korea. LC 94-18288. 1994. text 75.00 *(0-312-12223-3)* St Martin.

Moreira, Raymond, jt. auth. see Barreira, Joseph.

***Moreiras, Alberto D., et al, eds.** Nepantla: Views from South. 286p. 2000. pap. 10.00 *(0-8223-6482-4)* Duke.

Moreiro, Carlos Javier. Banking in Europe after 1992. LC 93-18024. 158p. 1993. 72.95 *(1-85521-362-1*, Pub. by Dartmth Pub) Ashgate Pub Co.

Morel. Chemistry in Practice. text. write for info. *(0-471-37116-5)* Wiley.

Morel & Buchner. Fragmenta Poetarum Latinorum. 3rd ed. Blansdorf, ed. (LAT.). 1995. 125.00 *(3-8154-1371-0*, T1371, Pub. by B G Teubner) U of Mich Pr.

Morel, A. Y., jt. auth. see Gordon, H. R.

Morel, Benedict A. Traite Des Degenerescences Physiques, Intellectuelles et Morales De L'espece Humaine, 2 vols. LC 75-16721. (Classics in Psychiatry Ser.). (FRE., Illus.). 1976. reprint ed. 62.95 *(0-405-07446-8)* Ayer.

Morel, Benoit, jt. ed. see Goodby, James E.

***Morel, Claude.** 15 Days of Prayer with Saint Francis de Sales. Hebert, Victoria & Sabourin, Denis, trs. from FRE. LC 99-46203. 128p. 2000. reprint ed. pap. 7.95 *(0-7648-0575-4)* Liguori Pubns.

Morel, Dominique, jt. auth. see Beguin, Gilles.

Morel, Edmund D. Affairs of West Africa. (Illus.). 382p. 1968. reprint ed. 39.50 *(0-7146-1702-4*, Pub. by F Cass Pubs) Intl Spec Bk.

— Black Man's Burden: The White Man in Africa from the Fifteenth Century to World War One. LC 74-81792. 240p. 1969. pap. 10.00 *(0-85345-115-X*, PB115X, Pub. by Monthly Rev) NYU Pr.

— King Leopold's Rule in Africa. LC 70-132078. 466p. 1971. reprint ed. lib. bdg. 35.00 *(0-8371-4647-X*, MKL&) Greenwood.

— Nigeria: Its Peoples & Its Problems. 3rd ed. (Illus.). 264p. 1968. reprint ed. 45.00 *(0-7146-1703-2*, BHA-01703, Pub. by F Cass Pubs) Intl Spec Bk.

— Red Rubber. LC 79-95442. (Studies in Russian Literature & Life: No. 100). 1970. reprint ed. lib. bdg. 75.00 *(0-8383-0995-X)* M S G Haskell Hse.

— Red Rubber: The Story of the Rubber Slave Trade Flourishing on the Congo in the Year of Grace 1906. 2nd ed. LC 71-76859. (Illus.). 213p. 1969. reprint ed. lib. bdg. 49.50 *(0-8371-1161-7*, MOR&, Greenwood Pr) Greenwood.

Morel, Francois M. & Hering, Janet G. Principles & Applications of Aquatic Chemistry. LC 92-18608. 608p. 1993. 79.95 *(0-471-54896-0)* Wiley.

Morel, Francois, jt. auth. see Carrez, Maurice.

Morel, Francois M. Principles of Aquatic Chemistry. LC 83-6840. (Wiley-Interscience Publications). 456p. reprint ed. pap. 141.40 *(0-7837-2404-7*, 204008900006) Bks Demand.

Morel, G. & Morel, M. Y. Les Oiseaux de Senegambie (The Birds of Senegambia) Notices et Cartes de Distribution (Information & Distribution Maps)Tr. of Birds of Senegambia - Information & Distribution Maps. (FRE.). 178p. 1990. pap. 22.00 *(2-7099-1012-8*, Pub. by LInstitut Francais) Balogh.

Morel, G., jt. auth. see Vernadat, F.

Morel, Gaud. Exploring Nature. Best, Clare et al, trs. LC 97-27529. (Illus.). 80p. (J). (gr. 2-9). 1998. lib. bdg. 23.95 *(0-88682-946-1*, Creat Educ) Creative Co.

— Nature's Timekeeper: The Tree. (Young Discovery Library). (Illus.). 40p. (J). (gr. k-6). 1993. lib. bdg. 2.99 *(1-56674-072-X*, HTS Bks) Forest Hse.

— Nature's Timekeeper: The Tree. Bogard, Vicki, tr. from FRE. LC 92-2710. (Illus.). 38p. (J). (gr. k-5). 1992. 5.95 *(0-944589-43-X)* Young Discovery Lib.

Morel, Gerard. Hybridization Techniques for Electron Microscopy. 368p. 1993. boxed set 141.95 *(0-8493-4414-X*, QH452) CRC Pr.

— Visualization of Nucleic Acids. LC 94-22190. 384p. 1995. boxed set 179.95 *(0-8493-4781-5)* CRC Pr.

Morel, Gerard, ed. Visualization of Receptors: Methods in Light & Electron Microscopy. LC 96-54597. 448p. 1997. boxed set 134.95 *(0-8493-2644-3)* CRC Pr.

***Morel, Janet.** Playing the Hand That's Dealt to You: A Guide for Parents of Children with Special Needs. LC 00-31190. 2000. write for info. *(1-887774-07-6)* Canmore Pr.

Morel, Jean-Michel & Solimini, Sergio. Variational Models for Image Segmentation. LC 94-36639. (Progress in Nonlinear Differential Equations & Their Applications Ser.: 14). (Illus.). xvi, 245p. 1994. 65.00 *(0-8176-3720-6)* Birkhauser.

***Morel, Jorge.** Homage to Latin Music - Salsa. 32p. 1999. pap. 14.95 *(0-7866-4728-0*, 98111BCD) Mel Bay.

— Latin American Rhythms for Guitar: Intermediate Level. 32p. 1997. pap. 17.95 incl. audio compact disk *(0-7866-2476-0*, 96214BCD) Mel Bay.

— Tangos & Milongas for Solo Guitar Bk/CD Set. 48p. 2000. pap. 17.95 *(0-7866-5249-7*, 098075BCD) Mel Bay.

Morel, Lin M. Heaven's Helpful Hints: (There's God in Your Soup) (Illus.). 117p. (Orig.). 1990. pap. 14.95 *(1-879672-50-2)* L Morel Assocs.

Morel, Linda, ed. see Goble, Phillip E.

***Morel, Lucas E.** Lincoln's Sacred Effort: Defining Religion's Role in American Self-Government. LC 99-53362. 272p. 2000. 70.00 *(0-7391-0105-6)*; pap. 23.95 *(0-7391-0106-4)* Lxngtn Bks.

Morel, M. Y., jt. auth. see Morel, G.

Morel, Mina D. Equine Reproductive Physiology: Breeding & Stud Management. (Illus.). 450p. 1993. text 49.95 *(0-85236-255-2*, Pub. by Farming Pr) Diamond Farm Bk.

Morel, P. Dynamic Meteorology: Lectures Delivered at the Centre Nationole d'Etudes Spatiales, Lannion, France, Aug. 7-Sept. 12, 1970. LC 72-78425. 621p. 1973. text 259.00 *(90-277-0344-2)* Kluwer Academic.

Morel-Seytoux, Hubert J., ed. Unsaturated Flow in Hydrologic Modeling: Theory & Practice. (C). 1989. text 260.00 *(0-7923-0211-7)* Kluwer Academic.

Morel-Seytoux, Hubert J., et al, eds. Modeling Hydrologic Processes. LC 78-68497. 1979. 35.00 *(0-918334-27-6)* WRP.

— Surface & Subsurface Hydrology. LC 78-68496. 1979. 35.00 *(0-918334-28-4)* WRP.

Morel, T. & Miller, J., eds. Aerodynamics of Transportation II. 89p. 1983. pap. text 24.00 *(0-317-03525-8*, H00282) ASME.

Morel, Thomas, ed. see Fluids Engineering Conference Staff.

Morelan, Bill. How to Stay Married for Life. (100 Hints Ser.). 160p. 1996. pap. 5.99 *(1-57757-003-0)* Honor Bks OK.

Morelan, Lyn, jt. auth. see Adams, David L.

Moreland & Reynolds. Three Views on Creation & Evolution. LC 98-33239. 1999. pap. 17.99 *(0-310-22017-3)* Zondervan.

Moreland, A. Dickens Landmarks in London. LC 72-6291. (Studies in Dickens: No. 52). (Illus.). 1972. reprint ed. lib. bdg. 75.00 *(0-8383-1625-5)* M S G Haskell Hse.

***Moreland, Betty D.** Dear Principal: A Behind-the-Scenes Peek at Humor in the Schoolhouse. viii, 62p. 1999. pap. 10.00 *(0-9676636-0-1)* B D Moreland.

Moreland, Carl & Bannister, David. Antique Maps. 3rd ed. (Illus.). 314p. (C). 1993. reprint ed. pap. 24.95 *(0-7148-2954-4*, Pub. by Phaidon Press) Phaidon Pr.

Moreland, Daniel, ed. see Hedges, Stoy.

Moreland, Donald E., et al, eds. Biochemical Responses Induced by Herbicides. LC 81-20645. (ACS Symposium Ser.: No. 181). 274p. 1982. 43.95 *(0-8412-0699-6)* Am Chemical.

— Biochemical Responses Induced by Herbicides. LC 81-20645. (ACS Symposium Ser.: Vol. 181). 285p. 1982. reprint ed. pap. 88.40 *(0-608-03106-2*, 206355900007) Bks Demand.

Moreland, Flloyd L., jt. auth. see Fleischer, Rita M.

Moreland, J. P., ed. The Creation Hypothesis: Scientific Evidence for an Intelligent Designer. LC 93-42724. 335p. (Orig.). 1994. pap. 13.99 *(0-8308-1698-4*, 1698) InterVarsity.

Moreland, J. P. & Geisler, Norman L. The Life & Death Debate: Moral Issues of Our Time. LC 90-37862. 192p. 1990. pap. 19.95 *(0-275-93702-X*, B3702, Praeger Pubs) Greenwood.

— The Life & Death Debate: Moral Issues of Our Time, 43. LC 90-37842. (Contributions in Philosophy Ser.: No. 43). 192p. 1990. 55.00 *(0-313-27556-4*, MOO/, Greenwood Pr) Greenwood.

An Asterisk (*) at the beginning of an entry indicates that the title is appearing for the first time.

Moreland, J. P. & Nielsen, Kai. Does God Exist? The Debate Between Theists & Atheists. LC 92-41375. 320p. (C). 1993. reprint ed. pap. 18.95 (*0-87975-823-6*) Prometheus Bks.

Moreland, J. P., jt. ed. see Wilkins, Michael J.

Moreland, James P. Love Your God with All Your Mind: The Role of Reason in the Life of the Soul. LC 97-2300. 249p. (Orig.). 1997. pap. 14.00 (*1-57683-016-0*) NavPress.

***Moreland, James P. & Rae, Scott B.** Body & Soul: Human Nature & the Crisis in Ethics. LC 99-86858. 350p. 2000. pap. 22.99 (*0-8308-1577-5*) InterVarsity.

Moreland, James P., jt. auth. see Craig, William L.

Moreland, James P., jt. auth. see Habermas, Gary R.

Moreland, Jennifer. The Renaissance, A. D. 1300-1600. (Learning Packets - History Ser.). (Illus.). 64p. (J). (gr. 1-8). 1992. ring bd. 18.00 (*0-913705-28-4*) Zephyr Pr AZ.

***Moreland, John.** Chelsea Gold: Award-Winning Gardens from the Chelsea Flower Show. 2000. 45.00 (*0-304-35431-7*, Pub. by Cassell) Sterling.

Moreland, Jonathan. Profit from Legal Insider Trading: Invest Today on Tomorrow's News. 224p. 2000. pap. 18.95 (*0-7931-2723-8*) Dearborn.

Moreland, Kim. The Medievalist Impulse in American Literature: Twain, Adams, Fitzgerald, & Hemingway. 320p. (C). 1996. text 42.50 (*0-8139-1658-5*) U Pr of Va.

Moreland, Laurence W., et al, eds. Blacks in Southern Politics. LC 87-15844. 312p. 1987. 69.50 (*0-275-92655-9*, C2655, Praeger Pubs) Greenwood.

— Contemporary Southern Political Attitudes & Behavior: Studies & Essays. LC 81-15694. 296p. 1982. 55.00 (*0-275-90864-X*, C0864, Praeger Pubs) Greenwood.

Moreland, Laurence W. & Steed, Robert P., eds. The 1996 Presidential Election in the South: Southern Party Systems in the 1990s. LC 97-19236. 264p. 1997. 59.95 (*0-275-95951-1*, Praeger Pubs) Greenwood.

Moreland, Laurence W., et al. 1988 Presidential Election in the South: Continuity Amidst Change in Southern Party Politics. LC 90-23761. 320p. 1991. 65.00 (*0-275-93145-5*, C3145, Praeger Pubs) Greenwood.

Moreland, Laurence W., ed. see Steed, Robert P.

Moreland, Lisa A., jt. auth. see Kaplan, Laura G.

Moreland, Marian H. & Moreland, Richard. Instant Christmas Pageant: The Not-So-Silent Night. Hawley, Jim, ed. LC 98-11937. (Illus.). 48p. (J). 1998. pap. 24.99 (*0-7644-2070-4*, Vital Ministry) Group Pub.

***Moreland, Marian H. & Moreland, Richard.** Instant Christmas Pageant: Wee Three Kings. 48p. 1999. pap. 24.99 incl. audio compact disk (*0-7644-2149-2*) Group Pub.

Moreland, Marylee M., jt. auth. see Temple, Gary L.

Moreland, Nancy, et al. Allied Health Reading Vocabulary Workbook. 2nd ed. 120p. 1994. pap. text, wbk. ed. 12.95 (*0-89641-225-3*) American Pr.

Moreland, Neil, jt. auth. see Birley, Graham.

***Moreland, Peggy.** Amor un Irresistible.Tr. of Irresistible Love. (SPA.). 2000. per. 3.50 (*0-373-35330-8*) Harlequin Bks.

Moreland, Peggy. Antiguos Amantes: The Rancher's Spittin' Image. (Deseo Ser.: No. 176).Tr. of Old Lovers. (SPA.). 1999. per. 3.50 (*0-373-35306-5*, 1-35306-9) Harlequin Bks.

— The Baby Doctor. (Desire Ser.). 1994. per. 2.99 (*0-373-05867-5*, 1-05867-6) Silhouette.

— Billionaire Bridegroom: Texas Cattleman's Club. (Desire Ser.: No. 1244). 1999. per. 3.75 (*0-373-76244-5*, 1-76244-2) Silhouette.

***Moreland, Peggy.** Groom of Fortune. 2001. mass mkt. 3.99 (*0-373-76336-0*) Silhouette.

— Hard Lovin' Man: (Texas Brides) (Desire Ser.: No. 1270). 2000. mass mkt. 4.25 (*0-373-76270-4*, 1-76270-7) Harlequin Bks.

— In Name Only. (Desire Ser.). 2000. mass mkt. 3.99 (*0-373-76313-1*, 1-76313-5) Silhouette.

Moreland, Peggy. A Little Texas Two-Step. 1997. per. 3.50 (*0-373-76090-6*, 1-76090-9) Silhouette.

— Lone Star Kind of Man. 1997. per. 3.50 (*0-373-76096-5*, 1-76096-6) Silhouette.

— Marry Me, Cowboy! (Desire Ser.: No. 1084). 1997. per. 3.50 (*0-373-76084-1*, 1-76084-2) Silhouette.

— Miss Lizzy's Legacy. (Desire Ser.). 1995. per. 3.25 (*0-373-05921-3*, 1-05921-1) Silhouette.

— The Rancher's Spittin' Image. (Desire Ser.). 1998. per. 3.75 (*0-373-76156-2*, 1-76156-8) Silhouette.

— The Restless Virgin. (Desire Ser.). 1998. per. 3.75 (*0-373-76163-5*, 1-76163-4) Silhouette.

***Moreland, Peggy.** Ride a Wild Heart. (Desire Ser.: Bk. 1306). 2000. mass mkt. 3.99 (*0-373-76306-9*, 1-76306-9) Silhouette.

Moreland, Peggy. Rugrats & Rawhide. 1997. per. 3.99 (*0-373-24084-8*, 1-24084-5) Silhouette.

— Seven Year Itch. (Desire Ser.). 1994. per. 2.99 (*0-373-05837-3*, 5-05837-5) Silhouette.

***Moreland, Peggy.** Slow Waltz Across Texas. (Desire Ser.: Vol. 1315). 2000. mass mkt. 3.99 (*0-373-76315-8*, 1-76315-0) Harlequin Bks.

Moreland, Peggy. A Sparkle in the Cowboy's Eyes. (Desire Ser.). 1998. per. 3.75 (*0-373-76168-6*, 1-76168-3) Silhouette.

— That McCloud Woman: Texas Brides. (Desire Ser.: Bk. 1227). 1999. per. 3.75 (*0-373-76227-5*, 1-76227-7) Silhouette.

— A Willful Marriage. (Desire Ser.). 1996. per. 3.50 (*0-373-76024-8*, 1-76024-8) Silhouette.

Moreland, R. S., ed. Regulation of Smooth Muscle Contraction. (Advances in Experimental Medicine & Biology Ser.: Vol. 304). (Illus.). 576p. (C). 1991. text 180.00 (*0-306-44041-5*, Kluwer Plenum) Kluwer Academic.

Moreland, Richard, jt. auth. see Moreland, Marian H.

Moreland, Richard C. Faulkner & Modernism: Revision & Rewriting. LC 90-12049. 270p. (Orig.). (C). 1990. pap. text 15.95 (*0-299-12504-1*) U of Wis Pr.

***Moreland, Richard C.** Learning from Difference: Teaching Morrison, Twain, Ellison, & Eliot. LC 99-18510. 192p. 1999. text 40.00 (*0-8142-0823-1*) Ohio St U Pr.

Moreland, Richard C. Learning from Difference: Teaching Morrison, Twain, Ellison & Eliot. LC 99-18510. 192p. 1999. pap. text 17.00 (*0-8142-5025-4*) Ohio St U Pr.

Moreland, William. India at the Death of Akbar: An Economic Study. (C). 1990. reprint ed. 12.50 (*81-85395-82-9*, Pub. by BR Pub) S Asia.

Moreland, William H. The Agrarian System of Moslem India. 314p. reprint ed. text 27.50 (*0-685-13416-4*) Coronet Bks.

— From Akbar to Aurangzeb: A Study in Indian Economic History. (C). 1990. 12.75 (*81-85395-83-7*, Pub. by BR Pub) S Asia.

— From Akbar to Aurangzeb: A Study in Indian Economic History. LC 77-180363. reprint ed. 47.50 (*0-404-56298-1*) AMS Pr.

— From Akbar to Aurangzeb: A Study in Indian Economic History. 372p. reprint ed. text 28.50 (*0-685-13417-2*) Coronet Bks.

— India at the Death of Akbar: An Economic Study. 339p. reprint ed. text 34.00 (*0-685-13418-0*) Coronet Bks.

Moreland, Willis D. & Goldenstein, Erwin H. Pioneers in Adult Education. (Illus.). 280p. 1985. text 38.95 (*0-8304-1082-1*) Burnham Inc.

Morelet, M., jt. auth. see Kiffer, E.

Morell, A., et al. IgG-Subklassen der Menschlichen Immunglobuline: Immunochemische Genetische, Biologische und Klinische Aspekte. (Illus.). 88p. 1975. pap. 25.25 (*3-8055-2153-7*) S Karger.

Morell, A., jt. auth. see Nydegger, U. E.

Morell, Bernard B., jt. auth. see Bittinger, Marvin L.

Morell, Carolyn M. Unwomanly Conduct: The Challenges of Intentional Childlessness. LC 93-45984. 240p. (C). 1994. pap. 18.99 (*0-415-90678-4*) Routledge.

Morell, H. Victorian Wooden Molding & Frame Designs: The 1887 Morell Catalog. 4th ed. (Illus.). 208p. 1991. reprint ed. pap. 13.95 (*0-486-26932-9*) Dover.

Morell, Hortensia R. Composicion Expresionista en "El Lugar sin Limites" de Jose Donoso. LC 85-1144. (UPREX, Estudios Literarios Ser.: No. 76). 122p. 1986. pap. 4.00 (*0-8477-0076-3*) U of PR Pr.

Morell, J. R. Algeria. 512p. 1984. 220.00 (*1-85077-017-4*, Pub. by Darf Pubs Ltd) St Mut.

Morell, Jane. Crime in Heaven. large type ed. (Large Print Ser.). 384p. 1997. 27.99 (*0-7089-3707-1*) Ulverscroft.

— The Score. large type ed. (Linford Romance Large Print Ser.). 352p. 1996. pap. 16.99 (*0-7089-7971-8*) Ulverscroft.

Morell, Jane. Sidewinder. large type ed. 352p. pap. 18.99 (*0-7089-5423-5*) Ulverscroft.

Morell, Jonathan A., jt. ed. see Hermalin, Jared A.

Morell, Martin, tr. see Yakubaitis, Eduard A.

Morell, Pierre, ed. Myelin. 2nd ed. LC 84-9975. (Illus.). 566p. (C). 1984. text 132.00 (*0-306-41540-2*, Kluwer Plenum) Kluwer Academic.

Morell, Robert C. & Eichhorn, John H. Patient Safety in Anesthetic Practice. LC 96-30949. 1996. text 69.00 (*0-443-07682-0*) Church.

Morell, Sarah K. Ivy Covered Towers. (Illus.). 70p. 1998. pap. 6.95 (*1-57502-684-8*, P01932) Morris Pubng.

Morell, Virginia. Ancestral Passions: The Leakey Family & the Quest for Humankind's Beginnings. (Illus.). 639p. 1995. 30.00 (*0-684-80192-2*) S&S Trade.

— Ancestral Passions: The Leakey Family & the Quest for Humankind's Beginnings. (Illus.). 624p. 1996. per. 16.00 (*0-684-82470-1*, Touchstone) S&S Trade Pap.

Morella, Constance, ed. Patent System & Modern Technology Needs: Meeting the Challenge of the 21st Century: Hearing Before the Committee on Science, U. S. House of Representatives. 54p. (C). 1998. reprint ed. text 25.00 (*0-7881-7068-6*) DIANE Pub.

Morella, Constance & Horn, Stephen, eds. Year 2000 Risks: What Are the Consequences of Information Technology Failure? 67p. (C). 1999. reprint ed. pap. text 20.00 (*0-7881-7851-2*) DIANE Pub.

Morella, Constance A., ed. The Global Dimensions of the Millennium Bug. (Illus.). 117p. 1999. reprint ed. pap. text 25.00 (*0-7881-8044-4*) DIANE Pub.

***Morella, Constance A., ed.** Technology in the Classroom: Panacea or Pandora's Box? - Congressional Hearings. 108p. (C). 1999. reprint ed. pap. text 25.00 (*0-7881-8319-2*) DIANE Pub.

Morella, Constance A. & Horn, Stephen, eds. Will Federal Government Computers Be Ready for the Year 2000? 106p. 1999. reprint ed. pap. text 25.00 (*0-7881-8043-6*) DIANE Pub.

Morella, Joe & Barey, Patricia. Simon & Garfunkel: Old Friends a Dual Biography. (Illus.). 256p. 1991. 19.95 (*1-55972-089-1*, Birch Ln Pr) Carol Pub Group.

Morella, Joe & Epstein, Edward Z. The Complete Films of Judy Garland. (Illus.). 204p. 1986. reprint ed. pap. 14.95 (*0-8065-1017-X*, Citadel Pr) Carol Pub Group.

Morella, Joe, et al. The Amazing Careers of Bob Hope. (Illus.). 1978. pap. 5.95 (*0-89508-000-1*) Rainbow Bks.

***Morellec, Frederic, photos by.** Asian Style. (Illus.). 144p. 2000. text 30.00 (*2-08-013680-1*, Pub. by Flammarion) Abbeville Pr.

Morellet, Andre. Prospectus d'un Nouveau Dictionnaire de Commerce. (Economistes Francais du XVIIIe Siecle Ser.). 1990. reprint ed. pap. 44.00 (*0-8115-3802-8*) Periodicals Srv.

Morelli, C., ed. see Kappelmeyer, O. & Haenel, Ralph.

Morelli, C. D. Basic Principles of Water Treatment. 272p. 1996. 60.00 (*0-927188-05-8*) Tall Oaks Pub.

Morelli, Claudia A. Reflections. 1998. pap. write for info. (*1-57553-774-5*) Watermrk Pr.

Morelli, Elizabeth, et al. After the Stork: Owner's Manual for the 1997 Model Year Baby. Stiles, Bink, ed. (Illus.). 240p. (Orig.). 1997. pap. 19.95 (*0-9658297-0-7*) Bink Productions.

— After the Stork: Owner's Manual for the 1998 Model Year Baby. Stiles, Bink, ed. (Illus.). 240p. 1997. pap. 19.95 (*0-9658297-1-5*) Bink Productions.

Morelli, Elizabeth A., ed. see Lonergan, Bernard J. F.

Morelli, Elizabeth A., jt. ed. see Morelli, Mark D.

Morelli, John. Voluntary Environmental Management: The Inevitable Future. LC 98-47480. 1999. 49.95 (*1-56670-344-1*, L1344) Lewis Pubs.

Morelli, M. Computers & Electronics Dictionary: Dizionario di Informatica e Degli Elaboratori Elettronici. 3rd ed. (ENG & ITA.). 231p. 1982. pap. 24.95 (*0-8288-0904-6*, M7821) Fr & Eur.

***Morelli, Marcello.** Royal Palaces. LC 99-38286. 1999. write for info. (*1-57145-219-2*) Advantage Pubs.

Morelli, Mark D. & Morelli, Elizabeth A., eds. The Lonergan Reader. (Lonergan Studies). 400p. 1996. pap. text 24.95 (*0-8020-7648-3*) U of Toronto Pr.

— The Lonergan Reader. (Longergan Studies). 624p. 1997. text 75.00 (*0-8020-4251-1*) U of Toronto Pr.

Morelli, Mark D., ed. see Lonergan, Bernard J. F.

Morelli, Patricia L., compiled by. United States Department of Agriculture Pomological Watercolor Collection Index. 211p. 1987. write for info. (*0-85964-206-2*) Chadwyck-Healey.

***Morelli, Ralph.** Java, Java, Java! Object-Oriented Problem Solving. LC 99-35621. 964p. 1999. pap. text 60.00 incl. cd-rom, audio compact disk (*0-13-011332-8*) P-H.

Morelli, Susan. Mrs. Funnywinkle. Weinberger, Jane, ed. LC 93-61196. (Illus.). 54p. (J). (ps-4). 1994. pap. 5.95 (*0-932433-62-6*) Windswept Hse.

Morelli, Ugo, ed. Handbook for the Seismic Evaluation of Buildings: A Prestandard, 1998. (Illus.). 360p. (C). 1999. pap. text 40.00 (*0-7881-7679-X*) DIANE Pub.

***Morelli, Ugo, ed.** Seismic Rehabilitation of Buildings: Strategic Plan 2005. (Illus.). 161p. (C). 1999. pap. text 35.00 (*0-7881-8381-8*) DIANE Pub.

Morelli, Val M. The Gates. (Renee Romance Ser.). 209p. 1993. pap. 5.95 (*0-9637810-0-6*) Not Aver Mind.

— Racing to the Moon. Spoon, ed. (Renee Romance Ser.). 266p. (Orig.). pap. 5.95 (*0-9637810-1-4*) Not Aver Mind.

Morello. Labman Microbiology Appl. Patient. 5th ed. 1997. 30.00 (*0-07-289071-1*) McGraw.

— Microbio Pat Care W/lm-wb&mm P. 6th ed. 1998. 89.50 (*0-07-228988-0*) McGraw.

— Microbiology in the Patient. 5th ed. 1994. 12.81 (*0-697-25097-0*, WCB McGr Hill) McGraw-H Hghr Educ.

Morello. Surgery of the Peripheral Nerves. (Illus.). 392p. 1988. text 275.00 (*88-299-0231-4*, Pub. by Piccin Nuova) Gordon & Breach.

Morello, et al. Microbiology: Applications to Patient Care. 6th ed. 1997. pap., wbk. ed., lab manual ed. 34.00 (*0-697-25766-5*, WCB McGr Hill) McGraw-H Hghr Educ.

***Morello, Celeste A.** The Philadelphia Italian Market Cookbook: The Tastes of South Ninth Street. LC 99-96482. (Illus.). 140p. 1999. pap. 24.95 (*0-9677334-0-5*) J & M.

Morello, G. & Pluchino, F. Surgery of Peripheral Nerves. (Surgical Technique Ser.: Vol. XIV). 392p. 1988. text 250.00 (*1-57235-043-1*) Piccin Nuova.

Morello, J. Master Studies: Drum. 96p. 1986. pap. 12.95 (*0-88188-748-X*, 06631474) H Leonard.

Morello, Josephine A., et al. Microbiology in Patient Care. 5th ed. 592p. (C). 1993. text, student ed. write for info. (*0-697-13784-8*, WCB McGr Hill) McGraw-H Hghr Educ.

— Microbiology in Patient Care. 6th ed. LC 97-14452. 576p. (C). 1997. text. write for info. (*0-697-25763-0*, WCB McGr Hill) McGraw-H Hghr Educ.

— Microbiology in Patient Care: Microbes in Motion. 5th ed. (C). 1995. text, student ed. write for info. (*0-697-34041-4*, WCB McGr Hill) McGraw-H Hghr Educ.

Morello, Michael J., jt. ed. see Mussinan, Cynthia J.

Morello, Sam Anthony. Lectio Divina: And the Practice of Tersian Prayer. LC 94-28368. (Pamphlet on American Writers Ser.). 32p. 1995. pap. 3.50 (*0-935216-24-3*) ICS Pubns.

Morelock, J. D. The Army Times Book of Great Land Battles: From the Civil War to the Gulf War. Boyne, Walter J., ed. LC 94-8373. 352p. 1994. pap. 29.95 (*0-425-14371-6*) Berkley Pub.

— Generals of the Ardennes: American Leadership in the Battle of the Bulge. 452p. 1994. per. 25.00 (*0-16-042069-5*) USGPO.

Morelock, J. D. & Boyne, Walter J., eds. The Army Times Book of Great Land Battles: From the Civil War to the Gulf War. 352p. 1999. reprint ed. pap. 15.95 (*0-425-16531-0*) Berkley Pub.

Morelock, Jack & Hubbard, Dennis K. Geological Oceanography. 576p. (C). 2002. 60.00 (*0-02-383532-X*, Macmillan Coll) P-H.

Morelos, Noel. Proceso de Produccion de Espacios y Estructuras en Teotihuacan. 285p. 1993. pap. 21.00 (*968-29-5105-4*, IN033) UPLAAP.

Morely, jt. auth. see Andrews.

***Morem, Bill.** The Art & Design of Dale J. Evers. (Illus.). 144p. 1999. 49.99 (*0-9676412-0-9*) ADDI Pubng CA.

Morem, Susan. How to Gain the Professional Edge: Achieve the Personal & Professional Image You Want. LC 96-79567. 177p. (Orig.). 1997. pap. 14.95 (*1-886656-04-5*) Better Books.

Moremen, John S., ed. Our Brothers' War. 152p. 1993. pap. 14.95 (*0-9624086-5-4*) Sulgrave Pr.

Moremen, John S., ed. see Smock, Frederick.

Moren, F., et al, eds. Aerosols in Medicine: Principles, Diagnosis, & Therapy. 2nd ed. LC 93-36576. 450p. 1993. 227.25 (*0-444-81332-2*) Elsevier.

Moren, Mary M. Wildflowers in a Kudzu World: Tales from a High School Guidance Office. LC 97-60033. (Illus.). 72p. 1997. pap. 7.95 (*0-932796-78-8*) Ed Media Corp.

***Morena, Gita.** The Wisdom of Oz. 235p. 2001. pap. 15.95 (*1-58394-036-7*) Frog Ltd CA.

Morena, Gita. The Wisdom of Oz. (Illus.). 225p. 1998. pap. 15.95 (*0-9663950-0-X*) Inner Connectns Pr.

Morena, John J. Advanced Composite Mold Making. LC 92-42441. 446p. (C). 1994. reprint ed. lib. bdg. 67.50 (*0-89464-825-X*) Krieger.

— Advanced Composites World Reference Dictionary. LC 96-49072. (Illus.). 100p. (C). 1997. 18.50 (*0-89464-991-4*) Krieger.

Morena, Miguel A. The Artistic History of Carlos Gardel: A Chronological Study with Filmography & Discography. (Latin American Music Ser.). 1980. lib. bdg. 75.00 (*0-8490-3059-5*) Gordon Pr.

Morena Torres, Felipa. Lexikon der Spanischen Redewendungen: Expresiones Idiomaticas, (GER & SPA.). 312p. 1990. 29.95 (*0-7859-8564-6*, 3927117498) Fr & Eur.

Morenberg. The Writer's Options: Lessons in Style & Arrangement. 6th ed. LC 98-22689. 250p. (C). 1998. pap. text 31.20 (*0-321-01585-1*) Addson-Wesley Educ.

***Morenberg & Sommers.** The Writer's Options: Lessons in Style & Arrangement. 6th ed. 104p. 1998. 12.00 (*0-321-40654-0*) Addson-Wesley Educ.

Morenberg, Max. Answer Key for Doing Grammar. 2nd ed. 72p. 1997. pap. text. write for info. (*0-19-511757-3*) OUP.

Morenberg, Max. Doing Grammar. 2nd ed. LC 96-26020. (Illus.). 288p. (C). 1997. pap. text 25.95 (*0-19-509783-1*) OUP.

Morenberg, Max, jt. ed. see Daiker, Donald A.

***Moreno, Alejandro.** Political Cleavages: Issues, Parties & the Consolidation of Democracy. LC 99-30615. 224p. 1999. text 65.00 (*0-8133-3550-7*) Westview.

Moreno, Antonio. Jung, Gods, & Modern Man. LC 73-122047. 288p. reprint ed. pap. 89.30 (*0-608-14234-4*, 202207300024) Bks Demand.

Moreno Baez, Enrique, ed. see De Montemayor, Jorge.

Moreno, Barry. Who Was Who at Ellis Island: A Survey. (Illus.). 150p. (Orig.). 1995. pap. 17.95 (*0-9646079-0-5*) Bellona Pr.

Moreno-Cabral, Carlos, et al. Manual of Postoperative Management in Adult Cardiac Surgery. (Illus.). 112p. 1988. pap. 29.00 (*0-683-06146-1*) Lppncott W & W.

Moreno, Carlos. Algebraic Curves over Finite Fields: Error-Correcting Codes & Exponential Sums. (Tracts in Mathematics Ser.: No. 97). 256p. (C). 1994. pap. text 30.95 (*0-521-45901-X*) Cambridge U Pr.

— Letter to Christopher Columbus: And Other Poems. 64p. (Orig.). 1993. pap. 4.95 (*1-880365-55-3*) Prof Pr NC.

Moreno, Carlos J. Advanced Analytic Number Theory Pt. 1: Ramification Theoretic Methods. LC 82-22620. (Contemporary Mathematics Ser.: No. 5). 190p. 1983. pap. 27.00 (*0-8218-5015-6*, CONM/15) Am Math.

— Advanced Analytic Number Theory Pt. 1: Ramification Theoretic Methods. LC 82-22620. (Contemporary Mathematics Ser.: No. 15). 199p. 1983. reprint ed. pap. 61.70 (*0-608-07819-0*, 205266400001) Bks Demand.

Moreno, Carlos Martinez, see Martinez Moreno, Carlos.

Moreno, Carmen, tr. see Gruber, Wilhelm.

Moreno, Dario. The Struggle for Peace in Central America. LC 93-36885. 264p. (C). 1994. 49.95 (*0-8130-1274-0*); pap. 19.95 (*0-8130-1275-9*) U Press Fla.

— U. S. Policy in Central America: The Endless Debate. 208p. (C). 1990. 49.95 (*0-8130-1005-5*); pap. 19.95 (*0-8130-1020-9*) U Press Fla.

Moreno de Alba, J. Algunas Minucias del Lenguaje. (Fondo 2000 Ser.). (SPA.). 1990. pap. 2.99 (*968-16-5058-1*, Pub. by Fondo) Continental Bk.

Moreno de Alba, Jose G. El Espanol en America (Spanish in America) 2nd ed. (SPA.). 248p. 1993. 17.99 (*968-16-4091-8*, Pub. by Fondo) Continental Bk.

— Minucias del Lenguaje (Details of the Language) (SPA.). 560p. 1992. pap. 19.99 (*968-16-3718-6*, Pub. by Fondo) Continental Bk.

Moreno De Alba, Jose G. Nuevas Minucias del Lenguaje (New Details of the Language) (SPA.). 435p. 1996. 30.99 (*968-16-4856-0*, Pub. by Fondo) Continental Bk.

Moreno-Duran, R. H. Finale Capriccoso con Madonna. (SPA.). 322p. 1983. pap. 9.00 (*84-85859-63-4*, 2017) Ediciones Norte.

— El Toque de Diana. (SPA.). 269p. 1981. pap. 8.50 (*84-85859-06-5*, 2009) Ediciones Norte.

Moreno, Elena. La Leyenda del Castillo, Level 1. (Leer en Espanol Ser.). (SPA.). (C). 1998. pap. 5.95 (*84-294-4044-5*) Santillana.

— El Misterio de la Llave, Level 1. (Leer en Espanol Ser.). (SPA.). (C). 1998. pap. 5.95 (*84-294-4040-2*) Santillana.

Moreno, Elena M. Hotels: International Design Portfolios. (Illus.). 216p. 1998. 44.99 (*1-56496-412-4*) Rockport Pubs.

Moreno, Enrique. Expanded Tunings in Contemporary Music: Theoretical Innovations & Practical Applications. LC 90-6025. (Studies in History & Interpretation of Music: Vol. 30). 156p. 1992. lib. bdg. 69.95 (*0-88946-485-5*) E Mellen.

Moreno, Fernando J., ed. see Universidad de Cantabria Staff, et al.

Moreno, Francisco J. Basic Principles of Politics. LC 97-78461. 250p. 1999. pap. 13.95 (*0-88739-209-1*) Creat Arts Bk.

— Between Faith & Reason. rev. ed. LC 97-41233. 128p. (C). 1997. pap. 20.95 (*0-7618-0952-X*) U Pr of Amer.

An Asterisk (*) at the beginning of an entry indicates that the title is appearing for the first time.

Moreno, G., et al. La Guia de Incafo de los Hongos de la Peninsula Iberica, 2 vols. (SPA., Illus.). 1276p. 1986. lib. bdg. 92.50 (*84-85389-44-1*) Lubrecht & Cramer.

Moreno, J. L. The Classics of Sociometry, Set Vols. XI-XVIII. pap. 110.00 (*0-685-22537-2*) Beacon Hse.

— Group Psychotherapy: A Symposium. pap. 16.00 (*0-685-06813-7*) Beacon Hse.

— Preludes to My Autobiography. 8.00 (*0-685-52594-5*) Beacon Hse.

— Psychodrama, 3 vols. Incl. Vol. 1. Collected Papers. pap. 20.00 Vol. 2. Foundations of Psychotherapy. 20.00 Vol. 3. Action-Therapy & Principles of Practice. 20.00 Vol. 3. Action-Therapy & Principles of Practice. pap. 19.00 write for info. (*0-318-51037-5*) Beacon Hse.

— Psychodrama & Sociodrama in American Education. 14.00 (*0-685-22536-4*) Beacon Hse.

— Sociometry, Experimental Method & the Science of Society. 16.00 (*0-685-06814-5*) Beacon Hse.

— Words of the Father. pap. 6.00 (*0-685-06818-8*) Beacon Hse.

Moreno, J. L., ed. Theater of Spontaneity. 3rd ed. 1983. pap. 15.00 (*0-685-42742-0*) Beacon Hse.

Moreno, J. M. Large Forest Fires. (Illus.). viii, 237p. 1998. pap. 69.50 (*90-73348-80-3*) Balogh.

Moreno, Jaime, ed. Analysis & Design of High-Rise Concrete Buildings. LC 86-72232. (American Concrete Institute Publication: No. SP-97). 336p. 1985. reprint ed. pap. 104.20 (*0-608-01429-X*, 206219100002) Bks Demand.

Moreno, Jaime H. & Lang, Tomas. Matrix Computations on Systolic-Type Arrays. LC 92-9868. (Kluwer International Series in Engineering & Computer Science: No. SECS 174). 320p. (C). 1992. text 139.50 (*0-7923-9237-X*) Kluwer Academic.

Moreno, Joanna, jt. auth. see Spitz, Karlheinz.

Moreno, Jonathan D. Deciding Together: Bioethics & Moral Consensus. (Illus.). 192p. 1995. text 29.95 (*0-19-509218-X*) OUP.

***Moreno, Jonathan D.** Undue Risk: Secret State Experiments on Humans. 368p. 2000. pap. text 17.95 (*0-415-92814-1*) Routledge.

— Undue Risk: Secret State Experiments on Humans. 2000. reprint ed. pap. 17.95 (*0-415-92835-4*) Routledge.

Moreno, Jonathan D., ed. Paying the Doctor: Health Policy & Physician Reimbursement. LC 90-37837. 208p. 1990. 52.95 (*0-86569-006-5*, T006, Auburn Hse) Greenwood.

Moreno, Jonathan D. & Glassner, Barry. Discourse in the Social Sciences: Strategies for Translating Models of Mental Illness, 40. LC 81-7092. (Contributions in Sociology Ser.: No. 40). (Illus.). 160p. 1981. 59.95 (*0-313-23159-1*, GLM/) Greenwood.

Moreno-Jones, Angelita. Outside the Box: An Unusual Guide for Business Owners. large type ed. (Orig.). 1997. pap. 14.95 (*0-9637441-5-1*) Kehori.

Moreno, Jorge, jt. auth. see Patino, Manny.

Moreno, Jose, tr. see Pfister, Marcus.

Moreno, Jose, tr. see Tripp, Valerie.

Moreno, Jose A. Barrios in Arms: Revolution in Santo Domingo. LC 68-12723. 240p. reprint ed. pap. 74.40 (*0-8357-5970-9*, 203190200077) Bks Demand.

Moreno, Jose F., ed. The Elusive Quest for Equality: 150 Years of Chicano/Chicana Education. LC 98-74040. (Illus.). 280p. 1998. pap. 22.95 (*0-916690-33-4*) Harvard Educ Rev.

Moreno, Jose M. & Oechel, Walter C., eds. The Role of Fire in Mediterranean-Type Ecosystems. LC 93-42622. (Ecological Studies). 1994. 105.00 (*0-387-94215-7*) Spr-Verlag.

***Moreno, Joseph.** Acting Your Inner Music. 1999. pap. 12.95 (*1-58106-012-2*) MMB Music.

***Moreno, Julie.** A New Owner's Guide to Pomeranians. 160p. 2000. 12.95 (*0-7938-2794-9*) TFH Pubns.

Moreno, Leonard. The Life of Jesus Christ, Vol. 1. 108p. (Orig.). 1992. pap. text 7.77 (*0-9631137-7-1*) Morenos Pub.

Moreno, Leonardo. Arqueologia de San Agustin: Pautas de Asentamiento Agustinianas en el Noroccidente de Saladoblanco (Huila) (SPA., Illus.). 144p. 1991. pap. 8.50 (*1-877812-16-1*, BR006) UPLAAP.

Moreno, Leonides. Of Stone & Tears. 1975. 2.00 (*0-912678-19-4*, Greenfld Rev Pr) Greenfld Rev Lit.

Moreno, Leslie B. Companeros: Activity Book in Spanish & English for Children. 144p. (YA). (gr. 7-11). 1983. pap. 5.95 (*0-917168-09-7*) Executive Comm.

Moreno, Luis, tr. see Shigo, Alex L.

***Moreno, M. R.** Siembras de Esperanza. (SPA.). 84p. 1999. write for info. (*92-806-3428-3*) U N I C E.

Moreno, Marco A. Historia de la Astronomia en Mexico. (Ciencia para Todos Ser.). (SPA.). pap. 6.99 (*968-16-4808-0*, Pub. by Fondo) Continental Bk.

— Odisea 1874 o el Primer Viaje Internacional. (Ciencia para Todos Ser.). (SPA.). pap. 6.99 (*968-16-4809-9*, Pub. by Fondo) Continental Bk.

Moreno, Maria L., jt. auth. see Marvel, Thomas.

Moreno, Mary. The Writer's Guide to Corporate Communications. LC 96-79674. 192p. (Orig.). 1997. pap. 18.95 (*1-880559-74-9*) Allworth Pr.

Moreno, Miguel A. How to Think Like a Scientist. 2nd ed. 112p. (C). 1992. 35.60 (*0-536-58173-8*) Pearson Custom.

Moreno, Nancy & Tharp, Barbara. Activities Guide for Teachers: Food & My World. Denk, James, ed. (My Health My World Ser.: Vol. 4). (Illus.). vi, 48p. pap. write for info. (*1-888997-36-2*) Baylor Coll Med.

— Explorations for Children & Adults: Food & My World. Denk, James, ed. (My Health My World Ser.: Vol. 4). (Illus.). 8p. (J). (ps-5). pap. write for info. (*1-888997-38-9*) Baylor Coll Med.

Moreno, Nancy, et al. Activities Guide for Teachers: Memory & Learning. rev. ed. (BrainLink Ser.: Vol. 4). (Illus.). vi, 40p. 1997. pap. write for info. (*1-888997-24-9*) Baylor Coll Med.

— Activities Guide for Teachers: Motor Highways. rev. ed. (BrainLink Ser.: Vol. 2). (Illus.). vi, 40p. 1997. pap. write for info. (*1-888997-22-2*) Baylor Coll Med.

Moreno, Nancy, et al. Activities Guide for Teachers: My Home Planet Earth. (My Health My World Ser.: Vol. 3). (Illus.). vi, 40p. 1998. pap. write for info. (*1-888997-35-4*) Baylor Coll Med.

Moreno, Nancy, et al. Activities Guide for Teachers: Sensory Signals. rev. ed. (BrainLink Ser.: Vol. 3). (Illus.). vi, 40p. 1997. pap. write for info. (*1-888997-23-0*, WOW Pubns) Baylor Coll Med.

Moreno, Nancy, et al. Exploraciones para Ninos y Adultos: Mi Mundo Bajo Techo. rev. ed. (My Health My World Ser.). (Illus.). 8p. (J). (gr. k-5). 1995. pap. write for info. (*1-888997-40-0*) Baylor Coll Med.

— Exploraciones para Ninos y Adultos (Explorations for Children & Adults) Brain Comparisons. rev. ed. (BrainLink Ser.). (SPA., Illus.). 8p. 1997. pap. write for info. (*1-888997-39-7*) Baylor Coll Med.

— Explorations for Children & Adults: Brain Comparisons. rev. ed. (BrainLink Ser.). (Illus.). 8p. 1997. pap. write for info. (*1-888997-25-7*) Baylor Coll Med.

— Explorations for Children & Adults: Memory & Learning. rev. ed. (BrainLink Ser.: Vol. 4). (Illus.). 8p. 1997. pap. write for info. (*1-888997-28-1*) Baylor Coll Med.

— Explorations for Children & Adults: Motor Highways. rev. ed. (BrainLink Ser.: Vol. 2). 8p. 1997. pap. write for info. (*1-888997-26-5*) Baylor Coll Med.

— Explorations for Children & Adults: My Home Planet Earth. rev. ed. (My Health My World Ser.: Vol. 3). (Illus.). 8p. 1997. pap. write for info. (*1-888997-33-8*) Baylor Coll Med.

— Explorations for Children & Adults: My World Indoors. rev. ed. (My Health My World Ser.). (Illus.). 8p. 1997. pap. write for info. (*1-888997-31-1*) Baylor Coll Med.

— Explorations for Children & Adults: Sensory Signals. rev. ed. (Illus.). 8p. 1997. pap. write for info. (*1-888997-27-3*) Baylor Coll Med.

— Explorations for Children & Adults: Water & My World. rev. ed. (My Health My World Ser.: Vol. 2). (Illus.). 8p. 1997. pap. write for info. (*1-888997-32-X*) Baylor Coll Med.

— My World Indoors: Activities Guide for Teachers. rev. ed. (My Health My World Ser.). (Illus.). vi, 48p. 1997. pap. write for info. (*1-888997-11-7*) Baylor Coll Med.

— Mystery of the Muddled Marsh. (My Health My World Ser.: Vol. 2). (Illus.). 36p. (J). (gr. k-5). 1996. write for info. (*1-888997-16-8*) Baylor Coll Med.

— Water & My World: Activities Guide for Teachers. rev. ed. (My Health My World Ser.: Vol. 2). (Illus.). vi, 40p. 1997. pap. write for info. (*1-888997-15-X*) Baylor Coll Med.

Moreno, Nancy P., et al. Sensory Signals. Activities Guide for Teachers. rev. ed. (BrainLink Ser.: Vol. 3). (Illus.). vi, 40p. 1995. pap., teacher ed. write for info. (*1-888997-09-5*) Baylor Coll Med.

Moreno, Paul D. From Direct Action to Affirmative Action: Fair Employment Law & Policy in America, 1933-1972. LC 96-50168. 312p. 1997. text 35.00 (*0-8071-2138-X*) La State U Pr.

***Moreno, Paul D.** From Direct Action to Affirmative Action: Fair Employment Law & Policy in America, 1933-1972. LC 96-50168. 328p. 1999. pap. text 12.95 (*0-8071-2383-8*) La State U Pr.

Moreno, Rich. The Nevada Trivia Book. 2nd rev. ed. LC 98-70069. (Illus.). 220p. 1998. pap. 10.95 (*1-889786-00-4*) Gem Guides Bk.

Moreno, Richard. The Backyard Traveler: Fifty-Four Outings in Northern Nevada. (Illus.). 268p. 1991. pap. 10.95 (*0-9631205-0-6*) Child Mus N Nev.

— The Backyard Traveler Returns: Sixty-Two Outings in Southern, Eastern & Historical Nevada. Mechan, Suzi, ed. (Illus.). 280p. (Orig.). 1992. pap. 10.95 (*0-9631205-1-4*) Child Mus N Nev.

— Food Festival Cookbook: The Great Nevada Food Festival Cookbook. Moore, David, ed. (Illus.). Date not set. pap. 4.95 (*1-890136-04-2*) Nevada Magazine.

— The Great Nevada Cookbook. (Illus.). 32p. 1993. pap. 4.95 (*1-890136-02-6*) Nevada Magazine.

— Great Nevada Day Hikes. 32p. 1996. pap. 4.95 (*1-890136-01-8*) Nevada Magazine.

***Moreno, Richard.** Historical Nevada Magazine: Outstanding Historical Features from the Pages of Nevada Magazine. LC 99-458949. (Illus.). 1998. pap. text 9.95 (*1-890136-06-9*) Nevada Magazine.

Moreno, Richard. Nevada's Living Ghost Towns. (Illus.). 32p. 1994. pap. 4.95 (*1-890136-03-4*) Nevada Magazine.

***Moreno, Richard.** Roadside History of Nevada. (Illus.). 368p. 2000. pap. 18.00 (*0-87842-410-5*) Mountain Pr.

Moreno, Richard, jt. auth. see Prosor, Larry.

Moreno Torres, Felipa. Sinonimos, Lexikon der Spanischen Synonyme. (GER & SPA.). 504p. 1992. 29.95 (*0-7859-8512-3*, 3860470191) Fr & Eur.

Moreno Valley Writers Guild Staff. Lure, Lore & Legends: A History of Northern New Mexico's Moreno Valley. Urban, Jack C., ed. LC 97-66712. (Illus.). 208p. (Orig.). 1997. pap. 12.95 (*0-9643161-7-X*) Columb Pub.

***Moreno, Zerka T., et al.** Psychodrama, Surplus Reality & the Art of Healing. LC 99-45591. 2000. write for info. (*0-415-22320-2*) Routledge.

Morenus, Richard. Crazy-White-Man. 1994. reprint ed. lib. bdg. 32.95 (*1-56849-315-0*) Buccaneer Bks.

Morenz, Siegfried. Egyptian Religion. Keep, Ann E., tr. LC 73-8401. 400p. 1973. text 55.00 (*0-8014-0782-6*) Cornell U Pr.

— Egyptian Religion. Keep, Ann E., tr. LC 73-8401. 400p. 1992. pap. text 19.95 (*0-8014-8029-9*) Cornell U Pr.

Moreo, Patrick J., et al. Front Office Operations & Night Audit Workbook, Vol. 1. (Illus.). 271p. (C). 1996. pap. text, wbk. ed. 49.00 (*0-13-398769-8*) P-H.

Morera, Dario. The Lyre & the Flute: Garcilaso & the Pastoral. (Monografias A Ser.: Vol. LXXXI). 128p. (C). 1982. 51.00 (*0-7293-0114-1*, Pub. by Tamesis Bks Ltd) Boydell & Brewer.

Morera, Esteve. Gramsci's Historicism: A Realist Interpretation. 192p. 1990. 45.00 (*0-685-26317-7*, A3710) Routledge.

Morere, Jean-Louis. Dictionnaire de Sciences Biologiques du College a L'Universite. (FRE.). 320p. 1991. pap. 69.95 (*0-7859-7978-6*, 2729841261) Fr & Eur.

Mores, Deb. Babies First Year. 1994. 20.00 (*0-517-59593-1*) Crown Pub Group.

Moresby, Lily & Beck, Adams. Then Ninth Vibration, & Other Stories. Reginald, R. & Menville, Douglas A., eds. LC 75-46251. (Supernatural & Occult Fiction Ser.). 1976. reprint ed. lib. bdg. 26.95 (*0-405-08111-1*) Ayer.

Moreschi, Robert W. Tort Liability Standards & the Firm's Response to Regulation. LC 90-44983. (Environment: Problems & Solutions Ser.: Vol. 22). 207p. 1990. text 25.00 (*0-8240-9299-6*) Garland.

Moreschini, ed. Apulei Platonici Madaurensis Vol. III: De Philosophia Libri. (LAT.). 1991. 59.50 (*3-519-01058-5*, T1058, Pub. by B G Teubner) U of Mich Pr.

Moreschini, ed. see Boethius, Anicius Manlius Severinus.

Moreschini, C. Poemata Arcana. Sykes, D. A., tr. (Theological Monographs). 310p. 1997. text 95.00 (*0-19-826732-0*) OUP.

Moreso, Josep J. Legal Indeterminacy & Constitutional Interpretation. LC 98-19233. (Law & Philosophy Library). xiii, 200 p. 1998. write for info. (*0-7923-5156-8*) Kluwer Academic.

Moret, Alexandre. The Nile & Egyptian Civilization. (African Studies). reprint ed. 50.00 (*0-938818-99-6*) ECA Assoc.

Moret-Bailly, L., jt. auth. see Laumon, G.

Moret, Bernard. Algorithms from P to NP: Design & Efficiency, Vol. I. 450p. (C). 1991. 46.00 (*0-8053-8008-6*) Benjamin-Cummings.

Moret, Bernard M. The Theory of Computation. LC 97-27356. 464p. (C). 1997. 76.00 (*0-201-25828-5*) Addison-Wesley.

Moret, Brigitte F. The Bear's Christmas. LC 98-11244. (Illus.). 32p. (J). (gr. 1-3). 1998. 15.95 (*1-55858-971-6*, Pub. by North-South Bks NYC); lib. bdg. 15.88 (*1-55858-972-4*, Pub. by North-South Bks NYC) Chronicle Bks.

Moret, P. R., et al, eds. Lactate: Physiologic, Methodologic & Pathologic Approach. (Illus.). 270p. 1980. 42.95 (*0-387-09829-1*) Spr-Verlag.

Moreta, Andes, jt. auth. see Murphy, Merilene M.

Moreto, Augustin. Spite for Spite: El Desden Con el Desden. Matthews, Dakin, tr. (Great Translations for Actors Ser.). 112p. 1995. pap. 11.95 (*1-57525-002-0*) Smith & Kraus.

Moreton, ed. see Robertson, J. D.

Moreton, C. A. Death in Practice. 249p. (C). 1989. 100.00 (*0-7223-2179-1*, Pub. by A H S Ltd) St Mut.

Moreton, C. E. The Townshends & Their World: Gentry, Law, & the Land in Norfolk C. 1450-1551. (Oxford Historical Monographs). (Illus.). 296p. 1992. 79.00 (*0-19-820299-7*) OUP.

***Moreton, Cole.** Hungry for Home: Leaving the Blaskets: A Journey from the Edge of Ireland. LC 00-25591. (Illus.). 288p. 2000. 23.95 (*0-670-89207-6*, Viking) Viking Penguin.

Moreton, Daniel. Animal Babies: A Counting Book. LC 98-18821. (Science Emergent Readers Ser.). (J). 1998. pap. 2.50 (*0-590-76164-1*) Scholastic Inc.

— La Cucaracha Martina: A Caribbean Folktale. LC 97-13631. (Illus.). 40p. (YA). (ps up). 1997. 14.95 (*1-890515-03-5*, Pub. by Turtle Bks) Publishers Group.

***Moreton, Daniel.** La Cucaracha Martina: A Caribbean Folktale. (Illus.). 40p. (YA). (ps up). 1999. pap. 7.95 (*1-890515-17-5*, Pub. by Turtle Bks) Publishers Group.

Moreton, Daniel. La Cucaracha Martina: Un Cuento Folklorico del Caribe. (SPA., Illus.). 40p. (YA). (ps up). 1997. 14.95 (*1-890515-04-3*, Pub. by Turtle Bks) Publishers Group.

***Moreton, Daniel.** La Cucaracha Martina: Un Cuento Folklorico del Caribe. Arisa, Miguel, tr. (SPA., Illus.). 40p. (YA). (ps up). 1999. pap. 7.95 (*1-890515-18-3*, Pub. by Turtle Bks) Publishers Group.

Moreton, Daniel. Day in Japan. LC 98-52726. 1999. pap. 10.01 (*0-439-04571-1*) Scholastic Inc.

***Moreton, Daniel & Berger, Samantha.** It's a Party. LC 98-38322. (Learning Center Emergent Readers Ser.). 1998. pap. 2.50 (*0-439-04587-8*) Scholastic Inc.

Moreton, Daniel & Chanko, Pamela. Snakes & Lizards. annuals LC 98-8008. (Science Emergent Readers Ser.). (J). 1998. 3.25 (*0-590-63900-5*) Scholastic Inc.

Moreton, Daniel, jt. auth. see Berger, Samantha.

Moreton, Daniel, jt. auth. see Canizares, Susan.

Moreton, Daniel, jt. auth. see Chanko, Pamela.

Moreton, Daniel, jt. auth. see Chessen, Betsey.

Moreton, Douglas. After You, Holmes. unabridged ed. Henry, Ian, ed. (Illus.). 140p. 1997. pap. 20.00 (*0-86025-287-6*, Pub. by I Henry Pubns) Empire Pub Srvs.

Moreton, Edwina & Segal, Gerald, eds. Soviet Strategy Toward Western Europe. 304p. (C). 1984. pap. text 19.95 (*0-04-330346-3*) Routledge.

Moreton, Gill, jt. auth. see McNamara, Sylvia.

Moreton, Gill, jt. auth. see McNamara, Sylvie.

Moreton-Macdonald, John R. History of France, 3 vols. LC 76-142245. reprint ed. 210.00 (*0-404-04430-1*) AMS Pr.

Moreton, Peter. Brushless Servomotors: A Practical Handbook. (Illus.). 208p. 2000. text 56.95 (*0-7506-3931-8*, Newnes) Buttrwrth-Heinemann.

Moreton, Pierre. MVP-FORTH File Management System. Haydon, Glen B., ed. (MVP-Forth Bks.: Vol. 5). 278p. (Orig.). 1984. pap. 30.00 (*0-317-56529-X*) Mntn View Pr.

Moreton, Robert & Chester, Myrvin. Transforming the Business: The IT Contribution. LC 96-27235. (Information Systems Ser.). 1996. pap. write for info. (*0-07-709243-0*) McGraw.

Moreton-Smith, K. E. Prediction of Temperature Gradients in Large Buildings. 1992. pap. 60.00 (*0-86022-330-2*, Pub. by Build Servs Info Assn) St Mut.

Moreton, T. Hugh. The Temple in History & Prophecy. 40p. (Orig.). 1992. pap. 2.50 (*1-879366-37-1*) Hearthstone OK.

Moreton, William. The Crown of Shakes. 160p. 1998. pap. write for info. (*0-7392-0021-6*, PO2775) Morris Pubng.

Moretta. American Promise. 1998. pap. text, student ed. 4.95 (*0-312-18248-1*) St Martin.

***Moretta, John.** William Pitt Ballinger: Texas Lawyer, Southern Statesman, 1825-1888. (Illus.). 2000. write for info. (*0-87611-177-0*) Tex St Hist Assn.

Moretta, John & Wilcox, David. Making the Most of "The American Promise" A Study Guide, Vol. I. 1998. pap. text, student ed. 23.95 (*0-312-11198-3*) St Martin.

— Testbank to Accompany "The American Promise" 1998. pap. text 13.33 (*0-312-17923-5*) St Martin.

Moretta, L., ed. Molecular Basis of NK Cell Recognition & Function. (Chemical Immunology Ser.: Vol. 64, 1996). (Illus.). xii, 184p. 1996. 172.25 (*3-8055-6332-9*) S Karger.

Moretti, E. C. & Mukhopadhyay, N. Current & Potential Future Industrial Practices for Reducing & Controlling Volatile Organic Compounds. LC 93-12704. (Center for Waste Reduction Technologies Ser.). 85p. 1993. 50.00 (*0-8169-0615-7*) Am Inst Chem Eng.

Moretti, Franco. Atlas of the European Novel 1800-1900. 192p. 1998. 25.00 (*1-85984-883-4*, Pub. by Verso) Norton.

— An Atlas of the European Novel 1800-1900. 1999. pap. text 18.00 (*1-85984-224-0*, Pub. by Verso) Norton.

— Modern Epic: The World-System from Goethe to Garcia Marquez. Hoare, Quintin, tr. from ITA. LC 95-43983. 272p. (C). 1996. 65.00 (*1-85984-934-2*, Pub. by Verso); pap. 22.00 (*1-85984-069-8*, Pub. by Verso) Norton.

— Signs Taken. 2nd ed. (C). 1997. pap. 19.00 (*1-85984-171-6*) Norton.

***Moretti, Franco.** The Way of the World: The Bildungsroman in European Culture. 288p. (C). 2000. pap. 20.00 (*1-85984-298-4*, Pub. by Verso) Norton.

Moretti, G. P., ed. Proceedings. (Series Entomologica: No. 20). 471p. 1981. lib. bdg. 230.00 (*90-6193-130-4*) Kluwer Academic.

Moretti, Laura, des. Battered Birds, Crated Herds: How We Treat the Animals We Eat. 64p. (Orig.). 1996. mass mkt. 4.95 (*0-9656377-0-0*) Farm Sanctuary.

Moretti, Laura A., ed. All Heaven in a Rage: Essays on the Eating of Animals. rev. ed. 80p. Date not set. pap. 9.95 (*1-884873-14-6*) My Bros Keeper.

Moretti, Mark, jt. auth. see Straczynski, J. Michael.

Moretti, Mickey, ed. see Engelbrecht, Charles V.

Moretti, Mike, jt. auth. see Ruffalo, Richard.

***Moretti, P. M.** Modern Vibrations Primer. LC 99-52988. 2000. write for info. (*0-8493-2038-0*) CRC Pr.

Moretti, Stephanie. The An Book. (Window on Words Ser.). (Illus.). 16p. (J). (ps-1). 1993. 18.95 (*1-879567-09-1*) Wonder Well.

— The At Book. (Window on Words Ser.). (Illus.). 18p. (J). (ps-1). 1991. 18.95 (*1-879567-08-3*, Valeria Bks) Wonder Well.

***Moretti, Stephanie.** The At Book: Window on Words. (Illus.). 30p. (J). (gr. k-1). 1999. reprint ed. text 20.00 (*0-7881-6733-2*) DIANE Pub.

Moretto, jt. auth. see Blicq.

Moretto, Gino. The Shroud: A Guide. LC 99-11635. (ENG.). 1999. 19.95 (*0-8091-3886-7*) Paulist Pr.

— The Shroud: A Guide. 80p. 1996. pap. 39.95 (*0-85439-531-8*, Pub. by St Paul Pubns) St Mut.

Moretto, Lisa A., jt. auth. see Blicq, Ron S.

Moretto, Lisa A., jt. auth. see Blicq, Ronald S.

Moretto, P. H., jt. auth. see Llabador, Y.

Moretz, Judith, ed. see Harrison, Chris.

Moretz, Judith, ed. see Harrison, Christopher L.

Morevski, Abraham. Shylock & Shakespeare. LC 67-19382. 112p. 1967. 6.95 (*0-87527-056-5*) Green.

— There & Back: Reminiscences & Ruminations of a Jew Who Was an Actor. Leftwich, Joseph, tr. from YID. LC 67-27245. (Illus.). 256p. 1967. 6.95 (*0-87527-057-3*) Green.

— There & Back Vol. 2: Reminiscences & Ruminations of a Jew Who Was an Actor. Dobkin, Eva Z., tr. from YID. LC 67-27245. (Illus.). 256p. 1991. 10.95 (*0-87527-501-X*) Green.

Morewedge, Parinz, ed. see Khamenei, Ayatollah S.

Morewedge, Parviz. Essays in Islamic Philosophy, Theology, & Mysticism. (Oneonta Philosophy Studies). 260p. (Orig.). (C). 1995. pap. 12.00 (*0-9633277-7-1*, Oneonta Philosophy) Global Pubns.

— Essays on the Philosophy of Nasir Al-Din Tusi. 1999. pap. 17.00 (*1-883058-29-5*, Nur) Global Pubns.

— Islamic Theology. 25p. 1993. 3.00 (*1-883058-11-2*, SAG&IP) Global Pubns.

— The Mystical Philosophy of Avicenna. (Nur Ser.). 250p. (Orig.). (C). 1998. pap. 17.00 (*1-883058-23-6*, Intl Medieval) Global Pubns.

— The Universal Message of Islamic Mysticism: A Theoretical Construct. 34p. 1993. 3.00 (*0-9633277-4-7*, SAG&IP) Global Pubns.

Morewedge, Parviz, ed. Islamic Philosophy & Mysticism. LC 80-14364. (Studies in Islamic Philosophy & Science). 256p. 1997. 50.00 (*0-88206-302-2*) Caravan Bks.

— Islamic Philosophy & Mysticism. 256p. 1996. 50.00 (*0-614-21227-8*, 1366) Kazi Pubns.

— Neoplatonism & Islamic Thought. LC 92-388. (Studies in Neoplatonism: Ancient & Modern: Vol. 5). 267p. 1992. text 19.50 (*0-7914-1335-7*) State U NY Pr.

— Philosophies of Existence: Ancient & Medieval. LC 81-66643. 352p. reprint ed. pap. 109.20 (*0-7837-5613-5*, 204551900005) Bks Demand.

Morewedge, Parviz, intro. Knowledge & Liberation in a Muslim World: An Introduction to Ismaili Philosophical Theology. (Ismaili Heriage Ser.). 132p. 1998. text 32.50 (*1-86064-217-9*, Pub. by I B T) St Martin.

Morewedge, Rosemarie T., ed. The Role of Woman in the Middle Ages. LC 74-23227. (Illus.). 195p. (C). 1975. text 22.50 (*0-87395-274-X*) State U NY Pr.

Morewedge, Rosmarie T. The Roles of Women in the Middle Ages: A Reassessment. 1998. pap. 17.00 (*1-883058-19-8*, Intl Medieval) Global Pubns.

Morewitz, S., ed. see Johnson, Joe B.

Morewitz, Stephen. Sexual Harassment & Social Change in American Society. LC 93-48393. 498p. 1996. 69.95 (*1-880921-77-4*); pap. 50.00 (*1-880921-76-6*) Austin & Winfield.

Morewitz, Stephen, jt. auth. see Livingston, Bruce.

Morewood, Steven, jt. auth. see Aldcroft, Derek H.

Morey, jt. auth. see Best.

Morey, Ann I. & Kitano, Margie K., eds. Multicultural Course Transformation in Higher Education: A Broader Truth. 312p. 1996. 38.00 (*0-205-16068-9*) Allyn.

Morey, Ann-Janine. Religion & Sexuality in American Fiction. (Cambridge Studies in American Literature & Culture: No. 57). 290p. (C). 1992. text 59.95 (*0-521-41676-0*) Cambridge U Pr.

— What Happened to Christopher: An American Family's Story of Shaken Baby Syndrome. LC 98-5368. 196p. 1998. 22.95 (*0-8093-2215-3*) S Ill U Pr.

Morey, Barbara, ed. see Ambrose, Paul V. & Algozzini, Joseph P.

Morey, Carl. Music in Canada: A Research & Information Guide. LC 96-29156. (Garland Reference Library of the Humanities). 304p. 1997. text 50.00 (*0-8153-1603-8*) Garland.

Morey, Cathy, ed. see Newlin, Lana S.

Morey, Clinton R. The Denial: A Play for Lent. 1980. 4.25 (*0-89536-412-3*, 0420) CSS OH.

Morey, Craig. Studio Nudes: Selected Photographs, 1989-1992. (Illus.). 80p. 1992. 25.00 (*0-9632813-0-5*) C Morey Photo.

***Morey, Daryl, et al, eds.** Knowledge Management: Classic & Contemporary Works. (Illus.). 450p. (C). 2001. 45.00 (*0-262-13384-9*) MIT Pr.

Morey, Doc. Phone Power: Increase Your Effectiveness Every Time You're on the Phone. LC 98-10417. Orig. Title: Techniques of Effective Telephone Communication. 128p. 1998. pap. 10.99 (*1-56414-366-X*) Career Pr Inc.

Morey, Earl W. Our God Reigns: An Inductive Approach to the Book of Revelation. 401p. (Orig.). 1992. pap. 18.95 (*0-9634717-0-8*) A Minis VA.

— Search the Scriptures: How to Study the Bible for Yourself. (Illus.). 333p. 1993. pap. 18.95 (*0-9634717-1-6*) A Minis VA.

Morey, Eileen. Eleanor Roosevelt. LC 97-6789. (Importance of Ser.). (Illus.). (J). (gr. 4-12). 1997. lib. bdg. 22.45 (*1-56006-086-7*) Lucent Bks.

Morey, Eileen, ed. Readings on the Scarlet Letter. LC 97-22684. (Literary Companion Ser.). 159p. (YA). (gr. 9-12). 1997. pap. 16.20 (*1-56510-756-X*); lib. bdg. 26.20 (*1-56510-757-8*) Greenhaven.

Morey, G. B., ed. Early Proterozoic Rocks of the Great Lakes Region. (IGC Field Trip Guidebooks Ser.). 72p. 1989. 13.00 (*0-87590-625-7*, T145) Am Geophysical.

Morey, G. B. & Hanson, Gilbert N., eds. Selected Studies of Archean Gneisses & Lower Proterozoic Rocks, Southern Canadian Shield. LC 80-67113. (Geological Society of America, Special Paper: No. 182). (Illus.). 181p. (Orig.). reprint ed. pap. 56.20 (*0-8357-3147-2*, 203941000012) Bks Demand.

Morey, G. B., et al. Bibliography of Minnesota Geology, 1951-1980. (Bulletin: No. 46). 1981. 10.00 (*0-934938-01-6*) Minn Geol Surv.

Morey, Grace K. & Clymer, R. Swinburne. Mystic Americanism: The Spiritual Heritage of America Revealed. 328p. 1975. 9.95 (*0-932785-33-6*) Philos Pub.

***Morey, James H.** Book & Verse. LC 99-6489. 408p. 1999. 34.95 (*0-252-02507-5*) U of Ill Pr.

Morey, James L., jt. auth. see Kirshner, Edward M.

Morey, Janet N. Famous Asian Americans. 1998. pap. 5.99 (*0-14-038435-9*) Viking Penguin.

— A Famous Hispanic American. 192p. 1999. pap. 5.99 (*0-14-038436-7*) Viking Penguin.

Morey, Janet N. Famous Mexican Americans. 1997. 11.09 (*0-606-11313-4*, Pub. by Turtleback) Demco.

Morey, Janet N. & Dunn, Wendy. Famous Hispanic Americans. LC 95-10670. (Illus.). 208p. (J). (gr. 5-9). 1996. 15.99 (*0-525-65190-X*, Dutton Child) Peng Put Young Read.

Morey, Kathy. Hawaii Trails: Walks, Strolls & Treks on the Big Island. LC 91-15130. (Illus.). 288p. 1992. pap. 13.95 (*0-89997-134-2*) Wilderness Pr.

— Hot Showers, Soft Beds, & Dayhikes in the Sierra: Walks & Strolls Near Lodgings. LC 96-35574. (Illus.). 256p. (Orig.). 1996. pap. 16.95 (*0-89997-163-6*) Wilderness Pr.

— Kauai Trails: Walks, Strolls, & Treks on the Garden Isle. 2nd ed. LC 97-3128. (Illus.). 234p. 1997. pap. 13.95 (*0-89997-214-4*) Wilderness Pr.

— Maui Trails: Walks, Strolls & Treks on the Valley Isle. 2nd ed. LC 96-6853. (Orig.). 1996. pap. 12.95 (*0-89997-196-2*) Wilderness Pr.

Morey, Kathy, jt. auth. see Wilderness Press Staff.

Morey, Leslie C. An Interpretive Guide to the Personality Assessment Inventory. LC 96-8181. 308p. 1996. 56.00 (*0-911907-22-X*) Psych Assess.

Morey, Philip R., et al, eds. Biological Contaminants in Indoor Environments. LC 90-21115. (Special Technical Publication Ser.: STP 1071). (Illus.). 260p. 1990. text 49.00 (*0-8031-1290-4*, \) ASTM.

— Biological Contaminants in Indoor Environments. LC 90-21115. (ASTM Special Technical Publication Ser.: No. 1071). (Illus.). 258p. reprint ed. pap. 80.00 (*0-608-10484-1*, 207111400009) Bks Demand.

Morey, Rita, ed. see Gill, George.

Morey, Rita, ed. see Milton, John.

Morey, Rita, ed. see Simmes, William.

***Morey, Robert.** Fearing God: The Key to the Tresure House of Heaven. 331p. 2000. pap. 21.00 (*1-891833-52-9*) Davidson Pr.

Morey, Robert. La Invasion Islamica. (SPA.). 208p. 1995. pap. 8.99 (*0-8254-1479-2*, Edit Portavoz) Kregel.

Morey, Robert A. Battle of the Gods: The Emerging God of the New Age. 324p. (Orig.). (C). 1989. pap. 9.95 (*0-925703-00-1*) Crown MA.

— Death & the Afterlife. LC 84-15682. 32p. 1984. text 16.99 (*0-87123-433-5*) Bethany Hse.

— Here Is Your God. (Orig.). (C). 1989. pap. write for info. (*0-925703-02-8*) Crown MA.

— How to Answer a Jehovah's Witness. LC 79-25502. 112p. (Orig.). 1980. pap. 7.99 (*0-87123-206-5*) Bethany Hse.

— How to Answer a Mormon. LC 82-24315. 128p. (Orig.). 1983. pap. 7.99 (*0-87123-260-X*) Bethany Hse.

— How to Keep Your Faith While in College. 144p. (Orig.). (C). 1989. pap. write for info. (*0-925703-03-6*) Crown MA.

— How to Keep Your Kids Drug Free. 128p. (Orig.). 1989. pap. write for info. (*0-925703-01-X*) Crown MA.

— Introduction to Defending the Faith. 2nd ed. 52p. (Orig.). 1989. reprint ed. pap. text. write for info. (*0-925703-09-5*) Crown MA.

— Islamic Invasion. 230p. 1992. reprint ed. pap. 9.99 (*0-89081-983-1*) Harvest Hse.

— The New Atheism & the Erosion of Freedom: How to Recognize & Combat the Hidden Influence of Secular Humanism & Unbelief in Today's Society. 176p. 1994. reprint ed. pap. 8.99 (*0-87552-362-5*) P & R Pubng.

— The Origins & Teachings of Freemasonry. 144p. (Orig.). 1990. pap. write for info. (*0-925703-28-1*) Crown MA.

— Reincarnation & Christianity. LC 80-24497. 64p. 1980. pap. 4.99 (*0-87123-493-9*) Bethany Hse.

— Studies in the Atonement. rev. ed. 320p. reprint ed. pap. write for info. (*0-925703-07-9*) Crown MA.

— The Trinity: Evidence & Issues. LC 96-60873. 580p. 1996. 24.99 (*0-529-10692-2*, TEI) World Publng.

— When Is It Right to Fight? A Penetrating Look at the Difficult Issues of Peace, Freedom & Responsiblity. 1994. reprint ed. pap. 8.99 (*0-87552-361-7*) P & R Pubng.

Morey, Shaun. Incredible Fishing Stories. White, Connie S., ed. LC 91-66632. (Illus.). 145p. (Orig.). 1991. pap. 12.95 (*0-9633691-0-5*) Incrdble Fish.

— Incredible Fishing Stories for Kids. LC 93-77082. (Illus.). 96p. (Orig.). (J). 1993. pap. 11.95 (*0-9633691-1-3*) Incrdble Fish.

— Kids' Incredible Fishing Stories. LC 96-6002. (Illus.). 128p. (YA). (gr. 3 up). 1999. pap. 7.95 (*0-7611-0450-X*, 10450) Workman Pub.

Morey, Sylvester M., ed. Can the Red Man Help the White Man. LC 80-83370. (Illus.). 130p. (gr. 7-12). 1970. pap. 4.95 (*0-913098-35-3*) Orion Society.

Morey, Walt. Death Walk. (Walt Morey Adventure Library). (Illus.). 176p. (YA). (gr. 5-12). 1991. 13.95 (*0-936085-18-5*) Blue Heron OR.

— Death Walk. 176p. (YA). 1993. pap. 7.95 (*0-936085-55-X*) Blue Heron OR.

— Death Walk. (Walt Morey Adventure Library Ser.). 1993. 13.05 (*0-606-12249-4*, Pub. by Turtleback) Demco.

— Gentle Ben. 192p. (J). (gr. 4 up). 1976. pap. 2.95 (*0-380-00743-6*, Avon Bks) Morrow Avon.

— Gentle Ben. (Illus.). 192p. (J). (gr. 5 up). 1992. pap. 4.99 (*0-14-036035-2*, PuffinBks) Peng Put Young Read.

— Gentle Ben. (J). 1992. 10.09 (*0-606-00460-2*, Pub. by Turtleback) Demco.

***Morey, Walt.** Gloomy Gus. 192p. (YA). (gr. 4 up). 1999. reprint ed. pap. 7.95 (*0-936085-46-0*, Pub. by Blue Heron OR) Consort Bk Sales.

Morey, Walt. Hero.Tr. of Lemon Meringue Dog. (J). 1995. 9.09 (*0-606-08548-3*, Pub. by Turtleback) Demco.

— Home Is the North. (Walt Morey Adventure Library). 180p. (YA). (gr. 4-9). 1989. reprint ed. pap. 7.95 (*0-936085-11-8*) Blue Heron OR.

— Kavik, the Wolf Dog. (J). 1997. 10.09 (*0-606-11534-X*, Pub. by Turtleback) Demco.

— Kavik, the Wolf Dog. (J). 1997. pap. 5.99 (*0-14-038423-5*) Viking Penguin.

— Scrub Dog of Alaska. (Walt Morey Adventure Library). (Illus.). 160p. (YA). (gr. 4-9). 1989. reprint ed. pap. 7.95 (*0-936085-13-4*) Blue Heron OR.

— Year of the Black Pony. (Walt Morey Adventure Library). (Illus.). 144p. (YA). (gr. 4-8). 1989. reprint ed. pap. 6.95 (*0-936085-14-2*, Pub. by Blue Heron OR) Consort Bk Sales.

Morey, William C. Outlines in Roman History. 1972. 59.95 (*0-8490-0789-5*) Gordon Pr.

— Outlines of Roman Law: Comprising Its Historical Growth & General Principles. 4th ed. xiii, 433p. 1985. reprint ed. 45.00 (*0-8377-0851-6*, Rothman) W S Hein.

Morf, Gustav. Polish Heritage of Joseph Conrad. LC 65-26452. (Studies in Conrad: No. 8). 1969. reprint ed. lib. bdg. 75.00 (*0-8383-0597-0*) M S G Haskell Hse.

Morf, Martin. Optimizing Work Performance: A Look Beyond the Bottom Line. LC 85-23232. 205p. 1986. 49.95 (*0-89930-143-6*, MWK/, Quorum Bks) Greenwood.

— The Work-Life Dichotomy: Prospects for Reintegrating People & Jobs. LC 88-35739. 211p. 1989. 57.95 (*0-89930-421-4*, MUP/, Quorum Bks) Greenwood.

Morfaux, L. M. Vocabulary of Philosophy & Humanist Sciences: Vocabulaire de la Philosophie et des Sciences Humaines. (FRE.). 392p. 1979. reprint ed. 34.95 (*0-7859-4857-0*) Fr & Eur.

Morfett, J. C., jt. auth. see Chadwick, Andrew J.

Morfett, John C., jt. auth. see Chadwick, Andrew.

***Morfey, Christopher.** The Dictionary of Acoustics. 400p. 2000. 64.95 (*0-12-506940-5*) Acad Pr.

Morfi, Fray J. History of Texas, Sixteen Seventy-Three to Seventeen Seventy-Nine, 2 pts. Castaneda, Carlos E., ed. LC 67-24718. (Quivira Society Publications, Vol. 6). 1967. reprint ed. 34.00 (*0-405-19053-0*) Ayer.

— History of Texas, 1673-1779, 2 vols. Castaneda, Carlos E., tr. & anno. by. 1935. 37.95 (*0-405-00076-6*) Ayer.

Morfi, Juan A. History of Texas, 1673-1779, 2 vols., Set. 1993. reprint ed. lib. bdg. 180.00 (*0-685-62348-3*) Rprt Serv.

Morfill, G. E., ed. Dust in Space & Comets: Proceedings of the Topical Meeting of the COSPAR Interdisciplinary Scientific Commission B (Meetings B1 & B2) of the COSPAR 25th Plenary Meeting, Graz, Austria, 25 June-7 July 1984. (Illus.). 324p. 1985. pap. 54.00 (*0-08-032745-1*, Pub. by PPL) Elsevier.

Morfill, G. E. & Buccheri, R., eds. Galactic Astrophysics & Gamma Ray Astronomy. 1983. text 211.50 (*90-277-1645-5*) Kluwer Academic.

Morfill, W. R. The Book of the Secrets of Enoch. 100p. 1997. reprint ed. pap. 12.50 (*0-7873-0622-3*) Hlth Research.

Morfill, W. R., ed. Ballads Relating Chiefly to the Reign of Queen Elizabeth, Vol. 2, Pt. 2. (Ballad Society Ser.). 57.50 AMS Pr.

Morfill, William R. Poland. LC 75-39494. (Select Bibliographies Reprint Ser.). 1977. reprint ed. 23.95 (*0-8369-9919-3*) Ayer.

Morfit, Christine A., jt. ed. see Moore, Sarah J.

Morford, Henry. The Days of Shoddy: A Novel of the Great Rebellion in 1861. LC 73-164571. (American Fiction Reprint Ser.). 1977. reprint ed. 35.95 (*0-8369-7048-9*) Ayer.

Morford, Jill P., et al, eds. Language Acquisition by Eye. LC 99-30894. 276p. 1999. 59.95 (*0-8058-2937-7*) L Erlbaum Assocs.

Morford, M. The Poet Lucan. (Bristol Classical Paperbacks Ser.). 104p. 1996. pap. text 25.95 (*1-85399-488-X*, Pub. by Brist Class Pr) Focus Pub-R Pullins.

Morford, Mark. Classical Mythology. 6th ed. (C). 1999. text. write for info. (*0-8013-1955-2*) Longman.

— Stoics & Neostoics: Rubens & the Circle of Lipsius. (Illus.). 256p. 1991. text 49.50 (*0-691-04081-8*, Pub. by Princeton U Pr) Cal Prin Full Svc.

***Morford, Mark P.** Classical Mythology. 6th ed. 704p. 1999. pap. 50.95 (*0-471-36891-1*) Wiley.

Morford, Mark P. & Lenardon, Robert J. Classical Mythology. 4th ed. 703p. (C). 1991. pap. text 33.95 (*0-8013-0465-2*, 78280) Longman.

***Morford, Mark P. & Lenardon, Robert J., eds.** Classical Mythology. 6th ed. (Illus.). 704p. (C). 2000. pap. 46.95 (*0-19-514338-8*) OUP.

Morford, T. C. Fifty Years Ago: A Brief History of the 29th Regiment New Jersey Volunteers in the Civil War. 60p. (C). 1990. reprint ed. pap. 9.00 (*0-944413-16-1*) Longstreet Hse.

Morford, Ted R. & Mauer, Shelley M. The Job World Instructor's Manual. 86p. 1987. 18.75 (*1-55549-012-3*) Ed Assocs KY.

— The Job World Workbook. 3rd ed. (Job World Ser.). 86p. (Orig.). 1987. 6.75 (*1-55549-013-1*) Ed Assocs KY.

Morford, V. J. Metals & Welding. rev. ed. (Illus.). 236p. 1987. spiral bd. 22.35 (*0-913163-19-8*, 170) Hobar Pubns.

Morfreds, Miriam G. & Newman, Sharon. Original Historical Mystery Anthology. 1997. mass mkt. write for info. (*0-614-18901-2*, Prime Crime) Berkley Pub.

Morga, Michael, jt. auth. see Alvarez, Tom.

Morga, Robert. Magic of the Demon Ewaz. Templar, Thorguard, ed. (Illus.). 110p. 1994. spiral bd. 8.00 (*1-883147-86-7*) Intern Guild ASRS.

Morgado, E. M., jt. ed. see Martins, J. P.

Morgado, Martin J. Junipero Serra. 1991. pap. 19.95 (*0-9627216-0-3*) Siempre Adelante.

Morgagni, Giambattista. Clinical Consultations: The Edition of Enrico Benassi (1935) rev. ed. Jarcho, Saul, tr. 450p. 1984. 25.00 (*0-317-04057-X*) F A Countway.

Morgaite, John-Paul. The Next Step, Pt. II. (Basic Christian Training Ser.). 64p. 1993. pap. 2.50 (*1-880322-03-X*) Champions Christ.

— Victory Christian Church Membership Manual. 41p. 1991. pap. 5.00 (*1-880322-01-3*) Champions Christ.

Morgall, Janine M. Technology Assessment: A Feminist Perspective. LC 93-9447. (Labor & Social Change Ser.). 288p. 1993. 69.95 (*1-56639-090-7*); pap. 22.95 (*1-56639-091-5*) Temple U Pr.

***Morgan.** Care & Management of Native Ponies. 2000. 45.00 (*0-85131-768-5*, Pub. by J A Allen) Trafalgar.

Morgan. Clinical Anesthesiology. 3rd ed. (C). 1999. pap. text 45.00 (*0-8385-1553-3*) Appleton & Lange.

— Community Mental Health: Practical Approaches to Long-Term Problems. 268p. 1993. pap. 44.75 (*1-56593-138-6*, 0450) Singular Publishing.

— Database Management Casebook. (C). 1998. pap. text 18.00 (*0-03-024622-9*) Harcourt Coll Pubs.

— Elements Structure. 2nd ed. (C). 1987. pap. 25.95 (*0-582-99485-3*, Pub. by Addison-Wesley) Longman.

— Environmental Science. 1992. teacher ed. 17.81 (*0-697-10833-3*) McGraw.

— Environmental Science. 1993. pap. 70.31 (*0-697-16358-X*) McGraw.

— Environmental Science. 2nd ed. 1999. pap. 45.00 (*0-697-21849-X*, WCB McGr Hill) McGrw-H Hghr Educ.

— Fund Life I: CB. (C). 1997. pap. text 40.31 (*0-201-35075-0*) Addison-Wesley.

***Morgan.** Geographic Information Systems in Public Health. 2000. 63.00 (*0-8342-1813-5*) Aspen Pub.

Morgan. Gilbert Legal Ethics. 7th ed. 1994. 18.95 (*0-15-900026-2*) Harcourt Legal.

— Harold Wilson: A Life. 625p. (C). 39.95 (*0-7453-0635-7*, Pub. by Pluto GBR) Stylus Pub VA.

— Ida Rowland Bellegard: Master Teacher & Scholar. (C). 1992. pap. text 16.00 (*0-07-043252-X*) McGraw.

***Morgan.** Idol More & Harder. 1999. pap. text 10.95 (*0-352-33437-1*) London Brdge.

Morgan. Immunological Techniques in Food Analysis. 250p. 1997. 1.00 (*0-12-506860-3*) Acad Pr.

— INV BIO: BIO 200 CB. (C). 1997. text 31.88 (*0-201-35077-7*) Addison-Wesley.

— Lab Mnl Custom Bio. (C). 1997. spiral bd., lab manual ed. 58.00 (*0-201-30733-2*) Addison-Wesley.

— The Life & Adventures of William Buckley. (Australian National University Press Ser.). 1996. write for info. (*0-08-033015-0*, Pergamon Pr) Elsevier.

— The National Experience. 8th ed. (C). 1993. pap. text 33.50 (*0-15-500734-3*, Pub. by Harcourt Coll Pubs) Harcourt.

— Navigating Cross-Cultural Ethics. LC 98-37850. xvi, 194p. 1998. 18.95 (*0-7506-9915-9*) Buttrwrth-Heinemann.

— Organizations in Society. 1997. pap. 24.95 (*0-333-43855-8*) St Martin.

— Point Set Theory. (Pure & Applied Mathematics Ser.: Vol. 131). (Illus.). 296p. 1989. text 155.00 (*0-8247-8178-3*) Dekker.

— Puritan Dilemma: The Story of John Winthorp. 2nd ed. 244p. 1998. pap. text 21.20 (*0-321-04369-3*) Addison-Wesley.

— The Responsive Reader. (C). 1995. pap., teacher ed. 26.75 (*0-15-502171-0*) Harcourt Coll Pubs.

— The Responsive Reader. (C). 1996. pap. text. write for info. (*0-15-501182-0*) Harcourt Coll Pubs.

— What Every Marriage Needs. LC 99-39407. 1999. 16.99 (*0-310-22698-8*) Zondervan.

Morgan, ed. Anatomy & Physiology Manual. (C). 1996. text. write for info. (*0-673-67601-3*) Addison-Wesley.

— World Politics: An Introduction. (C). 1992. write for info. (*0-673-38951-0*) Addison-Wesley.

***Morgan & Carter.** Biology. 1999. spiral bd., lab manual ed. 42.00 (*0-201-60925-8*) Addison-Wesley.

Morgan & Kerr. Louisiana Scenes: The Lower Mississippi Valley. 1962. 24.95 (*0-87511-088-6*) Claitors.

Morgan & Moore. Language Games & Centers. (Illus.). 112p. (J). (ps-1). 1998. pap., teacher ed. 14.95 (*1-55799-661-X*, 736) Evan-Moor Edu Pubs.

— Math Games & Centers. (Illus.). 112p. (J). (ps-1). 1998. pap., teacher ed. 14.95 (*1-55799-660-1*, 735) Evan-Moor Edu Pubs.

Morgan & Pritch. Destination Branding: Developing a Destination Proposition. 288p. Date not set. 65.95 (*0-7506-4994-1*) Buttrwrth-Heinemann.

Morgan & Silv. Moderates & Conservatives in West Europe. 1982. text 72.95 (*0-435-83615-3*) Ashgate Pub Co.

Morgan, et al. Managing Administration. (Public Administration & Public Policy Ser.: Vol. 26). (Illus.). 280p. 1984. text 95.00 (*0-8247-7096-X*) Dekker.

Morgan, jt. auth. see Moore.

Morgan, jt. auth. see Porter.

Morgan, jt. auth. see Richardson.

Morgan, ed. see Longus.

Morgan, tr. see Rubinstein, Anton.

Morgan, A. John. X-Ray Microanalysis in Electron Microscopy for Biologists. (Royal Microscopical Society Microscopy Handbooks Ser.). (Illus.). 72p. 1986. pap. 12.95 (*0-19-856409-0*) OUP.

Morgan, Aaron. Making Great Gingerbread Houses: Delicious Designs from Cabins to Castles, from Lighthouses to Treehouses. Blomgren, Paige G., ed. LC 99-29333. (Illus.). 128p. 1999. 24.95 (*1-57990-136-0*, Pub. by Lark Books) Random.

***Morgan, Aaron, ed.** You & God. (Biblical Living Ser.). 112p. 1999. pap. 4.99 (*0-88243-150-1*, 02-0150); pap., teacher ed. 6.99 (*0-88243-250-8*, 02-0250) Gospel Pub.

— You & Others. (Biblical Living Ser.). 112p. 1999. pap. 4.99 (*0-88243-151-X*, 02-0151); pap., teacher ed. 6.99 (*0-88243-251-6*, 02-0251) Gospel Pub.

— You & Your Family. (Biblical Living Ser.). 64p. 1999. pap., teacher ed. 6.99 (*0-88243-252-4*, 02-0252) Gospel Pub.

— You & Your Family. (Biblical Living Ser.). 112p. 1999. pap. 4.99 (*0-88243-152-8*, 02-0152) Gospel Pub.

— You & Your Priorities. (Biblical Living Ser.). 64p. 1999. pap., teacher ed. 6.99 (*0-88243-253-2*, 02-0253) Gospel Pub.

— You & Your Priorities. (Biblical Living Ser.). 112p. 1999. pap. 4.99 (*0-88243-153-6*, 02-0153) Gospel Pub.

Morgan, Adam. Eating the Big Fish: Culture, Socilty & Space. LC 98-28267. (Adweek Magazine Ser.). 304p. 1999. text 29.95 (*0-471-24209-8*) Wiley.

Morgan, Adrian. Toads & Toadstools: The Natural History, Mythology, & Cultural Oddities of This Strange Association. (Illus.). 224p. 1996. pap. 24.95 (*0-89087-777-7*) Ten Speed Pr.

Morgan, Adrian, jt. auth. see Morgan, Sally.

***MORGAN, AISHLING.** The Rake. (Orig.). 1999. mass mkt. 6.95 (*0-352-33434-7*) London Brdge.

An Asterisk (*) at the beginning of an entry indicates that the title is appearing for the first time.

Morgan, Alaistair. Antiques from the Garden. (Illus.). 1997. pap. 49.50 (0-614-27225-4) Antique Collect.

Morgan, Alastair. Improving Your Students' Learning. (Issues in Open & Distance Learning Ser.). 144p. 1993. pap. 25.00 (0-7494-0712-3, Kogan Pg Educ) Stylus Pub VA.

***Morgan, Albert T.** Yazoo: On the Picket Line of Freedom in the South: A Personal Narrative. 544p. 2000. pap. text 29.95 (1-57003-359-5) U of SC Pr.

Morgan, Albert W. Memories of Old Sunrise: Gold Mining on Alaska's Turnagain Arm 1897-1901. Buzzell, Rolfe G., ed. & intro. by. LC 94-68464. (Illus.). 125p. (Orig.). 1994. pap. 18.95 (1-878462-01-6) Cook Inlet Hist Soc.

Morgan, Aled, photos by. John Morgan's Wales: A Personal Anthology. (Illus.). 320p. (C). 1992. 75.00 (0-7154-0686-8, Pub. by C Davies Pubs) St Mut.

Morgan, Alexander. Vanilla Custard. (Illus.). 96p. (Orig.). 1987. pap. 10.00 (0-912449-23-3) Floating Island.

Morgan, Alice B., ed. see Hawes, Stephen.

Morgan, Alistair. Case Study Research in Distance Education. (C). 1991. pap. 24.00 (0-7300-1349-9, IDE806, Pub. by Deakin Univ) St Mut.

— Research into Student Learning in Distance Education. (C). 1991. pap. 24.00 (0-7300-1352-9, IDE806, Pub. by Deakin Univ) St Mut.

Morgan, Allan. Sadie & the Snowman. (Illus.). 32p. (J). (ps-2). 1987. pap. 2.50 (0-590-41826-2) Scholastic Inc.

— Tiens-Toi Bien, Mathieu! 24p. pap. (2-89021-316-1) La Courte Ech.

Morgan, Allen. Andrew & the Wild Bikes. (Illus.). 32p. (J). (ps-2). 1990. 12.95 (1-55037-083-9, Pub. by Annick); pap. 4.95 (1-55037-082-0, Pub. by Annick) Firefly Bks Ltd.

— El Barco de Camila (Nicole's Boat) (SPA., Illus.). 24p. (J). (ps-1). pap. 6.95 (980-257-040-0, Pub. by Ediciones Ekare) Kane-Miller Bk.

— Le Camion - Matthew & the Midnight Tow Truck. (Droles D'Histories Ser.). (FRE., Illus.). 24p. (J). (ps up). 1986. pap. 6.95 (2-89021-056-1, Pub. by La Courte Ech) Firefly Bks Ltd.

— Jessica Moffat's Silver Locket. unabridged ed. (Illus.). 32p. (J). (gr. 1 up). 1994. 12.95 (0-7737-2840-6) STDK.

— Jessica Moffat's Silver Locket. unabridged ed. (Illus.). 32p. (J). (gr. 1 up). 1996. pap. 7.95 (0-7737-5701-5) STDK.

— The Magic Hockey Skates. 32p. (J). (ps-3). 1994. pap. 6.95 (0-19-540851-9) OUP.

— The Magic Hockey Skates. unabridged ed. LC 98-226123. (Illus.). 32p. (J). (gr. k-3). 1996. pap. 8.95 (0-7737-5697-3) STDK.

— Mateo y la Grua de Medianoche. Langer, Shirley, tr.Tr. of Matthew & the Midnight Tow Truck. (SPA., Illus.). 32p. (YA). (ps up). 1991. pap. 5.95 (1-55037-190-8, Pub. by Annick) Firefly Bks Ltd.

— Mateo y los Pavos de Medianoche. Langer, Shirley, tr.Tr. of Matthew & the Midnight Turkeys. (SPA., Illus.). 32p. (YA). (ps up). 1991. pap. 5.95 (1-55037-188-6, Pub. by Annick) Firefly Bks Ltd.

— Matthew & the Midnight Ball Game. unabridged ed. LC 96-990105. (Illus.). 32p. (J). (ps-4). 1997. pap. 6.95 (0-7737-5853-4) STDK.

— Matthew & the Midnight Flood. LC 99-235869. (Matthew & the Midnight Ser.). (Illus.). 32p. (J). (ps up). 1998. pap. 6.95 (0-7737-5941-7) STDK.

— Matthew & the Midnight Money Van. (Illus.). 24p. (J). (ps-3). 1987. pap. 4.95 (0-920303-72-2, Pub. by Annick); lib. bdg. 14.95 (0-920303-75-7, Pub. by Annick) Firefly Bks Ltd.

— Matthew & the Midnight Money Van. (Annikins Ser.: Vol. 11). (Illus.). 32p. (J). (ps-2). 1991. pap. 0.99 (1-55037-194-0, Pub. by Annick) Firefly Bks Ltd.

— Matthew & the Midnight Pilot. unabridged ed. LC 96-990104. (Illus.). 32p. (J). (ps-4). 1997. pap. 6.99 (0-7737-5852-6) STDK.

***Morgan, Allen.** Matthew & the Midnight Pirates. LC 99-235877. (Matthew & the Midnight Ser.). (Illus.). 32p. (ps-3). 1998. pap. 6.99 (0-7737-5940-9) STDK.

Morgan, Allen. Matthew & the Midnight Tow Truck. (Illus.). 32p. (J). (ps-3). 1984. pap. 5.95 (0-920303-01-3, Pub. by Annick); lib. bdg. 14.95 (0-920303-00-5, Pub. by Annick) Firefly Bks Ltd.

— Matthew & the Midnight Tow Truck. (Annikins Ser.: Vol. 11). (Illus.). 24p. (J). (ps-2). 1991. pap. 0.99 (1-55037-192-4, Pub. by Annick) Firefly Bks Ltd.

— Matthew & the Midnight Turkeys. (Illus.). 24p. (J). (ps-3). 1985. pap. 4.95 (0-920303-37-4, Pub. by Annick); lib. bdg. 14.95 (0-920303-36-6, Pub. by Annick) Firefly Bks Ltd.

— Matthew & the Midnight Turkeys. (Annikins Ser.: Vol. 11). (Illus.). 24p. (J). (ps-2). 1991. pap. 0.99 (1-55037-193-2, Pub. by Annick) Firefly Bks Ltd.

— Nicole's Boat. (Annick Toddler Ser.). (Illus.). 24p. (J). (ps-1). 1986. 12.95 (0-920303-60-9, Pub. by Annick); pap. 4.95 (0-920303-61-7, Pub. by Annick) Firefly Bks Ltd.

***Morgan, Allen.** Nicole's Boat. rev. ed. 24p. (J). (ps-k). 2000. per. 5.95 (1-55037-630-6, Pub. by Annick Pr) Firefly Bks Ltd.

Morgan, Allen. Le Plombier. (FRE.). 24p. 1999. pap. write for info. (2-89021-362-5, Pub. by La Courte Ech) Firefly Bks Ltd.

Morgan, Allen. Sadie & the Snowman. (Illus.). 32p. (J). 1985. pap. 4.95 (0-919964-78-8) Kids Can Pr.

Morgan, Allen & Longval, Raymonde. En Avant, Pirates! 24p. (2-89021-340-4) La Courte Ech.

***Morgan, Allen & Martchenko, Michael.** Matthew & the Midnight Hospital. 32p. (J). (gr. k-3). 1999. pap. 6.95 (0-7737-6014-8) Genl Dist Srvs.

— Matthew & the Midnight Wrestlers. (Illus.). 32p. (J). 2000. pap. 6.99 (0-7737-6053-9, Stoddart Kids) Stoddart Publ.

***Morgan, Allen & Marton, Jirina.** Nicole's Boat. rev. ed. (Illus.). 24p. (J). (ps-k). 2000. lib. bdg. 15.95 (1-55037-631-4, Pub. by Annick Pr) Firefly Bks Ltd.

Morgan, Allen, et al. Du Courage, Mathieu! (FRE.). 24p. (2-89021-376-5) La Courte Ech.

Morgan, Alton C., Jr., jt. ed. see Foon, Kenneth F.

Morgan, Alun. Legends of Porthcawl & the Glamorgan Coast. 120p. (C). 1989. 45.00 (0-9504475-0-1, Pub. by D Brown & Sons Ltd) St Mut.

— Portcawl, Newton & Nottage: A Concise Illustrated History. 120p. (C). 1989. 59.00 (0-905928-73-3, Pub. by D Brown & Sons Ltd) St Mut.

Morgan, Alun, ed. The Breakwater. 190p. (C). 1989. pap. 35.00 (0-9500789-8-0, Pub. by D Brown & Sons Ltd) St Mut.

Morgan, Alun & Horricks, Raymond. Modern Jazz: A Survey of Developments since 1939. LC 77-8002. 240p. 1977. reprint ed. lib. bdg. 59.50 (0-8371-9674-4, MOMO, Greenwood Pr) Greenwood.

Morgan, Alun, jt. auth. see Game, Victor.

Morgan, Alun, ed. see Gammond, Peter & Fox, Charles.

Morgan, Andrew J., ed. Development of Epstein-Barr Virus Vaccine. (Medical Intelligence Unit Ser.). 105p. 1995. text 99.00 (1-57059-112-1) Landes Bioscience.

Morgan, Anita. Building on the Firm Foundation, Jesus Christ: A History of Pine Grove Baptist Church, Ruby, Louisiana, 1896-1996. LC 90-70298. 160p. 1996. 22.95 (1-57736-011-7) Providence Hse.

Morgan, Ann D., jt. auth. see Morgan, E. Victor.

Morgan, Ann L., ed. Contemporary Architects. 2nd ed. 1987. 149.00 (0-912289-26-0) St James Pr.

— Dear Stieglitz, Dear Love. LC 87-5030. (American Art Ser.). (Illus.). 536p. 1988. 85.00 (0-87413-292-4) U Delaware Pr.

Morgan, Anne. All Mixed Up: Big Book. large type ed. (Little Books & Big Bks.). (Illus.). 8p. (J). (gr. k-2). 1997. pap. text 19.47 (0-8215-0922-5) Sadlier.

Morgan, Anne, jt. auth. see High, Steven.

Morgan, Anne B. Shirazeh Houshiary: Turning Around the Centre. LC 93-61863. (Illus.). 24p. 1994. pap. 15.00 (0-929597-03-6) UMass Univ Gallery.

Morgan, Anne H. Prescription for Success: The Life & Values of Ewing Marion Kauffman. LC 95-23169. 438p. 1995. 22.95 (0-8362-0466-2) Andrews & McMeel.

— Robert S. Kerr: The Senate Years. LC 76-62514. (Illus.). 1980. pap. 14.95 (0-8061-1635-8) U of Okla Pr.

Morgan, Anne H. & Morgan, H. Wayne. Oklahoma: New Views of the Forty-Sixth State. LC 82-40327. (Illus.). 400p. 1982. 24.95 (0-8061-1651-X) U of Okla Pr.

Morgan, Anne H. & Strickland, Rennard, eds. Arizona Memories. LC 84-8853. 368p. 1984. pap. 114.10 (0-608-05645-6, 206609900006) Bks Demand.

Morgan, Anne H., jt. auth. see Morgan, H. Wayne.

Morgan, Annie L. Sunward I've Climbed: A Novel...Based on the True Story of Yvette Hamel & the 371st Fighter Group. LC 94-6583. (Illus.). 320p. 1994. 22.00 (1-881320-17-0, Black Belt) Black Belt Communs.

Morgan, Ardith, jt. auth. see Morgan, Herb.

Morgan, Arthur E. Community of the Future & the Future of Community. 1957. pap. 2.00 (0-910420-02-5) Comm Serv OH.

— Dams & Other Disasters: A Century of the Army Corps of Engineers in Civil Works. LC 74-172688. (Extending Horizons Ser.). 448p. (C). 1971. 7.50 (0-87558-066-1); pap. 3.95 (0-87558-094-7) Porter Sargent.

— Edward Bellamy. LC 73-16308. (Perspectives in American History Ser.: No. 18). (Illus.). 468p. 1974. reprint ed. lib. bdg. 49.50 (0-87991-346-0) Porcupine Pr.

— Great Community. 1946. pap. 1.00 (0-910420-03-3) Comm Serv OH.

— Industries for Small Communities. 1953. 4.00 (0-910420-19-X) Comm Serv OH.

— It Can Be Done in Home & Community. 1961. pap. 1.00 (0-910420 13 0) Comm Serv OH.

— The Long Road. 1962. 3.50 (0-910420-08-4); pap. 2.50 (0-910420-09-2) Comm Serv OH.

— Plagiarism in Utopia. 1944. pap. 1.00 (0-910420-16-5) Comm Serv OH.

— Scott & His Poetry. LC 79-120980. (Poetry & Life Ser.). reprint ed. 16.00 (0-404-52526-1) AMS Pr.

— Search for Purpose. 1957. 5.00 (0-910420-26-2) Comm Serv OH.

— Tendencies of Modern English Drama. LC 68-29233. (Essay Index Reprint Ser.). 1977. 21.95 (0-8369-1061-3) Ayer.

Morgan, Arthur E. & Szantho, Donald Harrington. The Small Community: Foundation of Democratic Life. LC 83-73240. 336p. 1984. reprint ed. pap. 10.00 (0-910420-28-9) Comm Serv OH.

Morgan, Arthur E., jt. auth. see Morgan, Griscom.

Morgan, Arthur E., jt. ed. see Morgan, Griscom.

Morgan, Arthur N., jt. auth. see La Farge, Oliver.

Morgan, Augustus De, see De Morgan, Augustus.

Morgan, Augustus De, see Smith, David E. & De Morgan, Augustus.

Morgan, Augustus De, see De Morgan, Augustus.

Morgan, Austen. Labour & Partition: The Belfast Working Class, 1905-1923. 280p. (C). 1987. 54.95 (0-7453-0326 9, Pub. by Pluto GBR) Stylus Pub VA.

Morgan, B., ed. Photoelectronic Image Devices: Proceedings of the 10th Symposium on Photoelectronic Image Devices, "The McGee Symposium" Held 6 September 1991 at Imperial College. (Institute of Physics Conference Ser.: No. 121). (Illus.). 456p. 1992. 182.00 (0-85498-411-9) IOP Pub.

Morgan, B. A., tr. see Von Kleist, Heinrich.

Morgan, B. J. Analysis of Quatal Response Data. 512p. (gr. 13). 1992. ring bd. 62.95 (0-412-31750-8, A4554, Chap & Hall CRC) CRC Pr.

— Elements of Simulation. (Illus.). 368p. (gr. 13). 1984. per. 58.95 (0-412-24590-6, NO. 6813, Chap & Hall CRC) CRC Pr.

Morgan, B. J. & North, P. M., eds. Statistics in Ornithology. LC 85-10052. (Lecture Notes in Statistics Ser.: Vol. 29). xxv, 418p. 1997. pap. 59.00 (0-387-96189-5) Spr-Verlag.

Morgan, B. L. Advanced Electronics Electron Physics. 1985. text 261.00 (0-12-014724-6) Acad Pr.

***Morgan, B. Paul, ed.** Complement Methods & Protocols. LC 99-58849. (Methods in Molecular Biology Ser.: Vol. 150). 280p. 2000. 79.50 (0-89603-654-5) Humana.

Morgan, B. Paul & Harris, Claire L., eds. Complement Regulatory Proteins. (Illus.). 382p. 1999. boxed set 99.95 (0-12-506965-0) Acad Pr.

Morgan, B. Q., tr. see Goethe, Johann Wolfgang Von.

Morgan, Barbara. Children's Zoo. 69p. 1994. pap. 18.00 (1-885156-11-1) Animas Quilts.

— Martha Graham: Sixteen Dances in Photographs. rev. ed. LC 80-81766. (Illus.). 168p. 1980. reprint ed. 125.00 (0-87100-176-4, 2176) Morgan.

— Prints, Drawings, Watercolors & Photographs. LC 88-62482. (Illus.). 128p. 1988. pap. 35.00 (0-87100-261-2) Morgan.

Morgan, Barbara, ed. Photomontage: Barbara Morgan. LC 80-81142. 64p. (Orig.). 1980. pap. 15.00 (0-87100-171-3) Morgan.

Morgan, Barbara & Patnaik, Deba P. Barbara Morgan. Martin, Lesley, ed. LC 98-86911. (Masters of Photography Ser.). (Illus.). 96p. 1998. 12.50 (0-89381-825-9) Aperture.

Morgan, Barbara K. Desserts. 36p. (Orig.). 1989. pap. 3.25 (0-940844-33-8) Wellspring.

— Potatoes. 36p. (Orig.). 1990. pap. 3.25 (0-940844-37-0) Wellspring.

***Morgan, Ben P.** The Governed of God: A Series of Transcribed Tapes By R. Brant Baker. LC 00-90928. 2000. 19.95 (0-533-13534-6) Vantage.

***Morgan, Bert, et al.** At the Track: The Golden Age of Horse Racing. LC 00-31706. (Illus.). 2001. write for info. (0-8118-2990-1) Chronicle Bks.

Morgan, Beth, ed. see Bordeaux, Darlene B.

Morgan, Beth, jt. ed. see Eidenbach, Peter L.

Morgan, Betsy & Jackson, Laura, eds. Going Home: Building Peace in El Salvador - The Story of. Repatriation. LC 91-10917. (Illus.). 160p. (Orig.). 1991. pap. 17.50 (0-945257-21-X) Apex Pr.

Morgan, Betsy Levonian & Korschgen, Ann J. Majoring in Psychology: Career Options for Undergraduates. LC 98-125166. 128p. (C). 1997. pap. text 9.00 (0-205-27525-7) Allyn.

***Morgan, Bettie, ed.** The Heritage of Wilcox County, Alabama. (Heritage of Alabama Ser.: Vol. 66). 320p. 2001. 50.00 (1-891647-67-9) Herit Pub Consult.

Morgan, Betty. The Professional Manicure Bible. LC 85-63875. (Illus.). 300p. 1985. pap. text 45.00 (0-936789-01-8) Ramif HI.

Morgan, Bill. The Beat Generation in New York: A Walking Tour of Jack Kerouac's City. LC 97-4114. (Illus.). 100p. (Orig.). 1997. per. 12.95 (0-87286-325-5) City Lights.

— Incredible Captures. 112p. (J). (gr. 4-7). 1993. pap. 2.95 (0-590-47142-2) Scholastic Inc.

— The Magic: Earvin Johnson. 136p. (J). (gr. 4-6). 1992. 2.95 (0-590-46050-1, 063) Scholastic Inc.

— Old Friends: Great Texas Courthouses. (Illus.). 160p. 1999. 55.00 (0-9667999-4-1) Landmark Publ.

Morgan, Bill. The Response to Allen Ginsberg, 1926-1994: A Bibliography of Secondary Sources, Vol. 23. LC 95-26449. 528p. 1996. lib. bdg. 85.00 (0-313-29536-0, Greenwood Pr) Greenwood.

Morgan, Bill. Trackings: The Body's Memory, the Heart's Fiction. 48p. 1998. pap. 5.00 (1-880743-08-6) Dead Metaphor.

— Trackings: The Body's Memory, the Heart's Fiction. 1998. pap. 4.95 (1-880743-09-4) Dead Metaphor.

— The Works of Allen Ginsberg, 1941-1994: A Descriptive Bibliography, 19. LC 94-41266. (Bibliographies & Indexes in American Literature Ser.: Vol. 19). 480p. 1995. lib. bdg. 79.50 (0-313-29389-9, Greenwood Pr) Greenwood.

Morgan, Bill, jt. auth. see Davis, Greg.

Morgan, Bill, ed. see Ginsberg, Allen.

Morgan, Blake. Day of the Lawless Gun. large type ed. (Dales Large Print Ser.). 208p. 1996. pap. 18.99 (1-85389-661-6, Dales) Ulverscroft.

Morgan, Bradford. The Millennium Crisis. LC 98-89502. 375p. 1998. text 25.00 (0-7388-0235-2); pap. text 15.00 (0-7388-0236-0) Xlibris Corp.

— Y2K: The Millennium Crisis. 360p. 1999. pap. text 12.95 (1-883697-10-7) Hara Pub.

Morgan, Bradley, ed. see Johnson, Anne J. & Cantor, George.

Morgan, Bradley J. Cyberhound's Web Guide: 9000 Sites with Bite. (Illus.). 1300p. 1996. 34.95 (0-7876-1017-8) Visible Ink Pr.

— Healthcare Career Directory - Nurses & Physicians. 2nd ed. Dupuis, Diane, ed. (Career Advisor Ser.). 1993. 17.95 (0-8103-9437-5, 089146) Visible Ink Pr.

— Magazine Careers Directory. 5th ed. Dupuis, Diane, ed. (Career Advisor Ser.). 1993. 17.95 (0-8103-9440-5, 089143) Visible Ink Pr.

— Newspapers Career Directory. 4th ed. Dupuis, Diane, ed. (Career Advisor Ser.). 1993. 17.95 (0-8103-9438-3, 089142) Visible Ink Pr.

— Public Relations Career Directory: A Practical One-Stop Guide to Getting a Job in Public Relations. 5th ed. Dupuis, Diane, ed. (Career Advisor Ser.). 1993. 17.95 (0-8103-9439-1, 089141) Visible Ink Pr.

— Radio Television Career Directory: A Practical One-Stop Guide to Getting a Job. 2nd ed. Dupuis, Diane, ed. (Career Advisor Ser.). 1993. 17.95 (0-8103-9441-3, 089144) Visible Ink Pr.

Morgan, Bradley J., ed. Advertising Career Directory. 5th ed. (Career Advisor Ser.). 300p. 1992. 39.00 (0-8103-5606-6, 101578) Visible Ink Pr.

— Book Publishing Career Directory. 5th ed. (Career Advisor Ser.). 300p. 1992. 39.00 (0-8103-5611-2, 101583) Visible Ink Pr.

— Magazines Career Directory: A Practical One-Stop Guide to Getting a Job in Public Relations. 5th ed. (Career Advisor Ser.). 300p. 1993. 39.00 (0-8103-5610-4, 101582) Gale.

— Marketing & Sales Career Directory. 4th ed. (Career Advisor Ser.). 300p. 1992. 39.00 (0-8103-5609-0, 101581) Visible Ink Pr.

— Travel & Hospitality Career Directory. 2nd ed. (Career Advisor Ser.). 300p. 1990. 29.95 (0-8103-5605-8, 101577) Visible Ink Pr.

Morgan, Bradley J., et al, eds. Film & Video Career Directory: A Practical, One-Step Guide to Getting a Job in Film & Video. (Career Advisor Ser.). 300p. 1994. 39.00 (0-8103-9159-7, M89334-101794) Gale.

Morgan, Bradley J. & Palmisano, Joseph M., eds. Computing & Software Career Directory. (Career Advisor Ser.). 300p. 1993. 39.00 (0-8103-9152-X, 101797) Gale.

— Computing & Software Career Directory. (Career Advisor Ser.). 300p. 1993. 17.95 (0-8103-9448-0, 089162) Visible Ink Pr.

— Environmental Career Directory. (Career Advisor Ser.). 300p. 1993. 17.95 (0-8103-9447-2, 089163) Visible Ink Pr.

— Healthcare Career Directory - Allied Health. (Career Advisor Ser.). 300p. 1993. 17.95 (0-8103-9449-9, 089167) Visible Ink Pr.

— Healthcare Career Directory - Medical-Technical. (Career Advisor Ser.). 300p. 1993. 17.95 (0-8103-9446-4) Visible Ink Pr.

— Psychology & Social Work Career Directory. (Career Advisor Ser.). 300p. 1993. 17.95 (0-8103-9445-6, 089164) Visible Ink Pr.

Morgan, Brandt, jt. auth. see Brown, Tom, Jr.

Morgan, Brandt, jt. auth. see Niederman, Sharon.

Morgan, Brendan. Sports Illustrated for Kids Game Time! An Inside Look at Football. Holder, Sherie, ed. 32p. (J). (gr. 2-8). 1999. pap. 3.99 (1-886749-65-5, Pub. by SI For Kids) Scholastic Inc.

Morgan, Bret, jt. auth. see Roth, Leland M.

Morgan, Brian. CORBA & Java: Where Distributed Objects Meet the Web. (Java Masters Ser.). 464p. 1998. pap. 44.95 (0-07-913749-0) McGraw.

— The ESL Classroom: Teaching, Critical Practice & Community Development. LC 98-229692. 128p. 1998. text 40.00 (0-8020-4334-8); pap. text 14.95 (0-8020-8154-1) U of Toronto Pr.

***Morgan, Brian.** Word Paintings. 1999. pap. write for info. (1-58235-185-6) Watermrk Pr.

Morgan, Brian D., jt. auth. see Levy, Lawrence.

Morgan, Brian L. Advances in Electronics & Electron Physics: Ninth Symposium on Photo-Electronic Image Devices, Vol. 74. Hawkes, Peter W., ed. 508p. 1988. text 205.00 (0-12-014674-6) Acad Pr.

Morgan, Brian L., ed. Advances in Electronics & Electron Physics, Vol. 64A. (Serial Publication Ser.). 1985. text 259.00 (0-12-014664-9) Acad Pr.

***Morgan, Bruce.** Strategy & Enterprise Value in the Relationship Economy. 352p. 1998. 34.95 (0-471-29284-2) Wiley.

Morgan, Bruce. What Is Your Company Worth? Building Value in the Relationship Economy. LC 97-34866. 320p. 1997. 34.95 (0-442-02625-0, VNR) Wiley.

Morgan, Bryan. Visual J++ 1.1 Unleashed. 2nd ed. LC 97-68206. 845p. 1997. 49.99 (1-57521-356-7) Sams.

Morgan, Buford. Quest for Quivera: Coronado's Exploration into Southern U. S. 189p. (YA). (gr. 7 up). 1990. 6.95 (0-89992-125-6); 12.95 (0-89992-325-9) Coun India Ed.

Morgan, Burton D. Mackinac to Miami: Exploring the Mississippi River. (Illus.). 96p. 1983. 45.00 (0-9609310-1-5) Summit Pub OH.

— Start at the Top. (Illus.). 131p. (C). 1982. 14.95 (0-9609310-0-7) Summit Pub OH.

***Morgan, Byron.** Applied Stochastic Modelling. (An Arnold Publication). 256p. 2000. pap. text 34.95 (0-340-74041-8, Pub. by E A) OUP.

Morgan, Byron J., ed. Statistics in Toxicology: A Volume in Memory of David A. Williams. LC 97-203011. (Royal Statistical Society Lecture Notes Ser.: No. 3). (Illus.). 244p. (C). 1996. text 65.00 (0-19-852329-7) OUP.

Morgan, C., et al, eds. On the Refinement Calculus. (Formal Approaches to Computing & Information Technology Ser.). 176p. 1994. reprint ed. 46.95 (3-540-19931-4) Spr-Verlag.

Morgan, C. Lloyd. Habit & Instinct. LC 73-2978. (Classics in Psychology Ser.). 1977. reprint ed. 25.95 (0-405-05150-6) Ayer.

— Introduction to Comparative Psychology, 2. LC 77-72191. (Contributions to the History of Psychology Ser.: Pt. D, Vol. II, Comparative Psychology). 240p. 1977. reprint ed. lib. bdg. 69.50 (0-313-26946-7, U6946, Greenwood Pr) Greenwood.

Morgan, C. Robert. Building an Optimizing Compiler. LC 98-122536. 472p. 1997. pap. text 59.95 (1-55558-179-X, Digital DEC) Buttrwrth-Heinemann.

Morgan, C. W. Morgan: A History of That Branch of the Morgan Family Beginning with James of New London & Continued Through Line of Col. Samuel & Sybil Huntington Morgan of Weathersfield, VT to 1911. 100p. 1991. reprint ed. pap. 15.00 (0-8328-1756-2) Higginson Bk Co.

M

An Asterisk (*) at the beginning of an entry indicates that the title is appearing for the first time.

Morgan, C. W., jt. ed. see Greenaway, David.

***Morgan, Cal.** 10 Foolish Fortune Hunters: The True Tale of a Female Marijuana Farmer. 320p. 1999. pap. 16.95 (*0-9674574-0-8*) Whatuworld.

Morgan, Cal, ed. see Wilson, Ian.

***Morgan, Candia.** Writing Mathematically: The Discourse of Investigation. LC 98-215171. x, 232p. 1998. pap. 26.95 (*0-7507-0810-7*) Taylor & Francis.

Morgan, Candia. Writing Mathematically: The Discourse of Investigation. LC 98-215171. 9. 232p. 1998. 85.00 (*0-7507-0811-5*, Falmer Pr) Taylor & Francis.

Morgan-Capner, Peter, ed. Current Topics in Clinical Virology. (Public Health Laboratory Service Publication). 314p. (C). 1992. pap. text 54.95 (*0-521-42710-X*) Cambridge U Pr.

Morgan, Carl H. The Layperson's Introduction to the New Testament. rev. ed. 1990. pap. 11.00 (*0-8170-1162-5*) Judson.

***Morgan, Carl O.** Crane Safety: A Guide to OSHA Compliance & Injury Prevention. LC 99-54937. 337p. 1999. pap. text 69.00 (*0-86587-687-8*, 687) Gov Insts.

***Morgan, Carol & Cain, Albane.** Foreign Language Culture Learning from a Dialogical Perspective. LC 00-30544. (Modern Languages Practice Ser.). 2000. pap. write for info. (*1-85359-498-9*) Taylor & Francis.

Morgan, Carol, jt. auth. see Byram, Michael.

Morgan, Carol E., ed. see Aptheker, Herbert.

Morgan, Carol M. & Levy, Doran J. Segmenting the Mature Market: Identifying, Targeting & Reaching America's Diverse, Booming Senior Markets. 300p. 1993. text 32.50 (*1-55738-448-7*, Irwn Prfssnl) McGraw-Hill Prof.

— Segmenting the Mature Market: Identifying, Targeting, & Reaching America's Diverse, Booming, Senior Markets. (Illus.). 363p. 1996. reprint ed. pap. 32.50 (*0-936889-41-1*) American Demo.

Morgan, Caroline, tr. see Dehousse.

Morgan, Carroll. Using Robots. 250p. 1985. 94.95 (*0-387-12584-1*) Spr-Verlag.

Morgan, Carroll & Vickers, Trevor, eds. On the Refinement Calculus. LC 92-40591. (Formal Applications of Computing & Information Technology Ser.). 1994. 49.95 (*0-387-19809-1*) Spr-Verlag.

Morgan, Carroll & Woodcock, J. C., eds. Refinement Workshop, Third: Organised by the Programming Research Group, Oxford & IBM UK Laboratories, Hursley Park, 9-11 January 1990. (Workshops in Computing Ser.). viii, 199p. 1991. pap. 40.00 (*0-387-19624-2*) Spr-Verlag.

Morgan, Carroll, et al. 3rd Refinement Workshop: Proceedings of the 3rd Refinement Workshop (organised By Bcs-facs & Sponsored by Ibm Uk Laboratories, Hursley Park & the Programming Research Group, University of Oxford) 9-11 January 1990, Hursley Park. LC 90-22992. (Workshops in Computing Ser.). vii, 197p. 1991. write for info. (*3-540-19624-2*) Spr-Verlag.

Morgan, Catherine. Athletes & Oracles: The Transformation of Olympia & Delphi in the Eighth Century B. C. (Illus.). 336p. (C). 1990. text 64.95 (*0-521-37451-0*) Cambridge U Pr.

***Morgan, Catherine A.** The Late Bronze Age Settlement & Early Iron Age Sanctuary. LC 99-48177. (Isthmia Ser.: Vol. 8). (Illus.). 566p. 1999. 100.00 (*0-87661-938-3*) Am Sch Athens.

Morgan, Catrin. Comfort Me with Apples. large type ed. (Magna General Fiction Ser.). 423p. 1992. 27.99 (*0-7505-0268-1*) Ulverscroft.

— Lily among Thorns. large type ed. 1993. 18.95 (*0-7505-0266-5*) Ulverscroft.

— Lily of the Valleys. large type ed. 1993. 18.95 (*0-7505-0264-9*) Ulverscroft.

Morgan, Cecil. The First Constitution of the State of Louisiana. fac. ed. LC 76-354043. (Historic New Orleans Collection Monograph). (Illus.). 147p. 1975. reprint ed. pap. 45.60 (*0-7837-7811-2*, 204756700007) Bks Demand.

Morgan, Cecilia. Public Men & Virtuous Women: The Gendered Languages of Religion & Politics in Upper Canada, 1791-1850. (Studies in Gender & History). 280p. 1997. text 55.00 (*0-8020-0725-2*); pap. text 18.95 (*0-8020-7671-8*) U of Toronto Pr.

Morgan, Charles. My Name Is Legion. (Literature Ser.). 346p. 1972. reprint ed. 39.00 (*0-403-01115-9*) Scholarly.

***Morgan, Charles & Splare, Joy.** Dragon Shadow: Skadus Drakon. 120p. (Orig.). 2000. pap. 10.00 (*0-9668392-0-X*) D C Morgan.

Morgan, Charles, ed. see Bellows, George.

Morgan, Charles J., jt. auth. see Siegel, Andrew F.

Morgan, Charles R. Gate of Hope. LC 88-63172. 230p. (Orig.). 1989. pap. 7.95 (*0-922753-01-6*) Pinnacle MO.

Morgan, Charlie. Earthworm Feeds & Feeding. 1978. pap. 8.00 (*0-914116-02-9*) Shields.

— Earthworm Selling & Shipping Guide. 1978. pap. 7.00 (*0-914116-01-0*) Shields.

— How to Raise, Store & Sell Nightcrawlers. 1984. pap. 6.00 (*0-914116-17-7*) Shields.

— Manual of Therapeutic Medications & Pesticides for Worm Growers. (Illus.). 1979. pap. 8.00 (*0-914116-16-9*) Shields.

— Profitable Earthworm Farming: Complete Manual of Worm Production, Storage, Selling & Shipping. 1975. pap. 8.00 (*0-914116-06-1*) Shields.

— Raising the African Nightcrawler. 1978. pap. 7.00 (*0-9600102-9-7*) Shields.

— The Worm Farm. 1962. pap. 7.00 (*0-914116-00-2*) Shields.

Morgan, Charlotte. One August Day. LC 97-23020. 196p. 1998. 24.00 (*0-9657639-1-9*) Van Neste.

— One August Day. 2nd rev. ed. 198p. 1998. pap. 16.00 (*0-9657639-5-1*) Van Neste.

Morgan, Charlotte E. Origin & History of the New York Employing Printers' Association. LC 68-58608. (Columbia University. Studies in the Social Sciences: No. 319). reprint ed. 27.50 (*0-404-51319-0*) AMS Pr.

Morgan, Cheryl. Dangerous Innocence. 137p. (Orig.). 1988. pap. 7.50 (*0-943487-09-9*) Sevgo Pr.

Morgan, Cheryl K. The Everglades. LC 89-5175. (Let's Take a Trip Ser.). (Illus.). 32p. (J). (gr. 3-6). 1990. pap. text 3.95 (*0-8167-1734-6*) Troll Communs.

Morgan, Chester. The Yanius Mystery. LC 96-61869. 313p. 1996. pap. 8.00 (*1-882194-26-8*) TN Valley Pub.

Morgan, Chester M. Redneck Liberal: Theodore G. Bilbo & the New Deal. LC 85-11023. 288p. 1985. pap. 89.30 (*0-7837-8516-X*, 204932500011) Bks Demand.

***Morgan, Chip.** Focused Interviewing. LC 99-42. 63p. 1999. spiral bd. 24.96 (*1-55212-291-3*) Trafford Pub.

Morgan, Chris. Future Man. (Illus.). 208p. 1979. 22.00 (*0-8290-0144-1*) Irvington.

— Future Man. (Illus.). 208p. 1987. reprint ed. pap. 6.95 (*0-8290-2117-5*) Irvington.

— Handwriting Analysis. 1996. 6.98 (*0-7858-0551-6*) Bk Sales Inc.

***Morgan, Chris & O'Reilly, Meg.** Assessing Open & Distance Learners. 192p. 1999. 59.95 (*0-7494-2875-9*, Kogan Pg Educ); pap. 29.95 (*0-7494-2878-3*, Kogan Pg Educ) Stylus Pub VA.

Morgan, Chris B. The Early Tax Records of Tallahatchie County, Mississippi, 1834-1851. LC 99-214353. 140p. (Orig.). 1997. pap. 20.00 (*1-885480-12-1*) Pioneer Pubng.

— Yalobusha County, Mississippi Original Land Entries, Bks. 1 & 2, 1833-1853. LC 99-214376. (Illus.). 198p. (Orig.). 1997. pap. 27.00 (*1-885480-14-8*) Pioneer Pubng.

Morgan, Chris B., ed. see Eskridge, William S.

Morgan, Chris J. Fortune Telling Kit, Including Accessories. LC 96-842. (Barron's Educational Ser.). 64p. 1996. 29.95 (*0-8120-8469-1*) Barron.

Morgan, Christine. Alabaster Village: Our Years in Transylvania. LC 96-50125. (Orig.). 1997. pap. 16.00 (*1-55896-350-2*, 5326, Skinner Hse Bks) Unitarian Univ.

— Curse of the Shadow Beasts. LC 98-85369. 192p. 1999. pap. 11.95 (*1-56315-188-X*, Pub. by SterlingHse) Natl Bk Netwk.

Morgan, Christine, jt. auth. see Gallagher, Patrick.

Morgan, Christopher. The Fire Jump & Other Poems. 79p. (C). 1989. 40.00 (*0-9502723-6-1*, Pub. by Brynmill Pr Ltd) St Mut.

— Muscle Bound. (Orig.). 1992. mass mkt. 4.95 (*1-56333-028-8*, Badboy) Masquerade.

— Steam Gauge. (Orig.). 1996. mass mkt. 6.50 (*1-56333-473-9*, Badboy) Masquerade.

Morgan, Christopher, ed. Sportsmen. (Orig.). 1996. mass mkt. 5.95 (*1-56333-385-6*, Badboy) Masquerade.

Morgan, Christopher, et al. Wizards & Their Wonders: Portraits in Computing. LC 97-33234. 1997. 49.95 (*0-89791-960-2*) Assn Compu Machinery.

Morgan, Christopher, jt. auth. see Van Devanter, Lynda.

***Morgan, Cindy.** Barefoot on Barbed Wire: Following God into the Unknown. 176p. 2001. pap. 9.99 (*0-7369-0095-0*) Harvest Hse.

Morgan, Claire, pseud. The Price of Salt. 276p. 1991. pap. 12.95 (*1-56280-003-5*) Naiad Pr.

— The Price of Salt. LC 75-12340. (Homosexuality Ser.). 1979. reprint ed. 19.95 (*0-405-07384-4*) Ayer.

Morgan, Clay. Idaho Unbound: A Scrapbook & Guide. Mitchell, Steve, ed. (Illus.). 248p. (Orig.). 1995. pap. 20.95 (*1-887504-00-1*) West Bound.

Morgan, Cleona. Daniel Meets a Lion. 1993. pap. 2.95 (*0-88494-885-4*) Bookcraft Inc.

Morgan, Cliff & Nicholson, Geoffrey. Beyond the Fields of Play: Cliff Morgan: An Autobiography. 288p. 1996. text 40.00 (*0-340-65741-3*, Pub. by Hodder & Stought Ltd) Trafalgar.

Morgan, Colette & Nickels, Trudy. Muppets. (Look & Find Ser.). (Illus.). 24p. (J). (gr. k-6). 1996. lib. bdg. 14.95 (*1-56674-178-5*, HTS Bks) Forest Hse.

Morgan, Colin & Morris, Glyn. Good Teaching & Learning: Pupils & Teachers Speak. LC 98-18442. 141p. 1998. 85.00 (*0-335-20263-2*); pap. 26.95 (*0-335-20262-4*) OpUniv Pr.

Morgan, Colin & Murgatroyd, Stephen. Total Quality Management in the Public Sector: An International Perspective. LC 93-24014. 208p. 1994. pap. 34.95 (*0-335-19102-9*) OpUniv Pr.

Morgan, Colin, jt. auth. see Murgatroyd, Stephen.

Morgan, Colin, jt. auth. see Riches, Colin R.

Morgan, Conway L. Expo: Trade Fair Stand Design. (Pro-Graphics Ser.). (Illus.). 160p. 1997. pap. 35.00 (*2-88046-263-0*, Rotovision) Watsn-Guptill.

— Jean Nouvel: The Elements of Architecture. LC 98-29130. (Illus.). 240p. 1998. pap. 25.00 (*0-7893-0226-8*, Pub. by Universe) St Martin.

— Logos: LOGO, Identity, Brand, Culture. (Pro-Graphics Ser.). (Illus.). 160p. 1998. pap. 35.00 (*2-88046-328-9*, Rotovision) Watsn-Guptill.

— Philippe Starck. LC 98-48499. (Illus.). 240p. 1999. pap. 25.00 (*0-7893-0227-6*, Pub. by Universe) St Martin.

— Sperone. (Illus.). 175p. 1997. 40.00 (*2-87660-191-5*, Pub. by Art Bks Intl) Partners Pubs Grp.

***Morgan, Conway Lloyd.** 20th Century Design. (Illus.). 192p. 2000. 29.95 (*0-7506-4651-9*, Architectural Pr) Buttrwrth-Heinemann.

Morgan, Conwy L. Emergent Evolution. 2nd ed. LC 77-27209. (Gifford Lectures: 1922). reprint ed. 42.50 (*0-404-60468-4*) AMS Pr.

Morgan, Conwy L. Habit & Instinct. 361p. 100.00 (*1-85506-684-X*) Thoemmes Pr.

Morgan, Conwy L. Life, Mind & Spirit. LC 77-27207. (Gifford Lectures: 1923). reprint ed. 32.50 (*0-404-60473-0*) AMS Pr.

Morgan, Craig D., et al. Bluebell Field Drill-Hole Database, Duchesne & Uintah Counties, Utah. (Circular Ser.: 90DF). 23p. (Orig.). 1995. pap. 5.95 (*1-55791-371-4*, C-90DF) Utah Geological Survey.

Morgan, Craig D., et al. Geological Considerations for Oil & Gas Drilling on State Potash Leases at Cane Creek Anticline, Grand & San Juan Counties, Utah. LC QE169.A322. (Circular Ser.: Vol. 84). (Illus.). 24p. 1991. pap. 4.00 (*1-55791-289-0*, C-84) Utah Geological Survey.

Morgan Creek Productions Staff. King & I. 1999. pap. text 3.50 (*0-590-68064-1*) Scholastic Inc.

— King & I: Deluxe Edition. 1999. pap. text 5.99 (*0-590-68066-8*) Scholastic Inc.

Morgan, Cynthia. If You Love Somebody Who Smokes: Confessions of a Nicotine Addict. LC 87-71061. 112p. (Orig.). 1987. pap. 5.95 (*0-933944-14-4*) City Miner Bks.

Morgan, D. Blessings of Home. gif. ed. LC 97-44462. (Illus.). 48p. 1998. 15.99 (*1-56507-803-9*) Harvest Hse.

— A Christmas to Remember. LC 98-204758. 48p. 1998. 15.99 (*1-56507-895-0*) Harvest Hse.

***Morgan, D.** Coming Home to You. 48p. 2000. 15.99 (*0-7369-0202-3*) Harvest Hse.

— A Friend Like You. LC 99-186315. 48p. 1999. 14.99 (*0-7369-0033-0*) Harvest Hse.

— Only Love Will Last. gif. ed. 48p. 2000. 14.99 (*0-7369-0338-0*) Harvest Hse.

Morgan, D. The Song of the Sea. LC 99-219267. (Illus.). 48p. 1999. 15.99 (*0-7369-0118-3*) Harvest Hse.

Morgan, D., jt. auth. see Pearce, David.

Morgan, D. Charles & Logghe, Craig. Advocatus Diaboli: Devil's Advocate. LC 98-92249. (Illus.). 100p. 1998. pap. 10.00 (*0-9668392-8-5*, 250) D C Morgan.

***Morgan, D. Densil.** The Span of the Cross: Christian Religion & Society in Wales 1914-2000. (Illus.). 304p. 2000. 50.00 (*0-7083-1616-6*, Pub. by U Wales Pr); pap. 29.95 (*0-7083-1571-2*, Pub. by U Wales Pr) Paul & Co Pubs.

Morgan, D. J., jt. ed. see Wickramasinghe, Nalin C.

Morgan, D. Lloyd, tr. see Nordenskiold, Gustaf E.

Morgan, D. O., ed. The Legacy of the Mongol Empire. 320p. 1997. 85.00 (*0-7007-0665-8*, Pub. by Curzon Pr Ltd) Paul & Co Pubs.

Morgan, D. P. Surface-Wave Devices for Signal Processing. (Studies in Electrical & Electronic Engineering: No. 19). 432p. 1991. reprint ed. pap. 67.50 (*0-444-88845-4*) Elsevier.

Morgan, D. P., tr. see Royer, D. & Dieulesaint, E.

Morgan, D. V. & Board, K. An Introduction to Semiconductor Microtechnology. 2nd ed. LC 89-70572. 222p. 1990. pap. 94.95 (*0-471-92478-4*) Wiley.

Morgan, D. V. & Williams, R. H., eds. Physics & Technology of Heterojunction Devices. (Materials & Devices Ser.: No. 8). 326p. 1991. 99.00 (*0-86341-204-1*, ED008Z) INSPEC Inc.

Morgan, D. V., jt. ed. see Howes, M. J.

Morgan, D. W. & Marshall, L. A. In Vivo Models of Inflammation. LC 99-11901. (Progress in Inflammatory Research Ser.). 360p. 1999. (*3-7643-5876-9*) Birkhauser.

Morgan, Dale L. The Great Salt Lake. (Illus.). 440p. 1995. pap. 14.95 (*0-87480-478-7*) U of Utah Pr.

— Humboldt, Highroad of the West. LC 70-146867. (Select Bibliographies Reprint Ser.). 1977. 26.95 (*0-8369-5634-6*) Ayer.

— Jedediah Smith & the Opening of the West. LC 53-10550. (Illus.). 470p. 1964. pap. 16.00 (*0-8032-5138-6*, Bison Books) U of Nebr Pr.

— The State of Deseret. LC 87-21632. 215p. reprint ed. pap. 66.70 (*0-7837-7063-4*, 204687500004) Bks Demand.

Morgan, Dale L., ed. Overland in 1846: Diaries & Letters of the California-Oregon Trail, 2 vols., 1. LC 93-8247. (Illus.). 475p. 1993. text 50.00 (*0-8032-3176-8*) U of Nebr Pr.

— Overland in 1846: Diaries & Letters of the California-Oregon Trail, 2 vols., 2. LC 93-8247. (Illus.). vii, 368p. 1993. text 50.00 (*0-8032-3177-6*) U of Nebr Pr.

— Overland in 1846: Diaries & Letters of the California-Oregon Trail, 2 vols., Vol. 1. LC 93-8247. (Illus.). 475p. 1993. pap. 19.95 (*0-8032-8200-1*, Bison Books) U of Nebr Pr.

— Overland in 1846: Diaries & Letters of the California-Oregon Trail, 2 vols., Vol. 2. LC 93-8247. (Illus.). vii, 368p. 1993. pap. 14.95 (*0-8032-8201-X*, Bison Books) U of Nebr Pr.

Morgan, Dale L., ed. see Anderson, William M.

***Morgan, Dana.** 7 Minute Cover Letters. (Illus.). 160p. 2000. pap. 10.95 (*0-7645-6082-4*) IDG Bks.

— 7 Minute Resumes. (Illus.). 160p. 2000. pap. text 10.95 (*0-02-863701-1*, Arco) Macmillan Gen Ref.

Morgan, Dana. 10 Minute Guide to Job Interviews. (Illus.). 160p. 1998. pap. 10.95 (*0-02-862136-0*, Arc) IDG Bks.

Morgan, Daniel P. & Jenson, William R. Teaching Behaviorally Disordered Students: Preferred Practices. 496p. (C). 1990. 105.00 (*0-675-20543-3*, Merrill Coll) P-H.

***Morgan, Darcy, et al.** Commercial Pricing. 55p. 1998. pap. 49.95 (*0-940343-95-9*, COMP) Natl Contract Mgmt.

Morgan, Dave. Door Slammers: The Chassis Book. (Illus.). 188p. (Orig.). reprint ed. pap. 30.00 (*0-9631217-0-7*) Lamplighter.

***Morgan, David.** The Beach. 2000. text 29.95 (*0-312-26558-1*) St Martin.

Morgan, David. The Capitol Press Corps: Newsmen & the Governing of New York State, 2. LC 77-84771. (Contributions in Political Science Ser.: No. 2). 177p. 1978. 52.95 (*0-8371-9883-6*, MCP/, Greenwood Pr) Greenwood.

***Morgan, David.** The Devious Dr. Franklin, Colonial Agent: Benjamin Franklin's Years in London. LC 99-52668. 1999. pap. 18.95 (*0-86554-674-6*) Mercer Univ Pr.

Morgan, David. Discovering Men. 240p. 1992. 39.95 (*0-04-445599-2*, A8163); pap. 15.95 (*0-04-445598-4*, A8164) Routledge.

— The European Parliament, Mass Media & the Search for Power & Influence. LC 99-71889. 102p. 1999. text 61.95 (*0-7546-1078-0*, Pub. by Ashgate Pub) Ashgate Pub Co.

— The Flacks of Washington: Government Information & the Public Agenda, 137. LC 85-5577. (Contributions in Political Science Ser.: No.137). (Illus.). 178p. 1986. 52.95 (*0-313-24856-7*, MFW/, Greenwood Pr) Greenwood.

— A Handbook of EMC Testing & Measurement. (IEE Electrical Measurement Ser.: No. 8). 320p. 1994. 149.00 (*0-86341-262-9*, Pub. by Peregrinus) Dist Unknown.

***Morgan, David.** Knowing the Score: Film Composers Talk about the Art, Craft, Blood, Sweat & Tears of Writing. (Masters in Film Ser.: No. 3). 288p. 2000. pap. 14.00 (*0-380-80482-4*, HarpEntertain) Morrow Avon.

Morgan, David. Medieval Persia 1040-1797. (History of the Near East Ser.). (Illus.). 197p. (C). 1989. pap. 47.00 (*0-582-49324-2*, 73578) Longman.

— The Mongols. 1990. pap. 31.95 (*0-631-17563-6*) Blackwell Pubs.

— Monty Python Speaks! LC 99-20146. (Masters in Film Ser.: Vol. 1). (Illus.). 352p. 1999. pap. 13.50 (*0-380-80479-4*, Avon Bks) Morrow Avon.

— Protestants & Pictures: Religion, Visual Culture & the Age of American Mass Production. LC 98-45312. (Illus.). 432p. 1999. 35.00 (*0-19-513029-4*) OUP.

— Sleep Secrets for Shift Workers & People with Off-Beat Schedules. LC 96-9961. 176p. 1996. pap. 15.95 (*1-57025-118-5*) Whole Person.

— Visual Piety: A History & Theory of Popular Religious Images. LC 97-14354. 283p. 1998. 40.00 (*0-520-20978-8*, Pub. by U CA Pr) Cal Prin Full Svc.

***Morgan, David.** Visual Piety: A History & Theory of Popular Religious Images. (Illus.). 265p. 1999. pap. 17.95 (*0-520-21932-5*, Pub. by U CA Pr) Cal Prin Full Svc.

Morgan, David. Whips & Whipmaking: With a Practical Introduction to Braiding. LC 72-78240. (Illus.). 139p. 1972. pap. 9.95 (*0-87033-270-8*) Cornell Maritime.

Morgan, David, ed. Icons of American Protestantism: The Art of Warner Sallman. LC 95-35800. (Illus.). 246p. 1996. 40.00 (*0-300-06342-3*) Yale U Pr.

Morgan, David & Benton, J. Edwin, eds. Intergovernmental Relations & Public Policy. 208p. (Orig.). 1985. pap. 15.00 (*0-918592-82-8*) Pol Studies.

***Morgan, David & Promey, Sally M.** The Visual Culture of American Religions. LC 00-34378. 2000. pap. write for info. (*0-520-22522-8*) U CA Pr.

Morgan, David & Stephenson, Geoffrey, eds. Suspicion & Silence: The Right to Silence in Criminal Investigations. LC 94-239004. 168p. 1994. text 38.00 (*1-85431-380-0*, Pub. by Blackstone Pr) Gaunt.

Morgan, David, jt. ed. see Scott, Sue.

***Morgan, David Gwynn.** Judging Judicial Activism. (Undercurrents Ser.). 72p. 2000. pap. 8.95 (*1-85918-229-1*, Pub. by Cork Univ) Stylus Pub VA.

Morgan, David H. Family Connections: An Introduction to Family Studies. 280p. 1996. suppl. ed. 60.95 (*0-7456-1078-1*, Pub. by Polity Pr); pap., suppl. ed. 25.95 (*0-7456-1079-X*, Pub. by Polity Pr) Blackwell Pubs.

Morgan, David H., jt. auth. see Hearn, Jeff.

Morgan, David J. The Mississippi River Delta: Legal-Geomorphologic Evaluation of Historic Shoreline Changes. (Geoscience & Man Ser.: Vol. 16). (Illus.). 104p. 1977. pap. 15.00 (*0-938909-15-0*) Geosci Pubns LSU.

— Patterns of Population Distribution: A Residential Preference Model & Its Dynamic. LC 78-18794. (University of Chicago, Department of Geography, Research Paper Ser.: No. 176). 217p. 1978. reprint ed. pap. 67.30 (*0-608-02271-3*, 206291200004) Bks Demand.

Morgan, David L. The Focus Group Guidebook. (Focus Group Kit Ser.: Vol. 1). 96p. 1997. pap. 13.95 (*0-7619-0818-8*) Sage.

— Focus Groups As Qualitative Research. (Qualitative Research Methods Ser.: Vol. 16). 96p. (C). 1988. text 24.00 (*0-8039-3208-1*); pap. text 10.50 (*0-8039-3209-X*) Sage.

— Focus Groups As Qualitative Research. 2nd ed. LC 96-25389. (Qualitative Research Methods Ser.: Vol. 16). 80p. 1997. 24.00 (*0-7619-0342-9*); pap. 10.50 (*0-7619-0343-7*) Sage.

— Planning & Designing Focus Group Research from Start to Finish. (Focus Group Kit Ser.: Vol. 2). 128p. 1997. pap. 16.95 (*0-7619-0817-X*) Sage.

Morgan, David L., ed. Successful Focus Groups: Advancing the State of the Art. LC 93-6872. (Focus Editions Ser.: Vol. 156). (Illus.). 320p. (C). 1993. text 59.95 (*0-8039-4873-5*); pap. text 26.00 (*0-8039-4874-3*) Sage.

Morgan, David L. & Krueger, Richard A., eds. Focus Group Kit, Vols. 1-6. LC 97-21135. 752p. 1997. 99.95 (*0-7619-0760-2*) Sage.

Morgan, David M. L., ed. Polyamine Protocols. LC 97-37499. (Methods in Molecular Biology Ser.: Vol. 79). (Illus.). 208p. 1997. 79.50 (*0-89603-448-8*) Humana.

Morgan, David P. Confessions of a Train-Watcher: Four Decades of Railroad Writing by David P. Morgan. Drury, George H., ed. LC 98-125240. (Illus.). 160p. 1997. 39.95 (*0-89024-306-9*, 01081, Kalmbach Books) Kalmbach.

An Asterisk (*) at the beginning of an entry indicates that the title is appearing for the first time.

Morgan, David P. & Scofield, Christopher L. Neural Networks & Speech Processing. (International Series in Engineering & Computer Science, VLSI, Computer Architecture, & Digital Screen Processing). 416p. (C). 1991. text 128.00 (*0-7923-9144-6*) Kluwer Academic.

Morgan, David P., jt. auth. see Balentine, Bruce.

Morgan, David R., ed. Urban Management. LC 72-8662. 183p. 1973. text 34.50 (*0-8422-5065-4*); pap. text 12.95 (*0-8422-0249-8*) Irvington.

Morgan, David R. & Caddy, David. Almost Alchemy. 52p. (C). 1988. 75.00 (*0-947612-31-9*, Pub. by Rivelin Grapheme Pr) St Mut.

Morgan, David R. & England, Robert E. Managing Urban America. 5th ed. LC 98-53700. (Illus.). 416p. (C). 1998. pap. text 32.95 (*1-56643-065-8*, Chatham House Pub) Seven Bridges.

Morgan, David R., et al. Oklahoma Politics & Policies: Governing the Sooner State. LC 90-13044. (Politics & Governments of the American States Ser.). xxviii, 264p. 1991. pap. text 25.00 (*0-8032-8136-6*) U of Nebr Pr.

— Oklahoma Politics & Policies: Governing the Sooner State. LC 90-13044. (Politics & Governments of the American States Ser.). xxviii, 264p. 1991. text 45.00 (*0-8032-3106-7*) U of Nebr Pr.

Morgan, David R., jt. ed. see Benton, J. Edwin.

Morgan, David T. The Devious Dr. Franklin, Colonial Agent: Benjamin Franklin's Years in London. 280p. 1996. 34.95 (*0-86554-525-1*, MUP/H395) Mercer Univ Pr.

— The New Crusades, the New Holy Land: Conflict in the Southern Baptist Convention, 1969-1991. LC 95-12245. 264p. (C). 1996. pap. text 24.95 (*0-8173-0804-0*) U of Ala Pr.

Morgan, David T. & Stafford, C. Russell, eds. Early Late Woodland Occupations in the Fall Creek Locality of the Mississippi Valley. LC 87-6584. (Kampsville Archeological Center Technical Reports: No. 3). (Illus.). 145p. (Orig.). 1987. pap. 7.95 (*0-942118-26-X*) Ctr Amer Arche.

Morgan, Deborah & Engler, Nick. How to Build Outdoor Structures. (Popular Science Ser.). (Illus.). 416p. (Orig.). 1987. pap. 21.95 (*0-8069-6742-0*) Sterling.

Morgan, Dennis. The Cardiff Story. 272p. (C). 1989. 90.00 (*0-7855-6867-0*, Pub. by D Brown & Sons Ltd) St Mut.

— Life in Process. (Personal Growth Bookshelf). 192p. 1993. 11.99 (*1-56476-125-8*, 6-3125, Victor Bks) Chariot Victor.

Morgan, Dennis, jt. auth. see Kuo, Sen.

Morgan, Dennis, ed. see Kaltenborn, Freddy M.

Morgan, Dennis L. The Complete Guide to Marketing a Small Business or Product Successfully. 269p. (Orig.). 1993. 29.95 (*0-9640823-0-6*) Morgan Mktg.

Morgan, Derek. Surrogacy & the Moral Economy. (Medico-Legal Issues Ser.). 1994. 59.95 (*1-85521-034-7*, Pub. by Dartmth Pub Co) Ashgate Pub Co.

Morgan, Derek, ed. Personal Injury. (C). 1991. text 22.00 (*1-85431-133-6*, Pub. by Blackstone Pr) Gaunt.

Morgan, Derek & Lee, Robert G., eds. Blackstone's Guide to the Human Fertilisation & Embryology Act, 1990: Abortion & Embryo Research, the New Law. 276p. (C). 1991. text 33.00 (*1-85431-105-0*, Pub. by Blackstone Pr) Gaunt.

Morgan, Diana. Chapel Hill. 256p. (Orig.). 1992. mass mkt. 4.99 (*0-446-35771-5*, Pub. by Warner Bks) Little.

— Christian Prespectives on Contemporary Issues. rev. ed. 96p. 1995. pap. 12.95 (*1-85311-110-4*, 819, Pub. by Canterbury Press Norwich) Morehouse Pub.

— The Lost Years. large type ed. (General Ser.). 464p. 1993. 27.99 (*0-7089-2882-X*) Ulverscroft.

Morgan, Diane. The Basset Hound Owner's Survival Guide. LC 97-28743. 212p. 1998. 24.95 (*0-87605-018-6*) Macmillan.

***Morgan, Diane.** Kant Trouble: The Obscurities of Enlightened. LC 99-44820. (Warwick Studies in European Philosophy Ser.). 224p. 2000. pap. write for info. (*0-415-18353-7*) Routledge.

— Siberian Huskies. LC 99-16718. (Complete Idiot's Guides (Lifestyle) Ser.). 1999. pap. text 14.95 (*1-58245-121-4*) Howell Bks.

Morgan, Diane. Understanding Your Horse's Lameness. LC 92-13128. (Illus.). 152p. 1992. 19.95 (*0-939481-26-X*) Half Halt Pr.

Morgan, Diane, et al. The Basic Gourmet: One Hundred Foolproof Recipes & Essential Techniques for the Beginning Cook. LC 94-18470. (Illus.). 168p. 1995. pap. 16.95 (*0-8118-0476-3*) Chronicle Bks.

— The Basic Gourmet Entertains: Foolproof Recipes & Manageable Menus for the Beginning Cook. LC 96-38846. 1997. pap. 17.95 (*0-8118-1428-9*) Chronicle Bks.

— Cooking for the Week: Leisurely Weekend Cooking for Easy Weekday Meals. LC 98-31674. (Illus.). 167p. 1999. pap. 18.95 (*0-8118-2128-5*) Chronicle Bks.

— Very Entertaining: Menus for Special Occasions. Lustburg, Lynn, ed. LC 89-81843. (Illus.). 174p. (Orig.). 1990. pap. 19.95 (*0-9620937-1-8*) Entertaining People.

Morgan, Don. Numerical Methods of DSP Systems in C. LC 97-1744. 352p. 1997. pap. 54.99 (*0-471-13232-2*) Wiley.

— Our Father: A Tribute to Dermot Morgan LC 99-158444. 206 p. 1998. 19.95 (*1-874597-96-0*) New Island Books.

— Practical DSP Modeling, Techniques & Programming in C. 442p. 1994. pap. 36.95 (*0-471-00606-8*); pap. 49.95 incl. disk (*0-471-00434-0*) Wiley.

Morgan, Don, jt. auth. see Lacy, Madison S.

Morgan, Donald G. Congress & the Constitution: A Study of Responsibility. LC 66-18252. 506p. reprint ed. pap. 156.90 (*0-608-30100-0*, 200524500051) Bks Demand.

Morgan, Donald P. Recognition & Management of Pesticide Poisonings. 4th ed. (Illus.). 207p. (C). 1996. pap. text 30.00 (*0-7881-3176-1*) DIANE Pub.

***Morgan, Donald W.** When Your World Is Coming Apart. 192p. (gr. 13). 2000. mass mkt. 5.99 (*0-8007-8677-7*) Chosen Bks.

Morgan, Dorothy H. & Aberdeen and North-East Scotland Family History Society Staff. The People of Crathie & Braemar (kindrocht) 1696: Taken from List of Pollable Persons in the Shires of Aberdeen 1696. LC 98-203450. 1998. write for info. (*1-900173-11-5*) Aberdeen & NE Scot.

***Morgan, Douglas.** Tiger Cruise. 288p. 2000. text 23.95 (*0-312-87042-6*) St Martin.

Morgan, E. Lo Que Toda Madre Necesita.Tr. of What Every Mom Needs. (SPA.). 1996. pap. 9.99 (*0-8297-0616-X*) Vida Pubs.

Morgan, E. B., jt. auth. see Andrews, C. F.

Morgan, E. Buford. Fruits of Murder. LC 99-61934. 365p. 1999. 25.00 (*0-7388-0386-3*); pap. 15.00 (*0-7388-0387-1*) Xlibris Corp.

Morgan, E. David, jt. ed. see Mandava, N. Bhushan.

Morgan, E. Sarah. Exposures: Essays by Missouri Women. unabridged ed. LC 96-46255. (Illus.). 160p. 1997. pap. 12.00 (*0-9617499-4-6*) Woods Colt Pr.

Morgan, E. Victor & Morgan, Ann D. The Economics of Public Policy. LC 78-182904. ix, 321p. 1972. write for info. (*0-85224-212-3*) Edinburgh U Pr.

Morgan, Edith, jt. auth. see Jasper, James M.

Morgan, Edmund, ed. see Wigglesworth, Michael.

Morgan, Edmund M., ed. Some Problems of Proof under the Anglo-American System of Litigation, 1955. LC 75-31438. (James S. Carpentier Lectures Ser.: 1955). 207p. 1976. reprint ed. lib. bdg. 35.00 (*0-8371-8517-3*, MOSP, Greenwood Pr) Greenwood.

Morgan, Edmund M., jt. auth. see Joughlin, Louis.

Morgan, Edmund S. American Slavery - American Freedom: The Ordeal of Colonial Virginia. 464p. 1995. pap. 14.95 (*0-393-31288-7*, Norton Paperbks) Norton.

— The Birth of the Republic, 1763-89. LC 92-8871. (Chicago History of American Civilization Ser.). 224p. (C). 1992. pap. text 11.00 (*0-226-53757-9*) U Ch Pr.

— The Birth of the Republic, 1763-89. rev. ed. LC 77-70169. (Chicago History of American Civilization Ser.). 1997. reprint ed. pap. text 7.95 (*0-226-53759-5*, CHAC14) U Ch Pr.

— The Birth of the Republic, 1763-89. 3rd ed. LC 92-8871. (Chicago History of American Civilization Ser.). 224p. (C). 1997. lib. bdg. 33.00 (*0-226-53756-0*) U Ch Pr.

— The Challenge of the American Revolution. (C). 1978. pap. 10.50 (*0-393-00876-2*) Norton.

— The Genius of George Washington. (Illus.). 104p. 1982. pap. 9.95 (*0-393-00060-5*) Norton.

— The Gentle Puritan: A Life of Ezra Stiles, 1727-1795. LC 62-8257. (Illus.). 508p. 1974. reprint ed. pap. 157.50 (*0-8357-3923-6*, 203665800004) Bks Demand.

— Inventing the People. 1989. pap. 12.95 (*0-393-30623-2*) Norton.

— The Meaning of Independence: John Adams, George Washington, Thomas Jefferson. LC 76-8438. (Richard Lectures for 1975, University of Virginia Ser.). 95p. reprint ed. pap. 30.00 (*0-7837-4227-4*, 204391400012) Bks Demand.

— The Puritan Family: Religion & Domestic Relations in Seventeenth-Century New England. LC 80-18819. 196p. 1980. reprint ed. lib. bdg. 57.50 (*0-313-22703-9*, MOPFA, Greenwood Pr) Greenwood.

— Virginians at Home: Family Life in the Eighteenth Century. LC 52-14250. (America Ser.: Vol. 2). (Illus.). 101p. (Orig.). 1952. 14.95 (*0-910412-52-9*) Colonial Williamsburg.

— Visible Saints: The History of a Puritan Idea. LC 63-9999. 168p. 1965. pap. text 10.95 (*0-8014-9041-3*) Cornell U Pr.

Morgan, Edmund S., ed. Puritan Family. rev. ed. 208p. 1942. pap. 13.50 (*0-06-131227-4*, TB1227, Torch) HarpC.

— Puritan Political Ideas, 1558 1794. LC 65-22347. (Orig.) 1965. pap. 7.35 (*0-672-60042-0*, AHS33, Bobbs) Macmillan.

Morgan, Edmund S. & Morgan, Helen M. The Stamp Act Crisis: Prologue to Revolution. LC 94-31357. (Institute of Early American History & Culture Ser.). 350p. 1995. pap. text 17.95 (*0-8078-4513-2*) U of NC Pr.

Morgan, Edna Q. John Adam Treutlen, Georgia's First Constitutional Governor - His Life, Real & Rumored. unabridged ed. LC 98-75823. (Illus.). 88p. 1998. write for info. (*0-9669559-0-0*) Hist Effingham.

Morgan, Edward B., jt. auth. see Davis, Edward H.

Morgan, Edward E., Jr. & Hiltner, John. Managing Aging & Human Service Agencies. LC 91-5227. 168p. 1992. 27.95 (*0-8261-7810-3*) Springer Pub.

Morgan, Edward H., jt. auth. see Warlick, Roger.

Morgan, Edward P. The '60s Experience: Hard Lessons about Modern America. (Illus.). 330p. 1991. 49.95 (*0-87722-805-1*) Temple U Pr.

— The '60s Experience: Hard Lessons about Modern America. 1992. pap. 22.95 (*1-56639-014-1*) Temple U Pr.

Morgan, Edward V. Theory & Practice of Central Banking, 1797-1913. 252p. 1965. 35.00 (*0-7146-1237-5*, Pub. by F Cass Pubs) Intl Spec Bk.

Morgan, Edwin. Collected Poems: Collected Poems. 608p. 1996. pap. 27.95 (*1-85754-188-X*, Pub. by Carcanet Pr) Paul & Co Pubs.

— Flower of Evil: Life of Charles Baudelaire. LC 75-114889. (Select Bibliographies Reprint Ser.). 1977. 21.95 (*0-8369-5293-6*) Ayer.

***Morgan, Edwin.** Snow & Other Guises. 160p. 2000. 14.95 (*1-85754-459-5*, Pub. by Carcanet Pr) Paul & Co Pubs.

Morgan, Edwin. Virtual & Other Realities. LC 98-209965. 128p. 1998. pap. 14.95 (*1-85754-347-5*, Pub. by Carcanet Pr) Paul & Co Pubs.

Morgan, Edwin, ed. Collins Albatross Book of Longer Poems: English & American Poetry from the Fourteenth Century to the Present Day. 736p. 1977. 20.95 (*0-8369-6051-3*) Ayer.

Morgan, Edwin, tr. see Racine, Jean.

Morgan, Edwin, tr. see Weores, Sandor.

Morgan, Efiona. Daughters of the Moon Tarot Deck: Tarot of the Goddess. (Illus.). 75p. 1996. 26.95 (*1-880130-04-1*) Daughters Moon.

Morgan, Eileen. Lust: Love & Longing. (Sin Series). (Illus.). 128p. 1999. 24.95 (*0-9669573-1-8*) Red Rock.

Morgan, Elaine. The Descent of the Child. 208p. 1995. 25.00 (*0-19-509895-1*) OUP.

— The Descent of the Child: Human Evolution from a New Perspective. 197p. (C). 1998. text 20.00 (*0-7881-5547-4*) DIANE Pub.

— The Descent of Woman: The Classic Study of Evolution. 4th ed. 288p. 1997. pap. 12.95 (*0-285-62700-7*, Pub. by Souvenir Pr Ltd) IPG Chicago.

— The Scars of Evolution: What Our Bodies Tell Us about Human Origin. (Illus.). 208p. 1994. reprint ed. pap. 13.95 (*0-19-509431-X*) OUP.

Morgan, Elaine & Davies, Stephen. Red Sea Pilot: Aden to Cyrpus. (Illus.). 280p. 1995. 125.00 (*0-85288-253-X*, Pub. by Laurie Norie & Wilson Ltd) St Mut.

Morgan, Elaine, jt. auth. see Davies, Stephen.

Morgan, Elemore. The Face of Louisiana. LC 78-86493. 176p. 1969. pap. 54.60 (*0-7837-8467-8*, 204927200010) Bks Demand.

— Five Days in Baton Rouge. 1951. pap. 2.50 (*1-57980-025-4*) Claitors.

Morgan, Elisa. Chronicles of Childhood: Recording Your Child's Spiritual Journey. 1996. 9.99 (*0-310-96450-4*) Zondervan.

— Meditations for Mothers: Moments with God amidst a Busy Nest. LC 98-32032. 2000. 14.99 (*0-310-22654-6*) Zondervan.

— Mom to Mom: Moving from Unspoken Questions to Quiet Confidence. 112p. 1996. 12.99 (*0-310-20396-1*) Zondervan.

— Mom to Mom: Moving from Unspoken Questions to Quiet Confidence. 112p. 1998. pap. 9.99 (*0-310-22557-4*) Zondervan.

***Morgan, Elisa.** What Every Child Needs. (Illus.). 2000. pap. 12.99 (*0-310-23271-6*) Zondervan.

Morgan, Elisa, ed. Heartfelt Devotions for Mom. gif. ed. LC 97-207196. 48p. 1997. 9.99 (*0-310-97052-0*) Zondervan.

***Morgan, Elisa, ed.** A Mother's Touch: The Difference a Mom Makes. (Illus.). 155p. 1999. pap. text 30.00 (*0-7881-6808-8*) DIANE Pub.

Morgan, Elisa & Kuykendall, Carol. What Every Child Needs: Daily Encouragement for Getting to the Heart of Mothering. 366p. (J). 1997. spiral bd. 9.99 (*0-310-97395-3*) Zondervan.

— What Every Child Needs: Getting to the Heart of Mothering. LC 97-21801. 256p. 1997. 15.99 (*0-310-21151-4*) Zondervan.

— What Every Mom Needs: Meet Your Nine Basic Needs (And Be a Better Mom) 224p. 1998. pap. 10.99 (*0-310-21920-5*) Zondervan.

Morgan, Elise N. The Angel of the Presence. (Meditation Ser.). 1922. pap. 6.95 (*0-87516-327-0*) DeVorss.

— Communion. (Meditation Ser.). 1928. pap. 6.95 (*0-87516-328-9*) DeVorss.

— The Illimitable One. (Meditation Ser.). 1934. pap. 6.95 (*0-87516-329-7*) DeVorss.

— Now, This Day. 1948. pap. 6.95 (*0-87516-330-0*) DeVorss.

— That We May Be Willing to Receive. (Meditation Ser.). 1938. pap. 6.95 (*0-87516-331-9*) DeVorss.

— The Way. (Meditation Ser.). 1972. pap. 6.95 (*0-87516-332-7*) DeVorss.

— Your Own Path: Written to Illumine the Way Through Meditation. (Meditation Ser.). 96p. 1985. pap. 6.95 (*0-87516-559-1*) DeVorss.

***Morgan, Elizabeth.** Sewing Church Linens: Convent Hemming & Simple Embroidery. rev. ed. LC 99-40451. (Illus.). 1999. 14.95 (*0-8192-1841-3*, 6288) Morehouse Pub.

Morgan, Elizabeth. To Save My Child: The Elizabeth Morgan Story. mass mkt. write for info. (*0-06-109599-0*, Harp PBks) HarpC.

Morgan, Elizabeth, ed. Socialist & Labor Songs of the 1930's. LC 96-77435. 88p. 1997. pap. 12.00 (*0-88286-230-8*) C H Kerr.

Morgan, Elizabeth D. Jane Long: A Child's Pictorial History. LC 92-17739. (Illus.). 104p. (J). (gr. 4-5). 1992. 12.95 (*0-89015-861-4*) Sunbelt Media.

— Mirabeau B. Lamar: President of Texas. LC 94-2641. (Illus.). 96p. (J). (gr. 4-5). 1995. 12.95 (*0-89015-963-7*, Eakin Pr) Sunbelt Media.

— Texas Christmas: As Celebrated under 6 Flags. LC 95-35770. (Illus.). 64p. (J). (gr. 5-6). 1995. 12.95 (*1-57168-067-5*, Eakin Pr) Sunbelt Media.

Morgan, Elizabeth M., et al. AgriScience Explorations. (Illus.). 1998. teacher ed. 12.95 (*0-8134-3125-5*, 3125) Interstate.

***Morgan, Elizabeth M., et al.** AgriScience Explorations. 2nd ed. LC 99-71694. (Illus.). viii, 518p. 2000. 74.95 (*0-8134-3189-1*) Interstate.

Morgan, Elizabeth S. The Governor of Desire: Poems. LC 92-37785. ix, 64p. (C). 1993. pap. 8.95 (*0-8071-1812-5*); text 15.95 (*0-8071-1811-7*) La State U Pr.

— On Long Mountain: Poems. LC 97-41958. 64p. 1998. pap. 11.95 (*0-8071-2253-X*) La State U Pr.

— Uncertain Seasons. 168p. 1996. pap. 15.95 (*0-8173-0865-2*) U of Ala Pr.

Morgan, Elmer. Sibling Rivalry in God's Family. 147p. (Orig.). 1993. pap. 5.95 (*1-56794-033-1*, C2292) Star Bible.

Morgan, Emma. A Stillness Built of Motion: Living with Tourette's. 2nd ed. (Illus.). (Orig.). 1996. reprint ed. pap. 7.00 (*0-9650733-4-3*, ECHO-003) Echolalia Pr.

Morgan, Eric. Defending Against the Enemy: Coping with Parkinson's Disease. LC 95-72727. 128p. (Orig.). 1997. pap. 12.95 (*0-936609-36-2*) QED Ft Bragg.

Morgan, Eric & Kopel, David. The Assault Weapon Panic: "Political Correctness" Takes Aim at the Constitution. (Issue Papers: No. 12-91). 66p. 1991. pap. text 8.00 (*1-57655-052-4*) Independ Inst.

Morgan, Ernest. Arthur Morgan Remembered. 1991. pap. 6.00 (*0-910420-31-9*) Comm Serv OH.

— Dealing Creatively with Death: A Manual of Death Education & Simple Burial. 10th ed. LC 83-71373. (Simple Burial Ser.). 168p. 1984. pap. 9.00 (*0-914064-19-3*) Zinn Pub Grp.

***Morgan, Ernest & Morgan, Jenifer.** Dealing Creatively with Death: A Manual of Death Education & Simple Burial. 14th rev. ed. 170p. 2001. pap. 12.95 (*0-942679-24-5*) Upper Access.

Morgan, F., jt. ed. see Vinogradoff, P.

Morgan, Faye. Riding the Gold Curve. 384p. 1994. 25.00 (*0-89672-326-7*) Tex Tech Univ Pr.

Morgan, Felix R. De Mujeres y Perros. LC 89-81221. (Coleccion Caniqui). (SPA., Illus.). 101p. (Orig.). 1990. pap. 9.95 (*0-89729-555-2*) Ediciones.

Morgan, Fiona. Daughters of the Moon Tarot: Tarot of the Goddess. (Illus.). 96p. 1991. reprint ed. pap. 9.95 (*1-880130-01-7*) Daughters Moon.

— Goddess Spirituality Book: Rituals, Holydays & Moon Magic. (Illus.). 194p. (Orig.). 1995. pap. 13.00 (*1-880130-06-8*) Daughters Moon.

— The Lesbian Erotic Cookbook. LC 98-71933. (Illus.). 218p. 1998. pap. 22.95 (*1-880130-08-4*) Daughters Moon.

— Mysteries of the Goddess: Astrology, Tarot & the Magical Arts. (Illus.). 194p. (Orig.). 1995. pap. 13.00 (*1-880130-37-8*) Daughters Moon.

Morgan, Fideles, jt. ed. see Lyons, Paddy.

Morgan, Fidelis, ed. The Female Tatler. 242p. (Orig.). 1992. pap. 6.95 (*0-460-87074-2*, Everyman's Classic Lib) Tuttle Pubng.

Morgan, Florette. Proper Me! The Way to Be. 70p. 1997. pap. 15.00 (*0-9653163-8-6*) Character Dev.

Morgan, Forrest, ed. The Collected Works of Walter Bagehot, 5 vols., Set. 2706p. (C). 1995. text, boxed set 655.00 (*0-415-13154-5*) Routledge.

Morgan, Forrest E. Living the Martial Way: A Manual for the Way a Modern Warrior Should Think. LC 92-16969. 320p. 1992. pap. 16.95 (*0-942637-76-3*) Barricade Bks.

***Morgan, Frank.** Calculus Lite. 2nd ed. LC 97-7245. (Illus.). 320p. (C). 1999. reprint ed. pap. text 28.00 (*1-56881-112-8*) AK Peters.

Morgan, Frank. Franham's War. large type ed. 168p. 1990. 18.95 (*0-7451-1146-7*, G K Hall Lrg Type) Mac Lib Ref.

***Morgan, Frank.** Geometric Measure Theory: A Beginner's Guide. 3rd ed. 400p. 2000. 69.95 (*0-12-506851-4*) Acad Pr.

— The Math Chat Book. LC 99-67970. 124p. 2000. pap. 19.95 (*0-88385-530-5*) Math Assn.

Morgan, Frank. Riemannian Geometry: A Beginner's Guide. 2nd rev. ed. LC 97-35094. (Illus.). 160p. (C). 1997. text 34.00 (*1-56881-073-3*) AK Peters.

Morgan, Frank, ed. Geometric Measure Theory: A Beginner's Guide. 2nd ed. (Illus.). 175p. 1995. text 37.00 (*0-12-506857-3*) Acad Pr.

***Morgan, Frank B.** Degrees & Other Awards Conferred by Degree- Granting Institutions: 1995-96. 71p. 1998. pap. 8.50 (*0-16-063677-9*) USGPO.

— Degrees & Other Awards Conferred by Institutions of Higher Education: 1993-94. 67p. 1996. pap. 4.75 (*0-16-048711-0*) USGPO.

— Degrees & Other Awards Conferred by Institutions of Higher Education: 1994-95. 69p. 1997. pap. 9.00 (*0-16-049233-5*) USGPO.

Morgan, Fred. Haunted Uwharries: Ghost Stories, Witch Tales & Other Strange Happenings from North America's Oldest Mountains. Bledsoe, Jerry, ed. LC 92-72657. (Illus.). 173p. 1992. pap. 10.95 (*1-878086-13-8*, Pub. by Down Home NC) Blair.

— Here & Now III: An Approach to Writing Through Perception. 3rd ed. 238p. (C). 1979. pap. text, teacher ed. 2.50 (*0-15-535625-9*) Harcourt Coll Pubs.

Morgan, Fred & Pohlman, Richard W. Education & Practice: The Critical Interface. (Illus.). 250p. 1993. pap. text 50.00 (*1-880250-02-0*) Assoc Comp Aid Des.

Morgan, Fred T. Ghost Tales of the Uwharries. LC 68-58501. 152p. 1991. pap. 7.95 (*0-89587-083-5*) Blair.

Morgan, Frederick. A Book of Change (Poems) LC 72-2214. 160p. 1972. 20.00 (*0-684-12950-7*); pap. 10.00 (*0-684-13962-6*) Hudson Rev.

— The Fountain & Other Fables. 66p. 1985. 20.00 (*0-931757-00-2*); pap. 15.00 (*0-931757-01-0*) Pterodactyl Pr.

— Northbrook. Poems. LC 81-14664. 88p. 1982. 14.95 (*0-252-00947-9*); 9.95 (*0-252-00948-7*) U of Ill Pr.

— Poems: New & Selected. LC 86-30844. 280p. 1987. 12.95 (*0-252-01434-0*); text 24.95 (*0-252-01433-2*) U of Ill Pr.

— Poems for Paula. 72p. (Orig.). 1995. 14.00 (*1-885266-14-6*); pap. 8.00 (*1-885266-18-9*) Story Line.

— Poems of the 2 Worlds. LC 76-51907. 132p. 1977. 14.95 (*0-252-00604-6*) U of Ill Pr.

— The Tarot of Cornelius Agrippa. LC 77-94782. (Illus.). 50p. (Orig.). 1978. pap. 75.00 (*0-915298-11-2*) Hudson Rev.

Morgan, Freeman E., Jr. Updated Morgan Genealogy: A History of James Morgan, 1607-1685, of New London, CT. LC 98-170982. (Illus.). 280p. 1998. pap. 30.50 (*0-7884-0870-4*, M564) Heritage Bk.

M

Morgan, G., ed. The Franklin's Tale. 1992. pap. 9.50 (*0-614-16251-3*, Pub. by Irish Acad Pr) Intl Spec Bk.
Morgan, G., et al. Child Care Handbook. (Illus.). 32p. 1988. reprint ed. write for info. (*0-9618201-1-X*) Work Family Direct.
Morgan, G., ed. see Casselberry, L. & Candy, F.
Morgan, G. Campbell. Basic Principles of the Christian Life. 89p. 1998. pap. 8.99 (*1-84030-016-7*) Emerald House Group Inc.
— El Corazon de Dios.Tr. of Hosea: The Heart & Holiness of God. (SPA.). 152p. 1992. pap. 3.75 (*0-8254-1494-6*, Edit Portavoz) Kregel.
— God's Last Word to Man. 1997. pap. text 8.99 (*1-898787-90-5*) Emerald House Group Inc.
— The Gospel According to John. Fang, Carl, tr. (G. Campbell Morgan's Expository Ser.). 1985. write for info. (*0-941598-94-2*); pap. write for info. (*0-941598-18-7*) Living Spring Pubns.
— The Gospel According to Luke. Chao, Lorna, tr. (G. Campbell Morgan's Expository Ser.). 1985. write for info. (*0-941598-95-0*) Living Spring Pubns.
— The Gospel According to Luke. Chao, Lorna Y., tr. (G. Campbell Morgan's Expository Ser.). 1985. pap. write for info. (*0-941598-17-9*) Living Spring Pubns.
— The Gospel According to Mark. Chan, Silas, tr. from ENG. (G. Campbell Morgan's Expository Ser.). (CHI.). 1984. write for info. (*0-941598-96-9*); pap. write for info. (*0-941598-16-0*) Living Spring Pubns.
— The Gospel According to Matthew. Chang, David, tr. from ENG. (G. Campbell Morgan's Expository Ser.). (CHI.). 1984. write for info. (*0-941598-97-7*); pap. write for info. (*0-941598-15-2*) Living Spring Pubns.
***Morgan, G. Campbell.** Hosea: The Heart & Holiness of God. 159p. 1998. pap. 15.00 (*1-57910-169-0*) Wipf & Stock.
Morgan, G. Campbell. Isaiah. Chao, Lorna Y., tr. (G. Campbell Morgan's Expository Ser.). 1985. write for info. (*0-941598-93-4*); pap. write for info. (*0-941598-20-9*) Living Spring Pubns.
— Jeremiah. Chan, Silas, tr. from CHI. (Morgan's Expository Ser.). 1987. write for info. (*0-941598-90-X*); pap. write for info. (*0-941598-42-X*) Living Spring Pubns.
***Morgan, G. Campbell.** Malachi's Message for Today. 131p. 1998. pap. 14.00 (*1-57910-176-3*) Wipf & Stock.
Morgan, G. Campbell. Me Han Defraudado! Orig. Title: Wherein!. (SPA.). 96p. 1992. mass mkt. 3.99 (*0-8254-1497-0*, Edit Portavoz) Kregel.
— Parables of the Kingdom. 221p. 1997. pap. 16.00 (*1-57910-089-9*) Wipf & Stock.
— Practice of Prayer. 1997. pap. text 7.99 (*1-898787-49-2*) Emerald House Group Inc.
— Preaching - Chinese Edition. Liu, John J., tr. (CHI.). 78p. 1997. pap. 5.00 (*1-56582-031-2*) Christ Renew Min.
— The Simple Things of the Christian Life. 1984. pap. 3.25 (*0-915374-40-4*) Rapids Christian.
***Morgan, G. Campbell.** Sunrise. (Classics Ser.). (Illus.). 85p. 1999. pap. 8.99 (*1-84030-057-4*) Emerald House Group Inc.
Morgan, G. Campbell. Survey of the Bible. (World Classic Library). 639p. 1994. reprint ed. 19.99 (*0-529-10061-4*, WCL1) World Pubing.
Morgan, G. Campbell. The Ten Commandments. 126p. 1997. pap. 8.99 (*1-898787-98-0*) Emerald House Group Inc.
***Morgan, G. Campbell.** The Ten Commandments. 126p. 1998. pap. 13.00 (*1-57910-175-5*) Wipf & Stock.
Morgan, G. Campbell & Spurgeon, Charles H. Understanding the Holy Spirit. (Classic Library). 500p. 1995. reprint ed. 19.99 (*0-529-10482-2*, UHS) World Pubing.
Morgan, G. Edward. Clinical Anesthesiology. 2nd ed. 1005p. (C). 1996. pap. text 54.95 (*0-8385-1381-6*, A1381-1, Apple Lange Med) McGraw.
Morgan, G. G., jt. ed. see Boim, L.
Morgan, G. G., ed. see Leith, Philip.
Morgan, G. J. What is Revival. 1998. pap. text 6.99 (*1-898787-30-1*) Ambassador Prodns Ltd.
Morgan, G. R., jt. ed. see Pauly, Daniel.
Morgan, Gareth. Athos Sixty. 144p. 1994. pap. 10.95 (*1-57087-069-1*) Prof Pr NC.
— Church Computing: A Strategy. (C). 1989. 49.00 (*1-870404-02-5*, Pub. by Jay Bks) St Mut.
— Creative Organization Theory: A Resource Book. 376p. (C). 1989. text 62.00 (*0-8039-3444-0*); pap. text 27.50 (*0-8039-3438-6*) Sage.
— Images of Organization. 432p. (C). 1986. text 58.00 (*0-8039-2830-0*); pap. text 28.00 (*0-8039-2831-9*) Sage.
— Images of Organization. 2nd ed. LC 96-35682. 1996. 59.95 (*0-7619-0631-2*) Sage.
Morgan, Gareth. Images of Organization. 2nd ed. LC 96-35682. 1996. pap. 28.00 (*0-7619-0632-0*) Sage.
Morgan, Gareth. Images of Organization: International Version. 486p. 1997. 59.95 (*0-7619-0633-9*); pap. 28.00 (*0-7619-0634-7*) Sage.
***Morgan, Gareth.** Images of Organization: The Executive Edition. 368p. 1998. pap. 25.95 (*0-7619-1752-7*) Sage.
Morgan, Gareth. Images of Organization - The Executive Edition. abr. ed. LC 98-10390. 349p. 1998. pap. 25.95 (*1-57675-038-8*) Berrett-Koehler.
— Imaginization: New Mindsets for Seeing, Organizing, & Managing. LC 97-21081. (Illus.). 350p. (Orig.). 1997. reprint ed. pap. 19.95 (*1-57675-026-4*) Berrett-Koehler.
— Imaginization: The Art of Creative Management. LC 93-12148. (Illus.). 320p. (C). 1993. text 45.00 (*0-8039-5299-6*) Sage.
— Riding the Waves of Change: Developing Managerial Competencies for a Turbulent World. LC 87-46337. (Management Ser.). 230p. 1988. text 32.95 (*1-55542-093-1*) Jossey-Bass.
Morgan, Gareth, ed. Beyond Method: Strategies for Social Research. 424p. 1983. 49.95 (*0-8039-1973-5*); pap. 22.50 (*0-8039-2078-4*) Sage.
Morgan, Gareth, jt. auth. see Harlow, Rosie.
Morgan, Gareth, jt. auth. see Maddix, Frank.
Morgan, Gary. There Was So Much Laughter. 50p. 1984. pap. 2.95 (*0-942424-03-4*) W Anglia Pubns.
Morgan, Genevieve. The Wedding Planner. 130p. 1996. 24.95 (*0-8118-0994-3*) Chronicle Bks.
Morgan, Genevieve, ed. Matisse: Artist Speaks, The. LC 95-25200. 96p. 1996. 16.95 (*0-00-255458-5*) Collins SF.
— Monet: The Artist Speaks. LC 95-38392. (Illus.). 96p. 1996. 16.95 (*0-00-225206-6*) Collins SF.
Morgan, Genevieve, jt. auth. see Morgan, Tom.
Morgan, Geoffrey. A Small Piece of Paradise. large type ed. (Dales Large Print Ser.). 1996. pap. 18.99 (*1-85389-634-9*, Dales) Ulverscroft.
— Soldier Bear. large type ed. (Magna Large Print Ser.). (Illus.). 200p. 1996. 27.99 (*0-7505-0961-9*) Ulverscroft.
— Tea with Mr. Timothy. 2nd large type ed. (Illus.). 111p. (J). 1993. 18.95 (*1-85695-300-9*, Pub. by ISIS Lrg Prnt) Transaction Pubs.
— A Touch of Magic. large type ed. (Dales Large Print Ser.). (Illus.). 234p. 1996. pap. 18.99 (*1-85389-636-5*) Ulverscroft.
— The White Dolphin. large type ed. 1996. pap. 18.99 (*1-85389-607-1*, Dales) Ulverscroft.
— A Window of Sky. large type ed. (Dales Large Print Ser.). 208p. 1996. pap. 18.99 (*1-85389-635-7*, Dales) Ulverscroft.
Morgan, George. Life of James Monroe. LC 76-106979. reprint ed. 74.50 (*0-404-00594-2*) AMS Pr.
Morgan, George, jt. auth. see Morgan, Peg.
Morgan, George, tr. see Tillman, Terry.
Morgan, George A. Speech & Society: The Christian Linguistic Social Philsophy of Eugen Rosenstock-Huessy. 192p. 1987. 24.95 (*0-8130-0852-2*) U Press Fla.
Morgan, George A., Jr. What Nietzsche Means. LC 74-2555. 408p. 1975. reprint ed. lib. bdg. 35.00 (*0-8371-7404-X*, MOWN, Greenwood Pr) Greenwood.
Morgan, George A. & Griego, Orlando V. Easy Use & Interpretation of SPSS 7.5 for Windows: Answering Research Question with Statistics. LC 98-11193. 250p. 1998. pap. write for info. (*0-8058-2959-8*) L Erlbaum Assocs.
***Morgan, George A., et al.** Using SPSS for Windows: An Introduction to Use & Interpretation in Research. 184p. 2000. pap. write for info. (*0-8058-3584-9*) L Erlbaum Assocs.
Morgan, George A., jt. auth. see Gliner, Jeffrey A.
Morgan, George A., jt. auth. see MacTurk, Robert H.
Morgan, George A., jt. ed. see MacTurk, Robert H.
Morgan, George H. Annals, Comprising Memoirs, Incidents, & Statistics of Harrisburg, from the Period of Its First Settlement (Pennsylvania) 446p. (Orig.). 1858. reprint ed. pap. text 29.00 (*1-55613-931-4*) Heritage Bk.
Morgan, George M. Alcock & Brown & the Boy in the Middle. LC 94-950201. (Illus.). 64p. (YA). (gr. 3 up). 1994. pap. 3.95 (*1-895387-20-5*) Creative Bk Pub.
Morgan, George T., Jr. & King, John O. The Woodlands: New Community Development, 1964-1983. LC 86-23081. (Illus.). 176p. 1987. 28.95 (*0-89096-306-1*) Tex A&M Univ Pr.
Morgan, George W. Genealogy Forum on America Online: A User's Guide. LC 98-41009. 288p. 1998. pap. 19.95 (*0-916489-87-6*) Ancestry.
— The Human Predicament: Dissolution & Wholeness. LC 68-23791. 368p. reprint ed. pap. 111.60 (*0-608-14773-7*, 202564100045) Bks Demand.
Morgan, Gerald. Anglo-Russian Rivalry in Central Asia 1810-1895. (Illus.). 284p. 1981. text 38.00 (*0-7146-3179-5*, Pub. by F Cass Pubs) Intl Spec Bk.
— Sir Gawain & the Green Knight & the Idea of Righteousness. (Dublin Studies in Medieval Renaissance Literature). 192p. 1991. 14.95 (*0-7165-2470-8*, Pub. by Irish Acad Pr) Intl Spec Bk.
— A Welsh House & It's Family: The Vaughans of Trawscoed. 1997. pap. 38.95 (*0-8464-4584-0*) Beekman Pubs.
— A Welsh House & Its Family: The Vaughans of Trawscoed. 1997. pap. 50.00 (*1-85902-472-6*, Pub. by Gomer Pr) St Mut.
Morgan, Geri, jt. auth. see Scoggin, Janet.
Morgan, Gillian. Book of Teddy Bear Making. 1998. 19.99 (*0-7858-0886-8*) Bk Sales Inc.
— The Complete Galley Slave. 144p. 1987. 40.00 (*0-85937-123-9*, Pub. by K Mason Pubns Ltd) St Mut.
***Morgan, Glenn.** Beyond Organizational Change. 2000. text 75.00 (*0-312-23188-1*) St Martin.
Morgan, Glenn & Engwall, Lars, eds. Regulation & Organisations: International Perspectives. LC 98-54691. (Advances in Management & Business Studies: No. 5). 256p. (C). (gr. 13). 1998. 85.00 (*0-415-18391-X*, D6293) Routledge.
Morgan, Gordon D. Toward an American Sociology: Questioning the European Construct. LC 96-20692. 216p. 1997. 59.95 (*0-275-94999-0*, Praeger Pubs) Greenwood.
Morgan, Gordon D. & Preston, Izola. The Edge of Campus: A Journal of the Black Experience at the University of Arkansas. LC 89-28619. 247p. 1990. pap. 12.00 (*1-55728-118-1*) U of Ark Pr.
Morgan, Griscom. The Community's Need for an Economy. 1969. pap. 1.00 (*0-910420-17-3*) Comm Serv OH.
— Compendium of Land Trust Documents. 37p. 1972. pap. 1.50 (*0-910420-18-1*) Comm Serv OH.
— Future of the Community Heritage. 1971. pap. 1.00 (*0-910420-04-1*) Comm Serv OH.
— Small Community, Population & the Economic Order. rev. ed. 1975. pap. 2.00 (*0-910420-22-X*) Comm Serv OH.
— Vitality & Civilization. 1947. pap. 1.00 (*0-910420-06-8*) Comm Serv OH.
Morgan, Griscom & Morgan, Arthur E. Future of Cities & Future of Man. 1993. pap. 5.00 (*0-910420-05-X*) Comm Serv OH.
Morgan, Griscom & Morgan, Arthur E., eds. Heritage of Community. rev. ed. (Orig.). 1971. pap. 2.00 (*0-910420-00-9*) Comm Serv OH.
Morgan, Griscom, et al. Human Scale in Schools. rev. ed. 1988. pap. 2.50 (*0-910420-29-7*) Comm Serv OH.
Morgan, Griscom, ed. see Community Service Editors.
Morgan Group, Inc. Staff. 1996 Directory GIS Education. LC 96-76028. 408p. 1996. pap. text 59.95 (*0-7872-2149-X*) Kendall-Hunt.
Morgan, Gwen & Veysey, Arthur. Poor Little Rich Boy: The Saga of America's Foremost Newspaper Dynasty - Col. Robert R. McCormick. LC 85-70124. (Illus.). 500p. 1985. pap. 15.00 (*0-916445-11-9*) Crossroads Comm.
Morgan, Gwen G. Managing the Day Care Dollars: A Financial Handbook. rev. ed. LC 82-50691. 112p. 1992. pap. 7.95 (*0-942820-02-9*) Steam Pr MA.
— The National State of Child Care Regulation, 1986. 250p. 1987. write for info. (*0-9618201-0-1*) Work Family Direct.
Morgan, Gwenda. The Hegemony of the Law: Richmond County, Virginia, 1642-1776. (Outstanding Studies in Early American History). 242p. 1989. reprint ed. 15.00 (*0-8240-6192-6*) Garland.
Morgan, Gwenda & Rushton, Peter. Rogues, Thieves & the Rule of Law: The Problems of Law Enforcement in North-East England, 1718-1820. LC 98-123339. 287p. 1998. 74.95 (*1-85728-116-0*, Pub. by UCL Pr Ltd) Taylor & Francis.
Morgan, Gwendolyn A. Medieval Balladry & the Courtly Tradition: Literature of Revolt & Assimilation. LC 92-28130. (American University Studies: English Language & Literature: Ser. IV, Vol. 160). 148p. 1993. 36.95 (*0-8204-2042-5*) P Lang Pubng.
Morgan, Gwendolyn A., ed. Medieval Ballads: Chivalry, Romance, & Everyday Life: A Critical Anthology. 226p. (C). 1996. pap. text 29.95 (*0-8204-3139-7*) P Lang Pubng.
Morgan, Gwyneth. Life in Medieval Village. 48p. 1975. pap. 11.95 (*0-521-20404-6*) Cambridge U Pr.
Morgan, H. G. Aids to Psychiatry. 3rd ed. (Illus.). 224p. 1989. pap. text 28.95 (*0-443-03928-3*) Church.
Morgan, H. G., jt. auth. see Williams, R.
Morgan, H. Wayne. Drugs in America: A Social History, 1800-1980. LC 81-14531. (Illus.). 248p. 1982. pap. 17.95 (*0-8156-2282-1*) Syracuse U Pr.
— Keepers of Culture: The Art-Thought of Kenyon Cox, Royal Cortissoz, & Frank Jewett Mather, Jr. LC 89-32669. (Illus.). 204p. 1989. 25.00 (*0-87338-390-7*) Kent St U Pr.
— Kenyon Cox, 1856-1919: A Life in American Art. LC 93-33967. (Illus.). 304p. (C). 1994. 32.00 (*0-87338-485-7*) Kent St U Pr.
— Yesterday's Addicts: American Society & Drug Abuse, 1865-1920. LC 73-7421. 220p. 1974. pap. 13.95 (*0-8061-1636-6*) U of Okla Pr.
Morgan, H. Wayne, ed. An American Art Student in Paris: The Letters of Kenyon Cox, 1877-1882. LC 86 4702. (Illus.). 226p. 1986. 35.00 (*0-87338-333-8*) Kent St U Pr.
— An Artist of the American Renaissance: The Letters of Kenyon Cox, 1883-1919. LC 95-1587. (Illus.). 224p. 1995. 35.00 (*0-87338-517-9*) Kent St U Pr.
— Victorian Culture in America, 1865-1914. LC 72-89722. (Primary Sources in American History Ser.). 1973. pap. text 7.95 (*0-88295-787-2*) Harlan Davidson.
Morgan, H. Wayne & Morgan, Anne H. Oklahoma: A History. (States & the Nation Ser.). (Illus.). 1984. pap. 7.95 (*0-393-30181-8*) Norton.
Morgan, H. Wayne, jt. auth. see Morgan, Anne H.
Morgan, Harriet P., ed. see National Research Council (U. S.), Committee on Mandatory Retirement in Higher Education Staff.
Morgan, Harry. Cognitive Style & Classroom Learning. LC 96-36357. 200p. 1997. 49.95 (*0-275-95684-9*, Praeger Pubs) Greenwood.
— Historical Perspectives on the Education of Black Children. LC 94-42843. 256p. 1995. 57.95 (*0-275-95071-9*, Praeger Pubs) Greenwood.
***Morgan, Harry.** The Imagination of Early Childhood Education. LC 98-38309. 272p. 1999. 59.95 (*0-89789-594-0*, Bergin & Garvey) Greenwood.
Morgan, Hazel, ed. Through Peter's Eyes. (C). 1990. pap. 24.00 (*0-85305-305-7*, Pub. by Arthur James) St Mut.
Morgan, Helen, ed. see Davis, Alvis O.
Morgan, Helen C. & Moorhead, Kelly J. Spirulina - Nature's Superfood. 43p. 1993. pap. 2.95 (*0-9637511-3-1*) Nutrex.
Morgan, Helen M., jt. auth. see Morgan, Edmund S.
Morgan, Henry, ed. Approaches to Prayer: A Resource Book for Groups & Individuals. LC 92-35257. (Illus.). 160p. (Orig.). 1993. pap. 11.95 (*0-8192-1599-6*) Morehouse Pub.
Morgan, Henry H. & Hollinshead, Ellen R. Four Pioneer Families of Minnesota & Their Puritan & Quaker Heritage: The Hollinshead, Baker, Rice, & Kneeland Families, Their Stories, Ancestries, & Descendants. LC 96-78578. (Illus.). ix, 311p. 1998. 50.00 (*0-9655639-0-1*, 001) Heptagon Pr.
Morgan, Henry J. The Canadian Legal Directory. (Biographical Reference Works). xii, 279p. 1989. reprint ed. 59.00 (*0-7812-0696-0*) Rprt Serv.
***Morgan, Herb & Morgan, Ardith.** Business Opportunities: Secrets Revealed. LC 99-95495. 320p. 2000. pap. 39.95 (*0-9674095-2-7*) Business Basics.
Morgan, Hilary. Burne-Jones, the Pre-Raphaelites & Their Century, 2 vols. (Illus.). (C). 1989. 195.00 (*0-7855-7123-X*) St Mut.
— Burne-Jones, the Pre-Raphaelites & Their Century, 2 Vols., Vol. 1: The Text. (Illus.). (C). 1989. write for info. (*1-872508-01-4*) St Mut.
— Burne-Jones, the Pre-Raphaelites & Their Century, 2 Vols., Vol. 2: The Plates. (Illus.). (C). 1989. write for info. (*1-872508-02-2*) St Mut.
Morgan, Hiram. Tyrone's Rebellion: The Outbreak of the Nine Years War in Tudor Ireland. (RHS Ser.: No. 0269-2244). (Illus.). 264p. 1999. pap. 29.95 (*0-85115-683-5*) Boydell & Brewer.
***Morgan, Hiram, ed.** Political Ideology in Ireland, 1541-1641. 256p. 2000. 55.00 (*1-85182-440-5*, Pub. by Four Cts Pr) Intl Spec Bk.
Morgan-Hopkin, Carol. Full Circle. 1997. pap. 29.95 (*0-8464-4577-8*) Beekman Pubs.
Morgan-Hopkin, Carole. Full Circle. 1997. pap. 30.00 (*1-85902-407-6*, Pub. by Gomer Pr) St Mut.
Morgan, Howard G. Death Wishes? The Understanding & Management of Deliberate Self-Harm. LC 79-1044. (Illus.). 182p. reprint ed. pap. 56.50 (*0-8357-3101-4*, 203935700012) Bks Demand.
Morgan, Howard M. & Morgan, John C. The God-Man of Galilee: Studies in Christian Living (Sermons) 100p. 1983. 4.95 (*0-913029-14-9*) Stevens Bk Pr.
Morgan, Howard W. From Hayes to McKinley: National Party Politics, 1877-1896. LC 69-17074. 678p. reprint ed. pap. 200.00 (*0-608-15201-3*, 202739200055) Bks Demand.
— William McKinley & His America. LC 63-19723. 623p. reprint ed. pap. 193.20 (*0-608-14263-8*, 202220700025) Bks Demand.
Morgan, Howard Wayne, ed. The Gilded Age. enl. rev. ed. LC 75-113203. 341p. reprint ed. pap. 105.80 (*0-608-15202-1*, 202739300055) Bks Demand.
Morgan, Hugh. Soviet Aces of World War II. (Aircraft of the Aces Ser.: No. 15). (Illus.). 96p. 1997. pap. 17.95 (*1-85532-632-9*, Pub. by Ospry) Motorbooks Intl.
Morgan, Hugh, ed. Adults with Autism: A Guide to Theory & Practice. (Illus.). 312p. (C). 1996. text 85.00 (*0-521-45070-5*); pap. text 37.95 (*0-521-45683-5*) Cambridge U Pr.
Morgan, Huw. Let Them Live. 1985. pap. 0.99 (*0-85234-199-7*, Pub. by Evangelical Pr) P & R Pubng.
Morgan, I. L., jt. ed. see Duggan, J. L.
Morgan, Ike, ed. FSU Football, 1998, Vol. 4. (Illus.). 100p. 1998. pap. 5.95 (*1-890881-00-7*) Talla Dem.
— FSU Football 1997. 3rd ed. (Illus.). 100p. 1997. pap. 5.95 (*0-9613040-8-1*) Talla Dem.
Morgan, Ike, et al, eds. FSU Football Magazine 1999. 96p. 1999. pap. 6.95 (*1-890881-02-3*) Talla Dem.
***Morgan, Ike, et al, eds.** FSU Football 2000. (FSU Football Ser.). (Illus.). 96p. 2000. pap. 6.95 (*1-890881-04-X*) Talla Dem.
Morgan, Ike, et al, eds. FSU 2 Times. 144p. 1999. pap. 14.95 (*1-890881-01-5*) Talla Dem.
***Morgan, Ike, et al, eds.** Perfect!, Vol. 1. (Illus.). 96p. 2000. pap. 4.63 (*1-890881-03-1*) Talla Dem.
Morgan, Irene R. The Joyous Discovery of Self. 60p. (Orig.) 1995. pap., spiral bd., wbk. ed. 20.00 (*1-889187-09-7*) Self-Empwrmnt.
Morgan, Iwan W. Beyond the Liberal Consensus: A Political History of the United States since 1965. LC 93-44098. 1994. pap. 21.95 (*0-312-12015-X*) St Martin.
— Deficit Government: Taxing & Spending in Modern America. LC 94-46129. (American Ways Ser.). 222p. 1995. 24.95 (*1-56663-081-9*, Pub. by I R Dee); pap. text 9.95 (*1-56663-082-7*, Pub. by I R Dee) Natl Bk Netwk.
Morgan, Iwan W. & Wynn, Neil A., eds. America's Century: Perspectives on Twentieth-Century American History. LC 91-29508. 340p. (C). 1993. 45.00 (*0-8419-1303-X*); pap. 19.95 (*0-8419-1304-8*) Holmes & Meier.
Morgan, J., et al. The L Squared Moduli Space & a Vanishing Theorem for Donaldson Polynomial Invariants. (Monographs in Geometry & Topology). 232p. (C). 1994. text 42.00 (*1-57146-006-3*) Intl Pr Boston.
Morgan, J., jt. auth. see Griffiths, P. A.
Morgan, J., jt. auth. see Turland, B. D.
Morgan, J. Brian. The Police Function & the Investigation of Crime. (Illus.). 201p. 1990. text 72.95 (*0-566-07127-4*) Ashgate Pub Co.
Morgan, J. Derald & Abdullah, Mohammed. Dielectric Engineering Practice in Power Apparatus. 450p. 1984. pap. text. write for info. (*0-317-05122-9*) Macmillan.
Morgan, J. Derald, jt. auth. see Matsch, Leander W.
Morgan, J. Jeffrey, jt. auth. see Morgan, James C.
Morgan, J. L. The Elite of the Fleet: Insignia of U. S. Naval Aviation. LC 90-81998. (Insignia Identification Ser.). (Illus.). 128p. 1990. 39.95 (*0-9626310-0-0*) Intl Trade Assn.
Morgan, J. M. Future Eden. 320p. 1992. mass mkt. 4.99 (*1-55817-653-5*, Pinncle Kensgtn) Kensgtn Pub Corp.
Morgan, J. R. & Stoneman, Richard, eds. Greek Fiction: The Greek Novel in Context. LC 93-28137. 272p. (C). 1994. pap. 24.99 (*0-415-08507-1*) Routledge.
— Greek Fiction: The Greek Novel in Context. LC 93-28137. 272p. (C). (gr. 13). 1994. 80.00 (*0-415-08506-3*) Routledge.
Morgan, J. T., ed. see Easter School in Agricultural Science (8th 1961, U.
Morgan, J. Tom, Jr. Kiss Impressions: My Love Affair with Lithography. LC 82-99983. 1983. 50.00 (*0-89938-014-X*) Tech & Ed Ctr Graph Arts RIT.
Morgan, J. W. California Impressions. Perkins, David, ed. (Illus.). 1886. 71.00 (*0-937048-46-1*) Santa Susana.

An Asterisk (*) at the beginning of an entry indicates that the title is appearing for the first time.

— A Product Formula for Surgery Obstructions. LC 78-4581. (Memoirs Ser.: No. 14/201). 90p. 1978. pap. 19.00 (*0-8218-2201-2*, MEMO/14/201) Am Math.

Morgan, Jack, ed. see Jewett, Sarah Orne.

Morgan, James. Application Cases in Management Information Systems. 2nd ed. 160p. (C). Date not set. pap. write for info. (*0-256-22056-5*) McGraw.

— Application Cases in Management Information Systems. 3rd ed. 160p. (C). Date not set. pap. 18.00 (*0-07-366257-7*) McGraw.

— Application Cases in MIS. 160p. (C). 1993. text, per. 22.95 incl. 5.25 hd (*0-256-13390-5*, Irwn McGrw-H) McGrw-H Hghr Educ.

***Morgan, James.** Distance to Moon. 336p. 2000. pap. 12.95 (*1-57322-816-8*, Riverhd Trade) Berkley Pub.

— The Distance to the Moon: A Road Trip into the American Dream. LC 98-54716. 304p. 1999. 24.95 (*1-57322-135-X*, Riverhead Books) Putnam Pub Group.

Morgan, James. The Last Generation. LC 99-24195. 4p. 1999. 24.95 (*1-57524-106-4*) Krieger.

Morgan, James, et al. Management Information Systems: With Application Cases & Internet Primer. 3rd ed. (C). 1996. text, pap. text 85.00 incl. 3.5 hd (*0-256-24678-5*, Irwn McGrw-H) McGrw-H Hghr Educ.

Morgan, James, jt. auth. see Kelley, Virginia C.

Morgan, James A., ed. Digest Shakespeareanae. LC 75-172743. (Shakespeare Society of New York. Publications: No. 4, Pts. 1 & 7). reprint ed. 37.50 (*0-404-04419-0*) AMS Pr.

— Mrs. Shakespeare's Second Marriage. LC 75-170138. (Shakespeare Society of New York. Publications: No. 14). reprint ed. 27.50 (*0-404-54214-X*) AMS Pr.

— Study in the Warwickshire Dialect. 3rd ed. LC 76-169927. (Shakespeare Society of New York. Publications: No. 10). reprint ed. 45.00 (*0-404-54210-7*) AMS Pr.

— Venus & Adonis: A Study in Warwickshire Dialect. LC 76-169261. (Shakespeare Society of New York. Publications: No. 2). reprint ed. 27.50 (*0-404-54202-6*) AMS Pr.

Morgan, James A., ed. see Shakespeare, William.

Morgan, James C. Jesus & Mastership: The Gospel According to Jesus of Nazareth, As Dictated Through James Coyle Morgan. 3rd ed. 389p. (C). 1997. pap. 14.95 (*1-878555-00-6*) Oakbridge Univ Pr.

— The New Book of Revelation: From John, the Disciple of Jesus the Christ, Through James Coyle Morgan. 100p. (Orig.). (C). 1991. pap. 9.95 (*1-878555-01-4*) Oakbridge Univ Pr.

Morgan, James C. & Morgan, J. Jeffrey. Cracking the Japanese Market: Strategies for Success in the New Global Economy. 288p. 1991. 32.95 (*0-02-921691-5*) Free Pr.

Morgan, James H., ed. Sampling Environmental Media, Vol. 128. LC 92-27603. (STP Ser.: No. 1282). (Illus.). 385p. 1996. text 79.00 (*0-8031-2043-5*, STP1282) ASTM.

Morgan, James J., jt. auth. see Stumm, Werner.

Morgan, James L. Arkansas Marriage Notices, 1819-1845. 86p. 1992. reprint ed. pap. 14.00 (*0-941765-78-4*) Arkansas Res.

— Arkansas Marriage Records, 1808-1835. LC 95-118214. 90p. 1994. reprint ed. pap. 15.00 (*0-941765-91-1*) Arkansas Res.

— Arkansas Newspaper Abstracts, 1819-1845. 364p. 1992. reprint ed. pap. 32.00 (*0-941765-73-3*) Arkansas Res.

— Arkansas Newspaper Index, 1819-1845. 100p. 1992. reprint ed. pap. 16.00 (*0-941765-75-X*) Arkansas Res.

— Arkansas Volunteers of 1836-1837. 81p. 1992. reprint ed. pap. 14.00 (*0-941765-79-2*) Arkansas Res.

— Census of the Territory of Arkansas, 1820 (Reconstructed) 108p. 1992. reprint ed. pap. 16.00 (*0-941765-77-6*) Arkansas Res.

— Families of Confederate Soldiers of Prairie County, Arkansas, 1861-1867. 53p. 1992. reprint ed. pap. 12.00 (*0-941765-82-2*) Arkansas Res.

— From Simple Input to Complex Grammar. (Learning, Development & Conceptual Change Ser.). (Illus.). 232p. 1986. 30.00 (*0-262-13217-6*, Bradford Bks) MIT Pr.

Morgan, James L. & Demuth, Katherine, eds. Signal To Syntax: Bootstrapping from Speech to Grammar in Early Acquisition. 500p. 1995. pap. 36.00 (*0-8058-1266-0*); text 69.95 (*0-8058-1265-2*) L Erlbaum Assocs.

Morgan, James L. & Thurman, Ted A. American Military Patch Guide: An Illustrated Reference to U. S. Army Shoulder Sleeve Insignia & Patches. LC 97-70469. (Illus.). 96p. 1997. 29.95 (*1-884452-33-7*); pap. 24.95 (*1-884452-32-9*) MOA Press.

Morgan, James L., jt. auth. see Morgan, Wayne R.

***Morgan, James Logan.** Marriage Records of Lawrence County, Arkansas, 1820-1850. 50p. 2000. pap. 12.00 (*1-56546-167-3*) Arkansas Res.

Morgan, James M. The Adorers of Dionysos, Bakchai. Pryse, tr. 164p. 1996. reprint ed. pap. 15.50 (*0-7873-0318-6*) Hlth Research.

Morgan, James N. & Duncan, Greg J. The Economics of Personal Choice. 272p. 1980. text 27.95 (*0-472-08007-5*, 08007) U of Mich Pr.

Morgan, James N., et al. Results from Two National Surveys of Philanthropic Activity. LC 79-53850. (Institute for Social Research, Research Report). 173p. (Orig.). reprint ed. pap. 53.70 (*0-7837-5254-7*, 204499100005) Bks Demand.

Morgan, James N., jt. auth. see Barfield, Richard E.

Morgan, James N., jt. auth. see Burpee, C. Gaye.

***Morgan, James P.** Plain Talk about Purchasing. 2000. pap. 37.00 (*0-9644791-3-3*, Purchasing Mag) Cahners Business.

Morgan, James P. & Shaver, Robert H., eds. Deltaic Sedimentation: Modern & Ancient. LC 72-191407. (Society of Economic Paleontologists & Mineralogists, Special Publication Ser.: No. 15). 332p. reprint ed. pap. 103.00 (*0-608-12953-4*, 202474000038) Bks Demand.

Morgan, James P., jt. auth. see Anderson, Ernest L.

Morgan, James P., jt. auth. see Stork, Ken.

***Morgan, Jamie & Lorenz, Mitzi.** Buffalo: The Style & Fashion of Ray Petri. 2000. 55.00 (*1-57687-091-X*, pwerHse Bks) pwerHse Cultrl.

Morgan, Jane. Conflict & Order: The Police & Labour Disputes in England & Wales 1900-1939. (Illus.). 326p. 1988. text 75.00 (*0-19-820128-1*) OUP.

Morgan, Jane & Morgan, Walter, eds. Soldier Poetry of the Second World War. LC 90-95632. xv, 182p. 1996. 19.95 (*0-88962-473-9*); pap. 14.95 (*0-88962-470-4*) Mosaic.

Morgan, Jane, jt. auth. see Claydon, Janet.

Morgan, Jane, ed. see Miller, Bob.

Morgan, Jason P., et al, eds. Mantle Flow & Melt Generation at Mid-Ocean Ridges. LC 93-812. (Geophysical Monograph Ser.: No. 71). 1993. 46.00 (*0-87590-035-6*) Am Geophysical.

Morgan, Jeanne B., jt. auth. see Witt, Beth.

Morgan, Jefferson, jt. auth. see Morgan, Jinx.

Morgan, Jeffrey R. & Yarmush, Martin L. Tissue Engineering Methods & Protocols. LC 98-11174. (Methods in Molecular Medicine Ser.: No. 18). (Illus.). 648p. 1998. 99.50 (*0-89603-516-6*) Humana.

Morgan, Jenifer, jt. auth. see Morgan, Ernest.

Morgan, Jenny. Film Researcher's Handbook: A Guide to Sources in North America, South America, Asia, Australasia. 472p. (C). 1996. 85.00 (*0-415-15123-6*) Routledge.

— Herbs for Horses No. 27: Threshold Picture Guide. (Illus.). 24p. (YA). 1993. pap. 12.00 (*1-872082-46-7*, Pub. by Kenilworth Pr) Half Halt Pr.

— Working with Horses: How to Obtain the Right Qualifications, Training & Job Opportunities. (Jobs & Careers Ser.). (Illus.). 96p. 1997. pap. 19.95 (*1-85703-320-5*, Pub. by How To Bks) Trans-Atl Phila.

Morgan, Jenny, jt. auth. see Graycar, Regina.

Morgan, Jerry L., jt. auth. see Green, Georgia M.

Morgan, Jessica & Medvedow, Jill. Collectors Collect Contemporary. (Illus.). 50p. 1999. pap. 25.00 (*0-910663-55-6*) ICA Inc.

Morgan, Jill. Afton of Castlethorpe. (J). 1999. pap. 3.99 (*0-679-88838-1*, Pub. by Random Bks Yng Read) Random.

— Blood Brothers. LC 96-16742. (Trophy Bk.). (Illus.). 128p. (J). (gr. 3-7). 1996. pap. 4.50 (*0-06-440562-1*, HarpTrophy) HarpC Child Bks.

— Mothers & Daughters. 1999. mass mkt. 5.99 (*0-451-19786-0*) NAL.

— Nora of Skye Aerie. (J). 1999. pap. 3.99 (*0-679-88837-3*, Pub. by Random Bks Yng Read) Random.

— Victorian Shadows, No. 1. 1996. pap. 4.99 (*0-679-87457-7*) Random.

— Victorian Shadows, No. 2. 1997. pap. 4.99 (*0-679-87458-5*) Random.

***Morgan, Jill, ed.** Mothers & Sons. 2000. pap. 14.95 (*0-451-20009-8*, Sig) NAL.

Morgan, Jill, ed. see Gabaldon, Diana, et al.

Morgan, Jill M. Blood Brothers. LC 96-16742. 1996. 9.60 (*0-606-09087-8*, Pub. by Turtleback) Demco.

— Till Death Do Us Part. 1999. mass mkt. 6.99 (*0-425-17197-3*) Berkley Pub.

Morgan, Jill M., ed. Mothers & Daughters: Celebrating the Gift of Love in Twelve New Stories. LC 97-32519. 256p. 1998. mass mkt. 14.95 (*0-451-19383-0*, Sig) NAL.

Morgan, Jim. Management for the Small Design Firm: Handling Your Practice, Personnel, Finances, & Projects. LC 97-7826. (Illus.). 176p. 1997. 45.00 (*0-8230-2967-0*) Watsn-Guptill.

Morgan, Jim, ed. see Rozum, Fred & Rozum, Mary.

Morgan, Jim, ed. see Tannock, Ian F. & Hill, Richard P.

Morgan, Jinx & Morgan, Jefferson. The Sugar Mill Caribbean Cookbook: Casual & Elegant Recipes Inspired by the Islands. LC 96-9929. (Illus.). 272p. 1996. pap. 14.95 (*1-55832-121-7*) Harvard Common Pr.

Morgan, Jo A. Fair Play: One Hundred Ninety-Nine of the Single Hottest Jocks in the NBA. JBJ Enterprises, Inc. Staff, ed. (NFL, Major League Baseball Ser.). 200p. (Orig.). 1992. pap. text 9.95 (*0-9631975-0-9*) J B J Ent.

— God's Unique Woman. 62p. 1996. pap. 4.95 (*0-89137-464-7*) Quality Pubns.

Morgan, Jo-Anne. Fair Play: One Hundred Ninety-Seven of the Hottest Single Athletes in the NBA. (Illus.). 160p. (Orig.). 1992. pap. write for info. (*0-318-69418-2*) J B J Ent.

Morgan, Joan. When Chickenheads Come Home to Roost. 240p. 2000. per. 12.00 (*0-684-86861-X*) S&S Trade.

— When Chickenheads Come Home to Roost: My Life as a Hip-Hop Feminist. LC 98-50135. 240p. 1999. 23.00 (*0-684-82262-8*) S&S Trade.

Morgan, Joe. The Official Book of the 1993 World Series: A Series to Remember: Toronto & Philadelphia, 1993. Hyman, Laurence J. & Rochmis, Jon, eds. LC 93-61703. 144p. 1993. 29.95 (*0-942627-19-9*) Woodford Pubng.

Morgan, Joe & Lally, Richard. Baseball for Dummies. LC 98-70137. (For Dummies Ser.). (Illus.). 432p. 1998. pap. 19.99 (*0-7645-5085-3*) IDG Bks.

***Morgan, Joe & Lally, Richard.** Baseball for Dummies. 2nd ed. (For Dummies Ser.). 432p. 2000. pap. 19.99 (*0-7645-5234-1*) IDG Bks.

Morgan, Joe & Lally, Richard. Long Balls, No Strikes: How Baseball Can Keep the Good Times Rolling. LC 99-33098. 288p. 1999. 25.00 (*0-609-60524-0*, Crown) Crown.

Morgan, Joe P. Radiology in Veterinary Orthopedics. LC 71-175464. 415p. reprint ed. pap. 128.70 (*0-608-16687-1*, 205619100055) Bks Demand.

***Morgan, Joe P.** Radiology of Veterinary Orthopedics: Features of Diagnosis. 2000. pap. 44.95 (*0-8138-0312-8*) Iowa St U Pr.

Morgan, Joe P., ed. Techniques of Veterinary Radiography. 5th ed. LC 92-41342. (Venture Series in Veterinary Medicine). (Illus.). 496p. (C). 1993. pap. text 74.95 (*0-8138-1727-7*) Iowa St U Pr.

Morgan, Joe P. & Leighton, Robert L. Radiology of Small Animal Fracture Management. LC 94-13109. (Illus.). 400p. 1994. text 83.00 (*0-7216-5455-X*, W B Saunders Co) Harcrt Hlth Sci Grp.

Morgan, Joe P. & Wolvekamp, W. T. An Atlas of Radiology of the Traumatized Dog & Cat. LC 94-22818. (Illus.). 240p. 1994. text 82.50 (*0-397-51483-2*) Lppncott W & W.

Morgan, Joe P., et al. Equine Radiography. (Venture Series in Veterinary Medicine). (Illus.). 384p. (C). 1991. text 92.95 (*0-8138-0257-1*) Iowa St U Pr.

Morgan, Joe R. Potato Branch: Sketches of Mountain Memories. LC 92-24274. 176p. 1992. 14.95 (*0-914875-20-5*) Bright Mtn Bks.

Morgan, John. The Bone-Duster. (QRL Poetry Bks.: Vol. XXI). 1980. 20.00 (*0-614-06380-9*) Quarterly Rev.

— A Discourse Upon the Institution of Medical Schools in America. LC 74-26276. (History, Philosophy & Sociology of Science Ser.). 1975. reprint ed. 16.95 (*0-405-06604-X*) Ayer.

— The Inside Passage. (Poetry Chapbook Ser.). 20p. (Orig.). 1985. pap. 7.00 (*0-937669-16-4*) Owl Creek Pr.

— The Log House in East Tennessee. LC 90-11912. 192p. 1990. pap. text 15.00 (*0-87049-653-0*) U of Tenn Pr.

***Morgan, John.** The Midnight Murder. large type ed. 312p. 2000. pap. 18.99 (*0-7089-5680-7*, Linford) Ulverscroft.

— Murderers Don't Smile. large type ed. 304p. 1999. pap. 18.99 (*0-7089-5597-5*, Linford) Ulverscroft.

Morgan, John, ed. An Easeful Death? Perspectives on Death, Dying & Euthanasia. LC 97-106308. 218p. 1996. pap. 34.00 (*1-86287-222-8*, Pub. by Federation Pr) Gaunt.

Morgan, John & Philp, J. R. You Can't Manage Alone: Practical Prayers for Conscientious Managers. 272p. 1986. pap. 14.99 (*0-310-33608-2*, 12766G) Zondervan.

Morgan, John & Rinvolucri, Mario. Once upon a Time: Using Stories in the Language Classroom. (Cambridge Handbooks for Language Teachers Ser.). 128p. 1984. pap. text 17.95 (*0-521-27262-9*) Cambridge U Pr.

Morgan, John & Welton, Peter. See What I Mean: An Introduction to Visual Communication. 2nd ed. 160p. 1992. pap. 18.95 (*0-340-55781-8*, A7066, Pub. by E A) St Martin.

Morgan, John, jt. auth. see Friedman, John.

Morgan, John, jt. auth. see Hess, Robert E.

Morgan, John, jt. auth. see Rinvolucri, Mario.

Morgan, John, jt. auth. see Sofie, Harold.

Morgan, John C., jt. auth. see Morgan, Howard M.

Morgan, John D., ed. The Dying & the Bereaved Teenager. LC 90-35058. 168p. (Orig.). (C). 1990. pap. 19.95 (*0-914783-44-0*) Charles.

— Ethical Issues in the Care of the Dying & Bereaved Aged. (Death, Value & Meaning Ser.). 356p. 1996. 46.95 (*0-89503-136-1*) Baywood Pub.

— Meeting the Needs of Our Clients Creatively: The Impact of Art & Culture on Caregiving. LC 99-12799. (Death, Value & Meaning Ser.). 320p. (C). 1999. text 48.95 (*0-89503-193-0*) Baywood Pub.

— Personal Care in an Impersonal World: A Multidimensional Look at Bereavement. LC 92-37430. (Death, Value & Meaning Ser.). 267p. 1993. text 37.95 (*0-89503-109-4*); pap. text 26.56 (*0-89503-110-8*) Baywood Pub.

— Readings in Thanatology. LC 96-36868. (Death, Value & Meaning Ser.). 589p. 1997. text 59.95 (*0-89503-149-3*) Baywood Pub.

— Young People & Death. LC 90-28402. 224p. (Orig.). 1991. pap. text 18.95 (*0-914783-49-1*) Charles.

Morgan, John D., jt. ed. see Doka, Kenneth J.

Morgan, John D., ed. see Dunne, Tad.

Morgan, John D., ed. see Fogarty, James A.

Morgan, John D., jt. ed. see Gilbert, Richard B.

Morgan, John D., ed. see Reed, Mary Lou.

Morgan, John H. Catholic Spirituality: A Guide for Protestants. LC 94-60405. 126p. (C). text 28.00 (*1-55605-238-3*) Wyndham Hall.

— From Freud to Frankl: Our Modern Search for Personal Meaning. LC 86-50580. 179p. (C). 1988. text 32.00 (*1-55605-062-3*); pap. text 16.00 (*0-932269-92-3*) Wyndham Hall.

— Good-Bye, Notre Dame: From Academic to Publisher (Making the Change & Living to Tell about It) 95p. 1998. pap. 16.00 (*1-55605-255-3*, Cloverdale) Wyndham Hall.

— Scholar, Priest, & Postor: Ministry Priorities among Clergy Today. LC 97-61551. 165p. 1999. pap. 20.00 (*1-55605-278-2*) Wyndham Hall.

— Women Priests: An Emerging Ministry in the Episcopal Church, 1960 to 1980. 185p. (C). 1985. pap. 16.00 (*0-932269-48-6*) Wyndham Hall.

Morgan, John H., intro. The Anglican Mind: A Theological Compendium of the Classic Statements (from the 17th Century) LC 90-50109. 500p. (C). 1990. pap. text 28.00 (*1-55605-147-6*) Wyndham Hall.

— The Anglican Mind: A Theological Compendium of the Classic Statements (From the 17th Century) LC 90-50109. 500p. (C). 1990. text 40.00 (*1-55605-148-4*) Wyndham Hall.

Morgan, John H., jt. auth. see Abraham, Francis.

Morgan, John H., jt. auth. see Barnes, William H.

Morgan, John J. & Webb, Ewing T. Making the Most of Your Life. LC 70-152199. (Essay Index Reprint Ser.). 1977. reprint ed. 23.95 (*0-8369-2248-4*) Ayer.

Morgan, John M., 4th & Bennett, Genevieve R. Directory of Colleges & Universities Offering GIS Courses. 70p. 1990. pap. 25.00 (*0-614-06095-8*, L333) Am Congrs Survey.

Morgan, John P. & Kagan, Doreen V., eds. Phenylpropanolamine: Risks, Benefits & Controversies, 5. LC 85-6590. (Clinical Pharmacology & Therapeutics Ser.: Vol. 5). 448p. 1985. 85.00 (*0-275-91336-8*, C1336, Praeger Pubs) Greenwood.

Morgan, John S. Business Faces the Urban Crisis. LC 74-86626. 264p. reprint ed. pap. 81.90 (*0-8357-7491-0*, 20518730013) Bks Demand.

— Getting a Job after Fifty. (Illus.). 276p. 1990. text 27.95 (*0-89433-311-9*, 8251); pap. text 14.95 (*0-8306-8251-1*) Petrocelli.

Morgan, John S. & Philp, J. R. You Can't Manage Alone. 256p. (Orig.). 1985. pap. 7.95 (*0-310-33602-3*, 12766P) Zondervan.

Morgan, John T. Land of Cotton. 1988. 13.95 (*0-9620539-0-2*) Morgan Academy.

Morgan, John W. The Seiberg-Witten Equations & Applications to the Topology of Smooth Four-Manifolds. LC 95-43748. (Mathematical Notes Ser.: Vol. 44). 130p. 1996. pap. text 19.95 (*0-691-02597-5*, Pub. by Princeton U Pr) Cal Prin Full Svc.

Morgan, John W. & O'Grady, Kieran G. Differential Topology of Complex Surfaces. (Lecture Notes in Mathematics Ser.: Vol. 1545). (Illus.). viii, 224p. 1993. pap. write for info. (*3-540-56674-0*) Spr-Verlag.

— Differential Topology of Complex Surfaces: Elliptic Surfaces with Pg Equals 1: Smooth Classification. LC 93-16063. (Lecture Notes in Mathematics Ser.: Vol. 1545). 1993. 45.95 (*0-387-56674-0*) Spr-Verlag.

Morgan, John W., jt. auth. see Friedman, Robert.

Morgan, Jon. Gaining a Yard: The Building of Baltimore's Football Stadium. (Illus.). 160p. 1998. 29.95 (*0-9649819-7-1*) Baltimore Sun.

— Glory for Sale: Fans, Dollars & the New NFL. Sjoerdsma, Ann, ed. 360p. (Orig.). 1997. pap. 19.95 (*0-9631246-5-X*) Bancroft MD.

Morgan, Joseph. The Physical Basis of Musical Sound. LC 78-5508. (Illus.). 168p. (Orig.). 1980. lib. bdg. 18.50 (*0-88275-656-7*) Krieger.

Morgan, Joseph G. The Vietnam Lobby: The American Friends of Vietnam, 1955-1975. LC 96-32708. 312p. (C). (gr. 13). 1997. 45.00 (*0-8078-2322-8*) U of NC Pr.

Morgan, Joseph M., jt. auth. see Morgan, Michael D.

Morgan, Joseph R. Hawaii: A Geography. (Geographies of the United States Ser.). 293p. (C). 1983. text 55.00 (*0-89158-942-2*) Westview.

— Hawaii: A Unique Geography. (Illus.). 256p. (C). 1996. pap. text 39.95 (*1-57306-021-6*) Bess Pr.

— Porpoises among the Whales: Small Navies in Asia & the Pacific. (Illus.). 48p. (Orig.). (C). 1994. pap. text 30.00 (*0-7881-0888-3*) DIANE Pub.

Morgan, Joseph R. & Valencia, Mark J., eds. Atlas for Marine Policy in East Asian Seas. LC 91-29923. (C). 1992. 195.00 (*0-520-07798-9*, Pub. by U CA Pr) Cal Prin Full Svc.

Morgan, Joyce. 96 Ways You Can Save Taxes in '96: Kansas City Edition. Gershon, Steve & Slabotsky, Scott, eds. 128p. (Orig.). Date not set. pap. 9.95 (*1-888303-03-4*) Loopholes Pr.

Morgan, Joyce V. Stanislavski's Encounter with Shakespeare: The Evolution of a Method. LC 83-17979. (Theater & Dramatic Studies: No. 14). (Illus.). 186p. reprint ed. pap. 57.70 (*0-8357-1485-3*, 207048500096) Bks Demand.

Morgan, Judith. An Art Text-Workbook: Calligraphy (Introduction) Wallace, Dorathye B., ed. (Illus.). 134p. (Orig.). 1990. pap., teacher ed. 15.95 (*0-914127-37-3*) Univ Class.

— An Art Text-Workbook: Calligraphy (Introduction) Wallace, Dorathye B., ed. (Illus.). 134p. (Orig.). (YA). (gr. 8-10). 1990. pap., student ed. 14.95 (*0-914127-31-4*) Univ Class.

— An Art Text-Workbook: Ceramics (Introduction) Wallace, Dorathye B., ed. (Illus.). 123p. (Orig.). (YA). (gr. 8-10). 1990. pap., student ed. 14.95 (*0-914127-24-1*) Univ Class.

— An Art Text-Workbook: Crafts (Introduction) Wallace, Dorathye B., ed. (Illus.). 157p. (Orig.). 1990. pap., teacher ed. 15.95 (*0-914127-38-1*) Univ Class.

— An Art Text-Workbook: Crafts (Introduction) Wallace, Dorathye B., ed. (Illus.). 157p. (Orig.). (YA). (gr. 8-10). 1990. pap., student ed. 14.95 (*0-914127-32-2*) Univ Class.

— An Art Text-Workbook: Drawing (Introduction) Wallace, Dorathye B., ed. (Illus.). 150p. (Orig.). (YA). (gr. 8-10). 1990. pap., teacher ed. 15.95 (*0-914127-52-7*); pap., student ed. 14.95 (*0-914127-51-9*) Univ Class.

— An Art Text-Workbook: Film Making (Introduction) Wallace, Dorathye B., ed. (Illus.). 146p. (Orig.). (YA). (gr. 8-10). 1990. pap., teacher ed. 15.95 (*0-914127-40-3*); pap., student ed. 14.95 (*0-914127-36-5*) Univ Class.

— Art Text-Workbook: General Art (Introduction) Wallace, Dorathye B., ed. (Illus.). 100p. (Orig.). (YA). (gr. 8-10). 1990. pap., teacher ed. 15.95 (*0-914127-53-5*); pap., student ed. 14.95 (*0-914127-54-3*) Univ Class.

— An Art Text-Workbook: Metalsmithing (Introduction) Wallace, Dorothy, ed. (Illus.). 142p. (Orig.). (YA). (gr. 8-10). 1990. pap., student ed. 14.95 (*0-914127-33-0*) Univ Class.

— An Art Text-Workbook: Metalsmithing (Introduction) Wallace, Dorothy, ed. (Illus.). 142p. (Orig.). 1990. pap., teacher ed. 15.95 (*0-914127-41-1*) Univ Class.

— An Art Text-Workbook: Painting (Introduction) Wallace, Dorathye B., ed. (Illus.). 127p. (Orig.). (YA). (gr. 8-10). 1990. pap., teacher ed. 15.95 (*0-914127-58-6*); pap., student ed. 14.95 (*0-914127-57-8*) Univ Class.

— An Art Text-Workbook: Photography (Introduction) Baird, Tate, ed. (Illus.). 178p. (Orig.). 1990. pap., teacher ed. 15.95 (*0-914127-42-X*) Univ Class.

M

— An Art Text-Workbook: Photography (Introduction) Baird, Tate, ed. (Illus.). 178p. (Orig.). (YA). (gr. 8-10). 1990. pap., student ed. 14.95 (*0-914127-23-3*) Univ Class.
— An Art Text-Workbook: Printmaking (Introduction) Wallace, Dorathye B., ed. (Illus.). 124p. (Orig.). (YA). (gr. 8-10). 1990. pap., teacher ed. 15.95 (*0-914127-28-4*); pap., student ed. 14.95 (*0-914127-27-6*) Univ Class.
— An Art Text-Workbook: Sculpture (Introduction) Wallace, Dorathye B., ed. (Orig.). 1990. pap., student ed. 14.95 (*0-914127-43-8*) Univ Class.
— An Art Text-Workbook: Sculpture (Introduction) Wallace, Dorathye B., ed. (Illus.). 113p. (Orig.). (YA). (gr. 8-10). 1990. pap., teacher ed. 15.95 (*0-914127-34-9*) Univ Class.
— An Art Text-Workbook: Weaving (Introduction) Wallace, Dorathye B., ed. (Illus.). 144p. (Orig.). (YA). (gr. 8-10). 1990. pap., teacher ed. 15.95 (*0-914127-62-4*); pap., student ed. 14.95 (*0-914127-61-6*) Univ Class.
— Investigating Bio Lab Mnl Cb. (C). 1997. pap. text, lab manual ed. 36.56 (*0-201-30462-7*) Addison-Wesley.
— Investigating Biology: An Annotated Lab Manual. 2nd ed. (C). 1996. spiral bd., lab manual ed. 68.44 (*0-8053-1946-8*) Benjamin-Cummings.
— Portrait of California. (Illus.). 80p. 1996. pap. text 12.95 (*1-55868-249-X*) Gr Arts Ctr Pub.

Morgan, Judith & De Zanger, Andre. The Tao of Living on Purpose. LC 98-85983. (Illus.). 130p. 1998. lib. bdg. 27.95 (*0-89334-285-8*, Humanics Trade) Humanics Ltd.

Morgan, Judith & Morgan, Neil. Dr. Seuss & Mr. Geisel: A Biography. LC 96-19313. (Illus.). 384p. 1996. pap. 22.00 (*0-306-80736-X*) Da Capo.

Morgan, Judith G. Investigating Biology. 3rd ed. 160p. (C). 1999. pap. text, suppl. ed. 11.33 (*0-8053-6557-5*) Benjamin-Cummings.

***Morgan, Judith G.** Investigating Biology. 3rd ed. 700p. (C). 1999. student ed., spiral bd. 54.00 (*0-8053-6556-7*) Benjamin-Cummings.

***Morgan, Julian.** Roller: A Dirt Road Sport. 2000. 19.95 (*0-942407-48-2*) Father & Son.

Morgan, Julie C. Model Airplane Racing. LC 78-172149. (Speed Sports Bks.). (Illus.). (YA). (gr. 7 up). 1972. 11.95 (*0-397-31295-4*) HarpC Child Bks.

Morgan, K. Socialist Historian Journal Issue 17. text 40.00 (*1-85489-118-9*) Rivers Oram.
— Socialist History Journal Issue 17. pap. text 17.50 (*1-85489-119-7*) Rivers Oram.

Morgan, K., et al. Interactive Technology in Health Care. LC 94-73352. 300p. (gr. 12). 1995. 80.00 (*90-5199-201-7*) IOS Press.

Morgan, K., jt. ed. see Westwood, J.

Morgan, K. L. Castledance: From the Chronicles of Fiarah. 1997. pap. text 12.95 (*1-890558-01-X*) Granite UT.

Morgan, K. L. Castledance Vol. I: From the Chronicles of Fiarah. LC 99-90035. 405p. 1997. pap. write for info. (*1-58308-176-3*, 81761) TriQuest.
— A Christmas Angel with Golden Spangles. LC 98-86378. (Illus.). 62p. 1999. pap. 5.95 (*1-58308-125-9*, 81259) TriQuest.
— Judges of Light Vol. II: From the Chronicles of Fiarah. LC 98-86377. (Illus.). 480p. 1998. pap. 15.95 (*1-58308-175-5*, 81754) TriQuest.
— Lodestar Vol. III: From the Chronicles of Fiarah. LC 99-90036. (Illus.). 618p. 2000. pap. 17.95 (*1-58308-177-1*, 81771) TriQuest.
— Love Isn't Love... Until. LC 99-67790. 84p. 1999. pap. write for info. (*1-58308-128-3*, 81283) TriQuest.
— Pioneer Ghost. LC 00-103153. 110p. 2000. pap. 8.95 (*1-58308-185-2*, 81852) TriQuest.

***Morgan, Karen, ed.** The Good Days. 192p. 1999. pap. 12.99 (*0-9672103-0-5*) Alliance Books.

Morgan, Karen, ed. see Jackson, Jeffrey.

Morgan, Karen, ed. see Willenzik, David S.

Morgan, Karen, ed. see Young, Stanford.

Morgan, Karen S., et al, eds. Global Healthcare Grid: The Transformation of Medicine Through Communication. LC 96-79462. (Studies in Health Technology & Informatics: --). 350p. (YA). (gr. 12). 1997. 98.00 (*90-5199-299-8*, 299-8) IOS Press.

Morgan, Karl Z. & Peterson, Ken M. The Angry Genie: One Man's Walk Through the Nuclear Age. LC 98-34766. 240p. 1998. 24.95 (*0-8061-3122-5*) U of Okla Pr.

Morgan, Kate. Keeping Baby Animals Safe: Big Book. large type ed. (Little Books & Big Bks.). (Illus.). 8p. (J). (ps-1). 1998. pap. text 19.89 (*0-8215-0865-2*) Sadlier.
— The Old School Dies. 240p. (Orig.). 1996. mass mkt. 5.99 (*0-425-15552-8*, Prime Crime) Berkley Pub.
— The Story of Things. (Illus.). 32p. (J). (gr. 3-7). 1991. 14.95 (*0-8027-6918-7*); lib. bdg. 15.85 (*0-8027-6919-5*) Walker & Co.

Morgan, Katherine R., ed. My Ever Dear Daughter, My Own Dear Mother: The Correspondence of Julia Stone Towne & Mary Julia Towne, 1868-1882. LC 96-24991. (Illus.). 328p. 1996. pap. 16.95 (*0-87745-564-3*); text 32.95 (*0-87745-563-5*) U of Iowa Pr.

Morgan, Kathleen. A Certain Magic. LC 99-28407. (Romances Ser.). 1999. pap. 25.95 (*0-7862-2088-0*, Five Star MI) Mac Lib Ref.

***Morgan, Kathleen.** Daughter of Joy. LC 99-25264. (Brides of Culdee Creek Ser.: Vol. 1). 336p. (gr. 9 up). 1999. pap. 10.99 (*0-8007-5718-1*) Revell.
— Daughter of Joy/Woman of Grace. 2000. pap. 11.99 (*0-8007-6458-7*) Revell.

Morgan, Kathleen. Demon Prince. 448p. (Orig.). 1997. mass mkt. 5.50 (*0-505-52234-9*, Love Spell) Dorchester Pub Co.
— Firesong. 1996. pap. 5.99 (*0-7860-0262-X*) Kensgtn Pub Corp.
— Firestar. 448p. (Orig.). 1997. mass mkt. 5.50 (*0-505-52218-7*, Love Spell) Dorchester Pub Co.
— Firestorm. 448p. 1995. mass mkt. 4.99 (*0-7860-0175-5*, Pinncle Kensgtn) Kensgtn Pub Corp.
— Heart's Surrender. 480p. 1994. mass mkt. 5.99 (*0-7860-0052-X*, Pinncle Kensgtn) Kensgtn Pub Corp.

***Morgan, Kathleen.** Heart's Surrender. LC 99-45470. 1999. 25.95 (*0-7862-2243-3*) Mac Lib Ref.

Morgan, Kathleen. The Heather & the Thistle. 288p. 1998. pap. 5.50 (*0-8217-5987-6*, Zebra Kensgtn) Kensgtn Pub Corp.
— Strands of Gold. (Faerie Tale Romance Ser.). 400p. (Orig.). 1997. mass mkt. 5.99 (*0-505-52239-X*, Love Spell) Dorchester Pub Co.
— Tales Plainly Told: The Eyewitness Narratives of Hemingway & Homer. (ENGL Ser.: Vol. 7). x, 90p. 1990. 50.00 (*0-938100-81-5*) Camden Hse.

***Morgan, Kathleen.** Woman of Grace, Vol. 2. LC 00-27187. (Brides of Culdee Creek Ser.: Vol. 2). 304p. (gr. 9 up). 2000. pap. 10.99 (*0-8007-5727-0*) Revell.

Morgan, Kathleen O'Leary. Alabama Crime Perspectives 1999. 22p. 1999. spiral bd. 19.00 (*0-7401-0100-5*) Morgan Quitno Corp.
— Alabama In Perspectives, 1999. 26p. 1999. spiral bd. 19.00 (*1-56692-950-4*) Morgan Quitno Corp.
— Alaska Crime Perspective, 1999. 22p. 1999. spiral bd. 19.00 (*0-7401-0101-3*) Morgan Quitno Corp.
— Alaska In Perspectives,1999. 26p. 1999. spiral bd. 19.00 (*1-56692-951-2*) Morgan Quitno Corp.
— Arizona Crime Perspectives 1999. 22p. 1999. spiral bd. 19.00 (*0-7401-0102-1*) Morgan Quitno Corp.
— Arizona in Perspectives, 1999. 26p. 1999. spiral bd. 19.00 (*1-56692-952-0*) Morgan Quitno Corp.
— Arkansas Crime Perspective, 1999. 22p. 1999. spiral bd. 19.00 (*0-7401-0103-X*) Morgan Quitno Corp.
— Arkansas Health Care in Perspective, 1999. 21p. 1999. spiral bd. 19.00 (*0-7401-0053-X*, M Quitno Pr) Morgan Quitno Corp.
— Arkansas in Perspective ,1999. 26p. 1999. spiral bd. 19.00 (*1-56692-953-9*) Morgan Quitno Corp.
— California Crime Perspectives 1999. 22p. 1999. spiral bd. 19.00 (*0-7401-0104-8*) Morgan Quitno Corp.
— California Health Care Perspective, 1999. 21p. 1999. spiral bd. 19.00 (*0-7401-0054-8*) Morgan Quitno Corp.
— California in Perspective, 1999. 26p. 1999. spiral bd. 19.00 (*1-56692-954-7*) Morgan Quitno Corp.

***Morgan, Kathleen O'Leary.** Campaigns & Elections Trends. 100p. 1999. pap. 50.00 (*0-7401-0009-2*, M Quitno Pr) Morgan Quitno Corp.
— Children at Risk Trends. 100p. 1999. pap. 50.00 (*0-7401-0006-8*, M Quitno Pr) Morgan Quitno Corp.

Morgan, Kathleen O'Leary. City Crime Rankings. 5th ed. 408p. 1999. per. 37.95 (*1-56692-331-X*) Morgan Quitno Corp.
— Colorado Crime Perspectives 1999. 22p. 1999. spiral bd. 19.00 (*0-7401-0105-6*) Morgan Quitno Corp.
— Colorado Health Care Perspective, 1999. 21p. 1999. spiral bd. 19.00 (*0-7401-0055-6*) Morgan Quitno Corp.
— Colorado in Perspective, 1999. 26p. 1999. spiral bd. 19.00 (*1-56692-955-5*) Morgan Quitno Corp.
— Connecticut Crime Perspectives 1999. 22p. 1999. spiral bd. 19.00 (*0-7401-0106-4*) Morgan Quitno Corp.
— Connecticut Health Care Perspective, 1999. 21p. 1999. spiral bd. 19.00 (*0-7401-0056-4*) Morgan Quitno Corp.
— Connecticut in Perspective, 1999. 26p. 1999. spiral bd. 19.00 (*1-56692-956-3*) Morgan Quitno Corp.

***Morgan, Kathleen O'Leary.** Crime State Rankings, 1999. 540p. 1999. per. 52.95 (*1-56692-334-4*) Morgan Quitno Corp.
— Crime Trends. 100p. 1998. pap. 50.00 (*1-56692-339-5*, M Quitno Pr) Morgan Quitno Corp.

Morgan, Kathleen O'Leary. Delaware Crime Perspectives 1999. 22p. 1999. spiral bd. 19.00 (*0-7401-0107-2*) Morgan Quitno Corp.
— Delaware Health Care Perspective, 1999. 21p. 1999. spiral bd. 19.00 (*0-7401-0057-2*) Morgan Quitno Corp.
— Delaware in Perspective, 1999. 26p. 1999. spiral bd. 19.00 (*1-56692-957-1*) Morgan Quitno Corp.

***Morgan, Kathleen O'Leary.** Education Finance Trends. 100p. 1999. pap. 50.00 (*0-7401-0007-6*, M Quitno Pr) Morgan Quitno Corp.
— Elementary & Secondary Education Trends. 100p. 1998. pap. 50.00 (*1-56692-340-9*, M Quitno Pr) Morgan Quitno Corp.
— Employment Trends. 100p. 1999. pap. 50.00 (*1-56692-348-4*, M Quitno Pr) Morgan Quitno Corp.
— Federal Government Finance Trends. 100p. 1998. pap. 50.00 (*1-56692-341-7*, M Quitno Pr) Morgan Quitno Corp.

Morgan, Kathleen O'Leary. Florida Crime Perspectives 1999. 22p. 1999. spiral bd. 19.00 (*0-7401-0108-0*) Morgan Quitno Corp.
— Florida in Perspective,1999. 26p. 1999. spiral bd. 19.00 (*1-56692-958-X*) Morgan Quitno Corp.
— Georgia Crime Perspectives 1999. 22p. 1999. spiral bd. 19.00 (*0-7401-0109-9*) Morgan Quitno Corp.
— Georgia in Perspective, 1999. 26p. 1999. spiral bd. 19.00 (*1-56692-959-8*) Morgan Quitno Corp.
— Hawaii Crime Perspectives 1999. 22p. 1999. spiral bd. 19.00 (*0-7401-0110-2*) Morgan Quitno Corp.

***Morgan, Kathleen O'Leary.** Health Care Trends. 100p. 1999. pap. 50.00 (*1-56692-344-1*, M Quitno Pr) Morgan Quitno Corp.
— Highway Transportation Trends. 100p. 1999. pap. 50.00 (*1-56692-345-X*, M Quitno Pr) Morgan Quitno Corp.
— Housing Trends. 100p. 2000. pap. 50.00 (*0-7401-0012-2*, M Quitno Pr) Morgan Quitno Corp.

Morgan, Kathleen O'Leary. Idaho Crime Perspective, 1999. 22p. 1999. spiral bd. 19.00 (*0-7401-0111-0*) Morgan Quitno Corp.
— Illinois Crime Perspectives 1999. 22p. 1999. spiral bd. 19.00 (*0-7401-0112-9*) Morgan Quitno Corp.
— Indiana Crime Perspectives 1999. 22p. 1999. spiral bd. 19.00 (*0-7401-0113-7*) Morgan Quitno Corp.
— Iowa Crime Perspectives 1999. 22p. 1999. spiral bd. 19.00 (*0-7401-0114-5*) Morgan Quitno Corp.
— Kansas Crime Perspectives,1999. 22p. 1999. spiral bd. 19.00 (*0-7401-0115-3*) Morgan Quitno Corp.
— Kentucky Crime Perspectives 1999. 22p. 1999. spiral bd. 19.00 (*0-7401-0116-1*) Morgan Quitno Corp.
— Louisiana Crime Perspectives, 1999. 22p. 1999. spiral bd. 19.00 (*0-7401-0117-X*) Morgan Quitno Corp.
— Maine Crime Perspectives, 1999. 22p. 1999. spiral bd. 19.00 (*0-7401-0118-8*) Morgan Quitno Corp.
— Maryland Crime Perspectives, 1999. 22p. 1999. spiral bd. 19.00 (*0-7401-0119-6*) Morgan Quitno Corp.
— Massachusetts Crime Perspectives, 1999. 22p. 1999. spiral bd. 19.00 (*0-7401-0120-X*) Morgan Quitno Corp.
— Michigan Crime Perspectives, 1999. 22p. 1999. spiral bd. 19.00 (*0-7401-0121-8*) Morgan Quitno Corp.
— Michigan Health Care Perspective, 1999. 21p. 1999. spiral bd. 19.00 (*0-7401-0071-8*) Morgan Quitno Corp.
— Minnesota Crime Perspectives, 1999. 22p. 1999. spiral bd. 19.00 (*0-7401-0122-6*) Morgan Quitno Corp.
— Minnesota Health Care Perspective, 1999. 21p. 1999. spiral bd. 19.00 (*0-7401-0072-6*) Morgan Quitno Corp.
— Mississippi Crime Perspectives, 1999. 22p. 1999. spiral bd. 19.00 (*0-7401-0123-4*) Morgan Quitno Corp.
— Mississippi Health Care Perspective, 1999. 21p. 1999. spiral bd. 19.00 (*0-7401-0073-4*) Morgan Quitno Corp.
— Missouri Crime Perspectives, 1999. 22p. 1999. spiral bd. 19.00 (*0-7401-0124-2*) Morgan Quitno Corp.
— Missouri Health Care Perspective, 1999. 21p. 1999. spiral bd. 19.00 (*0-7401-0074-2*) Morgan Quitno Corp.
— Montana Crime Perspectives,1999. 22p. 1999. spiral bd. 19.00 (*0-7401-0125-0*) Morgan Quitno Corp.
— Nebraska Crime Perspectives, 1999. 22p. 1999. spiral bd. 19.00 (*0-7401-0126-9*) Morgan Quitno Corp.
— Nebraska Health Care Perspective, 1999. 21p. 1999. spiral bd. 19.00 (*0-7401-0076-9*) Morgan Quitno Corp.
— Nevada Crime Perspectives, 1999. 22p. 1999. spiral bd. 19.00 (*0-7401-0127-7*) Morgan Quitno Corp.
— New Hampshire Crime Perspectives, 1999. 22p. 1999. spiral bd. 19.00 (*0-7401-0128-5*) Morgan Quitno Corp.
— New Hampshire Health Care Perspective, 1999. 21p. 1999. spiral bd. 19.00 (*0-7401-0078-5*) Morgan Quitno Corp.
— New Jersey Crime Perspectives, 1999. 22p. 1999. spiral bd. 19.00 (*0-7401-0129-3*) Morgan Quitno Corp.
— New Jersey Health Care Perspective, 1999. 21p. 1999. spiral bd. 19.00 (*0-7401-0079-3*) Morgan Quitno Corp.
— New Mexico Crime Perspectives, 1999. 22p. 1999. spiral bd. 19.00 (*0-7401-0130-7*) Morgan Quitno Corp.
— New Mexico Health Care Perspective, 1999. 21p. 1999. spiral bd. 19.00 (*0-7401-0080-7*) Morgan Quitno Corp.
— New York Crime Perspectives, 1999. 22p. 1999. spiral bd. 19.00 (*0-7401-0131-5*) Morgan Quitno Corp.
— New York Health Care Perspective, 1999. 21p. 1999. spiral bd. 19.00 (*0-7401-0081-5*) Morgan Quitno Corp.
— North Carolina Crime Perspective, 1999. 22p. 1999. spiral bd. 19.00 (*0-7401-0132-3*) Morgan Quitno Corp.
— North Carolina Health Care Perspective, 1999. 21p. 1999. spiral bd. 19.00 (*0-7401-0082-3*) Morgan Quitno Corp.
— North Dakota Crime Perspectives,1999. 22p. 1999. spiral bd. 19.00 (*0-7401-0133-1*) Morgan Quitno Corp.
— North Dakota Health Care Perspective, 1999. 21p. 1999. spiral bd. 19.00 (*0-7401-0083-1*) Morgan Quitno Corp.
— Ohio Crime Perspectives,1999. 22p. 1999. spiral bd. 19.00 (*0-7401-0134-X*) Morgan Quitno Corp.
— Oklahoma Crime Perspectives, 1999. 22p. 1999. spiral bd. 19.00 (*0-7401-0135-8*) Morgan Quitno Corp.
— Oklahoma Health Care Perspective, 1999. 21p. 1999. spiral bd. 19.00 (*0-7401-0085-8*) Morgan Quitno Corp.
— Oregon Crime Perspectives, 1999. 22p. 1999. spiral bd. 19.00 (*0-7401-0136-6*) Morgan Quitno Corp.

***Morgan, Kathleen O'Leary.** Oregon in Perspective, 1999. 26p. 1999. spiral bd. 19.00 (*1-56692-986-5*) Morgan Quitno Corp.
— Paying for Health Care Trends. 100p. 1999. pap. 50.00 (*0-7401-0010-6*, M Quitno Pr) Morgan Quitno Corp.

Morgan, Kathleen O'Leary. Pennsylvania Crime Perspectives, 1999. 22p. 1999. spiral bd. 19.00 (*0-7401-0137-4*) Morgan Quitno Corp.
— Pennsylvania Health Care Perspective, 1999. 21p. 1999. spiral bd. 19.00 (*0-7401-0087-4*) Morgan Quitno Corp.

***Morgan, Kathleen O'Leary.** Poverty & Social Welfare Trends. 100p. 1998. pap. 50.00 (*1-56692-342-5*, M Quitno Pr) Morgan Quitno Corp.
— Reproductive Heatlh Trends. 100p. 1999. pap. 50.00 (*0-7401-0008-4*, M Quitno Pr) Morgan Quitno Corp.

Morgan, Kathleen O'Leary. Rhode Island Crime Perspectives,1999. 22p. 1999. spiral bd. 19.00 (*0-7401-0138-2*) Morgan Quitno Corp.
— Rhode Island Health Care Perspective, 1999. 21p. 1999. spiral bd. 19.00 (*0-7401-0088-2*) Morgan Quitno Corp.

***Morgan, Kathleen O'Leary.** Senior Citizens: Trends. 100p. 2000. pap. 50.00 (*0-7401-0016-5*, M Quitno Pr) Morgan Quitno Corp.

Morgan, Kathleen O'Leary. South Carolina Crime Perspective, 1999. 22p. 1999. spiral bd. 19.00 (*0-7401-0139-0*) Morgan Quitno Corp.
— South Carolina Health Care Perspective, 1999. 21p. 1999. spiral bd. 19.00 (*0-7401-0089-0*) Morgan Quitno Corp.
— South Dakota Crime Perspectives,1999. 22p. 1999. spiral bd. 19.00 (*0-7401-0140-4*) Morgan Quitno Corp.
— South Dakota Health Care Perspective, 1999. 21p. 1999. spiral bd. 19.00 (*0-7401-0090-4*) Morgan Quitno Corp.

***Morgan, Kathleen O'Leary.** State & Local Government Finance Trends. 100p. 1998. pap. 50.00 (*1-56692-343-3*, M Quitno Pr) Morgan Quitno Corp.
— State Funding Priorities Trends. 100p. 2000. pap. 50.00 (*0-7401-0013-0*, M Quitno Pr) Morgan Quitno Corp.
— State Government Finance Trends. 100p. 1999. pap. 50.00 (*1-56692-346-8*, M Quitno Pr) Morgan Quitno Corp.
— State Tax Burden Trends. 100p. 2000. pap. 50.00 (*0-7401-0014-9*, M Quitno Pr) Morgan Quitno Corp.
— State Taxes Trends. 100p. 1999. pap. 50.00 (*1-56692-347-6*, M Quitno Pr) Morgan Quitno Corp.

Morgan, Kathleen O'Leary. Tennessee Crime Perspectives, 1999. 22p. 1999. spiral bd. 19.00 (*0-7401-0141-2*) Morgan Quitno Corp.
— Tennessee Health Care Perspective, 1999. 21p. 1999. spiral bd. 19.00 (*0-7401-0091-2*) Morgan Quitno Corp.
— Texas Crime Perspectives, 1999. 22p. 1999. spiral bd. 19.00 (*0-7401-0142-0*) Morgan Quitno Corp.
— Texas Health Care Perspectives1999. 21p. 1999. spiral bd. 19.00 (*0-7401-0092-0*) Morgan Quitno Corp.
— Utah Crime Perspectives, 1999. 22p. 1999. spiral bd. 19.00 (*0-7401-0143-9*) Morgan Quitno Corp.
— Utah Health Care Perspectives 1999. 21p. 1999. spiral bd. 19.00 (*0-7401-0093-9*) Morgan Quitno Corp.
— Vermont Crime Perspective, 1999. 22p. 1999. spiral bd. 19.00 (*0-7401-0144-7*) Morgan Quitno Corp.
— Vermont Health Care Perspectives 1999. 21p. 1999. spiral bd. 19.00 (*0-7401-0094-7*) Morgan Quitno Corp.
— Virginia Crime Perspectives, 1999. 22p. 1999. spiral bd. 19.00 (*0-7401-0145-5*) Morgan Quitno Corp.
— Virginia Health Care Perspective, 1999. 21p. 1999. spiral bd. 19.00 (*0-7401-0095-5*) Morgan Quitno Corp.

***Morgan, Kathleen O'Leary.** Vital Statistics Trends. 100p. 1999. pap. 50.00 (*1-56692-349-2*, M Quitno Pr) Morgan Quitno Corp.

Morgan, Kathleen O'Leary. Washington Crime Perspectives, 1999. 22p. 1999. spiral bd. 19.00 (*0-7401-0146-3*) Morgan Quitno Corp.
— Washington Health Care Perspective, 1999. 21p. 1999. spiral bd. 19.00 (*0-7401-0096-3*) Morgan Quitno Corp.

***Morgan, Kathleen O'Leary.** We the People - Population Trends. 100p. 1999. pap. 50.00 (*0-7401-0005-X*, M Quitno Pr) Morgan Quitno Corp.
— Wealth & Income Trends. 100p. 2000. pap. 50.00 (*0-7401-0011-4*, M Quitno Pr) Morgan Quitno Corp.
— Welfare Reform Trends. 100p. 2000. pap. 50.00 (*0-7401-0015-7*, M Quitno Pr) Morgan Quitno Corp.
— West Virginia Crime Perspectives,1999. 22p. 1999. spiral bd. 19.00 (*0-7401-0147-1*) Morgan Quitno Corp.

Morgan, Kathleen O'Leary. West Virginia Health Care Perspective, 1999. 21p. 1999. spiral bd. 19.00 (*0-7401-0097-1*) Morgan Quitno Corp.

***Morgan, Kathleen O'Leary.** Wisconsin Crime Perspectives, 1999. 22p. 1999. spiral bd. 19.00 (*0-7401-0148-X*) Morgan Quitno Corp.

Morgan, Kathleen O'Leary. Wisconsin Health Care Perspective, 1999. 21p. 1999. spiral bd. 19.00 (*0-7401-0098-X*) Morgan Quitno Corp.
— Wyoming Crime Perspectives,1999. 22p. 1999. spiral bd. 19.00 (*0-7401-0149-8*) Morgan Quitno Corp.
— Wyoming Health Care Perspectives 1999. 21p. 1999. spiral bd. 19.00 (*0-7401-0099-8*) Morgan Quitno Corp.

Morgan, Kathleen O'Leary, ed. Alaska Health Care in Perspective ,1999. 21p. 1999. spiral bd. 19.00 (*0-7401-0051-3*, M Quitno Pr) Morgan Quitno Corp.

***Morgan, Kathleen O'Leary, ed.** The Economy: Trends. 100p. 1998. pap. 50.00 (*1-56692-338-7*, M Quitno Pr) Morgan Quitno Corp.

Morgan, Kathleen O'Leary, ed. Georgia Health Care Perspective, 1999. 21p. 1999. spiral bd. 19.00 (*0-7401-0059-9*) Morgan Quitno Corp.
— Hawaii Health Care Perspective, 1999. 21p. 1999. spiral bd. 19.00 (*0-7401-0060-2*) Morgan Quitno Corp.
— Hawaii in Perspective, 1999. 26p. 1999. spiral bd. 19.00 (*1-56692-960-1*) Morgan Quitno Corp.
— Idaho Health Care Perspective, 1999. 21p. 1999. spiral bd. 19.00 (*0-7401-0061-0*) Morgan Quitno Corp.
— Idaho in Perspective, 1999. 26p. 1999. spiral bd. 19.00 (*1-56692-961-X*) Morgan Quitno Corp.
— Illinois Health Care Perspective, 1999. 21p. 1999. spiral bd. 19.00 (*0-7401-0062-9*) Morgan Quitno Corp.
— Illinois in Perspective, 1999. 26p. 1999. spiral bd. 19.00 (*1-56692-962-8*) Morgan Quitno Corp.
— Indiana Health Care Perspective,1999. 21p. 1999. spiral bd. 19.00 (*0-7401-0063-7*) Morgan Quitno Corp.
— Indiana in Perspective, 1999. 26p. 1999. spiral bd. 19.00 (*1-56692-963-6*) Morgan Quitno Corp.
— Iowa Health Care Perspective, 1999. 21p. 1999. spiral bd. 19.00 (*0-7401-0064-5*) Morgan Quitno Corp.
— Iowa in Perspective, 1999. 26p. 1999. spiral bd. 19.00 (*1-56692-964-4*) Morgan Quitno Corp.
— Kansas Health Care Perspective 1999. 21p. 1999. spiral bd. 19.00 (*0-7401-0065-3*) Morgan Quitno Corp.
— Kansas in Perspective, 1999. 26p. 1999. spiral bd. 19.00 (*1-56692-965-2*) Morgan Quitno Corp.
— Kentucky Health Care Perspective, 1999. 21p. 1999. spiral bd. 19.00 (*0-7401-0066-1*) Morgan Quitno Corp.

***Morgan, Kathleen O'Leary, ed.** Kentucky in Perspective, 1999. 26p. 1999. spiral bd. 19.00 (*1-56692-966-0*) Morgan Quitno Corp.

Morgan, Kathleen O'Leary, ed. Louisiana Health Care Perspective, 1999. 21p. 1999. spiral bd. 19.00 (*0-7401-0067-X*) Morgan Quitno Corp.

***Morgan, Kathleen O'Leary, ed.** Louisiana in Perspective, 1999. 26p. 1999. spiral bd. 19.00 (*1-56692-967-9*) Morgan Quitno Corp.

Morgan, Kathleen O'Leary, ed. Maine Health Care Perspective 1999. 21p. 1999. spiral bd. 19.00 (*0-7401-0068-8*) Morgan Quitno Corp.

***Morgan, Kathleen O'Leary, ed.** Maine in Perspective, 1999. 26p. 1999. spiral bd. 19.00 (*1-56692-968-7*) Morgan Quitno Corp.

Morgan, Kathleen O'Leary, ed. Maryland Health Care Perspective, 1999. 21p. 1999. spiral bd. 19.00 (*0-7401-0069-6*) Morgan Quitno Corp.

*Morgan, Kathleen O'Leary, ed. Maryland in Perspective, 1999. 26p. 1999. spiral bd. 19.00 (1-56692-969-5) Morgan Quitno Corp.

Morgan, Kathleen O'Leary, ed. Massachusetts Health Care Perspective, 1999. 21p. 1999. spiral bd. 19.00 (0-7401-0070-X) Morgan Quitno Corp.

*Morgan, Kathleen O'Leary, ed. Massachusetts in Perspective, 1999. 26p. 1999. spiral bd. 19.00 (1-56692-970-9) Morgan Quitno Corp.

Morgan, Kathleen O'Leary, ed. Michigan in Perspective, 1999. 26p. 1999. spiral bd. 19.00 (1-56692-971-7) Morgan Quitno Corp.

— Minnesota in Perspective, 1999. 26p. 1999. spiral bd. 19.00 (1-56692-972-5) Morgan Quitno Corp.

— Mississippi in Perspective, 1999. 26p. 1999. spiral bd. 19.00 (1-56692-973-3) Morgan Quitno Corp.

— Missouri in Perspective, 1999. 26p. 1999. spiral bd. 19.00 (1-56692-974-1) Morgan Quitno Corp.

— Montana Health Care Perspective, 1999. 21p. 1999. spiral bd. 19.00 (0-7401-0075-0) Morgan Quitno Corp.

— Montana in Perspective, 1999. 26p. 1999. spiral bd. 19.00 (1-56692-975-X) Morgan Quitno Corp.

— Nebraska in Perspective, 1999. 26p. 1999. spiral bd. 19.00 (1-56692-976-8) Morgan Quitno Corp.

*Morgan, Kathleen O'Leary, ed. Nevada Health Care Perspective, 1999. 21p. 1999. spiral bd. 19.00 (0-7401-0077-7) Morgan Quitno Corp.

Morgan, Kathleen O'Leary, ed. Nevada in Perspective, 1999. 26p. 1999. spiral bd. 19.00 (1-56692-977-6) Morgan Quitno Corp.

— New Hampshire in Perspective, 1999. 26p. 1999. spiral bd. 19.00 (1-56692-978-4) Morgan Quitno Corp.

— New Jersey in Perspective, 1999. 26p. 1999. spiral bd. 19.00 (1-56692-979-2) Morgan Quitno Corp.

— New Mexico in Perspective, 1999. 26p. 1999. spiral bd. 19.00 (1-56692-980-6) Morgan Quitno Corp.

— New York in Perspective, 1999. 26p. 1999. spiral bd. 19.00 (1-56692-981-4) Morgan Quitno Corp.

— North Carolina in Perspective, 1999. 26p. 1999. spiral bd. 19.00 (1-56692-982-2) Morgan Quitno Corp.

— North Dakota in Perspective, 1999. 26p. 1999. spiral bd. 19.00 (1-56692-983-0) Morgan Quitno Corp.

— Ohio in Perspective, 1999. 26p. 1999. spiral bd. 19.00 (1-56692-984-9) Morgan Quitno Corp.

— Oklahoma in Perspective, 1999. 26p. 1999. spiral bd. 19.00 (1-56692-985-7) Morgan Quitno Corp.

— Oregon Health Care Perspective 1999. 21p. 1999. spiral bd. 19.00 (0-7401-0086-6) Morgan Quitno Corp.

— Pennsylvania in Perspective 1999. 26p. 1999. spiral bd. 19.00 (1-56692-987-3) Morgan Quitno Corp.

— Rhode Island in Perspective, 1999. 26p. 1999. spiral bd. 19.00 (1-56692-988-1) Morgan Quitno Corp.

— South Carolina in Perspective, 1999. 26p. 1999. spiral bd. 19.00 (1-56692-989-X) Morgan Quitno Corp.

— South Dakota in Perspective, 1999. 26p. 1999. spiral bd. 19.00 (1-56692-990-3) Morgan Quitno Corp.

— Tennessee in Perspective, 1999. 26p. 1999. spiral bd. 19.00 (1-56692-991-1) Morgan Quitno Corp.

— Texas in Perspective, 1999. 26p. 1999. spiral bd. 19.00 (1-56692-992-X) Morgan Quitno Corp.

— Utah in Perspective, 1999. 26p. 1999. spiral bd. 19.00 (1-56692-993-8) Morgan Quitno Corp.

— Vermont in Perspective, 1999. 26p. 1999. spiral bd. 19.00 (1-56692-994-6) Morgan Quitno Corp.

— Virginia in Perspective, 1999. 26p. 1999. spiral bd. 19.00 (1-56692-995-4) Morgan Quitno Corp.

— Washington in Perspective, 1999. 26p. 1999. spiral bd. 19.00 (1-56692-996-2) Morgan Quitno Corp.

— West Virginia in Perspective, 1999. 26p. 1999. spiral bd. 19.00 (1-56692-997-0) Morgan Quitno Corp.

— Wisconsin in Perspective, 1999. 26p. 1999. spiral bd. 19.00 (1-56692-998-9) Morgan Quitno Corp.

— Wyoming in Perspective, 1999. 26p. 1999. spiral bd. 19.00 (1-56692-999-7) Morgan Quitno Corp.

Morgan, Kathleen O'Leary, et al, eds. City Crime Rankings Vol. I: Crime in Metropolitan America. 284p. (Orig.). 1995. pap. 19.95 (1-56692-307-7) Morgan Quitno Corp.

— City Crime Rankings Vol. II: Crime in Metropolitan America. 400p. (Orig.). 1996. lib. bdg. 34.95 (1-56692-309-3) Morgan Quitno Corp.

— Crime State Rankings, 1995. 544p. 1995. 67.95 (1-56692-305-0); pap. 43.95 (1-56692-301-8) Morgan Quitno Corp.

— Crime State Rankings, 1996. 512p. 1996. 49.95 (1-56692-311-5) Morgan Quitno Corp.

— Health Care State Rankings 1995. 540p. 1995. 67.95 (1-56692-306-9); pap. 43.95 (1-56692-302-6) Morgan Quitno Corp.

— Health Care State Rankings 1996. 540p. 1996. 49.95 (1-56692-312-3) Morgan Quitno Corp.

— State Rankings, 1995. 612p. 1995. 67.95 (1-56692-304-2); pap. 43.95 (1-56692-303-4) Morgan Quitno Corp.

— State Rankings, 1996. 608p. 1996. 49.95 (1-56692-310-7) Morgan Quitno Corp.

*Morgan, Kathleen O'Leary & Morgan, Scott E., eds. Alabama Crime in Perspective 2000. 22p. 2000. spiral bd. 19.00 (0-7401-0300-8) Morgan Quitno Corp.

Morgan, Kathleen O'Leary & Morgan, Scott E., eds. Alabama Crime Perspective, 1998. 20p. 1998. pap. 19.00 (1-56692-900-8) Morgan Quitno Corp.

*Morgan, Kathleen O'Leary & Morgan, Scott E., eds. Alabama Health Care in Perspective 1999. 21p. 1999. spiral bd. 19.00 (0-7401-0050-5) Morgan Quitno Corp.

— Alabama Health Care in Perspective 2000. 21p. 2000. spiral bd. 19.00 (0-7401-0200-1) Morgan Quitno Corp.

Morgan, Kathleen O'Leary & Morgan, Scott E., eds. Alabama Health Care Perspective, 1998. 20p. 1998. pap. 19.00 (1-56692-800-1) Morgan Quitno Corp.

— Alabama in Perspective, 1998. 24p. 1998. pap. 19.00 (1-56692-850-8) Morgan Quitno Corp.

*Morgan, Kathleen O'Leary & Morgan, Scott E., eds. Alabama in Perspective 2000. 26p. 2000. spiral bd. 19.00 (0-7401-0250-8) Morgan Quitno Corp.

— Alaska Crime in Perspective 2000. 22p. 2000. spiral bd. 19.00 (0-7401-0301-6) Morgan Quitno Corp.

Morgan, Kathleen O'Leary & Morgan, Scott E., eds. Alaska Crime Perspective, 1998. 20p. 1998. pap. 19.00 (1-56692-901-6) Morgan Quitno Corp.

*Morgan, Kathleen O'Leary & Morgan, Scott E., eds. Alaska Health Care in Perspective 2000. 21p. 2000. spiral bd. 19.00 (0-7401-0201-X) Morgan Quitno Corp.

Morgan, Kathleen O'Leary & Morgan, Scott E., eds. Alaska Health Care Perspective, 1998. 20p. 1998. pap. 19.00 (1-56692-801-X) Morgan Quitno Corp.

— Alaska in Perspective, 1998. 24p. 1998. pap. 19.00 (1-56692-851-6) Morgan Quitno Corp.

*Morgan, Kathleen O'Leary & Morgan, Scott E., eds. Alaska in Perspective 2000. 26p. 2000. spiral bd. 19.00 (0-7401-0251-6) Morgan Quitno Corp.

Morgan, Kathleen O'Leary & Morgan, Scott E., eds. America's Safest Places. LC 98-174996. 90p. 1996. pap. 7.95 (1-56692-319-0) Morgan Quitno Corp.

*Morgan, Kathleen O'Leary & Morgan, Scott E., eds. Arizona Crime in Perspective 2000. 22p. 2000. spiral bd. 19.00 (0-7401-0302-4) Morgan Quitno Corp.

Morgan, Kathleen O'Leary & Morgan, Scott E., eds. Arizona Crime Perspective, 1998. 20p. 1998. pap. 19.00 (1-56692-902-4) Morgan Quitno Corp.

*Morgan, Kathleen O'Leary & Morgan, Scott E., eds. Arizona Health Care in Perspective 1999. 21p. 1999. spiral bd. 19.00 (0-7401-0052-1) Morgan Quitno Corp.

— Arizona Health Care in Perspective 2000. 21p. 2000. spiral bd. 19.00 (0-7401-0202-8) Morgan Quitno Corp.

Morgan, Kathleen O'Leary & Morgan, Scott E., eds. Arizona Health Care Perspective, 1998. 20p. 1998. pap. 19.00 (1-56692-802-8) Morgan Quitno Corp.

— Arizona in Perspective, 1998. 24p. 1998. pap. 19.00 (1-56692-852-4) Morgan Quitno Corp.

*Morgan, Kathleen O'Leary & Morgan, Scott E., eds. Arizona in Perspective 2000. 26p. 2000. spiral bd. 19.00 (0-7401-0252-4) Morgan Quitno Corp.

— Arkansas Crime in Perspective 2000. 22p. 2000. spiral bd. 19.00 (0-7401-0303-2) Morgan Quitno Corp.

Morgan, Kathleen O'Leary & Morgan, Scott E., eds. Arkansas Crime Perspective, 1998. 20p. 1998. pap. 19.00 (1-56692-903-2) Morgan Quitno Corp.

*Morgan, Kathleen O'Leary & Morgan, Scott E., eds. Arkansas Health Care in Perspective 2000. 21p. 2000. spiral bd. 19.00 (0-7401-0203-6) Morgan Quitno Corp.

Morgan, Kathleen O'Leary & Morgan, Scott E., eds. Arkansas Health Care Perspective, 1998. 20p. 1998. pap. 19.00 (1-56692-803-6) Morgan Quitno Corp.

— Arkansas in Perspective, 1998. 24p. 1998. pap. 19.00 (1-56692-853-2) Morgan Quitno Corp.

*Morgan, Kathleen O'Leary & Morgan, Scott E., eds. Arkansas in Perspective 2000. 26p. 2000. spiral bd. 19.00 (0-7401-0253-2) Morgan Quitno Corp.

— California Crime in Perspective 2000. 22p. 2000. spiral bd. 19.00 (0-7401-0304-0) Morgan Quitno Corp.

Morgan, Kathleen O'Leary & Morgan, Scott E., eds. California Crime Perspective, 1998. 20p. 1998. pap. 19.00 (1-56692-904-0) Morgan Quitno Corp.

*Morgan, Kathleen O'Leary & Morgan, Scott E., eds. California Health Care in Perspective 2000. 21p. 2000. spiral bd. 19.00 (0-7401-0204-4) Morgan Quitno Corp.

Morgan, Kathleen O'Leary & Morgan, Scott E., eds. California Health Care Perspective, 1998. 20p. 1998. pap. 19.00 (1-56692-804-4) Morgan Quitno Corp.

— California in Perspective, 1998. 24p. 1998. pap. 19.00 (1-56692-854-0) Morgan Quitno Corp.

*Morgan, Kathleen O'Leary & Morgan, Scott E., eds. California in Perspective 2000. 26p. 2000. spiral bd. 19.00 (0-7401-0254-0) Morgan Quitno Corp.

Morgan, Kathleen O'Leary & Morgan, Scott E., eds. City Crime Rankings: Crime in Metropolitan America. 3rd ed. 400p. 1997. 37.95 (1-56692-315-8) Morgan Quitno Corp.

*Morgan, Kathleen O'Leary & Morgan, Scott E., eds. City Crime Rankings: Crime In Metropolitan America. 6th ed. 408p. 2000. per. 39.95 (0-7401-0003-3) Morgan Quitno Corp.

— Colorado Crime in Perspective 2000. 22p. 2000. spiral bd. 19.00 (0-7401-0305-9) Morgan Quitno Corp.

Morgan, Kathleen O'Leary & Morgan, Scott E., eds. Colorado Crime Perspective, 1998. 20p. 1998. pap. 19.00 (1-56692-905-9) Morgan Quitno Corp.

*Morgan, Kathleen O'Leary & Morgan, Scott E., eds. Colorado Health Care in Perspective 2000. 21p. 2000. spiral bd. 19.00 (0-7401-0205-2) Morgan Quitno Corp.

Morgan, Kathleen O'Leary & Morgan, Scott E., eds. Colorado Health Care Perspective, 1998. 20p. 1998. pap. 19.00 (1-56692-805-2) Morgan Quitno Corp.

— Colorado in Perspective, 1998. 24p. 1998. pap. 19.00 (1-56692-855-9) Morgan Quitno Corp.

*Morgan, Kathleen O'Leary & Morgan, Scott E., eds. Colorado in Perspective 2000. 26p. 2000. spiral bd. 19.00 (0-7401-0255-9) Morgan Quitno Corp.

— Connecticut Crime in Perspective 2000. 22p. 2000. spiral bd. 19.00 (0-7401-0306-7) Morgan Quitno Corp.

Morgan, Kathleen O'Leary & Morgan, Scott E., eds. Connecticut Crime Perspective, 1998. 20p. 1998. pap. 19.00 (1-56692-906-7) Morgan Quitno Corp.

*Morgan, Kathleen O'Leary & Morgan, Scott E., eds. Connecticut Health Care in Perspective 2000. 21p. 2000. spiral bd. 19.00 (0-7401-0206-0) Morgan Quitno Corp.

Morgan, Kathleen O'Leary & Morgan, Scott E., eds. Connecticut Health Care Perspective, 1998. 20p. 1998. pap. 19.00 (1-56692-806-0) Morgan Quitno Corp.

— Connecticut in Perspective, 1998. 24p. 1998. pap. 19.00 (1-56692-856-7) Morgan Quitno Corp.

*Morgan, Kathleen O'Leary & Morgan, Scott E., eds. Connecticut in Perspective 2000. 26p. 2000. spiral bd. 19.00 (0-7401-0256-7) Morgan Quitno Corp.

Morgan, Kathleen O'Leary & Morgan, Scott E., eds. Crime State Rankings, 1998. 540p. 1998. pap. 49.95 (1-56692-328-X) Morgan Quitno Corp.

— Crime State Rankings, 1997. 540p. 1997. 49.95 (1-56692-318-2) Morgan Quitno Corp.

*Morgan, Kathleen O'Leary & Morgan, Scott E., eds. Crime State Rankings 2000: Crime in the 50 United States. 540p. 2000. per. 52.95 (0-7401-0002-5) Morgan Quitno Corp.

— Delaware Crime in Perspective 2000. 22p. 2000. spiral bd. 19.00 (0-7401-0307-5) Morgan Quitno Corp.

Morgan, Kathleen O'Leary & Morgan, Scott E., eds. Delaware Crime Perspective, 1998. 20p. 1998. pap. 19.00 (1-56692-907-5) Morgan Quitno Corp.

*Morgan, Kathleen O'Leary & Morgan, Scott E., eds. Delaware Health Care in Perspective 2000. 21p. 2000. spiral bd. 19.00 (0-7401-0207-9) Morgan Quitno Corp.

Morgan, Kathleen O'Leary & Morgan, Scott E., eds. Delaware Health Care Perspective, 1998. 20p. 1998. pap. 19.00 (1-56692-807-9) Morgan Quitno Corp.

— Delaware in Perspective, 1998. 24p. 1998. pap. 19.00 (1-56692-857-5) Morgan Quitno Corp.

*Morgan, Kathleen O'Leary & Morgan, Scott E., eds. Delaware in Perspective 2000. 26p. 2000. spiral bd. 19.00 (0-7401-0257-5) Morgan Quitno Corp.

— Florida Crime in Perspective 2000. 22p. 2000. spiral bd. 19.00 (0-7401-0308-3) Morgan Quitno Corp.

Morgan, Kathleen O'Leary & Morgan, Scott E., eds. Florida Crime Perspective, 1998. 20p. 1998. pap. 19.00 (1-56692-908-3) Morgan Quitno Corp.

*Morgan, Kathleen O'Leary & Morgan, Scott E., eds. Florida Health Care in Perspective 1999. 21p. 1999. spiral bd. 19.00 (0-7401-0058-0) Morgan Quitno Corp.

— Florida Health Care in Perspective 2000. 21p. 2000. spiral bd. 19.00 (0-7401-0208-7) Morgan Quitno Corp.

Morgan, Kathleen O'Leary & Morgan, Scott E., eds. Florida Health Care Perspective, 1998. 20p. 1998. pap. 19.00 (1-56692-808-7) Morgan Quitno Corp.

— Florida in Perspective, 1998. 24p. 1998. pap. 19.00 (1-56692-858-3) Morgan Quitno Corp.

*Morgan, Kathleen O'Leary & Morgan, Scott E., eds. Florida in Perspective 2000. 26p. 2000. spiral bd. 19.00 (0-7401-0258-3) Morgan Quitno Corp.

— Georgia Crime in Perspective 2000. 22p. 2000. spiral bd. 19.00 (0-7401-0309-1) Morgan Quitno Corp.

Morgan, Kathleen O'Leary & Morgan, Scott E., eds. Georgia Crime Perspective, 1998. 20p. 1998. pap. 19.00 (1-56692-909-1) Morgan Quitno Corp.

*Morgan, Kathleen O'Leary & Morgan, Scott E., eds. Georgia Health Care in Perspective 2000. 21p. 2000. spiral bd. 19.00 (0-7401-0209-5) Morgan Quitno Corp.

Morgan, Kathleen O'Leary & Morgan, Scott E., eds. Georgia Health Care Perspective, 1998. 20p. 1998. pap. 19.00 (1-56692-809-5) Morgan Quitno Corp.

— Georgia in Perspective, 1998. 24p. 1998. pap. 19.00 (1-56692-859-1) Morgan Quitno Corp.

*Morgan, Kathleen O'Leary & Morgan, Scott E., eds. Georgia in Perspective 2000. 26p. 2000. spiral bd. 19.00 (0-7401-0259-1) Morgan Quitno Corp.

— Hawaii Crime in Perspective 2000. 22p. 2000. spiral bd. 19.00 (0-7401-0310-5) Morgan Quitno Corp.

Morgan, Kathleen O'Leary & Morgan, Scott E., eds. Hawaii Crime Perspective, 1998. 20p. 1998. pap. 19.00 (1-56692-910-5) Morgan Quitno Corp.

*Morgan, Kathleen O'Leary & Morgan, Scott E., eds. Hawaii Health Care in Perspective 2000. 21p. 2000. spiral bd. 19.00 (0-7401-0210-9) Morgan Quitno Corp.

Morgan, Kathleen O'Leary & Morgan, Scott E., eds. Hawaii Health Care Perspective, 1998. 20p. 1998. pap. 19.00 (1-56692-810-9) Morgan Quitno Corp.

— Hawaii in Perspective, 1998. 24p. 1998. pap. 19.00 (1-56692-860-5) Morgan Quitno Corp.

*Morgan, Kathleen O'Leary & Morgan, Scott E., eds. Hawaii in Perspective 2000. 26p. 2000. spiral bd. 19.00 (0-7401-0260-5) Morgan Quitno Corp.

Morgan, Kathleen O'Leary & Morgan, Scott E., eds. Health Care State Ranking, 1999. 540p. 1999. per. 52.95 (1-56692-333-6) Morgan Quitno Corp.

— Health Care State Rankings, 1998. 540p. 1998. pap. 49.95 (1-56692-330-1) Morgan Quitno Corp.

— Health Care State Rankings 1997. 540p. 1997. 49.95 (1-56692-317-4) Morgan Quitno Corp.

*Morgan, Kathleen O'Leary & Morgan, Scott E., eds. Health Care State Rankings 2000: Health Care in the 50 United States. 540p. 2000. per. 52.95 (0-7401-0001-7) Morgan Quitno Corp.

— Idaho Crime in Perspective 2000. 22p. 2000. spiral bd. 19.00 (0-7401-0311-3) Morgan Quitno Corp.

Morgan, Kathleen O'Leary & Morgan, Scott E., eds. Idaho Crime Perspective, 1998. 20p. 1998. pap. 19.00 (1-56692-911-3) Morgan Quitno Corp.

*Morgan, Kathleen O'Leary & Morgan, Scott E., eds. Idaho Health Care in Perspective 2000. 21p. 2000. spiral bd. 19.00 (0-7401-0211-7) Morgan Quitno Corp.

Morgan, Kathleen O'Leary & Morgan, Scott E., eds. Idaho Health Care Perspective, 1998. 20p. 1998. pap. 19.00 (1-56692-811-7) Morgan Quitno Corp.

— Idaho in Perspective, 1998. 24p. 1998. pap. 19.00 (1-56692-861-3) Morgan Quitno Corp.

*Morgan, Kathleen O'Leary & Morgan, Scott E., eds. Idaho in Perspective 2000. 26p. 2000. spiral bd. 19.00 (0-7401-0261-3) Morgan Quitno Corp.

— Illinois Crime in Perspective 2000. 22p. 2000. spiral bd. 19.00 (0-7401-0312-1) Morgan Quitno Corp.

Morgan, Kathleen O'Leary & Morgan, Scott E., eds. Illinois Crime Perspective, 1998. 20p. 1998. pap. 19.00 (1-56692-912-1) Morgan Quitno Corp.

*Morgan, Kathleen O'Leary & Morgan, Scott E., eds. Illinois Health Care in Perspective 2000. 21p. 2000. spiral bd. 19.00 (0-7401-0212-5) Morgan Quitno Corp.

Morgan, Kathleen O'Leary & Morgan, Scott E., eds. Illinois Health Care Perspective, 1998. 20p. 1998. pap. 19.00 (1-56692-812-5) Morgan Quitno Corp.

— Illinois in Perspective, 1998. 24p. 1998. pap. 19.00 (1-56692-862-1) Morgan Quitno Corp.

*Morgan, Kathleen O'Leary & Morgan, Scott E., eds. Illinois in Perspective 2000. 26p. 2000. spiral bd. 19.00 (0-7401-0262-1) Morgan Quitno Corp.

— Indiana Crime in Perspective 2000. 22p. 2000. spiral bd. 19.00 (0-7401-0313-X) Morgan Quitno Corp.

Morgan, Kathleen O'Leary & Morgan, Scott E., eds. Indiana Crime Perspective, 1998. 20p. 1998. pap. 19.00 (1-56692-913-X) Morgan Quitno Corp.

*Morgan, Kathleen O'Leary & Morgan, Scott E., eds. Indiana Health Care in Perspective 2000. 21p. 2000. spiral bd. 19.00 (0-7401-0213-3) Morgan Quitno Corp.

Morgan, Kathleen O'Leary & Morgan, Scott E., eds. Indiana Health Care Perspective, 1998. 20p. 1998. pap. 19.00 (1-56692-813-3) Morgan Quitno Corp.

— Indiana in Perspective, 1998. 24p. 1998. pap. 19.00 (1-56692-863-X) Morgan Quitno Corp.

*Morgan, Kathleen O'Leary & Morgan, Scott E., eds. Indiana in Perspective 2000. 26p. 2000. spiral bd. 19.00 (0-7401-0263-X) Morgan Quitno Corp.

— Iowa Crime in Perspective 2000. 22p. 2000. spiral bd. 19.00 (0-7401-0314-8) Morgan Quitno Corp.

Morgan, Kathleen O'Leary & Morgan, Scott E., eds. Iowa Crime Perspective, 1998. 20p. 1998. pap. 19.00 (1-56692-914-8) Morgan Quitno Corp.

*Morgan, Kathleen O'Leary & Morgan, Scott E., eds. Iowa Health Care in Perspective 2000. 21p. 2000. spiral bd. 19.00 (0-7401-0214-1) Morgan Quitno Corp.

Morgan, Kathleen O'Leary & Morgan, Scott E., eds. Iowa Health Care Perspective, 1998. 20p. 1998. pap. 19.00 (1-56692-814-1) Morgan Quitno Corp.

— Iowa in Perspective, 1998. 24p. 1998. pap. 19.00 (1-56692-864-8) Morgan Quitno Corp.

*Morgan, Kathleen O'Leary & Morgan, Scott E., eds. Iowa in Perspective 2000. 26p. 2000. spiral bd. 19.00 (0-7401-0264-8) Morgan Quitno Corp.

— Kansas Crime in Perspective 2000. 22p. 2000. spiral bd. (0-7401-0315-6) Morgan Quitno Corp.

Morgan, Kathleen O'Leary & Morgan, Scott E., eds. Kansas Crime Perspective, 1998. 20p. 1998. pap. 19.00 (1-56692-915-6) Morgan Quitno Corp.

*Morgan, Kathleen O'Leary & Morgan, Scott E., eds. Kansas Health Care in Perspective 2000. 21p. 2000. spiral bd. 19.00 (0-7401-0215-X) Morgan Quitno Corp.

Morgan, Kathleen O'Leary & Morgan, Scott E., eds. Kansas Health Care Perspective, 1998. 20p. 1998. pap. 19.00 (1-56692-815-X) Morgan Quitno Corp.

— Kansas in Perspective, 1998. 24p. 1998. pap. 19.00 (1-56692-865-6) Morgan Quitno Corp.

*Morgan, Kathleen O'Leary & Morgan, Scott E., eds. Kansas in Perspective 2000. 26p. 2000. spiral bd. 19.00 (0-7401-0265-6) Morgan Quitno Corp.

— Kentucky Crime in Perspective 2000. 22p. 2000. spiral bd. 19.00 (0-7401-0316-4) Morgan Quitno Corp.

Morgan, Kathleen O'Leary & Morgan, Scott E., eds. Kentucky Crime Perspective, 1998. 20p. 1998. pap. 19.00 (1-56692-916-4) Morgan Quitno Corp.

*Morgan, Kathleen O'Leary & Morgan, Scott E., eds. Kentucky Health Care in Perspective 2000. 21p. 2000. spiral bd. 19.00 (0-7401-0216-8) Morgan Quitno Corp.

Morgan, Kathleen O'Leary & Morgan, Scott E., eds. Kentucky Health Care Perspective, 1998. 20p. 1998. pap. 19.00 (1-56692-816-8) Morgan Quitno Corp.

— Kentucky in Perspective, 1998. 24p. 1998. pap. 19.00 (1-56692-866-4) Morgan Quitno Corp.

*Morgan, Kathleen O'Leary & Morgan, Scott E., eds. Kentucky in Perspective 2000. 26p. 2000. spiral bd. 19.00 (0-7401-0266-4) Morgan Quitno Corp.

— Louisiana Crime in Perspective 2000. 22p. 2000. spiral bd. 19.00 (0-7401-0317-2) Morgan Quitno Corp.

Morgan, Kathleen O'Leary & Morgan, Scott E., eds. Louisiana Crime Perspective, 1998. 20p. 1998. pap. 19.00 (1-56692-917-2) Morgan Quitno Corp.

*Morgan, Kathleen O'Leary & Morgan, Scott E., eds. Louisiana Health Care in Perspective 2000. 21p. 2000. spiral bd. 19.00 (0-7401-0217-6) Morgan Quitno Corp.

Morgan, Kathleen O'Leary & Morgan, Scott E., eds. Louisiana Health Care Perspective, 1998. 20p. 1998. pap. 19.00 (1-56692-817-6) Morgan Quitno Corp.

— Louisiana in Perspective, 1998. 24p. 1998. pap. 19.00 (1-56692-867-2) Morgan Quitno Corp.

*Morgan, Kathleen O'Leary & Morgan, Scott E., eds. Louisiana in Perspective 2000. 26p. 2000. spiral bd. 19.00 (0-7401-0267-2) Morgan Quitno Corp.

— Maine Crime in Perspective 2000. 22p. 2000. spiral bd. 19.00 (0-7401-0318-0) Morgan Quitno Corp.

Morgan, Kathleen O'Leary & Morgan, Scott E., eds. Maine Crime Perspective, 1998. 20p. 1998. pap. 19.00 (1-56692-918-0) Morgan Quitno Corp.

*Morgan, Kathleen O'Leary & Morgan, Scott E., eds. Maine Health Care in Perspective 2000. 21p. 2000. spiral bd. 19.00 (0-7401-0218-4) Morgan Quitno Corp.

Morgan, Kathleen O'Leary & Morgan, Scott E., eds. Maine Health Care Perspective, 1998. 20p. 1998. pap. 19.00 (1-56692-818-4) Morgan Quitno Corp.

— Maine in Perspective, 1998. 24p. 1998. pap. 19.00 (1-56692-868-0) Morgan Quitno Corp.

*Morgan, Kathleen O'Leary & Morgan, Scott E., eds. Maine In Perspective 2000. 26p. 2000. spiral bd. 19.00 (0-7401-0268-0) Morgan Quitno Corp.

— Maryland Crime in Perspective 2000. 22p. 2000. spiral bd. 19.00 (*0-7401-0319-9*) Morgan Quitno Corp.

Morgan, Kathleen O'Leary & Morgan, Scott E., eds. Maryland Crime Perspective, 1998. 20p. 1998. pap. 19.00 (*1-56692-919-9*) Morgan Quitno Corp.

***Morgan, Kathleen O'Leary & Morgan, Scott E., eds.** Maryland Health Care in Perspective 2000. 21p. 2000. spiral bd. 19.00 (*0-7401-0219-2*) Morgan Quitno Corp.

Morgan, Kathleen O'Leary & Morgan, Scott E., eds. Maryland Health Care Perspective, 1998. 20p. 1998. pap. 19.00 (*1-56692-819-2*) Morgan Quitno Corp.

— Maryland in Perspective, 1998. 24p. 1998. pap. 19.00 (*1-56692-869-9*) Morgan Quitno Corp.

***Morgan, Kathleen O'Leary & Morgan, Scott E., eds.** Maryland In Perspective 2000. 26p. 2000. spiral bd. 19.00 (*0-7401-0269-9*) Morgan Quitno Corp.

— Massachusetts Crime in Perspective 2000. 22p. 2000. spiral bd. 19.00 (*0-7401-0320-2*) Morgan Quitno Corp.

Morgan, Kathleen O'Leary & Morgan, Scott E., eds. Massachusetts Crime Perspective, 1998. 20p. 1998. pap. 19.00 (*1-56692-920-2*) Morgan Quitno Corp.

***Morgan, Kathleen O'Leary & Morgan, Scott E., eds.** Massachusetts Health Care in Perspective 2000. 21p. 2000. spiral bd. 19.00 (*0-7401-0220-6*) Morgan Quitno Corp.

Morgan, Kathleen O'Leary & Morgan, Scott E., eds. Massachusetts Health Care Perspective, 1998. 20p. 1998. pap. 19.00 (*1-56692-820-6*) Morgan Quitno Corp.

— Massachusetts in Perspective, 1998. 24p. 1998. pap. 19.00 (*1-56692-870-2*) Morgan Quitno Corp.

***Morgan, Kathleen O'Leary & Morgan, Scott E., eds.** Massachusetts In Perspective 2000. 26p. 2000. spiral bd. 19.00 (*0-7401-0270-2*) Morgan Quitno Corp.

— Michigan Crime in Perspective 2000. 22p. 2000. spiral bd. 19.00 (*0-7401-0321-0*) Morgan Quitno Corp.

Morgan, Kathleen O'Leary & Morgan, Scott E., eds. Michigan Crime Perspective, 1998. 20p. 1998. pap. 19.00 (*1-56692-921-0*) Morgan Quitno Corp.

***Morgan, Kathleen O'Leary & Morgan, Scott E., eds.** Michigan Health Care in Perspective 2000. 21p. 2000. spiral bd. 19.00 (*0-7401-0221-4*) Morgan Quitno Corp.

Morgan, Kathleen O'Leary & Morgan, Scott E., eds. Michigan Health Care Perspective, 1998. 20p. 1998. pap. 19.00 (*1-56692-821-4*) Morgan Quitno Corp.

— Michigan in Perspective, 1998. 24p. 1998. pap. 19.00 (*1-56692-871-0*) Morgan Quitno Corp.

***Morgan, Kathleen O'Leary & Morgan, Scott E., eds.** Michigan in Perspective 2000. 26p. 2000. spiral bd. 19.00 (*0-7401-0271-0*) Morgan Quitno Corp.

— Minnesota Crime in Perspective 2000. 22p. 2000. spiral bd. 19.00 (*0-7401-0322-9*) Morgan Quitno Corp.

Morgan, Kathleen O'Leary & Morgan, Scott E., eds. Minnesota Crime Perspective, 1998. 20p. 1998. pap. 19.00 (*1-56692-922-9*) Morgan Quitno Corp.

***Morgan, Kathleen O'Leary & Morgan, Scott E., eds.** Minnesota Health Care in Perspective 2000. 21p. 2000. spiral bd. 19.00 (*0-7401-0222-2*) Morgan Quitno Corp.

Morgan, Kathleen O'Leary & Morgan, Scott E., eds. Minnesota Health Care Perspective, 1998. 20p. 1998. pap. 19.00 (*1-56692-822-2*) Morgan Quitno Corp.

— Minnesota in Perspective, 1998. 24p. 1998. pap. 19.00 (*1-56692-872-9*) Morgan Quitno Corp.

***Morgan, Kathleen O'Leary & Morgan, Scott E., eds.** Minnesota in Perspective 2000. 26p. 2000. spiral bd. 19.00 (*0-7401-0272-9*) Morgan Quitno Corp.

— Mississippi Crime in Perspective 2000. 22p. 2000. spiral bd. 19.00 (*0-7401-0323-7*) Morgan Quitno Corp.

Morgan, Kathleen O'Leary & Morgan, Scott E., eds. Mississippi Crime Perspective, 1998. 20p. 1998. pap. 19.00 (*1-56692-923-7*) Morgan Quitno Corp.

***Morgan, Kathleen O'Leary & Morgan, Scott E., eds.** Mississippi Health Care in Perspective 2000. 21p. 2000. spiral bd. 19.00 (*0-7401-0223-0*) Morgan Quitno Corp.

Morgan, Kathleen O'Leary & Morgan, Scott E., eds. Mississippi Health Care Perspective, 1998. 20p. 1998. pap. 19.00 (*1-56692-823-0*) Morgan Quitno Corp.

— Mississippi in Perspective, 1998. 24p. 1998. pap. 19.00 (*1-56692-873-7*) Morgan Quitno Corp.

***Morgan, Kathleen O'Leary & Morgan, Scott E., eds.** Mississippi in Perspective 2000. 26p. 2000. spiral bd. 19.00 (*0-7401-0273-7*) Morgan Quitno Corp.

— Missouri Crime in Perspective 2000. 22p. 2000. spiral bd. 19.00 (*0-7401-0324-5*) Morgan Quitno Corp.

Morgan, Kathleen O'Leary & Morgan, Scott E., eds. Missouri Crime Perspective, 1998. 20p. 1998. pap. 19.00 (*1-56692-924-5*) Morgan Quitno Corp.

***Morgan, Kathleen O'Leary & Morgan, Scott E., eds.** Missouri Health Care in Perspective 2000. 21p. 2000. spiral bd. 19.00 (*0-7401-0224-9*) Morgan Quitno Corp.

Morgan, Kathleen O'Leary & Morgan, Scott E., eds. Missouri Health Care Perspective, 1998. 20p. 1998. pap. 19.00 (*1-56692-824-9*) Morgan Quitno Corp.

— Missouri in Perspective, 1998. 24p. 1998. pap. 19.00 (*1-56692-874-5*) Morgan Quitno Corp.

***Morgan, Kathleen O'Leary & Morgan, Scott E., eds.** Missouri in Perspective 2000. 26p. 2000. spiral bd. 19.00 (*0-7401-0274-5*) Morgan Quitno Corp.

— Montana Crime in Perspective 2000. 22p. 2000. spiral bd. 19.00 (*0-7401-0325-3*) Morgan Quitno Corp.

Morgan, Kathleen O'Leary & Morgan, Scott E., eds. Montana Crime Perspective, 1998. 20p. 1998. pap. 19.00 (*1-56692-925-3*) Morgan Quitno Corp.

***Morgan, Kathleen O'Leary & Morgan, Scott E., eds.** Montana Health Care in Perspective 2000. 21p. 2000. spiral bd. 19.00 (*0-7401-0225-7*) Morgan Quitno Corp.

Morgan, Kathleen O'Leary & Morgan, Scott E., eds. Montana Health Care Perspective, 1998. 20p. 1998. pap. 19.00 (*1-56692-825-7*) Morgan Quitno Corp.

— Montana in Perspective, 1998. 24p. 1998. pap. 19.00 (*1-56692-875-3*) Morgan Quitno Corp.

***Morgan, Kathleen O'Leary & Morgan, Scott E., eds.** Montana in Perspective 2000. 26p. 2000. spiral bd. 19.00 (*0-7401-0275-3*) Morgan Quitno Corp.

— Nebraska Crime in Perspective 2000. 22p. 2000. spiral bd. 19.00 (*0-7401-0326-1*) Morgan Quitno Corp.

Morgan, Kathleen O'Leary & Morgan, Scott E., eds. Nebraska Crime Perspective, 1998. 20p. 1998. pap. 19.00 (*1-56692-926-1*) Morgan Quitno Corp.

***Morgan, Kathleen O'Leary & Morgan, Scott E., eds.** Nebraska Health Care in Perspective 2000. 21p. 2000. spiral bd. 19.00 (*0-7401-0226-5*) Morgan Quitno Corp.

Morgan, Kathleen O'Leary & Morgan, Scott E., eds. Nebraska Health Care Perspective, 1998. 20p. 1998. pap. 19.00 (*1-56692-826-5*) Morgan Quitno Corp.

— Nebraska in Perspective, 1998. 24p. 1998. pap. 19.00 (*1-56692-876-1*) Morgan Quitno Corp.

***Morgan, Kathleen O'Leary & Morgan, Scott E., eds.** Nebraska in Perspective 2000. 26p. 2000. spiral bd. 19.00 (*0-7401-0276-1*) Morgan Quitno Corp.

— Nevada Crime in Perspective 2000. 22p. 2000. spiral bd. 19.00 (*0-7401-0327-X*) Morgan Quitno Corp.

Morgan, Kathleen O'Leary & Morgan, Scott E., eds. Nevada Crime Perspective, 1998. 20p. 1998. pap. 19.00 (*1-56692-927-X*) Morgan Quitno Corp.

***Morgan, Kathleen O'Leary & Morgan, Scott E., eds.** Nevada Health Care in Perspective 2000. 21p. 2000. spiral bd. 19.00 (*0-7401-0227-3*) Morgan Quitno Corp.

Morgan, Kathleen O'Leary & Morgan, Scott E., eds. Nevada Health Care Perspective, 1998. 20p. 1998. pap. 19.00 (*1-56692-827-3*) Morgan Quitno Corp.

— Nevada in Perspective, 1998. 24p. 1998. pap. 19.00 (*1-56692-877-X*) Morgan Quitno Corp.

***Morgan, Kathleen O'Leary & Morgan, Scott E., eds.** Nevada in Perspective 2000. 26p. 2000. spiral bd. 19.00 (*0-7401-0277-X*) Morgan Quitno Corp.

— New Hampshire Crime in Perspective 2000. 22p. 2000. spiral bd. 19.00 (*0-7401-0328-8*) Morgan Quitno Corp.

Morgan, Kathleen O'Leary & Morgan, Scott E., eds. New Hampshire Crime Perspective, 1998. 20p. 1998. pap. 19.00 (*1-56692-928-8*) Morgan Quitno Corp.

***Morgan, Kathleen O'Leary & Morgan, Scott E., eds.** New Hampshire Health Care in Perspective 2000. 21p. 2000. spiral bd. 19.00 (*0-7401-0228-1*) Morgan Quitno Corp.

Morgan, Kathleen O'Leary & Morgan, Scott E., eds. New Hampshire Health Care Perspective, 1998. 20p. 1998. pap. 19.00 (*1-56692-828-1*) Morgan Quitno Corp.

— New Hampshire in Perspective, 1998. 24p. 1998. pap. 19.00 (*1-56692-878-8*) Morgan Quitno Corp.

***Morgan, Kathleen O'Leary & Morgan, Scott E., eds.** New Hampshire in Perspective 2000. 26p. 2000. spiral bd. 19.00 (*0-7401-0278-8*) Morgan Quitno Corp.

— New Jersey Crime in Perspective 2000. 22p. 2000. spiral bd. 19.00 (*0-7401-0329-6*) Morgan Quitno Corp.

Morgan, Kathleen O'Leary & Morgan, Scott E., eds. New Jersey Crime Perspective, 1998. 20p. 1998. pap. 19.00 (*1-56692-929-6*) Morgan Quitno Corp.

***Morgan, Kathleen O'Leary & Morgan, Scott E., eds.** New Jersey Health Care in Perspective 2000. 21p. 2000. spiral bd. 19.00 (*0-7401-0229-X*) Morgan Quitno Corp.

Morgan, Kathleen O'Leary & Morgan, Scott E., eds. New Jersey Health Care Perspective, 1998. 20p. 1998. pap. 19.00 (*1-56692-829-X*) Morgan Quitno Corp.

— New Jersey in Perspective, 1998. 24p. 1998. pap. 19.00 (*1-56692-879-6*) Morgan Quitno Corp.

***Morgan, Kathleen O'Leary & Morgan, Scott E., eds.** New Jersey in Perspective 2000. 26p. 2000. spiral bd. 19.00 (*0-7401-0279-6*) Morgan Quitno Corp.

— New Mexico Crime in Perspective 2000. 22p. 2000. spiral bd. 19.00 (*0-7401-0330-X*) Morgan Quitno Corp.

Morgan, Kathleen O'Leary & Morgan, Scott E., eds. New Mexico Crime Perspective, 1998. 20p. 1998. pap. 19.00 (*1-56692-930-X*) Morgan Quitno Corp.

***Morgan, Kathleen O'Leary & Morgan, Scott E., eds.** New Mexico Health Care in Perspective 2000. 21p. 2000. spiral bd. 19.00 (*0-7401-0230-3*) Morgan Quitno Corp.

Morgan, Kathleen O'Leary & Morgan, Scott E., eds. New Mexico Health Care Perspective, 1998. 20p. 1998. pap. 19.00 (*1-56692-830-3*) Morgan Quitno Corp.

— New Mexico in Perspective, 1998. 24p. 1998. pap. 19.00 (*1-56692-880-X*) Morgan Quitno Corp.

***Morgan, Kathleen O'Leary & Morgan, Scott E., eds.** New Mexico in Perspective 2000. 26p. 2000. spiral bd. 19.00 (*0-7401-0280-X*) Morgan Quitno Corp.

— New York Crime in Perspective 2000. 22p. 2000. spiral bd. 19.00 (*0-7401-0331-8*) Morgan Quitno Corp.

Morgan, Kathleen O'Leary & Morgan, Scott E., eds. New York Crime Perspective, 1998. 20p. 1998. pap. 19.00 (*1-56692-931-8*) Morgan Quitno Corp.

***Morgan, Kathleen O'Leary & Morgan, Scott E., eds.** New York Health Care in Perspective 2000. 21p. 2000. spiral bd. 19.00 (*0-7401-0231-1*) Morgan Quitno Corp.

Morgan, Kathleen O'Leary & Morgan, Scott E., eds. New York Health Care Perspective, 1998. 20p. 1998. pap. 19.00 (*1-56692-831-1*) Morgan Quitno Corp.

— New York in Perspective, 1998. 24p. 1998. pap. 19.00 (*1-56692-881-8*) Morgan Quitno Corp.

***Morgan, Kathleen O'Leary & Morgan, Scott E., eds.** New York in Perspective 2000. 26p. 2000. spiral bd. 19.00 (*0-7401-0281-8*) Morgan Quitno Corp.

— North Carolina Crime in Perspective 2000. 22p. 2000. spiral bd. 19.00 (*0-7401-0332-6*) Morgan Quitno Corp.

Morgan, Kathleen O'Leary & Morgan, Scott E., eds. North Carolina Crime Perspective, 1998. 20p. 1998. pap. 19.00 (*1-56692-932-6*) Morgan Quitno Corp.

***Morgan, Kathleen O'Leary & Morgan, Scott E., eds.** North Carolina Health Care in Perspective 2000. 21p. 2000. spiral bd. 19.00 (*0-7401-0232-X*) Morgan Quitno Corp.

Morgan, Kathleen O'Leary & Morgan, Scott E., eds. North Carolina Health Care Perspective, 1998. 20p. 1998. pap. 19.00 (*1-56692-832-X*) Morgan Quitno Corp.

— North Carolina in Perspective, 1998. 24p. 1998. pap. 19.00 (*1-56692-882-6*) Morgan Quitno Corp.

***Morgan, Kathleen O'Leary & Morgan, Scott E., eds.** North Carolina in Perspective 2000. 26p. 2000. spiral bd. 19.00 (*0-7401-0282-6*) Morgan Quitno Corp.

— North Dakota Crime in Perspective 2000. 22p. 2000. spiral bd. 19.00 (*0-7401-0333-4*) Morgan Quitno Corp.

Morgan, Kathleen O'Leary & Morgan, Scott E., eds. North Dakota Crime Perspective, 1998. 20p. 1998. pap. 19.00 (*1-56692-933-4*) Morgan Quitno Corp.

***Morgan, Kathleen O'Leary & Morgan, Scott E., eds.** North Dakota Health Care in Perspective 2000. 21p. 2000. spiral bd. 19.00 (*0-7401-0233-8*) Morgan Quitno Corp.

Morgan, Kathleen O'Leary & Morgan, Scott E., eds. North Dakota Health Care Perspective, 1998. 20p. 1998. pap. 19.00 (*1-56692-833-8*) Morgan Quitno Corp.

— North Dakota in Perspective, 1998. 24p. 1998. pap. 19.00 (*1-56692-883-4*) Morgan Quitno Corp.

***Morgan, Kathleen O'Leary & Morgan, Scott E., eds.** North Dakota in Perspective 2000. 26p. 2000. spiral bd. 19.00 (*0-7401-0283-4*) Morgan Quitno Corp.

— Ohio Crime in Perspective 2000. 22p. 2000. spiral bd. 19.00 (*0-7401-0334-2*) Morgan Quitno Corp.

Morgan, Kathleen O'Leary & Morgan, Scott E., eds. Ohio Crime Perspective, 1998. 20p. 1998. pap. 19.00 (*1-56692-934-2*) Morgan Quitno Corp.

***Morgan, Kathleen O'Leary & Morgan, Scott E., eds.** Ohio Health Care in Perspective 1999. 21p. 1999. spiral bd. 19.00 (*0-7401-0084-X*) Morgan Quitno Corp.

— Ohio Health Care in Perspective 2000. 21p. 2000. spiral bd. 19.00 (*0-7401-0234-6*) Morgan Quitno Corp.

Morgan, Kathleen O'Leary & Morgan, Scott E., eds. Ohio Health Care Perspective, 1998. 20p. 1998. pap. 19.00 (*1-56692-834-6*) Morgan Quitno Corp.

— Ohio in Perspective, 1998. 24p. 1998. pap. 19.00 (*1-56692-884-2*) Morgan Quitno Corp.

***Morgan, Kathleen O'Leary & Morgan, Scott E., eds.** Ohio in Perspective 2000. 26p. 2000. spiral bd. 19.00 (*0-7401-0284-2*) Morgan Quitno Corp.

— Oklahoma Crime in Perspective 2000. 22p. 2000. spiral bd. 19.00 (*0-7401-0335-0*) Morgan Quitno Corp.

Morgan, Kathleen O'Leary & Morgan, Scott E., eds. Oklahoma Crime Perspective, 1998. 20p. 1998. pap. 19.00 (*1-56692-935-0*) Morgan Quitno Corp.

***Morgan, Kathleen O'Leary & Morgan, Scott E., eds.** Oklahoma Health Care in Perspective 2000. 21p. 2000. spiral bd. 19.00 (*0-7401-0235-4*) Morgan Quitno Corp.

Morgan, Kathleen O'Leary & Morgan, Scott E., eds. Oklahoma Health Care Perspective, 1998. 20p. 1998. pap. 19.00 (*1-56692-835-4*) Morgan Quitno Corp.

— Oklahoma in Perspective, 1998. 24p. 1998. pap. 19.00 (*1-56692-885-0*) Morgan Quitno Corp.

***Morgan, Kathleen O'Leary & Morgan, Scott E., eds.** Oklahoma in Perspective 2000. 26p. 2000. spiral bd. 19.00 (*0-7401-0285-0*) Morgan Quitno Corp.

— Oregon Crime in Perspective 2000. 22p. 2000. spiral bd. 19.00 (*0-7401-0336-9*) Morgan Quitno Corp.

Morgan, Kathleen O'Leary & Morgan, Scott E., eds. Oregon Crime Perspective, 1998. 20p. 1998. pap. 19.00 (*1-56692-936-9*) Morgan Quitno Corp.

***Morgan, Kathleen O'Leary & Morgan, Scott E., eds.** Oregon Health Care in Perspective 2000. 21p. 2000. spiral bd. 19.00 (*0-7401-0236-2*) Morgan Quitno Corp.

Morgan, Kathleen O'Leary & Morgan, Scott E., eds. Oregon Health Care Perspective, 1998. 20p. 1998. pap. 19.00 (*1-56692-836-2*) Morgan Quitno Corp.

— Oregon in Perspective, 1998. 24p. 1998. pap. 19.00 (*1-56692-886-9*) Morgan Quitno Corp.

***Morgan, Kathleen O'Leary & Morgan, Scott E., eds.** Oregon in Perspective 2000. 26p. 2000. spiral bd. 19.00 (*0-7401-0286-9*) Morgan Quitno Corp.

— Pennsylvania Crime in Perspective 2000. 22p. 2000. spiral bd. 19.00 (*0-7401-0337-7*) Morgan Quitno Corp.

Morgan, Kathleen O'Leary & Morgan, Scott E., eds. Pennsylvania Crime Perspective, 1998. 20p. 1998. pap. 19.00 (*1-56692-937-7*) Morgan Quitno Corp.

***Morgan, Kathleen O'Leary & Morgan, Scott E., eds.** Pennsylvania Health Care in Perspective 2000. 21p. 2000. spiral bd. 19.00 (*0-7401-0237-0*) Morgan Quitno Corp.

Morgan, Kathleen O'Leary & Morgan, Scott E., eds. Pennsylvania Health Care Perspective, 1998. 20p. 1998. pap. 19.00 (*1-56692-837-0*) Morgan Quitno Corp.

— Pennsylvania in Perspective, 1998. 24p. 1998. pap. 19.00 (*1-56692-887-7*) Morgan Quitno Corp.

***Morgan, Kathleen O'Leary & Morgan, Scott E., eds.** Pennsylvania in Perspective 2000. 26p. 2000. spiral bd. 19.00 (*0-7401-0287-7*) Morgan Quitno Corp.

— Rhode Island Crime in Perspective 2000. 22p. 2000. spiral bd. 19.00 (*0-7401-0338-5*) Morgan Quitno Corp.

Morgan, Kathleen O'Leary & Morgan, Scott E., eds. Rhode Island Crime Perspective, 1998. 20p. 1998. pap. 19.00 (*1-56692-938-5*) Morgan Quitno Corp.

***Morgan, Kathleen O'Leary & Morgan, Scott E., eds.** Rhode Island Health Care in Perspective 2000. 21p. 2000. spiral bd. 19.00 (*0-7401-0238-9*) Morgan Quitno Corp.

Morgan, Kathleen O'Leary & Morgan, Scott E., eds. Rhode Island Health Care Perspective, 1998. 20p. 1998. pap. 19.00 (*1-56692-838-9*) Morgan Quitno Corp.

— Rhode Island in Perspective, 1998. 24p. 1998. pap. 19.00 (*1-56692-888-5*) Morgan Quitno Corp.

***Morgan, Kathleen O'Leary & Morgan, Scott E., eds.** Rhode Island in Perspective 2000. 26p. 2000. spiral bd. 19.00 (*0-7401-0288-5*) Morgan Quitno Corp.

— South Carolina Crime in Perspective 2000. 22p. 2000. spiral bd. 19.00 (*0-7401-0339-3*) Morgan Quitno Corp.

Morgan, Kathleen O'Leary & Morgan, Scott E., eds. South Carolina Crime Perspective, 1998. 20p. 1998. pap. 19.00 (*1-56692-939-3*) Morgan Quitno Corp.

***Morgan, Kathleen O'Leary & Morgan, Scott E., eds.** South Carolina Health Care in Perspective 2000. 21p. 2000. spiral bd. 19.00 (*0-7401-0239-7*) Morgan Quitno Corp.

Morgan, Kathleen O'Leary & Morgan, Scott E., eds. South Carolina Health Care Perspective, 1998. 20p. 1998. pap. 19.00 (*1-56692-839-7*) Morgan Quitno Corp.

— South Carolina in Perspective, 1998. 24p. 1998. pap. 19.00 (*1-56692-889-3*) Morgan Quitno Corp.

***Morgan, Kathleen O'Leary & Morgan, Scott E., eds.** South Carolina in Perspective 2000. 26p. 2000. spiral bd. 19.00 (*0-7401-0289-3*) Morgan Quitno Corp.

— South Dakota Crime in Perspective 2000. 22p. 2000. spiral bd. 19.00 (*0-7401-0340-7*) Morgan Quitno Corp.

Morgan, Kathleen O'Leary & Morgan, Scott E., eds. South Dakota Crime Perspective, 1998. 20p. 1998. pap. 19.00 (*1-56692-940-7*) Morgan Quitno Corp.

***Morgan, Kathleen O'Leary & Morgan, Scott E., eds.** South Dakota Health Care in Perspective 2000. 21p. 2000. spiral bd. 19.00 (*0-7401-0240-0*) Morgan Quitno Corp.

Morgan, Kathleen O'Leary & Morgan, Scott E., eds. South Dakota Health Care Perspective, 1998. 20p. 1998. pap. 19.00 (*1-56692-840-0*) Morgan Quitno Corp.

— South Dakota in Perspective, 1998. 24p. 1998. pap. 19.00 (*1-56692-890-7*) Morgan Quitno Corp.

***Morgan, Kathleen O'Leary & Morgan, Scott E., eds.** South Dakota in Perspective 2000. 26p. 2000. spiral bd. 19.00 (*0-7401-0290-7*) Morgan Quitno Corp.

Morgan, Kathleen O'Leary & Morgan, Scott E., eds. State Ranking, 1999. 608p. 1999. per. 52.95 (*1-56692-332-8*) Morgan Quitno Corp.

— State Rankings, 1998. 608p. 1998. pap. 49.95 (*1-56692-329-8*) Morgan Quitno Corp.

***Morgan, Kathleen O'Leary & Morgan, Scott E., eds.** State Rankings 2000: A Statistical View of the 50 United States. 608p. 2000. per. 52.95 (*0-7401-0000-9*) Morgan Quitno Corp.

— Tennessee Crime in Perspective 2000. 22p. 2000. spiral bd. 19.00 (*0-7401-0341-5*) Morgan Quitno Corp.

Morgan, Kathleen O'Leary & Morgan, Scott E., eds. Tennessee Crime Perspective, 1998. 20p. 1998. pap. 19.00 (*1-56692-941-5*) Morgan Quitno Corp.

***Morgan, Kathleen O'Leary & Morgan, Scott E., eds.** Tennessee Health Care in Perspective 2000. 21p. 2000. spiral bd. 19.00 (*0-7401-0241-9*) Morgan Quitno Corp.

Morgan, Kathleen O'Leary & Morgan, Scott E., eds. Tennessee Health Care Perspective, 1998. 20p. 1998. pap. 19.00 (*1-56692-841-9*) Morgan Quitno Corp.

— Tennessee in Perspective, 1998. 24p. 1998. pap. 19.00 (*1-56692-891-5*) Morgan Quitno Corp.

***Morgan, Kathleen O'Leary & Morgan, Scott E., eds.** Texas Crime in Perspective 2000. 22p. 2000. spiral bd. 19.00 (*0-7401-0342-3*) Morgan Quitno Corp.

Morgan, Kathleen O'Leary & Morgan, Scott E., eds. Texas Crime Perspective, 1998. 20p. 1998. pap. 19.00 (*1-56692-942-3*) Morgan Quitno Corp.

***Morgan, Kathleen O'Leary & Morgan, Scott E., eds.** Texas Health Care in Perspective 2000. 21p. 2000. spiral bd. 19.00 (*0-7401-0242-7*) Morgan Quitno Corp.

Morgan, Kathleen O'Leary & Morgan, Scott E., eds. Texas Health Care Perspective, 1998. 20p. 1998. pap. 19.00 (*1-56692-842-7*) Morgan Quitno Corp.

— Texas in Perspective, 1998. 24p. 1998. pap. 19.00 (*1-56692-892-3*) Morgan Quitno Corp.

***Morgan, Kathleen O'Leary & Morgan, Scott E., eds.** Texas in Perspective 2000. 26p. 2000. spiral bd. 19.00 (*0-7401-0292-3*) Morgan Quitno Corp.

— Utah Crime in Perspective 2000. 22p. 2000. spiral bd. 19.00 (*0-7401-0343-1*) Morgan Quitno Corp.

Morgan, Kathleen O'Leary & Morgan, Scott E., eds. Utah Crime Perspective, 1998. 20p. 1998. pap. 19.00 (*1-56692-943-1*) Morgan Quitno Corp.

***Morgan, Kathleen O'Leary & Morgan, Scott E., eds.** Utah Health Care in Perspective 2000. 21p. 2000. spiral bd. 19.00 (*0-7401-0243-5*) Morgan Quitno Corp.

Morgan, Kathleen O'Leary & Morgan, Scott E., eds. Utah Health Care Perspective, 1998. 20p. 1998. pap. 19.00 (*1-56692-843-5*) Morgan Quitno Corp.

— Utah in Perspective, 1998. 24p. 1998. pap. 19.00 (*1-56692-893-1*) Morgan Quitno Corp.

***Morgan, Kathleen O'Leary & Morgan, Scott E., eds.** Utah in Perspective 2000. 26p. 2000. spiral bd. 19.00 (*0-7401-0293-1*) Morgan Quitno Corp.

— Vermont Crime in Perspective 2000. 22p. 2000. spiral bd. 19.00 (*0-7401-0344-X*) Morgan Quitno Corp.

Morgan, Kathleen O'Leary & Morgan, Scott E., eds. Vermont Crime Perspective, 1998. 20p. 1998. pap. 19.00 (*1-56692-944-X*) Morgan Quitno Corp.

***Morgan, Kathleen O'Leary & Morgan, Scott E., eds.** Vermont Health Care in Perspective 2000. 21p. 2000. spiral bd. 19.00 (*0-7401-0244-3*) Morgan Quitno Corp.

Morgan, Kathleen O'Leary & Morgan, Scott E., eds. Vermont Health Care Perspective, 1998. 20p. 1998. pap. 19.00 (*1-56692-844-3*) Morgan Quitno Corp.

— Vermont in Perspective, 1998. 24p. 1998. pap. 19.00 (*1-56692-894-X*) Morgan Quitno Corp.

***Morgan, Kathleen O'Leary & Morgan, Scott E., eds.** Vermont in Perspective 2000. 26p. 2000. spiral bd. 19.00 (*0-7401-0294-X*) Morgan Quitno Corp.

— Virginia Crime in Perspective 2000. 22p. 2000. spiral bd. 19.00 (*0-7401-0345-8*) Morgan Quitno Corp.

Morgan, Kathleen O'Leary & Morgan, Scott E., eds. Virginia Crime Perspective, 1998. 20p. 1998. pap. 19.00 (*1-56692-945-8*) Morgan Quitno Corp.

***Morgan, Kathleen O'Leary & Morgan, Scott E., eds.** Virginia Health Care in Perspective 2000. 21p. 2000. spiral bd. 19.00 (*0-7401-0245-1*) Morgan Quitno Corp.

Morgan, Kathleen O'Leary & Morgan, Scott E., eds. Virginia Health Care Perspective, 1998. 20p. 1998. pap. 19.00 (*1-56692-845-1*) Morgan Quitno Corp.
— Virginia in Perspective, 1998. 24p. 1998. pap. 19.00 (*1-56692-895-8*) Morgan Quitno Corp.
***Morgan, Kathleen O'Leary & Morgan, Scott E., eds.** Washington Crime in Perspective 2000. 22p. 2000. spiral bd. 19.00 (*0-7401-0346-6*) Morgan Quitno Corp.
Morgan, Kathleen O'Leary & Morgan, Scott E., eds. Washington Crime Perspective, 1998. 20p. 1998. pap. 19.00 (*1-56692-946-6*) Morgan Quitno Corp.
***Morgan, Kathleen O'Leary & Morgan, Scott E., eds.** Washington Health Care in Perspective 2000. 21p. 2000. spiral bd. 19.00 (*0-7401-0246-X*) Morgan Quitno Corp.
Morgan, Kathleen O'Leary & Morgan, Scott E., eds. Washington Health Care Perspective, 1998. 20p. 1998. pap. 19.00 (*1-56692-846-X*) Morgan Quitno Corp.
— Washington in Perspective, 1998. 24p. 1998. pap. 19.00 (*1-56692-896-6*) Morgan Quitno Corp.
***Morgan, Kathleen O'Leary & Morgan, Scott E., eds.** Washington in Perspective 2000. 26p. 2000. spiral bd. 19.00 (*0-7401-0296-6*) Morgan Quitno Corp.
— West Virginia Crime in Perspective 2000. 22p. 2000. spiral bd. 19.00 (*0-7401-0347-4*) Morgan Quitno Corp.
Morgan, Kathleen O'Leary & Morgan, Scott E., eds. West Virginia Crime Perspective, 1998. 20p. 1998. pap. 19.00 (*1-56692-947-4*) Morgan Quitno Corp.
***Morgan, Kathleen O'Leary & Morgan, Scott E., eds.** West Virginia Health Care in Perspective 2000. 21p. 2000. spiral bd. 19.00 (*0-7401-0247-8*) Morgan Quitno Corp.
Morgan, Kathleen O'Leary & Morgan, Scott E., eds. West Virginia Health Care Perspective, 1998. 20p. 1998. pap. 19.00 (*1-56692-847-8*) Morgan Quitno Corp.
— West Virginia in Perspective, 1998. 24p. 1998. pap. 19.00 (*1-56692-897-4*) Morgan Quitno Corp.
***Morgan, Kathleen O'Leary & Morgan, Scott E., eds.** Wisconscrime Crime in Perspective 2000. 22p. 2000. spiral bd. 19.00 (*0-7401-0348-2*) Morgan Quitno Corp.
Morgan, Kathleen O'Leary & Morgan, Scott E., eds. Wisconsin Crime Perspective, 1998. 20p. 1998. pap. 19.00 (*1-56692-948-2*) Morgan Quitno Corp.
***Morgan, Kathleen O'Leary & Morgan, Scott E., eds.** Wisconsin Health Care in Perspective 2000. 21p. 2000. spiral bd. 19.00 (*0-7401-0248-6*) Morgan Quitno Corp.
Morgan, Kathleen O'Leary & Morgan, Scott E., eds. Wisconsin Health Care Perspective, 1998. 20p. 1998. pap. 19.00 (*1-56692-848-6*) Morgan Quitno Corp.
— Wisconsin in Perspective, 1998. 24p. 1998. pap. 19.00 (*1-56692-898-2*) Morgan Quitno Corp.
***Morgan, Kathleen O'Leary & Morgan, Scott E., eds.** Wisconsin in Perspective 2000. 26p. 2000. spiral bd. 19.00 (*0-7401-0298-2*) Morgan Quitno Corp.
— Wyoming Crime in Perspective 2000. 22p. 2000. spiral bd. 19.00 (*0-7401-0349-0*) Morgan Quitno Corp.
Morgan, Kathleen O'Leary & Morgan, Scott E., eds. Wyoming Crime Perspective, 1998. 20p. 1998. pap. 19.00 (*1-56692-949-0*) Morgan Quitno Corp.
***Morgan, Kathleen O'Leary & Morgan, Scott E., eds.** Wyoming Health Care in Perspective 2000. 21p. 2000. spiral bd. 19.00 (*0-7401-0249-4*) Morgan Quitno Corp.
Morgan, Kathleen O'Leary & Morgan, Scott E., eds. Wyoming Health Care Perspective, 1998. 20p. 1998. pap. 19.00 (*1-56692-849-4*) Morgan Quitno Corp.
— Wyoming in Perspective, 1998. 24p. 1998. pap. 19.00 (*1-56692-899-0*) Morgan Quitno Corp.
***Morgan, Kathleen O'Leary & Morgan, Scott E., eds.** Wyoming in Perspective 2000. 26p. 2000. spiral bd. 19.00 (*0-7401-0299-0*) Morgan Quitno Corp.
***Morgan, Kathryn A.** Myth & Philosophy from the Pre-Socratics to Plato. LC 99-49056. 2000. write for info. (*0-521-62180-1*) Cambridge U Pr.
Morgan, Kathryn L. Children of Strangers: The Stories of a Black Family. LC 80 21144. 122p. 1981. pap. 16.95 (*0-87722-240-1*) Temple U Pr.
Morgan, Katrina, ed. see Clopper, Brian.
Morgan, Keith. Alternative Wicca. (Orig.). 1995. pap. 8.95 (*1-872189-46-6*, Pub. by Mandrake Pr) Holmes Pub.
— Charles Platt: The Artist As Architect. (American Monographs). (Illus.). 265p. 1985. 40.00 (*0-262-13188-9*) MIT Pr.
— Crystal Magic. (Orig.). 1996. pap. 7.95 (*1-872189-41-5*, Pub. by Mandrake Pr) Holmes Pub.
— Dowsing for Beginners. (Orig.). 1995. pap. 8.95 (*1-872189-12-1*, Pub. by Mandrake Pr) Holmes Pub.
— Easy Astral Projection. (Orig.). 1995. pap. 7.95 (*1-872189-81-4*, Pub. by Mandrake Pr) Holmes Pub.
— Essential Family Law. Bourne, Nicholas, ed. (Essential Law Ser.). 180p. 1995. pap. write for info. (*1-85941-128-2*, Pub. by Cavendish Pubng) Gaunt.
— The Harmonics of Wicca. (Orig.). 1993. pap. 8.95 (*1-872189-05-9*, Pub. by Mandrake Pr) Holmes Pub.
— Have You Been Cursed? (Orig.). 1995. pap. 7.95 (*1-872189-01-6*, Pub. by Mandrake Pr) Holmes Pub.
— The Horned God. (Orig.). 1994. pap. 8.95 (*1-872189-66-0*, Pub. by Mandrake Pr) Holmes Pub.
— Magic for Lovers. (Orig.). 1995. pap. 7.95 (*1-872189-07-5*, Pub. by Mandrake Pr) Holmes Pub.
— The Magickal Record. (Orig.). 1994. pap. 7.95 (*1-872189-35-0*, Pub. by Mandrake Pr) Holmes Pub.
— Making Magickal Incense & Ritual Perfumes. (Orig.). 1993. pap. 9.95 (*1-872189-02-4*, Pub. by Mandrake Pr) Holmes Pub.
— Making Magickal Tools & Ritual Equipment. (Orig.). 1994. pap. 9.95 (*1-872189-45-8*, Pub. by Mandrake Pr) Holmes Pub.
— Planet Magick. (Orig.). 1993. pap. 7.95 (*1-872189-11-3*, Pub. by Mandrake Pr) Holmes Pub.
— Read the Tarot Within 7 Days. (Orig.). 1994. pap. 7.95 (*1-872189-90-3*, Pub. by Mandrake Pr) Holmes Pub.
— Rune Magick. (Orig.). 1995. pap. 8.95 (*1-872189-55-5*, Pub. by Mandrake Pr) Holmes Pub.
— Simple Candle Magick. (Orig.). 1995. pap. 8.95 (*1-872189-61-X*, Pub. by Mandrake Pr) Holmes Pub.
— Simple Spells from a Witches' Spellbook. (Orig.). 1995. pap. 8.95 (*1-872189-75-X*, Pub. by Mandrake Pr) Holmes Pub.
— So You Want to Be a Witch. (Orig.). 1993. pap. 7.95 (*1-872189-51-2*, Pub. by Mandrake Pr) Holmes Pub.
— Tantric Tarot. (Orig.). 1995. pap. 8.95 (*1-872189-76-8*, Pub. by Mandrake Pr) Holmes Pub.
— Traditional Wicca. (Orig.). 1994. pap. 8.95 (*1-872189-25-3*, Pub. by Mandrake Pr) Holmes Pub.
— The Truth about Witchcraft. (Orig.). 1995. pap. 7.95 (*1-872189-65-2*, Pub. by Mandrake Pr) Holmes Pub.
— Wicca Awakens. (Orig.). 1995. pap. 8.95 (*1-872189-20-2*, Pub. by Mandrake Pr) Holmes Pub.
— A Witch's Kitchen. (Orig.). 1993. pap. 8.95 (*1-872189-21-0*, Pub. by Mandrake Pr) Holmes Pub.
Morgan, Keith, et al. Shaping an American Landscape: The Art & Architecture of Charles Platt. (Illus.). 1995. pap. 29.95 (*0-614-12960-5*) Hood Mus Art.
Morgan, Keith, jt. auth. see Miller, Naomi.
Morgan, Keith, jt. ed. see Lewis, Arnold.
Morgan, Keith N. Shaping an American Landscape: The Art & Architecture of Charles A. Platt. LC 94-31831. (Illus.). 213p. 1995. pap. 29.95 (*0-87451-705-2*); text 55.00 (*0-87451-704-4*) U Pr of New Eng.
Morgan, Kelly J., jt. auth. see Juricek, Kay.
Morgan, Kendall G. The Agency in Suite 309. 272p. 1998. 21.95 (*1-58244-001-8*) Rutledge Bks.
Morgan, Kenneth. Birth of Industrial Britain, 1750-1850: Economic Change. LC 98-42241. (Seminar Studies in History). 160p. 1999. pap. 14.66 (*0-582-29833-4*) Longman.
— The People's Peace: British History since 1945. 2nd ed. LC 98-30645. (Illus.). 624p. 1999. pap. 14.95 (*0-19-285350-3*) OUP.
— The Religion of the Hindus. 1987. reprint ed. 27.00 (*81-208-0387-6*, Pub. by Motilal Bnarsidass) S Asia.
Morgan, Kenneth & Schlepper, Almut, eds. Human Rights Have No Borders: Voices of Irish Poets. LC 98-235737. 176 p. :p. 1998. write for info. (*1-86023-079-2*) Martello Bks.
Morgan, Kenneth, ed. see Fisher, Jabez M.
Morgan, Kenneth J. Structured Programming in C. (C). 1995. 42.00 (*0-02-383972-4*, Macmillan Coll) P-H.
Morgan, Kenneth O. Callaghan: A Life. (Illus.). 800p. (C). 1998. 40.00 (*0-19-820216-4*) OUP.
***Morgan, Kenneth O.** Callaghan: A Life. (Illus.). 816p. 1999. pap. 24.95 (*0-19-285356-2*) OUP.
Morgan, Kenneth O. Consensus & Disunity: The Lloyd George Coalition Government, 1918 to 1922. (Illus.). 448p. 1979. text 79.00 (*0-19-822497-4*) OUP.
— Consensus & Disunity: The Lloyd George Coalition Government, 1918 to 1922. (Illus.). 448p. 1986. pap. text 27.50 (*0-19-822975-5*) OUP.
— David Lloyd George. LC 82-2988. 85p. 1982. reprint ed. lib. bdg. 55.00 (*0-313-23453-1*, MODG, Greenwood Pr) Greenwood.
— Labour in Power, 1945-1951. (Illus.). 564p. (C). 1985. pap. 21.00 (*0-19-285150-0*) OUP.
Morgan, Kenneth O. Labour People: Leaders & Lieutenants: Hardie to Kinnock. 2nd ed. 382p. pap. 15.95 (*0-19-285270-1*) OUP.
Morgan, Kenneth O. Modern Wales: Politics, Places & People. 492p. 1996. 75.00 (*0-7083-1317-5*, Pub. by Univ Wales Pr) Paul & Co Pubs.
— Rebirth of a Nation: Wales, 1880-1890. LC 97-34376. (Oxford History of Wales Ser.: Vol. VI). (Illus.). 480p. 1987. pap. text 19.95 (*0-19-821760-9*) OUP.
Morgan, Kenneth O., ed. The Oxford History of Britain. 2nd rev. ed. LC 98-30644. (Illus.). 772p. 1999. pap. 18.95 (*0-19-285349-X*) OUP.
— The Oxford Illustrated History of Britain. LC 83-21990. (Illus.). 654p. 1984. 49.95 (*0-19-822684-5*) OUP.
— The Oxford Illustrated History of Britain. LC 83-21990. (Illus.). 654p. 1986. pap. 26.50 (*0-19-285174-8*) OUP.
***Morgan, Kenneth O., ed.** The Oxford Illustrated History of Britain. (Illus.). 672p. 2001. pap. 24.95 (*0-19-289326-2*) OUP.
Morgan, Kenneth O., ed. see Corbishley, Mike, et al.
Morgan, Kenneth O., ed. see Salway, Peter & Blair, John.
Morgan, Kenneth W. Islam: The Straight Path. (C). 1987. 26.00 (*81-208-0403-1*, Pub. by Motilal Bnarsidass) S Asia.
— The Path of the Buddha: Buddhism Interpreted by Buddhists. 1986. 24.00 (*81-208-0030-3*, Pub. by Motilal Bnarsidass) S Asia.
— The Path of the Buddha: Buddhism Interpreted by Buddhists. 432p. 1986. reprint ed. 25.00 (*0-317-60576-3*, Pub. by Motilal Bnarsidass) S Asia.
— Reaching for the Moon: On Asian Religious Paths. LC 90-751. 207p. 1990. 20.50 (*0-89012-059-5*) Col U Pr.
Morgan, Kenneth W., ed. Islam the Straight Path: Islam Interpreted by Muslims. LC 58-9807. 463p. reprint ed. pap. 143.60 (*0-608-30486-7*, 201238300081) Bks Demand.
— The Religion of the Hindus: Interpreted by Hindus. LC 53-10466. 448p. reprint ed. 138.90 (*0-8357-9975-1*, 201562000095) Bks Demand.
Morgan, Kerry L. Real Choice, Real Freedom: In American Education. LC 97-28253. 312p. (C). 1997. 62.00 (*0-7618-0854-X*); pap. 36.50 (*0-7618-0855-8*) U Pr of Amer.
Morgan, Kevin. Regional Innovation Strategies: The Challenge for Less Favored Regions, 24. (Regional Policy & Development Ser.). 1998. pap. text 32.95 (*1-85302-699-9*) Taylor & Francis.
— Sleep & Aging: A Research-Based Guide to Sleep in Later Life. LC 87-45486. 160p. 1987. text 40.00 (*0-8018-3564-X*) Johns Hopkins.
Morgan, Kevin, ed. Gerontology: Responding to an Aging Society. 200p. 1992. 29.95 (*1-85302-117-2*) Taylor & Francis.
Morgan, Kevin, jt. auth. see Cooke, Philip.
Morgan, Kitty, jt. auth. see Littlefield, Kinney.
Morgan, Kristin. A Bride to Be. (Romance Ser.). 1995. per. 2.75 (*0-373-19055-7*, 1-19055-2) Silhouette.
— The Daddy & the Baby Doctor: Follow That Baby! 1998. per. 3.50 (*0-373-19333-5*, 1-19333-3) Silhouette.
— El Mejor Amigo, 164. (Harlequin Bianca - Harlequin Presents Ser.). 1999. per. 3.50 (*0-373-33514-8*) Harlequin Bks.
— First Comes Baby. (Romance Ser.: No. 845). 1992. per. 2.59 (*0-373-08845-0*, 5-08845-5) Silhouette.
— Having Gabriel's Baby. 1997. per. 3.25 (*0-373-19199-5*, 1-19199-8) Silhouette.
— Make Room for Baby. (Romance Ser.). 1995. per. 2.99 (*0-373-19084-0*, 1-19084-2) Silhouette.
— Rebel Dad: (Fabulous Fathers) (Romance Ser.). 1994. pap. 2.75 (*0-373-08982-1*, 5-08985-6) Silhouette.
— Shotgun Groom. 1998. per. 3.50 (*0-373-19291-6*, 1-19291-3) Silhouette.
— Welcome Home, Daddy! (Romance Ser.). 1996. per. 3.25 (*0-373-19150-2*, 1-19150-1) Silhouette.
— Who's That Baby? (Romance Ser.). 1993. per. 2.69 (*0-373-08929-5*, 5-08929-7) Silhouette.
Morgan, L. A., jt. auth. see Ehrhardt, H.
Morgan, L. H. Ancient Society: Or Researches in the Lines of Human Progress from Savagery Through Barbarism to Civilization. Leacock, E. G., ed. 1990. 20.00 (*0-8446-2611-2*) Peter Smith.
— The League of the Iroquois. (Illus.). 1990. 25.50 (*0-8446-2612-0*) Peter Smith.
Morgan, Lael. Art & Eskimo Power: The Life & Times of Alaskan Howard Rock. LC 88-24408. (Illus.). 260p. (YA). (gr. 9-12). 1988. pap. 16.95 (*0-945397-03-8*) Epicenter Pr.
— Earthquake Survival Manual: What to Do Before, During & after the "Big One" (Illus.). 160p. 1993. pap. 14.95 (*0-945397-20-8*) Epicenter Pr.
— Good Time Girls of the Alaska-Yukon Gold Rush. 2nd ed. Ummel, Christine, ed. (Illus.). 352p. 1999. reprint ed. pap. 17.95 (*0-945397-76-3*) Epicenter Pr.
Morgan, Lane. The Ethnic Market Food Guide. 272p. 1997. pap. 12.00 (*0-425-16130-7*) Berkley Pub.
Morgan, Lane, ed. Good Food Guide to Washington & Oregon: Discover the Finest, Freshest Foods Grown & Harvested in the Northwest. (Illus.). 320p. (Orig.). 1992. pap. 14.95 (*0-912365-50-1*) Sasquatch Bks.
Morgan, Lanier. Understanding & Modification of Delinquent Behavior. LC 84-90339. 1984. 15.00 (*0-87212-181-X*) Libra.
Understanding & Modification of Delinquent Behavior. rev. ed. LC 91-61814. 1992. 20.00 (*0-87212-251-4*) Libra.
Morgan, Larry A. The TI-82 Companion to Elementary Statistics. Berrisford, Julia, ed. (C). 1995. pap. text 12.00 (*0-201-87002-9*) Addison-Wesley.
Morgan, Laura W. Child Support Guidelines: Interpretation & Application. LC 96-31408. 710p. 1998. ring bd. 136.00 (*1-56706-283-0*) Aspen Law.
Morgan, Laurence A., et al. Biochemical & Resource Book. 2nd ed. LC 94-134. 1200p. 1994. pap. text 110.67 (*0-13-814443-5*) P-H.
Morgan, Lee. Dr. Johnson's "Own Dear Master" The Life of Henry Thrale. LC 97-52963. 304p. (C). 1998. 39.00 (*0-7618-1030-7*) U Pr of Amer.
— McMasters. 320p. (Orig.). 1995. mass mkt. 4.99 (*0-515-11632-7*, Jove) Berkley Pub.
— McMasters No. 2: Silver Creek Showdown. 192p. (Orig.). 1995. mass mkt. 3.99 (*0-515-11682-3*, Jove) Berkley Pub.
— McMasters No. 4: Big 70. 192p. (Orig.). 1995. mass mkt. 4.50 (*0-515-11765-X*, Jove) Berkley Pub.
— McMasters No. 6: Violent Sunday. 192p. (Orig.). 1996. mass mkt. 4.99 (*0-515-11842-7*, Jove) Berkley Pub.
— Plunder Valley. (McMasters Ser.: No. 3). 192p. (Orig.). 1995. mass mkt. 4.50 (*0-515-11731-5*, Jove) Berkley Pub.
Morgan, Lee & Cattaneo, Pietro. Abraham Lincoln. (What Made Them Great Ser.). (Illus.). 104p. (J). (gr. 5-8). 1990. lib. bdg. 12.95 (*0-382-09973-7*) Silver Burdett Pr.
Morgan, Lee & Solarino, Claudio. Christopher Columbus. (What Made Them Great Ser.). (Illus.). 104p. (J). (gr. 5-8). 1990. 12.95 (*0-382-09974-5*); pap. 5.95 (*0-382-24001-4*) Silver Burdett Pr.
Morgan, Len. Reflections of a Pilot. (Illus.). 224p. (Orig.). 1987. 16.95 (*0-8306-2098-2*); pap. 12.95 (*0-8306-2398-1*) McGraw-Hill Prof.
— Vectors: The Best of Len Morgan. 1991. 22.95 (*0-8306-2087-7*); pap. 14.95 (*0-8306-2083-4*) McGraw-Hill Prof.
Morgan, Lenore. Dragons & Stuff. LC 70-108725. (Illus.). 32p. (J). (gr. 2-4). 1970. lib. bdg. 9.95 (*0-87783-012-6*) Oddo.
— Dragons & Stuff. deluxe ed. LC 70-108725. (Illus.). 32p. (J). (gr. 2-4). 1970. pap. 3.94 (*0-87783-091-6*) Oddo.
— Peter's Pockets. LC 65-27622. (Illus.). 32p. (J). (gr. k-2). 1968. lib. bdg. 9.95 (*0-87783-029-0*) Oddo.
— Peter's Pockets. (Illus.). (J). (gr. k-2). 1978. pap. 1.25 (*0-89508-063-X*) Rainbow Bks.
Morgan, Les. Pulling Weeds. LC 88-93031. 124p. (Orig.). (J). (ps up). 1989. pap. 6.99 (*0-87509-414-7*) Chr Pubns.
— Taming the Lions in Your Life. LC 91-58677. 160p. (Orig.). (YA). (gr. 8-12). 1992. pap. 6.99 (*0-87509-479-1*) Chr Pubns.
Morgan, Leslie. Desert Lights. (Rapture Romance Ser.: No. 65). 192p. 1984. pap. 1.95 (*0-317-00765-3*, Sig) NAL.
Morgan, Leslie & Kunkel, Suzanne. Aging: The Social Context. LC 97-38527. (Illus.). 457p. 1998. text 45.95 (*0-8039-9087-1*) Pine Forge.
Morgan, Leslie A. After Marriage Ends: Economic Consequences for Midlife Women. (New Perspectives on Family Ser.). (Illus.). 240p. 1991. 48.00 (*0-8039-3548-X*); pap. 22.95 (*0-8039-3549-8*) Sage.
— After Marriage Ends: Economic Consequences for Midlife Women. LC 90-19472. (New Perspectives on Family Ser.). 179p. 1991. reprint ed. pap. 55.50 (*0-608-03816-4*, 206466600009) Bks Demand.
Morgan, Leslie A., et al. Small Board-&-Care Homes: Residential Care in Transition. LC 94-38059. (Illus.). 264p. 1995. text 47.50 (*0-8018-4996-9*) Johns Hopkins.
Morgan, Leslie Z., tr. see Ariosto, Ludovico.
Morgan, Lewis B., jt. auth. see Maslowski, Raymond M.
Morgan, Lewis Henry. The American Beaver & His Works. (Notable American Authors Ser.). 1999. reprint ed. lib. bdg. 125.00 (*0-7812-4587-7*) Rprt Serv.
— Ancient Society. 1974. lib. bdg. 150.00 (*0-87968-630-8*) Gordon Pr.
— Ancient Society. 1978. pap. 14.00 (*0-935534-02-4*) NY Labor News.
— Ancient Society. LC 85-1121. (Classics of Anthropology Ser.). 560p. 1985. reprint ed. pap. 23.95 (*0-8165-0924-7*) U of Ariz Pr.
— Ancient Society: Or Researches in Lines of Human Progress from Savagery Through Barbarism to Civilization. (Notable American Authors Ser.). 1999. reprint ed. lib. bdg. 125.00 (*0-7812-4589-3*) Rprt Serv.
— Houses & Houselife of the American Aborigines. (Notable American Authors Ser.). 1999. reprint ed. lib. bdg. 125.00 (*0-7812-4590-7*) Rprt Serv.
— The Indian Journals, 1859-62. LC 92-42188. (Illus.). 272p. 1993. reprint ed. pap. 10.95 (*0-486-27599-X*) Dover.
— The Indian Journals, Eighteen Fifty-Nine to Sixty-Two. White, Leslie Alvin & Walton, Clyde, eds. LC 58-10122. 269p. reprint ed. pap. 83.40 (*0-608-13965-3*, 205563300029) Bks Demand.
— Laws of Consanguinity & Descent of the Iroquois. (Notable American Authors Ser.). 1999. reprint ed. lib. bdg. 125.00 (*0-7812-4586-9*) Rprt Serv.
— The League of the Iroquois. 124p. 1995. write for info. (*1-57215-124-2*) World Pubns.
— The League of the Iroquois. (Illus.). 477p. 1984. reprint ed. pap. 14.95 (*0-8065-0917-1*, Citadel Pr) Carol Pub Group.
— The League of the Iroquois, 2 vols., Set. 1993. reprint ed. lib. bdg. 150.00 (*0-7812-5160-5*) Rprt Serv.
***Morgan, Lewis Henry.** A Study of the Houses of the American Aborigines: With Suggestions for the Exploration of the Ruins in New Mexico, Arizona, the Valley of the San Juan, & in Yucatan & Central America, under the Auspices of the Archaeological Institute. (LC History-America-E). 80p. 1999. reprint ed. lib. bdg. 69.00 (*0-7812-4287-8*) Rprt Serv.
Morgan, Lewis Henry. Systems of Consanguinity & Affinity of the Human Family. LC 96-53016. (Illus.). xxv, 604p. 1997. pap. text 40.00 (*0-8032-8230-3*, Bison Books) U of Nebr Pr.
— Systems of Consanguinity & Affinity of the Human Family. (Notable American Authors Ser.). 1999. reprint ed. lib. bdg. 125.00 (*0-7812-4588-5*) Rprt Serv.
***Morgan, Lily.** Beauty, Health & Happiness: A Way of Life. LC 99-91823. 366p. 2000. pap. 19.95 (*0-9669383-0-5*) Howard City.
Morgan, Linda. A Place We Call Home. 148p. 1999. pap. write for info. (*0-7392-0097-6*, PO2982) Morris Pubng.
Morgan, Linda A. Words for the Heart. LC 96-94558. 1996. pap. 6.95 (*0-7880-0903-6*, Fairway Pr) CSS OH.
***Morgan, Linda K. & Nunnelee, Janice, eds.** ARNA Core Curriculum for Radiologic Nursing. (Illus.). 372p. 1999. pap. text 110.00 (*0-9676280-0-8*) Amer Radiol.
***Morgan, Lisa.** How to Expedite Your Career Through Publishing. LC 99-90185. 220p. 1999. pap. 19.95 (*0-9670800-0-2*) IntelliPress.
Morgan, Lisa. Internet Commerce. (Illus.). 382p. (Orig.). 1995. pap. 32.00 (*1-56205-496-1*) New Riders Pub.
Morgan, Llewelyn. Patterns of Redemption in Virgil's Georgics. LC 98-44171. (Cambridge Classical Studies). 296p. (C). 1999. 59.95 (*0-521-65166-2*) Cambridge U Pr.
Morgan, Llyod. Century's Best Book on Design. 160p. 1995. pap. 34.50 (*0-419-19760-5*, E & FN Spon) Routledge.
Morgan, Lorrie. Forever Yours Faithfully Empty. 1997. write for info. (*0-345-42368-2*) Ballantine Pub Grp.
— Self-Help. 176p. 1995. mass mkt. 11.99 (*0-446-67192-4*, Pub. by Warner Bks) Little.
Morgan, Lorrie & Vecsey, George. Forever Yours, Faithfully. 1998. mass mkt. 6.99 (*0-345-42842-0*) Ballantine Pub Grp.
Morgan, Louise. Westward H-O-O-O-o-o-o-o-o! The Olivers. LC 89-61486. (Illus.). 208p. 1989. 24.95 (*0-8323-0472-7*) Binford Mort.
Morgan, Lucien. Dreams & Symbols: How to Understand the Meaning of Your Dreams. 1998. 16.98 (*1-880908-92-1*) Todtri Prods.
Morgan, Lyle. Homeopathic Medicine: First Aid & Emergency Care. 188p. (Orig.). 1989. pap. 10.95 (*0-89281-249-4*, Heal Arts VT) Inner Tradit.
Morgan, Lyle W. Homeopathic Treatment of Sports Injuries. LC 87-10161. 144p. 1987. pap. 9.95 (*0-89281-227-3*, Heal Arts VT) Inner Tradit.
Morgan, Lyle W., II. Homeopathy & Your Child: A Parent's Guide to Homeopathic Treatment from Infancy Through Adolescence. 128p. (Orig.). 1992. pap. 9.95 (*0-89281-330-X*) Inner Tradit.

M

An Asterisk (*) at the beginning of an entry indicates that the title is appearing for the first time.

Morgan, Lyle W. La Homeopatia y Su Hijo-Homeopathy & Your Child: Para Ninos Desde la Infancia Nasta la Adolescencia. (SPA.). 128p. 1995. pap. 9.95 (*0-89281-468-3*) Inner Tradit.

Morgan, Lynn M. Fetal Subjects, Feminist Positions. LC 99-12261. 1999. 49.95 (*0-8122-3496-0*) U of Pa Pr.

***Morgan, Lynn M., ed.** Fetal Subjects, Feminist Positions. LC 99-12261. (Illus.). 345p. 1999. pap. 26.50 (*0-8122-1689-X*) U of Pa Pr.

Morgan, M. Puget's Sound: A Narrative of Early Tacoma & the Southern Sound. LC 79-4844. (Illus.). 370p. 1981. pap. 17.50 (*0-295-95842-1*) U of Wash Pr.

Morgan, M., jt. auth. see Hake, H.

Morgan, M. G., ed. Energy & Man: Technical & Social Aspects of Energy. LC 74-27680. 536p. 1975. pap. 39.95 (*0-87942-042-1*, PP00513) Inst Electrical.

Morgan, M. Granger & Henrion, Max. Uncertainty: A Guide to Dealing with Uncertainty in Quantitative Risk & Policy Analysis. (Illus.). 344p. (C). 1990. text 59.95 (*0-521-36542-2*) Cambridge U Pr.

— Uncertainty: A Guide to Dealing with Uncertainty in Quantitative Risk & Policy Analysis. 344p. (C). 1992. pap. text 19.95 (*0-521-42744-4*) Cambridge U Pr.

Morgan, M. R. The Chronicle of Ernoul & the Continuations of William of Tyre. (Oxford Historical Monographs). 1974. 22.50 (*0-19-821851-6*) OUP.

Morgan, M. W., ed. see Warren, R. & della Rovere, G. Querci.

Morgan, Maggie. The Acceptable Face of Feminism. LC 97-124699. 224p. (C). 1996. pap. 25.00 (*0-85315-833-9*, Pub. by Lawrence & Wishart) NYU Pr.

Morgan, Mandy, jt. ed. see Kennedy, Robert.

Morgan, Mar Lou, jt. auth. see MacDonald, Kathryn.

Morgan, Marc S., jt. auth. see Johnson, Howard D.

Morgan, Marcia K. How to Interview Sexual Abuse Victims: With a Special Segment on Appropriate Use of Anatomical Dolls. (Interpersonal Violence: The Practice Ser.). 1994. pap. 21.50 (*0-8039-5289-9*) Sage.

— How to Interview Sexual Abuse Victims: With a Special Segment on Appropriate Use of Anatomical Dolls. (Interpersonal Violence: The Practice Ser.: Vol. 7). 1994. 48.00 (*0-8039-5288-0*) Sage.

— My Feelings. 2nd ed. (Illus.). (J). (ps-5). 1984. reprint ed. pap. text 4.95 (*0-930413-00-8*, TX-1-361-947) Migima Designs.

Morgan, Marcia K., jt. auth. see Friedemann, Virginia.

Morgan, Margaret. Color Decoration & Illumination for Calligraphy: Techniques & Projects. LC 96-41747. (Illus.). 96p. (Orig.). 1997. reprint ed. pap. text 12.95 (*0-486-29507-9*) Dover.

Morgan, Margery. The Well-Woman. (Illus.). 128p. (Orig.). 1993. pap. 9.95 (*0-563-36307-X*, BBC-Parkwest) Parkwest Pubns.

Morgan, Margery, jt. ed. see Page, Malcolm.

Morgan, Margery M., ed. see Shaw, George Bernard.

Morgan, Margie M. & Alford, Robbie M. We Knew You Wouldn't Remember, So We Wrote It Down: A Collection of Memories & Recipes from the Murry Girls. 1997. ring bd. 14.95 (*0-9658678-0-3*) Eagles Trning.

Morgan, Mariah, jt. auth. see Stewart, Mark.

Morgan, Marian & Preston, Izola. The Arkansas African-American Quizbook. 40p. (Orig.). 1993. pap. 10.00 (*0-938041-12-6*) Arc Pr AR.

Morgan, Marika L. Shunka: Life with an Arctic Wolf. (Illus.). 192p. 1996. reprint ed. pap. 15.00 (*1-880158-09-4*) J N Townsend.

Morgan, Marilyn. Alaska Alphabet: Stories & Activities. (Teaching Alaska Ser.: No. 1). (Illus.). 423p. (Orig.). (C). 1994. pap. text, teacher ed. 34.95 (*1-878051-18-0*) Circumpolar Pr.

***Morgan, Marilyn.** Careers in Criminology. 224p. (J). 2000. pap. 19.95 (*0-7373-0272-0*, 02720W, Pub. by Lowell Hse) NTC Contemp Pub Co.

Morgan, Marilyn S., jt. auth. see Steele, John E.

***Morgan, Marjorie.** National Identities & Travel in Victorian Britain. LC 00-41511. (Illus.). 2000. write for info. (*0-333-71999-9*, Macmillan UK) St & J.

Morgan, Mark & Ess, Dan. The Precision Farming Guide for Agriculturists: The Nuts & Bolts Guide to "Getting up to Speed" Fast & Effectively with This Exciting New Management Tool. Rawlins, Stephen L. et al, eds. (Agricultural Primer Ser.). (Illus.). 124p. 1997. pap. text 25.95 (*0-86691-245-2*, FP401NC) Deere & Co.

Morgan, Mark D. Ecology of Mysidacea. 1982. text 176.50 (*90-6193-761-2*) Kluwer Academic.

Morgan, Mark W., jt. auth. see Chang, Richard Y.

Morgan, Marlene J., jt. auth. see Lisak, Janet M.

Morgan, Marlo. Making the Message Mine. Grimme, Jeannette, ed. (Illus.). 115p. (Orig.). (YA). Date not set. pap. text. write for info. (*1-883473-01-2*) M M Co.

— Message from Forever: A Novel of Aboriginal Wisdom. LC 98-19903. 288p. 1998. 24.00 (*0-06-019107-4*, Cliff Street) HarperTrade.

***Morgan, Marlo.** Message from Forever: Rosenblat,&Barbara, Set. abr. ed. 1998. audio 18.00 (*0-694-51961-8*) HarperAudio.

Morgan, Marlo. Mutant Message Down Under. 208p. 1995. pap. 13.00 (*0-06-092631-7*, Perennial) HarperTrade.

— Mutant Message down Under. large type ed. LC 94-33225. 289p. 1994. lib. bdg. 21.95 (*0-7862-0330-7*) Thorndike Pr.

Morgan, Marlo. Mutant Message Down Under: Morgan,&Marlo. abr. ed. 1994. audio 18.00 (*0-694-51515-9*, CPN 2461) HarperAudio.

Morgan, Marlo. Mutant Message from Forever: A Novel of Aboriginal Wisdom. 336p. 1999. pap. 13.00 (*0-06-093026-8*) HarpC.

Morgan, Martha, jt. auth. see Fibush, Esther.

Morgan, Martha M. A Trip Across the Plains in 1849. 32p. 1983. pap. 7.95 (*0-87770-295-0*) Ye Galleon.

***Morgan, Mary.** Dangerous Moves, Vol. 32. 2000. mass mkt. 3.99 (*0-8217-6459-4*, Zebra Kensgtn) Kensgtn Pub Corp.

Morgan, Mary. The History of Econometric Ideas. (Historical Perspectives on Modern Economics Ser.). (Illus.). 312p. (C). 1991. pap. text 23.95 (*0-521-42465-8*) Cambridge U Pr.

— The House at the Edge of the Jungle. LC 98-44010. 224p. 1998. text 21.95 (*0-312-19898-1*) St Martin.

— Night Ride. LC 95-45779. (Illus.). (J). 1999. 16.00 (*0-689-80545-4*) Atheneum Yung Read.

— Night Ride. (J). 1997. 14.95 (*0-02-767460-6*) S&S Bks Yung.

— Patterns & Sources of Zuni Kachinas. 1989. 49.95 (*0-9601322-4-4*) Harmsen.

***Morgan, Mary.** Rosie Plush Individual Unit. (J). 1999. 5.99 (*0-7868-0488-2*, Pub. by Hyprn Child) Time Warner.

Morgan, Mary. Willful Neglect. 1998. per. 4.99 (*0-373-26297-3*, 1-26297-1, Mira Bks) Harlequin Bks.

— Willful Neglect. 256p. 1997. 22.95 (*0-312-15694-4*, Thomas Dunne) St Martin.

— Words from the Inner Spirit. Clark, Tyrone L. & Shidemantle, Lu Ann, eds. 62p. (Orig.). 1997. 4.95 (*0-9661372-0-5*) MGC-ERIE.

Morgan, Mary. The Pudgy Merry Christmas Book. (Pudgy Board Bks.). 18p. (J). (ps-3). 1989. bds. 3.50 (*0-448-02262-1*, G & D) Peng Put Young Read.

***Morgan, Mary & Morrison, Margaret, eds.** Models as Mediators: Perspectives on Natural & Social Science. LC 98-41630. (Ideas in Context Ser.: No. 52). (Illus.). 401p. (C). 1999. 64.95 (*0-521-65097-6*); pap. 24.95 (*0-521-65571-4*) Cambridge U Pr.

Morgan, Mary & Shermis, Michael. Critical Thinking, Reading & Writing. LC 89-49156. (Teaching Resources in the ERIC Database (TRIED) Ser.). 1989. pap. 14.95 (*0-927516-08-X*) ERIC-REC.

Morgan, Mary, ed. see Alano, Becky.

Morgan, Mary, ed. see Saint Louis Art Museum Staff.

Morgan, Mary H. How to Dress an Old-Fashioned Doll. LC 72-93612. Orig. Title: How to Dress a Doll. (Illus.). 95p. (J). (gr. 5-8). 1973. reprint ed. pap. 3.50 (*0-486-22912-2*) Dover.

Morgan, Mary M., compiled by. The Indiana 1820 Enumeration of Males. viii, 173p. 1988. 12.00 (*0-87195-010-3*) Ind Hist Soc.

Morgan, Mary S. From Interwar Pluralism to Postwar Neoclassicism. 1999. 59.95 (*0-8223-2335-4*) Duke.

Morgan, Mary S., jt. auth. see Den Butter, F. A. G.

Morgan, Mary S., jt. ed. see De Marchi, Neil.

Morgan, Mary S., jt. ed. see Hendry, David F.

Morgan, Maryanne, jt. auth. see Thompson, Simon B.

Morgan, Marycyliena, ed. Language & the Social Construction of Identity in Creole Situations. (Special Publications: Vol. 8). 148p. (Orig.). (C). 1994. pap. text 15.95 (*0-934934-40-1*) CAAS Pubns.

Morgan, Meg P., et al. Strategies for Technical Communication: A Collection of Teaching Tips. 105p. 1994. pap. text 30.00 (*0-914548-76-X*, 152-94) Soc Tech Comm.

Morgan, Melissa, jt. auth. see Chant, Ben.

Morgan, Melissa L. & Allee, Judith Waite. Homeschooling on a Shoestring: A Jam-Packed Guide. LC 97-43230. 376p. 1999. pap. 12.99 (*0-87788-546-X*, H Shaw Pubs) Waterbrook Pr.

Morgan, Melody. Abiding Hope. 368p. 1999. mass mkt. 5.50 (*0-8439-4493-5*) Dorchester Pub Co.

— Love & Honor. 320p. (Orig.). 1998. mass mkt. 4.99 (*0-8439-4341-6*, Leisure Bks) Dorchester Pub Co.

Morgan, Melvin D., jt. auth. see Volk, Michael D.

Morgan, Meredith W., jt. auth. see Rosenbloom, David.

Morgan, Meredith W., jt. ed. see Rosenbloom, Alfred J.

***Morgan, Michael.** Java 2 for Professional Developers. (Illus.). 762p. 1999. pap. 34.99 (*0-672-31697-8*) Sams.

Morgan, Michael. Lenin. 1972. 20.00 (*0-8214-0094-0*) Lib Soc Sci.

***Morgan, Michael.** Using Java 1.2. LC 98-84331. (Using... Ser.). 1998. pap. 29.99 (*0-7897-1627-5*) Que.

Morgan, Michael & Leggett, Susan, eds. Mainstream(s) & Margins: Cultural Politics in the 90s, 367. LC 95-37339. (Contributions in Political Science Ser.: No. 367). 264p. 1996. 65.00 (*0-313-29796-7*, Greenwood Pr) Greenwood.

Morgan, Michael & Shanahan, James L. Democracy Tango: Television, Adolescents, & Authoritarian Tensions in Argentina. Good, Leslie, ed. LC 95-13622. (Communication Ser.: Critical Studies in Communication). 256p. 1995. text 49.50 (*1-881303-90-X*); pap. text 21.95 (*1-881303-91-8*) Hampton Pr NJ.

Morgan, Michael, jt. auth. see Shanahan, Jim.

Morgan, Michael, ed. see Rutstein, Nathan.

Morgan, Michael, jt. ed. see Rutstein, Nathan.

Morgan, Michael, jt. ed. see Signorielli, Nancy.

Morgan, Michael D. & Morgan, Joseph M. Essentials of Weather. 200p. (C). 1996. pap. text 48.00 (*0-02-383811-6*, Macmillan Coll) P-H.

Morgan, Michael D., et al. Environmental Science: Managing Biological & Physical Resources, 3 vols., 2. 568p. (C). 1992. text. write for info. (*0-697-16308-3*) Brown & Benchmark.

— Environmental Science: Managing Biological & Physical Resources, 3 vols., 3. 568p. (C). 1992. text. write for info. (*0-697-16309-1*) Brown & Benchmark.

Morgan, Michael D., jt. auth. see Moran, Joseph M.

Morgan, Michael J. Molyneux's Question: Vision, Touch & the Philosophy of Perception. LC 76-54066. 222p. reprint ed. pap. 63.30 (*0-608-30648-7*, 2022463) Bks Demand.

Morgan, Michael J., ed. Carbohydrate Metabolism in Cultured Cells. LC 86-12170. (Illus.). 536p. (C). 1986. text 174.00 (*0-306-42240-9*, Kluwer Plenum) Kluwer Academic.

Morgan, Michael L. Dilemmas in Modern Jewish Thought: The Dialectics of Revelation & History. LC 92-7724. 224p. 1992. 9.95 (*0-253-33878-6*) Ind U Pr.

Morgan, Michael L., ed. Classics of Moral & Political Theory. 2nd ed. LC 96-48424. 1269p. (C). 1996. pap. text 29.95 (*0-87220-356-5*); lib. bdg. 55.00 (*0-87220-357-3*) Hackett Pub.

***Morgan, Michael L., ed.** A Holocaust Reader: Responses to the Nazi Extermination. 384p. 2000. 49.00 (*0-19-505957-3*); pap. 24.95 (*0-19-505958-1*) OUP.

Morgan, Michael V., ed. Michigan Drunk Driving Law & Practice. 2nd ed. LC 91-78184. 624p. 1992. ring bd. 95.00 (*0-685-65989-5*, 92-007) U MI Law CLE.

Morgan, Michaela. Bety Al Rescate (Helpful Betty to the Rescue) (SPA.). (J). (gr. 3-4). 1995. pap. 5.99 (*968-16-4569-3*, Pub. by Fondo) Continental Bk.

— Bety la Servicial Resuelve un Misterio (Helpful Betty Solves a Mystery) (SPA.). (J). (gr. 2). 1994. pap. 5.99 (*968-16-4570-7*, Pub. by Fondo) Continental Bk.

— Helpful Betty to the Rescue. LC 93-39885. (Illus.). (J). (gr. k-3). 1994. lib. bdg. 18.60 (*0-87614-831-3*, Carolrhoda) Lerner Pub.

***Morgan, Michaela & Carroll, Sara.** Sleepy Dreams. (Illus.). 4p. (J). 1998. bds. 14.98 (*1-58048-040-3*) Sandvik Pub.

Morgan, Michaela & Kemp, Moira. Helpful Betty Solves a Mystery. LC 93-39050. (J). (gr. k-3). 1994. lib. bdg. 18.60 (*0-87614-832-1*, Carolrhoda) Lerner Pub.

***Morgan, Michele.** Simple Wicca. (Simple Wisdom Ser.). (Illus.). 195p. 2000. 14.95 (*1-57324-199-7*) Conari Press.

Morgan, Michele A. Eat to Be Lean: A Step-by-Step Guide to a Healthy Eating Lifestyle. LC 96-95156. 144p. (Orig.). 1996. pap. 15.95 (*0-9655644-0-1*) Mainstream Pub.

Morgan, Mike. Netscape Plug in Developers Kit. LC 96-70765. 560p. 1996. pap. text 49.99 incl. cd-rom (*0-7897-0844-2*) Que.

— Using Netscape Suitespot 3, Vol. 1. 750p. 1997. 59.99 (*0-7897-1229-6*) Que.

— Using Netscape Suitespot 3, Vol. 2. 650p. 1997. 59.99 (*0-7897-1230-X*) Que.

Morgan, Millard. American Guide to Hotels, Motels, Resorts & Inns. (Western Edition Ser.). 180p. (Orig.). 1989. pap. 6.95 (*0-685-29015-8*) Guide Pr CA.

— American Guide to Hotels, Motels, Resorts & Inns: Central Edition. 180p. 1989. pap. 6.95 (*0-685-29018-2*) Guide Pr CA.

— American Guide to Hotels, Motels, Resorts & Inns: Eastern Edition. 180p. (Orig.). 1989. pap. 6.95 (*0-685-29017-4*) Guide Pr CA.

— American Guide to Hotels, Motels, Resorts & Inns: Southern Edition. 180p. (Orig.). 1989. pap. 6.95 (*0-685-29016-6*) Guide Pr CA.

Morgan, Moc. Trout & Salmon Flies of Wales. 1999. 34.95 (*0-8117-1611-2*) Stackpole.

Morgan, Mona M., ed. Growing up in Kilvert Country. 150p. (C). 1990. 30.00 (*0-86383-680-1*, Pub. by Gomer Pr) St Mut.

Morgan, Morris H., tr. see Pollio, Vitruvius.

Morgan, Moshe. A Guide to the Laws of Nidah. 137p. pap. 9.95 (*1-56062-304-7*) CIS Comm.

Morgan, Moshe. A Guide to the Laws of Sukkos. LC 94-68426. (Illus.). 400p. (C). 1994. 24.95 (*1-56062-275-X*) CIS Comm.

Morgan, Murray. Confederate Raider in the North Pacific: The Saga of the C.S.S. "Shenandoah," 1864-65. (Illus.). 344p. 1995. reprint ed. pap. 19.95 (*0-87422-123-4*) Wash St U Pr.

— The Last Wilderness. LC 76-41. 290p. 1976. pap. 12.95 (*0-295-95319-5*) U of Wash Pr.

— The Mill on the Boot: The Story of the St. Paul & Tacoma Lumber Company. LC 82-16107. (Illus.). 286p. 1982. 19.95 (*0-295-95949-5*) U of Wash Pr.

— The Mill on the Boot: The Story of the St. Paul & Tacoma Lumber Company. LC 82-16107. (Illus.). 296p. 1985. pap. 17.50 (*0-295-96273-9*) U of Wash Pr.

— The Mill on the Boot: The Story of the St. Paul & Tacoma Lumber Company. LC 82-16107. (Illus.). 286p. 1982. 19.95 (*0-685-38498-5*) Wash St Hist Soc.

— One Man's Gold Rush: A Klondike Album. rev. ed. LC 67-13109. (Illus.). 224p. (C). 1995. reprint ed. pap. 24.95 (*0-295-95187-7*) U of Wash Pr.

— Over Washington. Barnes, Beverley & Dow, Lesley, eds. (Wings over America Ser.). (Illus.). 256p. 1995. reprint ed. 45.00 (*1-887451-07-2*); reprint ed. pap. 35.00 (*1-887451-01-3*) Weldon Owen.

— Skid Road: An Informal Portrait of Seattle. rev. ed. LC 81-11701. (Illus.). 296p. 1982. reprint ed. pap. text 16.95 (*0-295-95846-4*) U of Wash Pr.

— The Viewless Winds. LC 89-16355. (Northwest Reprints Ser.). 240p. 1990. reprint ed. pap. 13.95 (*0-87071-505-4*); reprint ed. text 24.95 (*0-87071-504-6*) Oreg St U Pr.

Morgan, Murray, jt. auth. see Norden, Linda.

Morgan, Myfanwy, et al. Sociological Approaches to Health & Medicine. LC 85-48015. (Social Analysis Ser.). 297p. (C). 1985. 24.50 (*0-7099-1705-8*, Pub. by C Helm); pap. 11.50 (*0-7099-3514-5*, Pub. by C Helm) Routldge.

Morgan, N. G. Hormones & Cell Signalling. 208p. 1989. write for info. (*0-318-65444-X*); pap. write for info. (*0-335-15820-X*) OpUniv Pr.

Morgan, N. J. Printed in Germany, Bk. 1. 1989. pap. text 10.84 (*0-582-01450-6*, 78051) Longman.

— Printed in Germany, Bk. 2. 1989. pap. 10.84 (*0-685-32947-X*, 78050) Longman.

Morgan, Nancy, ed. see Dunn, Hampton.

Morgan, Neal. Karankawa County: Short Stories from a Corner of Texas. LC 89-48086. 152p. 1990. 17.95 (*0-89096-423-8*) Tex A&M Univ Pr.

— Play It from the Heart. vii, 345p. 1999. pap. 14.95 (*0-9671801-0-4*, 1) Sea Rim Bks.

Morgan, Neil, jt. auth. see Morgan, Judith.

Morgan, Nelson, jt. auth. see Gold, Ben.

Morgan, Nicholas. Secret Journeys: Theory & Practice in Reading Dickens. LC 91-55022. (Illus.). 152p. 1992. 29.50 (*0-8386-3447-8*) Fairleigh Dickinson.

Morgan, Nicholas, jt. ed. see Jones, Geoffrey.

***Morgan, Nicola.** Ancient Greece. LC 00-36934. (People Who Made History in Ser.). (Illus.). (J). 2000. write for info. (*0-7398-2747-2*) Raintree Steck-V.

Morgan, Nicola. Louis & the Night Sky. unabridged ed. LC 99-178828. (Illus.). 32p. (J). (ps-3). 1993. pap. 4.95 (*0-19-540970-1*) STDK.

Morgan, Nigel. Deadly Dwellings. (C). 1993. 45.00 (*1-873424-01-9*, Pub. by Mullion Bks) St Mut.

— The Lambeth Apocalypse: Collection of the Archbishop of Canterbury in Lambeth Palace Library, Set, MS 209. limited ed. (Illus.). 383p. 1990. text 3500.00 (*1-872501-55-9*) Gordon & Breach.

— Stage Lighting for Theatre Designers. 128p. (Orig.). 1995. pap. 21.95 (*0-435-08685-5*, 08685) Heinemann.

***Morgan, Nigel & Pritchard, Annette.** Advertising in Tourism & Leisure. 250p. 2000. 69.95 (*0-7506-4531-8*) Buttrwrth-Heinemann.

Morgan, Nigel & Pritchard, Annette. Tourism Promotion & Power: Creating Images, Creating Identities. LC 98-5757. 272p. 1998. 84.95 (*0-471-98341-1*) Wiley.

Morgan, Nigel, jt. auth. see Marks, Richard.

Morgan, Nigel J. & Pritchard, Annette. Power & Politics & the Seaside: The Development of Devon's Seaside Resorts in the Twentieth. (Illus.). 250p. 1998. text 75.00 (*0-85989-571-8*, Pub. by Univ Exeter Pr) Northwestern U Pr.

— Power & Politics & the Seaside: The Development of Devon's Seaside Resorts in the Twentieth Century. (Illus.). 250p. 1998. pap. text 29.95 (*0-85989-572-6*) Univ Exeter Pr.

Morgan, Nina. The Caribbean & the Gulf of Mexico. LC 96-8353. (Seas & Oceans Ser.). 48p. (J). (gr. 6-7). 1997. lib. bdg. 24.26 (*0-8172-4508-1*) Raintree Steck-V.

— Chemistry in Action: The Molecules of Everyday Life. (New Encyclopedia of Science Ser.). (Illus.). 160p. 1995. 39.95 (*0-19-521086-7*) OUP.

— Lasers. LC 96-44293. (20th Century Inventions Ser.). (Illus.). 48p. (J). (gr. 4-9). 1997. lib. bdg. 24.26 (*0-8172-4812-9*) Raintree Steck-V.

— Marine Technology Reference Book. (Illus.). 500p. 1990. 280.00 (*0-408-02784-3*) Buttrwrth-Heinemann.

— Mother Teresa: Saint of the Poor. 1998. pap. 7.95 (*0-8172-7848-6*) Raintree Steck-V.

— The North Sea & the Baltic Sea. LC 96-19443. (Seas & Oceans Ser.). 48p. (J). 1997. lib. bdg. 24.26 (*0-8172-4510-3*) Raintree Steck-V.

— Nuclear Power. LC 97-20302. (Twentieth Century Inventions Ser.). (Illus.). 48p. (J). (gr. 4-9). 1998. 24.26 (*0-8172-4818-8*) Raintree Steck-V.

— Technology in the Time of the Aztecs. LC 97-19066. (J). 1997. 25.69 (*0-8172-4878-1*) Raintree Steck-V.

Morgan, Noel G. Cell Signalling. LC 89-11931. (Molecular Cell Biology Ser.). 203p. 1990. pap. text 24.95 (*0-89862-518-1*) Guilford Pubns.

Morgan, Noja. Expressions from My Heart. 60p. 1993. 5.95 (*0-9622849-9-8*) Papito.

Morgan, Norah & Saxton, Juliana. Teaching Drama: A Mind of Many Wonders. 240p. (Orig.). 1987. pap. 48.50 (*0-7487-0243-1*, Pub. by S Thornes Pubs) Trans-Atl Phila.

Morgan, Oliver J. & Jordan, Merle, eds. Addiction & Spirituality: A Multidisciplinary Approach. LC 99-21210. 272p. 1999. pap. 27.99 (*0-8272-0023-4*, 985606, Pub. by Chalice Pr) Abingdon.

Morgan, Oliver J., jt. ed. see Cernera, Anthony J.

Morgan, Ora S., ed. Agricultural Systems of Middle Europe: A Symposium. LC 72-94470. reprint ed. 31.50 (*0-404-04434-4*) AMS Pr.

Morgan, P. & Odell, Edward W. Biopsy Pathology of the Oral Tissues. (Biopsy Pathology Ser.). 320p. 1997. text 75.00 (*0-412-54790-2*, Pub. by E A) OUP.

Morgan, P. H., jt. auth. see Carley, A. F.

Morgan, P. Lena, et al. The Educational Leader's Internship: Meeting New Standards. LC 96-60522. 239p. 1996. ring bd. 39.95 (*1-56676-444-0*) Scarecrow.

Morgan, Pat. Battle for the Seed. pap. 8.99 (*0-927936-09-7*) Vincom Pubng Co.

Morgan, Pat-Ann. The Munich Sabbatical. 256p. 1995. 24.95 (*0-947993-67-3*) Mlvrn Pubg Co.

Morgan, Patricia. Adoption & the Care of Children: The British & American Experience. (IEA Health & Welfare Unit Choice in Welfare Ser.: No. 42). 210p. 1998. pap. 26.50 (*0-255-36434-2*, Pub. by Inst Economic Affairs) Coronet Bks.

— Battle for the Seed. 112p. (Orig.). 1992. pap. 9.99 (*1-56043-099-0*) Destiny Image.

— Delinquent Fantasies. LC 78-309292. 1979. 21.00 (*0-85117-116-8*) Transatl Arts.

— Farewell to the Family? Public Policy & Family Breakdown in Britain & the U. S. A. LC 95-174909. (IEA Health & Welfare Unit Ser.: No. 21). 194p. 1995. pap. 26.50 (*0-255-36356-7*, Pub. by Inst Economic Affairs) Coronet Bks.

— How to Raise Children of Destiny. LC 95-100913. 210p. (Orig.). 1994. pap. 10.99 (*1-56043-134-2*) Destiny Image.

— Tell Me Again: The Cry of the Children. LC 96-208283. (Illus.). 144p. 1996. pap. 11.99 (*1-56043-180-6*) Destiny Image.

— Who Needs Parents? The Effects of Childcare & Early

M

Education on Children in Britain & the U. S. A. (Choice in Welfare Ser.: No. 31). 165p. 1996. pap. 26.50 (*0-255-36368-0*, Pub. by Inst Economic Affairs) Coronet Bks.

***Morgan, Patricia, et al.** Adoption: The Continuing Debate. (Choice in Welfare Ser.: Vol. 53). 160p. 1999. pap. 16.95 (*0-255-36456-3*, Pub. by Inst Economic Affairs) Coronet Bks.

Morgan, Patricia T. Tax Procedure & Tax Fraud in a Nutshell. (Nutshell Ser.). 400p. (C). 1990. reprint ed. pap. text 18.00 (*0-314-73300-0*) West Pub.

— Tax Procedure & Tax Fraud in a Nutshell. 2nd ed. LC 98-8134. (Nutshell Ser.). 400p. 1999. pap. 16.50 (*0-314-06586-5*) West Pub.

Morgan, Patrick A., jt. ed. see Kolodziej, Edward A.

Morgan, Patrick M. Arms Control in International Politics: Some Theoretical Reflections. (CISA Working Papers: No. 48). 34p. (Orig.). 1985. pap. 15.00 (*0-86682-061-2*) Ctr Intl Relations.

— Deterrence: A Conceptual Analysis. LC 76-51418. (Sage Library of Social Research: No. 40). 216p. 1977. reprint ed. pap. 67.00 (*0-608-01125-8*, 205942900001) Bks Demand.

— Theories & Approaches to International Politics. 4th ed. 314p. 1986. 39.95 (*0-88738-093-X*); pap. text 24.95 (*0-88738-630-X*) Transaction Pubs.

Morgan, Patrick M. & Nelson, Keith L., eds. Re-viewing the Cold War: Domestic Factors & Foreign Policy In the East-West Confrontation. LC 99-16056. 256p. 2000. pap. 24.95 (*0-275-96637-2*) Greenwood.

***Morgan, Patrick M. & Nelson, Keith L., eds.** Re-Viewing the Cold War: Domestic Factors & Foreign Policy in the East-West Confrontation. LC 99-16056. 256p. 2000. 69.50 (*0-275-96636-4*) Greenwood.

Morgan, Patrick M., jt. auth. see Knorr, Klaus.

Morgan, Patrick M., jt. auth. see Lake, David A.

Morgan, Patrick M., jt. ed. see Kolodziej, Edward A.

Morgan, Paul. Complement: Clinical Aspects & Relevance to Disease. 215p. 1991. text 62.00 (*0-12-506955-3*) Acad Pr.

***Morgan, Paul.** Natural Remedies for Allergies: Safe Self-Help Measures for Treating a Wide Range of Modern Allergies. 128p. 1999. reprint ed. text 25.00 (*0-7881-6783-9*) DIANE Pub.

— Natural Remedies for Hayfever: Self-Help Measures for Treating the Symptoms of Hayfever Naturally. (Illus.). 128p. 2000. text 27.00 (*0-7881-6983-1*) DIANE Pub.

***Morgan, Paul B.** K-9 Soldiers: Vietnam & After. LC 98-55569. (Illus.). 184p. 1999. pap. 13.95 (*1-55571-495-1*) PSI Resch.

— The Parrot's Beak: U. S. Operations in Cambodia. 150p. 2000. pap. 14.95 (*1-55571-543-5*, Pub. by PSI Resch) Midpt Trade.

Morgan, Paul W., jt. auth. see Barhydt, Fran.

Morgan, Peg & Morgan, George. The Morgan-Collins-Teeples Book: Idaho Pioneers. 82p. 1992. pap. 20.00 (*0-9634328-0-X*) Knit-Toons.

Morgan, Peggy & Braybrooke, Marcus, eds. Testing the Global Ethic: Voices from the Religions on Moral Values. (Illus.). 174p. (Orig.). 1998. pap. text 19.95 (*0-9637897-6-7*) CoNexus Pr.

Morgan, Peggy & Lawton, Clive, eds. Ethical Issues in Six Religious Traditions. 320p. 1996. pap. 24.50 (*0-7486-0709-9*, Pub. by Edinburgh U Pr) Col U Pr.

Morgan, Peggy, jt. auth. see Cole, W. Owen.

Morgan, Peirr, jt. auth. see Schaefer, Carole L.

Morgan, Peter. The Critical Idyll: Traditional Values & the French Revolution in Goethe's "Hermann und Dorothea" (GERM Ser.: Vol. 59). 186p. 1990. 55.00 (*0-938100-85-8*) Camden Hse.

— Original Porsche 911: The Guide to All Production Models 1963-98. (Illus.). 144p. 1998. 36.95 (*1-901432-16-5*, Bay View Bks) MBI Pubg.

— Original Porsche 924/944/968: The Guide to All Models 1975-95 Including Turbos & Limited Edition. (Illus.). 128p. 1998. 35.95 (*1-901432-05-X*, Bay View Bks) MBI Pubg.

***Morgan, Peter.** Porsche in Motorsport: Fifty Years on Track. (Illus.). 192p. 2000. 49.95 (*1-85960-659-8*, 130425AE, Pub. by Haynes Manuals) Motorbooks Intl.

— Porsche 917: The Winning Formula. (Illus.). 208p. 1999. 49.95 (*1-85960-633-4*, 129063AE, Pub. by Haynes Manuals) Motorbooks Intl.

Morgan, Peter & Nott, Susan. Development Control. 1988. 66.00 (*0-406-50250-1*, UK, MICHIE); pap. 40.00 (*0-406-50251-X*, U.K., MICHIE) LEXIS Pub.

Morgan, Peter F. The Poetic & Pictorial Elements in Works by 5 Writers in English - Milton, Pope, Wordsworth, Ruskin, Pound. LC 92-9968. (Illus.). 268p. 1992. lib. bdg. 89.95 (*0-7734-9503-7*) E Mellen.

Morgan, Peter W. & Reynolds, Glenn H. The Appearance of Impropriety: How the Ethics Wars Have Undermined America Government, Business & Society. LC 97-19251. 304p. 1997. 24.50 (*0-684-82764-6*) Free Pr.

Morgan, Philip. Italian Fascism. 1995. pap. 21.95 (*0-312-11566-0*) St Martin.

— Italian Fascism, 1919-1945. LC 94-29898. 1995. text 55.00 (*0-312-12321-3*) St Martin.

— Italian Fascism, 1919-1945. 1996. 45.00 (*0-333-53778-5*) St Martin.

Morgan, Philip D., ed. Diversity & Unity in Early North America. LC 93-16763. (Rewriting Histories Ser.). 296p. (C). 1993. pap. 24.99 (*0-415-08799-6*, B2412) Routledge.

Morgan, Philip D. & Omohundro Institute of Early American History & Cu. Slave Counterpoint: Black Culture in the Eighteenth-Century Chesapeake & Lowcountry. LC 97-40316. (Illus.). 736p. 1998. 55.00 (*0-8078-2409-7*); pap. 24.95 (*0-8078-4717-8*) U of NC Pr.

Morgan, Philip D., jt. ed. see Ammerman, David L.

Morgan, Philip D., jt. ed. see Bailyn, Bernard.

Morgan, Philip D., jt. ed. see Berlin, Ira.

Morgan, Philip I. Privatization & the Welfare State: Implications for Consumerism & the Workforce. (Illus.). 336p. 1995. text 83.95 (*1-85521-404-0*, Pub. by Dartmth Pub) Ashgate Pub Co.

Morgan, Phyllis S., jt. auth. see Gonzalez-T, Cesar A.

Morgan, Pierr. Sweet Porridge. Date not set. 14.95 (*0-399-21984-6*) Putnam Pub Group.

— The Turnip. (J). 1996. 11.15 (*0-606-12015-7*, Pub. by Turtleback) Demco.

Morgan, Prys. The History of the University of Wales 1939-1993, Vol. 3. LC 98-159131. (History of the University of Wales Ser.). 220p. 1997. 50.00 (*0-7083-1437-6*, Pub. by Univ Wales Pr) Paul & Co Pubs.

— Iolo Morganwg. LC 76-367703. (Writers of Wales Ser.). 98 p. 1975. write for info. (*0-7083-0609-8*) Univ Wales Pr.

Morgan, R. W. St. Paul in Britain. LC 83-73168. 128p. 1984. reprint ed. pap. 6.00 (*0-934666-12-1*) Artisan Pubs.

Morgan, Rachelle. Loving Linsey. 1999. mass mkt. 5.99 (*0-380-80040-3*, Avon Bks) Morrow Avon.

***Morgan, Rachelle.** Mustang Annie. 336p. 2000. mass mkt. 5.99 (*0-380-80921-4*) Morrow Avon.

Morgan, Rachelle. Wild Cat Cait. 1998. mass mkt. 5.99 (*0-380-80039-X*, Avon Bks) Morrow Avon.

Morgan, Rae, jt. auth. see Johnson, Margaret.

Morgan, Raleigh, Jr. The Regional French of County Beauce, Quebec. LC 74-78061. (Janua Linguarum, Series Practica: No. 177). 128p. 1975. pap. text 64.65 (*90-279-3107-0*) Mouton.

Morgan, Ray. Citizen Jerry Cohen: One Man's Life in Kansas City History. 247p. (Orig.). 1995. pap. 14.95 (*0-9646898-2-0*) Leathers Pub.

Morgan, Raye. Almost a Bride. (Desire Ser.: No. 717). 1992. per. 2.89 (*0-373-05717-2*, 5-05717-9) Harlequin Bks.

— Babies by the Busload. (Desire Ser.). 1996. per. 3.50 (*0-373-76022-1*, 1-76022-2) Silhouette.

— Babies on the Doorstep. 1994. per. 2.99 (*0-373-05886-1*, 1-05886-6) Harlequin Bks.

— Baby Dreams. (Desire Ser.). 1996. per. 3.50 (*0-373-75997-5*, 1-75997-6) Silhouette.

— Camino de los Suenos - The Way of the Dreams. (SPA.). 1997. per. 3.50 (*0-373-35194-1*, 1-35194-9) Harlequin Bks.

— Caution: Charm at Work. (Desire Ser.). 1993. per. 2.99 (*0-373-05807-1*, 5-05807-8) Silhouette.

— The Daddy Due Date. (Desire Ser.). 1994. per. 2.99 (*0-373-05843-8*, 5-05843-3) Silhouette.

— Un Deseo Hecho Realidad. (Deseo Ser.: No. 170). (SPA.). 1999. per. 3.50 (*0-373-35300-6*) Harlequin Bks.

— Una Estrella Inalcanzable: (An Unreachable Star) (Deseo Ser.: No. 129).Tr. of Unreachable Star. (SPA.). 1998. per. 3.50 (*0-373-35259-X*, 1-35259-0) Harlequin Bks.

— A Gift for Baby. (Desire Ser.: No. 1010). 1996. per. 3.50 (*0-373-76010-8*, 1-76010-7) Silhouette.

— The Hand-Picked Bride. (Desire Ser.: No. 1119). 1998. per. 3.50 (*0-373-76119-8*, 1-76119-6) Silhouette.

— Instant Dad. 1996. per. 3.50 (*0-373-76040-X*, 1-76040-4) Silhouette.

— Mala Reputacion: Yesterday's Outlas. (Deseo Ser.). (SPA.). 1996. per. 3.50 (*0-373-35169-0*, 1-35169-1) Harlequin Bks.

— Un Nino, un Regalo (A Gift for Baby) (Deseo Ser.).Tr. of A Baby, a Gift. (SPA.). 1997. per. 3.50 (*0-373-35212-3*, 1-35212-9) Harlequin Bks.

— No Hay Ley en el Amor: Wife by Contract. (Silhouette Deseo Ser.: Vol. 236).Tr. of There Is No Law in Love. (SPA.). 1998. per. 3.50 (*0-373-35236-0*, 1-35236-8) Harlequin Bks.

***Morgan, Raye.** Promoted--To Wife! (Romance Ser.: Bk. 1451). 2000. per. 3.50 (*0-373-19451-X*, 1-19451-3) Silhouette.

Morgan, Raye. Regreso Al Paraiso. (Silhouette Deseo Ser.: No. 148). 1996. per. 3.50 (*0-373-35148-8*, 1-35148-5) Harlequin Bks.

— Secret Dad. 1999. per. 3.75 (*0-373-76199-6*, Harlequin) Harlequin Bks.

— Sorry, the Bride Has Escaped. 1994. per. 2.99 (*0-373-05892-6*, 1-05892-4) Harlequin Bks.

— Wife by Contract. 1997. per. 3.50 (*0-373-76100-7*, 1-76100-6) Silhouette.

— Yesterday's Outlaw. (Desire Ser.). 1994. per. 2.99 (*0-373-05836-5*, 5-05836-7) Silhouette.

Morgan, Raymond F., et al. Reading for Success: A School-to-Work Approach. LC 95-24414. 1995. mass mkt. 22.95 (*0-538-63717-X*) S-W Pub.

Morgan, Raymond F., jt. auth. see Richardson, Judy S.

Morgan, Rebecca. Calming Upset Customers: Staying Effective During Unpleasant Situations. rev. ed. Hicks, Tony, ed. LC 95-83070. (Fifty-Minute Ser.). (Illus.). 79p. (Orig.). 1996. pap. 10.95 (*1-56052-384-0*) Crisp Pubns.

— Professional Selling: Practical Secrets for Successful Sales. Crisp, Michael G., ed. LC 87-72479. (Fifty-Minute Ser.). (Illus.). 91p. (Orig.). 1988. pap. 10.95 (*0-931961-42-4*) Crisp Pubns.

Morgan, Rebecca, ed. Ghost Ranch & Friends: A Cookbook. 2nd rev. ed. (Illus.). 400p. 1996. 15.00 (*0-9652025-0-X*) Ghost Ranch.

***Morgan, Rebecca & Braly, Ken, eds.** Speaking Successfully: 1001 Tips for Thriving in the Speaking Business. 193p. 1999. pap. 59.00 (*1-930039-00-X*) Morgan Seminar.

Morgan, Rebecca L. Life's Lessons: Insights & Information for a Richer Life. 1997. pap. 9.95 (*0-9660740-1-7*) Morgan Seminar.

— TurboTime: Maximizing Your Results Through Technology. 68p. 1996. pap. 19.95 (*0-9660740-0-9*) Morgan Seminar.

Morgan, Rhea V. Handbook of Small Animal Practice. LC 87-16821. 1281p. reprint ed. pap. 200.00 (*0-7837-2592-2*, 204275500006) Bks Demand.

— Handbook of Small Animal Practice. 3rd ed. LC 96-45945. (Illus.). 1210p. (C). 1997. text 149.00 (*0-7216-3329-3*) Harcourt.

Morgan, Rhodri. Cardiff-Half & Half a Capital. 80p. 1994. pap. 30.00 (*1-85902-112-3*, Pub. by Gomer Pr) St Mut.

— M. P. Cardiff - Half & Half a Capital. Stephens, Meic, ed. (Changing Wales Ser.). 80p. 1998. pap. 12.95 (*0-8464-4744-4*) Beekman Pubs.

Morgan, Richard. Bibliography of the Writings of Kenneth Patchen. 174p. 25.00 (*0-614-09422-4*) Appel.

***Morgan, Richard.** Fire in the Soul: A Prayerbook for the Later Years. Williams, Karen F., ed. LC 99-34605. 160p. 2000. pap. 12.00 (*0-8358-0879-3*) Upper Room Bks.

Morgan, Richard. Kenneth Patchen: An Annotated Descriptive Bibliography. 1978. 25.00 (*0-911858-36-9*) Appel.

***Morgan, Richard.** Sailing Away. 136p. 2000. pap. write for info. (*0-9668612-4-8*, Pub. by Lost Horse) SPD-Small Pr Dist.

Morgan, Richard, ed. see Patchen, Kenneth.

Morgan, Richard G., ed. Kenneth Patchen: A Collection of Essays. LC 77-78319. (Studies in Modern Literature: No. 2). (Illus.). 1977. lib. bdg. 29.50 (*0-404-16005-0*) AMS Pr.

Morgan, Richard J. A Guide to Historic Missions & Churches of the Arizona-Sonora Borderlands. LC 95-80598. (Illus.). 128p. 1995. per. 25.95 (*0-9648706-0-6*) Advent In Educ.

Morgan, Richard L. Autumn Wisdom: A Book of Readings. LC 95-60920. 192p. 1995. pap. 10.00 (*0-8358-0745-2*) Upper Room Bks.

— Beyond Retirement: Toward a Redirected Life. (Older Adult Issues Ser.). 50p. 1999. pap. 4.50 (*0-664-50083-8*) Geneva Press.

— From Grim to Green Pastures: Meditations for the Sick & Their Caregivers. LC 94-60662. 192p. 10.00 (*0-8358-0708-8*) Upper Room Bks.

— I Never Found That Rocking Chair: God's Call at Retirement. LC 92-61442. 144p. 1993. pap. 10.00 (*0-8358-0663-4*) Upper Room Bks.

— No Wrinkles on the Soul: A Book of Readings for Older Adults. 1990. pap. 9.95 (*0-687-60809-0*) Abingdon.

— No Wrinkles on the Soul: A Book of Readings for Older Adults. LC 89-51765. 1990. pap. text 10.00 (*0-8358-0610-3*) Upper Room Bks.

— Remembering Your Story: Leader's Guide. 48p. 1997. pap. 5.00 (*0-8358-0797-5*) Upper Room Bks.

— Remembering Your Story: Spiritual Autobiography. LC 96-5058. 160p. 1996. pap. 11.00 (*0-8358-0781-9*, UR781) Upper Room Bks.

— Saving Our Stories: A Legacy We Leave. (Older Adult Issues Ser.). 50p. 1999. pap. 4.50 (*0-664-50082-X*) Geneva Press.

— With Faces to the Evening Sun: Faith Stories from the Nursing Home. large type ed. Williams, Karen, ed. LC 97-33189. 192p. 1998. pap. 12.00 (*0-8358-0826-2*, UR826) Upper Room Bks.

Morgan, Robert. The Anger in Ernest & Ernestine. LC 90-214659. 72p. 1997. pap. text 9.95 (*0-88754-492-4*) Playwrights.

— The Balm of Gilead Tree: New & Selected Stories. LC 99-73466. 344p. 1999. pap. 17.95 (*0-917788-73-7*) Gnomon Pr.

— The Blue Valleys: A Collection of Stories. 176p. 1989. 15.95 (*0-934601-71-2*) Peachtree Pubs.

***Morgan, Robert.** The Blue Valleys: A Collection of Stories. 176p. 2000. per. 12.00 (*0-7432-0422-0*) Scribner.

Morgan, Robert. The Cadet Jumps into the Water. 1987. 4.50 (*0-614-18206-9*) Visual Studies.

***Morgan, Robert.** Gap Creek: The Story of a Marriage. LC 99-34995. 324p. 1999. 22.95 (*1-56512-242-9*, 72242) Algonquin Bks.

— Gap Creek: The Story of a Marriage. LC 99-34995. 324p. 2000. 22.95 (*1-56512-296-8*) Algonquin Bks.

— Gap Creek: The Story of a Marriage. 2000. pap. 12.00 (*0-7432-0363-1*) S&S Trade.

— Gap Creek: The Story of a Marriage. large type ed. LC 00-23380. (Basic Ser.). 528p. 2000. 30.95 (*0-7862-2545-9*) Thorndike Pr.

— Gap Creek: The Story of a Marriage. large type ed. LC 00-23380. (Basic Ser.). 2001. pap. 28.95 (*0-7862-2546-7*) Thorndike Pr.

Morgan, Robert. Good Measure: Essays, Interviews & Notes on Poetry. LC 92-34860. 192p. 1993. text 35.00 (*0-8071-1798-6*) La State U Pr.

— Groundwork. LC 79-55810. 1979. 18.50 (*0-917788-22-2*); pap. 12.50 (*0-917788-21-4*) Gnomon Pr.

— The Hinterlands. LC 99-12856. 356p. 1999. reprint ed. pap. 17.95 (*0-89587-178-5*) Blair.

— Land Diving: New Poems. LC 76-28168. viii, 70p. 1977. pap. 6.95 (*0-8071-0274-1*) La State U Pr.

***Morgan, Robert.** The Mountains Won't Remember Us: And Other Stories. 2000. pap. 12.00 (*0-7432-0421-2*, Scribner Pap Fic) S&S Trade Pap.

Morgan, Robert. The Mountains Won't Remember Us & Other Stories. 256p. 1992. 15.95 (*1-56145-049-9*) Peachtree Pubs.

— My Lamp Still Burns. 141p. (C). 1981. text 39.00 (*0-85088-504-3*, Pub. by Gomer Pr) St Mut.

— The Only Thing to Fear. 256p. 1994. mass mkt. 4.99 (*0-425-14468-2*, Prime Crime) Berkley Pub.

— Red Owl. 88p. (C). 1972. pap. 2.00 (*0-393-04136-0*) Norton.

— Romans. (New Testament Guides Ser.: No. 6). 164p. 1995. pap. 12.50 (*1-85075-739-9*, Pub. by Sheffield Acad) CUP Services.

— Sigodlin: Poems. LC 89-30431. (Wesleyan Poetry Ser.). 72p. 1990. pap. 12.95 (*0-8195-1180-3*, Wesleyan Univ Pr) U Pr of New Eng.

— Some Things Come Back. 256p. (Orig.). 1995. mass mkt. 4.99 (*0-425-14690-1*, Prime Crime) Berkley Pub.

— Source Readings Vol. 7: 20th Century. rev. ed. LC 98-106574. Vol. 7. (C). 1997. pap. text 21.75 (*0-393-96700-X*) Norton.

— Strizhov. (Illus.). 228p. 1998. write for info. (*0-9662641-0-X*) Global Curiosity.

***Morgan, Robert.** Topsoil Road: Poems. 64p. 2000. 22.50 (*0-8071-2612-8*); pap. 14.95 (*0-8071-2613-6*) La State U Pr.

Morgan, Robert. The Truest Pleasure. 1998. pap. 11.95 (*1-56512-222-4*) Algonquin Bks.

— Wild Peavines. 32p. (Orig.). 1996. pap. 10.00 (*0-917788-63-X*) Gnomon Pr.

Morgan, Robert A., jt. ed. see Choquette, Kent D.

Morgan, Robert B., jt. ed. see Berutti, Alfred.

Morgan, Robert C. Between Modernism & Conceptual Art: A Critical Response. LC 97-8174. 183p. 1997. 33.00 (*0-7864-0332-2*) McFarland & Co.

— Commentaries on the New Media Arts: Fluxus & Conceptual, Artists' Books, MailArt, Correspondence Art, Audio & Video Art. 64p. (Orig.). 1992. pap. 9.95 (*0-9635042-0-7*) Umbrella Assocs.

— Concept Decoratif Anti-Formalist Art of the Seventies. (Illus.). 28p. (Orig.). 1990. pap. 10.00 (*0-9624615-5-5*) Nahan Editions.

— Conceptual Art: An American Perspective. LC 93-45387. (Illus.). 216p. 1994. lib. bdg. 39.95 (*0-89950-950-9*) McFarland & Co.

— Dorothea Tanning "Messages" (Illus.). 24p. 1989. pap. write for info. (*0-9624615-7-1*) Nahan Editions.

— The End of the Art World. LC 98-72760. (Aesthetics Today Ser.). (Illus.). 256p. (Orig.). 1999. pap. 18.95 (*1-58115-010-5*) Allworth Pr.

***Morgan, Robert C.** Gary Hill. LC 00-21626. (PAJ Bks.). 384p. 2000. 48.00 (*0-8018-6401-1*) Johns Hopkins.

Morgan, Robert C. Lift High the Cross. LC 94-40486. 144p. (Orig.). 1995. pap. 11.95 (*0-687-21851-9*) Abingdon.

— Nancy Grossman, Ariane Lopez-Huici, Aura Rosenberg, Carolee Schneemann, Joan Semmel. (Illus.). 7p. 1989. pap. 2.00 (*0-9624615-6-3*) Nahan Editions.

Morgan, Robert C., intro. Franz Erhard Walther. (Illus.). 32p. (Orig.). 1988. pap. 12.00 (*0-929687-00-0*) E & C Zilkha Gal.

Morgan, Robert C., jt. auth. see Carmean, E. A., Jr.

Morgan, Robert C., jt. auth. see Hill, Gary.

Morgan, Robert F. The Adult Growth Examination: Test Manual for Measuring Body Age. 78p. 1994. student ed. 55.00 (*1-885679-00-9*) Morgan Fnd Pubs.

— Effective Verbal Adaptation (EVA) Test Manual for Personnel Selection & Screening: Executive & Professional Screening by Structured Scored Group Test Forms A&B. 70p. 1994. 85.00 (*1-885679-01-7*) Morgan Fnd Pubs.

— The Partners: A Three Act Play. 20p. (J). (gr. 6). 1994. pap. 20.00 (*1-885679-05-X*) Morgan Fnd Pubs.

— Uncas Slattery: A Two Act Play. 90p. 1994. pap. 34.00 (*1-885679-07-6*) Morgan Fnd Pubs.

Morgan, Robert F., ed. Iatrogenics in Professional Practice & Education: A Handbook - When Helping Hurts. 466p. 1994. pap. 30.00 (*1-885679-04-1*) Morgan Fnd Pubs.

Morgan, Robert F. & Wilson, Jane. Growing Younger - How to Measure & Change Your Body's Age: The Millenial Edition. rev. ed. (Illus.). 252p. 1999. pap. 74.00 (*1-885679-09-2*) Morgan Fnd Pubs.

Morgan, Robert F., ed. see Cooper, Linn, et al.

Morgan, Robert F., ed. see Roueche, Berton, et al.

Morgan, Robert J. Beyond Reasonable Doubt: Evidence for the Truth of Christianity. 96p. 1997. pap. text 9.95 (*0-910566-70-4*) Evang Trg Assn.

Beyond Reasonable Doubt: Evidence for the Truth of Christianity. (Illus.). 90p. 1997. ring bd. 24.95 (*0-910566-71-2*) Evang Trg Assn.

— From This Verse: 365 Scriptures That Changed the World. LC 98-15633. 1998. 14.99 (*0-7852-1393-7*) Nelson.

— James Madison on the Constitution & the Bill of Rights, 48. LC 88-10243. (Contributions in Legal Studies: No. 48). 235p. 1988. 57.95 (*0-313-26394-9*, MJM/, Greenwood Pr) Greenwood.

— On This Day: 365 Inspiring Stories about Saints, Martyrs & Heroes. LC 97-8956. 384p. 1997. 14.99 (*0-7852-1162-4*) Nelson.

— Tiny Talks: A Book of Devotions for Small Children. (Illus.). 160p. (J). (ps-2). 1996. 10.99 (*0-7852-7562-2*) Nelson.

***Morgan, Robert J.** Treasury of Stories, Illustrations & Quotes from A to Z. (Illus.). 544p. 2000. pap. 19.99 (*0-7852-4479-4*) Nelson.

Morgan, Robert M. Ten Thousand Goodbyes: Lifetime Reflections of a Traveling Man. LC 97-75415. (Illus.). 176p. 1997. pap. 17.95 (*0-9633818-9-X*) Premiere Edits.

— Water & the Land: A History of Irrigation in America. Shank, Bruce M., ed. (Illus.). 200p. 1993. 36.95 (*0-935030-02-6*) Irrigation.

Morgan, Robert P. Anthology of Twentieth Century Music. LC 91-24904. (C). 1992. pap. text 43.25 (*0-393-95284-3*) Norton.

Morgan, Robert P. & Barton, John. Biblical Interpretation. 352p. (C). 1988. pap. text 21.00 (*0-19-213257-1*) OUP.

Morgan, Robert P., jt. auth. see Norton Staff.

Morgan, Robert P., ed. see Cone, Edward T.

Morgan, Roberta, ed. see Despierres, G.

Morgan, Robin. Anatomy of Freedom: Feminism in Four Dimensions. 2nd ed. 1994. pap. 10.95 (*0-393-31161-9*) Norton.

— The Anatomy of Freedom: Feminism in Four Dimensions. 2nd ed. 1995. 21.50 (*0-8446-6853-2*) Peter Smith.

M

An Asterisk (*) at the beginning of an entry indicates that the title is appearing for the first time.

Morgan, Robin. Hot January. pap. 12.00 (*0-393-32106-1*) Norton.
— Hot January. LC 99-25137. 128p. 1999. text 22.50 (*0-393-04801-2*) Norton.
Morgan, Robin. The Mer-Child: A Legend for Children & Other Adults. LC 91-3246. (Illus.). 64p. (YA). 1991. 8.95 (*1-55861-054-5*) Feminist Pr.
— The Mer-Child: A Legend for Children & Other Adults. LC 91-3246. (Illus.). 64p. (YA). (gr. 3 up). 1991. 17.95 (*1-55861-053-7*) Feminist Pr.
***Morgan, Robin.** Saturday's Child: A Memoir. 416p. 2000. 27.95 (*0-393-05015-7*) Norton.
— Sisterhood Is Powerful: An Anthology of Writings from the Women's Liberation Movement. 2000. pap. 19.95 (*1-55861-247-5*) Feminist Pr.
Morgan, Robin. Upstairs in the Garden. 1991. pap. 9.95 (*0-393-30760-3*) Norton.
Morgan, Robin, ed. Sisterhood Is Global: The International Women's Movement Anthology. LC 96-38456. 832p. 1996. pap. 24.95 (*1-55861-160-6*) Feminist Pr.
Morgan, Robin & Perry, George, eds. The Book of Film Biographies: A Pictorial Guide. LC 97-37134. (Illus.). 256p. (Orig.). 1997. pap. 17.95 (*0-88064-185-1*) Fromm Intl Pub.
Morgan, Robin K. Case Studies in Child & Adolescent Psychopathology. LC 98-27727. 123p. 1998. pap. text 23.20 (*0-13-079604-2*) P-H.
Morgan, Rockie J., jt. auth. see Holt, William H.
Morgan, Rod. Prisons: The Politics of Reform. (Conflict & Change in Britain Ser.: A New Audit Ser.). (C). 1997. pap. 25.00 (*0-485-80108-6*, Pub. by Athlone Pr); text 65.00 (*0-485-80008-X*, Pub. by Athlone Pr) Humanities.
***Morgan, Rod & Evans, Malcolm E.** Protecting Prisoners: The Standards of the European Committee for the Prevention of Torture in Context. LC 99-16151. 320p. 1999. text 90.00 (*0-19-829821-8*) OUP.
Morgan, Rod & Newburn, Tim. The Future of Policing. LC 96-53053. (Illus.). 232p. 1997. text 52.00 (*0-19-876441-3*) OUP.
Morgan, Rod, jt. auth. see Evans, Malcolm.
Morgan, Rod, jt. ed. see Clarkson, C. M.
Morgan, Rodwell. Meet Corn Island. Meet Corn Island: The History of Corn Island in Relation to the Ebenezer Baptist Church. LC 97-104194. 214p. (Orig.). 1996. pap. 14.95 (*1-57502-314-8*, P01063) Morris Pubng.
Morgan, Roger & Silvestri, Stefano. Moderates & Conservatives in Western Europe. LC 83-5662. 288p. 1983. 37.50 (*0-8386-3201-7*) Fairleigh Dickinson.
Morgan, Ronald B. & Smith, Jack E. Staffing the New Workplace: Selecting & Promoting for Quality Improvement. (Illus.). 540p. 1996. text 40.00 (*0-87389-361-1*, H0865) ASQ Qual Pr.
Morgan, Ronald E. Southern Thunder: A Story of the Civil War, 1861-1865. LC 95-71272. 288p. (Orig.). 1996. pap. 12.00 (*1-884570-42-9*) Research Triangle.
Morgan, Ronald E., jt. auth. see Iler, Don C.
Morgan, Ronald R., et al. Enhancing Learning in Training & Adult Education. LC 95-43763. 384p. 1998. 65.00 (*0-275-95016-6*, Praeger Pubs); pap. 24.95 (*0-275-95911-2*, Praeger Pubs) Greenwood.
***Morgan, Ronald R., et al.** Rethinking Creativity. (Fastback Ser.: No. 458). 44p. 2000. pap. 3.00 (*0-87367-658-0*) Phi Delta Kappa.
Morgan, Ronald R., jt. auth. see Miller, Steven I.
Morgan, Rosemarie. Far from the Madding Crowd. 496p. 2000. pap. 7.95 (*0-14-043521-2*) Viking Penguin.
— Women & Sexuality in the Novels of Thomas Hardy. 224p. 1988. text 45.00 (*0-415-00268-0*) Routledge.
***Morgan, Rosemarie, ed.** The Hardy Review Occasional Series, Vol. 1. 40p. 1999. pap. 15.00 (*0-9669176-1-8*) T Hardy Assoc.
Morgan, Rosemarie A., ed. The Hardy Review, Vol. 1. 2nd ed. (Illus.). 160p. 1999. 25.00 (*0-9669176-0-X*, 199) T Hardy Assoc.
Morgan, Rosemary. A Hunger for the Flying. 1998. pap. 14.95 (*1-886094-89-6*) R Morgan.
Morgan, Rosie, et al, eds. The Heritage of Coosa County, Alabama. (Heritage of Alabama Ser.: No. 19). (Illus.). 300p. 1999. 55.00 (*1-891647-32-6*) Herit Pub Consult.
Morgan, Rowland. In the Next Three Seconds. LC 96-38480. (Illus.). 32p. (J). (gr. 3-7). 1997. 14.99 (*0-525-67551-5*, Dutton Child) Peng Put Young Read.
***Morgan, Rowland.** In the Next Three Seconds: Predictions for the Millennium. (Illus.). (J). 1999. 12.34 (*0-606-18411-2*) Turtleback.
Morgan, Rowland. In the Next Three Seconds: Predictions for the Millennium, Vol. 1. 1999. pap. 6.99 (*0-14-056624-4*, PuffinBks) Peng Put Young Read.
Morgan, Roy, jt. auth. see Peters, Ellis.
Morgan, Roy, ed. see Access Innovations, Inc. Staff.
Morgan, Royston P. Soil Conservation Problems & Prospects. 576p. (C). 1992. write for info. (*0-7855-2628-5*, Pub. by Intl Bk Distr) St Mut.
Morgan, Royston P. Soil Erosion & Conservation. 2nd ed. 198p. (C). 1996. pap. 50.00 (*0-582-24492-7*) Addison-Wesley.
Morgan, Royston P., jt. ed. see Chisci, G.
Morgan, Royston P., ed. see International Conference on Soil Conservation & Ma.
Morgan, S. Helping Relationships in Mental Health. (Illus.). 216p. (Orig.). (C). 1996. pap. text 39.95 (*1-56593-437-7*, 1106) Singular Publishing.
Morgan, S. J., jt. auth. see Darling, D. C.
Morgan, S. Keith & Seaton, Anthony. Occupational Lung Diseases. 3rd ed. LC 94-19777. (Illus.). 624p. 1995. text 97.00 (*0-7216-4671-9*, W B Saunders Co) Harcrt Hlth Sci Grp.
Morgan, Salley. Energy. (Illus.). (J). 1997. write for info. (*0-237-51774-4*) EVN1 UK.
Morgan, Sally. Acid Rain. LC 98-52903. 1999. 20.25 (*0-531-14567-0*) Watts.
— Animals & Their World. (Young Discoverers Ser.). (Illus.). 32p. (J). (gr. 1-4). 1995. lib. bdg. 13.90 (*0-7534-5035-6*) LKC.
— Animals & Their World. (Young Discoverers Ser.). (Illus.). 32p. (J). (gr. 1-4). 1996. pap. 7.95 (*0-7534-5034-8*) LKC.
***Morgan, Sally.** Animals as Friends. (Animals That Help Us Ser.). (Illus.). (J). 2000. pap. 6.95 (*0-531-15403-3*) Watts.
Morgan, Sally. Animals as Friends: A Head Keeper Remembers London Zoo. LC 99-12039. 2000. 20.00 (*0-531-14563-8*) Watts.
— Animals Helping with Special Needs LC 99-11430. (Help Us Ser.). 2000. 20.00 (*0-531-14564-6*) Watts.
— Animals on the Farm LC 99-14188. (Animals that Help Us Ser.). 2000. 20.00 (*0-531-14565-4*) Watts.
***Morgan, Sally.** Animals on the Farm. (Animals That Help Us Ser.). (Illus.). (J). 2000. pap. 6.95 (*0-531-15407-6*) Watts.
Morgan, Sally. Butterflies, Bugs, & Worms. LC 96-963. (Young Discoverers Ser.). (Illus.). 32p. (J). (gr. 1-4). 1996. 13.90 (*0-7534-5037-2*); pap. 6.95 (*0-7534-5036-4*) LKC.
***Morgan, Sally.** Care about Education: A Joint Training Curriculum for Supporting Children in Public. 112p. 2000. spiral bd. 67.50 (*1-900990-46-6*, Pub. by Natl Childrens Bur) Paul & Co Pubs.
Morgan, Sally. Changing Climate. LC 99-15833. 1999. 20.25 (*0-531-14568-9*) Watts.
— Circles & Spheres. (World of Shapes Ser.). (Illus.). 32p. (J). 1994. lib. bdg. 21.40 (*1-56847-235-8*) Raintree Steck-V.
Morgan, Sally. Colour & Communication. (J). 1993. write for info. (*0-237-51274-2*) EVN1 UK.
— Designs in Science Set. 1994. 118.65 (*0-8160-3180-0*) Facts on File.
Morgan, Sally. Ecology & Environment: The Cycles of Life. (New Encyclopedia of Science Ser.). (Illus.). 160p. 1995. 39.95 (*0-19-521140-5*) OUP.
***Morgan, Sally.** Energy. (Future Tech Ser.). (J). 1999. 15.95 (*1-929298-42-0*, Pub. by Thameside Pr) Smart Apple.
Morgan, Sally. Flowers, Trees, & Fruits. LC 96-964. (Young Discoverers Ser.). (Illus.). 32p. (J). (gr. 1-4). 1996. pap. 7.95 (*0-7534-5032-1*) LKC.
— Homes & Cities: Living for the Future. LC 97-7788. (Living for the Future Ser.). 32p. (J). 1998. 18.00 (*0-531-14478-X*) Watts.
— The Human Body. LC 96-14811. (Young Discoverers Ser.). (Illus.). 32p. (J). (gr. 1-4). 1996. 13.90 (*0-7534-5031-3*); pap. 7.95 (*0-7534-5030-5*) LKC.
— Ozone Hole LC 98-51696. (Earth Watch Ser.). 1999. 20.25 (*0-531-14569-7*) Watts.
***Morgan, Sally.** Read about Hurricanes. (Read about Ser.). (Illus.). 32p. (J). (gr. 2-4). 2000. 17.90 (*0-7613-1174-2*, Copper Beech Bks) Millbrook Pr.
Morgan, Sally. Saving the Rain Forest. LC 98-49133. (Earth Watch Ser.). (J). (gr. 3-7). 1999. lib. bdg. 20.25 (*0-531-14570-0*) Watts.
— Spirals. (World of Shapes Ser.). (Illus.). 32p. (J). 1995. lib. bdg. 21.40 (*1-56847-278-1*) Raintree Steck-V.
— Squares & Cubes. (World of Shapes Ser.). (Illus.). 32p. (J). 1994. lib. bdg. 21.40 (*1-56847-234-X*) Raintree Steck-V.
— Tourism in Balance. LC 97-6479. (Living for the Future Ser.). 32p. (J). 1998. 18.50 (*0-531-14476-3*) Watts.
— Triangles & Pyramids. LC 94-31055. (World of Shapes Ser.). (Illus.). 32p. (J). 1995. lib. bdg. 21.40 (*1-56847-277-3*) Raintree Steck-V.
Morgan, Sally & Bancroft, Bronwyn. In Your Dreams. LC 99-204635. (Illus.). 32p. 1997. pap. 9.95 (*1-86368-201-5*, Pub. by Fremantle Arts) Intl Spec Bk.
— Just a Little Brown Dog. LC 97-190474. (Illus.). 32p. 1997. pap. 9.95 (*1-86368-173-6*, Pub. by Fremantle Arts) Intl Spec Bk.
Morgan, Sally & Lalor, Paule. World Food. LC 97-7255. (Living for the Future Ser.). 32p. (J). 1998. 18.50 (*0-531-14477-1*) Watts.
Morgan, Sally & Morgan, Adrian. Colour in Art & Advertising. (Wonderful World of Colour Ser.). (Illus.). 48p. (YA). (gr. 7-10). 1994. write for info. (*0-237-51277-7*) EVN1 UK.
— Materials. LC 93-31722. (Designs in Science Ser.). (Illus.). 48p. (J). (gr. 4-9). 1994. 16.95 (*0-8160-2985-7*) Facts on File.
— Movement. LC 93-20162. (Illus.). 48p. (J). (gr. 4-9). 1993. 16.95 (*0-8160-2979-2*) Facts on File.
— Structures. LC 93-20164. (Illus.). 48p. (J). (gr. 4-9). 1993. 16.95 (*0-8160-2983-0*) Facts on File.
— Technology in Action. (Designs in Science Ser.). (Illus.). 48p. (YA). (gr. 5-9). 1994. 16.95 (*0-8160-3126-6*) Facts on File.
— Using Energy. LC 93-20407. (Designs in Science Ser.). (Illus.). 48p. (J). (gr. 4-9). 1993. 16.95 (*0-8160-2984-9*) Facts on File.
— Using Light. LC 93-21535. (Designs in Science Ser.). (Illus.). 48p. (J). (gr. 4-9). 1993. 16.95 (*0-8160-2980-6*) Facts on File.
— Using Sound. LC 93-31720. (Designs in Science Ser.). (Illus.). 48p. (J). (gr. 4-9). 1994. 16.95 (*0-8160-2981-4*) Facts on File.
— Water. LC 93-31721. (Designs in Science Ser.). (Illus.). 48p. (J). (gr. 4-9). 1994. 16.95 (*0-8160-2982-2*) Facts on File.
Morgan, Sally, jt. auth. see Harlow, Rosie.
Morgan, Sally, ed. see Montgomery, L. M.
Morgan, Sam B. & Okwumabua, Theresa M., eds. Child & Adolescent Disorders: Developmental & Health Psychology Perspectives. 480p. 1990. 99.95 (*0-8058-0514-1*) L Erlbaum Assocs.
Morgan, Sampson. Clean Culture: The New Soil Science. Bernard, Raymond W., ed. 1996. spiral bd. 10.00 (*0-7873-1005-0*) Hlth Research.
— How to Make the Most of the Land. 100p. 1974. reprint ed. spiral bd. 11.50 (*0-7873-0624-X*) Hlth Research.
Morgan, Sandy. We Did it in Mount Dora: A Cook Book by Cal & Maria Lawton. 300p. 1998. reprint ed. 18.95 (*0-9668283-0-5*, 24346) C & M Lawton.
Morgan, Sarah. Bread. (Illus.). 120p. 1975. 19.95 (*0-88426-042-9*) Encino Pr.
— The Civil War Diary of Sarah Morgan. East, Charles, ed. LC 91-2161. 688p. 1991. 34.95 (*0-8203-1357-2*) U of Ga Pr.
— Dining with the Cattle Barrons. 1981. 13.95 (*0-87244-064-8*) Texian.
— Sarah Morgan: The Civil War Diary of a Southern Woman. East, Charles, ed. LC 92-21798. (Illus.). 672p. 1992. pap. 16.00 (*0-671-78503-6*, Touchstone) S&S Trade Pap.
Morgan, Sarah J. & Okerstrom, Dennis. The Endangered Earth: Readings for Writers: Examination Copy. 496p. (C). 1991. pap. text. write for info. (*0-205-13496-3*, H3496-0) Allyn.
Morgan, Sarah J., jt. auth. see Okerstrom, Dennis.
Morgan, Sarah L., ed. see Weinsier, Roland L.
***Morgan, Scott E., ed.** Tennessee in Perspective 2000. 26p. 2000. spiral bd. 19.00 (*0-7401-0291-5*) Morgan Quitno Corp.
— Virginia in Perspective 2000. 26p. 2000. spiral bd. 19.00 (*0-7401-0295-8*) Morgan Quitno Corp.
— West Virginia in Perspective 2000. 26p. 2000. spiral bd. 19.00 (*0-7401-0296-6*) Morgan Quitno Corp.
Morgan, Scott E., jt. ed. see Morgan, Kathleen O'Leary.
Morgan, Scott M. & Colson, Elizabeth, eds. People in Upheaval. LC 86-33354. 228p. 1987. 19.50 (*0-934733-17-1*); pap. 14.50 (*0-934733-16-3*) CMS.
Morgan, Seth A. Manual for the Laboratory Assistant. pap. 4.95 (*0-89741-007-6*) Gila River.
Morgan, Sharon. Land Settlement in Early Tasmania: Creating an Antipodean England. (Studies in Australian History). 224p. (C). 1992. text 59.95 (*0-521-39031-1*) Cambridge U Pr.
Morgan, Sharon Drew. Selling with Integrity: Reinventing Sales Through Collaboration, Respect, & Serving. (Illus.). 225p. 1997. 24.95 (*1-57675-017-5*) Berrett-Koehler.
Morgan, Sharon R. At Risk Youth in Crises: A Team Approach in the Schools. 2nd ed. LC 93-41948. 268p. (C). 1994. pap. text 31.00 (*0-89079-574-6*, 6719) PRO-ED.
— Children in Crisis: A Team Approach in the Schools. LC 90-20860. 253p. (Orig.). (C). 1985. pap. text 28.00 (*0-89079-289-5*, 1747) PRO-ED.
Morgan, Sharon R. & Reinhart, Jo A. Interventions for Students with Emotional Disorders. LC 89-29103. 212p. (C). 1991. text 36.00 (*0-89079-296-8*, 1592) PRO-ED.
Morgan, Sherman F. The Aviation Humor of 1987. LC 87-91286. 128p. (Orig.). (C). 1987. pap. 5.95 (*0-944792-00-6*) Pendragon TX.
— Classic Aviation Humor Bk. II. 1989. pap. 5.95 (*0-944792-01-4*) Pendragon TX.
— Good Sticks. LC 89-92016. 364p. 1991. 19.95 (*0-944792-02-2*) Pendragon TX.
— Old Planes, Young Men & Red Wooden Shoes. 227p. (Orig.). 1993. pap. 10.00 (*0-944792-26-X*) Pendragon TX.
— Sherm Morgan's Classic Aviation Humor, Bk. III. 1992. pap. 6.95 (*1-881001-06-7*) Pendragon TX.
Morgan, Speer. The Assemblers. 304p. 1989. reprint ed. pap. 3.95 (*0-373-97098-6*) Harlequin Bks.
Morgan, Speer. The Freshour Cylinders. LC 98-26668. 245p. 1998. 23.00 (*1-878448-84-6*) MacMurray & Beck.
***Morgan, Speer.** The Freshour Cylinders. 345p. 2000. pap. 13.00 (*1-878448-99-4*) MacMurray & Beck.
Morgan, Speer, et al. The Best of the Missouri Review: Fiction, 1978-1990. 336p. (Orig.). 1991. pap. 18.95 (*0-8262-0784-7*); text 35.00 (*0-8262-0773-1*) U of Mo Pr.
Morgan, Stacy T. Adventure in the Caribbean. (Ruby Slippers School Ser.: Vol. 1). (Illus.). 8p. (Orig.). (J). (gr. 2-5). 1996. pap. 3.99 (*1-55661-600-7*, Hampshire MN) Bethany Hse.
— The Belgium Book Mystery. (Ruby Slippers School Ser.: Vol. 2). (Illus.). 8p. (Orig.). (J). (gr. 2-5). 1996. pap. 3.99 (*1-55661-601-5*, Hampshire MN) Bethany Hse.
— The British Bear Caper. (Ruby Slippers School Ser.: No. 4). 8p. (J). 1996. pap. 3.99 (*1-55661-603-1*) Bethany Hse.
— The Cuddlers. LC 92-75695. (Illus.). 1993. 12.95 (*0-912500-41-7*) La Leche.
— Escape from Egypt. LC 96-25229. (Ruby Slippers School Ser.: No. 3). 64p. (J). (gr. 2-5). 1996. pap. 3.99 (*1-55661-602-3*) Bethany Hse.
— Journey to Japan, Vol. 5. LC 97-4671. (Ruby Slippers School Ser.). 8p. (J). (gr. 2-5). 1997. pap. 3.99 (*1-55661-604-X*) Bethany Hse.
— New Zealand Shake-Up, Vol. 6. LC 97-4706. (Ruby Slippers School Ser.). 8p. (J). (gr. 2-5). 1997. pap. 3.99 (*1-55661-605-8*) Bethany Hse.
Morgan, Stacy Towle. Ruby Slippers, Vols. 1-6. (Ruby Slippers School Ser.). (J). 1997. pap., boxed set 23.99 (*0-7642-8154-2*, 258154) Bethany Hse.
Morgan Stanley Staff. Internet Advertising Report. (Illus.). 160p. 1997. pap. 18.00 (*0-88730-882-1*, HarpBusn) HarpInfo.
Morgan, Stephanie, tr. see Sellato, Bernard.
Morgan, Stephen H. Touring Eastern Canada. LC 98-67239. (Touring... Ser.). 372p. 1999. pap. 18.95 (*0-8442-1028-5*, 10285) NTC Contemp Pub Co.
Morgan, Stephen L., jt. auth. see Deming, Stanley N.
Morgan, Steve. Performance Assessment in Academic Libraries. LC 94-45209. 224p. 1995. 89.50 (*0-7201-2188-4*) Continuum.
Morgan, Steven & Grunfeld, Jean-Pierre, eds. Inherited Disorders of the Kidney: Investigation & Management. LC 98-21523. (Oxford Clinical Nephrology Ser.). (Illus.). 644p. 1998. text 198.50 (*0-19-262473-3*) OUP.
Morgan, Stuart. Martin Kippenberger: Heavy Madel. (Illus.). 112p. 1992. pap. 35.00 (*1-56466-014-1*) Archer Fields.
Morgan, Stuart, contrib. by. Damien Hirst: No Sense of Absolute Corruption. (Illus.). 126p. 1996. pap. 50.00 (*1-880154-08-0*) Gagosian Gallery.
Morgan, Stuart & Morris, Frances. Rites of Passage: Art for the End of the Century. (Illus.). 136p. 1996. pap. 40.00 (*1-85437-156-8*, Pub. by Tate Gallery) U of Wash Pr.
Morgan, Stuart, jt. auth. see Hunt, Ian.
Morgan, Stuart, jt. contrib. by see Deitch, Jeffrey.
Morgan, Susan. In the Meantime: Character & Perception in Jane Austen's Fiction. LC 79-21357. 220p. reprint ed. pap. 68.20 (*0-608-09483-8*, 205428300005) Bks Demand.
— Martin Munkacsi: An Aperture Monograph. (Illus.). 80p. 1992. 53.00 (*0-89381-516-0*) Aperture.
— Place Matters: Victorian Women's Travel Books on Southeast Asia. 350p. (C). 1996. text 50.00 (*0-8135-2248-X*); pap. text 19.95 (*0-8135-2249-8*) Rutgers U Pr.
Morgan, Susan, jt. auth. see Pryer, Ada.
Morgan, Susan, jt. auth. see Weston, Cole.
Morgan, Susan, ed. see North, Marianne.
Morgan, Susan B. Ladybug. 1989. 4.95 (*0-945603-01-0*) Dinnerman Bks.
— Smooth & Round in the Ground. 1989. 4.95 (*0-945603-04-5*) Dinnerman Bks.
Morgan, Susan K. Geologic Tours of Northern Utah. (Miscellaneous Publication of the Utah Geological Survey Ser.: Vol. 92-1). (Illus.). 98p. (Orig.). 1992. pap. 6.00 (*1-55791-317-X*, MP92-1) Utah Geological Survey.
Morgan, Susanah. The Sorcerer's Confession, Vol. 1. LC 97-76005. 360p. 1998. pap. 14.00 (*0-9661816-0-3*) Meresu Bks.
Morgan, Sydney O. Lady Morgan's Memoirs, 2 vols., Set. LC 76-37705. (Women of Letters Ser.). reprint ed. 145.00 (*0-404-56793-2*) AMS Pr.
— Missionary: An Indian Tale, 3 vols. in 1. LC 80-20308. 208p. 1980. reprint ed. 50.00 (*0-8201-1358-1*) Schol Facsimiles.
— The O'Briens & the O'Flahertys: A National Tale, 4 vols., 2 bks., Set. LC 79-8175. reprint ed. 84.50 (*0-404-62055-8*) AMS Pr.
— O'Donnel: A National Tale, 3 vols., 2 bks., Set. LC 79-8176. reprint ed. 84.50 (*0-404-62060-4*) AMS Pr.
— The Wild Irish Girl: A National Tale. LC 79-8177. reprint ed. 44.50 (*0-404-62064-7*) AMS Pr.
Morgan, T., jt. ed. see Horster, M. F.
Morgan, T. Clifton. Untying the Knot of War: A Bargaining Theory of International Crises. 232p. (C). 1994. text 52.50 (*0-472-10277-X*, 10277) U of Mich Pr.
Morgan, T. J., jt. ed. see Cisneros, C.
Morgan, T. R., jt. auth. see Slater, R. H.
Morgan-Tamosunas, Rikki, jt. ed. see Jordan, Barry.
Morgan-Tamosunas, Rikki, jt. ed. see Jordon, Barry.
Morgan, Ted. Literary Outlaw: The Life & Times of William S. Burroughs. (Illus.). 1990. pap. 12.95 (*0-380-70882-5*, Avon Bks) Morrow Avon.
— Maugham. LC 80-26890. (Touchstone Book Ser.). xxi, 711p. 1981. 9.95 (*0-671-42811-X*) S&S Trade.
— Wilderness at Dawn: The Settling of the North American Continent. 544p. 1994. per. 15.00 (*0-671-88237-6*, Touchstone) S&S Trade Pap.
Morgan, Teresa. Dya son the Farm with Annette & Samuel. (Illus.). 196p. (J). (gr. 3-6). 1987. 8.30 (*0-7399-0082-X*, 2116) Rod & Staff.
Morgan, Teresa. Literate Education in the Hellenistic & Roman Worlds. LC 98-13857. (Cambridge Classical Studies). (Illus.). 382p. (C). 1999. text 64.95 (*0-521-58466-3*) Cambridge U Pr.
Morgan, Terrell A., et al, eds. Language & Language Use: Studies in Spanish. (Illus.). 346p. (Orig.). (C). 1988. pap. text 29.50 (*0-8191-6698-7*); lib. bdg. 52.50 (*0-8191-6697-9*) U Pr of Amer.
Morgan, Terrell A., jt. ed. see Laeufer, Christiane.
***Morgan, Terri.** Gabrielle Reece: Volleyball's Model Athlete. LC 98-32265. 64p. 1999. pap. text 5.95 (*0-8225-9828-0*) Lerner Pub.
— Gabrielle Reece: Volleyball's Model Athlete. LC 98-32265. (Illus.). 80p. (YA). (ps-3). 1999. 21.27 (*0-8225-3667-6*, LernerSports) Lerner Pub.
— Gabrielle Reece: Volleyball's Model Athlete. (Illus.). (J). 1999. 11.30 (*0-606-18819-3*) Turtleback.
Morgan, Terri. Junior Seau: High-Voltage Linebacker. LC 96-13113. (Illus.). 64p. (J). 1997. pap. 5.95 (*0-8225-9746-2*, Lerner Publctns) Lerner Pub.
— Photography: Take Your Best Shot. (Illus.). 72p. (YA). (gr. 5 up). 1991. pap. 8.95 (*0-8225-9605-9*, Lerner Publctns) Lerner Pub.
— Ruthie Bolton-Holifield: Sharpshooting Playmaker. LC 98-27822. 64p. (YA). (gr. 4-9). 1999. 21.27 (*0-8225-3666-8*) Lerner Pub.
— Ruthie Bolton-holifield; Sharpshooting Playmaker, 64p. 1999. pap. text 5.95 (*0-8225-9827-2*) Lerner Pub.
Morgan, Terri & Thaler, Shmuel. Photography: Take Your Best Shot. (Media Workshop Ser.). 80p. (YA). (gr. 5 up). 1991. lib. bdg. 21.27 (*0-8225-2302-7*, Lerner Publctns) Lerner Pub.
— Steve Young: Complete Quarterback. (Achievers Ser.). (Illus.). 64p. 1995. pap. 5.95 (*0-8225-9716-0*, Lerner Publctns) Lerner Pub.

An Asterisk (*) at the beginning of an entry indicates that the title is appearing for the first time.

Morgan, Terri & Thaler, Shmuel. Steve Young: Complete Quarterback. (Achievers Ser.). (J). 1995. lib. bdg. 19.95 (*0-8225-2886-X*, Lerner Publctns) Lerner Pub.

Morgan, Terri & Thaler, Shuel. Chris Mullin: Sure Shot. LC 94-2704. (Achievers Ser.). (Illus.). 64p. (J). (gr. 4-9). 1994. pap. 5.95 (*0-8225-9664-4*, Lerner Publctns); lib. bdg. 19.93 (*0-8225-2882-7*, Lerner Publctns) Lerner Pub.

Morgan, Terri & Thornley, Stew. Junior Seau: High-Voltage Linebacker. LC 96-13113. (J). 1996. 19.93 (*0-8225-2896-7*, Lerner Publctns) Lerner Pub.

Morgan, Terri, tr. see Liu, Yuzeng.

Morgan, Terry, jt. auth. see Shonkwiler, John W.

Morgan, Tesni. Country Matters. (Orig.). 1997. mass mkt. 5.95 (*0-352-33174-7*, Pub. by BLA4) London Brdge.

— Dangerous Consequences. (Orig.). 1997. mass mkt. 5.95 (*0-352-33185-2*, Pub. by BLA4) London Brdge.

— Masque of Passion. 1998. mass mkt. 5.95 (*0-352-33259-X*, Pub. by BLA4) London Brdge.

— The Ties That Bind. 1999. mass mkt. 6.95 (*0-352-33438-X*) London Brdge.

Morgan, Thais, jt. ed. see Henricksen, Bruce.

Morgan, Thais E., ed. Men Writing the Feminine: Literature, Theory, & the Question of Genders. LC 93-43224. 207p. (C). 1994. text 49.50 (*0-7914-1993-2*); pap. text 16.95 (*0-7914-1994-0*) State U NY Pr.

— Victorian Sages & Cultural Discourse: Renegotiating Gender & Power. LC 90-30977. (Illus.). 320p. (C). 1990. text 45.00 (*0-8135-1600-5*); pap. text 18.00 (*0-8135-1601-3*) Rutgers U Pr.

Morgan, Thais E., tr. see Genette, Gerard.

Morgan, Theodore & Spoelstra, Nyle, eds. Economic Interdependence in Southeast Asia: Proceedings of a Conference Held at Bangkok, 1967. LC 68-9021. 442p. reprint ed. pap. 137.10 (*0-608-13889-4*, 202372500033) Bks Demand.

Morgan, Theron, ed. see Taylor, Lynn E.

***Morgan, Thomas.** Handbook of the Origin of Place-Names in Wales & Monmouthshire. xxii,224p. 2000. cd-rom 19.95 (*1-58211-234-7*) Quintin Pub RI.

Morgan, Thomas B. Speaking of Cardinals. LC 70-134119. (Essay Index Reprint Ser.). 1977. 20.95 (*0-8369-2002-3*) Ayer.

Morgan, Thomas D. Antitrust Law, Teacher's Manual to Accompany Cases & Materials on. (American Casebook Ser.). 150p. 1994. pap. text. write for info. (*0-314-04199-0*) West Pub.

— Cases & Materials on Antitrust Law & Its Origins. LC 93-50856. (American Casebook Ser.). 915p. (C). 1994. 60.00 (*0-314-03343-2*) West Pub.

— 1996 Selected Standards on Professional Responsibility Including California Rules. Rotunda, Ronald D., ed. 623p. 1995. 17.95 (*1-56662-336-7*) West Pub.

Morgan, Thomas D. & Rotunda, Ronald D. 1998 Selected Standards on Professional Responsibility Including California Rules. 648p. 1997. pap. write for info. (*1-56662-515-7*) Foundation Pr.

— Problems & Materials on Professional Responsibility: Problems & Materials. 6th ed. (University Casebook Ser.). 598p. 1995. text 38.50 (*1-56662-254-9*) Foundation Pr.

— Professional Responsibility, Problems & Materials On. 5th ed. 571p. 1990. text 34.50 (*0-88277-861-7*) Foundation Pr.

— Professional Responsibility, Revised Teacher's Manual to Accompany. 5th ed. (University Casebook Ser.). 363p. 1993. pap. text. write for info. (*1-56662-123-2*) Foundation Pr.

— Professional Responsibility, Selected Standards on, 1997. 639p. (C). 1996. pap. text. write for info. (*1-56662-501-7*) Foundation Pr.

— Selected Standards on Professional Responsibility, Including California Rules. 613p. (C). 1994. pap. text 16.95 (*1-56662-250-6*) Foundation Pr.

— Selected Standards on Professional Responsibility, Including California Rules, 1994. 5th ed. 607p. 1991. pap. text. write for info. (*1-56662-141-0*) Foundation Pr.

— Teacher's Manual to Accompany Problems & Materials on Professional Responsibility. 6th ed. (University Casebook Ser.). 340p. 1995. pap. text, teacher ed. write for info. (*1-56662-264-6*) Foundation Pr.

Morgan, Thomas D., et al. Cases & Materials on Economic Regulation of Business: Cases & Materials. 2nd ed. (American Casebook Ser.). 666p. (C). 1985. text 47.00 (*0-314-89739-9*) West Pub.

Morgan, Thomas L. & Barlow, William. From Cakewalks to Concert Halls: An Illustrated History of African American Popular Music from 1895 to 1930. LC 92-8996. (Illus.). 132p. 1992. 32.50 (*1-880216-06-X*, Elliott Clark) Black Belt Communs.

— From Cakewalks to Concert Halls: An Illustrated History of African American Popular Music from 1895 to 1930. (Illus.). 132p. 1993. reprint ed. pap. 21.95 (*1-880216-17-5*, Elliott Clark) Black Belt Communs.

Morgan, Thomas S. Juvenile Law & Practice. (Illus.). 678p. write for info. (*0-318-59331-9*) West Pub.

Morgan, Thomas S. & Eagles, Charles W. Study Guide, 1. pap. 12.00 (*0-393-97066-3*) Norton.

— Study Guide, 2. pap. 12.00 (*0-393-97068-X*) Norton.

Morgan, Todd. Elvis: His Life in Pictures. (Illus.). 144p. 1997. 19.98 (*0-89660-082-3*, Artabras) Abbeville Pr.

— Elvis: His Life in Pictures. LC 96-40903. (Tiny Folio Ser.). (Illus.). 288p. 1997. pap. 5.95 (*0-7892-0509-2*) Abbeville Pr.

Morgan, Tom. Not of Our Time. Pickup, Ronald, ed. (Illus.). 124p. (Orig.). 1989. pap. text 10.00 (*0-9623094-0-0*) GlenHill Prodns.

— Saints: A Visual Almanac of the Virtuous, Pure, Praiseworthy, & Good. LC 94-7244. (Illus.). 176p. 1994. 16.95 (*0-8118-0549-2*) Chronicle Bks.

— South African Nautical Almanac, 1997. 112p. 1997. pap. 159.95 (*0-949989-66-5*, Pub. by Laurie Norie & Wilson Ltd) St Mut.

Morgan, Tom, ed. Aspects of Complexity in Recent British Music. (Contemporary Music Review Ser.: Vol. 13, Pt. 1). 247p. 1995. pap. text 29.00 (*3-7186-5574-8*, ECU33, Harwood Acad Pubs) Gordon & Breach.

Morgan, Tom & Morgan, Genevieve. The Devil: A Visual Guide to the Demonic, Evil, Scurrilous, & Bad. 176p. 1996. 17.95 (*0-8118-1176-X*) Chronicle Bks.

Morgan, Tracy. Michael's Wife. (Temptation Ser.). 1993. per. 2.99 (*0-373-25530-6*, 1-25530-6) Harlequin Bks.

Morgan, Trevor. Physiology Through Questions. 200p. 1996. pap. text 25.00 (*0-07-470196-7*) McGraw-Hill HPD.

***Morgan, Trevor & McMullen, Bruce.** Regulatory Reform in Argentina's Natural Gas Sector. 80p. 1999. pap. 75.00 (*92-64-17019-7*, 61 1999 02 1 P, Pub. by Org for Econ) OECD.

Morgan, Trudy J. Alex Best & Friends. LC 94-37947. (J). 1994. pap. 5.99 (*0-8280-0849-3*) Review & Herald.

— Facing the Music. LC 95-7755. (YA). (gr. 7-10). 1995. pap. 5.99 (*0-8280-0880-9*) Review & Herald.

— Who Loves Alex Best? LC 93-35925. (J). 1994. pap. 5.99 (*0-8280-0736-5*) Review & Herald.

— Who Loves Alex Best? LC 95-51102. 1996. pap. 5.99 (*0-8280-1063-3*) Review & Herald.

Morgan, Una. The Cricket Match. 16p. 1999. pap. 6.00 (*0-8059-4495-8*) Dorrance.

Morgan, Valerie, jt. auth. see Dunn, Seamus.

Morgan, Vance G. Foundations of Cartesian Ethics. LC 98-54407. 1998. write for info. (*1-57392-291-9*, Humanity Bks) Prometheus Bks.

***Morgan-Vanroyen, Mary & Publications International, Ltd. Editorial Staff.** Little Miss Muffet. LC 98-176778. (J). 1998. write for info. (*0-7853-2633-2*) Pubns Intl Ltd.

Morgan, W. B., et al, eds. Tropical Resources: Ecology & Development. (Resource Management & Optimization Ser.). iv, 306p. 1990. pap. text 64.00 (*3-7186-0514-7*) Gordon & Breach.

Morgan, W. B., jt. auth. see Moss, R. P.

Morgan, W. B., jt. ed. see Billet, M. L.

Morgan, W. B., ed. see Fluids Engineering Conference Symposium on Cavity Flows Staff.

Morgan, W. H. La Administracion En Extension. pap. 3.10 (*0-8477-2209-0*) U of PR Pr.

Morgan, W. John. Curricular Issues for the Nineteen Nineties. (C). 1989. 50.00 (*1-85041-059-3*, Pub. by Univ Nottingham) St Mut.

Morgan, W. John & Coates, Ken. The Notts Coalfield & the British Miners Strike. 1989. pap. 21.00 (*1-85041-034-8*) U of Nottingham.

Morgan, W. John & Preston, Peter, eds. Raymond Williams: Politics, Education, Letters. LC 92-34122. 232p. 1993. text 45.00 (*0-312-08357-2*) St Martin.

Morgan, W. John, jt. auth. see Coates, K.

Morgan, W. John, jt. ed. see Hake, B. J.

Morgan, W. John, jt. ed. see Hake, Barry.

Morgan, W. M. Freemasonry Exposition: Exposition & Illustrations of Freemasonry. 110p. 1992. reprint ed. pap. 9.95 (*1-881316-93-9*) A&B Bks.

Morgan, W. Max, jt. auth. see Thomas, Gordon.

Morgan, W. P. Piety: Partial History of James Duncan Piety, His Forebears & Descendants, 1796-1948. (Illus.). 150p. 1994. reprint ed. pap. 23.00 (*0-8328-4232-X*); reprint ed. lib. bdg. 33.00 (*0-8328-4231-1*) Higginson Bk Co.

Morgan, W. Roy. Fat Suction. 1985. 19.95 (*0-918227-00-3*) Body Sculpt.

Morgan, Walter, jt ed. see Morgan, Jane.

Morgan, Walter L. & Gordon, Gary D. Communications Satellite Handbook. LC 88-6077. 944p. 1989. 198.00 (*0-471-31603-2*) Wiley.

Morgan, Walter L. & Rouffet, Denis. Business Earth Stations for Telecommunications. LC 87-29055. (Telecommunications Ser.). 234p. 1988. 138.00 (*0-471-63556-1*) Wiley.

Morgan, Walter L., jt. auth. see Gordon, Gary D.

Morgan, Wayne R. & Morgan, James L. The Coppers: Personal Chronicles of the Columbus, Ohio, Police Department. Date not set. 23.95 (*0-9669547-1-8*) Ascrybe.

Morgan, Weal & Hugh, John. German Jet Aces of World War 2 - Aircraft of the Aces. (Aircraft of the Aces Ser.: No. 17). (Illus.). 96p. 1997. pap. 17.95 (*1-85532-634-5*, Pub. by Ospry) Motorbooks Intl.

***Morgan, Wendy.** Ask Me Again, Vol. 59. 2000. mass mkt. 3.99 (*0-8217-6669-4*) Kensgtn Pub Corp.

Morgan, Wendy. Critical Literacy in the Classroom: The Art of the Possible. LC 96-46525. 232p. (C). 1997. 70.00 (*0-415-14247-4*); pap. 22.99 (*0-415-14248-2*) Routledge.

***Morgan, Wendy.** Loving Max, Vol. 13. (Zebra Bouquet Ser.). 1999. mass mkt. 3.99 (*0-8217-6348-2*, Zebra Kensgtn) Kensgtn Pub Corp.

Morgan, Wendy. Ned Kelly Reconstructed. LC 93-48705. 160p. (J). 1995. pap. 21.95 (*0-521-43783-0*) Cambridge U Pr.

— Obsession. 320p. 1996. mass mkt. 4.99 (*0-8217-5120-4*, Zebra Kensgtn) Kensgtn Pub Corp.

Morgan, Wendy, jt. auth. see Bunce, Vincent.

Morgan, Willard. From Critic to Convert: A Skeptic Questions His Way to Mormonism. 1995. 16.98 (*0-88290-517-1*, 1056) Horizon Utah.

Morgan, William. Collegiate Gothic: The Architecture of Rhodes College. (Illus.). 106p. 1995. 30.00 (*0-87233-118-0*) Bauhan.

— Freemasonry Exposed. 13.00 (*0-911164-10-3*) Powner.

***Morgan, William.** Freemasonry Exposed: Illustrations of Masonry. 110p. 1998. pap. 5.00 (*0-944379-14-1*) CPA Bk Pub.

Morgan, William. How to Help Your Child Learn to Read. 1978. 2.50 (*0-685-66030-3*) Delta Sales.

— Louisville: Architecture & the Urban Environment. LC 79-631. 1979. 15.00 (*0-87233-050-8*) Bauhan.

— Morgan's Freemasonry Exposed & Explained. 131p. 1998. reprint ed. pap. 14.50 (*0-7873-0623-1*) Hlth Research.

— Navajo Coyote Tales. Thompson, Hildegard, ed. & tr. by. LC 88-72048. (Illus.). 50p. (J). (gr. 2 up). 1988. reprint ed. pap. 8.95 (*0-941270-52-1*) Ancient City Pr.

Morgan, William, photos by. Portals: New England Doorways. (Illus.). 1981. pap. 4.75 (*0-87233-057-5*) Bauhan.

Morgan, William, jt. auth. see Young, Robert.

Morgan, William, jt. ed. see Brask, Per.

Morgan, William, ed. see Heikkinen, Mikko & Komonen, Markku.

Morgan, William, ed. see McCormick, Thomas J.

Morgan, William, tr. see Crowder, Jack L., et al.

Morgan, William, Sr., jt. auth. see Young, Robert W.

Morgan, William B., ed. see International Symposium on Cavitation Inception St.

Morgan, William D. & Kennedy, Charles S. The U. S. Consul at Work, 275. LC 90-19910. (Contributions in Political Science Ser.: No. 275). 272p. 1991. 65.00 (*0-313-27796-6*, MUW/, Greenwood Pr) Greenwood.

Morgan, William H. Personal Reminiscences of the War of 1861-5. LC 74-146868. (Select Bibliographies Reprint Ser.). 1977. reprint ed. 19.95 (*0-8369-5635-4*) Ayer.

Morgan, William J. Leftist Theories of Sport: A Critique & Reconstruction. LC 93-24135. (Sport & Society Ser.). 288p. 1994. text 49.50 (*0-252-02068-5*); pap. text 17.95 (*0-252-06361-9*) U of Ill Pr.

Morgan, William J., Jr. Supervision & Management of Quantity Food Preparation. 4th ed. LC 94-78475. (Illus.). (C). 1994. 42.00 (*0-8211-1262-7*) McCutchan.

***Morgan, William J., et al, eds.** The Ethics of Sports. 432p. 2000. write for info. (*0-7360-3643-1*) Human Kinetics.

Morgan, William J. & Meier, Klaus V. Philosophic Inquiry in Sport. 2nd rev. ed. LC 95-10920. (Illus.). 456p. 1995. pap. text 47.00 (*0-87322-716-6*, BMOR0716) Human Kinetics.

Morgan, William N. Ancient Architecture of the Southwest. LC 93-21256. (Illus.). 320p. (C). 1994. 60.00 (*0-292-75159-1*) U of Tex Pr.

— Precolumbian Architecture in the Eastern United States. LC 98-29504. (Ripley P. Bullen Ser.). (Illus.). xiv, 272 p. (Orig.). 1999. pap. 19.95 (*0-8130-1659-2*) U Press Fla.

— Prehistoric Architecture in Micronesia. (Illus.). 180p. 1988. 60.00 (*0-292-76506-1*) U of Tex Pr.

Morgan, William P., ed. Physical Activity & Mental Health. LC 96-20373. (Series in Health Psychology & Behavioral Medicine). 288p. 1996. 59.95 (*1-56032-365-5*) Taylor & Francis.

Morgan, William P. & Goldston, Stephen E. Exercise & Mental Health. (Series in Health Psychology & Behavioral Medicine). 196p. 1987. 56.95 (*0-89116-564-9*) Hemisp Pub.

Morgan, William T. East Africa. LC 74-161775. (Geographies for Advanced Study Ser.). (Illus.). 430p. 1976. reprint ed. pap. 133.30 (*0-608-08185-X*, 203033600068) Bks Demand.

— Salt Lantern: Traces of an American Family. LC 97-17333. (American Land & Life Ser.). (Illus.). 200p. 1997. pap. 15.95 (*0-87745-614-3*); text 29.95 (*0-87745-613-5*) U of Iowa Pr.

Morgan, William T., jt. auth. see Brinkman, Marilyn S.

Morgan, William T., jt. auth. see Stamp, L. Dudley.

Morgan, William T., jt. auth. see Young, Robert W.

Morgan, William W. Retinal Transmitters & Modulators: Models for the Brain, Vol. 2. LC 84-12068. 176p. 1984. 105.00 (*0-8493-5692-X*, QP479) Franklin.

Morgan, William W., ed. Retinal Transmitters & Modulators: Models for the Brain, Vol. I. 176p. 1985. 132.00 (*0-8493-5691-1*, QP479) CRC Pr.

Morgan, William W., ed. see Fisher, Donald W.

Morgan-Williams, Louise. I Can Sing En Francais: Fun Songs for Learning French. (I Can Sing Songbooks Ser.). (FRE., Illus.). 32p. (J). (gr. 4-7). 1993. pap. 12.95 incl. audio (*0-8442-1459-0*, 14590, Passprt Bks) NTC Contemp Pub Co.

— I Can Sing En Espanol! Fun Songs for Learning Spanish. (SPA., Illus.). 32p. (J). (gr. 4-7). 1995. pap. 8.95 (*0-8442-7168-3*, 71683, Natl Textbk Co) NTC Contemp Pub Co.

— I Can Sing In Espanol: Fun Songs for Learning Spanish. (SPA.). 32p. (J). (gr. 4-7). 1993. pap. 12.95 incl. audio (*0-8442-7172-1*, 71721) NTC Contemp Pub Co.

— I Can Sing In Francais! Fun Songs for Learning French. (I Can Sing Songbooks Ser.). (FRE., Illus.). 32p. (J). (gr. 4-7). 1994. pap. 9.95 incl. audio (*0-8442-1457-4*, 14574, Passprt Bks) NTC Contemp Pub Co.

Morgan, Winifred. An American Icon: Brother Jonathan & American Identity. LC 86-40597. (Illus.). 224p. 1988. 32.50 (*0-87413-307-6*) U Delaware Pr.

Morgan, Winona L. The Family Meets the Depression: A Study of a Group of Highly Selected Families, Vol. 19. LC 79-141550. (Child Welfare Ser.). (Illus.). 126p. (C). 1972. reprint ed. lib. bdg. 22.50 (*0-8371-5897-4*, CWMF, Greenwood Pr) Greenwood.

Morgan-Witts, Max, jt. auth. see Thomas, Gordon.

Morgan, Wyn, jt. ed. see Sapsford, David.

Morgan-Wynne, John E., jt. auth. see Davies, Gwynne H.

Morgane, Peter J. & Panksepp, Jaak, eds. Anatomy of the Hypothalamus. LC 79-23335. (Handbook of the Hypothalamus Ser.: No. 1). 746p. 1979. reprint ed. pap. 200.00 (*0-608-01325-0*, 206206800001) Bks Demand.

— Behavioral Studies of the Hypothalamus, Pt. A. LC 80-22563. (Handbook of the Hypothalamus Ser.: No. 3). 517p. 1980. pap. 160.30 (*0-608-01322-6*, 206206600001) Bks Demand.

— Behavioral Studies of the Hypothalamus, Pt. B. LC 80-22563. (Handbook of the Hypothalamus Ser.: No. 3). 480p. 1981. pap. 148.80 (*0-608-01323-4*, 206206600002) Bks Demand.

— Physiology of the Hypothalamus. LC 80-17602. (Handbook of the Hypothalamus Ser.: No. 2). 700p. 1980. reprint ed. pap. 200.00 (*0-608-01324-2*, 206206700001) Bks Demand.

Morganett, Rosemarie S. Skills for Living: Group Counseling Activities for Elementary Students. LC 94-65700. 238p. (Orig.). 1994. pap. text 25.95 (*0-87822-347-9*, 4761) Res Press.

— Skills for Living Vol. 1: Group Counseling Activities for Young Adolescents. LC 89-61588. 298p. 1989. pap. text 25.95 (*0-87822-318-5*, 3184) Res Press.

Morgani, Giambattista. The Clinical Consultations of Giambattista Morgagni: The Edition of Enrico Benassi, 1935. Jarcho, Saul, tr. from ITA. & intro. by. c, 450p. 1984. 25.00 (*0-88135-103-2*, Sci Hist) Watson Pub Intl.

Morgann, Maurice. Essay on the Dramatic Character of Sir John Falstaff. Gill, William A., ed. LC 72-109657. (Select Bibliographies Reprint Ser.). 1977. 20.95 (*0-8369-5266-9*) Ayer.

— Essay on the Dramatic Character of Sir John Falstaff. LC 79-115363. reprint ed. 29.50 (*0-404-04435-2*) AMS Pr.

Morgano, M., ed. The U. K. Finance Directory: A Directory of Sources of U. K. Corporate Finance. 600p. 1990. 695.00 (*0-86010-342-0*, Pub. by Graham & Trotman); pap. 425.00 (*0-86010-341-2*, Pub. by Graham & Trotman) St Mut.

Morganroth, Joel, ed. Congestive Heart Failure: Proceedings of Symposium on New Drugs & Devices, October 30-31, 1986, Philadelphia, PA. (Developments in Cardiovascular Medicine Ser.). (C). 1987. text 138.00 (*0-89838-955-0*) Kluwer Academic.

— The Evaluation of New Antiarrhythmic Drugs. 340p. 1981. text 126.50 (*90-247-2474-0*) Kluwer Academic.

Morganroth, Joel, et al, eds. Noninvasive Cardiac Imaging. LC 82-11095. (Illus.). 458p. reprint ed. pap. 142.00 (*0-8357-7624-7*, 205694700096) Bks Demand.

Morganroth, Joel & Moore, E. Neil. The Evaluation of Beta Blocker & Calcium Antagonist Drugs. 1982. text 176.50 (*90-247-2642-5*) Kluwer Academic.

— Sudden Cardiac Death & Congestive Heart Failure. 1983. text 158.50 (*0-89838-580-6*) Kluwer Academic.

Morganroth, Joel & Moore, E. Neil, eds. Cardiac Arrhythmias: New Therapeutic Drugs & Devices. (Developments in Cardiovascular Medicine Ser.). 1985. text 132.00 (*0-89838-716-7*) Kluwer Academic.

— Interventions in the Acute Phase of Myocardial Infarction. 320p. 1984. text 108.00 (*0-89838-659-4*) Kluwer Academic.

— Risk-Benefit Analysis for the Use & Approval of Thrombolytic, Antiarrhythmic, & Hypolipidemic Agents. (C). 1989. text 145.00 (*0-7923-0294-X*) Kluwer Academic.

— Use & Approval of Antihypertensive Agents & Surrogate Endpoints for the Approval of Drugs Affecting Antiarrhythmic Heart Failure & Hypolipidemia: Proceedings of the Tenth Annual Symposium on New Drugs & Devices, Oct. 31-Nov. 1, 1989. (C). 1990. text 133.50 (*0-7923-0756-9*) Kluwer Academic.

Morgans, Jim E., ed. see Heldt, Morris.

Morgans, W. M. Outlines of Paint Technology. 3rd ed. 503p. 1990. 275.00 (*0-470-21654-9*) Wiley.

Morgans, William. Illustrations of Masonry by One of the Fraternity Who Has Devoted Thirty Years to the Subject. Obaba, Al I., ed. 1991. pap. text 23.00 (*0-916157-96-2*) African Islam Miss Pubns.

Morganstern, Anne. Gothic Tombs of Kinship in France, the Low Countries & England. LC 98-41261. 2000. 60.00 (*0-271-01859-3*) Pa St U Pr.

Morganstern, James. The Fort at Dereagfzi & Other Material Remains in Its Vicinity: From Antiquity to the Middle Ages. LC 93-205965. (Istanbuler Forschungen Ser.). xii, 181p. 1993. write for info. (*3-8030-1761-0*) E J Wasmuth.

***Morganstern, Mimi.** The Good Food ABC Book. unabridged ed. LC 00-132865. (Illus.). vi, 28p. (J). (ps-3). 2000. per. 5.95 (*0-9700522-1-9*) M Morganstern.

— The Good Food ABC-Read-Along with Mimi: A Fun Nutritional Headstart Pack. (J). (ps-3). 2000. per. 8.99 incl. audio (*0-9700522-2-7*) M Morganstern.

— The House at Hemlock Farms. unabridged ed. LC 00-132864. (Illus.). vi, 54p. (J). (gr. 3-6). 2000. per. 5.95 (*0-9700522-3-5*) M Morganstern.

— The House at Hemlock Farms-"Read-Along with Mimi" A Cool Chapterbook-Package. LC 00-132864. (Illus.). vi, 54p. (J). (gr. 3-6). 2000. per. 9.99 incl. audio (*0-9700522-4-3*) M Morganstern.

Morganstern, Mindy. Real Rules for Girls: Notes from the Hippest Aunt You Never Had. (Illus.). 128p. (J). 2000. pap. 15.95 (*0-9659754-5-2*, Pub. by Girl Pr) LPC Group.

Morganstern, Stanley, jt. auth. see Sowald, Beatrice K.

Morganstern, Stanley, jt. ed. see Sowald, Beatrice K.

Morganstern, Steven. Overcoming Impotence: Doctor's Guide to Regaining Sexual Vitality. 2nd ed. (C). 1994. pap. 15.95 (*0-13-146978-9*) P-H.

— The Prostate Sourcebook: Everything You Need to Know. 252p. 1994. reprint ed. pap. 12.95 (*1-56565-117-0*) Lowell Hse.

Morganstern, Steven & Abrahams, Allen. The Prostate Sourcebook. 3rd ed. LC 99-188320. 272p. 1998. pap. 16.00 (*1-56565-817-X*, 0871XW, Pub. by Lowell Hse) NTC Contemp Pub Co.

Morganstern, Steven, jt. auth. see Teitelbaum, Michael.

Morgante, Amy, ed. Buddhist Perspectives on the Earth Charter, Vol. 1. 91p. 1997. pap. text 3.00 (*1-887917-04-7*) Boston RCFT-FC.

Morgante, Amy, jt. ed. see Casey, Helen M.

Morgante, Amy, ed. see Geissler, Rex.

Morgante, Amy, jt. ed. see Hays, Michael.

M

An Asterisk (*) at the beginning of an entry indicates that the title is appearing for the first time.

Morgante, John-Paul. First Things First, Pt. 1. (Basic Christian Training Ser.). 64p. 1991. pap. 2.50 (*1-880322-02-1*) Champions Christ.
— Follow-Up Manual. 50p. 1991. pap. 5.00 (*1-880322-00-5*) Champions Christ.
Morganthal, Deborah, ed. see Sturges, Norma.
***Morganthal, J. P. & la Forge, Bill.** Enterprise Application Integration with XML & Java. LC 99-58839. (XML Ser.). 400p. 2000. pap. 44.99 (*0-13-085135-3*) P-H.
Morganti, Rafaella O. & Couch, Warrick J., eds. Looking Deep in the Southern Sky: Proceedings of the ESO/Australia Workshop Held at Sydney, Australia, 10-12 December, 1997. 2nd ed. LC 98-32280. (ESO Astrophysics Symposia Ser.). (Illus.). xxi, 336p. 1999. 49.95 (*3-540-65286-8*) Spr-Verlag.
Morgantown Energy Technology Center Staff, ed. Proceedings of the Fuel Cell '96 Review Meeting (Aug. 1996) (Fuel Cell Information Ser.: Vol.IX). (Illus.). 272p. 1997. lib. bdg. 145.00 (*0-89934-338-4*, BT969) Bus Tech Bks.
Morgareidge, Kenneth, ed. see Zahourek, Jon.
Morgart, Marie. Visions in Verse. 1998. pap. write for info. (*1-57553-625-0*) Watermrk Pr.
Morgen, Howard. Fingerstyle Jazz Images Xmas. 32p. 1996. 17.95 incl. audio compact disk (*0-7866-2600-3*, 94409BCD) Mel Bay.
— Paul Simon for Fingerstyle Jazz Guitar. (Illus.). 88p. 1998. pap. text 24.95 (*0-8256-3317-6*, PS11436) Music Sales.
— 10 from Guitar Player. Stang, Aaron, ed. 72p. (Orig.). (YA). 1992. pap. text 12.95 (*0-89898-575-7*, F3216GTX) Wrner Bros.
Morgen, Hugh & Seibel, Jurgen. Combat Kills: Victory in the Skies. (Illus.). 200p. 1997. 39.95 (*1-85260-536-7*) Haynes Manuals.
Morgen, Kenneth B. Getting Simon: Two Gay Doctors' Journey to Fatherhood. LC 95-13177. 232p. (Orig.). 1995. pap. 14.95 (*1-883647-04-5*, Bramble Bks) Bramble Co.
Morgen, Sandra, ed. Gender & Anthropology. 1989. 20.00 (*0-913167-33-9*) Am Anthro Assn.
Morgen, Sandra, jt. ed. see Bookman, Ann.
Morgen, Sharon D. Sales on the Line: Meeting the Business Demands of the '90s Through Phone Partnering. 248p. (Orig.). 1993. pap. 14.95 (*1-55552-047-2*) Metamorphous Pr.
***Morgen, Sharon D.** Selling with Integrity: Reinventing Sales Through Collaboration, Respect & Serving. 1999. reprint ed. pap. 12.95 (*0-425-17156-6*) Berkley Pub.
Morgenbesser, Mel & Nehls, Nadine. Joint Custody: An Alternative for Divorcing Families. LC 80-22182. (Illus.). 176p. 1981. text 31.95 (*0-88229-620-5*) Burnham Inc.
Morgenbesser, Sidney, ed. see Dewey, John.
Morgenfrug, Rudolph A., jt. auth. see Dominy, Arthur L.
Morgenroth, Barbara. Best 50 Cherry Recipes. LC 98-216504. (Best 50 Ser.). 1998. pap. text 4.95 (*1-55867-197-8*) Bristol Pub Ent CA.
Morgenroth, Barbara, jt. auth. see Layman, Teresa.
Morgenroth, Chris & Battien, Pauline. Footprints in the Olympics: An Autobiography. (Illus.). 215p. 1991. pap. 16.95 (*0-87770-478-3*) Ye Galleon.
Morgenroth, Hermann & Najock, Dietmar, eds. Priapea - Concordantiae In Corpus Priapeorum et In Pervigilium Veneris. (Alpha-Omega, Reihe A Ser.: Bd. LIX). (LAT.). 181p. 1983. 52.50 (*3-487-07328-5*) G Olms Pubs.
— Vergilius - Concordantia in Appendicem Vergilianam. (Alpha-Omega, Reihe A Ser.: Bd. LXVIII). (GER.). x, 542p. 1992. write for info. (*3-487-09592-0*) G Olms Pubs.
Morgenroth, Joyce. Dance Improvisations. LC 86-19318. (Illus.). 160p. (C). 1987. pap. 16.95 (*0-8229-5386-2*); text 29.95 (*0-8229-3550-3*) U of Pittsburgh Pr.
Morgenroth, Kate. Kill Me First. LC 98-30752. 272p. 1999. 24.00 (*0-06-019275-5*) HarpC.
***Morgenroth, Kate.** Kill Me First. 384p. 2000. mass mkt. 6.99 (*0-06-109774-8*) HarpC.
— Kill Me First: Australian Edition. 288p. 1999. pap. 15.00 (*0-06-103010-4*) HarpC.
— Kill Me First: Buckley,&Betty. abr. ed. 1999. audio 18.00 (*0-694-52213-9*) HarperAudio.
Morgenroth, Klaus & Glaser, Rosemarie, contrib. by. Terminologie und Nomenklatur: Ein Dichotomischer Ansatz Zur Strukturellen Differenzierung der Fachlexik. (Leipziger Fachsprachen-Studien Ser.: No. 11). 197p. 1996. 42.95 (*3-631-49329-0*) P Lang Pubng.
Morgenroth, Konrad & Newhouse, M. The Surfactant System of the Lungs. viii, 112p. (C). 1988. lib. bdg. 79.25 (*3-11-011387-2*) De Gruyter.
— Das Surfactantsystem der Lunge. viii, 110p. (C). 1986. lib. bdg. 79.25 (*3-11-011015-6*) De Gruyter.
Morgens, Frank. Years at the Edge of Existence Vol. XV: War Memoirs, 1939-1945. LC 96-15576. (Studies in the Shoah). (Illus.). 208p. (C). 1996. lib. bdg. 42.50 (*0-7618-0332-7*) U Pr of Amer.
Morgensen, Gunnar V., jt. ed. see Atkinson, A. B.
Morgensen, O. E. Positron Annihilation in Chemistry. LC 94-27490. (Chemical Physics Ser.). 1994. 108.95 (*0-387-57853-6*) Spr-Verlag.
Morgenstein. Accounting. 2nd ed. (C). 1997. pap. text 28.50 (*0-15-504524-5*) HarBrace.
— Principles of Accounting. 2nd ed. (C). 1997. pap. text 50.00 (*0-15-504508-3*) Harcourt Coll Pubs.
Morgenstein, Melvin. Career Accounting Fundamentals. 559p. (C). 1988. student ed. write for info. incl. disk (*0-318-64534-3*); student ed. 5.50 (*0-15-505782-0*); disk. write for info. (*0-318-64533-5*) Dryden Pr.
Morgenstein, Rod & Mattingly, Rick. Drumset Musician. 80p. 1997. pap. 19.95 (*0-7935-6554-5*) H Leonard.
Morgenstern. Alle Galgenlieder. (GER.). (C). 1947. 13.95 (*0-8442-2741-2*, X2741-2) NTC Contemp Pub Co.
— Alle Galgenlieder. unabridged ed. (World Classic Literature Ser.). (GER.). pap. 7.95 (*3-89507-017-3*, Pub. by Bookking Intl) Distribks Inc.
Morgenstern, Barbara L., jt. auth. see Mirabito, Michael M.
Morgenstern, Barbara L., jt. auth. see Mirabito, Michael M. A.
Morgenstern, Christian. Lullabies, Lyrics & Gallows Songs. LC 94-40351. (Illus.). 48p. (J). (gr. 2-4). 1995. 16.95 (*1-55858-364-5*, Pub. by North-South Bks NYC) Chronicle Bks.
Morgenstern, Claudia, jt. ed. see Calleo, David P.
Morgenstern, Dan. Jazz People. (Illus.). 301p. 1993. reprint ed. pap. 24.50 (*0-306-80527-8*) Da Capo.
— Jazz People. (Illus.). 1978. reprint ed. pap. text 19.95 (*0-13-511352-0*) P-H.
Morgenstern, Dan, jt. auth. see Graham, Charles.
Morgenstern, E. Kristian. Geographic Variation in Forest Trees: Genetic Basis & Application of Knowledge in Silviculture. LC 97-125754. (Illus.). 176p. 1996. 75.00 (*0-7748-0579-X*) U of Wash Pr.
Morgenstern, Felice. International Conflicts of Labour Law: A Survey of the Law Applicable to the International Employment Relation. 2nd ed. ix, 129p. 1986. text 24.75 (*92-2-103593-X*) Intl Labour Office.
— Legal Problems of International Organizations. 163p. (C). 1986. 140.00 (*0-906496-24-1*, Pub. by Grotius Pubns Ltd) St Mut.
Morgenstern, George. Pearl Harbor: The Story of the Secret War. LC 42-1121. xx, 425p. (Orig.). 1991. reprint ed. pap. 8.95 (*0-939484-38-2*, 0978, Inst Hist Rev) Legion Survival.
Morgenstern, Henrike. Unterlassene Hilfeleistung, Solidaritat und Recht. (Rechtsphilosophische Schriften Ser.: Bd. 5). (GER.). 141p. 1997. 32.95 (*3-631-31496-5*) P Lang Pubng.
Morgenstern, I., jt. ed. see Van Hemmen, J. L.
Morgenstern, Julie. Organizing from the Inside Out: The Foolproof System for Organizing Your Home, Your Office & Your Life. LC 98-16292. (Illus.). 256p. 1998. pap. 15.00 (*0-8050-5649-1*, Owl) H Holt & Co.
***Morgenstern, Julie.** Organizing from the Inside Out for the New World of Work. 2001. pap. 14.00 (*0-8050-6470-2*) H Holt & Co.
— Time Management from the Inside Out: The Fool-Proof System for Taking Control of Your Schedule--And Your Life. 288p. 2000. pap. 15.00 (*0-8050-6469-9*, Owl) H Holt & Co.
Morgenstern, Michael. Como Hacerle Amor A Una Mujer. (SPA.). 167p. 1997. pap. text 11.98 (*968-13-1687-8*) Libros Fronteras.
Morgenstern, Michael. How to Make Love to a Woman. 160p. 1989. 7.99 (*0-517-60525-2*) Random Hse Value.
Morgenstern, Mira. The Politics of Ambiguity: Self, Culture, & Society in the Works of Jean-Jacques Rousseau. LC 95-44174. 1996. 45.00 (*0-271-01572-1*); pap. 18.95 (*0-271-01573-X*) Pa St U Pr.
Morgenstern, Oskar. International Financial Transactions & Business Cycles. (Studies in Business Cycles: No. 8). 671p. 1959. reprint ed. 160.00 (*0-87014-091-4*) Natl Bur Econ Res.
Morgenstern, Oskar, jt. auth. see Kemmerer, Edwin W.
Morgenstern, Oskar, jt. auth. see Von Neumann, John.
Morgenstern, Richard D., ed. Economic Analyses at EPA: Assessing Regulatory Impact. LC 97-14606. 480p. 1997. pap. 49.95 (*0-915707-83-7*) Resources Future.
Morgenstern, Sam, jt. auth. see Barlow, Harold.
Morgenstern, Steve. Win New Clients & Grow. 224p. 1996. pap. 20.00 (*0-679-76088-1*) Random.
Morgenstern, Susie. Oukele la Tele. (Folio - Cadet Bleu Ser.: No. 190). (FRE., Illus.). 54p. (J). (gr. 1-5). 1991. pap. 9.95 (*2-07-031190-2*) Schoenhof.
***Morgenstern, Susie Hoch.** Secret Letters from 0 to 10. (Illus.). 144p. (YA). (gr. 4-7). 2000. pap. 4.99 (*0-14-130819-2*, PuffinBks) Peng Put Young Read.
Morgenstern, W., et al, eds. Mathematical Modelling with Chernobyl Registry Data: Registry & Concepts. 110p. 1995. 21.95 (*3-540-60411-1*) Spr-Verlag.
Morgentaler. Dickens & Heredity. LC 99-22231. 2000. text 59.95 (*0-312-22493-1*) St Martin.
Morgentaler, Abraham. The Male Body: A Physician's Guide to What Every Man Should Know About His Sexual Health. LC 93-18035. 192p. 1993. pap. 10.00 (*0-671-86426-2*) S&S Trade.
Morgenthal, jt. auth. see Bougie.
Morgenthal, Deborah. The Book of Christian Crafts: 50 Beautiful Projects That Celebrate Christian Themes. LC 97-15487. (Illus.). 144p. 1997. 18.95 (*1-57990-008-9*, Pub. by Lark Books) Random.
— A Crafter's Book of Angels. LC 95-6210. (Illus.). 160p. 1995. 27.95 (*0-8069-3156-6*) Lark Books.
— A Crafter's Book of Angels. (Illus.). 160p. 1996. pap. 17.95 (*0-8069-3157-4*) Sterling.
***Morgenthal, Deborah.** A Crafter's Book of Angels. (Illus.). 160p. 2000. reprint ed. 25.00 (*0-7881-9214-0*) DIANE Pub.
— Creative Candleholders. 1999. write for info. (*1-57790-147-9*) Book Tech.
— Creative Candleholders: From Elegant to Whimsical, 60 Projects to Suit Every Style. LC 99-20195. 128p. 1999. pap. 16.95 (*1-57990-147-6*, Pub. by Lark Books) Random.
— Creative Candleholders: From Elegant to Whimsical, 60 Projects to Suit Every Style. LC 99-20195. (Illus.). 128p. 1999. pap. text 27.95 (*1-57990-128-X*) Lark Books.
Morgenthal, Deborah. Making Great Lamps: 50 Illuminating Projects, Techniques & Ideas. LC 98-21475. (Illus.). 144p. 1998. 26.95 (*1-57990-057-7*, Pub. by Lark Books) Random.
— The Ultimate T-Shirt Book: Creating Your Own Unique Designs. LC 97-29342. (Illus.). 144p. 1998. pap. 14.95 (*1-57990-017-8*, Pub. by Lark Books) Random.
— Wreaths Around the House: More Than 80 Distinctive Wreaths to Make, Enjoy & Give as Gifts. LC 93-39715. (Illus.). 144p. 1994. 27.95 (*0-8069-0712-6*) Sterling.
Morgenthal, Deborah. The Ultimate Birdhouse Book. 128p. 1998. pap. 14.95 (*0-8069-9935-7*) Sterling.
***Morgenthal, Deborah & Kilby, Janice Eaton.** The Metal Craft Book: 50 Easy & Beautiful Projects from Copper, Tin, Brass, Aluminum & More. LC 00-37110. (Illus.). 128p. 2000. write for info. (*1-57990-170-0*, Pub. by Lark Books) Sterling.
Morgenthal, Deborah & Rich, Chris. The Complete Book of Nature Craft Techniques: Hints, Tips & Tools for Every Kind of Nature Craft. (Illus.). 256p. 1996. 27.95 (*0-87596-714-0*) Rodale Pr Inc.
Morgenthal, Deborah, ed. see Acero, Raul.
Morgenthal, Deborah, ed. see Coney, Norma.
Morgenthal, Deborah, ed. see Cooper, Kathy.
Morgenthal, Deborah, ed. see Hopkin, Bart.
Morgenthal, Deborah, ed. see Mack, Daniel.
Morgenthal, Deborah, ed. see Miessmer, Andreas.
Morgenthal, Deborah, ed. see Reurs, Catherine.
Morgenthal, Deborah, ed. see Summitt.
Morgenthal, Deborah, ed. see Widess, Jim & Summit, Ginger.
Morgenthal, Jeffrey. Building Distributed Java Applications. (Illus.). 388p. 1997. pap. text 44.95 incl. cd-rom (*0-07-913679-6*) McGraw.
Morgenthaler, C., ed. see Morgenthaler, Stephan & Franscini, Stefano.
Morgenthaler, Fritz. Homosexuality, Heterosexuality, Perversion. Moor, Paul, ed. Aebi, Andreas, tr. from GER. 160p. 1988. 27.50 (*0-88163-060-8*) Analytic Pr.
Morgenthaler, George W. Planning Challenges of the 70's in the Public Domain, 15th Annual AAS Meeting, Jun. 17-20, 1969, Denver, CO. Burnsnali, William J. et al, eds. (Science & Technology Ser.: Vol. 22). (Illus.). 504p. 1970. 40.00 (*0-87703-050-2*, Am Astronaut Soc) Univelt Inc.
Morgenthaler, George W., ed. Exploration of Mars Symposium, Jun. 6-7, 1963, Denver, CO. LC 57-43769. (Advances in the Astronautical Sciences Ser.: Vol. 15). 634p. 1963. 45.00 (*0-87703-016-2*, Am Astronaut Soc) Univelt Inc.
— Future Space Program & Impact on Range & Network Development Symposium, Mar. 22-24, 1967, Las Cruces, NM. (Science & Technology Ser.: Vol. 15). 588p. 1967. 40.00 (*0-87703-043-X*, Am Astronaut Soc) Univelt Inc.
— Unmanned Exploration of the Solar System Symposium, Feb. 8-10, 1965, Denver CO. LC 57-43769. (Advances in the Astronautical Sciences Ser.: Vol. 19). 1000p. 1965. 45.00 (*0-87703-021-9*, Am Astronaut Soc) Univelt Inc.
Morgenthaler, George W., et al, eds. Aerospace Century XXI, 33rd AAS Annual Meeting, Oct. 26-29, 1986, Boulder, CO, 3 pts. LC 57-43769. (Advances in the Astronautical Sciences Ser.: Vol. 64). (Illus.). 1988. 225.00 (*0-87703-276-9*, Am Astronaut Soc); pap. 180.00 (*0-87703-277-7*, Am Astronaut Soc) Univelt Inc.
— Aerospace Century XXI: Space Flight Technologies, Pt. 2. LC 57-43769. (Advances in the Astronautical Sciences Ser.: Vol. 64). (Illus.). 608p. 1988. 75.00 (*0-87703-280-7*, Am Astronaut Soc); pap. 60.00 (*0-87703-283-1*, Am Astronaut Soc) Univelt Inc.
— Aerospace Century XXI: Space Missions & Policy, Pt. 1. LC 57-43769. (Advances in the Astronautical Sciences Ser.: Vol. 64). (Illus.). 686p. 1988. 75.00 (*0-87703-279-3*, Am Astronaut Soc); pap. 60.00 (*0-87703-282-3*, Am Astronaut Soc) Univelt Inc.
— Aerospace Century XXI: Space Sciences, Applications, & Commercial Developments, Pt. 3. LC 57-43769. (Advances in the Astronautical Sciences Ser.: Vol. 64). (Illus.). 724p. 1988. 75.00 (*0-87703-281-5*, Am Astronaut Soc); pap. 60.00 (*0-87703-284-X*, Am Astronaut Soc) Univelt Inc.
— Space Shuttle Payloads (AAS/AAAS Symposium) Dec. 27-28, 1972, Washington, D.C. AAS/AAAS Symposium, Washington, D. C., Dec. 27-28, 1972. (Science & Technology Ser.: Vol. 30). 532p. 1973. 40.00 (*0-87703-063-4*, Am Astronaut Soc) Univelt Inc.
Morgenthaler, George W. & Greyber, Howard D., eds. Astronomy from a Space Platform (AAS/AAAS Symposium) Dec. 27-28, 1971, Philadelphia, PA: AAS/AAAS Symposium, Philadelphia, PA, Dec. 27-28, 1971. (Science & Technology Ser.: Vol. 28). 416p. 1972. 35.00 (*0-87703-061-8*, Am Astronaut Soc) Univelt Inc.
Morgenthaler, George W. & Hollstein, Manfred, eds. Space Shuttle & Spacelab Utilization, What Are the Near-Term & Long-Term Benefits for Mankind?, 16th Goddard Memorial Symposium, 24th Annual AAS Meeting, March 8-10, 1978: Near-Term & Long-Term Benefits for Mankind, Pt. 1. LC 57-43769. (Advances in the Astronautical Sciences Ser.: Vol. 37). 400p. 1978. 40.00 (*0-87703-096-0*, Am Astronaut Soc) Univelt Inc.
— Space Shuttle & Spacelab Utilization, What Are the Near-Term & Long-Term Benefits for Mankind?, 16th Goddard Memorial Symposium, 24th Annual AAS Meeting, March 8-10, 1978: Near-Term & Long-Term Benefits for Mankind, Pt. 2. LC 57-43769. (Advances in the Astronautical Sciences Ser.: Vol. 37). 465p. 1978. 45.00 (*0-87703-097-9*, Am Astronaut Soc) Univelt Inc.
Morgenthaler, George W. & Jacobs, Horace, eds. Manned Lunar Flight (AAS/AAAS Symposium) Dec. 19, 1961, Denver, CO: Proceedings of the AAA/AAAS Symposium, Denver, CO, Dec. 19, 1961. LC 57-43769. (Advances in the Astronautical Sciences Ser.: Vol. 10). 310p. 1963. 35.00 (*0-87703-011-1*, Am Astronaut Soc) Univelt Inc.
Morgenthaler, George W. & Morra, Robert G., eds. Planning Challenges of the 70's in Space, 15th Annual AAS Meeting, Jun. 17-20, 1969, Denver CO. LC 57-43769. (Advances in the Astronautical Sciences Ser.: Vol. 26). (Illus.). 470p. 1970. 35.00 (*0-87703-053-7*, Am Astronaut Soc) Univelt Inc.
Morgenthaler, George W. & Silver, Aaron N., eds. Energy Delta, Supply vs. Demand, (AAS/AAAS Symposium) Feb. 25-27, 1974, San Francisco, CA. (Science & Technology Ser.: Vol. 35). 604p. 1976. 35.00 (*0-87703-070-7*, Am Astronaut Soc); pap. 25.00 (*0-87703-082-0*, Am Astronaut Soc) Univelt Inc.
Morgenthaler, Hans R. The Early Sketches of German Architect Erich Mendelsohn (1887-1953) No Compromise with Reality. LC 92-14574. 168p. 1992. 79.95 (*0-7734-9535-5*) E Mellen.
Morgenthaler, J. J., ed. Virus Inactivation in Plasma Products. (Current Studies in Hematology & Blood Transfusion: No. 56). (Illus.). x, 158p. 1988. 123.50 (*3-8055-4836-2*) S Karger.
Morgenthaler, John & Lenard, Lane. 5HTP - The Natural Alternative to Prozac. (Illus.). 40p. 1998. pap. 3.95 (*0-9627418-4-1*) Smart Pubns CA.
***Morgenthaler, John & Simms, Mia.** The Smart Guide to Low Carb Anti Aging Cooking. (Smart Guide Ser.). (Illus.). 120p. 2000. pap. 9.95 (*1-890572-05-5*, Pub. by Smart Pubns CA) Publishers Group.
Morgenthaler, John, et al. Better Sex Through Chemistry: A Guide to the New Prosexual Drugs & Nutrients. LC 94-74007. 224p. 1995. pap. 14.95 (*0-9627418-2-5*) Smart Pubns CA.
— The Smart Guide to Better Sex: From Andro to Zinc... Supplements & Herbs to Fire up Your Life. LC 99-60249. (Illus.). 128p. 1999. pap. 9.95 (*1-890572-01-2*) Smart Pubns CA.
Morgenthaler, John, jt. auth. see Dean, Ward.
Morgenthaler, John, jt. auth. see Simms, Mia.
Morgenthaler, John, jt. auth. see Wright, Jonathan V.
Morgenthaler, S., et al, eds. New Directions in Statistical Data Analysis & Robustness. LC 93-8952. (Monte Verita, Proceedings of the Centro Stefano Franciscini Ascona Ser.). 284p. 1993. 79.50 (*0-8176-2923-8*) Birkhauser.
Morgenthaler, S. & Tukey, John W., eds. Configural Polysampling: A Route to Practical Robustness. LC 90-13052. (Series in Probability & Mathematics). 228p. 1991. 119.95 (*0-471-52372-0*) Wiley.
Morgenthaler, Sally. Worship Evangelism. Date not set. pap. 16.99 (*0-310-22649-X*) Zondervan.
— Worship Evangelism: Inviting Unbelievers into the Presence of God. 224p. 1995. 22.99 (*0-310-48561-4*) Zondervan.
***Morgenthaler, Sasha.** Sasha Dolls. (Illus.). 120p. 2000. 55.00 (*3-7165-1073-4*, Pub. by Benteli Verlag) Antique Collect.
Morgenthaler, Shirley K., ed. Exploring Children's Spiritual Formation: Foundational Issues. 332p. 1999. pap. write for info. (*1-893989-00-3*) Pillars Pr.
Morgenthaler, Stephan & Franscini, Stefano. Conference on Statistical Science Honouring the Bicentennial of Stefano Franscini's Birth: Ascona, November 18-20, 1996. Morgenthaler, C. & Ronchetti, Elvezio, eds. LC 97-34596. (Monte Verita Ser.). 239p. 1997. 68.00 (*3-7643-5707-X*) Spr-Verlag.
Morgenthaler, Walter. Madness & Art: The Life & Works of Adolf Wolfli. Esman, Aaron H., tr. from GER. & intro. by. LC 91-46761. (Texts & Contexts Ser.). (Illus.). xviii, 156p. 1992. text 60.00 (*0-8032-3156-3*) U of Nebr Pr.
Morgenthau, Hans J. The Decline of Democratic Politics. LC 62-18111. (Politics in the Twentieth Century Ser.: Vol. 1). 443p. 1962. reprint ed. pap. 137.40 (*0-608-09968-6*, 2020126) Bks Demand.
— The Impasse of American Foreign Policy. LC 62-18111. (Politics in the Twentieth Century Ser.: Vol. 2). 573p. 1962. reprint ed. pap. 177.70 (*0-608-09969-4*, 200739500062) Bks Demand.
— In Defense of the National Interest: A Critical Examination of American Foreign Policy. LC 82-18295. 306p. (C). 1983. reprint ed. pap. text 22.00 (*0-8191-2846-5*) U Pr of Amer.
— Politics among Nations. 6th rev. ed. Thompson, Kenneth W., ed. 688p. (C). 1985. 76.56 (*0-07-554469-5*) McGraw.
— Politics in the Twentieth Century. LC 62-18111. 1962. 45.00 (*0-226-53824-9*) U Ch Pr.
— The Purpose of American Politics. LC 82-20057. 382p. (C). 1983. reprint ed. pap. text 27.00 (*0-8191-2847-3*) U Pr of Amer.
— The Restoration of American Politics. LC 74-83960. (Politics in the Twentieth Century Ser.: Vol. 3). 284p. 1962. reprint ed. pap. 88.10 (*0-608-09970-8*, 202196000026) Bks Demand.
Morgenthau, Hans J., ed. Crossroad Papers. (C). 1965. pap. 3.47 (*0-393-00284-5*) Norton.
Morgenthau, Hans J., ed. Peace, Security & the United Nations. LC 72-10841. (Essay Index Reprint Ser.). 1977. reprint ed. 18.95 (*0-8369-7232-5*) Ayer.
Morgenthau, Hans J. & Thompson, Kenneth W. Politics among Nations: The Struggle for Power & Peace. 448p. (C). 1992. pap. 34.69 (*0-07-043306-2*) McGraw.
Morgenthau, Hans W. Scientific Man vs. Power Politics. (Midway Reprint Ser.). 256p. 1998. reprint ed. pap. text 16.95 (*0-226-53826-5*) U Ch Pr.
Morgenthau, Henry, et al. The Morgenthau Diaries. LC 99-30853. (Research Collections in American Politics). 1995. write for info. incl. mic. film (*1-55655-563-6*) U Pubns Amer.
Morgenthau, Henry, et al. The Presidential Diaries of Henry Morgenthau, Jr., 1938-1945. LC 86-892370. (The Presidential Documents Ser.). 2 p. 1982. write for info. (*0-89093-350-2*) U Pubns Amer.

An Asterisk (*) at the beginning of an entry indicates that the title is appearing for the first time.

Morgenthau, Hans J. The Twilight of International Morality. (Reprint Series in Social Sciences). (C). 1993. reprint ed. pap. text 5.00 (*0-8290-2765-3*, PS-211) Irvington.

Morgenthau, Ruth S. Pride Without Prejudice: The Life of John O. Pastore. (Illus.). 201p. 1989. 30.00 (*0-932840-05-1*) RI Hist Soc.

Morgner, Irmtraud. The Life & Adventures of Trobadora Beatrice As Chronicled by Her Minstrel Laura: A Novel in Thirteen Books & Seven Intermezzos. Clausen, Jeanette, tr. from GER. & intro. by. Von Erde, Silke, intro. LC 99-52824. (European Women Writers Ser.). 544p. 2000. text 65.00 (*0-8032-3203-9*); pap. text 25.00 (*0-8032-8260-5*) U of Nebr Pr.

Morgovsky, Joel, jt. auth. see Deakin, Maureen.

Morgret, Charles O. Brosnan: The Railroads' Messiah, Vols. I & II. LC 94-90817. 1996. 70.00 (*0-533-11376-8*) Vantage.

Morgridge, Barbara G., ed. see Hamsun, Knut.

Morgridge, Tashia. Award-Winning Activities for All Curriculum Areas. 1990. pap. 10.99 (*0-8224-7336-4*) Fearon Teacher Aids.

Morgulis, Mikhail, jt. auth. see Marshall, Melissa Rose.

Morhange-Begue, Claude. Chamberet: Recollections from an Ordinary Childhood. Wainhouse, Austryn, tr. from FRE. LC 87-81087. 130p. 1987. 25.95 (*0-910395-25-X*); pap. 9.95 (*0-910395-26-8*) Marlboro Pr.

***Morhange-Begue, Claude.** Chamberet: Recollections from an Ordinary Childhood. LC 00-36859. 136p. 2000. pap. 16.95 (*0-8101-6077-3*) Northwestern U Pr.

Morhard, Anton. Die Gerichtliche Berufung Im Kanonischen Recht: Eine Analyse des Klassischen Remedium Iuris. (Adnotationes in ius Canonicum Ser.: Bd. 1). (GER.). 242p. 1995. 44.95 (*3-631-49013-5*) P Lang Pubng.

Morholt, Evelyn & Brandwein, Paul F. A Sourcebook for the Biological Sciences. 3rd ed. 813p. (C). 1986. text 61.00 (*0-15-582852-5*, Pub. by Harcourt Coll Pubs) Harcourt.

Morhous, Henry C. Reminiscences of the 123rd Regiment, N.Y.S.V., Giving a Complete History of Its Three Years Service in the War. (Illus.). 220p. 1995. 30.00 (*1-881868-01-X*) Wash Cnty Hist.

Mori. Race & Ethnicity. pap. text 12.27 (*0-395-97379-1*) HM.

Mori, A. & Satoh, T., eds. Molecular Aspects of Asian Medicines Vol. 1: The Orient. 1996. 69.95 (*0-915340-20-8*) PJD Pubns.

Mori, Akitane, et al. Guanidines Vol. 2: Further Explorations of the Biological & Clinical Significance. (Illus.). 380p. 1989. 105.00 (*0-306-43223-4*, Plenum Trade) Perseus Pubng.

***Mori, Aoi.** Toni Morrison & Womanist Discourse. (Modern American Literature Ser.: Vol. 16). 176p. 1999. reprint ed. pap. text 31.95 (*0-8204-4960-1*) P Lang Pubng.

Mori, Barbara L. Americans Studying the Traditional Japanese Art of the Tea Ceremony. LC 92-4379. 216p. 1992. lib. bdg. 89.95 (*0-7734-9853-2*) E Mellen.

Mori, Brian R. Dreams of Flight. 1984. pap. 3.25 (*0-8222-0333-2*) Dramatists Play.

Mori, Catherine A., jt. auth. see Hawley, R. Scott.

Mori, H. & Miyake, A., eds. New Aspects of Physiology & Pathology of Luteal Phase: Journal: Hormone Research, Vol. 37, Suppl. 1, 1992. (Illus.). iv, 80p. 1992. pap. 36.75 (*3-8055-5625-X*) S Karger.

Mori, H. & Yoshimura, Y., eds. Local Regulators in the Ovary - Paracrine & Autocrine Control. (Journal: Hormone Research Ser.: Vol. 41, Suppl. 1, 1994). (Illus.). iv, 68p. 1994. pap. 31.50 (*3-8055-5994-1*) S Karger.

Mori, H., jt. ed. see Yasumatsu, K.

Mori, Hana, et al. Jirohattan. Kurosaki, Tamiko & Crowe, Elizabeth, trs. from JPN. LC 93-72833. (Illus.). 80p. (Orig.). (YA). (gr. 4-8). 1993. pap. 6.95 (*1-880188-69-4*) Bess Pr.

Mori, Hazime & Kuramoto, Yoshiki. Dissipative Structures & Chaos. Paquette, G. C., tr. LC 98-3125. (Illus.). 350p. 1997. 74.95 (*3-540-62744-8*) Spr-Verlag.

Mori, Hiromi. Immigration Policy & Foreign Workers in Japan. LC 96-26630. 243p. 1996. text 65.00 (*0-312-16401-7*) St Martin.

Mori, Hiroyuki, ed. Estrogen-Dependent Tumors: Conference on the Treatment of Hormone-Dependent Tumors, Tokyo, January 1998. (Oncology Ser.: Vol. 55, Suppl. 1). (Illus.). iv, 60p. 1998. pap. 24.50 (*3-8055-6768-5*) S Karger.

Mori, Hisashi. Sculpture of the Kamakura Period. Eickmann, Katherine A., tr. LC 73-88470. (Heibonsha Survey of Japanese Art Ser.: Vol. 11). (Illus.). 176p. 1974. 20.00 (*0-8348-1017-4*) Weatherhill.

***Mori, Jennifer.** Britain in the Age of the French Revolution: 1785 - 1820. 272p. 2000. pap. 24.00 (*0-582-23852-8*) Longman.

— Supplementing the Age of the French Revolution: 1785 - 1820. 256p. 2001. 79.95 (*0-582-23851-X*) Longman.

Mori, Jennifer. William Pitt & the French Revolution, 1785-1795. LC 97-10963. 320p. 1997. text 55.00 (*0-312-17308-3*) St Martin.

Mori, Joseph E., jt. auth. see Pahler, Arnold J.

Mori, Joyce. Applique Patterns from Native American Beadwork Designs. LC 93-44235. (Illus.). 96p. 1994. 14.95 (*0-89145-826-3*, 3790, Am Quilters Soc) Collector Bks.

— Create a Quilt: New Easy, Fast Design Method for Blocks & Quilts. LC 98-87357. (Illus.). 128p. 1999. pap. 19.95 (*0-87341-620-1*, DHOQ) Krause Pubns.

— Crosses of Many Cultures: Designs for Applique. LC 98-18377. 64p. 1998. pap. 11.95 (*0-8192-1751-4*) Morehouse Pub.

— Native American Designs for Quilting. LC 98-27956. 80p. 1998. pap. 15.95 (*1-57432-710-0*) Collector Bks.

— The Ultimate Scrap Quilt: The Complete Guide to Constructed Fabric. LC 97-73029. (Illus.). 128p. 1997. pap. 21.95 (*0-8019-8925-6*, USQ) Krause Pubns.

Mori, Joyce & Myerberg, Cynthia. Dye It! Paint It! Quilt It! Making & Using One-of-a-Kind Fabrics in Quilts. LC 95-53849. 160p. 1996. pap. 22.95 (*0-8019-8737-7*) Krause Pubns.

— Dyeing to Quilt: Quick Direct-Dye Methods for Quilt Makers. LC 96-33622. (Illus.). 128p. 1997. pap. 24.95 (*0-8442-2626-2*, Quilt Dgst Pr) NTC Contemp Pub Co.

Mori, K., ed. MRI of the Central Nervous System: A Pathology Atlas. (Illus.). ix, 241p. 1991. 176.00 (*0-387-70069-2*) Spr-Verlag.

Mori, Kenjiro & Asian & Oceanic Society for Intravenous Anesthesia Staff. New Balanced Anesthesia: Proceedings of the First Congress of the Asian & Oceanic Society for Intravenous Anesthesia, Kyoto, 25-27 February, 1998. LC 98-38399. (International Congress Ser.). 1998. 184.00 (*0-444-50009-X*) Elsevier.

Mori, Kyoko. The Dream of Water. 288p. 1996. reprint ed. pap. 10.00 (*0-449-91043-1*) Fawcett.

— The Dream of Water: A Memoir. 88p. 1995. 22.50 (*0-8050-3260-6*) H Holt & Co.

— Fallout. 96p. (Orig.). 1994. pap. 7.95 (*1-882688-04-X*) Tia Chucha Pr.

— One Bird. (YA). (gr. 7 up). 1996. mass mkt. 4.50 (*0-449-70453-X*) Fawcett.

— Polite Lies: On Being a Woman Caught Between Cultures. 258p. 1999. pap. 11.95 (*0-449-00428-7*) Fawcett.

— Polite Lies: On Being a Woman Caught Between Cultures. LC 97-10445. 256p. 1998. text 22.50 (*0-8050-4079-X*) St Martin.

— Shizuko's Daughter. 240p. (J). 1994. mass mkt. 4.50 (*0-449-70433-5*, Juniper) Fawcett.

— Shizuko's Daughter. LC 92-26956. 240p. (YA). (gr. 7 up). 1995. 15.95 (*0-8050-2557-X*, Bks Young Read) H Holt & Co.

— Shizuko's Daughter. (J). 1994. 9.60 (*0-606-07153-9*, Pub. by Turtleback) Demco.

***Mori, Kyoko.** Stone Field, True Arrow: A Novel. LC 00-20408. 288p. 2000. 24.00 (*0-8050-4080-3*, Metropol Bks) H Holt & Co.

Mori, Lori De, see De Mori, Lori.

Mori, M., et al, eds. The LEC Rat: A New Model for Hepatitis & Liver Cancer. (Illus.). 360p. 1992. 212.00 (*0-387-70079-X*) Spr-Verlag.

***Mori, Mariko.** Dream Temple. 250p. 2000. 120.00 (*88-87029-11-3*) Fondazione Prada.

Mori, Maryellen Toman, tr. see Abe, Kobo.

Mori, Masahiko. Histochemistry of the Salivary Glands. LC 90-15070. (Illus.). 288p. 1991. 171.00 (*0-8493-6244-X*, QM576, CRC Reprint) Franklin.

Mori, Masahiko, ed. see Shrestha, Prashanta.

Mori, Masahiro. The Buddha in the Robot: A Robot Engineer's Thoughts on Science & Religion. Terry, Charles S., tr. 192p. 1981. pap. 11.95 (*4-333-01002-0*, Pub. by Kosei Pub Co) Tuttle Pubng.

Mori, Masaki. Epic Grandeur: Toward a Comparative Poetics of the Epic. LC 96-3486. (SUNY Series, The Margins of Literature). 192p. (C). 1996. text 57.50 (*0-7914-3201-7*); pap. text 18.95 (*0-7914-3202-5*) State U NY Pr.

Mori, Masatake, jt. ed. see Zhi, Zhongci.

Mori, Michael T. & Welder, W. Dean. The PCMCIA Developer's Guide. 2nd ed. LC 94-93969. (Illus.). 618p. (C). 1995. pap. 89.95 (*0-9640342-1-2*) Sycard Tech.

— The PCMCIA Developer's Guide. 3rd ed. (Illus.). 710p. 1999. pap. 89.95 (*0-9640342-2-0*) Sycard Tech.

Mori Ogai, pseud. The Incident at Sakai & Other Stories. Dilworth, David A., ed. LC 76-58462. (Unesco Collection of Representative Works, Series of Translations from the Literature of the Union of Soviet Socialist Republics: No. 1). (Illus.). 240p. reprint ed. pap. 74.40 (*0-8357-6154-1*, 203464300090) Bks Demand.

— Saiki Koi & Other Stories. Dilworth, David & Rimer, J. Thomas, eds. LC 77-4455. (Historical Literature of Mori Ogai Ser.: No. 2). 210p. 1977. reprint ed. pap. 65.10 (*0-608-04394-X*, 206517500001) Bks Demand.

— Vita Sexualis. Goldstein, Sanford & Ninomiya, Kazuji, trs. LC 72-79020. 156p. 1972. pap. 9.95 (*0-8048-1048-6*) Tuttle Pubng.

— The Wild Geese. Goldstein, Sanford & Ochiai, Kingo, trs. from JPN. LC 59-14087. 119p. 1974. pap. 8.95 (*0-8048-1070-2*) Tuttle Pubng.

— The Wild Goose (Gan) LC 95-17764. (Michigan Monograph Series in Japanese Studies: No. 14). 166p. 1995. 28.95 (*0-939512-70-X*) U MI Japan.

— The Wild Goose (Gan) Watson, Burton, tr. LC 95-17764. (Michigan Monograph Series in Japanese Studies: No. 14). 166p. 1995. pap. 14.95 (*0-939512-71-8*) U MI Japan.

— Youth & Other Stories. Rimer, J. Thomas, ed. LC 93-38737. (SHAPS Library of Translations). 576p. 1994. text 39.00 (*0-8248-1600-5*) UH Pr.

Mori, Renato De, see De Mori, Renato, ed.

Mori, Renato De, see Laface, P. & De Mori, Renato, eds.

Mori Rintaro, see Mori Ogai, pseud.

***Mori, S. & Barth, H. G.** Size Exclusion Chromatography. LC 99-34564. (Springer Laboratory Ser.). (Illus.). 300p. 1999. 106.00 (*3-540-65635-9*) Spr-Verlag.

Mori, S., jt. auth. see Furtado, J. I.

Mori, Scott A. Guide to the Vascular Plants of Central French Guiana. LC 96-3016. (Memoirs Ser.: Vol. 76, No. 1). 1997. 50.00 (*0-89327-398-8*) NY Botanical.

— The Lecythidaceae of a Lowland Neotropical Forest: La Fumee Mountain French Guiana. LC 87-11182. (Memoirs Ser.: Vol. 44). (Illus.). 190p. 1987. pap. 27.75 (*0-89327-315-5*) NY Botanical.

Mori, Scott A. & Lepsch-Cunha, Nadja. The Lecythidaceae of a Central Amazonian Moist Forest. LC 95-37040. (Memoirs Ser.: Vol. 75). (Illus.). 55p. (Orig.). 1995. pap. text 12.50 (*0-89327-396-1*) NY Botanical.

Mori, Scott A., jt. auth. see Mitchell, J.

Mori, Scott A., jt. auth. see Prance, Ghillean T.

Mori, Shunji. Optical Character Recognition. LC 98-23908. (Microwave & Optical Engineering Ser.). 560p. 1999. 125.00 (*0-471-30819-6*, Wiley-Interscience) Wiley.

Mori, Syuiti & Yamamoto, G., eds. Productivity of Communities in Japanese Inland Waters. LC 77-377170. (JIBP Synthesis Ser.: No. 10). 444p. 1975. reprint ed. pap. 137.70 (*0-608-01248-3*, 206193600001) Bks Demand.

Mori, Takao & Nagasawa, Hiroshi, eds. Toxicity of Hormones in Perinatal Life. 208p. 1988. 114.00 (*0-8493-6862-6*, RG627, CRC Reprint) Franklin.

Mori, Takeo & Milenkovic, Dragen. Secrets of Japanese Astrology: The Science of Kigaku. Robinson, Patricia, tr. from CZE. LC 92-46664. (ENG & JPN., Illus.). 144p. 1993. pap. 9.95 (*0-8348-0290-2*, Tengu Bks) Weatherhill.

***Mori, Toshio.** Unfinished Message: Selected Works of Toshio Mori. (California Legacy Ser.). 256p. 2000. pap. 15.95 (*1-890771-35-X*) Heyday Bks.

Mori, Toshio & Inada, Lawson F. Yokohama, California. LC 84-21987. 176p. (Orig.). 1985. reprint ed. pap. 14.95 (*0-295-96167-8*) U of Wash Pr.

Mori, Wendy, ed. Antivirals. (Illus.). (Orig.). 1997. pap. write for info. (*1-57936-042-4*) IBC USA.

— Biochip Arrays & Integrated Devices for Clinical Diagnostics. (IBC Library Ser.). (Illus.). (Orig.). 1997. pap. write for info. (*1-57936-040-8*) IBC USA.

— Bioinformatics & the Effective Use of the Internet for Rapid Drug Discovery. (Illus.). (Orig.). 1997. pap. write for info. (*1-57936-043-2*) IBC USA.

— Ischemic Stroke III. (Illus.). (Orig.). 1997. pap. write for info. (*1-57936-041-6*) IBC USA.

— Natural Products Drug Discovery: New Technologies to Increase Efficiency & Speed. (Illus.). (Orig.). 1997. pap. write for info. (*1-57936-044-0*) IBC USA.

— Oligonucleotide & Gene Therapy-Base Antisense Therapeutics. (IBC Library Ser.). (Illus.). (Orig.). 1997. pap. write for info. (*1-57936-039-4*) IBC USA.

— Pharmacokinetic/Pharmacodynamic Analysis II. (Illus.). (Orig.). 1997. pap. write for info. (*1-57936-045-9*) IBC USA.

Mori, Y. & Yang, W., eds. Thermal Engineering Joint Conference: Proceedings of the ASME-JSME, 4 vols., 1. 2005p. 1983. pap. text 10.00 (*0-317-02653-4*, I00158A) ASME.

— Thermal Engineering Joint Conference: Proceedings of the ASME-JSME, 4 vols., 2. 2005p. 1983. pap. text 10.00 (*0-317-02654-2*, I00158B) ASME.

— Thermal Engineering Joint Conference: Proceedings of the ASME-JSME, 4 vols., 3. 2005p. 1983. pap. text 10.00 (*0-317-02655-0*, I00158C) ASME.

— Thermal Engineering Joint Conference: Proceedings of the ASME-JSME, 4 vols., 4. 2005p. 1983. pap. text 10.00 (*0-317-02656-9*, I00158D) ASME.

— Thermal Engineering Joint Conference: Proceedings of the ASME-JSME, 4 vols., Set. 2005p. 1983. pap. text 30.00 (*0-317-02652-6*, I00158) ASME.

Mori, Yasuo & Yang, Wen-Jei, eds. Heat Transfer in High Technology & Power Engineering. (Illus.). 602p. 1986. 185.00 (*0-89116-645-9*) Hemisp Pub.

Mori, Yasuo, jt. ed. see Hatta, Keizo.

Moriah. Abused Beyond Words: The Healing Journey of Reclaiming Our Inner Power & Peace. 1998. 39.95 (*1-892268-02-7*); pap. 24.95 (*1-892268-01-9*) Pathways United Pubns.

***Morian, D. A., et al.** Maintaining Flexible Pavements: The Long Term Pavewment Performance Experiment SPS-3, 5-Year Data Analysis. (Illus.). 223p. (C). 1999. pap. text 35.00 (*0-7881-7588-2*) DIANE Pub.

Moriarity, Brian, jt. auth. see Roland, Harold E.

Moriarity, Cay & Palmer, Julia. St. Anthony's DRG Optimizer. Kukucka, Regina M. & Swann, Keith, eds. 363p. (C). 129.00 (*1-56329-366-8*) St Anthony Pub.

Moriarity, Cay & Palmer, Julia, eds. St. Anthony's DRG Optimizer (OPT) rev. ed. 400p. 1997. pap. 149.00 (*1-56329-497-4*) St Anthony Pub.

Moriarity, David M. Psychic Energy & Aggression. 188p. (C). 1991. pap. 32.50 (*0-87527-486-2*) Green.

Moriarity, Gene M., jt. auth. see O'Flynn, Michael F.

Moriarity, Michael. The Voyeur. 1998. 20.50 (*0-684-80426-3*) S&S Trade.

Moriarity, Pat. Popcorn Pimps. 72p. 1996. pap. 8.95 (*1-56097-254-8*, Pub. by Fantagraph Bks) Seven Hills Bk.

Moriarity, S., et al. Cost Accounting. 3rd ed. 1117p. 1991. text 58.00 incl. 5.25 hd (*0-471-54729-8*); text 58.00 incl. 3.5 hd (*0-471-54730-1*); text 52.00 (*0-471-54924-X*) Wiley.

Moriarity, Shane, ed. Joint Cost Allocations. 1981. 14.95 (*0-317-02579-1*) U OK Ctr Econ.

— Laboratory Market Research. 222p. 1986. 15.00 (*0-931880-05-X*) U OK Ctr Econ.

Moriarity, Shane & Allen, Carl P. Cost Accounting. 2nd ed. 1091p. (C). 1987. pap. text 10.00 (*0-471-60426-7*); pap. text 10.00 (*0-471-60427-5*) Wiley.

— Cost Accounting. 2nd ed. 1091p. (C). 1987. pap. text 10.00 (*0-471-60652-9*) Wiley.

Moriarity, Shane & Joyce, Edward, eds. Decision Making & Accounting: Current Research. 217p. 1984. 14.95 (*0-931880-04-1*) U OK Ctr Econ.

Moriarity, Stephen R. Fritz Kaeser: A Life in Photography. LC 98-24610. (Illus.). 1998. 49.95 (*0-268-02852-4*) U of Notre Dame Pr.

Moriarty. Key Facts in Diabetes. 1994. pap. text 12.95 (*0-443-04828-2*, W B Saunders Co) Harcrt Hlth Sci Grp.

Moriarty, Alice E., jt. auth. see Murphy, Lois B.

Moriarty, Andrea & Diamond, Christine. Kids Take L. A. 260p. 1999. pap. 15.95 (*0-9660893-2-4*, Pub. by Book Happy Bks) IPG Chicago.

Moriarty, Andrea, jt. auth. see Diamond, Christine.

Moriarty, Anthony. The Psychology of Adolescent Satanism: A Guide for Parents, Counselors, Clergy, & Teachers. LC 92-12731. 168p. 1992. 39.95 (*0-275-94307-0*, C4307, Praeger Pubs) Greenwood.

Moriarty, Anthony R. & Field, Mark W. Police Officer Selection: A Handbook for Law Enforcement Administrators. LC 94-17514. (Illus.). 372p. (C). 1994. 80.95 (*0-398-05922-5*); pap. 47.95 (*0-398-05970-5*) C C Thomas.

Moriarty, Brian, jt. auth. see Roland, Harold E.

Moriarty, Catherine, ed. The Voice of the Middle Ages: In Personal Letters, 1100-1500. (Illus.). 352p. 1991. 29.95 (*0-87226-343-6*, P Bedrick Books) NTC Contemp Pub Co.

— The Voice of the Middle Ages: In Personal Letters, 1100-1500. (Illus.). 352p. 1991. pap. 12.95 (*0-87226-252-9*, P Bedrick Books) NTC Contemp Pub Co.

Moriarty, Christine. Kids Take New York. LC 98-149359. 320p. 1997. pap. 15.95 (*0-9660893-0-8*) Book Happy Bks.

Moriarty, Christopher. Down The Dodder. (Illus.). 186p. 1998. pap. 14.95 (*0-86327-286-X*, Pub. by Wolfhound Press) Irish Amer Bk.

— Exploring Dublin: Wildlife, Parks, Waterways. LC 97-189911. (Illus.). 218p. 1998. pap. 14.95 (*0-86327-590-7*, Pub. by Wolfhound Press) Irish Amer Bk.

M

Moriarty, D. J. & Pullin, Roger S., eds. Detritus & Microbial Ecology in Aquaculture. (Conference Proceedings Ser.: No. 14). 1987. pap. 28.50 (*971-10-2229-X*, Pub. by ICLARM) Intl Spec Bk.

Moriarty, Dan. Happiness Is Subbing Everyday. 10p. (Orig.). (C). 1993. pap. text 6.00 (*0-614-28289-6*) D Moriarty.

Moriarty, Daniel P. How to Help Your Kids Through College. 1978. pap. 2.00 (*0-933968-01-9*) D Moriarty.

— How to Raise Money at Church Without Sales or Bingo. 1977. pap. 4.00 (*0-933968-00-0*) D Moriarty.

— Ten Ways to Lobby Your Representatives from Home. 1979. pap. 2.00 (*0-933968-03-5*) D Moriarty.

Moriarty, David M. King Phillip's War. 425p. (Orig.). (C). Date not set. pap. 32.50 (*0-87527-493-5*) Green.

— The Loss of Loved Ones. 2nd ed. LC 79-50189. 312p. 1983. 27.50 (*0-87527-161-8*) Green.

— Rudolf Hess, Deputy Fuhrer: A Psychological Study. (Illus.). 325p. (Orig.). (C). pap. 35.00 (*0-87527-489-7*) Green.

— The Stranger: A Psychological Study of Adolf Hitler. (Illus.). 302p. (Orig.). 1993. pap. text 27.50 (*0-87527-491-9*) Green.

Moriarty, Dorothy. Dorothy: A Nurse's Memoirs 1889-1989. large type ed. (Illus.). 368p. 1992. 27.99 (*0-7089-2591-X*) Ulverscroft.

Moriarty, Ernest T. One Day into Twenty Three. 164p. (Orig.). 1987. pap. text 14.50 (*0-9620139-0-0*) E T Moriarty.

Moriarty, F. Ecotoxicology: The Study of Pollutants in Ecosystems. 2nd ed. 289p. 1988. text 83.00 (*0-12-506761-5*); pap. text 41.00 (*0-12-506762-3*) Acad Pr.

Moriarty, Frank. Bold As Love: The Jimi Hendrix Experience. 120p. 1996. 19.98 (*1-56799-385-0*, MetroBooks) M Friedman Pub Grp Inc.

— Bruce Springsteen. LC 98-3053. (Illus.). 120p. 1998. 19.98 (*1-56799-652-3*, MetroBooks) M Friedman Pub Grp Inc.

***Moriarty, Frank.** Dale Earnhardt. LC 00-20556. (Illus.). 96p. 2000. 12.98 (*1-56799-965-4*, Friedman-Fairfax) M Friedman Pub Grp Inc.

— Dale Jarrett. (Illus.). 96p. 2000. 12.98 (*1-58663-048-2*) M Friedman Pub Grp Inc.

Moriarty, Frank. Ecotoxicology: The Study of Pollutants in Ecosystems. 3rd ed. (Illus.). 350p. 1999. pap. 49.95 (*0-12-506763-1*) Acad Pr.

— Encyclopedia of Stock Car Racing. LC 99-17987. (Illus.). 228p. 1998. 22.98 (*1-56799-459-8*, Friedman-Fairfax) M Friedman Pub Grp Inc.

***Moriarty, Frank.** Jeff Gordon: The Inside Track. LC 99-13357. (Illus.). 96p. 1999. 13.98 (*1-56799-851-8*) M Friedman Pub Grp Inc.

Moriarty, Frank. Johnny Cash. LC 97-13034. (Illus.). 120p. 1997. 19.98 (*1-56799-488-1*, MetroBooks) M Friedman Pub Grp Inc.

***Moriarty, Frank.** Supercars: The Story of the Dodge Charger Daytona & Plymouth SuperBird. (Illus.). 160p. 1999. pap. 24.95 (*1-57427-106-7*) Howell Pr VA.

— Superstars of Stock Car Racing. LC 99-32608. 1999. pap. text 12.98 (*1-56799-881-X*, MetroBooks) M Friedman Pub Grp Inc.

Moriarty, G. Andrews. Gilbert. The Gilberts of Clare & Colchester. 19p. 1997. reprint ed. pap. 5.00 (*0-8328-8738-2*); reprint ed. lib. bdg. 15.00 (*0-8328-8737-4*) Higginson Bk Co.

Moriarty, G. P. Dean Swift & His Writings. LC 70-130247. (English Literature Ser.: No. 33). 1970. reprint ed. lib. bdg. 75.00 (*0-8383-1137-7*) M S G Haskell Hse.

Moriarty, Gene, jt. auth. see Nekoogar, Farzad.

Moriarty, Gerald P., tr. from FRE. The Paris Law Courts: Sketches of Men & Manners. viii, 293p. 1999. reprint ed. 95.00 (*1-56169-496-7*) Gaunt.

— Paris Law Courts: Sketches of Men & Manners. (Illus.). viii, 293p. 1987. reprint ed. 42.50 (*0-8377-2434-1*, Rothman) W S Hein.

Moriarty, J., jt. auth. see Cruetz, E.

Moriarty, J. M. Ground Attack - Vietnam: The Marines Who Controlled the Skies. (Orig.). 1993. mass mkt. 5.99 (0-8041-1065-4) Ivy Books.

Moriarty, Jane C. Psychological & Scientific Evidence in Criminal Trials, 2 vols. LC 95-52656. 1996. ring bd. write for info. (0-8366-1005-9) West Group.

Moriarty, John. Diction: Italian, Latin, French, German . . . the Sounds & 81 Exercises for Singing Them. LC 74-17158. 1975. pap. 29.95 (0-911318-09-7) E C Schirmer.

***Moriarty, John.** Dreamtime. 2nd rev. ed. 288p. 1999. pap. 24.95 (1-901866-31-9, Pub. by Lilliput Pr) Irish Bks Media.

Moriarty, John. Turtle Was Gone a Long Time, 3. LC 96-170722. (Turtle Was Gone a Long Time Ser.). 1999. 39.95 (1-901866-02-5, Liplop) Goodfellow.

— Turtle Was Gone a Long Time: Crossing the Kedron. LC 96-170722. 242p. 1997. 34.95 (1-874675-63-5) Dufour.

— Turtle Was Gone a Long Time: The Horeshead Nebula Neighing. LC 96-170722. 288p. 1997. 39.95 (1-874675-90-2) Dufour.

Moriarty, John D. Psychiatric Treatment Is Much More Than Psychotherapy. 300p. 1993. 24.00 (0-9633747-0-2); pap. 16.95 (0-9633747-1-0) SoCal Med Pr.

Moriarty, John J., et al. Minnesota's Amphibians & Reptiles: Proceedings of a Symposium. 75p. 1997. pap. 9.95 (1-885209-08-8) Serpents Tale.

Moriarty, John J., jt. auth. see Oldfield, Barney.

Moriarty, John P. & McNeily, Curtlan R. Regulation of Financial Planners. LC 91-26315. (Securities Law Ser.). 1991. ring bd. 145.00 (0-87632-816-8) West Group.

Moriarty, Kathleen M. A Shaker Sampler Coloring Book. 2nd ed. (Illus.). 30p. (J). (gr. k-6). 1991. pap. 4.95 (0-915836-15-7) United Soc Shakers.

Moriarty, Laura. L' Archiviste. (Illus.). 32p. 1991. pap. 8.00 (84-87467-10-5) SPD-Small Pr Dist.

***Moriarty, Laura.** The Case. 100p. 1999. 11.50 (1-882022-36-X, Pub. by O Bks) SPD-Small Pr Dist.

Moriarty, Laura. Cunning: A Novel. LC 98-44412. 55p. 1999. pap. 10.00 (1-881471-30-6) S Duyvil.

— Like Roads. Dienstfrey, Pat, ed. LC 89-49484. 64p. (Orig.). (C). 1990. pap. text 8.00 (0-932716-24-5) Kelsey St Pr.

***Moriarty, Laura.** Nude Memoir. 88p. 2000. pap. 9.00 (1-928650-07-4, Pub. by Krupskaya) SPD-Small Pr Dist.

Moriarty, Laura. Rondeaux. LC 90-61555. (Roof Bks.). 88p. (Orig.). 1990. pap. text 8.00 (0-937804-39-8) Segue NYC.

— Spicer's City. (Poetry New York Pamphlet Ser.: Vol. 3). 30p. 1998. pap. 5.00 (0-923389-15-6) Meet Eyes Bind.

— Symmetry. Chadwick, Cydney, ed. 124p. (Orig.). 1996. pap. 9.95 (1-880713-04-7, Pub. by AVEC Bks) SPD-Small Pr Dist.

Moriarty, Laura, et al. An Avec Sampler, 1997. Chadwick, Cydney, ed. 66p. 1997. 8.50 (1-880713-10-1) AVEC Bks.

Moriarty, Laura, jt. auth. see Jerin, Robert.

Moriarty, Laura J. & Carter, David L., eds. Criminal Justice Technology in the 21st Century. LC 98-29807. 300p. 1998. text 59.95 (0-398-06902-6); pap. text 46.95 (0-398-06903-4) C C Thomas.

Moriarty, Laura J. & Jerin, Robert A. Current Issues in Victimology Research. LC 98-88619. 304p. 1998. pap. 25.00 (0-89089-861-8) Carolina Acad Pr.

Moriarty, Laura J., jt. auth. see McConnell, Elizabeth Huffmaster.

Moriarty, Linda P. Ni'ihau Shell Leis. LC 86-50306. (Illus.). 104p. 1986. 39.95 (0-8248-0998-X, Kolowalu Bk) UH Pr.

Moriarty, Marilyn F. Moses Unchained. LC 97-40787. 192p. 1998. 22.95 (0-8203-1985-6) U of Ga Pr.

Moriarty, Marilyn F. Writing Science Thru Critical Thinking. (Illus.). 236p. (C). 1995. pap. text 17.50 (0-86720-490-7) JB Pubns.

Moriarty, Marilyn F. Writing Science Thru Critical Thinking. (Philosophy Ser.). 232p. 1996. pap. 30.00 (0-86720-510-5) Jones & Bartlett.

Moriarty, Michael. The Liturgical Revolution: Prayer Book Revision & Associated Parishes : A Generation of Change in the Episcopal Church. LC 96-71102. 1996. write for info. (0-89869-203-2) Church Pub Inc.

— The Perfect 10: The Blessings of Following God's Commandments in a Post Modern World. LC 99-19135. 256p. 2000. pap. 12.99 (0-310-22764-X) Zondervan.

— Roland Barthes. LC 90-72070. (Key Contemporary Thinkers Ser.). 280p. 1992. 42.50 (0-8047-1932-2); pap. 14.95 (0-8047-1933-0) Stanford U Pr.

Moriarty, Michael E. Semiotics of World Literature. LC 96-25764. (Studies in Comparative Literature: Vol. 21). 340p. 1996. text 99.95 (0-7734-8776-X) E Mellen.

Moriarty, Patricia, ed. see Boloz, Sigmund A.

Moriarty, Patrick J. Evening Prayers, Morning Promises: Understanding 12 Step Spirituality. LC 89-37966. 160p. (Orig.). pap. 7.95 (0-934125-14-7) Hazelden.

Moriarty, Phyllis A., jt. auth. see Dreier, Susan.

Moriarty, Richard. N. Y., Understanding the Penal Law. 1998. teacher ed. 25.95 (0-87526-424-7) Gould.

Moriarty, Richard C. New York Understanding the Penal Law. 190p. 1994. ring bd. 25.95 (0-87526-416-6) Gould.

Moriarty, Rowland T., Jr., et al, eds. Business Marketing Strategy: Cases, Concepts, & Applications. LC 94-22561. (Marketing Ser.). 864p. (C). 1994. text 72.95 (0-256-16911-X, Irwn McGrw-H) McGrw-H Hghr Educ.

Moriarty, Sandra & Burnett, John. Introduction to Marketing Communications: An Integrated Approach. LC 97-38237. 659p. 1997. 97.00 (0-13-269085-3) P-H.

Moriarty, Sandra & Duncan, Tom. Creating & Delivering Winning Advertising & Marketing Presentations. (Illus.). 160p. 1996. pap. 22.95 (0-8442-3531-8, NTC Business Bks) NTC Contemp Pub Co.

— How to Create & Deliver Winning Advertising Presentations. 144p. 1994. pap. 19.95 (0-8442-3196-7, NTC Business Bks) NTC Contemp Pub Co.

Moriarty-Schieven, Cindy. In Celebration of Life. (Illus.). 154p. 1991. pap. 19.95 (0-87527-474-9) Green.

Moriarty, Tim. Vampire Nights. 1989. mass mkt. 3.95 (1-55817-180-0, Pinncle Kensgtn) Kensgtn Pub Corp.

Moriarty, Tim, jt. auth. see Boyle, Tish.

Moriarty, Timothy, jt. auth. see Boyle, Tish.

Moriarty, Timothy, jt. auth. see Boyle, Trish.

Morice, A. K., ed. Clinical Pulmonary Hypertension. (Portland Press Research Monographs: Vol. 8). (Illus.). 292p. 1995. text 136.00 (1-85578-074-7, Pub. by Portland Pr Ltd) Ashgate Pub Co.

Morice, Dave. The Adventures of Dr. Alphabet: 104 Unusual Ways to Write Poetry in the Classroom & the Community. (Illus.). 276p. 1995. pap. 17.95 (0-915924-44-7) Tchrs & Writers Coll.

— How to Make Poetry Comics. 64p. 1983. pap. 5.95 (0-915924-31-5) Tchrs & Writers Coll.

— Quicksand Through the Hourglass. LC 79-25714. (Illus.). 57p. (Orig.). 1979. pap. 9.00 (0-915124-27-0) Coffee Hse.

Morice, E. Diccionario de Estadistica. (SPA.). 220p. 1975. pap. 18.50 (0-8288-5808-X, S50210) Fr & Eur.

***Morice, Henri.** God's Providence Explained: How the Lord Fashions Each Moment & Each Event to Care for You & Draw You Closer to Him. LC 99-44834. Orig. Title: The Gospel of Divine Providence. 172p. 1999. reprint ed. pap. 14.95 (1-928832-01-6) Sophia Inst Pr.

Morichon, David. Pollution? No Problem! LC 98-5690. (J). 1998. pap. write for info. (0-7613-0434-7); lib. bdg. 21.90 (0-7613-1260-9) Millbrook Pr.

***Morici, Peter.** Antitrust in the Global Trading System: Reconciling U. S., Japanese & EU Approaches. (Illus.). iii, 141p. 2000. pap. 19.95 (1-888773-01-4) Econ Strategy.

Morici, Peter. Free Trade in the Americas. LC 94-7627. (Orig.). 1994. pap. 8.95 (0-87078-187-1) Century Foundation.

— A New Special Relationship: Free Trade & U. S.-Canada Economic Relations in the . . . 153p. 1991. pap. 23.95 (0-88645-132-9, Pub. by Inst Res Pub) Ashgate Pub Co.

— Trade Talks with Mexico: A Time for Realism. 124p. (Orig.). 1991. pap. text 15.00 (0-89068-110-4, CIR 22 (NPA253)) Natl Planning.

Morici, Peter, ed. Making Free Trade Work: The Canada - U. S. Agreement. LC 89-71317. 198p. 1990. reprint ed. pap. 61.40 (0-608-02006-0, 206266200003) Bks Demand.

Morici, Peter & Megna, Laura L. Canada-United States Trade & Economic Interdependence. (Canadian-U. S. Prospect Ser.). 64p. 1980. pap. 5.00 (0-88806-072-6) Natl Planning.

— U. S. Economic Policies Affecting Industrial Trade: A Quantitative Assessment. LC 83-60013. (Committee on Changing International Realities Ser.). 140p. (Orig.). 1983. pap. 12.00 (0-89068-068-X, CIR-13) Natl Planning.

Morici, Peter, jt. auth. see Mutti, John.

Morick, Harold. Challenges to Empiricism. LC 72-10731. 339p. (C). 1980. reprint ed. 34.95 (0-915144-89-1); reprint ed. pap. text 14.95 (0-915144-90-5) Hackett Pub.

Moriconi, M. Dictionnaire de la Mode, A a Z. (FRE.). 1998. 79.95 (0-320-00292-6) Fr & Eur.

Moricz, Szigmond & Vizinczey, Stephen. Be Faithful Unto Death. (Central European Classics Ser.). 336p. (C). 1996. pap. 16.95 (1-85866-060-2) Ctrl Europ Univ.

***Moricz, Zsigmond.** Relations. LC 98-142137. 240p. 1999. pap. 21.00 (963-13-4289-1, Pub. by Corvina Bks) St Mut.

Moriearty, Scott C. & Rubin, Laurie F. Representing Clients Before MCAD in Employment Cases. LC 95-78280. 104p. 1995. pap. text 59.00 (1-57589-019-4, 96-15.10-QC) Mass CLE.

Moriei, Peter, et al. Canadian Industrial Policy. LC 82-81566. 116p. (Orig.). 1982. pap. 10.00 (0-89068-063-9) Natl Planning.

Moriello. Clinical Handbook of Small Animals. 2000. pap. text. write for info. (0-7216-6092-4, W B Saunders Co) Harcrt Hlth Sci Grp.

***Moriello.** Veterinary Dermatology. 256p. 2001. pap. 25.00 (0-7506-7299-4) Buttrwrth-Heinemann.

Moriello, K. A. & Mason, I. S. Handbook of Small Animal Dermatology. LC 94-18014. (Pergamon Veterinary Handbook Ser.: No. 11). 1995. 80.00 (0-08-042281-0, Pergamon Pr); pap. 60.00 (0-08-042280-2, Pergamon Pr) Elsevier.

Morier, Henri. Dictionnaire de Poetique et de Rhetorique. 4th ed. (FRE.). 1320p. 1989. 350.00 (0-7859-0469-7, 2130400973) Fr & Eur.

— Dictionnaire Poetique, Rhetorique. (FRE.). 1998. 395.00 (0-320-00218-7) Fr & Eur.

Morier, J. The Adventure of Hajji Baba of Ispahan. 464p. 1987. 125.00 (1-85077-145-6, Pub. by Darf Pubs Ltd) St Mut.

Morier, James. Sargozasht-e Haji Baba-Ye Isfahani Haji Baba-Ye Isfahani. Isfahani, Mirza H., tr. (Bibliotheca Iranica Ser.: No. 9). Orig. Title: The Adventures of Haji Baba of Isphahan. (PER., Illus.). 432p. (Orig.). 1996. pap. text 24.95 (1-56859-042-3) Mazda Pubs.

Mories, John, contrib. by. 100+ Essential Guitar Chords. 1996. 9.95 (0-7119-3935-7, AM 91816) Omnibus NY.

Moriet, Marie-Therese. Dictionnaire Etymologique des Noms de Famille. (FRE.). 1120p. 1991. 150.00 (0-8288-9497-3) Fr & Eur.

Morigaki, K. Physics of Amorphous Semiconductors. 300p. 1997. text 55.00 (981-02-1381-6) World Scientific Pub.

Morigi, Paolo. Raccolta di un Amatore: D'arte Primtiva. (ENG, FRE, GER & ITA., Illus.). 475p. 1980. lib. bdg. 195.00 (0-87817-286-6) Hacker.

Moriguchi, Shigeichi. Software Excellence: A Total Quality Management Guide. LC 96-50309. (Illus.). 640p. 1997. 90.00 (1-56327-050-1) Productivity Inc.

Moriguchi, Yasuhiko, tr. see Chomei, Kamo.

Morihara, Bonnie V., jt. auth. see McSwain, Mary E.

Morihisa, John M., ed. Brain Imaging in Psychiatry. LC 84-6303. (Clinical Insights Ser.). 103p. reprint ed. pap. 32.00 (0-8357-7812-6, 203618400002) Bks Demand.

Morii, H., ed. Calcium-Regulating Hormones Vol. 1: Role in Disease & Aging. (Contributions to Nephrology Ser.: Vol. 90). (Illus.). xiv, 230p. 1991. 49.75 (3-8055-5371-4) S Karger.

— Calcium-Regulating Hormones Vol. II: Calcium Transport, Bone Metabolism & New Drugs. (Contributions to Nephrology Ser.: Vol. 91). (Illus.). viii, 152p. 1991. 49.75 (3-8055-5372-2) S Karger.

Morik, K., ed. Knowledge Representation & Organization in Machine Learning. (Lecture Notes in Artificial Intelligence Ser.: Vol. 347). 319p. 1989. 40.00 (0-387-50768-X) Spr-Verlag.

***Morik, Katharina, et al.** Making Robots Smarter: Combining Sensing & Action Through Robot Learning. LC 99-32645. 269p. 1999. write for info. (0-7923-8562-4) Kluwer Academic.

Morik, Katherina, et al. Knowledge Acquisition & Machine Learning. (Knowledge Based Systems Ser.). (Illus.). 320p. 1993. text 65.00 (0-12-506230-3) Acad Pr.

Morikawa, Hidemasa. Zaibatsu: The Rise & Fall of Family Enterprise Groups in Japan. 283p. 1992. 52.50 (0-86008-488-4, Pub. by U of Tokyo) Col U Pr.

Morikawa, Jun. Japan & Africa: Big Business & Diplomacy. LC 96-47286. 1996. write for info. (0-86543-576-6); pap. write for info. (0-86543-577-4) Africa World.

Morike, Eduard. Morike: Poems. Thomas, Lionel, ed. (Bristol German Texts Ser.). (GER.). 152p. 1960. 14.95 (0-631-01660-0) Blackwell Pubs.

— Mozart Auf der Reise Nach Prag. unabridged ed. (World Classic Literature Ser.). (GER.). pap. 5.95 (3-89507-018-1, Pub. by Bookking Intl) Distribks Inc.

— Mozart's Journey to Prague & Selected Poems. Luke, David, tr. from GER. 240p. 1997. 55.00 (1-870352-82-3, Pub. by Libris) Paul & Co Pubs.

Morikuni, James J. & Kang, Sung-Mo. Computer-Aided Design of Optoelectronic Integrated Circuits & Systems. 351p. 1997. 60.00 (0-8194-2614-8) SPIE.

Morill, Terrence C., ed. Lanthanide Shift Reagents for Stereochemical Analysis. 206p. 1987. pap. 105.00 (0-471-18650-3) Wiley.

Morillo & Pavkovic. Expanding Encounters. (History Ser.). 2002. pap. 41.00 (0-534-57276-6) Wadsworth Pub.

Morillo Caballero, Manuel, notes. Romancero. (Clasicos Esenciales Ser.). (SPA.). (C). 1998. pap. 9.95 (84-294-4558-7) Santillana.

Morillo, Carlos A., et al. The Wolff-Parkinson-White Syndrome. LC 96-36747. (Clinical Approaches to Tachyarrhythmias Ser.: Vol. 6). (Illus.). 58p. 1996. 24.00 (0-87993-660-6) Futura Pub.

Morillo, Carolyn R. Contingent Creatures: A Reward Event Theory of Motivation. 206p. (C). 1995. pap. text 22.95 (0-8226-3041-9); lib. bdg. 59.50 (0-8226-3040-0) Littlefield.

Morillo, Stephen. Warfare under the Anglo-Norman Kings, 1066-1135. (Illus.). 218p. 1997. pap. 29.95 (0-85115-689-4) Boydell & Brewer.

Morillo, Stephen, ed. The Battle of Hastings: Sources & Interpretations. LC 95-14358. (Warfare in History: Sources & Interpretations Ser.: vol. 1). (Illus.). 264p. 1998. pap. 29.95 (0-85115-619-3) Boydell & Brewer.

Morimitsu, Phil. In the Company of ECK Masters. 288p. 1988. pap. 12.00 (1-57043-058-6) Eckankar.

Morimitsu, Tamotsu. Cholesteatoma & Anterior Tympanotomy. LC 97-20738. (Illus.). x, 118p. 1997. 76.00 (4-431-70197-4) Spr-Verlag.

Morimore, Peter & Mortimore, Jo. The Primary Head: Roles, Responsibilities & Reflections. 144p. 1991. pap. 27.00 (1-85396-140-X, Pub. by P Chapman) Taylor & Francis.

— The Secondary Head: Roles, Responsibilities & Reflections. 176p. 1991. pap. 27.00 (1-85396-141-8, Pub. by P Chapman) Taylor & Francis.

Morimoto, Anri. Jonathan Edwards & the Catholic Vision of Salvation. LC 94-40824. 200p. 1995. pap. 35.00 (0-271-01453-9) Pa St U Pr.

Morimoto, Hikaru, tr. see Tatematsu, Wahei.

***Morimoto, Hiroaki, ed.** Photomask & X-Ray Mask Technology VI. 642p. 1999. pap. text 120.00 (0-8194-3230-X) SPIE.

Morimoto, Isao, tr. see Morimoto, Junko.

***Morimoto, Junko.** Negotiating Agreement & Disagreement in Japanese: Connective Expressions & Turn Construction. LC 99-40505. (Studies in Discourse & Grammar: Vol. 8). xii, 240p. 1999. 75.00 (1-55619-374-2) J Benjamins Pubng.

— The Two Bullies. Morimoto, Isao, tr. from JPN. LC 98-41774. (Illus.). 32p. (J). (ps-2). 1999. 17.00 (0-517-80061-6, Pub. by Crown Bks Yng Read); lib. bdg. 18.99 (0-517-80062-4, Pub. by Crown Bks Yng Read) Random.

Morimoto, Junko, jt. auth. see Martin, Rafe.

Morimoto, Kiyo, ed. see Burkle, Candace R. & Marshak, David.

Morimoto, Kiyo, ed. see Tobin, Catherine.

Morimoto, Kokichi. The Standard of Living in Japan. LC 78-63963. (Johns Hopkins University. Studies in the Social Sciences. Thirtieth Ser. 1912: No. 2). reprint ed. 32.50 (0-404-61210-5) AMS Pr.

Morimoto, M. & Kawai, T. Structure of Solutions of Differential Equations. 550p. 1996. text 128.00 (981-02-2321-8) World Scientific Pub.

Morimoto, M., jt. ed. see Bony, J. M.

Morimoto, Mitsuo. Analytic Functionals on the Sphere Analytic Functionals on the Sphere. LC 98-23076. (Translations of Mathematical Monographs). 170p. 1998. 65.00 (0-8218-0585-1, MMONO-MORIMOTO2) Am Math.

— An Introduction to Sato's Hyperfunctions. LC 93-21490. (Translations of Mathematical Monographs: Vol. 129).Tr. of Sato Chokansu Nyumon. 273p. 1993. text 49.00 (0-8218-4571-3, MMONO/129) Am Math.

Morimoto, Rand. Deploying Microsoft Exchange Server 5: The Authoritative Guide to Planning, Running & Fine-Tuning Your Exchange Rollout. LC 97-176756. 1997. pap. text 39.99 (0-07-882314-5) Osborne-McGraw.

— Exchange Server 6. 752p. 1998. pap. 39.99 (0-07-882472-9) McGraw.

— Windows NT 5 Design & Migration. 1998. pap. 44.99 (0-07-211918-7) Osborne-McGraw.

***Morimoto, Rand.** Windows 2000 Design & Migration. 563p. 1999. pap. 44.99 (0-07-212205-6) McGraw.

Morimoto, Richard I., et al, eds. Stress Proteins in Biology & Medicine. LC 89-23926. (Cold Spring Harbor Monographs: No. 19). (Illus.). 460p. 1990. reprint ed. pap. 142.60 (0-608-00930-X, 206172400011) Bks Demand.

Morimoto, Toshifumi, et al, eds. Brain & Oral Functions: Oral Motor Function & Dysfunction: Selected Papers from the Osaka International Oral Physiology Symposium on Brain & Oral Function, Osaka, 3-5 September 1994. LC 95-8197. (International Congress Ser.: No. 1079). 662p. 1995. 282.25 (0-444-81963-0) Elsevier.

Morimoto, Toyotomi. Japanese Americans & Cultural Continuity: Maintaining Language & Heritage. LC 96-40289. (Studies in the History of Education: Vol. 5). (Illus.). 192p. 1997. text 44.00 (0-8153-1767-0, SS990) Garland.

Morimoto, Tsuyoshi, jt. auth. see Kurematsu, Akira.

Morimura, Stephanie Forman, jt. auth. see Crowell, Todd.

Morin. Dismissal: There Is No Easy Way - But There Is a Better Way. 1995. pap. 9.95 (1-880030-48-9) DBM Pub.

— The Eye in Pediatric Disease. (Illus.). 400p. 1991. 60.00 (0-8016-3553-5) Mosby Inc.

Morin, Alexander J. Science Policy & Politics. 208p. (C). 1992. pap. text 22.40 (0-13-795246-5) P-H.

Morin, Alice. Newspaper Theatre. (J). (gr. 1-8). 1989. pap. 8.99 (0-8224-6349-0) Fearon Teacher Aids.

— Nicotine Management: Air Cigarettes. (Illus.). 66p. 1997. pap. 5.95 (0-9658854-0-2) Los Abuelos.

***Morin, Alice.** Teach Conflict Resolution with Puppets. (Illus.). 107p. 1999. pap. 14.95 (0-9658854-3-7) Los Abuelos.

Morin, Alice. Three Plays in Two Languages: Tres Obras Drammaticas en Dos Idiomas. Farber, Irene, tr. LC 99-216309. (ENG & SPA., Illus.). 61p. (YA). (gr. 6-12). 1997. spiral bd. 14.95 (0-9658854-1-0) Los Abuelos.

— What Makes Teachers Laugh? Administrators! (Illus.). 157p. 1998. pap. 10.95 (0-9658854-2-9) Los Abuelos.

Morin, Ann M. Her Excellency. (Twayne's Oral History Ser.: No. 14). (Illus.). 336p. 1994. per. 14.95 (0-8057-9142-6, Twyne) Mac Lib Ref.

— Her Excellency. (Twayne's Oral History Ser.: No. 14). (Illus.). 336p. 1994. 27.95 (0-8057-9118-3, Twyne) Mac Lib Ref.

Morin, Beatrice, jt. auth. see Colin, Eric.

Morin, Carol, jt. auth. see Meisels, Alexander.

Morin, Carole. Dead Glamorous: The Autobiography of Seduction & Self-Destruction. LC 96-27413. 190p. 1997. 23.95 (0-87951-750-6, Pub. by Overlook Pr) Penguin Putnam.

— Lampshades. LC 98-10744. 192p. 1998. 21.95 (0-87951-857-X, Pub. by Overlook Pr) Penguin Putnam.

Morin Center for Banking Law Studies Staff. Annual Review of Banking Law. 1987. boxed set 400.00 (0-614-05779-5, MICHIE) LEXIS Pub.

— Annual Review of Banking Law, 11 vols. 1997. 400.00 (0-327-01016-9, 80132, MICHIE) LEXIS Pub.

— Annual Review of Banking Law, Vols. 6-13, Set. 1992. text 400.00 (0-88063-162-7, 80132-10, MICHIE) LEXIS Pub.

— Annual Review of Banking Law, Vol. 6. 500p. 1987. 50.00 (0-88063-168-6, 80138-10, MICHIE) LEXIS Pub.

— Annual Review of Banking Law, Vol. 8. 700p. 1989. 50.00 (0-88063-273-9, 80140-10, MICHIE) LEXIS Pub.

— Annual Review of Banking Law, Vol. 9. 700p. 1990. 50.00 (0-88063-394-8, 80141-10, MICHIE) LEXIS Pub.

— Annual Review of Banking Law, Vol. 10. 270p. 1991. boxed set 80.00 (0-88063-782-X, 80142-10, MICHIE) LEXIS Pub.

Morin, Charles M. Insomnia: Psychological Assessment & Management. LC 93-6564. (Treatment Manuals for Practitioners Ser.). 238p. 1996. pap. text 22.00 (1-57230-120-1) Guilford Pubns.

Morin, Christopher. Cities of Lightning: The Iconography of Thunderbeings in the Oriental Traditions. 250p. 2000. pap. 24.95 (0-9660203-0-8) C Morin.

Morin, Dominique. How to Understand God. (Adult Christian Formation Program Ser.). (Illus.). 144p. (Orig.). 1990. pap. 12.95 (0-8245-1047-X) Crossroad NY.

Morin, Douglas J. No Less Zeal: A Spiritual Guide for Catholic Lay People. LC 92-34242. 156p. (Orig.). 1993. pap. 7.95 (0-8189-0631-6) Alba.

Morin, Drake B. The Drake Beam Morin Guide to Retirement Planning. 141p. 1994. pap. 10.95 (1-880030-28-4) DBM Pub.

— Managing Diversity in the Global Workplace. 1995. pap. 10.95 (1-880030-37-3) DBM Pub.

An Asterisk (*) at the beginning of an entry indicates that the title is appearing for the first time.

M

Morison, Alexander. The Physiognomy of Mental Diseases. 2nd ed. LC 75-16723. (Classics in Psychiatry Ser.). (Illus.). 1976. reprint ed. 23.95 (*0-405-07447-6*) Ayer.
Morison, B. J. The Martini Effect. LC 92-31610. (Little Maine Murder Ser.). 1992. 17.95 (*0-945980-38-8*) Nrth Country Pr.
— Port & a Star Boarder. LC 84-24. 244p. 1984. 12.95 (*0-89621-081-2*) Nrth Country Pr.
— Reality & Dream: A Christmas Story. LC 85-20870. (Illus.). 63p. (Orig.). 1985. pap. 3.95 (*0-89621-096-0*) Nrth Country Pr.
— The Voyage of the Chianti. LC 87-24888. 300p. 1987. 15.95 (*0-89621-110-X*); pap. 8.95 (*0-89621-112-6*) Nrth Country Pr.
***Morison, Bill & Morison, Melissa.** The Odyssey. (Illus.). 48p. (YA). (gr. 3 up). 1998. pap. write for info. (*0-88388-207-8*) Bellerophon Bks.
Morison, C. People from Bethlehem. 1995. 2.99 (*0-906731-35-6*, Pub. by Christian Focus) Spring Arbor Dist.
— People from Jericho. 1995. 2.99 (*0-906731-36-4*, Pub. by Christian Focus) Spring Arbor Dist.
— People from Jerusalem. 1995. 2.99 (*0-906731-52-6*, Pub. by Christian Focus) Spring Arbor Dist.
— People from Samaria. 1995. 2.99 (*0-906731-53-4*, Pub. by Christian Focus) Spring Arbor Dist.
Morison, Elting E. Men, Machines, & Modern Times. 1968. pap. text 14.50 (*0-262-63018-4*) MIT Pr.
Morison, Frank. Who Moved the Stone? 193p. 1987. pap. 10.99 (*0-310-29561-0*, 10373P) Zondervan.
***Morison, George Abbot.** Nathanial Morison & His Descendents. 2nd ed. (Illus.). 248p. 2000. per. write for info. (*0-9654497-9-3*) Transit Pub.
Morison, George S. The New Epoch: As Developed by the Manufacture of Power. LC 72-5064. (Technology & Society Ser.). (Illus.). 148p. 1972. reprint ed. 15.95 (*0-405-04715-0*) Ayer.
Morison, J. D. & Clarke, A. S. ELLA 2000: A Language for Electronic System Design. LC 93-1998. 1993. write for info. (*0-07-707821-7*) McGraw.
Morison, James C. The Life & Times of St. Bernard of Clairvaux. 1977. lib. bdg. 59.95 (*0-8490-2162-6*) Gordon Pr.
***Morison, John.** Ethnic & National Issues in Russian & East European History. LC 00-27323. 2000. write for info. (*0-312-23477-5*) St Martin.
Morison, John, ed. The Czech & Slovak Experience. LC 92-4308. 256p. 1992. text 65.00 (*0-312-07992-3*) St Martin.
— Eastern Europe & the West. LC 92-2776. (Selected Papers from the Fourth World Congress for Soviet & East European Studies, Harrogate, 1990). 296p. 1992. text 69.95 (*0-312-08040-9*) St Martin.
Morison, John & Bell, Christine, eds. Tall Stories? Reading Law & Literature. LC 96-1351. (Applied Legal Philosophy Ser.). (Illus.). 292p. 1996. 87.95 (*1-85521-741-4*, Pub. by Dartmth Pub) Ashgate Pub Co.
Morison, John & Leith, Philip. The Barrister's World: And the Nature of Law. 256p. 1991. 123.00 (*0-335-09396-5*); pap. 41.95 (*0-335-09395-7*) OpUniv Pr.
Morison, John, jt. auth. see Livingstone, Stephen.
Morison, John, jt. ed. see McDermott, Kevin.
Morison, John E. Foetal & Neonatal Pathology. 3rd ed. LC 72-500929. (Illus.). 655p. reprint ed. pap. 200.00 (*0-608-14725-7*, 202572600046) Bks Demand.
Morison, John H. The Great Poets As Religious Teachers. LC 72-286. (Essay Index Reprint Ser.). 1977. reprint ed. 19.95 (*0-8369-2809-1*) Ayer.
Morison, M., et al. Staff Development in Tomorrow's Finance Industry, 1989. 146p. (C). 1990. pap. 125.00 (*0-85297-262-8*, Pub. by Chartered Bank) St Mut.
Morison, Melissa, jt. auth. see Morison, Bill.
Morison, Moya. Color Guide to the Nursing Management of Wounds. 2nd ed. 1997. pap. text 31.95 (*0-7234-2557-4*, Pub. by Wolfe Pub) Mosby Inc.
— Family Perspectives on Bed Wetting in Young People. (Developments in Nursing & Health Care Ser.). 240p. 1996. 72.95 (*1-85972-346-2*, Pub. by Avebry) Ashgate Pub Co.
Morison, Patrick H. Forgive! As the Lord Forgave You. LC 87-6961. 32p. 1987. pap. 1.99 (*0-87552-293-9*) P & R Pubng.
Morison, Richard. An Exhortation to Styre All Englyshe Men to the Defense of Theyr Countreye. LC 79-38211. (English Experience Ser.: No. 476). 64p. 1972. reprint ed. 20.00 (*90-221-0476-1*) Walter J Johnson.
— Humanist Scholarship & Public Order: Two Tracts Against the Pilgrimage of Grace, & a Collection of Related Contemporary Documents. Berkowitz, David S., ed. LC 79-89983. 280p. 1984. text 39.50 (*0-918016-01-0*) Folger Bks.
— An Invective Agenste Treason. LC 72-38212. (English Experience Ser.: No. 477). 104p. 1972. reprint ed. 25.00 (*90-221-0477-X*) Walter J Johnson.
Morison, Samuel Eliot. Admiral of the Ocean Sea. (Illus.). 1941. 45.00 (*0-316-58354-5*) Little.
— Admiral of the Ocean Sea: A Life of Christopher Columbus. (Illus.). 720p. 1997. 12.98 (*1-56731-143-1*, MJF Bks) Fine Comms.
— Breve Historia de los Estados Unidos (A Concise History of the American Republic) 3rd ed. (SPA.). 1015p. 1988. 42.99 (*968-16-0489-X*, Pub. by Fondo) Continental Bk.
— Builders of the Bay Colony. LC 75-41198. reprint ed. 26.45 (*0-404-14741-0*) AMS Pr.
— Christopher Columbus, Mariner. (Illus.). 192p. (YA). (gr. 9-12). 1983. pap. 11.95 (*0-452-00992-8*, Mer) NAL.
— The Conservative American Revolution. (George Rogers Clark Lecture April 22, 1975 Ser.: Inaugural). (Illus.). 48p. 1985. reprint ed. lib. bdg. 22.50 (*0-8191-4875-X*) U Pr of Amer.
— The European Discovery of America, 2 vols., Vol. 1, The Northern Voyages A. D. 500-1600. LC 93-20183. (Illus.). 736p. (C). 1993. pap. 19.95 (*0-19-508271-0*) OUP.
— The European Discovery of America: The Southern Voyages. (Illus.). 820p. 1974. text 39.95 (*0-19-501823-0*) OUP.
— The European Discovery of America: The Southern Voyages, 1492-1616, 2 vols., Vol. 2. LC 93-20183. (Illus.). 776p. (C). 1993. pap. 19.95 (*0-19-508272-9*) OUP.
— Founding of Harvard College. LC 35-4941. (Illus.). 453p. 1935. text 43.00 (*0-674-31450-6*) HUP.
— The Founding of Harvard College. LC 95-16667. (Illus.). 592p. (Orig.). (C). 1995. reprint ed. pap. text 19.95 (*0-674-31451-4*) HUP.
— Freedom in Contemporary Society. LC 69-17586. (Essay Index Reprint Ser.). 1977. 17.95 (*0-8369-0049-9*) Ayer.
— The Great Explorers: The European Discovery of America. (Illus.). 784p. 1986. pap. 21.95 (*0-19-504222-0*) OUP.
— History of the United States Naval Operations in World War Two, 15 vols., Set. Incl. Vol. 1. Battle of the Atlantic, 1939-1943. 434p. (gr. 8). 1947. 50.00 (*0-316-58301-4*); Vol. 3. Rising Sun in the Pacific, 1931-April 1942. 411p. (gr. 8). 1948. 50.00 (*0-316-58303-0*); Vol. 6. Breaking the Bismarck's Barrier, 22 July 1942-May 1944. 463p. (gr. 8). 1950. 50.00 (*0-316-58306-5*); Vol. 7. Aleutians, Gilberts & Marshalls, June 1942 - April 1944. 369p. (gr. 8). 1951. 50.00 (*0-316-58307-3*); Vol. 9. Sicily-Salerno-Anzio, January 1943-June 1944. 413p. (gr. 8). 1954. 50.00 (*0-316-58316-2*); Vol. 11. Invasion of France & Germany, 1944-1945. 360p. (gr. 8). 1957. 50.00 (*0-316-58311-1*); Vol. 15. Supplement & General Index. 373p. (gr. 8). 1962. 50.00 (*0-316-58315-4*); (Illus.). (gr. 8). 1966. 750.00 (*0-316-58300-6*) Little.
— History of U. S. Naval Operations in World War II, 14 vols. (Illus.). 1960. write for info. (*0-614-26219-4*) Little.
— The Intellectual Life of Colonial New England. LC 79-20246. 288p. 1980. reprint ed. lib. bdg. 35.00 (*0-313-22032-8*, MOIL, Greenwood Pr) Greenwood.
— John Paul Jones: A Sailor's Biography. LC 89-13423. (Classics of Naval Literature Ser.). 300p. 1990. 32.95 (*0-87021-323-7*) Naval Inst Pr.
***Morison, Samuel Eliot.** John Paul Jones: A Sailor's Biography. 1999. pap. 21.95 (*1-55750-410-5*) Naval Inst Pr.
Morison, Samuel Eliot. The Maritime History of Massachusetts, 1783-1860. LC 79-5422. 433p. 1979. reprint ed. pap. text 20.00 (*0-930350-04-9*) NE U Pr.
— The Oxford History of the American People: Prehistory to 1789, Vol. 1. (Illus.). 422p. 1994. pap. 15.95 (*0-452-01130-2*, Mer) NAL.
— The Oxford History of the American People: 1789 Through the Reconstruction, Vol. II. (Illus.). 540p. 1994. pap. 15.95 (*0-452-01131-0*, Mer) NAL.
— The Oxford History of the American People: 1869 Through the Death of John F. Kennedy, Vol. III. (Illus.). 520p. 1994. pap. 15.95 (*0-452-01132-9*, Mer) NAL.
— The Ropemakers of Plymouth: A History of the Plymouth Cordage Company, 1824-1949. LC 75-41772. (Companies & Men: Business Enterprises in America Ser.). (Illus.). 1976. reprint ed. 23.95 (*0-405-08086-7*) Ayer.
— Three Centuries of Harvard. 520p. 1986. pap. 19.95 (*0-674-88891-X*) Belknap Pr.
— Two Ocean War, Vol. 1. 611p. 1989. pap. 23.95 (*0-316-58352-9*) Little.
— The Two-Ocean War: A Short History of the United States Navy in the Second World War. (Illus.). 672p. 1997. pap. text 14.99 (*1-57866-003-3*) Galahad Bks.
Morison, Samuel Eliot, ed. Sources & Documents Illustrating the American Revolution, 1764-1788, & the Formation of the Federal Constitution. 2nd ed. 424p. (YA). (gr. 9 up). 1965. pap. text 23.95 (*0-19-500262-8*) OUP.
Morison, Samuel Eliot, et al. A Concise History of the American Republic, 2 vols. 2nd ed. LC 82-3621. (Illus.). 878p. 1983. pap. text 44.95 (*0-19-503180-6*); pap. text 32.95 (*0-19-503181-4*); pap. text 32.95 (*0-19-503182-2*) OUP.
— The Growth of the American Republic, 2 vols., 1. 7th ed. (Illus.). 948p. 1980. text 44.95 (*0-19-502593-8*) OUP.
— The Growth of the American Republic, 2 vols., 2. 7th ed. (Illus.). 946p. 1980. text 44.95 (*0-19-502594-6*) OUP.
Morison, Samuel Eliot, ed. see Bradford, William.
Morison, Samuel Eliot, ed. see Parkman, Francis.
Morison, Samuel Eliot, tr. see Columbus, Christopher.
Morison, Samuel L. Guide to Naval Mine Warfare. Schomisch, Jeff W., ed. LC 96-215984. (Illus.). 432p. (Orig.). 1995. pap. 247.00 (*0-935453-68-7*) Pasha Pubns.
Morison, Samuel L., intro. United States Naval Vessels: The Official United States Navy Reference Manual Prepared by the Division of Naval Intelligence, 1 September 1945. (Illus.). 672p. 1996. 75.00 (*0-7643-0090-3*) Schiffer.
Morison, Samuel L. & Rowe, John S. Warships of the US Navy LC 85-167600. 242 p. 1983. write for info. (*0-7106-0206-5*) Janes Info Group.
Morison, Samuel L., jt. auth. see Polmar, Norman.
Morison, Stanley. Early Italian Writing Books: Renaissance to Baroque. 220p. 1991. 65.00 (*0-87923-880-1*) Godine.
— German Incunabula in the British Museum. LC 73-143358. (Illus.). 1975. reprint ed. 150.00 (*0-87817-077-4*) Hacker.
— Letterforms. rev. ed. LC 96-18636. (Illus.). 128p. 1997. pap. 19.95 (*0-88179-136-9*) Hartley & Marks.
— The Likeness of Thomas More: An Iconographical Survey of Three Centuries. Barker, Nicolas, ed. LC 64-4266. 134p. reprint ed. pap. 41.60 (*0-7837-5614-3*, 204552100005) Bks Demand.
— A Tally of Types. Crutchley, Brooke, ed. LC 95-35330. 144p. 1999. pap. 15.95 (*1-56792-004-7*) Godine.
Morison, Tom. Pounce: Cochon's Billions. 248p. 1997. pap. 12.95 (*1-55212-095-3*, No. 97-0017) Trafford Pub.
Morison, W. & Sappideen, C. M. Torts: Commentary & Materials. 8th ed. 1993. 130.00 (*0-455-21172-8*, Pub. by LawBk Co); pap. 94.00 (*0-455-21173-6*, Pub. by LawBk Co) Gaunt.
Morison, Warwick L. Phototherapy & Photochemotherapy of Skin Disease. 2nd ed. 304p. 1990. text 89.00 (*0-88167-723-X*) Lppncott W & W.
Morison, William J., jt. auth. see Cox, Dwayne.
Morisot, Berthe. Morisot Diary. 64p. pap. 1.00 (*0-486-27642-2*) Dover.
Morisseau-Leroy, Felix. Dyakout 1, 2, 3, 4. (CRP., Illus.). 177p. 1992. pap. text 11.95 (*0-944987-69-9*) Haitiana Pubns.
Morisseau-Leroy, Felix, et al. First Works of Caribbean Writers. (B. E. Ser.: No. 111). 1970. 25.00 (*0-8115-3042-6*) Periodicals Srv.
Morisseau-Leroy, Nirva, et al. Oracle8i SQLJ Programming. 557p. 1999. 49.99 (*0-07-212160-2*) McGraw.
Morisseau, Roland. Poesies, 1960-1961. (FRE.). 170p. 1993. pap. write for info. (*2-89135-042-1*) Guernica Editions.
— La Promeneuse au Jasmin. (Collection Voix: No. 7). (FRE.). 70p. 1988. pap. write for info. (*2-89135-021-9*) Guernica Editions.
Morisset, R. & Kurstak, Edward, eds. Advances in Sexually Transmitted Diseases: Diagnosis & Treatment. 237p. 1986. lib. bdg. 110.00 (*90-6764-059-X*, Pub. by VSP) Coronet Bks.
Morissett, Jean, ed. Growth of the Gastrointestinal Test. 240p. 1990. lib. bdg. 149.00 (*0-8493-4617-7*, R) CRC Pr.
Morissette, Alanis. Jagged Little Pill. 96p. 1996. otabind 19.95 (*0-7935-5883-2*) H Leonard.
Morita, Akio, et al. Made in Japan: Akio Morita & Sony. 1989. pap. 9.95 (*0-317-02806-5*) NAL.
Morita, James, tr. see Hara, Shiro.
Morita, James R. Kaneko Mitsuharu. (World Authors Ser.). 1980. 24.95 (*0-8057-6397-X*) Macmillan.
Morita, K., ed. Applied Fourier Transforms. LC 94-76401. 433p. (gr. 12). 1995. 93.00 (*90-5199-166-5*) IOS Press.
Morita, K. & Nagata, J., eds. Topics in General Topology. (Mathematical Library: No. 41). 748p. 1989. 313.00 (*0-444-70455-8*, North Holland) Elsevier.
Morita, Kahanano'eau, jt. illus. see Kahalio'umi, 'Umi.
Morita, Kiyoko. Book of Incense; Enjoying the Traditional Art of Japanese Scents. 1999. pap. text 9.95 (*4-7700-2389-8*) Kodansha Intl.
Morita, M., et al, eds. Nuclear Weak Process & Nuclear Structure. 622p. (C). 1989. text 151.00 (*981-02-0007-2*) World Scientific Pub.
Morita, Nagayoshi, et al. Integral Equation Methods for Electromagnetics. LC 91-29864. (Artech House Antenna Library). 354p. 1990. reprint ed. pap. 109.80 (*0-608-01347-1*, 206208700002) Bks Demand.
Morita, Noritada, ed. Economic Cooperation in the Greater Mekong Subregion: Facing the Challenges. (Illus.). 226p. (C). 1999. pap. text 30.00 (*0-7881-7671-4*) DIANE Pub.
Morita, Richard Y. Bacteria in Oligotrophic Environments: Starvation-Survival Life Styles. LC 96-50399. (Microbiology Ser.). (Illus.). 608p. 1997. write for info. (*0-412-10661-2*) Kluwer Academic.
Morita, S., jt. ed. see Matsumoto, Y.
Morita, Shoma. Morita Therapy & the True Nature of Anxiety-Based Disorders (Shinkeishitsu) LeVine, Peg, ed. Kondo, Akihisa, tr. LC 97-35187. (Illus.). 160p. (C). 1998. text 52.50 (*0-7914-3765-5*); pap. text 17.95 (*0-7914-3766-3*) State U NY Pr.
Morita, Y., ed. Recent Progress of Pineal Research - 40 Years after Discovery of Melatonin: Asia Pacific Meeting, Hamamatsu, March, 1997: Proceedings. (Biological Signals Ser.: Vol. 6, Nos. 4-6, 1997). (Illus.). 139p. 1998. pap. 50.50 (*3-8055-6638-7*) S Karger.
Moritani, Mineo. A Theoretical Study of Milton's Art, Vol. 1. 1986. 22.50 (*4-7952-6810-X*) World Univ AZ.
— A Theoretical Study of Milton's Art: An Interpretation of Paradise Lost, Vol. 1. 338p. 1986. 22.50 (*0-941902-03-X*) World Univ AZ.
— A Theoretical Study of Milton's Art: An Interpretation of Paradise Lost, Vol. 2. 151p. 1986. pap. 12.00 (*0-614-29775-3*) World Univ AZ.
Moritsch, Andreas, jt. auth. see Barker, Thomas M.
Moritsugu, Kim. Looks Perfect. 220p. 1996. pap. 14.95 (*0-86492-196-9*, Pub. by Goose Ln Edits) Genl Dist Srvs.
Moritz, A. F. Mahoning. LC 95-123824. (Illus.). 112p. 1994. pap. 11.95 (*0-919626-73-4*, Pub. by Brick Bks) Genl Dist Srvs.
— Song of Fear. 80p. 1992. pap. 10.95 (*0-919626-57-2*, Pub. by Brick Bks) Genl Dist Srvs.
Moritz, A. F. & Moritz, Theresa A. Leacock: A Biography LC 85-169746. 363 p. 1985. write for info. (*0-7737-2027-8*) Stoddart Publ.
Moritz, Cynthia. About Cancer. LC 93-37166. (For Your Information Ser.). 1993. 8.95 (*1-56420-031-0*); audio 16.00 (*1-56420-032-9*) New Readers.
Moritz, Dennis. Something to Hold Onto: Nine Theater Pieces. 1995. pap. 8.00 (*0-935992-01-4*) United Art Bks.
Moritz, Derry A., jt. ed. see Kim, Mija.
***Moritz, E. Katia.** Forms for Helping Children with OCD. (Best Practices in Short-Term Therapy Ser.: Vol. 2). (Illus.). 103p. 1998. pap. 29.95 (*1-882732-73-1*, 61549) Childswork.
***Moritz, E. Katia & Jablonsky, Jennifer.** Blink, Blink, Clop, Clop: Why Do We Do Things We Can't Stop?: An OCD Storybook. (Illus.). 61p. (J). (gr. k-7). 1998. pap. 15.95 (*1-882732-72-3*, 63604) Childswork.
Moritz, Fred. Be Ye Holy: The Call to Christian Separation. LC 93-50169. 144p. 1994. pap. 10.95 (*0-89084-737-1*, 078212) Bob Jones Univ.
***Moritz, Fred.** Contending for the Faith. LC 00-38455. 2000. pap. write for info. (*1-57924-361-4*) Bob Jones Univ.
Moritz, Helmut, jt. auth. see Heiskanen, Weikko A.
Moritz, John, ed. see McCrary, Jim.
Moritz, Karl P. Anton Reiser. unabridged ed. (World Classic Literature Ser.). (GER.). pap. 7.95 (*3-89507-011-4*, Pub. by Bookking Intl) Distribks Inc.
— Anton Reiser: A Psychological Novel. Russell, John R., tr. & intro. by. (GERM Ser.). 286p. (C). 1996. 60.00 (*1-57113-046-2*) Camden Hse.
— Grammatisches Worterbuch der Deutschen Sprache. (GER.). xlviii, 1600p. 1996. reprint ed. 360.00 (*3-487-03157-4*) G Olms Pubs.
Moritz, L. A. Grain-Mills & Flour in Classical Antiquity. Finley, Moses, ed. LC 79-4994. (Ancient Economic History Ser.). (Illus.). 1979. reprint ed. lib. bdg. 35.95 (*0-405-12381-7*) Ayer.
Moritz, Lena. Trade & Industrial Policies in the New South Africa. 61p. 1994. pap. 24.00 (*91-7106-355-2*) Coronet Bks.
Moritz, Patricia, jt. auth. see Gordner, Ronald L.
Moritz, Patricia M. Argentina. LC 98-15466. (Dropping in On Ser.). (J). 1998. 19.93 (*0-86593-491-6*) Rourke Corp.
— Costa Rica. LC 98-15467. (Dropping in on Ser.). (J). 1998. 19.93 (*0-86593-495-9*) Rourke Corp.
— Puerto Rico. LC 98-15473. (Dropping in on Ser.). (J). 1998. 19.93 (*0-86593-492-4*) Rourke Corp.
— Saudi Arabia. LC 98-15230. (Dropping in on Ser.). (J). 1998. (*0-86593-494-0*) Rourke Corp.
— South Africa. LC 98-15462. (Dropping in on Ser.). 32p. (J). 1998. 19.93 (*0-86593-493-2*) Rourke Corp.
Moritz, Robert, et al. Sponging: A Guide to Living off Those You Love. (Illus.). 112p. 1995. pap. 9.95 (*1-886186-00-6*) Dune Rd Bks.
Moritz, Robert E. Memorabilia Mathematics: The Philomath's Quotation Book. (Spectrum Ser.). 440p. 1993. reprint ed. pap. text 29.95 (*0-88385-321-3*, MEMO) Math Assn.
Moritz, Robin F. & Southwick, Edward E. Bees as Superorganisms: An Evolutionary Reality. LC 92-14560. (Illus.). 304p. 1992. 129.00 (*3-540-54821-1*); 156.95 (*0-387-54821-1*) Spr-Verlag.
Moritz, Theresa A., jt. auth. see Allen, Judson B.
Moritz, Theresa A., jt. auth. see Moritz, A. F.
Moritz, Thorsten. A Profound Mystery: The Use of the Old Testament in Ephesians. (Novum Testamentum, Supplements Ser.: No. 85). xiv, 252p. 1996. 101.50 (*90-04-10556-5*) Brill Academic Pubs.
Moritz, Tom, jt. ed. see Wilson, Sam.
Moriwaki, A. Banking Dictionary. (ENG & JPN.). 1990. lib. bdg. 85.00 (*0-8288-3900-X*, F117170) Fr & Eur.
Moriwaki, Glenda. Love for Priscilla. (Illus.). 28p. (Orig.). (J). (ps-3). 1991. pap. 4.95 (*0-9627956-7-4*) Meadora Pub.
Moriwaki, Toshimichi, jt. ed. see Hocken, Robert J.
Moriya, T. Spin Fluctuations in Itinerant Electron Magnetism. (Solid-State Sciences Ser.: Vol. 56). (Illus.). 260p. 1985. 88.95 (*0-387-15422-1*) Spr-Verlag.
Moriya, T., ed. Electron Correlation & Magnetism in Narrow Band Systems. (Solid-State Sciences Ser.: Vol. 29). (Illus.). 257p. 1981. 68.95 (*0-387-10767-3*) Spr-Verlag.
Moriyama, Iwao, et al. Cardiovascular Diseases in the United States. LC 73-154498. (Vital & Health Statistics Monographs, American Public Health Association). (Illus.). 524p. 1971. 45.00 (*0-674-09640-1*) HUP.
Moriyama, Tae. Tokyo Adventures: Glimpses of the City in Bygone Eras. Garvey, Bob & Garvey, Reiko, trs. (Illus.). 376p. 1993. 19.95 (*4-07-975842-1*, Pub. by Shufunomoto Co Ltd) Tuttle Pubng.
— Weekend Adventures Outside Tokyo: Travel with a Historical Twist. (Illus.). 358p. (Orig.). 1990. pap. 19.95 (*4-07-975049-8*, Pub. by Shufunomoto Co Ltd) Tuttle Pubng.
Moriyasu, ed. see Yoshikawa, Eiji.
Moriyasu, K. An Elementary Primer for Gauge Theory. 192p. 1983. text 41.00 (*9971-950-83-9*); pap. text 21.00 (*9971-950-94-4*) World Scientific Pub.
Moriyasu, Ushio. The Ume Plum's Secrets. 1992. per. 4.50 (*0-916508-40-4*) Happiness Pr.
***Moriz, Bert.** Pocket Guide to Preventing Process Plant Materials Mix-Ups. LC 00-25085. 180p. 2000. pap. 30.00 (*0-88415-344-4*) Gulf Pub.
Morize, Andre. Problems & Methods of Literary History. LC 66-13475. 1922. 28.00 (*0-8196-0168-3*) Biblo.
Morizio, Diane. So, You Want to Do Bread Dough Art. 1992. student ed. 8.95 (*0-9632807-6-7*) J&D Ent.
Morizot, Pierre. School of Chartres. 1987. pap. 6.95 (*0-916786-97-8*, Saint George Pubns) R Steiner Col.
Mork. History Civilization Combined. 9th ed. 1996. pap. text. write for info. (*0-13-228347-6*) Allyn.
***Mork, Gretchen.** Five Minute Phonics. (Illus.). (J). 1999. pap. 12.00 (*0-9666477-0-X*) Wild Pony Pubg.
Morkel, D. W., jt. auth. see Snyman, C. R.
Morkel, Pieter, jt. compiled by see Boshoff, Eben.
***Morken, Hubert & Formicola, Jo R.** Politics of School Choice. LC 99-36303. 416p. 1999. pap. 24.95 (*0-8476-9721-5*); text 70.00 (*0-8476-9720-7*) Rowman.
Morken, Hubert, jt. ed. see Formicola, Jo.
Morken, Ken E., ed. The Bazaar Book for Festivals & Craft Fairs in Greater Washington State for 1991. (Illus.). 192p. 1990. 19.00 (*0-685-39514-6*) Capital WA.

M

An Asterisk (*) at the beginning of an entry indicates that the title is appearing for the first time.

Morkert, A. S. Once upon a (Life) Time: Stories from Western Montana, 1908-1960. 96p. (Orig.). 1990. pap. text. write for info. (0-9620902-6-3) Vernon Print & Pub.

Morkholm, Otto. Early Hellenistic Coinage from the Accession of Alexander to the Peace of Apamaea (336-188 BC) Grierson, Philip & Westermark, Ulla, eds. (Illus.). 295p. (C). 1991. text 115.00 (0-521-39504-6) Cambridge U Pr.

Morkholm, Otto & Waggoner, Nancy M., eds. Greek Numismatics & Archaeology: Essays in Honor of Margaret Thompson. (Editions NR, 1979 Ser.). 326p. 1994. 75.00 (0-685-72018-7) Am Numismatic.

***Morkoc, H.** Nitride Semiconductors & Devices. LC 99-14665. (Materials Science Ser.: Vol. 32). (Illus.). xxii, 475p. 1999. 116.00 (3-540-64038-X) Spr-Verlag.

Morkot, Robert. Egypt. 3rd ed. (Illus.). 336p. 1997. pap. 19.95 (0-8442-4754-5, 47545, Passprt Bks) NTC Contemp Pub Co.

Morkot, Robert. Egypt. 4th ed. pap. 23.95 (962-217-654-2) China Guides.

Morkot, Robert. Egypt: Gift of the Nile. 2nd ed. (Illus.). 320p. 1995. pap. 16.95 (0-8442-9665-1, Passprt Bks) NTC Contemp Pub Co.

— Penguin Historical Atlas of Ancient Greece. 2000. pap. 8.00 (0-14-051335-3) Viking Penguin.

Morkot, Robert G. The Black Pharaohs: Egypt's Nubian Rulers. (Illus.). 352p. 1999. 63.00 (0-948695-23-4, Pub. by Rubicon Pr); pap. 39.50 (0-948695-24-2, Pub. by Rubicon Pr) David Brown.

Morkovine, Sergey, ed. Russian Cookbook. (Illus.). 32p. (Orig.). 1994. pap. 4.99 (0-9643971-2-9) Isometry.

Morkovkin, V. Lexical Basis of the Russian Language: Learner's Dictionary. (RUS.). 1168p. (C). 1984. 95.00 (0-7855-6671-6, Pub. by Collets) St Mut.

Morkovkina, V. V., jt. auth. see Denisova, P. N.

Morkovsky, Christine, tr. see Dussel, Enrique D.

Morkre, Morris E. & Kelly, Kenneth H. Effects of Unfair Imports on Domestic Industries: U. S. Antidumping & Countervailing Duty Cases, 1980 to 1988. (Illus.). 120p. (Orig.). (C). 1994. pap. text 40.00 (0-7881-1174-4) DIANE Pub.

Morlacchi, Francesco. Tebaldo Ed Isolina. (Italian Opera Ser., 1810-1840: Vol. 24). 260p. 1990. text 30.00 (0-8240-6573-5) Garland.

Morlan, Don M. & Tuttle, George E., Jr. Specific Situations in Effective Oral Communication. (gr. 12). 1977. teacher ed. 3.33 (0-672-61411-1, Bobbs); pap. 9.50 (0-672-61410-3, Bobbs) Macmillan.

Morlan, George K. America's Heritage from John Stuart Mill. LC 72-987. reprint ed. 20.00 (0-404-04436-0) AMS Pr.

Morlan, John E., jt. auth. see Espinosa, Leonard J.

Morlan, Joseph, jt. auth. see Fisher, Chris C.

Morlan, Michael. American Automobile Collections & Museums: A Guide to U. S. Exhibits. (American Travel Themes Ser.). (Illus.). 256p. (Orig.). 1992. pap. 15.95 (1-878446-10-X) Bon A Tirer Pub.

— Kitty Hawk to NASA: A Guide to U. S. Air & Space Museums & Exhibits. (American Travel Themes Ser.). (Illus.). 304p. (Orig.). 1991. pap. 15.95 (1-878446-04-5, A&S-1) Bon A Tirer Pub.

Morlan, Mike. Tecumseh L-Head Engine Repair Manual. LC 93-61211. 240p. 1994. pap. 12.95 (0-89287-617-4, H105) Intertec Pub.

Morlan, Richard E., jt. auth. see Dyck, Ian.

Morlan, Robert L. Political Prairie Fire: The Nonpartisan League, 1915-1922. LC 74-9275. (Illus.). 408p. 1974. reprint ed. lib. bdg. 35.00 (0-8371-7639-5, MOPF, Greenwood Pr) Greenwood.

Morlan, Terry H., ed. Energy Forecasting. 57p. 1985. 3.00 (0-87262-498-6) Am Soc Civil Eng.

Morland, Alanna. Leopard Lord. 272p. 1999. mass mkt. 5.99 (0-441-00606-X) Ace Bks.

— Shackle & Sword. 1999. reprint ed. mass mkt. 5.99 (0-441-00646-9) Ace Bks.

***Morland, Andrew.** Caterpillar Bulldozers & Tractors Calendar 2001. (Illus.). 12p. 2000. pap. 10.95 (0-89658-477-1) Voyageur Pr.

Morland, Andrew. Classic American Farm Tractors. LC 97-20151. (Illus.). 120p. 1997. pap. 15.95 (0-7603-0445-9) MBI Pubg.

— Farm Tractors. LC 93-17026. (Enthusiast Color Ser.). (Illus.). 96p. 1993. pap. 13.95 (0-87938-824-2) MBI Pubg.

— Ford & Fordson Tractors. (Enthusiast Color Ser.). (Illus.). 96p. 1995. pap. 13.95 (0-7603-0044-5) MBI Pubg.

— Harley Davidson. 80p. 1991. 9.99 (0-517-06683-1) Random Hse Value.

***Morland, Andrew.** Harley-Davidson Legends Calendar 2001. (Illus.). 26p. 2000. pap. 10.95 (0-89658-476-3) Voyageur Pr.

Morland, Andrew. Modern American Farm Tractors. (Enthusiast Color Ser.). (Illus.). 96p. 1994. pap. 13.95 (0-87938-926-5) MBI Pubg.

— Modern Farm Tractors. LC 97-6042. (Enthusiast Color Ser.). (Illus.). 96p. 1997. pap. 13.95 (0-7603-0155-7) MBI Pubg.

— Triumph Triples. (Osprey Colour Library). (Illus.). 128p. 1995. pap. 15.95 (1-85532-428-8) MBI Pubg.

— Vintage American Farm Tractors. (Enthusiast Color Ser.). (Illus.). 96p. 1997. pap. 13.95 (0-7603-0147-6) MBI Pubg.

***Morland, Andrew, photos by.** Vintage Ford Tractors: The Ultimate Tribute to Ford, Fordson & Ferguson Tractors. LC 99-86895. (Illus.). 160p. 2000. pap. 19.95 (0-89658-478-X) Voyageur Pr.

Morland, Andrew & Baldwin, Nick. Case Tractors. (Enthusiast Color Ser.). (Illus.). 96p. 1996. pap. 12.95 (0-7603-0093-3) MBI Pubg.

Morland, Andrew & Henshaw. Allis Chalmers Tractors. LC 97-6043. (Enthusiast Color Ser.). (Illus.). 96p. 1997. pap. 13.95 (0-7603-0108-5) MBI Pubg.

Morland, Andrew & Henshaw, Peter. The History of American Custom Motorcycles. (Illus.). 128p. 1997. pap. 18.95 (1-85532-614-0, Pub. by Ospry) Motorbooks Intl.

Morland, Andrew & Wendel, Charles H. Allis Chalmers Tractors. (Farmer Tractor Color History Ser.). (Illus.). 128p. 1992. pap. 21.95 (0-87938-628-2) MBI Pubg.

— Massey Tractors. (Farm Tractor Color History Ser.). (Illus.). 128p. 1992. pap. 21.95 (0-87938-618-5) MBI Pubg.

— Minneapolis-Moline Tractors, 1870 to 1969. (Farm Tractor Color History Ser.). (Illus.). 128p. 1990. pap. 21.95 (0-87938-468-9) MBI Pubg.

Morland, Andrew, jt. auth. see Pripps, Robert N.

Morland, Cary. Because Their Hearts Were Pure: or The Secret of the Mine. 1952. pap. 5.25 (0-8222-0102-X) Dramatists Play.

Morland, David. Demanding the Impossible? Human Nature & Politics in Nineteenth-Century Social Anarchism. LC 97-1672. (Anarchist Studies). 256p. 1998. 89.50 (0-304-33685-8); pap. 27.95 (0-304-33687-4) Continuum.

Morland, Harold, tr. see Borges, Jorge Luis.

Morland, J. Kenneth. Social Problems in the United States. LC 74-22542. (Illus.). 694p. reprint ed. pap. 200.00 (0-608-30682-7, 201251500081) Bks Demand.

Morland, J. Kenneth, jt. auth. see Williams, John E.

Morland, John, et al. Classroom Learning Centers. LC 73-77592. 1973. pap., teacher ed. 9.99 (0-8224-1410-4) Fearon Teacher Aids.

Morland, John K. Millways of Kent. 1958. pap. 14.95 (0-8084-0219-6) NCUP.

Morland, Margaret W. Gift of Jade: Poems by Margaret Ward Morland. Cavalieri, Grace, ed. 100p. 1998. pap. text 10.00 (0-938572-21-0) Bunny Crocodile.

Morland, Miles. A Walk Across France. Orig. Title: Miles Away. 256p. 1994. reprint ed. pap. 10.00 (0-449-90945-X) Fawcett.

Morland, Nigel. That Nice Miss Smith. large type ed. 1990. 27.99 (0-7089-2337-2) Ulverscroft.

Morlands, Andrew, jt. auth. see Pripps, Robert A.

Morle, James. Building Large-Scale Databases: Scaling Oracle 8i:Building Highly Scalable OLTP System Architectures. LC 99-51334. 576p. (C). 1999. pap. text 44.95 incl. cd-rom (0-201-32574-8) Addison-Wesley.

Morledge, Richard A. It's a Great Day in the Kingdom! A Five-Day-a-Week Devotional Compiled from the Sermons of Richard A. Morledge. Borasky, Leslie W., ed. 260p. (Orig.). 1996. pap. 14.95 (0-9648288-0-4) RAM Pr PA.

Morler, Patty, jt. auth. see Mattia, Jan B.

Morlet, M. Dictionnaire Etymologique des Noms de Famille. 2nd ed. (FRE.). 1997. 125.00 (0-320-00461-9) Fr & Eur.

Morley. Getting Started: Internet-NETSC. (C). 1997. pap. text 6.75 (0-03-020447-X) Harcourt Coll Pubs.

— Getting Started: Web Page Design with Microsoft Front page 97. (C). 1998. pap. text 42.00 (0-03-025079-X, Pub. by Harcourt Coll Pubs) Harcourt.

— Getting Started: Web Page Design with Microsoft Front page 98. 1998. pap. text 40.50 (0-03-027189-4) Dryden Press.

— Getting Started with a Computer. (C). 1997. pap. text, teacher ed. 42.00 (0-03-020362-7) Harcourt Coll Pubs.

— Getting Started with Computers. 2nd ed. LC 98-87086. (Illus.). 100p. (C). 1998. pap. 26.50 (0-03-022251-6, Pub. by Harcourt Coll Pubs) Harcourt.

— Getting Startedhardware Conce. 1997. 6.75 (0-03-020448-8) H Holt & Co.

Morley. Organising Feminisms. LC 98-20861. 1999. pap. 21.95 (0-312-21678-5) St Martin.

***Morley.** Organising Feminisms. LC 98-20861. 1999. text 65.00 (0-312-21676-9) St Martin.

Morley, jt. auth. see Davies.

Morley, jt. auth. see Lerski.

Morley, Andrew, jt. auth. see Baglee, Christopher.

Morley, Austin, jt. auth. see Morley, Linda.

Morley-Ball, Joyce A. Weary but Not Worn. LC 98-91409. 1998. pap. 8.95 (0-533-12660-6) Vantage.

Morley, Barry. Beyond Consensus: Salvaging Sense of the Meeting. LC 73-84214. 32p. (Orig.). 1993. pap. 4.00 (0-87574-307-2) Pendle Hill.

Morley, Becky, jt. ed. see Mullender, Audrey.

Morley, Bob, jt. auth. see Davies, Samuel.

Morley, C. B. Hymenoptera: Ichueumonidae: 1 Ichneumones Deltoidei, Vol. 3. (Illus.). xxxvi, 536p. 1973. reprint ed. 25.00 (0-88065-162-8) Scholarly Pubns.

***Morley, C. K., ed.** Geoscience of Rift Systems - Evolution of East Africa. (Studies in Geology: No. 44). (Illus.). 281p. 1999. ring bd. 134.00 (0-89181-051-X, 571) AAPG.

Morley, Carol. Dots & Spots. LC 92-24526. (Willa Perlman Bks.). (Illus.). 32p. (J). (ps-3). 1993. 14.00 (0-06-021526-7); lib. bdg. 13.89 (0-06-021527-5) HarpC Child Bks.

— A Spider & a Pig. LC 92-53215. (J). 1993. 14.95 (0-316-58405-3) Little.

***Morley, Carol & Wilde, Liz.** Body: 100 Tips for a Better Body. LC 00-34355. (Handbag Honeys Ser.). (Illus.). 112p. 2000. 9.95 (0-7370-0085-6) Time-Life Educ.

— Faces: 100 Makeup Moves. LC 00-34354. (Handbag Honeys Ser.). (Illus.). 112p. 2000. 9.95 (0-7370-0086-4) Time-Life Educ.

— Hands & Feet: 100 Pampering Tricks. LC 00-34358. (Handbag Honeys Ser.). (Illus.). 112p. 2000. 9.95 (0-7370-0088-0) Time-Life Educ.

Morley, Carol, jt. auth. see Wilde, Liz.

Morley, Carolyn A. Transformation, Miracles, & Mischief: The Mountain Priest Plays of Kyogen. (Cornell East Asia Ser.: No. 62). (Illus.). 248p. (Orig.). (C). 1993. pap. 14.45 (0-939657-62-7) Cornell East Asia Pgm.

Morley, Chris. Spiders. LC 98-84145. (Totally Amazing Ser.). 32p. 1998. pap. 5.99 (0-307-20160-0, Goldn Books) Gldn Bks Pub Co.

Morley, Christine & Orbell, Carole. Me & My Pet Cat. LC 96-60459. (Me & My Pet Ser.). (Illus.). 32p. (J). (gr. 1-5). 1997. 10.00 (0-7166-1749-8) World Bk.

— Me & My Pet Dog. LC 96-60458. (Me & My Pet Ser.). (Illus.). 32p. (J). (gr. 1-5). 1997. write for info. (0-7166-1747-1) World Bk.

— Me & My Pet Fish. LC 96-50421. (Me & My Pet Ser.). (Illus.). 32p. (J). (gr. k-4). 1997. write for info. (0-7166-1795-1) World Bk.

— Me & My Pet Rabbit. LC 96-50420. (Me & My Pet Ser.). (Illus.). 32p. (J). (gr. 1-4). 1997. write for info. (0-7166-1797-8) World Bk.

Morley, Christopher. Christopher Morley's New York. LC 88-81015. (Illus.). xiv, 379p. 1988. 19.95 (0-8232-1214-9) Fordham.

— Christopher Morley's Philadelphia. Kalfus, Ken, ed. LC 90-80081. (Illus.). xvi, 329p. (C). 1990. pap. 16.00 (0-8232-1270-X) Fordham.

— The Haunted Bookshop. 22.95 (0-88411-887-8) Amereon Ltd.

— The Haunted Bookshop. (Illus.). 240p. 1992. reprint ed. pap. 13.95 (1-879923-02-5) Booksellers Pub.

— Kitty Foyle. 25.95 (0-88411-888-6) Amereon Ltd.

— Kitty Foyle. 1993. reprint ed. lib. bdg. 89.00 (0-7812-5493-0) Rprt Serv.

— Parnassus on Wheels. 1976. 18.95 (0-8488-0594-1) Amereon Ltd.

— Parnassus on Wheels. (Illus.). 150p. 1992. reprint ed. pap. 12.95 (1-879923-01-7) Booksellers Pub.

— Parnassus on Wheels: The Haunted Bookshop. LC 98-85931. 200p. 1998. reprint ed. pap. 12.00 (1-892323-10-9) Vivisphere.

— Plum Pudding. 256p. 22.95 (0-8488-2491-1) Amereon Ltd.

— Prefaces Without Books: Prefaces & Introductions to Thirty Books. Abromson, Herman, ed. LC 76-14891. (Illus.). 1970. 15.00 (0-87959-062-9) U of Tex H Ransom Ctr.

— Travels in Philadelphia. 1993. reprint ed. lib. bdg. 89.00 (0-7812-5492-2) Rprt Serv.

Morley, Christopher D. Ironing Board. LC 68-8483. (Essay Index Reprint Ser.). 1977. 20.95 (0-8369-0718-3) Ayer.

— Thunder on the Left. (Classics Ser.: No. 68). 276p. 1995. 21.95 (1-55713-013-2) Sun & Moon CA.

— Thunder on the Left. (Sun & Moon Classics Ser.: No. 68). 276p. 1995. pap. 12.95 (1-55713-190-2) Sun & Moon CA.

— Thunder on the Left. LC 83-45821. reprint ed. 27.00 (0-404-20185-7) AMS Pr.

Morley, Cindy L. How to Get the Most Out of Meetings. LC 94-28351. 1994. pap. 8.95 (0-87120-231-X) ASCD.

Morley, Cindy L., jt. auth. see Ohle, Nancy.

Morley College for Working Men & Women, London Sta. Science To-Day & To-Morrow, Compiled from a Series of Lectures Delivered at Morley College. LC 67-30231. (Essay Index Reprint Ser.). 1977. 19.95 (0-8369-0857-0) Ayer.

Morley, Dan. BSA Gold Star - Portrait of a Motorcycling Legend. (Illus.). 128p. 1998. 24.95 (1-85915-094-2, Pub. by Windrow & Green) Motorbooks Intl.

Morley, David. Family Television: Cultural Power & Domestic Leisure. 178p. 1988. pap. 14.95 (0-906890-73-X) Routledge.

***Morley, David.** Home Territories: Media, Mobility & Identity. LC 00-35316. 2000. write for info. (0-415-15765-X) Routledge.

Morley, David. Television, Audiences, & Cultural Studies. LC 92-10404. 336p. (C). (gr. 13). 1992. pap. 22.99 (0-415-05445-1, A7921) Routledge.

Morley, David & Brunsdon, Charlotte. The Nationwide Television Studies LC 99-20335. (Research in Cultural & Media Studies). ix, 326 p. 1999. write for info. (0-415-14879-0) Routledge.

Morley, David & Chen, Kuan-Hsing, eds. Stuart Hall: Critical Dialogues in Cultural Studies. LC 95-16455. 544p. 1996. pap. 22.99 (0-415-08804-6) Routledge.

— Stuart Hall: Critical Dialogues in Cultural Studies. LC 95-16455. (Comedia Ser.). 544p. (C). 1996. 80.00 (0-415-08803-8) Routledge.

Morley, David & Robins, Kevin. Spaces of Identity: Global Media, Electronic Landscapes & Cultural Boundaries. LC 94-42068. (International Library of Sociology Ser.). 224p. (C). 1995. pap. 22.99 (0-415-09597-2) Routledge.

Morley, Deborah. I Have Seen Jesus. LC 96-90186. 1996. 16.95 (0-533-11933-2) Vantage.

***Morley, Deborah.** Introduction to the World Wide Web & Web Pages. 1998. pap. 7.50 (0-15-567838-8) Harcourt.

Morley, Diane, jt. auth. see Job, Barbara.

Morley, Don. BSA: Classic Motorcycles. (Osprey Colour Library). (Illus.). 128p. 1991. pap. 15.95 (1-85532-118-1, Pub. by Ospry) Motorbooks Intl.

Morley, Donna. Choices That Lead to Godliness. LC 98-52540. 240p. 1999. pap. 12.99 (1-58134-062-1) Crossway Bks.

Morley, E. & Hines, P. Designer's Guide to Manufacturing Processes. (Illus.). 320p. 1999. pap. 42.50 (0-7487-4337-5, Pub. by S Thornes Pubs) Trans Atl Phila.

Morley, Edith J. Life & Times of Henry Crabb Robinson. LC 71-115396. 1970. reprint ed. 32.50 (0-404-05368-8) AMS Pr.

Morley, Edith J., ed. see Robinson, Henry C.

Morley, F. H., ed. Grazing Animals. (World Animal Science Ser.: Vol. 1B). 412p. 1981. 215.50 (0-444-41835-0) Elsevier.

Morley, Felix. Freedom & Federalism. LC 80-82575. 352p. 1981. 12.00 (0-913966-86-X); pap. 5.50 (0-913966-87-8) Liberty Fund.

Morley, Felix, ed. Aspects of the Depression. LC 68-22932. (Essay Index Reprint Ser.). 1977. 17.95 (0-8369-0719-1) Ayer.

— Essays on Individuality. LC 76-30745. 1977. 12.00 (0-913966-27-4); pap. 5.50 (0-913966-28-2) Liberty Fund.

Morley-Fletcher, Hugo. Christie's Pictorial History of European Pottery. 1988. 65.00 (0-7148-8009-4, Pub. by Phaidon Press) Phaidon Pr.

Morley-Fletcher, Hugo, ed. Techniques of the World's Greatest Masters of Pottery & Ceramics. 192p. 1997. 17.98 (0-7858-0745-4) Bk Sales Inc.

Morley, Fran & Skarmeas, Nancy, eds. Hymns of Faith & Inspiration. (Illus.). 160p. 1991. 24.95 (0-8249-4041-5) Ideals.

Morley, Fran, jt. ed. see Skarmeas, Nancy.

***Morley, G. David.** Syntax in Functional Grammar: An Introduction to Lexicogrammar in Systemic Linguistics. LC 00-21925. 2000. pap. write for info. (0-8264-4735-X) Continuum.

Morley, Geoffrey. Smuggling in Hampshire & Dorset, 1700-1850. 224p. 1987. pap. 35.00 (0-905392-24-8) St Mut.

Morley, George. Shakespeare's Greenwood: The Customs in the Country, the Language, the Superstitions. LC 70-185021. (Studies in Shakespeare: No. 24). 289p. 1972. reprint ed. lib. bdg. 75.00 (0-8383-1381-7) M S G Haskell Hse.

Morley, Helena. The Diary of "Helena Morley" Bishop, Elizabeth, tr. 282p. 1995. pap. text 13.00 (0-374-52435-1, Noonday) FS&G.

Morley, Henry. Ideal Commonwealths. 490p. 1998. reprint ed. pap. 29.95 (0-7661-0209-2) Kessinger Pub.

— The Life of Henry Cornelius Agrippa: Doctor & Knight, Commonly Known As a Magician. 342p. 1993. reprint ed. pap. 24.95 (1-56459-388-6) Kessinger Pub.

— Mediaeval Tales (1884) 260p. 1998. reprint ed. pap. 17.95 (0-7661-0162-2) Kessinger Pub.

Morley, Hilda. Cloudless at First. 302p. 1989. pap. 12.95 (0-918825-72-5) Moyer Bell.

— To Hold in My Hand: Selected Poems, 1955-1983. LC 83-40199. 233p. 1983. text 27.50 (0-935296-46-8, Pub. by Sheep Meadow) U Pr of New Eng.

— The Turning. 193p. Date not set. pap. 14.95 (1-55921-230-6, Asphodel Pr) Moyer Bell.

— The Turning. LC 96-44931. 247p. 1998. 24.95 (1-55921-202-0, Asphodel Pr) Moyer Bell.

Morley, Iris. Proud Paladin. LC 70-144164. (Short Story Index Reprint Ser.). 1977. reprint ed. 20.95 (0-8369-3779-1) Ayer.

Morley, J., jt. ed. see Bray, M. A.

Morley, J. E. & Korenman, Stanley G., eds. Endocrinology & Metabolism in the Elderly. (Current Issues in Endocrinology & Metabolism Ser.). (Illus.). 592p. 1992. 150.00 (0-86542-148-X) Blackwell Sci.

Morley, J. S., jt. ed. see Andrews, P. R.

Morley, J. W., ed. Neural Aspects of Tactile Sensation. 1996. write for info. (0-614-17933-5) Elsevier.

— Neural Aspects of Tactile Sensation. LC 98-209962. 366p. 1998. 122.50 (0-444-82282-8) Elsevier.

Morley, Jacqueline. Across America: The Story of Lewis & Clark. (Expedition Ser.). (Illus.). 32p. (J). (gr. 3-7). 1999. pap. text 7.95 (0-531-15342-8) Watts.

— Egyptian Myths. LC 99-44979. 64p. 1999. 22.50 (0-87226-589-7, 65897B, P Bedrick Books) NTC Contemp Pub Co.

— An Egyptian Pyramid. (Inside Story Ser.). (Illus.). 48p. (YA). (gr. 5 up). 1993. pap. 10.95 (0-87226-255-3, 62553B, P Bedrick Books) NTC Contemp Pub Co.

— An Egyptian Pyramid: Inside Story. (Inside Story Ser.). (Illus.). 48p. (YA). (gr. 5 up). 1991. 18.95 (0-87226-346-0, 63460B, P Bedrick Books) NTC Contemp Pub Co.

— Entertainment: Screen, Stage & Stars. (Timelines Ser.). (Illus.). 48p. (J). (gr. 5-8). 1994. pap. 7.95 (0-531-15710-5); lib. bdg. 24.00 (0-531-14311-2) Watts.

— Exploring North America. LC 96-1926. (Voyages of Discovery Ser.). (Illus.). 48p. (YA). (gr. 4-7). 1996. 18.95 (0-87226-488-2, 64882B, P Bedrick Books) NTC Contemp Pub Co.

— First Facts about the Ancient Egyptians. LC 96-25045. (First Facts Ser.). (Illus.). 32p. (YA). (gr. 4 up). 1996. 14.95 (0-87226-495-5, 64955B, P Bedrick Books) NTC Contemp Pub Co.

— First Facts about the Vikings. LC 96-12301. (First Facts Ser.). (Illus.). 32p. (YA). (gr. 4 up). 1996. 14.95 (0-87226-497-1, 64971B, P Bedrick Books) NTC Contemp Pub Co.

— How Would You Survive As a Viking? LC 94-26161. (How Would You Survive? Ser.). (Illus.). 48p. (J). (gr. 5-8). 1995. lib. bdg. 23.00 (0-531-14344-9) Watts.

— How Would You Survive As an Ancient Egyptian? LC 94-26157. (How Would You Survive? Ser.). (Illus.). 48p. (J). (gr. 5-8). 1995. lib. bdg. 23.00 (0-531-14345-7) Watts.

— How Would You Survive As an Ancient Egyptian? LC 94-26157. (How Would You Survive? Ser.). (Illus.). 48p. (J). (gr. 5-8). 1996. pap. 7.95 (0-531-15303-7) Watts.

— How Would You Survive in the American West? LC 95-17603. (How Would You Survive? Ser.). (Illus.). 48p. (J). (gr. 5-8). 1996. lib. bdg. 24.00 (0-531-14382-1) Watts.

— How Would You Survive in the American West? (How Would You Survive? Ser.). 32p. (J). 1997. pap. 7.95 (0-531-15308-8) Watts.

M

*__Morley, Jacqueline.__ The Living Roman Fort. (Magnifications Ser.). 48p. (YA). (gr. 3 up). 2000. 18.95 (*0-87226-650-8*, P Bedrick Books) NTC Contemp Pub Co.

— The Living Tomb. (Magnifications Ser.). (Illus.). (YA). 2000. 18.95 (*0-87226-651-6*, P Bedrick Books) NTC Contemp Pub Co.

Morley, Jacqueline. A Renaissance Town. LC 96-33261. (Inside Story Ser.). (Illus.). 48p. (YA). (gr. 4-7). 1996. lib. bdg. 18.95 (*0-87226-276-6*, 62766B, P Bedrick Books) NTC Contemp Pub Co.

— Shakespeare's Theater. LC 94-16386. (Inside Story Ser.). (Illus.). 48p. (YA). (gr. 4-7). 1994. lib. bdg. 18.95 (*0-87226-309-6*, 63096B, P Bedrick Books) NTC Contemp Pub Co.

— So You Want to Be an Egyptian Princess. LC 98-27983. (So You Want to Be... Ser.). 32p. (J). (gr. 3-6). 1999. lib. bdg. 18.90 (*0-7613-1422-9*, Copper Beech Bks) Millbrook Pr.

— A Viking Town. LC 98-52918. (Metropolis Ser.). 45p. (J). (gr. 4-6). 1999. write for info. (*0-531-14530-1*) Watts.

*__Morley, Jacqueline.__ Viking Town. (Metropolis Ser.). (Illus.). (J). 2000. pap. 8.95 (*0-531-15380-0*) Watts.

Morley, Jacqueline & James, John. A Roman Villa: Inside Story. LC 92-15279. (Illus.). 48p. (YA). (gr. 4-7). 1992. lib. bdg. 18.95 (*0-87226-360-6*, 63614B, P Bedrick Books) NTC Contemp Pub Co.

Morley, Jacqueline & Salariya, David. Across America: The Story of Lewis & Clark. LC 97-34692. (Expedition Ser.). (Illus.). (J). 1998. 21.00 (*0-531-14455-0*) Watts.

Morley, James, ed. Deterrent Diplomacy: Japan, Germany & the U. S. S. R., 1935-1940. LC 75-25524. (Japan's Road to the Pacific War Ser.). 380p. reprint ed. pap. 117.80 (*0-608-12655-1*, 202510900042) Bks Demand.

Morley, James, jt. ed. see Olkowski, Dorothea.

Morley, James M. Muir Woods: The Ancient Redwood Forest near San Francisco. 2nd ed. 1992. pap. 10.95 (*0-938765-53-1*) Smith Novelty.

Morley, James W. Driven by Growth: Political Change in the Asia-Pacific Region. rev. ed. LC 98-16632. 408p. (C). (gr. 13). 1998. text 68.95 (*0-7656-0351-9*, East Gate Bk) M E Sharpe.

— Driven by Growth: Political Change in the Asia-Pacific Region. rev. ed. LC 98-16632. (Illus.). 408p. (C). (gr. 13). 1998. pap. text 24.95 (*0-7656-0352-7*, East Gate Bk) M E Sharpe.

— Japan & Korea: America's Allies in the Pacific. LC 81-4196. (Illus.). 152p. 1981. reprint ed. lib. bdg. 55.00 (*0-313-23033-1*, MOJK, Greenwood Pr) Greenwood.

— The Japanese Thrust into Siberia, 1918. LC 75-38115. (Select Bibliographies Reprint Ser.). 1980. reprint ed. 28.95 (*0-8369-9966-5*) Ayer.

Morley, James W., ed. Driven by Growth: Political Change in the Asia-Pacific Region. LC 91-28995. 382p. (gr. 13). 1992. text 83.95 (*1-56324-013-0*, East Gate Bk); pap. text 32.95 (*1-56324-014-9*, East Gate Bk) M E Sharpe.

— Forecast for Japan: Security in the 1970s. LC 71-37578. 255p. 1972. reprint ed. pap. 79.10 (*0-7837-8594-1*, 204940900011) Bks Demand.

— Japan's Road to the Pacific War: Japan Erupts (Selected Translations from Taiheiyo senso e no michi: Kaisen Gaiko shi), Vol. 4. LC 83-27320. (Studies of the East Asian Institute). 384p. 1984. text 69.00 (*0-231-05782-2*) Col U Pr.

— Japan's Road to the Pacific War: Japan's Negotiations with the United States, 1941. LC 94-1392. (Japan's Road to the Pacific War Ser.). 1994. 64.50 (*0-231-08024-7*) Col U Pr.

Morley, James W. & Nishihara, Masashi, eds. Vietnam Joins the World. LC 96-39809. 260p. (C). (gr. 13). 1997. text 69.95 (*1-56324-974-X*, East Gate Bk); pap. text 23.95 (*1-56324-975-8*, East Gate Bk) M E Sharpe.

Morley, Jane, et al, eds. Isis Cumulative Index, 1953-1982. 168p. 1985. pap. text 15.00 (*0-934235-01-5*); lib. bdg. 36.00 (*0-934235-00-7*) Hist Sci Soc.

Morley, Janet. All Desires Known. expanded ed. LC 93-45039. 128p. 1994. pap. 10.95 (*0-8192-1610-0*) Morehouse Pub.

Morley, Janet, ed. Bread of Tomorrow: Prayers for the Church Year. LC 92-5619. 192p. 1992. pap. 10.00 (*0-88344-831-9*) Orbis Bks.

Morley, Janet, et al, eds. Celebrating Women: The New Edition. 168p. 1995. pap. 13.95 (*0-8192-1652-6*) Morehouse Pub.

Morley, Jim, ed. PFD Wedding Design Manual. (Illus.). 104p. (C). 1993. text 30.95 (*0-944074-02-2*) AFS Education.

— Professional Floral Design Manual. (Illus.). 72p. (C). 1989. text 24.95 (*0-944074-01-4*) AFS Education.

Morley, Jim, ed. see American Floral Services, Inc. Staff.

Morley, Jim, ed. see American Floral Services Staff.

Morley, Joan. Consonants in Context Bk. 1: Rapid Review of Vowel & Prosodic Contexts. 88p. (C). 1991. pap. text 11.95 (*0-472-08127-6*, 08127) U of Mich Pr.

— Consonants in Context Bk. 2: Intensive Consonant Pronunciation Practice. 376p. (C). 1991. pap. text 18.95 (*0-472-08128-4*, 08128) U of Mich Pr.

— Consonants in Context Bk. 3: Extempore Speaking Practice. 136p. 1991. pap. text 14.95 (*0-472-08129-2*, 08129) U of Mich Pr.

Morley, Joan. Improving Aural Comprehension. LC 70-185904. (Illus.). 312p. (C). 1984. 150.00 incl. audio (*0-472-00200-7*, 00200) U of Mich Pr.

Morley, Joan. Improving Aural Comprehension's Student's Workbook: Teacher's Book of Readings. LC 70-185904. 312p. 1972. teacher ed. 12.95 (*0-472-08666-9*, 08666); pap. text, student ed. 16.95 (*0-472-08665-0*, 08665) U of Mich Pr.

— Improving Spoken English. LC 76-49151. 368p. 1979. pap. text 18.95 (*0-472-08660-X*, 08660) U of Mich Pr.

Morley, Joan. Improving Spoken English: An Intensive Personalized Program in Perception, Pronunciation, Practice in Context. LC 76-49151. (Illus.). 368p. (C). 1979. 150.00 incl. audio (*0-472-00206-6*, 00206) U of Mich Pr.

Morley, Joan. Listening Dictation: Understanding English Sentence Structure. 152p. 1976. pap. text 12.95 (*0-472-08667-7*, 08667) U of Mich Pr.

Morley, Joan. Listening Dictation: Understanding English Sentence Structure. LC 73-31050. (Illus.). 152p. (C). 1984. audio 85.00 U of Mich Pr.

— Rapid Review of Vowel & Prosodic Contexts. LC 91-65159. (Illus.). 88p. (C). 1993. 50.00 incl. audio (*0-472-00234-1*, 00234) U of Mich Pr.

Morley, Joan, ed. Pronunciation Pedagogy & Theory: New Views, New Directions. 115p. 1994. pap. 15.95 (*0-939791-55-2*) Tchrs Eng Spkrs.

Morley, John. Biographical Studies. 1977. 23.95 (*0-8369-1186-5*) Ayer.

— Burke. LC 68-58388. (English Men of Letters Ser.). reprint ed. 27.50 (*0-404-51720-X*) AMS Pr.

— Colonial Postscript: The Diary of a District Officer. (Illus.). 200p. 1992. text 39.50 (*1-85043-526-X*, Pub. by I B T) St Martin.

— The History of Furniture: Twenty-Five Centuries of Style & Design in the Western Tradition. LC 99-65084. (Illus.). 352p. 1999. 75.00 (*0-8212-2624-X*, Pub. by Bulfinch Pr) Little.

— The Life of William Ewart Gladstone, 3 vols., Set. LC 70-145193. 1966p. 1972. reprint ed. 125.00 (*0-403-01117-5*) Scholarly.

— Recollections, 2 vols., Set. LC 75-30034. reprint ed. 95.00 (*0-404-14080-7*) AMS Pr.

— Regency Design, 1790-1840: Gardens, Buildings, Interiors, Furniture. LC 92-28364. (Illus.). 448p. 1993. 150.00 (*0-8109-3768-9*, Pub. by Abrams) Time Warner.

Morley, John. Scriptwriting for High-Impact Videos: Imaginative Approaches to Delivering Factual Information. 272p. (C). 1991. 31.75 (*0-534-15066-7*) Wadsworth Pub.

Morley, John, ed. Beta Adrenoceptors in Asthma. (Perspectives in Asthma Ser.). 1984. text 83.00 (*0-12-506440-3*) Acad Pr.

— Preventive Therapy in Asthma. (Perspectives in Asthma Ser.: Vol. 5). (Illus.). 300p. (C). 1991. text 83.00 (*0-12-506448-9*) Acad Pr.

Morley, John & Colditz, I., eds. Eosinophils in Asthma. (Perspectives in Asthma Ser.: No. 4). 300p. 1989. text 83.00 (*0-12-506452-7*) Acad Pr.

Morley, John & Rainsford, Kim D., eds. Pharmacology of Asthma. (Agents & Actions Supplements Ser.: Vol. 13). 228p. 1983. 87.50 (*0-8176-1503-2*) Birkhauser.

Morley, John, ed. see Ainger, Alfred.

Morley, John, ed. see Black, William.

Morley, John, ed. see Church, Richard W.

Morley, John, ed. see Courthope, William J.

Morley, John, ed. see Dobson, Austin.

Morley, John, ed. see Dowden, Edward.

Morley, John, ed. see Fowler, Thomas.

Morley, John, ed. see Froude, James A.

Morley, John, ed. see Gosse, Edmund W.

Morley, John, jt. ed. see Hansel, Trevor T.

Morley, John, ed. see Hutton, Richard H.

Morley, John, ed. see Huxley, Thomas Henry.

Morley, John, ed. see James, Henry.

Morley, John, ed. see Masson, David.

Morley, John, ed. see Minto, William.

Morley, John, ed. see Nichol, John.

Morley, John, ed. see Saintsbury, George E.

Morley, John, ed. see Shairp, John C.

Morley, John, ed. see Smith, Goldwin A.

Morley, John, ed. see Stephen, Leslie.

Morley, John, ed. see Traill, H. D.

Morley, John, ed. see Trollope, Anthony.

Morley, John, ed. see Ward, Adolphus W.

Morley, John E., ed. Annual Review of Gerontology & Geriatrics Vol. 15: Focus on Nutrition. (Annual Review of Gerontology & Geriatrics Ser.). (Illus.). 280p. 1995. 54.00 (*0-8261-6497-8*) Springer Pub.

Morley, John E., et al, eds. Geriatric Nutrition: A Comprehensive Review. 2nd ed. LC 95-3911. (Illus.). 416p. 1995. text 107.00 (*0-7817-0169-4*) Lppncott W & W.

— Memory Function & Aging-Related Disorders. LC 91-5089. 352p. 1992. 48.95 (*0-8261-7710-7*) Springer Pub.

*__Morley, John E. & van den Berg, Lucretia, eds.__ Endocrinology of Aging. LC 99-31970. (Contemporary Endocrinology Ser.: Vol. 20). 280p. 1999. 99.50 (*0-89603-756-8*) Humana.

Morley, John M. Critical Miscellanies. LC 68-29234. (Essay Index Reprint Ser.). 1977. reprint ed. 25.95 (*0-8369-2417-7*) Ayer.

— Edmund Burke: A Historical Study. Mayer, J. P., ed. LC 78-67372. (European Political Thought Ser.). 1980. reprint ed. lib. bdg. 25.95 (*0-405-11722-1*) Ayer.

— The Life of William Ewart Gladstone, 3 Vols, Set. LC 68-57630. (Illus.). 1971. reprint ed. lib. bdg. 125.00 (*0-8371-0576-5*, MOWG) Greenwood.

— The Life of William Ewart Gladstone, Vol. 1. LC 68-57630. 1971. lib. bdg. 45.00 (*0-8371-3146-4*, Greenwood Pr) Greenwood.

— The Life of William Ewart Gladstone, 3 vols., Vol. 1. LC 68-57630. (Illus.). 1971. reprint ed. lib. bdg. 24.00 (*0-313-21287-2*, MOWA) Greenwood.

— The Life of William Ewart Gladstone, 3 Vols, Vol. 2. LC 68-57630. (Illus.). 1971. reprint ed. lib. bdg. 45.00 (*0-8371-0827-6*, MOWB) Greenwood.

— The Life of William Ewart Gladstone, 3 Vols, Vol. 3. LC 68-57630. (Illus.). 1971. reprint ed. lib. bdg. 45.00 (*0-8371-0828-4*, MOWC) Greenwood.

— Oracles on Man & Government. LC 68-22933. (Essay Index Reprint Ser.). 1977. reprint ed. 19.95 (*0-8369-0720-5*) Ayer.

— Walpole. LC 76-110858. 251p. 1971. reprint ed. lib. bdg. 65.00 (*0-8371-4527-9*, MOHW, Greenwood Pr) Greenwood.

Morley, John M., ed. English Men of Letters, 41 vols. LC 77-166037. reprint ed. lib. bdg. write for info. (*0-404-51700-5*) AMS Pr.

Morley, John T. Secular Socialists: The CCF-NDP in Ontario, a Biography. LC 85-160769. (Illus.). 283p. reprint ed. pap. 87.80 (*0-7837-6906-7*, 204673600003) Bks Demand.

Morley, John V. Rousseau & His Era. 700p. 1996. reprint ed. pap. 49.95 (*1-56459-578-1*) Kessinger Pub.

Morley, Judith. Miss Laughinghouse & the Reluctant Mystic: The Collected Poems of Judith Morley. (Orig.). 1995. pap. 12.00 (*0-9628181-6-X*) Black Thistle Pr.

Morley, Kevin, jt. auth. see Linton, Ian.

Morley, Laurene S. Hors d'Oeuvres: Easy Elegance. Petruzzini, Diane M., ed. (Orig.). 1986. pap. 6.95 (*0-9617473-0-7*) Creative Cookery.

Morley, Linda & Morley, Austin. The Four Seasons of Home: The Collected Letters of Austin Warren Morley. LC 97-92628. (Illus.). 53p. 1998. pap. 15.00 (*0-9660850-0-0*) Old Erie Pr.

Morley, Louise. School Effectiveness: Fracturing the Discourse. LC 99-28040. (Master Classes in Education Ser.). 176p. 1999. pap. text 24.95 (*0-7507-0847-6*, Falmer Pr) Taylor & Francis.

Morley, Louise & Rassool, Naz. School Effectiveness: Fracturing the Discourse. LC 99-28040. 176p. 1999. 79.95 (*0-7507-0848-4*, Falmer Pr) Taylor & Francis.

Morley, Louise & Walsh, Val, eds. Feminist Academics: Creative Agents for Change. LC 95-1200. (Gender & Society Ser.). 240p. 1995. 85.00 (*0-7484-0299-3*); pap. 29.95 (*0-7484-0300-0*) Taylor & Francis.

Morley, Louise, jt. ed. see Walsh, Val.

Morley, Lynda T. Let's Go! A Guide to Outings & Adventures in Dallas - Ft. Worth with Children Ages 1-5. 2nd rev. ed. LC 97-94060. 200p. 1998. pap. 15.95 (*0-9662888-0-7*) Morley Pr.

*__Morley, Lynda T.__ Lynda Morley's Outings & Adventures with Children Ages 1-5. 3rd rev. ed. 370p. (Orig.). 1999. pap. 17.95 (*0-9662888-1-5*) Morley Pr.

*__Morley, Marjorie.__ Farm in Condo Country. 130p. 2000. pap. 12.50 (*0-944920-36-5*) Bellowing Ark Pr.

Morley, Mary, jt. auth. see Jenkins, Clare.

*__Morley, Michael.__ Building with Structural Insulated Panels (Sips) Strength & Energy Efficiency Through Structure. (Illus.). 2000. 34.95 (*1-56158-351-0*) Taunton.

Morley, Michael. The Collaboration Between Brecht & Weill. Albright, Daniel, ed. 300p. Date not set. text 45.00 (*0-8153-2752-8*) Garland.

— How to Manage Your Global Reputation: A Guide to the Dynamics of International Public Relations. LC 98-13360. 172p. 1998. text 40.00 (*0-8147-5616-6*) NYU Pr.

Morley, Michael F. Ratio Analysis. 64p. 1984. pap. write for info. (*0-85258-233-1*) Thomson Learn.

Morley, Michael S. The Linear IC Handbook. (Illus.). 624p. 1986. 49.50 (*0-8306-0472-3*, NO. 2672) McGraw-Hill Prof.

Morley, Morris, jt. auth. see Petras, James.

Morley, Morris H. Imperial State & Revolution: The United States & Cuba, 1952-1986. 588p. 1988. pap. text 26.95 (*0-521-35762-4*) Cambridge U Pr.

— Washington, Somoza, & the Sandinistas: State & Regime in U. S. Policy Toward Nicaragua, 1969-1981. LC 93-34540. 455p. (C). 1994. text 85.00 (*0-521-45081-0*) Cambridge U Pr.

Morley, Morris H., ed. Crisis & Confrontation: Ronald Reagan's Foreign Policy. 264p. 1988. 68.00 (*0-8476-7432-0*, CR7432) Rowman.

Morley-Mower, Geoffrey. Cabell under Fire. 1974. lib. bdg. 250.00 (*0-87700-214-2*) Revisionist Pr.

*__Morley-Mower, Geoffrey.__ Flying Blind. 2000. 25.00 (*1-881325-40-7*) Yucca Tree Pr.

Morley-Mower, Geoffrey. Messerschmitt Roulette: The Western Desert, 1941-42. LC 93-85728. (Illus.). 1993. 24.95 (*1-883809-01-0*) Specialty Pr.

Morley, N. T. The Appointment. 1998. mass mkt. 6.95 (*1-56333-667-7*) Masquerade.

— The Circle. 1998. mass mkt. 6.95 (*1-56333-627-8*) Masquerade.

— Contract. 1998. mass mkt. 6.95 (*1-56333-575-1*) Masquerade.

— The Library. 1998. mass mkt. 6.95 (*1-56333-683-9*) Masquerade.

— The Limousine. (Orig.). 1997. mass mkt. 6.95 (*1-56333-555-7*) Masquerade.

— The Office. 1998. mass mkt. 6.95 (*1-56333-616-2*) Masquerade.

— The Secretary. 1998. mass mkt. 6.95 (*1-56333-690-1*) Masquerade.

*__Morley, Neville.__ Ancient History: Key Themes & Approaches. LC 99-47074. (Key Guides Ser.). 256p. 2000. pap. 18.95 (*0-415-16509-1*) Routledge.

Morley, Neville. Metropolis & Hinterland: The City of Rome & the Italian Economy, 200 BC-AD 200. LC 95-51652. 222p. (C). 1996. text 54.95 (*0-521-56006-3*) Cambridge U Pr.

*__Morley, Neville.__ Writing Ancient History. LC 99-28001. 1999. pap. 14.95 (*0-8014-8633-5*) Cornell U Pr.

*__Morley, Neville, ed.__ Ancient History: Key Themes & Approaches. LC 99-47074. 256p. (C). 2000. text 65.00 (*0-415-16508-3*) Routledge.

Morley, P., jt. auth. see Barnett, E.

Morley, Patricia. As Though Life Mattered: Leo Kennedy's Story. LC 93-90597. (Illus.). 264p. 1994. 49.95 (*0-7735-1147-4*, Pub. by McG-Queens Univ Pr) CUP Services.

— Margaret Laurence: The Long Journey Home. rev. ed. 200p. (C). 1991. reprint ed. pap. text 24.95 (*0-7735-0856-2*, Pub. by McG-Queens Univ Pr) CUP Services.

— My Other Family: An Artist-Wife in Singapore, 1946-48. (Illus.). 160p. 1994. text 39.50 (*1-85043-823-4*, Pub. by I B T) St Martin.

Morley, Patricia A. The Immoral Moralists: Hugh Maclennan & Leonard Cohen. LC 74-156053. 144 p. 1972. write for info. (*0-7720-0555-9*) Irwin Publ.

— The Mountain Is Moving: Japanese Women's Lives. LC 98-53302. 240p. 1999. text 28.50 (*0-8147-5626-3*) NYU Pr.

— The Mystery of Unity: Theme & Technique in the Novels of Patrick White. LC 77-188136. 261p. reprint ed. pap. 81.00 (*0-7837-6932-6*, 204676100003) Bks Demand.

Morley, Patrick. The Man in the Mirror: Solving the 24 Problems Men Face. LC 97-21288. 320p. 1997. pap. 12.99 (*0-310-21768-7*) Zondervan.

— The Man in the Mirror: Solving the 24 Problems Men Face. 2000. mass mkt. 7.99 (*0-310-23493-X*) Zondervan.

Morley, Patrick. Second Wind for the Second Half. LC 98-37484. 1999. 19.99 (*0-310-22132-3*) Zondervan.

Morley, Patrick. The Seven Seasons of a Man's Life... Crisis & Renewal. 144p. 1996. pap. text 5.95 (*0-8054-9787-0*, LifeWy Press) LifeWay Christian.

— The Seven Seasons of a Man's Life... Rebuilding. 144p. 1996. pap. text 5.95 (*0-8054-9786-2*, LifeWy Press) LifeWay Christian.

— The Seven Seasons of a Man's Life... Reflection & Building. 144p. 1996. pap. text 5.95 (*0-8054-9788-9*, LifeWy Press) LifeWay Christian.

— The Seven Seasons of a Man's Life... Suffering & Success. 144p. 1996. pap. text 5.95 (*0-8054-9785-4*, LifeWy Press) LifeWay Christian.

— Ten Secrets for the Man in the Mirror. LC 99-39363. 2000. 16.99 (*0-310-22897-2*) Zondervan.

— This Is the American Forces Network: The Anglo-American Battle of the Air Waves in World War II. LC 00-32622. 200p. 2000. 62.00 (*0-275-96901-0*, Praeger Pubs) Greenwood.

Morley, Patrick. What Husbands Wish Wives Knew. 1997. pap. 10.99 (*0-310-21866-7*) Zondervan.

Morley, Patrick M. Devotions for Couples: Refreshing Moments for Busy Couples Who Want More Intimacy in Their Relationships. LC 97-37030. 244p. 1997. 16.99 (*0-310-21765-2*) Zondervan.

*__Morley, Patrick M.__ The Rest of Your Life: A Road Map for Christians Who Want a Deeper Understanding of What to Believe & How to Live It. LC 97-32777. 320p. 1998. pap. 12.99 (*0-310-21767-9*) Zondervan.

Morley, Patrick M. The Seven Seasons of a Man's Life: Examining the Unique Challenges Men Face. LC 97-22998. 284p. 1997. 19.99 (*0-310-22019-X*) Zondervan.

— Walking with God in the Details of Life. LC 97-45148. 320p. 1998. pap. 12.99 (*0-310-21766-0*) Zondervan.

— What Husbands Wish Their Wives Knew about Men. 1999. pap. text 9.99 (*0-8297-1972-5*) Vida Pubs.

— What Husbands Wish Their Wives Knew about Men. LC 97-37316. 240p. 1998. 16.99 (*0-310-21414-9*) Zondervan.

— What Husbands Wish Wives Knew. 2000. pap. 12.99 (*0-310-22909-X*) Zondervan.

Morley, Paul, jt. auth. see Whitfield, James F.

Morley, Robert. Around the World in 81 Years. large type ed. 196p. 1991. 19.95 (*1-85089-307-1*, Pub. by ISIS Lrg Prnt); 19.95 (*1-85089-235-0*, Pub. by ISIS Lrg Prnt) Transaction Pubs.

*__Morley, Robert J.__ Origin & Evolution of Tropical Rain Forests. LC 99-29654. 272p. 2000. 140.00 (*0-471-98326-8*) Wiley.

Morley, S., et al. Industrial & Business Space Development: A Practical Guide to Implementation. 350p. 1989. 67.50 (*0-685-24722-8*, E & FN Spon) Routledge.

Morley, S. Griswold. The Covered Bridges of California. 1992. reprint ed. lib. bdg. 75.00 (*0-7812-5066-8*) Rprt Serv.

Morley, S. Griswold, ed. Spanish Ballads. 1977. lib. bdg. 59.95 (*0-8490-2647-4*) Gordon Pr.

Morley, S. Griswold & Hills, E. C. Modern Spanish Lyric. 1972. 59.95 (*0-8490-0652-X*) Gordon Pr.

Morley, Sam. Ninety-Nine Years of Navy: From Victoria to VJ Day Through Three Pairs of Eyes. 1995. 19.95 (*1-899163-07-7*) Cimino Pub Grp.

Morley, Samuel A. Poverty & Inequality in Latin America: Past Evidence, Future Prospects, Vol. 13. LC 94-35166. (Policy Essay Ser.). (Orig.). 1994. pap. 13.95 (*1-56517-020-2*) Overseas Dev Council.

— Poverty & Inequality in Latin America: The Impact of Adjustment & Recovery. 288p. 1995. text 42.50 (*0-8018-5064-9*) Johns Hopkins.

Morley, Sheridan. Audrey Hepburn: A Celebration. (Illus.). 192p. 1995. pap. 15.95 (*1-85793-267-6*, Pub. by Pavilion Bks Ltd) Trafalgar.

*__Morley, Sheridan.__ Dirk Bogarde: Rank Outsider. (Illus.). 192p. 2000. pap. 22.95 (*0-7475-4698-3*, Pub. by Blmsbury Pub) Trafalgar.

Morley, Sheridan. Elizabeth Taylor. (Legends Ser.). 156p. 1999. pap. 9.95 (*1-55783-339-7*) Applause Theatre Bk Pubs.

— Elizabeth Taylor: A Celebration. 19.95 (*0-685-39949-4*, M Joseph) Viking Penguin.

— Katharine Hepburn. (Legends Ser.). (Illus.). 156p. 1999. pap. 9.95 (*1-55783-340-0*) Applause Theatre Bk Pubs.

An Asterisk (*) at the beginning of an entry indicates that the title is appearing for the first time.

— Odd Man Out: James Mason. large type ed. 316p. 1990. 19.95 (*1-85089-376-4*, Pub. by ISIS Lrg Prnt) Transaction Pubs.
— Oscar Wilde. (Illus.). 160p. 1998. pap. 18.95 (*1-55783-330-3*) Applause Theatre Bk Pubs.
***Morley, Sheridan.** Private Lives of Noel & Gertie. 365p. 1999. pap. 27.95 (*1-84002-091-1*, Pub. by Theatre Comm) Consort Bk Sales.
— Quotable Oscar Wilde. (Illus.). 2000. 4.95 (*0-7624-0573-2*) Running Pr.
Morley, Sheridan. Robert, My Father. (Illus.). 240p. 1994. 34.95 (*0-297-81329-3*, Pub. by Weidenfeld & Nicolson) Trafalgar.
— Robert, My Father. large type ed. 24.95 (*1-85695-323-8*, Pub. by ISIS Lrg Prnt) Transaction Pubs.
— Shall We Dance? The Life of Ginger Rogers. 96p. 1995. text 19.95 (*0-312-14149-1*) St Martin.
Morley, Sheridan & Leon, Ruth. Gene Kelly: A Celebration. (Illus.). 168p. 1998. pap. 19.95 (*1-86205-072-4*, Pub. by Pavilion Bks Ltd) Trafalgar.
***Morley, Sheridan & Leon, Ruth.** Hey, Mr. Producer! The Musical World of Cameron Mackintosh. LC 98-87601. (Illus.). 192p. 1998. 35.00 (*0-8230-8816-2*, Billboard Bks) Watsn-Guptill.
Morley, Sheridan & Leon, Ruth. Judy Garland: Beyond the Rainbow. 172p. 1999. 29.95 (*1-55970-491-8*, Pub. by Arcade Pub Inc) Time Warner.
***Morley, Sheridan & Leon, Ruth.** Judy Garland: Beyond the Rainbow. 2000. pap. 19.95 (*1-55970-525-6*, Pub. by Arcade Pub Inc) Time Warner.
Morley, Sheridan & Leon, Ruth. Marilyn Monroe. (Get a Life...Pocket Biographies Ser.). (Illus.). 1997. pap. 9.95 (*0-7509-1510-2*, Pub. by Sutton Pub Ltd) Intl Pubs Mktg.
Morley, Sheridan, jt. ed. see Payn, Graham.
Morley, Simon. William Scott: Paintings & Drawings. LC 98-205063. (Illus.). 120p. 1998. pap. 29.95 (*1-85894-066-4*, Pub. by Merrell Holberton) U of Wash Pr.
Morley, Susan, jt. auth. see Tullio, Paolo.
Morley, Sylvanus G. The Inscriptions at Copan. LC 77-11506. (Carnegie Institution of Washington. Publications: No. 219). reprint ed. 57.00 (*0-404-16271-1*) AMS Pr.
— The Inscriptions of Peten, 5 vols. in 6. LC 77-11510. (Carnegie Institution of Washington. Publications: No. 437). reprint ed. 253.00 (*0-404-16290-8*) AMS Pr.
— Introduction to the Study of Maya Hieroglyphs. (Bureau of American Ethnology Bulletins Ser.). 284p. 1995. lib. bdg. 89.00 (*0-7812-4057-3*) Rprt Serv.
— An Introduction to the Study of the Maya Hieroglyphs. LC 74-82503. (Illus.). 284p. 1975. reprint ed. pap. 9.95 (*0-486-23108-9*) Dover.
— An Introduction to the Study of the Maya Hieroglyphs. 1988. reprint ed. lib. bdg. 75.00 (*0-685-21387-0*) Rprt Serv.
Morley, Sylvanus G., ed. Spanish Ballads. LC 78-137068. 226p. 1977. reprint ed. lib. bdg. 55.00 (*0-8371-5531-2*, MOSB, Greenwood Pr) Greenwood.
Morley, Sylvanus G. & Brainerd, George W. The Ancient Maya. 4th rev. ed. LC 81-85451. (Illus.). xx, 708p. 1983. 45.00 (*0-8047-1137-2*); pap. 19.95 (*0-8047-1288-3*) Stanford U Pr.
Morley, Sylvanus G., tr. see De Cervantes Saavedra, Miguel.
Morley, Thomas. Memecyleae. LC 76-13371. (Flora Neotropica Monographs: No. 15). (Illus.). 295p. 1976. pap. 22.00 (*0-89327-000-8*) NY Botanical.
Morley, Thomas, jt. auth. see Ownbey, Gerald B.
Morley, Thomas F. Discipline Through Virtue: A Discipline Approach That Assists Teachers & Parents in the Effective Use of "The Book of Virtues" 256p. 1995. pap. 14.95 (*0-9649031-0-5*) ThoMax.
Morley, William F. The Atlantic Provinces: Newfoundland, Nova Scotia, New Brunswick, Prince Edward Island. LC 68-90634. (Canadian Local Histories to 1950: A Bibliography Ser.: No. 1). 183p. reprint ed. pap. 56.80 (*0-8357-8031-7*, 203402000088) Bks Demand.
Morley, William F., jt. auth. see Beaulieu, Andre.
Morley, William F., ed. see Waldon, Freda F.
Morley, William H., jt. auth. see Douglas, Christina A.
Morling, Malena. Ocean Avenue. LC 98-66495. 1999. 22.00 (*0-932826-70-9*) New Issues MI.
— Ocean Avenue: (Poems) LC 98-66595. (Poetry Ser.). 64p. 1999. pap. 12.00 (*0-932826-68-7*) WMU Poetry & Prose.
Morlino, Leonardo. Democracy Between Consolidation & Crisis: Parties, Groups, & Citizens in Southern Europe. (Oxford Studies in Democratization). (Illus.). 406p. 1998. text 85.00 (*0-19-828082-3*) OUP.
Morlock, Daniel J. Escapes! Confessions of an Escape Artist. (My Favorite Ser.). (YA). 1995. 19.99 (*0-9649646-1-9*) Morlock Assocs.
— Magic Tricks for Kids Vol. 1: Everyday Objects. (My Favorite Ser.). (J). 1995. 14.99 (*0-9649646-0-0*) Morlock Assocs.
Morlock, Henry, jt. auth. see Harless, Marion.
Morlock, Laura L., jt. auth. see Frank, Richard G.
Morlot, Jan C., ed. Climate Change: Mobilising Global Effort. 200p. 1997. pap. 38.00 (*92-64-15675-5*, 97-97-21-1, Pub. by Org for Econ) OECD.
Morman, Edward T., ed. Efficiency, Science Management, & Hospital Standardization: An Anthology of Sources. (Medical Care in the United States Ser.). 288p. 1989. reprint ed. text 25.00 (*0-8240-8338-5*) Garland.
Morman, Jean M. Art: Tempo of Today. rev. ed. (Illus.). 1978. text 17.20 (*0-912242-14-0*) Art Educ.
Morman, Paul, tr. see De La Barre, Poullain.
Morman, Vanessa. Ten Years Hard Labor: Racism in the Military. 353p. 1993. pap. 15.95 (*1-891601-00-8*) Ladies Caliber.
Mormando, Franco. The Preacher's Demons: Bernardino of Siena & the Social Underworld of Early Renaissance Italy. LC 98-40505. 1999. 29.00 (*0-226-53854-0*) U Ch Pr.
Mormando, Franco, ed. Saints & Sinners: Caravaggio & the Baroque Image. LC 98-68410. (Illus.). 235p. 1999. pap. 40.00 (*1-892850-00-1*) McMullen Mus Art.
Mormann, W. H. CAD/CIM in Aesthetic Dentistry: CEREC 10 Year Anniversary Symposium; Proceedings. 663p. 1996. 84.00 (*3-87652-653-1*, RK21) Quint Pub Co.
Mormann, W. H., ed. International Symposium on Computer Restorations: State of the Art of the CEREC-Method. (Illus.). 632p. (Orig.). 1991. pap. text 56.00 (*0-86715-163-3*, B1633) Quint Pub Co.
Mormile, Mario. Dictionnaire Commercial: Francais-Italien, Italien-Francais. (FRE & ITA.). 1978. lib. bdg. 125.00 (*0-7859-3907-5*) Fr & Eur.
Mormino, Gary R. Immigrants on the Hill: Italian-Americans in St. Louis, 1882-1982. (Illus.). 304p. 1986. text 24.95 (*0-252-01261-5*) U of Ill Pr.
Mormino, Gary R. & Pozzetta, George E. The Immigrant World of Ybor City: Italians & Their Latin Neighbors in Tampa, 1885-1985. LC 98-35756. 384p. 1998. reprint ed. pap. 17.95 (*0-8130-1630-4*) U Press Fla.
Mormino, Gary R., jt. ed. see Henderson, Ann L.
Mormon Festival of Arts Staff, et al. Mormon Arts: Featuring Articles & Art Work by Mormon Artists & Authors. LC 72-93467. 1972. write for info. (*0-8425-0094-4*, BYU Press) Brigham.
Mormon, Paul J. Noel Aubert de Verse: A Study in the Concept of Toleration. LC 87-21643. (Texts & Studies in Religion: Vol. 32). 290p. 1986. lib. bdg. 89.95 (*0-88946-822-2*) E Mellen.
Mormons, Boris A. Sports Varieties - Studies of Exercise Using Human Saliva As a Diagnostic Instrument: Index of New Information & Bibliography. 150p. 1997. 47.50 (*0-7883-0988-9*); pap. 44.50 (*0-7883-0989-7*) ABBE Pubs Assn.
Mormont, Marc, et al, eds. Transport & Risk Communication: Belgium, Portugal & The Netherlands. LC 97-29373. (GER.). 344p. 1997. pap. 57.95 (*3-631-31700-X*) P Lang Pubng.
— Transport & Risk Communication: Belgium, Portugal & The Netherlands. LC 97-29373. (Illus.). 344p. 1997. pap. 57.95 (*0-8204-3277-6*) P Lang Pubng.
Mormorio, Diego. Tazio Secchiaroli: First of the Paparazzi. Bonfante-Warren, Alexandra, tr. from ITA. LC 98-42771. (Illus.). 264p. 1999. 49.50 (*0-8109-4177-5*, Pub. by Abrams) Time Warner.
Morn, Frank. Academic Politics & History of Criminal Justice Education, 46. LC 94-18557. (Contributions in Criminology & Penology Ser.: No. 46). 256p. 1995. 59.95 (*0-313-29316-3*, Greenwood Pr) Greenwood.
— The Eye That Never Sleeps: A History of the Pinkerton National Detective Agency. LC 81-47776. 255p. reprint ed. pap. 79.10 (*0-8357-3959-7*, 205705500004) Bks Demand.
— Foundations of Criminal Investigations. LC 99-28283. 326p. 2000. pap. 28.00 (*0-89089-874-X*) Carolina Acad Pr.
Morn, September B. Calming Touch & Massage. (Proper Puppy Guides Ser.: Vol. 4). (Illus.). 16p. (Orig.). 1996. pap. text 3.75 (*0-9633884-5-2*) Pawprince Pr.
— Cooperation Games: Fun Training Your Puppy. (Proper Puppy Guides Ser.: Vol. 6). (Illus.). 16p. (Orig.). 1996. pap. text 3.75 (*0-9633884-7-9*) Pawprince Pr.
— Crate-Den Training: A Safe & Private Space for Your Dog, Vol. 2. (Illus.). 16p. 1995. pap. text 3.75 (*0-9633884-3-6*) Pawprince Pr.
— Crimes & Punishments. (Proper Puppy Guides Ser.: Vol. 5). (Illus.). 16p. (Orig.). 1996. pap. text 3.75 (*0-9633884-6-0*) Pawprince Pr.
— Dogs Love to Please... We Teach Them How! The Safe & Gentle Guide to Dog Obedience Through Interspecies Communication. 4th rev. ed. (Illus.). 248p. 1994. pap., per. 15.95 (*0-9633884-1-X*) Pawprince Pr.
— House Training: An Owner's Guide to a Happy, Healthy Pet. LC 98-42792. 126p. 1999. text 12.95 (*1-58245-010-2*) Howell Bks.
***Morn, September B.** Labrador Retriever. LC 99-31346. (Training Your Dog Ser.). 176p. 1999. pap. text 11.95 (*0-7641-0992-8*) Barron.
Morn, September B. My, What Sharp Teeth: Chewing & Biting Problems, Vol. 3. (Illus.). 16p. 1996. pap. text 3.75 (*0-9633884-4-4*) Pawprince Pr.
— Positive Potty Training: The Quick Guide to a Dry Floor in Three Weeks or Less, Vol. 1. 16p. 1995. pap. text 3.75 (*0-9633884-2-8*) Pawprince Pr.
— The Proper Puppy Guides: Six Handbooks for Raising a Proper Puppy, 6 booklets, Set. (Illus.). 96p. (Orig.). 1996. pap. 18.00 (*0-9633884-8-7*) Pawprince Pr.
Morn, September B., ed. The Best of the Best - 1995: A Celebration of Fine Dog Writing. (Illus.). 208p. (Orig.). 1996. pap. text 20.00 (*0-9633884-9-5*) Pawprince Pr.
Mornand, Pierre. In the Forest of the Golden Dragon: A Biography of the Artist, Domjan. LC 73-76776. (ENG & FRE., Illus.). 128p. 1973. 40.00 (*0-933652-04-6*) Domjan Studio.
Mornay, Philippe De, see De Mornay, Philippe.
***Morneau.** Creating Active Server Pages. (Programming Ser.). (C). 2000. pap. 49.95 (*0-619-01525-X*) Course Tech.
— A Guide to Solution's Architecture. 2nd ed. (Programming Language Ser.). (C). 1999. text 43.25 (*0-619-01644-2*) Course Tech.
— A Guide to Solutions Architecture, 1st Printing with CD. (Programming Ser.). (C). 1999. pap. 57.95 (*0-619-01653-1*) Course Tech.
Morneau, Claude. Martinique: Ulysses Travel Guide. 3rd ed. Ulysses Travel Guide Staff, ed. (Illus.). 256p. 1998. 17.95 (*2-89464-136-2*) Globe Pequot.
***Morneau, Keith.** MCSD Architectures Exam Prep. LC 99-32121. 1999. write for info. (*1-57610-413-3*) W S Hein.
Morneau, Renney E. Berlin. LC 98-88052. (Images of America Ser.). (Illus.). 128p. 1998. pap. 16.99 (*0-7524-0914-X*) Arcadia Publng.
Morneau, Robert. Gift, Mystery & Calling: Prayers & Reflections. Koch, Carl, ed. 111p. 1994. pap. 6.95 (*0-88489-346-4*); spiral bd. 8.95 (*0-88489-355-3*) St Marys.
— Humility Vol. 3: 31 Reflections on Christian Virtue. Koch, Carl, ed. (Thirty-One Reflections on Christian Virtue Ser.). 96p. (Orig.). 1997. pap. 6.95 (*0-88489-425-8*) St Marys.
Morneau, Robert, jt. ed. see Siegfried, Regina.
Morneau, Robert F. Ashes to Easter: Lenten Meditations. 120p. 1997. pap. 9.95 (*0-8245-1720-2*) Crossroad NY.
— C.S. Lewis: Yielding to a Pursuing God. (Retreat with Ser.). 1999. pap. text 8.95 (*0-86716-328-3*) St Anthony Mess Pr.
— Fathoming Bethlehem: Advent Meditations. LC 97-15538. 120p. 1997. 12.95 (*0-8245-1689-3*) Crossroad NY.
— The Gift. LC 94-78138. 32p. (J). (gr. k-4). 1995. text 16.00 (*0-9642140-6-7*) Kodomo Pr.
***Morneau, Robert F.** The Gift. LC 99-87454. 32p. (J). (gr. 3-7). 2000. 14.95 (*0-8091-6673-9*) Paulist Pr.
Morneau, Robert F. Growing in Joy: 31 Reflections on Christian Virtue. LC 99-174501. (Growing in Abundance Ser.). 96p. 1998. pap. 7.95 (*0-88489-541-6*) St Marys.
— Mantras from a Poet: Jessica Powers. LC 90-64032. 134p. (Orig.). 1991. pap. 8.95 (*1-55612-420-1*, LL1420) Sheed & Ward WI.
— Paths to Prayer: Prayerful Insights from the Catechism. 160p. 1997. pap. 9.95 (*0-86716-326-7*) St Anthony Mess Pr.
***Morneau, Robert F.** Poetry as Prayer Vol. 3: Jessica Powers. (Illus.). 145p. 2000. pap. 8.95 (*0-8198-5921-4*) Pauline Bks.
Morneau, Robert F. A Retreat with Jessica Powers: Loving a Passionate God. 104p. 1995. pap. 7.95 (*0-86716-236-8*) St Anthony Mess Pr.
— Spiritual Aids for Those in Renew: Ponderings, Poems & Promises. LC 84-12299. 111p. (Orig.). 1984. pap. 4.50 (*0-8189-0473-9*) Alba.
— Spiritual Direction: Principles & Practices. 144p. (Orig.). 1992. pap. 12.95 (*0-8245-1202-2*) Crossroad NY.
— There Is a Season: An Inspirational Journal. LC 84-11622. (Illus.). 175p. 1986. 18.95 (*0-13-914755-1*, Busn); 9.95 (*0-13-914706-3*, Busn) P-H.
Morneau, Robert F., ed. Children's Book of Classic Catholic Prayers. LC 99-41548. (Illus.). 32p. (J). (ps-3). 2000. 5.95 (*0-8091-6666-6*) Paulist Pr.
***Morneau, Robet F.** From Resurrection to Pentecost: Easter Season Meditations. LC 99-50924. 144p. 2000. 12.95 (*0-8245-1855-1*, Pub. by Crossroad NY) Natl Bk Netwk.
Morneau, Roger. The Incredible Power of Prayer. LC 97-35817. 144p. (Orig.). 1997. pap. 1.99 (*0-8280-1329-2*) Review & Herald.
Morneau, Roger J. Beware of Angels: Deceptions in the Last Days LC 97-166753. 189p. 1997. write for info. (*0-8280-1300-4*) Review & Herald.
Morneau, Roger J. More Incredible Answers to Prayer. LC 93-18276. 1993. pap. 7.99 (*0-8280-0719-5*) Review & Herald.
— When You Need Incredible Answers to Prayer. LC 95-19379. 1995. pap. 7.99 (*0-8280-0976-7*) Review & Herald.
***Mornell, Pierre.** Games Companies Play: A Job-Hunter's Guide to Playing Smart & Winning Big in the High-Stakes Hiring Game. LC 00-26736. (Illus.). 192p. 2000. 24.95 (*1-58008-183-5*) Ten Speed Pr.
Mornell, Pierre. Hiring Smart: How to Predict Winners & Losers in the Incredibly Expensive People-Reading Game. LC 97-40126. (Illus.). 226p. 1998. 24.95 (*0-89815-972-5*) Ten Speed Pr.
Morner, Kathleen & Rausch, Ralph. From Absurd to Zeitgeist: The Compact Guide to Literary Terms. LC 97-15379. (Illus.). 256p. 1997. 12.95 (*0-8442-0401-3*, 04013) NTC Contemp Pub Co.
— NTC's Dictionary of Literary Terms. (Illus.). 304p. 1993. 16.95 (*0-8442-5465-7*, 54657, Natl Textbk Co) NTC Contemp Pub Co.
— NTC's Dictionary of Literary Terms. LC 98-7223. (Illus.). 304p. 1995. pap. 12.95 (*0-8442-5464-9*, 54649, Natl Textbk Co) NTC Contemp Pub Co.
Morner, M., jt. ed. see Emmer, P. C.
Morner, Magnus. The Andean Past: Land, Societies & Conflicts. LC 83-23136. 316p. reprint ed. pap. 98.00 (*0-7837-0421-6*, 204074400018) Bks Demand.
— Region & State in Latin America's Past. LC 92-28774. (Johns Hopkins Symposia in Comparative History Ser.: No. 21). (Illus.). 159p. 1993. reprint ed. pap. 49.30 (*0-608-06708-3*, 206690500009) Bks Demand.
Morner, Magnus & Svensson, Thommy, eds. The History of the Third World in Nordic Research. (Acta Regiae Societatis Scientiarum Humaniora Ser.: No. 25). 202p. (Orig.). 1986. pap. text 83.50 (*91-85252-36-0*, Pub. by Vetenskaps) Coronet Bks.
Morner, Nils-Axel, ed. Earth Rheology, Isostasy & Eustasy: Proceedings of Earth Rheology & Late Cenozoic Isostatic Movements an Interdisciplinary Symposium Held in Stockholm, Sweden, July 31-August 8, 1977. LC 79-1473. (Geodynamics Project: Scientific Report Ser.: No. 49). (Illus.). 621p. reprint ed. pap. 192.60 (*0-608-18417-9*, 203041500069) Bks Demand.
Morner, Nils-Axel & Karlen, W., eds. Climatic Changes on a Yearly to Millennial Basis. 1984. text 270.00 (*90-277-1779-6*) Kluwer Academic.
Morning, Barbara. Grandfather's Shirt. Johnson, Joy, ed. (Illus.). 16p. (J). (ps-2). 1996. pap. 4.95 (*1-56123-074-X*) Centering Corp.
Morning Call Staff, ed. Looking Back: A Pictorial Look at the Lehigh Valley, 1850 to 1920. LC 98-66246. (Illus.). 152p. 1998. 24.95 (*0-9664197-0-7*) Morning Call.
Morninghouse, Sundaira. Habari Gani? What's the News? LC 92-12272. (Illus.). 32p. (J). (gr. k-4). 1992. 14.95 (*0-940880-39-3*) Open Hand.
— Nightfeathers: Black Goose Rhymes. LC 89-63264. (Illus.). 32p. (J). (gr. 1-4). 1989. 9.95 (*0-940880-27-X*); pap. text 4.95 (*0-940880-28-8*) Open Hand.
Morningland Publications, Inc. Staff. Healing: As It Is, 2 vols., Set. (Illus.). 320p. (Orig.). 1981. pap. 10.00 (*0-935146-59-8*) Morningland.
— Morningland Astrology Chart Construction. (Illus.). 100p. (Orig.). 1980. pap., spiral bd. 3.50 (*0-935146-10-5*) Morningland.
Morningland Publications, Inc. Staff & Donato, Gopi G. Lord Jupiter. (Astrology Ser.). (Illus.). 283p. (Orig.). 1980. pap. 6.95 (*0-935146-50-4*) Morningland.
Morningland Publications, Inc. Staff, ed. see Donato, Gopi G.
Morningland Publications, Inc. Staff, ed. see Donato, Sri.
Morningland Publications, Inc. Staff, ed. see Donato, Sri & Donato, Gopi G.
Morningland Publications, Inc. Staff, ed. see Gyan, Gopi.
Morningland Publications, Inc. Staff, ed. see Kamazi, I.
Morningland Publications, Inc. Staff, ed. see Patricia.
Morningland Publications, Inc. Staff, ed. see Sri, Patricia.
***Morningstar.** In the Spirit. 1998. audio 10.99 (*7-5124-0183-3*) Destiny Image.
— Prepare the Way. 1998. audio 10.99 (*7-5124-0169-8*) Destiny Image.
Morningstar. U. S. Equities 6-7: Update 3. 4th ed. 1997. 29.25 (*0-256-24609-2*) McGraw.
— U. S. Equittes on Floppy: 1995-96 Edition User's Manual. 3rd ed. 120p. (C). 1995. 37.95 (*0-256-18734-7*, Irwn McGrw-H) McGrw-H Hghr Educ.
***Morningstar, Amadea.** The Ayurvedic Cookbook: A Personalized Guide to Good Nutrition & Health. Desai, Urmila, ed. 350p. 1999. 112.00 (*81-208-1176-3*, Pub. by Motilal Bnarsidass) St Mut.
Morningstar, Amadea. Ayurvedic Cooking for Westerners: Familiar Western Food Prepared with Ayurvedic Principles. LC 94-79592. 395p. (Orig.). 1995. pap. 19.95 (*0-914955-14-4*) Lotus Pr.
Morningstar, Amadea & Desai, Urmila. The Ayurvedic Cookbook. LC 90-35806. 340p. (Orig.). (C). 1990. pap. 17.95 (*0-914955-06-3*) Lotus Pr.
Morningstar, Amadea, jt. auth. see Gagnon, Daniel.
Morningstar, D. Isis. 75 Easy Trips into the Southern Sierras. LC 99-187909. (Illus.). 96p. 1998. pap. write for info. (*1-57579-128-5*) Pine Hill Pr.
Morningstar, Gersh, jt. auth. see Tropman, John E.
Morningstar Inc. Staff. Morningstar Closed-End Fund 250: 1996 Edition. 2nd ed. 1996. 35.00 (*0-7863-0538-X*, Irwn Prfssnl) McGraw-Hill Prof.
***Morningstar Inc. Staff.** Morningstar 500. 2000-2001 Edition. 600p. 2000. pap. 39.95 (*0-07-135774-2*) McGraw.
Morningstar Inc. Staff. Morningstar Mutual Fund 500: An In-Depth Look at 500 Select Mutual Funds from the Leading Authority in Mutual-Fund Analysis, 1996 Edition. 4th ed. 525p. 1996. 35.00 (*0-7863-0539-8*, Irwn Prfssnl) McGraw-Hill Prof.
— Morningstar Mutual Fund 500: 1999-2000 Edition. 1999. pap. text 35.00 (*0-07-134948-0*) McGraw.
Morningstar, Jean. Christian Clip Art. 64p. 1997. pap. 24.95 (*1-58051-000-0*, LL2000) Sheed & Ward WI.
— Christian Clip Art. 64p. 1997. pap. 24.95 (*1-58051-001-9*, LL2001) Sheed & Ward WI.
Morningstar, Jim. Breathing in Light & Love: Your Call to Breath & Body Mastery. 224p. (Orig.). 1994. pap. text 10.00 (*0-9604856-2-7*) Transform Inc.
— Family Awakening in Body, Mind & Spirit. 60p. 1984. pap. 6.00 (*0-9604856-1-9*) Transform Inc.
— Spiritual Psychology: A Course for Renewalin Body, Mind & Spirit. rev. ed. (Illus.). 140p. 1999. pap. 18.00 (*0-9604856-3-5*) Transform Inc.
— Spiritual Psychology: A New Age Course for Body, Mind & Spirit. 2nd ed. (Illus.). 119p. (C). 1981. pap. 10.00 (*0-9604856-0-0*) Transform Inc.
Morningstar, Louise R. Journey Through Brain Trauma: A Mother's Story of Her Daughter's Recovery. LC 98-11005. 208p. 1998. pap. text 12.95 (*0-87833-988-4*) Taylor Pub.
***Morningstar, Rani, ed.** Living with a Jack Russell Terrier. (Living with a Pet Ser.). (Illus.). 128p. 2000. 14.95 (*0-7641-5261-0*) Barron.
Morningstar, Sally. Ayurveda: Traditional Indian Healing for Harmony & Health. (Illus.). 64p. 1999. 9.95 (*1-85967-897-1*) Anness Pub.
***Morningstar, Sally.** Health & Well-being: Ayurveda. 64p. 2000. pap. 6.95 (*1-84215-171-1*) Anness Pub.
— Love Magic. LC 00-28504. (Illus.). 128p. 2000. pap. 14.95 (*0-8069-2781-X*) Sterling.
— Moon Wisdom: A Guide For Life. 64p. 2000. pap. 6.95 (*1-84215-125-8*) Anness Pub.
— Spellweaving: A Book of Spells & Practical Magic. (New Life Library). 1999. 11.95 (*0-7548-0191-8*, Lorenz Bks) Anness Pub.
***Morningstar Staff.** Fly Me Like the Wind. 1998. audio 10.99 (*7-5124-0197-3*) Destiny Image.
Morningstar Staff. The Morningstar Mutual Fund 500: 1998 Edition. 626p. 1998. pap. 35.00 (*0-07-043431-X*) McGraw.
Mornis, Risa. An Herbal Feast. LC 98-11633. (Illus.). 264p. 1998. pap. 16.95 (*0-87983-801-9*, 38019K, Keats Publng) NTC Contemp Pub Co.
Morns, Jan. Dakota & the Wolf Pack. (Friends of the Forest Adventure Bks.). (Illus.). (J). (ps-8). 1994. 16.95 (*0-9641742-0-0*) Pequot Pubng.

M

An Asterisk (*) at the beginning of an entry indicates that the title is appearing for the first time.

***Moro, Andrea.** Dynamic Antisymmetry. (Linguistic Inquiry Monographs: No. 38). 148p. 2000. 45.00 (*0-262-13375-X*) MIT Pr.

— Dynamic Antisymmetry. (Linguistic Inquiry Monographs: No. 38). 148p. (C). 2000. pap. 18.00 (*0-262-63201-2*) MIT Pr.

Moro, Andrea. The Raising of Predicates: Predicative Noun Phrases & the Theory of Clause Structure. (Cambridge Studies in Linguistics: No. 80). 328p. 1997. text 64.95 (*0-521-56233-3*) Cambridge U Pr.

Moro, Cesar. Love till Death. Lefevre, Frances, tr.Tr. of Amour a Mort. 140p. 1971. 25.00 (*0-931106-05-2*) TVRT.

— The Scandalous Life of Cesar Moro in His Own Words: Peruvian Surrealist Poetry. Ward, Philip, tr. (Modern Poets Ser.: Vol. 6). 1976. pap. 5.95 (*0-902675-73-7*) Oleander Pr.

Moro, Christiane, et al, eds. Outils et Signes: Perspectives Actuelles de la Theorie de Vygotski. (Exploration Ser.). (FRE., Illus.). vi, 221p. 1997. 36.95 (*3-906757-88-9*, Pub. by P Lang) P Lang Pubng.

Moro, Concepcion, jt. ed. see Farre, Jeronimo.

Moro, Elena, tr. see Carmichael, Clay.

Moro, Elena, tr. see Masurel, Claire.

Moro, Ginger H. European Designer Jewelry. LC 95-2180. (Illus.). 304p. (Orig.). 1995. 79.95 (*0-88740-823-0*) Schiffer.

Moro, Lillam, ed. see Fornes, Leopoldo.

Moro-Oka, Y., et al, eds. III-V Hydrogen Absorbing Materials - Catalytic Materials: Materials Research Society International Symposium Proceedings - IMAM-2. 396p. 1989. text 17.50 (*1-55899-031-3*, IMAM-2) Materials Res.

Moro, Oscar P. Rios y Palmas: Poesias. LC 85-80622. (Coleccion Espejo de Paciencia). (SPA.). 127p. (Orig.). 1985. pap. 8.95 (*0-89729-377-0*) Ediciones.

Moro, Oscar P. & Perez, Dario E. Lira Criolla (Decimas Cubanas) LC 86-83149. (Coleccion Espejo de Paciencia). 85p. (Orig.). 1987. pap. 9.95 (*0-89729-430-0*) Ediciones.

Moro, Polo. La Pelicula. LC 95-60608. (Coleccion Caniqui). (SPA.). 72p. (Orig.). 1995. pap. 9.95 (*0-89729-759-8*) Ediciones.

Moro, Polo, ed. A Flote. LC 96-83824. (Coleccion Hispanica - Literaria: No. 7). (SPA.). 128p. (Orig.). 1996. pap. 12.00 (*0-89729-797-0*) Ediciones.

Moro, Renata & Cesareo, Roberto. XRF & PIXE Applications in Life Science. 348p. (C). 1990. text 113.00 (*981-02-0079-X*) World Scientific Pub.

Moro, Ruben O. The History of the South Atlantic Conflict: The War for the Malvinas. LC 88-38300. 376p. 1989. 75.00 (*0-275-93081-5*, C3081, Praeger Pubs) Greenwood.

Moro, Ruth J. Angels in Our Midst: A Naturalistic Embrace of the Miraculous. unabridged ed. LC 97-170853. (Illus.). 64p. (Orig.). 1997. pap. 9.95 (*0-9656881-0-0*) Pebble Pr CA.

Moro, T. Diccionario Juridico. (SPA.). 1010p. 1994. 110.00 (*84-239-5988-0*, Pub. by Espasa Calpe) IBD Ltd.

Moro, Wendy, jt. auth. see Barrett, Ann.

Morof, Howard, et al. 96 Ways You Can Save Taxes in '96: Southeastern Michigan Edition. 128p. (Orig.). Date not set. pap. 9.95 (*1-888303-01-8*) Loopholes Pr.

Moroff, Diane L. Fornes: Theater in the Present Tense. LC 96-10153. 168p. (C). 1996. text 39.50 (*0-472-10726-7*, 10726) U of Mich Pr.

Moroi, Y. Micelles: Theoretical & Applied Aspects. (Illus.). 264p. (C). 1992. text 69.50 (*0-306-43996-4*, Kluwer Plenum) Kluwer Academic.

Moroji, T., ed. The Biology of Schizophrenia: Proceedings of the 7th International Symposium of the Tokyo Institute of Psychiatry, Tokyo, Japan, October 19-20, 1992. LC 94-3420. (Developments in Psychiatry Ser.). 284p. 1994. 194.50 (*0-444-81772-7*) Elsevier.

Morokoff, William J., jt. auth. see Kersch, Alfred.

Morokuma, Keiji, jt. ed. see Truhlar, Donald G.

Morokuma, Keiji, jt. ed. see Van Leeuwen, Piet W.

Moron Arroyo, Ciriaco, ed. see Unamuno, Miguel de.

Moron, Guillermo. Breve Historia Contemporanea de Venezuela. (SPA.). 366p. 1994. pap. 12.99 (*968-16-4207-4*, Pub. by Fondo) Continental Bk.

— History of Venezuela. Street, John, tr. from SPA. 268p. 1964. 69.50 (*0-614-00156-0*) Elliots Bks.

Morone. Winning in High-Tech Markets. 280p. 1993. 34.95 (*0-07-103386-6*) McGraw.

Morone, James A. The Democratic Wish: Popular Participation & the Limits of American Government. LC 90-80250. 402p. 1992. reprint ed. pap. 17.00 (*0-465-01602-2*, Pub. by Basic) HarpC.

— The Democratic Wish: Popular Participation & the Limits of American Government. rev. ed. LC 97-80178. 416p. 1998. pap. 18.00 (*0-300-07465-4*) Yale U Pr.

Morone, James A. & Belkin, Gary S., eds. The Politics of Health Care Reform: Lessons from the Past, Prospects for the Future. LC 94-10005. 552p. 1994. text 54.95 (*0-8223-1461-4*); pap. text 21.95 (*0-8223-1489-4*) Duke.

Morone, John J. & Hilbush, Mark R. Experiencing Artificial Intelligence: An Interactive Approach for the Apple. (Illus.). 190p. (Orig.). 1987. pap. 36.95 (*0-8306-2860-6*, 2860C) McGraw-Hill Prof.

— Experiencing Artificial Intelligence: An Interactive Approach for the IBM PC. (Illus.). 190p. (Orig.). 1987. pap. 29.95 incl. disk (*0-8306-2830-4*, 2830C) McGraw-Hill Prof.

Morone, Joseph & Woodhouse, Edward J. The Demise of American Nuclear Power: Learning from the Failure of a Politically Unsafe Technology. LC 88-39306. 168p. (C). 1989. 9.00 (*0-300-04448-8*); pap. 9.00 (*0-300-04449-6*) Yale U Pr.

Morone, Joseph G. Winning in High-Tech Markets: The Role of General Management. LC 92-15842. 304p. (C). 1993. 29.95 (*0-87584-325-5*) Harvard Busn.

Morone, Joseph G. & Woodhouse, Edward J. Averting Catastrophe: Strategies for Regulating Risky Technologies. (Illus.). 224p. 1986. pap. 15.95 (*0-520-05754-6*, Pub. by U CA Pr) Cal Prin Full Svc.

Moroney, Chris. Babe: A Pig for All Seasons. (J). 1998. 5.99 (*0-679-89442-X*) Random.

Moroney, John R. Exploration, Development, & Production: Texas Oil & Gas, 1970-1995. LC 97-31943. (Contemporary Studies in Economic & Financial Analysis Ser.: Vol. 82). 205p. 1997. 78.50 (*0-7623-0310-7*) Jai Pr.

Moroney, John R., ed. Advances in the Economics of Energy & Resources. (Advances in the Economics of Energy & Resources Ser.: Vol. 3). 274p. 1981. 73.25 (*0-89232-175-X*) Jai Pr.

— Advances in the Economics of Energy & Resources, Vol. 10. 1997. 73.25 (*0-7623-0129-5*) Jai Pr.

— Advances in the Economics of Energy & Resources, Vol. 11. Date not set. 73.25 (*0-7623-0304-2*) Jai Pr.

— Advances in the Economics of Energy & Resources: Energy Prices & Production, Vol. 8. 194p. 1994. 73.25 (*1-55938-465-4*) Jai Pr.

— Advances in the Economics of Energy & Resources Vol. 4: Formal Energy & Resource Models. (Advances in the Economics of Energy & Resources Ser.: Vol. 4). 275p. 1982. 73.25 (*0-89232-215-2*) Jai Pr.

— Advances in the Economics of Energy & Resources Vol. 5: Econometric Models of the Demand for Energy. (Advances in the Economics of Energy & Resources Ser.: Vol. 5). 210p. 1984. 73.25 (*0-89232-327-2*) Jai Pr.

— Advances in the Economics of Energy & Resources Vol. 7: Energy, Growth, & the Environment. 275p. 1992. 73.25 (*0-89232-947-5*) Jai Pr.

— Advances in the Economics of Energy & Resources Vol. 9: Sustainable Economic Growth. 241p. 1995. 73.25 (*1-55938-922-2*) Jai Pr.

Moroney, John R. & Khazzoom, J. Daniel, eds. Advances in the Economics of Energy & Resources Suppl. 1: An Econometric Model of Fuel Economy & Single-Vehicle Highway Fatalities. LC 94-10836. (Advances in the Economics of Energy & Resources Ser.). 184p. 1994. suppl. ed. 73.25 (*1-55938-738-6*) Jai Pr.

Moroney, John R. & Pindyke, Robert S., eds. Advances in the Economics of Energy & Resources Vol. 2: The Production & Pricing of Energy Resources. (Advances in the Economics of Energy & Resources Ser.: Vol. 2). 250p. 1979. 73.25 (*0-89232-079-6*) Jai Pr.

Moroney, Lynn. Moontellers: Myths of the Moon from Around the World. LC 95-2418. (Illus.). 32p. (J). (ps-3). 1995. lib. bdg. 14.95 (*0-87358-601-8*, Rising Moon Bks) Northland AZ.

Moroney, Lynn & Ata, Te. Viborita de Cascabel. Alarcon, Francisco X., tr. LC 89-14832. (ENG & SPA., Illus.). 32p. (YA). (ps-3). 1996. pap. 7.95 (*0-89239-140-5*) Childrens Book Pr.

Moroney, Paul. Issues in the Implementation of Digital Feedback Compensators. (Signal Processing, Optimization, & Control Ser.). (Illus.). 224p. 1983. 37.50 (*0-262-13185-4*) MIT Pr.

Moroney, Robert. The Family & the State: Considerations for Social Policy. LC 75-45230. 154p. reprint ed. pap. 47.80 (*0-608-13222-5*, 202526200043) Bks Demand.

Moroney, Robert M. Shared Responsibility: Families & Social Policy. Whittaker, James K., ed. LC 85-20950. (Modern Applications of Social Work Ser.). (Illus.). 229p. 1986. pap. text 25.95 (*0-202-36042-3*); lib. bdg. 48.95 (*0-202-36041-5*) Aldine de Gruyter.

Moroney, Robert M. & Krysik, Judy. Social Policy & Social Work: Critical Essays on the Welfare State. 2nd ed. LC 97-46375. (Modern Applications of Social Work Ser.). 317p. 1998. pap. text 28.95 (*0-202-36114-4*); lib. bdg. 53.95 (*0-202-36113-6*) Aldine de Gruyter.

Moroney, Robert M., et al. Caring & Competent Caregivers. LC 97-19748. 200p. 1998. 40.00 (*0-8203-1951-1*); pap. 18.00 (*0-8203-1952-X*) U of Ga Pr.

***Moroney, Stephen K.** The Noetic Effects of Sin: An Historical & Contemporary Exploration of How Sin Affects Our Thinking. LC 99-48063. 176p. 1999. 55.00 (*0-7391-0018-1*) Lxngtn Bks.

Moroney, Tracey. First Christmas. 1999. 4.99 (*0-7847-1051-1*) Standard Pub.

***Moroney, Tracey.** Follow the Star. 1999. 4.99 (*0-7847-1050-3*) Standard Pub.

Moroney, Tracey. Goldilocks & the Three Bears. (J). 1999. 7.99 (*1-56799-899-2*) M Friedman Pub Grp Inc.

— Little Red Riding Hood. (J). 1999. 7.99 (*1-56799-898-4*) M Friedman Pub Grp Inc.

Morong, Bill. Yo - Pho's: Young Photographers. Berk, Judy, ed. (Illus.). 145p. 1989. 29.95 (*0-923486-00-3*) F-Stop Pubns.

Moroni, Ercole, jt. auth. see Ellis, Kally.

Moroni, F., et al, eds. Metatropic Glutamate Receptors & Brain Function. (Portland Press Proceedings Ser.: Vol. 12). 318p. 1998. text 110.50 (*1-85578-117-4*, Pub. by Portland Pr Ltd) Ashgate Pub Co.

Moroni, Giancarlo. My Hands Held Out to You: The Use of Body & Hands in Prayer. 112p. 1994. pap. 35.00 (*0-86012-194-1*, Pub. by Srch Pr) St Mut.

Morony, Michael G. Agricultural Production & Pastoralism. 114.95 (*0-86078-706-0*) Ashgate Pub Co.

Morony, Michael G. Iraq after the Muslim Conquest. LC 83-42569. (Illus.). 720p. 1983. reprint ed. pap. 200.00 (*0-8357-3848-5*, 203658100004) Bks Demand.

Morony, Michael G. Manufacturing Mining & Labour. 114.95 (*0-86078-707-9*) Ashgate Pub Co.

Morony, Michael G., tr. The History of al-Tabari Vol. 18: Between Civil Wars: The Caliphate of Mu'awiyah, A. D. 661-680, A. H. 40-60. LC 85-2823. (SUNY Series in Near Eastern Studies). 261p. (C). 1986. text 49.50 (*0-87395-933-7*) State U NY Pr.

— The History of al-Tabari Vol. 18: Between Civil Wars: The Caliphate of Mu'awiyah, A. D. 661-680, A. H. 40-60. LC 85-2823. (SUNY Series in Near Eastern Studies). 261p. (C). 1987. pap. text 22.95 (*0-88706-314-4*) State U NY Pr.

Morony, Michael G., tr. see Al-Tabari.

Morosan, Vladimir. Choral Performance in Pre-Revolutionary Russia. LC 86-1266. (Illus.). xxi, 376p. 1994. pap. 39.00 (*0-9629460-2-8*) Musica Russica.

Morosan, Vladimir, ed. One Thousand Years of Russian Church Music, 988-1988. LC 89-63652. (Monuments of Russian Sacred Music Ser.). (ENG & RUS., Illus.). xlviii, 774p. 1991. lib. bdg. 129.00 (*0-9629460-0-1*) Musica Russica.

Morosan, Vladimir, ed. see Tchaikovsky, Peter Illich.

Morosani, Roopa, ed. see Ananda Yogi, Gururaj.

Morosanu, C. E. Thin Films by Chemical Vapour Deposition. (Thin Films Science & Technology Ser.: Vol. 7). 718p. 1990. 296.50 (*0-444-98801-7*, TFS 7) Elsevier.

Morosanu, Gheorghe. Nonlinear Evolution Equations & Applications. (C). 1988. text 211.50 (*90-277-2486-5*) Kluwer Academic.

***Morosawa, S., et al.** Holomorphic Dynamics. LC 99-14417. (Cambridge Studies in Advanced Mathematics: No. 66). (Illus.). 344p. (C). 2000. 69.95 (*0-521-66258-3*) Cambridge U Pr.

Morosco, Anthony B. Prosecution & Defense of Sex Crimes. 1976. 250.00 (*0-8205-1562-0*) Bender.

Morosco, Beatrice. Hodsdon. "The Restless Ones" A Family History (of the Hodsdon Family of Minnesota) (Illus.). 299p. 1998. reprint ed. pap. 45.00 (*0-8328-9156-8*); reprint ed. lib. bdg. 55.00 (*0-8328-9155-X*) Higginson Bk Co.

Morosini. Managing Cultural Differences: Effective Strategy & Execution Across Cultures in Global Corporate Alliances. LC 97-30782. (International Business & Management Ser.). 300p. 1998. 67.00 (*0-08-042762-6*, Pergamon Pr) Elsevier.

***Moroso, Pam.** New Cuisine Alternatives Vol. 1: Cream Puff Volcanoes & Chocolate Roller Blades. Castellanos, Laura, ed. (Illus.). 132p. 2000. pap. 12.95 (*0-9678804-0-8*, Pub. by Buckaroo) I P D.

Morosoff, Anna Grimaldi, see Grimaldi Morosoff, Anna.

***Moroson, Harold & Fisher, Murray.** Code Blue: True Stories of Wrongful Death & Injuries. 272p. 2000. mass mkt. 6.50 (*0-312-97510-4*, St Martins Paperbacks) St Martin.

Morot-Sir, Edouard. The Imagination of Reference: Meditating the Linguistic Condition. LC 92-22881. (University of Florida Humanities Monographs: No. 67). 184p. 1993. 49.95 (*0-8130-1171-X*) U Press Fla.

— The Imagination of Reference II: Perceiving, Indicating, Naming. 240p. 1995. 49.95 (*0-8130-1406-9*) U Press Fla.

Morowitz, David, ed. see Wechsberg, Joseph.

Morowitz, Harold & Singer, Jerome L. The Mind, the Brain & Complex Adaptive Systems. 256p. (C). 1995. pap. 38.00 (*0-201-40986-0*) Addison-Wesley.

Morowitz, Harold & Singer, Jerome L., eds. The Mind, the Brain & Complex Adaptive Systems. LC 94-44256. (Proceedings: Vol. 22). 237p. (C). 1995. 61.00 (*0-201-40988-7*) Addison-Wesley.

Morowitz, Harold J. Cosmic Joy & Local Pain: Musings of a Mystic Scientist. LC 86-26020. 1987. 18.95 (*0-684-18443-5*) Ox Bow.

— Ego Niches: An Ecological View of Organizational Behavior. LC 76-48588. (Illus.). 96p. 1977. pap. 8.95 (*0-918024-01-3*) Ox Bow.

— Energy Flow in Biology. LC 79-89841. 1979. pap. 14.00 (*0-918024-13-7*) Ox Bow.

— Entropy & the Magic Flute. (Illus.). 240p. 1996. reprint ed. pap. 13.95 (*0-19-511134-6*) OUP.

— Foundations of Bioenergetics. 1978. 55.00 (*0-12-507250-3*) Ox Bow.

— The Kindly Dr. Guillotin & Other Essays on Science & Life. 224p. 1998. pap. 12.50 (*1-887178-95-3*) Ox Bow.

— Mayonnaise & the Origin of Life: Thoughts of Minds & Molecules. LC 90-25713. vii, 244p. 1991. reprint ed. pap. 14.95 (*0-918024-82-X*) Ox Bow.

— The Thermodynamics of Pizza. 258p. (Orig.). 1992. reprint ed. pap. 14.95 (*0-8135-1774-5*) Rutgers U Pr.

— The Wine of Life: And Other Essays on Societies, Energy & Living Things. LC 79-16404. 1979. 18.95 (*0-312-88227-0*) Ox Bow.

Morowitz, Harold J. & Trefil, James S. The Facts of Life: Science & the Abortion Controversy. (Illus.). 192p. 1994. reprint ed. pap. 9.95 (*0-19-509046-2*) OUP.

***Morowski, Philip.** Science Bought & Sold. 1999. pap. text 28.00 (*0-226-53857-5*); lib. bdg. 70.00 (*0-226-53856-7*) U Ch Pr.

Moroy, T., jt. auth. see Sedlacek, H. H.

Moroz. Atlas: Student Study Book. 1990. pap. text. write for info. (*0-582-87067-4*, Pub. by Addison-Wesley) Longman.

Moroz, Andrew R., jt. auth. see Salembier, G. E.

Moroz, B. Z. Analytic Arithmetic in Algebraic Number Fields. (Lecture Notes in Mathematics Ser.: Vol. 1205). vii, 177p. 1986. 34.95 (*0-387-16784-6*) Spr-Verlag.

Moroz, George. Hercules: The Complete Myths of a Legendary Hero. LC 97-207328. 144p. (YA). 1997. mass mkt. 3.99 (*0-440-22732-1*) Dell.

Moroz, Georges. Hercules: The Twelve Labors of a Legendary Hero. abr. ed. 1998. pap. 3.99 (*0-440-41521-7*) Dell.

Moroz, Georges, jt. auth. see Sanvoisin, Eric.

Moroz, Georges, tr. see Sanvoisin, Eric.

Morozov. Above & Beyond: From Soviet General to Ukrainian Statebuilder. 1996. 29.95 (*0-614-19849-6*) HUP.

Morozov, jt. auth. see Elion, Herbert A.

***Morozov, A. Yu & Olshanetsky, M. A., eds.** Moscow Seminar in Mathematical Physics. LC 91-640741. (Translations Ser.: Ser. 2, Vol. 191, No. 43). 299p. 1999. 110.00 (*0-8218-1388-9*) Am Math.

***Morozov, Albert D., et al.** Invariant Sets for Windows. LC 99-51493. 260p. 1999. 56.00 (*981-02-4071-6*) World Scientific Pub.

Morozov, Boris, ed. Documents on Soviet Jewish Emigration. LC 98-52748. (Cummings Center Ser.: Vol. 14). 250p. 1999. 75.00 (*0-7146-4911-2*) F Cass Pubs.

Morozov, Kostiantyn P. Above & Beyond: From Soviet General to Ukrainian Statebuilder. (Ukrainian Research Institute Publications Ser.). (Illus.). 250p. 2000. 29.95 (*0-916458-77-6*) Harvard Ukrainian.

Morozov, Kostiantyn P., et al. The Military Tradition in Ukrainian History: Its Role in the Construction of Ukraine's Armed Forces. (Papers in Ukrainian Studies). (Illus.). 93p. 1995. pap. text 5.00 (*0-916458-73-3*) Harvard Ukrainian.

***Morozov, Nikita F. & Petrov, Y.** Dynamics of Fracture Problems of Solids. Stenkin, V., tr. from RUS. LC 99-49193. (Foundations of Engineering Mechanics Ser.). (Illus.). viii, 104p. 2000. 52.00 (*3-540-64274-9*) Spr-Verlag.

Morozov, P. V., ed. Research on the Viral Hypothesis of Mental Disorders. (Advances in Biological Psychiatry Ser.: Vol. 12). (Illus.). x, 178p. 1983. pap. 79.25 (*3-8055-3706-9*) S Karger.

Morozov, V. A. Methods for Solving Incorrectly Posed Problems. Nashed, Z., ed. Aries, A. B., tr. from RUS. (Illus.). 270p. 1984. 95.95 (*0-387-96059-7*) Spr-Verlag.

— Regularization Methods for Ill-Proposed Problems. 272p. 1993. 81.00 (*0-8493-9311-6*) CRC Pr.

Morozowich, Walter, jt. ed. see Tsuji, Kiyoski.

Morozumi, Atsuko. Un Gorila: Un Libro Para Aprender a Contar. 1996. 10.15 (*0-606-10961-7*, Pub. by Turtleback) Demco.

— Un Gorila - One Gorilla. LC 49-244520. (SPA.). 32p. (J). (ps-3). 1996. pap. 4.95 (*0-374-48061-3*) FS&G.

— One Gorilla. 32p. 1990. 14.95 (*0-385-25255-2*) Doubleday.

***Morozumi, Atsuko.** Helping Daddy. (Baby Bunny Board Bks.). (Illus.). 6p. (J). 2000. 4.99 (*0-375-80593-1*) Knopf.

— In the Park. (Baby Bunny Board Bks.). (Illus.). 6p. (J). 2000. 4.99 (*0-375-80591-5*, Pub. by Knopf Bks Yng Read) Random.

— Mi Amigo Gorila (My Friend Gorilla) Guibert, Rita, tr.Tr. of My Friend Gorilla. (Illus.). 32p. (J). (ps-k). 1999. text 5.95 (*0-374-44831-0*, Mirasol) FS&G.

Morozumi, Atsuko. My Friend Gorilla. LC 97-60546. (Illus.). (J). (ps-k). 1998. text 15.00 (*0-374-35458-8*) FS&G.

— One Gorilla. 32p. 1993. pap. 7.50 (*0-385-25410-5*) Doubleday.

— One Gorilla. LC 89-46577. (Illus.). 32p. (J). (ps). 1993. pap. 4.95 (*0-374-45646-1*, Sunburst Bks) FS&G.

— One Gorilla: A Counting Book. LC 89-46577. (Illus.). 26p. (J). (ps-1). 1990. 15.00 (*0-374-35644-0*) FS&G.

— One Gorilla, A Counting Book. 1993. 10.15 (*0-606-05524-X*, Pub. by Turtleback) Demco.

***Morozumi, Atsuko.** Playing. (Baby Bunny Board Bks.). (Illus.). 6p. (J). 2000. 4.99 (*0-375-80592-3*, Pub. by Knopf Bks Yng Read) Random.

— Time for Bed. (Baby Bunny Board Bks.). (Illus.). 6p. (J). 2000. 4.99 (*0-375-80594-X*, Pub. by Knopf Bks Yng Read) Random.

Morozumi, Atsuko & Price. Reindeer Christmas. (Illus.). 32p. 1995. mass mkt. 9.95 (*0-385-25547-0*) Doubleday.

Morozuoi & Price. The Reindeer Christmas. (Illus.). 32p. 1993. 18.95 (*0-385-25401-6*) Doubleday.

***Morozzi, C., et al.** Contemporary Italian Furniture Design. (Illus.). 240p. 2000. 79.95 (*88-7685-087-2*, Pub. by LArchivolto) Bks Nippan.

Morozzi, Christina, jt. auth. see Branzi, Andrea.

Morpeau, Louis. Anthologie d'un Siecle de Poesie Haitienne, 1817-1925, avec une Etude sur la Muse Haitienne d'Expression Franciase et une Etude sur la Muse Haitienne d'Expression Creole. (B. E. Ser.: No. 10). (FRE.). 1925. 35.00 (*0-8115-2961-4*) Periodicals Srv.

Morpeth, Robert, jt. auth. see Donaldson, Gordon.

Morphet, Edgar L. The Measurement & Interpretation of School Building Utilization. LC 75-177084. (Columbia University. Teachers College. Contributions to Education Ser.: No. 264). reprint ed. 37.50 (*0-404-55264-1*) AMS Pr.

***Morphet, Richard, ed.** Encounters: New Art from Old. (Illus.). 360p. 2000. 49.95 (*0-300-08481-1*) Yale U Pr.

Morpheus. No Lover Ever Dies. (Illus.). 80p. 1985. 11.99 (*0-9604512-1-8*) Mortal Pr.

Morphew, Carol, jt. auth. see Jacob, Bernard.

Morphew, Launa D. Mama, Buy Me a China Doll. LC 96-42012. 1997. write for info. (*1-56763-314-5*); pap. write for info. (*1-56763-315-3*) Ozark Pub.

Morphew, Melissa. The Garden Where All Loves End: Winner. Iddings, Kathleen, ed. LC 97-70019. (National Poetry Book Ser.). (Illus.). 80p. (Orig.). (C). 1997. pap. 10.00 (*0-931721-13-X*, 500) La Jolla Poets.

Morphew, Valerie N. Checking, Counting, & Other Strange Signs: OCD, the Secret Disorder. LC 97-93528. (Orig.). 1997. pap. write for info. (*0-9658324-0-6*) Mtns Fair Pr.

— Investigations in Science - Kindergarten Bk. I: Virginia Edition. (Illus.). 136p. 1998. ring bd. 22.50 (*0-9658324-1-4*) Mtns Fair Pr.

An Asterisk (*) at the beginning of an entry indicates that the title is appearing for the first time.

Morphy, Guillermo. Les Luthistes Espagnols du XVIe Siecle, 2 vols in 1. (FRE & GER., Illus.). 306p. 1967. reprint ed. lib. bdg. 95.00 (*0-8450-1008-5*) Broude.
Morphy, H. Animals into Art. 350p. 1988. text 90.00 (*0-04-445030-3*) Routledge.
Morphy, H., jt. ed. see Harrison, G. A.
Morphy, Howard. Aboriginal Art. LC 99-187473. (Illus.). 448p. 1998. pap. 22.95 (*0-7148-3752-0*, Pub. by Phaidon Press) Phaidon Pr.
— Ancestral Connections: Art & an Aboriginal System of Knowledge. (Illus.). 348p. 1991. pap. text 22.95 (*0-226-53866-4*) U Ch Pr.
— Ancestral Connections: Art & an Aboriginal System of Knowledge. (Illus.). 348p. 1992. lib. bdg. 55.00 (*0-226-53865-6*) U Ch Pr.
***Morphy, Howard & Boles, Margo Smith, eds.** Art from the Land: Dialogues with the Kluge-Ruhe Collection of Australian Aboriginal Art. (Illus.). 266p. 2000. pap. 40.00 (*0-646-37087-1*) U Pr of Va.
Morphy, Howard, jt. auth. see Banks, Marcus.
Morpurgo, J. E., ed. Charles Lamb (1775-1834) Charles Lamb & Elia. pap. write for info. (*1-85754-003-4*, Pub. by Carcanet Pr) Paul & Co Pubs.
Morpurgo, J. E., ed. & intro. see Allingham, Margery.
Morpurgo, M. Red Eyes at Night. (Illus.). (J). text 19.95 (*0-340-68752-5*, Pub. by Hodder & Stought Ltd); mass mkt. 7.95 (*0-340-68753-3*, Pub. by Hodder & Stought Ltd) Trafalgar.
Morpurgo, M., et al, eds. Pulmonary Circulation. (Current Topics in Rehabilitation Ser.). 192p. 1990. 69.95 (*0-387-19542-4*) Spr-Verlag.
Morpurgo, Mario. Pulmonary Embolism. LC 93-46951. (Lung Biology in Health & Disease Ser.: Vol. 75). (Illus.). 360p. 1994. text 180.00 (*0-8247-9178-9*) Dekker.
***Morpurgo, Michael.** Animal Stories. LC 99-34906. 224p. (J). (gr. 4-9). 1999. pap. 6.95 (*0-7534-5191-3*) LKC.
— Animal Stories. LC 99-34906. 224p. (YA). (gr. 4-9). 1999. 14.95 (*0-7534-5216-2*) LKC.
Morpurgo, Michael. Arthur: High King of Britain. LC 93-33620. (Illus.). 144p. (J). (gr. 4-9). 1995. 22.00 (*0-15-200080-1*) Harcourt.
— Blodin the Beast. LC 96-111371. (Illus.). 32p. (J). (gr. 2 up). 1995. 8.00 (*1-55591-211-7*) Fulcrum Pub.
— The Butterfly Lion. LC 96-52797. (Illus.). 96p. (J). (gr. 3-7). 1997. 14.99 (*0-670-87461-2*) Viking Penguin.
— Farm Boy. (Illus.). 74p. (YA). 1999. pap. 16.95 (*1-86205-192-5*, Pub. by Pavilion Bks Ltd) Trafalgar.
— The Ghost of Grania O'Malley. 181p. (J). (gr. 3-7). 1996. 15.99 (*0-670-86861-2*, Viking Child) Peng Put Young Read.
— Joan of Arc of Domremy. LC 97-51435. 23p. 1999. 23.00 (*0-15-201736-4*, Harcourt Child Bks) Harcourt.
***Morpurgo, Michael.** Kensuke's Kingdom. large type ed. (Illus.). (J). 2000. pap. write for info. (*0-7540-6096-9*) Chivers N Amer.
Morpurgo, Michael. Mr. Nobody's Eyes. 1999. pap. 3.95 (*0-14-034265-6*, Viking) Viking Penguin.
***Morpurgo, Michael.** Rainbow Bear. (J). 1999. write for info. (*0-385-60017-8*) BDD Bks Young Read.
— Waiting for Anya. (J). 1997. 10.09 (*0-606-12044-0*, Pub. by Turtleback) Demco.
Morpurgo, Michael. Waiting for Anya. LC 90-50560. 176p. (gr. 5-9). 1997. pap. 4.99 (*0-14-038431-6*) Viking Penguin.
— The War of Jenkin's Ear. LC 94-7602. 176p. (J). (gr. 3-7). 1995. 16.95 (*0-399-22735-0*, Philomel) Peng Put Young Read.
— The War of Jenkin's Ear. 176p. (YA). (gr. 7 up). 1997. pap. 5.95 (*0-698-11550-3*, PapStar) Peng Put Young Read.
Morpurgo, Michael. The War of Jenkin's Ear. LC 94-7602. (J). 1997. 11.05 (*0-606-12050-5*, Pub. by Turtleback) Demco.
— Wombat Goes Walk-About. LC 99-47082. (Illus.). 32p. (J). (ps-3). 2000. 16.99 (*0-7636-1168-9*) Candlewick Pr.
Morpurgo, Michael. Wreck of Zanzibar. 1999. pap. 5.99 (*0-14-038190-2*) Viking Penguin.
***Morpurgo, Michael, compiled by.** The Kingfisher Book of Great Boy Stories: A Treasury of Classics from Children's Literature. (Illus.). 160p. (J). 2000. 19.95 (*0-7534-5320-7*) LKC.
Morpurgo, Michael, ed. Beyond the Rainbow Warrior: A Collection of Stories to Celebrate 25 Years of Greenpeace. (Illus.). 144p. (J). (gr. 5-9). 1998. pap. 17.95 (*1-86205-035-X*, Pub. by Pavilion Bks Ltd) Trafalgar.
— Ghostly Haunts. (Illus.). 160p. (YA). 1996. pap. 16.95 (*1-85793-883-6*, Pub. by Pavilion Bks Ltd) Trafalgar.
***Morpurgo, Michael & Birmingham, Christian.** The Silver Swan. LC 99-58468. 32p. (J). (ps-3). 2000. 16.99 (*0-8037-2543-4*) Peng Put Young Read.
Morqmarco, Federico & Morqmarco, Stephen. Italian Pride: 101 Reasons to Be Proud Your Italian. LC 99-12773. (Illus.). 208p. 1999. 14.95 (*1-55972-512-5*, Birch Ln Pr) Carol Pub Group.
Morqmarco, Stephen, jt. auth. see Morqmarco, Federico.
Morr, Kenyon. Kingdom of Sorrow. (King's Quest Ser.: No. 2). 336p. (Orig.). 1996. mass mkt. 5.99 (*1-57297-033-2*) Blvd Books.
— See No Weevil. (King's Quest Ser.). 1996. mass mkt. 5.99 (*1-57297-174-6*) Blvd Books.
Morr, Mary L. & Irmiter, Theodore F. Introductory Foods: A Laboratory Manual. 6th ed. LC 94-23805. (Illus.). 320p. (C). 1995. pap., lab manual ed. 36.60 (*0-02-384142-7*, Macmillan Coll) P-H.
Morra, Isabella. Canzoniere: A Bilingual Edition. Mitchell, Irene M., ed. & tr. by. LC 98-15710. (Crossing Ser.: No. 2). (ENG & ITA.). 72p. 1998. pap. 9.00 (*1-884419-18-6*) Bordighera.
Morra, Joanne. Translating Algeria: Parallax 7, Vol. 7. (Parallax Ser.). 1999. pap. text 26.95 (*0-7484-0832-0*) Taylor & Francis.
Morra, Marco. Water in Biotechnological Surface. text. write for info. (*0-471-49041-5*) Wiley.
Morra, Marion & Potts, Eve. Choices: Realistic Alternatives in Cancer Treatment. rev. ed. 976p. 1980. pap. 12.95 (*0-380-75308-1*, Avon Bks) Morrow Avon.
Morra, Marion & Potts, Eve. Choices Revised & Update. 2nd rev. ed. LC 94-14927. 976p. 1994. pap. 15.00 (*0-380-77620-0*, Avon Bks) Morrow Avon.
Morra, Marion & Potts, Eve. Prostate Cancer Answ. Bk. LC 96-5684. 93p. 1996. pap. 12.50 (*0-380-78564-1*, Avon Bks) Morrow Avon.
— Triumph: Getting Back to Normal When You Have Cancer. 304p. 1990. pap. 9.95 (*0-380-75503-3*, Avon Bks) Morrow Avon.
Morra, Marion, jt. auth. see Potts, Eve.
Morra, Mike. Genetic Based Democracy: Rising Out of the Dark Age of Egalitarist America. LC 98-183956. 140p. 1998. lib. bdg. 49.00 (*1-56072-544-3*) Nova Sci Pubs.
Morra, Robert G., jt. ed. see Morgenthaler, George W.
Morrah, Patrick. Restoration England. LC 79-317995. 252p. reprint ed. pap. 78.20 (*0-608-15679-5*, 203199500077) Bks Demand.
Morral, Peter. Mental Health Nursing & Social Control. LC 98-153098. v, 164p. 1998. write for info. (*1-86156-050-8*) Whurr Pub.
Morral, J. E., ed. see International Symposium on Boron Steels (September.
Morral, Sheila. Fate Is Powerful. 38p. 1998. pap. 5.00 (*0-7872-4476-7*) Kendall-Hunt.
Morrall. Jorg Brue: The Elder. 113.95 (*1-84014-608-7*) Ashgate Pub Co.
Morrall, E. J., ed. The Goodli History of the Ladye Lucres of Scene & of Her Lover Eurialus No. 308. LC 96-229679. (Early English Text Society-Original Ser.). (Illus.). 116p. 1996. text 75.00 (*0-19-722311-7*) OUP.
Morrall, John B. Political Thought in Medieval Times. (Medieval Academy Reprints for Teaching Ser.). 1980. reprint ed. pap. text 12.95 (*0-8020-6413-2*) U of Toronto Pr.
— Political Thought in Medieval Times. 3rd ed. LC 72-187548. (History Ser.). 154p. 1971. write for info. (*0-09-107680-3*) Hutchinson.
Morrall, John B., jt. auth. see Ehler, Sidney Z.
Morrall, June. The Coburn Mystery: Northern California's Unsolved Murder. LC 92-81071. (Illus.). 228p. (Orig.). 1992. pap. write for info. (*0-9602088-1-X*) Moonbeam CA.
— Costside Memories: Motoring South of San Francisco, 1850-1950. Mannett, Luana, ed. (Illus.). 176p. (Orig.). 1994. write for info. (*0-9602088-2-8*) Moonbeam CA.
— Half Moon Bay Memories: The Coastside's Colorful Past. (Illus.). 176p. 1987. reprint ed. pap. 12.95 (*0-9602088-0-1*) Moonbeam CA.
***Morrall, Shiela.** Be A Winner: The Winner You Were Born to Be. LC 99-62278. 134p. (J). 1999. per. 9.00 (*0-7872-5959-4*) Kendall-Hunt.
Morrall, Shiela. Called to Make a Difference: A Book of Poetry. 128p. 1998. per. 10.00 (*0-7872-3267-X*) Kendall-Hunt.
Morray, David. An Ayyubid Notable & His World: Ibn Al-Adim & Aleppo as Portrayed in His Biological Dictionary of People Associated with the City. LC 93-47288. (Islamic History & Civilization, Studies & Texts Ser.: Vol. 5). xii, 335p. 1994. 112.50 (*90-04-09956-5*) Brill Academic Pubs.
Morray, J. P. Project Kuzbas: American Workers in Siberia, 1921-1926. LC 83-12607. (Illus.). 204p. 1983. pap. 4.75 (*0-7178-0606-5*) Intl Pubs Co.
Morray, Jeffrey P. Pediatric Intensive Care. (Illus.). 581p. (C). 1992. pap. text 115.00 (*0-8385-7800-4*, A7800-4, Apple Lange Med) McGraw.
***Morray-Jones, Christopher R.** A Transparent Illusion. LC 99-28682. 1999. write for info. (*90-04-11337-1*) Brill Academic Pubs.
Morray, Joseph P. From Yalta to Disarmament: Cold War Debate. LC 73-19225. 368p. 1974. reprint ed. lib. bdg. 39.75 (*0-8371-7306-X*, MOYD, Greenwood Pr) Greenwood.
— Grand Disillusion: Fracois Mitterrand & the French Left. LC 96-32466. 184p. 1997. 57.95 (*0-275-95735-7*, Praeger Pubs) Greenwood.
Morre, D. J., et al, eds. Molecular Mechanisms of Membrane Traffic. LC 93-1200. 1993. 219.95 (*0-387-53096-7*) Spr-Verlag.
Morre, Roger, jt. auth. see Day, Chris.
Morreale. Excellence in Public Speaking. (C). 1997. pap. text, teacher ed. 42.00 (*0-15-505472-4*) Harcourt Coll Pubs.
***Morreale, et al.** Human Communication. 2000. pap., student ed., wbk. ed. 17.00 (*0-534-56625-1*) Wadsworth Pub.
***Morreale, Ben.** Italian Americans: The Immigrant Experience. (Illus.). 240p. 2000. 60.00 (*0-88363-126-1*) H L Levin.
Morreale, Ben. The Loss of the Miraculous. LC 95-82276. (Prose Ser.: No. 32). 150p. (C). 1997. pap. 13.00 (*1-55071-019-2*) Guernica Editions.
***Morreale, Ben.** Sicily - The Hallowed Land: A Memoir. Cipolla, Gaetano, ed. (Sicilian Studies: Vol. 5). 220p. 2000. pap. 18.00 (*1-881901-23-8*) LEGAS.
Morreale, Ben, jt. auth. see Mangione, Jerre.
Morreale, Don. Complete Guide to Buddhist America. LC 97-29992. 1998. pap. 23.95 (*1-57062-270-1*, Pub. by Shambhala Pubns) Random.
Morreale, Joanne. A New Beginning: A Textual Frame Analysis of the Political Campaign Film. LC 90-9904. (SUNY Series in Speech Communication). 154p. (C). 1991. pap. text 18.95 (*0-7914-0609-1*) State U NY Pr.
— The Presidential Campaign Film: A Critical History. LC 93-20129. (Praeger Series in Political Communication). 224p. 1993. 65.00 (*0-275-93882-4*, C3882, Praeger Pubs) Greenwood.
— The Presidential Campaign Film: A Critical History. LC 93-20129. 224p. 1996. pap. 21.95 (*0-275-95580-X*, Praeger Pubs) Greenwood.
Morreale, Marie. Barbie, Television Reporter: In the Spotlight. (Little Golden Storybks.). (Illus.). 24p. (J). (ps-3). 1998. 2.29 (*0-307-98863-5*, 98863, Goldn Books) Gldn Bks Pub Co.
— Cleopatra Mini Edition. 1999. 4.95 (*0-8362-9273-1*) Andrews & McMeel.
***Morreale, Marie.** Hanging with the Backstreet Boys: An Unauthorized Biography. LC 99-160618. 99p. (J). (gr. 4-7). 1999. pap. 3.99 (*0-439-04532-0*) Scholastic Inc.
Morreale, Marie. Hercules: The Legendary Journey Scrapbook. (J). (gr. 4-7). 1996. pap. text 3.99 (*0-590-87104-8*) Scholastic Inc.
Morreale, Marie & Johns, Michael A. Totally Taylor: Hanson's Heartthrob. (J). (gr. 4-7). 1998. pap. text 3.99 (*0-590-02449-3*) Scholastic Inc.
Morreale, Marie T. Hanson Brothers Biography. (gr. 3-7). 1997. pap. 3.99 (*0-590-10683-X*) Scholastic Inc.
Morreale, Sherwyn P., et al, eds. The Competent Speaker Speech Evaluation Form. 65p. (Orig.). (C). 1993. pap. text 18.50 (*0-944811-13-2*) Natl Comm Assn.
Morreale, Sherwyn P. & Bovee, Courtland L. Excellence in Public Speaking. LC 97-71992. 528p. (C). 1997. pap. text 46.50 (*0-15-502182-6*, Pub. by Harcourt Coll Pubs) Harcourt.
***Morreale, Sherwyn P., et al.** Human Communication. (Speech & Theater Ser.). (C). 2000. text 19.00 (*0-534-56623-5*) Wadsworth Pub.
— Human Communication: Motivation, Knowledge & Skills. LC 00-32500. 2001. write for info. (*0-534-56619-7*) Wadsworth Pub.
— Interviewing Module: Human Communication. (Speech & Theater Ser.). (C). 2000. text 5.00 (*0-534-56624-3*) Wadsworth Pub.
Morreale, Vin, Jr. Breaking & Entering. 1994. pap. 5.60 (*0-87129-284-X*, B75) Dramatic Pub.
— Burning up the Stage: Monologues, Audition Pieces & Short Scenes for Actors from Six to Seventy. 371p. 1998. pap. 19.95 (*0-87129-865-1*, B87) Dramatic Pub.
— The Day the Woods Were One. (Orig.). (J). (gr. 3 up). 1985. pap. 6.00 (*0-88734-507-7*) Players Pr.
— The Happy Holidays Collection: Seven Christmas Comedies for Children. 96p. (J). (gr. 1 up). 1997. pap. 3.50 (*0-87129-755-8*, H44) Dramatic Pub.
— It'll All Come Out in the Wash: Playscript. (Orig.). 1985. pap. 6.00 (*0-88734-207-8*) Players Pr.
— Southern Discomfort - Twelve Short Southern Scenes. 80p. 1998. pap. 5.60 (*0-87129-827-9*, SC2) Dramatic Pub.
Uncool. 41p. (YA) (gr. 10 up). 1998. pap. 3.50 (*0-87129-828-7*, U24) Dramatic Pub.
Morreall, John. Comedy, Tragedy & Religion. LC 98-51495. 192p. (C). 1999. text 49.50 (*0-7914-4205-5*); pap. text 16.95 (*0-7914-4206-3*) State U NY Pr.
— Humor Works. LC 97-183409. 1997. pap. text 24.95 (*0-87425-400-0*) HRD Press.
— Taking Laughter Seriously. LC 82-5858. 144p. (C). 1983. text 64.50 (*0-87395-642-7*); pap. text 21.95 (*0-87395-643-5*) State U NY Pr.
Morreau, Jacqueline. Jacqueline Morreau. LC 86-4000. (Drawings & Graphics Ser.). (Illus.). 192p. 1986. 34.50 (*0-8108-1888-4*) Scarecrow.
Morreau, Jacqueline, jt. auth. see Kent, Sarah.
Morreau, Michael, jt. ed. see Fuhrmann, A.
Morreau, Michael, tr. see Gamut, L. T.
Morreim, E. Haavi. Balancing Act: The New Medical Ethics of Medicine's New Economics. LC 94-37058. 224p. 1995. pap. 17.95 (*0-87840-584-4*) Georgetown U Pr.
— Balancing Act: The New Medical Ethics of Medicine's New Economics. 196p. (C). 1991. lib. bdg. 102.00 (*0-7923-1170-1*, Pub. by Kluwer Academic) Kluwer Academic.
Morrel, B. B., jt. ed. see Conway, John B.
Morrell, Anne. Techniques of Indian Embroidery. 144p. 1995. pap. 18.95 (*1-883010-08-X*) Interweave.
Morrell, Bernard B., jt. auth. see Bittinger, Marvin L.
Morrell, Brad. Nirvana: Classic Rock Reads. (Classic Rock Read Ser.). (Illus.). 144p. pap. 16.95 (*0-7119-5221-3*, OP 47792) Omnibus NY.
— Nirvana & the Sound of Seattle. (Illus.). 96p. pap. 19.95 (*0-7119-3492-4*, OP 47326) Omnibus NY.
— The Story of Pearl Jam. (Illus.). 64p. 1997. pap. 11.95 (*0-8256-1572-0*, OP 47858) Omnibus NY.
Morrell, Carl A., ed. see Dexter, Seymour.
Morrell, Carol, ed. Grammar of Dissent: Poetry & Prose of Dionne Brand, Claire Harris & M. Nourbese Philip. 256p. 1994. pap. 14.95 (*0-86492-141-1*) Goose Ln Eds.
Morrell, David. Assumed Identity. 512p. 1994. mass mkt. 6.50 (*0-446-60070-9*, Pub. by Warner Bks) Little.
— Assumed Identity. abr. ed. 1993. audio. write for info. (*1-55800-913-2*, Dove Audio) NewStar Media.
— Assumed Identity. 1999. reprint ed. mass mkt. 3.99 (*0-446-60749-5*) Warner Bks.
***Morrell, David.** Black Evening. 345p. 2000. 40.00 (*1-881475-85-9*) Cemetery Dance.
— Black Evening: Tales of Dark Suspense. 480p. 2000. mass mkt. 7.50 (*0-446-60864-5*, Pub. by Warner Bks) Little.
Morrell, David. Blood Oath Vol. 1. 1994. mass mkt. 6.50 (*0-312-95345-3*) St Martin.
— The Brotherhood of the Rose. 352p. 1985. mass mkt. 5.95 (*0-449-20661-0*, Crest) Fawcett.
— The Brotherhood of the Rose. large type ed. 496p. 1987. 27.99 (*0-7089-8381-2*, Charnwood) Ulverscroft.
***Morrell, David.** Burnt Sienna. LC 00-39638. (Illus.). 2000. pap. write for info. (*0-7838-9087-7*, G K Hall & Co) Mac Lib Ref.
— Burnt Sienna. LC 99-36274. 400p. 2000. 24.95 (*0-446-51964-2*, Pub. by Warner Bks) Little.
Morrell, David. The Covenant of the Flame. 480p. 1992. mass mkt. 6.99 (*0-446-36292-1*, Pub. by Warner Bks) Little.
— The Covenant of the Flame. 1999. reprint ed. mass mkt. 3.99 (*0-446-60752-5*) Warner Bks.
— Desperate Measures. 512p. 1995. mass mkt. 6.99 (*0-446-60239-6*, Pub. by Warner Bks) Little.
— Desperate Measures. 1999. reprint ed. mass mkt. 3.99 (*0-446-60750-9*) Warner Bks.
— Double Image. LC 97-32283. 448p. 1998. 25.00 (*0-446-51963-4*, Pub. by Warner Bks) Little.
— Double Image. Warner, ed. 528p. 1999. mass mkt. 7.50 (*0-446-60696-0*, Pub. by Warner Bks) Little.
— Double Image. large type ed. LC 98-13745. 639p. 1998. 27.95 (*0-7838-0144-0*, G K Hall Lrg Type) Mac Lib Ref.
— Extreme Denial. 480p. 1997. mass mkt. 6.99 (*0-446-60396-1*, Pub. by Warner Bks) Little.
— Extreme Denial. large type ed. 673p. 1996. 26.95 (*0-7862-0699-3*) Thorndike Pr.
— The Fifth Profession. 512p. 1991. mass mkt. 6.99 (*0-446-36087-2*, Pub. by Warner Bks) Little.
— The Fifth Profession. 1999. reprint ed. mass mkt. 3.99 (*0-446-60751-7*) Warner Bks.
***Morrell, David.** Fireflies. LC 99-19499. 256p. 1999. mass mkt. 12.99 (*0-446-67590-3*, Pub. by Warner Bks) Little.
— First Blood. 320p. 2000. mass mkt. 6.99 (*0-446-36440-1*, Pub. by Warner Bks) Little.
Morrell, David. The Fraternity of the Stone. 1986. mass mkt. 6.99 (*0-449-20973-3*) Fawcett.
— The Fraternity of the Stone. large type ed. 560p. 1987. 11.50 (*0-7089-8397-9*, Charnwood) Ulverscroft.
— Last Reveille. 272p. 1994. mass mkt. 5.99 (*0-446-36442-8*, Pub. by Warner Bks) Little.
***Morrell, David.** The League of Night & Fog. 480p. 2000. mass mkt. 6.99 (*0-446-60754-1*, Pub. by Warner Bks) Little.
Morrell, David. The League of Night & Fog. large type ed. 532p. 1989. 27.99 (*0-7089-1936-7*) Ulverscroft.
— Testament. 352p. 1993. mass mkt. 5.99 (*0-446-36448-7*, Pub. by Warner Bks) Little.
— The Totem. 384p. 1995. mass mkt. 6.50 (*0-446-36446-0*, Pub. by Warner Bks) Little.
— The Totem Complete & Unaltered. deluxe ed. (Illus.). 1994. 24.95 (*1-880418-26-6*) D M Grant.
— The Totem Complete & Unaltered: (complete & unaltered) (Illus.). 1994. boxed set 100.00 (*1-880418-25-8*) D M Grant.
Morrell, David Cameron. The Art of General Practice. (Illus.). 168p. 1991. 45.00 (*0-19-261988-8*) OUP.
***Morrell, Doug.** Painters Have More Fun Than People. (Illus.). 211p. 1999. 14.95 (*1-891029-48-7*) Henderson Pub.
Morrell, Douglas & Smith, J. Daniel. The Disciple's Journal. (Illus.). 228p. (Orig.). 1996. pap. 15.00 (*0-9651908-0-3*) Narrow Rd.
Morrell, Ed. El Texto de Oro de las Sagradas Escrituras. Hilliker, Gary, ed. (SPA.). 24p. 1994. 0.50 (*1-879892-46-4*) Editorial Bautista.
Morrell, F., ed. Kindling & Synaptic Plasticity: The Legacy of Graham Goddard. xvi, 304p. 1991. 127.50 (*0-8176-3466-5*) Birkhauser.
***Morrell, Frances.** Continent Isolated: A Study of the European Dimension in the National Curriculum in England. 2000. pap. 16.00 (*0-901573-49-3*) Fed Trust Ed Res.
Morrell, Gordon W. Britain Confronts the Stalin Revolution: Anglo-Soviet Relations & the Metro-Vickers Crisis. (Illus.). x, 204p. (C). 1995. text 34.95 (*0-88920-250-8*) W Laurier U Pr.
Morrell, Herbert & Hackett, Jeff. Oliver Tractors. LC 97-13151. (Illus.). 160p. 1997. 29.95 (*0-7603-0356-8*) MBI Pubg.
Morrell, J. Gentlemen of Science: Early Correspondence of the British Association for the Advancement of Science. (Camden Fourth Ser.: No. 30). 382p. 27.00 (*0-86193-103-3*) David Brown.
Morrell, J. M., ed. Four English Comedies. 416p. 1982. pap. 11.95 (*0-14-043158-6*, Penguin Classics) Viking Penguin.
Morrell, J. M., jt. auth. see Betteridge, D.
Morrell, Jack. Science at Oxford: Transforming an Arts University. LC 97-7976. (Illus.). 494p. 1998. text 105.00 (*0-19-820657-7*) OUP.
— Science, Culture & Politics in Britain, 1750-1870. LC 96-52706. (Collected Studies: Vol. CS567). 352p. 1997. 106.95 (*0-86078-633-1*, Q127.G4M67, Pub. by Variorum) Ashgate Pub Co.
Morrell, James R. Spiritism & the Beginnings of Christianity. 87p. 1996. reprint ed. spiral bd. 8.00 (*0-7873-0625-8*) Hlth Research.
— Spiritism & the Beginnings of Christianity. 96p. 1996. reprint ed. pap. 7.95 (*1-56459-680-X*) Kessinger Pub.
Morrell, Jeffrey J., jt. auth. see Zabel, Robert A.
Morrell, Jessica P. Getting It Write: Effective Writing in the Workplace. (Illus.). 16p. (Orig.). 1996. pap. 3.00 (*1-884241-35-2*, SPSO020) Energeia Pub.
— Grant Writing Basics. (Illus.). 16p. (Orig.). 1996. pap. 3.00 (*1-884241-39-5*, EWO010) Energeia Pub.
— Marketing Words: The Writer's Guide to Marketing Income. 8p. (Orig.). 1996. pap. 2.50 (*1-884241-40-9*, EWO020) Energeia Pub.
— The Ten Commandments of Good Writing. (Illus.). 8p. (Orig.). 1995. pap. 2.50 (*1-884241-55-7*, SPS0317) Energeia Pub.

M

— Writing Out the Storm. LC 98-29891. 160p. 1998. pap. 14.95 (*1-888054-26-3*, 54263, Starbound Pub) Collectors Pr.

Morrell, K. J., et al. A Manual of Immunocytochemical Techniques. (Illus.). 208p. 1997. text. write for info. (*0-443-04861-4*) Church.

Morrell, L. C., ed. Holloway - Amiss - Leavell Family. 62p. 1994. reprint ed. pap. 13.00 (*0-8328-4135-8*) Higginson Bk Co.

***Morrell, Linton.** Steel Storage. 710p. 1999. write for info. (*0-7541-0593-8*, Pub. by Minerva Pr) Unity Dist.

Morrell, Louis. Morrell Future of Dollar Worldres. Sys. 160p. 1981. pap. 34.95 (*0-408-10675-1*) Buttrwrth-Heinemann.

Morrell, Louis, ed. It's Your Future: Financial Planning for Retirement. 2nd ed. 16p. 1992. 4.00 (*1-878240-14-5*) Coll & U Personnel.

Morrell, Louis R. Retirement Plan Alternatives: The Role of the Business Officer. LC 94-20948. 1994. 25.00 (*0-915164-95-7*) NACUBO.

***Morrell, Margot & Capparell, Stephanie.** Shackleton's Way: Leadership Lessons from the Great Antarctic Explorer. (Illus.). 224p. 2001. 24.95 (*0-670-89196-7*, Viking) Viking Penguin.

***Morrell, Mary.** Angels in High-Top Sneakers: And Other Stories to Stir the Soul. 2000. pap. 12.95 (*0-8294-1557-2*) Loyola Pr.

M

Morrell, Pam, tr. see Orloff, Erica & Baker, JoAnn.

Morrell, Pam, tr. see Pedder, Nancy Shank.

Morrell, Patrick. Design of Reinforced Concrete Elements. (Illus.). 1977. pap. 26.95 (*0-8464-0320-X*) Beekman Pubs.

Morrell, Peter. Air Transport, Vol. II-2. (Single Market Review Ser.). 1998. 70.00 (*0-7494-2314-5*) Kogan Page Ltd.

Morrell, Peter S. Airline Finance. LC 97-19613. 240p. 1997. text 77.95 (*0-291-39845-6*, Pub. by Ashgate Pub) Ashgate Pub Co.

Morrell, Robert E. Early Kamakura Buddhism: A Minority Report. Heisig, James A., ed. LC 87-70058. (Nanzan Studies in Religion & Culture). (Illus.). 200p. 1987. 30.00 (*0-89581-849-3*) Asian Humanities.

— Sand & Pebbles: The Tales of Muju Ichien, a Voice for Pluralism in Kamakura Buddhism. LC 84-16348. (SUNY Series in Buddhist Studies). 383p. (C). 1985. text 64.50 (*0-88706-059-5*); pap. text 21.95 (*0-88706-060-9*) State U NY Pr.

***Morrell, Robert J.** Become Empowered Customers: Food for Thought. LC 99-93986. 2000. pap. 7.95 (*0-533-13209-6*) Vantage.

Morrell, Sydney. Spheres of Influence. LC 70-142672. (Essay Index Reprint Ser.). 1977. 23.95 (*0-8369-2197-6*) Ayer.

Morrell, Thomas. The Card of Your Name: And the Ancient Symbology Hidden Within. 88p. 1998. spiral bd. 15.95 (*0-9665163-1-1*) Awakening IA.

— Planetary Progressions in the Mystic Quadrates. (Illus.). 90p. 1997. spiral bd. 15.95 (*0-9665163-0-3*) Awakening IA.

Morrell, W. H. Gunsmoke & the Spirit. 220p. 1996. pap. 5.95 (*0-917820-06-1*) Grist Mill.

Morrell, W. P. Gold Rushes. 2nd ed. LC 67-23287. (Illus.). 1968. 18.95 (*0-8023-1140-7*) Dufour.

Morrell, Z. N. Flowers & Fruits from the Wilderness: Or Thirty-Six Years in Texas & Two Winters in Honduras. LC 76-12002. (Illus.). 494p. 1976. reprint ed. pap. 10.95 (*0-918954-17-7*) Baylor Univ Pr.

Morren, George E. The Miyanmin: Human Ecology of a Papua New Guinea Society. LC 85-20817. (Studies in Cultural Anthropology: Vol. 9). (Illus.). 373p. 1986. reprint ed. pap. 115.70 (*0-608-07368-7*, 206759600009) Bks Demand.

Morrera, George, ed. see Weyand, Clinton.

Morresi, Angelo C., jt. auth. see Cheremisinoff, Paul N.

Morresi, Angelo C., jt. auth. see Cheremisinoff, Paul N.

Morressy, John. The Juggler. LC 95-33489. 261p. (YA). (gr. 6 up). 1995. 16.95 (*0-8050-4217-2*) H Holt & Co.

— The Juggler. LC 98-15524. 272p. (YA). (gr. 7-12). 1998. pap. 5.95 (*0-06-447174-8*) HarpC.

— Juggler. 1998. 10.05 (*0-606-13545-6*, Pub. by Turtleback) Demco.

***Morretta, Teresa M. & Ambrosini, Michelle.** Practical Approaches for Teaching Reading & Writing in Middle Schools. 2000. pap., teacher ed. 19.95 (*0-87207-266-5*, 266) Intl Reading.

Morrey. Two Thousand Year Book of Orthopaedics. 2000. 83.00 (*0-8151-0978-4*, 31714) Mosby Inc.

Morrey-Bailey, Alice. Stellarian. LC 86-81777. 158p. 1986. 10.98 (*0-88290-279-2*) Horizon Utah.

Morrey, Bernard F. The Elbow & Its Disorders. 2nd ed. (Illus.). 944p. 1993. text 199.00 (*0-7216-6794-5*, W B Saunders Co) Harcrt Hlth Sci Grp.

— Elbow & Its Disorders. 3rd ed. LC 99-33416. (Illus.). 925p. 2000. text. write for info. (*0-7216-7752-5*, W B Saunders Co) Harcrt Hlth Sci Grp.

Morrey, Bernard F., ed. Biological, Material, & Mechanical Considerations of Joint Replacement. LC 93-20466. (Bristol-Myers - Squibb-Zimmer Orthopaedic Research Symposia Ser.). 480p. 1993. text 103.00 (*0-7817-0008-6*) Lppncott W & W.

— Biological, Material & Mechanical Considerations of Joint Replacement. LC 93-20466. (Bristol-Myers Squibb/Zimmer Orthopaedic Symposium Ser.). (Illus.). 494p. reprint ed. pap. 153.20 (*0-608-09723-3*, 206988900007) Bks Demand.

— The Elbow. LC 93-4630. (Master Techniques in Orthopaedic Surgery Ser.). (Illus.). 368p. 1993. text 189.00 (*0-7817-0036-1*) Lppncott W & W.

— Joint Replacement Arthroplasty. (Illus.). 1252p. 1991. text 240.00 (*0-443-08725-3*) Church.

— Reconstructive Surgery of the Joints, 2 vols., Set. 2nd rev. ed. LC 95-44399. Orig. Title: Joint Replacement Arthroplasty. 1876p. 1995. text 350.00 (*0-443-08982-5*) Church.

Morrey, C. B., Jr., ed. Partial Differential Equations. LC 50-1183. (Proceedings of Symposia in Pure Mathematics Ser.: Vol. 4). 169p. 1961. reprint ed. pap. 38.00 (*0-8218-1404-4*, PSPUM/4) Am Math.

Morrey, Charles B., Jr. Multiple Integrals in the Calculus of Variations. (Grundlehren der Mathematischen Wissenschaften Ser.: Vol. 130). 1966. 126.95 (*0-387-03524-9*) Spr-Verlag.

Morrey, Charles B., Jr., jt. auth. see Protter, Murray H.

Morrical, Guy. Geometry Flipper 2. 49p. (YA). (gr. 9 up). 1994. 6.95 (*1-878383-28-0*) C Lee Pubns.

Morrical, Guy & Churchill, Eric R. Geometry Flipper 1. 49p. (YA). (gr. 7 up). 1989. reprint ed. 6.95 (*1-878383-04-3*) C Lee Pubns.

Morrice, Ken. For All I Know. 80p. 1989. pap. 21.00 (*0-08-025756-9*, Pub. by Mercat Pr Bks) St Mut.

— The Scampering Marmoset. 60p. 1990. pap. text 12.00 (*0-08-040927-X*, Pub. by Aberdeen U Pr) Macmillan.

Morrice, Ken, ed. When Truth Is Known. 72p. 1986. pap. text 5.75 (*0-08-032451-7*, R140, K150, Pergamon Pr) Elsevier.

***Morrice, Peter.** Golf Magazine Complete Guide to Golf. 2000. 29.95 (*1-58574-138-8*) Lyons Pr.

Morrice, Peter. The Golf Magazine Full Swing Handbook. LC 99-86540. 2000. pap. 12.95 (*1-55821-937-4*) Lyons Pr.

— The Golf Magazine Putting Handbook. 2000. pap. 12.95 (*1-55821-939-0*) Lyons Pr.

— The Golf Magazine Short Game Handbook. LC 99-86543. 2000. pap. 12.95 (*1-55821-938-2*) Lyons Pr.

Morrice, Polly Alison. Tale of Two Cities (Dickens) (Barron's Book Notes Ser.). (C). 1984. pap. 3.95 (*0-8120-3444-9*) Barron.

Morrice, Thomas. An Apology for Schoole-Masters. LC 76-57401. (English Experience Ser.: No. 817). 1977. reprint ed. lib. bdg. 20.00 (*90-221-0817-1*) Walter J Johnson.

Morrice, William G. The Durham New Testament Greek Course: A Three Month Introduction. 127p. 1993. reprint ed. pap. 12.99 (*0-85364-556-6*, Pub. by Paternoster Pub) OM Literature.

— Hidden Sayings of Jesus: Words Attributed to Jesus Outside the Four Gospels. 248p. (Orig.). 1997. pap. 16.95 (*1-56563-289-3*) Hendrickson MA.

— Joy in the New Testament. 144p. (Orig.). 1982. pap. 13.50 (*0-85364-340-7*) Attic Pr.

Morries, Gilbert. House Winslow. 1997. boxed set 49.99 (*0-7642-8149-6*) Bethany Hse.

Morrill. How to Study Sociology Booklet. 5th ed. 32p. (C). 1998. pap. text 8.00 (*0-321-02450-8*) Addson-Wesley Educ.

— Readings for Introductory Sociology. (C). 2000. pap. text (*0-321-03924-6*) Addson-Wesley Educ.

— Revolt in the Provinces: The People of England & the Tragedies of War, 1630-1648. 2nd ed. LC 98-52957. 232p. (C). 1998. pap. 25.66 (*0-582-25488-4*) Longman.

— Student Success Practice Tests. 5th ed. 128p. (C). 1999. pap. text 8.00 (*0-321-02448-6*) Addson-Wesley Educ.

***Morrill.** The Systematic Identification of Organic Compounds: Solutions Manual. 7th ed. 257p. 1998. pap. text 30.95 (*0-471-16135-7*) Wiley.

Morrill, Bruce, jt. auth. see Anderson, E. Byron.

***Morrill, Bruce T.** Anamnesis as Dangerous Memory: Political & Liturgical Theology in Dialogue. 224p. 2000. pap. text 27.95 (*0-8146-6183-1*, Pueblo Bks) Liturgical Pr.

Morrill, Bruce T., ed. see Cooke, Bernard J.

Morrill, Calvin. The Executive Way: Conflict Management in Corporations. LC 94-33344. 350p. 1995. 29.95 (*0-226-53873-7*) U Ch Pr.

— The Executive Way: Conflict Management in Corporations. xxii, 328p. 1996. pap. 17.95 (*0-226-53874-5*) U Ch Pr.

***Morrill, Calvin.** Youth Conflict. 2000. pap. 17.00 (*0-226-53876-1*); lib. bdg. 50.00 (*0-226-53875-3*) U Ch Pr.

***Morrill, Dan.** Southern Campaigns of the American Revolution. (Illus.). 235p. 1999. 32.95 (*1-877853-21-6*) Nautical & Aviation.

Morrill, Dexter, compiled by. Woody Herman: A Guide to the Big Band Recordings, 1936-1987. 40. LC 90-13989. (Discographies Ser.: No. 40). 144p. 1990. lib. bdg. 45.00 (*0-313-27756-7*, MGJ/, Greenwood Pr) Greenwood.

Morrill, Donald. At the Bottom of the Sky: Poems by Donald Morrill. LC 98-16341. 80p. 1998. pap. 11.00 (*0-922811-36-9*) Mid-List.

— A Stranger's Neighborhood. LC 97-21157. (Emerging Writers in Creative Nonfiction Ser.). 220p. 1998. 24.95 (*0-8207-0280-3*); pap. 16.95 (*0-8207-0281-1*) Duquesne.

Morrill, Elizabeth, ed. see Huang, Yu Cheng.

Morrill, George P. The Blake Streak Vol. 1: A Tale of War, Mutiny & Love. LC 97-90773. 442p. (C). 1998. 26.00 (*0-9658979-0-7*, 1) Worthington Krantz.

Morrill, Georgiana L., ed. Speculum Guidonis de Warewyke. (EETS, ES Ser.: No. 75). 1974. reprint ed. 54.00 (*0-527-00277-1*) Periodicals Srv.

Morrill, Glyn V. Type Logical Grammar: Categorical Logic of Signs. 332p. 1994. pap. text 65.00 (*0-7923-3226-1*, Pub. by Kluwer Academic); lib. bdg. 116.00 (*0-7923-3095-1*, Pub. by Kluwer Academic) Kluwer Academic.

Morrill, Irene P., ed. Canoeing the Charles. LC 97-159618. (Illus.). 101p. 1996. 24.95 (*1-884186-03-3*) Hollis Pub.

Morrill, J. S. The Revolt of the Provinces: Conservatives & Radicals in the English Civil War, 1630-1650. LC 79-41544. 234 p. 1980. pap. write for info. (*0-582-49704-3*) Longman.

Morrill, James L. The Ongoing State University. LC 60-9636. 153p. reprint ed. pap. 47.50 (*0-608-14127-5*, 205589200039) Bks Demand.

Morrill, Jennifer, jt. auth. see Mapes, Martha.

Morrill, John. The Nature of the English Revolution. LC 92-25941. 480p. (C). 1992. text 62.95 (*0-582-08941-7*, 79647) Longman.

— Oliver Cromwell & the English Revolution. 300p. (C). 1990. pap. 48.00 (*0-582-01675-4*, 78528) Addison-Wesley.

— The Oxford Illustrated History of Tudor & Stuart Britain. (Illus.). 1996. 39.95 (*0-614-96822-4*) OUP.

***Morrill, John, ed.** The Oxford Illustrated History of Tudor & Stuart Britain. (Oxford Illustrated Histories Ser.). (Illus.). 536p. 2001. pap. 26.50 (*0-19-289327-0*) OUP.

Morrill, John, ed. Revolution & Restoration. (History Today Bk.). (Illus.). 160p. 1993. pap. 22.95 (*1-85585-137-7*, Pub. by Collins & Br) Trafalgar.

— The Scottish National Covenant in Its British Context, 1638-51. 240p. 1991. 68.00 (*0-7486-0203-8*, Pub. by Edinburgh U Pr) Col U Pr.

Morrill, John, et al, eds. Public Duty & Private Conscience in Seventeenth-Century England: Essays Presented to G. E. Aylmer. LC 92-32519. (Illus.). 362p. 1993. text 59.00 (*0-19-820229-6*, Clarendon Pr) OUP.

Morrill, John, jt. auth. see Du Pont, Peter.

Morrill, John, jt. auth. see Wilson, Alex.

Morrill, John, ed. see Britain, Stuart.

Morrill, John, jt. ed. see Caldecott, Stratford.

Morrill, John, ed. see Cunningham, Hugh.

Morrill, John, ed. see Jones, Norman.

***Morrill, Judi S.** Science, Physiology & Nutrition for the Nonscientist. (Illus.). 2000. pap. 24.95 (*0-9657951-8-7*) Orange Grove.

Morrill, Judi S., et al. Are You Eating Right? Analyze Your Diet Using the Nutrient Content of More Than 5,000 Foods. 4th rev. ed. (Illus.). 352p. 1997. pap. 29.95 (*0-9657951-9-5*) Orange Grove.

Morrill, Judi S., jt. auth. see Deutsch, Ronald M.

Morrill, Pat. Real Deals in Washington Auctions, Vol. 1. (Illus.). 181p. 1998. mass mkt. 29.70 (*0-9668331-0-4*) Harbor Light.

Morrill, Penny C. Mexican Silver: Twentieth Century Handwrought Jewelry & Metalwork. LC 94-65616. (Illus.). 272p. 1994. 59.95 (*0-88740-610-6*) Schiffer.

— Silver Masters of Mexico: Hector Aguilar & the Taller Borda. LC 96-1894. 224p. (gr. 10-13). 1996. 49.95 (*0-88740-961-X*) Schiffer.

Morrill, Penny C. & Berk, Carole A. Mexican Silver: 20th Century Handwrought Jewelry & Metalwork. 2nd rev. ed. (Illus.). 272p. 1999. 59.95 (*0-7643-0663-4*) Schiffer.

Morrill, Richard, et al. Spatial Diffusion. LC 87-62683. (Scientific Geography Ser.: No. 10). (Illus.). 86p. 1988. reprint ed. pap. 30.00 (*0-608-04319-2*, 206509800012) Bks Demand.

Morrill, Richard L. Political Redistricting & Geographic Theory. Knight, C. Gregory, ed. LC 81-69235. (Resource Publications in Geography). (Orig.). 1981. pap. 15.00 (*0-89291-159-X*) Assn Am Geographers.

— Teaching Values in College. LC 80-8003. (Jossey-Bass Series in Higher Education). 191p. reprint ed. pap. 59.30 (*0-8357-4692-5*, 205234700008) Bks Demand.

***Morrill, Rowena.** The Art of Rowena. (Illus.). 2000. 29.95 (*1-85585-778-2*, Pub. by Paper Tiger) Sterling.

Morrill, Sibley S. The Texas Cannibals: or Why Father Serra Came to California. 28p. 1964. 5.00 (*0-910740-04-6*) Holmes.

Morrill, Terence C. Lanthanide Shift Reagents in Stereochemical Analysis, Vol. 5. (Illus.). 193p. 1987. 65.00 (*0-89573-119-3*, Wiley-VCH) Wiley.

Morrill, Wendell L. Insect Pests of Small Grains. LC 95-76088. (Illus.). 172p. 1995. 65.00 (*0-89054-200-7*) Am Phytopathol Soc.

Morrione, Thomas J., ed. see Blumer, Herbert.

Morris. At the Head of the Class. 1995. per. 15.95 (*0-8057-9130-2*, Twyne) Mac Lib Ref.

— Bob Fosse. 1997. 24.95 (*0-8057-9325-9*, Twyne) Mac Lib Ref.

— Canadian Nurses & the Law. 205p. 1991. boxed set 50.00 (*0-409-80190-9*, MICHIE) LEXIS Pub.

— Changing Children's Behavior. (C). 2000. pap. 64.00 (*0-205-28906-1*, Longwood Div) Allyn.

— Contemporary Psychology & Effective Behavior. 7th ed. 208p. (C). 1997. text, student ed. 30.00 (*0-673-38955-3*) Addison-Wesley Educ.

***Morris.** Darwins Five Theories of Evolution: Controversy & New Discoveries. 2000. pap. text. write for info. (*0-7167-4094-X*, Pub. by W H Freeman) VHPS.

Morris. Delphi Programming Made Simple. 200p. Date not set. pap. text. write for info. (*0-7506-3246-1*) Buttrwrth-Heinemann.

***Morris.** Dictionary of Financial Terms. (Illus.). 160p. 2000. 15.95 (*0-07-135903-6*, McGrw-H College) McGrw-H Hghr Educ.

Morris. Digital Electronics. (Electrical Engineering Ser.). 1993. pap. 31.95 (*0-340-55638-2*, VNR) Wiley.

— Excel for Windows 3.1 Made Simple. 160p. Date not set. pap. text 19.95 (*0-7506-2070-6*) Buttrwrth-Heinemann.

— Excel for Windows 95 Made Simple. 160p. Date not set. pap. text 19.95 (*0-7506-2816-2*) Buttrwrth-Heinemann.

Morris. First Certifcate Workbook. 1997. pap. write for info. (*0-17-556920-7*, Pub. by ITP Nelson) Thomson Learn.

Morris. History Urban Form. 3rd ed. 432p. 1996. pap. 56.00 (*0-582-30154-8*) Addison-Wesley.

***Morris.** Human Anatomy & Physiology 1. 1998. pap. text, lab manual ed. 33.60 (*0-201-38787-5*) Addison-Wesley.

Morris. Infinity. 1996. pap. 14.00 (*0-8050-4780-8*) St Martin.

— Kidney Transplantation. 5th ed. (C). 2000. text. write for info. (*0-7216-8297-9*, W B Saunders Co) Harcrt Hlth Sci Grp.

— Lab Exer Human Ana & Phys. (C). 1998. spiral bd., lab manual ed. 32.00 (*0-201-43460-1*) Addison-Wesley.

— Lincoln Reading Dictionary. 1990. pap. 13.25 (*0-15-321129-6*) Harcourt Schl Pubs.

— Lotus Notes 1-2-3 5.0 for Windows Made Simple. 160p. Date not set. pap. text 19.95 (*0-7506-2307-1*) Buttrwrth-Heinemann.

— Manwatching. pap. 18.95 (*0-586-04887-1*) HarpC.

***Morris.** Mergers & Acquisitions: Business Strategies for Accountants: 1999 Cumulative Supplement. 224p. 1999. pap. 69.00 (*0-471-29911-1*) Wiley.

Morris. Moscow Boy. (J). 1995. 14.95 (*0-689-31657-7*) Atheneum Yung Read.

— New York Cases in Business Law. (LA - Business Law Ser.). 1993. pap. 21.50 (*0-314-00494-7*) West Pub.

— Nixon Bio, Vol. II. 1995. 26.95 (*0-8050-1365-2*) H Holt & Co.

— Pre-Feeding Skills. 1998. pap. 65.00 (*0-12-784568-2*) Acad Pr.

Morris. Psychology. 9th ed. 1996. text. write for info. (*0-13-443136-7*) Allyn.

— Psychology. 9th ed. 1996. text. write for info. (*0-13-443144-8*) Allyn.

Morris. Psychology: An Introduction S-Cart. 10th ed. 1999. 63.00 (*0-13-020663-6*) P-H.

— The Psychology of Memory, Vol. 2. (C). 1993. lib. bdg. 125.00 (*0-8147-5494-5*) NYU Pr.

— The Psychology of Memory, Vol. 3. (C). 1993. lib. bdg. 125.00 (*0-8147-5495-3*) NYU Pr.

Morris. Raman & Infrared Chemical Imaging. 400p. write for info. (*0-471-24674-3*) Wiley.

Morris. Social Divisions: Economic Decline & Social Structural Change. 224p. 1995. 65.00 (*1-85728-201-9*, Pub. by UCL Pr Ltd); pap. 24.95 (*1-85728-202-7*, Pub. by UCL Pr Ltd) Taylor & Francis.

***Morris.** Software Industry Accounting: 1998 Special Report. 48p. 1998. pap. 60.00 (*0-471-29872-7*) Wiley.

Morris. Spanish Methodology pap. text. write for info. (*0-471-37203-X*); pap. text, wbk. ed. write for info. (*0-471-37202-1*) Wiley.

— Sport Psychology: Theory, Applications & Issues. 672p. 1998. text 48.00 (*0-471-33549-5*) Wiley.

— Step Forward! Unit 1: A Christian 12-Step Program to Lose Weight. 1998. pap., wbk. ed. 10.95 (*0-687-08736-8*) Abingdon.

— Step Forward! Unit 2: A Christian 12-Step Program to Lose Weight - & Keep It Off! 1998. pap., wbk. ed. 10.95 (*0-687-08756-2*) Abingdon.

— Supplement Real Estate Tax '81. 1981. 15.00 (*0-316-58393-6*, Aspen Law & Bus) Aspen Pub.

— Taste the Good Life: Nebraska Cookbook. 1992. pap., ring bd. 10.95 (*0-9631249-0-0*, Cookbks by Morris) Morris Pubng.

— Theories of Personality. (C). 1998. pap. text 12.00 (*0-201-45674-5*, Prentice Hall) P-H.

— Three Works. (C). 1968. pap. 16.50 (*0-85315-170-9*, Pub. by Lawrence & Wishart) NYU Pr.

— Webquester: Social Problems. 2nd ed. 150p. 1999. spiral bd. 13.13 (*0-07-235615-4*) McGraw.

Morris. World Famous Vidalia Sweet Onion Cookbook. 1992. pap. 12.95 (*0-9644537-0-3*) Morris Farms.

Morris, ed. Contemporary Psychology & Effective Behavior. 8th ed. (C). 1999. text. write for info. (*0-321-01188-0*) Addison-Wesley Educ.

Morris & Larkin. Introduction to Psychology. 2nd ed. 112p. 1998. pap. text 22.00 (*0-536-01201-6*) S&S Trade.

Morris & Martin. On-Line Fault Detection & Supervision in the Chemical Process. LC 96-41804. (IPPV IFAC Postprint Ser.). 246p. 1996. pap. 71.00 (*0-08-042607-7*, Pergamon Pr) Elsevier.

Morris & Mishkin, Frederic S. On Laws in Courts. 1965. text 27.00 (*0-88277-360-7*) Foundation Pr.

Morris & Nott. Well Women. 70.95 (*1-84014-720-2*) Ashgate Pub Co.

Morris & Tilney. Transplantation Reviews, Vol. 2. 2nd ed. 240p. 1988. text 83.00 (*0-7216-2869-9*, W B Saunders Co) Harcrt Hlth Sci Grp.

— Transplantation Reviews, Vol. 3. (Illus.). 240p. 1989. text 92.00 (*0-7216-3288-2*, W B Saunders Co) Harcrt Hlth Sci Grp.

Morris, jt. auth. see Boyle.

Morris, jt. auth. see Daye.

Morris, jt. auth. see Dunn.

Morris, jt. auth. see Maloof.

Morris, jt. auth. see Oakland.

Morris, jt. auth. see Perkins.

Morris, jt. auth. see Shaff.

Morris, James A. Art of Conversation: The Magic Key to Personal & Social Popularity. 1976. 19.95 (*0-13-046698-0*) P-H.

— Art of Conversation: The Magic Key to Personal & Social Popularity. 192p. 1986. per. 10.00 (*0-671-63275-2*) S&S Trade.

Morris, A. & Tarling, Donald H., eds. Palaeomagnetism & Tectonics of the Mediterranean Region. (Geological Society Special Publication: Series 105). (Illus.). vi, 432p. 1996. 110.00 (*1-897799-55-1*, 269, Pub. by Geol Soc Pub Hse) AAPG.

Morris, A., jt. auth. see Gardiner, G.

Morris, A. I. & Bancewicz, J. Handbook of Gastro-Esophageal Disease. (Illus.). 288p. 1998. pap. write for info. (*0-443-05387-1*) Church.

Morris, A. I. & Quest, Barry. Design - the Modern Law & Practice. 1987. 132.00 (*0-406-10320-8*, U.K., MICHIE) LEXIS Pub.

Morris, A. I., jt. auth. see Quest, Barry.

Morris, A. K., ed. Wallace Stevens: Imagination & Faith. 334p. 1997. pap. 19.95 (*0-691-00249-5*, Pub. by Princeton U Pr) Cal Prin Full Svc.

Morris, A. L. & Barras, R. C., eds. Air Quality Meteorology & Atmospheric Ozone - STP 653. 639p. 1978. 55.00 (*0-8031-0275-5*, STP653) ASTM.

Morris, A. V., jt. auth. see Collinson, William E.

Morris, Adalaide K. Sound States: Innovative Poetics & Acoustical Technologies. LC 97-9884. 368p. (gr. 13). 1998. pap. 24.95 (*0-8078-4670-8*); lib. bdg. 55.00 (*0-8078-2364-3*) U of NC Pr.

— Wallace Stevens: Imagination & Faith. LC 73-2495. (Princeton Essays in Literature Ser.). 218p. 1974. reprint ed. pap. 67.60 (*0-7837-9288-3*, 206002700004) Bks Demand.

Morris, Alan. Between Earth & Sky. LC 97-45446. (Guardians of the North Ser.). 288p. 1998. pap. 8.99 (*1-55661-695-3*) Bethany Hse.

— Between Earth & Sky. large type ed. LC 98-42037. 1999. 24.95 (*0-7862-1692-1*) Thorndike Pr.

— Bright Sword of Justice. large type ed. LC 98-4365. 1998. 22.95 (*0-7862-1470-8*, G K Hall Lrg Type) Mac Lib Ref.

— Bright Sword of Justice, Vol. 3. LC 97-21021. (Guardians of the North Ser.). 256p. 1997. pap. 8.99 (*1-55661-694-5*) Bethany Hse.

— By Honor Bound. LC 96-4442. (Guardians of the North Ser.: Bk. 1). 288p. 1996. pap. 8.99 (*1-55661-692-9*) Bethany Hse.

— By Honor Bound. large type ed. LC 97-44892. (Guardians of the North Ser.). 583p. 1998. 22.95 (*0-7862-1300-0*) Thorndike Pr.

— Collaboration & Resistance Reviewed: Writers & 'la Mode Retro' in Post-Gaullist France. 210p. 1992. 19.50 (*0-85496-634-X*) Berg Pubs.

— Heart of Valor. LC 96-45771. (Guardians of the North Ser.: Bk. 2). 256p. 1996. pap. 8.99 (*1-55661-693-7*) Bethany Hse.

— Honor Bound, Heart of Valor & Bright Sword of Justice, 3 vols. (Guardians of the North Ser.). 1997. boxed set 26.99 (*0-7642-8152-6*) Bethany Hse.

— Patrick Modiano. Flower, John E., ed. (New Directions in European Writing Ser.). 256p. 1996. 55.00 (*1-85973-098-1*); pap. 19.50 (*1-85973-004-3*) Berg Pubs.

— Wings of Healing. LC 99-6631. (Guardians of the North Ser.). 320p. 1999. pap. 8.99 (*1-55661-696-1*) Bethany Hse.

***Morris, Alan.** Wings of Healing. large type ed. LC 99-58242. (Christian Fiction Ser.). 2000. 24.95 (*0-7862-2378-2*) Thorndike Pr.

Morris, Alan & Morris, Gilbert. Tracks of Deceit. LC 95-46656. (Katy Steele Adventures Ser.: No. 1). 256p. 1996. pap. 10.99 (*0-8423-2039-3*) Tyndale Hse.

— Tracks of Deceit. large type ed. LC 98-11019. (Katy Steele Adventures Ser.). 1998. 22.95 (*0-7862-1412-0*) Thorndike Pr.

Morris, Alan, jt. auth. see Dent, Robert.

Morris, Alan B. Heart of Valor. large type ed. LC 98-10005. 1998. 22.95 (*0-7862-1406-6*) Mac Lib Ref.

Morris, Alan S. Measurement & Calibration Requirements for Quality Assurance to ISO 9000. LC 97-22234. (Series in Quality & Reliability Engineering). 404p. 1998. 94.95 (*0-471-97685-7*) Wiley.

Morris, Albert. Learning to Learn from Text. 2nd ed. (C). 1993. pap. text. write for info. (*0-201-53933-0*) Addison-Wesley.

Morris, Aldon & Mueller, Carol M., eds. Frontiers in Social Movement Theory. 400p. (C). 1992. pap. 25.00 (*0-300-05486-6*) Yale U Pr.

Morris, Aldon D. The Origins of the Civil Rights Movement: Black Communities Organizing for Change. 1986. pap. 16.95 (*0-02-922130-7*) Free Pr.

Morris, Aldyth. Captain James Cook. LC 94-48698. (Illus.). 1995. pap. 8.95 (*0-8248-1670-6*) UH Pr.

— Damien. LC 79-22915. 44p. 1980. pap. 7.95 (*0-8248-1323-5*) UH Pr.

— Lili'uokalani. LC 93-3717. (Illus.). 88p. (C). 1993. pap. 9.95 (*0-8248-1543-2*) UH Pr.

— Robert Louis Stevenson - Appointment on Moloka'i. LC 94-48702. (Illus.). 60p. 1995. pap. 8.95 (*0-8248-1671-4*) UH Pr.

Morris, Alfred & Sizer, John. Resources & Higher Education. 226p. 1983. 29.00 (*0-900868-90-2*) OpUniv Pr.

Morris, Alison, jt. auth. see Giller, Henri.

Morris, Alistair. Antiques from the Garden. LC 97-156529. (Illus.). 260p. 1996. 49.50 (*1-870673-17-4*, Pub. by Garden Art Pr) Antique Collect.

***Morris, Alistair.** Antiques from the Garden. LC 99-494994. (Antique Collectors' Club Ser.). (Illus.). 288p. 1999. 49.50 (*1-870673-33-6*, Pub. by Garden Art Pr) Antique Collect.

Morris, Alistair & Gardiner, Gordon. Automobilia of Europe: Reference & Price Guide. (Illus.). 256p. 1992. reprint ed. 49.50 (*1-85149-163-5*) Antique Collect.

Morris, Allen. The Florida Handbook. 26th ed. (Biennial Ser.). (Illus.). 700p. 1997. 34.95 (*0-9616000-6-3*) Peninsular Pub Co.

— The Florida Handbook, 1991-1992. (Illus.). 720p. 1991. text 37.95 (*0-9616000-3-9*) Peninsular Pub Co.

— The Florida Handbook, 1993-1994. (Illus.). 725p. reprint ed. text 37.95 (*0-9616000-4-7*) Peninsular Pub Co.

— The Florida Handbook, 1995-96. 25th ed. (Illus.). 700p. 1995. text 38.95 (*0-9616000-5-5*) Peninsular Pub Co.

— Florida Place Names: Alachua to Zolfo Springs. Morris, Joan P., ed. LC 95-294. (Illus.). 292p. 1995. 21.95 (*1-56164-084-0*) Pineapple Pr.

Morris, Allen, jt. auth. see Zalzala, Ali.

Morris, Allison. Family Group Conferences: Perspectives on Policy & Practice. Galaway, Burt et al, eds. 250p. (Orig.). 1996. pap. text 30.00 (*1-86287-201-5*, Criminal Justice) Willow Tree NY.

Morris, Alton C., ed. Folksongs of Florida: A Florida Sand Dollar Book. 488p. 1990. pap. 19.95 (*0-8130-0983-9*) U Press Fla.

Morris, Alton C., jt. auth. see Bloodworth, Bertha E.

Morris, Andrew. ULTIMA VII Clue Book: Key to the Black Gate. (Illus.). 64p. (Orig.). 1992. pap. 14.95 (*0-929373-09-X*) Origin Syst.

Morris, Andrew, ed. Houghton Hall: The Prime Minister, the Empress & the Hermitage. (Illus.). 176p. 1996. 70.00 (*0-85667-438-9*, Pub. by P Wilson) Scala Books.

Morris, Andrew, jt. auth. see Hobbs, Sheri.

Morris, Ann. The Animal Book. LC 95-13804. (World's Family Ser.). (Illus.). 32p. (J). (gr. 1 up). 1995. pap. 5.95 (*0-382-24703-5*); lib. bdg. 15.95 (*0-382-24702-7*) Silver Burdett Pr.

— Baby Book. (Illus.). 32p. (J). 1995. 13.95 (*0-382-24698-5*) Silver Burdett Pr.

— The Baby Book. (World's Family Ser.). (Illus.). 32p. (J). 1995. pap. 5.95 (*0-382-24700-0*); lib. bdg. 15.95 (*0-382-24699-3*) Silver Burdett Pr.

— Bread, Bread, Bread. LC 82-26677. (Illus.). 32p. (J). (ps-2). 1989. 16.00 (*0-688-06334-9*); lib. bdg. 15.93 (*0-688-06335-7*) Lothrop.

Morris, Ann. Bread, Bread, Bread. 1993. 10.15 (*0-606-05171-6*, Pub. by Turtleback) Demco.

Morris, Ann. Bread, Bread, Bread. LC 92-25547. (Illus.). 32p. (J). (ps-3). 1993. reprint ed. mass mkt. 4.95 (*0-688-12275-2*, Wm Morrow) Morrow Avon.

Morris, Ann. Bread, Bread, Bread Big Book. (Illus.). 32p. (J). (gr. k up). 1993. pap. 18.95 (*0-688-12939-0*, Wm Morrow) Morrow Avon.

Morris, Ann. The Daddy Book. (Illus.). 32p. (J). 1995. 13.95 (*0-382-24695-0*); pap. 5.95 (*0-382-24697-7*); lib. bdg. 15.95 (*0-382-24696-9*) Silver Burdett Pr.

***Morris, Ann.** Families. LC 99-37036. (Illus.). 32p. (YA). (ps-3). 2000. 15.95 (*0-688-17198-2*); 15.89 (*0-688-17199-0*) Morrow Avon.

Morris, Ann. The Grandma Book. LC 98-12310. (World's Family Ser.). (Illus.). (J). 1998. 20.00 (*0-382-42161-2*); lib. bdg. 18.95 (*0-382-39838-6*) Silver Burdett Pr.

— Grandma Book. LC 98-12310. (World's Family Ser.). (Illus.). (J). 1998. pap. 5.95 (*0-382-39840-8*) Silver Burdett Pr.

— The Grandpa Book. LC 98-12306. (World's Family Ser.). (Illus.). (J). 1998. 20.00 (*0-382-42162-0*); pap. 9.00 (*0-382-39843-2*) Silver Burdett Pr.

— Grandpa Book. LC 98-12306. (World's Family Ser.). (Illus.). (J). 1998. lib. bdg. 18.95 (*0-382-39841-6*) Silver Burdett Pr.

— Hats, Hats, Hats. LC 88-26676. (Illus.). 32p. (J). (ps-2). 1989. 16.00 (*0-688-06338-1*) Lothrop.

— Hats, Hats, Hats. (J). 1993. 10.15 (*0-606-05342-5*, Pub. by Turtleback) Demco.

Morris, Ann. Hats, Hats, Hats. LC 92-25548. (Illus.). 32p. (J). (ps up). 1993. reprint ed. mass mkt. 6.95 (*0-688-12274-4*, Wm Morrow) Morrow Avon.

— Hats, Hats, Hats Big Book. (Illus.). 32p. (J). (ps up). 1993. pap. 18.95 (*0-688-12938-2*, Wm Morrow) Morrow Avon.

Morris, Ann. Houses & Homes. LC 92-1365. (Illus.). 32p. (J). (ps-2). 1992. 17.00 (*0-688-10168-2*); lib. bdg. 16.93 (*0-688-10169-0*) Lothrop.

— Houses & Homes. 1994. 10.15 (*0-606-07672-7*, Pub. by Turtleback) Demco.

— Houses & Homes. LC 92-1365. (Illus.). 32p. (J). (gr. k up). 1995. reprint ed. mass mkt. 4.95 (*0-688-13578-1*, Wm Morrow) Morrow Avon.

— I Am Six. LC 94-30495. (Illus.). (J). 1995. 13.95 (*0-382-24686-1*); pap. 5.95 (*0-382-24688-8*); lib. bdg. 15.95 (*0-382-24759-0*) Silver Burdett Pr.

— Just One Seed. (ESL Theme Links Ser.). (Illus.). (J). (gr. k-3). 1993. 35.00 (*1-56334-307-X*); audio 10.50 (*1-56334-306-1*) Hampton-Brown.

— Just One Seed Theme Link. (Illus.). (J). (gr. k 3). 1993. 99.50 (*1-56334-308-8*) Hampton-Brown.

— Karate Boy. (Illus.). 32p. (J). (gr. 1-4). 1996. 15.99 (*0-525-45337-7*, Dutton Child) Peng Put Young Read.

— Light the Candle! Bang the Drum! A Book of Holidays from Around the World. LC 97-5373. (Illus.). 32p. (J). (gr. k-2). 1997. 15.99 (*0-525-45639-2*, Dutton Child) Peng Put Young Read.

— Little Ballerinas. (All Aboard Reading Ser.). (Illus.). 32p. (Orig.). (J). (ps-3). 1997. pap. 2.99 (*0-448-41607-7*, G & D) Peng Put Young Read.

— Little Skaters. LC 97-18136. (All Aboard Bks.). (Illus.). 32p. (J). (ps-3). 1997. pap. text 2.95 (*0-448-41734-0*, G & D) Peng Put Young Read.

— Little Skaters. 1997. 8.15 (*0-606-12758-5*, Pub. by Turtleback) Demco.

— Loving. (Illus.). 32p. (J). 1990. 16.00 (*0-688-06340-3*); lib. bdg. 15.93 (*0-688-06341-1*) Lothrop.

Morris, Ann. Loving. LC 90-33844. 1994. 10.15 (*0-606-06547-4*, Pub. by Turtleback) Demco.

Morris, Ann. Loving. Cohn, Amy, ed. LC 90-33844. (Illus.). 32p. (J). (ps-3). 1994. reprint ed. mass mkt. 4.95 (*0-688-13613-3*, Wm Morrow) Morrow Avon.

— Machines. 2nd ed. (Let Me Read Ser.). (Illus.). 16p. (J). (ps). 1995. bds. 2.95 (*0-673-36268-X*, GoodYrBooks) Addison-Wesley Educ.

— The Mommy Book. LC 95-12237. (World's Family Ser.). (Illus.). 32p. (J). (gr. k-1). 1950. lib. bdg. 22.00 (*0-382-24693-4*) Silver Burdett Pr.

— The Mommy Book. LC 95-12237. (World's Family Ser.). (Illus.). 32p. (J). (gr. k-1). 1995. 13.95 (*0-382-24692-6*); pap. 5.95 (*0-382-24694-2*) Silver Burdett Pr.

Morris, Ann. On the Go. LC 90-33842. 1994. 10.15 (*0-606-06635-7*, Pub. by Turtleback) Demco.

— On the Go. Cohn, Amy, ed. LC 90-33842. (Illus.). 32p. (J). (gr. k up). 1994. reprint ed. mass mkt. 5.95 (*0-688-13637-0*, Wm Morrow) Morrow Avon.

— Play. LC 97-15728. (J). 1998. lib. bdg. 14.93 (*0-688-14553-1*) Lothrop.

Morris, Ann. Play. LC 97-15728. (Illus.). 32p. (J). 1998. 15.00 (*0-688-14552-3*) Lothrop.

***Morris, Ann.** Second Chances: The Adoption Experience. LC 99-41638. 1999. pap. 19.95 (*1-85302-783-9*) Jessica Kingsley.

Morris, Ann. Shoes, Shoes, Shoes. LC 94-46649. (Illus.). 32p. (J). (gr. k-2). 1995. lib. bdg. 14.93 (*0-688-13667-2*) Lothrop.

— Shoes, Shoes, Shoes. LC 94-46649. (Illus.). 32p. (J). (ps-3). 1995. 15.00 (*0-688-13666-4*) Lothrop.

— Shoes, Shoes, Shoes. 32p. (J). 1998. mass mkt. 4.95 (*0-688-16166-9*, Wm Morrow) Morrow Avon.

— Sleepy, Sleepy. LC 85-45333. (Illus.). 16p. (J). (ps). 1986. 3.50 (*0-694-00075-2*) HarpC Child Bks.

— Teamwork. LC 98-46996. 1999. lib. bdg. 15.93 (*0-688-16995-3*) Lothrop.

— Tengo Seis Anos. (SPA., Illus.). 32p. (J). (gr. 1-3). 1996. pap. 5.95 (*0-382-39317-1*); lib. bdg. 15.95 (*0-382-39316-3*) Silver Burdett Pr.

— Tools. (ESL Theme Links Ser.). (Illus.). 24p. 1993. teacher ed. 15.00 (*1-56334-302-9*); teacher ed., student ed. 10.50 incl. audio (*1-56334-303-7*); teacher ed., student ed. 35.00 (*1-56334-304-5*); teacher ed., student ed. 99.50 (*1-56334-305-3*) Hampton-Brown.

— Tools. LC 92-3871. (Illus.). 32p. (J). (ps-3). 1982. 16.00 (*0-688-10170-4*) Lothrop.

— Tools. 32p. (J). 1998. mass mkt. 4.95 (*0-688-16165-0*, Wm Morrow) Morrow Avon.

— Tools: Big Book. (ESL Theme Links Ser.). (Illus.). 24p. 1993. pap. text 29.95 (*1-56334-300-2*) Hampton-Brown.

— Tools: Small Book. (ESL Theme Links Ser.). (Illus.). 24p. 1993. pap. text 6.00 (*1-56334-301-0*) Hampton-Brown.

— Weddings. LC 94-48040. (Illus.). 32p. (J). (gr. k-2). 1995. 15.00 (*0-688-13272-3*); lib. bdg. 14.93 (*0-688-13273-1*) Lothrop.

— Work. LC 97-21607. 1998. lib. bdg. 14.93 (*0-688-14867-0*) Lothrop.

— Work. LC 97-21607. (Illus.). 32p. 1998. 15.00 (*0-688-14866-2*) Lothrop.

— Yay, Team. LC 98-46996. 1999. 16.00 (*0-688-16551-6*) Lothrop.

Morris, Ann, ed. Lift Every Voice & Sing: St. Louis African Americans in the Twentieth Century. LC 99-36741. (Illus.). 240p. 2000. pap. 29.95 (*0-8262-1253-0*) U of Mo Pr.

Morris, Ann & Ambrose, Henrietta. North Webster: A Photographic History of a Black Community. LC 93-9619. (Illus.). 208p. 1993. 36.95 (*0-253-33895-6*); pap. 19.95 (*0-253-28601-8*) Ind U Pr.

Morris, Ann R. Winesburg, Ohio Notes. (Cliffs Notes Ser.). 64p. (Orig.). (C). 1974. pap. text 4.95 (*0-8220-1382-7*, Cliff) IDG Bks.

Morris, Ann R., jt. auth. see Dunn, Margaret M.

Morris, Anne, ed. Application of Expert Systems in Library & Information Centres. 247p. 1991. 65.00 (*0-86291-276-8*) Bowker-Saur.

Morris, Anne & Dyer, Hilary. Human Aspects of Library Automation. 2nd ed. LC 97-28407. 384p. 1998. 96.95 (*0-566-07504-0*, Pub. by Gower) Ashgate Pub Co.

Morris, Anne & Nott, Susan. All My Worldly Goods: A Feminist Perspective on the Legal Regulation of Wealth. LC 95-19399. (Illus.). 320p. 1995. text 87.95 (*1-85521-370-2*, Pub. by Dartmth Pub) Ashgate Pub Co.

***Morris, Anne & O'Donnell, Theresa.** Feminist Perspectives on Employment Law. 254p. 1999. pap. 36.00 (*1-85941-481-8*, Pub. by Cavendish Pubng) Gaunt.

Morris, Anne, jt. ed. see Jones, Michael.

Morris, Anne E., jt. ed. see Jones, Michael A.

Morris, Anneliese. Tee-Up Michigan Golf Guides, 1996: North Edition. 1996. pap. 8.95 (*1-879152-03-7*) Unicorn Grap Commns.

— Tee-Up Michigan Golf Guides, 1996: Southeast Edition. 1996. pap. 8.95 (*1-879152-04-5*) Unicorn Grap Commns.

— Tee-Up Michigan Golf Guides, 1996: Southwest Edition. 1996. pap. 8.95 (*1-879152-05-3*) Unicorn Grap Commns.

Morris, Anthony. ICH in Gastroenterology. (C). (gr. 13). 1994. 28.00 (*0-8151-6222-7*, 22884) Mosby Inc.

***Morris, Arthur.** The Art of Bird Photography. LC 97-46935. 160p. 1998. 35.00 (*0-8174-3303-1*, Amphoto) Watsn-Guptill.

Morris, Arthur. Bird Photography: Pure & Simple. LC 97-30092. (Illus.). 64p. 1997. pap. 9.95 (*1-890309-55-9*) Tern Bk Co.

— Geography & Development. LC 98-123263. 1998. 69.95 (*1-85728-080-6*, Pub. by UCL Pr Ltd); pap. 22.95 (*1-85728-081-4*, Pub. by UCL Pr Ltd) Taylor & Francis.

— Shorebirds: Beautiful Beachcombers. LC 96-7188. (Wildlife Ser.). (Illus.). 160p. (Orig.). 1996. pap. 14.95 (*1-55971-567-7*, NorthWord Pr) Creat Pub Intl.

Morris, Arthur S. Latin America: Economic Development & Regional Differentiation. 256p. (C). 1981. text 56.00 (*0-389-20194-4*, N6976) B&N Imports.

— South America. 3rd ed. (Illus.). 285p. 1991. pap. text 36.00 (*0-340-40607-0*, Pub. by Hodder & Stought Ltd) Lubrecht & Cramer.

Morris, Arthur S. & Lowder, Stella, eds. Decentralization in Latin America: An Evaluation. LC 91-17806. 240p. 1992. 59.95 (*0-275-94021-7*, C4021, Praeger Pubs) Greenwood.

Morris, Arval A. The Constitution & American Public Education. LC 89-62026. 652p. 1989. lib. bdg. 45.00 (*0-89089-348-9*) Carolina Acad Pr.

Morris, Aubrey R. The Haygoods of Mars Hill. unabridged ed. (Illus.). vi, 950p. 1996. 55.00 (*0-614-21800-4*) A R Morris.

Morris, B. J., jt. ed. see Wisden, W.

***Morris, Barbara.** Different Passions: The Desires of Hell to the Lust of Heaven. 176p. 2000. pap. 15.00 (*0-8059-4774-4*) Dorrance.

— The Golden Decade. 1999. pap. write for info. (*1-58235-245-3*) Watermrk Pr.

Morris, Barbara. Trim a Tree. LC 89-81054. (Illus.). 106p. (Orig.). 1989. pap. 9.95 (*0-944419-22-4*) Everett Inc.

Morris, Barbara, jt. auth. see Ball, Michelle.

Morris, Barbara, jt. ed. see Vernon, Kathleen M.

Morris, Barbara A., jt. auth. see Morris, Wesley.

Morris, Barbara B. The Kennedy Center: An Insider's Guide to Washington's Liveliest Memorial. LC 94-1836. (Illus.). 120p. 1994. pap. 10.95 (*0-939009-79-X*, EPM) Howell Pr VA.

Morris, Barbara H. Moving for Seniors. (Illus.). 42p. 1998. wbk. ed. 10.95 (*0-9671239-0-9*) Smooth Transitns.

***Morris, Barry.** The Audience Will: Companion Text. 96p. (C). 2000. per. 24.95 (*0-7872-7341-4*) Kendall-Hunt.

Morris, Barry. The Domestication of Resistance: The Dhan-Gadi & the Australian State. LC 88-39473. (Explorations in Anthropology Ser.). (Illus.). 262p. 1989. 19.50 (*0-85496-271-9*) Berg Pubs.

Morris, Benny. The Birth of the Palestinian Refugee Problem, 1947-1949. (Cambridge Middle East Library: No. 15). 400p. 1989. pap. text 24.95 (*0-521-33889-1*) Cambridge U Pr.

— Israel's Border Wars, 1949-1956: Arab Infiltration, Israeli Retaliation, & the Countdown to the Suez War. (Illus.). 472p. 1994. text 49.95 (*0-19-827850-0*) OUP.

— Israel's Border Wars, 1949-1956: Arab Infiltration, Israeli Retaliation, & the Countdown to the Suez War. 2nd ed. (Illus.). 486p. 1997. reprint ed. pap. text 49.95 (*0-19-829262-7*) OUP.

— 1948 & After: Israel & the Palestinians. (Illus.). 304p. 1991. 75.00 (*0-19-828784-4*) OUP.

— Righteous Victims: A History of the Zionist-Arab Conflict, 1881-1998. LC 98-42774. 1999. write for info. (*0-679-74475-4*) Knopf.

— Righteous Victims: A History of the Zionist-Arab Conflict, 1881-1999. LC 98-42774. 725p. 1999. 40.00 (*0-679-42120-3*) Knopf.

— The Roots of Appeasement: The British Weekly Press & Nazi Germany During the 1930s. 1991. text 45.00 (*0-7146-3417-4*, Pub. by F Cass Pubs) Intl Spec Bk.

Morris, Bernadine. Valentino. LC 96-60682. 80p. 1996. text 18.95 (*0-7893-0066-4*) St Martin.

Morris, Bernard, jt. auth. see Wilstead, John.

Morris, Bernard S. Imperialism & Revolution: An Essay for Radicals. LC 73-81164. (Midland Bks.: No. 170). 93p. reprint ed. pap. 30.00 (*0-8357-9217-X*, 201763200007) Bks Demand.

Morris, Bert. A Friendly Game? The Textbook for Protecting Yourself from Being Cheated at Poker. Gordon, Kenneth, ed. (Illus.). 123p. (Orig.). 1996. pap. 17.95 (*0-9654623-0-7*, 10117) Eleven Bar Seven.

Morris, Bertram. Aesthetic Process. LC 75-12900. (Northwestern University. Humanities Ser.: No. 8). reprint ed. 25.00 (*0-404-50708-5*) AMS Pr.

Morris, Beryl. Biotechnology. LC 93-41597. (Science & Our Future Ser.). (J). 1995. pap. 17.95 (*0-521-43785-7*) Cambridge U Pr.

— Training & Development for Women: Library Training Guide. 64p. 1993. pap. 35.00 (*1-85604-080-1*, LAP0801, Pub. by Library Association) Bernan Associates.

Morris, Betty. Falling, I Find Wings. LC 97-93908. 464p. 1998. pap. 12.95 (*0-9666055-1-9*) Mayflower Pr DC. Falling, I Find Wings is a novel of intimate conversations of four lively women confiding in Martha Kaufman, their conscientious psychiatrist. Each Wednesday afternoon starts with dreamy Elinor, a single mother needing love & money while raising teenagers, followed by another single mother, over-confident Billie, who mistreats her son. Next is poet Ursula, starving for recognition & facing the impending loss of her sight. Last of the day is ambitious artist Sandy, She loves David & is happily pregnant with his child, but determined on a career, not marriage. Martha, who had known her as a girl, is tempted to risk professional censure & treat her as a daughter. The problems they face include career obligations, effects of divorce on children, impulsive sex, abortion, runaways & confused expectations of men & women about marriage. Martha's conventional aims for them crash. She inaugurates different treatment which fails when she includes fairness to men. Finally she demands commitment to wider, more rigorous soul-searching. Written with a light touch, the premise is that both therapy & feminism can help prevent a fall into despair. Overall, this is a literary fiction with common sense & refreshing humor. ***Publisher Paid Annotation.***

Morris, Betty J., et al. Administering the School Library Media Center. 3rd ed. 567p. 1992. 50.00 (*0-8352-3092-9*) Bowker.

Morris, Bill. All Soul's Day. 336p. 1998. mass mkt. 6.99 (*0-380-79116-1*, Avon Bks) Morrow Avon.

— All Souls' Day: A Novel. LC 96-46834. 1997. mass mkt. 23.00 (*0-380-97453-3*, Avon Bks) Morrow Avon.

— The Astral Zoo. 190p. (Orig.). 1995. pap. 11.95 (*0-9639775-1-2*) New Sun Pubns.

M

An Asterisk (*) at the beginning of an entry indicates that the title is appearing for the first time.

— Chas E. Morris: Montana's Historic Photographer. (Illus.). 24p. (Orig.). 1997. pap. 10.00 (*0-944551-18-1*) Sundance Pr TX.

Morris, Bob. Koheleth Speaks! Ecclesiastes 3 & 4. 28p. (Orig.). 1997. 2.50 (*1-880573-32-6*) Bible Search Pubns.

Morris, Bonnie. Bulletin Board Ideas. 48p. (Orig.). 1991. pap. 6.95 (*0-687-04553-3*) Abingdon.

Morris, Bonnie J. Eden Built by Eves: The Culture of Women's Music Festivals. LC 98-54780. 360p. 1999. pap. 15.95 (*1-55583-477-9*, Pub. by Alyson Pubns) Consort Bk Sales.

***Morris, Bonnie J.** Girl Reel. LC 00-22571. 192p. 2000. pap. 14.95 (*1-56689-094-2*, Pub. by Coffee Hse) Consort Bk Sales.

Morris, Bonnie J. The High School Scene in the Fifties: Voices from West L. A. LC 96-41449. 144p. 1997. 49.95 (*0-89789-494-4*, Bergin & Garvey) Greenwood.

— Lubavitcher Women in America: Identity & Activism in the Postwar Era. LC 97-28021. 192p. (C). 1998. text 44.50 (*0-7914-3799-X*); pap. text 14.95 (*0-7914-3800-7*) State U NY Pr.

Morris, Brenda G. The Gift Bearers: A Sculptural Interpretation of Christmas Traditions Through the Centuries. LC 94-96636. (Illus.). 100p. 1995. 29.95 (*0-9643930-0-X*) Brenmor Bks.

***Morris, Brian.** Animals & Ancestors: An Ethnography. 256p. 2000. 65.00 (*1-85973-486-3*); pap. 22.50 (*1-85973-491-X*) Berg Pubs.

Morris, Brian. Anthropological Studies of Religion: An Introductory Text. (Illus.). 384p. 1987. pap. text 19.95 (*0-521-33991-X*) Cambridge U Pr.

— Anthropology of the Self: The Individual in Cultural Perspective. LC 94-9670. (Onthropology, Culture & Society Ser.). 192p. (C). 1994. 59.95 (*0-7453-0857-0*, Pub. by Pluto GBR); pap. 19.95 (*0-7453-0858-9*, Pub. by Pluto GBR) Stylus Pub VA.

— Bakunin: The Philosophy of Freedom. LC 93-70390. 159p. (Orig.). 1993. text 47.99 (*1-895431-67-0*, Pub. by Black Rose); pap. text 18.95 (*1-895431-66-2*, Pub. by Black Rose) Consort Bk Sales.

— Common Mushrooms of Malawi. 108p. (C). 1987. pap. text 31.80 (*82-90724-00-4*) Lubrecht & Cramer.

— In Favour of Circumcision. 72p. 1999. pap. 16.95 (*0-86840-537-X*, Pub. by New South Wales Univ Pr) Intl Spec Bk.

***Morris, Brian.** The Power of Animals: An Ethnography. (Illus.). 2000. pap. 19.50 (*1-85973-225-9*, Pub. by Berg Pubs) NYU Pr.

— The Power of Animals: Malawian Culture & Mammalian Life. LC 99-165884. 4p. 1998. 65.00 (*1-85973-220-8*, Pub. by Berg Pubs) NYU Pr.

Morris, Brian. Tide Race. (C). 1976. pap. 20.00 (*0-85088-420-9*, Pub. by Gomer Pr) St Mut.

— Western Conceptions of the Individual. 506p. 1991. 75.00 (*0-85496-698-6*) Berg Pubs.

— Western Conceptions of the Individual. 506p. (C). 1991. pap. 19.50 (*0-85496-801-6*, Pub. by Berg Pubs) NYU Pr.

Morris, Brian & Msonthi, Jerome. Chewa Medical Botany Part 1: A Study of Herbalism in Southern Malawi. 568p. 1995. text 84.95 (*3-8258-2637-6*) Transaction Pubs.

Morris, Brian, et al. The European Community, 1991-1992 Vol. XXXVI: The Professional Reference Book for Business, Media & Government. 3rd ed. (Illus.). 348p. 1992. 127.35 (*3-11-012760-1*) De Gruyter.

Morris, Brian, ed. see Ford, John.

Morris, Brian, ed. see Shakespeare, William.

Morris, Brian, ed. see Tourneur, Cyril.

Morris, Brian J., jt. ed. see Davies, R. Wayne.

Morris, Bridget. St. Birgitta of Sweden. LC 98-52188. (Illus.). 224p. 1999. 60.00 (*0-85115-727-0*) Boydell & Brewer.

Morris, Bruce. HTML in Action. 288p. 39.95 incl. cd-rom (*1-57235-948-X*) Microsoft.

Morris, Bruce. Rock Climber's Guide to Skyline Boulevard: Featuring Castle Rock State Park, Sanborn-Skyline County Park & Midpeninsula Regional Open Space District Preserves. 3rd rev. ed. (Illus.). 144p. pap. 19.95 (*0-9650234-2-7*) MorComm Pr.

Morris, Bruce. Sport Climber's Guide to Skyline Boulevard: Featuring Castle Rock State Park, Sanborn Skyline County Park & Mid-Peninsula Regional Open Space District Preserves. expanded ed. (Illus.). 123p. 1995. 17.50 (*0-9650234-1-9*) MorComm Pr.

— Sport Climber's Guide to the Castle Rock Area: Featuring Stevens Canyon Boulder, Summit & Indian Rocks, the Western Addition, & Castle Rock Falls. (Illus.). 64p. (Orig.). 1992. pap. 10.95 (*0-9650234-0-0*) MorComm Pr.

Morris, Bruce B. Prime Time Network Serials: Episode Guides, Casts & Credits for 37 Continuing Television Dramas, 1964-1993. LC 96-31166. (Illus.). 847p. 1997. lib. bdg. 95.00 (*0-7864-0164-8*) McFarland & Co.

Morris, Bruce C., jt. auth. see Wells, Donna K.

Morris, Bruce R. The Economics of the Special Taxation of Chain Stores. Bruchey, Stuart & Carosso, Vincent P., eds. LC 78-18971. (Small Business Enterprise in America Ser.). (Illus.). 1979. lib. bdg. 25.95 (*0-405-11474-5*) Ayer.

Morris, Burnis R. Covering Nonprofit Organizations & Their People: A Journalist's Guide. LC 98-210161. (Illus.). 80p. (C). 1997. pap. 15.00 (*0-929556-12-7*) Ind Sector.

— Nonprofit News Coverage: A Guide for Journalists. (Illus.). 64p. (Orig.). 1993. pap. 12.00 (*0-929556-13-5*, P91) Ind Sector.

Morris, C. Comentario Biblico del Continente Nuevo - New Continent Bible Commentary: Marcos. (SPA.). pap. 8.99 (*0-685-74917-7*, 498638) Editorial Unilit.

— The True History of Mexico. 1976. lib. bdg. 59.95 (*0-8490-2772-1*) Gordon Pr.

Morris, C., ed. Academic Press Dictionary of Science & Technology. (Illus.). 2432p. 1992. text 93.00 (*0-12-200400-0*) Acad Pr.

Morris, C. B. This Loving Darkness: Silent Films & Spanish Writers 1920 - 1936. 1980. 39.50 (*0-19-713440-8*) OUP.

Morris, C. Brian. Son of Andalusia: The Lyrical Landscapes of Federico Garcia Lorca. LC 97-4748. (Illus.). 488p. 1997. 39.95 (*0-8265-1288-7*) Vanderbilt U Pr.

Morris, C. G., jt. ed. see Halsey, W. D.

Morris, C. J. Gurkhas: An Ethnology. (C). 1993. text 11.00 (*81-85418-98-5*, Pub. by Low Price) S Asia.

Morris, C. J., jt. ed. see Catterall, Peter.

Morris, C. Robert, jt. auth. see Morris, Clarence R.

Morris, Calvin S. Reverdy C. Ransom: Black Advocate of the Social Gospel. 212p. (Orig.). (C). 1990. lib. bdg. 44.50 (*0-8191-7766-0*) U Pr of Amer.

Morris, Campbell. Best Jumbo Paper Aircraft. LC 92-40581. (Illus.). 32p. (Orig.). 1993. pap. 6.95 (*0-399-51801-0*, Perigee Bks) Berkley Pub.

— The Best Paper Aircraft. (Illus.). 64p. (Orig.). 1986. pap. 7.95 (*0-399-51301-9*, Perigee Bks) Berkley Pub.

— Fold Your Own Dinosaurs. LC 92-32894. (Illus.). 48p. (Orig.). (J). 1993. pap. 7.95 (*0-399-51794-4*, Perigee Bks) Berkley Pub.

— More Best Paper Aircraft. (Illus.). 32p. 1988. pap. 6.95 (*0-399-51446-5*, Perigee Bks) Berkley Pub.

— Skybusters. 40p. (gr. 4-7). 1995. pap. 2.99 (*0-590-22285-6*) Scholastic Inc.

— Spacebusters. 40p. (gr. 4-6). 1995. pap. 2.99 (*0-590-22284-8*) Scholastic Inc.

— Three D Magic Portfolio. 1995. pap. 15.95 (*0-8050-3755-1*) H Holt & Co.

Morris, Carla D. & Morris, Steven R. How to Index Your Local Newspaper Using WordPerfect or Microsoft Word for Windows. LC 95-21810. xvii, 167p. 1995. pap. text 40.00 incl. disk (*1-56308-305-1*) Libs Unl.

Morris, Carlos. Comentario Biblico del Continente Nuevo: Marcos.Tr. of New Continent Bible Commentary: Marcos. (SPA.). 281p. 1992. pap. write for info. (*0-614-27005-7*) Editorial Unilit.

Morris, Carlos A. Comentario Biblico Continente Nuevo: Marcos.Tr. of New Continent Bible Commentary: Mark. (SPA.). 281p. 1992. 9.99 (*1-56063-269-0*, 498637) Editorial Unilit.

Morris, Carol. Sweet Uprisings. (Illus.). 18p. (Orig.). 1990. pap. 5.00 (*0-9608802-7-5*) Years Pr.

Morris, Carol, ed. see Hurst, John A.

Morris, Carole, ed. see Bessent Bryd, Helen.

Morris, Carroll. A Suzuki Parent's Diary. 88p. 1984. pap. text 10.95 (*0-87487-590-0*) Summy-Birchard.

Morris, Catherine. Willem de Kooning. 1999. 12.95 (*0-8362-1933-3*) Andrews & McMeel.

Morris, Cecilia, jt. auth. see Marshall, Ian.

Morris, Cedric, tr. see Henning, Harald, Jr., et al.

Morris, Celia. Fanny Wright: Rebel in America. (Illus.). 352p. 1992. pap. text 16.95 (*0-252-06249-3*) U of Ill Pr.

***Morris, Celia.** Finding Celia's Place. LC 00-37804. (Illus.). 352p. 2000. 29.95 (*0-89096-963-9*) Tex A&M Univ Pr.

Morris, Celia. Storming the Statehouse: Running for Governor with Ann Richards & Dianne Feinstein. (Illus.). 352p. 1992. text 25.00 (*0-684-19328-0*) S&S Trade.

Morris, Ceridwen, jt. auth. see Robinson, Bill.

Morris, Chandra, ed. see Reid, Shell.

Morris, Charles. American Catholic. 1998. pap. 15.00 (*0-679-74221-2*) Vin Bks.

— The Aryan Race. abr. ed. 280p. 1998. pap. 18.00 (*1-878465-33-3*) Scott-Townsend Pubs.

— Aryan Sun-Myths: The Origins of Religions. 177p. 1996. reprint ed. pap. 14.00 (*0-7873-1267-3*) Hlth Research.

— Aryan Sun-Myths the Origin of Religions (1889) 192p. 1996. reprint ed. pap. 13.95 (*1-56459-893-4*) Kessinger Pub.

Morris, Charles & Coleman, James C. Contemporary Psychology & Effective Behavior, 7th Edition. 7th ed. 546p. (C). 1997. 67.60 (*0-673-46051-7*) Addson-Wesley Educ.

***Morris, Charles E., III & Browne, Stephen H.** Readings on the Rhetoric of Social Protest. 544p. 2001. pap. text. write for info. (*1-891136-06-2*) Strata Pub Co.

Morris, Charles G. Psychology: An Introduction. 10th ed. LC 98-14514. 724p. 1998. 78.67 (*0-13-676537-8*) P-H.

— Signification & Significance: A Study of the Relations of Signs & Values. 1968. pap. text 12.00 (*0-262-63014-1*) MIT Pr.

Morris, Charles G. & Maisto, Albert. Understanding Psychology. 4th ed. LC 98-5654. 615p. (C). 1998. pap. text 58.00 (*0-13-676529-7*) P-H.

***Morris, Charles G. & Maisto, Albert A.** Understanding Psychology Without Mind Matters. 5th ed. 608p. 2000. pap. 52.00 (*0-13-029073-4*) P-H.

Morris, Charles J., ed. American Labor Policy: A Critical Appraisal of the National Labor Relations Act. LC 86-32706. 483p. 1987. reprint ed. pap. 149.80 (*0-608-04261-7*, 206501600012) Bks Demand.

***Morris, Charles R.** Health Care & the U. S. Economy. 2000. pap. 9.95 (*0-87078-441-2*) Century Foundation.

Morris, Charles R. Locke, Berkeley, Hume. LC 79-17847. 174p. 1979. reprint ed. lib. bdg. 38.50 (*0-313-22091-3*, MOLO, Greenwood Pr) Greenwood.

— Money, Greed & Risk: Why Financial Crises & Crashes Happen. LC 98-32144. 297p. 1999. 25.00 (*0-8129-3173-4*, Times Business) Random.

Morris, Charles W. Logical Positivism, Pragmatism & Scientific Empiricism. LC 75-3285. reprint ed. 29.50 (*0-404-59273-2*) AMS Pr.

— Paths of Life: Preface to a World Religion. LC 72-94732. 228p. 1993. pap. text 2.25 (*0-226-53879-6*, P541) U Ch Pr.

— Symbolism & Reality: A Study in the Nature of Mind. LC 86-17602. (Foundations of Semiotics Ser.: No. 15). xxv, 128p. (C). 1993. 53.00 (*90-272-3287-3*) J Benjamins Pubng Co.

— Varieties of Human Value. LC 56-6641. (Midway Reprint Ser.: 1973). 225p. reprint ed. 69.80 (*0-8357-9660-4*, 201698900005) Bks Demand.

***Morris, Charles W. & Morris, Janet E.** Jesus in the Midst of Success: Standing Faithful in Seasons of Abundance. 224p. 2000. pap. 12.99 (*0-8054-1978-0*) Broadman.

Morris, Charles W., jt. auth. see Dean, James D.

Morris, Charles W., ed. see Mead, George Herbert.

Morris, Chris. Locoland. LC 97-68996. 176p. 1998. pap. 13.50 (*0-88739-163-X*) Creat Arts Bk.

— So You Have to Write an Essay. 88p. (C). 1995. spiral bd. 19.95 (*0-7872-0821-3*, 41082101) Kendall-Hunt.

Morris, Chris, et al. Weapons of Mass Destruction: Nonlethality, Information Warfare, & Airpower in the Age of Chaos. (Illus.). 35p. (Orig.). (C). 1995. pap. text 20.00 (*0-7881-1670-3*) DIANE Pub.

Morris, Christine. Tracing Your Ancestors. 1999. 16.99 (*1-84100-140-6*) Quadrillion Media.

Morris, Christine, jt ed. see Goodison, Lucy.

Morris, Christopher. Becoming Southern: The Evolution of a Way of Life, Warren County & Vicksburg. LC 93-37916. (Illus.). 288p. 1995. text 52.00 (*0-19-508366-0*) OUP.

— Becoming Southern: The Evolution of A Way of Life, Warren County & Vicksburg, Mississippi, 1760-1860. (Illus.). 258p. 1999. pap. 19.95 (*0-19-513421-4*) OUP.

— Models of Misrepresentation: On the Fiction of E. L. Doctorow. LC 91-3730. 1991. text 35.00 (*0-87805-524-X*) U Pr of Miss.

— The Oxford Book of Tudor Anthems. (Illus.). 360p. 1978. pap. 17.95 (*0-19-353325-1*) OUP.

— The Social Contract Theorists: Critical Essays on Hobbes, Locke & Rousseau. LC 98-37119. (Critical Essays on the Classics Ser.). 208p. 1998. text 57.95 (*0-8476-8906-9*) Rowman.

Morris, Christopher, ed. Anthems for Choirs Four. 206p. 1976. pap. 16.95 (*0-19-353018-X*) OUP.

— The Social Contract Theorists: Critical Essays on Hobbes, Locke & Rousseau. LC 98-37119. (Critical Essays on the Classics Ser.: No. 102). 208p. 1998. pap. 16.95 (*0-8476-8907-7*) Rowman.

Morris, Christopher, et al, eds. The HBJ Student Thesaurus. (Illus.). 312p. (J). (gr. 2-7). 1991. 14.95 (*0-15-232880-7*) Harcourt.

Morris, Christopher & Reinhardt, Steven G., eds. Southern Writers & Their Worlds. LC 97-49598. 176p. 1998. pap. text 11.95 (*0-8071-2274-2*) La State U Pr.

— Southern Writers & Their Worlds. LC 95-39356. (Walter Prescott Webb Memorial Lectures: No. 29). 176p. 1996. 24.95 (*0-89096-692-3*) Tex A&M Univ Pr.

Morris, Christopher, jt. ed. see Haynes, Sam W.

Morris, Christopher D., et al, eds. The Viking Age in Caithness, Orkney, & the North Atlantic. (Illus.). 528p. 1993. 45.00 (*0-7486-0430-8*, Pub. by Edinburgh U Pr) Col U Pr.

Morris, Christopher D., jt. auth. see Batey, Colleen E.

Morris, Christopher D., ed. see Doctorow, E. L.

Morris, Christopher G. The Harcourt Brace Student Thesaurus. Harcourt Brace, ed. LC 89-26916. (Illus.). 320p. (J). (gr. 3-7). 1994. 18.00 (*0-15-200186-7*, Harcourt Child Bks) Harcourt.

Morris, Christopher W. An Essay on the Modern State. LC 97-20458. (Illus.). 304p. (C). 1998. text 54.95 (*0-521-49625-X*) Cambridge U Pr.

Morris, Christopher W., jt. ed. see Coleman, Jules L.

Morris, Christopher W., jt. ed. see Frey, R. G.

Morris, Cindy E., ed. see Nguyen, Christophe, et al.

Morris, Claire E. Slam: A New Way to Tell the Truth. 55p. 1999. 9.95 (*1-57077-972-4*) Titlewaves.

Morris, Clara S. De, see De Morris, Clara S.

Morris, Clare. Quantitative Approaches in Business Studies. 4th ed. 480p. (Orig.). 1996. pap. 57.50 (*0-273-61697-8*, Pub. by Pitman Pub) Trans-Atl Phila.

***Morris, Clare.** Quantitative Approaches in Business Studies. 5th ed. 512p. (Orig.). 1999. pap. 57.50 (*0-273-63828-9*, Pub. by F T P-H) Trans-Atl Phila.

Morris, Clarence. How Lawyers Think. xiv, 144p. 1994. reprint ed. 35.00 (*0-8377-2475-9*, Rothman) W S Hein.

Morris, Clarence, ed. Great Legal Philosophers: Selected Readings in Jurisprudence. LC 57-11955. 582p. 1971. reprint ed. pap. 22.95 (*0-8122-1008-5*) U of Pa Pr.

Morris, Clarence R., intro. Trends in Modern American Society. LC 86-22762. (Benjamin Franklin Lectures of the University of Pennsylvania, 7th Series). 191p. 1986. reprint ed. lib. bdg. 55.00 (*0-313-22106-5*, MOTM, Greenwood Pr) Greenwood.

Morris, Clarence R. & Morris, C. Robert. Morris on Torts. 2nd ed. LC 80-170. (University Textbook Ser.). 443p. 1980. text 25.95 (*0-88277-002-0*) Foundation Pr.

Morris, Clarice. Classroom Experiments in Hair Structure & Chemistry. (Illus.). 1990. pap. 37.95 (*0-87350-068-7*) Milady Pub.

Morris, Clarine. Enoch, One of Santa's Elves. (Illus.). 16p. (J). (ps-5). 1995. pap. 2.50 (*0-9650312-0-9*) Cosmo Starr.

***Morris, Clarine.** Hoot. (Illus.). 12p. (J). (ps-3). 2000. pap. 3.00 (*0-9650312-1-7*) Cosmo Starr.

— I Have a Toothache. (Illus.). 12p. (J). (ps-7). 2000. pap. 3.00 (*0-9650312-5-X*) Cosmo Starr.

— Mommie Star. (Illus.). (J). (ps-10). 2000. pap. 3.00 (*0-9650312-3-3*) Cosmo Starr.

— The Obstinate Bear. (Illus.). 12p. (J). 2000. pap. 3.00 (*0-9650312-8-4*) Cosmo Starr.

— Reno. (Illus.). 12p. (J). (ps-5). 2000. pap. 3.00 (*0-9650312-4-1*) Cosmo Starr.

— Sam, the Hippo No One Wanted. (Illus.). (J). (ps-7). 2000. pap. 3.00 (*0-9650312-9-2*) Cosmo Starr.

Morris, Claud. The Last Inch: A Middle East Odyssey. (Illus.). 280p. 1996. 59.50 (*0-7103-0552-4*, Pub. by Kegan Paul Intl) Col U Pr.

Morris, Clayton L., jt. auth. see Haskel, Marilyn L.

Morris, Colin. The Discovery of the Individual, 1051-1200. (Medieval Academy Reprints for Teaching Ser.). 188p. 1987. reprint ed. pap. text 10.95 (*0-8020-6665-8*) U of Toronto Pr.

— Medieval Media: Mass Communication in the Making of Europe: An Inaugural Lecture Delivered At the University, 14th March 1972. LC 73-166842. 16 p. 1972. write for info. (*0-85432-084-9*) Univ of Southampton.

— The Papal Monarchy: The Western Church from 1050 to 1250. (Oxford History of the Christian Church Ser.). 690p. 1991. reprint ed. pap. text 39.95 (*0-19-826925-0*, 12306) OUP.

Morris, Colton G. & Cave, Hugh B. Fightin'est Ship: The Story of the Cruiser Helena in World War II. LC 79-20662. 1981. reprint ed. 17.95 (*0-89201-083-5*) Zenger Pub.

Morris, Constance L., tr. see Celarie, Henriette.

Morris, Corbyn. Essay Towards Fixing the True Standards of Wit & Humor. LC 70-172747. reprint ed. 29.50 (*0-404-04501-4*) AMS Pr.

Morris, Corliss. Behind the Badge: A Policewoman's Ordeal. 254p. (Orig.). 1990. pap. 4.95 (*1-879331-09-8*) Marciel Pub & Print.

— With Love to the Monsters under My Bed. 2nd ed. (Illus.). 60p. (Orig.). reprint ed. pap. 7.95 (*1-879331-08-X*) Marciel Pub & Print.

Morris County Historical Soc. Staff. Tours in Historic Morris County. (Illus.). 298p. 1977. reprint ed. pap. 5.00 (*0-614-29778-8*) M C H S.

Morris, Craig & Hagen, Adriana von. The Inka Empire & Its Andean Origins. (Illus.). 252p. 1993. 75.00 (*1-55859-556-2*) Abbeville Pr.

Morris, Craig, jt. auth. see Von Hagen, Adriana.

Morris, Curtis. Skillet & Trophy Fishing Texas. (Illus.). 256p. (Orig.). 1989. pap. text 10.95 (*1-877740-00-4*) Nel-Mar Pub.

Morris, Curtis L., jt. auth. see Morris, Vivian Gunn.

Morris, Cynthia, jt. auth. see Vila, Bryan.

Morris, Cynthia, jt. ed. see Vila, Bryan.

Morris, Cynthia T. & Adelman, Irma. Comparative Patterns of Economic Development, 1850-1914. LC 87-45480. (Johns Hopkins Studies in Development). 592p. reprint ed. pap. 183.60 (*0-608-07406-3*, 206763300009) Bks Demand.

Morris, Cynthia T., jt. auth. see Adelman, Irma.

Morris, D. Babywatching. 1992. write for info. (*0-224-03259-3*, Pub. by Random) Random House.

— Sword Life. (J). 1997. mass mkt. 8.95 (*0-340-67298-6*, Pub. by Hodder & Stought Ltd) Trafalgar.

Morris, D. World Markets for Spun Yarns: Forecasts to 2000. 1994. pap. 531.00 (*0-614-20917-X*, Pub. by Textile Inst) St Mut.

Morris, D. & Stogdon, A. World Markets for Cotton: Forecasts to 2000. 1995. pap. 531.00 (*0-85058-860-X*, Pub. by Textile Inst) St Mut.

Morris, D. & Tunney, D. World Markets for Textured Yarns: Forecasts to 2000. 1995. pap. 531.00 (*0-85058-859-6*, Pub. by Textile Inst) St Mut.

Morris, D. Bryant. Write a Research Paper in Six Easy Steps. Jennings, Margarette, ed. 69p. (Orig.). 1996. pap. 9.95 (*0-9653791-0-8*) JenPrint Publns.

Morris, D. G., ed. Mechanical Behaviour of Nanostructured Materials. (Materials Science Foundation Ser.: Vol. 2). (Illus.). 100p. (C). 48.00 (*0-87849-797-8*, Pub. by Trans T Pub) Enfield Pubs NH.

Morris, D. Hampton. Stephane Mallarme, Twentieth-Century Criticism, 1972-1979. LC 89-34656. (Romance Monographs: No. 48). 1989. pap. 22.00 (*84-599-2717-2*) Romance.

Morris, D. L., et al. Hepatic Metastases: Diagnosis & Management. Onik, Gary M., ed. LC 95-7176. (Illus.). 224p. 1996. text 115.00 (*0-7506-0879-X*) Buttrwrth-Heinemann.

Morris, D. M. Hunting Trophy Whitetails. (Illus.). 483p. 1997. 29.95 (*1-57157-105-1*) Safari Pr.

Morris, D. S., jt. auth. see Haigh, R. H.

Morris, D. W., et al, eds. Patterns in the Structure of Mammalian Communities. LC 89-32598. (Special Publications: No. 28). iv, 266p. (C). 1989. 30.00 (*0-89672-173-6*); pap. 20.00 (*0-89672-174-4*) Tex Tech Univ Pr.

Morris, Dan & Morris, Inez. The Complete Fish Cookbook. LC 73-161249. 1972. 10.00 (*0-672-51421-4*, Bobbs) Macmillan.

— The Complete Fish Cookbook. rev. ed. 436p. 1989. reprint ed. pap. 16.95 (*0-88317-155-4*) Stoeger Pub Co.

Morris, Daniel. Painless Publishing. (Illus.). 60p. (C). 1988. write for info. (*0-318-62977-1*) Osage Pr.

— Presque Isle. (Illus.). 102p. (Orig.). 1988. pap. write for info. (*0-318-62978-X*) Osage Pr.

— The Writings of William Carlos Williams: Publicity for the Self. 224p. 1995. text 34.95 (*0-8262-1002-3*) U of Mo Pr.

Morris, Daniel A. Federal Tort Claims, 1 vol. 1993. ring bd. 135.00 (*0-685-68851-8*) West Group.

Morris, Daniel C. & Brandon, Joel. Just Don't Do It: The Contrarian Manager's Guide to Challenging Popular Business Theories. LC 97-9048. 268p. 1997. 24.95 (*0-07-043184-1*) McGraw.

Morris, Daniel R. From Heaven to Hell: Imagery of Earth, Air, Water & Fire in the Novels of Georges Bernanos. (American University Studies: Romance Languages & Literature: Ser. II, Vol. 86). X, 332p. (C). 1988. text 41.95 (*0-8204-0691-0*) P Lang Pubng.

An Asterisk (*) at the beginning of an entry indicates that the title is appearing for the first time.

Morris, Danney E. & Olsen, Charles M. Discerning God's Will Together: A Spiritual Practice for the Church. 1997. pap. 11.95 (*1-56699-177-3*, AL180) Alban Inst.

***Morris, Danny E., ed.** A Life That Really Matters: The Story of the John Wesley Great Experiment. LC 99-64723. 110p. 1999. 12.95 (*1-57736-155-5*) Providence Hse.

Morris, Danny E. & Olsen, Charles M. Discerning God's Will Together: A Spiritual Practice for the Church. Donigian, George, ed. LC 96-43229. 144p. 1997. pap. 12.00 (*0-8358-0808-4*, UR808) Upper Room Bks.

Morris, Daphne K., jt. auth. see Averill, Lloyd J.

Morris, Darlene. House of Seven Gables Notes. (Cliffs Notes Ser.). 64p. 1964. pap. 4.95 (*0-8220-0595-6*, Cliff) IDG Bks.

Morris, Darrell. Case Studies in Teaching Beginning Readers: The Howard Street Tutoring Manual. LC 92-71181. (Illus.). 258p. (Orig.). (C). 1992. pap. text 23.00 (*0-9632376-0-8*) Fieldstream.

— The Howard Street Tutoring Manual: Teaching At-Risk Readers in the Primary Grades. 2nd ed. LC 98-32002. 242p. 1999. pap. text 25.00 (*1-57230-444-8*) Guilford Pubns.

Morris, Dave. Buried Treasure. 1990. pap. 5.95 (*0-440-80179-6*) BDD Bks Young Read.

***Morris, Dave.** Last Flight of the Liberators: The Seventh Flag over Texas. 222p. 2000. pap. 18.00 (*0-7388-2077-6*) Xlibris Corp.

Morris, Dave. Teenage Mutant Ninja Turtles, 5 vols. (J). (gr. 4-7). 1990. boxed set 14.75 (*0-440-36030-7*) Dell.

Morris, David. Advanced Strategies for Trophy Whitetails. 2nd ed. (Illus.). 352p. 1998. 29.95 (*1-57157-112-4*) Safari Pr.

— Dalesmen of the Mississippi. (C). 1990. 90.00 (*1-85072-062-2*, Pub. by W Sessions) St Mut.

— The End of Marriage: The Development of European Divorce Law 1550-1970. 1971. 22.95 (*0-8464-0375-7*) Beekman Pubs.

— Getting from Here to There: Building a Rational Transportation System. 9p. (Orig.). 1992. pap. 4.50 (*0-917582-28-4*) Inst Local Self Re.

— A Gift from America: The First 50 Years of CARE. LC 95-82235. 142p. 1996. 29.95 (*1-56352-285-3*) Longstreet.

— A Lifestyle of Worship: Making Worship a Joyful, Reviving Part of Your Everyday Experience. LC 98-40567. 1998. pap. 9.99 (*0-8307-2199-1*, Renew) Gospel Lght.

— Locating Trophy Whitetail. Boddington, Craig, ed. (Whitetail Secrets Ser.: No. 8). (Illus.). 151p. 1996. 19.95 (*1-56416-158-7*) Derrydale Pr.

— Self-Reliant Cities: Energy & the Transformation of Urban America. LC 81-18301. (Illus.). 256p. 1982. 19.95 (*0-87156-296-0*, Pub. by Sierra) Random.

Morris, David. The Swale: A History of the Holy River of St. Paulinus. 1995. pap. 45.00 (*1-85072-152-1*, Pub. by W Sessions) St Mut.

***Morris, David.** The Swale: A History of the Holy River of St. Paulinus. 1999. pap. 27.00 (*1-85072-173-4*, Pub. by W Sessions) St Mut.

Morris, David, et al, eds. Cancer: A Comprehensive Clinical Guide. 321p. 1998. pap. text 25.00 (*90-5702-216-8*, ECU32, Harwood Acad Pubs) Gordon & Breach.

Morris, David & Abeles, Tom. Substituting Agricultural Materials for Petroleum-Based Industrial Products. LC 86-21350. 33p. 1986. 20.00 (*0-917582-46-2*) Inst Local Self Re.

Morris, David & Ahmed, Irshad. The Carbohydrate Economy: Making Chemicals & Industrial Materials from Plant Matter. LC 92-18177. (Illus.). 66p. 1992. pap. text 25.00 (*0-917582-25-X*) Inst Local Self Re.

Morris, David & Kearsley, John, eds. Cancer: A Comprehensive Clinical Guide. 321p. 1998. text 75.00 (*90-5702-215-X*, ECU83, Harwood Acad Pubs) Gordon & Breach.

Morris, David & Platt, Brenda A. Garbage Disposal Economics: A Statistical Snapshot. LC 87-4182. (Illus.). 110p. 1987. pap. 20.00 (*0-917582-44-6*) Inst Local Self Re.

Morris, David, et al. Getting the Most from Our Materials: Making New Jersy the State of the Art. LC 91-22240. (Illus.). 85p. (Orig.). 1991. pap. text 25.00 (*0-917582-33-0*) Inst Local Self Re.

Morris, David, jt. auth. see Ahmed, Irshad.

Morris, David, ed. see Idol, Dick, et al.

Morris, David B. Alexander Pope: The Genius of Sense. LC 83-18577. 384p. reprint ed. pap. 119.10 (*0-7837-4474-9*, 204418200001) Bks Demand.

— The Culture of Pain. LC 90-11305. (Illus.). 354p. 1991. 45.00 (*0-520-07266-9*, Pub. by U CA Pr) Cal Prin Full Svc.

— The Culture of Pain. 1993. pap. 17.95 (*0-520-08276-1*, Pub. by U CA Pr) Cal Prin Full Svc.

— Earth Warrior: Overboard with Paul Watson & the Sea Shepherd Conservation Society. LC 94-37952. (Illus.). 224p. 1995. pap. 14.95 (*1-55591-203-6*) Fulcrum Pub.

Morris, David B. Illness & Culture in the Postmodern Age. LC 98-7092. 360p. 1998. 27.50 (*0-520-20869-2*, Pub. by U CA Pr); write for info. (*0-520-21441-2*) U CA Pr.

***Morris, David B.** Illness & Culture in the Postmodern Age. LC 98-7092. (Illus.). 360p. 2000. pap. 17.95 (*0-520-22689-5*) U CA Pr.

Morris, David G., jt. auth. see Webb, G. L.

Morris, David J., Jr. Market Power & Business Strategy: In Search of the Unified Organization. LC 95-50742. 224p. 1996. 57.95 (*1-56720-045-1*, Quorum Bks) Greenwood.

Morris, David J. Pulse Code Formats for Fiber Optical Data Communication. (Optical Engineering Ser.: Vol. 5). (Illus.). 224p. 1983. text 135.00 (*0-8247-7067-6*) Dekker.

Morris, David R. & Harford, Joe B. MRNA Metabolism & Post-Transcriptional Gene Regulation. LC 96-39030. (Modern Cell Biology Ser.). 354p. 1997. 135.00 (*0-471-14206-9*) Wiley.

Morris, David R. & Marton, Laurence J., eds. Polyamines in Biology & Medicine. LC 81-9757. (Biochemistry of Disease Ser.: No. 8). 477p. reprint ed. pap. 147.90 (*0-7837-3362-3*, 204332000008) Bks Demand.

Morris, Debbie. Forgiving the Dead Man Walking. Date not set. pap. 8.99 (*0-8297-0860-X*) Vida Pubs.

Morris, Debbie & Lewis, Gregg. Forgiving the Dead Man Walking: Only One Woman Can Tell the Entire Story. LC 98-17616. 256p. 1998. 19.99 (*0-310-22265-6*) HarpC.

— Forgiving the Dead Man Walking: Only One Woman Can Tell the Entire Story. 256p. 1999. pap. 12.99 (*0-310-23187-6*) HarpC.

Morris, Deborah. Adrift in the Atlantic. (Real Kids Real Adventures Ser.: No. 7). (J). 1998. mass mkt. 4.50 (*0-425-16190-0*) Berkley Pub.

***Morris, Deborah.** Apartment Fire. 2nd ed. (Real Kids, Real Adventures Ser.: Vol. 8). 112p. (YA). (gr. 4-7). 2000. reprint ed. pap. 4.99 (*1-928591-07-8*, Pub. by Adventure Ink) Midpt Trade.

Morris, Deborah. Explosion! (Real Kids Real Adventures: Vol.). (J). 1998. mass mkt. 4.50 (*0-425-16429-2*, JAM) Berkley Pub.

— Firestorm. (Real Kids Real Adventures Ser.: No. 6). 112p. (J). 1998. mass mkt. 4.50 (*0-425-16154-4*) Berkley Pub.

— A Lightning Strike. (Real Kids Real Adventures Ser.: No. 5). 112p. (J). (gr. 3-7). 1997. mass mkt. 3.99 (*0-425-16117-X*) Berkley Pub.

***Morris, Deborah.** Real Kids, Real Adventures: Bear Attack, Hero on Blanco River, Tornado. 2nd ed. 101p. (YA). (gr. 3-12). 2000. reprint ed. pap. 4.99 (*1-928591-04-3*, Pub. by Adventure Ink) Midpt Trade.

— Real Kids, Real Adventures: Mountain Lion!, Scouts Honor, Race for Rescue. 2nd ed. 112p. (YA). (gr. 3-12). 2000. reprint ed. pap. 4.99 (*1-928591-06-X*, Pub. by Adventure Ink) Midpt Trade.

Morris, Deborah. Real Kids, Real Adventures: Over the Edge. LC 97-5391. (Real Kids, Real Adventures Ser.). 112p. (J). 1997. mass mkt. 3.99 (*0-425-15975-2*) Berkley Pub.

***Morris, Deborah.** Real Kids, Real Adventures: Runaway School Bus, Abandon Ship! & Poison Gas. 2nd ed. 100p. (YA). (gr. 3-12). 2000. reprint ed. pap. 4.99 (*1-928591-09-4*, Pub. by Adventure Ink) Midpt Trade.

— Real Kids, Real Adventures: Shark Attack. 2nd ed. 100p. (YA). (gr. 3-12). 2000. reprint ed. pap. 4.99 (*1-928591-05-1*, Pub. by Adventure Ink) Midpt Trade.

Morris, Deborah. Real Kids, Real Adventures: Tornado. LC 97-5391. (Real Kids, Real Adventures Ser.). 112p. (J). 1997. mass mkt. 3.99 (*0-425-16043-2*) Berkley Pub.

***Morris, Deborah.** Real Kids, Real Adventures: Whirlpool, Kidnapped, Over the Edge. 2nd ed. 103p. (YA). (gr. 3-12). 2000. reprint ed. pap. 4.99 (*1-928591-13-2*, Pub. by Adventure Ink) Midpt Trade.

Morris, Deborah. Real Kids, Real Adventures No. 1: Shark Attack. (Real Kids, Real Adventures Ser.). 112p. (J). 1997. mass mkt. 3.99 (*0-425-15938-8*) Berkley Pub.

***Morris, Deborah.** Real Kids, Real Adventures No. 5: Earthquake. 104p. (YA). (gr. 3 up). 2000. pap. 4.99 (*1-928591-03-5*, Pub. by Adventure Ink) Midpt Trade.

— Real Kids, Real Adventures No. 6: Christmas Day Crash. 102p. (YA). (gr. 3 up). 2000. pap. 4.99 (*1-928591-08-6*, Pub. by Adventure Ink) Midpt Trade.

— Real Kids, Real Adventures No. 7: Long Way Home. 104p. (YA). (gr. 3 up). 2000. pap. 4.99 (*1-928591-02-7*, Pub. by Adventure Ink) Midpt Trade.

— Real Kids, Real Adventures No. 9: Lost Hiker. 100p. (YA). (gr. 3 up). 2000. pap. 4.99 (*1-928591-01-9*, Pub. by Adventure Ink) Midpt Trade.

— Real Kids, Real Adventures No. 10: Safety Net. 104p. (YA). (gr. 3 up). 2000. pap. 4.99 (*1-928591-00-0*, Pub. by Adventure Ink) Midpt Trade.

— Real Kids, Real Adventures No. 12: Train Track Rescue. 104p. (YA). (gr. 3 up). 2000. reprint ed. pap. 4.99 (*1-928591-14-0*, Pub. by Adventure Ink) Midpt Trade.

Morris, Deborah. Runaway Balloon. (Real Kids Real Adventures Ser.). (J). 1998. mass mkt. 4.50 (*0-425-16236-2*) Berkley Pub.

— Runaway School Bus. (Real Kids Real Adventures Ser.: No. 4). 112p. (J). (gr. 3-7). 1997. mass mkt. 3.99 (*0-425-16086-6*) Berkley Pub.

— Trapped in a Glacier. (Real Kids, Real Adventures Ser.: No. 10). 192p. (J). 1998. pap. 4.50 (*0-425-16578-7*, JAM) Berkley Pub.

Morris, Debra. Schools: An Education in Charity Law. (Illus.). 288p. 1996. 83.95 (*1-85521-444-X*, Pub. by Dartmth Pub) Ashgate Pub Co.

***Morris, Delyth & Williams, Glyn, eds.** Language Planning & Language Use. 304p. 2000. 55.00 (*0-7083-1579-8*, Pub. by U Wales Pr) Paul & Co Pubs.

Morris, Dennis. Bob Marley: Rebel with a Cause. 160p. 1999. pap. text 19.95 (*0-85965-268-8*) Publishers Group.

— Destroy: A Photographic Record of the Sex Pistols, 1977. (Illus.). 192p. 1998. pap. 29.95 (*1-871592-74-7*) Creation Books.

***Morris, Dennis.** Pictures: Oasis in Japan, 1995. (Illus.). 2000. pap. 14.95 (*1-902588-03-7*) Glitter Bks.

— Pictures: Oasis 1995. 72p. 1999. pap. 14.95 (*1-902588-04-5*, Pub. by Glitter Bks) Subterranean Co.

Morris, Derek J., ed. The Economic System in the United Kingdom. 3rd ed. (UGC Series in Economics). (Illus.). 960p. 1985. 45.00 (*0-19-877224-6*); pap. 19.95 (*0-19-877235-1*) OUP.

Morris, Derek J., jt. auth. see Hay, Donald A.

Morris, Derrick & Tamm, Boris, eds. Concise Encyclopedia of Software Engineering. LC 92-27942. (Advances in Systems Control & Information Engineering Ser.). 414p. 1992. 288.50 (*0-08-036214-1*, Pergamon Pr) Elsevier.

Morris, Derrick, et al. Object Oriented Computer Systems Engineering. LC 96-5191. (Applied Computing Ser.). 320p. 1996. pap. 34.95 (*3-540-76020-2*) Spr-Verlag.

Morris, Desmond. The Art of Ancient Cyprus. (Illus.). 368p. 1990. text 75.00 (*0-7148-2280-9*) Phaidon Pr.

***Morris, Desmond.** Body Guards: Protective Amulets & Charms. (Illus.). 224p. 1999. text 29.95 (*1-86204-572-0*, Pub. by Element MA) Penguin Putnam.

— Body Guards: Protective Amulets & Charms. 2001. reprint ed. pap. 18.95 (*1-86204-573-9*) Element MA.

— Cat Breeds of the World. LC 99-10008. 256p. 1999. 25.95 (*0-670-88639-4*, Viking) Viking Penguin.

Morris, Desmond. Catwatching. 1993. pap. 8.00 (*0-517-88053-9*, Crown) Crown Pub Group.

— CatWorld: A Feline Encyclopedia. LC 96-28314. (Illus.). 496p. 1997. 29.95 (*0-670-10006-4*) Viking Penguin.

— Dogwatching. 1993. pap. 8.00 (*0-517-88055-5*, Crown) Crown Pub Group.

— Horsewatching. (Illus.). 1989. 15.00 (*0-517-57267-2*, Crown) Crown Pub Group.

— The Human Animal. large type ed. 24.95 (*1-85695-048-4*, Pub. by ISIS Lrg Prnt) Transaction Pubs.

Morris, Desmond. Human Sexes. pap. write for info. (*0-312-20053-6*) St Martin.

Morris, Desmond. Human Sexes. LC 98-15122. (Illus.). 256p. 1998. text 24.95 (*0-312-18311-9*) St Martin.

— The Human Zoo: A Zoologist's Study of the Urban Animal. Turner, Philip, ed. LC 95-81946. (Kodansha Globe Ser.). 272p. 1996. pap. 13.00 (*1-56836-104-1*, Kodansha Globe) Kodansha.

— Illustrated Dogwatching. (Illus.). 144p. 1996. 19.99 (*0-517-15997-X*) Random Hse Value.

— Illustrated Horsewatching. (Illus.). 144p. 1999. pap. 19.95 (*1-57715-094-5*) Knckerbocker.

— Intimate Behaviour. 272p. 1997. pap. 15.00 (*1-56836-163-7*, Kodansha Globe) Kodansha.

— Naked Ape. 208p. 20.95 (*0-8488-2684-1*) Amereon Ltd.

— Naked Ape. 256p. 1999. pap. 11.95 (*0-385-33430-3*) Delta Alpha.

— Pocket Guide to Manwatching. pap. 9.95 (*0-586-05628-9*) HarpC.

— The Secret Surrealist: The Paintings of Desmond Morris. (Illus.). 112p. 1990. text 29.95 (*0-7148-2448-8*) Phaidon Pr.

***Morris, Diana.** Altitude of Excellence: Six Breakthrough Communication Strategies to Help You Achieve & Succeed, 5 vols. (Personal Excellence Library). 90p. 2000. spiral bd. 99.00 (*1-891019-18-X*) Morris Communs.

Morris, Diana. Blockbuster: Breakthrough Writing Tips & Tactics. 1998. pap. write for info. (*1-891019-07-4*) Morris Communs.

— Increase Your I. Q. (Irresistibility Quotient) 1998. pap. write for info. (*1-891019-03-1*) Morris Communs.

— Power Line Vol. 1: Know Your Communications Goal; Make It a Win-Win. 1998. pap. write for info. (*1-891019-11-2*) Morris Communs.

— Power Line Vol. 2: Power-Up Your Listening Skills. 1998. pap. write for info. (*1-891019-06-6*) Morris Communs.

— Power Line Vol. 3: Accentuate the Positive. 1998. pap. write for info. (*1-891019-12-0*) Morris Communs.

— Power Line Vol. 4: Beware the Power of Self-Talk. 1998. pap. write for info. (*1-891019-13-9*) Morris Communs.

— Power Line Vol. 5: Keep Your Cool in Hot Situations. 1998. pap. write for info. (*1-891019-04-X*) Morris Communs.

— Power Line Vol. 6: Build Your Credibility Muscle. 1998. pap. write for info. (*1-891019-05-8*) Morris Communs.

— Power Lines: How to Communicate with Power & Precision. LC 97-72784. 92p. (Orig.). 1997. pap. write for info. (*1-891019-00-7*) Morris Communs.

— Powerlines: A Completely Practical Guide to Communicating with Confidence & Power. 2nd ed. LC 98-65602. Orig. Title: Powerlines - How to Communicate with Power & Precision. 150p. 1998. pap. 16.95 (*1-891019-08-2*) Morris Communs.

Morris, Diana, intro. Miriam Laufer: A Retrospective. LC 81-66864. (Illus.). 80p. 1981. pap. text 12.95 (*0-940220-04-0*) Asylums Pr-Language.

Morris, Diane H., jt. auth. see Boyle, Mari.

Morris, Dick. Behind the Oval Office: Winning the Presidency in the Nineties. LC 99-168749. 688p. 1998. pap. 14.95 (*1-58063-053-7*, Pub. by Renaissance) St Martin.

***Morris, Dick.** The New Prince. 256p. 2000. pap. text 15.95 (*1-58063-147-9*) Renaissance.

Morris, Dick. The New Prince: Machiavelli Updated for the 21st Century. LC 99-21767. 240p. 1999. 21.95 (*1-58063-079-0*) Renaissance.

***Morris, Dick.** Vote.Com: How Big-Money Lobbyists & the Media Are Losing Their Influence & the Internet Is Giving Power Back to the People. 256p. 2000. pap. 15.95 (*1-58063-163-0*) Renaissance.

— VOTE.COM: How Big-Money Lobbyists & the Media Are Losing Their Influence & the Internet Is Giving Power to the People. LC 99-67457. 256p. 1999. 22.95 (*1-58063-105-3*) Renaissance.

Morris, Dirk. Government Debt in International Financial Markets. 220p. 1992. 54.00 (*0-86187-994-5*, Pub. by P P Pubs) Cassell & Continuum.

Morris-Dobie, Claire. Slam: A New Way to Tell the Truth. Federhofer-Stark, Sherri, ed. (Illus.). 64p. (J). (gr. 5-10). 1998. pap. 6.95 (*0-9668242-0-2*) Morris Commun.

Morris, Dolly L. Flower Drying Handbook: Includes Complete Microwave Drying Instructions. LC 95-37898. (Illus.). 96p. 1996. 19.95 (*0-8069-4878-7*) Sterling.

— Flower Drying Handbook: Includes Complete Microwave Drying Instructions. (Illus.). 96p. 1997. pap. 9.95 (*0-8069-4879-5*) Sterling.

Morris, Donald. Dewey & the Behavioristic Context of Ethics. 184p. 1996. 69.95 (*1-57309-041-7*); pap. 49.95 (*1-57309-040-9*) Intl Scholars.

Morris, Donald, jt. auth. see Jamieson, Paul.

Morris, Donald F. Small Local Governments & Information Management. 17p. (Orig.). 1984. pap. 2.00 (*1-55719-078-X*) U NE CPAR.

Morris, Donald R. The Washing of the Spears: The Rise & Fall of the Zulu Nation. LC 98-20022. (Illus.). 655p. 1998. reprint ed. pap. 19.95 (*0-306-80866-8*) Da Capo.

***Morris, Donna S.** Furniture Repairs from A-Z: A Quick Reference Guide of Tips & Techniques. vii, 128p. 2000. pap. 14.95 (*0-9665673-4-X*) Phoenix Pr Ltd.

Morris, Donna S. More Than 100 Furniture Repairs You Can Do Yourself: A Practical Handbook for Anyone Who Buys, Sells, or Owns Furniture. LC 98-91678. (Illus.). xv, 272p. 1998. pap. 24.95 (*0-9665673-3-1*) Phoenix Pr Ltd.

Morris, Doris, ed. see Sweet, Orville K.

Morris, Dorothy. A Garland of Green Gold. large type ed. 224p. 1992. pap. 16.99 (*0-7089-7189-X*) Ulverscroft.

— None of Your Black Business. LC 90-82800. 105p. (Orig.). (C). 1991. pap. 12.95 (*0-9627732-0-4*) Dell-Morse.

***Morris, Dorothy K.** Secret Sins of the Mother: A Novel. Finton, Kenneth H. & Thompson, Chaya, eds. LC 99-90153. 248p. 1999. 24.95 (*1-892977-03-6*) H T Commun.

Morris-Dotson, Cynthia E. In This World but Not of This World: Different Enough to Make a Difference. LC 97-91929. 116p. 1997. pap. write for info. (*0-9658508-0-3*) CeSalAlve.

***Morris, Doug.** Italy Guide. 3rd ed. 936p. 2000. pap. text 19.95 (*1-892975-31-9*) Open Rd Pub.

Morris, Douglas E. Rome & Southern Italy Guide. 2nd ed. 256p. 1998. pap. 14.95 (*1-883323-85-1*) Open Rd Pub.

Morris, Dwight & Gamache, Murielle E. Handbook of Campaign Spending: Money in the 1992 Congressional Races. LC 93-50217. 570p. 1994. 149.95 (*0-87187-997-2*) Congr Quarterly.

Morris, E. Techniques in Litigation. 4th ed. 381p. 1993. pap. 56.00 (*0-7021-2615-2*, Pub. by Juta & Co) Gaunt.

Morris, E. & Sadler, T. Our Rainforests & the Issues. (Illus.). 54p. (J). (gr. 6-11). 1992. pap. 16.95 (*0-643-05141-4*, Pub. by CSIRO) Accents Pubns.

Morris E. Fine Symposium Staff. Morris E. Fine Symposium, October 8-11, 1990, Detroit, MI: TMS Fall Meeting. Liaw, Peter K. et al, eds. LC 90-64027. (Illus.). 522p. 1991. reprint ed. pap. 161.90 (*0-608-02493-7*, 206313700004) Bks Demand.

Morris, E. K. & Braukmann, C. J. Behavioral Approaches to Crime & Delinquency: A Handbook of Application, Research, & Concepts. LC 87-29081. (Illus.). 652p. (C). 1988. 95.00 (*0-306-42632-3*, Plenum Trade) Perseus Pubng.

***Morris, E. M.** My Enemy, My Patient. LC 00-91498. 2000. pap. 12.95 (*0-533-13584-2*) Vantage.

Morris, Earl H. The House of the Great Kiva at the Aztec Ruin. LC 96-13209. 1996. pap. 3.95 (*1-877856-57-6*) SW Pks Mnmts.

— The Temple of the Warriors: The Adventure of Exploring & Restoring a Masterpiece of Native American Architecture in the Ruined City of Chichen Itza, Yucatan. LC 76-44764. (Illus.). reprint ed. 55.00 (*0-404-15871-4*) AMS Pr.

Morris, Earl H., et al. The Temple of the Warriors at Chichen Itza, Yucatan, 2 vols., Set. LC 77-11511. (Carnegie Institution of Washington. Publications: No. 406). reprint ed. 104.50 (*0-404-16280-0*) AMS Pr.

Morris, Ed. Garth Brooks, Platinum Cowboy. LC 92-43645. 1992. pap. 10.95 (*0-312-08788-8*) St Martin.

***Morris, Edmund.** Dutch. 2000. pap. 16.95 (*0-375-75645-0*) Modern Lib NY.

— Dutch: A Memoir of Ronald Reagan. LC 98-39600. (Illus.). 874p. 1999. 35.00 incl. audio (*0-394-55508-2*) Random.

Morris, Edmund. The Rise of Theodore Roosevelt. 896p. 1986. pap. 16.00 (*0-345-33902-9*) Ballantine Pub Grp.

— Ten Acres Enough: The Small Farm Dream Is Possible. 2nd ed. Miller, Lynn R., ed. 247p. 1996. reprint ed. 19.95 (*1-885210-03-5*); reprint ed. pap. 11.95 (*1-885210-02-7*) Small Farmers.

— The Wooden Dish. 1956. pap. 5.25 (*0-8222-1276-5*) Dramatists Play.

Morris, Edward. The Walker Art Gallery. (Illus.). 96p. 1994. 30.00 (*1-85759-036-8*) Scala Books.

Morris, Edward & Roberts, Emma. The Liverpool Academy & Other Exhibitions of Contemporary Art in Liverpool, 1774-1867: A History & Index of Artists & Works Exhibited. LC 98-188913. 600p. 1997. 124.95 (*0-85323-672-0*, Pub. by Liverpool Univ Pr) Intl Spec Bk.

Morris, Edward A. The Demagogue's Disease. LC 79-64157. (Illus.). 1979. 7.95 (*0-934062-00-5*); pap. 4.95 (*0-934062-01-3*) World Wide Prods.

— Evolution to Sainthood. LC 94-60845. 1997. pap. 4.50 (*0-934062-03-X*) World Wide Prods.

Morris, Edward K., jt. ed. see Todd, James T.

Morris, Edwin L. Fish, Fiber, & Fitness: Magic Keys to a Healthy, Vigorous, Happy Life. McKinney, Aubrey R., ed. (Adventures in Science Ser.). (Illus.). 160p. 1989. 24.95 (*0-914587-05-6*) Helix Pr.

Morris, Eileen. Crafts Kids Can Eat, Play with, or Wear. (J). (gr. k-3). 1991. pap. 12.99 (*0-86653-979-4*) Fearon Teacher Aids.

***Morris, Elaine L.** A Valentine Book for Honey Bee. (Illus.). 12p. (J). (ps-5). 2000. pap. 3.98 (*1-930977-00-X*) Cosmo Starr.

Morris, Elaine L., jt. ed. see Fitzpatrick, A. P.

M

Morris, Eleanor. Country Roads of Texas. LC 94-4403. (Country Roads Ser.). (Illus.). 120p. 1994. pap. 9.95 (1-56626-100-7, Cntry Rds Pr) NTC Contemp Pub Co.
— Country Roads of Texas: Drives, Day Trips, & Weekend Excursions. 2nd ed. LC 98-34145. (Country Roads of... Ser.). (Illus.). 144p. 1999. pap. 12.95 (1-56626-107-4, 61074, Cntry Rds Pr) NTC Contemp Pub Co.
— Country Towns of Texas. (Illus.). 120p. 1996. pap. 9.95 (1-56626-146-5) Fodors Travel.
***Morris, Eleanor.** The Texas Hill Country Book: A Complete Guide Including Austin & San Antonio. 2nd rev. ed. LC 99-57103. (Great Destinations Ser.). 352p. 2000. pap. 18.95 (1-58157-017-1, Pub. by Berkshire Hse) Natl Bk Netwk.
Morris, Eleanor, et al. City Smart Guidebook: Austin. 2nd ed. (Illus.). 216p. 1999. pap. 13.95 (1-56261-503-3, City Smart) Avalon Travel.
Morris, Eleanor S. British Planning & Urban Design: Principles & Policies in the 20th Century. 1996. pap. write for info. (0-582-23496-4) Addison-Wesley.
— Recommended Country Inns: The Southwest. 7th ed. 356p. 1999. pap. text 16.95 (0-7627-0300-8) Globe Pequot.
— The Texas Hill Country Book: A Complete Guide with Sections on Austin & San Antonio. LC 96-18635. (Great Destinations Ser.). (Illus.). 320p. 1997. pap. 17.95 (0-936399-84-8) Berkshire Hse.
Morris, Elias C. Sermons, Addresses & Reminiscences & Important Correspondence, with a Picture Gallery of Eminent Ministers & Scholars. Gaustad, Edwin S., ed. LC 79-52598. (Baptist Tradition Ser.). (Illus.). 1980. reprint ed. lib. bdg. 30.95 (0-405-12465-1) Ayer.
***Morris, Elisabeth.** Essential Paris. (AAA Essential Guides Ser.). 128p. 2000. pap. 8.95 (0-658-00380-1, 003801, Passprt Bks) NTC Contemp Pub Co.
Morris, Elisabeth. Paris. 2nd rev. ed. LC 99-179930. (Thomas Cook Travellers Ser.). 192p. 1996. write for info. (0-7495-1353-5, Pub. by Auto Assn Guides) Hunter NJ.
— Paris. 4th ed. (Passport's Illustrated Travel Guides from Thomas Cook Ser.). (Illus.). 192p. 1999. pap. 14.95 (0-658-00034-9, 000349, Passprt Bks) NTC Contemp Pub Co.
Morris, Elizabeth. Days Out & Other Papers. LC 67-26767. (Essay Index Reprint Ser.). 1977. 18.95 (0-8369-0721-3) Ayer.
— Jonathan Papers. LC 70-152200. (Essay Index Reprint Ser.). 1977. reprint ed. 20.95 (0-8369-2249-2) Ayer.
— More Jonathan Papers. LC 68-8484. (Essay Index Reprint Ser.). 1977. 19.95 (0-8369-0722-1) Ayer.
— Paris. 2nd ed. LC 94-67813. (Illustrated Travel Guides from Thomas Cook Ser.). (Illus.). 192p. (Orig.). 1994. pap. 12.95 (0-8442-9048-3, Passprt Bks) NTC Contemp Pub Co.
Morris, Elizabeth A. Basketmaker Caves in the Prayer Rock District, Northeastern Arizona. LC 79-20149. (Anthropological Papers: No. 35). 158p. 1980. pap. 16.95 (0-8165-0499-7) U of Ariz Pr.
***Morris, Elizabeth Ann.** Stained & Decorative Glass. (Illus.). 2000. 12.99 (0-7858-1175-3) Bk Sales Inc.
Morris, Elizabeth H. Personal Traits & Success in Teaching. LC 76-177087. (Columbia University. Teachers College. Contributions to Education Ser.: No. 342). reprint ed. 37.50 (0-404-55342-7) AMS Pr.
Morris, Ellen, compiled by. Monmouth County, New Jersey: Families of Color in 1880. (New Jersey, 1880: Afro-Americans & Native Americans Ser.). (Illus.). 134p. 1992. pap. 20.00 (0-317-04688-8) Morris Genealog Lib.
***Morris, Ellen K. & Levin, Edward S.** The Art of Publishers' Bookbinding: 1815-1915. (Illus.). 127p. 2000. 75.00 (0-915148-21-8) Wm Dailey.
***Morris, Ellen K., et al.** The Art of Publishers' Bookbindings, 1815-1915. LC 00-29430. (Illus.). 127p. 2000. pap. 37.50 (0-915148-22-6) Wm Dailey.
Morris, Ellen M. & Pasteris, Jill D., eds. Mantle Metasomatism & Alkaline Magmatism. LC 87-17390. (Geological Society of America Ser.: Vol. 215). (Illus.). 393p. 1987. reprint ed. pap. 121.90 (0-608-07741-0, 206782900010) Bks Demand.
Morris, Eric. Acting from the Ultimate Consciousness. 1992. pap. 11.95 (0-9629709-1-3) Ermor Enter.
— Acting, Imaging, & the Unconscious. LC 98-19463. 1998. 18.95 (0-9629709-4-8) Ermor Enter.
— Being & Doing: A Workbook for Actors. 190p. 1990. pap. text 12.95 (0-9629709-0-5) Ermor Enter.
***Morris, Eric.** Corregidor: The American Alamo of World War II. 2000. reprint ed. pap. 19.95 (0-8154-1085-9, Pub. by Cooper Sq) Natl Bk Netwk.
Morris, Eric. Irreverent Acting. (Orig.). 1992. pap. 11.95 (0-9629709-2-1) Ermor Enter.
— No Acting Please. 1995. pap. text 11.95 (0-9629709-3-X) Ermor Enter.
Morris, Eric, jt. auth. see Hoe, Alan.
Morris, Eugene J., et al. New York Practice Guide: Real Estate, 5 vols. 1986. ring bd. 760.00 (0-8205-1523-X) Bender.
Morris, Evan. The Book Lover's Guide to the Internet. rev. ed. 304p. 1998. pap. 12.95 (0-449-00227-6) Fawcett.
— The Booklover's Guide to the Internet. (Illus.). 256p. 1996. pap. 12.95 (0-449-91070-9) Fawcett.
***Morris, Evan.** The Word Detective. 288p. 2000. 17.95 (1-56512-239-9) Algonquin Bks.
Morris, Evelyn L. Emotions from the Heart. LC 98-90629. 1999. pap. 8.95 (0-533-12869-2) Vantage.
***Morris, Ewan.** Our Own Devices. (New Directions in Irish History Ser.). (Illus.). 240p. 2000. 45.00 (0-7165-2663-8, Pub. by Irish Acad,Pr) Intl Spec Bk.
Morris, F. C., jt. ed. see Levin, D. L.
Morris, Floyd. One Hundred Ninety-Eight Easy Wood Projects. 96p. 1989. pap. 13.28 (0-87006-629-3) Goodheart.
Morris, Frances. Chris Burden. 1999. pap. text 19.95 (1-85437-286-6, Pub. by Tate Gallery) U of Wash Pr.
Morris, Frances, jt. auth. see Clouzot, Henri.
Morris, Frances, jt. auth. see Morgan, Stuart.
Morris, Frances C., jt. auth. see Levin, Daniel L.
Morris, Francis. ECG Interpretation for Emergency Medicine: A Self Assessment Guide. LC 97-25514. 160p. 1997. pap. text 35.00 (0-7506-3019-1) Buttrwrth-Heinemann.
Morris, Francis, et al. Accident & Emergency Data & Drug Guide. 119p. 1995. pap. text 30.00 (0-7506-2035-8) Buttrwrth-Heinemann.
Morris, Frank T. Finches of Australia: A Folio. (Illus.). 124p. 65.00 (0-7018-1000-9) Eastview.
Morris, Fred P. How to Sharpen Your Listening to God Skills. LC 97-61560. 96p. 1998. pap. 8.99 (1-57921-051-1, Pub. by WinePress Pub) BookWorld.
Morris, Frederick M. Bishop Pike: Ham, Heretic, or Hero. LC 67-28381. 32p. reprint ed. pap. 30.00 (0-8357-7278-0, 201293400083) Bks Demand.
Morris, G. Laying down the Law. 3rd ed. 352p. 1992. pap. 51.00 (0-409-30541-3, Austral, MICHIE) LEXIS Pub.
Morris, G., et al. Laying down the Law. 4th ed. LC 97-179793. 424p. 1995. pap. write for info. (0-409-30952-4, MICHIE) LEXIS Pub.
Morris, G. H. & Chenail, Ronald U., eds. The Talk of the Clinic: Exploration in the Analysis of Medical & Therapeutic Discourse. (Communication Ser.). 344p. 1995. pap. 34.50 (0-8058-1373-X); text 79.95 (0-8058-1372-1) L Erlbaum Assocs.
Morris, G. S. & Stiehl, Jim. Changing Kids' Games. 2nd rev. ed. LC 98-27142. (Illus.). 148p. (J). 1998. pap. text 17.00 (0-88011-691-9, BMOR0691) Human Kinetics.
— Physical Education: From Intent to Action. 464p. (C). 1985. 54.00 (0-675-20115-2, Merrill Coll) P-H.
Morris, Gabrielle. At the Head of the Class. 1995. 29.95 (0-8057-9129-9, Twyne) Mac Lib Ref.
Morris, Gareth. Flute Technique: New Edition. (Illus.). 76p. 1992. pap. text 21.95 (0-19-318432-X) OUP.
Morris, Gareth, jt. ed. see Rose, A. H.
Morris, Gary, ed. Friends for Life. LC 98-16824. (Illus.). 48p. 1998. pap. 8.95 (0-88396-465-1) Blue Mtn Art.
— I Love You, Mom: A Collection of Poems from Blue Mountain Arts. LC 97-9945. 48p. 1998. pap. 8.95 (0-88396-449-X) Blue Mtn Art.
— I Love You, Mom, Special Edition: A Collection of Poems. LC 98-30608. (Illus.). 64p. 1998. 16.95 (0-88396-475-9) Blue Mtn Art.
— This Valentine's Day, I Love You More Than Words Can Say. LC 98-8697. (Illus.). 48p. 1998. pap. 7.95 (0-88396-470-8) Blue Mtn Art.
— This Valentine's Day, I Promise You All My Love. LC 95-36006. 64p. 1995. 16.95 (0-88396-421-X) Blue Mtn Art.
— To My Child: We May No Longer Live in the Same House, but You're Always in My Heart. LC 98-30719. (Illus.). 64p. 1998. 16.95 (0-88396-474-0) Blue Mtn Art.
— To My Child: We May No Longer Live in the Same House, but You're Always in My Heart: A Collection of Poems from Blue Mountain Arts. LC 97-9936. (Illus.). 48p. 1997. pap. 8.95 (0-88396-447-3) Blue Mtn Art.
***Morris, Gary, ed.** With God by Your Side... You Never Have to Be Alone. LC 99-16857. (Illus.). 64p. 1999. 16.95 (0-88396-526-7, H5267) Blue Mtn Art.
Morris, Gary, ed. With God by Your Side You Never Have to Be Alone: A Collection of Poems. LC 98-6911. (Illus.). 48p. 1998. pap. 8.95 (0-88396-468-6) Blue Mtn Art.
Morris, Gay, ed. Moving Words: Re-Writing Dance. (Illus.). 360p. (C). 1996. 90.00 (0-415-12542-1); pap. 27.99 (0-415-12543-X) Routledge.
Morris, Gene, jt. auth. see Morris, Michael H.
Morris, Geoffrey. The Rise of the Labour Movement. 128p. (C). 1986. 55.00 (0-7855-2154-2) St Mut.
Morris, Geoffrey & Ashton, Dennis. Training Sessions on Occupational Safety. 400p. 1998. ring bd. 393.95 (0-566-07910-0, Pub. by Gower) Ashgate Pub Co.
Morris, Geoffrey, jt. auth. see Everard, K. B.
Morris, Geoffrey, jt. auth. see King, Howard.
Morris, George. Rebellion in the Unions: A Handbook for Rank & File Action. LC 74-173354. 160p. 1971. pap. 2.75 (0-685-23466-5) New Outlook.
— Social Democrats - U. S. A. in the Service of Reaction: A Record of Racism, Low Wages, Bureaucracy & Betrayal of Socialism. 1976. pap. 0.50 (0-87898-119-5) New Outlook.
Morris, George, et al. Russian Face to Face Level 1: Beginning Assessment Package. (C). Date not set. 105.95 (0-8442-4323-X, X4323-X) NTC Contemp Pub Co.
Morris, George, jt. auth. see Fox, Eddie.
Morris, George E. & Fox, H.Eddie. Faith-Sharing: Dynamic Christian Witnessing by Invitation. expanded rev. ed. LC 96-84197. 160p. 1996. pap. 15.95 (0-88177-158-9, DR158) Discipleship Res.
Morris, George E., jt. ed. see Fox, H. Eddie.
Morris, George G. & Foutz, Susan L. Lynchburg in the Civil War. (Virginia Civil War Battles & Leaders Ser.). (Illus.). 146p. 1984. 19.95 (0-930919-11-4) H E Howard.
Morris, George H. Hunter Seat Equitation. 3rd ed. 224p. 1985. 32.50 (0-385-41368-8) Doubleday.
Morris, George S. British Thought & Thinkers: From John of Salisbury & Roger Bacon to John Stuart Mill & Herbert Spencer. 1977. lib. bdg. 59.95 (0-8490-1557-X) Gordon Pr.
— Hegel's Philosophy of the State & of History: An Exposition. 2nd ed. LC 75-3287. reprint ed. 32.50 (0-404-59275-9) AMS Pr.
Morris, George S., tr. see Ueberweg, Friedrich.
Morris, George W., et al. Russian: Face to Face: Beginning. (RUS.). (YA). 1993. student ed. 13.95 (0-8442-4307-8, Natl Textbk Co) NTC Contemp Pub Co.
— Russian: Face to Face: Beginning. (RUS.). 496p. (YA). 1994. teacher ed. 46.50 (0-8442-4302-7, Natl Textbk Co) NTC Contemp Pub Co.
— Russian: Face to Face: Beginning. (RUS.). 200p. (YA). 1994. student ed. 9.95 (0-8442-4301-9, Natl Textbk Co) NTC Contemp Pub Co.
— Russian: Face to Face: Beginning. (RUS.). 496p. (YA). 1995. text 39.50 (0-8442-4300-0, Natl Textbk Co) NTC Contemp Pub Co.
— Russian: Face to Face: Beginning. (RUS.). (YA). 1995. audio 40.00 (0-8442-4303-5, Natl Textbk Co) NTC Contemp Pub Co.
Morris, Gerald. Prophecy, Poetry & Hosea. (JSOT Supplement Ser.: No. 219). 167p. 1996. 52.50 (1-85075-599-X, Pub. by Sheffield Acad) CUP Services.
***Morris, Gerald.** The Savage Damsel & the Dwarf. LC 99-16457. 224p. (YA). 2000. 15.00 (0-395-97126-8) HM.
Morris, Gerald. The Squire, His Knight & His Lady. LC 98-28718. 240p. (J). (gr. 5-9). 1999. 15.00 (0-395-91211-3) HM.
***Morris, Gerald.** The Squire's Tale. (Illus.). 224p. (YA). (gr. 7-12). 2000. mass mkt. 4.50 (0-440-22823-9, LLL BDD) BDD Bks Young Read.
Morris, Gerald. The Squire's Tale. LC 97-12447. 224p. (J). (gr. 7-12). 1998. 15.00 (0-395-86959-5) HM.
Morris, Gerald E. & Howland, Llewellyn, III. Yachting in America: A Bibliography. x, 398p. 1991. 29.95 (0-913372-49-8) Mystic Seaport.
***Morris, Gerard.** Windows NT Server Lab Manual. (Illus.). 256p. (C). 1999. pap. text 23.10 (1-57676-047-2) Scott Jones Pubng.
Morris, Gilbert. All That Glitters. LC 99-15297. 384p. 1999. 19.99 (1-58134-107-5) Crossway Bks.
— Arrow of the Almighty, Vol. 4. LC 97-21200. (Liberty Bell Ser.). 34p. 1997. pap. 9.99 (1-55661-568-X) Bethany Hse.
— Attack of the Amazons. LC 97-147223. (Seven Sleepers Ser.: No. 8). (J). 1996. pap. 5.99 (0-8024-3691-9, 612) Moody.
— The Battle of Lookout Mountain. LC 97-147254. (Bonnets & Bugles Ser.: No. 7). (J). (gr. 5-10). pap. 5.99 (0-8024-0917-2, 564) Moody.
Morris, Gilbert. Beginning of Sorrows: Emmeshed By Evil.... How Long Before America Is No More. Date not set. pap. text 12.99 (0-7852-7003-5) Nelson.
Morris, Gilbert. Beneath the Mockingbird's Wings, Vol. 4. LC 99-50633. (Spirit of Appalachia Ser.). 320p. 1999. pap. text 10.99 (1-55661-888-3) Bethany Hse.
— Beyond the Quiet Hills. LC 97-33829. (Spirit of Appalachia Ser.: No. 2). 352p. 1997. pap. 10.99 (1-55661-886-7) Bethany Hse.
— Beyond the River. LC 99-21835. (Far Fields Ser.). 1999. 24.95 (0-7862-1968-8, G K Hall & Co) Mac Lib Ref.
— Blockade Runner. LC 96-207833. (Bonnets & Bugles Ser.: No. 5). (J). (gr. 5-9). pap. 5.99 (0-8024-0915-6, 565) Moody.
— Boomtown, No. 4. 261p. 1992. pap. 9.99 (0-8423-7789-1) Tyndale Hse.
— Bring the Boys Home. (Bonnets & Bugles Ser.: No. 10). 128p. (J). (gr. 5-9). 1997. pap. 5.99 (0-8024-0920-2, 3) Moody.
***Morris, Gilbert.** The Buried Jewels, Vol. 2. (Too Smart Jones Ser.: Vol. 2). (Illus.). 125p. (J). (gr. 2-7). 1999. pap. 5.99 (0-8024-4026-6) Moody.
Morris, Gilbert. The Captive Bride. LC 87-15782. (House of Winslow Ser.: Bk. 2). 24p. (Orig.). 1987. pap. 9.99 (0-87123-978-7) Bethany Hse.
— Caves That Time Forgot. LC 95-221032. (Seven Sleepers Ser.: No. 4). (J). pap. 5.99 (0-8024-3684-6, 613) Moody.
— Chariots in the Smoke. LC 96-43215. (Appomattox Saga Ser.: No. 9). 350p. 1997. pap. 10.99 (0-8423-5553-7) Tyndale Hse.
***Morris, Gilbert.** City of the Cyborgs, Vol. 3. (Seven Sleepers the Lost Chronicles Ser.: Vol. 4). (Illus.). 144p. (J). (gr. 7-12). 2000. pap. 5.99 (0-8024-3670-6) Moody.
— Command the Sun. LC 99-50484. (Liberty Bell Ser.: 7). 2000. pap. 9.99 (1-55661-571-X) Bethany Hse.
Morris, Gilbert. A Covenant of Love. LC 92-5584. (Appomattox Saga Ser.: Vol. 1). 361p. 1992. pap. 10.99 (0-8423-5497-2) Tyndale Hse.
— The Crossed Sabres. (House of Winslow Ser.: No. 13). 32p. (Orig.). 1993. pap. 9.99 (1-55661-309-1) Bethany Hse.
— The Dangerous Voyage. LC 95-9620. (The Time Navigators Ser.: Vol. 1). 16p. (J). (gr. 4-6). 1995. pap. 5.99 (1-55661-395-4) Bethany Hse.
— Dixie & Bandit. LC 99-192099. (Dixie Morris Animal Adventure Ser.: No. 6). 128p. (J). (gr. 4-7). 1998. pap. 5.99 (0-8024-3368-5) Moody.
— Dixie & Blizzard. (Dixie Morris Animal Adventure Ser.: No. 9). (Illus.). 159p. (J). (gr. 4-7). 1999. pap. 5.99 (0-8024-3371-5) Moody.
— Dixie & Champ. (Dixie Morris Animal Adventure Ser.: No. 7). (Illus.). 185p. (J). (gr. 2-5). 1999. pap. 5.99 (0-8024-3369-3) Moody.
— Dixie & Dolly. (Dixie Morris Animal Adventure Ser.: No. 3). (J). (gr. 4-7). 1998. pap. 5.99 (0-8024-3365-0) Moody.
— Dixie & Flash. (Dixie Morris Animal Adventure Ser.: No. 10). (Illus.). 160p. (J). (gr. 4-7). 1999. pap. 5.99 (0-8024-3372-3) Moody.
— Dixie & Ivan. LC 98-206085. (Dixie Morris Animal Adventure Ser.: No. 5). (Illus.). 128p. (J). (gr. 4-7). 1998. pap. 5.99 (0-8024-3367-7) Moody.
— Dixie & Jumbo. (Dixie Morris Animal Adventure Ser.: No. 1). (Orig.). (J). (gr. 4-7). 1998. pap. 5.99 (0-8024-3363-4) Moody.
— Dixie & Perry. (Dixie Morris Animal Adventure Ser.: No. 8). (J). (gr. 4-7). 1999. pap. 5.99 (0-8024-3370-7) Moody.
— Dixie & Sandy. (Dixie Morris Animal Adventure Ser.: No. 4). (Orig.). (J). (gr. 4-7). 1998. pap. 5.99 (0-8024-3366-9) Moody.
— Dixie & Stripes. LC 98-155529. (Dixie Morris Animal Adventure Ser.: No. 2). (J). (gr. 4-7). 1998. pap. 5.99 (0-8024-3364-2) Moody.
— The Dixie Widow. (House of Winslow Ser.: Bk. 9). 32p. (Orig.). 1991. pap. 9.99 (1-55661-115-3) Bethany Hse.
— Drummer Boy at Bull Run. LC 96-167666. (Bonnets & Bugles Ser.: No. 1). (J). (gr. 5-9). pap. 5.99 (0-8024-0911-3, 566) Moody.
***Morris, Gilbert.** Edge of Honor. LC 99-89972. 400p. 2000. 16.99 (0-310-22589-2) Zondervan.
Morris, Gilbert. Empress of the Underworld. LC 96-207830. (Seven Sleepers Ser.: No. 6). (J). pap. 5.99 (0-8024-3686-2, 614) Moody.
— Encounter at Cold Harbor. LC 98-131575. (Bonnets & Bugles Ser.: No. 8). 160p. (J). 1997. pap. 5.99 (0-8024-0918-0, 567) Moody.
— Escape with the Dream Maker. LC 97-147264. (Seven Sleepers Ser.: No. 9). 168p. (J). 1997. pap. 5.99 (0-8024-3692-7, 615) Moody.
***Morris, Gilbert.** Fallen Stars, Bitter Waters. (Omega Trilogy Ser.: Vol. 2). 2000. pap. write for info. (0-7852-7001-9) Nelson.
Morris, Gilbert. Fields of Glory. (Wakefield Dynasty Ser.: Vol. 4). 1996. pap. 11.99 (0-8423-6229-0) Tyndale Hse.
— The Final Adversary. LC 92-16172. (House of Winslow Ser.: Bk. 12). 304p. (Orig.). 1992. pap. 9.99 (1-55661-261-3) Bethany Hse.
— The Final Kingdom. LC 97-202558. (Seven Sleepers Ser.: No. 10). (Illus.). 168p. (J). 1997. pap. 5.99 (0-8024-3693-5, 616) Moody.
— Fire over Atlanta. LC 98-108278. (Bonnets & Bugles Ser.: No. 9). 168p. (J). 1997. pap. 5.99 (0-8024-0919-9, 568) Moody.
— Flight of the Eagles. (Seven Sleepers Ser.: No. 1). (J). pap. 5.99 (0-8024-3681-1, 617) Moody.
***Morris, Gilbert.** Flying Cavalier. LC 99-6518. (House of Winslow Ser.). 288p. 1999. 9.99 (0-7642-2115-9) Bethany Hse.
Morris, Gilbert. The Gallant Boys of Gettysburg. LC 97-147271. (Bonnets & Bugles Ser.: No. 6). (J). (gr. 5-9). pap. 5.99 (0-8024-0916-4, 569) Moody.
— The Gallant Outlaw. LC 93-45364. (House of Winslow Ser.: No. 15). 288p. 1994. pap. 9.99 (1-55661-311-3) Bethany Hse.
— The Gate of His Enemies. LC 92-17784. (Appomattox Sage Ser.). 337p. 1992. 10.99 (0-8423-1069-X) Tyndale Hse.
— Gates of Neptune. (Seven Sleepers Ser.: No. 2). 180p. (J). pap. 5.99 (0-8024-3682-X, 618) Moody.
— A Gathering of Eagles. LC 98-20311. (Wakefield Dynasty Ser.). 1998. pap. 11.99 (0-8423-6237-1) Tyndale Hse.
— The Gentle Rebel. LC 88-18712. (House of Winslow Ser.: Vol. 4). 288p. (Orig.). 1988. pap. 9.99 (1-55661-006-8) Bethany Hse.
***Morris, Gilbert.** Glorious Prodigal. (House of Winslow Ser.: Vol. 24). (Illus.). 320p. (J). 2000. pap. 9.99 (0-7642-2116-7) Bethany Hse.
— Growing Little Women for Younger Girls. 2000. pap. 12.99 (0-8024-2942-4) Moody.
Morris, Gilbert. The Holy Warrior. (House of Winslow Ser.: Vol. 6). 288p. (Orig.). 1989. pap. 9.99 (1-55661-054-8) Bethany Hse.
— The Honorable Imposter. (House of Winslow Ser.: No. 1). 336p. 1987. pap. 9.99 (0-87123-933-7) Bethany Hse.
— House of Winslow, 4 vols. (House of Winslow Ser.). (Orig.). (YA). 1992. boxed set 49.99 (1-55661-768-2) Bethany Hse.
— House of Winslow, 5 vols., Vol. 1-5. (Orig.). 1992. boxed set 49.99 (1-55661-767-4) Bethany Hse.
— The House of Winslow, Vols. 11-15. (House of Winslow Ser.). 1994. pap., boxed set 49.99 (1-55661-782-8, 252782) Bethany Hse.
***Morris, Gilbert.** How to Write & Sell a Christian Novel. (Illus.). 1999. pap. 12.00 (1-892525-17-8) ACW Press.
Morris, Gilbert. The Indentured Heart. LC 87-34128. (House of Winslow Ser.: Vol. 3). 288p. 1988. pap. 9.99 (1-55661-003-3) Bethany Hse.
— The Iron Lady. LC 96-10058. (House of Winslow Ser.: Vol. 19). 32p. 1996. pap. 9.99 (1-55661-687-2) Bethany Hse.
— The Iron Lady. large type ed. LC 97-16328. (Inspirational Ser.). 522p. 1997. lib. bdg. 23.95 (0-7838-8221-1, G K Hall Lrg Type) Mac Lib Ref.
— Jeweled Spur. LC 94-27179. (House of Winslow Ser.). 34p. 1994. pap. 9.99 (1-55661-392-X) Bethany Hse.
***Morris, Gilbert.** Journey to Freedom. LC 00-9044. (Illus.). 272p. (J). (gr. 4-7). 2000. 12.99 (1-58134-191-1) Crossway Bks.
Morris, Gilbert. Land of the Shadow. LC 93-13781. (Appomattox Saga Ser.: Vol. 4). 338p. 1993. 10.99 (0-8423-5742-4) Tyndale Hse.
— The Last Confederate. (House of Winslow Ser.: Vol. 8). 336p. (Orig.). 1990. pap. 9.99 (1-55661-109-9) Bethany Hse.
— Liberty Bell. (Liberty Bell Ser.: Vols. 1-3). 1996. boxed set 29.99 (0-7642-8084-8) Bethany Hse.
— Lone Wolf. LC 95-7541. (Reno Western Saga Ser.: Vol. 6). 236p. 1995. pap. 7.99 (0-8423-1997-2) Tyndale Hse.
***Morris, Gilbert.** One by One. (A Dani Ross Mystery Ser.). Orig. Title: Guilt by Association. 288p. 2000. reprint ed. pap. 11.99 (1-58134-192-X) Crossway Bks.

An Asterisk (*) at the beginning of an entry indicates that the title is appearing for the first time.

Morris, Gilbert. Out of the Whirlwind. LC 93-35507. (Appomattox Saga Ser.: No. 5). (Illus.). 316p. 1994. pap. 8.99 (*0-8423-1658-2*) Tyndale Hse.

— The Pool Party Thief, Vol. 1. (Too Smart Jones Ser.: Vol. 1). (Illus.). 115p. (J). (gr. 2-7). 1999. pap. 5.99 (*0-8024-4025-8*) Moody.

— The Quality of Mercy. LC 93-32432. (Danielle Ross Mystery Ser.). 312p. (gr. 10). 1993. pap. 9.99 (*0-8007-5474-3*) Revell.

— Race Against Time. LC 97-21024. (Time Navigators Ser.: Bk. 3). 144p. (J). (gr. 6-9). 1997. pap. 5.99 (*1-55661-397-0*) Bethany Hse.

— The Ramparts of Heaven. LC 96-32142. (The Wakefield Dynasty Ser.: No. 5). 400p. 1997. pap. 10.99 (*0-8423-6233-9*) Tyndale Hse.

— The Reluctant Bridegroom. (House of Winslow Ser.: Vol. 7). 34p. (Orig.). 1990. pap. 9.99 (*1-55661-069-6*) Bethany Hse.

— The Remnant. LC 96-72369. (Far Fields Ser.: Bk. 2). 192p. 1997. pap. 9.95 (*0-914984-91-8*) Starburst.

***Morris, Gilbert.** The Remnant. large type ed. LC 99-38126. 255p. 1999. 23.95 (*0-7862-2144-5*) Mac Lib Ref.

Morris, Gilbert. Reno. LC 92-9438. (Jim Reno Westerns Ser.: Vol. 1). 258p. 1992. 9.99 (*0-8423-1058-4*) Tyndale Hse.

— Ride the Wild River. LC 92-9437. (Jim Reno Westerns Ser.: No. 3). Orig. Title: The Runaway. 339p. 1992. 9.99 (*0-8423-5795-5*) Tyndale Hse.

***Morris, Gilbert.** The Right Hand of God. LC 99-6388. Vol. 6. 320p. 1999. pap. text 9.99 (*1-55661-570-1*) Bethany Hse.

Morris, Gilbert. Rimrock. LC 92-9439. (Jim Reno Westerns Ser.: Vol. 2). 257p. 1992. 7.99 (*0-8423-1059-2*) Tyndale Hse.

— The Rough Rider. large type ed. LC 96-20904. 458p. 1996. lib. bdg. 22.95 (*0-7838-1853-X*, G K Hall Lrg Type) Mac Lib Ref.

— The Rough Rider, Vol. 18. LC 95-45280. (House of Winslow Ser.). 34p. 1995. pap. 9.99 (*1-55661-394-6*) Bethany Hse.

— The Saintly Buccaneer. LC 88-33337. (House of Winslow Ser.: Vol. 5). 34p. (Orig.). 1989. pap. 9.99 (*1-55661-048-3*) Bethany Hse.

***Morris, Gilbert.** Savage Game of Lord Zarak. LC 99-58292. (Seven Sleepers the Lost Chronicles Ser.). (YA). 2000. pap. 5.99 (*0-8024-3668-4*) Moody.

Morris, Gilbert. Secret of Richmond Manor. LC 95-221031. (Bonnets & Bugles Ser.: No. 3). (J). (gr. 5-9). pap. 5.99 (*0-8024-0913-X*, 570) Moody.

— The Shadow of His Wings. LC 94-28708. (Appomattox Saga Ser.: Vol. 6). 352p. 1994. pap. 10.99 (*0-8423-5987-7*) Tyndale Hse.

— The Shadow Portrait. LC 97-45452. (House of Winslow Ser.). 32p. 1998. pap. 9.99 (*1-55661-689-9*) Bethany Hse.

— The Shield of Honor. LC 94-45604. (Wakefield Dynasty Ser.: Vol. 3). 400p. 1995. pap. 11.99 (*0-8423-5930-3*) Tyndale Hse.

— The Silver Star, Vol. 20. LC 97-4647. (House of Winslow Ser.). 336p. 1997. pap. 9.99 (*1-55661-688-0*) Bethany Hse.

— The Soldier Boy's Discovery. LC 96-207835. (Bonnets & Bugles Ser.: No. 4). (J). (gr. 5-9). pap. 5.99 (*0-8024-0914-8*, 571) Moody.

— Song in a Strange Land. (Liberty Bell Ser.: Vol. 2). 32p. (Orig.). 1996. pap. 9.99 (*1-55661-566-3*) Bethany Hse.

— The Song of Princes. LC 97-22665. (The Wakefield Dynasty Ser.). 1997. pap. 11.99 (*0-8423-6234-7*) Tyndale Hse.

— Sound the Trumpet. (Liberty Bell Ser.: Bk. 1). 32p. 1995. pap. 9.99 (*1-55661-565-5*) Bethany Hse.

***Morris, Gilbert.** The Spell of the Crystal Chair. LC 99-58291. (Seven Sleepers the Lost Chronicles Ser.). (J). 2000. pap. 5.99 (*0-8024-3667-6*) Moody.

Morris, Gilbert. The Spirit of Appalachia. 1998. boxed set 32.99 (*0-7642-8386-3*) Bethany Hse.

— Stars in Their Courses, Vol. 8. LC 95-35086. (Appomattox Saga Ser.). 350p. 1995. pap. 10.99 (*0-8423-1674-4*) Tyndale Hse.

***Morris, Gilbert.** Strange Creatures of Dr. Korbo. (Seven Sleepers the Lost Chronicles Ser.: Vol. 3). 2000. pap. 5.99 (*0-8024-3669-2*) Moody.

Morris, Gilbert. Sword of Camelot. (Seven Sleepers Ser.: No. 3). (J). pap. 5.99 (*0-8024-3683-8*, 619) Moody.

***Morris, Gilbert.** Then There Were Two. LC 00-8983. (Dani Ross Mystery Ser.: Vol. 2). 288p. 2000. pap. 11.99 (*1-58134-193-8*) Crossway Bks.

— Through a Glass Darkly. LC 00-23516. (Inspirational Ser.). 2000. 28.95 (*0-7838-9009-5*, G K Hall Lrg Type) Mac Lib Ref.

— Through a Glass Darkly: A Novel. LC 99-6387. 288p. 1999. pap. 10.99 (*1-55661-145-5*) Bethany Hse.

— Too Smart Jones & the Cat's Secret. (Gilbert Morris Mysteries Ser.: Vol. 6). (J). 2000. pap. 5.99 (*0-8024-4030-4*) Moody.

— Too Smart Jones & the Dangerous Woman. (Gilbert Morris Mysteries Ser.: Vol. 4). (J). 2000. pap. 5.99 (*0-8024-4028-2*) Moody.

— Too Smart Jones & the Disappearing Dogs. (Gilbert Morris Mysteries Ser.: Vol. 3). (J). 2000. pap. 5.99 (*0-8024-4027-4*) Moody.

— Too Smart Jones & the Mysterious Artist. Vol. 8. (J). 2000. pap. 5.99 (*0-8024-4034-7*) Moody.

— Too Smart Jones & the Spooky Mansion. Vol. 7. 2000. pap. 5.99 (*0-8024-4033-9*) Moody.

— Too Smart Jones & the Stolen Bicycle. (Gilbert Morris Mysteries Ser.: Vol. 9). 128p. (J). (gr. 4-7). 2000. pap. 5.99 (*0-8024-4031-2*) Moody.

— Too Smart Jones & the Stranger in the Cave. (Gilbert Morris Mysteries Ser.: Vol. 5). (J). 2000. pap. 5.99 (*0-8024-4029-0*) Moody.

— Too Smart Jones & the Wilderness Mystery. (Gilbert Morris Mysteries Ser.: Vol. 10). 128p. (J). (gr. 4-7). 2000. pap. 5.99 (*0-8024-4032-0*) Moody.

Morris, Gilbert. Tread upon the Lion. (Liberty Bell Ser.: No. 3). 34p. 1996. pap. 9.99 (*1-55661-567-1*) Bethany Hse.

— The Union Belle. (House of Winslow Ser.: No. 11). 336p. (Orig.). 1992. pap. 9.99 (*1-55661-186-2*) Bethany Hse.

— The Valiant Gunman. LC 93-2416. (House of Winslow Ser.: Bk. 14). 32p. 1993. pap. 9.99 (*1-55661-310-5*) Bethany Hse.

— Valley Justice. LC 94-26129. (Reno Western Saga Ser.: Vol. 5). 256p. 1995. 7.99 (*0-8423-7756-5*) Tyndale Hse.

— Vanishing Clues. (Time Navigators Ser.: Vol. 2). 144p. (J). (gr. 6-9). 1996. pap. 5.99 (*1-55661-396-2*) Bethany Hse.

— Voyage of the Dolphin. LC 97-147222. (Seven Sleepers Ser.: No. 7). (J). pap. 5.99 (*0-8024-3687-0*, 620) Moody.

— Voyagers to Freedom. (The House of Winslow Ser.). 1997. 12.99 (*0-88486-167-8*) Arrowood Pr.

— Wall of Fire. LC 94-43872. (Appomattox Saga Ser.: Vol. 7). 352p. 1995. 10.99 (*0-8423-8126-0*) Tyndale Hse.

— Where Honor Dwells. LC 92-36469. (Appomattox Ser.: No. 3). 355p. 1993. pap. 10.99 (*0-8423-6799-3*) Tyndale Hse.

— White Hunter. (House of Winslow Ser.). 32p. 1999. pap. 9.99 (*1-55661-909-X*) Bethany Hse.

— Wind from the Wilderness. (Liberty Bell Ser.). 288p. 1998. pap. 9.99 (*1-55661-569-8*) Bethany Hse.

— The Winds of God. LC 94-28712. (Wakefield Dynasty Ser.: No. 2). 422p. 1994. pap. 11.99 (*0-8423-7953-3*) Tyndale Hse.

— Winged Raiders of the Desert. (Seven Sleepers Ser.: No. 5). (J). pap. 5.99 (*0-8024-3685-4*, 621) Moody.

— Witness in Heaven. LC 98-3705. (Appomattox Saga Ser.). 1998. pap. 8.99 (*0-8423-5552-9*) Tyndale Hse.

— Wounded Yankee. (House of Winslow Ser.: Bk. 10). 34p. (Orig.). 1991. pap. 9.99 (*1-55661-116-1*) Bethany Hse.

— Yankee Belles in Dixie. LC 95-171397. (Bonnets & Bugles Ser.: No. 2). (J). (gr. 5-9). pap. 5.99 (*0-8024-0912-1*, 572) Moody.

— The Yukon Queen. (House of Winslow Ser.: Bk. 17). 288p. (J). 1995. pap. 9.99 (*1-55661-393-8*) Bethany Hse.

Morris, Gilbert, ed. The Sword of Truth. LC 94-7013. (Wakefield Dynasty Ser.). 422p. 1994. pap. 8.99 (*0-8423-6228-2*) Tyndale Hse.

Morris, Gilbert & Ferguson, J. Landon. Above the Clouds. LC 99-16862. (Chronicles of the Golden Frontier Ser.: Bk. 3). 319p. 1999. pap. 11.99 (*1-58134-108-3*) Crossway Bks.

— Riches Untold. LC 98-17250. (Chronicles of the Golden Frontier Ser.: Vol. 1). 368p. 1998. pap. 11.99 (*1-58134-014-1*) Crossway Bks.

***Morris, Gilbert & Ferguson, J. Landon.** The Silver Thread. (Chronicles of the Golden Frontier Ser.: Bk. 4). 320p. 2000. pap. 11.99 (*1-58134-212-8*) Crossway Bks.

Morris, Gilbert & Ferguson, J. Landon. Unseen Riches. LC 98-51867. (Chronicles of the Golden Frontier Ser.: Bk. 2). 368p. 1999. pap. 11.99 (*1-58134-022-2*) Crossway Bks.

Morris, Gilbert & Funderburtk, Bobby. Beyond the River. LC 93-84016. (Far Fields Ser.: No. 1). 288p. 1994. pap. 8.95 (*0-914984-51-9*) Starburst.

***Morris, Gilbert & McCarver, Aaron.** Among the King's Soldiers. (Spirit of Appalachia Ser.: Vol. 3). 320p. 1998. pap. 10.99 (*1-55661-887-5*) Bethany Hse.

Morris, Gilbert & McCarver, Aaron. Over the Misty Mountains. LC 96-45907. (Spirit of Appalachia Ser.). 352p. 1997. pap. 10.99 (*1-55661-885-9*) Bethany Hse.

***Morris, Gilbert & Meeks, Dan, 2nd.** Attack of the Denebian Starship. (Daystar Voyages Ser.: No. 10). (Illus.). (YA). (gr. 5-8). 2000. pap. 5.99 (*0-8024-4114-9*) Moody.

Morris, Gilbert & Meeks, Dan, 2nd. Dangers of the Rainbow Nebula. 7th ed. (Daystar Voyages Ser.: No. 7). 143p. (YA). (gr. 5-8). 1999. pap. 5.99 (*0-8024-4111-4*) Moody.

— Dark Spell Over Morlandria. (Daystar Voyages Ser.: No. 4). (YA). (gr. 5-8). 1998. pap. 5.99 (*0-8024-4108-4*) Moody.

— Escape from The Red Comet. (Daystar Voyages Ser.: No. 3). (YA). (gr. 5-8). 1998. pap. 5.99 (*0-8024-4107-6*) Moody.

***Morris, Gilbert & Meeks, Dan, 2nd.** Frozen Space Pilot, Vol. 8. (Daystar Voyages Ser.: No. 8). (YA). (gr. 5-8). 1999. pap. 5.99 (*0-8024-4112-2*) Moody.

Morris, Gilbert & Meeks, Dan, 2nd. Invasion of the Killer Locusts. (Daystar Voyages Ser.: No. 6). 140p. (YA). (gr. 5-8). 1999. pap. 5.99 (*0-8024-4110-6*) Moody.

— Revenge of the Space Pirate. LC 99-182080. (Daystar Voyages Ser.: No. 5). 160p. (YA). (gr. 5-8). 1998. pap. 5.99 (*0-8024-4109-2*) Moody.

— Secret of the Planet Makon. (Daystar Voyages Ser.: No. 1). (YA). (gr. 5-8). 1998. pap. 5.99 (*0-8024-4105-X*) Moody.

***Morris, Gilbert & Meeks, Dan, 2nd.** White Dragon of Sharnu, Vol. 9. (Daystar Voyages Ser.: No. 9). (YA). (gr. 5-8). 1999. pap. 5.99 (*0-8024-4113-0*) Moody.

Morris, Gilbert & Meeks, Dan, 2nd. Wizards of the Galaxy. (Daystar Voyages Ser.: No. 2). (Orig.). (YA). 1998. pap. 5.99 (*0-8024-4106-8*) Moody.

***Morris, Gilbert & Morris, Lynn.** Driven with the Wind. (Cheney Duvall, MD Ser.: 8). 320p. 1999. pap. 10.99 (*1-55661-699-6*) Bethany Hse.

Morris, Gilbert & Morris, Lynn. Shadow of the Mountain. LC 94-32698. (Cheney Duvall, M. D. Ser.: No. 2). 336p. 1994. pap. 9.99 (*1-55661-423-3*) Bethany Hse.

Morris, Gilbert, et al. The Beginning of Sorrows. (Omega Trilogy Ser.: No. 1). 192p. 1999. pap. 12.99 (*0-7852-7000-0*) Nelson.

Morris, Gilbert, jt. auth. see Morris, Alan.

Morris, Gilbert, jt. auth. see Morris, Lynn.

Morris, Gillian S. & Deakin, Simon. Labour Law. 1995. pap. text. write for info. (*0-406-01025-0*, UK, MICHIE) LEXIS Pub.

Morris, Gillian S., jt. auth. see Fredman, Sandra.

Morris, Glen. Country Roads of North Carolina. LC 94-14329. (Country Roads Ser.). (Illus.). 140p. (Orig.). 1994. pap. 9.95 (*1-56626-067-1*, Cntry Rds Pr) NTC Contemp Pub Co.

Morris, Glen T. & Ryser, Rudolph C. Indian Self-Governance: Perspectives on the Political Status of Indian Nations in the United States of America. Minugh, Carol J., ed. (Fourth World Papers Ser.). (Illus.). vi, 135p. 1989. pap. 15.00 (*1-893710-00-9*) Ctr for World Studies.

Morris, Glenda, jt. auth. see Early, Howard.

***Morris, Glenn.** Martial Arts Madness: A User's Guide to the Esoteric Martial Arts. LC 98-36693. 1999. pap. text 14.95 (*1-883319-77-3*) Frog Ltd CA.

Morris, Glenn. North Carolina Beaches. LC 97-31528. (Illus.). 312p. 1998. pap. 18.95 (*0-8078-4683-X*) U of NC Pr.

— Path Notes of an American Ninja Master. LC 93-8031. 264p. (Orig.). 1993. pap. 16.95 (*1-55643-157-0*) North Atlantic.

— Shadow Strategies of an American Ninja Master. LC 95-923. 250p. (Orig.). (C). 1995. pap. 16.95 (*1-883319-29-3*) Frog Ltd CA.

— Small Gardens. LC 98-27336. (Taylor's Weekend Gardening Guides Ser.). 128p. 1999. pap. 14.00 (*0-395-86643-X*) HM.

***Morris, Glenn.** Small Gardens: How to Get the Most Impact from the Least Space. 1999. 25.25 (*0-8446-6996-2*) Peter Smith.

Morris, Glenn E., ed. Epitope Mapping Protocols. (Methods in Molecular Biology Ser.: Vol. 66). 432p. 1996. 79.50 (*0-89603-375-9*) Humana.

Morris, Glyn, jt. auth. see Morgan, Colin.

Morris, Gordon. EDP Auditing Guide. 1992. text 175.00 (*1-55520-206-3*, Irwn Prfssnl) McGraw-Hill Prof.

Morris, Gordon, ed. Shaw's Directory of Courts. (C). 1988. pap. 110.00 (*0-7219-0983-3*, Pub. by Scientific) St Mut.

— Shaw's Directory of Courts in the United Kingdom. (C). 1987. pap. 85.00 (*0-7219-0980-9*, Pub. by Scientific) St Mut.

Morris, Gouverneur. Diary of the French Revolution, 2 vols. Davenport, Beatrix C., ed. LC 70-110859. (Illus.). 1972. reprint ed. lib. bdg. 75.00 (*0-8371-4528-7*, MOFR) Greenwood.

— Diary of the French Revolution, 2 Vols., Set. Davenport, Beatrix C., ed. LC 71-157348. (Select Bibliographies Reprint Ser.). 1977. reprint ed. 72.95 (*0-8369-5809-8*) Ayer.

— Diary of the French Revolution, 2 vols, Vol. 1. Davenport, Beatrix C., ed. LC 70-110859. (Illus.). 1972. reprint ed. lib. bdg. 45.00 (*0-8371-4529-5*, MOFS) Greenwood.

— Diary of the French Revolution, 2 vols, Vol. 2. Davenport, Beatrix C., ed. LC 70-110859. (Illus.). 1972. reprint ed. lib. bdg. 45.00 (*0-8371-4530-9*, MOFT) Greenwood.

— Footprint, & Other Stories. LC 70-142270. (Short Story Index Reprint Ser.). 1977. 23.95 (*0-8369-3754-6*) Ayer.

— Incandescent Lily, & Other Stories. LC 73-142271. (Short Story Index Reprint Ser.). 1977. 20.95 (*0-8369-3755-4*) Ayer.

***Morris, Grace K.** How to Choose Stocks That Will Out Perform the Market (2000) 75p. 1999. pap. 48.50 (*0-9673224-0-5*) Astro Economics Inc.

Morris, Grant H. & Snyder, Allen C. Mental Disorder in the Criminal Process: Stan Stress & the Vietnam-Sports Conspiracy, 72. LC 92-21355. (Contributions in Legal Studies: No. 72). 324p. 1993. 65.00 (*0-313-28761-9*, GM8761, Greenwood Pr) Greenwood.

Morris, Greggory. Basketball Basics. LC 75-34142. (Illus.). (J). (gr. 2-6). 1979. 6.95 (*0-13-072256-1*) Simon & Schuster.

Morris, Gregory, et al. Bogey Golfer's Guide to Public Golf Courses in Southeast Michigan. (Illus.). 324p. (Orig.). 1995. pap. 13.95 (*0-9649822-0-X*) HMZ Pubng.

Morris, Gregory, jt. auth. see Baldwin, Dean R.

Morris, Gregory K. Zon. 367p. (Orig.). 1995. pap. text 14.99 (*0-9648617-0-4*) ThreeTG Pr.

Morris, Gregory L. Candlestick Charting Explained: Timeless Techniques for Trading Stocks & Futures. 2nd ed. 1995. per. 35.00 (*1-55738-891-1*, Irwn Prfssnl) McGraw-Hill Prof.

Morris, Gregory L. Frank Bergon. LC 97-70322. (Western Writers Ser: Vol. 126). 1997. pap. 4.95 (*0-88430-125-7*) Boise St U W Writ Ser.

Morris, Gregory L. Talking up a Storm: Voices of the New West. LC 93-46326. (Illus.). xix, 246p. 1994. pap. 12.00 (*0-8032-8224-9*, Bison Books) U of Nebr Pr.

Morris, Gregory L. & Jiahua, Fan. Reservoir Sedimentation Handbook: Design & Management of Dams, Reservoirs, & Watersheds for Sustainable Use. (Illus.). 848p. 1997. 95.00 (*0-07-043302-X*) McGraw.

Morris, Guy V. Airborne Pulsed Doppler Radar. LC 88-8094. (Artech House Radar Library). (Illus.). 460p. 1988. reprint ed. pap. 142.60 (*0-608-00573-8*, 206145600009) Bks Demand.

Morris, H. C., jt. ed. see Lam, Lui.

Morris, H. H. Demystifying the Congregational Budget. LC 88-70759. 62p. (Orig.). 1988. pap. 6.95 (*1-56699-066-1*, OD75) Alban Inst.

***Morris, H. Jerry.** Barnwell County, South Carolina. (Images of America Ser.). (Illus.). 128p. 1999. pap. 18.99 (*0-7524-1341-4*) Arcadia Publng.

Morris, H. R., ed. see Symposium on Advances in Mass Spectrometry Soft Io.

Morris, Hal. How to Stop Foreclosure. 192p. 1983. 14.95 (*0-8253-0146-7*) Beaufort Bks NY.

Morris-Hale, Walter. Conflict & Harmony in Multi-Ethnic Societies: An International Perspective. (Major Concepts in Politics & Political Theory Ser.: Vol. 9). 360p. (C). 1996. pap. text 39.95 (*0-8204-2837-X*) P Lang Pubng.

Morris, Harold. Duplamente Perdoado.Tr. of Twice Pardoned. (POR.). 240p. 1990. pap. 9.95 (*0-8297-1629-7*) Vida Pubs.

— The Law of the Harvest: An Inspirational & Instructional Guide to Help Today's Teenagers Take Charge of Their Lives LC 98-90158. 112p. (YA). 1998. write for info. (*0-9662718-1-5*) Nantucket Publ.

— Unshackled, Vol. 1. LC 98-90159. 336p. 1998. 24.99 (*0-9662718-0-7*) Nantucket Publ.

Morris, Harry. Birth, & Copulation, & Death. LC 79-94804. 68p. reprint ed. pap. 30.00 (*0-7837-5079-X*, 204477700004) Bks Demand.

— Last Things in Shakespeare. LC 85-1453. (Illus.). 360p. 1985. reprint ed. pap. 111.60 (*0-608-04493-8*, 206523800001) Bks Demand.

— Richard Barnfield: Colin's Child. LC 63-63443. (Florida State University Studies: No. 38). 217p. reprint ed. pap. 67.30 (*0-7837-4928-7*, 204459400004) Bks Demand.

— The Sorrowful City. LC 65-29103. 63p. 1965. reprint ed. pap. 30.00 (*0-608-04491-1*, 206523600001) Bks Demand.

Morris, Helen. Can You Do This? large type ed. (Illus.). 8p. (J). (gr. k-3). 1999. pap. text 14.50 (*1-58084-154-6*) Lower Kuskokwim.

— Enemni (My House) large type ed. (ESK., Illus.). 8p. (J). (gr. k-3). 1999. pap. text 17.00 (*1-58084-158-9*) Lower Kuskokwim.

— Enka (My House) large type ed. (ESK., Illus.). 8p. (J). (gr. k-3). 1999. pap. text 17.00 (*1-58084-159-7*) Lower Kuskokwim.

— Kuaten-qa Pituten? (Can You Do This?) large type ed. (ESK., Illus.). 8p. (J). (gr. k-3). 1999. pap. text. write for info. (*1-58084-156-2*) Lower Kuskokwim.

— My House. large type ed. (Illus.). 8p. (J). (gr. k-3). 1999. pap. text 17.00 (*1-58084-157-0*) Lower Kuskokwim.

— Portrait of a Chef. (Midway Reprint Ser.). (Illus.). xii, 222p. 1993. reprint ed. pap. text 7.95 (*0-226-54000-6*) U Ch Pr.

— The Stencilled Home: 13 Themed Room Styles. LC 98-43319. (Illus.). 192p. 1999. 32.50 (*0-87951-915-0*, Pub. by Overlook Pr) Penguin Putnam.

— Waten-qaa Piyagngauten? (Can You Do This?) large type ed. (ESK., Illus.). 8p. (J). (gr. k-3). 1999. pap. text. write for info. (*1-58084-155-4*) Lower Kuskokwim.

***Morris, Henriette Hampton.** Sisters in Love. LC 99-46889. 300p. 1999. 20.00 (*1-887714-49-9*) Summerhse Pr.

— Sisters in Love. 2000. 20.00 (*1-57003-391-9*) U of SC Pr.

Morris, Henry. Amostra de Salmos. Orig. Title: Sampling the Psalms. (POR.). 180p. 1986. pap. 7.95 (*0-8297-0698-4*) Vida Pubs.

— The Bible, Science & Creation. 1991. pap. 1.99 (*0-8474-0868-X*) Back to Bible.

***Morris, Henry.** Biblical Creationism: What Each Book of the Bible Teaches about Creation & the Flood. LC 00-100197. 276p. 2000. pap. 12.99 (*0-89051-293-0*) Master Bks.

— Defending the Faith: Upholding Biblical Christianity & the Genesis Record. LC 99-66473. 256p. 1999. pap. 11.99 (*0-89051-324-4*) Master Bks.

Morris, Henry. The Heavens Declare the Glory of God. LC 97-60498. 384p. 1997. 14.99 (*0-529-10829-1*, HVN10) World Publng.

***Morris, Henry.** Long War Against God: The History & Impact of the Creation/Evolution Conflict. LC 00-100214. 344p. 2000. pap. 13.99 (*0-89051-291-4*) Master Bks.

— Remarkable Record of Job. LC 00-100213. 150p. 2000. pap. 8.99 (*0-89051-292-2*) Master Bks.

Morris, Henry, ed. Proceedings of the 10th Annual Control Engineering Conference: Held As Part of the Control Engineering Conference & Exposition, O'Hare Exposition Center, Rosemont, IL May 21-23, 1991. (Illus.). 500p. (Orig.). (C). 1991. pap. write for info. (*0-914331-60-4*, Control Engrng) Cahners Busn Des Plaines.

Morris, Henry F. Some Perspectives of East African History. 27p. 1970. write for info. (*91-7106-004-9*, Pub. by Nordic Africa) Transaction Pubs.

Morris, Henry L., jt. auth. see Phillips, Arthur.

Morris, Henry M. The Beginning of the World. LC 93-168745. 184p. 1991. reprint ed. pap. 8.95 (*0-89051-162-4*) Master Bks.

— The Bible Has the Answer. 260p. (YA). (gr. 10). 1971. pap. 11.99 (*0-8010-5905-4*) Baker Bks.

— The Biblical Basis of Modern Science. LC 84-72122. 520p. 1985. 29.99 (*0-8010-6178-4*) Baker Bks.

— Christian Education for the Real World. LC 77-78017. 296p. 1991. reprint ed. pap. 10.95 (*0-89051-160-8*) Master Bks.

— Creation & the Second Coming. LC 92-221626. 194p. 1991. pap. 10.95 (*0-89051-163-2*) Master Bks.

— Evolution & the Modern Christian. 1967. pap. 4.99 (*0-87552-337-4*) P & R Pubng.

— The Genesis Record: A Scientific & Devotional Commentary on the Book of Beginnings. LC 76-2265. 720p. 1976. 29.99 (*0-8010-6004-4*) Baker Bks.

***Morris, Henry M.** God Who is Real. 2000. pap. 9.99 (*0-89051-299-X*) Master Bks.

Morris, Henry M. Many Infallible Proofs: Evidences for the Christian Faith. LC 74-81484. 400p. 1997. pap. 11.95 (*0-89051-005-9*) Master Bks.

— Men of Science, Men of God. rev. ed. LC 82-70271. (Illus.). 107p. (YA). (gr. 7 up). 1988. pap. 7.95 (*0-89051-080-6*) Master Bks.

— The Revelation Record. 521p. 1983. 24.99 (*0-8423-5511-1*) Tyndale Hse.

— Science & the Bible. expanded rev. ed. pap. 9.99 (*0-8024-0656-4*, 278) Moody.
— Scientific Creationism. LC 74-14160. 281p. 1998. pap. 10.95 (*0-89051-003-2*) Master Bks.
— Scientific Creationism - Chinese Edition. Han, Paul, tr. (CHI.). 223p. 1997. pap. 8.50 (*1-56582-039-8*) Christ Renew Min.
— That Their Words May Be Used Against Them. LC 97-75947. 488p. 1998. boxed set 21.95 (*0-89051-228-0*) Master Bks.
Morris, Henry M., ed. Proceedings of the 9th Annual Control Engineering Conference: Held as Part of the Control Engineering Conference & Exposition, O'Hare Exposition Center, Rosemont, Illinois, May 22-24, 1990. (Illus.). 500p. (Orig.). (C). 1990. pap. text 120.00 (*0-914331-59-0*, Control Engrng) Cahners Busn Des Plaines.
Morris, Henry M., et al, eds. Advanced Control in Computer Integrated Manufacturing. (Proceedings of the 13th. Annual Advanced Control Conference). 200p. 1987. 30.00 (*0-931682-23-1*) Purdue U Pubns.
Morris, Henry M. & Clark, Martin E. The Bible Has the Answer. rev. ed. LC 76-20206. 394p. 1996. pap. 11.95 (*0-89051-018-0*) Master Bks.
Morris, Henry M. & Morris, John M. The Modern Creation Trilogy: Scripture & Creation; Science & Creation; Society & Creation, 3 vols. 1996. pap. 34.95 incl. cd-rom (*0-89051-216-7*, MCTSTP) Master Bks.
Morris, Henry M. & Parker, Gary. What Is Creation Science? rev. ed. LC 82-70114. (Illus.). 332p. 1987. pap. 11.95 (*0-89051-081-4*) Master Bks.
Morris, Henry M. & Wiggert, James M. Applied Hydraulics in Engineering. 2nd ed. 640p. 1972. text 103.95 (*0-471-06669-9*); pap. text, suppl. ed. 3.00 (*0-471-07503-5*) Wiley.
Morris, Henry M., jt. auth. see Whitcomb, John C.
Morris, Henry M., jt. auth. see Whitcomb, John C., Jr.
Morris, Henry M., jt. auth. see Whitcomb, John C.
***Morris, Herbert.** What Was Lost: Poems. LC 99-87231. 128p. 2000. text 21.00 (*1-58243-064-0*, Pub. by Counterpt DC) HarpC.
Morris, Herbert, ed. Freedom & Responsibility: Readings in Philosophy & Law. LC 61-8469. 557p. 1961. reprint ed. pap. 30.00 (*0-7837-2163-3*, 204246900004) Bks Demand.
Morris, Holly. A Different Angle: Fly Fishing Stories by Women. (Orig.). 1996. pap. 12.00 (*0-425-15134-4*) Berkley Pub.
Morris, Holly, ed. A Different Angle: Fly Fishing Stories by Women. (Illus.). 232p. (Orig.). 1998. mass mkt. 6.99 (*0-425-16187-0*) Berkley Pub.
— A Different Angle: Fly Fishing Stories by Women. LC 94-39386. 288p. (Orig.). 1995. 22.95 (*1-878067-63-X*) Seal Pr WA.
— Uncommon Waters: Women Write about Fishing. 2nd rev. ed. LC 91-21455. (Adventura Bks.). (Illus.). 320p. (Orig.). 1998. pap. 18.95 (*1-878067-76-1*) Seal Pr WA.
Morris, Humphrey, jt. ed. see Smith, Joseph H.
Morris, Huw & Willey, Brian. The Corporate Environment: A Guide for Human Resource Managers. 320p. (Orig.). 1996. pap. 64.50 (*0-273-61604-8*, Pub. by Pitman Pub) Trans-Atl Phila.
Morris, I., jt. auth. see Powell, B. B.
Morris, Ian. Archaeology as Cultural History: Words & Things in Iron Age Greece. LC 99-19855. (Social Archaeology Ser.). (Illus.). 400p. 1999. pap. text 34.95 (*0-631-19602-1*) Blackwell Pubs.
***Morris, Ian.** Archaeology as Cultural History: Words & Things in Iron Age Greece. LC 99-19855. (Social Archaeology Ser.). (Illus.). 400p. (C). 1999. text 69.95 (*0-631-17409-5*) Blackwell Pubs.
Morris, Ian. Death-Ritual & Social Structure in Classical Antiquity. (Key Themes in Ancient History Ser.). (Illus.). 284p. (C). 1992. pap. text 22.95 (*0-521-37611-4*) Cambridge U Pr.
Morris, Ian, ed. Classical Greece: Ancient Histories & Modern Archaeologies. LC 93-6625. (New Directions in Archaeology Ser.). (Illus.). 258p. (C). 1994. pap. text 23.95 (*0-521-45678-9*) Cambridge U Pr.
Morris, Ian, jt. auth. see Ross, Sydney.
Morris, Inez, jt. auth. see Morris, Dan.
Morris, Irvin. From the Glittering World: A Navajo Story. LC 96-31861. (American Indian Literature & Critical Studies Ser.: No. 22). (Illus.). 272p. 1997. 24.95 (*0-8061-2895-X*) U of Okla Pr.
***Morris, Irvin.** From the Glittering World: A Navajo Story. 272p. 2000. pap. text 12.95 (*0-8061-3242-6*) U of Okla Pr.
Morris, Irvin, jt. ed. see Eteitly, Henry.
Morris, Irwin L. Congress, the President & the Federal Reserve: The Politics of American Monetary Policymaking. LC 99-15912. 190p. 2000. text 39.50 (*0-472-10995-2*, 10995) U of Mich Pr.
Morris, Ivan. Modern Japanese Stories: An Anthology. LC 61-11971. (Illus.). 512p. 1977. pap. 16.95 (*0-8048-1226-8*) Tuttle Pubng.
— The Nobility of Failure: Tragic Heroes in the History of Japan. (Noonday Ser.). 500p. 1988. pap. 17.00 (*0-374-52120-4*) FS&G.
— The World of the Shining Prince: Court Life in Ancient Japan. De Angelis, Paul, ed. LC 94-14929. 352p. 1994. pap. 15.00 (*1-56836-029-0*) Kodansha.
Morris, Ivan, ed. Madly Singing in the Mountains: An Appreciation & Anthology of Arthur Waley. 404p. 1981. reprint ed. pap. 9.95 (*0-916870-35-9*) Creat Arts Bk.
Morris, Ivan, tr. from JPN. The Pillow Book of Sei Shonagon. 411p. 1991. pap. text 19.00 (*0-231-07337-2*) Col U Pr.
Morris, Ivan, ed. & tr. see Saikaku, Ihara.
Morris, Ivan, tr. see Mishima, Yukio, pseud.
Morris, Ivan, tr. see Oe, Kenzaburo, ed.
Morris, Ivan, tr. see Ooka, Shohei.
Morris, Ivan, tr. see Osaragi, Jiro.
Morris, Ivan, tr. see Sarashina, Lady.
Morris, Ivan, tr. & intro. see Sarashina, Lady.
Morris, J., ed. Computer Architecture '98: Proceedings of the 3rd Australasian Computer Architecture Conference - ACAC'98. 250p. 1998. pap. 59.95 (*981-3083-93-X*) Spr-Verlag.
***Morris, J., ed.** Computer Architecture '99: Proceedings of the 4th Australasian Conference on Computer Architecture (ACAC'99) 270p. 1999. 69.95 (*981-4021-57-1*) Spr-Verlag.
***Morris, J. & Morton, P.** Through the Classroom Window. large type unabridged ed. 2000. 25.95 (*0-7531-5705-5*, 157055, Pub. by ISIS Lrg Prnt) ISIS Pub.
Morris, J. A. & Baloyra, Enrique A. Conflict & Change in Cuba. LC 93-2426. 347p. 1993. pap. 10.95 (*0-8263-1465-1*) U of NM Pr.
Morris, J. Bayard, tr. Hernando Cortes: Five Letters. Orig. Title: Hernando Cortes Five Letters, 1519-1526. (C). 1991. pap. 13.95 (*0-393-09877-X*) Norton.
Morris, J. Bayard, tr. see Cortes, Hernan.
Morris, J. C., tr. see Lilie, Ralph-J.
Morris, J. E. The Felt Genealogy: A Record of the Descendants of George Felt of Casco Bay. 568p. 1989. reprint ed. pap. 87.00 (*0-8328-0543-2*); reprint ed. lib. bdg. 97.00 (*0-8328-0542-4*) Higginson Bk Co.
— The Welsh Wars of Edward I. (History Paperback Ser.). 352p. 1998. 70.00 (*0-7509-1168-9*, Pub. by Sutton Pub Ltd); pap. 24.95 (*0-7509-1824-1*, Pub. by Sutton Pub Ltd) Intl Pubs Mktg.
Morris, J. F. A Genealogical & Historical Register of the Descendants of Edward Morris of Roxbury, Massachusetts, & Woodstock, Connecticut. (Illus.). 423p. 1989. reprint ed. pap. 66.50 (*0-8328-0883-0*); reprint ed. lib. bdg. 76.50 (*0-8328-0882-2*) Higginson Bk Co.
Morris, J. G., et al, eds. Aluminum Alloys for Packaging: Proceedings of a Symposium Sponsored by the Structural Materials Division (SMD), Non-Ferrous Metals Committee, Held at Materials Week '92 in Chicago, IL, November 1-5, 1992. LC 93-78188. 407p. 1993. reprint ed. pap. 126.20 (*0-608-03820-2*, 206278200004) Bks Demand.
— Aluminum Alloys for Packaging II: A Collection of Papers from the 1996 TMS Annual Meeting & Exhibition in Anaheim, California, February 4-8, 1996. (Illus.). 273p. 1996. 100.00 (*0-87339-292-2*, 2922) Minerals Metals.
Morris, J. G., ed. see Metallurgical Society of AIME Staff.
Morris, J. G., ed. see Minerals, Metals & Materials Society Staff.
Morris, J. Gareth, jt. ed. see Rose, A. H.
Morris, J. H. & North, P. M. Cases & Materials on Private International Law. 786p. 1984. pap. text 68.00 (*0-406-25265-3*, UK, MICHIE) LEXIS Pub.
Morris, J. L., jt. auth. see Rushforth, J. M.
Morris, J. M., et al, eds. Fourth Refinement Workshop: Proceedings of the 4th Refinement Workshop Organised by BCS-FACS 9-11 January 1991, Cambridge, UK. (Workshops in Computing Ser.). (Illus.). viii, 479p. 1991. 59.00 (*0-387-19657-9*) Spr-Verlag.
Morris, J. N. Religion & Urban Change: Croydon, 1840-1914. LC 92-27759. (Royal Historical Society: Studies in History: No. 65). (Illus.). 248p. (C). 1993. 75.00 (*0-86193-222-6*, Royal Historical Soc) Boydell & Brewer.
Morris, J. R. Year 2000 Personal Protection Guide: How to Protect Your Assets, Identity, & Credit from the Upcoming Millenium Bug Computer Crisis. 2nd rev. ed. 178p. 1999. pap. 21.95 (*0-9663988-6-6*) Sterlingmoor Pub.
— Year 2000: Personal Protection Guide - How to Protect Your Assets, Identity, & Credit from the "Millennium Bug" Computer Crisis. LC 98-85167. (Illus.). 220p. 1998. pap. 21.95 (*0-9663988-3-1*) Sterlingmoor Pub.
Morris, J. S., jt. auth. see Friedman, Manis.
Morris, J. Scott. Real Estate Tax Forms. LC 80-84025. 1981. 65.00 (*0-316-58382-0*, Aspen Law & Bus) Aspen Pub.
— Real Estate Tax Planning. 1977. 65.00 (*0-316-58390-1*, Aspen Law & Bus) Aspen Pub.
Morris, Jack. Crime Analysis Charting. (Illus.). 116p. 1994. pap. 17.00 (*0-912479-01-9*) Palmer Pr.
— The Criminal Intelligence File. (Illus.). 100p. 1992. 20.00 (*0-912479-00-0*) Palmer Pr.
— The Deadly Routine. LC 80-82429. (Illus.). 154p. 1980. pap. 17.00 (*0-912479-04-3*) Palmer Pr.
— Master Criminals among the Gypsies. (Illus.). 200p. 1994. text 20.00 (*0-912479-11-6*) Palmer Pr.
— Police Informant Management. LC 83-63214. (Illus.). 95p. 1983. pap. 15.00 (*0-912479-02-7*) Palmer Pr.
Morris, Jack, jt. auth. see Frost, Charles C.
Morris, Jack J. Disaster Zone - U.S.A. LC 90-85799. 192p. (Orig.). 1991. pap. text. write for info. (*0-9628670-0-4*) Avanti Pub Hse.
Morris, Jackie. Bears, Bears & More Bears. LC 94-42980. (Illus.). 32p. (J). (ps-2). 1995. 12.95 (*0-8120-6516-6*); pap. 4.95 (*0-8120-9349-6*) Barron.
— Bears, Bears & More Bears. 1995. 10.15 (*0-606-08696-X*, Pub. by Turtleback) Demco.
Morris, Jackie. Stories from the Stars: Greek Myths of the Zodiac. (Abbeville Anthologies Ser.). 80p. (J). (ps-3). 1996. pap. 10.98 (*0-89660-105-6*, Artabras) Abbeville Pr.
Morris, Jackie, jt. auth. see Lewis, Sian.
***Morris, Jaclynn & Fair, Paul L.** From Me to You: The Reluctant Writer's Guide to Powerful, Personal Messages. 192p. 2000. pap. 14.99 (*1-58297-004-1*, Wrtrs Digest Bks) F & W Pubns Inc.
Morris, James. Heaven's Command: An Imperial Progress. LC 79-24327. (Illus.). 564p. 1980. pap. 16.00 (*0-15-640006-5*, Harvest Bks) Harcourt.
— Pax Britannica: The Climax of an Empire. LC 79-24725. (Illus.). 552p. 1980. pap. 16.00 (*0-15-671466-3*, Harvest Bks) Harcourt.
— The World of Venice. rev. ed. LC 73-18461. (Illus.). 336p. (C). 1995. reprint ed. pap. 15.00 (*0-15-698356-7*, Harvest Bks) Harcourt.
Morris, James, jt. auth. see Kish, Joseph L.
Morris, James A. History of U. S. Navy: An Illustrated History. 1984. 14.98 (*0-671-06980-2*) S&S Trade.
Morris, James C. The Pattern. LC 96-61875. 144p. (Orig.). 1997. pap. 10.99 (*1-883893-93-3*) WinePress Pub.
Morris, James E., ed. Electronics Packaging Forum: Multichip Module Technology Issues. LC 93-23146. (Illus.). 400p. 1993. text 79.95 (*0-7803-0439-X*, PC03368) Inst Electrical.
Morris, James E., et al. Village, Town & District Courts in New York. LC 95-80836. 700p. 1995. text. write for info. (*0-7620-0016-3*); pap. text. write for info. (*0-7620-0017-1*) West Group.
Morris, James G., ed. see AIME, Metallurgical Society Staff.
Morris, James H., jt. ed. see Esiri, Margaret M.
Morris, James M. America's Armed Forces: A History. 2nd ed. LC 95-19261. 408p. 1995. pap. text 56.00 (*0-13-310780-9*) P-H.
— Jailhouse Journalism: The Fourth Estate Behind Bars. LC 97-40846. (Illus.). 261p. 1998. lib. bdg. 39.95 (*0-7864-0420-5*) McFarland & Co.
Morris, James M., ed. Legacies of Woodrow Wilson. LC 94-47449. 1995. pap. write for info. (*0-943875-70-6*) W Wilson Ctr Pr.
— On Mozart. (Woodrow Wilson Center Press Ser.). (Illus.). 260p. (C). 1994. text 54.95 (*0-521-47065-X*); pap. text 18.95 (*0-521-47661-5*) Cambridge U Pr.
Morris, James M. & Adler, Laura, eds. Grant Seekers Guide. 5th rev. ed. 600p. 1998. pap. 39.95 (*1-55921-220-9*) Moyer Bell.
Morris, James M. & Kearns, Patricia M. Historical Dictionary of the United States Navy. LC 97-44805. (Historical Dictionaries of War, Revolution, & Civil Unrest Ser.: No. 4). 488p. 1998. 85.00 (*0-8108-3406-5*) Scarecrow.
Morris, James M., ed. see Jefferson, Thomas.
Morris, James O. Conflict Within the AFL, Vol. 10--10. LC 73-22506. (Cornell Studies in Industrial & Labor Relations: Vol. 10). 319p. 1974. reprint ed. lib. bdg. 75.00 (*0-8371-6371-4*, MOCA, Greenwood Pr) Greenwood.
Morris, James P. History of the U. S. Army. 1987. 14.98 (*0-671-08191-8*) S&S Trade.
Morris, James W. K. N. Pepper. LC 73-166813. 1971. reprint ed. 29.00 (*0-403-01458-1*) Scholarly.
Morris, Jan. Among the Cities. LC 85-13739. 410p. 1985. text 25.00 (*0-19-520489-1*) OUP.
Morris, Jan. Building Hong Kong. (Illus.). 124p. 1997. 40.00 (*962-7283-04-5*, Pub. by FormAsia) Weatherhill.
Morris, Jan. Conundrum. LC 87-8668. 192p. 1995. pap. 9.95 (*0-8050-0361-4*, Owl) H Holt & Co.
***Morris, Jan.** Coronation Everest. LC 99-59691. (Illus.). 150p. 2000. reprint ed. pap. 14.95 (*1-58080-047-5*) Burford Bks.
Morris, Jan. Fifty Years of Europe: An Album. LC 97-19926. 384p. 1997. 24.00 (*0-679-41610-2*) Villard Books.
— Fifty Years of Europe: An Album LC 99-174813. 376 p. 1997. write for info. (*0-670-86387-4*) Viking Penguin.
— Hong Kong. LC 97-139297. 1997. pap. 15.00 (*0-679-77648-6*) Random.
— Hong Kong. 1989. pap. 15.00 (*0-679-72486-9*) Vin Bks.
— Lincoln. 1999. 0.00 (*0-375-50159-2*) Random.
***Morris, Jan.** Lincoln: A Foreigner's Quest. LC 99-48516. 208p. 2000. 23.00 (*0-684-85515-1*) S&S Trade.
— Lincoln, a Foreigner's Quest. LC 00-37745. 2000. pap. write for info. (*0-7862-2624-2*) Thorndike Pr.
Morris, Jan. Manhattan 'Forty-Five. 288p. 1990. reprint ed. pap. 9.95 (*0-19-506664-2*) OUP.
— Manhattan, 1945. LC 98-12937. 286p. 1998. reprint ed. pap. 15.95 (*0-8018-5957-3*) Johns Hopkins.
— Over Europe. Earley, Mary-Dawn & Frasier, Jane, eds. (Illus.). 288p. 1995. reprint ed. 45.00 (*1-887451-00-5*) Wldon Owen Ref.
— Oxford. 3rd ed. (Illus.). 304p. 1988. pap. 13.95 (*0-19-282065-6*) OUP.
— The Princeship of Wales. Stephens, Meic, ed. (Changing Wales Ser.). 32p. 1995. pap. 11.95 (*0-8464-4717-7*) Beekman Pubs.
Morris, Jan, et al. Hong Kong: Return to the Heart of the Dragon: A Photographic & Literary Tribute to Hong Kong & Macau. (Illus.). 288p. 1995. 40.00 (*0-7892-0040-6*, Cross Riv Pr) Abbeville Pr.
Morris, Jane. Duke - Symes Familiy. (Illus.). 264p. 1996. reprint ed. pap. 41.00 (*0-8328-5404-2*); reprint ed. lib. bdg. 51.00 (*0-8328-5403-4*) Higginson Bk Co.
Morris, Jane A. Not in My Backyard: The Handbook. LC 94-8052. 300p. (Orig.). 1994. pap. 14.95 (*0-9624945-7-7*) Silvercat Pubns.
Morris, Janet. Facing AD/HD: A Survival Guide for Parents of Children with Attention Deficit/Hyperactivity Disorder. LC 98-66602. 232p. 1998. pap. text 14.95 (*0-87822-381-9*) Res Press.
Morris, Janet & Drake, David. Active Measures. 1985. pap. 3.95 (*0-671-55945-1*) S&S Trade.
Morris, Janet E., jt. auth. see Morris, Charles W.
***Morris, Janita.** The Soapmaker: Natural Handmade Soap from Your Kitchen. (Illus.). 128p. 2000. pap. 19.95 (*0-8230-4866-7*) Watsn-Guptill.
Morris, Jeannie. Brian Piccolo: A Short Season. 25th ed. (Illus.). 159p. 1995. pap. 12.95 (*1-56625-024-2*) Bonus Books.
Morris, Jeff. Petroleum Geology & Reservoirs: Oil Well Servicing & Workover, Lesson 2. 2nd ed. (Illus.). 116p. (Orig.). 1992. pap. text 16.00 (*0-88698-156-5*, 3.70220) PETEX.
Morris, Jeff, et al. Practical Petroleum Geology. Leecraft, Jodie, ed. (Illus.). 234p. (Orig.). 1985. pap. text 35.00 (*0-88698-097-6*, 1.00210) PETEX.
Morris, Jeffrey, ed. see Lincoln, Abraham.
Morris, Jeffrey B. The FDR Way. LC 95-12575. (Great Presidential Decisions Ser.). (Illus.). (J). (gr. 5 up). 1996. lib. bdg. 23.93 (*0-8225-2929-7*, Lerner Publctns) Lerner Pub.
— The Jefferson Way. LC 94-923. (Great Presidential Decisions Ser.). (Illus.). 112p. (YA). (gr. 5 up). 1994. lib. bdg. 23.93 (*0-8225-2926-2*, Lerner Publctns) Lerner Pub.
— The Reagan Way. LC 94-24644. (Illus.). 124p. (J). (gr. 6-9). 1995. lib. bdg. 23.93 (*0-8225-2931-9*, Lerner Publctns) Lerner Pub.
— The Truman Way. (Great Presidential Decisions Ser.). (Illus.). 128p. (YA). (gr. 5 up). 1994. lib. bdg. 23.93 (*0-8225-2927-0*, Lerner Publctns) Lerner Pub.
— The Washington Way. (Great Presidential Decisions Ser.). (Illus.). 128p. (J). (gr. 5 up). 1994. lib. bdg. 23.93 (*0-8225-2928-9*, Lerner Publctns) Lerner Pub.
Morris, Jeffrey B. & Martin, George W. Making Sure We Are True to Our Founders: The Association of the Bar of the City of New York, 1970-95. LC 96-53943. 1997. 30.00 (*0-8232-1738-8*) Fordham.
Morris, Jeffrey B., jt. ed. see Morris, Richard B.
Morris, Jeffrey W., jt. auth. see Drake, William.
Morris, Jeffrey W., jt. auth. see Whaley, Douglas J.
Morris, Jenny. Encounters with Strangers. 240p. 1999. pap. 17.95 (*0-7043-4400-9*, Pub. by Womens Press) Trafalgar.
***Morris, Jenny.** Having Someone Who Cares? Barriers to Change in the Public Care of Children. 72p. 2000. pap. 19.95 (*1-900990-56-3*, Pub. by Natl Childrens Bur) Paul & Co Pubs.
Morris, Jenny. The Shape of Things to Come? User-Led Social Services. 1994. pap. 35.00 (*0-902789-94-5*, Pub. by Natl Inst Soc Work) St Mut.
— Women Workers & the Sweated Trades: The Origins of Minimum Wage Legislation. 256p. 1986. text 78.95 (*0-566-05188-5*, Pub. by Avebry) Ashgate Pub Co.
Morris, Jenny, ed. Able Lives: Women's Experience of Paralysis. 240p. pap. 15.95 (*0-7043-4155-7*, Pub. by Womens Press) Trafalgar.
— Alone Together: Voices of Single Mothers. 224p. pap. 13.95 (*0-7043-4293-6*, Pub. by Womens Press) Trafalgar.
Morris, Jerry. Boston Globe Guide to Boston. 4th ed. LC 98-8782. 1998. pap. 14.95 (*0-7627-0326-1*) Globe Pequot.
***Morris, Jerry.** Boston Globe Guide to Boston. 5th ed. (Illus.). 2001. pap. 14.95 (*0-7627-0806-9*) Globe Pequot.
Morris, Jerry. Guide to Cape Cod. 4th ed. LC 97-52955. (Illus.). 256p. 1998. pap. 12.95 (*0-7627-0178-1*) Globe Pequot.
***Morris, Jerry.** Guide to Cape Cod: Everything You Need to Know to Enjoy One of New England's... 5th ed. (Illus.). 240p. 2000. pap. 13.95 (*0-7627-0647-3*) Globe Pequot.
Morris, Jerry. New England under Sail: A Guide to Sailing Ships, Ferries & Historic Vessels. LC 92-72758. (Under Sail Ser.). (Illus.). 140p. (Orig.). 1993. pap. 12.95 (*1-56626-013-2*, Cntry Rds Pr) NTC Contemp Pub Co.
Morris, Jerry A. Practicing Psychology in Rural Settings: Hospital Privileges & Collaborative Care. LC 97-25216. (Illus.). 159p. 1997. pap. text 19.95 (*1-55798-452-2*) Am Psychol.
Morris, Jill. Creative Breakthroughs: Tap the Power of Your Unconscious Mind. 272p. (Orig.). 1992. mass mkt. 12.99 (*0-446-39217-0*, Pub. by Warner Bks) Little.
Morris, Jim. War Story. 308p. 1994. text 29.95 (*0-87364-147-7*) Paladin Pr.
***Morris, Jim.** War Story. 2000. mass mkt. 6.99 (*0-312-97592-9*) St Martin.
Morris, Jim, jt. auth. see Gitell, Seth A.
Morris, Jim, jt. auth. see Robey, Jim.
Morris, Jim, jt. auth. see Stebben, Gregg.
Morris, Jo. No More Peanuts. (C). 1988. 21.00 (*0-946088-08-X*, Pub. by NCCL) St Mut.
Morris, Joan M., jt. auth. see Grimes, Michael D.
Morris, Joan P. & Warner, Lee H., eds. The Photographs of Alvan S. Harper: Tallahassee, 1885-1910. LC 82-24765. (Illus.). 152p. 1983. 39.95 (*0-8130-0737-2*) U Press Fla.
Morris, Joan P., ed. see Morris, Allen.
Morris, Joe A. Deadline Every Minute: The Story of the United Press. LC 69-10137. 356p. 1968. reprint ed. lib. bdg. 69.50 (*0-8371-0175-1*, MOUP, Greenwood Pr) Greenwood.
Morris, Joe L., jt. auth. see Collins, James C.
Morris, John. The Age of Arthur: A History of the British Isles from 350 to 650. LC 73-174522. xviii, 665 p. 1973. write for info. (*0-297-17601-3*) Trafalgar.
— Daddy, Is There Really a God? LC 97-73935. (Illus.). 32p. (J). 1997. boxed set 11.95 (*0-89051-188-8*) Master Bks.
***Morris, John.** Dinosaurs, The Lost World & You. 48p. 1999. pap. 3.99 (*0-89051-256-6*) Master Bks.
Morris, John. Earth Roads. 2nd ed. 336p. 1995. 51.95 (*1-85628-989-3*, Pub. by Avebry) Ashgate Pub Co.
— From Coronado to Escalante: The Explorers of the Spanish Southwest. Goetzmann, William H., ed. (World Explorers Ser.). (Illus.). 120p. (YA). (gr. 5 up). 1992. lib. bdg. 19.95 (*0-7910-1300-6*) Chelsea Hse.
— Health & Safety: A Guide for the Newly Appointed. LC 97-202668. (Management Skills Ser.). (Illus.). 160p. 1997. pap. 25.95 (*0-304-70120-3*) Continuum.

An Asterisk (*) at the beginning of an entry indicates that the title is appearing for the first time.

*__Morris, John.__ How Firm a Foundation in Scripture & Song. LC 99-66474. 256p. 1999. pap. 11.99 (*0-89051-322-8*) Master Bks.

Morris, John. Managing the Library Fire Risk. 2nd rev. ed. LC 78-22603. (Illus.). 1979. 15.50 (*0-9602278-1-4*) J Morris.

— Noah's Ark, Noah's Flood: Lots of Water, Lots of Mud. LC 98-66306. (Illus.). 32p. (J). 1998. boxed set 11.99 (*0-89051-234-5*) Master Bks.

*__Morris, John.__ Weapons of Our Warfare: 20 Key Issues for Creationists LC 99-188712. 47 p. 1998. write for info. (*0-932766-52-8*, Inst Creation) Master Bks.

Morris, John. The Welsh Wars of Edward I: Medieval Military History. LC 68-25253. (British History Ser.: No. 30). 1969. reprint ed. lib. bdg. 75.00 (*0-8383-0221-1*) M S G Haskell Hse.

Morris, John, ed. Exploring Stereotyped Images in Victorian & Twentieth-Century Literature & Society. LC 93-29916. 304p. 1993. pap. 79.95 (*0-7734-9325-5*) E Mellen.

Morris, John & Ham, Kenneth. What Really Happened to Dinosaurs? LC 92-201970. (Illus.). 32p. (J). (ps-2). 1990. boxed set 10.95 (*0-89051-159-4*) Master Bks.

Morris, John & McGee, Willie. "Bullet Bob" Comes to Louisville: And Other Tales from a Baseball Life. LC 98-30818. (Illus.). 196p. 1999. 22.00 (*1-888698-20-9*) Diamond Communications.

Morris, John, et al. Quality Care in the Nursing Home. LC 96-17375. 900p. (gr. 13). 1996. text 54.95 (*0-8151-4222-6*, 26266) Mosby Inc.

Morris, John, jt. auth. see Cornelius, R. M.

Morris, John, jt. auth. see Dunn, Ruben J.

Morris, John A. September Moon. LC 97-90463. 1998. pap. 8.95 (*0-533-12415-8*) Vantage.

Morris, John B., jt. auth. see MacKinnon, Pamela C.

Morris, John C. Applied Electronics. (Electrical Engineering Ser.). 1997. pap. 23.95 (*0-340-65284-5*, VNR) Wiley.

Morris, John C., ed. Handbook of Dementing Illnesses. LC 93-38090. (Neurological Disease & Therapy Ser.: Vol. 22). (Illus.). 688p. 1993. text 190.00 (*0-8247-8837-0*) Dekker.

Morris, John D. Geology Book. LC 99-67332. (Wonders of Creation Ser.). (Illus.). Date not set. boxed set 15.99 (*0-89051-281-7*) Master Bks.

Morris, John D. Noah's Ark & the Ararat Adventure. rev. ed. LC 93-80508. (Illus.). 64p. (J). (gr. 3-5). 1994. boxed set 13.95 (*0-89051-166-7*) Master Bks.

*__Morris, John D.__ Sword of the Border: Major General Jacob Jennings Brown, 1775-1828. LC 99-48634. 2000. 35.00 (*0-87338-659-0*) Kent St U Pr.

— Trip to the Ocean. LC 99-69399. (Illus.). 40p. (J). Date not set. boxed set 11.99 (*0-89051-285-X*) Master Bks.

Morris, John D. The Young Earth. LC 94-96176. 308p. 1994. pap. 14.95 (*0-89051-174-8*, YOUEAR) Master Bks.

Morris, John D., ed. Abraham's Family: A Man of Faith. 36p. 1998. pap. 7.99 (*0-89051-243-4*) Master Bks.

— Creation: When God Made the World. 36p. 1998. pap. 7.99 (*0-89051-242-6*) Master Bks.

Morris, John E. Bontecou: The Ancestry of Daniel Bontecou of Springfield, Massachusetts: A Record of Forty Successive Generations, Extending Through Thirteen Centuries. 271p. 1995. reprint ed. pap. 41.00 (*0-8328-4902-2*); reprint ed. lib. bdg. 51.00 (*0-8328-4901-4*) Higginson Bk Co.

— Bontecou Genealogy: A Records of the Descendants of Pierre Bontecou, Huguenot Refugee from France, in the Lines of His Sons. (Illus.). 271p. 1994. reprint ed. pap. 43.00 (*0-8328-4255-9*); reprint ed. lib. bdg. 53.00 (*0-8328-4256-7*) Higginson Bk Co.

— The Welsh Wars of Edward I. LC 96-7110. (Medieval Military Library). (Illus.). 352p. 1995. pap. 14.95 (*0-938289-68-3*, 289683) Combined Pub.

Morris, John F., jt. auth. see Mackinnon, Pamela C.

Morris, John G. L. The Neurology Short Case. 128p. 1992. pap. text 14.95 (*0-340-54923-8*, Pub. by E A) OUP.

Morris, John M. El Llano Estacado: Exploration & Imagination on the High Plains of Texas & New Mexico, 1536-1860. LC 96-40185. 400p. 1997. 39.95 (*0-87611-154-1*) Tex St Hist Assn.

Morris, John M., jt. auth. see Morris, Henry M.

Morris, John R. Landlord & Tenant. (Lecture Notes...Ser.). 392p. 1995. pap. 34.00 (*1-85941-045-6*, Pub. by Cavendish Pubng) Gaunt.

Morris, John S. Bean Street. LC 77-79214. (Lost Roads Poetry Ser.: No. 4). 1978. pap. 3.00 (*0-918786-07-X*) Lost Roads.

Morris, John T., jt. ed. see Tuman, John P.

Morris, John W. The Charismatic Movement. 43p. 1984. pap. 5.00 (*0-916586-72-3*, Pub. by Holy Cross Orthodox) BookWorld.

— Ghost Towns of Oklahoma. LC 77-22439. (Illus.). 1978. pap. 17.95 (*0-8061-1420-7*) U of Okla Pr.

— Orthodox Fundamentalists: A Critical View. LC 98-67944. 103p. 1998. pap. 10.95 (*1-880971-40-2*) Light&Life Pub Co MN.

Morris, John W., et al. Historical Atlas of Oklahoma. 3rd ed. LC 86-40077. (Illus.). 208p. 1986. 37.95 (*0-8061-1991-8*); pap. 19.95 (*0-8061-2001-0*) U of Okla Pr.

Morris, Johnathan, et al. Working for the Japanese: The Economic & Social Consequences of Japanese Investment in Wales. LC 93-14561. (Illus.). 180p. (C). 1993. text 65.00 (*0-485-11438-0*, Pub. by Athlone Pr) Humanities.

Morris, Johnny. Just Like You & Me. 1985. 35.00 (*0-900873-66-3*, Pub. by Bishopsgate Pr Ltd) St Mut.

Morris, Jonathan. The Political Economy of Shopkeeping in Milan, 1886-1922. (Past & Present Publications). (Illus.). 328p. (C). 1993. text 69.95 (*0-521-39119-9*) Cambridge U Pr.

Morris, Jonathan, jt. ed. see Blyton, Paul.

Morris, Jonathan, jt. ed. see Lumley, Robert.

Morris, Jonathan, ed. see Shakespeare, William.

Morris Jones, John, jt. ed. see Rhys, John.

Morris-Jones, W. H. Politics Mainly Indian. 392p. 1978. 19.95 (*0-318-36605-3*) Asia Bk Corp.

Morris-Jones, W. H., ed. From Rhodesia to Zimbabwe: Behind & Beyond Lancaster House. (Studies in Commonwealth Politics & History: No. 9). (Illus.). 123p. 1980. 39.50 (*0-7146-3167-1*, Pub. by F Cass Pubs) Intl Spec Bk.

Morris-Jones, W. H., jt. auth. see Dasgupta, Biplab.

Morris-Jones, W. H., jt. ed. see Madden, A. F.

Morris, Joodi, intro. From Wimberley's Kitchens: A Small Town in Texas. 1993. spiral bd. 4.95 (*0-9636364-0-5*) Wimb Chamb Com.

*__Morris, Joseph, et al.__ It Can Be Done: Poems of Inspiration. rev. ed. LC 00-131816. 240p. 2000. reprint ed. pap. 10.95 (*0-9679393-0-5*) Double Moon.

*__Morris, Joseph M.__ Mergers & Acquisitions: Business Strategies for Accountants. 2nd ed. LC 99-54858. (M & A Library). 432p. 2000. text 125.00 (*0-471-38187-X*) Wiley.

— Software Industry Accounting. 2nd ed. LC 99-37988. 496p. 2000. text 140.00 (*0-471-24958-0*) Wiley.

Morris, Joseph M. & Graff, Richard P. Joint Ventures: Business Strategies for Accountants. LC 97-31046. 316p. 1998. 125.00 (*0-471-57018-4*) Wiley.

Morris, Joyce J. Reiki - Hands That Heal. rev. ed. (Illus.). 200p. (Orig.). 1996. pap. 22.00 (*1-888196-22-X*) Ctr Bkstore.

Morris, Joyce J. & Morris, William R. Reiki Hands That Heal. LC 98-45654. (Illus.). 200p. 1999. pap. 19.95 (*1-57863-118-1*) Weiser.

Morris, Juddi. At Home with the Presidents. LC 98-54096. (Illus.). 172p. (J). (gr. 5-9). 1999. pap. 12.95 (*0-471-25300-6*) Wiley.

— The Harvey Girls: The Women Who Civilized the West. 144p. (YA). (gr. 4 up). 1994. 15.95 (*0-8027-8302-3*); lib. bdg. 16.85 (*0-8027-8303-1*) Walker & Co.

— Tending the Fire: The Story of Maria Martinez. LC 97-12009. 120p. (J). (gr. 3-6). 1997. pap. 6.95 (*0-87358-654-9*, Rising Moon Bks); lib. bdg. 12.95 (*0-87358-665-4*, Rising Moon Bks) Northland AZ.

Morris, Judith, jt. auth. see Gasson, Andrew.

Morris, Judy, jt. auth. see Lindenberger, Jan.

Morris, Judy K. The Kid Who Ran for Principal. LC 89-2729. 224p. (J). (gr. 3-7). 1989. 12.95 (*0-397-32359-X*) HarpC Child Bks.

— Kid Who Ran for Principal. LC 89-2729. 224p. (J). (gr. 3-7). 1989. 12.89 (*0-397-32360-3*) HarpC Child Bks.

Morris, Judy K. Nightwalkers. LC 96-16241. (Illus.). 144p. (J). (gr. 3-7). 1996. 14.95 (*0-06-027200-7*) HarpC Child Bks.

Morris, Judy L. & Gibbins, Ian L. Autonomic Innervation of the Skin. (Autonomic Nervous System Ser.). 432p. 1997. text 120.00 (*90-5702-235-4*, Harwood Acad Pubs) Gordon & Breach.

Morris, Julian. Green Goods? Consumers, Product Labels & the Environment. (IEA Studies on the Environment: No. 8). 110p. 1997. pap. 26.50 (*0-255-36441-5*, Pub. by Inst Economic Affairs) Coronet Bks.

*__Morris, Julian.__ Risk & the Precautionary Principle. 320p. 2000. pap. 29.95 (*0-7506-4683-7*) Buttrwrth-Heinemann.

Morris, Julian, ed. Climate Change: Challenging the Conventional Wisdom. (IEA Studies on the Environment: No. 10). 112p. 1997. pap. 32.50 (*0-255-36443-1*, Pub. by Inst Economic Affairs) Coronet Bks.

Morris, Julian, jt. auth. see Bate, Roger.

Morris, Julianna. Baby Talk. (Romance Ser.). 1995. per. 2.99 (*0-373-19097-2*, 1-19097-4) Silhouette.

*__Morris, Julianna.__ Callie, Get Your Groom. (Romance Ser.). 2000. per. 3.50 (*0-373-19436-6*) Silhouette.

Morris, Julianna. Une Chance de Bonheur. (Horizon Ser.). (FRE.). 1998. mass mkt. 3.50 (*0-373-39486-1*, 1-39486-5) Harlequin Bks.

*__Morris, Julianna.__ Charada.Tr. of Charade. (ENG & SPA.). 2000. per. 3.50 (*0-373-33542-3*) Harlequin Bks.

Morris, Julianna. Daddy Woke up Married. 1997. per. 3.25 (*0-373-19252-5*, 1-19252-5) Silhouette.

— Dr. Dad. (Romance Ser.: No. 1278). 1998. per. 3.50 (*0-373-19278-9*, 1-19278-0) Silhouette.

— Family of Three. (Romance Ser.). 1996. per. 3.25 (*0-373-19178-2*, 1-19178-2) Silhouette.

*__Morris, Julianna.__ Jodi's Mail-Order Man. (Romance Ser.: Bk. 1460). 2000. mass mkt. 3.50 (*0-373-19460-9*, 1-19460-4) Silhouette.

Morris, Julianna. The Marriage Stempede: Wrangers & Lace. (Romance Ser.: No. 1375). 1999. per. 3.50 (*0-373-19375-0*, 1-19375-4) Silhouette.

Morris, Julie. Step Forward! Unit 1: A Christian 12-Step Program to Lose Weight - And Keep It Off! - Leader's Guide, Unit 1. 1998. pap., teacher ed. 14.95 (*0-687-08746-5*) Abingdon.

— Step Forward! Unit 2: A Christian 12-Step Program to Lose Weight - And Keep It Off! - Leader's Guide, Unit 2. 1998. pap., teacher ed. 14.95 (*0-687-08766-X*) Abingdon.

— Step Forward! Unit 3: A Christian 12-Step Program to Lose Weight - & Keep It Off! 1998. pap., wbk. ed. 10.95 (*0-687-08776-7*) Abingdon.

— Step Forward! Unit 3: A Christian 12-Step Program to Lose Weight - And Keep It Off! - Leader's Guide, Unit 3. 1998. pap., teacher ed. 14.95 (*0-687-08786-4*) Abingdon.

— Step Forward! Unit 4: A Christian 12-Step Program to Lose Weight - & Keep It Off! 1998. pap., wbk. ed. 10.95 (*0-687-08796-1*) Abingdon.

— Step Forward! Unit 4: A Christian 12-Step Program to Lose Weight - And Keep It Off! - Leader's Guide, Unit 4. 1998. pap., teacher ed. 14.95 (*0-687-08806-2*) Abingdon.

Morris, June. Sexfacts: The Handbook for Healthy Sexuality. (Illus.). 44p. (Orig.). 1995. pap. 10.95 (*0-85572-244-4*) Seven Hills Bk.

— Sextalk. 1995. pap. 40.00 (*0-86431-151-6*, Pub. by Aust Council Educ Res) St Mut.

— Sextalk for Parents of Young Children. 120p. 1996. pap. 50.00 (*0-86431-201-6*, Pub. by Aust Council Educ Res) St Mut.

Morris, June, jt. auth. see Mannison, Mary.

Morris, June, jt. auth. see Schmidt, Mary M.

Morris, Justin, jt. auth. see McCoubrey, H.

Morris, Karen, ed. The Ultimate Monologue Index. 2nd ed. 285p. 1999. pap. 19.95 (*1-57525-183-3*) Smith & Kraus.

Morris, Karen, jt. auth. see Reid, Andrew.

Morris, Karen S. & Craker, Lyle E. Herb Gardens in America: A Visitor's Guide. 191p. (Orig.). 1991. pap. 9.95 (*0-9629868-0-1*) HSMP Pr.

Morris, Karl, jt. auth. see Alder, Harry.

*__Morris, Karyn.__ The Kids Can Press Jumbo Book of Gardening. unabridged ed. (Illus.). 256p. (YA). (gr. 3 up). 2000. pap. 14.95 (*1-55074-690-1*, Pub. by Kids Can Pr) Genl Dist Srvs.

Morris, Kate. Artificial Flower Arranger's Companion. 1995. write for info. (*0-7858-0312-2*) Bk Sales Inc.

*__Morris, Kate.__ British Techniques of Public Relations & Propaganda for Mobilizing East & Central Africa During World War II. LC 00-20028. (Studies in British History: Vol. 61). 488p. 2000. text 109.95 (*0-7734-7805-1*) E Mellen.

Morris, Katherine. Sorceress or Witch: The Image of Gender in Medieval Iceland & Northern Europe. 262p. (C). 1991. pap. text 32.50 (*0-8191-8257-5*); lib. bdg. 57.50 (*0-8191-8256-7*) U Pr of Amer.

Morris, Katherine, ed. Odyssey of Exile: Jewish Women Flee the Nazis for Brazil. LC 95-39736. (Illus.). 264p. 1996. 39.95 (*0-8143-2562-9*); pap. 19.95 (*0-8143-2563-7*) Wayne St U Pr.

Morris, Katherine, et al. Database Management Systems in Engineering. (Illus.). 54p. (Orig.). (C). 1994. pap. text 40.00 (*1-56806-363-6*) DIANE Pub.

Morris, Katherine, jt. auth. see Baker, Gordon.

Morris, Katherine, ed. & tr. see Grunbaum, Irene, et al.

Morris, Kathleen E. Speaking in Whispers: African-American Lesbian Erotica. LC 96-22395. 168p. (Orig.). 1996. pap. 11.95 (*1-879427-28-1*) Third Side Pr.

Morris, Kathleen V. & Hodgkin, John E. Pulmonary Rehabilitation Program Administration & Patient Education Manual. LC 96-3798. 432p. 1996. 135.00 (*0-8342-0754-0*) Aspen Pub.

Morris-Keitel, Helen G. Identity in Transition: The Images of Working-Class Women in Social Prose of the Vormarz (1840-1848) (North American Studies in Nineteenth-Century German Literature: Vol. 15). VIII, 208p. (C). 1995. text 60.95 (*0-8204-2256-8*) P Lang Pubng.

Morris-Keitel, Peter. Die Verbrechensthematik im Modernen Roman. Hermand, Jost, ed. LC 89-12146. (German Life & Civilization Ser.: Vol. 4). 210p. 1989. text 42.95 (*0-8204-1106-X*) P Lang Pubng.

*__Morris-Keitel, Peter & Niedermeier, Michael, eds.__ Okologie und Literatur. (German Life & Civilization Ser.: Vol. 33). (GER.). 224p. (C). 2000. 49.95 (*0-8204-4872-9*) P Lang Pubng.

Morris, Keith. The Story of the Canadian Pacific Railway. Bruchey, Stuart, ed. LC 80-1332. (Railroads Ser.). (Illus.). 1981. reprint ed. lib. bdg. 20.95 (*0-405-13806-7*) Ayer.

Morris, Kelly, ed. see Zafran, Eric M. & Ackerman, Gerald M.

Morris, Kelly Scott, jt. see Crowther, Terence G.

Morris, Kenneth. Book of the Three Dragons. Reginald, R. & Melville, Douglas, eds. LC 77-84257. (Lost Race & Adult Fantasy Ser.). 1978. reprint ed. lib. bdg. 23.95 (*0-405-11001-4*) Ayer.

— Collected Stories. 1995. pap. 13.95 (*0-312-89029-X*) Orb NYC.

— The Dragon Path: The Collected Tales of Kenneth Morris. 384p. 1995. 23.95 (*0-312-85309-2*) Tor Bks.

Morris, Kenneth & Inverson, Harris L. Golden Threads in the Tapestry of History. (Illus.). 54p. 1975. reprint ed. pap. 8.95 (*0-913004-27-8*) Point Loma Pub.

Morris, Kenneth E. Bonhoeffer's Ethic of Discipleship: A Study in Social Psychology, Political Thought, & Religion. LC 85-31949. 160p. 1986. 27.50 (*0-271-00428-2*) Pa St U Pr.

— Jimmy Carter: An American Moralist. LC 96-6350. 432p. 1996. 29.95 (*0-8203-1862-0*) U of Ga Pr.

— Jimmy Carter, American Moralist. LC 96-6350. 432p. 1997. pap. 19.95 (*0-8203-1949-X*) U of Ga Pr.

Morris, Kenneth G. Ghost of Revivals Past. 90p. (Orig.). 1996. pap. 5.95 (*1-57502-213-3*, D0853) Morris Pubng.

Morris, Kenneth L. The Grant Procurement Guide: Step by Step Procedures for Procuring Grants, Loans, & Contracts. Thorpe, Yelta, ed. LC 95-80268. 68p. (C). 1995. pap. 9.95 (*0-9648987-0-5*) KLM & Assocs.

Morris, Kenneth M. Asian Wall Street Journal Guide to Understanding Money & Investing in Asia. LC 99-196371. 160p. 1998. pap. 14.95 (*0-684-84650-0*, Fireside) S&S Trade Pap.

*__Morris, Kenneth M.__ Essential Guide to Your 401(K) 2000. pap. 14.95 (*0-07-135904-4*) McGraw.

Morris, Kenneth M. User's Guide to the Information Age. (Orig.). 1999. pap. text 14.95 (*0-07-134947-2*) McGraw.

— The Wall Street Journal Guide to Planning Your Financial Future: The Easy-to-Read Guide to Planning for Retirement. rev. ed. LC 99-199643. (Wall Street Journal Guides Ser.). 192p. 1998. per. 14.95 (*0-684-85724-3*, Fireside) S&S Trade Pap.

— The Wall Street Journal Guide to Understanding Personal Finance. LC 96-30011. 1997. pap. 18.95 incl. disk (*0-684-83362-X*) S&S Trade.

Morris, Kenneth M. & Morris, Virginia B. Guide to Understanding Money & Investing. rev. ed. (Wall Street Journal Guides Ser.). (Illus.). 160p. 1999. per. 15.95 (*0-684-86902-0*, Fireside) S&S Trade Pap.

— The Wall Street Journal Guide to Understanding Money & Investing. LC 95-126362. 155p. 1994. pap. 15.95 (*0-671-89451-X*, Fireside) S&S Trade Pap.

Morris, Kenneth M. & Siegel, Alan M. The Wall Street Journal Guide to Planning Your Financial Future: The Easy-to-Read Guide to Lifetime Planning for Retirement. 176p. 1995. per. 14.95 (*0-684-80202-3*, Fireside) S&S Trade Pap.

— The Wall Street Journal Guide to Understanding Personal Finance. LC 96-30011. (Illus.). 176p. 1997. per. 14.95 (*0-684-83361-1*) S&S Trade.

Morris, Kenneth M. & Siegel, Aland M. The Wall Street Journal Guide to Understanding Personal Finance. 176p. 1993. pap. 14.95 (*0-671-87964-2*, Fireside) S&S Trade Pap.

Morris, Kenneth M., et al. The Wall Street Journal Guide to Understanding Your Taxes: An Easy-to-Understand, Easy-to-Use Primer That Takes the Mystery Out of Income Taxes. LC 95-126385. 128p. 1995. pap. 14.95 (*0-671-50235-2*, Fireside) S&S Trade Pap.

Morris, Kevin L. The Image of the Middle Ages in Romantic & Victorian Literature. 272p. 1984. 45.00 (*0-7099-3511-0*, Pub. by C Helm) Routldge.

Morris, Kim. Molly in the Middle. LC 98-34281. (Real Kids Readers Ser.). (Illus.). 48p. (J). (gr. 1-3). 1999. pap. 3.99 (*0-7613-2084-9*, Copper Beech Bks); lib. bdg. 17.90 (*0-7613-2059-8*, Copper Beech Bks) Millbrook Pr.

Morris, Kim, ed. see Wright, Mary H.

Morris, Kimberly & Baum, L. Frank. The Wizard of Oz. LC 98-45494. (J). 1999. write for info. (*0-7894-4444-5*) DK Pub Inc.

Morris, Kirsten A., ed. Control of Flexible Structures. LC 93-11354. (Fields Institute Communications Ser.: Vol. 2). 243p. 1993. text 82.00 (*0-8218-9201-0*, FIC/2) Am Math.

Morris, L. The Poetry of Edwin Arlington Robinson. LC 73-92976. (Studies in Poetry: No. 38). (C). 1969. reprint ed. lib. bdg. 75.00 (*0-8383-0996-8*) M S G Haskell Hse.

Morris, L. A. Communicating Therapeutic Risks. (Recent Research in Psychology Ser.). xii, 186p. 1989. 64.95 (*0-387-97192-0*, 3675) Spr-Verlag.

Morris, L. Allen. A Legacy Lived: Your Enduring Influence for Future Generations. 2nd rev. ed. Thompson, Barbara R. et al, eds. Orig. Title: Dreams, Deals, Dividends & Donuts. 139p. 1998. pap. text 10.00 (*0-9640852-7-5*, 1006) Look Gl Bks.

Morris, L. Delyte, jt. auth. see Johnson, Pamela.

Morris, L. J., jt. auth. see Horne, M. R.

Morris, Lacey M., jt. ed. see Verlenden, Jeanne S.

Morris, Langdon. Managing the Evolving Corporation. (Industrial Engineering Ser.). 238p. 1994. text 26.95 (*0-442-01906-8*, VNR) Wiley.

Morris, Langdon. Managing the Evolving Corporation. (Industrial Engineering Ser.). 238p. 1994. 26.95 (*0-471-28651-6*, VNR) Wiley.

Morris, Langdon, jt. auth. see Miller, William L.

Morris, Larry A. The Male Heterosexual. 272p. 1996. 45.00 (*0-8039-5639-8*); pap. 19.95 (*0-8039-5640-1*) Sage.

Morris, Larry E. Industrial Stress Injuries: Dynamic Understanding, Clinical Illustrations & Logical Management. 185p. (C). 1989. 35.00 (*0-685-26951-5*) Bourne & Atherton Pubns.

Morris, Laurel, jt. auth. see Montgomery, Bob.

Morris, Laurence. Pilgrim's Progress (Retold for Children) (J). (gr. 1-5). 1993. mass mkt. 5.99 (*0-87508-747-7*) Chr Lit.

Morris, Lawrence J., jt. auth. see Johnson, Robert W.

*__Morris-Lee, James.__ Real-Time Marketing: Creating Competitive Advantage with Digital Print Communication. (Illus.). 220p. (C). 2000. pap. text 35.00 (*0-88362-299-8*) GATFPress.

Morris, Lennise G. God Speaks Through Trials. (Illus.). 75p. 1996. pap. 10.00 (*0-9651334-0-0*) Germaine Publns.

— War & Violence, Eternal Life or Death. LC 97-94292. 100p. 1998. pap. 9.00 (*0-9651334-1-9*) Germaine Publns.

Morris, Leon. Apostolic Preaching of the Cross. 1955. pap. 15.00 (*0-8028-1512-X*) Eerdmans.

— The Atonement. LC 83-20649. 219p. (Orig.). 1984. pap. 15.99 (*0-87784-826-2*, 826) InterVarsity.

*__Morris, Leon.__ The Cross in the New Testament. 456p. 1999. pap. 24.00 (*0-8028-1730-0*) Eerdmans.

Morris, Leon. The Cross of Jesus. LC 88-371. 126p. reprint ed. pap. 39.10 (*0-7837-6565-7*, 204613000011) Bks Demand.

— The Cross of Jesus. (Biblical Classics Library: Vol. 8). x, 118p. 1994. reprint ed. mass mkt. 5.99 (*0-85364-628-7*, Pub. by Paternoster Pub) OM Literature.

— The Epistle to the Romans. (The Pillar New Testament Commentary Ser.). 640p. 1988. 34.00 (*0-8028-3636-4*) Eerdmans.

— First & Second Thessalonians. rev. ed. Tasker, Randolph V., ed. (Tyndale New Testament Commentaries Ser.). 160p. 1984. pap. 12.00 (*0-8028-0034-3*) Eerdmans.

— First Corinthians. rev. ed. Tasker, Randolph V., ed. (Tyndale New Testament Commentaries Ser.). 224p. 1986. pap. 13.00 (*0-8028-0064-5*) Eerdmans.

M

An Asterisk (*) at the beginning of an entry indicates that the title is appearing for the first time.

— Galatians: Paul's Charter of Christian Freedom. LC 96-17460. 160p. 1996. 16.99 (*0-8308-1420-5*, 1420) InterVarsity.

— The Gospel According to John. rev. ed. (New International Commentary on the New Testament Ser.). 846p. 1971. 45.00 (*0-8028-2504-4*) Eerdmans.

— The Gospel According to Matthew. LC 92-15806. (Pillar New Testament Commentary Ser.). xvi, 782p. 1992. text 42.00 (*0-8028-3696-8*) Eerdmans.

— The Gospel According to St. Luke. rev. ed. (Tyndale New Testament Commentaries Ser.). 1988. pap. 14.00 (*0-8028-0419-5*) Eerdmans.

— Hebrews: Bible Study Commentary. 1983. pap. 6.99 (*0-310-45183-3*, 12390P) Zondervan.

— New Testament Theology. 448p. 1986. 20.95 (*0-310-45570-7*, 12391) Zondervan.

— New Testament Theology. 368p. 1990. pap. 19.99 (*0-310-45571-5*) Zondervan.

— Revelation. rev. ed. (Tyndale New Testament Commentaries Ser.). 1987. pap. text 13.00 (*0-8028-0273-7*) Eerdmans.

Morris, Leon, et al. The Expositor's Bible Commentary, Vol. 12. 1986. 34.99 (*0-88469-198-5*) BMH Bks.

Morris, Leon, jt. auth. see Cundall, Arthur E.

Morris, Leon, jt. auth. see Perkins, Ginny.

Morris, Leon, ed. see Bruce, F. F.

Morris, Leon, ed. see Cole, R. Alan.

Morris, Leon, ed. see France, Richard.

Morris, Leon, ed. see Guthrie, Donald.

Morris, Leslie A. Rosenbach Abroad: In Pursuit of Books in Private Collections. (Illus.). 64 p. 1988. pap. 12.50 (*0-939084-22-8*) R Mus & Lib.

— Rosenbach Redux: Further Book Adventures in England & Ireland. (Illus.). 111p. 1989. pap. 15.00 (*0-939084-25-2*) R Mus & Lib.

Morris, Leslie A., et al. John Keats, 1795-1995. (Illus.). 126p. (Orig.). 1995. pap. 15.00 (*0-914630-17-2*) Houghton Lib.

Morris, Leslie R. Interlibrary Loan Policies Directory. 6th rev. ed. LC 99-24663. 1250p. 1999. pap. 195.00 (*1-55570-347-X*) Neal-Schuman.

Morris, Leslie R., et al, eds. Choosing a Bibliographic Utility: User Views of Current Choices. 130p. (Orig.). 1990. pap. text 45.00 (*1-55570-044-6*) Neal-Schuman.

Morris, Lester. Did You Knows of England. x, 286p. 1998. pap. 14.00 (*0-9662214-3-5*) Brit Connect.

Morris, Lewis. The Papers of Lewis Morris. LC 73-117885. (Select Bibliographies Reprint Ser.). 1977. reprint ed. 25.95 (*0-8369-5338-X*) Ayer.

Morris, Libby V. & Little, Catherine J. Georgia's Health Professions: A Decade of Change 1985-1995. 111p. 1996. pap. 5.00 (*1-880647-05-2*) U GA Inst High Educ.

Morris, Libby V. & Parker, Sammy. Multiculturalism in Academe: A Source Book. LC 95-26398. (Source Books on Education: Vol. 47). 200p. 1996. text 39.00 (*0-8153-1798-0*, SS980) Garland.

Morris, Libby V., jt. auth. see Wimberley, Ronald C.

Morris, Linda, tr. see Kruglikov, Alexander.

Morris, Linda A. Women's Humor in the Age of Gentility: The Life & Works of Frances Miriam Whitcher. (Illus.). 256p. 1992. text 37.95 (*0-8156-2562-6*) Syracuse U Pr.

Morris, Linda A., ed. American Women Humorists: Critical Essays. LC 93-21788. (Studies in Humor: Vol. 4). 480p. 1993. text 25.00 (*0-8153-0622-9*, H1500) Garland.

Morris, Lisa R., jt. auth. see Schulz, Linda.

Morris, Lloyd. Incredible New York: High Life & Low Life of the Last Hundred Years. LC 75-1862. (Leisure Class in America Ser.). (Illus.). 1975. reprint ed. 26.95 (*0-405-06928-6*) Ayer.

— The Poetry of Edwin Arlington Robinson. LC 70-99664. (Select Bibliographies Reprint Ser.). 1977. 20.95 (*0-8369-5093-3*) Ayer.

Morris, Lloyd & Whitall, W. Van. The Poetry of Edwin Arlington Robinson: An Essay in Appreciation. LC 70-99664. (Select Bibliographies Reprint Ser.). 116p. reprint ed. 16.50 (*0-8290-0486-6*) Irvington.

Morris, Lloyd R. Incredible New York: High Life & Low Life from 1850-1950. 370p. (C). 1996. pap. 17.95 (*0-8156-0334-7*, MOINP) Syracuse U Pr.

— Not So Long Ago. (History - United States Ser.). 504p. 1993. reprint ed. lib. bdg. 99.00 (*0-7812-4845-0*) Rprt Serv.

— The Rebellious Puritan: Portrait of Mr. Hawthorne. (BCL1-PS American Literature Ser.). 369p. 1992. reprint ed. lib. bdg. 89.00 (*0-7812-6730-7*) Rprt Serv.

Morris, Llyn E. The Country Garage. (Album Ser.: No. 129). (Illus.). 32p. 4.75 (*0-85263-711-X*, Pub. by Shire Pubns) Parkwest Pubns.

Morris, Lois B., jt. auth. see Gold, Mark S.

Morris, Lois B., jt. auth. see Oldham, John M.

Morris, Lorenzo. One Third of a Nation. 1997. pap. text 54.00 (*0-88258-170-8*) Howard U Pr.

Morris, Lorenzo, ed. The Social & Political Implications of the 1984 Jesse Jackson Presidential Campaign. LC 89-27476. (Praeger Series in Political Economy). 288p. 1990. 62.95 (*0-275-92785-7*, C2785, Praeger Pubs) Greenwood.

Morris, Lorenzo & Bailey, Ura J. One-Third of a Nation: African American Perspectives, Vol. II. (Illus.). 504p. (C). 1997. pap. text 29.95 (*0-88258-168-6*, MOOT2P) Howard U Pr.

Morris, Lorenzo & Bailey, Ura J., eds. One-Third of a Nation: African American Perspectives. LC 99-34930. (Illus.). 504p. (C). 1999. pap. text 29.95 (*0-88258-167-8*, MOOT1P) Howard U Pr.

Morris, Louis A. The Morris, Arnold & Related Families. (Illus.). 288p. 1985. 25.00 (*0-89308-550-2*) Southern Hist Pr.

Morris, Louis A., et al, eds. Product Labeling & Health Risks. LC 80-22728. (Banbury Report: Vol. 6). 344p. 1980. reprint ed. pap. 106.70 (*0-608-01801-5*, 206245400003) Bks Demand.

Morris, Louise. The Crucifixion & the Resurrection of Jesus. 94p. 1993. spiral bd. 10.00 (*0-7873-0626-6*) Hlth Research.

— Stronger Than the Strong. 160p. (Orig.). 1998. pap. 7.99 (*0-87508-496-6*, 496) Chr Lit.

— Stronger Than the Strong: Jesus Sets a Tribal People of Thailand Free from Satan's Tyrranical Rule. (Illus.). 160p. 1998. pap. 8.99 (*981-3009-14-4*) OMF Bks.

Morris, Louise, jt. auth. see Maxwell, Hu.

Morris, Lucy W., ed. Old Rail Fence Corners: Frontier Tales Told by Minnesota Pioneers. xxi, 344p. 1976. reprint ed. pap. 14.95 (*0-87351-109-3*, Borealis Book) Minn Hist.

Morris, Lydia. The Workings of the Household: A U. S.-U. K. Comparison. (Family Life Ser.). (Illus.). 260p. 1990. pap. text 28.95 (*0-7456-0442-0*) Blackwell Pubs.

— The Workings of the Household: A U. S.-U. K. Comparison. (Family Life Ser.). (Illus.). 260p. 1990. text 64.95 (*0-7456-0441-2*) Blackwell Pubs.

Morris, Lydia & Lyon, E. Stina, eds. Gender Relations in Public & Private: New Research Perspectives. 1996. text 65.00 (*0-312-12869-X*) St Martin.

Morris, Lyle L. The Single Salary Schedule: An Analysis & Evaluation. LC 72-177086. (Columbia University. Teachers College. Contributions to Education Ser.: No. 413). reprint ed. 37.50 (*0-404-55413-X*) AMS Pr.

Morris, Lynda & Radford, Robert. AIA: The Story of the Artists International Association 1933-1953. 96p. 1983. 50.00 (*0-905836-35-9*, Pub. by Museum Modern Art) St Mut.

Morris, Lynn. The Balcony. LC 97-21008. (Portraits Ser.). 256p. 1997. pap. 8.99 (*1-55661-981-2*) Bethany Hse.

***Morris, Lynn.** The Balcony. large type ed. LC 99-33699. 1999. 23.95 (*0-7862-2146-1*) Mac Lib Ref.

Morris, Lynn. Cheney Duvall, M. D. Ser. Vols. 1-4: Stars for a Light, Shadow of the Mountain, A City Not Forsaken, 4 vols., Set. 1996. boxed set 39.99 (*0-7642-8027-9*) Bethany Hse.

— The Stars for a Light. LC 98-56123. 1999. 23.95 (*0-7862-1828-2*) Mac Lib Ref.

— Verity's Bane. 2000. pap. 10.99 (*0-310-22792-5*) Zondervan.

Morris, Lynn & Morris, Gilbert. A City Not Forsaken. large type ed. LC 96-46326. (Inspirational Ser.). 498p. 1997. lib. bdg. 23.95 (*0-7838-2025-9*, G K Hall Lrg Type) Mac Lib Ref.

***Morris, Lynn & Morris, Gilbert.** A City Not Forsaken, Bk. 3. 2000. 23.95 (*0-7862-2227-1*) Macmillan.

Morris, Lynn & Morris, Gilbert. In the Twilight, in the Evening. 1998. 22.95 (*0-7862-1365-5*) Five Star.

— In the Twilight, in the Evening, 6. LC 97-33844. 32p. 1997. pap. 10.99 (*1-55661-427-6*) Bethany Hse.

— Island of the Innocent. (Cheney Duvall, M. D. Ser.: Bk. 7). 32p. 1998. pap. 10.99 (*1-55661-698-8*) Bethany Hse.

***Morris, Lynn & Morris, Gilbert.** Island of the Innocent. LC 99-87869. 2000. 24.95 (*0-7862-2442-8*) Five Star.

Morris, Lynn & Morris, Gilbert. The Secret Place of Thunder. (Cheney Duvall M. D. Ser.: No. 5). 336p. 1996. pap. 10.99 (*1-55661-426-8*) Bethany Hse.

— The Secret Place of Thunder. large type ed. LC 98-21635. 1998. 20.00 (*0-7862-1514-3*) Thorndike Pr.

— Shadow of the Mountains. LC 99-22269. (Christian Fiction Ser.). 1999. 23.95 (*0-7862-2089-9*, Five Star MI) Mac Lib Ref.

— Shadow of the Mountains. large type ed. 481p. 1995. 21.95 (*0-7838-1489-5*, G K Hall Lrg Type) Mac Lib Ref.

— The Stars for a Light. LC 94-4892. (Cheney Duvall, M. D. Ser.: Bk. 1). 32p. 1994. pap. 10.99 (*1-55661-422-5*) Bethany Hse.

— Toward the Sunrising. LC 95-43937. (Cheney Duvall, M.D. Ser.: Vol. 4). 368p. 1996. pap. 10.99 (*1-55661-425-X*) Bethany Hse.

— Toward the Sunrising. LC 98-5790. 1998. 22.95 (*0-7862-1436-8*) Thorndike Pr.

Morris, Lynn, et al. A City Not Forsaken. (M. D. Ser.: Bk. 3). 336p. 1995. pap. 10.99 (*1-55661-424-1*) Bethany Hse.

Morris, Lynn, jt. auth. see Morris, Gilbert.

Morris, Lynn A., ed. Research about Leisure: Past, Present & Future. 2nd ed. 1994. pap. 24.95 (*0-915611-96-1*) Sagamore Pub.

Morris, Lynn L. & Fitz-Gibbon, Carol T. Evaluator's Handbook. LC 78-58658. (Program Evaluation Kit Ser.: No. 1). (Illus.). 133p. reprint ed. pap. 41.30 (*0-8357-4832-4*, 203776900009) Bks Demand.

— How to Deal with Goals & Objectives. LC 78-57012. (Program Evaluation Kit Ser.: No. 2). (Illus.). 78p. reprint ed. pap. 30.00 (*0-8357-4833-2*, 203777000009) Bks Demand.

— How to Measure Achievement. LC 78-58656. (Program Evaluation Kit Ser.). (Illus.). 159p. reprint ed. pap. 49.30 (*0-8357-4835-9*, 203777200009) Bks Demand.

— How to Measure Program Implementation. LC 78-58656. (Program Evaluation Kit Ser.). (Illus.). 140p. reprint ed. pap. 43.40 (*0-8357-4834-0*, 203777100009) Bks Demand.

Morris, Lynn L., et al. How to Communicate Evaluation Findings. 2nd ed. (Program Evaluation Kit Ser.: Vol. 9). 64p. (C). 1987. pap. text 13.95 (*0-8039-3134-4*) Sage.

— How to Measure Performance & Use Tests. 2nd ed. (Program Evaluation Kit Ser.: Vol. 7). 176p. (C). 1987. text 13.95 (*0-8039-3132-8*) Sage.

Morris, Lynn L., jt. auth. see Fitz-Gibbon, Carol T.

Morris, M., et al. The Scientific Management of Temperate Communities for Conservation. 1991. pap. 65.00 (*0-632-03186-7*) Blackwell Sci.

Morris, M., jt. auth. see Handcock, M.

Morris, M. C., jt. auth. see Bosschere, Jean de.

Morris, M. D., jt. auth. see Albern, William F.

Morris, M. E. Biostrike. 416p. (Orig.). 1996. mass mkt. 5.99 (*0-380-77889-0*, Avon Bks) Morrow Avon.

— Eye of the Storm. (Orig.). 1996. mass mkt. 5.99 (*0-380-00214-0*, Avon Bks) Morrow Avon.

— Stealth. 352p. (Orig.). 1996. mass mkt. 5.99 (*0-380-78488-2*, Avon Bks) Morrow Avon.

Morris, M. F. History of the Development of Constitutional & Civil Liberty: Being a Series of Eight Lectures Delivered Before the Post-Graduate Classes of the University of Georgetown. 261p. 1995. reprint ed. 37.50 (*0-8377-2479-1*, Rothman) W S Hein.

— An Introduction to the History of the Development of Law. 315p. 1997. reprint ed. 94.00 (*1-56169-251-4*) Gaunt.

— Introduction to the History of the Development of Law. 315p. 1982. reprint ed. 36.00 (*0-8377-0844-3*, Rothman) W S Hein.

Morris, M. G. Romilly's Visits to Wales, 1827-1854. 1997. 59.95 (*0-8464-4585-9*) Beekman Pubs.

— Romilly's Visits to Wales, 1827-1854. 1997. 60.00 (*1-85902-454-8*, Pub. by Gomer Pr) St Mut.

Morris, M. J. & Carrol, B. F., eds. Turbulent Flows, 1993. LC 87-71097. (FED Ser.: Vol. 155). 189p. 1993. pap. 40.00 (*0-7918-0963-3*, H00795) ASME.

Morris, M. J. & Carroll, B. F., eds. Turbulent Flows, 1994. LC 87-71097. (Fluid Engineering Division Conference Ser.: Vol. 188). 83p. 1994. pap. 30.00 (*0-7918-1371-1*) ASME.

Morris, M. J., jt. ed. see Parekh, D. E.

Morris, M. M. Fellows: Joseph & Philena (Elton) Fellows: Their Ancestors & Descendants. (Illus.). 404p. 1993. reprint ed. pap. 61.00 (*0-8328-3311-8*); reprint ed. lib. bdg. 71.00 (*0-8328-3310-X*) Higginson Bk Co.

Morris, M. Wayne. Stalin's Famine & Roosevelt's Recognition of Russia. LC 93-45822. 234p. (C). 1994. lib. bdg. 39.50 (*0-8191-9379-8*) U Pr of Amer.

Morris Machine Works Company Staff. Morris Machine Works Catalogue of 1885: Boilers & Engines. (Illus.). 20p. 1998. reprint ed. pap. 25.00 (*0-87556-866-1*) Saifer.

Morris, Manuel, compiled by. The Recorded Performances of Gerard Souzay: A Discography, 41. LC 90-13978. (Discographies Ser.: No. 41). 260p. 1990. lib. bdg. 57.95 (*0-313-27392-8*, MGG/, Greenwood Pr) Greenwood.

***Morris, Marcia A.** The Literature of Roguery in Seventeenth & Eighteenth-Century Russia. LC 00-8054. (Studies in Russian Literature & Theory). 2000. 79.95 (*0-8101-1753-3*) Northwestern U Pr.

Morris, Marcia A. Saints & Revolutionaries: The Ascetic Hero in Russian Fiction. LC 92-279. 256p. (C). 1993. text 64.50 (*0-7914-1299-7*); pap. text 21.95 (*0-7914-1300-4*) State U NY Pr.

Morris, Margaret. Georgia O'Keeffe: Selected Paintings & Works on Paper. LC 86-60906. (Illus.). 90p. (Orig.). 1986. pap. 20.00 (*0-935037-14-4*) G Peters Gallery.

— Leon Gaspard: Exhibition of Paintings. (Illus.). 31p. 1984. pap. 10.00 (*0-935037-08-X*) G Peters Gallery.

— Private Journal of Margaret Morris, Kept During a Portion of the Revolutionary War. Decker, Peter, ed. LC 71-77107. (Eyewitness Accounts of the American Revolution Ser.). 1977. reprint ed. 16.95 (*0-405-01168-7*) Ayer.

Morris, Margaret H. My Meadow. (Illus.). 144p. (Orig.). 1996. pap. 14.95 (*0-9632687-6-7*) PenRose Pub.

Morris, Margaret L. Irvins, Doaks, Logans & McCampbells of Virginia & Kentucky. 121p. 1996. reprint ed. pap. 19.00 (*0-8328-5242-2*); reprint ed. lib. bdg. 29.00 (*0-8328-5241-4*) Higginson Bk Co.

Morris, Maria. Teach Yourself Italian Verbs. (ITA., Illus.). 256p. 1995. pap. 8.95 (*0-8442-3637-3*, Teach Yrslf) NTC Contemp Pub Co.

Morris, Marianne. Sins of the Father. LC 92-42184. 1993. pap. 10.99 (*0-8163-1146-3*) Pacific Pr Pub Assn.

***Morris, Marie.** The Complete Idiot's Travel Guide to Boston. (Complete Idiot's Travel Guide Ser.). (Illus.). 288p. 1999. pap. 15.95 (*0-02-862912-4*) Macmillan Gen Ref.

Morris, Marie. Frommer's Boston '99. 228p. 1998. 14.95 (*0-02-862228-6*, Pub. by Macmillan) S&S Trade.

***Morris, Marie.** Frommer's Boston 2001. (Illus.). 304p. 2000. pap. 14.99 (*0-02-863743-7*) Macmillan Gen Ref.

Morris, Marie. Frommer's Boston '97. 1997. 12.95 (*0-02-861135-7*) Macmillan.

***Morris, Marilyn.** ABC's of the Birds & Bees: For Parents of Toddlers to Teens. LC 99-75678. 322p. 1999. pap. 17.95 (*1-881636-91-7*, Pub. by Windsor Hse Pub Grp) Baker & Taylor.

— ABCs of the Birds & Bees: For Parents of Toddlers to Teens. (Illus.). 336p. 2000. pap. 17.95 (*0-9648113-5-9*, 0620) Charles Rivr Pub.

Morris, Marilyn. The British Monarchy & the French Revolution. LC 97-16330. 256p. 1998. 28.50 (*0-300-07144-2*) Yale U Pr.

— Choices: That Lead to Lifelong Success. 2nd rev. ed. LC 99-71115. (Illus.). 165p. 1999. pap. 18.95 (*1-881636-74-7*) Windsor Hse Pub Grp.

— Choices That Lead to Lifelong Success, Set. Incl. Parent Manual. 128p. 1998. pap. text 49.95 (*0-9648113-2-4*); Student Workbook. 64p. (YA). 1998. pap. text, wbk. ed. 49.95 (*0-9648113-3-2*); Smith, Greg, ed. (Illus.). 240p. (YA). 1998. pap. text 49.95 (*0-9648113-1-6*); 1998. pap. text. write for info. (*0-9648113-4-0*) Charles Rivr Pub.

***Morris, Marilyn.** Teens, Sex & Choices. (Illus.). 224p. (YA). (gr. 6 up). 2000. pap. 13.95 (*0-9648113-6-7*, 0723) Charles Rivr Pub.

Morris, Marion E. The Sand Crabs. LC 99-60899. 192p. 1999. 16.00 (*1-891954-30-X*) Russell Dean.

Morris, Mark. Ireland: Emerald Isle. (Illus.). 288p. 1995. pap. 16.95 (*0-8442-9669-4*, 96694) NTC Contemp Pub Co.

— Moon Handbooks: Atlantic Canada: New Brunswick, Nova Scotia, Prince Edward Island, Newfoundland & Labrador. 2nd rev. ed. Vol. 2. (Illus.). 490p. 1999. pap. 18.95 (*1-56691-114-1*, Moon Handbks) Avalon Travel.

Morris, Mark, ed. The Center of the Galaxy. (C). 1989. pap. text 101.50 (*0-7923-0222-2*); lib. bdg. 234.00 (*0-7923-0221-4*) Kluwer Academic.

Morris, Mark & Zuckerson, Ben, eds. Mass Loss from Red Giants. 1985. text 167.00 (*90-277-2075-4*) Kluwer Academic.

Morris, Mark S. How to Become a Professional Bartender: Plus: the New up-to-Date List of Todays Most Popular Drink Recipes. (Illus.). 96p. (Orig.). 1992. pap. 9.95 (*0-9632492-0-7*) Morris Ent.

Morris, Mark W., jt. auth. see Daye, Charles E.

Morris, Marla, et al, eds. How We Work. LC 98-38982. XVII, 279p. 1999. 29.95 (*0-8204-4102-3*) P Lang Pubng.

Morris, Marlene B. The Flying Gourmet: Just Plane Good. LC 88-90622. (Illus.). 300p. (Orig.). 1988. pap. 14.95 (*0-9620398-0-2*) M & M Pubns.

Morris, Marshall. Saying & Meaning in Puerto Rico: Some Problems in the Ethnography of Discourse. (Language & Communication Library: Vol. 1). 186p. 1981. text 79.00 (*0-08-025822-0*, CRC Reprint) Franklin.

Morris, Marshall, ed. Translation & the Law. (American Translators Association Scholarly Monograph Ser.: Vol. VIII). viii, 334p. 1995. lib. bdg. 75.00 (*1-55619-627-X*) J Benjamins Pubng Co.

Morris, Martha. Katherine & the Garbage Dump. (Illus.). 24p. (J). (gr. 1-4). 1992. 12.95 (*0-929005-39-2*, Pub. by Sec Story Pr) LPC InBook.

***Morris, Martin.** Rethinking the Communicative Turn: Adorno, Habermas & the Problem of Communicative Freedom. (C). 2000. pap. text 19.95 (*0-7914-4798-7*) State U NY Pr.

— Rethinking the Communicative Turn: Adorno, Habermas & the Problem of Communicative Freedom. (C). 2001. text 59.50 (*0-7914-4797-9*) State U NY Pr.

Morris, Martin, ed. German Dis/Continuities, Vol. 96, No. 4. 225p. 1998. pap. 12.00 (*0-8223-6455-7*) Duke.

***Morris, Mary.** Acts of God. 256p. 2000. text 23.00 (*0-312-24663-3*) St Martin.

Morris, Mary. Angels & Aliens: A Journey West. LC 98-43015. 260p. 1998. text 23.00 (*0-312-19949-X*, Picador USA) St Martin.

***Morris, Mary.** Angels & Aliens: A Journey West. 272p. 2000. pap. 13.00 (*0-312-20429-9*, Picador USA) St Martin.

Morris, Mary. HTML for Fun & Profit. LC 96-144843. 336p. (C). 1995. pap. 39.95 incl. cd-rom (*0-13-242488-6*) P-H.

— Lifeguard. LC 98-19831. 192p. 1998. pap. 12.00 (*0-312-18694-0*) St Martin.

— Maiden Voyages. 1993. pap. 14.00 (*0-679-74030-9*) McKay.

— Night Sky. LC 97-799. 288p. 1997. pap. 13.00 (*0-312-15609-X*) St Martin.

— Nothing to Declare: Memoirs of a Woman Traveling Alone. LC 98-46693. 304p. 1998. pap. 13.00 (*0-312-19941-4*) St Martin.

— Nothing to Declare: Memoirs of a Woman Traveling Alone. large type ed. (General Ser.). 355p. 1989. lib. bdg. 19.95 (*0-8161-4730-2*, G K Hall Lrg Type) Mac Lib Ref.

Morris, Mary & McCann, Sally. Every Sewer's Guide to the Perfect Fit: Customizing Your Patterns for a Sensational Look. Orig. Title: Everybody's Guide to the Perfect Fit. (Illus.). 144p. 1999. pap. text 25.00 (*0-7881-6294-2*) DIANE Pub.

— Every Sewer's Guide to the Perfect Fit: Customizing Your Patterns for a Sensational Look. Matthews, Kate, ed. LC 97-6496. Orig. Title: Everybody's Guide to the Perfect Fit. (Illus.). 144p. 1997. 27.95 (*1-887374-43-4*, Pub. by Lark Books) Random.

Morris, Mary, jt. auth. see Morris, William.

Morris, Mary A., ed. Glorious Liqueurs: 150 Recipes for Spirited Desserts, Drinks, & Gifts of Food. 200p. 1996. reprint ed. pap. 14.95 (*0-9627403-7-3*) Lake Isle Pr.

Morris, Mary E. New Political Realities & the Gulf: Egypt, Syria, & Jordan. LC 92-46989. 1993. pap. 13.00 (*0-8330-1315-7*, MR-127-AF) Rand Corp.

— The Persistence of External Interest in the Middle East. LC 93-31042. 1994. pap. 15.00 (*0-8330-1486-2*, MR-318-DAG) Rand Corp.

Morris, Mary E. & Hinrichs, Randy J. Web Page Design: A Different Multimedia. 336p. (C). 1996. pap. text 24.95 (*0-13-239880-X*) P-H.

Morris, Mary E., et al. HTML for Fun & Profit. 3rd ed. LC 98-131503. 400p. (C). 1997. pap. 39.95 incl. cd-rom (*0-13-079672-7*) P-H.

Morris, Mary M. A Dangerous Woman. 1997. pap. 12.95 (*0-14-027211-9*, Penguin Bks) Viking Penguin.

— Vanished. 1997. pap. 12.95 (*0-14-027210-0*) Viking Penguin.

***Morris, Mary McGarry.** Fiona Range. LC 00-39918. 2000. write for info. (*1-56895-882-X*) Wheeler Pub.

— Fiona Range: A Novel. 418p. 2000. 24.95 (*0-670-89156-8*, Viking) Viking Penguin.

Morris, Mary McGarry. Songs in Ordinary Time. 740p. 1996. pap. 13.95 (*0-14-024482-4*, Penguin Bks) Viking Penguin.

Morris, Mary S., ed. see Schelle, Johann.

Morris, Maryke, jt. ed. see Crawford, Doreen.

Morris, Mathilde. Dreams & Nightmares of a German War Bride. LC 98-199768. 380p. 1998. pap. 19.95 (*1-57502-889-1*, PO2443) Morris Pubng.

Morris, May, ed. Collected Works of William Morris: Introductions by His Daughter, May Morris, 24 vols., Set. 8748p. (C). (gr. 13). 1992. 2475.00 (*0-415-07972-1*, B0563) Routledge.

An Asterisk (*) at the beginning of an entry indicates that the title is appearing for the first time.

Morris-McKinsey, Jill, ed. Religiously Speaking: Plays & Poems for Children's Church. 48p. (Orig.). (J). 1992. pap. 7.98 (*1-877588-03-2*) Creatively Yours.

Morris, Meaghan. Too Soon Too Late: History in Popular Culture. LC 97-47773. (Theories of Contemporary Culture Ser.: Vol. 22). (Illus.). 352p. 1998. 39.95 (*0-253-33395-4*); pap. 19.95 (*0-253-21188-3*) Ind U Pr.

Morris, Meaghan, jt. ed. see Frow, John.

Morris, Melvin. George Washington on Stamps, Vol. 132. LC 99-168715. (Illus.). 65p. 1997. pap. 12.00 (*0-935991-29-8*) Am Topical Assn.

***Morris, Melvin, ed.** Abraham Lincoln on Worldwide Stamps. LC 99-183142. (American Topical Association Handbook Ser.). 69p. 1998. pap. text 12.00 (*0-935991-32-8*) Am Topical Assn.

Morris, Michael. The Good & the True. LC 92-462. (Oxford Philosophical Monographs). 350p. 1992. text 75.00 (*0-19-823944-0*, Clarendon Pr) OUP.

***Morris, Michael.** Timberframe Plan Book. (Illus.). 128p. 2000. pap. 24.95 (*0-87905-976-1*) Gibbs Smith Pub.

Morris, Michael, tr. from SPA. Contemporary Basque Fiction: An Anthology. LC 90-11921. (Basque Ser.). 112p. 1990. 17.95 (*0-87417-158-X*) U of Nev Pr.

Morris, Michael & Williamson, John B. Poverty & Public Policy: An Analysis of Federal Intervention Efforts, 3. LC 86-398. (Studies in Social Welfare Policies & Programs: No. 3). 248p. 1986. 59.95 (*0-313-24942-3*, MPV/, Greenwood Pr) Greenwood.

Morris, Michael A. Caribbean Maritime Security. LC 93-3841. 270p. 1994. text 69.95 (*0-312-12057-5*) St Martin.

— The Strait of Magellan. (C). 1989. lib. bdg. 110.00 (*0-7923-0181-1*) Kluwer Academic.

Morris, Michael D. Microscopic & Spectroscopic Imaging of the Chemical State. (Practical Spectroscopy Ser.: Vol. 16). (Illus.). 504p. 1993. text 225.00 (*0-8247-9104-5*) Dekker.

***Morris, Michael D., ed.** Biomedical Applications of Raman Spectroscopy. 258p. 1999. pap. text 84.00 (*0-8194-3078-1*) SPIE.

***Morris, Michael E.** The Hunter's Log Book. 105p. 2000. spiral bd. 14.99 (*0-615-11227-7*) Awesome Advent.

Morris, Michael G., jt. auth. see Collins, N. Mark.

Morris, Michael H. Entrepreneurial Intensity: Sustainable Advantages for Individuals, Organizations & Societies. LC 97-31518. 192p. 1998. 59.95 (*0-89930-975-5*, Quorum Bks) Greenwood.

Morris, Michael H. & Morris, Gene. Market-Oriented Pricing: Strategies for Management. LC 89-10712. 218p. 1990. 62.95 (*0-89930-402-8*, MBY/, Greenwood Pr) Greenwood.

Morris, Michael L., ed. Maize Seed Industries in Developing Countries. LC 97-40583. 404p. 1998. pap. text 29.95 (*1-55587-790-7*); lib. bdg. 59.95 (*1-55587-789-3*) L Rienner.

Morris, Michael L., et al. Wheat Production in Bangladesh: Technological, Economic, & Policy Issues, Vol. 106. LC 97-36834. (Research Report Ser.). 1997. write for info. (*0-89629-109-X*) Intl Food Policy.

Morris, Michael P. The Bringing of Wonder: Trade & the Indians of the Southeast, 1700-1783, 36. LC 98-28290. (Contributions in Comparative Colonial Studies: Vol. 36). 176p. 1999. 55.00 (*0-313-30843-8*, Greenwood Pr) Greenwood.

Morris, Michele. Cowboy Life: A Saddlebag Guide for Dudes, Tenderfeet, & Cowpunchers Everywhere. 1993. pap. 12.00 (*0-671-86682-6*, Fireside) S&S Trade Pap.

Morris, Michele R. Mieux Ecrire en Francais: Livret du Professeur. 2nd ed. LC 88-21287. 323p. (Orig.). (C). 1988. pap., teacher ed. 5.00 (*0-87840-226-8*) Georgetown U Pr.

— Mieux Ecrire en Francais: Manuel de Composition et Guide Pratique a l'Usage des Etudiants Anglophones. 2nd ed. LC 88-21287. 323p. (Orig.). (C). 1988. pap. text 14.95 (*0-87840-225-X*) Georgetown U Pr.

Morris, Michele R., ed. Images of America in Revolutionary France. LC 90-3689. (ENG & FRE., Illus.). 225p. (Orig.). 1990. 21.95 (*0-87840-497-X*) Georgetown U Pr.

Morris, Michelle, jt. auth. see O'Donnell, Michael.

Morris, Mike, jt. auth. see Webster, Charlie.

Morris, Milton D. Immigration-The Beleaguered Bureaucracy. LC 84-22962. 150p. 1985. 29.95 (*0-8157-5838-3*); pap. 11.95 (*0-8157-5837-5*) Brookings.

Morris, Milton D., et al. Curbing Illegal Immigration. LC 82-70892. 38p. 1982. pap. 7.95 (*0-8157-5839-1*) Brookings.

Morris, Miranda. Pink Triangle: The Gay Law Reform Debate in Tasmania. (Illus.). xii, 135p. 1995. pap. 26.95 (*0-86840-135-8*, Pub. by New South Wales Univ Pr) Intl Spec Bk.

Morris, Monica B. Last-Chance Children: Growing up with Older Parents. 176p. 1988. 23.00 (*0-231-06694-5*) Col U Pr.

Morris, Morris D. Measuring the Condition of the World's Poor: The Physical Quality of Life Index. LC 79-16613. 190p. 1979. pap. 5.95 (*0-08-023889-0*) Overseas Dev Council.

Morris—orris, WadeWade, jt. illus. see Rankin, Jonathan P.

Morris, Myrle. You, Too, Can Be Forgiven. 208p. 1978. mass mkt. 5.99 (*0-88368-082-3*) Whitaker Hse.

Morris, Myron M. Merry Christmas Maze. (Illus.). 64p. 1997. pap. 2.50 (*0-89375-073-5*) NAL.

— Monster Mazes. 1997. pap. 1.25 (*0-89375-072-7*) NAL.

Morris, N. Hawaii. LC 93-188118. (World Bibliographical Ser.). 360p. 1993. lib. bdg. 91.50 (*1-85109-175-0*) ABC-CLIO.

Morris, N. Ronald, jt. ed. see Cappuccinelli, Piero.

Morris, Nanci A. Just for the Halibut. 75p. spiral bd. 8.00 (*1-57833-088-2*) Todd Commns.

Morris, Nancy. Puerto Rico: Culture, Politics, & Identity. LC 95-14416. (Illus.). 224p. 1995. 57.95 (*0-275-95228-2*, Praeger Pubs); pap. 19.95 (*0-275-95452-8*, Praeger Pubs) Greenwood.

Morris, Neil. Cars. LC 96-30009. (Traveling Through Time Ser.). (J). 1997. 18.95 (*0-382-39787-8*) Silver Burdett Pr.

— Cars. LC 96-30009. (Traveling Through Time Ser.). (J). (gr. 5). 1997. pap. 8.95 (*0-382-39788-6*) Silver Burdett Pr.

— Caves. LC 96-30859. (The World's Top Ten Ser.). (Illus.). 32p. (J). 1997. lib. bdg. 22.83 (*0-8172-4346-1*) Raintree Steck-V.

— Cities. LC 96-30119. (World's Top Ten Ser.). (Illus.). 32p. (J). 1997. lib. bdg. 22.83 (*0-8172-4344-5*) Raintree Steck-V.

— Deserts. (World's Top Ten Ser.). (Illus.). 32p. (J). 1997. lib. bdg. 24.26 (*0-8172-4341-0*) Raintree Steck-V.

— Earthquakes. (Natural Disasters Ser.). (Illus.). 32p. (YA). (gr. 5 up). 1999. pap. 5.95 (*0-7641-1059-4*) Barron.

***Morris, Neil.** Hurricanes & Tornadoes. (Natural Disasters Ser.). (Illus.). 32p. (YA). (gr. 5 up). 1999. pap. 5.95 (*0-7641-1060-8*) Barron.

Morris, Neil. Islands. LC 96-11580. (World's Top Ten Ser.). (Illus.). 32p. (J). 1997. lib. bdg. 22.83 (*0-8172-4340-2*) Raintree Steck-V.

— Lakes. LC 96-27639. (The World's Top Ten Ser.). (Illus.). 32p. (J). 1997. lib. bdg. 22.83 (*0-8172-4345-3*) Raintree Steck-V.

— Mountain Ranges. LC 96-4091. (World's Top Ten Ser.). (Illus.). 32p. (J). 1997. lib. bdg. 22.83 (*0-8172-4339-9*) Raintree Steck-V.

— Oceans & Seas. LC 96-27638. (World's Top Ten Ser.). (Illus.). 32p. (J). 1997. lib. bdg. 22.83 (*0-8172-4343-7*) Raintree Steck-V.

— Planes. LC 97-21773. (Traveling Through Time Ser.). 1997. 18.95 (*0-382-39791-6*) Silver Burdett Pr.

— Planes. LC 97-21773. (Traveling Through Time Ser.). (J). (gr. 5). 1997. pap. 8.95 (*0-382-39792-4*) Silver Burdett Pr.

— Rivers. LC 96-642. (World's Top Ten Ser.). (Illus.). 32p. (J). 1997. lib. bdg. 22.83 (*0-8172-4338-0*) Raintree Steck-V.

— Ships. LC 97-12533. (J). 1997. 18.95 (*0-382-39789-4*) Silver Burdett Pr.

— Ships. LC 97-12533. (J). (gr. 5). 1997. pap. 8.95 (*0-382-39790-8*) Silver Burdett Pr.

— Trains Traveling Through Time. LC 96-51499. (J). 1997. pap. write for info. (*0-382-39794-0*); lib. bdg. 18.95 (*0-382-39793-2*) Silver Burdett Pr.

— Wonders of Our World, 10 vols., Set. (Illus.). (J). (gr. 2-7). 1995. pap. 34.75 (*0-86505-848-2*); lib. bdg. 89.75 (*0-86505-836-9*) Crabtree Pub Co.

Morris, Neil. Wonders of Our World Series, 10 bks. Incl. Caves. (Illus.). 32p. (J). (gr. 2-7). 1995. pap. 6.95 (*0-86505-842-3*); Caves. (Illus.). 32p. (J). (gr. 2-7). 1995. lib. bdg. 20.60 (*0-86505-830-X*); Deserts. (Illus.). 32p. (J). (gr. 2-7). 1995. lib. bdg. 20.60 (*0-86505-827-X*); Deserts. LC 95-23440. (Illus.). 32p. (J). (gr. 1-4). 1995. pap. 6.95 (*0-86505-839-3*); Earthquakes. LC 98-93071. (Illus.). 32p. (J). (gr. 1-7). 1998. pap. 6.95 (*0-86505-844-X*); Earthquakes. LC 98-3306. (Illus.). 32p. (J). (gr. 2-7). 1998. lib. bdg. 20.60 (*0-86505-832-6*); Forests. LC 98-10766. (Illus.). 32p. (J). (gr. 2-7). 1998. pap. 6.95 (*0-86505-845-8*); Forests. LC 98-10766. (Illus.). 32p. (J). (gr. 2-7). 1998. lib. bdg. 20.60 (*0-86505-833-4*); Hurricanes & Tornados. LC 98-93032. (Illus.). 32p. (J). (gr. 4-11). 1998. pap. 6.95 (*0-86505-843-1*); Hurricanes & Tornados. LC 98-11203. (Illus.). 32p. (J). (gr. 2-7). 1998. lib. bdg. 20.60 (*0-86505-831-8*); Mountains. LC 95-23442. (Illus.). 32p. (J). (gr. 1-4). 1995. pap. 6.95 (*0-86505-841-5*); Mountains. (Illus.). 32p. (J). (gr. 2-7). 1995. lib. bdg. 20.60 (*0-86505-829-6*); Oceans. LC 95-31007. (Illus.). 32p. (J). (gr. 1-4). 1995. pap. 6.95 (*0-86505-840-7*); Oceans. (Illus.). 32p. (J). (gr. 2-7). 1995. lib. bdg. 20.60 (*0-86505-828-8*); Rivers & Lakes. LC 98-11202. (Illus.). 32p. (J). (gr. 8-12). 1998. pap. 6.95 (*0-86505-846-6*); Rivers & Lakes. LC 98-11202. (Illus.). 32p. (J). (gr. 2-7). 1998. lib. bdg. 20.60 (*0-86505-834-2*); Rocks & Minerals. LC 98-93072. (Illus.). 32p. (J). (gr. 4-7). 1998. pap. 6.95 (*0-86505-847-4*); Rocks & Minerals. LC 98-3307. (Illus.). 32p. (J). (gr. 2-7). 1998. lib. bdg. 20.60 (*0-86505-835-0*); Volcanoes. (Illus.). 32p. (J). (gr. 2-7). 1995. pap. 6.95 (*0-86505-838-5*); Volcanoes. (Illus.). 32p. (J). (gr. 2-7). 1995. lib. bdg. 20.60 (*0-86505-826-1*); (Illus.). (J). Set pap. 69.50 (*0-86505-849-0*); Set lib. bdg. 206.00 (*0-86505-837-7*) Crabtree Pub Co.

Morris, Neil. Wonders of the World Atlas. LC 98-10046. (Illus.). 48p. (J). (gr. 3-8). 1999. write for info. (*0-7166-9600-2*) World Bk.

Morris, Neil & Melling, David. My First Monolingual English Words. LC 98-37176. (My First ...Words to See Ser.). 48p. (J). 1999. 11.95 (*0-8442-2405-7*, 24057, Passprt Bks) NTC Contemp Pub Co.

***Morris, Neil & Morris, Roswitha, eds.** The Oxford Cartoon-Strip German Vocabulary Builder. (Illus.). 80p. 2000. pap. 11.95 (*0-19-860305-3*) OUP.

Morris, Neil & Morris, Roswitha, eds. The Oxford Starter German Dictionary. LC 96-43637. 376p. 1997. pap. 8.95 (*0-19-860033-X*) OUP.

Morris, Neil, jt. auth. see Cox, Reg.

Morris, Neil, jt. auth. see Morris, Ting.

Morris, Noel. Electrical & Electronic Engineering Principles. (Illus.). 420p. (Orig.). 1994. pap. 42.50 (*0-582-09815-7*, Pub. by Addison-Wesley) Trans-Atl Phila.

— Mastering Electrical Engineering. 2nd ed. 1991. 30.00 (*0-07-043295-3*) McGraw-Hill Prof.

Morris, Noel M. Circuitos Electricos. (SPA.). (C). 1993. pap. text 24.66 (*0-201-60149-4*) Addison-Wesley.

***Morris, Norene.** Tumbleweeds. 464p. 2000. pap. 4.97 (*1-57748-827-X*) Barbour Pub.

Morris, Norman, ed. see International Congress of Psychosomatic Obstetrics.

Morris, Norval. The Brothel Boy & Other Parables of the Law. 352p. 1994. reprint ed. pap. 15.95 (*0-19-509386-0*) OUP.

— The Future of Imprisonment. LC 74-13920. (Studies in Crime & Justice). xiv, 144p. 1993. pap. text 3.95 (*0-226-53906-7*) U Ch Pr.

— The Future of Imprisonment. LC 74-13920. (Studies in Crime & Justice). xiv, 144p. 1994. lib. bdg. 12.50 (*0-226-53905-9*) U Ch Pr.

— The Habitual Criminal. LC 72-9831. 395p. 1973. reprint ed. lib. bdg. 83.50 (*0-8371-6601-2*, MOHC, Greenwood Pr) Greenwood.

— Madness & the Criminal Law. LC 82-13435. (Studies in Crime & Justice). 168p. (C). 1995. pap. text 8.95 (*0-226-53908-3*) U Ch Pr.

— Madness & the Criminal Law. LC 82-13435. (Studies in Crime & Justice). 237p. (C). 1998. lib. bdg. 24.00 (*0-226-53907-5*) U Ch Pr.

Morris, Norval & Hawkins, Gordon J. The Honest Politican's Guide to Crime Control. LC 76-101467. 284p. 1972. pap. text 8.95 (*0-226-53902-4*, P460) U Ch Pr.

— Honest Politician's Guide to Crime Control. LC 76-101467. 1995. lib. bdg. 21.00 (*0-226-53901-6*) U Ch Pr.

— Letter to the President on Crime Control. LC 76-54657. 1993. pap. text 1.95 (*0-226-53998-9*) U Ch Pr.

Morris, Norval & Rothman, David J., eds. The Oxford History of the Prison: The Practice of Punishment in Western Society. (Illus.). 512p. 1995. 49.95 (*0-19-506153-5*) OUP.

— The Oxford History of the Prison: The Practice of Punishment in Western Society. (Illus.). 448p. 1997. pap. 19.95 (*0-19-511814-6*) OUP.

Morris, Norval & Tonry, Michael H. Between Prison & Probation: Intermediate Punishments in a Rational Sentencing System. (Illus.). 304p. 1991. reprint ed. pap. 11.95 (*0-19-507138-7*) OUP.

— Crime & Justice: An Annual Review of Research, Vol. 11. 480p. (C). 1981. reprint ed. lib. bdg. 23.50 (*0-226-53957-1*) U Ch Pr.

— Crime & Justice: An Annual Review of Research, Vol. 11. 480p. (C). 1981. reprint ed. pap. text 10.00 (*0-226-53959-8*) U Ch Pr.

Morris, Norval & Tonry, Michael H., eds. Crime & Justice: An Annual Review of Research, Vol. 1. 360p. 1979. lib. bdg. 17.00 (*0-226-53955-5*, P903) U Ch Pr.

— Crime & Justice: An Annual Review of Research, Vol. 1. 360p. 1980. pap. text 8.50 (*0-226-53956-3*, P903) U Ch Pr.

Morris, Norval, jt. auth. see Tonry, Michael H.

Morris, Norval, jt. ed. see Tonry, Michael H.

Morris-Olson, Melissa. Survival Strategies for Christian Colleges & Universities: A Leader's Guide to Managing in Turbulent Times. LC 97-171908. 122p. 1996. pap. 14.50 (*0-9652730-0-8*) Coal Christian Coll.

Morris, Oradel N. I Hear the Song of the Houmas: J'Entends la Chanson des Houmas. LC 88-92449. (Gens de la Louisiane - Peoples of Louisiana Ser.: Bk. 2). (ENG & FRE., Illus.). 160p. 1992. 29.95 (*0-944064-04-3*) Paupieres Pub.

— Little Angel Dancer. (Illus.). (Orig.). (J). (gr. 1-8). 1999. pap. write for info. (*0-944064-06-X*) Paupieres Pub.

— Le Monde Acadien de Ti-Jean. LC 81-107884. (Gens de la Louisiane - Peoples of Louisiana Ser.: Bk. 1).Tr. of Cajun World of Ti-Jean. (ENG & FRE., Illus.). 81p. (J). (gr. k-8). 1980. reprint ed. 8.95 (*0-944064-01-9*) Paupieres Pub.

— Le Reve de Ti-Jean: (Ti-Jean's Dream) (ENG & FRE.). (Orig.). 1983. pap. 4.50 (*0-944064-02-7*) Paupieres Pub.

Morris, Owen, ed. The 'Chymick Bookes' . . . of Sir Owen Wynne of Gwydir Vol. 4: Libri Pertinentes: An Annotated Catalogue. (Medieval & Renaissance Texts & Studies: Vol. 178). 68p. 1997. pap. 10.00 (*0-86698-220-5*, MR178) MRTS.

Morris, P. A. The Hedgehog. (Illus.). 14p. 1989. pap. 5.25 (*0-85263-958-9*, Pub. by Shire Pubns) Parkwest Pubns.

Morris, P. E. The Psychology of Memory, Vol. 1. (C). 1993. lib. bdg. 125.00 (*0-8147-5493-7*) NYU Pr.

Morris, P. J., jt. ed. see Mossman, S. T.

Morris, P. R. A History of the World Semiconductor Industry. (History of Technology Ser.: No. 12). 160p. 1990. 72.00 (*0-86341-227-0*, HT012) INSPEC Inc.

Morris, Pam. Bleak House. Martin, Graham, ed. (Open Guides to Literature Ser.). 112p. 1991. 102.50 (*0-335-09029-X*); pap. 27.95 (*0-335-09028-1*) OpUniv Pr.

— Literature & Feminism: An Introduction. LC 92-41839. 220p. 1993. pap. 26.95 (*0-631-18421-X*) Blackwell Pubs.

Morris, Pam, ed. The Bakhtin Reader: Selected Writings of Bakhtin, Medvedev, Voloshinov. (An Arnold Publication). 272p. 1997. pap. text 18.95 (*0-340-59267-2*, B3437, Pub. by E A) OUP.

Morris, Pamela. Book of the Horse. 1996. 6.98 (*0-7858-0544-3*) Bk Sales Inc.

Morris, Pamela, jt. auth. see Webster, Dottie.

Morris, Pamela, tr. see Bernanos, Georges.

Morris, Pat. Hedgehogs. (Illus.). 124p. text 19.95 (*0-905483-28-6*, Pub. by Whittet Bks) Diamond Farm Bk.

Morris, Pat, jt. auth. see Burgis, Mary J.

Morris, Pat, ed. see Schaub, Janette.

Morris, Patricia, jt. auth. see Brody, Helen.

Morris, Patricia J. & Muir, Jeannette T. Worth Doing Twice: Creating Quilts from Old Tops. LC 98-87382. (Illus.). 128p. 1999. per. 19.95 (*0-87341-706-2*) Krause Pubns.

Morris, Patricia M., et al. Trying to Take Root: Sustainable Agriculture in the U. S. Heartland. (Illus.). 94p. (Orig.). 1992. pap. 15.00 (*1-881360-00-8*) Public Voice.

Morris, Patricia R., jt. auth. see Persico, John, Jr.

Morris, Patricia S. & Berry, Margaret A. Stepping into Research! A Complete Research Skills Activities Program for Grades 5-12. 352p. 1990. pap. text 34.95 (*0-87628-800-X*) Ctr Appl Res.

Morris, Patricia S., jt. auth. see Berry, Margaret A.

***Morris, Patrick.** Nonlinear Editing. LC 99-32801. 224p. 1999. pap. 29.95 (*0-240-51564-1*, Focal) Buttrwrth-Heinemann.

Morris, Patrick F. Anaconda Montana: Copper Smelting Boom Town on the Western Frontier. LC 96-93090. (Illus.). v, 327p. (Orig.). 1997. pap. 16.95 (*0-9657209-2-6*) Swann Pub.

Morris, Paul. The Hong Kong School Curriculum. 2nd ed. 182p. 1996. pap. 33.50 (*962-209-412-0*, Pub. by HK Univ Pr) Coronet Bks.

***Morris, Paul.** A Practical Guide to Fund-Raising in Schools. LC 99-87277. 208p. 2000. write for info. (*0-415-22957-X*) Routledge.

Morris, Paul. Telling Jews about Jesus. 1994. pap. text 8.99 (*0-946462-32-1*, Pub. by Evangelical Pr) P & R Pubng.

— A Walk in the Garden: Biblical, Iconographical & Literary Images of Eden. Sawyer, Deborah, ed. (Journal for the Study of the Old Testament Supplement Ser.: No. 136). 220p. (C). 1992. 65.00 (*1-85075-338-5*, Pub. by Sheffield Acad) CUP Services.

Morris, Paul & Sweeting, Anthony, eds. Education & Development in East Asia. LC 95-1545. (Reference Books in International Education: Vol. 31). (Illus.). 312p. 1995. text 66.00 (*0-8153-1598-8*, SS942) Garland.

Morris, Paul & Williamson, John, eds. Teacher Education in the Asia-Pacific Region: A Comparative Study. LC 99-39999. (Reference Books in International Education: Vol. 48). (Illus.). 350p. 1999. 65.00 (*0-8153-1856-1*) Garland.

Morris, Paul, jt. ed. see Marsh, Colin J.

Morris, Paul C. Maritime Nantucket. LC 96-77311. (Illus.). 272p. 1996. 40.00 (*0-936972-16-5*) Lower Cape.

— Maritime Sketches. LC 85-50662. (Illus.). 88p. 1985. pap. 10.00 (*0-936972-07-6*) Lower Cape.

— A Portrait of a Ship, the Benj. F. Packard. LC 87-80164. (Illus.). 200p. 1987. 30.00 (*0-936972-09-2*) Lower Cape.

— Schooners & Schooner Barges. LC 84-81110. (Illus.). 160p. 1984. 30.00 (*0-936972-06-8*) Lower Cape.

Morris, Paul C. & Morin, Joseph F. The Island Steamers: A Chronology of Steam Transportation to & from the Offshore Islands of Martha's Vineyard & Nantucket. 2nd ed. Towne, Sumner A., Jr., ed. LC 77-79090. (Illus.). 196p. 1977. pap. 11.95 (*0-686-28900-5*) Nantucket Nautical.

Morris, Paul C. & Quinn, William P. Shipwrecks in New York Waters. (Illus.). 240p. 1989. 34.95 (*0-940160-44-7*) Parnassus Imprints.

— Shipwrecks in New York Waters: A Chronology of Ship Disasters from Montauk Point to Barnegat Inlet from the 1880s to the 1930s. (Illus.). 246p. 1999. reprint ed. pap. text 30.00 (*0-7881-6207-1*) DIANE Pub.

Morris, Paul J., II & Tchudi, Stephen. The New Literacy: Moving Beyond the 3Rs. LC 98-33552. 288p. 1998. pap. text 20.00 (*0-9663233-4-3*, 323343) Calendar Islands.

Morris, Paul J. & Tchudi, Stephen N. The New Literacy: Moving Beyond the 3 Rs. LC 96-25189. 1996. 30.95 (*0-7879-0292-6*) Jossey-Bass.

Morris, Paul L. Secrets of More Powerful Personal Prayer: Gaining Assurance Through Greater Faith. 174p. 1996. pap. 11.95 (*0-9645356-3-7*) Morris-Lee Pub.

Morris, Paula. Auditing 426 Handouts. 93p. (C). 1997. pap. 10.00 (*1-886855-82-X*) Tavenner Pub.

Morris, Paulette, jt. auth. see Skellington, Richard.

Morris, Pearse. Practical Neuroangiography. LC 97-3874. (Illus.). 400p. 1997. 99.00 (*0-683-30020-2*) Lppncott W & W.

Morris, Percy A. Field Guide to Atlantic Coast Shells. 3rd ed. LC 72-75612. (Illus.). 1973. 15.95 (*0-685-02290-0*) HM.

Morris, Percy A., jt. auth. see Abbott, R. Tucker.

Morris, Peter. Advanced MS Visual Basic. LC 97-26386. 900p. 1997. pap. text 39.99 (*1-57231-414-1*) Microsoft.

— David Cronenberg: A Delicate Balance. LC 94-211006. (Illus.). 160p. 1994. pap. 9.95 (*1-55022-191-4*) LPC InBook.

— Embattled Shadows: A History of Canadian Cinema, 1895-1939. (Illus.). 368p. 1992. reprint ed. pap. 24.95 (*0-7735-0323-4*, Pub. by McG-Queens Univ Pr) CUP Services.

— Fountains Dyed Blue for a Day. Hathaway, Michael, ed. 56p. (Orig.). 1992. pap. 10.00 (*0-943795-21-4*) Chiron Rev.

— French Politics Today. LC 93-40663. 1994. text 18.95 (*0-7190-3764-6*, Pub. by Manchester Univ Pr) St Martin.

***Morris, Peter.** Herbs for Magic & Ritual: A Beginner's Guide. (Headway Guides for Beginners Ser.). (Illus.). 96p. 2000. pap. 11.95 (*0-340-74255-0*, Pub. by Headway) Trafalgar.

Morris, Peter. Introduction to Game Theory. LC 94-6515. (Universitext Ser.). (Illus.). 230p. 1996. 29.95 (*0-387-94284-X*) Spr-Verlag.

Morris, Peter, ed. Cantonese Love Songs: An English Translation of Jiu Ji-yung's Cantonese Songs of the Early 19th Century. 216p. (C). 1992. pap. text 27.50 (*962-209-284-5*, Pub. by HK Univ Pr) Coronet Bks.

— Modelling Cognition. LC 86-28229. (Illus.). 325p. 1987. reprint ed. pap. 100.80 (*0-608-05289-2*, 206582700001) Bks Demand.

***Morris, Peter & Bryce, James.** Cereal Biotechnology. 256p. 2001. text 170.00 (*1-85573-498-2*, Pub. by Woodhead Pubng) Am Educ Systs.

M

An Asterisk (*) at the beginning of an entry indicates that the title is appearing for the first time.

Morris, Peter & Gruneberg, Michael M., eds. Theoretical Aspects of Memory, Vol. 2. 2nd ed. LC 93-27616. (Illus.). 304p. (C). 1994. pap. 24.99 (*0-415-06958-0*, B3706) Routledge.

Morris, Peter & Hawkins, Frank. Birds of Madagascar: A Photographic Guide. LC 98-86266. (Illus.). 224p. 1998. 40.00 (*0-300-07755-6*) Yale U Pr.

Morris, Peter & Jacobs, Daniel. Tunisia. 5th ed. (Rough Guide Ser.). (Illus.). 466p. (Orig.). 1998. pap. 17.95 (*1-85828-336-1*, Pub. by Rough Guides) Penguin Putnam.

Morris, Peter & Therivel, Riki, eds. Methods of Environment Impact Assessment. 256p. 1994. 75.00 (*1-85728-214-0*, Pub. by UCL Pr Ltd); pap. 27.50 (*1-85728-215-9*, Pub. by UCL Pr Ltd) Taylor & Francis.

Morris, Peter, jt. auth. see Cornick, Martyn.

Morris, Peter, jt. auth. see Kavanagh, Dennis A.

Morris, Peter, jt. auth. see McDonald, Malcolm.

Morris, Peter, jt. auth. see McDonald, Malcolm H.

Morris, Peter, jt. auth. see Oakland, John.

Morris, Peter, jt. ed. see Foden, David.

Morris, Peter, ed. see Williams, Trevor I.

Morris, Peter, tr. see Berstein, Serge.

Morris, Peter, tr. see Sadoul, Georges.

Morris, Peter A., ed. Netherlands International Law Review: Index, Vols. I-XXX. (C). 1991. lib. bdg. 135.50 (*0-7923-0906-5*) Kluwer Academic.

Morris, Peter E. & Conway, Martin E., eds. The Psychology of Memory, 3 vols. LC 92-45221. (International Library of Critical Writings in Business History). (C). 1993. lib. bdg. 375.00 (*0-8147-5496-1*) NYU Pr.

Morris, Peter E. & Hampson, Peter J. Understanding Cognitive Psychology. Smith, Peter K., ed. (Basic Psychology Ser.). (Illus.). 399p. (C). 1995. 70.95 (*0-631-15749-2*); pap. 28.95 (*0-631-15751-4*) Blackwell Pubs.

***Morris, Peter J.** Aliens Amongst Us. (Guides for Beginners Ser.). (Illus.). 96p. 2000. pap. 11.95 (*0-340-75833-3*, Pub. by Headway) Trafalgar.

Morris, Peter J. Kidney Transplantation. 4th ed. (Illus.). 576p. 1994. text 175.00 (*0-7216-4557-7*, W B Saunders Co) Harcrt Hlth Sci Grp.

— Polymer Pioneers: A Popular History of the Science & Technology of Large Molecules. (BCHOC Publication Ser.: No. 5). (Illus.). 88p. (Orig.). 1986. pap. 12.00 (*0-941901-03-3*, TP1116.M67 1986) Chem Heritage Fnd.

Morris, Peter J. & Malt, Ronald A., eds. The Oxford Textbook of Surgery. (Illus.). cd-rom 300.00 (*0-614-19712-0*, OP916195WE) OUP.

— The Oxford Textbook of Surgery. (Illus.). 1994. text 225.00 (*0-19-261800-8*) OUP.

Morris, Peter J. & Warlow, Charles P., eds. Transient Ischemic Attacks. LC 82-9668. (Science & Practice of Surgery Ser.: No. 3). (Illus.). 430p. reprint ed. pap. 133.30 (*0-7837-0923-4*, 204122800019) Bks Demand.

Morris, Peter M. The Days of Visitation: A Practical & Statistical Study of the Parishes of the Diocese of Swansea & Brecon Based on the Returns to the Visitation Questionnaire of Bishop Vaughan from 1977 to 1987. LC 89-48075. (Welsh Studies: Vol. 2). 272p. 1990. lib. bdg. 89.95 (*0-88946-065-5*) E Mellen.

Morris, Peter M. & James, Edward. A Critical Word Book of Leviticus, Numbers, Deuteronomy. (Computer Bible Ser.: Vol. 8). 1975. pap. 59.95 (*0-935106-13-8*) E Mellen.

— A Critical Word Book of the Pentateuch. (Computer Bible Ser.: Vol. 17). 1980. pap. 99.95 (*0-935106-03-0*) E Mellen.

Morris, Philip, ed. see White, Marjorie L. & Lewis, Peirce.

Morris, Philip A. Vulcan & His Times. LC 95-81571. (Illus.). 64p. (Orig.). 1995. pap. 9.95 (*0-943994-20-9*) Birmingham Hist Soc.

Morris, Philip A. & White, Marjorie L., eds. Designs on Birmingham: A Landscape History of a Southern City & Its Suburbs. (Illus.). (Orig.). 1989. 29.95 (*0-943994-14-4*); pap. 16.95 (*0-943994-15-2*) Birmingham Hist Soc.

Morris, Philip A., jt. auth. see White, Marjorie L.

Morris, Philip A., jt. ed. see White, Marjorie L.

Morris-Pierce, Elizabeth. Onward! Through the Fog! Six Dialogues Following the Example of Christ Through Lent. LC 98-44906. 88p. 1999. pap. 8.50 (*0-7880-1310-6*) CSS OH.

Morris Publishing Company Staff. The Mormon Trail Cookbook: Endeavors, Struggles & Cooking Traditions of the Mormon Pioneers. Feely, Dawn et al, eds. (Illus.). 194p. 1997. 10.95 (*1-57502-476-4*, Cookbks by Morris) Morris Pubng.

Morris, R. Artificial Worlds: Computers, Complexity & the Riddle of Life. LC 99-17912. (Illus.). 200p. (C). 1999. 25.95 (*0-306-46002-5*, Kluwer Plenum) Kluwer Academic.

— Ocean Life. (Mysteries & Marvels Ser.). (Illus.). 32p. (J). (gr. 3-7). 1983. text 5.95 (*0-86020-753-6*, Usborne) EDC.

— Ocean Life. (Mysteries & Marvels Ser.). (Illus.). 32p. (J). (gr. 3-7). 1999. lib. bdg. 14.95 (*0-88110-149-4*, Usborne) EDC.

— The Works of Edmund Spencer. 1988. reprint ed. lib. bdg. 99.00 (*0-7812-0237-X*) Rprt Serv.

Morris, R., ed. The Blickiling Homilies, Pts. I-III. (EETS, OS Ser.: Vols. 58 & 63, 73). 1874. 55.00 (*0-8115-3354-9*) Periodicals Srv.

— Chaucer's Translation of Boethius's 'de Consolatione Philosophiae' (EETS Extra Ser.: Vol. 5). 1969. reprint ed. 30.00 (*0-19-722503-9*, Pub. by EETS) Boydell & Brewer.

— Cursor Mundi Vol. I: Text 11.1-4954, Vol. I. (EETS Original Ser.: Vol. 57). 1963. reprint ed. 20.00 (*0-19-722057-6*, Pub. by EETS) Boydell & Brewer.

— Cursor Mundi Vol. I: Text 11.1-4954, Vol. II. (EETS Original Ser.: Vol. 57). 1966. reprint ed. 20.00 (*0-19-722059-2*, Pub. by EETS) Boydell & Brewer.

— Cursor Mundi Vol. I: Text 11.1-4954, Vol. III. (EETS Original Ser.: Vol. 57). 1966. reprint ed. 20.00 (*0-19-722062-2*, Pub. by EETS) Boydell & Brewer.

— Cursor Mundi Vol. I: Text 11.1-4954, Vol. IV. (EETS Original Ser.: Vol. 57). 1966. reprint ed. 20.00 (*0-19-722066-5*, Pub. by EETS) Boydell & Brewer.

— Cursor Mundi Vol. I: Text 11.1-4954, Vol. V. (EETS Original Ser.: Vol. 57). 1966. reprint ed. 20.00 (*0-19-722068-1*, Pub. by EETS) Boydell & Brewer.

— Cursor Mundi Vol. I: Text 11.1-4954, Vol. VI. (EETS Original Ser.: Vol. 57). 1963. reprint ed. 20.00 (*0-19-722099-1*, Pub. by EETS) Boydell & Brewer.

— Cursor Mundi Vol. I: Text 11.1-4954, Vol. VII. (EETS Original Ser.: Vol. 57). 1963. reprint ed. 20.00 (*0-19-722101-7*, Pub. by EETS) Boydell & Brewer.

— Early English Alliterative Poems. (EETS, OS Ser.: Vol. 1). 1972. reprint ed. 30.00 (*0-8115-3340-9*) Periodicals Srv.

— Early English Alliterative Poems from Ms. Cotton Nero Ax. (EETS Original Ser.: Vol. 1). 1965. reprint ed. 30.00 (*0-19-722001-0*, Pub. by EETS) Boydell & Brewer.

— Story of Genesis & Exodus. (EETS Original Ser.: Vol. 7). 1996. reprint ed. 54.00 (*0-85991-801-7*, Pub. by EETS) Boydell & Brewer.

— The Story of Genesis & Exodus: An Early English Song. (EETS, OS Ser.: No. 7). 1974. reprint ed. 54.00 (*0-527-00006-X*) Periodicals Srv.

Morris, R., et al, eds. Acid Toxicity & Aquatic Animals. (Society for Experimental Biology Seminar Ser.: No. 34). 296p. 1989. text 95.00 (*0-521-33435-7*) Cambridge U Pr.

— Health-Related Water Microbiology, 1996: Selected Proceedings of the IAWQ 8th International Symposium on Health-Related Water Microbiology 1996, Held in Mallorca, Spain, 6-10 October 1996. 482p. 1997. pap. 255.00 (*0-08-043300-6*, Pergamon Pr) Elsevier.

— Health-Related Water Microbiology 1994: Selected Proceedings of the International Symposium Organized by the IAWQ Specialist Group on Health-Related Water Microbiology as Part of Water Quality International 1994, 17th Biennial Conference of the IAWQ, Budapest, Hungary, Held July 24-30, 1994. (Water Science & Technology Ser.). (Illus.). 488p. 1995. pap. 206.25 (*0-08-042655-7*, Pergamon Pr) Elsevier.

Morris, R. & Payne, R. An Anthology of Machine Postal Markings. 5. Billings, Bart, ed. (Illus.). 83p. 1994. pap. 12.50 (*1-880065-08-8*) Machine Cancel Soc.

— The Columbia Story: Early History, Etc. of the Columbia Postal Supply Co. (Illus.). 244p. 1994. pap. 21.00 (*1-880065-09-6*) Machine Cancel Soc.

Morris, R., jt. auth. see Cork, Barbara.

Morris, R. A. & Andre, J., eds. Raster Imaging & Digital Typography II. (Cambridge Series on Electronic Publishing). (Illus.). 229p. (C). 1991. text 74.95 (*0-521-41764-3*) Cambridge U Pr.

Morris, R. G., ed. Parallel Distributed Processing: Implications for Psychology & Neurobiology. (Illus.). 352p. 1990. 75.00 (*0-19-852178-2*) OUP.

Morris, R. J. & Rodger, Richard, eds. Victorial City 1820-1914. LC 92-28232. (Readers in Urban History Ser.). (C). 1993. text 55.50 (*0-582-05133-9*, 79760) Longman.

— Victorian City 1820-1914. LC 92-28232. (Readers in Urban History Ser.). (C). 1993. pap. text 29.95 (*0-582-05132-0*, 79759) Longman.

Morris, R. J., jt. auth. see Langton, John.

Morris, R. J., jt. ed. see Fraser, Hamish.

Morris, R. O. Sixteenth Century Anthem Book. 6th ed. 122p. 1988. pap. 13.50 (*0-19-353407-X*) OUP.

Morris, R. W., et al, eds. Health-Related Water Microbiology 1992. (Water Science & Technology Ser.: Vol. 27). 500p. 1993. pap. 231.00 (*0-08-042207-1*, Pergamon Pr) Elsevier.

Morris, R. Winston & Goldstein, Edward R., eds. The Tuba Source Book. LC 94-48097. 992p. 1995. 79.95 (*0-253-32889-6*) Ind U Pr.

***Morris, Rachel & Clements, Luke, eds.** Gaining Ground: Law Reform for Gypsies & Travellers. (Illus.). 176p. 1999. pap. 33.95 (*0-900458-98-4*, Pub. by Univ of Herfordshire) Bold Strummer Ltd.

Morris, Ralph. The Life & Astonishing Adventures of John Daniel. LC 74-16398. (Science Fiction Ser.). (Illus.). 276p. 1975. reprint ed. 26.95 (*0-405-06307-5*) Ayer.

Morris, Ralph C. Air Conditioning Cutter's Ready Reference. rev. ed. LC 73-148571. (Illus.). 363p. 1971. 27.95 (*0-912524-02-2*) Busn News.

Morris, Randall C. Process Philosophy & Political Ideology: The Social & Political Thought of Alfred North Whitehead & Charles Hartshorne. LC 89-49229. 289p. (C). 1991. pap. text 21.95 (*0-7914-0416-1*) State U NY Pr.

Morris, Raymond N. Behind the Jester's Mask: Canadian Editorial Cartoons about Dominant & Minority Groups 1960-1979. 230p. 1989. text 40.00 (*0-8020-5806-X*) U of Toronto Pr.

— The Carnivalization of Politics: Quebec Cartoons on Relations with Canada, England & France, 1960-1979. (Illus.). 160p. 1995. 55.00 (*0-7735-1318-3*, Pub. by McG-Queens Univ Pr) CUP Services.

Morris, Reg & Payne, Rob. American Service Markings. 2nd ed. 102p. 1992. pap. 10.00 (*1-880065-02-9*) Machine Cancel Soc.

Morris, Reg & Payne, Robert J. Barr-Fyke Machines & Postal Markings, 3 vols., Set. (Illus.). 116p. 1990. pap. 26.00 (*0-9621481-4-8*); pap. 26.00 (*0-9621481-5-6*); pap. 26.00 (*0-9621481-6-4*) Machine Cancel Soc.

— Groth-Constantine Machines & Postal Markings. (Illus.). 95p. (Orig.). 1990. pap. text 7.00 (*0-9621481-1-3*) Machine Cancel Soc.

— Hampden: Machines & Postal Markings. 206p. (C). 1991. pap. 17.50 (*1-880065-01-0*) Machine Cancel Soc.

— Perfection Mechanical Hand Stamp Machine. (Illus.). 63p. 1991. pap. 8.00 (*0-9621481-9-9*) Machine Cancel Soc.

— Pneumatic: Machines & Postal Markings. 176p. (C). 1992. pap. 15.00 (*1-880065-00-2*) Machine Cancel Soc.

Morris, Reg, ed. see Billings, Bart.

Morris, Reginald O. Figured Harmony at the Keyboard, 2 vols., Vol. 1. 62p. 1968. 17.50 (*0-19-321471-7*) OUP.

— Figured Harmony at the Keyboard, 2 vols., Vol. 2. 30p. 1968. 14.95 (*0-19-321472-5*) OUP.

— Introduction to Counterpoint: Music Book Index. 55p. 1993. reprint ed. lib. bdg. 69.00 (*0-7812-9677-3*) Rprt Serv.

Morris, Reginald O. & Ferguson, Howard. Preparatory Exercises in Score Reading. 116p. 1968. 21.95 (*0-19-321475-X*) OUP.

Morris, Richard. Achilles in the Quantum Universe: The Definitive History of Infinity. LC 96-49772. 1997. 25.00 (*0-8050-4779-4*) H Holt & Co.

— Assyrians. 112p. (Orig.). 1991. pap. 10.95 (*0-912292-92-X*) Smith.

— Cosmic Questions: Galactic Halos, Cold Dark Matter & the End of Time. LC 93-13373. 208p. 1995. pap. 16.95 (*0-471-13296-9*) Wiley.

— Early Warning Indicators of Corporate Failure: A Critical Review of Previous Research & Further Empirical Evidence. LC 97-73608. 440p. 1997. 101.95 (*1-85972-565-1*, Pub. by Ashgate Pub) Ashgate Pub Co.

— Misshapen Banana. 1990. pap. 3.50 (*0-938979-36-1*) EG Bksellers.

— Sinners, Lovers, & Heroes: An Essay on Memorializing in Three American Cultures. LC 97-13019. (SUNY Series, Communication & the Struggle for Identity in Postmodernity). 237p. (C). 1997. pap. text 18.95 (*0-7914-3494-X*) State U NY Pr.

— Sinners, Lovers, & Heroes: An Essay on Memorializing in Three American Cultures. LC 97-13019. (SUNY Series, Communication & the Struggle for Identity in Postmodernity). 237p. (C). 1997. text 56.50 (*0-7914-3493-1*) State U NY Pr.

— The Universe, the Eleventh Dimension & Everything: What We Know & How We Know It. LC 99-37643. (Illus.). 208p. 1999. pap. 14.95 (*1-56858-140-8*) FWEW.

Morris, Richard, ed. Labor & Management. LC 76-183137. (Great Contemporary Issues Ser.). (Illus.). 500p. (C). 1973. 30.00 (*0-685-41643-7*) Ayer.

— Legends of the Holy Rood: Symbols of the Passion & Cross-Poems. (EETS, OS Ser.: No. 46). 1969. reprint ed. 54.00 (*0-527-00043-4*) Periodicals Srv.

— Old English Homilies & Homiletic Treatises, Pts. I & II. (EETS, OS Ser.: No. 29 & 34). 1974. reprint ed. 55.00 (*0-527-00029-9*) Periodicals Srv.

— Old English Homilies of the 13th Century. (EETS, OS Series II: No. 53). 1974. reprint ed. 50.00 (*0-527-00048-5*) Periodicals Srv.

— Old English Miscellany Containing a Bestiary, Etc. (EETS, OS Ser.: No. 49). 1974. reprint ed. 55.00 (*0-527-00045-0*) Periodicals Srv.

— The Puggala-Pannatti. LC 78-70109. reprint ed. 42.50 (*0-404-17359-4*) AMS Pr.

Morris, Richard, et al, eds. Cultural Legacies of Vietnam: Uses of the Past in the Present. LC 90-971. (Communication & Information Science Ser.). 256p. (C). 1990. pap. 39.50 (*0-89391-713-3*); text 73.25 (*0-89391-635-8*) Ablx Pub.

Morris, Richard & Colman, Hila. Thoroughly Modern Millie. 17.95 (*0-88411-449-X*) Amereon Ltd.

Morris, Richard & Orthwein, Jayne. Advanced Technology Program Focused Learning: Competition 98-09: Adaptive Learning Systems. (Illus.). 55p. 1999. reprint ed. pap. text 20.00 (*0-7881-7582-3*) DIANE Pub.

Morris, Richard, jt. ed. see Addyman, Peter.

Morris, Richard, ed. see Buddhavamsa.

Morris, Richard, ed. see Chaucer, Geoffrey.

Morris, Richard, ed. see Granger, James R., Jr.

Morris, Richard A. Old Russian Ways: Cultural Variations among Three Russian Groups in Oregon. LC 91-8067. (Immigrant Communities & Ethnic Minorities in the U. S. & Canada Ser.: No. 74). 1991. 64.50 (*0-404-19484-2*) AMS Pr.

Morris, Richard B. The American Revolution: A Short History. LC 78-24604. (Anvil Ser.). 192p. 1979. reprint ed. pap. text 11.50 (*0-88275-812-8*) Krieger.

— Basic Documents in American History. LC 80-12822. (Anvil Ser.). 194p. 1980. reprint ed. pap. text 11.50 (*0-89874-202-1*) Krieger.

— Basic Documents on the Confederation & Constitution. LC 84-28908. 254p. (C). 1985. reprint ed. pap. 14.50 (*0-89874-839-9*) Krieger.

— Independence. LC 81-607080. (Official National Park Handbook Ser.: No. 115). 1982. pap. 4.50 (*0-912627-12-3*) Natl Park Serv.

Morris, Richard B., ed. Labor & Management. LC 76-183137. (Great Contemporary Issues Ser.). (Illus.). 500p. (C). 1973. 27.95 (*0-405-04163-2*) Ayer.

Morris, Richard B., et al, eds. Dissertations in American Biography Series, 38 bks. 1982. write for info. (*0-318-50808-7*) Ayer.

Morris, Richard B. & Morris, Jeffrey B., eds. Encyclopedia of American History: Seventh Edition. 7th ed. LC 81-47668. (Illus.). 1296p. 1996. 60.00 (*0-06-270055-3*, Harper Ref) HarpC.

Morris, Richard B., jt. ed. see Commager, Henry S.

Morris, Richard B., jt. ed. see Leab, Daniel J.

Morris, Richard B., ed. see Thomas, Emory M.

Morris, Richard E., jt. auth. see Ferris, Robert G.

Morris, Richard J. & Kratochwill, Thomas R., eds. The Practice of Child Therapy. (General Psychology Ser.: No. 124). (Illus.). 360p. 1983. text 100.00 (*0-08-028033-1*, Pergamon Pr); pap. text 40.00 (*0-08-028032-3*, Pergamon Pr) Elsevier.

***Morris, Richard J. & Kratochwill, Thomas R., eds.** The Practice of Child Therapy. 3rd ed. LC 97-18367. 496p. (C). 1998. pap. text 79.00 (*0-205-16818-3*) Allyn.

Morris, Richard J., jt. auth. see Kratochwill, Thomas R.

Morris, Richard J., jt. ed. see Kratochwill, Thomas R.

Morris, Richard K. John P. Holland, 1841-1914: Inventor of the Modern Submarine. Still, William N., Jr., ed. LC 97-24118. (Studies in Maritime History). (Illus.). 245p. 1998. pap. 16.95 (*1-57003-236-X*) U of SC Pr.

— John P. Holland, 1841-1914. LC 79-6120. (Navies & Men Ser.). (Illus.). 1980. reprint ed. lib. bdg. 23.95 (*0-405-13048-1*) Ayer.

Morris, Richard R. The Framing of the Federal Constitution. (Illus.). 111p. 1997. reprint ed. pap. text 25.00 (*0-7881-4616-5*) DIANE Pub.

Morris, Richard S. Bum Rap on America's Cities: The Real Cause of Urban Decay. 204p. 1980. pap. text 25.76 (*0-13-089219-X*) P-H.

Morris, Rob. Freemasonry in the Holy Land or Handmarks of Hiram's Builders. 610p. 1997. reprint ed. pap. 45.00 (*0-7661-0024-3*) Kessinger Pub.

— The Lights & Shadows of Freemasonry Consisting of Masonic Tales, Songs & Sketches. 394p. 1997. reprint ed. pap. 29.95 (*0-7661-0018-9*) Kessinger Pub.

— The Poetry of Freemasonry. 416p. 1997. reprint ed. pap. 35.00 (*0-7661-0032-4*) Kessinger Pub.

Morris, Rob, jt. auth. see Gunderson, Steve.

Morris, Rob, jt. auth. see Mackey, Albert G.

Morris, Robert. Continuous Project Altered Daily: The Writings of Robert Morris. (October Ser.). (Illus.). 338p. 1994. 55.00 (*0-262-13294-X*) MIT Pr.

— Continuous Project Altered Daily: The Writings of Robert Morris. (Illus.). 338p. 1995. pap. text 27.50 (*0-262-63163-6*, Bradford Bks) MIT Pr.

— The Faithful Slave. LC 72-1562. (Black Heritage Library Collection). (Illus.). 1977. reprint ed. 17.95 (*0-8369-9039-0*) Ayer.

— Freemasonry in the Holy Land: Handmarks of Hiram's Builders. Davis, Moshe, ed. LC 77-70731. (America & the Holy Land Ser.). (Illus.). 1977. reprint ed. lib. bdg. 51.95 (*0-405-10270-4*) Ayer.

***Morris, Robert.** Making Skin-on-Frame Boats. (Illus.). 320p. 2000. pap. 24.95 (*0-88179-191-1*, Pub. by Hartley & Marks) Andrews & McMeel.

Morris, Robert. Our Globe under Siege III. 200p. 1988. pap. 9.95 (*0-936676-75-2*) Inst Achieve Human Pot.

— Papers of Robert Morris, 1781-1784. Gallagher, Mary & Nuxoll, Elizabeth, eds. (Pittsburgh Series in Bibliography: Vol. 9). (Illus.). 1703p. 1999. text 90.00 (*0-8229-3999-1*) U of Pittsburgh Pr.

— Papers of Robert Morris, 1781-1784, Vols. 1-9. 1703p. 1999. text 460.00 (*0-8229-4088-4*) U of Pittsburgh Pr.

Morris, Robert. Social Policy of the American Welfare State: An Introduction to Policy Analysis. (Boehm Ser.). (C). 1979. text 17.50 (*0-06-044618-8*) Allyn.

Morris, Robert. Toward a Caring Society. 1974. 2.50 (*0-686-09284-8*) Univ Bk Serv.

— The Truth about the American Flag. LC 76-12730. (Illus.). 1976. 10.80 (*0-9601476-1-6*) Wynnehaven.

— The Truth about the American Flag. LC 76-12730. (Illus.). 1976. pap. 7.65 (*0-9601476-2-4*) Wynnehaven.

— The Truth about the Betsy Ross Story. LC 82-70798. (Illus.). 1982. 15.95 (*0-9601476-3-2*); pap. 12.95 (*0-9601476-4-0*) Wynnehaven.

Morris, Robert, ed. Deep Blue vs. Kasparov: The Significance for Artificial Intelligence. (Technical Reports: No. WS-97-04). 68p. 1997. spiral bd. 25.00 (*1-57735-031-6*) AAAI Pr.

— Umbral Calculus & Hopf Algebras. LC 81-22756. (Contemporary Mathematics Ser.: Vol. 6). 84p. 1982. pap. 17.00 (*0-8218-5003-2*, CONM/6) Am Math.

Morris, Robert, et al. Personal Assistance: The Future of Home Care. LC 98-5933. 205p. 1998. 48.00 (*0-8018-5902-6*); pap. 18.95 (*0-8018-5903-4*) Johns Hopkins.

Morris, Robert, jt. auth. see Denton, Sally.

Morris, Robert, jt. auth. see Hansan, John E.

Morris, Robert, jt. auth. see Hopps, June G.

Morris, Robert, ed. see Conference on Umbral Calculus & Hopf Algebras, 197.

Morris, Robert, jt. ed. see Hansan, John E.

Morris, Robert, ed. see International Workshop on Temporal Representation & Reasoning Staff, et al.

Morris, Robert A. Dolphin. (I Can Read Bks.). (Illus.). (J). (gr. 2-4). 1975. 6.93 (*0-06-024337-6*, 659490) HarpC.

— Dolphin. LC 75-6292. (I Can Read Bks.). (Illus.). 64p. (J). (gr. 2-4). 1983. pap. 3.75 (*0-06-444043-5*) HarpC Child Bks.

— Dolphin. (I Can Read Bks.). (J). (gr. 2-4). 1975. 8.95 (*0-606-03210-X*, Pub. by Turtleback) Demco.

— Flights of Memory: A Collection of Poems by Robert A. Morris. 90p. 1998. pap. write for info. (*0-7392-0010-0*, P02748) Morris Pubng.

Morris, Robert A., ed. see Ring Theory Conference Staff.

Morris, Robert, Associates Staff. Controlling Credit Department Functions. LC 86-5115. (Illus.). 52p. (Orig.). 1986. pap. text 32.00 (*0-936742-29-1*) Robt Morris Assocs.

Morris, Robert B. Principles of Dental Treatment Planning. LC 82-15370. 252p. reprint ed. pap. 78.20 (*0-7837-2731-3*, 204311100006) Bks Demand.

***Morris, Robert C.** The Environmental Case for Nuclear Power: Economic, Medical & Political Considerations. LC 99-42981. 208p. 2000. pap. 16.95 (*1-55778-780-8*) Paragon Hse.

An Asterisk (*) at the beginning of an entry indicates that the title is appearing for the first time.

Morris, Robert C. Reading, Riting & Reconstruction: The Education of Freedmen in the South, 1861-1870. LC 80-25370. (Illus.). (C). 1995. 33.95 (*0-226-53928-8*) U Ch Pr.

Morris, Robert C., ed. Freedmen's Schools & Textbooks: Black Education in the South, 1861-1870, 6 vols., Set. Incl. Vol. 1. 62.50 (*0-404-60761-6*); Vol. 2. 62.50 (*0-404-60762-4*); Vol. 3. 62.50 (*0-404-60763-2*); Vol. 4. 37.50 (*0-404-60764-0*); Vol. 5. 42.50 (*0-404-60765-9*); Vol. 6. 37.50 (*0-404-60766-7*); reprint ed. 305.00 (*0-404-19519-9*) AMS Pr.

— Using What We Know about At-Risk Youth: Lessons from the Field. LC 94-60208. 272p. 1994. pap. 29.95 (*1-56676-147-6*) Scarecrow.

Morris, Robert C. & Schultz, Nelda, eds. A Resource Guide for Working with Youth at Risk. 263p. 1996. pap. 24.95 (*1-56676-098-4*) Scarecrow.

***Morris, Robert G.** Diplomatic Circles: A Foreign Service Novel. 304p. 1999. 16.95 (*0-7414-0228-9*) Buy Books.

Morris, Robert H., et al. Intertidal Invertebrates of California. LC 77-92946. (Illus.). 690p. 1980. 79.50 (*0-8047-1045-7*) Stanford U Pr.

Morris, Robert J. The Contemporary Peruvian Theatre. (Graduate Studies: No. 15). 98p. (Orig.). 1977. pap. 9.00 (*0-89672-025-X*) Tex Tech Univ Pr.

Morris, Robert K. Paradoxes of Order: Some Perspectives on the Fiction of V. S. Naipaul. LC 74-23752. (Literary Frontiers Ser.). 112p. 1975. pap. 12.95 (*0-8262-0172-5*) U of Mo Pr.

Morris, Robert K., ed. Old Lines, New Forces: Essays on the Contemporary British Novel, 1960-1970. LC 75-18243. 211p. 1976. 32.50 (*0-8386-1771-9*) Fairleigh Dickinson.

Morris, Robert L., ed. Perspectives in Psychical Research Series, 34 vols. 1975. 1049.00 (*0-405-07020-9*) Ayer.

Morris, Robert L., jt. auth. see Wiseman, Richard.

***Morris, Robert V.** Tradition & Valor: A Family Journey. (Illus.). 128p. 1999. pap. 18.95 (*0-89745-237-2*) Sunflower U Pr.

Morris, Roberta A., et al. Doing Legal Research: A Guide for Social Scientists & Mental Health Professionals. LC 96-35664. (Applied Social Research Methods Ser.: Vol. 43). 139p. 1996. 42.00 (*0-8039-3428-9*); pap. 18.95 (*0-8039-3429-7*) Sage.

Morris, Robin, jt. auth. see Miller, Edgar.

Morris, Robin D., jt. auth. see Horchler, Joani N.

Morris, Robin G., ed. Cognitive Neuropsychology of Alzheimer-Type Dementia. (Illus.). 370p. 1997. text 89.50 (*0-19-852343-2*) OUP.

Morris, Robin R., jt. auth. see Horchler, Joani N.

***Morris, Robyn C.** Flexible Benefits Answer Book, 1. 600p. 1999. boxed set 125.00 (*0-7355-0487-3*) Panel Pubs.

Morris, Rod, ed. see Alcorn, Randy.

Morris, Roderick C., ed. see Boito, Camillo.

Morris, Rodler F. From Weimar Philosemite to Nazi Apologist: The Case of Walter Bloem. LC 88-14751. (Studies in German Thought & History: Vol. 7). 264p. 1988. lib. bdg. 89.95 (*0-88946-349-2*) E Mellen.

Morris, Roger. Atlantic Seafaring: Ten Centuries of Exploration & Trade in the North Atlantic. 1992. 34.95 (*0-07-043298-8*) McGraw.

— Devil's Butcher Shop: The New Mexico Prison Uprising. LC 88-4005. 268p. 1988. reprint ed. pap. 17.95 (*0-8263-1062-1*) U of NM Pr.

— Partners in Power, Vol. 1. 1997. pap. 12.95 (*0-8050-5219-4*) H Holt & Co.

— Partners in Power: The Clintons & Their America. 512p. 1995. 27.50 (*0-8050-2804-8*) H Holt & Co.

— Partners in Power: The Clintons & Their America. 1999. pap. text 17.95 (*0-89526-302-5*) Regnery Pub.

— Richard Milhous Nixon: The Rise of an American Politician. LC 89-7451. (Illus.). 89p. 1995. 29.95 (*0-8050-1121-8*); pap. 15.95 (*0-8050-1834-4*, Owl) H Holt & Co.

Morris, Roland, jt. auth. see U. S. Department of State Staff.

***Morris, Ron N.** Handbook of Handwriting & Handprinting Analysis. (Illus.). 300p. 2000. 69.95 (*0-12-507640-1*) Acad Pr.

Morris, Ronald A., et al. Federal Taxation of Real Estate. LC 89-50355. 468p. 1989. text 10.00 (*0-318-42523-8*, J1-1467) PLI.

Morris, Ronald W. Values in Sexuality Education: A Philosophical Study. 132p. (Orig.). 1994. pap. text 19.50 (*0-8191-9557-X*); lib. bdg. 41.00 (*0-8191-9556-1*) U Pr of Amer.

***Morris, Rosalind C.** In the Place of Origins: Modernity & Its Mediums in Northern Thailand. LC 99-42577. (Body, Commodity, Text Ser.). 392p. 2000. pap. 21.95 (*0-8223-2517-9*) Duke.

Morris, Rosemary. Monks & Laymen in Byzantium, 843-1118. (Illus.). 252p. (C). 1995. text 69.95 (*0-521-26558-4*) Cambridge U Pr.

Morris, Rosemary, tr. see Farge, Arlette.

Morris, Rosemary, tr. see Latouche, Serge.

Morris, Rosemary, tr. see Lestringant, Frank.

Morris, Rosemary, tr. see Pinguet, Maurice.

Morris, Rosie. The Lilly Pond Family. (Illus.). (J). (gr. 3-6). 2000. pap. 6.95 (*0-533-12309-7*) Vantage.

Morris, Roswitha, jt. ed. see Morris, Neil.

Morris, Roy, Jr. Ambrose Bierce: Alone in Bad Company. LC 98-33467. 320p. 1999. pap. 15.95 (*0-19-512628-9*) OUP.

***Morris, Roy.** The Better Angel: Walt Whitman in the Civil War. LC 99-86210. 288p. 2000. 27.50 (*0-19-512482-0*) OUP.

Morris, Roy. Sheridan. 1994. 26.00 (*0-8446-6753-6*) Peter Smith.

Morris, Roy, Jr. Sheridan: The Life & Wars of General Phil Sheridan. LC 92-50621. (Civil War Library). 1993. pap. 16.00 (*0-679-74398-7*) Vin Bks.

***Morris, Rupert.** Business Writing. 194p. 1999. pap. 13.95 (*0-7528-2077-X*, Pub. by Orion Pubng Grp) Trafalgar.

Morris, Rupert. The Right Way to Write: How to Write Effective Letters, Reports, Memos & E-Mail. 1999. pap. 16.95 (*0-7499-1878-0*, Pub. by Piatkus Bks) London Brdge.

Morris, Ruth. Crumbling Walls: Why Prisons Fail. 166p. 1996. pap. 9.95 (*0-88962-410-0*) Mosaic.

Morris, Ruth & Heffren, Colleen. Street People Speak. (Illus.). 96p. 1995. pap. 9.95 (*0-88962-364-3*) Mosaic.

Morris, S. Brent. Magic Tricks, Card Shuffling, & Dynamic Computer Memories. LC 97-74358. (Spectrum Ser.). (Illus.). 150p. 1998. pap. text 28.95 (*0-88385-527-5*, CARDS/JR) Math Assn.

Morris, S. Conway, et al, eds. The Origins & Relationships of Lower Invertebrates. (Illus.). 1985. 125.00 (*0-19-857181-X*) OUP.

Morris, Sallie. Asian Cooking. (Practical Encyclopedia of ... Ser.). 1999. 35.00 (*0-7548-0193-4*, Lorenz Bks) Anness Pub.

— The Chinese Restaurant Menu Recipes. (Illus.). 192p. (Orig.). 1996. pap. 24.50 (*0-572-01776-6*, Pub. by W Foulsham) Trans-Atl Phila.

— New Guide to Spices. 1998. 12.98 (*1-84038-073-X*) Random.

***Morris, Sallie & Mackley, Lesley.** The Spice Book. 2000. pap. 19.95 (*1-84215-026-X*) Anness Pub.

Morris, Sallie & Mackley, Lesley. The Spice Ingredients Cookbook: A Definitive Guide to Spices, Spice Blends & Aromatic Seeds & How to Use Them in the Kitchen - with 100 Classic & Contemporary Recipes. (Illus.). 256p. 1998. 32.50 (*1-85967-372-4*, Lorenz Bks) Anness Pub.

Morris, Sally A., et al. Giving Thanks in Song & Prayer: Hymn Tunes of Sally Ann Morris. 104p. 1998. spiral bd. 16.95 (*1-57999-033-9*, G-4930) GIA Pubns.

Morris, Sally M. Favorite Seafood Recipes: Enjoy Your Restaurant Favorites at Home. rev. ed. (Illus.). 176p. 1989. pap. 8.95 (*1-55867-000-9*, Nitty Gritty Ckbks) Bristol Pub Ent CA.

Morris, Samuel C. Cancer Risk Assessment: A Quantitative Approach. (Occupational Safety & Health Ser.: Vol. 20). (Illus.). 416p. 1990. text 160.00 (*0-8247-8239-9*) Dekker.

Morris, Samuel M. Health Care Financing in the United States: Index of New Information with Authors & Subjects. rev. ed. LC 96-3652. 133p. 1996. 47.50 (*0-7883-1064-X*); pap. 44.50 (*0-7883-1065-8*) ABBE Pubs Assn.

— Medical Treatment of Self & Hypochondria: Index of Modern Authors & Subjects with Guide for Rapid Research. LC 90-56315. 160p. 1991. 47.50 (*1-55914-414-9*); pap. 44.50 (*1-55914-415-7*) ABBE Pubs Assn.

— Phobias & Disorders: Index of Modern Information. LC 88-47614. 150p. 1988. 47.50 (*0-88164-834-5*); pap. 44.50 (*0-88164-835-3*) ABBE Pubs Assn.

***Morris, Sandra.** The Beauty Manual: How to Look Your Best Ever. (Illus.). 2000. pap. 18.95 (*0-7373-0505-3*, Pub. by Lowell Hse) NTC Contemp Pub Co.

Morris, Sandra. Catwalk: Inside the World of the Supermodels. (Illus.). 96p. 1996. 20.00 (*0-7893-0056-7*, Pub. by Universe) St Martin.

— The Model Manual: Everything You Need to Know about Modelling. (Illus.). 200p. 1997. 24.95 (*0-297-83585-8*, Pub. by Weidenfeld & Nicolson) Trafalgar.

Morris, Sandra K., jt. auth. see Bunzel, Mark J.

***Morris, Sandra L.** Training in a Manila Envelope: A Guide to Facilitating an Early Childhood Self-Study Course. (Illus.). 40p. 2000. write for info. (*0-9676799-1-5*) Child Cre.

Morris, Sandra L., jt. auth. see Harper-Whalen, Susan.

Morris, Sarah P. Daidalos & the Origins of Greek Art. (Illus.). 498p. 1992. pap. text 35.00 (*0-691-00160-X*, Pub. by Princeton U Pr) Cal Prin Full Svc.

Morris, Sarah P., jt. ed. see Carter, Jane B.

Morris, Saundra, jt. ed. see Porte, Joel.

Morris, Scott. Go Big Red: Recipes & Traditions from the Hearts of Huskers. LC 92-64319. 248p. 1992. 16.95 (*0-9631249-2-7*, Cookbks by Morris) Morris Pubng.

— The Oregon Trail Cookbook: A Historical View of Cooking, Traveling & Surviving on the Trail. LC 93-78500. 200p. 1993. 10.95 (*0-9631249-3-5*, Cookbks by Morris) Morris Pubng.

***Morris, Scott.** The Total View of Taftly: A Novel. LC 99-89072. 208p. 2000. 18.95 (*1-892514-70-2*) Hill St Pr.

Morris, Scott, contrib. by. Collecting My Favorite Recipes. 136p. 1992. ring bd. 9.95 (*0-9631249-1-9*, Cookbks by Morris) Morris Pubng.

Morris, Scott, ed. Agriculture & Vegetation of the World. LC 92-22290. (Using & Understanding Maps Ser.). (Illus.). 48p. (YA). (gr. 5 up). 1993. lib. bdg. 17.95 (*0-7910-1804-0*) Chelsea Hse.

— The Economy of the World. LC 92-22291. (Using & Understanding Maps Ser.). (Illus.). 48p. (YA). (gr. 5 up). 1993. lib. bdg. 17.95 (*0-7910-1809-1*) Chelsea Hse.

— The Endangered World. LC 92-22289. (Using & Understanding Maps Ser.). (Illus.). 48p. (YA). (gr. 5 up). 1993. lib. bdg. 17.95 (*0-7910-1806-7*) Chelsea Hse.

— Industry of the World. LC 92-22288. (Using & Understanding Maps Ser.). (Illus.). 48p. (YA). (gr. 5 up). 1993. lib. bdg. 17.95 (*0-7910-1807-5*) Chelsea Hse.

— Languages of the World. LC 92-22287. (Using & Understanding Maps Ser.). (Illus.). 48p. (YA). (gr. 5 up). 1993. lib. bdg. 17.95 (*0-7910-1811-3*) Chelsea Hse.

— The Military World. LC 92-22286. (Using & Understanding Maps Ser.). (Illus.). 48p. (YA). (gr. 5 up). 1993. lib. bdg. 17.95 (*0-7910-1808-3*) Chelsea Hse.

***Morris, Scott, ed.** New Opportunities for Older Workers: A Statement on National Policy. 56p. 2000. pap. text 20.00 (*0-7881-8972-7*) DIANE Pub.

Morris, Scott, ed. The Physical World. LC 92-22285. (Using & Understanding Maps Ser.). (Illus.). 48p. (YA). (gr. 5 up). 1993. lib. bdg. 17.95 (*0-7910-1801-6*) Chelsea Hse.

— The Political World. LC 92-22284. (Using & Understanding Maps Ser.). (Illus.). 48p. (YA). (gr. 5 up). 1993. lib. bdg. 17.95 (*0-7910-1802-4*) Chelsea Hse.

— Populations of the World. LC 92-22283. (Using & Understanding Maps Ser.). (Illus.). 48p. (YA). (gr. 5 up). 1993. lib. bdg. 17.95 (*0-7910-1805-9*) Chelsea Hse.

— Using & Understanding Maps, 10 vols., Set. (Illus.). 48p. (YA). (gr. 5 up). 1994. lib. bdg. 179.50 (*0-7910-1800-8*) Chelsea Hse.

Morris, Sherry, jt. auth. see Hobson, Ginny.

Morris, Shirley, ed. Thoughts. (C). 1989. 30.00 (*0-7223-2352-2*, Pub. by A H S Ltd) St Mut.

Morris, Sidney. If This Isn't Love! LC 94-62042. (Gay Play Script Ser.). (Illus.). 101p. 1995. pap. 7.95 (*1-886586-01-2*) T n T Class.

Morris, Sidney A., jt. auth. see Hofmann, Karl H.

Morris, Skip. The Art of Tying the Bass Fly. LC 97-152980. (Illus.). 88p. 1997. spiral bd. 29.95 (*1-57188-076-3*) F Amato Pubns.

— The Art of Tying the Dry Fly. (Illus.). 112p. (Orig.). 1993. 39.95 (*1-878175-37-8*); pap. 29.95 (*1-878175-36-X*) F Amato Pubns.

— The Art of Tying the Nymph. (Illus.). 112p. 1994. spiral bd. 29.95 (*1-878175-51-3*) F Amato Pubns.

— Concise Handbook of Fly Tying. LC 96-157735. (Illus.). 32p. 1995. pap. 7.95 (*1-57188-035-6*) F Amato Pubns.

— The Custom Graphite Fly Rod: Design & Construction. (Illus.). 112p. 1989. 24.95 (*1-55821-011-3*) Lyons Pr.

— Fly Proportion Chart. (Illus.). 1994. pap. 3.95 (*1-878175-69-6*) F Amato Pubns.

— Fly Tying Made Clear & Simple. (Illus.). 80p. 1992. 29.95 (*1-878175-14-9*); spiral bd. 19.95 (*1-878175-13-0*) F Amato Pubns.

Morris, Skip. Fly Tying Made Clear & Simple. 1993. 26.95 incl. VHS (*1-878175-66-1*) F Amato Pubns.

Morris, Skip. Tying Foam Flies. (Illus.). 48p. 1994. 29.95 (*1-878175-90-4*); pap. 16.95 (*1-878175-89-0*) F Amato Pubns.

***Morris, Skip & Chan, Brian.** Morris & Chan on Fly Fishing Trout Lakes. (Illus.). 96p. 1999. 39.95 (*1-57188-182-4*); pap. 24.95 (*1-57188-181-6*) F Amato Pubns.

Morris, Sonia, ed. see Hryhorenko, Hrytsko & Ukrainka, Lesja.

Morris, Sonia, ed. see Kobylianska, Olha, et al.

Morris, Sonia, ed. see Pehilka, Olena, et al.

***Morris, Stefan, des.** Robbie Williams: Illustrated Biography. (Illus.). 48p. 1998. pap. 12.95 (*0-7119-6934-5*, OP48083) Omnibus NY.

Morris, Stephanie, jt. auth. see Crilly, Eileen.

Morris, Stephanie A., jt. auth. see McMahon, A. Michael.

Morris, Stephen. Excel for Windows 95 Clear & Simple. (Clear & Simple Ser.). 150p. 1996. pap. text 10.95 (*0-7506-9802-0*, Digital DEC) Buttrwrth-Heinemann.

— Health Economics for Nurses: An Introductory Guide. LC 97-41281. (Nursing Ser.). 296p. 1997. pap. 54.00 (*0-13-255993-5*) P-H.

— Newnes File Formats Pocket Book. 352p. 2000. text 22.95 (*0-7506-3423-5*) Buttrwrth-Heinemann.

— Object Oriented Programming with Windows 95 & NT. LC 98-39800. 450p. 1999. pap. text 44.95 (*1-55558-193-5*, Digital DEC) Buttrwrth-Heinemann.

— PC Printers Pocket Book. LC 92-166290. 336p. 1992. pap. 104.20 (*0-608-04991-3*, 206560900004) Bks Demand.

Morris, Stephen, ed. see Young, William.

Morris, Stephen D. Corruption & Politics in Contemporary Mexico. LC 90-47510. 224p. 1991. pap. text 19.95 (*0-8173-0525-4*) U of Ala Pr.

— Political Reformism in Mexico: An Overview of Contemporary Mexican Politics. LC 95-3472. 262p. 1995. pap. text 19.95 (*1-55587-594-7*); lib. bdg. 49.95 (*1-55587-572-6*) L Rienner.

Morris, Stephen J. Why Vietnam Invaded Cambodia: Political Culture & the Causes of War. (Illus.). 315p. 1998. pap. 18.95 (*0-8047-3050-4*) Stanford U Pr.

— Why Vietnam Invaded Cambodia: Political Culture & the Causes of War. LC DS556.8.M69 1999. (Illus.). 280p. 1999. 49.50 (*0-8047-3049-0*) Stanford U Pr.

Morris, Steve & Willcocks, Graham. Preventing Accidents & Illness at Work. 300p. 1995. pap. 47.50 (*0-273-61687-0*, Pub. by Pitman Pub) Trans-Atl Phila.

Morris, Steve, et al. How to Lead a Winning Team: An Action Guide. 192p. 1995. pap. 47.50 (*0-273-61093-7*, Pub. by Pitman Pub) Trans-Atl Phila.

— The Knowledge Manager. 250p. 1996. pap. write for info. (*0-273-62535-7*, Pub. by F T P H) Trans-Atl Phila.

Morris, Steve, jt. auth. see Willcocks, Graham.

Morris, Steve, ed. see Metelsky, Robert M.

Morris, Steven R., jt. auth. see Morris, Carla D.

Morris-Stiff, Gareth J. Clinical Cases for the MRCs & AFRCs. LC 98-2837. (Illus.). 200p. 1998. pap. text. write for info. (*0-340-69268-5*, Pub. by E A) St Martin.

Morris, Sue. Watt Pottery Identification & Value Guide. 160p. 1996. 19.95 (*0-89145-527-2*, 3327) Collector Bks.

Morris, Sue, ed. see Rowe, William.

Morris, Susan. Game Creations: Kid Created & Kid Approved Games & Activities. (Illus.). 128p. (Orig.). 1996. pap. 9.95 (*0-945872-11-9*) Great Activities Pub Co.

— Thomas Girtin (1775-1802) LC 85-51651. (Illus.). 79p. (Orig.). 1986. pap. 12.00 (*0-930606-50-7*) Yale Ctr Brit Art.

— A Traveler's Guide to Pioneer Jewish Cemeteries of the California Gold Rush. LC 95-80185. (Illus.). 107p. (Orig.). 1996. pap. 12.95 (*0-943376-63-7*) Magnes Mus.

Morris, Susan, jt. auth. see McCarthy, Bernice.

Morris, Susan V., jt. auth. see Shaw, Margaret.

Morris, Suzanne. Galveston: A Novel. 1976. 12.95 (*0-385-11534-2*) Doubleday.

Morris, Suzanne E. & Klein, Marsha D. Pre-Feeding Skills: A Comprehensive Resource for Feeding Development. (Illus.). 414p. 1987. pap. text 65.00 (*0-7616-7406-3*) Commun Skill.

Morris-Suzuki, Tessa. Beyond Computopia: Information, Automation & Democracy in Japan. (Japanese Studies). 280p. 1988. lib. bdg. 59.95 (*0-7103-0293-2*, A2124) Routledge.

— Re-Inventing Japan: Time, Space, Nation. LC 97-41873. (Japan in the Modern World Ser.). 256p. (C). (gr. 13). 1997. pap. text 19.95 (*0-7656-0082-X*, East Gate Bk) M E Sharpe.

— Re-Inventing Japan: Time, Space, Nation. LC 97-41873. (Japan in the Modern World Ser.). 240p. (C). (gr. 13). 1997. text 59.95 (*0-7656-0081-1*, East Gate Bk) M E Sharpe.

— The Technological Transformation of Japan from the Seventeenth to the Twenty-First Century. LC 94-10310. (Illus.). 314p. (C). 1994. pap. text 21.95 (*0-521-42492-5*) Cambridge U Pr.

Morris-Suzuki, Tessa & Takuro, Seiyama, eds. Japanese Capitalism since 1945: Critical Perspectives. LC 89-4297. 256p. (C). (gr. 13). 1990. text 79.95 (*0-87332-551-6*, East Gate Bk) M E Sharpe.

Morris-Suzuki, Tessa & Takuro, Seiyama, eds. Japanese Capitalism since 1945: Critical Perspectives. LC 89-4297. 256p. (C). (gr. 13). 1990. pap. text 42.95 (*0-87332-834-5*, East Gate Bk) M E Sharpe.

Morris, Sylvia. Biography of Clare Booth Luce, Vol. 2. write for info. (*0-679-45711-9*) Random.

Morris, Sylvia, ed. Use of Group Services in Permanency Planning for Children. LC 82-23389. (Social Work with Groups Ser.: Vol. 5, No. 4). 109p. 1983. text 32.95 (*0-86656-199-4*) Haworth Pr.

Morris, Sylvia J. Rage for Fame: The Ascent of Clare Boothe Luce. LC 96-43084. (Illus.). 561p. 1997. 30.00 (*0-394-57555-5*) Random.

Morris, T., jt. ed. see Watson, M.

Morris, T. A. Europe & England in the Sixteenth Century. LC 97-13192. 376p. (C). 1998. 80.00 (*0-415-15040-X*) Routledge.

— Europe & England in the Sixteenth Century. LC 97-13192. (Illus.). 376p. (C). 1998. pap. 25.99 (*0-415-15041-8*) Routledge.

***Morris, T. A.** Tudor Government. LC 98-33199. (Questions & Analysis in History Ser.). 160p. (C). 1999. pap. write for info. (*0-415-19149-1*) Routledge.

Morris, T. H., jt. auth. see Garner, Ann.

***Morris, T. R.** Experimental Design & Analysis in Animal Sciences. 224p. 1999. pap. text 40.00 (*0-85199-349-4*) OUP.

Morris, T. S. The Tucker Genealogy: A Record of Gilbert Ruggles & Evelina Christina (Snyder) Tucker, Their Ancestors & Descendants. (Illus.). 305p. 1989. reprint ed. pap. 45.50 (*0-8328-1187-4*); reprint ed. lib. bdg. 53.50 (*0-8328-1186-6*) Higginson Bk Co.

Morris, Ted. Snapshot. 345p. (C). 1990. pap. 35.00 (*0-7855-2639-0*, Pub. by IMMEL Pubng) St Mut.

Morris, Terence. The Criminal Area: A Study in Social Ecology. LC 85-8015. (International Library of Sociology & Social Reconstruction). 202p. 1985. reprint ed. lib. bdg. 75.00 (*0-313-24427-8*, MCRA, Greenwood Pr) Greenwood.

Morris, Terry. No Justice, No Peace: From Emmett Till - Rodney King. 128p. (Orig.). 1993. pap. 10.95 (*0-9635878-0-3*) Africentric.

Morris, Terry R. United States Army Air Service: Wing Badges - Uniforms & Insignia, 1913-1918. 128p. 1996. 39.95 (*1-888722-06-1*) S A Duff.

***Morris, Thomas D.** Free Men All: The Personal Liberty Laws of the North, 1780-1861. LC 00-39109. 2000. write for info. (*1-58477-107-0*) Lawbk Exchange.

Morris, Thomas D. Free Men All: The Personal Liberty Laws of the North, 1780-1861. LC 73-8126. 272p. reprint ed. pap. 84.40 (*0-608-08788-2*, 206942700004) Bks Demand.

— Southern Slavery & the Law, 1619-1860. LC 95-6565. (Studies in Legal History). 592p. 1996. 29.95 (*0-8078-2238-8*) U of NC Pr.

— Southern Slavery & the Law, 1619-1860. LC 95-6565. (Studies in Legal History). 592p. 1999. pap. 24.95 (*0-8078-4817-4*) U of NC Pr.

Morris, Thomas H. Prayer Celebrations for the Liturgical Year. LC 98-119997. (Illus.). 64p. (J). (gr. 7-9). 1998. pap. text 6.00 (*0-8215-5640-1*) Sadlier.

— The RCIA: Transforming the Church: A Resource for Pastoral Implementation. rev. ed. LC 97-28822. 304p. 1998. pap. 14.95 (*0-8091-3758-5*, 3758-5) Paulist Pr.

— Walking Together in Faith: A Workbook for Sponsors of Christian Initiation. 224p. 1992. pap. 14.95 (*0-8091-3289-3*) Paulist Pr.

Morris, Thomas H. & Coffey, Kathy. Anointed & Sealed with the Spirit Vol. 1: Leader's Guide. 2nd rev. ed. DeVries, Dirk & Mueller, Steve, eds. 112p. 1999. teacher ed. 14.95 (*1-889108-64-2*) Liv Good News.

Morris, Thomas R. The Virginia Supreme Court: An Institutional & Political Analysis. LC 75-1158. 207p. reprint ed. pap. 64.20 (*0-8357-2714-9*, 203982800013) Bks Demand.

Morris, Thomas R., jt. ed. see Cooper, Weldon.

Morris, Thomas V. Making Sense of It All: Pascal & the Meaning of Life. 224p. (Orig.). 1992. pap. 14.00 (*0-8028-0652-X*) Eerdmans.

— Our Idea of God. LC 90-19145. 216p. (C). 1991. text 15.00 (*0-268-01504-X*) U of Notre Dame Pr.

— Our Idea of God: An Introduction to Philosophical Theology. 192p. 1998. pap. 21.95 (*1-57383-101-8*, Regent Coll Pub) Regent College.

M

Morris, Thomas V., ed. Divine & Human Action: Essays in the Metaphysics of Theism. LC 88-47738. 368p. 1988. 49.95 (*0-8014-2197-7*) Cornell U Pr.

— Divine & Human Action: Essays in the Metaphysics of Theism. LC 88-47738. 375p. reprint ed. pap. 116.30 (*0-608-20927-9*, 207202600003) Bks Demand.

— God & the Philosophers: The Reconciliation of Faith & Reason. 304p. 1996. reprint ed. pap. 16.95 (*0-19-510119-7*) OUP.

— Philosophy & the Christian Faith. LC 87-40618. (Studies in Philosophy of Religion: No. 5). 336p. (C). 1990. text 37.00 (*0-268-01570-8*); pap. text 17.50 (*0-268-01571-6*) U of Notre Dame Pr.

Morris, Thomas W. The International Dictionary of Accounting Acronyms. (Illus.). 275p. 1998. 45.00 (*0-8144-0474-X*) AMACOM.

— The International Dictionary of Accounting Acronyms. (Illus.). 247p. 1997. 45.00 (*1-888998-47-4*) Glenlake Pub.

Morris, Thomas W., ed. International Dictionary of Accounting Acronyms. LC 99-482830. 275p. 1999. lib. bdg. 45.00 (*1-884964-56-7*) Fitzroy Dearborn.

***Morris, Tim.** Multimedia Systems: Delivering, Generating & Interacting with Multimedia. LC 00-37377. (Applied Computing Ser.). 2000. write for info. (*1-85233-248-4*) Spr-Verlag.

— Western Pacific Trackside with Bob Larson. (Illus.). 128p. 1999. 54.95 (*1-58248-022-2*) Morning NJ.

Morris, Timothy. Becoming Canonical in American Poetry. LC 94-12411. 192p. 1995. text 34.95 (*0-252-02136-3*); pap. text 12.95 (*0-252-06428-3*) U of Ill Pr.

— The Despairing Developer: Diary of an Aid Worker in the Middle East. 224p. 1991. 49.95 (*1-85043-486-7*, Pub. by I B T); text 16.95 (*1-85043-350-X*, Pub. by I B T) St Martin.

— Despairing Developer: Diary of an Aid Worker in the Middle East, Vol. 1. 1958. pap. 19.95 (*1-85043-322-4*) St Martin.

— Making the Team: The Cultural Work of Baseball Fiction. LC 96-10131. 208p. 1997. text 34.95 (*0-252-02294-7*) U of Ill Pr.

— Making The Team: The Cultural Work Of Baseball Fiction. LC 96-10131. 208p. 1997. 13.95 (*0-252-06597-2*) U of Ill Pr.

***Morris, Timothy.** You're Only Young Twice: Children's Literature & Film. LC 99-6617. 200p. (J). 2000. 24.95 (*0-252-02532-6*) U of Ill Pr.

Morris, Ting & Morris, Neil. Dinosaurs. LC 92-32915. (Sticky Fingers Ser.). 32p. (J). (gr. 2-4). 1993. lib. bdg. 20.00 (*0-531-14258-2*) Watts.

— Rain Forest. LC 93-26686. (Sticky Fingers Ser.). (Illus.). 32p. (J). (gr. 2-4). 1994. lib. bdg. 20.00 (*0-531-14281-7*) Watts.

***Morris, Tom.** Adventures of Your Life. 1999. text 25.00 (*0-8050-6143-6*) St Martin.

Morris, Tom. Bursting the Foundations: A Bibliographical Primer on the Criticism of Culture. LC 81-82009. (Paunch Ser.: No. 55-56). (Illus.). 164p. 1981. pap. 7.00 (*0-9602478-5-8*) Paunch.

— If Aristotle Ran General Motors. 240p. 1998. pap. 13.95 (*0-8050-5253-4*) H Holt & Co.

— If Aristotle Ran General Motors: A New Path of Wisdom for the Life of Business & the Business of Life. LC 97-204. 256p. 1997. 25.00 (*0-8050-5252-6*) H Holt & Co.

— Philosophy for Dummies. (For Dummies Ser.). 384p. 1999. pap. 19.99 (*0-7645-5153-1*, Dummies Trade Pr) IDG Bks.

— True Success: A New Philosophy of Excellence. 288p. (Orig.). 1995. pap. 14.95 (*0-425-14615-4*) Berkley Pub.

Morris, Tom, jt. auth. see Miles, John.

Morris, Tomy. A Treasury of Ghost Stories. LC 96-1907. 160p. (J). (gr. k-4). 1996. 6.95 (*0-7534-5027-5*) LKC.

Morris, Tony. Jonah & the Whale. (Now You Can Read Bible Stories Ser.). 24p. (J). 1994. 3.98 (*0-86112-784-6*) Brimax Bks.

— Stories from the Bible. (J). (gr. k-3). 1995. 9.98 (*1-85854-365-7*) Brimax Bks.

Morris, Tony, jt. auth. see Frank, Penny.

Morris, Tracie. Intermission. 126p. 1999. pap. 11.00 (*1-887128-30-1*) Soft Skull Pr.

Morris Trumbauer, Jean. Created & Called: Discovering our Gifts for Abundant Living. LC 98-43491. 1998. write for info. (*0-8066-3899-0*) Augsburg Fortress.

Morris, V. Dixon, tr. see Soshitsu Sen.

***Morris, V J.** Atomic Force Microscopy for Biologists. 1999. 51.00 (*1-86094-199-0*) World Scientific Pub.

Morris, V. J., jt. auth. see Jennings, B. R.

Morris, Valerie. Dancing on the Edge. 200p. 1996. pap. 9.95 (*1-888342-03-X*) Flying Pig.

— Homeworks: Giving Birth at Home with a Midwife. 149p. 1995. pap. 14.95 (*1-888342-00-5*) Flying Pig.

— Simple Plants: Traditional Medicinal Herbs of Northern Illinois. 84p. 1994. pap. 9.95 (*1-888342-01-3*) Flying Pig.

— Simple Plants: Traditional Medicinal Herbs of Northern Illinois. rev. ed. 100p. 1996. pap. text 12.95 (*1-888342-02-1*) Flying Pig.

Morris, Valerie B., jt. ed. see Pankratz, David B.

Morris, Van C. Deaning: Middle Management in Academe. LC 80-26119. 192p. 1981. text 24.95 (*0-252-00871-5*) U of Ill Pr.

— Existentialism in Education: What It Means. (Illus.). 163p. (C). 1990. reprint ed. pap. text 15.95 (*0-88133-497-9*) Waveland Pr.

Morris, Van Cleave & Pai, Young. Philosophy & the American School: An Introduction to the Philosophy of Education. 2nd ed. LC 93-4902. 490p. 1994. pap. 41.00 (*0-8191-9005-5*) U Pr of Amer.

Morris, Victor P. Oregon's Experience with Minimum Wage Legislation. LC 68-58609. (Columbia University. Studies in the Social Sciences: No. 320). reprint ed. 27.50 (*0-404-51320-4*) AMS Pr.

Morris, Vince. Zanshin: Meditation & the Mind in Modern Martial Arts. LC 92-1758. (Illus.). 108p. 1992. pap. 8.95 (*0-87728-756-2*) Weiser.

Morris, Virginia. Double Jeopardy: Women Who Kill in Victorian Fiction. LC 90-32879. 192p. 1990. text 24.95 (*0-8131-1751-8*) U Pr of Ky.

— How to Care for Aging Parents: A Complete Guide. LC 94-19321. (Illus.). 544p. (Orig.). 1996. pap. 15.95 (*1-56305-435-3*, 3435) Workman Pub.

Morris, Virginia & Scharf, Michael. An Insider's Guide to the International Criminal Tribunal for the Former Yugoslavia: A Documentary History & Analysis, 2 Vols. LC 94-23553. 501p. 1995. lib. bdg. 165.00 (*0-941320-92-8*) Transnatl Pubs.

Morris, Virginia & Scharf, Michael P. The International Criminal Tribunal for Rwanda, 2 vols. LC 97-44363. 1998. 225.00 (*1-57105-038-8*) Transnatl Pubs.

Morris, Virginia B. Creating Retirement Income. LC 99-197355. 156p. 1998. 14.95 (*0-07-134525-6*) McGraw.

— Creating Retirement Income. 1999. 89.70 (*0-07-134547-7*) McGraw.

— Crime & Punishment (Dostoevski) (Barron's Book Notes Ser.). (C). 1984. pap. 2.50 (*0-8120-3409-0*) Barron.

— A Woman's Guide to Investing. 1999. 89.70 (*0-07-134546-9*) McGraw.

***Morris, Virginia B.** A Woman's Guide to Investing. rev. ed. (Illus.). 159p. 1999. 14.95 (*0-07-134524-8*) McGraw.

Morris, Virginia B. Woman's Guide to Investing: Straight Talk Guide with the Information & the Inspiration You Need. LC 97-149372. 159p. 1997. pap. text 14.95 (*0-9650932-0-4*) Lghtbulb Pr.

Morris, Virginia B., jt. auth. see Morris, Kenneth M.

Morris, Vivian G., jt. auth. see Jaisinghani, Vijay T.

Morris, Vivian Gunn & Morris, Curtis L. Creating Caring & Nurturing Educational Environments For African American Children. LC 99-29574. 240p. 2000. 59.95 (*0-89789-689-0*, Bergin & Garvey) Greenwood.

Morris, W. The Collected Letters of William Morris: 1889-1892, Vol. 3. Kelvin, N., ed. 440p. 1996. text 45.00 (*0-691-06601-9*, Pub. by Princeton U Pr) Cal Prin Full Svc.

Morris, W. A., et al, eds. The English Government at Work, 1327-1336, Vol. 2 Fiscal Administration. (Medieval Academy Bks.: No. 48). 1968. reprint ed. 25.00 (*0-910956-22-7*) Medieval Acad.

Morris, W. A., jt. ed. see Willard, J. F.

Morris, W. H. Old Time Violin Melodies, Bk. 1. 25p. 1992. pap. 10.00 (*0-9637812-1-9*) MO St Old Time.

Morris, W. N. Mood. (Social Psychology Ser.). (Illus.). 248p. 1989. 96.95 (*0-387-96978-0*) Spr-Verlag.

Morris, W. R. Legacy of Buford Pusser: A Pictorial History of the "Walking Tall" Sheriff. LC 94-61035. (Illus.). 144p. Date not set. 29.95 (*1-56311-164-0*) Turner Pub KY.

— The Twelfth of August: Biography of "Walking Tall" Sheriff Buford Pusser. expanded ed. 1994. 19.95 (*0-9634779-9-4*) Cherokee Pr.

Morris, W. S., et al. History Thirty-First Regiment Illinois Volunteers Organized by John A. Logan. 302p. 1991. reprint ed. 24.95 (*0-9623990-5-1*); reprint ed. pap. 12.95 (*0-9623990-4-3*) Crossfire Pr.

— History 31st Regiment Illinois Volunteers Organized by John A. Logan. LC 97-28956. (Shawnee Classics). 1998. 14.95 (*0-8093-2184-X*) S Ill U Pr.

Morris, W. Sidney. Carmina Latina. (C). 1982. pap. text 39.00 (*0-900269-13-8*, Pub. by Old Vicarage) St Mut.

Morris, Walter F. Handmade Money: Latin American Artisans in the Marketplace. LC 96-49911. 1996. write for info. (*0-8270-3699-X*) OAS.

Morris, Warren B. The Revisionist Historians & German War Guilt. 1976. lib. bdg. 250.00 (*0-87700-257-6*) Revisionist Pr.

— The Road to Olmutz: The Political Career of Joseph Maria Von Radowitz. 1975. lib. bdg. 250.00 (*0-87700-230-4*) Revisionist Pr.

Morris, Wesley. Toward a New Historicism. LC 77-166384. 277p. 1972. reprint ed. pap. 85.90 (*0-7837-9394-4*, 206013900004) Bks Demand.

Morris, Wesley & Morris, Barbara A. Reading Faulkner. LC 89-4806. (Wisconsin Project on American Writers Ser.). 304p. (C). 1989. text 24.95 (*0-299-12220-4*) U of Wis Pr.

***Morris, William.** Art & Society: Lectures & Essays by William Morris. Zabel, Gary, ed. 174p. 1999. reprint ed. pap. text 17.00 (*0-7881-6202-0*) DIANE Pub.

Morris, William. The Collected Letters of William Morris, Vol. 1. LC 82-47604. (Illus.). 690p. reprint ed. pap. 200.00 (*0-608-06296-0*, 206665800001) Bks Demand.

— Collected Letters of William Morris, Vol. 4. Kelvin, Norman, ed. 392p. (C). 1996. text 45.00 (*0-691-04422-8*, Pub. by Princeton U Pr) Cal Prin Full Svc.

— Collected Works. 1973. 600.00 (*0-87968-895-5*) Gordon Pr.

***Morris, William.** The Collected Works of William Morris, 24 vols. Incl. Aeneids of Virgil. 1999. reprint ed. lib. bdg. 88.00 (*1-58201-455-8*); Defence of Guenevere, The Hollow Land. 1999. reprint ed. lib. bdg. 88.00 (*1-58201-445-0*); Earthly Paradise, a Poem. 1999. reprint ed. lib. bdg. 88.00 (*1-58201-448-5*); Hopes & Fears for Art, Lectures on Art & Industry. 1999. reprint ed. lib. bdg. 88.00 (*1-58201-466-3*); House of the Wolfings, The Story of the Glittering Plain. 1999. reprint ed. lib. bdg. 88.00 (*1-58201-458-2*); Journals of Travel in Iceland. 1999. reprint ed. lib. bdg. 88.00 (*1-58201-452-3*); Life & Death of Jason. 1999. reprint ed. lib. bdg. 88.00 (*1-58201-446-9*); Love Is Enough, Poems by the Way. 1999. reprint ed. lib. bdg. 88.00 (*1-58201-453-1*); News from Nowhere, A Dream of John Ball, A King's Lesson. 1999. reprint ed. lib. bdg. 88.00 (*1-58201-460-4*); Odyssey of Homer, Done into English Verse. 1999. reprint ed. lib. bdg. 88.00 (*1-58201-457-4*); Roots of the Mountains. 1999. reprint ed. lib. bdg. 88.00 (*1-58201-459-0*); Scenes from the Fall of Troy & Other Poems & Fragments. 1999. reprint ed. lib. bdg. 88.00 (*1-58201-468-X*); Signs of Change, Lectures on Socialism. 1999. reprint ed. lib. bdg. 88.00 (*1-58201-467-1*); Story of Grettir the Strong, The Story of the Volsungs & Niblungs. 500p. 1999. reprint ed. lib. bdg. 88.00 (*1-58201-451-5*); Story of Sigurd the Volsung & The Fall of the Niblungs. 1999. reprint ed. lib. bdg. 88.00 (*1-58201-456-6*); Sundering Flood, Unfinished Romances. 1999. reprint ed. lib. bdg. 88.00 (*1-58201-465-5*); Three Northern Love Stories, The Tale of Beowulf. 1999. reprint ed. lib. bdg. 88.00 (*1-58201-454-X*); Water of the Wondrous Isles. 1999. reprint ed. lib. bdg. 88.00 (*1-58201-464-7*); Wood Beyond the World, Child Christoph,r, Old French Romances. 1999. reprint ed. lib. bdg. 88.00 (*1-58201-461-2*); Pt. 1. Earthly Paradise, a Poem. 1999. reprint ed. lib. bdg. 88.00 (*1-58201-447-7*); Pt. 1. Well at the World's End. 1999. reprint ed. lib. bdg. 88.00 (*1-58201-462-0*); Pt. 2. Well at the World's End. 1999. reprint ed. lib. bdg. 88.00 (*1-58201-463-9*); Pt. 3. Earthly Paradise, a Poem. 1999. reprint ed. lib. bdg. 88.00 (*1-58201-449-3*); Pt. 4. Earthly Paradise, a Poem. 1999. reprint ed. lib. bdg. 88.00 (*1-58201-450-7*); 1999. reprint ed. Set lib. bdg. 2112.00 (*1-58201-444-2*) Classic Bks.

Morris, William. The Collected Works of William Morris, 24 vols., Set. (BCL1-PR English Literature Ser.). 1992. reprint ed. lib. bdg. 1800.00 (*0-7812-7608-X*) Rprt Serv.

— The Earthly Paradise, 2 vols., Set. Boos, Florence S., ed. LC 98-35345. (Illus.). 1639p. 1998. 275.00 (*0-8153-2104-X*) Garland.

— Golden Wings & Other Stories. (Forgotten Fantasy Classic Ser.: Vol. 8), xvi, 169 p. 1976. pap. 5.95 (*0-87877-107-7*, F-107) Newcastle Pub.

— The Letters of William Morris to His Family & Friends. Henderson, Philip, ed. LC 75-41199. reprint ed. 69.50 (*0-404-14711-9*) AMS Pr.

***Morris, William.** Morris Design for Honeysuckle. (William Morris Lined Ser.). 160p. 1999. 12.95 (*1-55156-086-0*, Pub. by Paperblank) Andrews & McMeel.

— Morris Design for Iris Journal. 160p. 1999. 12.95 (*1-55156-085-2*, Pub. by Paperblank) Andrews & McMeel.

— Morris Design for Windrush. (William Morris Lined Ser.). 160p. 1999. 12.95 (*1-55156-087-9*, Pub. by Paperblank) Andrews & McMeel.

Morris, William. News from Nowhere. Kumar, Krishan, ed. (Cambridge Texts in the History of Political Thought Ser.). 263p. (C). 1995. text 59.95 (*0-521-42007-5*); pap. text 19.95 (*0-521-42233-7*) Cambridge U Pr.

— News from Nowhere. Redmond, James, ed. (English Texts Ser.). 1972. pap. 10.95 (*0-7100-6756-9*, Routledge Thoemms) Routledge.

— News from Nowhere & Other Writings. Wilmer, Clive, ed. & intro. by. 480p. 1994. pap. 12.95 (*0-14-043330-9*, Penguin Classics) Viking Penguin.

— Old French Romances, Done into English. LC 75-113680. (Short Story Index Reprint Ser.). 1977. 19.95 (*0-8369-3409-1*) Ayer.

— Ornamentation & Illustrations from the Kelmscott Chaucer. 128p. 1973. pap. 8.95 (*0-486-22970-X*) Dover.

Morris, William. Stoked. 350p. 1994. pap. 19.95 (*0-9639775-0-4*) New Sun Pubns.

Morris, William. Stories in Prose, Stories in Verse, Shorter Poems, Lectures & Essays. Cole, G. D., ed. LC 75-41200. reprint ed. 94.50 (*0-404-14690-2*) AMS Pr.

— Three Works. Morton, A. L., ed. 404p. 1987. reprint ed. pap. 4.95 (*0-7178-0202-7*) Intl Pubs Co.

— True, Free Spirit: The Biography of Chas. E. Morris, Historic Western Photographer. (Illus.). 170p. 1997. 49.95 (*0-9645626-3-4*) Dallywelter Pr.

— The Unpublished Lectures of William Morris. LC 69-19307. 332p. reprint ed. pap. 103.00 (*0-7837-3609-6*, 204347500009) Bks Demand.

— The Well at the World's End. LC 97-183478. (Pocket Classics Ser.). 592p. 1996. pap. 13.95 (*0-7509-1207-3*, Pub. by Sutton Pub Ltd) Intl Pubs Mktg.

— The Widow's House by the Great Water. Timo, Helen, ed. 64p. (Orig.). (C). 1991. pap. 8.50 (*0-931332-07-9*) Wm Morris Soc.

— William Morris Full-Color Patterns & Design. (Illus.). 48p. 1988. reprint ed. pap. 8.95 (*0-486-25645-6*) Dover.

— William Morris on Art & Socialism. LC 99-37652. 2000. pap. text 10.95 (*0-486-40904-X*) Dover.

— The Wood Beyond the World. 261p. 1972. reprint ed. pap. 12.95 (*0-486-22791-X*) Dover.

Morris, William & Magnusson, Magnus. Icelandic Journals. LC 97-206425. 187p. 1997. 24.95 (*1-899197-25-7*) Dufour.

Morris, William & Morris, Mary. Morris Dictionary of Word & Phrase Origins. 2nd ed. LC 87-45651. 688p. 1988. 38.00 (*0-06-015862-X*) HarperTrade.

Morris, William & Ward, Colin. A Factory As It Might Be the Factory We Never Had. (Illus.). 32p. (Orig.). 1995. pap. 4.00 (*0-907123-21-X*, Pub. by Five Leaves) AK Pr Dist.

Morris, William, jt. ed. see Fulford, William.

Morris, William C., jt. auth. see Sashkin, Marshall.

Morris, William D. Heat Transfer & Fluid Flow in Rotating Coolant Channels. LC 82-139168. (Mechanical Engineering Research Studies Ser.: No. 2). (Illus.). 244p. reprint ed. pap. 75.70 (*0-8357-6139-8*, 203423100089) Bks Demand.

Morris, William J., Jr. Short Audit Case: The Valley Publishing Company. 8th ed. (Illus.). 359p. (Orig.). (C). 1998. pap. text 33.00 (*0-912503-12-2*) Armond-Dalton.

Morris, William O. Hannibal. LC 73-14457. (Heroes of the Nations Ser.). reprint ed. 45.00 (*0-404-58275-3*) AMS Pr.

— Moltke: A Biographical & Critical Study. LC 68-25254. (World History Ser.: No. 48). 1969. reprint ed. lib. bdg. 75.00 (*0-8383-0222-X*) M S G Haskell Hse.

— Napoleon. LC 73-14458. (Heroes of the Nations Ser.). reprint ed. 30.00 (*0-404-58276-1*) AMS Pr.

— Wellington. LC 73-14459. (Heroes of the Nations Ser.). reprint ed. 30.00 (*0-404-58277-X*) AMS Pr.

Morris, William Otis. The Dentist's Legal Advisor. LC 95-103734. 544p. (C). (gr. 13). 1994. text 51.95 (*0-8151-5867-X*, 25104) Mosby Inc.

Morris, William R., jt. auth. see Morris, Joyce J.

Morris, William T., jt. auth. see Sink, D. Scott.

Morris, Willie. After All, It's Only a Game. LC 92-19542. (Author & Artist Ser.). (Illus.). 100p. 1992. 25.00 (*0-87805-600-9*) U Pr of Miss.

— Chimes at Midnight. 2001. write for info. (*0-679-45013-0*) Random.

— The Courting of Marcus Dupree. LC 92-27510. 464p. 1992. reprint ed. pap. 17.95 (*0-87805-585-1*) U Pr of Miss.

— Good Old Boy: A Delta Boyhood. LC 80-52627. 143p. 1980. pap. 10.95 (*0-916242-10-2*) Yoknapatawpha.

— Good Old Boy & the Witch of Yazoo. 2nd ed. 164p. (J). (gr. 7-10). 1998. pap. 10.95 (*0-916242-67-6*) Yoknapatawpha.

***Morris, Willie.** James Jones: A Friendship. LC 99-37821. 288p. 2000. pap. text 17.95 (*0-252-06837-8*) U of Ill Pr.

Morris, Willie. The Last of the Southern Girls. LC 94-209598. (Voices of the South Ser.). 304p. 1994. pap. 16.95 (*0-8071-1956-3*) La State U Pr.

***Morris, Willie.** My Cat Spit McGee. (J). 2000. pap. 11.00 (*0-375-70693-3*, Pub. by Knopf Bks Yng Read) Random.

— My Cat Spit McGee. LC 99-31086. 144p. 1999. 18.95 (*0-375-50321-8*) Random.

— My Cat Spit McGee. large type ed. LC 99-54228. 1999. 23.95 (*1-57490-247-4*, Beeler LP Bks) T T Beeler.

— My Dog Skip. 1996. 15.35 (*0-606-14278-9*) Turtleback.

Morris, Willie. My Dog Skip. 144p. 1996. pap. 10.00 (*0-679-76722-3*) Vin Bks.

— My Dog Skip. large type ed. LC 98-8369. 122p. 1998. 21.95 (*1-57490-154-0*, Beeler LP Bks) T T Beeler.

***Morris, Willie.** My Mississippi. (Illus.). 256p. 2000. 37.00 (*1-57806-193-8*) U Pr of Miss.

— My Mississippi. limited ed. (Illus.). 256p. 2000. 100.00 (*1-57806-309-4*) U Pr of Miss.

— North Toward Home. LC 99-57733. 1999. 28.00 (*1-57806-266-7*) U Pr of Miss.

— North Toward Home. (Rediscovery Ser.). 448p. 2000. pap. 14.00 (*0-375-72460-5*) Vin Bks.

Morris, Willie. A Prayer for the Opening of the Little League Season. LC 94-14471. (Illus.). 32p. 1995. 15.00 (*0-15-200892-6*) Harcourt.

— A Prayer for the Opening of the Little League Season. LC 94-14471. (Illus.). 32p. (J). 1999. pap. 5.00 (*0-15-201724-0*) Harcourt.

— Terrains of the Heart: And Other Essays on Home. LC 81-50423. xiii, 265p. 1998. reprint ed. pap. 15.95 (*0-916242-23-4*) Yoknapatawpha.

Morris, Willie, ed. American Classrooms: Photographs by Catherine Wagner. (Illus.). 96p. (Orig.). 1988. pap. 37.95 (*0-89381-338-9*) Aperture.

***Morris, Willie, et al.** Eudora Welty: Writers' Reflections upon First Reading Welty. McHaney, Pearl A., ed. LC 98-75334. 118p. 1999. 16.95 (*1-892514-16-8*) Hill St Pr.

Morris, Winifred. What If the Shark Wears Tennis Shoes? (Illus.). (J). (ps-3). 1995. mass mkt. 4.95 (*0-689-71894-2*) Aladdin.

— What If the Shark Wears Tennis Shoes? LC 89-38150. (Illus.). 32p. (J). (gr. k-3). 1990. 13.95 (*0-689-31587-2*) Atheneum Yung Read.

Morris, Winifred. What If the Shark Wears Tennis Shoes? 1995. 10.15 (*0-606-08363-4*, Pub. by Turtleback) Demco.

Morris, Winnifred. Liar. LC 96-2465. 176p. (YA). 1996. 15.95 (*0-8027-8461-5*) Walker & Co.

Morris, Woodrow W. The Greatest of These: Quotations on Fundamental Truths of Charity - The Teaching of Freemasonry. (Illus.). xiv, 111p. 1985. 10.00 (*0-88053-080-4*, M 328) Macoy Pub.

Morris, Wright. Conversations with Wright Morris: Critical Views & Responses. Knoll, Robert E., ed. LC 76-25497. 329p. reprint ed. pap. 102.00 (*0-7837-6028-0*, 204584000008) Bks Demand.

— The Field of Vision. 1997. reprint ed. lib. bdg. 35.95 (*1-56849-687-7*) Buccaneer Bks.

— The Home Place. LC 99-19703. (Illus.). 200p. 1998. pap. 12.00 (*0-8032-8252-4*) U of Nebr Pr.

— The Loneliness of the Long Distance Writer: The Works of Love & the Huge Season. LC 95-47580. 575p. (Orig.). (C). 1996. 30.00 (*0-87685-991-0*); pap. 17.50 (*0-87685-990-2*) Black Sparrow.

— The Loneliness of the Long Distance Writer: The Works of Love & the Huge Season, signed ed. deluxe ed. LC 95-47580. 575p. (Orig.). (C). 1996. 40.00 (*0-87685-992-9*) Black Sparrow.

— Photographs & Words. Alinder, James, ed. LC 82-82471. (Illus.). 120p. 1982. 50.00 (*0-933286-28-7*) Frnds Photography.

***Morris, Wright.** Plains Song: For Female Voices. (Illus.). 237p. 2000. pap. 14.00 (*0-8032-8267-2*, Bison Books) U of Nebr Pr.

Morris, Wright. Three Easy Pieces. LC 93-35699. 328p. (Orig.). (C). 1993. 25.00 (*0-87685-924-4*); pap. 15.00 (*0-87685-923-6*) Black Sparrow.

An Asterisk (*) at the beginning of an entry indicates that the title is appearing for the first time.

— Three Easy Pieces, signed ed. deluxe ed. LC 93-35699. 328p. (Orig.). (C). 1993. 35.00 (*0-87685-925-2*) Black Sparrow.

— Time Pieces: Word & Image. (Writers & Artists on Photography Ser.). (Illus.). 126p. 1989. pap. 22.95 (*0-89381-382-6*) Aperture.

— Time Pieces: Word & Image. (Writers & Artists on Photography Ser.). (Illus.). 126p. 1989. 53.00 (*0-89381-381-8*) Aperture.

— Two for the Road. LC 94-38984. 304p. (Orig.). (C). 1994. 25.00 (*0-87685-945-7*); pap. 15.00 (*0-87685-944-9*) Black Sparrow.

— Two for the Road, signed ed. deluxe ed. LC 94-38984. 304p. (Orig.). (C). 1994. 40.00 (*0-87685-946-5*) Black Sparrow.

— Writing My Life: An Autobiography. LC 93-13802. 484p. (Orig.). (C). 1993. pap. 15.00 (*0-87685-908-2*) Black Sparrow.

Morris-Wu, Eleanor B. Human Efflorescence: A Study in Man's Evolutionary & Historical Development. 352p. (C). 1983. 27.50 (*0-87527-323-8*) Green.

Morris, Yao N. Amanmere: The Natural Blueprint for Sexual Relationships. (Illus.). 312p. 1997. pap. 23.00 (*0-9643263-1-0*) Blck River Pr.

Morris, Yolanda L. Introspective Journey. 1998. pap. write for info. (*1-57553-966-7*) Watermrk Pr.

Morris, Yvon. I Love Myself Weight Loss Program. 51p. 1996. pap. 9.98 (*1-888139-00-5*) Y Morris Carib.

— Prosperity for Beginners. 51p. 1996. pap. 9.98 (*1-888139-02-1*) Y Morris Carib.

— Quitters Are Winners: New 30 Day Stop Smoking Plan. 51p. 1996. pap. 9.98 (*1-888139-04-8*) Y Morris Carib.

— Stress Management Manual. 55p. 1995. pap. 9.98 (*1-888139-03-X*) Y Morris Carib.

— Your Good Health - Thank God. 51p. 1996. pap. 9.98 (*1-888139-01-3*) Y Morris Carib.

Morrisby, Edwin. Unpackaged Tours: World Travels off the Beaten Track. (Illus.). 400p. 1988. 17.95 (*0-8008-7939-2*) Taplinger.

Morrisey. Introductory Metalworking. (Tech & Industrial Education Ser.). 1983. text 25.95 (*0-538-33710-9*); teacher ed. 8.00 (*0-538-33712-5*) S-W Pub.

— Primary Social Studies. 1991. pap. text. write for info. (*0-582-07515-7*, Pub. by Addison-Wesley) Longman.

Morrisey, Brendan. Yorktown, 1781. (Campaign Ser.: Vol. 47). (Illus.). 96p. 1997. 15.95 (*1-85532-688-4*, Pub. by Ospry) Stackpole.

Morrisey, George L. Appraisal & Development Through Objectives & Results. (Illus.). 1972. pap. text 9.95 (*0-201-04834-5*) Addison-Wesley.

Morrisey, George L. Effective Business & Technical Presentations. 2nd ed. LC 74-24920. 224p. 1975. pap. text 15.95 (*0-201-04828-0*) Addison-Wesley.

— Loud & Clear: How to Prepare & Deliver Effective Business & Technical Presentations. 4th ed. LC 97-10309. 1997. pap. 15.00 (*0-201-12793-8*) Addison-Wesley.

— Morrisey on Planning Vol. 1: A Guide to Strategic Thinking: Building Your Planning Foundation. 143p. 1995. 24.50 (*0-7879-0168-7*) Jossey-Bass.

— Morrisey on Planning Vol. 2: Guide to Long-Range Planning: Creating Your Strategic Journey, Vol. II. (Management Ser.). 135p. 1995. 24.50 (*0-7879-0169-5*) Jossey-Bass.

— Morrisey on Planning Vol. 3: Guide to Tactical Planning: Producing Your Short-Term Results, Vol. #III. 158p. 1995. 24.95 (*0-7879-0170-9*) Jossey-Bass.

— Morrisey on Planning Series, 3 vols., Set. 1995. 59.00 (*0-7879-0115-6*) Jossey-Bass.

— Performance Appraisals in Business Industry: Keys to Effective Supervision. 1983. teacher ed. write for info. (*0-201-13982-0*); pap. write for info. (*0-201-04831-0*) Addison-Wesley.

— Performance Appraisals in the Public Sector: Key to Effective Supervision. (Illus.). 160p. 1983. pap. write for info. (*0-201-04847-7*) Addison-Wesley.

Morrisey, George L. & Sechrest, Thomas L. Effective Business & Technical Presentations. 3rd ed. LC 87-1814. (Illus.). 163p. 1987. pap. 21.95 (*0-201-15852-3*) Addison-Wesley.

Morrisey, George L., et al. The Executive Guide to Operational Planning. LC 87-45508. (Management Ser.). 157p. 1987. text 26.95 (*1-55542-064-8*) Jossey-Bass.

Morrisey, John. The Lake District. LC 95-72837. (Passport's Regional Guides of Great Britain Ser.). (Illus.). 128p. 1996. pap. 12.95 (*0-8442-4879-7*, 48797, Passprt Bks) NTC Contemp Pub Co.

Morrisey, Michael. Managed Care & Changing Health Care Markets. LC 97-43998. 1998. 39.95 (*0-8447-4038-1*); pap. 16.95 (*0-8447-4039-X*) Am Enterprise.

Morrisey, Michael A. Cost Shifting in Health Care: Separating Evidence from Rhetoric. LC 94-14605. 1994. 19.95 (*0-8447-3860-3*, AEI Pr) Am Enterprise.

Morrisey, Patricia A. Disability Etiquette in the Workplace: Special Legi-Slate Edition. 64p. 1993. pap. text. write for info. (*1-880955-02-4*) Legi-Slate.

Morrisey, Thomas J., jt. auth. see Miller, Rex.

Morrisey, Will. Culture in the Commercial Republic. 290p. (C). 1996. lib. bdg. 42.00 (*0-7618-0291-6*) U Pr of Amer.

— A Political Approach to Pacifism, Bk. 1. LC 95-12482. (Studies in World Peace: Vol. 6a). 472p. 1996. 109.95 (*0-7734-8910-X*) E Mellen.

— A Political Approach to Pacifism, Bk. 2. LC 95-12482. (Studies in World Peace: Vol. 6b). 460p. 1996. 109.95 (*0-7734-8912-6*) E Mellen.

Morrisey, Will, jt. auth. see Eidelberg, Paul.

Morrisey, William, jt. auth. see Harmon, Paul.

Morrish, Allan H. Canted Antiferromagnetism: Hematite. LC 94-35067. 208p. 1995. text 46.00 (*981-02-2007-3*) World Scientific Pub.

Morrish, Donald & Miller, Richard K. Genetic Regulation of Placental Development, & Immunology. LC 98-2599. (Trophoblast Research Ser.: Vol. 11). (Illus.). 408p. 1998. 120.00 (*1-58046-032-1*) U of Rochester.

***Morrish, George.** New Light from the Ancient Greek Bible. 2nd ed. (GRE.). 297p. 1998. pap. 8.95 (*0-86585-001-1*) Wm Carey Intl.

Morrish, Ivor. The Dark Twin: A Study of Evil - And Good. (Illus.). 1980p. 1999. pap. 9.95 (*0-8464-4953-6*) Beekman Pubs.

— Jane Austen & the Interplay of Character. LC 98-54271. 190p. 1999. pap. 29.95 (*0-485-12142-5*, Pub. by Athlone Pr) Transaction Pubs.

Morrish, John. The Fender Amp Book: A Complete History of Fender Amplifiers. (Illus.). 96p. 1995. 17.95 (*0-87930-345-X*) Miller Freeman.

— Magazine Editing. LC 96-7410. (Illus.). 288p. (C). 1996. 100.00 (*0-415-15263-1*); pap. 29.99 (*0-415-13672-5*) Routledge.

Morrish, John, ed. The Classical Guitar: A Complete History. limited ed. (Illus.). 132p. 1997. 75.00 (*0-87930-502-9*) Miller Freeman.

Morrish, Robert & Enfantino, Peter, eds. Quick Chills II: The Best Horror Fiction from the Specialty Press. (Quick Chills Ser.: Vol. II). (Illus.). 356p. 1992. 35.00 (*0-9631367-3-9*) Deadline Pr.

Morrish, Ronald G. Secrets of Discipline: For Parents & Teachers. 146p. 1998. pap. text 12.95 (*0-9681131-0-9*, Pub. by Woodstream Publ) Assoc Pubs Grp.

Morrish, Sheri, jt. auth. see Matthie-Jacobs, Linda.

Morrish, William R. Civilizing Terrains: Mountains, Mounds & Mesas. (Illus.). 102p. (C). 1990. pap. text 25.00 (*0-9625974-0-6*) Design Ctr Amer Urban Land.

***Morrish, William R. & Brown, Catherine R.** Planning to Stay: Learning to See the Physical Features in Your Neighborhood. (Illus.). 120p. 2000. pap. 19.95 (*1-57131-246-3*) Milkweed Ed.

Morrish, William R. & Brown, Catherine R. Planning to Stay: Learning to See the Physical Features of Your Neighborhood. LC 94-25402. (Illus.). 120p. 1994. pap. 16.95 (*1-57131-203-X*) Milkweed Ed.

Morrish, William Rees. Civilizing Terrains: Mountains, Mounds & Mesas. (Illus.). 116p. 1996. pap. 22.50 (*0-9651144-1-4*, Pub. by W K Stout) RAM Publications.

Morrison. Abell's Exploration. 7th ed. (C). 1994. pap. text, teacher ed. 33.75 (*0-03-001053-5*) Harcourt Coll Pubs.

— Abell's Realm of the Universe. 6th ed. (C). 1996. pap. text 39.00 (*0-03-005203-3*, Pub. by Harcourt Coll Pubs) Harcourt.

— Abell's Realm of the Universe. 6th ed. (C). 1997. pap. text, teacher ed. 26.75 (*0-03-016084-7*) Harcourt Coll Pubs.

— Abell's Realm of the Universe. 6th ed. (C). 1998. pap. text, teacher ed., suppl. ed. 28.00 (*0-03-016087-1*) Harcourt Coll Pubs.

— As If. 2000. pap. write for info. (*0-312-19539-7*) St Martin.

— Calculus: From Graphical, Numerical & Symbolic Points of View. (C). 1995. pap. text 19.00 (*0-03-016333-1*) Harcourt Coll Pubs.

— Child Development. 2nd ed. (Early Childhood Education Ser.). 1995. pap., teacher ed. 12.00 (*0-8273-4585-2*) Delmar.

— Child Development. 2nd ed. (Early Childhood Education Ser.). 1995. text 21.95 (*0-8273-4584-4*, VNR) Wiley.

— Creativity Advertising. 1998. 45.74 (*0-256-16912-8*) McGraw.

— Frontiers of Astronomy. 2nd ed. (C). 1995. pap. text, teacher ed. 33.75 (*0-03-093937-2*) Harcourt Coll Pubs.

***Morrison.** A Guide to Oracle 8. 2nd ed. (Miscellaneous/ Catalogs Ser.). 1999. pap. 48.95 (*0-619-00027-9*) Course Tech.

— A Guide to Using Oracle. (C). 1998. 31.00 (*0-7600-4992-0*) Thomson Learn.

Morrison. Hospitality & Travel Marketing. (Food & Hospitality Ser.). 1989. pap., teacher ed. 14.00 (*0-8273-2939-3*) Delmar.

— Hospitality & Travel Marketing. 2nd ed. (Hospitality, Travel & Tourism Ser.). 128p. 1996. teacher ed. 15.00 (*0-8273-7467-4*) Delmar.

***Morrison.** Hospitality & Travel Marketing. 3rd ed. (C). 2000. pap. 41.25 (*0-7668-1605-2*) Delmar.

Morrison. Hospitality Travel & Tourism Dictionary. (Food & Hospitality Ser.). (C). 2000. mass mkt. 29.95 (*0-7668-0785-1*) Delmar.

— Hospitality Unlimited. (Food & Hospitality Ser.). 1992. teacher ed. 8.50 (*0-8273-4026-5*) Delmar.

— International Design Yearbook 14, No. 14. (Illus.). 240p. 1999. 85.00 (*0-7892-0511-4*) Abbeville Pr.

— Management of Change. (GC - Principles of Management Ser.). 1997. pap. 35.00 (*0-7895-0708-0*) Course Tech.

***Morrison.** Management of the Voice & Its Disorders. 2nd ed. 2000. pap. 54.95 (*0-7693-0054-5*) Thomson Learn.

— Management of Voice Disorders. 1998. pap. 57.95 (*0-7693-0003-0*) Course Tech.

— Microsoft Office 2000. 2000. pap. 44.95 (*0-538-72412-9*) Thomson Learn.

Morrison. Microsoft Word 7.0 for Windows 95: Complete Course. LC 96-323. (DF - Computer Applications Ser.). 1996. mass mkt. 51.95 (*0-538-71519-7*) S-W Pub.

— Microsoft Word 7.0 for Windows 95: Tutorial & Applications. LC 96-12649. (DF - Computer Applications Ser.). 1996. mass mkt. 39.95 (*0-538-71522-7*) S-W Pub.

— Microsoft Word 7.0 for Windows 95: Tutorial & Applications. (DF - Computer Applications Ser.). 1996. mass mkt., student ed. 37.95 (*0-538-71524-3*) S-W Pub.

— Microsoft Word 6.0 for Windows - A Practical Approach. (DF - Computer Applications Ser.). (C). 1994. mass mkt. 44.95 (*0-538-71275-9*) S-W Pub.

— Microsoft Word 6.0 Mac: Tutorial & Applications. (DF - Computer Applications Ser.). 1995. mass mkt. 36.95 (*0-538-64914-3*) S-W Pub.

— Mise en Pratique: Manuel de Grammaire et d'Expression Ecrite. 3rd ed. 544p. (Orig.). 2000. pap. 59.95 (*0-201-61449-9*) Addison-Wesley.

***Morrison.** MS Office 2000. 2000. pap., wbk. ed. 12.95 (*0-538-72415-3*) Thomson Learn.

Morrison. MS Word 97 for Windows: Tutorial & Application. (DF - Computer Applications Ser.). (C). 1997. mass mkt. 41.95 (*0-538-71923-0*) S-W Pub.

— Negotiations Set. 508p. 1994. 50.00 (*0-89464-925-6*) Krieger.

— Organic Chemistry. 7th ed. 2000. pap. text, student ed., suppl. ed. 46.67 (*0-13-800160-X*) P-H.

***Morrison.** Organic Chemistry. 7th ed. 2000. pap. text, teacher ed. write for info. (*0-13-800210-X*) P-H.

Morrison. Practical Approach to Microsoft 97 for Windows. (DF - Computer Applications Ser.). 1997. mass mkt. 53.95 (*0-538-71927-3*) S-W Pub.

***Morrison.** Teaching in America. 2nd ed. LC 99-30805. 608p. 1999. pap. text 59.00 (*0-205-30345-5*, Longwood Div) Allyn.

Morrison. Understanding Patients. (C). 1995. pap. text 19.00 (*0-7020-1718-3*) Harcourt.

Morrison & Lewis. Microsoft Word Six for Windows: Tutorial & Application. 1995. 46.50 (*0-538-64763-9*) Thomson Learn.

Morrison & Michelle. Foundations of Mental Health Nursing. LC 96-42058. (Illus.). 592p. (C). (gr. 13). 1997. pap. text 29.95 (*0-8151-6964-7*, 27246) Mosby Inc.

Morrison, et al. Integrated Computer Tech. Clss., 1. 379p. 1998. pap. text 59.00 (*0-13-270000-X*) P-H.

— Powers of Ten: About the Relative Size of Things in the Universe. LC 82-5504. (Scientific American Library). (Illus.). 164p. (C). 1991. VHS 39.95 (*0-7167-5029-5*) W H Freeman.

Morrison, jt. auth. see Marshall.

Morrison, jt. auth. see Mill.

Morrison, jt. auth. see Pine.

Morrison, jt. auth. see Starks, Kay Johnston.

Morrison, ed. see Cinthio.

Morrison & Foerster Staff. CA Employer's Guide to Employee Handbook & Personnel Policy Manual. 1989. ring bd. 125.00 (*0-8205-1072-6*) Bender.

Morrison, A. J., tr. see Schlegel, Friedrich von.

Morrison, Adrian R. Progress Psychbiology & Physiological Psychology, Vol. 17. Fluharty, Steven J., ed. (Illus.). 208p. (C). 1998. boxed set 99.95 (*0-12-542117-6*) Acad Pr.

Morrison, Adrian R., jt. ed. see Epstein, Alan N.

Morrison, Al H., ed. see Gregory, Eve S., et al.

Morrison, Al H., ed. see O'Clery, Helen.

Morrison, Al H., ed. see Tilton, Matt.

Morrison, Alan B., ed. Fundamentals of American Law. LC 96-214352. 734p. 1996. text 75.00 (*0-19-876404-9*); pap. text 39.95 (*0-19-876405-7*) OUP.

Morrison, Alan S. Screening in Chronic Disease. 2nd ed. (Monographs in Epidemiology & Biostatistics: No. 19). (Illus.). 272p. 1992. text 49.50 (*0-19-506390-2*) OUP.

Morrison, Alastair. Fair Land Sarawak. (Studies on Southeast Asia: No. 13). (Illus.). 196p. (Orig.). 1993. pap. text 16.00 (*0-87727-712-5*) Cornell SE Asia.

Morrison, Alastair M. Hospitality & Travel Marketing. (Food & Hospitality Ser.). xi, 532 p. 1989. pap. 39.95 (*0-8273-2938-5*) Delmar.

— Hospitality & Travel Marketing. 2nd ed. LC 95-19700. (Food & Hospitality Ser.). 592p. (C). 1995. mass mkt. 65.95 (*0-8273-6620-5*) Delmar.

Morrison, Alec, ed. The Impossible Art of Golf: An Anthology of Golf Writing. 328p. 1994. 35.00 (*0-19-211698-3*) OUP.

Morrison, Alex, ed. The Changing Face of Peacekeeping: Proceedings of Peacekeeping '93. 243p. (Orig.). (C). 1994. pap. text 45.00 (*0-7881-1286-4*) DIANE Pub.

— Peacekeeping, Peacemaking or War: International Security Enforcement. 159p. 1994. reprint ed. pap. text 40.00 (*0-7881-1287-2*) DIANE Pub.

Morrison, Alex, jt. auth. see Jessop, David A.

Morrison, Alex, jt. ed. see Moore, John Norton.

Morrison, Alex, jt. ed. see Pollard, Tony.

Morrison, Alexander B. The Dawning of a Brighter Day. LC 90-35883. (Illus.). 149p. 1990. 9.95 (*0-87579-338-X*) Deseret Bk.

— Visions of Zion. LC 93-36628. vii, 139p. 1993. 12.95 (*0-87579-788-1*) Deseret Bk.

— Zion: A Light in the Darkness. LC 97-11004. ix, 134p. 1997. 16.95 (*1-57345-260-2*) Deseret Bk.

***Morrison, Alexandrea.** Oracle SQL Interactive Workbook. (Interactive Workbook Ser.). 544p. 2000. pap. text, wbk. ed. 39.99 (*0-13-015745-7*) P-H.

Morrison, Alfred. Guide for Justices of the Peace, 2 vols., Set. 3rd ed. 1967. reprint ed. 95.00 (*0-89941-618-7*, 501900) W S Hein.

Morrison, Alice M. & Morrison, Janet S. Descendants of James & Jennet Morrison of Rocky River. LC 96-75662. (Illus.). 762p. 1996. 60.00 (*1-888858-02-8*) Morrison Fmly.

— Descendants of John & Mary Morrison of Rocky River. LC 96-75660. (Illus.). 488p. 1996. 45.00 (*1-888858-00-1*) Morrison Fmly.

— Descendants of Robert & Sarah Morrison of Rocky River. LC 96-75661. (Illus.). 309p. 1996. 30.00 (*1-888858-01-X*) Morrison Fmly.

Morrison, Alison. Entrepreneurship: An International Perspective. 320p. 1998. pap. text 41.95 (*0-7506-3825-7*) Buttrwrth-Heinemann.

***Morrison, Alison.** Franchising Hospitality Services. (Illus.). 296p. 2000. pap. 37.95 (*0-7506-4772-8*) Buttrwrth-Heinemann.

Morrison, Alison. New Pressed Flower Designs. 1999. 14.95 (*1-85391-548-3*) Merehurst Ltd.

Morrison, Alison & Rimmington, Michael. Entrepreneurship in the Hospitality, Tourism & Leisure Industries. LC 00-265114. (Illus.). 250p. 1998. pap. 34.95 (*0-7506-4097-9*) Buttrwrth-Heinemann.

Morrison, Alison, jt. auth. see Wearne, Neil.

Morrison, Alison, jt. ed. see Lashley, Conrad.

Morrison, Allan. Haud Yer Wheesht! Your Scottish Granny's Favorite Sayings. 96p. 1999. pap. 7.95 (*1-897784-60-0*, Pub. by N Wilson Pubng) Interlink Pub.

— "Whaur's Yer Wullie Shakespeare Noo!" Scotland's Millennium Souvenir. LC 99-216074. 1999. pap. 7.95 (*1-897784-49-X*) Interlink Pub.

— "Ye Cannae Shove Yer Granny Aff a Bus!" Scots Grandchildren on Their Grannies. 1999. pap. 7.95 (*1-897784-81-3*) Interlink Pub.

Morrison, Allen. Latin America by Streetcar: A Pictorial Survey of Urban Rail Transport South of the U. S. A. LC 96-83892. (Illus.). 200p. 1996. 30.00 (*0-9622348-3-4*) Bonde Pr.

— The Tramways of Chile, 1858-1978. LC 92-73238. (Illus.). 144p. (Orig.). 1992. pap. 20.00 (*0-9622348-2-6*) Bonde Pr.

Morrison, Allen J. Strategies in Global Industries: How U. S. Businesses Compete. LC 89-24370. 216p. 1990. 62.95 (*0-89930-528-8*, MBG/, Greenwood Pr) Greenwood.

Morrison, Allen J., jt. ed. see Lecraw, Donald J.

Morrison, Alwyn R. Thoughts to Dwell On. LC 94-69160. 125p. 1995. pap. 9.95 (*0-9643939-0-5*) Shepard Edge.

Morrison, Andrea P., ed. Justice for Natives: Searching for Common Ground. LC 98-186068. (Illus.). 352p. 1994. 65.00 (*0-7735-1635-2*, Pub. by McG-Queens Univ Pr) CUP Services.

— Justice for Natives: Searching for Common Ground. LC 98-186068. (Illus.). 352p. 1994. pap. 22.95 (*0-7735-1645-X*, Pub. by McG-Queens Univ Pr) CUP Services.

***Morrison, Andrew.** Too Close to Home: Domestic Violence in Latin America. LC 99-71775. (Illus.). 206p. 1999. pap. text 24.95 (*1-886938-44-X*) Johns Hopkins.

Morrison, Andrew & Biehl, Maria Loreto. Too Close to Home: Domestic Violence in the Americas. LC 99-198138. 220p. 1999. pap. text 24.95 (*1-886938-43-1*) IADB.

Morrison, Andrew, jt. ed. see Lansky, Melvin R.

Morrison, Andrew L. The Antidepressant Sourcebook: A User's Guide for Patients & Families. LC 99-29949. 304p. 1999. pap. 12.95 (*0-385-49665-6*, Anchor NY) Doubleday.

Morrison, Andrew P. The Culture of Shame. LC 98-16681. 240p. 1998. reprint ed. pap. 25.00 (*0-7657-0174-X*) Aronson.

— Shame: The Underside of Narcissism. LC 89-37655. 226p. 1997. pap. text 29.95 (*0-88163-280-5*) Analytic Pr.

Morrison, Andrew P., ed. Essential Papers on Narcissism. (Essential Papers in Psychoanalysis). 496p. (C). 1986. pap. text 27.50 (*0-8147-5395-7*) NYU Pr.

***Morrison, Andrew R. & Biehl, Maria Loreto, eds.** El Costo del Silencio: El Violencia Domestica en las Americas. (SPA.). 245p. 1999. 24.95 (*1-886938-55-5*) IADB.

Morrison, Ann. Manuals Set (DCM & MCC) 2nd rev. ed. 1994. 485.00 (*0-614-05008-1*, MSET) Capitol Publns.

Morrison, Ann M. Developing Leadership Diversity in Organizations. (Philip Morris Lectures on Business & Society Ser.). 25p. 1993. pap. write for info. (*1-884663-02-8*) Baruch Coll Cty U.

— The New Leaders: Leadership Diversity in America. (Management Ser.). 352p. 1996. reprint ed. mass mkt. 18.50 (*0-7879-0184-9*) Jossey-Bass.

Morrison, Ann M., et al, eds. Making Diversity Happen: Controversies & Solutions. LC 93-40166. (Special Reports; No. 320G). 127p. 1993. pap. text 20.00 (*0-912879-72-6*) Ctr Creat Leader.

Morrison, Ann M. & Crabtree, Kristen M. Developing Diversity in Organizations: A Digest of Selected Literature. LC 93-144970. (Special Reports: No. 317G). 138p. 1992. pap. text 12.50 (*0-912879-70-X*) Ctr Creat Leader.

Morrison, Ann M., et al. Breaking the Glass Ceiling: Can Women Reach the Top of America's Largest Corporations? 2nd rev. ed. (Illus.). 1992. 19.95 (*0-201-63214-4*) Addison-Wesley.

— A Glass Ceiling Survey: Benchmarking Barriers & Practices. 45p. 1995. pap. text 15.00 (*1-882197-10-0*) Ctr Creat Leader.

— Performance Appraisal on the Line. 160p. pap. 15.00 (*0-912879-93-9*) Ctr Creat Leader.

Morrison, Arthur. Child of Jago. 240p. 1996. pap. 7.95 (*0-460-87772-0*, Everyman's Classic Lib) Tuttle Pubng.

— A Child of the Jago. (Victorian Classics Ser.). 208p. 1995. pap. 10.00 (*0-89733-392-6*) Academy Chi Pubs.

— Chronicles of Martin Hewitt. LC 74-144165. (Short Story Index Reprint Ser.). 1977. reprint ed. 18.95 (*0-8369-3780-5*) Ayer.

— Martin Hewitt, Investigator. LC 75-32769. (Literature of Mystery & Detection Ser.). (Illus.). 1976. reprint ed. 19.95 (*0-405-07888-9*) Ayer.

— Red Triangle. LC 75-116962. (Short Story Index Reprint Ser.). 1977. 21.95 (*0-8369-3466-0*) Ayer.

— Tales of Mean Streets. LC 96-42400. 175p. 1997. pap. text 11.00 (*0-89733-440-X*) Academy Chi Pubs.

— Tales of Mean Streets. LC 78-128742. (Short Story Index Reprint Ser.). 1977. 19.95 (*0-8369-3633-7*) Ayer.

Morrison, Barrie M. Political Centers & Cultural Regions in Early Bengal. LC 76-92469. (Monographs: No. 25). xii, 189p. 1969. 17.00 (*0-8165-0154-8*) Assn Asian Studies.

Morrison, Beverly H., jt. ed. see Bakker, Martinus A.

M

Morrison, Bill. Cheyenne Noon. large type ed. (Linford Western Large Print Ser.). 224p. 1998. pap. 17.99 (*0-7089-5271-2*, Linford) Ulverscroft.
— A Dollar from the Stage. large type ed. (Linford Western Large Print Ser.). 288p. 1997. pap. 16.99 (*0-7089-5047-7*) Ulverscroft.
— River Gold. large type ed. 192p. 1998. pap. 17.99 (*0-7089-5381-6*, Linford) Ulverscroft.
— Roswell Walks among Us. Kane, Nathan & Harkins, Tim, trs. (Illus.). 128p. 1997. pap. 12.95 (*0-9642999-9-2*) Bongo Enter.
— The Wooden Gun. large type ed. (Linford Western Library). 1995. pap. 16.99 (*0-7089-7769-3*, Linford) Ulverscroft.
Morrison, Bill, jt. auth. see Coates, Ken.
Morrison, Blake. And When Did You Last See Your Father? 1996. pap. 12.00 (*0-614-12561-8*, Picador USA) St Martin.
— And When Did You Last See Your Father? A Son's Memoir of Love & Loss. 224p. 1996. pap. 12.00 (*0-312-14273-0*, Picador USA) St Martin.
— As If: A Crime, a Trial, a Question of Childhood. LC 97-20438. 224p. 1997. text 21.00 (*0-312-16777-6*, Picador USA) St Martin.
Morrison, Blake. Penguin Book of Contemporary British Verse. pap. 15.95 (*0-14-058552-4*, Pub. by Pnguin Bks Ltd) Trafalgar.
Morrison, Blake. The Yellow House. LC 93-36274. (Illus.). 32p. (J). (ps up). 1994. pap. 4.99 (*1-56402-385-0*) Candlewick Pr.
— The Yellow House. (Illus.). 32p. (J). (ps-3). 1987. 12.95 (*0-15-299820-9*, Harcourt Child Bks) Harcourt.
Morrison, Blake & Rego, Paula. Pendle Witches. 54p. 1996. 49.95 (*1-900564-45-9*, Pub. by Enitha Pr) Dufour.
Morrison, Bob, jt. auth. see Levey, Jane.
Morrison, Bradley G. & Dalgleish, Julie G. Waiting in the Wings: A Larger Audience for the Arts & How to Develop It. rev. ed. LC 92-33800. 178p. 1992. pap. 15.95 (*1-879903-03-2*) Am for the Arts.
Morrison, Brenda, intro. S. C. Yuan. LC 94-72075. 200p. (Orig.). 1994. write for info. (*1-885666-06-3*); pap. write for info. (*1-885666-07-1*) Carmel Art.
Morrison, Brian, jt. auth. see Fink, Howard.
Morrison, Brian, jt. auth. see Patterson, Gordon.
Morrison, Bryce. Liszt. (Illustrated Lives of the Great Composers Ser.). (Illus.). 112p. 1989. pap. 17.95 (*0-7119-1682-9*, OP44999) Omnibus NY.
Morrison, C. L. Defilement. LC 78-64744. (Illus.). 1979. 24.95 (*0-932508-02-2*) Seven Oaks.
Morrison, C. L., ed. Pithy Sayings from FORMAT Interviews, Vol. I. 1979. pap. 4.95 (*0-932508-06-5*) Seven Oaks.
— Pithy Sayings from FORMAT Interviews, Vol. II. 1980. pap. 4.95 (*0-932508-07-3*) Seven Oaks.
Morrison, Carol. How to Build a Long-Lasting Fire: Writing Poems from Your Life. LC 96-271. 256p. 1996. pap. write for info. (*0-8442-5935-7*) NTC Contemp Pub Co.
— How to Build a Long-Lasting Fire: Writing Poems from Your Life. 1997. pap., teacher ed. 20.95 (*0-8442-5936-5*) NTC Contemp Pub Co.
Morrison, Carol M. Histology of the Atlantic Cod, Gadus Morhua Pt. IV: An Atlas, Eleutheroembryo & Larvae. 469p. 1993. 62.50 (*0-660-57482-9*) NRC Res Pr.
Morrison, Catherine, jt. auth. see Murray, John.
***Morrison, Catherine J.** Cost Structure & the Measurement of Economic Performance: Productivity, Utilization, Cost Economics & Related Performance Indicators LC 98-48311. 1999. write for info. (*0-7923-8403-2*) Kluwer Academic.
Morrison, Catherine W., jt. auth. see Morrison, John.

Morrison, Charles. The Fairfax Line: A Profile in History & Geography. (Illus.). 32p. 1974. pap. 3.95 (*0-87012-085-9*) McClain.

Morrison, Charles C. An Essay on the Relations Between Labor & Capital. LC 70-38273. (Evolution of Capitalism Ser.). 348p. 1979. reprint ed. 26.95 (*0-405-04128-4*) Ayer.
— Outlawry of War: A Constructive Policy for World Peace. LC 71-147607. (Library of War & Peace; Kellogg Pact & the Outlawry of War). 1972. lib. bdg. 46.00 (*0-8240-0367-5*) Garland.
— Unfinished Reformation. LC 68-20322. (Essay Index Reprint Ser.). 1977. 20.95 (*0-8369-0723-X*) Ayer.
Morrison, Charles E. Japan, the United States & a Changing Southeast Asia. (Illus.). 82p. (Orig.). 1985. pap. text 8.50 (*0-8191-4595-5*) U Pr of Amer.
Morrison, Charles E., ed. Asia-Pacific Report Nineteen Eighty-Seven thru Nineteen Eighty-Eight: Trends, Issues, Challenges. LC 87-20074. vi, 84p. 1987. pap. 10.00 (*0-86638-098-1*) EW Ctr HI.
— Asia-Pacific Report, 1986: Trends, Issues, Challenges. LC 85-27538. viii, 104p. 1986. pap. 10.00 (*0-86638-071-X*) EW Ctr HI.
— Japan, China & the Newly Industrialized Economies of East Asia, 1989. 1990. 5.00 (*0-685-34498-3*) Southern Ctr Intl Stud.
Morrison, Charles E., ed. Threats to Security in East Asia-Pacific. 221p. (C). 1983. text 27.95 (*0-317-91349-2*) Pac Forum.
Morrison, Charles E. & Dernberger, Robert F., eds. Asia-Pacific Report, 1989: Focus: China in the Reform Era. LC 89-1103. vi, 126p. 1989. pap. 15.00 (*0-86638-111-2*) EW Ctr HI.
Morrison, Charles E., et al. Community Building with Pacific Asia: A Report to the Trilateral Commission. LC 97-20421. (A Report to the Trilateral Commission Ser.). 123p. 1997. pap. 9.00 (*0-930503-75-9*) Trilateral Comm.
Morrison, Charles E., jt. auth. see Aggarwal, Vinod K.
Morrison, Charles E., jt. ed. see Aggarwal, Vinod K.
Morrison, Chris. PC Care Manual. 1991. 24.95 (*0-8306-6650-8*) McGraw-Hill Prof.
Morrison, Chris & Stover, T. Commodore Care Manual: 64 System. 1991. 24.95 (*0-8306-6432-7*) McGraw-Hill Prof.
Morrison, Chris & Stover, Teresa S. Apple Care Manual. 1991. 24.95 incl. 5.25 hd (*0-8306-4252-8*) McGraw-Hill Prof.
— Commodore Care Manual: Diagnosing & Maintaining Your 64 or 128 System. (Illus.). 224p. 1988. pap. 16.95 (*0-8306-3141-0*, 3141) McGraw-Hill Prof.
— Commodore Care Manual: 128 System. 1991. 24.95 (*0-8306-6433-5*) McGraw-Hill Prof.
— PC Care Manual: Diagnosing & Maintaining Your MS-DOS CP-M or Macintosh System. LC 87-26235. (Illus.). 224p. 1987. 24.95 (*0-8306-0991-1*, 2991) McGraw-Hill Prof.
Morrison, Clinton D., jt. tr. see Lammers, Wayne.
Morrison, Clyde A. Crystal Fields for Transition-Metal Ions in Laser Host Materials. LC 92-15276. viii, 190p. 1992. 91.95 (*0-387-55465-3*) Spr-Verlag.
Morrison, Colin, intro. Christmas in Ireland. 96p. 1998. 14.95 (*1-57098-245-7*, R Rinehart Intl) Roberts Rinehart.
***Morrison, Connie.** Microsoft Office 2000 Basics. LC 00-37415. (Illus.). 2000. write for info. (*0-538-72413-7*) Sth-Wstrn College.
Morrison, Connie. Microsoft Word: Easy Reference Guides for IBM & Macintosh. 1991. text, mass mkt. 7.95 incl. mac hd (*0-538-61758-6*); text, mass mkt. 7.95 incl. disk (*0-538-61757-8*) S-W Pub.
— Microsoft Word 5.1 - Macintosh: Easy Reference Guide. LC 93-19714. 1994. mass mkt. 7.95 (*0-538-62676-3*) S-W Pub.
— Microsoft Word for Windows 2.0: Easy Reference Guide. LC 93-33039. 1995. mass mkt. 9.95 (*0-538-63383-2*) S-W Pub.
***Morrison, Connie & Cable, Sandra.** Microsoft Office 2000: Advanced Course. LC 99-23145. 752p. 1999. pap. 54.95 (*0-538-68829-7*) Sth-Wstrn College.
Morrison, Connie & Jaehne, Julie S. Integrated Applications: A Visual Approach. (Illus.). 324p. 1998. spiral bd. 35.95 (*1-57426-109-6*) Computer Lit Pr.
Morrison, Connie, et al. Microsoft Office 2000: Advanced Tutorial. (Computer Applications Ser.). 1999. pap., wbk. ed. 12.95 (*0-538-68830-0*) S-W Pub.
Morrison, Connie, jt. auth. see Jaehne, Julie.
Morrison, Connie, jt. auth. see Pasewark, William.
Morrison, Craig. Go Cat Go! Rockabilly Music & Its Makers. LC 95-41807. (Music in American Life Ser.). (Illus.). 336p. 1996. 29.95 (*0-252-02207-6*); pap. 17.95 (*0-252-06538-7*) U of Ill Pr.
***Morrison, Craig.** 2 Samuel. (Berit Olam (The Everlasting Covenant) Ser.). 2000. 0.00 (*0-8146-5043-0*) Liturgical Pr.
Morrison, Craig, jt. auth. see Knudson, Duane.
Morrison, Craig E., ed. see Murphy, Roland E.
Morrison, Crystal D. Trial of Cristobal Colon: An Historical Play. LC 93-84327. 160p. (Orig.). 1996. pap. 15.98 (*1-879289-04-0*) Native Sun Pubs.
Morrison, D. & Anderson, C. Ford & Austin's Principles of Corporations Law: Workbook to 7th Edition. 184p. 1995. pap., wbk. ed. write for info. (*0-409-31112-X*, MICHIE) LEXIS Pub.
Morrison, D., jt. ed. see Chapman, C. P.
Morrison, D. C., ed. Organizing Early Experience: Imagination & Cognition in Childhood. 247p. 1988. pap. 31.95 (*0-89503-051-9*) Baywood Pub.
Morrison, D. H., ed. Treasury of Song for the Home Circle (1882) 550p. 1998. reprint ed. pap. 35.00 (*0-7661-0642-X*) Kessinger Pub.
Morrison, Dane. A Praying People: Massachusett Acculturation & the Failure of the Puritan Mission, 1600-1690. 2nd rev. ed. (American Indian Studies: Vol. 2). XXXI, 273p. (C). 1998. reprint ed. pap. text 32.95 (*0-8204-4191-0*) P Lang Pubng.
Morrison, Dane, ed. American Indian Studies: An Interdisciplinary Approach to Contemporary Issues. LC 96-50438. (Illus.). 430p. (C). 1997. text 59.95 (*0-8204-3101-X*) P Lang Pubng.
Morrison, Daniel. Trading Peasants & Urbanization in Eighteenth-Century Russia: The Central Industrial Region. (Modern European History Ser.). 440p. 1987. text 15.00 (*0-8240-8059-9*) Garland.
Morrison, Dannell C. Pee Yew Bartholomew: A Story about Divorce. LC 96-79869. 16p. (Orig.). (J). (gr. 5-8). 1997. pap. 5.95 (*1-57543-028-2*) Mar Co Prods.
Morrison, Danny. On the Back of the Swallow. 256p. (Orig.). 1996. pap. 14.95 (*1-57098-101-9*) Roberts Rinehart.
— West Belfast: A Novel. LC 95-71037. 255p. 1995. pap. 12.95 (*1-57098-043-8*) Roberts Rinehart.
— The Wrong Man: A Novel. 208p. 1997. pap. 12.95 (*1-57098-102-7*) Roberts Rinehart.
Morrison, Daryl. Guide to the Manuscript Collections, Holt-Atherton Department of Special Collections. Walker, Donald B. & Ford, Jonene, trs. (Illus.). 195p. (Orig.). 1995. pap. 25.00 (*0-614-14706-9*) Holt-Atherton.
***Morrison, David.** Beyond Gay. LC 99-70512. 288p. 1999. pap. 14.95 (*0-87973-690-9*) Our Sunday Visitor.
Morrison, David. Exploring Planetary Worlds. LC 92-46641. (Scientific American Library). 1993. text 32.95 (*0-7167-5043-0*) W H Freeman.
— FRONTIERS OF ASTRONOMY 2/E. 2nd ed. LC 93-86196. (C). 1994. pap. text 68.50 (*0-03-093933-X*) Harcourt Coll Pubs.
— Heroes, Antiheroes & the Holocaust: American Jewry & Historical Choice. LC 95-76846. 344p. 1995. 24.95 (*0-9646886-0-3*) Milah.
***Morrison, David.** Lies, Israel's Secret Service & the Rabin Murder. 284p. 2000. 24.95 (*965-229-241-9*, Pub. by Gefen Pub Hse) Gefen Bks.
Morrison, David. Me & My Monkey. Date not set. write for info. (*0-385-48274-4*) Doubleday.
Morrison, David & Germain, Georges-Hebert. The Real World of Engineering: Case Histories 41-65. (Illus.). 50.00 (*0-614-05208-4*) ASFE.
Morrison, David & Owen, Tobias C. The Planetary System. 2nd ed. Berrisford, Julie, ed. (Illus.). 570p. (C). 1992. 91.00 (*0-201-55450-X*) Addison-Wesley.
Morrison, David, jt. ed. see Friedman, Robert.
Morrison, David A. Caribou Hunters in the Western Arctic: Zooarchaeology of the Rita-Claire & Bison Skull Sites. (Mercury Ser.: ASC No. 157). (Illus.). 100p. 1998. pap. 14.95 (*0-660-15973-2*) U of Wash Pr.
Morrison, David A. The Diamond Jenness Collections from Bering Strait. (Mercury Ser.: ASC No. 144). (Illus.). 184p. 1994. pap. 19.95 (*0-660-12922-1*, Pub. by CN Mus Civilization) U of Wash Pr.
Morrison, David A. & Germain, Georges-Hebert. The Inuit: Glimpses of an Arctic Past. (Illus.). 160p. 1995. 27.95 (*0-660-14038-1*, Pub. by CN Mus Civilization) U of Wash Pr.
Morrison, David A. & Pilon, Jean-Luc, eds. Threads of Arctic Prehistory: Papers in Honour of William E. Taylor, Jr. LC 95-206685. (Mercury Ser.: ASC No. 149). (Illus.). 434p. 1994. pap. 29.95 (*0-660-50751-X*, Pub. by CN Mus Civilization) U of Wash Pr.
Morrison, David C. Bacterial Endotoxic Lipopolysaccarides, 2 vols., 1. 480p. 1992. lib. bdg. 225.00 (*0-8493-6787-5*, QP632) CRC Pr.
Morrison, David C., ed. Bacterial Endotoxic Lipopolysaccarides, 2 vols., 2. 480p. 1992. lib. bdg. 225.00 (*0-8493-6788-3*) CRC Pr.
Morrison, David C., jt. auth. see Prince, Frank A.
Morrison, David D. The Cast Iron Eagles of Grand Central Station. Diehl, Lorraine B., ed. LC 99-204164. (Illus.). 32p. 1998. pap. 14.95 (*0-945089-01-5*) Cannon Ball.
— Long Island Rail Road Steam Locomotive Pictorial. Valenti, Linda A., ed. LC 87-36821. (Illus.). 60p. (Orig.). 1987. pap. 9.95 (*0-945089-00-7*) Cannon Ball.
Morrison, David E. & Tumbler, Howard. Journalists at War: The Dynamic of News Reporting During the Falklands Conflict. 384p. 1988. text 49.95 (*0-8039-8057-4*); pap. text 18.95 (*0-8039-8058-2*) Sage.
Morrison, David J., jt. auth. see Martin, Edmund F.
Morrison, David J., jt. auth. see Slywotzky, Adrian J.
Morrison, David R. Aid & Ebb Tide: A History of CIDA & Canadian Development Assistance. LC 97-932446. 624p. 1998. 65.00 (*0-88920-304-0*) W Laurier U Pr.
Morrison, Deborah. IBM's Official Guide to Building a Better Web. LC 95-79926. 384p. 1995. pap. 29.99 (*1-56884-599-5*) IDG Bks.
— Os/2 Warp Internet Express. 256p. 1995. pap. 24.99 (*1-56884-465-4*) IDG Bks.
Morrison, Delores. Inspirations: Poems of Faith. 72p. 1999. pap. 8.00 (*0-8059-4716-7*) Dorrance.
Morrison, Dennis. Secret Society of the Shamans - Mystery Religions of the North American Indians Revealed. (Illus.). 112p. 1992. 12.95 (*0-938294-44-X*) Inner Light.
Morrison, Denton E., jt. ed. see Ghosh, Pradip K.
Morrison, Diana. A Glossary of Sanskrit: From the Spiritual Tradition of India. LC 77-27959. (SAN.). 40p. 1977. pap. 4.00 (*0-915132-12-5*) Nilgiri Pr.
Morrison, Diane, ed. American Indian Studies: An Interdisciplinary Approach to Contemporary Issues. 2nd ed. LC 96-50438. 456p. 1997. pap. 29.95 (*0-8204-3916-9*) P Lang Pubng.
Morrison, Don, ed. Model Personnel Policies for Business. 180p. ring bd. 49.00 (*0-927160-09-9*) Sound Resc Mgmt.
Morrison, Don A. Employee Performance Planning & Review System. (Illus.). (Orig.). (C). 1988. pap. 39.00 (*0-317-93480-5*) Sound Resc Mgmt.
— Employee Performance Planning & Review System: Effective Performance Management. (Illus.). (C). 1989. 49.00 (*0-927160-02-1*) Sound Resc Mgmt.
— Employee Performance Planning & Review System: Effective Performance Management. (Illus.). 165p. 1993. ring bd. 49.00 (*0-927160-07-2*) Sound Resc Mgmt.
— Model Job Descriptions for Business. 400p. ring bd. 139.00 (*0-927160-10-2*) Sound Resc Mgmt.
— Risk Management & Loss Control Manual: For Local Government. (Illus.). 267p. (Orig.). (C). 1988. pap. 49.00 (*0-317-93481-3*) Sound Resc Mgmt.
— Risk Management & Loss Control Manual: For Local Government. (Illus.). 267p. (Orig.). (C). 1989. 59.00 (*0-927160-00-5*); pap. 49.00 (*0-685-25550-6*) Sound Resc Mgmt.
— Strategic & Economic Development Planning: A Handbook for Local Government. (Illus.). 80p. (C). 1989. 24.00 (*0-927160-01-3*) Sound Resc Mgmt.
— Strategic Planning: A "How-To" Manual for Local Government. (Illus.). 85p. (Orig.). (C). 1988. pap. 19.00 (*0-317-93482-1*) Sound Resc Mgmt.
Morrison, Don A., ed. Model Governing Body Rules of Procedure. 30p. student ed. 29.00 (*0-927160-05-6*) Sound Resc Mgmt.
Morrison, Don A. & Gilliland, Jenifer. Morrison's Essential Recruitment & Selection Guide: For a Post-ADA Environment. (Illus.). 270p. 1993. ring bd. 7.00 (*0-927160-08-0*) Sound Resc Mgmt.
— Survival Kit for Local Government Managers. (Illus.). 133p. ring bd. 49.00 (*0-927160-06-4*) Sound Resc Mgmt.
Morrison, Donald. Mikhail S. Gorbachev: An Intimate Biography. pap. 4.50 (*0-318-50012-4*, Sig) NAL.
Morrison, Donald, ed. Mikhail S. Gorbachev: An Intimate Biography. 288p. 1988. 14.95 (*0-317-70076-6*, Sig) NAL.
Morrison, Donald C. & Ryan, John L., eds. Novel Therapeutic Strategies in the Treatment of Sepsis. (Infectious Disease & Therapy Ser.: Vol. 19). (Illus.). 392p. 1995. text 165.00 (*0-8247-9661-6*) Dekker.
Morrison, Donald F. Multivariate Statistical Methods. 3rd ed. 560p. (C). 1989. text 69.74 (*0-07-043187-6*) McGraw.
Morrison, Donald G., et al. Black Africa: A Comparative Handbook. 2nd ed. LC 89-2879. (Illus.). 768p. 1989. 249.50 incl. disk (*0-8290-2477-8*); text 169.50 (*0-8290-2466-2*) Irvington.
— Understanding Black Africa: Data & Analysis of Social Change & Nation Building. LC 88-33052. (Illus.). 253p. (C). 1989. text 39.50 (*0-8290-2228-7*); pap. text 22.95 (*0-8290-1371-7*) Irvington.
— Understanding Black Africa: Data & Analysis of Social Change & Nation Building. LC 88-33052. 255p. 1988. 39.50 (*0-88702-052-6*) Washington Inst Pr.
Morrison, Donald R., compiled by. Bibliography of Editions, Translations, & Commentary on Xenophon's Socratic Writings 1600-Present. 120p. 1988. 15.00 (*0-935225-02-1*) Mathesis Pubns.
Morrison, Donald W. Personal Problem Solving in the Classroom: The Reality Technique. LC 76-28419. 200p. reprint ed. pap. 62.00 (*0-608-10826-X*, 201584800097) Bks Demand.
***Morrison, Dorothy.** Bud, Blossom & Leaf: The Magical Herb Gardener's Handbook. 2001. pap. 14.95 (*1-56718-443-X*) Llewellyn Pubns.
Morrison, Dorothy. Everyday Magic: Spells & Rituals for Modern Living. LC 98-6861. (Illus.). 320p. (Orig.). 1998. pap. 9.95 (*1-56718-469-3*) Llewellyn Pubns.
— In Praise of the Crone: A Celebration of Feminine Maturity. LC 98-42216. (Illus.). 288p. 1999. 14.95 (*1-56718-468-5*) Llewellyn Pubns.
— Magical Needlework. LC 97-52214. (Illus.). 244p. (Orig.). 1998. pap. 17.95 (*1-56718-470-7*) Llewellyn Pubns.
***Morrison, Dorothy.** Outpost: John McLoughlin & the Far Northwest. LC 98-3162. (Illus.). 1998. 35.00 (*0-87595-267-4*) Oregon Hist.
Morrison, Dorothy. The Rise of Modern China. 1988. pap. text 13.98 (*0-05-004183-5*, 78260) Longman.
***Morrison, Dorothy.** Yule: A Celebration of Warmth & Light. 2000. pap. 14.95 (*1-56718-496-0*) Llewellyn Pubns.
Morrison, Dorothy N. Chief Sarah: Sarah Winnemucca's Fight for Indian Rights. (Eager Beaver Bks.). (Illus.). 190p. (J). (gr. 4 up). 1990. reprint ed. pap. 8.95 (*0-87595-204-6*) Oregon Hist.
— The Eagle & the Fort: The Story of John McLoughlin. (Illus.). 192p. 1984. reprint ed. pap. 8.95 (*0-87595-167-8*) Oregon Hist.
— Ladies Were Not Expected: Abigail Scott Duniway & Women's Rights. (Illus.). 148p. (J). (gr. 4 up). 1996. reprint ed. pap. 8.95 (*0-87595-166-X*) Oregon Hist.
— Whisper Again. 208p. (J). (gr. 2-9). 1989. reprint ed. pap. 2.95 (*0-8167-1307-3*) Troll Communs.
— Whisper Goodbye. 1992. 8.05 (*0-606-12605-8*, Pub. by Turtleback) Demco.
Morrison, Douglas R., ed. Prions & Brain Diseases in Animals & Humans. LC 98-12133. (NATO ASI Ser.: No. 295). (Illus.). 372p. (C). 1998. text 125.00 (*0-306-45825-X*, Kluwer Plenum) Kluwer Academic.
***Morrison, Douglas Wyeth.** Nutritional Healing: Body, Mind, & Spirit. 300p. 2001. pap. 27.50 (*1-55643-362-X*) North Atlantic.
Morrison, Douglass Andrew & Serruys, Patrick W., eds. Medically Refractory Rest Angina. (Illus.). 480p. 1992. text 190.00 (*0-8247-8630-0*) Dekker.
Morrison, Ed. Rugby: A Referee's Guide. 1996. pap. 13.95 (*0-00-218754-X*, Pub. by HarpC) Trafalgar.
Morrison, Eileen E., jt. auth. see Schroeder, Rick E.
Morrison, Elizabeth, ed. see Cambridge, Ada.
Morrison, Elizabeth, ed. see Garzarelli, Bernadette.
Morrison, Elizabeth, jt. ed. see Purcell, Randall B.
Morrison, Ellen E. The Church That Keeps Memories Alive: The Story of Christ Church, Alexandria, Virginia. 2nd rev. ed. LC 79-114253. (Illus.). 12p. 1979. pap. 1.75 (*0-9622537-0-7*) Morielle Pr.
— Gentle Man of Destiny: A Portrait of Robert E. Lee. 2nd rev. ed. LC 80-201289. (Illus.). 16p. 1984. pap. 1.75 (*0-9622537-1-5*) Morielle Pr.
— Guardian of the Forest: A History of Smokey Bear & the Cooperative Forest Fire Prevention Program. 3rd rev. ed. LC 96-75436. (Illus.). 224p. 1996. lib. bdg. 18.95 (*0-9622537-5-8*) Morielle Pr.
— Lady of Legend: The Mystery of the Female Stranger of Gadsby's Tavern. 2nd rev. ed. LC 87-460803. (Illus.). 16p. 1986. pap. 1.75 (*0-9622537-2-3*) Morielle Pr.
— The Smokey Bear Story. LC 94-73401. (Illus.). 64p. (J). (gr. 1 up). 1995. lib. bdg. 15.95 (*0-9622537-4-X*) Morielle Pr.
Morrison, Emily K. Leadership Skills: Developing Volunteers for Organizational Success. LC 94-9333. 240p. (Orig.). 1994. pap. 17.95 (*1-55561-066-8*) Fisher Bks.
Morrison, Emmeline. No More Such Days. large type ed. 368p. 1985. 27.99 (*0-7089-1352-0*) Ulverscroft.
Morrison, Ernest. The City on the Hill: History of the Harrisburg State Hospital. 262p. 1995. 25.00 (*0-9644246-0-6*); pap. 10.00 (*0-9644246-1-4*) Hist Committ HSH.
— J. Horace McFarland: A Thorn for Beauty. (Illus.). 350p. 1995. 19.95 (*0-89271-063-2*, 0424) Pa Hist & Mus.
Morrison, F. J., jt. ed. see Siegel, L. S.
***Morrison, Faith A.** Understanding Rheology. (Topics in Chemical Engineering Ser.). (Illus.). 656p. (C). 2000. text 95.00 (*0-19-514166-0*) OUP.

An Asterisk (*) at the beginning of an entry indicates that the title is appearing for the first time.

Morrison, Foster. The Art of Modeling Dynamic Systems: Forecasting for Chaos, Randomness, & Determinism. (Scientific & Technical Computation Ser.). 384p. 1991. 110.00 (*0-471-52004-7*) Wiley.

Morrison Foster, Elaine, et al. Stories in Stained Glass: To Teach the Providence of God : The Making & Meaning of the Stained Glass Windows in the New York Avenue Presbyterian Church, Washington, D. C. LC 98-70066. 120 p. 1998. write for info. (*1-880774-24-0*) Ferguson.

***Morrison, Francesca.** Sydney. (Architecture Guides Ser.). 320p. 1998. pap. 5.95 (*3-89508-645-2*, 520208) Konemann.

***Morrison, Fred L. & Wolfrum, Rhudiger.** International, Regional & National Environmental Law. LC 00-32735. 2000. write for info. (*90-411-8845-2*) Kluwer Law Intl.

Morrison, Fred W. Equalization of the Financial Burden of Education among Counties in North Carolina: A Study of the Equalizing Fund. LC 73-177089. (Columbia University. Teachers College. Contributions to Education Ser.: No. 184). reprint ed. 37.50 (*0-404-55184-X*) AMS Pr.

Morrison, G. The Mystery Play. Kahan, Bob, ed. (Illus.). 80p. 1995. mass mkt. 9.95 (*1-56389-189-1*, Pub. by DC Comics) Time Warner.

Morrison, G. A., Jr. King: Clement King of Marshfield, MA, 1668, & His Descendants. (Illus.). 65p. 1994. reprint ed. pap. 13.00 (*0-8328-4338-5*); reprint ed. lib. bdg. 23.00 (*0-8328-4337-7*) Higginson Bk Co.

Morrison, G. E. The Correspondence of G. E. Morrison, 2 vols., Set. Lo Hui-Min, ed. LC 74-31805. 825p. 1978. text 265.00 (*0-521-08779-1*) Cambridge U Pr.

Morrison, G. H. Morrison: Genealogy of the Descendants of John Morrison & Prudence Gwyn. 31p. 1994. reprint ed. pap. 6.00 (*0-8328-4163-3*) Higginson Bk Co.

Morrison, G. L., et al, eds. Fluid Measurement & Instrumentation - 1995 Vol. 211: Fluid Measurement & Instrumentation - 1995. LC 86-70582. (1995 ASME/JSME Fluids Engineering Conference Ser.: FED-Vol. 211). 164p. 1995. 88.00 (*0-7918-1466-1*, G00961) ASME.

***Morrison, Gail & Hark, Lisa.** Medical Nutrition & Disease. 2nd ed. LC 99-24988. (Illus.). 1999. pap. 34.95 (*0-632-04339-3*) Blackwell Sci.

Morrison, Gail, jt. auth. see Hark, Lisa.

Morrison, Gary, et al. Financial Success with Quicken for Macintosh. (Illus.). (Orig.). 1996. pap. 25.00 (*1-56830-252-5*) Hayden.

Morrison, Gary R. Your Kids, Their Future: Every Parents Guide to Helping Your Child Become Employable. rev. ed. LC 98-91256. 230p. 1999. pap. 15.00 (*0-9662651-0-6*) Landon Sols.

Morrison, Gavin. The Heyday of Leeds Holbeck & Its Locomotives. pap. 26.95 (*0-7110-2225-9*) Spec Mkting Intl.

Morrison, Gayle. To Move the World: Louis G. Gregory & the Advancement of Racial Unity in America. (Illus.). 399p. (C). 1983. pap. 13.95 (*0-87743-171-X*) Bahai.

Morrison, Gayle L. The Sky Is Falling: An Oral History of the CIA's Evacuation of the Hmong from Laos. LC 98-34811. (Illus.). 232p. 1998. lib. bdg. 39.95 (*0-7864-0512-0*) McFarland & Co.

Morrison, George. The Emergent Years: Independent Ireland 1922-62 LC 85-107056. 184p. 1984. write for info. (*0-7171-1341-8*) Gill & MacMill.

***Morrison, George.** Savour of Ireland: A Photographic & Gastronomic Tour of Ireland a Century Ago. (Illus.). 127p. 1999. reprint ed. pap. text 17.00 (*0-7881-6669-7*) DIANE Pub.

Morrison, George. Turning the Feather Around: My Life in Art. LC 97-44821. (Midwest Reflections Ser.). 205p. 1998. pap. 24.95 (*0-87351-360-6*) Minn Hist.

Morrison, George, photos by. The Irish Civil War: A Photographic Record. (Illus.). 288p. 1998. 35.00 (*1-57098-252-X*) Roberts Rinehart.

Morrison, George, jt. auth. see FitzGibbon, Theodora.

Morrison, George H. Highways of the Heart: A Series of Sermons. LC 93-37827. 208p. 1993. pap. 10.99 (*0-8254-3290-1*) Kregel.

— Meditations on the Gospels. LC 96-84208. (Walk in the Word Ser.). 714p. 1996. reprint ed. 24.99 (*0-89957-214-6*) AMG Pubs.

— More Meditations on the New Testament & Psalms. LC 96-85657. (Walk in the Word Ser.). 652p. 1996. 24.99 (*0-89957-215-4*) AMG Pubs.

— The Weaving of Glory. 208p. 1994. pap. 10.99 (*0-8254-3291-X*) Kregel.

— Wind on the Heath: Sunday Evening Sermons from a Glasgow Pulpit. LC 93-37826. 176p. 1993. pap. 10.99 (*0-8254-3289-8*) Kregel.

— The Wings of the Morning. 192p. 1994. pap. 10.99 (*0-8254-3288-X*) Kregel.

Morrison, George R. Liquidity Preferences of Commercial Banks. LC 66-13882. (Chicago University Economics Research Center Studies). 175p. reprint ed. pap. 54.30 (*0-608-10208-3*, 202013000016) Bks Demand.

Morrison, George S. Contemporary Curriculum. LC 92-35298. 544p. 1993. pap. text 54.00 (*0-205-14523-X*) Allyn.

— Early Childhood Education Today. 7th ed. LC 97-19920. 580p. (C). 1997. 69.00 (*0-13-749979-5*) P-H.

— Fundamentals of Early Childhood Education. 2nd ed. LC 99-32554. 400p. 1999. pap. text 48.00 (*0-13-012095-2*) P-H.

— World of Child Development. (Early Childhood Education Ser.). 1990. pap., student ed. 16.00 (*0-8273-3118-5*) Delmar.

— World of Child Development. (Early Childhood Education Ser.). 1990. teacher ed. 12.95 (*0-8273-3117-7*, VNR) Wiley.

— World of Child Development. (Early Childhood Education Ser.). 1990. 49.95 (*0-8273-3116-9*, VNR) Wiley.

Morrison, Glenn H. The Morrisons: They Came to the Land That Hudgin Drains. LC 93-81022. (Orig.). 1994. pap. 15.95 (*0-9640081-0-6*) G H Morrison.

Morrison, Golda L. Poems for the Purpose. Pacitti, Aleen M., ed. (Illus.). 136p. 1996. pap. text 4.95 (*0-9643424-2-1*) A J Morrison.

Morrison, Gordon. Oak Tree. LC 98-55148. 32p. (J). 1999. 16.00 (*0-395-95644-7*) HM.

Morrison, Gordon. Bald Eagle. LC 97-42007. 30p. 1998. 16.00 (*0-395-87328-2*) HM.

Morrison, Gordon, jt. auth. see Walton, Richard K.

Morrison, Grant. Batman: Arkham Asylum. Berger, Karen, ed. (Illus.). 128p. 1997. mass mkt. 14.95 (*0-930289-56-0*, Pub. by Warner Bks) Little.

***Morrison, Grant.** Batman: Gothic. Hill, Michael, ed. LC 94-223037. 128p. 1998. pap. 12.95 (*1-56389-028-3*, Pub. by DC Comics) Time Warner.

Morrison, Grant. DC One Million. (Illus.). 208p. 1999. pap. text 14.95 (*1-56389-525-0*, Pub. by DC Comics) Time Warner.

— Doom Patrol: Crawling from the Wreckage. Kahan, Bob, ed. (Illus.). 192p. 1992. pap. 19.95 (*1-56389-034-8*, Pub. by DC Comics) Time Warner.

***Morrison, Grant.** Invisible: Bloody Hell Amer **wrong Isbn Use 1563894440. LC 99-176947. 1998. mass mkt. write for info. (*1-56389-440-8*) Warner Bks.

— The Invisibles. (Invisibles Ser.). 224p. (J). 2000. pap. text 19.95 (*1-56389-600-1*, Pub. by DC Comics) Time Warner.

Morrison, Grant. The Invisibles: Bloody Hell in America. Kahan, Bob, ed. (Illus.). 104p. 1998. pap. text 12.95 (*1-56389-444-0*, Pub. by DC Comics) Time Warner.

— The Invisibles: Counting to None. (Illus.). 240p. 1999. pap. text 19.95 (*1-56389-489-0*, Pub. by DC Comics) Time Warner.

— The Invisibles: Say You Want a Revolution. LC 96-232414. (Illus.). 224p. 1996. mass mkt. 19.95 (*1-56389-267-7*, Pub. by DC Comics) Time Warner.

— Isaac Bronson & the Search for System in American Capitalism, 1789-1838. (Dissertations in American Economic History Ser.). 1978. 39.95 (*0-405-11050-2*) Ayer.

— J L A: American Dreams. LC 98-130879. (JLA Ser.). (Illus.). 112p. 1998. pap. text 7.95 (*1-56389-394-0*, Pub. by DC Comics) Time Warner.

— J L A: New World Order. LC 98-103950. (JLA Ser.). (Illus.). 96p. 1997. pap. text 5.95 (*1-56389-369-X*, Pub. by DC Comics) Time Warner.

— J L A: Rock of Ages. LC 98-222986. (JLA Ser.). (Illus.). 160p. 1998. pap. text 9.95 (*1-56389-416-5*, Pub. by DC Comics) Time Warner.

— JLA: Earth II. 96p. 2000. 24.95 (*1-56389-575-7*, Pub. by DC Comics) Time Warner.

— JLA: Justice for All. 232p. 1999. pap. text 14.95 (*1-56389-511-0*, Pub. by DC Comics) Time Warner.

— JLA Wild C. A. T. S. Semeiks, Val & Conrad, Kevin, eds. LC 98-101868. (Illus.). 64p. 1997. pap. 5.95 (*1-56389-366-5*) DC Comics.

— Kill Your Boyfriend. LC 99-205431. (Illus.). 64p. 1998. pap. 5.95 (*1-56389-453-X*) DC Comics.

Morrison, Grant & Janson, Klaus. Batman Gothic. (Illus.). (Orig.). 1992. mass mkt. 12.99 (*0-446-39428-9*, Pub. by Warner Bks) Little.

Morrison, Grant & McKeon, David. Batman: Arkham Asylum. 1990. mass mkt. 14.95 (*0-446-39189-1*, Pub. by Warner Bks) Little.

***Morrison, Grant & Miller, Mark.** Secret Origins Featuring JLA. (Illus.). 160p. 1999. pap. text 14.95 (*1-56389-542-0*, Pub. by DC Comics) Time Warner.

Morrison, Grant & Waid, Mark. Justice League America: Strength in Numbers. LC 99-176042. (Illus.). 224p. (J). 1998. pap. text 12.95 (*1-56389-435-1*, Pub. by DC Comics) Time Warner.

Morrison, Grant, et al. Spawn, Vol. 4. (Illus.). 128p. 1997. pap. 9.95 (*1-887279-52-0*) Image Comics.

Morrison, Greg, jt. auth. see Forstchen, William R.

Morrison, Greg, jt. auth. see Fortschen, William R.

Morrison, Gregory B. The Modern Technique of the Pistol. LC 91-72644. 175p. 1991. write for info. (*0-9621342-3-6*) Gunsite Trng Ctr.

Morrison, H. C. Remarkable Conversions & Striking Illustrations. pap. 3.99 (*0-88019-102-3*) Schmul Pub Co.

***Morrison, H. C.** The Two Lawyers: A Story of the Times. 120p. 1998. pap. 7.99 (*0-88019-384-0*) Schmul Pub Co.

Morrison, Harry. Bioorganic Photochemistry, Vol. 1, Photochemistry & the Nucleic Acids, Vol. 1, Photochemistry and the Nucleic Acids. LC 89-14837. 437p. 1990. 125.00 (*0-471-62987-1*) Wiley.

Morrison, Harry, ed. Biological Applications of Photochemical Switches. LC 89-14837. 316p. 1993. 120.00 (*0-471-57293-4*) Wiley.

Morrison, Heather & Sarajedini, Ata, eds. Formation of the Galactic Halo...Inside & Out. (ASP Conference Series Proceedings: Vol. 92). 557p. 1996. 34.00 (*1-886733-13-9*) Astron Soc Pacific.

Morrison, Henry C. The Practice of Teaching in the Secondary School. rev. ed. LC 31-9855. 698p. reprint ed. pap. 200.00 (*0-608-13401-5*, 202410100035) Bks Demand.

— School & Commonwealth. LC 73-142673. (Essay Index Reprint Ser.). 1977. 20.95 (*0-8369-2063-5*) Ayer.

Morrison, Howard. American Encounters. (Illus.). 80p. (Orig.). 1992. pap. write for info. (*0-929847-05-9*) Natl Mus Am.

Morrison, Howard Alexander, jt. auth. see Klapthor, Margaret Brown.

***Morrison, Hugh.** Acting Skills. 2nd rev. ed. (Illus.). 192p. 1999. pap. 17.95 (*0-7136-4932-1*, Pub. by A & C Blk) Midpt Trade.

Morrison, Hugh. Directing in the Theatre. LC 73-83996. 1974. pap. 10.95 (*0-87830-587-4*, Thtre Arts Bks) Routledge.

— Early American Architecture: From the First Colonial Settlements to the National Period. (Illus.). 640p. 1987. reprint ed. pap. 15.95 (*0-486-25492-5*) Dover.

— Louis Sullivan: Prophet of Modern Architecture. rev. ed. LC 97-46562. 352p. 1998. pap. 30.00 (*0-393-73023-9*) Norton.

Morrison, Hugh A. List of Books & of Articles in Periodicals Relating to Interoceanic Canal & Railway Routes. 174p. 1988. reprint ed. 15.00 (*0-913129-21-6*) La Tienda.

Morrison, I. & Schmid, G. The Second Curve. Date not set. write for info. (*0-449-91262-0*) Fawcett.

Morrison, I. & Scmid, G. The Second Curve. 1997. pap. 14.00 (*0-345-40788-1*) Ballantine Pub Grp.

Morrison, I., jt. auth. see Harris, J.

Morrison, I., jt. auth. see Harris, Joe.

Morrison, Ian. Golf. rev. ed. (Play the Game Ser.). (Illus.). 80p. 1994. pap. 8.95 (*0-7137-2442-0*, Pub. by Blandford Pr) Sterling.

— Health Care in the New Millennium: Vision, Values & Leadership. LC 99-44361. 256p. 1999. 39.95 (*0-7879-5115-3*) Jossey-Bass.

— Landscape Lake Dwellings: Lake Dwellings in a Landscape. 80p. (Orig.). 1988. pap. 16.50 (*0-85224-472-X*, Pub. by Edinburgh U Pr) Col U Pr.

— Play the Game: Golf. 1998. pap. 10.95 (*0-7063-7686-2*, Pub. by WrLock) Sterling.

Morrison, Ian. The Second Curve: Managing the Velocity of Change. 288p. 1996. 25.00 (*0-614-96347-8*) Ballantine Pub Grp.

***Morrison, Ian.** The Second Curve: Managing the Velocity of Change. 272p. 2000. text 25.00 (*0-7881-9178-0*) DIANE Pub.

Morrison, Ian & Shetland/Viking Archaeological Expedition Staff. The North Sea Earls: The Shetland Viking Archaeological Expedition. LC 74-152952. 148p. 1973. write for info. (*0-85614-028-7*, Pub. by GT Foulis) Haynes Manuals.

Morrison, Ian A., et al. Continuing Care Retirement Communities: Political, Social & Financial Issues. LC 85-8669. (Journal of Housing for the Elderly: Vol. 3, No. 1-2). 188p. 1986. text 49.95 (*0-86656-384-9*) Haworth Pr.

Morrison, Ian M., ed. Advances in Plant Cell Biochemistry & Biotechnology, Vol. 1. 274p. 1992. 109.50 (*1-55938-357-7*) Jai Pr.

Morrison, Irma L., jt. auth. see Freedman, Alan.

Morrison, Ivy, jt. auth. see Ludwig, Ray.

Morrison, J., jt. auth. see Lindgren, I.

Morrison, J. A. Martin Luther: The Great Reformer. McHugh, Michael J., ed. (Illus.). 108p. (YA). (gr. 6-12). 1994. pap. text 3.95 (*1-930092-16-4*, CLP29915) Christian Liberty.

Morrison, J. Cayce. The Puerto Rican Study, 1953-1957. Cortes, Carlos E., ed. LC 79-6217. (Hispanics in the United States Ser.). (Illus.). 1981. reprint ed. lib. bdg. 31.95 (*0-405-13165-8*) Ayer.

Morrison, J. F., jt. ed. see Torrens, M. J.

Morrison, J. H., jt. auth. see Peters, A.

***Morrison, J. S., et al.** The Athenian Trireme: The History & Reconstruction of an Ancient Greek Warship. (Illus.). 336p. 2000. 69.95 (*0-521-56419-0*) Cambridge U Pr.

— The Athenian Trireme: The History & Reconstruction of an Ancient Greek Warship. 2nd ed. (Illus.). 336p. 2000. pap. 24.95 (*0-521-56456-5*) Cambridge U Pr.

***Morrison, Jack.** Ravensbruck: Everyday Life in a Women's Concentration Camp. LC 99-85963. (Illus.). 380p. 2000. pap. 22.95 (*1-55876-219-1*) Wiener Pubs Inc.

— Ravensbruck: Everyday Life in a Women's Concentration Camp, 1939-45. LC 99-85963. (Illus.). 400p. 2000. 49.95 (*1-55876-218-3*) Wiener Pubs Inc.

Morrison, James. DSM-IV Made Easy: The Clinician's Guide to Diagnosis. LC 94-34302. 594p. 1995. lib. bdg. 49.00 (*0-89862-568-8*) Guilford Pubns.

— Kinzua & Corydon. (Images of America Ser.). (Illus.). 128p. 1998. pap. 16.99 (*0-7524-0955-7*) Arcadia Publng.

— Passport to Hollywood: Hollywood Films, European Directors. LC 98-13702. (Series in Postmodern Culture). (Illus.). 320p. (C). 1998. text 65.50 (*0-7914-3937-2*); pap. text 21.95 (*0-7914-3938-0*) State U NY Pr.

Morrison, James. When Psychological Problems Mask Medical Disorders: A Guide for Psychotherapists. LC 97-17253. 221p. 1997. 30.00 (*1-57230-180-5*, C0180) Guilford Pubns.

— When Psychological Problems Mask Medical Disorders: A Guide for Psychotherapists. 221p. 1999. pap. text 18.95 (*1-57230-539-8*, C0539) Guilford Pubns.

Morrison, James, et al, eds. The First Interview: Revised for DSM-IV. 317p. 1994. lib. bdg. 39.00 (*0-89862-569-6*) Guilford Pubns.

***Morrison, James & Anders, Thomas F.** Interviewing Children & Adolescents: Skills & Strategies for Effective DSM-IV Diagnosis. LC 99-43058. 450p. 1999. lib. bdg. 45.00 (*1-57230-501-0*, CO501) Guilford Pubns.

Morrison, James & Munoz, Rodrigo A. Boarding Time: A Psychiatry Candidate's Guide to Part II of the ABPN Examination. 2nd ed. 256p. 1995. pap. text 29.95 (*0-88048 722 4*, 8722) Am Psychiatric.

***Morrison, James & Taub, Stewart.** The Mission, The Method, This Magic: The Insight on Network Marketing. large type ed. 184p. 2000. pap. 19.95 (*0-9676131-0-8*) Millennium DE.

Morrison, James, jt. auth. see Morrison, Rob.

Morrison, James C. Meaning & Truth in Wittgenstein's Tractatus. LC 68-15536. (Janua Linguarum, Series Minor: No. 64). 1968. pap. text 35.40 (*90-279-0592-4*) Mouton.

Morrison, James D., ed. Asymmetric Synthesis, Vol. 5: Chiral Catalysis. 1985. text 184.00 (*0-12-507705-X*) Acad Pr.

Morrison, James D. & Mosher, Harry S. Asymmetric Organic Reactions. LC 75-21608. 465p. 1976. reprint ed. pap. 16.95 (*0-8412-0296-6*) Am Chemical.

Morrison, James E. Twenty-Four Early American Country Dances: Cotillions & Reels for the Year 1976. LC 76-3969. (Illus.). 72p. 1976. spiral bd. 14.00 (*0-917024-04-4*) Country Dance and Song.

Morrison, James F. The Polish People's Republic. LC 68-18209. (Integration & Community Building in Eastern Europe Ser.: No. 2). 184p. reprint ed. pap. 57.10 (*0-608-10161-3*, 200228000012) Bks Demand.

Morrison, James H. The Human Side of Management. (Business Ser). (Illus.). 1971. pap. text 11.95 (*0-201-04839-6*) Addison-Wesley.

Morrison, James H. Missionary Heroes of Africa. LC 79-89010. 267p. 1969. reprint ed. lib. bdg. 59.50 (*0-8371-1738-0*, MOM&) Greenwood.

Morrison, James L. The Best School: West Point, 1833-1866. LC 98-13132. 1998. pap. 18.00 (*0-87338-612-4*) Kent St U Pr.

— The Best School in the World: West Point, the Pre-Civil War Years, 1833-1866. LC 85-12625. 267p. reprint ed. pap. 82.80 (*0-7837-1982-5*, 204225600002) Bks Demand.

— The Healing of America: Welfare Reform in the Cyber Economy. LC 97-61059. (Illus.). 288p. 1997. text 69.95 (*1-85972-666-6*, Pub. by Ashgate Pub) Ashgate Pub Co.

Morrison, James L., Jr. Memoirs of Henry Heth, 6. LC 72-820. (Contributions in Military History Ser.: No. 6). 303p. 1974. 42.95 (*0-8371-6389-7*, MHH/, Greenwood Pr) Greenwood.

Morrison, James L., et al, eds. Applying Methods & Techniques of Futures Research. LC 82-84194. (New Directions for Institutional Research Ser.: No. IR 39). 1983. pap. 22.00 (*0-87589-957-9*) Jossey-Bass.

Morrison, James L., et al. Futures Research & the Strategic Planning Process: Implications for Higher Education. LC 85-61908. (ASHE-ERIC Higher Education Reports: No. 84-9). (Illus.). 141p. (Orig.). 1985. pap. 24.00 (*0-913317-18-7*) GWU Grad Schl E&HD.

Morrison, James L., jt. auth. see Ashley, William C.

Morrison, James O. Math, the Exciting Language. 120p. 1986. pap. text 6.50 (*0-935920-42-0*, Ntl Pubs Blck) P-H.

***Morrison, James P.** Fog Slow to Clear. 71p. 1999. pap. 10.95 (*1-891980-01-7*) Spectral Prods.

Morrison, James P. Idle Wheels. 119p. 1997. pap. 8.95 (*1-891980-00-9*) Spectral Prods.

Morrison, James R. & Munoz, Rodrigo. Boarding Time: A Psychiatry Candidate's Guide to Part II of the ABPN Examination. LC 90-564. 173p. reprint ed. pap. 53.70 (*0-608-02021-4*, 206267700003) Bks Demand.

Morrison, James V. Homeric Misdirection: False Predictions in the Iliad. LC 92-27449. (Monographs in Classical Antiquity). 184p. (C). 1992. text 39.50 (*0-472-10352-0*, 10352) U of Mich Pr.

Morrison, James W. Cdp, Certificate in Data Processing Examination LC 76-44248. (Arco Professional Career Examination Ser.). 640 p. 1976. write for info. (*0-668-04032-7*, Arco) Macmillan Gen Ref.

— Cdp, Certificate in Data Processing Examination LC 80-16390. (Arco Professional Career Examination Ser.). 349 p. 1980. write for info. (*0-668-04922-7*, Arco) Macmillan Gen Ref.

Morrison, Jan. A Safe Place: Beyond Sexual Abuse. 216p. (Orig.). (YA). 1990. pap. 7.99 (*0-87788-747-0*, H Shaw Pubs) Waterbrook Pr.

Morrison, Janet S., jt. auth. see Morrison, Alice M.

***Morrison, Jasper.** A World Without Words: Social Construction of Children Born Deaf & Blind. 1999. pap. 14.95 (*3-907044-82-7*) Lars Muller.

Morrison, Jaydene. Coping with ADD-ADHD: Attention Deficit Disorder - Attention Deficit Hyperactivity Disorder. (Coping Skills Library). (YA). 1998. pap. 6.95 (*1-56838-184-0*, 1156A) Hazelden.

Morrison, Jaydene, jt. auth. see Clayton, Lawrence.

Morrison, Jeffrey. Winckelmann & the Notion of Aesthetic Education. LC 95-46832. (Modern Languages & Literature Monographs). 284p. (C). 1996. text 90.00 (*0-19-815912-9*, Clarendon Pr) OUP.

Morrison, Jim. The American Night: The Writings of Jim Morrison, Vol. 2. LC 90-50901. Vol. 2. 224p. 1991. pap. 11.00 (*0-679-73462-7*) Vin Bks.

— Bloody Rain. 354p. (Orig.). 1996. pap. 9.95 (*1-881636-02-X*) Windsor Hse Pub Grp.

— 45 Acres of Fun & Tears. 145p. 1989. pap. 10.95 (*0-86492-112-8*, Pub. by Goose Ln Edits) Genl Dist Srvs.

— The Lords & the New Creatures. LC 74-107256. 142p. 1971. pap. 10.00 (*0-671-21044-0*, Touchstone) S&S Trade Pap.

— Wilderness: The Lost Writings of Jim Morrison, Vol. 1. 1989. pap. 12.00 (*0-679-72622-5*) Vin Bks.

Morrison, Joan. ShareHouse Blues. 160p. (C). 1990. pap. 40.00 (*0-86439-002-5*, Pub. by Boolarong Pubns) St Mut.

Morrison, Joan, jt. auth. see Zabusky, Charlotte F.

Morrison, Joel L. & Wortman, Kathryn, eds. Implementing the Spatial Data Transfer Standard. (Cartography & Geographic Information Systems Journal Ser.: Vol. 19, No. 5). 64p. 1992. 20.00 (*0-614-06099-0*, AC195) Am Congrs Survey.

Morrison, John. Greek & Roman Oared Warships 399-30 B.C. (Monographs: No. 62). (Illus.). 420p. 1996. 120.00 (*0-614-21810-1*, Pub. by Oxbow Bks) David Brown.

— Greek & Roman Oared Warships 399-30 B.C. (Oxbow Monographs in Archaeology: No. 62). (Illus.). 420p. 1996. 120.00 (*1-900188-07-4*, Pub. by Oxbow Bks) David Brown.

M

— The Happy Warrior. 160p. (C). 1990. 27.00 (*0-947087-08-7*, Pub. by Pascoe Pub) St Mut.

Morrison, John & Morrison, Catherine W. Mavericks: The Lives & Battles of Montana's Political Legends. LC 96-52420. 310p. 1997. 34.95 (*0-89301-199-1*) U of Idaho Pr.

Morrison, John & Williams, R. T. Greek Oared Ships 900-322 B.C. (Illus.). 390p. 1999. 75.00 (*1-900188-18-X*, Pub. by Oxbow Bks) David Brown.

Morrison, John, jt. auth. see Albrecht, Steven.

Morrison, John, jt. auth. see Greenhill, Basil.

Morrison, John, jt. ed. see Mizrahi, Terry.

Morrison, John A. The Deacon of Dobbinsville. 64p. pap. 1.50 (*0-686-29146-8*) Faith Pub Hse.

— The Educational Philosophy of St. John Bosco. LC 79-54817. viii, 258p. (Orig.). 1997. reprint ed. pap. 12.50 (*0-89944-050-9*, 050-9) Salesiana Pubs.

Morrison, John C., jt. auth. see Smith, Philip H.

Morrison, John D. Knowledge of the Self-Revealing God in the Thought of Thomas Forsyth Torrance. LC 96-31805. (Issues in Systematic Theology Ser.: Vol. 2). XVI, 386p. (C). 1997. pap. 58.95 (*0-8204-3341-1*) P Lang Pubng.

Morrison, John H. History of American Steam Navigation, 2 vols. 1977. lib. bdg. 200.00 (*0-8490-1965-6*) Gordon Pr.

— History of New York Ship Yards. (Illus.). 165p. 1997. reprint ed. lib. bdg. 26.50 (*0-8328-6094-8*) Higginson Bk Co.

— History of Steam Navigation. (Illus.). 1967. reprint ed. 30.00 (*0-87266-023-0*) Argosy.

Morrison, John H., et al. Clairvoyance: Reweaving the Fabric of Community for Black Folk. LC 98-84559. 227p. 1998. write for info. (*0-9663205-0-6*) New Thinking.

Morrison, John L. Alexander Campbell: Educating the Moral Person. 238p. pap. 9.99 (*0-89900-584-5*) College Pr Pub.

Morrison, John S. & Williams, R. T. Ared Ships, 900 - 322 B.C. LC 67-19504. 397p. reprint ed. pap. 113.20 (*0-608-13039-7*, 2024499) Bks Demand.

Morrison, Joseph L. Governor O. Max Gardner: A Power in North Carolina & New Deal Washington. LC 74-132253. (Illus.). 340p. reprint ed. pap. 105.40 (*0-8357-3865-5*, 203659700004) Bks Demand.

Morrison, Joyce. Fruit & Flower Fantasies. 76p. 1993. pap. 10.50 (*1-56770-277-5*) S Scheewe Pubns.

— Fruit & Flower Fantasy, Vol. 2. (Illus.). 1997. pap. 10.50 (*1-56770-382-8*) S Scheewe Pubns.

Morrison, Judith. The Book of Ayurveda: A Holistic Approach to Health & Longevity. 192p. 1995. per. 15.00 (*0-684-80017-9*) S&S Trade.

Morrison, K. F., ed. see Gregorovius, Ferdinand.

Morrison, Karin. Compassion Seeds. 101p. (Orig.). 1994. pap. 6.95 (*0-9645283-0-4*) K Morrison.

Morrison, Karl F. Conversion & Text: The Cases of Augustine of Hippo, Herman-Judah, & Constantine Tsatsos. 208p. 1992. pap. text 19.50 (*0-8139-1393-4*) U Pr of Va.

— Holiness & Politics in Early Medieval Thought. (Collected Studies: No. CS219). 302p. (C). 1985. reprint ed. lib. bdg. 109.95 (*0-86078-167-4*, Pub. by Variorum) Ashgate Pub Co.

— I Am You: The Hermeneutics of Empathy in Western Literature, Theology, & Art. LC 87-36042. 393p. 1988. reprint ed. pap. 121.90 (*0-608-06484-X*, 206678100009) Bks Demand.

***Morrison, Karl F.** Imperial Lives & Letters of the Eleventh Century. 2000. 45.00 (*0-231-12120-2*); pap. text 15.50 (*0-231-12121-0*) Col U Pr.

Morrison, Karl F. Understanding Conversion. LC 91-26971. 272p. reprint ed. pap. 84.40 (*0-608-08549-9*, 206907200002) Bks Demand.

Morrison, Karl F., jt. auth. see Gregorovius, Ferdinand A.

Morrison, Kathleen D. Fields of Victory: Vijayanagara & the Course of Intensification. LC 95-78982. (Contributions Ser.: Vol. 53). (Illus.). 201p. 1995. per. 27.00 (*1-882744-04-7*) U CA Arch Res Fac.

***Morrison, Kathleen D.** Fields of Victory: Vijayanagara & the Course of Intensification. 2nd ed. (Illus.). 2000. reprint ed. 59.50 (*81-215-0918-1*, Pub. by M Manoharial) S Asia.

Morrison, Kathy & Reader, Alice. Beginning Science. (Early Childhood Science Ser.). 80p. 1987. 9.95 (*0-317-58254-2*) Denison.

Morrison, Kathy, jt. ed. see Diffily, Deborah.

Morrison, Keith. Implementing Cross-Curricular Themes. LC 94-224866. 160p. 1994. pap. 29.00 (*1-85346-313-2*, Pub. by David Fulton) Taylor & Francis.

Morrison, Keith & Ridley, Ken. Curriculum Planning & the Primary School. 208p. (C). 1988. 45.00 (*1-85396-009-8*, Pub. by P Chapman) St Mut.

Morrison, Ken, ed. see Klusacek, Allan.

Morrison, Kenneth. Marx, Durkheim, Weber: Formations of Modern Social Thought. LC 95-235612. 352p. 1995. 69.95 (*0-8039-7562-7*); pap. 21.95 (*0-8039-7563-5*) Sage.

Morrison, Kenneth & Thompson, Marcia. Feeling Good about Me. Sorenson, Don L., ed. LC 79-55664. (Illus.). 224p. (Orig.). 1980. pap. text 8.95 (*0-932796-05-2*) Ed Media Corp.

Morrison, Kevin M. Speed Measurement in Traffic Law Enforcement from Radar to Laser. (Illus.). 107p. (C). 1994. pap. text 24.95 (*1-884566-17-0*) Inst Police Tech.

***Morrison, Kimberly, ed.** Stop the Pain: Step-by-Step Emergency Relief Made Easy. (Illus.). 1999. pap. 9.95 (*0-943629-43-8*) Swan Pub.

Morrison, Kristin. Canters & Chronicles: The Use of Narrative in the Plays of Samuel Beckett & Harold Pinter. LC 82-16086. viii, 228p. (C). 1995. 24.00 (*0-226-54130-4*) U Ch Pr.

— Canters & Chronicles: The Use of Narrative in the Plays of Samuel Beckett & Harold Pinter. LC 82-16086. viii, 240p. (C). 1996. pap. text 11.95 (*0-226-54131-2*) U Ch Pr.

— William Trevor. (Twayne's English Authors Ser.). 208p. 1993. 32.00 (*0-8057-7032-1*) Macmillan.

Morrison, L. A. The History of the Sinclair Family in Europe & America for 1100 Years. (Illus.). 453p. 1989. reprint ed. pap. 68.00 (*0-8328-1075-4*); reprint ed. lib. bdg. 76.00 (*0-8328-1074-6*) Higginson Bk Co.

Morrison, L. V. & Gilmore, G. F., eds. Galactic & Solar System Optical Astrometry: Proceedings of the Royal Greenwich Observatory & the Institute of Astronomy Workshop Held in Cambridge, June 21-24, 1993. LC 94-9034. (Illus.). 359p. (C). 1994. text 64.95 (*0-521-46240-1*) Cambridge U Pr.

Morrison, Laura L. & DeCiani, Gina. Legal Ethics For Paralegals. LC 94-27670. (Paralegal). 368p. (C). 1994. mass mkt. 48.95 (*0-314-04173-7*) West Pub.

Morrison, Laura M. Integration in Thought & Behavior: A Neuropsychological Theory. LC 81-83785. (Illus.). 357p. 1984. pap. 24.95 (*0-937638-00-5*) Harbor Pub.

Morrison, Leger. TFB - Typewriting for Business. 208p. 1985. reprint ed. student ed. 5.00 (*0-935920-35-8*, Ntl Pubs Blck); reprint ed. pap. text 11.50 (*0-935920-34-X*, Ntl Pubs Blck) P-H.

Morrison, Leger & Birt, Robert F. Illustrated Guide for Term Papers, Reports, Theses, & Dissertations, with Index & Rules for Punctuation & for Expression of Numbers. enl. ed. (Illus.). ix, 102p. (C). 1971. pap. text 5.25 (*0-911593-02-0*) Morrison Pub Co.

Morrison, Leger R. & Birt, Robert F. End-of-Line Division Manual. xx, 342p. (Orig.). (C). 1972. pap. text 9.50 (*0-911593-03-9*) Morrison Pub Co.

— Guide to Confused Words. xxvi, 272p. (Orig.). (C). 1972. pap. 7.85 (*0-911593-04-7*) Morrison Pub Co.

Morrison, Leonard A. History of the Alison or Allison Family in Europe & America, A. D. 1135 to 1893. (Illus.). 328p. 1988. reprint ed. pap. 49.00 (*0-8328-0115-1*); reprint ed. lib. bdg. 57.00 (*0-8328-0114-3*) Higginson Bk Co.

— The History of Windham, New Hampshire, 1719-1883, with the History & Genealogy of Its First Settlers. (Illus.). 862p. 1988. reprint ed. lib. bdg. 88.00 (*0-8328-0056-2*, NH0028) Higginson Bk Co.

Morrison, Lillian. At the Crack of the Bat. LC 91-28946. 1992. 11.15 (*0-606-06191-6*, Pub. by Turtleback) Demco.

— I Scream, You Scream: A Feast of Food Rhymes. LC 97-19796. (Illus.). 96p. (J). (gr. k-3). 1997. 12.95 (*0-87483-495-3*) August Hse.

— Slam Dunk: Poems about Basketball, Vol. 1. (Illus.). 64p. 1995. 15.95 (*0-7868-0054-2*) DK Pub Inc.

Morrison, Lillian. Slam Dunk, Basketball Poems. LC 94-14620. 1995. 11.15 (*0-606-11850-0*, Pub. by Turtleback) Demco.

Morrison, Lillian. Whistling the Morning in New Poems by Lillian Morrison: New Poems. LC 91-91409. (Illus.). 40p. (J). 1992. lib. bdg. 16.95 (*1-56397-035-X*, Wordsong) Boyds Mills Pr.

Morrison, Lillian, ed. Best Wishes, Amen: A New Collection of Autograph Verses. LC 74-2456. (Illus.). 224p. (J). (gr. 1-8). 1974. 12.95 (*0-690-00579-2*) HarpC Child Bks.

— Sprints & Distances: Sports in Poetry & the Poetry in Sport. LC 65-14906. (Illus.). 224p. (J). (gr. 4-7). 1990. lib. bdg. 13.89 (*0-690-04840-8*) HarpC Child Bks.

— Yours Till Niagara Falls: A Book of Autograph Verses. LC 89-82520. (Trophy Nonfiction Bk.). (Illus.). 192p. (J). (gr. 3-7). 1990. pap. 4.95 (*0-06-446104-1*, HarpTrophy); lib. bdg. 11.89 (*0-690-04876-9*) HarpC Child Bks.

***Morrison, Lillian & Boyajian, Ann.** More Spice Than Sugar: Poems about Feisty Females. LC 00-31947. 2001. write for info. (*0-618-06892-9*) HM.

Morrison, Liz, jt. auth. see Devereux, Sue.

Morrison, Louis. Monarch Notes on Tolkien's Fellowship of the Ring. 1975. 3.25 (*0-671-00971-0*, Arco) Macmillan Gen Ref.

Morrison, Louise D. Geography of the Heart: A Memoir. 240p. 1977. per. 1.50 (*0-671-00983-4*, WSP) PB.

Morrison, Lowell. The Fawn's Gift: A Lakota Legend. (Illus.). 32p. (J). 1995. pap. 6.95 (*1-56189-396-X*, 85214) Amer Educ Pub.

Morrison, M. Chicago Blackhawks, 1960-61, Vol. 5. 1997. pap. 10.00 (*1-894014-04-9*) Hockey Info Servs.

Morrison, M. Writing Sociology Essays. 1985. pap. text. write for info. (*0-582-35490-0*, Pub. by Addison-Wesley) Longman.

Morrison, M., jt. ed. see Jessop, J.

Morrison, M. A. & Owen, D. I., eds. In Honor of Ernest R. Lacheman on His Seventy-Fifth Birthday, April 29, 1981. LC 81-15123. (Studies on the Civilization & Culture of Nuzi & the Hurrians Ser.). xxi, 496p. 1981. text 69.50 (*0-931464-08-0*) Eisenbrauns.

Morrison, M. A., jt. ed. see Owen, D. I.

Morrison, M. E. Directory of Traditional Latin Masses, 1994-1995. 80p. (Orig.). 1994. pap. 10.00 (*1-883511-05-4*) Veritas Pr CA.

Morrison, M. E., ed. The Official Catholic Directory of Traditional Latin Masses & Resource Book, 1999. 4th rev. ed. 124p. 1999. pap. 10.00 (*1-883511-12-7*) Veritas Pr CA.

Morrison, M. E. S., jt. auth. see Lind, Edna M.

Morrison, M. Robert & Stamps, Robert F. DSM-IV Internet Companion. LC 98-9971. 500p. 1998. pap. 30.00 (*0-393-70267-7*) Norton.

Morrison, Madison. Happening. (C). 1997. text. write for info. (*81-207-1989-1*) Sterling Pubs.

***Morrison, Madison.** Or. 100p. 1999. pap. 9.00 (*81-86847-02-2*) Tiger Moon Pubns.

Morrison, Malcolm. Classical Acting. 1996. pap. 14.95 (*0-435-07019-3*) Heinemann.

— Clear Speech: Practical Speech Correction & Voice Improvement. (Illus.). 84p. 1997. pap. 10.95 (*0-435-07033-9*) Heinemann.

Morrison, Malcolm, ed. see Turner, J. Clifford.

Morrison, Margaret. Hello Out There. 128p. 1992. pap. 5.95 (*1-57087-104-3*) Prof Pr NC.

***Morrison, Margaret.** Unifying Scientific Theories: Physical Concepts & Mathematical Structures. (Illus.). 336p. (C). 2000. text 59.95 (*0-521-65216-2*) Cambridge U Pr.

Morrison, Margaret, jt. ed. see Morgan, Mary.

Morrison, Margaret N. A Simplified Guide to Using Statistical Techniques with Computer Applications. LC 86-3242. 206p. 1986. text 29.95 (*0-13-810185-X*, Busn) P-H.

Morrison, Marion. Amazon Rain Forest: And Its People. (Illus.). 1993. 24.26 (*0-8172-4672-X*) Raintree Steck-V.

Morrison, Marion. The Amazon Rain Forest & Its People. LC 93-20410. (People & Places Ser.). (Illus.). 48p. (YA). (gr. 5-8). 1993. lib. bdg. 24.26 (*1-56847-087-8*) Raintree Steck-V.

— Brazil. LC 96-30747. (Country Insights Ser.). (J). 1997. lib. bdg. 25.69 (*0-8172-4785-8*) Raintree Steck-V.

— Colombia. LC 98-19307. (Enchantment of the World Ser.). (Illus.). 144p. (YA). (gr. 5-9). 1999. write for info. (*0-516-21106-4*) Childrens.

— Costa Rica. 2nd ed. LC 97-40665. (Enchantment of the World Second Ser.). 144 p. (J). 1998. lib. bdg. 32.00 (*0-516-20469-6*) Childrens.

***Morrison, Marion.** Cuba. LC 98-28173. (Enchantment of the World Ser.). 144p. (YA). (gr. 5-9). 1999. 32.00 (*0-516-21051-3*) Childrens.

Morrison, Marion. Cuba. LC 97-18042. (Country Insights Ser.). 1998. 25.69 (*0-8172-4796-3*) Raintree Steck-V.

Morrison, Marion. Focus on Mexico. (Illus.). (J). 1994. write for info. (*0-237-51440-0*) EVN1 UK.

Morrison, Marion. Guide to Argentina. (World Guides Ser.). (Illus.). 32p. (J). (gr. 2-6). 1998. lib. bdg. 21.27 (*1-884756-57-3*) Davidson Titles.

***Morrison, Marion.** Guide to Brazil. rev. ed. (World Guides Ser.). (Illus.). 32p. (gr. 2-6). 1999. lib. bdg. 21.27 (*1-884756-39-5*) Davidson Titles.

— Guide to Costa Rica. (World Guides Ser.). (Illus.). 32p. (J). (gr. 2-6). 2000. lib. bdg. 21.27 (*1-884756-67-0*) Davidson Titles.

— Guide to Peru. rev. ed. (World Guides Ser.). (Illus.). 32p. (gr. 2-6). 1999. lib. bdg. 21.27 (*1-884756-52-2*) Davidson Titles.

Morrison, Marion. A History of the Ninth Regiment Illinois Volunteer Infantry, with the Regimental Roster. LC 96-46355. (Shawnee Classics Ser.). 1997. pap. 12.95 (*0-8093-2042-8*) S Ill U Pr.

— A History of the Ninth Regiment Illinois Volunteer Infantry, with the Regimental Roster. LC 96-46355. (Shawnee Classics Ser.). (Illus.). 152p. 1997. reprint ed. 29.95 (*0-8093-2043-6*) S Ill U Pr.

— Indians of the Andes. (Original People Ser.). (Illus.). 48p. (J). (gr. 4-8). 1987. 12.50 (*0-685-67605-6*) Rourke Corp.

— Indians of the Andes. (Original People Ser.). (Illus.). 48p. (J). (gr. 4-8). 1987. lib. bdg. 16.67 (*0-86625-260-6*) Rourke Pubns.

— Mexico & Central America. LC 94-37192. (Places & People Ser.). 32p. (J). (gr. 5-8). 1995. lib. bdg. 20.80 (*0-531-14366-X*) Watts.

— Mexico & Central America. (Places & People Ser.). (Illus.). 32p. (J). (gr. 5-8). 1996. reprint ed. pap. 6.95 (*0-531-15288-X*) Watts.

— Paraguay: Major World Nations. LC 99-13779. (Illus.). 144p. 1999. 19.95 (*0-7910-5393-8*) Chelsea Hse.

— Peru LC 99-17871. (Enchantment of the World Ser.). (J). 2000. 32.00 (*0-516-21545-0*) Childrens.

— Venezuela: Major World Nations. LC 98-6934. (Major World Nations Ser.). (Illus.). 144p. (YA). (gr. 5 up). 1999. lib. bdg. 19.95 (*0-7910-4972-8*) Chelsea Hse.

Morrison, Marjorie, jt. auth. see Chennells, Prue.

Morrison, Mark. Sea Kings of the Purple Towns. (Elric Roleplaying Game Ser.). (Illus.). 1993. pap. 18.95 (*1-56882-000-3*, 2114) Chaosium.

— Waterfall Walks & Drives in Georgia, Alabama & Tennessee. (Illus.). 176p. (Orig.). 1996. pap. 9.95 (*0-9636070-2-2*) H F Pub GA.

— Waterfall Walks & Drives in the Great Smoky Mountains & the Western Carolinas. (Illus.). 176p. 1999. pap. 9.95 (*0-9636070-3-0*) H F Pub GA.

— Waterfall Walks & Drives in the Western Carolinas. (Illus.). 128p. (Orig.). 1994. pap. 8.95 (*0-9636070-1-4*) H F Pub GA.

Morrison, Mark, et al. Sailing on the Seas of Fate: Ships, Seafaring, Sailors. (Elric Roleplaying Game Ser.). (Illus.). 80p. (Orig.). 1996. pap. 12.95 (*1-56882-022-4*, 2906) Chaosium.

— Sorcerers of Pan Tang. (Stormbringer Roleplaying Game System Ser.). (Illus.). 128p. (Orig.). 1991. pap. 18.95 (*0-933635-79-6*, 2112) Chaosium.

Morrison, Marlene, jt. ed. see Galloway, Shiela.

Morrison, Martha & Brown, Stephen F. Judaism. (World Religions Ser.). (Illus.). 128p. (J). (gr. 4-9). 1991. 19.95 (*0-8160-2444-8*) Facts on File.

Morrison, Martin E., ed. Directory of Traditional Latin Masses: The Official Directory for the U. S. & Canada 1997. 96p. (Orig.). 1996. pap. 9.95 (*1-883511-07-0*) Veritas Pr CA.

— Directory of Traditional Latin Masses, 1998: United States & Canada. 111p. 1997. pap. 10.00 (*1-883511-10-0*) Veritas Pr CA.

***Morrison, Marvin L.** Morrison's Sound-It-Out Speller: A Phonic Key to English. rev. ed. McRann, Penelope Kister, ed. xiv, 1069p. (YA). (gr. 5 up). 2000. 39.95 (*0-9678068-0-1*) Stone Cloud.

Morrison, Marvin L. Word Finder: The Phonic Key to the Dictionary. rev. ed. LC 86-61846. 408p. 1987. pap. 17.95 (*0-9608376-1-2*) Pilot Light.

Morrison, Mary. Christmas Jewelry. LC 98-86374. (Illus.). 160p. (Orig.). 1999. pap. 19.95 (*0-7643-0638-3*) Schiffer.

— Snow Babies, Santas & Elves: Collecting Christmas Bisque Figures. LC 95-85213. (Illus.). 160p. 1993. pap. 29.95 (*0-88740-493-6*) Schiffer.

Morrison, Mary, ed. see Ibsen, Henrik.

***Morrison, Mary B.** The Art of Finding Your Soul Mate: Five Key Elements. LC 00-91379. 2000. pap. 4.95 (*0-9674001-4-7*) Booga Bear.

— Family, Friends, Lovers & Others. 2000. pap. write for info. (*0-9674001-2-0*) Booga Bear.

— Justice Just Us Just Me. LC 99-93468. 101p. 1999. pap. 12.95 (*0-9674001-0-4*) Booga Bear.

— Kiss Me: Now Tell Me You Love Me. Date not set. write for info. (*0-9674001-5-5*) Booga Bear.

— Never Again Once More. Date not set. write for info. (*0-9674001-6-3*) Booga Bear.

— Soul Mates Dissipate. Malone, Susan M. & Haskins, Scott, eds. LC 00-90416. 276p. 2000. pap. 14.95 (*0-9674001-3-9*) Booga Bear.

Morrison, Mary C. Approaching the Gospels Together: A Leaders' Guide to Group Gospels Study. LC 86-62204. (Orig.). 1993. pap. 15.00 (*0-87574-910-0*, 6305) Pendle Hill.

Morrison, Mary C. A Fresh Look at the Gospels. LC 78-51385. 32p. (Orig.). 1978. pap. 1.00 (*0-87574-219-X*) Pendle Hill.

Morrison, Mary C. The Journal & the Journey. LC 81-85559. 32p. (Orig.). 1982. pap. 4.00 (*0-87574-242-4*) Pendle Hill.

***Morrison, Mary C.** Let Evening Come: Reflections on Aging. LC 97-19578. 144p. 1998. 14.95 (*0-385-49086-0*) Doubleday.

Morrison, Mary C. Re-Conciliation: The Hidden Hyphen. LC 74-24007. 24p. (Orig.). 1974. pap. 4.00 (*0-87574-198-3*) Pendle Hill.

Morrison, Mary C. The Way of the Cross. LC 85-60516. 32p. (Orig.). 1985. pap. 1.00 (*0-87574-260-2*) Pendle Hill.

Morrison, Mary C. Without Nightfall upon the Spirit: Reflections on Aging. LC 93-85962. 32p. 1994. pap. 4.00 (*0-87574-311-0*) Pendle Hill.

Morrison, Mary C., jt. auth. see Bonfield, Lynn A.

Morrison, Mary C., ed. see Law, William.

Morrison, Mary E., ed. Adaptations & Acting Versions. (Shakespeariana Ser.). xiii, 64p. (Orig.). 1990. 15.00 (*0-8357-0931-0*) Univ Microfilms.

— Alan Barbour's Screen Facts & Screen Nostalgia Illustrated Collection. (Guide to the Microfiche Collection). 11p. (Orig.). 1987. 10.00 (*0-685-46000-2*) Univ Microfilms.

— Albany Medical Center Inaugural Theses, 1839-1891. (Guide to the Microfiche Collection). 218p. 1989. 15.00 (*0-8357-0870-5*) Univ Microfilms.

— Crime & Juvenile Delinquency, 1984-1985: A Bibliographic Guide. iv, 42p. 1986. 30.00 (*0-8357-0704-0*) Univ Microfilms.

— Crime & Juvenile Delinquency, 1986: A Bibliographic Guide. iv, 42p. 1986. 30.00 (*0-8357-0720-2*) Univ Microfilms.

— Crime & Juvenile Delinquency, 1987: A Bibliographic Guide. iv, 40p. 1987. 30.00 (*0-8357-0755-5*) Univ Microfilms.

— Crime & Juvenile Delinquency, 1988: A Bibliographic Guide. iv, 42p. (Orig.). 1989. 30.00 (*0-8357-0802-0*) Univ Microfilms.

— Folklore, Superstition & Witchcraft in Shakespeare's Time. (Shakespeariana Ser.). x, 41p. (Orig.). 1989. 15.00 (*0-8357-0875-6*) Univ Microfilms.

— An Index to the Abstracts on Crime & Juvenile Delinquency, 1986. viii, 324p. 1987. 120.00 (*0-8357-0716-4*) Univ Microfilms.

— An Index to the Abstracts on Crime & Juvenile Delinquency, 1987. ix, 298p. 1988. 120.00 (*0-8357-0829-2*) Univ Microfilms.

— An Index to the Abstracts on Crime & Juvenile Delinquency 1988. v, 350p. (Orig.). 1990. pap. 250.00 (*0-8357-2121-3*) Univ Microfilms.

— An Index to the Abstracts on Crime & Juvenile Deliquency 1983-1984. 435p. 1986. 120.00 (*0-8357-0701-6*) Univ Microfilms.

— The John M. Echols Collection, Cornell University: Selections on the Vietnam War. (Guide to the Microfiche Collection: Unit 1). v, 59p. (Orig.). 1989. 20.00 (*0-8357-0881-0*) Univ Microfilms.

— The John M. Echols Collection, Cornell University: Selections on the Vietnam War. (Guide to the Microfiche Collection Ser.: Unit 2). v, 64p. (Orig.). 1989. 20.00 (*0-8357-0891-8*) Univ Microfilms.

— MusiCache: An Index to the Microfiche Collection. iv, 216p. reprint ed. 40.00 (*0-8357-0927-2*) Univ Microfilms.

— Prose Fiction of Shakespeare's Time. (Shakespeariana Ser.). xiii, 35p. (Orig.). 1989. 15.00 (*0-8357-0888-8*) Univ Microfilms.

— The Pulitzer Prizes in Journalism, 1917-1985: A Guide to the Microfilm Edition. 187p. 1986. 70.00 (*0-8357-0709-1*) Univ Microfilms.

— Rehabilitation & Handicapped Literature, 1982-1985 Update: A Bibliographic Guide to the Microfiche Collection. (Orig.). 1987. 20.00 (*0-8357-0732-6*) Univ Microfilms.

— Working Papers in Economics. (Guide to the Microfiche Collection: Ser. 1). v, 110p. 1989. 20.00 (*0-8357-0882-9*) Univ Microfilms.

— Working Papers in Economics. (Guide to the Microfiche Collection: Ser. 2). v, 95p. 1989. 20.00 (*0-8357-0890-X*) Univ Microfilms.

An Asterisk (*) at the beginning of an entry indicates that the title is appearing for the first time.

***Morrison, Mary F., ed.** Hormones, Gender & the Aging Brain: The Endocrine Basis of Geriatric Psychiatry. LC RC451.4.A5H67 2000. (Illus.). 368p. (C). 2000. 95.00 (*0-521-65304-5*) Cambridge U Pr.

Morrison, Mary G. The Tragedies of G. B. Giraldi Cinthio: The Transformation of Narrative Source into Stage Play. LC 97-10516. (Studies in Italian Literature: No. 4). (Illus.). 412p. 1997. text 109.95 (*0-7734-8636-4*) E Mellen.

Morrison, Mary G., ed. see Garnier, Robert.

***Morrison, M.E., ed.** The Official Catholic Directory of Traditional Latin Masses & Resource Book, 2000. 116p. 2000. pap. 10.00 (*1-883511-14-3*) Veritas Pr CA.

Morrison, Melanie. The Grace of Coming Home: Spirituality, Sexuality & the Struggle for Justice. LC 95-18070. 112p. (Orig.). 1995. pap. 11.95 (*0-8298-1071-4*) Pilgrim OH.

Morrison, Michael. Complete Idiot's Guide to Java 1.2. LC 98-86972. (Complete Idiot's Guide Ser.). 1998. pap. text 19.99 (*0-7897-1804-9*) Que.

— Complete Idiot's Guide to Java 2. LC 99-63009. 336p. 1999. pap. text 16.99 (*0-7897-2131-7*) Que.

— Java 1.1 Unleashed. 1997. 69.99 (*1-57521-361-3*) Sams.

— Presenting JavaBeans. LC 96-72398. 352p. 1997. 35.00 (*1-57521-287-0*) Sams.

— Teach Yourself Internet Game Programming with Java in 21 Days. LC 96-68596. 456p. 1996. 39.99 (*1-57521-148-3*) Sams.

— Teach Yourself MFC 6 in 24 Hours. LC 98-88866. (Teach Yourself Ser.). 1999. pap. text 24.99 (*0-672-31553-X*) Sams.

Morrison, Michael & Weems, Randy. Windows 95 Game Developer's Guide Using the Game SDK. LC 95-74786. (Illus.). 624p. (Orig.). 1995. 49.99 (*0-672-30661-1*) Sams.

Morrison, Michael, jt. auth. see Lemay, Laura.

Morrison, Michael, ed. see Bartholomew, Terese T. & Kao, Mayching.

Morrison, Michael, ed. see Kim, Kumja P. & Black, Kay E.

Morrison, Michael, ed. see Kim, Kumja P. & Lee, Margaret.

***Morrison, Michael A.** The Human Tradition in Antebellum America. LC 00-27911. (#7 in the Human Tradition in America Series: Vol. 7). 272p. 2000. 50.00 (*0-8420-2834-X*) Scholarly Res Inc.

Morrison, Michael A. John Barrymore, Shakespearean Actor. LC 97-12183. (Studies in American Theatre & Drama: Vol. 10). (Illus.). 416p. (C). 1997. 34.95 (*0-521-62028-7*) Cambridge U Pr.

***Morrison, Michael A.** John Barrymore, Shakespearean Actor. (Cambridge Studies in American Theatre & Drama: No. 10). (Illus.). 416p. (C). 1999. pap. text 19.95 (*0-521-62979-9*) Cambridge U Pr.

Morrison, Michael A. Slavery & the American West: The Eclipse of Manifest Destiny & the Coming of the Civil War. LC 96-23855. 396p. 1999. pap. 19.95 (*0-8078-4796-8*) U of NC Pr.

— Slavery & the American West: The Eclipse of Manifest Destiny & the Coming of the Civil War. LC 96-23855. 448p. (C). 1999. pap. 55.00 (*0-8078-2319-8*) U of NC Pr.

— Understanding Quantum Physics: A User's Manual, Vol. I. 624p. (C). 1990. 90.00 (*0-13-747908-5*) P-H.

***Morrison, Michael A., ed.** The Human Tradition in Antebellum America. 272p. 2000. 18.95 (*0-8420-2835-8*) Scholarly Res Inc.

Morrison, Michael A., ed. Trajectories of the Fantastic: Selected Essays from the Fourteenth International Conference on the Fantastic in the Arts, 70. LC 96-8428. (Contributions to the Study of Science Fiction & Fantasy: Vol. 70). 248p. 1997. 59.95 (*0-313-29646-4*, Greenwood Pr) Greenwood.

Morrison, Michael A., et al. Understanding More Quantum Physics, Vol. 1. 272p. (C). 1991. pap. 22.00 (*0-13-928300-5*, 530502) P-H.

— Wildlife-Habitat Relationships: Concepts & Applications. 2nd ed. LC 97-9445. (Illus.). 416p. 1998. 34.95 (*0-299-15640-0*) U of Wis Pr.

Morrison, Michael A., ed. see Gray, Ralph D.

Morrison, Michael A., jt. ed. see Gray, Ralph D.

Morrison, Michael D., intro. Fugitives from Justice: The Notebook of Texas Ranger Sergeant James B. Gillett. LC 95-40117. (Illus.). 288p. 1997. 24.95 (*1-880510-37-5*) State House Pr.

— Fugitives from Justice: The Notebook of Texas Ranger Sergeant James B. Gillett. LC 95-40117. (Illus.). x, 274p. 1997. pap. 17.95 (*1-880510-38-3*) State House Pr.

— Fugitives from Justice: The Notebook of Texas Ranger Sergeant James B. Gillett. deluxe limited ed. (Illus.). 288p. 1997. 100.00 (*1-880510-39-1*) State House Pr.

Morrison, Michael J. First Time Manager. 2nd ed. (Business & Management Ser.). 1999. pap. 17.95 (*0-7494-1386-7*) Kogan Page Ltd.

Morrison, Michael L., et al. Literature on Wildlife Research in the Madrean Archipelago, 1800s-1994. 62p. 1997. reprint ed. 13.20 (*0-89904-614-2*, Wildlife Resrch Grp); reprint ed. pap. 7.20 (*0-89904-615-0*, Wildlife Resrch Grp) Crumb Elbow Pub.

Morrison, Mike. ESPN-Information Please-Sports Almanac. Brown, Gerry, ed. (ESPN Information Please Sports Almanac Ser.). (Illus.). 960p. 1998. pap. 11.99 (*0-7868-8366-9*, Pub. by Hyperion) Little.

— Using Blackbird: Special Edition. LC 96-68040. 900p. 1997. pap. text 49.99 incl. cd-rom (*0-7897-0762-4*) Que.

Morrison, Mike, jt. auth. see Brown, Gerry.

Morrison, Minion K. Black Political Mobilization, Leadership, Power, & Mass Behavior. LC 86-30051. (SUNY Series in Afro-American Studies). 303p. (C). 1987. text 64.50 (*0-88706-515-5*) State U NY Pr.

— Ethnicity & Political Integration: The Case of Ashanti, Ghana. LC 82-23239. (Foreign & Comparative Studies Program, African Ser.: No. 38). (Orig.). (C). 1982. pap. text 8.00 (*0-915984-59-8*) Syracuse U Foreign Comp.

Morrison, Minion K., et al, eds. Housing the Urban Poor in Africa. LC 82-21636. (Foreign & Comparative Studies Program, African Ser.: No. 37). (Orig.). (C). 1982. pap. text 8.00 (*0-915984-61-X*) Syracuse U Foreign Comp.

Morrison, Morris. Prologue & Performances. 32p. 1972. write for info. (*0-318-64130-5*) Poets Pr.

Morrison, Morris R. Poetry As Therapy. LC 86-15281. 229p. 1987. 35.95 (*0-89885-312-5*, Kluwer Acad Hman Sci) Kluwer Academic.

***Morrison, Morrison.** Creating Data-Driven Web Sites. (Programming Ser.). (C). 2000. pap. 49.95 (*0-619-01556-X*) Course Tech.

Morrison, Murray D., et al. Management of Voice Disorders. LC 93-32952. (Illus.). 288p. 1993. text 59.50 (*0-412-35090-4*, Pub. by E A) OUP.

Morrison, Nancy B. The Gowk Storm. (Classics Ser.). 192p. 1994. pap. 9.95 (*0-86241-222-6*, Pub. by Canongate Books) Interlink Pub.

Morrison, Nannette E. Echoes of Valor. (Illus.). 172p. 1994. pap. 14.95 (*0-9663108-0-2*) Echo Effects.

— Thundering Silence. 138p. 1996. pap. 14.95 (*0-9663108-1-0*) Echo Effects.

— Warrior Poets & Warrior Saints. (Illus.). 170p. 1998. pap. 15.95 (*0-9663108-2-9*, Pub. by Echo Effects) New Leaf Dist.

Morrison, Neil, jt. auth. see Moore, John.

Morrison, Norman. Introduction to Fourier Analysis: With Full-System FFT Disk. 592p. 1994. text 115.00 incl. disk (*0-471-01737-X*) Wiley.

— Introduction to Fourier Analysis, Solutions Manual. 240p. 1995. pap., teacher ed. 29.50 (*0-471-12848-1*) Wiley.

***Morrison, Nyla Y.** Minna Cooks Caribbean: A Calorie Counter's Guide. 2nd rev. ed. (Illus.). 124p. 2000. spiral bd. 14.95 (*0-9701777-1-2*) Morrison Artistic.

Morrison, Pam, jt. auth. see Light, H. Wayne.

***Morrison, Park.** A Guide to Maine Golf Courses. LC 99-87083. 288p. 2000. pap. 15.95 (*0-89272-494-3*) Down East.

Morrison, Paul. The Poetics of Fascism: Ezra Pound, T. S. Eliot, Paul de Man. 192p. 1996. text 45.00 (*0-19-508085-8*) OUP.

— Sexual Subjects. (Idologies of Desire Ser.). (Illus.). 320p. Date not set. 35.00 (*0-19-507986-8*); pap. 14.95 (*0-19-507987-6*) OUP.

Morrison, Paul & Burnard, Philip, eds. Aspects of Forensic Psychiatric Nursing. 183p. 1992. 69.95 (*1-85628-371-2*, Pub. by Avebry) Ashgate Pub Co.

Morrison, Paul D., ed. Placer Gold Deposits of the Sierra Nevada. LC 97-60923. (Illus.). 192p. (Orig.). 1997. pap. 10.95 (*0-935182-97-7*) Gem Guides Bk.

Morrison, Paul D., ed. see Butler, Gail.

Morrison, Peggy G. Touchstones for a New Millennium: The Ground Rules for Working Relationships. LC 97-90122. 1997. pap. text 24.95 (*0-9658170-5-9*) Windansea Pr.

Morrison, Penelope, jt. auth. see Morrison, Rob.

Morrison, Perry, jt. auth. see Forester, Tom.

Morrison, Peter A., ed. see Beale, Calvin L.

Morrison, Philip. Nothing Is Too Wonderful to Be True. LC 94-17906. (Masters of Modern Physics Ser.). 1994. 34.95 (*1-56396-363-9*) Spr-Verlag.

Morrison, Philip & Morrison, Phylis. Primary Science: Symbol Or Substance? 20p. (Orig.). (C). 1984. pap. 3.00 (*0-317-45086-7*) City Coll Wk.

Morrison, Philip & Tsipis, Kosta. Reason Enough to Hope: America & the World of the Twenty-First Century. LC 98-23561. (Illus.). 228p. 1998. 25.00 (*0-262-13344-X*) MIT Pr.

Morrison, Philip, et al. Powers of Ten: About the Relative Size of Things in the Universe. LC 82-5504. (Illus.). 159p. (C). 1994. pap. 19.95 (*0-7167-6008-8*) W H Freeman.

Morrison, Phylis, jt. auth. see Morrison, Philip.

Morrison, Phylis S., jt. auth. see Holden, Alan.

Morrison, R. & Kennedy, Jessie. Advances in Databases: 14th British National Conference on Databases, Edinburgh, Scotland United Kingdom, July 1996 - Proceedings, Vol. 1094. LC 96-26228. (Lecture Notes in Computer Science Ser.). 234p. 1996. pap. 43.00 (*3-540-61442-7*) Spr-Verlag.

Morrison, R., jt. auth. see Davie, J. T.

Morrison, R., jt. auth. see Sommerville, Ian.

Morrison, R. B., ed. Quaternary Nonglacial Geology: Conterminous U. S. (DNAG, Geology of North America Ser.: Vol. K2). 670p. 1991. 42.50 (*0-8137-5215-9*) Geol Soc.

Morrison, R. H. All I Have Is a Fountain. 64p. 1995. pap. 9.00 (*1-880286-24-6*) Singular Speech Pr.

— The Voice of the Hands. 56p. 1997. pap. 7.50 (*1-880286-35-1*) Singular Speech Pr.

Morrison, R. H., tr. Poems from Mandelstam. LC 88-46184. 120p. 1990. 26.50 (*0-8386-3382-X*) Fairleigh Dickinson.

Morrison, R. L. & Bellack, A. S. Medical Factors & Psychological Disorders: A Handbook for Psychologists. LC 87-7903. (Illus.). 392p. (C). 1987. 90.00 (*0-306-42425-8*, Plenum Trade) Perseus Pubng.

Morrison, R. S. Mining Rights in Colorado. 331p. 1996. 85.00 (*1-56169-216-6*) Gaunt.

Morrison, Ralph. Grounding & Shielding in Instrumentation, 1. 4th ed. LC 97-26394. 201p. 1998. 68.50 (*0-471-24518-6*, Wiley-Interscience) Wiley.

— Instrumentation Fundamentals & Applications. LC 83-21696. 157p. reprint ed. pap. 48.70 (*0-7837-2810-7*, 205766200006) Bks Demand.

— Noise & Other Interfering Signals. LC 91-15226. 160p. 1991. 99.95 (*0-471-54288-1*) Wiley.

— Solving Interference Problems in Electronics. LC 95-12074. 224p. 1995. 68.95 (*0-471-12796-5*, Wiley-Interscience) Wiley.

Morrison, Ralph, et al. Grounding & Shielding in Facilities. LC 89-38142. 256p. 1990. 135.00 (*0-471-83807-1*) Wiley.

Morrison-Reed, Mark D. & James, Jacqui, eds. Been in the Storm So Long: A Meditation Manual. 64p. 1991. pap. 6.00 (*1-55896-202-6*, Skinner Hse Bks) Unitarian Univ.

Morrison-Reed, Mark D. & Young, Andrew J. Black Pioneers in a White Denomination. 3rd ed. LC 94-32438. 1994. pap. 15.00 (*1-55896-250-6*, Skinner Hse Bks) Unitarian Univ.

Morrison, Reg. The Spirit in the Gene: Humanity's Proud Illusion & the Laws of Nature. LC 99-28205. 288p. 1999. 25.00 (*0-8014-3651-6*) Cornell U Pr.

Morrison, Reg, jt. auth. see Goldsberry, Steven.

Morrison, Richard E. Scientists, Engineers & Technicians in Manufacturing Industries. (Illus.). 129p. (Orig.). (C). 1995. pap. text 30.00 (*0-7881-2414-5*) DIANE Pub.

Morrison, Richard G., jt. auth. see Findlay, James V.

Morrison, Rob. X-Rays. LC 93-28983. (Voyages Ser.). (Illus.). (J). 1994. 4.25 (*0-383-03789-1*) SRA McGraw.

Morrison, Rob & Morrison, James. Monsters! Just Imagine. LC 93-26927. (Voyages Ser.). (Illus.). (J). 1994. 4.25 (*0-383-03763-8*) SRA McGraw.

Morrison, Rob & Morrison, Penelope. Snorkels for Tadpoles. LC 93-28967. (Voyages Ser.). (Illus.). (J). 1994. 4.25 (*0-383-03775-1*) SRA McGraw.

Morrison, Robert, et al. High Stakes to High Risk: The Strange Story of Resorts International & the Taj Mahal. 1994. 21.95 (*0-317-05740-5*) Lake Erie Pr.

— Petroleum Hydrocarbon Contamination: Legal & Technical Considerations. 332p. 1998. pap. 99.73 (*1-890501-02-6*) Argent Commns.

Morrison, Robert, ed. see Polidori, John W.

***Morrison, Robert D.** Environmental Forensics. LC 99-39051. 256p. 1999. per. 39.95 (*0-8493-0001-0*); boxed set 79.95 (*0-8493-2058-5*) CRC Pr.

Morrison, Robert D. Ground Water Monitoring: Procedures, Equipment & Applications. (Illus.). 132p. (C). 1983. text 33.00 (*0-9611060-0-X*, 83-070805) Timco Mfg.

Morrison, Robert F. & Adams, Jerome, eds. Contemporary Career Development Issues. 192p. 1991. text 29.95 (*0-8058-0945-7*) L Erlbaum Assocs.

Morrison, Robert G. Nietzsche & Buddhism: A Study in Nihilism & Ironic Affinities. LC 96-53341. 260p. 1997. text 62.00 (*0-19-823556-9*) OUP.

— Nietzsche & Buddhism: A Study in Nihilism & Ironic Affinities. 260p. 1999. pap. text 24.95 (*0-19-823865-7*) OUP.

Morrison, Robert H. Internal Administrative Organization in Teachers Colleges. LC 78-177090. (Columbia University. Teachers College. Contributions to Education Ser.: No. 592). reprint ed. 37.50 (*0-404-55592-6*) AMS Pr.

Morrison, Robert M., et al. Business Interruption Insurance: Its Theory & Practice. LC 85-63188. 392 p. 1986. write for info. (*0-87218-331-9*) Natl Underwriter.

***Morrison, Robert R.** Lope De Vega & the Comedia De Santos. LC 99-45899. (Iberica Ser.: Vol. 33). 432p. (C). 2000. 66.95 (*0-8204-4856-7*) P Lang Pubng.

Morrison, Robert S. Handbook for Manufacturing Entrepreneurs. LC 73-91212. (Illus.). 1973. pap. 12.50 (*0-912400-09-9*) Western Res Pr.

— Inflation Can Be Stopped. LC 73-91213. (Illus.). 1973. 4.95 (*0-912400-05-6*); pap. 2.00 (*0-912400-04-8*) Western Res Pr.

— The Real War on Inflation Has Not Begun. LC 82-5057. (Illus.). 1982. 15.00 (*0-912400-25-0*); pap. 9.50 (*0-912400-26-9*) Western Res Pr.

Morrison, Robert T. Organic Chemistry. 4th ed. 1982. pap. text 30.60 (*0-205-17802-2*) Allyn.

Morrison, Robert T. & Boyd, A. W. Organic Chemistry. 5th ed. 1987. pap., student ed. 35.00 (*0-685-18128-6*, H8454-4); write for info. (*0-318-61878-8*, H0524-2); trans. 70.00 (*0-685-18129-4*, H0525-9) P-H.

— Organic Chemistry. 6th ed. (C). 1992. pap. text, student ed. 52.00 (*0-13-643677-3*) P-H.

Morrison, Robert T. & Boyd, Robert K. Organic Chemistry. 6th ed. 1360p. 1992. 114.00 (*0-13-643669-2*) P-H.

Morrison, Robert T. & Boyd, Robert N. Organic Chemistry. 4th ed. 1408p. (C). 1982. text 48.00 (*0-205-05838-8*, EDP 685838) Allyn.

— Organic Chemistry. 4th ed. (C). 1983. pap. text 11.20 (*0-205-07984-9*) Allyn.

— Organic Chemistry. 6th ed. (C). 1992. 62.00 (*0-205-12042-3*, Macmillan Coll) P-H.

— Organic Chemistry. 7th ed. 1998. text 85.33 (*0-13-267816-0*) P-H.

Morrison, Rodney J. Portugal: Revolutionary Change in an Open Economy. LC 81-2099. 200p. (C). 1981. 39.95 (*0-86569-077-4*, Auburn Hse) Greenwood.

Morrison, Roger. Desktop Companion: To Physical Pathology. unabridged ed. 1998. text 75.00 (*0-9635368-2-6*) Hahnemann Clinic.

— Desktop Guide: To Keynotes & Confirmatory Symptoms. 448p. 1993. 68.00 (*0-9635368-0-X*) Hahnemann Clinic.

Morrison, Ron, jt. ed. see Albano, Antonio.

Morrison, Ron, ed. see Jordan, Mickey & Atkinson, Malcolm P.

Morrison, Roy. Ecological Democracy. LC 95-8991. 280p. (C). 1995. 40.00 (*0-89608-514-7*) South End Pr.

— Ecological Democracy. LC 95-8991. 280p. (C). 1995. pap. 16.00 (*0-89608-513-9*) South End Pr.

— The Loggers of Warner. (Poetry Ser.). (Illus.). 96p. 1999. pap. 9.95 (*0-9658903-1-7*) Writers Pubg Coop.

— We Build the Road As We Travel: Mondragon a Cooperative Social System. rev. ed. (Illus.). 290p. 1997. pap. 19.95 (*0-9658903-0-9*) Writers Pubg Coop.

Morrison, Rusane. Summer Patchwork. 1976. 1.50 (*0-685-79010-X*) Oyez.

Morrison, Ruth. Batman Masterpieces: Portraits of the Dark Knight & His World. LC 98-8484. (Illus.). 208p. 1998. 40.00 (*0-8230-0461-9*) Watsn-Guptill.

Morrison, Ruth & Radtke, Dawn D. From Worry to Wellness: Twenty-One People Who Changed Their Lives. LC 90-70559. 192p. (Orig.). 1990. pap. 7.95 (*0-89622-443-0*) Twenty-Third.

Morrison, S. R. The Chemical Physics of Surfaces. 2nd ed. LC 90-42068. (Illus.). 456p. (C). 1990. text 85.00 (*0-306-43549-7*, Kluwer Plenum) Kluwer Academic.

— Electrochemistry at Semiconductor & Oxidized Metal Electrodes. LC 80-20416. (Illus.). 416p. (C). 1980. text 120.00 (*0-306-40524-5*, Kluwer Plenum) Kluwer Academic.

Morrison, S. Roy, jt. auth. see Madou, Marc J.

Morrison, Sally. Cross Creek Kitchens: Seasonal Recipes & Reflections. (Illus.). 224p. 1983. 24.95 (*0-937404-50-0*) Triad Pub FL.

Morrison, Sara. God Does Smile. 192p. 1997. pap. 14.95 (*1-55630-876-0*) Brentwood Comm.

Morrison, Sarah L. Modern Witch's Book of Herbs & Healing. LC 97-52341. 208p. 1998. pap. text 10.95 (*0-8065-1961-4*, Citadel Pr) Carol Pub Group.

— The Modern Witch's Book of Home Remedies. 204p. 1991. pap. 8.95 (*0-8065-1265-2*, Citadel Pr) Carol Pub Group.

— The Modern Witch's Book of Symbols. LC 97-218435. (Illus.). 224p. 1997. pap. text 9.95 (*0-8065-1909-6*, Citadel Pr) Carol Pub Group.

— The Modern Witch's Dreambook. 1990. pap. 7.95 (*0-8065-1203-2*, Citadel Pr) Carol Pub Group.

— The Modern Witch's Guide to Magic & Spells. LC 97-45629. 192p. 1998. pap. 12.00 (*0-8065-1963-0*, Citadel Pr) Carol Pub Group.

Morrison, Sarah L. Modern Witch's Spellbook. 1994. 8.95 (*0-679-50264-5*) McKay.

Morrison, Sarah L. The Modern Witch's Spellbook, Bk. I. LC 71-135588. 256p. 1973. reprint ed. pap. 12.00 (*0-8065-0372-6*) Carol Pub Group.

— The New Modern Witch's Dreambook. rev. ed. LC 93-43437. Orig. Title: The Modern Witch's Dreambook. 240p. 1994. reprint ed. 8.95 (*0-8065-1471-X*, Citadel Pr) Carol Pub Group.

Morrison, Scott. The Code Book of America, Pocket Size: Fourth Edition. 4th ed. (Illus.). 96p. (Orig.). 1997. pap. 5.95 (*0-929150-65-1*) Castalia CA.

— Nobel Santuary. 288p. 1990. 22.95 (*0-385-25249-8*) Doubleday.

— The Official Code Book of America. 3rd rev. ed. Sutherland, Rebecca & Terris, Anastasia, eds. 96p. 1996. reprint ed. pap. 6.95 (*0-929150-56-2*) Castalia CA.

— The Official Code Book of America: Pocket Size. Pocket Size. 2nd rev. ed. Sutherland, Rebecca & Terris, Anastasia, eds. (Illus.). 96p. (Orig.). 1996. reprint ed. pap. 5.95 (*0-929150-51-1*) Castalia CA.

— Open & Innocent: The Gentle, Passionate Art of Not-Knowing. 3rd rev. ed. 108p. 1998. pap. 9.00 (*1-882496-11-6*, 003) Twnty Frst Cntry Ren.

***Morrison, Scott.** Wayne Gretzky: The Great Goodbye. LC 99-492063. 96p. 1999. pap. 14.99 (*1-55263-099-4*, Pub. by Key Porter) Firefly Bks Ltd.

Morrison, Scott, ed. The Official Code Book of America: Pocket Size. 3rd ed. 96p. (Orig.). 1996. pap. 5.95 (*0-929150-57-0*) Castalia CA.

Morrison, Scott, ed. The Code Book of America. 2nd ed. (Illus.). (Orig.). 1995. pap. 6.95 (*0-929150-50-3*) Castalia CA.

Morrison, Scott, ed. see Cerutti, Stephen.

Morrison, Shelly. Western Americana Catalogue Prices: 19,000 Price Entries on Non-Texas Western Americana Offered for Sale in 1997, Vol. II. 250p. 1998. 38.50 (*0-926158-30-9*) Prototype Career Media.

Morrison, Shelly O. Texana Catalogue Prices, 1998 Vol. 13: 11,000 Price Entries on Texas Material Offered for Sale in 1995. 136p. (Orig.). 1996. pap. 38.50 (*0-926158-25-2*) W M Morrison.

Morrison, Shelly O., ed. see Ross, Lawrence S.

Morrison, Shirley L. The Pearl & the Princes. LC 84-23349. vi, 170p. 1985. 14.95 (*0-9613978-0-2*); pap. 7.95 (*0-9613978-1-0*) Laurel Pr.

Morrison, Slade, jt. auth. see Morrison, Toni.

Morrison, Sol. The World's Greatest Book of Chicken Jokes & Other Fowl Humor. (Illus.). 124p. (Orig.). 1995. pap. 9.95 (*0-940861-57-7*) Poetry Ctr Pr.

Morrison, Stanley, jt. auth. see Fairman, Charles.

Morrison, Steven A., jt. auth. see Winston, Clifford M.

Morrison, Susan. Arkansas Wildlife. LC 80-52076. 64p. 1980. 14.95 (*0-914546-32-5*) Rose Pub.

Morrison, Susan, et al. Critical Thinking & Test Item Writing. unabridged ed. Boyd, Donna, ed. (Illus.). (C). 1996. pap. text 29.95 (*0-9656678-0-4*) Health Educ.

Morrison, Susan Dudley, see Dudley Morrison, Susan.

***Morrison, Susan Signe.** Women Pilgrims in Late Medieval England. LC 99-87891. 2000. 85.00 (*0-415-22180-3*) Routledge.

Morrison, Susanna. Seasonal Wreaths: Over Thirty Simple, Stylish Ideas. (Illus.). 128p. 1997. 27.50 (*1-57076-094-2*, Trafalgar Sq Pub) Trafalgar.

Morrison, T. J. Functional Analysis. 288p. 2000. 84.95 (*0-471-37214-5*) Wiley.

Morrison, Taylor. Antonio's Apprenticeship: Painting a Fresco in Renaissance Italy. LC 95-4871. (Illus.). 32p. (J). (gr. 4-6). 1996. 15.95 (*0-8234-1213-X*) Holiday.

— Cheetah. LC 97-16683. 32p. (J). (gr. 2-3). 1998. 15.95 (*0-8050-5121-X*) H Holt & Co.

*Morrison, Taylor. Civil War Artist. LC 97-52738. (Illus.). 32p. (J). (gr. 1-5). 1998. 16.00 (0-395-91426-4) HM.
Morrison, Taylor. The Neptune Fountain: The Apprenticeship of a Renaissance Sculptor. LC 96-41735. (Illus.). 32p. (J). (gr. 4-6). 1997. lib. bdg. 15.95 (0-8234-1293-8) Holiday.
Morrison, Terri. The International Traveller's Guide to Doing Business in Europe. (Orig.). 1997. pap. 14.95 (0-614-28132-6) Macmillan USA.
— International Traveller's Guide to Doing Business in Europe. LC 97-71166. 342p. 1997. 16.95 (0-02-861756-8) Macmillan.
— The International Traveller's Guide to Doing Business in Latin America. 1997. pap. 14.95 (0-614-28133-4) Macmillan USA.
— International Traveller's Guide to Doing Business in Latin America. LC 97-71165. 384p. 1997. 16.95 (0-02-861755-X) Macmillan.
Morrison, Terri & Conaway, Wayne A. Spanish for the Business Traveler. (ENG & SPA.). 1996. 21.95 incl. audio (0-8120-8399-7) Barron.
*Morrison, Terri, et al. Dun & Bradstreet's Guide to Doing Business Around the World. rev. ed. 512p. 1999. 28.00 (0-7352-0108-0) PH Pr.
Morrison, Terri, et al. Dun & Bradstreet's International Guide. LC 96-40929. 352p. (C). 1996. pap. text 26.00 (0-13-531484-4) P-H.
*Morrison, Terri, et al. Kiss, Bow or Shake Hands: How to Do Business in Sixty Countries. (Illus.). 438p. 2000. reprint ed. pap. text 20.00 (0-7881-9227-2) DIANE Pub.
Morrison, Terri, et al. Kiss Bow or Shake Hands: How to Do Business in 60 Countries. LC 94-24539. 438p. 1994. pap. 19.95 (1-55850-444-3) Adams Media.
— The World Holiday & Time Zone Guide, 1999. LC 98-83118. (Illus.). 156p. 1999. pap. 9.95 (1-886284-47-4) Chandler Hse.
Morrison, Terry. The Five Senses. 1995. 3.95 (1-55708-482-3, MCT1013) McDonald Pub Co.
— Wild Animals. 1995. 3.95 (1-55708-483-1, T1014) McDonald Pub Co.
Morrison, Theodore. Chautauqua. LC 74-75614. 1977. pap. text 6.95 (0-226-54063-4, P737) U Ch Pr.
Morrison, Theodore, ed. see Chaucer, Geoffrey.
Morrison, Tom. More Root Beer Advertising & Collectibles. LC 97-68111. (Schiffer Book for Collectors Ser.). (Illus.). 160p. 1997. pap. 29.95 (0-7643-0042-3) Schiffer.
— Root Beer Advertising & Collectibles. LC 92-60625. (Illus.). 128p. 1992. pap. 24.95 (0-88740-421-9) Schiffer.
— To Fly Through the Air: The Experience of Learning to Fly. LC 91-8191. 200p. 1991. 29.95 (0-8138-0348-9) Iowa St U Pr.
— Weather for the New Pilot. LC 91-19260. (Illus.). 186p. 1991. 21.95 (0-8138-1773-0) Iowa St U Pr.
Morrison, Toni. Beloved. Bloom, Harold, ed. LC 98-22245. (Modern Critical Interpretations Ser.). 223p. 1999. 34.95 (0-7910-5132-3) Chelsea Hse.
— Beloved. LC 87-46157. 275p. 1987. 27.50 (0-394-53597-9) Knopf.
*Morrison, Toni. Beloved. LC 86-46157. 322p. 1998. 16.95 (0-375-40273-X) Knopf.
Morrison, Toni. Beloved. (C). 1997. pap. text. write for info. (0-8013-3148-X) Longman.
— Beloved. LC 88-5185. 288p. 1988. pap. write for info. (0-452-26446-4) NAL.
— Beloved. 1991. mass mkt. 5.99 (0-451-15659-5) NAL.
Morrison, Toni. Beloved. 1987. 15.10 (0-606-04046-3, Pub. by Turtleback) Demco.
Morrison, Toni. Beloved. (Penguin Great Books of the 20th Century Ser.). (Illus.). 288p. 2000. pap. 14.95 (0-14-028340-4) Viking Penguin.
— Beloved. gif. ed. 1998. 16.95 (0-375-40562-3) Knopf.
— Beloved. large type ed. LC 98-26241. 379p. 1998. pap. 19.95 (0-375-70414-0) Random Hse Lrg Prnt.
— Beloved. LC 88-5185. 275p. 1998. reprint ed. pap. 12.95 (0-452-28062-1) NAL.
*Morrison, Toni. The Big Box. LC 98-51948. (Illus.). 48p. (J). (gr. 3-7). 1999. lib. bdg. 20.49 (0-7868-2364-X, Pub. by Disney Pr) Little.
— The Big Box. 32p. (J). (gr. 2-6). 2005. mass mkt. 4.99 (0-7868-1291-5, Pub. by Disney Pr) Little.
Morrison, Toni. The Bluest Eye. Bloom, Harold, ed. LC 98-53872. (Modern Critical Interpretations Ser.). viii, 270p. 1999. 34.95 (0-7910-5191-9) Chelsea Hse.
*Morrison, Toni. The Bluest Eye. LC 94-14448. 215p. 2000. pap. 12.95 (0-452-28219-5, Plume) Dutton Plume.
Morrison, Toni. The Bluest Eye. LC 93-43124. 215p. 1993. 24.00 (0-679-43373-2) Knopf.
— The Bluest Eye. LC 94-14448. 215p. 1994. pap. write for info. (0-452-27305-6, Prentice Hall) P-H.
Morrison, Toni. The Bluest Eye. 224p. 1993. 15.00 (0-375-41155-0) Random.
Morrison, Toni. The Bluest Eye. LC 94-14448. 215p. 1994. 18.30 (0-606-06940-2, Pub. by Turtleback) Demco.
*Morrison, Toni. The Bluest Eye. large type ed. LC 99-47629. (G. K. Hall Core Ser.). 253p. 1999. 28.95 (0-7838-8815-5, G K Hall Lrg Type) Mac Lib Ref.
Morrison, Toni. Book of Mean People. 48p. (J). 2001. 15.99 (0-7868-0540-4, Pub. by Disney Pr) Time Warner.
— Conversations with Toni Morrison. Taylor-Guthrie, Danille K., ed. LC 93-44738. (Literary Conversations Ser.). xvii, 293 p. 1994. pap. 17.00 (0-87805-692-0) U Pr of Miss.
— The Dancing Mind: Speech Upon Acceptance of the National Book Foundation Medal for Distinguished Contribution to American Letters on the Sixth of November, Nineteen Ninety-Six. LC 97-108387. 17p. 1996. 15.00 (0-375-40032-X) Random.
— Jazz. 229p. 1993. pap. 11.95 (0-452-26965-2, Plume) Dutton Plume.
Morrison, Toni. Jazz. 1992. write for info. (0-394-22282-2) Knopf.
Morrison, Toni. Jazz. 229p. 1992. 21.00 (0-685-53430-8) Knopf.
— Jazz. 1992. 26.00 (0-679-41167-4) McKay.
— Jazz. 1993. pap. 5.99 (0-451-17780-0, Sig) NAL.
— Jazz. large type ed. LC 92-35901. (General Ser.). 312p. 1993. lib. bdg. 22.95 (0-8161-5624-7, G K Hall Lrg Type) Mac Lib Ref.
Morrison, Toni. The Nobel Lecture in Literature, 1993. LC 94-75096. 1994. 20.00 (0-679-43437-2) Knopf.
Morrison, Toni. Paradise. LC 97-80913. 318p. 1999. pap. 13.95 (0-452-28039-7, Plume) Dutton Plume.
— Paradise. LC 97-80913. 320p. 1997. 25.00 (0-679-43374-0) Knopf.
— Paradise. large type enl. ed. LC 97-31896. 453p. 1997. pap. 25.00 (0-375-70217-2) Random.
— Playing in the Dark: Whiteness & the Literary Imagination. LC 91-39671 . (Massey Lectures). xiii, 91p. 1992. 14.95 (0-674-67377-8) HUP.
— Playing in the Dark: Whiteness & the Literary Imagination. LC 92-50581. xiii, 91 p. 1993. pap. 10.00 (0-679-74542-4) Vin Bks.
— Song of Solomon. LC 87-5809. 337p. 1987. pap. 12.95 (0-452-26011-6) Dutton Plume.
— Song of Solomon. LC 96-101651. 362p. 1995. 20.00 (0-679-44504-8) Knopf.
— Song of Solomon. LC 77-874. 337p. 1977. 18.95 (0-394-49784-8) Random Hse Value.
Morrison, Toni. Song of Solomon. (Plume Contemporary Fiction Ser.). 1987. 17.05 (0-606-05092-2, Pub. by Turtleback) Demco.
Morrison, Toni. Song of Solomon. 1995. reprint ed. lib. bdg. 24.95 (1-56849-632-X) Buccaneer Bks.
— Song of Solomon: Modern Critical Interpretations. Bloom, Harold, ed. LC 98-52919. (Modern Critical Interpretations Ser.). 176p. 1999. 34.95 (0-7910-5193-5) Chelsea Hse.
— Song of Solomon/Beloved/Jazz. 3, Set. 1998. pap., boxed set 37.00 (0-452-15562-2) NAL.
— Sula. LC 73-7278. 174p. 1973. 25.00 (0-394-48044-9) Knopf.
— Sula. LC 87-15237. 174p. 1987. pap. 11.95 (0-452-26349-2) NAL.
— Sula: Modern Critical Interpretations. Bloom, Harold, ed. LC 98-50188. (Modern Critical Interpretations Ser.). 176p. 1999. 34.95 (0-7910-5194-3) Chelsea Hse.
— Tar Baby. LC 80-22821. 320p. 1981. 26.00 (0-394-42329-1) Knopf.
— Tar Baby. 305p. 1982. pap. 12.95 (0-452-26479-0, Prentice Hall) P-H.
Morrison, Toni. Tar Baby. 1983. 16.05 (0-606-01962-6, Pub. by Turtleback) Demco.
— Toni Morrison: Paradise/Beloved/Song of Solomon, 3 vols. 1999. boxed set 39.85 (0-452-15640-8, Plume) Dutton Plume.
Morrison, Toni, ed. Race-ing Justice, En-Gendering Power: Essays on Anita Hill, Clarence Thomas, & the Construction of Social Reality. LC 92-54119. (Illus.). xxx,475p. (Orig.). 1992. pap. 15.00 (0-679-74145-3) Pantheon.
Morrison, Toni & Lacour, Claudia Brodsky, eds. Birth of a Nation'hood: Gaze, Script & Spectacle in the O. J. Simpson case. xxviii, 418 p. 1997. pap. 15.00 (0-679-75893-3) Pantheon.
Morrison, Toni & Morrison, Slade. The Big Box. LC 98-51948. (Illus.). 48p. (J). (gr. 3-7). 1999. 19.99 (0-7868-0416-5, Pub. by Disney Pr) Time Warner.
Morrison, Toni, jt. auth. see Center for Learning Network Staff.
Morrison, Toni, ed. see Baldwin, James.
Morrison, Toni, ed. see Newton, Huey P.
Morrison, Tony. Pathways to the Gods: The Mystery of the Andes Lines. (Illus.). 254p. 1983. reprint ed. pap. 9.95 (0-89733-282-2) Academy Chi Pubs.
Morrison, Tony, et al, eds. Sexual Offending Against Children: Assessment & Treatment of Male Abusers. LC 94-1687. 240p. (C). 1994. pap. 25.99 (0-415-05505-9, B4373) Routledge.
Morrison, Tony, jt. auth. see Horwath, Jan.
Morrison Treseler, Kathleen, jt. auth. see Tresseler, Patrick.
Morrison, Trevor P. The Art of Computerized Measurement: Includes One Computer Disk. LC 97-5784. (Illus.). 298p. 1998. text 95.00 (0-19-856542-9); pap. text 38.00 (0-19-856541-0) OUP.
Morrison, Van. Van Morrison: Autobiography. 1999. pap. 25.00 (0-670-83408-4) Viking Penguin.
— Van Morrison: Autobiography. 384p. 2000. pap. 8.95 (0-14-013274-0) Viking Penguin.
Morrison, Venetia. The Art of George Stubbs. 1997. pap. text 25.95 (1-57715-022-8) Knckerbocker.
Morrison, Veronique, et al, eds. Tout a Fait Francais. (FRE., Illus.). 198p. (C). 1979. pap. 26.50 (0-393-09005-1) Norton.
Morrison, Vicki F. For the Birds. 52p. 1994. pap. 12.95 (0-936459-27-1) Stained Glass.
— The Stained Glass Village. (Illus.). 52p. 1993. pap. 12.95 (0-936459-21-2) Stained Glass.
Morrison, W. L. The System of Law & Courts Governing New South Wales. 2nd ed. 1985. pap. 71.00 (0-409-49263-9, AT, MICHIE) LEXIS Pub.
Morrison, Wallace B. Cancer in Dogs & Cats: Medical & Surgical Management. LC 98-10796. (Illus.). 550p. 1997. 99.95 (0-683-06105-4) Lppncott W & W.
Morrison, Wayne. Jurisprudence: From the Greeks to Post-Modernism. LC 97-161581. 576p. 1997. pap. 48.00 (1-85941-134-7, Pub. by Cavendish Pubng) Gaunt.
Morrison, Wayne A., jt. auth. see O'Brien, Bernard M.
Morrison, Wayne J. Theoretical Criminology: From Modernity to Post-Modernism. 535p. 1995. 54.00 (1-85941-221-1, Pub. by Cavendish Pubng); pap. 34.00 (1-85941-220-3, Pub. by Cavendish Pubng) Gaunt.
Morrison, Wendy. Treats Nutritional Treats: A Dynamite Cookbook for Nutritional Sweet Treats, Drinks, Breads & Muffins, Vol. 1. 72p. 1980. spiral bd. write for info. (0-920490-05-0) Detselig Ents.
Morrison, Wilbur H. Adventure Guide to the Sierra Nevada. (Adventure Guides Ser.). (Illus.). 300p. 1998. pap. 15.95 (1-55650-845-X) Hunter NJ.
— Catskills & Adirondacks Adventure Guide. (Adventure Guides Ser.). (Illus.). 224p. (Orig.). 1995. pap. 9.95 (1-55650-681-3) Hunter NJ.
— Donald W. Douglas: A Heart with Wings. LC 90-48685. (Illus.). 280p. 1991. 32.95 (0-8138-1834-6) Iowa St U Pr.
— Hellbirds: The Story of the B-29's in Combat. LC 79-20016. 1981. reprint ed. 17.95 (0-89201-062-2) Zenger Pub.
*Morrison, Wilbur H. Pilots, Man Your Planes! The History of Naval Aviation. LC 99-10941. (Illus.). 462p. 1999. 33.95 (1-55571-466-8) PSI Resch.
Morrison, William. Broadway Theatres: History & Architecture. LC 99-14611. (Illus.). 176p. 1998. pap. 16.95 (0-486-40244-4) Dover.
— Confession of William Morrison: The Rocky Mountain Trapper & the Narrative of His Wife. 30p. 1995. pap. 4.95 (0-87770-550-X) Ye Galleon.
Morrison, William, jt. auth. see Coates, Ken.
Morrison, William D. Juvenile Offenders. LC 70-172589. (Criminology, Law Enforcement, & Social Problems Ser.: No. 179). 1975. 10.00 (0-87585-179-7) Patterson Smith.
— Juvenile Offenders. LC 75-156029. reprint ed. 27.50 (0-404-09130-X) AMS Pr.
Morrison, William F. The Prenegotiation Planning Book. LC 91-32393. 272p. (C). 1992. reprint ed. lib. bdg. 33.50 (0-89464-671-0) Krieger.
Morrison, William F. & Calero, Henry H. The Human Side of Negotiations. LC 92-47483. 236p. (C). 1994. 32.50 (0-89464-836-5) Krieger.
Morrison, William J., ed. see Wourms, John P., et al.
Morrison, William J., ed. see Wright, James E., et al.
Morrison, William R. True North: The Yukon & Northwest Territories. (Illustrated History of Canada Ser.). (Illus.). 216p. 1998. 35.00 (0-19-541045-9) OUP.
Morrison, William R. & Coates, Kenneth A. Working the North: Labor & the Northwest Defense Projects, 1942-1946. LC 93-41687. (Illus.). xiv, 270p. 1994. 30.00 (0-912006-72-2); pap. 20.00 (0-912006-73-0) U of Alaska Pr.
Morrison, Yordis M. Heart-Talk: How to Break the Silence in Your Personal Relationships. 120p. 1998. pap. 13.95 (0-9666603-0-7) Natural High Bks.
— You Are Okay: Its Normal to Have Good & Bad Feelings. (Illus.). (J). (gr. 2-5). 1999. pap. 9.50 (0-9666603-1-5) Natural High Bks.
Morrisroe, Patricia. Mapplethorpe: A Biography. LC 96-43819. (Illus.). 512p. 1997. reprint ed. pap. 16.95 (0-306-80766-1) Da Capo.
Morriss, Andrew, jt. ed. see Meiners, Roger.
Morriss, Frances C., jt. auth. see Levin, Daniel L.
Morriss, Francis C., jt. auth. see Levin, Daniel L.
*Morriss, Frank. Saints in Verse. LC 99-74626. 80p. 2000. pap. 14.95 (1-892668-14-9) Prospect Pr.
Morriss, Frank, ed. A Christmas Celebration: The Wanderer's Christmas Anthology. LC 83-51146. 334p. 1983. 14.95 (0-915245-00-0) Wanderer Pr.
Morriss, James E., jt. auth. see Boyle, Joan M.
Morriss-Kay, Gillian, ed. Retinoids in Normal Development & Teratogenesis. (Illus.). 320p. 1992. 95.00 (0-19-854770-6) OUP.
Morriss, Mack. South Pacific Diary, 1942-1943. Day, Ronnie, ed. LC 95-44095. (Illus.). 256p. 1996. text 22.50 (0-8131-1969-3) U Pr of Ky.
Morriss, Margaret S. Colonial Trade of Maryland, 1689-1715. LC 76-49477. (Perspectives in American History Ser.: No. 46). viii, 157p. 1976. reprint ed. lib. bdg. 29.50 (0-87991-370-3) Porcupine Pr.
Morriss, Richard. Attention Disorders in Children: School-Based Assessment, Diagnosis, & Treatment. 1996. 49.50 (0-87424-314-9, W-314A) Western Psych.
*Morriss, Richard K. Archaeology of Buildings. (Illus.). 176p. 1999. pap. 24.99 (0-7524-1429-1, Pub. by Tempus Pubng) Arcadia Publng.
— Archaeology of Railways. (Illus.). 208p. 1999. 32.50 (0-7524-1430-5, Pub. by Tempus Pubng) Arcadia Publng.
Morriss, Richard K. The Buildings of Bath. (Buildings of...Ser.). (Illus.). 128p. 1993. pap. 13.95 (0-7509-0256-6, Pub. by Sutton Pub Ltd) Intl Pubs Mktg.
— The Buildings of Warwick. (Buildings of...Ser.). (Illus.). 128p. (Orig.). 1994. pap. 13.95 (0-7509-0558-1, Pub. by Sutton Pub Ltd) Intl Pubs Mktg.
— The Buildings of Worcester. (Buildings of...Ser.). (Illus.). 128p. (Orig.). 1994. pap. 13.95 (0-7509-0557-3, Pub. by Sutton Pub Ltd) Intl Pubs Mktg.
Morriss, Roger. Cockburn & the British Navy in Transition: Admiral Sir George Cockburn, 1722-1853. (Illus.). 400p. 1998. 70.00 (0-85989-526-2, Pub. by Univ Exeter Pr) Northwestern U Pr.
— Cockburn & the British Navy in Transition: Admiral Sir George Cockburn, 1772-1853. Still, William N., Jr., ed. LC 97-33915. (Studies in Maritime History). 300p. 1998. lib. bdg. 39.95 (1-57003-253-X) U of SC Pr.
— Nelson: The Life & Letters of a Hero. (Illustrated Letters Ser.). (Illus.). 160p. 1996. 24.95 (1-85585-274-8, Pub. by Collins & Br) Trafalgar.
— Nelson - The Life & Letters of a Hero. (Illus.). 160p. 1998. pap. 17.95 (1-85585-299-3, Pub. by Collins & Br) Trafalgar.
Morriss, Roger & Bursey, Peter, compiled by. Guide to British Naval Papers in North America. LC 94-2456. 416p. 1995. 150.00 (0-7201-2162-0) Continuum.
Morriss, S. Brian. Industrial Automation: Components & Control. LC 93-49739. 1994. 67.24 (0-02-802331-5) Glencoe.
*Morriss, S. Brian. Programmable Logic Controllers. LC 99-12358. (Illus.). 735p. 1999. 98.00 (0-13-095565-5, Prentice Hall) P-H.
Morrisseau, Calvin. Into the Daylight: A Wholistic Approach to Healing. (Illus.). 112p. 1998. text 40.00 (0-8020-4341-0); pap. text 14.95 (0-8020-8162-2) U of Toronto Pr.
Morrissett. CPA Firm Information & Records Management 1995. annuals 95th ed. (C). 1995. pap. text 79.00 (0-15-602497-7, Pub. by Harcourt Coll Pubs) Harcourt.
Morrissett, Christine, jt. auth. see Fenton, Erfert.
Morrissett, Irving, ed. Social Studies in the 1980s. fac. ed. LC 82-72766. (Report of Project SPAN Ser.). 159p. 1982. reprint ed. pap. 49.30 (0-608-01032-4, 208250800011) Bks Demand.
Morrissette, Bruce. Novel & Film: Essays in Two Genres. LC 85-995. (Illus.). xii, 182p. 1985. pap. text 10.95 (0-226-54024-3) U Ch Pr.
— Novel & Film: Essays in Two Genres. LC 85-995. (Illus.). xii, 194p. 1985. lib. bdg. 31.50 (0-226-54023-5) U Ch Pr.
Morrissette, Gabriel & Shainblum, Mark. Kentucky Revised Statutes Annotated: Official Edition. 64p. write for info. (0-614-05875-9, MICHIE) LEXIS Pub.
Morrissette, Nan H. Setting up a Bank Records Management Program. LC 92-37466. 192p. 1993. 59.95 (0-89930-748-5, MTX/, Quorum Bks) Greenwood.
*Morrissette, Paul. Loser Dies: A Satire. 215p. 2000. pap. 14.95 (0-7414-0376-5) Buy Books.
Morrissey. Longman Atlas for Caribbean Examination. 1991. pap. text. write for info. (0-582-07284-0, Pub. by Addison-Wesley) Longman.
— Our Island Jamaica. Date not set. pap. text. write for info. (0-582-05602-0, Pub. by Addison-Wesley) Longman.
Morrissey, Brendan. Boston 1775. (Campaign Ser.). (Illus.). 96p. 1994. pap. 14.95 (1-85532-362-1, 9531, Pub. by Ospry) Stackpole.
*Morrissey, Brendan. Saratoga 1777. (Campaign Ser.: Vol. 67). 2000. pap. 17.95 (1-85532-862-3) Ospry.
— Saratoga 1777. (Illus.). 96p. 2000. pap. 17.95 (1-84176-033-1) Ospry.
Morrissey, Brian. Ultimate Learning States Vol. 1: Exploring Intellectual Performance with Brainwave Technology. (Illus.). 102p. 1996. 27.95 (0-9651721-4-7) Self Study Systs.
Morrissey, Charles T. Vermont Bicentennial & History. 1984. pap. 9.95 (0-393-30223-7) Norton.
Morrissey, Dean. Chapter Book, No. 2. (J). Date not set. 15.95 (0-06-028583-4); lib. bdg. 15.89 (0-06-028584-2) HarpC Child Bks.
— The Christmas Ship. LC 99-27598. 40p. (J). (gr. k-4). 2000. 16.95 (0-06-028575-3); lib. bdg. 16.89 (0-06-028576-1) HarpC Child Bks.
Morrissey, Dean. The Great Kettles: A Tale of Time. LC 97-5749. (Illus.). 40p. (J). 1997. 17.95 (0-8109-3396-9, Pub. by Abrams) Time Warner.
Morrissey, Dean. Jack & the Beanstalk. 32p. (gr. k-4). 15.95 (0-06-028579-6) HarpC.
— Jack & the Beanstalk. 32p. (J). (gr. k-4). 15.89 (0-06-028580-X) HarpC.
— The Moon Robber. mass mkt. 5.95 (0-06-442113-9) HarpC.
— The Moon Robber. Date not set. lib. bdg. 15.89 (0-06-028582-6) HarpC Child Bks.
— The Moon Robber. (J). Date not set. 15.95 (0-06-028581-8) HarpC Child Bks.
Morrissey, Dean. Ship of Dreams. (Illus.). 37p. (J). 1994. 17.95 (0-8109-3848-0, Pub. by Abrams) Time Warner.
Morrissey, Dean, tr. see Doyle, Arthur Conan.
Morrissey, Di. Tears of the Moon. 672p. 1998. mass mkt. 6.50 (0-06-101314-5) HarpC.
Morrissey, Dianne J. Reflections of a Young Woman. 1978. pap. 4.95 (0-686-24550-4) Aaron-Jenkins.
Morrissey, Gerard. The Crisis of Dissent. 128p. (Orig.). 1985. pap. 5.95 (0-931888-19-0) Christendom Pr.
— Defending the Papacy. 96p. (Orig.). 1984. pap. 5.95 (0-931888-15-8) Christendom Pr.
— For the Love of Mary: Defending the Church from Anti-Marianism. Date not set. write for info. (0-9659770-0-5) AUFP.
— The Hardest Cross: Doctrine & Vatican Policy. 216p. (Orig.). 1995. pap. 7.95 (0-931888-58-1) Christendom Pr.
— What the Catholic Faithful Can Do. 128p. (Orig.). 1987. pap. 5.95 (0-931888-23-9) Christendom Pr.
Morrissey, Helena. International Securitisation. 650p. 1992. 132.00 (1-873446-30-6) Am Educ Systs.
Morrissey, Jake, ed. see Podrebarac, Charles.
Morrissey, Jane F., jt. ed. see Canales, Maria C.
*Morrissey, John F. Time Tells: Poems. 2000. pap. 7.95 (0-533-13254-1) Vantage.
Morrissey, Joseph. Research in Community & Mental Health, Vol. 9. Greenley, James R., ed. 1998. 73.25 (1-55938-140-X) Jai Pr.
Morrissey, Katherine G. Mental Territories: Mapping the Inland Empire. LC 97-23223. (Illus.). 240p. 1997. pap. 18.95 (0-8014-8326-3); text 45.00 (0-8014-3250-2) Cornell U Pr.
Morrissey, Kevin, jt. auth. see Bluestein, Barry.
Morrissey, Kim. Batoche. (Illus.). 96p. 1989. pap. 8.95 (0-919926-91-6, Pub. by Coteau) Genl Dist Srvs.
— Clever Paint: The Rosettis in Love. 90p. 1998. pap. 13.95 (0-88754-552-1) Playwrights.
— Dora: A Case of Hysteria. 64p. 1994. pap. 12.95 (1-85459-295-5, Pub. by N Hern Bks) Theatre Comm.

M

An Asterisk (*) at the beginning of an entry indicates that the title is appearing for the first time.

Morrissey, Kim. Poems for Men Who Dream of Lolita. 80p. 1992. text 19.95 (1-55050-030-9, Pub. by Coteau) Genl Dist Srvs.

Morrissey, Kim. Poems for Men Who Dream of Lolita. 72p. 1992. pap. 8.95 (1-55050-029-5, Pub. by Coteau) Genl Dist Srvs.

***Morrissey, Kirkie.** At Jesus' Feet. 2000. pap. 6.00 (1-57683-182-5) NavPress.

— Responsive Heart: Cultivating a Life-Long Love for God. 2000. pap. 6.00 (1-57683-181-7) NavPress.

Morrissey, Kirkie. A Woman's Workshop on Forgiveness. (Woman's Workshop Ser.). 160p. 1982. mass mkt. 6.99 (0-310-44931-6, 16245P) Zondervan.

Morrissey, Lee, ed. The Kitchen Turns 20: A Retrospective Anthology. (Illus.). 120p. (Orig.). 1992. pap. 10.00 (0-9634456-1-8) Kitchen Ctr.

Morrissey, Lynn D., compiled by. Seasons of a Woman's Heart: A Daybook of Stories & Inspiration. LC 98-83167. 304p. 1999. 18.95 (1-892016-03-6) Starburst.

***Morrissey, Lynn D., ed.** Treasures of a Woman's Heart: A Daybook of Stories & Inspiration. 304p. 2000. 18.95 (1-892016-25-7, Pub. by Starburst) Natl Bk Netwk.

Morrissey, Maria & Mitchell, Jack. VersaCAD Corporation's Training Guide: 2D & 3D Tutorials. (Orig.). (C). 1989. pap., teacher ed. 21.00 (0-8273-3563-6) Delmar.

Morrissey, Mary M. Building Your Field of Dreams. 304p. 1997. pap. 12.95 (0-553-37814-7) Bantam.

— When I Can't, God Can: A Daily Walk in Faith. 380p. 1999. pap. 7.95 (1-886491-23-2); pap. 16.95 incl. audio (1-886491-24-0) Tiger Mtn Pr.

***Morrissey, Michael.** Flamingo Anthology of New Zealand Short Stories. 501p. 2000. pap. 15.95 (1-86950-335-X) HarpC.

Morrissey, Michael D., jt. ed. see Kellermann, Gunter.

Morrissey, Michael P. Consciousness & Transcendence: The Theology of Eric Voegelin. LC 92-50159. (C). 1994. text 48.50 (0-268-00793-4) U of Notre Dame Pr.

Morrissey, Michael T. & Pollnac, Richard B., eds. Aspects of Small-Scale Fisheries Development. 154p. (C). 1989. pap. 7.00 (1-882027-00-0) URI ICMRD.

Morrissey, Michael T., jt. ed. see Sylvia, Gilbert.

***Morrissey, Mike & Gaffikin, Frank.** City Visions: Imagining Place, Enfranchising People. LC 99-22541. 250p. 1999. 59.95 (0-7453-1356-6, Pub. by Pluto GBR); pap. 24.95 (0-7453-1351-5, Pub. by Pluto GBR) Stylus Pub VA.

Morrissey, Mike & Gaffikin, Frank. Northern Ireland: The Thatcher Years. LC 89-25027. (Illus.). 160p. (C). 1990. pap. 15.00 (0-86232-907-8, Pub. by Zed Books); text 45.00 (0-86232-906-X, Pub. by Zed Books) St Martin.

Morrissey, Mike, jt. ed. see Gaffikin, Frank.

Morrissey, Muriel E. Amelia Earhart. (Illus.). 1977. pap. 4.95 (0-88388-044-X) Bellerophon Bks.

Morrissey, Muriel E. & Osborne, Carol L. Amelia, My Courageous Sister: Biography of Amelia Earhart. (Biography Ser.). (Illus.). 312p. 1987. 23.95 (0-940997-00-2) Aviation Archives.

Morrissey, Oliver & Stewart, Frances, eds. Economic & Political Reform in Developing Countries. LC 95-2568. 224p. 1995. text 75.00 (0-312-12606-9) St Martin.

Morrissey, Oliver, et al. British Aid & International Trade: Aid Policy Making, 1979-89. LC 92-11902. (Public Policy & Management Ser.). 1992. 118.00 (0-335-15652-5) OpUniv Pr.

Morrissey, Oliver, jt. ed. see Lloyd, Tim.

Morrissey, Oliver, jt. ed. see McGillivray, Mark.

Morrissey, Patricia. Disability Etiquette in the Workplace. 38p. 1991. 20.00 (0-916559-35-1, 2032-TM-4045) EPF.

Morrissey, Patricia A. ADA News & Regulations: For the Private Sector. 350p. 1993. 350.00 (1-880955-01-6) Legi-Slate.

— Human Resource Executive's Survival Guide to the Americans with Disabilities Act. LC 91-38253. 500p. 1992. ring bd. 135.00 (0-934753-63-6) LRP Pubns.

— A Primer for Corporate America on Civil Rights for the Disabled. LC 91-25397. 139p. (Orig.). 1991. pap. 12.95 (0-934753-49-0) LRP Pubns.

Morrissey, Paul F. Let Someone Hold You: The Journey of a Hospice Priest. LC 93-45874. 240p. (Orig.). 1994. pap. 16.95 (0-8245-1408-4) Crossroad NY.

Morrissey, Paulette. Anyone Can Antique. (Fast, Fun & Easy Ser.: Bk. 4). (Illus.). 18p. 1996. spiral bd. 9.95 (1-893502-03-1) Morrissey Co.

— Beyond the Basics. (Fast, Fun & Easy Ser.: Bk. 5). (Illus.). 19p. 1998. spiral bd. 9.95 (1-893502-04-X) Morrissey Co.

***Morrissey, Paulette.** Button Buddies: Crocheted Stuffed Animals with Button Joints. (Illus.). 20p. 2000. 15.95 (1-893502-15-5) Morrissey Co.

Morrissey, Paulette. Foolproof Drybrushing. (Fast, Fun & Easy Ser.: Bk. 3). (Illus.). 18p. 1996. spiral bd. 9.95 (1-893502-02-3) Morrissey Co.

***Morrissey, Paulette.** Greeting Bears for All Occasions: Send a Bear... Instead of a Card! (Illus.). (YA). (gr. 3 up). 1999. spiral bd. 8.95 (1-893502-12-0) Morrissey Co.

— Maggie & Keisha - Best Friends: Complete Patterns for Two Cloth Dolls & Their Wardrobes. (Illus.). 39p. 1999. spiral bd. 13.95 (1-893502-09-0) Morrissey Co.

Morrissey, Paulette. Make a Family - Make Their Wardrobe. (Illus.). 1999. spiral bd. 15.95 (1-893502-10-4) Morrissey Co.

***Morrissey, Paulette.** Make Their Furnishings - Make Their Home: A Complete House & all the Furnishings for the "Make a Family" Set of Dolls. (Illus.). 1999. spiral bd. 15.95 (1-893502-13-9) Morrissey Co.

Morrissey, Paulette. Mastering the Basics. (Fast, Fun & Easy Ser.: Bk. 1). (Illus.). 21p. 1996. spiral bd. 9.95 (1-893502-00-7) Morrissey Co.

— A Non-Fired Technique: How to Paint Bisque Dolls. (Illus.). 28p. 1997. spiral bd. 9.95 (1-893502-06-6) Morrissey Co.

— Perfect Eyes. (Fast, Fun & Easy Ser.: Bk. 2). (Illus.). 22p. 1996. spiral bd. 9.95 (1-893502-01-5) Morrissey Co.

— Project Journal. (Fast, Fun & Easy Ser.: Bk. 6). (Illus.). 28p. 1996. spiral bd. 8.95 (1-893502-05-8) Morrissey Co.

***Morrissey, Paulette.** Simply Kid's Cloth Dolls. (Illus.). 49p. 1999. spiral bd. 14.95 (1-893502-11-2) Morrissey Co.

— A Trio of Teddies to Crochet. (Illus.). 1999. spiral bd. 8.95 (1-893502-08-2) Morrissey Co.

Morrissey, Paulette. You Can Do It! Sell Your Own Crafts. (Illus.). 45p. 1998. spiral bd. 17.95 (1-893502-07-4) Morrissey Co.

Morrissey, Peter. The Young Ice Skater. LC 98-11936. (Young Enthusiast Ser.). 40p. (J). (gr. 3-8). 1998. pap. 15.95 (0-7894-3422-9) DK Pub Inc.

***Morrissey, Peter.** Young Ice Skater. LC 99-50019. (Young Enthusiast Ser.). (J). (gr. 3-7). 2000. 9.95 (0-7894-5427-0) DK Pub Inc.

Morrissey, Peter & Young, James. Figure Skating School: A Profesisonally Structured Course from Basic Steps to Advanced Techniques. (Illus.). 128p. 1999. reprint ed. pap. text 20.00 (0-7881-6408-2) DIANE Pub.

Morrissey, Peter, jt. auth. see Young, James.

Morrissey, Sally. Mud Stoves & Strawberry Jam. 240p. pap. 14.95 (0-9643963-0-0) R Paul Pr.

Morrissey, Susan K. Heralds of Revolution: Russian Students & the Mythologies of Radicalism. LC 97-2262. (Illus.). 304p. 1998. text 45.00 (0-19-511544-9) OUP.

Morrissey, Thomas. As One Sent: Peter Kenney 1779-1841: His Mission in Ireland & North America. (Illus.). 529p. 1996. text 54.95 (0-8132-0880-7) Cath U Pr.

— A Man Called Hughes. 512p. 1989. 75.00 (1-85390-138-5, Pub. by Veritas Pubns) St Mut.

***Morrissey, Thomas F.** Between the Lines: Photographs from the National Vietnam Veterans Memorial. LC 99-87050. (Illus.). 128p. 2000. text 34.95 (0-8156-0591-9) Syracuse U Pr.

Morrissey, Thomas J. Towards a National University: William Delaney Sj (1835-1924) 128p. 1997. 27.95 (0-86327-012-3, Pub. by Wolfhound Press) Irish Amer Bk.

Morrisson, Bill. Love Song for Ulster. 192p. 1994. pap. 19.95 (1-85459-260-2, Pub. by N Hern Bks) Theatre Comm.

Morrisson, Cecile. La Monnaie et Finances a Byzance: Analyses, Techniques. (Collected Studies: CS 461). 352p. 1994. 115.95 (0-86078-401-0, Pub. by Variorum) Ashgate Pub Co.

Morrisson, Clovis C. The Dynamics of Development in the European Human Rights Convention System. 192p. 1981. lib. bdg. 101.00 (90-247-2546-1) Kluwer Academic.

***Morrisson, Mark.** The Public Face of Modernism: Little Magazines, Audiences & Reception, 1905-1920. LC 00-8425. (Illus.). 2000. write for info. (0-299-16924-3) U of Wis Pr.

Morrissy, Raymond T. Atlas of Pediatric Orthopaedic Surgery. 2nd ed. 876p. 1996. text 446.00 (0-397-51824-2) Lppncott W & W.

— Atlas of Pediatric Orthopaedic Surgery. 2nd ed. (Illus.). 858p. 1996. text 215.00 (0-397-51515-4) Lppncott W & W.

Morrissy, Raymond T. & Weinstein, Stuart L. Atlas of Pediatric Orthopaedic Surgery. 3rd ed. 850p. text 199.00 (0-7817-2095-8) Lppncott W & W.

— Lovell & Winter's Pediatric Orthopaedics. 5th ed. 1552p. text. write for info. (0-7817-2580-1); text. write for info. (0-7817-2581-X); text 275.00 (0-7817-2582-8) Lppncott W & W.

Morrissy, Raymond T. & Weinstein, Stuart L., eds. Lovell & Winter's Pediatric Orthopaedics, 2 vols., Set. 4th ed. LC 95-31125. 1334p. 1995. text 293.00 (0-397-51397-6) Lppncott W & W.

— Lovell & Winter's Pediatric Orthopaedics, Vol. 1. LC 95-31125. 1995. write for info. (0-397-51598-7) Lppncott W & W.

— Lovell & Winter's Pediatric Orthopaedics, Vol. 2. LC 95-31125. 1995. write for info. (0-397-51599-5) Lppncott W & W.

Morritt, Hope. Rivers of Oil: The Founding of the North-American Petroleum Industry. (Illus.). 254p. 1993. pap. 19.95 (1-55082-088-5, Pub. by Quarry Pr) LPC InBook.

— Women & Computer Based Technologies: A Feminist Perspective. LC 97-1652. 202p. 1997. 44.50 (0-7618-0711-X); pap. 28.50 (0-7618-0712-8) U Pr of Amer.

Morro, A., jt. auth. see Caviglia, G.

Morro, Angelo, jt. auth. see Fabrizio, Mauro.

Morrocco, John. Air Power Unleashed: The Air War, 1968-1975. Boston Publishing Company Editors, ed. (Illus.). 192p. 1985. 16.30 (0-201-11268-X) Addison-Wesley.

Morrogh, Michael M. The Irish Century: A Photographic History of the Last Hundred Years. (Illus.). 244p. 1998. 45.00 (1-57098-237-6, R Rinehart Intl) Roberts Rinehart.

Morron, Bradford, ed. Conjunctions Fifteen: Biannual Volumes of New Writing. (Illus.). 415p. (Orig.). (C). 1991. pap. 9.95 (0-685-49112-9) Random.

Morrone, Francis. An Architectural Guidebook to Philadelphia. LC 98-50531. (Illus.). 256p. 1999. pap. 21.95 (0-87905-890-0) Gibbs Smith Pub.

— The Night Before Christmas in New York City. LC 94-220441. (Illus.). 60p. 1994. 5.95 (0-87905-615-0) Gibbs Smith Pub.

Morrone, Francis & Iska, James. The Architectural Guidebook to New York City. rev. expanded ed. LC 97-33086. (Illus.). 432p. 1998. pap. 21.95 (0-87905-841-2) Gibbs Smith Pub.

Morrone, Joan. Addicted. LC 85-82145. 125p. (Orig.). 1986. pap. 6.00 (0-9616771-0-4) J & R Pub.

— The Age of Reason: A Scientific Study of the Evolutionary Potential of Man - The Revelation of Cosmic Consciousness. (Illus.). 72p. (Orig.). 1988. pap. 8.50 (0-9616771-1-2) J & R Pub.

Morrone, John, ed. Grants & Awards Available to American Writers, 1998-99. 20th ed. 224p. 1998. pap. 15.00 (0-934638-15-2) PEN Am Ctr.

Morrone, Osvaldo, jt. ed. see Zuloaga, Fernando O.

Morrone, Wenda Wardell. Year 2000 Killers: Terrorism by Computer. LC 99-19881. 1999. 23.95 (0-312-20622-4, Thomas Dunne) St Martin.

Morroni, Mario. Production Process & Technical Change. (Illus.). 234p. (C). 1992. text 54.95 (0-521-41001-0) Cambridge U Pr.

Morrow. Cooking without Heat. Date not set. pap. text. write for info. (0-582-05853-8) Longman.

— Gardening in & Out. 1990. pap. text. write for info. (0-582-05851-1, Pub. by Addison-Wesley) Longman.

— Getting Ahead in English. Date not set. pap. text. write for info. (0-582-05870-8, Pub. by Addison-Wesley) Longman.

— Getting Ahead in Science. Date not set. pap. text. write for info. (0-582-05868-6, Pub. by Addison-Wesley) Longman.

Morrow. Make Things Without Needles. Date not set. pap. text. write for info. (0-582-05852-X, Pub. by Addison-Wesley) Longman.

Morrow. Republc if U Can Keep It. LC 98-56094. 482p. 1999. pap. 36.00 (0-13-095067-X) S&S Trade.

— Towering Jehovah. 1994. pap. 5.99 (0-09-926301-7) Random.

— The Woman Angler: An Introductory Handbook For Women Who Want to Fish. 1999. pap. 12.95 (0-312-20444-2) St Martin.

Morrow, et al. 1997 Year Book of Obstetrics & Gynecology & Women's Health. (Illus.). 728p. (C). (gr. 13). 1997. text 79.00 (0-8151-6019-4, 22714) Mosby Inc.

Morrow, Abbie C., ed. Sweet Smelling Myrrh: The Autobiography of Madame Guyon. abr. ed. 192p. 1996. reprint ed. pap. 10.99 (0-88019-348-4) Schmul Pub Co.

Morrow, Ann. Highness: The Maharajahs of India. large type ed. (Illus.). 448p. 1987. 27.99 (0-7089-8441-X) Ulverscroft.

— Princess. large type ed. 541p. 1992. 27.99 (0-7505-0398-X, Pub. by Mgna Lrg Print) Ulverscroft.

Morrow, Ann, jt. auth. see Cerulean, Susan.

Morrow, Arthur E. & Morrow, Edith M. Two Morrow's Legacy. (Illus.). 1988. 10.95 (0-9620550-0-X) Dodson Assocs.

***Morrow, Baiba & Morrow, Pat, photos by.** Footsteps in the Clouds. (Illus.). 160p. 2000. pap. 18.95 (1-55192-226-6) Raincoast Bk.

Morrow, Baiba, jt. auth. see Morrow, Pat.

Morrow, Baker H. Best Plants for NM Gardens & Landscapes: Keyed to Cities & Regions in New Mexico & Adjacent Areas. LC 95-4331. (Illus.). 267p. 1995. pap. 24.95 (0-8263-1595-X) U of NM Pr.

Morrow, Baker H., ed. A Harvest of Reluctant Souls: The Memorial of Fray Alonso de Benavides, 1630. LC 96-2750. (Illus.). 128p. 1996. 24.95 (0-87081-385-4) Univ Pr Colo.

Morrow, Baker H. & Price, V. B., eds. Anasazi Architecture & American Design. LC 96-25381. (Illus.). 220p. 1997. pap. 19.95 (0-8263-1779-0) U of NM Pr.

Morrow, Barbara, jt. ed. see Humeston, Barbara.

Morrow, Barbara Briggs, see Briggs Morrow, Barbara.

Morrow, Barbara O. From Ben-Hur to Sister Carrie: Remembering the Lives & Works of Five Indiana Authors. LC 95-77507. (Illus.). 200p. 1995. 21.95 (1-878208-60-8) Guild Pr IN.

Morrow, Betty, jt. ed. see Enarson, Elaine H.

Morrow, Blaine V. Dial Up! Gale's Bulletin Board Locator. 1081p. 1995. 49.00 (0-7876-0364-3) Gale.

Morrow, Bradford. The Almanac Branch. 288p. 1992. pap. 8.95 (0-393-30921-5) Norton.

***Morrow, Bradford.** American Fiction: States of the Art, Vol. 34. 2000. pap. 15.00 (0-941964-50-7) Conjunctions.

Morrow, Bradford. Come Sunday. 416p. 1996. pap. 12.95 (0-14-024756-4, Viking) Viking Penguin.

— Conjunctions No. 22, No. 22. (Illus.). 320p. 1994. pap. 10.00 (0-679-75581-0) Random.

***Morrow, Bradford.** Conjunctions 32, Eye to Eye. 1999. pap. text 12.00 (0-941964-48-5) Conjunctions.

— Conjunctions 23: New World Writing. 1994. pap. 10.00 (0-679-75820-8) Random.

Morrow, Bradford. Giovanni's Gift. LC 96-34024. 325p. 1998. pap. 12.95 (0-14-026293-8) Viking Penguin.

— Secular Psalms, Vol. 28. 360p. 1997. pap. text 12.00 (0-941964-44-2) Conjunctions.

Morrow, Bradford, ed. Conjunction: Bi-Annual Volumes of New Writing, Vol. 16. 360p. 1991. pap. 12.00 (0-941964-33-7) Conjunctions.

— Conjunctions: Bi-Annual Volumes of New Writing, Vol. 8. (Illus.). 272p. 1985. pap. 12.00 (0-941964-17-5) Conjunctions.

— Conjunctions: Bi-Annual Volumes of New Writing, Vol. 9. (Illus.). 296p. 1986. pap. 12.00 (0-941964-15-9) Conjunctions.

— Conjunctions: Bi-Annual Volumes of New Writing, Vol. 11. (Illus.). 296p. 1988. pap. 12.00 (0-941964-23-X) Conjunctions.

— Conjunctions: Bi-Annual Volumes of New Writing, Vol. 12. 312p. 1988. 25.00 (0-684-58712-2); pap. 12.00 (0-941964-26-4) Conjunctions.

— Conjunctions: Bi-Annual Volumes of New Writing, Vol. 13. 288p. 1989. pap. 12.00 (0-941964-30-2) Conjunctions.

— Conjunctions: Bi-Annual Volumes of New Writing, Vol. 14. 296p. 1989. pap. 12.00 (0-941964-31-0) Conjunctions.

— Conjunctions: Bi-Annual Volumes of New Writing, Vol. 15. 424p. 1990. pap. 12.00 (0-941964-32-9) Conjunctions.

— Conjunctions: Bi-Annual Volumes of New Writing, Vol. 17. 424p. 1991. pap. 12.00 (0-941964-34-5) Conjunctions.

— Conjunctions: Bi-Annual Volumes of New Writing, Vol. 19. 336p. 1992. pap. 12.00 (0-941964-36-1) Conjunctions.

— Conjunctions: 1. (Bi-Annual Volumes of New Writing Ser.). (Illus.). 320p. 1981. pap. 9.00 (0-941964-01-9) Conjunctions.

— Conjunctions: 3. (Bi-Annual Volumes of New Writing Ser.). (Illus.). 232p. 1982. pap. 12.00 (0-941964-05-1) Conjunctions.

— Conjunctions: 4. (Bi-Annual Volumes of New Writing Ser.). (Illus.). 232p. 1983. pap. 12.00 (0-941964-07-8) Conjunctions.

— Conjunctions: 5. (Bi-Annual Volumes of New Writing Ser.). (Illus.). 248p. (C). 1983. pap. 12.00 (0-941964-09-4) Conjunctions.

— Conjunctions: 6. (Bi-Annual Volumes of New Writing Ser.). (Illus.). 320p. 1984. pap. 12.00 (0-941964-11-6) Conjunctions.

— Conjunctions: 7. (Bi-Annual Volumes of New Writing Ser.). (Illus.). 284p. 1985. pap. 12.00 (0-941964-13-2) Conjunctions.

— Conjunctions Vol. 20: Fables, Yarns, Fairy Tales. 376p. 1992. pap. 12.00 (0-941964-35-3) Conjunctions.

— Conjunctions Vol. 20: Unfinished Business. 352p. 1993. pap. 12.00 (0-941964-37-X) Conjunctions.

— Conjunctions Vol. 21: The Credos Issue. 352p. 1994. pap. 12.00 (0-941964-38-8) Conjunctions.

— Conjunctions Vol. 22: The Novellas Issue. 384p. 1994. pap. 12.00 (0-941964-39-6) Conjunctions.

— Conjunctions Vol. 23: New World Writing. 336p. 1994. pap. 12.00 (0-941964-40-X) Conjunctions.

— Conjunctions Vol. 24: Critical Mass. 344p. 1995. pap. 12.00 (0-941964-29-9) Conjunctions.

Morrow, Bradford, ed. Conjunctions - 35: American Poetry: States of the Art. Date not set. pap. 12.00 (0-941964-51-5, Pub. by Conjunctions) Consort Bk Sales.

— Crossing Over: The Millennial Issue. (Conjunctions Ser.: No. 33). (Illus.). 411p. 2000. pap. 12.00 (0-941964-49-3, Pub. by Conjunctions) SPD-Small Pr Dist.

Morrow, Bradford, ed. Paper Airplane: The Thirtieth Issue. (Illus.). 385p. 1998. pap. 12.00 (0-941964-46-9) Conjunctions.

Morrow, Bradford, et al, eds. Conjunctions: Bi-Annual Volumes of New Writing, Vol. 10. (Conjunctions--Bi-Annual Volumes of New Writing Ser.). (Illus.). 320p. 1987. pap. 12.00 (0-941964-21-3) Conjunctions.

Morrow, Bradford & Antoni, Robert, eds. Conjunctions Vol. 27: The Archipelago. 1996. write for info. (0-614-18180-1) Bard Coll Pubns.

Morrow, Bradford & Constantine, Peter, eds. Radical Shadows: Previously Untranslated & Unpublished Works by 19th & 20th Century Masters. 1998. pap. 12.00 (0-941964-47-7, Pub. by Conjunctions) Consort Bk Sales.

Morrow, Bradford & Cooney, Seamus. A Bibliography of the Black Sparrow Press, 1966-1978. LC 80-24229. (Illus.). 302p. 1981. 40.00 (0-87685-465-X) Black Sparrow.

Morrow, Bradford & Lafourcade, Bernard. A Bibliography of the Writings of Wyndham Lewis. LC 78-12751. (Illus.). 350p. 1978. 40.00 (0-87685-419-6) Black Sparrow.

Morrow, Bradford, jt. auth. see Dowell, Coleman.

Morrow, Bradford, jt. ed. see Antoni, Robert.

Morrow, Bradford, ed. see Bellen, Martine.

Morrow, Bradford, ed. see Rexroth, Kenneth.

Morrow, Bruce & Rowell, Charles H., eds. Shades: An Anthology of Fiction by Gay Men of African Descent. LC 95-48795. 400p. (Orig.). 1996. pap. 12.00 (0-380-78305-3, Avon Bks) Morrow Avon.

Morrow, C. P. Synopsis of Gynecologic Oncology. 5th ed. Schmitt, William, ed. LC 98-21396. 736p. 1998. text 120.00 (0-443-07509-3, W B Saunders Co) Harcrt Hlth Sci Grp.

Morrow, C. Paul, et al, eds. Recent Clinical Developments in Gynecologic Oncology. LC 83-3312. (Progress in Cancer Research & Therapy Ser.: No. 24). (Illus.). 233p. 1983. reprint ed. pap. 72.30 (0-7837-9517-3, 206026600005) Bks Demand.

Morrow, C. Paul & Curtin, John P. Gynecologic Cancer Surgery. LC 96-17074. (Illus.). 824p. 1995. text 195.00 (0-443-08970-1) Church.

Morrow, C. Paul & Townsend, Duane E. Synopsis of Gynecologic Oncology. 3rd ed. LC 87-2112. (Illus.). 602p. reprint ed. pap. 186.70 (0-7837-6248-8, 204596000010) Bks Demand.

Morrow, Carol A. Peace Therapy. LC 94-96664. 80p. 1995. pap. 4.95 (0-87029-273-0) Abbey.

— Trust-in-God Therapy. LC 98-73408. (Illus.). 88p. 1998. pap. 4.95 (0-87029-322-2, 20119) Abbey.

Morrow, Carol Ann. A Retreat with Anthony of Padua: Finding Our Way. (Retreat with Ser.). 102p. 1999. pap. 8.95 (0-86716-310-0, B3100) St Anthony Mess Pr.

Morrow, Charlene & Perl, Teri, eds. Notable Women in Mathematics: A Biographical Dictionary. LC 97-18598. (Illus.). 320p. (YA). (gr. 9 up). 1998. 49.95 (0-313-29131-4, Greenwood Pr) Greenwood.

M

M

Morrow, Charles T. Shock & Vibration Engineering. LC 63-7556. 404p. reprint ed. pap. 125.30 (*0-608-30875-7*, 201195600080) Bks Demand.

***Morrow, Christine.** Stir It Up: Reggae Album Cover Art. LC 99-31751. (Illus.). 120p. 1999. pap. 24.95 (*0-8118-2616-3*) Chronicle Bks.

Morrow, Christine, jt. auth. see Picton, Bernard.

***Morrow, Curtis.** Return of the African-American. LC 99-42759. 1999. 19.95 (*1-56072-717-9*) Nova Sci Pubs.

Morrow, Curtis. What's a Commie Ever Done to Black People? A Korean War Memoir of Fighting in the U.S. Army's Last All Negro Unit. LC 96-53102. (Illus.). 144p. 1997. 26.50 (*0-7864-0333-0*) McFarland & Co.

Morrow, Danny R. Silhouette of a Saint: Albert Pepper. 1985. 5.95 (*0-86544-027-1*) Salv Army Suppl South.

Morrow, David A. Current Therapy in Theriogenology Vol. 2: Diagnosis, Treatment & Prevention of Reproductive Diseases in Small & Large Animals. 2nd ed. (Illus.). 1143p. 1986. text 163.00 (*0-7216-6580-2*, W B Saunders Co) Harcrt Hlth Sci Grp.

***Morrow, David C.** Behind the Big Lady: Recollections of Legs Bar. 72p. 2000. pap. 20.00 (*0-9641836-8-4*); spiral bd. 20.00 (*0-9641836-7-6*) Textar Media.

Morrow, David C. How Women Manipulate. 40p. (Orig.). 1996. pap. 6.00 (*0-9641836-3-3*) Textar Media.

— The Immolated Sovereign. 10p. (Orig.). 1997. pap. 6.00 (*0-9641836-4-1*) Textar Media.

— The Once & Future Nerd. 20p. (Orig.). 1994. pap. 5.00 (*0-9641836-0-9*) Textar Media.

— Reverend R. R. Morrow, Jr. 35p. 1999. pap. 10.00 (*0-9641836-6-8*) Textar Media.

— Shondan Language. 20p. (Orig.). 1995. pap. 5.00 (*0-9641836-2-5*) Textar Media.

— Thomas Morrow: Pioneer of Alabama & Texas. 18p. (Orig.). 1994. pap. 18.00 (*0-9641836-1-7*) Textar Media.

— West from Emmaus. 14p. 1998. pap. 3.00 (*0-9641836-5-X*) Textar Media.

Morrow, Don, et al. A Concise History of Sport in Canada. (Illus.). 400p. 1990. pap. text 21.00 (*0-19-540693-1*) OUP.

Morrow, Duncan, jt. auth. see Aughey, Arthur.

Morrow, Ed. Born This Day: A Daily Celebration of Famous Beginnings. (Illus.). 324p. 1995. pap. 12.95 (*0-8065-1648-8*, Citadel Pr) Carol Pub Group.

***Morrow, Ed.** Born This Day: A Daily Celebration of Famous Beginnings. 407p. 1999. reprint ed. pap. 13.00 (*0-7881-6666-2*) DIANE Pub.

Morrow, Ed. The Grim Reaper's Book of Days: A Cautionary Record of Famous, Infamous & Unconventional Exits. (Illus.). 256p. 1992. pap. 9.95 (*0-8065-1364-0*, Citadel Pr) Carol Pub Group.

Morrow, Edith M., jt. auth. see Morrow, Arthur E.

***Morrow, Edwin P.** Letters: Text Library System. 1999. per. write for info. (*1-893717-04-6*) Finan Plan.

Morrow, Edwin P. Personal Coaching for Financial Advisors. (Illus.). 36p. (C). 1999. 14.00 (*1-893717-01-1*) Finan Plan.

Morrow, Edwin P. Web-Based Marketing for Financial Advisors. (C). Date not set. per. 14.00 (*1-893717-03-8*) Finan Plan.

Morrow, Edwin P. & Kelvin, Jeffrey B. Complete Millenium Preparation Guide. (Illus.). 242p. 1998. ring bd. 385.00 (*1-893717-00-3*) Finan Plan.

Morrow, Ellen P. The Desperate Woman's Guide to Fitness. LC 97-93484. (Illus.). 172p. 1997. pap. 9.95 (*0-9656964-4-8*) Bench Pr Calif.

Morrow, Felix. Revolution & Counter-Revolution in Spain. 2nd ed. LC 74-80372. 262p. 1974. reprint ed. lib. bdg. 50.00 (*0-87348-401-0*) Pathfinder NY.

— Revolution & Counter-Revolution in Spain. 2nd ed. LC 74-80372. 262p. 1974. reprint ed. pap. 17.95 (*0-87348-402-9*) Pathfinder NY.

Morrow, France. Unleashing Our Unknown Selves: An Inquiry into the Future of Feminity & Masculinity. LC 90-39262. 288p. 1990. 65.00 (*0-275-93587-6*, C3587, Praeger Pubs); pap. 22.95 (*0-275-93837-9*, B3837, Praeger Pubs) Greenwood.

Morrow, G. J. & Yang, W. S., eds. Probability Models in Mathematical Physics: Proceedings of the Conference on Probability Models in Mathematical Physics, Colorado Springs, May 16-24, 1990. 252p. 1991. text 104.00 (*981-02-0394-2*) World Scientific Pub.

Morrow, Gertrude. The Compassionate School: A Practical Guide to Educating Abused & Traumatized Children. 250p. (C). 1987. text 27.95 (*0-13-154742-9*) P-H.

Morrow, Glenn R. Plato's Cretan City: A Historical Interpretation of the Laws. 646p. 1993. pap. text 29.95 (*0-691-02484-7*, Pub. by Princeton U Pr) Cal Prin Full Svc.

— Plato's Law of Slavery in Its Relation to Greek Law. LC 75-13283. (History of Ideas in Ancient Greece Ser.). 1976. reprint ed. 15.95 (*0-405-07325-9*) Ayer.

Morrow, Glenn R., tr. see Proclus.

Morrow, Gray & Caragonne, George. Doctor Dare. pap. 16.95 (*1-56097-344-7*, Pub. by Fantagraph Bks) Seven Hills Bk.

Morrow, H. W. Statics & Strength of Materials. 3rd ed. LC 97-11183. 608p. 1997. 86.00 (*0-13-453201-5*) P-H.

***Morrow, Henry W.** Corpses of Angels. 120p. 2000. pap. 12.50 (*0-941017-61-3*) Bombshelter Pr.

Morrow, Honore. On to Oregon! (Illus.). (J). (gr. 4-7). 1946. reprint ed. 16.00 (*0-688-21639-0*, Wm Morrow) Morrow Avon.

— On to Oregon! LC 90-19554. (Illus.). 240p. (J). (gr. 5-9). 1991. reprint ed. pap. 4.95 (*0-688-10494-0*, Wm Morrow) Morrow Avon.

Morrow, Honore W. Splendor of God. 26.95 (*0-89190-310-0*) Amereon Ltd.

Morrow, I. F., tr. see Von Salomon, Ernst.

Morrow, Ian F., tr. see Kees, Herman.

Morrow, Ian F., tr. see Paleoloque, Maurice.

Morrow, James. Bible Stories for Adults. LC 95-36805. 244p. 1996. 22.00 (*0-15-100192-8*); pap. 12.00 (*0-15-600244-2*, Harvest Bks) Harcourt.

— Blameless in Abaddon. 2nd ed. 416p. 1997. pap. 13.00 (*0-15-600505-0*, Harvest Bks) Harcourt.

— City of Truth. LC 92-43161. 128p. 1993. pap. 7.95 (*0-15-618042-1*) Harcourt.

— The Eternal Footman. LC 99-25684. 400p. 1999. 24.00 (*0-15-129325-2*) Harcourt.

***Morrow, James.** The Eternal Footman. 368p. 2000. pap. 14.00 (*0-15-601081-X*) Harcourt.

Morrow, James. Nebula Awards No. 27: SFWA's Choices for the Best Science Fiction & Fantasy of the Year. LC 83-647399. 1993. 24.95 (*0-15-164935-9*) Harcourt.

— Only Begotten Daughter. 312p. 1996. pap. 12.00 (*0-15-600243-4*, Harvest Bks) Harcourt.

***Morrow, James.** Shard of the Afflicted House. 1999. pap. write for info. (*1-58235-184-8*) Watermrk Pr.

Morrow, James. This Is the Way the World Ends. LC 85-24773. 336p. 1995. pap. 12.00 (*0-15-600208-6*) Harcourt.

— Towing Jehovah. LC 93-35022. 1994. 23.95 (*0-15-190919-9*) Harcourt.

— Towing Jehovah. LC 93-35022. 384p. 1995. pap. 13.00 (*0-15-600210-8*) Harcourt.

Morrow, James, ed. Nebula Awards No. 26: SFWA's Choices for the Best Science Fiction & Fantasy of the Year. 1992. 24.95 (*0-15-164934-0*, Harvest Bks); pap. 12.95 (*0-15-665472-5*, Harvest Bks) Harcourt.

Morrow, James, jt. auth. see Paradoxa Staff.

Morrow, James A., jt. auth. see Curtis, Edward B.

Morrow, James D. Game Theory for Political Scientists. LC 94-9256. 646p. 1994. text 35.00 (*0-691-03430-3*, Pub. by Princeton U Pr) Cal Prin Full Svc.

***Morrow, James R., Jr., et al.** Doing Sport Psychology. LC 99-86726. (Illus.). 384p. 2000. 55.00 (*0-7360-3188-X*) Human Kinetics.

Morrow, Jean & Miles, Ruth H. Walkway to the Future: Implementing the NCTM Standards at the K-4 Level. (Illus.). 1996. text. write for info. (*0-614-19586-1*, G196) Janson Pubns.

Morrow, Jodie B. & Lebov, Myrna. Not Just a Secretary: Using the Job to Get Ahead. LC 82-24744. (General Trade Bks.). 182p. 1984. pap. 12.95 (*0-471-87060-9*, 1-999) Wiley.

Morrow, John. The History of Political Thought: A Thematic Introduction. LC 97-23354. 464p. 1998. text 60.00 (*0-8147-5448-1*) NYU Pr.

— The History of Political Thought: A Thematic Introduction. 464p. 1998. pap. text 22.50 (*0-8147-5597-6*) NYU Pr.

— Young England: The "New" Generation. LC 98-53992. (Illus.). 192p. 1998. 56.00 (*0-7185-0145-4*); pap. 25.95 (*0-7185-0146-2*) Continuum.

Morrow, John, et al. Autoimmune Rheumatic Disease. 2nd ed. LC 98-28029. (Illus.). 288p. 1999. text 75.00 (*0-19-262883-6*) OUP.

Morrow, John, jt. auth. see Francis, Mark.

Morrow, John H. Building German Airpower, 1909-1914. LC 76-15287. 164p. reprint ed. pap. 50.90 (*0-8357-7466-X*, 202317100032) Bks Demand.

— German Air Power in World War I. LC 81-11588. 289p. reprint ed. pap. 89.60 (*0-7837-6466-9*, 204647000001) Bks Demand.

Morrow, John H., Jr. The Great War in the Air: Military Aviation from 1909 to 1921. LC 92-17437. (History of Aviation Ser.). (Illus.). 464p. 1993. 37.50 (*1-56098-238-1*) Smithsonian.

Morrow, John H., Jr. & Rogers, Earl, eds. A Yankee Ace in the RAF: The World War I Letters of Captain Bogart Rogers. LC 87-16161. (Modern War Studies). (Illus.). 256p. 1996. 24.95 (*0-7006-0798-6*) U Pr of KS.

Morrow, John H., ed. see Rivkin, Arnold.

Morrow, Judy G. The Best Thing about My Teacher: Notes of Appreciation from Students. LC 98-37670. 128p. 1999. pap. 5.99 (*0-8054-1661-7*) Broadman.

— Boomerabilia: I Remember. LC 98-6675. 128p. 1998. pap. 5.99 (*0-8054-1275-1*) Broadman.

— I Wish I Could Fly: When Kids Make a Wish. LC 98-37762. 128p. 1999. pap. 5.99 (*0-8054-1662-5*) Broadman.

— Life Is Too Short to Live Only for the Weekends: And 199 Other Timely Reminders for Joyful Living. LC 98-16684. 128p. 1998. pap. 5.99 (*0-8054-1244-1*) Broadman.

Morrow, Judy G. & Gordon, Nancy. Silent Cradle: Understanding in Time of Pregnancy Loss. 216p. 1998. pap. 11.95 (*0-89367-225-4*) Light & Life Comm.

Morrow, Katherine D. Greek Footwear & the Dating of Sculpture. LC 84-40500. (Illus.). 272p. 1986. text 40.00 (*0-299-10190-8*) U of Wis Pr.

— Greek Footwear & the Dating of Sculpture. LC 84-40500. (Wisconsin Studies in Classics). (Illus.). 263p. reprint ed. pap. 81.60 (*0-608-07015-7*, 206722200009) Bks Demand.

Morrow, Lance. Heart. 1995. 22.95 (*0-614-15434-0*) Warner Bks.

Morrow, Laura, jt. ed. see Atkins, G. Douglas.

Morrow, Laurie. Trout Tales & Other Angling Stories. LC 95-61183. 1995. 29.00 (*1-885106-16-5*) Wild Adven Pr.

Morrow, Laurie, ed. Cold Noses & Warm Hearts: Beloved Dog Stories by Great Authors. LC 96-41386. (Illus.). 232p. 1996. 25.00 (*1-57223-066-5*, 0665) Willow Creek Pr.

Morrow, Laurie, jt. auth. see Smith, Steve.

Morrow, Laurie, ed. see Ford, Corey.

***Morrow, Lesley M.** Getting Ready to Read with Mother Goose. (Illus.). 160p. 1999. pap., teacher ed. 49.50 (*0-8215-6951-1*) Sadlier.

— Getting Ready to Read with Mother Goose. (Illus.). 72p. (J). (ps-k). 1999. pap. 6.57 (*0-8215-6950-3*) Sadlier.

Morrow, Lesley M. The Literacy Center: Contexts for Reading & Writing. (Illus.). 240p. (Orig.). (C). 1997. pap. text 22.50 (*1-57110-022-9*) Stenhse Pubs.

— Literacy Development in the Early Years. 3rd ed. LC 96-10711. 418p. 1996. pap. text 51.00 (*0-205-17442-6*) P-H.

Morrow, Lesley M., ed. Family Literacy Connections in Schools & Communities. 280p. 1995. pap. 22.95 (*0-87207-127-8*) Intl Reading.

— A Survey of Family Literacy in the United States. 140p. 1995. pap. 14.95 (*0-87207-131-6*) Intl Reading.

Morrow, Lesley M., et al, eds. Resources in Early Literacy Development: An Annotated Bibliography. LC 92-28410. 58p. 1992. reprint ed. pap. 30.00 (*0-608-03472-X*, 206418200008) Bks Demand.

Morrow, Lesley M. & Walker, Barbara J. The Reading Team: A Handbook for Volunteer Tutors K-3. 40p. 1997. pap. 14.95 (*0-87207-185-5*, 185) Intl Reading.

Morrow, Lesley M., et al. Literacy Instruction in Half- & Whole-Day Kindergarten: Research to Practice. LC 98-12319. (Literacy Studies Ser.). 1998. pap. 24.95 (*0-87207-188-X*, 188) Intl Reading.

Morrow, Lesley M., jt. ed. see Strickland, Dorothy S.

Morrow, Lesley M., jt. ed. see Walker, Barbara.

***Morrow, Lesley Mandel, et al, contrib. by.** Discovering God's Child: A Faith Development Program for Three Year Olds. (Discovering God Ser.). (Illus.). 128p. (J). (ps). 1999. pap. 11.25 (*0-8215-2450-X*) Sadlier.

— Discovering God's Child, Guide: A Faith Development Program for Three Year Olds. (Discovering God Ser.). (Illus.). 212p. 1999. teacher ed., spiral bd. 24.99 (*0-8215-2451-8*) Sadlier.

— Discovering God's Loved: A Faith Development Program for Five Year Olds. rev. ed. (Discovering God Ser.). (Illus.). 128p. (J). (gr. k-1). 1999. pap. text 11.25 (*0-8215-2470-4*) Sadlier.

— Discovering God's World: A Faith Development Program for Four Year Olds. rev. ed. (Discovering God Ser.). (Illus.). 128p. (J). (ps-k). 1999. pap. text 11.25 (*0-8215-2460-7*) Sadlier.

Morrow, Lesley Mandel, jt. auth. see Strickland, Dorothy S.

Morrow, Linda, ed. see Adams, Faye.

Morrow, Linda, ed. see Deveraux, Jude.

Morrow, Lorna J., ed. The Teaching & Learning of Algorithms in School Mathematics: 1998 Yearbook. LC 98-3128. (Illus.). 256p. 1998. 27.00 (*0-87353-440-9*) NCTM.

Morrow, Lorna J., jt. ed. see Rowan, Thomas E.

***Morrow, Louis L.** My Catholic Faith: A Manual of Religion. (Illus.). 415p. (YA). (gr. 6 up). 2000. 39.95 (*0-9639032-6-8*) Sarto Hse.

***Morrow, Lynn & Myers-Phinney, Linda.** Shepherd of the Hills Country: Tourism Transforms the Ozarks, 1880s-1930s. LC 99-31450. 1999. pap. 24.00 (*1-55728-574-8*) U of Ark Pr.

Morrow, Lynn, jt. ed. see Keefe, James F.

***Morrow, Man.** The Greys: A Story of Hope for the Future. 283p. 2000. pap. 10.95 (*0-9701098-0-6*) Wheelchair Pubng.

Morrow, Marilyn, et al. Practicing the Application of Health Education Skill & Competencies. (Health Science Ser.). 400p. 1997. pap. 28.75 (*0-7637-0353-0*) Jones & Bartlett.

Morrow, Mary F. Sarah Winnemucca. (Raintree-Rivilo American Indian Stories Ser.). (Illus.). 32p. (J). (gr. 4-7). 1990. pap. 4.95 (*0-8114-4095-8*) Raintree Steck-V.

— Sarah Winnemucca: Paiute Native American Indian Stories. (Raintree-Rivilo American Indian Stories Ser.). 1996. 10.15 (*0-606-12504-3*, Pub. by Turtleback) Demco.

Morrow, Mary S. Concert Life in Haydn's Vienna: Aspects of a Developing Musical & Social Institution. LC 88-23385. (Sociology of Music Ser.: No. 7). (Illus.). 500p. 1989. lib. bdg. 47.00 (*0-918728-83-5*) Pendragon NY.

— German Music Criticism in the Late Eighteenth Century: Aesthetic Issues in Instrumental Music. LC 96-41039. 268p. (C). 1997. text 64.95 (*0-521-58227-X*) Cambridge U Pr.

Morrow, Muriel M., tr. see Paleoloque, Maurice.

Morrow, Nancy. Dreadful Games: The Play of Desire in the Nineteenth-Century Novel. LC 87-35902. 209p. 1988. 24.00 (*0-87338-358-3*) Kent St U Pr.

Morrow, Nancy & Clark, Marlene, eds. Currents of Inquiry: Readings for Academic Writing. LC 97-36270. xxvii, 496p. 1997. pap. text 34.95 (*1-55934-818-6*, 1818) Mayfield Pub.

Morrow, Nancy, ed. see Overlook Hospital Auxilary Staff.

Morrow, Nell. The Movie Mom's Guide to Family Movies. 1997. pap. 12.00 (*0-614-28117-2*, Avon Bks) Morrow Avon.

Morrow, Norma L. Being a Medical Transcriptionist. 208p. 1991. pap. text 37.80 (*0-89303-082-1*) P-H.

Morrow, Norman, ed. Interfacial Phenomena in Petroleum Recovery. (Surfactant Science Ser.: Vol. 36). (Illus.). 464p. 1990. text 199.00 (*0-8247-8385-9*) Dekker.

Morrow, Norman R. Proceedings of the 3rd International Symposium on Reservoir Wettability & Its Effect on Oil Recovery. (Illus.). viii, 200p. 1996. 50.00 (*0-941570-17-7*) U of Wyoming.

Morrow, Ord L. Gigantes Al Acecho. (SPA.). 136p. 1995. mass mkt. 4.99 (*0-8254-1481-4*, Edit Portavoz) Kregel.

Morrow, Pat & Morrow, Baiba. The Yukon. (Illus.). 128p. 1998. pap. 24.95 (*1-55209-108-2*) Firefly Bks Ltd.

Morrow, Pat, jt. photos by see Morrow, Baiba.

Morrow, Patrick. Bret Harte. LC 72-619588. (Western Writers Ser.: No. 5). (Illus.). 51p. (Orig.). (C). 1972. pap. 4.95 (*0-88430-004-8*) Boise St U W Writ Ser.

Morrow, Patrick, tr. Porcelain Butterfly. 1972. pap. 2.00 (*0-88031-005-7*) Invisible-Red Hill.

Morrow, Patrick D. Katherine Mansfield's Fiction. LC 92-74783. 1993. 29.95 (*0-87972-563-X*); pap. 10.95 (*0-87972-564-8*) Bowling Green Univ Popular Press.

— The Popular & the Serious in Select Twentieth-Century American Novels. LC 92-4342. 162p. 1992. lib. bdg. 79.95 (*0-7734-9496-0*) E Mellen.

— Post-Colonial Essays on South Pacific Literature. LC 97-49145. 200p. 1998. text 79.95 (*0-7734-8474-4*) E Mellen.

Morrow, Phyllis & Schneider, William, eds. When Our Words Return: Writing, Hearing, & Remembering Oral Traditions of Alaska & the Yukon. LC 95-32445. (C). 1995. 36.95 (*0-87421-199-9*); pap. 19.95 (*0-87421-195-6*) Utah St U Pr.

Morrow, R. H., jt. ed. see Vaughan, J. P.

Morrow, Ralph E. Washington University in St. Louis: A History. LC 96-6388. 757p. 1996. 69.95 (*1-883982-10-3*) MO Hist Soc.

Morrow, Raymond A. & Brown, David A. Critical Theory & Methodology: Interpretive Structuralism As a Research Program. LC 94-10888. (Contemporary Social Theory Ser.: Vol. 3). 320p. 1994. 62.00 (*0-8039-4682-1*); pap. 28.50 (*0-8039-4683-X*) Sage.

Morrow, Raymond A. & Torres, Carlos A., eds. Social Theory & Education: A Critique of Theories of Social & Cultural Reproduction. LC 94-3956. (SUNY Series, Teacher Empowerment & School Reform). 517p. (C). 1995. pap. text 24.95 (*0-7914-2252-6*) State U NY Pr.

***Morrow, Rebecca.** The 2000 Managing 401(K) Plans Yearbook. (Illus.). 200p. 1999. pap. 199.00 (*1-58673-004-5*) IOMA.

Morrow, Rob, photos by. Northern Exposures. (Illus.). 96p. (J). 1994. pap. 9.70 (*0-7868-6064-2*, Pub. by Hyperion) Time Warner.

Morrow, Robert. Immigration: Blessing or Burden? LC 97-3708. 144p. (J). (gr. 6-10). 1997. lib. bdg. 21.27 (*0-8225-2613-1*) Lerner Pub.

Morrow, Robert, ed. Dental Laboratory Procedures: Complete Dentures, 1. 600p. (C). (gr. 13). 1985. text 99.95 (*0-8016-3519-5*, 03519) Mosby Inc.

— The Indoor Air Quality Directory, 1992-1993. 375p. (Orig.). 1992. pap. 75.00 (*0-9633003-1-8*) IAQ Pubns.

— Lead Tech '92 Proceedings: Solutions for a Nation at Risk, 1992-1993. (Illus.). 650p. 1992. pap. 50.00 (*0-9633003-3-4*) IAQ Pubns.

Morrow, Rodger, ed. see Ryder, Thomas.

Morrow, Rosemary. Earth User's Guide to Permaculture. (Illus.). 144p. (Orig.). 1994. pap. 15.95 (*0-86417-514-0*, Pub. by Kangaroo Pr) Seven Hills Bk.

***Morrow, Rosemary.** Earth Users Guide to Permaculture. 152p. 2000. pap. 13.00 (*0-684-87201-3*) S&S Trade.

Morrow, Rosemary. Earthuser's Guide to Permaculture Teacher's Notes: Teacher's Notes. (Illus.). 128p. 1997. pap., teacher ed. 16.95 (*0-86417-800-X*, Pub. by Kangaroo Pr) Seven Hills Bk.

Morrow, Roy W. & Crain, Jeffrey S., eds. Applications of Inductively Coupled Plasma-Mass Spectrometry to Radionuclide Determinations, Vol. 2. LC 95-47789. (STP Ser.: No. 1344). (Illus.). 155p. 1998. pap. text 54.00 (*0-8031-2496-1*, STP1344) ASTM.

Morrow, Roy W., jt. ed. see Crain, Jeffrey S.

Morrow, S. Rex, jt. ed. see Fravel, Mark, Jr.

Morrow, Sandra. The Art of the Show: An Introduction to the Study of Exposition Management. unabridged ed. LC 97-73359. (Illus.). 400p. (Orig.). 1997. pap. text 49.95 (*0-9657982-0-8*) IAEM.

Morrow, Sue A. The Beginning of Wisdom: Sermons for Pentecost Middle Third. LC 92-45764. (Cycle B First Lesson Texts Ser.). 1993. pap. 7.50 (*1-55673-614-2*, 9339) CSS OH.

Morrow, Susan Brind. The Names of Things: Life Language, & Beginning in the Egyptian Desert. 240p. 1998. pap. 13.00 (*1-57322-680-7*, Riverhead Books) Putnam Pub Group.

***Morrow, Susan Swick, ed.** Lovies: Cherished Objects of Affection. (Illus.). 50p. 2000. pap. 19.95 (*0-9700122-0-9*) S S Morrow.

Morrow, T. B., et al, eds. Fluid Measurement & Instrumentation, 1994. LC 86-70582. (Fluid Engineering Division Conference Ser.: Vol. 183). 109p. 1994. pap. 35.00 (*0-7918-1366-5*) ASME.

— Industrial & Environmental Application of Fluid Mechanics 1994. LC 92-54703. (Fluid Engineering Division Conference Ser.: Vol. 186). 197p. 1994. pap. 37.50 (*0-7918-1369-X*) ASME.

Morrow, T. B., jt. ed. see Bajura, R. A.

***Morrow, Terry.** Walking Together. 1999. pap. write for info. (*1-58235-285-2*) Watermrk Pr.

Morrow, Theodore, tr. see Libanio, J. B.

Morrow, Theresa. Seattle Survival Guide III: The Essential Handbook for Urban Living. 3rd ed. LC 96-19980. (Illus.). 384p. (Orig.). 1996. reprint ed. pap. 19.95 (*1-57061-089-4*) Sasquatch Bks.

— Seattle Survival Guide II: The Essential Handbook for City Living. 2nd rev. ed. (Illus.). 420p. 1993. pap. 17.95 (*0-912365-84-6*) Sasquatch Bks.

Morrow, Thomas J., jt. auth. see Kennedy, Joyce L.

Morrow, Thomas R., ed. see Hetrick, Joyce.

***Morrow, Tom.** Shotgun Care & Maintenance: An Orvis Field Guide, 1. (Illus.). 128p. 2000. 16.95 (*1-57223-316-8*) Willow Creek Pr.

Morrow, Virginia. Understanding Families: Children's Perspectives. 76p. 1998. pap. 17.00 (*1-900990-27-X*, Pub. by Natl Childrens Bur) Paul & Co Pubs.

Morrow, Wanda. Ave & Vale. 1998. pap. write for info. (*1-58235-021-3*) Watermrk Pr.

Morrs, Hein & Palomba, Rossella, eds. Population, Family, & Welfare: A Comparative Survey of European Attitudes, Vol. 1. (Illus.). 314p. 1995. text 69.00 (*0-19-828846-8*) OUP.

An Asterisk (*) at the beginning of an entry indicates that the title is appearing for the first time.

Mors, Walter B. & Rizzini, Carlos T. Useful Plants of Brazil. LC 66-17891. 181p. reprint ed. pap. 56.20 (0-608-13511-9, 201629300003) Bks Demand.

Mors, Walter B., et al. Medicinal Plants of Brazil. DeFilipps, Robert A., ed. (Medicinal Plants of the World Ser.: No. 6). (Illus.). Date not set. write for info. (0-917256-42-5) Ref Pubns.

Mors, Walter P. Consumer Credit Finance Charges: Rate Information & Quotation. (Financial Research Program II: Studies in Consumer Installment Financing: No. 12). 150p. 1965. 39.30 (0-87014-128-7) Natl Bur Econ Res.

Morsak, Louis C., jt. auth. see Faussner, Hans C.

Morsbach, Helmut. Simple Etiquette in Japan. 1988. pap. 20.00 (0-904404-46-3, Pub. by P Norbury Pubns Ltd) St Mut.

— Simple Guide to Japan: Customs & Etiquette. 3rd ed. 1997. pap. text. write for info. (1-86034-021-0, Pub. by MAGI1 UK) Midpt Trade.

Morsbach, Helmut & Stach, Babett, eds. Posters of GDR Films, 1945-1990. (Film-Television-Sound Archive Ser.: Vol. 2). 149p. 1991. lib. bdg. 60.00 (3-598-22591-1) K G Saur Verlag.

Morsbach, Helmut, et al. Remembering the Katakana. 96p. 1990. pap., suppl. ed. 8.00 (0-87040-860-7) Japan Pubns USA.

Morsberger, Robert & Lesser, Stephen, eds. American Screenwriters. (Dictionary of Literary Biography Ser.: Vol. 26). (Illus.). 400p. 1984. text 155.00 (0-8103-0917-3) Gale.

Morsch, Gary & Hall, Eddy. Ministry: It's Not Just for Ministers. 128p. (Orig.). 1993. pap. 8.99 (0-8341-1510-7) Beacon Hill.

Morsch, Gary & Nelson, Dean. Heart & Soul. LC 97-26956. 180p. 1997. per. 13.99 (0-8341-1681-2) Beacon Hill.

Morsch, Gary, jt. auth. see Hall, Eddy.

Morsch, Lucille M. Check List of New Jersey Imprints, 1784-1800. 1939. 25.00 (0-527-01906-2) Periodicals Srv.

Morschauser, Joseph, III, jt. auth. see Becton, F. Julian.

Morschauser, Scott. Threat-Formulae in Ancient Egypt. xvi, 268p. (Orig.). 1991. pap. 72.00 (0-9613805-5-1) Halgo Inc.

Morschauser, Scott, jt. ed. see Kort, Ann.

Morscher, E. W., ed. Endoprosthetics: Commemorative Volume for Dr. Otto Frey-Zund. LC 95-30520. (Illus.). 432p. 1995. 152.00 (3-540-58499-4) Spr-Verlag.

Morscher, Edgar, et al, eds. Applied Ethics in a Troubled World. LC 97-51864. (Philosophical Studies). 315p. 1998. write for info. (0-7923-4965-2) Kluwer Academic.

Morse. Age of Virtue. LC 99-18157. 1999. text 65.00 (0-312-22353-6) St Martin.

— Classic Rock Stories: The Stories behind the Greatest Songs of All Time. 2nd ed. LC 98-14747. (Illus.). 212p. (YA). 1998. pap. 12.95 (0-312-18067-5) St Martin.

— Mangerial Accounting: Ready Notes. 1997. pap., student ed. 24.69 (0-256-19594-3) McGraw.

— Methods of Theoretical Physics, Vol. 2. 1999. 22.50 (0-07-043353-4) McGraw.

— Nursing Research. 2nd ed. 208p. 1995. pap. 37.95 (1-56593-586-1, 1194) Singular Publishing.

— Practical Guide to Teaching in the Fire Service. LC 98-14459. 1998. pap. 12.95 (0-7668-0432-1) Delmar.

Morse & Davis. Cash Flow & Financial Statement Analysis. (AQ - Managerial Accounting Ser.). 1995. pap., suppl. ed. 12.95 (0-538-85605-X) S-W Pub.

— Management Accounting: A Strategic Approach. (AB - Accounting Principles Ser.). (C). 1995. mass mkt., student ed. 21.95 (0-538-84491-4) S-W Pub.

— Management Accounting: A Strategic Approach. (AQ - Managerial Accounting Ser.). 1996. text 5.95 (0-538-86265-3) S-W Pub.

Morse & Stoiber, Richard E., eds. Crystal Identification with the Polarizing Microscope. LC 93-27087. (Illus.). 304p. (C). (gr. 13). 1994. text 83.95 (0-412-04821-3) Chapman & Hall.

***Morse, et al.** Cash Flow & finance Statement Analysis Strategic Approach: Management Accounting. 2nd ed. (SWC-Accounting Ser.). 1999. pap. 13.00 (0-324-00805-8) Sth-Wstrn College.

Morse, jt. auth. see Dyckman, Thomas R.

Morse, jt. auth. see Long.

Morse, A. Reynolds. The Quest for Redonda. (Illus.). 160p. 1986. pap. 10.00 (0-317-39306-5) Reynolds Morse.

— The Works of M. P. Shiel, 2 vols., Vol. 2, Pts. 1 & 2. rev. ed. Orig. Title: Works of M. P. Shiel, a Study in Bibliography 1948. (Illus.). 864p. 1980. 90.00 (0-686-62335-5); pap. 65.00 (0-686-62336-3); 75.00 (0-685-04347-9) Reynolds Morse.

Morse, A. S., ed. Control Using Logic-Based Switching. LC 96-44550. (Lecture Notes in Control & Information Sciences: Vol. 222). (Illus.). 280p. 1996. pap. 54.00 (3-540-76097-0) Spr-Verlag.

Morse, Abner. Genealogical Register of the Inhabitants & History of the Town of Sherborn & Hollister, Ma. (Illus.). 340p. 1993. reprint ed. lib. bdg. 39.00 (0-8328-2889-0) Higginson Bk Co.

— Grout from "Genealogy of Several Ancient Puritans" (Illus.). 61p. 1997. reprint ed. pap. 12.00 (0-8328-8850-8); reprint ed. lib. bdg. 22.00 (0-8328-8849-4) Higginson Bk Co.

Morse, Albert L. The Tattooists. Walsh, John A., ed. (Illus.). 1977. 100.00 (0-918320-01-1) A L Morse.

Morse, Alexander P. Treatise on Citizenship: By Birth & by Naturalization with Reference to the Law of Nations, Roman Civil Law, Law of the United States of America & the Law of France - Including Provisions in the Federal Constitution, & in the Several State Constitutions, in Respect of Citizenship; Together with Decisions Thereon of the Federal & State Courts. LC 97-1953. xxviii, 385p. 1997. reprint ed. 55.00 (0-8377-2483-X, Rothman) W S Hein.

Morse, Ann. America's Newcomers: Employment & Training Programs for Refugees & Immigrants. 18p. 1993. 10.00 (1-55516-927-9, 9360) Natl Conf State Legis.

Morse, Ann, ed. America's Newcomers: An Immigrant Policy Handbook. LC 95-620352. 108p. 1994. 35.00 (1-55516-996-1, 9366) Natl Conf State Legis.

Morse, Ann & Dunlap, Jonathan C. America's Newcomers: Community Relations & Ethnic Diversity. 20p. 1994. 10.00 (1-55516-995-3, 9365) Natl Conf State Legis.

***Morse, Ann, et al.** America's Newcomers: Mending the Safety Net for Immigrants. LC 98-219028. ix, 77 p. 1998. write for info. (1-55516-707-1) Natl Conf State Legis.

Morse, Anne N. & Morse, Samuel C., texts. Bridge of Fire: Two Potters East & West. (Illus.). 24p. 1992. 5.00 (0-916746-16-X) Springfield Lib & Mus.

Morse, Anthony P., jt. auth. see Kenyon, Hewitt.

Morse, Arthur D. While Six Million Died: A Chronicle of American Apathy. 420p. 1998. pap. 16.95 (0-87951-836-7, Pub. by Overlook Pr) Penguin Putnam.

Morse, Arthur L. Understanding Reality: The Past... The Present... The Future. LC 98-94892. 160p. 1999. 24.95 (0-9669269-0-0); pap. 14.95 (0-9669269-1-9) Artsbks.

Morse, Birgit Faber, jt. auth. see Rouse, Irving.

Morse-Boycott, Desmond L. Lead, Kindly Light. LC 70-107728. (Essay Index Reprint Ser.). 1977. 18.95 (0-8369-1529-1) Ayer.

Morse, C. G., jt. auth. see Rubino-Sammartano, M.

Morse, C. Scott. Soulwind TPB Vol. 1: The Kid from Planet Earth. (Illus.). 144p. 1997. pap. 9.95 (1-887279-64-4) Image Comics.

Morse, C. Wesley. Environmental Consultation. LC 83-24802. 193p. 1984. 57.95 (0-275-91233-7, C1233, Praeger Pubs) Greenwood.

Morse, Carl & Larkin, Joan, eds. Gay & Lesbian Poetry in Our Time. (Stonewall Inn Editions Ser.). 432p. 1989. pap. 15.95 (0-312-03836-4) St Martin.

Morse, Carlton E. Killer at the Wheel. 400p. 1987. 16.95 (0-940249-01-4) Seven Stones Pr.

— A Lavish of Sin. 224p. 1987. 14.95 (0-940249-02-2) Seven Stones Pr.

— One Man's Family Album. (Illus.). 160p. (Orig.). 1988. pap. 8.95 (0-940249-05-7) Seven Stones Pr.

— Stuff the Lady's Hatbox. (I Love a Mystery Novel Ser.). 342p. (Orig.). 1988. 16.95 (0-940249-03-0); pap. 9.95 (0-940249-04-9) Seven Stones Pr.

Morse, Carmel L. Audio-Visual Primer. LC 82-84727. (Illus.). 75p. (Orig.). 1983. pap. 5.95 (0-911997-00-8) Backwoods Pubns.

Morse, Chandler, jt. auth. see Barnett, Harold J.

Morse, Chandler, ed. see Copeland, Morris A.

Morse, Charlotte C., et al, eds. Uses of Manuscripts in Literary Studies: Essays in Memory of Judson Boyce Allen. (Studies in Medieval Culture: No. 31). 1992. pap. 15.00 (1-879288-14-1); boxed set 35.00 (1-879288-13-3) Medieval Inst.

Morse, Christopher. Not Every Spirit: A Dogmatics of Christian Disbelief. LC 93-45865. 432p. (C). 1994. pap. 24.00 (1-56338-087-0) TPI PA.

***Morse, Christopher Hill.** Ragged Mountain Revelry. large type ed. (Illus.). 74p. (YA). (gr. 1-12). 2000. pap. 25.00 (0-9678775-0-4) Oculus Pr.

Morse, Christopher J., jt. auth. see Klein, Irving J.

Morse-Cluley, Elizabeth & Read, Richard. Webster's New World Power Vocabulary. 2nd ed. LC 93-47434. 256p. (Orig.). 1994. 10.00 (0-671-88821-8) Prntice Hall Bks.

Morse, Constance. Music & Music-Makers. LC 68-54363. (Essay Index Reprint Ser.). 1977. 22.95 (0-8369-0724-8) Ayer.

Morse, D., et al, eds. Guide to Prosthetic Cardiac Valves. (Illus.). xvi, 362p. 1985. 240.00 (0-387-96123-2) Spr-Verlag.

Morse, D. R. & Pollack, R. L. The Stress-Free, Anti-Aging Diet. (Stress in Modern Society Ser.: No. 19). 1989. 32.50 (0-404-63270-X) AMS Pr.

Morse, Dale & Zimmerman, Jerold. Managerial Accounting. 104p. (C). 1997. text 22.50 (0-256-26479-1, Irwn McGrw-H) McGrw-H Hghr Educ.

Morse, Dale & Zimmerman, Jerold L. Managerial Accounting. LC 96-46238. 864p. (C). 1996. text 70.95 (0-256-18955-2, Irwn McGrw-H) McGrw-H Hghr Educ.

Morse, Dan, photos by. Albert Bierstadt's West. (Illus.). 90p. 1997. pap. 25.00 (0-935037-90-X) G Peters Gallery.

— Carol Mothner: Theatre of Dolls. LC 93-84654. (Illus.). 16p. 1993. pap. 10.00 (0-935037-50-0) G Peters Gallery.

— Nicolai Fechin: Across Two Continents. LC 78-58003. (Illus.). 84p. 1997. pap. 25.00 (0-935037-87-X) G Peters Gallery.

— Rediscovering the Landscape of the Americas. (Illus.). 111p. (Orig.). 1996. pap. 19.95 (0-935037-95-0) G Peters Gallery.

— Willard Nash, an American Cezanne. (Illus.). 88p. (Orig.). 1997. pap. 25.00 (0-935037-92-6) G Peters Gallery.

Morse, Dan F. Sloan: A Paleoindian Dalton Cemetery in Arkansas. LC 96-54013. (Series in Archaeological Inquiry). (Illus.). 208p. 1997. text 70.00 (1-56098-712-X) Smithsonian.

— The Steuben Village & Mounds: A Multicomponent Late Hopewell Site in Illinois. LC 64-7124. (Anthropological Papers: No. 21). (Illus.). 176p. reprint ed. 54.60 (0-8357-9613-2, 201118200073) Bks Demand.

Morse, Dan F., ed. see Lucas Powell, Mary.

Morse, Daniel P., Jr. The History of the Fiftieth Aero Squadron. (Great War Ser.: No. 6). (Illus.). 110p. 1990. reprint ed. 29.95 (0-89839-151-2) Battery Pr.

Morse, David. American Romanticism, Vol. 2. LC 85-13424. 144p. 1986. 52.00 (0-389-20587-7, N8145 3) B&N Imports.

— High Victorian Culture. LC 92-18942. 568p. (C). 1992. text 60.00 (0-8147-5487-2) NYU Pr.

— High Victorian Culture. LC 92-18942. (C). 1993. pap. text 20.00 (0-8147-5504-6) NYU Pr.

— Perspectives on Romanticism: A Transformational Analysis. 324p. 1981. 45.00 (0-389-20164-2, N6934) B&N Imports.

Morse, David, intro. CyberDictionary: Your Guide to the Wired World. LC 96-216402. 300p. 1996. pap. 17.95 (1-888232-04-8) Knowldge Exchange.

Morse, David E. The Iron Bridge. LC 97-27849. 448p. 1998. 25.00 (0-15-100259-2) Harcourt.

Morse, David H., ed. Acquisitions in Health Sciences Libraries. LC 96-46948. (Current Practice in Health Sciences Librarianship Ser.: Vol. 5). 256p. 1996. 39.50 (0-8108-3052-3) Scarecrow.

Morse, David L., ed. see Voegelin, Eric.

***Morse, Davis.** Management Accounting: A Strategic Approach. 2nd ed. LC 99-29552. (SWC-Accounting Ser.). 704p. 1999. 106.95 (0-538-87889-4) Thomson Learn.

Morse, Dean. The Peripheral Worker. LC 73-76251. 222p. reprint ed. pap. 68.90 (0-608-15858-5, 203071700070) Bks Demand.

Morse, Dean & Gray, Susan. Early Retirement: Boon or Bane?, a Study of Three Large Corporations. LC 79-54970. (Conservation of Human Resources Ser.: No. 14). (Illus.). 154p. 1981. text 38.50 (0-916672-44-1) Rowman.

Morse, Dean W. Pride Against Prejudice: Work in the Lives of Older Blacks & Young Puerto Ricans. LC 78-65534. (Conservation of Human Resources Ser.: No. 9), 254p. 1981. text 38.50 (0-916672-67-0) Rowman.

Morse, Dean W., et al. Life after Early Retirement: The Experiences of Lower Level Workers. LC 81-70970. (Conservation of Human Resources Ser.: Vol. 17). 206p. 1983. text 53.50 (0-916672-62-X) Rowman.

Morse, Deborah D., jt. ed. see Barreca, Regina.

Morse, Donald, ed. see Scherr, Barry J.

Morse, Donald E., ed. The Fantastic in World Literature & the Arts: Selected Essays from the Fifth International Conference on the Fantastic in the Arts, 28. LC 87-7424. (Contributions to the Study of Science Fiction & Fantasy Ser.: No. 28). 264p. 1987. 69.50 (0-313-25526-1, MFA/) Greenwood.

Morse, Donald E., et al, eds. The Celebration of the Fantastic: Selected Papers from the Tenth Anniversary International Conference on the Fantastic in the Arts, 49. LC 91-37133. (Contributions to the Study of Science Fiction & Fantasy Ser.: No. 49). 328p. 1992. 65.00 (0-313-27814-8, MFO/, Greenwood Pr) Greenwood.

— A Small Nation's Contribution to the World: Essays on Anglo-Irish Literature & Language. (Irish Literary Studies Ser.). 250p. (C). 1994. lib. bdg. 59.00 (0-86140-375-4, Pub. by Smyth) B&N Imports.

Morse, Donald E. & Csilla, Bertha, eds. More Real Than Reality: The Fantastic in Irish Literature & the Arts, 45. LC 90-47537. (Contributions to the Study of Science Fiction & Fantasy Ser.: No. 45). 288p. 1991. 59.95 (0-313-26612-3, MFM/, Greenwood Pr) Greenwood.

***Morse, Donald R.** Searching for Eternity: A Scientist's Spiritual Journey to Overcome Death Anxiety. 420p. 2000. pap. 29.95 (0-940829-27-4) Eagle Wing Bks.

Morse, Donald R. & Pollack, Robert L. Nutrition, Stress & Aging: An Holistic Approach. LC 87-45805. (Stress in Modern Society Ser.: No. 17). 1988. 32.50 (0-404-63268-8) AMS Pr.

Morse, Douglass H. American Warblers: An Ecological & Behavioral Perspective. LC 89-31622. (Illus.). 384p. 1980. 48.95 (0-674-03035-4) HUP.

— Behavioral Mechanisms in Ecology. LC 80-12130. 391p. 1980. 46.50 (0-674-06460-7) HUP.

— Behavioral Mechanisms in Ecology. LC 80-12130. 391p. 1982. pap. 18.95 (0-674-06461-5) HUP.

Morse, Edgar & Curran, Thomas, eds. Silver in the Golden State: Images & Essays Celebrating the History & Art of Silver in California. (Artisans & the Arts Ser.). (Illus.). 130p. 1986. lib. bdg. 43.00 (0-8026-0021-2) Univ Pub Assocs.

Morse, Edward L. Foreign Policy & Interdependence in Gaullist France. LC 72-5391. 351p. 1973. reprint ed. pap. 108.90 (0-7837-9395-2, 206014000004) Bks Demand.

Morse, Edward L., ed. see Morse, Samuel F.

Morse, Edward S. Catalogue of the Morse Collection of Japanese Pottery. LC 77-83037. (Illus.). 544p. 1979. reprint ed. boxed set 60.00 (0-8048-1299-3) Tuttle Pubng.

***Morse, Edward S.** Glimpses of China & Chinese Homes. 225p. 2000. text 110.00 (0-7103-0703-9) Col U Pr.

Morse, Edward S. Glimpses of China & Chinese Homes. (Illus.). 216p. 1993. reprint ed. lib. bdg. 35.00 (0-8328-3102-6) Higginson Bk Co.

— Japan, Day by Day. LC 90-47731. (Illus.). 908p. 1990. reprint ed. 39.95 (0-87797-190-0) Cherokee.

— Japanese Homes & Their Surroundings. (Illus.). 372p. 1961. reprint ed. pap. 9.95 (0-486-20746-3) Dover.

— Japanese Homes & Their Surroundings. LC 76-157262. (Illus.). 408p. 1971. reprint ed. pap. 16.95 (0-8048-0998-4) Tuttle Pubng.

Morse, Edward S. Was Middle America Peopled from Asia? (LC History-America-E). 1898. reprint ed. lib. bdg. 79.00 (0-7812-4392-0) Rprt Serv.

Morse, Elisabeth, jt. ed. see Hollingsworth, Dorothy.

Morse, Eric. Friday the Thirteenth: Jason's Curse. (Tales from Camp Crystal Lake Ser.: Bk. 2). 192p. (Orig.). (YA). 1994. mass mkt. 3.99 (0-425-14339-2) Berkley Pub.

— Friday the Thirteenth: Mother's Day. (Tales from Camp Crystal Lake Ser.: Bk. 1). 192p. (Orig.). (YA). 1994. mass mkt. 3.50 (0-425-14292-2) Berkley Pub.

— Friday the Thirteenth Bk. 4: Tales from Camp Crystal Lake: Road Trip. 192p. (Orig.). (YA). (gr. 7 up). 1994. mass mkt. 3.50 (0-425-14383-X) Berkley Pub.

Morse, Eric W. Freshwater Saga: Memoirs of a Lifetime of Wilderness Canoeing. 1987. pap. 12.95 (0-8020-6657-7) U of Toronto Pr.

— Fur Trade Canoe Routes of Canada: Then & Now. rev. ed. (Illus.). 1979. pap. 12.95 (0-8020-6384-5) U of Toronto Pr.

— Fur Trade Canoe Routes of Canada: Then & Now. 2nd ed. LC 80-478235. (Canadian University Paperbooks Ser.: 239). 136p. reprint ed. pap. 42.20 (0-608-13754-5, 205547700022) Bks Demand.

Morse, F. L. Thomaston Scrapbook, 2 vols. in 1. (Illus.). 512p. 1997. write for info. (0-89725-330-2, 1852, Penobscot Pr) Picton Pr.

Morse, Flo. The Shakers & the World's People. LC 87-8223. (Illus.). 399p. 1987. reprint ed. pap. 19.95 (0-87451-426-6) U Pr of New Eng.

— The Story of the Shakers. LC 85-31430. (Illus.). 128p. 1986. pap. 10.00 (0-88150-062-3, Pub. by Countryman) Norton.

Morse, Flo & Newton, Vincent, eds. A Young Shaker's Guide to Good Manners: A Facsimile of a Juvenile Guide, or Manual of Good Manners, 1844. fac. ed. LC 98-12026. (Illus.). 72p. 1998. 14.95 (0-88150-418-1, Pub. by Countryman) Norton.

Morse, G. Company Law, Charlesworth. (C). 1987. 100.00 (0-7855-4251-5, Pub. by Witherby & Co) St Mut.

Morse, Gary A. Therapist As Supervisor & Coach. LC 98-23837. 311p. 1998. pap. text 35.00 (0-7506-7095-9) Buttrwrth-Heinemann.

Morse, Geoffrey, jt. auth. see Whittaker, Andrew M.

Morse, George P. America Twice Betrayed: Reversing Fifty Years of Government Security Failure. LC 95-14067. 376p. 1995. 23.50 (0-910155-32-1) Bartleby Pr.

Morse, George P. The Mass: Its Mysteries Revealed. 61p. (YA). (gr. 4 up). pap. 7.95 (0-9672595-0-9) Caths Comitd Pope.

Morse, George W. Retention & Expansion of Existing Businesses: Theory & Practice in Business Visitation Programs. LC 89-11070. (Illus.). 214p. 1990. text 39.95 (0-8138-0133-8) Iowa St U Pr.

Morse, Gertrude. The Dogs May Bark: But the Caravan Moves On. Morse, Helen, ed. 428p. 1998. pap. 19.99 (0-89900-671-X) College Pr Pub.

Morse, Gladys K. A Potpourri of Pleasantries. Bickford, Gail H., ed. (Illus.). 60p. (Orig.). 1993. pap. 6.00 (0-945069-01-4) Freedom Pr Assocs.

Morse, Gordon. My Maui. pap. 9.95 (1-885129-09-2) My Island.

— Pugets. 1995. pap. text 11.95 (1-885129-05-X) My Island.

Morse, H. Newcomb. The Thinkers. 270p. (C). 1994. lib. bdg. 38.00 (0-8191-9666-5) U Pr of Amer.

Morse, Harriet. Gardening in the Shade. LC 81-23231. (Illus.). 242p. 1982. pap. 13.95 (0-917304-16-0) Timber.

Morse, Harriet K. Elizabethan Pageantry. LC 68-56511. (Illus.). 128p. 1972. reprint ed. 27.95 (0-405-08798-5, Pub. by Blom Pubns) Ayer.

Morse, Harry N. Graphic Description of Pacific Coast Outlaws: Thrilling Exploits of Their Arch-Enemy, Sheriff Harry N. Morse. (Great West & Indian Ser.: Vol. 11). (Illus.). 1990. 23.95 (0-87026-074-X) Westernlore.

Morse, Helen, ed. see Morse, Gertrude.

Morse, Henry. Practical Guide to Teaching Adults. LC 98-37515. (Electrical Trades Ser.). 65p. 1998. pap. text 12.95 (0-7668-1134-4) Delmar.

— Suicide: An Essay on Comparative Moral Statistics. LC 74-25770. (European Sociology Ser.). 402p. 1975. reprint ed. 29.95 (0-405-06524-8) Ayer.

Morse, Howard H. Historic Old Rhinebeck, Echoes of Two Centuries: A Hudson River & Post Road Colonial Town...Historical, Genealogical, Biographical, Traditional. (Illus.). 448p. 1997. reprint ed. lib. bdg. 47.00 (0-8328-6210-X) Higginson Bk Co.

Morse, Howard H. & Kelly, Arthur C. Historic Old Rhinebeck, Echoes of Two Centuries: A Hudson River & Post Road Colonial Town. LC 77-368871. (Illus.). 509p. 1977. reprint ed. lib. bdg. 26.00 (1-56012-035-5, 34) Kinship Rhinebeck.

Morse, Ivan E. & Tse, Francis L. Measurement & Instrumentations in Engineering Principles & Basic Laboratory Experiments. (Mechanical Engineering Ser.: Vol. 67). (Illus.). 784p. 1989. text 85.00 (0-8247-8086-8) Dekker.

Morse, J. G., ed. Industry-University Advanced Materials Conference: Proceedings of a Conference. LC 87-1716. (Illus.). 410p. reprint ed. pap. 127.10 (0-608-17833-0, 203259000080) Bks Demand.

Morse, J. H. & Leavitt, Emily W. Morse Genealogy, Being a Revision of the Memorial of the Morse Publication by Abner Morse in 1850, 2 vols. in 1. 596p. 1989. reprint ed. pap. 90.00 (0-8328-0885-7); reprint ed. lib. bdg. 98.00 (0-8328-0884-9) Higginson Bk Co.

Morse, J. M., ed. Cross-Cultural Nursing: Anthropological Approaches to Nursing. vi, 144p. 1989. pap. text 35.00 (2-88124-383-5) Gordon & Breach.

Morse, J. N., ed. Organizations: Multiple Agents with Multiple Criteria, Newark, 1980. Proceedings. (Lecture Notes in Economics & Mathematical Systems Ser.: Vol. 190). (Illus.). 509p. 1981. 55.50 (0-387-10821-1) Spr-Verlag.

Morse, J. Thomas, et al. The Feeling Fun House: Feelings: Dealing with Feelings. Gouge, Betty et al, eds. LC 85-45423. (KidSkills Interpersonal Skill Ser.). (Illus.). 45p. (J). (gr. 2-3). 1985. lib. bdg. 9.95 (0-934275-03-3) Fam Skills.

— An Island Adventure: Self-Esteem: Being a Friend to

M

Myself. Gouge, Betty et al, eds. LC 85-45429. (KidSkills Interpersonal Skill Ser.). (Illus.). 47p. (J). (gr. 2-3). 1985. lib. bdg. 9.95 (*0-934275-01-7*) Fam Skills.

— Kid Skills Interpersonal Skill Series: An Island Adventure: Self-Esteem: Being A Friend to Myself. unabridged ed. LC 85-45429. (KidSkills Interpersonal Skill Ser.). (J). (gr. 1-3). 1985. 13.95 incl. audio (*0-934275-14-9*) Fam Skills.

— Lair of the Jade Tiger: Friendship: Keeping Friends. Gouge, Betty et al, eds. LC 85-81270. (KidSkills Interpersonal Skill Ser.). (Illus.). 48p. (J). (gr. 2-3). 1986. lib. bdg. 9.95 (*0-934275-07-6*) Fam Skills.

— The Land of Listening: Listening: Getting & Giving Attention. Gouge, Betty et al, eds. LC 85-45429. (KidSkills Interpersonal Skill Ser.). (Illus.). 45p. (J). (gr. 2-3). 1985. lib. bdg. 9.95 (*0-934275-00-9*) Fam Skills.

— A Lasting Friend: Friendship: Making Friends. Gouge, Betty et al, eds. LC 85-45422. (KidSkills Interpersonal Skill Ser.). (Illus.). 45p. (J). (gr. 2-3). 1985. lib. bdg. 9.95 (*0-934275-06-8*) Fam Skills.

Morse, J. Thomas, ed. see Gouge, Betty, et al.

Morse, J. W. & Mackenzie, Fred T., eds. Geochemistry & Sedimentary Carbonates No. 48: Developments in Sedimentology. 696p. 1990. 184.75 (*0-444-87391-0*); pap. 87.25 (*0-444-88781-4*) Elsevier.

Morse, James K. Jedidiah Morse: A Champion of New England Orthodoxy. LC 39-11247. reprint ed. 20.00 (*0-404-04504-9*) AMS Pr.

Morse, Jane C., ed. Beatrix Potter's Americans: Selected Letters. LC 81-7258. (Illus.). 232p. 1982. 35.95 (*0-87675-282-2*) Horn Bk.

Morse, Jane L. Off to College, 1998: A Guide for College Bound Students. 68p. 1998. pap. text 3.00 (*0-9654246-1-8*) Dees Comm.

Morse, Janice M. Preventing Patient Falls. 200p. 1996. 46.00 (*0-7619-0592-8*); pap. 21.95 (*0-7619-0593-6*) Sage.

Morse, Janice M., ed. Completing a Qualitative Project: Details & Dialogue. LC 97-4679. 432p. 1997. 58.00 (*0-7619-0600-2*); pap. 27.95 (*0-7619-0601-0*) Sage.

— Critical Issues in Qualitative Research Methods. (C). 1993. text 58.00 (*0-8039-5042-X*); pap. text 26.95 (*0-8039-5043-8*) Sage.

— Qualitative Health Research. (Illus.). 272p. (C). 1992. 58.00 (*0-8039-4774-7*) Sage.

— Qualitative Nursing Research: A Contemporary Dialogue. rev. ed. (Illus.). 360p. (C). 1990. text 52.00 (*0-8039-4078-5*); pap. text 24.50 (*0-8039-4079-3*) Sage.

Morse, Janice M. & Field, Peggy A. Qualitative Research Methods. 2nd ed. (Illus.). 304p. 1995. pap. 26.00 (*0-8039-7327-6*) Sage.

— Qualitative Research Methods for Health Professionals. 2nd ed. LC 95-11488. (Illus.). 254p. 1995. 54.00 (*0-8039-7326-8*) Sage.

Morse, Janice M. & Johnson, Joy L., eds. The Illness Experience: Expressions of Suffering. (Illus.). 320p. 1991. 48.00 (*0-8039-4053-X*); pap. 22.95 (*0-8039-4054-8*) Sage.

Morse, Jedidiah. American Gazetteer. LC 71-146409. (First American Frontier Ser.). (Illus.). 1971. reprint ed. 52.95 (*0-405-02871-7*) Ayer.

— American Gazetteer, 1797. 629p. 1979. 23.20 (*0-686-27821-6*) Bookmark.

— American Geography: Or, a View of the Present Situation of the United States of America. LC 70-125754. (American Environmental Studies). 1976. reprint ed. 33.95 (*0-405-02680-3*) Ayer.

— A Report to the Secretary of War of the U. S. on Indian Affairs. LC 70-108516. (Illus.). 400p. 1972. reprint ed. 69.00 (*0-403-00345-8*) Scholarly.

Morse, Jennifer. Apprentice to Power: A Woman's Awakening. 272p. (Orig.). 1996. pap. 13.95 (*0-9650958-1-9*) Acacia Pubng.

Morse, Jeremy. Do We Know Where We're Going? LC HG3881.Z677. (Per Jacobsson Lecture Ser.: Vol. 1985). 40p. reprint ed. pap. 30.00 (*0-608-08771-8*, 206941000004) Bks Demand.

— Sabemos Adonde Nos Dirigimos? LC HG3881.M677. (Conferencia Per Jacobsson de 1985 Ser.). (SPA.). 44p. reprint ed. pap. 30.00 (*0-608-08773-4*, 206941200004) Bks Demand.

— Savons-Nous ou Nous Allons? LC HG3881.M677. (Fondation Per Jacobsson Conference de 1985 Ser.). (FRE.). 44p. reprint ed. pap. 30.00 (*0-608-08772-6*, 206941100004) Bks Demand.

Morse, Jerome G. & Olerud, Lesley A. Industry-University Advanced Materials Conference Two, 1989: Proceedings. (Illus.). 888p. 1989. pap. text 25.00 (*0-9624027-0-2*) Advan Mat Inst.

Morse, Jill, jt. auth. see Whetsell-Mitchell, Juliann.

Morse, Jim. Big Band Era. Skogen, Kirsten, ed. (Illus.). 120p. (Orig.). 1992. 5.95 (*1-881550-00-1*) Hiawatha Pubs.

***Morse, Jim.** Minnesota Free: The State's Best No-Charge Attractions. 271p. 1998. pap. 14.95 (*0-931714-78-8*, Pub. by Nodin Pr) Bookmen Inc.

Morse, Joan M., jt. ed. see Ansell, Dorothy I.

Morse, John C., ed. Trichoptera, 4th International Symposium: Proceedings: Clemson, South Carolina, 11-16 July 1983. (Entomologica Ser.: No. 30). 512p. 1984. lib. bdg. 212.50 (*90-6193-003-0*) Kluwer Academic.

Morse, John D. Old Master Paintings in North America. (Illus.). 256p. 1996. pap. 19.95 (*0-89659-050-X*) Abbeville Pr.

Morse, John T., Jr. Abraham Lincoln, 2 vols. LC 73-128958. (American Statesmen Ser.: Nos. 25, 26). reprint ed. 95.00 (*0-404-50892-8*) AMS Pr.

— Benjamin Franklin. LC 74-128926. (American Statesmen Ser.: No. 1). reprint ed. 49.50 (*0-404-50851-0*) AMS Pr.

— Famous Trials: The Tichborne Claimant - Troppmann - Prince Pierre Bonaparte - Mrs. Wharton. v, 342p. 1993. reprint ed. 37.50 (*0-8377-2444-9*, Rothman) W S Hein.

— John Adams. LC 79-128970. (American Statesmen Ser.: No. 6). reprint ed. 45.00 (*0-404-50856-1*) AMS Pr.

— John Quincy Adams. LC 77-128967. (American Statesmen Ser.: No. 15). reprint ed. 45.00 (*0-404-50866-9*) AMS Pr.

— Thomas Jefferson. Schlesinger, Arthur Meier, Jr., ed. LC 96-50448. (American Statesmen Ser.). 500p. 1997. lib. bdg. 34.95 (*0-7910-4545-5*, Chelsea Juniors) Chelsea Hse.

— Thomas Jefferson. LC 77-128975. (American Statesmen Ser.: No. 11). reprint ed. 45.00 (*0-404-50861-8*) AMS Pr.

Morse, John T., Jr., intro. Diary of Gideon Welles, Secretary of the Navy under Lincoln & Johnson Vol. I: 1861 to 1864. (Illus.). 549p. 1995. reprint ed. lib. bdg. 62.50 (*0-8328-4501-9*) Higginson Bk Co.

— Diary of Gideon Welles, Secretary of the Navy under Lincoln & Johnson Vol. II: 1864 to 1866. (Illus.). 653p. 1995. reprint ed. lib. bdg. 72.50 (*0-8328-4500-0*) Higginson Bk Co.

— Diary of Gideon Welles, Secretary of the Navy under Lincoln & Johnson Vol. III: 1867 to 1869. (Illus.). 671p. 1995. reprint ed. lib. bdg. 75.00 (*0-8328-4499-3*) Higginson Bk Co.

Morse, John T., Jr., ed. see Adams, Charles F.

Morse, John T., Jr., ed. see Burton, Theodore E.

Morse, John T., Jr., ed. see Coolidge, Louis A.

Morse, John T., ed. see Gay, Sydney H.

Morse, John T., Jr., ed. see Gilman, Daniel C.

Morse, John T., Jr., ed. see Hart, Albert B.

Morse, John T., Jr., ed. see Hosmer, James K.

Morse, John T., Jr., ed. see Lodge, Henry C.

Morse, John T., Jr., ed. see Lothrop, Thorton K.

Morse, John T., Jr., ed. see Magruder, Allan B.

Morse, John T., Jr., ed. see McCall, Samuel W.

Morse, John T., Jr., ed. see McLaughlin, Andrew C.

Morse, John T., Jr., ed. see Pellew, George.

Morse, John T., Jr., ed. see Roosevelt, Theodore.

Morse, John T., Jr., ed. see Schurz, Carl.

Morse, John T., Jr., ed. see Shepard, Edward M.

Morse, John T., Jr., ed. see Smith, Theodore C.

Morse, John T., Jr., ed. see Stanwood, Edward.

Morse, John T., Jr., ed. see Stevens, John A.

Morse, John T., Jr., ed. see Storey, Moorfield.

Morse, John T., Jr., ed. see Sumner, William G.

Morse, John T., Jr., ed. see Thayer, William R.

Morse, John T., Jr., ed. see Tyler, Moses C.

Morse, John T., Jr., ed. see Von Holst, Hermann E.

Morse, Johnathan. Word by Word: The Language of Memory. LC 89-23931. (Illus.). 272p. 1990. 37.50 (*0-8014-2383-X*) Cornell U Pr.

***Morse, Jon, et al, eds.** ETA Carinae at the Millennium. (Conference Series Proceedings: Vol. 179). 382p. 1999. text 52.00 (*1-58381-003-X*) Astron Soc Pacific.

— Ultraviolet - Optical Space Astronomy Beyond HST, Vol. 164. LC 99-61102. (ASP Conference Series Proceedings). 468p. (C). 1999. text 52.00 (*1-886733-85-6*) Astron Soc Pacific.

Morse, Jonathan. Word by Word: The Language of Memory. LC 89-23931. 277p. reprint ed. pap. 85.90 (*0-608-20928-7*, 207202700003) Bks Demand.

Morse, Joseph E. Virginia's Country Stores: A Quiet Passing. LC 96-47597. (Illus.). 128p. 1997. 24.95 (*1-880664-19-4*) E M Pr.

Morse, Joyce S., jt. ed. see Roth, Shirley P.

Morse, Kay. Stolen Recipes & Saucy Stories: Best Girlfriend's Cookbook. LC 97-7693. (Illus.). 206p. 1998. 19.95 (*1-885221-89-4*) BookPartners.

Morse, Kendall. Stories Told in the Kitchen. LC 81-8775. (Illus.). 95p. (Orig.). 1981. pap. 4.95 (*0-945980-19-1*) Nrth Country Pr.

Morse, Kenneth. Move in Our Midst: Looking at Worship in the Life of the Church. LC 77-6411. 159p. 1977. reprint ed. pap. 49.30 (*0-608-02166-0*, 206283500004) Bks Demand.

Morse, Kenneth I. Listen to the Sunrise: Hymns & Prayers. LC 92-191169. 112p. (Orig.). 1991. reprint ed. pap. 34.80 (*0-608-04179-3*, 206491400011) Bks Demand.

Morse, Kenneth J. Preaching in a Tavern & 129 Other Surprising Stories from Brethren Life. LC 96-51491. 1997. pap. 14.95 (*0-87178-005-4*) Brethren.

Morse, Kitty. A Biblical Feast: Food from Biblical Times for Today. LC 98-10101. Orig. Title: Cooking with Jesus - Food from Biblical Times for Today. (Illus.). 128p. 1998. pap. 14.95 (*0-89815-965-2*) Ten Speed Pr.

— The California Farm Cookbook. LC 93-14992. (Illus.). 304p. 1993. text 26.95 (*0-88289-911-2*) Pelican.

— Cooking at the Kasbah: Recipes from My Moroccan Kitchen. LC 98-11490. (Illus.). 156p. 1998. pap. 22.95 (*0-8118-1503-X*) Chronicle Bks.

***Morse, Kitty.** Couscous: Fresh & Flavorful Contemporary Recipes. LC 99-49814. (Illus.). 120p. 2000. pap. 16.95 (*0-8118-2401-2*) Chronicle Bks.

Morse, Kitty. Edible Flowers: A Kitchen Companion. (Illus.). 80p. 1995. 12.95 (*0-89815-754-4*) Ten Speed Pr.

— The Vegetarian Table: North Africa. LC 95-31834. (Illus.). 168p. 1996. 22.95 (*0-8118-0694-4*) Chronicle Bks.

Morse, L. E. & Henifin, M. S., eds. Rare Plant Conservation: Geographic Data Organization. LC 80-19361. 377p. 1981. pap. 25.00 (*0-89327-223-X*) NY Botanical.

Morse, Laurie, jt. auth. see Greising, David.

Morse, Lawrence. Writing the Economics Paper. 1981. pap. text 6.95 (*0-8120-2113-4*) Barron.

Morse, Lawrence B. Statistics for Business & Economics: Back to Basics, 3.5 IBM. (C). 1997. pap. 9.00 (*0-06-501661-0*) Addson-Wesley Educ.

***Morse, Leigh A., frwd.** Eli Nadelman: The Late Work. (Illus.). 75p. 1999. 30.00 (*1-58821-026-X*) Salander OReilly.

Morse, Linda H., jt. ed. see Herington, Thomas N.

Morse, M., et al, eds. The Banks & the Public. (C). 1989. 60.00 (*0-85297-060-9*, Pub. by Chartered Bank) St Mut.

Morse, Margaret. Virtualities: Television, Media Art, & Cyberculture. LC 97-40901. (Theories of Contemporary Culture Ser.: Vol. 21). (Illus.). 304p. 1998. 39.95 (*0-253-33382-2*); pap. 19.95 (*0-253-21177-8*) Ind U Pr.

Morse, Margaret, ed. see Junior League of Elmira, Inc. Staff.

Morse, Marjorie J. Selected Papers. (Illus.). 882p. 1981. 129.95 (*0-387-90532-4*) Spr-Verlag.

Morse, Mark E., ed. Handbook for Massachusetts Selectmen. 3rd rev. ed. 106p. 1998. pap. 35.00 (*0-9621064-0-2*) MA Municipal Assn.

Morse, Marston. The Calculus of Variations in the Large. 8th ed. LC 34-40909. (Colloquium Publications: Vol. 18). 368p. 1934. reprint ed. pap. 55.00 (*0-8218-1018-9*, COLL/18) Am Math.

— Global Variational Analysis: Weierstrass Integrals on a Riemannian Manifold. LC 76-836. (Mathematical Notes Ser.: No. 16). 269p. 1976. reprint ed. pap. 83.40 (*0-608-06607-9*, 206680400009) Bks Demand.

— Topological Methods in the Theory of Functions of a Complex Variable. (Annals of Mathematics Studies). 1947. 25.00 (*0-527-02731-6*) Periodicals Srv.

— Variational Analysis: Critical Extremals & Sturmian Extensions. LC 72-8368. (Pure & Applied Mathematics Ser.). 272p. reprint ed. 84.40 (*0-8357-9998-0*, 201952300012) Bks Demand.

Morse, Mary. Women Changing Science: Voices from a Field in Transition. (Illus.). 303p. (C). 1995. 27.95 (*0-306-45081-X*, Plenum Trade) Perseus Pubng.

Morse, Melvin. Closer to the Light. 1997. pap. 12.00 (*0-449-00120-2*) Fawcett.

— Closer to the Light: Learning from Near Death Experiences of Children. 1991. mass mkt. 5.99 (*0-8041-0832-3*) Ivy Books.

— Parting Visions. 1995. mass mkt. 5.99 (*0-8041-1366-1*) Ivy Books.

Morse, Melvin & Perry, Paul. Where God Lives: The Science of the Paranormal & How Our Brains Are Linked to the Universe. 208p. 2000. 22.00 (*0-06-017504-4*, Cliff Street) HarperTrade.

Morse, Melvin L. & Perry, Paul J. Closer to the Light: Learning from the Near-Death Experiences of Children. large type ed. (General Ser.). 293p. 1991. lib. bdg. 21.95 (*0-8161-5183-0*, G K Hall Lrg Type) Mac Lib Ref.

Morse, Merrill. The Ministry to the Single Person. (Ministry Ser.). 56p. 1988. pap. text 1.95 (*0-8146-1586-4*) Liturgical Pr.

Morse, Michael L., jt. auth. see Montell, William L.

Morse, Michal. Decorate a Doll's House. (Illus.). 1999. 35.00 (*1-55821-972-2*) Lyons Pr.

— Furnish a Doll's House. (Illus.). 112p. 1994. reprint ed. pap. 19.95 (*0-89024-259-3*, 12155) Kalmbach.

Morse, Nancy. A Child of His Own. (Intimate Moments Ser.). 1997. per. 3.99 (*0-373-07773-4*, 1-07773-4) Silhouette.

— The Mom Who Came to Stay. 1995. per. 3.75 (*0-373-07683-5*, 1-07683-5) Silhouette.

Morse, Nancy C. Satisfactions in White-Collar Job. Stein, Leon, ed. LC 77-70518. (Illus.). 1977. reprint ed. lib. bdg. 23.95 (*0-405-10187-2*) Ayer.

***Morse, Nancy L.** Cubeo Grammar: Studies in the Languages of Columbia 5. (Publications in Linguistics). 212p. 1999. pap. 29.00 (*1-55671-044-5*) S I L Intl.

Morse, Pamela, jt. ed. see Hall, Rand.

Morse, Peter. Hokusai: One Hundred Poets. LC 88-25175. (Illus.). 222p. 1989. 80.00 (*0-8076-1213-8*) Braziller.

— The Illustrated Bartsch Vol. 2-1, Commentary: Netherlandish Artists - Anthonie Waterloo. (C). 1992. lib. bdg. 149.00 (*0-89835-101-4*) Abaris Bks.

***Morse, Peter.** John Sloan's Print's: A Catalogue Raisonne of the Etchings, Lithographs & Posters. 416p. 2000. 175.00 (*1-55660-308-8*) A Wofsy Fine Arts.

Morse, Peter, jt. ed. see Leach, Mark C.

Morse, Philip M. In at the Beginnings: A Physicist's Life. LC 76-40010. 1976. 35.00 (*0-262-13124-2*) MIT Pr.

— Vibration & Sound. LC 81-68618. 468p. 1981. 33.00 (*0-88318-287-4*) Acoustical Soc Am.

Morse, Philip M. & Feshbach, Herman. Methods of Theoretical Physics, 2 vols. (International Series in Pure & Applied Physics). (Illus.). (C). 1953. 144.69 (*0-07-043317-8*) McGraw.

— Methods of Theoretical Physics, 2 vols., Vol. 1. (International Series in Pure & Applied Physics). (Illus.). (C). 1953. 144.69 (*0-07-043316-X*) McGraw.

Morse, Philip M. & Ingard, K. Uno. Theoretical Acoustics. 960p. 1986. pap. text 49.50 (*0-691-02401-4*, Pub. by Princeton U Pr) Cal Prin Full Svc.

***Morse, Philip M. & Kimball, George E.** Methods of Operations Research LC 98-85163. vii, 158 p. 1998. write for info. (*0-930473-07-8*) Military Opera Res.

Morse, Philip M. & Kimball, George E. Methods of Operations Research. LC 80-83558. (Illus.). 179p. 1980. reprint ed. 25.95 (*0-932146-03-1*) Peninsula CA.

Morse, Philip S. & Ivey, Allen E. Face to Face: Communication & Conflict Resolution in the Schools. LC 96-5103. 112p. 1996. pap. 16.95 (*0-8039-6308-4*) Corwin Pr.

— Face to Face: Communication & Conflict Resolution in the Schools. LC 96-5103. 112p. 1996. 39.95 (*0-8039-6307-6*) Corwin Pr.

Morse, Richard, et al, eds. Grassroots Horizons: Connecting Participatory Development Initiatives East & West. 394p. 1995. pap. 30.50 (*1-85339-290-1*, Pub. by Intermed Tech) Stylus Pub VA.

Morse, Richard L. Truth in Savings with Centsible Interest & Morse Rate Tables. iv, 104p. (Orig.). 1992. pap. 11.95 (*1-881331-00-8*) Family Econ Trust.

Morse, Richard M. New World Soundings: Culture & Ideology in the Americas. LC 89-1730. (Johns Hopkins Studies in Atlantic History & Culture). 312p. reprint ed. pap. 96.80 (*0-608-08795-5*, 206943400004) Bks Demand.

Morse, Richard M., ed. Haiti's Future: Views of Twelve Haitian Leaders. LC 87-30533. (Woodrow Wilson Center Perspectives Ser.). (Illus.). 144p. (Orig.). (C). 1988. pap. text 12.00 (*0-943875-03-X*); lib. bdg. 29.25 (*0-943875-06-4*) W Wilson Ctr Pr.

Morse, Richard M. & Hardoy, Jorge E., eds. Rethinking the Latin American City. (Woodrow Wilson Center Press Ser.). 190p. 1992. text 27.50 (*0-943875-43-9*) Johns Hopkins.

***Morse, Robert, et al.** 25 Mountain Bike Tours in Massachusetts: From Cape Cod to the Connecticut River. 2nd ed. LC 99-58149. (Illus.). 224p. 2000. pap. 15.95 (*0-88150-456-4*, Pub. by Countryman) Norton.

Morse, Robert E. Evocation of Virgil in Tolkien's Art. LC 86-71230. 80p. (Orig.). 1986. 19.00 (*0-86516-175-5*); pap. 9.00 (*0-86516-176-3*) Bolchazy-Carducci.

— Fabulae Latinae. (LAT.). 36p. (Orig.). (YA). (gr. 9-12). 1992. pap., spiral bd. 2.50 (*0-939507-42-0*, B729) Amer Classical.

Morse, Robert S. 25 Mountain Bike Tours in Massachusetts: From the Connecticut River to the Atlantic Coast. LC 91-15374. (25 Mountain Bike Tours Ser.). 176p. 1991. pap. 12.00 (*0-88150-191-3*, Pub. by Countryman) Norton.

***Morse, Roger.** The Last Nazi. 440p. 1999. 28.00 (*0-9671046-0-2*) N Bushwick Inc.

Morse, Roger & Flottum, Kim, eds. The ABC & XYZ of Bee Culture: An Encyclopedia of Beekeeping. 40th rev. ed. (Illus.). 528p. 1990. 30.00 (*0-936028-01-7*) A I Root.

— Honey Bee Pests, Predators & Diseases. 3rd rev. ed. (Illus.). 575p. 1997. 40.00 (*0-936028-10-6*) A I Root.

Morse, Roger A. Making Mead (Honey Wine) History, Recipes, Methods & Equipment. (Illus.). 128p. 1992. reprint ed. pap. text 10.95 (*1-878075-04-7*) Wicwas Pr.

— The New Complete Guide to Beekeeping. LC 94-3657. (Illus.). 208p. 1994. pap. 17.00 (*0-88150-315-0*, Pub. by Countryman) Norton.

— Rearing Queen Honey Bees. 2nd rev. ed. (Illus.). 128p. 1997. pap. text 14.95 (*1-878075-05-5*) Wicwas Pr.

***Morse, Roger A.** Richard Archbold & the Archbold Biological Station. LC 99-41986. (Illus.). 128p. 2000. 29.95 (*0-8130-1761-0*) U Press Fla.

Morse, Ronald A., ed. Japan & the Middle East in Alliance Politics. LC 86-1512. (Illus.). 124p. (Orig.). 1986. pap. text 22.00 (*0-8191-5266-8*) U Pr of Amer.

— Korean Studies in America: Options for the Future. LC 83-13996. 164p. (Orig.). 1983. pap. text 25.50 (*0-8191-3409-0*) U Pr of Amer.

— The Politics of Japan's Energy Strategy. (Research Papers & Policy: No. 3). (Orig.). 1981. pap. 7.00 (*0-912966-45-9*) IEAS.

— Southeast Asian Studies: Options for the Future. Report of a Conference at the Wilson Center March 1984. 192p. (Orig.). 1985. pap. text 23.00 (*0-8191-4318-9*); lib. bdg. 55.50 (*0-8191-4317-0*) U Pr of Amer.

— U. S.-Japan Relations: An Agenda for the Future. LC 88-36667. 80p. (Orig.). (C). 1989. pap. text 15.00 (*0-8191-7349-5*); lib. bdg. 29.00 (*0-8191-7348-7*) U Pr of Amer.

Morse, Ronald A., et al, eds. Burma: A Study Guide. LC 88-5441. 332p. (C). 1988. text 43.50 (*0-943875-04-8*) W Wilson Ctr Pr.

Morse, Ronald A., jt. auth. see Coleman, Edwin J.

Morse, Rory. My Guardian Angels. unabridged ed. (Illus.). 60p. 1997. spiral bd. 15.00 (*1-929326-49-1*) Hal Bar Pubg.

Morse, Russell A., Jr. Tax Sales Manual, 1984-85. 32p. 1984. pap. 17.50 (*0-943714-01-X*) Cmdrs-Rusty's.

— Tax Sales Manual, 1983-84. (Mining District Record Ser.). 8p. 1983. pap. 25.00 (*0-943714-00-1*) Cmdrs-Rusty's.

Morse, Rusty. The Armchair Quarterback's Guide to the Football Cards of the Denver Broncos. (Illus.). 24p. (Orig.). 1986. pap. 3.00 (*0-943714-02-8*) Cmdrs-Rusty's.

Morse, Ruth. Truth & Convention in the Middle Ages: Medieval Rhetoric & Representation. (Illus.). 309p. (C). 1990. text 69.95 (*0-521-30211-0*) Cambridge U Pr.

Morse, S. A. Basalts & Phase Diagrams: An Introduction to the Quantitative Use of Phase Diagrams in Igneous Petrology. LC 93-33966. 510p. (C). 1994. text 61.50 (*0-89464-857-8*) Krieger.

Morse, Samuel C., jt. text see Morse, Anne N.

Morse, Samuel F. Foreign Conspiracy Against the Liberties of the United States: The Numbers of Brutus. LC 76-46090. (Anti-Movements in America Ser.). 1977. lib. bdg. 20.95 (*0-405-09963-0*) Ayer.

— Imminent Dangers to the Free Institutions of the United States Through Foreign Immigration & the Present State of the Naturalization Laws. LC 69-18785. (American Immigration Collection. Series 1). 1969. reprint ed. 13.95 (*0-405-00533-4*) Ayer.

— Samuel F. B. Morse: His Letters & Journals, 2 vols. Morse, Edward L., ed. LC 76-75279. (Library of American Art). (Illus.). 1080p. 1973. reprint ed. lib. bdg. 110.00 (*0-306-71304-7*) Da Capo.

— Samuel French Morse Collected Poems. Rotella, Guy, ed. 355p. 1995. 35.00 (*0-943373-34-4*); pap. 19.95 (*0-943373-35-2*) Natl Poet Foun.

Morse, Sarah & Quinn Roberts, Donna. Moving Mom & Dad: Why, Where, How & When to Help Your Parents Relocate. rev. ed. (Lanier Guides). 256p. 1998. pap. 14.95 (*0-89087-868-4*) Celestial Arts.

Morse, Sarah, jt. auth. see Cross, David.

An Asterisk (*) at the beginning of an entry indicates that the title is appearing for the first time.

***Morse, Scott.** The August Ones. Rich, Jamie S., ed. (Soulwind Ser.: Vol. V). (Illus.). 96p. 2001. pap. 8.50 (*1-929998-02-3*) Oni Pr Inc.

— Infamous Transit Vagrants. (Soulwind Ser.). (Illus.). 2000. pap. 11.95 (*0-9667127-7-3*) Oni Pr Inc.

— Kid from Planet Earth. (Soulwind Ser.: Vol. 2). (Illus.). 104p. (J). 2000. pap. 8.50 (*0-9667127-6-5*) Oni Pr Inc.

Morse, Scott. Littlegreyman. (Illus.). 96p. (Orig.). 1997. pap. 6.95 (*1-887279-55-5*) Image Comics.

***Morse, Scott.** Smack Dab. (Illus.). 96p. 2000. pap. 8.50 (*0-9700387-1-2*) Crazyfish.

— Volcanic Revolver. 1999. pap. 9.95 (*0-9667127-5-7*) Oni Pr Inc.

— The Way Things Never Happened. Rich, Jamie S., ed. (Soulwind Ser.: Vol. IV). (Illus.). 96p. 2000. pap. 8.50 (*1-929998-01-5*) Oni Pr Inc.

Morse, Sidney. Freemasonry in the American Revolution. 134p. 1992. reprint ed. pap. 12.95 (*1-56459-047-X*) Kessinger Pub.

Morse, Stearns A., jt. auth. see Stoiber, Richard E.

Morse, Stephen. Successful Product Management. 2nd ed. (Marketing in Action Ser.). 150p. 1998. pap. 30.00 (*0-7494-2702-7*) Kogan Page Ltd.

Morse, Stephen & Buhler, William. Integrated Pest Management: Ideals & Realities in Developing Countries. LC 97-16388. 1997. 49.95 (*1-55587-685-4*) L Rienner.

Morse, Stephen & Stoking, Michael, eds. People & Environment: Development for the Future. 215p. 1996. pap. 25.95 (*0-7748-0546-3*) U of Wash Pr.

Morse, Stephen, jt. auth. see Shapiro, Michael H.

Morse, Stephen S. Emerging Viruses. (Illus.). 352p. (C). 1996. pap. text 29.95 (*0-19-510484-6*) OUP.

Morse, Stephen S., ed. Evolutionary Biology of Viruses. LC 93-29820. 368p. 1993. text 75.00 (*0-7817-0119-8*) Lppncott W & W.

Morse, Steve. Open Ears. LC 97-185850. (Illus.). 125p. (YA). pap. 14.95 (*0-89524-884-0*, 02503101) Cherry Lane.

Morse, Suzanne W. Renewing Civic Capacity: Preparing Students for Service & Citizenship. Fife, Jonathan D., ed. & frwd. by. LC 89-63528. (ASHE-ERIC Higher Education Reports: No. 89-8). 133p. (Orig.). (C). 1990. pap. 24.00 (*0-9623882-7-0*) GWU Grad Schl E&HD.

Morse, Ted. Longman Guide to the Advanced Placement Examination in United States History. 2nd ed. LC 94-112381. 1994. text 18.16 (*0-8013-1143-8*) Addison-Wesley.

Morse, Theoda M. & White, Charles. A Genealogical History of the Families of Morrill, Maine. (Illus.). 461p. 1992. reprint ed. lib. bdg. 48.00 (*0-8328-2335-X*) Higginson Bk Co.

Morse, Theoda M., ed. see Robinson, Timothy W.

Morse, Theodore F. Excellence in United States History. 1986. pap. text 12.81 (*0-88334-193-X*, 76158) Longman.

Morse, Tim. Yesstories. 3rd ed. (Illus.). 192p. 1996. pap. 15.95 (*0-312-14453-9*) St Martin.

Morse, Virginia, jt. auth. see Nottage, Cindy.

Morse, Virginia, jt. auth. see Sheldon, Cindy.

Morse, Wayne J. & Roth, Harold P. Cost Accounting: Lab Manual. 3rd ed. LC 85-6153. 1040p. (C). 1986. pap. text 80.00 (*0-201-13998-7*) Addison-Wesley.

— Cost Accounting: Processing, Evaluating, & Using Cost Data. 3rd ed. LC 85-6153. 1040p. (C). 1986. teacher ed. write for info. (*0-201-13997-9*); text 51.95 (*0-201-13995-2*); student ed. 24.75 (*0-201-13996-0*); write for info. (*0-201-13979-0*); 27.95 (*0-201-13745-3*) Addison-Wesley.

Morse, Wayne J., et al. Management Accounting. (C). 1986. pap. text. write for info. (*0-201-15870-1*) Addison-Wesley.

— Management Accounting. 3rd ed. (Illus.). 896p. (C). 1991. text 61.25 (*0-201-52827-4*) Addison-Wesley.

Morse, Wayne L. & Beattie, Ronald H. Survey of the Administration of Criminal Justice in Oregon: Final Report on 1771 Felony Cases in Multnomah County Report Number One. LC 74-3838. (Criminal Justice in America Ser.). 1974. reprint ed. 24.95 (*0-405-06155-2*) Ayer.

Morse, Whit, jt. auth. see Firestone, Linda.

Morse, William C. Crisis Intervention in Residential Treatment: The Clinical Innovations of Fritz Redl. LC 91-25834. (Residential Treatment for Children & Youth Ser.). (Illus.). 107p. 1991. lib. bdg. 29.95 (*1-56024-215-9*) Haworth Pr.

— The Education & Treatment of Socioemotionally Impaired Children & Youth. LC 85-2842. (Illus.). 384p. 1985. text 45.00 (*0-8156-2268-6*); pap. text 16.95 (*0-8156-2269-4*) Syracuse U Pr.

Morse, William C., ed. Humanistic Teaching for Exceptional Children: An Introduction to Special Education. (Illus.). 344p. (C). 1979. pap. 16.95 (*0-8156-2215-5*) Syracuse U Pr.

Morse, William C., et al. Studies in Psychology of Reading, No. 4-- LC 68-54427. (Michigan University Monographs in Education: No. 4). 188p. 1968. reprint ed. lib. bdg. 35.00 (*0-8371-0176-X*, MOPR, Greenwood Pr) Greenwood.

Morse, William E., jt. auth. see Russel, J. C.

Morse, William R. Chinese Medicine. LC 75-23661. (Clio Medica Ser.: 11). (Illus.). reprint ed. 36.00 (*0-404-58911-1*) AMS Pr.

Morse, William S. A Country Life. LC 94-43017. (Illus.). 136p. (Orig.). 1995. pap. 9.95 (*0-9642213-1-4*) Moose Cntry.

— A Mix of Years. LC 97-26811. 1997. pap. 20.00 (*0-9642213-5-7*) Moose Cntry.

Morse, Winifred A., ed. see Vec Staff & Delmar Staff.

***Morse/Davis/Hartgraves.** Management Account: Strategic Approach. 2nd ed. 1999. pap., student ed. 21.25 (*0-324-00804-X*) Thomson Learn.

***Morse/McNamara.** Visions of Sustainability. 264p. 2000. 69.95 (*1-84014-867-5*) Ashgate Pub Co.

Morselli, Mario. Amadeo Avogadro. 1984. text 206.50 (*90-277-1624-2*) Kluwer Academic.

Morselli, Paolo L., jt. ed. see Schmidt, Dieter A.

Morselli, Raffaella. Collezionisti e Quadrerie Nella Bologna del Seicento. Sones, Anna C., ed. LC 98-16671. (Documents for the History of Collecting Ser.). (Illus.). 730p. 1998. 100.00 (*0-89236-531-5*, Pub. by J P Getty Trust) OUP.

Morseth, Ellen & Center for Pastoral Life & Ministry of the Diocese, des. Call to Leadership: Transforming the Local Church. 96p. 1995. 39.95 (*1-55612-616-6*, LL1616) Sheed & Ward WI.

***Morseth, Michele.** The People of the Volcanoes, Puyulek Pu'irtug! Aniakchaik National Monument & Preserve Ethnographic Overview & Assessment. Norris, Frank & Sucec, Margaret, eds. (Illus.). 206p. 1998. pap. write for info. (*0-941555-05-4*) Natl Pk AK.

Morshead, E. D., tr. see Aeschylus.

Morshead, Ian. The Life & Murder of Henry Morshead: A True Story of the Raj. (Illus.). 220p. 1982. 27.00 (*0-900891-76-9*) Oleander Pr.

Morshead, O. F., ed. see Pepys, Samuel.

Morshead, Richard W. Patterns of Educational Practice: Theories of Curriculum. 352p. 1995. pap. 28.00 (*0-87650-318-0*) Pierian.

Morshen, Nikolai. Sobranie Stikhov. (Modern Russian Literature & Culture, Studies & Text: Vol. 37). (RUS.). 269p. (Orig.). 1996. pap. 20.00 (*1-57201-024-X*) Berkeley Slavic.

Morsi, Pamela. Courting Miss Hattie. 304p. 1991. mass mkt. 5.99 (*0-553-29000-2*) Bantam.

— Garters. 336p. 1992. mass mkt. 5.99 (*0-515-10895-2*, Jove) Berkley Pub.

— Garters. large type ed. LC 93-18606. 488p. 1993. lib. bdg. 20.95 (*1-56054-725-1*) Thorndike Pr.

— Heaven Sent. 352p. 1991. mass mkt. 5.99 (*0-553-28944-6*) Bantam.

***Morsi, Pamela.** Here Comes the Bride. 384p. 2000. mass mkt. 6.99 (*0-06-101366-8*, Avon Bks) Morrow Avon.

Morsi, Pamela. The Love Charm. 384p. 1996. mass mkt. 5.99 (*0-380-78641-9*, Avon Bks) Morrow Avon.

***Morsi, Pamela.** The Love Charm. large type ed. LC 98-24628. 424 p. 1998. 25.95 (*0-7838-0307-9*, G K Hall & Co) Mac Lib Ref.

Morsi, Pamela. Marrying Stone. 336p. 1994. mass mkt. 5.50 (*0-515-11431-6*, Jove) Berkley Pub.

— No Ordinary Princess. 400p. 1997. mass mkt. 5.99 (*0-380-78643-5*, Avon Bks) Morrow Avon.

— No Ordinary Princess. large type ed. LC 98-24001. (Large Print Bks.). 1998. 25.95 (*1-56895-519-7*) Wheeler Pub.

— Runabout. 304p. (Orig.). 1994. mass mkt. 4.99 (*0-515-11305-0*, Jove) Berkley Pub.

— Runabout. large type ed. LC 94-32215. 400p. (Orig.). 1994. pap. 18.95 (*0-7838-1126-8*, G K Hall Lrg Type) Mac Lib Ref.

— Sealed with a Kiss. 400p. 1998. mass mkt. 5.99 (*0-380-79638-4*, Avon Bks) Morrow Avon.

— Simple Jess. 336p. (Orig.). 1996. mass mkt. 6.50 (*0-515-11837-0*, Jove) Berkley Pub.

— Something Shady. 336p. (Orig.). 1995. mass mkt. 5.99 (*0-515-11628-9*, Jove) Berkley Pub.

— Sweetwood Bride. 416p. 1999. mass mkt. 6.99 (*0-06-101365-X*) HarpC.

***Morsi, Pamela.** Sweetwood Bride. large type ed. LC 00-22870. 2000. 25.95 (*1-56895-855-2*) Wheeler Pub.

Morsi, Pamela. Wild Oats. 336p. 1993. mass mkt. 5.99 (*0-515-11185-6*, Jove) Berkley Pub.

— Wild Oats. large type ed. LC 93-37210. 571p. 1994. lib. bdg. 17.95 (*0-7862-0099-5*) Thorndike Pr.

Morsiani, Mario. Epidemiology & Screening of Diabetes. LC 88-7249. 320p. 1989. 163.00 (*0-8493-4971-0*, RC660, CRC Reprint) Franklin.

Morsink, Deborah H. Tournants: Conversation en Culture. LC 92-24486. (C). 1992. pap. text 26.00 (*0-13-927682-3*) P-H.

Morsink, Hubert, jt. ed. see Allen, Tim.

Morsink, Johannes. The Universal Declaration of Human Rights: Origins & Intent. LC 98-41468. (Pennsylvania Studies in Human Rights). 1999. 49.95 (*0-8122-3474-X*) U of Pa Pr.

Morsink, Robert L. Foreign Direct Investment & Corporate Networking: A Framework for Spatial Analysis of Investment Conditions. LC 98-27886. (New Horizons in International Business Ser.). 272p. 1998. 85.00 (*1-85898-983-3*) E Elgar.

Morskaya, Larisa. Za Grekhi Roditelei (For the Parents Sins) Povesti I Rasskazy (Novels & Stories) (Illus.). 224p. (C). 1991. pap. 14.00 (*0-911971-55-6*) Effect Pub.

Morsman, Edgar M., Jr. The Art of Commercial Lending. LC 97-24752. 150p. (Orig.). 1997. pap. write for info. (*1-57070-017-6*) Robt Morris Assocs.

— Commercial Loan Portfolio Management. Behr, Joan H., ed. LC 93-16711. (Illus.). 136p. 1993. pap. text 64.00 (*0-936742-95-X*, 31181) Robt Morris Assocs.

— Effective Loan Management. LC 81-84671. (Illus.). 224p. 1982. text 65.00 (*0-936742-06-2*) Robt Morris Assocs.

— The Postmistress of Saddlestring, Wyoming. LC 98-205298. (Illus.). xi, 90p. 1998. pap. 14.95 (*0-9664438-0-2*) E M Morsman.

Morson, Basil C., ed. Alimentary Tract. 3rd ed. (Symmers Systemic Pathology Ser.: Vol. 3). (Illus.). 472p. 1987. text 209.00 (*0-443-03095-2*) Church.

Morson, Caroline, tr. see Ethievant, Catherine.

Morson, Caroline, tr. see Poor Clares of Poligny Staff & Elizabeth.

Morson, Caroline, tr. see Vintrou, Francoise.

Morson, Gary S. The Boundaries of Genre: Dostoevsky's "Diary of a Writer" & the Traditions of Literary Utopia. 219p. 1988. pap. 14.95 (*0-8101-0811-9*) Northwestern U Pr.

— Hidden in Plain View: Narrative & Creative Potentials in 'War & Peace' LC 87-6471. 336p. 1987. 47.50 (*0-8047-1387-1*); pap. 15.95 (*0-8047-1718-4*) Stanford U Pr.

— Narrative & Freedom: The Shadows of Time. LC 94-7065. 336p. 1994. 35.00 (*0-300-05882-9*) Yale U Pr.

— Narrative & Freedom: The Shadows of Time. 336p. 1996. pap. 17.00 (*0-300-06875-1*) Yale U Pr.

Morson, Gary S., ed. Bakhtin: Essays & Dialogues on His Work. LC 85-24624. xiv, 206p. 1986. pap. text 14.00 (*0-226-54133-9*); lib. bdg. 28.00 (*0-226-54132-0*) U Ch Pr.

— Literature & History: Theoretical Problems & Russian Case Studies. LC 85-27843. 352p. 1986. 47.50 (*0-8047-1302-2*) Stanford U Pr.

Morson, Gary S. & Emerson, Caryl. Mikhail Bakhtin: Creation of a Prosaics. LC 90-39855. 560p. 1990. 57.50 (*0-8047-1821-0*); pap. 18.95 (*0-8047-1822-9*) Stanford U Pr.

Morson, Gary S. & Emerson, Caryl, eds. Rethinking Bakhtin: Extensions & Challenges. (Studies in Russian Literature & Theory). 330p. 1989. pap. 18.95 (*0-8101-0810-0*) Northwestern U Pr.

Morson, Gary S., jt. ed. see Allen, Elizabeth C.

Morson, Ian. Falconer & the Face of God. 1997. mass mkt. 5.99 (*0-312-96410-2*) St Martin.

— Falconer & the Great Beast: A Medieval Oxford Mystery. LC 99-14510. (Illus.). 220p. (YA). 1999. text 21.95 (*0-312-20543-0*) St Martin.

— Falconer's Crusade. 1996. mass mkt. 4.99 (*0-312-95697-5*, Pub. by Tor Bks) St Martin.

— Falconer's Judgement. (Dead Letter Mysteries Ser.). 1997. mass mkt. 5.99 (*0-312-96151-0*) St Martin.

— A Psalm for Falconer, Vol. 1. Date not set. write for info. (*0-312-96534-6*) Tor Bks.

Morson, Jamie, jt. ed. see Kalb, Marion.

Morson, John. Christ the Way: The Christology of Guerric of Igny. (Cistercian Studies: N0.25). 1978. 3.00 (*0-87907-825-1*) Cistercian Pubns.

Morson, Lillian I. Morson's English Guide for Court Reporters. 400p. 1997. pap. text. write for info. (*0-9657932-0-6*); pap. text, teacher ed. write for info. (*0-9657932-1-4*) Morson Guide.

***Morss, Christopher.** Helena to Vicksburg, A Civil War Odessey: The Personal Diary of Joshua Whittington Underhill, Surgeon, 46th Regiment, Indiana Volunteer Infantry, 23 October 1862 - 21 July 1863. 341p. 2000. 27.95 (*1-882063-49-X*) Cottage Pr MA.

Morss, John R. Growing Critical: Alternatives to Developmental Psychology. LC 95-8132. (Critical Psychology Ser.). 184p. (C). 1995. 80.00 (*0-415-06108-3*); pap. 25.99 (*0-415-06109-1*) Routledge.

Morss, L. R., jt. ed. see Meyer, G.

Morss, Lester R. Rare Earths, 1991 Proceedings of The 19th Rare Earth Research Conference, Lexington, Kentucky, July 14-19, 1991. 1992. write for info. (*0-444-75088-6*) Elsevier.

Morss, Lester R. Rare Earths, 1991: Proceedings of the 19th Rare Earth Research Conference, Lexington, Kentucky, July 14-19, 1991. 1992. write for info. (*0-444-75089-4*) Elsevier.

Morss, Lester R. & Fuger, Jean, eds. Transuranium Elements: A Half Century. LC 92-7475. (Illus.). 562p. 1992. text 110.00 (*0-8412-2219-3*, Pub. by Am Chemical) OUP.

Morss, Noel. Ancient Culture of the Fremont River in Utah. (HUPMP Ser.: Vol. 12, No. 3). 1931. 30.00 (*0-527-01226-2*) Periodicals Srv.

— Archaeological Explorations on the Middle Chinlee. LC 28-11557. (American Anthropological Association Memoirs Ser.). 1927. pap. 25.00 (*0-527-00533-9*) Periodicals Srv.

— Notes on the Archaeology of the Kaibito & Rainbow Plateaus in Arizona. (Harvard University Peabody Museum of Archaeology & Ethnology Papers: Vol. 12, No. 3). 1974. reprint ed. pap. 30.00 (*0-527-01225-4*) Periodicals Srv.

Morss, Willard N. & Herren, Janet M. Stolen Princess: A Northwest Indian Legend. LC 83-82920. (Illus.). 79p. (Orig.). (J). (gr. 4-8). 1983. pap. 8.95 (*0-9613025-0-X*) J M Herren.

Morstein, Mona. The Childhood of Sherlock Holmes Bk. 1: The Butler's Tale. LC 99-41708. 368p. 2000. pap. 24.95 (*1-880090-79-1*) Galde Pr.

Morstein, Petra Von, see Von Morstein, Petra.

Morstyn, George & Kaye, A. H., eds. Phototherapy of Cancer. x, 224p. 1990. text 198.00 (*3-7186-0510-4*) Gordon & Breach.

Morstyn, George & Sheridan, William, eds. Cell Therapy: Stem Cell Transplantation, Gene Therapy, & Cellular Immunotherapy. (Cancer Ser.). (Illus.). 646p. (C). 1996. text 115.00 (*0-521-47315-2*) Cambridge U Pr.

Morsy, E. Aloe Vera Science & Technology 1996-1997, 4 vols. 10th ed. 200p. 1997. pap. 95.00 (*0-937425-30-3*) C I T A Intl.

Morsy, E. M. Aloe Vera, Science & Technology, 1998-1999. 120p. 1999. pap. 75.00 (*0-937425-33-8*) C I T A Intl.

— Aloe Vera Science & Technology, 1997-1998. 70p. 1998. pap. 55.00 (*0-937425-32-X*) C I T A Intl.

Morsy, Esam M. Aloe Vera, Science & Technology, 1980-1993. 7th ed. (Illus.). 579p. 1993. pap. text 285.00 (*0-937425-26-5*) C I T A Intl.

— Science & Technology, 1993-1995. 8th ed. 120p. (Orig.). 1995. pap. 95.00 (*0-937425-27-3*) C I T A Intl.

Morsy, Esam M., ed. For Formulation Chemists Only, 3 vols., Set. (F2CO Ser.). (Illus.). 144p. 1991. pap. 285.00 (*0-685-52445-0*) C I T A Intl.

— For Formulation Chemists Only, Vol. 1. (F2CO Ser.). 150p. 1991. pap. text 95.00 (*0-937425-02-8*) C I T A Intl.

— For Formulation Chemists Only, 3 vols., Vol. 2. (F2CO Ser.). (Illus.). 144p. 1991. pap. 95.00 (*0-937425-14-1*) C I T A Intl.

— For Formulation Chemists Only, Vol. 2. (F2CO Ser.). 148p. 1992. pap. text 95.00 (*0-937425-03-6*) C I T A Intl.

Morsy, Zaghloul, ed. The Challenge of Illiteracy: From Reflection to Action. LC 94-32885. (IBE Studies on Education: Vol. 1). 352p. 1994. text 50.00 (*0-8153-1854-5*, SS995) Garland.

Morsy, Zaghloul & Altbach, Philip G., eds. Higher Education in an International Perspective: Critical Issues. LC 95-26399. (IBE Studies in Education: Vol. 03). 232p. 1996. reprint ed. text 51.00 (*0-8153-2336-0*, SS1102) Garland.

Morsy, Zhagloul & Altbach, Philip G., eds. Higher Education in International Perspective: Toward the 21st Century. 250p. 1993. text 37.50 (*0-89891-066-8*) Advent Bks Div.

Mort, D. M. Developmental Concordance & Discordance During Puberty & Early Adolescence. (SRCD Ser.: Vol. 18, No. 1). 1953. 25.00 (*0-527-01557-1*) Periodicals Srv.

Mort, David. Sources of Unofficial U. K. Statistics. 3rd ed. LC 96-51905. 480p. 1997. text 109.95 (*0-566-07672-1*, Pub. by Gower) Ashgate Pub Co.

— U. K. Statistics: A Guide for Business Users. 300p. 1992. 76.95 (*0-566-02971-5*, Pub. by Gower) Ashgate Pub Co.

***Mort, David & Lunn, Wendy.** Sources of Unofficial U. K. Statistics. 4th ed. LC 99-49655. 200p. 2000. 113.95 (*0-566-08236-5*, Pub. by Gower) Ashgate Pub Co.

Mort, David & Woolley, Marcus. Counties & Regions of the U. K. 3rd ed. 200p. 1994. 76.95 (*0-566-02972-3*, Pub. by Gower) Ashgate Pub Co.

Mort, F. Sexual Geographies. pap. text 19.50 (*0-85315-896-7*) Lawrence & Wishart.

Mort, Frank. Cultures of Consumption: Commerce, Masculinities & Social Space. LC 95-21633. (Comedia Ser.). (Illus.). 288p. (C). 1996. 80.00 (*0-415-03051-X*); pap. 24.99 (*0-415-03052-8*) Routledge.

— Dangerous Sexualities: Medicomoral Politics in England since 1830. 2nd ed. LC 99-32888. (Illus.). 320p. (C). 1999. 80.00 (*0-415-16733-7*); pap. 24.99 (*0-415-16734-5*) Routledge.

Mort, J. & Jansen, F. Plasma Deposited Thin Films. LC 86-23264. 256p. 1986. reprint ed. 146.00 (*0-8493-5119-7*, CRC Reprint) Franklin.

***Mort, Janet.** A Passion for Our Grandchildren: Our Families Need Us... NOW. LC 99-32. (Illus.). 297p. 1999. spiral bd. 19.46 (*1-55212-281-6*) Trafford Pub.

Mort, Jo-Ann, ed. Not Your Father's Union Movement: Inside the AFL-CIO. 240p. 1998. 60.00 (*1-85984-889-3*, Pub. by Verso); pap. 20.00 (*1-85984-286-0*, Pub. by Verso) Norton.

***Mort, John.** Soldier in Paradise. LC 99-29858. 192p. 1999. 19.95 (*0-87074-440-2*) SMU Press.

Mort, John. Tanks: Vietnam Stories. LC 85-73391. 88p. 1986. pap. 8.95 (*0-933532-55-5*) BkMk.

— The Walnut King: And Other Stories. 184p. (Orig.). 1990. pap. 8.00 (*0-9617499-2-X*) Woods Colt Pr.

Mort, S. R. Coins of the Hapsburg Emperors & Related Issues 1619-1919. (Illus.). 1998. reprint ed. pap. 20.00 (*0-942666-15-1*) S J Durst.

Mort, S. W. Bluewater Seamanship. (C). 1987. 42.00 (*0-85174-403-6*) St Mut.

Mort, Simon. The Minutes. 128p. 1991. text 56.95 (*0-566-02708-9*, Pub. by Gower) Ashgate Pub Co.

— Professional Report Writing. 300p. 1992. 69.95 (*0-566-02712-7*, Pub. by Gower) Ashgate Pub Co.

— Professional Report Writing. 240p. 1995. pap. 33.95 (*0-566-07669-1*, Pub. by Gower) Ashgate Pub Co.

Mort, Terry. The Reasonable Art of Fly Fishing. (Illus.). 240p. 1998. pap. 24.95 (*1-55821-683-9*) Lyons Pr.

Mort, Terry A. Systematic Selling: How to Influence the Buying Decision Process. LC 77-5937. 198p. reprint ed. pap. 61.40 (*0-608-12837-6*, 202355200033) Bks Demand.

Mortalsin, Mary. Celibacy Is Hard, Right? 1994. mass mkt. 4.99 (*0-671-52422-4*) PB.

Morte, Michael W. La, see La Morte, Michael W.

Morteani, Giulio, ed. Prehistoric Gold in Europe - Mines, Metallurgy & Manufacture: Proceedings of the NATO Advanced Research Workshop, Seeon, Germany, September 27-October 1, 1993. LC 94-23902. (NATO ASI Ser.: Series E, Applied Sciences: Vol. 280). 632p. (C). 1994. text 378.00 (*0-7923-3255-5*) Kluwer Academic.

Mortelier, Christiane, tr. see Thiercelin, Louis.

Mortelmans, L. Scintigraphic Evaluation of Coronary Thrombolysis. No. 25. 148p. (Orig.). 1990. pap. 39.50 (*90-6186-370-8*, Pub. by Leuven Univ) Coronet Bks.

Morten, Baker E. The First Step to Recovery. 200p. 1992. pap. text 19.95 (*0-9633004-3-1*) Integ Pub DC.

— Unlock Your Happiness. LC 93-80792. 104p. 1994. pap. 10.95 (*0-9633004-8-2*) Integ Pub DC.

Mortensen, Klaus P. The Time of Unrememberable Being: Wordsworth & the Sublime, 1787-1805. LC 99-159322. (Illus.). 208p. 1999. 35.00 (*87-7289-443-1*, Pub. by Mus Tusculanum) Paul & Co Pubs.

Mortensen, A. Russell, jt. ed. see Mulder, William.

Mortensen, Andreas, jt. auth. see Suresh, Subra.

Mortensen, Benjamin F. The Diary of a Frontline Chaplain. LC 97-67055. (Illus.). 208p. 1997. 14.95 (*1-56236-983-0*, Pub. by Aspen Bks) Origin Bk Sales.

Mortensen, Brita M. & Downs, Brian W. Strindberg: An Introduction to His Life & Work. 246p. reprint ed. pap. 70.20 (*0-608-10302-0*, 2051420) Bks Demand.

Mortensen, C. David. Miscommunication: Finding Our Way. LC 96-35714. 368p. 1997. pap. 21.95 (*0-8039-7376-4*) Sage.
— Problematic Communication: The Construction of Invisible Walls. LC 93-23671. 256p. 1994. 55.00 (*0-275-94632-0*, Praeger Pubs) Greenwood.
— Violence & Communication: Public Reactions to an Attempted Presidential Assassination. (Illus.). 232p. (Orig.). (C). 1988. pap. text 22.00 (*0-8191-6688-X*) U Pr of Amer.

Mortensen, C. David & Ayres, Carter M. Miscommunication: Finding Our Way. LC 96-35714. 368p. 1997. 46.00 (*0-8039-7375-6*) Sage.

Mortensen, Carl E. The Healing of America, Vol. 1. 55p. 1993. pap. 7.95 (*0-9636251-0-1*) C E Mortensen.

***Mortensen, Charles A.** A Reference Grammar of Northern Embera Languages: Studies in the Languages of Columbia. (Publications in Linguistics). 212p. 1999. pap. 29.00 (*1-55671-081-X*) S I L Intl.

Mortensen, Chris. Inconsistent Mathematics. LC 94-37996. (Mathematics & Its Applications Ser.: Vol.312). 168p. 1994. lib. bdg. 102.00 (*0-7923-3186-9*, Pub. by Kluwer Academic) Kluwer Academic.

Mortensen, Colin, jt. auth. see Kirberger, Kimberly.

Mortensen, Daniel B. Pattern for Joint Operations: World War 2 Close Air Support, North Africa. LC 87-19335. (Illus.). 104p. 1987. pap. 7.50 (*0-16-001963-X*, 008-029-00161-6) USGPO.

***Mortensen, Daniel R., et al.** Airpower & Ground Armies: Essays on the Evolution of Anglo-American Air Doctrine 1940-1943. LC 97-46744. (Illus.). 224p. 1998. pap. 13.00 (*1-58566-047-7*) Air Univ.

Mortensen, Danny, jt. auth. see Norris, Bob.

Mortensen, Donald G. & Schmuller, Alan M. Guidance in Today's Schools. 3rd ed. LC 75-35989. 564p. reprint ed. pap. 174.90 (*0-608-10801-4*, 205539700017) Bks Demand.

Mortensen, Douglas L., jt. auth. see Root, Jack B., Sr.

Mortensen, E., ed. Nutrient Dynamics & Biological Structure in Shallow Freshwater & Brackish Lakes. LC 93-47528. (Developments in Hydrobiology Ser.: No. 94). 528p. (C). 1994. text 403.50 (*0-7923-2677-6*) Kluwer Academic.

Mortensen, Enok. Danish-American Life & Letters: A Bibliography. Scott, Franklyn D., ed. LC 78-15200. (Scandinavians in America Ser.). 1979. reprint ed. lib. bdg. 15.95 (*0-405-11652-7*) Ayer.

Mortensen, Inge Demant. Nomads of Luristan & Their Material Culture. LC 93-60435. (Carlsberg Nomad Ser.). (Illus.). 496p. 1993. 50.00 (*0-500-01572-4*, Pub. by Thames Hudson) Norton.

Mortensen, Jorgan, ed. The Future of Pensions in the European Community. 231p. 1992. 37.00 (*1-85753-057-8*, Pub. by Brasseys) Brasseys.

Mortensen, Jorgen, ed. Improving Economic & Social Cohesion in the European Community. LC 94-1155. 1994. text 79.95 (*0-312-12174-1*) St Martin.

Mortensen, Joshua, jt. auth. see Francy, Claire E.

Mortensen, Karen. Form & Content in Children's Human Figure Drawings. 256p. (C). 1991. text 45.00 (*0-8147-5456-2*) NYU Pr.
— Form & Content in Children's Human Figure Drawings. 256p. (C). 1993. pap. text 18.50 (*0-8147-5500-3*) NYU Pr.

Mortensen, Kay S., jt. auth. see Allen, Dell K.

Mortensen, Kell, jt. ed. see Brown, Wyn.

***Mortensen, Lance.** OCP, Oracle8i DBO Study Guide. 512p. 2000. 49.99 (*0-7821-2686-3*) Sybex.

Mortensen, Lance. SMS 1.2. (MCSE Test Success Ser.). 1998. pap. text 24.99 (*0-7821-2336-8*) Sybex.
— Windows 98: Covers Exam 70-098. LC 98-88330. (MCSE Exam Notes Ser.). 416p. 1998. pap. text 19.99 (*0-7821-2421-6*) Sybex.
— Windows 98 Study Guide. LC 98-87090. (Mcse). xxx, 784p. 1998. student ed. 49.99 (*0-7821-2373-2*) Sybex.

Mortensen, Lance & Heldman, William. Systems Management Server 2 Study Guide. 2nd ed. LC 99-62995. (MCSE Ser.). (Illus.). 804p. 1999. 49.99 incl. cd-rom (*0-7821-2413-5*) Sybex.

***Mortensen, Lance & Sawtell, Rick.** SQL Server 7 Administration Study Guide. 2nd ed. LC 99-61298. 736p. 1999. student ed. 49.99 (*0-7821-2382-1*) Sybex.
— Windows 95 Study Guide. 2nd ed. LC 98-84651. (MCSE Ser.). 832p. 1998. student ed. 49.99 (*0-7821-2256-6*) Sybex.

Mortensen, Lance, et al. MCSE SQL Server 6.5 Administration Study Guide. LC 97-80468. 672p. 1997. pap. text 49.99 (*0-7821-2172-1*) Sybex.

Mortensen, Michael E. Geometric Modeling. 216p. 1985. pap. text, student ed., suppl. ed. 50.00 (*0-471-81872-0*) Wiley.

Mortensen, Preben. Art in the Social Order: The Making of the Modern Conception of Art. LC 96-15473. 213p. (C). 1997. text 59.50 (*0-7914-3277-7*); pap. text 19.95 (*0-7914-3278-5*) State U NY Pr.

Mortensen, Richard E. Random Signals & Systems. LC 86-19007. (Illus.). 247p. reprint ed. pap. 76.60 (*0-7837-3528-6*, 205786400008) Bks Demand.

Mortensen, Robert K. In the Cause of Progress: A History of the New Mexico Cattle Growers Association. (Illus.). 128p. 1983. 17.95 (*0-9627417-2-8*) Athena NM.

Mortensen, Viggo. Recent Forgeries. (Illus.). 110p. 1998. pap. 25.00 incl. cd-rom (*1-889195-32-4*, Pub. by Smart Art Pr) RAM Publications.

Mortensen, Viggo & Sorensen, Robert C., eds. Free Will & Determinism: Papers from an Interdisciplinary Research Conference, 1986. 214p. (Orig.). (C). 1987. pap. 25.00 (*87-7288-095-3*, Pub. by Aarhus Univ Pr) David Brown.

Mortensen, William. Monsters & Madonnas. LC 72-9220. (Literature of Photography Ser.). 1977. reprint ed. 18.95 (*0-405-04927-7*) Ayer.

***Mortensen, William, et al.** William Mortensen: A Revival. LC 98-72304. (Illus.). 1998. write for info. (*0-938262-33-5*) Ctr Creat Photog.

Mortenson, Barbara J. Jardin de Amadores (1611) LC 97-27180. (Critical Editions of Spanish Artistic Ballads (Romanceros Artisticos) 1580-1650 Ser.: Vol. 1). (SPA.). 500p. 1997. text 109.95 (*0-7734-8623-2*) E Mellen.

Mortenson, Kenneth E. Variable Capacitance Diodes: The Operation & Characterization of Varactor, Charge Storage & PIN Diodes for RF & Microwave Applications. LC 74-189395. (Modern Frontiers in Applied Science Ser.). 142p. reprint ed. pap. 44.10 (*0-608-14597-1*, 202505300041) Bks Demand.

Mortenson, Kenneth E. & Borrego, Jose M. Design, Performance, & Applications of Microwave Semiconductor Control Components. LC 70-189394. (Modern Frontiers in Applied Science Ser.). (Illus.). 294p. reprint ed. pap. 91.20 (*0-8357-4176-1*, 203695400006) Bks Demand.

Mortenson, Michael E. Computer Graphics: An Introduction to the Mathematics & Geometry. (Illus.). 396p. (C). 1989. 36.95 (*0-8311-1182-8*) Indus Pr.
— Computer Graphics Handbook. (Illus.). 272p. 1990. 29.95 (*0-8311-1002-3*) Indus Pr.
— Geometric Modeling. 2nd ed. LC 96-21242. 544p. 1997. 69.99 (*0-471-12957-7*) Wiley.
— Geometric Transformations. (Illus.). 384p. (C). 1995. 59.95 (*0-8311-3057-1*) Indus Pr.
— Mathematics for Computer Graphics Applications: An Introduction to the Mathematics & Geometry Of Cad/cam, Geometric Modeling, Scientific Visualization, & Other CG Applications. 2nd ed. LC 99-10096. (Illus.). 416p. 1999. text 39.95 (*0-8311-3111-X*) Indus Pr.

Mortenson, Ray. Meadowland. LC 83-80569. (Illus.). 80p. 1983. 25.00 (*0-912810-40-8*) Lustrum Pr.

Mortenson, Rita. R. Atkinson Fox, His Life & Work. LC 84-52506. 159p. 1999. 22.95 (*0-87069-437-5*) L-W Inc.

***Mortenson, Tom.** Standard Catalog of Sports Autographs. (Illus.). 160p. 2000. pap. 21.95 (*0-87341-944-8*, SPAU1) Krause Pubns.
— 2000 Standard Catalog of Sports Memorabilia. LC 99-63751. (Illus.). 496p. 1999. pap. 21.95 (*0-87341-781-X*) Krause Pubns.

Mortenson, Vernon. God Made It Grow: The History of T. E. A. M. (Illus.). 1024p. (Orig.). 1994. pap. text 19.95 (*0-87808-257-3*, WCL257-3) William Carey Lib.

Morter, M. T., Jr. Chiropractic Physiology: A Review of Scientific Principles As Related to the Chiropractic Adjustment with Emphasis on the Bio Energetic Synchronization Technique. LC 88-70369. 120p. 1988. 32.00 (*0-944994-01-6*) BEST Research.
— Correlative Urinalysis: The Body Knows Best. LC 87-51116. 150p. 1988. 32.00 (*0-944994-00-8*) BEST Research.
— Correlative Urinalysis: The Body Knows Best. LC 87-51116. 200p. 1988. pap. 32.00 (*0-944994-02-4*) BEST Research.
— The Healing Field. 146p. (Orig.). 1991. pap. 24.95 (*0-944994-03-2*) BEST Research.

Morter, M. Ted, Jr. An Apple a Day? Is It Enough Today? 2nd rev. ed. 1997. 19.95 (*0-944994-10-5*) BEST Research.
— Dynamic Health Revised: Using Your Own Beliefs, Thoughts & Memory to Create a Healthy Body. 2nd rev. ed. LC 98-107007. 1997. 19.95 (*0-944994-09-1*) BEST Research.
— Exercise or Diet? LC 97-221805. 1997. 19.95 (*0-944994-11-3*) BEST Research.

***Morter, M. Ted, Jr.** PH You Potential for Health. 2nd rev. ed. 1999. pap. 5.00 (*0-944994-13-X*) Morris Pubng.

Mortgage Bankers Assn. of America Staff. Introduction to Real Estate Law Correspondence Course. 55p. (C). 1995. pap. 270.00 (*1-57599-002-4*) Mortgage Bankers.
— Processing Government Loans. 260p. (C). 1997. pap. 145.00 (*1-57599-015-6*) Mortgage Bankers.

Mortgage Bankers Association of America Staff. Advanced Loan Processing. 250p. (C). 1997. pap. 270.00 (*1-57599-021-0*) Mortgage Bankers.
— Basics of Mortgage-Backed Securities Correspondence Course. rev. ed. 325p. (C). 1998. pap. 270.00 (*1-57599-041-5*) Mortgage Bankers.
— Collection Department Responsibilities & Operations Correspondence Course. rev. ed. 230p. (C). 1998. pap. 270.00 (*1-57599-032-6*) Mortgage Bankers.
— Commercial Real Estate Mortgage Servicing Correspondence Course. rev. ed. 300p. (C). 1998. pap. 270.00 (*1-57599-035-0*) Mortgage Bankers.
— Conventional Loan Processing. rev. ed. 185p. (C). 1997. pap. 270.00 (*1-57599-048-2*) Mortgage Bankers.
— Escrow Department Procedures & Responsibilities Correspondence Course. rev. ed. 200p. (C). 1998. pap. 270.00 (*1-57599-031-8*) Mortgage Bankers.
— FHA/VA Foreclosures & Claims Procedures Correspondence Course. rev. ed. 230p. (C). 1998. pap. 270.00 (*1-57599-033-4*) Mortgage Bankers.
— Fundamentals of Underwriting Commercial Real Estate Correspondence Course. rev. ed. 225p. (C). 1998. pap. 270.00 (*1-57599-038-5*) Mortgage Bankers.
— Introduction to Alternative Lending Programs Correspondence Course. 225p. (C). 1998. pap. 270.00 (*1-57599-027-X*) Mortgage Bankers.
— Introduction to Mortgage Banking. rev. ed. 300p. (C). 1998. pap. 270.00 (*1-57599-044-X*) Mortgage Bankers.
— Loss Mitigation. rev. ed. 175p. (C). 1997. pap. 270.00 (*1-57599-049-0*) Mortgage Bankers.
— Management Skills Correspondence Course. 450p. (C). 1997. pap. 410.00 (*1-57599-028-8*) Mortgage Bankers.
— Mortgage Loan Origination Correspondence Course: Keys to Success in the Mortgage Banking Industry. rev. ed. 260p. (C). 1998. pap. 270.00 (*1-57599-029-6*) Mortgage Bankers.
— Mortgage Loan Underwriting Correspondence Course. rev. ed. 280p. (C). 1998. pap. 270.00 (*1-57599-030-X*) Mortgage Bankers.
— Real Estate Law. 95p. (C). 1997. pap., wbk. ed. 270.00 (*1-57599-026-1*) Mortgage Bankers.
— Regulatory Compliance Correspondence Course. 195p. (C). 1999. pap. write for info. (*1-57599-020-2*) Mortgage Bankers.
— Residential Secondary Mortgage Market Correspondence Course. rev. ed. 190p. (C). 1997. pap. 270.00 (*1-57599-037-7*) Mortgage Bankers.
— Understanding Real Estate Appraisal Correspondence Course. rev. ed. 150p. (C). 1998. pap. 270.00 (*1-57599-036-9*) Mortgage Bankers.
— Underwriting the Self-Employed Borrower Correspondence Course. rev. ed. 150p. (C). 1998. pap. 270.00 (*1-57599-039-3*) Mortgage Bankers.

Morth, Margaret, jt. auth. see Johnson, Pattie J.

Morthier, Geert & Vankwikelberge, Patrick. Handbook of Distributed Feedback Laser Diodes. LC 97-4213. (Optoelectronics Engineering Ser.). 315p. 1997. 103.00 (*0-89006-607-8*) Artech Hse.

Mortier, K. M. & Orszulik, S. T., eds. Chemistry & Technology of Lubricants. LC 91-44485. 302p. 1992. 110.00 (*1-56081-594-9*, Wiley-VCH) Wiley.

Mortier, R. M. & Orszulik, S. T. Chemistry & Technology of Lubricants. 2nd ed. 1996. text. write for info. (*0-7514-0246-X*) Kluwer Academic.

Mortier, R. Shamms. Amiga Desktop Videography. (Illus.). (Orig.). 1991. pap. 39.95 (*0-944500-62-5*) MichTron.

***Mortier, R. Shamms.** Bryce 4 F/X & Design. LC 99-35765. (Illus.). 338p. 1999. write for info. incl. cd-rom (*1-57610-482-6*) Coriolis Grp.
— Creating 3D Comix. (Illus.). 600p. 2000. pap. 49.95 (*1-886801-92-4*) Chrles River Media.

Mortier, R. Shamms. Freehand Effects Magic. 240p. 1997. pap. text 39.99 incl. cd-rom (*1-56830-362-9*) Hayden.

***Mortier, R. Shamms.** Mastering Pixels: 3D: A Comprehensive Guide. LC 00-101316. (Illus.). 450p. 2000. pap. 49.95 incl. audio compact disk (*0-12-508040-9*) Morgan Kaufmann.
— The Poser 4 Handbook. (Illus.). 532p. 1999. pap. 49.95 incl. cd-rom (*1-886801-93-2*) Chrles River Media.

***Mortier, Shamms.** Advanced Bryce Creations: PhotoRealistic 3D Worlds. (Illus.). 500p. 2000. pap. 54.95 incl. cd-rom (*1-58450-035-2*) Chrles River Media.

Mortier, Shamms. The Bryce 3D Handbook. (Illus.). 400p. 1998. pap. 49.95 (*1-886801-58-4*) Chrles River Media.
— GIF Animation Web Magic. 1997. pap. text 39.99 incl. cd-rom (*1-56830-353-X*) Hayden.
— PageMaker 6.5 Complete. LC 96-78099. 928p. 1997. 45.00 (*1-56830-331-9*) Hayden.
— The Poser 3 Handbook. (Illus.). 450p. 1998. pap. 49.95 (*1-886801-90-8*, 1-886801-90-8) Chrles River Media.

Mortiere, Michael D. Principles of Primary Wound Management: A Guide to the Fundamentals. LC 96-94515. (Illus.). 96p. (Orig.). 1996. pap. text 16.00 (*0-9652878-0-7*) Clifton Pub.

Mortifee, Ann, jt. auth. see Robbins, John.

Mortillaro, Nicholas A. The Pathophysiology of the Microcirculation. 305p. 1994. lib. bdg. 239.00 (*0-8493-4547-2*, RC700) CRC Pr.

Mortimer. The Owl & the Pussycat. (Illus.). 32p. (J). (ps-4). Date not set. 15.95 (*0-06-027228-7*); lib. bdg. 15.89 (*0-06-027229-5*) HarpC.
— Phrasal Verbs. Date not set. pap. text. write for info. (*0-582-52217-X*, Pub. by Addison-Wesley) Longman.

Mortimer, A. M. & Rix, K. J., eds. The Psychopathology of Perception: Proceedings of the Third Leeds Psychopathology Symposium, September 1988 - Psychopathology Journal, Vol. 24, No. 6. (Illus.). 36p. 1991. pap. 55.00 (*3-8055-5536-9*) S Karger.

***Mortimer, Anthony R.** Variable Passions: A Reading of Shakespeare's Venus & Adonis LC 99-30572. (Studies in the Renaissance). 1999. write for info. (*0-404-62336-0*) AMS Pr.

Mortimer, Armine K. The Gentlest Law: Roland Barthes's the Pleasure of the Text. (American University Studies: General Literature: Ser. XIX, Vol. 22). XIII, 254p. (C). 1989. text 38.95 (*0-8204-0944-8*) P Lang Pubng.
— Plotting to Kill. LC 90-19208. (Writing about Women Ser.: Vol. 1). XIV, 222p. (C). 1991. text 41.95 (*0-8204-1435-2*) P Lang Pubng.

***Mortimer, Armine Kotin.** Writing Realism: Representations of Reality in French Literature. LC 00-8409. 256p. 2000. 42.50 (*0-8018-6478-X*) Johns Hopkins.

Mortimer, Barbara A. Hollywood's Frontier Captives: Cultural Anxiety & the Captivity Plot in American Film. LC 99-14195. (Studies in American Popular History & Culture). 192p. 1999. 50.00 (*0-8153-3116-9*) Garland.

Mortimer, Brian, jt. auth. see Dixon, John D.

Mortimer, Bunny, jt. auth. see Mortimer, John.

Mortimer, C. H. The Oxygen Content of Air-Saturated Fresh Waters, & Aids in Calculating Percentage Saturation. (International Association of Theoretical & Applied Limnology, Communications Ser.: No. 6). (Illus.). 20p. 1956. pap. 15.00 (*3-510-52006-8*, Pub. by E Schweizerbartsche) Balogh.
— The Oxygen Content of Air-Saturated Fresh Waters over Ranges of Temperature & Atmospheric Pressure of Limnological Interest. (International Association of Theoretical & Applied Limnology, Communications Ser.: No. 22). (Illus.). 23p. 1981. pap. 15.00 (*3-510-52022-X*, Pub. by E Schweizerbartsche) Balogh.
— A Review of Temperature Measurement in Limnology. (International Association of Theoretical & Applied Limnology, Communications Ser.: No. 1). (Illus.). 25p. 1969. reprint ed. pap. 15.00 (*3-510-52001-7*, Pub. by E Schweizerbartsche) Balogh.

Mortimer, C. H. & Moore, W. H. The Use of Thermistors for the Measurement of Lake Temperatures. rev. ed. (International Association of Theoretical & Applied Limnology, Communications Ser.: No. 2). (Illus.). v, 42p. 1970. reprint ed. pap. 15.00 (*3-510-52002-5*, Pub. by E Schweizerbartsche) Balogh.

***Mortimer, Carole.** Bound by Contract. (Presents Ser.: Vol. 2130). 2000. mass mkt. 3.99 (*0-373-12130-X*, 1-12130-0) Harlequin Bks.

Mortimer, Carole. A Christmas Affair. 1990. per. 2.50 (*0-373-11325-0*) Harlequin Bks.

***Mortimer, Carole.** Un Coeur Indomptable. (FRE.). 2000. mass mkt. 3.99 (*0-373-34812-6*) Harlequin Bks.

Mortimer, Carole. Darkness into Light. large type ed. (Nightingale Series Large Print Bks.). 233p. 1991. pap. 14.95 (*0-8161-5179-2*, G K Hall Lrg Type) Mac Lib Ref.
— The Diamond Bride: Nanny Wanted! (Presents Ser.: Vol. 1966). 1998. per. 3.75 (*0-373-11966-6*, 1-11966-8) Harlequin Bks.
— Elusive Obsession. (Presents Ser.). 1994. per. 2.99 (*0-373-11631-4*, 1-11631-8) Harlequin Bks.
— Elusive Obsession. large type ed. (Harlequin Ser.). 1993. lib. bdg. 19.95 (*0-263-13413-X*) Thorndike Pr.
— Fated Attraction. 1994. per. 2.99 (*0-373-11689-6*, 1-11689-6) Harlequin Bks.
— Fated Attraction. large type ed. 1992. reprint ed. 18.95 (*0-263-13031-2*) Mac Lib Ref.
— Glass Slippers & Unicorns. large type ed. (Nightingale Series Large Print Bks.). 226p. 1991. pap. 14.95 (*0-8161-5187-3*, G K Hall Lrg Type) Mac Lib Ref.
— Gracious Lady. 1994. per. 2.99 (*0-373-11657-8*, 1-11657-3) Harlequin Bks.
— El Hombre de Sus Suenos: (The Man of Her Dreams) (Bianca Ser.: No. 131).Tr. of Man of Her Dreams. (SPA.). 1998. per. 3.50 (*0-373-33481-8*, 1-33481-2) Harlequin Bks.
— Hunter's Moon: (Presents Plus) (Presents Ser.). 1994. per. 2.99 (*0-373-11703-5*, 1-11703-5) Harlequin Bks.
— The Jilted Bridegroom. (Presents Ser.). 1993. per. 2.99 (*0-373-11559-8*, 1-11559-1) Harlequin Bks.
— Joined by Marriage: Top Author. (Presents Ser.: Vol. 1977). 1998. per. 3.75 (*0-373-11977-1*, 1-11977-5) Harlequin Bks.
— Just One Night. 1988. pap. 3.50 (*0-373-83206-0*) Harlequin Bks.

***Mortimer, Carole.** Man to Marry. (Presents Ser.). 2000. mass mkt. 3.99 (*0-373-12086-9*) Harlequin Bks.
— Man to Marry. large type ed. (Thorndike Harlequin Romance Ser.). 2000. 22.95 (*0-263-16286-9*) Mills & Boon.

Mortimer, Carole. A Marriage to Remember: Top Author. (Presents Ser.: No. 1929). 1998. per. 3.50 (*0-373-11929-1*, 1-11929-6) Harlequin Bks.
— Married by Christmas: (Top Author) 1998. per. 3.75 (*0-373-11995-X*, 1-11995-7) Harlequin Bks.
— Memories of the Past. (Presents Ser.: No. 451). 1992. per. 2.89 (*0-373-11451-6*, 1-11451-1) Harlequin Bks.
— Memories of the Past. large type ed. 1991. reprint ed. lib. bdg. 18.95 (*0-263-12686-2*) Mac Lib Ref.
— Mother of the Bride. (Presents Plus Ser.). 1993. per. 2.99 (*0-373-11607-1*, 1-11607-8) Harlequin Bks.
— Mother of the Bride. large type ed. (Harlequin Ser.). 1993. reprint ed. lib. bdg. 18.95 (*0-263-13266-8*) Mac Lib Ref.
— Mujer de un Solo Hombre - One-Man Woman. (SPA.). 1997. per. 3.50 (*0-373-33415-X*, 1-33415-0) Harlequin Bks.

***Mortimer, Carole.** Noel en Robe Blanche. (Azur Ser.: No. 807). (FRE.). 2000. mass mkt. 3.99 (*0-373-34807-X*, 1-34807-7, Harlequin French) Harlequin Bks.

Mortimer, Carole. The One & Only. LC 95-23063. (Presents Ser.). 186p. 1996. per. 3.50 (*0-373-11793-0*, 1-11793-6) Harlequin Bks.
— One-Man Woman. 1997. per. 3.50 (*0-373-11863-5*, 1-11863-7) Harlequin Bks.
— One-Man Woman. large type ed. (Harlequin Romance Ser.). 1997. 20.95 (*0-263-14971-4*) Mac Lib Ref.
— Private Lives: Presents Plus. (Presents Ser.). 1993. per. 2.99 (*0-373-11583-0*, 1-11583-1) Harlequin Bks.
— Return Engagement. large type ed. (Harlequin Ser.). 1994. lib. bdg. 19.95 (*0-263-13717-1*) Thorndike Pr.
— Return Engagement: (Presents Plus) (Presents Ser.). 1994. per. 2.99 (*0-373-11671-3*, 1-11671-4) Harlequin Bks.
— A Rogue & a Pirate. large type ed. (Magna Large Print Ser.). 1994. 27.99 (*0-7505-0741-1*, Pub. by Mgna Lrg Print) Ulverscroft.
— Romance of a Lifetime. (Presents Ser.: No. 468). 1992. per. 2.89 (*0-373-11468-0*, 1-11468-5) Harlequin Bks.
— Romance of a Lifetime. large type ed. 285p. 1992. reprint ed. 18.95 (*0-263-12812-1*) Thorndike Pr.
— Saving Grace. (Presents Ser.). 1993. per. 2.89 (*0-373-11543-1*, 1-11543-5) Harlequin Bks.
— Saving Grace. large type ed. 1992. reprint ed. 18.95 (*0-263-13090-8*) Mac Lib Ref.
— Un Serment Inoubliable. (Azur Ser.: No. 750). (FRE.). 1999. mass mkt. 3.50 (*0-373-34750-2*, 1-34750-9) Harlequin Bks.

***Mortimer, Carole.** Their Engagement Is Announced. 2000. mass mkt. 3.99 (*0-373-12098-2*) Harlequin Bks.

Mortimer, Carole. To Be a Bridegroom. (Romance Ser.). 1999. per. 3.75 (*0-373-12051-6*, 1-12051-8) Harlequin Bks.
— To Be a Bridegroom. large type ed. (Harlequin Ser.). 1999. 21.95 (*0-263-16105-6*, Pub. by Mills & Boon) Ulverscroft.
— To Be a Husband: Bachelor Brothers. 1999. per. 3.75 (*0-373-12043-5*, 1-12043-5) Harlequin Bks.

***Mortimer, Carole.** To Be a Husband: Bachelor Brothers. (Harlequin Ser.). 1999. 21.95 (*0-263-16084-X*) Mills & Boon.

An Asterisk (*) at the beginning of an entry indicates that the title is appearing for the first time.

Mortimer, Carole. To Woo a Wife: Bachelor Brothers. (Presents Ser.: Bk. 2039). 1999. per. 3.75 (*0-373-12039-7*, 1-12039-3) Harlequin Bks.
— To Woo a Wife: Bachelor Brothers. 1999. 21.95 (*0-263-16059-9*, G K Hall & Co) Mac Lib Ref.
— Two's Company. (Harlequin Presents Ser.: No. 1823). 1996. per. 3.50 (*0-373-11823-6*, 1-11823-1) Harlequin Bks.
— Two's Company. large type ed. (Harlequin Romance Ser.). 1996. 20.95 (*0-263-14552-2*) Mac Lib Ref.
— Le Visage du Passe. (Azur Ser.). (FRE.). 1994. pap. 3.50 (*0-373-34433-3*, 1-34433-2) Harlequin Bks.
— War of Love: (Presents Plus) LC 95-4587. (Presents Ser.). 186p. 1995. per. 3.25 (*0-373-11727-2*, 1-11727-4) Harlequin Bks.
— Wildest Dreams. (Presents Ser.: No. 1894). 1997. per. 3.50 (*0-373-11894-5*, 1-11894-2) Harlequin Bks.
— Wildest Dreams. large type ed. (Harlequin Ser.). 1998. 20.95 (*0-263-15322-3*) Thorndike Pr.
***Mortimer, Carole.** A Yuletide Seduction, large type ed. (Harlequin Romance Ser.). 2000. 22.95 (*0-263-16410-1*) Mills & Boon.
Mortimer, Carole, jt. auth. see Jordan, Penny.
Mortimer, Carole, jt. auth. see Neels, Betty A.
Mortimer, Charles E. Chemistry. 5th ed. 1983. pap., student ed. 8.75 (*0-534-02728-8*) Wadsworth Pub.
— Chemistry: A Concept Approach - Answer Book. 4th ed. (Chemistry Ser.). 1979. pap. 1.75 (*0-534-25547-7*) Wadsworth Pub.
— Chemistry: A Concept Approach - Solutions Manual. 4th ed. (Chemistry Ser.). 1979. pap. 3.75 (*0-534-25546-9*) Wadsworth Pub.
— Chemistry: A Conceptual Approach. 3rd ed. 1975. pap. text 20.75 (*0-534-30162-2*) Wadsworth Pub.
— Chemistry: A Conceptual Approach. 4th ed. (Chemistry Ser.). 1979. pap. 26.00 (*0-534-25545-0*) Wadsworth Pub.
Mortimer, Charlotte. Marrying by Lot. 1993. reprint ed. lib. bdg. 89.00 (*0-7812-5494-9*) Rprt Serv.
Mortimer, Colin. Elements of Pronounciation. 104p. 1985. pap. text 14.95 (*0-521-26938-5*) Cambridge U Pr.
— Elements of Pronounciation, Set. 100p. 1985. pap. 62.95 (*0-521-26334-4*) Cambridge U Pr.
Mortimer, Curt. Dinosaur Journal: Making Sense of a Young Son's Death. LC 96-14724. (Illus.). 187p. (Orig.). 1996. pap. 10.95 (*0-940895-19-6*) Cornerstone IL.
Mortimer, Curtiss. Chicago in Adagio: A Cornerstone Press Poetry Chapbook. Peterson, Patrick, ed. LC 97-162559. 32p. 1996. pap. 5.00 (*0-940895-30-7*) Cornerstone IL.
Mortimer, D., jt. auth. see McNicol, S. B.
Mortimer, D., jt. ed. see Jansen, R.
Mortimer, David. Practical Laboratory Andrology. LC 92-48921. (Illus.). 416p. 1994. text 75.00 (*0-19-506595-6*) OUP.
***Mortimer, Edward.** People, Nation & State: The Meaning of Ethnicity & Nationalism. 1999. pap. text 19.95 (*1-86064-401-5*, Pub. by I B T) St Martin.
Mortimer, Edward A., Jr., jt. auth. see Plotkin, Stanley A.
Mortimer, Eunice. Working with the Elderly. Davies, Martin, ed. (Community Care Practice Handbook Ser.: No. 9). vi, 91p. (Orig.). (C). 1982. pap. text 16.95 (*0-566-05171-0*) Ashgate Pub Co.
Mortimer, Gail L. Daughter of the Swan: Legacies of Love & Knowledge in Eudora Welty's Fiction. LC 93-41117. 264p. 1994. 40.00 (*0-8203-1633-4*) U of Ga Pr.
Mortimer, George. Observations & Remarks Made During a Voyage to the Islands of Teneriffe, Amsterdam, Maria's Islands near Van Dieman's Land, Otaheita, Sandwich Islands, Owyhee, the Fox Islands on the Northwest Coast of America, Tinian, & From Thence to Canton, in the Brig. 80p. 1989. 22.50 (*0-87770-456-2*) Ye Galleon.
Mortimer, Halina, et al. Logic of Induction. 168p. 1988. text 41.95 (*0-470-21234-9*) P-H.
Mortimer, James, et al, eds. The Aging Motor System, 3. LC 82-598. 258p. 1982. 59.95 (*0-275-90865-8*, C0865, Praeger Pubs) Greenwood.
Mortimer, James, tr. see Dreyfus, Alfred.
Mortimer, James W., jt. auth. see Hurst, W. J.
Mortimer, Jeanne A. Marine Turtles in the Republic of the Seychelles: Status & Management : Report on Project 1809 (1981-1984) LC 86-123064. vii, 80 p. 1984. write for info. (*2-88032-901-9*, Pub. by IUCN) Island Pr.
***Mortimer, Jeff, retold by.** Learning Curves: Hits, Misses & Home Runs. xviii, 416p. 1999. 29.95 (*1-879094-65-7*) Momentum Bks.
Mortimer, Jeylan T. Changing Attitudes Toward Work. (Studies in Productivity: Highlights of the Literature Ser.: Vol. 11). 55p. 1979. pap. 55.00 (*0-08-029492-8*) Work in Amer.
Mortimer, Jeylan T. & Finch, Michael D., eds. Adolescents, Work & Families: An Intergenerational Development Analysis. LC 96-10001. (Understanding Families Ser.: Vol. 6). 240p. 1996. 48.00 (*0-8039-5124-8*); pap. 21.95 (*0-8039-5125-6*) Sage.
Mortimer, Jeylan T., et al. Work, Family, & Personality: Transition to Adulthood. Platt, Gerald, ed. LC 85-20951. (Modern Sociology Ser.). 272p. 1986. text 73.25 (*0-89391-293-X*) Ablx Pub.
Mortimer, Jeylan T., jt. auth. see Call, Kathleen T.
Mortimer, Jeylan T., jt. ed. see Petersen, Anne C.
Mortimer, John. The Best of Rumpole. LC 93-1063. 288p. 1994. reprint ed. pap. 12.95 (*0-14-017684-5*, Penguin Bks) Viking Penguin.
— Character Parts. 1986. text. write for info. (*0-670-81124-6*) Viking Penguin.
— Charade. 1976. 20.95 (*0-8488-0595-X*) Amereon Ltd.
— Clinging to the Wreckage: A Part of Life. LC 83-13078. 224p. 1984. pap. 11.95 (*0-14-006860-0*, Penguin Bks) Viking Penguin.
— Dunster. large type ed. LC 94-26347. 407p. 1994. pap. 19.95 (*0-8161-7476-8*, G K Hall Lrg Type) Mac Lib Ref.
— Felix in the Underwood. 256p. 1998. pap. 12.95 (*0-14-027496-0*) Viking Penguin.
— A First Rumpole Omnibus. (Crime Monthly Ser.). 560p. 1984. pap. 16.95 (*0-14-006768-X*, Penguin Bks) Viking Penguin.
— Murderers & Other Friends: Another Part of Life. 272p. 1996. pap. 11.95 (*0-14-024800-5*, Viking) Viking Penguin.
— Paradise Postponed. 384p. 1986. pap. 12.95 (*0-14-009864-X*, Penguin Bks) Viking Penguin.
— Rumpole a la Carte. 256p. 1991. reprint ed. pap. 10.95 (*0-14-015609-7*, Penguin Bks) Viking Penguin.
— Rumpole & the Age of Miracles. 1989. pap. 10.95 (*0-14-013116-7*, Penguin Bks) Viking Penguin.
— Rumpole & the Age of Miracles. large type ed. 1995. pap. 19.95 (*0-7838-1188-8*, G K Hall Lrg Type) Mac Lib Ref.
— Rumpole & the Angel of Death. 1995. 22.95 (*0-614-96276-5*, Viking) Viking Penguin.
— Rumpole & the Angel of Death. 272p. 1997. reprint ed. pap. 9.95 (*0-14-026314-4*) Viking Penguin.
— Rumpole & the Golden Thread. 256p. 1984. pap. 9.95 (*0-14-025014-X*, Penguin Classics) Viking Penguin.
— Rumpole for the Defense. 192p. 1984. pap. 9.95 (*0-14-025013-1*) Viking Penguin.
— Rumpole of the Bailey. 17.95 (*0-89190-275-9*) Amereon Ltd.
— Rumpole of the Bailey. 208p. 1980. pap. 9.95 (*0-14-025012-3*) Viking Penguin.
— Rumpole on Trial. large type ed. LC 93-7198. 380p. 1993. lib. bdg. 21.95 (*1-56054-727-8*) Thorndike Pr.
— Rumpole on Trial. 256p. 1993. reprint ed. pap. 10.00 (*0-14-017510-5*, Penguin Bks) Viking Penguin.
— Rumpole's Last Case. 1990. pap. 10.95 (*0-14-012695-3*, Penguin Bks) Viking Penguin.
— Rumpole's Return. 18.95 (*0-89190-277-5*) Amereon Ltd.
— Rumpole's Return. 160p. 1982. pap. 9.95 (*0-14-024698-3*, Penguin Classics) Viking Penguin.
— The Second Rumpole Omnibus: Rumpole & the Golden Thread, Rumpole for the Defence & Rumpole's Last Case. 672p. 1988. pap. 16.95 (*0-14-008958-6*, Penguin Bks) Viking Penguin.
— The Sound of Trumpets. LC 98-38968. 256p. 1999. 23.95 (*0-670-87861-8*) Viking Penguin.
***Mortimer, John.** The Sound of Trumpets. 288p. 1999. pap. 12.95 (*0-14-028851-1*) Viking Penguin.
Mortimer, John. The Sound of Trumpets. large type ed. LC 99-35097. 405p. 1999. pap. 26.95 (*0-7838-8716-7*) Mac Lib Ref.
— Summer's Lease. 288p. 1991. pap. 11.95 (*0-14-015827-8*, Penguin Bks) Viking Penguin.
— The Third Rumpole Omnibus: Rumpole a la Carte, Rumpole on Trial, Rumpole & the Angel of Death. LC 98-139485. 768p. 1998. pap. 16.95 (*0-14-025741-1*, Penguin Bks) Viking Penguin.
— Titmuss Regained. 288p. 1991. pap. 12.95 (*0-14-014921-X*, Penguin Bks) Viking Penguin.
— The Trials of Rumpole. 20.95 (*0-89190-276-7*) Amereon Ltd.
— The Trials of Rumpole. 208p. 1981. pap. 9.95 (*0-14-024697-5*, Penguin Bks) Viking Penguin.
Mortimer, John & Mortimer, Bunny. Shelter & Shade: Creating a Healthy & Profitable Environment for Your Livestock with Trees. LC 96-18694. (Illus.). 160p. 1996. pap. 20.00 (*0-9632460-4-6*) Green Park.
Mortimer, John & Rooks, Brian. The International Robot Industry Report. (Illus.). 260p. 1987. 180.95 (*0-387-16353-0*) Spr-Verlag.
Mortimer, John, ed. see Ingersoll Engineers Staff.
Mortimer, Katharine. Sting of the Wasp. 224p. 1987. 17.95 (*0-88191-047-3*) Freundlich.
Mortimer, Kenneth P. & McConnell, T. R. Sharing Authority Effectively. LC 76-50721. (Jossey-Bass Series in Higher Education). 344p. reprint ed. pap. 106.70 (*0-8357-4913-4*, 203784300009) Bks Demand.
Mortimer, Kenneth P., et al. Flexibility in Academic Staffing: Effective Policies & Practices. Fife, Jonathan D., ed. & frwd. by. LC 85-72832. (ASHE-ERIC Higher Education Reports: No. 85-1). 121p. (Orig.). 1985. pap. 24.00 (*0-913317-20-9*) GWU Grad Schl E&HD.
***Mortimer, Martin.** The English Glass Chandelier. (Illus.). 200p. 2000. 89.50 (*1-85149-328-X*) Antique Collect.
Mortimer, Martin, jt. auth. see Cousens, Roger.
***Mortimer, Mary.** Learn Descriptive Cataloging. LC 99-46644. (Library Basics Ser.: No. 3). 256p. 2000. reprint ed. pap. 35.00 (*0-8108-3693-9*) Scarecrow.
— Learn Dewey Decimal Classification. 21st ed. LC 99-40185. (Library Basics Ser.: No. 2). 145p. 1999. pap. 24.50 (*0-8108-3694-7*) Scarecrow.
Mortimer, Maxwell & Namorato, Cono. Third Annual Tax Shelter Controversies: The IRS, Justice & SEC Crack Down. write for info. (*0-318-58298-8*) Harcourt.
***Mortimer, Maya.** Meeting the Sensei: The Role of the Master in Shirakaba Writers. LC 99-56875. (Japanese Studies Library). 308p. 2000. 78.00 (*90-04-11655-9*) Brill Academic Pubs.
***Mortimer, Mildred, ed.** Maghrebian Mosaic: A Literature in Transition. 320p. 2000. lib. bdg. 59.95 (*0-89410-888-3*, Three Contnts) L Rienner.
Mortimer, Mildred, tr. see Sebbar, Leila.
Mortimer, Mildred P. Journeys Through the French African Novel. LC 90-4416. (Studies in African Literature). 230p. (Orig.). (C). 1990. pap. text 18.50 (*0-435-08042-3*, 08042) Heinemann.
Mortimer, Mildred P., et al, eds. The Literature of Africa & the African Continuum. LC 84-51450. (African Literature Association Annuals Ser.). 140p. (Orig.). 1988. 22.00 (*0-89410-460-8*); pap. 14.00 (*0-89410-461-6*) Cornell AS&RC.
Mortimer, Monty. Competition Training for Horse & Rider. (Illus.). 60p. 1997. pap. 19.95 (*0-7153-0473-9*, Pub. by D & C Pub) Sterling.
— The Riding Instructor's Handbook. LC 97-218495. (Illus.). 144p. 1997. pap. 14.95 (*0-7153-0622-7*) Sterling.
***Mortimer, P.** Broke Through Britan. 1999. pap. text 17.95 (*1-84018-163-X*, Pub. by Mainstream Pubng) Trafalgar.
Mortimer, Pamela. Blue Jazz Moon. (Illus.). 62p. (Orig.). 1996. pap. 5.00 (*0-9632399-2-9*) Premier PA.
Mortimer, Pamela, ed. see Long, David M.
Mortimer, Penelope. Queen Mother: An Alternative Portrait of Her Life & Times. LC 96-164692. (Illus.). 320p. 1996. pap. 16.95 (*0-233-98972-2*, Pub. by Andre Deutsch) Trafalgar.
Mortimer, Raymond, intro. Cheri & the Last of Cheri. (Twentieth-Century Classics Ser.). 256p. 1995. pap. 11.95 (*0-14-018317-5*, Penguin Bks) Viking Penguin.
— The Vagabond. LC 00-3268. (Twentieth-Century Classics Ser.). 192p. 1995. pap. 10.95 (*0-14-018325-6*, Penguin Classics) Viking Penguin.
Mortimer, Raymond, jt. auth. see Todd, Dorothy.
Mortimer, Rex. Indonesian Communism Under Sukarno: Ideology & Politics, 1959-1965. LC 73-19372. 448p. 1974. text 57.50 (*0-8014-0825-3*) Cornell U Pr.
Mortimer, Richard. Angevin England, 1154 - 1258. Chibnall, Marjorie, ed. (History of Medieval Britain Ser.). (Illus.). 272p. 1996. pap. 22.95 (*0-631-20284-6*) Blackwell Pubs.
— Angevin England, 1154-1258. Chibnall, Marjorie, ed. (History of Medieval Britain Ser.). (Illus.). 256p. 1994. 48.95 (*0-631-16388-3*) Blackwell Pubs.
— Leiston Abbey Cartulary & Butley Priory Charters. (Suffolk Charters Ser.: No. I). 187p. 1979. 45.00 (*0-85115-106-X*) Boydell & Brewer.
Mortimer, Richard, ed. Charters of St. Bartholomew's Priory, Sudbury. LC 96-217542. (Suffolk Charters Ser.: Vol. 15). (Illus.). 128p. (C). 1996. 45.00 (*0-85115-574-X*) Boydell & Brewer.
Mortimer, Richard, jt. auth. see Harper-Bill, Christopher.
Mortimer, Richard, jt. ed. see Harper-Bill, Christopher.
Mortimer, Richard, jt. ed. see Harvey, Anthony.
Mortimer, Robert G. The Calculus of Physics. LC 92-40711. 1993. 13.75 (*0-8053-4650-3*) Benjamin-Cummings.
— Mathematics for Physical Chemistry. 2nd ed. LC 98-89310. (Illus.). 456p. (C). 1999. pap. 35.00 (*0-12-508340-8*) Acad Pr.
***Mortimer, Robert G.** Physical Chemistry. 2nd ed. 960p. 2000. 89.95 (*0-12-508345-9*) Acad Pr.
Mortimer, Ruth. French 16th Century Books, 2 vols., Vol. I & II. (Illustrated Books of the Renaissance). (Illus.). 730p. 1998. reprint ed. boxed set 275.00 (*0-8150-0000-6*) Wittenborn Art.
— Italian 16th Century Books, 2 vols., Vols. I & II. rev. ed. (Illustrated Books of the Renaissance). (Illus.). 840p. 1998. boxed set 295.00 (*0-8150-0001-4*) Wittenborn Art.
Mortimer, Ruth, intro. The Selma Erving Collection: Modern Illustrated Books. 60p. 1977. pap. 7.00 (*0-87391-037-0*) Smith Coll Mus Art.
Mortimer, Sheila. Fred the Frog. (Illus.). 32p. (J). (ps-2). 1995. 8.95 (*0-7078-0235-0*, Pub. by Natl Trust) Trafalgar.
Mortimer, Steve, jt. auth. see Desborough, James.
Mortimer, Stuart. Techniques of Spiral Work: A Practical Guide to the Craft of Making Twists by Hand. LC 95-34339. (Illus.). 176p. 1996. pap. 24.95 (*0-941936-34-1*) Linden Pub Fresno.
Mortimer, W. Golden. Peru & the History of Coca: Divine Plant of the Incas. 1976. lib. bdg. 75.00 (*0-8490-0821-2*) Gordon Pr.
Mortimer, William G. Peru: History of Coca, "the Divine Plant" of the Incas. LC 74-15120. reprint ed. 69.50 (*0-404-11980-8*) AMS Pr.
Mortimore, Claudia. Immigration & Adoption. 128p. 1994. pap. 16.00 (*1-85856-012-8*, Trentham Bks) Stylus Pub VA.
Mortimore, Denise. Complete Illustrated Guide to Nutritional Healing. LC 98-21697. (Illus.). 224p. 1998. pap. text 24.95 (*1-86204-176-8*, Pub. by Element MA) Penguin Putnam.
***Mortimore, Denise.** The Complete Illustrated Guide to Vitamins & Minerals: A Practical Approach to a Healthy Diet & Safe Supplements. (Illus.). 2000. pap. 24.95 (*1-86204-453-8*, Pub. by Element MA) Penguin Putnam.
Mortimore, Denise. Healing Foods. (In a Nutshell Ser.). (Illus.). 64p. 1999. 7.95 (*1-86204-381-7*, Pub. by Element MA) Penguin Putnam.
— Nutritional Healing. LC 98-20386. (In a Nutshell Ser.). (Illus.). 64p. 1998. 7.95 (*1-86204-245-4*, Pub. by Element MA) Penguin Putnam.
Mortimore, James. Babylon 5 Security Manual. LC PN1992.77.B24M67. 176p. 1998. pap. 18.95 (*0-345-42453-0*, Del Rey) Ballantine Pub Grp.
Mortimore, Jim. Bel Tempest. 1998. pap. 5.95 (*0-563-40593-7*) BBC.
***Mortimore, Jim.** Campaign. (Doctor Who Ser.). 288p. 2000. mass mkt. 6.95 (*0-563-55593-9*) BBC Bks.
Mortimore, Jim. Cracker: Mad Woman in the Attic. LC 96-20779. 256p. 1996. 21.95 (*0-312-14576-4*) St Martin.
— Eye of Heaven. (Doctor Who Ser.). 1998. pap. 5.95 (*0-563-40567-8*) BBC.
— The Sword of Forever. (New Adventures Ser.). 1998. mass mkt. 5.95 (*0-426-20526-X*, Pub. by Virgin Bks) London Brdge.
Mortimore, Jim, jt. auth. see Leonard, Paul.
Mortimore, Jo, jt. auth. see Morimore, Peter.
Mortimore, Michael. Roots in the African Dust: Sustaining the Drylands. LC 97-42897. (Illus.). 236p. (C). 1998. 59.95 (*0-521-45173-6*); pap. 21.95 (*0-521-45785-8*) Cambridge U Pr.
Mortimore, Michael & Adams, W. M. Working the Sahel: Environment & Society in Northern Nigeria. LC 98-34516. (Global Environmental Change Ser.). 1999. write for info. (*0-415-14096-X*) Routledge.
Mortimore, Peter. The Road to Improvement: Reflections on School Effectiveness. LC 98-33633. 396p. 1998. pap. 39.00 (*90-265-1526-X*) Swets.
— The Road to Improvement: Reflections on School Effectiveness. LC 98-33633. 396p. 1998. 97.00 (*90-265-1525-1*) Swets.
Mortimore, Peter & Little, Viv, eds. Living Education: Essays in Honor of John Tomlinson. 288p. 1997. pap. 49.95 (*1-85396-348-8*, Pub. by P Chapman) Taylor & Francis.
Mortimore, Peter, et al. Managing Associate Staff: Innovation in Primary & Secondary Schools. 192p. 1993. pap. 37.50 (*1-85396-231-7*, Pub. by P Chapman) Taylor & Francis.
— School Matters: The Junior Years. 314p. 1988. pap. 22.00 (*0-7291-0194-0*, Pub. by P Chapman) Taylor & Francis.
Mortimore, Roger, jt. auth. see Leonard, R. L.
Mortimore, S. E. Cracker: The Mad Woman in the Attic, Vol. 1. 1998. mass mkt. 5.99 (*0-312-96337-8*) St Martin.
Mortimore, Sara, jt. auth. see Mayes, Tony.
Mortis, Joseph, ed. see Society of Biological Psychiatry Staff.
Mortiz, Patricia M. Columbia. LC 98-16608. (Dropping in on Ser.). (J). 1998. (*0-86593-496-7*) Rourke Corp.
Mortland, Carol A., jt. ed. see Haines, David W.
Mortland, Donald, ed. see Colcord, Lincoln.
Mortley, Raoul. The Idea of Universal History from Hellenistic Philosophy to Early Christian Historiography. LC 96-506. (Texts & Studies in Religion: Vol. 67). 244p. 1996. text 89.95 (*0-7734-8787-5*) E Mellen.
— Womanhood the Feminine in Ancient Hellenism Gnosticism Christianity & Islam. 1981. 25.00 (*0-85668-912-2*, Pub. by Aris & Phillips); pap. 18.50 (*0-85668-913-0*, Pub. by Aris & Phillips) David Brown.
Mortlock, Robert P. Evolution of Metabolic Function. 352p. 1992. lib. bdg. 189.00 (*0-8493-8863-5*) CRC Pr.
Mortlock, Robert P., ed. Microorganisms As Model Systems for Studying Evolution. LC 84-17938. (Monographs in Evolutionary Biology). 344p. 1984. 95.00 (*0-306-41788-X*, Plenum Trade) Perseus Pubng.
Mortman, Doris. The Lucky Ones. LC 96-80069. 407p. 1997. 22.95 (*1-57566-204-3*) Kensgtn Pub Corp.
— The Lucky Ones. 480p. 1998. pap. 6.99 (*0-8217-5920-5*, Zebra Kensgtn) Kensgtn Pub Corp.
— The Lucky Ones. large type ed. LC 97-47191. (Large Print Bks.). 1998. pap. 23.95 (*1-56895-532-4*) Wheeler Pub.
— Out of Nowhere. LC 97-75385. 480p. 1998. text 23.95 (*1-57566-301-5*, Knsington) Kensgtn Pub Corp.
— Out of Nowhere, 1. 544p. 1999. mass mkt. 6.99 (*0-8217-6253-2*) Kensgtn Pub Corp.
— True Colors. 1996. mass mkt. 6.99 (*0-8041-1111-1*) Ivy Books.
***Mortola, Jacopo P. A.** Respiratory Physiology of Newborn Mammals: A Comparative Perspective. LC 00-9834. (Illus.). 2001. write for info. (*0-8018-6497-6*) Johns Hopkins.
Morton. Contemporary Composers. 2nd ed. 1200p. 2002. 160.00 (*1-55862-238-1*) St James Pr.
— Forecasting Module 3" - Parsifal Workbench. (GC - Principles of Management Ser.). (C). 1998. pap. 29.95 (*0-87709-535-3*) S-W Pub.
— Home Rule & Irish Question. (C). 1980. pap. text 13.50 (*0-582-35215-0*) Addison-Wesley.
— Inventory Module 3 - Parsifal Workbench. (GC - Principles of Management Ser.). (C). 1998. pap. 29.95 (*0-87709-537-X*) S-W Pub.
Morton. Managing Operations Emerging Companies. 1984. 21.95 (*0-201-15860-4*) Addison-Wesley.
Morton. Production & Operations Management. (GC - Principles of Management Ser.). 720p. (C). 1999. 83.95 (*0-87709-524-8*) Course Tech.
— Project Management Module+Software - Parsifal Workbench. (GC - Principles of Management Ser.). (C). 1998. pap. 29.95 (*0-87709-531-0*) S-W Pub.
— Public Relations Publications. (Communications Ser.). 1919. pap. 30.00 (*0-534-52209-2*) Brooks-Cole.
— Scheduling Module 3" - Parsifal Workbench. (GC - Principles of Management Ser.). (C). 1998. pap. 29.95 (*0-87709-533-7*) S-W Pub.
— Sea Trials. LC 99-36354. 1999. text 23.95 (*0-312-20908-8*) St Martin.
Morton, jt. auth. see Enright.
Morton, jt. auth. see Perry.
Morton, James. Easy Rock Drum Charts. 44p. 1996. pap. 7.95 (*0-7866-0458-1*, 95442) Mel Bay.
Morton, A. A., jt. auth. see Broderick, M.
Morton, A. C., et al, eds. Developments in Sedimentary Provenance Studies. (Geological Society Special Publications Classic: No. 57). (Illus.). 376p. 1996. 34.00 (*1-897799-53-5*, 259, Pub. by Geol Soc Pub Hse) AAPG.
— Geology of the Brent Group. (Geological Society Special Publications: No. 61). (Illus.). vi, 506p. (C). 1992. 125.00 (*0-903317-68-0*, 263, Pub. by Geol Soc Pub Hse) AAPG.
Morton, A. H., ed. see Membre, Michele.
Morton, A. L., ed. The Political Writings of William Morris. rev. ed. 259p. 1973. text 9.95 (*0-85315-586-0*, Pub. by Lawrence & Wishart) NYU Pr.
Morton, A. L., ed. The Political Writings of William Morris. 246p. (C). 1973. pap. 9.95 (*0-85315-257-8*, Pub. by Lawrence & Wishart) NYU Pr.
Morton, A. L., ed. see Morris, William.

M

Morton, A. Q. The Gathering of the Gospels: From Papyrus to Printout. LC 97-12634. (Mellen Biblical Studies: No. 53). 152p. 1997. text 69.95 (*0-7734-2427-X*, Mellen Biblical Pr) E Mellen.

— The Making of Mark. LC 95-32755. (Biblical Press Ser.: Vol. 41). 112p. 1996. text 59.95 (*0-7734-2393-1*, Mellen Biblical Pr) E Mellen.

Morton, A. Q. & Michaelson, Sidney. A Critical Concordance to the Acts of the Apostles. (Computer Bible Ser.: Vol. 7). 1976. pap. 89.95 (*0-935106-14-6*) E Mellen.

Morton, A. Q., et al. A Critical Concordance to I & II Corinthians. (Computer Bible Ser.: Vol. 19). 1979. pap. 119.95 (*0-935106-01-4*) E Mellen.

— A Critical Concordance to I, II Thessalonians. Baird, J. Arthur & Freedman, David N., eds. (Computer Bible Ser.: Vol. 26). 136p. 1983. pap. 69.95 (*0-935106-21-9*) E Mellen.

— A Critical Concordance to the Epistle of Paul to the Galatians. Baird, J. Arthur & Freedman, David, eds. (Computer Bible Ser.: Vol. 21). 1980. pap. text 69.95 (*0-935106-16-2*) E Mellen.

— Critical Concordance to the Letter of Paul to the Colossians. Baird, J. Arthur & Thompson, David, eds. (Computer Bible Ser.: Vol. 24). 1981. pap. text 49.95 (*0-935106-19-7*) E Mellen.

— A Critical Concordance to the Letter of Paul to the Ephesians. Baird, J. Arthur & Freedman, David, eds. (Computer Bible Ser.: Vol. 22). 1980. pap. text 59.95 (*0-935106-17-0*) E Mellen.

— Critical Concordance to the Letter of Paul to the Philippians. Baird, J. Arthur & Thompson, David, eds. (Computer Bible Ser.: Vol. 23). 1980. pap. text 49.95 (*0-935106-18-9*) E Mellen.

— Critical Concordance to the Letter of Paul to the Romans. Baird, J. Arthur & Freedman, David Noel, eds. (Computer Bible Ser.: Vol. 13). 1977. pap. 99.95 (*0-935106-08-1*) E Mellen.

— A Critical Concordance to the Pastoral Epistles, I, II Timothy, Titus, Philemon. Baird, J. Arthur & Freedman, David N., eds. (Computer Bible Ser.: Vol. 25). 1982. pap. 89.95 (*0-935106-20-0*) E Mellen.

Morton, Adam. A Guide Through the Theory of Knowledge. 2nd ed. LC 97-3879. (Illus.). 224p. (C). 1997. text 52.95 (*0-631-20004-5*); pap. text 21.95 (*0-631-20005-3*) Blackwell Pubs.

— Philosophy in Practice: An Introduction to the Main Question. (Illus.). 500p. (C). 1996. 87.95 (*0-631-18864-9*); pap. 36.95 (*0-631-18865-7*) Blackwell Pubs.

Morton, Adam & Stich, Stephen P., eds. Beracerrax & His Critics. LC 95-25841. (Philosophers & Their Cities Ser.: Vol. 8). (Illus.). 300p. (C). 1996. 60.95 (*0-631-19268-9*) Blackwell Pubs.

Morton, Alan. The Complete Directory to Science Fiction, Fantasy & Horror Television Series: A Comprehensive Guide to the First 50 Years, 1946 to 1996. 992p. (Orig.). 1997. pap. 29.95 (*0-9657358-0-X*, Other Wrlds) A Morton.

Morton, Alan Q. & Wess, Jane A. Public & Private Science: The King George III Collection. (Illus.). 720p. 1993. 125.00 (*0-19-856392-2*) OUP.

Morton, Aleksander & Morton, H. Neurons & Symbols: The Stuff That Mind Is Made Of. (ITCP-UK Computer Science Ser.). 272p. (C). 1993. mass mkt. 46.95 (*0-412-46090-4*) Chapman & Hall.

Morton, Alexander C. The Official Guide to Airline Careers. write for info. (*0-318-59582-6*) S&S Trade.

Morton, Alexandra. Siwiti: A Whale's Story. (Illus.). 48p. (Orig.). (YA). (gr. 8-12). 1991. pap. 9.95 (*0-920501-97-4*) Orca Bk Pubs.

Morton, Alexandra, photos by. In the Company of Whales: From the Diary of a Whale Watcher. (Illus.). 64p. (J). (ps-2). 1999. pap. 9.95 (*1-55143-058-4*) Orca Bk Pubs.

Morton, Alice, tr. see De Heusch, Luc.

Morton, Allen D. Financial Management. (Test Yourself Ser.). (Illus.). 192p. 1998. pap. 12.95 (*0-8442-2386-7*) NTC Contemp Pub Co.

Morton, Alvin. A Noble Spirit. (Illus.). 272p. 1998. 43.00 (*0-8059-4463-X*) Dorrance.

Morton, Andrew. Diana: Her New Life. 1995. mass mkt. 6.50 (*0-671-53434-3*) PB.

— Diana: Her New Life. 1995. mass mkt. 7.50 (*0-671-53398-3*, PB Trade Paper) PB.

— Diana: Her New Life. 1994. 23.00 (*0-684-80009-8*) S&S Trade.

— Diana: Her New Life. large type ed. LC 95-2572. (Illus.). 285p. 1995. lib. bdg. 25.95 (*0-7862-0425-7*) Thorndike Pr.

— Diana: Her True Story in Her Own Words. Rubenstein, Julie & Peters, Sally, eds. 288p. 1992. per. 7.50 (*0-671-79878-2*) PB.

— Diana: Her True Story in Her Own Words. LC 99-204436. 1997. 22.45 (*0-684-85080-X*) S&S Trade.

— Diana: Her True Story in Her Own Words. 1992. 12.60 (*0-606-13330-5*, Pub. by Turtleback) Demco.

— Diana: Her True Story in Her Own Words. large type ed. 304p. 1993. reprint ed. 21.95 (*1-56054-608-5*) Thorndike Pr.

— Diana: Her True Story in Her Own Words. large type ed. 304p. 1993. reprint ed. lib. bdg. 14.95 (*1-56054-889-4*) Thorndike Pr.

— Diana: Her True Story in Her Own Words. rev. ed. 1998. per. 7.99 (*0-671-02412-4*) PB.

— Diana: Sa Vrai Histoire. 1999. pap. 15.95 (*2-266-05516-X*) Presses Pocket.

— Moi: The Making of an African Statesman. (Illus.). 224p. 1999. 29.95 (*1-85479-253-9*, Pub. by M OMara) Trafalgar.

— Monica's Story. LC 99-190557. (Illus.). 288p. 1999. text 24.95 (*0-312-24091-0*) St Martin.

— Monica's Story. (Illus.). 385p. 1999. mass mkt. 6.99 (*0-312-97362-4*, St Martins Paperbacks) St Martin.

***Morton, Andrew.** Monica's Story. ed. 2000. text. write for info. (*0-312-26365-1*) St Martin.

Morton, Andrew. Monica's Story. large type ed. LC 99-33154. 1999. 28.95 (*0-7862-2051-1*) Thorndike Pr.

***Morton, Andrew.** Monica's Story: Van&Dyck, Jennifer. abr. ed. 1999. audio 18.00 (*0-694-52193-0*) HarperAudio.

Morton, Andrew. Tree Heritage of Britain & Ireland: A Guide to the Famous Trees of Britain & Ireland. LC 98-191153. 208p. 1998. write for info. (*1-85310-559-7*) Swan Hill Pr.

— The Wealth of the Windsors. (Illus.). 192p. 1994. reprint ed. pap. 10.45 (*1-55970-261-3*, Pub. by Arcade Pub Inc) Time Warner.

Morton, Andrew, tr. see Pu, Ning.

Morton, Andrew R. Food-Calorie Intake & Effects on Diet, Energy & Metabolism: Index of New Information with Authors & Subjects. rev. ed. LC 94-34922. 163p. 1997. 47.50 (*0-7883-0444-5*); pap. 44.50 (*0-7883-0445-3*) ABBE Pubs Assn.

— Food Contamination: Medical Subject Analysis with Bibliography. LC 87-47612. 160p. 1987. 47.50 (*0-88164-536-2*); pap. 44.50 (*0-88164-537-0*) ABBE Pubs Assn.

***Morton, Anne.** Education & the State from 1833. LC 98-150754. (Readers' Guides Ser.: No. 18). 216p. 1999. pap. 24.00 (*1-873162-33-2*, Pub. by PRO Pubns) Midpt Trade.

Morton, Anne. The Office Management Manual: A Guide for Secretaries, Administrative Assistants, & Other Office Professionals. 2nd ed. (Reference Ser.). 336p. (Orig.). 1990. pap. 9.95 (*0-88908-537-4*) Self-Counsel Pr.

— The Secretary's Friend: The Office Management Manual. LC 86-45541. 256p. 1986. 14.95 (*0-933051-16-6*) Lowen Pub.

— The Secretary's Friend: The Office Management Manual. 2nd rev. ed. 256p. 1987. pap. 9.95 (*0-933051-33-6*) Lowen Pub.

Morton, Annie, et al. Great Special Events & Activities. LC 91-65991. 112p. 1991. pap. 16.95 (*0-910251-45-2*) Venture Pub PA.

Morton, Arthur. Animal Farms & More. (Illus.). (J). (gr. k-3). 1995. 12.50 (*1-57842-002-4*) Delmas Creat.

— Los Animales Articos. Aguilar, Angelita L., tr. (SPA.). (J). (gr. k-3). 1995. 12.50 (*1-57842-015-6*) Delmas Creat.

— Animales de Africa. Rodrigues-Kalson, Patricia, tr. (SPA.). (J). (gr. k-3). 1993. 12.50 (*1-57842-001-6*) Delmas Creat.

— Los Animales de la Granja. Aguilar, Angelita L., tr. (SPA.). (J). (gr. k-3). 1995. 12.50 (*1-57842-039-3*) Delmas Creat.

— Animales Del Bosque. Aguilar, Angelita L., tr. (SPA.). (J). (gr. k-3). 1994. 12.50 (*1-57842-005-9*) Delmas Creat.

— Animales Del Bosque Libro II. Aguilar, Angelita L., tr. (SPA.). (J). (gr. k-3). 1996. 12.50 (*1-57842-007-5*) Delmas Creat.

— Animales del Oceano. Aguilar, Angelita L., tr. (SPA.). (J). (gr. k-3). 1994. 12.50 (*1-57842-062-8*) Delmas Creat.

— Animales Nocturnos. Aguilar, Angelita L., tr. (SPA.). (J). (gr. k-3). 1994. 12.50 (*1-57842-058-X*) Delmas Creat.

— Los Animalitos de la Playa. Aguilar, Angelita L., tr. (SPA.). (J). (gr. k-3). 1995. 12.50 (*1-57842-011-3*) Delmas Creat.

— Animals All Around. (Illus.). (J). (gr. k-3). 1992. write for info. (*1-57842-004-0*) Delmas Creat.

— Animals All Around, Bk. II. (Illus.). (J). (gr. k-3). 1992. 12.50 (*1-57842-006-7*) Delmas Creat.

— Animals' Defense. (Illus.). (J). (gr. k-3). 1995. 12.50 (*1-57842-008-3*) Delmas Creat.

— Animals Galore at the Seashore. Phantha, Manny, tr. (LAO.). (J). (gr. k-3). 1995. 12.50 (*1-57842-013-X*) Delmas Creat.

— Arctic Animals. (Illus.). (J). (gr. k-3). 1995. 12.50 (*1-57842-014-8*) Delmas Creat.

— Aves del Jardin. Aguilar, Angelita L., tr. (SPA.). (J). (gr. k-3). 1994. 12.50 (*1-57842-017-2*) Delmas Creat.

— Backyard Birds. (Illus.). (J). (gr. k-3). 1993. 12.50 (*1-57842-016-4*) Delmas Creat.

— Bears Wild & Tame. Phantha, Manny, tr. (LAO.). (J). (gr. k-3). 1995. 12.50 (*1-57842-022-9*) Delmas Creat.

— Bears Wild & Tame. Thach, Suon, tr. (CAM.). (J). (gr. k-3). 1995. 12.50 (*1-57842-023-7*) Delmas Creat.

— Bird Nests. (Illus.). (J). (gr. k-3). 1994. 12.50 (*1-57842-024-5*) Delmas Creat.

— A Book of Opposites. Phantha, Manny, tr. (LAO.). (J). (gr. k-3). 1995. 12.50 (*1-57842-103-9*) Delmas Creat.

— Caterpillar to Butterfly. (Illus.). (J). (gr. k-3). 1992. 12.50 (*1-57842-026-1*) Delmas Creat.

— Caterpillar to Butterfly. Phanta, Manny, tr. (LAO.). (J). (gr. k-3). 1995. 12.50 (*1-57842-029-6*) Delmas Creat.

— Caterpillar to Butterfly. Thach, Suon, tr. (CAM.). (J). (gr. k-3). 1994. 12.50 (*1-57842-030-X*) Delmas Creat.

— Caterpillar to Moth. (Illus.). (J). (gr. k-3). 1994. 12.50 (*1-57842-031-8*) Delmas Creat.

— Caterpillar to Moth. Thach, Suon, tr. (CAM.). (J). (gr. k-3). 1995. 12.50 (*1-57842-033-4*) Delmas Creat.

— Las Culebras. Aguilar, Angelita L., tr. (SPA.). (J). (gr. k-3). 1995. 12.50 (*1-57842-083-0*) Delmas Creat.

— De Oruga a Mariposa. Rodriguez-Kalson, Patricia, tr. (SPA.). (J). (gr. k-3). 1993. 12.50 (*1-57842-027-X*) Delmas Creat.

— De Oruga a Mariposa Nocturna. Aguilar, Angelita L., tr. (SPA.). (J). (gr. k-3). 1994. 12.50 (*1-57842-032-6*) Delmas Creat.

— De Semilla a una Planta. Rodriguez-Kalson, Patricia, tr. (SPA.). (J). (gr. k-3). 1993. 12.50 (*1-57842-074-1*) Delmas Creat.

— La Defensa de los Animales. Aguilar, Angelita L., tr. (SPA.). (J). (gr. k-3). 1995. 12.50 (*1-57842-009-1*) Delmas Creat.

— Dlais Qua Thab Dlais Nyig (Hmong) Thao, Yer J., tr. (J). (gr. k-3). 1995. 12.50 (*1-57842-021-0*) Delmas Creat.

— Earthworms. (Illus.). (J). (gr. k-3). 1995. 12.50 (*1-57842-036-9*) Delmas Creat.

— Farm Animals. (Illus.). (J). (gr. k-3). 1995. 12.50 (*1-57842-038-5*) Delmas Creat.

— Grow, Tadpole, Grow. Phantha, Manny, tr. (LAO.). (J). (gr. k-3). 1994. 12.50 (*1-57842-043-1*) Delmas Creat.

— Grow, Tadpole, Grow. Thach, Suon, tr. (CAM.). (J). (gr. k-3). 1994. 12.50 (*1-57842-044-X*) Delmas Creat.

— Los Gusanos de Sede. Aguilar, Angelita L., tr. (SPA.). (J). (gr. k-3). 1995. 12.50 (*1-57842-081-4*) Delmas Creat.

— Hay Muchos Tipos de Aranas! Aguilar, Angelita L., tr. (SPA.). (J). (gr. k-3). 1994. 12.50 (*1-57842-085-7*) Delmas Creat.

— Helpful Bats. (Illus.). (J). (gr. k-3). 1992. 12.50 (*1-57842-045-8*) Delmas Creat.

— Helpful Bats. Phantha, Manny, tr. (LAO.). (J). (gr. k-3). 1995. 12.50 (*1-57842-048-2*) Delmas Creat.

— Helpful Bats. Thach, Suon, tr. (CAM.). (J). (gr. k-3). 1994. 12.50 (*1-57842-049-0*) Delmas Creat.

— Kaab Laug Saab Thab Kaab Laug Tsuv Yog Yaam Tsaj Txawv Tshoaj (Hmong) Thao, Yer J., tr. (J). (gr. k-3). 1995. 12.50 (*1-57842-086-5*) Delmas Creat.

— Kaab Tsuag Nyuam Plhis Ua Npauj Npaim (Hmong) Thao, Yer J., tr. (J). (gr. k-3). 1993. 12.50 (*1-57842-028-8*) Delmas Creat.

— Ladybugs, True Beetles. (Illus.). (J). (gr. k-3). 1994. 12.50 (*1-57842-050-4*) Delmas Creat.

— Life of a Salmon. (Illus.). (J). (gr. k-3). 1994. 12.50 (*1-57842-052-0*) Delmas Creat.

— Life of a Salmon. Thach, Suon, tr. (CAM.). (J). (gr. k-3). 1995. 12.50 (*1-57842-054-7*) Delmas Creat.

— Las Lombrices. Aguilar, Angelita L., tr. (SPA., Illus.). (J). (gr. k-3). 1995. 12.50 (*1-57842-037-7*) Delmas Creat.

— Mamiferos del Oceano. Aguilar, Angelita L., tr. (SPA.). (J). (gr. k-3). 1994. 12.50 (*1-57842-066-0*) Delmas Creat.

— Las Mariquitas Son Verdaderos Escarabajos. Aguilar, Angelita L., tr. (SPA., Illus.). (J). (gr. k-3). 1996. 12.50 (*1-57842-051-2*) Delmas Creat.

— Marsupiales, Bebes de Bolsa. Aguilar, Angelita L., tr. (SPA.). (J). (gr. k-3). 1995. 12.50 (*1-57842-056-3*) Delmas Creat.

— Marsupials, Pouch Babies. (Illus.). (J). (gr. k-3). 1995. 12.50 (*1-57842-055-5*) Delmas Creat.

— Murcielagos Serviciales. Aguilar, Angelita, tr. (SPA.). (J). (gr. k-3). 1994. 12.50 (*1-57842-046-6*) Delmas Creat.

— Nidos de Pajoros. Aguilar, Angelita L., tr. (SPA.). (J). (gr. k-3). 1994. 12.50 (*1-57842-025-3*) Delmas Creat.

— Night Prowlers. (Illus.). (J). (gr. k-3). 1992. 12.50 (*1-57842-057-1*) Delmas Creat.

— Night Prowlers. Thach, Suon, tr. (CAM.). (J). (gr. k-3). 1994. 12.50 (*1-57842-060-1*) Delmas Creat.

— Noob Tawg Tau Hlub Ua Ntsoj Tsuag (Hmong) Thao, Yer J., tr. (J). (gr. k-3). 1994. 12.50 (*1-57842-075-X*) Delmas Creat.

— Noog Nyob Tsua Tog Vaaj Tog Tsev (Hmong) Thao, Yer J., tr. (J). (gr. k-3). 1995. 12.50 (*1-57842-018-0*) Delmas Creat.

— Ntsoj Tsuag Xyoob Ntoo Tsua Koj Thab Kuv (Hmong) Thao, Yer J., tr. (J). (gr. k-3). 1994. 12.50 (*1-57842-071-7*) Delmas Creat.

— Ocean Animals. (Illus.). (J). (gr. k-3). 1993. 12.50 (*1-57842-061-X*) Delmas Creat.

— Ocean Animals. Thach, Suon, tr. (CAM.). (J). (gr. k-3). 1995. 12.50 (*1-57842-064-4*) Delmas Creat.

— Ocean Mammals. (Illus.). (J). (gr. k-3). 1993. 12.50 (*1-57842-065-2*) Delmas Creat.

— Los Osos Salvajes y Mansos. Aguilar, Angelita L., tr. (SPA.). (J). (gr. k-3). 1994. 12.50 (*1-57842-020-2*) Delmas Creat.

— Penguins, Model Parents. (Illus.). (J). (gr. k-3). 1994. 12.50 (*1-57842-067-9*) Delmas Creat.

— Los Pinguinos Son Padres Modelos. Aguilar, Angelita L., tr. (SPA.). (J). (gr. k-3). 1994. 12.50 (*1-57842-068-7*) Delmas Creat.

— Plantas para Ti y para Mi. Rodriguez-Kalson, Patricia, tr. (SPA.). (J). (gr. k-3). 1993. 12.50 (*1-57842-070-9*) Delmas Creat.

— Plants for You & Me. (Illus.). (J). (gr. k-3). 1992. 12.50 (*1-57842-069-5*) Delmas Creat.

— Plants for You & Me. Thach, Suon, tr. (CAM.). (J). (gr. k-3). 1995. 12.50 (*1-57842-072-5*) Delmas Creat.

— Puav Paab Tau Ntau Yaam (Hmong) Thao, Yer J., tr. (J). (gr. k-3). 1994. 12.50 (*1-57842-047-4*) Delmas Creat.

— Seed to Plant. (Illus.). (J). (gr. k-3). 1992. 12.50 (*1-57842-073-3*) Delmas Creat.

— Seed to Plant. Phantha, Manny, tr. (LAO.). (J). (gr. k-3). 1994. 12.50 (*1-57842-076-8*) Delmas Creat.

— Seed to Plant. Thach, Suon, tr. (CAM.). (J). (gr. k-3). 1994. 12.50 (*1-57842-077-6*) Delmas Creat.

— Silkworms. (Illus.). (J). (gr. k-3). 1995. 12.50 (*1-57842-080-6*) Delmas Creat.

— Snakes. (Illus.). (J). (gr. k-3). 1996. 12.50 (*1-57842-082-2*) Delmas Creat.

— Spiders Are Unique. (Illus.). (J). (gr. k-3). 1992. 12.50 (*1-57842-084-9*) Delmas Creat.

— Spiders Are Unique. Phantha, Manny, tr. (LAO.). (J). (gr. k-3). 1995. 12.50 (*1-57842-087-3*) Delmas Creat.

— Spiders Are Unique. Thach, Suon, tr. (CAM.). (J). (gr. k-3). 1994. 12.50 (*1-57842-088-1*) Delmas Creat.

— Las Tortugas Son Huerfanas Al Nacer. Aguilar, Angelita L., tr. (SPA.). (J). (gr. k-3). 1995. 12.50 (*1-57842-090-3*) Delmas Creat.

— Tsaj Mo Ntuj (Hmong) Thao, Yer J., tr. (J). (gr. k-3). 1995. 12.50 (*1-57842-059-8*) Delmas Creat.

— Tsaj Nyob Tsua Huv Dlej Hav TXWV (Hmong) Thao, Yer J., tr. (J). (gr. k-3). 1995. 12.50 (*1-57842-063-6*) Delmas Creat.

— Tsaj Txhu Nyob Tsua Ntsua Dleg (Hmong) Thao, Yer J., tr. (J). (gr. k-3). 1994. write for info. (*1-57842-012-1*) Delmas Creat.

— Turtles, Orphans at Birth. (Illus.). (J). (gr. k-3). 1994. 12.50 (*1-57842-089-X*) Delmas Creat.

— La Vida de un Salmon. Aguilar, Angelita L., tr. (SPA.). (J). (gr. k-3). 1994. 12.50 (*1-57842-053-9*) Delmas Creat.

Morton, Arthur L. British Labour Movement. (C). 1979. pap. 19.50 (*0-85315-286-1*, Pub. by Lawrence & Wishart) NYU Pr.

— Everlasting Gospel. (Studies in Blake: No. 3). 1958. pap. 39.95 (*0-8383-0098-7*) M S G Haskell Hse.

— History & the Imagination: The Selected Writings of A. L. Morton. (C). 1990. text 40.00 (*0-85315-719-7*, Pub. by Lawrence & Wishart) NYU Pr.

— A People's History of England. 2nd ed. 588p. (C). 1989. pap. 19.50 (*0-85315-723-5*, Pub. by Lawrence & Wishart) NYU Pr.

Morton, Arthur L. & Tate, George. The British Labour Movement, 1770-1920: A Political History. LC 74-25892. 313p. 1975. reprint ed. lib. bdg. 35.00 (*0-8371-7865-7*, MOBL, Greenwood Pr) Greenwood.

Morton, B., ed. The Marine Flora & Fauna of Hong Kong & Southern China III: Proceedings of the 4th International Workshop on the Marine Flora & Fauna of Hong Kong, Hong Kong, April 11-29, 1989, 2 vols. 928p. 1992. pap. 197.00 (*90-73348-17-X*, Pub. by Backhuys Pubs) Balogh.

Morton, B. A. How Women Win the Auto Repair Game. LC 95-71129. 216p. 1996. pap. text 23.95 (*0-9648217-4-5*) CarSmart Pubns.

Morton, Ballard. Gladly Learn: Leadership: Learning, Teaching & Practicing. 260p. 1997. 22.95 (*1-889937-08-8*) Crescent Hill Bks.

Morton, Blaise, jt. ed. see Lasiecka, Irena.

Morton, Brian. Asian Marine Biology, Vol. 1. Marine Biological Association of Hong Kong Staff, ed. (Illus.). 192p. (C). 1984. pap. 39.95 (*962-209-113-X*, Pub. by HK Univ Pr) Coronet Bks.

— Asian Marine Biology, Vol. 2. Marine Biological Association of Hong Kong Staff, ed. (Illus.). 152p. (C). 1985. pap. 39.95 (*962-209-126-1*, Pub. by HK Univ Pr) Coronet Bks.

— Asian Marine Biology, Vol. 3. Marine Biological Association of Hong Kong Staff, ed. (Illus.). 192p. (C). 1986. pap. 39.95 (*962-209-187-3*, Pub. by HK Univ Pr) Coronet Bks.

— Asian Marine Biology, Vol. 4. Marine Biological Association of Hong Kong Staff, ed. (Illus.). 170p. (C). 1987. pap. 39.95 (*962-209-198-9*, Pub. by HK Univ Pr) Coronet Bks.

— Asian Marine Biology, Vol. 5. Marine Biological Association of Hong Kong Staff, ed. (Illus.). 146p. (C). 1988. pap. 39.95 (*962-209-218-7*, Pub. by HK Univ Pr) Coronet Bks.

— Asian Marine Biology, Vol. 6. Marine Biological Association of Hong Kong Staff, ed. (Illus.). 256p. (C). 1989. pap. 39.95 (*962-209-240-3*, Pub. by HK Univ Pr) Coronet Bks.

— Asian Marine Biology, Vol. 7. Marine Biological Association of Hong Kong Staff, ed. (Illus.). 214p. (C). 1990. pap. 39.95 (*962-209-273-X*, Pub. by HK Univ Pr) Coronet Bks.

— Asian Marine Biology, Vol. 8. Marine Biological Association of Hong Kong Staff, ed. (Illus.). 232p. (C). 1991. pap. 39.95 (*962-209-297-7*, Pub. by HK Univ Pr) Coronet Bks.

— Asian Marine Biology, Vol. 9. Marine Biological Association of Hong Kong Staff, ed. (Illus.). 352p. 1992. pap. 39.95 (*962-209-323-X*, Pub. by HK Univ Pr) Coronet Bks.

— The Bivalvia: Proceedings of a Memorial Symposium in Honour of Sir Charles Maurice Yonge. 364p. (C). 1990. pap. text 67.50 (*962-209-254-3*, Pub. by HK Univ Pr) Coronet Bks.

***Morton, Brian.** The Dylanist. 2000. pap. 13.95 (*0-425-17226-0*) Berkley Pub.

Morton, Brian. The Marine Biology of the South China Sea, 2 vols. 772p. 1994. pap. 125.00 (*962-209-356-6*, Pub. by HK Univ Pr) Coronet Bks.

— Partnerships in the Sea: Hong Kong's Marine Symbioses. (Illus.). 140p. 1988. 49.50 (*962-209-211-X*, Pub. by HK Univ Pr) Coronet Bks.

— Starting Out in the Even. large type ed. LC 98-14066. 1998. 24.95 (*0-7862-1451-1*) Thorndike Pr.

***Morton, Brian.** Starting Out in the Evening. 325p. 1999. reprint ed. pap. 12.95 (*0-425-16869-7*) Berkley Pub.

Morton, Brian, compiled by. A Bibliography of Hong Kong Marine Science: 1842-1990. 148p. (C). 1990. pap. text 39.50 (*962-209-275-6*, Pub. by HK Univ Pr) Coronet Bks.

***Morton, Brian, ed.** Asian Marine Biology, 1998, Vol. 15. 184p. 1999. pap. (*962-209-500-3*) HK Univ Pr.

Morton, Brian, ed. Blackwell Guide to Recorded Contemporary Music. (Blackwell Guides Ser.). 352p. 1996. 56.95 (*0-631-18881-9*) Blackwell Pubs.

— The Malacofauna of Hong Kong & Southern China II, 2 vols. 700p. (C). 1985. pap. text 127.50 (*962-209-120-2*, Pub. by HK Univ Pr) Coronet Bks.

— The Malacofauna of Hong Kong & Southern China III. 524p. 1994. pap. 87.50 (*962-209-365-5*, Pub. by HK Univ Pr) Coronet Bks.

— The Marine Biology of the South China Sea III, 2 vols. (Illus.). 704p. 1998. pap. 99.50 (*962-209-461-9*, Pub. by HK Univ Pr) Coronet Bks.

— The Marine Flora & Fauna of Hong Kong & Southern China 11, 3 vols., Set. 1322p. (C). 1990. pap. text 257.50 (*962-209-241-1*, Pub. by HK Univ Pr) Coronet Bks.

— The Marine Flora & Fauna of Hong Kong & Southern China III: Proceedings of the 4th International Workshop

An Asterisk (*) at the beginning of an entry indicates that the title is appearing for the first time.

on the Marine Flora & Fauna of Hong Kong, Hong Kong, April 11-29, 1989, 2 vols. (Illus.). 928p. 1993. pap. 225.00 (*962-209-293-4*, Pub. by HK Univ Pr) Coronet Bks.

— The Marine Flora & Fauna of Hong Kong & Southern China IV, Vol. IV. 540p. (Orig.). 1997. pap. 99.50 (*962-209-437-6*, Pub. by HK Univ Pr) Coronet Bks.

Morton, Brian, et al, eds. Asian Marine Biology, No. 13. (Illus.). 166p. 1997. pap. 39.95 (*962-209-447-3*, Pub. by HK Univ Pr) Coronet Bks.

Morton, Brian & Collins, Pamela, eds. Contemporary Composers. 1019p. 1992. 160.00 (*1-55862-085-0*, 200105) St James Pr.

Morton, Brian, jt. auth. see Britton, Joseph C.

Morton, Brian, ed. see International Marine Biological Workshop Staff.

Morton, Brian, jt. ed. see Marine Biological Association of Hong Kong Staff.

Morton, Brian, tr. see Lie, Jonas.

Morton, Brian N. Americans in London: A Street-By-Street Guide. LC 86-6621. (Illus.). 296p. 1986. pap. 12.95 (*0-688-06555-4*) Olivia & Hill.

— Americans in Paris: An Anecdotal Street Guide. (Illus.). 313p. 1986. 20.00 (*0-934034-06-0*); pap. 12.95 (*0-934034-05-2*) Olivia & Hill.

Morton, Brian N. & Spinelli, Donald C. Beaumarchais: A Bibliography. xxiv, 374p. 1988. 50.00 (*0-934034-08-7*) Olivia & Hill.

Morton, Brian N., ed. see De Beaumarchais, Pierre.

Morton, Brian N., ed. see De Beaumarchais, Pierre-Augustin C.

Morton, Bruce. John Gould Fletcher: A Bibliography. LC 79-10877. (Serif Series, Bibliographies & Checklists: No. 37). 219p. reprint ed. pap. 67.90 (*0-7837-0295-7*, 204061600018) Bks Demand.

Morton, Bruce, compiled by. Halley's Comet, Seventeen Fifty-Five to Nineteen Eighty-Four: A Bibliography. LC 84-19716. (Illus.). 280p. 1985. lib. bdg. 36.95 (*0-313-24022-1*, MOH/, Greenwood Pr) Greenwood.

Morton, C., jt. auth. see Morton, I. D.

Morton, C., jt. auth. see Morton, Ian D.

Morton, C. W. Pilots Die Faster. LC 97-6271. 1997. text 21.95 (*0-312-15624-3*) St Martin.

Morton, C. W. & Mobley, Jack. Rage Sleep. LC 98-7900. 304p. 1998. 22.95 (*0-312-19321-1*, Thomas Dunne) St Martin.

Morton, Carl. A Book of Opposites. (Illus.). (J). (gr. k-3). 1995. 12.50 (*1-57842-100-4*) Delmas Creat.

— El Libro de Contrarios. Aguilar, Angelita L., tr. (SPA.). (J). (gr. k-3). 1995. 12.50 (*1-57842-101-2*) Delmas Creat.

— Phooj Ntawv Qha Txuj Cov Lug Ntxeev los Yog Lug Tsov (Hmong) Thao, Yer J., tr. (J). (gr. k-3). 1995. 12.50 (*1-57842-102-0*) Delmas Creat.

Morton, Carl. Five Toes: Mother Goose. (J). (gr. k-1). 1992. 7.50 (*1-57842-099-7*) Delmas Creat.

— Little Bo-Peep: Mother Goose. (J). (gr. k-1). 1992. 7.50 (*1-57842-097-0*) Delmas Creat.

— Mother Goose. (J). (gr. k-1). 1992. 10.00 (*1-57842-092-X*) Delmas Creat.

— Mother Goose III. (J). (gr. k-1). 1992. 10.00 (*1-57842-094-6*) Delmas Creat.

— Mother Goose II. (J). (gr. k-1). 1992. 10.00 (*1-57842-093-8*) Delmas Creat.

— Old Mother Hubbard: Mother Goose. (J). (gr. k-1). 1992. 10.00 (*1-57842-095-4*) Delmas Creat.

— One, Two, Buckle My Shoe: Mother Goose. (J). (gr. k-1). 1992. 10.00 (*1-57842-098-9*) Delmas Creat.

— Robin Red Breast: Mother Goose. (J). (gr. k-1). 1992. 7.50 (*1-57842-096-2*) Delmas Creat.

Morton, Carlos. At Risk. LC 97-13870. (Carlos Morton Collection). (YA). 1997. pap. 5.00 (*0-88734-442-9*) Players Pr.

— Los Dorados: Playscript. Landes, William A., ed. LC 90-53688. 30p. (Orig.). 1991. pap. 5.00 (*0-88734-321-X*) Players Pr.

— The Drop-Out. Landes, William-Alan, ed. LC 96-39957. 55p. (Orig.). (YA). (gr. 6-12). 1997. pap. 5.00 (*0-88734-443-7*) Players Pr.

— Drug-O. Landes, William-Alan, ed. LC 96-39709. 55p. (Orig.). (YA). (gr. 6-12). 1997. pap. 6.00 (*0-88734-444-5*) Players Pr.

— Los Fatherless. Landes, William-Alan, ed. LC 96-39713. 55p. (Orig.). (YA). (gr. 6-12). 1997. pap. 5.00 (*0-88734-376-7*) Players Pr.

— El Jardin. LC 90-53686. 34p. (Orig.). 1991. pap. 5.00 (*0-88734-320-1*) Players Pr.

— Johnny Tenorio. LC 93-19387. 1993. pap. 5.00 (*0-88734-339-2*) Players Pr.

— Johnny Tenorio & Other Plays. LC 91-40493. 192p. 1992. pap. 11.00 (*1-55885-047-3*, Pub. by Arte Publico) Empire Pub Srvs.

— The Many Deaths of Danny Rosales: And Other Plays. LC 82-72277. 160p. (Orig.). (C). 1983. pap. 10.00 (*0-934770-16-6*) Arte Publico.

— The Many Deaths of Danny Rosales: Playscript. LC 90-53684. 50p. (Orig.). 1991. pap. 6.00 (*0-88734-232-9*) Players Pr.

— The Miser of Mexico. LC 93-19388. (Orig.). 1993. pap. 6.00 (*0-88734-270-1*) Players Pr.

— Pancho Diablo. LC 93-15620. 1993. pap. 5.00 (*0-88734-340-6*) Players Pr.

— Rancho Hollywood. LC 90-53687. 50p. (Orig.). 1991. pap. 6.00 (*0-88734-233-7*) Players Pr.

***Morton, Carlos.** Rancho Hollywood Y Otras Obras Del Teatro Chicano. LC 99-27468. (SPA., Illus.). 160p. 2000. 12.95 (*1-55885-289-1*) Arte Publico.

Morton, Carlos. The Savior. LC 93-15619. 1993. pap. 6.00 (*0-88734-271-X*) Players Pr.

Morton, Carlos, tr. from SPA. The Fickle Finger of Lady Death & Other Plays. (Taft Memorial Fund & University of Cincinnati Studies in Latin American, Chicano & U. S. Latino Theatre: Vol. 5). 152p. (Orig.). (C). 1996. pap. text 32.95 (*0-614-13327-0*) P Lang Pubng.

Morton, Charles. Charles Morton's Compendium Physicae. Hornberger, Theodore, ed. LC QC0017.. (Publications - Colonial Society of Massachusetts: Vol. 33). 277p. reprint ed. pap. 85.90 (*0-7837-0267-1*, 204057600017) Bks Demand.

***Morton, Charles F.** The Word That Rhymes Every Time Version 1.0 Raw Edition: GodWare Instructs His Kids with Care. 17p. 1999. pap. 7.99 (*0-9677079-0-0*) B I T S.

— The Word That Rhymes Every Time Version 2.0 Raw Edition: GodWare Instructs His Kids with Care. 18p. 1999. pap. 7.99 (*0-9677079-1-9*) B I T S.

— The Word That Rhymes Every Time Version 3.0 Raw Edition: GodWare Instructs His Kids with Care. 18p. 1999. pap. 7.99 (*0-9677079-2-7*) B I T S.

Morton, Chris & Beverly, Don. School District Instructional Computer-Use Evaluation Manual. LC 88-24682. (Illus.). 61p. 1989. pap. 24.95 (*0-87778-214-8*) Educ Tech Pubns.

Morton, Chris & Thomas, Ceri L. The Mystery of the Crystal Skulls: A Real-Life Detective Story of the Ancient World. LC 98-23740. (Illus.). 400p. 1998. pap. 22.00 (*1-879181-54-1*) Bear & Co.

Morton, Christine. Picnic Farm. LC 97-10880. (Illus.). 32p. (J). 1998. lib. bdg. 15.95 (*0-8234-1332-2*) Holiday.

Morton, Chuck & Morton, E. Lynn. Ferrets. 2nd rev. ed. Vriends, Matthew M., ed. LC 94-37728. (Complete Pet Owner's Manual Ser.). 1995. pap. 6.95 (*0-8120-9021-7*) Barron.

Morton, Chuck, jt. auth. see Morton, E. Lynn.

Morton, Colin. How to Be Born Again. 96p. 1992. pap. 12.95 (*1-55082-036-2*, Pub. by Quarry Pr) LPC InBook.

— The Merzbook: Kurt Schwitters Poems. 80p. 1987. pap. 12.95 (*0-919627-46-3*, Pub. by Quarry Pr) LPC InBook.

— Oceans Apart. LC 95-183786. 192p. 1995. pap. 16.95 (*1-55082-136-9*, Pub. by Quarry Pr) LPC InBook.

Morton, Colin B., jt. auth. see Death, Chuck.

***Morton-Cooper, Alison.** Action Research in Health Care. LC 99-87086. 2000. write for info. (*0-632-04091-2*) Blackwell Sci.

Morton-Cooper, Alison & Palmer, Anne. Mentoring & Preceptorship: A Guide to Support Roles in Clinical Practice. LC 93-19829. 192p. 1993. pap. 24.95 (*0-632-03596-X*) Blackwell Sci.

Morton-Cooper, Alison, et al. Excellence in Health Care Management. LC 96-21528. 256p. (Orig.). 1996. pap. text 29.95 (*0-632-04032-7*) Blackwell Sci.

Morton, Craig, jt. auth. see Garber, Julie.

Morton, D. Morton: The Mortons & Their Kin: A Genealogy & a Source Book. 899p. 1992. reprint ed. pap. 119.00 (*0-8328-2298-1*); reprint ed. lib. bdg. 129.00 (*0-8328-2297-3*) Higginson Bk Co.

Morton, Danelle, jt. auth. see Shirley, Donna.

Morton, Daniel O. Memoir of Rev. Levi Parsons: Late Missionary to Palestine. Davis, Moshe, ed. (America & the Holy Land Ser.). 1977. reprint ed. lib. bdg. 36.95 (*0-405-10271-2*) Ayer.

Morton, David. Off the Record: The Technology & Culture of Sound Recording in America. LC 99-27914. 180p. 2000. pap. 22.00 (*0-8135-2747-3*) Rutgers U Pr.

— Photo Atlas for Anatomy & Physiology. LC 97-202725. (Biology Ser.). 1997. pap. 33.95 (*0-534-51716-1*) Wadsworth Pub.

Morton, David, ed. Selected Reports in Ethnomusicology, Vol. II, No. 2. LC 75-24270. (Illus.). xii, 259p. (Orig.). 1975. pap. text 9.50 (*0-88287-005-X*) UCLA Dept Ethnom.

— Shorter Modern Poems, 1900-1931. LC 74-116411. (Granger Index Reprint Ser.). 1977. 15.95 (*0-8369-6152-8*) Ayer.

Morton, David & Perry, James W. Photo Atlas for Biology. (Biology Ser.). 1995. 20.95 (*0-534-23556-5*) Wadsworth Pub.

Morton, David A. How to Qualify for Social Security Disability: And Protect Your Rights. LC 92-93518. 224p. (Orig.). 1992. pap. 15.00 (*0-9634464-0-1*) Fine Bks.

Morton, David A., III. Medical Proof of Social Securities Disability. LC 83-16800. 585p. (C). 1983. reprint ed. text. write for info. (*0-314-72082-0*) West Pub.

Morton, David A., 3rd. Medical Proof of Social Securities Disability: 1995-1996 Supplement. (Miscellaneous Treatise Ser.). 400p. (C). 1995. pap. text, suppl. ed. write for info. (*0-314-08334-0*) West Pub.

***Morton, David A.** Nolo's Guide to Social Security Disability: Getting & Keeping Your Benefits. LC 99-57186. 2000. 29.95 (*0-87337-574-2*) Nolo com.

Morton, David C. & Wolfe, Charles K. DeFord Bailey: A Black Star in Early Country Music. LC 90-22519. (Illus.). 224p. (C). 1993. pap. 14.95 (*0-87049-792-8*) U of Tenn Pr.

Morton, David E. Poems of a Lifetime. 1999. pap. write for info. (*1-58235-075-2*) Watermrk Pr.

***Morton, David L.** A History of Electronic Entertainment Since 1945. 84p. 1999. pap. text 11.95 (*0-7803-9936-6*) Inst Electrical.

Morton, David L. Off the Record: The Technology & Culture of Sound Recording in America. LC 99-27914. (Illus.). 180p. 2000. text 50.00 (*0-8135-2746-5*) Rutgers U Pr.

Morton, Davis L. Traveler's Guide to the Great Art Treasures of Europe. 575p. 1987. 55.00 (*0-8161-8733-9*, Hall Reference) Macmillan.

Morton, Delma. African Animals. (Illus.). (J). (gr. k-3). 1992. 12.50 (*1-57842-000-8*) Delmas Creat.

— Animales en los Charcos de la Playa. Aguilar, Angelita L., tr. (SPA.). (J). (gr. k-3). 1995. 12.50 (*1-57842-116-0*) Delmas Creat.

— Animals Galore at the Seashore. (Illus.). (J). (gr. k-3). 1994. 12.50 (*1-57842-010-5*) Delmas Creat.

— Animals Galore in the Tide Pool. (Illus.). (J). (gr. k-3). 1992. 12.50 (*1-57842-115-2*) Delmas Creat.

— Las Aves de la Playa. Aguilar, Angelita L., tr. (SPA.). (J). (gr. k-3). 1994. 12.50 (*1-57842-079-2*) Delmas Creat.

— Bears Wild & Tame. (Illus.). (J). (gr. k-3). 1992. 12.50 (*1-57842-019-9*) Delmas Creat.

— The Busy Book. (Illus.). (J). (gr. k-3). 1989. 12.50 (*1-57842-104-7*) Delmas Creat.

— Counting Color Word Book. (Illus.). (J). (gr. k-2). 1989. 12.50 (*1-57842-108-X*) Delmas Creat.

— Counting Color Word Book. Phantha, Manny, tr. (LAO.). (J). (gr. k-2). 1994. 12.50 (*1-57842-111-X*) Delmas Creat.

— Counting Color Word Book. Thach, Suon, tr. (CAM.). (J). (gr. k-2). 1995. 12.50 (*1-57842-112-8*) Delmas Creat.

— Dinosaur, What Was Your Name? (Illus.). (J). (gr. k-3). 1993. 12.50 (*1-57842-034-2*) Delmas Creat.

— Dinosaurio, Como Te Han Nombrado? Rodriguez-Kalson, Patricia, tr. (SPA.). (J). (gr. k-3). 1993. 12.50 (*1-57842-035-0*) Delmas Creat.

— El Libro de Colores y Numeros. Rodriguez-Kalson, Patricia, tr. (SPA.). (J). (gr. k-2). 1993. 12.50 (*1-57842-109-8*) Delmas Creat.

— More, Where Have You Been? (Illus.). (J). (gr. k-3). 1989. 12.50 (*1-57842-114-4*) Delmas Creat.

— Shore Birds. (Illus.). (J). (gr. k-3). 1991. 12.50 (*1-57842-078-4*) Delmas Creat.

— Where Have You Been? (Illus.). (J). (gr. k-3). 1989. 12.50 (*1-57842-113-6*) Delmas Creat.

— Yog Phoo Ntawv Suav Xim Thab Thag Xim (Hmong) Thao, Yer J., tr. (J). (gr. k-2). 1993. 12.50 (*1-57842-110-1*) Delmas Creat.

***Morton, Desmond.** Canada: A Millennium Portrait. (Illus.). 106p. 1999. pap. 16.95 (*0-88866-647-0*) Edgar Kent.

— A Military History of Canada: From Champlain to Kosovo. 4th rev. ed. 368p. 2000. pap. 24.99 (*0-7710-6514-0*) McCland & Stewart.

Morton, Desmond. Ministers & Generals: Politics & the Canadian Militia, 1868-1904. LC 79-135208. 272p. reprint ed. pap. 84.40 (*0-608-30834-X*, 201437400090) Bks Demand.

— A Peculiar Kind of Politics: Canada's Overseas Ministry in the First World War. 280p. 1982. text 30.00 (*0-8020-5586-9*) U of Toronto Pr.

— A Short History of Canada. expanded ed. 351p. 1995. pap. 14.95 (*0-7710-6516-7*) McCland & Stewart.

— Short History of Canada. 3rd rev. ed. LC 98-115201. 348p. 1998. pap. text 15.95 (*0-7710-6517-5*) McCland & Stewart.

Morton, Desmond. The United Nations: Its History & the Canadians Who Shaped It. (Illus.). 64p. (J). 1995. pap. 18.95 (*1-55074-222-1*) Kids Can Pr.

Morton, Desmond. Working People: An Illustrated History of the Canadian Labour Movement. 4th ed. (Illus.). 420p. 1999. pap. 24.95 (*0-7735-1801-0*) McG-Queens Univ Pr.

Morton, Desmond & Wright, Glenn. Winning the Second Battle: Canadian Veterans & the Return to Civilian Life, 1915-1930. 328p. 1987. pap. 18.95 (*0-8020-6634-8*); text 45.00 (*0-8020-5705-5*) U of Toronto Pr.

Morton, Don & Tsunoi, Naoko. The Best of Tokyo. rev. ed. (Illus.). 208p. 1993. pap. 12.95 (*0-8048-1919-X*) Tuttle Pubng.

Morton, Donald. Material Queer: A Lesbigay Cultural Studies Reader. (Queer Critique Ser.). 416p. (C). 1996. pap. 32.00 (*0-8133-1927-7*, Pub. by Westview) HarpC.

Morton, Donald & Zavarzadeh, Mas'ud, eds. Theory - Pedagogy - Politics: Texts for Change. 264p. 1991. text 29.95 (*0-252-01761-7*); pap. text 12.50 (*0-252-06157-8*) U of Ill Pr.

Morton, Donald, jt. auth. see Zavarzadeh, Mas'ud.

***Morton, Dorothy R.** Jesus: A Reassessment. 60p. 1999. pap. 25.00 (*1-85072-231-5*, Pub. by W Sessions) St Mut.

Morton, Douglas R., Jr., jt. ed. see Pike, John E.

Morton, E. D., jt. auth. see Simmonds, A. T.

***Morton, E. Lynn & Morton, Chuck.** Ferrets: Everything about Purchase, Care, Nutrition, Diseases, Behavior & Breeding. rev. ed. LC 00-25042. (Illus.). 2000. 6.95 (*0-7641-1050-0*) Barron.

Morton, E. Lynn, jt. auth. see Morton, Chuck.

Morton, E. Reginald. Essentials of Medical Electricity. 1991. lib. bdg. 88.95 (*0-8490-5014-6*) Gordon Pr.

Morton, E. Susan & Grigsby, R. Kevin. Advancing Family Preservation Practice. (Focus Editions Ser.: Vol. 150). (Illus.). 196p. (C). 1992. 59.95 (*0-8039-4570-1*); pap. 26.00 (*0-8039-4571-X*) Sage.

***Morton, Edward J., ed.** Radiation Sources & Radiation Interactions. 160p. 1999. pap. text 50.00 (*0-8194-3257-1*) SPIE.

Morton, Eugene S., jt. auth. see Owings, Donald H.

Morton, F. L. Pro-Choice vs. Pro-Life: The Abortion Debate in Canada. LC 92-34959. (Illus.). 371p. 1993. pap. 21.95 (*0-8061-2522-5*) U of Okla Pr.

Morton, F. L., jt. auth. see Knopff, Ranier.

Morton, Fred, et al. Historical Dictionary of Botswana. LC 89-36098. (African Historical Dictionaries Ser.: No. 44). (Illus.). 244p. 1989. 31.00 (*0-8108-2224-5*) Scarecrow.

Morton, Frederic. A Nervous Splendor: Vienna, 1888-1889. 340p. 1980. pap. 13.95 (*0-14-005667-X*, Penguin Bks) Viking Penguin.

— The Rothschilds: Portrait of a Dynasty. LC 98-14815. 352p. 1998. pap. 16.00 (*1-56836-220-X*) Kodansha.

Morton, Friedrich. In the Land of the Quetzal Feather. (Illus.). 1960. 10.00 (*0-8159-5807-2*) Devin.

Morton, George. How to Become a Medical Transcriptionist: A Career for the 21st Century. LC 98-96009. 150p. 1998. pap. 12.95 (*0-9663470-0-5*) Med Lang Dev.

Morton, George, ed. see Riegel, E. C.

Morton, George A. & Malloch, D. Macleod. Law & Laughter: Illustrated with Portraits of Eminent Members of Bench & Bar. (Illus.). 1989. reprint ed. 38.50 (*0-8377-2439-2*, Rothman) W S Hein.

Morton, Gerald W. A Biography of Mildmay Fane, Second Earl of Westmorland (1601-1666) The Unknown Cavalier. LC 90-24436. (Studies in British History: Vol. 22). (Illus.). 168p. 1991. lib. bdg. 79.95 (*0-88946-261-5*) E Mellen.

— A Short Guide to Business Writing. (C). 1996. pap. text 26.00 (*0-15-501635-0*, Pub. by Harcourt Coll Pubs) Harcourt.

Morton, Gerald W., jt. ed. see Helgeson, Karin P.

Morton, Glenn R. Adam, Apes, & Anthropology: Finding the Soul of Fossil Man. (Illus.). 203p. 1997. pap. text 22.00 (*0-9648227-2-5*) DMD Pubng.

— Foundation, Fall & Flood: A Harmonization of Genesis & Science. 165p. (C). 1995. pap. text 17.00 (*0-9648227-0-9*) DMD Pubng.

— Foundation, Fall & Flood: A Harmonization of Genesis & Science. 2nd ed. (Illus.). 171p. 1995. pap. text 17.00 (*0-9648227-1-7*) DMD Pubng.

***Morton, Glenn R.** Foundation, Fall & Flood: A Harmonization of Genesis & Science. 3rd ed. (Illus.). (C). 1999. pap. 20.00 (*0-9648227-3-3*) DMD Pubng.

Morton, Grace, jt. auth. see Morton, Lucy.

Morton, H., jt. auth. see Morton, Aleksander.

Morton, H. V. In Search of England. (Illus.). 288p. 1984. 9.95 (*0-396-08378-1*, Pub. by Turtleback) Demco.

Morton, Harold. Flying for God: Into the Son. 208p. (C). 1990. pap. text 35.00 (*0-7855-5978-7*) St Mut.

Morton, Helen. Becoming Tongan: An Ethnography of Childhood. LC 95-41374. 1996. pap. text 23.00 (*0-8248-1795-8*) UH Pr.

— Highlights: Eighty Years Worth Living. (Illus.). 272p. 1989. pap. 17.95 (*0-933858-05-1*) Kennebec River.

Morton, Helen, jt. auth. see Aleksander, Igor.

Morton, Henry. Electric Lighting: Underwriter's Standard Requirements of 1882. (Illus.). 65p. 1998. pap. 25.00 (*0-87556-865-3*) Saifer.

Morton, Henry W. & Stuart, Robert C., eds. The Contemporary Soviet City. LC 83-8543. 276p. (gr. 13). 1984. pap. text 65.95 (*0-87332-254-1*) M E Sharpe.

Morton, Henry W. & Stuart, Robert C., eds. The Contemporary Soviet City. LC 83-8543. 276p. 1984. reprint ed. pap. 85.60 (*0-7837-9952-7*, 206067900006) Bks Demand.

Morton, Herbert. Tyngsborough. (Images of America Ser.). 128p. 1996. pap. 16.99 (*0-7524-0295-1*) Arcadia Publng.

Morton, Herbert C. The Story of Webster's Third: Philip Gove's Controversial Dictionary & Its Critics. (Illus.). 348p. (C). 1994. text 39.95 (*0-521-46146-4*) Cambridge U Pr.

— The Story of Webster's Third: Philip Gove's Controversial Dictionary & Its Critics. (Illus.). 348p. (C). 1995. pap. text 18.95 (*0-521-55869-7*) Cambridge U Pr.

Morton, Herbert C. & Price, Anne J. The ACLS Survey of Scholars: Final Report of Views on Publications, Computers, & Libraries. (Illus.). 148p. (Orig.). (C). 1989. pap. text 23.00 (*0-8191-7261-8*) Am Coun Lrnd Soc.

Morton, Hugh, jt. photos by see Donnan, Bob.

Morton, I. D. & Lenges, J., eds. Education & Training in Food Science. 240p. 1991. 135.00 (*1-85573-273-4*) Am Educ Systs.

Morton, I. D. & MacLeod, A. J., eds. Food Flavours Pt. C: The Flavour of Fruits. (Developments in Food Science Ser.: 3C). 372p. 1990. 216.75 (*0-444-87362-7*) Elsevier.

Morton, I. D. & Morton, C. Elsevier's Dictionary of Food Science & Technology. (ENG, FRE, GER & SPA.). 208p. 1990. 195.00 (*0-8288-9213-X*, M7929) Fr & Eur.

***Morton, Ian & Hall, Judith.** Dictionary of Pharmacological Agents: Properties & Synonyms. LC 99-42527. 1999. write for info. (*0-7514-0499-3*) Kluwer Academic.

Morton, Ian D. & Morton, C. Elsevier's Dictionary of Food Science & Technology. (ENG, FRE, GER, LAT & SPA.). 214p. 1980. 137.25 (*0-444-41559-9*) Elsevier.

Morton, Ira. The Galloping Ghost: Biography of Harold "Red" Grange, First Football Superstar. (Illus.). 1984. 10.50 (*0-916445-04-6*) Crossroads Comm.

Morton, Ira, afterword by. The Red Grange Story: An Autobiography. LC 93-11212. (Illus.). 232p. 1993. reprint ed. 11.95 (*0-252-06329-5*) U of Ill Pr.

Morton, J. Criminal Justice Act, 1987: A Commentary. (Criminal Law Guides Ser.). 128p. 1988. pap. 34.00 (*0-08-033088-6*, Pergamon Pr) Elsevier.

— A Guide to Sentencing. (Waterlow Criminal Law Guide Ser.). 160p. 1990. pap. 29.95 (*0-08-040117-1*, Pergamon Pr) Elsevier.

Morton, J. & Matthewman, R. Livestock Extension Policy. 1998. pap. 60.00 (*0-85954-484-2*, Pub. by Nat Res Inst) St Mut.

Morton, J., et al. Livestock Production Extension: Issues, Case Studies & Policy Options. 1997. pap. 60.00 (*0-85954-480-X*, Pub. by Nat Res Inst) St Mut.

Morton, J., jt. auth. see Duckers, L. J.

Morton, J., jt. auth. see Gillett, W. B.

Morton, J., jt. auth. see Hall, D. O.

Morton, J., jt. auth. see McNelis, B.

Morton, J., jt. auth. see Rosenfeld, J. L.

Morton, J., jt. ed. see Duckers, L. J.

Morton, J., jt. ed. see McNelis, B.

Morton, J. B. Brumaire: The Rise of Bonaparte. (Select Bibliographies Reprint Ser.). 1977. reprint ed. 25.95 (*0-518-19075-7*) Ayer.

— Hilaire Belloc: A Memoir. 1984. lib. bdg. 90.00 (*0-8490-3236-9*) Gordon Pr.

Morton, J. E. Urban Mortgage Lending: Comparative Markets & Experience. (Financial Research Program IV: Studies in Urban Mortgage Financing: No. 6). 212p. 1956. reprint ed. 55.20 (*0-87014-144-9*) Natl Bur Econ Res.

Morton, J. Y. Adding Animals, Big bk. Yoko Mia Hirano, ed. (Early Math Ser.). (Illus.). 16p. (J). (ps-1). 1997. pap. 16.95 (*1-56784-951-2*) Newbridge Educ.

— Adding Animals, Mini-bk. Yoko Mia Hirano, ed. (Early Math Ser.). (Illus.). 16p. (J). (ps-1). 1997. pap. 3.16 (*1-56784-976-8*) Newbridge Educ.

Morton, Jackson. The View from the States: Public Law 94-171 Redistricting Data from the Year 2000 Census. (Illus.). 39p. 1998. reprint ed. pap. text 20.00 (*0-7881-7382-0*) DIANE Pub.

Morton, Jacqueline. English Grammar for Students of French: The Study Guide for Those Learning French. 4th ed. LC 96-39834. 176p. (C). 1997. pap. text, student ed. 12.95 (*0-934034-29-X*) Olivia & Hill.

— French Slang. (FRE.). 1995. pap. 9.95 incl. audio (*0-934034-27-3*) Olivia & Hill.

— French Slang: The Key to Spoken French. 32p. 1995. pap. 10.95 incl. audio (*0-934034-28-1*) Olivia & Hill.

Morton, Jacqueline, ed. see Cruise, Edwina.

Morton, Jacqueline, ed. see Levenson, Ana & Eggly, Susan.

Morton, Jacqueline, ed. see Primorac, Karen & Adorni, Sergio.

Morton, Jacqueline, ed. see Simon, Mutsuko E.

Morton, Jacqueline, ed. see Zorach, Cecile & Melin, Charlotte.

Morton, James. Anthology of Rock Drumming. 128p. 1982. spiral bd. 14.95 (*0-87166-861-0*, 93802) Mel Bay.

— Easiest Drum Set Book. 28p. 1990. pap. 3.95 (*1-56222-027-6*, 94494) Mel Bay.

— Investing with the Grand Masters: Investment Strategies of Britain's Most Successful Investors. 256p. 1996. 35.00 (*0-273-62536-5*) F T P-H.

— Killer-Fillers. 42p. 1997. 17.95 incl. audio compact disk (*0-7866-2766-2*, 93687BCD) Mel Bay.

— Killer Fillers. 42p. 1980. pap. 5.95 (*0-87166-379-1*, 93687) Mel Bay.

— The Poverty of Nations: The Aid Dilemma at the Heart of Africa. LC 95-62319. 272p. 1996. text 24.50 (*1-86064-034-6*, Pub. by I B T) St Martin.

— Rock Studies for Drum Set. 28p. 1997. 9.95 incl. audio compact disk (*0-7866-2709-3*, 94379BCD) Mel Bay.

— The Sandwich & the Plumber. (Illus.). 32p. 1998. pap. write for info. (*1-57579-093-9*) Pine Hill Pr.

— The Who's Who of Unsolved Murders. (Illus.). 300p. 1996. 24.95 (*1-85626-163-8*, Pub. by Cathie Kyle) Trafalgar.

— You Can Teach Yourself Drums. 96p. 1990. pap. 9.95 (*1-56222-033-0*, 94495) Mel Bay.

— You Can Teach Yourself Drums. 1991. pap. 18.95 incl. audio (*1-56222-518-9*, 94495P) Mel Bay.

— You Can Teach Yourself Drums. 1991. audio 9.98 (*1-56222-034-9*, 94495C) Mel Bay.

— You Can Teach Yourself Drums. 96p. 1998. 17.95 incl. audio compact disk (*0-7866-4517-2*, 94495BCD) Mel Bay.

Morton, James, ed. Ancren Riwle, a Treatise on the Rules & Duties of Monastic Life from a Semi-Saxon MS. of the Thirteenth Century. LC 72-158250. (Camden Society, London. Publications, First Ser.: No. 1). reprint ed. 115.00 (*0-404-50157-5*) AMS Pr.

— The Financial Times Global Guide to Investing: The Secrets of the World's Leading Investment Gurus. LC 96-147055. 600p. 1995. 75.00 (*0-273-61414-2*) F T P-H.

Morton, James, jt. auth. see Carskadden, Jeff.

Morton, James P., jt. auth. see Sandys, Edwina.

Morton, Jane. Devotions for the Sandbox Set: 40 Lively Learning Times for Little Ones. LC 96-37757. 94p. (J). (ps-k). 1997. 11.99 (*1-56476-599-7*, Chariot Bks) Chariot Victor.

— No Place for Cal. 112p. (Orig.). (J). 1989. pap. 2.75 (*0-380-75548-3*, Avon Bks) Morrow Avon.

— Noah's Amazing Ark. (Illus.). 6p. (J). 1994. 5.99 (*1-56476-170-3*, 6-3170, Victor Bks) Chariot Victor.

***Morton, Jane & Dreier, Ted.** Moozie's Kind Adventure. deluxe ed. LC 99-90526. (Moozie Adventures Ser.). (Illus.). 28p. (J). (gr. k-2). 1999. 14.95 (*0-9662268-1-X*) Best Frnds Bks.

Morton, Jane, jt. auth. see Preston, Marianne K.

Morton, Jane W. & Preston, Marianne K. Fresh Herb Pocket Cookbook. 1997. pap. text 3.25 (*1-883283-10-8*) Brick Tower.

Morton, Janice. Complete Preparation for Childbirth: A Self Help Manual for Expectant Parents. 240p. (C). 1990. pap. text 37.50 (*962-209-220-9*, Pub. by HK Univ Pr) Coronet Bks.

Morton, Jeffrey S. The International Law Commission of the United Nations. LC 98-58086. (Illus.). 224p. 2000. 29.95 (*1-57003-170-3*) U of SC Pr.

Morton, Jera M. Artisans: Glass: An Inspirational Portfolio. (Illus.). 144p. 1999. spiral bd. 19.95 (*0-8230-0305-1*) Watsn-Guptill.

Morton, Jerome H., jt. auth. see Kennedy, Rosa L.

Morton, Jerry. Back to Algansee: Stories of Now & Then. (Illus.). 112p. (Orig.). 1993. mass mkt. 6.95 (*0-9655400-2-2*) J Lee Pr.

— Footprints & Friends: Conversations from Hat Creek to Nirvana. (Illus.). 112p. 1988. mass mkt. 5.95 (*0-9655400-1-4*) J Lee Pr.

— Romania. (Illus.). 112p. (Orig.). 1996. pap. 24.95 (*0-9655400-3-0*) J Lee Pr.

— Yesterday in Hodunk: Voices from the Michigan Countryside. (Illus.). 96p. 1985. mass mkt. 4.95 (*0-9655400-0-6*) J Lee Pr.

Morton, Jessica G. Kids on the Net: Conducting Internet Research in K-5 Classrooms. LC 98-26658. (Beeline Ser.). 1998. pap. 9.95 (*0-325-00021-2*) Heinemann.

Morton, Jim, jt. auth. see Dotz, Warren.

Morton, Joann B., ed. Change, Challenge, & Choices: Women's Role in Modern Corrections. (Illus.). 117p. 1991. 17.50 (*0-929310-54-3*, 322) Am Correctional.

— Complex Challenges, Collaborative Solutions: Programming for Adult & Juvenile Female Offenders. LC 98-12160. 240p. 1998. pap. 29.95 (*1-56991-081-2*) Am Correctional.

Morton, Joelle, ed. see Simpson, Christopher.

Morton, John. Airline Liveries: Past & Present. LC 99-30756. (Illus.). 112p. 1999. pap. 24.95 (*0-7603-0743-1*, Pub. by MBI Pubg) Motorbooks Intl.

***Morton, John.** The Blessings Already Are. 1999. 25.00 (*0-914829-67-X*) Mandeville LA.

Morton, John. Jetliner Glory: Airliner Liveries. LC 97-52158. (Illus.). 112p. 1997. pap. 24.95 (*0-7603-0515-3*) MBI Pubg.

— Lost Airlines Liveries: Airline Color Schemes of the Past. LC 97-118432. 112p. 1996. pap. text 21.95 (*0-7603-0258-8*) MBI Pubg.

***Morton, John.** PIC: Your Personal Introductory Course. 384p. 2001. pap. 26.95 (*0-7506-5038-9*, Newnes) Buttrwrth-Heinemann.

Morton, John. Your Personal Introductory Course. LC 99-172626. (Illus.). 208p. 1999. pap. text 26.95 (*0-7506-3932-6*, Newnes) Buttrwrth-Heinemann.

Morton, John, ed. Biological & Social Factors in Psycholinguistics. LC 70-137819. (Illus.). 215p. reprint ed. 66.70 (*0-8357-9666-3*, 201492400093) Bks Demand.

***Morton, John K.** Charter Airlines: Their Aircraft & Colors. (Illus.). 112p. 2000. pap. 24.95 (*1-84037-098-X*, 130150AE, Pub. by Airlife Publishing) Motorbooks Intl.

— Miami Airport. (Illus.). 112p. 1999. pap. 15.95 (*1-84037-061-0*, Pub. by Airlife Publishing) Motorbooks Intl.

Morton, John N. Morton Family Tree: Chauncy Morton & Betsy Pike: Their Ancestry & Descent. (Illus.). 125p. 1995. reprint ed. pap. 33.00 (*0-8328-4930-8*); reprint ed. lib. bdg. 23.00 (*0-8328-4929-4*) Higginson Bk Co.

***Morton, John O.** It Ain't Gonna Work: The "Real" Oakland, 2 vols. in 1. deluxe ed. Morton, Linda J., ed. 380p. (C). 1998. 22.00 (*0-9700881-0-8*) ST John.

— One to a 100: Manuscript Printing & Bookbinding Design. 45p. 2000. 5.95 (*0-9700881-1-6*) ST John.

Morton, John W. The Artillery of Nathan Bedford Forrest's Cavalry. 374p. 1909. 35.00 (*1-56013-008-3*) Olde Soldier Bks.

— The Artillery of Nathan Bedford Forrest's Cavalry. 374p. 1994. pap. 12.95 (*0-89176-042-3*, Bellum Edits) R Bemis Pub.

Morton, Joseph W., Jr., ed. Sparks from the Camp Fire: Tales of the Old Veterans. unabridged ed. LC 96-44046. (Illus.). xiii, 648p. (C). 1996. reprint ed. 44.95 (*1-889881-06-6*) Old Bks Pub.

Morton, Joyce. Legal Office Procedures. 4th ed. LC 97-25108. 406p. 1997. pap. text 51.00 (*0-13-261017-5*) P-H.

***Morton, Joyce.** Legal Office Procedures. 5th ed. LC 00-24719. 400p. 2000. pap. 44.67 (*0-13-015597-7*) P-H.

Morton, Jude, jt. ed. see Jones, Lisa.

Morton, Julia F. Atlas of Medicinal Plants of Middle America: Bahamas to Yucatan, 2 vols. fac. ed. (Illus.). 1454p. 1981. 229.95 (*0-398-04036-2*) C C Thomas.

— Fruits of Warm Climates. Dowling, Curtis F., ed. (Illus.). 559p. 1987. 100.00 (*0-9610184-1-0*) AgScience.

— Major Medicinal Plants: Botany, Culture & Uses. fac. ed. (Illus.). 448p. 1977. 99.95 (*0-398-03673-X*) C C Thomas.

— Plants Poisonous to People in Florida. LC 81-71614. 1995. pap. 19.95 (*0-87024-336-5*) U of Miami Pr.

— Plants Poisonous to People in Florida & Other Warm Areas. 2nd rev. ed. LC 81-71614. (Illus.). 170p. 1982. pap. 19.75 (*0-9610184-0-2*) ECHO Inc.

Morton, K. W., ed. International Conference on Numerical Methods in Fluid Dynamics, Twelfth: Proceedings of the Conference Held at the University of Oxford, England, on 9-13 July 1990. (Lecture Notes in Physics Ser.: Vol. 371). xiv, 562p. 1991. 77.00 (*0-387-53619-1*) Spr-Verlag.

Morton, K. W. & Baines, M. J. Numerical Methods for Fluid Dynamics II. 2nd ed. (Institute of Mathematics & Its Applications Conference Series, New Ser.: New Series 7). (Illus.). 679p. 1986. 95.00 (*0-19-853610-0*) OUP.

— Numerical Methods for Fluid Dynamics V. LC 95-49215. (Illus.). 650p. (C). 1996. text 90.00 (*0-19-851480-8*, Clarendon Pr) OUP.

Morton, K. W. & Baines, M. J., eds. Numerical Methods for Fluid Dynamics III. (Institute of Mathematics & Its Applications Conference Series, New Ser.: New Series 17). (Illus.). 552p. 1989. 98.00 (*0-19-853632-1*) OUP.

Morton, K. W. & Mayers, D. F. Numerical Solution of Partial Differential Equations. (Illus.). 239p. (C). 1995. text 69.95 (*0-521-41855-0*); pap. text 25.95 (*0-521-42922-6*) Cambridge U Pr.

Morton, K.W., jt. auth. see Richtmyer, Robert D.

Morton, K. W., jt. ed. see Baines, M. J.

Morton, Keith S., photos by. Country Living Seasons at Seven Gates Farm. LC 96-6776. (Illus.). 224p. 1996. 30.00 (*0-688-14466-7*, Hearst) Hearst Commns.

Morton, L. L. A Make-Believe Face: Growing up "Born-Again" Inside the Religious Right. unabridged ed. 250p. (Orig.). 1993. pap. 7.95 (*0-9634673-0-1*) Indep-Hse Pr.

Morton, Larry, jt. auth. see Appleby, Martha.

Morton, Laura, jt. auth. see Henner, Marilu.

Morton, Laura, jt. auth. see Lanza, Louis.

Morton, Laura, jt. auth. see Lunden, Joan.

Morton, Laura, jt. auth. see Springer, Jerry.

Morton, Leah, pseud. I Am a Woman & a Jew. (American Biography Ser.). 362p. 1991. reprint ed. lib. bdg. 79.00 (*0-7812-8364-7*) Rprt Serv.

Morton, Leith. Divided Self: A Biography of Arishma Takeo. 288p. (Orig.). 1989. pap. text 24.95 (*0-04-378006-7*, Pub. by Allen & Unwin Pty) Paul & Co Pubs.

Morton, Leith, ed. from JPN. Seven Stories of Modern Japan. Clarke, H. D. et al, trs. from JPN. (University of Sydney East Asian Ser.: No. 5). 96p. 1991. pap. text 16.00 (*0-9590735-9-0*, Pub. by Wild Peony Pty) UH Pr.

Morton, Leith, tr. see Kusano, Shimpei.

Morton, Lena Beatrice. The Influence of the Sea Upon English Literature from the Anglo-Saxon to the Victorian Period. 1974. lib. bdg. 250.00 (*0-87700-223-1*) Revisionist Pr.

Morton, Leslie T. & Moore, Robert J. A Bibliography of Medical & Biomedical Biography. 2nd ed. LC 94-8284. 333p. 1994. 131.95 (*0-85967-981-0*, Pub. by Scolar Pr) Ashgate Pub Co.

— A Chronology of Medicine & Related Sciences. LC 96-42257. 800p. 1997. text 131.95 (*1-85928-215-6*, Pub. by Scolar Pr) Ashgate Pub Co.

Morton, Leslie T. & Wright, Derek J. How to Use a Medical Library. 7th ed. LC 89-54537. 94p. 1990. reprint ed. pap. 30.00 (*0-608-07772-0*, 206786000010) Bks Demand.

Morton, Linda J., ed. see Morton, John O.

***Morton, Lois.** Health Care Restructuring: Market Theory vs. Civil Society. 210p. 2000. 67.00 (*0-86569-303-X*, Auburn Hse) Greenwood.

Morton, Lois W., jt. auth. see Baskin, Maria M.

Morton, Lone. Get Dressed, Robbie (Habille-Toi, Robbie) Jansen, Jacqueline, tr. (ENG & FRE., Illus.). 28p. (YA). (ps-3). 1998. 6.95 (*0-7641-5128-2*) Barron.

— Get Dressed, Robbie (Vistete, Roberto) (ENG & SPA., Illus.). 28p. (J). (ps-3). 1998. 6.95 (*0-7641-5129-0*) Barron.

— Goodnight Everyone (Bonne Nuit a Tous) Bougard, Marie-Therese, tr. LC 94-2434. (Language Learning Story Books: I Can Read Spanish - I Can Read French). (ENG & FRE., Illus.). 28p. (J). (ps up). 1994. 6.95 (*0-8120-6453-4*) Barron.

— Goodnight Everyone (Buenas Noches a Todos) LC 94-2433. (Language Learning Story Books: I Can Read Spanish - I Can Read French). (ENG & SPA., Illus.). 28p. (J). (ps up). 1994. 6.95 (*0-8120-6452-6*) Barron.

— Happy Birthday (Bon Anniversaire) (FRE., Illus.). 28p. (J). (ps up). 1996. 6.95 (*0-8120-6581-6*) Barron.

— Happy Birthday (Feliz Cumpleanos) (SPA., Illus.). 28p. (J). (ps up). 1996. 6.95 (*0-8120-6582-4*) Barron.

— I'm Too Big (Je Suis Trop Gros) Helie, Ide M., tr. from FRE. LC 94-561. (Language Learning Story Books: I Can Read Spanish - I Can Read French). (ENG & FRE., Illus.). 28p. (J). (ps up). 1994. 6.95 (*0-8120-6454-2*) Barron.

— I'm Too Big (Soy Demasiado Grande) LC 94-563. (Language Learning Story Books: I Can Read Spanish - I Can Read French). (ENG & SPA., Illus.). 28p. (J). (ps up). 1994. 6.95 (*0-8120-6451-8*) Barron.

— My First Design Book: Projects to Make with Stencil Shapes. (Illus.). 24p. (J). (gr. 1-4). 1993. pap. 4.95 (*0-8120-1744-7*) Barron.

Morton, Lone & Risk, Mary. Goodnight Everyone: English-French Version: Bonne Nuit a Tous. (I Can Read French Ser.). (ENG & FRE.). (J). (ps up). 1998. 9.95 incl. audio (*0-7641-7188-7*) Barron.

— Goodnight Everyone: English-Spanish Version: Buenas Noches a Todos. (I Can Read Spanish Ser.). (ENG & SPA.). (J). (ps up). 1998. 9.95 incl. audio (*0-7641-7191-7*) Barron.

— Happy Birthday: English-French Version: Bon Anniversaire. (I Can Read French Ser.). (ENG & FRE.). (J). (ps up). 1998. 9.95 incl. audio (*0-7641-7187-9*) Barron.

— Happy Birthday: English-Spanish Version: Feliz Cumpleanos. (I Can Read Spanish Ser.). (ENG & SPA.). (J). (ps up). 1998. 9.95 incl. audio (*0-7641-7192-5*) Barron.

— I'm Too Big: English-French Version: Je Suis Trop Gros. (I Can Read French Ser.). (ENG & FRE.), (J). (ps up). 1998. pap. 9.95 incl. audio (*0-7641-7189-5*) Barron.

— I'm Too Big: English-Spanish Version: Soy Demasiado Grande. (I Can Read Spanish Ser.). (ENG & SPA.). (J). (ps up). 1998. pap. 9.95 incl. audio (*0-7641-7193-3*) Barron.

Morton, Lone, jt. auth. see Bruzzone, Catherine.

Morton, Louis. Robert Carter of Nomini Hall: A Virginia Tobacco Planter of the 18th Century. LC 83-45824. 1983. reprint ed. 31.00 (*0-404-20187-3*) AMS Pr.

Morton, Lucie T. Winegrowing in Eastern America: An Illustrated Guide to Viniculture East of the Rockies. LC 85-47696. (Illus.). 219p. reprint ed. pap. 67.90 (*0-608-20929-5*, 207202800003) Bks Demand.

Morton, Lucy & Morton, Grace. Cloth Marionettes: Sewing, Stringing, Staging. (Illus.). 96p. (Orig.). 1984. pap. 10.95 (*0-938432-20-6*) Mother Earth.

Morton, Lyman. Yucatan Cookbook: Recipes & Tales. (Cookbook Ser.). (Illus.). 256p. 1996. pap. 24.95 (*1-878610-51-1*) Red Crane Bks.

Morton, Lynne, jt. auth. see Schneider, Stephen H.

Morton, Malvin, ed. Can Public Welfare Keep Pace? LC 76-89859. 189p. reprint ed. pap. 58.60 (*0-8357-7985-8*, 203071300070) Bks Demand.

***Morton, Margaret.** Fragile Dwelling. (Illus.). 160p. 2000. 40.00 (*0-89381-915-8*) Aperture.

Morton, Margaret. The Tunnel: The Underground Homeless of New York City. (Architecture of Despair Ser.). (Illus.). 1996. 40.00 (*0-300-06538-8*); pap. 20.00 (*0-300-06559-0*) Yale U Pr.

Morton, Margaret, jt. auth. see Balmori, Diana.

Morton, Marian. Emma Goldman. (Twayne's Twentieth Century American Biography Ser.). 200p. 1992. pap. 15.95 (*0-8057-7794-6*) Macmillan.

Morton, Marian J. Women in Cleveland: An Illustrated History. LC 94-48852. (Encyclopedia of Cleveland History Ser.). (Illus.). 224p. 1995. 39.95 (*0-253-32896-9*); pap. 29.95 (*0-253-20972-2*) Ind U Pr.

Morton, Marian J. & Duncan, Russell, eds. First Person Past: American Autobiographies since 1877, Vol. II. (Illus.). 232p. (C). 1994. pap. text 16.50 (*1-881089-29-0*) Brandywine Press.

— First Person Past: American Autobiographies to 1877, Vol. I. (Illus.). 272p. (Orig.). (C). 1994. pap. text 14.90 (*1-881089-22-3*) Brandywine Press.

Morton, Marian J., jt. auth. see Frey, Sylvia R.

Morton, Marilyn, ed. Manitoba: A Color Guidebook. (Illus.). 200p. 1995. pap. 19.95 (*0-88780-322-9*, Pub. by Formac Publ Co) Seven Hills Bk.

Morton, Mark & Noble, Gail. The End: Closing Words for a Millennium. 1999. pap. 24.95 (*0-921368-83-6*) Genl Dist Srvs.

***Morton, Mark A.** Hop Up, Vol. 1. (Illus.). 128p. 2000. pap. 12.95 (*0-9675570-0-3*, 130151AE, Pub. by Hop Up Prod) Motorbooks Intl.

***Morton, Marsha & Schmunk, Peter L.** The Arts Entwined: Music & Painting in the Nineteenth Century. LC 99-34397. (Reference Library of the Humanities). 1999. write for info. (*0-8153-3156-8*) Garland.

Morton, Mary & Morton, Michael. 5 Steps to Selecting the Best Alternative Medicine: A Guide to Complementary & Integrative Healthcare. LC 96-36134. 352p. 1996. pap. 16.95 (*1-880032-94-5*) New Wrld Lib.

Morton, Mary G., jt. auth. see Bowron, Edgar Peters.

Morton, Maurice. Rubber Technology. 3rd ed. (Illus.). 1987. text 62.95 (*0-442-26422-4*) Chapman & Hall.

Morton, Maurice, ed. Rubber Technology. 3rd ed. 125.50 (*0-412-53950-0*) Chapman & Bkman.

Morton, Michael, jt. auth. see Morton, Mary.

Morton, Michael M. Herder & the Poetics of Thought: Unity & Diversity in "On Diligence in Several Learned Languages" LC 88-7697. 208p. 1989. lib. bdg. 35.00 (*0-271-00663-3*) Pa St U Pr.

Morton, Michael S., ed. The Corporation of the 1990s: Information Technology & Organizational Transformation. (Illus.). 352p. 1991. 35.00 (*0-19-506358-9*) OUP.

Morton, Michael S., jt. ed. see Allen, Thomas J.

Morton, Miriam, ed. Russian Plays for Young Audiences. 401p. 1977. 13.95 (*0-932720-62-5*); pap. 9.95 (*0-932720-61-7*) New Plays Inc.

Morton, Moira. Blossoming Romance. large type ed. (Linford Romance Library). 256p. 1989. pap. 16.99 (*0-7089-6693-4*, Linford) Ulverscroft.

Morton, N. E., et al. Methods in Genetic Epidemiology. (Contributions to Epidemiology & Biostatistics Ser.: Vol. 4). (Illus.). x, 262p. 1983. pap. 131.25 (*3-8055-3668-2*) S Karger.

Morton, N. S. Assisting the Anaesthetist. (Illus.). 264p. 1997. text 79.50 (*0-19-262444-X*) OUP.

***Morton, N. S.** More Case Presentations in Paediatric & Intensive Care. 160p. 2000. pap. text 28.50 (*0-7506-4215-7*) Buttrwrth-Heinemann.

Morton, N. S., ed. Assisting the Anaesthetist. (Illus.). 264p. 1997. pap. text 39.95 (*0-19-262443-1*) OUP.

Morton, N. S., et al, eds. Stabilization & Transport of the Critically Ill. (Illus.). 256p. 1996. write for info. (*0-443-05176-3*) Church.

Morton, N. S. & Raine, P. A., eds. Pediatric Day Case Surgery. (Illus.). 130p. 1994. text 69.50 (*0-19-262256-0*) OUP.

Morton, Nathaniel. New England's Memorial. LC 38-10717. 232p. 1979. reprint ed. 50.00 (*0-8201-1184-8*) Schol Facsimiles.

— New England's Memorial: Also Excerpts from Governor Bradford's History of Plymouth Colony & His Dialogue Prince's Chronology, & Governor Winslow's Visit to Massasoit. xxiv, 515p. 1997. reprint ed. pap. 36.00 (*0-7884-0705-8*, M567) Heritage Bk.

Morton, Neil S., ed. Paediatric Intensive Care. (Illus.). 310p. 1997. text 65.00 (*0-19-262511-X*) OUP.

Morton, Nelle. The Journey Is Home. LC 85-42342. 285p. 1986. reprint ed. pap. 16.50 (*0-8070-1133-9*, BP 718) Beacon Pr.

***Morton, Oren F.** Annals of Bath County, Virginia. 208p. 1999. reprint ed. pap. 25.00 (*0-8063-4642-6*, Pub. by Clearfield Co) ACCESS Pubs Network.

Morton, Oren F. Centennial Hitory of Alleghany County. (Illus.). 232p. 1997. reprint ed. lib. bdg. 29.50 (*0-8328-6511-7*) Higginson Bk Co.

— A History of Highland County, Virginia: With New 112-Page Index to Names. LC 78-8816. (Illus.). 532p. 1997. reprint ed. pap. 45.00 (*0-8063-7963-4*, Pub. by Clearfield Co) ACCESS Pubs Network.

— A History of Monroe County, West Virginia. LC 73-16338. (Illus.). 510p. 1998. reprint ed. pap. 40.00 (*0-8063-0592-4*) Clearfield Co.

— History of Monroe County, West Virginia. (Illus.). 510p. 1993. reprint ed. lib. bdg. 52.50 (*0-8328-2940-4*) Higginson Bk Co.

— A History of Pendleton County, West Virginia. (Illus.). 493p. 2000. reprint ed. pap. write for info. (*0-8063-0593-2*, 3905, Pub. by Clearfield Co) ACCESS Pubs Network.

***Morton, Oren F.** A History of Rockbridge County, Virginia. (Illus.). 574p. 1999. reprint ed. pap. 47.50 (*0-8063-7991-X*, 3910, Pub. by Clearfield Co) ACCESS Pubs Network.

Morton, Oren F. A History of Rockbridge County, Virginia. (Illus.). 582p. 1998. reprint ed. pap. 41.00 (*0-7884-1026-1*, M568) Heritage Bk.

An Asterisk (*) at the beginning of an entry indicates that the title is appearing for the first time.

— A History of Rockbridge County, Virginia. 574p. 1994. reprint ed. lib. bdg. 59.50 (*0-8328-4258-3*) Higginson Bk Co.

Morton, Oren F. & Cole, J. R. History of Preston County, 2 vols. (Illus.). 887p. 1997. reprint ed. lib. bdg. 89.00 (*0-8328-6951-1*) Higginson Bk Co.

Morton, Oren F. & Cole, J. R. A History of Preston County, West Virginia, 2 vols. 888p. 1997. reprint ed. pap. 85.00 (*0-8063-4689-2*) Clearfield Co.

Morton, Owen F. History of Preston County, Pt. I. 2nd ed. 564p. 1915. reprint ed. 40.00 (*0-87012-625-3*) McClain.

Morton, P., jt. auth. see Brittain, A.

Morton, P., jt. auth. see Morris, J.

Morton, P. H., ed. Surface Engineering & Heat Treatment: Past, Present & Future. 384p. 1992. pap. 70.00 (*0-901716-01-4*, Pub. by Inst Materials) Ashgate Pub Co.

Morton, Pamela. Basics of Disco Dancing. (Illus.). 56p. 1982. pap. text 9.95 (*0-89641-092-7*) American Pr.

— The Basics of Square Dancing. (Illus.). 67p. 1981. pap. text 9.95 (*0-89641-084-6*) American Pr.

Morton, Pat. Architect: Work in Progress. LC 97-42047. 1997. pap. text 35.00 (*1-885254-72-5*, Pub. by Monacelli Pr) Penguin Putnam.

Morton, Pat & Fox, Marcia R. The First-Job Hunt Survival Guide: Winning Advice on Choosing & Getting the Job You Want. (Career Works). 176p. 1995. pap. 11.95 (*1-880030-44-6*) DBM Pub.

Morton, Pat & Fox, Marcia R., eds. Job Search 101: Getting Started on Your Career Path. LC 97-5426. (Illus.). 224p. (Orig.). 1997. pap. 12.95 (*1-56370-314-9*) JIST Works.

Morton, Pat, jt. auth. see Stirling, Bob.

Morton, Patricia. Disfigured Images: The Historical Assault on Afro-American Women. LC 90-20540. (Contributions in Afro-American & African Studies: No. 144). 192p. 1991. pap. 18.95 (*0-275-93885-9*, B3885, Praeger Pubs) Greenwood.

— Disfigured Images: The Historical Assault on Afro-American Women, 144. LC 90-20701. (Contributions in Afro-American & African Studies: No. 144). 192p. 1991. 49.95 (*0-313-27296-4*, MBW/, Greenwood Pr) Greenwood.

Morton, Patricia, ed. Discovering the Women in Slavery: Emancipating Perspectives on the American Past. LC 95-14154. (Illus.). x, 320p. 1996. pap. 20.00 (*0-8203-1757-8*) U of Ga Pr.

— Discovering the Women in Slavery: Emancipating Perspectives on the American Past. LC 95-14154. (Illus.). x, 320p. 1996. 40.00 (*0-8203-1756-X*) U of Ga Pr.

***Morton, Patricia A.** Hybrid Modernities: Architecture & Representation at the 1931 Colonial Exposition, Paris. (Illus.). 352p. 2000. 40.00 (*0-262-13362-8*) MIT Pr.

Morton, Patricia G. Health Assessment in Nursing. 2nd ed. (Illus.). 681p. 1993. 49.95 (*0-8036-0010-0*) Davis Co.

Morton, Patricia G., et al, eds. Davis's Clinical Guide to Health Assessment. 2nd ed. (Illus.). 340p. (C). 1995. pap. text 31.95 (*0-8036-0119-0*) Davis Co.

Morton, Paul. It's Time for the Outpouring. 1994. pap. 8.00 (*0-927936-59-3*) Vincom Pubng Co.

— Why Kingdoms Fall: When Man's Thinking Prevails Over God's Voice. 1999. pap. text 8.99 (*1-57778-078-7*) Albury Pub.

Morton, Peg. Walk with Me. LC 97-69936. 1997. write for info. (*0-87574-333-1*) Pendle Hill.

Morton, Peggy Klein. Harmony Form & Expr. 1990. 4.95 (*1-55708-252-9*, MCR868) McDonald Pub Co.

— Rhythm & Melody. 1990. 4.95 (*1-55708-251-0*, R867) McDonald Pub Co.

Morton, Peter. Fire Across the Desert: Woomera & the Anglo-Australian Joint Project, 1946-1980. (Illus.). 575p. 1997. reprint ed. pap. 71.95 (*0-644-47500-5*, Pub. by Aust Gov Pub) Accents Pubns.

— An Institutional Theory of Law: Keeping Law in Its Place. LC 97-35700. 428p. 1998. text 95.00 (*0-19-825825-9*) OUP.

Morton, Peter, ed. see Baker, Chuck.

Morton, Peter A. An Historical Introduction to the Philosophy of Mind: Readings with Commentary. 1996. pap. 32.95 (*1-55111-087-3*) Broadview Pr.

Morton, Phyllis D., jt. ed. see Ballam, Harry.

Morton Press Staff. Chicago Works: A Collection of Chicago Author's Best Stories. Levy, Laurie, ed. 270p. (Orig.). 1990. 18.95 (*0-9625446-0-4*); pap. 10.00 (*0-9625446-1-2*) Morton Pr.

Morton, R. A. & Ayers, W. B., Jr. Plio-Pleistocene Genetic Sequences of the Southwestern Louisiana Continental Shelf & Slope RIO 210: Geologic Framework, Sedimentary Facies, & Hydrocarbon Distribution. (Illus.). 74p. 1992. pap. 7.00 (*0-317-05177-6*, RI 210) Bur Econ Geology.

Morton, R. A. & McGowen, J. H. Modern Depositional Environments of the Texas Coast. (Guidebook Ser.: GB 20). (Illus.). 167p. 1980. reprint ed. pap. 4.50 (*0-318-03129-9*) Bur Econ Geology.

Morton, R. A., et al. Continuity & Internal Properties of Gulf Coast Sandstones & Their Implications for Geopressured Fluid Production. (Reports of Investigations: RI 132). (Illus.). 70p. 1983. pap. 3.00 (*0-318-03287-2*) Bur Econ Geology.

Morton, R. A., jt. auth. see Paine, J. G.

***Morton, Rachel.** One Island Many Faiths: The Experience of Religion in Britain. LC 99-66193. (Illus.). 160p. 2000. 27.50 (*0-500-01987-8*, Pub. by Thames Hudson) Norton.

Morton, Ralph, tr. see Satoh, Akira.

Morton, Rebecca B. Learning by Voting: Sequential Choices in Presidential Primaries & Other Elections. (Illus.). 180p. (C). text 44.50 (*0-472-11129-9*, 11129) U of Mich Pr.

— Methods & Models: A Guide to the Empirical Analysis of Formal Models in Political Science. LC 98-49519. 336p. (C). 1999. 59.95 (*0-521-63300-1*); pap. 22.95 (*0-521-63394-X*) Cambridge U Pr.

Morton, Richard. Anne Sexton's Poetry of Redemption. LC 88-39019. (Studies in Art & Religious Interpretation: Vol. 11). 150p. 1988. lib. bdg. 69.95 (*0-88946-563-0*) E Mellen.

Morton, Richard A. Justice & Humanity: The Politics of Edward F. Dunn. LC 96-20415. 240p. (C). 1997. 34.95 (*0-8093-2095-9*) S Ill U Pr.

Morton, Richard F. An English Doctor in America. LC 97-20252. 186p. 1997. pap. 12.00 (*0-87034-127-8*) Fraser Pub Co.

***Morton, Richard F., et al.** A Study Guide to Epidemiology & Biostatistics. 2000. 35.00 (*0-8342-1758-9*) Aspen Pub.

Morton, Richard F., et al. A Study Guide to Epidemiology & Biostatistics. 4th rev. ed. 224p. 1995. pap., student ed. 33.00 (*0-8342-0740-0*) Aspen Pub.

Morton, Richard L. Struggle Against Tyranny & the Beginning of a New Era: Virginia, 1677-1699. LC F 0229.M67. (Jamestown 350th Anniversary Historical Booklet Ser.: No. 9). 90p. reprint ed. pap. 30.00 (*0-7837-2023-8*, 204229800002) Bks Demand.

Morton, Robert. Robert Morton: The Collected Works. Atlas, Allan, ed. (Masters & Monuments of the Renaissance Ser.: Vol. 2). (Illus.). xxxvi, 105p. 1982. pap. 50.00 (*0-8450-7302-8*) Broude.

Morton, Robert, et al. Living with the Texas Shore. LC 83-1753. (Living with the Shore Ser.). (Illus.). xii, 180p. (C). 1983. pap. 16.95 (*0-8223-0500-3*) Duke.

Morton, Robert J., jt. auth. see Karmark, C. J.

***Morton, Ron & Gawboy, Carl.** Talking Rocks: Geology & 10,000 Years of Native American Tradition in the Lake Superior Region. LC 99-6701. (Illus.). 224p. 1999. pap. 16.95 (*1-57025-142-8*) Pfeifer-Hamilton.

Morton, Ron & Lloyd, John, eds. The Health-Promoting Primary School. 160p. 1994. pap. 24.95 (*1-85346-325-6*, Pub. by David Fulton) Taylor & Francis.

Morton, Ron L. Music of the Earth: Volcanoes, Earthquakes, & Other Geological Wonders. (Illus.). 326p. (C). 1996. 28.95 (*0-306-45263-4*, Plenum Trade) Perseus Pubng.

Morton, Rosemary & Phillips, Barbara. Accidents & Emergencies in Children. 2nd ed. (Handbooks in Emergency Medicine Ser.: No. 15). (Illus.). 282p. 1996. text 84.50 (*0-19-262720-1*); pap. text 47.50 (*0-19-262719-8*) OUP.

Morton, Ruth. Interior Design: The Home-Its Furnishing & Equipment. Zinkus, Dan & Newman, Carol, eds. (Illus.). 184p. (Orig.). (gr. 9-12). 1979. pap. text 18.60 (*0-07-043426-3*) McGraw.

Morton, Ruth, et al. The Home, It's Furnishings & Equipment. 1979. text 33.96 (*0-07-043417-4*) McGraw.

***Morton, S. & Rolph, J., eds.** Public Policy & Statistics: Case Studies from RAND. LC 00-20827. (Illus.). 304p. 2000. 49.95 (*0 387 98777 0*) Spr-Verlag.

Morton, S., jt. auth. see Duxbury, R.

***Morton, Samuel G.** An Inquiry into the Distinctive Characteristics of the Aboriginal Race of America. (LC History-America-E). 48p. 1999. reprint ed. lib. bdg. 69.00 (*0-7812-4265-7*) Rprt Serv.

— Some Observations on the Ethnography & Archaeology of the American Aborigines. (LC History-America-E). 19p. 1999. reprint ed. lib. bdg. 69.00 (*0-7812-4266-5*) Rprt Serv.

Morton, Sarah W. My Mind & Its Thoughts, in Sketches, Fragments, & Essays. LC 74-28388. 336p. 1975. reprint ed. lib. bdg. 50.00 (*0-8201-1150-3*) Schol Facsimiles.

Morton, Sean D. Area 51: Nightmare in Dreamland. (Illus.). 240p. 1997. 21.95 (*0-87131-826-1*) M Evans.

Morton, Sharon E., ed. Heaven - Fact Or Fiction. 2nd rev. ed. 49p. 1990. reprint ed. pap. 6.95 (*0-9628047-0-3*) T J Simmons.

Morton, Suzanne. Ideal Surroundings: Domestic Life in a Working-Class Suburb in the 1920s. (Studies in Gender & History). (Illus.). 200p. 1995. text 40.00 (*0-8020-0474-1*); pap. text 17.95 (*0-8020-7575-4*) U of Toronto Pr.

Morton, T. C. Light Beyond the Darkness. LC 96-93139. 270p. (Orig.). 1997. pap. 12.95 (*0-9657118-0-3*) Solid Rock MN.

Morton, Thomas D. & Salus, Marsha K. Supervising Child Protective Services Caseworkers. 86p. (Orig.). (C). 1995. pap. text 25.00 (*0-7881-1920-6*) DIANE Pub.

Morton, Thomas E. & Pentico, David W. Heuristic Scheduling Systems: With Applications to Production Systems & Project Management. LC 92-37963. (Series in Engineering & Technology Management). 720p. 1993. 140.00 (*0-471-57819-3*) Wiley.

Morton, Thomas G. The History of the Pennsylvania Hospital, 1751-1895. LC 73-2408. (Mental Illness & Social Policy; the American Experience Ser.). 1973. reprint ed. 48.95 (*0-405-05218-9*) Ayer.

— New English Canaan or New Canaan. LC 73-141136. (Research Library of Colonial Americana: Personal Narratives & Promotional Literature). 196p. 1972. reprint ed. 23.95 (*0-405-03309-5*) Ayer.

Morton, Thomas H., Jr., et al. Principles of Biopsy: A Self-Instructional Guide, Bk. 8. 3rd rev. ed. (Illus.). 94p. 1983. pap. 14.95 (*0-89939-081-1*) Stoma Pr.

Morton-Thompson, Diana & Woods, Arnold M., eds. Development Geology Reference Manual. (Methods in Exploration Ser.: No. 10). (Illus.). xv, 550p. 1993. ring bd. 96.00 (*0-89181-660-7*, 612) AAPG.

***Morton, Timothy.** The Poetics of Spice: Romantic Consumerism & the Exotic. LC 99-87472. (Illus.). 328p. 2000. write for info. (*0-521-77146-3*) Cambridge U Pr.

— Radical Food: The Culture & Politics of Eating & Drinking, 1790-1820. LC 99-86630. (Illus.). 2000. write for info. (*0-415-14870-7*) Routledge.

Morton, Timothy. Shelley & the Revolution in Taste: The Body & the Natural World. (Studies in Romanticism: No. 10). (Illus.). 313p. (C). 1995. text 64.95 (*0-521-47135-4*) Cambridge U Pr.

Morton, Tom. Altered Mates: The Man Question. 336p. 1998. pap. 16.95 (*1-86448-333-4*, Pub. by Allen & Unwin Pty) Paul & Co Pubs.

— Cooperative Learning & Social Studies. 220p. 1996. pap. text 25.00 (*1-879097-32-X*) Kagan Cooperative.

— Hell's Golfer: A Good Walk Spoiled. (Illus.). 208p. 1996. 29.95 (*1-85158-656-3*, Pub. by Mainstream Pubng) Trafalgar.

Morton, Tom J. Texas Real Estate Finance. 5th ed. LC 94-6528. 379p. 1994. 39.95 (*0-7931-1020-3*, 1557-1705) Dearborn.

Morton, Verne. Images of Rural Life: Photographs of Verne Morton, DeWitt Historical Society of Tompkins County. LC 83-10376. (York State Book Ser.). (Illus.). 252p. 1984. reprint ed. pap. 78.20 (*0-608-06958-2*, 206716600009) Bks Demand.

***Morton, Virginia B.** Marching Through Culpepper: A Novel of Culpepper, Virginia - Crossroads of the Civil War. LC 00-103914. (Illus.). xiv, 520p. (C). 2000. 27.99 (*0-615-11642-6*) Edgehill Bks.

Morton, W. Morton, the Stem of Morton: Collection of Genealogical Notes Respecting the Family of Morton, Chiefly Seated in the Wapentake of Strafford-cum-Tickhill, S. Yorkshire. 311p. 1995. lib. bdg. 57.50 (*0-8328-4450-0*) Higginson Bk Co.

— Morton, the Stem of Morton: Collection of Genealogical Notes Respecting the Family of Morton, Chiefly Seated in the Wapentake of Strafford-cum-Tickhill, S. Yorkshire. 311p. 1995. reprint ed. pap. 47.50 (*0-8328-4451-9*) Higginson Bk Co.

Morton, W. E. Physical Properties of Textile Fibres. 660p. 1975. 125.00 (*0-7855-7212-0*) St Mut.

Morton, W. E. & Hearle, John W. Physical Properties of Textile Fibres. 3rd ed. 1997. 250.00 (*1-870812-41-7*, Pub. by Textile Inst) St Mut.

Morton, W. L., ed. see Begg, Alexander.

Morton, W. Scott. China: Its History & Culture. 3rd ed. 324p. (C). 1995. pap. 14.95 (*0-07-043424-7*) McGraw.

— Japan: Its History & Culture. 3rd ed. 311p. (C). 1994. pap. 12.95 (*0-07-043423-9*) McGraw.

Morton, Walter A. British Finance, 1930-1940. Wilkins, Mira, ed. LC 78-3942. (International Finance Ser.). (Illus.). 1979. reprint ed. lib. bdg. 35.95 (*0-405-11242-4*) Ayer.

Morton, Ward M. Woman Suffrage in Mexico. LC 62-20735. (Illus.). 174p. reprint ed. pap. 54.00 (*0-8357-6721-3*, 203535600095) Bks Demand.

Morton, William C. The Harmony of Verse. LC 68-85787. 245p. reprint ed. pap. 76.00 (*0-608-30115-9*, 201437500089) Bks Demand.

Morton, William Lewis. The Canadian Identity. 2nd ed. 1972. pap. text 13.95 (*0 8020-6139-7*) U of Toronto Pr

— The Canadian Identity. 2nd ed. LC 73-187505. 174p. 1972. reprint ed. pap. 54.00 (*0-608-01974-7*, 206262900003) Bks Demand.

— Henry Youle Hind, Eighteen Twenty-Three to Nineteen Eight. LC 81-113864. (Canadian Biographical Studies: No. 7). 171p. reprint ed. pap. 53.10 (*0-608-12877-5*, 202365300033) Bks Demand.

— Manitoba: A History. LC 67-4598. 561p. reprint ed. pap. 174.00 (*0-608-12876-7*, 202365400033) Bks Demand.

Morton-Williams, Jean. Interviewer Approaches. LC 93-20002. 250p. 1993. 72.95 (*1-85521-339-7*, Pub. by Dartmth Pub) Ashgate Pub Co.

Morton-Williams, Peter, ed. see Bradbury, R. E.

Morton-Young, Tommie. After-School & Parent Education Programs for At-Risk Youths & Their Families: A Guide to Organizing & Operating a Community-Based Center for Basic Educational Skills Reinforcement, Homework Assistance, Cultural Enrichment & a Parent Involvement Focus. LC 94-38716. (Illus.). 144p. (C). 1995. text 39.95 (*0-398-05961-6*); pap. text 27.95 (*0-398-05962-4*) C C Thomas.

Mortonson, Kenneth A. The Advent Instructor: Reflections on Christmas Symbolism. (Illus.). 1995. pap. 7.95 (*0-7880-0562-6*) CSS OH.

— Lent Instructor: Reflections & Symbols. LC 95-94163. 1997. pap. text 6.95 (*1-55673-993-1*) CSS OH.

— Open My Eyes: More Children's Object Lessons by Kenneth Mortonson. LC 95-41492. 124p. 1996. pap. 11.50 (*0-7880-0566-9*, Fairway Pr) CSS OH.

— That Seeing, They May Believe: Children's Object Lessons. LC 93-18007. 1993. pap. 10.95 (*1-55673-652-5*, 9352) CSS OH.

Mortreux, Andre & Petit, Francis, eds. Industrial Applications of Homogeneous Catalysis. (C). 1987. text 201.00 (*90-277-2520-9*) Kluwer Academic.

Mortsell, Anders. Neutral Pion Production in Proton-Proton Collisions Close to the Kinematical Threshold. (Uppsala Dissertations from the Faculty of Science Ser.: No. 6). (Illus.). 102p. 1995. pap. 37.50 (*91-554-3525-4*) Coronet Bks.

Mortvedt, John J., et al. Fertilizer Technology & Application. (Illus.). 200p. (C). 1999. pap. text 29.25 (*1-892829-03-7*) Meister Pub Co.

Mortz, John R. How to Moonlight with Your Computer. rev. ed. 356p. 1990. pap. 39.95 (*0-9623722-3-4*) Amer Inst Comput Tech.

— Insider Secrets for the Desktop Publisher: How to Turn Your PC into an 89,378 Dollars per Year Profit Center. 1990. pap. write for info. (*0-9623722-4-2*) Amer Inst Comput Tech.

— Make Money Moonlighting! The Four Best Ways to Earn Money with Your Computer & the Four Traps to Avoid. 121p. 1989. pap. 9.95 (*0-9623722-2-6*) Amer Inst Comput Tech.

Mortzfeld, Peter. Katalog der Graphischen Portrats in der Herzog August Bibliothek Wolfenbuttel, 40 vols., Set. Bibliothek, Herzog A., ed. (Portraitsammlung Series A). 1986. lib. bdg. 6500.00 (*3-598-31480-9*) K G Saur Verlag.

Morus, Iwan R. Frankenstein's Children: Electricity, Exhibition, & Experiment in Early-Nineteenth-Century London. LC 98-9451. 353p. 1998. text 45.00 (*0-691-05952-7*, Pub. by Princeton U Pr) Cal Prin Full Svc.

Moruzzi, G. & Strumia, F. The Hanle Effect & Level-Crossing Spectroscopy. (Physics of Atoms & Molecules Ser.). (Illus.). 388p. (C). 1991. text 120.00 (*0-306-43630-2*, Kluwer Plenum) Kluwer Academic.

Moruzzi, Giovanni, et al, eds. Microwave, Infrared, & Laser Transitions of Methanol: Atlas of Assigned Lines from 0 to 1258 CM. LC 95-23097. 544p. 1995. boxed set 254.95 (*0-8493-2478-5*, 2478) CRC Pr.

Moruzzi, Giuseppe, jt. auth. see Dow, Robert.

Moruzzi, James M. Nazi Trials: A Soldier's Story of Terror. Klein, Irving J. et al, eds. LC 95-22231. 224p. (Orig.). 1995. pap. 15.95 (*0-938993-23-2*) Coral Gables Pub.

Moruzzi, V. L. & Sommers, C. B. Calculated Electronic Properties of Ordered Alloys. 448p. (C). 1995. text 86.00 (*981-02-1918-0*) World Scientific Pub.

Morvan, Christiane. Dictionnaire Cegos. (ENG & FRE.). 1986. 89.95 (*0-7859-8642-1*, 271240307X) Fr & Eur.

Morvan, J. M. & Verstraelen, L. Geometry & Topology of Submanifolds. 260p. (C). 1989. text 92.00 (*9971-5-0932-6*) World Scientific Pub.

***Morvan, Jean-David & Buchet, Philippe.** Wake. 2001. pap. 9.95 (*1-56163-267-8*) NBM.

Morvan, M., et al, eds. STACS 98: Proceedings of the 15th Annual Symposium on Theoretical Aspects of Computer Science, Paris, France, February 25-27, 1998, Vol. 137. LC 98-3118. (Lecture Notes in Computer Science Ser.: Vol. 1373). xv, 630p. 1998. pap. 89.00 (*3-540-64230-7*) Spr-Verlag.

Morvan, Michael, jt. ed. see Bouchitte, Vincent.

Morvan, Michel, jt. auth. see Reischuk, R. Udiger.

Morvan, P. Cegos Dictionary: Definition of Micro - Computer & Electronic Vocabulary: Dictionnaire Cegos: Definition Du Vocabulaire Micro-Informatique - Electronique. (ENG & FRE.). 322p. 1986. 65.00 (*0-8288-1375-2*, M8340) Fr & Eur.

— Dictionnaire Informatique, A a Z. (FRE.). 351p. 1996. 36.95 (*0-320-00642-5*) Fr & Eur.

***Morvant, Mark C.** Biochemistry Lab Manual. (C). 1999. pap. text 11.94 (*1-56870-364-3*) RonJon Pub.

Morvant, Mark C., jt. auth. see Halterman, Ronald L.

***Morville, Peter, et al.** The Internet Searcher's Handbook: Locating Information, People & Software. 2nd rev. ed. LC 99-38213. 165p. 1999. pap. 45.00 (*1-55570-359-3*) Neal-Schuman.

Morville, Peter, jt. auth. see Rosenfeld, Louis.

Morvillo, Nancy & Schmidt, Matthew. The MCAT Biology Book. (Illus.). 416p. (C). 2000. pap. 29.95 (*1-889057-08-8*) Nova Pr.

Morvillo, Robert G., jt. ed. see Obermaier, Otto G.

Morway, Richard J., ed. Classic Brain Teasers of the Twentieth Century Vols. 1 & 2: A Selection of the Best Puzzles in Logic, Math, & Deductive Reasoning, Vol. 1. 48p. 1992. pap. 2.95 (*0-9632528-0-1*) Madisn Hse NH.

— Classic Brain Teasers of the Twentieth Century Vols. 1 & 2: A Selection of the Best Puzzles in Logic, Math, & Deductive Reasoning, Vol. 2. 48p. 1992. pap. 2.95 (*0-9632528-1-X*) Madisn Hse NH.

Morwitz, Ernst, tr. see George, Stefan.

***Morwood, Carolyn.** The Blessing File: A Lyn Blessing Crime Thriller. 1999. pap. 15.95 (*0-7043-4586-2*, Pub. by Womens Press) Trafalgar.

Morwood, James. A Dictionary of Latin Words & Phrases. 240p. 1998. 18.95 (*0-19-860229-4*) OUP.

— A Latin Grammar. 256p. 1999. pap. 12.95 (*0-19-860277-4*) OUP.

— The Pocket Oxford Latin Dictionary. (Illus.). 368p. 1995. reprint ed. pap. 11.95 (*0-19-864228-8*) OUP.

Morwood, James, ed. A Dictionary of Latin Words & Phrases. 240p. 1998. pap. 12.95 (*0-19-860109-3*) OUP.

— The Oxford Latin Dictionary. 704p. 1998. pap. 6.95 (*0-19-860139-5*) OUP.

***Morwood, James, ed.** The Pocket Oxford Latin Dictionary. 368p. 2000. pap. 11.95 (*0-19-860283-9*) OUP.

Morwood, James & Crane, David, eds. Sheridan Studies. (Illus.). 217p. (C). 1996. text 59.95 (*0-521-46466-8*) Cambridge U Pr.

Morwood, James & Warman, Mark. Our Greek & Latin Roots. Phinney, Ed, ed. (Awareness of Language Ser.). (Illus.). 56p. (C). 1990. pap. text 9.95 (*0-521-37841-9*) Cambridge U Pr.

Morwood, James, jt. auth. see Balme, Maurice.

Morwood, James, jt. auth. see Balme, Maurice G.

Morwood, James, ed. see Euripides.

Morwood, James, ed. see Euripides Staff.

Morwood, James, jt. ed. see Woodhouse, S. E.

Morwood, James, ed. & tr. see Euripides.

Morwood, James, tr. see Euripides.

Morwood, James H., jt. auth. see Balme, Maurice G.

Morwood, James H., ed. see Apuleius, Lucius.

Morwood, Michael. Tomorrow's Catholic: Understanding God & Jesus in a New Millennium. LC 97-60030. 160p. (Orig.). 1997. pap. 9.95 (*0-89622-724-3*) Twenty-Third.

Morwood, Peter. Rules of Engagement. (Star Trek Ser.: No. 48). 288p. 1990. pap. 4.50 (*0-685-28839-0*); per. 4.99 (*0-671-66129-9*) PB.

— Seaquest DSV: The Novel. 1993. mass mkt. 4.99 (*0-441-00037-1*) Ace Bks.

Morwood, Peter, jt. auth. see Duane, Diane.

Morwood, Peter, jt. auth. see Duane E., Diane.

M

***Morwyn.** The Complete Book of Psychic Arts: Divination Practices from Around the World. LC 99-45050. 264p. 1999. pap. 14.95 (*1-56718-236-4*) Llewellyn Pubns.

Morwyn. Secrets of a Witch's Coven. Alexander, Skye, ed. LC 88-50422. (Illus.). 400p. 1988. pap. 19.95 (*0-914918-80-X*, Whitford) Schiffer.

— Web of Light: Rites for Witches in the New Age. 256p. 1996. pap. 19.95 (*0-924608-17-X*, Whitford) Schiffer.

— Witch's Brew: Secrets of Scents. LC 95-68972. (Illus.). 256p. (YA). (gr. 10-13). 1993. pap. 16.95 (*0-924608-19-6*, Whitford) Schiffer.

Morwyng, P., tr. see Gesner, Conrad.

Moryganov, A. P., ed. Textile Chemistry: Theory, Technology & Equipment. LC 97-190948. 305p. (C). 1997. lib. bdg. 115.00 (*1-56072-439-0*) Nova Sci Pubs.

Morykan, Dana G. The Official Price Guide to Country Antiques & Collectibles. 4th ed. 640p. (Orig.). 1999. pap. 15.95 (*0-676-60165-0*) Hse Collectbls.

Morykan, Dana G. & Rinker, Harry L. Warman's Country Antiques & Collectibles. 3rd ed. LC 96-5629. 336p. 1996. pap. 19.95 (*0-87069-743-9*, Wllce-Homestd) Krause Pubns.

Moryson, Fynes. An Itinerary. LC 70-38150. (English Experience Ser.: No. 387). 1971. reprint ed. 175.00 (*90-221-0387-0*) Walter J Johnson.

— Shakespeare's Europe. rev. ed. LC 66-12287. (Illus.). 570p. 1972. 38.95 (*0-405-08799-3*, Pub. by Blom Pubns) Ayer.

Moryson, M. Testing for Random Walk Coefficients in Regression & State Space Models. LC 98-36670. (Contributions to Statistics Ser.). (Illus.). xvi, 317p. 1998. pap. 73.00 (*3-7908-1132-7*) Spr-Verlag.

Morzenti, Alida. Captive Raptor Management: Common Raptors of the United States. 95p. 1997. pap. 18.00 (*0-9660923-1-7*) Wldlfe Pubns.

— Captive Raptor Management: Common Raptors of the United States. 2nd rev. ed. (Illus.). 124p. (C). 1998. pap. 18.00 (*0-9660923-6-8*) Wldlfe Pubns.

Morzer, Bruyns & Wolff, W. J., eds. Nature Conservation: Management & Physical Planning in the Wadden Sea Area. 164p. 1983. pap. 71.00 (*90-6191-061-7*, Pub. by A A Balkema) Ashgate Pub Co.

Morzik, Fritz. German Air Force Airlift Operations. LC 68-22555. (German Air Force in World War 2 Ser.). (Illus.). 1968. reprint ed. 24.95 (*0-405-00042-1*) Ayer.

Morzinski, Mary. The Linguistic Influence of Polish on Joseph Conrad's Style. 200p. 1995. 29.50 (*0-88033-309-X*, 412, Pub. by East Eur Monographs) Col U Pr.

Morzoeff, Nicholas. Silent Poetry: Deafness, Sign, & Visual Culture in Modern France. LC 94-42545. 320p. 1995. text 35.00 (*0-691-03789-2*, Pub. by Princeton U Pr) Cal Prin Full Svc.

Mos, Leendert P., et al, eds. Annals of Theoretical Psychology, Vol. 2. LC 84-644088. 390p. 1984. 85.00 (*0-306-41692-1*, Plenum Trade) Perseus Pubng.

— Annals of Theoretical Psychology, Vol. 4. LC 84-644088. (Illus.). 420p. (C). 1986. 114.00 (*0-306-42327-8*, Plenum Trade) Perseus Pubng.

Mos, Leendert P. & Royce, Joseph R., eds. Annals of Theoretical Psychology, Vol. 1. LC 84-644088. 346p. 1984. 85.00 (*0-306-41327-2*, Plenum Trade) Perseus Pubng.

Mos, Leendert P., jt. auth. see Robinson, D. N.

Mos, Leendert P., jt. auth. see Van Geert, P.

Mos, Leendert P., jt. ed. see Madsen, K. B.

Mos, Leendert P., jt. ed. see Royce, Joseph R.

Mos, Leendert P., jt. ed. see Staats, Arthur W.

Mosaic Software Inc. Staff. The Twin Educational Version. (Illus.). 208p. (C). 1987. pap. text 22.60 (*0-13-935370-4*) P-H.

Mosak, Harold H. A Child's Guide to Parent Rearing. LC 80-66084. (Illus.). 79p. (Orig.). (C). 1980. pap. text 3.50 (*0-918560-27-6*) Adler Sch Prof Psy.

— On Purpose: Collected Papers. LC 76-42942. 1977. pap. 14.95 (*0-918560-19-5*) Adler Sch Prof Psy.

Mosak, Harold H. & Maniacci, Michael P. A Primer of Adlerian Psychology: The Analytic-Behavioral-Cognitive Psychology of Alfred Adler. LC 99-25738. 1999. 27.95 (*1-58391-003-4*) Brunner-Mazel.

— Tactics in Counseling & Psychotherapy. LC 98-65651. 200p. (C). 1998. pap. text 27.50 (*0-87581-417-4*, TCP) F E Peacock Pubs.

Mosak, Richard D. Banach Algebras. LC 75-25957. (Chicago Lectures in Mathematics). 180p. 1975. pap. text 7.00 (*0-226-54204-1*) U Ch Pr.

Mosala, Itumeleng J. & Tlhagale, Buti, eds. Hammering Swords into Ploughshares: Essays in Honor of Archbishop Mpilo Desmond Tutu. LC 87-5242. 314p. reprint ed. pap. 97.40 (*0-8357-4370-5*, 203719900007) Bks Demand.

— The Unquestionable Right to Be Free: Black Theology from South Africa. LC 87-102501. 224p. 1986. reprint ed. pap. 69.50 (*0-7837-9813-X*, 206054200005) Bks Demand.

Mosala, Itumeleng J., jt. ed. see Tlhagale, Buti.

***Mosallam, Ayman S., ed.** Innovative Systems for Seismic Repair & Rehabilitation of Structure: Design & Applications. LC 00-101387. 240p. 2000. text 149.95 (*1-56676-964-7*) Technomic.

Mosallan, K. H., jt. auth. see Chen, Wai-Fah.

Mosatche, Harriet S. & Unger, Karen. Too Old for This, Too Young for That! Your Survival Guide for the Middle-School Years. LC 99-46773. (Illus.). 200p. (YA). (gr. 5-9). 2000. pap. 14.95 (*1-57542-067-8*) Free Spirit Pub.

Mosbach, Klaus, ed. Immobilized Enzymes & Cells, Pt. B. (Methods in Enzymology Ser.: Vol. 135). 675p. 1987. text 167.00 (*0-12-182035-1*) Acad Pr.

Mosbach, Klaus, et al, eds. Immobilized Enzymes & Cells, Vol. 137, Pt. D. (Methods in Enzymology Ser.: Vol. 137). 767p. 1988. text 159.00 (*0-12-182037-8*) Acad Pr.

Mosbacher, E., tr. see Giglio, Giovanni.

Mosbacher, Eric, tr. see Aichinger, Ilse.

Mosbacher, Eric, tr. see Perutz, Leo.

Mosbacher, Eric, tr. see Silone, Ignazio.

Mosbacher, Eric, tr. see Strasser, Otto.

***Mosbacher, Georgette.** It Takes Money, Honey: A Get-Smart Guide to Total Financial Freedom. 304p. 2000. pap. 13.00 (*0-06-098747-2*) HarpC.

Mosbacher, Georgette. It Takes Money, Honey: A Get-Smart Guide to Total Financial Freedom. LC 98-42935. 304p. 1999. 24.00 (*0-06-039236-3*, ReganBks) HarperTrade.

***Mosbacher, Georgette.** It Takes Money, Honey: A Get-Smart Guide to Total Financial Freedom, Set. abr. ed. 1999. audio 18.00 (*0-694-51912-X*, CPN2732, Pub. by HarperAudio) Lndmrk Audiobks.

***Mosbacher, Kathi.** Adventurous Palate - Houston: The Intrepid Gourmet's Guide to Unique Restaurants. 368p. 1998. pap. 14.95 (*0-914373-45-5*, 73455) Gulf Pub.

Mosback, Gerald & Mosback, Vivienne. Practical Faster Reading. 132p. 1977. pap. text 12.95 (*0-521-21346-0*) Cambridge U Pr.

Mosback, Vivienne, jt. auth. see Mosback, Gerald.

Mosberg, Michael. Guide to Researching the International Principle of Self-Determination. LC 97-80512. Vol. 29. 1997. 42.00 (*1-57588-401-1*, 311480) W S Hein.

Mosbrooker, Michael. Implementation of Project Management. 2nd ed. 1999. write for info. (*0-201-52388-4*) Addison-Wesley.

Mosbrugger, V. The Tree Habit in Land Plants: A Functional Comparison of Trunk Construction with a Brief Introduction into the Biomechanics of Trees. Bhattacharji, S. et al, eds. (Lecture Notes in Earth Sciences Ser.: Vol. 28). v, 161p. 1990. 32.95 (*0-387-52374-X*) Spr-Verlag.

Mosburg, Earl R. Dictionary of Spoken Nepali: Nepali-English, English-Nepali, with Phrases & Grammar Reference Notes. (ENG & NEP.). viii, 111p. (Orig.). 1991. pap. 14.95 (*0-9629545-2-7*) E R Mosburg.

Mosby. Ace Pathology. (Illus.). 624p. 1997. pap. text 29.95 incl. disk (*0-8151-9428-5*, 28948) Mosby Inc.

— Cardiopulmonary Physical Therapy. 3rd ed. 1997. text, student ed. 15.95 (*0-8151-4887-9*) Mosby Inc.

***Mosby.** Managing Major Diseases: Pulmonary Disorders. 4th ed. LC 99-10468. 1999. text 29.95 (*0-323-00855-0*) Harcourt.

Mosby. Medical Dictionary, English-Spanish/Spanish-English. (ENG & SPA.). 370p. 1996. 95.00 (*0-7859-9644-3*) Fr & Eur.

***Mosby.** Mosby's Nursing Drug Database, 1999. 1998. pap. 39.95 (*0-323-00659-0*) Mosby Inc.

Mosby. Mosby's Quick Review: Neuroscience. 350p. 1999. text. write for info. incl. cd-rom (*0-323-00836-4*) Mosby Inc.

— Radiographic Imaging Study Guide. (Radiographic Instructional Ser.). (Illus.). 176p. (C). 1998. student ed. write for info. (*0-8151-5408-9*) Mosby Inc.

— Rapid Review: Step 1. 2001. text. write for info. (*0-323-00841-0*) Harcourt.

— Surefire Documentation. 448p. 1998. text 36.95 (*0-323-00431-8*, Pub. by Harcourt Coll Pubs) Harcourt.

***Mosby.** 2000 Mosby's Genrx: Book. 10th ed. 1504p. 1999. text 49.95 (*0-323-00627-2*) Mosby Inc.

Mosby, C. V. Encyclopedia Mosby de Medicina y Enfermeria, 3 vols., Set. (SPA.). 1990. 495.00 (*0-8288-8235-5*, 8477642184) Fr & Eur.

— Mosby's Home Health Nursing Pocket Consultant. LC 95-136742. (Illus.). 352p. (C). (gr. 13). 1994. spiral bd. 29.95 (*0-8151-6125-5*, 25341) Mosby Inc.

Mosby, C. V., jt. auth. see Ajn.

Mosby, C. V., jt. auth. see Anderson, Kenneth N.

Mosby, C. V., Company Staff. Cardiac Disorders. LC 98-40594. (Managing Major Diseases Ser.). 1999. write for info. (*0-323-00741-4*) Mosby Inc.

Mosby Editorial Staff. Mosby Buyer's Guide to Ten Essential Herbs. 96p. 1997. pap. text 10.00 (*1-57857-004-2*) Mosby Consmer Hlth.

— Mosby's Tour Guide to Alternative Medicine. 160p. 1997. pap. text 10.00 (*1-57857-003-4*) Mosby Consmer Hlth.

Mosby Editorial Staff, ed. Mosby's Spanish/English-English/Spanish Medical Dictionary. (ENG & SPA.). 1996. 275.00 (*0-7859-9704-0*) Fr & Eur.

Mosby, George, Jr. Population. 1983. pap. 7.00 (*0-914610-35-X*) Hanging Loose.

Mosby, Jack & Dapkus, Dave. Alaska Paddling Guide. 3rd rev. ed. LC 86-11669. (Illus.). 113p. 1992. pap. 7.95 (*0-9608550-2-5*) J & R Enter.

Mosby, John S. Memoirs from John S. Mosby. (Great Commanders Ser.). 432p. 1998. reprint ed. 30.00 (*1-56515-015-5*) Collect Reprints.

— Mosby's Memoirs. LC 94-69016. 1995. pap. 14.95 (*1-879941-27-9*) J S Sanders.

— Mosby's War Reminiscences. 264p. 1997. pap. text 12.95 (*1-887269-09-6*) J Culler & Sons.

— Stuart's Cavalry in the Gettysburg Campaign. 228p. 1987. reprint ed. 25.00 (*0-942211-28-6*) Olde Soldier Bks.

Mosby, John S., jt. ed. see Gardner, Seth.

Mosby, Katherine. Private Altars. 384p. 1996. mass mkt. 6.99 (*0-425-15236-7*) Berkley Pub.

***Mosby, Katherine.** Private Altars. 2000. 13.95 (*0-425-17126-4*) Berkley Pub.

Mosby Lifeline Staff. Healthcare Basics Cd-Rom for Windows Single Site License. 400p. 1996. pap. text 195.00 (*0-8151-5561-1*) Mosby Inc.

Mosby Medical Library Staff. 2001 Year Book of Dermatology. 2001. text 81.00 (*0-323-00448-2*) Mosby Inc.

— 2002 Year Book of Dermatology. 2002. text 81.00 (*0-323-00449-0*) Mosby Inc.

— 2000 Year Book of Dermatology. 2000. text 81.00 (*0-323-00447-4*) Mosby Inc.

Mosby Staff. Ace Step 3 (Mac) (Illus.). 416p. (C). (gr. 13). 1996. pap. text 38.00 incl. disk, mac hd (*0-8151-2756-1*, 28975) Mosby Inc.

— Ace the Boards Pharmacology (Mac) 450p. (C). (gr. 13). 1996. text 30.00 incl. disk, mac hd (*0-8151-3152-6*, 28953) Mosby Inc.

— Anatomy. 1997. pap. text 2.00 (*0-8151-8601-0*) Mosby Inc.

— Arrhythmias. LC 98-47836. (Managing Major Diseases Ser.). 1999. 29.95 (*0-323-00854-2*) Mosby Inc.

Mosby Staff. Case Management Practice Guidelines. (Illus.). 160p. (C). (gr. 13). 1995. text 71.95 (*0-8151-9010-7*, 29088) Mosby Inc.

Mosby Staff. A Celebration of Chiropractic. 24p. (gr. 13). 1995. text 17.95 (*0-8151-6556-0*) Mosby Inc.

— FOR Radiation Imaging. 1998. text 1150.00 (*0-8151-6948-5*) Mosby Inc.

— Mosby Patient Teaching Guides. (C). (gr. 13). 1996. 160.00 incl. disk (*0-8151-8557-X*, 28720) Mosby Inc.

— Mosby Patient Teaching Guides for Health Promotion. 32p. (C). (gr. 13). 1997. pap. text 24.95 (*0-8151-2574-7*, 31313) Mosby Inc.

— Mosby's Comprehensive Bookmarks to Internet Resources. (gr. 13). 1996. write for info. (*0-8151-4816-X*, 30462) Mosby Inc.

***Mosby Staff.** Mosby's Patient Carelink. 160p. 1998. write for info. (*0-8151-4457-1*) Mosby Inc.

Mosby Staff. Mosby's Patient Teaching Guides. (C). (gr. 13). 1994. spiral bd. 52.95 (*0-8151-5862-9*, 25114) Mosby Inc.

***Mosby Staff.** Mosby's Patient Teaching Guides: Update 3, Update 3. (Illus.). 40p. 1998. write for info. (*0-323-00073-8*) Mosby Inc.

— Mosby's Patient Teaching Guides with Updates 2 & 3. 1998. write for info. (*0-323-00227-7*) Mosby Inc.

— Mosby's Patient Teaching Guides with Updates 2 & 3: Tips. 1998. write for info. (*0-8151-6196-4*) Mosby Inc.

Mosby Staff. Mosby's Primary Care Patient Teaching Guides. 2nd rev. ed. Date not set. ring bd. 39.95 (*0-8151-8399-2*) Mosby Inc.

— Mosby's Psychiatric Nursing Study Guide: Instructor's Resource Manual. (C). (gr. 13). 1997. text. write for info. (*0-8151-2131-8*, 30751) Mosby Inc.

— Mosby's Success in Medicine: Anatomy (Ibm) (Illus.). 480p. (C). (gr. 13). 1996. pap. text 29.95 incl. 3.5 hd (*0-8151-8974-5*, 29056) Mosby Inc.

— Mosby's Success in Medicine: Biochemistry (Ibm) 400p. (C). (gr. 13). 1996. pap. text 29.95 (*0-8151-8985-0*, 29062) Mosby Inc.

— Mosby's Success in Medicine: Physiology (IBM) (Illus.). 304p. (C). (gr. 13). 1996. pap. text 29.95 (*0-8151-8914-1*, 29046) Mosby Inc.

— Patient Teaching Guides. 30p. 1996. text, suppl. ed. 19.95 (*0-8151-6907-8*) Mosby Inc.

— Patient Teaching Guides on Disk. 200p. 1996. text 99.95 (*0-8151-8551-0*) Mosby Inc.

— Physical Exam of the Neurologic System. 1995. 595.00 (*0-8151-6135-2*) Mosby Inc.

— Radiobiology & Radiation Protection Study Guide. (Radiographic Instructional Ser.). (Illus.). 200p. 1998. student ed. write for info. (*0-8151-5423-2*) Mosby Inc.

— Radiologic Physics Study Guide: Study Guide. (Radiographic Instructional Ser.). (Illus.). 208p. 1997. student ed. write for info. (*0-8151-5405-4*) Mosby Inc.

— Radiology & Physics. 1997. text 1150.00 (*0-8151-6947-7*) Mosby Inc.

Mosby Staff & Mauger, Gaston. Ocular Drug Handbook. 320p. (C). (gr. 13). 1996. text 35.95 (*0-8151-6910-8*, 27119) Mosby Inc.

Mosby Staff, jt. auth. see Ajn.

Mosby Year Book Publishing Staff. Mosby's Dental Drug Reference. 4th ed. 1998. pap. 33.95 (*0-323-00501-2*) Mosby Inc.

Mosby-Year Book Staff. Expert Rapid Response. LC 98-20962. 1998. 140.00 (*0-323-00377-X*) Mosby Inc.

Mosby Year Book Staff. Mosby's Medical Terminology Instructor's Resource Library. (Illus.). 281p. 1994. pap. text. write for info. (*0-8151-5887-4*, 24525) Mosby Inc.

***Mosby Year Book Staff.** Patient Genrx. 1999. pap. text 99.00 (*0-8151-3752-4*) Mosby Inc.

Mosby Year Books Staff. Mosby's Ace the Boards: General Clinical Sciences. LC 98-51164. 336p. (C). (gr. 13). 1999. pap. text 28.95 (*0-8151-3715-X*, 31410) Mosby Inc.

— Patient Genrx in Spanish. (SPA.). 1999. pap. text 99.00 (*0-8151-3754-0*) Mosby Inc.

Mosby Yearbook, Inc. Staff. Mosby's Genrx Retail Direct Mail 1998. (C). 1997. text 69.95 (*0-8151-4418-0*, 30812) Mosby Inc.

Mosca, Edoardo. Optimal, Predictive, & Adaptive Control. LC 94-6082. 480p. 1994. text 67.00 (*0-13-847609-8*) P-H.

Mosca, Gaetano. Partiti e Sindacati Nella Crisi Del Regime Parlamentare: Parties & Labor Unions in the Crisis of the Parliamentary Regime. LC 74-25771. (European Sociology Ser.). 348p. 1975. reprint ed. 28.95 (*0-405-06525-6*) Ayer.

— The Ruling Class. Livingston, Arthur, ed. Kahn, Hannah D., tr. from ITA. LC 80-17230.Tr. of Elementi Di Scienza Politica. 514p. 1980. reprint ed. lib. bdg. 45.50 (*0-313-22617-2*, MORU, Greenwood Pr) Greenwood.

Mosca, Gene & Gautreau, Ronald. Physics: For Scientists & Engineers, Vol. 1. 4th ed. 2000. student ed. write for info. (*1-57259-511-6*) Worth.

Mosca, Giammaria, jt. auth. see Schulz, Anne M.

Mosca, Mark. Hole in the Heart. LC 94-220167. (Mystery on the Monterey Peninsula Ser.). 240p. (Orig.). 1994. pap. 9.95 (*0-9617681-7-7*) Otter B Bks.

Moscardini, A. O. & Robson, E. H. Information Transmission, Reception & Security: Mathematical & Computer Modelling for the Communications Industry. (Mathematics & Its Applications Ser.). 214p. 1988. 92.95 (*0-470-21024-9*) P-H.

Moscardini, A. O., jt. auth. see Cross, M.

Moscardini, A. O., jt. ed. see Esroy, Yasar.

Moscardo, Gianna. Making Visitors Mindful: Principles for Creating Sustainable Visitor Experience Through. (Advances in Tourism Applications Ser.: Vol. 2). (Illus.). 224p. 1999. pap. 16.95 (*1-57167-259-1*) Sagamore Pub.

Moscardo, Gianna, jt. ed. see Laws, Eric.

Moscatelli, Robert G. Too Soon Old, Too Late Smart: How to Get Control of Your Money (Before Your Money Gets Control of You) LC 94-96692. (Illus.). 294p. (Orig.). 14.95 (*0-9643601-0-1*) Blck Knight.

Moscati, Sabatino. The Celts. rev. ed. Frey, Otto H. et al, eds. (Illus.). 720p. 1999. pap. 35.00 (*0-8478-2193-5*, Pub. by Rizzoli Intl) St Martin.

Moscati, Sabatino, ed. The Phoenicians. (Illus.). 672p. 1999. pap. 35.00 (*0-8478-2194-3*, Pub. by Rizzoli Intl) St Martin.

Moscato, Donald R. Building Financial Decision-Making Models: An Introduction to Principles & Procedures. LC 80-65704. 160p. reprint ed. pap. 49.60 (*0-8357-7465-1*, 202358100033) Bks Demand.

Moscato, Michael & LeBlanc, Leslie. The United States of America vs. One Book Entitled Ulysses by James Joyce: Documents & Commentary : 50-Year Retrospective. LC 83-25929. 482p. 1984. lib. bdg. 79.50 (*0-313-27065-1*, U7065) Greenwood.

Mosch, Susan Von, see Von Mosch, Susan.

Mosch, W., jt. auth. see Arora, R.

Mosch, W., jt. auth. see Hauschild, W.

Moschandreas, Maria. Business Economics. LC 93-38120. 384p. (C). 1994. pap. 32.95 (*0-415-10910-8*) Thomson Learn.

— Business Economics. LC 93-38120. 384p. (C). (gr. 13). 1994. pap. 86.95 (*0-415-10909-4*) Thomson Learn.

— Business Economics. 2nd ed. (ITBP Textbooks Ser.). 1999. pap. text 22.99 (*1-86152-399-8*) Thomson Learn.

Moschea, Pat, jt. auth. see Rinder, Lenore.

Moscheles, Felix, ed. see Mendelssohn, Felix.

Moscheles, Felix, ed. & tr. see Mendelssohn, Felix.

Moscheles, Ignaz & Kann, Hans. Piano Concerto No. 3 in G Minor, Op. 58 Two-Piano Score. LC 79-155179. (Illus.). (Orig.). 1971. pap. 6.50 (*0-912028-03-3*) Music Treasure.

Moschella, David C. Waves of Power: Dynamics of Global Technology Leadership, 1964-2010. LC 96-49652. 240p. 1997. 29.95 (*0-8144-0379-4*) AMACOM.

Moschella, Samuel L. & Hurley, Harry J. Dermatology, 2 vols., Set. 3rd ed. (Illus.). 2767p. 1992. text 350.00 (*0-7216-3263-7*, W B Saunders Co) Harcrt Hlth Sci Grp.

Moscherosch, Johann M., pseud. Visiones de Don Quevedo, 2 vols. in 1. xliv, 976p. 1974. reprint ed. write for info. (*3-487-05288-1*) G Olms Pubs.

***Moschetta, Evelyn.** Marriage Spirit: Finding the Passion & Joy of Soul Centered Love. LC 97-40029. (Illus.). 320p. 2000. per. 13.00 (*0-684-85198-9*) S&S Trade.

Moschetta, Evelyn, jt. auth. see Moschetta, Paul.

Moschetta, Paul & Moschetta, Evelyn. The Marriage Spirit: Finding the Passion & Joy of Soul-Centered Love. LC 97-40029. 288p. 1998. 22.50 (*0-684-83450-2*) S&S Trade.

Moschinsky, George. U Sviti Mystets'kykh Chariv (Fascinating Corners in the World of Art) (UKR., Illus.). 323p. 1963. 23.95 (*0-938103-09-1*) ZZYZX Pub.

Moschis, George P. Gerontographics: Life-Stage Segmentation for Marketing Strategy Development. LC 95-51412. 192p. 1996. 59.95 (*1-56720-062-1*, Quorum Bks) Greenwood.

Moschis, George P. Marketing Strategies for the Mature Market. LC 94-8542. 216p. 1994. 59.95 (*0-89930-887-2*, Quorum Bks) Greenwood.

Moschis, George P. Marketing to Older Consumers: A Handbook of Information for Strategy Development. LC 91-47642. 352p. 1992. 69.50 (*0-89930-764-7*, MOV, Quorum Bks) Greenwood.

***Moschis, George P., et al.** The Maturing Marketplace: Buying Habits of Baby Boomers & Their Parents. LC 99-36602. (Illus.). 320p. 2000. 67.50 (*1-56720-344-2*, Q344, Quorum Bks) Greenwood.

Moschonas, Andreas. Education & Training in the European Union. LC 97-41409. (Illus.). 170p. 1998. 67.95 (*1-84014-067-4*, LA622.M67, Pub. by Ashgate Pub) Ashgate Pub Co.

Moschonas, Andreas, jt. auth. see Kourvetaris, George A.

Moschos, John. The Spiritual Meadow (Pratum Spirituale) Wortley, John, tr. from LAT. & intro. by. (Cistercian Studies). 261p. 1992. pap. 17.95 (*0-87907-539-2*) Cistercian Pubns.

Moschovakis, Yiannis N. Notes on Set Theory. LC 93-35825. (University Texts in Mathematics Ser.). (Illus.). 272p. 1994. 39.95 (*0-387-94180-0*) Spr-Verlag.

Moschovakis, Yiannis N., jt. ed. see Kechris, A. S.

Moschovitis, Christos J. P., et al. History of the Internet: A Chronology, 1843 to the Present. LC 99-13275. (Illus.). 312p. 1999. lib. bdg. 65.00 (*1-57607-118-9*) ABC-CLIO.

Moschovitis Group, Inc. Staff. Philosophers & Religious Leaders. Von Dehsen, Christian, ed. LC 99-45394. (Lives & Legacies Ser.: Vol. 2). (Illus.). 246p. 1999. boxed set 69.95 (*1-57356-152-5*) Oryx Pr.

***Moschovitis Group, Inc. Staff.** Statistical Handbook on Consumption & Wealth in the United States. Kaul, Chandrika & Tomaselli-Moschovitis, Valerie, eds. LC 99-38530. (Statistical Handbook Ser.). (Illus.). 308p. 1999. boxed set 65.00 (*1-57356-251-3*) Oryx Pr.

An Asterisk (*) at the beginning of an entry indicates that the title is appearing for the first time.

Moschovitis Group, Inc. Staff. Statistical Handbook on Death & Dying in the United States. (Statistical Handbook Ser.). (Illus.). 344p. 1999. text 65.00 (*1-57356-265-3*) Oryx Pr.

Moschovitis Group Staff. Atlas Of Modern American Culture: Baby Boom to the 21st Century. (Illus.). 240p. 1999. lib. bdg. 115.00 (*0-02-865008-5*) Macmillan.

— Atlas of Modern American Culture: Baby Boom to 21st Century. 2000. per. 35.00 (*0-02-865007-7*) Macmillan.

Moschus. Europa. (GER.). xii, 144p. 1991. write for info. (*0-318-70420-X*) G Olms Pubs.

— Moschus Europa. (Altertumswissenschaftliche Texte und Studien: Vol. 19). (GER.). xii, 144p. 1991. pap. text 20.00 (*3-487-09432-0*) G Olms Pubs.

Moschus, John. Spiritual Meadow: The Pratum Spirituale. 1981. pap. 1.25 (*0-89981-100-0*) Eastern Orthodox.

Moschwitzer, Albrecht. Parat Lexikon Elektronik. (GER.). 1000p. 1993. 225.00 (*0-7859-8415-1*, 3527281533) Fr & Eur.

— Semiconductor Devices, Circuits & Systems. (Monographs in Electrical & Electronic Engineering). (Illus.). 368p. 1991. 85.00 (*0-19-859374-0*) OUP.

Moschytz, G. M. S., ed. MOS Switched-Capacitor Filters: Analysis & Design. LC 84-9055. 512p. 1986. 79.95 (*0-87942-177-0*, PC01701) Inst Electrical.

Moschytz, George S. & Horn, P. Active Filter Design Handbook: For Use with Programmable Pocket Calculators & Minicomputers. LC 80-40845. (Illus.). 324p. reprint ed. pap. 100.50 (*0-7837-6732-3*, 204636000011) Bks Demand.

Moschzisker, Felix Von, see Von Moschzisker, Felix.

Moschzisker, Robert Von, see Von Moschzisker, Robert.

Moscinski, Sharon. Tracing Our English Roots. LC 94-26925. (American Origins Ser.). (Illus.). 48p. (J). (gr. 4-7). 1995. 12.95 (*1-56261-188-7*, J Muir) Avalon Travel.

— Tracing Our Irish Roots. LC 93-2070. (American Origins Ser.). (Illus.). 48p. (J). 1993. text 12.95 (*1-56261-148-8*, J Muir) Avalon Travel.

Moscinski, Sharon. Tracing Our Polish Roots. LC 93-50732. (American Origins Ser.). (Illus.). 48p. (J). (gr. 4-7). 1994. 12.95 (*1-56261-161-5*, J Muir) Avalon Travel.

Mosco, Maisie. For Love & Duty. 416p. 1992. mass mkt. 5.50 (*0-06-100395-6*, Harp PBks) HarpC.

— New Beginnings. large type ed. (General Fiction Ser.). 400p. 1992. 27.99 (*0-7089-8657-9*) Ulverscroft.

— Out of the Ashes. large type ed. (Charnwood Library). 1991. 27.99 (*0-7089-8559-9*, Charnwood) Ulverscroft.

Mosco, Marilena. Pitti Palace: The Palace & Its Art. (Illus.). 96p. 1997. 30.00 (*1-85759-133-X*) Antique Collect.

— The Pitti Palace, Florence: A Souvenir Guide to the Palace & Its Art. (Illus.). 96p. 1997. 30.00 (*0-85667-469-9*) Scala Books.

Mosco, Umberto, ed. see Fabes, Eugene, et al.

Mosco, Vincent. Doing It Right with Computer Communication: A Case Study of the United Services Automobile Association. unabridged ed. LC 95-138763. (Illus.). 31p. (Orig.). 1994. pap. text. write for info. (*1-879716-20-8*, P-94-9) Ctr Info Policy.

— The Pay-per-Society: Computers & Communication in the Information Age. Dervin, Brenda, ed. LC 89-6665. (Communication & Information Science Ser.). 224p. (Orig.). (C). 1989. pap. 39.50 (*0-89391-604-8*) Ablx Pub.

— The Political Economy of Communication: Rethinking & Renewal. LC 98-2647. (Media, Culture & Society Ser.). (Illus.). 336p. 1996. 75.00 (*0-8039-8560-6*); pap. 26.95 (*0-8039-8561-4*) Sage.

— Pushbutton Fantasies: Critical Perspectives on Videotex & Information Technology. Voigt, Melvin J., ed. LC 82-11601. (Communication & Information Science Ser.). 240p. (C). 1982. pap. 39.50 (*0-89391-132-1*); text 73.25 (*0-89391-125-9*) Ablx Pub.

— Will Computer Communication End Geography? unabridged ed. (Illus.). 42p. (Orig.). 1995. pap. text. write for info. (*1-879716-30-5*, P-95-4) Ctr Info Policy.

Mosco, Vincent & Voigt, Melvin J., eds. Policy Research in Telecommunications: Proceedings from the 11th Annual Telecommunications Policy Research Conference. LC 83-12340. (Communication & Information Science Ser.). 472p. 1984. text 82.50 (*0-89391-260-3*) Ablx Pub.

Mosco, Vincent & Wasko, Janet, eds. Changing Patterns of Communication Control. LC 82-11592. (Critical Communications Review Ser.: Vol. 2). 320p. 1984. text 78.50 (*0-89391-153-4*) Ablx Pub.

— The Critical Communication Review Vol. 1: Labor, the Working Class & Media. LC 82-11592. 340p. 1983. pap. 49.50 (*0-89391-212-3*) Ablx Pub.

— The Political Economy of Information. LC 87-40369. (Studies in Communication & Society). 368p. (C). 1988. pap. text 12.95 (*0-299-11574-7*) U of Wis Pr.

— Popular Culture & Media Events. LC 82-11592. (Critical Communications Review Ser.: Vol. 3). 336p. 1985. text 78.50 (*0-89391-279-4*) Ablx Pub.

Mosco, Vincent, jt. auth. see Wasko, Janet.

Moscoe, Mike. The First Casualty. 336p. 1999. pap. 5.99 (*0-441-00593-4*) Ace Bks.

— First Dawn. (Lost Millenium Ser.: Bk. 1). 280p. 1996. mass mkt. 5.99 (*0-441-00392-3*) Ace Bks.

— The Lost Millennium: Second Fire. 320p. 1997. mass mkt. 5.99 (*0-441-00458-X*) Ace Bks.

— The Lost Millennium III: Lost Days. 1998. mass mkt. 5.99 (*0-441-00510-1*) Ace Bks.

***Moscoe, Mike.** The Price of Peace. 2000. mass mkt. 5.99 (*0-441-00695-7*) Ace Bks.

Moscona, A. A., jt. auth. see Moscona, Aron A.

Moscona, Aron, ed. The Cell Surface in Development. LC 74-7308. 348p. reprint ed. 107.90 (*0-608-16127-6*, 201519700092) Bks Demand.

Moscona, Aron A. & Moscona, A. A. Introductory Concepts in Developmental Biology. LC 78-7946. (Illus.). 1994. lib. bdg. 25.00 (*0-226-53476-6*) U Ch Pr.

Mosconi, Gail, jt. auth. see Foge, Leslie.

Mosconi, William, jt. auth. see McNair, Carol J.

Mosconi, Willie. Willie Mosconi on Pocket Billiards. 1995. pap. 9.00 (*0-517-88428-3*) Random.

— Winning Pocket Billiards. 1995. pap. 9.00 (*0-517-88427-5*) Random.

Moscoso, Americo, tr. see Lindsey, Michael, et al.

Moscotti, Albert D. British Policy & the Nationalist Movement in Burma, 1917-1937. LC 73-86163. (Asian Studies at Hawaii: No. 11). 281p. reprint ed. pap. 87.20 (*0-8357-7426-0*, 202703000053) Bks Demand.

Moscove. Accounting Information Systems. 5th ed. 416p. 1996. pap. text, teacher ed. 40.00 (*0-471-13663-8*) Wiley.

— Cost Accounting, 6 vols. 6th ed. (C). 1989. pap. text, teacher ed., suppl. ed. 4.36 (*0-395-44708-9*) HM.

Moscove, Stephen A. & Wright, Arnold M. Cost Accounting with Managerial Applications. 6th ed. LC 88-81349. 1989. text 49.16 (*0-318-36900-1*) HM.

Moscove, Stephen A., et al. Core Concepts of Accounting Information Systems. 6th ed. LC 98-41571. 496p. 1999. pap. 61.95 (*0-471-28304-5*) Wiley.

— Cost Accounting: With Managerial Applications. 5th ed. LC 84-80701. 928p. (C). 1985. 6.36 (*0-685-09608-4*) HM.

Moscovich, Ivan. The Magic Cylinder Book: Hidden Pictures to Color & Discover. (J). 1991. pap. 7.95 (*0-906212-67-7*, Pub. by Tarquin Pubns) Parkwest Pubns.

***Moscovich, Ivan.** Mindgames. 2000. 95.20 (*0-7611-2083-1*) Workman Pub.

— Mindgames. (MindGames Ser.). (Illus.). 24p. 2000. 5.95 (*0-7611-2018-1*) Workman Pub.

Moscovich, Ivan. Mind's Eye Geometry. (Illus.). (J). 1996. pap. 8.50 (*0-906212-98-7*, Pub. by Tarquin Pubns) Parkwest Pubns.

***Moscovich, Ivan.** Probability Games. (MindGames Ser.). (Illus.). 24p. 2000. 5.95 (*0-7611-2017-3*) Workman Pub.

Moscovich, Ivan. Puzzling Reflections: Test Your Thinking Powers with Mirror-Cubes. (J). 1991. pap. 6.95 (*0-906212-72-3*, Pub. by Tarquin Pubns) Parkwest Pubns.

— The Think Tank. LC 98-136319. (Illus.). 32p. (J). (gr. 4-7). 1998. 24.95 (*0-7894-2429-0*) DK Pub Inc.

Moscovici, Claudia. Erotisms. LC 96-12905. 152p. (C). 1996. pap. text 23.50 (*0-7618-0313-0*); lib. bdg. 43.50 (*0-7618-0312-2*) U Pr of Amer.

— From Sex Objects to Sexual Subjects. LC 96-30437. 190p. (C). 1996. 65.00 (*0-415-91810-3*); pap. 17.99 (*0-415-91811-1*) Routledge.

***Moscovici, Claudia.** Gender & Citizenship: The Dialectics of Subject-Citizenship in Nineteenth Century French Literature & Culture. LC 99-87268. 144p. 2000. text 65.00 (*0-8476-9694-4*); pap. text 18.95 (*0-8476-9695-2*) Rowman.

— Persuals into (Post) Modern Thought. LC 99-88671. 120p. 2000. 24.50 (*0-7618-1615-1*) U Pr of Amer.

Moscovici, S., jt. auth. see Graumann, Carl F.

Moscovici, S., jt. ed. see Graumann, Carl F.

Moscovici, Serge. The Invention of Society: Psychological Explanations for Social Phenomena. Leigh, Sue, ed. Halls, W. D., tr. from FRE. 360p. 1996. pap. 33.95 (*0-7456-1839-1*) Blackwell Pubs.

***Moscovici, Serge.** Social Representations. Duveen, Gerard, ed. 2001. 67.95 (*0-7456-2225-9*, Pub. by Polity Pr); pap. 32.95 (*0-7456-2226-7*, Pub. by Polity Pr) Blackwell Pubs.

— Social Representations: Studies in Social Psychology. 1999. pap. text 18.50 (*0-8147-5630-1*) NYU Pr.

***Moscovici, Serge.** Social Representations: Studies in Social Psychology. 240p. 1999. text 50.00 (*0-8147-5629-8*) NYU Pr.

Moscovici, Serge, et al, eds. Perspectives on Minority Influence. (European Studies in Social Psychology). 272p. 1985. text 64.95 (*0-521-24695-4*) Cambridge U Pr.

Moscovici, Serge & Doise, Willem. Conflict & Consensus: A General Theory of Collective Decisions. 240p. 1994. 69.95 (*0-8039-8456-1*); pap. 17.99 (*0-8039-8457-X*) Sage.

Moscovit, Andrei, pseud. The Seventh Wife. Olcott, Anthony, tr. from RUS. 468p. 1994. 23.00 (*1-880909-16-2*) Baskerville.

Moscovitch, Allan & Drover, Glenn, eds. Inequality: Essays on the Political Economy of Social Welfare. (Studies in the Political Economy of Canada). 408p. 1981. pap. 15.95 (*0-8020-6426-4*) U of Toronto Pr.

***Moscovitch, Arlene.** Egypt the Culture. LC 99-16637. (Lands, Peoples, & Cultures Ser.). (Illus.). 32p. (YA). (gr. 4-9). 1999. pap. 7.95 (*0-86505-314-6*); lib. bdg. 20.60 (*0-86505-234-4*) Crabtree Pub Co.

— Egypt the Culture. (Lands, Peoples, & Cultures Ser.). (Illus.). (J). 1989. 13.40 (*0-606-18053-2*) Turtleback.

Moscovitch, Arlene. Egypt the Land. (Lands, Peoples & Cultures Ser.). (Illus.). 32p. (YA). (gr. 4-9). 1999. lib. bdg. 20.60 (*0-86505-232-8*) Crabtree Pub Co.

***Moscovitch, Arlene.** Egypt the Land. LC 99-16591. (Lands, Peoples & Cultures Ser.). (Illus.). 32p. (YA). (gr. 4-9). 1999. pap. 7.95 (*0-86505-312-X*) Crabtree Pub Co.

— Egypt the People. LC 99-16638. (Lands, Peoples & Cultures Ser.). (Illus.). 32p. (YA). (gr. 4-9). 1999. pap. 7.95 (*0-86505-313-8*); lib. bdg. 20.60 (*0-86505-233-6*) Crabtree Pub Co.

Moscovitch, Edward. Mental Retardation Programs: How Does Massachusetts Compare? (Pioneer Paper Ser.: No. 4). 100p. (Orig.). 1991. pap. 10.00 (*0-929930-06-1*) Pioneer Inst.

— Special Education: Good Intentions Gone Awry. (Pioneer Paper Ser.: No. 8). 165p. 1993. pap. 10.00 (*0-929930-10-X*) Pioneer Inst.

Moscovitch, Morris, ed. Infant Memory: Its Relation to Normal & Pathological Memory in Humans & Other Animals. LC 84-9844. (Advances in the Study of Communication & Affect Ser.: Vol. 9). 236p. 1984. 65.00 (*0-306-41588-7*, Plenum Trade) Perseus Pubng.

Moscovitch, Morris, jt. ed. see Kanwisher, Nancy.

Moscovitz, Judy. The Dieter's Companion: How to Make Any Diet Work. 192p. (Orig.). 1989. mass mkt. 6.95 (*0-380-75460-6*, Avon Bks) Morrow Avon.

— The Rice Diet Report. 224p. 1987. mass mkt. 5.99 (*0-380-70286-X*, Avon Bks) Morrow Avon.

Moscow, Alvin. Building a Business: The Jim Walter Story. LC 95-33449. (Illus.). 340p. 1995. 24.95 (*1-56164-087-5*); pap. 14.95 (*1-56164-092-1*) Pineapple Pr.

Moscow, Alvin, jt. auth. see Geneen, Harold.

Moscow, Alvin, jt. auth. see Hearst, Patricia C.

Moscow, Bradford. Book of New York Firsts. 1982. 9.95 (*0-02-080960-3*, Collier S&S) S&S Trade.

Moscow, Henry. The Book of New York Firsts: Unusual, Arcane, & Fascinating Facts in the Life of New York City. LC 94-39250. (Illus.). 133p. 1995. pap. 14.95 (*0-8156-0308-8*) Syracuse U Pr.

— The Street Book: An Encyclopedia of Manhattan's Street Names & Their Origins. 2nd ed. LC 78-66990. (Illus.). 119p. 1990. pap. 16.95 (*0-8232-1275-0*) Fordham.

Moscow Museum of Art & Industry Staff. Medieval Russian Ornament in Full Color: From Illuminated Manuscripts. LC 94-32632. (Pictorial Archive Ser.). (Illus.). 112p. 1994. pap. 21.95 (*0-486-28258-9*) Dover.

Moscow Synod Staff, ed. Bogojavlenije Gospodnje.Tr. of Theophany. 194p. reprint ed. pap. 8.00 (*0-317-29167-X*) Holy Trinity.

— Preobrazhenije Gospodnje.Tr. of Transfiguration of the Lord. 128p. pap. 6.00 (*0-317-29169-6*) Holy Trinity.

Moscow, Vsesoiuznyi Nauchno-issledovatel'skii Inst. New Data on Rare Element Mineralogy (Authorized Translation from the Russian) Ginzburg, A. I., ed. LC 61-18756. 144p. reprint ed. pap. 44.70 (*0-608-11392-1*, 200336800021) Bks Demand.

Moscowitz. From Story to Movie to Critique. 202p. 1998. pap. text 25.00 (*0-536-01862-6*) Pearson Custom.

Moscowitz, David S. Amulet of the Salkti. (Illus.). 1984. 6.95 (*0-940244-20-9*) Flying Buffalo.

Moscowitz, Ellyn. Legal Research & Writing for Paralegals. LC 93-72659. 315p. (C). 1993. pap. 29.95 (*0-87084-132-7*) Anderson Pub Co.

Moscowitz, Gary, ed. see Schacter, Vicki.

Moscowitz, Harold, ed. see Bdolak, Levanah S.

***Moscowitz, John E.** Critical Approaches to Writing about Film. LC 99-31977. 212p. 1999. pap. text 23.60 (*0-13-083707-5*) P-H.

Moscowitz, Mark, ed. see American Bookworks Staff & Peterson's Guides Staff.

Moscowitz, Mark, ed. see Carris, Joan D.

Moscowitz, Mark, ed. see Crystal, Michael R.

Moscowitz, Raymond. Stuffy: The Life of Newspaper Pioneer Basil "Stuffy" Walters. LC 82-50. (Illus.). 213p. 1982. reprint ed. pap. 66.10 (*0-608-00130-9*, 206091100006) Bks Demand.

Moscrip, F. A., jt. auth. see Battin, George W.

Moscrop. A Sinhalese-English - English-Sinhalese Dictionary. rev. ed. (ENG & SNH.). 336p. 1992. 49.95 (*0-8288-6986-3*) Fr & Eur.

Moscrop, J. E., jt. auth. see Robbins, J.

Moscrop, John J. Measuring Jerusalem: The Palestine Exploration Fund & British Interests in the Holy Land LC 99-29412. 1999. 74.95 (*0-7185-0220-5*) Leicester U Pr.

Moscrop, T. A Sinhalese-English - English-Sinhalese Dictionary. (ENG & SNH.). 335p. 1992. 31.00 (*0-7859-8920-X*) Fr & Eur.

Moscucci, Ornella. The Science of Woman: Gynaecology & Gender in England, 1800-1929. (History of Medicine Ser.). (Illus.). 288p. (C). 1993. pap. text 22.95 (*0-521-44795-X*) Cambridge U Pr.

Mosdell, jt. auth. see Malone.

***Mosdell, Chris.** Splatter Head. 288p. 2000. pap. 16.00 (*1-893722-02-3*, Emersons Eye Pr) Bent Light.

Mose, D. G., jt. auth. see Bickford, Marion E.

***Mose, Ingo.** Sanfter Tourismus. (Gessellschaft, Raum, Umwelt (Society, Space, Environment): Vol. 1).Tr. of Eco Tourism. (GER.). 181p. 1998. pap. text 23.00 (*90-5708-024-9*, Verlag Fakultas) Gordon & Breach.

— Sanfter Tourismus (Eco Tourism) (Gessellschaft, Raum, Umwelt (Society, Space, Environment): Vol. 1). (GER.). 181p. 1998. text 35.00 (*90-5708-023-0*, Verlag Fakultas) Gordon & Breach.

Mose, Kenrick E. Defamiliarization in the Work of Gabriel Garcia Marquez from 1947-1967. LC 89-9406. (Hispanic Literature Ser.). 350p. 1989. lib. bdg. 99.95 (*0-88946-387-5*) E Mellen.

— Shades of Darkness: Poems. LC 92-40838. 1993. pap. 14.95 (*0-7734-0029-X*, Mellen Poetry Pr) E Mellen.

Mosedale, F. Philosophy & Science: The Wide Range of Interaction. (C). 1979. pap. text 43.60 (*0-13-662577-0*) P-H.

Mosegaard-Hansen, Maj-Britt. The Function of Discourse Particles: A Study with Special Reference to Spoken Standard French. LC 97-46674. (Pragmatics & Beyond New Ser.: Vol. 53). (FRE.). xii, 418p. (C). 1998. 85.00 (*1-55619-815-9*) J Benjamins Pubng Co.

Mosekilde, ed. European Simulation Multiconference, 1991 Proceedings. 968p. 1991. pap. 150.00 (*0-911801-92-8*, ESM91-1) Soc Computer Sim.

Mosekilde, E. & Mosekilde, L. Complexity, Chaos & Biological Evolution. (NATO ASI Ser.: Vol. 270). (Illus.). 446p. (C). 1991. text 130.00 (*0-306-44026-1*, Kluwer Plenum) Kluwer Academic.

Mosekilde, Erik & Mouritsen, Ole G. Modeling the Dynamics of Living Systems: Nonlinear Phenomena & Pattern Formation. (Series in Synergetics: Vol. 65). 1994. write for info. (*0-387-58480-3*); 75.95 (*3-540-58480-3*) Spr-Verlag.

Mosekilde, L., jt. auth. see Mosekilde, E.

Mosel, Arlene. The Funny Little Woman. LC 75-179046. (Illus.). (J). (ps-3). 1993. pap. 5.99 (*0-14-054753-3*, PuffinBks) Peng Put Young Read.

— Funny Little Woman. LC 75-179046. (J). 1986. 11.19 (*0-606-03787-X*, Pub. by Turtleback) Demco.

— Tikki Tikki Tembo. LC 68-11839. (Illus.). (J). (ps-2). 1995. 14.95 (*0-8050-0662-1*, Bks Young Read); pap. 18.95 (*0-8050-2345-3*, Bks Young Read) H Holt & Co.

— Tikki Tikki Tembo. Alonso, Liwayway, tr. LC 68-11839. (Illus.). 48p. (J). 1994. 14.95 (*1-880507-13-7*) Lectorum Pubns.

— Tikki Tikki Tembo. (J). 1968. 11.15 (*0-606-04377-2*, Pub. by Turtleback) Demco.

Mosel, Doug, jt. auth. see Gift, Robert G.

Mosel, Tad. All the Way Home. 1961. 15.00 (*0-8392-1003-5*) Astor-Honor.

— Impromptu. 1961. pap. 3.25 (*0-8222-0557-2*) Dramatists Play.

— That's Where the Town's Going. 1963. pap. 5.25 (*0-8222-1130-0*) Dramatists Play.

Mosel, U. Fields, Symmetries & Quarks. 5th enl. rev. ed. Balian, R. et al, eds. (Texts & Monographs in Physics Ser.). (Illus.). xiv, 310p. 1999. 59.95 (*3-540-65235-3*) Spr-Verlag.

Moselage, John. The Lawhorn Site, Vol. 24. Bray, Robert T., ed. (Missouri Archaeologist Ser.). (Illus.). 110p. (Orig.). 1962. pap. 3.50 (*0-943414-40-7*) MO Arch Soc.

Moseler, Claudius. Liegenschaftskonversion in Rheinland-Pfalz: Geographische Untersuchung Zu Den Entwicklungschancen Bei Der Umnutzung Aufgelassener Militarischer Liegenschaften. (Illus.). 246p. 1998. 45.95 (*3-631-33480-X*) P Lang Pubng.

Moselev, George. The Consolidation of the South China Frontier. LC 73-170719. (Center for Chinese Studies). 206p. reprint ed. pap. 63.90 (*0-608-15845-3*, 203144200074) Bks Demand.

Moseley. Exercising English, Bk. 3. 1994. pap. text. write for info. (*0-582-91623-2*, Pub. by Addison-Wesley) Longman.

— Interactions, 2 vols. (C). 1993. pap., teacher ed. 2.76 (*0-395-67560-X*) HM.

— Interactions, 2 vols. alternate ed. LC 93-78684. (C). 1993. pap. 31.56 (*0-395-67559-6*) HM.

— Interactions, 2 vols. 2nd ed. LC 93-78684. (C). 1993. pap. text 30.36 (*0-395-67558-8*) HM.

— Interactions, 3 vols. 3rd ed. LC 96-76937. (C). 1997. pap. text 30.36 (*0-395-78294-5*) HM.

***Moseley, Ann.** Interactions. 4th ed. 1999. pap. text 26.07 (*0-395-95841-5*) HM.

Moseley, Ann. Ole Edvart Rolvaag. LC 87-70033. (Western Writers Ser.: No. 80). (Illus.). 52p. (Orig.). 1987. pap. 4.95 (*0-88430-079-X*) Boise St U W Writ Ser.

Moseley, Ann & Harris, Jeanette. Interactions: A Thematic Reader, 3 vols. 3rd ed. (C). 1997. text, teacher ed. 29.16 (*0-395-84071-6*) HM.

Moseley, Ann, jt. auth. see Harris, Jeanette.

Moseley, Antony. Learn Visual dBASE 5.5 for Windows in a Day. (Popular Applications Ser.). 136p. 1996. pap. 15.95 incl. disk (*1-55622-469-9*) Wordware Pub.

Moseley, Barbara, jt. ed. see McKee, Gwen.

Moseley, Charles. A Century of Emblems: Curiously Culled & Delightfully Displayed. An Introductory Anthology. (Illus.). 321p. 1990. text 78.95 (*0-85967-750-8*, Pub. by Scolar Pr) Ashgate Pub Co.

— J. R. R. Tolkien. (Writers & Their Works). 96p. (Orig.). 1997. pap. 22.50 (*0-7463-0749-7*, Pub. by Northcote House) Trans-Atl Phila.

Moseley, Charles, tr. & intro. see Mandeville, John.

Moseley, Charles J., et al, eds. Beacham's Guide to Environmental Issues & Sources, 5 vols., Set. LC 92-42027. 1993. 240.00 (*0-933833-31-8*) Beacham Pub Corp.

Moseley, Christopher. Colloquial Estonian. LC 93-11594. (Colloquials Ser.). (Illus.). 240p. (gr. 13). 1994. pap. 22.99 (*0-415-08743-0*) Routledge.

— Colloquial Estonian. LC 93-11594. (Colloquials Ser.). 240p. (C). (gr. 13). 1994. pap. 49.99 incl. audio (*0-415-08745-7*) Routledge.

— Colloquial Latvian: A Complete Language Course. (Colloquials Ser.). (C). 1996. audio 27.99 (*0-415-11798-4*) Routledge.

— Colloquial Latvian: A Complete Language Course. (Colloquials Ser.). (Illus.). 276p. 1996. 49.99 incl. audio (*0-415-11799-2*); pap. 25.99 (*0-415-11797-6*) Routledge.

Moseley, Christopher, ed. From Baltic Shores: Short Stories from Denmark, Estonia, Finland, Latvia, Lithuania, Sweden. 256p. 1995. pap. 24.00 (*1-870041-25-9*, Pub. by Norvik Pr) Dufour.

Moseley, Christopher, tr. see Gronow, Pekka & Saunio, Ilpo.

Moseley, Dan, ed. Joyful Giving: Sermons on Stewardship. LC 97-9555. 120p. (Orig.). 1997. pap. 14.99 (*0-8272-1711-0*) Chalice Pr.

Moseley, Dana. A Fiesta at Twilight. LC 92-81048. 1993. 18.95 (*0-87212-258-1*) Libra.

Moseley, Doug & Moseley, Naomi. Making Your Second Marriage a First-Class Success: A Couple's Guide. LC 98-22822. 256p. 1998. per. 15.95 (*0-7615-1424-4*) Prima Pub.

Moseley, Douglas, jt. auth. see Moseley, Naomi.

M

Moseley, Edward H. & Clark, Paul C. Historical Dictionary of the United States-Mexican War. LC 97-11302. (Historical Dictionaries of Religions, Philosophies, & Movements Ser.: No. 2). 1997. 59.00 (0-8108-3334-4) Scarecrow.

Moseley, Edward H. & Huck, Eugene R., eds. Militarists, Merchants & Missionaries: United States Expansion in Middle America. LC 68-14556. 184p. reprint ed. 57.10 (0-8357-9620-5, 205045000081) Bks Demand.

Moseley, Edward H. & Terry, Edward D., eds. Yucatan, a World Apart. LC 79-26492. (Illus.). 347p. 1980. reprint ed. pap. 107.60 (0-608-01677-2, 206233300002) Bks Demand.

Moseley, Edward H., jt. ed. see Baklanoff, Eric N.

Moseley, Eva S., ed. Women, Information & the Future: Collecting & Sharing Resources Worldwide. LC 95-8890. 296p. 1995. pap. 20.00 (0-917846-67-2) Highsmith Pr.

Moseley, Fred, ed. Heterodox Economic Theories: True or False? LC 94-49056. 168p. 1995. 85.00 (1-85278-841-0) E Elgar.

— Marx's Method in Capital: A Reexamination. LC 92-22220. 240p. (C). 1993. text 45.00 (0-391-03785-4) Humanities.

Moseley, Fred, et al, eds. The Imperiled Economy Bk. 2: Through the Safety Net. 272p. (Orig.). (C). 1988. pap. 14.00 (0-85345-900-2, Pub. by Monthly Rev) NYU Pr.

Moseley, Fred & Campbell, Martha. New Investigations of Marx's Method. LC 99-10402. 1999. write for info. (1-57392-364-8, Humanity Bks) Prometheus Bks.

Moseley, Fred & Campbell, Martha, eds. New Investigations of Marx's Method. LC 96-48493. 212p. (C). 1997. text 45.00 (0-391-04021-9) Humanities.

Moseley, Fred B. & Wolfe, Edward N., eds. International Perspectives on Profitability & Accumulation. (New Directions in Modern Economics Ser.). 336p. 1992. text 95.00 (1-85278-557-8) E Elgar.

Moseley, G. C. Leather Goods Manufacture: Methods & Processes. 340p. 1986. reprint ed. pap. text 25.00 (0-87556-389-9) Saifer.

Moseley, George. Sino-Soviet Cultural Frontier: The Ili Kazakh Autonomous Chou. LC 67-827. (East Asian Monographs: No. 22). (Illus.). 171p. 1966. pap. 20.00 (0-674-80925-4) HUP.

Moseley, George B. & Moseley, George B., III. Managed Care Strategies: A Physician Practice Desk Reference. LC 98-32278. 609p. 1999. 79.00 (0-8342-0735-4, 07354) Aspen Pub.

Moseley, George B., III, jt. auth. see Moseley, George B.

Moseley, H. F., ed. see Hermodsson, Ivan.

Moseley, Henry Gwyn Jeffreys. The Mechanical Principles of Engineering & Architecture. (Industrial Antiquities Ser.). (Illus.). 656p. 1998. reprint ed. pap. 240.00 (1-85297-017-0, Pub. by Archival Facs) St Mut.

— Non-Ionizing Radiation Microwaves, Ultraviolet & Laser Radiation. (Medical Physics Handbook Ser.: No. 18). (Illus.). 308p. 1988. 124.00 (0-85274-166-9) IOP Pub.

Moseley, Henry N. Notes by a Naturalist. rev. ed. LC 72-1710. Orig. Title: Notes by a Naturalist on the Challenger. (Illus.). reprint ed. 65.00 (0-404-08159-2) AMS Pr.

Moseley, Herbert F. Recurrent Dislocation of the Shoulder. LC RD0557.M6. 175p. reprint ed. pap. 54.30 (0-608-12129-0, 202382400034) Bks Demand.

Moseley, James G. A Complex Inheritance: The Idea of Self-Transcendence in the Theology of Henry James, Sr., & the Novels of Henry James. LC 75-8955. (American Academy of Religion. Dissertation Ser.: No. 4). 179p. reprint ed. pap. 55.50 (0-7837-5469-8, 204523400005) Bks Demand.

— A Cultural History of Religion in America, 2. LC 80-23609. (Contributions to the Study of Religion Ser.: No. 2). 183p. 1981. 52.95 (0-313-22479-X, MRA/, Greenwood Pr) Greenwood.

Moseley, James W. UFO Crash Secrets at Wright-Patterson Air Force Base. 100p. 1992. 15.00 (0-938294-71-7) Inner Light.

Moseley, Julia W., ed. see Daniels-Moseley, Julia.

Moseley, K. A., jt. auth. see Bennison, G. M.

***Moseley, Keith.** The Bible Alphabet: Pop-up Book. 10p. (J). 1998. 19.99 (0-8054-1288-3) Broadman.

Moseley, L. G., et al. Pascal in Practice: Using the Language. (Computers & Their Applications Ser.). 274p. 1987. pap. text 34.95 (0-470-20779-5) P-H.

Moseley, Leslie & Nobleman, Marc T. Felix Activity Book. LC 97-165039. (Illus.). 144p. (Orig.). (J). 1996. pap. 12.95 (0-7892-0174-7, Abbeville Kids) Abbeville Pr.

Moseley, Lloyd W. Customer Relations: The Road to Greater Profits. rev. ed. LC 72-85929. (Illus.). 1990. pap. 36.95 (0-912016-79-5) Lebhar Friedman.

Moseley, Lonnie E. Excel X Macro & VBA Handbook. 1996. pap. text 44.99 incl. cd-rom (0-7821-1950-6) Sybex.

Moseley, Lonnie E. & Boodey, David M. Mastering Microsoft Office 97 Professional Edition. 2nd ed. LC 96-71022. 1216p. 1996. pap. text 39.99 (0-7821-1925-5) Sybex.

***Moseley, M. P., ed.** Ground Improvement. 228p. (C). (gr. 13). 1998. text 150.00 (0-7514-0073-4) B Acad & Prof.

Moseley, Margaret. Bonita Faye. 240p. 1997. mass mkt. 5.99 (0-06-101189-4, Harp PBks) HarpC.

— Bonita Faye. 178p. 1996. 20.00 (0-9637629-4-X) Three Forks.

— The Fourth Steven. 257p. 1998. mass mkt. 5.99 (0-425-16406-3, Prime Crime) Berkley Pub.

— Grinning in His Mashed Potatoes. 292p. 1999. mass mkt. 6.50 (0-425-16982-0, Prime Crime) Berkley Pub.

***Moseley, Margaret.** A Little Traveling Music, Please. 2000. mass mkt. 6.50 (0-425-17551-0, Prime Crime) Berkley Pub.

Moseley, Mary. The Bahamas Handbook. 1976. lib. bdg. 69.95 (0-8490-1472-7) Gordon Pr.

Moseley, Mary J. & Bally, Scott J., eds. Communication Therapy: An Integrated Approach to Aural Rehabilitation. LC 96-16866. 404p. 1996. text 59.95 (1-56368-054-8) Gallaudet Univ Pr.

Moseley, Merritt. David Lodge: How Far Can You Go? LC 89-29632. (Milford Ser.: Popular Writers of Today: Vol. 16). viii, 112p. 1991. pap. 17.00 (0-8095-5229-9) Millefleurs.

— Understanding Julian Barnes. LC 96-25197. (Understanding Contemporary British Literature Ser.). 200p. 1997. text 29.95 (1-57003-140-1) U of SC Pr.

— Understanding Kingsley Amis. LC 92-37274. (Understanding Contemporary British Literature Ser.). 201p. (C). 1993. text 29.95 (0-87249-861-1) U of SC Pr.

Moseley, Merritt, ed. Proceedings of the 1991 Asheville Institute on General Education. 87p. (Orig.). 1992. pap. 15.00 (0-911696-54-7) Assn Am Coll.

Moseley, Michael, jt. auth. see Kucharczyk, John.

Moseley, Michael E. The Incas & Their Ancestors: The Archaeology of Peru. LC 91-65309. (Illus.). 272p. 1993. pap. 19.95 (0-500-27723-0, Pub. by Thames Hudson) Norton.

Moseley, Michael E. & Cordy-Collins, Alana, eds. Northern Dynasties: Kingship & Statecraft in Chimor: Symposium at Dumbarton Oaks, October 12 & 13, 1985. LC 89-23336. (Illus.). 560p. 1990. 40.00 (0-88402-180-7, MCND) Dumbarton Oaks.

***Moseley, N. Allan.** Worldviews at War! The Biblical Worldview & Its Place in Society. 2000. 21.00 (1-891833-53-7) Davidson Pr.

Moseley, Naomi & Moseley, Douglas. Dancing in the Dark: The Shadow Side of Intimate Relationship. Niendorff, John S., ed. LC 93-85994. 252p. 1994. pap. 14.95 (1-880823-08-X) N Star Pubns.

Moseley, Naomi, jt. auth. see Moseley, Doug.

Moseley, Nicholas, ed. see Plautus, Titus Maccius.

Moseley, P. T., et al, eds. Techniques & Mechanisms in Gas Sensing. (Sensors Ser.). (Illus.). 408p. 1991. 168.00 (0-7503-0074-4) IOP Pub.

Moseley, P. T. & Tofield, B. C., eds. Solid State Gas Sensors. (Sensors Ser.). (Illus.). 264p. 1987. 128.00 (0-85274-514-1) IOP Pub.

Moseley, Philip, jt. auth. see Murray, Merrick.

***Moseley, Ray.** Mussolini's Shadow: The Double Life of Count Galeazzo Ciano. LC 99-34242. (Illus.). 302p. 2000. 29.95 (0-300-07917-6) Yale U Pr.

Moseley, Romney M. Becoming a Self Before God: Critical Transformations. 1991. pap. 15.95 (0-687-02504-4) Abingdon.

Moseley, Romney M., et al. 1993 Manual for Faith Development Research. 2nd rev. ed. De Nicola, Karen B., ed. 126p. (C). 1993. ring bd. 30.00 (0-9621113-2-5) Emory U Ctr Faith.

Moseley, Ron W. Yeshua: A Guide to the Real Jesus & the Original Church. 214p. 1998. pap. 12.99 (1-880226-68-5) M J Pubs.

***Moseley, Roy.** Evergreen: Victor Saville in His Own Words. LC 99-48562. (Illus.). 272p. 2000. 29.95 (0-8093-2315-X) S Ill U Pr.

Moseley, Roy, jt. auth. see Higham, Charles.

Moseley, Rufus. Manifest Victory. 1985. pap. 9.95 (0-910924-92-9) Macalester.

— Perfect Everything. 230p. pap. 7.95 (0-910924-29-5) Macalester.

Moseley, S. Kelley. Managing Seniors Housing. LC 88-61093. (Illus.). 214p. 1988. pap. 7.50 (0-86718-323-3) Home Builder.

Moseley, Spencer & Reed, Gervais. Walter F. Isaacs: An Artist in America, 1886-1964. LC 74-28489. (Index of Art in the Pacific Northwest Ser.: No. 8). (Illus.). 124p. 1982. 20.00 (0-295-95950-9) U of Wash Pr.

Moseley, Spencer & Rogers, Millard B. Wendell Brazeau: A Search for Form. LC 76-49167. (Index of Art in the Pacific Northwest Ser.: No. 12). (Illus.). 96p. 1977. 16.50 (0-295-95555-4); pap. 8.95 (0-295-95546-5) U of Wash Pr.

***Moseley, Stuart.** The First Christmas. (J). 1999. 14.99 (0-8054-2034-7) Broadman.

Moseley, Tom. Clarion Program for Dummies: Windows Edition. LC 95-81818. (For Dummies Ser.). 384p. 1996. pap. 24.99 (1-56884-334-8) IDG Bks.

Moseley, William W., et al, compiled by. Spanish Literature, 1500-1700: A Bibliography of Golden Age Studies in Spanish & English, 1925-1980, 3. LC 84-8965. (Bibliographies & Indexes in World Literature Ser.: No. 3). 765p. 1984. lib. bdg. 115.00 (0-313-21491-3, MSL/) Greenwood.

Moseley, Willie G. Classic Guitars, U. S. A. A Primer for the Vintage Guitar Collector. LC 91-70519. (Illus.). 160p. (C). 1992. pap. 19.95 (0-931759-52-8, 00000139) Centerstream Pub.

— Executive Rock: A Fan's Perspective on the Evolution of Popular Music since 1950. 224p. 1996. pap. 9.95 (0-7935-6695-9, 00330236) H Leonard.

— Executive Rock: A Fan's Perspective on the Evolution of Popular Music since 1950. (Illus.). 228p. 1996. pap. 9.95 (1-884883-04-4) Vintage Guitar.

— Guitar People. (Illus.). 300p. (Orig.). 1997. pap. 19.95 (1-884883-06-0) Vintage Guitar.

— Stellas & Stratocasters. (Illus.). 292p. 1994. pap. 19.95 (0-7935-3492-5, HL00330115) H Leonard.

— Stellas & Stratocasters. LC 94-222242. 292p. 1994. pap. 19.95 (1-884883-00-1) Vintage Guitar.

Mosely, Donald C., et al. Supervisory Management: The Art of Empowering & Developing People. 3rd ed. LC 92-24127. (C). 1992. mass mkt. 39.00 (0-538-82246-5) S-W Pub.

Mosely Education Commission. Reports of the Mosely Education Commission to the United States of America, October-December, 1903. LC 73-89223. (American Education: Its Men, Institutions, & Ideas. Series 1: Its Men, Institutions & Ideas, Ser. 1). 1978. reprint ed. 20.95 (0-405-01445-7) Ayer.

Mosely, F. & Meredith, Sue. Help Your Child Learn, Number Skills. (Parents' Guides Ser.). (Illus.). 48p. 1999. lib. bdg. 14.95 (0-88110-412-4, Usborne) EDC.

Mosely, F., et al. Help Your Child Learn, Number Skills. (Parents' Guides Ser.). (Illus.). 48p. 1990. pap. 6.95 (0-7460-0314-5, Usborne) EDC.

Mosely Industrial Commission. Reports of the Delegates of the Mosely Industrial Commission to the United States of America, Oct.-Dec., 1902. LC 73-2526. (Big Business; Economic Power in a Free Society Ser.). 1973. reprint ed. 19.95 (0-405-05105-0) Ayer.

Mosely, Jane, ed. see Lynch, Daniel.

***Mosely, Keith.** Beauty Mouse & The Beast. 1999. 8.95 (90-76048-24-X) Abbeville Pr.

— Cindy Mouse. 1999. 8.95 (90-76048-25-8) Abbeville Pr.

— Robinson Mouse. 1999. 8.95 (90-76048-26-6) Abbeville Pr.

— Snow Mouse & The Seven Moles. 1999. 8.95 (90-76048-23-1) Abbeville Pr.

Mosely Lesch, Ann. The Sudan: Contested National Identities. LC 98-34099. (Indiana Series in Arab & Islamic Studies). (Illus.). 336p. 1998. 39.95 (0-253-33432-2); pap. 19.95 (0-253-21227-8) Ind U Pr.

***Mosely, Nicholas.** Catastophe Practice. LC 88-30391. 342p. 2001. 12.95 (1-56478-252-2) Dalkey Arch.

— Serpent. LC 89-35214. 192p. 2000. pap. 11.95 (1-56478-244-1, Pub. by Dalkey Arch) Chicago Distribution Ctr.

Mosely, Pixie Anne, jt. ed. see Arant, Wendi.

Moseman, C. M. & Brother Staff. Mosemans' Illustrated Catalog of Horse Furnishing Goods: An Unabridged Republication of the Fifth Edition. (Illus.). 320p. 1987. reprint ed. pap. 19.95 (0-486-25381-3) Dover.

Mosemann, John H. Russell's Hell vs. the Bible Hell. 15p. 1988. reprint ed. pap. 0.95 (1-883858-54-2) Witness CA.

Mosenson, Cecil. From the "Pit" to the Rose Garden. (Illus.). (Orig.). 1991. pap. 11.95 (0-9629935-1-4) Woodruff PA.

— Mr. Principal, Your Activity Period Sucks. (Illus.). (Orig.). 1991. pap. 11.95 (0-9629935-0-6) Woodruff PA.

Mosenthal. Cockpit Companion. 20p. 1998. pap. 10.95 (1-898660-34-4) Motorbooks Intl.

Mosenthal, Basil. Young Sailor: An Introduction to Sailing & the Sea. (Illus.). 48p. (YA). (gr. 8 up). 1993. 13.95 (0-924486-61-9) Sheridan.

Mosenthal, Peter B. Understanding Reading. (C). 1994. write for info. (0-582-28482-1) Addison-Wesley.

Mosenthal, Peter B., ed. Visual Literacy. (Advances in Reading/Language Research Ser.: Vol. 7). Date not set. 78.50 (0-7623-0264-X) Jai Pr.

Mosenthal, Salomon R. Von, see Von Mosenthal, Salomon R.

Mosenthal, William T. Concepts in Gross Anatomy: A Review for the USMLE Step 1. LC 96-47926. (USMLE Concepts Ser.). 260p. 1997. pap. 26.95 (1-85070-928-9) Prthnon Pub.

— Review Questions for Neuroanatomy: Structural & Functional. LC 96-2843. (Review Questions Ser.). 134p. 1996. pap. 19.95 (1-85070-653-0) Prthnon Pub.

— Textbook of Neuroanatomy: With an Atlas & Dissection Guide. (Illus.). 528p. (C). 1995. pap. text 32.95 (1-85070-587-9) Prthnon Pub.

***Moser.** Buried Pipe Design. 2nd ed. (Illus.). 420p. 2000. 79.95 (0-07-043503-0) McGrw-H Hghr Educ.

Moser. Drive. (J). 1998. 16.00 (0-671-89105-7) S&S Bks Yung.

— Stories from the Old Testament, Vol 2. (J). 1998. 16.00 (0-671-88662-2) S&S Bks Yung.

— Stories from the Old Testament, Vol 3. (J). 1998. 16.00 (0-671-88663-0) S&S Bks Yung.

— Stories from the Old Testament, Vol 4. (J). 1998. 16.00 (0-671-88664-9) S&S Bks Yung.

Moser. Survey Methods in Social Investigation. 1971. 20.95 (0-435-82604-2) Ashgate Pub Co.

Moser & Watters. Creating America: Reading & Writing Arguments. 2nd ed. LC 98-39877. 556p. (C). 1998. pap. text 39.20 (0-13-081421-0) P-H.

Moser, et al. Insel der Endemiten. (Bibliotheca Diatomologica Ser.: Band 38). (Illus.). 470p. 1998. 142.00 (3-443-57029-1, Pub. by Gebruder Borntraeger) Balogh.

Moser, jt. auth. see Riegel.

Moser, Rupert, jt. auth. see Blickle, Peter.

Moser & Kalton. Survey Methods in Social Investigation. 1985. pap. 35.95 (1-85521-472-5) Ashgate Pub Co.

Moser, A. Bioprocess Technology - Kinetics & Reactors. (Illus.). 455p. 1988. 277.00 (0-387-96603-X) Spr-Verlag.

***Moser, Adolph.** Don't Fall Apart on Saturdays! The Children's Divorce-Survival Book. 61p. (gr. 4-7). 2000. write for info. (0-933849-77-X, Pub. by Landmark Edns) Baker & Taylor.

Moser, Adolph J. Don't Despair on Thursdays! The Children's Grief-Management Book. Thatch, Nancy R., ed. LC 95-8653. (Emotional Impact Ser.). (Illus.). 60p. (J). (gr. k-8). 1995. lib. bdg. 15.95 (0-933849-60-5) Landmark Edns.

— Don't Feed the Monster on Tuesdays! The Children's Self-Esteem Book. Thatch, Nancy R., ed. LC 91-12941. (Emotional Impact Ser.). (Illus.). 55p. (J). (gr. k-12). 1991. lib. bdg. 15.95 (0-933849-38-9) Landmark Edns.

— Don't Pop Your Cork on Mondays! The Children's Anti-Stress Book. LC 88-13912. (Emotional Impact Ser.). (Illus.). 48p. (J). (gr. k up). 1988. lib. bdg. 15.95 (0-933849-18-4) Landmark Edns.

— Don't Rant & Rave on Wednesdays! The Children's Anger-Control Book. Thatch, Nancy R., ed. LC 94-22775. (Emotional Impact Ser.). (Illus.). 61p. (J). 1994. lib. bdg. 15.95 (0-933849-54-0) Landmark Edns.

— Don't Tell a Whopper on Fridays! The Children's Truth-Control Book. Thatch, Nancy R., ed. LC 99-17406. (Emotional Impact Ser.). (Illus.). 61p. (J). (gr. k-9). 1999. lib. bdg. 15.95 (0-933849-76-1) Landmark Edns.

Moser, Andreas. Pharmacology of Endogenous Neurotoxins. LC 97-12361. 1997. 120.00 (0-8176-3993-4) Birkhauser.

— Pharmacology of Endogenous Neurotoxins. LC 97-12361. (Illus.). 328p. 1997. 99.95 (3-7643-3993-4) Spr-Verlag.

Moser, Antonio & Leers, Bernardino. Moral Theology: Dead Ends & Alternatives. Burns, Paul, tr. from POR. LC 90-187473. (Theology & Liberation Ser.).Tr. of Teologia Moral: Impasses e Alternativas. 256p. reprint ed. pap. 79.40 (0-608-20245-2, 207150400012) Bks Demand.

— Moral Theology: Dead Ends & Ways Forward. 256p. 1994. pap. 30.00 (0-86012-171-2, Pub. by Srch Pr) St Mut.

Moser, Barry. Fly! A Brief History of Flight Illustrated. LC 92-30960. (Willa Perlman Bks.). (Illus.). 56p. (J). (gr. 1 up). 1993. lib. bdg. 15.89 (0-06-022894-6) HarpC Child Bks.

— Gold Rush: Twenty-Five Wood Engravings on a Theme of the Discovery & Mining of Gold in America, Africa & Australia. limited ed. (Illus.). 32p. (C). 1985. 600.00 (0-923980-02-4) Arundel Pr.

— Good & Perfect Gifts: A Retelling of O. Henry's The Gift of the Magi. LC 94-39168. (Illus.). 32p. (J). (gr. k-3). 1997. 14.95 (0-316-58543-2) Little.

— The Holly Tree. 32p. (J). 1997. write for info. (0-316-58544-0) Little.

***Moser, Barry.** In the Face of Presumptions: Essays, Speeches & Incidental Writings. Renaud, Jessica, ed. (Illus.). 224p. 2000. 30.00 (1-56792-126-4) Godine.

— Moser Untitled Bow A. (J). Date not set. write for info. (0-688-16764-0) Morrow Avon.

— Moser Untitled Bow B. (J). Date not set. write for info. (0-688-16765-9) Morrow Avon.

***Moser, Barry.** Mad Hatter. (Barry Moser Ser.). 160p. 1998. 9.95 (1-55156-080-1, Pub. by Paperblank) Andrews & McMeel.

— March Hare. (Barry Moser Ser.). 160p. 1998. 9.95 (1-55156-081-X, Pub. by Paperblank) Andrews & McMeel.

Moser, Barry. Queen of Hearts Journal. (Barry Moser Ser.). 160p. 1998. 9.95 (1-55156-082-8) Paperblank.

— Sixty Years of American Poetry: Celebrating the Anniversary of the Academy of American Poets. expanded rev. ed. LC 96-10854. 360p. 1996. 35.00 (0-8109-4464-2, Pub. by Abrams) Time Warner.

***Moser, Barry.** White Rabbit Journal. (Barry Moser Ser.). 160p. 1998. 9.95 (1-55156-083-6, Pub. by Paperblank) Andrews & McMeel.

***Moser, Barry.** Great Ghost Stories. LC 98-4885. 240p. (J). (gr. 4-7). 1998. 22.00 (0-688-14587-6, Wm Morrow) Morrow Avon.

***Moser, Barry.** The Holy Bible. LC 99-36629. 102p. 1999. 65.00 (0-670-88797-8) Studio Bks.

Moser, Barry, jt. auth. see Harper, Isabelle.

Moser, Barry, jt. illus. see San Souci, Robert D.

Moser, Barry K. Linear Models: A Mean Model Approach. LC 96-33930. (Probability & Mathematical Statistics Ser.). (Illus.). 228p. 1996. text 49.95 (0-12-508465-X) Acad Pr.

Moser, Beverly & Ohnesorg, Stephanie. A Guide to Language Immersion Weekends for Undergraduates. 25p. 1997. ring bd. 8.00 (0-942017-59-5, 04-64654) Amer Assn Teach German.

Moser, Beverly, et al. Schemata. LC 95-82111. 304p. (C). 1996. pap. text 32.00 (0-03-010104-2) Holt R&W.

Moser, Britta A. Politische Autobiographien in der Fruhen Amerikanischen Republik: Benjamin Franklin, John Adams, Thomas Jefferson und James Monroe. (Europaische Hochschulschriften, Reihe 14: No. 329). 387p. 1997. 63.95 (3-631-31034-X) P Lang Pubng.

Moser, Cara, jt. auth. see Harper, Dan.

Moser, Carolin O. N., et al. Mainstreaming Gender & Development in the World Bank: Progress & Recommendations. LC 98-39050. (Environmentally & Socially Sustainable Development: Social Development Ser.). 48p. 1999. pap. 22.00 (0-8213-4262-2, 14262) World Bank.

Moser, Caroline. Gender Planning & Development: Theory, Practice & Training. LC 92-37648. 240p. (C). 1993. pap. 27.99 (0-415-05621-7, A5978) Routledge.

— Household Responses to Poverty & Vulnerability Vol. 1: Confronting Crisis in Cisne Dos, Guayaquil, Ecuador. (Urban Management Programme Policy Papers: No. 21). 160p. 1997. pap. 22.00 (0-8213-3847-1, 13847) World Bank.

Moser, Caroline & Holland, Jeremy. Household Responses to Poverty & Vulnerability Vol. 4: Confronting Crisis in Chawama, Lusaka, Zambia. (Urban Management Programme Policy Papers: No. 24). 136p. 1997. pap. 22.00 (0-8213-3850-1, 13850) World Bank.

— Urban Poverty & Violence in Jamaica. LC 96-40537. 56p. 1997. pap. 22.00 (0-8213-3870-6, 13870) World Bank.

Moser, Caroline & McIlwaine, Cathy. Household Responses to Poverty & Vulnerability Vol. 2: Confronting Crisis in Angyalfold, Budapest, Hungary. (Urban Management Programme Policy Papers: No. 22). 120p. 1997. pap. 22.00 (0-8213-3848-X, 13848) World Bank.

— Household Responses to Poverty & Vulnerability Vol. 3: Confronting Crisis in Commonwealth, Metro Manila, Philippines. (Urban Management Programme Policy Papers: No. 23). 136p. 1997. pap. 22.00 (0-8213-3849-8, 13849) World Bank.

An Asterisk (*) at the beginning of an entry indicates that the title is appearing for the first time.

Moser, Caroline & Peake, Linda, eds. Women, Human Settlements, & Housing. 256p. (C). 1988. text 55.00 (0-422-61860-8, Pub. by Tavistock); pap. text 14.95 (0-422-61980-9, Pub. by Tavistock) Routledge.

Moser, Caroline O. Confronting Crisis: A Comparative Study of Household Responses to Poverty & Vulnerability in Four Poor Urban Communities. LC 95-52826. (Environmentally Sustainable Development Studies & Monographs Ser.: No. 8). 114p. 1996. pap. 22.00 (0-8213-3562-6, 13562) World Bank.

— Confronting Crisis: A Summary of Household Responses to Poverty & Vulnerability in Four, Poor Urban Communities. (Environmentally Sustainable Development Studies & Monographs Ser.). (FRE & SPA.). 32p. 1996. pap. 22.00 (0-8213-3561-8, 13561) World Bank.

— Confronting Crisis: A Summary of Household Responses to Poverty & Vulnerability in Four, Poor Urban Communities. (FRE.). 36p. 1996. pap. 22.00 (0-8213-3570-7, 13570); pap. 22.00 (0-8213-3571-5, 13571) World Bank.

Moser, Caroline O., ed. Community Participation in Urban Projects in the Third World. (Progress in Planning Ser.: No. 32). (Illus.). 68p. 1990. pap. 30.00 (0-08-040159-7, Pergamon Pr) Elsevier.

***Moser, Charles.** Health Care Without Shame: A Handbook for The Sexually Diverse & Their Caregivers. 1999. pap. text 11.95 (1-890159-12-3) Greenery Pr.

Moser, Charles & Madeson, J. J. Bound to Be Free: The SM Experience. LC 73-17887. 216p. 1998. reprint ed. pap. 15.95 (0-8264-1047-2) Continuum.

Moser, Charles, et al. Russia: The Spirit of Nationalism. LC 77-126039. (Review of National Literatures Ser.: Vol. 3, No. 1). 264p. 1972. pap. 6.95 (0-918680-60-3) Griffon House.

Moser, Charles A. Esthetics As Nightmare: Russian Literary Theory, 1855-1870. LC 88-19505. 324p. 1989. reprint ed. pap. 100.50 (0-608-06476-9, 206677300009) Bks Demand.

— A History of Bulgarian Literature 1865-1944. LC 76-170000. (Slavistic Printings & Reprintings Ser.: No. 112). 282p. 1972. text 67.70 (90-279-2008-7) Mouton.

— Pisemsky: A Provincial Realist. LC 78-78521. 283p. reprint ed. pap. 87.80 (0-7837-5938-X, 204573700007) Bks Demand.

Moser, Charles A. & Rollberg, P. And Meaning for a Life Entire. LC 99-169956. 510 p. 1997. write for info. (0-89357-249-7) Slavica.

Moser, Charlotte. Clyde Connell: The Art & Life of a Louisiana Woman. (Illus.). 94p. 1991. pap. 19.95 (0-292-71141-7) U of Tex Pr.

Moser, Christopher L. Basketry of the Indians of California, 3 vols. Incl. Native American Basketry of Central California. (Illus.). 323p. (Orig.). 1986. pap., boxed set 30.00 (0-935661-12-3); Native American Basketry of Southern California. (Illus.). 363p. 1993. pap., boxed set 45.00 (0-935661-20-4); Northern California Indian Basketry. (Illus.). 363p. 1989. pap., boxed set 30.00 (0-935661-18-2); 1993. Set boxed set 130.00 (0-935661-22-0) Riverside Mus Pr.

Moser, Claus A. Statistics & Economic Policy. LC 77-357499. (Mercantile Credit Lecture Ser.). 31p. 1974. Price not set. (0-7049-0253-2) Univ of Reading.

Moser, Cora. Illustrated Bible for Children. (Illus.). (J). 2000. 25.00 (0-689-80576-4) S&S Childrens.

Moser, Curtis C. How to Save Thousands When You Buy a Mobile Home. rev. ed. 96p. pap. 14.95 (0-9628152-0-9) CCM Advrtsng.

Moser, David A., jt. auth. see Haimes, Yacov Y.

Moser, Diane, jt. auth. see Spangenburg, Ray.

Moser, Diane K. & Spangenburg, Ray. Opening the Space Frontier. (Space Exploration Ser.). (Illus.). 136p. (YA). 1989. 22.95 (0-8160-1848-0) Facts on File.

Moser, Diane K. & Spangenburg, Ray. Early Settlements. LC 97-27453. (American Historic Places Ser.). (Illus.). 1998. 19.95 (0-8160-3405-2) Facts on File.

Moser, Diane K. & Spangenburg, Raymond. Political & Social Movements. LC 97-28096. (American Historic Places Ser.). (Illus.). 130p. (YA). (gr. 7-12). 1998. 19.95 (0-8160-3404-4) Facts on File.

Moser, Diane K., jt. auth. see Spangenburg, Ray.

Moser, Dietz-Ruediger. Die Tannhaeuser Legende. (Fabula Supplement Ser.: Vol. 4). (C). 1977. 80.00 (3-11-005957-6) De Gruyter.

Moser, Edward P. Politically Correct American History. 1996. 10.00 (0-614-97105-5) Crown Pub Group.

— Politically Correct Guide to American History, 000. LC 98-50014. 1999. pap. 10.00 (0-609-80188-0) Three Rivers Pr.

— Politically Correct Guide to the Bible, 000. 1999. pap. 10.00 (0-609-80187-2) Three Rivers Pr.

Moser, Erwin. The Crow in the Snow & Other Bedtime Stories. Agee, Joel, tr. from GER. LC 86-10740. (Illus.). 48p. (J). (ps up). 1986. 10.95 (0-915361-49-3) Lambda Pubs.

— Wilma the Elephant. Agee, Joel, tr. LC 86-1145. (J). (gr. 3-8). 1986. 9.95 (0-915361-45-0) Lambda Pubs.

Moser, Frank H. & Thomas, Arthur L. The Phthalocyanines, Vol. I. 248p. 1983. 137.00 (0-8493-5677-6, QD441, CRC Reprint) Franklin.

— The Phthalocyanines, Vol. II. 184p. 1983. 100.00 (0-8493-5678-4, CRC Reprint) Franklin.

Moser, G. & Woodbridge, H. C. Ruben Dario y "El Cojo Ilustrado" 69p. 1.00 (0-318-22350-3) Hispanic Inst.

Moser, Gary G., et al. Nigeria: Experience with Structural Adjustment. LC 97-1966. (Occasional Papers). 1997. write for info. (1-55775-630-9) Intl Monetary.

Moser, Gerald. A New Bibliography of the Lusophone Literatures of Africa. 2nd rev. ed. LC 93-19931. (Bibliographical Research in African Literatures Ser.: No. 2). 432p. 1993. 90.00 (1-873836-85-6, Pub. by H Zell Pubs) Seven Hills Bk.

Moser, Gerald M. Changing Africa: The First Literary Generation of Independent Cape Verde. LC 92-72961. (Transactions Ser.: Vol. 82, Pt. 4). (Illus.). 102p. (C). 1992. pap. 15.00 (0-87169-824-2, T824-MOG) Am Philos.

***Moser, Gerd.** SAP R/3 Interfacing Using BAPIs: A Practical Guide to Working Within the SAP Business Framework. 150p. 1998. 70.00 incl. cd-rom (3-528-05694-0) Morgan Kaufmann.

Moser, Gerd, et al. Neukaledonien: Diatomeenflora Einer Tropeninsel. Revision der Collection Maillard & Untersuchung Neuen Materials. (Bibliotheca Diatomologica Ser.: Vol. 32). (GER., Illus.). 341p. 1995. pap. 140.00 (0-614-97986-2, Pub. by Gebruder Borntraeger) Balogh.

Moser, Gert, jt. auth. see Lange-Bertalot, H.

Moser, Grant, ed. see Clans, Heather M.

Moser, Greg. Winning the Race: The Greg Moser Story. (Illus.). 320p. 1998. 21.95 (0-9663857-0-5) C Burns DDS.

Moser, H. & Rauert, W. Isotopenmethoden in der Hydrologie. (Lehrbuch der Hydrogeologie Ser.). xx, 400p. 1980. 82.00 (3-443-01012-1, Pub. by Gebruder Borntraeger) Balogh.

Moser, H. Geoffrey. Dawn Fish. LC 78-56849. 1979. 6.95 (0-87212-109-7) Libra.

Moser, H. O. A History of Delano, Pennsylvania. (Illus.). 227p. 1993. reprint ed. lib. bdg. 33.00 (0-8328-3549-8) Higginson Bk Co.

Moser, Hans J. Paul Hofhaimer: Ein Lied- und Orgelmeister des Deutschen Humanismus. ix, 231p. 1966. write for info. (0-318-71931-2) G Olms Pubs.

Moser, Harold D., et al, eds. The Papers of Andrew Jackson: Guide & Index to the Microfilm Editions. LC 86-33831. 343p. 1987. 50.00 (0-8420-4007-2) Scholarly Res Inc.

— The Papers of Andrew Jackson, 1816-1820, Vol. 4. LC 79-15078. (Illus.). 676p. (C). 1993. text 60.00 (0-87049-778-2) U of Tenn Pr.

— The Papers of Andrew Jackson, 1821-1824: 1821-1824, Vol. 5. LC 79-15078. 664p. 1996. text 60.00 (0-87049-897-5) U of Tenn Pr.

— The Papers of Andrew Jackson, 1814-1815, Vol. 3. LC 79-15078. (Illus.). 648p. 1991. text 60.00 (0-87049-650-6) U of Tenn Pr.

Moser, Harold D., et al. The Papers of Andrew Jackson, 1804-1813, Vol. 2. LC 79-15078. (Andrew Jackson Ser.). 664p. (C). 1985. 60.00 (0-87049-441-4) U of Tenn Pr.

Moser, Harold D., ed. see Webster, Daniel.

Moser, Hugo W., jt. auth. see Bruyn, George W.

Moser, J. Alcohol Policies in National Health & Development Planning. (WHO Offset Publications: No. 89). 102p. 1985. 11.00 (92-4-170089-0) World Health.

— Problems & Programmes Related to Alcohol & Drug Dependence in 33 Countries. (Offset Publications: No. 6). 1974. pap. text 20.00 (92-4-170006-8, 1120006) World Health.

Moser, J., jt. auth. see Rootman, I.

Moser, James, jt. ed. see Stevens, Tracy.

Moser, James D. & Stevens, Tracy, eds. International Motion Picture Almanac. annuals 68th ed. 700p. 1997. text 109.00 (0-900610-57-3) Quigley Pub Co.

— International Television & Video Almanac. annuals 42nd ed. 700p. 1997. text 109.00 (0-900610-58-1) Quigley Pub Co.

Moser, Joann. Singular Impressions: The Monotype in America. LC 96-39416. (Illus.). 224p. 1997. 65.00 (1-56098-737-5) Smithsonian.

Moser, Joann & Dreishpoon, Douglas. Drawn Across the Century: Highlights from the Dillard Collection of Art on Paper. Barkley, Miriam & Doll, Nancy, eds. write for info. (1-890949 01 3) UNC Greensboro.

Moser, Johann, ed. & tr. see Aquinas, Thomas, Saint.

Moser, Johann J. Von der Deutschen Reichsstande Landen, Deren Landstanden, Unterthanen, Landesfreyheiten, Beschwerden, Schulden und Zusammenkunfften. (GER.). 1531p. 1977. reprint ed. write for info. (3-487-06275-5) G Olms Pubs.

Moser, John E. Twisting the Lion's Tail: The Persistence of Anglophobia in American Politics, 1921-1948. LC 98-13175. 263p. 1998. text 45.00 (0-8147-5615-8) NYU Pr.

Moser, Jorg G., ed. Photodynamic Tumor Therapy: 2nd & 3rd Generation Photosensitizers. (Illus.). 240p. 1998. text 49.00 (90-5699-139-6, ECU63, Harwood Acad Pubs) Gordon & Breach.

Moser, Juelich W., jt. auth. see Moser, M.

Moser, Juergen K., jt. auth. see Siegel, C. L.

Moser, Juergen K., jt. auth. see Siegel, Carl L.

Moser, Jurgen, ed. Fritz John: Collected Papers, 2 vols., Vol. I. (Contemporary Mathematicians Ser.). 648p. 1980. 137.50 (0-8176-3266-2) Birkhauser.

— Fritz John: Collected Papers, 2 vols., Vol. II. (Contemporary Mathematicians Ser.). 760p. 1980. 137.50 (0-8176-3267-0) Birkhauser.

Moser, Jurgen & Kyner, Walter T. Lectures on Hamiltonian Systems, & Rigorous & Formal Stability of Orbits about an Oblate Planet. LC 52-42839. (Memoirs Ser.: No. 1/81). 87p. 1989. reprint ed. pap. 19.00 (0-8218-1281-5, MEMO/1/81) Am Math.

Moser, Jurgen, jt. auth. see Kyner, Walter T.

Moser, K. Pulmonary Vascular Diseases. (Lung Biology in Health & Disease Ser.: Vol. 14). (Illus.). 728p. 1979. text 250.00 (0-8247-6609-1) Dekker.

Moser, Kay. Celebration! 2nd rev. ed. LC 93-1662. 302p. 1998. reprint ed. pap. 14.00 (1-890236-22-5, 420, Celebration Classics) Seton St Clare.

— Counterfeit Legacy. LC 97-66262. 359p. 1997. pap. 14.00 (1-890236-38-1, 425, Celebration Classics) Seton St Clare.

Moser, Kenneth M., jt. ed. see Bordow, Richard A.

Moser, Kit, jt. auth. see Spangenburg, Ray.

Moser, Koloman. Turn-of-the-Century Viennese Patterns & Designs. LC 98-26290. (Illus.). 64p. 1998. pap. 11.95 (0-486-40269-X) Dover.

Moser, L. E., et al. Cool Season Farage Grasses. (Agronomy Monograph Ser.: Vol. 34). 841p. 1996. 54.00 (0-89118-130-X) Am Soc Agron.

Moser, Leslie E. Crack, Cocaine, Methamphetamine & Ice: What Every One of Us Must Know about These Public Enemies. 336p. 1990. 19.95 (1-878938-00-2) Mlti-Media Prodns.

— Older & Growing: Your Eternal Life Beginning Now. 1990. 14.95 (1-878938-01-0) Mlti-Media Prodns.

Moser, M. Microstructures of Ceramics: Structures & Properties of Grinding Tools. 364p. (C). 1980. 105.00 (963-05-1576-8, Pub. by Akade Kiado) St Mut.

Moser, M. & Horak, E. Cortinarius Fr. und Nahe Verwandte Gottungen in Suedamerika. 1975. 162.50 (3-7682-5452-6) Lubrecht & Cramer.

Moser, M. & Juelich, W. Farbatlas der Basidiomyceten (Color Atlas of Basidiomycetes), Fasc. 3. (ENG, FRE, GER & ITA., Illus.). 30p. 1986. ring bd. 64.00 (3-437-30513-1) Lubrecht & Cramer.

Moser, M. & Moser, Juelich W. Farbatlas der Basidiomyceten: Fasc. 1 & 2.Tr. of Color Atlas of Basidiomycetes. (FRE, GER & ITA., Illus.). 93p. 1985. 130.00 (3-437-30438-0) Lubrecht & Cramer.

Moser, M. Theresa, jt. ed. see Donahue, James.

Moser, Madeline. Ever Heard of an Aardwolf? LC 95-37878. (Illus.). 40p. (J). (ps-5). 1996. 16.00 (0-15-200474-2) Harcourt.

Moser, Margaret & Crawford, Bill. Rock Stars Do the Dumbest Things. LC 98-17774. (Illus.). 256p. 1998. pap. 12.95 (1-58063-023-5) Renaissance.

***Moser, Margaret, et al.** Movie Stars Do the Dumbest Things. LC 99-36450. 304p. 1999. pap. 14.95 (1-58063-107-X) Renaissance.

***Moser, Marvin.** Clinical Management of Hypertension. 4th rev. ed. 238p. 1999. pap. text 19.95 (1-884735-54-1) Prof Comms.

Moser, Marvin. Heart-Healthy Cooking for All Seasons. 1997. per. 15.00 (0-671-88519-7) PB.

— Myths, Misconceptions & Heroics: The Story of the Treatment of Hypertension from the 1930's. 68p. 1997. pap. 22.00 (0-9626020-4-3) Le Jacq Commns.

— Tibetan for Windows. (Illus.). 29p. 1998. spiral bd. 60.00 incl. disk (0-9662348-0-4) Tibetan For Windows.

Moser, Marvin & Becker, Brenda L. Week by Week to a Strong Heart. 336p. 1994. mass mkt. 5.50 (0-380-72089-2, Avon Bks) Morrow Avon.

Moser, Marvin, et al. Heart-Healthy Cooking for All Seasons. Rubenstein, Julie, ed. (Illus.). 256p. 1996. 25.00 (0-671-88520-0, PB Hardcover) PB.

Moser, Mary A., ed. Immersed in Technology Art & Virtual Environments. (Illus.). 368p. 1997. reprint ed. pap. text 22.50 (0-262-63183-0) MIT Pr.

Moser, Mary A. & MacLeod, Douglas, eds. Immersed in Technology: Art & Virtual Environments. (Leonardo Book Ser.). (Illus.). 367p. 1996. 40.00 (0-262-13314-8) MIT Pr.

Moser, Mary B., jt. auth. see Felger, Richard S.

Moser, Mary E., ed. Etruscan Pottery: The Meeting of Greece & Etruria. (Illus.). 66p. 1984. pap. 10.00 (0-614-23979-6) U Museum Pubns.

Moser, Maynard. Jacob Gould Schurman: Scholar, Political Activist & Ambassador of Good Will, 1892-1942. 1981. 30.95 (0-405-14100-9) Ayer.

Moser, Meinhard. Die Pilze Mitteleuropas Vol. 4: Die Gattung Phlegmacium (Schleimkoepfe) (Illus.). 1960. 143.00 (3-7682-0523-1) Lubrecht & Cramer.

— The Polypores, Boletes & Agarica. Kibby, Geoffrey & Rayner, R., trs. from GER. (Illus.). 355p. (C). 1983. text 72.50 (0-916422 13 7) Mad River.

Moser-Mercer, Barbara, jt. ed. see Lambert, Sylvie.

Moser, Michael E. & Finlayson, Max, eds. Wetlands. (Illus.). 224p. 1991. 45.00 (0-8160-2556-8) Facts on File.

Moser, Michael J. & Change, Jessie T., eds. Foreign Trade Investment & the Law in the People's Republic of China. 2nd ed. LC 87-11272. 616p. 1987. pap. text 49.95 (0-19-584058-5) OUP.

Moser, Michael J. & Moser, Yeone W. Foreigners Within the Gates: The Legations at Peking. LC 92-39882. (Illus.). 172p. 1993. text 35.00 (0-19-585702-X) OUP.

***Moser, Michael J. & Zee, Winston K.** China Tax Guide. 3rd ed. LC 99-32999. (Illus.). 428p. 1999. text 65.00 (0-19-590610-1) OUP.

Moser, Nancy. Expecting: Celebrating the Waiting & the Wonder. LC 98-27139. 80p. 1998. pap. 5.99 (0-87788-610-5, H Shaw Pubs) Waterbrook Pr.

***Moser, Nancy.** The Invitation. (Mustard Seed Ser.: Vol. 1). 432p. 1999. pap. 11.99 (1-57673-352-1) Multnomah Pubs.

Moser, Nancy. Motherhood: A Celebration of Blessings & Blunders. LC 97-157265. 1997. pap. text 5.99 (0-87788-564-8, H Shaw Pubs) Waterbrook Pr.

— The Quest. LC 99-22049. (Mustard Seed Ser.: Vol. 2). 400p. 1999. pap. 11.99 (1-57673-410-2) Multnomah Pubs.

***Moser, Nancy.** The Temptation. LC 00-8508. (Mustard Seed Ser.: Vol. 3). 2000. 12.99 (1-57673-734-9) Multnomah Pubs.

Moser, Nell. A Simple Guidebook for Mortgage Loans. 135p. 1998. mass mkt. 12.95 (1-57532-101-7) Press-Tige Pub.

Moser, Norman. El Grito del Norte & Other Stories: Stories, Tales & Fables. (New 80's Bk.). (Illus.). 172p. (Orig.). 1983. pap. 6.00 (0-941442-02-0) Illuminations Pr.

— Open Season: Selected Poems. (New 80's Bk.). (Illus.). 60p. (Orig.). 1980. 3.00 (0-686-29369-X) Illuminations Pr.

Moser, Norman, ed. The Shorter Plays & Scenarios of Norm Moser. 48p. (Orig.). 1981. pap. 3.00 (0-941442-00-4) Illuminations Pr.

Moser, Paul K. Empirical Justification. 258p. 1985. pap. text 61.50 (90-277-2042-8, D Reidel); lib. bdg. 114.50 (90-277-2041-X, D Reidel) Kluwer Academic.

— Empirical Knowledge: Readings in Contemporary Epistemology. LC 86-3197. 296p. (C). 1986. pap. 21.95 (0-8476-7493-2) Rowman.

— Philosophy after Objectivity: Making Sense in Perspective. LC 92-38864. 280p. 1993. text 65.00 (0-19-508109-9) OUP.

— Philosophy after Objectivity: Making Sense in Perspective. 280p. 1999. pap. 19.95 (0-19-513094-4) OUP.

Moser, Paul K., ed. Empirical Knowledge: Readings in Contemporary Epistemology. 2nd ed. 480p. 1996. pap. text 28.95 (0-8476-8204-8); lib. bdg. 73.00 (0-8476-8203-X) Rowman.

***Moser, Paul K. & Carson, Thomas L., eds.** Moral Relativism: A Reader. LC 99-55853. 320p. 2000. text 45.00 (0-19-513129-0); pap. text 24.95 (0-19-513130-4) OUP.

Moser, Paul K. & Mulder, Dwayne. Contemporary Approaches to Philosophy. (Illus.). 450p. (Orig.). (C). 1993. pap. text 23.80 (0-02-384171-0, Macmillan Coll) P-H.

Moser, Paul K. & Trout, J. D., eds. Contemporary Materialism: A Reader. LC 94-32686. 400p. (C). 1995. pap. 29.99 (0-415-10864-0, B7041) Routledge.

Moser, Paul K. & Vander Nat, Arnold. Human Knowledge: Classical & Contemporary Approaches. 2nd ed. 480p. (C). 1995. text 67.00 (0-19-508626-0); pap. text 32.95 (0-19-508625-2) OUP.

Moser, Paul K., et al. The Theory of Knowledge: A Thematic Introduction. LC 96-52985. 224p. (C). 1997. text 50.00 (0-19-509465-4); pap. text 23.95 (0-19-509466-2) OUP.

Moser, Paul K., jt. ed. see Carson, Thomas L.

***Moser, Peter.** The Political Economy of Democratic Institutions. LC 99-88523. (Locke Institute Ser.). 208p. 2000. 85.00 (1-85898-966-3) E Elgar.

***Moser, Peter Daniel.** Decision Rules in European Union. LC 99-48154. 352p. 2000. text 75.00 (0-312-23029-X) St Martin.

***Moser-Puangsuwan, Yeshua & Weber, Thomas.** Nonviolent Intervention Across Borders: A Recurrent Vision. LC 99-88960. 2000. 20.00 (1-880309-11-4) S M Matsunaga.

Moser, Richard. The New Winter Soldiers: GI & Veteran Dissent During the Vietnam Era. (Sights on the Sixties Ser.). (Illus.). 300p. (C). 1996. text 50.00 (0-8135-2241-2) Rutgers U Pr.

***Moser, Robert G.** Unexpected Outcomes: Electoral Systems, Political Parties, & Representation in Russia. (Pitt Ser. in Russian & East European Studies). 191p. 2001. pap. 19.95 (0-8229-5746-9) U of Pittsburgh Pr.

Moser, Robert V. Different Views for Christian Thinking. 72p. 1988. 6.95 (0-9621065-0-X) R V Moser.

Moser, Rodney L. Primary Care for Physician Assistants: PreTest Self-Assessment & Review. (Illus.). 207p. 1998. pap. 34.00 (0-07-052406-8) McGraw-Hill HPD.

Moser, Rodney L., ed. Primary Care for Physician Assistants. LC 97-50437. (Illus.). 641p. 1998. text 65.00 (0-07-043491-3) McGraw-Hill HPD.

Moser, Ronald, jt. auth. see Fischer, Robert.

***Moser, Royce.** Effective Management of Occupational & Environmental Health & Safety Programs: A Practical Guide. 2nd ed. LC 99-21243. 1999. 80.00 (1-883595-25-8) OEM Health.

Moser, Sally, et al. Needles: Southern Sierra Rock Climbing. (Southern Sierra Rock Climbing Ser.). (Illus.). 230p. (Orig.). 1992. pap. 20.00 (0-934641-43-9) Falcon Pub Inc.

— Sequoia Kings Canyon. (Southern Sierra Rock Climbing Ser.). (Illus.). 312p. (Orig.). 1993. pap. 25.00 (0-934641-51-X) Falcon Pub Inc.

Moser, Sally, jt. auth. see Vernon, Greg.

Moser, Sally, ed. see Bridwell, Jim & Peall, Keith.

Moser-Simpson, Stacy, ed. see Jaffee, Dwight & Spiegel, Matt.

Moser, Stephanie. Ancestral Images: The Iconography of Human Origins. LC 98-9890. (Illus.). 224p. 1998. 39.95 (0-8014-3549-8) Cornell U Pr.

Moser, Susanne. Human Driving Forces & Their Impacts on Land Use/Land Cover. (Active Learning Modules on the Human Dimensions of Global Change Ser.). (Illus.). 190p. (C). 1997. pap., teacher ed. 20.00 (0-89291-233-2); pap., student ed., wbk. ed. 8.75 (0-89291-234-0) Assn Am Geographers.

Moser, Susanne & Hanson, Susan. Notes on Active Pedagogy: A Supplement to the Active Learning Modules Produce by the AAG/CCG2. (Active Learning Modules on the Human Dimensions of Global Change Ser.). (Illus.). 30p. (C). 1997. pap. text 3.00 (0-89291-228-6) Assn Am Geographers.

***Moser, Teresa.** An Odd Body: Church, Witness & Culture in 1 & 2 Corinthians. (Good Ground Ser.: No. 2, Pt. 7). 47p. 2000. pap. 5.95 (0-87303-366-3) Faith & Life.

Moser, Thomas. How to Build Shaker Furniture. LC 76-46809. (Illus.). 224p. 1980. pap. 16.95 (0-8069-8392-2) Sterling.

— Measured Shop Drawings for American Furniture. LC 84-26872. (Illus.). 328p. 1988. pap. 21.95 (0-8069-6792-7) Sterling.

Moser, Thomas C. The Life in the Fiction of Ford Madox Ford. LC 80-7548. 370p. reprint ed. pap. 114.70 (0-8357-4645-3, 203757600008) Bks Demand.

Moser, Thomas C., ed. see Conrad, Joseph.

An Asterisk (*) at the beginning of an entry indicates that the title is appearing for the first time.

Moser, U. & Von Zeppelia, I., eds. Cognitive-Affective Processes: New Ways of Psychoanalytic Modeling. (Monographien der Breuninger-Stiffung Stuttgart Ser.). (Illus.). vii, 183p. 1991. 62.95 (*0-387-53993-X*) Spr-Verlag.

Moser, W. O., jt. auth. see Coxeter, H. S.

Moser, W. R. & Pfeffer, R., eds. Honoring the Eightieth Birthday of John Happel: Special Issues of the Journal Chemical Engineering Communications, 2 vols., Set. ii, 566p. 1989. pap. text 1001.00 (*2-88124-380-0*) Gordon & Breach.

***Moser-Wellman, Annette.** The Five Faces of Genius. 2001. 23.95 (*0-670-89477-X*, Viking) Viking Penguin.

Moser, William D. A Three-Hour Service for Good Friday: Reflections from the Cross. LC 97-29590. 54p. 1997. pap. 6.95 (*0-7880-1136-7*) CSS OH.

Moser, William D., ed. see Giusto, Joan M.

Moser, William R., ed. Advanced Catalysts & Nanostructured Materials: Modern Synthetic Methods. LC 96-3066. (Illus.). 592p. 1996. text 85.00 (*0-12-508460-9*) Acad Pr.

— Catalysis of Organic Reactions. LC 81-15172. (Chemical Industries Ser.: Vol. 5). (Illus.). 496p. 1981. text 215.00 (*0-8247-1341-9*) Dekker.

Moser, William R. & Slocum, Donald W., eds. Homogeneous Transition Metal Catalyzed Reactions: Developed from a Symposium. LC 92-356. (Advances in Chemistry Ser.: No. 230). (Illus.). 640p. 1992. reprint ed. pap. 198.40 (*0-608-03969-1*, 205256100011) Bks Demand.

Moser, Yeone W., jt. auth. see Moser, Michael J.

Moserova, J. & Houskova, E. The Healing & Treatment of Skin Defects. (Illus.). viii, 163p. 1989. 65.25 (*3-8055-4704-8*) S Karger.

Moses. Introduction to the Human Body. 3rd ed. (C). Date not set. write for info. (*0-06-501394-8*) Addson-Wesley Educ.

***Moses.** Selections from "the Philosophy & Opinions of Marcus Garvey" 1999. text 39.95 (*0-312-12253-5*) St Martin.

Moses. The South Carolina Probate Practice Manual. 1990. 125.00 (*0-685-46188-2*, NO. 421) SC Bar CLE.

Moses, jt. auth. see Hirohashi.

Moses, jt. auth. see Nikola-Lisa, W.

Moses, Laurie, ed. Insect & Disease Control Guide. rev. ed. (Illus.). 604p. (C). 1998. pap. 54.00 (*1-892829-01-0*) Meister Pub Co.

Moses, A. D. Matthew's Transfiguration Story & Jewish-Christian Controversy. LC 96-132445. (JSNT Supplement Ser.: No. 122). 294p. 1996. 85.00 (*1-85075-576-0*, Pub. by Sheffield Acad) CUP Services.

Moses, A. J. & Basak, Amitava, eds. Nonlinear Electromagnetic Systems. LC 95-8175. (Studies in Applied Electromagnetics & Mechanics: Vol. 10). 900p. (YA). (gr. 12). 1996. 150.00 (*90-5199-251-3*, 251-3) IOS Press.

Moses, A. M., ed. see International Conference on the Neurohypophysis St.

Moses, Abayomi. U. S. Law Schools: A Directory of Courses & Other Special Programs Available at the American Law Schools. LC 81-52882. 180p. 1981. 14.00 (*0-9606958-0-X*); pap. 11.00 (*0-9606958-1-8*) Sekoni Pubs.

Moses, Albert L. The South Carolina Probate Practice Manual. 1990. ring bd. 125.00 (*0-943856-33-7*, 421) SC Bar CLE.

Moses, Allen J. Controversy in Temporomandibular Disorders: A Clinicians' Guide to Critical Thinking. (Illus.). vi, 172p. (Orig.). 1997. pap. text 70.00 (*0-9654416-0-1*) Futa Bk Pubs.

Moses, Amy. At the Zoo. (Field Trips Ser.). (Illus.). 32p. (J). (gr. 1-4). 1997. lib. bdg. 21.36 (*1-56766-287-0*) Childs World.

— Doctors Help People. (Community Helpers Ser.). (Illus.). 32p. (J). (gr. k-3). 1996. lib. bdg. 21.36 (*1-56766-304-4*) Childs World.

— Hospital. LC 96-5242. (Field Trips Ser.). (Illus.). 32p. (J). (gr. 1-4). 1997. lib. bdg. 21.36 (*1-56766-291-9*) Childs World.

— If I Were an Ant. LC 92-12947. (Rookie Readers Ser.). (Illus.). 32p. (J). (ps-2). 1992. lib. bdg. 17.00 (*0-516-02011-0*) Childrens.

— If I Were an Ant. LC 92-12947. (Rookie Readers Ser.). (Illus.). 32p. (J). (ps-3). 1993. pap. 4.95 (*0-516-42011-9*) Childrens.

Moses, Amy. Zookeepers Care for Animals. LC 96-6141. (Community Helpers Ser.). (Illus.). 32p. (J). (gr. k-3). 1996. lib. bdg. 21.36 (*1-56766-303-6*) Childs World.

Moses, Barbara. Career Intelligence: Mastering the New Work & Personal Realities. LC 98-232931. 272p. 1997. 24.95 (*0-7737-3016-8*) Stoddart Publ.

— Career Intelligence: The 12 New Rules for Work & Life Success. LC 98-21727. 300p. 1998. reprint ed. pap. 15.95 (*1-57675-048-5*) Berrett-Koehler.

— Discover Seashores: A Discovery Book. (Illus.). 32p. (J). (gr. 5-7). 1995. pap. 3.75 (*0-915992-72-8*) Eastern National.

***Moses, Barbara.** The Good News about Careers: How You'll Be Working in the Next Decade. LC 99-49949. 256p. 2000. 25.00 (*0-7879-5269-9*) Jossey-Bass.

— The Good News about Careers: How You'll Be Working in the Next Decade. 246p. 2000. pap. 22.95 (*0-7737-6117-9*) Stoddart Publ.

***Moses, Barbara & National Council of Teachers of Mathematics Staff.** Algebraic Thinking, Grades K-12: Readings from NCTM's School-Based Journals & Other Publications. LC 99-41986. 456p. 1999. pap. 31.95 (*0-87353-474-3*, 701E1) NCTM.

Moses, Bernard. The Railway Revolution in Mexico. 1976. lib. bdg. 59.95 (*0-8490-2499-4*) Gordon Pr.

Moses, Beth. It's All Well & Good: A Wholistic Guidebeeok to Relaxation & Wellness. (Illus.). 196p. 1997. pap. 14.95 (*0-89917-946-0*) Tichenor Pub.

Moses, Beth Silverman, jt. auth. see Magura, Stephen.

Moses, Brian. Hippopotamus Dancing & Other Poems. LC 93-43968. 48p. (J). 1994. 16.95 (*0-521-44141-2*) Cambridge U Pr.

***Moses, Brian.** Munching, Crunching, Sniffing & Snooping. LC 99-20404. (Eyewitness Readers). 32p. (J). (gr. 1-3). 1999. 3.95 (*0-7894-4752-5*); 12.95 (*0-7894-4753-3*) DK Pub Inc.

Moses, Brian. Tengo Celos (I'm Jealous) (Mis Emociones/My Emotions Ser.). 1997. pap. text 7.95 (*950-24-0640-0*) Lectorum Pubns.

— Tengo Miedo (I'm Scared) (Mis Emociones/My Emotions Ser.). 1997. pap. text 7.95 (*950-24-0639-7*) Lectorum Pubns.

— Tengo Rabia (I'm Angry) (Mis Emociones/My Emotions Ser.). 1997. pap. text 7.95 (*950-24-0641-9*) Lectorum Pubns.

***Moses, Brian & Sirret, Dawn.** Winking, Blinking, Wiggling & Wagging. LC 99-44161. (Eyewitness Readers). (Illus.). 32p. (J). (gr. 1-3). 2000. 12.95 (*0-7894-5414-9*, D K Ink); pap. 3.95 (*0-7894-5413-0*, D K Ink) DK Pub Inc.

Moses, Bruce E. How to Market Yourself, Yourself! The Executive Job Changing Guide Book. LC 79-63505. (Illus.). 1979. 14.95 (*0-9602540-0-5*) Pro-Search.

Moses, Carole. Melville's Use of Spenser. (American University Studies: American Literature: Ser. XXIV, Vol. 6). 235p. (C). 1989. text 39.95 (*0-8204-0832-8*) P Lang Pubng.

— Process, Purpose, Practice: A Basic Writer's Guide. 411p. (C). 1991. teacher ed. 2.66 (*0-669-19819-6*); pap. text 36.76 (*0-669-19818-8*); teacher ed. 37.96 (*0-669-24709-X*) HM Trade Div.

Moses, Catherine. Real Life in Castro's Cuba. LC 99-24812. (Latin American Silhouettes Ser.). 184p. 1999. pap. 18.95 (*0-8420-2837-4*) Scholarly Res Inc.

***Moses, Catherine.** Real Life in Castro's Cuba. LC 99-24812. (Latin American Silhouettes Ser.). 184p. 1999. 55.00 (*0-8420-2836-6*) Scholarly Res Inc.

***Moses, Cathy.** Dissenting Fictions: Identity & Resistance in the Contemporary American Novel. (Literary Criticism & Cultural Theory Ser.). 160p. 2000. 60.00 (*0-8153-3653-5*) Garland.

Moses, Claire G. French Feminism in the 19th Century. LC 83-18040. 311p. (C). 1985. text 64.50 (*0-87395-859-4*); pap. text 21.95 (*0-87395-860-8*) State U NY Pr.

Moses, Claire G. & Hartmann, Heidi, eds. U. S. Women in Struggle: A Feminist Studies Anthology. (Women in American History Ser.). 464p. 1995. text 49.95 (*0-252-02166-5*); pap. text 19.95 (*0-252-06462-3*) U of Ill Pr.

Moses, Claire G. & Rabine, Leslie W. Movement & Meaning: Creativity & Interpretation in Ballet & Mime. LC 92-42841. (Illus.). 32p. (C). 1993. pap. 19.95 (*0-253-20818-1*, MB-818) Ind U Pr.

Moses, Daniel D. & Goldie, Terry, eds. An Anthology of Canadian Native Literature in English. 2nd ed. 448p. 1998. text 29.95 (*0-19-541282-6*) OUP.

***Moses, Dolores C.** Family Matters. 372p. 2000. pap. 16.95 (*0-9678153-0-4*) Cherry St Pubs.

Moses, Don V., et al. Face to Face with an Orchestra. LC 85-63337. (Orig.). 1987. pap. text 19.95 (*0-911009-06-X*) Prestige Pubns.

Moses, Don V., jt. auth. see Demaree, Robert W., Jr.

***Moses, Dushawn.** L. I. F. E. Living It from Experience. (Illus.). 196p. 2000. pap. 19.95 (*0-9676743-0-1*) Allwrite Grp.

Moses, Ed. Nine Sisters Dancing. 248p. (Orig.). 1996. pap. 12.95 (*1-56474-162-1*) Fithian Pr.

Moses, Edward M. West Point Battle Heroes, the Medal of Honor: An Historical Sketchbook. LC 99-93273. (Illus.). 113p. 1999. 19.95 (*0-9648939-8-3*) Moses Getz.

— West Point, the Making of Leaders: An Historical Sketchbook. rev. ed. LC 95-95174. (Illus.). 88p. (YA). (gr. 10 up). 1996. 19.95 (*0-9648939-9-1*) Moses Getz.

Moses, Edward P. & Warda, Mark. How to Make a Georgia Will. 3rd ed. (Legal Survival Guides Ser.). 96p. 1998. pap. 12.95 (*1-57248-075-0*) Sourcebks.

Moses, Elbert R., Jr. Adventure in Reasoning. 80p. 1988. 15.00 (*0-9621305-0-8*) Moses Pubns.

Moses, Elbert R. Beating the Odds: A Mini Autobiography. (Illus.). 50p. (Orig.). (YA). 1992. pap. text 3.95 (*0-922484-03-1*) Poligion Pub.

Moses, Elbert R. & Peters, Claude D. In Pursuit of Life. unabridged ed. LC 83-90115. 100p. (Orig.). 1996. pap. 9.95 (*0-9621305-1-6*) Moses Pubns.

Moses, Elissa. The $100 Billion Allowance: Getting Your Share of the Global Teen Market. LC 00-36494. 256p. 2000. 29.95 (*0-471-29848-4*) Wiley.

Moses, Gavriel. The Nickel Was for the Movies - Film in the Novel: Pirandello to Pulg. LC 93-16283. 1994. 48.00 (*0-520-07943-4*, Pub. by U CA Pr) Cal Prin Full Svc.

Moses, George. Those Good Old Days in the Black Hills. 120p. (Orig.). 1991. pap. text. write for info. (*0-913062-01-4*) Fenwyn Pr.

Moses, Grace E. Rooster Strut on the Suwannee & Two Short Stories. LC 88-3458. 149p. 1988. 13.75 (*0-930950-15-1*); pap. 8.75 (*0-930950-16-X*) Nopoly Pr.

***Moses, Grace M.** The Welsh Lineage of John Lewis (1592-1657), Emigrant to Gloucester, Virginia. rev. ed. 68p. 1998. pap. 11.00 (*0-8063-4542-X*) Clearfield Co.

Moses, Greg. Revolution of Conscience: Martin Luther King, Jr., & the Philosophy of Nonviolence. LC 96-35442. (Critical Perspectives Ser.). 238p. 1996. lib. bdg. 33.95 (*1-57230-169-4*, 0169) Guilford Pubns.

— Revolution of Conscience: Martin Luther King, Jr., & the Philosophy of Nonviolence. 238p. 1998. pap. text 17.95 (*1-57230-407-3*) Guilford Pubns.

Moses, H. & Patterson, C. H. Research Readings in Rehabilitation Counseling. 1973. pap. 9.80 (*0-87563-054-5*) Stipes.

Moses, H., jt. auth. see Kay, I.

Moses, H., jt. auth. see Patterson, C. H.

Moses, H. Vincent & Turney, Celena, eds. Our Families/Our Stories: From the African American Community, Riverside, California. (Illus.). 20p. (Orig.). 1997. mass mkt. 5.00 (*0-935661-25-5*) Riverside Mus Pr.

Moses, H. Vincent, jt. auth. see Focht, Brenda B.

Moses, H. Weston, et al. A Practical Guide to Cardiac Pacing. 4th ed. LC 94-3383. 256p. 1995. pap. text 39.00 (*0-316-58552-1*, Little Brwn Med Div) Lppncott W & W.

Moses, H. Weston, et al. A Practical Guide to Cardiac Pacing. 5th ed. 224p. pap. text 39.95 (*0-7817-1956-9*) Lppncott W & W.

Moses, Halsey H. Law of Mandamus & the Practice Connected with It: With an Appendix of Forms. iv, 268p. 1981. reprint ed. 43.00 (*0-8377-0838-9*, Rothman) W S Hein.

***Moses, Harry M.** It's So Easy When You Know How. 1999. pap. 12.00 (*1-886578-06-0*) New Thoughts.

Moses, Hazel. Playing with Words. (Illus.). 28p. (J). (gr. 1-4). 1996. spiral bd. 4.50 (*0-9653867-0-8*) Wrking Print.

Moses, Henry C. Inside College: New Freedom, New Responsibility. 240p. (C). 1990. pap. 10.95 (*0-87447-383-7*) College Bd.

Moses-Hrushovski, Rena. Deployment: Hiding Behind Power Struggles As a Character Defense. LC 94-98. 344p. 1994. 60.00 (*1-56821-042-6*) Aronson.

Moses-Hrushovski, Rena, jt. ed. see Rangell, Leo.

Moses, Ingrid. Academic Staff Evaluation & Development: A University Case Study. LC 87-30074. (Illus.). 318p. (Orig.). (C). 1988. pap. text 32.95 (*0-7022-2117-1*, Pub. by Univ Queensland Pr) Intl Spec Bk.

Moses, Ingrid & Roe, Ernest. Heads & Chairs: Managing Academic Departments. 1990. pap. 29.95 (*0-7022-2263-1*, Pub. by Univ Queensland Pr) Intl Spec Bk.

Moses, J. Forecasting College & University Revenues. 121p. 1997. pap. 130.00 (*1-57440-003-7*) Primary Research.

Moses, James. Children's Publishing, Media & Entertainment. 252p. 265.00 (*0-9626749-7-4*) Primary Research.

— How to Estimate the Local, Regional & National Markets for Employer-Paid Tuition. 75p. 1998. per. 85.00 (*1-57440-011-8*) Primary Research.

— Reference & Professional Information Business: A Study of Reference, Professional, Scientific, Technical, Directory & Database Publishing, 1990 Edition. 218p. 1991. ring bd. 125.00 (*0-9626749-1-5*) Primary Research.

— The Reference Book & Technology Report. 218p. 1990. per. write for info. (*0-9626749-0-7*) Primary Research.

Moses, James & Bois, Gary. Evaluating the College: Performance Assessment in Higher Education. 135p. 1998. per. 57.50 (*1-57440-010-X*) Primary Research.

Moses, James & Flicek, Joseph. Free Markets Emerge in the Electric Power Industry: Bottom Line Consequences for American Corporations, Utilities & Their Investors, Government Agencies & Other Producers & Consumers of Electricity. 178p. (Orig.). 1995. pap. 68.50 (*0-926674-99-4*) Primary Research.

Moses, James & Katos, Demetrios. The Corporate - Business Library Budget & Materials Expenditure Report. 100p. 1991. ring bd. 145.00 (*0-9626749-2-3*) Primary Research.

Moses, James & Park, Peter. The Public Library Budget & Materials Expenditure Report. 150p. 1991. ring bd. 95.00 (*0-9626749-3-1*) Primary Research.

Moses, James & Strickland, Winifred G. The German Shepherd Today: A Complete Reference for the German Shepherd Owner. rev. ed. LC 73-19044. (Illus.). 460p. 1988. 24.95 (*0-02-614990-7*) Howell Bks.

Moses, James & Weinstein, Jay. Restructuring Higher Education: Cost Containment & Productivity Enhancement Efforts of North American Colleges & Universities. 1997. pap. 59.50 (*1-57440-006-1*) Primary Research.

Moses, James, et al. The Adult & Continuing Education Business Report. 156p. Date not set. 295.00 (*1-57440-007-X*) Primary Research.

— The Survey of Distance Learning Programs in Higher Education. 132p. 1997. per. 85.00 (*1-57440-008-8*) Primary Research.

Moses, James, jt. auth. see Flicek, Joseph.

Moses, James A., jt. auth. see Strickland, Winifred G.

Moses, James A., jt. ed. see Maruish, Mark E.

Moses, Jeff, jt. auth. see Hallam, Kerry.

Moses, Jeff, jt. auth. see Welch, Bill.

Moses, Jeffrey. Oneness: Great Principles Shared by All Religions. 128p. 1992. pap. 9.00 (*0-449-90760-0*, Columbine) Fawcett.

Moses, Jeffrey S., jt. auth. see Harris, George A.

***Moses, Jennifer.** Food & Whine: Confessions of a New Millennium Mom. 224p. 2000. pap. 12.00 (*0-684-86562-9*) S&S Trade.

— Food & Whine: Confessions of an End-of-the-Millennium Mom, 1. LC 98-51154. 224p. 1999. 22.00 (*0-684-84837-6*) S&S Trade.

Moses, Joel C., jt. auth. see Rasmussen, Jorgen S.

Moses, John. The Desert: An Anthology for Lent. LC 97-37678. 176p. 1998. pap. 12.95 (*0-8192-1728-X*) Morehouse Pub.

— The Sacrifice of God: A Holistic Theory of Atonement. 246p. 1994. pap. 21.95 (*1-85311-056-6*, 856, Pub. by Canterbury Press Norwich) Morehouse Pub.

— Trade Unionism in Germany from Bismarck to Hitler, 1869-1933, 2 vols. Incl. Vol. 1. Eighteen Sixty-Nine to Nineteen Eighteen. 314p. 1982. 53.00 (*0-389-20072-7*, 06843); Vol. 2. 1919-1933. 295p. 1982. 50.00 (*0-389-20073-5*, 06844); 1982. 25.00 (*0-685-00695-6*) B&N Imports.

***Moses, John A. & Pugsley, Christopher.** The German Empire & Britain's Pacific Dominions, 1871-1919: Essays on the Role of Australia & New Zealand in World Politics in the Age of Imperialism. LC 00-34154. 2000. pap. write for info. (*1-930053-00-2*) Regina Bks.

Moses, John G. & Nassar, Eugene P. Annotated Index to the "Syrian World," 1926-1932. Rosenblatt, Judith, ed. LC 93-80115. (Illus.). xiii, 129p. 1994. spiral bd. 18.00 (*0-932833-13-6*) Immig His Res.

***Moses, Jonathon W.** Open States in the Global Economy: The Political Economy of Small-State Macroeconomic Management. LC 99-53014. 2000. text 69.95 (*0-312-23106-7*) St Martin.

Moses, Joseph & Sepulveda, Lou. The Consumer's Guide to Wireless Security: How To Purchase the Best Security System for Your Home. LC 96-47048. (Illus.). 240p. 1997. 29.95 (*0-07-043492-1*); pap. 19.95 (*0-07-043493-X*) McGraw.

Moses, Julian M. & De Luca, Giuseppe. American Celebrity Recordings 1900-1925. 3rd ed. LC 93-78789. 208p. 1993. pap. 12.95 (*0-9632903-1-2*) Monarch Rec Ent.

Moses, Kate, jt. ed. see Peri, Camille.

Moses, Kathy. It's a Child's World: The Complete Guide to Day-Care; an Operational Manual for Providers, an Informational Guide for Parents. (Illus.). 184p. (Orig.). 1989. pap. 11.95 (*0-942323-06-8*) N Amer Heritage Pr.

— Outsider Art of the South. LC 98-43877. (Illus.). 240p. 1999. 59.95 (*0-7643-0729-0*) Schiffer.

Moses, L. G. The Indian Man: A Biography of James Mooney. LC 83-6481. (Illus.). 320p. 1984. text 29.95 (*0-252-01040-X*) U of Ill Pr.

— Wild West Shows & the Images of American Indians, 1883-1933. LC 95-32450. (Illus.). 364p. (C). 1996. 39.95 (*0-8263-1685-9*) U of NM Pr.

— Wild West Shows & the Images of American Indians, 1883-1933. (Illus.). 364p. 1999. pap. 18.95 (*0-8263-2089-9*) U of NM Pr.

Moses, Larry W. The Political Role of Mongol Buddhism. LC 81-622859. (Uralic & Altaic Ser.: Vol. 133). x, 299p. 1977. 15.00 (*0-933070-01-2*) Res Inst Inner Asian Studies.

Moses, Larry W. & Halkovic, Stephen A., Jr. Introduction to Mongolian History & Culture. LC 86-620695. (Uralic & Altaic Ser.: Vol. 149). 305p. (Orig.). (C). 1985. pap. 10.00 (*0-933070-18-7*) Res Inst Inner Asian Studies.

Moses, Larry W., ed. see Halkovic, Stephen A., Jr.

Moses, Laurie, ed. Farm Chemicals Handbook, Vol. 85. rev. ed. (Illus.). 990p. (C). 1999. pap. 92.00 (*1-892829-02-9*) Meister Pub Co.

Moses, Leon N. & Lindstrom, Dan, eds. Transportation of Hazardous Materials: Issues in Law, Social Science, & Engineering Ser. LC 93-20447. 368p. (C). 1993. lib. bdg. 134.00 (*0-7923-9340-6*) Kluwer Academic.

Moses, Leon N. & Savage, Ian, eds. Transportation Safety in an Age of Deregulation. (Illus.). 368p. 1989. text 75.00 (*0-19-505797-X*) OUP.

Moses, Libby, jt. auth. see Scalisi, Danny.

Moses, Lincoln E., jt. auth. see Chernoff, Herman.

Moses, Lois, jt. ed. see Williams, Kimmika.

Moses, Lucille, jt. auth. see Osborne, Susan Titus.

Moses, Marion. Cosecha Dolorosa: Campesinos y Pesticidas, Parte I Trabajadores en el Fil. Abello, Elizabeth, tr. from ENG. (SPA., Illus.). 120p. 1992. teacher ed. 10.00 (*1-881510-02-6*) Pesticide Educ Ctr.

— Cosecha Dolorosa: Campesinos y Pesticidas, Parte II Mezcladores, Cargadores, Aplicadores. Abello, Elizabeth, tr. from ENG. (SPA., Illus.). 120p. 1992. teacher ed. 10.00 (*1-881510-04-2*) Pesticide Educ Ctr.

— Designer Poisons: How to Protect Your Health & Home from Toxic Pesticides. (Illus.). 412p. (Orig.). 1995. pap. 19.95 (*1-881510-15-8*) Pesticide Educ Ctr.

— Harvest of Sorrow: Farm Workers & Pesticides, Part I Field Workers. (Illus.). 72p. 1992. student ed. 10.00 (*1-881510-01-8*) Pesticide Educ Ctr.

— Harvest of Sorrow: Farm Workers & Pesticides, Part II Mixers, Loaders, Applicators. (Illus.). 72p. 1992. student ed. 10.00 (*1-881510-03-4*) Pesticide Educ Ctr.

Moses, Michael, ed. & photos by see Bizar, Jodi.

Moses, Michael A., et al. Hom Operations Management Software for Windows: Gaining Competitive Advantage from Operations. LC 98-52770. 1999. write for info. (*0-07-366262-3*) McGraw.

Moses, Michael R. A Dragon's Song. (Illus.). 56p. 1997. 25.00 (*0-944551-19-X*) Sundance Pr TX.

Moses, Michael R., photos by. The Mission Trail. (Illus.). 24p. (Orig.). 1997. pap. 10.00 (*0-944551-14-9*) Sundance Pr TX.

Moses, Michael V. The Novel & the Globalization of Culture. 272p. 1995. pap. text 24.95 (*0-19-508952-9*) OUP.

Moses, Monte C., jt. auth. see Whitaker, Kathryn S.

Moses, Montrose. American Theater As Seen by Its Critics, 1752-1934. 391p. 1993. reprint ed. lib. bdg. 89.00 (*0-7812-5279-2*) Rprt Serv.

— Fabulous Forrest. 1993. reprint ed. lib. bdg. 89.00 (*0-7812-5495-7*) Rprt Serv.

Moses, Montrose J. American Dramatist. rev. ed. LC 64-14706. (Illus.). 1972. 24.95 (*0-405-08800-0*, Pub. by Blom Pubns) Ayer.

— Fabulous Forrest: The Record of an American Actor. LC 72-91909. (Illus.). 1972. reprint ed. 24.95 (*0-405-08801-9*, Pub. by Blom Pubns) Ayer.

— Famous Actor-Families in America. LC 68-58994. (Illus.). 341p. 1972. reprint ed. 23.95 (*0-405-08802-7*, Pub. by Blom Pubns) Ayer.

— The Life of Heinrich Conried. Farkas, Andrew, ed. LC 76-29959. (Opera Biographies Ser.). (Illus.). 1977. reprint ed. lib. bdg. 35.95 (*0-405-09699-2*) Ayer.
— Representative Plays by American Dramatists. 1972. 132.00 (*0-685-43147-9*, 1026) Ayer.
— Representative Plays by American Dramatists, 3 vols. (BCL1-PS American Literature Ser.). 1992. reprint ed. lib. bdg. 225.00 (*0-7812-6654-8*) Rprt Serv.
Moses, Montrose J., ed. Representative Plays by American Dramatists, 3 vols., Vol. 1. LC 64-14707. 678p. 1911. reprint ed. 145.95 (*0-405-08803-5*) Ayer.
— Representative Plays by American Dramatists, 3 vols., Vol. 2. 823p. 1972. 48.95 (*0-405-08805-1*) Ayer.
— Representative Plays by American Dramatists, 3 vols., Vol. 3. LC 64-14707. 926p. 1972. 48.95 (*0-405-08806-X*) Ayer.
— Representatives Plays by America Dramatists, Vol. 1. 678p. 1972. 48.95 (*0-405-08804-3*) Ayer.
Moses, Montrose J., tr. see Maeterlinck, Maurice.
Moses, Moses. Groaning, Travailing, & Weeping. LC 94-90412. 65p. 1996. 10.95 (*0-533-11236-2*) Vantage.
Moses, Nelson, jt. auth. see Klein, Harriet B.
Moses, Norton H. Lynching & Vigilantism in the United States: An Annotated Bibliography, 34. LC 96-44068. (Bibliographies & Indexes in American History Ser.: Vol. 34). 464p. 1997. lib. bdg. 85.00 (*0-313-30177-8*, Greenwood Pr) Greenwood.
Moses of Khoren. Patmowt'iwn Hayots: History of the Armenians. Thomson, Robert W., ed. LC 81-3869. (Classical Armenian Texts Ser.). 488p. 1981. reprint ed. 50.00 (*0-88206-032-5*) Caravan Bks.
Moses, R. E. & Summers, William C., eds. DNA Replication & Mutagenesis. (Illus.). 515p. 1988. 49.00 (*1-55581-003-9*) ASM Pr.
Moses, R. T., jt. auth. see Sellin, R. H.
Moses, Rafael, ed. Persistent Shadows of the Holocaust: The Meaning to Those Not Directly Affected. 288p. 1993. 42.50 (*0-8236-4062-0*) Intl Univs Pr.
Moses, Robert. Civil Service of Great Britain. LC 14-2375. (Columbia University. Studies in the Social Sciences: No. 139). reprint ed. 34.50 (*0-404-51139-2*) AMS Pr.
Moses, Robert, ed. The AMC Classic Movie Companion. LC 99-24551. (Illus.). 640p. 1999. pap. 19.95 (*0-7868-8394-4*, Pub. by Hyperion) Time Warner.
Moses, Robert, ed. & intro. see Light, Ken.
***Moses, Robert P. & Cobb, Charles E., Jr.** Radical Equations: Organizing Math Literacy in America's Schools. 2001. 21.00 (*0-8070-3126-7*) Beacon Pr.
Moses, Russell L. Freeing the Hostages: Reexamining U. S.-Iranian Negotiations & Soviet Policy. LC 95-23144. (Pitt Series in Policy & Institutional). 470p. (C). 1996. text 45.00 (*0-8229-3919-3*) U of Pittsburgh Pr.
— Mediation & Private Contacts in the Iran Hostage Crisis, April 1980-January 1981. (Pew Case Studies in International Affairs). 94p. (C). 1989. pap. text 3.50 (*1-56927-316-2*) Geo U Inst Dplmcy.
Moses, Sheila, jt. auth. see Gregory, Dick.
Moses, Stanley, ed. Enduring Visions: The Legacy of Bertram Gross. 280p. 1995. write for info. (*0-9649519-0-8*) Bttrfly Pr.
Moses, Stanley, jt. auth. see Margolis, Edwin.
Moses, Stephane. System & Revelation: The Philosophy of Franz Rosenzweig. Tihanyi, Catherine, tr. LC 91-29532. 318p. 1992. 39.95 (*0-8143-2128-3*) Wayne St U Pr.
Moses, Stephane, ed. see Cohen, Hermann.
Moses, Vincent. Oranges for Health - California for Wealth: The Billion-Dollar Navel & the California Dream. (Illus.). vii, 34p. (Orig.). 1992. pap. 6.00 (*0-9603586-1-7*) Chaffey Commun Cult Ctr.
Moses, Vivian. Exploiting Biotechnology. viii, 332p. 1995. text 71.00 (*3-7186-5570-5*, Harwood Acad Pubs); pap. text 18.00 (*3-7186-5571-3*, Harwood Acad Pubs) Gordon & Breach.
Moses, Vivian, ed. Biotechnology: The Science & the Business. xiv, 596p. 1991. text 275.00 (*3-7186-5094-0*, Harwood Acad Pubs); pap. text 77.00 (*3-7186-5111-4*, Harwood Acad Pubs) Gordon & Breach.
Moses, Vivian, jt. ed. see Springham, Derek G.
Moses, W. R. Double View. (Inland Seas Ser.: No. 3). 1984. pap. 10.00 (*1-55780-083-9*) Juniper Pr ME.
— Edges. (Juniper Bks.: No. 60). 1994. pap. 9.00 (*1-55780-143-6*) Juniper Pr ME.
— Tu Fu Poems. (WNJ Ser.: Vol. 31). 30p. 1997. pap. 12.00 (*1-55780-177-0*) Juniper Pr ME.
Moses, W. Stainton. Direct Spirit Writing (Psychography) A Treatise on One of the Objective Forms: Psychic or Spiritual Phenomena. 152p. 1996. reprint ed. spiral bd. 13.00 (*0-7873-0627-4*) Hlth Research.
***Moses, Will.** Legend of Sleepy Hollow. 1999. pap. 6.99 (*0-698-11648-8*, PapStar) Peng Put Young Read.
Moses, Will. Silent Night. LC 96-18585. (Illus.). 40p. (J). (ps up). 1997. 16.95 (*0-399-23100-5*, Philomel) Peng Put Young Read.
Moses, William F. A Guide to American State & Local Laws on South Africa: 1991 Edition. Voorhes, Meg, ed. 116p. 1991. reprint ed. pap. 25.00 (*0-931035-89-9*) IRRC Inc DC.
— A Guide to American State & Local Laws on South Africa: 1992 Edition. 156p. (Orig.). 1992. pap. 35.00 (*0-931035-99-6*) IRRC Inc DC.
— A Guide to American State & Local Laws on South Africa: 1993 Edition. 160p. (Orig.). 1993. pap. 45.00 (*1-879775-06-9*) IRRC Inc DC.
Moses, William S. Spirit Teachings Through the Mediumship of William Stainton Moses. LC 75-36910. (Occult Ser.). 1976. reprint ed. 26.95 (*0-405-07968-0*) Ayer.
Moses, Wilson J. Afrotopia: The Roots of African American Popular History. LC 97-43389. (Studies in American Literature & Culture: No. 118). 288p. (C). 1998. pap. 17.95 (*0-521-47941-X*); text 54.95 (*0-521-47408-6*) Cambridge U Pr.
— Black Messiahs & Uncle Toms: Social & Literary Manipulations of a Religious Myth. (C). 1993. pap. 16.95 (*0-271-00933-0*) Pa St U Pr.
Moses, Wilson J. The Golden Age of Black Nationalism, 1850-1925. (Illus.). 348p. 1988. pap. text 11.95 (*0-19-520639-8*) OUP.
Moses, Wilson J. Liberian Dreams: Back-to-Africa Narratives from the 1850s. LC 97-37112. 1998. pap. 16.95 (*0-271-01711-2*) Pa St U Pr.
— The Wings of Ethiopia: Studies in African-American Life & Letters. LC 90-4020. 303p. 1990. reprint ed. pap. 94.00 (*0-608-00135-X*, 206091600006) Bks Demand.
Moses, Wilson J., ed. Classical Black Nationalism: From the American Revolution to Marcus Garvey. 257p. (C). 1996. text 50.00 (*0-8147-5524-0*); pap. text 18.50 (*0-8147-5533-X*) NYU Pr.
Moses, Wilson J., ed. see Centeno, Miguel A.
Moses, Wilson J., ed. see Crummell, Alexander.
Moses, Yoram, ed. Theoretical Aspects of Reasoning about Knowledge: Proceedings of the 4th Conference (TARK 1992), Monterey, California, March 22-25, 1992. LC 92-12306. 329p. (C). 1998. pap. text 39.95 (*1-55860-243-7*) Morgan Kaufmann.
Moseson, Rich, ed. The New Ham Survival Guide. (Illus.). 16p. (Orig.). 1995. mass mkt. 1.00 (*0-943016-12-6*) CQ Commns Inc.
Mosey, Anne C. Activities Therapy. LC 73-79286. 205p. 1973. text 30.00 (*0-911216-41-3*) Lppncott W & W.
— Applied Scientific Inquiry in the Health Professions: An Epistemological Orientation. 2nd ed. (Illus.). 400p. (Orig.). 1996. pap. text 55.00 (*1-56900-032-8*) Am Occup Therapy.
— Occupational Therapy: Configuration of a Profession. 186p. 1986. text 50.00 (*0-89004-699-9*) Lppncott W & W.
— Psychosocial Components of Occupational Therapy. 624p. 1986. text 53.00 (*0-89004-334-5*) Lppncott W & W.
Mosey, David & Murdoch, John, eds. Butterworths Building & Engineering Contracts: A Construction Practitioners' Guide. 1994. write for info. (*0-406-04949-1*, BBEC1, MICHIE) LEXIS Pub.
Mosgrove, George D. Kentucky Cavaliers in Dixie: Reminiscences of a Confederate Cavalryman. LC 98-51565. (Illus.). xiii, 282p. 1999. pap. 15.00 (*0-8032-8253-2*) U of Nebr Pr.
***Mosha, R. Sambuli.** The Heartbeat of Indigenous Africa: A Study of the Chagga Educational System. LC 99-35514. (Indigenous Knowledge & Schooling Ser.: Vol. 3). 288p. 1999. 65.00 (*0-8153-3464-8*); pap. 24.95 (*0-8153-3618-7*) Garland.
Moshansky, Mozelle. Mendelssohn. (Illustrated Lives of the Great Composers Ser.). (Illus.). 144p. 1996. 17.95 (*0-7119-0252-6*, OP 42381) Omnibus NY.
Moshaver, Ziba, jt. ed. see Hakimian, Hassan.
Moshe, Beth. Judaism's Truth Answers the Missionaries. 276p. 1987. 24.95 (*0-8197-0520-9*); pap. 16.95 (*0-8197-0515-2*) Bloch.
Moshe, Carmilly-Weinberger. Fear of Art. 249p. 1986. lib. bdg. 39.95 (*0-8352-2241-1*) Bowker.
Moshe, Davis, jt. ed. see Fink, Reuben.
Moshe, Karp, ed. see International Beilinson Symposium Staff.
***Moshe, Ma'oz & Nusseibeh, Sari.** Jerusalem: Points Beyond Friction & Beyond. LC 00-21563. (Illus.). 2000. write for info. (*90-411-8843-6*) Kluwer Law Intl.
Moshe Oppen, Menachem. The Laws of Tahara. LC 94-72545. (Pictorial Avodah Ser.: Vol. 5). (Illus.). 170p. 16.95 (*1-56062-269-5*) CIS Comm.
— A Twist of the Tongue, 2 Vols. (Illus.). 123p. 10.95 (*1-56062-009-9*) CIS Comm.
— A Twist of the Tongue, Vol. 1. (Illus.). 119p. (YA). 10.95 (*0-935063-31-5*); pap. 7.95 (*0-935063-32-3*) CIS Comm.
— A Twist of the Tongue, Vol. 2. (Illus.). 123p. pap. 7.95 (*1-56062-010-2*) CIS Comm.
Moshe, Rami B., tr. from HEB. "What's Wrong with the 'Mental Health' System & What Can Be Done about It" 36p. 1998. pap. 3.00 (*1-58429-028-5*) Rational Isl.
Moshe, Rami B., tr. see Jackins, Harvey, et al.
Moshe, S. L., jt. auth. see Corcoran, M. E.
***Mosheim, Lorenz J.** Anderweitiger Versuch einer Unpartheiischen und Gruendlichen Ketzergeschichte, Vol. 2. Mulsow, Martin, ed. (GER.). 500p. 1998. reprint ed. 145.00 (*3-487-10660-4*, Pub. by G Olms Verlag) Lubrecht & Cramer.
Moshell, Michael. Computer Power. 224p. 1982. text, student ed. 18.80 (*0-07-065773-4*) McGraw.
Moshenberg, Daniel, tr. see Virilio, Paul.
Mosher, jt. auth. see Kansas State University Staff.
Mosher, jt. auth. see Stark.
Mosher, Arthur T. Technical Co-Operation in Latin-American Agriculture. LC 75-26310. (World Food Supply Ser.). (Illus.). 1976. reprint ed. 40.95 (*0-405-07788-2*) Ayer.
Mosher-Ashley, Pearl M. & Barnett, Phyllis W. A Life Worth Living: Practical Strategies for Reducing Depression in Older Adults. 2nd ed. LC 97-1679. 384p. (Orig.). 1997. pap. 31.95 (*1-878812-03-3*) Hlth Prof Pr.
Mosher, Bill. Visionaries. LC 95-17030. 200p. 1995. 18.00 (*1-57075-024-6*) Orbis Bks.
— Visionaries. LC 95-17030. (Illus.). 176p. reprint ed. pap. 54.60 (*0-608-20268-1*, 207152700012) Bks Demand.
Mosher, Bob, et al. Training for Results: Teaching Adults to Be Independant, Assertive Learners. 2nd rev. ed. (Illus.). vii, 138p. (Orig.). 1996. pap. 19.95 (*1-889176-00-1*) Element K.
Mosher, Clelia D. The Mosher Survey. MaHood, James & Wanburg, Kristine, eds. LC 79-48014. 490p. 1980. lib. bdg. 30.95 (*0-405-13090-2*) Ayer.
Mosher, David L., tr. see Augustine, Saint.
***Mosher, Dennis.** The Little Tree Without a Name. 2000. 10.95 (*0-533-13250-9*) Vantage.
Mosher, Edith A. & Williams, Nella D. From Indian Legends to the Modern Bookshelf. 1931. 12.50 (*0-911586-24-5*) Wahr.
Mosher, Edith K., jt. auth. see Bailey, Stephen K.
Mosher, Elizabeth M. Swanville, ME Vital Records of, Prior to 1892. (Illus.). 209p. 1998. lib. bdg. 59.50 (*0-929539-27-3*, 1127) Picton Pr.
— Vital Records of Appleton - Knox County, ME Prior to 1892. 246p. 1993. 65.00 (*0-929539-65-6*, 1165) Picton Pr.
— Vital Records of Appleton - Knox County, ME Prior to 1892: Facsimile Edition. (Illus.). 603p. 1993. 99.50 (*0-89725-162-8*, 1510) Picton Pr.
— Vital Records of Lincolnville, Maine. (Illus.). 394p. 1993. lib. bdg. 75.00 (*0-89725-098-2*, 1130) Picton Pr.
— Vital Records of Searsport, Waldo County, Maine Prior to 1892. 352p. 1993. lib. bdg. 75.00 (*0-89725-135-0*, 1448) Picton Pr.
— Vital Records of Unity, Maine Prior to 1892. 1995. lib. bdg. 65.00 (*0-89725-219-5*, 1596) Picton Pr.
— Vital Records of Vinalhaven, Maine Prior to 1892. LC 97-183561. 328p. 1994. lib. bdg. 75.00 (*0-89725-212-8*, 1465) Picton Pr.
Mosher, Elizabeth M., compiled by. Thorndike, ME Vital Records, Prior to 1892. 229p. 1998. lib. bdg. 55.00 (*0-89725-097-4*, 14175) Picton Pr.
— Vital Records of Carmel, Maine Prior to 1892. 141p. 1993. lib. bdg. 35.00 (*0-89725-124-5*) Picton Pr.
Mosher, Elizabeth M., compiled by. Vital Records of Prospect, Maine Prior to 1892. 476p. 1998. pap. 39.50 (*0-89725-356-6*, 1886) Picton Pr.
Mosher, Elizabeth M., ed. Records of Rev. Edward F. Cutter of Maine, 1833-1856. LC 88-63777. 96p. 1989. 20.00 (*0-929539-19-2*, 1119) Picton Pr.
Mosher, Elizabeth M., tr. Marriage Records of Waldo County, Maine Prior to 1892. 634p. 1990. lib. bdg. 95.00 (*0-929539-20-6*, 1120) Picton Pr.
— Northport, ME Vital Records of Typescript Prior to 1892. 207p. 1995. 65.00 (*0-89725-232-2*, 1613) Picton Pr.
— Vital Records of Freedom, Waldo County, Maine Prior to 1892. (Illus.). 194p. 1991. lib. bdg. 65.00 (*0-929539-81-8*, 1181) Picton Pr.
Mosher, Eunice D. Olympics, 2004? Ask Yia Yia & Pa Pou. large type ed. Caso, Adolph, ed. LC 97-53260. (Illus.). 32p. (J). (ps-3). 1998. pap. 9.95 (*0-8283-2033-0*) Branden Bks.
Mosher, Fred & Schneider, David I. Handbook of BASIC for the Commodore 64. (Illus.). 350p. 14.95 (*0-317-12840-X*) P-H.
Mosher, Frederick C. Democracy & the Public Service. (Public Administration & Democracy Ser.). 1968. 12.95 (*0-19-500031-5*) OUP.
— Democracy & the Public Service. 2nd ed. (Public Administration & Democracy Ser.). (Illus.). 268p. (C). 1982. text 22.95 (*0-19-503018-4*) OUP.
— Some Views from the Campus. LC 87-8193. (Papers on Presidential Transitions & Foreign Policy: Vol. IV). 128p. (Orig.). (C). 1987. lib. bdg. 35.50 (*0-8191-6331-7*, Pub. by White Miller Center) U Pr of Amer.
— Tale of Two Agencies: A Comparative Analysis of the General Accounting Office & the Office of Management & Budget. LC 83-10634. (Miller Center Series on the American Presidency). xxvi, 219p. 1986. pap. text 16.95 (*0-8071-1305-0*) La State U Pr.
Mosher, Frederick C., ed. American Public Administration: Past, Present, Future. LC 74-17916. 312p. 1975. pap. text 19.95 (*0-8173-4829-8*) U of Ala Pr.
— Basic Documents of American Public Administration, 1776-1950. LC 76-13866. 225p. (C). 1976. text 30.00 (*0-8419-0275-5*) Holmes & Meier.
— The President Needs Help: Proceedings of a Conference Held on January 15, 1987. (Miller Center Tenth Anniversary Commemorative Publication, 1975-1985). 98p. (Orig.). (C). 1988. lib. bdg. 29.50 (*0-8191-6780-0*, Pub. by White Miller Center) U Pr of Amer.
Mosher, Frederick C., ed. & intro. see Price, Don K. & Evans, Robert H.
Mosher, Frederick D. The GAO: The Quest for Accountability in American Government. 1979. pap. text 15.00 (*0-89158-459-5*) Westview.
Mosher, Harold F., jt. ed. see Bosinelli, Rosa M.
Mosher, Harry S., jt. auth. see Morrison, James D.
Mosher, Howard Frank. Disappearances. LC 77-22083. 320p. 1984. reprint ed. pap. 14.95 (*0-87923-524-1*) Godine.
***Mosher, Howard Frank.** The Fall of the Year: A Novel. LC 99-28502. 288p. 1999. 24.00 (*0-395-98416-5*) HM.
— The Fall of the Year: A Novel. 288p. 2000. pap. 13.00 (*0-618-08236-0*, Mariner Bks) HM.
Mosher, Howard Frank. Marie Blythe: A Novel. (Contemporay American Fiction Ser.). 464p. 1989. pap. 12.95 (*0-14-007659-X*, Penguin Bks) Viking Penguin.
— North Country: A Personal Journey Through the Borderland. 272p. 1998. pap. 13.00 (*0-395-90139-1*, Mariner Bks) HM.
— A Stranger in the Kingdom. 432p. 1990. pap. 13.95 (*0-385-31263-6*, Delta Trade) Dell.
— Where the Rivers Flow North. (Contemporay American Fiction Ser.). 224p. 1989. pap. 12.95 (*0-14-007748-0*, Penguin Bks) Viking Penguin.
Mosher, Howard Frank, ed. see Bennett, Reginald.
Mosher, J. Randolph. The Birth of Mass Politics in Spain: Lerrouxismo in Barcelona, 1901-1909. Payne, Stanley G., ed. LC 91-12679. (Modern European History Ser.). 472p. 1991. text 30.00 (*0-8240-2545-8*) Garland.
***Mosher, Jake.** The Last Buffalo Hunter. 2000. 24.95 (*1-56792-146-9*) Godine.
Mosher, James F. Liquor Liability Law, 2 vols. 1987. ring bd. 280.00 (*0-8205-1498-5*) Bender.
— Responsible Beverage Service: An Implementation Handbook for Communities. (Illus.). 108p. (Orig.). 1991. pap. 15.00 (*1-879552-37-X*) SCRDP.
Mosher, Jerry, ed. see Ashmore, Nancy V.
Mosher, John. Unavoidable Germans: Art vs. Politics & the Consequences. 402p. 1997. 49.50 (*0-7618-0647-4*) U Pr of Amer.
Mosher, Joseph A. Exemplum in the Early Religious & Didactic Literature of England. LC 11-32391. reprint ed. 32.50 (*0-404-04505-7*) AMS Pr.
Mosher, Kiki. Learning about Bravery from the Life of Harriet Tubman. (Character Building Bk.: Set 2). (Illus.). 24p. (J). (gr. k-4). 1996. lib. bdg. 15.93 (*0-8239-2424-6*, PowerKids) Rosen Group.
— Learning about Compassion from the Life of Florence Nightingale. LC 96-3511. (Character Building Bk.: Set 2). (Illus.). 24p. (J). (gr. k-4). 1996. lib. bdg. 15.93 (*0-8239-2423-8*, PowerKids) Rosen Group.
— Learning about Fairness from the Life of Susan B. Anthony. LC 96-16089. (Character Building Bk.: Set 2). (Illus.). 24p. (J). (gr. k-4). 1996. lib. bdg. 15.93 (*0-8239-2422-X*, PowerKids) Rosen Group.
— Learning about Honesty from the Life of Abraham Lincoln. LC 96-15666. (Character Building Bk.: Set 2). (Illus.). 24p. (J). (gr. k-4). 1996. lib. bdg. 15.93 (*0-8239-2420-3*, PowerKids) Rosen Group.
— Learning about Leadership from the Life of George Washington. LC 96-15670. (Character Building Bk.: Set 2). (Illus.). 24p. (J). (gr. k-4). 1996. lib. bdg. 15.93 (*0-8239-2421-1*, PowerKids) Rosen Group.
Mosher, Kimberley, jt. auth. see Zehner, Judith.
Mosher, Linda L. Going Home: Memories of West Virginia. 1992. pap. 7.50 (*1-880631-01-6*) Shuffaloff Bks.
Mosher, Loren R. & Burti, Lorenzo. Community Mental Health: A Practical Guide. 224p. (C). 1994. pap. 17.00 (*0-393-70165-4*) Norton.
Mosher, Loren R., jt. auth. see Gunderson, John G.
Mosher, Lucinda A. Religion & Society: The Role of Compassion, Selfless Service, & Social Justice in Five Major Faith Traditions. (Illus.). 175p. (Orig.). (YA). (gr. 8-12). 1996. pap. text 23.50 (*1-881678-56-3*) CSEE.
Mosher, Lynn. Manufacturing Processes: Course Outline Lab Activity Manual. 62p. (C). 1998. per. 18.95 (*0-7872-5159-3*, 41515901) Kendall-Hunt.
Mosher, Merrill H. John Freeman of Norfolk County, VA: His Descendants in North Carolina & Virginia & Other Colonial N.C. Freeman Families. (Illus.). 236p. (Orig.). 1994. pap. text 18.50 (*0-7884-0109-2*) Heritage Bk.
***Mosher, Michael.** Creating Web, Graphics, Audio & Video. 2000. pap. 40.00 (*0-13-088614-9*) P-H.
Mosher, Nicole M. Le Texte Visualise: Le Calligramme de l'Epoque Alexandrine a l'Epoque Cubiste. (American University Studies: Romance Languages & Literature: Ser. II, Vol. 119). 188p. (C). 1990. text 42.95 (*0-8204-0924-3*) P Lang Pubng.
Mosher, Paul W., ed. Title Key Word & Author Index to Psychoanalytic Journals. 1988. 38.00 (*0-318-32967-0*) Am Psychoanalytic.
Mosher, R. A., et al. The Dynamics of Electrophoresis. (Electrophoresis Library). (Illus.). 236p. 1991. 198.00 (*3-527-28379-X*, Wiley-VCH) Wiley.
Mosher, Ralph, ed. Moral Education: A First Generation of Research & Development. LC 80-18607. 412p. 1980. 42.95 (*0-275-90528-4*, C0528, Praeger Pubs) Greenwood.
Mosher, Ralph, Jr. & Kenny, Robert A. Preparing for Citizenship: Teaching Youth to Live Democratically. LC 94-6379. 216p. 1994. pap. 19.95 (*0-275-95096-4*, Praeger Pubs) Greenwood.
Mosher, Ralph, et al. Preparing for Citizenship: Teaching Youth to Live Democratically. LC 94-6379. 216p. 1994. 59.95 (*0-275-94606-1*, Praeger Pubs) Greenwood.
Mosher, Ralph L., ed. see Day, James M.
Mosher, Randy. The Brewer's Companion: Being a Complete Compendium of Brewing Knowlege. 2nd rev. ed. (Illus.). Date not set. pap. 19.95 (*0-9640410-1-4*) Alephenalia.
Mosher, Richard. The Taxi Navigator. LC 96-11687. 144p. (J). (gr. 3-7). 1996. 15.95 (*0-399-23104-8*, Philomel) Peng Put Young Read.
Mosher, Steve. God's Power, Jesus' Faith & World Mission: A Study in Romans. LC 95-48103. 360p. 1996. pap. 19.99 (*0-8361-9031-9*) Herald Pr.
Mosher, Steven W. Hegemon: China's Plan to Dominate Asia & the World. LC 00-28283. 265p. 2000. 24.95 (*1-893554-08-2*) Encounter Bks.
Mosher, Steven W., ed. Korea in the 1990s: Prospects for Unification. 172p. (C). 1992. text 34.95 (*1-56000-010-4*) Transaction Pubs.
— The United States & the Republic of China: Democratic Friends, Strategic Allies & Economic Partners. 176p. (C). 1991. text 39.95 (*0-88738-410-2*) Transaction Pubs.
Mosher, Sue. The Microsoft Exchange User's Handbook. LC 96-45905. (Illus.). 692p. (Orig.). 1997. pap. 49.95 incl. cd-rom (*1-882419-52-9*) News Four-Hund.
— The Microsoft Outlook E-Mail & Fax Guide. LC 97-33936. 450p. 1997. pap. 39.95 (*1-882419-82-0*) News Four-Hund.
***Mosher, Sue.** Microsoft Outlook 2000: E-Mail & Fax Guide. (Illus.). 1999. pap. text 39.95 (*1-55558-235-4*, Digital DEC) Buttrwrth-Heinemann.
Mosher, Terry, jt. ed. see Freed, Josh.
Mosher, Terry W. Harsh: The Life, Times & Philosophy of Hall of Fame Coach Marv Harshman. 166p. 1994. 21.50 (*0-9639827-0-2*) Mo Bks.
Mosher, William J. U. S. S. Wilkes "The Lucky Ship" LC 96-80007. (Illus.). 464p. 1997. 35.00 (*1-881851-10-9*) Genealogy Pub.
Moshi, Humphrey & Biermann, Werner, eds. Contextualizing Poverty in Tanzania: Historical Origins, Policy Failures & Recent Trends. 208p. 1996. pap. text 24.95 (*3-8258-3027-6*) Transaction Pubs.

M

An Asterisk (*) at the beginning of an entry indicates that the title is appearing for the first time.

Moshi, Humphrey, jt. ed. see Biermann, Werner.

Moshi, Lioba, et al. Mwalimu Wa Kiswahili: A Language Teaching Manual. 123p. 1998. pap. text, teacher ed. 22.00 (*1-883058-61-9*) Global Pubns.

Moshi, Lioba, jt. ed. see Mufwene, Salikoko S.

Moshi, Lioba J. Mazoezi Ya Kiswahili: Kitabu Cha Wanafunzi Wa Mwaka Wa Kwanza: Swahili Exercises: A Workbook for First Year Students. LC 88-27671. 244p. (Orig.). (C). 1989. pap. text 26.50 (*0-8191-7215-4*) U Pr of Amer.

Moshier. Methods & Programs for Mathematical Functions. 1990. pap. write for info. (*0-318-68280-X*) P-H.

Moshier, Stephen L. Methods & Programs for Mathematical Functions. 1989. text 59.95 (*0-470-21609-3*) P-H.

Moshimer, Joan. The Complete Book of Rug Hooking. (Illus.). 176p. 1989. pap. 12.95 (*0-486-25945-5*) Dover.

Moshinskie. Fluids & Shock, a Computerized Review. (C). 1995. 36.00 (*0-8359-4904-4*) Prntice Hall Bks.

Moshinskiy, David. Things You Know That Are Not So: A Digest of Erroneous Popular Wisdom. LC 95-94457. (Illus.). 162p. 1995. pap. 12.95 (*0-7880-0611-8*, Fairway Pr) CSS OH.

Moshinsky, George. Behind the Masonic Curtain: The Soviet Attack on Masonry. (Illus.). 61p. (Orig.). 1986. pap. 10.95 (*0-938103-00-8*) ZZYZX Pub.

— For the Love of Freedom: The Soviet Occupation of Bessarabia, 1940. Chang, M., ed. 347p. 1997. 29.95 (*0-614-30081-9*) ZZYZX Pub.

— General Erich Ludendorff: The Nazi Persecution of Masonry, Vol. I. (Illus.). 380p. 1996. 39.95 (*0-938103-02-4*) ZZYZX Pub.

Moshinsky, George, tr. see Meshko, Oksana.

Moshinsky, M. Group Theory & the Many-Body Problem. vi, 182p. 1968. text 195.00 (*0-677-01740-5*) Gordon & Breach.

Moshinsky, M. Harmonic Oscillator in Modern Physics: From Atoms to Quarks. (Documents on Modern Physics Ser.). 100p. 1969. text 142.00 (*0-677-02450-9*) Gordon & Breach.

Moshinsky, Marcos & Smirnov, Yuri F. The Harmonic Oscillator in Modern Physics: From Atoms to Quarks. 2nd expanded rev. ed. (Contemporary Concepts in Physics Ser.). 400p. 1996. text 51.00 (*3-7186-0620-8*); pap. text 22.00 (*3-7186-0621-6*) Gordon & Breach.

Moshiri, Farnoosh. At the Wall of the Almighty. LC 99-21087. 508p. 1999. pap. 16.00 (*1-56656-315-1*) Interlink Pub.

Moshiri, Gerald A. Constructed Wetlands for Water Quality Improvement. 656p. 1993. lib. bdg. 95.00 (*0-87371-550-0*, L550) Lewis Pubs.

Moshiri, Leila. Colloquial Persian. 2nd ed. 228p. 1988. pap. 20.99 (*0-415-00886-7*, A1402) Routledge.

— Colloquial Persian 2E. (Colloquials Ser.). 1989. pap. 17.95 incl. audio (*0-415-00887-5*, A1406) Routledge.

— Colloquial Persian 2E, Set. 2nd ed. (Colloquials Ser.). 200p. 1988. pap. 29.95 incl. audio (*0-415-02618-0*, A2659) Routledge.

Moshkin, V. A., ed. Castor. Dhote, R. K., tr. from RUS. 329p. (C). 1986. text 95.00 (*90-6191-466-3*, Pub. by A A Balkema) Ashgate Pub Co.

Moshkov, Mikhail M., jt. auth. see Jardine, L. J.

Moshkovich, Helen M., jt. auth. see Larichev, Oleg I.

Moshkovitz, Moshe. Dictionary of Television & Audiovisual Terminology. LC 98-2945. 183p. 1998. lib. bdg. 39.95 (*0-7864-0440-X*) McFarland & Co.

***Moshkovitz, Moshe.** The Virtual Studio: Technology & Techniques. (Illus.). 224p. 2000. pap. 49.95 (*0-240-80425-2*, Focal) Buttrwrth-Heinemann.

Moshman, David. Adolescents Psychological Development: Rationality, Morality, & Identity. LC 98-54349. 152p. 1999. 39.95 (*0-8058-2857-5*); pap. 16.50 (*0-8058-2858-3*) L Erlbaum Assocs.

— Children, Education, & the First Amendment: A Psycholegal Analysis. LC 88-29094. (Children & the Law Ser.). 237p. 1989. reprint ed. pap. 73.50 (*0-608-01855-4*, 206250500003) Bks Demand.

Moshos. Data Communications. (West Engineering Ser.). 1989. text 64.95 (*0-534-93833-7*) PWS Pubs.

Moshy, Roger E., jt. auth. see Friedman, Ellis H.

Mosich, Donna M. WordPerfect 4.2 Macros. 1991. 24.95 (*0-8306-6651-6*) McGraw-Hill Prof.

— WordPerfect 5.0: New Features & Advanced Techniques. (Illus.). 300p. 1988. 29.95 (*0-8306-3084-8*, 3084) McGraw-Hill Prof.

Mosich, Donna M., et al. Advanced Turbo C Programmer's Guide. LC 88-27907. 339p. 1988. pap. 21.95 (*0-471-63742-4*) Wiley.

— WordPerfect Macros: The Windows Version. 576p. 1992. pap. 29.95 (*0-8306-2501-1*, 3945, Windcrest) TAB Bks.

Mosier, Alice & Pace, Frank J. Medical Records Technology. LC 74-18676. (Allied Health Ser.). 1975. pap. 9.95 (*0-672-61396-4*, Bobbs) Macmillan.

Mosier, C. H. Practice & Procedure in Magistrates Courts. 216p. 1986. 104.00 (*1-85190-013-6*, Pub. by Fourmat Pub) St Mut.

Mosier, Dan L. The H. A. Coal Mine: Chronicles of a Coal Mine in Hayward, Cal. 2nd rev. ed. 27p. (Orig.). 1979. pap. 2.95 (*1-889064-00-9*) Mines Rd Bks.

— Name Index for the Centennial Year Book of Alameda County, California. 59p. 1999. pap. 9.95 (*1-889064-06-8*) Mines Rd Bks.

Mosier, Dan L. & Finney, Page. Dublin Gold. (Illus.). 18p. (Orig.). 1980. pap. 2.95 (*1-889064-01-7*) Mines Rd Bks.

Mosier, Dan L. & Williams, Earle E. History of Tesla, a California Coal Mining Town. LC 98-91374. (Illus.). 380p. (Orig.). 1999. pap. 29.95 (*1-889064-04-1*) Mines Rd Bks.

Mosier, Dan L., jt. auth. see Mosier, Page.

Mosier, Dewey & Mosier, Nola, eds. Tales of the Trinity: By Major Horace Bell. LC 83-5128. 55p. 1983. pap. 5.95 (*0-9607054-1-4*) Trinity Cty Hist Soc.

Mosier, Elizabeth. My Life as a Girl. LC 98-8688. 193p. (YA). (gr. 7-12). 1999. lib. bdg. 18.99 (*0-679-99035-6*) Random.

***Mosier, Elizabeth.** My Life as a Girl. 208p. (YA). (gr. 7-12). 2000. pap. 4.99 (*0-375-80194-4*, Pub. by Random Bks Yng Read) Random.

Mosier, Elizabeth. My Life As a Girl. LC 98-8688. 212p. (YA). (gr. 7-12). 1999. 17.00 (*0-679-89035-1*, Pub. by Random Bks Yng Read) Random.

***Mosier, John.** The Myth of the Great War. 2001. write for info. (*0-06-019676-9*) HarpC.

Mosier, K. C., II. For New Believers: The Most Important Facts I Know about Christianity. 1998. pap. 8.95 (*0-533-12705-X*) Vantage.

Mosier, Nola, jt. ed. see Mosier, Dewey.

Mosier, Page & Mosier, Dan L. Alameda County Place Names. (Illus.). 130p. (Orig.). 1986. pap. 9.95 (*1-889064-02-5*) Mines Rd Bks.

Mosier, Sally. Expectations Cookbook: Low Fat & No Fat Recipes. 1996. pap. 15.95 (*0-9651423-0-2*) Expectations.

— Food for the Soul. LC 97-204873. 288p. 1997. pap. 15.00 (*1-57566-209-4*, Knsington) Kensgtn Pub Corp.

Mosier, Tim D. Twisters in the Heartland. LC 98-24664. 200p. 1998. 18.95 (*1-58141-002-6*) Rivercross Pub.

Mosig, John. The Australian Yabby Farmer. 2nd rev. ed. 224p. (Orig.). pap. 39.95 (*0-643-06367-6*, Pub. by CSIRO) Accents Pubns.

Mosiman, Bille Sue. Death in Dixie. 1998. mass mkt. 5.99 (*0-425-16298-2*, Prime Crime) Berkley Pub.

***Mosiman, Billie S.** Red Moon Rising. 2001. mass mkt. 6.99 (*0-88677-955-3*, Pub. by DAW Bks) Penguin Putnam.

Mosiman, Billie S. Widow. 384p. (Orig.). 1995. mass mkt. 5.99 (*0-425-14683-9*) Berkley Pub.

— Wireman. 272p. 1997. reprint ed. mass mkt. 4.50 (*0-8439-4338-6*, Leisure Bks) Dorchester Pub Co.

Mosiman, Billie S. & Greenberg, Martin H., eds. August Is a Good Time for Killing: And Other Blood-Curdling Stories of Murder in the East. LC 98-4796. 224p. 1998. pap. 9.95 (*1-55853-576-4*) Rutledge Hill Pr.

— Blowout in Little Man Flats: And Other Spine-Tingling Stories of Murder in the West. LC 98-4798. 224p. 1998. pap. 9.95 (*1-55853-573-X*) Rutledge Hill Pr.

— The Fifth Grave: And Other Terrifying Tales of Homicide in the Heartland. LC 98-4797. 224p. 1998. pap. 9.95 (*1-55853-574-8*) Rutledge Hill Pr.

— Never Shake a Family Tree: And Other Heart-Stopping Tales of Murder in New England. LC 98-4799. 224p. 1998. pap. 9.95 (*1-55853-577-2*) Rutledge Hill Pr.

Mosimann, Anton. The Essential Mosimann. (Illus.). 160p. 1994. 50.00 (*0-09-175379-1*, Pub. by Ebury Pr) Trafalgar.

Mosimann, E. A., jt. compiled by see Callery, B. G.

Mosin, V. A., intro. Greek Charters of Serbian Rulers. 696p. (C). 1974. reprint ed. lib. bdg. 133.95 (*0-902089-65-X*, Pub. by Variorum) Ashgate Pub Co.

Mosin, Vladimir. Anchor Watermarks. (Monumenta Chartae Papyraceae Ser.: 13). (Illus.). 540p. (C). 1973. text 139.50 (*90-5356-225-7*, Pub. by Amsterdam U Pr) U of Mich Pr.

Mosing, Lisa. Sharpening Your Image: How to Get, Keep & Expand a Healthcare Business. 238p. 1992. pap. 29.95 (*0-9633990-0-4*) Nutrition Wks.

Mosiondz, Peter, Jr. Successful Stamp Dealing: Tried & Tested Tips & Techniques. LC 95-61760. 120p. 1996. pap. 12.95 (*0-87341-452-7*) Krause Pubns.

Mosk, Carl. Competition & Cooperation in Japanese Labour Markets. LC 95-4170. (Studies in the Modern Japanese Economy). 1995. text 75.00 (*0-312-12683-2*) St Martin.

— Making Health Work: Human Growth in Modern Japan. (Studies in Demography: Vol. 8). (Illus.). 174p. (C). 1996. 48.00 (*0-520-08315-6*, Pub. by U CA Pr) Cal Prin Full Svc.

Mosk, Sanford A. Land Tenure Problems in the Santa Fe Railroad Grant Area. Bruchey, Stuart, ed. LC 80-1333. (Railroads Ser.). (Illus.). 1981. reprint ed. lib. bdg. 15.95 (*0-405-13807-5*) Ayer.

Moskal, Jeanne. Blake, Ethics, & Forgiveness. LC 93-11799. 240p. (C). 1994. text 34.95 (*0-8173-0678-1*) U of Ala Pr.

***Moskalenko, S. A. & Snoke, D. W.** Bose-Einstein Condensation of Excitons & Biexcitons: And Coherent Nonlinear Optics with Excitons. LC 98-44874. (Illus.). 416p. 2000. 85.00 (*0-521-58099-4*) Cambridge U Pr.

Moskaleva, Raisa, ed. see Gozun, Alla.

Moskalew, W. Formular Language & Poetic Design in the Aeneid. 1982. pap. 49.00 (*90-04-06580-6*, MNS, 73) Brill Academic Pubs.

Moskaliuk, Stepan S. Group Theoretical Methods in Physics: Proceedings of the Eleventh International Hutsulian Workshop Held in Rakhiv, Ukraine, Oct. 1992. (Monographs in Physics). 280p. (C). 1995. lib. bdg. 80.00 (*0-911767-74-6*) Hadronic Pr Inc.

Moskaliuk, Stepan S., ed. Methods in Mathematical Physics: Proceedings of the 12th International Hutsulian Workshop. 469p. (C). 1998. pap. text 80.00 (*1-57485-027-X*) Hadronic Pr Inc.

Moskau, Linda, jt. auth. see Moskau, Mike.

Moskau, Mike & Moskau, Linda. Solid Black & White Answers to Life's Questions. 206p. (Orig.). 1998. pap. 7.77 (*0-9640404-8-4*) Harvard House.

Moskhos, John. Spiritual Meadow. 93p. Date not set. pap. write for info. (*1-879038-49-8*, 9018) Synaxis Pr.

Moskin, J. Robert. The Meaning of CAPHE: A Report on the First Five Years of the Consortium for the Advancement of Private Higher Education. ix, 147p. (Orig.). 1990. 3.00 (*1-879994-01-1*) Consortium Advan.

— Report from Jerusalem: City at the Crossroads. LC 77-79877. (Illus.). 64p. 1977. pap. 1.50 (*0-87495-013-9*) Am Jewish Comm.

— U. S. Marine Corps Story. 916p. 1992. pap. 29.95 (*0-316-58558-0*) Little.

Moskin, J. Robert, jt. auth. see Vitullo-Martin, Julia.

Moskin, J. Robert, jt. ed. see Simmons, Edwin H.

Moskin, Julia, jt. auth. see Palomino, Rafael.

Moskin, Marietta D. Day of the Blizzard. (J). 1999. pap. 1.50 (*0-590-30092-X*) Scholastic Inc.

***Moskin, Marietta D.** I Am Rosemarie. 258p. 1999. 24.95 (*0-7351-0225-2*); pap. 12.95 (*0-7351-0226-0*) Replica Bks.

Moskin, Marietta D. Margaret Thatcher. (In Focus Biographies Ser.). (Illus.). 128p. (J). 1990. lib. bdg. 13.98 (*0-671-69632-7*, Julian Messner) Silver Burdett Pr.

— Margaret Thatcher. (In Focus Biographies Ser.). (Illus.). 128p. (YA). (gr. 9). 1990. pap. 7.95 (*0-671-69633-5*, Julian Messner) Silver Burdett Pr.

Moskin, Nancy, tr. see Cao, Guanlong.

Mosking, Dian-Marie, ed. Management & Organisation: Relational Alternatives to Individualism. 256p. 1995. 78.95 (*1-85972-167-2*, Pub. by Avebry) Ashgate Pub Co.

Moskoff, William. The Bread of Affliction: The Food Supply in the U. S. S. R. During World War II. (Cambridge Russian, Soviet & Post-Soviet Studies: No. 76). (Illus.). 272p. (C). 1990. text 85.00 (*0-521-37499-5*) Cambridge U Pr.

Moskoff, William. Hard Times: Impoverishment & Protest in the Perestroika Years: The Soviet Union 1985-1991. LC 93-20098. 260p. (C). (gr. 13). 1993. pap. text 35.95 (*1-56324-214-1*) M E Sharpe.

Moskoff, William. Hard Times:Impoverishment & Protest in the Perestroika Years: The Soviet Union 1985-1991. LC 93-20098. 260p. (C). (gr. 13). 1993. text 85.95 (*1-56324-213-3*) M E Sharpe.

Moskoff, William, ed. Perestroika in the Countryside: Agricultural Reform in the Gorbachev Era. LC 90-8603. 144p. (gr. 13). 1990. text 85.95 (*0-87332-767-5*) M E Sharpe.

Moskoff, William, jt. auth. see Jones, Anthony.

Moskoff, William, jt. ed. see Jones, Anthony.

Moskoff, William, jt. ed. see Linz, Susan J.

Moskop, John C. Divine Omniscience & Human Freedom: Thomas Aquinas & Charles Hartshorne. LC 84-1172. xviii, 105p. 1984. text 14.95 (*0-86554-123-X*, MUP/H102) Mercer Univ Pr.

Moskop, John C. & Kopelman, Loretta M., eds. Ethics & Critical Care Medicine. (Philosophy & Medicine Ser.: No. 19). 256p. 1985. text 107.00 (*90-277-1820-2*) Kluwer Academic.

Moskop, John C., jt. auth. see Kopelman, Loretta M.

Moskop, John C., jt. ed. see Kopelman, Loretta M.

Moskop, Ruth W., tr. see Delkeskamp-Hayes, Corinna & Cutter, Mary A., eds.

Moskos, Charles & Butler, John S. All That We Can Be: Black Leadership & Racial Integration the Army Way. 224p. 1997. pap. 13.00 (*0-465-00113-0*, Pub. by Basic) HarpC.

Moskos, Charles C. Greek Americans: Struggle & Success. enl. rev. ed. 176p. 1989. pap. 24.95 (*0-88738-778-0*) Transaction Pubs.

Moskos, Charles C., Jr. Peace Soldiers: The Sociology of a United Nations Military Force. 1992. lib. bdg. 12.50 (*0-226-54225-4*) U Ch Pr.

Moskos, Charles C., II & Chambers, John W., eds. The New Conscientious Objection: From Sacred to Secular Resistance. LC 92-20615. (Illus.). 296p. 1993. pap. text 29.95 (*0-19-507955-8*) OUP.

Moskos, Charles C., et al. The Postmodern Military: Armed Forces after the Cold War. LC 99-48791. 304p. (C). 1999. text 45.00 (*0-19-513328-5*); pap. text 29.95 (*0-19-513329-3*) OUP.

Moskos, Charles C., jt. ed. see Georgakas, Dan.

Moskosky, Susan, ed. Women's Health Care Nurse Practitioner Certification Review Guide. LC 95-33625. 500p. (C). 1995. pap. text 52.00 (*1-878028-13-8*) Hlth Lead Assoc.

Moskovitch, Morris, jt. ed. see Umlita, Carlo.

Moskovits, Malka. The World That Crumbled. LC 93-6758. 1993. pap. 13.95 (*0-89604-155-7*, Holocaust Library) US Holocaust.

Moskovits, Martin, ed. Science & Society: The John C. Polanyi Nobel Laureates Lectures. 168p. 1997. pap. 13.95 (*0-88784-589-4*, Pub. by Hse of Anansi Pr) Genl Dist Srvs.

Moskovits, Martin, ed. Science & Society. (John C. Polanyi Nobel Laureates Lectures). 168p. 1995. 19.95 (*0-88784-170-8*, Pub. by Hse of Anansi Pr) Genl Dist Srvs.

Moskovitz, David, et al. Full Environmental Disclosure for Electricity: Tracking & Reporting Key Information. Harrington, Cheryl, ed. LC 98-124558. 31p. 1997. 15.00 (*1-55516-586-9*, 4126) Natl Conf State Legis.

Moskovitz, Denise P., ed. Chicago Ancestor File, 1974-1984. 381p. 1985. pap. 8.00 (*1-881125-08-4*) Chi Geneal Soc.

Moskovitz, Jack. Artist As Autist. (Illus.). 59p. (Orig.). 1989. pap. 3.00 (*0-926935-14-3*) Runaway Spoon.

— Isis Slices. (Illus.). 31p. (Orig.). 1992. pap. 3.00 (*0-926935-66-6*) Runaway Spoon.

Moskovitz, Myron. California Eviction Defense Manual: June 1994 Update. 2nd ed. Dworin, Christopher D., ed. LC 93-71542. 362p. 1994. 33.00 (*0-88124-772-3*, RE-32081) Cont Ed Bar-CA.

***Moskovitz, Myron.** Cases & Problems in California Criminal Law. LC 99-18633. 824p. (C). 1999. 53.95 (*0-87084-351-6*) Anderson Pub Co.

Moskovitz, Myron. Cases & Problems in Criminal Law. 4th ed. (Anthology Ser.). 810p. (C). 1998. 57.95 (*0-87084-244-7*) Anderson Pub Co.

— Cases & Problems in Criminal Procedure: The Courtroom. 2nd ed. LC 98-14631. (Casebook Seriesills Ser.). 1998. 57.00 (*0-8205-3116-2*) Bender.

— Cases & Problems in Criminal Procedure: The Police. 2nd ed. LC 98-14632. (Analysis & Skills Ser.). 1998. 57.00 (*0-8205-3115-4*) Bender.

Moskovitz, Myron. Winning an Appeal,1995. 3rd ed. 1995. text 20.00 (*1-55834-265-6*) Bender.

Moskovitz, Myron & Bishop, Catherine M. California Eviction Defense Manual. 2nd ed. Chapin, John K., ed. LC 93-71542. 180p. 1997. ring bd. 43.00 (*0-7626-0117-5*, RE-32084) Cont Ed Bar-CA.

— California Eviction Defense Manual: 5/98 Update, 2 vols. 2nd ed. Millner, Dianne, ed. LC 93-71542. 516p. 1998. ring bd. 60.00 (*0-7626-0228-7*, RE-32085) Cont Ed Bar-CA.

Moskovitz, Myron & Schur, Dara L. California Eviction Defense Manual. 2 vols. 2nd ed. Chapin, John K., ed. LC 93-71542. 310p. 1996. ring bd. 43.00 (*0-7626-0021-7*, RE-32083) Cont Ed Bar-CA.

Moskovitz, Myron & Warner, Ralph E. Tenants' Rights. 14th ed. LC 99-13951. 272p. 1999. pap. 21.95 (*0-87337-520-3*) Nolo com.

— Tenant's Rights: California Edition. 13th rev. ed. Stewart, Marcia, ed. LC 95-39119. (Illus.). 272p. 1997. pap. 19.95 (*0-87337-377-4*) Nolo com.

Moskovitz, Myron, et al. California Eviction Defense Manual, Set, Vols. 1 & 2. 2nd ed. Dworin, Christopher D., ed. LC 93-71542. 1082p. 1993. 155.00 (*0-88124-636-0*, RE-32080) Cont Ed Bar-CA.

***Moskovitz, Myron, et al.** California Eviction Defense Manual: May 2000 Update, 2. 2nd ed. Maly, Bonnie C., ed. 1238p. 2000. 89.00 (*0-7626-0432-8*, RE-32087) Cont Ed Bar-CA.

— California Eviction Defense Manual - 5-99 Update. Maly, Bonnie C., ed. LC 93-71542. 476p. 1999. ring bd. 72.00 (*0-7626-0329-1*, RE-32086) Cont Ed Bar-CA.

— California Landlord-Tenant Practice. 2nd ed. Sherlin, Johanna, ed. LC 97-67674. 780p. 1997. ring bd. 179.00 (*0-7626-0065-9*, RE-32690) Cont Ed Bar-CA.

***Moskovitz, Patti.** The Complete Bar/Bat Mitzvah Book: Everything You Need to Plan a Meaningful Celebration. LC 99-59748. 240p. 2000. pap. 17.99 (*1-56414-463-1*) Career Pr Inc.

Moskovitz, Patti, jt. ed. see Berkowitz, Allan.

Moskovitz, Richard A. Lost in the Mirror: An Inside Look at Borderline Personality Disorder. 208p. (Orig.). 1996. pap. 12.95 (*0-87833-936-1*) Taylor Pub.

Moskow, Shirley, ed. see Booth, Robert.

Moskow, Shirley B. Emma's World: An Intimate Look at Lives Touched by the Civil War Era. 294p. 1990. pap. 17.00 (*0-88282-191-1*) New Horizon NJ.

Moskow, Shirley B., ed. Hunan Hand & Other Ailments: Letters to the New England Journal of Medicine. 1987. 15.95 (*0-316-58533-5*, Little Brwn Med Div) Lppncott W & W.

Moskow, Shirley Blotnick, ed. see Frost, Jack.

Moskowitz. Osteoarthritis. 2nd ed. 1992. text 170.00 (*0-7216-6581-0*, W B Saunders Co) Harcrt Hlth Sci Grp.

Moskowitz, et al. Shiel in Diverse Hands: A Collection of Essays. LC 82-61695. 501p. 1983. pap. 32.50 (*0-685-04346-0*) Reynolds Morse.

Moskowitz, Addie A., jt. auth. see Laskin, Pamela L.

Moskowitz, Anita F. Nicola Pisano's Arca di San Domenico & Its Legacy. LC 92-35574. (College Art Association Monographs on the Fine Arts: Vol. L). (Illus.). 160p. (C). 1994. 65.00 (*0-271-00946-2*) Pa St U Pr.

— The Sculpture of Andrea & Nino Pisano. (Illus.). 608p. 1987. text 245.00 (*0-521-30754-6*) Cambridge U Pr.

***Moskowitz, Anita Fiderer.** Italian Gothic Sculpture: C. 1250-c. 1400. LC 99-57210. (Illus.). 432p. (C). 2000. text. write for info. (*0-521-44483-7*) Cambridge U Pr.

Moskowitz, Bette Ann. Do I Know You? Living Through the End of a Parent's Life. LC 97-38240. 208p. 1998. 20.00 (*1-56836-210-2*) Kodansha.

Moskowitz, Dan, jt. ed. see Kozzumi, Luci.

Moskowitz, Daniel, ed. The 1998 Health Network & Alliance Sourcebook. (Illus.). 642p. 1997. pap. 250.00 (*1-57987-042-2*) Faulkner & Gray.

Moskowitz, Daniel, jt. ed. see Koizumi, Luci.

Moskowitz, Daniel B., ed. 1999 Health Network & Alliance Sourcebook: Purchasing & Selling Strategies for Payers & Providers, Including Blue Book Network, Coalition & Alliance Directories. (Illus.). 544p. 1998. pap. 265.00 (*1-57987-099-6*) Faulkner & Gray.

Moskowitz, Daniel B., jt. ed. see Koizumi, Luci S.

Moskowitz, David & Ivens, Kathy. OS/2 Power Tools. 400p. 1989. pap. 44.95 incl. disk (*0-13-643065-1*) P-H.

***Moskowitz, Eva S.** Therapy Nation: America's Obsession with Emotional Well-Being. LC 00-8987. 2001. write for info. (*0-8018-6403-8*) Johns Hopkins.

Moskowitz, Faye. And the Bridge Is Love: Life Stories. LC 91-14217. 160p. 1993. pap. 12.00 (*0-8070-6327-4*) Beacon Pr.

— A Leak in the Heart: Tales from a Woman's Life. LC 84-48298. 176p. 1987. pap. 12.95 (*0-87923-659-0*) Godine.

— Whoever Finds This, I Love You. 224p. 1988. pap. 11.95 (*0-87923-936-0*) Godine.

Moskowitz, Faye, ed. Her Face in the Mirror: Jewish Women on Mothers & Daughters. 336p. (C). 1995. pap. 18.00 (*0-8070-3615-3*) Beacon Pr.

Moskowitz, Francine & Moskowitz, Robert. Parenting Your Aging Parents. LC 90-92272. 304p. 1991. 21.95 (*0-9624415-0-3*) Key Pubns Woodland Hills.

Moskowitz, Gertrude. Caring & Sharing in the Foreign Language Class: A Sourcebook on Humanistic Techniques. 360p. (C). 1978. mass mkt. 28.95 (*0-8384-2771-5*, Newbury) Heinle & Heinle.

Moskowitz, H. R. New Directions for Product Testing & Sensory Analysis of Foods. 370p. 1985. 73.00 (*0-917678-18-4*) Food & Nut Pr.

— Product Testing & Sensory Evaluation of Foods: Marketing & R&D Approaches. 605p. 1983. 87.00 (*0-917678-16-8*) Food & Nut Pr.

Moskowitz, H. R., et al, eds. Sensation & Measurement: Papers in Honor of S. S. Stevens. LC 74-77966. 550p. 1974. text 226.00 (*90-277-0474-0*) Kluwer Academic.

Moskowitz, H. R. & Warren, Craig, eds. Odor Quality & Chemical Structure. LC 80-28633. (ACS Symposium Ser.: No. 148). 1981. 38.95 (*0-8412-0607-4*) Am Chemical.

Moskowitz, Harvey S. & Lindbloom, Carl G. The Illustrated Book of Development Definitions. (Illus.). 263p. 1981. pap. text 18.95 (*0-88285-070-9*) Transaction Pubs.

— The New Illustrated Book of Development Definitions. LC 92-19394. 328p. (C). 1993. pap. 29.95 (*0-88285-144-6*) Ctr Urban Pol Res.

Moskowitz, Howard, ed. Applied Sensory Analysis of Foods, Vol. I. 272p. 1988. lib. bdg. 210.00 (*0-8493-6705-0*, TX546) CRC Pr.

— Applied Sensory Analysis of Foods, Vol. II. 192p. 1988. lib. bdg. 210.00 (*0-8493-6706-9*, TX546) CRC Pr.

Moskowitz, Howard R. Consumer Testing & Evaluation of Personal Care Products. (Cosmetic Science & Technology Ser.: No. 14). (Illus.). 512p. 1995. text 180.00 (*0-8247-9367-6*) Dekker.

— Cosmetic Product Testing: A Modern Psychophysical Approach. LC 84-17660. (Cosmetic Science & Technology Ser.: No. 3). 477p. reprint ed. pap. 147.90 (*0-7837-2025-4*, 205245100002) Bks Demand.

— Food Concepts & Products: Just in Time Development. LC 93-71709. (Publications in Food Science & Nutrition Ser.). 502p. 1995. 159.95 (*0-917678-32-X*, 67832X) Technomic.

— Food Texture. (Food Science & Technology Ser.: Vol. 22). (Illus.). 352p. 1987. text 185.00 (*0-8247-7585-6*) Dekker.

Moskowitz, Howard R. & Warren, Craig B., eds. Odor Quality & Chemical Structure: Based on a Symposium. LC 80-28633. (ACS Symposium Ser.: Vol. 148). 252p. 1981. reprint ed. pap. 78.20 (*0-608-03034-1*, 206348700007) Bks Demand.

Moskowitz, Ira & Collier, John. Patterns & Ceremonials of the Indians of the Southwest. unabridged ed. LC 95-6513. (Illus.). 192p. 1995. reprint ed. pap. text 14.95 (*0-486-28692-4*) Dover.

Moskowitz, Jane M., jt. auth. see Bloomfield, Brynna C.

Moskowitz, Joel. The Paper Machine Series, Vol 2: The Working Piston Engine. 96p. 1986. pap. 79.50 (*0-671-93855-X*) S&S Trade.

Moskowitz, Ken. Greater Washington Area Bicycle Atlas. 3rd rev. ed. (Illus.). 254p. 1985. pap. 9.95 (*0-9614892-0-0*) Potomac Area.

Moskowitz, Lester R. Permanent Magnet & Application Handbook. 2nd ed. LC 85-5629. (Illus.). 970p. (C). 1995. 149.50 (*0-89464-768-7*) Krieger.

Moskowitz, Melissa. The Jews for Jesus Family Cookbook. pap. 11.00 (*1-881022-14-5*) Purple Pomegranate.

Moskowitz, Michael, et al, eds. The Neurobiological & Developmental Basis for Psychotherapeutic Intervention. LC 97-23572. (Illus.). 288p. 1997. text 50.00 (*0-7657-0097-2*) Aronson.

Moskowitz, Michael, jt. ed. see Ellman, Steven J.

Moskowitz, Michael A. & Caplan, Louis R., eds. Cerebrovascular Diseases: Nineteenth Princeton Stroke Conference. 552p. 1995. text 185.00 (*0-7506-9603-6*) Buttrwrth-Heinemann.

Moskowitz, Milton. The Global Marketplace: One Hundred & Two of the Most Influential Companies Outside of America. 1988. 22.50 (*0-317-66939-7*, Scribners Ref) Mac Lib Ref.

Moskowitz, Milton, jt. auth. see Levering, Robert.

Moskowitz, Moses. The Roots & Reaches of United Nations Actions & Decisions. LC 80 51741. 220p. 1980 lib bdg. 67.50 (*90-286-0140-6*) Kluwer Academic.

Moskowitz, Nachama S. Original Bulletin Boards on Jewish Themes. xii, 477 p. 1986. pap. 13.50 (*0-86705-019-5*) A R E Pub.

Moskowitz, Nachama Skolnik. A Bridge to Prayer - The Jewish Worship Workbook Vol. 1: God, Prayer & the Shema. (J). (gr. 4-6). 1988. pap. text 7.00 (*0-8074-0417-9*, 123594) UAHC.

— A Bridge to Prayer - The Jewish Worship Workbook Vol. 2: The Amidah, Torah Service & Concluding Prayers. (Illus.). 144p. (J). (gr. 6-7). 1989. pap. text 7.00 (*0-8074-0432-2*, 123596) UAHC.

— Games, Games & More Games: Fun for Jewish Learning. 306p. (J). (gr. 4-6). 1994. pap. 8.00 (*0-8074-0504-3*, 201000) UAHC.

Moskowitz, Nathan. Molecular Modulation of Chemical Presynaptic Neurotransmission. 258p. 1985. 65.00 (*0-275-91320-1*, C1320, Praeger Pubs) Greenwood.

Moskowitz, Rachel. Job Outlook in Brief, 1994-2005. 43p. 1997. pap. 5.25 (*0-16-054438-6*) USGPO.

Moskowitz, Reed C. Your Healing Mind. 304p. 1993. reprint ed. pap. 10.00 (*0-380-71470-1*, Avon Bks) Morrow Avon.

Moskowitz, Richard. Homeopathic Medicines for Pregnancy & Childbirth. 300p. (Orig.). 1992. pap. 16.95 (*1-55643-137-6*) North Atlantic.

Moskowitz, Robert. How to Organize Your Work & Your Life. 2nd rev. ed. LC 92-27756. 304p. 1981. pap. 14.95 (*0-385-42480-9*) Doubleday.

— Out on Your Own. 216p. 1997. ring bd. 21.95 (*0-9624415-3-8*) Key Pubns Woodland Hills.

Moskowitz, Robert, jt. auth. see Moskowitz, Francine.

Moskowitz, S. Electronic Transformers. 275p. 2000. 2500.00 (*0-614-06126-1*, LE609) Lead Edge Reports.

— Mini-Mills vs. Integrated & Foreign Producers. 183p. 1998. 2500.00 (*0-945235-63-1*) Lead Edge Reports.

***Moskowitz, S.** The Power U. S. Transformer Industry. 250p. 2000. ring bd. 2500.00 (*0-317-55172-8*) Lead Edge Reports.

Moskowitz, Sam. After All These Years. 96p. 1991. pap. 5.95 (*0-910619-07-7*) Niekas Pubns.

— History of the Movement 1854-1890. (Illus.). 1980. 15.00 (*0-937986-40-2*) D M Grant.

Moskowitz, Sam. Horrors Unknown: Newly Discovered Masterpieces by Great Names in Fantastic Terror. LC 70-155734. x, 214 p. (J). 1971. write for info. (*0-8027-5534-8*) Walker & Co.

Moskowitz, Sam, ed. A. Merritt: Reflections in the Moon Pool. 1985. 20.00 (*1-880418-13-4*) D M Grant.

Moskowitz, Seymour. Thermodynamics of the Future. 2 vols. (Illus.). 257p. (C). 1989. reprint ed. text 300.00 (*0-9630456-2-8*); reprint ed. pap. text 275.00 (*0-9630456-5-2*) S Moskowitz.

— Thermodynamics of the Future, Vol. 1. (Illus.). 257p. (C). 1989. reprint ed. text 160.00 (*0-9630456-0-1*); reprint ed. pap. text 150.00 (*0-9630456-3-6*) S Moskowitz.

— Thermodynamics of the Future, Vol. 2. (Illus.). 257p. (C). 1989. reprint ed. text 160.00 (*0-9630456-1-X*); reprint ed. pap. text 150.00 (*0-9630456-4-4*) S Moskowitz.

Moskowitz, Seymour H., et al. New York Trial Guide, 5 vols., Set. 1990. 475.00 (*0-8205-1599-X*, 599) Bender.

Moskuina, Tamara. Secrets of the Soviet Skaters: Off-Ice Training Methods. Copley-Graves, L., ed. (Illus.). 1998. pap. 40.00 (*1-882849-03-5*) Platoro Pr.

Moslander, Marie. Life's Path Unfolding. 200p. 1994. pap. 12.95 (*1-884954-00-6*) Evergreen WA.

Mosle, Mira & Crisler, Shirley. In the Midst of His People: The Authorized Biography of Bishop Maurice J. Dingman. LC 94-26663. (Illus.). 300p. (Orig.). 1994. pap. 14.95 (*0-945213-13-1*) Rudi Pub.

***Mosleh, A.** Modeling Common-Cause Failures in Probabilistic Risk Assessment. 203p. 1998. per. 17.00 (*0-16-062974-8*) USGPO.

Mosleh, A. & Bari, R. A., eds. Probabilistic Safety Assessment & Management, 4 vols. LC 98-37885. lviii, 2934p. 1998. 375.00 incl. cd-rom (*3-540-76262-0*) Spr-Verlag.

Moslen, Mary Trinen. Free Radical Mechanisms of Tissue Injury. 240p. 1992. lib. bdg. 139.00 (*0-8493-5161-8*, RB170) CRC Pr.

Mosler, Axel M., jt. auth. see Droste, Thorston.

Mosler, David & Catley, Bob. America & Americans in Australia. LC 98-6858. 224p. 1998. 59.95 (*0-275-96252-0*, Praeger Pubs) Greenwood.

***Mosler, David & Catley, Bob.** Global America: Imposing Liberalism on a Recalcitrant World. LC 99-54746. 2000. write for info. (*0-275-96662-3*, Praeger Pubs) Greenwood.

Mosler, H., ed. see International Symposium on the Judicial Settlement.

Mosler, Hermann. The International Society As a Legal Community. LC 80-50454. (Collected Courses, the Hague Academy of International Law: Vol. 140, 1974-IV). 327p. 1980. pap. text 63.00 (*90-286-0080-9*) Kluwer Academic.

Mosler, K. & Scarsini, Marco, eds. Stochastic Orders & Decision under Risk. LC 91-77909. (IMS Lecture Notes - Monographs: Vol. 19). xiv, 392p. 1992. pap. 30.00 (*0-940600-26-9*) Inst Math.

Mosler, Karl C. Cinitnous Location of Transportation Networks. (Texts & Monographs in Economics & Mathematical Systems). (Illus.). x, 158p. 1987. 49.95 (*0-387-17297-1*) Spr-Verlag.

Mosler, Karl C. & Scarsini, Marco. Stochastic Orders & Applications: A Classified Bibliography. (Lecture Notes in Economics & Mathematical Systems Ser.: Vol. 401). vi, 379p. 1993. pap. write for info. (*3-540-56956-1*) Spr-Verlag.

— Stochastic Orders & Applications: A Classified Biography. LC 93-8817. (Lecture Notes in Economics & Mathematical Systems Ser.: Vol. 401). 1993. pap. 65.00 (*0-387-56956-1*) Spr-Verlag.

Mosley. Supervisory Management. 4th ed. LC 96-24986. (GC - Principles of Management Ser.). 1996. mass mkt. 75.95 (*0-538-85560-6*) S-W Pub.

— Supervisory Management. 4th ed. (GC - Principles of Management Ser.). 1996. mass mkt., student ed. 15.95 (*0-538-85561-4*) S-W Pub.

— When I Go to Work I Feel Guilt. 1998. pap. 15.00 (*0-7225-3431-0*, 833607Q) Thorsons PA.

Mosley & Megginson, David. Supervisory Management: Art of Empowering. 3rd ed. (GC - Principles of Management Ser.). (C). 1992. mass mkt., student ed. 17.00 (*0-538-82247-3*) S-W Pub.

Mosley & Moore. Partnering. (GC - Principles of Management Ser.). 1997. text 29.95 (*0-538-84442-6*) S-W Pub.

Mosley, Albert. Introduction to Logic. (C). 1989. pap. text 28.60 (*0-536-57394-8*) Pearson Custom.

Mosley, Albert G. African Philosophy: Selected Readings. LC 95-2731. 416p. (C). 1995. pap. text 52.00 (*0-02-384181-8*, Macmillan Coll) P-H.

Mosley, Albert G. & Capaldi, Nicholas. Affirmative Action: Social Justice or Unfair Preference? (Point/Counterpoint Ser.: Vol. 94). 150p. 1996. pap. text 17.95 (*0-8476-8302-8*); lib. bdg. 51.00 (*0-8476-8301-X*) Rowman.

Mosley, C. Debrett's Guide to Bereavement. 1995. mass mkt. 17.95 (*0-7472-4425-1*, Pub. by Headline Bk Pub) Trafalgar.

Mosley, Charles, ed. Burke's Peerage & Baronetage, 2 vols. 106th ed. 3400p. 1999. lib. bdg. 395.00 (*1-57958-083-1*) Fitzroy Dearborn.

Mosley, Christopher. Colloquial Estonian. LC 93-11594. (Colloquials Ser.). 27p. (C). (gr. 13). 1994. 29.99 incl. audio (*0-415-08744-9*) Routledge.

Mosley, Christopher & Asher, R. E., eds. Atlas of the World's Languages. (Illus.). 372p. (C). (gr. 13). 1993. 675.00 (*0-415-01925-7*, A7190) Routledge.

Mosley, Daniel J. Case Implementation Reference Guide. (C). 2001. 39.00 (*0-13-177353-4*, Macmillan Coll) P-H.

— Client Server Software Testing on the Desktop & the Web Top. LC 99-26488. (Illus.). 342p. (C). 1999. 46.00 (*0-13-183880-6*) P-H.

Mosley, David L. Gesture, Sign & Song: An Interdisciplinary Approach to Schumann's Liederkreis Opus 39. LC 89-32372. (New Connections: Studies in Interdisciplinarity: Vol. 3). (Illus.). 214p. (C). 1990. text 46.95 (*0-8204-1102-7*) P Lang Pubng.

Mosley, Diana. A European Diary: Notes from the 1950s & 1960s. Guinness, Jasper, ed. 80p. 1990. 50.00 (*0-930126-29-7*) Typographeum.

— The Writing of Rebecca West. 48p. 1986. 40.00 (*0-930126-18-1*) Typographeum.

Mosley, Don & Hollyday, Joyce. With Our Own Eyes. LC 96-24455. 304p. 1996. pap. 12.99 (*0-8361-9050-5*) Herald Pr.

Mosley, Donald C., et al. Management: Leadership in Action. 5th ed. LC 95-8641. Orig. Title: Management: Concepts & Applications. (Illus.). 672p. (C). 1997. text 87.00 (*0-673-99264-0*) Addson-Wesley Educ.

***Mosley, Donald C., et al.** Supervisory Management: The Art of Empowering & Developing People. 5th ed. LC 00-33859. 2001. write for info. (*0-324-02127-5*) Sth-Wstrn College.

***Mosley, Douglas & Mosley, Naomi.** The Shadow Side of Intimate Relationships: What's Going on Behind the Scenes. (Illus.). 295p. 2000. pap. 15.95 (*1-880823-22-5*, Pub. by N Star Pubns) Midpt Trade.

Mosley, Francis. The Dinosaur Eggs. (Illus.). 30p. (J). (ps-2). 1992. pap. 5.95 (*0-8120-4959-4*) Barron.

Mosley, Francis. Myths & Legends. LC 93-11878. (Story Library). 260p. (Orig.). (J). (gr. 1 up). 1994. pap. 7.95 (*1-85697-975-X*) LKC.

Mosley-Howard, Susan. Human Development in Education. 144p. (C). 1995. pap. text, spiral bd. 23.95 (*0-7872-1035-8*) Kendall-Hunt.

Mosley, Hugh G., jt. auth. see Koning, J. De.

***Mosley, Ivo.** Chistmas in Africa: An Erotic Fable. 2000. pap. 3.95 (*1-86092-018-7*, Pub. by Travelman Pub) IPG Chicago.

— Dumbing Down: Culture, Politics & the Mass Media. 2000. pap. text 19.95 (*0-907845-65-7*, Pub. by Imprint Acad) Philos Document.

Mosley, J. G. Palliation in Malignant Disease. (Illus.). 170p. 1988. text 60.00 (*0-443-03690-X*) Church.

Mosley, J. R., Sr. Biblical Explanation of the Church's Covenant: Preaching from the Covenant. 1990. pap. text. write for info. (*0-9627958-2-8*) J R Mosleys Pr.

— Christian Men's Union Brotherhood Guide. 51p. 1990. pap. text 3.50 (*0-9627958-0-1*, TXU 371-442) J R Mosleys Pr.

Mosley, J. R. Ordination for Deacons. 4p. (Orig.). 1997. pap. 4.00 (*0-9627958-3-6*) J R Mosleys Pr.

Mosley, J. R., Sr. Resolutions for Funeral, Welcome Addresses, & Responses for Special Occasions & Annual Days. 1990. pap. text 2.50 (*0-9627958-1-X*) J R Mosleys Pr.

Mosley, J. R. What to Do with Grief: Grief Viewed from a Christian Perspective. 29p. 1999. pap. write for info. (*0-9627958-4-4*) J R Mosleys Pr.

Mosley, James L. Snore No More. (Modern Technology & Information Ser.). (Illus.). 80p. 4.95 (*0-685-51586-9*) Son Rise Pubns.

— Snore No More: How to Make Your Family Members Stop Snoring. 2nd rev. ed. (Illus.). 180p. 1997. pap. 12.95 (*0-936369-67-1*) Son-Rise Pubns.

Mosley, Janice, jt. auth. see Breeden, Terri.

Mosley, Jean B. Seeds on the Wind. 220p. 1994. text 25.00 (*0-9642039-0-1*) Concord Printing.

***Mosley, Jenny.** Quality Circle Time in the Secondary School: A Handbook of Good Practice. (Illus.). 160p. 1999. pap. 29.95 (*1-85346-616-6*) David Fulton.

Mosley, Jenny, jt. auth. see Gillibrand, Eileen.

Mosley, John. The Christmas Star. (Illus.). 76p. (Orig.). 1988. pap. 3.95 (*0-919874-0-5*) Griffith Observ.

— Stargazing for Advanced Beginners: A User-Friendly Guide for Locating Stars, Planets & Other Deep-Space Objects. LC 98-6316. (Illus.). 144p. 1998. pap. 18.00 (*1-56565-960-0*, 09600W, Pub. by Lowell Hse) NTC Contemp Pub Co.

— Stargazing for Beginners: A User-Friendly Guide for Locating & Understanding Constellations. LC 97-35739. (Illus.). 128p. 1997. pap. 17.00 (*1-56565-821-3*, 08213W, Pub. by Lowell Hse) NTC Contemp Pub Co.

— The Ultimate Guide to the Sky. 80p. (J). Date not set. pap. 9.95 (*1-56565-596-6*, 05855W, Pub. by Lowell Hse) NTC Contemp Pub Co.

Mosley, K. F. The Human Dilemma. 128p. 1984. 35.00 (*0-7212-0658-1*, Pub. by Regency Pr GBR) St Mut.

Mosley, Kim. Study Guide for Photo/Imaging. 4th ed. 44p. (C). 1997. pap. text 6.00 (*0-88196-010-1*) Oak Woods Media.

Mosley, Leonard. Duel for Kilimanjaro. 21.95 (*0-89190-158-2*) Amereon Ltd.

***Mosley, Leonard.** Lindbergh: A Biography. 2000. pap. 12.95 (*0-486-40964-3*) Dover.

Mosley, M. Berries! Berries! Berries! (Illus.). 176p. 1997. spiral bd. 5.95 (*1-57166-086-0*) Hearts N Tummies.

— Nuts! Nuts! Nuts! (Illus.). 176p. 1997. spiral bd. 5.95 (*1-57166-091-7*) Hearts N Tummies.

— Peaches! Peaches! Peaches! (Illus.). 176p. 1997. spiral bd. 5.95 (*1-57166-088-7*) Hearts N Tummies.

— Pumpkins! Pumpkins! Pumpkins! (Illus.). 176p. 1997. spiral bd. 5.95 (*1-57166-087-9*) Hearts N Tummies.

Mosley, Marilyn C. Dachshund Tails Down the Yukon. (Dachshund Tails Ser.: No. 3). (Illus.). 112p. (Orig.). (J). (gr. 5). 1988. pap. 5.95 (*0-9614850-2-7*) M C Mosley.

— Dachshund Tails North. LC 82-90167. (Dachshund Tails Ser.: No. 1). (Illus.). 50p. (Orig.). (J). (gr. 5). 1982. pap. 4.95 (*0-9614850-0-0*) M C Mosley.

— Dachshund Tails up the Inside Passage. LC 84-90672. (Dachshund Tails Ser.: No. 2). (Illus.). 95p. (Orig.). (J). (gr. 5). 1984. pap. 4.95 (*0-9614850-1-9*) M C Mosley.

Mosley, Marilyn C., et al, eds. Alaskan Ferry Tales for Children. LC 89-80605. (Illus.). 112p. (Orig.). (J). 1989. pap. 6.95 (*0-9614850-3-5*) M C Mosley.

Mosley, Melissa M. Community Planning Kit. (Illus.). 240p. (Orig.). 1997. write for info. (*0-614-23616-9*) Quixote.

— Family Planning Kit for in-Home Elder Care. (Illus.). 240p. (Orig.). 1996. pap. write for info. (*0-614-23617-7*) Quixote.

Mosley, Naomi, jt. auth. see Mosley, Douglas.

Mosley, Nicholas. Accident. LC 85-72479. 198p. 1985. reprint ed. pap. 11.95 (*0-916583-11-2*) Dalkey Arch.

— Assassins. rev. ed. LC 96-51795. 256p. 1997. reprint ed. pap. 12.95 (*1-56478-152-6*) Dalkey Arch.

— Catastrophe Practice. rev. ed. LC 88-30391. 342p. 1989. 19.95 (*0-916583-35-X*) Dalkey Arch.

— Children of Darkness & Light. LC 96-51797. 248p. 1997. pap. 13.95 (*1-56478-151-8*) Dalkey Arch.

— Efforts at Truth. LC 94-37597. 345p. 1995. 22.95 (*1-56478-075-9*) Dalkey Arch.

— Hopeful Monsters. A Novel. LC 91-13076. 551p. 1991. 21.95 (*0-916583-85-6*) Dalkey Arch.

***Mosley, Nicholas.** Hopeful Monsters: A Novel. LC 00-20968. 551p. 2000. pap. 14.95 (*1-56478-242-5*, Pub. by Dalkey Arch) Chicago Distribution Ctr.

— Imago Bird. LC 00-20971. 186p. 2000. pap. 11.95 (*1-56478-243-3*, Pub. by Dalkey Arch) Chicago Distribution Ctr.

Mosley, Nicholas. Imago Bird. rev. ed. LC 88-30392. 180p. 1989. 19.95 (*0-916583-36-8*) Dalkey Arch.

— Impossible Object. LC 85-72480. 219p. 1985. reprint ed. pap. 9.95 (*0-916583-09-0*) Dalkey Arch.

— Judith. 298p. 1992. reprint ed. pap. 10.95 (*0-916583-77-5*) Dalkey Arch.

— Judith. rev. ed. LC 90-3636. 298p. 1991. 19.95 (*0-916583-69-4*) Dalkey Arch.

— Natalie Natalia. 2nd rev. ed. LC 96-132. 278p. 1996. pap. 12.95 (*1-56478-086-4*) Dalkey Arch.

— Rules of the Game - Beyond the Pale: Memoirs of Sir Oswald Mosley & Family. LC 90-14042. (Illus.). 600p. 1991. 27.50 (*0-916583-75-9*) Dalkey Arch.

— Serpent. rev. ed. LC 89-35214. 190p. 1990. 19.95 (*0-916583-49-X*) Dalkey Arch.

Mosley, O. Policy & Debate. 1972. 59.95 (*0-8490-0869-7*) Gordon Pr.

— Tomorrow We Live. 1973. 59.95 (*0-8490-1221-X*) Gordon Pr.

Mosley, Oswald. Two Germans of Genius. 44p. 1987. 30.00 (*0-930126-22-X*) Typographeum.

Mosley, Oswald & Quill, Michael. Revolution by Reason & Other Essays. LC 97-42852. (Studies in British History: Vol. 45). 320p. 1997. 99.95 (*0-7734-8429-9*) E Mellen.

Mosley, Oswald E. The Alternative. 1972. 59.95 (*0-87968-592-1*) Gordon Pr.

Mosley, Pat & Crocker, John. Sensor Materials. LC 96-20098. (Sensors Ser.). (Illus.). 196p. 1996. 150.00 (*0-7503-0015-9*) IOP Pub.

Mosley, Patrick A. The Lighter Side of Stained Glass. (Illus.). 90p. 1984. pap. 6.95 (*0-917661-00-1*) P Mosley.

Mosley, Paul. Conditionality As Bargaining Process: Structural-Adjustment Lending. LC 87-25806. (Essays in International Finance Ser.: No. 168). 40p. 1987. pap. text 10.00 (*0-88165-075-7*) Princeton U Int Finan Econ.

— Foreign Aid: Its Defense & Reform. LC 86-23400. 280p. 1987. 36.00 (*0-8131-1608-2*) U Pr of Ky.

— The Making of Economic Policy: Theory & Evidence from Britain & the United States since 1945. LC 83-40518. 240p. 1984. text 29.95 (*0-312-50688-0*) St Martin.

Mosley, Paul, et al. Aid & Power: The World Bank & Policy-Based Lending, Vol. 1. 2nd ed. LC 95-19175. 368p. (C). 1995. pap. 29.99 (*0-415-13210-X*) Routledge.

— Aid & Power: The World Bank & Policy-Based Lending, Vol. 1. 2nd ed. LC 95-19175. 368p. (C). (gr. 13). 1995. 100.00 (*0-415-13209-6*) Routledge.

— Aid & Power Vol. 2: The World Bank & Policy-Based Lending. 416p. 1991. 89.95 (*0-415-06077-X*, A5485) Routledge.

***Mosley, Philip.** Split Screen: Belgian Cinema & Cultural Identity. (C). 2000. pap. text 23.95 (*0-7914-4748-0*) State U NY Pr.

— Split Screen: Belgian Cinema & Cultural Identity. (C). 2000. text 71.50 (*0-7914-4747-2*) State U NY Pr.

Mosley, Philip, ed. Georges Rodenbach: Critical Essays. LC 95-17061. (Illus.). 208p. 1996. 34.50 (*0-8386-3588-1*) Fairleigh Dickinson.

Mosley, Philip, tr. see Rodenbach, Georges.

Mosley, Philip, tr. see Vaes, Guy.

Mosley, Pixey Anne, jt. ed. see Arant, Wendi.

Mosley, R. J., tr. see Moiseev, Yu V. & Zaikov, G. E.

Mosley, R. K. Westminster Workshop: A Student's Guide to British Government. 249p. 1985. pap. text 20.00 (*0-08-031835-5*, Pergamon Pr) Elsevier.

Mosley, Rosa M. Tame Your Tongue! Learn English Using the Bible, Vol. 1. (Illus.). vii, 123p. (Orig.). 1997. pap. text 25.00 (*0-9657229-0-2*) ROSAL Intl.

Mosley, Shawn. The Breaking Point. 130p. (Orig.). 1996. pap. 7.95 (*1-885342-06-3*) Creative Ways.

Mosley, Stephen. Deepen My Heart: Making Room for the Fullness of God. LC 98-13668. 224p. (Orig.). 1998. pap. 10.99 (*0-8280-1285-7*) Review & Herald.

M

Mosley, Steven. Burned Out on Being Good: What to Do if Your Religion Is Wearing You Out. Robinson, Glen, ed. LC 97-35337. 156p. 1998. pap. 8.99 (*0-8163-1578-7*) Pacific Pr Pub Assn.
— If Only God Would Answer. LC 97-132417. 208p. 1998. pap. 9.99 (*0-8280-1254-7*) Review & Herald.

Mosley, Steven, jt. auth. see Finley, Mark.

Mosley, Steven R. Deepen My Heart. LC 98-13668. 1998. 10.99 (*0-8280-1256-3*) Review & Herald.

***Mosley, Steven R.** Your Religion Is Too Small: Breaking Out of a Small View of Faith. Thomas, Jerry D., ed. LC 00-23567. 191p. 2000. pap. 11.99 (*0-8163-1782-8*) Pacific Pr Pub Assn.

Mosley, Steven R., jt. auth. see Finley, Mark.

Mosley, Thomas E. Marketing Your Invention. 2nd ed. LC 97-2315. 1997. pap. 22.95 (*1-57410-072-6*, 6100-1702) Dearborn.

Mosley, W. H. & Bungey, J. H. Reinforced Concrete Design. 3rd ed. (Illus.). 399p. (C). 1987. pap. text 31.50 (*0-333-45183-X*) Scholium Intl.
— Reinforced Concrete Design. 4th ed. (Civil Engineering Ser.). (Illus.). 401p. (C). 1991. pap. text 32.50 (*0-333-53718-1*) Scholium Intl.

Mosley, W. H., jt. auth. see Hulse, R.

M

Mosley, Walter. Always Outnumbered, Always Outgunned. LC 96-54870. 224p. 1997. 23.00 (*0-393-04539-0*) Norton.
— Always Outnumbered, Always Outgunned. 208p. 1998. per. 14.00 (*0-671-01499-4*) S&S Trade.
— Always Outnumbered, Always Outgunned. large type ed. LC 97-38618. 360p. 1998. 28.95 (*0-7862-1268-3*) Mac Lib Ref.
— Black Betty. LC 94-6839. 255p. 1994. 19.95 (*0-393-03644-8*) Norton.
— Black Betty. 368p. 1995. per. 6.50 (*0-671-88427-1*, Pocket Books) PB.
— Black Betty. 344p. 1997. per. 14.00 (*0-671-01983-X*) PB.
— Black Betty. large type ed. LC 94-5385. 520p. 1994. lib. bdg. 23.95 (*0-7862-0323-4*) Thorndike Pr.
— Blue Light. LC 98-18975. 304p. (gr. 8). 1998. 24.00 (*0-316-57098-2*) Little.
— Blue Light. 400p. 1999. mass mkt. 6.99 (*0-446-60692-8*, Pub. by Warner Bks) Little.
— Blue Light. LC 99-10600. 1999. write for info. (*1-56895-639-8*) Wheeler Pub.
— Devil in a Blue Dress. LC 89-25503. 219p. 1990. 19.95 (*0-393-02854-2*) Norton.
— Devil in a Blue Dress. 1997. per. 14.00 (*0-671-01982-1*) PB.
— Devil in a Blue Dress, abr. ed. (Easy Rawlins Mystery Ser.). 1993. audio 16.95 (*1-55927-238-4*, 390653, Pub. by Audio Renaissance) Lndmrk Audiobks.
— Devil in a Blue Dress. large type ed. LC 93-16667. 336p. 1993. lib. bdg. 20.95 (*1-56054-722-7*) Thorndike Pr.
— Devil in a Blue Dress. Ryan, Kevin, ed. 240p. 1995. reprint ed. mass mkt. 6.50 (*0-671-51142-4*) PB.
— Gone Fishin' An Easy Rawlins Novel. 244p. 1998. per. 6.50 (*0-671-01011-5*) PB.
— Gone Fishin' An Easy Rawlins Novel. large type ed. LC 97-4107. (Americana Series). 202p. 1997. 27.95 (*0-7862-1060-5*) Thorndike Pr.
— Gone Fishin' An Easy Rawlins Novel. 256p. 1999. reprint ed. pap. 14.00 (*0-671-02746-8*, PB Trade Paper) PB.
— A Little Yellow Dog: An Easy Rawlins Mystery. LC 96-4231. 300p. 1996. 23.00 (*0-393-03924-2*) Norton.
— A Little Yellow Dog: An Easy Rawlins Mystery. 1997. per. 6.50 (*0-671-88429-8*) PB.
— A Little Yellow Dog: An Easy Rawlins Mystery. 1997. per. 14.00 (*0-671-01986-4*, PB Trade Paper) PB.
— A Little Yellow Dog: An Easy Rawlins Mystery. large type ed. LC 96-24353. 1996. 26.95 (*0-7862-0810-4*) Thorndike Pr.

Mosley, Walter. A Little Yellow Dog: An Easy Rawlins Mystery. limited ed. 100.00 (*0-393-03978-1*) Norton.

Mosley, Walter. The Man in My Basement. 2000. write for info. (*0-316-57082-6*) Little.
— A Red Death. LC 90-23660. 284p. 1991. 19.95 (*0-393-02998-0*) Norton.
— A Red Death. 1997. per. 14.00 (*0-671-01984-8*) PB.
— A Red Death. large type ed. LC 93-18588. 41p. 1993. lib. bdg. 21.95 (*1-56054-723-5*) Thorndike Pr.
— A Red Death. Chelius, Jane, ed. 256p. 1992. reprint ed. mass mkt. 6.50 (*0-671-74989-7*) PB.
— Red Death Promotion with Yellow Dog. (An Easy Rawlins Mystery Ser.). 1997. per. 3.99 (*0-671-01006-9*, Pocket Books) PB.
— RL's Dream. 288p. 1995. 22.00 (*0-393-03802-5*) Norton.
— RL's Dream. 272p. 1996. pap. 14.00 (*0-671-88428-X*) PB.
— RL's Dream. 1996. pap. 12.00 (*0-614-97796-7*, WSP) PB.

***Mosley, Walter.** Walkin' the Dog. LC 99-16407. 272p. (gr. 8). 1999. 24.95 (*0-316-96620-7*) Little.

Mosley, Walter. Walkin' the Dog. 2000. 14.95 (*0-316-57054-0*) Little.

***Mosley, Walter.** Walkin' the Dog. 288p. 2000. pap. 13.95 (*0-316-88171-6*, Back Bay) Little.
— Walkin' the Dog. large type ed. LC 99-89945. 370p. 2000. 31.95 (*0-7838-8961-5*, G K Hall Lrg Type) Mac Lib Ref.
— Walkin' the Dog. large type ed. LC 99-89945. 2000. pap. 29.95 (*0-7838-8962-3*, G K Hall & Co) Mac Lib Ref.

Mosley, Walter. White Butterfly. LC 91-44700. 256p. 1992. 19.95 (*0-393-03366-X*) Norton.
— White Butterfly. 1997. per. 14.00 (*0-671-01985-6*) PB.
— White Butterfly. large type ed. LC 93-16668. 389p. 1993. lib. bdg. 20.95 (*1-56054-724-3*) Thorndike Pr.
— White Butterfly. Chelius, Jane, ed. 394p. 1993. reprint ed. mass mkt. 6.50 (*0-671-86787-3*) PB.

***Mosley, Walter.** Workin' on the Chain Gang: Shaking off the Dead Hand of History. LC 99-16196. (Library of Contemporary Thought). 128p. 2000. 16.95 (*0-345-43069-7*) Ballantine Pub Grp.

Mosley, Walter, et al, eds. Black Genius: African American Solutions to African American Problems. LC 98-39663. (Illus.). 320p. 1999. 24.95 (*0-393-04701-6*) Norton.
— Black Genius: African American Solutions to African American Problems. 320p. 2000. pap. 14.95 (*0-393-31978-4*, Norton Paperbks) Norton.

Mosley, William. What Color Was Jesus? (Illus.). 67p. 1987. pap. 9.95 (*0-913543-09-8*) African Am Imag.

Moslow, T. F., jt. auth. see Rhodes, E. G.

Mosman, Chesley A. The Rough Side of War: The Civil War Journal of Chesley A. Mosman, 1st Lieutenant, Company D, 59th Illinois Volunteer Infantry Regiment, 1862-1866. (Illus.). 448p. 1987. 25.00 (*0-940591-06-5*) Basin Pub.

Mosman, Karen, ed. see Connolly, et al.

Mosman, Richard A. This Irritating World We Live In. (Illus.). 1989. pap. write for info. (*0-318-65828-3*) R A Mosman.

Mosmann, Charles. Evaluating Instructional Computing: Measuring Needs & Resources for Computing in Higher Education. 88p. 1977. 12.00 (*0-318-14018-7*) EDUCOM.

Mosmann, Charles J. Academic Computers in Service. LC 72-13602. (Jossey-Bass Higher Education Ser.). 202p. reprint ed. pap. 62.70 (*0-8357-5027-2*, 202566500045) Bks Demand.

Mosmann, Charles J., ed. Statewide Computing Systems: Coordinating Academic Computer Planning. LC 74-24337. (Books in Library & Information Science: Vol. 10). 215p. reprint ed. pap. 66.70 (*0-608-17052-6*, 202711900054) Bks Demand.

Mosmiller, Thomas E., jt. ed. see Kimmel, Michael S.

Mosnaim, Aron D. & Wolf, Marion E., eds. Noncatecholic Phenylethylamines Pt. 1: Phenylethylamine: Biological Mechanisms & Clinical Aspects. LC 77-26130. (Modern Pharmacology-Toxicology Ser.: No. 12). (Illus.). 552p. 1978. reprint ed. pap. 171.20 (*0-608-01192-4*, 206076800001) Bks Demand.
— Noncatecholic Phenylethylamines Pt. 2: Phenylethanolamine, Tyramines, & Octapamine. LC 77-26130. (Modern Pharmacology-Toxicology Ser.: No. 12). (Illus.). 383p. 1980. reprint ed. pap. 118.80 (*0-608-00253-4*, 206076800002) Bks Demand.

Mosnaim, Aron D., jt. ed. see Wolf, Marion E.

Mosner, Elizabeth M., ed. Vital Records of Knox, Maine Prior to 1892. 183p. 1996. 65.00 (*0-89725-277-2*, 1776) Picton Pr.

Mosocco, Ronald A. The Chronological Tracking of the American Civil War per the Official Records of the War of the Rebellion. 2nd rev. ed. LC 94-76315. (Illus.). 464p. (C). 1995. lib. bdg. 39.95 (*0-9641675-9-X*) James River.

Mosolov, Peter Petrovich, jt. auth. see Maslov, V. P.

Mosonyi, Emil. Water Power Development, Vol. 1. 1074p. (C). 1987. 350.00 (*0-569-09084-9*, Pub. by Collets) St Mut.
— Water Power Development, Vol. 2. 748p. (C). 1965. 350.00 (*0-7855-4956-0*, Pub. by Collets) St Mut.
— Water Power Development Vol. 1: Low Head Power Plants, Vol. 1. 1074p. (C). 1995. pap. 495.00 (*963-05-4271-4*, Pub. by Akade Kiado) St Mut.
— Water Power Development Vol. II, Pts. A & B: High Head Power Plants. 1091p. (C). 1991. pap. 595.00 (*963-05-5885-8*, Pub. by Akade Kiado) St Mut.

Mosotf, Zachary Mumbo, tr. see Doyle, Arthur Conan.

Mosquera, Cristobal. Poesias Ineditas de Cristobal Mosquera. Diaz Plaja, Guillermo, ed. (SPA.). 239p. 1968. pap. 100.00 (*0-614-00213-3*) Elliots Bks.

Mosquera, Gerardo, ed. Beyond the Fantastic: Contemporary Art Criticism from Latin America. LC 95-82047. (Illus.). 352p. 1996. pap. text 26.95 (*0-262-63172-5*) MIT Pr.

Mosquera, Gerardo, jt. auth. see Zeitlin, Marilyn A.

Moss. Design of Digital Systems. 7th ed. 1997. pap. text, lab manual ed. 25.35 (*0-13-745894-0*) P-H.
— Emma's Journal. LC 98-27974. 56p. (J). (gr. 3-5). 1999. 15.00 (*0-15-202025-X*) Harcourt.
— Java 1999. write for info. (*0-07-135187-6*) McGraw.
— Noninvasive Electrocardiology. 1995. text 65.00 (*0-7020-1925-9*, W B Saunders Co) Harcrt Hlth Sci Grp.
— Operating Costs & Energy Management in Buildings. LC 97-65933. (Illus.). 200p. (C). 1997. pap. 45.00 (*0-419-21770-3*, E & FN Spon) Routledge.

***Moss.** Rose's Journal. 2001. write for info. (*0-15-202423-9*) Harcourt.

Moss. The Town House. 1995. 39.95 (*0-8050-1398-9*) H Holt & Co.

Moss & Johnston. Collaborations Inter High, 4. (Global ESL/ELT Ser.). 112p. (J). 1996. pap. 14.95 (*0-8384-6634-6*); pap., wbk. ed. 9.95 (*0-8384-6635-4*) Heinle & Heinle.
— Collaborations Inter High, 4. (Global ESL/ELT Ser.). (J). 1997. suppl. ed. 57.95 (*0-8384-6638-9*); text, suppl. ed. 50.95 (*0-8384-6641-9*) Heinle & Heinle.
— Collaborations Inter High, 4. (Global ESL/ELT Ser.). (J). 1997. mass mkt., teacher ed. 18.95 (*0-8384-6643-5*) Heinle & Heinle.

Moss, jt. auth. see Pierce.

Moss & Yale Staff. Employment Opportunity. LC 99-48716. 266p. 1999. pap. text 37.33 (*0-205-29800-1*) Allyn.

Moss, Abigail J. Plan & Operation of the National Employer Health Insurance Survey LC 99-25082. (DHHS Publication Ser.). 1999. write for info. (*0-8406-0553-6*) Natl Ctr Health Stats.

Moss, Adrian. HIV & AIDS: Management by the Primary Care Team. (Practical Guides for General Practice Ser.: No. 16). 112p. 1992. pap. text 21.95 (*0-19-262216-1*) OUP.

Moss, Alan. Beginner's Guide to Still Life Drawing. 1993. 12.98 (*1-55521-852-0*) Bk Sales Inc.

***Moss, Alan L. & Yale, Donald G.** Employment Opportunity: Outlook, Reason & Reality. 260p. (C). 1999. 28.00 incl. cd-rom (*0-13-018203-6*) P-H.

Moss, Albert A., et al, eds. Computed Tomography of the Body: With Magnetic Resonance Imaging, 3 vols. 2nd ed. (Illus.). 1477p. 1991. text 299.00 (*0-7216-2415-4*, W B Saunders Co) Harcrt Hlth Sci Grp.
— Computed Tomography of the Body Vol. 1: With Magnetic Resonance Imaging: Thorax & Neck. 2nd ed. (Illus.). 492p. 1991. text 155.00 (*0-7216-4358-2*, W B Saunders Co) Harcrt Hlth Sci Grp.
— Computed Tomography of the Body Vol. 2: With Magnetic Resonance Imaging: Bone & Joint, Vol. 2. 2nd ed. (Illus.). 492p. 1991. text 75.00 (*0-7216-4359-0*, W B Saunders Co) Harcrt Hlth Sci Grp.
— Computed Tomography of the Body Vol. 3: With Magnetic Resonance Imaging: Abdomen, Vol. 3. 2nd ed. (Illus.). 493p. 1991. text 199.00 (*0-7216-4503-8*, W B Saunders Co) Harcrt Hlth Sci Grp.

Moss, Alfred A. The American Negro Academy: Voice of the Talented Tenth. fac. ed. LC 80-18026. 349p. 1981. reprint ed. pap. 108.20 (*0-7837-7806-6*, 204756200007) Bks Demand.

Moss, Alfred A., Jr. From Slavery to Freedom: A History of Negro Americans. 7th ed. (C). 1994. pap., student ed. 13.75 (*0-07-021908-7*) McGraw.

Moss, Alfred A., Jr., jt. auth. see Anderson, Eric.

Moss, Alfred A., Jr., jt. auth. see Franklin, John H.

Moss, Alfred A., Jr., jt. ed. see Anderson, Eric.

Moss, Alison, ed. Catalogue of British Official Publications Not Published by HMSO, 1983. 500p. 1984. lib. bdg. write for info. (*0-85964-132-5*) Chadwyck-Healey.

Moss, Alwyn, ed. see Moss, Ann E.

Moss, Ambler H., Jr., ed. Assessments of the North American Free Trade Agreement: Assessments of the North American Free Trade Agreement. LC 93-39473. 120p. (C). 1995. pap. 16.95 (*1-56000-730-3*, Pub. by U Miami N-S Ctr) L Rienner.

Moss, Andy, ed. see Clement, Richard.

Moss, Anita & Stott, Don. The Family of Stories: An Anthology of Children's Literature. 672p. (C). 1986. pap. text 53.00 (*0-03-921832-5*, Pub. by Harcourt Coll Pubs) Harcourt.

***Moss, Ann.** Latin Commentaries on Ovid from the Renaissance. LC 98-46745. (Library of Renaissance Humanism). 1998. write for info. (*1-893009-02-5*) Summertown.

Moss, Ann. Printed Commonplace-Books & the Structuring of Renaissance Thought. 358p. (C). 1996. text 85.00 (*0-19-815908-0*) OUP.

Moss, Ann E. Friends of Tinkle the Cat Rescue Club. Moss, Alwyn, ed. LC 90-24192. (Illus.). 96p. 1991. pap. 8.95 (*0-936015-27-6*) Pocahontas Pr.

Moss, Anne, jt. auth. see Church, Nancy.

Moss, Anne, jt. auth. see Zimmer-Loew, Helene.

Moss, Austin P., ed. Wines & Vines of Napa County: Coles' Insider's Guide. (Insiders Guide Ser.). (Illus.). 280p. (Orig.). 1991. pap. 11.95 (*0-929635-06-X*) Cole Pub Co Inc.
— The Wines & Vines of Sonoma County. LC 90-1763. (Insiders Guide Ser.). 280p. (Orig.). 1990. pap. 9.95 (*0-929635-01-9*) Cole Pub Co Inc.

Moss, B. Ecology of Fresh Waters: Man & Medium. 2nd ed. (Illus.). 432p. 1988. pap. text 49.95 (*0-632-01642-6*) Blackwell Sci.

***Moss, B.** Ecology of Fresh Waters: Man & Medium, Past to Future. 3rd ed. LC 97-35549. (Illus.). 557p. 1998. pap. 49.95 (*0-632-03512-9*) Blackwell Sci.

Moss, Barbara G., jt. ed. see Collins, Martha D.

***Moss, Barbara Robinette.** Change Me into Zeus' Daughter. 2000. 24.00 (*0-7432-0218-X*) Scribner.

Moss, Basil. Tales of the Wichitas. LC 97-41841. 224p. 1998. 25.95 (*0-89672-390-9*) Tex Tech Univ Pr.

***Moss, Bernard H.** Single European Currency National. 2000. text 21.95 (*0-312-23031-1*) St Martin.

Moss, Beverly J. Literacy Across Communities. Farr, Marcia, ed. LC 94-7395. (Written Language Ser.). 240p. (C). 1994. text 47.50 (*1-881303-61-6*); pap. text 21.95 (*1-881303-62-4*) Hampton Pr NJ.

Moss, Bill, jt. auth. see Applewhaite, Charles.

***Moss, Bobby G.** Roster of the Loyalists in the Battle of Kings Mountain LC 98-90635. xviii, 162p. 1998. write for info. (*0-9626172-4-5*) Scotia Hibernia Pr.

Moss, Bobby G., jt. auth. see Hopper, C. G., Jr.

Moss, C., jt. auth. see Savin, J. A.

Moss, Carol. Science in Mesopotamia. (Illus.). 64p. (J). (gr. 4-6). 1999. pap. 8.95 (*0-531-15930-2*) Watts.

***Moss, Carolyn J.** Pen Photographs of Charles Dicken's Readings: Taken from Life. LC 97-61395. (Illus.). xx, 101p. (C). 1998. 28.50 (*0-87875-495-4*) Whitston Pub.

Moss, Carolyn J., ed. Kate Field: Selected Letters. LC 96-10190. (Illus.). 304p. (C). 1996. 49.95 (*0-8093-2078-9*) S Ill U Pr.

Moss, Carolyn J., jt. auth. see Moss, Sidney P.

Moss, Carolyn J., jt. auth. see Moss, Sydney P.

Moss, Charlotte. Creating Room. 1999. pap. 14.95 (*0-14-025659-8*) Viking Penguin.
— Passion for Detail. 192p. 1991. 42.50 (*0-385-26760-6*) Doubleday.
— Room Service: A Step-by-Step Guide to Accessorizing Your Home. LC 94-16052. (Illus.). 144p. 1995. 29.95 (*0-670-84799-2*, Viking Studio) Studio Bks.

Moss, Charlotte, ed. The Poetry of Home. (Illus.). 152p. 1998. 29.95 (*0-9669503-0-5*, Boxwood Press) CM Retail.

Moss, Cheryl T., et al. Healthy Hair Care Tips for Today's Black Woman. (Illus.). 130p. 1999. pap. 13.99 (*0-9671491-0-X*) Talley Pubg.

Moss, Claude S. Dreams, Images & Fantasy: A Semantic Differential Casebook. LC 79-105543. 317p. reprint ed. pap. 98.30 (*0-608-30237-6*, 202278100029) Bks Demand.

Moss, Cynthia. Elephant Memories. large type ed. (Charnwood Library). (Illus.). 448p. 1992. 27.99 (*0-7089-8638-2*) Ulverscroft.

***Moss, Cynthia.** Elephant Memories: Thirteen Years in the Life of an Elephant Family. (Illus.). 1999. pap. 18.00 (*0-226-54237-8*) U Ch Pr.

Moss, Cynthia. Little Big Ears. LC 96-7404. (Illus.). 40p. (J). (gr. k-5). 1996. per. 17.00 (*0-689-80031-2*) S&S Bks Yung.
— Portraits in the Wild: Animal Behavior in East Africa. LC 81-23092. (Illus.). 1996. pap. 15.95 (*0-226-54233-5*) U Ch Pr.

Moss, D. W. & Butterworth, P. J. Enzymology & Medicine. (Illus.). 1974. pap. text 60.00 (*0-272-00094-9*) St Mut.

Moss, Danny, ed. Public Relations in Practice: A Casebook. 240p. (C). (gr. 13). 1990. pap. 65.00 (*0-415-05528-8*, A4893) Thomson Learn.

Moss, Danny & McManus, Toby. Public Relations Research: An International Perspective. 256p. 1997. pap. 74.95 (*0-415-10995-7*) Thomson Learn.

***Moss, Danny, et al.** Perspectives on Public Relations Research. LC 99-16205. (Advances in Management & Business Studies). 232p. 1999. 90.00 (*0-415-21767-9*) Routledge.

Moss, David. The Song of David: The Moss Haggadah, 2. (ENG & HEB., Illus.). 340p. 1987. pap. write for info. (*0-9624473-2-3*) Bet Alpha Editions.
— The Song of David: The Moss Haggadah, I. (ENG & HEB., Illus.). 340p. 1987. write for info. (*0-9624473-1-5*) Bet Alpha Editions.
— The Song of David: The Moss Haggadah, Set, Vols. 1 & 2. deluxe limited ed. LC 87-206430. (ENG & HEB., Illus.). 340p. 1987. pap. 6500.00 (*0-9624473-0-7*) Bet Alpha Editions.

Moss, David, jt. ed. see Misztal, Barbara A.

Moss, David A. Socializing Security: Progressive-Era Economists & the Origins of American Social Policy. LC 95-20652. 256p. (C). 1995. text 43.00 (*0-674-81502-5*) HUP.

Moss, David J. Thomas Attwood: The Biography of a Radical. 400p. 1990. text 65.00 (*0-7735-0708-6*, Pub. by McG-Queens Univ Pr) CUP Services.

Moss, Deborah. Lee, the Rabbit with Epilepsy. LC 88-40249. (Illus.). 32p. (J). (ps up). 1989. lib. bdg. 12.95 (*0-933149-32-8*) Woodbine House.
— Shelley, the Hyperactive Turtle. LC 88-40248. (Illus.). 24p. (J). (ps-3). 1989. lib. bdg. 12.95 (*0-933149-31-X*) Woodbine House.

Moss, Dena Simone. The Joffrey School's Book of Ballet Fitness. LC 98-23501. (Illus.). 256p. 1999. pap. 21.95 (*0-312-19470-6*, St Martin Griffin) St Martin.

Moss, Dennis R. Pressure Vessel Design Manual. 2nd ed. LC 97-24025. 1997. 115.00 (*0-88415-647-8*, 5647) Gulf Pub.
— Pressure Vessel Design Manual: Illustrated Procedures for Solving Every Major Pressure Vessel Design Problem. LC 87-360. (Illus.). 236p. 1987. 89.00 (*0-87201-719-2*, 1719) Gulf Pub.

Moss, Donald, ed. Humanistic Psychology: A Historical & Biographical Sourcebook. LC 97-32965. (Schools of Psychological Thought Ser.). 480p. 1999. lib. bdg. 95.00 (*0-313-29158-6*, Greenwood Pr) Greenwood.

Moss, Donald W. & Rosalki, Sydney B., eds. Enzyme Tests in Diagnosis. (Illus.). 272p. 1996. pap. text 55.00 (*0-340-55245-X*, Pub. by E A) OUP.

Moss, Donna. How I Praise You! 150 Little Psalms in Song. LC 98-96170. (Illus.). 240p. (J). (ps-8). 1998. otabind 15.95 (*0-9663809-2-4*) Apex Pubg Svcs.

Moss, E. H. Flora of Alberta. 2nd ed. (Illus.). 704p. 1983. text 70.00 (*0-8020-2508-0*) U of Toronto Pr.

***Moss, Edna J.** Basic Keyboarding for Medical Office Assistant, IML. 2nd ed. 100p. 1999. teacher ed. 14.95 (*0-7668-0924-2*) Delmar.

Moss, Edna J. Basic Keyboarding for the Medical Office Assistant. 2nd ed. LC 98-53985. (Medical Assisting Ser.). (C). 1999. pap. 32.95 (*0-7668-0923-4*) Delmar.

Moss, Edward. The Grammar of Consciousness: An Exploration of Tacit Knowing. LC 94-18454. 256p. 1995. text 59.95 (*0-312-12222-5*) St Martin.

Moss, Elaine. From Morn to Midnight. LC 77-2548. (Illus.). (J). (gr. k-3). 1977. 10.25 (*0-690-01393-0*) HarpC Child Bks.

Moss, Elizabeth. Domestic Novelists in the Old South: Defenders of Southern Culture. LC 91-40827. (Southern Literary Studies). 272p. (C). 1992. text 37.50 (*0-8071-1730-7*) La State U Pr.

***Moss, Ellen Feinman & Lee, Charmaine.** Best Excuse. 1999. pap. text 5.95 (*0-9683303-0-4*) TUM.

Moss, Eric O. Eric Owen Moss. (Architectural Monographs: No. 29). (Illus.). 144p. 1993. pap. 38.00 (*1-85490-190-7*) Academy Ed UK.
— Eric Owen Moss. (Architectural Monographs: No. 29). (Illus.). 144p. 1993. 55.00 (*1-85490-189-3*, Pub. by Wiley) Wiley.

Moss, Eric O. & Vidler, Anthony. Eric Owen Moss: Buildings & Projects 2. (Illus.). 224p. 1996. 60.00 (*0-8478-1909-4*, Pub. by Rizzoli Intl); pap. 40.00 (*0-8478-1910-8*, Pub. by Rizzoli Intl) St Martin.

Moss, Eric Owen. Gnostic Architecture. (Illus.). 160p. 1999. pap. 45.00 (*1-58093-019-0*, Pub. by Monacelli Pr) Penguin Putnam.

Moss, Ezra H. & Packer, John G. Flora of Alberta: A Manual of Flowering Plants, Conifers, Ferns, & Fern Allies Found Growing Without Cultivation in the

An Asterisk (*) at the beginning of an entry indicates that the title is appearing for the first time.

Province of Alberta, Canada. 2nd ed. LC 84-179310. (Illus.). 701p. reprint ed. pap. 200.00 (*0-8357-8132-1*, 203398800088) Bks Demand.

Moss, F. Teaching Literature in the Elementary Grades: A Thematic Approach. 304p. (C). 1996. pap. text 33.95 (*0-926842-55-2*) CG Pubs Inc.

***Moss, Francis.** The Rosenberg Espionage Case. LC 99-31389. (Famous Trials Ser.). (Illus.). 128p. (YA). (gr. 6-9). 2000. lib. bdg. 23.70 (*1-56006-578-8*) Lucent Bks.

Moss, Francis, jt. auth. see Pedersen, Ted.

Moss, Frank. How Anyone Can Prosper & Get Wealthy Trading Country Land. 8th ed. 120p. 1996. pap. 21.95 (*1-56150-168-9*) Intl Wealth.

— How Anyone Can Prosper & Get Wealthy Trading Country Land. 9th ed. 120p. 1998. pap. 21.95 (*1-56150-218-9*) Intl Wealth.

— How Anyone Can Prosper & Get Wealthy Trading Country Land. 10th ed. 120p. 1999. pap. 21.95 (*1-56150-269-3*) Intl Wealth.

***Moss, Frank.** How Anyone Can Prosper & Get Wealthy Trading Country Land. 11th ed. 120p. 2000. pap. 21.95 (*1-56150-329-0*) Intl Wealth.

Moss, Frank, ed. Story of the Riot: Persecution of Negroes by Roughs & Policemen, in the City of New York, August, Nineteen Hundred. LC 73-90186. (Mass Violence in America Ser.). 1976. reprint ed. 21.95 (*0-405-01329-9*) Ayer.

Moss, Frank & McClintock, P. V., eds. Noise in Nonlinear Dynamical Systems Vol. 3: Experiments & Simulation. (Illus.). 296p. (C). 1989. text 120.00 (*0-521-35265-7*) Cambridge U Pr.

Moss, G. M., et al. Military Ballistics: A Basic Manual. (Land Warfare: Brassey's New Battlefield Weapons & Technology Ser.: Vol. 12). (Illus.). 230p. 1994. pap. 21.95 (*1-85753-084-5*, Pub. by Brasseys) Brasseys.

***Moss, G. P. & Roe, A. D.** Highland Gold & Silversmiths. (Illus.). 180p. 1999. 49.95 (*1-901663-25-6*, 3256, Pub. by Natl Mus Scotland) A Schwartz & Co.

***Moss, Gary.** Eyecare Business Management Standards of Performance. 352p. 2000. pap. 25.00 (*0-7506-7238-2*) Buttrwrth-Heinemann.

Moss, Gene R. Healthcare Reform D. O. A. Why Politics Will Destroy Healthcare & How One Physician's Plan Can Prevent It. 206p. 1994. pap. 14.95 (*0-9639747-0-X*) Behav Med Assocs.

Moss, Geoff, ed. The Basics of Special Needs: A Routledge - Special Children Survival Guide for the Classroom Teacher. (Illus.). 304p. (C). 1998. ring bd. 75.00 (*0-415-11865-4*, D6021) Routledge.

Moss, George. America in the Twentieth Century. 4th ed. LC 99-13326. 657p. (C). 1999. pap. text 48.67 (*0-13-083370-3*) P-H.

***Moss, George.** Moving On: The American People since 1945. 2nd ed. LC 00-20144. 480p. 2000. pap. 36.00 (*0 13 017191-3*) P-H.

— Native Justice. LC 99-93632. 1999. pap. 10.95 (*0-533-13094-8*) Vantage.

Moss, George D. Moving On: The American People since 1945. LC 93-27288. 432p. 1994. pap. text 37.60 (*0-13-606138-9*) P-H.

— The Rise of Modern America: A History of the Amrican People, 1890-1945. LC 94-36595. 400p. 1994. pap. text 32.00 (*0-13-181587-3*) P-H.

— Vietnam: An American Ordeal. 3rd ed. LC 97-34013. 512p. (C). 1997. pap. text 34.00 (*0-13-897083-1*) P-H.

— A Vietnam Reader: Sources & Essays. 352p. (C). 1990. pap. text 52.00 (*0-13-946625-8*) P-H.

Moss, George H., Jr. Double Exposure Two: Stereographic Views of the Jersey Shore (1859-1910) & Their Relationship to Pioneer Photography. LC 95-71818. (Illus.). 200p. 1995. 29.95 (*0-912396-07-5*) Ploughshare Pr.

— Steamboat to the Shore: A Pictorial History of the Steamboat Era in Monmouth County New Jersey. LC 66-28794. (Illus.). 102p. 1991. reprint ed. 29.95 (*0-912396-02-4*) Ploughshare Pr.

Moss, George H., Jr. & Schnitzspahn, Karen L. Those Innocent Years - 1898-1914: Images of the Jersey Shore from the Pach Photographic Collection. (Illus.). 160p. 1997. reprint ed. pap. 25.95 (*0-912396-08-3*) Ploughshare Pr.

Moss, Glenn & Obery, Ingrid, eds. South Africa Contemporary Analysis. 650p. 1990. lib. bdg. 82.00 (*0-905450-42-6*, Pub. by H Zell Pubs) Seven Hills Bk.

— South African Review, No. 4. 599p. (Orig.). 1988. pap. text 25.95 (*0-86975-335-5*, Pub. by Ravan Pr) Ohio U Pr.

— South African Review No. 6: From "Red Friday" to Codesa. xxi, 508p. (C). 1993. pap. text 24.95 (*0-86975-418-1*, Pub. by Ravan Pr) Ohio U Pr.

Moss, Graham & McKee, Barry. Spitfires & Polished Metal: Restoring the Classic Fighter. LC 99-27103. (Illus.). 144p. 1999. pap. 24.95 (*0-7603-0741-5*, Pub. by MBI Pubg) Motorbooks Intl.

Moss, Graveyard. Graveyard Moss Is Still Alive. 48p. (Orig.). (YA). (gr. 9). 1988. pap. 5.00 (*0-945237-00-6*) Morgan Virginia Pub.

Moss, Gregory R., jt. auth. see McMorrow, Debra B.

Moss, Guy B. Enforcing Security Interests in Personal Property. LC 92-81052. 62p. 1992. pap. text 45.00 (*0-944490-47-6*) Mass CLE.

Moss, H., jt. auth. see Domoryad, A.

Moss, H. P. One Alaskan's Potpourri Vol. 2: A Collection of Frontier Stories: The Homestead Years. LC 97-60982. (Illus.). 240p. (Orig.). 1997. pap. 14.95 (*0-9653074-1-7*) Eagle Riv.

Moss, Halina, tr. see Vorob'ev, Nikolai N.

Moss, Harold. Collected Essays on Egyptology. (Illus.). (Orig.). 1998. pap. write for info. (*1-890173-05-3*, CES) P Shoemaker.

— Politics, Religion, & Sex: All the Things You're Not Supposed to Talk: Performers' Edition. (Illus.). 100p. (Orig.). 1997. pap. 7.00 (*1-890173-01-0*, Pasigram) P Shoemaker.

— Politics, Religion, & Sex: All the Things You're Not Supposed to Talk: Reader's Edition. 2nd ed. (Illus.). 150p. (Orig.). 1996. pap. 10.95 (*1-890173-00-2*, Pasigram) P Shoemaker.

— Words from a Silent Man: Collected Short Writings & Photographs. (Illus.). (Orig.). 1998. pap. 11.95 (*1-890173-02-9*, Pasigram) P Shoemaker.

Moss, Harry W., Jr. The Book of the Few: Genesis: A Secular Interpretation of Biblical Creation. Moss, Steve, ed. LC 96-44023. (Illus.). 72p. 1997. pap. 10.00 (*1-880284-25-1*) J Daniel.

Moss, Helen. Big Bend. LC 82-600156. (Official National Park Handbook Ser.: No. 119). 1983. pap. 6.00 (*0-912627-15-8*) Natl Park Serv.

— Silky, the Woods Cat. (Illus.). 80p. (J). (gr. 2-4). 1993. 10.95 (*0-89015-867-3*) Sunbelt Media.

Moss, Henry S. The Birth of the Middle Ages, 395-814. LC 80-24038. (Illus.). 291p. 1980. reprint ed. lib. bdg. 69.50 (*0-313-22708-X*, MOBM, Greenwood Pr) Greenwood.

Moss, Howard. Instant Lives And More. (Illus.). 112p. 1998. reprint ed. pap. 11.00 (*0-88001-586-1*) HarpC.

***Moss, Howard & Motta, Vanna.** Using Italian Synonyms. 600p. (C). 2000. write for info. (*0-521-47506-6*); pap. write for info. (*0-521-47573-2*) Cambridge U Pr.

Moss, Howard, jt. auth. see Kagan, Jerome.

Moss, Howard A., ed. see Hess, Robert, et al.

Moss, Hugh. By Imperial Command, 2 vols., Set. (Illus.). 272p. 1976. 225.00 (*0-905298-00-4*, Pub. by Bamboo Pub) Antique Collect.

— By Imperial Command: An Intro to Ch'ing Imperial Painted Enamels, 2 vols., Set. (Illus.). 250p. 1976. 350.00 (*0-87556-740-1*) Saifer.

Moss, Hugh, et al. The Art of the Chinese Snuff Bottle: The J & J Collection, 2 vols., Set. LC 93-4947. (Illus.). 800p. 1994. boxed set 250.00 (*0-8348-0289-9*) Weatherhill.

Moss, Hugh, ed. see Holden, Rachelle R.

Moss, Hunter V., ed. see Compton, Eric N.

Moss, I. G. Quantum Theory, Black Holes & Inflation. 174p. 1996. 98.00 (*0-471-95736-4*) Wiley.

Moss, Ian S., ed. see Smith, Adam.

Moss, Irvin & Foster, Mark. Home Run in the Rockies: The History of Baseball in Colorado. 144p. 1994. text. write for info. (*0-9641818-0-0*) H I Moss.

Moss, J., et al. Bacterial Toxins & Virulence Factors in Disease Vol. 8. LC 94-47040. (Handbook Natural Toxins Ser.: Vol. 8). (Illus.). 664p. 1995. text 210.00 (*0-8247-9381-1*) Dekker.

Moss, James N., jt. ed. see Scott, Carl D.

Moss, Jane, jt. auth. see Weiss, Jonathan.

Moss, Janice, jt. auth. see Southwestern Legal Foundation Staff.

Moss, Jason & Kottler, Jeffrey. The Last Victim: A True-Life Journey into the Mind of the Serial Killer. LC 98-34908. (Illus.). 288p. 1999. 24.00 (*0-446-52340-2*, Pub. by Warner Bks) Little.

***Moss, Jason & Kottler, Jeffrey.** The Last Victim: A True-Life Journey into the Mind of the Serial Killer. 294p. 2000. mass mkt. 6.99 (*0-446-60827-0*, Pub. by Warner Bks) Little.

Moss, Jean. The Jean Moss Book of World Knits. LC 97-24049. (Illus.). 128p. 1997. 27.95 (*1-56158-198-4*, 070330) Taunton.

Moss, Jean D. Novelties in the Heavens: Rhetoric & Science in the Copernican Controversy. LC 92-21608. 368p. (C). 1993. pap. text 17.95 (*0-226-54235-1*) U Ch Pr.

— Novelties in the Heavens: Rhetoric & Science in the Copernican Controversy. LC 92-21608. 368p. (C). 1993. lib. bdg. 49.95 (*0-226-54234-3*) U Ch Pr.

Moss, Jean D., ed. Rhetoric & Praxis: The Contribution of Classical Rhetoric to Practical Reasoning. LC 85-25449. 184p. reprint ed. pap. 57.10 (*0-7837-4631-8*, 204435400002) Bks Demand.

Moss, Jeffrey. Bone Poems. LC 97-15743. (Illus.). 96p. (J). 1997. 14.95 (*0-7611-0884-X*) Workman Pub.

— The Butterfly Jar. (Illus.). 128p. (J). (ps up). 1989. 17.95 (*0-553-05704-9*) Bantam.

Moss, Jeffrey, jt. auth. see Werbach, Melvyn R.

***Moss, Jenny Jackson & Dixon, Amy.** Cajun Night after Christmas. LC 99-85962. (Illus.). (J). 2000. 14.95 (*1-56554-779-9*) Pelican.

Moss, Joel, ed. ADP-Ribosylation: Metabolic Effects & Regulatory Functions. LC 94-21849. 256p. (C). 1994. text 268.00 (*0-7923-2951-1*) Kluwer Academic.

— Lam & Other Diseases Characterized by Smooth Muscle Proliferation. LC 99-11317. (Lung Biology in Health & Disease Ser.). (Illus.). 640p. 1999. text 225.00 (*0-8247-0214-X*) Dekker.

Moss, Joel & Vaughan, Martha, eds. ADP-Ribosylating Toxins & G Proteins: Insights into Signal Transduction. LC 89-18549. 585p. reprint ed. pap. 181.40 (*0-608-08628-2*, 206915100003) Bks Demand.

Moss, John. Enduring Dreams: An Explorations of Arctic Landscape. 1997. pap. text 14.95 (*0-88784-596-7*) Genl Dist Srvs.

— Introduction to Data Processing. 1978. 45.00 (*0-905897-25-0*) St Mut.

***Moss, John.** Invisible among the Ruins: Field Notes of a Canadian in Ireland. 176p. 2000. pap. write for info. (*1-896951-19-8*, Pub. by Cormor Bks) Genl Dist Srvs.

— The Paradox of Meaning: Cultural Poetics & Critical Fictions. 224p. 1999. pap. 16.95 (*0-88801-230-6*) Turnstone Pr.

Moss, John, ed. The Canadian Novel: Beginnings, Vol. 2. (Illus.). 216p. 1985. 17.95 (*0-920053-15-7*, Pub. by NC Ltd); pap. 12.95 (*0-920053-17-3*, Pub. by NC Ltd) U of Toronto Pr.

— The Canadian Novel: Here & Now, Vol. 1. (Illus.). 204p. 1978. pap. 12.95 (*0-920053-04-1*, Pub. by NC Ltd) U of Toronto Pr.

— The Canadian Novel: Here & Now, Vol. 1. (Illus.). 204p. 1984. 17.95 (*0-920053-06-8*, Pub. by NC Ltd) U of Toronto Pr.

— The Canadian Novel: Modern Times, Vol. 3. (Illus.). 204p. 1983. pap. 12.95 (*0-919601-90-1*, Pub. by NC Ltd) U of Toronto Pr.

— The Canadian Novel: Present Tense, Vol. 4. (Illus.). 224p. 1985. pap. 12.95 (*0-919601-65-0*, Pub. by NC Ltd) U of Toronto Pr.

— The Canadian Novel: Present Tense, Vol. 4. (Illus.). 224p. 1985. pap. 17.95 (*0-919601-67-7*, Pub. by NC Ltd) U of Toronto Pr.

Moss, John, jt. auth. see Davison, Jon.

Moss, John R. & Ragsdale, Elizabeth S. Enhancing Self-Esteem for Exceptional Leaners. 1994. pap. 29.95 (*0-937660-18-3*) PIP.

Moss, John R. & Skelton, Louise. Developing Self-Concept for Exceptional Learners: A Handbook. rev. ed. (C). 1977. pap. 7.00 (*0-937660-05-1*) PIP.

Moss, John R., et al. A College Level Program for Learning Disabled Students. (C). 1980. pap. 15.95 (*0-937660-01-9*) PIP.

Moss, John R., jt. ed. see Fielding, P. M.

Moss-Jones, John. Automating Managers. 1991. text 47.50 (*0-86187-837-X*, Pub. by P P Pubs) Cassell & Continuum.

Moss, Joseph. A Manual of Classical Bibliography, 2 vols., Set. 2nd ed. LC 76-101049. reprint ed. lib. bdg. 193.00 (*0-8046-0714-1*) Irvington.

Moss, Joy. Using Literature in the Middle Grades: A Thematic Approach. 252p. (J). (gr. 3-8). 1994. text 36.95 (*0-926842-38-2*) CG Pubs Inc.

Moss, Joy F. Focus on Literature: A Context for Literacy Learning. LC 89-22804. 272p. (Orig.). (C). 1990. pap. text 19.95 (*0-913461-17-2*, 26) R Owen Pubs.

Moss, Joyce & Valestuk, Lorraine. World Literature & Its Times Vol. 1: Profiles of Notable Literary Works & the Historical Events That Influenced Them. LC 99-29292. (Illus.). 562p. 1999. 105.00 (*0-7876-3726-2*, GML00299-113374, Gale Res Intl) Gale.

Moss, Joyce & Wilson, George. Literature & Its Times: Profiles of 300 Notable Literary Works & the Historical Events That Influenced Them, 5 vols. 2500p. 1997. 395.00 (*0-7876-0606-5*, GML00198-109703) Gale.

Moss, Joyce & Wilson, George. Profiles in World History: British World Influence to Seeking Alternatives to Capitalism (1750-1900), 8 vols. (Profiles in World History Ser.: Vol. 5). 246p. (J). 1995. text 39.00 (*0-7876-0469-0*, 5 of 8, UXL) Gale.

— Profiles in World History: Significant Events & the People Who Shaped Them, 8 vols. (Profiles in World History Ser.). 1968p. (J). 1995. text 270.00 (*0-7876-0464-X*, UXL) Gale.

— Profiles in World History Vol. 1: Beginnings of Civilization to Expansion of World Powers (3100-200 B.C.), 8 vols. (Profiles in World History Ser.: Vol. 1). 246p. (J). 1995. text 39.00 (*0-7876-0465-8*, 1 of 8, UXL) Gale.

— Profiles in World History Vol. 2: Experimenting with Governments to Viking Invasion of England (200 B. C. - A. D. 1066), 8 vols. (Profiles in World History Ser.: Vol. 2). 246p. (J). 1995. text 39.00 (*0-7876-0466-6*, 2 of 8, UXL) Gale.

— Profiles in World History Vol. 3: The Crusades to Building Empires in the Americas, 8 vols. (Profiles in World History Ser.: Vol. 3). 246p. (J). 1995. text 39.00 (*0-7876-0467-4*, 3 of 8, UXL) Gale.

— Profiles in World History Vol. 4: The Age of Discovery to Industrial Revolution (1400-1830) (Profiles in American History Ser.: Vol. 4). 246p. (J). 1995. text 39.00 (*0-7876-0468-2*, UXL) Gale.

— Profiles in World History Vol. 6. Social Reform to World Wars (1880-1945), 8 vols. (Profiles in World History Ser.: Vol. 6). 246p. (J). 1995. text 39.00 (*0-7876-0470-4*, 6 of 8, UXL) Gale.

— Profiles in World History Vol. 7: Reshaping Europe to Cold War (1945-1970), 8 vols. (Profiles in World History Ser.: Vol. 7). 246p. (J). 1995. text 39.00 (*0-7876-0471-2*, 7 of 8, UXL) Gale.

— Profiles in World History Vol. 8: Middle East Crisis to Innovations in Technology (1960-1995), 8 vols. (Profiles in World History Ser.: Vol. 8). 246p. (J). 1995. text 39.00 (*0-7876-0472-0*, 8 of 8, UXL) Gale.

Moss, Joyce & Wilson, George, eds. Peoples of the World: Latin Americans. 1989. 55.00 (*0-8103-7445-5*) Gale.

— Peoples of the World: North Americans, Vol. 2. 441p. 1990. 55.00 (*0-8103-7768-3*, 100732-M94800) Gale.

Moss, Joyce, jt. auth. see Wilson, George.

Moss, Julian V. Upgrading, Maintaining, & Servicing IBM PC's & Compatibles. Leventhal, Lance A., ed. LC 92-24227. (Lance A. Leventhal Microtrend Ser.). 400p. (Orig.). 1992. pap. 29.95 (*0-915391-70-8*) Slawson Comm.

Moss, K. Heat & Mass Transfer in Building Services Design. LC 98-168614. 1998. pap. 37.99 (*0-419-22650-8*) Thomson Learn.

Moss, Karen. Altered Egos. Boberg, Scott, ed. LC 94-67738. (Illus.). 84p. (Orig.). 1994. pap. 25.00 (*0-9624941-2-7*) SM Mus Art.

Moss, Karen, et al, contrib. by. Kim Abele: Encyclopedia Persona, A-Z. LC 93-20828. (Illus.). 110p. 1993. 30.00 (*0-911291-22-9*, Pub. by Fellows Cont Art) RAM Publications.

Moss, Karen, ed. see Drew, Nancy, et al.

Moss, Karen, ed. see Kohl, Jeanette, et al.

Moss, Karl. Java Servlets. 445p. 1998. pap. 44.95 incl. cd-rom (*0-07-913779-2*) McGraw.

***Moss, Karl.** Java Servlets. 2nd ed. (Enterprise Computing Ser.). (Illus.). 576p. 1999. pap. 49.99 (*0-07-135188-4*) Osborne-McGraw.

Moss, Kary L. Rights of Women & Girls. (American Civil Liberties Union Handbooks Ser.). 1998. 14.09 (*0-606-13742-4*, Pub. by Turtleback) Demco.

Moss, Kary L., ed. Man-Made Medicine: Women's Health, Public Policy & Reform. LC 96-21855. 304p. 1996. text 49.95 (*0-8223-1811-3*); pap. text 15.95 (*0-8223-1816-4*) Duke.

Moss, Kate. Kate: The Kate Moss Book. (Illus.). 144p. 1997. pap. 12.95 (*0-7893-0101-6*, Pub. by Universe) St Martin.

— Kate Moss: The Kate Moss Book. (Illus.). 144p. 1995. pap. 22.50 (*0-7893-0005-2*, Pub. by Universe) St Martin.

Moss, Kate & Peri, Camille, eds. Mothers Who Think: Tales of Real Life Parenthood. LC 98-48168. 282p. 1999. 22.95 (*0-375-50269-6*) Villard Books.

Moss, Kathlyn & Scherer, Alice. The Beadwork. (Illus.). 112p. 1992. 29.95 (*0-8109-3670-4*, Pub. by Abrams) Time Warner.

Moss, Kathy & Arbogast, Susanne L. Nurse's Manual of Infectious Diseases: Little, Brown's Infectious Diseases Fact Finder. LC 96-28013. 258p. 1996. spiral bd. 34.95 (*0-316-58513-0*, Little Brwn Med Div) Lppncott W & W.

Moss, Katrina R. Medium Secure Psychiatric Provision in the Private Sector. LC 98-73023. 168p. 1998. text 59.95 (*1-84014-310-X*, Pub. by Ashgate Pub) Ashgate Pub Co.

Moss, Kay K. Southern Folk Medicine, 1750-1820: 1750-1820. LC 98-40223. 224p. 1999. 29.95 (*1-57003-289-0*) U of SC Pr.

Moss, Kenneth B. Technology & the Future Strategic Environment. 194p. 1992. pap. text 18.75 (*0-943875-24-2*) W Wilson Ctr Pr.

Moss, Kevin, ed. Out of the Blue: Russia's Hidden Gay Literature - An Anthology. (Illus.). 416p. 1996. 50.00 (*0-940567-19-9*); pap. 19.95 (*0-940567-20-2*) Gay Sunshine.

***Moss, Kevin L.** Network Administrator's Survival Guide. 1999. pap. text 59.99 (*0-07-913786-5*) McGraw.

Moss, Larry. Twisting History: Lessons in Balloon Sculpting. LC TT926.M67 1995. (Illus.). 110p. 1995. pap. text 14.95 (*0-9648497-3-9*, Pub. by Fooled Ya) Parma Pubng.

Moss, Laurence S. Mountifort Longfield: Ireland's First Professor of Political Economy. LC 75-34003. 240p. 1976. 14.95 (*0-916054-02-0*) Jameson Bks.

Moss, Laurence S., ed. Joseph A. Schumpeter, Historian of Economic Thought. LC 95-40590. (Perspectives on the History of Economic Thought Ser.). 336p. (C). 1996. 90.00 (*0-415-13353-X*) Routledge.

Moss, Laurence S., ed. see Grice-Hutchinson, Marjorie.

Moss, Lawrence S., et al, eds. Logic, Language & Computation, Vol. 2. (Lecture Notes Ser.: Vol. 91). 440p. (C). 1999. text 64.95 (*1-57586-181-X*); pap. text 26.95 (*1-57586-180-1*) CSLI.

Moss, Lawrence S., jt. auth. see Barwise, Jon.

Moss, Leonard. Arthur Miller. rev. ed. (United States Authors Ser.: No. 115). 200p. 1980. 21.95 (*0-8057-7311-8*, Twyne) Mac Lib Ref.

***Moss, Leonard.** The Excess of Heroism in Tragic Drama. LC 99-88037. 240p. 2000. 49.95 (*0-8130-1759-9*) U Press Fla.

Moss, Leonard. Henry Miller. (United States Authors Ser.: No. 115). 168p. 1990. 28.95 (*0-8057-7607-9*) Macmillan.

Moss, Lisa Braver. Celebrating Family: Our Lifelong Bonds with Parents & Siblings. LC 98-52202. 240p. 1999. pap. 13.95 (*1-885171-30-7*) Wldcat Canyon.

***Moss, Lloyd.** Our Marching Band. LC 99-37284. (Illus.). (J). 2001. write for info. (*0-399-23335-0*) Putnam Pub Group.

Moss, Lloyd. Zin! Zin! Zin! A Violin. LC 93-37902. (Illus.). 32p. (J). (ps-3). 1995. 16.00 (*0-671-88239-2*) S&S Bks Yung.

***Moss, Lloyd.** Zin Zin Zin! a Violin. (J). (gr. k-3). 2000. per. 6.99 (*0-689-83524-8*) Aladdin.

Moss, M. Caring for Old Master Paintings. 1994. 37.50 (*0-7165-2531-3*, Pub. by Irish Acad Pr) Intl Spec Bk.

***Moss, M.** Ugly Menorah. 2000. pap. write for info. (*0-374-48047-8*) FS&G.

Moss, M. E. Benedetto Croce: Essays on Literature & Literary Criticism. LC 89-4627. 244p. (C). 1990. pap. text 21.95 (*0-7914-0201-0*) State U NY Pr.

— Benedetto Croce Reconsidered: Truth & Error in Theories of Art, Literature, & History. LC 86-22399. 164p. 1987. reprint ed. pap. 50.90 (*0-608-02326-4*, 206296700004) Bks Demand.

Moss, M. O., jt. auth. see Adams, M. R.

Moss, M. O., jt. auth. see Smith, John E.

Moss, M. O., jt. ed. see Adams, M. R.

Moss, Mae T. Reengineering of Operative & Invasive Services: Preparing for the Capitated Dollar. LC 96-2940. 240p. 1996. spiral bd. 79.00 (*0-8342-0850-4*, 20850) Aspen Pub.

Moss, Maria J. A Poetical Cook-Book. 144p. 1972. 3.95 (*0-405-02213-1*) Arno Press.

***Moss, Marie.** Hello Kitty: The Girl, the Story, the Book. 2000. 17.95 (*0-8109-3444-2*, Pub. by Abrams) Time Warner.

Moss, Marion. Removing Your Mask: No More Hiding from Your Truth. Warden, Rosemary & Hubbard, Richard, eds. (Illus.). 320p. (Orig.). 1992. pap. 13.95 (*0-9631341-0-8*) Orion Pub.

Moss, Marissa. After-School Monster. (Picture Puffin Ser.). (YA). 1993. 10.19 (*0-606-05108-2*, Pub. by Turtleback) Demco.

***Moss, Marissa.** The All-New Amelia: And Brighter Than Bright Amelia. LC 99-27033. (J). 1999. pap. text 5.95 (*1-56247-822-2*) Pleasant Co.

M

— The All-New Amelia: And Brighter Than Bright Amelia. LC 99-27033. (J). (gr. 3-5). 1999. text 12.95 (*1-56247-840-0*) Pleasant Co.

Moss, Marissa. Amelia Hits the Road. LC 98-40673. (J). 1999. pap. text 5.95 (*1-56247-790-0*) Pleasant Co.

— Amelia Hits the Road. LC 98-40673. 40p. (J). (gr. 4-7). 1999. text 12.95 (*1-56247-791-9*) Pleasant Co.

— Amelia Hits the Road. LC 97-446. (Illus.). 40p. (J). (gr. 2-7). 1997. 14.95 (*1-883672-57-0*) Tricycle Pr.

— Amelia Takes Command. LC 98-40672. 40p. (J). (gr. 4-7). 1999. text 12.95 (*1-56247-789-7*) Pleasant Co.

— Amelia Takes Command. LC 98-40672. (Illus.). 40p. (J). (gr. 3-7). 1999. pap. 5.95 (*1-56247-788-9*) Pleasant Co.

— Amelia Takes Command. LC 97-50168. (Illus.). 40p. (J). (gr. 3-5). 1998. 14.95 (*1-883672-70-8*) Tricycle Pr.

***Moss, Marissa.** Amelia Works It Out. LC 99-89850. 2000. pap. write for info. (*1-58485-080-9*) Paragon Hse.

Moss, Marissa. Amelia Writes Again! LC 98-40670. 32p. (gr. 4-7). 1999. text 12.95 (*1-56247-787-0*) Pleasant Co.

— Amelia Writes Again! LC 98-40670. (Amelia (American Girl) Ser.). (Illus.). 32p. (J). (gr. 4-7). 1999. pap. 5.95 (*1-56247-786-2*) Pleasant Co.

— Amelia Writes Again! LC 95-52874. (Illus.). 32p. (J). (gr. 2-7). 1996. 14.00 (*1-883672-42-2*) Tricycle Pr.

***Moss, Marissa.** Amelia's Card Game. (Illus.). (YA). (gr. 3-7). 2000. 5.95 (*1-58485-163-5*) Pleasant Co.

— Amelia's Family Ties. (Illus.). (J). 2000. 11.30 (*0-606-18352-3*) Turtleback.

Moss, Marissa. Amelia's Notebook. LC 98-40671. 32p. (J). (gr. 4-7). 1999. 12.95 (*1-56247-785-4*) Pleasant Co.

— Amelia's Notebook. LC 98-40671. (Illus.). (J). (gr. 3-7). 1999. pap. 5.95 (*1-56247-784-6*) Pleasant Co.

— Amelia's Notebook. LC 94-5382. (Illus.). 32p. (J). (gr. 2-7). 1995. 14.00 (*1-883672-18-X*) Tricycle Pr.

***Moss, Marissa.** Amelia's Notebook. (Illus.). (J). 1999. 11.30 (*0-606-18353-1*) Turtleback.

Moss, Marissa. Dr. Amelia's Boredom Survival Guide: First Aid for Rainy Days, Boring Errands, Waiting Rooms, Whatever! LC 98-54758. (Illus.). 63p. (YA). (gr. 3 up). 1999. pap. text 5.95 (*1-56247-794-3*) Pleasant Co.

***Moss, Marissa.** Hannah's Journal: The Story of an Immigrant Girl. LC 99-35651. (Young American Voices Ser.). (Illus.). 56p. (J). (gr. 4-7). 2000. 15.00 (*0-15-202155-8*, Harcourt Child Bks) Harcourt.

— Luv, Amelia - Luv, Nadia. (J). 1999. pap. text 7.95 (*1-56247-823-0*) Pleasant Co.

— Luv, Amelia - Luv, Nadia. (American Girl Backpack Bks.). (Illus.). 32p. (J). (ps-3). 1999. 14.95 (*1-56247-839-7*) Pleasant Co.

Moss, Marissa. Mel's Diner. LC 93-38683. (Illus.). 32p. (J). (gr. k-3). 1996. 13.95 (*0-8167-3460-7*) BridgeWater.

— Mel's Diner. LC 93-38683. (Illus.). 32p. (J). (gr. k-3). 1996. pap. 4.95 (*0-8167-3461-5*) Troll Communs.

— Mel's Diner. 1994. 10.05 (*0-606-09607-8*, Pub. by Turtleback) Demco.

— My Notebook: (With Help from Amelia) (Amelia (American Girl) Ser.). (Illus.). 48p. (J). (gr. 3-7). 1999. pap. 5.95 (*1-56247-792-7*) Pleasant Co.

— My Notebook (with Help from Amelia) (Illus.). 48p. (J). (gr. 2-7). 1997. pap. 9.95 (*1-883672-47-3*) Tricycle Pr.

— Rachel's Journal: The Story of a Pioneer Girl. LC 97-28234. (Illus.). 48p. (J). (gr. 3-5). 1998. 15.00 (*0-15-201806-9*) Harcourt.

— Rachel's Journal: The Story of a Pioneer Girl. (J). 2001. pap. write for info. (*0-15-202168-X*) Harcourt.

— Regina's Big Mistake. (Illus.). 32p. (J). (gr. k-3). 1990. 16.00 (*0-395-55330-X*) HM.

— Regina's Big Mistake. LC 90-32740. (Illus.). 32p. (J). (gr. k-3). 1995. pap. 6.95 (*0-395-70093-0*, Sandpiper) HM.

— Regina's Big Mistake. (J). 1990. 12.40 (*0-606-08068-6*) Turtleback.

— True Heart. LC 95-50866. (Illus.). 32p. (J). (gr. k-4). 1999. 16.00 (*0-15-201344-X*) Harcourt.

— The Ugly Menorah. LC 95-33260. (Illus.). 32p. (J). (ps-3). 1996. 14.00 (*0-374-38027-9*) FS&G.

Moss, Mark, ed. see Gillette, Steve.

Moss, Mark B., jt. ed. see Albert, Marilyn S.

Moss, Martha. Photography Books Index: A Subject Guide to Photo Anthologies, Vol. 1. LC 79-26938. 298p. 1980. lib. bdg. 26.50 (*0-8108-1283-5*) Scarecrow.

— Photography Books Index: A Subject Guide to Photo Anthologies, Vol. II. LC 84-23652. 276p. 1985. 25.00 (*0-8108-1773-X*) Scarecrow.

Moss, Marvin A. Applying TQM to Product Design & Development. (Quality & Reliability Ser.: Vol. 46). (Illus.). 440p. 1995. text 110.00 (*0-8247-9677-2*) Dekker.

— Designing for Minimal Maintenance Expense: The Practical Application of Reliability & Maintainability. (Quality & Reliability Ser.: Vol. 1). (Illus.). 184p. 1985. text 77.50 (*0-8247-7314-4*) Dekker.

Moss, Maureen. A Survival Guide for the Groom to Be or How Not to Let Sex Become a Fond Memory. Meyer, Beth, ed. (Illus.). 128p. (Orig.). 1996. pap. 9.95 (*0-9651310-1-7*) Constant Concepts.

Moss, Maurice, tr. see Moreau, Claude.

Moss, Michael. An Invaluable Treasure: A History of the TSB. (Illus.). 336p. 1994. 55.00 (*0-297-81118-5*, Pub. by Weidenfeld & Nicolson) Trafalgar.

Moss, Michael H., et al. Histology: A Text & Atlas. 3rd ed. (Illus.). 704p. 1994. 53.00 (*0-683-07369-9*) Lppncott W & W.

Moss, Millicent. The Sunshine Box: Millie's Fanciful Journey to Hope. LC 96-37890. (Millie's Fanciful Journey to Hope Ser.). (Illus.). 96p. (J). (gr. 3-9). 1998. 12.99 (*1-57673-132-4*, Gold n Honey) Zondervan.

Moss, Milton, ed. Measurement of Economic & Social Performance. (Studies in Income & Wealth: No. 38). 615p. 1973. 159.90 (*0-87014-259-3*) Natl Bur Econ Res.

Moss, Milton, ed. see Conference on the Measurement of Economic & Social.

***Moss, Miriam.** Arctic Song. LC 98-46372. (Illus.). 32p. (J). (gr. k-3). 1999. 15.95 (*0-8167-6069-1*) BrdgeWater.

— Arctic Song. (Illus.). 32p. (J). (ps-3). 2000. pap. 5.95 (*0-8167-6519-7*) Troll Communs.

Moss, Miriam. Be Positive. LC 92-26717. (Staying Healthy Ser.). (Illus.). 32p. (J). (gr. 6). 1993. lib. bdg. 13.95 (*0-89686-786-2*, Crstwood Hse) Silver Burdett Pr.

— Eat Well. LC 92-28738. (Staying Healthy Ser.). (Illus.). 32p. (J). (gr. 6). 1993. lib. bdg. 13.95 (*0-89686-785-4*, Crstwood Hse) Silver Burdett Pr.

— Fashion Designer. LC 90-48323. (Fashion World Ser.). (Illus.). 32p. (J). (gr. 5-6). 1991. text 13.95 (*0-89686-621-1*, Crstwood Hse) Silver Burdett Pr.

— Fashion Model. LC 90-15082. (Fashion World Ser.). (Illus.). 32p. (J). (gr. 5-6). 1991. lib. bdg. 13.95 (*0-89686-609-2*, Crstwood Hse) Silver Burdett Pr.

— Fashion Photographer. LC 90-15059. (Fashion World Ser.). (Illus.). 32p. (J). (gr. 5-6). 1991. lib. bdg. 13.95 (*0-89686-608-4*, Crstwood Hse) Silver Burdett Pr.

— Jigsaw. LC 96-42480. (Illus.). 32p. (J). (gr. k-4). 1997. 15.95 (*0-7613-0074-0*); lib. bdg. 22.40 (*0-7613-0044-9*) Millbrook Pr.

— Keep Fit. LC 92-13916. (Staying Healthy Ser.). (Illus.). 32p. (J). (gr. 6). 1993. lib. bdg. 13.95 (*0-89686-788-9*, Crstwood Hse) Silver Burdett Pr.

— Street Fashion. LC 90-48913. (Fashion World Ser.). (Illus.). 32p. (J). (gr. 5-6). 1991. lib. bdg. 13.95 (*0-89686-611-4*, Crstwood Hse) Silver Burdett Pr.

***Moss, Miriam.** This Is the Tree. LC 99-49003. (Illus.). (J). 2000. 14.95 (*0-916291-98-7*) Kane-Miller Bk.

Moss, Murphy, jt. auth. see Coffey, Mary A.

Moss, Nancy L. De, see DeMoss, Nancy L.

Moss, Nathaniel. Ron Kovic: The Paralyzed U. S. Marine Who Became an Antiwar Activist. LC 93-16373. (Great Achievers Ser.). (Illus.). 120p. (YA). (gr. 5 up). 1994. lib. bdg. 19.95 (*0-7910-2076-2*) Chelsea Hse.

Moss, Norman. British-American Language Dictionary. 174p. 1989. 12.95 (*0-8442-9105-6*, Natl Textbk Co) NTC Contemp Pub Co.

— British-American Language Dictionary. 174p. 1990. pap. 7.95 (*0-8442-9104-8*, Natl Textbk Co) NTC Contemp Pub Co.

— British-English Language Dictionary: For More Effective Communication Between Americans & Britons. 2nd ed. (Illus.). 192p. 1991. 14.95 (*0-8442-9115-3*, Natl Textbk Co) NTC Contemp Pub Co.

— British-English Language Dictionary: For More Effective Communication Between Americans & Britons. 2nd ed. (Illus.). 192p. 1995. pap. 9.95 (*0-8442-9116-1*, 91161, Natl Textbk Co) NTC Contemp Pub Co.

— Travel Guide to British/American English. (Illus.). 172p. 1994. pap. 4.95 (*0-8442-9512-4*, 95124, Passprt Bks) NTC Contemp Pub Co.

Moss, P. Buckley. The Etchings of P. Buckley Moss. Henderson, Malcolm & Henderson, Jaikie, eds. (Illus.). 114p. 1988. 58.00 (*0-9626627-0-4*) Shenandoah Pub.

— P. Buckley Moss, The People's Artist: An Autobiography. Henderson, Malcolm et al, eds. (Illus.). 103p. 1989. lib. bdg. 12.00 (*0-9626627-1-2*) Shenandoah Pub.

Moss, Pamela, jt. auth. see Strike, Kenneth A.

Moss, Pamela A., jt. auth. see Strike, Kenneth A.

***Moss, Pamela J.** Placing Autobiography in Geography. LC 00-38780. (Space, Place & Society Ser.). 2000. 19.95 (*0-8156-2848-X*) Syracuse U Pr.

Moss, Peter. Hong Kong Handover: Signed, Sealed & Delivered. (Illus.). 60p. 1998. 31.00 (*962-7283-22-3*, Pub. by FormAsia) Weatherhill.

***Moss, Peter.** Hong Kong Style. (Illus.). 120p. 1999. 38.00 (*962-7283-25-8*, Pub. by FormAsia) Weatherhill.

— Skylines. 132p. 1999. 51.00 (*962-7283-26-6*, Pub. by FormAsia) Weatherhill.

Moss, Peter & Pence, Alan R., eds. Valuing Quality in Early Childhood Services: New Approaches to Defining Quality. (Early Childhood Education Ser.). 192p. (C). 1994. pap. text 19.95 (*0-8077-3431-4*) Tchrs Coll.

Moss, Peter & Penn, Helen. Transforming Nursery Education. 192p. 1996. pap. 24.95 (*1-85396-308-9*, Pub. by P Chapman) Taylor & Francis.

Moss, Peter, jt. auth. see Cluskey, William M.

Moss, Peter, jt. auth. see McClusky, William.

Moss, Peter J., jt. ed. see Gupta, Ajaya K.

***Moss, Philip & Tilly, Chris.** Stories Employers Tell: Race, Skill, & Hiring in America. 250p. 2001. 29.95 (*0-87154-609-4*) Russell Sage.

Moss, R., ed. Transport of Animals Intended for Breeding, Production & Slaughter. 1982. text 121.50 (*90-247-2679-4*) Kluwer Academic.

Moss, R., et al. Animal Population Dynamics. LC 82-9531. 1982. 7.50 (*0-412-22240-X*, NO. 2297) Chapman & Hall.

Moss, R. P. & Morgan, W. B. Fuelwood & Rural Energy Production & Supply in Humid Tropics: Report for the UNU with Special Reference to Tropical Africa & South East Asia, Vol. 4. (Natural Resources & the Environment Ser.). (Illus.). 234p. 1981. text 90.00 (*0-907567-03-7*, Tycooly Pub) Weidner & Sons.

Moss, Ralph W. Alternative Medicine Online: A Guide to Natural Remedies on the Internet. LC 97-22650. 208p. 1997. pap. 12.95 (*1-881025-10-1*) Equinox Pr.

***Moss, Ralph W.** Antioxidants Against Cancer. LC 99-57585. (Ralph Moss on Cancer Ser.). (Illus.). 2000. pap. 9.95 (*1-881025-28-4*) Equinox Pr.

Moss, Ralph W. The Cancer Industry: The Classic Expose on the Cancer Establishment. pap. 14.95 (*1-55778-439-6*) Equinox Pr.

— The Cancer Industry: The Classic Expose on the Cancer Establishment. LC 96-84574. 41p. 1996. pap. 16.95 (*1-881025-09-8*) Equinox Pr.

— Cancer Therapy: The Independent Consumer's Guide to Non-Toxic Treatment & Prevention. 41p. 1993. pap. 19.95 (*1-881025-06-3*) Equinox Pr.

— Herbs Against Cancer. LC 98-26261. 1998. pap. text 16.95 (*1-881025-40-3*) Equinox Pr.

— Questioning Chemotherapy: A Critique of the Use of Toxic Drugs in the Treatment of Cancer. LC 95-11440. 1995. 19.95 (*1-881025-25-X*) Equinox Pr.

Moss, Ralph W., jt. auth. see Randolph, Theron G.

Moss, Ray, jt. ed. see Gabel, Detlaf.

Moss Rehabilitation Center Staff, jt. auth. see Kardon Institute Staff.

Moss, Richard. The Black Butterfly: An Invitation to Radical Aliveness. LC 86-11773. 320p. (Orig.). 1995. pap. 14.95 (*0-89087-475-1*) Celestial Arts.

— The I That Is We: Awakening to Higher Energies Through Unconditional Love. LC 81-65713. 240p. 1995. pap. 12.95 (*0-89087-327-5*) Celestial Arts.

— Words That Shine Both Ways: Reflections That Reconnect Us to Our True Nature. deluxe ed. LC 97-77336. 152p. 1997. 17.00 (*0-9659820-0-9*) Enneas Pubns.

Moss, Richard, ed. see Muensterberg, Hugo.

Moss, Richard B., ed. Cystic Fibrosis: Infection, Immunopathology & Host Response. 262p. 1990. 89.50 (*0-89603-192-6*) Humana.

Moss, Richard J. The Life of Jedidiah Morse: A Station of Peculiar Exposure. LC 94-28143. (Illus.). 192p. (C). 1995. text 28.00 (*0-87049-868-1*) U of Tenn Pr.

Moss, Richard L. The Dermatology Office Manual. (Office Manual Ser.). 221p. 1995. 149.50 (*1-890018-07-4*) Anadem Pubng.

Moss, Richard M. The Second Miracle: Intimacy, Spirituality, & Conscious Relationships. LC 95-17541. 236p. 1995. pap. 12.95 (*0-89087-765-3*) Celestial Arts.

Moss, R.Lawrence, et al. Case Studies in Pediatric Surgery. 384p. (C). 2000. 65.00 (*0-8385-1548-7*) McGraw.

Moss, Robert. The Abridger. 12.95 (*1-55517-044-7*) CFI Dist.

Moss, Robert. Capstone of Faith. 163p. pap. 9.95 (*1-55517-200-8*) CFI Dist.

— Capstone of Faith. 176p. 1995. pap. 10.95 (*1-55517-174-5*) CFI Dist.

— Conscious Dreaming. 384p. 1996. 16.00 (*0-517-88710-X*, Crown) Crown Pub Group.

Moss, Robert. The Covenant Coat. pap. 12.95 (*1-55517-348-9*) CFI Dist.

Moss, Robert. Dreamgates: An Explorer's Guide to Worlds of Soul, Imagination, & Life Beyond Death. LC 97-45984. 368p. 1998. pap. 14.00 (*0-609-80216-X*) Crown Pub Group.

***Moss, Robert.** Dreaming True: How To Dream Your Future & Change Your Life for the Better. 400p. 2000. pap. 14.95 (*0-671-78530-3*) PB.

Moss, Robert. The Films of Carol Reed. LC 85-17512. 256p. 1987. text 45.50 (*0-231-05984-1*) Col U Pr.

— Fire along the Sky. 416p. 1995. 5.99 (*0-8125-3536-7*, Pub. by Forge NYC) St Martin.

— The Firekeeper. 1996. pap. 6.99 (*0-614-98055-0*) Forge NYC.

— Firekeeper, Vol. 1. 1996. mass mkt. 6.99 (*0-8125-4847-7*, Pub. by Tor Bks) St Martin.

Moss, Robert. I, Nephi. pap. 9.95 (*1-55517-198-2*) CFI Dist.

Moss, Robert. Interpreter. 1998. mass mkt. 6.99 (*0-8125-4848-5*, Pub. by Forge NYC) St Martin.

Moss, Robert. Soldiers 'n Saints. pap. 14.98 (*1-55517-319-5*) CFI Dist.

— That I Were an Angel. 9.95 (*1-55517-032-3*) CFI Dist.

— Title of Liberty. 10.95 (*1-55517-199-0*) CFI Dist.

— Valiant Witness. pap. 12.95 (*1-55517-344-6*) CFI Dist.

Moss, Robert, jt. auth. see Mahler, Walter R.

Moss, Robert A. The Brain & the Bible: Is Psychology Compatible with Christianity? 108p. 1993. pap. 8.95 (*0-9638848-1-6*) R A Moss.

— Understanding Emptiness: The Think - Feel Conflict. 128p. 1993. pap. 9.95 (*0-9638848-0-8*) R A Moss.

Moss, Robert A. & Dunlap, Helen D. Why Johnny Can't Concentrate: Coping with Attention Deficit Problems. rev. ed. LC 95-35807. 272p. 1995. pap. 14.95 (*0-553-37541-5*) Bantam.

Moss, Robert A. & Wertheimer, David. Notes on Teaching the Bible (Old Testament & Mark) (YA). (gr. 9-12). 1981. teacher ed. 16.25 (*1-881678-12-1*) CSEE.

Moss, Robert D. The Art of Ship & Boat Handling. Kimel, Neal, ed. LC 93-206641. (Illus.). 150p. 1991. 49.95 (*1-883121-00-0*) Onboard Marine.

Moss, Robert G. Avoiding Y2Kaos: Preparing for the Non-Negotiable Deadline. Huelsing, Susie, ed. (Illus.). 72p. 1999. pap. 29.95 (*0-9669533-0-4*) Year Two Thou.

Moss, Robert H. A Reader's Book of Mormon Digest. pap. 11.95 (*1-55517-337-3*) CFI Dist.

Moss, Roberta. Makin' Buckskin Clothes. 1982. 7.50 (*0-913150-48-7*) Pioneer Pr.

Moss, Roger W. For Historic Buildings: A Guide to Selecting Reproduction: Lighting, Vol. 3. LC 87-36012. (Historic Interiors Ser.). (Illus.). 192p. 1995. pap. 29.95 (*0-471-14399-5*) Wiley.

— Philadelphia Victorian: The Building of the Athenaeum. LC 98-10906. (Illus.). 169p. 1998. pap. 35.00 (*0-916530-16-7*) Athenaeum Phila.

— Philadelphia Victorian: The Building of the Athenaeum. limited ed. LC 98-10906. (Illus.). 169p. 1998. 75.00 (*0-916530-15-9*) Athenaeum Phila.

Moss, Roger W., ed. Paint in America: The Colors of Historic Buildings. 320p. 1995. pap. 19.95 (*0-471-14411-8*) Wiley.

— Paint in America: The Colors of Historic Buildings. LC 96-18763. (Illus.). 320p. 1995. 39.95 (*0-471-14410-X*) Wiley.

Moss, Roger W. & Crane, Tom. Historic Houses of Philadelphia: A Tour of the Region's Museum Homes. LC 98-10934. 1998. pap. 19.95 (*0-8122-1647-4*) U of Pa Pr.

— Historic Houses of Philadelphia: A Tour of the Region's Museum Homes. LC 98-10934. (Illus.). 256p. 1998. 34.95 (*0-8122-3438-3*) U of Pa Pr.

Moss, Roger W. & Winkler, Gail C. Victorian Exterior Decoration: How to Paint Your 19th Century American House Historically. LC 86-15014. (Illus.). 1995. pap. 19.95 (*0-8050-2313-5*, Owl) H Holt & Co.

— Victorian Interior Decoration: American Interiors, 1830-1900. (Illus.). 272p. 1995. pap. 19.95 (*0-8050-2312-7*, Owl) H Holt & Co.

Moss, Roger W., jt. auth. see Winkler, Gail C.

Moss-Rogers, Lorraine. Sessions: A Single Continuous Course or Period of Lessons Studies. 210p. 1998. pap. 12.95 (*0-7392-0024-0*, PO2782) Morris Pubng.

Moss, Ronald L. My Dearest Love: Love Letters from Him to Her. 142p. (Orig.). 1996. pap. 14.95 (*0-9655693-0-6*) Moss & Moss.

Moss, Rose. The Schoolmaster. (Writers Ser.). 239p. 1995. reprint ed. pap. text 12.95 (*0-86975-470-X*, Pub. by Ravan Pr) Ohio U Pr.

Moss, Roy L. The Lord's Portion: A Scriptural View of Tithing. LC 96-13479. 96p. 1996. pap. 5.99 (*1-56722-191-2*) Word Aflame.

***Moss, S., et al, eds.** Fundamental Mechanisms of Low-Energy-Beam-Modified Surface Growth & Processing Vol. 585: Materials Research Society Symposium Proceedings. 2000. text 86.00 (*1-55899-493-9*) Materials Res.

Moss, S. E., ed. The Annexins: An Important Family of Calcium & Phospholipid-Binding Proteins. (Portland Press Research Monographs: Vol. 2). 173p. (C). 1992. 85.00 (*1-85578-008-9*, Pub. by Portland Pr Ltd) Ashgate Pub Co.

Moss, S. J. & Ledwith, A., eds. The Chemistry of the Semiconductor Industry. (Illus.). 352p. 1987. mass mkt. 166.50 (*0-412-01321-5*, 9953, Chap & Hall NY) Chapman & Hall.

Moss-Salentijn, Letty & Hendricks-Klyvert, Marlene. Dental & Oral Tissues: An Introduction. 3rd ed. LC 89-13713. (Illus.). 327p. 1990. pap. text 35.95 (*0-8121-1320-9*) Lppncott W & W.

Moss, Sally. Peter's Painting. LC 95-8704. (Illus.). 24p. (J). (ps-2). 1995. 13.95 (*1-57255-013-9*) Mondo Pubng.

Moss, Sanford. Natural History of the Antarctic Peninsula. (Illus.). 256p. 1990. pap. text 21.50 (*0-231-06269-9*) Col U Pr.

Moss, Scott & Rae, John, eds. Artificial Intelligence & Economic Analysis: Prospects & Problems. 280p. 1992. 95.00 (*1-85278-685-X*) E Elgar.

Moss, Sidney P. Charles Dickens' Quarrel with America. LC 82-50401. xii, 356p. 1984. 38.50 (*0-87875-255-2*) Whitston Pub.

— Poe's Major Crisis: His Libel Suit & New York's Literary World. LC 74-100089. 256p. reprint ed. pap. 79.40 (*0-608-11984-9*, 202342400033) Bks Demand.

***Moss, Sidney P. & Moss, Carolyn J.** American Episodes Involving Charles Dickens. LC 98-60852. (Illus.). x, 164p. 1999. 28.50 (*0-87875-504-7*) Whitston Pub.

Moss, Sidney P. & Moss, Carolyn J. Charles Dickens & His Chicago Relatives: A Documentary Narrative. LC 93-60503. (Illus.). xvi, 191p. 1994. 35.00 (*0-87875-444-X*) Whitston Pub.

— Dickens, Trollope, Jefferson: Three Anglo-American Encounters. LC 99-71001. (Illus.). xii, 84p. 2000. 22.50 (*0-87875-512-8*) Whitston Pub.

Moss, Stanley. Asleep in the Garden: New & Selected Poems. LC 97-32666. 160p. 1997. 20.00 (*1-888363-63-0*) Seven Stories.

Moss, Stanley, ed. Interviews & Encounters with Stanley Kunitz. LC 92-19621. 259p. (C). 1993. text 27.50 (*0-935296-79-4*, Pub. by Sheep Meadow) U Pr of New Eng.

Moss, Stephen. Growing up Cavity-Free: A Parent's Guide to Prevention. (Illus.). 147p. (Orig.). 1993. pap. 18.00 (*0-86715-256-7*) Quint Pub Co.

Moss, Stephen & Kushner, Jeffrey N. Purchasing Managed Care Services for Alcohol & Other Drug Treatment: Essential Elements & Policy Issues. (Illus.). 58p. (C). 1997. reprint ed. pap. text 30.00 (*0-7881-4035-3*) DIANE Pub.

Moss, Steve. World's Shortest Stories. 224p. 21.95 (*0-8488-2668-X*) Amereon Ltd.

Moss, Steve, ed. The World's Shortest Stories: Murder, Love, Horror & Suspense. LC 97-66805. 238p. 1998. pap. 7.95 (*0-7624-0300-4*) Running Pr.

***Moss, Steve & Daniel, John M., eds.** The World's Shortest Stories of Love & Death: Passion - Suspicion - Betrayal - Revenge - All This & More. 2000. pap. 7.95 (*0-7624-0698-4*) Running Pr.

Moss, Steve, ed. see Moss, Harry W., Jr.

Moss, Steven D., jt. auth. see Casteel, David A.

Moss, Stirling. Jenks a Passion for Motorsport: The Words & Life of Denis Jenkinson. (Illus.). 224p. 1997. 39.95 (*1-899870-22-9*, Pub. by Motor Racing) Motorbooks Intl.

Moss, Sue, jt. ed. see Chamberlain, Jocelyn.

Moss, Susan. Keep Your Breasts: Preventing Breast Cancer the Natural Way. LC 94-92245. (Illus.). 306p. 1994. reprint ed. pap. 19.95 (*0-9642329-0-1*) Res Pubns CA.

— Keep Your Breasts: Preventing Breast Cancer the Natural Way. 5th ed. LC 94-92245. 316p. 1998. pap. text 19.95 (*0-9642329-1-X*) Res Pubns CA.

Moss, Susan, ed. see Harris, Judith P.

Moss, Sydney P. & Moss, Carolyn J. The Charles Dickens-Thomas Powell Vendetta: The Story in Documents. LC 95-62175. xiv, 151p. 1996. 28.50 (*0-87875-475-X*) Whitston Pub.

Moss, Sylvia. Cities in Motion. LC 87-5003. (National Poetry Ser.). 72p. 1987. 9.95 (*0-252-01436-7*) U of Ill Pr.

An Asterisk (*) at the beginning of an entry indicates that the title is appearing for the first time.

— Cities in Motion: Poems. LC 87-5003. (National Poetry Ser.). 69p. 1987. reprint ed. pap. 30.00 (0-7837-8081-8, 204783400008) Bks Demand.
— Costumes & Chemistry: A Guide to Materials & Applications. (Illus.). 320p. 2000. pap. write for info. (0-89676-214-9, Costume & Fashion Pr) QSMG Ltd.
Moss, Sylvia, jt. auth. see Tubbs, Stewart L.
Moss, T. S., et al, eds. Progress in Quantum Electronics, Vol. 8. (Illus.). 278p. 1985. 140.00 (0-08-031718-9, Pub. by PPL) Elsevier.
— Progress in Quantum Electronics, Vol. 9. (Illus.). 346p. 126.00 (0-08-034010-5, Pub. by PPL) Elsevier.
Moss, T. S. & Stenholm, Stig. Progress in Quantum Electronics, Vol. 6, Complete. (Illus.). 292p. 1981. 88.00 (0-08-028387-X, Pergamon Pr) Elsevier.
Moss, T. S., jt. ed. see Balkanski, M.
Moss, T. S., jt. ed. see Kneubuhl, Fritz K.
Moss, T. S., jt. ed. see Landsberg, Peter T.
Moss, T. S., jt. ed. see Schultz, G.
Moss, Terry. American History to the 1960s Study Partner. LC 94-77897. (Final Exam Ser.). 77p. 1994. pap. 5.49 (1-885962-54-1) Lincoln Lrning.
— Art History Study Partner. (Final Exam Ser.). 76p. 1996. pap. 5.49 (1-885962-67-3) Lincoln Lrning.
— Food & Drink Blaster! LC 94-77895. (Nutshell Ser.). 50p. 1994. pap. 4.95 (1-885962-50-9) Lincoln Lrning.
— Geography & Travel Blaster! LC 94-77901. (Nutshell Ser.). 60p. 1994. pap. 4.95 (1-885962-53-3) Lincoln Lrning.
— Literature Study Partner. LC 94-77900. (Final Exam Ser.). 68p. 1994. pap. 5.49 (1-885962-57-6) Lincoln Lrning.
— Myth & Legend Study Partner. (Final Exam Ser.). 72p. 1996. pap. 5.49 (1-885962-66-5) Lincoln Lrning.
— Photography Blaster! LC 94-77896. (Nutshell Ser.). 52p. 1994. pap. 4.95 (1-885962-51-7) Lincoln Lrning.
— Space . . . the Final Exam. (Final Exam Ser.). (Illus.). 68p. (Orig.). 1997. pap. 5.49 (1-885962-60-6) Lincoln Lrning.
— Weight Training & Total Fitness Blaster! LC 94-77894. (Nutshell Ser.). 53p. 1994. pap. 4.95 (1-885962-52-5) Lincoln Lrning.
— World History, 1600-1960 Study Partner. LC 94-77899. (Final Exam Ser.). 77p. 1994. pap. 5.49 (1-885962-55-X) Lincoln Lrning.
— World History to 1700 Study Partner. LC 94-77898. (Final Exam Ser.). 60p. 1994. pap. 4.95 (1-885962-56-8) Lincoln Lrning.
Moss, Thomas C. Fiscal Year Nineteen Seventy-Six Rating Factors: HUD Community Development Grant Program Non-Metropolitan Communities. 8p. (Orig.). 1975. pap. 1.00 (1-55719-024-0) U NE CPAR.
Moss, Thomas C. & O'Connor, Micheal G. Community Development Needs in Rural Nebraska & Iowa. 16p. (Orig.). 1975. pap. 1.50 (1-55719-026-7) U NE CPAR.
Moss, Thomas H., jt. ed. see Lunstedt, Sven B.
Moss, Thylias. At Redbones. (CSU Poetry Ser.: No. XXIX). 56p. (Orig.). 1990. pap. 7.00 (0-914946-73-0) Cleveland St Univ Poetry Ctr.
— Hosiery Seams on a Bowlegged Woman. (Orig.). pap. 4.50 (0-318-18369-2) League Bks.
— I Want to Be. 1998. 11.19 (0-606-13511-1, Pub. by Turtleback) Demco.
— Last Chance for the Tarzan Holler. LC 97-24005. 117p. 1998. 24.00 (0-89255-229-8) Persea Bks.
— Last Chance for the Tarzan Holler: Poems. 128p. 1999. reprint ed. pap. 14.00 (0-89255-243-3, Pub. by Persea Bks) Norton.
— Pyramid of Bone. Rowell, Charles H., ed. LC 88-25855. (Callaloo Poetry Ser.). ix, 56p. 1989. pap. 10.95 (0-8139-1202-4) U Pr of Va.
— Rainbow Remnants in Rock Bottom Ghetto Sky: Poems. LC 90-23770. (National Poetry Ser.: 1990). 72p. (Orig.). 1991. pap. 9.95 (0-89255-157-7) Persea Bks.
— Small Congregations: New & Selected Poems. LC 92-15683. 158p. 1999. 22.95 (0-88001-289-7); pap. 12.00 (0-88001-363-X) HarpC.
— The Tale of a Sky-Blue Dress. LC 98-17552. 272p. 1998. mass mkt. 23.00 (0-380-97550-5, Avon Bks) Morrow Avon.
***Moss, Thylias.** Tale of a Sky-Blue Dress. 288p. 1999. reprint ed. pap. 13.50 (0-380-79362-8, Avon Bks) Morrow Avon.
Moss, Tim H., et al. Intra-Operative Diagnosis of CNS Tumors. LC 97-9708. (An Arnold Publication). (Illus.). 202p. 1997. text 145.00 (0-340-67737-6) OUP.
***Moss, Tom, ed.** DNA-Protein Interactions: Principles & Protocols. 2nd ed. (Methods in Molecular Biology Ser.: Vol. 148). 550p. 2000. 125.00 (0-89603-625-1); spiral bd. 89.50 (0-89603-671-5) Humana.
Moss, Trevor S., et al. Semiconductor Opto-Electronics. LC 73-167813. 453p. reprint ed. pap. 140.50 (0-608-14827-X, 202573500046) Bks Demand.
Moss, Veronica A., jt. auth. see Sims, Ruth.
Moss, Vladimir A. The Saints of Anglo-Saxon England. (Orig.). 1992. pap. write for info. (0-913026-33-6) St Nectarios.
— The Saints of Anglo-Saxon England, Vol. I. LC 92-82557. (Illus.). 112p. (Orig.). 1992. pap. 8.50 (0-913026-32-8) St Nectarios.
— The Saints of Anglo-Saxon England, Vol. II. (Illus.). 128p. (Orig.). 1993. pap. 8.50 (0-913026-34-4) St Nectarios.
— The Saints of Anglo-Saxon England, Vol. III. (Illus.). (Orig.). 1996. pap. 8.50 (0-913026-35-2) St Nectarios.
Moss-Vreeland, Patricia, jt. auth. see Mittelman, Karen S.
Moss, W. From Page to Screen: Children's & Young Adult Books on Film & Video. 450p. 1992. 60.00 (0-8103-7893-0) Gale.
— Peoples of the World: Africa South Sahara 1, Vol. 3. 443p. 1991. 55.00 (0-8103-7942-2) Gale.
— Peoples of the World: The Middle East & North Africa, Vol. 4. 437p. 1991. 55.00 (0-8103-7941-4) Gale.
Moss, W. & Wilson. Peoples of the World: Eastern Europe & the Post-Soviet Republics, Vol. 5. 550p. 1992. 55.00 (0-8103-8867-7, 101509) Gale.
— Peoples of the World: Western Europeans, Vol. 6. 438p. 1993. 55.00 (0-8103-8868-5, 101510) Gale.
Moss, W. & Wilson, George. Peoples of the World: Asians & Pacific Islanders, Vol. 7. 550p. 1993. 55.00 (0-8103-8866-9, 101508) Gale.
Moss, W. Stanley. Ill Met by Moonlight. LC 98-10092. (Illus.). 192p. 1998. pap. 14.95 (1-58080-060-2) Burford Bks.
— Ill Met by Moonlight. LC 97-11128. 1997. pap. write for info. (1-55821-550-6) Lyons Pr.
Moss, Walter. A History of Russia. LC 96-34845. 624p. (C). 1996. pap. 37.19 (0-07-043480-8) McGraw.
— A History of Russia, Vol. 2. LC 96-34845. 576p. (C). 1996. pap. 37.19 (0-07-043482-4) McGraw.
***Moss, Walter G., et al.** The Twentieth Century: Readings in Global History. LC 98-41745. 384p. 1999. pap., teacher ed. 20.50 (0-07-289324-9, McGrw-H College) McGrw-H Hghr Educ.
Moss, Wayne F. Know-It-All Guide to the Trinity Alps. 2nd ed. LC 81-80959. (Illus.). 144p. 1982. pap. 7.95 (0-9606162-0-9) Mossart.
— The Trinity Alps Companion: Hiking Trails & Fishing Tales in the California Wilderness. LC 97-26472. (Illus.). 254p. (Orig.). 1997. pap. 14.95 (0-9639705-3-4) Ecopress.
Moss, William. Confederate Broadside Poems: An Annotated Descriptive Bibliography. (Illus.). 225p. 1988. lib. bdg. 59.95 (0-313-27704-4) Greenwood.
— Corporation Report, 2020. (Cyberpunk Ser.). (Illus.). 88p. (Orig.). 1991. pap. 10.00 (0-614-02724-1, CP3111) Talsorian.
— Corporation Report, 2020, Vol. 2. (Cyberpunk Ser.). (Illus.). 80p. (Orig.). 1992. pap. 10.00 (0-937279-20-X, CP3151) Talsorian.
— Corporation Report, 2020, Vol. 3. (Cyberpunk Ser.). (Illus.). 88p. (Orig.). 1992. pap. 10.00 (0-937279-24-2, CP3161) Talsorian.
— Land of the Free. (Cyberpunk Ser.). (Illus.). 120p. (Orig.). 1994. pap., boxed set 18.00 (0-937279-38-2, CP3231) Talsorian.
— Tales of the Forlorn Hope. (Cyberpunk Ser.). (Illus.). 104p. (Orig.). 1992. pap. 10.00 (0-937279-21-8, CP3121) Talsorian.
Moss, William, et al. Solo of Fortune. (Cyberpunk Ser.). (Illus.). 80p. 1989. student ed. 10.00 (0-937279-06-4, CP 3101) Talsorian.
Moss, William A. 10-Minute Card Games. LC 95-22505. (Illus.). 96p. 1995. pap. 4.95 (0-8069-3847-1) Sterling.
Moss, William M., jt. auth. see AVSC Staff.
Moss, William R. School Desegregation, Enough Is Enough. 216p. 1992. 19.95 (0-9634115-0-0) Danmo Pub Co.
Mossa, Joann, jt. auth. see Henry, James.
Mossavar-Rahmani, Bijan, ed. Natural Gas Trade in Transition. LC 87-81051. (International Energy Studies: No. 1). x, 91p. (Orig.). 1987. pap. 16.50 (0-942781-00-7) Harvard EEPC.
Mossbe, Daniel, et al. Real-Time Systems Education II: June 8, 1997, Montreal, Canada. LC 97-76881. viii, 125 p. 1997. write for info. (0-8186-8256-6) IEEE Comp Soc.
Mossberg, Barbara A. Emily Dickinson: When a Writer is a Daughter. LC 80-8633. 224p. reprint ed. pap. 69.50 (0-7837-3721-1, 205789900009) Bks Demand.
Mossberg, Christer L. Scandinavian Immigrant Literature. (Western Writers Ser.: No. 47). (Illus.). 52p. (Orig.). 1981. pap. 4.95 (0-88430-071-4) Boise St U W Writ Ser.
***Mossberg, Lena L., ed.** Evaluation of Events: Scandinavian Experience. LC 99-58762. (Illus.). 174p. 2000. text 38.00 (1-882345-41-X) Cognizant Comm.
— Evaluation of Events: Scandinavian Experience. LC 99-58762. (Illus.). 174p. (C). 2000. text 45.00 (1-882345-40-1) Cognizant Comm.
Mossberg, Walter S. The Information. 1996. write for info. (0-8129-2599-8, Times Bks) Crown Pub Group.
***Mossberger, Karen.** The Politics of Ideas & the Spread of Enterprise Zones. LC 00-26360. (American Governance & Public Policy Ser.). 288p. 2000. text 60.00 (0-87840-800-2); pap. text 24.95 (0-87840-801-0) Georgetown U Pr.
Mosse, Claude. Alexander II & the Modernization of Russia. 1992. text 65.00 (1-85043-513-8, Pub. by I B T) St Martin.
— Dictionnaire de la Civilisation Grecque. (FRE.). 512p. 1992. 125.00 (0-7859-8173-X, 2870274416) Fr & Eur.
— Dictionnaire de la Civilisation Grecque. (FRE.). 1998. reprint ed. 59.95 (0-320-00364-7) Fr & Eur.
— Fin de la Democratie Atheniennes: Aspects Sociaux et Politiques du Declin de la Cite Grecque au Ie Siecle avant J.-C. la Vie Economique d'Athenes au Ie Siecle: Crise ou Renouveau? Finley, Moses, ed. LC 79-4995. (Ancient Economic History Ser.). (FRE.). 1979. reprint ed. lib. bdg. 48.95 (0-405-12382-5) Ayer.
Mosse, David, et al. Development As Process: Concepts & Methods for Working with Complexity. LC 97-32107. 208p. (C). 1998. 75.00 (0-415-18605-6) Routledge.
Mosse, Fernand. Handbook of Middle English. rev. ed. Walker, James A., tr. LC 68-17255. (Illus.). 519p. (C). 1969. reprint ed. 39.95 (0-8018-0478-7) Johns Hopkins.
Mosse, George. Confronting History: A Memoir. LC 99-6425. (Illus.). 224p. 1999. text 27.95 (0-299-16580-9) U of Wis Pr.
Mosse, George L. Confronting the Nation: Jewish & Western Nationalism. LC 93-17227. (Tauber Institute for the Study of European Jewry Ser.: No.16). 232p. Date not set. reprint ed. pap. 72.00 (0-608-20686-5, 207179300002) Bks Demand.
— The Crisis of German Ideology: Intellectual Origins of the Third Reich. LC 97-26819. x, 373p. 1998. reprint ed. pap. 15.95 (0-86527-426-6) Fertig.
— Culture of Western Europe: The Nineteenth & Twentieth Centuries. 3rd ed. 438p. (C). 1988. pap. 35.00 (0-8133-0623-X, Pub. by Westview) HarpC.
— Fallen Soldiers: Reshaping the Memory of the World Wars. (Illus.). 272p. 1991. reprint ed. pap. 13.95 (0-19-507139-5) OUP.
— The Fascist Revolution: Toward a General Theory of Fascism. LC 98-16770. 248p. 1999. 35.00 (0-86527-432-0) Fertig.
***Mosse, George L.** The Fascist Revolution: Toward a General Theory of Fascism. LC 98-16770. 248p. 2000. reprint ed. pap. 13.95 (0-86527-435-5) Fertig.
Mosse, George L. German Jews Beyond Judaism. 98p. 1997. reprint ed. pap. 16.95 (0-87820-053-3) Hebrew Union Coll Pr.
— Germans & Jews: The Right, the Left & the Search for a 'Third Force' in Pre-Nazi Germany. LC 68-9631. 1970. 35.00 (0-86527-081-3) Fertig.
— The Image of Man: The Creation of Modern Masculinity. (Illus.). 240p. 1996. 27.50 (0-19-510101-4) OUP.
— The Image of Man: The Creation of Modern Masculinity. (Studies in the History of Sexuality Ser.). (Illus.). 240p. 1998. reprint ed. pap. 17.95 (0-19-512660-2) OUP.
— Masses & Man: Nationalist & Fascist Perceptions of Reality. LC 80-15399. xi, 362p. 1980. 45.00 (0-86527-334-0) Fertig.
— Masses & Man: Nationalist & Fascist Perceptions of Reality. LC 87-6131. 374p. 1987. reprint ed. pap. 18.95 (0-8143-1895-9) Wayne St U Pr.
— Nationalism & Sexuality: Respectability & Abnormal Sexuality in Modern Europe. 1997. reprint ed. pap. 13.95 (0-86527-429-0) Fertig.
— Nationalism & Sexuality: Respectabilty & Abnormal Sexuality in Modern Europe. LC 84-6082. (Illus.). 256p. 1985. 40.00 (0-86527-350-2) Fertig.
— The Nationalization of the Masses: Political Symbolism & Mass Movements in Germany, from the Napoleonic Wars Through the Third Reich. LC 91-55260. (Illus.). 272p. 1991. pap. text 16.95 (0-8014-9978-X) Cornell U Pr.
— The Nationalization of the Masses: Political Symbolism & Mass Movements in Germany, from the Napoleonic Wars Through the Third Reich. (Illus.). xiv, 272p. 2000. pap. 13.95 (0-86527-431-2) Fertig.
— Nazism: An Historical & Comparative Analysis. 160p. 1998. 32.95 (0-7658-0684-3) Transaction Pubs.
— The Reformation. rev. ed. (Illus.). 64p. (C). 1991. pap. text 2.25 (1-877891-02-9) Paperbook Pr Inc.
— Toward the Final Solution: A History of European Racism. LC 77-24356. (Illus.). 1978. 40.00 (0-86527-194-1) Fertig.
— Toward the Final Solution: A History of European Racism. (Illus.). xvi, 277p. 1997. reprint ed. pap. 14.95 (0-86527-428-2) Fertig.
Mosse, George L., ed. Police Forces in History. LC 74-84258. 344p. reprint ed. pap. 106.70 (0-608-14199-2, 202193500026) Bks Demand.
Mosse, George L., jt. auth. see Reinharz, Jehuda.
Mosse, George L., jt. ed. see Laqueur, Walter.
Mosse, George L., jt. ed. see Vago, Bela.
Mosse, Hilda L. The Complete Handbook of Children's Reading Disorders: You Can Prevent or Correct Learning Disorders. 2nd ed. (Illus.). 714p. (Orig.). 1987. pap. text 34.95 (0-942311-00-0) Riggs Inst Pr.
Mosse, Hilde. You Can Prevent or Correct Learning Disorders: The Complete Handbook of Children's Reading Disorders. 732p. (C). 1989. reprint ed. pap. text 34.95 (0-8077-2983-3) Tchrs Coll.
Mosse, Julia C. India: Paths to Development. (C). 1991. pap. text 21.00 (0-85598-153-9, Pub. by Oxfam Pubns) St Mut.
Mosse, Julia Cleves. Half the World, Half the Chance: An Introduction to Gender & Development. (Illus.). 240p. (C). 1992. pap. 15.95 (0-85598-186-5, Pub. by Oxfam Pub) Stylus Pub VA.
— India: Paths to Development. 2nd ed. (Country Profiles Ser.). (Illus.). 64p. (C). 1993. pap. 9.95 (0-85598-224-1, Pub. by Oxfam Pub) Stylus Pub VA.
***Mosse, Nicholas.** Country Living Irish Country: Decorating with Pottery, Fabric & Furniture. LC 98-8320. 144p. 1999. 25.00 (0-688-16501-X, Hearst) Hearst Commns.
Mosse, Roberto & Sontheimer, Leigh E. Performance Monitoring Indicators Handbook. LC 96-27346. (Technical Papers: No. 334). 54p. 1996. pap. 22.00 (0-8213-3731-9, 13731) World Bank.
Mosse, W. E. Alexander the Second & the Modernization of Russia. 200p. 1992. 39.50 (0-685-51843-4, Pub. by I B T) St Martin.
— Economic History of Russia, 1856-1914. 300p. 1996. text 19.95 (1-86064-066-4, Pub. by I B T) St Martin.
Mosse, W. E. The German-Jewish Economic Elite, 1820-1935: A Socio-Cultural Profile. (Illus.). 380p. 1989. text 85.00 (0-19-822990-9) OUP.
Mosse, W. E. Jews in the German Economy: The German-Jewish Economic Elite, 1820-1935. LC 86-18080. 370p. 1987. 79.00 (0-19-821967-9) OUP.
Mosse, Werner E., et al, eds. Second Chance. xii, 654p. 1991. 115.00 (3-16-145741-2, Pub. by JCB Mohr) Coronet Bks.
Mosse, Werner E., et al. Revolution & Evolution 1848 in German-Jewish History. 443p. 1981. lib. bdg. 110.00 (3-16-743752-9, Pub. by JCB Mohr) Coronet Bks.
Mossein, Seyyed. Islamic-Christian Dialogue: Problems & Obstacles to Be Overcome. (Occasional Papers Ser.). iii, 28p. 1998. pap. 3.95 (1-929218-06-0) Georgetwn U Ctr Muslim.
Mossek, M. Palestine Immigration Policy under Sir Herbert Samuel: British, Zionist & Arab Attitudes. 197p. 1978. 45.00 (0-7146-3096-9, Pub. by F Cass Pubs) Intl Spec Bk.
Mossel, Bob. Atlas of South Australia. 148p. (C). 1989. text 135.00 (0-89771-032-0, Pub. by Bob Mossel) St Mut.
— Learning & Other Things: The History of Education in South Australia. 496p. (C). 1989. pap. text 60.00 (0-89771-025-8, Pub. by Bob Mossel) St Mut.
— Light Aircraft Adventure into PNG. (C). 1989. pap. text 45.00 (0-89771-019-3, Pub. by Bob Mossel) St Mut.
— Where No Road Goes. 104p. (C). 1989. text 75.00 (0-89771-017-7, Pub. by Bob Mossel) St Mut.
Mossel, Bob & Kuhne, D. Beyond Lake Eyre. 112p. (C). 1989. text 80.00 (0-89771-016-9, Pub. by Bob Mossel) St Mut.
Mossel, Bob, et al. The Great 1974, Filling of Lake Eyre. 136p. (C). 1989. pap. text 45.00 (0-89771-034-7, Pub. by Bob Mossel) St Mut.
Mossel, Bob, jt. auth. see Kotwicki, V.
Mossel, David A., et al. Essentials of the Microbiology of Foods: A Textbook of Advanced Studies. LC 91-13719. 736p. 1996. 275.00 (0-471-93036-9) Wiley.
Mossell, N. F. The Work of the Afro-American Woman. LC 72-161270. (Black Heritage Library Collection). 1977. reprint ed. 27.95 (0-8369-8829-9) Ayer.
— The Work of the Afro-American Woman. (Schomburg Library of Nineteenth-Century Black Women Writers). 224p. 1988. reprint ed. text 32.00 (0-19-505265-X) OUP.
— The Work of the Afro-American Woman. (Schomburg Library of Nineteenth-Century Black Women Writers). 224p. 1990. reprint ed. pap. 9.95 (0-19-506326-0) OUP.

M

Mossenb, Ock. Modular Programming Languages: Joint Modular Languages Conference, JML '97, Linz, Austria, March 19-21, 1997: Proceedings. LC 97-6964. (Lecture Notes in Computer Science Ser.: Vol. 120). 1997. pap. 61.00 (3-540-62599-2) Spr-Verlag.
Mossenbock, Hanspeter. Object-Oriented Programming in Oberon-2. Bach, Robert, tr. from GER. LC 93-10033.Tr. of Objektorientierte Programmierung in Oberon-2. (Illus.). 278p. 1993. pap. text 39.00 (0-387-56411-X) Spr-Verlag.
— Object-Oriented Programming in Oberon-2. 2nd ed. Bach, Robert, tr. (Illus.). 280p. 1995. 49.95 (3-540-60062-0) Spr-Verlag.
Mossenson, David. Hebrew, Israelite, Jew: The History of the Jews of Western Australia. 9.95 (0-85564-314-5, Pub. by Univ of West Aust Pr) Intl Spec Bk.
— State Education in Western Australia, 1829-1960. LC 75-157278. 187p. 1971. write for info. (0-85564-047-2) Intl Spec Bk.
Mosser, David, jt. auth. see Laney, Joan.
Mosser, Marjorie. Good Maine Food. 424p. 1978. reprint ed. pap. 12.95 (0-89272-038-7) Down East.
***Mosser, Monique & Tyssot, Georges.** The History of Garden Design: The Western Tradition. LC 99-67034. (Illus.). 543p. 2000. pap. 44.95 (0-500-28206-4, Pub. by Thames Hudson) Norton.
Mosseri, Remy, jt. auth. see Sadoc, Jean-Francois.
Mosses, Peter D. Action Semantics. (Tracts in Theoretical Computer Science Ser.: No. 26). 392p. (C). 1992. text 59.95 (0-521-40347-2) Cambridge U Pr.
Mosses, Peter D., ed. see Sixth International Joint Conference on Theory & P, et al.
Mossetto, Gianfranco. Aesthetics & Economics. LC 93-15476. 232p. (C). 1993. lib. bdg. 152.50 (0-7923-2296-7, Pub. by Kluwer Academic) Kluwer Academic.
Mossetto, Gianfranco, jt. text see Costantini, Paolo.
Mosseveld, C. J. P. M. Van, see Van Mosseveld, C. J. P. M.
Mosshammer, ed. Syncelli, Georgii. (GRE.). 1984. 105.00 (3-322-00199-7, T1890, Pub. by B G Teubner) U of Mich Pr.
Mosshammer, Alden A. The Chronicle of Eusebius & Greek Chronographic Tradition. LC 76-1029. 366p. 1979. 40.00 (0-8387-1939-2) Bucknell U Pr.
Mossholder, Ray. Kids Are a Plus. 1995. pap. 10.99 (0-88419-357-8) Creation House.
Mossi, John & Toolan, Suzanne. Canticles & Gathering Prayers. 150p. 1989. spiral bd. 10.95 (0-88489-228-X) St Marys.
Mossialios Kanavos. Structure of the International Market for Pharmaceuticals. 63.95 (1-85521-622-1) Ashgate Pub Co.
Mossialos, Elias & Le Grand, Julian, eds. Health Care & Cost Containment in the European Union. LC 98-44661. 600p. 1999. text 105.95 (1-84014-403-3, Pub. by Ashgate Pub) Ashgate Pub Co.
Mossialos, Elias, jt. auth. see Meetsos, Achilleas.
Mossiker, Frances. Madame de Sevigne: A Life & Letters. LC 85-4096. 560p. 1985. reprint ed. pap. text 27.00 (0-231-06153-6) Col U Pr.
— Pocahontas: The Life & the Legend. LC 95-43815. (Illus.). 424p. 1996. reprint ed. pap. 15.95 (0-306-80699-1) Da Capo.
Mossin, Albert C. Selling Performance & Contentment in Relation to School Background. LC 79-177093. (Columbia University. Teachers College. Contributions to Education Ser.: No. 952). reprint ed. 37.50 (0-404-55952-2) AMS Pr.
Mossin, Henrik, tr. see Sloek, Johannes.
***Mossinger, Ingrid, ed.** European Textile Design in the 1920s. (Illus.). 1999. 55.00 (3-908161-61-4) Abbeville Pr.
Mossinger, Rosemarie. Woodleaf Legacy: The Story of California Gold Rush Town. rev. ed. Chapman, Jean, ed. LC 94-77982. (Illus.). 180p. (YA). (gr. 5 up). 1995. pap. 22.95 (0-9621940-4-2) C Mautz Pubng.
Mossinger, Rosemarie, ed. see Rowe, Jeremy.
Mossinghoff, Michael J., jt. auth. see Blachman, Nancy R.
Mosslacher, Egon. Breeding & Caring for Chinchillas. (Illus.). 128p. 1989. 17.95 (0-86622-804-7, PS-850) TFH Pubns.

Mossle, Klaus P. Extraterritoriale Beweisbeschaffung im Internationalen Wirtschaftsrecht: Eine Vergleichende Untersuchung unter Besonderer Berucksichtigung des Amerikanischen & Deutschen Rechts. (GER.). 533p. 1990. pap. 116.00 (*3-7890-1888-0*, Pub. by Nomos Verlags) Intl Bk Import.

Mossman, B. C. & Stark, M. W. The Lasting Salute: Civil & Military Funerals, 1921-1969. (Illus.). 428p. (Orig.). (C). 1995. pap. text 60.00 (*0-7881-2072-7*) DIANE Pub.

Mossman, B. T. & Begin, R. O., eds. Effects of Mineral Dusts on Cells. (NATO ASI Series H: Vol. 30). (Illus.). 155p. 1989. 171.95 (*0-387-50422-2*, 3117) Spr-Verlag.

Mossman, Billy C. United States Army in the Korean War: Ebb & Flow, Nov. 1950-July 1951. LC 89-600137. (Illus.). 569p. 1990. per. 36.00 (*0-16-023487-5*, 008029002116) USGPO.

Mossman, Brooke T., jt. ed. see Guthrie, George D., Jr.

Mossman, Carol A. The Narrative Matrix: Stendhal's "Le Rouge & le Noir" LC 84-80768. (French Forum Monographs: No. 53). 177p. (Orig.). 1984. pap. 13.45 (*0-917058-53-4*) French Forum.

— Politics & Narratives of Birth: Gynocolonization from Rousseau to Zola. (Cambridge Studies in French: No. 41). 271p. (C). 1993. text 69.95 (*0-521-41586-1*) Cambridge U Pr.

Mossman, Harland W. Vertebrate Fetal Membranes Comparative Ontogeny & Morphology: Evolution: Phylogenetic Significance, Basic Functions: Research Opportunities. 400p. 1987. text 100.00 (*0-8135-1132-1*) Rutgers U Pr.

Mossman, Jennifer, ed. Pseudonyms & Nicknames Dictionary, 2 vols., Set. 3rd ed. 2207p. 1986. 239.00 (*0-8103-0541-0*) Gale.

Mossman, Judith, ed. Plutarch & His Intellectual World: Essays on Plutarch. 250p. 1997. 49.50 (*0-7156-2778-3*, Pub. by Classical Pr) David Brown.

Mossman, Keith. Pip Book. 128p. pap. 12.95 (*0-14-046255-4*, Pub. by Pnguin Bks Ltd) Trafalgar.

Mossman, Kenny, ed. see Bloodworth, Bryan & Cushman, Roger.

Mossman, Lois Coffey. Changing Conception Relative to the Planning of Lessons. LC 72-177094. (Columbia University. Teachers College. Contributions to Education Ser.: No. 147). reprint ed. 37.50 (*0-404-55147-5*) AMS Pr.

Mossman, M. Samba Larue Sextet. 1995. pap. text 20.00 (*0-7935-4837-3*, 00000508) H Leonard.

Mossman, Marilyn. Introduction to Logo, Bk. 1. Schroeder, Bonnie, ed. 1989. pap. text 5.95 (*1-56177-109-0*, 402-1) CES Compu-Tech.

— Introduction to Logo, Bk. 2. Schroeder, Bonnie, ed. (Illus.). 1989. pap. text 5.95 (*1-56177-110-4*, 402-2) CES Compu-Tech.

— Introduction to Logo: Lab Pack 1. Schroeder, Bonnie, ed. (Illus.). teacher ed., student ed. 199.95 incl. disk (*1-56177-113-9*, L402-1) CES Compu-Tech.

— Introduction to Logo: Lab Pack 2. Schroeder, Bonnie, ed. (Illus.). teacher ed., student ed. 199.95 incl. disk (*1-56177-114-7*, L402-2) CES Compu-Tech.

— Introduction to Logo: Teacher Edition, Pt. 1. Schroeder, Bonnie, ed. (Illus.). 1989. teacher ed. 19.95 (*1-56177-115-5*, TE402-1) CES Compu-Tech.

— Introduction to Logo: Teacher Edition, Pt. 2. Schroeder, Bonnie, ed. (Illus.). 1989. teacher ed. 19.95 (*1-56177-116-3*, TE402-2) CES Compu-Tech.

— Introduction to Word Processing: Course Code 182-N. Schroeder, Bonnie, ed. (Illus.). 141p. (Orig.). (J). (gr. 4). 1989. pap. text 8.95 (*0-917531-59-0*) CES Compu-Tech.

— Introduction to Word Processing: Lab Pack. Schroeder, Bonnie, ed. (Illus.). teacher ed., student ed. 179.95 incl. disk (*1-56177-053-1*, L182); teacher ed., student ed. 8.95 incl. 5.25 hd (*1-56177-052-3*, D-182) CES Compu-Tech.

— Skill Builders: Lab Pack 1. Schroeder, Bonnie, ed. (Illus.). teacher ed. 19.95 (*1-56177-123-6*, TE492-1); teacher ed., student ed. 199.95 incl. disk (*1-56177-121-X*, L492-1); student ed. 5.95 (*1-56177-117-1*, 492-1) CES Compu-Tech.

— Skill Builders: Lab Pack 2. Schroeder, Bonnie, ed. (Illus.). teacher ed. 19.95 (*1-56177-124-4*, TE492-2); teacher ed., student ed. 199.95 incl. disk (*1-56177-122-8*, L492-2); student ed. 5.95 (*1-56177-118-X*) CES Compu-Tech.

Mossman, Marilyn & Roberts, Diane. Introduction to Word Processing: Course Code 182-N. Schroeder, Bonnie, ed. (Illus.). 150p. (Orig.). 1989. teacher ed. 19.95 (*0-917531-75-2*) CES Compu-Tech.

Mossman, Philip. Money of the American Colonies & Confederation: A Numismatic, Economic & Historical Correlation. (Numismatic Studies: No. 20). (Illus.). 312p. 1993. 100.00 (*0-89722-249-0*) Am Numismatic.

Mossman, S. T. & Morris, P. J., eds. The Development of Plastics. 120p. 1994. 68.00 (*0-85186-575-5*, R6575) CRC Pr.

***Mossman, Susan.** Early Plastics: Perspectives, 1850-1950. (Illus.). 256p. 2000. pap. text 41.95 (*0-7185-0237-X*) Leicester U Pr.

Mossman, Susan, ed. Early Plastics: Perspectives, 1850-1950. (Illus.). 256p. 1996. text 89.50 (*0-7185-0020-2*) Bks Intl VA.

Mossman, Tam. Seven Strategies in Every Best-Seller: A 186-Page Guide to Extraordinarily Successful Writing. 192p. (Orig.). 1998. pap. 19.95 (*0-9632947-1-7*) Tiger Maple Pr.

Mossman, Tam, ed. Answers from a Grander Self. 221p. (Orig.). 1993. pap. 12.95 (*0-9632947-0-9*) Tiger Maple Pr.

Mossman, Thomas L., jt. auth. see Bavaro, Joseph J.

***Mossmen, Tam.** Eight Strategies in Every Best-Seller: A Definitive Guide to Extraordinarily Successful Writing. 2nd rev. ed. 240p. 1999. pap. 14.95 (*1-893302-05-9*) Dandelion Bks.

Mossner, Ernest C. Bishop Butler & the Age of Reason. LC 69-13247. 1972. reprint ed. 18.95 (*0-405-08807-8*, Pub. by Blom Pubns) Ayer.

— The Forgotten Hume: Le Bon David (1943 Edition) 276p. 1996. reprint ed. 48.00 (*1-85506-069-8*) Bks Intl VA.

Mossner, Ernest C., ed. see Smith, Adam.

Mossner, Ernest C., ed. & intro. see Hume, David.

Mossoba, Magdi M., ed. Spectral Medthods in Food Analysis: Instrumentation & Applications. LC 98-45744. (Illus.). 488p. 1998. text 165.00 (*0-8247-0223-9*) Dekker.

Mossoba, Magdi M., jt. auth. see McDonald, Richard E.

Mossop, R. T. History of Western Medicine in Zimbabwe. LC 97-43750. (Studies in African Health & Medicine: Vol. 9). (Illus.). 624p. 1998. text 129.95 (*0-7734-8536-8*) E Mellen.

Mosston, Muska & Ashworth, Sara. Teaching Physical Education. 4th ed. 256p. (C). 1993. pap. text 58.00 (*0-02-384183-4*, Macmillan Coll) P-H.

Most. Littlest Dinosaurs: Mini-Book. (J). 1995. 4.95 (*0-15-200381-9*, Harcourt Child Bks) Harcourt.

— Where to Look for a Dinosaur: Mini-Book. (J). 1995. 4.95 (*0-15-200379-7*, Harcourt Child Bks) Harcourt.

Most, Benjamin A. Changing Authoritarian Rule & Public Policy in Argentina, 1930-1970. LC 90-42342. (GSIS Monograph in World Affairs). 206p. 1990. lib. bdg. 25.00 (*1-55587-246-8*) L Rienner.

Most, Benjamin A. & Starr, Harvey. Inquiry, Logic & International Politics. Kegley, Charles W., Jr. & Puchala, Donald J., eds. LC 88-33984. (Studies in International Relations). 244p. 1989. pap. text 21.95 (*0-87249-630-9*) U of SC Pr.

***Most, Bernard.** ABC T-Rex. LC 98-51128. 32p. (J). 2000. 15.00 (*0-15-202007-1*, Harcourt Child Bks) Harcourt.

Most, Bernard. Catbirds & Dogfish. LC 94-17839. (J). (ps-3). 1995. pap. 5.00 (*0-15-200779-2*) Harcourt.

— Catbirds & Dogfish. LC 94-17839. (Illus.). 32p. (J). (ps-3). 1995. 13.00 (*0-15-292844-8*) Harcourt.

— Catbirds & Dogfish. 1995. 10.20 (*0-606-07352-3*, Pub. by Turtleback) Demco.

— Catch Me If You Can! LC 98-15569. (Green Light Readers Ser.). (Illus.). 20p. (J). 1999. pap. 3.95 (*0-15-202001-2*) Harcourt.

— Catch Me If You Can! (Green Light Readers Ser.). 20p. (J). 2000. 10.95 (*0-15-202351-8*) Harcourt.

— Cock-a-Doodle-Moo! LC 95-36097. (Illus.). 40p. (J). (ps-2). 1996. pap. 13.00 (*0-15-201252-4*, Red Wagon Bks) Harcourt.

— The Cow That Went Oink. LC 89-39896. (Illus.). 32p. (J). (ps-3). 1990. 13.00 (*0-15-220195-5*) Harcourt.

— Cow That Went Oink. LC 89-39896. (Big Bks.). (Illus.). 32p. (J). (ps-3). 1991. pap. 23.95 (*0-15-220196-3*, Harcourt Child Bks) Harcourt.

— Dinosaur Cousins? LC 86-18485. (Illus.). 40p. (J). (ps-3). 1990. pap. 6.00 (*0-15-223498-5*, Voyager Bks) Harcourt.

— A Dinosaur Named after Me. D'Andrade, Diane, ed. LC 90-36272. (Illus.). 32p. (J). (ps-3). 1991. 12.95 (*0-15-223494-2*) Harcourt.

— Dinosaur Named After Me. 1991. 10.20 (*0-606-07435-X*, Pub. by Turtleback) Demco.

— A Dinosaur Named after Me. abr. ed. LC 90-36272. (Illus.). 32p. (J). (ps-3). 1995. pap. 5.00 (*0-15-223493-4*, Voyager Bks) Harcourt.

— Dinosaur Questions. LC 94-42630. (Illus.). 40p. (J). (ps-3). 1995. 16.00 (*0-15-292885-5*, Harcourt Child Bks) Harcourt.

— Four & Twenty Dinosaurs. LC 98-15869. (Illus.). 32p. (J). 1999. pap. 6.00 (*0-15-201959-6*) Harcourt.

— Happy Holidaysaurus! LC 91-19832. (Illus.). 32p. (J). (ps-3). 1992. 13.95 (*0-15-233386-X*, Harcourt Child Bks) Harcourt.

— Hippopotamus Hunt. abr. ed. LC 93-39988. (Illus.). 32p. (J). (ps-3). 1994. 14.95 (*0-15-234520-5*) Harcourt.

— How Big Were the Dinosaurs? LC 93-19152. (Illus.). 24p. (J). (ps-3). 1994. 16.00 (*0-15-236800-0*, Harcourt Child Bks) Harcourt.

— How Big Were the Dinosaurs? LC 93-19152. (Illus.). 24p. (J). (ps-3). 1995. pap. 6.00 (*0-15-200852-7*, Voyager Bks) Harcourt.

— How Big Were the Dinosaurs? 1996. pap. text 6.35 (*0-382-33658-5*) Silver Burdett Pr.

— How Big Were the Dinosaurs? 1995. 11.20 (*0-606-07673-5*, Pub. by Turtleback) Demco.

— If the Dinosaurs Came Back. LC 77-23911. (Illus.). 32p. (J). (ps-2). 1984. pap. 6.00 (*0-15-238021-3*, Voyager Bks) Harcourt.

— If the Dinosaurs Came Back. LC 95-215704. (Illus.). 32p. (J). (ps-2). 1995. pap. 5.00 (*0-15-200380-0*, Red Wagon Bks) Harcourt.

— If the Dinosaurs Came Back. (J). 1978. 11.20 (*0-606-04256-3*, Pub. by Turtleback) Demco.

— If the Dinosaurs Came Back. abr. ed. LC 77-23911. (Illus.). 32p. (J). (ps-2). 1978. 16.00 (*0-15-238020-5*, Harcourt Child Bks) Harcourt.

— If the Dinosaurs Came Back. LC 77-23911. (Big Bks.). (Illus.). 32p. (J). (ps-2). 1991. reprint ed. pap. 23.95 (*0-15-238022-1*) Harcourt.

— If the Dinosaurs Came Back, Set. unabridged ed. (Illus.). (J). (gr. k-3). 1991. pap. 15.95 incl. audio (*0-87499-236-2*); pap., teacher ed. 37.95 incl. audio (*0-87499-238-9*) Live Oak Media.

— The Littlest Dinosaurs. LC 88-30063. (Illus.). 32p. (J). (ps-2). 1993. pap. 5.95 (*0-15-248126-5*) Harcourt.

— The Littlest Dinosaurs, 4 bks., Set. (Illus.). (J). (gr. 1-6). 1993. pap., teacher ed. 33.95 incl. audio (*0-87499-193-5*) Live Oak Media.

— The Littlest Dinosaurs, Set. unabridged ed. (Illus.). (J). (gr. 1-6). 1993. pap. 15.95 incl. audio (*0-87499-191-9*) Live Oak Media.

— Moo-Ha! LC 96-10591. (Illus.). 20p. (J). 1997. pap. 5.95 (*0-15-201248-6*) Harcourt.

— My Very Own Octopus. D'Andrade, Diane, ed. LC 80-12786. (Illus.). 32p. (J). (ps-3). 1991. pap. 6.00 (*0-15-256345-8*, Voyager Bks) Harcourt.

— Oink-Ha! LC 96-10592. (Illus.). 20p. (J). 1997. pap. 5.95 (*0-15-201249-4*) Harcourt.

— Pair of Protoceratops. LC 96-26358. (Illus.). 36p. (J). (ps-3). 1998. 11.00 (*0-15-201443-8*) Harcourt.

— Peek a Moo. LC 97-33042. (Illus.). 20p. (J). 1998. 5.95 (*0-15-201251-6*, Harcourt Child Bks) Harcourt.

— Pets in Trumpets & Other Word-Play Riddles. LC 90-23873. (Illus.). 32p. (J). (ps-3). 1991. 12.95 (*0-15-261210-6*, Harcourt Child Bks) Harcourt.

— Row Row Row Your Goat. LC 97-33043. (Illus.). 20p. (J). 1998. pap. 5.95 (*0-15-201250-8*, Harcourt Child Bks) Harcourt.

— There's an Ant in Anthony. LC 79-23089. (Illus.). 32p. (J). (ps-3). 1992. mass mkt. 4.95 (*0-688-11513-6*, Wm Morrow) Morrow Avon.

— There's an Ant in Anthony. (J). 1992. 9.15 (*0-606-01324-5*, Pub. by Turtleback) Demco.

— Trio of Triceratops. LC 96-23701. (Illus.). 36p. (J). 1998. 11.00 (*0-15-201448-9*) Harcourt.

— La Vaca Que Decia Oink (The Cow That Went Oink) Mlawer, Teresa, tr. from ENG. (SPA., Illus.). 32p. (J). 1994. 12.95 (*1-880507-14-5*) Lectorum Pubns.

— The Very Boastful Kangaroo. LC 98-55234. 20p. (J). 1999. 10.95 (*0-15-202349-6*, Harcourt Child Bks) Harcourt.

— The Very Boastful Kangaroo. LC 98-55234. (Green Light Readers Ser.). 20p. (J). 1999. pap. 3.95 (*0-15-202266-X*) Harcourt.

— Whatever Happened to the Dinosaurs? LC 84-37795. (Voyager Picture Bks.). (Illus.). 32p. (J). (ps-3). 1987. pap. 4.95 (*0-15-295296-9*, Voyager Bks) Harcourt.

— Whatever Happened to the Dinosaurs? LC 84-37795. (Illus.). 32p. (J). (ps). 1995. pap. 5.00 (*0-15-200378-9*, Red Wagon Bks) Harcourt.

— Whatever Happened to the Dinosaurs? abr. ed. LC 84-3779. (Illus.). 32p. (J). (ps-3). 1984. 16.00 (*0-15-295295-0*, Harcourt Child Bks) Harcourt.

— Where to Look for a Dinosaur. LC 92-19443. (Illus.). 32p. (J). (gr. k-3). 1993. 13.00 (*0-15-295616-6*, Harcourt Child Bks) Harcourt.

— Where to Look for a Dinosaur. LC 92-19443. (Illus.). 32p. (J). 1997. pap. 5.00 (*0-15-201504-3*, Voyager Bks) Harcourt.

— Where to Look for a Dinosaur. (J). 1997. 10.20 (*0-606-12086-6*, Pub. by Turtleback) Demco.

— Z-Z-Zoink! LC 98-2823. (Illus.). 32p. (J). (ps-1). 1999. 13.00 (*0-15-292845-6*) Harcourt.

— Zoodles. LC 91-33490. (Illus.). 32p. (J). (gr. k-3). 1992. 13.95 (*0-15-299969-8*, Harcourt Child Bks) Harcourt.

— Zoodles. LC 91-33490. (Illus.). 32p. (J). (ps-3). 1994. pap. 19.95 (*0-15-200071-2*, Harcourt Child Bks) Harcourt.

Most, Bernard, ed. The Cow That Went Oink. 93rd ed. 1998. pap. text 10.75 (*0-15-300312-X*, Harcourt Child Bks) Harcourt.

Most, Bernard & Freeman, Don. The Little Dinosaurs. unabridged ed. (Illus.). (J). (gr. k-1). 1993. 22.95 incl. audio (*0-87499-192-7*) Live Oak Media.

Most, Bruce W. Bonded for Murder: A Ruby Dark Mystery. 1996. mass mkt. 5.99 (*0-312-96051-4*) St Martin.

— Missing Bonds, Vol. 1. 288p. 1997. mass mkt. 5.99 (*0-312-96273-8*) St Martin.

Most, Clark F. Experimental Organic Chemistry. LC 87-21653. 608p. 1988. text 84.95 (*0-471-82043-1*) Wiley.

Most, Clark F. & Zubrick, James W. Experimental Organic Chemistry A Student's Guide to Techniques. 4th ed. 1008p. 1997. text, student ed. 118.90 (*0-471-28299-5*) Wiley.

Most, Daniel L., jt. auth. see Noe, George T.

***Most, Doug.** Always in Our Hearts: The Story of Amy Grossberg, Brain Peterson, The Pregnancy They Hid & the Baby They Killed. 312p. 2000. mass mkt. 6.50 (*0-312-97309-8*) St Martin.

Most, Doug. Always in Our Hearts: The Story of Amy Grossberg, Brian Peterson, & the Baby They Didn't Want. LC 98-32047. (Illus.). 280p. 1999. 22.95 (*0-9654733-5-X*) Record Bks.

Most, Friederike. Coal Mine Portraits. (Illus.). 144p. 1997. 45.00 (*3-908162-89-0*) Dist Art Pubs.

Most, Glenn W., ed. see Conte, Gian B.

Most, Glenn W., jt. ed. see Laks, Andre.

Most, Glenn W., tr. see Conte, Gian Biagio.

Most, J. Science of Revolutionary Warfare: A Guide for Would-Be Anarchists. (Anarchists & Anarchism Ser.). 1990. lib. bdg. 250.00 (*0-87700-887-6*) Revisionist Pr.

Most, Johann. Science of Revolutionary Warfare. (Explosives, Incendiaries & Demolitions Ser.: No. 2). 1990. lib. bdg. 79.95 (*0-8490-3993-2*) Gordon Pr.

Most, John. Revolutionaire Kriegswissenschaft. (History of Political Violence Ser.). 1985. reprint ed. lib. bdg. 30.00 (*0-527-41194-9*) Periodicals Srv.

Most, Johnny. Feelings: Private Thoughts & Poems. LC 92-71501. (Illus.). 104p. (Orig.). 1992. pap. 13.95 (*0-9632856-0-2*) Charm Pub Co.

— High Above Courtside: My Life with the Boston Celtics. 1992. write for info. (*0-201-15758-6*) Addison-Wesley.

Most, Kenneth S. The Future of the Accounting Profession: A Global Perspective. LC 92-34945. 240p. 1993. 62.95 (*0-89930-726-4*, MUT, Quorum Bks) Greenwood.

Most, Kenneth S. & Lewis, Ronald J. Accompany Cost Accounting. LC 81-6688. (Accounting Ser.). 650p. (C). 1987. pap. text 15.95 (*0-471-84242-7*) P-H.

Most, Kenneth S., jt. auth. see Chang, Lucia S.

Most, Kenneth S., jt. ed. see Doupnik, Timothy S.

Most, Kenneth S., tr. see Schmalenbach, Eugen.

Most, Philippe. Dictionnaire de Medecine du Sport. (FRE.). 274p. 1987. pap. 95.00 (*0-7859-7828-3*, 2225810176) Fr & Eur.

Most, Robert, jt. ed. see Zeidner, Moshe.

Most, Sam. Jazz Improvisation. rev. ed. Cavalier, Debbie, ed. 128p. (C). 1996. pap. text 19.95 (*1-57623-654-4*, EL96122CD) Wrner Bros.

Most, William G. Catholic Apologetics Today: Answers to Modern Critics: Does It Make Sense to Believe? LC 86-50853. 272p. (C). 1992. pap. 9.00 (*0-89555-305-8*) TAN Bks Pubs.

— The Consciousness of Christ. LC 80-68761. 232p. (Orig.). 1980. pap. text 6.95 (*0-931888-03-4*) Christendom Pr.

— Free from All Error: Authorship, Inerrancy, Historicity of Scripture, Church Teaching, & Modern Scripture Scholars. 179p. (Orig.). 1985. pap. 11.95 (*0-913382-51-5*, 101-31) Marytown Pr.

— The Heart Has Its Reasons: The Sacred Heart of Jesus & the Immaculate Heart of Mary. 35p. (Orig.). 1985. pap. 1.50 (*0-913382-50-7*, 105-40) Marytown Pr.

— Our Father's Plan: God's Arrangements & Our Response. 276p. 1993. reprint ed. pap. 7.95 (*0-931888-50-6*) Christendom Pr.

— The Thought of St. Paul: A Commentary on the Pauline Epistles. 301p. (Orig.). 1994. pap. 14.95 (*0-931888-56-5*) Christendom Pr.

Mostaedi, Arian, jt. auth. see Broto, Carles.

Mostaedi, Arian, ed. see Broto, Carles.

Mostaert, Antoine & Cleaves, Francis W., eds. Les Lettres de 1289 et 1305 des Ilkhan Argun et Oljeitu A. Philippe Le Bel. LC 62-19219. (Harvard-Yenching Institute, Scripta Mongolica Ser.: No. 1). (FRE., Illus.). 111p. 1962. pap. 10.00 (*0-674-52850-6*) HUP.

***Mostafa, Joshua.** Letters & Mailing. LC 99-54212. (Essential Computers Ser.). 72p. 2000. pap. text 6.95 (*0-7894-5529-3*, D K Ink) DK Pub Inc.

Mostafa, Sobhy M., ed. Anaesthesia for Ophthalmic Surgery. (Illus.). 352p. 1992. 89.50 (*0-19-261960-8*) OUP.

Mostafavi, Mohsen & Leatherbarrow, David. On Weathering: The Life of Buildings in Time. (Illus.). 139p. 1993. 31.50 (*0-262-13291-5*); pap. text 16.95 (*0-262-63144-X*) MIT Pr.

Mostafavi, Mohsen, jt. auth. see Fardjadi, Homa.

Mostafawy, Schoole. Die Flucht Nach Agypten. (Europaische Hochschulschriften Ser.: Reihe 28, Vol. 316). (Illus.). 304p. 1998. pap. 56.95 (*3-631-32566-5*) P Lang Pubng.

Mostaghaci, Hamid, ed. Advanced Ceramic Materials: Applications of Advanced Material in a High-Tech Society I. LC 97-169376. (Key Engineering Materials Ser.: Vols. 122-124). (Illus.). 590p. (C). 1997. 236.00 (*0-87849-745-5*, Pub. by Trans T Pub) Enfield Pubs NH.

Mostecky, Vaclav, jt. auth. see Ruggles, Melville J.

Mosteller, F. & Wallace, D. L. Applied Bayesian & Classical Inference: The Case of the Federalist Papers. 2nd ed. LC 84-5489. (Series in Statistics). (Illus.). 290p. 1984. 72.95 (*0-387-90991-5*) Spr-Verlag.

Mosteller, Frederick. Fifty Challenging Problems in Probability with Solutions. viii, 88p. 1987. reprint ed. pap. text 4.95 (*0-486-65355-2*) Dover.

Mosteller, Frederick & Tukey, John W. Data Analysis & Regression: A Second Course in Statistics. LC 76-15465. (Behavioral Science Ser.). 608p. (C). 1977. 103.00 (*0-201-04854-X*) Addison-Wesley.

Mosteller, Frederick, jt. ed. see Bailar, John C., III.

Mosteller, Frederick, jt. ed. see Frazier, Howard S.

Mosteller, Frederick, jt. ed. see Lovie, A. D.

Mosteller, Frederick, jt. ed. see Warren, Kenneth S.

Mosteller, Juliette. Living, Loving & Enduring: A Journey to Love. 80p. (Orig.). 1996. pap. 9.95 (*1-887798-04-8*) WriteMore Pubns.

Mosteller, Lee. Survival English Three, Bk. 3. 192p. 1994. pap. text 19.33 (*0-13-878166-4*) P-H.

— Survival English 3A. 2nd ed. 1994. write for info. (*0-13-017005-4*) P-H.

Mosteller, Lee & Haight, Michele A. Survival English: English Through Conversations, Bk. 2B. (Illus.). 128p. 1988. pap. text 5.25 (*0-13-879263-1*) P-H.

Mosteller, Lee & Paul, Bobbi. Survival English, Bk. 1. 2nd ed. 272p. 1993. pap. text 19.33 (*0-13-016635-9*) P-H.

— Survival English, Bk. 1B. 2nd ed. 144p. 1993. pap. text 12.80 (*0-13-016601-4*) P-H.

Mosteller, Lee & Paul, Bobbi. Survival English: English Through Conversations, BK. 1B. (Illus.). 128p. (C). 1988. pap. text 9.60 (*0-13-879222-4*) P-H.

Mosteller, Lee & Paul, Bobbi. Survival English: English Through Conversations, Bk. 2. 2nd ed. 240p. 1994. pap. text 19.33 (*0-13-016650-2*) P-H.

— Survival English 2A. 2nd ed. 1994. pap. write for info. (*0-13-016619-7*) P-H.

— Survival English 2B. 2nd ed. 1994. pap. write for info. (*0-13-016627-8*) P-H.

— Survivinal English, Bk 1A. 2nd ed. 144p. 1993. pap. text 12.80 (*0-13-016593-X*) P-H.

Mosteller, Robert P., et al. North Carolina Evidentiary Foundation. LC 98-85075. 1998. text 80.00 (*0-327-00114-3*, 60110-10) LEXIS Pub.

Mosteller, Sue. A Place to Hold My Shaky Heart: Reflections from Life in a Community. LC 98-72904. 128p. 1998. pap. 12.95 (*0-8245-1763-6*, Crsrd) Crossroad NY.

Mosten, Forrest S. The Complete Guide to Mediation. LC 96-27951. 1996. pap. 124.95 (*1-57073-348-1*) Amer Bar Assn.

Mostepanenko, Vladimir & Trunov, N. N. The Casimir Effect & Its Applications. Znajek, R. L., tr. LC 97-162442. (Illus.). 212p. (C). 1997. text 100.00 (*0-19-853998-3*) OUP.

Moster, Mary B. Cuando el Medico Dice: Es Cancer. (Serie Guia de Bolsillo - Pocket Guides Ser.).Tr. of When the Doctor Says "It's Cancer". (SPA.). 90p. 1987. pap. 2.79 (*0-8423-6515-X*, 498042) Editorial Unilit.

Moster, Mary B., ed. see Lingeman, James E., et al.

Mostern, Kenneth. Autobiography & Black Identity Politics: Racialization in Twentieth-Century America. LC 98-36538. (Cultural Margins Ser.: Vol. 7). 300p. (C). 1999. text 54.95 (*0-521-64114-4*); pap. text 19.95 (*0-521-64679-0*) Cambridge U Pr.

Mostert. Dutch-English, English-Dutch Medical Dictionary. 3rd ed. (DUT & ENG.). 206p. 1990. 75.00 (*0-7859-7519-5*, 9031310786) Fr & Eur.

Mostert, Erik. Commissions for Environmental Impact Assessment: Their Contribution to the Effectiveness of Environmental Impact Assessment. xi, 311p. (Orig.). 1995. pap. 59.50 (*90-407-1169-0*, Pub. by Delft U Pr) Coronet Bks.

Mostert, Frederick. Mostert: Famous & Well-Known Marks. 1996. write for info. (*0-406-99734-9*, MFWKM, MICHIE) LEXIS Pub.

Mostert, Marco, jt. ed. see Barral, Xavier.

Mostert, Mark P. Interprofessional Collaboration in Education. LC 97-36026. 304p. 1997. pap. text 40.00 (*0-205-16689-X*) Allyn.

Mostert, Mark P. Interprofessional Collaboration in Schools: Practical Action in the Classroom: Instructor's Manual with Test Bank. 144p. (C). 1997. pap. text, teacher ed. write for info. (*0-205-27791-8*, T7791-1) Allyn.

Mostert, Mary. Coming Home: Families Can Stop the Unraveling of America. LC 96-12060. (Illus.). 166p. 1996. pap. 13.00 (*1-882723-26-0*, Pub. by Gold Leaf Pr) Origin Bk Sales.

***Mostert, Natasha.** The Midnight Side: A Novel. LC 00-25931. 256p. 2001. 24.00 (*0-688-17385-3*, Wm Morrow) Morrow Avon.

Mostert, Paul S., jt. auth. see Hofmann, Karl H.

Mosteshar, Cherry. Unveiled, Vol. 1. 1997. mass mkt. 6.99 (*0-312-96288-6*) St Martin.

— Unveiled: One Woman's Nightmare in Iran. (Illus.). 353p. 1998. text 24.00 (*0-7881-5803-1*) DIANE Pub.

Mosteshar, Sai'd. Mosteshar on Telecommunications: Regulation in the European Community. (European Business Law & Practice Ser.). 448p. (C). 1993. lib. bdg. 145.00 (*1-85333-756-0*, Pub. by Graham & Trotman) Kluwer Academic.

Mosteshar, Sai'd, ed. Research & Invention in Outer Space: Liability & Intellectual Property Rights. LC 95-44. 1995. lib. bdg. 151.00 (*0-7923-2982-1*, Pub. by M Nijhoff) Kluwer Academic.

***Mostia, William L.** Troubleshooting. LC 99-42403. 2000. 40.00 (*1-55617-705-4*) ISA.

Mosto, Alvise Ca Da, see Ca da Mosto, Alvise.

Mostofi, Abdollah. The Administrative & Social History of the Qajar Period, 3 vols. Mostofi-Glenn, Nayer, tr. from PER. LC 97-40041. (Illus.). 1347p. 1997. 89.00 (*1-56859-041-5*) Mazda Pubs.

Mostofi, F. K., et al. Histological Typing of Kidney Tumours. 2nd ed. LC 97-30425. (International Histological Classification of Tumors Ser.). (Illus.). 120p. 1997. pap. 69.95 (*3-540-63199-2*) Spr-Verlag.

— Histological Typing of Testis Tumours. 2nd ed. LC 97-30424. (International Histological Classification of Tumors Ser.). (Illus.). xi, 132p. 1997. pap. 74.00 (*3-540-63374-X*) Spr-Verlag.

***Mostofi, F. K., et al.** Histological Typing of Urinary Bladder Tumours. 2nd ed. LC 99-36795. (World Health Organization Ser.). xiv, 104p. 1999. pap. 76.00 (*3-540-64063-0*) Spr-Verlag.

Mostofi-Glenn, Nayer, tr. see Mostofi, Abdollah.

Mostofsky, David I. & Barlow, David H. The Management of Anxiety in Medical Disorders. LC 99-32656. 418p. (C). 2000. 62.50 (*0-205-28704-2*, Macmillan Coll) P-H.

Mostofsky, David I. & Lomranz, Jacob, eds. Handbook of Pain & Aging. LC 97-16599. (Series in Adult Development & Aging). 408p. (C). 1997. 65.00 (*0-306-45458-0*, Plenum Trade) Perseus Pubng.

Mostofsky, David I. & Loyning, Yngve, eds. The Neurobehavioral Treatment of Epilepsy. 352p. 1993. text 69.95 (*0-8058-1106-0*) L Erlbaum Assocs.

Mostofsky, David I. & Piedmont, Ralph L. Therapeutic Practice in Behavioral Medicine: A Selective Guide to Assessment, Treatment, Clinical Issues, & Therapies for Specific Disorders. LC 84-43031. (Joint Publication in the Jossey-Bass Social & Behavioral Science Series & the Jossey-Bass Health Ser.). 380p. reprint ed. pap. 117.80 (*0-7837-2536-1*, 204269500006) Bks Demand.

Mostofsky, David I. & Yehuda, Shlomo, eds. Handbook of Essential Fatty Acid Biology: Biochemistry, Physiology & Behavioral Neurobiology. LC 96-50976. (Illus.). 480p. 1997. 145.00 (*0-89603-365-1*) Humana.

Mostofsky, David I., jt. ed. see Yehuda, Shlomo.

Mostoller, Dwight E., et al. Ready-to-Use Computer Literacy Activities Kits, Level I, Level I. 64p. (J). (gr. 4-6). 1987. student ed. 5.95 (*0-317-66399-2*) P-H.

— Ready-to-Use Computer Literacy Activities Kits Level II, Level Two. 64p. (J). (gr. 7-10). 1987. student ed. 5.95 (*0-317-66401-8*) P-H.

Mostoller, Ed. Deer Hunting: The Guide to Doing It Right. LC 94-38740. (Illus.). 97p. 1994. 16.95 (*1-885018-00-2*); pap. 9.95 (*1-885018-01-0*) Logo Press.

Moston, Doug. Coming to Terms with Acting: An Instructive Glossary: What You Need to Know to Understand It, Discuss It, Deal with It, & Do It. 216p. (Orig.). 1993. pap. 16.95 (*0-89676-121-5*, Drama Pubs) QSMG Ltd.

Moston, Stephen, jt. auth. see Engleberg-Moston, Estella.

Mostov, Julie. Power, Process & Popular Sovereignty. 256p. (C). 1992. 49.95 (*0-87722-970-8*) Temple U Pr.

Mostow, Carole, jt. auth. see Garwin, Arthur.

Mostow, Debra. All about Reptiles. (J). 1995. pap. 1.95 (*0-590-48722-1*) Scholastic Inc.

Mostow, G. & Caldi, D., eds. Proceedings of the Gibbs Symposium, Yale University, May 15-17, 1989. LC 90-37667. 321p. 1990. text 68.00 (*0-8218-0157-0*, GIBBS) Am Math.

Mostow, G. D., ed. see Pure Mathematics Symposium Staff.

Mostow, G. Daniel, jt. auth. see Deligne, Pierre.

Mostow, Joshua S. Pictures of the Heart: The Hyakunin Isshu in Word & Image. LC 95-30185. (Illus.). 640p. 1996. text 48.00 (*0-8248-1705-2*) UH Pr.

Mostow, Mark A. Continuous Cohomology of Spaces with Two Topologies. LC 76-25187. (Memoirs of the American Mathematical Society Ser.: No. 7/175). 142p. 1976. pap. 22.00 (*0-8218-2175-X*, MEMO 7/175) Am Math.

Mostowski, Andrej. Sentences Undecidable in Formalized Arithmetic: An Exposition of the Theory of Kurt Godel. LC 82-11886. (Studies in Logic & the Foundations of Mathematics). 117p. 1982. reprint ed. lib. bdg. 35.00 (*0-313-23151-6*, MOSU) Greenwood.

Mostowskiu, Paul A. Wake up, America: My Four Years in Hell. LC 97-91327. 315p. 1998. 24.95 (*0-533-12641-X*) Vantage.

Mostowy, Jan G. Podhale: A Companion Guide to the Polish Highlands. De Gorgey, Maria, tr. from POL. (Illus.). 276p. 1997. 19.95 (*0-7818-0522-8*, 652) Hippocrene Bks.

Mostwin, Danuta. The Transplanted Family: A Study of Social Adjustment of the Polish Immigrant Family to the United States after the Second World War. Cordasco, Francesco, ed. LC 80-881. (American Ethnic Groups Ser.). 1981. lib. bdg. 42.95 (*0-405-13442-8*) Ayer.

***Mostyn, Bobbie.** Where Are the Men? 712 Places You Haven't Thought to Look. LC 99-95481. 224p. 1999. pap. 14.95 (*0-9673969-0-5*) InData Group.

Mostyn, David. Captain Daylight. (Illus.). 64p. (J). (ps-3). pap. 7.95 (*0-14-036469-2*, Pub. by Pnguin Bks Ltd) Trafalgar.

— Captain Daylight's Birthday Bash. (Illus.). (J). 1996. pap. 7.95 (*0-14-037633-X*, Pub. by Pnguin Bks Ltd) Trafalgar.

Mostyn, David, jt. auth. see Smart Alec Staff.

Mostyn, Trevor. Coming of Age in the Middle East. 256p. 1987. 35.00 (*0-7103-0208-8*) Routledge.

Mosvick, Roger K. & Nelson, Robert B. We've Got to Start Meeting Like This: A Guide to Successful Business Meeting Management. 312p. (Orig.). 1995. pap. 14.95 (*1-57112-069-6*, P0696) JIST Works.

Moszkowski, M. Fifteen Etudes de Virtousite Opus 72: For The Piano. 68p. 1986. pap. 8.95 (*0-7935-5202-8*, 50261830) H Leonard.

Moszynska, Anna. Abstract Art. LC 89-51347. (World of Art Ser.). (Illus.). 1990. pap. 14.95 (*0-500-20237-0*, Pub. by Thames Hudson) Norton.

Moszynska, W., jt. auth. see Chernetsov, Valeriui.

Moszynski, Jerzy R., ed. see American Society of Mechanical Engineers Staff.

Mota, A. Teixeira & Hair, P. E., eds. East of Mina: Afro-European Relations on the Gold Coast in the 1550s & 1560s. LC 90-146629. (Studies in African Sources: No. 3). 107p. (Orig.). 1989. pap. 22.00 (*0-942615-05-0*) U Wis African Stud.

Mota, Clarice Novaes de, see Novaes de Mota, Clarice.

Mota-Hernandez, F., ed. Seminar on Kidney Diseases in Children. (Journal: Paediatrician: Vol. 8, No. 5-6, 1979). 1979. pap. 57.50 (*3-8055-0344-X*) S Karger.

Mota, Miguel, ed. see Lowry, Malcolm & Fitzgerald, F. Scott.

Mota Soares, Carlos A., ed. Computer Aided Optimal Design: Structural & Mechanical Systems. (NATO Asi Series F: Vol. 27). 1045p. 1987. 180.95 (*0-387-17598-9*) Spr-Verlag.

Mota Soares, Carlos A., jt. ed. see Bendse, Martin P.

Motaal, Doaa A., jt. auth. see Volpi, Elena.

Motala, Ziyad. Constitutional Options for A Democratic South Africa: A Comparative Perspective. LC 94-6680. 1994. 21.95 (*0-88258-187-2*) Howard U Pr.

Motamed, Hosein A. Anatomy, Radiology, & Kinesiology of Hand-Unit. 2nd ed. LC 81-90206. (Illus.). 344p. 2000. reprint ed. 250.00 (*0-910161-06-2*) Motamed Med Pub.

— Surgery of Hand Unit in Adults & Children, 2 vols. Incl. Vol. I. LC 77-78228. (Illus.). 2000. reprint ed. Not sold separately (*0-910161-03-8*); Vol. II. LC 77-78228. (Illus.). 2000. reprint ed. Not sold separately (*0-910161-04-6*); LC 77-78228. reprint ed. 450.00 (*0-910161-02-X*) Motamed Med Pub.

***Motamedi, M. E. & Goering, Rolf, eds.** Miniaturized Systems with Micro-Optics & MEMS. 434p. 1999. pap. text 92.00 (*0-8194-3475-2*) SPIE.

Motamedi, M. Edward, et al, eds. Miniaturized Systems with Micro-Optics & Micromechanics II, Vol. 3008. LC 97-175321. 382p. 1997. 89.00 (*0-8194-2419-6*) SPIE.

Motamedi, M. Edward & Bailey, Wayne, eds. Microelectronic Structures & MEMS for Optical Processing II, Vol. 2881. 226p. 1996. 56.00 (*0-8194-2279-7*) SPIE.

Motamedi, M. Edward & Goering, Rolf, eds. Miniaturized Systems with Micro-Optics & Micromechanics III, Vol. 3276. LC 98-226760. 290p. 1998. 69.00 (*0-8194-2715-2*) SPIE.

Motamedi, M. Edward & Herzig, Hans P., eds. Microelectronic Structures & MEMS for Optical Processing III, Vol. 3226. LC 98-122103. 220p. 1997. 59.00 (*0-8194-2658-X*) SPIE.

Motamedi, M. Edward, jt. ed. see Herzig, Hans P.

***Motamen-Samadian, Sima & Celso, Garrido N.** Emerging Markets, Past & Present Experiences & Future Prospects LC 99-39493. 2000. text 59.95 (*0-312-22898-8*) St Martin.

Motamen-Scobie, Homa. European Monetary Union: The Way Forward. LC 97-14248. 224p. (C). 1998. 75.00 (*0-415-17408-2*) Routledge.

Motapanyane, Virginia, ed. see Black, James R.

Motard-Noar, Martine. Les Fictions d'Helene Cixous: Une Autre Langue de Femme. LC 91-70279. (French Forum Monographs: No. 73). (FRE.). 208p. (Orig.). 1991. pap. 14.95 (*0-917058-77-1*) French Forum.

Motard, Rudolphe L. & Joseph, Babu, eds. Wavelet Applications in Chemical Engineering. LC 94-13695. (International Series in Engineering & Computer Science, VLSI, Computer Architecture, & Digital Screen Processing: Vol. 272). 344p. (C). 1994. text 148.50 (*0-7923-9461-5*) Kluwer Academic.

***Motavalli, Jim.** Forward Drive: The Race to Build "Clean" Cars for the Future. LC 99-32154. 272p. 2000. 25.00 (*1-57805-035-9*, Pub. by Sierra) Random.

Motazedi, Robert. Building & Flying RC Sailplanes & Electric Gliders. Emmerich, Michael, ed. LC 93-28719. (Illus.). 88p. (Orig.). 1993. per. 11.95 (*0-89024-179-1*, 12125) Kalmbach.

Motchenbacher, C. D. & Connelly, J. A. Low Noise Electronic System Design. LC 92-39598. 448p. 1993. 104.95 (*0-471-57742-1*) Wiley.

Motchkavitz, Leslie, jt. auth. see McKerns, Dorothy.

Mote, Jr., et al, eds. Skiing Trauma & Safety, Vol. 10. 408p. 1996. 149.00 (*0-8031-2022-2*, STP1266) ASTM.

Mote, Ashley. The Glory Days of Cricket: The Extraordinary Story of Broadhalfpenny Down. (Illus.). 434p. 1999. 39.95 (*1-86105-111-5*, Pub. by Robson Bks) Parkwest Pubns.

Mote, C. Daniel. Skiing Trauma & Safety: International Symposium, STP 1104, 8th. LC 89-14984. (Special Technical Publication Ser.). (Illus.). 463p. 1991. pap. text 113.00 (*0-8031-1405-2*, STP1104) ASTM.

Mote, C. Daniel, jt. ed. see Johnson, Robert J.

Mote, Dave. Children's Literature Review, Vol. 2. LC 96-20634. 500p. 1996. 130.00 (*1-55862-216-0*) St James Pr.

***Mote, Frederick W.** Imperial China, 900-1800. LC 99-31840. 1440p. 2000. 39.95 (*0-674-44515-5*) HUP.

Mote, Frederick W. Intellectual Foundations of China. 2nd ed. 144p. (C). 1988. pap. 20.63 (*0-07-554030-4*) McGraw.

Mote, Frederick W. & Twitchett, Denis C., eds. The Cambridge History of China Vol. 7: The Ming Dynasty, 1368-1644. (Illus.). 1008p. 1988. text 159.95 (*0-521-24332-7*) Cambridge U Pr.

Mote, Frederick W., jt. ed. see Twitchett, Denis.

Mote, Max, jt. ed. see Itzkowitz, Norman.

Mote, Patricia M. Dorothy Fuldheim: FIRST First Lady of Television News. LC 97-11135. (Illus.). 256p. 1997. 22.95 (*0-9633083-5-1*) Quixote Pubns.

Mote, Patricia M., jt. auth. see Hall, Alma D.

***Mote, Philip W. & O'Neill, Alan.** Numerical Modeling of the Global Atmosphere in the Climate System. LC 00-37056. (NATO ASI Ser.). 2000. write for info. (*0-7923-6301-9*, Kluwer Plenum) Kluwer Academic.

Mote, Victor L. Siberia: Worlds Apart. LC 98-14843. (Series on the Post-Soviet Republics). 256p. 1998. pap. text 25.00 (*0-8133-1837-8*, Pub. by Westview) HarpC.

Moteka, Patricia, ed. see Brom, Elgar.

Motekaitis, Ramumas J., jt. auth. see Martell, A. E.

Motekaitis, Ramumas J., jt. auth. see Martell, Arthur E.

***Moten, Fred.** Arkansas. 44p. 1999. pap. 5.00 (*0-9674857-1-1*) Pressed Wafer Pr.

***Moten, Matthew.** The Delafield Commission & the American Military Profession. LC 99-53768. 288p. 2000. 47.95 (*0-89096-925-6*) Tex A&M Univ Pr.

Motes, Martin R. Vandas: Their Botany, History & Culture. LC 96-32199. 188p. 1997. 32.95 (*0-88192-376-1*) Timber.

***Motes, Mary.** Kosova Kosovo: Prelude to War, 1966-1999. unabridged ed. Fehrman, Jan, ed. (Illus.). xiii, 307p. 1999. 24.95 (*0-9674343-0-0*); pap. 14.95 (*0-9674343-1-9*) Redland Pr.

Motgomery, Mark, ed. see Meier, Marcie.

***Motha, Philip & Yuen, Belinda.** Singapore Real Property Guide. 4th ed. LC 99-912557. (Illus.). 600p. 1999. 99.50 (*9971-69-224-4*, Pub. by Sngapore Univ Pr) Coronet Bks.

Mothander, Bjorn, et al. Farm Implements for Small-Scale Farmers in Tanzania. (Scandinavian Institute of African Studies). (Illus.). 214p. (Orig.). 1989. pap. 41.00 (*91-7106-290-4*) Coronet Bks.

Mothayne, Anthere L. Substantial Justice. 230p. 1999. pap. write for info. (*0-7392-0187-5*, PO3159) Morris Pubng.

Mothe, Gordon De La, see De La Mothe, Gordon.

Mother. Commentaries on the Dhammapada.Tr. of Commentaires sur le Dhammapada. (FRE.). 118p. 1995. pap. 5.00 (*81-7058-133-8*, Pub. by SAA) E-W Cultural Ctr.

— Conversations, 1929, 1930-1931.Tr. of Entretiens, 1929, 1930-1931. (FRE.). 181p. 1989. pap. 5.00 (*81-7058-131-1*, Pub. by SAA) E-W Cultural Ctr.

***Mother.** Education, Pt. 1.Tr. of Education. (FRE.). 205p. 1998. pap. 6.95 (*81-7058-132-X*, Pub. by SAA) E-W Cultural Ctr.

— Education, Pt. 2.Tr. of Education. (FRE.). 245p. 1994. pap. 4.95 (*81-7058-198-2*, Pub. by SAA) E-W Cultural Ctr.

— Education, Pt. 3.Tr. of Education. (FRE.). 151p. 1997. pap. 4.95 (*81-7058-199-0*, Pub. by SAA) E-W Cultural Ctr.

Mother. Flowers: Their Spiritual Significance. Vijay, ed. (Illus.). 96p. 1998. pap. 7.95 (*81-7060-028-6*, Pub. by SAA) E-W Cultural Ctr.

— Flowers & Their Messages. 4th ed. (Illus.). 309p. 1996. pap. 19.95 (*81-7058-297-0*, Pub. by SAA) E-W Cultural Ctr.

— Health & Healing in Yoga. 305p. 1989. pap. 7.95 (*81-7058-023-4*, Pub. by SAA) E-W Cultural Ctr.

Mother. Ideal Child. 6th ed.Tr. of L'Enfant Ideal. (FRE.). 16p. 1997. pap. 0.50 (*81-7058-494-9*, Pub. by SAA) E-W Cultural Ctr.

Mother. The Lesson of Life. 180p. 1985. pap. 6.00 (*0-89071-322-7*, Pub. by SAA) Acrpls Bks CO.

Mother. The Lesson of Life. 182p. 1997. pap. 6.95 (*81-7058-474-4*, Pub. by SAA) E-W Cultural Ctr.

Mother. The Life Divine: The Mother's Talks. 154p. (Orig.). 1989. pap. 4.95 (*0-317-99972-9*, Pub. by Sri Aurob Ashram Trust) Acrpls Bks CO.

— Mantras of the Mother. 1983. 5.00 (*0-89071-319-7*, Pub. by SAA) Acrpls Bks CO.

Mother. Mantras of the Mother. 2nd ed. 276p. 1994. 4.95 (*81-7058-179-6*, Pub. by SAA) E-W Cultural Ctr.

— The Mother on Herself. 2nd ed. 46p. 1998. pap. 2.50 (*81-7058-172-9*, Pub. by SAA) E-W Cultural Ctr.

— Notes on the Way.Tr. of Notes sur le Chemin. (FRE.). 347p. 1995. pap. 6.50 (*81-7058-376-4*, Pub. by SAA) E-W Cultural Ctr.

— On Thoughts & Aphorisms. 2nd ed. 362p. 1998. pap. 15.95 (*81-7058-528-7*, Pub. by SAA) E-W Cultural Ctr.

— Prayers & Meditations. 2nd ed.Tr. of Prieres et Meditations. (FRE.). 381p. 1997. pap. 14.50 (*81-7058-052-8*, Pub. by SAA) E-W Cultural Ctr.

— Questions & Answers 1953. 2nd ed. 417p. 1998. pap. 24.95 (*81-7058-519-8*, Pub. by SAA) E-W Cultural Ctr.

Mother. The Sunlit Path.Tr. of Voie Ensoleillee. (FRE.). 194p. 1998. pap. 7.25 (*81-7058-025-0*, Pub. by SAA) E-W Cultural Ctr.

Mother. The Supreme Discovery. 9th ed.Tr. of Decouverte Supreme. (FRE.). 18p. 1996. pap. 0.75 (*81-7058-287-3*, Pub. by SAA) E-W Cultural Ctr.

Mother. Tales of All Times. Orig. Title: Youth's Noble Path. (Illus.). 138p. (J). (gr. 3-8). 1983. pap. 4.95 (*0-89071-321-9*, Pub. by SAA) Acrpls Bks CO.

— Three Plays. 101p. (Orig.). 1989. pap. 3.95 (*0-317-99973-7*, Pub. by Sri Aurob Ashram Trust) Acrpls Bks CO.

Mother, jt. auth. see Aurobindo, Sri.

Mother, jt. auth. see Satprem Staff.

Mother, jt. auth. see Sri Aurobindo.

Mother & Satprem. Mother's Agenda, 1966, Vol. 7. LC 80-472990. 340p. 1991. pap. 12.50 (*0-938710-13-3*) Inst Evolutionary.

***Mother Agnes of Jesus.** The Last Conversations of St. Therese. 152p. 1998. reprint ed. 15.00 (*0-911845-72-0*) Neumann Pr.

Mother Agnes of Jesus, ed. see St. Therese of Lisieux.

Mother Angelica. Mother Angelica's Answers, Not Promises. 1991. per. 6.50 (*0-671-74673-1*) PB.

Mother Columba Hart, tr. Hadewijch: The Complete Works. LC 80-84500. (Classics of Western Spirituality Ser.). 440p. 1981. pap. 24.95 (*0-8091-2297-9*) Paulist Pr.

Mother Connec. Homespun Fun. LC 96-25605. (Illus.). 256p. 1996. pap. 11.95 (*0-312-14617-5*) St Martin.

Mother Earth News Editors. The Abundant Vegetable Garden: A Handbook for Success. (Illus.). 224p. (Orig.). 1985. pap. 19.95 (*0-938432-28-1*) Mother Earth.

— The Backcountry Handbook: An Illustrated Guide to the Techniques & Joys of the Wilderness Experience. 1989. pap. 11.95 (*0-671-65795-X*, Fireside) S&S Trade Pap.

— The Fresh Foods Country Cookbook. (Illus.). 196p. (Orig.). 1984. pap. 17.95 (*0-938432-23-0*) Mother Earth.

— How to Convert Your Vehicle to Propane. Hoffman, Robert, ed. 50p. (Orig.). 1981. pap. 7.50 (*0-938432-01-X*) Mother Earth.

— Living on Less. (Illus.). (Orig.). 1984. pap. 14.95 (*0-938432-07-9*) Mother Earth.

— Mother's Homebuilding & Shelter Guide. Miner, Robert, ed. (Illus.). 200p. 1983. pap. text 15.95 (*0-938432-15-X*) Mother Earth.

— Mother's One Hundred & One Workshop Projects. (Illus.). 208p. 1984. pap. 14.95 (*0-938432-06-0*) Mother Earth.

— The Rural Living Handbook: An Illustrated Guide to Practical Country Skills. 1989. pap. 11.95 (*0-671-65794-1*, Fireside) S&S Trade Pap.

Mother Earth News Editors & Davis, William C. Mother's Energy Efficiency Book: Heat, Light, Power. (Illus.). 250p. 1983. 17.95 (*0-938432-22-2*) Mother Earth.

Mother Earth News Editors & Kerley, Michael R., eds. The Mother Earth News Alcohol Fuel Handbook. (Illus.). 120p. (Orig.). 1980. pap. 12.95 (*0-938432-00-1*) Mother Earth.

Mother Earth News Staff. Living on Less: An Authoritive Guide to Affordable Food, Fuel, & Shelter. Vivian, John, ed. (Illus.). 287p. 1998. pap. 19.95 (*0-9660494-0-3*, Pub. by Sussex Pubs) Chelsea Green Pub.

Mother Goof, pseud. The Sheep Who Was Allergic to Wool. LC 92-60096. (Illus.). 32p. (J). (gr. 3 up). 1992. 8.95 (*0-9623184-1-8*) Sunflower Hill.

Mother Goose. Mother Goose Nursery Rhymes: Super Chubby Books. LC 84-72862. (Illus.). 32p. (J). (ps up). 1984. 4.99 (*0-671-49878-9*) S&S Trade.

Mother Goose Staff. Mother Goose in Hieroglyphics. Bleiler, Everett F., ed. 64p. 1973. pap. 4.95 (*0-486-20745-5*) Dover.

Mother Immaculata. Consecration & the Spirit of Carmel. LC 82-72203. (Living Meditation & Prayerbook Ser.). (Illus.). 270p. (Orig.). 1985. pap. text 6.00 (*0-932406-08-4*) AFC.

Mother Katherine, tr. The Vigils for the Services of Pentecost & the Ascension. 2nd ed. (Library of Orthodox Thinking). 43p. 1996. pap. 5.00 (*0-920669-32-8*, Pub. by Peregrina Pubng) Cistercian Pubns.

Mother Katherine & Mother Thekla, trs. The Great Canon (of) St Andrew of Crete: And, The Life of St. Mary of Egypt. 2nd ed. (Library of Orthodox Thinking). 161p. 1997. pap. 15.00 (*0-920669-26-3*, Pub. by Peregrina Pubng) Cistercian Pubns.

— The Life of St. Mary of Egypt. 2nd ed. (Library of Orthodox Thinking). 39p. 1997. pap. 4.00 (*0-920669-25-5*, Pub. by Peregrina Pubng) Cistercian Pubns.

Mother Love. Forgive or Forget: Never Underestimate the Power of Forgiveness. Bolden, Tonya, ed. & abr. by. LC 99-34892. 187p. 1999. 22.95 (*0-06-019450-2*) HarpC.

M

An Asterisk (*) at the beginning of an entry indicates that the title is appearing for the first time.

Mother M. Angelica. Mother Angelica's Answers, Not Promises. LC 96-77717. 275p. 1996. 15.95 (*0-89870-606-8*) Ignatius Pr.

Mother Maria. George Herbert: Aspects of His Theology. 2nd ed. (Library of Orthodox Thinking). 41p. 1996. pap. 5.00 (*0-920669-36-0*, Pub. by Peregrina Pubng) Cistercian Pubns.

— An Introduction to the Divine Liturgy: An Explanation of the Liturgy of St. John Chrysostom. 1989. pap. 4.95 (*0-937032-66-2*) Light&Life Pub Co MN.

— The Two Temples: The Loneliness of God's Saints. 2nd ed. (Library of Orthodox Thinking). 27p. 1996. pap. 5.00 (*0-920669-27-1*, Pub. by Peregrina Pubng) Cistercian Pubns.

Mother Maria Gysi. Amos: Prophet of God. 2nd ed. (Library of Orthodox Thinking). 72p. 1996. pap. 6.00 (*0-920669-38-7*, Pub. by Peregrina Pubng) Cistercian Pubns.

— Eastern Spirituality. 2nd ed. (Library of Orthodox Thinking). 43p. 1996. pap. 5.00 (*0-920669-33-6*, Pub. by Peregrina Pubng) Cistercian Pubns.

— Evil in the New Testament. 2nd ed. (Library of Orthodox Thinking). 63p. 1996. pap. 7.00 (*0-920669-40-9*, Pub. by Peregrina Pubng) Cistercian Pubns.

— The Hidden Treasure. 2nd ed. (Library of Orthodox Thinking). 80p. 1991. pap. 9.00 (*0-920669-23-9*, Pub. by Peregrina Pubng) Cistercian Pubns.

— Introduction to the Divine Liturgy. 2nd ed. (Library of Orthodox Thinking). 42p. 1997. pap. 5.00 (*0-920669-39-5*, Pub. by Peregrina Pubng) Cistercian Pubns.

— The Potential of Orthodox Thinking. 2nd ed. (Library of Orthodox Thinking). 24p. 1998. pap. 4.00 (*0-920669-21-2*, Pub. by Peregrina Pubng) Cistercian Pubns.

— Realism of the Orthodox Faith. 2nd ed. (Library of Orthodox Thinking). 23p. 1996. pap. 4.00 (*0-920669-31-X*, Pub. by Peregrina Pubng) Cistercian Pubns.

— Sceptrum Regale: Life Towards the Transcent. 2nd ed. (Library of Orthodox Thinking). 51p. 1996. pap. 5.00 (*0-920669-30-1*, Pub. by Peregrina Pubng) Cistercian Pubns.

Mother Mary, jt. auth. see Van Hubbard, Ileah.

Mother Mary, jt. tr. see Ware, Kallistos T.

Mother Mary Francis. Walled in Light: St. Colette. 247p. 1985. pap. 9.50 (*0-8199-0889-4*, Frncscn Herld) Franciscan Pr.

Mother Mary Francis, tr. see St. Colette.

Mother Meera. Bringing down the Light: Journey of a Soul after Death. LC 89-13577. (ENG, FRE & GER., Illus.). 64p. 1990. 29.95 (*0-9622973-2-1*) Meeramma Pubns.

Mother Ruth. In Wisdom Thou Hast Made Them. Galanter, Patricia, ed. (Illus.). 141p. 1986. 15.95 (*0-937431-01-X*) Adams Bannister Cox.

Mother Teresa of Calcutta. The Best Gift Is Love: Meditations. Lovett, Sean-Patrick, ed. LC 92-42958. Orig. Title: A Way of Love. (Illus.). 121p. 1993. reprint ed. pap. 8.99 (*0-89283-814-0*, Charis) Servant.

Mother Teresa of Calcutta. The Blessings of Love. 128p. 1996. pap. 6.99 (*0-89283-975-9*) Servant.

— Everything Starts from Prayer: Mother Teresa's Meditations on Spiritual Life for People of All Faiths. Stern, Anthony, ed. LC 98-11855. (Illus.). 170p. 1998. 17.95 (*1-883991-25-0*) Whte Cloud Pr.

***Mother Teresa of Calcutta.** Everything Starts from Prayer: Mother Teresa's Meditations on Spiritual Life for People of All Faiths. Stern, Anthony, ed. 176p. 2000. pap. 12.95 (*1-883991-37-4*, Pub. by Whte Cloud Pr) SCB Distributors.

— Heart of Joy: The Transforming Power of Self-Giving. 149p. (Orig.). 1987. pap. 6.99 (*0-89283-342-4*) Servant.

Mother Teresa of Calcutta. In My Own Words. large type ed. 1996. lib. bdg. 20.95 (*0-7838-1835-1*, G K Hall Lrg Type) Mac Lib Ref.

— In the Silence of the Heart: Meditations by Mother Teresa. 1994. pap. text 5.95 (*0-687-85547-0*) Abingdon.

— Jesus, the Word to Be Spoken. large type ed. (Large Print Inspirational Ser.). (Orig.). 1987. pap. 9.95 (*0-8027-2574-0*) Walker & Co.

— Jesus, the Word to Be Spoken: Prayers & Meditations for Every Day of the Year. 1998. pap. 9.99 (*1-56955-073-5*) Servant.

***Mother Teresa of Calcutta.** The Joy in Loving: A Guide to Daily Living. LC 99-46847. 448p. 2000. pap. 13.95 (*0-14-019607-2*) Viking Penguin.

Mother Teresa of Calcutta. Loving Jesus. 166p. 1991. pap. 6.99 (*0-89283-676-8*, Charis) Servant.

— Meditations from a Simple Path: Mother Teresa. 96p. 1996. 10.00 (*0-345-40699-0*) Ballantine Pub Grp.

— Mother Teresa. LC 97-38584. 128p. 1997. 5.99 (*0-517-20169-0*) Random Hse Value.

— Mother Teresa: In My Own Words. LC 97-38338. (Illus.). 128p. 1997. pap. 8.00 (*0-7648-0200-3*) Liguori Pubns.

***Mother Teresa of Calcutta.** Mother Teresa: No Greater Love. 224p. 2000. 6.98 (*1-56731-401-5*, MJF Bks) Fine Comms.

Mother Teresa of Calcutta. A Mother Teresa Treasury: Mother Teresa of Calcutta, 3 vols. Incl. Vol. 1. Gift for God. LC 85-42786. 96p. Vol. 2. Love of Christ. LC 85-42786. 128p. 1985. Vol. 3. Life in the Spirit. LC 85-42786. 96p. 1985. LC 85-42786. 1985. 32.95 (*0-06-068228-0*) Harper SF.

— No Greater Love. 1997. 21.00 (*0-614-28615-8*) New World.

— One Heart Full of Love. Gonzalez-Balado, Jose L., ed. 170p. 1988. pap. 6.99 (*0-89283-393-9*) Servant.

— Orar. 1999. pap. text 9.95 (*84-08-02841-3*) Planeta.

— Seeking the Heart of God: Reflections on Prayer. LC 92-54257. 112p. 1993. 12.00 (*0-06-068238-8*, Pub. by Harper SF) HarpC.

— A Simple Path. large type ed. 464p. 1995. 23.00 (*0-679-44231-6*) Random Hse Lrg Prnt.

***Mother Teresa of Calcutta.** Stories Told by Mother Teresa. (Illus.). (ps up). 2000. pap. 7.95 (*1-84207-010-X*) Element MA.

— Thirsting for God: A Yearbook of Prayers & Meditations. 2000. mass mkt. 6.99 (*1-56955-227-4*) Servant.

Mother Teresa of Calcutta. Total Surrender. large type ed. DeVananda, Angelo, ed. LC 93-8541. (EasyRead Type Ser.). 160p. (Orig.). 1993. reprint ed. pap. 8.95 (*0-8027-2676-3*) Walker & Co.

— Total Surrender. rev. ed. Devananda, Angelo, ed. 158p. (C). 1989. pap. 6.99 (*0-89283-651-2*, Charis) Servant.

— Words to Love By. LC 82-73373. (Illus.). 80p. (Orig.). 1983. pap. 9.95 (*0-87793-261-1*) Ave Maria.

— Words to Love By. large type ed. 96p. (Orig.). 1985. reprint ed. pap. 6.95 (*0-8027-2478-7*) Walker & Co.

Mother Teresa of Calcutta & Roger of Taize. Meditations on the Way of the Cross. LC 86-9313. (Illus.). 64p. (Orig.). 1998. reprint ed. pap. 7.95 (*0-8298-0585-0*) Pilgrim OH.

Mother Teresa of Calcutta, et al. No Greater Love. large type ed. LC 97-43988. 240p. 1998. pap. 14.95 (*0-8027-2727-1*) Walker & Co.

Mother Thais. Zhitija Russkikh Svatikh, v 2 tom, 2 vols., 1. LC 82-81204.Tr. of Lives of the Russian Saints. pap. 10.00 (*0-88465-012-X*) Holy Trinity.

— Zhitija Russkikh Svatikh, v 2 tom, 2 vols., 2. LC 82-81204.Tr. of Lives of the Russian Saints. pap. 13.00 (*0-88465-020-0*) Holy Trinity.

Mother, The. Flowers & Their Messages. LC 92-70607. (Illus.). 309p. 1992. pap. 29.95 (*0-941524-68-X*) Lotus Pr.

— Search for the Soul: In Everyday Living. LC 89-85343. 162p. (Orig.). (C). 1990. pap. 8.95 (*0-941524-57-4*) Lotus Pr.

— The Soul & Its Powers. LC 92-70605. 147p. (Orig.). 1992. pap. 9.95 (*0-941524-67-1*) Lotus Pr.

Mother, The, jt. auth. see Aurobindo, Sri.

Mother Thekla. The Blessing of Ikons: Prayers for the Blessing of Ikons. 1988. pap. 1.95 (*0-937032-60-3*) Light&Life Pub Co MN.

— Can Wisdom Be Taught? 2nd ed. (Library of Orthodox Thinking). 33p. 1997. pap. 4.00 (*0-920669-29-8*, Pub. by Peregrina Pubng) Cistercian Pubns.

— Expression of Faith. 2nd ed. LC 98-7008. (Library of Orthodox Thinking). (Illus.). 23p. 1997. pap. 4.00 (*0-920669-28-X*, Pub. by Peregrina Pubng) Cistercian Pubns.

— The Monastery of the Assumption: A History. (The Library of Othodox Thinking). 30p. 1991. pap. 4.00 (*0-920669-22-0*, Pub. by Peregrina Pubng) Cistercian Pubns.

Mother Thekla, tr. The Blessing of Ikons. 2nd ed. (Library of Orthodox Thinking). 29p. 1996. pap. 4.00 (*0-920669-37-9*, Pub. by Peregrina Pubng) Cistercian Pubns.

— The Service of Vespers: Introduction & Translation for Reference. 2nd ed. (Library of Orthodox Thinking). 54p. 1998. pap. 7.00 (*0-920669-35-2*, Pub. by Peregrina Pubng) Cistercian Pubns.

Mother Thekla, jt. tr. see Mother Katherine.

Mothering Magazine Staff, ed. see Pedersen, Anne.

***Mothers' Aid Staff.** Our Baby's First Seven Years: A Record Book. 7th ed. Brown, Liza, ed. (Illus.). 76p. 2000. 40.00 (*0-970301l-0-3*) Mothers Aid.

Mothers of NBA. Mothers of the NBA Cookbook. 1998. pap. write for info. (*0-375-75098-3*) Villard Books.

Mothers of Pre-Schoolers Int'l Staff. New Moms' Practical Parenting Tips. 1997. pap. 6.99 (*0-614-28112-1*) Zondervan.

***Mothershed, Jack.** Th'were Knights Before Christmases. (Illus.). ii, 40p. 1998. 19.95 (*1-893359-49-2*) Winward Ways.

***Mothersill, C. & Austin, B.** Aquatic Invertebrate Cell Culture. LC 00-44577. (Books in Food Science). 2001. write for info. (*1-85233-646-3*) Spr-Verlag.

Mothersill, C. & Seymour, C., eds. New Developments in Fundamental & Applied Radiobiology. 460p. 1991. 95.00 (*0-7484-0020-6*, Pub. by Tay Francis Ltd) Taylor & Francis.

Mothersill, Mary. Beauty Restored. 438p. (C). 1991. reprint ed. pap. text 19.95 (*0-937431-04-4*) Adams Bannister Cox.

Mothersole, Peter L. & White, Norman W. Broadcast Data Systems: Teletext & RDS. (Illus.). 158p. 1990. pap. 32.95 (*0-240-51354-1*, Focal) Buttrwrth-Heinemann.

— Broadcast Data Systems: Teletext & RDS. LC 90-33586. (Illus.). 158p. reprint ed. pap. 49.00 (*0-608-06249-9*, 206657800008) Bks Demand.

***Motherwell, David.** Life on Sunnyside Farm. Spears-Stewart, Reta & Keckridge, Gina, eds. LC 99-95239. (Illus.). 227p. 1999. 19.95 (*1-892477-19-X*); pap. 14.95 (*1-892477-13-0*) Barnabs Pub.

***Motherwell, Robert.** The Collected Writings of Robert Motherwell. Terenzio, Stephanie, ed. LC 99-14459. (Documents of Twentieth Century Art Ser.). 360p. 1999. pap. 19.95 (*0-520-22179-6*, Pub. by U CA Pr) Cal Prin Full Svc.

Motherwell, Robert, ed. The Dada Painters & Poets: An Anthology. 2nd ed. LC 88-10349. (Paperbacks in AA History Ser.). (Illus.). 464p. 1989. reprint ed. pap. 24.95 (*0-674-18500-5*) HUP.

Motherwell, Robert. Robert Motherwell: Collage Prints 1984. 32p. 1984. pap. 8.00 (*0-614-13077-8*) Tyler Graphics Ltd.

— Robert Motherwell: Color Etchings 1984. 16p. pap. 8.00 (*0-614-13078-6*) Tyler Graphics Ltd.

— Robert Motherwell: El Negro. 16p. pap. 10.00 (*0-614-13076-X*) Tyler Graphics Ltd.

Motherwell, W. B. & Crich, D. Free-Radical Chain Reactions in Organic Synthesis. (Best Synthetic Methods Ser.). (Illus.). 268p. 1991. text 128.00 (*0-12-508760-8*) Acad Pr.

Motherwell, William, ed. Rob Stene's Dream, a Poem. LC 70-173003. (Maitland Club, Glasgow. Publications: No. 52). reprint ed. 37.50 (*0-404-53033-8*) AMS Pr.

Mothner, Carol. Carol Mothner: Promises. (Illus.). 14p. 1997. pap. 10.00 (*0-935037-91-8*) G Peters Gallery.

Mothner, Carol, intro. Carol Mothner: Private Places. LC 90-61446. (Illus.). 24p. 1990. pap. 10.00 (*0-935037-32-2*) G Peters Gallery.

Motier, Donald. Just Friends: A Novel & Two Short Stories. LC 84-62218. 119p. 1984. 5.00 (*0-9614048-0-9*) Phaedrus.

Motil, John. Digital Systems Fundamentals. xx, 490p. (C). 1983. reprint ed. pap. text 22.00 (*0-917930-65-7*) Ridgeview.

Motin, Susan Hubbs, see Hauptman, Robert & Hubbs Motin, Susan, eds.

Motion, Andrew. Keats. LC 97-76775. (Illus.). 636p. 1998. text 35.00 (*0-374-18100-4*) FS&G.

— Keats. 1999. pap. 18.00 (*0-226-54240-8*) U Ch Pr.

— Philip Larkin: A Writer's Life. LC 93-71731. 570p. 1993. 35.00 (*0-374-23168-0*) FS&G.

— Philip Larkin: A Writer's Life. 574p. 1994. pap. 13.00 (*0-374-52407-6*) FS&G.

— The Price of Everything. 128p. (Orig.). 1995. pap. 11.95 (*0-571-16900-7*) Faber & Faber.

— Selected Poems, 1976-1997. 160p. 1999. pap. 16.95 (*0-571-19504-0*) Faber & Faber.

***Motion, Andrew.** Wainewright the Poisoner. LC 99-89445. (Illus.). 272p. 2000. 26.00 (*0-375-40209-8*) Knopf.

Motion, Andrew, intro. Selected Poems. 240p. 1994. 7.50 (*0-460-87458-6*, Everyman's Classic Lib) Tuttle Pubng.

Motion Picture Producers & Distributors of America, jt. auth. see National Conference on Motion Pictures Staff.

Motion, Tim. Jazz Portraits: An Eye for the Sound: Images of Jazz & Jazz Musicians LC 99-193429. 128 p. 1995. write for info. (*0-86101-827-3*, Pub. by Salamander) Combined Pub.

***Motivala, Baman.** Oracle Forms: Interactive Workbook. 467p. 2000. pap., wbk. ed. 39.99 (*0-13-015808-9*) P-H.

Motivational Dialogues Central Council Staff. How to Turn-on to Life: Reach Way Beyond Money. LC 85-61067. 148p. 1988. teacher ed. 4.00 (*0-317-89801-9*); pap. 8.00 (*0-317-89800-0*); lib. bdg. 11.00 (*0-317-89799-3*) Mahon Pr.

Motizuki, Kazuko, ed. Structural Phase in Transitions in Layered Transition Metal Compounds. 1986. text 218.00 (*90-277-2171-8*) Kluwer Academic.

Motlagh, Cyrus K. Structuring Uncertainties in Long-Range Power Planning. LC 76-620019. (MSU Public Utilities Papers: No. 1976). 183p. reprint ed. pap. 56.80 (*0-7837-6267-4*, 204597900010) Bks Demand.

Motlagh, Hushidar H. I Shall Come Again. 486p. 1992. 34.95 (*0-937661-00-7*); pap. 24.95 (*0-937661-01-5*) Global Persp.

Motley. Today's French Theatre. (Yale French Studies). 1954. 25.00 (*0-527-01722-1*) Periodicals Srv.

Motley, Christie M. Child Support Enforcement: Strong Leadership Required to Maximize Benefits of Automated Systems. (Illus.). 79p. (C). 1997. pap. text 25.00 (*0-7881-4740-4*) DIANE Pub.

Motley, Constance Baker. Equal Justice under Law: An Autobiography. LC 98-15129. (Illus.). 400p. 1998. text 25.00 (*0-374-14865-1*) FS&G.

***Motley, Constance Baker.** Equal Justice under Law: An Autobiography. (Illus.). 288p. 1999. pap. 14.00 (*0-374-52618-4*) FS&G.

Motley, Edward M., jt. auth. see Qasim, Syed R.

***Motley, Ellavea Garrett.** The Role of the Teacher in Orientation & Mobility Services for the Blind & Visually Impaired. (Illus.). 120p. 2000. pap. 14.00 (*0-8059-4798-1*) Dorrance.

Motley Fool Staff & Gardner, Tom. The Foolish Four: How to Crush Your Mutual Funds in 15 Minutes a Year. unabridged ed. 148p. 1998. pap. 15.00 (*1-892547-01-5*) Motley Fool.

Motley, James, jt. auth. see Hamilton, James.

Motley, James B. Protect Yourself, Your Family, Your Home: Checklists Against Crime. 192p. 1994. pap. 9.95 (*0-02-881074-0*) Brasseys.

— U. S. Strategy to Counter Domestic Political Terrorism. 124p. (C). 1993. pap. text 25.00 (*1-56806-847-6*) DIANE Pub.

Motley, James B. & Bluhm, Raymond K. The Soldier's Guidebook. (Association of the U. S. Army Book Ser.). (Illus.). 424p. 1995. 24.95 (*0-02-881035-X*); pap. 7.20 (*1-57488-067-5*) Brasseys.

Motley, James B., jt. auth. see Bluhm, Raymond K., Jr.

Motley, John J. & Kelly, Philip R. Now Hear This! Histories of U. S. Ships in World War II. LC 79-18703. 1980. reprint ed. 30.00 (*0-89201-057-6*) Zenger Pub.

Motley, John L. Merry-Mount: A Romance of the Massachusetts Colony, 2 vols., Set. LC 78-64081. reprint ed. 75.00 (*0-404-17290-3*) AMS Pr.

— The Rise of the Dutch Republic, 3 vols. unabridged ed. (Classic Reprint Ser.). (Illus.). 1545p. 1997. reprint ed. 150.00 (*0-936128-62-3*) De Young Pr.

— The Writings of John Lothrop Motley, 17 vols, Set. Curtis, George W., ed. Incl. 1. Rise of the Dutch Republic. 67.50 (*0-404-04521-9*); 2. Rise of the Dutch Republic. 67.50 (*0-404-04522-7*); 3. Rise of the Dutch Republic. 67.50 (*0-404-04523-5*); 4. Rise of the Dutch Republic. 67.50 (*0-404-04524-3*); 5. Rise of the Dutch Republic. 67.50 (*0-404-04525-1*); 6. History of the United Netherlands. 67.50 (*0-404-04526-X*); 7. History of the United Netherlands. 67.50 (*0-404-04527-8*); 8. History of the United Netherlands. 67.50 (*0-404-04528-6*); 9. History of the United Netherlands. 67.50 (*0-404-04529-4*); 10. History of the United Netherlands. 67.50 (*0-404-04530-8*); 11. History of the United Netherlands. 67.50 (*0-404-04531-6*); 12. Life & Death of John of Barneveld, Advocate of Holland, with a View of the Primary Causes & Movements of the Thirty Years' War. 67.50 (*0-404-04532-4*); 13. Life & Death of John of Barneveld, Advocate of Holland, with a View of the Primary Causes & Movements of the Thirty Years' War. 67.50 (*0-404-04533-2*); 14. Life & Death of John of Barneveld, Advocate of Holland, with a View of the Primary Causes & Movements of the Thirty Years' War. 67.50 (*0-404-04534-0*); 15. Correspondence. 67.50 (*0-404-04535-9*); 16. Correspondence. 67.50 (*0-404-04536-7*); 17. Correspondence. 67.50 (*0-404-04537-5*); reprint ed. 552.50 (*0-685-00418-X*) AMS Pr.

Motley, Lynne. The Cat Lover's Guide to Products & Resources for Felines in the Home & Alley. (Illus.). 220p. (Orig.). 1996. pap. 22.00 (*0-9631233-7-8*) Allium Pr.

Motley, Marion, ed. see Stone, Sarah H.

Motley, Mark. Becoming a French Aristocrat: The Education of the Court Nobility, 1580-1715. 262p. (C). 1990. text 45.00 (*0-691-05547-5*, Pub. by Princeton U Pr) Cal Prin Full Svc.

Motley, Mary P. Africa, Its Empires, Nations, & People: A Reader for Young Adults. LC 72-96720. (Illus.). 165p. reprint ed. pap. 51.20 (*0-7837-3592-8*, 204345600009) Bks Demand.

Motley, Mary P., compiled by. The Invisible Soldier: The Experience of the Black Soldier, World War II. LC 87-26370. (Illus.). 366p. (C). 1987. pap. 19.95 (*0-8143-1961-0*) Wayne St U Pr.

Motley, Mary P., ed. The Invisible Soldier: The Experience of the Black Soldier, World War I. LC 75-29420. (Illus.). 364p. reprint ed. pap. 112.90 (*0-608-10518-X*, 2054429) Bks Demand.

Motley, Michael E. & Farrington, Lester C. Test & Evaluation: DOD Has Been Slow in Improving Testing of Software Intensive Systems. (Illus.). 56p. (C). 1997. reprint ed. pap. text 30.00 (*0-7881-4132-5*) DIANE Pub.

Motley, Michael E., et al. U. S. Postal Service: Issues Related to Governance of the Postal Service. (Illus.). 56p. (C). 1998. pap. text 20.00 (*0-7881-7533-5*) DIANE Pub.

Motley, Michael E., ed. see Anderson, Teresa L., et al.

Motley, Michael T. Overcoming Your Fear of Public Speaking. (C). 1994. pap. text 18.25 (*0-07-043521-9*) McGraw.

Motley, Robert J. Business Communication. 378p. (C). 1993. pap. text, student ed. 29.00 (*0-15-500252-X*) Dryden Pr.

Motley, Willard. Knock on Any Door. 515p. 1989. reprint ed. pap. text 18.00 (*0-87580-543-4*) N Ill U Pr.

— We Fished All Night. LC 73-18875. reprint ed. 39.50 (*0-404-11370-2*) AMS Pr.

Motley, Wilma E. Ethics, Jurisprudence & History for the Dental Hygienist. 3rd ed. LC 82-23926. 227p. reprint ed. pap. 70.40 (*0-7837-2732-1*, 204311200006) Bks Demand.

Motlhabi, Mokgethi B. Challenge to Apartheid: Toward a Morally Defensible Strategy. LC 88-7157. 255p. reprint ed. pap. 79.10 (*0-7837-0521-2*, 204084500018) Bks Demand.

Motlmann, Jurgen, jt. ed. see Kuschel, Karl-Joseph.

Motloch, J. L., jt. auth. see Landphair, H. C.

Motloch, John. Intro to Landscape Design. 1990. text 46.95 (*0-442-23688-3*, VNR) Wiley.

— Introduction to Landscape Design. 464p. 1990. pap. 59.95 (*0-471-28897-7*, VNR) Wiley.

Motlow, James & Gillenkirk, Jeff. Bitter Melon: Inside America's Last Rural Chinese Town. 2nd ed. (Illus.). 144p. 1993. pap. 19.95 (*0-930588-58-4*) Heyday Bks.

Motmans, Kris, jt. ed. see Michiels, Luc.

Moto, Susan & Van Kaam, Adrian. Epiphany Manual on the Art & Discipline: A Fresh Approach to the Ancient Practice of Spiritual Direction. LC 98-190554. 115p. 1998. pap. text 15.00 (*1-880982-09-9*) Epiphany Assn.

Motobayashi, T. Heavy Ion Collisions. 500p. 1995. text 108.00 (*981-02-2207-6*) World Scientific Pub.

Motocourse Editors, ed. Motocourse Official History: 50 Years of the FIM Road Racing World Championships. (Illus.). 208p. 1999. 59.95 (*1-874557-83-7*) Hazelton Publishing.

Motoda, H., ed. see Lu, H. J.

Motoda, Hiroshi & Lee, Hing- Yan, eds. PRICAI '98: Topics in Artificial Intelligence: Proceedings of the 5th Pacific Rim International Conference on Artificial Singapore, November 22-27, 1998. LC 98-48078. xix, 646p. 1998. pap. 95.00 (*3-540-65271-X*) Spr-Verlag.

Motoda, Hiroshi, jt. auth. see Liu, Huan.

Motohashi, Y. Sieve Methods & Prime Numbers Theory. (Tata Institute Lectures on Mathematics). xi, 205p. 1984. 26.95 (*0-387-12281-8*) Spr-Verlag.

— Spectral Theory of the Riemann Zeta-Function. (Cambridge Tracts in Mathematics Ser.: No. 127). 238p. (C). 1997. text 52.95 (*0-521-44520-5*) Cambridge U Pr.

Motohashi, Y., ed. Analytic Number Theory. LC 98-108272. (London Mathematical Society Lecture Note Ser.: Vol. 247). (Illus.). 392p. (C). 1997. pap. text 47.95 (*0-521-62512-2*) Cambridge U Pr.

Motoki. Karate Girl. Verre, Tom, ed. (Eros Graphic Novel Ser.: No. 7). (Illus.). 96p. (Orig.). 1993. pap. 12.95 (*1-56097-206-8*) Fantagraph Bks.

Motoki. Karate Girl Tengu Wars. Vol. 30. pap. 13.95 (*1-56097-237-8*) Seven Hills Bk.

Motoki, S. & Saito, T. The Chemistry of Thione S-Imides, Vol. 4. 26p. 1984. pap. text 38.00 (*3-7186-0271-7*) Gordon & Breach.

An Asterisk (*) at the beginning of an entry indicates that the title is appearing for the first time.

Motolinia, Toribio. History of the Indians of New Spain, New Series, No. 4-- Foster, Elizabeth A., tr. LC 73-8449. (Illus.). 294p. 1970. reprint ed. lib. bdg. 35.00 (*0-8371-6977-1*, MONS, Greenwood Pr) Greenwood.

Motomora, Mitchell. Happy Birthday! (Real Readers Ser.: Level Red). (Illus.). 32p. (J). (gr. 1-4). 1989. pap. 4.95 (*0-8114-6706-6*) Raintree Steck-V.

— Lazy Jack & the Silent Princess. (Real Reading Ser.: Level Green). (Illus.). 32p. (J). (gr. 1-4). 1989. pap. 4.95 (*0-8114-6726-0*) Raintree Steck-V.

— Lazy Jack & the Silent Princess. (Real Readers Ser.: Level Green). (Illus.). 32p. (J). (ps-3). 1989. lib. bdg. 21.40 (*0-8172-3529-9*) Raintree Steck-V.

— Momotaro. (Real Reading Ser.). (J). (ps). 1993. pap. 4.95 (*0-8114-6714-7*) Raintree Steck-V.

— Specs: The True Story of Baseball Player George Toporcer. (Ready-Set-Read Ser.). (Illus.). 32p. (J). (ps-3). 1990. lib. bdg. 21.40 (*0-8172-3585-X*) Raintree Steck-V.

— Specs: The True Story of Baseball Player George Toporcer. 28p. (J). (ps-3). 1995. pap. text 4.95 (*0-8114-6746-5*) Raintree Steck-V.

Motomura, Hiroshi, et al. Immigration & Nationality Laws of the United States, Selected Statutes, Regulations & Forms: 1997 Edition. annuals 7th ed. (Miscellaneous Ser.). 809p. (C). 1997. pap. text, suppl. ed. write for info. (*0-314-22643-5*) West Pub.

***Motono, Eiichi.** Conflict & Cooperation in Sino-British Business, 1860-1911: The Impact of Pro-British Commercial Network in Shanghai LC 99-16580. (St. Antony's Ser.). 1999. text 69.95 (*0-312-22497-4*) St Martin.

Motooka, Tohru & Kitsuregawa, Masaru. The Fifth Generation Computer: The Japanese Challenge. Apps, F. R., tr. LC 85-12290. (Illus.). 130p. reprint ed. pap. 40.30 (*0-8357-4603-8*, 203753600008) Bks Demand.

Motooka, Wendy. The Age of Reasons: Quixotism, Sentimentalism & Political Economy in Eighteenth-Century Britain. LC 97-45073. 296p. (C). 1998. 85.00 (*0-415-17941-6*) Routledge.

Motor Information Staff. Imported Wiring Diagram Manual. 1997. pap. 98.00 (*0-87851-960-2*, Hearst) Hearst Commns.

— Imported Wiring Diagram Manual. 1998. pap. 136.00 (*0-87851-985-8*, Hearst) Hearst Commns.

— 1997 Domestic Wiring Diagram. 1998. pap. 136.00 (*0-87851-983-1*, Hearst) Hearst Commns.

Motor Vehicle Manufacturers Association of the Uni. Automobiles of America: Milestones, Pioneers, Roll Call, Highlights. 4th rev. ed. LC 73-19838. 304p. reprint ed. pap. 94.30 (*0-8357-5919-9*, 203101600073) Bks Demand.

***Motorboating & Sailing Editors.** The New Boatkeeper: Motorboating & Sailing's Authoritative Guide to Maintenance, Repair & Improvement. Gladstone, Bernard, ed. & intro. by. LC 99-20867. (Illus.). 305p. 1999. pap. 14.00 (*0-380-79934-0*, Avon Bks) Morrow Avon.

***Motorbooks International Staff.** Haynes Jeep Wrangler, 1987-1999. 2000. pap. 17.95 (*1-56392-367-X*) Iconografix.

Motorbooks Staff. Automobile Year, 1997-98, No. 45. 1998. 54.95 (*2-88324-048-5*, Pub. by J R Piccard) Motorbooks Intl.

***Motorbooks Staff.** Haynes Yamaha YFS200 Blaster: 1988 Thru 1998. LC 98-86346. (Illus.). 128p. 1999. pap. text 23.95 (*1-56392-317-3*, 129356AM, Pub. by Haynes Manuals) Motorbooks Intl.

Motorbooks Staff. Mille Miglia: The Postwar Years. 1998. 29.95 (*88-7911-188-4*) Giorgio Nada Editore.

***Motorbooks Staff.** 1999 Indy Review: Complete Coverage of the 1998 Indy Racing League Season, Vol. 9. (Illus.). 160p. 1999. 24.95 (*0-7603-0774-1*, 129030AP, Pub. by MBI Pubg) Motorbooks Intl.

***Motorbooks Staff & Shapiro, Larry.** Pumpers: Workhorse Fire Engines. LC 99-37654. (Illus.). 128p. 1999. pap. text 21.95 (*0-7603-0672-9*, 128966AP, Pub. by MBI Pubg) Motorbooks Intl.

— Special Police Vehicles. LC 99-37653. (Illus.). 96p. 1999. pap. text 14.95 (*0-7603-0670-2*, 128962AP, Pub. by MBI Pubg) Motorbooks Intl.

Motorcycle Mechanics Institute Staff. The Complete Guide to Motorcycle Mechanics. 2nd ed. LC 93-14849. 378p. (C). 1993. pap. text 86.00 (*0-13-225889-7*) Prntice Hall Bks.

Motorcycle, Michael. Hairline Lifeline. LC 97-91304. (Illus.). 96p. 1998. 18.98 (*0-9661981-5-8*) Sanctum Pr.

Motorcycle Safety Foundation Staff. Motorcycling Excellence: The Motorcycle Safety Foundation's Guide to Skills, Knowledge, & Strategies for Riding Right. (Illus.). 176p. 1995. pap. 24.95 (*1-884313-01-9*) Whitehorse NH.

Motorcyclist Magazine Editors. Complete Idiot's Guide to Motorcycles. 352p. 1998. pap. text 17.95 (*0-02-862416-5*) Macmillan Gen Ref.

Motorola Codex Staff. Basics Book of ISDN. (Illus.). 56p. 1991. pap. text 16.95 (*0-201-56368-1*) Addison-Wesley.

— The Basics Book of OSI & Networking Management. (Illus.). 80p. (C). 1992. pap. text 15.95 (*0-201-56371-1*) Addison-Wesley.

Motorola Codex Staff. The Basics Book of X.25 Packet Switching. 96p. 1991. pap. text 11.95 (*0-201-56373-8*) Addison-Wesley.

Motorola, Inc. Staff. M68000 8-, 16-, 32-Bit Microprocessor's: Programmer's Reference Manual. 5th ed. 240p. 1986. 26.95 (*0-13-541475-X*) P-H.

— MC68000 8- 16- 32-Bit Microprocessor User's Manual. 7th ed. 368p. 1989. pap. 22.95 (*0-13-567074-8*) P-H.

— MC 68020 32-Bit Microprocessor User's Manual. (Illus.). 448p. 1984. pap. 18.95 (*0-13-541467-9*) P-H.

— MC68020 32-Bit Microprocessor User's Manual. 2nd ed. 464p. 1986. 21.95 (*0-13-566860-3*) P-H.

Motorola Museum of Electronics Staff. Motorola: A Journey Through Time & Technology. (Illus.). 96p. 1994. 50.00 (*1-56946-005-1*); 35.00 (*1-56946-008-6*); pap. 25.00 (*1-56946-011-6*) Motorola Univ.

— Motorola: A Journey Through Time & Technology. (SPA., Illus.). 96p. (C). 1994. pap. 25.00 (*1-56946-012-4*); pap. text 25.00 (*1-56946-013-2*) Motorola Univ.

— Motorola: A Journey Through Time & Technology. (CHI., Illus.). 96p. (YA). 1994. 35.00 (*1-56946-006-X*); pap. text 25.00 (*1-56946-010-8*) Motorola Univ.

Motorola UNIX Staff. UNIX System 5 Calls & Library Functions: Reference Manual for Motorola Processors. 1104p. (C). 1992. pap. 48.80 (*0-13-035841-X*) P-H.

Motosof, Eli, ed. see Schneersohn, Shmuel.

Motovilova, jt. auth. see Mitrokhina, V. I.

Motowidlo, Stephan J., jt. ed. see Borman, Walter C.

Motoyama, Etsuro K. Smith's Anesthesia for Infants & Children. 6th ed. Davis, Peter J., ed. (Illus.). 1024p. (C). (gr. 13). 1995. text 139.00 (*0-8151-5937-4*, 23779) Mosby Inc.

Motoyama, Hiroshi. Karma & Reincarnation. 160p. (Orig.). 1993. pap. 10.00 (*0-380-77213-2*, Avon Bks) Morrow Avon.

***Motoyama, Hiroshi.** Karma & Reincarnation: The Key to Spiritual Evolution & Enlightment. 2000. pap. 12.95 (*0-7499-1916-7*) Piatkus Bks.

Motoyama, Hiroshi. Theories of the Chakras: Bridge to Higher Consciousness. LC 81-51165. 350p. 1995. pap. 12.00 (*0-8356-0551-5*, Quest) Theos Pub Hse.

— Toward a Superconsciousness: Meditational Theory & Practice. Nagatomo, Shigenori & Ames, Clifford R., trs. LC 89-81298. (Illus.). 164p. (Orig.). 1990. reprint ed. pap. 50.90 (*0-608-01784-1*, 206244200003) Bks Demand.

Motoyama, N., jt. ed. see Kuhr, R. J.

Motoyama, Sho. Illustrated Survey of Japanese Monster Figures: 1966-71, 1. 1999. pap. text 27.95 (*4-7663-3220-2*) Green Arrow.

Motoyama, Yukihiko. Proliferating Talent: Essays on Politics, Thought, & Education in the Meiji Era. Elisonas, J. S. & Rubinger, Richard, eds. LC 97-779. 440p. 1997. text 48.00 (*0-8248-1846-6*) UH Pr.

Motoyama, Yukihiko, jt. auth. see Holzman, Donald.

Motoyoshi, Akiko & Houser, Michael. BBC Japanese Phrase Book. (BBC Phrase Bks.). (Illus.). 192p. 1995. pap. 5.95 (*0-8442-9173-0*, 91730) NTC Contemp Pub Co.

— Japan: The All-in-One Travel & Language Guide. LC 97-42537. (Get Around in . . . Ser.). (JPN., Illus.). 128p. 1998. pap. 8.95 (*0-8442-0156-1*, 01561, Passprt Bks); pap. 19.95 incl. audio (*0-8442-0191-X*, 0191X, Passprt Bks) NTC Contemp Pub Co.

***Motoyoshi, Michelle.** Filipinos in California. (California Cultures Ser.). (Illus.). 64p. (J). (gr. 4-8). 1999. pap. text 14.95 (*1-884925-92-8*) Toucan Valley.

— The Japanese in California. (California Cultures Ser.). (Illus.). 64p. (J). (gr. 4-8). 1999. pap. text 14.95 (*1-884925-90-1*) Toucan Valley.

— Mexicans in California. (California Cultures Ser.). (Illus.). 64p. (J). (gr. 4-8). 1999. pap. text 14.95 (*1-884925-91-X*) Toucan Valley.

Motreanu, D. Minimax Theorems & Qualitative Properties of the Solutions of Hemivariational Inequalities. LC 98-45178. (Nonconvex Optimization & Its Applications Ser.). 12p. 1999. 156.00 (*0-7923-5456-7*) Kluwer Academic.

***Motreanu, D. & Pavel, N. H.** Tangency, Flow Invariance for Differential Equations & Optimization Problems LC 99-22025. (Monographs & Textbooks in Pure & Applied Mathematics). (Illus.). 504p. 1999. text 195.00 (*0-8247-7341-1*) Dekker.

Motro, Amihai, ed. Uncertainty Management in Information Systems: From Needs to Solutions. 480p. (C). 1996. text 163.50 (*0-7923-9803-3*) Kluwer Academic.

***Motsau, T. D.** Mfana Mischief. (Illus.). 73p. 1999. pap. 9.00 (*0-627-02220-0*, Pub. by J L Van Schaik) BHB Intl.

Motsch, Markus F., ed. Lessing Yearbook IV. 247p. 1972. 12.50 (*0-318-20524-6*, 6741) Lessing Soc.

Motsett, C. B. If It Wasn't for the People This Job Would Be Fun! Coaching for Buy-In & Results. LC 97-98461. 160p. 1997. per. 19.95 (*1-57444-202-3*) St Lucie Pr.

Motseyoef, ed. see Seals, David.

Motseyoef, tr. see Seals, David.

***Motsinger, Thomas N., et al, eds.** Archaeology in West-Central Arizona: Proceedings of the 1996 Arizona Archaeological Council Prescott Conference. (Illus.). 259p. 2000. pap. 29.95 (*0-927579-18-9*) Sharlot Hall Mus Pr.

Motsonelidze, N. S. Stability & Seismic Resistance of Buttress Dams. Kothekar, V. S., tr. from RUS. 293p. (C). 1987. text 116.00 (*90-6191-490-6*, Pub. by A A Balkema) Ashgate Pub Co.

— Stability & Seismic Resistance of Buttress Dams. 278p. (C). 1987. 30.00 (*81-204-0207-3*, Pub. by Oxford IBH) S Asia.

Mott. Harrap's Tintin Illustrated Spanish Dictionary. 1994. 25.00 (*0-245-60361-1*, Harraps IN) Macmillan Gen Ref.

Mott, ed. Breakthru: Writing & Language Skills. 1989. pap. 10.57 (*0-8092-4237-0*) NTC Contemp Pub Co.

Mott & Kajikawa, Kimiko. Sweet Dreams: How Animals Sleep. LC 98-16637. (J). (ps-2). 1999. 15.95 (*0-8050-5890-7*) H Holt & Co.

Mott, jt. auth. see Dougherty.

Mott, jt. auth. see Opper.

***Mott, Anita L.** Mosser - Musser Family. 227p. 1999. pap. 24.00 (*0-7884-1187-X*, M577) Heritage Bk.

Mott, Barbara & Mott, Elizabeth. Mott's Miniature Furniture Workshop Manual: Techniques & Patterns for 144 Miniature Masterpieces. 2nd rev. ed. (Illus.). 216p. 1995. pap. 19.95 (*1-56523-052-3*) Fox Chapel Pub.

Mott, Brian & Rion, Rosana. Harrap's Tintin Illustrated Spanish Dictionary: English-Spanish - Spanish-English. (SPA., Illus.). 448p. 1993. 25.00 (*0-671-84869-0*, Harraps IN) Macmillan Gen Ref.

Mott, Carol Wilder & Weakland, John H. Rigor & Imagination: Essays on Human Communication from the Interactional View. LC 81-83995. 432p. 1981. 69.50 (*0-275-90741-4*, C0741, Praeger Pubs) Greenwood.

Mott, Chapman & Hill, Tessa. Amazing Earth Adventures: A Kid's Guide to Preserving the Planet. (J). 1992. pap. 2.75 (*0-590-45560-5*) Scholastic Inc.

Mott, Donald R. & Saunders, Cheryl M. Stephen Spielberg. (Twayne's Filmmakers Ser.). 216p. 1988. pap. 16.95 (*0-8057-9311-9*) Macmillan.

Mott, Elizabeth, jt. auth. see Mott, Barbara.

Mott, Elliott R. Cycling Possibilities: Course Guides for the Wasatch Front Bicyclist. (Illus.). 114p. 1993. pap. 8.95 (*0-9626322-3-6*) Roosevelt & Torrey.

— Cycling Possibilities Vol. 1: Course Guide for the Salt Lake Bicyclist. (Illus.). 88p. 1990. pap. 8.95 (*0-9626322-1-X*) Roosevelt & Torrey.

— Cycling Possibilities Vol. 2: Course Guides for the Northern Utah Bicyclist. (Illus.). 96p. 1991. pap. 8.95 (*0-9626322-2-8*) Roosevelt & Torrey.

Mott, Evelyn Clarke. Balloon Ride. (Illus.). 32p. (J). (ps-1). 1991. 13.95 (*0-8027-8124-1*); lib. bdg. 14.85 (*0-8027-8126-8*) Walker & Co.

— Steam Train Ride. (Illus.). 1999. pap. text 13.35 (*0-7857-6534-4*) Econo-Clad Bks.

Mott, Evelyn Clarke. Steam Train Ride. 1995. 10.15 (*0-606-09897-6*, Pub. by Turtleback) Demco.

— Steam Train Ride. (Illus.). 32p. (J). (gr. 4-8). 1991. 13.95 (*0-8027-6995-0*); lib. bdg. 14.85 (*0-8027-6996-9*) Walker & Co.

— Steam Train Ride. LC 90-49223. (Illus.). 32p. (J). (ps-3). 1995. pap. 5.95 (*0-8027-7452-0*) Walker & Co.

Mott, Frank L. A History of American Magazines. LC 39-2823. 950p. reprint ed. pap. 200.00 (*0-7837-4086-7*, 205745800001) Bks Demand.

— A History of American Magazines, Vol. 2. LC 39-2823. (Illus.). 660p. reprint ed. pap. 200.00 (*0-7837-3069-1*, 205745800002) Bks Demand.

— A History of American Magazines, Vol. 3. LC 39-2823. (Illus.). 683p. reprint ed. pap. 200.00 (*0-7837-3070-5*, 205745800003) Bks Demand.

— A History of American Magazines, Vol. 4. LC 39-2823. 890p. reprint ed. pap. 200.00 (*0-7837-4087-5*, 205745800004) Bks Demand.

— A History of American Magazines, Vol. 5. LC 39-2823. 613p. reprint ed. pap. 190.10 (*0-7837-4088-3*, 205745800005) Bks Demand.

Mott, Frank L., ed. The Employment Revolution: Young American Women of the 1970's. 256p. 1982. 35.00 (*0-262-13186-2*) MIT Pr.

— Journalism in Wartime. LC 84-696. 216p. (C). 1984. reprint ed. lib. bdg. 55.00 (*0-313-24458-8*, MOJW, Greenwood Pr) Greenwood.

Mott, George F. & Lambert, Richard D., eds. Urban Change & the Planning Syndrome. LC 72-93250. (Annals of the American Academy of Political & Social Science Ser.: No. 405). 250p. (C). 1973. 28.00 (*0-685-00185-7*, 87761); pap. 18.00 (*0-87761-157-2*) Am Acad Pol Soc Sci.

Mott, Graham. Investment Appraisal. 3rd ed. 196p. 1997. pap. 44.50 (*0-7121-1074-7*, Pub. by Pitman Pub) Trans-Atl Phila.

Mott, Harold. Antennas for Radar & Communications: A Polarimetric Approach. LC 92-9240. (Series in Microwave & Optical Engineering). 544p. 1992. 148.00 (*0-471-57538-0*) Wiley.

— Polarization in Antennas & Radar. LC 86-1349. 320p. 1986. 162.50 (*0-471-01167-3*) Wiley.

Mott, Harold & Boerner, Wolfgang M., eds. Wideband Interferometric Sensing & Imaging Polarimetry, Vol. 3120. LC 98-145673. 410p. 1997. 69.00 (*0-8194-2542-7*) SPIE.

Mott, Helen, jt. ed. see Quinn, Brian.

Mott Hospital Staff. Ann Arbor's Cookin' Betz, Ann & Ronald McDonald House Staff, eds. 368p. (Orig.). 1985. pap. 10.00 (*0-9618208-0-2*) Ronald McDonald Hse.

Mott Iron Works Staff. Mott's Illustrated Catalog of Victorian Plumbing Fixtures for Bathrooms & Kitchens. (Illus.). 288p. 1988. reprint ed. pap. 15.95 (*0-486-25526-3*) Dover.

Mott, J. J., jt. ed. see Tothill, J. C.

Mott, Jack R., jt. auth. see Gogg, Thomas J.

Mott, Jacolyn A., ed. The American Paintings in the Pennsylvania Academy of the Fine Arts: An Illustrated Checklist. (Illus.). 204p. (Orig.). 1989. pap. 30.00 (*0-943836-11-5*) Penn Acad Art.

Mott, Jacolyn A., ed. see Danly, Susan.

Mott, Jacolyn A., ed. see Fresella-Lee, Nancy.

Mott, Jim, jt. auth. see Kopriva, Don.

Mott, Joan, ed. Pre-GED Writing & Language Skills. 1987. pap. 10.57 (*0-8092-4898-0*) NTC Contemp Pub Co.

Mott, Joanna, tr. see Paris, Ginette.

Mott, John R. The Evangelization of the World in This Generation. LC 76-38457. (Religion in America, Ser. 2). 258p. 1972. reprint ed. 19.95 (*0-405-04078-4*) Ayer.

Mott, John R., et al. Student Mission Power: Report of the First International Convention of the Student Volunteer Movement for Foreign Missions, 1891. LC 79-92013. 235p. 1979. reprint ed. pap. 7.95 (*0-87808-736-2*) William Carey Lib.

Mott, K. & Chen, M. Progress in Assessment of Morbidity Due to Schistosomiasis: Reviews of Recent Literature. (Document Published by WHO Parasitic Diseases Programme Ser.). 56p. 1989. pap. text 20.00 (*0-9510869-4-4*) World Health.

Mott, Kathleen O. Leadership Skills for the Nurse Manager: Restructuring the Role of Management in Today's... LC 96-7876. 240p. 1996. pap. 32.50 (*0-7863-0860-5*, Irwn Prfssnl) McGraw-Hill Prof.

***Mott, Kenneth F.** The Supreme Court & the Living Constitution. 240p. 1999. pap. text 17.50 (*1-891877-05-4*) Sheron Ent.

Mott, Lawrence. To the Credit of the Sea. LC 78-150555. (Short Story Index Reprint Ser.). 1977. reprint ed. 21.95 (*0-8369-3852-6*) Ayer.

— White Darkness: And Other Stories of the Great Northwest. LC 74-150554. (Short Story Index Reprint Ser.). (Illus.). 1977. reprint ed. 23.95 (*0-8369-3851-8*) Ayer.

Mott, Lawrence V. The Development of the Rudder: A Technological Tale. LC 96-8051. (Studies in Nautical Archaeology: No. 3). (Illus.). 224p. (Orig.). 1996. pap. 19.95 (*0-89096-723-7*) Tex A&M Univ Pr.

Mott, Lawrie. Our Children at Risk: The 5 Worst Environmental Threats to Their Health. (Illus.). 124p. 1997. pap. 14.00 (*1-893340-11-2*) Natl Resources Defense Coun.

Mott, Lawrie & Snyder, Karen. Pesticide Alert: A Guide to Pesticides in Fruits & Vegetables. 128p. 1987. 6.95 (*0-318-39812-5*) Natl Resources Defense Coun.

— Pesticide Alert: A Guide to Pesticides in Fruits & Vegetables. LC 87-42965. (Illus.). 128p. 1988. pap. 6.95 (*0-87156-726-1*, Pub. by Sierra) Random.

Mott, Leslie C. Engineering Drawing & Construction. 2nd ed. (Illus.). 1977. pap. 14.95 (*0-19-859114-4*) OUP.

Mott, Lewis F. System of Courtly Love. LC 65-26458. (Studies in Comparative Literature: No. 35). (C). 1969. reprint ed. lib. bdg. 75.00 (*0-8383-0599-7*) M S G Haskell Hse.

Mott, Luiz. Epidemic of Hate: Violations of the Human Rights of Gay Men, Lesbians & Transvestites. (Illus.). 85p. 1996. pap. 12.00 (*1-884955-04-5*) Intl Gay & Lesbian.

Mott, Margaret, ed. see MacCubbin, Tom.

Mott-McDonald Associates Staff. Using Title XX to Serve Children & Youth. LC 76-357536. 80p. reprint ed. pap. 30.00 (*0-608-14387-1*, 201937500011) Bks Demand.

Mott, Michael. Corday. rev. ed. (International-Visions Ser.). (Illus.). 84p. 1995. pap. 9.45 (*0-938872-21-4*) Black Buzzard.

— The Seven Mountains of Thomas Merton. (Illus.). 720p. 1993. pap. 24.00 (*0-15-680681-9*) Harcourt.

— Woman & the Sea: Selected Poems by Michael Mott. Beacham, Walton, ed. 272p. (Orig.). 1999. pap. 17.95 (*0-938078-48-8*) Anhinga Pr.

***Mott, Pat.** Orange County 2000 - The Millennium Book. unabridged ed. (Illus.). 256p. 1999. 49.95 (*0-9670270-0-4*, Pub. by Orange Coast Kom) Sunbelt Pubns.

Mott, Peter, jt. ed. see Neimark, Peninah Rhodes.

***Mott, Robert L.** Applied Fluid Mechanics. 5th ed. LC 99-46580. (Illus.). 597p. 2000. 87.00 (*0-13-023120-7*) P-H.

Mott, Robert L. Applied Strength of Materials. 3rd ed. 641p. 1995. 105.00 (*0-13-376278-5*) P-H.

— Machine Elements & Mechanics. 3rd ed. LC 98-34439. 852p. 1998. 105.00 (*0-13-841446-7*) P-H.

***Mott, Robert L.** Radio Live! Television Live! Those Golden Days When Horses Were Coconuts. (Illus.). 240p. 2000. 45.00 (*0-7864-0816-2*) McFarland & Co.

Mott, Robert L. Radio Sound Effects: Who Did It, & How, in the Era of Live Broadcasting. LC 92-50313. (Illus.). 303p. 1993. lib. bdg. 42.50 (*0-89950-747-6*) McFarland & Co.

Mott, Rodney L. The Due Process of Law. LC 72-165604. (American Constitutional & Legal History Ser). 702p. 1973. reprint ed. lib. bdg. 85.00 (*0-306-70225-8*) Da Capo.

Mott, Sandra R. Handbook of Child Health Nursing. 1986. pap. text 15.96 (*0-201-13699-6*) Addison-Wesley.

— Nursing Care for Children. 2nd ed. Hunter, Debra, ed. 1907p. (C). 1990. pap. text 9.95 (*0-201-52924-6*) Addison-Wesley.

— Nursing Care of Children & Families. 2nd ed. Hunter, Debra, ed. 1907p. (C). 1990. text 78.75 (*0-201-12923-X*); student ed. write for info. (*0-201-12924-8*) Addison-Wesley.

Mott, Sandra R., jt. auth. see James.

Mott, Sandra R., jt. auth. see James, Susan R.

Mott, Sarah. InService Education: Its Effect on the Ability of an Extended Care Facility to Meet the Outcome Standards. (Research Monographs: No. 10). 1983. pap. 21.00 (*0-7300-2046-0*, Pub. by Deakin Univ) St Mut.

Mott, Sarah & Riggs, Ann, eds. Elderly People - Their Need for an Participation in Social Interactions (Dinroo) (Research Monographs: No. 5). 73p. 1993. pap. 33.00 (*0-7300-1521-1*, Pub. by Deakin Univ) St Mut.

Mott, Sir Nevill Francis. A Life in Science. 198p. 1995. pap. 29.95 (*0-7484-0434-1*, Pub. by Tay Francis Ltd) Taylor & Francis.

— Metal-Insulator Transitions. 2nd rev. ed. 296p. 1990. 121.00 (*0-85066-783-6*) Taylor & Francis.

Mott, Sir Nevill Francis, ed. Workshop on Oxidation Processes, Vol. 55, No. 6. (Philosophical Magazine Ser.). 1987. pap. 34.00 (*0-85066-930-8*) Taylor & Francis.

— Workshop on Oxidation Processes II, Vol. 55, No. 6. (Philosophical Magazine Ser.). 1987. pap. 34.00 (*0-85066-917-0*) Taylor & Francis.

Mott, Sir Nevill Francis, ed. Science in the Making: Scientific Development As Chronicled by Historic Papers in the Philosophical Magazine with Commentaries & Illustrations, Vol. 2: 1851-1900. 448p. 1997. 99.00 (*0-7484-0642-5*, Pub. by Tay Francis Ltd) Taylor & Francis.

M

Mott, Sir Nevill Francis & Alexandrov, A. S. High Temperature Superconductors & Other Superfluids. 250p. 1995. 49.50 (0-7484-0309-4, Pub. by Tay Francis Ltd) Taylor & Francis.

Mott, Sir Nevill Francis & Alexandrov, A. S., eds. Sir Nevill Mott: 65 Years in Physics. LC 95-18277. (Series in 20th Century Physics: Vol. 12). 750p. 1995. text 99.00 (981-02-2237-8); pap. text 51.00 (981-02-2252-1) World Scientific Pub.

Mott, Sir Nevill Francis & Jones, H. Theory of the Properties of Metals & Alloys. 326p. 1958. pap. 10.95 (0-486-60456-X) Dover.

Mott, Sir Nevill Francis, jt. auth. see Alexandrov, A. S.

Mott-Smith, Geoffrey. Mathematical Puzzles for Beginners & Enthusiasts. 2nd ed. (Illus.). 248p. 1954. pap. 7.95 (0-486-20198-8) Dover.

Mott-Smith, Geoffrey, jt. auth. see Morehead, Albert H.

Mott-Smith, Geoffrey, jt. ed. see Morehead, Albert H.

Mott, Stephen C. Biblical Ethics & Social Change. 262p. 1982. pap. text 21.95 (0-19-502948-8) OUP.

— Political Visions: A Christian Analysis. LC 92-25045. (Illus.). 352p. 1993. pap. text 35.00 (0-19-508138-2) OUP.

Mott, Steve & Lutz, Susan. The College Survival Instruction Book. LC 96-20939. Orig. Title: The Original College Adventure Aide. 128p. (Orig.). 1996. pap. 6.99 (1-56414-248-5) Career Pr Inc.

Mott, Sue. A Girl's Guide to Ball Games. (Illus.). 192p. 1997. 35.00 (1-85158-868-X, Pub. by Mainstream Pubng) Trafalgar.

Mott, Thomas B. Myron T. Herrick, Friend of France. 1993. reprint ed. lib. bdg. 89.00 (0-7812-5392-6) Rprt Serv.

— Twenty Years As Military Attache. Kohn, Richard H., ed. LC 78-22390. (American Military Experience Ser.). 1980. reprint ed. lib. bdg. 25.95 (0-405-11867-8) Ayer.

Mott, Troy, jt. auth. see O'Reilly, Tim.

Mott, Troy, ed. see Kent, Dorothy.

Mott, Troy, ed. see Leonhard, Woody & Deegan, Peter.

Mott, Troy, ed. see Syroid, Tom & Leuf, Bo.

Mott, Troy S., ed. see O'Quinn, Donnie.

Mott, Vincent, jt. auth. see Chirovsky, Nicholas L.

Mott, Vincent L. How to Play Drums. (Self Improvement Ser.). 96p. (Orig.). 1985. pap. text 7.95 (0-8494-1550-0, 85-10) Hansen Ed Mus.

Mott, W. King, Jr. The Third Way: Economic Justice According to John Paul II. 200p. 1998. 37.00 (0-7618-1265-2) U Pr of Amer.

***Mott, Wesley T.** American Renaissance in New England. LC 00-26759. (Dictionary of Literary Biography Ser.: No. 2). (Illus.). 400p. 2000. text 204.75 (0-7876-3132-9) Gale.

Mott, Wesley T. The Strains of Eloquence: Emerson & His Sermons. LC 88-28123. 288p. 1989. lib. bdg. 37.50 (0-271-00660-9) Pa St U Pr.

Mott, Wesley T., ed. Biographical Dictionary of Transcendentalism. LC 95-45187. 336p. 1996. lib. bdg. 85.00 (0-313-28836-4, Greenwood Pr) Greenwood.

— Encyclopedia of Transcendentalism. LC 95-40030. 320p. 1996. lib. bdg. 79.50 (0-313-29924-2, Greenwood Pr) Greenwood.

Mott, Wesley T. & Burkholder, Robert E., eds. Emersonian Circles: Essays in Honor of Joel Myerson. LC 96-34805. 296p. 1997. 60.00 (1-878822-72-1) Univ Rochester Pr.

Mott, Wesley T., ed. see Emerson, Ralph Waldo.

Mott, William H., IV. The Economic Basis of Peace: Linkages Between Economic Growth & International Conflict, 187. LC 96-51138. (Contributions in Economics & Economic History Ser.: Vol. 187). 320p. 1997. 65.00 (0-313-30366-5, Greenwood Pr) Greenwood.

— Military Assistance: An Operational Perspective, 170. LC 98-17532. (Contributions in Military Studies Ser.: No. 170). 384p. 1999. 65.00 (0-313-30729-6, GM0729, Greenwood Pr) Greenwood.

Mott, William H., et al, contrib. by. Laser Satellite Communication & the Telecommunications Industry: The Status, the Problem, & the Opportunity. LC 99-27547. 328p. 2000. 69.50 (1-56720-329-9, Quorum Bks) Greenwood.

Motta, Glenda, jt. auth. see Phillips, Robert.

***Motta, Hau'oli & Wilson, William H.** He Mau Hana Ka'u E Hana Ai. (HAW., Illus.). 24p. (J). (gr. k). 1999. pap. 6.95 incl. audio (1-58191-079-7) Aha Punana Leo.

Motta, Jack J. & Tennant, Jeffrey L. College Prep Mathematics Worktext, Vol. 1. 240p. (C). 1996. pap. text 25.14 (0-7872-2338-7) Kendall-Hunt.

Motta, Jake La, see La Motta, Jake.

Motta, Janice C. Impact! Adult Literacy & Language, Bk. 3. 1982. pap. text, teacher ed. 9.07 (0-201-05317-9) Addison-Wesley.

Motta, Janice C. & Riley, K. Breakthrough to Literacy, 3 bks., Bk. 1. 1981. pap. write for info. (0-318-50127-9); pap., teacher ed. write for info. (0-318-50128-7) Addison-Wesley.

— Breakthrough to Literacy, 3 bks., Bk. 2. 1981. teacher ed. write for info. (0-318-50130-9); write for info. (0-318-50129-5) Addison-Wesley.

— Breakthrough to Literacy, 3 bks., Bk. 3. 1981. write for info. (0-318-50131-7) Addison-Wesley.

— Impact! Adult Literacy & Language Skills, Bk. 1. 1982. pap. text. write for info. (0-318-56708-3) Addison-Wesley.

— Impact! Adult Literacy & Language Skills, Bk. 2. 1982. pap. text. write for info. (0-318-56710-5) Addison-Wesley.

— Impact! Adult Literacy & Language Skills, Bk. 3. 1982. write for info. (0-318-56712-1) Addison-Wesley.

— Impact! Adult Literacy & Language Skills, No. I. 1982. teacher ed. write for info. (0-318-56709-1) Addison-Wesley.

— Impact! Adult Literacy & Language Skills, No. II. 1982. teacher ed. write for info. (0-318-56711-3) Addison-Wesley.

— Impact! Adult Literacy & Language Skills, No. III. 1982. teacher ed. write for info. (0-318-56713-X) Addison-Wesley.

Motta, Marcella, ed. Brain Endocrinology. 2nd ed. LC 91-14199. (Comprehensive Endocrinology Ser.). (Illus.). 496p. 1991. reprint ed. pap. 153.80 (0-608-07219-2, 206744400009) Bks Demand.

— The Endocrine Functions of the Brain. fac. ed. LC 77-84553. (Comprehensive Endocrinology Ser.). (Illus.). 492p. pap. 152.60 (0-7837-7292-0, 204701400005) Bks Demand.

Motta, Marcella & Serio, Mario, eds. Sex Hormones & Antihormones in Endocrine Dependent Pathology: Proceedings of an International Symposium, Milano, 10-14 April 1994. LC 94-32151. (International Congress Ser.: Vol. 1064). 448p. 1994. 233.50 (0-444-81879-0) Elsevier.

Motta, Marcella, ed. see International Symposium on Androgens & Antiandroge.

Motta, P. Color Atlas of Microscopic Anatomy. 268p. 1990. text 40.00 (1-57235-011-3, Pub. by Piccin Nuova) Gordon & Breach.

Motta, P. Color Atlas of Microscopic Anatomy. (Illus.). 268p. 1990. text. write for info. (88-299-0082-6, Pub. by Piccin Nuova) Gordon & Breach.

Motta, P. M. Basic, Clinical & Surgical Nephrology. DiDio, L. J., ed. (Developments in Nephrology Ser.). 1985. text 186.00 (0-89838-698-5) Kluwer Academic.

Motta, P. M., ed. Biopathology of the Liver: An Ultrastructural Approach. (C). 1988. text 254.00 (0-7462-0049-8) Kluwer Academic.

— Ultrastructure of Endocrine Cells & Tissues: Electron Microscopy in Biology & Medicine. 1983. text 240.00 (0-89838-568-7) Kluwer Academic.

Motta, P. M., et al, eds. Scanning Electron Microscopy of Vascular Casts: Methods & Applications. (Electron Microscopy in Biology & Medicine Ser.). 416p. (C). 1992. text 350.50 (0-7923-1297-X) Kluwer Academic.

Motta, P. M. & Didio, L. J., eds. Basic & Clinical Hepatology. 200p. 1981. text 191.50 (90-247-2404-X) Kluwer Academic.

Motta, P. M. & Fujita, Hisao, eds. Ultrastructure of the Digestive Tract. (Electron Microscopy in Biology & Medicine Ser.). (C). 1988. text 197.00 (0-89838-893-7) Kluwer Academic.

Motta, P. M. & Hafez, E. S., eds. Biology of the Ovary. (Developments in Obstetrics & Gynecology Ser.: No. 2). 345p. 1980. text 234.00 (90-247-2316-7) Kluwer Academic.

Motta, P. M., jt. ed. see Bonucci, E.

Motta, P. M., jt. ed. see Ruggeri, A.

Motta, Philip J. The Butterflyfishes: Success on the Coral Reef. (Developments in Environmental Biology of Fishes Ser.). (C). 1989. text 213.50 (0-7923-0168-4) Kluwer Academic.

Motta, Pietro M., ed. Ultrastructure of Smooth Muscle. (Electron Microscopy in Biology & Medicine Ser.). (C). 1990. text 242.00 (0-7923-0480-2) Kluwer Academic.

Motta, Pietro M., jt. ed. see Riva, Alessandro.

Motta, Pietro M., jt. ed. see Van Blerkom, Jonathan.

Motta, Sheree, jt. auth. see Adamse, Michael.

Motta, Vanna, jt. auth. see Moss, Howard.

Motta, William. 50 Years of Road & Track: The Art of the Automobile. LC 97-12594. (Illus.). 264p. 1997. 39.95 (0-7603-0398-3) MBI Pubg.

Mottahedeh, Patricia E., ed. Out of Noah's Ark: Animals in Ancient Art from the Leo Mildenberg Collection.Tr. of Aus Noahs Arche. (Illus.). 196p. 1997. text 35.00 (3-8053-2347-6) P Zabern.

Mottahedeh, Roy. Loyalty & Leadership in an Early Islamic Society. rev. ed. 239p. 1998. pap. text 24.50 (1-86064-181-4) I B T.

***Mottahedeh, Roy.** Mantle of the Prophet. 2000. pap. 25.95 (1-85168-234-1, Pub. by Onewrld Pubns) Penguin Putnam.

Mottahedeh, Roy P., jt. auth. see Laiou, Angeliki E.

Mottale, Morris M. The Arms Buildup in the Persian Gulf. 244p. (Orig.). (C). 1986. pap. text 24.00 (0-8191-5203-X) U Pr of Amer.

— Iran: The Political Sociology of the Islamic Revolution. LC 94-35179. 82p. (Orig.). (C). 1995. pap. text 17.50 (0-8191-9743-2) U Pr of Amer.

Mottana, A. & Barragato, F., eds. Absorption Spectroscopy in Mineralogy: First European Meeting, Academia Nazionale del Lincei, Palazzo Corsini, Rome, Italy, 4-7 Oct., 1989. 294p. 1990. 147.00 (0-444-88799-7) Elsevier.

Mottana, Annibale. Guide to Minerals & Rocks: Guia de Minerales y Rocas. 6th ed. (SPA.). 608p. 1991. write for info. (0-7859-4933-X) Fr & Eur.

Motte, Andrew, tr. see Newton, Sir Isaac.

Motte, Dean De la, see De la Motte, Dean.

Motte, Ellen N. La, see La Motte, Ellen N.

Motte, Fouque De La, see De La Motte, Fouque.

Motte Fouque, Friedrich De La, see De La Motte Fouque, Friedrich.

Motte, Ganzague. Homilies for Sundays of the Year: Cycle A. Drury, John, tr. from FRE. 352p. 1974. 10.00 (0-8199-0461-9, Frncscn Herld) Franciscan Pr.

Motte, Geoff A. & Stout, Thomas M. Chartwork & Marine Nagivation: For Fishermen & Boat Operators. LC 83-46037. (Illus.). 187p. reprint ed. pap. 58.00 (0-7837-6296-8, 204601100010) Bks Demand.

Motte Green, Catherine De, see De Motte Green, Catherine.

Motte-Haber, Helga De La, see Flesch, Martin & De La Motte-Haber, Helga.

Motte, Helga De la, see De la Motte, Helga.

Motte, Jochen. Biblische Theologie Nach Walther Zimmerli: Darstellung und Wurdigung der Alttestamentlichen Theologie Walther Zimmerlis und der Sich Aus Ihr Ergebenden Perspektive Zum Neuen Testament in Systematisch-Theologischer Sicht. (Europaische Hochschulschriften Ser.: Reihe 23, Bd. 521). (GER.). XV, 211p. 1994. 39.95 (3-631-48078-4) P Lang Pubng.

Motte, Mary, ed. see SEDOS Research Seminar on the Future of Mission St.

Motte, Warren. Small Worlds: Minimalism in Contemporary French Literature. LC 98-26165. (Stages Ser.). ix, 212p. 1999. text 45.00 (0-8032-3202-0) U of Nebr Pr.

Motte, Warren F. Playtexts: Ludics in Contemporary Literature. LC 94-19827. (Stages Ser.). ix, 233p. 1995. text 40.00 (0-8032-3181-4) U of Nebr Pr.

— Questioning Edmond Jabes. LC 89-14642. 202p. 1990. reprint ed. pap. 62.70 (0-7837-8897-5, 204960800001) Bks Demand.

Motte, Warren F., Jr., ed. Oulipo: A Primer of Potential Literature. LC 97-51428. 224p. 1998. pap. 14.95 (1-56478-187-9) Dalkey Arch.

Motte, Warren F., Jr. & Prince, Gerald, eds. Alteratives. LC 93-76190. (French Forum Monographs: No. 82). 229p. (Orig.). 1993. pap. 17.95 (0-917058-87-9) French Forum.

Motte, Warren F. Jr. The Poetics of Experiment: A Study of the Work of George Perec. LC 83-81599. (French Forum Monographs: No. 51). 163p. (Orig.). 1984. pap. 12.95 (0-917058-51-8) French Forum.

Mottel, William, et al. Industrial Safety Is Good Business: The Dupont Story. 200p. 1995. pap. 60.95 (0-442-01842-8, VNR) Wiley.

Mottel, William J., et al. Industrial Safety Is Good Business: The DuPont Story. (Industrial Health & Safety Ser.). 256p. 1995. 74.95 (0-471-28628-1, VNR) Wiley.

Mottelay, Paul F. Bibliographical History of Electricity & Magnetism. (Illus.). 693p. 1991. reprint ed. 85.00 (1-888262-54-0) Martino Pubng.

Mottelay, Paul F., ed. Bibliographical History of Electricity & Magnetism. LC 74-26277. (History, Philosophy & Sociology of Science Ser.). (Illus.). 1975. reprint ed. 52.95 (0-405-06605-8) Ayer.

Mottelson, Ben R., jt. auth. see Bohr, Aage.

Motter & Dupre. The Heart of the Beast. Berger, K., ed. LC 94-231889. (Illus.). 96p. pap. 14.95 (1-56389-168-9, Vertigo) DC Comics.

Motter, Alton M. Ecumenism 101: A Handbook about the Ecumenical Movement. 88p. (Orig.). 1997. pap. 6.95 (0-88028-175-8, 1394) Forward Movement.

Motter, Alton M., ed. Preaching about Death: Eighteen Sermons Dealing with the Experience of Death from the Christian Perspective. LC 74-26336. 94p. reprint ed. pap. 30.00 (0-608-16838-6, 202686200052) Bks Demand.

Motter, Charlott. Star, Sky, Alexandra, & Majesty. (Illus.). 32p. (J). (gr. 4-6). 1997. pap. 8.00 (0-8059-4216-5) Dorrance.

Motter, Charlott L. Reiki? A Healing Art? Yes! (Illus.). 64p. 1999. pap. 15.00 (0-8059-4527-X) Dorrance.

Motter, D. & Askwith, M. The Prisoner: Shattered Visage. Bruning, Richard & Carlson, KC, eds. (Illus.). 208p. 1990. pap. 19.95 (0-930289-53-6) DC Comics.

Motter, Dean. The Prisoner: Shattered Visage. 1991. mass mkt. 14.95 (0-446-39245-6, Pub. by Warner Bks) Little.

— Terminal City. (Illus.). 232p. 1997. pap. text 19.95 (1-56389-391-6, Pub. by DC Comics) Time Warner.

Motter, Dean, ed. see Coleridge, Samuel Taylor.

Motter, Dean, ed. see Hernandez, Gilbert & Hernandez, Jaime.

Motter, Dean, jt illus. see Friedman, Michael Jan.

Motter, Wendell & Foster, Charles A. Finite Mathematics with Applications: Florida Edition. (Illus.). 640p. 1990. write for info. (0-912675-87-X); pap. text 48.95 (0-912675-82-9) Ardsley.

Motterlini, Matteo, ed. see Lakatos, Imre & Feyerabend, Paul K.

Mottern, Nicholas. Suffering Strong: The Journal of a Westerner in Ethiopia, the Sudan, Eritrea & Chad. (Current Issues Ser.: No. 3). (Illus.). 110p. 1987. 12.95 (0-932415-30-X); pap. 5.95 (0-932415-31-8) Red Sea Pr.

Mottershead, Allen. Electronic Devices & Circuits: An Introduction. LC 72-93687. 655p. reprint ed. pap. 200.00 (0-608-16130-6, 200775600064) Bks Demand.

— Introduction to Electricity & Electronics: Conventional Current Version. 2nd ed. LC 85-26306. 380p. 1986. pap. text 22.95 (0-471-84080-7) P-H.

Mottershead, J., ed. Suetonius: Claudius. 190p. 1986. 20.95 (0-86292-080-9, Pub. by Brist Class Pr) Focus Pub-R Pullins.

Mottershead, J. E., ed. Modern Practice in Stress & Vibration Analysis. (Proceedings of Conference, University of Liverpool, 3-5 April 1989 Ser.). 350p. 1989. pap. 40.00 (0-08-037523-5, Pub. by Pergamon Repr) Franklin.

Mottershead, J. E., jt. auth. see Friswell, M. I.

Mottesi, A. Atrevete a Dar Amor. (Serie Realidades - Realities Ser.).Tr. of Dare to Give Love. (SPA.). 1.99 (1-56063-099-X, 498144) Editorial Unilit.

Mottesi, A. H. Calles Rectas, Sendero Torcido (Straight Streets Crooked Path) (SPA.). 1.79 (0-685-74906-1, 498505) Editorial Unilit.

— De Inspiracion. LC 97-212383. (Momentos Ser.).Tr. of Of Inspiration. (SPA.). 1993. pap. 12.99 (0-8423-6450-1, 498508) Tyndale Hse.

— De Pleno Gozo. (Serie Momentos - Moments Ser.).Tr. of Of Great Joy. (SPA.). 34p. 1993. pap. 1.79 (0-8423-6349-1, 498507) Editorial Unilit.

— Dia del Bien, Dia del Mal.Tr. of Good Day, Bad Day. (SPA.). 1.79 (0-685-74927-4, 498506) Editorial Unilit.

— Escogiendo Caminos.Tr. of Choosing a Path. (SPA.). 1.99 (0-685-74934-7, 498502) Editorial Unilit.

— Eternidad, Tiempo, Vanidad (Eternity, Time, Vanity) (SPA.). 1.99 (0-685-74935-5, 498504) Editorial Unilit.

— Frente a un Problema (Facing the Problem) (SPA.). 1.79 (0-685-74938-X, 498503) Editorial Unilit.

— La Lus de la Casa (The Light of the Home) (SPA.). 1.79 (0-685-74950-9, 498501) Editorial Unilit.

Mottesi, Alberto. America: Five Hundred Anos Despues. (SPA.). 164p. (Orig.). 1992. pap. 10.95 (0-9633528-0-6) A Mottesi Evang Assn.

— En Su Presencia.Tr. of In His Presence. (SPA.). 372p. 1988. pap. 8.99 (0-945792-19-0, 498509) Editorial Unilit.

— El Poder de Su Presenciq.Tr. of Power of His Presence. (SPA.). 240p. 1997. pap. 9.99 (0-88113-464-3) Caribe Betania.

Mottesi, Alberto & Mottesi, Noemi. Salvemos la Familia (Let's Save the Family) (What You Need to Know about ... in 12 Lessons Ser.). (SPA.). 192p. 12.99 (0-88113-548-8) Caribe Betania.

Mottesi, Noemi, jt. auth. see Mottesi, Alberto.

Mottessi, Noemi. El Aborto: Cartas a una Amiga. (Serie Realidades - Realities Ser.).Tr. of Abortion: Letters to a Friend. (SPA.). 28p. 1994. 1.99 (1-56063-157-0, 498147) Editorial Unilit.

Motteux, Peter A., jt. auth. see Eccles, John C.

Motteux, Peter A., tr. see De Cervantes Saavedra, Miguel.

Mottice, Robert N. & Hardt, John P., eds. China's Economic Future: Challenges to U. S. Policy. (Illus.). 530p. (C). 1998. pap. text 50.00 (0-7881-4932-6) DIANE Pub.

Mottier, V. Eronique, jt. auth. see Carver, Terrell.

Mottin, Marie-France, jt. auth. see Dumont, Rene.

Mottinger, Lyle D., et al. Appleseeds. 42p. (Orig.). 1987. pap. text 7.00 (0-937652-35-0) Natl Art Ed.

Mottl, Felix, ed. see Wagner, Richard.

Mottla, Gabriel V. New York Evidence-Proof of Cases, 2 vols. 2nd ed. LC 66-275456. 1658p. 190.00 (0-317-00483-2) West Group.

— New York Evidence-Proof of Cases, 2 vols. 2nd ed. LC 66-275456. 1658p. 1993. suppl. ed. 89.50 (0-317-03184-8) West Group.

— Proof of Cases in Massachusetts, 2 vols. 2nd ed. LC 66-24570. 1780p. 1993. suppl. ed. 60.00 (0-317-03185-6) West Group.

— Proof of Cases in Massachusetts, 2 vols. 3rd ed. LC 66-24570. 1780p. 220.00 (0-317-00489-1) West Group.

***Mottley, Chuck.** The Turnaround: From 0-10 to 10-0. LC 99-96398. (Illus.). 223p. 1999. pap. 19.95 (0-9674689-1-4) Jubilee Pubg Inc.

Mottman, Edward, jt. auth. see Mann, W. Edward.

Mottmann, Jurgen, et al. A Passion for God's Reign: Theology, Christian Learning, & the Christian Self. Volf, Miroslav, ed. LC 97-38349. 120p. 1998. pap. 12.00 (0-8028-4494-4) Eerdmans.

Motto, Anna Lydia & Clark, John R. Essays on Seneca. LC 93-7340. (Studien zur Klassischen Philologie: No. 79). 264p. 1993. 49.00 (3-631-45687-5) P Lang Pubng.

— Senecan Tragedy. 367p. 1988. 128.00 (90-256-0920-1, Pub. by AM Hakkert) BookLink Distributors.

Motto, Anna Lydia & Clark, John R., eds. Senecan Tragedy. 372p. 1989. pap. 98.00 (90-256-0959-7, Pub. by AM Hakkert) BookLink Distributors.

Motto, Anna Lydia, et al. Veritas Amicitiaeque Causa: Essays in Honor of Anna Lydia Motto & John R. Clark. LC PA26.M69V47 1999. 1999. pap. 45.00 (0-86516-454-1) Bolchazy-Carducci.

***Motto, Carmine J.** In Crime's Way: A Generation of Secret Service Adventures. 336p. 1999. boxed set 22.50 (0-8493-2259-6) CRC Pr.

— Undercover. 2nd ed. LC 99-462595. (Illus.). 224p. 1999. boxed set 49.95 (0-8493-1365-1) CRC Pr.

Motto, Jerome A., et al. Standards for Suicide Prevention & Crisis Centers. LC 73-17029. 114p. 1974. 32.95 (0-87705-105-4, Kluwer Acad Hman Sci) Kluwer Academic.

Mottola, Anthony & St. Ignatius of Loyola. Spiritual Exercises of St. Ignatius. 208p. 1964. pap. 9.95 (0-385-02436-3, D170, Image Bks) Doubleday.

Mottola, Charles. When I Look for You: A Collection of Poems. 170p. 1998. pap. 18.00 (1-57502-863-8, PO2355) Morris Pubng.

Mottola, Emil, jt. ed. see Mattis, Michael.

Mottola, H. A., ed. Henry Freisher: "Talanta" Issue. (Illus.). 160p. 1985. pap. 31.00 (0-08-032639-0, Pub. by PPL) Elsevier.

Mottola, Horacio A. Kinetic Aspects of Analytical Chemistry. LC 87-26344. (Chemical Analysis Ser.). 285p. 1988. 195.00 (0-471-83676-1) Wiley.

Motton, Gregory. Ambulance & Downfall. (Oberon Bks.). 128p. 1997. pap. 16.95 (1-870259-61-0) Theatre Comm.

— Motton: Plays Three. 204p. 1999. pap. 18.95 (1-84002-021-0, Pub. by Theatre Comm) Consort Bk Sales.

— Motton: Plays 2. (Oberon Bks.). 256p. 1998. pap. 18.95 (1-84002-020-2) Theatre Comm.

Motton, Gregory, tr. see Buchner, Georg.

Mottoni, P. De, see Li, T. T. & De Mottoni, P.

Mottram, Bob. Salt-Water Salmon Angling. (Illus.). 140p. 1990. pap. 9.95 (0-936608-89-7) F Amato Pubns.

Mottram, D. Drugs in Sports. 2nd ed. 304p. (C). 1995. pap. 35.00 (0-419-18890-8) Routledge.

Mottram, D. S., jt. ed. see Taylor, A.

Mottram, Eric. Blood on the Nash Ambassador: Investigations in American Culture. 1989. 19.95 (0-09-182364-1, Pub. by Hutchinson) Trafalgar.

— Hyderabad Depositions, 1984-1986. LC 98-177656. 122p. 1997. pap. 14.95 (3-7052-0140-9, Pub. by Poetry Salzburg) Intl Spec Bk.

Mottram, J. Toby & Shaw, Christopher T. Using Finite Elements in Mechanical Design. 1996. write for info. (0-07-709093-4) McGraw.

An Asterisk (*) at the beginning of an entry indicates that the title is appearing for the first time.

*Mottram, James. Coen Brothers. 2000. 21.95 (1-57488-273-2) Brasseys.
Mottram, R. F. Human Nutrition. 3rd ed. 179p. 1979. pap. 30.00 (0-917678-09-5) Food & Nut Pr.
Mottram, R. F., jt. auth. see Moffat, D. B.
Mottram, Ralph H. Armistice & Other Memories: Forming a Pendant to the 'Spanish Farm Trilogy' LC 79-160946. (Short Story Index Reprint Ser.). 1977. reprint ed. 19.95 (0-8369-3925-5) Ayer.
Mottram, Ron. The Danish Cinema Before Dreyer. LC 87-16125. 315p. 1988. 31.00 (0-8108-2035-8) Scarecrow.
Mottram, William. The True Story of George Eliot. LC 72-3376. (English Literature Ser.: No. 33). 1972. reprint ed. lib. bdg. 75.00 (0-8383-1508-9) M S G Haskell Hse.
Mottran, J. The Gangster Movie from A to Z. (Illus.). 192p. 1999. pap. text 21.95 (0-7134-8276-1) B T Burch.
Mottu, Philippe. The Story of Caux. (Illus.). 1963. 8.95 (0-901269-03-4) Grosvenor USA.
Motture, Peta, jt. ed. see Currie, Stuart.
Motulsky, A. G., jt. auth. see Vogel, F.
Motulsky, Arno G., jt. ed. see Goodman, Richard M.
Motulsky, Harvey. Intuitive Biostatistics. (Illus.). 408p. (C). 1995. pap. text 29.95 (0-19-508607-4) OUP.
Motulsky, Helen. In My Fashion. LC 97-222452. (Orig.). 1996. pap. 9.95 (1-886094-52-7) Chicago Spectrum.
Motum, John, ed. The Putnam Aeronautical Review, Vol. 1. LC 89-61978. (Illus.). 256p. 1990. 47.95 (0-87021-610-4) Naval Inst Pr.
— The Putnam Aeronautical Review, Vol. II. (Illus.). 256p. 1991. 47.95 (1-55750-676-0) Naval Inst Pr.
Motumura, Hirsohi, et al. Immigration & Nationality Laws of the United States, Selected Statutes, Regulations & Forms, 1998. (Miscellaneous Ser.). 850p. 1998. pap. text 18.00 (0-314-23333-4) West Pub.
Motus, Cecile L. Hiligaynon Dictionary. LC 73-152469. (University of Hawaii, Honolulu. Pacific & Asian Linguistics Institute Ser.). 337p. reprint ed. pap. 104.50 (0-608-11000-0, 200770900063) Bks Demand.
— Hiligaynon Lessons. LC 78-152470. (University of Hawaii, Honolulu. Pacific & Asian Linguistics Institute Ser.). 454p. reprint ed. pap. 140.80 (0-608-11034-5, 201722000004) Bks Demand.
Motus, L. & Narita, S., eds. Distributed Computer Control Systems 1989. (IFAC Workshop Ser.: No. 9005). 148p. 1990. 71.75 (0-08-037870-6, Pergamon Pr) Elsevier.
Motus, Leo & Rodd, Michael G. Timing Analysis of Real-Time Software: A Practical Approach to the Specification & Design of Real-Time. LC 94-28551. 226p. 1994. pap. text 51.25 (0-08-042025-7, Pergamon Pr) Elsevier.
Motwani, P. Chess under the Microscope. (Illus.). 256p. 1999. pap. text 17.95 (0-7134-8390 3) B T B.
Motwani, Paul. C.O.O.L. Chess: Creative Original Opening Lines. LC 97-71872. (New American Batsford Chess Library). 192p. (Orig.). 1997. pap. 22.50 (1-879479-51-6) ICE WA.
Motwani, Prem. A Dictionary of Loanwords Usage: Katakana-English. (ENG & JPN.). 258p. 1991. 125.00 (0-828-7340-2) Fr & Eur.
Motwani, Rajeev & Raghavan, Prabhakar. Randomized Algorithms. 492p. (C). 1995. text 47.95 (0-521-47465-5) Cambridge U Pr.
Motyer, J. Alec. After Death. 1996. 9.99 (1-85792-170-4, Pub. by Christian Focus); pap. 9.99 (0-906731-70-4, Pub. by Christian Focus) Spring Arbor Dist.
— Isaiah. LC 99-21941. (Tyndale Old Testament Commentaries Ser.: Vol. 18). 416p. 1999. 19.99 (0-8308-1434-5, 1434); pap. 12.99 (0-87784-244-2, 244) InterVarsity.
— El Mensaje de Filipenses.Tr. of Message of Philippians. (SPA.). 240p. 1993. pap. 1.99 (0-8254-1486-5, Edit Portavoz) Kregel.
*Motyer, J. Alec. The Prophecy of Isaiah: An Introduction & Commentary. LC 93-17815. 544p. 1999. pap. 19.99 (0-8308-1593-7, 1593) InterVarsity.
Motyer, J. Alec & Wenham, Gordon J. New Bible Commentary. 4th enl. rev. ed. LC 94-4076. (Illus.). 1340p. 1994. 39.99 (0-8308-1442-6, 1442) InterVarsity.
Motyer, S. Remember Jesus. Date not set. 7.99 (1-85792-153-4, Pub. by Christian Focus) Spring Arbor Dist.
*Motyer, Stephen. Who's Who in the Bible. (Illus.). 64p. (gr. 3-7). 1999. 14.99 (0-8423-3656-7) Tyndale Hse.
Motyer, Stephen. Your Father the Devil: A New Approach to John & 'the Jews' (Biblical & Theological Monographs). xiii, 260p. 1997. reprint ed. pap. 35.00 (0-85364-832-8, Pub. by Paternoster Pub) OM Literature.
Motyka-Sanders, Jan, ed. Philolakon: Lakonian Studies in Honour of Hector Catling. (Illus.). 334p. 1992. 68.00 (0-904887-10-3, Pub. by Brit Sch Athens) David Brown.
Motyka, W. Annotated Bibliography of Russian Language Publications on Accounting, 1736-1917, 2 vols. 848p. 1993. write for info. (0-318-70046-8); write for info. (0-318-70047-6) Garland.
— Annotated Bibliography of Russian Language Publications on Accounting, 1736-1917, 2 vols., Set. LC 93-2711. (New Works in Accounting History). (RUS & ENG.). 848p. 1993. text 20.00 (0-8153-1247-4) Garland.
Motyl, Alexander J. Dilemmas of Independence: Ukraine after Totalitarianism. LC 93-16966. 200p. 1993. pap. 17.95 (0-87609-131-1) Coun Foreign.
— The Post-Soviet Nations: Perspectives on the Demise of the U. S. S. R. 322p. 1995. pap. 19.50 (0-231-07895-1) Col U Pr.
— Revolutions, Nations, Empires: Conceptual Limits & Theoretical Possibilities. LC 99-17430. 224p. 1999. pap. 18.50 (0-231-11431-1) Col U Pr.
*Motyl, Alexander J. Revolutions, Nations, Empires: Conceptual Limits & Theoretical Possibilities. LC 99-17430. 224p. 1999. 45.00 (0-231-11430-3) Col U Pr.
Motyl, Alexander J. Sovietology, Rationality, Nationality: Coming to Grips with Nationalism in the U. S. S. R. 1990. text 46.00 (0-231-07326-7) Col U Pr.
— Will the Non-Russians Rebel? State, Ethnicity, & Stability in the U. S. S. R. LC 86-24386. (Cornell Studies in Soviet History & Science). 224p. (C). 1987. 32.50 (0-8014-1947-6) Cornell U Pr.
*Motyl, Alexander J., ed. Encyclopedia of Nationalism, 2 vols. 1400p. 2000. 425.00 (0-12-227230-7) Acad Pr.
Motyl, Alexander J., ed. The Post-Soviet Nations: Perspectives in the Demise of the U. S. S. R. 360p. 1992. text 50.00 (0-231-07894-3) Col U Pr.
— Thinking Theoretically About Soviet Nationalities. 288p. 1992. text 57.50 (0-231-07512-X) Col U Pr.
— Thinking Theoretically about Soviet Nationalities: History & Comparison in the Study of the U. S. S. R. LC 91-31877. (Studies of the Harriman Institute). 284p. (C). 1995. pap. 18.50 (0-231-07513-8) Col U Pr.
Motyl-Mudretzkyj, Irene & Hahn-Raabe, Claudia, eds. Die Deutschstunde, 1995 Fall Vol. II: Ein TV-Magazin fur Amerikanische Deutschlehrer. (GER., Illus.). 100p. 1997. spiral bd. 4.00 (0-942017-40-4, 36-644534-2) Amer Assn Teach German.
— Die Deutschstunde, 1995 Spring: Ein TV-Magazin fur Amerikanische Deutschlehrer. (GER., Illus.). 42p. 1997. spiral bd. 4.00 (0-942017-39-0, 36-644534-1) Amer Assn Teach German.
— Die Deutschstunde, 1996 Fall Vol. IV: Ein TV-Magazin fur AmerikanischeDeutschlehrer, Vol. IV. (GER., Illus.). 48p. 1997. spiral bd. 4.00 (0-942017-42-0, 36-644534-4) Amer Assn Teach German.
— Die Deutschstunde, 1996 Spring Vol. III: Ein TV-Magazin fur Amerikanische Deutschlehrer. (GER., Illus.). 128p. 1997. spiral bd. 4.00 (0-942017-41-2, 36-644534-3) Amer Assn Teach German.
Motyl-Mudretzkyj, Irenen & Whiteman, Johanna. Deutsche Welle: Aktuelle Fernsehsendungen im Kommunikativen Unterricht. (GER.). 150p. (C). 1995. pap. text, teacher ed. 12.00 (0-942017-21-8) Amer Assn Teach German.
*Motz, Annabelle B. The Psychology of Female Violence: Crimes Against the Body. LC 00-42499. 2000. pap. write for info. (0-415-12675-4) Routledge.
Motz, H., jt. auth. see Luchini, P.
Motz, Julie. Hands of Life: From the Operating Room to Your Home, an Energy Healer Reveals the Secrets of Using Your Body's Own Energy Medicine for Healing, Recovery, & Transformation. LC 98-23077. 320p. 1998. 24.95 (0-553-10714-3) Bantam.
*Motz, Julie. Hands of Life: Use Your Body's Own Energy Medicine for Healing, Recovery & Transformation. 320p. 2000. pap. 14.95 (0-553-37929-9) Bantam.
Motz, Julie. Rescue 911 Family First Aid & Emergency Care Book: Simple Step-by-Step Guide. 1996. mass mkt. 5.99 (0-671-52514-X, PB Trade Paper) PB.
Motz, L. & Weaver, J. H. The Concepts of Science: From Newton to Einstein. LC 87-38493. (Illus.). 446p. (C). 1988. 23.50 (0-306-42872-5, Plenum Trade) Perseus Pubng.
— The Story of Mathematics. (Illus.). 366p. (C). 1993. 25.95 (0-306-44508-5, Plenum Trade) Perseus Pubng.
— The Story of Physics. LC 88-33655. (Illus.). 428p. (C). 1989. 24.50 (0-306-43076-2, Plenum Trade) Perseus Pubng.
Motz, Lloyd & Weaver, Jefferson H. The Story of Astronomy. LC 95-41138. (Illus.). 398p. (C). 1995. 28.95 (0-306-45090-9, Plenum Trade) Perseus Pubng.
— Story of Mathematics. 368p. 1995. pap. 14.00 (0-380-72458-8, Avon Bks) Morrow Avon.
— The Story of Physics. 432p. 1992. pap. 12.50 (0-380-71725-5, Avon Bks) Morrow Avon.
Motz, Lloyd & Weaver, Jefferson H., eds. Conquering Mathematics: From Arithmetic to Calculus. LC 91-9329. (Illus.). 320p. (C). 1991. 24.95 (0-306-43768-6, Plenum Trade) Perseus Pubng.
Motz, Lotte. The Faces of the Goddess. LC 95-41494. (Illus.). 288p. 1997. 35.00 (0-19-508967-7) OUP.
Motz, Marilyn F. & Browne, Pat, eds. Making the American Home: Middle-Class Women & Domestic Material Culture, 1840-1940. LC 88-70387. (Illus.). 212p. (C). 1988. 33.95 (0-87972-433-1); pap. 16.95 (0-87972-434-X) Bowling Green Univ Popular Press.
Motzki. Hadith. 109.95 (0-86078-704-4) Ashgate Pub Co.
*Motzki, Harald. The Biography of Muhammad: The Issue of the Sources. LC 99-41850. (Islamic History & Civilization Ser.). (Illus.). 352p. 2000. 58.50 (90-04-11513-7) Brill Academic Pubs.
Motzkin, Gabriel. Time & Transcendence: Secular History, the Catholic Reaction, & the Rediscovery of the Future. LC 92-10249. (Philosophical Studies in Contemporary Culture: Vol. 1). 320p. (C). 1992. lib. bdg. 166.50 (0-7923-1773-4, Pub. by Kluwer Academic) Kluwer Academic.
*Motzkin, Linda. Aleph Isn't Tough: An Introduction to Hebrew for Adults. Person, Hara, ed. (C). 2000. 12.00 (0-8074-0725-9) UAHC.
— Aleph Isn't Tough: Teacher's Edition. Vol. 1. (C). 2000. teacher ed. 16.00 (0-8074-0726-7) UAHC.
Motzkin, Linda, jt. auth. see Resnikoff, Irene.
Motzkin, T. S., ed. see Pure Mathematics Symposium Staff.
Motzwadi, Stan. Soweto: Portrait of a City. (Illus.). 144p. (C). 1989. 130.00 (0-7855-4046-6) St Mut.
Mou, Shela, jt. auth. see Caldwell, Linda.
Mou-Lam, Wong, jt. tr. see Price, A. F.
Mou-Tuan Huang, et al. Food Phytochemicals for Cancer Prevention: Fruits & Vegetables. LC 93-33775. (ACS Symposium Ser.: Vol. 546). 426p. 1994. text 110.00 (0-8412-2768-3, Pub. by Am Chemical) OUP.
Moua, Jean, tr. see Coburn, Jewell R., et al.
Moua, Mitt, tr. see Smalley, William A., et al.
Moua, Xe S., tr. see Zhang, Song N.
Moua, Xe Susane, tr. see Kraus, Robert & Chen, Debby.
Mouat, et al, eds. Wordweavers. 93p. (Orig.). 1986. pap. write for info. (0-917557-02-6) Wyo Writers.
Mouat, David A. & Hutchinson, Charles F., eds. Desertification in Developed Countries - Why Can't We Control It? Proceedings of the International Symposium & Workshop Held in Tucson, Arizona, U. S. A. 24-29 October 1994. LC 95-48178. 360p. (C). 1996. text 161.50 (0-7923-3919-3) Kluwer Academic.
Mouat, Frederick J. Rough Notes of a Trip to Reunion, Mauritius & Ceylon. LC 98-904956. vi, 139p. 1997. write for info. (81-206-0221-8) Asian Educ Servs.
Mouat, Jeremy. Roaring Days: Rossland's Mines & the History of British Columbia. (Illus.). 256p. 1996. pap. 25.95 (0-7748-0519-6) U of Wash Pr.
Mouat, Marty, jt. auth. see Petrino, Bob.
Mouat, Ricardo G. Jose Donoso: Impostura e Impostacion. (SPA.). 277p. 1983. pap. 12.00 (0-685-08346-2, 3005) Ediciones Norte.
*Moubayed, Sami M. Damascus Between Democracy & Dictatorship. 248p. 2000. 37.50 (0-7618-1744-1) U Pr of Amer.
Moubray, George A. De, see De Moubray, George A.
Moubray House Publishing Ltd. Staff. Daniel Defoe's Scotland. (Illus.). (C). 1991. pap. 90.00 (0-948473-19-3) St Mut.
— Scottish Interiors Series, 4 vols. (Illus.). 384p. (C). 1989. 35.00 (0-948473-06-1); 35.00 (0-948473-05-3); 35.00 (0-948473-04-5); 35.00 (0-948473-07-X) St Mut.
— Scottish Interiors Series, 4 vols., Set. (Illus.). 384p. (C). 1989. 140.00 (0-7855-5968-X) St Mut.
Moubray, John. Reliability-Centered Maintenance. 2nd ed. LC 97-8176. 448p. 1997. 49.95 (0-8311-3078-4) Indus Pr.
— Reliability-Centred Maintenance. 2nd ed. 440p. 1999. text 69.95 (0-7506-3358-1) Buttrwrth-Heinemann.
Mouchel, J. M., jt. auth. see Garnier, Josette.
Mouchet, Jean-Paul & Mitchell, Alan. Abnormal Pressure While Drilling. 264p. (C). 1989. 160.00 (2-901026-28-1, Pub. by Edits Technip) Enfield Pubs NH.
Mouchet, Paulette. Horseback Riding Trails of Southern California, Vol. I. LC 95-92581. (Illus.). 128p. (Orig.). 1995. pap. 14.95 (0-9647945-0-0) Crown Valley Pr.
— Horseback Riding Trails of Southern California, Vol. II. LC 95-92581. (Illus.). 160p. (Orig.). 1996. pap. 16.95 (0-9647945-1-9) Crown Valley Pr.
Moudgil, jt. auth. see Somasundaran, P.
Moudgil, Brij M. & Somasundaran, P., eds. Dispersion & Aggregation: Fundamentals & Applications. (Engineering Foundation Conference Proceedings Ser.). 584p. 1994. 50.00 (0-939204-51-7, P-79) Am Inst Chem Eng.
Moudgil, Virinder K., ed. Molecular Mechanism of Steroid Hormone Action: Recent Advances. (Illus.). xii, 824p. 1985. 223.10 (3-11-010118-1) De Gruyter.
— Recent Advances in Steroid Hormone Action. 552p. (C). 1987. lib. bdg. 207.70 (3-11-010762-7) De Gruyter.
— Receptor Phosphorylation. LC 88-4339. 400p. 1989. 220.00 (0-8493-6318-7, QP552, CRC Reprint) Franklin.
— Steroid Hormone Receptors: Basic & Clinical Aspects. LC 93-33850. (Hormones in Health & Disease Ser.). 1993. 87.00 (0-8176-3694-3) Birkhauser.
— Steroid Receptors in Health & Disease. LC 88-22477. (Serono Symposia U. S. A. Ser.). (Illus.). 346p. 1988. 95.00 (0-306-42987-X, Plenum Trade) Perseus Pubng.
Moudiotis, George. Traditional Greek Cooking: The Food & Wines of Greece. (Illus.). 240p. 1998. 21.95 (1 85964-117-2, Pub. by Garnet-Ithaca) LPC InBook.
*Moudon, Anne Vernez. Parcel Based GIS. 416p. 2000. text 79.95 (0-471-37163-7) Wiley.
Moudon, Anne Vernez, ed. Public Streets for Public Use. (Illus.). 352p. 1991. pap. text 38.50 (0-231-07599-5) Col U Pr.
Moudud, Hasna J. Women in China. 94p. 1980. 17.95 (0-7069-1084-2) Asia Bk Corp.
*Moudud, Jamee K. Government Spending in a Growing Economy. (Public Policy Brief Highlights Ser.: Vol. 52A). 6p. 1999. pap. write for info. (0-941276-71-6) J Levy.
— Government Spending in a Growing Economy: Fiscal Policy & Growth Cycles. (Public Policy Brief Ser.: Vol. 52). 40p. 1999. pap. write for info. (0-941276-70-8) J Levy.
Mouel, J. L. Le, see Le Mouel, J. L.
Mouer, Ross E. & Sugimoto, Yoshio. Images of Japanese Society: A Study in the Structure of Social Reality. (Japanese Studies). 600p. 1985. 65.00 (0-7103-0078-6) Routledge.
— Images of Japanese Society: A Study in the Structure of Social Reality. 552p. 1990. pap. 25.00 (0-7103-0379-3, A4425) Routledge.
Mouer, Ross E. & Sugimoto, Yoshio, eds. Constructs for Understanding Japan. 250p. 1989. text 69.50 (0 7103-0209-6) Routledge.
Moufang, Christoph, ed. Katholische Katechismen des 16 Jahrhunderts in Deutscher Sprache. l, 626p. 1964. reprint ed. write for info. (0-318-71847-2) G Olms Pubs.
Mouffe, Barbara S., ed. see Hawthorne, Nathaniel.
*Mouffe, Chantal. The Challenge of Carl Schmitt. 1999. pap. 20.00 (1-85984-244-5, Pub. by Verso) Norton.
— Challenge of Carl Schmitt. 1999. 60.00 (1-85984-704-8, Pub. by Verso) Norton.
— The Democratic Paradox. (Phronesis Ser.). 192p. 2000. 60.00 (1-85984-758-7, Pub. by Verso) Norton.
— The Democratic Paradox. (Phronesis Ser.). 192p. (C). 2000. pap. 19.00 (1-85984-279-8, Pub. by Verso) Norton.
Mouffe, Chantal. The Return of the Political. 240p. (C). 1993. pap. 19.00 (0-86091-651-0, B2512, Pub. by Verso) Norton.
— The Return of the Political. 240p. (C). (gr. 13). 1993. 19.00 (0-86091-486-0, B2508, Pub. by Verso) Norton.
Mouffe, Chantal, ed. Dimensions of Radical Democracy: Pluralism, Citizenship, Community. (Phronesis Ser.). 336p. (C). 1992. 60.00 (0-86091-344-9, Pub. by Verso) Norton.
Mouffe, Chantal, jt. auth. see Laclau, Ernesto.
Mouffe, Chantal, ed. see Critchley, Simon, et al.
Mouflet, Djoniba. Joneeba: Workout to the Dance & Drums of Africa. 160p. 2000. pap. 17.95 (1-57826-049-3, Pub. by Hatherleigh) Norton.
Mouftah, Hussein T. & Elmirghani, Jaafar M. H. Photonic Switching Technology: Systems & Networks. LC 98-7873. 612p. 1998. 99.95 (0-7803-4707-2) Inst Electrical.
Mougalian, Susan, ed. see Brown, James C.
Mougayar, Walid. How to Be a Successful Computer Consultant: Expanded & Revised. 4th expanded ed. LC 97-46907. (Illus.). 416p. 1998. pap. 21.95 (0-07-058029-4) McGraw.
— Opening Digital Markets: Battle Plans & Business Strategies for Internet Commerce. 2nd ed. LC 97-41318. (Illus.). 336p. 1997. 24.95 (0-07-043542-1) McGraw.
Mougayar, Walid, jt. auth. see Simon, Alan R.
Mougeon, Raymond & Beniak, Edouard. The Case of French in Ontario, Canada. (Oxford Studies in Language Contact). 256p. 1991. text 80.00 (0-19-824827-X) OUP.
*Moughalian, Ray. Healthcare Safety Sourcebook. Orig. Title: MOHR's Guide. (Illus.). 202p. 2000. pap. text 99.00 (1-57839-069-9) Opus Communs.
*Moughtin, Cliff. Urban Design: Street & Square. 2nd ed. LC 99-44873. (Illus.). 238p. 1999. pap. text 47.95 (0-7506-4274-2) Buttrwrth-Heinemann.
Moughtin, James C. Urban Design: Green Dimensions. (Illus.). 224p. 2000. text 62.95 (0-7506-2659-3) Buttrwrth-Heinemann.
— Urban Design: Street & Square. (Illus.). 224p. 1992. 79.95 (0-7506-0416-6) Buttrwrth-Heinemann.
*Mouginis-Mark, Peter J., et al, eds. Remote Sensing of Active Volcanism. LC 99-462162. (Geophysical Monograph Ser.: Vol. 116). 274p. 2000. 66.00 (0-87590-099-2) Am Geophysical.
Mouhammed, Adil H. Introductory Mathematical Economics. LC 99-28965. 260p. 1999. text 39.95 (0-7656-0459-0) M E Sharpe.
— Quantitative Methods for Business & Economics. LC 99-28683. (Illus.). 392p. 1999. text 48.95 (0-7656-0458-2) M E Sharpe.
Mouhot, Henri. Travels in Siam, Cambodia & Laos, 1858-1860, 2 vols. (Oxford in Asia Hardback Reprints Ser.). (Illus.). 632p. 1991. 69.00 (0-19-588951-7) OUP.
Mouilleron-Becar, Claude, jt. auth. see Bruno, A.
Mouilloron-Becar, jt. auth. see Bruno, A.
Mouines, C. Ulises, jt. ed. see Balzer, Wolfgang.
Moukarim, Moustafa F. Al-Kiama "The Life After" The Sequences Leading to the Impending Battle of Armageddon & the Commencement of Judgment Day. LC 96-90754. 87p. 1997. pap. 10.95 (0-533-12164-7) Vantage.
— Hamza: Strive for a Wiser Life. LC 97-90223. 1997. pap. 12.95 (0-533-12321-6) Vantage.
*Moukeli, Pierre, ed. Actes du 3e Colloque Africain Sur La Recherche en Informatique (1996) Proceedings of the 3rd African Conference on Research in Computer Science. (Illus.). 894p. 1999. pap. text 50.00 (0-7881-7650-1) DIANE Pub.
Moukwa, Mosongo, et al, eds. Cement-Based Materials: Present, Future, & Environmental Aspects. LC 93-33157. (Ceramic Transactions Ser.: No. 37). 202p. 1993. 74.00 (0-944904-68-8, CT037) Am Ceramic.
Moulaert, F. & Todtling, F., eds. The Geography of Advanced Producer Services in Europe. (Progress in Planning Ser.: Vol. 43). 280p. 1995. pap. 132.25 (0-08-042631-X, Pergamon Pr) Elsevier.
*Moulaert, Frank. Globalization & Integration Area Development in European Cities. (Oxford Geographical & Environmental Studies). (Illus.). 230p. 2000. text 65.00 (0-19-924113-9) OUP.
Moulaert, Frank & Salinas, Wilson. Regional Analysis & the New International Division of Labor. (Studies in Applied Regional Science). 1982. lib. bdg. 73.50 (0-89838-107-X) Kluwer Academic.
Moulaert, Frank & Scott, Allen J. Cities, Enterprises & Society on the Eve of the 21st Century: A State of Knowledge. LC 96-20079. (Illus.). 256p. 1997. 95.00 (1-85567-404-1) Bks Intl VA.
Moulaert, Frank, jt. ed. see Daniels, Peter W.
Moulakis, Athanasios. Beyond Utility: Liberal Education for a Technological Age. LC 93-27212. 184p. (C). 1993. text 24.95 (0-8262-0929-7) U of Mo Pr.
— Reason & Practice of a Republican State: Francesco Guicciardini's "How to Bring Order to Popular Government" LC 98-6588. 176p. 1998. pap. 21.95 (0-8476-8994-8) Rowman.
— Republican Realism in Renaissance Florence: Francesco Guicciardini's "Discorso di Logrogno" LC 98-6588. 192p. 1998. 53.00 (0-8476-8993-X) Rowman.
— Simone Weil & the Politics of Self-Denial. Hein, Ruth, tr. LC 97-38830. 280p. 1998. 34.95 (0-8262-1162-3) U of Mo Pr.
*Moulakis, Athanasios. World of the Polis. (Collected Works of Eric Voegelin: Vol. 15). 2000. 39.95 (0-8262-1283-2) U of Mo Pr.

M

Moulakis, Athanasios, ed. Legitimacy-Legitimate: Proceedings of the Conference Held in Florence, June 3-4, 1982 (Actes de Colloque de Florence 3 et 4 June 1982) (European University Institute, Series C (Political & Social Science): No. 3). vi, 105p. 1985. 36.55 (*3-11-010063-0*) De Gruyter.

— The Promise of History: Essays in Political Philosophy. (European University Institute, Series C (Political & Social Science): No. 2). vi, 206p. 1985. 69.25 (*3-11-010043-6*) De Gruyter.

— Technology & Responsibility: Essays Presented on the Occasion of the Centenary of the College of Engineering & Applied Science, University of Colorado, Boulder. LC 93-61149. (Illus.). 155p. 1993. 17.00 (*0-918714-39-7*) Intl Res Ctr Energy.

Moulakis, Athanasios, ed. & intro. see Voegelin, Eric.

Mouland, Dennis J. Ethics for the Professional Surveyor: A Collection of Thoughts. 165p. 1996. pap. 30.00 (*0-910845-57-3*) Landmark Ent.

Mouland, Michael. The Complete Idiot's Guide to Hiking, Camping & the Great Outdoors. LC 95-83361. (Complete Idiot's Guide Ser.). 332p. 1996. pap. 16.95 (*0-02-861100-4*) Macmillan Gen Ref.

— The Complete Idiot's Guide to Hiking, Camping & the Great Outdoors. 2nd ed. LC 99-62282. (Illus.). 352p. 1999. pap. text 16.95 (*0-02-863186-2*, Pub. by Macmillan Gen Ref) S&S Trade.

Mould, Charles, ed. see Boalch, Donald H.

Mould, Chris. Frankenstein. 32p. 1997. pap. 4.99 (*0-19-272340-5*) OUP.

— Frankenstein. LC PZ7.M85895Fr 1997. 32p. (J). (gr. 2). 1998. 17.95 (*0-19-279020-X*) OUP.

Mould, George. Manchester Memories. 132p. (C). 1988. 85.00 (*0-900963-41-7*, Pub. by T Dalton) St Mut.

Mould, Owen, ed. see Montana, Denby.

***Mould, Patrick.** Chef Patrick Mould: Recipes from a Chef. 160p. 1999. 19.95 (*0-9673971-0-3*) Louisiana Culinary.

Mould, R. F. A Century of X-Rays & Radioactivity in Medicine with Emphasis on Photographic Records of the Early Years. (Illus.). 236p. 1993. 105.00 (*0-7503-0224-0*) IOP Pub.

— Introductory Medical Statistics. 3rd expanded rev. ed. LC 98-176710. (Medical Science Ser.). (Illus.). 350p. 1998. pap. 49.00 (*0-7503-0513-4*) IOP Pub.

Mould, Richard A. Basic Relativity. LC 93-38098. (Illus.). 450p. 1994. reprint ed. 49.95 (*0-387-94188-6*) Spr-Verlag.

Mould, Richard F. Chernobyl: The Real Story. 256p. 1988. text 123.00 (*0-08-035718-0*, Pub. by Pergamon Repr) Franklin.

— Mould's Medical Anecdotes: Omnibus Edition. LC 96-9553. (Illus.). 496p. 1996. pap. 35.00 (*0-7503-0390-5*) IOP Pub.

— Radiation Protection in Hospitals. (Medical Science Ser.). (Illus.). 224p. 1985. 100.00 (*0-85274-802-7*) IOP Pub.

Mould, Richard F., ed. see International Conference on International Strategi.

Mould, Richard F., ed. see International Working Party for Treatment of Cance.

Mould, Richard F., ed. see Intl. Conf. on Intl. Strategies for the Eradicatio.

Mould, Richard F., ed. see Workshop on the Use of Computers in Data Handling.

Mould, William A., jt. ed. see Tappan, Donald W.

Moulden, T. H. Fundamentals of Transonic Flow. 350p. (C). 1991. reprint ed. 59.50 (*0-89464-441-6*) Krieger.

Moulder. Social Problems of the Modern World. LC 99-58514. (Sociology - Intro Level Ser.). 2000. pap. 33.95 (*0-534-56682-0*) Wadsworth Pub.

Moulder, Bennett. A Guide to the Common Spiders of Illinois. (Popular Science Ser.: Vol. X). (Illus.). 125p. (J). (ps-12). 1992. pap. 10.00 (*0-89792-135-6*) Ill St Museum.

Moulder, Bob. Cavaliers & Roundheads: The Story of the English Civil War With Pull-Up Scenes. 1997. pap. 10.95 (*1-899618-02-3*, Pub. by Tarquin Pubns) Parkwest Pubns.

Moulder, D. S. & Williamson, P., eds. Estuarine & Coastal Pollution: Detection, Research & Control: Proceedings of an IAWPRC Conference Held in Plymouth, 16-19 July 1985: 364p. 1986. pap. 105.00 (*0-08-033669-8*, Pergamon Pr) Elsevier.

Moulder, Evelina, ed. The Municipal Year Book, 1995. (Illus.). 416p. 1995. text 79.95 (*0-87326-970-5*, 41001) Intl City-Cnty Mgt.

— The Municipal Year Book, 1994. (Illus.). 416p. 1994. 79.95 (*0-87326-969-1*) Intl City-Cnty Mgt.

— The Municipal Year Book, 1996. (Illus.). 338p. 1996. 79.95 (*0-87326-971-3*, 42023) Intl City-Cnty Mgt.

— The Municipal Year Book, 1993. (Illus.). 416p. 1993. 79.95 (*0-87326-968-3*) Intl City-Cnty Mgt.

— The Municipal Year Book, 1992. (Illus.). 416p. 1992. 77.50 (*0-87326-967-5*) Intl City-Cnty Mgt.

Moulder, Evelina, ed. see Gustafson, Katharine H.

***Moulder, Evelina R. & International City/County Management Association Staff.** Profile of the City Council, 1996. LC 98-217153. (Special Data Issue Ser.). 85p. 1998. write for info. (*0-87326-811-3*) Intl City-Cnty Mgt.

Moulder, Evelina R., ed. see Martin, Lawrence L.

Moulder, James W., ed. Intracellular Parasitism. 288p. 1989. lib. bdg. 225.00 (*0-8493-5065-4*, QR171) CRC Pr.

Moulder, John F., et al. Handbook of X-ray Photoelectron Spectroscopy: A Reference Book of Standard Spectra for Identification & Interpretation of XPS Data. Chastain, Jill, ed. LC 92-61338. (Illus.). 275p. 1992. 290.00 (*0-9627026-2-5*) Perkin-Elmer.

Moulder, Robert, jt. auth. see McCrory, Martin.

Moulds, A. J., jt. see Hopcroft, Keith.

Moulds, JoAnn M. & Laird-Fryer, Barbara, eds. Blood Groups: Ch-Rg, Kn-McC-Yk, Cromer. LC 92-49706. 66p. 1992. 43.00 (*1-56395-009-X*) Am Assn Blood.

Moulds, JoAnn M. & Woods, Laura L. Blood Groups: P, I, Sda & Pr. LC 91-4870. (Illus.). 151p. (C). 1991. text 40.00 (*1-56395-002-2*) Am Assn Blood.

Moulds, Kristine. Generations of Sowers Sharing the Word: A Centennial History of Concordia College, Seward, Nebraska. LC 93-48402. 1994. write for info. (*0-89865-887-X*) Donning Co.

Moulds, Maxwell. A Guide to Australian Cicadas. (Illus.). 217p. 1990. 39.95 (*0-86840-139-0*, Pub. by New South Wales Univ Pr) Intl Spec Bk.

Moule, C. F. D. The Holy Spirit. 126p. 1997. pap. 14.00 (*1-57910-035-X*) Wipf & Stock.

Moule, Charles F. The Epistles of Paul the Apostle to the Colossians & to Philemon. (Cambridge Greek New Testament Ser.). 170p. (C). 1957. pap. text 21.95 (*0-521-09236-1*) Cambridge U Pr.

— Gospel According to Mark. (Cambridge Bible Commentary on the New English Bible, New Testament Ser.). 134p. (Orig.). (C). 1965. pap. text 20.95 (*0-521-09288-4*) Cambridge U Pr.

— Idiom Book of New Testament Greek. 2nd ed. 246p. (C). 1959. pap. text 24.95 (*0-521-09237-X*) Cambridge U Pr.

Moule, Charles F. & Farmer, William R., eds. Christian History & Interpretation: Studies Presented to John Knox. LC 67-15306. 464p. reprint ed. pap. 132.30 (*0-608-30483-2*, 2022449) Bks Demand.

Moule, Charles F., jt. ed. see Bammel, E.

Moule, H. Charles Simeon. 1997. pap. 11.99 (*1-85792-310-3*, Pub. by Christian Focus) Spring Arbor Dist.

Moule, H. E., jt. auth. see Darlow, T. H.

Moule, Handley C. Ephesian Studies. 1982. pap. 5.95 (*0-87508-363-3*) Chr Lit.

***Moule, Handley C.** Holy Spirit: Veni Creator. 1999. pap. text 9.99 (*1-85792-442-8*) Christian Focus.

Moule, Handley C. The Second Epistle to the Corinthians. 1979. pap. 5.95 (*0-87508-359-5*) Chr Lit.

— Studies in Hebrews. LC 77-79181. (Kregel Popular Commentary Ser.). 128p. 1977. pap. 7.99 (*0-8254-3223-5*) Kregel.

— Studies in Second Timothy. LC 77-79182. (Kregel Popular Commentary Ser.). 192p. 1977. pap. 8.99 (*0-8254-3219-7*) Kregel.

— Thoughts for Sunday. LC 97-71385. (Walk in the Word Ser.). 482p. 1997. reprint ed. pap. 24.99 (*0-89957-216-2*) AMG Pubs.

***Moule, Handley C. G.** Veni Creator. 269p. 1999. pap. 24.00 (*1-57910-292-1*) Wipf & Stock.

Moule, William R. God's Arms Around Us. LC 90-21982. (Illus.). 400p. 1990. reprint ed. 19.95 (*0-931892-60-0*) B Dolphin Pub.

— A Little Moule History: 1890's-1937. LC 90-22041. (Illus.). 624p. 1990. 24.95 (*0-931892-61-9*) B Dolphin Pub.

Moules, Joan. Passionate Enchantment. large type ed. (Linford Romance Library). 320p. 1989. pap. 16.99 (*0-7089-6648-9*, Linford) Ulverscroft.

— Richer Than Diamonds. large type ed. 1990. pap. 16.99 (*0-7089-6931-3*) Ulverscroft.

Moules, Tina & Ramsay, Joan. Textbook of Children's Nursing. (Illus.). 544p. 1998. pap. 59.50 (*0-7487-3340-X*, Pub. by S Thornes Pubs) Trans-Atl Phila.

Moulijn, J. A., et al, eds. Catalysis: An Integrated Approach to Homogeneous, Heterogeneous & Industrial Catalysis. (Studies in Surface Science & Catalysis: Vol. 79). 478p. 1993. 205.00 (*0-444-89229-X*) Elsevier.

Moulijn, J. A., jt. ed. see Figueiredo, J. L.

Moulijn, Jacob A., jt. auth. see Cybulski, Andrzej.

Moulik, Achala. Earth Is But a Star. 1997. pap. 18.50 (*81-7476-182-9*, Pub. by UBS Pubs) S Asia.

Moulik, Sunanda. Grasses & Bamboos of India. 1994. pap. 300.00 (*81-7233-073-1*, Pub. by Scientific Pubs) St Mut.

Moulik, T., ed. Food Energy Nexus & Ecosystems. (C). 1988. 47.50 (*81-204-0362-2*, Pub. by Oxford IBH) S Asia.

Moulik, T. K. & Purushotham, P. Technology Transfer in Rural Industries: Cases & Analysis. 1986. 18.50 (*0-86132-124-3*, Pub. by Popular Prakashan) S Asia.

Moulik, T. K., jt. ed. see Streefkerek, Hein.

Moulin, Annie. Peasantry & Society in France since 1789. Cleary, M. C. & Cleary, M. F., trs. (Illus.). 271p. (C). 1991. text 59.95 (*0-521-39534-8*); pap. text 19.95 (*0-521-39577-1*) Cambridge U Pr.

Moulin, Daniel De, see De Moulin, Daniel.

Moulin-Eckart, Richard D. Cosima Wagner, 2 vols., Set. Phillips, Catherine A., tr. from GER. LC 81-1500. (Music Ser.). (Illus.). 1981. reprint ed. lib. bdg. 110.00 (*0-306-76102-5*) Da Capo.

Moulin, Herve. Axioms of Cooperative Decision-Making. (Econometric Society Monographs: No. 15). (Illus.). 352p. 1988. text 90.00 (*0-521-36055-2*) Cambridge U Pr.

— Axioms of Cooperative Decision-Making. (Econometric Society Monographs: No. 15). (Illus.). 346p. (C). 1991. pap. text 30.95 (*0-521-42458-5*) Cambridge U Pr.

— Cooperative Microeconomics: A Game-Theoretic Introduction. LC 95-3606. 440p. 1995. text 55.00 (*0-691-03481-8*, Pub. by Princeton U Pr) Cal Prin Full Svc.

Moulin, Herve, ed. Game Theory for the Social Sciences. rev. ed. LC 86-5439. 256p. (C). 1986. pap. text 22.50 (*0-8147-5431-7*) NYU Pr.

Moulin, Thomas, jt. auth. see DeNevi, Don.

Moulinie, Henri. De Bonald: La Vie, la Carriere Politique, la Doctrine. Mayer, J. P., ed. LC 78-67373. (European Political Thought Ser.). (FRE.). 1980. reprint ed. lib. bdg. 35.95 (*0-405-11723-X*) Ayer.

Moulinier, Louis. Le Pur et l'Impur dans la Pensee des Grecs d'Homere a Aristote. LC 75-10642. (Ancient Religion & Mythology Ser.). (FRE.). 1976. reprint ed. 47.95 (*0-405-07260-0*) Ayer.

Moulinier, M. B. Haviland - Lounsbury - Moulinier Genealogy & Memoirs. 169p. 1994. reprint ed. pap. 25.00 (*0-8328-4124-2*); reprint ed. lib. bdg. 35.00 (*0-8328-4123-4*) Higginson Bk Co.

Moullade, M. & Nairn, Alan E. The Phanerozoic Geology of the World, Vol. I. (Palaeozoic Ser.: Pt. A). 430p. 1991. 255.75 (*0-444-87384-8*) Elsevier.

Moullade, M. & Nairn, Alan E., eds. The Phanerozoic Geology of the World: The Mesozoic, Vol. 2A. 530p. 1978. 273.00 (*0-444-41671-4*) Elsevier.

— The Phanerozoic Geology of the World: The Mesozoic, Vol. 2B. 450p. 1983. 264.25 (*0-444-41672-2*, I-343-83) Elsevier.

Moullade, M., jt. ed. see Nairn, Alan E.

Moullagaliev, A., tr. see Borokov, A. A.

Moulnier, ed. see De Chateaubriand, Francois-Rene.

Moulou, Patrick. Les Tablatures par l'Image. Lefferts, Michael, ed. (FRE.). 48p. (Orig.). (C). 1997. pap. text 19.95 (*0-7692-1313-8*, 01010322) Wrner Bros.

Mouloua, Mustapha & Koonce, Jefferson M., eds. Human-Automation Interaction: Research & Practice. LC 97-140. 326p. 1997. write for info. (*0-8058-2841-9*) L Erlbaum Assocs.

Mouloua, Mustapha, jt. ed. see Parasuraman, Raja.

Mouloua, Mustapha, jt. ed. see Scerbo, Mark W.

Moulson, A. J., jt. auth. see Herbert, J.

Moulsworth, Martha. My Name Was Martha: A Renaissance Woman's Autobiographical Poem. Evans, Robert C. & Wiedemann, Barbara, eds. LC 93-27167. 117p. (C). 1993. lib. bdg. 22.50 (*0-933951-53-1*) Locust Hill Pr.

Moult, Thomas. The Best Poems of 1922. LC 78-74821. (Granger Poetry Library). (Illus.). 1979. reprint ed. 20.00 (*0-89609-140-6*) Roth Pub Inc.

Moult, Thomas, ed. The Best Poems of 1923. LC 78-74822. (Granger Poetry Library). (Illus.). 1979. reprint ed. 20.00 (*0-89609-141-4*) Roth Pub Inc.

— Best Poems of 1924. LC 79-50845. (Granger Poetry Library). (Illus.). 1979. reprint ed. 20.00 (*0-89609-163-5*) Roth Pub Inc.

— Best Poems of 1926. LC 79-50846. (Granger Poetry Library). (Illus.). 1979. reprint ed. 20.00 (*0-89609-164-3*) Roth Pub Inc.

— Best Poems of 1931. LC 78-73492. (Granger Poetry Library). (Illus.). 1979. reprint ed. 20.00 (*0-89609-118-X*) Roth Pub Inc.

— Best Poems of 1932. LC 78-73493. (Granger Poetry Library). (Illus.). 1979. reprint ed. 20.00 (*0-89609-119-8*) Roth Pub Inc.

***Moulthrop, Glenna Hammer.** Mother Teresa: Living in Love: A Compilation of Mother Teresa's Teaching on Love. LC 99-88406. 112p. 2000. 12.95 (*0-9668774-1-1*) TowleHse Pubg.

Moulthrop, James S., jt. ed. see Shuler, Scott.

Moulton, jt. auth. see Bellow, Gay.

Moulton, jt. auth. see Wittmeyer.

Moulton, A., et al, eds. Centennial History of Harrison, Containing the Celebration of 1905 & Historical & Biographical Matter. (Illus.). 727p. 1995. reprint ed. lib. bdg. 75.00 (*0-8328-4595-7*) Higginson Bk Co.

Moulton, Anthony L., ed. Congenital Heart Surgery: Current Techniques & Controversies. LC 83-21342. (Illus.). 347p. 1984. text 97.50 (*0-941022-00-5*) Davies Pubng.

Moulton, Augustus F. Grandfather Tales of Scarborough. (Illus.). 209p. 1997. reprint ed. lib. bdg. 29.00 (*0-8328-5911-7*) Higginson Bk Co.

***Moulton, Augustus F.** Maine Historical Sketches. (Illus.). 313p. 2000. pap. 24.00 (*0-7884-1490-9*, 1490) Heritage Bk.

Moulton, Augustus F. Old Prouts Neck. (Illus.). 119p. 1997. reprint ed. pap. 15.00 (*0-8328-5901-X*) Higginson Bk Co.

Moulton, Bea, jt. auth. see Bellow, Gary.

Moulton, Beth. King Arthur. (Illus.). 32p. (J). (gr. k up). 1997. pap. 14.95 (*1-886201-10-2*) Nana Banana.

Moulton, Bruce A. Bridal Shower Journal. (Illus.). 22p. 1995. 16.95 (*0-9633573-2-8*) Lakeland Color.

— Our Honeymoon: A Journal of Romantic Memories. 1994. 7.95 (*0-9633573-1-X*) Lakeland Color.

— Vacation Getaway: A Journal of Your Travel Memories. 36p. 1992. 6.95 (*0-9633573-0-1*) Lakeland Color.

Moulton, C., ed. see Moulton, H. W.

Moulton, C. W. Lion in the Fire. LC 96-86151. 100p. (Orig.). 1996. pap. 12.95 (*0-9653938-0-1*) Fresno Poets.

Moulton, Candy. Roadside History of Nebraska. LC 97-22949. 450p. 1997. 30.00 (*0-87842-348-6*); pap. text 18.00 (*0-87842-347-8*) Mountain Pr.

— Roadside History of Wyoming. Greer, Dan, ed. LC 95-22419. (Roadside History Ser.). (Illus.). 440p. 1995. 30.00 (*0-87842-315-X*); pap. 18.00 (*0-87842-316-8*) Mountain Pr.

— The Writer's Guide to Everyday Life in the Wild West from 1840-1900. LC 98-48127. (Everyday Life Ser.). (Illus.). 336p. 1999. 18.99 (*0-89879-870-1*, 10600, Wrtrs Digest Bks) F & W Pubns Inc.

Moulton, Candy & Kern, Ben. Wagon Wheels: A Contemporary Journey on the Oregon Trail. (Illus.). 256p. (Orig.). 1996. 24.95 (*0-931271-37-1*); pap. 14.95 (*0-931271-36-3*) Hi Plains Pr.

Moulton, Candy V. The Grand Encampment: Settling the High Country. LC 97-11732. (Illus.). 240p. 1997. pap. 17.95 (*0-931271-44-4*) Hi Plains Pr.

— Legacy of the Tetons: Homesteading in Jackson Hole. LC 95-105717. 237p. (Orig.). 1994. pap. 15.95 (*0-9634839-4-3*) Tamarack Bks.

Moulton, Candy V. & Moulton, Flossie. Steamboat, Legendary Bucking Horse: His Life & Times, & the Cowboys Who Tried to Tame Him. LC 92-8507. 1992. pap. 11.95 (*0-931271-19-3*) Hi Plains Pr.

Moulton, Candy V., jt. auth. see Adare, Sierra.

Moulton, Carroll. Ancient Greece & Rome, 3. LC 98-13728. 1998. 90.00 (*0-684-80505-7*) S&S Trade.

Moulton, Carroll, ed. Ancient Greece & Rome. 1998. 90.00 (*0-684-80503-0*) S&S Trade.

— Ancient Greece & Rome, 2. LC 98-13728. 1998. 90.00 (*0-684-80504-9*) S&S Trade.

— Ancient Greece & Rome, 4. LC 98-13728. 1998. 90.00 (*0-684-80506-5*) S&S Trade.

— Ancient Greece & Rome: An Encyclopedia for Students, 4 vols. LC 98-13728. (Illus.). 752p. (YA). (gr. 8). 1998. 375.00 (*0-684-80507-3*) S&S Trade.

Moulton, Charles W. The Library of Literary Criticism of English & American Authors, 8 vols. 1990. 360.00 (*0-8446-1318-5*) Peter Smith.

— The Library of Literary Criticism of English & American Authors, 8 vols., Set. (BCL1-PR English Literature Ser.). 1992. reprint ed. lib. bdg. 600.00 (*0-7812-7004-9*) Rprt Serv.

Moulton, Dwayne. The Mystery of the Pink Waterfall. LC 80-84116. (Illus.). 192p. (J). (gr. 3-8). 1980. 14.95 (*0-9605236-0-X*) Pandoras Treasures.

Moulton, Dwayne, ed. see Idaho Writer's League Staff.

Moulton, Faye S. Adventuring into Vermont's Past. LC 90-80145. (Illus.). 84p. (Orig.). 1990. pap. 8.95 (*0-914960-81-4*) Academy Bks.

Moulton, Flossie, jt. auth. see Moulton, Candy V.

Moulton, Forest R. An Introduction to Celestial Mechanics. 437p. 1984. reprint ed. pap. 12.95 (*0-486-64687-4*) Dover.

Moulton, Gary. American Encounters: Lewis & Clark, the People, & the Land. (Illus.). 32p. (Orig.). 1991. pap. text 10.00 (*0-938932-03-9*) U Nebr CFGPS.

— Lewis & Clark & the Route to the Pacific. Goetzmann, William H., ed. (World Explorers Ser.). (Illus.). 120p. (YA). (gr. 5 up). 1991. lib. bdg. 19.95 (*0-7910-1327-8*) Chelsea Hse.

Moulton, Gary, ed. Herbarium of the Lewis & Clark Expedition. LC 98-53495. (Journals of the Lewis & Clark Expedition Ser.). (Illus.). 357p. 1999. 75.00 (*0-8032-2931-3*) U of Nebr Pr.

Moulton, Gary, ed. see Lewis, Meriwether & Clark, William.

Moulton, Gary E. John Ross, Cherokee Chief. LC 76-1146. (Brown Thrasher Bks.). 292p. 1986. reprint ed. pap. 15.95 (*0-8203-0888-9*) U of Ga Pr.

Moulton, Gary E., ed. see Lewis, Meriwether & Clark, William.

Moulton, Gwen, jt. auth. see Crim, Sarah.

Moulton, H. Fletcher, ed. Trial of Steinie Morrison. (Notable British Trials Ser.). xxxi, 282p. 1995. reprint ed. 95.00 (*1-56169-163-1*) Gaunt.

Moulton, H. J. Houdini's History of Magic in Boston, 1792-1915. (Illus.). 176p. 1983. 35.00 (*0-916638-27-8*) Meyerbooks.

Moulton, H. W. Moulton Annals. Moulton, C., ed. (Illus.). 454p. 1989. reprint ed. pap. 68.00 (*0-8328-0889-X*); reprint ed. lib. bdg. 76.00 (*0-8328-0888-1*) Higginson Bk Co.

Moulton, Harland B. From Superiority to Parity: The United States & the Strategic Arms Race, 1961-1971. LC 79-140920. 333p. 1973. 55.00 (*0-8371-5822-2*, MNS/, Greenwood Pr) Greenwood.

Moulton, Harold G. Financial Organization & the Economic System. LC 75-2652. (Wall Street & the Security Market Ser.). 1975. reprint ed. 46.95 (*0-405-06977-4*) Ayer.

— The Financial Organization of Society. LC 75-2653. (Wall Street & the Security Market Ser.). 1975. reprint ed. 65.95 (*0-405-06978-2*) Ayer.

— The Formation of Capital. LC 75-2654. (Wall Street & the Security Market Ser.). 1975. reprint ed. 23.95 (*0-405-06979-0*) Ayer.

Moulton, Harold G. & Ko, Junichi. Japan: An Economic & Financial Appraisal. LC 77-97886. reprint ed. 49.50 (*0-404-04507-3*) AMS Pr.

Moulton, Harold G., et al. Capital Expansion, Employment & Economic Stability. LC 75-2655. (Wall Street & the Security Market Ser.). 1975. reprint ed. 35.95 (*0-405-06980-4*) Ayer.

— The Recovery Problem in the United States. LC 73-176337. (FDR & the Era of the New Deal Ser.). (Illus.). 1972. reprint ed. lib. bdg. 85.00 (*0-306-70421-8*) Da Capo.

Moulton, Harold K., ed. The Moulton's Analytical Greek Lexicon Revised. rev. ed. (GRE.). 1967. 25.95 (*0-310-20280-9*, 6257) Zondervan.

Moulton, Harper W. & Fickel, Arthur A. Executive Development: Preparing for the 21st Century. (Illus.). 224p. 1993. text 45.00 (*0-19-507465-3*) OUP.

***Moulton, Ian Frederick.** Before Pornography: Erotic Writing in Early Modern England. (Studies in the History of Sexuality). (Illus.). 304p. 2000. text 49.95 (*0-19-513709-4*) OUP.

Moulton, James H. Early Zoroastrianism: Lectures Delivered at Oxford & in London, February to May, 1912. LC 77-27517. (Hibbert Lectures). reprint ed. 55.00 (*0-404-60414-5*) AMS Pr.

— Grammar of New Testament Greek, Vol. I. 320p. 1985. 49.95 (*0-567-01011-2*, Pub. by T & T Clark) Bks Intl VA.

— Grammar of New Testament Greek Vol. 4: Style. 184p. 1976. 39.95 (*0-567-01018-X*, Pub. by T & T Clark) Bks Intl VA.

— The Treasure of the Magi: A Story of Modern Zoroastrianism. LC 73-173004. reprint ed. 41.50 (*0-404-04508-1*) AMS Pr.

An Asterisk (*) at the beginning of an entry indicates that the title is appearing for the first time.

— The Treasure of the Magi: A Study of Modern Zoroastrianism. 1973. lib. bdg. 59.95 (*0-8490-2759-4*) Gordon Pr.
— The Treasure of the Magi: A Study of Modern Zoroastrianism. 280p. 1996. reprint ed. pap. 24.95 (*1-56459-612-5*) Kessinger Pub.
Moulton, James H., jt. auth. see Milligan, G.

Moulton, Janice & Robinson, George. Scaling the Dragon. LC 94-71584. 260p. (Orig.). 1994. pap. 19.95 (*0-940121-29-8*, P209, Cross Roads Bks) Cross Cultural Pubns.
The authors portray here the delights & problems of two Americans living in contemporary China. In this country where people once ate rats to survive, capitalism has introduced color television & electronic pianos. Where a communist economy thrives, its citizens nevertheless have become street entrepreneurs & are moving into a life incorporating advertising, incentive programs & even income tax. The authors show how their expectations & anticipations could not begin to touch the reality of life in China. They made friends; & they made enemies; & they learned to recognize the difference. They understand China to the degree that some Chinese professors would like to think that "they are really Chinese." *Publisher Paid Annotation.*

Moulton, Janice & Robinson, George M. Organization of Language. LC 80-19052. 400p. 1981. pap. text 29.95 (*0-521-29851-2*) Cambridge U Pr.
Moulton, Jeanne M. Animation Rurale: Education for Rural Development. 249p. (Orig.). (C). 1977. pap. 6.00 (*0-932288-48-0*) Ctr Intl Ed U of MA.
Moulton, Jenni K. Essential German Dictionary. 2nd ed. (GER.). 1997. mass mkt. 3.99 (*0-345-41080-7*) Ballantine Pub Grp.
Moulton, Jenni K., jt. auth. see Moulton, William G.
Moulton, Jeremy, jt. auth. see Moulton, Peter.
Moulton, Joy W. Genealogical Resources in English Repositories. LC 87-82876. (Illus.). 648p. 1988. 45.00 (*0-944485-00-6*) Hampton OH.
— Supplement to Genealogical Resources in English Repositories. (Orig.). (C). 1992. pap. text 4.75 (*0-944485-01-4*) Hampton OH.
Moulton, L. Rozelle, jt. auth. see Fad, Kathleen M.
Moulton, LeArta. The Herb Walk Reference Manual. 99p. 1993. 8.95 (*0-935596-19-4*) LM Pubns.
Moulton, LeArta & Bingham, Rita. The Quick Wholesome Foods Recipe Booklet. 1991. pap. 2.75 (*0-935596-29-1*) LM Pubns.
Moulton, LeArta A. The Amazing Wheat Book: Recipes & Instructions for Making Wheat Meat, Seasoning Mixes, Whole Wheat Breads, Pastries & Snacks. 2nd rev. ed. (Illus.). 223p. 1997. pap. 15.95 (*0-935596-13-5*) LM Pubns.
Moulton, Lynda W. Data Bases for Special Libraries: A Strategic Guide to Information Management. LC 91-11338. (Library Management Collection). 176p. 1991. lib. bdg. 52.95 (*0-313-27369-3*, MOI/, Greenwood Pr) Greenwood.
Moulton, Margaret. Western Gardener's Journal: A Three-Year Almanac. (Illus.). 176p. 1998. spiral bd. 19.95 (*0-8118-1876-4*) Chronicle Bks.
***Moulton, Mark K.** Snowman Named Just Bob. (Illus.). (J). 1999. pap. 18.00 (*0-7412-0283-2*) Lang Graphics Ltd.
Moulton, Michael & Sanderson, James. Wildlife Issues in a Changing World. (Illus.). 368p. (Orig.). (C). 1996. per. 39.95 (*1-57444-068-3*) St Lucie Pr.
Moulton, Michael, jt. auth. see Sanderson, James.
Moulton, Nancy. Dark Desires. 352p. 1988. pap. 3.95 (*0-380-75419-3*, Avon Bks) Morrow Avon.
— Defiant Heart. 368p. (Orig.). 1989. pap. 3.95 (*0-380-75730-3*, Avon Bks) Morrow Avon.
***Moulton, Patrice & Harper, Linda.** Outside Looking in: When Someone You Love Is in Therapy. LC 99-24827. 160p. 1999. 20.00 (*1-884444-57-1*) Safer Soc.
Moulton, Paul C. The Best Ticket in Town: A History of the Norfolk Forum. LC 98-43054. 1998. write for info. (*0-9653759-6-X*) Hallmark Publng.
Moulton, Peter. A+ Certification. 992p. 1999. 49.99 incl. cd-rom (*0-13-084316-4*, Pub. by P-H) S&S Trade.
***Moulton, Peter & Moulton, Jeremy.** A+ Certification: The Complete Video Course. 959p. 1999. pap. 80.00 (*0-13-086188-X*) P-H.
***Moulton, Peter, et al.** A+ Certification. 1999. 129.99 incl. VHS (*0-13-086138-3*) P-H.
Moulton, Phillips P. The Living Witness of John Woolman. LC 72-94969. 36p. (Orig.). 1973. 4.00 (*0-87574-187-8*) Pendle Hill.
— Violence, or Aggressive Nonviolent Resistance. LC 76-170019. (Orig.). 1971. pap. 4.00 (*0-87574-178-9*) Pendle Hill.
Moulton, Phillips P., ed. The Journal & Major Essays of John Woolman. LC 71-171970. 336p. 1989. pap. 15.00 (*0-944350-10-0*) Friends United.
Moulton, Richard G. The Literary Study of the Bible. LC 70-4534. 1898. 59.00 (*0-403-00113-7*) Scholarly.
— The Literary Study of the Bible. 1988. reprint ed. lib. bdg. 59.00 (*0-7812-0552-2*) Rprt Serv.
— Shakespeare As a Dramatic Artist. (BCL1-PR English Literature Ser.). 443p. 1992. reprint ed. lib. bdg. 99.00 (*0-7812-7303-X*) Rprt Serv.
Moulton, Ron & Lloyd, Pat. Kites: A Practical Handbook for the Modern Kite Flyer. rev. ed. (Illus.). 256p. (Orig.). 1997. pap. 34.00 (*1-85486-143-3*, Pub. by Nexus Special Interests) Trans-Atl Phila.
***Moulton, Sandra.** Mastering Domino R5. (Mastering Ser.). 704p. 2000. pap. 39.99 (*0-7821-2678-2*) Sybex.
Moulton, Sara & Anderson, Jean. The Good Morning America Cut the Calories Cookbook: 120 Delicious Low-Fat, Low-Cal Recipes from Our Viewers - With Additional Recipes by Sara Moulton & Emeril Lagasse. rev. ed. LC 95-14024. 256p. 2000. 24.95 (*0-7868-6163-0*, Pub. by Hyperion) Time Warner.
Moulton, Stephen R., 2nd & Stewart, Kenneth W. Caddisflies (Trichoptera) of the Interior Highlands of North America. (Memoirs of the American Entomological Institute Ser.: Vol. 56). (Illus.). 313p. (C). 1996. 40.00 (*1-887988-00-9*) Am Entomol Inst.
Moulton, Thomas. Porter As a Portion of Maines: Its Settlement, Etc. (Illus.). 96p. 1997. reprint ed. pap. 19.00 (*0-8328-5898-6*) Higginson Bk Co.
Moulton, W. F., et al, eds. A Concordance to the Greek Testament. 5th ed. 1126p. 1997. text 59.99 (*0-8010-2152-9*) Baker Bks.
— A Concordance to the Greek Testament. 5th ed. (GRE.). 1120p. 1978. 59.95 (*0-567-01021-X*, Pub. by T & T Clark) Bks Intl VA.
Moulton, William G. A Linguistic Guide to Language Learning. 2nd ed. xii, 140p. (Orig.). 1970. pap. 10.00 (*0-87352-027-0*, E3000) Modern Lang.
— Sounds of English & German. LC 62-20024. (Orig.). 1992. pap. text 9.95 (*0-226-54309-9*) U Ch Pr.
— Swiss German Dialect & Romance Patois. (LD Ser.: No. 34). 1941. pap. 25.00 (*0-527-00780-3*) Periodicals Srv.
Moulton, William G. & Moulton, Jenni K. Spoken German. LC 76-416. (Spoken Language Ser.). 290p. 1971. pap. 90.00 incl. audio (*0-87950-097-2*) Spoken Lang Serv.
Moulton, William G. & Moulton, Jenni K. Spoken German. LC 76-416. (Spoken Language Ser.). 290p. 1971. audio 75.00 (*0-87950-096-4*) Spoken Lang Serv.
Moulton, William G. & Moulton, Jenni K. Spoken German, Units 1-12. LC 76-416. (Spoken Language Ser.). 290p. 1971. pap. 15.00 (*0-87950-091-3*) Spoken Lang Serv.
Moultrie, Keith, jt. auth. see Gould, Nick.
Moultrie Service League Staff. Southern Settings: Creating Delightful Masterpieces. LC 96-172440. (Illus.). 1996. 17.95 (*0-9651477-0-3*) Moultrie Srv.
Moultrie, William. Memoirs of the American Revolution, So Far As It Related to the States of North & South Carolina & Georgia. LC 67-29045. (Eyewitness Accounts of the American Revolution Ser.). 1979. reprint ed. 36.95 (*0-405-01139-3*) Ayer.
Moultrup, David J. Husbands, Wives & Lovers: The Emotional System of the Extramarital Affair. LC 89-71492. (Family Therapy Ser.). 278p. 1990. lib. bdg. 33.95 (*0-89862-105-4*) Guilford Pubns.
***Mouly, Francoise & Weschler, Lawrence.** Covering the New Yorker: Cutting-Edge Covers from a Literary Institution. (Illus.). 2000. 50.00 (*0-7892-0657-9*) Abbeville Pr.
Mouly, Michel & Pautet, Marie-Bernadette. The GSM System for Mobile Communications. 701p. (C). 1992. 139.95 (*0-945592-15-9*) Telecom Pubng.
Mouly, Ruth W. The Religious Right & Israel: The Politics of Armageddon. (Midwest Research Monographs: No. 2). 47p. 1985. pap. 4.50 (*0-915987-01-5*) Political Rsch Assocs.
Mouly, V. Suchitra & Sankaran, Jayaram K. Organizational Ethnography: An Illustrative Application in the Study of Indian R & D Settings. LC 94-33425. 180p. 1995. text 22.95 (*0-8039-9211-4*) Sage.
Moulyn, Adrian C. The Meaning of Suffering: An Interpretation of Human Existence from the Viewpoint of Time, 22. LC 82-6171. (Contributions in Philosophy Ser.: No. 22). (Illus.). 336p. 1982. 65.00 (*0-313-22233-9*, MOS/, Greenwood Pr) Greenwood.
— Mind-Body: A Pluralistic Interpretation of Mind Body Interaction under the Guidelines of Time, Space, & Movement, 46. LC 90-47286. (Contributions in Philosophy Ser.: No. 46). 192p. 1991. 62.95 (*0-313-27351-0*, MMU/, Greenwood Pr) Greenwood.
Mounce, Donnelleigh, ed. see Howard, Marlene.
Mounce, Eva D., jt. auth. see Gums, Bonnie L.
Mounce, H. O. Hume's Naturalism. LC 98-35364. 1999. 75.00 (*0-415-19124-6*); pap. 25.99 (*0-415-19125-4*) Routledge.
— The Two Pragmatisms: From Peirce to Rorty. LC 96-21878. 256p. (C). 1997. pap. 25.99 (*0-415-15283-6*) Routledge.
— Wittgenstein's Tractatus: An Introduction. LC 81-40474. viii, 136p. (C). 1981. reprint ed. pap. text 7.95 (*0-226-54319-6*) U Ch Pr.
— Wittgenstein's Tractatus: An Introduction. LC 81-40474. viii, 144p. (C). 1989. reprint ed. pap. text 13.95 (*0-226-54321-8*) U Ch Pr.
Mounce, Howard. The Two Pragmatisms: From Peirce to Rorty. LC 96-21878. 256p. (C). 1997. 80.00 (*0-415-15282-8*) Routledge.
Mounce, John & ITE Transportation Council Staff. Student Chapter Manual. 2nd rev. ed. 41p. 1998. pap. text. write for info. (*0-935403-27-2*, PP-011B) Inst Trans Eng.
Mounce, Robert H. The Book of Revelation. LC 97-25322. (New International Commentary on the New Testament Ser.). 1997. 44.00 (*0-8028-2537-0*) Eerdmans.
— Matthew. (New International Biblical Commentary Ser.). 288p. 1991. pap. 11.95 (*0-943575-18-4*) Hendrickson MA.
— Romans. LC 95-17311. (New American Commentary: Vol. 27). 304p. 1995. 27.99 (*0-8054-0127-X*) Broadman.
— What Are We Waiting For? A Commentary on Revelation. fac. ed. LC 91-45243. 151p. 1992. reprint ed. pap. 46.90 (*0-7837-7967-4*, 204772300008) Bks Demand.
Mounce, William. Pastoral Epistles. (Word Biblical Commentary Ser.: Vol. 46). 592p. 1999. 32.99 (*0-8499-0245-2*) Word Pub.
Mounce, William D. Analytical Lexicon to the Greek New Testament. 608p. 1993. 42.99 (*0-310-54210-3*) Zondervan.
Mounce, William D. Basics of Biblical Greek. 480p. 1999. 37.99 (*0-310-23211-2*) HarpC.
— Basics of Biblical Greek: Grammar. (ENG & GRE.). 464p. 1993. 29.99 (*0-310-59800-1*) Zondervan.
— Basics of Biblical Greek: Workbook. (ENG & GRE.). 192p. 1993. pap., wbk. ed. 17.99 (*0-310-40091-0*) Zondervan.
— A Graded Reader of Biblical Greek: Companion to Basics of Biblical Greek & Greek Grammar Beyond the Basics. 256p. 1996. pap. 16.99 (*0-310-20582-4*) Zondervan.
Mounce, William D., jt. ed. see Hughes, John J.
Mound, L. A. Bear Essentials of Love. pap. text 6.00 (*0-9626732-0-X*) Vision Dists.
Mound, Laurence A. Amazing Insects. LC 92-26735. (Eyewitness Juniors Ser.: No. 26). (Illus.). 32p. (J). (ps-3). 1993. pap. 9.99 (*0-679-83925-9*, Pub. by Knopf Bks Yng Read) Random.
— Amazing Insects. (Eyewitness Juniors Ser.: No. 26). (J). (ps-3). 1993. 15.19 (*0-606-05273-9*, Pub. by Turtleback) Demco.
— Insectos - Insects: Eyewitness Book. 1995. 18.95 (*84-372-3727-0*) Santillana.
Mound, Laurence A. & Brooks, Stephen. Insects. LC 94-31842. (DK Pockets Ser.). (Illus.). 128p. (YA). (gr. 7 up). 1995. pap. 6.95 (*1-56458-887-4*) DK Pub Inc.
Mound, Laurence A. & Kibby, Geoffrey. Thysanoptera: An Identification Guide. 2nd ed. LC 98-29659. (CABI Publishing Ser.). (Illus.). 76p. 1998. spiral bd. 35.00 (*0-85199-211-0*) OUP.
Mound, Laurence A. & Marullo, Rita. The Thrips of Central & South America: An Introduction (Insecta: Thysanoptera) Gupta, Virendra K., ed. LC 96-1387. (Memoirs on Entomology, International Ser.: No. 6). (Illus.). 1996. 65.00 (*1-56665-061-5*) Assoc Pubs FL.
Mound, Laurence A., et al. Psocoptera, Phthiraptera, Thysanoptera. (Zoological Catalogue of Australia Ser.: Vol. 26). 418p. 1996. 79.95 (*0-643-05703-X*, Pub. by CSIRO) Accents Pubns.
***Mound, Lawrence.** Insect. (Eyewitness Books). (Illus.). (J). (gr. 4-7). 2000. 19.99 (*0-7894-6566-3*) DK Pub Inc.
— Insect. (Eyewitness Books). (J). (gr. 4-7). 2000. 15.95 (*0-7894-5816-0*) DK Pub Inc.
Mound, Linda. Understanding People & Organisations: An Introduction to Organisational Behaviour. (Illus.). 352p. 1999. pap. 49.50 (*0-7487-2404-4*, Pub. by S Thornes Pubs) Trans-Atl Phila.
Mounier, Emmanuel. Personalism. Mairet, Philip, tr. LC 75-122050. 1970. reprint ed. pap. 8.00 (*0-268-00434-X*) U of Notre Dame Pr.
Mounier, Emmanuel, ed. see Maritain, Jacques.
Mounier, J. P., jt. ed. see Gomella, C.
Mounier, Jean J. On the Influence Attributed to Philosophers, Free-Masons, & to the Illuminati, on the Revolution of France. LC 74-13148. 280p. 1974. reprint ed. 50.00 (*0-8201-1135-X*) Schol Facsimiles.
Mounier, Margie, tr. Le Temps Universel. unabridged ed. LC 95-72719.Tr. of Universal Time. (FRE., Illus.). 36p. (Orig.). 1995. pap. 15.00 (*1-888457-00-7*) Photo Do Not Bend.
Mounin, Georges. Diccionario de Linguistica. (SPA.). 32.95 (*0-7859-0895-1*, S-50062) Fr & Eur.
— Dictionnaire de la Linguistique. (FRE.). 346p. 1974. 105.00 (*0-7859-7741-4*, 2130331335) Fr & Eur.
— Dictionnaire de la Linguistique. (FRE.). 384p. 1993. pap. 31.95 (*0-7859-8625-1*, 213044881x) Fr & Eur.
— Semiotic Praxis: Studies in Pertinence & in the Means of Expression & Communication. Tihanyi, Catherine, tr. (Topics in Contemporary Semiotics Ser.).Tr. of Fr.. 226p. 1985. 59.50 (*0-306-41767-7*, Plenum Trade) Perseus Pubng.
Mounsey, Augustus H. Satsuma Rebellion: An Episode of Modern Japanese History. LC 79-65367. (Studies in Japanese History & Civilization). 294p. 1979. reprint ed. lib. bdg. 69.50 (*0-313-26993-9*, U6993, Greenwood Pr) Greenwood.
Mount. Mount Washington in Winter, 1870-1871. (Illus.). 363p. 1993. reprint ed. pap. text 21.00 (*1-55613-891-1*) Heritage Bk.
Mount, Balfour M., jt. ed. see Ajemian, Ina.
Mount, Charles M. Designer Interiors. (Illus.). 160p. 1995. 29.95 (*0-86636-346-7*) PBC Intl Inc.
Mount, Christopher. Stenberg Brothers: Constructing a Revolution in Soviet Design. LC 97-70100. (Illus.). 96p. (Orig.). 1997. pap. 19.95 (*0-87070-051-0*, 0-8109-6173-3, Pub. by Mus of Modern Art) Abrams.
***Mount, Dana.** Directions to a Story. 82p. 1999. pap. write for info. (*0-9662645-9-2*) D Mount.
Mount, Dana. A Story. 89p. 1998. pap. 3.00 (*0-9662645-8-4*) D Mount.
***Mount, Dana.** A Story & Directions to a Story. 82p. 1998. pap. write for info. (*0-9662645-0-9*) D Mount.
***Mount Diablo Interpretive Association Staff.** The Mount Diablo Guide: Mount Diablo Interpretive Association. (Illus.). 160p. 2000. pap. write for info. (*1-893163-07-5*, Pub. by Berkeley Hills) Publishers Group.
Mount, Ellis. Creative Planning of Special Library Facilities. LC 88-24633. (Haworth Series in Special Librarianship: No. 1). 197p. 1988. pap. text 19.95 (*0-86656-804-2*) Haworth Pr.
— Creative Planning of Special Library Facilities. LC 88-24633. (Haworth Series in Special Librarianship: No. 1). 197p. 1988. text 39.95 (*0-86656-697-X*) Haworth Pr.
— Milestones in Science & Technology: The Ready Reference Guide to Discoveries, Inventions, & Facts. 2nd ed. LC 93-25679. (Illus.). 216p. 1993. 39.50 (*0-89774-671-6*) Oryx Pr.
— Sci-Tech Libraries Serving Societies & Institutions. (Science & Technology Libraries: Vol. 7, No. 2). 149p. 1987. 29.95 (*0-86656-618-X*) Haworth Pr.
— Special Libraries & Information Centers: An Introductory Text. LC 83-571. (Illus.). 200p. 1983. reprint ed. pap. 62.00 (*0-8357-6428-1*, 203579600097) Bks Demand.
— University Science & Engineering Libraries, 49. 2nd ed. LC 84-6530. (Contributions in Librarianship & Information Science Ser.: No. 49). (Illus.). 303p. 1985. 59.95 (*0-313-23949-5*, MOU/, Greenwood Pr) Greenwood.
Mount, Ellis, ed. Adaptation of Turnkey Computer Systems in Sci-Tech Libraries. LC 88-23593. (Science & Technology Libraries: Vol. 9, No. 1). (Illus.). 116p. 1989. text 29.95 (*0-86656-859-X*) Haworth Pr.
— Alternative Careers in Sci-Tech Information Service. (Science & Technology Libraries: Vol. 7, No. 4). 154p. 1987. 39.95 (*0-86656-694-5*) Haworth Pr.
— Cataloging & Indexing in Sci-Tech Libraries. (Science & Technology Libraries: Vol. 2, No. 3). 86p. 1982. pap. text 24.95 (*0-86656-204-4*) Haworth Pr.
— Collection Development in Sci-Tech Libraries. LC 83-22478. (Science & Technology Libraries: Vol. 4, No. 2). 138p. 1984. text 29.95 (*0-86656-279-6*) Haworth Pr.
— Collection Management in Sci-Tech Libraries. (Science & Technology Libraries: Vol. 9, No. 3). 125p. 1989. 29.95 (*0-86656-933-2*) Haworth Pr.
— Current Awareness Services in Sci-Tech Libraries. (Science & Technology Libraries: Vol. 2, No. 1). 80p. 1982. pap. 22.95 (*0-86656-113-7*) Haworth Pr.
— Data Manipulation in Sci-Tech Libraries. LC 85-5569. (Science & Technology Libraries: Vol. 5, No. 4). 131p. 1985. text 3.95 (*0-86656-441-1*) Haworth Pr.
— Document Delivery for Sci-Tech Libraries. (Science & Technology Libraries: Vol. 2, No. 4). 127p. 1982. pap. text 29.95 (*0-86656-200-1*) Haworth Pr.
— End-User Training for Sci-Tech Databases. LC 89-27971. (Science & Technology Libraries: Vol. 10, No. 1). (Illus.). 128p. 1990. text 4.95 (*0-86656-963-4*) Haworth Pr.
— Expanding Technologies - Expanding Careers: Librarianship in Transition. 155p. (Orig.). 1997. pap. 45.00 (*0-87111-465-8*) SLA.
— Fee-Based Services in Sci-Tech Libraries. LC 84-19186. (Science & Technology Libraries: Vol. 5, No. 2). xii, 105 p. 1985. text 29.95 (*0-86656-326-1*) Haworth Pr.
— Innovations in Planning Facilities for Sci-Tech Libraries. (Science & Technology Libraries: Vol. 7, No. 1). 158p. 1986. 29.95 (*0-86656-592-2*) Haworth Pr.
— Libraries Serving Science-Oriented & Vocational High Schools. LC 88-6597. (Science & Technology Libraries: Vol. 8, No. 3). (Illus.). 134p. 1989. text 4.95 (*0-86656-792-5*) Haworth Pr.
— Management of Sci-Tech Libraries. LC 84-6615. (Science & Technology Libraries: Vol. 4, Nos. 3-4). 169p. 1984. text 39.95 (*0-86656-280-X*); pap. text 19.95 (*0-86656-284-2*) Haworth Pr.
— Monographs in Sci-Tech Libraries. LC 82-23435. (Science & Technology Libraries: Vol. 3, No. 3). 101p. 1983. text 29.95 (*0-86656-218-4*) Haworth Pr.
— Networking in Sci-Tech Libraries & Information Centers. (Science & Technology Libraries: Vol. 1, No. 2). 119p. 1981. pap. text 29.95 (*0-917724-72-0*) Haworth Pr.
— One Hundred Years of Sci-Tech Libraries: A Brief History. LC 87-34567. (Science & Technology Libraries: Vol. 8, No. 1). (Illus.). 193p. 1988. text 39.95 (*0-86656-745-3*) Haworth Pr.
— Online vs. Manual Searching in Sci-Tech Libraries. (Science & Technology Libraries: Vol. 3, No. 1). 83p. 1982. pap. text 29.95 (*0-86656-203-6*) Haworth Pr.
— Opening New Doors: Alternative Careers for Librarians. LC 92-38494. 1992. 39.00 (*0-87111-408-9*) SLA.
— Planning Facilities for Sci-Tech Libraries. LC 83-8570. (Science & Technology Libraries: Vol. 3, No. 4). 121p. 1983. text 29.95 (*0-86656-237-0*) Haworth Pr.
— Planning for Online Search Services in Sci-Tech Libraries. (Science & Technology Libraries: Vol. 1, No. 1). 142p. 1981. pap. text 29.95 (*0-917724-73-9*) Haworth Pr.
— Planning the Special Library: A Project of the New York Chapter, SLA. Blueprint for the '70s: A Seminar on Library Planning (1971: New York) LC 72-85956. (Special Libraries Association Monographs: No. 4). 128p. reprint ed. pap. 39.70 (*0-608-16444-5*, 202675600052) Bks Demand.
— Preservation & Conservation of Sci-Tech Materials. LC 86-33540. (Science & Technology Libraries: Vol. 7, No. 3). 171p. 1987. text 5.95 (*0-86656-650-3*) Haworth Pr.
— Relation of Sci-Tech Information to Environmental Studies. LC 89-71657. (Science & Technology Libraries: Vol. 10, No. 2). 155p. 1990. text 4.95 (*0-86656-988-X*) Haworth Pr.
— Role of Computers in Sci-Tech Libraries. LC 86-7619. (Science & Technology Libraries: Vol. 6, No. 4). 145p. 1986. 4.95 (*0-86656-577-9*) Haworth Pr.
— The Role of Conference Literature in Sci-Tech Libraries. (Science & Technology Libraries: Vol. 9, No. 2). 146p. 1989. 29.95 (*0-86656-780-1*) Haworth Pr.
— Role of Maps in Sci-Tech Libraries. LC 84-27919. (Science & Technology Libraries: Vol. 5, No. 3). 122p. 1985. text 29.95 (*0-86656-395-4*) Haworth Pr.
— Role of Patents in Sci-Tech Libraries. LC 82-2885. (Science & Technology Libraries: Vol. 2, No. 2). 97p. 1982. pap. text 29.95 (*0-86656-114-5*) Haworth Pr.
— Role of Serials in Sci-Tech Libraries. LC 83-12682. (Science & Technology Libraries: Vol. 4, No. 1). 109p. 1983. text 29.95 (*0-86656-260-5*) Haworth Pr.

M

— Role of Standards in Sci-Tech Libraries. LC 90-4306. (Science & Technology Libraries: Vol. 10, No. 3). 127p. 1990. text 29.95 (*1-56024-021-0*) Haworth Pr.

— Role of Technical Reports in Sci-Tech Libraries. LC 81-7231. (Science & Technology Libraries: Vol. 1, No. 4). 82p. 1982. pap. 29.95 (*0-917724-74-7*) Haworth Pr.

— The Role of Trade Literature in Sci-Tech Libraries. LC 90-4806. (Science & Technology Libraries: Vol. 10, No. 4). 135p. 1990. text 29.95 (*1-56024-038-5*) Haworth Pr.

— Role of Translations in Sci-Tech Libraries. LC 82-23353. (Science & Technology Libraries: Vol. 3, No. 2). 94p. 1983. 29.95 (*0-86656-217-6*) Haworth Pr.

— Sci-Tech Libraries in Museums & Aquariums. LC 85-16436. (Science & Technology Libraries: Vol. 6, Nos. 1-2). 204p. 1985. text 6.95 (*0-86656-484-5*) Haworth Pr.

— Sci-Tech Libraries Servng Zoological Gardens. LC 88-17548. (Science & Technology Libraries: Vol. 8, No. 4). (Illus.). 111p. 1989. text 3.95 (*0-86656-837-9*) Haworth Pr.

— Sci-Tech Library Networks Within Organizations. LC 88-540. (Science & Technology Libraries: Vol. 8, No. 2). (Illus.). 162p. 1988. text 29.95 (*0-86656-747-X*) Haworth Pr.

— Serving End-Users in Sci-Tech Libraries. LC 84-10789. (Science & Technology Libraries: Vol. 5, No. 1). 122p. 1984. text 29.95 (*0-86656-327-X*) Haworth Pr.

— Training of Sci-Tech Librarians & Library Users. LC 81-6975. (Science & Technology Libraries: Vol. 1, No. 3). 72p. 1981. pap. text 22.95 (*0-917724-75-5*) Haworth Pr.

— Weeding of Collections in Sci-Tech Libraries. LC 85-27010. (Science & Technology Libraries: Vol. 6, No. 3). 164p. 1986. text 39.95 (*0-86656-552-3*) Haworth Pr.

Mount, Ellis, intro. Sci-Tech Archives & Manuscript Collections. LC 89-19779. (Science & Technology Libraries: Vol. 9, No. 4). (Illus.). 144p. 1989. text 32.95 (*0-86656-950-2*) Haworth Pr.

Mount, Ellis & Kovacs, Beatrice. Using Science & Technology Information Sources. LC 90-21836. 200p. 1991. pap. 26.95 (*0-89774-593-0*) Oryx Pr.

***Mount, Ellis & Massoud, Renee.** Special Libraries & Information Centers: An Introductory Text. 4th ed. 334p. 1999. 49.00 incl. audio (*0-87111-501-8*) SLA.

Mount, Ellis & Newman, Wilda B. Top Secret-Trade Secret: Accessing & Safeguarding Restricted Information. LC 85-19864. 214p. 1985. pap. text 45.00 (*0-918212-90-1*) Neal-Schuman.

***Mount, Eric, Jr.** Covenant, Community & the Common Good: An Interpretation of Christian Ethics. LC 99-34475. 192p. (C). 1999. pap. 19.95 (*0-8298-1355-1*) Pilgrim OH.

Mount, Ferdinand. Jem (And Sam) 432p. 1999. 25.95 (*0-7867-0649-X*) Carroll & Graf.

***Mount, Ferdinand.** Jem & Sam. 432p. 2000. pap. 13.95 (*0-7867-0745-3*, Pub. by Carroll & Graf) Publishers Group.

Mount, Ferdinand. Of Love & Asthma. 1995. pap. 7.99 (*0-7493-2188-1*) Buttrwrth-Heinemann.

— The Subversive Family: An Alternative History of Love & Marriage. LC 92-30779. 300p. 1992. 24.95 (*0-02-921992-2*) Free Pr.

— Umbrella. 224p. 1995. pap. 7.99 (*0-7493-2193-8*) Buttrwrth-Heinemann.

Mount, Ferdinand, intro. Communism: A TLS Companion. LC 92-44913. (TLS Companions Ser.). xxviii, 350p. (C). 1993. pap. 16.50 (*0-226-54324-2*); lib. bdg. 49.50 (*0-226-54323-4*) U Ch Pr.

Mount, Franklin M. How to Incorporate & Start a Business in California. LC 97-11174. 320p. 1996. pap. 16.95 (*1-55850-586-5*) Adams Media.

Mount, Graeme S. The Sudbury Region: An Illustrated History. LC 86-5653. (Illus.). 144p. 1986. 24.95 (*0-89781-177-1*) Am Historical Pr.

Mount, Graeme S., jt. auth. see Mahant, Edelgard.

Mount, Graeme S., jt. auth. see Randall, Stephen J.

Mount, Guy. Coyote's Big Penis & Other Stories. 80p. 1989. per. 5.95 (*0-9604462-5-7*) Sweetlight.

— How Steelhead Lost His Stripes: A Children's Story & Coloring Book. (Illus.). (J). (gr. k-6). 1984. pap. 3.00 (*0-9604462-1-4*) Sweetlight.

— Lady Ocean: A Love Story for Children. (Illus.). (J). (gr. k-6). 1986. pap. 3.00 (*0-9604462-2-2*) Sweetlight.

— The Marijuana Mystery: A Novel. 168p. 1993. per. 9.95 (*0-9604462-8-1*) Sweetlight.

Mount, Guy, compiled by. The Peyote Book: A Study of Native Medicine. 3rd ed. 144p. 1993. per. 9.95 (*0-9604462-3-0*) Sweetlight.

Mount, Guy, ed. Serrano Songs & Stories. 48p. 1993. 4.95 (*0-9604462-7-3*) Sweetlight.

Mount, Guy, jt. auth. see Modesto, Ruby.

Mount, Guy, ed. see Bello, Joan.

Mount, Harry, ed. see Reynolds, Joshua.

Mount Holyoke College Staff. Those Having Torches. LC 68-57335. (Essay Index Reprint Ser.). 1977. 18.95 (*0-8369-0716-7*) Ayer.

Mount, J. A. Mount: History & Genealogy Record of the Mount & Flippin Families. 120p. 1991. reprint ed. pap. 21.00 (*0-8328-1821-6*); reprint ed. lib. bdg. 31.00 (*0-8328-1820-8*) Higginson Bk Co.

Mount, Jeffrey F. California Rivers & Streams: The Conflict Between Fluvial Process & Land Use. LC 95-10822. (Illus.). 376p. 1995. 55.00 (*0-520-20192-2*, Pub. by U CA Pr); pap. 22.50 (*0-520-20250-3*, Pub. by U CA Pr) Cal Prin Full Svc.

Mount, Jenny, ed. see Harrison, John M.

Mount, Kay H., jt. ed. see Salmon, Shirley J.

Mount, Kevin, jt. auth. see Little, Michael.

Mount, L. E., ed. see Easter School of Agricultural Science (20th: 1973:.

Mount, Richard T., tr. see De Berceo, Gonzalo.

Mount, Robert H. The Reptiles & Amphibians of Alabama. LC 95-46581. (Illus.). 368p. 1980. pap. 19.95 (*0-8173-0054-6*) U of Ala Pr.

Mount, Robert H., jt. auth. see Schwaner, Terry D.

Mount San Antonio College Philosophy Group Staff, ed. Plato's Cave Vol. 1: Interviews with the Wise. 60p. (Orig.). 1992. pap. 9.95 (*1-56543-012-3*) Mt SA Coll Philos.

Mount Sinai Hospital (New York, N. Y.) Staff, jt. auth. see Bauer, Joel J.

Mount, Steven R., jt. auth. see Lindmier, Thomas A.

Mount, Timothy, jt. auth. see Dore, Mohammed.

Mount, Timothy, jt. auth. see In, Francis.

Mount, Tom. The Greatest Adventure: Photography. (Illus.). 200p. pap. 24.95 (*0-915539-01-2*) IANTD.

— Technical Diver Encyclopedia. unabridged ed. (Illus.). iv, 270p. 1998. pap. text 59.95 (*0-915539-04-7*) IANTD.

Mount, Tom & Ikehara, Akira J. The New Practical Diving: A Complete Manual for Compressed Air Divers. LC 79-52941. (Illus.). 200p. 1980. reprint ed. pap. 19.95 (*0-87024-300-4*) U of Miami Pr.

Mount, Tom & Schaeffer, Patti. The Complete Guide to Underwater Modeling. (Illus.). 80p. pap. 10.95 (*0-915539-00-4*) IANTD.

Mount Vernon Hospital Auxilary Staff. Cardinal Cuisine. 1988. 14.95 (*0-9619391-0-9*) Mount Vernon Hospital Auxilary.

Mount Zion Baptist Church Historical Committee. Joy & Jubilee Through Jesus: The Birth & Growth of Mount Zion Missionary Baptist Church. LC 98-68033. (Illus.). 168p. 1998. 24.95 (*1-57736-123-7*) Providence Hse.

Mountain. Celtic Encyclopedia. 1995. write for info. (*0-8069-0383-X*) Sterling.

Mountain, Alan. The Dive Sites of Mauritius. LC 97-67404. (Dive Sites of . . . Ser.). (Illus.). 136p. 1997. pap. 24.95 (*0-8442-4859-2*, 48592, Passprt Bks) NTC Contemp Pub Co.

— The Diver's Handbook. LC 96-49471. (Illus.). 160p. 1997. pap. 24.95 (*1-55821-552-2*) Lyons Pr.

Mountain, Alan G. Wild South Africa. LC 98-17954. (Illus.). 208p. 1998. 40.00 (*0-262-13347-4*) MIT Pr.

Mountain Bike Magazine Editors & Bicycling Magazine Editors. Mountain Bike Magazine's Complete Guide to Mountain Biking Skills: Expert Tips on Conquering Curves, Corners, Dips, Descents, Hills, Water Hazards, & Other All-Terrain Challenges. (Illus.). 224p. 1996. pap. 14.95 (*0-87596-300-5*) Rodale Pr Inc.

Mountain Bike Magazine Editors, jt. auth. see Bicycling Magazine Editors.

Mountain, Charles M. Hymn Canticles for the Church Year: New Lyrics for Traditional Hymns. LC 96-38665. 298p. (Orig.). 1997. pap. 26.95 (*0-7880-1002-6*) CSS OH.

— The Liturgical Witness of the New Testament: 14 Worship Services Drawn from the New Testament. LC 95-41228. 266p. (Orig.). 1996. pap. 18.50 (*0-7880-0714-9*) CSS OH.

Mountain, Colleen. Daily Pacifiers for Busy Moms: Lighthearted Encouragement for Young Mothers of Young Children. LC 98-206895. 179p. 1998. pap. 10.99 (*0-88965-144-2*, Pub. by Horizon Books) Chr Pubns.

Mountain Dreamer, Oriah. The Invitation. LC 98-45903. 144p. 1999. 18.00 (*0-06-251584-5*, Pub. by Harper SF) HarpC.

***Mountain Dreamer, Oriah.** The Invitation. LC 98-45903. 1999. pap. write for info. (*0-06-251585-3*) Harper SF.

Mountain, Harry. The Celtic Encyclopedia, 5 vols. LC 98-20788. (Illus.). 1370p. 1998. pap. 130.00 (*1-58112-889-4*) Upublish.

Mountain, Kathleen, ed. see Thurman, Beverly J.

Mountain, Kathleen B. The Gift: Journey to the Self Through Psychotherapy. LC 98-70642. 288p. 1998. 24.95 (*0-9663271-0-1*) Inner Passages.

Mountain, Lee. Bobby Bear & Uncle Sam's Riddle. (Bobby Bear Ser.). (Illus.). 32p. (J). (ps-1). 1988. lib. bdg. 11.45 (*0-87783-221-8*) Oddo.

***Mountain, Lee.** Early 3 Rs: How to Lead Beginners into Reading, Writing & Arithme-TALK. LC 99-38043. 128p. 1999. pap. write for info. (*0-8058-3400-1*) L Erlbaum Assocs.

Mountain, Lee. Jungle Trip. (Attention Span Stories Ser). (Illus.). 48p. (Orig.). (J). (gr. 6-9). 1978. pap. text 8.65 (*0-89061-148-3*, 584, Jamestwn Pub) NTC Contemp Pub Co.

— Sports Trip. (Attention Span Stories Ser). (Illus.). 48p. (Orig.). 1978. pap. text 8.65 (*0-89061-147-5*, 583, Jamestwn Pub) NTC Contemp Pub Co.

— Star Trip. (Attention Span Stories Ser). (Illus.). 48p. (Orig.). 1978. pap. text 8.65 (*0-89061-149-1*, 585, Jamestwn Pub) NTC Contemp Pub Co.

— Survival Trip. (Attention Span Stories Ser). (Illus.). 48p. (Orig.). 1978. pap. text 8.65 (*0-89061-146-7*, 582, Jamestwn Pub) NTC Contemp Pub Co.

— Time Trip. (Attention Span Stories Ser.). (Illus.). 48p. (Orig.). 1978. pap. text 8.65 (*0-89061-145-9*, 581, Jamestwn Pub) NTC Contemp Pub Co.

— Uncle Sam & the Flag. LC 77-83633. (Illus.). 32p. (J). (gr. 2-3). 1978. lib. bdg. 9.95 (*0-87783-145-9*) Oddo.

— Uncle Sam & the Flag. deluxe ed. LC 77-83633. (Illus.). 32p. (J). (gr. 2-3). 1978. pap. 3.94 (*0-87783-148-3*) Oddo.

Mountain, Lee, et al. Jamestown Heritage Reader: Pocketful of Posiers. (Illus.). 80p. (J). (gr. 1). 1994. pap. 6.50 (*0-89061-949-2*, Jamestwn Pub) NTC Contemp Pub Co.

Mountain, Lee, jt. auth. see Crawley, Sharon J.

Mountain, Rick. The Eyes of Aspen. Carrington, W. G. & Cross, W. J., eds. LC 98-65114. 325p. 1998. pap. 14.95 (*1-888701-06-4*) Jarrett Pr.

Mountain State Association of Bed & Breakfasts Sta, contrib. by. Good Morning West Virginia! Travel Guide & Recipe Collection. LC 97-60129. (Illus.). 160p. (Orig.). 1997. pap. 12.95 (*1-883651-05-0*) Winters IN.

Mountain State Press Staff, ed. see Weaver, Samuel R.

Mountain Top Historical Society Staff. Kaaterskill: From the Catskill Mountain House to the Hudson River School. LC 98-122606. (Illus.). 120p. (Orig.). 1993. pap. 13.95 (*0-9628523-8-4*) Blk Dome Pr.

Mountaine, Trevor. Eden's Guide: (Evidence for & Control of Our Miraculous Power) LC 92-74816. 256p. (Orig.). 1993. pap. 15.00 (*1-882478-00-2*) Heyberg Media.

***Mountaineers Books Staff.** Mountaineering 2000. 1999. 11.99 (*0-89886-634-0*) Mountaineers.

Mountaineers Staff. First Aid Pamphlet. 36p. 1996. 1.10 (*0-89886-070-9*) Mountaineers.

— The Ten Essentials for Travel in the Outdoors. (Illus.). 36p. 1993. pap. 2.95 (*0-89886-374-0*) Mountaineers.

Mountaineers Staff, jt. auth. see Graydon, Don.

Mountaingrove, Jean & Menefee, Christine, eds. WomanSpirit Index: A Comprehensive Guide to a Decade of Women's Spirituality, 1974-1984. (Illus.). 120p. (Orig.). 1989. spiral bd. 13.95 (*0-9621035-1-9*) WomanSpirit.

Mountainwater, Shekhinah. Ariadne's Thread: A Workbook of Goddess Magic. (Illus.). 384p. 1991. pap. 16.95 (*0-89594-475-8*) Crossing Pr.

Mountbatten, Louis. South-East Asia, 1943-1945. 280p. 1987. 125.00 (*0-7855-2712-5*, Pub. by Himalayan Bks) St Mut.

Mountbatten, Marco L. An Introduction to Polo. 188p. (C). 1990. 100.00 (*0-85131-142-3*, Pub. by J A Allen) St Mut.

Mountcastle, John W. Flame On! U. S. Incendiary Weapons, 1918-1945. LC 98-53329. (Illus.). 220p. 1999. 29.95 (*1-57249-166-3*) White Mane Pub.

Mountcastle, Maxine. Poems "From Deep Within" LC 94-96059. 56p. 1994. lib. bdg. 5.00 (*0-9639403-0-9*) Maish & Mountcastle.

Mountcastle, V. B., jt. ed. see Deecke, L.

Mountcastle, Vernon B. Perceptual Neuroscience: The Cerebral Cortex. LC 98-15241. (Illus.). 448 p. 1998. 59.95 (*0-674-66188-5*) HUP.

Mountcastle, William D., jt. auth. see McGee, Robert S.

Mountcastle, William W. Science Fantasy Voices & Visions of Cosmic Religion. LC 96-10674. 172p. 1996. pap. text 26.00 (*0-7618-0297-5*); lib. bdg. 46.00 (*0-7618-0296-7*) U Pr of Amer.

Mounteney, S. N., jt. auth. see Naylor, D.

Mountford. The Art of Entertainment. 184p. 1991. 25.00 (*0-88188-889-3*, 08602480) H Leonard.

Mountford, A. J., jt. ed. see Mackay, Ronald.

Mountford, E. R. Barry Railway: Plans of Locomotives, Wagons & Coaches. 80p. (C). 1985. 39.00 (*0-85361-355-9*) St Mut.

— Cardiff Railway. 176p. (C). 1985. 65.00 (*0-85361-347-8*) St Mut.

— A Register of G. W. R. Absorbed Coaching Stock, 1922-1923. 80p. (C). 1985. 39.00 (*0-85361-235-8*) St Mut.

Mountford, Frances. A Commoners' Cottage: The Story of a Surrey Cottage. LC 97-207798. (Illus.). 160p. 1997. pap. 22.95 (*0-7509-0987-0*, Pub. by Sutton Pub Ltd) Intl Pubs Mktg.

— Heartbreak Farm: A Farmer & His Farm in Wartime. LC 97-178947. (Illus.). 160p. 1997. 31.95 (*0-7509-1390-8*, Pub. by Sutton Pub Ltd) Intl Pubs Mktg.

Mountford, Helen, jt. auth. see Keppler, Jan Horst.

Mountford, J. F. Bradley's Arnold Latin Prose Composition. (College Classical Ser.). (gr. 11-12). 1992. reprint ed. 32.50 (*0-89241-344-1*); reprint ed. pap. text 20.00 (*0-89241-119-8*) Caratzas.

Mountford, J. F., et al, eds. Glossaria Latina, Bd. I: Glossarium Ansileubi Sive Librum Glossarum. xxi, 1990p. 1965. reprint ed. write for info. (*0-318-71131-1*) G Olms Pubs.

— Glossaria Latina, Bd. II: Arma, Abavus Philoxenus. xxi, 1990p. 1965. reprint ed. write for info. (*0-318-71132-X*) G Olms Pubs.

— Glossaria Latina, Bd. III: Abstrusa, Abolita. xxi, 1990p. 1965. reprint ed. write for info. (*0-318-71133-8*) G Olms Pubs.

— Glossaria Latina, Bd. V: (Abba, AA) xxi, 1990p. 1965. reprint ed. write for info. (*0-318-71135-4*) G Olms Pubs.

— Glossaria Latina, 5 vols., Set. xxi, 1990p. 1965. reprint ed. write for info. (*0-318-71130-3*) G Olms Pubs.

Mountford, James F. & Schultz, Joseph T. Index Rerum et Nominum in Scholiis Servii et Aelii Donati Tractatorum. 205p. 1963. reprint ed. write for info. (*0-318-71180-X*) G Olms Pubs.

Mountford, Kathi & Horsted, Kim. Law. 170p. 1990. 160.00 (*0-900239-48-4*, Pub. by Chartered Bank) St Mut.

Mountfort, Douglas O. & Orpin, Colin G., eds. Anaerobic Fungi: Biology, Ecology & Function. (Mycology Ser.: Vol. 12). (Illus.). 304p. 1994. text 150.00 (*0-8247-8948-2*) Dekker.

Mountfort, G. Wild India: The Wild Life & Scenery of India & Nepal. (C). 1991. 105.00 (*0-7855-0222-X*, Pub. by Ratna Pustak Bhandar) St Mut.

Mountfort, Guy. Wild India: The Wildlife & Scenery of India & Nepal. (Illus.). 208p. 1991. 39.95 (*0-262-13276-1*) MIT Pr.

Mountfort, Guy, jt. auth. see Peterson.

Mountfort, William. The Life & Death of Doctor Faustus, Made into a Farce. LC 92-22711. (Augustan Reprints Ser.: No. 157). 1972. reprint ed. 14.50 (*0-404-70157-4*, PR3605) AMS Pr.

— Plays of William Mountfort. LC 77-21660. 280p. 1977. 50.00 (*0-8201-1292-5*) Schol Facsimiles.

***Mountin, Thomas E.** The Last Mogul. 2001. text 27.50 (*0-8050-6186-X*) St Martin.

— The Last Mogul. 2002. text 15.95 (*0-8050-6187-8*) St Martin.

***Mountjoy, Jesse T., et al.** Non-Profit Corporations in Kentucky. 3rd ed. 188p. 1999. pap. 43.00 (*1-58757-023-8*, BM030) Univ of KY.

Mountjoy, Joseph B. & Brockington, Donald L., eds. El Auge y la Caida del Clasico en el Mexico Central. 288p. 1987. pap. 7.00 (*968-36-0427-7*, UN017) UPLAAP.

Mountjoy, P. A. Mycenaean Athens. (Studies in Mediterranean Archaeology & Literature: No. 127). (Illus.). 140p. 1995. pap. 45.00 (*91-7081-073-7*, Pub. by P Astroms) Coronet Bks.

— Mycenaean Decorated Pottery: A Guide to Identification. (Studies in Mediterranean Archaeology: Vol. LXXIII). (Illus.). 241p. (Orig.). 1986. pap. 125.00 (*91-86098-32-2*, Pub. by P Astroms) Coronet Bks.

Mountjoy, Penelope. Mycenaean Pottery: An Introduction. (Illus.). 215p. 1993. pap. 32.00 (*0-947816-36-4*, Pub. by Oxford Univ Comm Arch) David Brown.

Mountjoy-Pepka, Vincent. Democracy for Americans: A Real Plan to Reinvent the Government. LC 94-75124. 256p. (Orig.). 1994. pap. 12.00 (*0-9639883-8-7*) Kick Pr.

Mountjoy, Richard D. 100 Years of Bell Telephone. LC 95-31133. (Illus.). 176p. (Orig.). 1995. pap. 29.95 (*0-88740-872-9*) Schiffer.

Mountmorres. History of the Principal Transactions of the Irish Parliament from 1634-1666. LC 78-174186. 1978. reprint ed. 125.00 (*0-7165-2010-9*) W S Hein.

Mountney, G. J. Poultry Egg & Meat Production. (Illus.). 300p. (C). 1987. text 54.95 (*0-442-27497-1*) Chapman & Hall.

Mountney, George J., pref. Poultry Products Technology. (Illus.). 368p. 1989. reprint ed. pap. 39.95 (*1-56022-001-5*) Haworth Jrnl Co-Edits.

Mountney, George J. & Gould, Wilbur A. Practical Food Microbiology & Technology. 3rd ed. 364p. (C). 1992. reprint ed. lib. bdg. 74.50 (*0-89464-673-7*) Krieger.

Mountney, George J. & Parkhurst, Carmen R., eds. Poultry Products Technology. 3rd ed. LC 94-48542. (Illus.). 446p. (C). 1995. 129.95 (*1-56022-856-3*, TS1986) Haworth Jrnl Co-Edits.

Mountrose, Jane, jt. auth. see Mountrose, Phillip.

Mountrose, Phillip. Getting Thru to Kids: Problem Solving with Children Ages 6 to 18. LC 96-9538. (Getting Thru Ser.: No. 1). (Illus.). 140p. (Orig.). 1997. pap. 11.95 (*0-9653787-7-2*) Holstc Communs.

— Tips & Tools for Getting Thru to Kids: Innovative Approaches for Preschoolers to Teens. LC 98-93530. (Getting Thru Ser.: Vol. 2). (Illus.). 228p. 1999. pap. 12.95 (*0-9653787-4-8*) Holstc Communs.

***Mountrose, Phillip & Mountrose, Jane.** Getting Thru to Your Emotions with EFT: Tap into Your Hidden Potential with the Emotional Freedom Techniques. LC 99-95415. (Getting Thru Ser.: No. 3). (Illus.). 275p. 1999. pap. 13.95 (*0-9653787-6-4*) Holstc Communs.

— Getting Thru to Your Soul: The Four Keys to Living Your Divine Purpose. LC 00-190043. (Getting Thru Ser.: Vol. 4). (Illus.). 300p. 2000. pap. 14.95 (*0-9653787-0-5*, Pub. by Holstc Communs) Midpt Trade.

Mounts, Harry C., Jr., jt. auth. see Bateman, Ronald S.

Mounts, Jackqueline J. Helping Our Young People Connect with God. 60p. 1997. pap. 6.00 (*1-57502-583-3*, PO1674) Morris Pubng.

Mounts, Willard. The Pioneer & the Prairie Lawyer: Boone & Lincoln Family Historical & Biographical Heritage. Manuscripts International Staff, ed. LC 91-72847. (Illus.). 224p. (Orig.). 1992. pap. 14.95 (*0-9630038-0-1*) Ginwill Pub.

— The Pioneer & the Prairie Lawyer: Historical & Biographical - Boone & Lincoln Family Heritage. LC 91-72847. (Illus.). 224p. 1992. reprint ed. pap. 14.95 (*0-9630038-1-X*) Ginwill Pub.

— The Rugged Southern Appalachia. Brandhorst, Beatrice, ed. LC 96-80009. (Illus.). 192p. (Orig.). 1997. pap., per. 14.95 (*0-9630038-2-8*) Ginwill Pub.

Mountziaris, T. J., et al, eds. Gas-Phase Surface Chemistry in Electronic Materials Processing Vol. 334: Materials Research Society Symposium Proceedings. LC 94-9632. 553p. 1994. text 30.00 (*1-55899-233-2*) Materials Res.

Mour, Stanley I. American Jazz Musicians. LC 97-27173. (Collective Biographies Ser.). (Illus.). 128p. (YA). (gr. 6 up). 1998. lib. bdg. 20.95 (*0-7660-1027-9*) Enslow Pubs.

***Moura, Ann.** Green Witchcraft III: The Manual. (Illus.). 264p. 2000. pap. 12.95 (*1-56718-688-2*) Llewellyn Pubns.

Moura, Ann. Green Witchcraft II: Balancing Light & Shadows. (Illus.). 288p. 1999. pap. 12.95 (*1-56718-689-0*, K689) Llewellyn Pubns.

***Moura, Ann.** Origins of Modern Witchcraft: The Evolution of a World Religion. 2000. pap. 14.95 (*1-56718-648-3*) Llewellyn Pubns.

Moura Castro, Claudio De, see De Moura Castro, Claudio, ed.

Moura Castro, Claudio De, see Espinola, Viola & De Moura Castro, Claudio, eds.

Moura, Eduardo C. How to Determine Sample Size & Estimate Failure Rate in Life Testing. (Basic "How to" Ser.: Vol. 15). (Illus.). 98p. 1991. pap. 26.00 (*0-87389-112-0*, T3515) ASQ Qual Pr.

Moura, Jose M. & Lourtie, Isabel M., eds. Acoustic Signal Processing for Ocean Exploration: Proceedings of the NATO Advanced Study Institute on Acoustic Signal Processing for Ocean Exploration, Funchal, Madeira, Portugal, July 26-August 7, 1992. LC 92-43800. (NATO Advanced Study Institutes Series C, Mathematical & Physical Sciences: No. 388). 1993. text 385.00 (*0-7923-2133-2*) Kluwer Academic.

Moura, Jose M., jt. ed. see Bucy, Richard S.

Moura, Lincoln. Computer Graphics & Image Processing in Medicine. 1993. pap. text 120.00 (*2-88124-892-6*) Gordon & Breach.

M

An Asterisk (*) at the beginning of an entry indicates that the title is appearing for the first time.

Mourad. Nursing Care of Adults with Orthopaedic Conditions. 2nd ed. LC 87-279. 576p. 1989. text 41.95 (*0-8273-4315-9*) Delmar.
Mourad, Leona A. American Nursing Review for NCLEX-PN. 3rd ed. LC 97-25002. 560p. 1997. 27.95 incl. disk (*0-87434-924-9*) Springhouse Corp.
— Orthopaedic Nursing. LC 94-16955. (Plans of Care for Specialty Practice Ser.). 360p. (C). 1994. pap. 32.75 (*0-8273-5944-6*) Delmar.
Mourad, Roger P., Jr. Postmodern Philosophical Critique & the Pursuit of Knowledge in Higher Education. LC 97-217. (Critical Studies in Education & Culture Ser.). 136p. 1997. 52.95 (*0-89789-488-X*, Bergin & Garvey); pap. 18.95 (*0-89789-554-1*, Bergin & Garvey) Greenwood.
Mourad, Samiha & Zorian, Yervant. Principles of Testing Electronic Circuits. LC 99-52179. 400p. 2000. 79.95 (*0-471-31931-7*) Wiley.
Mourad, Samiha, jt. auth. see Chan, Pak K.
Mouradian, George. Armenian InfoText. LC 95-94023. (Illus.). 342p. (Orig.). 1995. pap. 15.00 (*0-9634509-2-1*) Bookshelf Pubs.
***Mouradian, George.** Handbook of QS-9000 Tools & Equipment Certification. LC 99-89646. 252p. 2000. 49.00 (*0-7680-0527-2*, R-265) Soc Auto Engineers.
***Mouradian, M. Maral, ed.** Parkinson's Disease. 350p. 2000. 99.50 (*0-89603-761-4*) Humana.
Mouradian, Ted. Best in Life: A Guide to Managing Your Relationships with Others in Your Workplace & Especially with Yourself. LC . (Your Mapp Ser.: Vol. 1). (Illus.). 168p. 1997. reprint ed. pap. 14.00 (*0-921411-55-3*) Genl Dist Srvs.
— JC & Me. (Your Mapp Ser.). 2000. 12.00 (*1-896647-35-9*) Genl Dist Srvs.
Mourant, A. E. Blood Relations: Blood Groups & Anthropology. (Illus.). 154p. 1985. pap. 16.95 (*0-19-857631-5*) OUP.
Mourant, Arthur E., et al. The Distribution of the Human Blood Groups, & Other Polymorphisms. 2nd ed. LC 76-364647. (Oxford Monographs on Medical Genetics). 1071p. reprint ed. pap. 200.00 (*0-608-18697-X*, 202706700053) Bks Demand.
Mourant, John A., jt. auth. see Harshbarger, Luther H.
Mourant, John A., tr. see Augustine, Saint.
Mourao, A. M., et al, eds. New Worlds in Astroparticle Physics: Proceedings of the International Workshop Faro, Portugal 8-10 September, 1996. LC 98-215439. 430p. 1998. 94.00 (*981-02-3389-2*) World Scientific Pub.
***Mourao, Ana M., et al, eds.** New Worlds in Astroparticle Physics: Proceedings of the Second International Workshop. 500p. 1999. 108.00 (*981-02-4087-2*) World Scientific Pub.
Mouras, Melanie, ed. see Keyes, Frank E., Jr.
Mouravieff, A. N. A History of the Church of Russia. Blackmore, R. W., tr. from RUS. 448p. (C). 1988. reprint ed. 16.95 (*1-878997-09-2*) St Tikhons Pr.
Mouravieff, B., tr. & intro. see Mouravieff, Boris & D'Oncieu, Manek.
Mouravieff, Boris. Gnosis, Vol. I, Exoteric Cycle: Study & Commentaries on the Esoteric Tradition of Eastern Orthodoxy. Amis, Robin & Wissa, S. A., trs. from FRE. (Illus.). 106p. (Orig.). (C). 1990. pap. text 29.95 (*1-872292-10-0*) Praxis Inst.
— Gnosis, Vol. II, Mesoteric Cycle: Study & Commentaries on the Esoteric Tradition of Eastern Orthodoxy. Amis, Robin, ed. & tr. by. from FRE. D'Oncley, Manek, tr. from FRE. (Illus.). 106p. (Orig.). (C). 1992. pap. text 29.95 (*1-872292-11-9*) Praxis Inst.
Mouravieff, Boris & D'Oncieu, Manek. Gnosis, Vol. III: Esoteric Cycle. Amis, Robin, ed. Mouravieff, B., tr. & intro. by. Amis, R., intro. (Studies & Commentary on the Esoteric Tradition of Eastern Orthodoxy: Vol. 3). (Illus.). 106p. (Orig.) (C). 1993. pap. text 29.95 (*1-872292-12-7*) Praxis Inst.
Mourby, Adrian. Whatever Happened To . . . ? The Ultimate Sequels Book. 1998. 10.95 (*0-285-63401-1*, Pub. by Souvenir Pr Ltd) IPG Chicago.
Mourdoukoutas, Panos. Collective Entrepreneurship in a Globalizing Economy. LC 99-10408. 168p. 1999. 55.00 (*1-56720-289-6*, Quorum Bks) Greenwood.
— The Experiment. 188p. (Orig.). 1995. pap. 11.99 (*0-87411-693-7*) Copley Pub.
— The Global Corporation: The Decolonization of American Business. LC 98-24564. 160p. 1999. 55.00 (*1-56720-241-1*, Quorum Bks) Greenwood.
— How to Compete in the Japanese Market: Adapt, Develop, Promote. 152p. (Orig.). (C). 1995. pap. text 26.95 (*0-87411-771-2*) Copley Pub.
— Japan's Turn: The Interchange in Economic Leadership. LC 92-42461. 244p. (C). 1993. 55.00 (*0-8191-9036-5*); pap. text 27.50 (*0-8191-9298-8*) U Pr of Amer.
Mourdoukoutas, Panos & Papayani, John. Beating the Market: How to Win the Wall Street Game. Orig. Title: When to Buy Stocks, Bonds, & Gold. 163p. (Orig.). 1997. pap. 25.00 (*0-87411-840-9*) Copley Pub.
Mourdoukoutas, Panos, jt. see Arayama, Yuko.
Mourdoukoutas, Panos, jt. auth. see Arayama, Yuko.
Moure, Erin. Domestic Fuel. 108p. (Orig.). 1985. pap. 8.95 (*0-88784-143-0*, Pub. by Hse of Anansi Pr) Genl Dist Srvs.
***Moure, Erin.** A Frame of the Book. 2000. pap. 12.95 (*1-55713-402-2*) Sun & Moon CA.
Moure, Erin. The Green Word: Selected Poems. 92p. (C). 1994. pap. (*0-19-541077-7*) OUP.
— Search Procedures. 160p. (Orig.). 1996. pap. 12.95 (*0-88784-575-4*, Pub. by Hse of Anansi Pr) Genl Dist Srvs.
— Sheepish Beauty, Civilian Love. 136p. (Orig.). 1992. pap. 9.95 (*1-55065-028-9*, Pub. by Vehicule Pr) Genl Dist Srvs.
— Wanted Alive. 111p. (Orig.). 1983. pap. 8.95 (*0-88784-097-3*, Pub. by Hse of Anansi Pr) Genl Dist Srvs.
Moure, Gloria. Marcel Duchamp. LC 88-42716. (Twentieth Century Artists Ser.). (Illus.). 128p. 1988. 27.50 (*0-8478-0978-1*, Pub. by Rizzoli Intl) St Martin.
Moure, Kenneth. Managing the Franc Poincare, 1928-1936: Economic Understanding & Political Constraint in French Monetary Policy, 1928-1936. (Studies in Monetary & Financial History). 318p. (C). 1991. text 89.95 (*0-521-39458-9*) Cambridge U Pr.
Moure, M. Petit Moure: Dictionnaire de L'Histoire. (FRE.). 1998. 125.00 (*0-320-00280-2*) Fr & Eur.
***Moure, Nancy.** The World of Zarh Pritchard: The Naturalist Poet. Weir, Christine, ed. (Illus.). 64p. 1999. pap. text 20.00 (*1-886394-02-4*) W A Karges.
Moure, Nancy D. California Art: 450 Years of Painting & Other Media. LC 98-233186. (Illus.). 560p. 1998. 95.00 (*0-9614622-4-8*); pap. text 85.00 (*0-9614622-5-6*) Dustin Pubns.
— Los Angeles Painters of the 1920s. (Illus.). 40p. 1972. 2.00 (*0-915478-29-3*) Montgomery Gallery.
— Partners in Illusion: Albert Binford & William J. McCloskey. Bryant, Jacqueline, ed. 120p. (C). 1996. pap. 24.95 (*0-9633959-4-7*) Bowers Mus.
— Publications in Southern California Art 1, 2, & 3, 3 vols. in 1. rev. ed. Incl. Vol. 1. Index to the California Watercolor Society Exhibitions 1921-1954. 1984. (*0-9614622-1-3*); Vol. 2. Index to Artists Clubs & Exhibitions in Los Angeles Before 1930. 1984. (*0-9614622-2-1*); Vol. 3. Dictionary of Art & Artists in Southern California Before 1930. 1984. (*0-9614622-3-X*); 525p. 1984. 80.00 (*0-9614622-0-5*) Dustin Pubns.
— William L. Sonntag, Artist of the Ideal. (Illus.). 157p. 1980. 65.00 (*0-318-01276-6*) Goldfld Pub.
— William Louis Sonntag: Artist of the Ideal. (Illus.). 157p. 1980. text 65.00 (*0-686-35887-2*) Goldfld Pub.
— William Louis Sonntag: Artist of the Ideal. deluxe limited ed. (Illus.). 157p. 1980. 125.00 (*0-686-37195-X*) Goldfld Pub.
Moure, Nancy D. & Goldfield, Edward. Edgar Payne 1882-1947. (Illus.). 82p. 1987. 65.00 (*0-9617802-0-7*) Goldfld Pub.
Moure, Nancy D., et al. Publications in Southern California Art 4, 5, 6. 546p. 1999. pap. write for info. (*0-9614622-6-4*) Dustin Pubns.
Moureau, Magdeleine. Dictionary of Drilling & Boreholes: English-French, French-English. (ENG & FRE.). 436p. 1990. 89.95 (*0-8288-3188-2*, 2710805928); 175.00 (*0-7859-7936-0*, 2710805928) Fr & Eur.
— Dictionary of Petroleum Technology: English-French - French-English. (ENG & FRE.). 1991. lib. bdg. 325.00 (*0-8288-3189-0*) Fr & Eur.
Moureau, Magdeleine & Brace, Gerald. Comprehensive Dictionary of Petroleum Science & Technology: English-French, French-English. (ENG & FRE.). 1040p. 1993. 350.00 (*0-7859-7134-3*, 2710806487) Fr & Eur.
— Dictionary of Drilling & Boreholes: English-French, French-English. (ENG & FRE.). 436p. 1990. 149.50 (*2-7108-0592-8*) IBD Ltd.
— Dictionary of Petroleum Technology: English-French, French-English. (ENG & FRE.). 988p. 1979. 650.00 (*2-7108-0361-5*, Pub. by Edits Technip) Enfield Pubs NH.
Moureau, Magdeleine & Rouge, Janine. Dictionnaire Technique des Termes Utilises dans l'Industrie du Petrole, Anglais-Francais, Francais-Anglais.Tr. of English-French, French-English Dictionary of the Petroleum Industry. (ENG & FRE.). 914p. 1977. 325.00 (*0-8288-5394-0*, M6419) Fr & Eur.
Moureau, P. Dictionary Gascon/French/Gascon. (FRE.). 162p. 1997. 49.95 (*0-320-00481-3*) Fr & Eur.
Mourelatos, Alexander P., ed. The Pre-Socratics: A Collection of Critical Essays. 580p. 1993. pap. text 22.95 (*0-691-02088-4*, Pub. by Princeton U Pr) Cal Prin Full Svc.
Mourell, M. Butterworths Student Companions: Real Property. 1992. pap. 17.00 (*0-409-30396-8*, Austral, MICHIE) LEXIS Pub.
Mourelle, Don F. The Voyage of the Sonora in 1775. 150p. 1988. 32.50 (*0-87770-402-3*) Ye Galleon.
Mouret, Francois J., ed. see Montaigne, Michel de.
Mouret, Jean-Noel. Knives of the World. 1994. 17.98 (*1-55521-993-4*) Bk Sales Inc.
— Rifles of the World. 144p. 1994. 17.98 (*1-55521-997-7*) Bk Sales Inc.
Mourey, Gabriel, et al. Art Nouveau Jewelry & Fans. (Illus.). 149p. 1998. reprint ed. pap. 9.95 (*0-486-22961-0*) Dover.
Mouri, Allahyar. The International Law of Expropriation As Reflected in the Work of the Iran-U. S. Claims Tribunal. LC 93-44433. (Developments in International Law Ser.: No. 17). 612p. (C). 1994. lib. bdg. 221.00 (*0-7923-2654-7*) Kluwer Academic.
Mourides, Jo Ann, jt. auth. see Harvey, John F.
Mourik, Aad Van, see Molle, Willem & Van Mourik, Aad.
Mourik, J. A. Van, see Van Mourik, J. A., ed.
Mouriquand, Jacqueline, et al. Diagnosis of Non-Palpable Breast Lesions: Ultrasonographical Controlled Fine Needle Aspiration. LC 93-13055. (Illus.). x, 72p. 1993. 75.00 (*3-8055-5747-7*) S Karger.
Mouritsen, Jan, jt. ed. see Munro, Rolland.
Mouritsen, Laurel. For Love & Zion. LC 96-49277. 1997. pap. 11.95 (*1-57734-066-3*, 01112732) Covenant Comms.
— The Passageway. 1996. pap. 9.95 (*1-55503-688-0*, 01111663) Covenant Comms.
Mouritsen, Ole G. Computer Studies of Phase Transitions & Critical Phenomena. (Computational Physics Ser.). (Illus.). 210p. 1984. 75.95 (*0-387-13397-6*) Spr-Verlag.
Mouritsen, Ole G., jt. auth. see Mosekilde, Erik.
Mouritzen, Hans. External Danger & Democracy: Old Nordic Lessons & New European Challenges. LC 96-44641. (Illus.). 173p. 1996. 72.95 (*1-85521-885-2*, Pub. by Dartmth Pub) Ashgate Pub Co.
— Finlandization: Towards a General Theory of Adaptive Politics. 463p. 1988. text 101.95 (*0-566-05656-9*, Pub. by Dartmth Pub) Ashgate Pub Co.
— The International Civil Service: A Study of Bureaucracy: International Organizations. 192p. 1990. text 77.95 (*1-85521-163-7*, Pub. by Dartmth Pub) Ashgate Pub Co.
Mouritzen, Hans, ed. Bordering Russia: Theory & Prospects for Europe's Baltic Rim. LC 97-39119. (Illus.). 326p. 1998. text 72.95 (*1-85521-959-X*, Pub. by Ashgate Pub) Ashgate Pub Co.
Mouritzen, Hans, et al. European Integration & National Adaptations: A Theoretical Inquiry. LC 95-48995. (Illus.). 337p. (C). 1996. lib. bdg. 115.00 (*1-56072-291-6*) Nova Sci Pubs.
Mouritzen, Poul E., ed. Managing Cities in Austerity: Urban Fiscal Stress in Ten Western Countries. (Urban Innovation Ser.: Vol. 2). 256p. 1992. 59.95 (*0-8039-8632-7*) Sage.
Mourlot, Fernand, et al. Miro Litografo, 4 vols., Set. (SPA., Illus.). 926p. 1981. 1900.00 (*1-55660-227-8*) A Wofsy Fine Arts.
***Mourmouras, I. A. & Arghyrou, M. G.** Monetary Policy at the European Periphery: Greek Experience & Lessons for EU Candidates. Addison, J. T. et al, eds. (European & Transatlantic Studies). xvi, 218p. 2000. (*3-540-66932-9*) Spr-Verlag.
Mourning Dove. Coyote Stories. Guie, Heister D., ed. & illus. by. LC 76-43793. reprint ed. 39.50 (*0-404-15648-7*) AMS Pr.
Mourning Dove. Coyote Stories. Guie, Heister D., ed. LC 89-28956. (Illus.). xviii, 246p. 1990. reprint ed. pap. text 9.95 (*0-8032-8169-2*, Bison Books) U of Nebr Pr.
Mourning Dove. Mourning Dove: A Salishan Autobiography. Miller, Jay, ed. LC 89-14780. (American Indian Lives Ser.). (Illus.). xl, 267p. 1990. text 45.00 (*0-8032-3119-9*) U of Nebr Pr.
Mourning Dove Staff, intro. Cogewea, the Half Blood. LC 80-29687. (Illus.). 302p. 1981. pap. 11.95 (*0-8032-8110-2*, Bison Books) U of Nebr Pr.
***Mouro, Gladys.** An American Nurse Amidst Chaos, 1975-1998. 217p. 2000. text 24.95 (*0-8156-6099-5*) Syracuse U Pr.
Mourot, Jean, jt. auth. see De Chateaubriand, Rene.
Mourou, G. A., et al, eds. Picosescond Electronics & Optoelectronics. (Electrophysics Ser.: Vol. 21). (Illus.). x, 258p. 1988. text 59.40 (*0-387-15884-7*) Spr-Verlag.
Mouroulis, Pantazis. Visual Instrumentation Handbook: Principles of Optical Design. LC 98-49404. (Illus.). 430p. 1999. 89.95 (*0-07-043561-8*) McGraw.
Mouroulis, Pantazis & MacDonald, John. Geometrical Optics & Optical Design. (Oxford Series in Optical & Imaging Sciences). (Illus.). 368p. (C). 1996. text 88.00 (*0-19-508931-6*) OUP.
Mourrain, Jacques, tr. see Baudrillard, Jean.
Mourre, Michel. Dictionnaire Encyclopedique d'Histoire, 5 vols. (FRE.). 5884p. 1996. pap. 350.00 (*0-7859-9495-5*) Fr & Eur.
— Dictionnaire Encyclopedique d'Histoire: Encyclopedic Dictionary of History, 8 vols., Set. (FRE.). 5480p. 1978. 595.00 (*0-8288-5194-8*, M6420) Fr & Eur.
— Le Petit Mourre: Dictionnaire de l'Histoire. (FRE.). 1990. lib. bdg. 125.00 (*0-7859-3953-9*) Fr & Eur.
— Universal Dictionary of History: Dictionnaire d'Histoire Universelle. (FRE.). 1981. 125.00 (*0-8288-1489-9*, F700) Fr & Eur.
Moursand, David G. & Duris, Charles S. Elementary Theory & Application of Numerical Analysis. 308p. 1988. pap. 9.95 (*0-486-65754-X*) Dover.
***Moursund, Beth.** Magic: The Gathering - Official Encyclopedia; The Complete Card Guide, 1. (Illus.). 224p. 2000. pap. 23.95 (*1-56025-214-6*, Thunders Mouth) Avalon NY.
— Magic: The Gathering - Official Encyclopedia; The Complete Card Guide, 2. (Illus.). 144p. 2000. pap. 23.95 (*1-56025-221-9*, Thunders Mouth) Avalon NY.
— Magic Vol. 4: The Gathering - Official Encyclopedia. (Illus.). 192p. 1999. pap. 23.95 (*1-56025-211-1*, Thunders Mouth) Avalon NY.
Moursund, Beth. Magic: The Gathering: The Official Guide to Portal - Cards, Strategies & Techniques. LC 98-156057. (Illus.). 64p. 1997. pap. text 10.95 (*1-56025-152-2*, Thunders Mouth) Avalon NY.
— Magic: The Gathering: The Official Guide to Tempest - Cards, Strategies & Techniques. (Illus.). 124p. 1998. pap. 16.95 (*1-56025-157-3*, Thunders Mouth) Avalon NY.
— Magic: The Gathering: The Official Strategy Guide - The Color Illustrated Guide to Winning Play. (Illus.). 126p. (Orig.). 1997. pap. 16.95 (*1-56025-149-2*, Thunders Mouth) Avalon NY.
— Magic: The Gathering Vol. 3: The Official Encyclopedia. (Magic Ser.: Vol. 3). (Illus.). 128p. 1998. pap. 22.95 (*1-56025-189-1*, Thunders Mouth) Avalon NY.
— The Official Magic: The Gathering Strategies & Secrets. 1997. pap. 19.99 (*0-614-28536-4*, Strategies & Secrets) Sybex.
Moursund, Beth & Justice, Mark. Magic: The Gathering: The Official Advanced Strategy Guide. (Magic Ser.). (Illus.). 128p. 1998. pap. 17.95 (*1-56025-199-9*, Thunders Mouth) Avalon NY.
Moursund, David, jt. auth. see Yoder, Sharon.
***Moursund, David G.** Project-Based Learning Using Information Technology. LC 99-236301. (Illus.). 160p. 1998. spiral bd. 24.95 (*1-56484-145-6*) Intl Society Tech Educ.
Moursund, Janet. The Process of Counseling & Therapy. 3rd ed. LC 92-12024. 240p. (C). 1992. pap. 33.40 (*0-13-720657-7*) P-H.
***Moursund, Janet, et al.** Beyond Empathy: A Therapy of Contact-in-Relationship. LC 99-20272. 380p. 1999. 44.95 (*0-87630-963-5*) Brunner-Mazel.
Moursund, Janet, jt. auth. see Erskine, Richard.
Moursund, Janet, jt. auth. see Kranzler, Gerald.
Moursund, Janet P., jt. auth. see Erskine, Richard G.
Mousa, Issam S. The Arab Image in the U. S. Press, Vol. 1. LC 83-49021. (American University Studies: Communications: Ser. XV). 201p. (Orig.). 1984. pap. text 19.00 (*0-8204-0069-6*) P Lang Pubng.
Mousa, S. A., ed. Role in Health & Diseases. (Biotechnology Intelligence Unit Ser.). (Illus.). 248p. 1998. 179.00 (*3-540-64714-7*) Spr-Verlag.
***Mousa, Shaker A.** Angiogenesis Inhibitors & Stimulators: Potential Therapeutic Implications. (Medical Intelligence Unit Ser.). 194p. 1999. (*1-57059-613-1*) Landes Bioscience.
Mousa, Shaker A. Cell Adhesion Molecules & Matrix Proteins: Role in Health & Diseases. LC 98-7739. (Biotechnology Intelligence Unit Ser.). 1998. write for info. (*1-57059-541-0*) Landes Bioscience.
Mousalimas, S. A. The Transition from Shamanism to Russian Orthodoxy in Alaska. LC 94-36777. 272p. (C). 1995. 49.95 (*1-57181-006-4*) Berghahn Bks.
Mousalimas, S. A., ed. Arctic Ecology & Identity. (Istor Bks.: Vol. 4). (Illus.). 176p. 1997. write for info. (*963-05-6629-X*, Pub. by Akade Kiado) Intl Spec Bk.
Mousavi. Hazaras of Afghanistan. LC 97-2704. 288p. 1997. text 59.95 (*0-312-17386-5*) St Martin.
Mousavizadeh, Nader, ed. The Black Book of Bosnia: The Consequences of Appeasement. 240p. 1995. pap. 12.50 (*0-465-09835-5*, Pub. by Basic) HarpC.
Mouse, Clement. A Visit from Saint Nicholas: And Santa Mouse, Too! 32p. (J). 1998. reprint ed. pap. 10.01 (*0-7868-1176-5*) Hyprn Child.
Mouse, Stanley. Freehand: The Art of Stanley Mouse. Williams, Roger, ed. LC 92-32048. (Illus.). 128p. (Orig.). 1993. 39.95 (*0-943389-12-7*); pap. 24.95 (*0-943389-11-9*) Snow Lion-SLG Bks.
Mouse, Timothy D., tr. see Tudor, Tasha.
Mouse Works Staff. Adventure Slip. (J). 1997. 31.92 (*1-57082-709-5*, Pub. by Mouse Works) Little.
— Aladdin. (J). 1995. 7.98 (*1-57082-030-9*, Pub. by Mouse Works) Time Warner.
— Aladdin - Peter Pan, 2. 75th anniversary ed. 1998. 9.99 (*0-7364-0086-9*) Mouse Works.
***Mouse Works Staff.** Ariel's Cake. LC 99-220647. 20p. (J). (ps-1). 1998. 4.98 (*1-57082-821-0*, Pub. by Mouse Works) Time Warner.
Mouse Works Staff. Ballerina Minnie. LC 99-161658. 12p. (J). 1998. 4.99 (*1-57082-893-8*, Pub. by Mouse Works) Time Warner.
— Bambi. Baker, Liza, ed. (Disney's Read-Aloud Storybooks Ser.). (Illus.). 64p. (ps-2). 1999. 6.99 (*0-7364-0121-0*, Pub. by Mouse Works) Time Warner.
— Barnyard Tales. LC 97-215279. 5p. (J). 1997. 7.98 (*1-57082-670-6*, Pub. by Mouse Works) Time Warner.
— Beauty & the Beast. (SPA.). 64p. 1999. write for info. (*0-7364-0127-X*, Pub. by Mouse Works) Little.
— Beauty & the Beast. 64p. (J). 1999. 5.99 (*0-7364-0125-3*, Pub. by Mouse Works) Time Warner.
Mouse Works Staff. Beauty & the Beast: The Enchanted Christmas. LC 97-216099. 24p. (J). 1997. 6.98 (*1-57082-729-X*, Pub. by Mouse Works) Time Warner.
Mouse Works Staff. Beauty & the Beast: The Hidden Halo. LC 98-100413. (Illus.). 18p. (J). 1997. 3.98 (*1-57082-673-0*, Pub. by Mouse Works) Time Warner.
— Beauty & the Beast & The Aristocats, 2 vols. 75th anniversary ed. 1998. 9.99 (*0-7364-0092-3*) Mouse Works.
— Birthday Present for Piglet. 24p. (J). 1996. 9.98 (*1-57082-354-5*, Pub. by Mouse Works) Time Warner.
Mouse Works Staff. Blackberry Surprise. 10p. (J). (ps-k). 1994. write for info. (*1-57082-967-5*) Mouse Works.
Mouse Works Staff. Blue Ribon Day. 24p. (J). 1998. 7.98 (*1-57082-878-4*, Pub. by Mouse Works) Time Warner.
— Boo to You, Winnie the Pooh! LC 98-197720. (Pooh Ser.). 5p. (J). 1998. 4.99 (*1-57082-752-4*, Pub. by Mouse Works) Time Warner.
— Bravest Blossom. 5p. (J). 1998. 5.98 (*1-57082-675-7*, Pub. by Mouse Works) Time Warner.
— Bug's Life. LC 99-161343. (Illus.). 96p. (J). 1998. 7.99 (*1-57082-979-9*, Pub. by Mouse Works) Time Warner.
— Christmas Stocking. LC 97-222168. 5p. (J). 1997. 5.98 (*1-57082-717-6*, Pub. by Mouse Works) Time Warner.
— Christmas Stocking. (Standard Characters Ser.). (J). 1998. 2.98 (*1-57082-817-2*, Pub. by Mouse Works) Little.
— Christmas Tree. (Pooh Ser.). 8p. (J). 1998. 2.99 (*1-57082-818-0*, Pub. by Mouse Works) Time Warner.
— Christmas Wreath. (Pooh Ser.). (J). 1998. 2.98 (*1-57082-819-9*) Mouse Works.
Mouse Works Staff. Cinderella: Meet the Characters. LC 96-127094. (Illus.). 20p. (J). 1995. 5.98 (*1-57082-290-5*) Mouse Works.
Mouse Works Staff. Colorful Picnic. LC 98-170286. 16p. (J). 1998. 3.98 (*1-57082-748-6*, Pub. by Mouse Works) Time Warner.
— Cooking with Pooh: Yummy Tummy Cookie Cutter Treats, with Four Cookie Cutters. (Illus.). 24p. (J). 1995. 9.98 (*1-57082-261-1*, Pub. by Mouse Works) Time Warner.
— Daring Adventures. (J). 1997. 19.98 (*1-57082-857-1*) Mouse Works.
***Mouse Works Staff.** Dinosaur. (Disney's Read-Aloud Storybooks Ser.). (SPA.). 64p. (J). (gr. k-2). 2000. 6.99 (*0-7364-1001-5*, Pub. by Mouse Works) Time Warner.
Mouse Works Staff. Disney Anytime Stories, Vol. 1. LC 96-219756. (J). 1996. 9.98 (*1-57082-408-8*) Little.

M

— Disney Trivia. (J). 1997. 2.98 (*1-57082-759-1*, Pub. by Mouse Works) Time Warner.
— Disney's Make Your Own Paper Airplane. 40p. 1999. pap. 7.99 (*0-7364-0134-2*, Pub. by Mouse Works) Time Warner.
— Disney's The Jungle Book. LC 97-224835. (Illus.). 96p. (J). (ps-4). 1995. 7.98 (*1-57082-293-X*, Pub. by Mouse Works) Time Warner.
— Dizzy Duck. LC 97-162906. 9p. (J). 1997. 4.98 (*1-57082-575-0*, Pub. by Mouse Works) Time Warner.
Mouse Works Staff. Djali's Jolly Day. LC 97-128629. 9p. (J). 1996. 6.98 (*1-57082-324-3*) Mouse Works.
Mouse Works Staff. Dumbo Classic Friendly Tale. 10p. 1999. 6.99 (*0-7364-1012-0*, Pub. by Mouse Works) Time Warner.
— Enchanted Eve. 5p. (J). 1996. 9.98 (*1-57082-504-1*, Pub. by Mouse Works) Time Warner.
— First Lullabye. (J). 1998. 4.98 (*1-57082-714-1*, Pub. by Mouse Works) Little.
***Mouse Works Staff.** First Words. (J). 1998. 4.98 (*1-57082-712-5*, Pub. by Mouse Works) Little.
— Foam Book 1: Foam Bath Book. 6p. (J). 2000. 7.99 (*0-7364-1053-8*, Pub. by Hyprn Ppbks) Little.
Mouse Works Staff. Follow the Leader. LC 97-220832. (Illus.). 18p. (J). 1997. 3.98 (*1-57082-628-5*, Pub. by Mouse Works) Time Warner.
— A Friend Is: A Friend Is... (Illus.). 24p. (J). 1995. 5.98 (*1-57082-292-1*, Pub. by Mouse Works) Little.
— George of the Jungle: Movie Storybook. LC 97-214400. (Illus.). (J). 1997. 6.98 (*1-57082-635-8*, Pub. by Mouse Works) Time Warner.
— Go to Sleep! LC 97-221518. (Illus.). 18p. (J). 1997. 3.98 (*1-57082-674-9*, Pub. by Mouse Works) Time Warner.
— Good Friends. LC 97-138562. (J). 1997. 3.98 (*1-57082-566-1*, Pub. by Mouse Works) Time Warner.
— The Great Mouse Detective. (J). 1997. 7.98 (*1-57082-754-0*, Pub. by Mouse Works) Time Warner.
— Happy Birthday, Hercules! LC 97-184239. (J). 1997. 3.98 (*1-57082-540-8*, Pub. by Mouse Works) Time Warner.
— Happy Days. LC 98-144004. (J). 1998. 7.98 (*1-57082-723-0*, Pub. by Mouse Works) Time Warner.
— Happy Halloween! LC 99-162513. (Standard Characters Ser.). (Illus.). (J). 1998. 8.99 (*1-57082-749-4*, Pub. by Mouse Works) Time Warner.
— Heroes & Friends. (J). 1997. 31.92 (*1-57082-772-9*, Pub. by Mouse Works) Little.
— Hide & Seek. LC 98-106545. (Illus.). 10p. (J). 1997. 6.98 (*1-57082-689-7*, Pub. by Mouse Works) Time Warner.
— Honey of a Day. 18p. (J). 1998. 3.98 (*1-57082-791-5*, Pub. by Mouse Works) Time Warner.
— The Hunchback of Notre Dame. LC 96-217825. 96p. (J). 1996. 7.98 (*1-57082-173-9*, Pub. by Mouse Works); 5.98 (*1-57082-273-5*, Pub. by Mouse Works) Little.
— Hungry Pig. LC 97-162899. 9p. (J). 1997. 4.98 (*1-57082-573-4*, Pub. by Mouse Works) Time Warner.
— I See the Moon. LC 96-165063. (Illus.). 12p. (J). 1995. 5.98 (*1-57082-231-X*, Pub. by Mouse Works) Time Warner.
— I See the Sun. LC 96-127605. (Illus.). 10p. (J). 1995. 5.98 (*1-57082-234-4*, Pub. by Mouse Works) Time Warner.
— Ice-Skating Champ. (J). 1997. 8.98 (*1-57082-852-0*, Pub. by Mouse Works) Time Warner.
— Island Rescue. 24p. (J). 1998. 7.98 (*1-57082-879-2*, Pub. by Mouse Works) Time Warner.
— It's Tigger Time. LC 96-127590. (Illus.). 12p. (J). 1995. 6.98 (*1-57082-266-2*, Pub. by Mouse Works) Time Warner.
— El Jorodado de Notre Dame. 96p. (J). 1996. 7.98 (*1-57082-267-0*, Pub. by Mouse Works) Little.
Mouse Works Staff. The Jungle Book Little Library. LC 97-220414. (J). (ps-3). 1997. 5.98 (*1-57082-861-X*, Pub. by Mouse Works) Little.
Mouse Works Staff. The Jungle Book/Bambi, 2 vols. 75th anniversary ed. 1998. write for info. (*0-7364-0090-7*) Mouse Works.
— Knock-Knock Jokes. LC 98-133266. (J). 1997. 2.98 (*1-57082-760-5*, Pub. by Mouse Works) Time Warner.
— The Lady & the Tramp. (J). 1997. 7.98 (*1-57082-728-1*, Pub. by Mouse Works) Time Warner.
— El Libro de la Selva (The Jungle Book) (SPA.). 96p. (J). 1996. 7.98 (*1-57082-511-4*, Pub. by Mouse Works) Time Warner.
— Lion King. (Disney's Read-Aloud Storybooks Ser.). (Illus.). 64p. (J). (ps-2). 1999. 6.99 (*0-7364-0123-7*, Pub. by Mouse Works) Time Warner.
— The Little Mermaid: Seek & See. LC 98-206168. 24p. (J). 1998. 3.98 (*1-57082-936-5*, Pub. by Mouse Works) Time Warner.
— Lucky Classis Friendly Tale. 10p. 1999. 6.99 (*0-7364-1010-4*, Pub. by Mouse Works) Time Warner.
— Luke Skywalker. LC 98-127247. (Star Wars Ser.). (J). 1998. 6.98 (*1-57082-824-5*, Pub. by Mouse Works) Time Warner.
— Marie: Classic Friendly Tale. 10p. 1999. bds. 6.99 (*0-7364-1013-9*, Pub. by Mouse Works) Time Warner.
— Me & Dad. (J). 1995. 6.98 (*1-57082-191-7*, Pub. by Mouse Works) Little.
— Merry Christmas to You! (J). 1999. 7.98 (*1-57082-940-3*, Pub. by Mouse Works) Little.
— Mickey's Christmas. LC 98-226119. (Mickey Mouse Ser.). 5p. (J). 1998. 8.99 (*1-57082-757-5*, Pub. by Mouse Works) Time Warner.
— Mickey's Christmas Candy Cane. LC 98-232698. (Standard Characters Ser.). 8p. (J). 1998. 2.99 (*1-57082-820-2*, Pub. by Mouse Works) Time Warner.
— Mickey's Christmas Carol. (J). 1995. 7.98 (*1-57082-005-8*, Pub. by Mouse Works) Time Warner.
— Millenium Falcon. 4p. (J). 1997. 4.98 (*1-57082-640-4*, Pub. by Mouse Works) Time Warner.
— Missing Music. (Illus.). 18p. (J). 1997. 3.98 (*1-57082-672-2*, Pub. by Mouse Works) Time Warner.
— Mulan. 24p. (J). 1998. 3.98 (*1-57082-925-X*, Pub. by Mouse Works) Time Warner.
— Mulan - Lady & the Tramp, 2. 75th anniversary ed. 1998. 9.99 (*0-7364-0089-3*) Mouse Works.
— Mulan Classic Storybook. LC 99-162498. (Mulan Ser.). 96p. (J). 1998. 7.98 (*1-57082-864-4*, Pub. by Mouse Works) Time Warner.
— Mulan Spanish Classic Storybook. (Mulan Ser.). (SPA.). 96p. (J). 1998. 7.98 (*1-57082-865-2*, Pub. by Mouse Works) Time Warner.
— My First Peek-a-Boo Game. (Disney Babies Ser.). (J). 1998. 4.98 (*1-57082-713-3*, Pub. by Mouse Works) Little.
— My First Picnic. 5p. (J). 1997. 6.98 (*1-57082-569-6*, Pub. by Mouse Works) Time Warner.
Mouse Works Staff. My Gingerbread House. LC 97-222171. 5p. (J). 1997. 5.98 (*1-57082-718-4*, Pub. by Mouse Works) Time Warner.
Mouse Works Staff. My Town. LC 97-216088. 9p. (J). 1997. 5.98 (*1-57082-715-X*, Pub. by Mouse Works) Time Warner.
Mouse Works Staff. Night Time Mystery. (Illus.). 10p. (J). (ps-k). 1994. bds. write for info. (*1-57082-968-3*) Mouse Works.
Mouse Works Staff. Noisy Night. LC 98-121356. 16p. (J). 1998. 3.98 (*1-57082-746-X*, Pub. by Mouse Works) Time Warner.
— Oh, Brother! It's the Easter Bunny! (Pooh Ser.). (J). (ps). 1998. 7.98 (*1-57082-773-7*, Pub. by Mouse Works) Time Warner.
— On the Go! (Illus.). 10p. (J). 1997. 7.98 (*1-57082-637-4*, Pub. by Mouse Works) Time Warner.
— On the Ice, Vol. 1. (J). 1996. 8.98 (*1-57082-405-3*) Little.
— 101 Dalmatians. (Illus.). 96p. (J). 1995. 7.98 (*1-57082-365-0*, Pub. by Mouse Works) Time Warner.
— 101 Dalmatians. 5p. (J). 1996. 5.98 (*1-57082-079-1*, Pub. by Mouse Works) Little.
— 101 Dalmatians. (Disney's Read-Aloud Storybooks Ser.). 64p. 1999. 6.99 (*0-7364-0112-1*, Pub. by Mouse Works) Time Warner.
***Mouse Works Staff.** 101 Dalmatians/The Lion King, 2 vols. 75th anniversary ed. (Illus.). (J). (ps-3). 1998. 9.99 (*0-7364-0085-0*) Mouse Works.
Mouse Works Staff. Perfect Dress. LC 96-135924. (Illus.). 24p. (J). 1995. 9.98 (*1-57082-271-9*, Pub. by Mouse Works) Little.
— The Perfect Picnic Spot. LC 97-162788. (J). 1997. 3.98 (*1-57082-564-5*, Pub. by Mouse Works) Time Warner.
— Peter Pan. LC 98-177059. (Peter Pan Ser.). (J). 1998. 3.98 (*1-57082-926-8*, Pub. by Mouse Works) Time Warner.
— Piglet Tales. LC 99-159402. (Illus.). 5p. (J). 1997. 6.99 (*1-57082-691-9*, Pub. by Mouse Works) Time Warner.
— Pinocchio - Toy Story, 2. 75th anniversary ed. 1998. 9.99 (*0-7364-0088-5*) Mouse Works.
— Pooh: Eeyore Friendly Tales. LC 99-159402. (Friendly Tales Ser.). (Illus.). 5p. (J). 1997. 6.99 (*1-57082-690-0*, Pub. by Mouse Works) Time Warner.
— Pooh: Good Friends-The Perfect Picnic Spot-A Walk in the Woods-Who Hid the Honey? (Pooh Ser.). (J). 1998. 9.98 (*1-57082-725-7*, Pub. by Mouse Works) Time Warner.
— Pooh Anytime, Vol. 1. LC 96-227568. 61p. (J). 1996. 9.98 (*1-57082-409-6*) Little.
— Pooh Flip Book. 40p. (J). 1997. 2.98 (*1-57082-411-8*) Little.
— Pooh Friendly Tales With Plush. LC 99-159402. (Pooh Ser.). (Illus.). 5p. (J). 1997. bds. 6.99 (*1-57082-692-7*, Pub. by Mouse Works) Time Warner.
— Pooh Loves You: Pooh Friendly Tale Ser., 1. LC 99-195600. 10p. 1999. 6.99 (*0-7364-0102-4*, Pub. by Mouse Works) Time Warner.
— Pooh's Popping Opposites, Pop-Up Book. (Illus.). 5p. (J). 1996. 7.98 (*1-57082-328-6*, Pub. by Mouse Works) Time Warner.
— Puppy Love. LC 97-120424. 5p. (J). 1997. 5.98 (*1-57082-554-8*, Pub. by Mouse Works) Time Warner.
— Real Treasure: A Real Treasure. LC 97-162932. (Illus.). (J). 1995. 5.98 (*1-57082-276-X*, Pub. by Mouse Works) Time Warner.
Mouse Works Staff. A Reel Fishy Story. (Illus.). 10p. (ps-k). 1994. write for info. (*1-57082-969-1*) Mouse Works.
Mouse Works Staff. Rescue Han Solo. LC 99-161401. (J). 1998. 6.98 (*1-57082-823-7*, Pub. by Mouse Works) Time Warner.
— The Rescuers. (Illus.). 96p. (J). 1997. 7.98 (*1-57082-755-9*, Pub. by Mouse Works) Time Warner.
— Robin Hood. (J). 1997. 7.98 (*1-57082-756-7*, Pub. by Mouse Works) Time Warner.
— Romance Slip. (J). 1997. 31.92 (*1-57082-708-7*, Pub. by Mouse Works) Little.
Mouse Works Staff. Roo's Big Adventure. (Illus.). 10p. (ps-k). 1994. bds. write for info. (*1-57082-970-5*) Mouse Works.
Mouse Works Staff. Santa Pooh Friendly Tales. (Winnie the Pooh Staff). (J). 1998. 6.99 (*1-57082-858-X*, Pub. by Mouse Works) Time Warner.
— Santa Roo: Peek-a-Pooh. LC 96-220305. 10p. (J). 1996. 6.98 (*1-57082-331-6*, Pub. by Mouse Works) Time Warner.
— Santa's Helpers Storybook. 24p. (J). 1995. 5.98 (*1-57082-321-9*, Pub. by Mouse Works) Time Warner.
— Scary Seek & See. (Illus.). (J). 1998. 3.98 (*1-57082-240-9*, Pub. by Mouse Works) Little.
— Ship Shapes. 7p. (J). 1997. 5.98 (*1-57082-710-9*, Pub. by Mouse Works) Time Warner.
— Silly Sheep. LC 97-162904. 9p. (J). 1997. 4.98 (*1-57082-574-2*, Pub. by Mouse Works) Time Warner.
— Simba Classic Friendly Tale. 10p. 1999. 6.99 (*0-7364-1011-2*, Pub. by Mouse Works) Time Warner.
— Simba Pride. 10p. (J). 1998. 3.99 (*1-57082-747-8*, Pub. by Mouse Works) Time Warner.
— Simba's Pride. 96p. (J). 1998. 7.99 (*1-57082-890-3*, Pub. by Mouse Works) Time Warner.
— Sleeping Beauty: Storybook, Vol. 1. LC 97-226320. (J). 1997. 7.98 (*1-57082-731-1*, Pub. by Mouse Works) Time Warner.
— Sleeping Beauty/The Little Mermaid, 2 vols. 75th anniversary ed. 1998. 9.99 (*0-7364-0091-5*) Mouse Works.
— Sleepytime Friendship Box: One, Two, Pooh's Looking for You/Winnie the Pooh's Sleepytime Hum/Poo, 4 vols. 10p. 1999. boxed set 9.99 (*0-7364-0145-8*, Pub. by Mouse Works) Time Warner.
— Snow White & the Seven Dwarfs. (Disney's Read-Aloud Storybooks Ser.). (Illus.). 64p. (J). (ps-2). 1999. 6.99 (*0-7364-0122-9*, Pub. by Mouse Works) Time Warner.
— Snow White & the Seven Dwarfs - Cinderella, 2. 75th anniversary ed. 1998. 9.99 (*0-7364-0087-7*, Pub. by Mouse Works) Little.
— So Many Surprises!, Vol. 1. LC 97-203051. (Illus.). 10p. (J). 1997. 7.98 (*1-57082-638-2*, Pub. by Mouse Works) Time Warner.
***Mouse Works Staff.** Standard Characters Friendly Tales Pack Out Box Set. (J). 1999. 27.96 (*0-7364-0042-7*, Pub. by Mouse Works) Time Warner.
Mouse Works Staff. Tigger Tales. LC 99-159402. (Illus.). 5p. (J). 1997. 6.99 (*1-57082-693-5*, Pub. by Mouse Works) Time Warner.
— Topsy Turvy Day, Pop-Up Book. LC 96-217859. (Illus.). 5p. (J). 1996. 6.98 (*1-57082-294-8*, Pub. by Mouse Works) Little.
— Touch of Magic. (J). 1997. 31.92 (*1-57082-793-1*, Pub. by Mouse Works) Little.
— Toy Story. 24p. (J). 1996. 6.98 (*1-57082-278-6*, Pub. by Mouse Works) Time Warner.
— Toy Story Word Books. LC 96-232881. (Illus.). (J). 1995. 6.98 (*1-57082-291-3*, Pub. by Mouse Works) Time Warner.
— Tuck Me In, Vol. 1. (J). 1997. 7.98 (*1-57082-874-1*, Pub. by Mouse Works) Little.
— 26-in-One. (J). 1998. 9.99 (*1-57082-875-X*, Pub. by Mouse Works) Time Warner.
— Walk in Woods. LC 97-162798. (J). 1997. 3.98 (*1-57082-563-7*, Pub. by Mouse Works) Time Warner.
— What's a Bear to Wear? (Illus.). 10p. (J). 1997. 7.98 (*1-57082-676-5*, Pub. by Mouse Works) Time Warner.
— Where's Piglet? LC 97-113320. (Illus.). 12p. (J). (ps). 1995. 6.98 (*1-57082-262-X*, Pub. by Mouse Works) Time Warner.
— Who Hid Honey? LC 97-162804. (J). 1997. 3.98 (*1-57082-565-3*, Pub. by Mouse Works) Time Warner.
— Winnie the Pooh. (Winnie the Pooh Ser.). 20p. (J). 1998. 4.99 (*1-57082-789-3*, Pub. by Mouse Works) Time Warner.
— Winnie the Pooh's ABC. LC 98-232702. (Disney Babies Ser.). 18p. (J). 1998. 4.99 (*1-57082-779-6*, Pub. by Mouse Works) Time Warner.
— Winnie the Pooh's Big Book of First Words, Vol. 1. 48p. 1999. text 12.99 (*0-7364-0142-3*, Pub. by Mouse Works) Time Warner.
Mouse Works Staff, jt. auth. see Disney Staff.
Mouseglib, Pomfret & Pulver, Kathryn. I'd Do It All over Again. LC 96-91019. 1996. 16.95 (*0-533-11854-9*) Vantage.
Mouser, Barbara, jt. auth. see Mouser, Bill.
***Mouser, Barbara K.** Five Aspects of Femininity for Young Women: Leader's Guide. 200p. 2000. pap. 12.00 (*1-929656-04-1*) Intl Council Gender Studs.
***Mouser, Barbara K. & Fisher, Priscilla.** Five Aspects of Femininity for Young Women: A Biblical Theology of Womanhood. 164p. (YA). (gr. 9 up). 2000. pap. 15.00 (*1-929656-03-3*) Intl Council Gender Studs.
Mouser, Bill. Aspects of a Man. LC 95-237310. 224p. 1995. pap. 10.00 (*1-883893-15-1*) WinePress Pub.
Mouser, Bill & Mouser, Barbara. Aspects of a Woman. LC 95-231079. (Illus.). 450p. 1995. 10.00 (*1-883893-16-X*) WinePress Pub.
Mouser, Bruce L., ed. Journal of James Watt: Expedition to Timbo, Capital of the Fula Empire in 1794. 1994. write for info. (*0-942615-25-5*) U Wis African Stud.
Mouser, G. W., jt. auth. see Brown, Robert E.
Mouser, Jeffrey D. Welding Codes, Standards & Specifications. LC 97-37604. (Illus.). 398p. 1997. 74.95 (*0-07-043550-2*) McGraw.
Mouser, William. Proverbs: Learning to Live Wisely. (LifeGuide Bible Studies). 95p. (Orig.). 1990. pap., wbk. ed. 4.99 (*0-8308-1026-9*, 1026) InterVarsity.
Mousework Staff. Alice in Wonderland. (Illus.). (J). 1997. 7.98 (*1-57082-795-8*, Pub. by Mouse Works) Time Warner.
— Beauty & the Beast: Classic Storybook, Vol. 1. (J). 1996. 7.98 (*1-57082-034-1*, Pub. by Mouse Works) Time Warner.
— Dumbo. (Illus.). (J). 1997. 7.98 (*1-57082-798-2*, Pub. by Mouse Works) Little.
— Farmer Mickey. (Disney's Ser.). 12p. (J). 1998. 4.99 (*1-57082-892-X*, Pub. by Mouse Works) Time Warner.
— The Great Mouse Mystery. (Illus.). (J). 1997. 7.98 (*1-57082-805-9*, Pub. by Mouse Works) Little.
— Many Adventures of Winnie the Pooh. LC 99-159377. (Illus.). 96p. (J). 1998. 7.98 (*1-57082-804-0*, Pub. by Mouse Works) Time Warner.
— Mickey Mouse's Xmas Carol. (J). 1997. 7.98 (*1-57082-799-0*, Pub. by Mouse Works) Little.
— Peter Pan. (Illus.). (J). 1997. 7.98 (*1-57082-801-6*, Pub. by Mouse Works) Time Warner.
Mousework Staff. Pinocchio. (Illus.). (J). 1997. 7.98 (*1-57082-806-7*, Pub. by Mouse Works) Little.
Mousework Staff. Rescuers. (Illus.). (J). 1997. 7.98 (*1-57082-807-5*, Pub. by Mouse Works) Little.
— Simba Faces Danger. LC 99-209619. 18p. (J). 1998. 2.99 (*1-57082-993-4*, Pub. by Mouse Works) Time Warner.
— Tarzan. (SPA., Illus.). 64p. (J). (ps-2). 1999. 7.99 (*0-7364-0057-5*, Pub. by Mouse Works) Time Warner.
Mouseworks. Painting Eggs. (J). 1998. 3.98 (*1-57082-777-X*, Pub. by Mouse Works) Little.
Mouseworks Staff. Aladdin. (J). 1997. 7.98 (*1-57082-794-X*, Pub. by Mouse Works) Time Warner.
— Aladdin. (SPA., Illus.). (J). 1997. write for info. (*1-57082-809-1*) Mouse Works.
***Mouseworks Staff.** Alice in Wonderland/Classic. 2002. 7.99 (*1-57082-976-4*, Pub. by Mouse Works) Time Warner.
Mouseworks Staff. Ariel's Sea. LC 97-212112. (J). 1997. 5.98 (*1-57082-629-3*, Pub. by Mouse Works) Time Warner.
— Aristocats. (J). 1997. 7.98 (*1-57082-780-X*, Pub. by Mouse Works) Little.
Mouseworks Staff. Bambi. (Spanish Classics Ser.). (Illus.). (J). 1996. 7.98 (*1-57082-402-9*, Pub. by Mouse Works) Little.
Mouseworks Staff. Beauty & the Beast. (Spanish Classics Ser.). (Illus.). (J). 1997. write for info. (*1-57082-810-5*); 7.98 (*1-57082-870-9*, Pub. by Mouse Works) Little.
***Mouseworks Staff.** Beauty & the Beast Spanish Read Aloud Storybook Classic La Bella Y La Bestia. 64p. (J). 1999. 6.99 (*0-7364-0141-5*) Disney Pr.
Mouseworks Staff. La Bella y la Bestia. rev. ed.Tr. of Beauty & the Beast. (SPA., Illus.). 96p. (J). 1998. 7.99 (*0-7364-0078-8*, Pub. by Mouse Works) Little.
***Mouseworks Staff.** Blanca Nieves y Los Enamos. (SPA., Illus.). 96p. (J). 1998. 7.99 (*0-7364-0079-6*, Pub. by Mouse Works) Little.
— Bug Life. 96p. (J). 1998. 7.99 (*1-57082-980-2*, Pub. by Mouse Works) Time Warner.
Mouseworks Staff. A Bugs Life: Can You Find the Difference? LC 99-162323. (Seek & See Ser.). (Illus.). 24p. (J). (gr. k-3). 1998. pap. 3.99 (*1-57082-937-3*, Pub. by Mouse Works) Time Warner.
***Mouseworks Staff.** Busy Book: Pooh's Knock Three Times. 7th ed. (Illus.). 12p. (J). (ps). 2000. pap. text 6.99 (*0-7364-1004-X*, Pub. by Mouse Works) Time Warner.
Mouseworks Staff. Butter's First Words. 8p. 1999. bds. 3.50 (*0-7364-0184-9*, Pub. by Mouse Works) Time Warner.
***Mouseworks Staff.** Buzz Book Pal. 18p. (J). 1999. 8.99 (*0-7364-0117-2*, Pub. by Disney Pr) Time Warner.
Mouseworks Staff. Cinderella. (Classics Ser.). (Illus.). (J). 1997. 7.99 (*1-57082-797-4*, Pub. by Mouse Works) Time Warner.
— Cinderella: Read Aloud. 64p. (J). 1999. 6.99 (*0-7364-0124-5*, Pub. by Mouse Works) Time Warner.
— Darth Vader. 8p. (J). 1997. 6.98 (*1-57082-611-0*, Pub. by Mouse Works) Time Warner.
***Mouseworks Staff.** Dinosaur. (Read-Aloud Storybook Ser.). 64p. (J). (gr. k-2). 2000. 6.99 (*0-7364-1000-7*, Pub. by Mouse Works) Time Warner.
— Disney's Easy to Read Stories. (J). 2000. 11.99 (*0-7364-0167-9*, Pub. by Mouse Works) Time Warner.
Mouseworks Staff. Disney's I Believe in Me. LC 98-228680. (Illus.). 8p. (J). 1998. 3.99 (*1-57082-954-3*, Pub. by Mouse Works) Time Warner.
***Mouseworks Staff.** Disney's Make Your Own Christmas Cards. 40p. (J). 2000. 7.99 (*0-7364-1015-5*, Pub. by Disney Pr) Time Warner.
— Disney's Make Your Own Halloween Adventure. 40p. (J). 2000. 7.99 (*0-7364-1014-7*, Pub. by Disney Pr) Time Warner.
Mouseworks Staff. Disney's Pooh's Five Little Honeypots. LC 98-235174. (Illus.). (J). 1998. 6.99 (*1-57082-941-1*, Pub. by Mouse Works) Time Warner.
— Disney's Red & Blue & Pooh Shapes, Too! LC 99-162319. (Pooh Busy Bks.). (Illus.). 12p. (J). 1998. 6.99 (*1-57082-944-6*, Pub. by Mouse Works) Time Warner.
***Mouseworks Staff.** Disney's Winnie the Pooh's Feelings: Learn & Grow. (Illus.). 18p. (J). (ps). 2000. pap. text 4.99 (*0-7364-1008-2*, Pub. by Mouse Works) Time Warner.
— Disney's Winnie the Pooh's Senses: Learn & Grow. (Illus.). 18p. (J). (ps). 2000. pap. text 4.99 (*0-7364-1009-0*, Pub. by Mouse Works) Time Warner.
Mouseworks Staff. Donald Duck. LC 99-161550. (Friendly Tales Ser.). (Illus.). 5p. (J). 1998. 6.99 (*1-57082-927-6*, Pub. by Mouse Works) Time Warner.
— Doug's Composition Book. 1999. pap. 2.99 (*0-7364-0182-2*, Pub. by Mouse Works) Time Warner.
— Dumbo Classic Storybook. rev. ed. 96p. (J). 1998. 7.99 (*0-7364-0022-2*, Pub. by Mouse Works) Little.
***Mouseworks Staff.** Dumbo Read Aloud Storybook. 64p. (J). 2000. 6.99 (*0-7364-1052-X*, Pub. by Hyperion) Time Warner.
Mouseworks Staff. The Easter Bunny. LC PZ8.3.T63Eas 1998. (J). 1998. 2.98 (*1-57082-775-3*, Pub. by Mouse Works) Time Warner.
— Easter Dinner. (J). 1998. 3.98 (*1-57082-776-1*, Pub. by Mouse Works) Little.
— Fantasia Flip Book. (Illus.). 40p. (J). 2000. 3.95 (*0-7364-0093-1*, Pub. by Mouse Works) Time Warner.
— Flubber. (J). 1997. 6.98 (*1-57082-607-2*) Mouse Works.
***Mouseworks Staff.** Foam Book Foam Bath Book Friendship Book. 2nd ed. 6p. (J). 2000. 7.99 (*0-7364-1054-6*, Pub. by Hyprn Ppbks) Little.
Mouseworks Staff. Gifts Galore. LC 98-170289. 16p. (J). 1998. 3.98 (*1-57082-790-7*, Pub. by Mouse Works) Time Warner.
— Goofy. (Friendly Tales Ser.). (Illus.). 10p. (J). (ps). 1998. 6.99 (*1-57082-928-4*, Pub. by Mouse Works) Time Warner.
***Mouseworks Staff.** Happy Easter, Pooh! Friendly Tales. (Illus.). 10p. (J). (ps-k). 2000. pap. text 6.99 (*0-7364-1056-2*, Pub. by Hyperion) Time Warner.

An Asterisk (*) at the beginning of an entry indicates that the title is appearing for the first time.

— Happy Graduation, Pooh! Friendly Tales. (Illus.). 10p. (J). (ps-k). 2000. pap. text 6.99 (*0-7364-1057-0*, Pub. by Hyperion) Time Warner.

Mouseworks Staff. Hats! Hats! LC 98-162526. 16p. (J). 1998. 3.98 (*1-57082-750-8*, Pub. by Mouse Works) Time Warner.

— Holiday Gift. 24p. (J). 1997. 9.98 (*1-57082-623-4*, Pub. by Mouse Works) Time Warner.

***Mouseworks Staff.** I Love You, Pooh! (Keepsake Photo Storybks.). 10p. (J). 2000. bds. 6.99 (*0-7364-0190-3*, Pub. by Mouse Works) Time Warner.

Mouseworks Staff. It's Easter All Around! LC 98-132587. (J). 1998. 7.98 (*1-57082-774-5*, Pub. by Mouse Works) Time Warner.

— It's Hard to Share: Little Lessons for Bambi. (Illus.). 8p. (J). 1998. 3.99 (*1-57082-953-5*, Pub. by Mouse Works) Time Warner.

— Jungle Animals. (Tarzan Touch & Feel Bks.). (Illus.). 10p. (J). 1999. 6.99 (*0-7364-0071-0*, Pub. by Mouse Works) Time Warner.

Mouseworks Staff. Key Chain Books 12 Copy Clip Strip. (J). 1997. 35.76 (*1-57082-831-8*) Little.

Mouseworks Staff. Lady & the Tramp. (Spanish Classics Ser.). (Illus.). (J). 1997. 7.98 (*1-57082-871-7*, Pub. by Mouse Works) Little.

— The Lady & the Tramp: We're All Different. (Illus.). (J). 1999. 2.99 (*0-7364-0044-3*, Pub. by Mouse Works) Little.

— The Lady & the Tramp Easy Reader. 48p. (J). 1998. 3.95 (*0-7364-0039-7*, Pub. by Mouse Works) Time Warner.

— Learn & Draw with Mickey. 22p. (J). 1999. 12.99 (*0-7364-0101-6*, Pub. by Mouse Works) Time Warner.

***Mouseworks Staff.** Learn & Grow Carry Along. (J). 1999. 9.99 (*0-7364-0181-4*, Pub. by Mouse Works) Little.

— Lion King. (Seek & See Ser.). (Illus.). 24p. (J). 1998. 3.99 (*1-57082-938-1*, Pub. by Mouse Works) Time Warner.

Mouseworks Staff. The Lion King: Spanish Read Aloud. (SPA., Illus.). 64p. (ps-2). 1999. pap. 6.99 (*0-7364-0138-5*, Pub. by Mouse Works) Time Warner.

— The Little Mermaid. (Spanish Classics Ser.).Tr. of Lille havfrue. (Illus.). (J). 1997. write for info. (*1-57082-872-5*) Mouse Works.

***Mouseworks Staff.** Love U Mama. 10p. (J). 1999. bds. 6.99 (*1-57082-985-3*, Pub. by Mouse Works) Time Warner.

Mouseworks Staff. Merry Christmas to You! (Pooh Ser.). 5p. (J). 1998. 7.98 (*0-7364-0026-5*, Pub. by Mouse Works) Time Warner.

— Mickey & Friends Roly Poly. 1998. 9.99 (*0-7364-0035-4*, Pub. by Mouse Works) Little.

— Mickey Mouse's Christmas. 64p. 1999. 6.99 (*0-7364-0126-1*, Pub. by Mouse Works) Little.

— Mickey's Friendly Tale, Vol. 1. 10p. 1999. 6.74 (*0-7364-0176-8*, Pub. by Mouse Works) Time Warner.

— Mickey's Things That Go Word. 48p. (J). 1999. 12.99 (*0-7364-0114-8*, Pub. by Mouse Works) Time Warner.

— Mickey's Toon Town. (Illus.). (J). 1999. bds. write for info. (*0-7364-0063-X*) Mouse Works.

— Micky Mouse. (Friendly Tales Ser.). (Illus.). (J). 1998. 6.99 (*1-57082-929-2*, Pub. by Mouse Works) Time Warner.

— Minnie Mouse. LC 99-161550. (Friendly Tales Ser.). (Illus.). (J). 1998. 6.99 (*1-57082-930-6*, Pub. by Mouse Works) Time Warner.

— Night-Night, Roo. LC 99-162657. 18p. (J). 1998. 3.99 (*1-57082-984-5*, Pub. by Mouse Works) Time Warner.

***Mouseworks Staff.** Noodle Dance! Chunky Roly Poly. 16p. (J). 1999. 3.50 (*0-7364-0011-7*, Pub. by Mouse Works) Time Warner.

Mouseworks Staff. Oliver & Company. (Classics Ser.). (Illus.). (J). 1997. write for info. (*1-57082-800-8*) Mouse Works.

***Mouseworks Staff.** 102 Dalmations. abr. ed. (Read-Aloud Storybook Ser.). 64p. (J). (ps-2). 2000. 6.99 (*0-7364-0195-4*) Mouse Works.

— 102 Dalmatians: Colorful Pups. (Lift the Flaps Bks.). 10p. (J). (ps). 2000. 4.99 (*0-7364-0228-4*, Pub. by Mouse Works) Time Warner.

Mouseworks Staff. Peanut's Shapes. 8p. (J). 1999. 3.50 (*0-7364-0183-0*, Pub. by Mouse Works) Time Warner.

— Peter Pan. (J). 1999. 4.99 (*0-7364-0045-1*, Pub. by Mouse Works) Little.

— Piglet's up & down Day. LC 98-106124. (Illus.). 5p. (J). (ps). 1997. 7.98 (*1-57082-613-7*, Pub. by Mouse Works) Time Warner.

— Pongo's in Love. (101 Dalmations Ser.). 9p. (J). 1998. 8.98 (*1-57082-539-4*, Pub. by Mouse Works) Time Warner.

***Mouseworks Staff.** Pooh. (My Very First Cloth Book Ser.). (J). 1999. 6.99 (*0-7364-0177-6*, Pub. by Disney Pr) Little.

Mouseworks Staff. Pooh: Cook with Components. (J). 1996. write for info. (*1-57082-459-2*, Pub. by Mouse Works) Little.

— Pooh Counting. LC 98-235635. (J). 1997. 9.98 (*1-57082-620-X*, Pub. by Mouse Works) Time Warner.

Mouseworks Staff. Pooh Flat Pack: Flndr Pb. 9.98 (*1-57082-744-3*, Pub. by Mouse Works) Time Warner.

— Pooh Friendly Tales. (J). 1999. boxed set 27.96 (*0-7364-0041-9*, Pub. by Mouse Works) Time Warner.

— Pooh Loves Christmas! A Winnie the Pooh Photo Album & Storybook. (Keepsake Photo Storybks.). 10p. (J). 2000. bds. 6.99 (*0-7364-0191-1*, Pub. by Mouse Works) Time Warner.

— Pooh Movie Tree House Book: Freindship Book. 8p. (J). (ps-3). 2000. 16.99 (*0-7364-1049-X*, Pub. by Hyperion) Time Warner.

Mouseworks Staff. Pooh Storybook Treasury. LC 97-170388. (Illus.). (J). 1997. 14.98 (*1-57082-722-2*, Pub. by Mouse Works) Time Warner.

— Pooh's Pitter Patter Splash. (Pooh Busy Bks.). (Illus.). 12p. (J). 1999. bds. 6.99 (*1-57082-943-8*, Pub. by Mouse Works) Time Warner.

— R2-D2's Missing. (J). 1997. 6.98 (*1-57082-612-9*, Pub. by Mouse Works) Time Warner.

— The Rescuers. (J). 1997. 7.98 (*1-57082-050-3*, Pub. by Mouse Works) Little.

— Robin Hood. (J). 1997. 7.98 (*1-57082-808-3*, Pub. by Mouse Works) Little.

— Rolie Polie Olie Teapot Carry. 5p. (J). Date not set. 6.99 (*0-7364-0166-0*, Pub. by Mouse Works) Time Warner.

— Rotten Egg. LC 98-140482. (J). 1998. 2.98 (*1-57082-778-8*, Pub. by Mouse Works) Time Warner.

— Santa Mickey Friendly Tales. (J). 1998. 6.99 (*1-57082-974-8*, Pub. by Mouse Works) Little.

***Mouseworks Staff.** Santa Minnie Friendly Tales. (J). 1998. 6.99 (*1-57082-975-6*, Pub. by Mouse Works) Little.

Mouseworks Staff. Snow White. (Classics Ser.). (Illus.). (J). 1997. write for info. (*1-57082-802-4*); write for info. (*1-57082-811-3*) Mouse Works.

— Snow White Classic. rev. ed. 7.99 (*1-57082-977-2*, Pub. by Mouse Works) Little.

Mouseworks Staff. Star Wars: Flip Book Collection. (Star Wars Ser.). (J). 1997. 6.49 (*1-57082-580-7*, Pub. by Mouse Works) Time Warner.

Mouseworks Staff. The Sword in the Stone. (Classics Ser.). (J). 1997. 7.98 (*1-57082-803-2*, Pub. by Mouse Works) Time Warner.

***Mouseworks Staff.** Tarzan. LC 99-231395. (Illus.). 8p. (J). (ps). 1999. 2.99 (*0-7364-0048-6*, Pub. by Mouse Works) Time Warner.

Mouseworks Staff. Tarzan. (Illus.). 64p. (J). (ps-2). 1999. 6.99 (*0-7364-0047-8*, Pub. by Mouse Works) Time Warner.

***Mouseworks Staff.** Tickle Me, Pooh! (Winnie the Pooh Touch & Feel Ser.). 12p. (J). 2000. 8.99 (*0-7364-1019-8*, Pub. by Mouse Works) Time Warner.

— Tigger. (My Very First Cloth Book Ser.). (J). 1999. 6.99 (*0-7364-0178-4*, Pub. by Disney Pr) Little.

Mouseworks Staff. Toy Story: Read Aloud. 64p. (J). 1999. 6.99 (*0-7364-0120-2*, Pub. by Mouse Works) Time Warner.

— Toy Story II: Punchout Play. 1999. 8.99 (*0-7364-0175-X*, Pub. by Mouse Works) Time Warner.

— Toy Story II: Spanish Read. (SPA.). 64p. 1999. write for info. (*0-7364-0128-8*, Pub. by Mouse Works) Little.

— Toy Story II: Tab Book. 14p. 1999. 7.99 (*0-7364-0171-7*, Pub. by Mouse Works) Time Warner.

— Toy Story II. 64p. 1999. 6.99 (*0-7364-0151-2*, Pub. by Mouse Works); pap. 3.99 (*0-7364-0169-5*, Pub. by Mouse Works) Time Warner.

— Toy Story II: Lift the Flap. 10p. 1999. 4.99 (*0-7364-0179-2*, Pub. by Mouse Works) Time Warner.

— Toy Story 2: Sheriff Woody & the Roundup Gang Friendship Box, 4 vols. (YA). 1999. bds. 9.99 (*0-7364-0170-9*, Pub. by Mouse Works) Time Warner.

— Toy Story II Green Army Men. (J). 1999. 9.99 (*0-7364-0174-1*, Pub. by Mouse Works) Little.

***Mouseworks Staff.** Toy Story 2: A Read-aloud Storybook. 1999. 6.99 (*0-7364-0140-7*, Pub. by Mouse Works) Time Warner.

— Toy Story 2: Find the Flag. (J). 1999. 4.99 (*0-7364-1042-2*, Pub. by Disney Pr) Little.

— Toy Story 2: Flip. 96p. (J). 1999. 3.99 (*0-7364-1044-9*, Pub. by Disney Pr) Little.

— Toy Story 2: Let's Play. 10p. (J). 1999. 11.99 (*0-7364-1043-0*, Pub. by Disney Pr) Little.

— Toy Story 2: Let's Play. 10p. 1999. 11.99 (*0-7364-0186-5*, Pub. by Mouse Works) Time Warner.

Mouseworks Staff. Welcome to Rolie Polie Olie's. 6p. 1999. 8.99 (*0-7364-0165-2*, Pub. by Mouse Works) Time Warner.

***Mouseworks Staff.** Who's Our Mommy Pooh? Discovery Lift the Flap. 14p. (J). 2000. 5.99 (*0-7364-1059-7*) Little.

Mouseworks Staff. Whose Face? Pooh's Face! (Pooh Busy Bks.). (Illus.). 12p. (J). 1998. 6.99 (*1-57082-942-X*, Pub. by Mouse Works) Time Warner.

***Mouseworks Staff.** Winnie the Pooh Easy-to-Read Stories. (Illus.). 192p. (J). (ps-3). 2000. 9.99 (*0-7364-1050-3*, Pub. by Mouse Works) Time Warner.

Mouseworks Staff. The Winnie-the-Pooh Read Aloud Collection: Winnie-the-Pooh & Some Bees - Eeyore Has a Birthday - Piglet Is Entirely Surrounded by Water. 64p. 1999. 12.99 (*0-7364-0109-1*, Pub. by Mouse Works) Time Warner.

— Winnie the Pooh Spanish Read. 48p. 1999. pap. 4.99 (*0-7364-0108-3*, Pub. by Mouse Works) Little.

***Mouseworks Staff.** Winnie the Pooh's Book of Friendship. (Illus.). 32p. (J). 2000. 12.99 (*0-7868-3286-X*, Pub. by Disney Pr) Time Warner.

Mouseworks Staff. Winnie-the-Pooh's Friendly Adventures. (Disney's Read-Aloud Storybooks Ser.). 64p. (J). 1999. 6.99 (*0-7364-0107-5*, Pub. by Mouse Works) Time Warner.

***Mouseworks Staff.** Winnie the Pooh's Holiday Hummables. 14p. (J). (ps-k). 2000. bds. 7.99 (*0-7364-1060-0*, Pub. by Mouse Works) Time Warner.

— Winnie the Pooh's Touch & Feel Book. 2nd ed. 10p. (J). Date not set. 6.99 (*0-7364-1021-X*, Pub. by Hyperion) Little.

— Woody Book Pal. 18p. (J). 1999. 8.99 (*0-7364-0116-4*, Pub. by Disney Pr) Time Warner.

Mouseworks Staff. Xmas Surprise. 9p. (J). 1997. 10.98 (*1-57082-627-7*, Pub. by Mouse Works) Time Warner.

Mouseworks Staff & Alexander, Lloyd. Black Cauldron Classic. (Chronicles of Prydain Ser.). (J). 1997. write for info. (*1-57082-796-6*) Mouse Works.

Mouseworks Staff & Kassirer, Sue. Where Are the Bugs? LC 99-159364. (Lift the Flaps Bks.). (Illus.). 10p. (J). 1998. bds. 4.99 (*1-57082-958-6*, Pub. by Mouse Works) Time Warner.

Mouseworks Staff, et al. Mickey's Christmas Carol. LC 99-158608. (Little Library). (J). 1997. 5.98 (*1-57082-720-6*, Pub. by Mouse Works) Little.

Moushabeck, Michel, jt. ed. see Bennis, Phyllis.

Moushine, Naomi, jt. auth. see Friesem, Ricky.

***Mousley, Andy.** Renaissance Drama & Contemporary Literary Theory. LC 99-56334. 2000. pap. write for info. (*0-312-23174-1*) St Martin.

— Renaissance Drama & Contemporary Literary Theory. LC 99-56334. 2000. write for info. (*0-312-23173-3*) St Martin.

Mousley, Judith & Marks, Genee. Discourses in Mathematics. 112p. (C). 1991. pap. 60.00 (*0-7300-1291-3*, ECT403, Pub. by Deakin Univ) St Mut.

***Mousli, Lilian.** Gruesome Alphabet. (Illus.). 32p. 1999. pap. 7.95 (*0-943151-01-5*) Slave Labor Bks.

Mousnier, Roland. Peasant Uprisings in 17th-Century France, Russia, & China. Pearce, Brian, tr. LC 76-884549. (Great Revolutions Ser.: 1). 381p. reprint ed. pap. 118.20 (*0-608-11933-4*, 202331400032) Bks Demand.

Mousnier, Roland E. The Institutions of France under the Absolute Monarchy, 1598-1789: Society & the State, Vol. 1. Pearce, Brian, tr. from FRE. LC 78-26857. 804p. 1979. reprint ed. lib. bdg. 66.00 (*0-226-54327-7*) U Ch Pr.

— The Institutions of France under the Absolute Monarchy, 1598-1789: The Organs of State & Society, Vol. II. Goldhammer, Arthur, tr. from FRE. LC 78-26857. 716p. (C). 1984. 66.00 (*0-226-54328-5*) U Ch Pr.

Mousourakis, George. Criminal Responsibility & Partial Excuses. LC 98-24988. 222p. 1998. text 59.95 (*1-85521-943-3*, KD7890.M68, Pub. by Ashgate Pub) Ashgate Pub Co.

Moussa, Effat A. Computer Integrated Probability & Mathematical Statistics for Science & Management. rev. ed. 924p. 1993. per. 75.95 (*0-8403-8753-9*) Kendall-Hunt.

Moussa, Helene. Storm & Sanctuary: The Journey of Ethiopian & Eritrean Women Refugees. LC 94-120367. xiv, 284 p. 1993. write for info. (*1-895247-08-X*) Artemis Enter.

Moussa-Mahmoud, Fatma, tr. see Mahfouz, Naguib.

Moussa, Naima. Nutrient Gene Interactions, 001. 2000. ring bd. write for info. (*0-8493-2216-2*) CRC Pr.

Moussalli, Ahmad S. Islamic Fundamentalism: Myths & Realities. 400p. 1998. 40.00 (*0-86372-232-6*, Pub. by Garnet-Ithaca) LPC InBook.

— Moderate & Radical Islamic Fundamentalism: The Quest for Modernity, Legitimacy, & the Islamic State. LC 98-36151. 1999. 50.00 (*0-8130-1658-4*) U Press Fla.

— Radical Islamic Fundamentalism: The Ideological & Political Discourse of Sayyid Qutb. 326p. (C). 1993. pap. text 20.00 (*0-8156-6089-8*) Syracuse U Pr.

Moussalli, Amhad. Historical Dictionary of Islamic Fundamentalist Movements in the Arab World, Iran & Turkey. Woronoff, Jon, ed. LC 98-45879. (Religions, Philosophies & Movements Ser.: No. 23). 504p. 1999. 75.00 (*0-8108-3609-2*) Scarecrow.

Moussalli, Stephanie D. Sanctuary's Case Against America: How the Cities of Refuge Help Ortega. (Issue Papers: No. 7-88). 13p. 1988. pap. text 8.00 (*1-57655-023-0*) Independ Inst.

Moussavi, Fakhreddin, compiled by. Guide to the Hanna Collection & Related Archival Materials at the Hoover Institution on War, Revolution & Peace on the Role of Education in Twentieth-Century Society. (Bibliography Ser.: No. 64). 250p. 1982. lib. bdg. 19.95 (*0-8179-2641-0*) Hoover Inst Pr.

Moussay, G. Dictionary Minangkabau Indonesian-Francais. (FRE.). 1328p. 1995. 275.00 (*0-320-00946-7*) Fr & Eur.

Mousseau, Timothy A. & Fox, Charles W., eds. Maternal Effects as Adaptations. (Illus.). 400p. 1998. text 65.00 (*0-19-511163-X*) OUP.

Mousseau, Timothy A., et al. Adaptive Genetic Variation in the Wild. LC 99-13844. 288p. 2000. text 60.00 (*0-19-512183-X*) OUP.

Mousset & Dupuis, Hector. Dictionnaire Francais-Tamoul.Tr. of French-Tamil Dictionary. (FRE & TAM.). 1253p. 1990. 150.00 (*0-8288-1108-3*, M223) Fr & Eur.

Mousset-Jones, Pierre F. Mine Ventilation: Second Us-addendum. 1985. 104.00 (*90-6191-648-8*) Ashgate Pub Co.

Mousset-Jones, Pierre F., ed. Mine Ventilation: U. S. Mine Ventilation Symposium, Reno, Nevada, 2nd, 23-25 September 1985, Vol. 1. (C). 1985. text 188.00 (*90-6191-611-9*, Pub. by A A Balkema) Ashgate Pub Co.

Moussinac, Leon, compiled by. The New Movement in the Theatre. LC 65-19619. (Illus.). 1972. reprint ed. 82.95 (*0-405-08808-6*, Pub. by Blom Pubns) Ayer.

Moussiopoulos, N. & Ebel, A., eds. Air Pollution III: Observation & Simulation of Air Pollution: Results from SANA & EUMAC. 152p. 1995. 61.00 (*1-85312-444-3*) Computational Mech MA.

Moussiopoulos, N., jt. ed. see Power, H.

Moussis, Nicholas. Access to European Union. 6th ed. 550p. 1996. pap. 86.00 (*2-930066-22-9*) Paul & Co Pubs.

— Access to European Union. 7th ed. LC 97-215623. 550p. 1997. pap. 88.00 (*2-930066-39-3*, Pub. by Euroconfidential) Paul & Co Pubs.

— Handbook of European Union. 3rd ed. 370p. 1997. pap. 40.00 (*2-930119-11-X*, Pub. by Euroconfidential) Paul & Co Pubs.

— Handbook of European Union. 5th ed. LC 99-461790. (Euroconfidential Collection). 360p. 1998. pap. 35.00 (*2-930119-20-9*, Pub. by Euroconfidential) Paul & Co Pubs.

Moussorgsky, Modest P. Boris Godunov in Full Score: (Rimsky-Korsakov Version) 784p. 1987. pap. 32.95 (*0-486-25321-X*) Dover.

— Pictures at an Exhibition & Other Works for Piano. 224p. 1990. pap. 12.95 (*0-486-26515-3*) Dover.

— Selected Songs. 144p. (Orig.). 1994. pap. 9.95 (*0-486-28089-6*) Dover.

***Moust, Hans.** Guild Guitar Book: The Company & the Instruments, 1952-1977. (Illus.). 184p. 1999. per. 39.95 (*0-634-00966-4*) H Leonard.

Moustafa, Margaret. Beyond Traditional Phonics: Research Discoveries & Reading Instruction. LC 97-22907. 1997. pap. 15.00 (*0-435-07247-1*) Heinemann.

Moustafa, Margaret, jt. auth. see Dombey, Henrietta.

Moustakas, Clark. Being-In, Being-For, Being-With. LC 95-7080. 1995. 50.00 (*1-56821-537-1*) Aronson.

— Existential Psychotherapy & the Interpretations of Dreams. LC 93-40807. 232p. 1994. 45.00 (*1-56821-180-5*) Aronson.

— Existential Psychotherapy & the Interpretations of Dreams. LC 93-40807. 232p. 1995. reprint ed. pap. 40.00 (*1-56821-771-4*) Aronson.

— Heuristic Research: Design, Methodology, & Applications. 160p. (C). 1990. 46.00 (*0-8039-3881-0*); pap. 19.95 (*0-8039-3882-9*) Sage.

— Phenomenological Research Methods. LC 94-7355. 240p. 1994. 52.00 (*0-8039-5798-X*); pap. 24.00 (*0-8039-5799-8*) Sage.

— Relationship Play Therapy. LC 96-9434. 232p. 1997. 45.00 (*0-7657-0029-8*) Aronson.

***Moustakas, T. D., et al, eds.** III-V Nitride Materials & Processes III. LC 99-62683. 230p. 1999. 46.00 (*1-56677-212-5*, PV 98-18) Electrochem Soc.

Moustakas, T. D., et al, eds. III-V Nitride Materials & Processes. LC 95-83750. (Proceedings Ser.: Vol. 96-11). (Illus.). 234p. 1996. 46.00 (*1-56677-163-3*) Electrochem Soc.

Moustakas, T. D., jt. ed. see Pankove, Jacques I.

Moustakas, Theodore D., jt. ed. see Pankove, Jacques.

Moustaki, Georges. En Ballades, Tome 1. (FRE., Illus.). 200p. 1996. pap. 49.95 (*2-86808-103-7*) Intl Scholars.

— En Ballades, Tome 2. (Illus.). 200p. 1996. pap. 49.95 (*2-86808-104-5*) Intl Scholars.

Moustiers, Pierre. L' Hiver d'un Gentilhomme. (FRE.). 1975. pap. 11.95 (*0-7859-4046-4*) Fr & Eur.

— La Paroi. (FRE.). 224p. 1969. pap. 15.95 (*0-7859-3961-X*, 2070246590) Fr & Eur.

Mout, M. E., et al, eds. Erasmianism: Idea & Reality: Proceedings of the Colloquium, Amsterdam, The Netherlands, 19-21 September, 1996. 208p. 1997. pap. 43.00 (*0-444-85821-0*, North Holland) Elsevier.

Moutafakis, NIcholas J. The Logics of Preference: A Study of Prohairetic Logics in Twentieth Century Philosophy. 296p. (C). 1987. text 139.00 (*90-277-2591-8*, D Reidel) Kluwer Academic.

Moutafchieva, Vera P. Agrarian Relations in the Ottoman Empire in the Fifteenth & Sixteenth Centuries. (East European Monographs: No. 251). 245p. 1988. text 46.50 (*0-88033-148-8*, Pub. by East Eur Monographs) Col U Pr.

Moutal, Patrick. Comparative Study of Selected Hindustani Ragas on Contemporary Practice. (C). 1991. text 38.00 (*0-685-50093-4*, Pub. by M Manoharial) S Asia.

— Hindustani Raga-S Index. (Illus.). 340p. (C). 1991. 29.50 (*81-215-0525-9*, Pub. by Munshiram) Coronet Bks.

Moutaouakil, Ahmed. Pragmatic Functions in Functional Grammar of Arabic. (Functional Grammar Ser.: No. 8). xi, 156p. 1989. pap. 38.50 (*90-6765-271-7*) Mouton.

Moutet, Fernand. Golden Chord. Barkan, Stanley H., ed. Festinger, Nancy, tr. (Review Chapbook Ser.: No. 17: Provencal Poetry 1).Tr. of Provencal & Eng.. 16p. 1981. 15.00 (*0-89304-840-2*, CCC144); pap. 5.00 (*0-89304-816-X*); audio 10.00 (*0-89304-841-0*) Cross-Cultrl NY.

***Mouthaan, Ton J.** Semiconductor Devices Explained. LC 99-30067. 346p. 2000. 74.95 (*0-471-98854-5*) Wiley.

Mouthaan, Ton J. & Salm, Cora. Microelectronics Education: Proceedings of the 2nd European Workshop Held in Noordwijkerhout, the Netherlands, 14-15 May 1998. LC 98-21506. 298p. 1998. write for info. (*0-7923-5107-X*) Kluwer Academic.

Mouthany, J. R. English Without Teacher & Dictionary: English-Arabic. 237p. 1988. pap. 14.95 (*0-86685-058-9*, LDL0589) Intl Bk Ctr.

Mouthier, Annie. Dictionnaire des Termes Juridiques et Commerciaux. (FRE.). 227p. 1991. pap. 39.95 (*0-7859-8645-6*, 273280102x) Fr & Eur.

— Encyclopedie de SARL. 260p. 1993. pap. 59.95 (*0-7859-5639-5*, 2732801070) Fr & Eur.

***Moutinho, L.** Strategic Management in Tourism. LC 99-59381. (CABI Publishing Ser.). 450p. 1999. pap. text 45.00 (*0-85199-282-X*) OUP.

Moutinho, L., jt. auth. see Phillips, P.

Moutinho, Louis. Cases in Marketing Management. 2nd ed. LC 95-158530. 416p. (C). 1995. pap. text 53.00 (*0-201-62744-2*) Addison-Wesley.

Moutinho, Luiz & Evans, Martin. Applied Marketing Research. LC 92-17238. (C). 1992. pap. text 34.00 (*0-201-56504-8*) Addison-Wesley.

Moutinho, Luiz, et al. Computer Modelling & Expert Systems in Marketing. LC 94-7100. 224p. (C). 1994. pap. 81.95 (*0-415-08983-2*, B4539) Thomson Learn.

— Expert Systems in Tourism Marketing. LC 95-560. (Issues in Tourism Ser.). 224p. 1996. pap. 49.95 (*0-415-09316-3*) Thomson Learn.

— Quantitative Analysis in Marketing Management. LC 97-49694. 1998. text 93.00 (*0-471-96339-9*) Wiley.

— Quantitative Analysis in Marketing Management. LC 97-49694. 342p. 2000. pap. 47.00 (*0-471-96430-1*) Wiley.

M

Moutloub, Ahmed. A Dictionary of Clothes in Lisan al-'Arab. (ARA.). 142p. 1995. 24.95 (*0-86685-652-8*, LDL6528, Pub. by Librairie du Liban) Intl Bk Ctr.

Mouton, Boyce. Beyond the Veil. 158p. 1987. pap. 5.99 (*0-89900-314-1*) College Pr Pub.

Mouton, Boyce, ed. see Pratt, Michael C.

Mouton, Donald, ed. see De La Salle, John B.

Mouton, Donald, ed. see Maillefer, Francois-Elie & D'Auge, Bernard.

Mouton, Francois. Collins Watch Guide: Whales, Dolphins & Seals. (Illus.). 1997. pap. 11.95 (*0-00-220089-9*, Pub. by HarpC) Trafalgar.

Mouton, Jane S. & Blake, Robert R. Synergogy: A New Strategy for Education, Training, & Development. LC 83-23898. (Joint Publication in the Jossey-Bass Management Series & the Jossey-Bass Social & Behavioral Science Ser.). 206p. reprint ed. pap. 63.90 (*0-7837-2549-3*, 204270800006) Bks Demand.

Mouton, Jane S., jt. auth. see Blake, Robert R.

Mouton, Jean. Le Regard d'Hermann. unabridged ed. LC 99-161510.Tr. of Hermann's Gaze. (ENG & FRE.). 136p. 1998. pap. 18.00 (*0-9645677-3-3*) Starbks.

Mouton, John, jt. auth. see Householder, Jerry.

Moutos, Thomas, jt. auth. see Hart, Robert A.

Moutoussamy-Ashe, Jeanne. Viewfinders: Black Women Photographers. (Illus.). 200p. 1993. 39.95 (*0-86316-159-6*); pap. 19.95 (*0-86316-158-8*) Writers & Readers.

***Moutra, Billye J.** Dear Jesus. 1999. pap. text 0.00 (*0-9663213-0-8*) Educ Solns.

Moutran, Julie. Science Teacher's Almanac: Practical Ideas & Activities for Every Month of the School Year. 336p. 1992. pap. text 29.95 (*0-87628-809-3*) Ctr Appl Res.

Moutsatson, Peter & Straub, Joseph T. Management Fundamentals. 442p. (C). 1998. pap. text 43.95 (*1-56226-417-6*) CAT Pub.

***Moutsatsos, Kiki F.** Onassis Women: Kaye,&Judy, Set. 1998. audio 18.00 (*0-694-52117-5*) HarperAudio.

***Moutsatsos, Kiki F. & Karas, Phyllis.** The Onassis Women: An Eyewitness Account. LC 98-17129. (Illus.). 304p. 1998. 25.95 (*0-399-14443-9*, G P Putnam) Peng Put Young Read.

Moutschen, Jean. Introduction to Genetic Toxicology. LC 84-11868. (Wiley-Interscience Publications). 202p. reprint ed. pap. 62.70 (*0-8357-6940-2*, 203799900009) Bks Demand.

Moutsopoulos, Evanqhelos, jt. ed. see Gruender, C. David.

Mouw, Gene H. The Bible Condensed: Written in Current American. Mouw, Lynne A., ed. LC 89-92099. 144p. (Orig.). (C). 1989. pap. 8.95 (*0-9624551-0-5*) Mouw.

Mouw, Lynne A., ed. see Mouw, Gene H.

Mouw, Richard J. The God Who Commands: A Study in Divine Command Ethics. LC 89-40385. (C). 1991. pap. 13.00 (*0-268-01021-8*) U of Notre Dame Pr.

— Smell of Sawdust. 14.99 (*0-310-23196-5*) HarpC.

— Uncommon Decency: Christian Civility in an Uncivil World. LC 92-5680. 192p. (Orig.). 1992. pap. 10.99 (*0-8308-1825-1*) InterVarsity.

Mouy, Paul. Le Developpment de la Physique Cartesienne 1646-1712 (the Development of Cartesian Physics) Cohen, I. Bernard, ed. LC 80-2138. (Development of Science Ser.). (FRE.). 1981. reprint ed. lib. bdg. 33.95 (*0-405-13893-8*) Ayer.

Mouyelo-Katoula, Michel & Munnsa, Kantilal. Comparison of Price Levels & Economic Aggregates 1993: The Results of 22 African Countries. 378p. 1996. pap. 35.00 (*92-827-6742-6*, CA93-95-079-2AC, Pub. by Comm Europ Commun) Bernan Associates.

Mouzannar, Ibrahim. Tabbakh al Lebanie: Lebanese Cooking. (ARA., Illus.). 200p. 16.95 (*0-86685-278-6*, LDL2786, Pub. by Librairie du Liban) Intl Bk Ctr.

Mouzelis, Nicos. Sociological Theory: What Went Wrong?: Diagnosis & Remedies. LC 94-44296. 256p. (C). 1995. pap. 24.99 (*0-415-07694-3*) Routledge.

— Sociological Theory: What Went Wrong?: Diagnosis & Remedies. LC 94-44296. 256p. (C). (gr. 13). 1995. 80.00 (*0-415-12720-3*) Routledge.

Mouzelis, Nicos P. Back to Sociological Theory: The Construction of Social Orders. LC 91-9240. 1993. pap. 20.95 (*0-312-10361-1*) St Martin.

— Modern Greece: Facets of Underdevelopment. LC 78-312273. 222p. (C). 1980. 39.50 (*0-8419-0357-3*) Holmes & Meier.

— Organisation & Bureaucracy: An Analysis of Modern Theories. LC 68-11361. 239p. 1967. pap. text 25.95 (*0-202-30078-1*) Aldine de Gruyter.

***Mouzon, D. C.** Office & Ministry of - APOSTLE. 69p. 2000. pap. write for info. (*1-929740-01-8*) Faith Love & Truth.

— The Spirit of "Envy" 32p. 2000. pap. write for info. (*1-929740-03-4*) Faith Love & Truth.

— The Truth about "Ahab & Jezebel" 28p. 1999. pap. write for info. (*1-929740-00-X*) Faith Love & Truth.

— Understanding the Basics of - "DELIVERANCE" 23p. 2000. pap. write for info. (*1-929740-02-6*) Faith Love & Truth.

***Mouzon, Stephen A.** Architectural Elements: Traditional Construction Details. (Illus.). 2000. pap. 199.95 (*0-07-136350-5*) McGraw.

***Mouzos, Jenny.** Femicide: The Killing of Women in Australia 1989-1998. (Research & Public Policy Series: Vol. 18). 45p. 1999. pap. text 75.00 (*0-642-24117-1*, Pub. by Aust Inst Criminology) St Mut.

Movat, H. Z., ed. Leukocyte Emigration & Its Sequelae. (Illus.). vi, 186p. 1987. 121.00 (*3-8055-4489-8*) S Karger.

Movchan, A. B. & Movchan, N. V. Mathematical Modelling of Solids with Nonregular Boundaries. Bellomo, N., ed. LC 95-23090. (Mathematical Modelling Ser.). 352p. 1995. boxed set 99.95 (*0-8493-8338-2*, 8338) CRC Pr.

Movchan, N. V., jt. auth. see Movchan, A. B.

Movement for a Peoples Assembly Staff. The Los Angeles Rebellion Against Racism. 1992. pap. 2.50 (*0-89567-104-2*) World View Forum.

Movenkamp, Herbert, jt. auth. see Kurtz, Sheldon F.

Movius, Hallam L. Early Man & Pleistocene Stratigraphy in Southern & Eastern Asia. (HU PMP Ser.: Vol. 19, No. 3). (Illus.). 1944. 28.00 (*0-527-01249-1*) Periodicals Srv.

Movius, Hallam L., jt. auth. see Howe, B.

Movius, Hallam L., Jr., ed. see Bricker, Harvey M., Jr. & David, Nicholas.

Movius, Phyllis D., jt. auth. see Romig, Ella M.

Movsesian, Ara J. How to Write Love Letters & Love Poems. LC 84-147625. (Illus.). 310p. 1983. pap. 12.95 (*0-916919-00-5*) Electric Pr.

— Love Poems for Cards & Letters. LC 88-81507. (Illus.). 90p. 1988. pap. 9.95 (*0-916919-60-9*) Electric Pr.

***Movsesian, Ara John.** Pearls of Love: How to Write Love Letters & Love Poems. 307p. 1999. reprint ed. pap. text 13.00 (*0-7881-6593-3*) DIANE Pub.

Movsessian, Alexander, see Shirvanzadeh, pseud.

Movshon, J. Anthony, jt. ed. see Landy, Michael S.

Movshovitz-Hadar, Nitsa & Webb, John. One Equals Zero: And Other Mathematical Surprises. LC 98-232540. (Illus.). xvi, 168p. (YA). (gr. 9-12). 1998. pap. text 13.95 (*1-55953-309-9*) Key Curr Pr.

Movshovitz, Howie, ed. Mike Leigh: Interviews. LC 99-44200. (Conversations with Filmmakers Ser.). 256p. 2000. 45.00 (*1-57806-067-2*) U Pr of Miss.

Movshovitz, Howie & Brunette, Peter, eds. Mike Leigh: Interviews. LC 99-44200. (Conversations with Filmmakers Ser.). 256p. 2000. pap. 18.00 (*1-57806-068-0*) U Pr of Miss.

Movsovic, M. I. Technical & Vocational Education in the U. S. S. R. A Bibliographical Survey (UNESCO) (Education Studies & Documents: No. 30). 1974. reprint ed. pap. 25.00 (*0-8115-1354-8*) Periodicals Srv.

Mow, V. C., et al, eds. Biomechanics of Diarthrodial Joints, 2 vols., Vol. I. (Illus.). xix, 450p. 1990. 93.95 (*0-387-97378-8*) Spr-Verlag.

— Biomechanics of Diarthrodial Joints, 2 vols., Vol. II. (Illus.). xx, 464p. 1990. 93.95 (*0-387-97379-6*) Spr-Verlag.

Mow, Van C., et al, eds. Knee Meniscus: Basic & Clinical Foundations. LC 91-45669. (Illus.). 204p. reprint ed. pap. 63.30 (*0-608-09760-8*, 206993300007) Bks Demand.

Mow, Van C. & Hayes, Wilson C., eds. Basic Orthopaedic Biomechanics. 2nd ed. LC 97-1336. 560p. 1997. text 89.00 (*0-397-51684-3*) Lppncott W & W.

Mow, Van C., et al. Knee Meniscus: Basic & Clinical Foundations. 208p. 1992. text 93.50 (*0-88167-895-3*) Lppncott W & W.

Mowad, Linda & Ruhle, Diane C. The Handbook of Emergency Nursing: A Nursing Process Approach. 391p. (C). 1992. pap. text 43.95 (*0-8385-3600-X*, A3600-2, Apple Lange Med) McGraw.

Mowaljarlai, David & Malnic, Jutta. Yorro Yorro - Aboriginal Creation & the Renewal of Nature: The Art & Stories of the People of the Australian Kimberley. LC 93-78292. (Illus.). 248p. (Orig.). 1993. pap. 19.95 (*0-89281-460-8*) Inner Tradit.

Mowat. Liver Disorders in Childhood. 508p. 1998. pap. text 100.00 (*0-7506-4200-9*) Buttrwrth-Heinemann.

— Owls in the Family. rev. ed. 1989. pap. 6.99 (*0-7710-6693-7*) McCland & Stewart.

Mowat, Alex P. Liver Disorders in Childhood. 3rd ed. (Illus.). 496p. 1994. 160.00 (*0-7506-1039-5*) Buttrwrth-Heinemann.

Mowat, Alexander, jt. auth. see Mowat, William.

Mowat, Barbara, ed. see Shakespeare, William.

***Mowat, Barbara A. & Werstine, Paul.** A Midsummer Night's Dream. 1999. per. 8.95 (*0-671-04290-4*) S&S Trade.

— Othello. 1999. per. 9.95 (*0-671-04289-0*) S&S Trade.

— Romeo & Juliet. 1999. per. 9.95 (*0-671-04288-2*) S&S Trade.

Mowat, Barbara A., ed. see Luke, Helen M.

Mowat, Barbara A., ed. see Shakespeare Association Staff.

Mowat, Barbara A., ed. see Shakespeare, William.

Mowat-Brown, George. The Rover. (Album Ser.: No. 282). (Illus.). 32p. 1989. pap. 6.25 (*0-7478-0154-1*, Pub. by Shire Pubns) Parkwest Pubns.

Mowat, Charles. Britain Between the Wars, Nineteen Eighteen to Nineteen Forty. LC 55-5139. 704p. reprint ed. pap. 200.00 (*0-8357-7411-2*, 202406000035) Bks Demand.

Mowat, Claire. The French Isles. 112p. 1995. mass mkt. 4.99 (*0-7704-2719-7*) Bantam.

— Girl from Away. 96p. 1993. pap. 4.99 (*0-7704-2571-2*) Bantam.

Mowat, Farley. Aftermath: Travels in a Postwar World. (Illus.). 240p. 1996. 22.95 (*1-57098-103-5*) Roberts Rinehart.

— Aftermath: Travels in a Postwar World. 240p. 1997. pap. 14.95 (*1-57098-173-6*) Roberts Rinehart.

— And No Birds Sang. 21.95 (*0-89190-821-8*) Amereon Ltd.

— The Black Joke. 1987. mass mkt. 6.99 (*0-7710-6679-1*) McCland & Stewart.

— The Boat Who Wouldn't Float. 208p. (YA). 1984. mass mkt. 4.99 (*0-553-27788-X*) Bantam.

— Born Naked: The Early Adventures of the Author of "Never Cry Wolf" 272p. 1994. mass mkt. 6.99 (*0-7704-2617-4*) Bantam.

— Born Naked: The Early Adventures of the Author of Never Cry Wolf. 272p. 1995. pap. 12.00 (*0-395-73528-9*) HM.

— Born Naked: The Early Adventures of the Author of "Never Cry Wolf" large type ed. LC 94-31743. 1994. pap. 19.95 (*1-56895-076-4*) Wheeler Pub.

— The Curse of the Viking Grave. 1987. mass mkt. 6.99 (*0-7710-6680-5*) McCland & Stewart.

— The Dog Who Wouldn't Be. 21.95 (*0-89190-819-6*) Amereon Ltd.

— The Dog Who Wouldn't Be. 224p. (YA). 1984. mass mkt. 4.99 (*0-553-27928-9*) Bantam.

— The Dog Who Wouldn't Be. 208p. 1984. pap. 6.99 (*0-7704-2265-9*) Bantam.

***Mowat, Farley.** The Farfarers: Before the Norse. LC 99-43310. 377p. 2000. pap. 16.00 (*1-883642-56-6*, Pub. by Steerforth Pr) Publishers Group.

Mowat, Farley. The Farley Mowat Reader. (Illus.). 192p. 1997. 24.95 (*1-57098-175-2*) Roberts Rinehart.

— Grey Seas Under. 256p. 1981. mass mkt. 5.99 (*0-7704-2333-7*) Bantam.

— Lost in the Barrens. 208p. (YA). 1985. mass mkt. 5.50 (*0-553-27525-9*, Starfire BDD) BDD Bks Young Read.

— Lost in the Barrens. 1987. mass mkt. 6.99 (*0-7710-6681-3*) McCland & Stewart.

— Lost in the Barrens. 1956. 9.09 (*0-606-00513-7*, Pub. by Turtleback) Demco.

— Mowat Adventure Stories. 1987. mass mkt. 20.99 (*0-7710-6682-1*) McCland & Stewart.

— My Father's Son. 384p. 1993. mass mkt. 7.99 (*0-7704-2576-3*) Bantam.

— Never Cry Wolf. 19.95 (*0-89190-823-4*) Amereon Ltd.

— Never Cry Wolf. 176p. 1983. mass mkt. 5.99 (*0-553-27396-5*) Bantam.

— Never Cry Wolf. 176p. 1985. pap. 6.99 (*0-7704-2137-7*) Bantam.

Mowat, Farley. Never Cry Wolf. (J). 1979. 10.60 (*0-606-02207-4*, Pub. by Turtleback) Demco.

Mowat, Farley. The Newfoundland: A Personal Voyage of Discovery. 448p. 1990. pap. 7.99 (*0-7704-2419-8*) Bantam.

— Owls in the Family. 1976. 21.95 (*0-89190-820-X*) Amereon Ltd.

— Owls in the Family. 96p. (J). 1996. pap. 4.50 (*0-440-41361-3*) BDD Bks Young Read.

Mowat, Farley. Owls in the Family. (J). 1996. 9.19 (*0-606-02220-1*, Pub. by Turtleback) Demco.

Mowat, Farley. People of the Deer. 25.95 (*0-89190-818-8*) Amereon Ltd.

— People Of The Deer. 304p. 1984. mass mkt. 5.99 (*0-7704-2254-3*) Bantam.

— Rescue the Earth! Conversations with the Green Crusaders. 282p. 1998. pap. text 15.00 (*0-7881-5961-5*) DIANE Pub.

— Sea of Slaughter: A Chronicle of the Destruction of Animal Life in the North Atlantic. Brooks, Cristen, ed. LC 96-21050. (Illus.). 446p. 1996. reprint ed. pap. 13.95 (*1-57630-019-6*, Chapters Bks) HM.

— Sibir. 1990. mass mkt. 6.95 (*0-7710-6691-0*) McCland & Stewart.

— Three Farley Mowat Classics, 3 vols. 1993. mass mkt. 21.99 (*0-7710-6698-8*) McCland & Stewart.

— Virgunga: The Passion of Dian Fossey. 448p. 1988. mass mkt. 7.99 (*0-7704-2257-8*) Bantam.

— A Whale for the Killing. 21.95 (*0-89190-822-6*) Amereon Ltd.

— A Whale for the Killing. 224p. 1984. mass mkt. 5.99 (*0-7704-2331-0*) Bantam.

Mowat, Farley. Whale for the Killing. (J). 1972. 10.60 (*0-606-02387-9*, Pub. by Turtleback) Demco.

Mowat, Farley. Woman in the Mists: The Story of Dian Fossey & the Mountain Gorillas of Africa. LC 87-40166. 400p. 1988. mass mkt. 11.99 (*0-446-38720-7*, Pub. by Warner Bks) Little.

Mowat, J. L., ed. Alphita, a Medico-Botanical Glossary. (Anecdota Oxoniensia Ser.: No. 2). 1988. reprint ed. 67.40 (*0-404-63952-6*) AMS Pr.

Mowat, J. L., ed. see Mirfeld, John.

Mowat, Keith, jt. ed. see Curtis, Mike.

Mowat, Linda. Casava & Chica: Bread & Beer of the Amazonian Indians. (Ethnography Ser.: No. 11). (Illus.). 64p. 1989. pap. 10.50 (*0-7478-0008-1*, Pub. by Shire Pubns) Parkwest Pubns.

Mowat, R. C. Decline & Renewal: Europe - Ancient & Modern. 1991. 35.95 (*0-9517695-0-2*, Pub. by New Cherwell) Intl Spec Bk.

— Modern Prophetic Voices: From Kierkegaard to Buchman. (Orig.). 1994. pap. 12.95 (*0-9517695-6-1*, Pub. by New Cherwell); pap. 12.95 (*0-9517695-4-5*, Pub. by New Cherwell) Intl Spec Bk.

Mowat, Robert B. Americans in England. LC 79-99642. (Essay Index Reprint Ser.). 1977. 28.95 (*0-8369-1423-6*) Ayer.

— International Relations. LC 67-22105. (Essay Index Reprint Ser.). 1977. 17.95 (*0-8369-0725-6*) Ayer.

Mowat, Robert J. The Logboats of Scotland. (Oxbow Monographs in Archaeology: No. 68). (Illus.). 166p. 1996. pap. 40.00 (*1-900188-11-2*, Pub. by Oxbow Bks) David Brown.

Mowat, Susan. The Port of Leith. 470p. (C). 1996. pap. 60.00 (*0-85976-403-6*, Pub. by J Donald) St Mut.

Mowat, William & Mowat, Alexander. A Treatise on Stair Building & Hand Railing. LC 85-6916. 390p. 1985. reprint ed. pap. 26.95 (*0-941936-02-3*) Linden Pub Fresno.

Mowatt, Anna C. Autobiography of an Actress. Baxter, Annette K., ed. LC 79-8807. (Signal Lives Ser.). (Illus.). 1980. reprint ed. lib. bdg. 50.95 (*0-405-12853-3*) Ayer.

— Fashion: Or, Life in New York. Meserve, Walter J., ed. & intro. by. (On Stage, America! Ser.). 53p. 1996. spiral bd. 4.95 (*0-937657-26-3*) Feedbk Theabks & Prospero.

Mowatt, Barbara A., ed. see Shakespeare, William.

Mowatt, D. G. & Secker, Hugh. The Nibelungenlied: An Interpretative Commentary. LC 68-83851. 152p. reprint ed. pap. 47.20 (*0-8357-4145-1*, 203691800006) Bks Demand.

Mowatt, Don, frwd. Out of Isak Dinesen in Africa: Karen Blixen's Untold Story. 2nd rev. ed. LC 98-72165. (Illus.). 440p. 1998. 35.00 (*0-9643893-8-X*, SAN 298-6043) Coulsong List.

Mowatt, Geoffry S. The Rainbow Through the Rain: A Tale of a Japanese Prisoner of War. (Illus.). 155p. 1996. pap. 14.95 (*0-9517695-9-6*, Pub. by New Cherwell) Intl Spec Bk.

Mowatt, John J., ed. The Ukrainians in Rhode Island: Faith & Determination. (Rhode Island Ethnic Heritage Pamphlet Ser.). (Illus.). (Orig.). 1988. pap. 6.75 (*0-917012-90-9*) RI Pubns Soc.

Mowbray, Andrew, ed. see Campbell, Archibald.

Mowbray, Carol T., et al, eds. Women & Mental Health: New Directions for Change. LC 84-19228. (Women & Therapy Ser.: Vol. 3, Nos. 3-4). 202p. 1985. text 6.95 (*0-86656-331-8*); pap. text 19.95 (*0-86656-437-3*) Haworth Pr.

Mowbray, Carol T, et al, eds. Women & Mental Health: New Directions for Change. LC 84-22454. (Women & Therapy Ser.: Vol. 3, Nos. 3 & 4). 202p. 1985. pap. text 19.95 (*0-918393-13-2*, Harrington Park) Haworth Pr.

Mowbray, Carol T. & International Association of Phychosocial Rehabilitation Services. Consumers as Providers in Psychiatric Rehabilitation. LC 98-226152. xvii, 525p. 1997. write for info. (*0-9655843-1-3*) Intl Assn Psych.

Mowbray, Donald. Authority & Community in the Middle Ages. 2000. 82.00 (*0-7509-1867-5*) Bks Intl VA.

Mowbray, E. Andrew. The American Eagle-Pommel Sword: The Early Years, 1793-1830. 2nd ed. LC 88-61132. (Illus.). 244p. 1997. 65.00 (*0-917218-74-4*) A Mowbray.

Mowbray, George, jt. auth. see Rutman, Leonard.

Mowbray, James F. Post Viral Fatigue Syndrome. Jenkins, Rachel, ed. LC 90-13138. 502p. 1993. pap. 176.95 (*0-471-93879-3*, Wiley-Liss) Wiley.

Mowbray, James F., jt. ed. see Jenkins, Rachel.

Mowbray, Jay H., ed. Sinking of the Titanic: Eyewitness Accounts. LC 98-3690. (Illus.). 320p. pap. 6.95 (*0-486-40298-3*) Dover.

Mowbray, John. Plot Pak: Precalculus Tutorials with Computer Graphics. (Software Ser.). 191p. (C). 1987. pap. text 53.95 incl. disk (*0-534-07542-8*) PWS Pubs.

Mowbray, Robert. Maximizing the Profitability of Law Firms. 134p. 1997. pap. 44.00 (*1-85431-597-8*, Pub. by Blackstone Pr) Gaunt.

Mowbray, Stuart C., ed. American Swords: From the Philip Medicus Collection. LC 97-76111. (Illus.). 272p. 1998. 55.00 (*0-917218-78-7*) A Mowbray.

***Mowbray, Stuart C., ed.** Civil War Arms Purchases & Deliveries. LC 99-76266. 312p. 2000. 35.00 (*0-917218-89-2*) A Mowbray.

Mowbray, Stuart C. & Heroux, Jennifer, eds. Civil War Arms Makers & Their Contracts: A Facsimile Reprint of the Report by the Commission on Ordnance & Ordnance Stores, 1862. LC 97-75489. 599p. 1998. 39.50 (*0-917218-77-9*) A Mowbray.

Mowbray, Thomas. An Introduction to Corba. LC 97-16075. 400p. (C). 1997. pap. 47.95 (*0-201-89540-4*) Addison-Wesley.

***Mowbray, Thomas J.** Software Architecture: A Programmer's Field Manual. (Software Architecture & Engineering Ser.). 400p. 2000. pap. 45.00 (*1-57870-152-X*) New Riders Pub.

Mowbray, Thomas J. & Malveau, Raphael C. CORBA Design Patterns. LC 96-44734. 352p. 1997. pap., pap. text 54.95 incl. cd-rom (*0-471-15882-8*) Wiley.

Mowbray, Thomas J. & Zahavi, Ron. The Essential CORBA: Systems Integration Using Distributed Objects. LC 95-50760. 336p. 1995. 54.99 (*0-471-10611-9*) Wiley.

***Mowbray, Tom & Malveau, Raphael C.** Software Architecture: A Programmer's Field Manual. 2000. 49.00 (*0-13-027407-0*) P-H.

Mowbray, William W. The Eastern Shore Baseball League. LC 88-32224. (Illus.). 208p. 1989. reprint ed. pap. 64.50 (*0-608-04099-1*, 206483100011) Bks Demand.

— Powerboat Racing on the Chesapeake. LC 95-44185. (Illus.). 127p. 1995. pap. 16.95 (*0-87033-473-5*, Tidewtr Pubs) Cornell Maritime.

Mowday, L. La Trampa.Tr. of Snare. (SPA.). 276p. pap. 8.99 (*1-56063-554-1*, 498588) Editorial Unilit.

Mowday, Lois. La Trampa.Tr. of Snare. Date not set. write for info. (*0-614-26584-3*) Editorial Unilit.

Mowe, Rosalind. South East Asian Specialties: A Culinary Journey Through Singapore, Malaysia, & Indonesia. (Culinary Recipes Ser.). (Illus.). 320p. 1999. 19.95 (*3-89508-909-5*, 520350) Konemann.

Mowell, Barry D. Internet Resources for World Geography: A Reference Guide & Workbook. 96p. (C). per. write for info. (*0-7872-6729-5*) Kendall-Hunt.

Mowell, Barry D. World Travel Guide: A Resource for Travel & Information. LC 99-20889. (Illus.). 454p. 1999. pap. 19.95 (*1-55571-494-3*) PSI Resch.

Mowen, jt. auth. see Hansen.

Mowen, Carol & Mowen, Gregg. Focus on Independent Study. Romano, Louis G., ed. 16p. 1990. pap. text. write for info. (*0-318-72649-1*) MI Middle Educ.

Mowen, Gregg, jt. auth. see Mowen, Carol.

Mowen, John C. Judgement Calls: Making Good Decisions in Difficult Situations. 304p. 1994. pap. 12.00 (*0-671-89883-3*, Fireside) S&S Trade Pap.

***Mowen, John C.** The 3M Model of Motivation & Personality: Theory & Empirical Applications to Consumer Behavior. LC 99-47406. 336p. 1999. 110.00 (*0-7923-8543-8*) Kluwer Academic.

Mowen, John C. & Minor, Michael. Consumer Behavior. 5th ed. LC 97-3101. 696p. 1997. 92.00 (*0-13-737115-2*) P-H.

***Mowen, John C. & Minor, Michael.** Consumer Behavior: A Framework. 352p. 2000. pap. 51.33 (*0-13-016972-2*, Prentice Hall) P-H.

An Asterisk (*) at the beginning of an entry indicates that the title is appearing for the first time.

M

An Asterisk (*) at the beginning of an entry indicates that the title is appearing for the first time.

— The Dandy Dollhouse Stories. (Illus.). 73p. 1993. 16.95 (*1-878208-30-6*) Guild Pr IN.
— The Dandy Dollhouse Stories: The Mexican Dollhouse. LC 96-75159. (Illus.). 90p. (J). (gr. 4-6). 1996. 16.95 (*1-878208-80-2*) Guild Pr IN.
— The Dandy Dollhouse Stories: Twenty Years Later. LC 94-78046. 92p. (J). 1994. 16.95 (*1-878208-51-9*) Guild Pr IN.
— For the Love of Music: A Legacy of Teaching. 80p. 1992. pap. 8.95 (*1-878208-18-7*) Guild Pr IN.
— Travel Impressions: The Discovery of Golden Civilizations. LC 96-78246. 75p. (Orig.). 1996. pap. 8.95 (*1-878208-93-4*) Guild Pr IN.
Moxley, Ray. Building Management by Professionals. LC 92-2429. (Butterworth Architecture Management Guides Ser.). (Illus.). 191p. reprint ed. pap. 59.30 (*0-608-04415-6*, 206519600001) Bks Demand.
Moxley, Richard T., jt. ed. see Griggs, Robert C.
Moxley, Robert, jt. ed. see Kalb, Gilbert.
Moxley, Roy. Writing & Reading in Early Childhood: A Functional Approach. LC 81-9686. (Illus.). 290p. 1982. 39.95 (*0-87778-180-X*) Educ Tech Pubns.
Moxley, Roy A. Continuous Improvement of Instruction: Instructional Design with Frequent Measurement & Postitive Evaluation (Pre-K) 236p. (C). 1994. text 27.87 (*1-884802-00-1*); pap. text 20.76 (*1-884802-01-X*) NextPrint.

M

***Moxley, Russ S.** Leadership & Spirit: Breathing New Vitality & Energy into Individuals & Organizations. LC 99-6656. 256p. 1999. 30.95 (*0-7879-0949-1*) Jossey-Bass.
Moxley, Sheila. ABCD: An Alphabet Book of Cats & Dogs. (J). 2000. write for info. (*0-316-59240-4*) Little.
Moxley, Sheila. The Arabian Nights. LC 94-9137. 160p. (YA). (gr. 5 up). 1994. 19.95 (*0-531-06868-4*) Orchard Bks Watts.
— Skip Across the Ocean: Nursery Rhymes from Around the World. LC 94-48739. 48p. (J). (ps-1). 1996. 15.95 (*0-531-09455-3*) Orchard Bks Watts.
Moxley, Susan. Play with Papier-Mache. LC 94-14247. (Play with Crafts Ser.). 24p. (J). (ps-2). 1995. lib. bdg. 19.95 (*0-87614-865-8*, Carolrhoda) Lerner Pub.
Moxley, Wright. Red Snow. 422p. 28.95 (*0-8488-2626-4*) Amereon Ltd.
Moxly, S. H. Coastal Tables: For Use in Sight of Land. (C). 1987. 40.00 (*0-85174-128-2*) St Mut.
Moxnes, Halvor. Constructing Early Christian Families: Family as Social Reality & Metaphor. LC 96-44657. (Illus.). 288p. (C). 1997. 80.00 (*0-415-14638-0*); pap. 25.99 (*0-415-14639-9*) Routledge.
***Moxon-Browne.** Building a Better Team. 1998. pap. 33.95 (*0-566-08007-9*) Ashgate Pub Co.
Moxon-Browne, Edward. Nation, Class & Creed in Northern Ireland. 224p. (Orig.). 1983. 69.95 (*0-566-00607-3*) Ashgate Pub Co.
Moxon-Browne, Edward, ed. European Terrorism. Vol. 3. LC 93-6399. (International Library of Terrorism: No. 3). 501p. 1994. 50.00 (*0-8161-7335-4*, G K Hall & Co) Mac Lib Ref.
***Moxon-Browne, Edward, ed.** Who Are the Europeans Now? 240p. 1999. text 69.95 (*1-84014-429-7*, Pub. by Ashgate Pub) Ashgate Pub Co.
Moxon, Geoffrey. The Raven's Wing. large type ed. (General Ser.). 416p. 1993. 27.99 (*0-7089-2883-8*) Ulverscroft.
— The Red Knight. large type ed. 1990. 27.99 (*0-7089-2286-4*) Ulverscroft.
Moxon, Joseph. Mechanic Exercises: or The Doctrine of Handy-Works. (Illus.). 352p. 1989. reprint ed. pap. 25.00 (*1-879335-85-9*) Astragal Pr.
Moxon, Karen A., jt. auth. see Chapin, John K.
Moxon, P. R. Gundogs: Training & Field Trials. 16th ed. (Illus.). 176p. 1997. 35.95 (*1-85310-585-6*, Pub. by Swan Hill Pr) Voyageur Pr.
— Training the Roughshooter's Dog. (Illus.). 158p. 1994. 28.95 (*1-85310-501-5*, Pub. by Swan Hill Pr) Voyageur Pr.
Moxon, Richard W. Offshore Production in the Less Developed Countries: A Case Study of Multinationality in the Electronics Industry. LC HD0069.F6M68. (New York University, Institute of Finance, Bulletin Ser.: No. 98-99, July, 1974). 95p. reprint ed. pap. 30.00 (*0-608-17459-9*, 202993300066) Bks Demand.
Moy. Animal Addresses. Date not set. pap. text. write for info. (*0-582-87034-8*, Pub. by Addison-Wesley) Longman.
Moy & Usatine. Color Atlas of Office Skin Surgery. LC 97-42561. (Illus.). 336p. (C). (gr. 13). 1998. text 69.95 (*0-8151-7362-8*, 28047) Mosby Inc.
Moy, Amelyn C. Business Guide to Singapore. LC 98-140098. 300p. 1997. pap. 17.95 (*981-00-6793-3*, Pub. by Select Bks) Weatherhill.
Moy, Caryl, jt. auth. see Nunnally, Elam.
Moy, Celeste M. & Moy-Savings Publications Committee. Value in The Village: A Savings & Investment Club Guide for African-americans. LC 97-78332. 90p. 1998. write for info. (*0-9663016-0-9*) Moy-Savings.
Moy, Doug H. Living Trusts: After the 1997 Taxpayer Relief Act. 2nd ed. LC 98-17438. 425p. 1998. pap. text 39.95 incl. disk (*0-471-29027-0*) Wiley.
***Moy, Doug H.** Wealth Preservation: How to Start & Develop an Estate Planning Practice. LC 98-5037. 464p. 1998. 80.00 (*0-471-12259-9*) Wiley.
Moy, Henry, intro. Treasures of Beloit College: 100 Works from the Logan Museum of Anthropology & the Wright Museum of Art. (Illus.). 100p. (Orig.). 1995. pap. 12.95 (*1-884941-03-6*) Beloit Coll.
Moy, J. Erik, jt. auth. see Theodore, Louis.
Moy, James S. Marginal Sights: Staging the Chinese in America. LC 93-17415. (Studies in Theatre History & Culture). (Illus.). 172p. 1993. text 29.95 (*0-87745-427-2*) U of Iowa Pr.
— Marginal Sights: Staging the Chinese in America. LC 93-17415. (Studies in Theatre History & Culture). (Illus.). 172p. 1993. reprint ed. pap. text 14.95 (*0-87745-448-5*) U of Iowa Pr.
Moy, Jean O., tr. & intro. see Inoue, Yasushi.
Moy, John T. OSPF: Anatomy of an Internet Routing Protocol. LC 97-39463. 368p. (C). 1998. 47.95 (*0-201-63472-4*) Addison-Wesley.
— OSPF Complete Implementation. (C). 2000. 44.95 incl. cd-rom (*0-201-30966-1*) Addison-Wesley.
Moy, Laurence S., jt. auth. see Cranfield, Arthur.
Moy, Mark M. The EMTALA Answer Book. LC 99-25465. 160p. 1998. pap. 39.00 (*0-8342-1088-6*, 10886) Aspen Pub.
***Moy, Mark M.** The Emtala Answer Book. 2nd ed. LC 00-33183. 2000. write for info. (*0-8342-1877-1*) Aspen Pub.
***Moy, Patricia & Pfau, Michael.** With Malice Toward All? The Media & Public Confidence in Democratic Institutions. LC 99-46408. (Praeger Series in Political Communication). 240p. 2000. write for info. (*0-275-96433-7*, Praeger Pubs) Greenwood.
Moy, Ronald L. Atlas of Cutaneous Facial Flaps & Grafts: A Differential Diagnosis of Wound Closures. LC 89-13856. 224p. 1990. text 98.50 (*0-8121-1313-6*) Lppncott W & W.
— Practical Management of Skin Cancer. LC 98-30093. (Illus.). 288p. 1998. text 125.00 (*0-397-51604-5*) Lppncott W & W.
Moy, Ronald L., abr. Study Guide for Statistics for Buisness & Financial Economics. 300p. 1999. pap. 28.00 (*981-02-3831-2*) World Scientific Pub.
Moy, Ronald L., jt. ed. see Lask, Gary P.
***Moy, Roy G., ed.** Helping Employers Comply with the ADA: An Assessment of How the United Ststes Equal Emplyment Opportunity Commission is Enforcing. (Illus.). 312p. (C). 2000. reprint ed. pap. text 35.00 (*0-7881-8623-X*) DIANE Pub.
***Moy, Ruby G., ed.** Helping State & Local Governments Comply with the ADA: An Assessment of How the United States Department of Justice Is Enforcing. 167p. (C). 2000. reprint ed. pap. text 30.00 (*0-7881-8662-0*) DIANE Pub.
Moy-Savings Publications Committee, jt. auth. see Moy, Celeste M.
Moya, Antonio P. De la Divina Proporcion. (SPA.). 259p. 1981. pap. 7.75 (*84-85859-14-6*, 2010) Ediciones Norte.
Moya, Carlos J. Philosophy of Action. 1990. pap. 26.95 (*0-7456-0747-0*) Blackwell Pubs.
Moya, Carol J. A Guide to Austin Private Schools. 2nd rev. ed. 1997. pap. 29.95 (*0-9652814-1-8*) Austin Priv Schl.
Moya, Isabel M. Cartas Con Mi Guia. LC 95-61700. (SPA., Illus.). 86p. (Orig.). 1995. pap. 10.95 (*1-882573-06-4*, Zinnia Bks) Serena Bay.
Moya, J. Perez. Estrategia Gestion y Habilidades Directivas. (SPA.). 335p. 1996. pap. 26.50 (*84-7978-280-3*, Pub. by Ediciones Diaz) IBD Ltd.
Moya, Jose. Al Este de Broadway. 2nd rev. ed. LC 98-93930. (SPA.). 256p. Date not set. pap. 14.95 (*0-9668578-0-1*) Ediciones MC.
Moya, Jose. Al Este de Broadway. 3rd rev. ed. (SPA.). Date not set. 21.95 (*0-9668578-1-X*) Ediciones MC.
Moya, Jose C. Cousins & Strangers: Spanish Immigrants in Buenos Aires, 1850-1930. LC 96-26731. 586p. 1997. 55.00 (*0-520-07229-4*, Pub. by U CA Pr); pap. 25.00 (*0-520-21526-5*, Pub. by U CA Pr) Cal Prin Full Svc.
Moya, Olga & Fono, Andrew L. Federal Enviromental Law: The User's Guide. LC 97-130575. (Paralegal). 425p. (C). 1997. pap. text 14.25 (*0-314-03721-7*) West Pub.
***Moya, Paula M. L. & Hames-Garcia, Michael P., eds.** Reclaiming Identity: Realist Theory & the Predicament of Postmodernism. 382p. 2000. 60.00 (*0-520-22348-9*) U CA Pr.
***Moya, Paula M. L. & Hames-Garcia, Michael Roy, eds.** Reclaiming Identity: Realist Theory & the Predicament of Postmodernism. LC 00-22788. (Illus.). 382p. 2000. pap. 24.95 (*0-520-22349-7*, Pub. by U CA Pr) Cal Prin Full Svc.
Moyad, Mark A. The ABC's of Advanced Prostate Cancer. LC 99-14167. (Illus.). 325p. 2000. 24.95 (*1-886947-68-6*) Sleepng Bear.
— The ABC's of Nutrition & Supplements for Prostate Cancer. LC 99-18425. (Illus.). 275p. 2000. 24.95 (*1-886947-69-4*) Sleepng Bear.
Moyad, Mark A. & Oesterling, Joseph E. The ABCs of Prostate Cancer. (Illus.). 196p. 1996. pap. text 19.95 (*1-886569-06-1*) J W Edwards.
Moyad, Mark A., jt. auth. see Oesterling, Joseph E.
Moyal, Georges J., ed. Rene Descartes: Critical Assessments, 4 vols., Set. (Illus.). 1696p. (C). (gr. 13). 1991. text, boxed set 655.00 (*0-415-02528-0*, A5795) Routledge.
Moyal, Henri M., tr. see Nebot, Didier.
***Moyano, Maria Elena.** The Autobiography of Maria Elena Moyano: The Life & Death of a Peruvian Activist. Miloslavich Tupac, Diana, ed. & anno. by. LC 00-26805. (Illus.). 2000. 34.95 (*0-8130-1810-2*) U Press Fla.
Moyano, Maria J. Argentina's Lost Patrol: Armed Struggle, 1969-1979. LC 94-35509. 1995. 27.50 (*0-300-06122-6*) Yale U Pr.
Moyano, Pilar. Fernando Villalon: El Poeta y Su Obra. 1990. 46.50 (*0-916379-80-9*) Scripta.
Moyar, Mark. Phoenix & the Birds of Prey: The CIA's Secret Campaign to Destroy the Viet Cong. (Illus.). 464p. 1997. 29.95 (*1-55750-593-4*) Naval Inst Pr.
***Moybe, Lemuel A. & Kapadia, Asha Seth.** Difference Equations with Public Health Applications. LC 00-40473. (Biostatistics Ser.). 2000. write for info. (*0-8247-0447-9*) Dekker.
Moyd, Glenda. Silent Heart. LC 98-86240. 48p. 1998. pap. text 7.95 (*1-56167-451-6*, Five Star Spec Ed) Am Literary Pr.
Moyd, Olin P. Preaching & Practical Theology: An African American Perspective. LC 94-9198. 1994. 9.95 (*0-910683-23-9*) Townsnd-Pr.
— The Sacred Art: Preaching & Theology in the African American Tradition. 160p. 1995. pap. 14.00 (*0-8170-1220-6*) Judson.
Moye. Feldman Pathways Psychology. 1993. teacher ed. 30.00 (*0-07-020799-2*) McGraw.
— Law of Business Organization. 5th ed. LC 98-8350. (Paralegal Ser.). 976p. (C). 1998. pap. text 82.95 (*0-314-12806-9*) Delmar.
— Law of Business Organization. 5th ed. 264p. 1998. pap. text, teacher ed. 15.95 (*0-7668-0391-0*) Delmar.
Moye, A. Tom. The Depth of His Love. LC 97-73691. (Orig.). 1997. pap. 8.99 (*0-88270-697-7*, Logos NJ) Bridge-Logos.
Moye, H. Anson. Analysis of Pesticide Residues. LC 90-33710. 478p. (C). 1990. reprint ed. 89.50 (*0-89464-330-4*) Krieger.
Moye, Jerry. Praying with the Saints: Julian of Norwich & Saint Francis of Assissi. (Reclaiming the Sacred Ser.: No. 1). 128p. 1996. pap. 13.00 (*1-57312-036-7*) Smyth & Helwys.
***Moye, John E.** Colorado Business Organization Forms, Issue 1. 250p. 1999. ring bd. write for info. (*0-327-01577-2*, 8033921) LEXIS Pub.
Moye, John E. Colorado Corporate Forms, 2 vols., Set. 2nd ed. 1878p. 1994. spiral bd. 269.00 (*0-250-47236-8*, 80301-10, MICHIE) LEXIS Pub.
— Law Of Business Organization 3. 3rd ed. Tubb, ed. (SWC-Business Law). 692p. (C). 1989. mass mkt. 54.75 (*0-314-47359-9*) West Pub.
— The Law of Business Organizations. 4th ed. Hannan, ed. LC 93-33053. 700p. (C). 1994. mass mkt. 55.25 (*0-314-01219-2*) West Pub.
Moye, John E. Loan Documentation for Lawyers. 129p. 1993. pap. 125.00 (*0-943380-88-X*) PEG MN.
— Loan Documentation Manual. 1999. write for info. (*1-58012-053-9*) James Pub Santa Ana.
***Moye, L.** Statistical Reasoning in Medicine: The Intuitive P Value Primer. (Illus.). 224p. 2000. pap. 35.00 (*0-387-98933-1*) Spr-Verlag.
Moye, Valerie B. Conditions That Support Transfer for Change. 50p. 1997. pap. 9.95 (*1-57517-043-4*) SkyLght.
***Moyer.** Contemporary Financial Management Fundamentals. (SWC-General Business Ser.). (C). 2001. text, student ed. 18.50 (*0-324-05880-2*) Sth-Wstrn College.
***Moyer & McGuigan.** Contemporary Financial Management. 8th ed. (SWC-Finance Ser.). 2000. pap. 67.00 (*0-324-00894-5*) Sth-Wstrn College.
Moyer, et al. Introduction to Finance: Financial Institutions & Markets. (SWC-Economics Ser.). 2001. pap. 64.50 (*0-324-02424-X*) Thomson Learn.
— Introdution to Finance: Financial Institutions & Markets. (SWC-Economics Ser.). 2001. pap. 30.00 (*0-324-02426-6*) Thomson Learn.
Moyer, jt. auth. see Harris.
Moyer, jt. auth. see Hugenberg.
Moyer, Alan & Berggoetz, Glen. 101 Drills to Improve Your Golf Game. (Illus.). 224p. 1999. pap. 16.95 (*1-58382-035-3*) Sports Masters.
Moyer, Albert E. Joseph Henry: The Rise of an American Scientist. LC 97-20686. (Illus.). 416p. 1997. text 45.00 (*1-56098-776-6*) Smithsonian.
— A Scientist's Voice in American Culture: Simon Newcomb & the Rhetoric of Scientific Method. (C). 1992. 48.00 (*0-520-07689-3*, Pub. by U CA Pr) Cal Prin Full Svc.
***Moyer, Alma.** The Empty Places. 1999. pap. write for info. (*1-58235-315-8*) Watermrk Pr.
Moyer, Ann, ed. see Lewis, Laura.
Moyer, Ann E. Musica Scientia: Musical Scholarship in the Italian Renaissance. LC 91-55057. (Illus.). 336p. 1992. text 49.95 (*0-8014-2426-7*) Cornell U Pr.
***Moyer, Bernadette.** Bare Breasted Heart: Poetry of Life, Love, Pain & Gain. 88p. 1999. pap. 18.95 (*0-9666183-1-9*) Two Bee-A-TwinBee.
Moyer, Bernadette A. Angel Stacey Earth Angel to Guardian Angel - Daddy in Heaven, It Is Me, Your Daughter. (Illus.). 96p. (J). (ps-6). 1998. pap. 20.95 (*0-9666183-9-4*) Two Bee-A-TwinBee.
***Moyer, Bernadette A.** Bee an Artist & Bee Creative: Sketch Book. (Illus.). 50p. (J). (gr. k-12). 1999. spiral bd. 12.95 (*0-9666183-6-X*) Two Bee-A-TwinBee.
Moyer, Bernadette A. But . . . We Are Twins. large type ed. (Illus.). 16p. (J). (ps-4). 1998. pap. 3.85 (*0-9666183-8-6*) Two Bee-A-TwinBee.
***Moyer, Bernedette A., creator.** Caesar Salad & I Like It! A Copulation of Poetry for Children & by Children. (Illus.). 80p. (J). (gr. 1-12). 1999. pap. 11.95 (*0-9666183-3-5*) Two Bee-A-TwinBee.
Moyer, Charles A. Comparing Surface Failure Modes in Bearings & Gears: Appearances vs. Mechanisms. (Nineteen Ninety-One Fall Technical Meeting Ser.: Vol. 91FTM6). (Illus.). 11p. 1991. pap. text 30.00 (*1-55589-603-0*) AGMA.
— Power Density Development: The Role of Improved Line Contact Performance. (Nineteen Eighty-Nine Fall Technical Meeting Ser.: Vol. 89FTM3). (Illus.). 10p. 1989. pap. text 30.00 (*1-55589-538-7*) AGMA.
— The Role of Reliability for Bearings & Gears. (Nineteen Ninety-Two Fall Technical Meeting Ser.: Vol. 92FTM8). (Illus.). 7p. 1992. pap. text 30.00 (*1-55589-588-3*) AGMA.
Moyer, Charles A., jt. auth. see Haager, P. L.
***Moyer, Charles R.** Contemporary Financial Management. 8th ed. (SWC-Finance Ser.). 2000. pap., student ed. 20.50 (*0-324-05258-8*) Sth-Wstrn College.
Moyer, Chris. Special Edition Using FileMaker Pro 3 for the Mac. (Illus.). 575p. (Orig.). 1996. pap. 34.99 (*0-7897-0662-8*) Que.
Moyer, Chris & Bowers, Bob. Advanced FileMaker Pro 4.0 Developer's Guide. 750p. (C). 1999. pap. 49.95 (*0-12-509365-9*) Morgan Kaufmann.
Moyer, Christine M. Serenity to the End: A Collection of Photos & Verse. (Illus.). 50p. (Orig.). pap. 9.95 (*1-886453-02-0*) Candleberry Pr.
— Simple Things to the Believer: A Collection of Photos & Verse. (Illus.). 53p. (Orig.). 1994. pap. 9.95 (*1-886453-00-4*) Candleberry Pr.
Moyer, Christine M., ed. The Journey to Deliverance: A Collection of Photos & Verse. (Illus.). 50p. (Orig.). pap. 9.95 (*1-886453-01-2*) Candleberry Pr.
Moyer, Craig A. & Francis, Michael A. Hazard Communication Handbook: A Right-to-Know Compliance Guide, 1993. 1991. pap. 90.00 (*0-87632-888-5*) West Group.
Moyer, Craig A. & Trimarche, Gregory D. Brownfields: A Practical Guide to the Cleanup, Transfer, & Redevelopment of Contaminated Property. 503p. 1997. pap. 179.00 (*1-890501-01-8*) Argent Commns.
Moyer, D. David & Fisher, Kenneth P. Land Parcel Identifiers for Information Systems. LC 73-91110. 465p. 1973. 25.00 (*0-910058-59-8*, 304860); pap. 20.00 (*0-910058-58-X*, 304860) W S Hein.
Moyer, Darienne, tr. see Berand, Yves & Colli, Jean-Claude.
***Moyer, Dennis K.** Fraktur Writings & Folk Art Drawings of the Schwenkfelder Library Collection. Wetzell, Willard, ed. (Illus.). 1998. 65.00 (*0-935980-12-1*) Schwenkfelder Lib.
Moyer, Don, ed. 1999 Wine Watch Guide. 128p. 1998. pap. 9.95 (*0-9667459-0-6*, WWG1999) AMS Press.
***Moyer, Don, ed.** 2000 Wine Watch Guide. (Illus.). 132p. 1999. pap. 9.95 (*0-9667459-1-4*, WWG2000) AMS Press.
***Moyer, Duane.** Creating True Wealth: Christian Youth Entrepreneurship. (Illus.). 144p. (YA). (gr. 7-12). 1999. pap. 25.00 (*0-9668337-1-6*) Youth Business.
Moyer, Ellen. Arthritis: Questions You Have...Answers You Need. rev. ed. LC 96-47270. 192p. 1997. pap. 12.95 (*1-882606-52-3*) Peoples Med Soc.
— Cholesterol & Triglycerides: Questions You Have--Answers You Need. 192p. 1995. pap. 10.95 (*1-882606-51-5*) Peoples Med Soc.
— Vitamins & Minerals: Questions You Have - Answers You Need. LC 93-30754. 224p. 1993. pap. 10.95 (*1-882606-05-1*) Peoples Med Soc.
Moyer, F. Special Forces Foreign Weapons Handbook. 1986. lib. bdg. 79.95 (*0-8490-3663-1*) Gordon Pr.
***Moyer, Florence.** Rainbow's End. 2000. mass mkt. 4.99 (*0-8217-6480-2*, Zebra Kensgtn) Kensgtn Pub Corp.
Moyer, Frank A. Special Forces Foreign Weapons Handbook. 1987. pap. 14.95 (*0-8065-1044-7*, Citadel Pr) Carol Pub Group.
Moyer Frounfelker, Grace. As a Little Child. LC 98-23543. (Illus.). 144p. 1998. pap. 8.99 (*0-8361-9089-0*) Herald Pr.
Moyer, H. Wayne. Agricultural Policy Reform: Politics & Process in the EC & U. S. A. LC 89-48550. (Illus.). 256p. 1990. text 46.95 (*0-8138-1371-9*) Iowa St U Pr.
Moyer, Imogene. The Changing Roles of Women in the Criminal Justice System: Offenders, Victims, & Professionals. 2nd rev. ed. (Illus.). 367p. (C). 1992. pap. text 22.95 (*0-88133-654-8*) Waveland Pr.
Moyer, Inez. Responding to Infants. LC 83-71345. 200p. (Orig.). (J). (ps). 1983. pap. 18.95 (*0-513-01769-0*) Denison.
Moyer, J. H., jt. auth. see Armstrong, T. E.
Moyer, J. W., jt. auth. see Clark, C. A.
Moyer, James C., jt. auth. see Matthews, Victor H.
Moyer, Janet L. The Landscape Lighting Book. LC 91-44393. 304p. 1992. 90.00 (*0-471-52726-2*) Wiley.
Moyer, Joan, ed. see Association for Childhood Education International Staff.
Moyer, Joan P., et al. The Child-Centered Kindergarten. 1987. pap. 1.50 (*0-87173-115-0*) ACEI.
Moyer, John W. Practical Taxidermy. 2nd ed. LC 92-4770. 158p. 1992. reprint ed. lib. bdg. 23.50 (*0-89464-743-1*) Krieger.
Moyer, Joyce, ed. see Gould, James P.
Moyer, K. E. Violence & Aggression: A Physiological Perspective. LC 86-4987. 237p. 1987. pap. text 14.95 (*0-943852-19-6*) Prof World Peace.
Moyer, Larry R. Larry Moyer's How to Book: On Personal Evangelism. LC 98-17621. 128p. 1998. pap. text 7.99 (*0-8254-3179-4*) Kregel.
Moyer, Laurence. Victory Must Be Ours: Germany in the Great War, 1914-1918. (Illus.). 397p. 1995. 52.50 (*0-85052-439-3*, Pub. by Leo Cooper) Trans-Atl Phila.
***Moyer, Linda L. & Willes, Burl.** Undiscovered Islands of the Mediterranean. (Illus.). 220p. 1999. reprint ed. pap. text 15.00 (*0-7881-6373-6*) DIANE Pub.
Moyer, Lloyd K. The Holy Rosary of Mary, the Beloved: A Devotional to Mary Magdalene. LC 92-80734. (Illus.). 67p. (Orig.). 1992. pap., per. 16.95 (*0-9631507-0-7*) Sophia Pr VT.
Moyer, Mark V., et al. Florida Fresh Water Plants: A Handbook of Common Aquatic Plants in Florida Lakes. (Illus.). 280p. (Orig.). 1996. pap. 35.00 (*0-916287-19-X*) Univ Fla Food.
Moyer, Marshall M. Rollo Bones, Canine Hypnotist. LC 97-44304. (Illus.). 32p. (J). (gr. k-3). 1998. 14.95 (*1-883672-65-1*) Tricycle Pr.
Moyer, Miriam W. Demands of Love. (Illus.). 152p. 1978. 7.15 (*0-7399-0164-8*, 2200) Rod & Staff.
Moyer, Nancy. Escape from the Killing Fields: One Girl Who Survived the Cambodian Holocaust. 224p. (Orig.). 1991. pap. 9.99 (*0-310-53891-2*) Zondervan.

An Asterisk (*) at the beginning of an entry indicates that the title is appearing for the first time.

Moyer, Page E. The ABCs of a Really Good Speech: For Managers, Ministers, & Most of the Rest of Us Who Are Less Than Confident Speakers. LC 89-82274. (Illus.). 120p. (Orig.). 1990. pap. 12.95 (*0-9625294-0-0*) Circle NY.

Moyer, Patrick, jt. auth. see Paesler, Michael.

***Moyer, Patsy.** Doll Values: Antique to Modern. 4th ed. (Illus.). 368p. 2000. pap. 12.95 (*1-57432-161-7*) Collector Bks.

Moyer, Patsy. Modern Collectible Dolls: Identification & Value Guide, Vol. II. LC 97-183190. 232p. 1998. 19.95 (*1-57432-053-X*, 5050) Collector Bks.

— Modern Collectible Dolls Identification & Value Guide. 3rd ed. LC 97-183190. 224p. 1999. 24.95 (*1-57432-117-X*) Collector Bks.

***Moyer, Patsy.** Modern Collectible Dolls Identification & Value Guide. 4th ed. (Illus.). 272p. 2000. 24.95 (*1-57432-174-9*) Collector Bks.

Moyer, Philip D., jt. auth. see Namestka, Keith B.

Moyer, R. Charles. Contemporary Financial Management. 6th ed. (SWC-Finance). (C). 1994. pap., student ed. 17.50 (*0-314-05462-6*) S-W Pub.

Moyer, R. Charles, et al. Contemporary Financial Management. 6th ed. LC 94-21326. 880p. (C). 1994. mass mkt. 62.25 (*0-314-04342-X*) West Pub.

— Contemporary Financial Management. 7th ed. LC 97-22789. 1997. mass mkt. 93.95 (*0-538-87776-6*) S-W Pub.

— Contemporary Financial Management, 5th. 5th ed. Schiller, ed. (SWC-Finance). 841p. (C). 1991. mass mkt. 65.50 (*0-314-91348-3*) West Pub.

— Managerial Economics: Readings, Cases & Exercises. 261p. 1979. pap. text 37.00 (*0-8299-0157-4*); pap. text. write for info. (*0-314-43376-7*) West Pub.

Moyer, R. Charles, jt. auth. see McGuigan, James R.

Moyer, R. Larry. Dear God, I'm Ticked Off: Answering the Spiritual Complaints & Concerns of Others. LC 98-53733. 144p. 1999. pap. 8.99 (*0-8254-3175-1*) Kregel.

— Free & Clear: Understanding & Communicating God's Offer of Eternal Life. LC 96-3420. 272p. 1997. pap. 12.99 (*0-8254-3177-8*) Kregel.

***Moyer, R. Larry.** 31 Days to Contagious Living: A Daily Devotional Guide on Modeling Christ to Others. 2000. pap. 6.99 (*0-8254-3174-3*) Kregel.

Moyer, R. Larry. 31 Days with the Master Fisherman: A Daily Devotional on Bringing Others to Christ. LC 96-2940. 96p. 1997. pap. 5.99 (*0-8254-3178-6*) Kregel.

Moyer, R. Larry. Welcome to the Family: Understanding Your New Relationship to God & Others. 64p. 1996. pap. 5.99 (*0-8254-3176-X*) Kregel.

Moyer, Reed. Competition in the Midwestern Coal Industry. (Economic Studies: No. 122). (Illus.). 238p. 1964. 16.50 (*0-674-15400-2*) HUP.

Moyer, Reed, et al. Macro Marketing. 2nd ed. LC 77-26816. (Wiley Hamilton Series in Marketing). (Illus.). 213p. reprint ed. pap. 66.10 (*0-608-10690-9*, 202018600016) Bks Demand.

Moyer, Robert. Love So Amazing. 1997. pap. 5.99 (*0-907927-54-8*) Emerald House Group Inc.

Moyer, Robert E. & Ayres, Frank, Jr. Schaum's Outline of Trigonometry. 3rd ed. LC 98-40457. (Illus.). 208p. 1998. pap., student ed. 14.95 (*0-07-006893-3*) McGraw.

Moyer, Robert E., jt. auth. see Ayres, Frank, Jr.

Moyer, Robert M., jt. auth. see Bargmann, Dale.

Moyer, Roert E., jt. auth. see Siegel, Murray R.

Moyer, Ronald L. American Actors, 1861-1910: An Annotated Biography. LC 79-64229. xvi, 268p. 1979. 47.00 (*0-87875-167-X*) Whitston Pub.

Moyer, Ruth C., jt. auth. see Meyer, Louis.

Moyer, Steve, jt. ed. see Benson, John.

Moyer, Susan L. Silk Painting: The Artist's Guide to Gutta & Wax Resist Techniques. (Illus.). 144p. 1991. pap. 24.95 (*0-8230-4828-4*) Watsn-Guptill.

— Silk Painting for Fashion & Fine Art: Techniques for Making Ties, Scarves, Dresses, Decorative Pillows & Fine Art Paintings. (Illus.). 144p. 1995. pap. 24.95 (*0-8230-4831-4*) Watsn-Guptill.

Moyer, Terry J. Crescendo. (YA). 1995. 15.98 (*0-88290-527-9*, 1059) Horizon Utah.

— Have I Got a Story for You! 160p. (Orig.). 1996. pap. 12.98 (*0-88290-574-0*, 1061) Horizon Utah.

***Moyer, Virginia A., et al, eds.** Evidence Based Pediatrics & Child Health. (Illus.). 383p. 2000. 49.00 (*0-7279-1424-3*) BMJ Pub.

Moyer, Willard, et al. The Witchery of Sleep: An Anthology. 1977. lib. bdg. 59.95 (*0-8490-2828-0*) Gordon Pr.

Moyers, et al. Standards of Human Occlusal Development. (Craniofacial Growth Ser.: Vol. 5). (Illus.). 371p. 1976. 65.00 (*0-929921-03-8*) UM CHGD.

***Moyers, Bill.** Fooling with Words. 2000. pap. write for info. (*0-688-17792-1*, Quil) HarperTrade.

— Fooling with Words: A Celebration of Poets & Their Craft. LC 99-34965. 304p. 1999. 20.00 (*0-688-17346-2*, Quil) HarperTrade.

Moyers, Bill. Genesis: A Living Conversation. (Illus.). 400p. 1997. pap. 21.95 (*0-385-49043-7*, Main St Bks) Doubleday.

— Healing & the Mind. Flowers, Betty Sue, ed. LC 92-31074. 384p. 1993. 25.00 (*0-385-46870-9*) Doubleday.

— Healing & the Mind. LC 92-31074. 384p. 1995. pap. 19.95 (*0-385-47687-6*) Doubleday.

Moyers, Bill. The Language of Life: A Festival of Poets. (Illus.). 480p. 1996. pap., mass mkt. 21.95 incl. audio (*0-385-48410-0*) Doubleday.

Moyers, Bill. The Secret Government: The Constitution in Crisis. 2nd ed. Kytle, Calvin, ed. LC 89-70131. 131p. 1990. 16.95 (*0-932020-61-5*) Seven Locks Pr.

— The Secret Government: The Constitution in Crisis. 2nd ed. Kytle, Calvin, ed. LC 89-70131. 131p. 1990. pap. 9.95 (*0-932020-60-7*) Seven Locks Pr.

— Talking about Genesis. 112p. 1996. pap. 5.95 (*0-385-48580-8*, Main St Bks) Doubleday.

— World of Ideas, Vol. II. 304p. 1990. pap. 22.95 (*0-385-41665-2*) Doubleday.

— A World of Ideas: Conversations with Thoughtful Men & Women about American Life Today & the Ideas Shaping Our Future. 528p. 1989. pap. 27.50 (*0-385-26346-5*) Doubleday.

Moyers, Bill & Beckett, Wendy. Sister Wendy in Conversation with Bill Moyers: The Complete Conversation. Johnson, Karen, ed. 96p. 1997. pap. 11.95 (*1-57807-077-5*) WGBH.

Moyers, Bill, jt. auth. see Campbell, Joseph.

Moyers, Bill, jt. auth. see Center for Investigative Reporting Staff.

Moyers, Dwayne, jt. auth. see Beroff, Art.

Moyers, Penelope A. Substance Abuse: A Multidimensional Assessment & Treatment Approach. LC 88-43456. (Illus.). 216p. (C). 1992. pap. 24.00 (*1-55642-084-6*) SLACK Inc.

Moyers, Richard L. & Enright, Kathleen P. A Snapshot of America's Nonprofit Boards: Results of the NCNB Nonprofit Governance Survey, Vol. 146. 2nd ed. 24p. 1997. pap. 19.00 (*0-925299-74-X*) Natl Ctr Nonprofit.

Moyers, Susan. Garlic in Health, History & World Cuisine. LC 96-70120. (Illus.). 270p. (Orig.). 1996. pap. 16.95 (*0-9654236-0-3*) Suncoast Pr.

Moyers, Tony L. Wanderings: Exploring Moral Landscapes Past & Present. LC 96-34285. 276p. 1996. pap. text 34.00 (*0-7618-0486-2*) U Pr of Amer.

Moyers, William, jt. auth. see Lee, Katie.

Moyes, Adrian. Common Ground. 98p. (C). 1987. pap. text 35.00 (*0-85598-078-8*, Pub. by Oxfam Pubns) St Mut.

Moyes, Bill. Successful Radio Promotions. (Illus.). 150p. 1988. pap. 40.00 (*0-89324-048-6*, 3234) Natl Assn Broadcasters.

Moyes, Canon. Why Catholics Pray to the Blessed Virgin Mary: An Incident in Catholic Life. (Compact Study Ser.). 15p. (Orig.). 1993. pap. 1.95 (*0-935952-94-2*) Angelus Pr.

Moyes, Norman B. Battle Eye: A History of American Combat Photography. LC 95-51982. (Illus.). 144p. 1996. 17.98 (*1-56799-287-0*, MetroBooks) M Friedman Pub Grp Inc.

Moyes, Patricia. Angel Death. LC 80-1396. 240p. 1995. pap. 4.95 (*0-8050-0505-6*, Owl) H Holt & Co.

— Black Girl, White Girl. LC 89-7440. 224p. 1995. pap. 4.95 (*0-8050-1149-8*, Owl) H Holt & Co.

— Black Widower. LC 85-8493. 224p. 1995. pap. 4.95 (*0-8050-0243-X*, Owl) H Holt & Co.

— The Coconut Killings. LC 76-29910. 224p. 1995. pap. 5.95 (*0-8050-0754-7*, Owl) H Holt & Co.

— The Curious Affair of the Third Dog. LC 85-17610. 224p. 1995. pap. 4.95 (*0-8050-0503-X*, Owl) H Holt & Co.

— Dead Men Don't Ski. LC 84-6732. 288p. 1995. pap. 5.95 (*0-8050-0705-9*, Owl) H Holt & Co.

— Death & the Dutch Uncle. LC 82-23259. 256p. 1995. pap. 5.95 (*0-8050-0506-4*, Owl) H Holt & Co.

— Death on the Agenda. LC 84-6750. 192p. 1995. pap. 4.95 (*0-8050-0507-2*, Owl) H Holt & Co.

— Down among the Dead Men. LC 86-9834. 240p. 1995. pap. 5.95 (*0-8050-0117-4*, Owl) H Holt & Co.

— Falling Star. LC 81-7030. 256p. (Orig.). 1995. pap. 5.95 (*0-8050-0755-5*, Owl) H Holt & Co.

— How to Talk to Your Cat. (Illus.). 128p. 1995. pap. 9.95 (*0-8050-1645-7*, Owl) H Holt & Co.

— How to Talk to Your Cat. LC 92-44737. (Illus.). 128p. 1993. 6.99 (*0-517-09296-4*) Random Hse Value.

— Johnny under Ground: An Inspector Henry Tibbett Mystery. LC 66-10121. 256p. 1995. pap. 5.95 (*0-8050-0270-7*, Owl) H Holt & Co.

— Just Pockets: Sewing Techniques & Design Ideas. LC 97-13757. (Orig.). 1997. pap. 19.95 (*1-56158-170-4*, 070321) Taunton.

— Many Deadly Returns: An Inspector Henry Tibbett Mystery. LC 87-15015. 256p. 1995. pap. 5.95 (*0-8050-0598-6*, Owl) H Holt & Co.

— Murder a la Mode. LC 63-12604. 224p. 1995. pap. 5.95 (*0-8050-0706-7*, Owl) H Holt & Co.

— Murder Fantastical. LC 84-6752. 256p. 1995. pap. 5.95 (*0-8050-0504-8*, Owl) H Holt & Co.

— Night Ferry to Death. LC 85-5567. 192p. 1995. pap. 5.95 (*0-8050-0116-6*, Owl) H Holt & Co.

— Season of Snows & Sins. LC 74-155526. 224p. 1995. pap. 5.95 (*0-8050-0849-7*, Owl) H Holt & Co.

— Sewing Basics: Creating a Stylish Wardrobe with Step-by-Step Techniques. LC 98-55587. 1999. pap. 24.95 (*1-56158-266-2*) Taunton.

— A Six-Letter Word for Death. LC 82-18738. 252p. 1995. pap. 5.95 (*0-8050-0244-8*, Owl) H Holt & Co.

— To Kill a Coconut. large type ed. 336p. 1981. 27.99 (*0-7089-0632-X*) Ulverscroft.

— Twice in a Blue Moon. 1995. pap. 5.95 (*0-8050-2948-6*) H Holt & Co.

— Twice in a Blue Moon. large type ed. LC 93-47393. 266p. 1994. lib. bdg. 20.95 (*0-7862-0168-1*) Thorndike Pr.

— Who Is Simon Warwick? LC 78-53951. 176p. 1995. pap. 5.95 (*0-8050-0719-9*, Owl) H Holt & Co.

— Who Killed Father Christmas? And Other Unseasonable Demises. LC 96-214369. 278p. (Orig.). 1996. pap. 16.00 (*1-885941-09-9*) Crippen & Landru.

— Who Killed Father Christmas? And Other Unseasonable Demises. deluxe limited ed. 278p. (Orig.). 1996. 40.00 (*1-885941-08-0*) Crippen & Landru.

Moyes, Robert. Victoria: The Insider's Guide. 2nd rev. ed. LC 97-65297. (Illus.). 128p. 1997. pap. 5.95 (*1-55143-079-7*) Orca Bk Pubs.

Moyise, Steve. Introduction to Biblical Studies. LC 98-163887. 96p. 1998. pap. 16.50 (*0-304-70091-6*) Continuum.

***Moyise, Steve, ed.** The Old Testament in the New Testament: Essays in Honour of J. L. North. (Journal for the Study of the New Testament, Supplement Ser.: No. 189). 304p. 2000. 82.00 (*1-84127-061-X*, Pub. by Sheffield Acad) CUP Services.

Moyise, Steve, jt. auth. see Marsh, Clive.

Moyise, Steve P. The Old Testament in the Book of Revelation. (JSNT Supplement Ser.: Vol. 115). 173p. 1995. 52.50 (*1-85075-554-X*, Pub. by Sheffield Acad) CUP Services.

Moylan, Brian J. Works Rally Mechanic - Tales of the BMC/BL-Works Rally Department, 1955-1979. (Illus.). 160p. 1998. 34.95 (*1-874105-97-9*, Pub. by Vloce Pub) Motorbooks Intl.

Moylan, Bridget. Glacier's Grandest: A Pictorial History of the Hotels & Chalets of Glacier National Park. LC 94-67154. (Illus.). 92p. 1995. pap. 9.95 (*0-929521-89-7*) Pictorial Hist.

***Moylan, D. C.** The Case of the Antenatus in Scotland Claiming as Heir in England: Being a Report of the Case of Birtwhistle vs. Vardeill. 81p. 1999. reprint ed. 30.00 (*1-56169-550-5*, 18135) Gaunt.

Moylan, David J., jt. auth. see Coia, Lawrence R.

Moylan, Margaret F. Symphony in Counterpoint: An Overture to Hope. 7p. 1994. pap. 5.95 (*0-9642109-0-8*) Parkinsonian.

Moylan, Michele & Stiles, Lane, eds. Reading Books: Essays on the Material Text & Literature in America. LC 96-8322. (Studies in Print Culture & the History of the Book). (Illus.). 296p. (C). 1997. 50.00 (*1-55849-062-0*); pap. 17.95 (*1-55849-063-9*) U of Mass Pr.

Moylan, Peter J. Assembly Language for Engineers. (Computers & Their Applications Ser.). 220p. 1987. text 52.95 (*0-470-20908-9*) P-H.

Moylan, Terry, ed. Johnny O'Leary of Sliabh Luachra: Dance Music from the Cork-Kerry Border. (Illus.). 232p. (Orig.). 1994. pap. 33.95 (*1-874675-42-2*, Pub. by Lilliput Pr) Irish Bks Media.

Moylan, Tom. Demand the Impossible: Science Fiction & the Utopian Imagination. 256p. 1987. 39.95 (*0-317-54027-0*, 1125) Routledge.

***Moylan, Tom.** Scraps of the Untainted Sky: Science Fiction, Utopia, Dystopia. (Cultural Studies Ser.). 340p. 2000. pap. 30.00 (*0-8133-9768-5*) Westview.

Moylan, Tom, jt. ed. see Daniel, Jamie O.

Moylan, William M. The Art of Recording. (Illus.). 300p. 1992. text 49.95 (*0-442-00669-1*, VNR) Wiley.

Moyle, Evelyn W., jt. auth. see Moyle, John B.

Moyle, J. B. The Contract of Sale in the Civil Law: With References to the Laws of England Scotland & France. LC 93-79720. 292p. 1994. reprint ed. 80.00 (*1-56169-078-3*) Gaunt.

— Imperatoris Iustiniani Institutionum: Libri Quattuor. 4th ed. LC 93-79719. 690p. 1994. reprint ed. 170.00 (*1-56169-077-5*) Gaunt.

***Moyle, J. B.** Institutes of Justinian. 4th ed. vii, 220p. 1999. 70.00 (*1-56169-469-X*) Gaunt.

Moyle, James H. Mormon Democrat: The Religious & Political Memoirs of James Henry Moyle. limited ed. Sessions, Gene A., ed. LC 94-40560. (Significant Mormon Diaries Ser.: No. 8). (Illus.). 407p. 1998. 85.00 (*1-56085-023-X*) Signature Bks.

Moyle, John B. & Moyle, Evelyn W. Northland Wild Flowers. LC 76-55173. (Illus.). 246p. 1984. pap. 18.95 (*0-8166-1355-9*) U of Minn Pr.

Moyle, John T., jt. auth. see Davey, Andrew.

Moyle, John T. B., et al, eds. Pulse Oxlmetry: Principles & Practice Series. rev. ed. (Illus.). 140p. 1998. pap. text 31.95 (*0-7279-1235-6*) Login Brothers Bk Co.

Moyle, Natalie. The Turkish Minstrel Tale Tradition. LC 90-3620. (Harvard Dissertations in Folklore & Oral Literature Ser.). 244p. 1990. reprint ed. text 20.00 (*0-8240-2673-X*) Garland.

Moyle, Peter B. Fish: An Enthusiast's Guide. (Illus.). 278p. 1995. pap. 14.95 (*0-520-20165-5*, Pub. by U CA Pr) Cal Prin Full Svc.

Moyle, Peter B. & Cech, Joseph J. Fishes: An Introduction to Ichthyology 4th ed. LC 99-28580. 612p. 1999. 86.67 (*0-13-011282-8*) P-H.

Moyle, Peter B., et al. Distribution & Ecology of Stream Fishes of the Sacramento-San Joaquin Drainage System, California. LC 81-13072. (University of California Publications in Zoology: No. 115). 266p. 1982. pap. 82.50 (*0-7837-7495-8*, 204921700010) Bks Demand.

Moyle, Peter B., jt. ed. see Schreck, C. B.

***Moyle, Philippa.** My Favorite Bible Stories. LC 98-60694. (Read Aloud Ser.). (Illus.). 20p. (J). (ps-3). 1998. bds. 9.98 incl. audio (*0-7651-0694-9*) Smithmark.

Moyle, Richard. Polynesian Sound-Producing Instruments. (Ethnography Ser.: No. 20). (Illus.). 64p. 1990. pap. 10.50 (*0-7478-0095-2*, Pub. by Shire Pubns) Parkwest Pubns.

Moyles, Janet R. Just Playing? The Role & Status of Play in Early Childhood Education. 192p. 1989. pap. 28.95 (*0-335-09564-X*) OpUniv Pr.

— Organizing for Learning in the Primary Classroom: A Balanced Approach to Classroom Management. LC 92-5706. 208p. 1993. 103.95 (*0-335-15660-6*); pap. 28.95 (*0-335-15659-2*) Taylor & Francis.

Moyles, Janet R., ed. Beginning Teaching: Beginning Learning in Primary Education. LC 95-1199. 268p. 1995. 104.95 (*0-335-19436-2*) OpUniv Pr.

— Beginning Teaching, Beginning Learning in Primary Education. LC 95-1199. 192p. 1995. pap. 27.95 (*0-335-19435-4*) OpUniv Pr.

— The Excellence of Play. LC 93-25317. 192p. 1994. pap. 22.95 (*0-335-19068-5*) OpUniv Pr.

Moyles, Janet R. & Hargreaves, Linda. The Primary Curriculum: Learning from International Perspectives. LC 97-17424. 240p. (C). 1998. pap. 22.99 (*0-415-15832-X*) Routledge.

Moyles, Lois. Alleluia Chorus. LC 78-68471. 1979. 7.95 (*0-913506-10-9*) Woolmer-Brotherson.

Moyles, R. G. A Bibliography of Salvation Army Literature in English, 1865-1987: Mightier than the Sword. LC 88-8964. (Texts & Studies in Religion: Vol. 38). 250p. 1988. lib. bdg. 89.95 (*0-88946-827-3*) E Mellen.

— Improved by Cultivation: An Anthology of English Canadian Prose to 1914. LC 95-108875. 400p. 1994. pap. 22.95 (*1-55111-049-0*) Broadview Pr.

— The Text of Paradise Lost: A Study in Editorial Procedure. 198p. 1985. text 30.00 (*0-8020-5634-2*) U of Toronto Pr.

Moyles, R. G. & Owram, Doug. Imperial Dreams & Colonial Realities: British Views of Canada, 1880-1914. (Illus.). 278p. 1988. text 29.95 (*0-8020-2675-3*) U of Toronto Pr.

Moyles, R. G., jt. ed. see Demers, R. A.

Moyles, R. G., jt. ed. see Djwa, Sandra.

Moylett, Helen, jt. ed. see Abbott, Lesley.

Moynaham, Brian. Rasputin: The Saint Who Sinned. LC 97-5025. (Illus.). 400p. 1997. 30.00 (*0-679-41930-6*) Random.

Moynahan, Brian. Airport International. 1991. pap. text. write for info. (*0-00-370138-7*) Addison-Wesley.

***Moynahan, Brian.** Rasputin: The Saint Who Sinned. LC 99-45454. 432p. 1999. pap. text 16.00 (*0-306-80930-3*, Pub. by Da Capo) HarpC.

Moynahan, Brian. The Russian Century: A History of the Last 100 Years. (Illus.). 256p. 1995. pap. 15.95 (*0-679-76436-4*) Random.

***Moynahan, Jean Ann.** Captain of Hearts. LC 99-91306. 192p. 2000. 18.95 (*0-8034-9393-2*, Avalon Bks) Bouregy.

Moynahan, John K. Designing an Effective Sales Compensation Program. LC 79-54844. 222p. reprint ed. pap. 68.90 (*0-608-12231-9*, 202389100034) Bks Demand.

— The Sales Compensation Handbook. 400p. 1991. 69.95 (*0-8144-0110-4*) AMACOM.

Moynahan, Juliam. Anglo-Irish: The Literary Imagination in a Hyphenated Culture. LC 94-19545. 222p. 1995. text 32.50 (*0-691-03757-4*, Pub. by Princeton U Pr) Cal Prin Full Svc.

Moynahan, Julian. Vladimir Nabokov. LC 71-633325. (University of Minnesota Pamphlets on American Writers Ser.: No. 96). 47p. (Orig.). reprint ed. pap. 30.00 (*0-7837-2871-9*, 205758400006) Bks Demand.

Moynahan, Michael E. Once upon a Miracle: Drama for Worship & Religious Education. LC 92-41325. 224p. 1993. pap. 12.95 (*0-8091-3361-X*) Paulist Pr.

Moynahan, Michael E. Once upon a Mystery: What Happens Next? LC 98-23004. 208p. 1998. pap. 14.95 (*0-8091-3791-7*) Paulist Pr.

Moynahan, Ruth B., et al, eds. So Much to Be Done: Women Settlers on the Mining & Ranching Frontier. 2nd enl. ed. LC 98-15057. (Women in the West Ser.). (Illus.). xxii, 354p. 1998. pap. 16.95 (*0-8032-8248-6*, Bison Books) U of Nebr Pr.

Moyne, Ernest J. Raising the Wind: The Legend of Lapland & Finland Wizards in Literature. Kime, Wayne R., ed. (Illus.). 224p. 1981. 34.50 (*0-87413-146-4*) U Delaware Pr.

Moyne, Ernest J., ed. Alexandra Gripensberg's "A Half Year in the New World" Miscellaneous Sketches of Travel in the United States (1888) 225p. 20.00 (*0-87413-100-6*) U Delaware Pr.

Moyne, John & Books, Coleman, trs. Open Secret. 96p. 1996. pap. 9.00 (*0-614-21325-8*, 924) Kazi Pubns.

Moyne, John, tr. see Barks, Coleman.

Moyne, John, jt. tr. see Barks, Coleman.

Moyne, John, jt. tr. see Books, Coleman.

Moyne, John, tr. see Rumi, Jalal Al-Din.

Moyne, John, tr. see Rumi, Melvana.

Moyne, John A. Rumi & Sufi Tradition. 91p. 1998. pap. 14.00 (*1-883058-98-8*) Global Pubns.

— Understanding Language: Man or Machine. (Foundations of Computer Science Ser.). 374p. 1985. 79.50 (*0-306-41970-X*, Plenum Trade) Perseus Pubng.

Moyne, Ron. A Star of Honor. LC 89-273. 1990. 21.95 (*0-87949-302-X*) Ashley Bks.

Moynes, jt. auth. see Riley.

***Moynes, Riley & Fallon, Nick.** Top Funds 2000: Building Your Mutual Fund Portfolio for the 21st Century. rev. ed. 216p. 2000. pap. text. write for info. (*0-201-68496-9*) Addison-Wesley.

Moynes, Riley & Friedman, Jack P. The Money Coach. LC 97-31312. 160p. 1998. pap. 12.95 (*0-7641-0579-5*) Barron.

Moynet, M. J. L' Envers du Theatre: Machines et Decorations. LC 76-174870. (FRE., Illus.). 1972. reprint ed. 26.95 (*0-405-08809-4*) Ayer.

***Moynier, John.** Avalanche Aware: Safe Travel in Avalanche Country. LC 98-26084. (How-To Ser.). 128p. 1998. pap. 6.95 (*1-56044-670-6*) Falcon Pub Inc.

Moynier, John. Avalanche Awareness: A Practical Guide to Safe Travel in Avalanche Terrain. (Illus.). 32p. (Orig.). 1993. pap. 4.95 (*0-934641-72-2*) Falcon Pub Inc.

— Back Country Skiing in the High Sierra. (Illus.). 189p. (Orig.). 1992. pap. 13.95 (*0-934641-44-7*) Falcon Pub Inc.

***Moynier, John.** Backcountry Skiing California's High Sierra. LC 99-27439. (Illus.). 200p. 1999. pap. 14.95 (*1-56044-913-6*) Falcon Pub Inc.

— Basic Essentials: Cross-Country Skiing. 2nd ed. LC 99-32267. (Illus.). 80p. 1999. pap. text 7.95 (*0-7627-0521-3*) Globe Pequot.

Moynier, John. The Basic Essentials of Mountaineering. LC 90-26009. (Basic Essentials Ser.). (Illus.). 72p. (Orig.). 1991. pap. 4.95 (*0-934802-65-3*) Globe Pequot.

— Mammoth Lakes. (Twelve Short Hikes Ser.). (Illus.). 32p. 1997. pap. 4.95 (*1-57540-091-X*) Falcon Pub Inc.

***Moynier, John.** Scenic Day Hikes in the Mammoth Lakes Area. (Illus.). 32p. 1999. pap. 6.00 (*0-9676116-0-1*) Maximus Pr.

Moynier, John & Fiddler, Claude. Sierra Classics: 100 Best Climbs in the High Sierra. (Illus.). 318p. (Orig.). 1993. pap. 25.00 (*0-934641-60-9*) Falcon Pub Inc.

***Moynier, John & Lewis, Martyn.** Bishop Area Rock Climbs. 2nd rev. ed. (Illus.). 104p. 1999. pap. 13.00 (*0-9676116-1-X*) Maximus Pr.

Moynier, John, jt. auth. see Lewis, Marty.

Moynihan. Congregation Doctrine Faith. write for info. (*0-06-254849-2*) HarpC.

Moynihan, Brendan. Trading on Expectations: Strategies to Pinpoint Trading Ranges, Trends & Reversals. LC 97-9276. (Wiley Finance Editions Ser.). 232p. 1997. 59.95 (*0-471-17782-2*) Wiley.

Moynihan, Brendan, jt. auth. see Patch, Cecilia.

Moynihan, Brendan, jt. auth. see Paul, Jim.

Moynihan, C. T., jt. ed. see Frischat, G. H.

Moynihan, C. T., jt. ed. see Lucas, J.

Moynihan, C. T., jt. ed. see Yamane, M.

Moynihan, Cornelius J. Introduction to Real Property: Introduction to the Law. 2nd ed. 239p. (C). 1987. reprint ed. 28.50 (*0-314-60555-X*) West Pub.

Moynihan, Daniel P. Came the Revolution: Argument in the Reagan Era. 336p. 1988. 17.95 (*0-15-115375-2*) Harcourt.

— Family & Nation. LC 85-27041. 160p. 1986. 12.95 (*0-15-130143-3*) Harcourt.

— Family & Nation. 244p. 1987. pap. 5.95 (*0-15-630140-7*, Harvest Bks) Harcourt.

— Loyalties. LC 83-22666. 112p. 1984. 9.95 (*0-15-154748-3*) Harcourt.

— Miles to Go: A Personal History of Social Policy. LC 96-8291. (Illus.). 245p. 1996. 22.95 (*0-674-57440-0*) HUP.

— Miles to Go: A Personal History of Social Policy. (Illus.). 256p. 1997. reprint ed. pap. 14.95 (*0-674-57441-9*) HUP.

— On the Law of Nations. 224p. 1990. text 33.95 (*0-674-63575-2*) HUP.

— On the Law of Nations. 224p. 1992. pap. text 10.95 (*0-674-63576-0*) HUP.

— Pandaemonium: Ethnicity in International Politics. LC 92-41370. 240p. 1993. 27.50 (*0-19-827787-3*) OUP.

Moynihan, Daniel P. & Combest, Larry. Secrecy: Report of the Commission on Protecting & Reducing Government Secrecy. (Illus.). 240p. 1997. pap. text 45.00 (*0-7881-4685-8*) DIANE Pub.

Moynihan, Daniel P., jt. auth. see Eberstadt, Nicholas.

Moynihan, Daniel P., jt. auth. see Glazer, Nathan.

Moynihan, Daniel P., jt. ed. see Denton, James S.

Moynihan, Daniel P., jt. ed. see Glazer, Nathan.

Moynihan, Daniel Patrick. Secrecy: The American Experience. LC 98-8144. (World Religions, Themes & Issues Ser.). (Illus.). 262p. 1998. 22.50 (*0-300-07756-4*) Yale U Pr.

— Secrecy: The American Experience. (Illus.). 272p. 1999. pap. 10.95 (*0-300-08079-4*) Yale U Pr.

Moynihan, James. Implementation Manual for the Healthcare Claim Payment Advice: Guidelines For... 2nd rev. ed. 200p. (C). 1996. ring bd. 95.00 (*1-55738-625-0*, Irwn Prfssnl) McGraw-Hill Prof.

Moynihan, James H. The Life of Archbishop John Ireland. LC 76-6358. (Irish Americans Ser.). (Illus.). 1976. reprint ed. 40.95 (*0-405-09351-9*) Ayer.

Moynihan, James J. Edi: A Guide for the Healthcare Professional. LC 93-16554. (Illus.). 98p. 1993. per. 24.95 (*1-882198-17-4*) Hlthcare Fin Mgmt.

— Implementation Manual for the 835 Health Care Claim-Payment - Advice. 175p. 1992. 74.95 (*0-930228-91-X*) Hlthcare Fin Mgmt.

— Implementation Manual for the 835 Health Care Claim Payment-Advice Supplement. 40p. 1992. 50.00 (*1-882198-12-3*) Hlthcare Fin Mgmt.

Moynihan, James J. & McLure, Marcia L. EDI: A Guide for Integrating Electronic Data Interchange in Today's Healthcare Facility. 216p. (C). 1995. text 45.00 (*1-55738-624-2*, Irwn Prfssnl) McGraw-Hill Prof.

Moynihan, Jeff. Father Aloyisius: Wonder Worker. LC 96-69105. 64p. (Orig.). 1996. pap. 2.95 (*1-882972-75-9*, 3531) Queenship Pub.

Moynihan, Jeffrey J. El Padre Juan Luis: Hacedor de Maravillas en America. (SPA.). 64p. 1997. pap. 2.95 (*1-57918-046-9*, 3531S) Queenship Pub.

Moynihan, Jenny, jt. auth. see Coleman, Clive.

Moynihan, Kenneth J. Can the Scholar's History Be the Public's History? (Lila Wallace-Reader's Digest Fund/American Antiquarian Society Lectures: No. 2). 12p. 1996. reprint ed. pap. 4.50 (*0-944026-69-9*) Am Antiquarian.

Moynihan, Martin. Communication & Noncommunication by Cephalopods. LC 84-47821. (Animal Communication Ser.). (Illus.). 154p. 1985. 35.00 (*0-253-31382-1*) Ind U Pr.

— Geographic Variation in Social Behavior & in Adaptations to Competition among Andean Birds. (Publications of the Nuttall Ornithological Club: No. 18). (Illus.). 162p. (C). 1979. 17.50 (*1-877973-28-9*) Nuttall Ornith.

— The New World Primates: Adaptive Radiation & the Evolution of Social Behavior, Languages & Intelligence. LC 75-3467. (Illus.). 273p. 1976. reprint ed. pap. 84.70 (*0-608-06642-7*, 206683900009) Bks Demand.

Moynihan, Martin, ed. & tr. see Lewis, C. S. & Calabria, Don G.

Moynihan, Martin H. The Social Regulation of Competition & Aggression in Animals. LC 97-53122. 208p. 1998. text 27.50 (*1-56098-788-X*) Smithsonian.

Moynihan, Michael. The Coming American Renaissance: How to Benefit from America's Economic Resurgence. LC 96-19657. 320p. 1996. 22.50 (*0-684-81207-X*) S&S Trade.

— War Correspondent. 256p. 1994. 24.95 (*0-85052-413-X*, Pub. by Leo Cooper) Trans-Atl Phila.

Moynihan, Michael & Soderlind, Didrik. Lords of Chaos: The Bloody Rise of the Satanic Metal Underground. LC 98-168794. (Illus.). 358p. 1997. pap. 16.95 (*0-922915-48-2*) Feral Hse.

Moynihan, Michael W. Attitudes of Americans on Coping with Interdependence: Findings of Opinion Research Organizations. 20p. 1976. pap. text 10.50 (*0-8191-5859-3*) U Pr of Amer.

Moynihan, Patricia M. Diabetes Youth Curriculum: A Toolbox for Educators: Resource & Activities Guide - "The Toolbox", Bk. 2. Raab, Patricia B., ed. LC 88-7112. (Illus.). 260p. 1988. ring bd. 55.00 (*0-937721-50-6*) Wiley.

Moynihan, Patricia M., et al. Diabetes Youth Curriculum Bk. 1: A Toolbox for Educators: The Curriculum. LC 88-7111. (Illus.). 136p. (Orig.). 1988. pap. text 95.00 (*0-937721-49-2*) Wiley.

Moynihan, Patricia M., jt. auth. see Haig, Broatch.

Moynihan, Patrick. Pandaemonium: Ethnicity in International Politics. 238p. 1994. reprint ed. pap. 8.95 (*0-19-827946-9*) OUP.

Moynihan, Robert, intro. The Necessary Learning: Liberal Arts & Sciences, Defense & Reform. LC 88-26185. 116p. (C). 1988. lib. bdg. 32.00 (*0-8191-7204-9*) U Pr of Amer.

Moynihan, Ruth B. Coming of Age: Four Centuries of Connecticut Women & Their Choices. Wilkie, Everett C., Jr., ed. (Illus.). 116p. (C). 1989. reprint ed. pap. write for info. (*0-940748-99-1*) Conn Hist Soc.

— Rebel for Rights: Abigail Scott Duniway. LC 83-1142. (Yale Historical Publications: No. 130). (Illus.). 320p. 1985. pap. 17.00 (*0-300-03478-4*) Yale U Pr.

Moynihan, Ruth B., et al, eds. Second to None: A Documentary History of American Women Vol. 1: From the Sixteenth Century to 1865. LC 93-14347. (Illus.). xx, 404p. 1994. pap. text 25.00 (*0-8032-8199-4*, Bison Books) U of Nebr Pr.

— Second to None: A Documentary History of American Women Vol. 2: From 1865 to the Present. LC 93-14347. (Illus.). xxii, 474p. (C). 1994. pap. text 25.00 (*0-8032-8204-4*, Bison Books) U of Nebr Pr.

— So Much to Be Done: Women Settlers on the Mining & Ranching Frontier. LC 89-22549. (Women in the West Ser.). (Illus.). xxii, 326p. 1990. text 45.00 (*0-8032-3134-2*) U of Nebr Pr.

Moynihan, T. P., jt. auth. see Smart, P.

***Moyo, Stella S., et al.** Privatization of Municipal Services in East Africa: A Governance Approach to Human Settlements Management. LC 99-889629. x, 100p. 1998. write for info. (*92-1-131386-4*) UN.

Moys. Manual of Law Librarians. (C). 1976. text 55.00 (*0-89158-637-7*) Westview.

Moys, Alan. Colloquial French: A Complete Language Course. LC 95-16104. (ENG & FRE., Illus.). 290p. (gr. 13). 1995. pap. 14.99 (*0-415-12089-6*) Routledge.

— Colloquial French: A Complete Language Course. LC 95-16104. (ENG & FRE.). 288p. (gr. 13). 1996. 27.99 incl. audio (*0-415-12091-8*) Routledge.

Moys, Elizabeth M., ed. Manual of Law Librarianship: The Use & Organization of Legal Literature. 2nd ed. (Professional Librarian Ser.). 952p. 1987. 70.00 (*0-8161-1854-X*, Hall Reference) Macmillan.

— Moys Classification & Thesaurus for Legal Materials. 3rd ed. 400p. 1991. 110.00 (*0-86291-903-7*) Bowker-Saur.

Moysan, Nelly. Teach Yourself French Vocabulary. (Teach Yourself Ser.). (ENG & FRE., Illus.). 192p. 1996. pap. 7.95 (*0-8442-3984-4*, Teach Yrslf) NTC Contemp Pub Co.

Moyse-Faurie, Claire. Dictionnaire Futunien-Francais. (FRE.). 1993. write for info. (*0-7859-8186-1*, 2-87723-070-8) Fr & Eur.

Moyse-Faurie, Claire & Joredie, Marie-Adele. Dictionnaire Xaracuu-Francais (Nouvelle-Caledonie) (FRE.). 1986. 75.00 (*0-7859-8235-3*, 2-906341-00-2) Fr & Eur.

Moyse, L. First Step in Flute Playing Bk. 1: 2 Flutes. 36p. 1986. pap. 4.95 (*0-7935-4409-2*, 50335410) H Leonard.

— Flutists Primer: Easy & Melodious Exercises 2nd Flute or Piano Optional. 36p. 1986. pap. 9.95 (*0-7935-5005-X*, 50333710) H Leonard.

— Forty Little Pieces in Progressive Order: For Beginner Flutists. 52p. 1986. pap. 8.95 (*0-7935-2552-7*, 50329130) H Leonard.

— Sixty-Five Little Pieces in Progressive Order for Beginner Flutists. 80p. 1988. pap. 12.95 (*0-7935-4814-4*, 50488965) H Leonard.

— Ten Pieces Bassoon & Piano: Opus 37 No. 5. 32p. 1991. pap. 9.95 (*0-7935-0640-9*, 50481111) H Leonard.

— Ten Pieces Clarinet & Piano: Opus 37 No. 3. 32p. 1991. pap. 8.95 (*0-7935-0641-7*, 50481110) H Leonard.

— Ten Pieces for Flute & Piano. 32p. 1991. pap. 8.95 (*0-7935-0643-3*, 50481279) H Leonard.

— Ten Pieces for Horn & Piano: Opus 37 No. 4. 24p. 1991. pap. 8.95 (*0-7935-0642-5*, 50481109) H Leonard.

— Ten Pieces for Oboe & Piano: Opus 37 No. 3. 24p. 1991. pap. 8.95 (*0-7935-0639-5*, 50481112) H Leonard.

— Young Flutist's Recital Book: 3 Centuries of Flute Music. 48p. 1986. pap. 7.95 (*0-7935-5103-X*, 50336720) H Leonard.

Moyse, Sarah. Chinese New Year. LC 97-27148. (Festivals Ser.). (Illus.). 32p. (J). (gr. 3-6). 1998. lib. bdg. 20.90 (*0-7613-0374-X*) Millbrook Pr.

Moyser, George & Wagstaff, Margaret, eds. Research Methods for Elite Studies. (Contemporary Social Research Ser.: No. 14). 240p. (C). 1987. text 55.00 (*0-04-312035-0*); pap. text 19.95 (*0-04-312036-9*) Routledge.

Moyser, George H., jt. auth. see Medhurst, Kenneth H.

Moysie, David. Memoirs of the Affairs of Scotland. LC 75-193018. (Bannatyne Club, Edinburgh. Publications: No. 39). reprint ed. 37.50 (*0-404-52925-9*) AMS Pr.

Mozafar, A. Plant Vitamins: Agronomic, Physiological & Nutritional Aspects. 432p. 1993. boxed set 249.00 (*0-8493-4734-3*) CRC Pr.

Mozafar, Mehdi. Authority in Islam: From Muhammad to Khomeini. LC 86-13070.Tr. of Pouvoic Islamique. 136p. (gr. 13). 1987. text 69.95 (*0-87332-388-2*) M E Sharpe.

Mozaffari, Mehdi. Fatwa: Violence & Discourtesy. (Illus.). 213p. 1998. pap. 18.95 (*87-7288-776-1*, Pub. by Aarhus Univ Pr) David Brown.

Mozaffari, Mehdi, ed. Security Politics in the Commonwealth of Independent State: The Southern Belt. LC 97-1718. 234p. 1997. text 65.00 (*0-312-17459-4*) St Martin.

Mozan. Racing Numerology: A Standard System of the Science of Numbers Applied to Horse Racing. 2nd ed. 103p. 1998. reprint ed. pap. 21.00 (*0-7873-0628-2*) Hlth Research.

Mozans, H. J. Woman in Science. LC 90-50964. (C). 1991. reprint ed. pap. text 17.50 (*0-268-01946-0*) U of Notre Dame Pr.

Mozart, Homer. Guppies. LC 98-7553. (Fish Ser.). (Illus.). 64p. (YA). (gr. 3 up). 1999. lib. bdg. 17.95 (*0-7910-5091-2*) Chelsea Hse.

— Guppies, Keeping & Breeding Them in Captivity: Keeping & Breeding Them in Captivity. (Illus.). 64p. 1996. pap. 6.95 (*0-7938-0358-6*, RE609) TFH Pubns.

Mozart, Leopold. A Treatise on the Fundamental Principles of Violin Playing. 2nd ed. Knocker, Editha, tr. (Early Music Ser.). (Illus.). 274p. (C). 1985. pap. text 45.00 (*0-19-318513-X*) OUP.

Mozart, Leopold, et al. Orchestral Music in Salzburg, 1750-1780. Eisen, Cliff, ed. (Recent Researches in Music of the Classic Era Ser.: Vol. RRC40). xxiii, 118p. 1994. pap. 45.00 (*0-89579-287-7*) A-R Eds.

Mozart, Wolfgang Amadeus. The Abduction from the Seraglio in Full Score. 320p. 1989. pap. 16.95 (*0-486-26004-6*) Dover.

— Classic Mozart. 32p. 1997. pap. 8.95 (*0-7935-8327-6*) H Leonard.

— La Clemenza di Tito. 192p. 1993. pap. 12.95 (*0-486-27540-X*) Dover.

— Complete Piano Trios & Quartets & Piano Quintet. 272p. 1991. pap. 13.95 (*0-486-26714-8*) Dover.

— Complete Serenades in Full Score Series I. 240p. 1990. pap. 12.95 (*0-486-26565-X*) Dover.

— Complete Sonatas & Variations for Violin & Piano, Ser. I. 224p. 1992. pap. 12.95 (*0-486-27299-0*) Dover.

— Complete Sonatas & Variations for Violin & Piano, Ser. II. 208p. 1992. pap. 13.95 (*0-486-27406-3*) Dover.

— Complete String Quartets. 277p. 1970. pap. 13.95 (*0-486-22372-8*) Dover.

— Complete String Quintets. 181p. 1978. reprint ed. pap. 9.95 (*0-486-23603-X*) Dover.

— Concerti for Wind Instruments in Full Score. 272p. 1987. pap. 13.95 (*0-486-25228-0*) Dover.

— Cosi Fan Tutte. John, Nicholas, ed. Browne, Marmaduke E., tr. from ITA. (English National Opera Guide Series: Bilingual Libretto, Articles: No. 22). (Illus.). 128p. 1984. pap. 9.95 (*0-7145-3882-5*) Riverrun NY.

— Cosi Fan Tutte: Libretto. 80p. 1986. pap. 4.95 (*0-7935-2619-1*, 50340000) H Leonard.

— Cosifan Tutte in Full Color. 448p. 1983. pap. 19.95 (*0-486-24528-4*) Dover.

— Don Giovanni. 1990. 19.50 (*0-8446-5069-2*) Peter Smith.

— Don Giovanni. John, Nicholas, ed. Platt, Norman & Sarti, Laura, trs. from ITA. (English National Opera Guide Series: Bilingual Libretto, Articles: No. 18). (Illus.). 128p. 1982. pap. 9.95 (*0-7145-3853-1*) Riverrun NY.

— Don Giovanni: Complete Orchestral & Vocal Score. Schunemann, Georg & Soldan, Kurt, eds. LC 73-91488. (Opera Libretto Ser.). 468p. 1977. reprint ed. pap. 19.95 (*0-486-23026-0*) Dover.

— Don Giovanni: Libretto. (ENG & ITA.). 84p. 1986. pap. 4.95 (*0-7935-2609-4*, 50340090) H Leonard.

— Don Giovanni Piano. 1998. pap. 7.95 (*963-8303-98-0*) Konemann.

— Favorite Opera Classics Vol. I: Mozart. 88p. 1998. pap. 7.95 (*963-8303-71-9*) Konemann.

— Favorite Opera Classics Vol. II: Mozart. 88p. 1998. pap. 7.95 (*963-8303-87-5*) Konemann.

— Idomeneo in Full Score. 384p. 1992. pap. 18.95 (*0-486-27108-0*) Dover.

Mozart, Wolfgang Amadeus. Later Symphonies. 285p. 1974. pap. 12.95 (*0-486-23052-X*) Dover.

Mozart, Wolfgang Amadeus. Letters of Wolfgang Amadeus Mozart. Mersman, Hans, ed. Bozman, M. M., tr. (Illus.). 276p. 1972. pap. 7.95 (*0-486-22859-2*) Dover.

***Mozart, Wolfgang Amadeus.** The Libretti of Mozart's Completed Operas, Vol. 2. LC 98-220275. (ITA, GER & ENG., Illus.). 1998. 75.00 (*1-878617-22-2*) Leyerle Pubns.

Mozart, Wolfgang Amadeus. The Magic Flute. LC 97-1348. (Illus.). 40p. (YA). (gr. 3 up). 1997. 17.95 (*0-8118-1003-8*) Chronicle Bks.

— The Magic Flute: Libretto.Tr. of Zauberflaute. 56p. 1986. pap. 4.95 (*0-7935-2864-X*, 50340050) H Leonard.

— The Magic Flute: 1791 Libretto by Emanuel Schikaneder. Eckelmeyer, Judith A., tr. & intro. by. LC 79-67268. xxix, 65p. 1980. lib. bdg. 39.95 (*0-88946-955-5*) E Mellen.

— The Marriage of Figaro. 144p. 1999. 19.98 (*1-57912-065-2*) Blck Dog & Leventhal.

— The Marriage of Figaro. John, Nicholas, ed. Dent, Edward, tr. from ITA. (English National Opera Guide Series: Bilingual Libretto, Articles: No. 17). (Illus.). 1982. pap. 9.95 (*0-7145-3771-3*) Riverrun NY.

— The Marriage of Figaro: Complete Orchestral Score. LC 78-67726. 448p. 1979. reprint ed. pap. 18.95 (*0-486-23751-6*) Dover.

— Melody Dicer. 32p. 1984. pap. 9.95 (*0-935474-09-9*) Carousel Pubns Ltd.

— Melody Dicer Manuscript Book. Mercuri, Carmela, ed. 32p. 1984. pap. text 4.95 (*0-935474-10-2*) Carousel Pubns Ltd.

— Mozart. 64p. 1996. pap. 9.95 (*0-7935-6737-8*) H Leonard.

— Mozart: Taschenpartitur, 2 vols. (Cloth Bound Pocket Ser.). 1999. boxed set 14.95 (*963-9155-50-0*) Konemann.

— Mozart Arias. 88p. 1996. pap. 16.95 incl. audio compact disk (*0-7935-6241-4*); pap. 16.95 incl. audio compact disk (*0-7935-6242-2*) H Leonard.

— Mozart for Guitar. 16p. 1984. pap. 4.95 (*0-7935-2705-8*) H Leonard.

— Mozart Masterpieces for Solo Piano: 19 Works. 128p. 1998. pap. 7.95 (*0-486-40408-0*) Dover.

— Mozart Piano Concerto in C Major. Kerman, Joseph, ed. (Critical Scores Ser.). (Illus.). (C). 1970. pap. text 16.75 (*0-393-09890-7*) Norton.

— Mozart Speaks: Views on Music, Musicians, & the World. 446p. 1995. 20.00 (*0-02-871356-7*, Schirmer Books) Mac Lib Ref.

— Mozart's Don Giovanni: Complete Italian Libretto. Bleiler, Ellen H., tr. (ITA.). 121p. 1985. pap. 2.95 (*0-486-24944-1*) Dover.

— Mozart/Twelve Songs, High Voice. Paton, John G., ed. 72p. (C). 1992. pap. 8.95 (*0-88284-497-0*, 3389) Alfred Pub.

— Mozart/Twelve Songs, Medium Voice. Paton, John G., ed. 72p. (C). 1992. pap. text 9.95 (*0-88284-498-9*, 3390) Alfred Pub.

— My First Book of Classics: Mozart. (Easy Classics Ser.). 1990. 6.95 (*0-685-32053-7*, H701) Hansen Ed Mus.

— Le Nozze di Figaro: Libretto.Tr. of Marriage of Figaro. (ITA.). 96p. 1986. pap. 4.95 (*0-7935-2592-6*, 50340080) H Leonard.

— Piano Concerto No. 26 in D Major ("Coronation"), K.537: The Autograph Score. 128p. 1991. pap. 12.95 (*0-486-26747-4*) Dover.

— Piano Concerto Nos. 20, 21 & 22: With Orchestral Reduction for Second Piano. 208p. 1995. pap. text 12.95 (*0-486-28435-2*) Dover.

— Piano Concertos Nos. 11-16 in Full Score. 256p. 1987. pap. 12.95 (*0-486-25468-2*) Dover.

— Piano Concertos, Nos. 17-22. 370p. 1978. pap. 16.95 (*0-486-23599-8*) Dover.

— Piano Concertos, Nos. 23-27. 310p. 1978. pap. 13.95 (*0-486-23600-5*) Dover.

***Mozart, Wolfgang Amadeus.** Piano Concertos Nos. 7-10 in Full Score: With Mozart's Cadenzas for Nos. 7 & 9. 2000. pap. 16.95 (*0-486-41165-6*) Dover.

Mozart, Wolfgang Amadeus. Practical Elements of Thorough-Bass. LC 76-27136. 1976. reprint ed. pap. 3.00 (*0-915282-04-6*) J Patelson Mus.

***Mozart, Wolfgang Amadeus.** Requiem, 1. 1999. pap. text 9.95 (*963-9059-90-0*) Konemann.

Mozart, Wolfgang Amadeus. Requiem in Full Score. 108p. 1989. pap. 8.95 (*0-486-25311-2*) Dover.

— Requiem, K626, in Full Score. 112p. Date not set. 3.95 (*0-486-40116-2*) Dover.

— Seven Great Opera Overtures in Full Score. 144p. pap. 13.95 (*0-486-40174-X*) Dover.

— Seventeen Divertimenti for Various Instruments. 241p. 1979. reprint ed. pap. 13.95 (*0-486-23862-8*) Dover.

— Six Masses in Full Score. 352p. 1992. pap. 17.95 (*0-486-27086-6*) Dover.

— Sonatas & Fantasies for Solo Piano. 272p. 1996. pap. 12.95 (*0-486-29222-3*) Dover.

— Sonatas, Phantasies & Rondi I. 224p. pap. 7.95 (*963-8303-00-X*) Konemann.

Mozart, Wolfgang Amadeus. Sonatas, Phantasies & Rondi II. 168p. pap. 7.95 (*963-8303-01-8*) Konemann.

Mozart, Wolfgang Amadeus. Step by Step-Mozart, 1. 1998. pap. text 7.95 (*963-9059-52-8*) Konemann.

— Symphonies Nos. 22-34 in Full Score. 288p. 1991. pap. 14.95 (*0-486-26675-3*) Dover.

— Symphony No. Thirty-Five in D, K. 385: The Haffner Symphony. 1968. pap. 8.00 (*0-19-385289-6*) OUP.

— Symphony No. 35, K385, "Haffner," Symphony No. 36, K425, "Linz" & Symphony No. 38, K504, "Prague" 128p. 1998. pap. 3.95 (*0-486-40420-X*) Dover.

— Symphony Number 40 in G Minor K550. 1998. 3.95 (*0-486-29849-3*, 741743Q) Dover.

— Variations, Rondos & Other Works for Piano. 208p. 1991. pap. 11.95 (*0-486-26882-9*) Dover.

— The Violin Concerti & the Sinfonia Concertante, K 364, in Full Score. 208p. 1986. pap. 12.95 (*0-486-25169-1*) Dover.

— Works for Piano Four Hands & Two Pianos. 160p. 1990. pap. 10.95 (*0-486-26501-3*) Dover.

— Die Zauberfloete. (GER.). 1998. pap. 7.95 (*963-8303-08-5*) Konemann.

***Mozart, Wolfgang Amadeus & Schikaneder, Emanuel.** The Magic Flute. LC 00-25259.Tr. of Zauberflote. (Illus.). 2000. 50.00 incl. cd-rom (*0-7892-0645-5*) Abbeville Pr.

Mozart, Wolfgang Amadeus, jt. auth. see Chrysostom, J.

Mozejko, Edward. Yordan Yovkov. 117p. 1984. pap. 14.95 (*0-89357-117-2*) Slavica.

Mozejko, Edward, et al, eds. Vasiliy Pavlovich Aksenov: A Writer in Quest of Himself. (Illus.). 272p. 1986. 27.95 (*0-89357-141-5*) Slavica.

Mozeleski, Paul M., ed. see Mozeleski, Peter A.

An Asterisk (*) at the beginning of an entry indicates that the title is appearing for the first time.

Mozeleski, Peter A. AIDS World Newsletter, Vol. 1, No. 1. Mozeleski, Paul M., ed. Dominguez, Rosie, ed. & tr. by. (YA). (gr. 6-12). 1991. pap. 2.50 (*1-880058-56-1*); pap. 2.50 (*1-880058-57-X*) Rubbers Bros Comics.

— AIDS World Newsletter, Vol. 1, No. 2. Mozeleski, Paul M., ed. Dominguez, Rosie, ed. & tr. by. (YA). (gr. 6-12). 1991. pap. 2.50 (*1-880058-58-8*); pap. 2.50 (*1-880058-59-6*) Rubbers Bros Comics.

— The Rubbers Bros. Comics, Vol. 1, No. 1. Mozeleski, Paul M. & Dominguez, Rosie, eds. Pagan, Margarita, tr. (Illus.). 16p. (YA). (gr. 6-12). 1990. pap. 2.50 (*1-880058-01-4*); pap. 2.50 (*1-880058-13-8*) Rubbers Bros Comics.

— The Rubbers Bros. Comics, Vol. 1, No. 2. Mozeleski, Paul M. & Dominguez, Rosie, eds. Pagan, Margarita, tr. (Illus.). 16p. (YA). (gr. 6-12). 1991. pap. 2.50 (*1-880058-02-2*); pap. 2.50 (*1-880058-14-6*) Rubbers Bros Comics.

— The Rubbers Bros. Comics, Vol. 1, No. 3. Mozeleski, Paul M. & Dominguez, Rosie, eds. Pagan, Margarita, tr. (Illus.). 16p. (YA). (gr. 6-12). 1992. pap. text 2.50 (*1-880058-03-0*); pap. text 2.50 (*1-880058-15-4*) Rubbers Bros Comics.

— The Rubbers Bros. Comics, Vol. 1, No. 4. Mozeleski, Paul M. & Dominguez, Rosie, eds. Castalanas, Guadalupe, tr. (SPA., Illus.). 16p. (YA). (gr. 6-12). 1992. pap. text 2.50 (*1-880058-16-2*) Rubbers Bros Comics.

— The Rubbers Bros. Comics, Vol. 1, No. 7. Mozeleski, Paul M. & Dominguez, Rosie, eds. (SPA., Illus.). 16p. (YA). (gr. 6-12). 1998. pap. 2.50 (*1-880058-07-3*) Rubbers Bros Comics.

— The Rubbers Bros. Comics, Vol. 1, Nos. 1-6. Mozeleski, Paul M. & Dominguez, Rosie, eds. (Illus.). (YA). (gr. 6-12). 1992. pap. 2.50 (*1-880058-00-6*) Rubbers Bros Comics.

— Rubbers Bros. Comics, When AIDS Strikes, AIDS World Newsletter: AIDS Talk Seminars, Activity. Mozeleski, Paul M. & Dominguez, Rosie, eds. (SPA.). (YA). (gr. 6-12). 1991. pap. 2.50 (*1-880058-18-9*) Rubbers Bros Comics.

— Rubbers Bros. Comics, When AIDS Strikes, AIDS World Newsletter: AIDS Talk Seminars, Comic. Mozeleski, Paul M. & Dominguez, Rosie, eds. (SPA.). (YA). (gr. 6-12). 1991. pap. 2.50 (*1-880058-05-7*); pap. 2.50 (*1-880058-17-0*) Rubbers Bros Comics.

— When AIDS Strikes. Mozeleski, Paul M. & Dominguez, Rosie, eds. (Illus.). 8p. (Orig.). (YA). (gr. 6-12). 1991. pap. 2.50 (*1-880058-85-5*) Rubbers Bros Comics.

— When AIDS Strikes, Vol. 1, Nos. 1 & 2. Mozeleski, Paul M., ed. Dominguez, Rosie, ed. & tr. by. (Illus.). 8p. (Orig.). (YA). (gr. 6-12). 1991. pap. 2.50 (*1-880058-84-7*) Rubbers Bros Comics.

Mozelle, Isaac. The Flowering Plants of Western India. 383p. 1989. 210.00 (*81-7158-039-4*, Pub. by Scientific Pubs) St Mut.

Mozelle, Shirley. Zack's Alligator. LC 88-32067. (I Can Read Bks.). (Illus.). 64p. (J). (gr. 1-3). 1995. pap. 3.95 (*0-06-444186-5*) HarpC Child Bks.

— Zack's Alligator. (I Can Read Bks.). (J). (gr. 1-3). 1995. 8.95 (*0-606-08413-4*, Pub. by Turtleback) Demco.

— Zack's Alligator Goes to School. LC 92-29871. (I Can Read Bks.). (Illus.). 64p. (J). (gr. 1-3). 1998. pap. 3.75 (*0-06-444248-9*) HarpC.

— Zack's Alligator Goes to School. (I Can Read Bks.). (Illus.). 64p. (J). (gr. 1-3). 1994. lib. bdg. 13.89 (*0-06-022888-1*) HarpC Child Bks.

— Zack's Alligator Goes to School. (I Can Read Bks.). (J). (gr. 1-3). 1998. 8.95 (*0-606-13942-7*, Pub. by Turtleback) Demco.

Mozena, James P., et al. Clinical Guideline Development: An Algorithm Approach. LC 95-39261. 176p. 1996. spiral bd. 79.00 (*0-8342-0734-6*, 20734) Aspen Pub.

— Stop Managing Costs: Designing Healthcare Organizations Around Core Business Systems LC 98-55718. 1999. write for info. (*0-87389-449-9*) ASQ Qual Pr.

Mozer, David. Bicycling in Africa: The Place in Between. rev. ed. (Illus.). 196p. 1989. pap. 14.95 (*0-9623052-0-0*) IBF WA.

Mozer, Michael C. The Perception of Multiple Objects: A Connectionist Approach. (Bradford Neural Network Modeling & Connectionism Ser.). 232p. 1991. 27.50 (*0-262-13270-2*, Bradford Bks) MIT Pr.

Mozes, Deborah B., jt. ed. see Bernstein, Julianne.

Mozes, Nava, et al, eds. Microbial Cell Surface Analysis: Structural & Physico-Chemical Methods. 368p. 1991. 95.00 (*0-89573-783-3*, Wiley-VCH) Wiley.

Mozeson, I. E. & Stavsky, Lois. Jerusalem Mosaic: Voices from the Holy City. LC 94-21439. (Illus.). 160p. (J). (gr. 7 up). 1994. mass mkt. 15.95 (*0-02-767651-X*, Four Winds Pr) S&S Childrens.

Mozeson, Isaac E. The Word: The Dictionary That Reveals the Hebrew Sources of English. LC 95-17239. 320p. 1995. pap. 40.00 (*1-56821-615-7*) Aronson.

Mozet, Nicole. George Sand, Ecrivain de Romans. (FRE.). 248p. 1997. pap. 69.95 (*2-86808-106-1*) Intl Scholars.

Mozet, Nicole, ed. see Sand, George.

Mozga, Ilsa A., tr. see Goetz-Stankiewicz, Marketa, ed.

Mozhaev, D. V., et al. English-Russian & Russian-English Dictionary of Forestry & Forest Industries. 2nd rev. ed. 864p. (C). 1998. 85.95 (*0-8285-5499-4*) Firebird NY.

***Mozian, Laurie Deutsch.** Foods That Fight Disease: A Simple Guide to Using & Understanding Phytonutrients to Protect Your Health. 2000. pap. text 13.95 (*1-58333-037-2*, Avery) Penguin Putnam.

Mozier, Jeanne. Tales, Too! Tales from the Springs. Walker, Robert L., ed. & intro. by. 150p. (Orig.). 1995. pap. write for info. (*0-938572-14-8*) Bunny Crocodile.

***Mozier, Jeanne.** Way Out in West Virginia: A Must-Have Guide to the Oddities & Wonders of the Mountain. LC 99-60065. (Illus.). 1999. pap. 12.95 (*1-891852-02-7*) Quarrier Pr.

Mozingo, David & Nee, Victor G., eds. State & Society in Contemporary China. LC 82-46010. 269p. 1983. pap. text 17.95 (*0-8014-9253-X*) Cornell U Pr.

Mozingo, Hugh N. Shrubs of the Great Basin: A Natural History. LC 86-7070. (Great Basin Ser.: No. 4). 364p. (Orig.). 1987. pap. 34.95 (*0-87417-112-1*) U of Nev Pr.

Mozingo, Julia. In a Family Way. 1996. per. 3.99 (*0-373-24062-7*, 1-24062-1) Silhouette.

Mozino, Jose M. Noticias de Nutka: An Account of Nootka Sound in 1792. LC 84-45542. (American Ethnological Society Monographs: No. 50). 1988. reprint ed. 35.00 (*0-404-62948-2*) AMS Pr.

— Noticias de Nutka: An Account of Nootka Sound in 1792. 2nd ed. Engstrand, Iris H., ed. & tr. by. from SPA. LC 90-50981. 200p. 1991. reprint ed. pap. 14.95 (*0-295-97103-7*) U of Wash Pr.

Mozley, E. N. The Theology of Albert Schweitzer. LC 73-16630. 108p. 1974. reprint ed. lib. bdg. 35.00 (*0-8371-7204-7*, SCTH, Greenwood Pr) Greenwood.

Mozley, J. H., tr. Argonautica. (Loeb Classical Library: No. 286). 482p. 1934. 18.95 (*0-674-99316-0*) HUP.

— Art of Love & Other Poems. (Loeb Classical Library: No. 232). 396p. 1979. text 18.95 (*0-674-99255-5*) HUP.

Mozley, Robert F. The Politics & Technology of Nuclear Proliferation. LC 98-12070. 1998. write for info. (*0-295-97725-6*) U of Wash Pr.

— The Politics & Technology of Nuclear Proliferation. LC 98-12070. (Illus.). 384p. 1998. pap. 25.00 (*0-295-97726-4*) U of Wash Pr.

— Uranium Enrichment & Other Technical Problems Relating to Nuclear Weapons Proliferation. 64p. (Orig.). 1994. pap. 9.00 (*0-935371-30-3*) CFISAC.

Mozolin, Viktor P. Property Law in Contemporary Russia. 174p. 1993. 40.00 (*0-935328-75-0*) Intl Law Inst.

— Property Law in Contemporary Russia. 174p. 1993. ring bd. 75.00 (*90-411-0994-3*) Kluwer Law Intl.

Mozorov, Vladimir, ed. Who's Who in Russia & the CIS Republics. 328p. 1995. 60.00 (*0-8050-2691-6*) H Holt & Co.

Mozqovoi, A. A. Fundamentals of Nematology: Ascaridata of Animals & Men. (C). 1986. 17.50 (*0-8364-2112-4*, Pub. by Oxford IBH) S Asia.

Mozsi, Ferenc. My Poempire: 50 Selected Poems. Hargitai, Peter, tr. 130p. 1997. write for info. (*963-85315-8-4*) Framo Pub.

Mozsik. Cell Injury & Protection in the Gastrointestinal Tract from Basic Sciences to Clinical Perspectives 1996. LC 97-212611. 1997. text 227.50 (*0-7923-8720-1*) Kluwer Academic.

Mozsik, G., et al, eds. Oxygen Free Radicals & Scavengers in the Natural Science. 356p. 1993. pap. 295.00 (*963-05-6589-7*, Pub. by Akade Kiado) St Mut.

Mozsik, G. Y., et al, contrib. by. Twenty-Five Years of Peptic Ulcer Research in Hungary: From Basic Sciences to Clinical Practice, 1971-1995. 448p. 1997. 234.00 (*963-05-7436-5*, Pub. by Akade Kiado) St Mut.

Mozsik, Gy, et al. Capsaicin-Sensitive Afferent Nerves in Gastric Mucosal Damage & Protection. 124p. 1997. pap. 108.00 (*963-05-7437-3*, Pub. by Akade Kiado) St Mut.

— Research on Dietary Fibres. 222p. (C). 1986. 75.00 (*963-05-4254-4*, Pub. by Akade Kiado) St Mut.

Mozsik, Gy, jt. auth. see Javor, T.

Mozumber, A. Fundamentals of Radiation Chemistry. LC 99-60404. (Illus.). 364p. 1999. text 95.00 (*0-12-509390-X*) Acad Pr.

Mozumdar, A. K. Today & Tomorrow. 2nd ed. 1979. pap. 5.95 (*0-87516-066-2*) DeVorss.

Mozur, Joseph P., Jr. Parables from the Past: The Prose Fiction of Chingiz Aitmatov. (Russian & East European Studies). 212p. (C). 1994. pap. 22.95 (*0-8229-5531-8*); text 59.95 (*0-8229-3791-3*) U of Pittsburgh Pr.

Mozzer-Mather, Susan, jt. auth. see Carroll, Cathryn.

Mozzillo, Mario. Things Are Out of Joint. 225p. 1995. 21.95 (*0-9644443-0-5*) Windsor House.

***Mozzochi, Charles J.** The Fermat Diary. LC 00-30629. 200p. 2000. 29.00 (*0-8218-2670-0*) Am Math.

***MP Ediciones Staff.** Curso Visual y Practico de Computacion: Aprendiendo PC, Facil, Rapido y Bien. (SPA.). 620p. 1999. pap. 78.00 (*987-9131-88-6*, Pub. by MP Ediciones) Am Wholesale.

— Curso Visual y Practico de Computacion: Aprendiendo PC, Facil, Rapido y Bien. 580p. 1999. pap. 78.00 (*987-526-006-1*, Pub. by MP Ediciones) Am Wholesale.

***MP Ediciones Staff, prod.** 111 Respuestas y Tips del Correo Electronico que Todo Usuario Debe Saber, en Espanol: 111 Answers & Tips on Internet E-mail in Spanish. 1999. pap. 15.90 (*987-526-004-5*, Pub. by MP Ediciones) Am Wholesale.

MP Ediciones Staff, ed. see Goldberger, Ricardo.

Mpanda, Samson. Geological Development of the East African Coastal Basin of Tanzania. (Stockholm Contributions in Geology 45(1): No. 45). (Illus.). 121p. 1998. pap. 47.50 (*91-22-01756-9*, Pub. by JCB Mohr) Coronet Bks.

Mphahlele, Es'kia. Afrika My Music. (Ravan Writers Ser.). 260p. 1995. reprint ed. pap. text 13.95 (*0-86975-484-X*, Pub. by Ravan Pr) Ohio U Pr.

— Afrika My Music: An Autobiography, 1957-1983. 260p. 1986. pap. text 13.95 (*0-86975-237-5*, Pub. by Ravan Pr) Ohio U Pr.

— Chirundu. 2nd ed. LC 95-198537. 172p. (Orig.). 1994. pap. text 14.95 (*0-86975-449-1*, Pub. by Ravan Pr) Ohio U Pr.

— Down Second Avenue: Growing up in a South African Ghetto. 1990. 22.00 (*0-8446-4451-X*) Peter Smith.

— Renewal Time. LC 88-61391. (Readers International Ser.). 225p. (Orig.). (C). 1988. 16.95 (*0-930523-55-5*); pap. 8.95 (*0-930523-56-3*) Readers Intl.

Mpho M'atsepo Nthunya. Singing Away the Hunger: Stories from a Life in Lesotho. Kendall, Limakatso, ed. LC 97-129010. 186p. 1997. pap. 22.00 (*0-86980-932-6*, Pub. by Univ Natal Pr) Intl Spec Bk.

Mpuila, F. Tshipamba. Biochemical, Mechanical & Functional Properties of the Ca(2 Plus) Hemeostasis in Renal Cells in Culture. No. 69. 149p. (Orig.). 1993. pap. 43.50 (*90-6186-556-5*, Pub. by Leuven Univ) Coronet Bks.

Mpuku, Herrick C. & Zyuulu, Ivan, eds. Contemporary Issues in Socio-Economic Reform in Zambia. LC 97-72078. (Making of Modern Africa Ser.). 160p. 1997. text 59.95 (*1-85972-442-6*, Pub. by Avebry) Ashgate Pub Co.

***MP4K Staff.** Untitled: (The Dot, a Dot, Dot) (Illus.). 4p. 2000. pap. 1000.00 (*0-9678655-2-2*, 1) M P Four K.

— Untitled: (The Dot, a Dot, Dot) (Illus.). 4p. 2000. pap. 100.00 (*0-9678655-9-X*, 2) M P Four K.

MQ Publications Staff. Chaucer. (Little Brown Notebooks Ser.). 1998. 9.99 (*1-84072-065-4*, Pub. by M Q Pubns) Watsn-Guptill.

— Chocolate. (Infatuations Ser.). 1998. 12.95 (*1-897954-61-1*, Pub. by Mus Quilts Pub) Sterling.

— Christmas Carols. 1998. 12.95 (*1-897954-99-9*, Pub. by Mus Quilts Pub) Sterling.

— Dickens. (Little Brown Notebooks Ser.). 1998. 9.99 (*1-84072-061-1*, Pub. by M Q Pubns) Watsn-Guptill.

— Discoveries. 1998. 12.95 (*1-897954-62-X*, Pub. by Mus Quilts Pub) Sterling.

— Gay Portraits. (Infatuations Ser.). 1998. 12.95 (*1-897954-85-9*, Pub. by Mus Quilts Pub) Sterling.

— Infatuation Astrology. (Infatuations Ser.). 1998. 12.95 (*1-897954-60-3*, Pub. by Mus Quilts Pub) Sterling.

— Lesbian Portraits. (Infatuations Ser.). 1998. 12.95 (*1-897954-92-1*, Pub. by Mus Quilts Pub) Sterling.

— Little House. (Little Brown Notebooks Ser.). 1998. 9.99 (*1-84072-064-6*, Pub. by M Q Pubns) Watsn-Guptill.

— Movies. (Infatuations Ser.). 1998. 12.95 (*1-897954-63-8*, Pub. by Mus Quilts Pub) Sterling.

— Opera. (Infatuations Ser.). 1998. 12.95 (*1-897954-64-6*, Pub. by Mus Quilts Pub) Sterling.

— Poetry. (Infatuations Ser.). (Illus.). 256p. 1998. 12.95 (*1-897954-65-4*, Pub. by Mus Quilts Pub) Sterling.

— Sherlock Holmes. (Little Brown Notebooks Ser.). 1998. 9.99 (*1-84072-062-X*, Pub. by M Q Pubns) Watsn-Guptill.

— Wine. (Infatuations Ser.). 1998. 12.95 (*1-897954-67-0*, Pub. by Mus Quilts Pub) Sterling.

MQ Publications Staff, ed. see Montgomery, L. M.

***MQP Creative Staff.** Best Friends. 2001. write for info. (*0-688-17702-6*, HarpRes) HarpInfo.

— Dog Days. 2001. write for info. (*0-688-17703-4*, HarpRes) HarpInfo.

— Kisses. LC 99-86296. (Illus.). 112p. 2000. 10.00 (*0-688-17700-X*, Hearst) Hearst Commns.

— Mothers & Babies. LC 99-87688. (Illus.). 112p. 2000. 10.00 (*0-688-17701-8*, Hearst) Hearst Commns.

M'Queen, James. Geographical Survey of Africa. 303p. reprint ed. 47.50 (*0-7146-1834-9*, Pub. by F Cass Pubs) Intl Spec Bk.

Mr. Fresh & the Supreme Rockers Staff. Breakdancing. 128p. 1984. pap. 2.95 (*0-380-88153-5*, Avon Bks) Morrow Avon.

Mr. J. More of the World's Dirty Jokes. 1980. pap. 5.95 (*0-8065-0710-1*, Citadel Pr) Carol Pub Group.

— Still More World's Best Dirty Jokes. 120p. 1998. pap. 6.95 (*0-00-638076-X*, Pub. by HarpC) Trafalgar.

Mr. J. The World's Best Dirty Jokes. 1985. mass mkt. 4.95 (*0-345-33106-0*) Ballantine Pub Grp.

— The World's Best Dirty Jokes. (Illus.). 160p. 1976. 7.95 (*0-8184-0223-7*) Carol Pub Group.

Mr. J. The World's Best Dirty Jokes. (Illus.). 136p. 1997. 5.98 (*0-89009-403-9*) Bk Sales Inc.

— The World's Best Dirty Jokes. 96p. 1998. pap. 6.95 (*0-00-637784-X*, Pub. by HarpC) Trafalgar.

***Mr. K.** Dirty Joke Book Guaranteed Highly Offensive. LC 99-38428. 1999. pap. text 9.95 (*0-8065-2126-0*) Carol Pub Group.

Mr. Mike Staff. Swimming in Chocolate: Poems & Drawings by Mr. Mike. (Illus.). 180p. (J). (gr. k-6). 1998. pap. 12.95 (*0-9658365-4-1*) Beetle Bug.

Mr. P. World's Best Yiddish Dirty Jokes. (Illus.). 128p. 1984. pap. 4.95 (*0-8065-0887-6*, Citadel Pr) Carol Pub Group.

***Mr Unzip Staff.** How to Screw the Post Office. LC 99-68334. (Illus.). 72p. 2000. pap. 8.00 (*1-55950-200-2*, 40089) Loompanics.

Mr. X. Fired? Fight Back! The No-Nonsense Guide for the Newly Fired, Downsized, Outplaced, Laid off & Those Who Are Worried about It. 192p. 1995. pap. 16.95 (*0-8144-7875-1*) AMACOM.

Mrabet, Mohammed. Big Mirror. Bowles, Paul, tr. 80p. 1990. pap. 10.95 (*0-7206-0730-2*, Pub. by P Owen Ltd) Dufour.

— The Boy Who Set the Fire & Other Stories. Bowles, Paul, tr. 144p. 1989. reprint ed. pap. 8.95 (*0-87286-230-5*) City Lights.

— The Chest. Bowles, Paul, tr. (ARA.). 120p. 1983. pap. 7.50 (*0-939180-18-9*) Tombouctou.

— The Chest. deluxe limited ed. Bowles, Paul, tr. (ARA.). 120p. 1983. 35.00 (*0-939180-21-9*) Tombouctou.

— Chocolate Creams & Dollars. Igliori, Paola, ed. Bowles, Paul, tr. from ARA. (Illus.). 192p. 1993. 29.95 (*0-9625119-6-X*) Inanout Pr.

— The Lemon. Bowles, Paul, tr. 192p. (Orig.). 1986. reprint ed. pap. 8.95 (*0-87286-181-3*) City Lights.

— Look & Move On. Bowles, Paul, tr. 128p. 1989. 30.00 (*0-7206-0756-6*, Pub. by P Owen Ltd) Dufour.

— Love with a Few Hairs. Bowles, Paul, tr. from ARA. 176p. 1986. reprint ed. pap. 8.95 (*0-87286-192-9*) City Lights.

— Marriage with Papers. Bowles, Paul, tr. LC 85-52107. 88p. (Orig.). 1986. pap. 6.00 (*0-939180-32-4*) Tombouctou.

— Marriage with Papers. deluxe ed. Bowles, Paul, tr. LC 85-52107. 88p. (Orig.). 1986. 35.00 (*0-939180-29-4*) Tombouctou.

— M'Hashish. Bowles, Paul, tr. LC 70-88228. (Orig.). 1969. pap. 8.95 (*0-87286-034-5*) City Lights.

Mracek, Jan. Technical Illustration & Graphics. (Illus.). 352p. (C). 1983. 34.00 (*0-685-05866-2*) P-H.

Mrachek, L. A., jt. auth. see Palmer, Claude I.

Mrachek, Leonard & Komschilies, Charles. Basic Technical College Mathematics. 2nd ed. 322p. (C). 1993. pap. text 38.20 (*0-13-891995-X*) P-H.

Mrad, Gabriela, ed. Agenda for Leadership, 1998. LC 98-13446. (Pioneer Paper Ser.). 180p. 1998. pap. 15.00 (*0-929930-19-3*) Pioneer Inst.

***Mrad, Nezih.** Effects of Wheel-Load Spatial Repeatibility on Road Damage: A Literature Review. (Illus.). 44p. (C). 2000. reprint ed. pap. text. write for info. (*0-7881-8568-3*) DIANE Pub.

Mraida, Carlos, jt. auth. see Deiros, Pablo A.

Mrak, Mojmir. The Succession of States in Respect to Treaties, State Property, Archives, & Debts. LC 98-50287. (Developments in International Law Ser.). 1999. 81.00 (*90-411-1145-X*) Kluwer Law Intl.

Mrak, Robert E., ed. Muscle Membranes in Diseases of Muscle. 168p. 1985. 99.00 (*0-8493-5622-9*, RC925, CRC Reprint) Franklin.

Mraovitch, Sima. Kako da Saberem Korake. Maljkovic-Petkovic, Djero et al, eds. (Biblioteka Jugoscvenska Diaspora Ser.). (CRO & SER., Illus.). 84p. (Orig.). 1982. 5.95 (*0-943898-04-8*); pap. 4.95 (*0-943898-05-6*) Gospic Realty.

Mraovtich. Neurophysiological Basis of Cerebral Blood Flow. 424p. 79.00 (*0-86196-272-9*, Pub. by J Libbey Med) Bks Intl VA.

Mraz, Barbara. Sacred Strands: How Eight Women Came to Their Ministries. 2nd ed. (Illus.). 152p. 1995. pap. 10.95 (*1-883477-05-0*) Lone Oak MN.

Mraz, Bohumir. Ingres: Dibujos. (Grandes Monografias). (SPA., Illus.). 200p. 1993. 150.00 (*84-343-0381-7*) Elliots Bks.

Mraz, Charles. Health & the Honeybee. LC 94-67746. (Illus.). 104p. 1995. pap. 12.95 (*0-9642485-0-6*) Queen City VT.

Mraz, John & Storey, Jaime V. Uprooted: Braceros in the Hermanos Mayo's Lense. LC 96-12337. 139p. 1996. pap. 18.95 (*1-55885-178-X*) Arte Publico.

***Mrazek, Robert J.** Stonewall's Gold. 1999. mass mkt. 4.99 (*0-312-97429-9*) St Martin.

— Stonewalls Gold: A Novel of the Civil War. (Illus.). 240p. 2000. pap. 12.95 (*0-312-25422-9*) St Martin.

Mrazek, James E. The Fall of Eben Emael: The Daring Airborne Assault That Sealed the Fate of France: May 1940. (Illus.). 208p. 1991. 19.93 (*0-89141-406-1*, Pub. by Presidio Pr) Natl Bk Netwk.

— The Fall of Eben Emael: The Daring Airborne Assault That Sealed the Fate of France: May 1940. (Illus.). 208p. 1999. pap. 14.95 (*0-89141-664-1*, Pub. by Presidio Pr) Natl Bk Netwk.

Mrazek, R., jt. ed. see Marcinkowski, T.

Mrazek, Rick, ed. Pathways to Partnerships: Coalitions for EE: Proceedings from NAAEE's 1993 Annual Conference in Big Sky, Montana. 516p. (Orig.). 1994. pap. 10.00 (*1-884008-19-4*) NAAEE.

Mrazek, Robert J. Stonewall's Gold. LC 98-36891. 240p. 1999. 22.95 (*0-312-20024-2*, Thomas Dunne) St Martin.

Mrazek, Rudolf. Sjahrir: Politics & Exile in Indonesia. (Studies on Southeast Asia: No. 14). (Orig.). 1994. pap. text 24.25 (*0-87727-713-3*) Cornell SE Asia.

Mrazik, et al. Plastic Design of Steel. LC 85-5623. 420p. 1987. text 116.00 (*0-470-20132-0*) P-H.

Mrazovich, Christine, ed. see Reninger, T.

Mrena, Clarita A. Foster Care: Agencies Face Challenges Securing Stable Homes for Children of Substance Abusers. (Illus.). 96p. 1999. pap. text 20.00 (*0-7881-7836-9*) DIANE Pub.

***Mrena, Clarita A.** Foster Care: Kinship Care Quality & Permanency Issues. (Illus.). 116p. (C). 1999. pap. text 25.00 (*0-7881-8426-1*) DIANE Pub.

Mrix, Evans M. Britain's Military Heritage. 1997. text 29.95 (*0-233-99150-6*, Pub. by Andre Deutsch) Trafalgar.

MRJ Tech Solutions Staff. Parallel Systems in the Data Warehouse. LC 97-34527. 416p. (C). 1997. 49.99 (*0-13-680604-X*) P-H.

Mrkvicka. Your Bank is Ripping You Off. 256p. 1999. pap. 13.95 (*0-312-24577-7*) St Martin.

Mrkvicka, Edward F., Jr. How to Become Number One: A Crash Course for Career Success. LC 91-90115. (Orig.). 1991. pap. 8.95 (*0-9628726-0-1*) Reliance Enter.

***Mrkvicka, Edward F.** J. K. Lasser's Pick Winning Stocks. 308p. 2000. pap. 16.95 (*0-471-39357-6*) Wiley.

Mrkvicka, Edward F. Your Bank Is Ripping You Off: How They're Doing It & How You Can Fight Back & Save a Fortune. LC 96-30824. 1997. pap. 12.95 (*0-312-15246-9*) St Martin.

MRM Staff. Pashto Newspaper Reader. LC 84-72437. iv, 246p. 1984. text 43.00 (*0-931745-04-7*) Dunwoody Pr.

M'Robert, P. Tour Through Part of the North Provinces of America. LC 67-29039. (Eyewitness Accounts of the American Revolution Ser.). 1979. reprint ed. 17.95 (*0-405-01136-9*) Ayer.

Mroch, Walter, et al. A Field Guide to Topaz & Associated Minerals of the Thomas Range, Utah. (Illus.). 114p. 1996. pap. 25.00 (*0-9674920-0-9*) H M Pubng.

Mroczkowska-Brand, Katarzyna, tr. see Kapuscinski, Ryszard.

M

Mroczkowski, Dennis P. U. S. Marines in the Persian Gulf, 1990-1991: With the 2D Marine Division in Desert Shield & Desert Storm. (Illus.). 107p. 1996. reprint ed. pap. text 30.00 (0-7881-3356-X) DIANE Pub.

— United States Marines in the Persian Gulf, 1990-1991: With the 2d Marine Division in Desert Shield & Desert Storm. 117p. 1993. per. 13.00 (0-16-041922-0) USGPO.

Mroczkowski, Robert S. Electronic Connector Handbook. (Illus.). 480p. 1997. 100.00 (0-07-041401-7) McGraw.

Mroczowski, P. J., ed. from LAT. Stephen Baron: De Regimine Principum: 1509. LC 90-6126. (Illus.). X, 167p. (C). 1990. text 54.95 (0-8204-0648-1) P Lang Pubng.

Mrode, R. A. Linear Models for the Prediction of Animal Breeding Values. (A CAB International Publication). 200p. 1996. text 75.00 (0-85198-996-9) OUP.

Mrofchak, Audrey. Sword of the Spirit. LC 97-65314. 250p. (Orig.). 1997. pap. text 9.95 (1-882972-95-3, 3601) Queenship Pub.

Mrogenda, Ute. Die Terrakottafiguren von Myrina: Eine Untersuchung Ihrer Moglichen Bedeutung und Funktion im Grabzusammenhang. (Europaische Hochschulschriften, Reihe 38: Bd. 63). (GER., Illus.). 200p. 1996. 42.95 (3-631-30962-7) P Lang Pubng.

Mrope, Angelous J., jt. auth. see Pinto, Rogerio F.

Mrowicki, Linda. Let's Work Safely! English Language Skills for Safety in the Workplace. (Illus.). 114p. (Orig.). 1984. pap. text 7.50 (0-916591-00-X); 4.50 (0-916591-01-8) Linmore Pub.

— Practice with Your Partner: Dictation Activities for Student-Student Interaction. 46p. 1987. pap. text 19.95 (0-9655910-9-3) Linmore Pub.

Mrowicki, Linda, ed. see Terdy, Dennis.

Mroz, Albert. The Illustrated Encyclopedia of American Trucks & Commercial Vehicles. LC 95-82431. (Illus.). 432p. 1996. pap. 34.95 (0-87341-368-7, AWT01) Krause Pubns.

Mroz, Glen, jt. auth. see Reed, David D.

Mroz, John Edwin. Beyond Security: Private Perceptions among Arabs & Israelis. LC 80-82857. (Illus.). 230p. 1981. text 46.00 (0-08-027517-6, Pergamon Pr); pap. text 20.00 (0-08-027516-8, Pergamon Pr) Elsevier.

— Beyond Security: Private Perceptions among Arabs & Israelis. 200p. 1980. 23.00 (0-685-11730-8); pap. 9.95 (0-937722-00-6) Intl Peace.

— Influence in Conflict: The Impact of Third Parties on the Arab-Israeli Dispute since 1973. 400p. 1987. text 44.01 (0-08-028797-2, Pergamon Pr); pap. text 16.51 (0-08-028796-4, Pergamon Pr) Elsevier.

Mroz, M. Divine Vengeance. LC 77-120130. (Studies in Shakespeare: No. 24). 1970. reprint ed. lib. bdg. 75.00 (0-8383-1091-5) M S G Haskell Hse.

Mroz, Ray. Called to Righteousness. LC 98-65639. 144p. 1998. pap. 12.95 (1-57197-118-1) Pentland Pr.

Mroz, Z., ed. see International Union of Theoretical & Applied Mecha.

Mroz, Zenon, et al, eds. Inelastic Behaviour of Structures under Variable Loads. LC 95-4010. (Solid Mechanics & Its Applications Ser.: Vol. 36). 496p. (C). 1995. text 239.50 (0-7923-3397-7) Kluwer Academic.

Mrozek, Donald J. Air Power & the Ground War in Vietnam: Ideas & Actions. (Illus.). 204p. 1988. pap. 9.00 (1-58566-015-9) Air Univ.

— The U. S. Air Force after Vietnam: Postwar Challenges & Potential for Responses. 133p. 1988. pap. 6.50 (1-58566-024-8) Air Univ.

Mrozek, Donald J., ed. Sport in the West. (Illus.). 71p. (Orig.). 1983. pap. 15.00 (0-89745-041-8) Sunflower U Pr.

Mrozek, Donald J., et al, eds. The Martin Marauder & the Franklin Allens: A Wartime Love Story. (Illus.). 544p. 1980. pap. 10.00 (0-89745-007-8) Sunflower U Pr.

Mrozek, Donald J., jt. ed. see Higham, Robin.

Mrozek, John. The Drug Screen Manual: The Tests, the Technology, the Risks, the Reality. LC 98-234088. 64p. 1998. pap. 15.00 (0-87364-982-6) Paladin Pr.

— The Y2K Computer Crash Scenario: What to Expect & How to Protect Your Assets, Your Credit, & Your Way of Life. LC 98-234800. 64p. 1998. pap. 17.00 (1-58160-006-2) Paladin Pr.

Mrozek, John P. & Schafer, Marilyn E. Chiropractic Research Abstracts Collection (CRAC) 1990, Vol. 4. 130p. 1991. 38.00 (0-683-01420-X) Lppncott W & W.

Mrozek-Orlowski, Mary, jt. ed. see Fishman, Maryanne.

Mrozek, Slawomir. Three Plays: Striptease, Repeat Performance, the Prophets. Gruenthal, Lola et al, trs. from POL. 168p. 1986. pap. 5.95 (0-936839-49-X) Applause Theatre Bk Pubs.

— Vatzlav. Manheim, Ralph, tr. from POL. 92p. 1986. pap. 5.95 (0-936839-50-3) Applause Theatre Bk Pubs.

Mroziewicz, B., et al. Physics of Semiconductor Lasers. 474p. 1991. 210.00 (0-444-98737-1, North Holland) Elsevier.

Mrozinska, T. Suesswasserflora von Mitteleuropa Band 14: Chlorophyta VI: Oedogoniophyceae: Oedogoniales. Pascher, A., ed. (GER., Illus.). 624p. 1985. lib. bdg. 103.00 (3-437-30413-5, Pub. by Gustav Fischer) Balogh.

Mrozinski, Ronald. Franciscan Prayer Life. 186p. 1983. 12.50 (0-8199-0795-2, Frncscn Herld) Franciscan Pr.

Mrozowski, Stephen A., et al. Living on the Boott: Historical Archaeology at the Boott Mills Boardinghouses of Lowell, Massachusetts. LC 95-52177. (Illus.). 112p. 1996. 40.00 (1-55849-034-5); pap. 13.95 (1-55849-035-3) U of Mass Pr.

Mrrchison, R., jt. auth. see Devine, T. M.

Mrs. Charles E. Cowman. Springs in the Valley. large type ed. 1990. kivar 12.95 (0-310-22517-5) Zondervan.

Mrs. Dragoo's 1995-96 Third Grade Class. Basketball Fever. large type ed. (WeWrite Kids! Ser.: No. 32). (Illus.). 45p. (J). (gr. 1-5). 1996. pap. 3.95 (1-57635-007-X) WeWrite.

Mrs. Gould's 1996-97 Third Grade Class, Rochester. The Pit. (WeWrite Kids! Ser.: No. 35). (Illus.). 50p. (J). (ps-4). 1997. pap. 3.95 (1-57635-011-8) WeWrite.

MRS International Meeting on Advanced Materials, F. Biosensors: May 31-June 1, 1988, Sunshine City, Ikebukuro, Tokyo, Japan. LC 90-174424. (Proceedings of the MRS International Meeting on Advanced Materials Ser.: No. 14). (Illus.). 268p. reprint ed. pap. 83.10 (0-7837-1931-0, 204214600001) Bks Demand.

— Superconductivity: May 31-June 3, 1988, Sunshine City, Ikebukuro, Tokyo, Japan. LC 90-174207. (Proceedings of the MRS International Meeting on Advanced Materials Ser.: No. 6). (Illus.). 1055p. reprint ed. pap. 200.00 (0-7837-1930-2, 204214500001) Bks Demand.

Mrs. Kern's 1995-96 Third Grade Class. Noot's Toupee Day. (WeWrite Kids! Ser.: No. 31). (Illus.). 50p. (J). (ps-4). 1996. pap. 3.95 (1-57635-004-5); lib. bdg. 18.95 (1-57635-003-7) WeWrite.

Mrs. Moose. Raymond Floyd Goes to Africa: or There Are No Bears in Africa. (Illus.). 32p. (J). (gr. 1-4). 1993. 14.95 (0-86543-375-5) Africa World.

Mrs. Richardson's & Mrs. Doyle's 5th Grade Class,. Prison - Not Me! large type unabridged ed. (WeWrite Kids! Ser.: No. 39). (Illus.). 45p. (J). (gr. 3-5). 1998. pap. 3.95 (1-57635-021-5) WeWrite.

Mrsny, Randall J., jt. ed. see Park, Kinam.

Mrugala, Ann. Woman Space. (Illus.). 54p. 1997. pap. 10.00 (0-9660097-1-1, LO8000-W08000) Adrian Dominican.

Mruk, Christopher J. Self-Esteem: Research, Theory & Practice. 2nd ed. LC 99-21028. (Illus.). 240p. 1999. text 39.95 (0-8261-8751-X) Springer Pub.

Mryglot, Gerard & Marks, Ted. How to Say Fabulous in 8 Different Languages: A Multilingual Phrasebook for Gay Men. 120p. 1995. pap. 9.95 (0-9646511-3-0) Translator Network.

Mrysiades, Kostas & Myrsiades, Linda, eds. Race-ing Representation: Voice, History, & Sexuality. LC 97-37072. (CULED Ser.). 288p. 1997. 58.00 (0-8476-8856-9); pap. 20.95 (0-8476-8857-7) Rowman.

Ms. Foundation for Women Staff, jt. auth. see Forsyth, Sondra.

Ms. Light's 1996-97 Fifth Grade LEAP Students. Frozen in a Dream. (WeWrite Kids! Ser.: No. 34). (Illus.). 50p. (J). (ps-4). 1997. pap. 3.95 (1-57635-010-X) WeWrite.

MSA Women's Committee. The Parents' Manual. 1990. pap. 4.00 (0-89259-093-9) Am Trust Pubns.

MSC Staff. MSC - Patran MSC - Nastran Preference Guide Vol. 1: Structural Analysis. rev. ed. (Illus.). 289p. 1997. pap. text 25.00 (1-58524-009-5) MacNeal-Schwendler.

— MSC - Patran MSC - Nastran Preference Guide Vol. 2: Thermal Analysis. rev. ed. (Illus.). 265p. 1997. pap. text 25.00 (1-58524-010-9) MacNeal-Schwendler.

MSFC Staff, jt. auth. see NASA Staff.

Mshengu, Thulani, et al. Asinamali! The Life of Msizi Dube/Impilo kaMsizi Dube. (Illus.). 88p. 1992. pap. 6.00 (0-86980-875-3, Pub. by Univ Natal Pr) Intl Spec Bk.

Mshigeni, K. E. Biology & Ecology of Benthic Marine Algae with Special Reference to Hypnea (Rhodophyta, Gigartinales: A Review of the Literature. (Bibliotheca Phycologica Ser.: No. 37). 1978. pap. 26.80 (3-7682-1166-5) Lubrecht & Cramer.

Mshimba, A., jt. ed. see Tutschke, W.

Mshimba, A. S. & Tutschke, W. Functional Analytic Methods in Complex Analysis & Applications to Partial Differential Equations. 392p. (C). 1990. text 113.00 (981-02-0186-9) World Scientific Pub.

***Mshomba, Richard E.** Africa in the Global Economy. LC 99-51382. 246p. 2000. 55.00 (1-55587-718-4); pap. 22.00 (1-55587-443-6) L Rienner.

Mshomba, Richard E. The Uncertainty of the International Coffee Agreement. (Pew Case Studies in International Affairs). 50p. (C). 1994. pap. 3.50 (1-56927-159-3) Geo U Inst Dplmcy.

MSI Staff. Ascension! An Analysis of the Art of Ascension As Taught by the Ishayas. 3rd ed. Ishaya, Dharani, ed. LC 95-61427. 193p. (Orig.). 1991. reprint ed. pap. 11.95 (0-931783-51-8) SFA Pubns.

— Enlightenment! The Yoga Sutras of Patanjali, a New Translation & Commentary. 2nd ed. Ishaya, Dharani, ed. LC 95-61425. 332p. (Orig.). 1995. reprint ed. pap. 15.95 (0-931783-17-8) SFA Pubns.

— Erster Donner: Abenteuervoller Entdeckungen. Ishaya, Ishvara, tr. 1998. pap. 12.95 (0-931783-27-5) SFA Pubns.

— First Thunder: An Adventure of Discovery. Ishaya, Dharani, ed. LC 94-74923. 279p. (Orig.). 1995. pap. 12.95 (0-931783-07-0) SFA Pubns.

— Primer Trueno (First Thunder) Una Aventura de Descubrimiento. Ishaya, Ambala, tr. pap. 12.95 (0-931783-23-2) SFA Pubns.

— Second Thunder: Seeking the Black Ishayas. 2nd ed. Ishaya, Dharani, ed. LC 95-61426. (Illus.). 387p. (Orig.). 1995. reprint ed. pap. 17.95 (0-931783-08-9) SFA Pubns.

— Third Thunder: The Fall of Etan - Orah, the Deathless Dancer. Ishaya, Dharani, ed. LC 97-65521. (Illus.). iii, 371p. (Orig.). 1997. pap. 17.95 (0-931783-09-7) SFA Pubns.

— Third Thunder: The Fall of Etan - Shamara, the Oblation Bearer. Ishaya, Dharani, ed. LC 97-65641. (Illus.). 400p. (Orig.). 1997. pap. 17.95 (0-931783-10-0) SFA Pubns.

— Third Thunder: The Fall of Etan - Swayam, the Father of Time. Ishaya, Dharani, ed. LC 97-65642. (Illus.). 400p. (Orig.). 1998. pap. 17.95 (0-931783-11-9) SFA Pubns.

Msika, Hangson, jt. auth. see Roscoe, Adrian.

Msimuko, Arthur, jt. ed. see Achola, Paul P. W.

Msiska, Mpalive. Wole Soyinka. Armstrong, Isobel & Loughrey, Bryan, eds. (Writers & Their Work Ser.). 1997. pap. 17.00 (0-7463-0811-6, Pub. by Northcote House) U Pr of Miss.

Msiska, Mpalive-Hangson & Hyland, Paul. Writing Africa Crosscurrents. LC 96-25811. (C). 1997. pap. text 30.00 (0-582-21418-1) Addison-Wesley.

— Writing Africa Crosscurrents. LC 96-25811. (C). 1997. text 62.81 (0-582-21419-X) Longman.

Msiska, O. V. & Costa-Pierce, B. A., eds. History, Status & Future of Common Carp (Cyprinus Carpio L.) (ICLARM Conference Proceedings Ser.: No. 40). 27p. 1993. write for info. (971-8709-37-1, Pub. by ICLARM) Intl Spec Bk.

Msiska, Stephen K. Golden Buttons: Christianity & Traditional Religion among the Tumbuka. 66p. 1998. 54.95 (1-57309-229-0, U Pr W Africa) Intl Scholars.

Msonthi, Jerome, jt. auth. see Morris, Brian.

MSSD English Department Staff. A Closer Look: The English Program at the Model Secondary School for the Deaf. Welsh-Charrier, Chic & Powers, Rachel, eds. (Illus.). 69p. 1996. pap. text, teacher ed. 9.95 (0-88095-207-5) Gallaudet U Pre Coll.

MSU (MREC), Michigan Recreation Educators Conso St. Recreation in Michigan. 176p. (C). 1995. per. 23.95 (0-7872-1397-7, 41139701) Kendall-Hunt.

Msukwa, Louis A., jt. auth. see Pelletier, David L.

Msumza, Luyanda K., ed. see Lembede, Anton M.

Msuya, John M. Nutrition Improvement Projects in Tanzania: Implementation, Determinants of Performance & Policy Implications. LC 99-25012. (Development Economics & Policy Ser.: Vol. 11). (Illus.). XX, 206p. 1999. pap. text 45.95 (0-8204-3639-9) P Lang Pubng.

MSW Publishing Co Staff, ed. see Grice, Donna C.

***Mt. Airy Regional Museum Staff.** Mount Airy. (Images of America Ser.). 128p. 1999. pap. 18.99 (0-7385-0105-0) Arcadia Publng.

Mt. Shasta, Peter, ed. & pref. see Ascended Masters Staff.

Mtewa, Mekki. Malawi: Democratic Theory & Public Policy. 137p. 1986. 18.95 (0-87047-004-3); pap. 13.95 (0-87047-005-1) Schenkman Bks Inc.

Mtewa, Mekki, ed. International Science & Technology: Philosophy, Theory & Policy. 220p. 1990. text 45.00 (0-312-03688-4) St Martin.

— Perspectives in International Development. 1987. 18.00 (0-8364-2063-2, Pub. by Allied Pubs) S Asia.

Mtshali, Oswald J. & Gordimer, Nadine. Sounds of a Cowhide Drum. LC 73-183198. 96p. 1972. 15.95 (0-89388-034-5); pap. 9.95 (0-89388-035-3) Okpaku Communications.

Mtshaulana, Patric M., et al, eds. Documents on International Law: Handbook for Law Students & Constitutional Lawyers. 325p. 1996. pap. 35.00 (0-7021-3532-1, Pub. by Juta & Co) Gaunt.

MTU Staff & Hugine, Andrew. PreCalculus: An Intuitive Approach-Michigan Technological University Customized Edition. 644p. (C). 1995. per. 46.14 (0-7872-1451-5) Kendall-Hunt.

MTV Editorial Staff. MTV's Road Rules: Road Trips. LC 96-220302. 1996. per. 18.00 (0-671-00374-7, MTV Bks) PB.

— MTV's Singled Out's Guide to Dating. LC 96-225044. 128p. 1996. per. 15.00 (0-671-00372-0, MTV Bks) PB.

MTV Staff. MTV's Travel Log. LC 98-195301. 1997. per. 12.00 (0-671-01533-8, PB Trade Paper) PB.

— The Real World Diaries. LC 96-217764. 1996. per. 18.00 (0-671-00373-9, MTV Bks) PB.

— Road Rules Book 2. 1997. per. 18.00 (0-671-01536-2, MTV Bks) PB.

Mtv Staff. Voters Guide to American Government. (C). 1996. pap. text 4.00 (0-205-26497-2) Allyn.

Mtwa, Percy, et al. Woza Albert! 80p. (C). 1988. pap. 9.95 (0-413-53000-0, A0323) Heinemann.

Mu Alpha Theta Staff. Mathematical Buds, Vol. II. 126p. 1981. 2.50 (0-940790-02-5) Mu Alpha Theta.

Mu, En-Chih, et al. Correlation of the Silurian Rocks of China. Berry, W. B., ed. LC 85-24729. (Geological Society of America Ser.: Vol. 202). (Illus.). 103p. 1986. reprint ed. pap. 32.00 (0-608-07731-3, 206781900010) Bks Demand.

Mu, Guoguang, et al, eds. International Conference on Holography & Optical Information Processing (ICHOIP'96), Vol. 2866. 552p. 1996. 99.00 (0-8194-2262-2) SPIE.

Mu, Rui & Guiguo, Wang, eds. Chinese Foreign Economic Law. 1990. 82.00 (0-935328-62-9) Intl Law Inst.

— Chinese Foreign Economic Law: Analysis & Commentary. 612p. 1989. ring bd. 125.00 (90-411-0985-4) Kluwer Law Intl.

Mu-Tsun, Lee. Small Cookbook - Soup! Soup! Soup! LC 96-102477. (CHI & ENG.). 80p. 1994. pap. 7.95 (0-941676-50-1) Wei-Chuan Pub.

— Small Cookbook - Tofu! Tofu! Tofu! LC 95-237714. (CHI & ENG.). 80p. 1994. pap. 7.95 (0-941676-49-8) Wei-Chuan Pub.

Mu, Yi, jt. ed. see Varadharajan, Vijay.

Muakasa, Sahar. Love Life Rhythm. LC 87-71849. (ARA & ENG.). 181p. 1987. 30.00 (0-944025-00-5) Advance Research.

Muakasa, Sahar, jt. auth. see Veenaskay.

Mu'Allakat. The Seven Poems Suspended in the Temple at Mecca. LC 73-12764. reprint ed. 27.50 (0-404-11238-2) AMS Pr.

Muamini, Therese. Beloved Son: Born with HIV. 192p. 1997. 24.95 (1-85375-205-3, Pub. by Prion) Trafalgar.

— Beloved Son: Born with HIV. 192p. 1997. pap. 9.95 (1-85375-202-9) Trafalgar.

Muammar Al Qathafi. The Green Book of Muammar Al Qathafi. 1982. lib. bdg. 250.00 (0-87700-451-X) Revisionist Pr.

Mu'asir, Nadwat I. & Al Haqq, Jad A. Abhath Nadwat Is'ham al Fikr al Islami fi al Iqtisad al Mu'asir: Proceedings of the Conference on the Contribution of Islamic Thought in Contemporary Economics. 2nd ed. (Silsilat Islamiyat al Ma'rifah: No. 11). 754p. 1993. 25.00 (1-56564-149-3); pap. 15.00 (1-56564-155-8) IIIT VA.

Muat, Rosemary, jt. contrib. by see Gellis, Marilyn.

Muata, Abhaya A. The Ausarian Resurrection: The Complete Myth of Shetaut Asar-Aset-Heru. unabridged ed. (Illus.). 183p. 1997. 29.99 (1-884564-12-7) Cruzian Mystic.

— The Blooming Lotus of Divine Love: The Process of Mystical Transformation & the Path of Divine Love. (Illus.). 225p. (Orig.). 1997. pap. 14.99 (1-884564-11-9) Cruzian Mystic.

— The Cycles of Time: The Mystical Origins & Destiny of the Soul. unabridged ed. (Illus.). (Orig.). 1997. pap. 14.99 (1-884564-13-5) Cruzian Mystic.

— Egyptian Proverbs: Tem T Tchaas. 160p. 1993. pap. 9.95 (1-884564-00-3) Cruzian Mystic.

— Egyptian Tantra Yoga: The Art of Sex Sublimation & Universal Consciousness. unabridged ed. (Illus.). 186p. (Orig.). 1997. pap. 15.99 (1-884564-03-8) Cruzian Mystic.

— The Egyptian Yoga Exercise Workout Book: The Movement of the Gods & Goddesses. unabridged ed. (Illus.). 104p. (Orig.). 1997. pap. 16.99 (1-884564-10-0) Cruzian Mystic.

— The Hidden Properties of Matter: Mystical Teachings of Memphite Theology. unabridged ed. (Illus.). 160p. (Orig.). 1997. pap. 14.99 (1-884564-07-0) Cruzian Mystic.

— Initiation into Egyptian Yoga: The Secrets of Sheti. unabridged ed. (Illus.). 145p. 1997. pap. 16.99 (1-884564-02-X) Cruzian Mystic.

— The Mystical Teachings of the Ausarian Resurrection. unabridged ed. (Illus.). 237p. (Orig.). 1997. pap. 15.99 (1-884564-22-4) Cruzian Mystic.

— Mysticism of Ushet Rekhat: Worship of the Goddess. unabridged ed. (Illus.). 64p. 1997. 9.99 (1-884564-18-6) Cruzian Mystic.

— The Serpent Power: The Yoga of Life Force Development for Spiritual Enlightenment. unabridged ed. (Illus.). 156p. (Orig.). 1997. pap. 15.99 (1-884564-19-4) Cruzian Mystic.

— The Way of the Sages: How to Understand & Practice Ancient Mystical Philosophy. unabridged ed. (Illus.). 160p. (Orig.). 1997. pap. 16.99 (1-884564-23-2) Cruzian Mystic.

— The Wisdom of Isis: God in the Universe, God in the Heart. unabridged ed. (Illus.). 136p. (Orig.). 1997. pap. 15.99 (1-884564-24-0) Cruzian Mystic.

— The Wisdom of Maati: The Path of Spiritual Enlightenment Through Virtuous Living. unabridged ed. (Illus.). 160p. (Orig.). 1997. pap. 15.99 (1-884564-20-8) Cruzian Mystic.

Muazzam, M. Ghulam. Ramadan Fasting & Medical Science. (C). 1991. 35.00 (0-7855-6718-6, Pub. by A H S Ltd); 40.00 (0-7223-2545-2, Pub. by A H S Ltd) St Mut.

Mubarak, Jamil A. From Bad Policy to Chaos in Somalia: How an Economy Fell Apart. LC 95-51426. 200p. 1996. 55.00 (0-275-95486-2, Praeger Pubs) Greenwood.

Mubarak, Mazin. Al-Rummani al-Nahawi fi Daw' Sharhihi li-Kitab Sibawayh. (ARA.). 472p. 1995. pap. 15.95 (1-57547-215-5) Dar Al-Fikr.

Mubarak, Muhammad A. Nizam al Islam al 'Aqa'idi fi al 'Asr al Hadith: The Credal System of Islam in the Modern Age. (Silsilat Rasa'il Islamiyat al Ma'rifah Ser.: No. 2). (ARA.). 44p. (Orig.). 1989. pap. 2.00 (1-56564-161-2) IIIT VA.

Mubarek, Helena. Trouble in Riddle City. (J). (gr. 4-9). 1992. pap. text 9.97 (0-937659-49-5) GCT.

Mucalov, Janice. Fight the Ticket in British Columbia. 7th ed. (Provincial Legal Ser.). 168p. (Orig.). 1995. pap. 9.95 (1-55180-032-2) Self-Counsel Pr.

Mucchielli, Jean-Louis, jt. ed. see Buckley, Peter J.

Mucci, Dallas. This Pair of Hands. 152p. (Orig.). 1988. pap. 8.99 (0-8341-1239-6) Beacon Hill.

Mucci, J. F., jt. auth. see March, N. H.

Mucciaroni, ed. The Political Economy of the United States. (C). 1998. text. write for info. (0-321-01157-0) Addson-Wesley Educ.

Mucciaroni, Gary. The Political Failure of Employment Policy, 1945-1982. LC 90-31987. (Political Science Ser.). 328p. 1991. pap. 19.95 (0-8229-5474-5) U of Pittsburgh Pr.

— Reversals of Fortune: Public Policy & Private Interests. 225p. (C). 1995. 38.95 (0-8157-5876-6); pap. 16.95 (0-8157-5875-8) Brookings.

Mucciaroni, Gary, ed. Whither Public Policy? Liberalism, Conservatism, & Social Change. (Orig.). 1990. pap. 15.00 (0-944285-21-X) Pol Studies.

Muccigrosso, Robert. Celebrating the New World: Chicago's Columbian Exposition of 1893. (American Ways Ser.). (Illus.). 224p. 1993. 24.95 (1-56663-013-4, Pub. by I R Dee); pap. text 11.95 (1-56663-014-2, Pub. by I R Dee) Natl Bk Netwk.

Muccigrosso, Robert, ed. Research Guide to American Historical Biography, Vol. 1-3. LC 88-19316. 1778p. 1988. lib. bdg. 195.00 (0-933833-09-1) Beacham Pub Corp.

Muccigrosso, Robert & Robbins, Ceila D. Manufacturing in America: A Legacy of Excellence. LC 95-38734. (Illus.). 160p. 1995. write for info. (0-944641-15-6) Greenwich Pub Group.

Muccigrosso, Robert, et al. Term Paper Resource Guide to Twentieth-Century United States History. LC 98-44592. 328p. 1999. 49.95 (0-313-30096-8, Greenwood Pr) Greenwood.

Muccigrosso, Robert, jt. ed. see Contosta, David R.

Muccini, Ugo. Palazzo Vecchio: Guide to the Building, the Apartments & the Collections. (Illus.). 128p. 1992. 19.95 (0-8161-0611-8, G K Hall & Co) Mac Lib Ref.

An Asterisk (*) at the beginning of an entry indicates that the title is appearing for the first time.

***Muccio, Edward A.** Decoration & Assembly of Plastic. LC 99-37114. 1999. write for info. (*0-87170-634-2*) ASM.

Muccio, Edward A. Plastic Part Technology. (Illus.). 304p. 1991. 94.00 (*0-87170-432-3*, 6901) ASM.

— Plastics Processing Technology. 323p. 1994. 87.00 (*0-87170-494-3*, 6614) ASM.

Muccio, Tom, jt. auth. see Marshall, Tom.

Mucciolo, Gary. Everything You Need to Know about Birth Control. rev. ed. (Illus.). 64p. (gr. 7-12). 1998. lib. bdg. 17.95 (*0-8239-2835-7*) Rosen Group.

Mucciolo, John M. Shakespeare's Universe: Renaissance Ideas & Conventions: Essays for W. R. Elton. LC 95-8834. 292p. 1996. 86.95 (*1-85928-193-1*, Pub. by Scolar Pr) Ashgate Pub Co.

Mucciolo, John M., jt. ed. see Elton, W. R.

Mucciolo, Louis. Eighty Something: Interviews with Senior Citizens Who Stay Involved. large type ed. (Illus.). 256p. 1992. 18.95 (*1-55972-149-9*, Birch Ln Pr) Carol Pub Group.

Mucciolo, Rich, jt. auth. see Mucciolo, Tom.

Mucciolo, Tom & Mucciolo, Rich. Purpose Movement Color: A Strategy for Effective Presentations. (Illus.). 80p. (Orig.). 1994. pap. 24.95 (*0-9647428-0-2*) MediaNet.

Much, Fred. The Pass after Class. rev. unabridged ed. LC 86-90709. 104p. (Orig.). 1987. pap. 5.95 (*0-9618053-0-7*) Fred Much.

Mucha, Alphonse M. Art Nouveau Figurative Designs. 48p. 1977. pap. 4.95 (*0-486-23444-4*) Dover.

— The Art Nouveau Style Book of Alphonse Mucha. (Illus.). 80p. 1980. pap. 11.95 (*0-486-24044-4*) Dover.

— Drawings of Mucha: Seventy Works. (Illus.). 72p. 1978. pap. 8.95 (*0-486-23672-2*) Dover.

— Mucha Art Nouveau Masterpieces, 2 vols. (Illus.). 1986. pap. text 20.90 (*0-486-25293-0*) Dover.

— Mucha's Figures Decoratives. Orig. Title: Figure Décoratives. (Illus.). 48p. 1981. reprint ed. pap. 8.95 (*0-486-24234-X*) Dover.

— Mucha's Floral Borders: Thirty Full-Color Art Nouveau Designs. (Illus.). 32p. (Orig.). 1985. pap. 6.95 (*0-486-24916-6*) Dover.

Mucha, Alphonse M., et al. Art Nouveau Designs in Color. (Illus.). 90p. (Orig.). 1974. pap. 10.95 (*0-486-22885-1*) Dover.

Mucha, Janusz. Everyday Life & Festivity in a Local Ethnic Community: Polish-Americans in South Bend, Indiana. 200p. 1996. 28.00 (*0-88033-338-3*, 441, Pub. by East Eur Monographs) Col U Pr.

Mucha, Janusz L., jt. ed. see Keen, Mike Forrest.

***Mucha, Jenusz.** Dominant Culture As a Foreign Culture: Dominant Groups in the Eyes of Minorities. 256p. 1998. text 35.00 (*0-88033-410-X*, 512, Pub. by East Eur Monographs) Col U Pr.

Mucha, Juanita, jt. auth. see Hanzak, Gary.

Mucha, Zak. The Beggars' Shore. 328p. 1999. pap. 12.95 (*0-9669476-0-6*, Pub. by Red Seventy-One) IPG Chicago.

***Muchal.** A Programmers Guide to Java Certification: A COmprehensive Primer. LC 99-40779. 800p. (C). 1999. pap. text 44.95 (*0-201-59614-8*) Addison-Wesley.

Muchall, William, jt. auth. see St. German, Christopher.

Muchembled, Robert. Popular Culture & Elite Culture in France, 1400-1750. LC 84-25078. 336p. reprint ed. pap. 104.20 (*0-7837-8813-4*, 204945900011) Bks Demand.

— La Sorciere au Village. (FRE.). 1991. pap. 15.95 (*0-7859-3979-2*) Fr & Eur.

Muchene, Barbara S. & Muchene, Munene. Suzanne's African Adventure: A Visit to Cucu's Land. Wagner, Shirley L., ed. LC 92-75821. (Illus.). 90p. (Orig.). (J). (gr. 3-6). 1993. pap. 9.95 (*1-878398-18-0*) Blue Note Pubns.

Muchene, Munene, jt. auth. see Muchene, Barbara S.

***Muchiki, Yoshiyuki.** Egyptian Proper Names & Loanwords in North-West Semitic. LC 99-40507. (Dissertation Ser.: No. 173). 357p. 1999. 48.00 (*0-88414-004-0*, 06 21 73, Pub. by Soc Biblical Lit) Scholars Pr GA.

Muchinsky. Psychology Applied to Work. 4th ed. (Psychology Ser.). 1993. pap., teacher ed. write for info. (*0-534-16622-9*) Brooks-Cole.

— Psychology Applied to Work. 6th ed. LC 99-26100. (Psychology Ser.). 1999. pap. text 87.95 (*0-534-36252-4*) Brooks-Cole.

— Psychology Applied to Work. 6th ed. (Psychology Ser.). 1999. mass mkt., wbk. ed. 14.00 (*0-534-36254-0*) Brooks-Cole.

Muchinsky, Paul M. People at Work: The New Millenium. (Psychology). 2001. mass mkt. 54.95 (*0-534-34848-3*) Brooks-Cole.

— Psychology Applied to Work. 2nd ed. 602p. (C). 1989. mass mkt. 38.50 (*0-534-10729-X*) Brooks-Cole.

— Psychology Applied to Work: An Introduction to Industrial & Organizational Psychology. 3rd ed. 650p. (C). 1990. mass mkt. 50.00 (*0-534-13032-1*) Brooks-Cole.

— Psychology Applied to Work: An Introduction to Industrial & Organizational Psychology. 4th ed. 738p. (C). 1993. text 47.50 (*0-534-16620-2*) Brooks-Cole.

— Psychology Applied to Work: An Introduction to Industrial & Organizational Psychology. 5th ed. 1996. mass mkt., teacher ed. write for info. (*0-534-34238-8*) Brooks-Cole.

— Psychology Applied to Work: An Introduction to Industrial & Organizational Psychology. 5th ed. LC 96-20143. (Psychology Ser.). 538p. (C). 1996. pap. 53.25 (*0-534-33876-3*) Brooks-Cole.

— Psychology Applied to Work: Student Exercise Book. 5th ed. (Psychology Ser.). 1996. mass mkt., wbk. ed. 18.00 (*0-534-34237-X*) Brooks-Cole.

Muchlberger, ed. Structure & Stratigraphy of Trans-Pecos Texas. (IGC Field Trip Guidebooks Ser.). 216p. 1989. 13.00 (*0-87590-574-9*, T317) Am Geophysical.

***Muchlinski, Peter.** Multinational Enterprises & the Law. 768p. 1999. pap. 74.95 (*0-631-21676-6*) Blackwell Pubs.

Muchlinski, Peter. Multinational Enterprises & the Law. 768p. (C). 1999. 110.95 (*0-631-17311-0*) Blackwell Pubs.

Muchman, Beatrice. Never to Be Forgotten: A Young Girl's Holocaust Memoir. LC 97-8828. 1997. 23.00 (*0-88125-598-X*) Ktav.

Muchmore, Clyde & Ellis, Harvey. Oklahoma Civil Procedure Forms. LC 98-67078. 1998. ring bd. 250.00 (*0-327-00197-6*, 82218-20) LEXIS Pub.

Muchmore, Clyde A. & Ellis, Harvey. Oklahoma Civil Procedure Forms, 2 vols. 1993. suppl. ed. 89.00 (*0-685-74633-X*, MICHIE) LEXIS Pub.

— Oklahoma Civil Procedure Forms, 2 vols., Set. 1000p. 1994. spiral bd. 250.00 (*0-87189-074-7*, 82216-10, MICHIE) LEXIS Pub.

Muchmore, Jo A. Johnny Rides Again. LC 94-19466. 128p. (J). (gr. 4-6). 1995. 14.95 (*0-8234-1156-7*) Holiday.

Muchmore, Jo Ann. Johnny Rides Again. 1997. 11.05 (*0-606-12746-1*, Pub. by Turtleback) Demco.

Muchmore, Lynn, jt. ed. see Beyle, Thad L.

Muchnic, Suzanne. Odd Man In: Norton Simon & the Pursuit of Culture. LC 98-2981. 339p. 1998. 29.95 (*0-520-20643-6*, Pub. by U CA Pr) Cal Prin Full Svc.

— Paul Darrow: A Retrospective. (Illus.). 62p. 1992. 15.00 (*0-685-62731-4*) Williamson Gallery.

Muchnic, Suzanne & Courtney, Julie. Mark Lere. (Illus.). 36p. (Orig.). 1986. pap. 4.00 (*0-939351-00-5*) Temple U Tyler Gal.

Muchnick, Barbara. The Laughing Horse. 58p. write for info. (*0-318-58342-9*) Just Fun Horse.

Muchnick, Bruce G. Clinical Medicine in Optometric Practice. (Illus.). 480p. (C). (gr. 13). 1994. text 64.00 (*0-8016-6306-7*, 06306) Mosby Inc.

Muchnick, Bruce G., jt. auth. see Gurwood, Andrew S.

Muchnick, Cynthia C. 101 Ways to Pop the Question: The Most Ingenious Ways to Say "Will You Marry Me?" - From Newlyweds Nationwide, Vol. 2. LC 97-116814. 176p. 1997. pap. 8.95 (*0-02-861513-1*, Arco) Macmillan Gen Ref.

— Will You Marry Me? The World's Most Romantic Proposals. 128p. 1995. 6.95 (*0-02-861048-2*) Macmillan.

Muchnick, Marc. Naked Management: Bare Essentials for Motivating the X-Generation at Work. 152p. 1996. per. 24.95 (*1-57444-061-6*) St Lucie Pr.

***Muchnick, Marlena Tanya.** Life Changing Testimonies of the Lord Jesus Christ. 230p. 1999. pap. 13.95 (*1-55517-394-2*) CFI Dist.

Muchnick, Marlena Tanya. Notes of a Jewish Convert to the LDS Church: Conversion of a Soul. 83p. 1998. mass mkt. 12.95 (*0-89716-803-8*, Peanut Btr Pubng) Elton-Wolf Pub.

Muchnick, S. S., jt. auth. see Jones, N. D.

Muchnick, S. S., ed. see Reisig, W.

Muchnick, Steven. Advanced Compiler Design & Implementation. LC 97-13063. 1000p. 1997. text 89.95 (*1-55860-320-4*) Morgan Kaufmann.

Muchnick, Steven S. & Jones, Neil D. Program Flow Analysis: Theory & Application. (Software Ser.). (Illus.). 448p. (C). 1981. 50.00 (*0-13-729681-9*) P-H.

Muchnick, V. B. & Shafarenko, A. V. Data Parallel Computing: The Language Dimension. (Illus.). 256p. 1996. mass mkt. 52.95 (*1-85032-179-5*) ITCP.

Muchnik, Michael. David Comes Home. (Illus.). 48p. (J). 1984. reprint ed. 7.00 (*0-8266-0350-5*, Merkos LInyonei Chinuch) Kehot Pubn Soc.

— The Double Decker Purple Shul Bus. (Illus.). 48p. (J). 1984. reprint ed. 7.00 (*0-8266-0352-1*, Merkos LInyonei Chinuch) Kehot Pubn Soc.

— Hershel's Houseboat. (Illus.). 48p. (J). 1984. reprint ed. 7.00 (*0-8266-0354-8*, Merkos LInyonei Chinuch) Kehot Pubn Soc.

— Leah & Leibel's Lighthouse. (Illus.). 48p. (J). 1984. reprint ed. 7.00 (*0-8266-0355-6*, Merkos LInyonei Chinuch) Kehot Pubn Soc.

— The Scribe Who Lived in a Tree. (Illus.). 48p. (J). 1984. reprint ed. 7.00 (*0-8266-0351-3*, Merkos LInyonei Chinuch) Kehot Pubn Soc.

— Tuvia's Train That Had No End. (Illus.). 48p. (J). 1984. reprint ed. 7.00 (*0-8266-0353-X*, Merkos LInyonei Chinuch) Kehot Pubn Soc.

Muchnik, Michoel. The Cuckoo Clock Castle of Shir. LC 79-55560. (Illus.). (J). (ps-3). 1980. 8.95 (*0-8197-0476-8*) Bloch.

Muchnik, S. S. & Schnupp, Peter. An Integrated Approach to Software Engineering. (Compass International Ser.). (Illus.). xiv, 375p. 1994. 54.95 (*0-387-97561-6*) Spr-Verlag.

Muchnik, S. S., ed. see Lins, Charles.

Muchnik Staff. Diccionario de Americanismos. (SPA.). 740p. 1985. pap. 65.00 (*0-7859-3459-6*, S12121) Fr & Eur.

Muchoney, Douglas M., et al. A Rapid Ecological Assessment of the Blue & John Crow Mountains National Park, Jamaica. Baker, Douglas S., ed. (Illus.). 90p. 1994. pap. 10.00 (*0-9624590-9-7*) Nature VA.

Muchow, Kenneth, et al. Digital Circuits. (Illus.). 480p. (C). 1987. student ed. 16.95 (*0-685-17183-3*) P-H.

Muchunsky, Paul M. Psychology Applied to Work: Student Workbook. 4th ed. (Psychology Ser.). 1993. pap., wbk. ed. 19.95 (*0-534-16623-7*) Brooks-Cole.

Mucina, L. & Dale, M. B., eds. Numerical Syntaxology: Proceedings of Part of the Symposium "Numerical Syndynamics" Held in Unovce Near Galanta, Slovakia, May 18-23, 1983. (Advances in Vegetation Science Ser.). (C). 1989. reprint ed. text 266.50 (*0-7923-0388-1*) Kluwer Academic.

Muck, Terry C., jt. ed. see Gross, Rita M.

Muck-Weymann, M., jt. auth. see Haerten, R.

Mucke, Dorothea E. Von, see Kelly, Veronica & Von Mucke, Dorothea E., eds.

Mucke, Dorothea E. Von, see Von Mucke, Dorothea E.

Mucke, Edith. Beginning in Triumph: A Memoir. LC 94-15569. 160p. 1994. pap. 9.95 (*0-87839-086-3*) North Star.

Muckelbust, Helmer, et al. Dyslexia & Reading Disabilities. 224p. 1972. text 29.50 (*0-8422-7005-1*) Irvington.

Muckenhoupt, Benjamin. Transplantation Theorems & Multiplier Theorems for Jacobi Series. LC 86-22270. (Memoirs of the American Mathematical Society Ser.: No. 64/356). 86p. 1986. pap. 18.00 (*0-8218-2418-X*, MEMO/64/356) Am Math.

Muckenhoupt, Benjamin, jt. auth. see Chanillo, Sagun.

***Muckenhoupt, Margaret.** Sigmund Freud: Explorer of the Unconscious. (Oxford Portraits in Science Ser.). (Illus.). 160p. 1999. pap. 11.95 (*0-19-513212-2*) OUP.

Muckenhoupt, Margaret. Sigmund Freud: Exploring the Unconscious. LC 95-42340. (Portraits in Science Ser.). (Illus.). 160p. (YA). 1997. 22.00 (*0-19-509933-8*) OUP.

Muckenstrum-Chavin, Bernadette, jt. auth. see Chavin, Remy.

Muckerman, Norman J., ed. see Saint Alphonsus Liquori.

Mucket, J. P., et al. Large Scale Structure in the Universe: Proceedings of the International Workshop. 380p. 1995. text 92.00 (*981-02-2342-0*) World Scientific Pub.

***Muckian.** One-day Mba in Finance & Accounting. 2000. 49.95 (*0-13-028459-9*) P-H.

— One-day Mba in Marketing. 2000. 49.95 (*0-13-028156-5*) P-H.

Muckian, Michael. Complete Idiot's Guide to Finance & Accounting. LC 97-71175. 320p. 1997. 16.95 (*0-02-861752-5*) Macmillan Gen Ref.

Muckian, Michael & Woods, John. The Business Letter Handbook: How to Write Effective Letters & Memos for Every Business Situation. 256p. 1996. pap. 10.95 (*1-55850-614-4*) Adams Media.

Muckian, Michael P. What Every Credit Union Executive Should Know about Marketing: The All in One Source for What . . . 1994. per. 149.00 (*1-55738-720-6*, Irwn Prfssnl) McGraw-Hill Prof.

***Muckian, Mike.** Prentice Hall's One-Day MBA in Finance & Accounting. 2000. pap. 20.00 (*0-7352-0148-X*) PH Pr.

Muckle, J., ed. Turgenev: Mumu. (Bristol Russian Texts Ser.). (RUS.). 112p. 1992. pap. 18.95 (*1-85399-270-4*, Pub. by Brist Class Pr) Focus Pub-R Pullins.

Muckle, James. Education in Russia Past & Present: An Introductory Study Guide & Select Bibliography. 1993. pap. 13.00 (*0-9517853-2-X*, Pub. by Bramcote Pr) Intl Spec Bk.

— A Gentlemen's Guide to Childcare. Conradson, Shari, ed. (Illus.). 18p. 1997. pap. 3.00 (*0-9620445-7-1*) KSJL Publishing.

— A Guide to the Soviet Curriculum: What the Russian Child Is Taught at School. 224p. 1988. lib. bdg. 57.50 (*0-7099-4667-8*) Routledge.

— How to Find Jobs Teaching Overseas. 2nd ed. Conradson, Shari, ed. LC 91-76506. (Illus.). 89p. 1992. pap. 7.95 (*0-9620445-5-5*) KSJL Publishing.

— Portrait of a Soviet School under Glasnost. LC 90-31927. 225p. 1990. text 39.95 (*0-312-04748-7*) St Martin.

Muckle, James, tr. see Leskov, Nikolai.

Muckle, James E. An American Abroad. Conradson, Diane & Conradson, Shari, eds. LC 92-71705. (Illus.). 99p. (Orig.). 1992. pap. 7.95 (*0-9620445-6-3*) KSJL Publishing.

— The Class Act Reading Game. 2nd rev. ed. 16p. 1992. pap. 3.00 (*0-9620445-3-9*) KSJL Publishing.

Muckle, Jim. A Self Publishing Success Story. Conradson, Shari, ed. (Illus.). 50p. (Orig.). 1990. pap. 5.00 (*0-9620445-4-7*) KSJL Publishing.

Muckle, Robert J. The First Nations of British Columbia: An Anthropological Survey. LC 98-167112. (Illus.). 146p. 1998. pap. text 19.95 (*0-7748-0663-X*) U of Wash Pr.

Muckle, W. C. Muckle's Naval Architecture. 2nd ed. (Marine Engineering Ser.). (Illus.). 400p. 1987. 110.00 (*0-408-00334-0*) Buttrwrth-Heinemann.

Muckler, Paul T. Website Tips for Smartiepants: 250+ How To's, Do's & Don'ts. LC 98-91294. 70p. 1998. pap. 7.95 (*0-9663611-0-5*) Martek Ltd.

Muckley, Robert L. Leyendas de Puerto Rico. (SPA.). 128p. 1993. pap. 15.50 (*0-8442-7275-2*) NTC Contemp Pub Co.

Muckley, Robert L. & Martinez-Santiago, Adela. Stories from Puerto Rico (Historias de Puerto Rico) LC 99-10181. (ENG & SPA.). 192p. 1998. pap. 11.95 (*0-8442-0402-1*, 04021, Teach Yrslf) NTC Contemp Pub Co.

Mucklow, J. C., jt. auth. see Charlton, Roger.

Mulchandani, N. H. Five Thousand Legal Maxims & Phrases with Meaning & Citations. (C). 1990. 30.00 (*0-89771-129-7*) St Mut.

Mucnik, jt. auth. see Humbaraci.

Muczynski, R. Duos for Flute & Clarinet. 16p. 1991. pap. 10.95 (*0-7935-0970-X*) H Leonard.

— Sonata for Flute & Piano Opus 14. 32p. 1986. pap. 15.95 (*0-7935-4437-8*, 50336120) H Leonard.

— Three Designs: For Three Timpani - Opus 11, No. 2. 1987. pap. 3.95 (*0-7935-5575-2*, 50353570) H Leonard.

Mud Flower Collective Staff. God's Fierce Whimsy: Christian Feminism & Theological Education. Heyward, Carter, ed. LC 84-26561. 240p. (Orig.). 1985. pap. 13.95 (*0-8298-0546-X*) Pilgrim OH.

Mudahar, Mohinder S. Kyrgyz Republic: Strategy for Rural Growth & Poverty Alleviation. LC 98-42156. (Discussion Paper Ser.: No. 394R). (ENG.). 143p. 1998. 25.00 (*0-8213-4326-2*, 14326) World Bank.

— Kyrgyz Republic: Strategy for Rural Growth & Poverty Alleviation (Russian) (Discussion Paper Ser.: No. 394R). 167p. 1998. 22.00 (*0-8213-4396-3*, 14396) World Bank.

Mudahar, Mohinder S. & Hignett, T. P. Energy & Fertilizer: Policy Implications & Options for Developing Countries (Executive Brief) (Technical Bulletin Ser.: No. T-19). (Illus.). 25p. (Orig.). 1981. pap. 4.00 (*0-88090-018-0*) Intl Fertilizer.

— Energy & Fertilizer: Policy Implications & Options for Developing Countries (Executive Brief) LC 82-6084. (Technical Bulletin Ser.: No. T-20). (Illus.). 241p. (Orig.). 1982. pap. 15.00 (*0-88090-019-9*) Intl Fertilizer.

Mudahar, Mohinder S. & Kanwar, J. S. Fertilizer Sulfur & Food Production. 1986. text 175.00 (*90-247-3243-3*) Kluwer Academic.

Mudahar, Mohinder S. & Kapusta, Edwin C. Fertilizer Marketing Systems & Policies in the Developing World. Roth, E. N., ed. LC 87-3152. (Technical Bulletin Ser.: No. T-33). 43p. (Orig.). 1987. pap. text 4.00 (*0-88090-059-8*) Intl Fertilizer.

Mudahar, Mohinder S., et al. Transforming Agricultural Research Systems in Transition Economies: The Case of Russia. LC 98-27892. (Discussion Paper Ser.: No. 396). 115p. 1998. pap. 22.00 (*0-8213-4313-0*, 14313) World Bank.

Mudahar, Mohinder S., jt. auth. see Johl, S. S.

Mudahar, Mohinder S., jt. auth. see Kanwar, J. S.

***Mudambi, Ram, et al, eds.** Rules & Reason: Perspectives on Constitutional Political Economy. (Illus.). 336p. 2000. write for info. (*0-521-65057-7*); pap. write for info. (*0-521-65959-0*) Cambridge U Pr.

Mudambi, Ram & Ricketts, Martin J. The Organisation of the Firm: International Business Perspectives. LC 97-8357. (Illus.). 232p. (C). 1997. 85.00 (*0-415-14298-9*) Routledge.

Mudambi, Ram, jt. auth. see Baum, Thomas.

Mudd. Pot for Pennies. 1998. pap. 19.95 (*0-9647858-3-8*) Trans-High Corp.

Mudd, Charles & Sillars, Malcolm O. Public Speaking: Content & Communication. 6th ed. (Illus.). 424p. (C). 1991. pap. text 24.95 (*0-88133-587-8*) Waveland Pr.

Mudd, Chris. Cholesterol & Your Health - the Great American Rip-Off!, Pt. 1. (Illus.). 170p. 1990. pap. write for info. (*0-9624515-1-7*) Am Lite Co.

Mudd, G. C. & France, J. M. Evaluation of Endurance Limit for Contact Stress in Gears with Particular Reference to Surface Hardened Gears. (Technical Papers). 19p. 1983. pap. text 30.00 (*1-55589-072-5*) AGMA.

Mudd, G. C. & Myers, E. J. Load Distribution Factors in Proposed AGMA & ISO Rating Procedures. (Technical Papers: Vol. P219.14). (Illus.). 21p. 1981. pap. text 30.00 (*1-55589-257-4*) AGMA.

Mudd, Harvey. A European Education. LC 85-22840. 87p. (Orig.). 1986. 14.00 (*0-87685-659-8*); pap. 8.50 (*0-87685-658-X*) Black Sparrow.

— A European Education, signed ed. deluxe ed. LC 85-22840. 87p. (Orig.). 1986. 25.00 (*0-87685-660-1*) Black Sparrow.

— The Plain of Smokes. LC 82-14792. (Illus.). 98p. (Orig.). (C). 1982. 14.00 (*0-87685-567-2*); pap. 6.50 (*0-87685-566-4*) Black Sparrow.

***Mudd, Jeffrey S.** Tumbleweed: Rites & Wrongs of Passage in a Left of Center Texas Town. viii, 243p. 2000. pap. 12.95 (*0-9679184-0-5*) Southpaw Bks.

***Mudd, Joseph A.** With Porter in North Missouri: A Chapter in the History of the War Between the States. (Illus.). 504p. 1999. reprint ed. pap. 19.95 (*1-929919-00-X*) Pr Camp Pope.

***Mudd, Leo.** Blue Light Special. 1999. pap. 11.95 (*1-886036-24-1*) Passages Pbg.

***Mudd, Mollie & Aspen Grants & Nonprofit Development Group Staff.** The Grantseeker's Handbook to Essential Internet Sites, 2000-2001. 243p. 2000. pap. 99.00 (*0-8342-1800-3*, 18003) Aspen Pub.

Mudd, Nancy. How to Do Your Own Divorce in Tennessee Vol. 1: (Uncontested, No Assest, No Children) 17p. (Orig.). 1996. pap. 12.00 (*0-9653953-0-8*) Consmer Advocates.

Mudd, Norman. In Defense of Aleister Crowley: An Open Letter to Lord Beaverbrook. 1993. pap. 4.95 (*1-55818-208-X*, Sure Fire) Holmes Pub.

Mudd, Roger. American Heritage Great Minds of History. LC 98-44710. 241p. 1999. 24.95 (*0-471-32715-8*) Wiley.

Mudd-Ruth, Maria. Fire Fighting: Behind the Scenes. LC 97-11233. (Illus.). 64p. (J). (gr. 3-5). 1998. 17.00 (*0-395-70129-5*) HM.

***Mudd-Ruth, Maria.** The Mississippi River. LC 99-49873. (Ecosystems of North America Ser.). (Illus.). (J). 2001. lib. bdg. 27.07 (*0-7614-0934-3*, Benchmark NY) Marshall Cavendish.

— The Pacific Coast. LC 00-20008. (Ecosystems of North America Ser.). (Illus.). (YA). 2001. 27.07 (*0-7614-0935-1*, Benchmark NY) Marshall Cavendish.

— The Tundra. LC 98-48646. (Ecosystems of North America Ser.). (gr. 4-7). 2000. lib. bdg. 27.07 (*0-7614-0902-5*, Benchmark NY) Marshall Cavendish.

Mudd, Samuel. Briggs' Information-Processing Model of the Binary Classification Task. 152p. (C). 1983. text 29.95 (*0-89859-291-7*) L Erlbaum Assocs.

***Mudd, Stephanie.** Tales for Topics: Linking Favourite Stories. (Illus.). 72p. 1999. pap. text 15.95 (*0-947882-25-1*) Belair Pubns Ltd.

Mudd, Stephanie & Mason, Hilary. In a Moment: Mini-Topics for Classroom, Substitute & Supply Teachers with Children from Five to Eight. 1995. pap. 15.95 (*0-947882-27-8*) Incentive Pubns.

Mudd, Steve. The Planet Beyond. 224p. 1990. mass mkt. 4.50 (*0-445-21047-8*, Pub. by Warner Bks) Little.

— Tangled Webs. (Questar Ser.). 256p. (Orig.). 1989. mass mkt. 3.95 (*0-445-20938-0*, Pub. by Warner Bks) Little.

Mudde, Cas. The Ideology of the Extreme Right. text. write for info. (*0-7190-5793-0*, Pub. by Manchester Univ Pr) St Martin.

Muddiman, David, jt. ed. see Black, Alistair.

An Asterisk (*) at the beginning of an entry indicates that the title is appearing for the first time.

Muddiman, J. G. The Bloody Assizes. (Notable British Trials Ser.). 250p. 1995. reprint ed. 79.00 (*1-56169-115-1*, 14625) Gaunt.

Muddiman, J. G., ed. Trial of King Charles the First. (Notable British Trials Ser.). xvii, 282p. 1995. reprint ed. 90.00 (*1-56169-114-3*) Gaunt.

Mudditt, B. Howard, ed. Christian Worship (Hymns) 716p. 1976. text 19.50 (*0-85364-194-3*) Attic Pr.

Muddle, B. C. Interfaces II. (Materials Science Forum: Vols. 189-190). (Illus.). 450p. (C). 1995. 200.00 (*0-87849-693-9*, Pub. by Trans T Pub) Enfield Pubs NH.

Muddle, B. C., ed. Martensitic Transformations. 714p. (C). 1990. text 241.00 (*0-87849-610-6*, Pub. by Trans T Pub) Enfield Pubs NH.

Muderlak, Ed. Parker Guns - The Old Reliable: A Concise History of the Famous American Shotgun Manufacturing. (Illus.). 325p. 1997. 40.00 (*1-57157-054-3*) Safari Pr.

***Muderlak, Ed.** When Ducks Were Plenty: The Golden Age of Waterfowling & Duck Hunting from 1840 Till 1920. (Illus.). 300p. 2000. 49.95 (*1-57157-090-X*) Safari Pr.

Mudfoot, Judyl. Masked Ball: Dreams & Disguises. 36p. (Orig.). 1986. pap. 10.00 (*0-930012-47-X*) J Mudfoot.

Mudford, Peter. Graham Greene. LC 96-209946. (Writers & Their Work Ser.). 95p. (Orig.). 1996. pap. text 15.00 (*0-7463-0758-6*, Pub. by Northcote House) U Pr of Miss.

M

Mudford, Peter, ed. Master Humphrey's Clock & Other Stories. (Everyman Paperback Classics). 224p. 1997. pap. 6.95 (*0-460-87654-6*, Everyman's Classic Lib) Tuttle Pubng.

Mudford, Peter, ed. see Butler, Samuel.

Mudford, Peter, ed. see Eliot, George, pseud.

Mudgal, jt. auth. see Vats.

Mudge. Heart Transplantation. 2000. text 135.00 (*0-7216-7786-X*, W B Saunders Co) Harcrt Hlth Sci Grp.

— Proceedings of the International Conference on Parallel Processing, Held 1992, Vol. 1. 320p. 1992. per. 79.95 (*0-8493-0781-3*) CRC Pr.

Mudge, Arthur E. Innovative Change: One Hundred One Case Histories. 163p. 1989. text 37.00 (*0-939332-19-1*) J Pohl Assocs.

— Successful Program Management: Sharpening the Competitive Edge. 216p. 1989. text 37.00 (*0-939332-18-3*) J Pohl Assocs.

— Value Engineering: A Systematic Approach. 286p. 1989. reprint ed. text 37.00 (*0-939332-17-5*) J Pohl Assocs.

Mudge, Bradford K. Sara Coleridge, a Victorian Daughter: Her Life & Essays. LC 88-37427. 312p. (C). 1989. 40.00 (*0-300-04443-7*) Yale U Pr.

***Mudge, Bradford K.** The Whore's Story: Women, Pornography & the British Novel, 1684-1830. LC 99-32571. (Ideologies of Desire Ser.). (Illus.). 272p. 2000. 35.00 (*0-19-513505-9*) OUP.

Mudge, Bradford K., ed. British Romantic Novelists, 1789-1832. LC 92-9153. (Dictionary of Literary Biography Ser.: Vol. 116). 400p. 1992. text 155.00 (*0-8103-7593-1*) Gale.

Mudge, Eugene T. The Social Philosophy of John Taylor of Carolina. LC 76-181960. reprint ed. 20.00 (*0-404-04515-4*) AMS Pr.

— The Social Philosophy of John Taylor of Caroline: A Study in Jeffersonian Democracy. (BCL1 - U. S. History Ser.). 227p. 1992. reprint ed. lib. bdg. 79.00 (*0-7812-6131-7*) Rprt Serv.

Mudge, Gilbert H., Jr. Manual Electr ISE, No. 2. 1986. 15.95 (*0-316-58919-5*) Little.

— Manual of Electrocardiography. 1986. spiral bd. 32.95 (*0-316-58918-7*, Little Brwn Med Div) Lppncott W & W.

Mudge-Grout, Christine, et al. Immunologic Disorders. (Illus.). 368p. (C). (gr. 13). 1992. text 36.00 (*0-8016-2775-3*, 02775) Mosby Inc.

Mudge, Isadore G. George Eliot Dictionary. LC 72-762. (Reference Ser.: No. 44). 1972. reprint ed. lib. bdg. 75.00 (*0-8383-1350-7*) M S G Haskell Hse.

— A George Eliot Dictionary. (BCL1-PR English Literature Ser.). 260p. 1992. reprint ed. lib. bdg. 79.00 (*0-7812-7526-1*) Rprt Serv.

Mudge, Jacqueline. Randy Savage: Story of the Wrestler They Call "Macho Man" LC 99-33772. (Illus.). 64p. 1999. 17.95 (*0-7910-5409-8*) Chelsea Hse.

***Mudge, Jacqueline.** Bret Hart: The Story of the Wrestler They Call "The Hitman" 1999. pap. text 9.95 Chehalem.

Mudge, Jacqueline. Bret Hart: The Story of the Wrestler They Call "The Hitman" LC 99-38097. (Illus.). 64p. 1999. 17.95 (*0-7910-5408-X*) Chelsea Hse.

— Bret Hart: The Story of the Wrestler They Call "The Hitman" LC 99-38097. (Wrestling Stars Ser.). (Illus.). 64p. (YA). (gr. 3 up). 1999. pap. 9.95 (*0-7910-5554-X*) Chelsea Hse.

***Mudge, Jacqueline.** Diamond Dallas Page. (Pro Wrestling Legends Ser.). 2000. 17.95 (*0-7910-5829-8*) Chelsea Hse.

— Diamond Dallas Page: The Story of the Wrestler They Call "Diamond Dallas Page" LC 00-21867. (Pro Wrestling Legends Ser.). 2000. pap. 8.95 (*0-7910-5830-1*) Chelsea Hse.

— Kevin Nash. (Pro Wrestling Legends Ser.). (YA). 2000. 17.95 (*0-7910-5827-1*) Chelsea Hse.

— Kevin Nash. LC 00-20729. (Pro Wrestling Legends Ser.). (Illus.). (YA). 2000. pap. 8.95 (*0-7910-5828-X*) Chelsea Hse.

Mudge, Jacqueline. Randy Savage: The Story of the Wrestler They Call "Macho Man" LC 99-33772. (Wrestling Stars Ser.). (Illus.). 64p. (YA). (gr. 3 up). 1999. pap. 8.95 (*0-7910-5555-8*) Chelsea Hse.

Mudge, Jean M. Chinese Export Porcelain for the American Trade, 1785-1835. LC 61-16518. (Illus.). 284p. 40.00 (*0-87413-102-2*) U Delaware Pr.

— Chinese Export Porcelain for the American Trade, 1785-1835. rev. ed. LC 79-4713. (Illus.). 300p. 1980. 55.00 (*0-87413-166-9*) U Delaware Pr.

Mudge, John T. The White Mountains: Names, Places, & Legends. 2nd ed. (Illus.). 222p. 1995. pap. 13.95 (*0-9633560-6-2*) Durand Pr.

Mudge, John T., ed. The Old Man's Reader: History & Legends of Franconia Notch. (Illus.). 231p. (Orig.). 1995. pap. 13.95 (*0-9633560-3-8*) Durand Pr.

Mudge, John T., ed. see Crawford, Lucy.

Mudge, Lewis S. The Church as Moral Community: Ecclesiology & Ethics in Ecumenical Debate. LC 98-15081. 176p. 1998. pap. 19.95 (*0-8264-1048-0*) Continuum.

— The Sense of a People: Toward a Church for the Human Future. LC 92-7926. 256p. 1992. pap. 18.00 (*1-56338-040-4*) TPI PA.

Mudge, Lewis S., ed. see Ricoeur, Paul.

Mudge, Stephen. Paris Rooms: Portfolios from 34 Interior Designers. 1999. 40.00 (*1-56496-499-X*) Rockport Pubs.

— Southern Rooms: Interior Design from Miami to Houston. 160p. 1999. 35.00 (*1-56496-598-8*) Rockport Pubs.

Mudge, Zachariah A. Sketches of Mission Life among the Indians of Oregon. 1983. 14.95 (*0-87770-308-6*) Ye Galleon.

Mudgett, Timothy B. Make the Fur Fly: A History of a Union Volunteer Division in the American Civil War. LC 97-26247. 188p. 1997. 24.95 (*1-57249-084-5*, Burd St Pr) White Mane Pub.

Mudibo-Piwang, Catherine & Frascino, Edward. A Visit from the Leopard: Memories of a Ugandan Childhood. LC 99-26992. (Illus.). 64p. (J). (gr. 2-6). 2000. 15.95 (*0-945912-27-7*) Pippin Pr.

Mudie & Cottom. The Management & Marketing of Services. 2nd ed. LC 99-461880. 306p. 1999. pap. text 34.95 (*0-7506-3594-0*) Buttrwrth-Heinemann.

Mudie, Colin, jt. auth. see Mudie, Rosemary.

Mudie, Peter. Marketing: An Analytical Framework & Perspect. LC 96-40334. 312p. 1997. pap. 55.00 (*0-13-357757-0*) P-H.

Mudie, Peter & Cottam, Angela. The Management & Marketing of Services. 250p. 1993. pap. text 44.95 (*0-7506-0789-0*) Buttrwrth-Heinemann.

Mudie, Peter & Thoms, Albie. Sydney Underground Movies UBU Films (1956-1970) LC 98-163952. (Illus.). 288p. 1997. pap. 44.95 (*0-86840-512-4*, Pub. by New South Wales Univ Pr) Intl Spec Bk.

Mudie, Rosemary & Mudie, Colin. Power Yachts. (Illus.). 1977. 29.95 (*0-8464-1298-5*) Beekman Pubs.

Mudimbe, V. Y. The Idea of Africa. LC 94-1183. (African Systems of Thought Ser.). 256p. 1994. 32.50 (*0-253-33898-0*); pap. 12.95 (*0-253-20872-6*) Ind U Pr.

— The Invention of Africa: Gnosis, Philosophy, & the Order of Knowledge. LC 87-45324. (African Systems of Thought Ser.). 256p. 1988. pap. 15.95 (*0-253-20468-2*, MB-468) Ind U Pr.

— Nations, Identities, Cultures. 1995. pap. text 10.00 (*0-8223-6428-X*) Duke.

— Parables & Fables: Exegesis, Textuality & Politics in Central Africa. LC 91-12498. (Illus.). 260p. (Orig.). (C). 1991. pap. 19.95 (*0-299-13064-9*); lib. bdg. 50.00 (*0-299-13060-6*) U of Wis Pr.

— The Rift. De Jager, Marjolijn, tr. LC 92-44511. 128p. 1993. 16.95 (*0-8166-2312-0*) U of Minn Pr.

— Tales of Faith: Religion As Political Performance in Central Africa. LC 97-10362. (Jordan Lectures in Comparative Religion: Vol. 18). 176p. 1997. 49.95 (*0-485-17418-9*, Pub. by Athlone Pr) Humanities.

Mudimbe, V. Y., ed. Nations, Identities, Cultures. LC 97-20054. 240p. 1997. pap. text 15.95 (*0-8223-2065-7*); lib. bdg. 45.95 (*0-8223-2052-5*) Duke.

— The Surreptitious Speech: "Presence Africaine" & the Politics of Otherness, 1947-1987. (Illus.). 490p. 1992. pap. text 24.95 (*0-226-54507-5*); lib. bdg. 71.50 (*0-226-54506-7*) U Ch Pr.

Mudliar, T. D. Property, a Constitutional Right. (C). 1988. 150.00 (*0-7855-4744-4*) St Mut.

***Mudloff, Thomas F. & Fellows, Ronald E.** Hieroglyphs for Travelers: What Do Those Little Pictures Mean? LC 99-91135. 120p. (J). 1999. spiral bd. 14.95 (*0-939968-02-9*) R E Fellows.

Mudore, John. Counting on Your Fingers Is Not Immoral Vol. 1: Hands-On Activities to Learn Fractions, Decimals, & Percent. Faye, Constance, ed. (Illus.). 168p. 1998. mass mkt., wbk. ed. 25.00 (*0-9636514-7-1*) Infinity Pubs.

— Counting on Your Fingers Is Not Immoral Vol. 2: Hands-On Activities to Learn Integers & Equations. Faye, Constance, ed. (Illus.). 144p. 1998. mass mkt., wbk. ed. 20.00 (*0-9636514-1-2*) Infinity Pubs.

— Making Math Matter: A Math Resource - Book for Middle & Secondary Teachers. LC 93-77825. 144p. (Orig.). 1994. pap. 20.00 (*0-9636514-8-X*) Infinity Pubs.

Mudrak, Myroslava M. The New Generation & Artistic Modernism in the Ukraine. LC 86-7043. (Studies in the Fine Arts: The Avant-Garde: No. 50). (Illus.). 294p. reprint ed. pap. 91.20 (*0-8357-1687-2*, 207051400097) Bks Demand.

Mudroch, Alena & Azcue, Jose. Manual of Aquatic Sediment Sampling. 240p. 1995. lib. bdg. 65.00 (*1-56670-029-9*, L1029) Lewis Pubs.

Mudroch, Alena & Azcue, Jose M. Manual of Bioassessment of Aquatic Sediment Quality. LC 98-229734. 1998. lib. bdg. 79.95 (*1-56670-343-3*) Lewis Pubs.

Mudroch, Alena & MacKnight, Scott D. Handbook of Techniques for Aquatic Sediments Sampling. LC 95-19446. (Illus.). 208p. 1991. lib. bdg. 133.00 (*0-8493-3587-6*, GC380) CRC Pr.

Mudroch, Alena & MacKnight, Scott D., eds. Handbook of Techniques for Aquatic Sediments Sampling. 2nd ed. LC 94-14255. 256p. 1994. lib. bdg. 85.00 (*1-56670-027-2*, L1027) Lewis Pubs.

Mudrooroo. Doin Wildcat. 208p. 17.95 (*0-947062-45-9*) Hyland Hse.

— Dr. Wooreddy's Prescription for Enduring the Ending of the World. 208p. pap. 12.95 (*0-947062-02-5*, Pub. by Hyland Hse) Seven Hills Bk.

— Garden of Gethsemane. (Illus.). 180p. 14.95 (*0-947062-66-1*, Pub. by Hyland Hse) Seven Hills Bk.

— The Indigenous Literature of Australia. 240p. pap. 16.95 (*1-86447-014-3*, Pub. by Hyland Hse) Seven Hills Bk.

— Long Live Sandawara. 208p. pap. 12.95 (*0-947062-01-7*) Hyland Hse.

— Pacific Highway Boo-Blooz. 1996. pap. 16.95 (*0-7022-2834-6*, Pub. by Univ Queensland Pr) Intl Spec Bk.

Mudrovic, W. Michael. Breaking New Ground: The Transgressive Poetics of Claudio Rodriguez. LC 98-39218. (ENG & SPA.). 584p. 1999. 69.50 (*0-934223-52-1*) Lehigh Univ Pr.

Mudugula, I. S. The Acarya: Sankara of Kaladi - a Story. (Illus.). 142p. 1985. 16.00 (*0-317-46523-6*, Pub. by Motilal Bnarsidass) S Asia.

Mudumbai, Srinivas. United States Foreign Policy Towards India, 1947-1954. 1985. 12.00 (*0-8364-1335-0*, Pub. by Manohar) S Asia.

Mueck, Thomas A. & Polaschek, Martin L. Index Data Structures in Object-Oriented Databases. LC 97-17631. (International Series on Advances in Database Systems). 1997. text 119.00 (*0-7923-9971-4*) Kluwer Academic.

Muecke, Douglas C., ed. see Horace.

Muecke, Kyoko, tr. see Yagi, Tokutaro.

Muecke, Stephen. No Road: Bitumen All the Way. LC 97-158779. 249p. 1997. pap. 16.95 (*1-86368-181-7*, Pub. by Fremantle Arts) Intl Spec Bk.

— Speaking into Space (Textual Spaces) Aboriginality & Cultural Studies. 1992. pap. 32.95 (*0-86840-101-3*, Pub. by New South Wales Univ Pr) Intl Spec Bk.

Muecke, Stephen, tr. see Gill, Jose.

Muegge, Kathrin, jt. ed. see Durum, Scott K.

***Mueggler, Erik.** The Age of Wild Ghosts: Memory, Violence, & Place in Southwest China. (Illus.). 361p. 2001. 50.00 (*0-520-22623-2*); pap. 19.95 (*0-520-22631-3*, Pub. by U CA Pr) Cal Prin Full Svc.

Muego, Benjamin N. Spectator Society: The Philippines under Martial Rule. LC 88-25304. (Monographs in International Studies, Southeast Asia Ser.: No. 77). 201p. 1986. pap. text 17.00 (*0-89680-138-1*) Ohio U Pr.

Muehl, Lois. Talkable Tales. (Illus.). 128p. 1993. 25.95 (*0-937857-44-0*, 1540) Speech Bin.

Muehl, Lois & Muehl, Siegmar. Trading Cultures in the Classroom: Two American Teachers in China. 288p. (Orig.). 1993. pap. 11.75 (*0-8248-1442-8*, Kolowalu Bk) UH Pr.

Muehl, Siegmar, jt. auth. see Muehl, Lois.

Muehlbauer, F. J. & Kaiser, W. J., eds. Expanding the Production & Use of Cool Season Food Legumes: Proceedings of the Second International Food Legume Research Conference on Pea, Lentil, Faba Bean, Chickpea, & Grasspea, Cairo, Egypt, 12-16 April 1992. LC 93-31539. (Current Plant Science & Biotechnology in Agriculture Ser.: Vol. 19). 1028p. (C). 1994. text 679.50 (*0-7923-2535-4*) Kluwer Academic.

Muehlbauer, Jen, jt. auth. see Degenhart, Curt.

Muehlberg, R. L. Jet Stream. (Breakup of America Ser.). vi, 130p. (Orig.). 1996. pap. 12.95 (*0-9653342-0-1*) Muehlberg Pr.

Muehlberg, R. Lee. Life Is Choices, Hope Is a Decision. ii, 86p. (Orig.). 1996. pap. 7.95 (*0-9653342-1-X*) Muehlberg Pr.

Muehlberger, W. R., jt. ed. see Henry, C. D.

Muehldorf, E. I., jt. auth. see Kim, J. C.

Muehlenberg, Ekkehard. Psalmenkommentare aus der Katenenueberlieferung, Vol. 1. LC 73-91808. (Patristische Texte und Studien: Band 15). (GER.). (C). 1974. 157.70 (*3-11-004182-0*) De Gruyter.

— Psalmenkommentare aus der Katenenueberlieferung, Vol. 2. (Patristische Texte und Studien: Vol. 16). (C). 1977. 157.70 (*3-11-005717-4*) De Gruyter.

— Psalmenkommentare aus der Katenenueberlieferung: Untersuchungen zu den Psalmenkatenen, Vol. 3. (Patristische Texte und Studien: No. 19). (C). 1978. 108.50 (*3-11-006959-8*) De Gruyter.

Muehlig, Linda, ed. see Chotner, Deborah, et al.

Muehling, Andreas. Karl Ludwig Schmidt: Und Wissenschaft ist Leben. (Arbeiten zur Kirchengeschichte Ser.: Vol. 66). (GER.). xi, 263p. (C). 1996. lib. bdg. 109.65 (*3-11-015442-0*) De Gruyter.

Muehling, Darrel D., ed. Proceedings of the Conference of the American Academy of Advertising, 1998. 1998. pap. 25.00 (*0-931030-21-8*) Am Acad Advert.

Muehlman, Sandra. Word Processing on Microcomputers: Legal Applications & Exercises. 256p. (C). 1989. pap. text. write for info. (*0-318-65463-6*) P-H.

Muehlman-Shortt, Sandra. Legal Word Processing Exercises. 192p. (C). 1991. pap. text 22.40 (*0-13-964545-4*, 180101) P-H.

Muehlmann, Robert G. Berkeley's Ontology. LC 92-17820. 320p. 1992. lib. bdg. 37.95 (*0-87220-146-5*) Hackett Pub.

Muehlmann, Robert G., ed. Berkeley's Metaphysics: Structural, Interpretive, & Critical Essays. 288p. 1995. 48.50 (*0-271-01427-X*) Pa St U Pr.

Muehlmatt, Ernest, jt. auth. see Schroeder, Roger.

Muehrcke, Jill, ed. Accounting & Financial Management. (Leadership Ser.). 115p. 1993. spiral bd. 35.00 (*0-614-07095-3*) Soc Nonprofit Org.

— Board Leadership & Governance. (Leadership Ser.). 106p. 1993. spiral bd. 35.00 (*0-614-07092-9*) Soc Nonprofit Org.

— Computers & Information Systems. (Leadership Ser.). 106p. 1993. spiral bd. 35.00 (*0-614-07093-7*) Soc Nonprofit Org.

— Enterprise (for Profit) Endeavors. (Leadership Ser.). 124p. 1993. spiral bd. 35.00 (*0-614-07094-5*) Soc Nonprofit Org.

— Fundraising & Resource Development, Vol. 1. (Leadership Ser.). 164p. 1990. spiral bd. 20.00 (*0-614-07096-1*) Soc Nonprofit Org.

— Fundraising & Resource Development, Vol. 2. (Leadership Ser.). 128p. 1993. spiral bd. 20.00 (*0-614-07097-X*) Soc Nonprofit Org.

— Law & Taxation, Vol. 1. (Leadership Ser.). 100p. 1990. spiral bd. 20.00 (*0-614-07098-8*) Soc Nonprofit Org.

— Law & Taxation, Vol. 2. (Leadership Ser.). 81p. 1993. spiral bd. 20.00 (*0-614-07099-6*) Soc Nonprofit Org.

— Management & Planning, Vol. 1. (Leadership Ser.). 123p. 1990. spiral bd. 20.00 (*0-614-07100-3*) Soc Nonprofit Org.

— Management & Planning, Vol. 2. (Leadership Ser.). 130p. 1993. spiral bd. 20.00 (*0-614-07101-1*) Soc Nonprofit Org.

— Marketing. (Leadership Ser.). 90p. 1993. spiral bd. 20.00 (*0-614-07103-8*) Soc Nonprofit Org.

— Nonprofit Start-Up Kit. 88p. 1995. pap. 35.00 (*0-614-18255-7*) Soc Nonprofit Org.

— Personnel & Human Resources Development, Vol. 1. (Leadership Ser.). 95p. 1990. spiral bd. 35.00 (*0-614-07105-4*) Soc Nonprofit Org.

— Personnel & Human Resources Development, Vol. 2. (Leadership Ser.). 72p. 1993. spiral bd. 35.00 (*0-614-07106-2*) Soc Nonprofit Org.

— PR & Communications. (Leadership Ser.). 93p. 1993. spiral bd. 35.00 (*0-614-07104-6*) Soc Nonprofit Org.

— Profiles in Excellence. (Leadership Ser.). 147p. 1993. spiral bd. 35.00 (*0-614-07102-X*) Soc Nonprofit Org.

— Volunteer Management. (Leadership Ser.). 75p. 1993. spiral bd. 35.00 (*0-614-07107-0*) Soc Nonprofit Org.

Muehrcke, Jill & Nelson, Andrea. Are You Sitting on a Gold Mine: Fundraising Self-Assessment Guide. (Illus.). 135p. 1995. spiral bd. 35.00 (*0-614-10168-9*) Soc Nonprofit Org.

Muehrcke, Juliana, jt. auth. see Muehrcke, Phillip.

Muehrcke, Juliana O., jt. auth. see Muehrcke, Phillip C.

Muehrcke, Phillip & Muehrcke, Juliana. Map Use: Reading, Analysis & Interpretation. 4th rev. ed. LC 97-73803. (Illus.). 648p. 1998. pap. text 40.00 (*0-9602978-4-7*) JP Pubns WI.

Muehrcke, Phillip C. Map Use: Reading, Analysis & Interpretation. 2nd ed. LC 78-70573. (Illus.). 525p. (C). 1986. pap. text 25.00 (*0-9602978-2-0*) JP Pubns WI.

Muehrcke, Phillip C. & Muehrcke, Juliana O. Map Use: Reading, Analysis & Interpretation. 3rd rev. ed. LC 92-71696. (Illus.). 600p. 1992. pap. text 40.00 (*0-9602978-3-9*) JP Pubns WI.

Muehrcke, Robert C., ed. see Micek, Joseph G.

Muehreke, Jill, ed. Volunteer Liability & Risk Management. 104p. 1997. pap. 35.00 (*0-614-30651-5*) Soc Nonprofit Org.

Muelder, Walter G. The Ethical Edge of Christian Theology: Forty Years of Communitarian Personalism. LC 83-21935. (Toronto Studies in Theology: Vol. 13). 435p. 1983. lib. bdg. 109.95 (*0-88946-754-4*) E Mellen.

Muelen, David L. Van der, see Van der Muelen, David L., ed.

Muelenberg, Matthew, ed. Food & Agribusiness Marketing in Europe. LC 93-34606. (Journal of International Food & Agribusiness Marketing Ser.: Vol. 5, Nos. 3 & 4). (Illus.). 209p. 1994. reprint ed. 49.95 (*1-56024-474-7*) Haworth Pr.

— Food & Agribusiness Marketing in Europe. LC 93-34606. (Journal of International Food & Agribusiness Marketing Ser.: Vol. 5, Nos. 3 & 4). 209p. 1995. reprint ed. pap. 24.95 (*1-56024-788-6*) Haworth Pr.

Muellbauer, John, jt. auth. see Deaton, Agnus.

Mueller. Communication & Aging. (C). 2000. text 25.95 (*0-205-28826-X*, Longwood Div) Allyn.

— Evidence. 1995. suppl. ed. 19.95 (*0-316-58903-9*, Aspen Law & Bus) Aspen Pub.

Mueller. Healing Humor. 176p. pap. 10.95 (*0-471-34788-4*) Wiley.

Mueller. Just Enough Algebra. LC 98-45578. 144p. (C). 1998. pap. text 23.00 (*0-201-50344-1*) Addison-Wesley.

***Mueller.** Lagrange & Lagrange County. (Images of America Ser.). 1999. pap. 18.99 (*0-7385-0191-3*) Arcadia Publng.

Mueller. Mod Evidence, Set. 1813p. 1995. 135.00 (*0-316-59002-9*, Aspen Law & Bus) Aspen Pub.

— Modern Evidence. 1995. 135.00 (*0-316-59000-2*) Little.

— Upgrding&repairing Pc. 8th ed. 1998. pap. text 81.99 (*1-58076-058-9*) Que Educ & Trng.

***Mueller.** Windows 2000 Programming Bible. LC 99-49493. (Bible Ser.). (Illus.). 1056p. 1999. pap. 49.99 (*0-7645-3312-6*) IDG Bks.

Mueller. Women & Heart Disease. 2000. text. write for info. (*0-443-07900-5*, W B Saunders Co) Harcrt Hlth Sci Grp.

Mueller & Williams. The CNA/CNE. 2nd ed. 1996. pap., student ed. 49.95 incl. cd-rom (*0-07-912922-6*) McGraw.

Mueller, et al. Missing Tablets & Unknown Oracles. 50p. 1996. pap. text 5.00 (*1-879665-20-4*) Cyborg Prods.

— Sichtwechsel NEU: Allgemeine Einfuehrung 1, 2, 3. (GER.). 48p. (Orig.). (C). 1995. pap. text 40.00 (*3-12-675022-2*, Pub. by Klett Edition) Intl Bk Import.

Mueller, jt. auth. see Choi.

Mueller, A. Perturbative QCD. (Advanced Series on Directions in Hep.: Vol. 5). 624p. 1989. text 110.00 (*9971-5-0564-9*); pap. text 40.00 (*9971-5-0565-7*) World Scientific Pub.

An Asterisk (*) at the beginning of an entry indicates that the title is appearing for the first time.

Mueller, A. & Diemann, E. Transition Metal Chemistry. (Illus.). 338p. 1981. pap. 90.00 (0-89573-039-1, Wiley-VCH) Wiley.
Mueller, A. C. My Good Shepherd Bible Story Book. LC 70-89876. 175p. (J). (gr. 3-5). 1969. bds. 15.99 (0-570-03400-0, 56-1126) Concordia.
Mueller, Alice & Mueller, Stephen. The Pocket Idiot's Guide to German. (Pocket Idiot's Guides Ser.). 184p. 1999. pap. 9.95 (0-02-863177-3) Macmillan Gen Ref.
Mueller, Amelia. Jeremy's Jack-O-Lantern. (Illus.). 24p. (Orig.). (J). (gr. k-3). 1992. pap. 5.95 (0-945530-06-4) Wordsworth KS.
— A Quiet Strength: The Susanna Ruth Krehbiel Story. LC 92-82738. 146p. 1992. pap. 2.50 (0-87303-201-2) Faith & Life.
Mueller, Arlene & Indelicato, Dorothy. Wine, Food & the Good Life. (Wine Cookbook Ser.). (Illus.). 128p. 1985. pap. 9.95 (0-932664-47-4) Wine Appreciation.
Mueller Associates, Inc. Staff. Waste Oil: Reclaiming Technology, Utilization & Disposal. LC 88-38438. (Pollution Technology Review Ser.: No. 166). (Illus.). 193p. 1989. 59.00 (0-8155-1193-0) Noyes.
Mueller, B. & Von Wichert, P., eds. Lung Surfactant: Basic Research in the Pathogenesis of Lung Disorders. (Progress in Respiratory Research Ser.: Vol. 27). (Illus.). x, 266p. 1994. 208.75 (3-8055-5837-6) S Karger.
Mueller, B. Jeanne, jt. auth. see Reinoehl, Richard.
Mueller, Barbara. International Advertising: Communicating Across Cultures. LC 95-17905. 340p. (C). 1995. 52.95 (0-534-19278-5) Wadsworth Pub.
Mueller, Barbara R., ed. The Congress Book, 1990. LC 40-2870. (Illus.). 198p. 1990. text 25.00 (0-929333-16-0) Am Philat Congr.
Mueller, Benito, ed. & tr. see Brentano, Franz.
Mueller, Bertha, tr. see Goethe, Johann Wolfgang Von.
Mueller, Betty A. Keeping Track: A Record of Your Dog's Progress in the Tracking Field. (Illus.). 1993. ring bd. 19.95 (1-888994-01-0) Howln Moon.
— Notebook Tracker: Maps for Tracking Dogs. 100p. 1996. spiral bd. 11.95 (1-888994-04-5) Howln Moon.
Mueller, Bill W., ed. The Steamboater's Handbook V: Steamboating. (Illus.). 288p. (Orig.). 1995. pap. 25.00 (0-933847-12-2) Wooden Porch Bks.
— The Steamboater's Handbook VI: Steamboating. (Illus.). 304p. 1996. pap. 25.00 (0-933847-14-9) Wooden Porch Bks.
Mueller, Bondell, ed. see Campadonica, Carol.
Mueller, C. Foundations of the Mathematical Theory of Electromagnetic Waves. rev. ed. Higgins, T. P., tr. LC 75-81586. (Grundlehren der Mathematischen Wissenschaften Ser.: Vol. 155). (Illus.). 1969. 79.00 (0-387-04506-6) Spr-Verlag.
Mueller, Carl R., tr. see Buchner, Georg.
Mueller, Carl R., tr. see Schnitzler, Arthur.
Mueller, Carl R., tr. see Strindberg, August.
Mueller, Carl Richard, jt. auth. see Wedekind, Frank.
Mueller, Carol M., ed. The Politics of the Gender Gap: The Social Construction of Political Influence. (Yearbooks in Women's Policy Studies: Vol. 12). 320p. (C). 1988. text 44.00 (0-8039-2732-0); pap. text 21.95 (0-8039-2733-9) Sage.
— The Politics of the Gender Gap: The Social Construction of Political Influence. LC 87-22454. (Sage Yearbooks in Women's Policy Studies: No. 12). 316p. reprint ed. pap. 98.00 (0-7837-6719-6, 204634600011) Bks Demand.
Mueller, Carol M., jt. ed. see Katzenstein, Mary F.
Mueller, Carol M., jt. ed. see Morris, Aldon.
Mueller, Carol S. Marketing Today's Fashion. 3rd ed. LC 94-17476. 320p. 1994. pap. text 85.00 (0-13-043001-3) P-H.
Mueller, Carolyn, ed. Periodicals of the Mid-West & West. LC 85-60590. 1986. 35.00 (0-87650-210-9) Pierian.
Mueller, Catherine L. Be Aware! Be Alert! LC 96-78275. (Illus.). 218p. (Orig.). (YA). (gr. 9). 1996. pap. 9.95 (0-9644799-1-5) Luth News.
Mueller, Charles, jt. auth. see Kim, Jae-On.
Mueller, Charles S. Almost Adult: Preteen Story Devotions. LC 92-27014. 160p. (Orig.). (J). (gr. 4-7). 1993. pap. 6.99 (0-570-04598-3, 12-3184) Concordia.
Mueller, Charles W., jt. auth. see Kim, Jae-On.
Mueller, Charles W., jt. auth. see Price, James L.
Mueller, Christine L. The Styrian Estates, 1740-1848: A Century of Transition. (Modern European History Ser.). 448p. 1987. text 15.00 (0-8240-8049-1) Garland.
Mueller, Christopher B. Evidence Text. LC 94-76922. 1392p. 1994. lib. bdg. 41.95 (0-316-58998-5, Aspen Law & Bus) Aspen Pub.
Mueller, Christopher B. & Kirkpatrick, Laird C. Evidence. LC 97-21818. (Aspen Roadmap Ser.). 1997. write for info. (1-56706-541-4, 65414) Aspen Law.
— Evidence. 2nd ed. LC 99-18723. 1368p. 1999. boxed set 43.95 (0-7355-0069-X) Panel Pubs.
*Mueller, Christopher B. & Kirkpatrick, Laird C. Evidence: Practice Under the Rules. 2nd ed. LC 99-21888. 1736p. 1999. boxed set 185.00 (0-7355-0447-4) Panel Pubs.
Mueller, Christopher B. & Kirkpatrick, Laird C. Evidence under the Rules. 3rd ed. LC 95-80627. 1052p. 1996. teacher ed. write for info. (0-316-58902-0, 89020) Aspen Law.
*Mueller, Christopher B. & Kirkpatrick, Laird C. Evidence under the Rules: Text, Cases & Problems. 4th ed. LC 99-54967. 2000. boxed set 68.00 (0-7355-1231-0) Panel Pubs.
— Federal Rules of Evidence: With Advisory Committe Notes, Legislative History, & Cases, 2000 Edition. annuals 465p. 2000. pap. text, suppl. ed. 26.95 (0-7355-1322-8, 13228) Panel Pubs.
Mueller, Christopher B. & Kirkpatrick, Laird C. Federal Rules of Evidence, with Advisory Committee Notes & Cases: 1997 Edition. 3rd ed. 550p. 1997. pap. write for info. (1-56706-567-8, 65678) Panel Pubs.
— Federal Rules of Evidence with Advisory Committee Notes & Legislative History. 1988. pap. 14.00 (0-316-58922-5, Aspen Law & Bus) Aspen Pub.
Mueller, Christopher B., jt. auth. see Louisell, David W.
Mueller, Cookie. Ask Dr. Mueller: The Writings of Cookie Mueller. LC 96-69698. 320p. (Orig.). (C). 1997. pap. 13.99 (1-85242-331-5, High Risk Bks) Serpents Tail.
— How to Get Rid of Pimples. (Illus.). 80p. (Orig.). 1984. pap. 6.00 (0-917061-19-5) Top Stories.
— Walking Through Clear Water in a Pool Painted Black. 150p. 1990. pap. 6.00 (0-936756-61-6) Autonomedia.
Mueller, Daniel. How Animals Mate. LC 98-31823. 224p. 1999. text 23.95 (0-87951-925-8, Pub. by Overlook Pr) Penguin Putnam.
*Mueller, Daniel. How Animals Mate. (Sewanee Writers Ser.). 2000. pap. 13.95 (1-58567-055-3, Pub. by Overlook Pr) Penguin Putnam.
*Mueller, Daniel & Groves, D. I. Potassic Igneous Rocks & Associated Gold-Copper Mineralization. 3rd rev. enl. ed. LC 99-40223. (Illus.). xiv, 252p. 1999. 79.95 (3-540-66371-1) Spr-Verlag.
Mueller, David L. Foundation of Karl Barth's Doctrine of Reconciliation: Jesus Christ Crucified & Risen. LC 91-262. (Toronto Studies in Theology: Vol. 53). 510p. 1991. lib. bdg. 119.95 (0-88946-583-5) E Mellen.
Mueller, Deirdre. Year 2000 Manual: Solutions & Basic Knowledge for the Non-Technical PC User. Korody, Marc & Hall, Jeremiah, eds. LC 98-73587. (Illus.). 92p. 1998. pap. 29.95 (0-9666209-0-9) IntelliSrce.
Mueller, Delbert. A Guide for Curriculum Writers. 308p. (C). 1992. pap. text 29.50 (0-8191-8399-7); lib. bdg. 64.50 (0-8191-8398-9) U Pr of Amer.
Mueller, Dennis. Constitutional Democracy. (Illus.). 400p. 1996. text 65.00 (0-19-509588-X) OUP.
Mueller, Dennis C. The Corporation: Growth, Diversification & Mergers. (Fundamentals of Pure & Applied Economics Ser.: Vol. 16). viii, 100p. 1987. pap. text 43.00 (3-7186-0357-8) Gordon & Breach.
— The Dynamics of Company Profits. (Illus.). 224p. (C). 1990. text 80.00 (0-521-38372-2) Cambridge U Pr.
— Profits in the Long Run. (Illus.). 400p. 1986. text 85.00 (0-521-30693-0) Cambridge U Pr.
— The Public Choice Approach to Politics. (Economists of the Twentieth Century Ser.). 552p. 1993. 110.00 (1-85278-805-4) E Elgar.
— Public Choice II. rev. ed. (Illus.). 544p. (C). 1989. pap. text 27.95 (0-521-37952-0) Cambridge U Pr.
— Public Choice II. rev. ed. (Illus.). 544p. (C). 1989. text 85.00 (0-521-37083-3) Cambridge U Pr.
Mueller, Dennis C., ed. Perspectives on Public Choice: A Handbook. (Illus.). 685p. (C). 1996. pap. text 31.95 (0-521-55654-6) Cambridge U Pr.
— Perspectives on Public Choice: A Handbook. (Illus.). 685p. (C). 1996. text 80.00 (0-521-55377-6) Cambridge U Pr.
— The Political Economy of Growth. LC 81-15955. (Illus.). 292p. reprint ed. pap. 90.60 (0-7837-5197-4, 205768100006) Bks Demand.
Mueller-Dombois, D., jt. ed. see Huettl, R. F.
Mueller-Dombois, Dieter & Fosberg, F. Raymond. Vegetation of the Tropical Pacific Islands, Vol. 132. LC 97-24026. (Ecological Studies). 880p. 1997. write for info. (0-387-98285-X); pap. write for info. (0-387-98313-9) Spr-Verlag.
Mueller, E. Menschen um Mueller: Textbuch. (GER., Illus.). 79p. (C). 1972. pap. text 17.25 (3-12-558500-7, Pub. by Klett Edition) Intl Bk Import.
— Menschen um Mueller: Textbuch. (GER., Illus.). (C). 1978. audio 33.25 (3-12-558570-8, Pub. by Klett Edition) Intl Bk Import.
*Mueller, Edward A. Queen of Sea Routes: The Merchant & Miners Transportation Company. Dunbaugh, Edwin L., ed. LC 99-57379. (Illus.). 185p. 2000. lib. bdg. 37.50 (1-930098-00-6) Purple Mnt Pr.
— St. Johns & Ocklawaha Rivers. (Images of America Ser.). (Illus.). 128p. 1999. pap. 18.99 (0-7385-0176-X) Arcadia Publng.
Mueller, Edward A. Upper Mississippi River Rafting Steamboats. LC 94-43491. (Illus.). 285p. 1995. text 44.95 (0-8214-1113-6) Ohio U Pr.
Mueller, Elaine A. Oh Boy! What Is It? Story Cookbook, Vol. 1. LC 85-61810. (Illus.). 128p. (Orig.). 1985. spiral bd. 14.95 (0-934713-00-6) Results Ent.
Mueller, Elizabeth F., tr. see Deforges, Regine.
Mueller, Eric & Schaul, Joe. I Once Knew an Indian. 1988. 15.00 (0-317-90578-3) Earnest Pubns.
Mueller, Erik T. Fluent French: Experiences of an English Speaker. 67p. 1998. spiral bd. 50.00 (0-9660746-2-9) Signiform.
— Natural Language Processing with ThoughtTreasure. 343p. 1997. spiral bd. 120.00 (0-9660746-0-2) Signiform.
*Mueller, Errol. The Mystical Rites of our Creator: Version 1.0. (HomeWorship 101 Ser.). 250p. 1999. pap. 15.00 (0-9675266-0-4) White Stone Comm.
Mueller, Erwin & Nolte, Oliver, eds. American Subsidiaries of German Firms 1992-1993 (Tochtergesellschaften Deutscher Unternehmen in Den U. S. A. 1992-1993) 20th ed. (ENG & GER.). 280p. 1992. 100.00 (0-86640-042-7) Manhattan Pub Co.
Mueller, Eva, et al. Technological Advance in an Expanding Economy: Its Impact on a Cross-Section of the Labor Force. LC 71-627965. 266p. reprint ed. pap. 82.50 (0-608-18057-2, 202913700058) Bks Demand.
Mueller, F. Max, tr. Dhammapada or Path of Virtue of the Lord Buddha. 135p. 1998. reprint ed. pap. 16.95 (0-7661-0595-4) Kessinger Pub.
Mueller, F. von, jt. auth. see Bentham, G.
Mueller, Ferdinand Von, see Von Mueller, Ferdinand.
Mueller, Frank. Struktur und Dynamik Von Flora und Vegetation (Gehoelz-, Saum-, Moos-, Flechtengesellschaften) Auf Lesesteinwaellen (Steinruecken) Im Erzgebirge. (Dissertationes Botanicae Ser.: Band 295). vi, 296p. 1998. pap. 77.00 (3-443-64207-1, Pub. by Gebruder Borntraeger) Balogh.
Mueller, Frank & Bestavros, Azer. Languages, Compilers, & Tools for Embedded Systems: ACM Sigplan Workshop Lectures '98, Motreal, Canada, June 9-12, 1998: Proceedings, Vol. 147. LC 98-41921. (Lecture Notes in Computer Science Ser.). 1998. pap. 49.00 (3-540-65075-X) Spr-Verlag.
Mueller, Frederick A., ed. see Spencer, William.
Mueller, Frederick O., et al. Catastrophic Injuries in High School & College Sports. LC 95-31210. (Sport Science Monographs: Vol. 8). (Illus.). 120p. (Orig.). 1995. pap. text 19.00 (0-87322-674-7, BMUE0674) Human Kinetics.
Mueller, Friedrich M. Anthropological Religion. LC 73-18822. (Gifford Lectures: 1891). 1975. reprint ed. 67.50 (0-404-11428-8) AMS Pr.
— Buddhist Texts from Japan, 3 pts. in 1 vol. LC 73-18824. (Illus.). reprint ed. 55.00 (0-404-11430-X) AMS Pr.
— A History of Ancient Sanskrit Literature. 2nd rev. ed. LC 73-18826. reprint ed. 76.50 (0-404-11437-7) AMS Pr.
— Last Essays. LC 73-18815. (Second Ser.). reprint ed. 55.00 (0-404-11439-3) AMS Pr.
— Last Essays: Essays on Language, Folklore & Other Subjects. LC 73-18828. (First Ser.). reprint ed. 55.00 (0-404-11438-5) AMS Pr.
— Lectures on the Origin & Growth of Religion As Illustrated by the Religions of India. LC 73-18816. reprint ed. 45.00 (0-404-11440-7) AMS Pr.
— The Life & Letters of the Right Honourable Friedrich Max Mueller, 2 vols., Set. LC 73-18820. (Illus.). reprint ed. 115.00 (0-404-11445-8) AMS Pr.
— Life & Religion. LC 73-18821. reprint ed. 39.50 (0-404-11448-2) AMS Pr.
— Natural Religion. LC 73-18810. (Gifford Lectures: 1888). reprint ed. 49.50 (0-404-11450-4) AMS Pr.
— Physical Religion. LC 73-18811. (Gifford Lectures: 1890). reprint ed. 44.50 (0-404-11451-2) AMS Pr.
— Ramakrishna, His Life & Sayings. LC 73-18812. reprint ed. 32.50 (0-404-11452-0) AMS Pr.
— Rig-Veda-Samhita: The Sacred Hymns of the Brahmans, 4 vols., Set. 2nd ed. LC 73-18831. 1892. 176.00 (0-404-11461-X) AMS Pr.
— The Science of Language, 2 vols. LC 73-18817. reprint ed. 155.00 (0-404-11441-5) AMS Pr.
— The Science of Thought. LC 73-18813. reprint ed. 69.50 (0-404-11453-9) AMS Pr.
— Selected Essays on Language, Mythology & Religion, 2 vols., Set. LC 73-18814. reprint ed. 145.00 (0-404-11456-3) AMS Pr.
— The Six Systems of Indian Philosophy. LC 73-18829. reprint ed. 44.50 (0-404-11459-8) AMS Pr.
— Theosophy: or Psychological Religion. LC 73-18830. (Gifford Lectures: 1892). reprint ed. 62.50 (0-404-14460-8) AMS Pr.
Mueller, G. Mikroradiographische Untersuchungen zur Mineralisation der Knochen Fruehgeborener und junger Saeuglinge 1980. (Journal: Acta Anatomica: Vol. 108, Suppl. 64). (Illus.). iv, 44p. 1981. pap. 39.25 (3-8055-1719-X) S Karger.
— Sedimentary Petrology Pt. 1: Methods in Sedimentary Petrology. xii, 283p. 1967. 29.00 (3-510-65006-9, Pub. by E Schweizerbartsche) Balogh.
Mueller, G. O. Comparative Criminal Law in the United States. (N. Y. U. Criminal Law Education & Research Center, Monograph Ser.: Vol. 4). (Illus.). 72p. 1970. reprint ed. pap. 18.50 (0-8377-0827-3, Rothman) W S Hein.
Mueller, G. O. & Buergenthal, T., trs. from GER. German Penal Code. (American Series of Foreign Penal Codes: Vol. 4). x, 177p. 1961. 40.00 (0-8377-0024-8, Rothman) W S Hein.
Mueller, G. O., et al. Delinquency & Puberty: Examination of a Juvenile Delinquency Fad. (N. Y. U. Criminal Law Education & Research Center, Monograph Ser.: Vol. 5). (Illus.). x, 123p. 1971. reprint ed. pap. 18.50 (0-8377-0830-3, Rothman) W S Hein.
Mueller, G. O., jt. ed. see Adler, Freda.
Mueller, G. O., jt. tr. see Moreau, J. F.
Mueller, Gary & Hughes, Allison, eds. Vision, 1994 Vol. 2: Harvard Students Look Ahead. LC 94-225525. xiv, 137p. (Orig.). 1994. pap. 10.95 (0-9641866-0-8) Dipylon Pr.
Mueller, Gene & Denyer, Bob. Never Let a Skinny Guy Make Sandwiches. (Illus.). 1994. pap. 14.95 (0-9640419-4-4) B&G MD.
Mueller, Gene & Mueller, Lynne. Year, 2000 Vol. 1: Your Personal Guide to Self & Family Protection. 84p. 1999. pap. 19.95 (0-9669410-0-4) G Two Ware.
Mueller, Gene, jt. auth. see Mitcham, Samuel W., Jr.
Mueller, George. Answers to Prayer. (Classics Ser.). mass mkt. 4.99 (0-8024-0565-7, 387) Moody.
*Mueller, Gerd. Electroluminescence. (Semiconductors & Semimetals Ser.: Vol. 64). (Illus.). 430p. 1999. 160.00 (0-12-752173-9) Acad Pr.
*Mueller, Gerd, ed. Electroluminescence II. Vol. 65. 300p. 2000. 160.00 (0-12-752174-7) Acad Pr.
Mueller, Gereon. A-Bar Syntax: A Study of Movement Types. LC 95-22184. (Studies in Generative Grammar: No. 42). x, 482p. (C). 1995. lib. bdg. 136.95 (3-11-014469-7) Mouton.
Mueller, Gerhard. Accounting: An International Perspective. 5th ed. 208p. 2000. pap. 34.06 (0-07-231638-1) McGraw.
Mueller, Gerhard, ed. Theologische Realenzyklopaedia Vol. 27: Politik/Politologie - Publizistik/Presse. (GER.). iv, 800p. (C). 1997. lib. bdg. 325.35 (3-11-015435-8) De Gruyter.
— Theologische Realenzyklopaedia Vol. 28: Puerstinger - Religionsphilosophie. (GER.). 800p. (C). 1997. lib. bdg. 325.35 (3-11-015580-X) De Gruyter.
— Theologische Realenzyklopaedie: Teil I, Band 1-17 und Registerband. (TRE Ser.). (GER.). (Orig.). (C). 1993. pap. text 750.00 (3-11-013898-0) De Gruyter.
Mueller, Gerhard, et al. Original Pronouncements, Vol. 1. 7th ed. (C). 1997. 56.50 (0-256-18105-5, Irwn McGrw-H) McGrw-H Hghr Educ.
Mueller, Gerhard G. & Kelly, Lauren. Introductory Financial Accounting. 3rd ed. 416p. (C). 1990. pap. text 54.80 (0-13-485616-3) P-H.
Mueller, Gerhard G., et al. Accounting: An International Perspective. LC 93-3989. 180p. 1993. text 30.00 (0-7863-0007-8, Irwn Prfssnl) McGraw-Hill Prof.
— Accounting: International Perspective. 4th ed. LC 96-17360. 224p. (C). 1996. text 27.25 (0-256-17082-7, Irwn McGrw-H) McGrw-H Hghr Educ.
Mueller, Gerhard G., jt. auth. see Choi, Frederick D. S.
Mueller, Gerhard G., jt. ed. see Choi, Frederick D. S.
Mueller, Gerhard O., jt. auth. see Adler, Freda.
Mueller, German, jt. auth. see Rodrigues-Filho, Saulo.
Mueller, Gregory, jt. auth. see Sanderson, Stephanie.
Mueller, Guntram & Brent, Ronald I. Just-in-Time Algebra & Trigonometry: For Students of Calculus. Guardino, Karen, ed. LC 96-43715. 181p. (C). 1996. pap. text 28.00 (0-201-41951-3) Addison-Wesley.
*Mueller, Guntram & Brent, Ronald I. Just-in-Time Algebra & Trigonometry: For Students of Calculus. 2nd ed. LC 00-35526. (Illus.). 2000. write for info. (0-201-66974-9) Addison-Wesley.
Mueller, Gus. Successful Conference: Programming Methods. 90p. (Orig.). 1982. pap. 10.00 (0-9614097-0-3) Fern Pubns.
Mueller, Gustar E. Philosophy of Literature. LC 72-14195. (Essay Index Reprint Ser.). 1977. reprint ed. 21.95 (0-518-10021-9) Ayer.
Mueller, Gustav E. Philosophy of Our Uncertainties: A Comment on the Uncertainties of Our Philosophies. LC 36-17433. 251p. reprint ed. pap. 77.90 (0-608-30644-4, 200483400047) Bks Demand.
Mueller, H. Der Eine und der Andere: Textbuch. (GER.). 55p. (C). 1975. pap. text 15.50 (3-12-558900-2, Pub. by Klett Edition) Intl Bk Import.
— Der Eine und die Andere: Textbuch mit Handreichungen. (GER.). 56p. (C). 1994. pap. text 15.50 (3-12-675420-1, Pub. by Klett Edition); audio 29.00 (3-12-675421-X, Pub. by Klett Edition) Intl Bk Import.
— Hoeren - Brummen - Sprechen: Angewandte Phonetik im Unterricht Deutsch als Fremdsprache: Begleitheft. (GER.). 38p. (C). 1992. pap. text 13.75 (3-12-675351-5, Pub. by Klett Edition) Intl Bk Import.
Mueller, H. & Weber, W., eds. Familial Cancer. (Illus.). xx, 292p. 1985. 161.00 (3-8055-4245-3) S Karger.
Mueller, H., jt. ed. see Yaksh, Tony L.
Mueller, H. Gustav & Geoffery, Virgina C., eds. Communication Disorders in Aging: Assessment & Management. fac. ed. LC 87-21084. (Illus.). 528p. 1994. pap. 163.70 (0-7837-7687-X, 204744100007) Bks Demand.
Mueller, H. Gustav & Hall, James W., III. Audiologists' Desk Reference Vol. 2: Singular, Vol. 2. (Illus.). 850p. 1998. pap. 79.95 (1-56593-711-2, 1398) Thomson Learn.
Mueller, H. Gustav & Hampton, Dennis. Programmable Hearing Aids: The Art & Science. 1997. 38.00 incl. audio (1-58041-009-X, 0112074) Am Speech Lang Hearing.
Mueller, H. Gustav, et al. Probe Microphone Measurements: Hearing Aid Selection & Assessment. (Illus.). 256p. (C). 1992. pap. 65.00 (1-879105-68-3, 0323) Thomson Learn.
Mueller, H. Gustav, jt. auth. see Hall, James W., III.
Mueller, H. N., III, jt. ed. see Steffens, Henry J.
Mueller, Hans M. Homiletik. (GER.). xvii, 442p. (C). 1995. 67.70 (3-11-013186-2) De Gruyter.
Mueller, Hans-Peter, ed. Bibel und Alter Orient: Altorientische Beitrage zum Alten Testament von Wolfram von Soden. (Beiheft zur Zeitschrift fuer die Alttestamentliche Wissenschaft Ser.: Band 162). xii, 224p. 1985. 92.35 (3-11-010091-6) De Gruyter.
Mueller, Hans R. Schulkinder unter Stress: Theoretische Ueberlegungen zum Stressmodell. Ritzel, G., ed. (Sozialmedizinische und Paedagogische Jugendkunde Ser.: Band 12). 140p. 1976. 21.00 (3-8055-2299-1) S Karger.
Mueller-Harvey, Irene, jt. ed. see Caygill, John C.
Mueller, Heiner. Germania. Lotringer, Sylvere, ed. Schutze, Bernard & Schutze, Carolind, trs. from GER. (Foreign Agents Ser.). 256p. (Orig.). (C). 1990. pap. text 6.00 (0-936756-63-2) Autonomedia.
Mueller, Heinz P., et al, eds. Law Librarianship: A Handbook, 2 vols. No. 19. 1983. write for info. (0-318-57950-2); write for info. (0-318-57951-0) W S Hein.
— Law Librarianship: A Handbook, 2 vols., Set. (AALL Publications Ser.: No. 19). 1983. 95.00 (0-8377-0116-3, Rothman) W S Hein.
Mueller, Helga. Hydrocarbons in the Freshwater Environment: A Literature Review. (Advances in Limnology Ser.: Vol. 24). (GER., Illus.). 69p. 1987. pap. text 25.00 (3-510-47022-2, Pub. by E Schweizerbartsche) Balogh.
Mueller, Henry R. Whig Party in Pennsylvania. LC 74-82233. (Columbia University. Studies in the Social Sciences: No. 230). reprint ed. 27.50 (0-404-51230-5) AMS Pr.

M

Mueller, Herbert C. Learning to Teach Through Playing: A Brass Method. (Illus.). 163p. 1991. pap. 27.50 (*1-56516-005-3*) H Leonard.

Mueller, Hilbert F. How to Cultivate Common Sense. rev. ed. LC 80-82006. (Illus.). 240p. 1980. pap. 5.00 (*0-937342-00-9*) Hawk-Island.

Mueller-Hill, Benno. Murderous Science: Elimination by Scientific Selection of Jews, Gypsies, & Others in Germany, 1933-1945. Fraser, George R., tr. from GER. LC 97-40085. (Illus.). 200p. (C). 1997. pap. 29.00 (*0-87969-531-5*) Cold Spring Harbor.

Mueller-Hillebrand, Burkhart H. German Tank Maintenance in World War II. (Center for Military History Publication German Report Series, DA Pam: No. 104-7). 50p. 1987. reprint ed. pap. 2.00 (*0-16-001965-6*, S/N 008-029-001) USGPO.

— German Tank Maintenance in World War II: An Historical Study. (Illus.), 44p. (Orig.). (C). 1994. pap. text 25.00 (*0-7881-1169-8*) DIANE Pub.

Mueller, Horst, jt. ed. see Claussen, Bernhard.

Mueller, Howard E. AIDS: A Christian Response. LC 96-173150. (Master's Touch Bible Study Ser.). 1996. pap. 4.50 (*0-570-09552-2*, 20-2593) Concordia.

Mueller, Hugo. Deutsch Bk. 1, Pt. 2: Intermediate German Lessons for Advanced Beginners, 2 vols. (ENG & GER.). 350p. 1967. 12.50 (*0-87559-207-4*) Shalom.

— Deutsch Bk. 3: Intermediate German Lessons for Advanced Beginners, 2 vols. (ENG & GER.). 246p. 1967. 12.50 (*0-87559-208-2*) Shalom.

Mueller, I. I., et al, eds. Global & Regional Geodynamics. (International Association of Geodesy Symposia Ser.: Vol. 101). xii, 349p. 1990. 94.95 (*0-387-97265-X*) Spr-Verlag.

— Sea Surface Topography & the Geoid. (International Association of Geodesy Symposia Ser.: Vol. 104). x, 187p. 1990. 79.95 (*0-387-97268-4*) Spr-Verlag.

Mueller, I. I. & Zerbini, S., eds. The Interdisciplinary Role of Space Geodesy. (Lecture Notes in Earth Sciences Ser.: Vol. 22). xv, 300p. 1989. 47.95 (*0-387-51161-X*) Spr-Verlag.

Mueller, I. I., jt. ed. see Colombo, Oscar.

Mueller, Ian. Philosophy of Mathematics & Deductive Structure in Euclid's "Elements" (Illus.). 400p. (C). 1981. 55.00 (*0-262-13163-3*) MIT Pr.

Mueller, Ian, tr. see Alexander of Aphrodisias.

Mueller, Ilze, tr. see Reinig, Christa.

***Mueller, Irene Kellar.** This & That, Pt. II. LC 99-96904. 176p. 1999. pap. 10.95 (*0-9668980-1-X*) Connection Pubns.

Mueller, Iris W. John Stuart Mill & French Thought. LC 68-58805. (Essay Index Reprint Ser.). 1977. 20.95 (*0-8369-0089-8*) Ayer.

Mueller, Ivan I. Introduction to Satellite Geodesy. LC 64-15693. (Illus.). 437p. reprint ed. pap. 135.50 (*0-608-30522-7*, 205127200093) Bks Demand.

Mueller, Ivan I. & Kolaczek, Barbara, eds. Developments in Astrometry & Their Impact on Astrophysics & Geodynamics: Proceedings of the 156th Symposium of the International Astronomical Union Held in Shanghai, China, September 15-19, 1992. LC 93-16750. 1993. lib. bdg. 163.00 (*0-7923-2237-1*) Kluwer Academic.

Mueller, Ivan J., ed. see Wycliffe, John.

Mueller, J., ed. Neurology & Psychiatry: A Meeting of Minds. (Illus.). xiv, 290p. 1989. 195.00 (*3-8055-4712-9*) S Karger.

Mueller, J. J. What Are They Saying about Theological Method? LC 84-61031. (What Are They Saying about...Ser.). 88p. (Orig.). 1985. pap. 5.95 (*0-8091-2657-5*) Paulist Pr.

Mueller, J. T., tr. see Walther, Carl F.

Mueller, J. Theodore, tr. see Luther, Martin.

Mueller, James R. The Five Fragments of the Apocryphon of Ezekiel: A Critical Study. LC 95-137360. (Journal for the Study of the Pseudepigrapha Supplement Ser.: No. 5). 196p. 1994. 57.50 (*1-85075-195-1*, Pub. by Sheffield Acad) CUP Services.

Mueller, James W. The Use of Sampling in Archaeological Survey. (Memoir Ser.: No. 28). 104p. 1974. 6.00 (*0-932839-07-X*) Soc Am Arch.

Mueller, James W., ed. Sampling in Archaeology. LC 74-26372. 300p. (C). 1975. pap. 18.95 (*0-8165-0482-2*) U of Ariz Pr.

Mueller, Janel. The Native Tongue & the Word: Developments in English Prose Style, 1380-1580. LC 83-15817. 512p. 1994. 27.50 (*0-226-54562-8*) U Ch Pr.

Mueller, Janel M., ed. see Donne, John.

Mueller, Jerome F. Plumbing Design & Installation Details. 1987. text 55.00 (*0-07-043963-X*) McGraw.

Mueller, Jerome F., jt. auth. see Hicks, Tyler Gregory.

Mueller, Jim. All the Presidents' Dogs. LC 95-94982. (Illus.). 112p. (Orig.). 1995. pap. 11.95 (*0-9645724-0-0*) Mueller Pub.

Mueller, Joan. Faithful Listening: Discernment in Everyday Life. 140p. (Orig.). 1996. pap. 14.95 (*1-55612-900-9*, LL1900) Sheed & Ward WI.

***Mueller, Joan.** Francis: A Novel. 272p. 2000. 21.95 (*0-88347-448-4*, Pub. by T More); pap. 17.95 (*0-88347-456-5*, Pub. by T More) BookWorld.

Mueller, Johannes. Enzymatische Regulation des Fruchtkoerperwachstums Bei Basidiomyceten: Entwicklung eines Modells Am Beispiel des Pleurotus Ostreatus (Jacq. Ex Fr.) Kummer. (Bibliotheca Mycologica: Vol. 106). (GER., Illus.). 186p. 1986. 48.00 (*3-443-59007-1*, Pub. by Gebruder Borntraeger) Balogh.

***Mueller, John.** Capitalism, Democracy & Ralph's Pretty Good Grocery. LC 99-17412. 1999. 29.95 (*0-691-00114-6*, Pub. by Princeton U Pr) Cal Prin Full Svc.

Mueller, John. Clipper Programmer's Guide. 1990. pap. 24.95 (*0-672-22734-7*, MICHIE) LEXIS Pub.

***Mueller, John.** COM+ Developer's Guide. (Professional's Developers Library). (Illus.). 2000. pap. 44.99 (*0-07-212086-X*) Osborne-McGraw.

— Complete Guide to Windows 2000 Server. (Peter Norton (Sams) Ser.). 800p. 2000. pap. 39.99 (*0-672-31777-X*) Sams.

— Netware 5 All-In-One CNA/CNE Certification Exam Guide. LC 99-38180. 1999. pap. 99.99 (*0-07-134778-X*) Osborne-McGraw.

Mueller, John. Oink: Heaven's Butcher. LC 96-36760. (Illus.). 112p. 1996. pap. 19.95 (*0-87816-529-0*) Kitchen Sink.

— Oink: Heaven's Butcher Collection. Garnier, Catherine, ed. LC 96-36760. (Illus.). 112p. 1998. 27.95 (*0-87816-531-2*) Kitchen Sink.

— Policy & Opinion in the Gulf War. LC 93-21226. 398p. 1994. pap. text 19.95 (*0-226-54565-2*) U Ch Pr.

— Policy & Opinion in the Gulf War. LC 93-21226. 398p. 1994. lib. bdg. 55.00 (*0-226-54564-4*) U Ch Pr.

— The Ultimate DOS Programmer's Manual. 2nd ed. 1993. 40.00 (*0-07-043965-6*) McGraw.

— The Ultimate DOS Programmer's Manual. 2nd ed. (Illus.). 880p. 1993. text 40.00 (*0-8306-4114-9*, 4221, Windcrest) TAB Bks.

Mueller, John & Wang, Wallace. Microsoft Macro 5.1. 1991. 24.95 (*0-8306-8691-6*) McGraw-Hill Prof.

— Ultimate DOS Programmers Manual. 1991. 29.95 (*0-8306-6752-0*); 29.95 (*0-8306-6753-9*) McGraw-Hill Prof.

Mueller, John & Williams, Robert. Novell Certification Handbook. 2nd ed. LC 96-5711. (Illus.). 1996. pap. 24.95 (*0-07-044365-3*) McGraw.

Mueller, John & Williams, Robert A. Novell Certification Handbook. 2nd ed. 1996. pap. write for info. (*0-07-044265-7*) McGraw.

Mueller, John, jt. auth. see Norton, Peter.

Mueller, John, jt. auth. see Peter Norton Computing Group Staff.

Mueller, John A., jt. auth. see Thomann, Robert V.

***Mueller, John E.** Peace, Prosperity & Politics. LC 99-46218. (Political Economy of Global Interdependence Ser.). 1999. 75.00 (*0-8133-6761-1*) Westview.

Mueller, John H. The American Symphony Orchestra: A Social History of Musical Taste. LC 76-8875. (Illus.). 437p. 1976. reprint ed. lib. bdg. 79.50 (*0-8371-8915-2*, MUAS, Greenwood Pr) Greenwood.

Mueller, John P. ActiveX from the Ground Up. LC 97-124844. 608p. 1996. pap. text 29.99 (*0-07-882264-5*) Osborne-McGraw.

— Visual C++ from the Ground Up. LC 97-184750. 1997. pap., pap. text 34.99 (*0-07-882307-2*) Osborne-McGraw.

Mueller, John P. & Gatlin, Anthony. The Complete Microsoft Certification Success Guide. 2nd ed. LC 97-3990. (Illus.). 283p. 1997. pap. text 39.95 incl. cd-rom (*0-07-913201-4*) McGraw.

Mueller, John Paul. Visual C++ 6 from the Ground Up. 2nd ed. LC 98-218282. (Illus.). 718p. 1998. pap. 34.99 (*0-07-882506-7*) Osborne-McGraw.

— Visual Studio 6: The Complete Reference. LC 99-201311. (The Complete Reference Ser.). 1008p. 1999. pap. text 49.99 (*0-07-882583-0*) Osborne-McGraw.

Mueller, John Paul & Williams, Robert A. CNA/CNE Study Guide. LC 97-26275. (Illus.). 900p. 1997. 59.95 (*0-07-913619-2*) McGraw.

Mueller, John Paul, jt. auth. see Sheldon, Thomas.

Mueller, John T. Great Missionaries to China. LC 73-38329. (Biography Index Reprint Ser.). 1977. reprint ed. 15.95 (*0-8369-8124-3*) Ayer.

— Great Missionaries to the Orient. LC 78-38330. (Biography Index Reprint Ser.). 1977. reprint ed. 18.95 (*0-8369-8125-1*) Ayer.

Mueller, John T., tr. see Pieper, Francis.

Mueller-Joseph, Laura & Petersen, Marie. Dental Hygiene Process: Diagnosis & Care Planning. LC 94-32214. 192p. (C). 1995. pap. 44.95 (*0-8273-5678-1*) Delmar.

Mueller, Joseph N. Guadalcanal 1942. (Campaign Ser.: No. 18). (Illus.). 96p. pap. 14.95 (*1-85532-253-6*, 9517, Pub. by Osprey) Stackpole.

***Mueller, Joseph N.** Guadalcanal 1942, Vol. 18. 1999. pap. text 17.95 (*1-85532-916-6*) Osprey.

Mueller, Juergen. Pieter Bruegel: Dutch Proverbs. (Illus.). 96p. 1999. pap. 9.99 (*3-8228-7057-9*) Taschen Amer.

***Mueller, Julie.** 101 Bodice Designs: Dress Ideas for Women, Children & Dolls. (Illus.). 53p. 1998. pap. 20.00 (*1-929867-00-X*) Acorn IL.

Mueller, K. A. & Benedek, G. Phase Separation in Cuprate Superconductors: Proceedings of the 3rd Workshop. 392p. 1993. text 109.00 (*981-02-1274-7*) World Scientific Pub.

Mueller, K. A. & Thomas, H., eds. Structural Phase Transitions, Vol. I. (Topics in Current Physics Ser.: Vol. 23). (Illus.). 190p. 1981. 44.95 (*0-387-10329-5*) Spr-Verlag.

Mueller, Karen. Beating Bully O'Brien. (J). (gr. 3-7). 1991. pap. 2.95 (*0-380-75935-7*, Avon Bks) Morrow Avon.

***Mueller, Karen.** Celtic Autoharp. 56p. 1999. pap. 19.95 incl. audio compact disk (*0-7866-0853-6*, 95529BCD) Mel Bay.

***Mueller, Karin Price.** Online Money Management. 336p. 2001. pap. 19.99 (*0-7356-1111-4*) Microsoft.

Mueller, Karl. Die Lebermoose Europas. 3rd ed. Herzog, T., ed. (Rabenhorst's Kryptogamenflora Ser.: No. 6/1). (GER., Illus.). 1365p. 1990. reprint ed. text 299.00 (*81-211-0049-6*, Pub. by Mahendra Pal Singh) Lubrecht & Cramer.

Mueller, Kate, ed. see McLure, John.

Mueller, Kate, jt. ed. see Mochizuki, Kiichi.

Mueller, Kate, ed. see Neary, Daniel A.

Mueller, Katherine, ed. see Mochizuki, Kiichi.

Mueller, Kimberly J. The Nuclear Power Issue: A Guide to Who's Doing What in the U. S. & Abroad. LC 79-52430. (Who's Doing What Ser.: No. 8). (Illus.). 106p. (Orig.). 1981. pap. 25.00 (*0-912102-44-6*) Cal Inst Public.

Mueller-Krumbhar, H., jt. ed. see Chernov, A. A.

Mueller, L., ed. Rock Mechanics. (CISM International Centre for Mechanical Sciences Ser.: Vol. 165). (Illus.). 390p. 1982. 65.95 (*0-387-81301-2*) Spr-Verlag.

Mueller, L., et al. The Coins of Alexander the Great. (Illus.). 173p. 1981. pap. 20.00 (*0-89005-382-0*) Ares.

Mueller, L. W., ed. Modern Day Poets & Authors. LC 77-81769. 1977. 6.50 (*0-8187-0029-7*) Harlo Press.

Mueller, Larry. Speed Train Your Own Bird Dog. LC 89-39933. (Illus.). 256p. (Orig.). 1990. pap. 19.95 (*0-8117-2304-6*) Stackpole.

— Speed Train Your Own Retriever: The Quick, Efficient, Proven System for Training a Finished Dog. LC 86-23109. (Illus.). 192p. (Orig.). 1987. pap. 19.95 (*0-8117-2201-5*) Stackpole.

Mueller, Laura M. Collector's Encyclopedia of Compacts: Carryalls & Face Powder Boxes. 1996. 24.95 (*0-89145-562-0*, 3722) Collector Bks.

— Collector's Encyclopedia of Compacts Vol. II: Carryalls & Face Powder Boxes, Identification & Values. (Collector's Encyclopedia Ser.). (Illus.). 344p. 1997. 24.95 (*0-89145-766-6*, 4854) Collector Bks.

***Mueller, Laurence D.** Stability in Model Populations. LC 00-38493. (Monographs in Population Biology: Vol. 31). (Illus.). 336p. 2000. 79.50 (*0-691-00732-2*) Princeton U Pr.

***Mueller, Laurence D. & Joshi, Amitabh.** Stability in Model Populations. LC 00-38493. (Monographs in Population Biology: Vol. 31). (Illus.). 336p. 2000. pap. 29.95 (*0-691-00733-0*) Princeton U Pr.

Mueller-Lauter, Wolfgang. Dostoevskijs Ideendialektik. 66p. (C). 1974. 11.55 (*3-11-005731-X*) De Gruyter.

Mueller-Lauter, Wolfgang & Pestalozzi, Karl, eds. Nietzsche Werke: Kritische Gesamtausgabe. (GER.). xvii, 1704p. (C). 1996. lib. bdg. 453.60 (*3-11-007774-4*) De Gruyter.

— Nietzsche Werke Two, Bd. 2-3: Kritische Gesamtausgabe, Bd. 2-3. (GER.). xii, 446p. (C). 1992. lib. bdg. 153.85 (*3-11-009922-5*); lib. bdg. 149.25 (*3-11-013915-4*) De Gruyter.

Mueller, Lavonne. Breaking the Prairie Wolf Code. 1986. pap. 5.25 (*0-8222-0148-8*) Dramatists Play.

— Little Victories. 1984. pap. 5.25 (*0-8222-0680-3*) Dramatists Play.

— The Mothers. LC 97-28472. 72p. 1997. write for info. (*1-55783-328-1*) Applause Theatre Bk Pubs.

Mueller, Lavonne, ed. Baseball Monologues. LC 96-14325. 160p. 1996. pap. 11.95 (*0-435-07021-5*) Heinemann.

— Monologues from the Road. LC 99-28940. (Orig.). 1999. pap. 12.95 (*0-325-00124-3*) Heinemann.

Mueller, Lavonne & Reynolds, Jerry D. Creative Writing: Forms & Techniques. 1990. pap., teacher ed. 12.66 (*0-8442-5366-9*) NTC Contemp Pub Co.

— Creative Writing: Forms & Techniques. (Illus.). 256p. 1994. pap. 14.95 (*0-8442-5365-0*, 53650, Natl Textbk Co) NTC Contemp Pub Co.

Mueller, Lavonne & Reynolds, Jerry D. Creative Writing: Forms & Techniques. (Illus.). 256p. 1995. 27.44 (*0-8442-5379-0*, 53790, Natl Textbk Co) NTC Contemp Pub Co.

Mueller, Lisel. Alive Together: New & Selected Poems. LC 96-23399. 232p. 1996. 24.95 (*0-8071-2127-4*); pap. 17.95 (*0-8071-2128-2*) La State U Pr.

— Dependencies. LC 97-46684. 64p. 1998. pap. 11.95 (*0-8071-2275-0*) La State U Pr.

— Learning to Play by Ear. (W.N.J. Ser.: No. 26). (Illus.). 80p. (Orig.). 1990. pap. 12.00 (*1-55780-138-X*) Juniper Pr ME.

— The Need to Hold Still: Poems. LC 79-20965. xii, 68p. 1980. pap. 12.95 (*0-8071-0670-4*) La State U Pr.

— The Private Life: Poems. LC 75-5350. 64p. 1976. pap. 11.95 (*0-8071-0171-0*) La State U Pr.

— Second Language. Poems. LC 86-7246. 72p. 1986. pap. 12.95 (*0-8071-1337-9*) La State U Pr.

— Voices from the Forest. (W.N.J. Ser.: No. 7). 1977. pap. 8.00 (*1-55780-056-1*) Juniper Pr ME.

— Waving from Shore. LC 89-12144. 64p. 1989. pap. 11.95 (*0-8071-1576-2*); text 15.95 (*0-8071-1575-4*) La State U Pr.

Mueller, Lisel, et al. Primavera IV. Heller, Janet R. et al, eds. LC 76-647540. (Illus.). (C). 1978. pap. 4.00 (*0-916980-04-9*) Primavera.

Mueller, Lisel, tr. see Kaschnitz, Marie L.

Mueller, Lisel, tr. see Kaschnitz, Mary L.

Mueller, Lothar W. How to Publish Your Own Book. LC 75-12222. (Illus.). 184p. 1976. 7.95 (*0-8187-0019-X*); pap. 5.95 (*0-8187-0017-3*) Harlo Press.

Mueller, Lothar W., ed. Harlo's Anthology of Modern-Day Poets & Authors - 1972. LC 72-95005. 128p. 1973. 6.00 (*0-8187-0010-6*) Harlo Press.

— Harlo's Anthology of Modern-Day Poets & Authors 1974. LC 74-27876. 152p. 1974. 6.00 (*0-8187-0016-5*) Harlo Press.

Mueller, Louise, ed. see Bunkowske, Bernice.

Mueller, Lovonne. Elvis Monologues. LC 97-24665. 1997. pap. 12.95 (*0-435-07044-4*) Heinemann.

Mueller, Lucian. De Re Metrica Poetarum Latinorum Praeter Plautum et Terentium, Libri VII. (GER.). xiv, 651p. 1967. reprint ed. write for info. incl. 3.5 hd (*0-318-70573-7*) G Olms Pubs.

— De Re Metrica Poetarum Latinorum Praeter Plautum et Terentium Libri VII. xiv, 651p. 1967. reprint ed. write for info. incl. 3.5 hd (*0-318-71182-6*) G Olms Pubs.

Mueller-Lutz, H. L. Diccionario de Seguros. (ENG, FRE, GER & SPA.). 282p. 1977. pap. 15.75 (*0-7859-0901-X*, S-50035) Fr & Eur.

Mueller-Lyer, Franz C. The Evolution of Modern Marriage: A Sociology of Sexual Relations. LC 72-11292. reprint ed. 37.50 (*0-404-57484-X*) AMS Pr.

Mueller, Lynne, jt. auth. see Mueller, Gene.

Mueller, M. Let's Color Korea: Traditional Games. 24p. (J). (gr. k-3). 1989. pap. 10.95 (*0-930878-95-7*) Hollym Intl.

Mueller, M. E., et al. Manual of Internal Fixation. 2nd rev. ed. LC 78-20743. (Illus.). 1979. 230.00 (*3-540-92113-3*) Spr-Verlag.

Mueller, Magda, jt. ed. see Herminghouse, Patricia A.

Mueller, Magda, jt. ed. see Herminghouse, Patricia.

***Mueller, Marge.** Essential San Juan Islands Guide. 3rd ed. (Illus.). 2000. pap. 14.95 (*1-881409-28-7*) Jhnstn Assocs.

Mueller, Marge. Washington State Parks: A Complete Recreation Guide. 2nd ed. LC 99-6431. 250p. 1999. pap. 16.95 (*0-89886-642-1*) Mountaineers.

***Mueller, Marge & Mueller, Ted.** British Columbia's Gulf Islands: Afoot & Afloat. (Afoot & Afloat Ser.). (Illus.). 272p. 2000. pap. 16.95 (*0-89886-612-X*) Mountaineers.

Mueller, Marge & Mueller, Ted. The Essential San Juan Islands Guide. 2nd ed. LC 96-14422. (Illus.). 288p. (Orig.). 1996. reprint ed. pap. 14.95 (*1-881409-15-5*) Jhnstn Assocs.

— Exploring Washington's Wild Areas: A Guide for Hikers, Backpackers, Climbers, XC Skiers, & Paddlers. (Illus.). 356p. 1994. pap. 16.95 (*0-89886-351-1*) Mountaineers.

— Fire, Faults & Floods: A Road & Trail Guide Exploring the Origins of the Columbia River Basin. LC 96-46352. (Northwest Naturalist Bks.). 1997. pap. 19.95 (*0-89301-206-8*) U of Idaho Pr.

— Guide to Washington's South Cascades' Volcanic Landscapes. (Illus.). 224p. 1995. pap. 12.95 (*0-89886-445-3*) Mountaineers.

— Middle Puget Sound & Hood Canal: Afoot & Afloat. 2nd rev. ed. LC 96-40917. (Afoot & Afloat Ser.). (Illus.), 224p. (Orig.). 1997. pap. 14.95 (*0-89886-498-4*) Mountaineers.

— North Puget Sound: Afoot & Afloat. 2nd rev. ed. (Afoot & Afloat Ser.). (Illus.). 224p. 1995. pap. 14.95 (*0-89886-435-6*) Mountaineers.

— The San Juan Islands Afoot & Afloat. 3rd ed. LC 94-44878. 224p. 1995. pap. 14.95 (*0-89886-434-8*) Mountaineers.

— Seattle's Lakes, Bays, & Waterways, Afoot & Afloat: Including the Eastside. LC 98-12172. (Afoot & Afloat Ser.). (Illus.). 224p. 1998. pap. 14.95 (*0-89886-553-0*) Mountaineers.

— South Puget Sound, Afoot & Afloat. 3rd ed. LC 95-46945. 224p. 1996. pap. 14.95 (*0-89886-465-8*) Mountaineers.

Mueller, Marge, jt. auth. see Diamond, Lynnell.

Mueller, Mark, ed. Mr. Moon & Miss Sun/The Herdsman & the Weaver. (Korean Folk Tales for Children Ser.: Vol. 2). (Illus.). 45p. (J). (gr. 2-5). 1990. lib. bdg. 10.95 (*0-930878-72-8*) Hollym Intl.

— The Woodcutter & the Heavenly Maiden/The Fire Dogs. (Korean Folk Tales for Children Ser.: Vol. 1.). (Illus.). 45p. (J). (gr. 2-5). 1990. lib. bdg. 10.95 (*0-930878-71-X*) Hollym Intl.

Mueller, Mark, jt. auth. see Vorhees, Duance.

Mueller, Marlies. Les Idees Politiques dans le Roman Heroique de 1630 a 1670. LC 84-81405. (Harvard Studies in Romance Languages: No. 40). 219p. 1984. pap. 15.00 (*0-940940-40-X*) Harvard U Romance Lang & Lit.

Mueller, Marnie. The Climate of the Country: A Novel. LC 94-2426. 318p. 1994. 19.95 (*1-880684-16-0*, Pub. by Curbstone) Consort Bk Sales.

— The Climate of the Country: A Novel. LC 98-24112. 308p. 1999. 24.95 (*1-880684-58-6*) Curbstone.

— Green Fires: Assault on Eden: A Novel of the Ecuadorian Rainforest. 318p. 1999. pap. 13.95 (*1-880684-59-4*, Pub. by Curbstone) Consort Bk Sales.

Mueller, Martin. Children of Oedipus & Other Essays on the Imitation of Greek Tragedy, 1550-1800. LC 79-26018. 296p. reprint ed. pap. 91.80 (*0-8357-8068-6*, 203407000088) Bks Demand.

— The Iliad. (Unwin Critical Library). 192p. (C). 1986. pap. text 10.95 (*0-04-800087-6*) Routledge.

Mueller, Martin, et al, eds. The Science of Biological Specimen Preparation for Microscopy & Microanalysis, 1985. (Proceedings of the Pfefferkorn Conference Ser.: No. 4). (Illus.). xii, 308p. 1986. text 46.00 (*0-931288-37-1*) Scanning Microscopy.

Mueller, Mary K. Taking Care of Me: The Habits of Happiness. 186p. (Orig.). 1997. pap. 12.95 (*0-9654372-0-5*) Insight Inc.

Mueller, Mary M., tr. see Caesarius of Arles, Saint.

Mueller, Melinda. Apocrypha. 34p. 1998. pap. 11.95 (*0-9652272-4-3*) Grey Spider.

Mueller, Michael. Motor City Muscle: High-Powered History of the American Muscle Car. LC 97-10100. (Illus.). 192p. 1997. 29.95 (*0-7603-0196-4*) MBI Pubg.

— The Sinner's Return to God: or The Prodigal Son. LC 82-74244. 224p. 1993. reprint ed. pap. 11.00 (*0-89555-205-1*) TAN Bks Pubs.

Mueller, Michael A., jt. auth. see Key, Timothy J.

Mueller, Mike. The American Pickup Truck. LC 99-11567. (Illus.). 160p. 1999. 29.95 (*0-7603-0473-4*) MBI Pubg.

— Chevelle 1964-1972. LC 93-13164. (Muscle Car Color History Ser.). (Illus.). 128p. 1993. pap. 21.95 (*0-87938-761-0*) MBI Pubg.

— Chevy 55-56-57. LC 93-17024. (Enthusiast Color Ser.). (Illus.). 96p. 1993. 13.95 (*0-87938-816-1*) MBI Pubg.

— Chevy Muscle Cars. (Enthusiast Color Ser.). (Illus.). 96p. 1994. pap. 13.95 (*0-87938-864-1*) MBI Pubg.

— Chrysler Muscle Cars. LC 93-13064. (Enthusiast Color Ser.). (Illus.). 96p. 1993. pap. 13.95 (*0-87938-817-X*) MBI Pubg.

— Classic Pickups of the 1950s. LC 99-28953. (Enthusiast Color Ser.). (Illus.). 96p. 1999. pap. 13.95 (*0-7603-0586-2*, Pub. by MBI Pubg) Motorbooks Intl.

An Asterisk (*) at the beginning of an entry indicates that the title is appearing for the first time.

— Corvette C5. LC 98-16421. (Color Tech Ser.). (Illus.). 128p. 1998. pap. text 17.95 (*0-7603-0457-2*) Motorbooks Intl.
— Corvette Milestones. LC 95-50570. (Enthusiast Color Ser.). (Illus.). 96p. 1996. pap. 13.95 (*0-7603-0095-X*) MBI Pubg.
***Mueller, Mike.** Corvette 1968-1982. LC 99-86043. (Sports Car Color History Ser.). 128p. 2000. pap. text 21.95 (*0-7603-0418-1*, 128961AP, Pub. by MBI Pubg) Motorbooks Intl.
Mueller, Mike. Corvette Sting Ray 1963-1967: The Glory Years of America's Sports Car. LC 94-26707. (Muscle Car Color History Ser.). (Illus.). 128p. 1994. pap. 21.95 (*0-87938-788-2*) MBI Pubg.
— Corvette, 1953-1962. LC 96-720. (Sports Car Color History Ser.). (Illus.). 128p. 1996. pap. 21.95 (*0-7603-0041-0*) MBI Pubg.
— Fifties American Cars. (Enthusiast Color Ser.). (Illus.). 96p. 1994. pap. 13.95 (*0-87938-924-9*) MBI Pubg.
— Fifties Muscle: The Dawn of High Performance. (Illus.). 128p. 1996. pap. 19.95 (*0-7603-0006-2*) MBI Pubg.
— Ford Muscle Cars. LC 93-13063. (Enthusiast Color Ser.). (Illus.). 96p. 1993. pap. 13.95 (*0-87938-815-3*) MBI Pubg.
— Ford Mustang. (Enthusiast Color Ser.). (Illus.). 96p. 1995. pap. 13.95 (*0-87938-990-7*) MBI Pubg.
— Illustrated Chevelle Buyer's Guide. (Illustrated Buyer's Guide Ser.). (Illus.). 160p. 1995. pap. 17.95 (*0-7603-0075-5*) MBI Pubg.
***Mueller, Mike.** Mustang, 1964-1/2-1973. (Illus.). 156p. 2000. 29.95 (*0-7603-0734-2*, 130124AP, Pub. by MBI Pubg) Motorbooks Intl.
Mueller, Mike. Pontiac Muscle Cars. (Enthusiast Color Ser.). (Illus.). 96p. 1994. pap. 13.95 (*0-87938-863-3*) MBI Pubg.
— Thunderbird Milestones. LC 98-31988. (Enthusiast Color Ser.). (Illus.). 96p. 1999. pap. 13.95 (*0-7603-0474-2*) MBI Pubg.
Mueller, Mike, jt. auth. see Brownell, Tom.
Mueller, Mike, jt. auth. see Bunn, Don.
Mueller, Mike, jt. auth. see Herd, Paul A.
Mueller, Mike, jt. auth. see Young, Anthony.
Mueller, Milton. Universal Service: Competition, Interconnection & Monopoly in the Making of the American Telephone System. LC 96-35151. (AEI Studies in Telecommunications Deregulation). (Illus.). 170p. 1996. 42.00 (*0-262-13327-X*) MIT Pr.
Mueller, Milton & Tan, Zixiang. China in the Information Age: Telecommunications & the Dilemmas of Reform, 169. LC 96-38365. (Washington Papers). 184p. 1996. 55.00 (*0-275-95828-0*, Praeger Pubs) Greenwood.
Mueller, Milton & Zixiang Tan. China in the Information Age: Telecommunications & the Dilemmas of Reform, 169. LC 96-38365. (Washington Papers). 184p. 1996. pap. 16.95 (*0-275-95829-9*, Praeger Pubs) Greenwood.
Mueller, Milton L. Telephone Companies in Paradise: A Case Study in Telecommunications Deregulation. 250p. (C). 1993. text 44.95 (*1-56000-103-8*) Transaction Pubs.
Mueller, Mokika. This Infinite Fraternity of Feeling: Gender, Genre & Homoerotic Crisis in Hawthorne's The Blithedale Romance & Melville's Pierre. LC 96-4204. 232p. 1996. 37.50 (*0-8386-3650-0*) Fairleigh Dickinson.
Mueller, Nancy. QuarkXPress 4.04 Made Easy. LC 99-13250. 314p. 1999. 34.95 incl. cd-rom (*1-881795-16-0*) Bellwether-Cross.
***Mueller, Nancy.** Work Worldwide: International Career Strategies for the Adventurous Job Seeker. LC 99-57943. 240p. 2000. pap. 14.95 (*1-56261-490-8*) Avalon Travel.
Mueller-Nelson, Gertrud. Clip Art for Celebrations & Service. 188p. 1992. pap. 15.95 (*0-8146-6083-5*, Pueblo Bks) Liturgical Pr.
— Clip Art for Feasts & Seasons. expanded ed. 224p. 1992. pap. 15.95 (*0-8146-6041-X*, Pueblo Bks) Liturgical Pr.
Mueller, Oswald, ed. & tr. see Roemer, Ferdinand.
Mueller, P. C. & Schiehlen, W. O. Forced Linear Vibrations. (CISM International Center for Mechanical Sciences, Courses & Lectures Ser.: Vol. 172). (Illus.). 1979. 31.95 (*0-387-81487-6*) Spr-Verlag.
Mueller, P. Henry. Perspective on Credit Risk. LC 88-436. (Illus.). 76p. 1988. pap. 43.00 (*0-936742-48-8*, 34131) Robt Morris Assocs.
Mueller, P. S. Shrink Wrap: More Than 200 Seriously Ridiculous Cartoons. (Illus.). 126p. 1992. pap. 6.95 (*0-930753-12-7*) Spect Ln Pr.
— The Spread of Terror: Plus Lots of Cartoons We Could Have Put on the Cover but Didn't. 122p. 1986. pap. 5.95 (*0-933893-15-9*) Bonus Books.
Mueller, P. S., jt. auth. see Schreiner, Dave.
Mueller, Pamela B. The Bumpedy Road. (Illus.). 111p. (YA). (gr. 3 up). 1999. pap. write for info. (*0-9685097-0-3*) Pamela Mueller.
Mueller, Paul & Mueller, Sage. The North Carolina Employment Guide, 1993. 153p. 1992. pap. 34.95 (*1-881803-01-5*); disk 69.95 (*0-685-61600-2*) Career Res.
Mueller, Peter. Diccionario Rioduero: Literatura, Vol. 1. (SPA.). 304p. 1977. 14.95 (*0-8288-5360-6*, S50164) Fr & Eur.
— Lexikon der Datenverarbeitung. (GER.). 1968. 55.00 (*0-7859-0836-6*, M-7265) Fr & Eur.
Mueller, Peter, jt. auth. see Loebel.
Mueller, Peter E. In Walks Jesus. (New Life Bible Studies). 1998. pap. text 5.50 (*0-570-09685-5*, 20-2477) Concordia.
Mueller, Peter O. Wortbildung des Nuernberger Frueneuhochdeutsch Bd. 1: Substantiv-Derivation in den Schriften Albrecht Duerers. (GER.). xx, 532p. (C). 1993. lib. bdg. 200.00 (*3-11-012815-2*) De Gruyter.
Mueller, Phyllis, ed. see Davis, Ren & Davis, Helen.
Mueller, Phyllis, ed. see Massengale, Dee.
Mueller, Phyllis, ed. see Massie, Marian.
Mueller, Phyllis, ed. see Purdy, A. Jane.
Mueller, R. F. & Saxena, Surendra K. Chemical Petrology: With Applications to the Terrestinal Planets & Meteorites. LC 76-26049. (Illus.). 1977. 161.00 (*0-387-90196-5*) Spr-Verlag.
Mueller, Ralph & Turk, Jerry. Report after Action: The Story of the 103rd Infantry Division. (Divisional Ser.: No. 1). (Illus.). 166p. 1978. reprint ed. 39.95 (*0-89839-010-9*) Battery Pr.
Mueller, Ralph A. Der Un teilbare Geist: Modularismus und Holismus in der Kognitionsforschung. (Foundations of Communication & Cognition Ser.). (GER.). xix, 443p. (C). 1991. lib. bdg. 152.35 (*3-11-012916-7*, 250-91) De Gruyter.
Mueller, Ralph O. Basic Principles of Structural Equation Modeling: An Introduction to LISREL & EQS, Vol. XXVIII. Fienberg, S. & Olkin, Ingram, eds. LC 95-15043. (Texts in Statistics Ser.). (Illus.). 229p. 1995. 43.95 (*0-387-94516-4*) Spr-Verlag.
Mueller, Reinhold C. The Procuratori Di San Marco & the Ventian Credit Market: A Study of the Development of Credit & Banking in the Trecento. Bruchey, Stuart, ed. LC 77-77181. (Dissertations in European Economic History Ser.). 1978. lib. bdg. 40.95 (*0-405-10794-3*) Ayer.
— The Venetian Money Market: Banks, Panics, & the Public Debt, 1200-1500. LC 96-36921. (Illus.). 568p. 1997. text 65.00 (*0-8018-5437-7*) Johns Hopkins.
Mueller, Reinhold C., jt. auth. see Lane, Frederic C.
Mueller, Reinhold C., ed. see Lane, Frederic C.
Mueller, Richard. Ghostbusters. 256p. 1989. pap. 3.95 (*0-8125-0382-1*, Pub. by Tor Bks) St Martin.
Mueller, Richard J. Instructional Psychology: Principles & Practices. 294p. (C). 1992. pap. text 18.80 (*0-87563-397-8*) Stipes.
Mueller, Robert. Air Force Bases Vol. 1: Active Air Force Bases Within the United States on 17 September 1982. 1990. write for info. (*0-912799-53-6*) AFH & MP.
— For People Just Like Us. Sherer, Michael L., ed. (Orig.). 1986. pap. 4.50 (*0-89536-834-X*, 6848) CSS OH.
Mueller, Robert, jt. auth. see Carter, Kit C.
Mueller, Robert, jt. auth. see Mueller, Roseanna.
Mueller, Robert, jt. ed. see Carter, Kit C.
Mueller, Robert A. Automated Microcode Synthesis. Stone, Harold, ed. LC 83-24095. (Computer Science: Computer Architecture & Design Ser.: No. 1). 134p. 1984. reprint ed. pap. 41.60 (*0-8357-1498-5*, 207040900088) Bks Demand.
Mueller, Robert A. & Lundberg, Dag B. Manual of Drug Interactions for Anesthesiology. LC 88-20410. 384p. reprint ed. pap. 119.10 (*0-7837-2564-7*, 204272300006) Bks Demand.
Mueller, Robert A. & Page, Rex L. Symbolic Computing with LISP & Prolog. LC 88-23414. 469p. 1988. pap. 73.95 (*0-471-60771-1*) Wiley.
Mueller, Robert F. & Young, Ian D. Emery's Elements of Medical Genetics. 10th ed. LC 97-35527. 1998. write for info. (*0-443-05951-9*) Church.
Mueller, Robert F., et al. Emery's Elements of Medical Genetics. 10th ed. LC 97-35527. (C). 1998. pap. text. write for info. (*0-443-05902-0*) Church.
Mueller, Robert F., jt. auth. see Emery, Alan E.
Mueller, Robert G., ed. West Germany under Construction: Politics, Society, & Culture in the Adenauer Era. LC 96-38008. (Social History, Popular Culture, & Politics in Germany Ser.). 472p. (C). 1997. text 59.50 (*0-472-09648-6*, 09648); pap. text 26.95 (*0-472-06648-X*, 06648) U of Mich Pr.
Mueller, Robert J. Seven Tell Their Story. Sherer, Michael L., ed. (Orig.). 1988. pap. 4.25 (*1-55673-019-5*, 8803) CSS OH.
Mueller, Robert K. Anchoring Points for Corporate Directors: Obeying the Unenforceable. LC 96-2214. 192p. 1996. 57.95 (*1-56720-068-0*, Quorum Bks) Greenwood.
— The Director's & Officer's Guide to Advisory Boards. LC 89-32858. 289p. 1990. 69.50 (*0-89930-467-2*, MDJ/, Quorum Bks) Greenwood.
Mueller, Robery A. & Lundberg, Dag B. Manual of Drug Interactions for Anesthesiology. 3rd ed. LC 96-29164. 1996. pap. text 42.00 (*0-443-07764-9*) Church.
Mueller, Rolf R. Festival & Fiction in Heinrich Wittenwiler's "Ring" A Study of the Narrative in Its Relation to the Traditional Topoi of Marriage, Folly, & Play. (German Language & Literature Monographs: No 3). viii, 155p. 1977. 39.00 (*90-272-0963-4*) J Benjamins Pubng Co.
Mueller, Rosawitha. Valie Export - Fragments of the Imagination. LC 94-6589. (Women Artists in Film Ser.). 256p. 1995. pap. 24.95 (*0-253-20925-0*) Ind U Pr.
***Mueller, Roseanna & Mueller, Robert.** Lagrange & Lagrange Park. (Images of America Ser.). 128p. 1999. pap. 18.99 (*0-7385-0260-X*) Arcadia Publng.
Mueller, Roseanna, tr. see De Montemayor, Jorge.
Mueller, Rosemary. Feeling of War 1991. (Illus.). 32p. (Orig.). 1992. pap. 11.95 (*0-9632214-0-X*) Piper-Davies.
Mueller, Ross A. Upper Midwest Flies That Catch Trout & How to Fish Them. LC 95-95017. (Illus.). 128p. 1995. pap. 114.95 (*0-9648047-0-0*) R Mueller.
Mueller, Roswitha. Bertolt Brecht & the Theory of Media. LC 88-33805. (Modern German Culture & Literature Ser.). 163p. 1989. reprint ed. pap. 50.60 (*0-608-03486-X*, 206420100008) Bks Demand.
— Valie Export - Fragments of the Imagination. LC 94-6589. (Women Artists in Film Ser.). 256p. 1995. 49.95 (*0-253-33906-5*) Ind U Pr.
Mueller, Sage, jt. auth. see Mueller, Paul.
Mueller-Schwefe, Gerhard. William Shakespeare: Welt-Werk-Wirkung. (Sammlung Goeschen Ser.: Vol. 2208). (C). 1978. 15.85 (*3-11-007545-8*) De Gruyter.
***Mueller, Scott.** A+ Certification Study Guide: Upgrading & Repairing PCs. 400p. 1999. pap. text 19.99 (*0-7897-2095-7*) Que.
Mueller, Scott. Mueller's Official Puppy Owner Manual. (Orig.). pap. text 4.95 (*0-9637183-0-4*) Bridgept Pub.
— Ultimate A+ Certification Kit. 1998. pap. text 99.99 (*0-7357-0071-0*) New Riders Pub.
— Upgrading & Repairing PCs. 3rd ed. (Illus.). 1254p. 1993. 34.95 (*1-56529-467-X*) Que.
— Upgrading & Repairing PCs. 6th ed. LC 96-69951. 1464p. 1996. 49.99 (*0-7897-0825-6*) Que.
— Upgrading & Repairing PCs. 6th ed. 1996. 65.00 incl. cd-rom (*0-7897-1053-6*) Que.
— Upgrading & Repairing PCs. 8th ed. LC 97-68686. 1200p. 1997. 49.99 incl. cd-rom (*0-7897-1295-4*) Macmillan.
— Upgrading & Repairing PCs. 11th ed. LC 98-87630. (Illus.). 1628p. 1999. 59.99 (*0-7897-1903-7*) Que.
***Mueller, Scott.** Upgrading & Repairing Pcs: 10th Anniversary Academic Edition. 10th ed. 1531p. 2001. pap. write for info. (*1-58076-289-1*) Que Educ & Trng.
Mueller, Scott. Upgrading & Repairing PCs Quick Reference. 2nd ed. LC 98-84691. (Scott Mueller Library Ser.). 1998. pap. 19.99 (*0-7897-1669-0*) Que.
***Mueller, Scott.** Upgrading & Repairing PCs with CD-ROM. 12th ed. 1650p. 2000. 49.99 (*0-7897-2303-4*) Que.
Mueller, Scott. Upgrading & Repairing Pieces Reference Ed. Technician's Portable. 320p. 1999. pap. text 19.99 (*0-7897-2096-5*) Que.
Mueller, Scott & Micro House Staff. Micro House PC Hardware Library. LC 98-84620. (Scott Muller Library). 1998. write for info. (*0-7897-1665-8*) Que.
Mueller, Scott & Zacker, Craig. Upgrading & Repairing Personal Computers. 9th annot. ed. LC 98-84282. 1998. pap. text 54.99 (*0-7897-1636-4*, Prentice Hall) P-H.
Mueller, Scott, et al. Killer PC Utilities. (Illus.). 1300p. (Orig.). 1993. 39.95 (*1-56529-328-2*) Que.
Mueller, Scott, jt. auth. see Que Education & Training Staff.
Mueller-Seyfarth, Winfried H., ed. see Mainlaender, Philipp.
Mueller, Sherry L. Careers in International Education, Exchange & Development: Selected Resources. LC 99-24190. 1999. write for info. (*0-912207-81-7*) NAFSA Washington.
Mueller-Shore, Margaret. An Independent Study Guide to Anatomy & Physiology to Prepare for ACT - PEP Exams or Other Challenge Exams. 272p. (C). 1994. text. write for info. (*0-697-24692-2*, WCB McGr Hill) McGrw-H Hghr Educ.
Mueller, Siegfried. Elektrische und Dieselelektrische Triebfahrzeuge. (GER., Illus.). 204p. 1979. 52.95 (*0-8176-1033-2*) Birkhauser.
Mueller, Stephen & Polhill, Dennis. Stop That Train: RTD's Light Rail Boondoggle Is on a Fast Track for Disaster. (Issue Papers: No. 2-94). 13p. 1994. pap. text 8.00 (*1-57655-062-1*) Independ Inst.
— Stop That Train Pt. II: A Reply to RTD. (Issue Paper #5-94 Ser.). 14p. 1994. pap. text 8.00 (*1-57655-133-4*) Independ Inst.
— Stop That Train Pt. II: A Reply to RTD. (Issue Papers: No. 5-94). 15p. 1994. pap. text 8.00 (*1-57655-060-5*) Independ Inst.
Mueller, Stephen, jt. auth. see Mueller, Alice.
***Mueller, Stephen R. & Polhill, Dennis.** Let Those Who Receive the Benefits Pay the Costs: An Analysis of the Colorado State Government's Flawed Plan. 1999. pap. write for info. (*1-57655-187-3*) Independ Inst.
Mueller, Stephen R. & Polhill, Dennis. Light Rail in Denver: Taking the Taxpayers for a Ride. (Issue Paper #4-97 Ser.). 17p. 1997. pap. text 8.00 (*1-57655-156-3*) Independ Inst.
Mueller, Steve. The Seeker's Guide to Reading the Bible: A Catholic View. LC 99-28198. (Seeker Ser.). 290p. 1999. pap. 11.95 (*0-8294-1345-6*) Loyola Pr.
***Mueller, Steve, ed.** First Eucharist & Beyond Vol. 1: Ongoing Initiation into Communion with Christ, Leaders' Guide. 56p. 2000. pap., teacher ed. 9.95 (*1-889108-78-2*) Liv Good News.
— First Eucharist & Beyond - Ongoing Initiation into Communion with Christ Vol. 2: Family Activity Book. (Illus.). 2000. pap. 5.95 (*1-889108-79-0*) Liv Good News.
— Growing in Friendship with Christ: Family Activity Book. (First Reconciliation & Beyond Ser.: Vol. 2). (Illus.). 40p. 2000. pap. 5.95 (*1-889108-77-4*) Liv Good News.
— Growing in Friendship with Christ: Leader's Guide. (First Reconciliation & Beyond Ser.: Vol. 1). 56p. 2000. pap., teacher ed. 9.95 (*1-889108-76-6*) Liv Good News.
Mueller, Steve, ed. see Morris, Thomas H. & Coffey, Kathy.
***Mueller, Steven.** The Germans of History. 210p. 2000. pap. 9.95 (*0-9702576-0-0*) Waldmann Pr.
Mueller, Ted, jt. auth. see Mueller, Marge.
Mueller, Theodore & Niedzielski, Henri. Basic French, 3 vols., Set. Incl. Introduction a la Culture. (FRE.). 1974. pap. text 3.10 (*0-89197-672-8*); Pratique de la grammaire. (FRE.). 1974. pap. text 8.20 (*0-89197-671-X*); Premiers Pas. (FRE.). 1974. pap. text 4.40 (*0-89197-670-1*); (FRE.). 1974. Set pap. text 15.70 (*0-89197-673-6*) Irvington.
Mueller, Tobin J. Danger, Dinosaurs! A Musical Comedy about the Evolution & Extinction of the Dinosaurs, Incl. audio tape. (Illus.). (J). (ps-8). 1990. pap. 14.95 incl. audio (*1-56213-003-X*) Ctr Stage Prodns.
— Music of the Planet: A Musical Journey about the World & Wonders of Our Solar System. (J). (ps-8). 1990. pap. 14.95 (*1-56213-017-X*) Ctr Stage Prodns.
— Say Yes! to Life: A Musical Drama about the Dangers Drugs Pose to the Joys of Living. (Illus.). (J). (gr. 4-9). 1990. pap. 14.95 (*1-56213-045-5*) Ctr Stage Prodns.
— The Sound of Money: A Musical Adventure about Economics & the Building of Community. (Illus.). (J). (ps-8). 14.95 incl. audio (*1-56213-031-5*) Ctr Stage Prodns.
— To Save the Planet: A Musical Fable about the Global Environment & What We Can Do to Help. (Illus.). 54p. (J). (gr. 4-9). 1991. 14.95 incl. audio (*1-56213-078-1*) Ctr Stage Prodns.
Mueller, Tobin J., jt. auth. see Pulaski High School Drama Club Staff.
Mueller, U., jt. ed. see Franke, W. W.
Mueller, Udo. Diccionario Rioduero Literatura, Vol. 2. (SPA.). 352p. 1978. 14.95 (*0-7859-5750-2*, 8422008602) Fr & Eur.
— Herder Literature Lexicon, Biographic Dictionary: Herder-Lexikon Literatur: Biographisches Woerterbuch, 2 vols. (GER.). 574p. 1981. 75.00 (*0-8288-1572-0*, M7442) Fr & Eur.
Mueller, Virginia. A Halloween Mask for Monster. Fay, Ann, ed. LC 86-1569. (Monster Bks.). (Illus.). 24p. (J). (ps-1). 1986. lib. bdg. 13.95 (*0-8075-3134-0*) A Whitman.
— Monster Goes to School. (Illus.). 24p. (J). (ps-1). 1997. reprint ed. pap. 4.95 (*0-8075-5265-8*) A Whitman.
— Monster's Birthday Hiccups. Levine, Abby, ed. LC 91-2118. (Illus.). 24p. (J). (ps-1). 1991. lib. bdg. 13.95 (*0-8075-5267-4*) A Whitman.
— Monster's Birthday Hiccups. (Illus.). 24p. (J). (ps-1). 1997. reprint ed. pap. 4.95 (*0-8075-5268-2*) A Whitman.
— What Is Faith? Beegle, Shirley, ed. (Happy Day Bks.). (Illus.). 24p. (J). (ps-3). 1994. reprint ed. pap. 1.99 (*0-7847-0265-9*, 04215) Standard Pub.
Mueller, Virginia, jt. auth. see Cupp, Peggy.
Mueller-Vollmer, Kurt. Translating Cultures, Translating Literatures: New Vistas & Approaches in Literary Studies. LC 98-60722. 1999. pap. text 17.95 (*0-8047-3544-1*) Stanford U Pr.
Mueller-Vollmer, Kurt, ed. Herder Today: Contributions from the International Herder Conference, Nov. 5-8, 1987, Stanford, California. xxiv, 451p. (C). 1990. lib. bdg. 144.65 (*3-11-011739-8*) De Gruyter.
Mueller-Vollmer, Kurt, jt. ed. see Muller-Vollmer, Kurt.
Mueller Von der Haegen, Anne. Giotto. (Masters of Italian Art Ser.). (Illus.). 140p. 1998. 19.95 (*3-8290-0249-1*, 520529) Konemann.
Mueller, W. The Knee: Form, Function, & Ligament Reconstruction. (Illus.). 314p. 1985. 250.00 (*0-387-11716-4*) Spr-Verlag.
— Manifolds with Cusps of Rank One. (Lecture Notes in Mathematics Ser.: Vol. 1244). xi, 158p. 1987. 34.95 (*0-387-17696-9*) Spr-Verlag.
Mueller, W., jt. ed. see Schattenkirchner, M.
Mueller, Walt. Understanding Today's Youth Culture. rev. expanded ed. LC 98-48838. 1998. pap. text 14.99 (*0-8423-7739-5*) Tyndale Hse.
— Understanding Today's Youth Culture Discussion Guide. 80p. 1995. 4.99 (*0-8423-7738-7*) Tyndale Hse.
Mueller, Walter. Grammatical Aids for Students of New Testament Greek. 1972. pap. 11.00 (*0-8028-1447-6*) Eerdmans.
Mueller, Walter W., jt. auth. see Jungraithmayr, Herrmann.
Mueller, Wayne. Revelation. LC 96-72092. (People's Bible Teachings Ser.). 229p. 1997. pap. 10.99 (*0-8100-0674-X*, 15N0577) Northwest Pub.
***Mueller, Wendy S.** The Birders Book: Journal Your Backyard Birds. vi, 116p. 2000. 15.95 (*0-9700390-0-X*) Potpourri Pr MN.
Mueller, Werner, et al. Geometrie & Physik. Academy of Sciences & Technology in Berlin Staff, ed. (Akademie der Wissenschaften zu Berlin, Forschungsbericht Ser.: No. 8). (GER., Illus.). vii, 192p. (Orig.). (C). 1993. pap. text 90.80 (*3-11-013944-8*) De Gruyter.
Mueller, Werner A. Nibelungenlied Today. LC 70-181961. (North Carolina. University. Studies in the Germanic Languages & Literatures: No. 34). reprint ed. 27.00 (*0-404-50934-7*) AMS Pr.
Mueller, Willard F. & Garoian, Leon. Changes in the Market Structure of Grocery Retailing. LC 86-18317. 225p. 1986. reprint ed. lib. bdg. 69.50 (*0-313-25222-X*, MUCM, Greenwood Pr) Greenwood.
Mueller-Wille, Christopher. Natural Landscape Amenities & Suburban Growth: Metropolitan Chicago, 1970-1980. LC 90-10818. (Geography Research Papers: Vol. 230). (Illus.). xii, 154p. 2000. pap. text 14.00 (*0-89065-136-1*) U Ch Pr.
Mueller, William B. How to Grow All of Your Own Food: A Natural Step-by-Step Method. (Illus.). 1976. 5.95 (*0-940536-00-5*) Big Toad Pr.
Mueller, William J. & Aniskiewicz, Albert S. Psychotherapeutic Intervention in Hysterical Disorders. LC 85-15. 300p. 1986. 50.00 (*0-87668-913-6*) Aronson.
Mueller, William M. & Shaw, Milton C., eds. Energetics in Metallurgical Phenomena, 4 vols., Vol. 2. x, 204p. 1965. text 274.00 (*0-677-01010-9*) Gordon & Breach.
Mueller, William M., ed. see Conference on Application of X-Ray Analysis (10th,.
Mueller, William M., ed. see Conference on Applications of X-Ray Analysis.
Mueller, William M., jt. ed. see McCall, James L.
Mueller, Wolfgang. Dichter-Helden in der DDR-Literatur der Siebziger Jahre. (DDR-Studien - East German Studies: Vol. 5). (GER.). 220p. (C). 1989. text 40.95 (*0-8204-0897-2*) P Lang Pubng.
— Das Gegenwort-Woerterbuch. (GER.). 352p. (C). 1997. lib. bdg. 124.50 (*3-11-014640-1*) De Gruyter.
Mueller, Wolfgang E. Albert Schweitzer's Kulturphilosophie Im Horizont Saekularer Ethik. (Theologische Bibliothek Toepelmann Ser.: Vol. 59). (GER.). ix, 331p. (C). 1993. lib. bdg. 113.85 (*3-11-013966-9*) De Gruyter.

M

Muellner, Carrie & Muellner, Jon. Bed, Breakfast & Bike Pacific Northwest: A Cycling Guide to Country Inns. LC 95-60718. (Illus.). 278p. (Orig.). 1995. pap. 14.95 (*0-933855-09-5*) Anacus Pr.

Muellner, Jon, jt. auth. see Muellner, Carrie.

Muellner, Leonard. The Anger of Achilles: "Menis" in Greek Epic. (Myth & Poetics Ser.). 240p. 1996. text 39.95 (*0-8014-3230-8*) Cornell U Pr.

Muellner, Leonard, jt. auth. see Walsh, Norman.

Muellner, Leonard, tr. see Bertin, Celia.

Muellner, Leonard, tr. see Detienne, Marcel.

Muellner, Leonard, tr. see Grmek, Mirko D.

Muellner, Mireille, tr. see Bertin, Celia.

Muellner, Mireille, tr. see Detienne, Marcel.

Muellner, Mireille, tr. see Grmek, Mirko D.

Muelver, Jerry. Creating Cool Web Pages with Perl. LC 96-77080. 416p. 1996. pap. 29.99 (*0-7645-3018-6*) IDG Bks.

Muench, Ann, jt. auth. see Madfes, Tania J.

Muench, Bruce. Stick Your Head under the Surface. (Illus.). ix, 189p. 1997. pap. 19.95 (*0-9659221-0-3*) Lake Mgmt Serv.

***Muench, Chris.** Windows CE Technology Tutorial: Solutions for the Developer. 544p. 2000. pap. 49.95 (*0-201-61642-4*) Addison-Wesley.

M

Muench, David. American Landscape. (Illus.). 208p. 1997. 24.99 (*0-88486-186-4*) Galahad Bks.

— Colorado: A Book of 30 Postcards, 1. 1995. pap. text 7.95 (*1-56313-753-4*) BrownTrout Pubs Inc.

— Hawaii Postcards. 1995. pap. text 8.95 (*1-56313-779-8*) BrownTrout Pubs Inc.

— Plateau Light. LC 98-26898. (Illus.). 1998. 39.95 (*1-55868-416-6*) Gr Arts Ctr Pub.

— Uncommon Places. LC 91-65. (Illus.). 166p. 1991. 39.95 (*0-917953-40-1*) Appalachian Trail.

Muench, David, photos by. Ancient America. (Illus.). 240p. 1997. pap. 29.95 (*1-57098-126-4*) Roberts Rinehart.

Muench, David, et al, photos by. Colorado. (Illus.). 112p. 1995. 25.95 (*1-56313-616-3*) BrownTrout Pubs Inc.

— Colorado: A Photographic Portfolio. (Illus.). 112p. 1995. pap. 17.95 (*1-56313-758-5*) BrownTrout Pubs Inc.

Muench, David, photos by. David Muench in Texas. LC 95-18915. (Illus.). 128p. 1995. 39.95 (*1-56313-757-7*) BrownTrout Pubs Inc.

— Images in Stone. (Illus.). 192p. 1995. 49.95 (*1-56313-442-X*) BrownTrout Pubs Inc.

— Images in Stone: Petroglyphs & Pictographs. limited ed. (Illus.). 192p. 1995. write for info. (*1-56313-604-X*) BrownTrout Pubs Inc.

Muench, David, et al, photos by. Michigan. (Illus.). 112p. 1995. pap. 17.95 (*1-56313-761-5*) BrownTrout Pubs Inc.

— Michigan: A Photographic Portfolio. (Illus.). 112p. 1995. 25.95 (*1-56313-760-7*) BrownTrout Pubs Inc.

Muench, David, photos by. Nature's America. rev. ed. (Illus.). 160p. 1995. pap. 24.95 (*1-57098-024-1*) Roberts Rinehart.

— New Mexico II: Photos of David Muench. (Illus.). 160p. 1991. 39.95 (*1-55868-048-9*) Gr Arts Ctr Pub.

— Portrait of Utah. LC 98-89045. (Illus.). 1999. pap. 12.95 (*1-55868-423-9*) Gr Arts Ctr Pub.

Muench, David & Flemmons, Jerry. Texas. 45.00 (*0-528-81105-3*) Rand McNally.

Muench, David & Muench, Marc. American Portfolios. limited ed. (Illus.). 168p. 1995. 125.00 (*1-56313-764-X*) BrownTrout Pubs Inc.

— American Portfolios: Three Wilderness Portfolios. (Illus.). 168p. 1995. 39.95 (*1-56313-441-1*) BrownTrout Pubs Inc.

***Muench, David & Muench, Marc, photos by.** California. LC 89-83846. (Illus.). 144p. 1999. text 39.95 (*1-55868-469-7*) Gr Arts Ctr Pub.

Muench, David & Muench, Marc, photos by. The Rockies. LC 97-70195. (Illus.). 208p. 1997. 50.00 (*1-55868-308-9*) Gr Arts Ctr Pub.

Muench, David, jt. auth. see Pike, Donald G.

Muench, David, jt. photos by see Reynolds, Robert.

Muench, Karl H. Genetic Medicine. (Illus.). 399p. (C). 1992. pap. text 45.00 (*0-8385-3121-0*, A3121-9, Apple Lange Med) McGraw.

Muench, Marc, photos by. Ski the Rockies. (Illus.). 144p. 1994. 39.95 (*1-55868-196-5*) Gr Arts Ctr Pub.

Muench, Marc, jt. auth. see Muench, David.

Muench, Marc, jt. photos by see Muench, David.

Muench, Steve, et al. Oracle: Forms Developer's Companion. 596p. (Orig.). (C). 1994. pap. text 44.50 (*0-9637526-5-0*) Maverick CA.

Muench, Teri & Pomerantz, Susan. Attn, A & R: A Step-by-Step Guide into the Recording Industry: For Artists & Songwriters. Feldstein, Sandy & Wilson, Patrick, eds. (Illus.). 124p. 1988. pap. 17.95 (*0-88284-361-3*, 2260) Alfred Pub.

Muenchhausen, Friedrich Von, see Von Muenchhausen, Friedrich.

Muenchner Rueckversicherungs-Gesellschaft Staff, jt. ed. see Allianz Versicherungs-AG Staff.

Muenchow, Charles, tr. see Westermann, Claus.

Muendel, Renate. George Meredith. (Twayne's English Authors Ser.: No. 434). 160p. 1986. 27.95 (*0-8057-6932-3*) Macmillan.

Muenscher, Walter C. Keys to Woody Plants. 6th rev. ed. (Comstock Bk.). (Illus.). 108p. 1950. pap. text 12.95 (*0-8014-0307-3*) Cornell U Pr.

— Weeds. 2nd ed. LC 79-48017. (Comstock Bk.). (Illus.). 560p. 1987. pap. text 24.95 (*0-8014-9417-6*) Cornell U Pr.

Muensterberg, Hugo. On the Witness Stand: Essays on Psychology & Crime. Moss, Richard, ed. LC 70-156030. reprint ed. 35.00 (*0-404-09180-6*) AMS Pr.

Muensterberger, Werner L. Collecting: An Unruly Passion: Psychological Perspectives. LC 95-31802. 320p. 1995. pap. 13.00 (*0-15-600253-1*, Harvest Bks) Harcourt.

— Collecting: An Unruly Passion: Psychological Perspectives. LC 93-2174. 203p. 1993. text 45.00 (*0-691-03361-7*, Pub. by Princeton U Pr) Cal Prin Full Svc.

— Vincent Van Gogh - Dessins, Pastels, Etudes. (FRE., Illus.). 106p. 1948. lib. bdg. 14.95 (*0-8288-3978-6*) Fr & Eur.

Muensterberger, Werner L., et al, eds. The Psychoanalytic Study of Society, 6 Vols., 1. LC BF0175.P75. 384p. 1960. reprint ed. pap. 119.10 (*0-608-08326-7*, 201045100070) Bks Demand.

— The Psychoanalytic Study of Society, 6 Vols., 2. LC BF0175.P75. 317p. 1960. reprint ed. pap. 98.30 (*0-608-08327-5*, 201045100071) Bks Demand.

— The Psychoanalytic Study of Society, 6 Vols., 3. LC BF0175.P75. 408p. reprint ed. pap. 126.50 (*0-608-08328-3*, 201045100072) Bks Demand.

— The Psychoanalytic Study of Society, 6 Vols., 5. LC BF0175.P75. 258p. 1960. reprint ed. pap. 80.00 (*0-608-08330-5*, 201045100074) Bks Demand.

— The Psychoanalytic Study of Society, 6 Vols., 6. LC BF0175.P75. 320p. reprint ed. pap. 99.20 (*0-608-08331-3*, 201045100075) Bks Demand.

— The Psychoanalytic Study of Society, Vol. 4. LC BF0175.P75. 350p. reprint ed. pap. 108.50 (*0-608-08329-1*, 201045100073) Bks Demand.

— The Psychoanalytic Study of Society, Vol. 8. LC 61-486. (Illus.). 1979. 50.00 (*0-300-02257-3*) Yale U Pr.

— The Psychoanalytic Study of Society, Vol. 10. (Muensterberger Ser.). 400p. 1983. text 39.95 (*0-88163-004-7*) Analytic Pr.

Muensterberger, Werner L. & Axelrad, S., eds. Psychoanalysis & the Social Sciences, Vol. 4. LC 47-12480. 295p. 1955. reprint ed. pap. 91.50 (*0-608-09996-1*, 201045200070) Bks Demand.

— Psychoanalysis & the Social Sciences, Vol. 5. LC 47-12480. 307p. 1955. reprint ed. pap. 95.20 (*0-608-09997-X*, 201045200071) Bks Demand.

Muentner, Carolyn. My Unicorn Thinks He Is Real: And Similar Confusions. 68p. 1982. reprint ed. 8.95 (*0-9606240-2-3*) Pearl-Win.

— The Wind Will Not Forget. 68p. 1983. 8.95 (*0-9606240-3-1*) Pearl-Win.

Muenzer, Clark S. Figures of Identity: Goethe's Novels & the Enigmatic Self. LC 83-43033. (Studies in German Literature). 176p. 1984. 30.00 (*0-271-00361-8*) Pa St U Pr.

Muer, Chuck. The Simply Great Cookbook, Vol. II. (Illus.). 165p. (Orig.). 1995. ring bd. 19.95 (*1-879094-38-X*) Momentum Bks.

— The Simply Great Cookbook: Recipes & the Experience of Fine Dining from the Kitchens of Chuck Muer. LC 92-15339. (Illus.). 166p. (Orig.). 1992. pap. 19.95 (*1-879094-13-4*) Momentum Bks.

Mueser, Anne M., jt. auth. see Verrilli, George E.

Mueser, Anne M., ed. see Russell, David, et al.

Mueser, Kim T. & Gingerich, Susan. Coping with Schizophrenia: A Guide for Families. LC 94-67043. 368p. 1994. pap. 15.95 (*1-879237-78-4*) New Harbinger.

Mueser, Kim T. & Glynn, Shirley M. Behavioral Family Therapy for Psychiatric Disorders. LC 98-68758. 346p. 1999. 49.95 (*1-57224-143-8*) New Harbinger.

***Mueser, Kim T. & Tarrier, Nicholas, eds.** Handbook of Social Functioning in Schizophrenia. LC 97-27797. 512p. (C). 1998. 75.00 (*0-205-16444-7*) Allyn.

Mueser, Roland. Long-Distance Hiking: Lessons from the Appalachian Trail. LC 97-21278. (Illus.). 192p. 1997. pap. 16.95 (*0-07-044458-7*) McGraw.

***Muessig, Carolyn A.** The Faces of Women in the Sermons of Jacques de Vitry. (Translations Ser.: Vol. 27). 216p. 1999. pap. 25.00 (*0-920669-59-X*, Pub. by Peregrina Pubng) Cistercian Pubns.

Muessig, Carolyn A., ed. Medieval Monastic Preaching. LC 98-36284. (Studies in Intellectual History: Vol. 90). (Illus.). xvi, 368p. 1998. 126.50 (*90-04-10883-1*) Brill Academic Pubs.

Muet, P. A., jt. auth. see Dagenais, M. G.

Muet, Pierre-Alain & Fonteneau, Alain. Reflation & Austerity: Economic Policy under Mitterand. Slater, Malcolm, tr. LC 89-28948.Tr. of La/Gauche Face a la Crise. 335p. 1991. 19.50 (*0-85496-644-7*) Berg Pubs.

Muether, John, jt. auth. see Hart, D. G.

Muether, John J., jt. auth. see Kepple, Robert J.

Muething, Eugenia. Nazareth along the Banks of the Ganges, 1947-1990. LC 97-74184. (Illus.). 272p. 1997. write for info. (*1-56469-035-0*); pap. write for info. (*1-56469-036-9*) Harmony Hse Pub.

Mueting, Donald, jt. auth. see Hawkins, Robert.

Muetterties, Earl L., jt. auth. see Jesson, J. P.

Muetterties, Earl L. & Knoth, Walter H. Polyhedral Boranes. LC 68-11437. 205p. reprint ed. pap. 63.60 (*0-608-18703-8*, 202710900054) Bks Demand.

Muetze. ABC der Optik. (GER.). 960p. 1991. 95.00 (*0-8288-6079-3*, M-7290) Fr & Eur.

***Muevihill, Michael.** Matrix, Vol. 10. (Shadowrun Ser.). 2000. pap. 22.00 (*1-55560-401-3*) FASA Corp.

Muezzino-Lu, A. & Williams, M. L., eds. Industrial Air Pollution: Assessment & Control. (NATO ASI Series G: Ecological Sciences: Vol. 31). x, 235p. 1992. 181.95 (*0-387-53098-3*) Spr-Verlag.

Mufarrij-Sherower, T. S., ed. see Sherower, Abbott W.

Mufassir, Sulaiman S. Jesus, a Prophet of Islam. 23p. (Orig.). (YA). (gr. 10-12). 1980. pap. 1.25 (*0-89259-089-0*) Am Trust Pubns.

Mufassir, Sulayman. Biblical Studies from a Muslim Perspective. Obaba, Al I., ed. 49p. (YA). 1991. pap. text 4.00 (*0-916157-61-X*) African Islam Miss Pubns.

Muff, Rolf. The Antimony Deposits in the Murchision Range of the Northeastern Transvaal, Republic of South Africa. (Monograph Series on Mineral Deposits: No. 16). x, 90p. 1978. 35.00 (*3-443-12016-4*, Pub. by Gebruder Borntraeger) Balogh.

***Muffat, Georg.** Georg Muffat on Performance Practice: The Texts from Florilegium Primum, Florilegium Secundum & Auserlesene Instrumentalmusik - A New Translation with Commentary. Wilson, David K., ed. & tr. by. 128p. 2000. pap. 24.95 (*0-253-21397-5*) Ind U Pr.

Muffat, Gottlieb. Seventy-Two Versetl Sammt Twelve Toccaten. fac. ed. (Monuments of Music & Music Literature in Facsimile, I Ser.: Vol. 18). 1967. lib. bdg. 50.00 (*0-8450-2018-8*) Broude.

Muffler, ed. South Cascades Arc Volcanism, California & Southern Oregon. (IGC Field Trip Guidebooks Ser.). 64p. 1989. 21.00 (*0-87590-563-3*, T312) Am Geophysical.

Muffler, L. J., jt. ed. see Rybach, L.

Muffling, Friedrich K. The Memoirs of Baron Von Muffling: A Prussian Officer in the Napoleonic Wars. LC 96-49843. (Napoleonic Library). 1997. write for info. (*1-85367-273-4*) Stackpole.

Muffoletto, Mary L., ed. see Backer, Lynne.

Muffoletto, Mary L., ed. see Backer, Lynne & Cline, Debbie.

Muffoletto, Mary L., ed. see Corwin, Patty & O'Callahan, Cheryl.

Muffoletto, Mary L., ed. see Dencker-Koenig, Karla.

Muffoletto, Mary L., ed. see Emmel, Ruth & Ruchelle, Marion.

Muffoletto, Mary L., ed. see Frankel, Sheila & Barbour, Barbara.

Muffoletto, Mary L., ed. see Rochelle, Marion & Emmel, Ruth.

***Muffoletto, Mary Lu.** Alphabetizing: Grades 2-4. (Illus.). 64p. 1998. pap., teacher ed. 6.95 (*1-889369-33-0*, TI0600) Teaching Ink.

— Tall Tales: Grades 4-6. (Illus.). 64p. 1997. pap., teacher ed. 6.95 (*1-889369-21-7*, TI0081) Teaching Ink.

— Winter Olympics: Grades 4-6. (Illus.). 64p. 1997. pap., teacher ed. 6.95 (*1-889369-23-3*, TI0091) Teaching Ink.

***Muffoletto, Mary Lu & Rochelle, Marion.** Ecology & Eco-Systems: Grades 4-6. (Illus.). 64p. 1998. pap., teacher ed. 6.95 (*1-889369-30-6*, TI0300) Teaching Ink.

Muffoletto, Mary Lu, jt. auth. see Rochelle, Marion.

Muffoletto, Robert & Knupfer, Nancy N. Computers in Education: Social, Political & Historical Perspectives. LC 93-9798. (Media, Education, Culture, Technology Ser.). 272p. 1993. text 52.50 (*1-881303-59-4*); pap. text 23.95 (*1-881303-60-8*) Hampton Pr NJ.

Muffs, Yochanan. Love & Joy: Law, Language, & Religion in Ancient Israel. (Jewish Theological Seminary of America Ser.). 240p. (Orig.). (C). 1995. pap. text 15.95 (*0-674-53932-X*) HUP.

— Love & Joy, Law, Language, & Religion in Ancient Israel. LC 92-11977. 1992. 29.95 (*0-674-53931-1*) Jewish Sem.

Mufoletto, Mary L., ed. see Dencker-Koenig, Karla.

Mufson, Daniel. Reza Abdoh. LC 98-49385. 1999. 38.00 (*0-8018-6123-3*) Johns Hopkins.

— Reza Abdoh. 1999. pap. 19.95 (*0-8018-6124-1*) Johns Hopkins.

Mufson, Laura, et al. Interpersonal Psychotherapy for Depressed Adolescents. LC 93-1429. 218p. 1993. lib. bdg. 30.00 (*0-89862-686-2*) Guilford Pubns.

Mufson, Maurice, jt. auth. see Neitch, Shirley M.

Mufson, Maurice A., ed. Pathophysiology: PreTest Self-Assessment & Review. LC 98-36684. (Basic Sciences: Pretest Self Assessment & Review Ser.). (Illus.). 250p. 1999. pap. text 18.95 (*0-07-052692-3*) McGraw-Hill HPD.

Mufson, Richard A. Just for Laughs. 70p. 1996. 9.95 (*0-9650381-0-6*) R Mufson.

Mufson, Susan & Kranz, Rachel. Straight Talk about Child Abuse. (Straight Talk Ser.). 112p. (YA). (gr. 6-12). 1991. 19.95 (*0-8160-2376-X*) Facts on File.

— Straight Talk about Date Rape. (Straight Talk Ser.). 128p. (YA). (gr. 6-12). 1993. 19.95 (*0-8160-2863-X*) Facts on File.

— Straight Talk about Date Rape. LC 98-105120. (Straight Talk Ser.). 128p. (YA). (gr. 6-12). 1997. reprint ed. pap. text 9.95 (*0-8160-3752-3*) Facts on File.

Mufti, G. J. & Galton, D. A., eds. The Myelodysplastic Syndromes. (Illus.). 256p. 1992. text 89.95 (*0-443-04083-4*) Church.

Mufti, G. J., jt. ed. see Schmalzi, F.

Mufti, Ghulam J., et al. An Atlas of Malignant Haematology: Cytology, Histology & Cytogenetics. 432p. 1996. sl. 124.00 (*0-397-51572-3*) Lppncott W & W.

— An Atlas of Malignant Haematology: Cytology, Histology & Cytogenetics. (Illus.). 432p. 1996. text 205.00 (*0-397-51400-X*) Lppncott W & W.

Mufti, Malik. Sovereign Creations: Pan-Arabism & Political Order in Syria & Iraq. 288p. 1996. text 35.00 (*0-8014-3168-9*) Cornell U Pr.

***Mufti, Mohammed H.** Healthcare Development Strategies in the Kingdom of Saudi Arabia. LC 99-53993. 2000. write for info. (*0-306-46314-8*, Kluwer Plenum) Kluwer Academic.

Muftic, Sead. Security Mechanisms for Computer Networks. 1989. text 47.95 (*0-470-21387-6*) P-H.

Muftic, Sead, Jr., et al. Security Architecture for Open Distributed Systems. (Communication & Distributed Systems Ser.). 298p. 1993. 140.00 (*0-471-93472-0*) Wiley.

Muftuler-Bac, Meltem. Turkey's Relations with a Changing Europe. LC 96-3411. (Europe in Change Ser.). 1996. text. write for info. (*0-7190-4234-8*) Manchester Univ Pr.

***Mufuka, Ken & Ricketson, William.** An Introduction to Western Civilization. 2nd rev. ed. Voice of Truths Staff, ed. 88p. 2000. pap. text 17.95 (*0-9666777-3-0*) Voice of Truths.

Mufwene, Salikoko S. African-American English: Structure, History & Usage. LC 97-37628. 328p. (C). 1998. 85.00 (*0-415-11732-1*) Routledge.

— African-American English: Structure, History, & Usage. LC 97-37628. 328p. (C). 1998. pap. 25.99 (*0-415-11733-X*) Routledge.

Mufwene, Salikoko S., ed. Africanisms in Afro-American Language Varieties. LC 92-8225. 576p. (C). 1993. 45.00 (*0-8203-1465-X*) U of Ga Pr.

Mufwene, Salikoko S., et al, eds. Papers from the 12th Regional Meeting of CLS, Vol. 1. 697p. 1976. pap. 7.00 (*0-614-16721-3*) Chicago Ling.

Mufwene, Salikoko S. & Moshi, Lioba, eds. Topics in African Linguistics: Papers from the XXI Annual Conference on African Linguistics, University of Georgia, April 1990. LC 93-5761. (Current Issues in Linguistic Theory Ser.: No. 100). x, 304p. 1993. 76.00 (*1-55619-553-2*) J Benjamins Pubng Co.

Muga, Bruce J. & Wilson, James F. Dynamic Analysis of Ocean Structures. LC 77-122021. (Ocean Technology Ser.). (Illus.). 389p. 1970. reprint ed. pap. 120.60 (*0-608-05476-3*, 206594500006) Bks Demand.

Mugaas, John N., et al. Metabolic Adaptation to Climate & Distribution of the Raccoon Procyon Lotor & Other Procyonidae. LC 93-3119. (Smithsonian Contributions to Zoology Ser.: No. 542). (Illus.). 38p. reprint ed. pap. 30.00 (*0-7837-5897-9*, 204568800007) Bks Demand.

Mugan, Daniel J., ed. Curriculum Guide to Venezuela, No. 5. 185p. (Orig.). 1989. teacher ed. 15.95 (*0-938305-04-2*) Assn Tchrs Latin Amer.

Mugan, Daniel J., ed. Curriculum Guide on Argentina. (Curriculum Guides on Latin America Ser.: No. 4). (Illus.). 225p. 1986. teacher ed. 14.50 (*0-938305-03-4*) Assn Tchrs Latin Amer.

— Curriculum Guide on Brazil. (Curriculum Guides on Latin America Ser.: No. 3). (Illus.). 230p. 1986. teacher ed. 14.50 (*0-938305-02-6*) Assn Tchrs Latin Amer.

— Curriculum Guide on Ecuador. (Curriculum Guides on Latin America Ser.: No. 2). (Illus.). 350p. 1984. reprint ed. teacher ed. 14.95 (*0-938305-01-8*) Assn Tchrs Latin Amer.

Mugane, John M. A Paradigmatic Grammar of Gikuyu. LC 96-38000. (Stanford Monographs in African Languages). 192p. (C). 1997. 36.95 (*1-57586-076-7*) CSLI.

Mugasha, Agasha. The Law of Multi-Bank Financing. 552p. 1998. text 65.00 (*0-7735-1628-X*, Pub. by McG-Queens Univ Pr) CUP Services.

Mugerauer, Robert. Heidegger's Language & Thinking. LC 86-27188. 232p. (C). 1990. pap. 18.50 (*0-391-03667-X*) Humanities.

— Interpretations on Behalf of Place: Environmental Displacements & Alternative Responses. LC 93-11617. (SUNY Series in Environmental & Architectural Phenomenology). (Illus.). 237p. (C). 1994. text 59.50 (*0-7914-1943-6*); pap. text 19.95 (*0-7914-1944-4*) State U NY Pr.

— Interpreting Environments: Traditions, Deconstruction, Hermeneutics. LC 95-8156. (Illus.). 244p. 1995. pap. 14.95 (*0-292-75189-3*); text 35.00 (*0-292-75178-8*) U of Tex Pr.

Mugerauer, Robert, jt. auth. see Alofsin, Anthony.

Mugerauer, Robert, jt. ed. see Seamon, David.

Mugerwa, M. N., jt. auth. see Blomen, L. J.

Mugford, Jane, et al. Violence Prevention in Practice: Australian Award-Winning Programs. LC 98-145395. 76 p. 1996. write for info. (*0-642-24024-8*) Aust Inst Criminology.

Mugford, Jane, jt. auth. see Asian and Pacific Conference of Correctional Administrators Staff.

Mugford, Miranda, jt. auth. see Macfarlane, Alison.

Mugford, Roger. Never Say No! The Complete Program for a Happier & More Cooperative Dog. LC 93-32929. 208p. 1994. pap. 12.00 (*0-399-51884-3*) Berkley Pub.

— Never Say No! The Complete Program for a Happier & More Cooperative Dog. LC 93-32929. (Illus.). 224p. 1994. 18.95 (*0-399-13947-8*, G P Putnam) Peng Put Young Read.

Mugford, Simon. Fantastic Cutaway Book of Rescue. LC 97-8022. (Illus.). 40p. (J). (gr. 3-6). 1997. pap. 9.95 (*0-7613-0630-7*, Copper Beech Bks); lib. bdg. 23.90 (*0-7613-0616-1*, Copper Beech Bks) Millbrook Pr.

***Mugg, Berthinia.** A Visit to Spitesville: A Murder Mystery. LC 99-91488. 1999. 25.00 (*0-7388-0828-8*); pap. 18.00 (*0-7388-0829-6*) Xlibris Corp.

Muggamin, Howard. The Jewish Americans. LC 95-19690. 120p. (YA). (gr. 5 up). 1995. lib. bdg. 19.95 (*0-7910-3365-1*) Chelsea Hse.

— The Jewish Americans. rev. ed. LC 95-19690. (Immigrant Experience Ser.). 120p. (YA). (gr. 5 up). 1995. pap. 9.95 (*0-7910-3387-2*) Chelsea Hse.

Mugge, Maximilian A., tr. see Nietzsche, Friedrich Wilhelm.

Mugge-Meiburg, Beth L. Words Chiseled into Marble: Artworks in the Prose Narratives of Conrad Ferdinand Meyer. LC 90-49695. (North American Studies in Nineteenth-Century German Literature: Vol. 9). 236p. (C). 1991. text 41.95 (*0-8204-1493-X*) P Lang Pubng.

Muggeridge, Malcolm. Chronicles of Wasted Time: An Autobiography. LC 88-38725. 558p. 1989. reprint ed. pap. 14.95 (*0-89526-762-4*) Regnery Pub.

— Earnest Atheist: A Study of Samuel Butler. LC 77-153491. (English Literature Ser.: No. 33). 1971. reprint ed. lib. bdg. 75.00 (*0-8383-1242-X*) M S G Haskell Hse.

— Something Beautiful for God: Mother Teresa of Calcutta. 160p. 1986. pap. 12.00 (*0-06-066043-0*, Pub. by Harper SF) HarpC.

An Asterisk (*) at the beginning of an entry indicates that the title is appearing for the first time.

— Something Beautiful for God: Mother Teresa of Calcutta. large type ed. (Large Print Inspirational Ser.). 174p. 1985. pap. 9.95 (*0-8027-2474-4*) Walker & Co.
Muggeridge, Malcolm, ed. see Ciano, Galeazzo.
Muggeridge, Richard, jt. auth. see Reed, Philip.
Muggeridge, Thomas M. Winter in Moscow. LC 87-9170. 270p. reprint ed. pap. 83.70 (*0-7837-3170-1*, 204280800006) Bks Demand.
Muggia, Franco M. Cancer Chemotherapy I. 1983. text 187.00 (*90-247-2713-8*) Kluwer Academic.
Muggia, Franco M., ed. Cancer Chemotherapy: Concepts, Clinical Investigations & Therapeutic Advances. (Cancer Treatment & Research Ser.). (C). 1988. text 160.50 (*0-89838-381-1*) Kluwer Academic.
— Concepts, Mechanisms, & New Targets for Chemotherapy. LC 95-17716. (Cancer Treatment & Research Ser.: Vol. 78). 256p. (C). 1995. text 212.00 (*0-7923-3525-2*) Kluwer Academic.
— Experimental & Clinical Progress in Cancer Chemotherapy. (Cancer Treatment & Research Ser.). 1985. text 146.50 (*0-89838-679-9*) Kluwer Academic.
— New Drugs, Concepts & Results in Cancer Chemotherapy. (Cancer Treatment & Research Ser.). 176p. (C). 1991. text 147.50 (*0-7923-1253-8*) Kluwer Academic.
Muggia, Franco M., et al, eds. Cancer Treatment & the Heart. LC 92-17266. (Johns Hopkins Series in Hematology/Oncology). (Illus.). 400p. reprint ed. pap. 124.00 (*0-608-08794-7*, 206943300004) Bks Demand.
Muggia, Franco M. & Rozencweig, Marcel, eds. Clinical Evaluation of Antitumor Therapy. (Developments in Oncology Ser.). 1986. text 139.50 (*0-89838-803-1*) Kluwer Academic.
— Lung Cancer: Progress in Therapeutic Research. fac. ed. LC 77-84552. (Progress in Cancer Research & Therapy Ser.: No. 11). (Illus.). 640p. pap. 198.40 (*0-7837-7179-7*, 204712000005) Bks Demand.
Muggia, Franco M., et al. Anthracycline Antibiotics in Cancer Therapy. 1982. text 226.00 (*90-247-2711-1*) Kluwer Academic.
Muggia, Franco M., jt. ed. see Mathe, G.
Mugglestone, jt. auth. see Brown.
Mugglestone, Lynda. "Talking Power" The Rise of Accent as Social Symbol. (Illus.). 362p. 1997. reprint ed. pap. text 28.00 (*0-19-823706-5*) OUP.
— Talking Proper: The Rise of Accent as Social Symbol. (Illus.). 368p. 1995. 59.00 (*0-19-823948-3*) OUP.
Mugglestone, Lynda, ed. Lexicography & the OED: Pioneers in the Untrodden Forest. (Oxford Studies in Lexicography & Lexicology). (Illus.). 480p. 2000. text 85.00 (*0-19-823784-7*) OUP.
Mugglestone, Lynda, ed. & intro. see Eliot, George, pseud.
***Muggleton, David.** Inside Subculture: The Postmodern Meaning of Style. (Dress, Body, Culture Ser.). (Illus.). 224p. 2000. 65.00 (*1-85973-347-6*, Pub. by Berg Pubs); pap. 19.50 (*1-85973-352-2*, Pub. by Berg Pubs) NYU Pr.
Muggleton, Stephen. Inductive Acquisition of Expert Systems. 1990. text 34.50 (*0-201-17561-4*) Addison-Wesley.
Muggleton, Stephen, ed. Inductive Logic Programming. (APIC Ser.). (Illus.). 576p. 1992. text 104.00 (*0-12-509715-8*) Acad Pr.
Muggleton, Stephen, et al, eds. Inductive Logic Programming: 6th International Workshop, ILP-96, Stockholm, Sweden, August 26-28, 1996, Selected Papers, Vol. 131. LC 97-36657. (Lecture Notes in Artificial Intelligence: Vol. 1314). viii, 397p. 1997. pap. 67.00 (*3-540-63494-0*) Spr-Verlag.
***Muggli, Glorianne.** Articles of Faith Activity Book. (Activity Bks.). (Illus.). 92p. (J). 1999. pap. 7.95 (*1-57665-061-8*) Muggli Graphics.
Muggli, Glorianne. As I Have Loved You Love One Another. (Illus.). 100p. (Orig.). 1995. pap. 8.95 (*1-57665-008-1*) Muggli Graphics.
***Muggli, Glorianne.** Book of Mormon. (Classroom Activity Book Ser.). (Illus.). 96p. (J). 1999. pap. 8.95 (*1-57665-062-6*) Muggli Graphics.
Muggli, Glorianne. Classroom Activity Book: Doctrine & Covenants & Church History. (Illus.). 100p. (Orig.). 1996. pap. 7.95 (*1-57665-025-1*) Muggli Graphics.
— Clips & Covers, Bk. 2. (Illus.). 80p. 1997. pap. 6.95 (*1-57665-038-3*) Muggli Graphics.
— Clips & Covers Bk. 1: Clip Art & Program Covers. (Clips & Covers Ser.). (Illus.). 96p. (Orig.). 1996. pap. 7.95 (*1-57665-016-2*) Muggli Graphics.
— Exaltation. (Classroom Activity Book Ser.). (Illus.). 80p. 1997. pap. 6.95 (*1-57665-037-5*) Muggli Graphics.
— General Conference Activity Book. (Gospel Games Puzzle Book). (Illus.). 52p. (Orig.). 1996. pap. 5.95 (*1-57665-018-9*) Muggli Graphics.
— Gospel Games No. 1: Presidents of the Church. (Gospel Games Puzzle Book). (Illus.). 96p. (Orig.). 1996. pap. 7.95 (*1-57665-017-0*) Muggli Graphics.
— Holiday Activity Book. (Gospel Games Ser.). (Illus.). (Orig.). 1996. pap. write for info. (*1-57665-019-7*) Muggli Graphics.
— I Can Choose the Right. (Primary Theme Bks.). (Illus.). 100p. (Orig.). 1996. pap. 8.95 (*1-57665-022-7*) Muggli Graphics.
— I Know the Scriptures Are True. (Primary Theme Book Ser.). (Illus.). 100p. 1997. pap. 8.95 (*1-57665-034-0*) Muggli Graphics.
***Muggli, Glorianne.** I'll Make & Keep My Baptismal Covenants. (Primary Theme Book Ser.). (Illus.). 100p. 1999. pap. 9.95 (*1-57665-055-3*) Muggli Graphics.
— Primary Idea Book. (Illus.). 64p. 1999. pap. 7.95 (*1-57665-056-1*) Muggli Graphics.
Muggli, Glorianne. Yo Puedo Escoger el Camino Correcto. Payne, Annie & Stevens, Lorena, trs. (Primary Theme Bks.).Tr. of I Can Choose the Right. (SPA., Illus.). 100p. (Orig.). 1996. pap. 8.95 (*1-57665-023-5*) Muggli Graphics.
Muggli, Glorianne & Muggli, Liesl. Gospel Games: Holiday Activity Book. (Gospel Games Activity Bks.). (Illus.). 80p. (Orig.). (J). 1996. pap. 6.95 (*1-57665-029-4*) Muggli Graphics.
Muggli, Glorianne, jt. auth. see Brown, Susan Taylor.
Muggli, Glorianne, jt. auth. see Grossnickle, Doris.
Muggli, Glorianne, jt. auth. see Hawkins, Starleen.
Muggli, Glorianne, jt. auth. see Nedreberg, Sherry.
Muggli, Glorianne, ed. see Brown, Susan C.
Muggli, Liesl, jt. auth. see Muggli, Glorianne.
Mughabghab, S. F., et al, eds. Neutron Cross Sections Vol. 1, Pt. B: Z - 61-100: Neutron Resonance Parameters & Thermal Cross Sections. 652p. 1984. text 133.00 (*0-12-509711-5*) Acad Pr.
***Mughal, Tariq I. & Goldman, John M.** Understanding Leukaemia & Related Cancers. (Illus.). 107p. 1999. pap. 24.95 (*0-632-05346-1*) Blackwell Sci.
Mughal Tent Project Staff. Shamiana: The Mughal Tent. 1999. pap. text 19.95 (*1-85177-307-X*) V&A Ent.
***Mughan, Anthony.** Media & the Presidentialization of Parliamentary Elections. LC 00-33291. 2000. write for info. (*0-312-23786-3*) St Martin.
Mughan, Anthony, jt. ed. see Gunther, Richard.
Mughan, Anthony, jt. ed. see Patterson, Samuel C.
Mughniyyah, Allamah M. The Hajj: According to the Five Schools of Islamic Jurisprudence. Qara'i, Ali Q., tr. from ARA. 96p. (C). 1989. pap. text 6.70 (*1-871031-09-5*) Abjad Bk.
Mughniyyah, Muhammad J. The Despotic Rulers: Ash Shiah Wa Hakimun. rev. ed. Wasi, S. M. & Aini, A. A., eds. Haq, M. Fazal, tr. from ARA. 274p. reprint ed. pap. 8.00 (*0-941724-46-8*) Islamic Seminary.
***Mughrabi, Hael, et al, eds.** Microstructures & Mechanical Properties of Metalic High Temperature Material. LC 99-203042. 580p. 1999. pap. 195.00 (*3-527-27142-2*) Wiley.
Mugica Berrondo, Placido. Diccionario Castellano - Vasco. (BAQ & SPA.). 1032p. 1987. 95.00 (*0-7859-3346-8*) Fr & Eur.
Mugica, Jacques, jt. auth. see Barold, S. Serge.
Mugika, Placido. Diccionario Castellano-Vasco. 4th ed. (SPA.). 1027p. 95.00 (*0-8288-6235-4*, S-50441) Fr & Eur.
Mugler, Charles. Dictionnaire Historique de la Terminologie Optique des Grecs. (FRE.). 460p. 1964. pap. 150.00 (*0-8288-6767-4*, M-6421); pap. 165.00 (*0-7859-7845-3*, 2252001674) Fr & Eur.
Mugler, Dale H., jt. auth. see Sterrett, Andrew.
Mugler, Dale H., ed. see Boas, Ralph P., Jr.
Mugler, Frederick. The Madrona Murders. LC 98-85385. 325p. 1998. 25.00 (*0-9663501-5-4*); pap. 15.00 (*0-7388-0023-6*) Xlibris Corp.
***Muglia, Sylvia J.** Internal Works. 2000. pap. 6.95 (*0-533-13248-7*) Vantage.
Muglia, V., ed. Enterprise Information Exchange: A Roadmap for Electronic Data Interchange for Manufacturing Companies. 188p. 1992. 17.50 (*0-87263-435-3*) SME.
Muglich, Heinz. Entstehung Betrieblicher Weiterbildungsstrukturen im Dritten Reich. (Studien zur Erwachsenenbildung: Bd. 13). (GER.). 210p. 1996. pap. 42.95 (*3-631-30453-6*) P Lang Pubng.
Mugnai, D., ed. see Ranfagni, A.
Mugnaini, Joseph A. The Hidden Elements of Drawing. LC 73-3944. (Illus.). 211p. reprint ed. pap. 65.50 (*0-608-11233-X*, 200634000058) Bks Demand.
Mugnier, Charlotte. The Paraprofessional & the Professional Job Structure. LC 80-12543. 163p. reprint ed. pap. 50.60 (*0-608-12589-X*, 202395100034) Bks Demand.
Mugnier, Marie-Laure & Chein, Michel, eds. Conceptual Structures. LC 98-29353. (Lecture Notes in Artificial Intelligence Ser.: Vol. 439). xiii, 439p. 1998. pap. 69.00 (*3-540-64791-0*) Spr-Verlag.
Mugno, Salvatore. Io Ho Mangiato le Fragole: Italian Essays. (ITA.). 89p. 1988. 10.00 (*0-89304-526-8*) Cross-Cultrl NY.
Mugo, Micere, et al. The Trial of Dedan Kimathi. (African Writers Ser.). 85p. (C). 1977. pap. 9.95 (*0-435-90191-5*, 90191) Heinemann.
Mugo, Phoebe, ed. Lodu's Escape: And Other Stories from Africa. (Illus.). 64p. (Orig.). (J). (gr. 3-5). 1994. pap. 6.95 (*0-377-00269-0*) Friendship Pr.
Mugrditchian, Hovhannes. To Armenians with Love: The Memoirs of a Patriot. Martin, Paul, ed. (Illus.). xviii, 206p. 1997. 14.95 (*0-9661815-0-6*) P Martin.
Mugridge. Elementary Algebra. (C). 1990. pap. text, student ed. 26.50 (*0-03-009413-5*) Harcourt Coll Pubs.
— Elementary Algebra. 2nd ed. (C). 1994. pap. text, teacher ed., suppl. ed. 37.50 (*0-03-072993-9*, Pub. by Harcourt Coll Pubs) Harcourt.
— Elementary Algebra. 2nd ed. (C). 1994. pap. text, teacher ed. 33.75 (*0-03-072992-0*) Harcourt Coll Pubs.
— Elementary Algebra: Prepared Tests. 2nd ed. (C). 1994. pap. text 40.00 (*0-03-072994-7*, Pub. by Harcourt Coll Pubs) Harcourt.
— Intermediate. 2nd ed. (C). 1994. pap. text, teacher ed. 40.00 (*0-03-004002-7*, Pub. by Harcourt Coll Pubs) Harcourt.
— Intermediate Algebra. 2nd ed. (C). 1994. pap. text, teacher ed. 33.75 (*0-03-072944-0*) Harcourt Coll Pubs.
— ST SM INTERM ALGEBRA 2E. 2nd ed. (C). 1994. pap. text, student ed. 25.00 (*0-03-072951-3*) Harcourt Coll Pubs.
Mugridge, Donald H. & Conover, Helen F. An Album of American Battle Art, 1755-1918. LC 72-6278. (Illus.). 340p. 1972. reprint ed. lib. bdg. 55.00 (*0-306-70523-0*) Da Capo.
Mugridge, Ian. The View from Xanadu: William Randolph Hearst & United States Foreign Policy. (Illus.). 232p. 1995. 60.00 (*0-7735-1281-0*, Pub. by McG-Queens Univ Pr); pap. 19.95 (*0-7735-1295-0*, Pub. by McG-Queens Univ Pr) CUP Services.
Mugridge, Ian, ed. Founding the Open Universities: Essays in Memory of G. Ram Reddy. LC 97-905298. (C). 1997. text. write for info. (*81-207-1974-3*) Sterling Pubs.
Mugridge, Ian & Kaufman, David, eds. Distance Education in Canada. 336p. 1986. 39.95 (*0-7099-4619-8*, Pub. by C Helm) Routldge.
Mugridge, Larry R. Elementary Algebra. annot. ed. 600p. (C). 1990. teacher ed. write for info. (*0-03-031442-9*) SCP.
— Intermediate Algebra. annot. ed. 896p. (C). 1991. teacher ed. write for info. (*0-03-031587-5*) SCP.
***Muguti, Elizabeth, et al.** Energy Efficiency for Small & Medium Enterprise. (Energy & Environment Technology Source Bks.). 72p. 1999. pap. 15.00 (*1-85339-446-7*, Pub. by Intermed Tech) Stylus Pub VA.
Muha, Thomas & Vernon, Maureen. If Your Divorce Is the Pits, Stop Digging: A Parent's Handbook. 1996. write for info. (*0-614-06627-1*) Lookng Glass.
— If Your Divorce Is the Pits, Stop Digging: The Group Leader's Guide. 1996. write for info. (*0-614-06628-X*) Lookng Glass.
Muhaiyaddeen, M. R. Come to the Secret Garden: Sufi Tales of Wisdom. LC 83-49210. (Illus.). 450p. (J). 1985. 23.00 (*0-914390-27-9*) Fellowship Pr PA.
— Come to the Secret Garden: Sufi Tales of Wisdom. 437p. (J). 1996. 24.95 (*0-614-20998-6*, 149) Kazi Pubns.
— Dhikr: The Remembrance of God. 2nd rev. ed. LC 99-17828. (Illus.). 250p. 1998. 16.00 (*0-914390-53-8*) Fellowship Pr PA.
— Gems of Widsom No. 4: Come to Prayer. 65p. (Orig.). 1995. pap. 6.00 (*0-914390-48-1*) Fellowship Pr PA.
— Gems of Wisdom No. 1: The Value of Good Qualities. 80p. 1992. pap. 6.00 (*0-914390-34-1*) Fellowship Pr PA.
— Gems of Wisdom No. 2: Beyond Mind & Desire. LC 93-6734. 80p. 1993. pap. 6.00 (*0-914390-36-8*) Fellowship Pr PA.
— Golden Words of a Sufi Sheikh. LC 82-11854. 472p. 1983. 23.00 (*0-914390-24-4*) Fellowship Pr PA.
— Guidebook to the True Secret of the Heart, Vol. 1. (Illus.). 230p. 1976. reprint ed. pap. 11.00 (*0-914390-07-4*) Fellowship Pr PA.
— Hajj: The Inner Pilgrimage. LC 98-12255. (Illus.). 170p. 1998. pap. 17.00 (*0-914390-52-X*); text 23.00 (*0-914390-51-1*) Fellowship Pr PA.
— Islam & World Peace: Explanations of a Sufi. LC 87-11921. 150p. 1987. 18.00 (*0-914390-30-9*); pap. 12.00 (*0-914390-25-2*) Fellowship Pr PA.
— My Love You My Children: One Hundred & One Stories for Children of All Ages. 475p. (J). 1996. 24.95 (*0-614-21036-4*, 868) Kazi Pubns.
— A Mystical Journey. LC 89-1102. 150p. 1990. 14.00 (*0-914390 28 7*); pap. 11.00 (*0-914390-29-5*) Fellowship Pr PA.
— Question of Life - Answers of Wisdom, Vol. 1. LC 90-3822. 350p. 1991. 23.00 (*0-914390-32-5*) Fellowship Pr PA.
— Sheikh & Disciple. LC 83-1565. (Illus.). 120p. 1983. 12.00 (*0-914390-26-0*) Fellowship Pr PA.
— A Song of Muhammad. LC 95-13365. 300p. 1996. pap. 17.00 (*0-914390-50-3*); text 23.00 (*0-914390-49-X*) Fellowship Pr PA.
— A Tasty Economical Cookbook, Vol. 2. (Illus.). 166p. 1983. spiral bd. 6.00 (*0-914390-22-8*) Fellowship Pr PA.
— To Die Before Death: The Sufi Way of Life. 260p. 1997. text 23.00 (*0-914390-37-6*) Fellowship Pr PA.
— To Die Before Death: The Sufi Way of Life. 260p. 1997. pap. 17.00 (*0-914390-39-2*) Fellowship Pr PA.
— Treasures of the Heart: Sufi Stories for Young Children. Steele, Christine, ed. Balamore, Usha, tr. (Illus.). 110p. (J). (ps). 1993. 15.00 (*0-914390-33-3*) Fellowship Pr PA.
— Treasures of the Heart: Sufi Stories for Young Children (Illus.). 97p. (J). 1996. 15.00 (*0-614-21043-7*, 1257) Kazi Pubns.
— Wisdom of the Divine, Vol. 2. 1972. pap. 8.00 (*0-914390-12-0*) Fellowship Pr PA.
— Wisdom of the Divine, Vol. 3. (Illus.). 1977. pap. 8.00 (*0-914390-40-6*) Fellowship Pr PA.
— Wisdom of the Divine, Vol. 4. (Illus.). 1988. pap. 8.00 (*0-914390-41-4*) Fellowship Pr PA.
— Wisdom of the Divine, 4 vols., Vols. 1-4. 90p. 1972. pap. 8.00 (*0-914390-00-7*) Fellowship Pr PA.
Muhajir, A. M., compiled by. Mystery of God. 328p. 1984. 19.95 (*0-900125-44-6*) Bahai.
Muhajir, M. R. Lessons from the Stories of the Quran. 1991. pap. 16.50 (*1-56744-120-3*) Kazi Pubns.
Muhaiyaddeen, M. R. Gem of Wisdom, No. 3: The Innermost Heart. 70p. (Orig.). 1994. pap. 6.00 (*0-914390-38-4*) Fellowship Pr PA.
Muhammad & Ali, Hazrat. Excellent Sayings of Muhammad & Ali. Campbell, Charles I., tr. from ARA. 1978. pap. 7.50 (*0-917220-02-1*) Khaneghah & Maktab.
Muhammad Abdullah & Al-Buraey, Muhammad. Administrative Development: An Islamic Perspective. 420p. 1986. pap. 80.00 (*0-7103-0059-X*, A3186); pap. 22.50 (*0-685-24717-1*, A3186) Routledge.
Muhammad, Adnan S. Adwa' 'ala Kitab al-Jihad fi al-Islam lil-Duktur Muhammad Sa id Ramadan al-Buti. 1994. pap. 1.95 (*1-57547-001-2*) Dar Al-Fikr.
— Al-Qira'ah Awwalan. 176p. 1993. pap. 1.95 (*1-57547-021-7*) Dar Al-Fikr.
Muhammad al-Ghazzali. Fatawa of Imam Al Ghazzali. 178p. (C). 1997. pap. 12.00 (*0-934905-80-0*, Library of Islam) Kazi Pubns.
Muhammad, Al-Hajj I. What Should You Do If You Are Arrested or Framed by the Cops? 32p. (Orig.). 1990. pap. 4.95 (*1-56411-034-6*) Untd Bros & Sis.
Muhammad al-Jamal, Shaykh. Al-Wird Ash-Shadhuliyyah. Students of Shaykh Muhammad, tr. from ARA. 120p. 1998. pap. 15.00 (*1-892595-05-2*) Sidi Muha Pr.
— The Deeper Meaning Behind the Pillars of Islam. Fawzia, Rosina, tr. from ARA. 206p. 1996. pap. 14.00 (*1-892595-03-6*) Sidi Muha Pr.
— Fruits from the Tree of Life. 265p. 1996. pap. 14.00 (*1-892595-01-X*) Sidi Muha Pr.
— Music of the Soul: Sufi Teachings. 2nd ed. 524p. 1996. pap. 29.95 (*1-892595-00-1*) Sidi Muha Pr.
— Stories of the Prophets. (Illus.). 359p. 1996. pap. 21.00 (*1-892595-02-8*) Sidi Muha Pr.
— The Taste of the Love. Al-Jamal, Mahmoud, tr. from ARA. 67p. 1998. pap. 15.00 (*1-892595-04-4*) Sidi Muha Pr.
Muhammad al-Tijani al-Samawi. Then I Was Guided. LC 91-66698. 232p. 1993. pap. 8.00 (*1-879402-06-8*, OO) Tahrike Tarsile Quran.
Muhammad, Amir N. Muslims in America: Seven Centuries of History, 1312-1998: Collections & Stories of American Muslims. LC 97-52570. 1998. 8.95 (*0-915957-78-7*) amana pubns.
Muhammad, Askia. Behind Enemy Lines: Marcus Garvey, Elijah Muhammad, Louis Farrakhan & Arabs in American White Media. unabridged ed. 144p. (Orig.). 1996. pap. 10.00 (*1-56411-152-0*, 4BBG0154) Untd Bros & Sis.
Muhammad 'Ata Ur-Rahim. Jesus Prophet of Islam. LC 91-66699. 246p. (Orig.). (C). reprint ed. pap. 14.95 (*1-879402-07-6*, 45A) Tahrike Tarsile Quran.
Muhammad bin Uthman Adh-Shahabi. The Major Sins in Islam. 550p. 1993. text 35.00 (*1-56744-489-X*) Kazi Pubns.
Muhammad, Bryan. Health & Grooming Tips for the Well-Made Man. (Illus.). 65p. (YA). (gr. 6 up). 1997. pap. 10.00 (*0-9662547-0-8*) B Muhammad.
Muhammad, Elijah. Blood Bath: The True Teaching of Malcolm X "Seldom Told" Hakim, Nasie, ed. 64p. 1995. pap. 6.95 (*1-884855-20-2*) Secretarius.
— Christianity vs. Islam. 72p. (Orig.). 1994. pap. text 7.95 (*1-884855-03-2*) Secretarius.
— The Fall of America. 265p. (Orig.). 1991. pap. 11.95 (*1-56411-107-5*) Untd Bros & Sis.
— The Fall of America. (Orig.). 1993. pap. 12.00 (*1-56411-168-7*) Untd Bros & Sis.
— The Fall of America. 288p. (Orig.). 1996. reprint ed. pap. 9.95 (*1-884855-18-0*) Secretarius.
— The History of Jesus' Birth, Death & What It Means to You & Me. 64p. 1995. pap. text 6.95 (*1-884855-07-5*) Secretarius.
— History of the Nation of Islam. 72p. 1995. pap. text 6.95 (*1-884855-06-7*) Secretarius.
— How to Eat to Live, Bk. I. 132p. 1996. reprint ed. pap. 7.95 (*1-884855-16-4*) Secretarius.
— How to Eat to Live, Bk. I. 123p. reprint ed. pap. 8.95 (*1-56411-019-2*) Untd Bros & Sis.
— How to Eat to Live, Bk. 2. 210p. 1996. reprint ed. pap. 8.95 (*1-884855-15-6*) Secretarius.
— How to Eat to Live, Bk. II. (Illus.). 200p. 1992. reprint ed. pap. 10.00 (*1-56411-020-6*) Untd Bros & Sis.
— Message to the Blackman in America. 356p. 25.00 (*1-56411-005-2*) Untd Bros & Sis.
— Message to the Blackman in America. 392p. 1996. reprint ed. pap. 9.95 (*1-884855-14-8*) Secretarius.
— The Mother Plane. 64p. 1995. pap. text 6.95 (*1-884855-08-3*) Secretarius.
— The Muslim Recipe Book for MGT/GCC: How to Cook What You Eat to Live. Khalifah, Reda F., ed. 1995. reprint ed. pap. 5.95 (*1-56411-082-6*, 4BBG0087) Untd Bros & Sis.
— 100 Answers to the Most Uncommon 100 Questions. 64p. 1995. pap. text 6.95 (*1-884855-09-1*) Secretarius.
— Our Saviour Has Arrived. 238p. 1996. reprint ed. pap. 9.95 (*1-884855-17-2*) Secretarius.
— Our Saviour Has Arrived. 226p. 1990. reprint ed. pap. 11.95 (*1-56411-021-4*) Untd Bros & Sis.
— The Science of Time: The Time & the Judgement. Hakim, Nasie, ed. 96p. (Orig.). 1997. pap. 7.95 (*1-884855-27-X*) Secretarius.
— The Secrets of Freemasonry. 64p. 1994. pap. text 6.95 (*1-884855-05-9*) Secretarius.
— The Supreme Wisdom, Vol. 1. 64p. 1997. reprint ed. pap. 5.95 (*1-884855-13-X*) Secretarius.
— The Supreme Wisdom, Vol. 2. 96p. 1957. pap. 6.95 (*1-56411-080-X*) Untd Bros & Sis.
— The Supreme Wisdom, Vol. 2. 96p. 1996. reprint ed. pap. 6.95 (*1-884855-19-9*) Secretarius.
— The Supreme Wisdom Bk. 1: Solution to the So-Called Negroes' Problem. 56p. 1957. pap. 4.95 (*1-56411-079-6*) Untd Bros & Sis.
— The Theology of Time. 551p. (Orig.). 1992. pap. 24.95 (*1-56411-025-7*) Untd Bros & Sis.
— The Theology of Time. 551p. (Orig.). 1992. 49.95 (*1-56411-032-X*) Untd Bros & Sis.
— The Theology of Time, Vol. I. 170p. (Orig.). 1992. pap. 10.00 (*1-56411-028-1*) Untd Bros & Sis.
— The Theology of Time: Secret Science of the Times. unabridged ed. Hakim, Nasir, ed. (Illus.). 392p. 1997. 25.00 (*1-884855-30-X*) Secretarius.
— The Tricknology of the Enemy. Hakim, Nasie, ed. 24p. (Orig.). 1997. pap. 3.95 (*1-884855-21-0*) Secretarius.
— The True History of Elijah Muhammad: Autobiographically Authoritative. LC 96-80510. 324p. 1997. 21.95 (*1-884855-11-3*) Secretarius.
— The True History of Jesus. 37p. (Orig.). 1992. pap. 6.95 (*1-56411-047-8*) Coal Remb Elijah.
— The True History of Jesus: Religion. 37p. 1992. pap. text 6.95 (*0-9632728-0-2*) Coal Remb Elijah.
— The True History of Master Fard Muhammad: Allah (God) in Person. 208p. 1996. 16.95 (*1-884855-10-5*) Secretarius.

M

An Asterisk (*) at the beginning of an entry indicates that the title is appearing for the first time.

— The True History of Master Fard Muhammad Allah (God) in Person. Hakim, Nasir, ed. 208p. 1996. reprint ed. pap. 10.00 (*1-884855-31-8*) Secretarius.

Muhammad, En. Pi. & Krishnankutty, Gita. The Eye of God: Deivathinte Kannu. LC 98-900495. (Studies in Military & Strategic History). xiii, 148 p. 1997. write for info. (*0-333-92321-9*) Macmillan Pr.

Muhammad, Fayz. Kabul under Siege: An Inside Account of the 1929 Uprising. McChesney, Robert D., ed. LC 98-29652. (Princeton Series on the Middle East Bernard Lewis & Heath Lowry Ser.). (Illus.). 196p. 1997. pap. 25.95 (*1-55876-155-1*); text 49.95 (*1-55876-154-3*) Wiener Pubs Inc.

Muhammad Fazl ur-Rahman Ansari. Quranic Foundations & Structure of Muslim Society, Set. Vols. I & II. 890p. 1993. text 85.00 (*0-614-16644-6*) Kazi Pubns.

— Quranic Foundations & Structure of Muslim Society, Vol. I. 445p. 1993. text. write for info. (*1-56744-485-7*) Kazi Pubns.

— Quranic Foundations & Structure of Muslim Society, Vol. II. 445p. 1993. text. write for info. (*1-56744-486-5*) Kazi Pubns.

Muhammad, Ghazi B. The Crisis of the Islamic World. 1997. pap. 9.50 (*1-901230-05-8*, Pub. by Islamic Wrld Report) Intl Spec Bk.

Muhammad, H. R. The Sacred Origin & Nature of Sports & Culture. LC 98-72995. 139p. 1998. pap. 16.95 (*1-887752-13-7*) Fons Vitae.

Muhammad, Hassan. The Reality of the Mother Plane. unabridged ed. (Illus.). 80p. (Orig.). 1997. pap. 6.95 (*1-56411-157-1*, 4BBG0158) Untd Bros & Sis.

***Muhammad Ibn, Abu Al-Walid.** Middle Commentary of Aristotle's de Anima. Ivry, Alfred L., ed. (Islamic Translation Ser.). (ARA & ENG.). 300p. 2000. 29.95 (*0-8425-2473-8*) Brigham.

Muhammad Ibn-Jusuf Al-Herewi. The Buhr-ool Juwahir (Bahr al-Gewahir) Mujeed, Hukem A., ed. 294p. reprint ed. write for info. (*0-318-71535-X*) G Olms Pubs.

Muhammad Ibn Musa, Al K. The Algebra of Mohammed Ben Musa, 2 pts. in 1. Rosen, Frederic, ed. & tr. by. from ARA. xvi, 208p. 1986. reprint ed. lib. bdg. 63.70 (*3-487-07722-1*) G Olms Pubs.

Muhammad Ibn Yahya, Shaikh. Necklaces of Gems (Qala'id al-Jawahir) Holland, Muhtar, tr. from ARA. 603p. 1998. pap. 29.95 (*1-882216-17-2*) Al-Baz Pub.

Muhammad Ibn Yusuf, Abu'Umar. History of the Governors of Egypt. Koenig, Nicholas A., ed. LC 70-180364. (Columbia University. Contributions to Oriental History & Philology Ser.: No. 2). reprint ed. 27.50 (*0-404-50532-5*) AMS Pr.

Muhammad Iqbal Siddiqi. Asharah Mubasharah. 200p. (Orig.). 1990. pap. 7.50 (*1-56744-223-4*) Kazi Pubns.

Muhammad, Isam. Give Yourself Good Credit: The 7 Easy Steps to Help You Repair Your Credit. 2nd ed. Harrell, Willie, ed. (Illus.). 175p. 1993. 29.95 (*0-9637870-0-4*) Credit-Master.

Muhammad, John. The Journal of Truth. unabridged ed. 152p. (Orig.). 1996. pap. 10.00 (*1-56411-150-4*, 4BBG152) Untd Bros & Sis.

***Muhammad, John F.** How to Be a Woman's Best Friend. (Illus.). vi, 134p. 1999. 15.00 (*0-9678853-0-2*, NC510) Doveseed Prod.

***Muhammad, Joy & Savage, Stephanie, eds.** Using Microsoft Internet Explorer 4.0: Module 1. (Illus.). 250p. 1998. pap. text 20.00 (*0-7423-0005-6*) ComputerPREP.

Muhammad, Kevin. Obesity, Diabetes, & How to Eat to Live. LC 97-61410. (Within the Pulse Ser.: Vol. 1). (Illus.). 110p. 1997. pap. 10.95 (*0-9658864-0-9*) Crescent Pub Grp.

Muhammad, Lateef. Welfare: A Novocain. Muhammad, Sabir K., ed. 75p. (Orig.). (C). 1991. lib. bdg. 5.00 (*0-9627663-1-3*) Designer Comns.

Muhammad, Mahdi Fard, see Fard Muhammad, Mahdi.

***Muhammad, Maryum.** My Dad Moved Yesterday. (J). (gr. k-2). 2000. 10.95 (*0-533-13230-4*) Vantage.

Muhammad, Mukhtar. Genesis of New American Leadership: The Third Resurrection - From Decentralization to Interdependence. (Illus.). 200p. 1999. 29.95 (*0-9672724-1-6*, Qalam Bks) FAMACO Pubs.

Muhammad, Mustafa A. Alif Lam Ra: The Path to the Hereafter. 196p. 1996. 21.95 (*1-887798-00-5*) WriteMore Pubns.

Muhammad, Poure. The Chronology of the Nation of Islam. (Illus.). 97p. 1996. pap. 10.95 (*0-9643128-1-6*) Honor E Muhammad.

Muhammad, Ramadan. God is in the Heavens of Your Mind Vol. I: Reality Consciousness. 72p. 1998. pap. 8.00 (*0-8059-4565-2*) Dorrance.

Muhammad, S. A., jt. auth. see Tax Practioners Association Staff.

Muhammad, S. Ifetayo. The Goals of a Polygamous Woman. 16p. (Orig.). (J). 1987. pap. 0.50 (*0-916157-11-3*) African Islam Miss Pubns.

— Vitamin A Through Zinc: An Alphabet of Good Health. 16p. (Orig.). (J). 1985. pap. 1.00 (*0-916157-13-X*) African Islam Miss Pubns.

Muhammad Sa id Ramadan al-Buti. Al-Islam Maladh Kul al-Mujtamaat'al-Insaniyah: Limadha? Wa-Kayfa? 280p. 1991. pap. 7.95 (*1-57547-005-5*) Dar Al-Fikr.

— Al-Jihad fi al-Islam: Kayfa Nafhamuh? Wa-Kayfa Numarisuh? 257p. 1993. pap. 7.95 (*1-57547-012-8*) Dar Al-Fikr.

— Al-Salafiyah Marhalah Zamaniyah Mubarakah La Madhhab Islami. 270p. 1988. pap. 6.95 (*1-57547-019-5*) Dar Al-Fikr.

— Fiqh al-Sirah al-Nabawiyah: Ma 'a Mujaz li-Tarikh al-Khilafah al-Rashidiyah. 592p. 1991. 9.95 (*1-57547-007-1*) Dar Al-Fikr.

— Hurriyat al-Insan fi Zill Ubudiyatih. (Hadha Huwa al-Islam Ser.). 128p. 1992. pap. 1.95 (*1-57547-015-2*) Dar Al-Fikr.

— Kubra al-Yaqiniyat al-Kawniyah: Wujud al-Khaliq wa-Wazifat al-Makhluq. 392p. 1983. pap. 9.95 (*1-57547-022-5*) Dar Al-Fikr.

— Madkhal ila Fahm al-Judhur Man Ana? Wa Limadha? Wa-ila-Ayn? (Hadha Huwa al-Islam Ser.). 128p. 1991. pap. 1.95 (*1-57547-016-0*) Dar Al-Fikr.

Muhammad, Sabir K. The Need for Logic in Religion among African Americans. (Orig.). 1990. pap. text 5.00 (*0-9627663-0-5*) Designer Comns.

Muhammad, Sabir K., ed. see Muhammad, Lateef.

Muhammad, Sayf A. Bani Unveiled, al- 156p. (Orig.). (C). 1995. pap. text 12.95 (*0-934905-55-X*) Kazi Pubns.

Muhammad, Shan. The Growth of Muslim Politics in India. (C). 1991. 28.00 (*81-7024-418-8*, Pub. by Ashish Pub Hse) S Asia.

Muhammad, Shaykh & Kabbani, Hisham. The Doctrine of the Ahl Al-Sunna vs. the Salafi Movement. 136p. (C). 1997. pap. 9.95 (*1-871031-77-X*) Abjad Bk.

Muhammad, Shaykh, et al. The Children of the Truth. 404p. 1998. pap. 30.00 (*1-892595-06-0*) Sidi Muha Pr.

Muhammad, Silis. Reparations Petition: For United Nations Assistance under Resolution 1503 (XLVIII) on Behalf of African-Americans in the United States of America. 23p. (Orig.). pap. 5.00 (*1-56411-083-4*) Untd Bros & Sis.

Muhammad, Tynnetta. Comer by Night. (Illus.). 128p. (Orig.). 1986. pap. 10.49 (*0-9643128-0-8*) Honor E Muhammad.

Muhammad, Umar B. The Theory & Practice of Market Law in Medieval Islam. Dien, M. Izzi, ed. 247p. (C). 1997. 99.00 (*0-906094-33-X*, Pub. by Gibb Memorial Trust) David Brown.

Muhammad, Yolanda. Egyptian Echoes: Contemporary Art Inspired by Ancient Monuments. 32p. 1993. 15.00 (*0-9635774-0-9*) Sun Cities Art.

Muhammad, Yolanda, ed. see Dow, JaneAnn.

Muhammad, Yunini M., jt. auth. see Guo, Li.

Muhammad Zafrulla Khan, tr. from ARA. Gardens of the Righteous: Riyadh As Salihin of Imam Nawawi. 2nd ed. LC 89-3225. 332p. 1989. reprint ed. 19.95 (*0-940793-27-X*, Olive Branch Pr) Interlink Pub.

Muhammadrashid. Microelectronic Circuits. LC 97-46066. (Electrical Engineering Ser.). (C). 1998. pap. 102.95 (*0-534-95174-0*) Wadsworth Pub.

— Microelectronic Circuits. (Electrical Engineering). 1999. pap., lab manual ed. 25.95 (*0-534-95173-2*) Wadsworth Pub.

***Muhammed, Joy.** Internet Enterprise Development. (Illus.). (YA). 1999. pap. write for info. (*0-7423-0370-5*, ACE60INEDKIT) ComputerPREP.

— Internet Security. (Illus.). (YA). 1999. pap. write for info. (*0-7423-0372-1*, ACE48INSCKIT) ComputerPREP.

— Web Server Administration. (Illus.). (YA). 1999. pap. write for info. (*0-7423-0371-3*, ACE30WSADKIT) ComputerPREP.

— Web Site Design. (Illus.). (YA). 1999. pap. write for info. (*0-7423-0368-3*, ACE30WSDNKIT) ComputerPREP.

***Muhammed, Joy, ed.** E-Commerce Professional. (Illus.). (YA). 1999. pap. write for info. (*0-7423-0374-8*, ACE30ECPFKIT) ComputerPREP.

— Internet Application Development. (Illus.). (YA). 1999. pap. write for info. (*0-7423-0369-1*, ACE60INADKIT) ComputerPREP.

— Internet Foundations. (Illus.). (YA). 1999. pap. write for info. (*0-7423-0367-5*, ACE30INFDKIT) ComputerPREP.

— Internetworking Professional. (Illus.). (YA). 1999. pap. write for info. (*0-7423-0373-X*, ACE42INPFKIT) ComputerPREP.

Muhandes, jt. auth. see Wahba, Magdi.

Muhanji, Cherry. Her. LC 90-47570. 220p. 1990. pap. 9.95 (*1-879960-02-8*); lib. bdg. 19.95 (*1-879960-03-6*) Aunt Lute Bks.

Muharyaddeen, M. R. Dhikr: The Remembrance of God. 2nd rev. ed. LC 99-17828. (Illus.). 250p. (Orig.). 1998. pap. 11.00 (*0-914390-54-6*) Fellowship Pr PA.

Muhawi, Ibrahim. Speak Bird, Speak Again: Palestinian Arab Folktales. 420p. 1996. pap. 18.50 (*0-614-21654-0*, 1156) Kazi Pubns.

Muhawi, Ibrahim & Kanaana, Sharif. Speak, Bird, Speak Again: Palestinian Arab Folktales. 512p. 1988. pap. 19.95 (*0-520-06292-2*, Pub. by U CA Pr) Cal Prin Full Svc.

Muhawi, Ibrahim, tr. see Darwish, Mahmoud.

Muhe, Richard, et al. Wristwatches: History of a Century's Development. rev. ed. LC 86-61198. (Illus.). 410p. 1996. 79.95 (*0-88740-070-1*) Schiffer.

Muhl, Barbara Mary. Along the Royal Road. (Anatomy of Spirituality Ser.: Vol. 2). 337p. 1992. reprint ed. pap. 24.95 (*1-880863-02-2*, ARR) Christus Pub.

— The Royal Road to Reality. 2nd rev. ed. (Anatomy of Spirituality Ser.: Vol. 1). 352p. (Orig.). 1995. reprint ed. pap. 24.95 (*1-880863-01-4*, RRR) Christus Pub.

— Script, Kid & Fantasyland: The Truth That Makes You Free. 350p. 1998. pap. text 20.95 (*1-880863-26-X*) Christus Pub.

— This Pilgrim's Progress: A Correspondence with Joel Goldsmith. 364p. (Orig.). 1991. reprint ed. pap. 24.95 (*1-880863-25-1*, TPP) Christus Pub.

***Muhlan, Claudia.** Stay Cool Mun. 128p. 1999. pap. 24.00 (*1-85608-224-5*, Pub. by Hunt GBR) St Mut.

Muhlbacher, F., et al, eds. Transplant International - Official Journal of the European Society for Organ Transplantation: Proceedings of the 7th ESOT Congress, Vienna, October 3-7, 1995, Suppl. 1. (Illus.). 530p. 1996. pap., suppl. ed. 157.00 (*3-540-61024-3*) Spr-Verlag.

Muhlbacher, J. R., et al. Oberon-2 Programming with Windows. LC 97-8043. 376p. 1997. pap. 49.95 incl. cd-rom (*3-540-62522-4*) Spr-Verlag.

Muhlbauer, Alfred, jt. auth. see Keller, Wolfgang.

Muhlbauer, Andre & Raal, J. D. Vapor-Liquid Equilibria Measurements & Calculations. (Series in Chemical & Mechanical Engineering). 200p. 1996. text 105.00 (*1-56032-550-X*) Taylor & Francis.

Muhlbauer, Gene & Dodder, Laura. The Losers: Gang Delinquency in an American Suburb. LC 82-25497. 138p. 1983. 65.00 (*0-275-91048-2*, C1048, Praeger Pubs) Greenwood.

Muhlbauer, W. Kent. Pipeline Risk Management Manual. LC 91-32612. (Illus.). 275p. 1992. reprint ed. pap. 85.30 (*0-608-04208-0*, 206494300011) Bks Demand.

— Pipeline Risk Management Manual. 2nd ed. (Illus.). 438p. 1996. 75.00 (*0-88415-668-0*, 5668) Gulf Pub.

Muhlberger, Detlef, ed. The Social Basis of European Fascist Movements. LC 87-14093. 384p. 1987. lib. bdg. 49.95 (*0-7099-3585-4*, Pub. by C Helm) Routldge.

Muhlberger, Richard. American Folk Marquetry: Masterpieces in Wood. (Illus.). 240p. 1998. 65.00 (*0-912161-07-8*) Mus Amer Folk.

***Muhlberger, Richard.** Charles Webster Hawthorne: Paintings & Watercolors. (Illus.). 112p. 2000. 40.00 (*0-295-97927-5*) U of Wash Pr.

Muhlberger, Richard. Mojo Hand: Recent Work by Richard Yarde. Keough, Jeffrey, ed. (Illus.). 12p. (Orig.). 1996. pap. 15.00 (*0-9628905-5-3*) MA Collge Art.

— Unseen Renoir, 1. 1999. 24.95 (*1-885440-46-4*) First Glance.

— The Unseen Van Gogh. (Illus.). 176p. 1998. 22.95 (*1-885440-28-6*) First Glance.

— What Makes a Van Gogh a Van Gogh? (Illus.). 48p. (YA). (gr. 5 up). 1993. 11.99 (*0-670-85198-1*, Viking Child) Peng Put Young Read.

Muhle, Peter. Agriculture-Forestry-Horticulture Dictionary: English-German.Tr. of Landwirtschaft, Forstwirtschaft, Gartenbau. (ENG & GER.). 732p. 1990. 225.00 (*0-7859-8516-6*, 3861170124); lib. bdg. 150.00 (*0-8288-3597-7*, F92570) Fr & Eur.

— Dictionary of Wood Science & Technology: English-German - German-English. 466p. 1992. 193.00 (*3-87097-157-6*, Pub. by O Brandstetter Verlag) IBD Ltd.

— Landwirtschaft - Forstwirtschaft - Gartenbau: Englisch - Deutsch. 1991. 150.00 (*0-8288-2481-9*) Fr & Eur.

— Wood Science Dictionary: English-German, German-English. (ENG & GER.). 460p. 1992. 190.00 (*0-7859-7067-3*) Fr & Eur.

Muhle, Peter, ed. German-English Dictionary of Agriculture, Forestry & Horticulture. (ENG & GER.). 731p. 1993. 168.00 (*0-7859-8774-6*) Fr & Eur.

Muhlebach, Richard F. & Alexander, Alan A. Business Strategies for Real Estate Management Companies. LC 97-15981. (Illus.). 428p. 1997. text 79.00 (*1-57203-053-4*, 720) Inst Real Estate.

Muhlebach, Richard F., jt. auth. see Alexander, Alan A.

Muhleck, Ralph. Zur Effektivitat der Forderung von Direktinvestitionen in Entwicklungslandern: Wirkungspotentiale von Investitionsanreizen der DEG. (GER., Illus.). 229p. 1996. 44.95 (*3-631-30869-8*) P Lang Pubng.

Muhleitner, Elke. Biographisches Lexikon der Psychoanalyse. (GER.). 400p. 1992. 125.00 (*0-7859-8542-5*, 3892955573) Fr & Eur.

Muhlemann, Hans R. Introduction to Oral Preventive Medicine. (Illus.). 253p. 1976. pap. text 32.00 (*3-87652-591-8*) Quint Pub Co.

Muhlenberg, E., ed. see Nyssenus, Gregorius.

Muhlenberg, Henry M. Pennsylvania-German in the Revolutionary War, 1775-1783. (Illus.). 542p. 1997. reprint ed. lib. bdg. 55.00 (*0-8328-6382-3*) Higginson Bk Co.

Muhlenburg, Heinrich M. The Correspondence of Heinrich Melchior Muhlenberg, 1748-1752, Vol. 2. Kleiner, John W. & Lehmann, Helmut T., eds. & trs. by. from GER. LC 93-86108. (Illus.). 316p. 1997. 39.50 (*0-89725-227-6*, 1494) Picton Pr.

Muhlenfeld, Elisabeth. Mary Boykin Chesnut: A Biography. LC 80-26610. (Southern Biography Ser.). (Illus.). 302p. (C). 1980. pap. 17.95 (*0-8071-1804-4*) La State U Pr.

Muhlenfeld, Elisabeth, jt. ed. see Woodward, C. Vann.

Muhlert, Jan K., frwd. Palmer Museum of Art Twenty-Fifth Anniversary, 1972-1997. (Illus.). 46p. 1997. pap. 5.00 (*0-911209-46-8*) Palmer Mus Art.

***Muhlfeld, Diane L., ed.** Best Behavior: Unleashing Your Dog's Instinct to Obey. (Good Dog Library). (Illus.). 208p. 2000. 26.95 (*1-879620-65-0*) Belvoir Pubns.

Muhlhaus, Hans B. Continuum Models for Materials with Microstructure. 492p. 1996. 180.00 (*0-471-95065-3*, Wiley-Interscience) Wiley.

Muhlhauser, Max, ed. Cooperative Computer-Aided Authoring & Learning: A Systems Approach. LC 94-37355. 368p. (C). 1994. text 133.50 (*0-7923-9527-1*) Kluwer Academic.

Muhlhausler, Peter. Linguistic Ecology: Language Change & Linguistic Imperialism in the Pacific Rim. 416th ed. (Politics of Language Ser.). 416p. (C). 1995. 75.00 (*0-415-05635-7*) Routledge.

Muhlhausler, Peter, jt. auth. see Fill, Alwin.

Muhll, Von der, see Von der Muhll, ed.

Muhlmann, Heiner. The Nature of Cultures: A Blueprint for a Theory of Culture Genetics. LC 96-20113. 160p. 1996. pap. 34.95 (*3-211-82800-1*) Spr-Verlag.

Muhlstein, ed. see Proust, Marcel.

Muhlstein, Anka. La Salle: Explorer of the North American Frontier. Wood, Willard, tr. from FRE. LC 94-47991. (Illus.). 256p. 1994. 22.45 (*1-55970-219-2*, Pub. by Arcade Pub Inc) Time Warner.

— La Salle: Explorer of the North American Frontier. Wood, Willard, tr. from FRE. LC 94-47991. (Illus.). 256p. 1995. pap. 11.45 (*1-55970-294-X*, Pub. by Arcade Pub Inc) Time Warner.

— A Taste for Freedom: The Life of Astolphe de Custine. unabridged ed. Waugh, Teresa, tr. from FRE. 320p. 1999. pap. 16.95 (*1-885983-41-7*, Pub. by Turtle Point Pr) Dist Art Pubs.

Muhly, James D. Copper & Tin: The Distribution of Mineral Resources & the Nature of the Metals Trade in the Bronze Age, Including Supplement. (Connecticut Academy of Arts & Sciences Ser., Trans.: Vol. 43). 380p. 1973. pap. 69.50 (*0-685-22879-7*) Elliots Bks.

Muhly, Paul S. & Solel, Baruch. Hilbert Modules over Operator Algebras. LC 95-373. (Memoirs of the American Mathematical Society Ser.: No. 559). 53p. 1995. pap. 28.00 (*0-8218-0346-8*, MEMO/117/559) Am Math.

Muhly, Paul S., jt. ed. see Jorgensen, Palle E.

Muhm, Don. The NFO: A Farm Belt Rebel. LC 98-89806. (Illus.). 400p. 2000. pap. 16.95 (*1-883477-30-1*); lib. bdg. 24.95 (*1-883477-29-8*) Lone Oak MN.

Muhm, Don, et al. The Farmers Union in Minnesota: More Than a Farm Organization. Howe, Ray, ed. LC 97-75133. (Illus.). 400p. 1998. lib. bdg. 21.95 (*1-883477-23-9*) Lone Oak MN.

***Muhni, Suntin Sunder.** Performing Indianness in New York City: Desi on the Hudson. LC 99-14194. 200p. 1999. 50.00 (*0-8153-3372-2*) Garland.

Muhr, Alan, jt. ed. see Dorfmann, Al.

Muhr, C., et al. Frontiers in European Radiology, Vol. 3. (Illus.). 140p. 1983. 79.95 (*0-387-11446-7*) Spr-Verlag.

Muhr, Ursula. Easter Egg Fun. (Illus.). 12p. (J). (ps up). 1996. 5.95 (*0-689-80609-4*) S&S Childrens.

Muhrer, Verle, jt. ed. see Whitehead, Fred.

Muhrhammer. TCP IP Tutorial & Technical Overview. 500p. 1998. pap. 64.00 (*0-13-020130-8*) P-H.

Muhs, Joachim F. How to Choose the Right Yacht. (Illus.). 128p. 1994. pap. 19.95 (*0-7136-3950-4*) Sheridan.

Mui, Ada C., et al. Long-Term Care & Ethnicity. LC 98-11157. 232p. 1998. 59.95 (*0-86569-232-7*, Auburn Hse) Greenwood.

Mui, Chunka, jt. auth. see Downes, Larry.

Mui, Hoh-cheung & Mui, Lorna H. Shops & Shopkeeping in Eighteenth-Century England. 400p. 1989. 65.00 (*0-7735-0620-9*, Pub. by McG-Queens Univ Pr) CUP Services.

Mui, Linda. When You Can't Find Your UNIX System Administrator. (Computer Science). 156p. 1995. pap. 17.95 (*1-56592-104-6*) Thomson Learn.

Mui, Linda & Pearce, Eric. X Window System Administrator's Guide, Vol. 8. O'Reilly, Tim, ed. (Computer Science). (Illus.). 372p. (Orig.). 1992. pap. 29.95 (*0-937175-83-8*) Thomson Learn.

Mui, Linda & Quercia, Valerie. X User Tools. O'Reilly, Tim, ed. (Illus.). 856p. (Orig.). 1994. pap. 49.95 (*1-56592-019-8*) Thomson Learn.

Mui, Linda, ed. see Blank-Edelman, David.

Mui, Linda, ed. see Descartes, Alligator & Bunce, Tim.

Mui, Linda, ed. see Eckstein, Robert.

Mui, Linda, ed. see Gundavaram, Shishir, et al.

Mui, Linda, ed. see Killelea, Patrick.

Mui, Linda, ed. see Leavitt, John.

Mui, Linda, ed. see Quercia, Valerie.

Mui, Linda, ed. see Rosenfeld, Louis & Morville, Peter.

Mui, Linda, ed. see Spainhour, Stephen & Eckstein, Robert.

Mui, Linda, ed. see Stein, Lincoln & MacEachern, Doug.

Mui, Linda, ed. see Vromans, Johan.

Mui, Linda, ed. see Walsh, Nancy.

Mui, Linda, ed. see Wong, Clinton.

Mui, Lorna H., jt. auth. see Mui, Hoh-cheung.

Mui, Peter, ed. see O'Reilly & Associates Staff & Cutler, Ellie.

Muia, Maria. The Last 30 Seconds. LC 98-86292. 325p. 1998. 25.00 (*0-7388-0055-4*); pap. 15.00 (*0-7388-0056-2*) Xlibris Corp.

Muia, Paul J. Esthetic Restorations: Improved Dentist-Laboratory Communication. LC 92-48524. (Illus.). 280p. 1993. text 110.00 (*0-86715-226-5*) Quint Pub Co.

Muijen, M., jt. ed. see Weller, M. P.

Muijen, Marie-Louise Van, see Van Muijen, Marie-Louise.

Muijres, Guus. Acoustic Waves in Cracked Media. (Illus.). 103p. 1998. pap. 39.50 (*90-407-1649-8*, Pub. by Delft U Pr) Coronet Bks.

Muilenberg, Michael L. Aerobiology. Burge, Harriet A., ed. 176p. 1996. lib. bdg. 49.95 (*1-56670-206-2*, L1206) Lewis Pubs.

Muilenburg, Grace & Swineford, Ada. Land of the Post Rock: Its Origins, History & People. LC 74-23833. (Illus.). xiv, 210p. 1975. pap. 12.95 (*0-7006-0194-5*) U Pr of KS.

Muiler, R., ed. see Popa, Constantin M.

Muillo. Enciclopedia Juvenil, 10 vols., Set. (SPA.). 1500p. (J). 1974. 295.00 (*0-8288-6034-3*, S50472) Fr & Eur.

Muilwijk, M. The Divine Kura Tribe: Kuravanci & Other Prabandhams. (Gonda Indological Studies: Vol. 4). xvi, 288p. 1996. pap. 72.00 (*90-6980-082-9*, Pub. by Egbert Forsten) Hodlder & Stoughton.

Muinzer, Genevieve. New to the U. K. A Guide to Your Life & Rights in the U. K. 224p. 1987. 35.00 (*0-7102-0852-9*, 08529, Routledge Thoemms) Routledge.

Muinzer, L. A., tr. see Carling, Finn.

Muinzer, Louis, tr. see Hauger, Torill T.

Muinzer, Louis A., tr. see Carling, Finn.

Muir. Developmental Psychology Reader. 1992. pap. text 13.40 (*0-536-58273-4*) Pearson Custom.

— Handbook of Veterinary Anesthesia. 3rd ed. 2000. text 49.95 (*0-323-00801-1*) Mosby Inc.

Muir & Hubbell, John A. E. Equine Anesthesia: Monitoring & Emergency Therapy. (Illus.). 528p. (C). (gr. 13). 1991. text 74.95 (*0-8016-3576-4*, 03576) Mosby Inc.

An Asterisk (*) at the beginning of an entry indicates that the title is appearing for the first time.

Muir, jt. auth. see Bartlet.

Muir, jt. auth. see Howard.

Muir, jt. ed. see Harper.

Muir, Ada. Healing Herbs & Health Foods of the Zodiac. LC 92-37676. (Illus.). 192p. 1999. mass mkt. 3.99 (*0-87542-575-5*) Llewellyn Pubns.

Muir, Albert E. The Technology Transfer System: Inventions - Marketing - Licensing - Patenting - Setting - Practice - Management - Policy. LC 97-93356. xiii, 241p. 1997. 24.95 (*0-9657597-6-8*) Latham Bk Pub.

Muir, Alexander. From Aberdeen to Ottawa in Eighteen Forty-Five: The Diary of Alexander Muir. Mackenzie, George A., ed. (Illus.). 116p. 1990. pap. text 12.00 (*0-08-037983-4*, Pub. by Aberdeen U Pr) Macmillan.

Muir, Alice J., jt. auth. see Hambly, Kenneth.

Muir, Allan, jt. ed. see Muir, Doris.

***Muir, Andrew.** Razor's Edge: Bob Dylan & the Never Ending Tour. (Illus.). 2000. pap. 18.95 (*1-900924-13-7*, Pub. by Helter Skelter) Interlink Pub.

Muir, B. J. Leod: Six Old English Poems: A Handbook. xxxvi, 162p. 1989. 43.00 (*2-88124-357-6*) Gordon & Breach.

Muir, Bernard J., ed. The Exeter Anthology of Old English Poetry: An Edition of Exeter Dean & Chapter. LC 95-149779. 1000p. 1995. text 90.00 (*0-85989-436-3*, Pub. by Univ Exeter Pr) Northwestern U Pr.

— The Exeter Book. 148p. 1992. text 39.00 (*0-85989-370-7*) Univ Exeter Pr.

Muir, Bernard J. & Turner, Andrew J., eds. Life of Saint Wilfrid: Edmer's Vita Sanci Wilfridi. (Exeter Medieval Texts & Studies). 304p. 1998. text 95.00 (*0-85989-597-1*) Univ Exeter Pr.

Muir, Bernard J., jt. ed. see Manion, Margaret M.

Muir, Bernice L. Pathophysiology: An Introduction to Mechanisms of Disease. 2nd ed. LC 87-25298. 685p. 1989. text 44.00 (*0-8273-4317-5*) Delmar.

Muir, Bill. Totally True. 1997. pap. 4.99 (*0-310-67649-5*) Zondervan.

Muir, Bryce & Muir, Margaret. Lawn Wars: Lawn Ornaments (A Field Guide) (Illus.). 32p. (Orig.). 1988. pap. 8.95 (*0-942396-55-3*) Blackberry ME.

Muir, Calum S. & Wagner, G. Directory of On-Going Research in Cancer Epidemiology, 1982. (IARC Scientific Publications: No. 46). 722p. 1986. pap. 32.00 (*0-19-723046-6*) OUP.

Muir, Calum S. & Wagner, G., eds. Directory of On-Going Research in Cancer Epidemiology, 1984. (IARC Scientific Publications: No. 62). 748p. 1985. pap. 26.50 (*0-19-723062-8*) OUP.

Muir, Calum S., ed. see Wagner, G.

Muir, Caroline, jt. auth. see Muir, Charles.

Muir, Charles & Muir, Caroline. Tantra: The Art of Conscious Loving. LC 88-7854. (Illus.). 144p. 1989. pap. 12.95 (*0-916515-86-9*) Mercury Hse Inc.

Muir, Chaun, jt. auth. see Haynes, J. H.

Muir, Daniel T., jt. auth. see Williams, Jon M.

Muir, Darwin & Slater, Alan, eds. Infant Development: The Essential Readings. (Essential Readings in Developmental Psychology Ser.). (Illus.). 256p. 1999. 59.95 (*0-631-21746-0*); pap. 24.95 (*0-631-21747-9*) Blackwell Pubs.

Muir, Darwin, jt. auth. see Slater, Alan.

***Muir, Diana.** Reflections in Bullough's Pond: Economy & Ecosystem in New England. LC 99-58013. (Revisiting New England Ser.). (Illus.). 320p. 2000. 26.00 (*0-87451-909-8*) U Pr of New Eng.

***Muir, Doris & Muir, Allan, eds.** Muir's Original Log Home Guide for Builders & Buyers. (Illus.). 260p. 1999. pap. 25.00 (*0-9677869-0-8*) G J Schroeder.

Muir, Dorothy T. Mount Vernon: The Civil War Years. 1993. pap. 10.95 (*0-931917-26-3*) Mt Vernon Ladies.

Muir, Douglas A. & Puzo, Michael J. Massachusetts Corporations. LC 79-92872. (Practice Systems Library Manual). 1993. suppl. ed. 69.50 (*0-317-03187-2*) West Group.

Muir, Douglas A., et al. Massachusetts Corporations. LC 79-92872. (Practice Systems Library Manual). Date not set. ring bd. 140.00 (*0-317-03186-4*, 68820, MICHIE) LEXIS Pub.

Muir, Douglas A., et al. Massachusetts Corporations: A Practice Systems Library Manual. 1981. ring bd. 140.00 (*0-327-00971-3*, 68820, MICHIE) LEXIS Pub.

— Massachusetts Corporations: 1999 Edition. 1000p. 1999. ring bd. 155.00 (*0-327-04910-3*, 6882011) LEXIS Pub.

Muir, Douglas A., et al. Massachusetts Corporations, 1998 Supplement. 150p. 1998. ring bd., suppl. ed. write for info. (*0-327-00550-5*, 6883012) LEXIS Pub.

Muir, E. The Politics of King Lear. LC 76-99171. (Studies in Shakespeare: No. 24). 1970. reprint ed. lib. bdg. 59.00 (*0-8383-0331-5*) M S G Haskell Hse.

***Muir, Eden.** Inside Form *Z: Guide to 3D Modeling & Rendering. 2nd ed. 1999. pap. 49.95 (*1-56690-189-8*, OnWord Pr) High Mtn.

Muir, Eden G. Inside Form-Z, 2. LC 98-17940. 450p. (C). 1998. pap. 49.95 (*1-56690-182-0*) Thomson Learn.

Muir, Edward. The Leopold Von Ranke Manuscript Collection of Syracuse University: The Complete Catalogue. 240p. 1983. text 75.00 (*0-8156-2294-5*) Syracuse U Pr.

— Mad Blood Stirring: Vendetta & Factions in Friuli During the Renaissance. LC 92-15211. 424p. 1993. text 49.95 (*0-8018-4446-0*) Johns Hopkins.

— Mad Blood Stirring: Vendetta in Renaissance Italy. abr. ed. LC 97-41775. (Illus.). 208p. 1998. pap. text 15.95 (*0-8018-5849-6*) Johns Hopkins.

— Ritual in Early Modern Europe. LC 96-50034. (New Approaches to European History Ser.: Vol. 11). (Illus.). 304p. (C). 1997. text 54.95 (*0-521-40169-0*); pap. text 17.95 (*0-521-40967-5*) Cambridge U Pr.

Muir, Edward & Ruggiero, Guido, eds. History from Crime. Curry, Corrada B. et al, trs. LC 93-32009. (Selections from Quaderni Storici Ser.). 1994. 38.50 (*0-8018-4732-X*); pap. 15.95 (*0-8018-4733-8*) Johns Hopkins.

— Microhistory & the Lost Peoples of Europe. LC 90-27638. (Selections from Quaderni Storici Ser.). 240p. 1991. text 38.50 (*0-8018-4182-8*); pap. text 15.95 (*0-8018-4183-6*) Johns Hopkins.

— Sex & Gender in Historical Perspective. Gallucci, Margaret A. et al, trs. LC 90-31730. (Selections from Quaderni Storici Ser.). (Illus.). 260p. reprint ed. pap. 80.60 (*0-608-07335-0*, 206756300009) Bks Demand.

Muir, Edwin. An Autobiography. (Classics Ser.). 320p. 1995. pap. 11.95 (*0-86241-423-7*, Pub. by Canongate Books) Interlink Pub.

— An Autobiography. (Memoir Ser.). 296p. (C). 1990. reprint ed. pap. 10.95 (*1-55597-128-8*) Graywolf.

— The Estate of Poetry. LC 92-39289. (Discovery Ser.). 144p. 1993. pap. 11.00 (*1-55597-182-2*) Graywolf.

— John Knox: Portrait of a Calvinist. LC 76-148892. (Select Bibliographies Reprint Ser.). 1977. reprint ed. 23.95 (*0-8369-5656-7*) Ayer.

— Latitudes. 322p. 1977. 21.95 (*0-8369-2665-X*) Ayer.

— The Politics of King Lear. 1972. 200.00 (*0-87968-032-6*) Gordon Pr.

— Scott & Scotland: The Predicament of the Scottish Writer. 114p. 1982. 13.95 (*0-904919-60-9*) Dufour.

— Scottish Journey: A Modern Classic. LC 96-167556. 250p. 1996. pap. 13.95 (*1-85158-841-8*, Pub. by Mainstream Pubng) Trafalgar.

— Transition: Essays on Contemporary Literature. 218p. 1977. 20.95 (*0-8369-2666-8*) Ayer.

— Transition: Essays on Contemporary Literature. (BCL1-PR English Literature Ser.). 218p. 1992. reprint ed. lib. bdg. 79.00 (*0-7812-7061-8*) Rprt Serv.

Muir, Edwin, tr. see Broch, Hermann.

Muir, Edwin, tr. see Kafka, Franz.

Muir, Elizabeth G. & Whiteley, Marilyn F., eds. Changing Roles of Women Within the Christian Church in Canada. (Illus.). 391p. 1995. text 60.00 (*0-8020-0669-8*); pap. text 24.95 (*0-8020-7623-8*) U of Toronto Pr.

***Muir, Frank.** A Kentish Lad. 2000. 29.95 (*0-593-03452-X*, Pub. by Transworld Publishers Ltd) Trafalgar.

— The Walpole Orange. 2000. pap. 8.95 (*0-552-14136-4*, Pub. by Transworld Publishers Ltd) Trafalgar.

Muir, Frank, ed. The Oxford Book of Humorous Prose. 1,196p. 1992. pap. 18.95 (*0-19-282959-9*) OUP.

Muir, Frank & Norden, Denis. Oh, My Word! 128p. 1981. 7.95 (*0-416-00811-9*, NO. 0235) Routledge.

Muir, Fredric J. A Reason for Hope: Liberation Theology Confronts a Liberal Faith. LC 93-86732. 160p. (Orig.). (C). 1994. pap. 10.00 (*0-931104-39-4*) SunInk Pubn.

Muir-Giles, G. & Clark-Wilson, Jo. Rehabilitation of the Severely Brain Injured Adult: A Practical Approach. 2nd ed. (Illus.). 272p. 1998. pap. 47.75 (*1-56593-319-2*, 0649) Singular Publishing.

Muir, Hazel. Larousse Dictionary of Scientists. LC 94-75739. 608p. 1996. pap. 16.95 (*0-7523-0036-9*) LKC.

Muir, Hazel, jt. ed. see Walker, Peter.

Muir, Helen. The Biltmore, Beacon for Miami. 3rd expanded rev. ed. LC 97-34407. 192p. 1998. pap. 19.95 (*0-9633461-8-0*) Valiant Pr.

— Celestial Seasonings. 1998. 216.00 (*0-671-71850-9*) S&S Trade.

— Frost in Florida: A Memoir. Seibel, Mark, ed. (Illus.). 208p. 1995. 19.95 (*0-9633461-6-4*) Valiant Pr.

***Muir, Helen.** Miami, U.S.A. An Expanded Edition. 2000. 24.95 (*0-8130-1831-5*) U Press Fla.

Muir, Holly J. Conducting a Preliminary Benchmarking Analysis: A Librarian's Guide. 32p. 1993. pap. text 24.00 (*1-884935-12-5*) Lib Benchmarking.

Conducting & Analyzing Benchmarking Data: A Librarian's Guide. 42p. 1994. pap. text 31.50 (*1-884935-15-X*) Lib Benchmarking.

— Developing Benchmarking Metrics: A Librarian's Guide. 48p. 1993. pap. text 36.00 (*1-884935-13-3*) Lib Benchmarking.

— Identifying Benchmarking Partners: Academic, Public & School Libraries. 35p. 1994. pap. text 26.25 (*1-884935-17-6*) Lib Benchmarking.

— Identifying Benchmarking Partners: Special Libraries. 66p. 1993. pap. text 49.50 (*1-884935-14-1*) Lib Benchmarking.

— Presenting Benchmarking Results: A Librarian's Guide. 44p. 1994. pap. text 33.00 (*1-884935-16-8*) Lib Benchmarking.

Muir, I. D. The Four-Axis Universal Stage, Vol. 49. LC 80-83455. (Illus.). 1981. 20.00 (*0-904962-08-3*) Microscope Pubns.

Muir, Ian. Plastic Surgery in Pedeatrics. 1988. 116.00 (*0-316-58944-6*, Little Brwn Med Div) Lppncott W & W.

***Muir, Ian, et al.** European Patent Law: Law & Procedure under the EPC & PCT. 382p. 1999. text 80.00 (*0-19-826875-0*) OUP.

Muir, J. Divided Loyalties, Shared Beliefs. 6.99 (*1-85792-100-3*, Pub. by Christian Focus) Spring Arbor Dist.

— Excel 5. 200p. 1995. pap. 70.00 (*1-85805-120-7*, Pub. by DP Publns) St Mut.

— More Than My Job's Worth. 6.99 (*1-85792-018-X*, Pub. by Christian Focus) Spring Arbor Dist.

— Windows & MS-DOS, Windows 3.1 & 95: MS-DOS 5 & 6. 200p. 1995. pap. 59.95 (*1-85805-124-X*, Pub. by DP Publns) St Mut.

Muir, J. E. & Roberts, Ronald. Recent Developments in Aquaculture, No. 4. (Illus.). 450p. 1993. 125.00 (*0-632-02898-X*) Blackwell Sci.

Muir, J. F., et al, eds. Pulmonary Rehabilitation. 261p. 1996. pap. text 43.00 (*0-7279-1022-1*, Pub. by BMJ Pub) Login Brothers Bk Co.

Muir, J. Gordon. Sex, Politics & the End of Morality. LC 97-75512. 320p. 1998. pap. 17.95 (*1-57197-090-8*) Pentland Pr.

Muir, J. V., ed. Homer: Odyssey IX. (Bristol Greek Texts Ser.). (GRE.). 79p. 1981. 16.95 (*0-906515-61-0*, Pub. by Brist Class Pr) Focus Pub-R Pullins.

Muir, J. V., jt. ed. see Easterling, P. E.

Muir, Jane. Of Men & Numbers: The Story of the Great Mathematicians. unabridged ed. (Illus.). 256p. 1996. reprint ed. pap. text 7.95 (*0-486-28973-7*) Dover.

Muir, Janette K. Introduction to Interpersonal & Small Group Communication Handbook. 160p. 1994. per. 17.95 (*0-8403-9744-5*) Kendall-Hunt.

— Introduction to Oral Communication Handbook. 96p. (C). 1994. 12.95 (*0-8403-9635-X*) Kendall-Hunt.

Muir, Janette K., ed. C-SPAN in the Communication Classroom: Theories & Application. LC 92-61675. 112p. (C). 1992. pap. text 2.50 (*0-944811-09-4*) Natl Comm Assn.

Muir, Janette K. & Muir, Star A. Foundations of Public Communication. 240p. 1994. per., wbk. ed. 37.95 (*0-8403-8920-5*) Kendall-Hunt.

Muir, Jeannette T., jt. auth. see Morris, Patricia J.

***Muir, Jeff & Roberts, Mark R.** Excavations at Wyndyke Furlong, Abingdon, Oxfordshire. (Illus.). 75p. 2000. pap. 18.95 (*0-947816-90-9*, Pub. by Oxford Univ Comm Arch) David Brown.

Muir, Jim. Little Girls Have to Sleep. LC 92-37456. (Illus.). (J). 1993. pap. 16.00 incl. audio (*1-881320-03-0*, Black Belt) Black Belt Communs.

Muir, John. All the World Over: Notes from Alaska. LC 95-25688. (Pathstone Editions Ser.). 96p. (Orig.). 1996. pap. 9.00 (*0-87156-853-5*, Pub. by Sierra) Random.

Muir, John. America's Wilderness: The Photographs of Ansel Adams with Writings by John Muir. LC 96-69256. (Illus.). 128p. 1997. 17.98 (*1-56138-744-4*, Courage) Running Pr.

— The Cruise of the Corwin: Journal of the Arctic Expedition of 1881. (Illus.). 320p. 2000. pap. 10.00 (*0-618-05701-3*) HM.

Muir, John. The Discovery of Glacier Bay, 1879. Jones, William R., ed. (Illus.). 16p. 1978. reprint ed. pap. 2.00 (*0-89646-045-2*) Vistabooks.

— Gentle, Wilderness: The Sierra Nevada. 168p. 1995. 24.98 (*0-88486-125-2*) Galahad Bks.

— How to Keep Your Volkswagen Alive: A Manual of Step-by-Step Procedures for the Complete Idiot. 18th rev. ed. LC 99-26236. (Illus.). 480p. 1999. pap. 25.00 (*1-56261-480-0*, J Muir) Avalon Travel.

— The Hummingbird of the California Waterfalls. Jones, William R., ed. (Illus.). 24p. 1977. reprint ed. pap. 2.00 (*0-89646-019-3*) Vistabooks.

— In the Heart of the California Alps. Jones, William R., ed. (Illus.). 24p. 1977. reprint ed. pap. 2.00 (*0-89646-026-6*) Vistabooks.

— John Muir: His Life & Letters & Other Writings. Gifford, Terry, ed. LC 96-221226. (Illus.). 900p. 1996. 38.00 (*0-89886-463-1*) Mountaineers.

— John Muir: The Eight Wilderness Discovery Books, 8 vols. LC 92-53740. 1056p. 1992. 38.00 (*0-89886-335-X*) Mountaineers.

— John Muir; To Yosemite & Beyond. Engberg, Robert & Wesling, Donald, eds. LC 98-6137. 171p. 1999. pap. text 12.95 (*0-87480-580-5*) U of Utah Pr.

— John of the Mountains: The Unpublished Journals of John Muir. (American Biography Ser.). 459p. 1991. reprint ed. lib. bdg. 89.00 (*0-7812-8292-6*) Rprt Serv.

— Letters from Alaska. Engberg, Robert & Merrell, Bruce, eds. LC 93-18845. (Illus.). 128p. (Orig.). (C). 1993. pap. 14.95 (*0-299-13954-9*); lib. bdg. 30.00 (*0-299-13950-6*) U of Wis Pr.

— Mountaineering Essays. Fleck, Richard, ed. LC 98-6137. 200p. 1997. pap. text 10.95 (*0-87480-544-9*) U of Utah Pr.

— The Mountains of California. LC 88-23938. (John Muir Library). (Illus.). 304p. 1989. pap. 10.00 (*0-87156-663-X*, Pub. by Sierra) Random.

— The Mountains of California. LC 92-43496. 264p. 1993. pap. 9.95 (*0-14-026661-5*) Viking Penguin.

— The Mountains of California. LC 90-47833. (Illus.). 406p. 1990. reprint ed. 34.95 (*0-87797-191-9*) Cherokee.

— The Mountains of California. 1992. reprint ed. lib. bdg. 75.00 (*0-7812-5067-6*) Rprt Serv.

— My First Summer in the Sierra. 1992. 22.50 (*0-8446-6523-1*) Peter Smith.

— My First Summer in the Sierra. LC 89-6081. (Illus.). 208p. 1990. pap. 10.00 (*0-87156-748-2*, Pub. by Sierra) Random.

— My First Summer in the Sierra. 336p. 1987. pap. 9.95 (*0-14-025570-2*) Viking Penguin.

— My First Summer in the Sierra. LC 90-47834. (Illus.). 361p. 1990. reprint ed. 34.95 (*0-87797-192-7*) Cherokee.

— My First Summer in the Sierra. (BCL1 - United States Local History Ser.). 353p. 1991. reprint ed. lib. bdg. 89.00 (*0-7812-6342-5*) Rprt Serv.

— My First Summer in the Sierras, 001. LC 98-16599. 336p. 1998. pap. 10.00 (*0-395-35351-3*) HM.

— Nature Writings. Cronon, William, ed. LC 96-9664. (Illus.). 888p. 1997. 35.00 (*1-883011-24-8*, Pub. by Library of America) Penguin Putnam.

— Northwest Passages: From the Pen of John Muir in California, Oregon, Washington & Alaska. LC 98-73725. (Illus.). 64p. 1998. reprint ed. 15.00 (*0-9633056-8-9*) Coldstream Pr.

— Our National Parks. LC 01-26282. Date not set. 10.00 (*0-403-00194-3*) Scholarly.

— Our National Parks. LC 90-45254. (John Muir Library). (Illus.). 296p. 1991. pap. 10.00 (*0-87156-626-5*, Pub. by Sierra) Random.

— Our National Parks. LC 70-120568. reprint ed. 22.50 (*0-404-04516-2*) AMS Pr.

— Our National Parks. 1988. reprint ed. lib. bdg. 49.00 (*0-7812-0771-1*) Rprt Serv.

— Our National Parks. LC 80-53957. 394p. 1981. reprint ed. 29.50 (*0-299-08590-2*); reprint ed. pap. 16.95 (*0-299-08594-5*) U of Wis Pr.

— Our Yosemite National Park. Jones, William R., ed. (Illus.). 96p. (Orig.). 1980. reprint ed. pap. 3.95 (*0-89646-061-4*) Vistabooks.

— The Proposed Yosemite National Park: Treasures & Features. Jones, William R., ed. (Illus.). 64p. 1976. reprint ed. pap. text 2.00 (*0-89646-003-7*) Vistabooks.

— Rambles of a Botanist among the Plants & Climates of California. (Illus.). 43p. 1974. 10.00 (*0-87093-301-9*) Dawsons.

— A Rival of the Yosemite: The Canon of the South Fork of King's River, California. Jones, William R., ed. (Illus.). 24p. 1977. reprint ed. pap. 2.00 (*0-89646-010-X*) Vistabooks.

— Sacred Summits: John Muir's Mountain Days. White, Graham, ed. & intro. by. 1998. pap. 13.95 (*0-86241-785-6*, Pub. by Canongate Books) Interlink Pub.

— Sierra Big Trees. abr. ed. Jones, William R., ed. (Illus.). 80p. 1981. reprint ed. pap. 4.95 (*0-89646-069-X*) Vistabooks.

— Songs & Seeds: A Journal with John Muir. 150p. 1996. pap. 12.00 (*0-945519-17-6*) Mountn Meadw Pr.

— Steep Trails. LC 93-25661. (John Muir Library). 304p. 1994. pap. 10.00 (*0-87156-535-8*, Pub. by Sierra) Random.

— Steep Trails. (BCL1 - United States Local History Ser.). 390p. 1991. reprint ed. lib. bdg. 89.00 (*0-7812-6326-3*) Rprt Serv.

— Stickeen. 74p. 1989. 8.95 (*1-55709-112-9*) Applewood.

— Stickeen. LC 90-84443. (Illus.). 96p. 1990. reprint ed. pap. 6.95 (*0-930588-48-7*) Heyday Bks.

— Stickeen: An Adventure with a Dog & a Glacier. (Illus.). 1978. reprint ed. pap. 3.95 (*0-89646-032-0*) Vistabooks.

— Stickeen: John Muir & the Brave Little Dog. LC 99-186602. (Illus.). 36p. (J). (ps-7). 1998. 16.95 (*1-883220-79-3*); pap. 7.95 (*1-883220-78-5*) Dawn CA.

— Story of My Boyhood & Youth. (Illus.). 246p. 1965. reprint ed. pap. 15.95 (*0-299-03654-5*) U of Wis Pr.

— Thomas Carlyle's Apprenticeship. LC 79-116797. (English Biography Ser.: No. 31). 1970. reprint ed. lib. bdg. 75.00 (*0-8383-1039-7*) M S G Haskell Hse.

— A Thousand-Mile Walk to the Gulf. LC 98-234890. 224p. 1998. pap. 10.00 (*0-395-90147-2*, Mariner Bks) HM.

— A Thousand-Mile Walk to the Gulf. LC 90-47830. (Illus.). 246p. 1990. reprint ed. 34.95 (*0-87797-193-5*) Cherokee.

— A Thousand-Mile Walk to the Gulf. (BCL1 - United States Local History Ser.). 219p. 1991. reprint ed. lib. bdg. 79.00 (*0-7812-6291-7*) Rprt Serv.

— A Thousand-Mile Walk to the Gulf. LC 91-30471. (John Muir Library). (Illus.). 160p. 1992. reprint ed. pap. 10.00 (*0-87156-591-9*, Pub. by Sierra) Random.

— Travels in Alaska. LC 98-11911. 368p. 1998. pap. 10.00 (*0-395-90148-0*, Mariner Bks) HM.

Muir, John. Travels in Alaska. 1993. pap. 10.95 (*0-14-026832-4*) Viking Penguin.

Muir, John. Travels in Alaska. LC 77-19358. (Illus.). reprint ed. 32.50 (*0-404-16075-1*) AMS Pr.

— Travels in Alaska. 1988. reprint ed. lib. bdg. 49.00 (*0-7812-0154-3*) Rprt Serv.

— Travels in Alaska. (BCL1 - United States Local History Ser.). 326p. 1991. reprint ed. lib. bdg. 89.00 (*0-7812-6345-X*) Rprt Serv.

— Travels in Alaska. LC 70-145196. 1915. reprint ed. 59.00 (*0-403-01120-5*) Scholarly.

— Travels in Alaska. LC 87-26311. (John Muir Library). 352p. 1988. reprint ed. pap. 10.00 (*0-87156-783-0*, Pub. by Sierra) Random.

***Muir, John.** The Velvet Monkey Wrench: Millennial Edition. (Legacy Edition Ser.). 256p. 2000. pap. 20.00 (*0-943734-39-8*) Ocean Tree Bks.

Muir, John. Wes Craven: The Art of Horror. LC 98-28223. (Illus.). 327p. 1998. lib. bdg. 45.00 (*0-7864-0576-7*) McFarland & Co.

— The Wild Sheep. Jones, William R., ed. (Illus.). 32p. 1977. reprint ed. pap. 2.00 (*0-89646-017-7*) Vistabooks.

— The Wilderness Journeys: My Boyhood & Youth - First Summer in the Sierra - 1000 Mile Walk - Stickeen - Travels in Alaska. 736p. 1996. pap. 14.95 (*0-86241-586-1*, Pub. by Canongate Books) Interlink Pub.

— The Yosemite. 1992. reprint ed. lib. bdg. 75.00 (*0-7812-5068-4*) Rprt Serv.

— The Yosemite. LC 87-23573. (John Muir Library). (Illus.). 288p. 1988. reprint ed. pap. 10.00 (*0-87156-782-2*, Pub. by Sierra) Random.

Muir, John, ed. An Inspector Recalls. 80p. 1990. pap. 21.00 (*1-898218-26-9*) St Mut.

***Muir, John & Cornell, Joseph Bharat.** My Life with Nature. LC 00-8827. 2000. pap. write for info. (*1-58469-009-7*) Dawn Pub Co.

Muir, John, jt. auth. see Austin, Mary.

Muir, John, jt. auth. see Kennedy, Michael P.

Muir, John G. Classroom Clangers. (Illus.). 64p. (C). 1989. 20.00 (*0-903065-49-5*, Pub. by G Wright Pub) St Mut.

— More Classroom Clangers. (Illus.). 64p. (C). 1989. 30.00 (*0-903065-54-1*, Pub. by G Wright Pub) St Mut.

Muir, John K. An Analytical Guide to Television's Battlestar Galactica. LC 98-38737. (Illus.). 244p. 1998. lib. bdg. 39.95 (*0-7864-0441-8*) McFarland & Co.

An Asterisk (*) at the beginning of an entry indicates that the title is appearing for the first time.

— A Critical History of Doctor Who on Television. LC 99-38016. (Illus.). 504p. 1999. lib. bdg. 65.00 (*0-7864-0442-6*) McFarland & Co.

— Exploring Space, 1999: An Episode Guide & Complete History of the Mid-1970s Science Fiction Television Series. LC 97-659. (Illus.). 222p. 1997. lib. bdg. 36.50 (*0-7864-0165-6*) McFarland & Co.

*__Muir, John K.__ A History & Critical Analysis of Blake's 7, the 1978-1981 British Television Space Adventure. LC 99-55344. (Illus.). 223p. 1999. lib. bdg. 38.50 (*0-7864-0600-3*) McFarland & Co.

*__Muir, John Kenneth.__ The Films of John Carpenter. LC 99-88930. (Illus.). 275p. 2000. 48.50 (*0-7864-0725-5*) McFarland & Co.

— Terror Television: American Series, 1970-1999. (Illus.). 640p. 2000. boxed set 75.00 (*0-7864-0890-1*) McFarland & Co.

*__Muir, Julia & Sidey, Anna.__ Textbook of Community Children's Nursing. LC 99-52566. 2000. text. write for info. (*0-443-06368-0*) Harcrt Hlth Sci Grp.

Muir, Karen L. The Strongest Part of the Family: A Study of Lao Refugee Women in Columbus, Ohio. LC 87-45782. (Immigrant Communities & Ethnic Minorities in the U. S. & Canada Ser.: No. 17). 1988. 38.50 (*0-404-19427-3*) AMS Pr.

Muir, Kenneth. Last Periods of Shakespeare, Racine, Ibsen. LC 60-9132. 126p. reprint ed. pap. 39.10 (*0-7837-3677-0*, 20435510009) Bks Demand.

— Shakespeare: Contrasts & Controversies. LC 85-994. 208p. 1985. 29.95 (*0-8061-1940-3*) U of Okla Pr.

— Shakespeare Survey, 40 vols., Set. 1986. 1600.00 (*0-7855-1202-0*) St Mut.

Muir, Kenneth, ed. Elizabethan Lyrics. LC 79-75715. (Granger Index Reprint Ser.). 1977. 19.95 (*0-8369-6032-7*) Ayer.

Muir, Kenneth, et al, eds. Shakespeare: Man of the Theater. LC 82-40346. (Illus.). 272p. 1983. 38.50 (*0-87413-217-7*) U Delaware Pr.

Muir, Kenneth, intro. The Romantic Period: Excluding the Novel, 1 of 7 vols. (Great Writers Library). 113p. pap. 6.00 (*0-312-34705-7*) Academy Chi Pubs.

Muir, Kenneth & O'Loughlin, Sean. The Voyage to Illyria: A New Study of Shakespeare. LC 79-128891. (Select Bibliographies Reprint Ser.). 1977. reprint ed. 19.95 (*0-8369-5511-0*) Ayer.

Muir, Kenneth & Wells, Stanley, eds. Aspects of King Lear: Articles Reprinted from Shakespeare Survey. LC 82-4344. (Illus.). 111p. reprint ed. pap. 31.70 (*0-8357-5797-8*, 2030611) Bks Demand.

Muir, Kenneth, ed. see Shakespeare, William.

Muir, Kenneth, tr. see Calderon de la Barca, Pedro.

Muir, Kerry, ed. Childsplay: A Collection of Scenes & Monologues for Children. (Illus.). 200p. (Orig.). (J). (gr. 3-6). 1995. pap. 12.95 (*0-87910-188-1*) Limelight Edns.

Muir-Leresche, Kay, jt. ed. see Valdes, Alberto.

Muir, Lucy. Highland Rivalry. (Regency Romance Ser.: No. 43). 1991. per. 2.75 (*0-373-31143-5*) Harlequin Bks.

Muir, Lynette R. The Biblical Drama of Medieval Europe. (Illus.). 344p. (C). 1995. text 64.95 (*0-521-41291-9*) Cambridge U Pr.

Muir, M. Kerr, jt. auth. see Wybar, K.

Muir, M. M. A History of Chemical Theories & Laws. LC 74-26279. (History, Philosophy & Sociology of Science Ser.). 1975. reprint ed. 41.95 (*0-405-06606-6*) Ayer.

— The Story of Alchemy & the Beginnings of Chemistry. 208p. 1992. reprint ed. pap. 18.95 (*1-56459-019-4*) Kessinger Pub.

Muir, M. M. P. The Alchemical Essence & the Chemical Element: An Episode in the Quest of the Unchanging (1894) 100p. 1998. reprint ed. pap. 16.95 (*0-7661-0176-2*) Kessinger Pub.

Muir, Malcolm, Jr. Black Shoes & Blue Water: Surface Warfare in the United States Navy, 1945-1975. LC 95-2964. (Contributions to Naval History Ser.: No. 6). 1995. pap. 19.00 (*0-945274-31-9*) Naval Hist Ctr.

— Black Shoes & Blue Water: Surface Warfare in the United States Navy, 1945-1975. (Illus.). 348p. 1999. reprint ed. pap. text 35.00 (*0-7881-7001-5*) DIANE Pub.

Muir, Malcolm. Black Shoes & Blue Water 1945-1975: Surface Warfare in the United States Navy. 364p. 1996. per. 19.00 (*0-16-045359-3*) USGPO.

*__Muir, Malcolm.__ Human Tradition in the World War II Era. (Human Tradition in America Ser.). (Illus.). 2000. 50.00 (*0-8420-2785-8*) Scholarly Res Inc.

*__Muir, Malcolm, ed.__ The Human Tradition in the World War II Era. LC 00-29700. 2000. pap. 18.95 (*0-8420-2786-6*) Scholarly Res Inc.

Muir, Marcie. Australian Children's Books Vol. 1: A Bibliography 1774-1972, 2 vols. (Miegunyah Press Ser.: No. 1:7). (Illus.). 1992. 150.00 (*0-522-84431-6*, Pub. by Melbourne Univ Pr) Paul & Co Pubs.

Muir, Margaret, jt. auth. see Muir, Bryce.

Muir, Marie A. The Environmental Contexts of AIDS. LC 90-7705. 232p. 1991. 55.00 (*0-275-93618-X*, C3618, Praeger Pubs) Greenwood.

Muir, Mary, jt. auth. see Clark, Charles T.

Muir, Matthew M. The Story of Alchemy & the Beginnings of Chemistry. LC 79-8618. reprint ed. 27.50 (*0-404-18482-0*) AMS Pr.

Muir, Michael. But How Do I Use Hyperstudio with Kids? Designing & Doing Curriculum Based Projects. LC 99-236287. (Illus.). 130p. 1997. spiral bd. 21.95 (*1-56484-116-2*) Intl Society Tech Educ.

Muir, Niki, jt. ed. see France, Jenny.

*__Muir, Patrick F.__ Stories to Entertain You... If You Get Bored on Your Wedding Night. 232p. 1999. pap. 12.95 (*0-9676060-0-4*, Pub. by PM Bk) Postal.

Muir, Patrick F. & Orban, Peter E., eds. Sensors & Controls for Intelligent Machining, Agile Manufacturing & Mechatronics, Vol. 3518. LC 99-200345. 1999. 69.00 (*0-8194-2979-1*) SPIE.

Muir, Pauline, jt. auth. see Welden, Dan.

Muir, Percy. Minding My Own Business: An Autobiography. (Illus.). 240p. 1991. reprint ed. 35.00 (*0-938768-28-X*) Oak Knoll.

Muir, R. M., jt. ed. see Addis, T. R.

Muir, Rae. All but the Queen of Hearts. (Historical Ser.: No. 369). 1997. per. 4.99 (*0-373-28969-3*, 1-28969-3) Harlequin Bks.

— Hawken's Wife. 1999. per. 4.99 (*0-373-29050-0*, Harlequin) Harlequin Bks.

— The Lieutenant's Lady. 298p. 1997. per. 4.99 (*0-373-28983-9*, 1-28983-4) Harlequin Bks.

— The Trail to Temptation. 1996. per. 4.99 (*0-373-28945-6*, 1-28945-3) Harlequin Bks.

— Twice a Bride. (Historical Ser.). 1998. per. 4.99 (*0-373-29014-4*, 1-29014-7) Harlequin Bks.

Muir, Ramsay. America the Golden. LC 73-13145. (Foreign Travelers in America, 1810-1935 Ser.). 156p. 1974. reprint ed. 15.95 (*0-405-05469-6*) Ayer.

Muir, Richard. The New Reading the Landscape: Fieldwork in Landscape History. (Illus.). 288p. 1999. 80.00 (*0-85989-579-3*); pap. 29.95 (*0-85989-580-7*) Univ Exeter Pr.

— Political Geography: A New Introduction. LC 97-5293. 352p. 1997. pap. text 39.95 (*0-470-23744-9*) Halsted Pr.

— The Yorkshire Countryside: A Landscape History. LC 98-149926. (Illus.). 256p. 1998. pap. 30.00 (*1-85331-198-7*, Pub. by Edinburgh U Pr) Col U Pr.

Muir, Richard & Paddison, Ronan. Politics, Geography & Behavior. 1981. pap. 13.95 (*0-416-31340-X*, NO. 3460) Routledge.

Muir, Robin. John Deakin. LC 97-8723. (Illus.). 144p. 1997. text 50.00 (*0-86565-988-5*) Vendome.

Muir, Robin, ed. Clifford Coffin: Photographs from Vogue 1945 to 1955. LC 97-65595. (Illus.). 140p. 1997. 60.00 (*1-55670-654-5*) Stewart Tabori & Chang.

Muir, Rory. Britain & the Defeat of Napoleon, 1807-1815. LC 95-32097. 466p. 1996. 50.00 (*0-300-06443-8*) Yale U Pr.

— Tactics & the Experience of Battle in the Age of Napoleon. LC 97-44386. 352p. 1998. 40.00 (*0-300-07385-2*) Yale U Pr.

*__Muir, Rory.__ Tactics & the Experience of Battle in the Age of Napoleon. 352p. 2000. pap. 16.95 (*0-300-08270-3*) Yale U Pr.

Muir, Roy & May, Jerry, eds. Developing an Effective Major Gift Program: From Managing Staff to Soliciting Gifts. 1993. pap. 41.50 (*0-89964-302-7*, 29002) Coun Adv & Supp Ed.

Muir, Russell & Saba, Joseph P. Improving State Enterprise Performance: The Role of Internal & External Incentives. LC 95-42147. (Technical Papers: Vol. 306). 192p. 1995. pap. 22.00 (*0-8213-3470-0*, 13470) World Bank.

Muir, Sarah. Saddlery & Horse Equipment: The Complete Illustrated Guide to Riding Tack. 1999. 22.95 (*1-85967-907-2*) Anness Pub.

Muir, Star. Communication Research Handbook. 152p. (C). 1998. per. 25.95 (*0-7872-5111-9*, 41511101) Kendall-Hunt.

Muir, Star A. & Veenendall, Thomas L., eds. Earthtalk: Communication Empowerment for Environmental Action. LC 95-34420. (Praeger Series in Political Communication). 256p. 1996. 65.00 (*0-275-95370-X*, Praeger Pubs) Greenwood.

Muir, Star A., jt. auth. see Kenner, Janette M.

Muir, Star A., jt. auth. see Muir, Janette K.

Muir, Stephen. Albert's Old Shoes. unabridged ed. (Illus.). 32p. (J). (ps-3). 1996. pap. 6.99 (*0-7737-5777-5*) STDK.

Muir, Steven C., jt. ed. see Coyle, J. Kevin.

Muir, Theda, ed. see Baxter, Ellen.

Muir, Tom & Rance, Brian. Collaborative Practice in the Built Environment. (Built Environment Series of Textbooks). (Illus.). 192p. (Orig.). (C). 1995. pap. 32.99 (*0-419-19560-2*, E & FN Spon) Routledge.

*__Muir, Tonya.__ Breaking Away: With Faltering Steps - Making Strides. (Illus.). 500p. 2000. pap. 21.99 (*0-9674196-4-6*, 005) Renaissance Alliance.

Muir, Vic. Lawn Bowls Straight from the Shoulder. 140p. (C). 1990. pap. 36.00 (*0-9589209-0-7*, Pub. by Boolarong Pubns) St Mut.

Muir, Virginia J. The One Year Bible Story Book. (Illus.). 384p. (YA). (gr. 5 up). 1988. 14.99 (*0-8423-2631-6*) Tyndale Hse.

Muir, W. The Caliphate. 624p. 1984. 280.00 (*1-85077-014-X*, Pub. by Darf Pubs Ltd) St Mut.

— Mahomet & Islam. 256p. 1986. 220.00 (*1-85077-085-9*, Pub. by Darf Pubs Ltd) St Mut.

Muir, W. M. & Hubbell, John T. Handbook of Veterinary Anesthesia. 2nd ed. LC 94-24404. (Illus.). 496p. (C). (gr. 13). 1994. text 54.00 (*0-8016-7656-8*, 07656) Mosby Inc.

Muir, Willa. Imagined Corners. (Classics Ser.). 282p. 1994. pap. 9.95 (*0-86241-140-8*, Pub. by Canongate Books) Interlink Pub.

— Imagined Selves. 720p. 1997. pap. 14.95 (*0-86241-605-1*, Pub. by Canongate Books) Interlink Pub.

Muir, Willa, tr. see Broch, Hermann.

Muir, Willa, tr. see Kafka, Franz.

Muir, William. Annals of the Early Caliphate from Original Sources. 1977. lib. bdg. 59.95 (*0-8490-1434-4*) Gordon Pr.

— The Caliphate: Its Rise, Decline, & Fall. LC 74-180365. reprint ed. 52.50 (*0-404-56305-8*) AMS Pr.

— The Life of Mohammad from Original Sources. rev. ed. Weir, Thomas H., ed. LC 78-180366. reprint ed. 57.50 (*0-404-56306-6*) AMS Pr.

— Life of St. Columba. 1997. pap. 4.95 (*0-89979-095-X*) British Am Bks.

— The Mameluke: or Slave Dynasty of Egypt, 1260-1517. LC 71-180367. reprint ed. 32.00 (*0-404-56307-4*) AMS Pr.

Muir, William, ed. Notices from the Local Records of Dysart. LC 73-164819. (Maitland Club, Glasgow. Publications: No. 73). reprint ed. 27.50 (*0-404-53110-5*) AMS Pr.

Muir, William & Kraus, Bernard. Marion: A History of the United States Watch Company. Fuller, Eugene T., ed. LC 85-61588. (Illus.). 218p. 1985. 24.15 (*0-9614984-0-4*) Natl Assn Watch & Clock.

Muir, William A. Christmas Traditions. LC 89-29237. 179p. 1992. reprint ed. lib. bdg. 42.00 (*1-55888-895-0*) Omnigraphics Inc.

Muir, William K. The Bully Pulpit: The Presidential Leadership of Ronald Reagan. 275p. 1992. 24.95 (*1-55815-167-2*) ICS Pr.

Muir, William K., Jr. Law & Attitude Change. LC 67-28851. 182p. 1985. reprint ed. pap. text 9.00 (*0-226-54628-4*) U Ch Pr.

— Legislature: California's School for Politics. LC 82-16128. xvi, 220p. 1995. pap. text 9.95 (*0-226-54626-8*) U Ch Pr.

— Police: Streetcorner Politicians. LC 76-8085. (Illus.). 318p. 1979. pap. text 14.95 (*0-226-54633-0*, P825) U Ch Pr.

Muir, Wilma, tr. see Kafka, Franz.

Muir Wood, A. M. Coastal Hydraulics. xii, 188p. 1969. text 274.00 (*0-677-61680-5*) Gordon & Breach.

*__Muir Wood, A. M.__ Tunnelling: Management by Design. LC 99-47534. (Illus.). 256p. 2000. 65.00 (*0-419-23200-1*, E & FN Spon) Routledge.

*__Muir-Wood, David.__ Geotechnical Modelling. (Applied Geotechnics Ser.). (Illus.). 352p. (Orig.). (C). 1999. pap. 40.00 (*0-419-23730-5*, E & FN Spon) Routledge.

Muirden, James. About the Universe? LC 94-27356. (How Do We Know? Ser.). (Illus.). 48p. (J). (gr. 4-8). 1995. lib. bdg. 24.26 (*0-8114-3884-8*) Raintree Steck-V.

— How to Use an Astronomical Telescope: A Beginner's Guide to Observing the Cosmos. 400p. 1988. per. 15.00 (*0-671-66404-2*, Fireside) S&S Trade Pap.

— Seeing Stars. LC 97-32577. (SuperSmarts Ser.). (Illus.). 24p. (J). (gr. 2-3). 1998. 11.99 (*0-7636-0373-2*) Candlewick Pr.

— Seeing Stars. LC 97-32577. (Supersmarts Ser.). (Illus.). 24p. (J). (gr. 2-5). 1998. 4.99 (*0-7636-0647-2*) Candlewick Pr.

— The Stars & Planets. (Visual Factfinders Ser.). (Illus.). 96p. (YA). (gr. 5 up). 1993. lib. bdg. 16.90 (*1-85697-693-9*, Kingfisher) LKC.

— Stars & Planets. LC 93-20104. (Visual Factfinders Ser.). (Illus.). 96p. (YA). (gr. 4-7). 1993. 15.90 (*1-85697-852-4*, Kingfisher) LKC.

Muirden, James, ed. Sky Watcher's Handbook: The Expert Reference Source for the Amateur Astronomer. LC 92-32996. (Illus.). 416p. 1998. reprint ed. text 35.00 (*0-7167-4502-X*) OUP.

Muirhead, B. W. The Development of Postwar Canadian Trade Policy: The Failure of the Anglo-European Option. 240p. 1992. 60.00 (*0-7735-0922-4*, Pub. by McG-Queens Univ Pr) CUP Services.

Muirhead, Brian & Simon, William L. High-Velocity Leadership: The Mars Pathfinder Approach to Faster, Better, Cheaper. LC HD57.7.M84 1999. 241p. 1999. 25.00 (*0-88730-974-7*, HarpBusn) HarpInfo.

Muirhead, Brian, jt. auth. see Pritchett, Price.

Muirhead, Bruce. Against the Odds: The Public Life & Times of Louis Rasminsky. (Illus.). 352p. 1999. text 45.00 (*0-8020-0629-9*) U of Toronto Pr.

Muirhead, C. Diary of a Bomb Aimer. 160p. (C). 1991. 75.00 (*0-946771-75-8*, Pub. by Spellmnt Pubs) St Mut.

Muirhead, Colin. Complete English Springer Spaniel. 1996. 24.95 (*1-86054-095-3*, Pub. by Ringpr Bks) Seven Hills Bk.

Muirhead, Deborah. A Practical Spelling Book. (Illus.). 60p. 1998. pap. write for info. (*0-89822-149-8*) Visual Studies.

Muirhead, Desmond. Walk Around the Old Course: The Many Faces of St. Andrews. LC 99-55588. 1999. 29.95 (*0-87833-158-1*) Taylor Pub.

Muirhead, Desmond & Rando, Guy L. Golf Course Development & Real Estate. LC 94-60767. 192p. 1994. pap. text 59.95 (*0-87420-762-2*, G09) Urban Land.

*__Muirhead, George.__ Central CT State University. (Images of America Ser.). 1999. pap. 18.99 (*0-7385-0160-3*) Arcadia Publng.

Muirhead, James. Historical Introduction to the Private Law of Rome. xxiv, 462p. 1998. reprint ed. 146.00 (*1-56169-418-5*) Gaunt.

— Historical Introduction to the Private Law of Rome. 2nd ed. Goudy, Henry, ed. & rev. by. xxv, 457p. 1998. reprint ed. 145.00 (*1-56169-397-9*) Gaunt.

— Historical Introduction to the Private Law of Rome. 2nd rev. ed. Goudy, Henry, ed. & rev. by. (Illus.). xxv, 457p. 1985. reprint ed. 47.50 (*0-8377-0821-4*, Rothman) W S Hein.

— The Institutes of Gaius & Rules of Ulpian: The Former from Studemund's Apograph of the Verona Codex. LC 93-79718. 658p. 1994. reprint ed. 160.00 (*1-56169-076-7*) Gaunt.

Muirhead, James F. America, the Land of Contrasts: A Briton's View of His American Kin. LC 74-87430. (American Scene Ser.). Orig. Title: Bodley Head. 1970. reprint ed. lib. bdg. 37.50 (*0-306-71576-7*) Da Capo.

Muirhead, James P. Life of James Watt. (Industrial Antiquities Ser.). (Illus.). 608p. 1998. reprint ed. pap. 240.00 (*1-85297-016-2*, Pub. by Archival Facs) St Mut.

Muirhead, John H. Coleridge As Philosopher: 1930 Edition. 288p. 1996. reprint ed. 60.00 (*1-85506-152-X*) Bks Intl VA.

— Rule & End in Morals. LC 74-99665. (Select Bibliographies Reprint Ser.). 1977. 19.95 (*0-8369-5094-1*) Ayer.

Muirhead, John S. An Outline of Roman Law. LC 97-74173. 199p. 1997. reprint ed. 66.00 (*1-56169-323-5*, 14644) Gaunt.

Muirhead, John W. A History of African-Americans in McLean County, Illinois, 1835-1975. 79p. 1998. pap. 10.00 (*0-943788-16-1*) McLean County.

Muirhead, Joy. Finding a Job in New Zealand: How to Discover Well Paid Work & a Great New Lifestyle. (Living & Working Abroad Ser.). 142p. 1996. pap. 19.95 (*1-85703-218-7*, Pub. by How To Bks) Trans-Atl Phila.

*__Muirhead, Joy.__ Getting a Job in New Zealand: Find Well-Paid Work & a Great New Lifestyle. 2nd ed. 144p. 2000. pap. 14.95 (*1-85703-577-1*, Pub. by How To Bks) Midpt Trade.

Muirhead, Robb J. Aspects of Multivariate Statistical Theory. LC 82-1912. (Probability & Mathematical Statistics Ser.). 704p. 1982. 259.95 (*0-471-09442-0*, Wiley-Interscience) Wiley.

Muirhead, Rust. Caroline & Dear Me's Christmas Tree. (Illus.). 48p. (J). (gr. 3-5). 1997. 12.95 (*1-888170-11-5*) Advent Quest.

Muirhead, Sara. I Was a Country Girl. (American Autobiography Ser.). 211p. 1995. reprint ed. lib. bdg. 79.00 (*0-7812-8598-4*) Rprt Serv.

Muirhead, Stuart. Crisis Banking in the East: The History of the Chartered Mercantile Bank of India, London & China, 1853-1893. Green, Edwin, ed. (Illus.). 302p. (C). 1996. text 86.95 (*1-85928-244-X*, Pub. by Scolar Pr) Ashgate Pub Co.

Muirhead, Thomas, jt. auth. see Maxwell, Robert.

Muirhead-Thomson, E. C. Behaviour Patterns of Blood-Sucking Flies. LC 81-21019. (Illus.). 240p. 1982. 110.00 (*0-08-025497-7*, Pub. by Pergamon Repr) Franklin.

Muirhead-Thomson, R. C., ed. Trap Responses of Flying Insects: The Influence of Trap Design on Capture Efficiency. (Illus.). 287p. 1991. text 83.00 (*0-12-509755-7*) Acad Pr.

Muirithe, Diarmaid O. A Dictionary of Anglo-Irish: Words & Phrases from Gaelic in the English of Ireland. 240p. 2000. 49.50 (*1-85182-197-X*, Pub. by Four Cts Pr) Intl Spec Bk.

*__Muirithe, Diarmaid O.__ A Dictionary of Anglo-Irish: Words & Phrases from Gaelic in the English of Ireland. 240p. 2000. pap. 29.95 (*1-85182-445-6*, Pub. by Four Cts Pr) Intl Spec Bk.

— The Words We Use. 144p. 1996. pap. 14.95 (*1-85182-220-8*, Pub. by Four Cts Pr) Intl Spec Bk.

*__Muirithe, Diarmaid O.__ The Words We Use. 96p. 1999. pap. 11.95 (*1-85182-466-9*, Pub. by Four Cts Pr) Intl Spec Bk.

Muirithe, Diarmaid O., jt. auth. see Dolan, T. P.

*__Muirithe, Diarmuid O. & Nutall, Deirdre, eds.__ The Folklore of County Wexford. 240p. 1999. boxed set 24.95 (*1-85182-453-7*, Pub. by Four Cts Pr) Intl Spec Bk.

Muise, D. A., ed. A Reader's Guide to Canadian History No. 1: Beginnings to Confederation. 256p. 1982. pap. text 14.95 (*0-8020-6442-6*) U of Toronto Pr.

Muise, D. A., jt. ed. see Forbes, E. R.

Muise, Jeff. Old Bob's Gift. LC 96-4929. (Illus.). 158p. (J). (gr. 4-12). 1996. pap. 12.95 (*1-885482-04-3*) Shawangunk Pr.

Muise, O., tr. see Walter, H.

Muise, Richard. R-C Car Painting & Finishing Techniques. (Illus.). 29p. 1992. pap. 9.95 (*0-911295-19-4*) Air Age.

Muisener, Philip P. Understanding & Treating Adolescent Substance Abuse. LC 93-32463. (Sourcebooks for the Human Services Ser.: Vol. 27). (C). 1993. text 56.00 (*0-8039-4275-3*) Sage.

Muiswinkel, W. B. Van, see Van Muiswinkel, W. B., ed.

Mujahid, Sharif A. Quaid-I-Azam Jinnah: Studies in Interpretation. (C). 1993. 22.00 (*81-85557-04-7*, Pub. by Low Price) S Asia.

Mujal-Leon, Eusebio. Communism & Political Change in Spain. LC 81-48616. 288p. 1983. 13.95 (*0-253-31389-9*) Ind U Pr.

— The Cuban University under the Revolution. (Occasional Papers: No. 25). 70p. (Orig.). (C). 1988. pap. 5.00 (*0-317-90486-8*) Cuban Amer Natl Fndtn.

— European Socialism & the Conflict in Central America, 138. LC 88-35952. (Washington Papers: No. 138). 144p. 1989. 49.95 (*0-275-93238-9*, C3238, Praeger Pubs); pap. 16.95 (*0-275-93239-7*, B3239, Praeger Pubs) Greenwood.

Mujal-Leon, Eusebio, ed. The U. S. S. R. & Latin America: A Developing Relationship. 288p. 1989. text 39.95 (*0-04-445165-2*) Routledge.

Mujal-Leon, Eusebio M., jt. ed. see Penniman, Howard R.

Mujeed, Hukem A., ed. see Muhammad Ibn-Jusuf Al-Herewi.

Mujica. Milenio: Mil Anos de Literatura Espanola. 400p. pap. text 58.95 (*0-471-24112-1*) Wiley.

Mujica, Barbara. Antologia de la Literatura Espanola: Edad Media. LC 90-28275. 260p. 1991. text 48.95 (*0-471-53693-8*) Wiley.

— Antologia de la Literatura Espanola, Renacimiento y Siglo de Oro, Vol. 2. LC 90-28274. 640p. 1991. text 55.95 (*0-471-53694-6*) Wiley.

— Antologia de la Literature Espanola - to 1681, 2 vols., Vol. 1. 99th ed. 900p. 1991. text 59.00 (*0-471-89028-6*) Wiley.

— The Deaths of Don Bernardo. (Mujer Latina Ser.). 365p. 1990. pap. 23.95 (*0-685-45619-6*) Floricanto Pr.

*__Mujica, Barbara.__ Frida: A Novel. 2000. 26.95 (*1-58567-074-X*, Pub. by Overlook Pr) Penguin Putnam.

Mujica, Barbara. Hispano Mundo. (C). 1998. text 40.50 (*0-03-013387-4*) Harcourt Coll Pubs.

An Asterisk (*) at the beginning of an entry indicates that the title is appearing for the first time.

— Iberian Pastoral Characters. 33.00 (*0-916379-17-5*) Scripta.
— El Proximo Paso. (C). 1996. text 55.00 (*0-03-013388-2*) Harcourt Coll Pubs.
— Sanchez Across the Street & Other Stories: Woldt Corporation. LC 96-86613. 138p. (Orig.). 1997. pap. 9.95 (*1-877978-75-2*, FLF Pr) FL Lit Foundation.
— Texto Y Vida: Introduccion a LA Literature Espanola. Vardy, Katherine L., ed. 608p. (C). 1990. text 69.00 (*0-03-013164-2*) Harcourt Coll Pubs.
— Texto y Vida: Introduccion a la Litteratura Hispano Americana. (SPA., Illus.). 608p. (C). 1992. text 69.00 (*0-03-026237-2*) Harcourt Coll Pubs.
Mujica, Barbara, compiled by. Premio Nobel: Once Grandes Escritores del Mundo Hispanico. LC 96-44386. (SPA.). 368p. 1997. pap. 24.95 (*0-87840-642-5*) Georgetown U Pr.
Mujica, Barbara, ed. Texto y Espectaculo: Selected Proceedings of the Symposium on Spanish Golden Age Theatre, March 11, 12, 13, 1987 the University of Texas at El Paso. LC 88-37834. 172p. (C). 1989. lib. bdg. 34.50 (*0-8191-7312-6*) U Pr of Amer.
Mujica, Barbara, et al, eds. Looking at the Comedia in the Year of the Quincentennial: Proceedings of the 1992 Symposium on Golden Age Drama at the University of Texas, El Paso, March 18-21. LC 93-2619. (ENG & SPA.). 1993. 62.50 (*0-8191-9249-X*); pap. 34.50 (*0-8191-9357-7*) U Pr of Amer.
***Mujica, Barbara & Florensa, Eva.** Antologia de la Literatura Espanola, Siglos XVIII y XIX. (SPA.). 522p. 1998. pap. 64.95 (*0-471-25573-4*) Wiley.
Mujica, Barbara & Stoll, Anita K., eds. El Texto Puesto en Escena. (SPA.). 208p. 1999. 54.00 (*1-85566-064-4*, Pub. by Tamesis Bks Ltd) Boydell & Brewer.
Mujica, Barbara, et al. Pasaporte: First Year Spanish. 2nd ed. 125p. 1984. pap. text 15.00 (*0-471-80161-5*) Wiley.
Mujica, Barbara L., et al. Pasaporte: First Year Spanish. 2nd ed. LC 84-125653. (ENG & SPA., Illus.). 475p. reprint ed. pap. 147.30 (*0-7837-3500-6*, 205783300008) Bks Demand.
Mujica, Francisco. History of the Skyscraper. LC 76-57764. (Architecture & Decorative Art Ser.). 1977. reprint ed. lib. bdg. 125.00 (*0-306-70862-0*) Da Capo.
Mujica, Sonia A. Rito, Simbolo e Historia en la Piramide de Akapana, Tiwanaku: Un Analisis de Ceramica Ceremonial Prehispanica. 248p. 1995. pap. 15.00 (*1-877812-43-9*, UC002) UPLAAP.
Mujumdar, Arun S. Advances in Drying, Vol. 1. 1980. 55.00 (*0-07-043975-3*) McGraw.
— Advances in Drying, Vol. 4. 421p. 1987. 195.00 (*0-89116-408-1*) Hemisp Pub.
— Advances in Transplant Procedure, Vol. 8. 1993. write for info. (*0-8493-9320-5*) CRC Pr.
— Drying of Solids. 536p. 1992. text 95.00 (*1-881570-03-7*) Science Pubs.
— Handbook of Industrial Drying, Vol. 1. 2nd expanded rev. ed. (Illus.). 730p. 1995. text 330.00 (*0-8247-8996-2*) Dekker.
— Handbook of Industrial Drying, Vol. 2. 2nd expanded rev. ed. (Illus.). 730p. 1995. text 330.00 (*0-8247-9644-6*) Dekker.
Mujumdar, Arun S., ed. Advances in Drying, Vol. 5. 375p. 1992. 115.00 (*0-89116-109-0*) Hemisp Pub.
— Drying 87. 237p. 1987. 215.00 (*0-89116-722-6*) Hemisp Pub.
Mujumdar, Arun S. & Mashelkar, R. A., eds. Advances in Transport Processes, Vol. 8. 280p. 1991. 275.00 (*0-89116-987-3*) Elsevier.
Mujumdar, Arun S. & Roques, Marlo, eds. Drying '89. (Illus.). 550p. 1990. 176.00 (*0-89116-749-8*) Hemisp Pub.
Mujumdar, Arun S., jt. auth. see Kudra, T.
Mujumdar, Arun S., jt. ed. see Turner, Ian.
Mukaffah. Kalilat wa Dumna. (ARA., Illus.). 347p. 1983. 19.95 (*0-86685-367-7*) Intl Bk Ctr.
Mukai, jt. auth. see Shimosato.
Mukai, Koji, jt. ed. see Hellier, Coel.
Mukai, Linda P. & Chan, Janis F. Living with Dying: A Personal Journey. 225p. (Orig.). 1996. pap. 12.95 (*0-9650961-0-6*) Butterfld Pr CA.
Mukai, Shigeru, jt. ed. see Mabuchi, Toshiki.
Mukai, Tsuyoshi, jt. ed. see Suzuki, Takashi.
Mukaiyama, Teruaki. Challenges in Synthetic Organic Chemistry. Baldwin, J. E., ed. (International Series of Monographs on Chemistry: No. 20). (Illus.). 234p. 1994. reprint ed. pap. text 40.00 (*0-19-855855-4*) OUP.
***Mukamal, Steven S. & Rothstein, Martin L.** U. S. Immigration Laws: Working, Living & Studying in America. 2nd ed. xxi, 382p. 1999. 85.00 (*1-57588-531-X*, 323460) W S Hein.
Mukamel, S., jt. ed. see Lefebvre, R.
Mukamel, Shaul. Principles of Nonlinear Optical Spectroscopy. (Oxford Series on Optical & Imaging Sciences: Vol. 6). (Illus.). 576p. (C). 1999. pap. text 55.00 (*0-19-513291-2*) OUP.
Mukand, Jon, ed. Articulations: The Body & Illness in Poetry. LC 94-16528. 452p. (Orig.). 1994. pap. 19.95 (*0-87745-478-7*) U of Iowa Pr.
Mukandala, Rwekaza S., jt. auth. see Grosh, Barbara.
Mukarovsky, Jan. On Poetic Language. Steiner, Peter & Burbank, John, trs. from CZE. 88p. 1976. pap. 21.00 (*90-316-0080-6*) J Benjamins Pubng Co.
— Structure, Sign, & Function: Selected Essays. Burbank, John & Steiner, Peter, eds. & trs. by. LC 77-76310. (Yale Russian & East European Studies: No. 14). 309p. reprint ed. pap. 95.80 (*0-8357-8336-7*, 203383600087) Bks Demand.
— The Word & Verbal Art: Selected Essays by Jan Mukarovsky. Burbank, John & Steiner, Peter, eds. & trs. by. LC 76-49733. (Yale Russian & East European Studies: No. 13). 256p. reprint ed. pap. 79.40 (*0-8357-8378-2*, 203383700087) Bks Demand.
Mukarram, Ahmed, jt. auth. see Limaye, Satu P.
Mukasa, Ham. Uganda's Katikiro in England. Millar, Ernest, tr. LC 74-152926. (Black Heritage Library Collection). 1977. 22.95 (*0-8369-8770-5*) Ayer.
Mukasa, Ham & Gikandi, Simon. Uganda's Katikiro in England. LC 98-18301. 256p. 2000. pap. 24.95 (*0-7190-5437-0*, Pub. by Manchester Univ Pr) St Martin.
Mukerjee, Dada. By His Grace: A Devotee's Story. (Illus.). 208p. 1990. pap. 12.95 (*0-9628878-7-0*) Hanuman Found.
— The Near & the Dear. (Illus.). 294p. 1996. pap. 12.95 (*1-887474-02-1*) Hanuman Found.
Mukerjee, M. Commentary on Customs Act with Rules & Notifications. (C). 1990. 275.00 (*0-89771-224-2*) St Mut.
Mukerjee, R., jt. auth. see Gupta, S.
Mukerjee, Rahul, jt. auth. see Chaudhuri.
Mukerjee, Rahul, jt. auth. see Dey, Aloke.
Mukerji, A. B. The Chamars of Uttar Pradesh: A Study in Social Geography. 155p. 1980. 12.95 (*0-318-36868-4*) Asia Bk Corp.
Mukerji, A. P. Doctrine & Practice of Yoga. reprint ed. 11.00 (*0-911662-23-5*) Yoga.
— Yoga Lessons for Developing Spiritual Consciousness. reprint ed. 11.00 (*0-911662-24-3*) Yoga.
Mukerji, Bithika. Life & Teachings of Sri Ma Anandamayi: A Bird on the Wing. LC 98-904654. (Sri Garib Das Oriental Ser.). viii, 347 p. 1998. write for info. (*81-7030-577-2*) Sri Satguru Pubns.
Mukerji, Bithika, jt. ed. see Sundararajan, J. K.
Mukerji, Chandra. Territorial Ambitions & the Gardens of Versailles. (Cultural Social Studies). (Illus.). 420p. (C). 1997. text 80.00 (*0-521-49675-6*); pap. text 34.95 (*0-521-59959-8*) Cambridge U Pr.
Mukerji, Chandra & Schudson, Michael, eds. Rethinking Popular Culture: Contemporary Perspectives in Cultural Studies. LC 90-39009. 512p. 1991. pap. 19.95 (*0-520-06893-9*, Pub. by U CA Pr) Cal Prin Full Svc.
Mukerji, D. G. Chitra, The Story of a Pigeon. 225p. (C). 1988. 50.00 (*1-85219-040-X*, Pub. by Bishopsgate Pr Ltd) St Mut.
Mukerji, Dhan G. Devotional Passages from the Hindu Bible. 58p. 1998. reprint ed. pap. 9.95 (*0-7661-0453-2*) Kessinger Pub.
— Gay-Neck: The Story of a Pigeon. LC 68-13419. (Illus.). 192p. (J). (gr. 4 up). 1968. 15.99 (*0-525-30400-2*, Dutton Child) Peng Put Young Read.
Mukerji, Jatin N., jt. ed. see Surles, Richard H., Jr.
Mukerji, K. G., ed. Concepts in Mycorrhizal Research. LC 95-48021. (Handbook of Vegetation Science Ser.: Vol. 19, Pt. 2). 1996. text 228.00 (*0-7923-3890-1*) Kluwer Academic.
Mukerji, K. G., et al, eds. Biotechnological Approaches in Biocontrol of Plant Pathogens. LC 99-17061. (Illus.). 260p. (C). 1999. text 115.00 (*0-306-46104-8*, Kluwer Plenum) Kluwer Academic.
Mukerji, K. G. & Garg, K. L., eds. Biocontrol of Plant Diseases, Vol. 1. LC 87-15826. 224p. 1988. 128.00 (*0-8493-4595-2*, SB732, CRC Reprint) Franklin.
— Biocontrol of Plant Diseases, Vol. II. 224p. 1988. 121.00 (*0-8493-4596-0*, SB732, CRC Reprint) Franklin.
***Mukerji, K. G., et al.** Mycorrhizal Biology. LC 99-49587. 340p. 2000. write for info. (*0-306-46294-X*, Kluwer Plenum) Kluwer Academic.
Mukerji, K. G., jt. auth. see Lakhanpal, T. N.
Mukerji, K. G., jt. ed. see Upadhyay, R. K.
Mukerji, Kiran, jt. auth. see Stulz, Roland.
Mukerji, P. N., tr. see Hariharananda, Swami A.
Mukerji, Rose, jt. auth. see Lasky, Lila.
Mukes, Martin J. & Miles, Daniel J. Miles Chart Display of Popular Music, Vol. 3. 400p. 1981. lib. bdg. 40.00 (*0-913920-04-5*) Convex Indus.
***Mukes, Robert.** Deliverance: From Living in Darkness to Walking in the Marvelous Light. Spectrum Marketing Group Staff, tr. & photos by by. 160p. 2000. pap. 14.99 (*0-9701799-0-1*) Renewed Mind Pub.
Mukesh, Doble, jt. auth. see Bhaduri, Sumit.
Mukh, Firma K. & Dastidar, Sachi G. Regional Disparities & Regional Development: Planning of West Bengal. (C). 1991. 24.00 (*0-8364-2645-2*, Pub. by Firma KLM) S Asia.
Mukhachev, Iu. Classes & the Class Struggle in the U. S. S. R. 1920's-1930's. 150p. (C). 1988. 40.00 (*0-7855-3892-5*) St Mut.
Mukharjee, B. N. Mass Media & Political Modernity. 168p. 1971. 15.95 (*0-318-37278-9*) Asia Bk Corp.
Mukharjee, M., ed. Considerations. 153p. 1977. 10.95 (*0-318-36945-1*) Asia Bk Corp.
Mukharjee, R. K. Society & Community in India. 155p. 1979. 12.95 (*0-318-36864-1*) Asia Bk Corp.
Mukharji, D. P. Sociology of Indian Culture. 239p. 1979. 18.95 (*0-318-36974-5*) Asia Bk Corp.
Mukharji, P. Hindu Women. 118p. 1980. 11.95 (*0-318-37062-X*) Asia Bk Corp.
***Mukharji, T. N.** Art Manufactures of India. 2000. reprint ed. 67.50 (*81-7305-176-3*, Pub. by Aryan Bks Intl) S Asia.
Mukherjea, A. & Pothoven, K. Real & Functional Analysis Pt. A: Real Analysis. 2nd ed. (Mathematical Concepts & Methods in Science & Engineering Ser.: Vol. 27). (Illus.). 372p. (C). 1984. text 105.00 (*0-306-41557-7*, Kluwer Plenum) Kluwer Academic.
Mukherjea, A. & Pothoven, K. Real & Functional Analysis Pt. B: Functional Analysis. 2nd ed. (Mathematical Concepts & Methods in Science & Engineering Ser.: Vol. 28). (Illus.). 286p. (C). 1985. text 95.00 (*0-306-41558-5*, Kluwer Plenum) Kluwer Academic.
Mukherjea, A., jt. auth. see Hognas, G.
Mukherjea, Ajita R. Parliamentary Procedure in India. 3rd ed. 396p. 1983. 37.50 (*0-19-561133-0*) OUP.
Mukherjea, Sushil. Historicity of Lord Jagannatha: A Socio-Historical Study. (C). 1989. 14.00 (*81-85195-17-X*, Pub. by Minerva) S Asia.
Mukherjee & Ramaswamy, T. N., eds. Facets of Mahatma Gandhi: Non-Violence & Satyagraha, 4 vols., Set. (C). 1994. 145.00 (*81-7100-669-8*, Pub. by Deep & Deep Pubns) S Asia.
Mukherjee, jt. auth. see Allen.
Mukherjee, A. Accountancy Problems. 1985. 85.00 (*0-7875-5072-8*, Pub. by Current Dist) St Mut.
— Postcolonialism My Living. 1998. pap. 21.95 (*0-920661-75-0*) TSAR Pubns.
— Towards a Non-Static Theory of Profit Maximization. 1990. 34.00 (*81-7017-274-8*, Pub. by Abhinav) S Asia.
Mukherjee, A., ed. Participatory Rural Appraisal: Methods & Applications in Rural Planning. 1995. 38.00 (*0-7069-8466-8*, Pub. by Vikas) S Asia.
Mukherjee, A. B., ed. Biochemistry, Molecular Biology & Physiology of Phospholipase A2 & Its Regulatory Factors. (Advances in Experimental Medicine & Biology Ser.: Vol. 279). (Illus.). 272p. (C). 1990. text 114.00 (*0-306-43699-X*, Kluwer Plenum) Kluwer Academic.
Mukherjee, A. K. Flora of Pachmarhi & Bori Reserves. (Flora of India Ser.: No. 3). 407p. 1984. text 40.00 (*0-945345-54-2*, Pub. by Mahendra Pal Singh) Lubrecht & Cramer.
Mukherjee, A. K., ed. see International Symposium on Rate Processes in Plast.
Mukherjee, A. K., jt. ed. see Mishra, Rajiv S.
Mukherjee, A. L. A Short Textbook of Otolaryngology. 1985. 65.00 (*0-7855-0825-2*, Pub. by Current Dist) St Mut.
Mukherjee, Ajoy. A Passage to Medicine Practical: Long, Short & Spot Cases, Charts, Skiagrams, E. C. G. Instruments & Drugs. 501p. 1997. pap. (*81-86793-31-3*) Current Bks Intl.
Mukherjee, Amitabha. Structural Adjustment Programme & Food Security: Hunger & Poverty in India. 373p. 1994. 87.95 (*1-85628-595-2*, Pub. by Avebry) Ashgate Pub Co.
— Women in Indian Life & Society. LC 98-901889. (C). 1996. 32.00 (*81-85094-97-7*, Pub. by Punthi Pus) S Asia.
Mukherjee, Amitava. Structural Adjustment Programme Putting the First Things, Poverty & Environment, Last: An Interim Analysis. 263p. 1994. pap. 225.00 (*81-85330-21-2*, Pub. by Print Hse) St Mut.
— Studies in Multilevel Planning Vol. I: Researches in Decentralisation with Special Reference to District Planning in India. Yugandhar, B. N., ed. 1990. 48.50 (*81-7026-158-9*, Pub. by Heritage IA) S Asia.
Mukherjee, Amitava & Agnihotri, V. K., eds. Environment & Development: Views from the East & the West. (C). 1993. 68.00 (*81-7022-788-7*, Pub. by Concept) S Asia.
Mukherjee, Aparna. British Colonial Policy in Burma: An Aspect of Colonialism in South East Asia, 1840-1885. 1988. 50.00 (*0-8364-2290-2*, Pub. by Abhinav) S Asia.
Mukherjee, Arun. Crime & Public Disorder in Colonical Bengal: 1861-1912. (C). 1995. 4.00 (*81-7074-167-X*, Pub. by KP Bagchi) S Asia.
— The Gospel of Wealth in the American Novel: The Rhetoric of Dreiser & Some of His Contemporaries. 240p. (C). 1987. 59.50 (*0-389-20681-4*, N8239) B&N Imports.
Mukherjee, Asoke, jt. auth. see Lieberman, Ronald.
Mukherjee, B. N. Coins & Currency Systems of Post-Gupta Bengal: (c. AD 550-700) (C). 1993. 19.50 (*81-215-0563-1*, Pub. by M Manoharial) Coronet Bks.
— External Trade of Early North-Eastern India. 124p. 1992. text 18.95 (*0-7069-6164-1*, Pub. by Vikas) S Asia.
— Mathura & Its Society: The Saka Pahlava Phase. 1981. 14.00 (*0-8364-1589-2*) S Asia.
— The Rise & Fall of the Kushana Empire. (C). 1988. 96.00 (*0-8364-2393-3*, Pub. by Firma KLM) S Asia.
Mukherjee, B. N., ed. East Indian Art Styles. 1985. 20.00 (*0-8364-1483-7*, Pub. by KP Bagchi) S Asia.
Mukherjee, Bhabananda. Structure & Kinship in Tribal India. 1981. 10.00 (*0-8364-0769-5*, Pub. by Minerva) S Asia.
***Mukherjee, Bharati.** Desirable Daughters 2002. pap. 13.95 (*0-7868-8515-7*, Pub. by Disney Pr) Time Warner.
Mukherjee, Bharati. The Holder of the World. 304p. 1994. reprint ed. pap. 12.00 (*0-449-90966-2*) Fawcett.
— Jasmine. 256p. 1999. reprint ed. pap. 12.00 (*0-8021-3630-3*, Grove) Grove-Atltic.
— Leave It to Me. 1998. pap. 12.95 (*0-449-00396-5*) Fawcett.
— Leave It to Me. LC 97-5833. 1997. 23.00 (*0-679-43427-5*) Knopf.
***Mukherjee, Bharati.** The Middleman & Other Stories. 208p. 1999. pap. 12.00 (*0-8021-3650-8*, Grove) Grove-Atltic.
Mukherjee, Bharati. Political Culture & Leadership in India. (C). 1991. 36.00 (*81-7099-320-2*, Pub. by Mittal Pubs Dist) S Asia.
— Regionalism in Indian Perspective. 1992. 13.00 (*81-7074-123-8*, Pub. by KP Bagchi) S Asia.
Mukherjee, Bharati, ed. Traditional Medicine. 420p. (C). 1993. text 45.00 (*1-881570-32-0*) Science Pubs.
Mukherjee, Bharati, jt. auth. see Blaise, Clark.
Mukherjee, Biswanath. Optical Communication Networks. LC 97-16145. (Computer Communications Ser.). (Illus.). 576p. 1997. 60.00 (*0-07-044435-8*) McGraw.
Mukherjee, Chandan, et al. Econometrics & Data Analysis for Developing Countries. LC 97-8284. (Priorities for Development Economics Ser.). 400p. (C). 1998. 125.00 (*0-415-09399-6*) Routledge.
— Econometrics & Data Analysis for Developing Countries. LC 97-8284. (Priorities for Development Economics Ser.). (Illus.). 496p. (C). 1998. pap. 39.99 (*0-415-09400-3*) Routledge.
Mukherjee, D. Applied Many-Body Methods in Spectroscopy & Electronic Structure. (Illus.). 304p. (C). 1992. text 95.00 (*0-306-44193-4*, Kluwer Plenum) Kluwer Academic.
Mukherjee, D., ed. Aspects of Many-Body Effects in Molecules & Extended Systems. (Lecture Notes in Chemistry Ser.: Vol. 50). viii, 565p. 1989. 103.95 (*0-387-50765-5*) Spr-Verlag.
Mukherjee, Dhurjati. Youth: Change & Challenge - India. 1977. 7.50 (*0-8364-0481-5*) S Asia.
Mukherjee, H. Plant Groups. (C). 1989. 100.00 (*0-89771-410-5*, Pub. by Current Dist) St Mut.
Mukherjee, Haridas & Mukherjee, Uma. Sri Aurobindo & the New Thought in Indian Politics. (C). 1997. 40.00 (*81-7102-058-5*, Pub. by Firma KLM) S Asia.
Mukherjee, Hena. The Early History of the East Indian Railway: 1845-1879. (C). 1994. text 28.50 (*81-7102-003-8*, Pub. by Firma KLM) S Asia.
Mukherjee, Jaya. Tagore & Radhakrishnan: A Study in Religious Perspective. 120p. 1992. 12.00 (*81-85078-79-3*, Pub. by Janaki) Nataraj Bks.
Mukherjee, Jugal Kishore. From Man Human to Man Divine: Sri Aurobindo's Vision of the Evolutionary Destiny of Man. 250p. 1991. 12.95 (*81-7058-233-4*, Pub. by SAA) E-W Cultural Ctr.
Mukherjee, K., jt. ed. see Mazumder, Jyoti.
Mukherjee, K. K., tr. see Bauer, Karl M.
Mukherjee, K. N., ed. see Minerals, Metals & Materials Society Staff.
***Mukherjee, Kali, ed.** Metallurgy/Materials Education Yearbook. 38th ed. 230p. 1999. pap. 45.00 (*0-87170-645-8*, 41352G) ASM.
Mukherjee, Kalyan K. Numerical Analysis. (C). 1989. 60.00 (*0-89771-396-6*, Pub. by Current Dist) St Mut.
Mukherjee, Kumar D. Handbook of Chromotography, Lipids, Vol. III. 544p. 1993. lib. bdg. 199.00 (*0-8493-3039-4*, QP751) CRC Pr.
Mukherjee, M. A Passage to Medicine Practice. (C). 1990. 75.00 (*0-7855-4669-3*, Pub. by Current Dist) St Mut.
— Selected Papers on National Income. (C). 1995. 34.00 (*81-7074-150-5*, Pub. by KP Bagchi) S Asia.
Mukherjee, Meenakshi. Jane Austen. Figes, Eva & King, Adele, eds. LC 90-48428. (Women Writers Ser.). 180p. 1991. text 29.95 (*0-312-05794-6*) St Martin.
***Mukherjee, Meenakshi.** The Perishable Empire: Essays on Indian Writing in English. 286p. 2000. text 24.95 (*0-19-565147-2*) OUP.
— Rushdie's Midnight's Children: A Book of Readings LC 99-932720. 227p. 1999. write for info. (*81-85753-28-8*, Pub. by Pencraft International) S Asia.
Mukherjee, Meenakshi, ed. Considerations: Twelve Studies in Indo-Anglian Writings. (C). 1977. 8.00 (*0-8364-0082-8*) S Asia.
Mukherjee, Nirmalangshu, ed. see Chomsky, Noam.
Mukherjee, P. K. & Constance, Lincoln. Umbelliferae (Abiaceae) of India. 288p. (C). 1992. text 75.00 (*1-881570-26-6*) Science Pubs.
Mukherjee, Prabhat. The History of Jagannath Temple. 1977. 14.50 (*0-8364-0414-9*) S Asia.
— The History of Medieval Vaishnavism in Orissa. 200p. 1986. reprint ed. 14.00 (*0-8364-1754-2*, Pub. by Manohar) S Asia.
— History of the Chaitanya Faith in Orissa. 1979. 14.00 (*0-8364-0547-1*) S Asia.
Mukherjee, Prabhati. Beyond the Four Varnas: The Untouchables in India. (C). 1988. 14.00 (*81-208-0459-7*, Pub. by Motilal Bnarsidass) S Asia.
Mukherjee, R. The Culture & Art of India. (Illus.). 1984. text 48.00 (*0-685-13648-5*) Coronet Bks.
— Family & Planning in India. 90p. 1976. 5.95 (*0-318-36834-X*) Asia Bk Corp.
Mukherjee, R. R. & Radhakrishnan, T. Long Vegetable Fibres. 81p. 1972. 100.00 (*0-7855-7203-1*) St Mut.
Mukherjee, Ramkrishna. The Quality of Life: Valuation in Social Research. 240p. (C). 1989. text 24.00 (*0-8039-9587-3*) Sage.
— The Rise & Fall of the East India Company: A Sociological Appraisal. LC 73-90082. 461p. reprint ed. pap. 143.00 (*0-7837-3919-2*, 204376700010) Bks Demand.
— Society, Culture, & Development. 272p. 1992. 29.95 (*0-8039-9102-9*) Sage.
— Sociology of Indian Sociology. 1980. write for info. (*0-8364-1453-5*, Pub. by Allied Pubs) S Asia.
— Systemic Sociology. (Illus.). 256p. (C). 1993. text 26.00 (*0-8039-9126-6*) Sage.
MukherJee, Ramkrishna. Uganda: An Historical Accident? Class, Nation, State Formation. LC 85-71370. 290p. 1985. 35.00 (*0-86543-015-2*); pap. 14.95 (*0-86543-016-0*) Africa World.
***Mukherjee, Ramkrishna & Mukherji, Partha N.** Methodology in Social Research: Dilemmas & Perspectives: Essays in Honor of Ramkrishna Mukherjee. LC 00-28268. 2000. pap. write for info. (*0-7619-9446-7*) Sage.
***Mukherjee, Roma.** Legal Status & Remedies for Women in India. 1998. 30.00 (*81-7100-997-2*) Deep & Deep Pubns.
Mukherjee, Roma. Women, Law & Free Legal Aid in India. LC 98-907463. 1998. 48.00 (*81-7629-098-X*, Pub. by Deep & Deep Pubns) S Asia.
***Mukherjee, Rudrangshu.** Spectre of Violence: The 1857 Kanpur Massacres. LC 98-908913. xiii, 217 p. 1998. 26.00 (*0-670-88359-X*, Viking) Viking Penguin.
Mukherjee, Rudrangshu, ed. The Penguin Gandhi Reader. 320p. 1995. pap. 13.95 (*0-14-023686-4*, Penguin Bks) Viking Penguin.

An Asterisk (*) at the beginning of an entry indicates that the title is appearing for the first time.

Mukherjee, Rudrangshu & Subramanian, Lakshmi, eds. Politics & Trade in the Indian Ocean World: Essays in Honour of Ashin Das Gupta. LC 98-915484. (Illus.). 290p. 1999. text 24.95 (*0-19-564420-4*) OUP.

Mukherjee, S., et al, eds. Nuclear Reaction Mechanism. 636p. (C). 1989. text 161.00 (*9971-5-0882-6*) World Scientific Pub.

Mukherjee, S. & Dagger, D. The Size of the Crime Problem in Australia. 2nd ed. 128p. 1990. pap. 25.00 (*0-642-14935-6*, Pub. by Aust Inst Criminology) Advent Bks Div.

Mukherjee, S. & Prasanna, A. R. Gravitation & Cosmology: Proceedings of the 15th IAGRG Conference, N. Bengal University, Nov. 4-7, 1989. 1992. write for info. (*81-224-0415-4*, Pub. by Wiley Estrn) Franklin.

Mukherjee, S., et al. Crime & Justice in Australia. 62p. 1990. pap. 30.00 (*0-642-14938-0*, Pub. by Aust Inst Criminology) Advent Bks Div.

Mukherjee, S., jt. auth. see Banerjee, P. K.

Mukherjee, S. K. Orchids. (C). 1988. 30.00 (*0-7855-3273-0*, Pub. by Scientific) St Mut.

Mukherjee, S. N. & Sydney Association for Studies in Society Staff. Citizen Historian: Exploration in Historiography. LC 98-915923. xiv, 148 p. 1996. write for info. (*81-7304-141-5*) Manohar.

Mukherjee, Sadhan. South Asia Media Handbook. (C). 1990. 19.50 (*81-7023-305-4*, Pub. by Allied Pubs) S Asia.

Mukherjee, Samir, jt. ed. see Tray, Amita.

Mukherjee, Sampat. Methods of Economic Investigation. (C). 1989. 55.00 (*0-89771-424-5*, Pub. by Current Dist) St Mut.

Mukherjee, Sampat, ed. Economic Environment of Business. (C). 1989. 60.00 (*0-89771-428-8*, Pub. by Current Dist) St Mut.

Mukherjee, Sandeep. Commentaries on Prevention of Corruption Act. (C). 1990. 65.00 (*0-89771-173-4*) St Mut.

Mukherjee, Sanjib K., jt. auth. see Goldman, Robert L.

Mukherjee, Satyanshu, et al, compiled by. A Statistical Profile of Crime in Australia. LC 98-145401. 96p. 1999. pap. 25.00 (*0-642-24033-7*, Pub. by Aust Inst Criminology) Advent Bks Div.

Mukherjee, Satyanshu & Graycar, Adam. Crime & Justice in Australia. 1997. 2nd ed. (Illus.). 108p. 1997. pap. 35.00 (*1-876067-08-X*, Pub. by Federation Pr) Gaunt.

Mukherjee, Satyanshu, et al. Juvenile Crime & Justice: Australia, 1997. LC 98-201086. 86p. 1999. pap. 25.00 (*0-642-24044-2*, Pub. by Aust Inst Criminology) Advent Bks Div.

Mukherjee, Satyanshu K. & Higgins, Karl. Violent Deaths & Firearms in Australia: Data & Trends. LC 98-145388. 96p. 1996. pap. 20.00 (*0-642-24017-5*, Pub. by Aust Inst Criminology) Advent Bks Div.

Mukherjee, Satyanshu Kumar & Carcach, Carlos. Repeat Victimisation in Australia: Extent, Correlates & Implications for Crime Prevention. LC 98-200907. x, 40 p. 1999. pap. 75.00 (*0-642-24057-4*, Pub. by Aust Inst Criminology) St Mut.

Mukherjee, Sipra. Indian Administration of Lord William Bentinck. (C). 1995. 18.00 (*81-7074-142-4*, Pub. by KP Bagchi) S Asia.

Mukherjee, Subrata. Gandhian Thought: Marxist Interpretation. (C). 1991. 21.50 (*0-685-50011-X*, Pub. by Deep & Deep Pubns) S Asia.

Mukherjee, Subrata & Ramaswamy, Suchila, eds. John Stuart Mill: The Subjection of Women. 1p. (C). 1995. 22.00 (*87-17-10080-1*, Pub. by Deep & Deep Pubns) S Asia.

***Mukherjee, Subrata & Ramaswamy, Sushila.** A History of Socialist Thought: From the Precursors to the Present. LC 00-33272. 2000. pap. write for info. (*0-7619-9465-3*) Sage.

Mukherjee, Subrata & Ramaswamy, Sushila, eds. John Stuart Mill, 1806-1873. (C). 1995. 58.00 (*81-7100-560-8*, Pub. by Deep & Deep Pubns) S Asia.

***Mukherjee, Subrata & Ramaswamy, Sushila, eds.** Mao Zedong: His Thoughts & Works. 1998. 36.00 (*81-7100-774-0*) Deep & Deep Pubns.

— Prince Peter Kropotkin: His Thoughts & Works. 1998. 78.00 (*81-7100-765-1*) Deep & Deep Pubns.

— Robert Owen: His Thoughts & Works. 1998. 46.00 (*81-7100-756-2*) Deep & Deep Pubns.

— Rusa Luxemburg: His Thoughts & Works. 1998. 32.00 (*81-7100-772-4*) Deep & Deep Pubns.

— Saint Simon: His Thoughts & Works. 1998. 34.00 (*81-7100-755-4*) Deep & Deep Pubns.

— Thomas More: His Thoughts & Works. 1998. 40.00 (*81-7100-750-3*) Deep & Deep Pubns.

— Vladimir Illyich Lenin: His Thoughts & Words. 1998. 72.00 (*81-7100-771-6*) Deep & Deep Pubns.

— Wilhelm Liebknecht: His Thoughts & Works. 1998. 44.00 (*81-7100-762-7*) Deep & Deep Pubns.

— William Godwin: His Thoughts & Works. 1998. 72.00 (*81-7100-754-6*) Deep & Deep Pubns.

— William Morris: His Thoughts & Works. 1998. 40.00 (*81-7100-763-5*) Deep & Deep Pubns.

Mukherjee, Subrata & Ramaswamy, Sushila, eds. Women in the 19th Century: Sphere, Condition & Duties. 1999. 26.50 (*81-7629-151-X*, Pub. by Deep & Deep Pubns) S Asia.

Mukherjee, Subrata, jt. auth. see Chandra, Abhijit.

Mukherjee, Sushil K. The Story of the Calcutta Theatre, 1753-1980. 1983. 32.00 (*0-8364-0994-9*, Pub. by KP Bagchi) S Asia.

Mukherjee, Uma, jt. auth. see Mukherjee, Haridas.

Mukherji, A. A Passage to Medicine Practical. (C). 1989. 75.00 (*0-89771-357-5*, Pub. by Current Dist) St Mut.

— Prescription Writing. (C). 1989. 40.00 (*0-89771-356-7*, Pub. by Current Dist) St Mut.

Mukherji, A. K. Analytical Chemistry of Zirconium & Hafnium. LC 71-109236. 1970. 157.00 (*0-08-006886-3*, Pub. by Pergamon Repr) Franklin.

Mukherji, Anjan. Walrasian & Non-Walrasian Equilibria: An Introduction to General Equilibrium Analysis. (Illus.). 256p. 1990. 72.00 (*0-19-877290-4*); pap. 35.00 (*0-19-877289-0*) OUP.

Mukherji, Arandita. Socio Economic Backwardness in Women. (C). 1987. 9.00 (*81-7024-096-4*, Pub. by Ashish Pub Hse) S Asia.

Mukherji, B. C. Vedanta & Tagore. 98p. 1994. pap. 113.00 (*81-85880-42-5*, Pub. by Print Hse) St Mut.

Mukherji, B. C., tr. see Rasajalanidhi.

Mukherji, Indrani. T. S. Eliot & Neo-Classical Poetry. (C). 1997. 20.00 (*81-7018-935-7*, Pub. by BR Pub) S Asia.

Mukherji, M. & Roychowdhury, R. Advanced Cost & Management Accountancy. (C). 1989. 135.00 (*0-89771-437-7*, Pub. by Current Dist) St Mut.

Mukherji, Nirmal, jt. ed. see Arora, Balveer.

Mukherji, P. N., jt. ed. see Oommen, T. K.

Mukherji, Partha N. From Left Extremism to Electoral Politics. 1984. 22.50 (*0-8364-1096-3*, Pub. by Manohar) S Asia.

Mukherji, Partha N., jt. auth. see Mukherjee, Ramkrishna.

Mukherji, Penny, jt. auth. see O'Dea, Teresa.

***Mukherji, Priyadarsi.** Chinese & Tibetan Societies Through Folk Literature. 1999. 38.00 (*81-7095-073-2*, Pub. by Lancer India) S Asia.

Mukherji, Runi B., jt. auth. see Adler, Leonore L.

Mukherji, S. K. College Botany, Vol. III. (C). 1989. 100.00 (*0-89771-415-6*, Pub. by Current Dist) St Mut.

***Mukherji, S. K. & Castelijns, J. A., eds.** Modern Head & Neck Imaging. (Medical Radiology Ser.). (Illus.). xvi, 248p. 2000. pap. 75.00 (*3-540-66344-4*) Spr-Verlag.

Mukherji, S. K., ed. see Baert, A. L., et al.

Mukherji, Santi L. The Philosophy of Man-Making. (C). 1989. 40.00 (*0-89771-452-0*, Pub. by Current Dist) St Mut.

Mukherji, Suresh K. & Castillo, Mauricio. Clinical Applications of MR Spectroscopy. LC 97-26486. 317p. 1998. 110.00 (*0-471-16178-0*, Wiley-Liss) Wiley.

Mukherji, Suresh K., jt. auth. see Castillo, Mauricio.

Mukhi, Sunita S., et al, eds. Bridges with Asia: Asian Americans in the United States: Summary Report. 50p. 1997. pap. write for info. (*0-87848-522-8*) Asia Soc.

***Mukhia, Harbans.** The Feudalism Debate. LC 99-938131. 1999. 32.00 (*81-7304-284-5*, Pub. by Manohar) S Asia.

Mukhia, Harbans. Perspectives on Medieval History. (C). 1993. 32.00 (*0-7069-6387-3*, Pub. by Vikas) S Asia.

Mukhia, Harbans, jt. ed. see Byres, T. J.

Mukhin, K. N. Experimental Nuclear Physics, Vols. 1-2. 1032p. (C). 1987. 235.00 (*0-685-46640-X*, Pub. by Collets) St Mut.

Mukhopadhaya, M. A Guide to Employees Providence Fund. (C). 1988. 95.00 (*0-7855-3670-1*) St Mut.

Mukhopadhyay, A., jt. auth. see Randhawa, G. S.

Mukhopadhyay, A. N. Handbook of Diseases of Sugar Beet, 2 Vols., Set. 467p. 1987. 240.00 (*0-8493-3130-7*, SB608) CRC Pr.

Mukhopadhyay, Amal K. & D. Gupta, Sobhanlal. India, Politics & Society Today & Tomorrow: Essays in Honour of Professor Amal Kumar Mukhopadhyay. LC 98-908800. viii, 272 p. 1998. write for info. (*81-7074-209-9*, Pub. by K P Bagchi) S Asia.

Mukhopadhyay, Amal K. & Raizada, Mohan K., eds. Tissue Renin-Angiotensin Systems: Current Concepts of Local Regulators in Reproductive & Endocrine Organs. (Advances in Experimental Medicine & Biology Ser.: Vol. 377). (Illus.). 470p. (C). 1995. text 130.00 (*0-306-45077-1*, Kluwer Plenum) Kluwer Academic.

Mukhopadhyay, B. Motivation in Education Management: Issues & Strategies. (C). 1995. write for info. (*81-207-1621-3*) Sterling Pubs.

Mukhopadhyay, Deepankar. Maverick Maestro Mrinal Sen. (C). 1995. 28.00 (*81-7223-213-6*, Pub. by Indus Pub) S Asia.

Mukhopadhyay, Durgadas. Culture, Performance & Communication. (C). 1989. 29.50 (*81-7018-565-3*, Pub. by BR Pub) S Asia.

— Religion, Philosophy & Literature of Bengal Vaishnavism. 1990. 17.50 (*81-7018-597-1*, Pub. by BR Pub) S Asia.

Mukhopadhyay, Durgadas, ed. In Praise of Krishna. (C). 1990. text 18.50 (*81-7018-546-7*, Pub. by BR Pub) S Asia.

Mukhopadhyay, M. Structures: Matrix & Finite Element. 3rd ed. 423p. 1993. 91.00 (*90-5410-234-9*, Pub. by A A Balkema) Ashgate Pub Co.

***Mukhopadhyay, Mamata.** Natural Extracts Using Supercritical Carbon Dioxide. LC 00-39733. (Illus.). 2000. pap. write for info. (*0-8493-0819-4*) Auerbach.

Mukhopadhyay, Marmar & Parhar, Madhu. Indian Education: Developments since Independence. LC 99-932144. 1999. 30.00 (*81-259-0692-4*, Pub. by Vikas) S Asia.

Mukhopadhyay, N., jt. auth. see Moretti, E. C.

***Mukhopadhyay, Nitis.** Probability & Statistical Inference. LC 00-22901. (Statistics). 665p. 2000. 95.00 (*0-8247-0379-0*) Dekker.

Mukhopadhyay, Nitis & Solanky, Tumulesh K. Multistage Selection & Ranking Procedures: Second-Order Asymptotics. LC 93-47524. (Statistics: Textbooks & Monographs: Vol. 142). (Illus.). 432p. 1994. text 150.00 (*0-8247-9078-2*) Dekker.

Mukhopadhyay, P., ed. Theory of Probability: An Introduction. (C). 1989. 60.00 (*0-89771-399-0*, Pub. by Current Dist) St Mut.

Mukhopadhyay, P., jt. auth. see Banerjee, S.

Mukhopadhyay, P. K. Organic Petrography & Organic Geochemistry of Texas Tertiary Coals in Relation to Depositional Environment & Hydrocarbon Generation. (Reports of Investigations: RI 188). (Illus.). 118p. 1989. pap. 9.00 (*0-317-03121-X*) Bur Econ Geology.

Mukhopadhyay, Pradyot K. Nyaya Theory of Linguistic Performance: A New Interpretation of Tattvacintamani. (Jadavpur Studies in Philosophy, Second Ser.). 1992. 25.00 (*81-7074-095-9*, Pub. by KP Bagchi) S Asia.

Mukhopadhyay, Prasanta K. & Dow, Wallace G. Vitrinite Reflectance As a Maturity Parameter: Applications & Limitations. LC 94-34670. (Symposium Ser.: No. 570). (Illus.). 306p. 1994. text 89.00 (*0-8412-2994-5*, Pub. by Am Chemical) OUP.

Mukhopadhyay, Purnachandra. Journey of the Upanishads to the West. 1987. 32.50 (*0-8364-2025-X*) S Asia.

Mukhopadhyay, Ranadhir, jt. auth. see Ghosh, Anil K.

Mukhopadhyay, S., jt. ed. see Oommen, T. R.

Mukhopadhyay, S. K. High-Performance Fibres. (Textile Progress Ser.: Vol. 25, Nos. 3/4). 1994. pap. 72.00 (*1-870812-66-2*, Pub. by Textile Inst) St Mut.

Mukhopadhyay, Samir, ed. Advances in Fibre Science. 218p. 1992. 130.00 (*1-870812-37-9*, Pub. by Textile Inst) St Mut.

Mukhopadhyay, Samir K. Permanent Settlement to Operation Barga. (C). 1994. text 16.00 (*0-614-04131-7*, Pub. by Minerva) S Asia.

Mukhopadhyay, Sampat. Corporate Planning & Policy. (C). 1989. 125.00 (*0-89771-438-5*, Pub. by Current Dist) St Mut.

Mukhopadhyay, Satya N. & Das, Dipak K. Oxygen Responses, Reactivities, & Measurements in Biosystems. LC 94-6561. 224p. 1994. lib. bdg. 179.00 (*0-8493-4730-0*) CRC Pr.

Mukhopadhyay, Subrata K. Cult of Goddess Sitala in Bengal: An Enquiry into Folk Culture. (C). 1994. text 19.50 (*81-7102-001-1*, Pub. by Firma KLM) S Asia.

Mukhopadhyay, Swapna. Women's Health, Public Policy, & Community Action. LC 98-900343. 192 p. 1998. write for info. (*81-7304-103-2*) Manohar.

***Mukhopadhyay, Swapna, ed.** In the Name of Justice: Women & Law in Society. LC 98-907375. 1998. 20.00 (*81-7304-129-6*, Pub. by Manohar) S Asia.

Mukhopadhyay, Swapna & Savithri, R. Poverty, Gender & Reproductive Choice: An Analysis of Linkages. LC 98-900602. 126 p. 1998. write for info. (*81-7304-106-7*) Manohar.

Mukhopadhyay, Tarun K. Feroze Gandhi: A Crusader in Parliament. (C). 1992. 18.00 (*81-7023-335-6*, Pub. by Allied Pubs) S Asia.

Mukhopadyay, M. Vibration, Dynamics & Structural Systems. (C). 1989. 20.00 (*81-204-0421-1*) S Asia.

Mukhopakhyaya, Mihir M. Sculptures of the Ganga-Yamuna Valley. 1986. 40.00 (*0-8364-1627-9*, Pub. by Abhinav) S Asia.

Mukhtar, Hasan. Pharmacology of the Skin. (Illus.). 448p. 1991. boxed set 125.00 (*0-8493-7292-5*, RL801) CRC Pr.

— Skin Cancer: Mechanisms & Human Relevance. 464p. 1994. boxed set 178.95 (*0-8493-7358-1*) CRC Pr.

Mukhtar, Syeda-Masooda, jt. ed. see Oakey, Ray.

Mukhtarov, E. I. & Zhizhin, G. N. Vibrational Spectra & Structures: A Series of Advances, Vol. 21. Durig, James R., ed. 466p. 1992. 266.00 (*0-444-89865-4*) Elsevier.

Mukjika, P. Diccionario Vasco-Castellano, 2 vols., Set.Tr. of Basque-Spanish Dictionary. (BAQ & SPA.). 1991. 195.00 (*0-8288-7253-8*, 8427112696) Fr & Eur.

Mukoda, Kuniko. The Name of the Flower: Stories. Matsumoto, Tomone, tr. from JPN. LC 93-6309. (Rock Spring Collection). 152p. (Orig.). 1993. pap. 10.95 (*1-880656-09-4*) Stone Bridge Pr.

Mukoh, Takao, tr. see Yamamoto, Tsunetomo.

Mukohata, Yasuo, ed. New Era in Bioenergetics. (Illus.). 308p. 1992. text 73.00 (*0-12-509854-5*) Acad Pr.

Mukoma, Kambuyi S. Basisgemeinden in Afrika: Die Negro-Afrikanische Ekklesiologie Am Beispiel Zaire. (Erfahrung und Theologie Ser.: Bd. 24). (GER., Illus.). 340p. 1994. 54.95 (*3-631-47329-X*) P Lang Pubng.

Mukomla, Supron. Thai Traditional Medical Massage. Mohn, Jerry, ed. & tr. by. (Illus.). 150p. 1999. pap. 19.95 (*0-9666377-3-9*) J Mohn Pr.

Mukonoweshuro, Eliphas G. Colonialism, Class Formation & Underdevelopment in Sierra Leone. 268p. (Orig.). (C). 1993. pap. text 28.50 (*0-8191-8283-4*); lib. bdg. 49.50 (*0-8191-8282-6*) U Pr of Amer.

Mukoyama, Kenichiro, jt. auth. see Sasa, Ryuji.

Mukta, Parita. Upholding the Common Life: The Community of Mirabai. (Illus.). 304p. 1995. 28.00 (*0-19-563115-3*) OUP.

— Upholding the Common Life: The Community of Mirabai. (Gender Studies). (Illus.). 288p. 1998. reprint ed. pap. text 11.95 (*0-19-564373-9*) OUP.

Muktananda, Swami. Bhagawan Nityananda of Ganeshpuri. LC 96-3550. 192p. 1996. pap. 12.95 (*0-911307-45-1*) SYDA Found.

— A Book for the Mind. 2nd ed. 40p. (Orig.). 1993. pap. 4.75 (*0-911307-71-0*) SYDA Found.

— Conversations with Swami Muktananda: The Early Years. 2nd ed. LC 97-52578. Orig. Title: Paramartha Katha Prasang: Spiritual Conversations with Swami Muktananda. (Illus.). 400p. 1998. pap. 14.95 (*0-911307-53-2*) SYDA Found.

— Does Death Really Exist? 2nd ed. LC 95-14439. 64p. 1995. pap. 8.95 (*0-911307-36-2*) SYDA Found.

— From the Finite to the Infinite. 2nd ed. LC 94-43555. 616p. 1994. pap. 16.95 (*0-911307-31-1*) SYDA Found.

— God Is with You. 2nd ed. 40p. (Orig.). 1993. pap. 4.75 (*0-911307-72-9*) SYDA Found.

— I Am That: The Science of Hamsa from the Vijnana Bhairava. rev. ed. LC 92-35416. 96p. 1992. reprint ed. pap. 8.95 (*0-914602-27-6*) SYDA Found.

— I Have Become Alive: Secrets of the Inner Journey. 2nd ed. Durgananda, Swami, ed. LC 91-31166. 240p. 1992. pap. 12.95 (*0-911307-26-5*) SYDA Found.

Muktananda, Swami. I Love You. 2nd ed. 40p. (Orig.). 1993. pap. 4.75 (*0-911307-73-7*) SYDA Found.

Muktananda, Swami. I Welcome You All with Love. 2nd ed. 40p. (Orig.). 1993. pap. 4.75 (*0-911307-65-6*) SYDA Found.

— Kundalini: Secret of Life. (C). 1995. reprint ed. 6.00 (*81-7476-038-5*, Pub. by UBS Pubs Dist) S Asia.

— Kundalini: The Secret of Life. 3rd ed. 80p. 1994. pap. 8.95 (*0-911307-34-6*) SYDA Found.

— Light on the Path. 3rd ed. LC 98-14242. 112p. 1994. pap. 8.95 (*0-911307-70-2*) SYDA Found.

— Mukteshwari. 2nd ed. LC 95-15966. 392p. 1995. pap. 12.95 (*0-911307-35-4*) SYDA Found.

— Mystery of the Mind. 2nd rev. ed. LC 81-50159. 72p. (Orig.). 1992. pap. 8.95 (*0-911307-51-6*) SYDA Found.

— Nothing Exists That Is Not Shiva: Commentaries on the Shiva Sutra, Vijnanabhairava, Gurugita, & Other Sacred Texts. LC 97-22811. 160p. (Orig.). 1997. pap. 12.95 (*0-911307-56-7*) SYDA Found.

***Muktananda, Swami.** Play of Consciousness: A Spiritual Autobiography. 3rd ed. Chidvilasananda, Gurumayi, tr. from HIN. & intro. by. LC 99-42868.Tr. of Chitshakti Vilas. (Illus.). 368p. 2000. pap. 15.95 (*0-911307-81-8*, 205570, Pub. by SYDA Found) Words Distrib.

Muktananda, Swami. Reflections of the Self: Poems of Spiritual Life. Chidvilasananda, Swami, tr. LC 80-50391. 200p. (Orig.). 1980. pap. 10.95 (*0-914602-50-0*) SYDA Found.

— Secret of the Siddhas. LC 80-53590. 264p. 1980. pap. 12.95 (*0-914602-52-7*) SYDA Found.

— Selected Essays. rev. ed. Zweig, Paul, ed. LC 95-47165. 216p. 1995. pap. 12.95 (*0-911307-37-0*) SYDA Found.

— The Self Is Already Attained. 2nd ed. 40p. 1993. pap. 4.75 (*0-911307-74-5*) SYDA Found.

— To Know the Knower. 44p. (Orig.). 1993. pap. 4.75 (*0-911307-75-3*) SYDA Found.

— Where Are You Going? A Guide to the Spiritual Journey. 3rd ed. LC 97-40699. 1994. pap. 12.95 (*0-911307-60-5*) SYDA Found.

Muktananda, Swami & Chidvilasananda, Swami, contrib. by. Resonate with Stillness: Daily Contemplations. LC 95-41463. 408p. 1995. pap. 14.95 (*0-911307-42-7*) SYDA Found.

Mukul, Malay & Mitra, Gautam. Geology of the Sheeprock Thrust Sheet, Central Utah - New Insights. (Miscellaneous Publication of the Utah Geological Survey Ser.: Vol. 98-1). (Illus.). 56p. 1998. pap. 7.95 (*1-55791-615-2*, MP-98-1) Utah Geological Survey.

***Mukund, Kanakalatha.** The Trading World of the Tamil Merchant: Evolution of Merchant Capitalism in the Coromandel. LC 99-938999. (Illus.). 1999. 20.00 (*81-250-1661-9*, Pub. by Orient Longman Ltd) S Asia.

Mukunda, N. World of Bohr & Dirac: Images of Twentieth Century Physics. (C). 1993. reprint ed. 10.00 (*81-224-0483-9*) S Asia.

Mukundan, Monisha, ed. The Namaste Book of Indian Short Stories, Vol. 1. (C). 1992. 14.00 (*81-85674-02-7*, Pub. by UBS Pubs Dist) S Asia.

— The Namaste Book of Indian Short Stories, Vol. I. LC 92-901235. (C). 1994. 9.00 (*81-85944-85-7*, Pub. by UBS Pubs Dist) S Asia.

Mukundan, R. Moment Functions in Image Analysis - Theory & Applications. 1998. 28.00 (*981-02-3524-0*) World Scientific Pub.

Mukurasi, Laeticia. Post Abolished: One Woman's Struggle for Employment Rights in Tanzania. (Cornell International Industrial & Labor Relations Reports: No. 19). 144p. 1991. 27.50 (*0-87546-702-4*, ILR Press); pap. 12.95 (*0-87546-703-2*, ILR Press) Cornell U Pr.

Mul, Jos De, see De Mul, Jos.

Mul, Sjaak De, see De Mul, Sjaak.

Mula, Tom. Jacob Marley's Christmas Carol. LC 95-38108. (Illus.). 116p. (J). (gr. 7). 1995. 10.00 (*1-55850-537-7*) Adams Media.

Mulac, Jim, jt. ed. see Sklar, Morty.

Mulac, Pamela, jt. auth. see Longman, A. Earl.

Mulaik, Stanley A., jt. ed. see Harlow, Lisa L.

***Mulak, J. & Gajek, Zbigniew.** The Effective Crystal Field Potential. LC 00-28030. 2000. write for info. (*0-08-043608-0*) Elsevier.

Mulak, Steven J. Brown Feathers: Waterfowling Tales & Upland Dreams. LC 87-7120. 224p. reprint ed. pap. 69.50 (*0-608-00475-8*, 206129400007) Bks Demand.

— Pointing Dogs Made Easy: How to Train, Nurture, & Appreciate Your Bird Dog. limited ed. Traux, Doug & DeLaurier, Art, Jr., eds. LC 95-31114. (Illus.). 184p. 1995. 25.00 (*0-924357-54-1*) Countrysport Pr.

— Wings of Thunder: New England Grouse Hunting Revisited. LC 98-37644. (Illus.). 208p. 1998. 30.00 (*0-924357-74-6*) Countrysport Pr.

Mulamoottil, George, et al, eds. Wetlands: Environmental Gradients, Boundaries, & Buffers: Proceedings of an International Symposium, April 22-23, 1994. LC 95-46404. 320p. 1996. lib. bdg. 75.00 (*1-56670-147-3*) Lewis Pubs.

Mulamoottil, George, et al. Constructed Wetlands for the Treatment of Landfill Leacheates. LC 98-23910. 304p. 1999. 69.95 (*1-56670-342-5*, L1342) Lewis Pubs.

Mulanax, Richard B. The Boer War in American Politics & Diplomacy. 248p. (Orig.). (C). 1994. lib. bdg. 48.00 (*0-8191-9356-9*) U Pr of Amer.

Mular, Andrew L. & Anderson, Mark A., eds. Design & Installation of Concentration & Dewatering Circuits. LC 85-63667. (Illus.). 852p. reprint ed. pap. 200.00 (*0-8357-6643-8*, 203531000094) Bks Demand.

M

An Asterisk (*) at the beginning of an entry indicates that the title is appearing for the first time.

Mular, Andrew L. & Bhappu, Roshan B., eds. Mineral Processing Plant Design. LC 77-26531. 897p. reprint ed. pap. 200.00 (*0-608-14285-9*, 201742000005) Bks Demand.

Mular, Andrew L. & Jergensen, Gerald V., eds. Design & Installation of Comminution Circuits. LC 82-71992. (Illus.). 1032p. reprint ed. pap. 200.00 (*0-8357-6642-X*, 203530900094) Bks Demand.

Mular, Andrew L., ed. see Mineral Processing Plant Design Symposium Staff.

Mular, Paul, jt. auth. see Carpentieri, Tony.

Mulari, Mary. Adventure in Applique. (Illus.). 44p. (Orig.). 1989. pap. 8.95 (*0-9613569-6-0*) Mary Prodns.

— Applique Design Collection. (Illus.). 56p. (Orig.). 1984. pap. 8.95 (*0-9613569-3-6*) Mary Prodns.

— Country Style Appliques. (Illus.). 42p. (Orig.). 1987. pap. 7.95 (*0-9613569-5-2*) Mary Prodns.

— Deluxe Designs: Designing with Ultrasuede & Other Special Fabrics. (Illus.). 48p. (Orig.). 1992. pap. 12.95 (*0-9613569-9-5*) Mary Prodns.

***Mulari, Mary.** Denim & Chambray with Style: Sewing Easy Accents for "Comfort" Clothes. LC 99-66539. (Illus.). 128p. 2000. pap. 19.95 (*0-87341-808-5*) Krause Pubns.

Mulari, Mary. Designer Sweatshirts. (Illus.). 44p. (Orig.). 1989. pap. 7.95 (*0-9613569-1-X*) Mary Prodns.

— Garments with Style: Adding Flair to Tops, Jackets, Vests, Dresses & More! LC 94-23783. (StarWear Ser.). (Illus.). 144p. 1995. pap. 17.95 (*0-8019-8640-0*) Krause Pubns.

— Mary Mulari Appliques with Style: Designs & Techniques with Fresh Attitude. LC 98-85566. (Illus.). 144p. 1998. pap. 15.95 (*0-87341-683-X*, MEAC) Krause Pubns.

— More Designer Sweatshirts. (Illus.). 60p. (Orig.). 1986. pap. 8.95 (*0-9613569-4-4*) Mary Prodns.

— More Sweatshirts with Style. LC 96-20440. (Illus.). 160p. 1996. pap. 19.95 (*0-8019-8759-8*) Krause Pubns.

— Sweatshirts with Style. LC 93-8197. (Illus.). 128p. 1993. pap. 15.95 (*0-8019-8392-4*) Krause Pubns.

Mulas, Francesco. Studies on Italian-American Literature. LC 95-496. 88p. 1995. pap. 14.50 (*0-934733-87-2*) CMS.

Mulase, Motohico, tr. see Kuga, Michio.

Mulathino, Paula. Origami. 80p. 1995. 10.98 (*0-7858-0262-2*) Bk Sales Inc.

Mulawka, E. J. African Grey Parrots. (Illus.). 128p. 1983. 23.95 (*0-86622-975-2*, PS-780) TFH Pubns.

Mulawka, Edward J. Yellow-Fronted Amazon Parrots. (Illus.). 160p. 12.95 (*0-86622-526-9*, PS-781) TFH Pubns.

Mulay, Regina. Mass Media, International Relations & Non-Alignment. 536p. 1987. 48.50 (*0-8364-2030-6*, Pub. by Deep & Deep Pubns) S Asia.

Mulay, S. P., jt. ed. see Ortega, A.

Mulbacher & Dahringer. International Marketing: A Global Perspective. (ITBP Acquisitions Ser.). 1999. pap. 24.99 (*1-86152-456-0*) Thomson Learn.

Mulbagala, K. V. The Popular Practice of Yoga. 238p. 1996. pap. 17.00 (*0-89540-295-5*, SB-295) Sun Pub.

Mulberg, Jon. Social Limits to Economic Theory. LC 94-47651. (Modern Economics Ser.). 325p. (C). 1995. pap. 29.99 (*0-415-12386-0*) Routledge.

***Mulberry, Keith.** Word 2000 Essentials Advanced with CD-ROM. 208p. (C). 1999. pap. text 18.67 incl. audio compact disk (*1-58076-305-7*, Prentice Hall) P-H.

— Word 2000 Essentials Basic with CD-ROM. 212p. (C). 1999. pap. text 18.67 incl. audio compact disk (*1-58076-092-9*, Prentice Hall) P-H.

Mulbery, Keith. Corel WordPerfect 7 for Windows 95: A Guide to Productivity. 640p. 1996. pap. 38.65 (*0-7600-4445-7*) Course Tech.

— Corel WordPerfect 7 for Windows 95: A Guide to Productivity, Review Pack. 10th ed. (C). 1996. 3.5 hd. write for info. (*0-7600-4446-5*) Course Tech.

— Corel WordPerfect 7 for Windows 95: Enhancing Productivity. 10th ed. 320p. (C). 1997. pap. 26.95 (*0-7600-5014-7*) Course Tech.

— Mastering & Using Microsoft Office 97: Professional Business Simulations. 96p. 1997. pap. write for info. (*0-7600-5045-7*) Course Tech.

***Mulbery, Keith.** Mous Essentials Word 2000. 2nd ed. 550p. 2000. pap. 45.33 (*0-13-019106-X*) P-H.

Mulbery, Keith. WordPerfect 6.1 for Windows - A Guide to Productivity, Incl. instr. resource kit, test bank, transparency. (Illus.). 888p. 1995. text, mass mkt. write for info. incl. 3.5 ld (*1-56527-236-6*) Course Tech.

Mulcahey, Dave, jt. auth. see Frank, Tom.

Mulcahy. Global Supply Chain Logistics. LC 99-31909. (Professional Engineering Ser.). 400p. 2000. 69.95 (*0-07-134867-0*) McGraw.

Mulcahy, Charles C., et al. Public Sector Labor Relations in Wisconsin. 620p. 1988. ring bd. 75.00 (*0-945574-03-7*) State Bar WI.

Mulcahy, D. B. Life of St. Kiaran the Elder of Seir. 1998. pap. 3.50 (*0-89979-107-7*) British Am Bks.

Mulcahy, D. L., et al, eds. Biotechnology & Ecology of Pollen. (Illus.). 700p. 1986. 141.00 (*0-387-96267-0*) Spr-Verlag.

Mulcahy, David E. Warehouse Distribution & Operations Handbook. 864p. 1993. 89.50 (*0-07-044002-6*) McGraw.

Mulcahy, David E., ed. Materials Handling Handbook. LC 98-22675. (Illus.). 768p. 1998. 99.50 (*0-07-044014-X*) McGraw.

Mulcahy, Greg. Constellation: A Novel. LC 96-2755. 160p. 1996. pap. 13.00 (*1-888105-13-5*) Avisson Pr.

***Mulcahy, Greg.** Drinking in Silence. 144p. 2000. pap. 15.00 (*1-888105-44-5*) Avisson Pr.

***Mulcahy, Joanne B.** Birth & Rebirth on an Alaskan Island: The Life of an Alutiiq Healer. LC 00-36881. 208p. 2001. pap. 24.95 (*0-8203-2253-9*) U of Ga Pr.

Mulcahy, John J., ed. Diagnosis & Management of Male Sexual Dysfunction. LC 96-22329. (Topics in Clinical Urology Ser.). (Illus.). 240p. 1997. 79.50 (*0-89640-322-X*) Igaku-Shoin.

Mulcahy, Kevin V., jt. auth. see Crabb, Cecil V.

Mulcahy, Kevin V., jt. ed. see Pankratz, David B.

Mulcahy, Linda, et al, eds. Medical Mishaps: Pieces of the Puzzle. LC 98-21881. 224p. 1998. 29.95 (*0-335-20258-6*) OpUniv Pr.

Mulcahy, Linda, et al. Medical Mishaps: Pieces of the Puzzle. LC 98-21881. 1998. 95.00 (*0-335-20259-4*) OpUniv Pr.

Mulcahy, Lucille. Dark Arrow. LC 94-39582. (Illus.). x, 209p. (J). (gr. 7 up). 1995. pap. 7.95 (*0-8032-8220-6*, Bison Books) U of Nebr Pr.

Mulcahy, Pat, ed. see Hirsch, E. D., Jr.

Mulcahy, Risteard. The Longterm Care of the Coronary Patient. (Illus.). 124p. (Orig.). 1992. pap. text 35.00 (*0-443-04673-5*) Church.

***Mulcahy, Rita.** PMP Exam Prep. 2nd rev. ed. (Illus.). 336p. 1999. pap. 89.00 (*1-890676-42-X*, Pub. by Beavers Pond) Bookman Bks.

Mulcahy, Robert. Diseases: Finding the Cure. LC 95-42739. (Innovators Ser.). (Illus.). 144p. (YA). (gr. 5-12). 1996. lib. bdg. 19.95 (*1-881508-28-5*) Oliver Pr MN.

— Medical Technology: Inventing the Instruments. LC 96-4939. (Innovators Ser.). (Illus.). 144p. (YA). (gr. 5-12). 1997. lib. bdg. 19.95 (*1-881508-34-X*) Oliver Pr MN.

Mulcahy, Robert F., et al, eds. Enhancing Learning & Thinking. LC 91-15556. 304p. 1991. 69.50 (*0-275-93666-X*, C3666, Praeger Pubs) Greenwood.

Mulcahy, Sylvia, tr. see Verdi, Giuseppe.

***Mulcaire-Jones, George.** The Bead System of Natural Family Planning. Garces, Soledad, tr.Tr. of Planificacion Familiar Natural - Sistema de Cuentas. (SPA., Illus.). 122p. 1999. ring bd. write for info. (*0-9673056-1-6*) Maternal Life.

— Windows to Ordinary Souls. unabridged ed. 91p. 1998. pap. 19.95 (*0-9673056-0-8*) Maternal Life.

Mulcaster, Richard. Positions Concerning the Training up of Children. Barker, William, ed. 696p. 1993. text 80.00 (*0-8020-2987-6*) U of Toronto Pr.

— Positions Wherein Those Primitive Circumstances Be Examined: Which Are Necessarie for the Training up of Children (1581 Edition) Stern, Jeffrey, ed. & intro. by. (Classics in Education Ser.). 308p. 1996. reprint ed. 80.00 (*1-85506-298-4*) Bks Intl VA.

Mulchandani, Ashok & Rogers, Kim, eds. Affinity Biosensors: Techniques & Protocols. LC 98-4566. (Methods in Biotechnology Ser.: Vol. 7). (Illus.). 264p. 1998. 79.50 (*0-89603-539-5*) Humana.

— Enzyme & Microbial Biosensors: Techniques & Protocols. LC 98-174557. (Methods in Biotechnology Ser.: Vol. 6). (Illus.). 284p. 1998. 79.50 (*0-89603-410-0*) Humana.

***Mulchandani, Ashok & Sadik, Omowunki A., eds.** Chemical & Biological Sensors for Environmental Monitoring Biosensors. (ACS Symposium Ser.: No. 762). (Illus.). 336p. 2000. text 115.00 (*0-8412-3687-9*, Pub. by Am Chemical) OUP.

Mulcherjee, S., jt. auth. see Daguer, D.

Mulchow, David & Mogel, William A. Energy Law & Transactions, 5 vols. 1990. ring bd. 630.00 (*0-8205-1336-9*) Bender.

Mulcrone, Patricia. Contemporary's Essential GED. LC 96-32038. 1996. pap. 13.00 (*0-8092-0905-5*) NTC Contemp Pub Co.

Mulcrone, Patricia, ed. Contemporary's GED: How to Prepare for the High School Equivalency Examination. rev. ed. (Illus.). 938p. 1994. pap. 13.50 (*0-8092-3777-6*) NTC Contemp Pub Co.

— Current Perspectives on Administration of Adult Education Programs. LC 85-644750. (New Directions for Adult & Continuing Education Ser.: No. ACE 60). 115p. (Orig.). 1994. pap. 22.00 (*1-55542-714-6*) Jossey-Bass.

Mulcrone, Patricia & Rainey, William. Contemporary's Complete Pre-GED. LC 96-43778. 1024p. 1996. pap. 13.50 (*0-8092-0930-6*) NTC Contemp Pub Co.

Mulcrone, Richard T., et al, eds. The Report of the Task Force on Juvenile Programming, Evaluation & Planning: State of Minnesota. 70p. 1998. pap. text 20.00 (*0-7881-4247-X*) DIANE Pub.

Mulder. Imported Foundation Stock of North American Arabian Horses, Vol. 1. rev. ed. 1991. 30.00 (*0-87505-361-0*) Borden.

Mulder, A. C., ed. Advanced Wastewater Treatment: Nutrient Removal & Anaerobic Processes. 224p. 1997. pap. write for info. (*0-08-043295-6*) Elsevier.

Mulder, A. C., jt. ed. see Knyn, T.

Mulder, Alfred E. Happiness Is: An Introduction to Christian Faith & Life. 2nd ed. LC 95-4929. 1995. pap. 4.95 (*1-56212-117-0*) CRC Pubns.

Mulder, B., et al, eds. Materials Science of the Cell Vol. 489: Materials Research Society Symposium Proceedings. (Materials Research Society Symposium Proceedings Ser.). 226p. 1998. text 80.00 (*1-55899-394-0*) Materials Res.

Mulder-Bakker, Anneke B., ed. Sanctity & Motherhood: Essays on Holy Mothers in the Middle Ages. LC 95-13824. (Garland Reference Library of the Humanities: Vols. 1767 & 14). (Illus.). 360p. 1995. text 69.00 (*0-8153-1425-6*, H1767) Garland.

***Mulder, Barry S., ed.** The Strategy & Design of the Effectiveness Monitoring Program for the Forest Plan. (Illus.). 138p. (C). 2000. pap. text 30.00 (*0-7881-8525-X*) DIANE Pub.

***Mulder, Britiany.** Christmas Wishes. 2000. 4.99 (*1-56245-404-8*) Great Quotations.

Mulder, C. J., jt. auth. see Tytgat, G. N.

Mulder, C. L. & De Bruin, E. J., eds. Psychosocial Interventions in Patients with Cancer & Coronary Heart Disease: Examples of Field Studies & Methodological Considerations. LC 93-19354. 96p. 1993. pap. 22.00 (*90-265-1349-6*) Swets.

Mulder, Carol J. Imported Foundation Stock of North American Arabian Horses, Vol. 1. limited rev. ed. (Illus.). 314p. 1991. 45.00 (*0-87505-360-2*) Borden.

— Imported Foundation Stock of North American Arabian Horses, Vol. 2. (Illus.). 431p. 1993. 39.00 (*0-87505-111-1*) Borden.

— Imported Foundation Stock of North American Arabian Horses, Vol. 3. (Illus.). 354p. 1995. 40.00 (*0-87505-365-3*) Borden.

Mulder, Chester O. Search the Scriptures, Old Testament Vol. 5: Joshua. 1965. pap. 1.99 (*0-8341-0032-0*) Beacon Hill.

Mulder, Chris J. & Tytgat, N. J., eds. Is Crohn's Disease a Mycobacterial Disease? 1992. text 81.00 (*0-7923-2026-3*) Kluwer Academic.

Mulder, Chris J., jt. ed. see Mearin, M. L.

Mulder, David. The Alchemy of Revolution: Gerrard Winstanley's Occultism & Seventeenth-Century English Communism. LC 89-34745. (American University Studies: History: Ser. IX, Vol. 77). XI, 364p. 1990. text 60.95 (*0-8204-1173-6*) P Lang Pubng.

Mulder, David P. Narrative Preaching: Stories from the Pulpit. LC 96-10519. (Illus.). 112p. 1996. 10.99 (*0-570-04861-3*, 12-3352) Concordia.

Mulder, Dennis M. & Cutshall, Mark. The Living Power of God's Word. 192p. 1996. pap. 14.99 (*0-8054-6080-2*, 4260-80) Broadman.

Mulder, Dwayne, jt. auth. see Moser, Paul K.

Mulder, E. F. De, see McCall, G. J. & De Mulder, E. F.

Mulder, Gerald J. Sulfation of Drugs & Related Compounds. 248p. 1981. 142.00 (*0-8493-5920-1*, RM301, CRC Reprint) Franklin.

Mulder, Gerard J., ed. Conjugation Reactions in Drug Metabolism: An Integral Approach. 300p. 1990. 148.00 (*0-85066-738-0*) Taylor & Francis.

***Mulder, Gerit D., et al.** Clinicians' Pocket Guide to Chronic Wound Repair. 4th ed. LC 98-29793. 1998. 12.95 (*0-87434-988-5*) Springhouse Corp.

***Mulder, Henk A. & Biesiot, Wouter.** Transition to a Sustainable Society: A Backcasting Approach to Modelling Energy & Ecology. LC 97-35436. (Advances in Ecological Economics Ser.). 320p. (C). 1998. 95.00 (*1-85898-731-8*) E Elgar.

Mulder, Henk L. & Kraft, V. Foundations for a Scientific Analysis of Value. Schneewind, Elizabeth H., tr. (Vienna Circle Collection: No. 15). 212p. 1981. lib. bdg. 112.00 (*90-277-1211-5*, D Reidel) Kluwer Academic.

Mulder, Henk L. & Van de Velde-Schlick, Barbara, eds. Moritz Schlick: Philosophical Papers, Vol. 2. (Vienna Circle Collection: No. 11). 572p. 1980. pap. text 115.00 (*90-277-0942-4*, D Reidel) Kluwer Academic.

— Moritz Schlick: Philosophical Papers, Vol. 2, 1925-1936 (Vienna Circle Collection: No. 11). 572p. 1980. lib. bdg. 182.50 (*90-277-0941-6*, D Reidel) Kluwer Academic.

Mulder, Henk L. & Van De Velde-Schlick, Barbara, eds. Moritz Schlick: Philosophical Papers, Vol. 1, 1909-1922, Vol. 1. (Vienna Circle Collection: No. 11). 414p. 1978. pap. text 78.50 (*90-277-0315-9*, D Reidel); lib. bdg. 158.50 (*90-277-0314-0*, D Reidel) Kluwer Academic.

Mulder, Henk L., ed. see Kraft, V.

Mulder, Henk L., ed. see Menger, Karl.

Mulder, Henk L., ed. see Schlick, Moritz.

***Mulder, J. D. & Van Liere, R., eds.** Virtual Environments 2000: Proceedings of the Eurographics Workshop in Amsterdam, The Netherlands, June 1-2, 2000. (Eurographics Ser.). (Illus.). x, 217p. 2000. pap. 54.95 (*3-211-83516-4*) Spr-Verlag.

Mulder, J. W. & Hervey, S. G. Theory of the Linguistic Sign. (Janua Linguarum, Ser. Minor: No. 136). 70p. (Orig.). 1972. pap. text 44.65 (*90-279-2187-3*) Mouton.

Mulder, Jan. Dynamic Translinear & Log-Domain Circuits: Analysis & Synthesis. LC 98-46087. (Series in Engineering & Computer Science). xii, 273p. 1999. 120.00 (*0-7923-8355-9*) Kluwer Academic.

— Foundations of Axiomatic Linguistics. (Trends in Linguistics, Studies & Monographs: No. 40). xii, 475p. (C). 1989. lib. bdg. 153.85 (*0-89925-323-7*) Mouton.

Mulder, Jan, jt. auth. see Serdijn, Wouter A.

Mulder, Jean G. Ergativity in Coast Tsimshian (Sm'algyax) LC 94-9526. (Publications in Linguistics Ser.: Vol. 124). 1994. 28.00 (*0-520-09788-2*, Pub. by U CA Pr) Cal Prin Full Svc.

Mulder, John M. Woodrow Wilson: The Years of Preparation. LC 77-72128. (Supplementary Volumes to the Papers of Woodrow Wilson). (Illus.). 334p. reprint ed. pap. 103.60 (*0-8357-6548-2*, 203591200097) Bks Demand.

Mulder, John M., et al, eds. The Organizational Revolution: Presbyterians & American Denominationalism. (Presbyterian Presence Ser.). 300p. (Orig.). 1991. pap. 24.95 (*0-664-25197-8*) Westminster John Knox.

Mulder, John M., et al. Woodrow Wilson: A Bibliography, 27. LC 97-22554. (Bibliographies of the Presidents of the United States Ser.: Vol. 27). 488p. 1997. lib. bdg. 95.00 (*0-313-28185-8*, Greenwood Pr) Greenwood.

Mulder, John R. Temple of the Mind: Education & Literary Taste in Seventeenth-Century England. LC 79-79059. 1969. 30.50 (*0-672-53602-1*) Irvington.

Mulder, John T., jt. ed. see Kerr, Hugh T.

Mulder, Kenneth W. Piracy - Days of Long Ago. 2nd rev. ed. Mulder, Sandra, ed. (Illus.). 88p. 1998. reprint ed. per. 14.95 (*1-889034-03-7*) Mulder Ent.

— Seminoles - Days of Long Ago. 2nd rev. ed. Mulder, Sandra, ed. (Illus.). 32p. 1996. 5.00 (*1-889034-01-0*) Mulder Ent.

— Tampa Bay - Days of Long Ago. 3rd ed. Mulder, Sandra, ed. (Illus.). 24p. 1990. 5.00 (*1-889034-02-9*) Mulder Ent.

Mulder-Krieger, T. & Verpoorte, R. Anthocyanins As Flower Pigments: Feasibilities for Flower Colour Modification. LC 93-11838. 164p. (C). 1993. pap. text 2549.00 (*0-7923-2465-X*) Kluwer Academic.

Mulder, L. J., et al, eds. Computers in Psychology: Application in Education, Research & Psychodiagnostics. 240p. 1991. 45.25 (*90-265-1170-1*) Swets.

Mulder, Linnea. Sarah & Puffle: A Story for Children about Diabetes. LC 92-25638. (Illus.). 32p. (J). 1992. pap. 8.95 (*0-945354-42-8*) Am Psychol.

Mulder, M. J. The Old Testament in Syriac According to the Peshitta Version Pt. III, Fasc. 3: Ezekiel. LC 78-339247. xxxvi, 113p. 1993. reprint ed. 79.00 (*90-04-07314-0*) Brill Academic Pubs.

Mulder, M. J., jt. ed. see Dirksen, P. B.

Mulder, Marcel. Basic Principles of Membrane Technology. 580p. (C). 1996. pap. text 65.00 (*0-7923-4248-8*); lib. bdg. 255.00 (*0-7923-4247-X*) Kluwer Academic.

Mulder, Mark. Group Structure, Motivation & Group Performance. (Psychology Ser.). (Illus.). 1963. text 14.65 (*3-10-800280-5*) Mouton.

Mulder, Martin, et al, eds. Corporate Training for Effective Performance. 288p. (C). 1995. lib. bdg. 91.00 (*0-7923-9599-9*) Kluwer Academic.

Mulder, Mary J. & Coyle, Richard. Come, Sing & Celebrate! (Orig.). 1988. pap. 4.25 (*1-55673-074-8*, 8871) CSS OH.

Mulder, Mauk. The Daily Power Game. (Quality of Working Life Ser.: No. 6). 1977. lib. bdg. 66.50 (*90-207-0707-8*) Kluwer Academic.

Mulder, Niels. Inside Indonesian Society: Cultural Change in Java. 240p. 1997. pap. 17.95 (*90-5496-026-4*, Pub. by Pepin Pr) Tuttle Pubng.

— Inside Southeast Asia: Religion, Everyday Life, Cultural Change. 164p. 1997. pap. 17.95 (*90-5496-028-0*, Pub. by Pepin Pr) Tuttle Pubng.

— Inside Thai Society: An Interpretation of Everyday Life. 192p. 1997. pap. 17.95 (*90-5496-027-2*, Pub. by Pepin Pr) Tuttle Pubng.

— Thai Images: The Culture of the Public World. LC 97-942544. 364p. 1998. pap. text 14.95 (*974-7100-44-4*) U of Wash Pr.

Mulder, Rev. Imported Foundation Stock of North American Arabian Horses, Vol. 2. limited ed. 1993. 45.00 (*0-87505-366-1*) Borden.

Mulder, Sandra, ed. see Mulder, Kenneth W.

Mulder, Timothy J. So You've Been Asked to... Lead in Prayer. 16p. 1996. pap. 0.95 (*1-56212-217-7*) CRC Pubns.

***Mulder, William.** Homeward to Zion: The Morman Migration from Scandinavia. (Illus.). 2000. pap. 16.95 (*0-8166-3674-5*) U of Minn Pr.

Mulder, William & Mortensen, A. Russell, eds. Among the Mormons. 482p. 1994. reprint ed. pap. 15.95 (*0-914740-36-9*) Western Epics.

Mulderig, Gerald P. The Heath Guide to Grammar & Usage. (C). text, teacher ed. 21.56 (*0-669-34133-9*) HM Trade Div.

— The Heath Guide to Grammar & Usage. 13th ed. (C). pap. text, wbk. ed. 19.16 (*0-669-34134-7*) HM Trade Div.

— The Heath Guide to Grammar & Usage. 13th ed. 160p. (C). 1994. pap. text 17.56 (*0-669-35378-7*) HM Trade Div.

— The Heath Guide to Writing the Research Paper. 216p. (C). 1992. pap. text 15.96 (*0-669-27704-5*) HM Trade Div.

— The Heath Guide to Writing the Research Paper. 2nd ed. 224p. (C). 1995. pap. text 17.16 (*0-669-35377-9*) HM Trade Div.

— The Heath Handbook. 13th ed. 800p. (C). 1995. pap. text 20.36 (*0-669-34131-2*) HM Trade Div.

Mulderig, Gerald P. & Elsbree, Langdon. The Heath Handbook. 12th ed. LC 89-85074. 771p. (C). 1990. text 20.36 (*0-669-17859-4*); teacher ed. 21.56 (*0-669-17860-8*); 2.66 (*0-669-17864-0*); 2.66 (*0-669-17862-4*); trans. write for info. (*0-318-66918-8*) HM Trade Div.

***Mulders, Annemieke.** Complex Magnetic Phenomena in Rare Earth Intermetallic Compounds. (Illus.). 118p. 1998. pap. 42.50 (*90-407-1696-X*, Pub. by Delft U Pr) Coronet Bks.

Mulders, M. A. Remote Sensing in Soil Science. (Developments in Soil Science Ser.: No. 15). 380p. 1987. 189.00 (*0-444-42783-X*) Elsevier.

Muldofsky, Peri. Will Smith. LC 98-85421. (Little Bks.). (Illus.). 80p. (J). 1998. 4.95 (*0-8362-7134-3*) Andrews & McMeel.

***Muldoon.** Architecture of Global Governance. 2000. pap. 35.00 (*0-8133-6844-8*, Pub. by Westview) HarpC.

Muldoon, Brian. The Heart of Conflict. 272p. 1997. pap. 14.00 (*0-399-51895-9*, Perigee Bks) Berkley Pub.

Muldoon, Herbert A. Law & Forensics: Index of New Information. 150p. 1998. 47.50 (*0-7883-2032-7*); pap. 44.50 (*0-7883-2033-5*) ABBE Pubs Assn.

Muldoon, James. The Americas in the Spanish World Order: The Justification for Conquest in the Seventeenth Century. LC 93-50529. 256p. (C). 1994. text 34.50 (*0-8122-3245-3*) U of Pa Pr.

— Canon Law, World Order & the Expansion of Europe. LC 98-6522. (Variorum Collected Studies: Vol. 612). 330p. 1998. text 89.95 (*0-86078-685-4*, LAW, Pub. by Ashgate Pub) Ashgate Pub Co.

Muldoon, James, ed. Varieties of Religious Conversion in the Middle Ages. LC 96-39216. 248p. 1997. 49.95 (*0-8130-1509-X*) U Press Fla.

Muldoon, James B. You Have No Courts with Any Sure Rule of Law: The Saga of the Supreme Judicial Court of Massachusetts. (Illus.). 353p. (Orig.). 1992. pap. 16.95 (*0-9632270-0-9*) Lookout Hill.

Muldoon, James P., ed. A Guide to Delegate Preparation, 1994-1995. 185p. 1994. pap. 10.00 (*1-880632-26-8*) UNA-USA.

Muldoon, James P., Jr., et al, eds. Multilateral Diplomacy & the United Nations Today. LC 98-20749. 272p. 1998. 65.00 (*0-8133-9959-9*, Pub. by Westview) HarpC.

***Muldoon, James P., Jr., et al, eds.** Multilateral Diplomacy & the United Nations Today. LC 98-20749. 272p. 1998. pap. text 26.00 (*0-8133-9958-0*, Pub. by Westview) HarpC.

Muldoon, Joseph A. The Facilitator's Guide for the Insight Class Program. 112p. 1988. teacher ed. 24.95 (*0-9613416-8-8*) Comm Intervention.

— Nobody's Fault, Everybody's Responsibility: What Parents Can Do When a Child Is Using Alcohol & Other Drugs. 48p. (Orig.). 1989. pap. 3.95 (*0-945485-09-3*) Comm Intervention.

Muldoon, Joseph A. & Crowley, James F. One Step Ahead: Early-Intervention Strategies for Adolescent Drug Problems. LC 85-73646. (Illus.). 180p. (Orig.). 1986. pap. 14.95 (*0-9613416-1-0*) Comm Intervention.

Muldoon, Kathleen M. Princess Pooh. Mathews, Judith, ed. LC 88-33978. (Illus.). 32p. (J). (gr. 2-5). 1989. lib. bdg. 14.95 (*0-8075-6627-6*) A Whitman.

Muldoon, Katie. How to Profit Through Catalog Marketing. Knudsen, Anne, ed. (Illus.). 416p. 1995. 89.95 (*0-8442-3572-5*, NTC Business Bks) NTC Contemp Pub Co.

Muldoon, Marilynn C., ed. see Muldoon, Virginia.

Muldoon, Maureen. The Abortion Debate in the United States & Canada: A Source Book. LC 91-3658. 256p. 1991. text 15.00 (*0-8240-5260-9*, SS648) Garland.

Muldoon, Maureen, ed. Abortion: An Annotated Indexed Bibliography. LC 79-91622. (Studies in Women & Religion: Vol. 3). 167p. 1980. lib. bdg. 79.95 (*0-88946-972-5*) E Mellen.

Muldoon, Paul. The Annals of Chile. LC 94-10874. 191p. 1994. text 21.00 (*0-374-10518-9*) FS&G.

— The Annals of Chile. 191p. 1995. pap. 10.00 (*0-374-52456-4*) FS&G.

— The Astrakhan Cloak. LC 92-51047. 112p. 1993. pap. 10.95 (*0-916390-54-3*) Wake Forest.

— Bandanna. 80p. 1999. pap. 13.00 (*0-571-19762-0*) Faber & Faber.

***Muldoon, Paul.** Collected Poems 1968-1998. 2002. text. write for info. (*0-374-12543-0*) FS&G.

Muldoon, Paul. Hay: Poems. LC 98-23285. 224p. 1998. text 22.00 (*0-374-16831-8*) FS&G.

***Muldoon, Paul.** Hay: Poems. 144p. 1999. pap. 13.00 (*0-374-52619-2*) FS&G.

Muldoon, Paul. Madoc: A Mystery. 1991. 19.95 (*0-374-19557-9*) FS&G.

— Madoc: A Mystery. 272p. 1992. pap. 12.00 (*0-374-52344-4*) FS&G.

— Meeting the British. LC 87-50181. 64p. (Orig.). 1987. pap. 6.95 (*0-916390-26-8*) Wake Forest.

— Mules & Early Poems. 72p. 1986. pap. 6.95 (*0-916390-22-5*) Wake Forest.

— The Prince of the Quotidian. LC 94-60895. 40p. 1994. pap. 5.95 (*0-916390-63-2*) Wake Forest.

— Quoof. LC 83-50028. 64p. 1983. pap. 6.95 (*0-916390-19-5*) Wake Forest.

— Selected Poems - Muldoon. 128p. 1987. pap. 16.50 (*0-88001-154-8*) HarpC.

Muldoon, Paul. Selected Poems, 1968-1986. 153p. 1993. pap. 12.00 (*0-374-52374-6*, Noonday) FS&G.

Muldoon, Paul. Shining Brow. LC 94-107918. 80p. (Orig.). 1993. pap. 13.95 (*0-571-16789-6*) Faber & Faber.

— Six Honest Serving Men. LC 95-182146. 50p. 1995. 22.95 (*1-85235-169-1*); pap. 12.95 (*1-85235-168-3*) Dufour.

Muldoon, Paul, ed. The Faber Book of Contemporary Irish Poetry. 416p. 1986. pap. 19.95 (*0-571-13761-X*) Faber & Faber.

***Muldoon, Paul, ed.** Ploughshares Spring 2000 Vol. 26: Poems & Stories Edited by Paul Muldoon. 226p. 2000. pap. 9.95 (*0-933277-28-8*) Ploughshares.

Muldoon, Paul & Doyle, Bill. Kerry Slides. LC 96-170834. 62p. 1997. 28.95 (*1-85235-190-X*) Dufour.

Muldoon, Paul, jt. auth. see Mausberg, Burkhard.

Muldoon, Paul, jt. auth. see Slides, Kerry.

Muldoon, Paul, tr. see Ni Dhomhnaill, Nwala.

Muldoon, Paul, tr. see Nuala Ni Dhomhnaill.

Muldoon, Robert L., jt. auth. see Jackson, George G.

Muldoon, Sylvan & Carrington, Hereward. The Projection of the Astral Body. (Illus.). 336p. 1973. reprint ed. pap. 12.95 (*0-87728-069-X*) Weiser.

Muldoon, Sylvan J. & Carrington, Hereward. The Projection of the Astral Body. (Collector's Library of the Unknown). 242p. 1990. reprint ed. write for info. (*0-8094-8062-X*); reprint ed. lib. bdg. write for info. (*0-8094-8063-8*) Time-Life.

Muldoon, Virginia. When Nancy Lived on Chestnut Street. Muldoon, Marilynn C., ed. (Illus.). 52p. 1982. pap. 3.95 (*0-940930-00-5*) Forsythe & Cromwell.

Muldowney, Mary S., tr. see Augustine, Saint.

Muldrew, Jessie. Focus on Creative Playmaking. Romano, Louis G., ed. 17p. 1989. pap. text. write for info. (*0-318-72650-5*) MI Middle Educ.

Muldrew, Karan, jt. auth. see Glusha, Laura.

Muldrew, Karen, jt. auth. see Glusha, Laura.

Muldrow, Diane. Barbie - Holiday Helpers. (Little Golden Bks.). 24p. (J). (ps-3). 1998. 2.29 (*0-307-96000-5*, 96000, Goldn Books) Gldn Bks Pub Co.

— Barbie Loves Her Sisters. (Golden Deluxe Super Shape Bks.). 16p. (J). (ps-3). 1997. pap. text 3.99 (*0-307-21100-2*, 21100, Goldn Books) Gldn Bks Pub Co.

***Muldrow, Diane.** Buzz Lightyear: Space Ranger. (Toy Story 2 Ser.). (Illus.). 24p. (J). 1999. 3.29 (*0-307-13325-7*, Goldn Books) Gldn Bks Pub Co.

Muldrow, Diane. The Chick Book. (Super Shape Bks.). 24p. (J). (ps-k). 1998. pap. text 3.29 (*0-307-10322-6*, 10322, Goldn Books) Gldn Bks Pub Co.

***Muldrow, Diane.** Counting Fun on the Farm. 12p. 1999. pap. 4.99 (*0-307-10665-9*, Whitman Coin) St Martin.

— Girls Can Do Anything. 12p. (Orig.). 1999. pap. text 4.99 (*0-307-10666-7*, Whitman Coin) St Martin.

Muldrow, Diane. Happy Book. 18p. (J). 1999. 13.95 (*0-590-10993-6*) Scholastic Inc.

— Haunted Halloween. LC 97-80828. (Mickey & Friends Ser.). 24p. (J). 1998. 2.29 (*0-307-96006-4*, 96006, Goldn Books) Gldn Bks Pub Co.

— I Am Barbie. LC 96-80410. (Sturdy Board Bks.). (Illus.). (J). (ps). 1997. 4.99 (*0-307-12043-0*, 12043, Goldn Books) Gldn Bks Pub Co.

***Muldrow, Diane.** Ice Skating Dreams. (Barbie Amazing Athlete Look-Look Bks.). (Illus.). 24p. (J). 1999. pap. 3.29 (*0-307-13255-2*, Goldn Books) Gldn Bks Pub Co.

Muldrow, Diane. Jingle Bells. LC 97-80244. (Little Golden Bks.). 24p. (J). 1998. 2.29 (*0-307-96020-X*, 96020, Goldn Books) Gldn Bks Pub Co.

— Kindness. LC 98-48390. 32p. 1999. lib. bdg. write for info. (*1-55916-233-3*) Rourke Bk Co.

— Lassie: The Great Escape. (Look-Look Bks.). (Illus.). 24p. (J). 1998. pap. 3.29 (*0-307-12986-1*, 12986, Goldn Books) Gldn Bks Pub Co.

***Muldrow, Diane.** Mickey Big Book. 48p. (J). 2000. 12.99 (*0-7364-1018-X*, Pub. by Disney Pr) Time Warner.

Muldrow, Diane. My Favorite Teacher. LC 97-76904. (Look-Look Bks.). (Illus.). 24p. (J). (ps-3). 1998. pap. 2.99 (*0-307-13180-7*, 13180, Goldn Books) Gldn Bks Pub Co.

— My First Barbie: A Colorful Beach Day. LC 97-74275. (Naptime Tales Ser.). (Illus.). 16p. (J). (ps). 1998. bds. 3.99 (*0-307-12994-2*, 12994, Goldn Books) Gldn Bks Pub Co.

— My First Barbie: Shapes at the Ballet. LC 97-74276. (Naptime Tales Ser.). (Illus.). 16p. (J). 1998. bds. 3.99 (*0-307-12993-4*, 12993, Goldn Books) Gldn Bks Pub Co.

— The New Counselor. LC 97-74561. (Super Shape Bks.). (Illus.). 24p. (J). 1998. pap. 3.29 (*0-307-10345-5*, 10345, Goldn Books) Gldn Bks Pub Co.

***Muldrow, Diane.** Woody's Round-Up. (Toy Story 2 Ser.). (Illus.). 24p. (J). 1999. 3.29 (*0-307-13326-5*, Goldn Books) Gldn Bks Pub Co.

***Muldrow, Diane & Brooks, Nan.** Undersea Animals. (Animals All Around Ser.). (Illus.). 18p. (J). (ps-1). 2000. bds. 5.99 (*1-57584-389-7*) Rdrs Digest.

Muldrow, George M., jt. auth. see Donker, Marjorie.

***Muldrow, Lycurgus.** The Common Sense Guide for Spirituality: How to Begin, Stay Focused, & Evolve Spiritually. 206p. 1999. pap. 16.95 (*0-9671961-0-8*, Pub. by Glden Eight Intl) ACCESS Pubs Network.

Muldrow, Ronald. Facing Wes - A Musical Tribute to Wes Montgomery: Intermediate Level. 120p. 1997. spiral bd. 14.95 (*0-7866-3052-3*, 96617) Mel Bay.

Mule, Harris M., jt. auth. see English, E. Philip.

Mule, Marty. Rolling Green: A Century of Tulane Football. (Illus.). 101p. 1993. 24.95 (*0-9639795-0-7*) Tulane U Athletic.

***Mule, Rosa.** Political Parties, Games & Redistribution. (Illus.). 222p. 2001. write for info. (*0-521-79008-5*); pap. write for info. (*0-521-79358-0*) Cambridge U Pr.

Mule, S. J. & Brill, Henry. Chemical & Biological Aspects of Drug Dependence. LC 72-191695. (Drug Dependence Ser.). 576p. 1972. 55.00 (*0-87819-011-2*, CRC Reprint) Franklin.

Mulej & Dyck. Self-Transformation of the Forgotten Four-Fifths. 408p. (C). 1997. 49.95 (*0-7872-4499-6*) Kendall-Hunt.

***Mulekwa, Charles.** Time of Fire. (Nick Hern Books, Drama Classics). 80p. 2000. pap. 16.95 (*1-85459-478-8*) Theatre Comm.

Mulenga. Knowledge, Vol. 1. 1998. pap. 25.00 (*1-85649-518-3*) St Martin.

— Knowledge, Vol. 1. 1998. pap. text 59.95 (*1-85649-517-5*, Pub. by Zed Books) St Martin.

Mulert, Laurie. Am I Fat? A Story about Dieting. LC 98-87031. (Illus.). 39p. 1998. pap. 5.95 (*1-57543-063-0*) Mar Co Prods.

Mulfinger, Dale. The Architecture of Edwin Lunde. LC 95-15039. (Illus.). xiii, 121p. 1995. pap. 45.00 (*0-87351-314-2*) Minn Hist.

Mulfinger, George, ed. Design & Origins in Astronomy. (Creation Research Society Monographs: No. 2). (Illus.). 152p. (Orig.). 1984. pap. 9.00 (*0-940384-03-5*) Creation Research.

Mulford, A. C. Boundaries & Landmarks. 1977. reprint ed. pap. 15.00 (*0-686-18920-5*, 611) CARBEN Survey.

Mulford, Beverley M. The Mulford Method: A Preschool Teaching Program. (Illus.). 96p. (C). teacher ed. write for info. (*0-9639125-0-X*) Mulford School.

***Mulford, Carla.** Teaching the Literatures of Early America. LC 99-47304. (Options for Teaching Ser.). 1999. pap. 22.00 (*0-87352-359-8*) Modern Lang.

***Mulford, Carla, ed.** Teaching the Literatures of Early America. LC 99-47304. 402p. 2000. 40.00 (*0-87352-358-X*) Modern Lang.

Mulford, Carla, ed. see Stockton, Annis B.

Mulford, Carla, ed. & intro. see Brown, William H. & Foster, Hannah W.

Mulford, Charles. Interorganizational Relations: Implications for Community Development. (Center for Policy Research Monographs: Vol. 4). 227p. 1984. 34.95 (*0-89885-147-5*, Kluwer Acad Hman Sci) Kluwer Academic.

Mulford, Charles W. CPS Financial Accounting Course Notebook. 2nd rev. ed. 292p. (C). 1995. text 15.95 (*0-256-21200-7*, Irwn McGrw-H) McGrw-H Hghr Educ.

Mulford, Charles W. & Comiskey, Eugene E. Financial Warnings. 10th ed. LC 95-48809. 496p. 1996. 112.00 (*0-471-12044-8*) Wiley.

Mulford, Charles W., jt. auth. see Comiskey, Eugene E.

Mulford, Clarence. Bar Twenty. (Hopalong Cassidy Ser.). 382p. 1974. reprint ed. lib. bdg. 27.95 (*0-88411-213-6*) Amereon Ltd.

— Bar Twenty Days. (Hopalong Cassidy Ser.). 412p. 1974. reprint ed. lib. bdg. 27.95 (*0-88411-214-4*) Amereon Ltd.

— Bar Twenty Three. (Hopalong Cassidy Ser). 1976. reprint ed. lib. bdg. 25.95 (*0-88411-227-6*) Amereon Ltd.

— Bar-20 Rides Again. Date not set. lib. bdg. 25.95 (*0-88411-215-2*, Aeonian Pr) Amereon Ltd.

— Coming of Cassidy. (Hopalong Cassidy Ser.). 438p. 1974. reprint ed. lib. bdg. 29.95 (*0-88411-216-0*) Amereon Ltd.

— Cottonwood Gulch. large type ed. (Hopalong Cassidy Ser.). 348p. 1974. reprint ed. lib. bdg. 25.95 (*0-88411-233-0*) Amereon Ltd.

Mulford, Clarence. Hopalong Cassidy. abr. ed. Kaye, Jocelyn, ed. 1993. pap. 12.95 incl. audio (*1-882071-38-7*) B&B Audio.

Mulford, Clarence. Hopalong Cassidy. 1976. reprint ed. lib. bdg. 27.95 (*0-88411-217-9*) Amereon Ltd.

— The Man from Bar Twenty. (Hopalong Cassidy Ser.). 1976. reprint ed. lib. bdg. 24.95 (*0-88411-229-2*) Amereon Ltd.

— Man from the Bar-20. 1995. pap. 4.99 (*0-8125-5050-1*, Pub. by Forge NYC) St Martin.

— Orphan. 308p. 1974. reprint ed. lib. bdg. 27.95 (*0-88411-225-X*) Amereon Ltd.

Mulford, Clarence E. Bar-20. LC 94-143941. 288p. 1992. mass mkt. 4.99 (*0-8125-2290-7*, Pub. by Tor Bks) St Martin.

Mulford, Clarence E. Bar-Twenty Days. 256p. 1993. mass mkt. 4.99 (*0-8125-3003-9*, Pub. by Tor Bks) St Martin.

— Bar-23. 1998. mass mkt. 5.99 (*0-8125-6771-4*, Pub. by Forge NYC) St Martin.

— Bring Me His Ears. (Hopalong Cassidy Ser.). 1976. reprint ed. 26.95 (*0-88411-228-4*) Amereon Ltd.

— Buck Peters, Ranchman. 320p. 1993. mass mkt. 4.99 (*0-8125-2499-3*, Pub. by Tor Bks) St Martin.

— Buck Peters, Ranchman. 1973. reprint ed. lib. bdg. 26.95 (*0-88411-202-0*) Amereon Ltd.

— Coming of Cassidy. (Hopalong Cassidy Ser.: No. 1). (Illus.). 288p. 1992. mass mkt. 4.99 (*0-8125-2291-5*, Pub. by Tor Bks) St Martin.

— H. C. & Eagle's Brood. large type ed. 1976. 24.95 (*0-88411-235-7*) Amereon Ltd.

— H. C. Returns. 1976. 24.95 (*0-88411-218-7*) Amereon Ltd.

— H. C. Serves Writ. 1976. 23.95 (*0-88411-220-9*) Amereon Ltd.

— H. C. Takes Cards. 1976. 23.95 (*0-88411-221-7*) Amereon Ltd.

— H. C.'s Protege. 1976. 25.95 (*0-88411-219-5*) Amereon Ltd.

— Hopalong Cassidy. (Illus.). 320p. 1992. mass mkt. 4.99 (*0-8125-2242-7*, Pub. by Tor Bks) St Martin.

— Johnny Nelson. 1976. 26.95 (*0-88411-222-5*) Amereon Ltd.

— Johnny Nelson. 304p. 1997. mass mkt. 5.99 (*0-8125-6766-8*, Pub. by Tor Bks) St Martin.

— Me an' Shorty. 1976. 23.95 (*0-88411-223-3*) Amereon Ltd.

— Mesquite Jenkins. large type ed. 1976. 24.95 (*0-88411-236-5*) Amereon Ltd.

— Mesquite Jenkins, Tumbleweed. 1976. 24.95 (*0-88411-224-1*) Amereon Ltd.

— On the Trail of the Tumbling T. 1976. 24.95 (*0-88411-209-8*) Amereon Ltd.

— The Round-Up. large type ed. Date not set. reprint ed. lib. bdg. 24.95 (*0-88411-238-1*, Aeonian Pr) Amereon Ltd.

— Rustler's Valley. large type ed. Date not set. reprint ed. lib. bdg. 25.95 (*0-88411-239-X*, Aeonian Pr) Amereon Ltd.

— Tex. 288p. 1999. mass mkt. 5.99 (*0-8125-6687-4*, Pub. by Tor Bks) St Martin.

— Tex. (Hopalong Cassidy Ser.). 1976. reprint ed. lib. bdg. 24.95 (*0-88411-226-8*) Amereon Ltd.

— Trail Dust. large type ed. Date not set. lib. bdg. 24.95 (*0-88411-240-3*, Aeonian Pr) Amereon Ltd.

Mulford, Elisha. The Nation: The Foundations of Civil Order & Political Life in the United States. LC 71-120327. xiv, 418p. 1971. reprint ed. 49.50 (*0-678-00705-5*) Kelley.

Mulford, Karen S. Arizona's Historic Escapes. LC 97-33225. (Illus.). (Orig.). 1997. pap. 12.95 (*0-89587-202-1*) Blair.

— Arizona's Historic Restaurants & Their Recipes. LC 95-32834. (Illus.). 1995. 16.95 (*0-89587-132-7*) Blair.

Mulford, Karen S., jt. auth. see O'Brien, Dawn.

Mulford, Nancy, ed. G Protein-Coupled Receptors: New Opportunities for Commercial Development. (Biomedical Library). 312p. 1996. pap. 895.00 (*1-57936-005-X*) IBC USA.

— Mucosal Immunization: Genetic Approaches & Adjuvants. (Biomedical Library). 436p. 1996. pap. 695.00 (*1-57936-008-4*) IBC USA.

— Natural Products: Rapid Utilization of Sources for Drug Discovery & Development. (Biomedical Library). 352p. 1995. pap. 795.00 (*1-57936-009-2*) IBC USA.

Mulford, O. J. Windmill Pointe: Lake Sainte Claire. 64p. 1998. reprint ed. lib. bdg. 69.00 (*0-7812-4801-9*) Rprt Serv.

***Mulford, Phil.** Absolute Beginners Bass Guitar. 40p. 1999. pap. text 11.95 (*0-7119-7427-6*, AM92616) Music Sales.

Mulford, Phil. Classic Metal Bass. 64p. 1997. pap. 14.95 incl. cd-rom (*0-7119-4505-5*) Omnibus NY.

— The Complete Bass Player Bk. 1. (Illus.). (Orig.). 1997. pap. 19.95 incl. audio compact disk (*0-7119-3440-1*, AM91109, Pub. by Wise Publns) Omnibus NY.

— The Complete Bass Player Bk. 2, Bk. 2. (Illus.). (Orig.). 1996. 19.95 (*0-7119-3441-X*, AM 91110, Pub. by Wise Publns) Omnibus NY.

— Fast Forward Metal Bass Styles. 64p. pap. 14.95 incl. audio compact disk (*0-7119-4504-7*) Omnibus NY.

— Rock Steady Bass Styles. 64p. pap. 14.95 incl. cd-rom (*0-7119-4501-2*) Omnibus NY.

Mulford, Philippa G. Emily Smiley Sings the Blues. (Emily Smiley Ser.: Vol. 3). (J). (gr. 2-6). 1998. mass mkt. 3.99 (*0-8125-6352-2*, Pub. by Tor Bks) St Martin.

— Emily Smiley Takes a Shot. (Emily Smiley Ser.: No. 2). (J). 1998. pap. 3.99 (*0-8125-6351-4*, Pub. by Tor Bks) St Martin.

— Everything I Hoped For. 192p. (Orig.). (YA). (gr. 8-12). 1990. pap. 2.95 (*0-380-76074-6*, Avon Bks) Morrow Avon.

***Mulford, Philippa G.** The Holly Sisters on Their Own. LC 97-24089. 158p. (J). (gr. 5-9). 1998. lib. bdg. 14.95 (*0-7614-5022-X*) Marshall Cavendish.

Mulford, Philippa G. Keys to Successful Stepmothering. LC 95-13018. (Parenting Keys Ser.). 144p. 1996. pap. 6.95 (*0-8120-9330-5*) Barron.

— Making Room for Katherine. LC 93-32268. 160p. (J). (gr. 5-9). 1994. mass mkt. 14.95 (*0-02-767652-8*, Mac Bks Young Read) S&S Childrens.

Mulford, Phillipa G. Emily Smiley & the Mean Queen. (J). 1997. pap. 4.99 (*0-8125-6350-6*, Pub. by Tor Bks) St Martin.

Mulford, Prentice. Gift of the Spirit. 1981. 300.00 (*0-8490-0235-4*) Gordon Pr.

— The Gift of the Spirit: A Selection from the Essays of Prentice Mulford. 267p. 1993. pap. 22.00 (*0-89540-261-0*, SB-261) Sun Pub.

— The Gift of Understanding. 288p. 1996. pap. 24.00 (*0-89540-296-3*, SB-296) Sun Pub.

— Thought Forces. 172p. 1984. pap. 17.00 (*0-89540-144-4*, SB-144) Sun Pub.

— Thoughts Are Things. 1991. lib. bdg. 79.95 (*0-8490-4293-3*) Gordon Pr.

— Thoughts Are Things. 171p. 1993. pap. 16.00 (*0-89540-232-7*, SB-232) Sun Pub.

— Thoughts Are Things. 171p. 1996. reprint ed. pap. 12.50 (*0-7873-0629-0*) Hlth Research.

— Thoughts Are Things. 176p. 1996. reprint ed. pap. 11.95 (*1-56459-673-7*) Kessinger Pub.

— Your Forces & How to Use Them. 100p. 1998. reprint ed. pap. 16.95 (*0-7661-0308-0*) Kessinger Pub.

Mulford, Uri. Pioneer Days & Later Times in Corning & Vicinity, 1789-1920. (Illus.). 528p. 1997. reprint ed. lib. bdg. 55.00 (*0-8328-6125-1*) Higginson Bk Co.

***Mulford, Wendy.** The East Anglia Sequence: Norfolk 1984 - Suffolk 1994. 64p. 1998. pap. 12.50 (*0-946904-71-5*, Pub. by Spec Diseases) SPD-Small Pr Dist.

Mulford, Wendy. Love Poems by Women. LC 90-82345. 320p. 1991. pap. 10.00 (*0-449-90538-1*, Columbine) Fawcett.

Mulford, Wendy, jt. auth. see Maitland, Sara.

Mulgan, Catherine. The Renaissance Monarchies, 1469-1558. LC 99-174432. (Perspectives in History Ser.). vii, 118p. (C). 1998. pap. 11.95 (*0-521-59870-2*) Cambridge U Pr.

Mulgan, G. J. Politics in an Antipolitical Age. 220p. 1994. pap. 26.95 (*0-7456-0813-2*) Blackwell Pubs.

Mulgan, Geoff. Connexity: How to Live in a Connected World. LC 97-30350. 288p. 1998. pap. 14.95 (*0-87584-850-8*) Harvard Busn.

Mulgan, John, jt. auth. see Bolitho, Hector.

Mulgan, Richard. Democracy & Power in New Zealand: A Study of New Zealand Politics. 2nd ed. 188p. 1989. pap. 19.95 (*0-19-558200-4*) OUP.

— Politics in New Zealand. 2nd rev. ed. 332p. 1997. pap. 24.95 (*1-86940-171-9*, Pub. by Auckland Univ) Paul & Co Pubs.

Mulgrew, Bernard & Cowan, Colin F. Adaptive Filters & Equalisers. (C). 1988. text 100.50 (*0-89838-285-8*) Kluwer Academic.

***Mulhall.** Bridging the Gap. 1999. pap. text 30.00 (*0-443-05984-5*) Harcourt.

Mulhall, A., jt. ed. see Hardey, M.

Mulhall, Brian E., jt. auth. see Parkinson, David H.

***Mulhall, Daniel.** A New Day Dawning: A Portrait of Ireland in 1900. LC 99-492098. (Illus.). 248p. 2000. 35.95 (*1-898256-65-9*, Pub. by Collins Press) Irish Bks Media.

Mulhall, John P., ed. Contemporary Diagnosis & Management of Urologic Emergencies. (Illus.). 230p. (C). 2000. pap. 29.50 (*1-884065-38-4*) Assocs in Med.

Mulhall, John P. & Goldstein, Irwin. Contemporary Diagnosis & Management of Male Impotence. (Illus.). 150p. 2000. pap. 29.95 (*1-884065-32-5*) Assocs in Med.

Mulhall, John W. America & the Founding of Israel: An Investigation of the Morality of America's Role. LC 94-62144. 270p. 1995. pap. 7.95 (*0-9645157-0-9*) Deshon Pr.

Mulhall, Michael G. The English in South America. Wilkins, Mira, ed. LC 76-29753. (European Business Ser.). (Illus.). 1977. reprint ed. lib. bdg. 57.95 (*0-405-09769-7*) Ayer.

Mulhall, Stephen. Routledge Philosophy Guidebook to Heidegger & Being & Time. LC 95-38893. (Philosophy Guidebooks Ser.). 224p. (C). 1996. 60.00 (*0-415-10092-5*); pap. 12.99 (*0-415-10093-3*) Routledge.

— Stanley Cavell: Philosophy's Recounting of the Ordinary. 376p. 1994. text 68.00 (*0-19-824074-0*) OUP.

— Stanley Cavell: Philosophy's Recounting of the Ordinary. 378p. 1999. pap. text 24.95 (*0-19-823850-9*) OUP.

An Asterisk (*) at the beginning of an entry indicates that the title is appearing for the first time.

Mulhall, Stephen, ed. The Cavell Reader. (Blackwell Readers Ser.). 352p. (C). 1996. 60.95 (*0-631-19742-7*); pap. 28.95 (*0-631-19743-5*) Blackwell Pubs.

Mulhall, Stephen & Swift, Adam, eds. Liberals & Communitarians. 2nd ed. 384p. (C). 1996. pap. 28.95 (*0-631-19819-9*) Blackwell Pubs.

Mulhausen, Harold L. & Alexander, James E. Korea: Memories of a U. S. Marine. (Illus.). 80p. 1995. pap. 7.50 (*0-939965-11-9*) Macedon Prod.

Mulhauser, Frederick L., ed. see Clough, Arthur H.

Mulhauser, Gregory R. Mind Out of Matter: Topics in the Physical Foundations of Consciousness & Cognition. LC 98-22509. (Studies in Cognitive Systems). 1998. 120.00 (*0-7923-5103-7*) Kluwer Academic.

Mulhauser, Ruth. Maurice Sceve. LC 76-28722. (Twayne's World Authors Ser.). 138p. (C). 1977. lib. bdg. 20.95 (*0-8057-6264-7*) Irvington.

Mulhearn, Daniel & Taibi, John. General Motors F Units the Locos: That Revolutionized Railroading. 1982. pap. 15.95 (*0-915276-39-9*) Quadrant Pr.

Mulhearn, Henry J. Graphing & Charting Simplified. 105p. 1976. pap. 12.95 (*0-87526-221-X*) Gould.

— Police Science Fundamentals. 1973rd ed. 220p. pap. 14.95 (*0-87526-160-4*) Gould.

Mulhearn, Robyn & Pippin, Aleta. Yikes!! My Butt's Falling, Vol. 1. LC 97-75124. 160p. 1998. pap. 9.95 (*0-9660546-1-X*) Inner Sources.

Mulhearn, Robyn, jt. auth. see Pippin, Aleta.

Mulherin, Jennifer. As You Like It: Shakespeare for Everyone. LC 90-478. (Illus.). 32p. (J). 1990. lib. bdg. 12.95 (*0-87226-339-8*, P Bedrick Books) NTC Contemp Pub Co.

Mulherin, Jennifer & Frost, Abigail. Best Loved Plays of Shakespeare. LC 00-100001. (Illus.). 160p. (YA). (gr. 5 up). 1999. 24.95 (*1-887734-62-7*) Star Brght Bks.

Mulhern, Chieko. Koda Rohan. LC 76-50541. (Twayne's World Authors Ser.). 178p. (C). 1977. lib. bdg. 17.95 (*0-8057-6272-8*) Irvington.

Mulhern, Chieko, tr. see Arai, Shinya.

Mulhern, Chieko I., ed. Heroic with Grace: Legendary Women of Japan. LC 90-28750. 344p. (C). (gr. 13). 1991. 69.95 (*0-87332-527-3*, East Gate Bk); pap. 25.95 (*0-87332-552-4*, East Gate Bk) M E Sharpe.

— Japanese Women Writers: A Bio-Critical Sourcebook. LC 94-617. 536p. 1994. lib. bdg. 105.00 (*0-313-25486-9*) Greenwood.

Mulhern, Florence. Crusader for the Least of These: The Story of the SPCA of Anne Arundel County. LC 96-32458. (Illus.). 128p. (Orig.). 1997. pap. 11.95 (*1-56474-201-6*) Fithian Pr.

Mulhern, Francis. Contemporary Marxist Literary Criticism: Longman Critical Readers. (C). 1992. text 61.25 (*0-582-05977-1*) Addison-Wesley.

***Mulhern, Francis.** Culture/Metaculture. LC 99-54750. (Illus.). 256p. 2000. pap. write for info. (*0-415-10230-8*) Routledge.

— Culture/Metaculture. LC 99-54750. (New Critical Idiom Ser.). 256p. (C). 2000. text. write for info. (*0-415-10229-4*) Routledge.

— The Present Lasts a Long Time: Essays in Cultural Politics. LC 98-42849. (Clitical Conditions Ser.: 7). 280p. 1998. pap. 30.00 (*0-268-03861-9*, Pub. by U of Notre Dame Pr) Chicago Distribution Ctr.

Mulhern, James. History of Secondary Education in Pennsylvania. LC 77-89208. (American Education: Its Men, Institutions, & Ideas. Series 1). 1970. reprint ed. 30.95 (*0-405-01447-3*) Ayer.

Mulhern, Kathleen, jt. auth. see Purdam, Stanley H.

Mulhern, Kathy. Finding God in the Craziness of Life Vol. 1: Prayers & Meditations on Tough Issues for Today's Teens, 5 vols. 48p. (Orig.). (YA). 1996. pap. 4.95 (*0-8192-8005-4*) Liv Good News.

— Finding God in the Craziness of Life Vol. 2: Prayers & Meditations on Tough Issues for Today's Teens, 5 vols. (Illus.). 48p. (Orig.). (YA). 1996. pap. 4.95 (*0-8192-8006-2*) Liv Good News.

— Finding God in the Craziness of Life Vol. 3: Prayers & Meditations on Tough Issues for Today's Teens, 5 vols. (Illus.). 48p. (Orig.). (YA). 1996. pap. 4.95 (*0-8192-8007-0*) Liv Good News.

— Finding God in the Craziness of Life Vol. 4: Prayers & Meditations on Tough Issues for Today's Teens, 5 vols. (Illus.). 48p. (Orig.). (YA). 1996. pap. 4.95 (*0-8192-8008-9*) Liv Good News.

— Finding God in the Craziness of Life Vol. 5: Prayers & Meditations on Tough Issues for Today's Teens, 5 vols. (Illus.). 48p. (Orig.). (YA). 1996. pap. 4.95 (*0-8192-8009-7*) Liv Good News.

Mulhern, Kathy, ed. see DeVries, Dirk.

Mulhern, Raymond K., jt. ed. see Bearison, David J.

Mulhern, Sean. Pupil Services: A Resource & Planning Guide. LC 95-621571. 115p. (C). 1995. pap. text 21.00 (*1-57337-016-9*) WI Dept Pub Instruct.

Mulhern, Sean, et al. Preventing Youth Violence & Aggression & Promoting Safety in Schools. 20p. (C). 1994. pap. text 9.00 (*1-57337-028-2*) WI Dept Pub Instruct.

Mulhern, Tom. Acoustic Instrument Amplification. 112p. 1997. pap. 17.95 (*0-7935 6701-7*) H Leonard.

Mulhern, Tom, ed. Bass Heroes: Styles, Stories & Secrets of 30 Great Bass Players. (Illus.). 208p. 1993. pap. 19.95 (*0-87930-274-7*) Miller Freeman.

Mulholland, jt. auth. see Gully.

***Mulholland, Catherine.** William Mulholland & the Rise of Los Angeles. LC 99-48289. (Illus.). 496p. 2000. 35.00 (*0-520-21724-1*, Pub. by U CA Pr) Cal Prin Full Svc.

Mulholland, David H. A Reading Guide to the Old Testament. iv, 261p. 1989. pap. 9.95 (*0-87579-283-9*) Deseret Bk.

Mulholland, David W. Hugging the Coast & More. (Illus.). 128p. 1999. pap. 12.95 (*1-929254-00-8*) Poetry Works.

***Mulholland, Dewey.** Mark's Story of Jesus: Messiah for All Nations. 224p. 1999. pap. 20.00 (*1-57910-251-4*) Wipf & Stock.

Mulholland, George, et al, eds. Global Growth of Technology: Is America Prepared? A Working Conference. (Illus.). 99p. (C). 1997. reprint ed. pap. text 25.00 (*0-7881-4732-3*) DIANE Pub.

Mulholland, Gerry C. Pocket Guide to 12 Lead ECG Interpretation. LC 97-42698. 1998. 19.95 (*0-683-40235-8*) Lppncott W & W.

Mulholland, Gloria. Summer Angel. (Illus.). 25p. (J). (gr. 4-7). 1998. 6.95 (*0-533-12409-3*) Vantage.

Mulholland, J. No Compromise & The Fool: Two Life-Centered Plays That Relate Biblical Themes to Contemporary Life. 1991. pap. text 8.99 (*0-00-528675-1*) Lillenas.

Mulholland, J. Derral, ed. Scientific Applications of Lunar Laser Ranging. (Astrophysics & Space Science Library: No. 62). 1977. lib. bdg. 117.50 (*90-277-0790-1*) Kluwer Academic.

Mulholland, J. Derral, jt. auth. see Evans, David S.

Mulholland, J. R. Heating, Ventilation & Air Conditioning Plant. 142p. 1970. 28.95 (*0-8464-1468-6*) Beekman Pubs.

Mulholland, James. No Compromise & The Fool: Two Life-Centered Plays That Relate Biblical Themes to Contemporary Life. 78p. 1987. 8.99 (*0-8341-9243-8*, MP-638) Lillenas.

Mulholland, Joan. Handbook of Persuasive Tactics: A Handbook of Strategies for Influencing Others Through Communication. LC 93-17210. 416p. (C). (gr. 13). 1993. 90.00 (*0-415-08930-1*, B0737) Routledge.

— Language of Negotiation: A Handbook of Practical Strategies for Improving Communication. 224p. (C). 1991. text 75.00 (*0-415-06040-0*, Pub. by Tavistock) Routldge.

Mulholland, John. Beware Familiar Spirits. LC 75-7388. (Perspectives in Psychical Research Ser.). 1975. reprint ed. 29.95 (*0-405-07036-5*) Ayer.

Mulholland, Joyce L., jt. auth. see Brown, Meta.

***Mulholland, Judie & Seltzer, Jerry.** Ekarma Y2kalendar: A Daily Planner for the Next Millennium. (Illus.). 176p. 1999. spiral bd. 34.95 (*0-905249-98-4*) Findhorn Pr.

Mulholland, Kenneth & Dyers, J. A. Pollution Prevention: Methodology, Technologies & Practices. LC 98-40828. (AIChE Originals Ser.). 330p. 1999. 175.00 (*0-8169-0782-X*, Q-7) Am Inst Chem Eng.

Mulholland, Kenneth, jt. auth. see Hulbert, Terry C.

Mulholland, Lisa, jt. ed. see Griffin, Kate.

Mulholland, M. Robert, Jr. Invitation to a Journey: A Road Map for Spiritual Formation. LC 93-3529. 173p. (Orig.). 1993. pap. 10.99 (*0-8308-1386-1*, 1386) InterVarsity.

Mulholland, M. Robert. Revelation: Holy Living in an Unholy World. 304p. 1990. 21.99 (*0-310-51740-0*) Zondervan.

— Shaped by the Word. LC 85-51241. 1985. pap. 11.00 (*0-8358-0519-0*) Upper Room Bks.

***Mulholland, Marc.** Northern Ireland at the Crossroads. LC 99-46717. 272p. 2000. text 69.95 (*0-312-22835-X*) St Martin.

Mulholland, Paul, ed. see Middleton, Thomas & Dekker, Thomas.

Mulholland, R. D. Introduction to the New Zealand Legal System. 7th ed. 352p. 1990. pap. 90.00 (*0-409-78895-3*, NZ, MICHIE) LEXIS Pub.

Mulholland, Rory, tr. see Korte, Peter & Seesslen, Georg, eds.

Mulholland, Rosemary. South Africa, 1948-1994. (History Programm Ser.). (Illus.). 64p. 1998. pap. 13.95 (*0-521-57678-4*) Cambridge U Pr.

Mulholland, S. C., jt. auth. see Rapp, G., Jr.

Mulholland, S. Grant, ed. Antibiotic Therapy in Urology. LC 95-39528. 232p. 1996. text 72.00 (*0-397-51586-3*) Lppncott W & W.

Mulholland, Shona, jt. auth. see James, Rebecca.

Mulholland, St. Clair A. The Story of the 116th Regiment Pennsylvania Infantry. 422p. 35.00 (*1-56013-005-9*) Olde Soldier Bks.

***Mulholland, Sylvia.** The Thirty-Two Teeth Smile. 2000. write for info. (*0-688-17072-2*, Wm Morrow) Morrow Avon.

Mulholland, T. B., jt. ed. see Evans, C. R.

Mulholland, W. D. Adirondack Campsites. 42p. 1993. reprint ed. lib. bdg. 69.00 (*0-7812-5258-X*) Rprt Serv.

— Catskill Campsites. 14p. 1993. reprint ed. lib. bdg. 69.00 (*0-7812-5259-8*) Rprt Serv.

— Catskill Trails. 34p. 1993. reprint ed. lib. bdg. 69.00 (*0-7812-5260-1*) Rprt Serv.

— Lake Placid Trails. 22p. 1993. reprint ed. lib. bdg. 69.00 (*0-7812-5261-X*) Rprt Serv.

Mulica, Barbara, jt. auth. see Damiani, Bruno.

Mulica, F. James. Dreamtech Vol. 1: A Powerful Tool to Record & Analyze Your Dreams. 110p. (YA). (gr. 7 up). 1997. pap. 49.95 incl. cd-rom (*0-9658424-2-8*) Dreamtech.

Mulick, James A., jt. ed. see Jacobson, John W.

Mulick, James A., jt. ed. see Matson, Johnny L.

Mulier, Filip, jt. auth. see Cherkassky, Vladimier S.

Mulisch, Harry. The Assault. 1986. 7.95 (*0-07-544991-9*) McGraw.

— The Assault. White, Claire, tr. from DUT. LC 84-22623. 192p. 1986. pap. 13.00 (*0-394-74420-9*) Pantheon.

— The Discovery of Heaven: A Novel. LC 96-12756. 736p. 1997. pap. 15.95 (*0-14-023937-5*) Viking Penguin.

— What Poetry Is. Barkan, Stanley H., ed. White, Claire Nicolas, tr. (Cross-Cultural Review Chapbook Ser.: No. 9:). (DUT & ENG.). 40p. 1981. 15.00 (*0-89304-875-5*, CCC133); pap. 5.00 (*0-89304-808-9*) Cross-Cultrl NY.

Mulkay, Michael. The Embryo Research Debate: Science & the Politics of Reproduction. (Cambridge Cultural Social Studies). 224p. (C). 1997. text 59.95 (*0-521-57180-4*); pap. text 19.95 (*0-521-57683-0*) Cambridge U Pr.

Mulkay, Michael. Functionalism Exchange & Theoretical Strategy. 1993. 63.95 (*0-7512-0103-0*) Ashgate Pub Co.

— Science & the Sociology of Knowledge. 1993. 56.95 (*0-7512-0104-9*) Ashgate Pub Co.

Mulkay, Michael. Sociological Pilgrimage. 256p. 1990. 65.00 (*0-335-09409-0*); pap. 21.00 (*0-335-09404-X*) OpUniv Pr.

— Sociology of Science: A Sociological Pilgrimage. LC 90-5275. (Science, Technology, & Society Ser.). (Illus.). 248p. 1991. 39.95 (*0-253-33933-2*) Ind U Pr.

— The Word & the World: Explorations in the Form of Sociological Analysis. 240p. (C). 1985. text 49.95 (*0-04-301196-9*); pap. text 19.95 (*0-04-301197-7*) Routledge.

Mulkay, Michael, ed. see Larrain, Jorge A.

Mulkay, Michael, jt. ed. see Outhwaite, William.

Mulkearn, Lois, ed. see Pownall, Thomas.

***Mulkeen.** Administrative Law. (Paralegal Ser.). (C). 2002. text 36.75 (*0-7668-1911-6*) Delmar.

— Introduction to Nurse Paralegalism. (Paralegal Ser.). (C). 2001. text 42.75 (*0-7668-1909-4*) Delmar.

Mulkeen, et al. Issues of Professional Preparation & Practice. Wendel, Frederick C., ed. 79p. (Orig.). (C). 1992. pap. text 7.00 (*1-55996-149-X*) Univ Council Educ Admin.

Mulkeen, Anne. Wild Thyme, Winter Lightning: The Symbolic Novels of L. P. Hartley. LC 73-18047. 209p. reprint ed. pap. 64.80 (*0-608-16065-2*, 203319700084) Bks Demand.

Mulkeen, Thomas A., et al, eds. Democratic Leadership: The Changing Context of Administrative Preparation. LC 93-42751. (Interpretive Perspectives on Education & Policy Ser.). 288p. 1994. pap. 39.50 (*1-56750-049-8*); text 73.25 (*0-89391-912-8*) Ablx Pub.

Mulken, Margot Van, see Van Reenen, Pieter T., ed.

Mulken, Margot Van, see Van Reenen, Pieter T. & Van Mulken, Margot, eds.

Mulkerin, Mary T. Gousha Atlas Carolinas. (Road Atlas Ser.). (Illus.). 64p. 1992. pap. 5.95 (*0-13-117722-2*, H M Gousha) Prntice Hall Bks.

***Mulkern, Dawn.** New Day, Better You: Navigating the Health Food Maze. LC 99-93366. Purdom, Misty, ed. 55p. 1999. pap. 12.95 (*1-929555-38-5*) Mulkern.

***Mulkern, Dawn & Vann, Andrea Bode.** Choose Great - Lose Weight: Real Food for Real People. 38p. 2000. 19.95 (*1-929555-39-3*) Mulkern.

Mulkern, John R. The Know-Nothing Party in Massachusetts: The Rise & Fall of a People's Party. (New England Studies). 300p. 1990. text 45.00 (*1-55553-071-0*) NE U Pr.

Mulkerne, D. D. & Andrews, M. E. Civil Service, Business & Industry Tests: Clerical & Stenographic. 2nd ed. 1983. text 14.56 (*0-07-043987-7*) McGraw.

Mulkerne, Donald J., Jr. Perfect Term Paper: Step-by-Step. LC 87-12630. 176p. 1988. pap. 9.95 (*0-385-24794-X*, Anchor NY) Doubleday.

Mulkerns, Val. Antiquities: A Sequence of Short Stories. LC 78-316473. 134 p. (J). 1978. write for info. (*0-233-96971-3*, Pub. by Andre Deutsch) Trafalgar.

— A Time Outworn. 9.95 (*0-8159-6905-8*) Devin.

Mulkers, Anne. Live Data Structures in Logic Programs. LC 93-19196. (Lecture Notes in Computer Science Ser.: Vol. 675). 1993. 39.95 (*0-387-56694-5*) Spr-Verlag.

Mulkey, Kent, jt. auth. see Chilcote, Kathy.

Mulkey, Lynn M. Seeing & Unseeing Social Structure: Sociology's Essential Insights. LC 94-49567. 138p. 1995. pap. text 23.00 (*0-205-14881-6*) Allyn.

Mulkey, Michael, jt. ed. see Gardiner, John.

***Mulkey, Rick.** Before the Age of Reason. 69p. 1998. pap. 10.00 (*1-877603-60-0*) Pecan Grove.

Mulkey, S. Wayne, jt. auth. see Cassell, Jack L.

Mulkey, Young J., ed. see Character Education Institute Staff.

Mulky, M. J., et al, eds. Industrial Research. (C). 1988. 36.00 (*0-8364-2432-8*, Pub. by Oxford IBH); 36.00 (*81-204-0286-3*, Pub. by Oxford IBH) S Asia.

Mulky, M. J., et al. Research in Industry. (C). 1987. 20.00 (*81-204-0273-1*, Pub. by Oxford IBH) S Asia.

Mull, Carol. Seven Hundred Fifty Over-the-Counter Stocks. LC 84-71342. 438p. 1986. 32.00 (*0-86690-279-1*, M2614-014) Am Fed Astrologers.

— Standard & Poor's 500. LC 83-72385. 100p. 1984. 33.00 (*0-86690-261-9*, M2400-014) Am Fed Astrologers.

Mull, Dave, ed. see Van Dam, Kevin.

Mull, David K. The Death of Old Man Hanson. 77p. (Orig.). (J). (gr. 5-9). 1995. pap. 5.00 (*0-88092-118-8*) Royal Fireworks.

Mull, J. Alexander & Boger, Gordon. Recollections of the Catawba Valley. LC 82-20721. 1983. 6.50 (*0-913239-05-4*) Appalach Consortium.

Mull, Kayla & Boldrick, Lorrie B. Pot-Bellied Pet Pigs: Mini-Pig Care & Training Manual. (Illus.). 154p. (Orig.). 1989. pap. 9.95 (*0-9624531-0-2*) All Pub.

Mull, Lucy. The Vegetarian Child: A Complete Guide for Parents. LC 96-1949. 224p. 1997. pap. 12.00 (*0-399-52271-9*, Perigee Bks) Berkley Pub.

Mull, Meghan, ed. see Charuhas, Chris.

Mull, Richard F., et al. Recreational Sport Management. 3rd rev. expanded ed. LC 96-44985. (Illus.). 344p. 1997. text 40.00 (*0-87322-808-1*, BMUL0808) Human Kinetics.

Mull, Thomas E. HVAC Systems Design & Applications Manual. LC 97-20717. 528p. 1997. 74.95 (*0-07-044451-X*) McGraw.

— Introduction to HVAC: How to Calculate Heating & Cooling Loads. LC 95-18689. 1995. 27.95 (*0-912524-84-7*) Busn News.

Mull, William P., jt. auth. see Howarth, Francis G.

Mulla, B., jt. auth. see Pollock, T.

Mulla, M. Code of Civil Procedure. (C). 1990. 115.00 (*0-89771-242-0*) St Mut.

— Code of Civil Procedure, 3 vols., Set. (C). 1990. 300.00 (*0-89771-241-2*) St Mut.

— The Indian Contract Act. (C). 1990. 65.00 (*0-89771-223-4*) St Mut.

— Principles of Hindu Law. (C). 1990. 100.00 (*0-89771-144-0*) St Mut.

— Principles of Mohammedan Law. (C). 1990. 85.00 (*0-89771-143-2*) St Mut.

Mullady, Brian T. The Meaning of the Term "Moral" in St. Thomas Aquinas. 144p. 1996. pap. 69.95 (*1-57309-190-1*, Cath Scholar Pr) Intl Scholars.

Mullahy. Student Study Guide for the Case Manager's Handbook. 15.00 (*0-8342-1140-8*, 11408) Aspen Pub.

Mullahy, Catherine M. The Case Manager's Handbook. 2nd ed. LC 98-5033. 448p. 1998. 49.00 (*0-8342-1073-8*, 10738) Aspen Pub.

— Essential Readings in Case Management. 2nd ed. LC 98-14420. 307p. 1998. 29.00 (*0-8342-1139-4*, 11394) Aspen Pub.

Mullahy, Patrick, ed. The Contributions of Harry Stack Sullivan. 242p. 1995. pap. 45.00 (*1-56821-560-6*) Aronson.

Mullaley, Robert C. History of the Mullaleys: A Twelve Hundred Year Journey from County Galway to Iowa. LC 93-91767. (Illus.). 214p. 1993. 45.00 (*0-9639174-0-4*) R C Mullaley.

Mullally. Peter of Spain Vol. 13: And Selected Anonymous Treatises. LC 64-17335. (Medieval Philosophical Texts in Translation Ser.). 156p. 1964. 15.00 (*0-87462-213-1*) Marquette.

***Mullally, David.** Order in the Court: A Writer's Guide to the Legal System. LC 99-46123. (Behind the Scenes Ser.). (Illus.). 288p. 1999. pap. 17.99 (*0-89879-858-2*, 10601, Wrtrs Digest Bks) F & W Pubns Inc.

Mullally, Evelyn. The Artist at Work: Narrative Technique in Chretien de Troyes. LC 88-71547. (Transactions Ser.: Vol. 78, Pt. 4). 240p. (Orig.). (C). 1988. pap. 30.00 (*0-87169-784-X*, T784-MUE) Am Philos.

Mullally, Evelyn, jt. ed. see Thompson, John.

Mullally, Frederic. Hitler Has Won. LC 76-352949. ix, 293p. (YA). 1975. write for info. (*0-333-18428-9*) Macmillan.

***Mullally, Frederic.** Primo: The Story of Man Mountain Carnera, World Heavyweight Champion. 210p. 1999. pap. 13.95 (*1-86105-242-1*) Robson.

Mullally, Linda. Hiking with Dogs. LC 99-24775. (Illus.). 128p. 1999. pap. 6.95 (*1-56044-817-2*) Falcon Pub Inc.

***Mullally, Matthew S.** Far from Home: Short Stories. 208p. 1999. pap. 10.00 (*0-9676516-0-3*) Brookeville Pr.

Mullally, Maureen, et al. Law & the Family in Ireland. LC 98-232274. xiv, 1465p. 1998. pap. 20.00 (*1-901657-09 4*, Pub. by Blackhall Pub) Gaunt.

Mullaly, Bob. Structural Social Work: Ideology, Theory & Practice. 2nd ed. LC HV40.M83 1997. 248p. 1998. pap. text 28.00 (*0-19-541245-1*) OUP.

Mullaly, Edward. Desperate Stages. 113p. 1987. pap. 7.95 (*0-86492-067-9*, Pub. by Goose Ln Edits) Genl Dist Srvs.

Mullaly, Edward J. Archibald MacLeish: A Checklist. LC 72-619620. (Serif Series: Bibliographies & Checklists: No. 26). 109p. reprint ed. pap. 33.80 (*0-8357-5576-2*, 203520300093) Bks Demand.

Mullaly, Paula A. Index to New Jersey School Law Decisions. write for info. (*0-318-61246-1*) NJ Schl Bds.

Mullan, Bob. Are Mothers Really Necessary? 224p. 1988. 60.00 (*1-85283-200-2*, Pub. by Boxtree); pap. 40.00 (*1-85283-210-X*, Pub. by Boxtree) St Mut.

— Consuming Television: Television & Its Audiences. LC 96-23777. 352p. 1997. text 66.95 (*0-631-20233-1*); pap. text 25.95 (*0-631-20234-X*) Blackwell Pubs.

— The Enid Blyton Story. 160p. 1988. 40.00 (*1-85283-201-0*, Pub. by Boxtree) St Mut.

— Mad to Be Normal: Conversations with R. D. Laing. 406p. (C). 1995. pap. 23.00 (*1-85343-395-0*, Pub. by Free Assoc Bks) NYU Pr.

— Modern Social Work in Search of a Soul: Felix Biestek: in the Service of Others. LC 97-6105. (Illus.). 332p. 1997. 59.95 (*1-57309-162-6*, Cath Scholar Pr); pap. 34.95 (*1-57309-161-8*, Cath Scholar Pr) Intl Scholars.

— Not a Pretty Picture: Ethnic Minority Views on Television. 128p. 1996. text 58.95 (*1-85972-498-1*, Pub. by Avebry) Ashgate Pub Co.

— The Self-Help Cascade. 200p. 1998. 55.00 (*1-85343-415-9*, Pub. by Free Assoc Bks) NYU Pr.

***Mullan, Bob.** The Self-Help Cascade. 200p. 1998. pap. 23.50 (*1-85343-416-7*, Pub. by Free Assoc Bks) NYU Pr.

Mullan, Bob. Zoo Culture. 2nd ed. LC 98-25075. 1998. pap. text 16.95 (*0-252-06762-2*) U of Ill Pr.

Mullan, Bob, ed. Memories of R. D. Laing. LC 97-185305. (Illus.). 352p. 1997. 99.50 (*0-304-70114-9*); pap. 37.50 (*0-304-70115-7*) Continuum.

— Sociologists on Sociology. LC 96-84695. 371p. 1996. 68.95 (*1-85972-316-0*, Pub. by Avebry) Ashgate Pub Co.

— Therapists on Therapy. 275p. (C). 1996. 55.00 (*1-85343-329-2*, Pub. by Free Assoc Bks) NYU Pr.

— Therapists on Therapy. 275p. (C). 1996. pap. 24.95 (*1-85343-331-4*, Pub. by Free Assoc Bks) NYU Pr.

Mullan, Bob & Marvin, Garry. Zoo Culture. 2nd ed. LC 98-25075. (Illus.). 210p. 1998. 39.95 (*0-252-02457-5*) U of Ill Pr.

Mullan, Brendan, ed. see Grummon, Phyllis T.

Mullan, C. S. Census of India, 1931 Vol. 3: Assam, 2 Vols., Part 1-Report, Part 2-Tables, Set. (C). 1992. reprint ed. 140.00 (*81-85425-93-0*, Pub. by Manohar) S Asia.

M

An Asterisk (*) at the beginning of an entry indicates that the title is appearing for the first time.

Mullan, D., et al, eds. Astrophysics in Antarctica. LC 89-46421. (AIP Conference Proceedings Ser.: No. 198). 288p. 1992. lib. bdg. 80.00 (*0-88318-398-6*) Am Inst Physics.

Mullan, D. J., jt. ed. see Byrne, P. B.

***Mullan, David.** Administrative Law. (Essentials of Canadian Law Ser.). 350p. 2000. pap. 34.95 (*1-55221-009-X*, Pub. by Irwin Law) Gaunt.

Mullan, David, ed. Religious Pluralism in the West: An Anthology. LC 97-14136. 440p. 1997. pap. text 68.95 (*0-631-20669-8*); pap. text 31.95 (*0-631-20670-1*) Blackwell Pubs.

***Mullan, David George.** Scottish Puritanism, 1590-1638. LC 99-45412. 400p. 2000. text 98.00 (*0-19-826997-8*) OUP.

Mullan, Desmond. The Definitive Fart Book: Gas Past, Present & Future. Carle, Cliff, ed. 64p. 1995. pap. 4.99 (*0-918259-65-7*) CCC Pubns.

***Mullan, Desmond.** Farting. Carle, Cliff, ed. 1998. pap. text 5.95 (*1-57644-082-6*) CCC Pubns.

Mullan, E. H. Mentality of the Arriving Immigrant. LC 77-129408. (American Immigration Collection. Series 2). (Illus.). 1970. reprint ed. 14.95 (*0-405-00562-8*) Ayer.

Mullan, John. Miners & Travelers Guide. Brown, Kimberly R. & Adams, Glen, eds. (Illus.). 178p. 1991. reprint ed. 19.95 (*0-87770-502-X*) Ye Galleon.

— Miner's & Travelers' Guide to Oregon, Washington, Idaho, Montana, Wyoming, & Colorado. LC 72-9461. (Far Western Frontier Ser.). (Illus.). 158p. 1978. reprint ed. 18.95 (*0-405-04989-7*) Ayer.

— Report on the Construction of a Military Road from Fort Walla Walla to Fort Benton. (Illus.). 183p. 1998. 29.95 (*0-87770-102-4*) Ye Galleon.

— Sentiment & Sociability: The Language of Feeling in the Eighteenth Century. 270p. 1990. reprint ed. pap. text 18.95 (*0-19-812252-7*) OUP.

***Mullan, John & Reid, Christopher, eds.** Eighteenth-Century Popular Culture. (Illus.). 304p. 2000. pap. 19.95 (*0-19-871135-2*); text 60.00 (*0-19-871134-4*) OUP.

Mullan, John, et al. Lives of the Great Romantics: Shelley, Byron & Wordsworth by Their Contemporaries, 3 vols., Set. LC 95-21350. 1250p. 1996. text 320.00 (*1-85196-270-0*, Pub. by Pickering & Chatto) Ashgate Pub Co.

— Lives of the Great Romantics II: By Their Contemporaries. LC 97-1345. 1997. pap. write for info. (*1-85196-371-5*, Pub. by Pickering & Chatto) Ashgate Pub Co.

— Lives of the Great Romantics II: By Their Contemporaries, 3 vols., Vol. 3. LC 97-1345. 1997. write for info. (*1-85196-372-3*, Pub. by Pickering & Chatto) Ashgate Pub Co.

Mullan, John, ed. see Defoe, Daniel.

***Mullan, Kenneth.** Blackstone's Pharmacy Law & Practice. 440p. 2000. pap. 43.50 (*1-85431-940-X*, Pub. by Blackstone Pr) Gaunt.

***Mullan, Phil.** Imaginary Time Bomb: Why an Ageing Population is Not a Social. 2000. text 39.50 (*1-86064-452-X*, Pub. by I B T) St Martin.

Mullane, Deirdre, compiled by. Words to Make My Dream Children Live: An African-American Book of Quotations. LC 94-32710. 448p. 1995. pap. 14.95 (*0-385-42244-X*, Anchor NY) Doubleday.

Mullane, Deirdre, ed. Crossing the Danger Water: Four Hundred Years of African-American Writing. LC 93-17194. 800p. 1993. pap. 17.50 (*0-385-42243-1*, Anchor NY) Doubleday.

Mullane, Janet, ed. Nineteenth-Century Literature Criticism, Vol. 18. 600p. 1988. 150.00 (*0-8103-5818-2*) Gale.

Mullane, Janet & Sherman, Laurie, eds. Nineteenth-Century Literature Criticism, Vol. 27. LC 84-643008. (Illus.). 511p. 1990. text 150.00 (*0-8103-5827-1*) Gale.

Mullane, Janet & Wilson, Bob, eds. Nineteenth-Century Literary Criticism, Vol. 23. 600p. 1989. text 150.00 (*0-8103-5823-9*) Gale.

— Nineteenth-Century Literary Criticism, Vol. 25. 500p. 1990. text 150.00 (*0-8103-5825-5*) Gale.

Mullane, Janet & Wilson, Bob, eds. Nineteenth-Century Literature Criticism, Vol. 19. 600p. 1988. 150.00 (*0-8103-5819-0*) Gale.

Mullane, Janet & Wilson, Bob, eds. Nineteenth-Century Literature Criticism, Vol. 22. 400p. 1989. text 150.00 (*0-8103-5822-0*) Gale.

Mullane, Janet & Wilson, Bob, eds. Nineteenth-Century Literature Criticism: Archives, Vol. 20. 1988. 150.00 (*0-8103-5820-4*) Gale.

Mullane, Janet & Wilson, Robert, eds. Nineteenth-Century Literature Criticism, Vol. 21. 400p. 1989. text 150.00 (*0-8103-5821-2*) Gale.

Mullane, Janet & Wilson, Robert T., eds. Nineteenth-Century Literature Criticism, Vol. 26. LC 84-643008. (Illus.). 511p. 1990. text 150.00 (*0-8103-5826-3*) Gale.

Mullane, Janet, et al. Nineteenth-Century Literary Criticism, Vol. 24. 500p. 1989. text 150.00 (*0-8103-5824-7*) Gale.

Mullane, Janet, jt. ed. see Abbey, Cherie D.

Mullane, R. Mike. Do Your Ears Pop in Space? & 500 Other Surprising Questions about Space Travel. LC 96-28544. 256p. 1997. pap. 14.95 (*0-471-15404-0*) Wiley.

— Lift Off! An Astronaut's Dream. LC 94-18122. (Illus.). (J). 1994. lib. bdg. 13.95 (*0-382-24663-2*) Silver Burdett Pr.

— Lift Off! An Astronaut's Dream. LC 94-18122. (Illus.). 114p. (J). (gr. 4). 1994. pap. 4.95 (*0-382-24664-0*) Silver Burdett Pr.

***Mullane, Stephen.** Discovering Whales of the East Coast. (Discovering Ser.). (Illus.). 64p. 2000. pap. 8.95 (*0-9672957-1-8*, Pub. by Elan Pub Inc) Book Warehse.

Mullaney, Aidan, tr. see Pazzelli, Raffaele.

Mullaney, Charles P., jt. auth. see Buccini, Eugene P.

Mullaney, Janet P., ed. Truthtellers of the Times: Interviews with Contemporary Women Poets. LC 98-21815. 120p. (C). 1998. pap. 14.95 (*0-472-06680-3*, 06680) U of Mich Pr.

— Truthtellers of the Times: Interviews with Contemporary Women Poets. LC 98-21815. 120p. (C). 1998. text 39.50 (*0-472-09680-X*, 09680) U of Mich Pr.

Mullaney, Jeanne, jt. auth. see Slick, Sam L.

Mullaney, John A. REITs: Building Profits with Real Estate Investment Trusts. LC 97-14586. (Investment Classics Ser.). (Illus.). 304p. 1997. 39.95 (*0-471-19324-0*) Wiley.

Mullaney, Marie M. Bibliographic Directory of the Governors of the United States, 1983-1988. LC 89-2273. 408p. 1989. lib. bdg. 85.00 (*0-313-28083-5*, MGX/, Greenwood Pr) Greenwood.

— Biographical Directory of the Governors of the United States, 1988-1993. LC 93-37875. 440p. 1994. lib. bdg. 85.00 (*0-313-28312-5*, Greenwood Pr) Greenwood.

Mullaney, Marie M., compiled by. American Governors & Gubernatorial Elections, 1979-1987. LC 88-13248. 104p. 1988. lib. bdg. 55.00 (*0-313-28092-4*, MGZ/, Greenwood Pr) Greenwood.

Mullaney, Stephen, jt. auth. see Vale, David.

Mullaney, Steven. The Place of the Stage: License, Play, & Power in Renaissance England. LC 87-17327. 192p. (Orig.). (C). 1995. pap. text 17.95 (*0-472-08346-5*, 08346) U of Mich Pr.

— The Place of the Stage: License, Play, & Power in Rennaissance England. (Illus.). 192p. 1988. 24.95 (*0-226-54760-1*) U Ch Pr.

— The Place of the Stage: License, Play, & Power in Renaissance England. (Illus.). 192p. 1994. pap. text 12.95 (*0-226-54761-2*) U Ch Pr.

Mullany, Nicholas, ed. Torts in the Nineties. 342p. 1996. 125.00 (*0-455-21437-9*, Pub. by LawBk Co) Gaunt.

Mullany, Peter. Monarch Notes on Marlowe's Dr. Faustus & Other Writings. (Orig.). (C). 3.95 (*0-671-00717-3*, Arco) Macmillan Gen Ref.

***Mullany, Peter.** Orphans. 1999. pap. 12.95 (*1-901680-30-4*) Screen Test Pub.

Mullard, Chris. Black Britain: With an Account of Recent Events at the Institute of Race Relations by Alexander Kirby. LC 73-331041. 194p. reprint ed. pap. 60.20 (*0-8357-7284-5*, 202318700032) Bks Demand.

— Race, Power & Resistance. 256p. 1985. 42.50 (*0-7100-9774-3*, Routledge Thoemms) Routledge.

***Mullard, Maurice.** New Labor. LC 00-40103. 2000. write for info. (*1-56072-824-8*) Nova Sci Pubs.

Mullard, Maurice. Policy Making in Britain: An Introduction. 240p. (C). 1995. pap. 24.99 (*0-415-10850-0*, C0052) Routledge.

— Policy Making in Britain: An Introduction. LC 94-48178. 240p. (C). (gr. 13). 1995. 85.00 (*0-415-10849-7*, C0051) Routledge.

Mullard, Maurice & Lee, Simon, eds. The Politics of Social Policy in Europe. LC 96-52265. 304p. 1997. 90.00 (*1-85898-367-3*) E Elgar.

Mullard, Maurice & Spicker, Paul. Policy Making in Britain. LC 97-53073. 240p. (C). 1998. 80.00 (*0-415-16540-7*) Routledge.

Mullard Technical Service Dept. Staff. Circuits for Audio Amplifiers. (Illus.). 144p. (Orig.). 1993. reprint ed. pap. 16.95 (*1-882580-03-6*) Audio Amateur.

Mullarkey, Barbara A. Bittersweet Aspartame: A Diet Delusion. 88p. (Orig.). 1992. pap. 11.00 (*0-944366-00-7*) Hlth Watch Bk.

— Bittersweet Aspartame, a Diet Delusion. 2nd ed. (Illus.). 86p. 1993. pap. 11.00 (*0-944366-01-5*) Hlth Watch Bk.

Mullarkey, James C., jt. ed. see Dolly, Edward D.

***Mullarkey, John.** Bergson & Philosophy: An Introduction. LC 99-57656. 224p. (C). 2000. pap. text 20.00 (*0-268-02161-9*, Pub. by U of Notre Dame Pr) Chicago Distribution Ctr.

Mullarkey, John. New Bergson. 208p. 1999. pap. 29.95 (*0-7190-5553-9*); text 69.95 (*0-7190-5380-3*) Manchester Univ Pr.

Mullarkey, Lisa G. Witch's Portraits. 192p. (J). (gr. 5-9). 1998. 15.99 (*0-8037-2337-7*, Dial Yng Read) Peng Put Young Read.

***Mullarney, Killian.** Birds of Europe. (Field Guides Ser.). 2000. 39.50 (*0-691-05053-8*, Pub. by Princeton U Pr) Cal Prin Full Svc.

***Mullay, Marilyn & Schlicke, Priscilla, eds.** Walford's Guide to Reference Material Vol. 1: Science & Technology. 387p. 1999. 269.00 (*1-85604-341-X*, Pub. by Library Association) Bernan Associates.

Mullay, Sandy, ed. The Edinburgh Encyclopedia. (Illus.). 416p. 1996. 39.95 (*1-85158-762-4*, Pub. by Mainstream Pubng) Trafalgar.

Mulle, Karen, jt. auth. see March, John S.

Mulleady, Geraldine. Counselling Drug Users about HIV & AIDS. 2nd ed. (Illus.). 224p. 1992. pap. 39.95 (*0-632-02939-0*) Blackwell Sci.

Mullejahns. Tex und Tetafont. (GER.). (C). 1991. text. write for info. (*0-201-55993-5*) Addison-Wesley.

Mullen. Black American African American: Vietnam Through the Gulf War. 2nd ed. (C). 1991. pap. text 31.80 (*0-536-58069-3*) Pearson Custom.

— Connections for Health. 4th ed. 1996. 79.06 (*0-697-21569-5*, WCB McGr Hill) McGrw-H Hghr Educ.

— Judicial Review in Scotland. 1996. pap. text 113.50 (*0-471-96614-2*) Wiley.

Mullen & Katz. Victoriana Photo Album. (Photo Albums Ser.). 12p. 1997. 9.99 (*0-88088-642-0*) Peter Pauper.

Mullen, et al. Connections for Health. 4th annot. ed. 1995. teacher ed. 26.87 (*0-697-25847-5*, WCB McGr Hill) McGrw-H Hghr Educ.

— Connections for Health. 5th ed. 1999. 34.74 (*0-697-29421-8*, WCB McGr Hill) McGrw-H Hghr Educ.

— Connections for Health: Ancillary Binder. 3rd ed. 1996. 31.74 (*0-697-21570-9*, WCB McGr Hill) McGrw-H Hghr Educ.

— Connections for Health: Course Planner. 4th ed. 1995. teacher ed. 26.87 (*0-697-21566-0*, WCB McGr Hill) McGrw-H Hghr Educ.

— Healthy Connections. 5th ed. 1999. student ed., wbk. ed. 13.12 (*0-697-29527-3*) McGraw.

— Menu - Connections for Healthy... 5th ed. 1999. 36.30 (*0-697-29420-X*) McGraw.

Mullen & Katz Staff. Traveler's Journal. (Guided Journals Ser.). 160p. 1998. 11.99 (*0-88088-202-6*) Peter Pauper.

Mullen, Andrew. Dugouts in the Ypres Salients. 1999. 45.00 (*0-85052-641-8*, 526418, Pub. by Leo Cooper) Combined Pub.

Mullen, Ann. Twin Justice . . . Shattered Dreams: A Mother Tells of the Heartbreaking Events That Preceded the Death of Her Twin Sons. Smith, Kathleen, ed. 128p. (Orig.). 1992. pap. 9.95 (*0-943135-14-1*, Grn Briar Patch) Gallagher Jordan.

Mullen, B. & Geothals, G. R., eds. Theories of Group Behavior. (Social Psychology Ser.). (Illus.). 255p. 1986. 86.95 (*0-387-96351-0*) Spr-Verlag.

Mullen, Barbara D. & McGinn, Kerry A. The Ostomy Book: Living Comfortably with Colostomies, Ileostomies & Urostomies. 2nd rev. ed. 252p. 1991. pap. 16.95 (*0-923521-12-7*) Bull Pub.

Mullen, Bill. Popular Fronts: Chicago & African-American Cultural Politics, 1935-46. LC 98-19740. 248p. 1999. pap. 16.95 (*0-252-06748-7*) U of Ill Pr.

— Popular Fronts: Chicago & African-American Cultural Politics, 1935-46. LC 98-19740. (Illus.). 242p. 1999. 39.95 (*0-252-02440-0*) U of Ill Pr.

Mullen, Bill, jt. ed. see Linkon, Sherry.

Mullen, Brian. Advanced BASIC Meta-Analysis. 1989. 184p. (C). 1989. 39.95 (*0-8058-0502-8*) LEA S&AM.

Mullen, Brian & Johnson, Craig. The Psychology of Consumer Behavior. 232p. 1990. 36.00 (*0-89859-857-5*) L Erlbaum Assocs.

— The Psychology of Consumer Behavior. 36p. 1990. teacher ed. write for info. (*0-8058-1165-6*) L Erlbaum Assocs.

Mullen, Candy & Lang, Audry, photos by. The Earth Is Still Our Mother. (Collection of Poetry: No. 1). (Illus.). 57p. 1997. pap. 7.95 (*0-9660458-0-7*) OM Publ.

Mullen, Carol, ed. Breaking the Circle of One: Redefining Mentorship in the Lives & Writings of Educators. LC 96-50060. (Counterpoints Ser.: Vol. 55). (Illus.). XXIII, 222p. (C). 1997. pap. text 29.95 (*0-8204-3758-1*) P Lang Pubng.

Mullen, Carol A. Imprisoned Selves: An Inquiry into Prisons & Academe. LC 96-43222. 276p. 1996. pap. text 32.50 (*0-7618-0553-2*); lib. bdg. 57.50 (*0-7618-0552-4*) U Pr of Amer.

***Mullen, Carol A. & Diamond, C. T., eds.** The Postmodern Educator: Arts-Based Inquiries & Teacher Development. LC 98-24674. (Counterpoints Ser.: Vol. 89). xxi, 466p. (C). 1999. pap. text 32.95 (*0-8204-4101-5*) P Lang Pubng.

Mullen, Chris. The Young Basketball Player. LC 95-14844. (Young Enthusiast Ser.). (Illus.). 40p. (J). (gr. 3-6). 1995. 15.95 (*0-7894-0220-3*, 5-70633) DK Pub Inc.

***Mullen, Christopher A. & Ryan, J. Atticus, eds.** Unrepresented Nations & Peoples Organization Vol. 3: Yearbook 1997. 494p. 1998. 140.00 (*90-411-1022-4*) Kluwer Law Intl.

Mullen, Conley E. Connections for Health Care. 4th ed. 1996. 20.62 (*0-697-21567-9*, WCB McGr Hill) McGrw-H Hghr Educ.

Mullen, Connell. Shrines of Our Lady. 176p. 1999. pap. 16.95 (*0-312-24327-8*) St Martin.

Mullen, Deborah C. Beyond Subjectivity & Representation: Perception, Expression & Creation in Nietzsche, Heidegger & Merleau-Ponty. LC 99-12972. 176p. 1999. 35.00 (*0-7618-1381-0*) U Pr of Amer.

Mullen, Denise & Rentz, Lisa T. The Insiders' Guide to Myrtle Beach & Grand Strand. 5th ed. (Insiders' Guide Travel Ser.). (Illus.). 333p. 1999. pap. 16.95 (*1-57380-063-5*, The Insiders Guide) Falcon Pub Inc.

Mullen, Dore. All We Know of Heaven. large type ed. 608p. 1985. 27.99 (*0-7089-1339-3*) Ulverscroft.

Mullen, E. Theodore, Jr. The Divine Council in Canaanite & Early Hebrew Literature. LC 80-10128. (Harvard Semitic Monographs: Vol. 24). 339p. reprint ed. pap. 105.10 (*0-608-08675-4*, 206919800003) Bks Demand.

Mullen, Edward J. Afro-Cuban Literature: Critical Junctures, 91. LC 97-45645. (Contributions to the Study of World Literature Ser.: Vol. 91). 256p. 1998. 55.00 (*0-313-30408-4*, Greenwood Pr) Greenwood.

— Carlos Pellicer. LC 77-1959. (Twayne's World Authors Ser.). 173p. (C). 1977. lib. bdg. 20.95 (*0-8057-6288-4*) Irvington.

— Critical Essays on Langston Hughes. (Critical Essays on American Literature Ser.). 211p. (C). 1986. 47.00 (*0-8161-8697-9*, G K Hall & Co) Mac Lib Ref.

Mullen, Edward J. & Darst, David H. Sendas Literarias: Hispanoamerica. 283p. (C). 1988. pap. 35.00 (*0-07-554129-7*) McGraw.

***Mullen, Edward J. & Garganigo, John F.** El Cuento Hispanico: A Graded Literary Anthology. 5th ed. (SPA & ENG.). 224p. (C). 1998. pap. 32.19 (*0-07-012331-4*) McGrw-H Hghr Educ.

Mullen, Edward J. & Garganigo, John F. El Cuento Hispanico, a Graded Literary Anthology, Primis Version. 1997. pap. text. write for info. (*0-07-217387-4*) McGraw.

Mullen, Edward J. & Garganigo, John F., eds. El Cuento Hispanico: A Graded Literary Anthology. 4th ed. (C). 1994. pap. text 25.25 (*0-07-043955-9*) McGraw.

Mullen, Edward J. & Magnabosco, Jennifer L., eds. Outcomes Measurement in the Human Services: Cross-Cutting Issues & Methods. LC 97-7824. 360p. (Orig.). (C). 1997. pap. text 36.95 (*0-87101-275-8*, 2758) Natl Assn Soc Wkrs.

Mullen, Edward J., jt. ed. see Hess, Peg M.

Mullen, Edwin & Griffith, Jane. Short Bike Rides in Connecticut: Rides for the Casual Cyclist. 6th ed. LC 97-46432. (Short Bike Rides Ser.). (Illus.). 144p. 1998. pap. 11.95 (*0-7627-0205-2*) Globe Pequot.

— Short Bike Rides on Cape Cod, Nantucket & the Vineyard. 7th ed. LC 98-54144. (Short Bike Rides Ser.). (Illus.). 160p. 1999. pap. text 10.95 (*0-7627-0436-5*) Globe Pequot.

Mullen, Frank, Jr. The Donner Party Chronicles: A Day-by-Day Account of a Doomed Wagon Train, 1846-1847. (Illus.). 380p. 1997. pap. 35.00 (*1-890591-01-7*) NV Humanities.

Mullen, G. L., jt. auth. see Lidl, Rudolf.

Mullen, Gail S. & Bothmer, Richard. The Quiz Book: 1729 Academic Questions to Challenge the Mind. 104p. 1990. pap. 14.95 (*0-936386-55-X*) Creative Learning.

Mullen, Gary L. & Shiue, Peter J., eds. Finite Fields - Theory, Applications & Algorithms: Proceedings of the Second International Conference on Finite Fields - Theory, Applications & Algorithms, August 17-21, 1993, Las Vegas, Nevada. LC 94-19971. (Contemporary Mathematics Ser.: Vol. 168). 402p. 1994. pap. 65.00 (*0-8218-5183-7*, CONM/168) Am Math.

— Finite Fields, Coding Theory, & Advances in Communications & Computing. LC 92-23503. (Lecture Notes in Pure & Applied Mathematics Ser.: Vol. 141). (Illus.). 480p. 1992. pap. text 185.00 (*0-8247-8805-2*) Dekker.

Mullen, Gary L., jt. auth. see Laywine, Charles F.

Mullen, Gary L., jt. ed. see Mullin, Ronald C.

Mullen, George D. Peace in the Middle East: Israeli-Palestinian Peace Proposal. (C). 1994. 19.95 (*1-881116-46-8*, Pub. by Black Forest Pr) Epic Bk Promo.

Mullen, Grant. Why Do I Feel So Down, When My Faith Should Lift Me Up? 1999. pap. 14.99 (*1-85240-246-6*, Renew) Gospel Lght.

Mullen, Harris. Confederate Generals at Gettysburg - A Field Guide: Who Was Who & What Did They Do. (Illus.). 52p. (Orig.). 1996. pap. 5.95 (*0-9646629-1-4*) High Water Pr.

— God Bless General Early. (Illus.). 320p. 1998. 25.00 (*0-9646629-2-2*) High Water Pr.

— 10 Incredible Mistakes Made at Gettysburg: A Review of the Battle & How Blunders by the Generals Shaped the Outcome. (Illus.). 32p. (Orig.). 1995. pap. text 5.95 (*0-9646629-0-6*) High Water Pr.

Mullen, Harryette. Freeing the Soul: Race, Subjectivity, & Difference in Slave Narratives. LC 99-24415. (Studies in American Literature & Culture: Vol. 113). 208p. (C). 1997. text 54.95 (*0-521-49751-5*); pap. text 16.95 (*0-521-49753-1*) Cambridge U Pr.

— Muse & Drudge. 88p. (Orig.). 1995. pap. 12.50 (*0-935162-15-1*) Singing Horse.

— S PeRM K T. 48p. (Orig.). 1992. pap. 8.00 (*0-935162-12-7*) Singing Horse.

Mullen, Inga E. German Realism in the United States: The American Reception of Meyer, Storm, Raabe, Keller & Fontane. (Studies in Modern German Literature: Vol. 6). X, 206p. (C). 1988. text 36.50 (*0-8204-0424-1*) P Lang Pubng.

Mullen, J., jt. auth. see Harrison, W.

Mullen, Jack. Behind the Shield. 352p. (Orig.). 1996. mass mkt. 5.99 (*0-380-78236-7*, Avon Bks) Morrow Avon.

Mullen, James X. The Simple Art of Greatness. 1999. pap. 9.95 (*0-14-023437-3*) Viking Penguin.

Mullen, Jane. A Complicated Situation: Stories. LC 98-36287. 176p. 1998. 19.95 (*0-87074-431-3*) SMU Press.

Mullen, Jean. Outsiders: American Short Stories for Students of English as a Second Language. (Illus.). 256p. (C). 1984. pap. text 31.80 (*0-13-645366-X*) P-H.

Mullen, Jim. It Takes a Village Idiot: Complicating the Simple Life. 1999. write for info. (*0-316-90458-9*) Little.

— It Takes a Village Idiot: Complicating the Simple Life. 224p. (gr. 8). 2000. 21.95 (*0-316-59045-2*) Little.

Mullen, Jo. Aspects: Beginner's Notebook. LC 85-71464. 90p. 1986. 10.50 (*0-86690-297-X*, M2357-014) Am Fed Astrologers.

— Astrology Beginner's Notebook. LC 83-73608. 80p. 1984. 9.50 (*0-86690-269-4*, M2531-014) Am Fed Astrologers.

***Mullen, John.** Basic Essentials: Snowboarding. 2nd ed. LC 99-44353. (Illus.). 80p. 1999. pap. text 7.95 (*0-7627-0523-X*) Globe Pequot.

Mullen, John. McMullen: Business Transfers & Employee Rights. 3rd ed. 1997. write for info. (*0-406-04467-8*, MBTE3, MICHIE) LEXIS Pub.

Mullen, John D. Hard Thinking: The Reintroduction of Logic to Everyday Life. 328p. 1995. pap. text 31.95 (*0-8476-8003-7*); lib. bdg. 71.50 (*0-8476-8002-9*) Rowman.

— Kierkegaard's Philosophy: Self Deception & Cowardice in the Present Age. LC 95-7348. 188p. (C). 1995. reprint ed. pap. 19.50 (*0-8191-9803-X*) U Pr of Amer.

Mullen, John D., jt. auth. see Roth, Byron M.

Mullen, Joseph, ed. Rural Poverty Alleviation: International Development Perspectives. 200p. 1995. 77.95 (*1-85628-864-1*, Pub. by Avebry) Ashgate Pub Co.

— Rural Poverty, Empowerment & Sustainable Livelihoods. (Institute for Development Policy & Management Ser.). 166p. 1999. text 61.95 (*1-85972-261-X*, Pub. by Ashgate Pub) Ashgate Pub Co.

Mullen, Joseph A., ed. see Skoryna, Stanley C.

An Asterisk (*) at the beginning of an entry indicates that the title is appearing for the first time.

***Mullen, Joseph B.** Psychic Secrets: Your Guide to Dreams, Hunches & Spirit Contact. LC 00-190723. 164p. 2000. 25.00 (*0-7388-1963-8*); pap. 18.00 (*0-7388-1964-6*) Xlibris Corp.
Mullen, K. & Ferenci, P., eds. Hepatic Encephalopathy. (Illus.). iv, 64p. 1996. pap. 21.75 (*3-8055-6358-2*) S Karger.
Mullen, K. & Wegner, G. Electronic Materials: The Oligomer Approach. LC TK7871.15.P6M85 1998. 628p. 1998. 225.00 (*3-527-29438-4*, Wiley-VCH) Wiley.
Mullen, Kathleen D. & Gold, Robert S. Connections for Health. 4th ed. 704p. (C). 1995. text. write for info. (*0-697-25794-0*) Brown & Benchmark.
Mullen, Kathleen D. & Horne, Deborah A. Connections for Health. 4th ed. 256p. (C). 1996. text, student ed., wbk. ed. 17.50 (*0-697-21568-7*) Brown & Benchmark.
Mullen, Kathleen D., et al. Connections for Health. 3rd ed. 624p. (C). 1993. write for info. (*0-697-17345-3*) Brown & Benchmark.
— Connections for Health. 4th ed. 624p. (C). 1995. text. write for info. (*0-697-21565-2*) Brown & Benchmark.
Mullen, Kenneth. Healthy Balance: A Qualitative Study of Men's Health Beliefs. 200p. 1993. 66.95 (*1-85628-548-0*, Pub. by Avebry) Ashgate Pub Co.
Mullen, Kevin J. Let Justice Be Done: Crime & Politics in Early San Francisco. LC 89-4750. (Wilbur S. Shepperson Series in History & Humanities). (Illus.). 336p. 1989. 24.95 (*0-87417-146-6*) U of Nev Pr.
Mullen, Laura. After I Was Dead: Poems. LC 98-36308. (Contemporary Poetry Ser.). 120p. 1999. pap. 15.95 (*0-8203-2096-X*) U of Ga Pr.
— The Surface. 88p. (Orig.). 1991. 10.95 (*0-252-06187-X*) U of Ill Pr.
***Mullen, Laura.** The Tales of Horror: A Flip-Book. Dienstfrey, Patricia & Corrigan, Erin, eds. LC 99-29444. 108p. 1999. pap. 12.00 (*0-932716-48-2*) Kelsey St Pr.
***Mullen, Lisa.** Champagne Wishes: Fun & Creative Ideas for the Romantically Challenged Male. Mann, Alicja, ed. & des. by. 56, VIIIp. (Orig.). 2000. pap. 8.75 (*0-9654360-2-0*) Word Studio.
Mullen, Margaret. An Arkansas Childhood: Growing up in the Athens of the Ozarks. (Illus.). 1989. 14.95 (*0-943099-06-4*) M & M Pr.
— Safe for Now. 88p. (Orig.). 1993. pap. 11.95 (*0-9627007-1-1*) Monday Pr CA.
Mullen, Marjorie, jt. auth. see Graham, Earl C.
Mullen, Mary C., jt. auth. see Shield, Jo E.
Mullen, Mary J. Wavelength. 240p. 1995. pap. 5.95 (*0-9645523-0-2*) Custom Media Design.
Mullen, Michael. Festival of Fools. pap. 5.95 (*0-86327-051-4*, Pub. by Wolfhound Press) Irish Amer Bk.
— The Four Masters. 153p. (YA). (gr. 5 up). 1992. pap. 9.95 (*1-85371-204-3*, Pub. by Poolbeg Pr) Dufour.
— Kelly: A Novel. 1997. pap. text 6.95 (*0-86327-070-0*) Irish Amer Bk.
— The Long March. 182p. 1997. pap. 7.95 (*1-85371-890-4*, Pub. by Poolbeg Pr) Dufour.
— Magus the Lollipop Man. (YA). 1997. pap. 4.95 (*0-86327-017-4*, Pub. by Wolfhound Press) Irish Amer Bk.
Mullen, Michael, et al. The First Christmas. 190p. (J). (gr. 4-7). 1994. pap. 12.95 (*1-85371-296-5*, Pub. by Poolbeg Pr) Dufour.
Mullen, Mike. First Steps: Laying a Firm Foundation. 32p. (Orig.). 1999. pap. 1.65 (*1-56794-130-3*, C-2455) Star Bible.
Mullen, Nate. Trade Secrets of Professional Landscape Lighting. (Illus.). 1998. 50.00 (*0-9670634-0-X*) Unique Pubg.
Mullen, Nina A., jt. auth. see Olsen, Laurie.
Mullen, Patricia. The Stone Movers. 368p. (Orig.). 1995. mass mkt. 5.50 (*0-446-60106-3*, Pub. by Warner Bks) Little.
Mullen, Patrick B. I Heard the Old Fishermen Say: Folklore of the Texas Gulf Coast. 2nd ed. 219p. 1988. reprint ed. pap. text 17.95 (*0-87421-139-5*) Utah St U Pr.
— Listening to Old Voices: Folklore, Life Stories, & the Elderly. (Folklore & Society Ser.). (Illus.). 312p. 1991. text 30.95 (*0-252-01808-7*) U of Ill Pr.
Mullen, Patrick B., jt. auth. see Lloyd, Timothy C.
***Mullen, Paul E., et al.** Stalkers & Their Victims. LC 99-44607. (Illus.). 352p. (C). 2000. pap. text 49.95 (*0-521-66950-2*) Cambridge U Pr.
Mullen, Paul E., jt. auth. see Fergusson, David M.
Mullen, Paul E., jt. auth. see White, Gregory L.
Mullen, Peg. Unfriendly Fire: A Mother's Memoir. LC 94-48108. (Singular Lives: The Iowa Series in North American Autobiography). (Illus.). 175p. 1995. 22.95 (*0-87745-506-6*); pap. 13.95 (*0-87745-507-4*) U of Iowa Pr.
Mullen, Peter. Country Matters. large type ed. 1996. pap. 18.99 (*1-85389-592-X*, Dales) Ulverscroft.
— Rural Rites. large type ed. (Dales Large Print Ser.). 1995. pap. 18.99 (*1-85389-593-8*, Dales) Ulverscroft.
— Shrines of Our Lady: A Guide to over Fifty of the World's Most Famous Marian Shrines. LC 98-21124. 184p. 1998. 23.95 (*0-312-19503-6*) St Martin.
Mullen, R. D., et al, eds. Philip K. Dick: Forty Articles on Philip K. Dick from Science-Fiction Studies. 320p. 1992. pap. 14.95 (*0-9633169-1-5*) SF-TH.
Mullen, Ray. Society & Sex Offenders. LC 98-25432. 196p. 1998. pap. 16.95 (*1-885373-14-7*) Emerald Ink.
Mullen, Richard. Anthony Trollope: A Victorian in His World. LC 91-16912. 767p. 1991. 45.00 (*0-913720-77-1*) Beil.
Mullen, Robbins. Wellness Testwell Conn For Hea. 1996. 22.00 (*0-697-35774-0*, WCB McGr Hill) McGr-H Hghr Educ.
Mullen, Robert. Americas. 224p. 1994. pap. 12.95 (*1-55050-063-5*, Pub. by Coteau) Genl Dist Srvs.
Mullen, Robert. Blacks in America's Wars. Date not set. pap. 9.95 (*0-87348-897-0*) Pathfinder NY.
— HTML Quick Reference. 240p. 1996. 19.99 (*0-7897-0867-1*) Que.
— Ten Minute Guide to Approach. LC 93-73710. 160p. 1994. 10.99 (*1-56761-407-8*, Alpha Ref) Macmillan Gen Ref.
Mullen, Robert, et al. Microsoft Office 97 Professional Quick Reference. LC 96-72201. 410p. 1997. pap. 19.99 (*0-7897-1061-7*) Que.
Mullen, Robert J. Architecture & Its Sculpture in Viceregal Mexico. LC 96-51256. (Illus.). 286p. 1997. pap. 24.95 (*0-292-75210-5*) U of Tex Pr.
— Architecture & Its Sculpture in Viceregal Mexico. LC 96-51256. (Illus.). 263p. 1997. 45.00 (*0-292-75209-1*) U of Tex Pr.
— The Architecture & Sculpture of Oaxaca: 1530's-1980's. LC 94-40915. (Monographs). (Illus.). 456p. (Orig.). (C). 1995. per. 60.00 (*0-87918-079-X*) ASU Lat Am St.
Mullen, Robert W. Blacks in America's Wars: The Shift in Attitudes from the Revolutionary War to Vietnam. LC 73-89091. (Illus.). 96p. 1973. reprint ed. 30.00 (*0-913460-30-3*) Pathfinder NY.
Mullen, Ruth, ed. see AVSC International Staff.
Mullen, Samuel. Critical Communications: Operations Guide to Business. 1995. 25.00 (*0-87814-466-8*) PennWell Bks.
— Emergency Planning Guide for Utilities. LC 93-49432. 250p. 1994. 49.95 (*0-87814-413-7*) PennWell Bks.
Mullen, Sherrie, jt. ed. see Oe, Emily.
Mullen, Sidney, jt. ed. see Jensen, Ferne.
Mullen, Sue. Creole Cooking. 1993. 12.98 (*1-55521-908-X*) Bk Sales Inc.
Mullen, Susan. Buggy Bear. (Illus.). 24p. (J). (ps-3). 1998. 16.95 (*0-9668658-0-4*) Family Buggy.
Mullen, Thomas. Laughing Out Loud & Other Religious Experiences. LC 83-3643. 133p. 1989. pap. 7.50 (*0-944350-11-9*) Friends United.
Mullen, Thomas, jt. ed. see Tverdohlebou, Stanislav.
Mullen, Tom. Living Longer & Other Sobering Possibilities. LC 96-14674. 118p. 1996. 10.00 (*0-944350-39-9*) Friends United.
— Where Two or Three Are Gathered, Someone Spills the Milk. LC 86-14322. 126p. 1986. reprint ed. pap. 8.00 (*0-913408-95-6*) Friends United.
Mullen, Tom J., ed. Butterworths Scottish Housing Law Handbook. 800p. 1992. pap. 135.00 (*0-406-11551-6*, UK, MICHIE) LEXIS Pub.
Mullen, W. Frank, et al, eds. The Government & Politics of Washington State. LC 79-101175. (Illus.). 228p. reprint ed. pap. 70.70 (*0-8357-4566-X*, 203747500008) Bks Demand.
Mullen, Wendell D. How to Model Your Ministry after the New Testament. (Illus.). 311p. 1994. pap. 12.95 (*0-9622191-5-0*) McElroy Pub.
Mullen, William. Choreia: Pindar & Dance. LC 81-47936. 291p. 1982. reprint ed. pap. 83.00 (*0-608-02738-3*, 2063403) Bks Demand.
Mullen, Yvonne. Computer Applications Calc - Spreadsheet Planner: Course Code 394-3. Schroeder, Bonnie, ed. (Illus.). 100p. (gr. 8). 1989. reprint ed. 19.95 (*0-917531-80-9*) CES Compu-Tech.
— Word Processing Teacher Edition: Course Code S04-2. Schroeder, Bonnie, ed. (Illus.). 80p. 1989. reprint ed. 15.00 (*0-917531-77-9*) CES Compu-Tech.
Mullen, Yvonne & Schroeder, Bonnie. BASIC Programming 1. (Illus.). 120p. 1989. reprint ed. teacher ed. 19.95 (*0-685-45805-9*, T303-1) CES Compu-Tech.
— BASIC Programming 1: Lab Pack, Pt. 1. Doheny, Catherine, ed. (Illus.). 179.95 (*1-56177-074-4*, L303-1); teacher ed. 19.95 (*0-685-45806-7*, T303-1) CES Compu-Tech.
— BASIC Programming 1: Lab Pack, Pt. 2. Doheny, Catherine, ed. (Illus.). 179.95 (*0-685-45807-5*, L303-2); 19.95 (*1-56177-077-9*, T303-2); disk 6.95 (*1-56177-072-8*, D303-1); disk 6.95 (*1-56177-073-6*, D303-2) CES Compu-Tech.
— Word Processing: Lab Pack. (Illus.). 1990. teacher ed., wbk. ed. 149.95 incl. disk (*1-56177-135-X*, L404) CES Compu-Tech.
Mullen, Yvonne & Weinman, Susan. Programming with Logo: Lab Pack. Schroeder, Bonnie, ed. (Illus.). 97p. 1990. teacher ed. 19.95 (*1-56177-100-7*, TE394-6); teacher ed., student ed. 149.95 incl. disk (*1-56177-099-X*, L394-6); disk 15.95 (*1-56177-098-1*, D394-6) CES Compu-Tech.
Mullen, Yvonne, jt. auth. see Weinman, Susan.

Mullenax, Foster. Capasheea's Leadmine. 200p. (Orig.). 1989. pap. 9.95 (*0-87012-484-6*) McClain.
A captivating, heartwarming story of two independent searches in the legendary lead mines in the northern mountains of West Virginia. One search is a manhunt for an elderly eccentric who has been missing for days. The other is a Brazilian expedition in pursuit of the big-eared bat. How the two parties combine & spin a tale of intrigue & suspense make Mullenax's second novel a must. *Publisher Paid Annotation.*

–Sugarlands. LC 80-82131. 422p. 1980. pap. 15.00 (*0-87012-387-4*) McClain.
Ever wonder what a friend or relative might have become had they finished high school & college? Elmer & Sylvia did neither, yet during their more than half a century as a team facing tragedies, reversals, disappointments & occasional successes they achieved true greatness. The Great Depression crushed Elmer like the grinding heel of the wood hick's corked shoe on a rattlesnake's head. His life as a timber beast with a worn-out portable sawmill, coal miner & his dream of owning his own mine produced a man of stature & self-worth achieved through the gift of high intelligence, intense desire to better his inherited lot & genuine love of life & family. From first to last page, SUGARLANDS is vivid account of what life was like for these poor struggling hill folks that gave in but never gave up. (Reprinted 1999) *Publisher Paid Annotation.*

Mullenax, Michelle, ed. see Ashcraft, Howard D.
Mullender, Audrey. Rethinking Domestic Violence: The Social Work & Probation Response. LC 96-2572. 336p. (C). 1996. 85.00 (*0-415-08054-1*); pap. 24.99 (*0-415-08055-X*) Routledge.
Mullender, Audrey & Kearn, Sarah. I'm Here Waiting: Birth Relatives Views on Part 11 of the Adoption Contact Register for England & Wales. 187p. 1997. pap. 60.00 (*1-873868-41-3*) BAAF.
Mullender, Audrey & Morley, Becky, eds. Children Living with Domestic Violence. LC 96-177859. 212p. pap. 29.95 (*1-871177-72-3*, Pub. by Whiting & Birch) Paul & Co Pubs.
— Children Living with Domestic Violence. LC 96-177859. 212p. 1994. 67.50 (*1-871177-71-5*, Pub. by Whiting & Birch) Paul & Co Pubs.
Mullender, Audrey & Ward, Dave. Self-Directed Groupwork: Users Take Action for Empowerment. 194p. 1992. pap. text 17.95 (*1-871177-11-1*, Pub. by Whiting & Birch) Paul & Co Pubs.
Mullender, Sape. Distributed Systems. 2nd ed. 580p. (C). 1993. 52.50 (*0-201-62427-3*) Addison-Wesley.
Mullendore, Richard H., jt. ed. see Bryan, William A.
Mullenheim-Rechberg, Burkard B. Von, see Von Mullenheim-Rechberg, Burkard B.
Mullenhoff, Karl. Altdeutsche Sprachproben. (GER.). viii, 150p. 1963. write for info. (*3-296-16800-1*, Pub. by Weidmann) Lubrecht & Cramer.
Mullenhoff, Karl & Scherer, Wilhelm. Denkmaler Deutscher Poesie und Prosa Aus Dem VIII.-XII. Jahrhundert Band II. (GER.). xliv, 322p. 1964. write for info. (*3-296-16901-6*, Pub. by Weidmann) Lubrecht & Cramer.
— Denkmaler Deutscher Poesie und Prosa Aus Dem VIII.-XII. Jahrhundert Band II: Anmerkungen. (GER.). ii, 492p. 1964. write for info. (*3-296-16902-4*, Pub. by Weidmann) Lubrecht & Cramer.
Mullenix, L., jt. auth. see Fink, H.
Mullenix, Linda S. Civil Procedure. LC 97-14975. (Aspen Roadmap Ser.). 1997. pap. text 21.95 (*1-56706-485-X*) Aspen Law.
***Mullenix, Linda S.** Civil Procedure-Mullenix. LC 98-219557. 1998. pap. 22.50 (*0-314-23230-3*) West Pub.
Mullenix, Linda S. Mass Tort Litigation: Cases & Materials (American Casebook Series) (Paralegal). 1160p. (C). 1996. text 55.00 (*0-314-06635-7*) West Pub.
— Mass Tort Litigation - Cases & Materials. (American Casebook Ser.). 208p. 1995. pap. text, teacher ed. write for info. (*0-314-09001-0*) West Pub.
Mullenix, Linda S., jt. auth. see Ward, Bernard J.
Mullenix, Matthew. American Kestrels in Modern Falconry. 2nd rev. ed. (Illus.). 90p. 1996. pap. 10.00 (*1-885054-04-1*) Eaglewing Pubng.
***Mullenneaux, Lisa.** Ni una Bomba Mas: Vieques vs. U. S. Navy. LC 00-190931. (Illus.). 164p. 2000. pap. 12.00 (*0-615-11307-9*) Penington Pr.
Mullennix, John W., jt. ed. see Johnson, Keith.
Mullens, John E. Schools & Staffing Survey: Recommendations for the Future. 250p. 1997. pap. 21.00 (*0-16-048961-X*) USGPO.
Mullens, Joseph. The Religious Aspects of Hindu Philosophy. (C). 1991. reprint ed. 32.00 (*81-7054-123-9*, Pub. by Classical Pubng) S Asia.
Mullens, Leonard. Lord Teach Us to Pray. 1963. pap. 1.00 (*0-686-75248-1*) Firm Foun Pub.
— Unity in Christ. 1958. 3.00 (*0-88027-053-5*) Firm Foun Pub.
Mullens, Robert L., jt. ed. see Rencis, Joseph J.
Mullensiefen, Wolfgang. Gefahrenabwehr und Gefahrerforschung Durch den Grundeigentumer: Eine Untersuchung Uber Reichweite und Grenzen der Polizeirechtlichen Zustandsverantwortlichkeit Im Falle von Boden- und Gewasserbelastungen. (Europaische Hochschulschriften Ser.: Reihe 2, Bd. 2207). (GER.). 224p. 1997. 44.95 (*3-631-32292-5*) P Lang Pubng.
Muller. Breve Diccionario de Filosofia: Brief Dictionary of Philosophy. (SPA.). 464p. 1977. 29.95 (*0-8288-5292-8*, S50199) Fr & Eur.
— Desktop Encyclopedia Networking. 1999. 295.00 (*0-07-134710-0*) McGraw.
— Desktop Encyclopedia Networking. LC 99-32794. 600p. 1999. 49.95 (*0-07-134711-9*) McGraw.
— Diccionario Aleman-Espanol, Espanol-Aleman. (GER & SPA.). 900p. 24.25 (*0-7859-0883-8*, S-50384) Fr & Eur.
— Dispersal Centers Terre. 1973. lib. bdg. 141.50 (*90-6193-203-3*, Pub. by M Nijhoff) Kluwer Academic.
— Duden Woerterbuch Vol. 8: Sinnverwandte. 2nd ed. (GER.). 800p. 1986. 59.95 (*0-7859-7224-2*, 3411209089) Fr & Eur.
MULLER. Hydroinformatics '96, Vol. 1. 1996. 91.00 (*90-5410-853-3*) Ashgate Pub Co.
— Hydroinformatics '96, Vol. 2. 1996. 91.00 (*90-5410-854-1*) Ashgate Pub Co.
Muller. McGraw-Hill Reader. 4th ed. 1991. teacher ed. 28.12 (*0-07-044029-8*) McGraw.
— The McGraw-Hill Reader. 7th ed. LC 99-33123. 672p. 1999. pap. 37.81 (*0-07-229294-6*) McGraw.
— Neotropische Okosysteme. 1976. lib. bdg. 121.50 (*90-6193-208-4*, Pub. by M Nijhoff) Kluwer Academic.
— Rituals of Fertility & the Sacrifice of Desire: Nazarite Women's Performance in South Africa. LC 99-17548. (Chicago Studies in Ethnomusicology). 272p. 1999. lib. bdg. 57.00 (*0-226-54819-8*) U Ch Pr.
— Rituals of Fertility & the Sacrifice of Desire: Nazarite Women's Performance in South Africa. LC 99-17548. (Chicago Studies in Ethnomusicology). 272p. 2000. pap. text 26.00 (*0-226-54820-1*) U Ch Pr.
Muller. The Short Prose Reader. 7th ed. 1993. 15.31 (*0-07-044250-9*) McGraw.
Muller, ed. Petronii. 4th ed. (LAT.). 1995. pap. 29.95 (*3-519-01580-3*, T1580, Pub. by B G Teubner) U of Mich Pr.
Muller & Haensch, Gunther. Handworterbuch Spanish to German. 9th ed. (GER & SPA.). 658p. 1996. 89.95 (*0-320-00671-9*) Fr & Eur.
Muller, et al. Autonomes und partnerschaftliches Lernen: Modelle und Beispiele us dem Fremdsprachen Unterricht. 208p. 1989. 26.25 (*3-468-49439-4*) Langenscheidt.
Muller, jt. auth. see Bock.
Muller, A. Interaction & Determination Attempt at Elaborating an Up-to-Date Theory of Determinancy in Natural Philosophy. 234p. (C). 1991. 90.00 (*963-05-5552-2*, Pub. by Akade Kiado) St Mut.
Muller, A., ed. International Association of Logopaedics & Phoniatrics, 19th Congress, Edinburgh 1983: Main Papers. (Journal: Folia Phoniatrica: Vol. 35, No. 1-2). 96p. 1983. pap. 31.50 (*3-8055-3729-8*) S Karger.
Muller, A., et al, eds. Electron & Proton Transfer in Chemistry & Biology. LC 92-14464. (Studies in Physical & Theoretical Chemistry: Vol. 78). 394p. 1992. 261.25 (*0-444-88862-4*) Elsevier.
Muller, A., jt. auth. see Morcay, Raoul.
Muller, A., jt. auth. see Sumer, B. Mutlu.
Muller, A. B., ed. see Magellanic Clouds Symposium Staff.
Muller, A. Charles, tr. The Sutra of Perfect Enlightenment: Korean Buddhism's Guide to Meditation (with Commentary by the Son Monk Kihwa) LC 98-39738. (SUNY Series in Korean Studies). 352p. (C). 1999. text 74.50 (*0-7914-4101-6*); pap. text 24.95 (*0-7914-4102-4*) State U NY Pr.
Muller, A. S. International Organizations & Their Host States: Aspects of Their Legal Relationship. LC 95-4844. (Legal Aspects of International Organization Ser.: Vol. 21). 1995. write for info. (*90-411-0080-6*) Kluwer Law Intl.
Muller, Achim, jt. ed. see Pope, Michael T.
Muller, Alberto. Monologo con Yolanda: Novela Sobre las Sombras de Una Isla. (Coleccion Caniqui). (SPA.). 126p. (Orig.). 1995. pap. 9.99 (*0-89729-782-2*) Ediciones.
Muller, Alberto & Suarez, Manuel L. Tierra Metalizada: Poemas. LC 85-82279. (SPA.). 62p. (Orig.) 1986. pap. 6.95 (*0-89729-385-1*) Ediciones.
Muller, Alexander. I: Western Civilization SG. 190p. (C). 1995. pap. text, per. 17.95 (*0-7872-0964-3*) Kendall-Hunt.
Muller, Alexander V., ed. Soloview, the Character of Old Russia. Vol. 24. 1987. pap. 15.00 (*0-87569-095-5*) Academic Intl.
***Muller, Alice.** Complete Idiot's Guide to Learning German. 2nd ed. (Complete Idiot's Guides (Lifestyle) Ser.). (GER & ENG.). 460p. 2000. pap. 16.95 (*0-02-863925-1*, Alpha Ref) Macmillan Gen Ref.
Muller, Andreas, ed. Discharge & Velocity Measurements: Proceedings of a Short Course, Zurich, 26-27 August 1987. 216p. (C). 1988. text 123.00 (*90-6191-782-4*, Pub. by A A Balkema) Ashgate Pub Co.
— Hydroinformatics 96: Proceedings of the Second International Conference, Zurich, 9-13 September 1996, 2 vols. (Illus.). 1000p. (C). 1996. 181.00 (*90-5410-852-5*, Pub. by A A Balkema) Ashgate Pub Co.
***Muller, Andreas, et al, eds.** Global Capitalism, Liberation Theology & the Social Sciences: An Analysis of the Contradictions of Modernity at the Turn of the Millennium. LC 99-24845. 312p. 1999. lib. bdg. 69.00 (*1-56072-679-2*) Nova Sci Pubs.
Muller, Antal. Quantum Mechanics: A Physical World Picture. LC 73-18062. 1974. 55.00 (*0-08-017936-3*, Pub. by Pergamon Repr) Franklin.
Muller Associates Inc. Staff, et al, compiled by. Handbook of Radon in Buildings: Detection, Safety, & Control. 266p. 1988. 76.95 (*0-89116-823-0*) Hemisp Pub.
Muller, Astrid. Wissen und Schreiben: Ergebnisse und Folgerungen Aus der Aufsatzstudie Ost. (GER.). 119p. 1997. 29.95 (*3-631-31737-9*) P Lang Pubng.
Muller, B. The Physics of the Quark-Gluon Plasma. (Lecture Notes in Physics Ser.: Vol. 225). vii, 142p. 1985. 18.95 (*0-387-15211-3*) Spr-Verlag.
— Wortschatz und Bedeutungsvermittlung. Neuner, Gerd, ed. (Fernstudienangebot Ser.). (GER.). 119p. 1996. 11.25 (*3-468-49672-9*) Langenscheidt.
Muller, B. & Fried, H. M. QCD Vacuum Structure: Proceedings of the Workshop on QCD Vacuum Structure & Its Applications. 388p. 1993. text 95.00 (*981-02-1280-1*) World Scientific Pub.
Muller, B. & Reinhardt, J. Neural Networks: An Introduction. Domany, E. et al, eds. (Physics of Neural Networks Ser.). (Illus.). xiii, 266p. 1991. reprint ed. text 49.00 incl. 5.25 hd (*0-387-52380-4*) Spr-Verlag.
Muller, B., jt. auth. see Fried, H. M.
Muller, B., jt. ed. see Fried, H. M.
Muller, Barbara. Florentine Embroidery. (Illus.). 96p. 1993. pap. 18.00 (*0-916896-54-4*) Lacis Pubns.
— Incognito. 90p. 1998. pap. 6.00 (*1-877603-48-1*) Pecan Grove.

M

Muller, Baron. The Adventures of a San Francisco Newsman. 100p. 1991. pap. 8.95 (*0-917583-21-3*) Lexikos.

Muller, Benito, jt. auth. see Bartsch, Ulrich.

Muller-Bergh, Klaus, jt. auth. see Gonzalez Echevarria, Roberto.

Muller, Bernd D., ed. Anders lernen im Fremdsprachen Unterricht: Experimente us der Praxis. 192p. 1988. 26.25 (*3-468-49436-X*) Langenscheidt.

***Muller, Berndt & Pisarski, Robert D., eds.** RHIC Physics & Beyond: Kay Kay Gee Day. (Conference Proceedings Ser.: Vol. 482). (Illus.). 178p. 1999. 68.00 (*1-56396-878-9*) Am Inst Physics.

Muller, Berndt, jt. auth. see Greiner, Walter.

Muller-Bierl, Maja. The Professional's Book of Budgerigars. T.F.H. Publications Staff, tr. from GER. (Illus.). 144p. 1991. lib. bdg. 11.95 (*0-86622-076-3*, TS-138) TFH Pubns.

Muller, Brenda, jt. auth. see Muller, Carrel.

Muller, Brigitte & Gunther, Horst H. A Complete Book of Reiki Healing: Heal Yourself, Others, & the World Around You. LC 94-47299. 1995. pap. 15.95 (*0-940795-16-7*) LifeRhythm.

Muller-Broich, Jan Dominik. Autodistributive Computer Software: Shareware, Freeware Und Public Domain Software Als Sonderformen der Softwareuberlassung eine Vertragliche Zuordnung Unter Besonderer Berucksichtigung Des 69d Abs. 1 Urhg. XXVIII, 242p. 1998. 48.95 (*3-631-33955-0*) P Lang Pubng.

M

Muller, Brunhild. Painting with Children. 48p. 1990. pap. 8.95 (*0-86315-048-9*, 1192, Pub. by Floris Bks) Anthroposophic.

Muller, C., ed. Ecology & Mental Health. (Journal: Psychiatria Clinica: Vol. 7, Nos. 4 & 5). 100p. 1975. 48.75 (*3-8055-2212-6*) S Karger.

Muller, C., ed. see Metochites, Theodorus.

Muller, C. F. Nachtrage zur Plautinischen Prosodie. (GER.). xvi, 159p. 1973. reprint ed. write for info. (*0-318-70442-0*) G Olms Pubs.

Muller, Carl. Spit & Polish LC 98-906476. 435 p. 1998. write for info. (*0-14-027023-X*) Penguin Books.

Muller, Carl F. Wilhelm. Nachtrage Zur Plautinischen Prosodie. xvi, 159p. 1973. reprint ed. write for info. (*0-318-71181-8*) G Olms Pubs.

— Plautinische Prosodie. (GER.). xvi, 159p. 1971. reprint ed. write for info. (*3-487-04085-9*) G Olms Pubs.

Muller, Carrel & Jacques, Ethel M. Dinosaur Discovery. (Illus.). 32p. (J). (gr. 3-6). 1987. student ed. 5.00 (*0-915785-02-1*) Bonjour Books.

Muller, Carrel & Muller, Brenda. Explore Louisiana. (Illus.). 32p. (J). (gr. 3 up). 1984. 5.50 (*0-915785-00-5*) Bonjour Books.

— Louisiana Indians. (Illus.). 64p. (J). (gr. 3 up). 1985. 7.50 (*0-915785-01-3*) Bonjour Books.

Muller, Catherine M. Marguerite Porete et Marguerite d'Oingt de l'Autre Cote du Miroir. (Currents in Comparative Romance Languages & Literatures Ser.: Vol. 72). (FRE.). XVI, 213p. (C). 1999. text 47.95 (*0-8204-4010-8*, 40108) P Lang Pubng.

Muller, Ch. The Art & Antiques Dictionary, Vol. 1. (ENG, FRE & GER.). 376p. 1982. 125.00 (*0-8288-0950-X*, M14333) Fr & Eur.

Muller, Charlotte F. Health Care & Gender. LC 90-8383. 272p. 1990. text 45.00 (*0-87154-610-8*) Russell Sage.

— Health Care & Gender. (Illus.). 258p. 1992. pap. 14.95 (*0-87154-611-6*) Russell Sage.

— Light Metals Monopoly. LC 68-58611. (Columbia University. Studies in the Social Sciences: No. 519). reprint ed. 22.50 (*0-404-51519-3*) AMS Pr.

Muller, Christa, jt. auth. see Lafontaine, Oskar.

Muller, Christian. Entwicklung Eines Wissensbasierten Systems zur Unterstutzung Analytischer Prufungshandlungen im Rahmen der Jahresabschlubprufung, Vol. XXV. (Europaische Hochschulschriften: Reihe 5: Bd. 1974). (GER.). 300p. 1996. pap. 57.95 (*3-631-49636-2*) P Lang Pubng.

— Gerichtspraxis im Stadtstaat Cordoba: Zum Recht der Gesellschaft in Einer Mealikitisch-Islamischen Rechtstradition des 5./11. Jahrhunderts. LC 99-10661. (Studies in Islamic Law & Society). 489p. 1999. 135.50 (*90-04-11354-1*) Brill Academic Pubs.

***Muller, Christian.** Laminated Timber Construction. (ENG., Illus.). 200p. 2000. 65.00 (*3-7643-6267-7*, Pub. by Birkhauser) Princeton Arch.

Muller, Christian & Mellke, Hans, contrib. by. Durer, Holbein Grunewald. LC 99-36741. (Illus.). 432p. 1999. 75.00 (*3-7757-0848-0*, Pub. by Gerd Hatje) Dist Art Pubs.

Muller, Christiane & Grobety, Andre. Vivre l'Angeologie au Quotidien. LC 97-941404. (FRE., Illus.). 313p. 1997. 24.95 (*2-89466-013-8*) Edns Roseau.

***Muller, Christoph.** Jugendpsychiatrische Begutachtung von Straffalligen Jugendlichen: Diagnostische und Therapeutische Bedingungen und Moglichkeiten Forensischer Begutachtung in einer Durchgangsstation. (Europaische Hochschulschriften Ser.: Reihe 6). 135p. 1999. 18.95 (*3-906762-70-X*) P Lang Pubng.

Muller, Christoph A. Strategische Fuhrung Europaischer Mittelstandischer Unternehmen: Am Beispiel der Werkzeugmaschinenbranche. (GER., Illus.). 476p. 1995. 68.95 (*3-906755-43-6*) P Lang Pubng.

***Muller, Christopher.** Modelling Soil-Biosphere Interactions. LC 99-35159. (CABI Publishing Ser.). 220p. 1999. text 65.00 (*0-85199-353-2*, Pub. by C A B Intl) OUP.

Muller, Claude, jt. ed. see Attal, Pierre.

Muller, Courtney L., jt. auth. see Holt, Robert N.

Muller, Curt-Christian, ed. Diekholzen - Eine Ortschronik. (GER.). xi, 162p. 1992. write for info. (*3-487-09683-8*) G Olms Pubs.

Muller, Cynthia, et al. Colors & Shapes, 5 bks. (Apples for Teachers Ser.). 96p. 11.99 (*0-8224-0459-1*, FE0459) Fearon Teacher Aids.

— Kindergarten Homework Packet. (Apples for Teachers Ser.). 48p. (J). (ps). 4.99 (*0-8224-4150-0*, FE4150) Fearon Teacher Aids.

— Letters A-Z, 5 bks. (Apples for Teachers Ser.). 96p. 11.99 (*0-8224-0456-7*, FE0456) Fearon Teacher Aids.

— Numbers 0 to 10, 5 bks. (Apples for Teachers Ser.). 96p. 11.99 (*0-8224-0457-5*, FE0457) Fearon Teacher Aids.

— Time: Months, Holidays, Seasons, & Telling Time, 5 bks. (Apples for Teachers Ser.). 96p. 9.99 (*0-8224-0458-3*, FE0458) Fearon Teacher Aids.

Muller, D. Potassic Igneous Rocks & Associated Gold-Copper Mineralization. Neugebauer, H. J. et al, eds. (Lecture Notes in Earth Sciences Ser.: Vol. 56). (Illus.). xiv, 210p. 1995. 75.95 (*3-540-59116-8*) Spr-Verlag.

Muller, D. E. A Goya Oil Sketch for an Officer's Portrait. 1984. 1.50 (*0-87535-136-0*) Hispanic Soc.

Muller, Daniel & Groves, David I. Potassic Igneous Rocks & Associated Gold-Copper Mineralization. LC 95-10058. (Lecture Notes in Earth Sciences Ser.: Vol. 56). 1995. write for info. (*0-387-59116-8*) Spr-Verlag.

— Potassic Igneous Rocks & Associated Gold-Copper Mineralization. 2nd ed. LC 96-40254. (Lecture Notes in Earth Sciences Ser.: Vol. 56). (Illus.). 238p. 1997. pap. 78.95 (*3-540-62075-3*) Spr-Verlag.

Muller, Dave. Colorado Mountain Hikes for Everyone: Routes & Maps to 105 Named Summits. LC 87-92198. (Illus.). 196p. (Orig.). 1987. pap. 11.95 (*0-9619666-0-2*) D J Muller.

— Colorado Mountain Ski Tours & Hikes: A Year Round Guide. (Illus.). 224p. (Orig.). 1993. pap. 14.95 (*0-9619666-1-0*) D J Muller.

Muller, Dave, jt. auth. see Taylor, Jayne.

Muller, Dave J., et al, eds. Psychology & Law: Topics from an International Conference. LC 83-21684. 494p. reprint ed. pap. 153.20 (*0-7837-5204-0*, 204493200005) Bks Demand.

Muller, Dave J., et al. Nursing Children: Psychology, Research, & Practice. 2nd ed. LC 92-20109. 1992. 41.50 (*1-56593-023-1*, 0266) Thomson Learn.

Muller, Dave J., jt. ed. see Code, Chris.

Muller, David. Whitey. (Writers Ser.). 120p. 1995. reprint ed. pap. text 12.95 (*0-86975-468-8*, Pub. by Ravan Pr) Ohio U Pr.

Muller, David J., jt. auth. see Code, Chris.

Muller, Dieter. Dictionary of Microprocessor Systems: English-French-German-Russian. 4th ed. (ENG, FRE, GER & RUS.). 448p. 1990. 175.00 (*0-8288-0270-X*, M 13124) Fr & Eur.

Muller, E. Simplified Grammar of the Pali Language. (C). 1995. reprint ed. 18.00 (*81-206-1103-9*, Pub. by Asian Educ Servs) S Asia.

Muller, E., ed. see Come, B., et al.

Muller, E. E. & MacLeod, R. M., eds. Neuroendocrine Perspectives, Vol. 8. (Illus.). xiv, 182p. 1990. 117.00 (*0-387-97365-6*) Spr-Verlag.

— Neuroendocrine Perspectives, Vol. 9. (Illus.). xiv, 246p. 1991. 145.00 (*0-387-97524-1*) Spr-Verlag.

Muller, E. E., jt. auth. see Myller, E.

Muller, Earl C., jt. ed. see Carey, Patrick W.

Muller-Eberhard, H. J. & Miescher, Peter A., eds. Complement. (Illus.). vi, 480p. 1985. 111.00 (*0-387-15075-7*) Spr-Verlag.

Muller, Eddie. Dark City: The Lost World of Film Noir. 2nd ed. LC 98-5677. (Illus.). 208p. 1998. pap. 22.95 (*0-312-18076-4*, St Martin Griffin) St Martin.

***Muller, Eddie.** Dark City Dames. 2000. pap. 19.95 (*0-06-098854-1*) HarpC.

— Dark City Dames: The Wicked Women of Film Noir. 192p. 2000. 29.95 (*0-06-039369-6*) HarpC.

Muller, Eddie. Grindhouse. LC 96-26667. (Illus.). 144p. 1996. pap. 19.95 (*0-312-14609-4*) St Martin.

Muller, Edith A., ed. Highlights of Astronomy, 2 pts., Pt. 1. (International Astronomical Union Highlights Ser.). 1977. lib. bdg. 117.50 (*90-277-0849-5*) Kluwer Academic.

— Highlights of Astronomy, 2 pts., Pt. 1. (International Astronomical Union Highlights Ser.). 1977. pap. text 80.00 (*90-277-0830-4*) Kluwer Academic.

— Highlights of Astronomy, 2 pts., Pt. 2. (International Astronomical Union Highlights Ser.). 1977. lib. bdg. 129.50 (*90-277-0850-9*) Kluwer Academic.

— Highlights of Astronomy, 2 pts., Pt. 2. (International Astronomical Union Highlights Ser.). 1977. pap. text 88.00 (*90-277-0832-0*) Kluwer Academic.

— Reports on Astronomy, 3 pts., Pt. 1. (Transactions of the International Astronomical Union Ser.: Vol. XVII A). 1979. lib. bdg. 80.00 (*90-277-1005-8*) Kluwer Academic.

— Reports on Astronomy, 3 pts., Pt. 2. (Transactions of the International Astronomical Union Ser.: Vol. XVII A). 1979. lib. bdg. 80.00 (*90-277-1006-6*) Kluwer Academic.

— Reports on Astronomy, 3 pts., Pt. 3. (Transactions of the International Astronomical Union Ser.: Vol. XVII A). 1979. lib. bdg. 80.00 (*90-277-1007-4*) Kluwer Academic.

Muller, Edith A., ed. see International Astronomical Union Staff.

Muller, Edith Alice & Appenzeller, I. Remembering Edith Alice Muller. LC 97-48764. (Astrophysics & Space Science Library). 150p. 1998. 99.00 (*0-7923-4789-7*) Kluwer Academic.

Muller, Edmund & Bhattacharjee, Arun. India Wins Independence: A History of Modern India, 1707-1947: A Connected Historical Narration of India's Freedom Struggle. (C). 1988. 34.00 (*0-8364-2437-9*, Pub. by Ashish Pub Hse) S Asia.

— Subhas Chandra Bose & Indian Freedom Struggle. 1985. 17.50 (*0-8364-1452-7*, Pub. by Ashish Pub Hse) S Asia.

Muller, Eduard, ed. see Muller, Karl O.

Muller, Edward, ed. see Buddhaghosa.

Muller, Edward J. & Myatt, Robert L., Jr. Reading Architectural Working Drawings Vol. 2: Commercial Construction. 3rd ed. (Illus.). (C). 1988. pap. text 70.00 (*0-13-755794-9*) P-H.

Muller, Edward John & Grau, Philip A. Reading Architectural Working Drawings Vol. 1: Residential & Light Construction. 5th ed. LC 99-35374. 330p. (C). 1999. spiral bd. 68.00 (*0-13-979782-3*) P-H.

Muller, Edward John, et al. Architectural Drawing & Light Construction. 5th ed. LC 98-26035. 776p. 1998. 89.00 (*0-13-520529-8*) P-H.

Muller, Edward K., ed. A Concise Historical Atlas of Pennsylvania. 115p. 1989. pap. 32.95 (*0-87722-672-5*) Temple U Pr.

Muller, Edward N. Aggressive Political Participation. LC 78-70309. 316p. 1979. reprint ed. pap. 98.00 (*0-7837-9396-0*, 206014100004) Bks Demand.

Muller, Ekkehardt. Microstructural Analysis of Revelation 4-11. (Andrews University Seminary Doctoral Dissertation Ser.: Vol. 21). 788p. (Orig.). 1996. pap. 19.99 (*1-883925-11-8*) Andrews Univ Pr.

***Muller, Eric.** While You're Waiting for the Food to Come. LC 99-17168. (Illus.). 96p. (YA). (gr. 3-7). 1999. pap. 8.95 (*0-531-07144-8*) Orchard Bks Watts.

Muller, Eric. While You're Waiting for the Food to Come: A Tabletop Science Activity Book. LC 99-17168. (Illus.). 96p. (YA). (gr. 3 up). 1999. 15.95 (*0-531-30199-0*) Orchard Bks Watts.

Muller, Eric & Koehler, Barbara. Frailing the Five-String Banjo. 96p. 1973. spiral bd. 11.95 (*0-87166-878-5*, 93335) Mel Bay.

— Frailing the Five-String Banjo. 1993. 18.95 incl. audio (*0-7866-0913-3*, 93335P); audio 9.98 (*0-87166-756-8*, 93335C) Mel Bay.

Muller, Erich, et al. Science & Skiing. LC 97-145406. (Illus.). 640p. (C). 1996. 95.00 (*0-419-20850-X*, E & FN Spon) Routledge.

***Muller, Erich, et al.** Science in Elite Sport. LC 98-54129. (Illus.). 1999. write for info. (*0-419-24530-8*) Routledge.

Muller, Erich H., ed. see Handel, George Frideric.

Muller, Erich M., ed. see Schutz, Heinrich.

***Muller, Erik.** Vern Rutsala. LC 98-70945. (Western Writers Ser.: Vol. 132). 49p. 1998. 5.95 (*0-88430-131-1*) Boise St U W Writ Ser.

Muller, Erwin & Neuneck, Gotz. Abrustung & Konventionelle Stabilitat in Europa. (GER.). 203p. 1990. pap. 41.50 (*3-7890-1974-7*, Pub. by Nomos Verlags) Intl Bk Import.

Muller, Eugene W. Job Analysis Comparing the Tasks in State-Local Government Purchasing & Institutional Purchasing. Ketchum, Carol L., ed. 40p. (Orig.). (C). 1994. pap. text 20.00 (*0-945968-16-7*) Ctr Advanced Purchasing.

— Job Analysis Identifying the Tasks of Purchasing. Ketchum, Carol L., ed. LC 92-81840. 68p. (Orig.). (C). 1992. pap. text 20.00 (*0-945968-10-8*) Ctr Advanced Purchasing.

Muller, Eugenio E., et al, eds. Growth Hormone & Somatomedins During Lifespan. LC 93-19508. 1993. 174.00 (*0-387-56690-2*) Spr-Verlag.

Muller, Eugenio E. & Genazzani, Andrea R., eds. Central & Peripheral Endorphins: Basic & Clinical Aspects. fac. ed. LC 83-42986. (Frontiers in Neuroscience Ser.). (Illus.). 389p. pap. 120.60 (*0-7837-7534-2*, 204697000005) Bks Demand.

Muller, F. Atheneum Worterbuch: Aleman-Espanol, Espanol-Aleman. (GER & SPA.). 383p. 1979. pap. 9.95 (*0-8288-4719-3*, S35066) Fr & Eur.

Muller, F. & Leupelt, M., eds. Eco Targets, Goal Functions, & Orientors. LC 98-13139. (Illus.). xviii, 619p. 1998. 90.00 (*3-540-63679-X*) Spr-Verlag.

Muller, F. M. Seedlings of the North-Western European Lowland. 1978. text 221.50 (*90-6193-588-1*) Kluwer Academic.

— The Vedanta Philosophy. 182p. 1984. text 27.00 (*0-685-14047-4*) Coronet Bks.

Muller, F. Max. India: What Can It Teach Us? 2nd ed. (C). 1991. reprint ed. 20.00 (*81-215-0394-9*, Pub. by M Manoharial) Coronet Bks.

— My Indian Friends. (Auld Lang Syne Second Ser.). (C). 1993. reprint ed. 18.50 (*81-206-0839-9*, Pub. by Asian Educ Servs) S Asia.

— Science of Thought (1909) 100p. 1998. reprint ed. pap. 16.95 (*0-7661-0370-6*) Kessinger Pub.

— Three Introductory Lectures on the Science of Thought. (C). 1988. reprint ed. 11.50 (*81-206-0423-7*, Pub. by Asian Educ Servs) S Asia.

— The Upanishads, 2 vols. 1974. lib. bdg. 500.00 (*0-8490-1252-X*) Gordon Pr.

— Upanishads, 2 vols., Vol. 1. 1962. reprint ed. text 9.95 (*0-486-20993-8*) Dover.

— Upanishads, 2 vols., Vol. 2. 1962. reprint ed. text 9.95 (*0-486-20992-X*) Dover.

Muller, F. Max, ed. Sacred Books of the East. 1998. reprint ed. text 2250.00 (*0-7007-0600-3*, Pub. by Curzon Pr Ltd) UH Pr.

— The Texts of Taoism, Vol. 1. Legge, James, tr. 396p. 1962. pap. 9.95 (*0-486-20990-3*) Dover.

— The Texts of Taoism, Vol. 2. Legge, James, tr. 396p. 1962. pap. 9.95 (*0-486-20991-1*) Dover.

Muller, F. Max & Oldenberg, Hermann. Vedic Hymns, 2 vols. 1974. lib. bdg. 500.00 (*0-685-01976-4*) Gordon Pr.

Muller, F. Max, ed. see Arya-Sura.

Muller, F. Max, ed. see Kasawara, Kenju.

Muller, Fabiola, jt. auth. see O'Rahilly, Ronan.

Muller-Fahrenholz, Geiko. God's Spirit: Transforming a World in Crisis. LC 97-37892. 176p. 1995. 19.95 (*0-8264-0824-9*) Continuum.

Muller-Fahrenholz, Geiko, ed. Partners in Life: The Handicapped & the Church. LC 80-473412. (Faith & Order Papers: No. 89). 188p. reprint ed. pap. 58.30 (*0-7837-6005-1*, 204581500008) Bks Demand.

Muller, Felix, jt. auth. see Jorgensen, Sven E.

Muller-Feyen, Carla. Engagierter Journalismus: Wilhelm Herzog und das Forum (1914-1929): Zeitgeschehen und Zeitgenossen Im Spiegel Einer Nonkonformistischen Zeitschrift. (GER.). 1997. 82.95 (*3-631-49960-4*) P Lang Pubng.

Muller, Filip. Eyewitness Auschwitz: Three Years in the Gas Chambers. LC 99-32041. (Illus.). 192p. 1999. pap. 12.95 (*1-56663-271-4*, Pub. by I R Dee) Natl Bk Netwk.

Muller, Florencia. La Ceramica de Cuicuilco B: Un Rescate Arqueologico. 285p. 1990. pap. 9.00 (*968-6068-54-6*, IN011) UPLAAP.

Muller, Florian. Public Relations: New British Photography. 1998. 29.95 (*3-89322-338-X*, Pub. by Edition Cantz) Dist Art Pubs.

Muller, Francis J. De Paroecia Domui Religiosae Commissa. x, 85p. 1956. pap. 3.50 (*1-57659-111-5*) Franciscan Inst.

Muller, Frank G. The Wall Paintings from the Oecus of the Villa of Publius Fannius Synistor in Boscoreale. (Iconological Studies in Roman Art: Vol. 2). (Illus.). x, 156p. 1994. lib. bdg. 57.00 (*90-5063-256-4*, Pub. by Gieben) J Benjamins Pubng Co.

Muller, Frank G., jt. ed. see Ahmad, Yusuf J.

Muller, Frank G. J. M. The Aldobrandini Wedding. (Iconological Studies in Roman Art: Vol. 3). (Illus.). xii, 208p. 1994. lib. bdg. 57.00 (*90-5063-266-1*, Pub. by Gieben) J Benjamins Pubng Co.

— The So-Called Peleus & Thetis Sarcophagus in the Villa Albani. (Iconological Studies in Roman Art: Vol. 1). (Illus.). 192p. 1994. lib. bdg. 57.00 (*90-5063-246-7*, Pub. by Gieben) J Benjamins Pubng Co.

Muller, Franz. Chemistry & Biochemistry of Flavoenzymes, Vol. 1. (Illus.). 448p. 1991. boxed set 275.00 (*0-8493-4393-3*, QP552) CRC Pr.

— Chemistry & Biochemistry of Flavoenzymes, Vol. 2. (Illus.). 520p. 1991. boxed set 275.00 (*0-8493-4394-1*, QP552) CRC Pr.

— Chemistry & Biochemistry of Flavoenzymes, Vol. 3. (Illus.). 680p. 1991. boxed set 250.00 (*0-8493-4395-X*, QP552) CRC Pr.

Muller, Frederick. La Comida: The Foods, Cooking & Traditions of the Upper Rio Grande. LC 94-42423. (Illus.). 194p. 1995. pap. 18.95 (*0-87108-842-8*) Pruett.

Muller, Frederik. Energy & Environment in Interregional Input-Output Models. (Studies in Applied Regional Science: Vol. 15). 1979. lib. bdg. 73.50 (*0-89838-002-2*) Kluwer Academic.

Muller, Friedrich A. Der Islam im Morgen-und Abendland, 2 vols. (Illus.). 1331p. reprint ed. write for info. (*0-318-71534-1*) G Olms Pubs.

Muller, Friedrich M. Biographies of Words & the Home of the Aryas. (C). 1987. reprint ed. 22.00 (*81-206-0299-4*, Pub. by Asian Educ Servs) S Asia.

— Comparative Mythology: An Essay. rev. ed. Dorson, Richard M., ed. LC 77-70612. (International Folklore Ser.). 1979. reprint ed. lib. bdg. 24.95 (*0-405-10111-2*) Ayer.

— Introduction to the Science of Religion. Bolle, Kees W., ed. LC 77-79145. (Mythology Ser.). 1978. lib. bdg. 35.95 (*0-405-10554-1*) Ayer.

Muller, G. H. Convection & Inhomogeneities in Crystal Growth from the Melt. (Crystals - Growth, Properties & Applications Ser.). 140p. 1988. 112.95 (*0-387-18603-4*) Spr-Verlag.

Muller, G. H. & Kruger, G., eds. Hector, Vol. II. (Illus.). 412p. 1988. 49.95 (*0-387-19137-2*) Spr-Verlag.

Muller, G. H. & Richter, M. M., eds. Models & Sets, Pt. 1. (Lecture Notes in Mathematics Ser.: Vol. 1103). viii, 484p. 1984. 59.95 (*0-387-13900-1*) Spr-Verlag.

Muller, G. H., ed. see Ebbinghaus, Heinz-Dieter.

Muller, G. H., ed. see Proof Theory Symposium Staff.

Muller-Gartner, Hans W., jt. ed. see Gulyas, Balazs.

Muller, Georg. Comparative World Data: A Statistical Handbook for Social Science. LC 88-45391. 504p. (C). 1989. 3.5 hd 95.00 (*0-8018-3805-3*) Johns Hopkins.

Muller, George. The Autobiography of George Muller. 237p. 1984. mass mkt. 5.99 (*0-88368-159-5*) Whitaker Hse.

— Faith in Action. Setran, David P., ed. & intro. by. (Collection of Classics Ser.). 74p. 1994. pap. text 2.95 (*1-879089-19-X*) B Graham Ctr.

***Muller, George.** Release the Power of Prayer. LC 99-55750. 1999. pap. 7.99 (*0-88368-352-0*) Whitaker Hse.

Muller, Gerald. With Life & Laughter: The Life of Father Pro. LC 96-2915. 160p. 1996. pap. 9.95 (*0-8198-8281-X*) Pauline Bks.

Muller-Gerbl, Magdalena. The Subchondral Bone Plate. Beck, F. et al, eds. LC 97-35147. (Advances in Anatomy, Embryology & Cell Biology Ser.). (Illus.). 142p. 1998. pap. 99.00 (*3-540-63673-0*) Spr-Verlag.

Muller, Gerda. Autumn. (Illus.). 12p. (J). (ps). Date not set. 10.95 (*0-86315-191-4*, 24193, Pub. by Floris Bks) Gryphon Hse.

— Spring. unabridged ed. (Illus.). 12p. (J). (ps). Date not set. 10.95 (*0-86315-193-0*, 29851, Pub. by Floris Bks) Gryphon Hse.

— Summer. (Illus.). 12p. (J). (ps). Date not set. 10.95 (*0-86315-194-9*, 20694, Pub. by Floris Bks) Gryphon Hse.

— Winter. (Illus.). 12p. (J). (ps). Date not set. 10.95 (*0-86315-192-2*, 24192, Pub. by Floris Bks) Gryphon Hse.

An Asterisk (*) at the beginning of an entry indicates that the title is appearing for the first time.

Muller, Gerhard. Keeping & Breeding Turtles. LC 99-212493. (Illus.). 160p. 1998. 22.95 (0-7938-0129-X, LR-104) TFH Pubns.
— Lexikon Technologie Metallverarbeitende Industri. 2nd ed. (GER.). 699p. 1992. 125.00 (0-7859-8694-4, 380855102x) Fr & Eur.
— Register zu Band 1-27. 384p. 1997. 76.00 (3-11-016088-9) De Gruyter.
Muller, Gerhard F. Bering's Voyages: The Reports From Russia. Urness, Carol, ed. & tr. by. LC 86-51585. (Rasmuson Library Historical Translation Ser.: Vol. III). (Illus.). 221p. (Orig.). 1986. pap. 15.00 (0-912006-22-6) U of Alaska Pr.
Muller, Gerhard J., ed. Medical Optical Tomography: Functional Imaging & Monitoring. LC 93-5546. 1993. pap. 110.00 (0-8194-1379-8, IS11) SPIE.
Muller, Gerhard J. & Roggan, Andre, eds. Laser-Induced Interstitial Thermotherapy. LC 95-12212. (Institute Ser.: Vol. PM25). 1995. 95.00 (0-8194-1859-5) SPIE.
Muller, Gerhard M., jt. auth. see Viswanath, V. S.
Muller, German. Lexikon Elektrotechnik. (GER.). 1994. 195.00 (0-7859-8416-X, 3527281541) Fr & Eur.
Muller, Gilbert H. Chester Himes. (Twayne's United States Authors Ser.: No. 553). 184p. 1989. text 20.95 (0-8057-7545-5, Twyne) Mac Lib Ref.
— Here & Now: Current Readings for Writers. LC 97-15994. 496p. 1997. pap. 31.88 (0-07-044372-6) McGraw.
***Muller, Gilbert H.** New Strangers in Paradise: The Immigrant Experience & Contemporary American Fiction. LC 99-24008. 288p. 1999. 29.95 (0-8131-2134-5) U Pr of Ky.
Muller, Gilbert H. The Short Prose Reader. 9th ed. LC 99-29905. 496p. 1999. pap. 30.94 (0-07-229263-6) McGraw.
Muller, Gilbert H., ed. The McGraw-Hill Reader: Issues Across the Disciplines. 6th ed. 752p. (C). 1996. pap. 31.25 (0-07-044009-3) McGraw.
Muller, Gilbert H. & Wiener, Harvey S. The Short Prose Reader 4th ed. LC 86-10408. xxi, 426p. 1987. write for info. (0-07-044021-2) McGraw.
Muller, Gilbert H. & Wiener, Harvey S. The Short Prose Reader. 8th ed. LC 96-24813. 512p. (C). 1996. pap. 30.06 (0-07-044016-6) McGraw.
***Muller, Gilbert H. & Wiener, Harvey S.** The Short Prose Reader 9th ed. LC 99-29905. 2000. write for info. (0-07-229264-4) McGraw.
Muller, Gilbert H. & Williams, John A. Ways in Approaches to Reading & Writing about Literature. LC 93-1666. 128p. (C). 1994. pap. 12.43 (0-07-044203-7) McGraw.
Muller, Gilbert H. & Williams, John A., compiled by. Bridges: Literature Across Cultures. LC 93-3954. 1142p. (C). 1993. pap. 40.00 (0-07-044216-9) McGraw.
Muller, Gilbert H. & Williams, John A., intros. The McGraw-Hill Introduction to Literature. 2nd ed. LC 94-17019. 1200p. (C). 1994. pap. 39.38 (0-07-044246-0) McGraw.
Muller-Goldingen, Christian, ed. see Aristotle.
Muller-Gotama, Franz. Grammatical Relations: A Cross-Linguistic Perspective on Their Syntax & Semantics. LC 94-3344. (Empirical Approaches to Language Typology Ser.: Vol. 11). x, 171p. 1994. 75.40 (3-11-013737-2) Mouton.
Muller, Gottfried H., jt. auth. see Bootz, Friedrich.
Muller, Gunther. Woerterbuecher der Biologie, Mikrobiologie: Dictionary of Biology, Microbiology. (GER.). 25p. 1980. 35.00 (0-8288-1221-7, M15333) Fr & Eur.
Muller, H., et al, eds. Hereditary Cancer: Second International Research Conference on Familial Cancer, Approaches to Familial Cancer in the 21st Century, Basel, September, 1995. LC 96-30501. (Illus.). xii, 234p. 1996. 137.50 (3-8055-6329-9) S Karger.
Muller, H., jt. auth. see Gachter, R.
Muller, H. G. An Introduction to Tropical Food Science. (Illus.). 328p. 1988. pap. text 38.95 (0-521-33686-4) Cambridge U Pr.
— An Introduction to Tropical Food Science. (Illus.). 328p. 1989. text 110.00 (0-521-33488-8) Cambridge U Pr.
Muller, H. G. & Fedorov, M. V., eds. Super-Intense Laser-Atom Physics IV: Proceedings of the NATO Advanced Research Workshop on Super-Intense Laser-Atom Physics, Moscow, Russia, August 5-9, 1995. LC 96-14544. (NATO ASI Ser.: Vol. 13). 1996. text 313.00 (0-7923-4048-5) Kluwer Academic.
Muller, H. H. Fiscal Policies in a General Equilibrium Model with Persistent Unemployment. (Lecture Notes in Economics & Mathematical Systems Ser.: Vol. 216). 92p. 1983. 28.00 (0-387-12316-4) Spr-Verlag.
***Muller, H. J. & Dieng, R., eds.** Computational Conflicts: Conflict Modeling for Distributed Intelligent Systems. LC 00-28512. (Illus.). 200p. 2000. pap. 49.00 (3-540-66799-7) Spr-Verlag.
Muller, H. J., ed. see Seneca, Lucius Annaeus.
Muller, H. Nicholas, III. From Ferment to Fatigue? 1870-1900: A New Look at the Neglected Winter of Vermont. (Occasional Papers: No. 7). 28p. (Orig.). 1984. pap. text 5.00 (0-944277-12-8, M8) U VT Ctr Rsch VT.
Muller, H. Nicholas, III, jt. auth. see Duffy, John J.
Muller, Hanns. Pocket Dictionary of Horseman's Terms in English, German, French & Spanish. (FRE.). 1971. 9.95 (0-685-00343-4) Transatl Arts.
Muller, Hans. Diccionario Lexicon, Aleman-Espanol, Espanol-Aleman: German-Spanish, Spanish-German Dictionary Lexicon. (GER & SPA.). 384p. 1977. pap. 14.95 (0-8288-5350-9, S31392) Fr & Eur.
Muller, Hans A. Sheep. (Complete Pet Owner's Manual Ser.). (Illus.). 1989. pap. 6.95 (0-8120-4091-0) Barron.
Muller, Hans-Peter. Mythos-Kerygma-Wahrheit: Gesammelte Aufsatze Zum Alten Testament in Seiner Umwelt und Zur Biblischen Theologie. (Beiheft zur Zeitschrift fuer die Alttestamentliche Wissenschaft Ser.: Band 200). (GER.). xiv, 319p. (C). 1991. lib. bdg. 101.55 (3-11-012885-3) De Gruyter.
Muller, Hans-Reinhard, tr. see Hatano, Emi & Hoashi, Jitsuo.
***Muller, Hans W.** Gold of the Pharaohs. LC 99-34191. (Illus.). 256p. 1999. 60.00 (0-8014-3725-3) Cornell U Pr.
Muller, Hansjorg. Anwendungsmoglichkeiten Chaostheoretischer bei der Analyse Okonomischer Prozesse. (GER., Illus.). XII, 231p. 1996. 44.95 (3-631-30425-0) P Lang Pubng.
Muller, Harald, ed. A European Non-Proliferation Policy: Prospects & Problems. (Illus.). 438p. 1987. 84.00 (0-19-829702-5) OUP.
Muller, Hausi A., et al, eds. Computer Aided Software Engineering. LC 96-31757. 216p. (C). 1996. text 150.00 (0-7923-9773-8) Kluwer Academic.
Muller, Heindrun. Ubungen Zur Dt. Sprache Two: Ubungen Zum Wortschatz. (Schulerduden-Ubungsbucher Ser.). 295p. 1988. 16.95 (3-411-01363-X, Pub. by Bibliogr Inst Brockhaus) Langenscheidt.
Muller, Heiner. The Battle: Plays, Prose, Poems. 176p. 1990. pap. 14.95 (1-55554-049-X) PAJ Pubns.
— Explosion of a Memory: And Other Writings. Weber, Carl, ed. & tr. by. (Illus.). 1989. 28.00 (1-55554-040-6); pap. 14.95 (1-55554-041-4) PAJ Pubns.
— Hamletmachine & Other Texts for the Stage. Weber, Carl, tr. LC 83-61193. 140p. 1984. pap. 14.95 (0-933826-45-1) PAJ Pubns.
Muller, Heiner & Schmidt, Jochen. Pina Bausch: Photographs by Detlef Erler. (Illus.). 152p. 1995. 55.00 (3-905514-18-4) Dist Art Pubs.
Muller, Heinrich. Juggernaut. (Orig.). 1981. mass mkt. 2.75 (0-89083-854-2, Zebra Kensgtn) Kensgtn Pub Corp.
— Lovis Corinth: The Late Graphic Work, Die Spate Graphik. rev. ed. (ENG & GER., Illus.). 224p. 1994. 150.00 (1-55660-171-9) A Wofsy Fine Arts.
***Muller, Heinrich.** Muller Journals Vol. 1, 1948-1950: The Washington Years. Douglas, Gregory, ed. (Illus.). 272p. 1999. 35.95 (0-912138-79-3) Bender Pub CA.
Muller, Heinz. Langenscheidt Spanish-German, German-Spanish Pocket Dictionary: Langenscheidt Handwoerterbuch Spanisch-Deutsch-Spanisch. (GER & SPA.). 1400p. 1987. 110.00 (0-8288-0352-8, S39871) Fr & Eur.
Muller, Heinz & Haensch, Guenther. Langenscheidt Spanish-German Pocket Dictionary: Langenscheidt Handwoerterbuch Spanisch-Deutsch. (GER & SPA.). 656p. 1987. 69.95 (0-8288-0351-X, F19592) Fr & Eur.
Muller, Heinz Konrad & Nau, Bernard. Fluid Sealing Technology: Principles & Applications. LC 98-4223. (Mechanical Engineering Ser.). (Illus.). 504p. 1998. text 185.00 (0-8247-9969-0) Dekker.
Muller, Helen. Jet Jewellery & Ornaments. (Illus.). 32p. 1989. pap. 6.25 (0-85263-503-6, Pub. by Shire Pubns) Parkwest Pubns.
Muller, Helen D., jt. auth. see McGovern, Edythe M.
Muller, Henry F. & Taylor, Pauline. A Chrestomathy of Vulgar Latin: With a Detailed Glossary & Bibliography. xvii, 315p. 1990. reprint ed. 54.60 incl. 3.5 hd (3-487-09378-2) G Olms Pubs.
Muller, Herbert J. The Children of Frankenstein: A Primer of Modern Technology & Human Values. LC 76-103926. 447p. reprint ed. pap. 138.60 (0-608-30966-4, 201763300007) Bks Demand.
— Religion & Freedom in the Modern World. LC 63-20911. 1993. pap. text 1.50 (0-226-54815-5, P193) U Ch Pr.
— Science & Criticism: The Humanistic Tradition in Contemporary Thought. 303p. 1977. 20.95 (0-8369-2327-8) Ayer.
— Thomas Wolfe. 1976. 21.95 (0-8488-1435-5) Amereon Ltd.
Muller, Herbert W. Epicyclic Drive Trains: Analysis, Synthesis, & Applications. Glover, John H., ed. Mannhardt, Werner G., tr. LC 81-114220. (Illus.). 374p. 1982. 79.95 (0-8143-1663-8) Wayne St U Pr.
Muller, Hermann. The Fertilisation of Flowers. Egerton, Frank N., 3rd, ed. Thompson, D'Arey W., tr. LC 77-74241. (History of Ecology Ser.). (Illus.). 1978. reprint ed. lib. bdg. 57.95 (0-405-10410-3) Ayer.
Muller, Hermann Joseph & Carlson, Elof A., eds. Man's Future Birthright: Essays on Science & Humanity. LC 79-171215. 164p. (C). 1973. text 24.50 (0-87395-097-6) State U NY Pr.
Muller, Hermann Joseph, jt. ed. see Weissenborn, Wilhelm.
Muller-Hermelink, H. K., et al, eds. Risk & Progression Factors in Carcinogenesis. LC 96-12853. (Recent Results in Cancer Research Ser.: Vol. 143). 392p. 1996. 157.00 (3-540-60953-9) Spr-Verlag.
Muller-Hermelink, Hans K., jt. ed. see Marx, Alexander.
Muller, Herta. The Land of Green Plums. Hofmann, Michael, tr. from GER. LC 98-28184. 256p. 1998. pap. 16.95 (0-8101-1597-2, Hydra Bks) Northwestern U Pr.
— The Land of Green Plums: A Novel. Hofmann, Michael, tr. 256p. 1995. 23.00 (0-8050-4295-4) H Holt & Co.
— Nadirs. Lug, Sieglinde, tr. from GER. LC 98-48347. (European Women Writers Ser.). 134p. 1999. 40.00 (0-8032-3197-0) U of Nebr Pr.
***Muller, Herta.** Nadirs. Lug, Sieglinde, tr. from GER. LC 98-48347. (European Women Writers Ser.). 134p. 1999. pap. 13.00 (0-8032-8254-0, Bison Books) U of Nebr Pr.
Muller, Herta. The Passport. 96p. 1992. pap. 7.95 (1-85242-139-8) Serpents Tail.
— Traveling on One Leg. Glajar, Valentina & Lefevere, Andre, trs. from GER. LC 98-34200. 176p. 1998. 24.95 (0-8101-1641-3, Hydra Bks) Northwestern U Pr.
Muller-Hill, Benno. The Lac Operon: A Short History of a Genetic Paradigm. LC 96-20965. ix, 207p. (Orig.). (C). 1996. pap. text 29.95 (3-11-014830-7) De Gruyter.
Muller-Hillebrand, Burkhart. Germany & Its Allies in World War II. LC 79-67365. 285p. 1980. lib. bdg. 45.00 (0-313-27066-X, U7066, Greenwood Pr) Greenwood.
Muller-Holtz, Henner, jt. auth. see Arndt, Helmut.
Muller, Horst F. & Henschel, Bernhard, contrib. by. Werner Krauss Das Wissenschaftliche Werk: Band 8: Sprachwissenschaft und Wortgeschichte. 658p. 1997. 116.00 (3-11-015136-7) De Gruyter.
Muller, Horst F., jt. contrib. by see Jehle, Peter.
Muller, Horst M. Sprache und Evolution: Grundlagen der Evolution und Ansatze einer Evolutionstheoretischen Sprachwissenschaft. (Grundlagen der Kommunikation & Kognition (Foundations of Communication & Cognition) Ser.). (Illus.). x, 137p. (C). 1990. lib. bdg. 98.50 (3-11-011041-5) De Gruyter.
***Muller, Humphrey.** Continental Drift: A Novel. 452p. 2000. pap. 21.95 (0-595-09543-7, Writers Club Pr) iUniversecom.
Muller-Idzerda, A. C. One Hundred Indoor Plants. (Illus.). 1959. 10.95 (0-87523-114-4) Emerson.
Muller, Ingo. Hitler's Justice: The Courts of the Third Reich. Schneider, Deborah L., tr. LC 90-39068. 368p. 1991. 41.50 (0-674-40418-1, MULHIT) HUP.
— Hitler's Justice: The Courts of the Third Reich. Schneider, Deborah L., tr. from GER. 368p. 1992. pap. 23.95 (0-674-40419-X) HUP.
Muller, Ingo & Ruggeri, Tommaso. Extended Thermodynamics. LC 92-26754. (Tracts in Natural Philosophy Ser.: Vol. 37). 230p. 1993. 75.95 (0-387-97922-0); write for info. (3-540-97922-0) Spr-Verlag.
Muller, Irmgard, ed. see Joas, Gunter.
Muller, Irmgard, ed. see Wiegand, Jens.
Muller, Isabelle. Lonely Planet Guadeloupe et ses Iles. (FRE.). 1997. 18.95 (2-84070-068-9) Lonely Planet.
Muller, J. Elementary Functions. 220p. 1997. write for info. (3-7643-3990-X) Birkhauser.
Muller, J. Mississippian Political Economy. LC 97-16721. (Interdisciplinary Contributions to Archaeology Ser.). (Illus.). 472p. (C). 1997. 95.00 (0-306-45529-3, Plenum Trade) Perseus Pubng.
Muller, J. Regulation of Aldostorone Biosynthesis. 2nd rev. ed. (Monographs on Endocrinology: Vol. 29). (Illus.). 300p. 1987. 158.00 (0-387-17907-0) Spr-Verlag.
Muller, J. C. Advances in Cartography. (International Cartographic Association Ser.). 252p. 1991. 129.25 (1-85166-603-6, Pergamon Pr) Elsevier.
Muller, J. M. Elementary Functions: Algorithms & Implementation. LC 97-20183. 285p. 1997. 59.95 (0-8176-3990-X) Birkhauser.
Muller, J. P. The Design of Intelligent Agents: A Layered Approach. LC 96-49596. (Lecture Notes in Artificial Intelligence Ser.: Vol. 1177). 227p. 1997. text 34.95 (3-540-62003-6) Spr-Verlag.
Muller, J. P. & Perram, John W., eds. Distributed Software Agents & Applications: 6th European Workshop on Modelling Autonomous Agents in a Multi-Agent World, MAAMAW'94, Odense,Denmark, August 3-5, 1994: Proceedings. LC 96-16990. (Lecture Notes in Computer Science Ser.: Vol. 1069). 219p. 1996. pap. 43.00 (3-540-61157-6) Spr-Verlag.
Muller, J. R., jt. ed. see Baker, John R.
Muller, J. W., tr. see Senefelder, Alois.
Muller, James A., ed. see Gardiner, Stephen.
Muller, James E., jt. ed. see Willich, Stefan N.
Muller, James W. The Revival of Constitutionalism. LC 87-30177. 276p. 1988. reprint ed. pap. 85.60 (0-7837-8908-4, 204961900001) Bks Demand.
Muller, James W., ed. Churchill As Peacemaker. LC 97-3851. (Woodrow Wilson Center Press Ser.). 358p. (C). 1997. text 64.95 (0-521-58314-4) Cambridge U Pr.
Muller, James W., ed. Churchill's "Iron Curtain" Speech Fifty Years Later. LC 99-35267. (Illus.). 200p. 1999. 27.50 (0-8262-1247-6) U of Mo Pr.
***Muller, Jan-Werner.** Another Country: German Intellectuals, Unification & National Identity. 256p. 2000. 27.50 (0-300-08388-2) Yale U Pr.
Muller, Jean. Dictionnaire Abrege des Imprimateurs Editeurs Francais du 16 Siecle. (FRE.). 150p. 1970. pap. 125.00 (0-7859-8525-5, 3873200309) Fr & Eur.
— Dictionnaire Abrege des Imprimateurs Editeurs Francais du 16 Siecle. 16th ed. 1970. write for info. (0-7859-8670-7, 3873200309) Fr & Eur.
Muller, Jean-Claude, et al, eds. GIS & Generalisation: Methodology & Practice. (GISDATA Ser.: No. 1). 224p. 1995. 85.00 (0-7484-0318-3, Pub. by Tay Francis Ltd); pap. 34.95 (0-7484-0319-1, Pub. by Tay Francis Ltd) Taylor & Francis.
Muller, Jenny. Income Distribution in the Agricultural Sector of Thailand. Heidhues, Franz, ed. (Development Economics & Policy Ser.: Vol. 8). (Illus.). 289p. 1996. pap. 54.95 (3-631-30920-1) P Lang Pubng.
— Income Distribution in the Agricultural Sector of Thailand: Empirical Analysis & Policy Options. Heidhues, Franz, ed. (Development Economics & Policy Ser.: Vol. 8). (Illus.). 289p. 1996. pap. 54.95 (0-8204-3234-2) P Lang Pubng.
Muller-Jerina, Alwin. Handbuch der Historischen Buchbestande in Deutschland Band 2.1: Niedersachsen A-G. Raabe, Paul, ed. (GER.). 276p. 1998. write for info. (3-487-09575-0) G Olms Pubs.
Muller, Jerry Z. Adam Smith in His Time & Ours: Designing the Decent Society. 180p. 1992. 27.95 (0-02-922234-6) Free Pr.
— Adam Smith in His Time & Ours: Designing the Decent Society. LC 95-13210. 263p. 1995. pap. text 15.95 (0-691-00161-8, Pub. by Princeton U Pr) Cal Prin Full Svc.
— Conservatism: An Anthology of Social & Political Thought from David Hume to the Present. LC 96-45563. 464p. 1997. text 59.50 (0-691-03712-4, Pub. by Princeton U Pr); pap. text 19.95 (0-691-03711-6, Pub. by Princeton U Pr) Cal Prin Full Svc.
— The Other God that Failed: Hans Freyer & the Deradicalization of German Conservatism. LC 87-18781. 465p. 1987. reprint ed. pap. 144.20 (0-608-02577-1, 206322300004) Bks Demand.
Muller, Jim. The Great Logo Adventure. (Illus.). 350p. 1998. pap. text 24.95 (0-9651934-6-2) Doone Publns.
Muller, Joan. Under the Cloak of Justice: The Work of Ned Cartledge. High, Steven, ed. (Illus.). 24p. 1994. 9.00 (0-935519-19-X) Anderson Gal.
Muller, Joanne, jt. auth. see Bailey, Susan P.
Muller, Jochen. Inwieweit Wird die Pressefreiheit in Indien Durch die Anwendung Von Contempt of Parliament Eingeschrankt? (Europaische Hochschulschriften Ser.: Reihe 2, Band 2378). (GER.). 193p. 1998. pap. 39.95 (3-631-32917-2) P Lang Pubng.
Muller, Johann G. Des Flavius Josephus Schrift Gegen Den Apion. 394p. 1969. reprint ed. write for info. (0-318-70978-3) G Olms Pubs.
Muller, Johannes. The Chambered Cairns of the Northern & Western Isles. 92p. 1988. pap. 14.00 (0-614-21833-0) David Brown.
— Die Wissenschaftlichen Vereine und Gesellschaften Deutschlands Im 19 Jahrhundert, 3 vols., Set. 1965. reprint ed. write for info. (0-318-71848-0) G Olms Pubs.
Muller, Johannes R. Regiomontanus: On Triangles - De Triangulis Omnimodis. Hughes, Barnabas, tr. & intro. by. LC 66-22861. (ENG & LAT.). 308p. 1967. reprint ed. pap. 95.50 (0-608-01882-1, 206253400003) Bks Demand.
Muller, John P. Beyond the Psychoanalytic Dyad: Developmental Semiotics in Freud, Peirce, & Lacan. LC 95-14600. 256p. (C). 1995. pap. 20.99 (0-415-91069-2) Routledge.
— Beyond the Psychoanalytic Dyad: Developmental Semiotics in Freud, Peirce, & Lacan. LC 95-14600. 256p. (C). 1995. 70.00 (0-415-91068-4) Routledge.
***Muller, John P. & Brent, Joseph.** Peirce, Semiotics & Psychoanalysis LC 99-41190. (Psychiatry & the Humanities Ser.). 2000. 38.00 (0-8018-6288-4) Johns Hopkins.
Muller, John P. & Richardson, William J. Lacan & Language: A Reader's Guide to "Ecrits" 443p. 1994. pap. 29.95 (0-8236-8129-7) Intl Univs Pr.
Muller, John P. & Richardson, William J., eds. The Purloined Poe: Lacan, Derrida, & Psychoanalytic Reading. LC 87-2760. 424p. 1988. pap. text 17.95 (0-8018-3293-4) Johns Hopkins.
Muller, Jon. Archaeology of the Lower Ohio River Valley. LC 85-15050. (New World Archaeological Record Ser.). 1986. pap. text 69.95 (0-12-510331-X) Acad Pr.
Muller, Jon. Mississippian Political Economy. LC 97-16721. (Interdisciplinary Contributions to Archaeology Ser.). (Illus.). 472p. (C). 1997. pap. 47.00 (0-306-45675-3, Plenum Trade) Perseus Pubng.
Muller, Jorge. Se Puede Confiar en Dios? large type ed.Tr. of God Can Be Trusted. (SPA.). 37p. 1989. pap. 2.99 (1-56063-341-7, 494026) Editorial Unilit.
Muller, Josef. Josef Muller-Brockmann Designer: A Pioneer of the International Style in Graphic Design. (Illus.). 264p. 1996. 50.00 (1-56898-063-9); pap. 35.00 (1-56898-062-0) Princeton Arch.
Muller, Joseph. The Star-Spangled Banner: Words & Music Issued Between 1814-1864. LC 79-169653. (Music Ser.). (Illus.). 1973. reprint ed. lib. bdg. 35.00 (0-306-70263-0) Da Capo.
***Muller, Judy.** Now This: Radio, Television... And the Real World. LC 99-87257. 256p. 2000. 23.95 (0-399-14619-9) Putnam Pub Group.
Muller, Julia. Words & Music in Henry Purcell's First Semi-Opera, Dioclesian: An Approach to Early Music Through Early Theatre. LC 90-5676. (Studies in History & Interpretation of Music: Vol. 28). 520p. 1990. lib. bdg. 119.95 (0-88946-495-2) E Mellen.
Muller, Jurgen, et al, eds. Mobile Telecommunications: Emerging European Markets. LC 94-37148. 323p. 1994. 83.00 (0-89006-796-1) Artech Hse.
Muller, Jurgen, jt. ed. see Foreman-Peck, James.
Muller, K., ed. Coastal Research in the Gulf of Bothnia. (Monographiae Biologicae: No. 45). 480p. 1982. text 282.00 (90-6193-098-7) Kluwer Academic.
***Muller, K., et al, eds.** Transformation of Social Security: Pensions in Central-Eastern Europe. LC 99-41025. (Contributions to Economics Ser.). x, 305p. 1999. pap. 75.00 (3-7908-1210-2) Spr-Verlag.
Muller, K. A. & Thomas, H., eds. Structural Phase Transitions 2. (Topics in Current Physics Ser.: Vol. 45). (Illus.). 192p. 1991. 49.95 (0-387-52238-7) Spr-Verlag.
Muller, K. A., jt. auth. see Sigmund, E.
Muller, K. A., jt. ed. see Bednorz, J. G.
Muller, K A., ed. see Sigmund, E.
Muller, K. H., jt. ed. see Hierholzer, G.
Muller, K. R., et al, eds. Chemical Waste. (Illus.). 370p. 1985. 257.95 (0-387-13246-5) Spr-Verlag.
Muller, Kal. Bali. 1991. pap. 15.95 (0-8442-9900-6, Passprt Bks) NTC Contemp Pub Co.
— Borneo: Journey into the Tropical Rain Forest. (Regional Guides of Indonesia Ser.). (Illus.). 204p. 1994. pap. 14.95 (0-8442-9904-9, Passprt Bks) NTC Contemp Pub Co.
— East of Bali: From Lombok to Timor. (Regional Guides of Indonesia Ser.). 1994. pap. 15.95 (0-8442-9905-7, Passprt Bks) NTC Contemp Pub Co.
— East of Bali: From Lombok to Timor. (Regional Guides of Indonesia Ser.). (Illus.). 322p. 1995. pap. 17.95 (0-8442-9949-9, 99499, Passprt Bks) NTC Contemp Pub Co.
— Indonesia in Color. (Illus.). 80p. 1992. pap. 9.95 (0-945971-26-5) Periplus.

M

An Asterisk (*) at the beginning of an entry indicates that the title is appearing for the first time.

— Indonesia in Colour. (Illus.). 1993. pap. 9.95 (*0-945971-97-4*); pap. 9.95 (*0-945971-93-1*); pap. text 9.95 (*0-945971-95-8*) Periplus.
— Indonesian New Guinea: Irian Jaya. 2nd ed. Pickell, David, ed. (Indonesia Travel Guides Ser.). (Illus.). 208p. 1994. pap. 19.95 (*0-945971-06-0*) Periplus.
— Indonesie. (Oog op de Wereld Ser.). (DUT., Illus.). 1990. pap. text 9.95 (*0-945971-27-3*) Periplus.
— Irian Jaya: Nieuw-Guinea. Oey, Eric, ed. Wassing, Rene & Wassing, Rita, trs. from ENG. (Indonesie Reisbibliotheek Ser.). (DUT.). 175p. 1991. 19.95 (*0-945971-19-2*) Periplus.
— Kalimantan: Borneo. Pickell, David, ed. Keers, Francien et al, trs. from ENG. (Indonesie Reisbibliotheek Ser.). (DUT.). 206p. 1991. pap. 19.95 (*0-945971-37-0*) Periplus.
— Kalimantan: Indonesian Borneo. Pickell, David, ed. 203p. 1995. pap. 19.95 (*962-593-045-0*) Periplus.
— Maluku: De Molukken. Pickell, David, ed. Pattiruhu, Maureen, tr. from ENG. (Indonesie Reisbibliotheek Ser.). (DUT.). 175p. 1991. pap. 19.95 (*0-945971-18-4*) Periplus.
— New Guinea. 2nd ed. LC 76-18466. (Regional Guides of Indonesia Ser.). (Illus.). 288p. 1994. pap. 15.95 (*0-8442-9898-0*, Passprt Bks) NTC Contemp Pub Co.
— New Guinea: Journey into the Stone Age. 3rd rev. ed. (Passport's Regional Guides of Indonesia Ser.). (Illus.). 208p. 1996. pap. 19.95 (*0-8442-8997-3*, 89973, Passprt Bks) NTC Contemp Pub Co.
— Spice Islands. 2nd ed. (Regional Guides of Indonesia Ser.). (Illus.). 288p. 1994. pap. 15.95 (*0-8442-9899-9*, Passprt Bks) NTC Contemp Pub Co.
— Spice Islands: Exotic Eastern Indonesia. 1992. pap. 12.95 (*0-8442-9902-2*, Passprt Bks) NTC Contemp Pub Co.
— Spice Islands: Exotic Eastern Indonesia. 3rd ed. (Passport's Regional Guides of Indonesia Ser.). (Illus.). 244p. 1997. pap. 19.95 (*0-8442-9909-X*, 9909X, Passprt Bks) NTC Contemp Pub Co.
— Spice Islands: The Moluccas. Pickell, David, ed. (Indonesia Travel Guides Ser.). (Illus.). 200p. 1993. pap. 19.95 (*0-945971-07-9*) Periplus.
— Underwater Indonesia: A Guide to the World's Greatest Diving. 2nd ed. Pickell, David, ed. 326p. 1995. pap. 19.95 (*962-593-029-9*) Periplus.
Muller, Kal, ed. Irian Jaya. 176p. 1991. pap. 37.50 (*0-945971-34-6*) Periplus.
— Maluku. 176p. 1991. pap. 37.50 (*0-945971-33-8*) Periplus.
— Nusa Tenggara. 296p. 1991. pap. 37.50 (*0-945971-36-2*) Periplus.
Muller, Karen, ed. Authority Control Symposium. (Occasional Papers: No. 6). (Illus.). 144p. (Orig.). 1987. pap. 20.00 (*0-942740-05-X*) Art Libs Soc.
***Muller, Karin.** Along the Inca Road: A Woman's Journey into an Ancient Empire. (Illus.). 304p. 2000. 26.00 (*0-7922-7685-X*) Natl Geog.
Muller, Karin. Hitchhiking Vietnam. LC 97-47233. (Illus.). 288p. 1998. 24.95 (*0-7627-0257-5*); pap. 14.95 (*0-7627-0243-5*) Globe Pequot.
Muller, Karl, et al, eds. Dictionary of Mission: Theology, History, Perspectives. rev. ed. Mansfield, Francis et al, trs. from GER. LC 97-23162. (American Society of Missiology Ser.: No. 24).Tr. of Lexikon der Missionstheologischer Grundergriffe. 544p. 1997. 50.00 (*1-57075-148-X*) Orbis Bks.
Muller, Karl O. Die Dorier, 2 vols., Set. (Geschichten Hellenischer Stamme und Stadte Ser.: Bd. II und III). xxiii, 1110p. 1989. reprint ed. write for info. (*3-487-09261-1*) G Olms Pubs.
— Introduction to a Scientific System of Mythology. Bolle, Kees W., ed. LC 77-79144. (Mythology Ser.). 1978. reprint ed. lib. bdg. 33.95 (*0-405-10553-3*) Ayer.
— Kleine Deutscshe Schriften Uber Religion, Kunst, Sprache und Literatur, Leben und Geschichte Des Alterthums, 2 vols., Set. Muller, Eduard, ed. xlix, 1321p. 1979. reprint ed. write for info. (*3-487-06757-9*) G Olms Pubs.
Muller-Karpe, H. Historia de la Edad de Piedra. (SPA.). 414p. 1993. 100.00 (*84-249-0332-3*) Elliots Bks.
Muller, Karsten. Secrets of Pawn Endings. 1999. pap. text 24.95 (*1-85744-255-5*) Cadgn Bks.
***Muller, Katharina.** The Political Economy of Pension Reform in Central-Eastern Europe. LC 99-44830. (Studies in Comparative Economic Systems). 240p. 2000. 80.00 (*1-84064-238-6*) E Elgar.
Muller, Kathleen, jt. auth. see Douglas, Jack.
Muller, Kathleen, ed. see Loomis, Patricia.
Muller, Kathleen, ed. see Peyton, Wes.
Muller, Kathleen, ed. see Rambo, Ralph.
Muller, Kathleen, ed. see Yu, Connie Y.
Muller, Kathryn, jt. auth. see Park, Jane.
Muller, Kenneth J., et al, eds. Neurobiology of the Leech. LC 81-68893. (Illus.). 330p. 1981. reprint ed. pap. 102.30 (*0-608-04088-6*, 206482000011) Bks Demand.
***Muller, Kerstin Andrea.** Produktverantwortung und Ihre Durchsetzung: Eine Kartellrechtliche Beurteilung von Selbstverpflichtungen Im Umweltrecht Aus Deutscher und Europaischer Sicht Unter Besonderer Berucksichtigung der Altautoentsorgung. (Frankfurter Wirtschaftsrechtliche Studien. : Bd. 31). 324p. 1999. 52.95 (*3-631-35399-5*) P Lang Pubng.
Muller-Kirsten, H. & Wiedemann, A., eds. Supersymmetry: An Introduction with Conceptual & Calculational Details. (Lecture Notes in Physics Ser.: Vol. 7). 608p. 1987. text 104.00 (*9971-5-0354-9*); pap. text 51.00 (*9971-5-0355-7*) World Scientific Pub.
Muller, Klaus. Wenn Ich "Ich" Sage: Studien zur Fundamentaltheologischen Relevanz Selbstbewubter Subjektivitat. (Regensburger Studien Zur Theologie Ser.: Bd. 46). (GER.). 671p. 1994. 87.95 (*3-631-47635-3*) P Lang Pubng.
Muller, Klaus-Jurgen, et al, eds. The Military in Politics & Society in France & Germany in the Twentieth Century. LC 94-46596. (German Historical Perspectives Ser.: Vol. 9). 176p. 1995. 37.50 (*0-85496-812-1*) Berg Pubs.
Muller, Klaus-Robert & Orr, Genevieve B., eds. How to Make Neural Networks Work: Tips & Tricks of the Trade. LC 98-49183. (Lecture Notes in Computer Science Ser.). 1999. pap. text 67.00 (*3-540-65311-2*) Spr-Verlag.
Muller, Kurt E. Language Competence: Implications for National Security, 119. LC 85-31240. (Washington Papers: No. 119). 181p. 1986. 55.00 (*0-275-92213-8*, C2213, Praeger Pubs); pap. 13.95 (*0-275-92214-6*, B2214, Praeger Pubs) Greenwood.
— Language Status in the Post-Cold-War Era. Tonkin, Humphrey, ed. LC 96-10297. (Papers of the Center for Research & Documentation on World Language Problems: Vol. 4). 166p. 1996. lib. bdg. 34.50 (*0-7618-0299-1*) U Pr of Amer.
Muller, Kurt E., ed. Languages As Barrier & Bridge. (Papers of the Center for Research & Documentation on World Language Problems). 140p. (Orig.). (C). 1992. lib. bdg. 45.00 (*0-8191-8670-8*) U Pr of Amer.
— Languages in Elementary Schools. 232p. 1989. pap. 10.00 (*0-944675-41-7*) Amer Forum.
Muller, Kurt E., jt. auth. see Benya, Rosemarie.
Muller, Lars. Constructions: Design Integral, Ruedi Baur & Associates. LC 99-202684. 1998. pap. text 35.00 (*3-907044-74-6*, Pub. by Lars Muller) Dist Art Pubs.
Muller, Lars, ed. ECM Sleeves of Desire: A Cover Story, ECM-Edition of Contemporary Music. (GER & ENG.). 320p. 1996. pap. 35.00 (*1-56898-064-7*) Princeton Arch.
***Muller, Lars, ed.** Helvetica: Homage to a Typeface. (Illus.). 160p. 2000. 30.00 (*3-907044-87-8*, Pub. by Lars Muller) Princeton Arch.
Muller, Lars, jt. ed. see Binet, Helene.
Muller, Lars, jt. ed. see Blaser, Werner.
Muller, Lars, ed. see Perrault, Dominique.
Muller, Lauren, ed. June Jordan's Poetry for the People: A Revolutionary Blueprint. LC 95-8470. (Illus.). 240p. (C). (gr. 13). 1995. pap. 18.99 (*0-415-91168-0*) Routledge.
Muller, Lauren & Blueprint Collective Staff, eds. June Jordan's Poetry for the People: A Revolutionary Blueprint. LC 95-8470. (Illus.). 240p. (C). 1995. 75.00 (*0-415-91167-2*) Routledge.
Muller-Lauter, Wolfgang. Nietzsche: His Philosophy of Contradictions & the Contradictions of His Philosophy. LC 98-25391. (International Nietzsche Studies). 296p. 1999. 39.95 (*0-252-02452-4*); pap. 21.95 (*0-252-06758-4*) U of Ill Pr.
— Nietzsche Als Herausforderung: Nietzsche-Interpretationen II. 312p. 1998. 99.00 (*3-11-013452-7*) De Gruyter.
— Uber Werden und Willen Zur Macht: Nietzche-Interpretationen I. 272p. 1998. 86.00 (*3-11-013451-9*) De Gruyter.
***Muller, Lawrence G. & Freeman, Laurence.** Wisdom Roads: Conversations with Remarkable Meditation Masters. LC 99-57184. 192p. 2000. pap. 19.95 (*0-8264-1234-3*) Continuum.
Muller, Leonard, tr. see Cohen, Marcel.
***Muller, Leos.** The Merchant Houses of Stockholm C. 1640-1800: A Comparative Study of Early-Modern Entrepreneurial Behaviour. LC 98-171209. (Studia Historica Upsaliensia Ser.: Vol. 188). (Illus.). 304p. 1998. pap. 62.50 (*91-554-4233-1*, Pub. by Almqvist Wiksell) Coronet Bks.
Muller, Liguori G., tr. see Augustinius, Aurelius.
Muller, Lillian. Feel Great, Be Beautiful over Forty: Inside Tips on How to Look Better, Be Healthier & Slow the Aging Process. abr. ed. 1996. 16.95 incl. audio (*1-882071-67-0*) B&B Audio.
Muller, Linda L. & Hamer, Jan. One, Two - Cycloaddition Reactions: The Formation of Three- & Four-Membered Heterocycles. LC 67-20265. 372p. reprint ed. pap. 115.40 (*0-7837-3459-X*, 205778500008) Bks Demand.
Muller-Lutz. Insurance Dictionary. (ENG, FRE, GER & SPA.). 304p. 1990. pap. 50.00 (*3-88487-210-9*, Pub. by V Versich) IBD Ltd.
Muller-Lutz, H. L. Insurance Dictionary. 3rd ed. (ENG, FRE, GER & SPA.). 281p. 1981. pap. 39.95 (*0-8288-0969-0*, M 7807) Fr & Eur.
Muller-Lux, William & Roltgen, Ingrid. Muller-Lux Drawings, 1958-1963. (Illus.). 184p. 1988. 65.00 (*0-9621943-0-1*) Sunrise AZ.
Muller, M. Consistent Classical Supergravity Theories. (Lecture Notes in Physics Ser.: Vol. 336). vi, 125p. 1989. 34.95 (*0-387-51427-9*, 3358) Spr-Verlag.
Muller, M., et al. Moment Mal!, Lehrbuch 1. (GER., Illus.). 128p. (C). 1996. pap. text 19.95 (*3-468-47751-1*) Langenscheidt.
— Moment Mal!, Level 1. (ENG, FRE & GER., Illus.). 128p. (C). 1996. pap. text 21.95 (*3-468-96940-6*); pap. text, wbk. ed. 18.95 (*3-468-96942-2*); pap. text, wbk. ed. 39.95 incl. audio compact disk (*3-468-96943-0*) Langenscheidt.
— Moment Mal!, Level 2. (ENG, FRE & GER., Illus.). 128p. (C). 1997. pap. text 21.95 (*3-468-96950-3*); pap. text, wbk. ed. 39.95 incl. audio compact disk (*3-468-96953-8*) Langenscheidt.
Muller, M., ed. see Scherer, W.
Muller, M., jt. ed. see Weissenborn.
Muller, M. E., et al, eds. Manual of Internal Fixation. 3rd rev. ed. (Illus.). 750p. 1995. 249.00 (*0-387-52523-8*) Spr-Verlag.
Muller, M. E. & Ganz, R., eds. Total Hip Prostheses. 1976. 263.00 (*0-387-92103-6*) Spr-Verlag.
Muller, M. E., et al. The Comprehensive Classification of Fractures of Long Bones. (Illus.). 220p. 1994. 89.00 (*0-387-18165-2*) Spr-Verlag.
Muller, M. J., et al, eds. Hormones & Nutrition in Obesity & Cachexia. (Illus.). 160p. 1990. 47.95 (*0-387-51637-9*) Spr-Verlag.
***Muller, M. W., et al, eds.** New Development in Approximation Theory: 2nd International Dortmund Meeting (IDoMAT) '98, February 23-27, 1998. LC 99-34585. (International Series of Numerical Mathematics: vol. 132). 240p. 1999. 119.00 (*3-7643-6143-3*, Pub. by Birkhauser) Spr-Verlag.
Muller, Manfred J. Selected Climatic Data for a Global Set of Standard Stations for Vegetation Science. 1982. text 282.00 (*90-6193-945-3*) Kluwer Academic.
Muller, Manuel Ruiz, jt. ed. see Bass, Susan Perkoff.
Muller, Marcel. Prefiguration et Structure Romanesque dans A la Recherche du Temps Perdu. LC 78-73096. (French Forum Monographs: No. 14). (Illus.). 95p. (Orig.). 1979. pap. 9.95 (*0-917058-13-5*) French Forum.
Muller, Marcel N., ed. Rhetorique. (Michigan Romance Studies: Vol. 13). 158p. 1993. pap. 15.00 (*0-939730-12-X*) Mich Romance.
Muller, Marcia. Ask the Cards a Question. 209p. 1990. reprint ed. mass mkt. 6.99 (*0-445-40849-9*, Pub. by Warner Bks) Little.
— Both Ends of the Night. 384p. 1998. mass mkt. 6.99 (*0-446-60550-6*, Pub. by Warner Bks) Little.
— Both Ends of the Night. large type ed. LC 97-21391. (Wheeler Large Print Book Ser.). 1997. pap. 23.95 (*1-56895-463-8*) Wheeler Pub.
— The Broken Promise Land: A Sharon McCone Mystery. 384p. 1997. mass mkt. 6.50 (*0-446-60410-0*, Pub. by Warner Bks) Little.
— The Cavalier in White. 1993. per. 3.99 (*0-373-83304-0*, 1-83304-5) Harlequin Bks.
— The Cheshire Cat's Eye. 207p. 1990. reprint ed. mass mkt. 6.99 (*0-445-40850-2*, Pub. by Warner Bks) Little.
— Dark Star. 1993. per. 3.99 (*0-373-83308-3*, 1-83308-6) Harlequin Bks.
— Edwin of the Iron Shoes. 224p. 1990. reprint ed. mass mkt. 5.99 (*0-445-40902-9*, Pub. by Warner Bks) Little.
— Eye of the Storm. 244p. 1989. mass mkt. 5.99 (*0-445-40625-9*, Pub. by Warner Bks) Little.
— Games to Keep the Dark Away. 215p. 1990. reprint ed. mass mkt. 5.99 (*0-445-40851-0*, Pub. by Warner Bks) Little.
— Games to Keep the Dark Away: A Sharon McCone Mystery. 160p. 1984. 10.95 (*0-312-31620-8*) St Martin.
— Leave a Message for Willie. 214p. 1990. mass mkt. 6.50 (*0-445-40900-2*, Pub. by Warner Bks) Little.
— The Legend of the Slain Soldiers. 192p. 1996. mass mkt. 5.99 (*0-446-40421-7*, Pub. by Warner Bks) Little.
Muller, Marcia. Lighthouse. pap. 4.50 (*0-7867-0885-9*) Carroll & Graf.
— Listen to the Silence. LC 99-87734. 304p. 2000. 24.95 (*0-89296-689-0*, Pub. by Mysterious Pr) Little.
— Listen to the Silence. large type ed. LC 00-39871. 2000. write for info. (*1-56895-908-7*) Wheeler Pub.
— McCone & Friends. 202p. 2000. pap. 16.00 (*1-885941-38-2*) Crippen & Landru.
— McCone & Friends. limited ed. 202p. 2000. 40.00 (*1-885941-37-4*) Crippen & Landru.
Muller, Marcia. The McCone Files. 248p. 1995. pap. 15.00 (*1-885941-05-6*) Crippen & Landru.
— Pennies on a Dead Woman's Eyes. 304p. 1992. 18.95 (*0-89296-454-5*) Mysterious Pr.
— Pennies on a Dead Woman's Eyes. 336p. 1993. mass mkt. 5.99 (*0-446-40033-5*, Pub. by Warner Bks) Little.
— The Shape of Dread. 288p. 1990. reprint ed. mass mkt. 5.99 (*0-445-40916-9*, Pub. by Warner Bks) Little.
— There Hangs the Knife. 1993. per. 3.99 (*0-373-83307-5*, 1-83307-8) Harlequin Bks.
— There's Nothing to Be Afraid Of. 218p. 1990. mass mkt. 6.99 (*0-445-40901-0*, Pub. by Warner Bks) Little.
— There's Something in a Sunday. 210p. 1990. mass mkt. 6.99 (*0-445-40865-0*, Pub. by Warner Bks) Little.
— Till the Butchers Cut Him Down. 1995. pap. write for info. (*0-446-40034-3*, Mysterious Paperbk) Warner Bks.
— Till the Butchers Cut Him Down. 336p. 1995. reprint ed. mass mkt. 5.99 (*0-446-60302-3*, Pub. by Warner Bks) Little.
— Trophies & Dead Things. 272p. 1991. reprint ed. mass mkt. 5.99 (*0-446-40039-4*, Pub. by Warner Bks) Little.
— A Walk Through the Fire. LC PS3563.U397W3 1999. 304p. 1999. 23.00 (*0-89296-688-2*, Pub. by Mysterious Pr) Little.
— A Walk Through the Fire. LC 99-26442. 1999. 27.95 (*0-7862-2001-5*) Thorndike Pr.
***Muller, Marcia.** A Walk Through the Fire. 2000. mass mkt. 6.99 (*0-446-60816-5*) Warner Bks.
Muller, Marcia. Where Echoes Live. 368p. 1992. mass mkt. 5.99 (*0-446-40161-7*, Pub. by Warner Bks) Little.
— While Other People Sleep. LC 98-13394. (Sharon McCone Mysteries Ser.). 344p. 1998. 22.50 (*0-89296-650-5*, Pub. by Mysterious Pr) Little.
— While Other People Sleep. 1999. mass mkt. 6.99 (*0-446-60721-5*, Pub. by Warner Bks) Little.
— While Other People Sleep. large type ed. LC 98-34900. 442p. 1999. 30.00 (*0-7862-1615-8*, G K Hall Lrg Type) Mac Lib Ref.
— A Wild & Lonely Place: A Sharon McCone Mystery. 336p. 1996. reprint ed. mass mkt. 6.50 (*0-446-60328-7*, Pub. by Warner Bks) Little.
— Wolf in the Shadows. 368p. 1993. 18.95 (*0-89296-525-8*) Mysterious Pr.
— Wolf in the Shadows. large type ed. LC 93-37404. (Cloak & Dagger Ser.). 548p. 1993. lib. bdg. 21.95 (*0-7862-0087-1*) Thorndike Pr.
— Wolf in the Shadows. 384p. 1994. reprint ed. mass mkt. 5.50 (*0-446-40383-0*, Pub. by Warner Bks) Little.
Muller, Marcia & Pronzini, Bill. Beyond the Grave. 240p. 1999. mass mkt. 5.95 (*0-7867-0650-3*) Carroll & Graf.
— Detective Duos. 448p. 1999. pap. 18.95 (*0-19-512910-5*) OUP.
— Double. 288p. 1995. mass mkt. 5.50 (*0-446-40413-6*, Pub. by Warner Bks) Little.
— The Lighthouse. (Mystery Scene Bk.). 304p. 1992. mass mkt. 4.50 (*0-88184-885-9*) Carroll & Graf.
Muller, Marcia & Pronzini, Bill, eds. Detective Duos. LC 97-10562. 448p. 1997. 30.00 (*0-19-510214-2*) OUP.
Muller, Marcia & Pronzinni, Bill. Duo. LC 98-42591. 220p. 1998. 21.95 (*0-7862-1657-3*) Five Star.
Muller, Marcia, ed. see Greenberg, Martin H.
Muller, Marianne. Grosse Lexikon der Gastronomie. 2nd ed. (GER.). 680p. 1991. 135.00 (*0-7859-8558-1*, 3925673393) Fr & Eur.
— A Part of My Life: Photographs. (Illus.). 128p. 1998. 39.95 (*3-931141-29-2*, 810201, Pub. by Scalo Pubs) Dist Art Pubs.
Muller, Marianne, et al. Great Napkin Folding & Table Decorations. LC 90-36204. (Illus.). 96p. (Orig.). 1990. pap. 12.95 (*0-8069-7384-6*) Sterling.
***Muller, Mark.** Prairie in Your Pocket: A Guide to Plants of the Tallgrass Prairie. (Illus.). 2000. pap. 8.95 (*0-87745-683-6*) U of Iowa Pr.
Muller, Mark, jt. auth. see Christiansen, Paul.
Muller-Markus, S. Protophysik: Entwurf einer Philosophie des Schopferischen. 1. Teil: Spezielle Relativitatstheorie. 438p. 1971. text 211.50 (*90-247-5106-3*) Kluwer Academic.
Muller, Mary. Encounter at Dawn. large type ed. 512p. 1983. 27.99 (*0-7089-1030-0*) Ulverscroft.
Muller, Mary B. & Neeld, Elizabeth H. Sister Bernadette: Cowboy Nun from Texas. (Illus.). 256p. (Orig.). 1991. pap. 14.95 (*0-937897-98-1*) Centerpoint Pr.
Muller, Mary L. Imagery of Dissent. (Illus.). 1989. pap. 10.00 (*0-932900-20-8*) Elvejhem Mus.
Muller, Mary M. Angels in Our Midst. 158p. 1998. pap. 14.98 (*0-88290-622-4*, 1085) Horizon Utah.
— A Town at Presque Isle: A Short History of Erie, Pennsylvania to 1980. (Illus.). 72p. 1991. pap. 6.95 (*1-883658-08-X*, 0313) Erie Cnty Hist.
Muller, Max. History of Ancient Sanskrit Literature: So Far As It Illustrates the Primitive Religion of the Brahmans. (C). 1993. reprint ed. 27.50 (*81-206-0554-3*, Pub. by Asian Educ Servs) S Asia.
— Life & Religion: An Aftermath from the Writings of the Right Honourable Professor F. Max Muller. 2nd ed. 237p. (Orig.). 1995. reprint ed. pap. 14.95 (*1-885395-10-8*) Book Tree.
— Philosophisches Woerterbuch. (GER.). 39.95 (*0-7859-8369-4*, 3451041510) Fr & Eur.
Muller, Max, ed. Sacred Book of the East: Vedic Hymns, 2 vols, Set. 1975. 600.00 (*0-8490-3963-0*) Krishna Pr.
— Sacred Books of China: Text of Taoism, 2 vols, Set. 1975. lib. bdg. 600.00 (*0-87968-298-1*) Krishna Pr.
— Sacred Books of the East, 50 vols., Set. 1987. 850.00 (*81-208-0289-6*, Pub. by Motilal Bnarsidass) S Asia.
Muller, Max, tr. The Upanishads, 2 vols. 1975. lib. bdg. 600.00 (*0-87968-548-4*) Krishna Pr.
Muller, Max & Halder, Alois. Small Dictionary of Philosophy: Kleines Philosophisches Woerterbuch. 12th ed. (GER.). 343p. 1985. pap. 19.95 (*0-8288-2279-4*, M7506) Fr & Eur.
Muller, Max F. Sacred Books of the East, 50 vols. 1997. 10000.00 (*81-7156-355-4*, Pub. by Print Hse) St Mut.
— The Vedanta Philosophy. 173p. 1985. 29.95 (*0-318-37034-4*) Asia Bk Corp.
Muller, Melissa. Anne Frank: The Biography. Kimber, Rita & Kimber, Robert, trs. LC 98-22923. (Illus.). 256p. 1998. 23.00 (*0-8050-5996-2*, Metropol Bks) H Holt & Co.
— Anne Frank: The Biography. Kimber, Robert, tr. 352p. 1999. pap. 14.00 (*0-8050-5997-0*, Owl) H Holt & Co.
Muller, Michael. Buro Komplett mit Word for Windows Reihe Losungen. (GER.). (C). 1991. text. write for info. (*0-201-55981-1*) Addison-Wesley.
— The Holy Sacrifice of the Mass. LC 90-71853. 589p. 1992. reprint ed. pap. 20.00 (*0-89555-437-2*) TAN Bks Pubs.
— Die Portfolio Verwaltung Excel Reihe Losungen. (GER.). (C). 1991. text. write for info. (*0-201-55978-1*) Addison-Wesley.
— Prayer-the Key to Salvation. LC 85-52207. 226p. 1992. reprint ed. pap. 7.50 (*0-89555-287-6*) TAN Bks Pubs.
— Das Private Finanzpaket Hit Works Reihe Losungen. (GER.). (C). 1991. text. write for info. (*0-201-55980-3*) Addison-Wesley.
— Terminplanung Excel Reihe Losungen. (GER.). (C). 1991. text. write for info. (*0-201-55948-X*) Addison-Wesley.
Muller, Miklos, jt. ed. see Marr, J. Joseph.
Muller, Mogens. The First Bible of the Church: A Plea for the Septuagint. LC 96-165214. (Journal for the Study of the Old Testament Supplement Ser.: No. 206, No. 1). 163p. 1996. 52.50 (*1-85075-571-X*, Pub. by Sheffield Acad) CUP Services.
Muller, N. WEBMASTER'S GD HTML S2. 1996. pap., pap. text 34.95 incl. disk (*0-07-912273-6*) McGraw.
Muller, N. F. & Dessing, R. P. European Drug Index. 2nd ed. 1380p. 1992. 353.75 (*0-444-89733-X*) Elsevier.
Muller, Nathan, jt. auth. see Davidson, Robert.
***Muller, Nathan J.** Bluetooth Demystified. (Demystified Ser.). 2000. pap. 49.95 (*0-07-136323-8*) McGraw.
Muller, Nathan J. The Desktop Encyclopedia of Telecommunications. LC 97-41307. (Illus.). 592p. 1998. pap. 49.95 (*0-07-044457-9*) McGraw.
***Muller, Nathan J.** Desktop Encyclopedia of Telecommunications. 2nd ed. (Telecommunications Ser.). (Illus.). 650p. 2000. pap. text 49.95 (*0-07-135893-5*) McGraw-Hill Prof.
Muller, Nathan J. Desktop Encyclopedia of the Internet: Internet Technology. LC 98-41081. 1998. 73.00 (*0-89006-729-5*) Artech Hse.
— Intelligent Hubs. LC 93-6111. 336p. 1993. 83.00 (*0-89006-698-1*) Artech Hse.

An Asterisk (*) at the beginning of an entry indicates that the title is appearing for the first time.

M

An Asterisk (*) at the beginning of an entry indicates that the title is appearing for the first time.

Muller, W. E. G., jt. ed. see Schroder, H.C.

Muller, W. G. Collecting Spatial Data: Optimum Design of Experiments for Random Fields. (Contributions to Statistics Ser.). xii, 186p. 1998. pap. 56.00 (*3-7908-1134-3*) Spr-Verlag.

Muller, W. G., jt. ed. see Kitsos, C. P.

Muller, W. H. Early History of the Supreme Court. xii, 117p. 1982. reprint ed. 38.00 (*0-8377-0845-1*, Rothman) W S Hein.

— Polaria: The Gift of the White Stone. (Illus.). 210p. (Orig.). 1996. pap. 14.95 (*0-914732-34-X*) Bro Life Inc.

Muller, W. Max. Egyptian Mythology & Indochinese Mythology. LC 63-19097. (Mythology of All Races Ser.: Vol. 12). (Illus.). reprint ed. 40.00 (*0-8154-0160-4*) Cooper Sq.

Muller, Walter, jt. ed. see Shavit, Yossi.

Muller-Warmuth, W. & Schollhorn, R., eds. Progress in Intercalation Research. LC 93-4586. (Physics & Chemistry of Materials with Low-Dimensional Structures Ser.: Vol. 17). 544p. 1993. text 336.00 (*0-7923-2357-2*) Kluwer Academic.

Muller, Wayne. History & Romance of Darners: Darn It!! (Illus.). 157p. (Orig.). 1994. pap. 19.95 (*0-89538-072-2*) L-W Inc.

— How, Then, Shall We Live? Four Simple Questions That Reveal the Beauty & Meaning of Our Lives. 304p. 1997. pap. 14.95 (*0-553-37505-9*) Bantam.

— Legacy of the Heart: The Spiritual Advantages of a Painful Childhood. 224p. 1992. pap. 20.00 (*0-671-76119-6*) S&S Trade.

— Legacy of the Heart: The Spiritual Advantages of a Painful Childhood. 224p. 1993. per. 11.00 (*0-671-79784-0*) S&S Trade Pap.

— Programming Using VAX Basic. 320p. 1985. pap. text 18.95 (*0-317-38895-9*) P-H.

***Muller, Wayne.** Sabbath: Finding Rest, Renewal & Delight in Our Busy Lives. 256p. 2000. pap. 14.95 (*0-553-38011-7*) Bantam.

Muller, Wayne. Sabbath: Restoring the Sacred Rhythm of Rest & Delight. LC 98-43982. 256p. 1999. 23.95 (*0-553-10672-4*) Bantam.

Muller, Wemer, et al. German 20mm Flak in World War II, 1939-1945. Force, Edward, tr. from GER. LC 95-215751. (Illus.). 48p. (Orig.). 1995. pap. 9.95 (*0-88740-758-7*) Schiffer.

Muller-Werdan, Ursula, et al. Cytokines & the Heart: Molecular Mechanisms of Septic Cardiomyopathy. LC 95-32356. (Medical Intelligence Unit Ser.). 231p. 1996. 99.00 (*1-57059-295-0*) Landes Bioscience.

Muller, Werner. America - The New World or the Old? Heritage, Anne & Kremmel, Paul, trs. from GER. (Illus.). 295p. 1990. pap. 61.00 (*3-631-40486-7*) P Lang Pubng.

— Captured Tanks in German Service: Small Tanks & Armored Tractors. LC 98-182509. 48p. 1998. pap. 9.95 (*0-7643-0573-5*) Schiffer.

— The 88mm Flak. Force, Edward, tr. from GER. LC 91-62751. (Illus.). 48p. 1991. pap. 9.95 (*0-88740-360-3*) Schiffer.

— The 88mm Flak. LC 98-131799. (Illus.). 48p. 1998. pap. 9.95 (*0-7643-0393-7*) Schiffer.

— German Flak in World War II. LC 97-80167.Tr. of Flak in Einsatz 1939-1945. (Illus.). 160p. 1998. 24.95 (*0-7643-0399-6*) Schiffer.

— German Medium Flak in Combat: Twenty Millimeter - Eighty-Eight Millimeter Flak. Force, Edward, tr. from GER. LC 91-62749. (Illus.). 48p. 1991. pap. 9.95 (*0-88740-351-4*) Schiffer.

— Ground Radar Systems of the Luftwaffe, 1939-1945. LC 98-184140. 48p. 1998. pap. 9.95 (*0-7643-0567-0*) Schiffer.

— The Heavy Flak Guns, 1933-1945. Force, Edward, tr. from GER. LC 90-61169. (Illus.). 140p. 1990. 24.95 (*0-88740-263-1*) Schiffer.

— Sound Locators, Fire Control Systems & Searchlights of the German Heavy Flak Units, 1939-1945. LC 98-182522. 48p. 1998. pap. 9.95 (*0-7643-0568-9*) Schiffer.

Muller, Werner A. Developmental Biology. 382p. 1996. 39.95 (*0-387-94718-3*) Spr-Verlag.

Muller Wiedemann, Hans, jt. auth. see Urieli, Baruch.

Muller-Wieland, Marcel. Geist und Tiefenbezug der Sprache. (GER.). 220p. 1989. write for info. (*3-487-09126-7*) G Olms Pubs.

— Gewalt und Sesshafte Verschuttung Erzieherische Grundlagen der Friedensfahigkeit. (Anstobe Zur Friedensarbeit Ser.: Vol. 12). (GER.). viii, 294p. 1995. write for info. (*3-487-09996-9*) G Olms Pubs.

— Sehende Liebe. (GER., Illus.). xiv, 230p. 1992. write for info. (*3-487-09502-5*) G Olms Pubs.

Muller, Will, ed. see Maple, Maude S.

Muller-Wille, Ludger, ed. see Boas, Franz.

Muller-Wille, Michael. Death & Burial in Medieval Europe. (Illus.). 71p. (Orig.). 1993. pap. 29.00 (*91-22-01575-2*) Coronet Bks.

Muller, William A. Secrets of Surf Fishing at Night. 140p. (Orig.). 1993. pap. 11.95 (*0-9625187-6-X*) Wavecrest Comns.

— Smallboat Fishing with the Experts. (With the Experts Ser.). (Illus.). 213p. 1988. text 16.95 (*0-9625187-2-7*) Wavecrest Comns.

— Surf Fishing for Stripers & Blues. (Illus.). 100p. 1991. 10.95 (*0-9625187-4-3*) Wavecrest Comns.

Muller, William A., ed. Science Manual: The Process & Communication. 78p. 1991. pap. text 10.95 (*0-9625187-3-5*) Wavecrest Comns.

Muller, William A. & Reina, Richard. Surf Fishing with the Experts. 2nd ed. (With the Experts Ser.). (Illus.). 242p. pap. 11.95 (*0-9625187-5-1*) Wavecrest Comns.

Muller, William A., jt. auth. see Reina, Richard.

Muller, William D. International Register of Research on British Politics, 1988. 7th ed. LC 88-27181. 336p. 1988. 99.95 (*0-88946-980-6*) E Mellen.

Muller, William D., ed. International Register of Research on British Politics. 8th ed. LC 89-640687. 472p. 1992. lib. bdg. 109.95 (*0-88946-571-1*) E Mellen.

Muller-Winkler, Claudia. Die Agyptischen Objekt-Amulette: Mit Publikation der Sammlung des Biblischen Instituts der Universitat Freiburg Schweiz, Ehemals Sammlung Fouad S. Matouk. (Orbis Biblicus et Orientalis Ser.: Vol. 5). (GER.). 560p. 1987. text 154.00 (*3-7278-0551-X*, Pub. by Presses Univ Fribourg) Eisenbrauns.

Muller-Wohlahrt, H W & Montag, H. J. Injured... What Now? How to Handle Sports Injuries. (Illus.). 160p. 1999. pap. 14.95 (*0-8038-9442-2*, Pub. by Hastings) Midpt Trade.

Muller, Wolfgang, ed. Printing: Technical Dictionary Of. 1020p. (C). 1981. 330.00 (*0-7855-5003-8*, Pub. by Collets) St Mut.

Muller, Wolfgang, jt. auth. see Khan, Nicholas.

Muller, Wolfgang, jt. ed. see Cosentino, Christine.

***Muller, Wolfgang C. & Kaare, Strom, eds.** Coalition Governments in Western Europe. (Comparative European Politics Ser.). 320p. 2000. text 72.00 (*0-19-829760-2*) OUP.

Muller, Wolfgang C. & Saalfeld, Thomas, eds. Members of Parliament in Western Europe: Roles & Behaviour. LC 97-764. 296p. 1997. 45.00 (*0-7146-4821-3*, Pub. by Irish Acad Pr); pap. 19.50 (*0-7146-4369-6*, Pub. by Irish Acad Pr) Intl Spec Bk.

Muller, Wolfgang C. & Wright, Vincent, eds. The State in Western Europe: Retreat or Redefinition? LC 94-22208. 199p. 1994. 39.50 (*0-7146-4594-X*, Pub. by F Cass Pubs) Intl Spec Bk.

Muller, Wolfgang C., jt. ed. see Luther, Kurt R.

Muller, Wolfgang C., jt. ed. see Strom, Kaare.

Muller, Wolfgang E., jt. auth. see Heumann, Jurgen.

Muller, Wolfgang H. Prinzipien Wirtschaftlichen Handelns & Ihre Anwendung: Umrib Einer Wirtschaftsphilosophie. (Illus.). 141p. 1996. 31.95 (*3-631-30477-3*) P Lang Pubng.

Muller, Wolfgang P. Huguccio: The Life, Works, & Thought of a Twelfth-Century Jurist. LC 93-1896. (Studies in Medieval & Early Modern Canon Law: Vol. 3). 320p. 1994. 59.95 (*0-8132-0787-8*) Cath U Pr.

Mullers, Josefine. Die Ehre der Himmlischen: Holderlins Patmos-Hymne und die Sprachwerdung des Gottlichen. (Europaische Hochschulschriften Ser.: Bd. 1639). (GER.). 150p. 1997. 32.95 (*3-631-32457-X*) P Lang Pubng.

Mullerson, R. A. Human Rights Diplomacy. LC 96-26289. 240p. (C). 1997. pap. 27.99 (*0-415-15391-3*) Routledge.

***Mullerson, R. A.** Ordering Anarchy: International Law in International Society. LC 00-41583. 2000. write for info. (*90-411-1408-4*) Kluwer Law Intl.

Mullerson, Rein. International Law, Rights & Politics: Developments in Eastern Europe & the CIS. LC 93-46093. (New International Relations Ser.). 224p. (C). 1994. pap. 27.99 (*0-415-11134-X*) Routledge.

Mullerson, Rein, et al, eds. Constitutional Reforms & International Law in Central & Eastern Europe. LC 97-32489. (Studies in Law). 372p. 1998. 136.50 (*90-411-0526-3*) Kluwer Law Intl.

Mullerus, Carolus, ed. Geographi Graeci Minores, 3 vols., Bd. 1 & 2. (GER.). ccviii, 1242p. 1990. reprint ed. write for info. (*0-318-70586-9*) G Olms Pubs.

— Geographi Graeci Minores, 3 vols., Bd. 3. (GER.). ccviii, 1242p. 1990. reprint ed. write for info. (*0-318-70587-7*) G Olms Pubs.

— Geographi Graeci Minores, 3 vols., Set. (GER.). ccviii, 1242p. 1990. reprint ed. write for info. (*3-487-09217-4*) G Olms Pubs.

Mullery, A. L., et al, eds. Intelligence in Services & Networks: Technology for Cooperative Competition: Fourth International Conference on Intelligence in Services & Networks: IS&N'97, Cernobbio, Italy, May 27-29, 1997, Proceedings. LC 97-24998. (Lecture Notes in Computer Science Ser.: No. 1238). xii, 480p. 1997. pap. 73.00 (*3-540-63135-6*) Spr-Verlag.

Mullet, J. Five Years Whaling Voyage, 1848-1853. 1977. 19.95 (*0-87770-182-2*) Ye Galleon.

Mullet, Kevin. Designing Visual Interfaces: Communication Oriented Techniques. 304p. (C). 1994. pap. 52.00 (*0-13-303389-9*) P-H.

Mullet, Rosa. Fall & Winter in North Carolina Forests. (Illus.). 244p. (YA). (gr. 7-10). 1982. pap. 7.50 (*0-7399-0120-6*, 2235) Rod & Staff.

Mullet, Rosa Mae. Spring & Summer in North Carolina Forests. (Illus.). 238p. (YA). (gr. 7-10). 1982. pap. 7.50 (*0-7399-0119-2*, 2405) Rod & Staff.

Mullett, D. L. Composite Floor Systems. LC 97-31335. 1998. 79.95 (*0-632-04143-9*) Blackwell Sci.

Mullett, G. M. Spider Woman Stories. LC 78-11556. 142p. 1979. pap. 11.95 (*0-8165-0621-3*) U of Ariz Pr.

Mullett, Gary M., jt. auth. see Noddings, Charles R.

Mullett, Margaret. Theophylacht of Ochrid: Reading the Letters of a Byzantine Archbishop. LC 95-50631. (Birmingham Byzantine & Ottoman Monographs: Vol. 2). 464p. 1997. 86.95 (*0-86078-549-1*, Pub. by Variorum) Ashgate Pub Co.

Mullett, Michael. James II & English Politics, 1678-1688. LC 93-23857. (Lancaster Pamphlets Ser.). 80p. (C). 1993. pap. 11.99 (*0-415-09042-3*, B2465) Routledge.

— New Light on George Fox, 1624-1691. 1999. pap. 24.00 (*1-85072-142-4*, Pub. by W Sessions) St Mut.

— Popular Culture & Popular Protest in Late Medieval & Early Modern Europe. 256p. 1987. lib. bdg. 49.95 (*0-7099-3566-8*, Pub. by C Helm) Routldge.

— The Reformation. (Rigby Interactive Library - History). (Illus.). 48p. (J). 1998. write for info. (*1-57572-011-6*) Heinemann Lib.

***Mullett, Michael A.** Catholic Reformation. LC 99-12908. 1999. pap. 22.99 (*0-415-18915-2*) Routledge.

***Mullett, Michael A.** Catholic Reformation. LC 99-12908. 304p. (C). 1999. text. write for info. (*0-415-18914-4*) Routledge.

Mullett, Michael A. Catholics in Britain & Ireland, 1558-1829. LC 97-53207. (Social History in Perspective Ser.). 1998. text 55.00 (*0-312-21397-2*) St Martin.

— John Bunyan in Context. LC 97-16025. 320p. (C). 1997. text 44.00 (*0-8207-0287-0*) Duquesne.

Mulley, Athol, jt. auth. see Sigley, Bill.

Mulley, Graham, ed. Everyday Aids & Appliances. (Illus.). 111p. 1989. pap. text 7.00 (*0-7279-0241-5*, Pub. by BMJ Pub) Login Brothers Bk Co.

Mulley, Raymond. Control System Documentation: Applying Symbols & Identification. LC 93-30757. (RMS Ser.). 232p. 1994. 48.00 (*1-55617-490-X*) ISA.

Mullholland, M. Robert. Shaped by the Word. 1985. pap. 9.95 (*0-687-61048-6*) Abingdon.

Mullholland, St. Clair A. Story of the 116th Regiment: Pennsylvania Volunteers in the War of Rebellion. Kohl, Lawrence F., ed. LC 95-39243. (Irish in the Civil War Ser.: 5). (Illus.). xxii, 480p. 1995. 30.00 (*0-8232-1606-3*) Fordham.

Mullians, Jonita, ed. see Sykes, Diane L. & D. B. & Associates Staff.

Mullica, Karyn, jt. auth. see Ausberger, Carolyn.

Mullican, Judith. Springtime on the Farm. large type ed. (Children's Booklets Ser.). (Illus.). 8p. (J). (ps-k). 1998. pap. 10.95 (*1-57332-121-4*) HighReach Lrning.

Mullican, Judy. Apples, Apples. (HRL Little Book Ser.). (Illus.). 8p. (J). (ps-k). 1997. pap. text 10.95 (*1-57332-079-X*) HighReach Lrning.

— Apples, Apples. large type ed. (HRL Big Book Ser.). (Illus.). 8p. (J). (ps-k). 1997. pap. text 10.95 (*1-57332-077-3*) HighReach Lrning.

Mullican, Judy. Bonnie's Beach Towel. (HRL Big Bks.). 8p. (J). (ps-k). 1994. pap. text 10.95 (*1-57332-008-0*) HighReach Lrning.

Mullican, Judy. By the Pond. (HRL Little Book Ser.). (Illus.). 8p. (Orig.). (J). (ps-k). 1997. pap. text 10.95 (*1-57332-075-7*) HighReach Lrning.

— By the Pond. large type ed. (HRL Big Bks.). (Illus.). 8p. (Orig.). (J). (ps-k). 1997. pap. text 10.95 (*1-57332-076-5*) HighReach Lrning.

— The Circus. (HRL Little Bks.). (Illus.). 8p. (Orig.). (J). (ps-k). 1996. pap. text 10.95 (*1-57332-029-3*) HighReach Lrning.

— The Circus. large type ed. (Big Bks.). (Illus.). 8p. (Orig.). (J). (ps-k). 1996. pap. text 10.95 (*1-57332-030-7*) HighReach Lrning.

— The Circus Is Coming to Town. large type ed. (HRL Big Bks.). (Illus.). 8p. (Orig.). (J). (ps-k). 1996. pap. text 10.95 (*1-57332-031-1*) HighReach Lrning.

— The Clean-up Day. large type ed. (HRL Big Bks.). (Illus.). 8p. (Orig.). (J). (ps-1). 1996. pap. text 10.95 (*1-57332-025-0*) HighReach Lrning.

— Connie Cow's Friends. large type ed. (HRL Cuddle Bks.). (Illus.). 6p. (J). (ps-k). 1999. pap. text 10.95 (*1-57332-137-0*) HighReach Lrning.

— The Day the Dinosaur Came to the Library. (HRL Big Bks.). (Illus.). 8p. (J). (ps-k). 1994. pap. text 10.95 (*1-57332-005-6*) HighReach Lrning.

— Down at the Seashore. large type ed. (Little Bks.). (Illus.). 8p. (Orig.). (J). (ps-k). 1996. pap. text 10.95 (*1-57332-031-5*); pap. text 10.95 (*1-57332-032-3*) HighReach Lrning.

— Families - Familias. Loomis, Linda, tr. (HRL Big Bks.). (SPA., Illus.). 8p. (Orig.). (J). (ps-k). 1995. pap. text 10.95 (*1-57332-055-2*) HighReach Lrning.

— The Fire. (HRL Little Bks.). (Illus.). 8p. (Orig.). (J). (ps-1). 1996. pap. text 10.95 (*1-57332-039-0*) HighReach Lrning.

— The Fire. large type ed. (HRL Big Bks.). (Illus.). 8p. (Orig.). (J). (ps-1). 1996. pap. text 10.95 (*1-57332-026-9*) HighReach Lrning.

— Fire in the Night. (HRL Little Bks.). (Illus.). 8p. (J). (ps-k). 1995. pap. 10.95 (*1-57332-021-8*) HighReach Lrning.

— Fire in the Night. large type ed. (HRL Big Bks.). (Illus.). 8p. (J). (ps-k). 1997. pap. text 10.95 (*1-57332-096-X*) HighReach Lrning.

— From Here to There. (Little Bks.). (Illus.). 8p. (Orig.). (J). (ps-k). 1996. pap. text 10.95 (*1-57332-027-7*) HighReach Lrning.

— From Here to There. large type ed. (HRL Big Bks.). (Illus.). 8p. (Orig.). (J). (ps-k). 1996. pap. text 10.95 (*1-57332-028-5*) HighReach Lrning.

— Going to Benny's. (HRL Big Bks.). (Illus.). 8p. (Orig.). (J). (ps-k). 1995. pap. text 10.95 (*1-57332-054-4*) HighReach Lrning.

— Healthy Foods. (HRL Little Bks.). (Illus.). 8p. (J). (ps-k). 1995. pap. text 10.95 (*1-57332-051-X*); pap. text 10.95 (*1-57332-052-8*) HighReach Lrning.

***Mullican, Judy.** Healthy Me. (CB Ser.). (Illus.). 7p. (J). (ps-1). 2000. pap. text 10.95 (*1-57332-158-3*) HighReach Lrning.

Mullican, Judy. Holidays. (HRL Little Bks.). (Illus.). 8p. (J). (ps). 1995. pap. 10.95 (*1-57332-022-6*); pap. 10.95 (*1-57332-023-4*) HighReach Lrning.

— Hooray for the U. S. A.! (HRL Little Bks.). (Illus.). 8p. (Orig.). (J). (ps-k). 1996. pap. text 10.95 (*1-57332-034-X*) HighReach Lrning.

— In the Desert. large type ed. (Cuddle Bks.). (Illus.). 10p. (J). (ps-k). 1998. pap. text 10.95 (*1-57332-119-2*) HighReach Lrning.

— In the Forest. large type ed. (Cuddle Bks.). (Illus.). 7p. (J). (ps-k). 1998. pap. text 10.95 (*1-57332-129-X*) HighReach Lrning.

***Mullican, Judy.** In the Meadow. large type ed. (CB Ser.). (Illus.). 7p. (J). (ps-1). 2000. pap. text 10.95 (*1-57332-142-7*) HighReach Lrning.

Mullican, Judy. In the Sunlight. large type ed. (Big Bks.). (Illus.). 8p. (J). (ps-k). 1998. pap. text 10.95 (*1-57332-115-X*); pap. text 10.95 (*1-57332-114-1*) HighReach Lrning.

— Inside the Big Red Barn. large type ed. (HRL Children's Bks.). (Illus.). 8p. (J). (ps-k). 1999. pap. text 10.95 (*1-57332-136-2*); pap. text 10.95 (*1-57332-135-4*) HighReach Lrning.

Mullican, Judy. The Jungle Band. (Big Bks.). (Illus.). 8p. (J). (ps-k). 1994. pap. text 10.95 (*1-57332-009-9*) HighReach Lrning.

Mullican, Judy. Kenny & the Poison. (HRL Big Bks.). (Illus.). 8p. (Orig.). (J). (ps-k). 1998. pap. text 10.95 (*1-57332-089-7*) HighReach Lrning.

— Kenny & the Poison. large type ed. (HRL Little Bks.). (Illus.). 8p. (Orig.). (J). (ps-k). 1998. pap. text 10.95 (*1-57332-088-9*) HighReach Lrning.

— Let's Go to the Balloon Show! (HRL Big Bks.). (Illus.). 8p. (J). (ps-k). 1994. pap. text 10.95 (*1-57332-004-8*) HighReach Lrning.

***Mullican, Judy.** Let's Have a Parade! large type ed. (HRL Cuddle Bks.). (Illus.). 7p. (J). (ps-k). 1999. pap. text 10.95 (*1-57332-139-7*) HighReach Lrning.

— Looking for a Book. large type ed. (BB Ser.). (Illus.). 8p. (J). (ps-1). 2000. pap. text 10.95 (*1-57332-165-6*); pap. text 10.95 (*1-57332-166-4*) HighReach Lrning.

Mullican, Judy. Lord Lenny Comes Home. large type ed. (HRL Big Bks.). (Illus.). 8p. (Orig.). (J). (ps-k). 1996. pap. text 10.95 (*1-57332-071-4*) HighReach Lrning.

— Magic Words. (HRL Little Bks.). (Illus.). 8p. (Orig.). (J). (ps up). 1997. pap. text 10.95 (*1-57332-053-6*) HighReach Lrning.

— Magic Words. large type ed. (HRL Big Bks.). (Illus.). 8p. (Orig.). (J). (ps-k). 1998. pap. text 10.95 (*1-57332-112-5*) HighReach Lrning.

— Marsha Gets Mad. (HRL Big Bks.). (Illus.). 8p. (J). (ps-k). 1995. pap. text 10.95 (*1-57332-013-7*) HighReach Lrning.

— Me! Me! Magnificent Me! large type ed. (HRL Little Bks.). (Illus.). 8p. (J). (ps-k). 1998. pap. text 10.95 (*1-57332-108-7*); pap. text 10.95 (*1-57332-109-5*) HighReach Lrning.

— Mr. Turkey. large type ed. (Cuddle Bks.). (Illus.). 7p. (J). (ps-k). 1998. pap. text 10.95 (*1-57332-126-5*) HighReach Lrning.

— Molly & the Snow. (HRL Little Bks.). (Illus.). 8p. (Orig.). (J). (ps). 1995. pap. text 10.95 (*1-57332-058-7*) HighReach Lrning.

— My Forest Friends. (Big Bks.). (Illus.). 8p. (J). (ps-k). 1994. pap. text 10.95 (*1-57332-003-X*) HighReach Lrning.

***Mullican, Judy.** My Forest Friends. large type ed. (LB Ser.). (Illus.). 8p. (J). (ps-1). 2000. pap. text 10.95 (*1-57332-172-9*); pap. text 10.95 (*1-57332-180-X*) HighReach Lrning.

— Our Very Own Rocket. (HBL Big Bks.). (Illus.). 8p. (J). (ps-k). 1994. pap. text 10.95 (*1-57332-010-2*) HighReach Lrning.

Mullican, Judy. Patty Helps Out. large type ed. (HRL Cuddle Bks.). (Illus.). 8p. (J). (ps-k). 1999. pap. text 10.95 (*1-57332-140-0*); pap. text 10.95 (*1-57332-141-9*) HighReach Lrning.

***Mullican, Judy.** People, People. large type ed. (CB Ser.). (Illus.). 6p. (J). (ps-k). 2000. pap. text 10.95 (*1-57332-159-1*) HighReach Lrning.

Mullican, Judy. Riding the Range. (HRL Big Bks.). (Illus.). 8p. (J). (ps-k). 1998. pap. text 10.95 (*1-57332-104-4*) HighReach Lrning.

— Riding the Range. large type ed. (HRL Little Bks.). (Illus.). 8p. (J). (ps-k). 1997. pap. text 10.95 (*1-57332-097-8*) HighReach Lrning.

— Springtime on the Farm. large type ed. (Big Bks.). (Illus.). 8p. (J). (ps-k). 1998. pap. text 10.95 (*1-57332-120-6*) HighReach Lrning.

***Mullican, Judy.** Story Time. large type ed. (CB Ser.). (Illus.). 7p. (J). (ps-1). 2000. pap. text 10.95 (*1-57332-171-0*) HighReach Lrning.

Mullican, Judy. Susie Plants a Seed. (Little Bks.). (Illus.). 8p. (Orig.). (J). (ps-k). 1995. pap. text 10.95 (*1-57332-065-X*); pap. text 10.95 (*1-57332-066-8*) HighReach Lrning.

— Things That Go. (Little Bks.). (Illus.). 8p. (Orig.). (J). (ps-k). 1995. pap. text 10.95 (*1-57332-063-3*) HighReach Lrning.

— Under the Sea. (HRL Big Bks.). (Illus.). 8p. (J). (ps-k). 1998. pap. text 10.95 (*1-57332-093-5*) HighReach Lrning.

— Under the Sea. large type ed. (HRL Little Bks.). (Illus.). 8p. (J). (ps-k). 1998. pap. text 10.95 (*1-57332-092-7*) HighReach Lrning.

***Mullican, Judy.** What Can Li Zhang Cook? large type ed. (BB Ser.). (Illus.). 8p. (J). (ps-k). 2000. pap. text 10.95 (*1-57332-160-5*); pap. text 10.95 (*1-57332-161-3*) HighReach Lrning.

Mullican, Judy. What Pet Should I Get? large type ed. (HRL Children's Bks.). (Illus.). 8p. (J). (ps-k). 1999. pap. text 10.95 (*1-57332-134-6*) HighReach Lrning.

***Mullican, Judy.** What Pet Should I Get? large type ed. (HRL Big Bks.). (Illus.). 8p. (J). (ps-k). 1999. pap. text 10.95 (*1-57332-132-X*) HighReach Lrning.

Mullican, Judy. What Will We Play Today? (HRL Big Bks.). (Illus.). 8p. (J). (ps-k). 1995. pap. text 10.95 (*1-57332-019-6*) HighReach Lrning.

— When I Grow Up. (HRL Little Bks.). (Illus.). 8p. (J). (ps-k). 1997. pap. text 10.95 (*1-57332-098-6*); pap. text 10.95 (*1-57332-099-4*) HighReach Lrning.

— Where We Live. (HRL Little Bks.). (Illus.). 8p. (Orig.). (J). (ps-1). 1996. pap. text 10.95 (*1-57332-040-4*) HighReach Lrning.

An Asterisk (*) at the beginning of an entry indicates that the title is appearing for the first time.

— Where We Live. large type ed. (HRL Big Bks.). (Illus.). 8p. (Orig.). (J). (ps-1). 1996. pap. text 10.95 (*1-57332-041-2*) HighReach Lrning.
— Who Am I? (HRL Little Bks.). (Illus.). 8p. (J). (ps-k). 1995. pap. text 10.95 (*1-57332-017-X*); pap. text 10.95 (*1-57332-018-8*) HighReach Lrning.
— Who Can? (HRL Big Bks.). (Illus.). 8p. (J). (ps-k). 1994. pap. text 10.95 (*1-57332-001-3*) HighReach Lrning.
— Who Can? (Quien Puede?) Loomis, Linda, tr. (HRL Big Bks.). (SPA., Illus.). 8p. (Orig.). (J). (ps-k). 1995. pap. text 10.95 (*1-57332-056-0*) HighReach Lrning.
***Mullican, Judy & Carroll, Ken, Jr.** Bedtime Stories. large type ed. (Cuddle Bks.). (Illus.). 6p. (J). (ps-k). 1999. pap. text 10.95 (*1-57332-147-8*) HighReach Lrning.
Mullican, Judy & Crowell, Knox. A Firefighter in Class. large type ed. (Little Book Ser.). (Illus.). 8p. (J). (ps-k). 1999. pap. text 10.95 (*1-57332-148-6*) HighReach Lrning.
***Mullican, Judy & Crowell, Knox.** A Firefighter in Class. large type ed. (Big Book Ser.). (Illus.). 8p. (J). (ps-k). 1999. pap. text 10.95 (*1-57332-143-5*) HighReach Lrning.
***Mullican, Judy & Linke, Don, Jr.** In the Fall. large type ed. (Cuddle Bks.). (Illus.). 6p. (J). (ps-k). 1999. pap. text 10.95 (*1-57332-146-X*) HighReach Lrning.
Mullican, Judy & Smith, Beth E. Four Little Turkeys. (HRL Little Bks.). (Illus.). 8p. (J). (ps-k). 1997. pap. text 10.95 (*1-57332-083-8*) HighReach Lrning.
Mullican, Judy, jt. auth. see Jerrell, Pam.
Mullican, Judy, jt. auth. see Smith, Beth E.
Mullican, Matt. Matt Mullican. 1994. 75.00 (*3-88375-189-8*, Pub. by Walther Konig) Dist Art Pubs.
— Matt Mullican World Frame. (Illus.). 222p. (Orig.). 1992. pap. text 35.00 (*1-879293-04-8*) Contemp Art Mus.
Mullican, W. F. & Senger, R. K. Hydrogeologic Investigations of Deep Ground-Water Flow in the Chihuahuan Desert, Texas, RIO 205. (Illus.). 60p. 1992. pap. 5.00 (*0-317-05172-5*, RI 205) Bur Econ Geology.
Mullick, jt. auth. see Moran.
Mullick, M. & Bhattacharyya, B. Technology of Machining Systems. (C). 1989. 50.00 (*0-89771-381-8*, Pub. by Current Dist) St Mut.
Mullick, Promatha N. History of the Vaisyas of Bengal. 169p. 1986. reprint ed. 22.00 (*0-8364-1633-3*, Pub. by Usha) S Asia.
Mullie, Sozef L. The Structural Principles of the Chinese Language, 3 vols. 1976. lib. bdg. 300.00 (*0-8490-2698-9*) Gordon Pr.
Mulligan. Microeconomic Theory: Applied Approach. (C). 1994. pap., student ed. 13.50 (*0-205-12273-6*, Macmillan Coll) P-H.
— Parental Priorities. LC 97-21621. 344p. 1997. pap. text 24.95 (*0-226-54840-6*); lib. bdg. 60.00 (*0-226-54839-2*) U Ch Pr.
Mulligan, Adair D. The Gunstock Parish: A History of Gilford, New Hampshire. LC 95-21214. (Illus.). 488p. 1995. 35.00 (*0-914659-74-X*) Phoenix Pub.
Mulligan, Allan. The Complete Guide to Developing & Marketing Your Own Seminar. 164p. 1984. pap. write for info. (*0-912551-00-3*) A Mulligan.
Mulligan, Ann, jt. auth. see Ahlfeld, David.
Mulligan, Barbara, ed. see Thomas, Tim.
Mulligan, David, ed. Environmental Management of the Australian Minerals & Energy Industries: Principles & Practice. LC 97-142329. 808p. 1999. reprint ed. 69.95 (*0-86840-383-0*) New South Wales Univ Pr.
***Mulligan, Donald E. & Knutson, Kraig.** Construction & Culture: A Built Environment. (Illus.). 260p. (C). 1999. text 34.95 (*0-87563-939-9*) Stipes.
Mulligan, E. Jeanne. Pencil Playground: A Creative Writing Curriculum. (Illus.). 1991. student ed. 29.95 (*0-9608502-0-1*) Estella Graphics.
Mulligan, Eileen M. Physiology: Pretest Self-Assessment & Review. 6th ed. LC 90-5599. vii, 195 p. 1991. write for info. (*0-07-051978-1*) McGraw-Hill HPD.
Mulligan, Elizabeth A. & Stone, Gene. Accounting & Financial Reporting in Life & Health Insurance Companies. LC 96-77388. (FLMI Insurance Education Program Ser.). 715p. text 69.95 (*0-939921-85-5*, Pub. by Life Office) PBD Inc.
Mulligan, Elizabeth A. & Stone, Gene. Comptabilite et Declarations Financieres des Compagnies d'Assurances de Personnes. Heeden, Vivian F., ed. (FLMI Insurance Education Program Ser.). (FRE.). 695p. (C). 1997. pap. text 88.00 (*1-57974-006-5*) Life Office.
Mulligan, Frank. A Lector's Guide to the Episcopal Eucharistic Lectionary. (Orig.). 1987. pap. 16.00 (*0-9618112-0-X*) St Marks Pr.
Mulligan, Geoff. Removing the Spam: E-Mail Processing & Filtering. LC 98-52144. (Networking Basics Ser.). 208p. (C). 1999. pap. text 19.95 (*0-201-37957-0*) Addison-Wesley.
Mulligan, Gerald & Agriculture Canada Staff. Common Weeds of Canada. (Illus.). 140p. (Orig.). 1987. pap. 16.95 (*0-920053-59-9*, Pub. by NC Ltd) U of Toronto Pr.
Mulligan, James. Riddle of Justice: A Monograph; Together with Suggestions for Much-Needed New Laws. xvi, 155p. 1983. reprint ed. 34.00 (*0-8377-0849-4*, Rothman) W S Hein.
Mulligan, James A. The Hanoi Commitment. LC 81-90096. (Illus.). 298p. 1981. 15.00 (*0-9606000-0-0*) RIF Mktg.
— The Hanoi Commitment. 5th ed. (Illus.). 298p. 1981. lib. bdg. 20.00 (*0-685-45814-8*) RIF Mktg.
Mulligan, James G. Managerial Economics: Strategy for Profit. 592p. 1989. teacher ed. write for info. (*0-318-63858-4*, H1973-0) P-H.
— Microeconomic Theory: Applied Approach. (C). 1999. 52.00 (*0-205-12276-0*, Macmillan Coll) P-H.
Mulligan, James J. Choose Life. LC 91-31394. 383p. 1991. pap. text 17.95 (*0-935372-31-8*) NCBC.
— Theologians & Authority Within the Living Church. LC 86-30542. 139p. (Orig.). 1987. pap. 13.95 (*0-935372-18-0*) NCBC.
Mulligan, Jessica M. Making Money with Online Entertainment: How to Create & Profit from Online Content. (Illus.). 320p. 1997. pap., pap. text 39.95 incl. cd-rom (*0-07-913177-8*) McGraw.
Mulligan, John. Shopping Cart Soldiers. LC 96-37883. 239p. 1997. 22.95 (*1-880684-48-9*) Curbstone.
— Shopping Cart Soldiers. LC 98-36814. 256p. 1999. per. 12.00 (*0-684-85605-0*, Scribner Pap Fic) S&S Trade Pap.
— Solaris Essential Reference. 267p. 1999. pap. 24.95 (*0-7357-0023-0*) New Riders Pub.
Mulligan, Joseph E. The Jesuit Martyrs of El Salvador: Celebrating the Anniversaries. (Illus.). 200p. (Orig.). (C). 1994. pap. 17.95 (*1-879175-15-0*) Fortkamp.
— The Nicaraguan Church & the Revolution. LC 90-63486. 320p. (Orig.). (C). 1991. pap. 17.95 (*1-55612-411-2*, LL1411) Sheed & Ward WI.
Mulligan, Joseph F., ed. Heinrich Rudolph Hertz (1857-1894) A Collection of Articles & Addresses. LC 93-34637. (Illus.). 465p. 1994. text 25.00 (*0-8153-1288-1*, H1697) Garland.
Mulligan, Joseph F. & Mulligan, Kevin T. The Mulligan Guide to Sports Journalism Careers. LC 98-8171. 352p. 1999. pap. 15.95 (*0-8442-4540-2*, 45402) NTC Contemp Pub Co.
Mulligan, Kate. Canal Parks, Museums & Characters of the Mid-Atlantic. (Illus.). 136p. 1999. pap. 13.95 (*0-9655552-1-6*) Wakefield Pr.
— Towns along the Towpath. LC 96-62086. (Illus.). 128p. (Orig.). 1997. pap. 14.00 (*0-9655552-0-8*) Wakefield Pr.
Mulligan, Kevin, ed. Language, Truth & Ontology. (Philosophical Studies in Philosophy). 224p. (C). 1992. lib. bdg. 146.50 (*0-7923-1509-X*, Pub. by Kluwer Academic) Kluwer Academic.
— Mind, Meaning & Metaphysics: The Philosophy & Theory of Language of Anton Marty. 304p. (C). 1990. lib. bdg. 191.50 (*0-7923-0578-7*, Pub. by Kluwer Academic) Kluwer Academic.
— Speech Act & Sachverhalt: Reinach & the Foundation of Realist Phenomenology. (Primary Sources in Phenomenology Ser.: Vol. 1). 356p. 1987. lib. bdg. 218.00 (*90-247-3427-4*, Pub. by M Nijhoff) Kluwer Academic.
Mulligan, Kevin T., jt. auth. see Mulligan, Joseph F.
Mulligan, Mark. Ghost of Black's Island: The Screenplay. (Illus.). 121p. (Orig.). (YA). (gr. 6-8). 1993. pap. 9.95 (*1-882444-01-9*) Blvd Bks FL.
— Manatee: The Screenplay. (Illus.). 121p. (Orig.). (YA). (gr. 9-12). 1993. pap. 9.95 (*1-882444-00-0*) Blvd Bks FL.
Mulligan, Michael E. Classic Radiological Signs: An Atlas & History. LC 96-13052. (Illus.). 208p. 1996. text 49.95 (*1-85070-664-6*) Prthnon Pub.
Mulligan, Patrick J. Dented Rose. 75p. 1993. pap. 5.95 (*0-9636104-0-6*) P J Mulligan.
Mulligan, Robert W., tr. see Aquinas, Thomas, Saint.
***Mulligan, Sarah A., et al.** Child Care Plus+ Curriculum on Inclusion: Practical Strategies for Early Childhood Programs. (Illus.). 307p. 2000. 60.00 (*0-9676799-0-7*) Child Cre.
Mulligan, Sarah A., ed. see Harper-Whalen, Susan & Morris, Sandra L.
Mulligan, Shawn M. Mulligan's Bar Guide: To Mixing, Serving & Otherwise Cinsuming Cocktails, Liqueurs & Shooters. 1998. pap. 3.95 (*0-00-215443-9*) Harper SF.
***Mulligan, Shawn M.** Mulligan's Bar Guide: To Mixing, Serving & Otherwise Consuming Cocktails, Liqueurs & Shooters. rev. ed. 88p. 2000. pap. 5.25 (*0-00-638579-6*) HarpC.
Mulligan, Shelia. Walk in Balance: The Path to Healthy, Happy, Harmonious Living. 224p. 1989. per. 11.00 (*0-671-76564-7*, Pub. by P-H) S&S Trade.
Mulligan, Shelia, jt. auth. see Nufer, Peter.
Mulligan, Steve, photos by. Living Landscapes of Kansas. LC 95-4636. (Illus.). 166p. (C). 1995. 29.95 (*0-7006-0727-7*) U Pr of KS.
— Terra Incognita. LC 97-39186. (Illus.). 64p. 1998. 35.00 (*0-7006-0887-7*) U Pr of KS.
***Mulligan, Therese.** The Photography of Alfred Stieglitz: Georgia O'Keeffe's Enduring Legacy. (Illus.). 2000. 29.95 (*0-935398-23-6*, Pub. by G Eastman Hse) U of NM Pr.
***Mulligan, Therese, ed.** Photographs: George Eastman House, Rochester, Ny. (Illus.). 768p. 1999. pap. text 29.99 (*3-8228-7073-0*) Benedikt Taschen.
Mulligan, Tim. The Traveler's Guide to the Hudson River Valley. 4th ed. LC 99-10623. 240p. 1999. pap. 15.95 (*0-375-75342-7*) Random.
Mulligan, Timothy. Neither Sharks Nor Wolves: The Men of Nazi Germany's U-Boat Arm, 1939-1945. LC 98-53659. (Illus.). 340p. 1999. 34.95 (*1-55750-594-2*) Naval Inst Pr.
Mulligan, Timothy O., compiled by. Guide to Records Relating to U. S. Participation in World War II Pt. II: Support & Supply. LC 98-7231. 1998. pap. 20.00 (*1-880875-16-0*, 200119) National Archives & Recs.
Mulligan, Timothy P. Lone Wolf: The Life & Death of U-Boat Ace Werner Henke. LC 93-20128. 288p. 1993. 39.95 (*0-275-93677-5*, C3677, Praeger Pubs) Greenwood.
— The Politics of Illusion & Empire: German Occupation Policy in the Soviet Union, Nineteen Forty-Two to Nineteen Forty Three. LC 87-32702. 220p. 1988. 57.95 (*0-275-92837-3*, C2837, Praeger Pubs) Greenwood.
Mulligan, Timothy P., compiled by. Guide to Records Relating to U. S. Military Participation in World War II Pt. I: Policy, Planning, Administration. 1996. pap. 15.00 (*1-880875-08-X*, 2000118) National Archives & Recs.
Mulligan, Vicki B. Children's Play: An Introduction for Care Providers. 256p. (C). 1996. pap. text 19.16 (*0-201-82979-7*) Addison-Wesley.
Mulligan, William, et al. The Aramco Reports on Al-Hasa & Oman 1950-1955, 4 vols., Set. (ARA & ENG., Illus.). 1200p. (C). 1990. reprint ed. lib. bdg. 395.00 (*1-85207-225-3*, Pub. by Archive Editions) N Ross.
Mulligan, William C. The Adventurous Gardener's Sourcebook of Rare & Unusual Plants. LC 92-12060. (Illus.). 1993. 40.00 (*0-671-75104-2*) S&S Trade.
— Complete Guide to North American Gardens: The Northeast, Vol. 1. 1991. pap. 15.95 (*0-316-59807-0*) Little.
— The Complete Guide to North American Gardens Vol. 2: The West Coast. (Illus.). 176p. 1998. pap. text 16.00 (*0-7881-5394-3*) DIANE Pub.
— The Lattice Gardener. LC 95-8158. (Illus.). 192p. 1995. pap. 35.00 (*0-02-587885-9*) Macmillan.
Mulligan, William H. Mulligan's Law: The Wit & Wisdom of William Hughes Mulligan. LC 97-38943. 246p. 1996. 25.00 (*0-8232-1718-3*) Fordham.
Mulligan, William H., Jr., ed. A Historical Dictionary of American Industrial Language. LC 87-37544. 320p. 1988. lib. bdg. 85.00 (*0-313-24171-6*, MAI/, Greenwood Pr) Greenwood.
Mulliken, R. S. Life of a Scientist. (Illus.). 180p. 1989. 86.95 (*0-387-50375-7*) Spr-Verlag.
Mulliken, Robert S. Selected Papers of Robert S. Mulliken. Hinze, J. & Ramsay, D. A., eds. LC 74-11633. xvi, 1120p. 1975. lib. bdg. 66.00 (*0-226-54847-3*) U Ch Pr.
Mulliken, Robert S. & Person, Willis B. Molecular Complexes: A Lecture & Reprint Volume. LC 71-84970. 516p. reprint ed. pap. 160.00 (*0-608-10196-6*, 200766600066) Bks Demand.
Mulliken, Todd. The State of Affairs: Why They Happen & How Love Can Be Restored. LC 98-60451. 128p. 1998. pap. 11.95 (*1-57921-113-5*, Pub. by WinePress Pub) BookWorld.
Mullikin, Lee. I'm Out of Here! Tips for Owners of Runaway Dogs. (Illus.). 32p. 1998. pap. 4.95 (*0-945199-11-2*) Double SS Pr.
***Mullin.** Crystalization. 576p. 2000. 135.00 (*0-7506-4833-3*) Buttrwrth-Heinemann.
Mullin. Electrical Wiring: Commerical. 9th ed. (Electrical Trades Ser.). 96p. 1996. teacher ed. 16.00 (*0-8273-6656-6*, VNR) Wiley.
— Electrical Wiring Residential 12E Transparency Masters. 128p. 1996. 12.95 (*0-8273-8376-2*) Delmar.
— House Wiring with the NEC IG. 80p. 1999. text, teacher ed. 16.00 (*0-8273-8351-7*) Delmar.
Mullin & Smith. Electrical Wiring - Commercial. 10th ed. LC 98-30058. 352p. 1998. text 53.95 (*0-7668-0179-9*) Delmar.
Mullin, jt. auth. see Smith.
Mullin, Amy S., ed. see American Chemical Society Staff.
Mullin, Ann & Clough, Jan. Drawing. 96p. (C). 1995. pap. text, per. 32.95 (*0-7872-1049-8*) Kendall-Hunt.
Mullin, Anna. Stand up & Be Counted. 1.50 (*0-687-50352-3*) Abingdon.
Mullin, B., jt. ed. see Lovold, S.
***Mullin, Bernard J., et al.** Sport Marketing. 2nd rev. ed. LC 99-41126. (Illus.). 456p. (C). 1999. 54.00 (*0-88011-877-6*) Human Kinetics.
Mullin Burton, Ann. An Everyname Index to "Some Descendants of James McCain, Sr. of Somerset County, New Jersey" 1952: McCain Index. 25p. 1999. pap. 8.00 (*0-937505-17-X*) Glyndwr Resc.
Mullin, Chris. Error of Judgement: The Truth about the Birmingham Bombings. 329p. 1990. pap. 11.95 (*1-85371-090-3*, Pub. by Poolbeg Pr) Dufour.
***Mullin, Chris.** Young Basketball Player. (Young Enthusiast Ser.). (J). (gr. 3-7). 2000. 9.95 (*0-7894-5426-2*) DK Pub Inc.
Mullin, Christopher A. & Scott, Jeffrey G., eds. Molecular Mechanisms of Insecticide Resistance: Diversity among Insects. LC 92-28366. (Symposium Ser.: No. 505). (Illus.). 322p. 1992. text 85.00 (*0-8412-2474-9*, Pub. by Am Chemical) OUP.
Mullin, Donald, compiled by. Victorian Actors & Actresses in Review: A Dictionary of Contemporary Views of Representative British & American Actors & Actresses, 1837-1901. LC 83-1407. (Illus.). 571p. 1983. lib. bdg. 65.00 (*0-313-23316-0*, MVA/) Greenwood.
— Victorian Plays: A Record of Significant Productions on the London Stage, 1837-1901, 4. LC 86-25718. (Bibliographies & Indexes in the Performing Arts Ser.: No. 4). 213p. 1987. lib. bdg. 75.00 (*0-313-24211-9*, MVP/) Greenwood.
Mullin, Eileen. The Essential Photoshop Book. (Essentials Ser.). 456p. 1996. per. 35.00 incl. cd-rom (*0-7615-0695-0*) Prima Pub.
— The Essential Photoshop 5 Book. 2nd ed. LC 98-66466. (Illus.). 500p. 1998. per. 24.99 (*0-7615-1396-5*) Prima Pub.
— Web Design Resources Directory. 1997. pap. 39.99 (*0-614-28475-7*, Lycos Pr) Que.
Mullin, Glenn H. The Fourteen Dalai Lamas: A Sacred Legacy of Reincarnation. Shepherd, Valerie, ed. LC 99-44923. (Illus.). 256p. 2000. 24.95 (*1-57416-039-7*) Clear Light.
***Mullin, Glenn H.** Fourteen Dalai Lamas: A Sacred Legacy of Reincarnation. LC 99-44923. (Illus.). 384p. 2000. pap. 19.95 (*1-57416-054-0*) Clear Light.
Mullin, Glenn H. Gems of Wisdom from the Seventh Dalai Lama. LC 99-48048. 171p. 2000. pap. 15.95 (*1-55939-132-4*) Snow Lion Pubns.
— Living in the Face of Death: The Tibetan Tradition. LC 98-14199. 238p. 1999. pap. 16.95 (*1-55939-100-6*) Snow Lion Pubns.
— Mystical Verses of a Mad Dalai Lama. LC 94-2560. 288p. 1994. pap. 14.00 (*0-8356-0700-3*, Quest) Theos Pub Hse.
— The Practice of Kalachakra. LC 91-27945. 352p. 1991. pap. 16.95 (*0-937938-95-5*) Snow Lion Pubns.
— Tibet Past & Present: Featuring Personal Sacred Objects of His Holiness the Dalai Lama. 1996. 27.00 (*1-56352-352-3*) Longstreet.
— Tibet Past & Present: Featuring Personal Sacred Objects of His Holiness the Dalai Lama. 1996. pap. text 16.95 (*1-56352-353-1*) Longstreet.
— Training the Mind in the Great Way. 174p. 1993. pap. 12.95 (*0-937938-96-3*) Snow Lion Pubns.
Mullin, Glenn H., tr. from TIB. Readings on the Six Yogas of Naropa. LC 97-18938. 200p. 1997. pap. 16.95 (*1-55939-074-3*) Snow Lion Pubns.
Mullin, Glenn H., ed. & tr. see Dalai Lama, VII.
Mullin, Glenn H., ed. & tr. see Dalai Lama XIV.
Mullin, J. B. & Stradling, R. A., eds. Narrow Gap Semiconductors, 1992: Proceedings of the 6th International Conference, University of Southampton, U. K., 19-23 July, 1992. (Illus.). 455p. 1993. 229.00 (*0-7503-0249-6*) IOP Pub.
Mullin, J. B., jt. auth. see Heinrich, H.
Mullin, J. B., jt. auth. see Miller, L. S.
***Mullin, James, et al, eds.** Science, Technology & Innovation in Chile. 180p. 2000. pap. 17.95 (*0-88936-911-9*, Pub. by IDRC Bks) Stylus Pub VA.
Mullin, James J., jt. auth. see Smith, Henry C.
Mullin, Jim T., jt. auth. see Bushnell, Ian W.
Mullin, John. Reports to the Hon. George Stoneman, Governor of California, on Certain Claims of the State of California Against the United States, November 1, 1878, to November 1, 1886. Bruchey, Stuart, ed. LC 78-56670. (Management of Public Lands in the U. S. Ser.). (Illus.). 1979. reprint ed. lib. bdg. 44.95 (*0-405-11345-5*) Ayer.
— Stay with Us: Praying as Disciples. (Spirit Life Ser.). 48p. (Orig.). 1995. pap. 3.95 (*1-878718-28-2*, Resurrection Pr) Catholic Bk Pub.
Mullin, Karen, jt. ed. see Barteck, Lynn.
Mullin, Kathy. ABCs of Home Schooling. (Illus.). 180p. (Orig.). 1994. pap. 14.95 (*1-57327-001-6*, M Pr CA) Busn Concepts.
Mullin, Kay. The Wondrous Land: The Faery Faith of Ireland. (Orig.). 1997. pap. 23.95 (*1-86163-010-7*, Pub. by Capall Bann Pubng) Holmes Pub.
Mullin, Lenore M., ed. Arrays, Functional Languages & Parallel Systems. 336p. (C). 1991. text 137.00 (*0-7923-9213-2*) Kluwer Academic.
Mullin, M., jt. auth. see ICSID Staff.
Mullin, Mark. Rapid Prototyping for Object. 240p. 1990. pap. text 22.95 (*0-201-55024-5*) Addison-Wesley.
Mullin, Mark H. Educating for the Twenty-First Century: The Challenge for Parents & Teachers. LC 91-635. 208p. 1993. pap. 14.95 (*1-56833-012-X*) Madison Bks UPA.
— Education for the 21st Century: Headmasters Looks Toward the Year 2000. 125p. 1991. 17.95 (*0-8191-8062-9*) Madison Bks UPA.
Mullin, Michael. Africa in America: Slave Acculturation & Resistance in the American South & the British. 432p. 1994. pap. text 17.95 (*0-252-06446-1*) U of Ill Pr.
— Design by Motley. LC 94-42667. (Illus.). 256p. 1996. 55.00 (*0-87413-569-9*) U Delaware Pr.
— Theatre at Stratford-upon-Avon: First Supplement, A Catalogue-Index to Productions of the Royal Shakespeare Company, 1979-1993, 17. LC 94-22456. (Bibliographies & Indexes in the Performing Arts Ser.: Vol. 17). 352p. 1994. lib. bdg. 99.50 (*0-313-25028-6*, Greenwood Pr) Greenwood.
Mullin, Michael, compiled by. Theatre at Stratford-Upon-Avon: A Catalogue-Index to Productions of the Shakespeare Memorial-Royal Shakespeare Theatre, 1879 to 1978, 2 vols. LC 79-8578. 1980. lib. bdg. 150.00 (*0-313-22126-X*, MSH/) Greenwood.
— Theatre at Stratford-Upon-Avon: A Catalogue-Index to Productions of the Shakespeare Memorial-Royal Shakespeare Theatre, 1879 to 1978, 2 vols., Vol. 1. LC 79-8578. 1980. lib. bdg. 85.00 (*0-313-22169-3*, MSH/1) Greenwood.
— Theatre at Stratford-Upon-Avon: A Catalogue-Index to Productions of the Shakespeare Memorial-Royal Shakespeare Theatre, 1879 to 1978, 2 vols., Vol. 2. LC 79-8578. 1980. lib. bdg. 85.00 (*0-313-22170-7*, MSH/2) Greenwood.
Mullin, Michael M. Webs & Scales: Physical & Ecological Processes in Marine Fish Recruitment. LC 93-10188. (Washington Sea Grant Ser.). 144p. 1993. 25.00 (*0-295-97244-0*); pap. 15.00 (*0-295-97245-9*) U of Wash Pr.
Mullin, Molly A. Merriweather's Reign. LC 94-2416. 1995. pap. 6.00 (*0-88734-239-6*) Players Pr.
Mullin, Molly A., jt. auth. see Blu, Susan.
***Mullin, Patrick J.** Prostate & Finasteride: Index of New Information with Authors, Subjects & References. rev. ed. LC 96-12486. 141p. 1999. 47.50 (*0-7883-2128-5*); pap. 44.50 (*0-7883-2129-3*) ABBE Pubs Assn.
Mullin, Penn. The Four Corners Mystery Series, 5 vols. Kratoville, Betty Lou, ed. (Illus.). 48p. (Orig.). (J). (gr. 4-11). 1997. pap. 17.00 (*1-57128-055-3*, 8055-3) High Noon Bks.
— High-Five Series: Whale Summer, Spirits of the Canyon & Trail to Danger, 3 bks. (Orig.). (J). (gr. 6-11). 1991. student ed. 10.00 (*0-87879-924-9*) High Noon Bks.
— High-Five Series: Whale Summer, Spirits of the Canyon & Trail to Danger, 3 bks., Set. (Orig.). (J). (gr. 6-11). 1991. pap. text 12.00 (*0-87879-913-3*) High Noon Bks.
— Message from Outer Space. Kratoville, Betty Lou, ed. (Meridian Bks.). (Illus.). 64p. (J). (gr. 3-9). 1989. lib. bdg. 4.95 (*0-87879-616-9*) High Noon Bks.

— Postcards from America Series: The White House Mystery, High Time in New York, Windy City Whirl, Trouble in the Black Hills, San Francisco Adventure. Kratoville, Betty Lou, ed. (Illus.). (Orig.). (J). (gr. 4-12). 1992. pap. 17.00 (*0-87879-957-5*, 957-5) High Noon Bks.
— Postcards from Europe Series, 5 bks. Kratoville, Betty Lou, ed. (Illus.). 48p. (J). (gr. 6-10). 1994. pap. text 17.00 (*0-87879-976-1*) High Noon Bks.
— Postcards from South America, 5 bks., Set. Kratoville, Betty Lou, ed. (Postcards Ser.). (Illus.). 48p. (Orig.). (J). (gr. 3-10). 1995. pap. text 17.00 (*1-57128-014-6*, 014-6) Acad Therapy.
— Trailblazers Series, 5 vols., Set. Kratoville, Betty L., ed. (Illus.). 48p. (YA). (gr. 4). 1999. pap. 17.00 (*1-57128-113-4*, 8113-4) Acad Therapy.
Mullin, Ray. Electrical Wiring Residential. 13th ed. LC 98-4135. (Illus.). 608p. 1998. text 54.95 (*0-8273-8607-9*) Delmar.
***Mullin, Ray.** Electrical Wiring Residential: Instructor's Guide. 13th ed. 96p. 1999. teacher ed. 18.95 (*0-8273-8608-7*) Delmar.
Mullin, Ray C. Electrical Wiring: Residential Plans. 11th ed. (Illus.). 1993. 15.50 (*0-8273-5774-5*) Delmar.
— Electrical Wiring - Res. 12th ed. (Electrical Trades Ser.). 96p. 1996. text, teacher ed. 16.95 (*0-8273-6843-7*) Delmar.
— Electrical Wiring - Residential. 11th ed. 1993. teacher ed. 15.00 (*0-8273-5096-1*) Delmar.
— Electrical Wiring - Residential. 11th ed. 504p. 1993. trans. 114.95 (*0-8273-5652-8*) Delmar.
— Electrical Wiring - Residential. 11th ed. 504p. 1993. text 41.95 (*0-8273-5795-8*) Delmar.
— Electrical Wiring-Residential. 9th ed. 304p. 1987. pap. 30.95 (*0-8273-2766-8*) Delmar.
— Electrical Wiring, Residential. 11th ed. 1993. pap. 40.50 (*0-8273-5095-3*) Delmar.
— Electrical Wiring, Residential. 12th ed. 608p. 1995. pap. 38.25 (*0-8273-6841-0*) Delmar.
— Electrical Wiring, Residential. 12th ed. 512p. 1995. pap. 43.50 (*0-8273-6842-9*) Delmar.
— Electrical Wiring Residential House Plan. 12th ed. (Electrical Trades Ser.). 1996. 16.95 (*0-8273-7442-9*) Delmar.
— House Wiring with the NEC. LC 98-4515. 352p. (C). 1999. pap. 27.95 (*0-8273-8350-9*) Delmar.
Mullin, Ray C. & Smith, Robert L. Electrical Wiring: Commercial. 7th ed. 256p. 1989. pap., teacher ed. 15.00 (*0-8273-4093-1*) Delmar.
— Electrical Wiring: Commercial. 7th ed. 256p. 1990. pap. text 29.50 (*0-8273-4092-3*) Delmar.
— Electrical Wiring: Commercial. 8th ed. LC 92-12939. 1993. pap. 30.50 (*0-8273-5093-7*) Delmar.
— Electrical Wiring: Commercial. 9th ed. LC 95-13501. 336p. 1995. pap. 36.00 (*0-8273-6655-8*) Delmar.
— Electrical Wiring - Commercial. 8th ed. 1993. teacher ed. 16.00 (*0-8273-5094-5*) Delmar.
Mullin, Ray C., jt. auth. see Sanders, Melvin K.
Mullin, Ray C., jt. auth. see Stauffer, H. Brooke.
Mullin, Rita, ed. see Sinclair, Upton.
Mullin, Rita T. Animalogy: Wierd & Wacky Animal Facts. LC 97-29170. (Illus.). (J). 1998. lib. bdg. 13.99 (*0-517-80001-2*) Crown Pub Group.
— Animalogy; Weird & Wacky Animal Facts. (Animal Planet Ser.). (J). 1998. 15.19 (*0-606-13133-7*, Pub. by Turtleback) Demco.
Mullin, Robert B. Episcopal Vision-American Reality: High Church Theology & Social Thought in Evangelical America. 247p. 1986. 37.50 (*0-300-03487-3*) Yale U Pr.
— Miracles & the Modern Religious Imagination. LC 96-13505. 336p. 1996. 35.00 (*0-300-06696-1*) Yale U Pr.
Mullin, Robert B., jt. auth. see Ahlstrom, Sydney E.
Mullin, Ronald C. & Mullen, Gary L., eds. Finite Fields: Theory, Applications & Algoritms. LC 98-38826. (Contemporary Mathematics Ser.: Vol. 225). 233p. 1998. pap. 49.00 (*0-8218-0817-6*) Am Math.
Mullin, Ronald C., jt. auth. see Gao, XuHong.
Mullin, Sue. Nuevo Cubano Cooking. 128p. 1993. 12.98 (*1-55521-906-3*) Bk Sales Inc.
— Salads. 128p. 1996. 12.98 (*0-7858-0554-0*) Bk Sales Inc.
***Mullin, Timothy J.** The Fighting Submachine Gun, Machine Pistol & Shotgun: A Hands-On Evaluation. (Illus.). 224p. 1999. pap. 35.00 (*1-58160-040-2*) Paladin Pr.
Mullin, Timothy J. Testing the War Weapons: Rifles & Light Machine Guns from Around the World. LC 98-116223. (Illus.). 432p. 1997. pap. 45.00 (*0-87364-943-5*) Paladin Pr.
Mullin, Tom, ed. The Nature of Chaos. LC 92-41598. (Illus.). 344p. 1993. pap. text 29.95 (*0-19-853954-1*, Clarendon Pr) OUP.
Mullin, Virginia L. Chemistry Experiments for Children. LC 68-9306. (Illus.). 96p. (J). (gr. 3-10). 1968. reprint ed. pap. 3.95 (*0-486-22031-1*) Dover.
Mullineaux, Donal R., jt. ed. see Lipman, Peter W.
Mulliner Box & Planing Co. Staff. Turn-of-the-Century Doors, Windows & Decorative Millwork: The Mulliner Catalog of 1893. LC 94-23833. Orig. Title: Combined Book of Sash, Doors, Blinds, Mouldings, Stair Work, Mantels & All Kinds of Interior & Exterior Finish. (Illus.). 336p. 1995. pap. text 13.95 (*0-486-28514-6*) Dover.
Mulliner, K. & The-Mulliner, Lian. Historical Dictionary of Singapore. LC 91-35697. (Asian Historical Dictionaries Ser.: No. 7). (Illus.). 285p. 1991. 42.00 (*0-8108-2504-X*) Scarecrow.
Mullineux, A. Financial Reform in Central & Eastern Europe. 314p. 1995. lib. bdg. 115.00 (*1-56072-231-2*) Nova Sci Pubs.
— Financial Reform in Central & Eastern Europe: Lessons from the 'West', Poland & Further East. 264p. 1995. lib. bdg. 125.00 (*1-56072-233-9*) Nova Sci Pubs.
Mullineux, A. W. The Business Cycle after Keynes: A Contemporary Analysis. LC 83-27160. 132p. 1984. 45.00 (*0-389-20453-6*, 08014) B&N Imports.
— Business Cycles & Financial Crisis. 176p. 1990. reprint ed. text 54.50 (*0-472-10181-1*, 10181) U of Mich Pr.
Mullineux, A. W. & Green, Christopher J. Economic Performance & Financial Sector Reform in Central & Eastern Europe: Capital Flows, Bank & Enterprise Restructuring. LC 98-17099. 336p. 1999. 100.00 (*1-85898-806-3*) E Elgar.
Mullineux, Andrew, ed. Financial Innovation, Banking & Monetary Aggregates. LC 95-42411. (Illus.). 224p. 1996. 90.00 (*1-85898-126-3*) E Elgar.
Mullineux, Andrew W., jt. ed. see Dickinson, David.
Mullineux, Andy. U. K. Banking after Deregulation. 192p. 1987. lib. bdg. 55.00 (*0-7099-4689-9*, Pub. by C Helm) Routldge.
Mullineux, Andy, et al. Business Cycles: Theory & Evidence. LC 92-26627. 208p. 1993. pap. 24.95 (*0-631-18567-4*) Blackwell Pubs.
Mullineux, Glen, ed. The Mathematics of Surfaces No.6, Vol. VI. LC 97-108428. (Institute of Mathematics & Its Applications Conference Series, New Ser.: No. 58). (Illus.). 584p. 1996. text 145.00 (*0-19-851198-1*) OUP.
Mullineux, Neil. The World Tyre Industry: A New Perspective to 2005. LC 98-129602. (Research Reports: No. R348). 1997. 945.00 (*0-85058-921-5*) Economist Intell.
Mullinex, Phyllis. Testing Programs for Behavior Toxicology Test Guides: Methodology & Interpretation of Data. 1989. 58.00 (*0-911131-21-3*) Specialist Journals.
Mulling, Judy C., ed. see Martin, Norman R.
Mulling, Sylvia S., jt. see Osburne, Andrea G.
Mulling, Sylvia S., jt. auth. see Osburne, Adrea G.
Mulling, Sylvia S., jt. auth. see Osburne, Andrea G.
Mullings, Christine, et al. New Technologies in the Humanities. 1996. 75.00 (*1-85739-113-6*) Bowker-Saur.
Mullings, Leith. On Our Own Terms: Race, Class & Gender in the Lives of African-American Women. LC 96-28853. 224p. (C). 1996. 75.00 (*0-415-91285-7*) Routledge.
— On Our Own Terms: Race, Class, & Gender in the Lives of African-American Women. 96-28853. 224p. (C). 1996. pap. 19.99 (*0-415-91286-5*) Routledge.
Mullings, Leith, jt. ed. see Marable, Manning.
Mullings, Pal. The Final Draw. LC 95-26798. 275p. 1996. 18.95 (*0-944957-57-9*) Rivercross Pub.
***Mullins, Lynne.** Noodles to Pasta: Fresh & Easy Recipes with Noodles. (Illus.). 2000. pap. text. write for info. (*0-7322-6752-8*) HarpC.
Mullins, A. F., Jr. Born Arming: Development & Military Power in New States. LC 86-23043. (ISIS Studies in International Security & Arms Control: Vol. 2). 168p. 1987. 35.00 (*0-8047-1375-8*) Stanford U Pr.
Mullins, Andrea. Adults on Mission Guide. Hansen, Susan, ed. 16p. (Orig.). 1996. pap. text 3.95 (*1-56309-170-4*, W964125) Womans Mission Union.
— Women on Mission Guide. Hansen, Susan, ed. 44p. (Orig.). 1995. pap. text 3.95 (*1-56309-109-7*, W954106) Womans Mission Union.
Mullins, Anne & Saunders, Cheryl. Economic Union in Federal Systems. 283p. 1994. 64.00 (*1-86287-123-X*, Pub. by Federation Pr) Gaunt.
Mullins, C. Daniel, jt. auth. see Hartzema, Abraham G.
Mullins, Carolyn. Life Skills Reading. 1985. pap. 10.95 (*0-87694-149-8*) Ed Design Inc.
Mullins, Carolyn J. A Parent's Guide to Youth Soccer. LC 83-80731. (Illus.). 144p. 1983. reprint ed. pap. 44.70 (*0-608-07060-2*, 206726600009) Bks Demand.
Mullins, Cecil J. Seining the Air for Sparrows. LC 88-31434. (Illus.). 52p. (Orig.). 1988. pap. 5.95 (*0-936015-15-2*) Pocahontas Pr.
Mullins, Charles E. & Mayer, David C. Congenital Heart Disease: A Diagrammatic Atlas. (Illus.). 394p. 1991. pap. 145.00 (*0-471-58817-2*, Wiley-Liss) Wiley.
Mullins, Colleen. Opening Day. 1998. 25.00 (*1-893125-04-1*) Womens Studio Wrkshop.
Mullins, Craig. Db2 Developer's Guide. 3rd ed. LC 97-67996. 1440p. 1997. 59.99 (*0-672-31168-2*) Sams.
Mullins, Craig S. DB2 Developer's Guide. 2nd ed. 1159p. (Orig.). 1994. 59.99 (*0-672-30512-7*) Sams.
Mullins, David, jt. auth. see Marsh, Alex.
***Mullins, Debra.** Donovan's Bed. 384p. 2000. mass mkt. 5.99 (*0-380-80774-2*, Avon Bks) Morrow Avon.
Mullins, Debra. Once a Mistress. 384p. 1999. mass mkt. 5.99 (*0-380-80444-1*, Avon Bks) Morrow Avon.
Mullins, Denvil. . . . And Ten to Go. LC 99-178094. 227p. (J). (gr. 4 up). 1998. 17.95 (*1-57072-051-7*) Overmountain Pr.
— The Cornfields of Coaley Creek: Tales from Southwest Virginia. 224p. (Orig.). 1994. pap. 9.95 (*1-57072-011-8*) Overmountain Pr.
— Echoes of Appalachia. 216p. (Orig.). 1995. pap. 9.95 (*1-57072-021-5*) Overmountain Pr.
Mullins, Denvil. Images of Yesterday. LC 98-225754. (Images of Yesterday Ser.: Vol. 5). 166p. 1997. pap. 12.95 (*1-57072-067-3*) Overmountain Pr.
Mullins, Denvil. Remember When. 168p. 1999. pap. 12.95 (*1-57072-090-8*) Overmountain Pr.
— The Road Back Home: Tales of Appalachia. 194p. (Orig.). 1996. pap. 9.95 (*1-57072-040-1*) Overmountain Pr.
— Times of Used to Be. 188p. 1993. pap. 9.95 (*1-57072-001-0*) Overmountain Pr.
Mullins, E. J. & McKnight, T. S., eds. Canadian Woods: Their Properties & Uses. 3rd ed. 400p. 1981. text 40.00 (*0-8020-2430-0*) U of Toronto Pr.
Mullins, E. L. Texts & Calendars: An Analytical Guide to Serial Publications, 1957-1982, Vol. 2. (Royal Historical Society Guides & Handbooks Ser.: No.12). 335p. 27.00 (*0-86193-100-9*) David Brown.
Mullins, Edgar Y. Baptist Beliefs. 1987. pap. 9.00 (*0-8170-1014-9*) Judson.
***Mullins, Edgar Young.** The Christian Religion in its Doctrinal Expression. 538p. 2000. pap. 42.00 (*1-57910-431-2*) Wipf & Stock.
Mullins, Edmund. Cornish Primitive: Alfred Wallis. (Illus.). 64p. 1994. 29.95 (*1-85793-274-9*, Pub. by Pavilion Bks Ltd) Trafalgar.
Mullins, Eustace C. This Difficult Individual: Ezra Pound. LC 78-64049. (Des Imagistes: Literature of the Imagist Movement Ser.). reprint ed. 31.00 (*0-404-17081-1*) AMS Pr.
***Mullins, Gary E.** Dancing the Beguine: A Memoir of Unwinding Romance. LC 00-190425. 389p. 2000. 25.00 (*0-7388-1687-6*); pap. 18.00 (*0-7388-1688-4*) Xlibris Corp.
Mullins, George H. Culturgrams: The Nations Around Us: The Americas & Europe. (Illus.). (C). 1997. pap. 80.00 (*0-89434-205-3*); pap. 35.00 (*0-89434-206-1*) Ferguson.
— Culturgrams Vol. II: The Nations Around Us: Middle East, Asia, Africa, & Pacific Areas. rev. ed. (Illus.). 160p. (C). 1998. pap. 45.00 (*0-89434-207-X*) Ferguson.
— The Third Walnut Tree: Was It An "Act of God"? LC 99-19292. 160p. 2000. pap. 12.95 (*1-56474-309-8*) Fithian Pr.
Mullins, George J., jt. auth. see Connolly, Francis M.
Mullins, Gerry. Dorothea Lange's Ireland. (Illus.). 122p. 1998. 29.95 (*1-57098-181-7*); pap. 19.95 (*1-57098-182-5*) Roberts Rinehart.
Mullins, H. T. & Eyles, N., eds. Subsurface Geologic Investigations of New York Finger Lakes: Implications for Late Quaternary Deglaciation & Environmental Change. LC 96-35721. (Special Papers: No. 311). 1996. pap. 35.00 (*0-8137-2311-6*) Geol Soc.
Mullins, Henry T. Carbonate Depositional Environments - Modern & Ancient Pt. 4: Periplatform Carbonates. Warme, John E. & Shanley, Keith W., eds. LC 85-22384. (Colorado School of Mines Quarterly Ser.: Vol. 81, No. 2, 1986). (Illus.). 63p. 1986. pap. text 20.00 (*0-918062-69-1*) Colo Sch Mines.
Mullins, Hugh A. Marine Insurance Digest. LC 59-15426. 308p. reprint ed. 95.50 (*0-8357-9073-8*, 201910500010) Bks Demand.
Mullins, I. J. Management & Organisational Behaviour. 546p. (C). 1989. 195.00 (*0-7855-5691-5*, Pub. by Inst Pur & Supply) St Mut.
Mullins, Jeff. Dating & Marriage: Avoiding Hell on Earth. LC 99-93331. 192p. 1999. pap. 11.95 (*0-9672886-0-6*) J Mullins.
Mullins, Joe. Hawaii's Volcanoes Legends & Facts. pap. 5.95 (*0-681-27872-2*) Booklines Hawaii.
Mullins, John D., jt. ed. see Lambert, John W.
Mullins, Johnny. City of Love. 213p. 1984. 7.45 (*0-89697-134-1*) Intl Univ Pr.
Mullins, Joleen W. Let's Cook, America: Traditional American Cooking. LC 91-91371. 265p. (Orig.). 1992. pap. text 14.95 (*0-9631418-0-5*) W Mullins Pubs.
Mullins, Joseph G. Hawaiian Journey. (Illus.). 128p. 1984. pap. 12.95 (*0-935180-04-4*) Mutual Pub HI.
Mullins, Judy C., ed. see Martin, Norman R.
Mullins, Kelly, ed. see Spon, Rogie.
Mullins, L. Tribute to Teddy Bear Artists, Series 2. 2nd ed. (Illus.). 160p. 1996. 29.95 (*0-87588-456-3*) Hobby Hse.
Mullins, L. J. Management & Organizational Behaviour. 546p. (C). 1989. 175.00 (*0-7855-4622-7*, Pub. by Inst Pur & Supply) St Mut.
Mullins, L. J., et al, eds. Annual Review of Biophysics & Bioengineering, Vol. 2. LC 79-188446. (Illus.). 1973. text 55.00 (*0-8243-1802-1*) Annual Reviews.
— Annual Review of Biophysics & Bioengineering, Vol. 3. LC 79-188446. (Illus.). 1974. text 55.00 (*0-8243-1803-X*) Annual Reviews.
— Annual Review of Biophysics & Bioengineering, Vol. 4. LC 79-188446. (Illus.). 1975. text 55.00 (*0-8243-1804-8*) Annual Reviews.
— Annual Review of Biophysics & Bioengineering, Vol. 5. LC 79-188446. (Illus.). 1976. text 55.00 (*0-8243-1805-6*) Annual Reviews.
— Annual Review of Biophysics & Bioengineering, Vol. 6. LC 79-188446. (Illus.). 1977. text 55.00 (*0-8243-1806-4*) Annual Reviews.
— Annual Review of Biophysics & Bioengineering, Vol. 7. LC 79-188446. (Illus.). 1978. text 55.00 (*0-8243-1807-2*) Annual Reviews.
— Annual Review of Biophysics & Bioengineering, Vol. 8. LC 79-188446. (Illus.). 1979. text 55.00 (*0-8243-1808-0*) Annual Reviews.
— Annual Review of Biophysics & Bioengineering, Vol. 9. LC 79-188446. (Illus.). 1980. text 55.00 (*0-8243-1809-9*) Annual Reviews.
— Annual Review of Biophysics & Bioengineering, Vol. 10. LC 79-188446. (Illus.). 1981. text 55.00 (*0-8243-1810-2*) Annual Reviews.
— Annual Review of Biophysics & Bioengineering, Vol. 11. LC 79-188446. (Illus.). 1982. text 55.00 (*0-8243-1811-0*) Annual Reviews.
— Annual Review of Biophysics & Bioengineering, Vol. 12. LC 79-188446. (Illus.). 1983. text 55.00 (*0-8243-1812-9*) Annual Reviews.
Mullins, Larry. Goal Setting for Women Only! (Illus.). 64p. 1984. pap. 5.95 (*0-912137-03-7*) Actionizing.
— Immature People With Power: How to Handle Them! LC 82-73202. (Illus.). 256p. 1983. 19.95 (*0-912137-00-2*); pap. 14.95 (*0-912137-01-0*) Actionizing.
— Sixty-Two Minutes That Will Change Your Life. (Illus.). 40p. 1983. pap. 4.95 (*0-912137-02-9*) Actionizing.
***Mullins, Laurie J.** Management & Organisational Behavior. 5th ed. (Illus.). 864p. 1999. pap. 59.50 (*0-273-63552-2*) F T P H.
Mullins, Leith, ed. Cities in the United States: Studies in Urban Anthropology. LC 87-5218. 368p. 1987. pap. text 23.50 (*0-231-05001-1*) Col U Pr.
Mullins, Lila. The Heavenly Connection: Reaching Spiritual Maturity. 128p. 1997. pap. 8.95 (*0-9650991-1-3*) Librom Pubng.
Mullins, Lila B. Pathway to Glory: Keys to Christian Living. (Illus.). 128p. (Orig.). 1996. pap. 7.95 (*0-9650991-0-5*) Librom Pubng.
Mullins, Linda. American Teddy Bear Artist Pattern Book. LC 98-226869. (Illus.). 96p. 1998. 24.95 (*0-87588-519-5*, H5455) Hobby Hse.
— American Teddy Bear Encyclopedia. LC 95-211422. (Illus.). 144p. 1995. 29.95 (*0-87588-432-6*) Hobby Hse.
***Mullins, Linda.** Creating Heirloom Teddy Bears, Vol. 2. Vol. 2. (Illus.). 96p. 2000. 24.95 (*0-87588-553-5*) Hobby Hse.
Mullins, Linda. Creating Heirloom Teddy Bears: The Complete Pattern Book. LC 96-142216. (Illus.). 96p. 1995. 24.95 (*0-87588-444-X*) Hobby Hse.
***Mullins, Linda.** Creating Miniature Teddy Bears: International Artists' Designs. (Illus.). 128p. 2000. 24.95 (*0-87588-584-5*) Hobby Hse.
— Linda Mullin's Teddy Bear & Friends Identification & Price Guide. (Illus.). 160p. 2000. 19.95 (*0-87588-580-2*) Hobby Hse.
Mullins, Linda. Teddy Bear - Tales & Patterns. 56p. 1997. 19.95 (*0-87588-492-X*, 5315) Hobby Hse.
— Teddy Bear Artists Postcards. (Illus.). 30p. 1995. pap. 6.95 (*0-87588-436-9*) Hobby Hse.
— Teddy Bears Past & Present, Vol. II. Vol. II. (Illus.). 255p. 1991. 25.00 (*0-87588-384-2*) Hobby Hse.
— Teddy Bears Past & Present: A Collector's Identification Guide, Vol. I. Vol. 1. (Illus.). 304p. 1986. 29.95 (*0-87588-264-1*, 3120) Hobby Hse.
— Tribute to Teddy Bear Artists. LC 95-146722. (Illus.). 144p. 1996. 29.95 (*0-87588-427-X*) Hobby Hse.
— Tribute to Teddy Bear Artists, Vol. 3. LC 99-204763. (Illus.). 144p. 1998. 29.95 (*0-87588-526-8*) Hobby Hse.
— Ultimate Handbook for Making Teddy Bears. LC 98-190360. (Illus.). 88p. 1998. pap. 14.95 (*0-87588-518-7*, H5461) Hobby Hse.
Mullins, Linda, jt. auth. see Simmons, Patricia L.
Mullins, Lisa. The Off to College Journal: An Inspirational & Interactive Journal for First-Year College Students. LC 98-30592. (Illus.). 170p. (Orig.). (C). 1999. pap. 9.95 (*1-56072-337-8*, Nova Kroshka Bks) Nova Sci Pubs.
Mullins, Lisa C., ed. Blueprints for America's Past. (Architectural Treasures of Early America Ser.). (Illus.). 224p. 1988. 19.95 (*0-918678-33-1*) Natl Hist Soc.
— Colonial Architecture of the Mid-Atlantic. (Architectural Treasures of Early America Ser.). (Illus.). 246p. 1987. 19.95 (*0-918678-23-4*) Natl Hist Soc.
— Early American Community Structures. (Architectural Treasures of Early America Ser.). 248p. 1988. 19.95 (*0-918678-29-3*) Natl Hist Soc.
— Early American Southern Homes. (Architectural Treasures of Early America Ser.). 248p. 1987. 19.95 (*0-918678-27-7*) Natl Hist Soc.
— Early Architecture of Rhode Island. (Architectural Treasures of Early America Ser.). 248p. 1987. 19.95 (*0-918678-25-0*) Natl Hist Soc.
— The Evolution of Colonial Architecture. (Architectural Treasures of Early America Ser.). 248p. 1988. 19.95 (*0-918678-28-5*) Natl Hist Soc.
— The Georgian Heritage. (Architectural Treasures of Early America Ser.). (Illus.). 224p. 1988. 19.95 (*0-918678-37-4*) Natl Hist Soc.
— Grandeur of the South. (Architectural Treasures of Early America Ser.). (Illus.). 224p. 1988. 19.95 (*0-918678-36-6*) Natl Hist Soc.
— Homes of New York & Connecticut. (Architectural Treasures of Early America Ser.). (Illus.). 245p. 1987. 19.95 (*0-918678-24-2*) Natl Hist Soc.
— New England by the Sea. (Architectural Treasures of Early America Ser.). (Illus.). 245p. 1987. 19.95 (*0-918678-22-6*) Natl Hist Soc.
— Regional Architecture of the Early South. (Architectural Treasures of Early America Ser.). (Illus.). 245p. 1987. 19.95 (*0-918678-21-8*) Natl Hist Soc.
— The Southern Tradition. (Architectural Treasures of Early America Ser.). (Illus.). 224p. 1988. 19.95 (*0-918678-34-X*) Natl Hist Soc.
— Styles of the Emerging Nation. (Architectural Treasures of Early America Ser.). (Illus.). 224p. 1988. 19.95 (*0-918678-35-8*) Natl Hist Soc.
— Survey of Early American Design. (Architectural Treasures of Early America Ser.). (Illus.). 248p. 1987. 19.95 (*0-918678-20-X*) Natl Hist Soc.
— Village Architecture of Early New England. (Architectural Treasures of Early America Ser.). 248p. 1987. 19.95 (*0-918678-26-9*) Natl Hist Soc.
Mullins, Lorin J. Ion Transport in Heart. LC 80-6272. 144p. 1981. reprint ed. pap. 44.70 (*0-608-00421-9*, 206113600007) Bks Demand.
Mullins, M., jt. auth. see Bary, N.
Mullins, M., jt. auth. see Kuhn, J.
Mullins, Marion D. The First Census of Texas, Eighteen Twenty-Nine to Eighteen Thirty-Six. 63p. 1959. 10.25 (*0-915156-22-9*, 22) Natl Genealogical.
— Republic of Texas Poll Lists for 1846. LC 73-17065. 189p. 1998. reprint ed. pap. 21.00 (*0-8063-0598-3*) Clearfield Co.
Mullins, Marion D., jt. auth. see Grammer, Norma R.
Mullins, Mark. Business, Loan & Real Property Forms, 3 vols., Set. 1994. 375.00 (*1-55834-140-4*, MICHIE) LEXIS Pub.

An Asterisk (*) at the beginning of an entry indicates that the title is appearing for the first time.

Mullins, Mark R. Christianity Made in Japan: A Study of Indigenous Movements. LC 98-35083. (Nanzan Library of Asian Religion & Culture). (Illus.). 278p. (C). 1998. text 48.00 (*0-8248-2114-9*); pap. text 24.95 (*0-8248-2132-7*) UH Pr.

— Religion & Society in Modern Japan. LC 93-23877. (Nanzan Studies in Asian Religions: Vol. 5). 256p. (C). 1993. text 30.00 (*0-89581-935-X*); pap. text 25.00 (*0-89581-936-8*) Asian Humanities.

— Religious Minorities in Canada: A Sociological Study of the Japanese Experience. LC 88-1703. (Canadian Studies: Vol. 4). 220p. 1989. lib. bdg. 89.95 (*0-88946-195-3*) E Mellen.

Mullins, Mark R. & Young, Richard F., eds. Perspectives on Christianity in Korea & Japan: The Gospel & Culture in East Asia. LC 95-35989. 1995. write for info. (*0-7734-8868-5*) E Mellen.

Mullins, Mary V., ed. see Wright, Ronald & Wright, Bonnie.

Mullins, Mattie. Judy: The Murder Of My Daughter, The Healing Of My Family. 1999. pap. text 13.95 (*1-891874-01-2*) Recover Comns.

***Mullins, Mattie.** Preachers Wives Tell All. 2000. pap. 13.95 (*1-891874-08-X*) Recover Comns.

— Preachers' Wives Tell All: Lively Tales & Tasty Recipes from Country Parsonage Kitchens. (Illus.). 2000. pap. 13.95 (*1-891874-04-7*) Recover Comns.

Mullins, Michael. Called to Be Saints: Christian Living in First Century Rome. 576p. 1989. 60.00 (*1-85390-177-6*, Pub. by Veritas Pubns) St Mut.

Mullins, Michael A. & Reed, Rowena. The Union Bookshelf: A Selected Civil War Bibliography. LC 82-71852. (Illus.). 100p. 1982. pap. text 25.00 (*0-916107-12-4*) Broadfoot.

Mullins, Michael G., et al. Biology of the Grapevine. (Biology of Horticultural Crops Ser.). (Illus.). 251p. (C). 1992. text 74.95 (*0-521-30507-1*) Cambridge U Pr.

Mullins, Nicholas. Science: Some Sociological Perspectives. LC 72-12826. (Studies in Sociology). 42p. (C). 1973. pap. text. write for info. (*0-672-61205-4*, Bobbs) Macmillan.

Mullins, Nicholas C. Social Networks among Biological Scientists. Zuckerman, Harriet & Merton, Robert K., eds. LC 79-6270. (Dissertations on Sociology Ser.). 1980. lib. bdg. 25.95 (*0-405-12983-1*) Ayer.

Mullins, O. C., jt. auth. see Sheu, E. Y.

Mullins, Oliver C. & Sheu, Eric Y., eds. Structures & Dynamics of Asphaltenes: Proceedings of the International Symposium on Asphaltenes at the Fine Particle Society Meeting in Chicago, Illinois, August 23-24, 1995, & the Symposium on Asphaltene & Resid Characterization Held in San Francisco, California, April 13-17, 1998. (Illus.). 448p. (C). 1998. text 150.00 (*0-306-45930-2*, Kluwer Plenum) Kluwer Academic.

Mullins, P. R. Race & Affluence: An Archaeology of African America & Consumer Culture. LC 99-12107. (Contributions to Global Archaeology Ser.). (Illus.). 217p. (C). 1999. 59.95 (*0-306-46089-0*, Plenum Trade) Perseus Pubng.

Mullins, Patricia. Dinosaur Encore. LC 92-19848. (Willa Perlman Bks.). (Illus.). 32p. (J). (ps-2). 1993. lib. bdg. 14.89 (*0-06-021073-7*) HarpC Child Bks.

— Dinosaur Encore. LC 92-19848. (Trophy Picture Bk.). (Illus.). 32p. (J). (ps-3). 1996. pap. 6.95 (*0-06-443465-6*, HarpTrophy) HarpC Child Bks.

— V for Vanishing: An Alphabet of Endangered Animals. LC 93-8181. (Illus.). 32p. (J). (ps-2). 1994. 15.00 (*0-06-023556-X*) HarpC Child Bks.

— V for Vanishing: An Alphabet of Endangered Animals. LC 93-8181. (Trophy Picture Bk.). (Illus.). 32p. (J). (ps-2). 1997. pap. 6.95 (*0-06-443471-0*, HarpTrophy) HarpC Child Bks.

— V for Vanishing: An Alphabet of Endangered Animals. (J). 1997. 12.15 (*0-606-12029-7*, Pub. by Turtleback) Demco.

***Mullins, Patricia.** One Horse Waiting for Me. LC 97-68018. 32p. (J). (ps-2). 1998. per. 16.00 (*0-689-81381-3*, 878849) S&S Bks Yung.

Mullins, Patricia A., jt. auth. see Alea, Pat.

Mullins, Patrick. Retreat from Africa. 115p. (C). 1989. text 49.00 (*1-872795-37-4*, Pub. by Pentland Pr) St Mut.

Mullins, Patrick J. Prostate Cancers - Prevention & Control: Index of New Information for Medicine, Science & Research with New Update of Progress. rev. ed. 151p. 1997. 47.50 (*0-7883-1616-8*); pap. 44.50 (*0-7883-1617-6*) ABBE Pubs Assn.

***Mullins, Renee.** Plum Purdy. (Illus.). 52p. 2000. pap. 10.95 (*1-57377-102-3*, 0-19884-02342) Easl Pubns.

Mullins, Reuben B. Pulling Leather: Being the Early Recollections of a Cowboy on the Wyoming Range, 1884-1889. Clayton, Lawrence, ed. LC 88-16491. (Illus.). 219p. (Orig.). 1988. pap. 11.95 (*0-931271-10-X*) Hi Plains Pr.

Mullins, Reverdy, jt. auth. see Fenker, Richard M., Jr.

Mullins, Rich. Rich Mullins: Home. Well, Chris, ed. 64p. 1998. pap. 9.95 (*0-9662478-0-9*) Voxcorp.

Mullins Rigdon, Anne. Southern Celebrations: A Cookbook from the Heart of a Caterer's Kitchen. LC 98-90346. 240p. 1999. 27.95 (*0-9665510-0-1*) Southern Celeb.

Mullins, Shirley S. Teaching Music: The Human Experience. 115p. (Orig.). 1985. pap. text 9.95 (*0-9616262-0-8*) Media Servs.

***Mullins, Stephen M.** Toby & Character Jugs of the 20th Century Companion Price Guide. (Illus.). 2000. pap. 17.95 (*1-928938-02-7*) K James Pubg.

Mullins, Stephen M., jt. auth. see Fastenau, David C.

Mullins, Steve, ed. see Bartelme, Tony & Hicks, Brian.

***Mullins, Tamela.** Jesus, Is His Name. 1999. pap. write for info. (*1-58235-171-6*) Watermrk Pr.

Mullins, Terry W. Staff Development Programs: A Guide to Evaluation. LC 94-21623. (Program Evaluation Guides for Schools Ser.). 112p. 1994. pap. 24.95 (*0-8039-6045-X*) Corwin Pr.

Mullins, Tom. Running Lightly: Poems for Young People. 1998. pap. text 12.95 (*1-85635-193-9*) Irish Amer Bk.

Mullins, Traci. Vitamminas para el Alma. (SPA.). 1998. 14.95 (*968-19-0435-4*) Santillana.

Mullins, Traci & Spangler, Ann. Vitamins for the Soul. LC 97-9324. 160p. 1997. 15.95 (*0-385-48738-X*) Doubleday.

— Vitamins for Your Soul: 200 Ways to Nurture Your Spiritual Life. large type ed. LC 97-41488. 123p. 1997. 23.95 (*0-7838-8330-7*, G K Hall & Co) Mac Lib Ref.

Mullins, Walter G. Strike Defense Manual. fac. ed. LC 80-14961. 152p. pap. 47.20 (*0-7837-7418-4*, 204721300006) Bks Demand.

Mullins, Wayman C. 1942: Issue in Doubt. LC 94-5234. 320p. 1994. 29.95 (*0-89015-968-8*) Sunbelt Media.

— A Sourcebook on Domestic & International Terrorism: An Analysis of Issues, Organizations, Tactics & Responses. 2nd ed. LC 96-30404. (Illus.). 610p. 1997. text 129.95 (*0-398-06722-8*); pap. text 99.95 (*0-398-06723-6*) C C Thomas.

Mullins, Wayman C., jt. auth. see McMains, Michael J.

Mullins, William & Allen, Phyllis. Student Housing: Architectural & Social Aspects. LC 76-159965. (Illus.). 1971. 94.50 (*0-89197-955-7*) Irvington.

Mullins, William J., jt. auth. see Brehm, John J.

***Mullins/Winn.** ACP: Pasta Perfect Inc. 1998. 3.00 (*0-324-01608-5*) Thomson Learn.

***Mullis, Angela & Kamper, David, eds.** Indian Gaming: Who Wins? LC 00-103282. (Native American Politics Ser.: Vol. 6). 190p. 2000. pap. 15.00 (*0-935626-53-0*, Pub. by U Cal AISC) Bookpeople.

Mullis, Clifford T., jt. auth. see Roberts, Richard A.

Mullis, Darrell, et al. The Accounting Game: Basic Accounting Fresh from the Lemonade Stand. LC 98-17214. (Illus.). 192p. 1998. pap. 16.95 (*1-57071-396-0*) Sourcebks.

Mullis, Ina V. & Martin, Michael O. Mathematics Achievement in Missouri & Oregon in an International Context: 1997 TIMSS Benchmarking. LC 98-86204. 200p. 1998. write for info. (*1-889938-10-6*) Intl Study Ctr.

— Mathematics & Science Achievement in the Final Year of Secondary School: IEA's Third International Mathematics & Science Study. LC 97-81365. 1998. pap. write for info. (*1-889938-08-4*) Intl Study Ctr.

Mullis, Ina V., et al. Mathematics Achievement in the Primary School Years: IEA's 3rd International Mathematics. LC 97-67235. 200p. (Orig.). 1997. pap. write for info. (*1-889938-04-1*) Intl Study Ctr.

Mullis, Ina V., et al. The State of Mathematics Achievement: NAEP's 1990 Assessment of the Nation & the Trial Assessment of the States (Complete Report) (Illus.). 532p. (Orig.). (C). 1993. pap. text 75.00 (*0 7881 0107 2*) DIANE Pub.

— The State of Mathematics Achievement: NAEP's 1990 Assessment of the Nation & the Trial Assessment of the States (Executive Summary) (Illus.). 42p. (Orig.). (C). 1993. pap. text 25.00 (*0-7881-0106-4*) DIANE Pub.

Mullis, Ina V., jt. auth. see Martin, Michael O.

Mullis, Ina V., jt. ed. see Martin, Michael O.

Mullis, Ina V. S. Report in Brief: NAEP 1992 Trends in Academic Progress, Achievement of United States Students in Science, 1969 to 1992; Mathematics, 1973 to 1992; Reading, 1971 to 1992; Writing, 1984 to 1992. 32p. 1994. pap. 2.50 (*0-16-045132-9*) USGPO.

Mullis, Kary B. Dancing Naked in the Mind Field. 240p. 1998. pap. 13.00 (*0-679-77400-9*) Vin Bks.

— Polymerase Chain Reaction. (Illus.). 458p. 1994. 49.50 (*0-8176-3750-8*) Birkhauser.

Mullis, Kary B. & Gibbs, Richard, eds. The Polymerase Chain Reaction: A Textbook. (Illus.). xxii, 458p. (C). 1994. 79.00 (*0-8176-3607-2*) Birkhauser.

Mullish, Henry. Modern Programming: FORTRAN IV. LC 68-3217. 144p. reprint ed. pap. 44.70 (*0-608-30968-0*, 201259100082) Bks Demand.

Mullish, Henry & Cooper, Herbert. The Spirit of "C" An Introduction to Modern Programming. 527p. (C). 1987. pap. text, teacher ed. write for info. (*0-314-35228-7*) West Pub.

Mullish, Henry, jt. auth. see Ebner, David.

Mulliss, Christine. Goodness! Eating Healthily. 63p. (C). 1977. pap. 9.95 (*0-8464-1014-1*) Beekman Pubs.

Mullia, M. S., et al. Distribution, Transport, & Fate of the Insecticides: Malathion & Parathion in the Environment. Gunther, Francis A., ed. (Residue Reviews Ser.: Vol. 30). (Illus.). 172p. 1981. 89.95 (*0-387-90634-7*) Spr-Verlag.

***Mullner, Ross M. & Jewell, Mark.** A Bibliography of Recent Works on Home Health Care. LC 00-32452. (Studies in Health & Human Services: Vol. 37). 200p. 2000. 79.95 (*0-7734-7763-2*) E Mellen.

Mullner, Ross M., jt. ed. see Brehm, Henry P.

Mullock, James & Leigh-Pollitt, Piers. The Data Protection Act 1998 Explained. (Point of Law Ser.). viii, 192p. 1999. 50.00 (*0-11-702336-1*, Pub. by Statnry Office) Balogh.

Mullock, Philip, jt. auth. see Aqvist.

Mulloney, Stephen. Traces of Thoreau: A Cape Cod Journey. LC 98-12874. (Illus.). 176p. 1998. text 42.50 (*1-55553-344-2*); pap. text 15.95 (*1-55553-343-4*) NE U Pr.

Mulloy, Diana. Enhanced Energy Recovery Industry Review. 251p. 1998. 1500.00 (*1-56965-511-1*, DOR97) BCC.

Mulloy, John J. Christianity & the Challenge of History. 275p. (Orig.). 1995. pap. 14.95 (*0-931888-61-1*) Christendom Pr.

Mulloy, John J., ed. see Dawson, Christopher.

Mulloy, Martin. Saudi Arabia: Major World Nations. LC 98-16320. (Major World Nations Ser.). (Illus.). 144p. (YA). (gr. 5 up). 1999. lib. bdg. 19.95 (*0-7910-4982-5*) Chelsea Hse.

— Syria: Major World Nations. LC 98-4307. (Major World Nations Ser.). (Illus.). 144p. (YA). (gr. 5 up). 1999. lib. bdg. 19.95 (*0-7910-4983-3*) Chelsea Hse.

Mulmuley, Ketan. Computational Geometry. LC 93-3138. 447p. (C). 1993. text 29.00 (*0-13-336363-5*) P-H.

Mulnix, Wolfe. Problem Book Molecular & Cellular Biology. 2nd ed. 2002. pap. 22.00 (*0-534-37531-6*) Thomson Learn.

Mulock, Dinah M. Little Lame Prince, Adventures of a Brownie. (J). 1976. 20.95 (*0-8488-1109-7*) Amereon Ltd.

Mulock, Miss. The Little Lame Prince. (Illus.). 116p. 1991. reprint ed. lib. bdg. 14.95 (*0-89966-762-7*) Buccaneer Bks.

Mulongey, K., et al, eds. Biological Nitrogen Fixation & Sustainability of Tropical Agriculture. 502p. 1992. 380.00 (*0-471-93560-3*) Wiley.

Mulpeter, Virginia A. & Rosenfield, Judith F. Program for the Assessment & Instruction of Swallowing (PAIS) 24p. (Orig.). (C). 1993. teacher ed. 55.00 (*0-937857-39-4*, 1529) Speech Bin.

Mulqueen, Maggie. On Our Own Terms: Redefining Competence & Femininity. LC 91-12245. 221p. (C). 1992. pap. text 21.95 (*0-7914-0952-X*) State U NY Pr.

Mulready, Sally, jt. auth. see Callaghan, Hugh.

Mulrenin, Paul E., jt. auth. see Goldsmith, Benedict I.

Mulrenin, Paul E., ed. see Members of the 455th Bomb Squadron Association.

Mulrennan, Monica E. A Casebook of Environmental Issues in Canada. 160p. 1997. pap. 21.95 (*0-471-19964-8*) Wiley.

Mulrine, Stephen, tr. see Chekhov, Anton.

Mulrine, Stephen, tr. see Gogol, Nikolai Vasilevich.

Mulrine, Stephen, tr. see Ostrovsky, Alexander.

Mulroney, Catherine, jt. auth. see Babad, Michael.

Mulroney, Merryl. Treasures of the Rainforest: An Introduction to the Endangered Forest Birds of Hawaii. LC 98-96888. (Illus.). 48p. (J). (gr. 3-6). 1999. pap. 8.95 (*0-9669569-0-7*) Peregrine.

Mulrooney, et al. Ophthalmology Pearls of Wisdom. (Pearls of Wisdom Ser.). 1999. pap. 88.00 (*1-890369-18-7*) Boston Medical.

***Mulrooney, C.** Come on with the Rain. 24p. 1999. pap. 3.95 (*1-930935-03-X*, Pick Pocket Pr) Phony Lid Pubns.

Mulrooney, J. Patrick. Paddies. LC 97-78449. 260p. 1999. pap. 16.50 (*0-88739-206-7*) Creat Arts Bk.

Mulrooney, Patrick. Paddies. LC 97-78449. 260p. 1999. 24.50 (*0-88739-194-X*) Creat Arts Bk.

***Mulrow, Cynthia D., ed.** Treatment of Depression - Newer Pharmacotherapies: Evidence Report - Technology Assessment. (Illus.). 365p. (C). 2000. pap. text 40.00 (*0-7881-8540-3*) DIANE Pub.

Mulrow, Cynthia D. & Cook, Deborah, eds. Systematic Reviews: Synthesis of Best Evidence for Health Care Decisions. LC 97-34983. 128p. 1998. pap. text 27.00 (*0-943126-66-5*) Amer Coll Phys.

Mulrow, P. J, jt. ed. see Ganten, D.

Mulroy. Regional Anesthesia: An Illustrated Procedural Guide. 2nd ed. LC 95-4493. (Illus.). 327p. 1995. pap. text 69.95 (*0-316-58906-3*, Little Brwn Med Div) Lppncott W & W.

Mulroy, Darrell & Tallent, Dinah. No Cuffs: Police Issues Teenagers Face. 91p. (Orig.). (YA). (gr. 7-12). 1995. pap. 6.95 (*1-57515-087-5*) PPI Pubng.

Mulroy, Darrell, jt. auth. see Santiago, Julio.

***Mulroy, David, tr.** Early Greek Lyric Poetry. LC 91-42973. (Illus.). 240p. (C). 1999. pap. text 18.95 (*0-472-08606-5*, 08606) U of Mich Pr.

Mulroy, David, tr. Early Greek Lyric Poetry: Translated with an Introduction & Commentary. LC 91-42973. 240p. (C). 1992. text 42.50 (*0-472-10296-6*, 10296) U of Mich Pr.

Mulroy, David, tr. & comment see Horace.

Mulroy, David D. Comites Catulli: Structured Vocabulary Lists for Catullus 1-60. LC 86-10984. 112p. (Orig.). (C). 1986. pap. text 17.00 (*0-8191-5449-0*) U Pr of Amer.

— Picturing the Tale: Chapters in the Study of the Use of Classical Myths by Painters & Sculptors. 92p. (C). 1995. pap. text 17.95 (*0-8403-7761-4*) Kendall-Hunt.

***Mulroy, Donna.** Reunion. LC 99-64036. 378p. 1999. pap. 16.95 (*0-89716-930-1*, Peanut Btr Pubng) Elton-Wolf Pub.

Mulroy, Elizabeth A. The New Uprooted: Single Mothers in Urban Life. LC 95-2084. 206p. 1995. 59.95 (*0-86569-038-3*, Auburn Hse); pap. 18.95 (*0-86569-039-1*, Auburn Hse) Greenwood.

Mulroy, Elizabeth A., ed. Women As Single Parents: Confronting Institutional Barriers in the Courts, the Workplace, & the Housing Market. LC 88-11920. 328p. 1988. 55.00 (*0-86569-176-2*, Auburn Hse) Greenwood.

Mulroy, Kevin. Freedom on the Border: The Seminole Maroons in Florida, the Indian Territory, Coahuila & Texas. LC 92-29135. (Illus.). 278p. 1993. 29.00 (*0-89672-250-3*) Tex Tech Univ Pr.

Mulroy, Kevin, ed. Western Amerykanski: Polish Poster Art & the Western. LC 98-52392. (Illus.). 229p. 1999. pap. 40.00 (*0-295-97813-9*) U of Wash Pr.

***Mulroy, Kevin, ed.** Western Amerykanski: Polish Poster Art & the Western. LC 98 52392. (Illus.). 229p. 1999. 60.00 (*0-295-97812-0*) U of Wash Pr.

Mulry, Ray C. In the Zone: Making Winning Moments Your Way of Life. (Illus.). 198p. (Orig.). 1996. pap. 12.95 (*0-915556-28-6*) Great Ocean.

Mulry, Terrence J., jt. auth. see Church, F. Forrester.

Mulryan, John. Through a Glass Darkly: Milton's Reinvention of the Mythological Tradition. LC 96-9980. (Language & Literature Ser.: Vol. 21). (Illus.). 350p. (C). 1996. text 48.00 (*0-8207-0267-6*) Duquesne.

Mulryan, John, ed. Milton & the Middle Ages. LC 81-694400. 192p. 1982. 29.50 (*0-8387-5036-2*) Bucknell U Pr.

Mulryan, Lenore H. Nagual in the Garden: Fantastic Animals in Mexican Ceramics. LC 95-49823. (Illus.). 156p. 1996. 50.00 (*0-930741-48-X*); pap. 29.00 (*0-930741-49-8*) UCLA Fowler Mus.

Mulryme, J. R., ed. see Middleton, Thomas.

Mulryne, J. R. & Shewring, Margaret, eds. Italian Renaissance Festivals & Their European Influence. LC 92-1736. (Illus.). 440p. 1992. text 99.95 (*0-7734-9608-4*) E Mellen.

— Theatre & Government under the Early Stuarts. LC 92-33796. 285p. (C). 1993. text 74.95 (*0-521-40159-3*) Cambridge U Pr.

Mulryne, J. R., ed. see Holderness, Graham.

Mulryne, J. R., ed. see Kyd, Thomas.

Mulryne, J. R., ed. see Middleton, Thomas.

Mulryne, J. R., ed. see Webster, John.

Mulryne, Ronnie & Shewring, Margaret, eds. Shakespeare's Globe Rebuilt. LC 97-178719. (Illus.). 192p. (C). 1997. pap. 20.95 (*0-521-59988-1*) Cambridge U Pr.

Mulsoon, Paul. Ireland: A Troubled Mirror, Issue 134. (Illus.). 1994. pap. 27.95 (*0-89381-566-7*) Aperture.

Mulsow, Martin, ed. see Mosheim, Lorenz J.

Multani, M. S. Physics of Clusters & Nanophase Materials. 850p. 1990. text 1571.00 (*0-677-26120-9*) Gordon & Breach.

Multani, M. S. & Gupta, L. C. Selected Topics in Superconductivity. LC 92-43565. (Frontiers in Solid State Sciences Ser.). 676p. 1993. pap. write for info. (*981-02-1202-X*); text 135.00 (*981-02-1201-1*) World Scientific Pub.

Multani, M. S., jt. auth. see Gupta, L. C.

Multatuli, pseud. Max Havelaar: Or the Coffee Auctions of the Dutch Trading Company. Edwards, Roy, tr. from DUT. LC 82-2043. (Library of the Indies). 400p. 1982. lib. bdg. 40.00 (*0-87023-359-9*) U of Mass Pr.

Multer, Kent. The Official Miva Web-Scripting Book: Shopping Carts, Feedback Forms, Guestbooks & More. LC 99-60719. (Illus.). 400p. 1999. pap. 34.95 (*0-9661032-1-1*, Pub. by Top Floor Pub) IPG Chicago.

Multer, Susan D. Singing Your Own Song: Using the Mind-Body Connection to Enhance Your Health. LC 94-23113. (Illus.). 96p. (Orig.). 1995. pap. 7.95 (*0-942963-51-2*) Distinctive Pub.

Multhauf, Robert P. Neptune's Gift: A History of Common Salt. LC 77-8688. (Johns Hopkins Studies in the History of Technology; New Ser.: No. 2). (Illus.). 344p. reprint ed. pap. 106.70 (*0-8357-4033-1*, 203672500005) Bks Demand.

— Neptune's Gift: A History of Common Salt. (Illus.). 326p. 1996. reprint ed. pap. text 19.95 (*0-8018-5469-5*) Johns Hopkins.

— The Origins of Chemistry. (Classics in the History & Philosophy of Science Ser.: Vol. 3). 424p. 1993. pap. text 64.00 (*2-88124-594-3*) Gordon & Breach.

Multhaup, Robert H., jt. auth. see Eschenbrenner, Gunther P.

Multi - AMP Institute Staff. Test Equipment. LC 93-20199. 241p. 1993. pap. 33.00 (*0-8273-4923-8*) Delmar.

Multi-Amp Institute Staff. Basic Electricity for Electricians. 256p. 1992. pap. 45.95 (*0-8273-4917-3*) Delmar.

— Industrial Instrumentation. Rader, Billie T., ed. (Illus.). (Orig.). (C). 1989. write for info. (*0-318-66525-5*) Multi-Amp Inst.

— Motors, Generators & Transformers. LC 94-20840. 512p. 1995. pap. 39.25 (*0-8273-4920-3*) Delmar.

— Motors, Generators & Transformers. LC 94-20840. 160p. 1995. text, teacher ed. 23.50 (*0-8273-4921-1*) Delmar.

Multi-Phase Flow & Heat Transfer Symposium Staff. Multiphase Transport: Fundamentals, Reactor Safety, Applications: Proceedings of the Multi-Phase Flow & Heat Transfer Symposium, 2nd, Miami Beach, April 16-18, 1979. 5 vols. Set. Veziroglu, T. Nejat, ed. LC 80-11157. (Illus.). 3932p. 1980. text 875.00 (*0-89116-159-7*) Hemisp Pub.

Multi-Resources Incorporation & Rollant, Paulette D. Mosby's Review Cards: Mental Health Nursing. 232p. 1997. text 22.95 (*0-8151-7378-4*, 28137) Mosby Inc.

Multi-Resources Incorporation, et al. Mosby's Review Cards: Marternity Women Health Nursing. 273p. 1997. text 22.95 (*0-8151-7382-2*, 28138) Mosby Inc.

Multi-Resources Incorporation Staff, et al. Mosby's Review Cards: Pediatric Nursing. 190p. 1997. text 22.95 (*0-8151-7377-6*, 28136) Mosby Inc.

Multiamp Institute Staff. Basic Electricity for Electricians. (Electrical Trades Ser.). 1992. teacher ed. 16.00 (*0-8273-4918-1*) Delmar.

***Multicultural Marketing Resources Staff.** The Source Book of Multicultural Exports, 2000-2001. (Illus.). 96p. 2000. pap. 59.95 (*0-9666315-2-8*) Multicult Mktg.

Multilateral Church Conversation in Scotland Staff. Deacons for Scotland. 88p. 1993. pap. 30.00 (*0-86153-125-6*) St Mut.

Multilateral Trade Negotiations, the Uruguay Trade. The Dunkel Draft from the GATT Secretariat: Multilateral Trade Negotiations - The Uruguay Round Track Negotiations Committee Draft Final Act Embodying the Results of the Uruguay Round of Multilateral Trade Negotiations. Institute for International Legal Information Staf, ed. LC 92-17248. 547p. 1992. reprint ed. 75.00 (*0-89941-799-X*, 307560) W S Hein.

Multim, Azimuth. Interactive Skills: Seneca S4. 1996. 35.74 (*0-07-847664-X*) McGraw.

Multimedia Development Services Staff. Accident Prevention Signs & Tags, 4 vols., Vol. 3, Module 2. (Safety, Health & Environmental Fundamentals Ser.). (Illus.). (Orig.). (C). 1996. pap. text 30.00 (*1-57431-119-0*); pap. text, teacher ed. 49.95 (*1-57431-120-4*) Tech Trng Systs.

M

— Basic Electrical Equipment. (Plant Fundamentals Ser.: Vol. XI, Module II). (Illus.). 1995. teacher ed. 49.95 (*1-57431-075-5*); student ed. 30.00 (*1-57431-035-6*) Tech Trng Systs.
— Basic Electricity. (Plant Fundamentals Ser.). (Illus.). 99p. (Orig.). 1995. student ed. 30.00 (*1-57431-007-0*) Tech Trng Systs.
— Basic Electricity, Vol. II, Module IV. (Plant Fundamentals Ser.). (Illus.). (Orig.). 1995. teacher ed. 49.95 (*1-57431-047-X*) Tech Trng Systs.
— Bloodborne Pathogens, 4 vols., Vol. 3, Module 3. (Safety, Health & Environmental Fundamentals Ser.). (Illus.). (Orig.). (C). 1996. pap. text, teacher ed. 49.95 (*1-57431-126-3*); pap. text, student ed. 30.00 (*1-57431-125-5*) Tech Trng Systs.
— Body Protection, 4 vols., Vol. 1, Module 4. (Safety, Health & Environmental Fundamentals Ser.). (Illus.). (Orig.). (C). 1996. pap. text 30.00 (*1-57431-111-5*); pap. text, teacher ed. 49.95 (*1-57431-112-3*) Tech Trng Systs.
— Bulk Materials Handling. (Plant Fundamentals Ser.: Vol. VI, Module III). (Illus.). 1995. teacher ed. 49.95 (*1-57431-060-7*); student ed. 30.00 (*1-57431-020-8*) Tech Trng Systs.
— Communication. (Plant Fundamentals Ser.). (Illus.). (Orig.). 1995. student ed. 30.00 (*1-57431-002-X*) Tech Trng Systs.
— Communication, Vol. 1, Module 2. (Illus.). (Orig.). 1995. teacher ed. 49.95 (*1-57431-042-9*) Tech Trng Systs.
— Compressors Vol. IV, Module II. (Plant Fundamentals Ser.). (Illus.). (Orig.). 1995. teacher ed. 49.95 (*1-57431-053-4*); student ed. 30.00 (*1-57431-013-5*) Tech Trng Systs.
— Confined Spaces, 4 vols., Vol. 1, Module 3. (Safety, Health & Environmental Fundamentals Ser.). (Illus.). (Orig.). (C). 1996. text, teacher ed. 49.95 (*1-57431-102-6*); pap. text 30.00 (*1-57431-101-8*) Tech Trng Systs.
— Continuous Improvement. (Plant Fundamentals Ser.: Vol. X, Module I). (Illus.). 1995. teacher ed. 49.95 (*1-57431-071-2*); student ed. 30.00 (*1-57431-031-3*) Tech Trng Systs.
— Control of Hazardous Energy Sources, 4 vols. (Safety, Health & Environmental Fundamentals Ser.). (Illus.). (Orig.). (C). 1996. pap. text, teacher ed. 49.95 (*1-57431-118-2*) Tech Trng Systs.
— Control of Hazardous Energy Sources, 4 vols., Vol. 2, Module 1. (Safety, Health & Environmental Fundamentals Ser.). (Illus.). (Orig.). (C). 1996. pap. text 30.00 (*1-57431-117-4*) Tech Trng Systs.
— Cooling Towers. (Plant Fundamentals Ser.). (Illus.). 49p. (Orig.). 1995. student ed. 30.00 (*1-57431-016-X*) Tech Trng Systs.
— Cooling Towers, Vol. V, Module II. (Illus.). (Orig.). 1995. teacher ed. 49.95 (*1-57431-056-9*) Tech Trng Systs.
— Crushing & Grinding. (Plant Fundamentals Ser.). (Illus.). (Orig.). 1995. student ed. 30.00 (*1-57431-018-6*) Tech Trng Systs.
— Crushing & Grinding, Vol. VI, Module I. (Illus.). (Orig.). 1995. teacher ed. 49.95 (*1-57431-058-5*) Tech Trng Systs.
— Distillation. (Plant Fundamentals Ser.: Vol. VII, Module IV). (Illus.). 1995. teacher ed. 49.95 (*1-57431-064-X*); student ed. 30.00 (*1-57431-024-0*) Tech Trng Systs.
— Distributed Control Systems. (Plant Fundamentals Ser.: Vol. VIII, Module III). (Illus.). 1995. teacher ed. 49.95 (*1-57431-067-4*); student ed. 30.00 (*1-57431-027-5*) Tech Trng Systs.
— Electrical Safety, 4 vols., Vol. 2, Module 2. (Safety, Health & Environmental Fundamentals Ser.). (Illus.). (Orig.). (C). 1996. text, teacher ed. 49.95 (*1-57431-130-1*); pap. text 30.00 (*1-57431-129-8*) Tech Trng Systs.
— Eye & Face Protection, 4 vols., Vol. 1, Module 1. (Safety, Health & Environmental Fundamentals Ser.). (Illus.). (Orig.). (C). 1996. text, teacher ed. 49.95 (*1-57431-104-2*); pap. text 30.00 (*1-57431-103-4*) Tech Trng Systs.
— Fire Protection, 4 vols., Vol. 4, Module 3. (Safety, Health & Environmental Fundamentals Ser.). (Illus.). (C). 1996. text, teacher ed. 49.95 (*1-57431-110-7*); pap. text 30.00 (*1-57431-109-3*) Tech Trng Systs.
— Fired Equipment, Vol. V, Module III. (Illus.). (Orig.). 1995. teacher ed. 49.95 (*1-57431-057-7*); student ed. 30.00 (*1-57431-017-8*) Tech Trng Systs.
— Hazcom, 4 vols., Vol. 3, Module 1. (Safety, Health & Environmental Fundamentals Ser.). (Illus.). (Orig.). (C). 1996. pap. text 30.00 (*1-57431-113-1*); pap. text, teacher ed. 49.95 (*1-57431-114-X*) Tech Trng Systs.
— Hazwoper, 4 vols., Vol. 4, Module 2. (Safety, Health & Environmental Fundamentals Ser.). (Illus.). (C). 1996. pap. text 30.00 (*1-57431-115-8*) Tech Trng Systs.
— Hazwoper - Chemical Protective Clothing, 4 vols., Vol. 4, Module 2. (Safety, Health & Environmental Fundamentals Ser.). (Illus.). (C). 1996. text, teacher ed. 49.95 (*1-57431-116-6*) Tech Trng Systs.
— Hearing Protection, 4 vols., Vol. 1, Module 3. (Safety, Health & Environmental Fundamentals Ser.). (Illus.). (Orig.). (C). 1996. text, teacher ed. 49.95 (*1-57431-108-5*); pap. text 30.00 (*1-57431-107-7*) Tech Trng Systs.
— Heat Exchangers, Vol. V, Module I. (Plant Fundamentals Ser.). (Illus.). (Orig.). 1995. teacher ed. 49.95 (*1-57431-055-0*); student ed. 30.00 (*1-57431-015-1*) Tech Trng Systs.
— Hot Work, 4 vols. (Safety, Health & Environmental Fundamentals Ser.). (Illus.). (Orig.). (C). 1996. text, teacher ed. 49.95 (*1-57431-132-8*); pap. text 30.00 (*1-57431-131-X*) Tech Trng Systs.
— Improving Human Performance in the Workplace. 190p. 1997. spiral bd. 39.95 (*1-57431-150-6*) Tech Trng Systs.
— Instrumentation. (Plant Fundamentals Ser.: Vol. VIII, Module II). (Illus.). 1995. teacher ed. 49.95 (*1-57431-066-6*); student ed. 30.00 (*1-57431-026-7*) Tech Trng Systs.
— Ionizing Radiation, 4 vols., Vol. 3, Module 4. (Safety, Health & Environmental Fundamentals Ser.). (Illus.). (Orig.). (C). 1996. text, teacher ed. 49.95 (*1-57431-128-X*); pap. text 30.00 (*1-57431-127-1*) Tech Trng Systs.
— ISO 9000. (Plant Fundamentals Ser.: Vol. X, Module III). (Illus.). 1995. teacher ed. 49.95 (*1-57431-073-9*); student ed. 30.00 (*1-57431-033-X*) Tech Trng Systs.
— Lubrication. (Plant Fundamentals Ser.: Vol. XI, Module III). (Illus.). 1995. teacher ed. 49.95 (*1-57431-076-3*); student ed. 30.00 (*1-57431-036-4*) Tech Trng Systs.
— Mixing. (Plant Fundamentals Ser.: Vol. VII, Module III). (Illus.). 1995. teacher ed. 49.95 (*1-57431-063-1*); student ed. 30.00 (*1-57431-023-2*) Tech Trng Systs.
— Piping, Vol. III, Module II. (Plant Fundamentals Ser.). (Illus.). (Orig.). 1995. teacher ed. 49.95 (*1-57431-049-6*) Tech Trng Systs.
— Piping V, Vol. III, Module II. (Plant Fundamentals Ser.). (Illus.). 46p. (Orig.). 1995. student ed. 30.00 (*1-57431-009-7*) Tech Trng Systs.
— Plant Fundamentals Instructor's Guides: A Performance-Based Training Series for the Process Industries, 12 Vols., Set. (Plant Fundamentals Ser.). (Illus.). (Orig.). 1995. teacher ed. 975.00 (*1-57431-040-2*) Tech Trng Systs.
— Prime Movers Vol. IV, Module III, Vol. I. (Plant Fundamentals Ser.). (Illus.). (Orig.). 1995. teacher ed. 49.95 (*1-57431-054-2*); student ed. 30.00 (*1-57431-014-3*) Tech Trng Systs.
— Problem Solving. (Plant Fundamentals Ser.). (Illus.). (Orig.). 1995. student ed. 30.00 (*1-57431-003-8*) Tech Trng Systs.
— Problem Solving, Vol. 1, Module III. (Illus.). (Orig.). 1995. teacher ed. 49.95 (*1-57431-043-7*) Tech Trng Systs.
— Process Chemistry. (Plant Fundamentals Ser.: Vol. II, Module II). (Illus.). 80p. 1995. student ed. 30.00 (*1-57431-005-4*) Tech Trng Systs.
— Process Chemistry, Vol. II, Module II. (Plant Fundamentals Ser.). (Illus.). (Orig.). 1995. teacher ed. 49.95 (*1-57431-045-3*) Tech Trng Systs.
— Process Control. (Plant Fundamentals Ser.: Vol. VIII, Module I). (Illus.). 1995. teacher ed. 49.95 (*1-57431-065-8*); student ed. 30.00 (*1-57431-025-9*) Tech Trng Systs.
— Process Math, Vol. II, Module I. (Plant Fundamentals Ser.). (Illus.). 92p. (Orig.). 1995. student ed. 30.00 (*1-57431-004-6*) Tech Trng Systs.
— Process Math Vol., Vol. II, Module I. (Plant Fundamentals Ser.). (Illus.). (Orig.). 1995. teacher ed. 49.95 (*1-57431-044-5*) Tech Trng Systs.
— The Process Operator. (Plant Fundamentals Ser.). (Illus.). (Orig.). 1995. student ed. 30.00 (*1-57431-001-1*) Tech Trng Systs.
— The Process Operator Vol., Vol. 1, Module 1. (Plant Fundamentals Ser.). (Illus.). (Orig.). 1995. teacher ed. 49.95 (*1-57431-041-0*) Tech Trng Systs.
— Process Physics. (Plant Fundamentals Ser.). (Illus.). 64p. (Orig.). 1995. student ed. 30.00 (*1-57431-006-2*) Tech Trng Systs.
— Process Physics Vol., Vol. II, Module III. (Plant Fundamentals Ser.). (Illus.). (Orig.). 1995. teacher ed. 49.95 (*1-57431-046-1*) Tech Trng Systs.
— Pumps. (Plant Fundamentals Ser.). (Illus.). 54p. (Orig.). 1995. student ed. 30.00 (*1-57431-012-7*) Tech Trng Systs.
— Pumps, Vol. IV, Module I. (Illus.). (Orig.). 1995. teacher ed. 49.95 (*1-57431-052-6*) Tech Trng Systs.
— Quality Principles. (Plant Fundamentals Ser.: Vol. XII, Module I). (Illus.). 1995. teacher ed. 49.95 (*1-57431-077-1*); student ed. 30.00 (*1-57431-037-2*) Tech Trng Systs.
— Quality Teams. (Plant Fundamentals Ser.: Vol. XII, Module III). (Illus.). 1995. teacher ed. 49.95 (*1-57431-079-8*); student ed. 30.00 (*1-57431-039-9*) Tech Trng Systs.
— Quality Tools. (Plant Fundamentals Ser.: Vol. XII, Module II). (Illus.). 1995. teacher ed. 49.95 (*1-57431-078-X*); student ed. 30.00 (*1-57431-038-0*) Tech Trng Systs.
— Reacting. (Plant Fundamentals Ser.: Vol. VII, Module I). (Illus.). 1995. teacher ed. 49.95 (*1-57431-061-5*); student ed. 30.00 (*1-57431-021-6*) Tech Trng Systs.
— Reading Drawings. (Plant Fundamentals Ser.: Vol. IX, Module I). (Illus.). 1995. teacher ed. 49.95 (*1-57431-068-2*); student ed. 30.00 (*1-57431-028-3*) Tech Trng Systs.
— Resource Conservation & Recovery Act (RCRA), 4 vols., Vol. 4, Module 1. (Safety, Health & Environmental Fundamentals Ser.). (Illus.). (Orig.). (C). 1996. text, teacher ed. 49.95 (*1-57431-122-0*); pap. text 30.00 (*1-57431-121-2*) Tech Trng Systs.
— Respiratory Protection, 4 vols., Vol. 1, Module 2. (Safety, Health & Environmental Fundamentals Ser.). (Illus.). (Orig.). (C). 1996. text, teacher ed. 49.95 (*1-57431-106-9*); pap. text 30.00 (*1-57431-105-0*) Tech Trng Systs.
— Separation. (Plant Fundamentals Ser.: Vol. VII, Module II). (Illus.). 1995. teacher ed. 49.95 (*1-57431-062-3*); student ed. 30.00 (*1-57431-022-4*) Tech Trng Systs.
— Spill Prevention, 4 vols., Vol. 4, Module 4. (Safety, Health & Environmental Fundamentals Ser.). (Illus.). (Orig.). (C). 1996. text, teacher ed. 49.95 (*1-57431-124-7*); pap. text 30.00 (*1-57431-123-9*) Tech Trng Systs.
— Statistical Process Control. (Plant Fundamentals Ser.: Vol. X, Module II). (Illus.). 1995. teacher ed. 49.95 (*1-57431-072-0*); student ed. 30.00 (*1-57431-032-1*) Tech Trng Systs.
— Steam Traps. (Plant Fundamentals Ser.). (Illus.). 62p. (Orig.). 1995. student ed. 30.00 (*1-57431-011-9*) Tech Trng Systs.
— Steam Traps, Vol. III, Module IV. (Illus.). (Orig.). 1995. teacher ed. 49.95 (*1-57431-051-8*) Tech Trng Systs.
— Tanks & Vessels. (Plant Fundamentals Ser.). (Illus.). 68p. (Orig.). 1995. student ed. 30.00 (*1-57431-008-9*) Tech Trng Systs.
— Tanks & Vessels Vol., Vol. III, Module I. (Plant Fundamentals Ser.). (Illus.). (Orig.). 1995. teacher ed. 49.95 (*1-57431-048-8*) Tech Trng Systs.
— Total Productive Maintenance. (Plant Fundamentals Ser.: Vol. XI, Module I). (Illus.). 1995. teacher ed. 49.95 (*1-57431-074-7*); student ed. 30.00 (*1-57431-034-8*) Tech Trng Systs.
— Using Procedure Information. (Plant Fundamentals Ser.: Vol. IX, Module III). (Illus.). 1995. teacher ed. 49.95 (*1-57431-070-4*); student ed. 30.00 (*1-57431-030-5*) Tech Trng Systs.
— Using Process Safety Information. (Plant Fundamentals Ser.: Vol. IX, Module II). (Illus.). 1995. teacher ed. 49.95 (*1-57431-069-0*); student ed. 30.00 (*1-57431-029-1*) Tech Trng Systs.
— Valves. (Plant Fundamentals Ser.). (Illus.). 90p. (Orig.). 1995. student ed. 30.00 (*1-57431-010-0*) Tech Trng Systs.
— Valves, Vol. III, Module III. (Illus.). (Orig.). 1995. teacher ed. 49.95 (*1-57431-050-X*) Tech Trng Systs.
— Workplace Basics, 8 vols. Incl. Vol. 8: Ethics in the Workplace. (Illus.). 39p. (Orig.). 1996. pap. text 25.00 (*1-57431-147-6*); Vol. 4: Problem Solving. (Illus.). 31p. (Orig.). 1996. pap. text 25.00 (*1-57431-139-5*); Vol. 3: Communication. (Illus.). 31p. (Orig.). 1996. pap. text 25.00 (*1-57431-137-9*); Vol. 5: Workplace Relations. 39p. (Orig.). 1996. pap. text 25.00 (*1-57431-141-7*); Vol. 2: Self Esteem & Motivation in the Workplace. (Illus.). 49p. (Orig.). 1996. pap. text 25.00 (*1-57431-135-2*); Vol. 1: Work Force 2000/Learning to Learn. (Illus.). 23p. (Orig.). 1996. pap. text 25.00 (*1-57431-133-6*); Vol. 6: Team Building. (Illus.). 31p. (Orig.). 1996. pap. text 25.00 (*1-57431-143-3*); Vol. 7: Goal Setting & Planning. (Illus.). 37p. (Orig.). 1996. pap. text 25.00 (*1-57431-145-X*); 59.95 (*1-57431-149-2*) Tech Trng Systs.

Multimedia Quay2 Staff. PageMill: Training on CD. 1996. pap. text 49.95 (*0-201-88616-2*) Peachpit Pr.

Multimedia Staff, jt. ed. see ACM Staff.

MultiMedia Telecommunications Association Staff. A Centrex Primer on a Growing Market. 63p. 1991. pap. 40.00 (*0-685-52644-5*, 260) MultiMedia Telecomm.
— EuroTelecom, 1992: A Report of Telecommunications in the European Common Market. 225p. 1990. pap. 698.00 (*0-940919-13-3*, 210) MultiMedia Telecomm.
— Industry Basics: Introduction to the History, Structure, & Technology of the Telecommunications Industry. 4th ed. 96p. 1991. pap. 40.00 (*0-940919-17-6*, 230) MultiMedia Telecomm.
— Interconnect Industry Review, 1992. (Illus.). 25p. (Orig.). pap. 53.00 (*0-940919-26-5*) MultiMedia Telecomm.
— Safety Resource Manual for the Telecommunications Industry. 125p. 1990. pap. 53.00 (*0-685-52630-5*, 225) MultiMedia Telecomm.
— Telecommunications Export Guide: A Directory of International Trade Data & Resources. 3rd ed. 210p. 1993. pap. 103.00 (*0-940919-31-1*) MultiMedia Telecomm.
— Telecommunications Source Book, 1993. 208p. 1993. pap. 53.00 (*0-940919-28-1*) MultiMedia Telecomm.

MultiMedia Telecommunications Association Staff, et al. Voice Messaging Industry Review, 1991. (Illus.). 60p. (Orig.). 1991. pap. 253.00 (*0-940919-23-0*) MultiMedia Telecomm.

Multiple Photograhers Staff, photos by. Kodak Gallery Award Collection Album. (Illus.). 100p. 1999. pap. 59.95 (*0-9658571-9-0*) Marathon NE.

Multiple Reserve Currency Study Group Staff. How Central Banks Manage Their Reserves. (Report Ser.). 52p. 1982. pap. 10.00 (*1-56708-050-2*) Grp of Thirty.

Multnomah Books Staff. Blessings from God. LC 96-211111. (Just the Right Words Ser.: No. 1). 144p. 1996. 12.99 (*0-88070-984-7*, Multnomah Bks) Multnomah Pubs.

Multon, J. L., ed. Analysis & Control Methods for Food & Agricultural Products, 4 Vols. Incl. Analysis of Food Constituents. LC 96-22646. 510p. 1997. 150.00 (*0-471-18966-9*); Analytical Techniques for Foods & Agricultural Products: Laboratory of Biochemical Applications. Linden, G., ed. 578p. 1995. 195.00 (*0-471-18609-0*); Microbiological Control for Foods & Agricultural Products. Bourgeois, C. M. & Leveau, J. Y., eds. 542p. 1995. 210.00 (*0-471-18600-7*, Wiley-VCH); Quality Control for Food & Agricultural Products. 300p. 1995. 165.00 (*0-471-18617-1*); 1p. 1997. Set pap. 545.00 (*0-471-19260-0*) Wiley.

Multon, J. L., ed. Analysis of Food Constituents. LC 96-22646. (Analysis & Control Methods for Foods & Agricultural Products Ser.). 400p. 1996. 150.00 (*1-56081-697-X*, Wiley-VCH) Wiley.
— Quality Control for Foods & Agricultural Products: General Principles & Legal Aspects. LC 94-39865. (Analysis & Control Methods for Foods & Agricultural Products Ser.). (Illus.). 300p. 1995. 125.00 (*1-56081-698-8*, Wiley-VCH) Wiley.

Multon, J. L., jt. ed. see Bureau, G.

Multon, J. L., jt. ed. see Simatos, D.

Mulukutla, P. S., ed. Reagents for Better Metallurgy. fac. ed. LC 93-86997. (Illus.). 373p. 1994. reprint ed. pap. 115.70 (*0-7837-8205-5*, 204796300009) Bks Demand.

Mulvaney. Growth & Developmental Biology of Meat Animals. 1995. write for info. (*0-8493-8758-2*) CRC Pr.

Mulvaney, Jay. Kennedy Weddings: A Family Album. 2nd ed. LC 99-15917. 192p. 1999. text 35.00 (*0-312-24208-5*) St Martin.

Mulvaney, John & Green, Neville. Commandant of Solitude: The Journals of Captain Collet Barker (1828-1831) (Miegunyah Press Ser.: No. 1:8). 1992. 49.95 (*0-522-84472-3*, Pub. by Melbourne Univ Pr) Paul & Co Pubs.

Mulvaney, John & Kamminga, Johan. Prehistory of Australia. LC 99-21564. (Illus.). 512p. 1999. pap. 27.95 (*1-56098-804-5*) Smithsonian.

***Mulvaney, Kathleen & Manassas Museum Systems Staff.** Manassas, Virginia: A Place of Passages. (Images of America Ser.). (Illus.). 128p. 1999. pap. 18.99 (*0-7385-0147-6*) Arcadia Publng.

***Mulvaney, Maureen G.** Any Kid Can Be a Super Star: Practical Parenting Strategies for Real Parents. Bruce, Carla, ed. 243p. 1999. pap. 19.95 (*0-9616923-9-1*) MGM Assocs.

Mulvaney, Rebekah M. & Nelson, Carlos I. Rastafari & Reggae: A Dictionary & Sourcebook. LC 90-3591. 272p. 1990. lib. bdg. 59.95 (*0-313-26071-0*, MVR/, Greenwood Pr) Greenwood.

Mulvaney, Robert, ed. see Simon, Yves.

Mulvaney, Robert J., jt. auth. see Gould, James A.

Mulvaney-Smith, Alison. Balancing Women: Time Management & Self-Esteem for Women. 1998. pap. text. write for info. (*0-7318-0605-0*) Simon & Schuster.

Mulvany, M. J., ed. Fourth International Symposium on Resistance Arteries, Warren, Vermont, January 1994: Abstracts. (Journal Ser.: Vol. 31, Suppl. 1, 1994). ii, 60p. 1993. pap. 26.25 (*3-8055-5919-4*) S Karger.
— International Symposium on Resistance Arteries, 3rd, Rebild, Skrping, Denmark, May 1991 Abstracts. (Journal: Blood Vessels: Vol. 28, No. 4, 1991). 80p. 1991. pap. 55.00 (*3-8055-5409-5*) S Karger.

Mulvany, M. J., et al, eds. Resistance Vessels: Physiology, Pharmacology & Hypertensive Pathology. (Mikrozirkulation in Forschung und Klinik; Progress in Applied Microcirculation Ser.: Vol. 8). (Illus.). x, 236p. 1985. pap. 121.75 (*3-8055-4052-3*) S Karger.

***Mulvany, Martha.** Story of the Beagle. LC 98-49410. (Dogs Throughout History Ser.). 24p. (J). 2000. lib. bdg. 18.60 (*0-8239-5518-4*) Rosen Group.
— Story of the Boxer. LC 98-49411. (Dogs Throughout History Ser.). 24p. (J). 2000. lib. bdg. 18.60 (*0-8239-5519-2*) Rosen Group.

Mulvany, Nancy C. Indexing Books. (Illus.). 336p. 1994. 32.00 (*0-226-55014-1*) U Ch Pr.

Mulvany, Nancy C., ed. Indexing, Providing Access to Information: Looking Back, Looking Ahead: The Proceedings of the 25th Annual Meeting of the American Society of Indexers. LC 93-25136. 161p. 1993. pap. text 35.00 (*0-936547-19-7*) Am Soc Index.

Mulvenon, James C. Professionalization of the Senior Chinese Officer Corps: Trends & Implications. LC 97-31081. 109p. 1997. pap. 15.00 (*0-8330-2543-0*, MR-901-OSD) Rand Corp.

Mulvenon, James C., ed. China Facts & Figures Annual Handbook, Vol. 23. 512p. 1998. 97.00 (*0-87569-202-8*) Academic Intl.

Mulvenon, James C. & Yang, Richard H., eds. The People's Liberation Army in the Information Age. (Illus.). ix, 288p. 1999. pap. 25.00 (*0-8330-2716-6*) Rand Corp.

***Mulvenon, James Charles.** Soldiers of Fortune: The Rise & Fall of the Chinese Military-Business Complex, 1978-1998. 320p. 2000. text 69.95 (*0-7656-0579-1*, East Gate Bk) M E Sharpe.

Mulvey, Cecilia, ed. see Vec Staff & Delmar Staff.

Mulvey, Christopher. Transatlantic Manners: Social Patterns in Nineteenth-Century Anglo-American Travel Literature. (Illus.). 255p. (C). 1990. text 64.95 (*0-521-30366-4*) Cambridge U Pr.

Mulvey, Deb, ed. We Had Everything but Money. LC 92-60979. 164p. 1992. 14.95 (*0-89821-099-2*, 11572) Reiman Pubns.
— We Pulled Together & Won! Personal Memories of the World War II Years. LC 93-84612. (Illus.). 164p. 1993. 14.95 (*0-89821-112-3*, 12300) Reiman Pubns.

Mulvey, Francis P., et al. Retirement Income: Implications of Demographic Trends for Social Security & Pension Reform. (Illus.). 56p. (C). 1998. text 20.00 (*0-7881-7547-5*) DIANE Pub.

Mulvey, J., jt. ed. see Brink, D. M.

Mulvey, Janemarie, jt. auth. see Moon, Marilyn.

Mulvey, Joanne & National School Services Staff. Involved Parenting from Birth to Age 7 LC 97-215919. x, 98 p. 1997. write for info. (*0-932957-19-6*) Natl School.

Mulvey, John M. & Ziemba, William T., eds. World Wide Asset & Liability Modeling. LC 99-172050. (Publications of the Newton Institute: Vol. 10). 680p. (C). 1998. text 95.00 (*0-521-57187-1*) Cambridge U Pr.

Mulvey, Kate & Richards, Melissa. Decades of Beauty: The Changing Image of Women, 1890s to 1990s. LC 98-25077. (Illus.). 208p. 1998. 34.95 (*0-8160-3920-8*, Checkmark) Facts on File.

Mulvey, Laura. Citizen Kane. (BFI Film Classics Ser.). (Illus.). 88p. 1993. pap. 10.95 (*0-85170-339-9*, Pub. by British Film Inst) Ind U Pr.
— Fetishism & Curiosity. LC 95-52638. (Perspectives Co-Published with the British Film Institute Ser.). 208p. (C). 1996. 39.95 (*0-253-33211-7*) Ind U Pr.
— Fetishism & Curiosity. LC 95-52638. (Perspectives Co-Published with the British Film Institute Ser.). 208p. (C). 1996. pap. 17.95 (*0-253-21019-4*) Ind U Pr.
— Jimmie Durham. LC 96-146318. (Contemporary Artists Ser.). (Illus.). 160p. (Orig.). 1995. pap. 29.95 (*0-7148-3348-7*, Pub. by Phaidon Press) Phaidon Pr.

An Asterisk (*) at the beginning of an entry indicates that the title is appearing for the first time.

— Visual & Other Pleasures. LC 88-9627. (Theories of Representation & Difference Ser.). 218p. (Orig.). 1989. 35.00 (*0-253-36226-1*); pap. 18.95 (*0-253-20494-1*, MB-494) Ind U Pr.

Mulvey, M. Priests of the Future: Formation & Communion. 1991. pap. 7.95 (*0-911782-84-2*) New City.

Mulvey, Mary D. French Catholic Missionaries in the Present United States (1604-1791) LC 73-3578. (Catholic University of America. Studies in Romance Languages & Literatures: No. 23). reprint ed. 32.50 (*0-404-57773-3*) AMS Pr.

Mulvey-Roberts, Marie. British Poets & Secret Societies. LC 89-201236. 181p. 1986. write for info. (*0-7099-2255-8*) C Helm.

— The Handbook to Gothic Literature. LC 97-48295. 350p. 1998. text 55.00 (*0-8147-5609-3*); pap. text 19.50 (*0-8147-5610-7*) NYU Pr.

Mulvey, T. & Webster, R. K., eds. Modern Physical Techniques in Materials Technology. (Harwell Ser.). (Illus.). (C). 1974. text 59.00 (*0-19-851708-4*) OUP.

Mulvey, T., ed. see Institute of Physics, Great Britain, Electron Micr.

Mulvey, Tom & Sheppard, Colin, eds. Advances in Optical & Electron Microscopy, Vol. 12. 376p. 1991. text 136.00 (*0-12-029912-7*) Acad Pr.

— Advances in Optical & Electron Microscopy, Vol. 13. (Illus.). 320p. 1994. text 110.00 (*0-12-029913-5*) Acad Pr.

— Advances in Optical & Electron Microscopy, Vol. 14. (Illus.). 320p. 1994. text 110.00 (*0-12-029914-3*) Acad Pr.

Mulvey, Tom, jt. auth. see Kazan, Benjamin.

Mulvey, Walt. Winning at Work: How to Be a Great Employee. LC 95-76235. 100p. 1995. pap. 10.00 (*1-883697-45-X*) Hara Pub.

Mulvey, William E. Soil & Rock Causing Engineering Geologic Problems in Utah. LC TN24.U8 A322. (Special Study Ser.: Vol. 80). (Illus.). 23p. 1992. pap. 9.00 (*1-55791-199-1*, SS-80) Utah Geological Survey.

Mulvey, William E. & Lund, William R. Geologic Evaluation of Wastewater Disposal in Bedrock, Duchesne County, Utah. LC TN24.U8 A322. (Special Study Ser.: Vol. 72). (Illus.). 20p. 1990. pap. 6.75 (*1-55791-191-6*, SS-72) Utah Geological Survey.

Mulvihill, Edward R., ed. see Sanchez-Silva, Jose M.

Mulvihill, James E., jt. ed. see Greenwald, Robert A.

Mulvihill, John J. Catalog of Human Cancer Genes: Mckusick's Mendelian Inheritance in Man for Clinical & Research Oncologists (ONCO-MIM) LC 98-54978. 240p. 1999. 125.00 (*0-8018-4799-0*) Johns Hopkins.

Mulvihill, John J., et al, eds. Genetics of Human Cancer. LC 75-44924. (Progress in Cancer Research & Therapy Ser.: No. 3). (Illus.). 541p. reprint ed. pap. 167.80 (*0-7837-7094-4*, 204691900004) Bks Demand.

Mulvihill, Margaret. St. Patrick's Daughter. 252p. 1995. pap. 10.95 (*0-340-59774-7*, Pub. by Hodder & Stought Ltd) Trafalgar.

***Mulvihill, Margaret.** Treasury of Saints & Martyrs. (Illus.). 80p. 1999. 19.99 (*0-670-88789-7*, Viking Child) Peng Put Young Read.

Mulvihill, Margaret, ed. People in the Past. LC 92-54483. (Picturepedia Ser.). (Illus.). (J). 1993. write for info. (*1-56458-217-5*) DK Pub Inc.

Mulvihill, Mary L. Human Diseases: A Systemic Approach. 4th ed. LC 94-8977. (C). 1994. pap. text 39.95 (*0-8385-3928-9*, A3928-7) Appleton & Lange.

Mulvihill, Maureen, ed. see Ephelia.

Mulvihill, Maureen E. Stuart Women of Letters. (Literature Reference Ser.). 450p. Date not set. text 65.00 (*0-8240-6316-3*) Garland.

Mulvihill, Robert F., jt. auth. see Farren, Sean.

Mulvihill, Robert F., jt. auth. see Kearney, Hugh F.

Mulvihill, William. God Is Blind. LC 95-77912. 317p. (Orig.). 1996. pap. 13.00 (*0-9645875-2-1*) Brickiln Pr.

— Meadow Lane. 142p. 1998. pap. 9.00 (*1-891380-01-X*) Brickiln Pr.

***Mulvihill, William.** Night of the Axe. 2nd ed. 168p. 1999. reprint ed. pap. 9.00 (*1-891380-07-9*) Brickiln Pr.

— Sagaponack. 167p. 1999. pap. 9.00 (*1-891380-04-4*) Brickiln Pr.

Mulvihill, William. The Sands of Kalahari. rev. ed. LC 60-8479. 246p. 1996. reprint ed. pap. 12.00 (*0-9645875-3-X*) Brickiln Pr.

— Sands of the Kalahari. 20.95 (*0-89190-869-2*) Amereon Ltd.

— Serengeti. rev. ed. LC 95-83396. 138p. 1996. pap. 12.00 (*0-9645875-4-8*) Brickiln Pr.

— South Fork Place Names: Some Informal Long Island History. 2nd rev. ed. LC 95-77332. 114p. (Orig.). 1997. pap. 8.00 (*0-9645875-1-3*) Brickiln Pr.

— Three Novels & a Story: Sagaponack, Ava, Speakeasy, Wrackline. LC 95-75653. 447p. (Orig.). 1996. pap. 16.00 (*0-9645875-0-5*) Brickiln Pr.

— The Tiger Heart. 126p. 1997. pap. 12.00 (*0-9645875-7-2*) Brickiln Pr.

— Wrackline. 1998. pap. 5.00 (*0-9645875-9-9*) Brickiln Pr.

Mulville, Frank. In Gramma's Wake: Girl Stella's Voyage to Cuba. 330p. 1970. pap. 12.50 (*0-87556-439-9*) Saifer.

— North Cross to Southern Cross. 1994. pap. text 14.95 (*1-85253-291-2*) Cimino Pub Grp.

— Rescue & Recovery: Iskra's Ordeal in the Western Isles. (Illus.). 180p. 1997. pap. 14.95 (*1-57409-038-0*) Sheridan.

— Schooner Integrity. (Illus.). 184p. 1992. pap. 14.95 (*0-85036-425-6*, Pub. by Seafarer Bks) Sheridan.

— Single-Handed Sailing. (Illus.). 192p. (Orig.). 1990. pap. 17.50 (*0-85036-410-8*) Sheridan.

Mulvoy, Mark. Sports Illustrated Golf. 1988. pap. 9.95 (*1-56800-036-7*, Pub. by Sports Illus Bks) Natl Bk Netwk.

— Sports Illustrated Golf: Play Like a Pro. LC 94-2072. 1993. pap. 12.95 (*1-56800-007-3*, Pub. by Sports Illus Bks) Natl Bk Netwk.

Muly, James D., jt. auth. see Wertime, Theodore A.

Mulys, jt. auth. see Detaille, Georges.

Mulzer, Johann. Organic Synthesis Highlights III. 460p. 1998. pap. 105.00 (*3-527-29500-3*, Wiley-VCH) Wiley.

Muma, John R. Cognitive Socialization: Clinical Implications: Cognition, Codification, Communication, Expression. LC 97-30925. 1997. text. write for info. (*0-8058-2094-9*); pap. text. write for info. (*0-8058-2095-7*) L Erlbaum Assocs.

Muma, Richard D. & Lyons, Barbara Ann. HIV Manual for Health Care Professionals. 2nd rev. ed. LC 96-41640. 501p. (C). 1999. pap. 23.95 (*0-8385-3773-1*, A3773-7, Apple Lange Med) McGraw.

— Patient Education: A Practical Approach. 381p. (C). 1996. pap. text 37.95 (*0-8385-2039-1*, A2039-4, Apple Lange Med) McGraw.

Mumaw, Catherine & Voran, Marilyn H. The Whole Thing. 24p. (J). (gr. 6-11). 1981. pap. 2.99 (*0-8361-1962-2*) Herald Pr.

***Mumaw, Evelyn King.** The Merging: A Story of Two Families & Their Child. 224p. 2000. 13.95 (*0-9665021-6-7*, DreamSeeker) Pandora PA.

Mumaw, John R. Answers to Anxiety. 1993. pap. 6.95 (*0-87813-551-0*) Christian Light.

— Assurance of Salvation. 1989. pap. 4.95 (*0-87813-955-9*) Christian Light.

Mumaw, Laura, ed. see Ling, Shao-Wen.

Mumayiz, Saleh A. & Schonfeld, Paul. Airport Modeling & Simulation: Conference Proceedings, August 17-20, 1997, Key Bridge Marriott Hotel, Arlington, Virginia. LC 98-37247. 352p. 1998. 49.00 (*0-7844-0397-X*) Am Soc Civil Eng.

Mumba, Nevers. Integrity with Fire. 1995. per. 8.95 (*0-927936-55-0*) Christ for the Nations.

Mumbru, J. & Fabra, R. Crystallinity Topics in the Synthetic Fibres. 1992. pap. 42.00 (*0-7855-2811-3*, Pub. by Textile Inst) St Mut.

Mumby, David G. Graduate School: Winning Strategies for Getting in with or Without Excellent Grades. 1. 256p. 1997. 19.95 (*0-9682173-4-6*) ProtoCALL Pub.

Mumby, Dennis K. Communication & Power in Organizations: Discourse, Ideology & Domination. Thayer, Lee, ed. LC 88-3356. (People, Communication, Organization Ser.). 208p. 1988. text 73.25 (*0-89391-480-0*) Ablx Pub.

— Communication & Power in Organizations: Discourse, Ideology, & Domination. Thayer, Lee, ed. LC 88-3356. (People, Communication, Organization Ser.). 208p. 1988. pap. 39.50 (*1-56750-160-5*) Ablx Pub.

— Narrative & Social Control: Critical Perspectives. (Annual Reviews of Communication Research Ser.: Vol. 21). (Illus.). 304p. (C). 1993. text 58.00 (*0-8039-4931-6*); pap. text 26.00 (*0-8039-4932-4*) Sage.

***Mumby, Jewell A., contrib. by.** To Mother with Love. 1998. pap. 10.00 (*0-9668412-0-4*) J A Mumby.

Mumcuoglu, Madeleine. Sambuco Black Elderberry Extract: A Breakthrough in the Treatment of Influenza Viruses. 16p. 1995. 2.50 (*0-9646056-0-0*) R S S Pub Inc.

Mumehiro, S., jt. ed. see Tanaka, H.

Mumenthaler, Mark. Neurologic Differential Diagnosis. 2nd ed. Appenzeller, Otto, tr. (GER., Illus.). 192p. (C). 1992. pap. text 47.00 (*0-86577-432-3*) Thieme Med Pubs.

— Neurology. 3rd ed. (Flexibook Ser.). (Illus.). 551p. (Orig.). 1990. text 29.90 (*0-86577-317-3*) Thieme Med Pubs.

Mumenthaler, Mark, ed. Treatment of Chronic Pain. 337p. 1990. text 176.00 (*3-7186-5026-6*, Harwood Acad Pubs); pap. text 114.00 (*3-7186-5027-4*, Harwood Acad Pubs) Gordon & Breach.

***Mumenthaler, Mark & Mattle, Heinrich.** Neurology. 4th ed. (Illus.). 950p. (Orig.). 2000. pap. 39.00 (*0-86577-936-8*) Thieme Med Pubs.

Mumenthaler, Mark & Schliack, H., eds. Peripheral Nerve Lesions: Diagnosis & Therapy. (Illus.). 464p. 1990. text 109.00 (*0-86577-361-0*) Thieme Med Pubs.

Mumey, Jack. The New Joy of Being Sober: A Book for Recovering Alcoholics & Those who love them. rev. ed. LC 94-28358. 240p. 1994. pap. 11.95 (*0-925190-31-4*) Fairview Press.

Mumey, Jack & Tinsley, Cynthia. Age Different Relationships: Finding Happiness with an Older or Younger Love. 176p. 1993. pap. 9.95 (*0-925190-65-9*) Fairview Press.

— Recharging Your Relationship: Finding the Fun Again! 224p. 1995. pap. 10.95 (*0-925190-34-9*) Fairview Press.

Mumey, Nolie. The Life of Jim Baker. 1976. 24.95 (*0-8488-0246-2*) Amereon Ltd.

Mumford. De Otra Mirada a la Guia - Take Another Look at Guidance. (SPA.). 184p. 1995. write for info. (*1-56063-555-X*) Editorial Unilit.

Mumford. Developing Top Managers. 242p. 1988. 74.95 (*0-566-02719-4*) Ashgate Pub Co.

— How Managers can Develop Managers. 1998. pap. 33.95 (*0-566-08009-5*) Ashgate Pub Co.

Mumford. The Lewis Mumford Reader. 1986. 14.95 (*0-07-545025-9*) McGraw.

Mumford & Jedynakiewicz. Principles of Endodontics. 1988. pap. text 54.00 (*1-85097-006-8*, 1569) Quint Pub Co.

Mumford, jt. auth. see Carson.

***Mumford, Alan.** Effective Learning. 96p. 2000. pap. 17.95 (*0-8464-5036-4*) Beekman Pubs.

Mumford, Alan. Gower Handbook of Management Development. 4th ed. 600p. 1995. 113.95 (*0-566-07445-1*, Pub. by Gower) Ashgate Pub Co.

— How Managers Can Develop Managers. 240p. 1993. 69.95 (*0-566-07403-6*, Pub. by Gower) Ashgate Pub Co.

— Learning at the Top. LC 95-790. 1995. 19.95 (*0-07-709066-7*) McGraw.

— Management Development: Strategies for Action. 304p. 2000. pap. 56.95 (*0-8464-5108-5*) Beekman Pubs.

Mumford, Alan. Management Development: Strategies for Action. 256p. (C). 1989. 110.00 (*0-85292-426-7*, Pub. by IPM Hse); 125.00 (*0-7855-4548-4*, Pub. by IPM Hse) St Mut.

— Management Development: Strategies for Action. 248p. (C). 1993. pap. text 79.00 (*0-85292-518-2*, Pub. by IPM Hse) St Mut.

Mumford, Alan, ed. Action Learning at Work. LC 96-46427. 430p. 1997. text 96.95 (*0-566-07890-2*, Pub. by Gower) Ashgate Pub Co.

Mumford, Amy R. It Hurts to Lose a Special Person. deluxe ed. (Accent Expressions Ser.). (Illus.). 24p. (Orig.). 1994. pap. 5.99 (*0-89636-093-8*, LifeJourney) Chariot Victor.

— It Only Hurts Between Paydays: A Handbook for Personal Money Management. rev. ed. LC 80-70679. 160p. 1992. pap. 8.99 (*0-89636-067-9*, LifeJourney) Chariot Victor.

Mumford, Andrew. Beginning Visual Interdev 7.0 Web Development. 800p. Date not set. pap. 39.99 (*1-86100-452-4*) Wrox Pr Inc.

— Beginning Web Development with Visual Interdev 6. (Beginning Ser.). 700p. 1999. pap. 39.99 (*1-86100-294-7*) Wrox Pr Inc.

Mumford, Anne & Henderson, Loften. The CGM Handbook. (Illus.). 480p. 1993. text 71.00 (*0-12-510560-6*) Acad Pr.

Mumford, Bob. The Purpose of Temptation. 1997. pap. 8.99 (*0-88270-674-8*) Bridge-Logos.

— Take Another Look at Guidance: Proven Methods to Help You Sail Through Life's Tough Choices. 192p. 1993. pap. 7.95 (*1-884004-01-6*) Lifechangers.

Mumford, C. J., jt. auth. see Carson, Phillip.

Mumford, Claire. The Nile. (Butterfly Bks.). 32p. (J). (gr. 3-5). 1983. 9.95 (*0-86685-447-9*) Intl Bk Ctr.

Mumford, Clive J. & Carson, Philop. Control of Industrial Chemical Hazards, 2 vols., Vol. 2. 1089p. 1989. text 247.00 (*0-470-20886-4*) Halsted Pr.

Mumford, Clive J., jt. auth. see Carson, P.

Mumford, Clive J., jt. auth. see Carson, P. A.

Mumford, D. The Red Book of Varieties & Schemes. (Lecture Notes in Mathematics Ser.: Vol. 1358). v, 309p. 1996. 52.95 (*3-387-50497-4*) Spr-Verlag.

Mumford, D., et al. Geometric Invariant Theory. 3rd enl. ed. (Ergebnisse der Mathematik und Ihrer Grenzgebiete Ser.: Vol. 2). 320p. 1993. write for info. (*3-540-56963-4*) Spr-Verlag.

— Geometric Invariant Theory. 3rd enl. ed. (Ergebnisse der Mathematik und Ihrer Grenzgebiete Ser.: Vol. 34). 320p. 1996. 98.00 (*0-387-56963-4*) Spr-Verlag.

— Tata Lectures on Theta III. (Progress in Mathematics Ser.: Vol. 97). vii, 202p. 1991. 55.00 (*0-8176-3440-1*) Birkhauser.

Mumford, D., jt. auth. see Nitzberg, M.

Mumford, D., jt. ed. see Artin, M.

Mumford, D., jt. ed. see Hironaka, H.

Mumford, David. Algebraic Geometry I: Complex Projective Varieties. 2nd ed. LC 94-39113. (Classics in Mathematics Ser.). 186p. 1995. 35.00 (*3-540-58657-1*) Spr-Verlag.

— Tata Lecture Notes on Theta Functions, Vol. 1. (Progress in Mathematics Ser.: Vol.43). 220p. 1994. 40.50 (*0-8176-3109-7*) Birkhauser.

— Tata Lecture Notes on Theta Functions, Vol. 2. (Progress in Mathematics Ser.: Vol.43). 200p. 1993. 42.50 (*0-8176-3110-0*) Birkhauser.

Mumford, David & Gordon, Bruce. Disneyland the Nickel Tour: A Postcard Journey Through 40 Years of the Happiest Place on Earth. (Illus.). 368p. 1995. 75.00 (*0-9646059-0-2*) Camphor Tree Pubs.

Mumford, David, et al. Indra's Pearls: An Atlas of Kleinian Groups. (Illus.). 512p. 2000. text 49.95 (*0-521-35253-3*) Cambridge U Pr.

— Two & Three-Dimensional Patterns of the Face. LC 98-37189. (Illus.). 264p. (C). 1999. text 48.00 (*1-56881-087-3*) AK Peters.

Mumford, David, jt. auth. see Smith, Peggy.

Mumford, David, jt. ed. see Artin, Michael.

Mumford, David B. The Red Book of Varieties & Schemes: Includes the Michigan Lectures (1974) on Curves & Their Jacobians. 2nd ed. Dold, A. & Eckmann, B., eds. LC 97-36240. (Lecture Notes in Mathematics: Vol. 1358). (Illus.). x, 304p. 1999. pap. 46.00 (*3-540-63293-X*) Spr-Verlag.

Mumford, E. Dangerous Decisions: Problem Solving in Tomorrow's World. LC 99-24210. (Illus.). 222p. (C). 1999. 49.95 (*0-306-46142-0*, Kluwer Plenum); pap. 27.50 (*0-306-46143-9*, Kluwer Plenum) Kluwer Academic.

— Values, Technology & Work. (Information Systems Ser.: No. 3). 328p. 1981. text 211.50 (*90-247-2562-3*) Kluwer Academic.

Mumford, Enid & Ward, T. B. Computers: Planning for People. (Modern Management Ser.). (Illus.). 176p. (C). 1968. pap. 25.00 (*0-8464-1177-6*) Beekman Pubs.

Mumford, Enid, jt. ed. see Cooper, Cary L.

***Mumford, Eric.** The CIAM Discourse on Urbanism, 1928-1960. LC 99-54625. (Illus.). 408p. 2000. 45.00 (*0-262-13364-4*) MIT Pr.

Mumford, Erika. Willow Water. 120p. (Orig.). 1988. pap. 7.95 (*0-9619960-1-3*) Every Other Thursday.

— Words for Myself. 48p. (Orig.). 1992. pap. 8.95 (*0-9619960-2-1*) Every Other Thursday.

Mumford, Esther H. Calabash: A Guide to the History, Culture, & Art of African Americans in Seattle & King County, Washington. (Illus.). 158p. (Orig.). 1993. pap. 9.95 (*0-9605670-7-0*) Ananse Pr.

— The Man Who Founded a Town. (Washington Biography Ser.). (Illus.). 32p. (Orig.). (J). (gr. 2-5). 1990. 8.95 (*0-9605670-2-X*); pap. 4.95 (*0-9605670-3-8*) Ananse Pr.

— Seattle's Black Victorians, 1852 to 1901. (Illus.). 253p. (Orig.). 1980. pap. 7.95 (*0-9605670-0-3*) Ananse Pr.

— Seven Stars & Orion: Reflections of the Past. (Illus.). 112p. (Orig.). 1986. pap. 7.95 (*0-9605670-1-1*) Ananse Pr.

Mumford, John, jt. auth. see Saraswati, Anandakapila.

Mumford, Jonn. A Chakra & Kundalini Workbook: Psycho-Spiritual Techniques for Health, Rejuvenation, Psychic Powers & Spiritual Realization. 2nd enl. rev. ed. LC 94-20282. (Illus.). 296p. 1999. pap., wbk. ed. 16.95 (*1-56718-473-1*) Llewellyn Pubns.

— Death: Beginning or End?: Methods for Immortality. LC 98-50288. (Illus.). 224p. 1999. 9.95 (*1-56718-476-6*, K476) Llewellyn Pubns.

— Ecstasy Through Tantra. 3rd ed. LC 87-45734. (Tantra & Sexual Arts Ser.). (Illus.). 190p. 1987. pap. 16.00 (*0-87542-494-5*) Llewellyn Pubns.

— Magical Tattwa Cards: A Complete System of Self-Development, Incl. 26 cards. LC 97-2899. (Illus.). 288p. 1999. 29.95 (*1-56718-472-3*) Llewellyn Pubns.

— The Mind Magic Kit. LC 97-44746. 128p. 1998. boxed set 15.95 (*1-56718-475-8*) Llewellyn Pubns.

Mumford, Kevin J. Interzones: Black-White Sex Districts in Chicago & New York. LC 96-26945. 248p. (C). 1997. pap. 17.50 (*0-231-10493-6*) Col U Pr.

— Interzones: Black White Sex Districts in Chicago & New York in the Early Twentieth Century. LC 96-26945. 1996. 52.00 (*0-231-10492-8*) Col U Pr.

Mumford, Laura S. Love & Ideology in the Afternoon: Soap Opera, Women, & Television Genre. LC 94-44239. (Arts & Politics of the Everyday Ser.). 176p. 1995. 27.95 (*0-253-32879-9*); pap. 12.95 (*0-253-20965-X*) Ind U Pr.

— Women's Issues: An Annotated Bibliography. (Magill Bibliographies Ser.). 163p. 1991. 42.00 (*0-8108-2806-5*) Scarecrow.

Mumford, Lewis. Art & Technics. LC 52-1930. (Bampton Lectures in America: No. 4). 62p. 1952. text 44.50 (*0-231-01903-3*) Col U Pr.

***Mumford, Lewis.** Art & Techniques. (Illus.). 2000. pap. text 15.50 (*0-231-12105-9*) Col U Pr.

Mumford, Lewis. Brown Decades. 266p. 1993. reprint ed. lib. bdg. 79.00 (*0-7812-5302-0*) Rprt Serv.

— The Brown Decades: A Study of the Arts in America, 1865-1895. 2nd ed. (Illus.). 128p. 1971. pap. 6.95 (*0-486-20200-3*) Dover.

Mumford, Lewis. The City in History: Its Origins, Its Transformations & Its Prospects. 720p. 1997. 12.98 (*1-56731-211-X*, MJF Bks) Fine Comms.

Mumford, Lewis. The City in History: Its Origins, Its Transformations & Its Prospects. LC 61-7689. (Illus.). 734p. 1968. reprint ed. pap. 27.00 (*0-15-618035-9*, Harvest Bks) Harcourt.

— The Culture of Cities. LC 80-23130. (Illus.). 586p. 1981. reprint ed. lib. bdg. 52.50 (*0-313-22746-2*, MUCC, Greenwood Pr) Greenwood.

— The Culture of Cities. LC 32-27277. (Illus.). 638p. 1970. reprint ed. pap. 24.00 (*0-15-623301-0*, Harvest Bks) Harcourt.

— From the Ground Up: Observations on Contemporary Architecture, Housing, Highway Building, & Civic Design. LC 56-13736. 264p. (Orig.). 1956. pap. 12.95 (*0-15-634019-4*, Harvest Bks) Harcourt.

— The Future of Technics & Civilization. 184p. 1986. reprint ed. pap. 7.50 (*0-900384-32-8*) Left Bank.

— Herman Melville. (BCL1-PS American Literature Ser.). 377p. 1992. reprint ed. lib. bdg. 89.00 (*0-7812-6797-8*) Rprt Serv.

— Herman Melville. 377p. 1993. reprint ed. lib. bdg. 89.00 (*0-7812-5280-6*) Rprt Serv.

— The Highway & the City. LC 80-22641. 246p. 1981. reprint ed. lib. bdg. 59.50 (*0-313-22747-0*, MUHC, Greenwood Pr) Greenwood.

— The Human Way Out. (C). 1958. pap. 4.00 (*0-87574-097-9*) Pendle Hill.

— Interpretations & Forecasts, 1922-1972: Studies in Literature, History, Biography, Technics, & Contemporary Society. LC 79-10266. 522p. 1979. pap. 5.95 (*0-15-644903-X*, Harvest Bks) Harcourt.

— Myth of the Machine. (Illus.). 1997. 14.98 (*1-56731-201-2*, MJF Bks) Fine Comms.

— Myth of the Machine, 2 vols. Incl. Vol. 1. Technics & Human Development. (Illus.). 384p. 1971. reprint ed. pap. 19.95 (*0-15-662341-2*, Harvest Bks); Vol. 2. Myth of the Machine. (Illus.). 544p. 1974. reprint ed. pap. 19.95 (*0-15-671610-0*, Harvest Bks); (Illus.). pap. write for info. (*0-318-52958-0*, Harvest Bks) Harcourt.

— Pentagon of Power: The Myth of the Machine, Vol. 2. LC 70-124836. (Illus.). 496p. 1970. 12.95 (*0-15-163974-4*) Harcourt.

— Roots of Contemporary American Architecture. LC 75-171490. 452p. 1972. reprint ed. pap. text 11.95 (*0-486-22072-9*) Dover.

— Sidewalk Critic: Lewis Mumford's Writings on New York. Wojtowicz, Robert, ed. LC 98-18843. (Illus.). 288p. 1998. 27.50 (*1-56898-133-3*) Princeton Arch.

— Sticks & Stones. 247p. 1993. reprint ed. lib. bdg. 79.00 (*0-7812-5301-2*) Rprt Serv.

— Sticks & Stones. rev. ed. (Illus.). 113p. 1955. pap. 5.95 (*0-486-20202-X*) Dover.

— The Story of Utopias. 1990. 24.00 (*0-8446-1319-3*) Peter Smith.

— Technics & Civilization. LC 63-19641. (Illus.). 536p. (C). 1963. pap. 23.00 (*0-15-688254-X*, Harvest Bks) Harcourt.

— The Transformations of Man. 1990. 22.00 (*0-8446-4590-7*) Peter Smith.

— Values for Survival: Essays, Addresses, & Letters on Politics & Education. LC 79-167387. (Essay Index Reprint Ser.). 1977. reprint ed. 22.95 (*0-8369-2704-4*) Ayer.

M

Mumford, Lewis, et al. Arts in Renewal. LC 70-84296. (Essay Index Reprint Ser.). 1977. 18.95 (*0-8369-1121-0*) Ayer.

Mumford, Lloyd R., Jr. Computer Consulting 101: A Beginner's How-To Guide to Becoming a Computer Consultant. Kaplan, Gale, ed. (Illus.). 104p. (C). 1995. write for info. (*0-9644847-2-2*) Lloyds Bridges.

Mumford, M. D., et al, eds. Patterns of Life History: The Ecology of Human Individuality. 512p. (C). 1990. text 125.00 (*0-8058-0225-8*) L Erlbaum Assocs.

Mumford, M. J. Philosophical Perspectives on Accounting: Essays in Honor of Edward Stamp. LC 92-18454. 256p. (C). (gr. 13). 1992. pap. 85.95 (*0-415-08093-2*, A9718) Thomson Learn.

Mumford, Marilyn R., jt. ed. see Swartzlander, Susan.

Mumford, Michael J., intro. Edward Stamp: Later Papers. (Foundations of Accounting Ser.: No. 18). 106p. 1988. text 10.00 (*0-8240-6133-0*) Garland.

Mumford, Monica G., jt. ed. see Fowler, Sandra M.

Mumford PTA Staff. The Monarch's Feast: A World of Recipes from the Mary Munford Community. (Illus.). 545p. 1997. pap. 17.95 (*0-9660007-0-6*) M Munford.

Mumford, R. E. Distribution of the Mammals of Indiana. (Indiana Academy of Science Monograph: No. 1). (Illus.). 114p. 1969. pap. 8.00 (*1-883362-02-4*) IN Acad Sci.

Mumford, Richard L. An American History Primer. 396p. (C). 1989. pap. text 29.50 (*0-15-502344-6*, Pub. by Harcourt Coll Pubs) Harcourt.

Mumford, Russell E. & Keller, Charles E. The Birds of Indiana. LC 83-49454. (Illus.). 400p. 1984. 59.95 (*0-253-10736-9*) Ind U Pr.

Mumford, S. D. Vasectomy: The Decision-Making Process. (Illus.). 1978. pap. 10.00 (*0-911302-33-6*) San Francisco Pr.

— Vasectomy Counseling. (Illus.). 1977. 15.00 (*0-911302-31-X*); pap. 5.00 (*0-317-58585-1*) San Francisco Pr.

Mumford, S. R. Himalayan Dialogue - Tibetan Lamas & Gurung Shamans in Nepals. (C). 1991. text 60.00 (*0-7855-0141-X*, Pub. by Ratna Pustak Bhandar) St Mut.

Mumford, Stephen. Dispositions. LC 98-3549. 262p. 1998. text 65.00 (*0-19-823611-5*) OUP.

Mumford, Stephen D. American Democracy & the Vatican: Population Growth & National Security. LC 84-72500. 268p. (Orig.). 1984. 11.95 (*0-931779-00-6*, Humanist Press); pap. 7.95 (*0-931779-01-4*, Humanist Press) Am Humanist.

— The Life & Death of NSSM 200: How the Destruction of Political Will Doomed a U. S. Population Policy. rev. ed. LC 96-70965. xxii, 579p. (Orig.). 1996. 39.00 (*0-937307-04-1*); pap. 32.00 (*0-937307-05-X*) CRPS.

— The Pope & the New Apocalypse: The Holy War Against Family Planning. (Illus.). 82p. (Orig.). 1986. 6.95 (*0-937307-00-9*); pap. 3.95 (*0-937307-01-7*) CRPS.

Mumford, Susan. The Complete Guide to Massage: A Step-by-Step Approach to Total Body Relaxation. 192p. 1996. pap. 16.95 (*0-452-27518-0*, Plume) Dutton Plume.

— Healing Massage. 128p. 1998. pap. 16.95 (*0-452-27994-1*, Plume) Dutton Plume.

Mumford, Thomas F., Jr., jt. auth. see Cheney, Daniel P.

Mumford, Thomas M. Horizontal Harmony of the Four Gospels in Parallel Columns: (King James Version) LC 90-6346. xiii, 169p. 1982. pap. 9.95 (*0-87747-942-9*) Deseret Bk.

Mumford, William W., et al. Noise Performance Factors in Communication Systems. LC 68-5234. (Illus.). 97p. reprint ed. pap. 30.10 (*0-608-10236-9*, 201007500068) Bks Demand.

Mumick, Inderpal S., jt. ed. see Gupta, Ashish.

Mu'Min, Ridgely A. Amen: The Secret Waters of the Great Pyramid. (Illus.). 196p. (Orig.). 1988. pap. 16.95 (*0-317-93345-0*); lib. bdg. 29.95 (*0-317-93344-2*) AM Distributors.

Mumion, William, jt. ed. see Hackett, Jeremiah.

***Mumm, Debbie.** Debbie Mumm's Quick Country Quilts for Every Room: Wall Quilts, Bed Quilts, & Coordinating Accessories Using Easy, Timesaving Techniques. (Illus.). 288p. 2000. pap. text 19.95 (*1-57954-264-6*) Rodale Pr Inc.

Mumm, Debbie. Debbie Mumm's Quick Country Quilts for Every Room: Wall Quilts, Bed Quilts, & Dozens of Coordinating Accessories for You to Make. LC 98-8914. (Illus.). 228p. 1998. text 29.95 (*0-87596-775-2*) Rodale Pr Inc.

— More Quick Country Quilting: Over Sixty New Fast & Fun Projects from the Author of Quick Country Quilting. (Illus.). 256p. 1996. pap. 14.95 (*0-87596-757-4*) Rodale Pr Inc.

— Quick Country Christmas Quilts. LC 95-9830. (Illus.). 256p. 1995. text 27.95 (*0-87596-653-5*) Rodale Pr Inc.

— Quick Country Christmas Quilts. (Illus.). 1998. pap. 16.95 (*0-87596-986-0*) Rodale Pr Inc.

— Quick Country Quilting: Over 80 Projects Featuring Easy, Timesaving Techniques. (Illus.). 256p. 1995. pap. 15.95 (*0-87596-741-8*) Rodale Pr Inc.

— Welcome Home. LC 98-20263. (Illus.). 128p. 1998. pap. 29.95 (*1-56477-235-7*, DB349) Martingale & Co.

Mumm, Debbie. Joined at the Heart: A Celebration of Friendship. LC 99-231903. (Cherished Moments Ser.). 48p. 1909. 12.99 (*1-57051-096-2*, 0962) Brownlow Pub Co.

— Seeds of Friendship, 1. LC 99-236693. 1998. 8.99 (*1-57051-098-9*) Brownlow Pub Co.

— Tea Time Friends. (Little Treasures Ser.). 64p. 1998. 5.99 (*1-57051-097-0*, 0970) Brownlow Pub Co.

Mumm, Robert C. Photometrics Handbook. 2nd rev. ed. (Illus.). 275p. (Orig.). (C). 1997. pap. 20.00 (*0-911747-37-0*) Broadway Pr.

Mumm, Susan. Stolen Daughters, Virgin Mothers: Anglican Sisterhoods in Victorian Britain. LC 97-34291. xv, 304 p. 1999. 75.00 (*0-7185-0151-9*) Bks Intl VA.

Mumm, Susan M. The Rituals Resource Book: Alternative Weddings, Funerals, Holidays & Other Rites of Passage. 2nd rev. ed. LC 97-112156. Orig. Title: Rituals for a New Age-Alternative Weddings, Funerals, Holidays, Etc. (1987). 285p. 1995. pap. 21.95 (*0-9619645-1-0*) A Yul Pub & Dist.

Mumma, Albert. Environmental Law: Meeting U. K. & E. C. Requirements. LC 95-5091. 1995. write for info. (*0-07-707952-3*) McGraw.

***Mumma, Howard.** Albert Camus & the Minister. LC 00-8354. 234p. 2000. pap. 15.95 (*1-55725-246-7*, 930-049, Pub. by Paraclete MA) BookWorld.

Mumma, J. D., ed. see Takehara, Jan C.

Mumma, Michael J. & Smith, Harlan J., eds. Astrophysics from the Moon. LC 90-55582. (AIP Conference Proceedings Ser.: No. 207). (Illus.). 696p. 1992. 85.00 (*0-88318-770-1*) Am Inst Physics.

Mumma, Ralph O., jt. ed. see Von Emon, Jeanette M.

***Mummaw, Stefan.** 72dpi: The Best of Online Interface Design. 240p. 2000. pap. 39.95 (*1-929685-01-7*) Muska Lipman.

Mumme, I. A. The Emerald. 158p. (C). 1989. text 45.00 (*0-89771-023-1*, Pub. by Bob Mossel) St Mut.

— The World of Sapphires. 212p. (C). 1989. pap. text 70.00 (*0-89771-027-4*, Pub. by Bob Mossel) St Mut.

Mumme, Jack. Risk Management for Dentists. 160p. 1997. 49.00 (*0-910167-38-9*) Comm Unltd CA.

Mumme, June. Play Next Play. 1998. pap. 19.95 (*1-57640-023-9*) Host Comns Inc.

Mumme, Patricia Y. The Srivaisnava Theological Dispute - Manavalamamuni & Bedanta Desika. (C). 1988. 25.00 (*0-8364-2453-0*, Pub. by New Era Pub) S Asia.

Mumme, Patricia Y., jt. ed. see Fort, Andrew O.

Mumme, Ronald L., jt. auth. see Koenig, Walter D.

Mumme, Stephen P. Apportioning Groundwater Beneath the U. S.-Mexico Border. (Research Reports: No. 45). 54p. (C). 1988. ring bd. 5.00 (*0-935391-79-7*, RR-45) UCSD Ctr US-Mex.

Mummert, J. Abiding in Christ. 1991. pap. 6.95 (*0-937032-79-4*) Light&Life Pub Co MN.

Mummert, John D. Sermon on the Mount. LC 98-42235. 78p. 1999. pap. 6.95 (*1-57249-146-9*, Burd St Pr) White Mane Pub.

Mummert, John R. & Bach, Jeff. Refugee Ministry in the Local Congregation. LC 91-42220. 128p. (Orig.). 1992. pap. 9.99 (*0-8361-3580-6*) Herald Pr.

Mummert, Luke. Ravishing & Heartfelt Poetic Insight. 1997. pap. 56.95 (*1-57553-638-2*) Watermrk Pr.

Mummery, A. F. & Hobson, John A. The Physiology of Industry: Being an Exposure of Certain Fallacies in Existing Theories of Economics. LC 87-17943. (Reprints of Economic Classics Ser.). xvii, 215p. 1989. reprint ed. 35.00 (*0-678-00673-3*) Kelley.

***Mummery, Sue.** Why 2000. (Illus.). (ps-3). 1999. pap. 0.00 (*1-85792-483-5*) Christian Focus.

Mummery, W. Kerry, jt. auth. see Sefton, Judy M.

Mummy, Patrick, jt. auth. see Johnson, Richard.

Mumper, Michael. Removing College Price Barriers: What Government Has Done & Why It Hasn't Worked. LC 95-797. (SUNY Series, Social Context of Education & SUNY Series, Teacher Empowerment & School Reform). 304p. (C). 1995. pap. text 24.95 (*0-7914-2704-8*) State U NY Pr.

— Removing College Price Barriers: What Government Has Done & Why It Hasn't Worked. LC 95-797. (SUNY Series, The Social Context of Education & SUNY Series, Teacher Empowerment & School Reform). 304p. (C). 1995. text 74.50 (*0-7914-2703-X*) State U NY Pr.

Mumpower, Carl. Vietnam: Coming All the Way Home. (Illus.). 112p. (Orig.). 1992. pap. 9.95 (*1-56664-008-3*) WorldComm.

Mumpower, Jeryl L. & Ilchman, Warren F., eds. New York State in the Year 2000. LC 87-6486. 572p. (C). 1988. text 34.50 (*0-88706-602-X*) State U NY Pr.

Mumps Development Committee. American National Standards for Information System - Programming Languages - MUMPS. 1990. 30.00 (*0-918118-37-9*) M Technol.

MUMPS Users' Group Staff. Proceedings of the MUMPS Users' Group Meeting. Faulkner, Judith R., ed. 1979. 20.00 (*0-918118-06-9*) M Technol.

— Proceedings of the MUMPS Users' Group Meeting, 1974. Zimmerman, Joan, ed. 1974. 20.00 (*0-918118-01-8*) M Technol.

— Proceedings of the MUMPS Users' Group Meeting, 1978. Zimmerman, Pat, ed. 1978. pap. 20.00 (*0-918118-05-0*) M Technol.

Mumpton, F. A. & Sand, Leonard B., eds. Natural Zeolites: Occurrence, Properties, Use. LC 77-30439. 546p. 1978. 375.00 (*0-08-021922-5*, Pergamon Pr) Elsevier.

Mumpton, Frederick A., jt. ed. see Mackinnon, I. D.

Mumtamayee, C. Rural Ecology. (C). 1989. 34.00 (*81-7024-231-2*, Pub. by Ashish Pub Hse) S Asia.

Mumtaz, Ali K. Scheduled Castes & Their Status in India. 276p. 1980. 23.50 (*0-940500-23-X*) Asia Bk Corp.

Mumtaz, Kamil K. Modernity & Tradition: Contemporary Architecture in Pakistan. LC 99-203964. (The Jubilee Ser.). (Illus.). 150p. 1999. text 35.00 (*0-19-577853-7*) OUP.

Mumtaz, Khavar & Mithra, Yameema. Pakistan: Tradition & Change. (Oxfam Country Profiles Ser.). (Illus.). 64p. 1996. pap. 9.95 (*0-85598-336-1*, Pub. by Oxfam Pub) Stylus Pub VA.

Mumtaz, Khawar, jt. ed. see Rupesinge, Kumar.

Mun, Seong K., jt. ed. see Kim, Yongmin.

Mun, J. & M'Baye, A. A., eds. Gallium Arsenide Technology in Europe. LC 94-15890. (Research Reports ESPRIT, Project Group Microelectronic Ser.: Vol. 1). viii, 388p. 1994. 56.95 (*0-387-57906-0*) Spr-Verlag.

Mun, Myong-dae & Pak, Tong-won. Kyongju: City of Millennial History. LC 98-87502. 228 p. 1998. 36.95 (*1-56591-094-X*) Hollym Intl.

Mun, Thomas. A Discourse of Trade. LC 30-21325. 39p. 1988. reprint ed. pap. 5.00 (*0-942153-22-7*) Entropy Conserv.

— A Discourse of Trade, from England unto the East-Indies. LC 68-30534. (Reprints of Economic Classics Ser.). 58p. 1971. reprint ed. 25.00 (*0-678-00873-6*) Kelley.

— A Discourse of Trade Unto the East Indies. LC 72-6257. (English Experience Ser.: No. 85). 58p. 1969. reprint ed. 25.00 (*90-221-0085-5*) Walter J Johnson.

— England's Treasure by Forraign Trade. LC 86-7467. (Reprints of Economic Classics Ser.). vii, 88p. 1986. reprint ed. 25.00 (*0-678-06274-9*) Kelley.

***Mun-Yol, Yi.** Our Twisted Hero. 2001. 21.95 (*0-7868-6670-5*, Pub. by Hyperion) Time Warner.

Munack, A. & Schugerl, K., eds. Computer Applications in Biotechnology: The 6th International Conference, Garmisch-Partenkirchen, Germany, May 14-17, 1995. (IFAC Postprint Ser.). 378p. 1995. pap. 82.25 (*0-08-042377-9*, Pergamon Pr) Elsevier.

Munack, A. & Tantau, H. J., eds. Mathematical & Control Applications in Agriculture & Horticulture, 1997: Proceedings of the 3rd IFAC Workshop, Hannover, Germany, 28 September-2 October 1997. 322p. 1998. pap. 76.50 (*0-08-043037-6*, Pergamon Pr) Elsevier.

Munafo. Psychology for the MRC Psych. LC 98-189084. 208p. 1998. pap. text 40.00 (*0-7506-3403-0*) Buttrwrth-Heinemann.

***Munafo, Marcus.** Chronic Pain: A Handbook for Nurses. (Illus.). 192p. 2000. pap. 35.00 (*0-7506-4120-7*) Buttrwrth-Heinemann.

Munafo, Marcus, jt. auth. see Horn, Sandra.

Munakata, Kiyohiko. Sacred Mountains in Chinese Art. (Illus.). 208p. (Orig.). 1991. pap. 39.95 (*0-252-06188-8*) U of Ill Pr.

Munakata, Kuniyoshi. Noh Othello in English & Japanese. (Illus.). 228p. 1998. 87.95 (*4-585-10025-3*, Pub. by Hokuseido Pr) Book East.

Munakata, Kuniyoshi & Guest, Michael, eds. Essentially Oriental: R. H. Blyth Selection. (Illus.). 355p. 1997. pap. 32.95 (*4-590-00954-4*, Pub. by Hokuseido Pr) Book East.

Munakata, Toshinori. Fundamentals of the New Artificial Intelligence: Beyond Traditional Paradigms. LC 97-24056. (Graduate Texts in Computer Science Ser.). (Illus.). 200p. 1997. 49.95 (*0-387-98302-3*) Spr-Verlag.

— Matrices & Linear Programming with Business Applications. LC 78-54198. 1979. teacher ed. 6.00 (*0-8162-6167-9*); text 36.95 (*0-8162-6166-0*) Holden-Day.

Munakata, Yuko, jt. auth. see O'Reilly, Randall C.

Munan, Heidi. Culture Shock! Malaysia. (Illus.). 239p. 1991. pap. 12.95 (*1-55868-070-5*) Gr Arts Ctr Pub.

Munari, Lorenzo, jt. auth. see Mathis, Wayne N.

Munas Vinas, Salvador & Farrell, Eugene F. The Technical Analysis of Renaissance Illuminated Manuscripts from the Historical Library of the University of Valencia (Estudio Tecnico de los Codices Miniados Renacentistas de la Biblioteca Historica de la Universidad de Valencia. LC 99-24622.Tr. of Estudio Tecnico de los Codices Miniados Historica de la Universidad de Valencia. (ENG & SPA., Illus.). 1999. pap. 15.00 (*1-891771-03-5*) Harvard Art Mus.

Munasinghe, Mohan. Energy Analysis & Policy. (Illus.). 315p. 1990. text 145.00 (*0-408-05634-7*) Buttrwrth-Heinemann.

— Environmental Economics & Sustainable Development. LC 92-42952. (Environment Papers: No. 3). 120p. 1993. pap. 22.00 (*0-8213-2352-0*, 12352) World Bank.

Munasinghe, Mohan, ed. Environmental Impacts of Macroeconomic & Sectoral Policies. LC 95-13305. 344p. 1997. pap. 40.00 (*0-8213-3225-2*) World Bank.

Munasinghe, Mohan, et al, eds. Conservation of West & Central African Rainforests. LC 92-26870. (Technical Paper, 1253-7494 Environment Ser.: No. 1). (ENG & FRE.). 366p. 1992. pap. 22.00 (*0-8213-2256-7*, 12256) World Bank.

— Defining & Measuring Sustainability: The Biogeophysical Foundations. LC 95-2865. 474p. 1995. pap. 29.00 (*0-8213-3134-5*, 13134) World Bank.

— Informal Settlements, Environmental Degradation, & Disaster Vulnerability: Turkey Case Study. 208p. 1995. pap. 22.00 (*0-8213-3397-6*, 13397) World Bank.

— Towards a Sustainable Urban Environment: The Rio de Janeiro Study. LC 93-6969. (Discussion Paper Ser.: No. 195). 185p. 1993. pap. 22.00 (*0-8213-2388-1*, 12388) World Bank.

Munasinghe, Mohan & McNeely, Jeffrey A. Protected Area Economics & Policy: Linking Conservation & Sustainable Development. LC 94-45272. 372p. 1995. pap. 22.00 (*0-8213-3132-9*, 13132) World Bank.

Munasinghe, Mohan & Meier, Peter. Energy Policy Analysis & Modelling. (Studies in Energy & the Environment). 371p. (C). 1993. text 69.95 (*0-521-36326-8*) Cambridge U Pr.

Munasinghe, Mohan & Warford, Jeremy J. Electricity Pricing: Theory & Case Studies. LC 81-47613. 400p. reprint ed. pap. 124.00 (*0-7837-4405-6*, 204414500012) Bks Demand.

Munasinghe, Mohan, et al. Global Climate Change: Economic & Policy Issues. 212p. 1996. pap. 22.00 (*0-8213-3402-6*, 13402) World Bank.

— Valuing Tropical Forests: Methodology & Case Study of Madagascar. (Environment Papers: No. 13). 76p. 1995. pap. 22.00 (*0-8213-3407-7*, 13407) World Bank.

Munasinghe, Mohan, jt. auth. see Guarnizo, Caroline.

Munasinghe, Mohan, jt. auth. see Jepma, Catrinus J.

Munasinghe, Mohan, jt. auth. see Meier, Peter.

Munasinghe, Mohan, jt. ed. see Hanna, Susan.

Munasinghe, Mohan, jt. ed. see King, Kenneth.

Munavvar, Mohamed. Ocean States: Archipelagic Regimes in the Law of the Sea. LC 94-13947. (Publications on Ocean Development: Vol. 22). 240p. (C). 1995. lib. bdg. 112.00 (*0-7923-2882-5*) Kluwer Academic.

Munawar, M. Phytoplankton Dynamics in the North American Great Lakes Vol. 2: Lakes Huron, Superior & Michigan. 275p. 1998. 110.00 (*0-614-23637-1*, Pub. by SPB Acad Pub) Balogh.

Munawar, M., ed. International Symposium on the Phycology of Large Lakes of the World: Proceedings, Held at the 1st International Congress, St. John's Newfoundland, Canada. (Advances in Limnology Ser.: Heft 25). (GER., Illus.). v, 256p. 1987. pap. 58.00 (*3-510-47023-0*, Pub. by E Schweizerbartsche) Balogh.

— Limnology & Fisheries of Georgian Bay & the North Channel Ecosystems. (Developments in Hydrobiology Ser.). 1988. text 245.00 (*90-6193-653-5*) Kluwer Academic.

Munawar, M., et al, eds. Environmental Bioassay Techniques & Their Application: Proceedings of the First International Conference Held in Lancaster, England, 11-14 July 1988. (C). 1990. text 463.00 (*0-7923-0498-5*) Kluwer Academic.

***Munawar, M., et al, eds.** State of Lake Erie - Past, Present & Future. (Ecovision World Monograph Ser.). (Illus.). 166p. 1999. 140.00 (*90-5782-018-8*, Pub. by Backhuys Pubs) Balogh.

Munawar, M. & Dave, G., eds. Developments & Progress in Sediment Quality Assessment: Rational Challenges & Strategies. (Ecovision World Monographs). (Illus.). xvi, 256p. 1997. 95.00 (*90-5103-133-5*, Pub. by SPB Acad Pub) Balogh.

Munawar, M. & Edsall, T., eds. Environmental Assessment & Habitat Evaluation of the Upper Great Lakes Connecting Channels. (Developments in Hydrobiology Ser.). (C). 1991. lib. bdg. 242.00 (*0-7923-1206-6*) Kluwer Academic.

Munawar, M. & Luotola, M. The Contaminants in the Nordic Ecosystem: The Dynamics, Processes & Fate. (Illus.). 276p. 1995. 100.00 (*90-5103-108-4*, Pub. by SPB Acad Pub) Balogh.

Munawar, M. & Talling, J. F., eds. Seasonality of Freshwater Phytoplankton. (Developments in Hydrobiology Ser.). 1986. text 221.50 (*90-6193-577-6*) Kluwer Academic.

Munawar, M., et al. Aquatic Ecosystems of China: Environmental & Toxicological Assessment. 1995. 45.00 (*90-5103-105-X*, Pub. by SPB Acad Pub) Balogh.

— Bioindicators of Environmental Health. (Ecovision World Monographs). 265p. 1995. 99.00 (*90-5103-116-5*, Pub. by SPB Acad Pub) Balogh.

— Lake Huron EcoSystem: Ecology, Fisheries & Management. 485p. 1995. 170.00 (*90-5103-117-3*, Pub. by SPB Acad Pub) Balogh.

— Phytoplankton Dynamics in the North American Great Lakes Vol. 1: Lakes Ontario, Erie, St. Clair. 275p. 1997. 110.00 (*90-5103-115-7*, Pub. by SPB Acad Pub) Balogh.

Munawar, M., jt. ed. see Murphy, T.

Munawwar, Muhammab I. Secrets of God's Mystical Oneness: Asrar Al-Towhid. 665p. 1996. pap. 28.00 (*0-614-21342-8*, 1401) Kazi Pubns.

Munawwar, Muhammad. Dimensions of Pakistan Movement. 367p. 1987. 39.95 (*1-56744-261-7*) Kazi Pubns.

***Munby, A. N. L.** The Alabaster Hand. xxii, 142p. 1999. 38.50 (*1-899562-83-4*) Ash-Tree.

Munby, Denys L. God & the Rich Society: A Study of Christians in a World of Abundance. LC 85-21886. 209p. 1985. reprint ed. lib. bdg. 59.50 (*0-313-24925-3*, MGRS, Greenwood Pr) Greenwood.

Munby, Hugh, et al, eds. Seeing Curriculum in a New Light: Essays from Science Education. 190p. 1984. reprint ed. pap. text 20.50 (*0-8191-4238-7*) U Pr of Amer.

Munby, Hugh, jt. ed. see Russell, Tom.

Munby, J., jt. auth. see Cunliffe, B. W.

Munby, John. Communicative Syllabus Design: A Sociolinguistic Model for Defining the Content of Purpose-Specific Language Programmes. 238p. 1981. pap. text 21.95 (*0-521-28294-2*) Cambridge U Pr.

Munby, Jonathan. Public Enemies, Public Heroes: Screening the Gangster from Little Caesar to Touch of Evil. LC 98-22151. (Illus.). 249p. 1999. pap. 16.00 (*0-226-55033-8*); lib. bdg. 45.00 (*0-226-55031-1*) U Ch Pr.

Munby, Julian, jt. ed. see Tatton-Brown, Tim.

Muncaster, Barbara. Learn Basic Business Math Using Calculations, Tests. (KH - Office Machines Ser.). 1985. 1.95 (*0-538-13543-3*) S-W Pub.

— Learning Basic Math & Business Math. 2nd ed. (MB - Business/Vocational Math Ser.). 1991. mass mkt. 25.95 (*0-538-60815-3*) S-W Pub.

Muncaster, Barbara & Prescott, Susan. Computer Calculator. LC 93-4198. 1994. mass mkt. 11.95 (*0-538-62332-2*) S-W Pub.

***Muncaster-Jewell, Penny.** Penny's Practical Guide to Advanced Projects. 250p. 1999. pap. 75.00 (*0-9672149-2-0*) Canstar.

— Penny's Practical Guide to PE-Design. (Illus.). 282p. 1997. pap. 75.00 (*0-9672149-0-4*) Canstar.

— Penny's Practical Guide to PE-Designs, Palette & Deco Wizard. 1999. pap. 75.00 (*0-9672149-1-2*) Canstar.

Muncaster, P. W. A Practical Guide to TIG (GTA) Welding. 144p. 1991. 108.00 (*1-85573-020-0*, Pub. by Woodhead Pubng) Am Educ Systs.

Muncaster, R. G., jt. auth. see Cohen, H.

An Asterisk (*) at the beginning of an entry indicates that the title is appearing for the first time.

***Muncaster, Ralph O.** Are There Hidden Codes in the Bibles? LC 99-88441. (Examine the Evidence Ser.). 48p. 2000. pap. 3.99 (*0-7369-0366-6*) Harvest Hse.
— Can Archaeology Prove the New Testament? (Examine the Evidence Ser.). 48p. 2000. pap. 3.99 (*0-7369-0367-4*) Harvest Hse.
— Can Archaeology Prove the Old Testament? (Examine the Evidence Ser.). 48p. 2000. pap. 3.99 (*0-7369-0356-9*) Harvest Hse.
— Can You Trust Your Bible? (Examine the Evidence Ser.). 48p. 2000. pap. 3.99 (*0-7369-0355-0*) Harvest Hse.
— Creation vs. Evolution: What Do the Latest Scientific Discoveries Reveal? (Examine the Evidence Ser.). 48p. 2000. pap. 3.99 (*0-7369-0351-8*) Harvest Hse.
— Does the Bible Predict the Future? (Examine the Evidence Ser.). 48p. 2000. pap. 3.99 (*0-7369-0353-4*) Harvest Hse.
— How Do We Know Jesus Is God? LC 99-53618. (Examine the Evidence Ser.). 48p. 2000. pap. 3.99 (*0-7369-0321-6*) Harvest Hse.
— Is the Bible Really a Message from God? (Reasons to Believe Ser.). 48p. 2000. pap. 3.99 (*0-7369-0352-6*) Harvest Hse.
— Science--Was the Bible Ahead of Its time? (Examine the Evidence Ser.). 48p. 2000. pap. 3.99 (*0-7369-0354-2*) Harvest Hse.
— What Is the Proof for the Resurrection? (Examine the Evidence Ser.). 48p. 2000. pap. 3.99 (*0-7369-0324-0*) Harvest Hse.
— What Really Happened Christmas Morning? (Examine the Evidence Ser.). 48p. 2000. pap. 3.99 (*0-7369-0323-2*) Harvest Hse.
— What Really Happens When You Die? (Examine the Evidence Ser.). 48p. 2000. pap. 3.99 (*0-7369-0365-8*) Harvest Hse.
Muncaster, Roger. A-Level Physics. 4th ed. 960p. (C). 1997. pap. 59.50 (*0-7478-1584-4*, Pub. by S Thornes Pubs) Trans-Atl Phila.
— A-Level Physics. 4th ed. 953p. 1997. pap. 57.50 (*0-7487-1584-3*, Pub. by S Thornes Pubs) Trans-Atl Phila.
— Astrophysics & Cosmology. 144p. 1997. pap. 29.50 (*0-7487-2865-1*, Pub. by S Thornes Pubs) Trans-Atl Phila.
— Medical Physics. (Illus.). 140p. 1998. pap. 34.50 (*0-7487-2324-2*) St Mut.
— Nuclear Physics & Fundamental Particles. 160p. 1998. pap. 34.50 (*0-7487-1805-2*) St Mut.
— Relativity & Quantum Physics. 140p. 1998. pap. 34.50 (*0-7487-1799-4*) St Mut.
Munce, R. H. Ruth. 117p. 1971. 3.95 (*0-914674-00-5*) Freelandia.
***Munce, Robert.** Grace Livingston Hill. large type ed. LC 99-45561. (G. K. Hall Paperback Ser.). 1999. pap. 21.95 (*0-7838-8797-3*, G K Hall Lrg Type) Mac Lib Ref.
Muncey, Donna E. & McQuillan, Patrick J. Reform & Resistance: An Ethnographic View of School Reform. LC 95-43603. 319p. 1996. 35.00 (*0-300-06108-0*) Yale U Pr.
Munch. Life Insurance, 1993. 1993. suppl. ed. 52.50 (*0-316-58961-6*, Aspen Law & Bus) Aspen Pub.
Munch, Christopher H., jt. auth. see Dorr, Robert C.
Munch, Edvard. Graphic Works of Edvard Munch. (Illus.). 90p. 1979. pap. 11.95 (*0-486-23765-6*) Dover.
***Munch, Edvard.** Munch. (Illus.). 2000. pap. 1.00 (*0-486-41066-8*) Dover.
Munch, Edward, et al. Surface & Illusion: Ten Portfolios. (Aperture Ser.: No. 145). 80p. 1997. pap. 27.95 (*0-89381-684-1*) Aperture.
Munch, Freidrich, tr. see Boernstein, Henry.
***Munch, Glenn R.** About Y2K: The Survival Handbook & Guide to Practical Preparations for the Year 2000 & Beyond! 156p. 1999. pap. 10.95 (*0-9621581-1-9*) Genmet Pub.
Munch, Glenn R. Getting It Together: The Practical Job Search Guide. 2nd rev. ed. (Illus.). 107p. (C). 1991. reprint ed. pap. text 9.95 (*0-685-24040-1*) Genmet Pub.
Munch, Guido, et al, eds. The Universe at Large: Key Issues in Astronomy & Cosmology. LC 96-28580. (Illus.). 460p. (C). 1997. text 85.00 (*0-521-55367-9*); pap. text 36.95 (*0-521-58944-4*) Cambridge U Pr.
Munch, Helen, ed. see Brookes, Gay & Withrow, Jean.
Munch, Helen, ed. see Haverson, Wayne W. & Haverson, Susan.
Munch, Helen, ed. see Kuntz, Laurie.
Munch, James C., Jr. Financial & Estate Planning with Life Insurance Products. 750p. 1989. 125.00 (*0-316-58941-1*, Aspen Law & Bus) Aspen Pub.
— Financial Planning Set. 1990. 125.00 (*0-316-58947-0*, Aspen Law & Bus) Aspen Pub.
— Life Insurance in Estate Planning. LC 80-84027. (C). 1981. text, suppl. ed. 80.00 (*0-316-58932-2*, Aspen Law & Bus) Aspen Pub.
Munch, Peter A. Norse Mythology, Legends of Gods & Heroes. Hustvedt, Sigurd B., tr. LC 74-112002. 1970. reprint ed. 49.50 (*0-404-04538-3*) AMS Pr.
— Sociology of Tristan da Cunha: Results of the Norwegian Scientific Expedition to Tristan da Cunha, 1937-1938. LC 77-87549. reprint ed. 30.00 (*0-404-16611-3*) AMS Pr.
Munch-Petersen, Thomas, tr. see Nissen, Henrik S., ed.
Munch, R., jt. ed. see Murthy, T. K.
***Munch, Richard.** Democracy at Work: A Comparative Sociology of Environmental Regulation in the United Kingdom, France, Germany & the United States. LC 00-29842. 288p. 2000. 65.00 (*0-275-96840-5*) Greenwood.
— The Ethics of Modernity: Formation & Transformation in Britain, France, Germany & the United States. LC 00-40305. (Legacies of Social Thought Ser.). 2000. pap. write for info. (*0-8476-9921-8*) Rowman.
Munch, Richard. Theory of Action: Towards a New Synthesis Going Beyond Parsons. 358p. (C). 1988. text 67.50 (*0-7102-1218-6*, Routledge Thoemms) Routledge.
— Understanding Modernity: Towards a New Perspective Going Beyond Durkheim & Webber. (International Library of Sociology Ser.). 356p. 1988. text 75.00 (*0-415-01283-X*) Routledge.
Munch, Richard & Smelser, Neil J., eds. Theory of Culture. 435p. 1994. pap. 19.95 (*0-520-07599-4*, Pub. by U CA Pr) Cal Prin Full Svc.
Munch, Richard W. Harry G. Traver: Legends of Terror. Hershey, Richard & Bush, Lee O., eds. (Roller Coaster Designers Ser.). (Illus.). 175p. (C). 1982. pap. 19.95 (*0-935408-02-9*) Amusement Pk Bks.
Munch, Rudolf. Prinzipien und Praxis des Englischen Unterrichts. (GER.). 2442p. 1972. 47.80 (*3-296-50600-4*, Pub. by Weidmann) Lubrecht & Cramer.
Munch, Victor C. De, see De Munch, Victor C.
Munch, William H., Jr. Homeless Mind. 288p. 1992. pap. 12.95 (*1-880977-03-6*) Watusi.
Munchausen, Baron. Gulliver Revived: Travels & Adventures. 141p. 1992. reprint ed. pap. text 25.00 (*0-87556-841-6*) Saifer.
Muncheryan, Hrand M. Laser & Optoelectronic Engineering. 336p. 1991. 132.00 (*1-56032-062-1*) Hemisp Pub.
— Principles & Practice of Laser Technology. (Illus.). 294p. 1983. 15.95 (*0-8306-0129-5*) McGraw-Hill Prof.
Munchow, L. & Reif, R. Recent Developments in the Nuclear Many Body Problems. 152p. (C). 1985. 70.00 (*0-7855-4965-X*, Pub. by Collets) St Mut.
Munchow, Michael, jt. ed. see Shamdasani, Sonu.
Muncie, John, et al, eds. Understanding the Family. 320p. 1995. 65.00 (*0-8039-7954-1*); pap. 21.95 (*0-8039-7955-X*) Sage.
Muncie, John & McLaughlin, Eugene. The Problem of Crime. 352p. 1996. 79.95 (*0-7619-5004-4*); pap. 29.95 (*0-7619-5005-2*) Sage.
Muncie, John, et al. Criminological Perspectives: A Reader. 560p. 1996. 85.00 (*0-7619-5002-8*); pap. 26.95 (*0-7619-5003-6*) Sage.
Muncie, John, jt. ed. see McLaughlin, Eugene.
Munck. Marx at 2000. LC 99-15594. 164p. 2000. text 65.00 (*0-312-22407-9*) St Martin.
Munck, De Silva. Postmodern Insurgencies. LC 99-15423. 2000. text 69.95 (*0-312-22629-2*) St Martin.
Munck, Gerardo L. Authoritarianism & Democratization: Soldiers & Workers in Argentina, 1976-1983. LC 98-7195. 1998. pap. 19.95 (*0-271-01808-9*) Pa St U Pr.
— Authoritarianism & Democratization: Soldiers & Workers in Argentina, 1976-1983. LC 98-7195. (Illus.). 384p. 1998. 55.00 (*0-271-01807-0*) Pa St U Pr.
Munck, Jorgen L. The Kornilov Revolt: A Critical Examination of Sources & Research. (Illus.). 176p. (Orig.). (C). 1987. pap. text 27.00 (*87-7288-040-6*, Pub. by Aarhus Univ Pr) David Brown.
Munck, Lars, jt. ed. see Pomeranz, Y.
Munck, Ronaldo. Critical Development Theory: Contributions to a New Paradigm. 217p. 1999. pap. 22.50 (*1-85649-638-4*) Zed Books.
— Critical Development Theory: Contributions to a New Paradigm. O'Hearn, Denis, ed. 217p. 1999. 55.00 (*1-85649-637-6*) Zed Books.
— The Difficult Dialogue: Marxism & Nationalism. 192p. (C). 1986. pap. 15.00 (*0-86232-494-7*, Pub. by Zed Books) St Martin.
— Latin America: The Transition of Democracy. LC 89-36323. 224p. (C). 1997. pap. 19.95 (*0-86232-819-5*, Pub. by St Martin) St Martin.
— The New International Labour Studies: An Introduction. LC 88-27566. 256p. (C). 1988. pap. 17.50 (*0-86232-587-0*, Pub. by Zed Books); text 49.95 (*0-86232-586-2*, Pub. by Zed Books) St Martin.
Munck, Ronaldo, jt. auth. see Jones, Anny Brooksbank.
Munck, Ronnie. Irish Economy: Results & Prospects. LC 92-45632. 178p. (C). 1993. 54.95 (*0-7453-0673-X*, Pub. by Pluto GBR); pap. 18.95 (*0-7453-0674-8*, Pub. by Pluto GBR) Stylus Pub VA.
***Munck, Thomas.** Enlightenment: A Comparative Social History, 1721-1794. 256p. 2000. pap. text 24.00 (*0-340-66325-1*, Pub. by E A) OUP.
— The Enlightenment: A Comparative Social History 1721-1794. (An Arnold Publication). 264p. 2000. text 65.00 (*0-340-66326-X*, Pub. by E A) OUP.
Munck, Thomas. Seventeenth Century Europe: State, Conflict & the Social Order in Europe 1598-1700. LC 89-10893. 480p. 1990. pap. 14.95 (*0-312-04012-1*) St Martin.
— Seventeenth Century Europe, 1598-1700: State, Conflict & the Social Order in Europe. 1990. pap. text 14.95 (*0-333-28641-3*) St Martin.
Munck, Thomas, jt. auth. see Mawdsley, Evan.
Muncy, Harold W., ed. Asphalt Emulsions, No. 1079. LC 89-49641. (Special Technical Publication Ser.). (Illus.). 122p. 1990. text 32.00 (*0-8031-1457-5*, STP1079) ASTM.
Muncy, John. Whatever Happened to the Wrath of God? 112p. (Orig.). 1995. pap. 6.95 (*0-9629625-5-4*) Ethnos.
Muncy, Lysbeth W. The Junker in the Prussian Administration under William II, 1888 1914. LC 70-80574. 1970. reprint ed. 40.00 (*0-86527-112-7*) Fertig.
Muncy, Mitchell S. & Budziszewski, J., eds. The End of Democracy? No. II: A Crisis of Legitimacy. LC 98-48483. 320p. 1999. pap. 12.95 (*1-890626-10-4*) Spence Pub.
Muncy, Patricia T. Complete Book of Illustrated Reading & Writing Activities for the Primary Grades: Over 330... 354p. 1995. pap. text 28.95 (*0-87628-269-9*) Ctr Appl Res.
— Hooked on Books! Activities & Projects That Make Kids Want to Read. LC 94-31460. (Illus.). 304p. 1994. pap. text 27.95 (*0-87628-411-X*) Ctr Appl Res.
— Springboards to Creative Thinking. LC 85-11389. 240p. 1985. pap. text 27.95 (*0-87628-775-5*) Ctr Appl Res.
Muncy, Robyn. Creating a Female Dominion in American Reform, 1890-1935. 240p. 1994. reprint ed. pap. text 18.95 (*0-19-508924-3*) OUP.
Muncy, Robyn, jt. auth. see Michel, Sonya.
Mund, jt. auth. see Dahal.
Mund, Ed, ed. see Birkland, Barbara J., et al.
Mund, Edward L., ed. see Fish, Harriet U.
Mund, Fred A. Keep the Music Ringing. 48p. 1979. pap. 4.99 (*0-8341-1026-1*) Nazarene.
Mund, Vernon A., jt. auth. see Wolf, Ronald H.
Munda, D. T. Zen Munchkins: Little Wisdoms. (Illus.). 104p. (Orig.). 1991. pap. 12.95 (*0-8048-1640-9*) Tuttle Pubng.
Munda, G. Multicriteria Evaluation in a Fuzzy Environment: Theory & Applications in Ecological Economics. (Contributions to Economics Ser.). (Illus.). xiv, 255p. 1995. pap. 71.00 (*3-7908-0892-X*) Spr-Verlag.
Munda, I. M. Survey of the Benthis Algal Vegetation of the Dyrafjordur, Northwest Iceland. (Offprint from Nova Hedwigia Ser.: No. 29). (Illus.). 1978. pap. text 30.00 (*3-7682-1201-7*) Lubrecht & Cramer.
Mundahl, John. Tales of Courage, Tales of Dreams: A Multicultural Reader. LC 92-42252. 176p. 1993. pap. text 14.58 (*0-201-53962-4*) Addison-Wesley.
Mundahl, Steve & Reider, Marge D. Beyond Betrayal. 312p. 1998. pap. 14.95 (*1-884707-97-1*) Lifestyles.
Mundal, Else, ed. see Fidjestol, Bjarne.
Mundale, Susan, ed. see Otis, Caroline H.
Munday. Custom Auto Electronics & Auto. 1998. 24.95 (*0-949398-73-X*, 861763Q, Pub. by Graffiti) Motorbooks Intl.
Munday, A., tr. from FRE. The Defence of Contraries. LC 72-188. (English Experience Ser.: No. 175). 1969. reprint ed. 25.00 (*90-221-0175-4*) Walter J Johnson.
Munday, A. R., jt. auth. see Peckett, C. W.
Munday, Anthony. The English Roman Life. Ayres, Phillip J., ed. (Studies in Tudor & Stewart Literature). (Illus.). 1980. 45.00 (*0-19-812635-2*) OUP.
— John-A-Kent & John-A-Cumber. LC 70-133714. (Tudor Facsimile Texts. Old English Plays Ser.: No. 58). reprint ed. 59.50 (*0-404-53358-2*) AMS Pr.
Munday, Anthony & Chettle, Henry. Death of Robert Earl of Huntington. LC 73-133712. (Tudor Facsimile Texts. Old English Plays Ser.: No. 95). reprint ed. 59.50 (*0-404-53395-7*) AMS Pr.
— The Downfall of Robert Earl of Huntington. LC 77-133713. (Tudor Facsimile Texts. Old English Plays Ser.: No. 94). 92p. 1970. reprint ed. 59.50 (*0-404-53394-9*) AMS Pr.
Munday, Anthony & Shakespeare, William. Sir Thomas More. LC 74-133715. (Tudor Facsimile Texts. Old English Plays Ser.: No. 65). reprint ed. 59.50 (*0-404-53365-5*) AMS Pr.
Munday, Brian & Ely, Peter. Social Care in Europe. 240p. 1996. pap. text 36.00 (*0-13-354193-2*) P-H.
Munday, Don. Tin Dog, Damper & Dust: A Shearer's Life. pap. 16.95 (*1-875560-06-8*, Pub. by Univ of West Aust Pr) Intl Spec Bk.
Munday, Ethel. The Yorkshire Terrier rev. ed. LC 77-374564. 173p. 1976. write for info. (*0-09-127580-6*) Arrow Bks.
Munday, Ethel & Munday, Vera. The Yorkshire Terrier rev. ed. LC 79-301557. 175p. 1978. write for info. (*0-09-134530-8*) Arrow Bks.
Munday, Godfrey B. The Life & Correspondence of the Late Admiral Lord Rodney, 2 vols., Set. LC 72-8677. (American Revolutionary Ser.). 970p. reprint ed. lib. bdg. 122.00 (*0-8398-1271-X*) Irvington.
Munday, John. E. W. Cooke, R. A., F. R. S., 1811-1880: A Man of His Time. LC 97-101521. (Illus.). 400p. 1996. 89.50 (*1-85149-222-4*) Antique Collect.
— Naval Cannon. (Album Ser.: No. 312). (Illus.). 32p. 1998. pap. 6.25 (*0-85263-844-2*, Pub. by Shire Pubns) Parkwest Pubns.
Munday, John & Wohlenhaus-Munday, Frances. Surviving the Death of a Child. 96p. 1995. pap. 12.00 (*0-664-25566-3*) Westminster John Knox.
***Munday, Laurie D.** Math for Meds: Dosages & Solutions. 8th rev. ed. LC 76-43259. (Illus.). 306p. 2000. pap. text 34.95 (*0-918082-09-9*, 30,000) WI Pubns Inc.
Munday, Laurie D., jt. auth. see Curren, Anna M.
Munday, Marianne. Data & Word Processing. rev. ed. (Opportunities in... Ser.). (Illus.). 160p. pap. 11.95 (*0-8442-4613-1*, 46131, Natl Textbk Co) NTC Contemp Pub Co.
— Opportunities in Data & Word Processing Careers. rev. ed. (Opportunities in... Ser.). (Illus.). 160p. 1996. 14.95 (*0-8442-4612-3*, 46123, Natl Textbk Co) NTC Contemp Pub Co.
Munday, Marianne F. Opportunities in Crafts Careers. (Illus.). 160p. 1987. 13.95 (*0-8442-6015-0*, VGM Career) NTC Contemp Pub Co.
— Opportunities in Crafts Careers. (Illus.). 160p. 1993. pap. 10.95 (*0-8442-6017-7*, VGM Career) NTC Contemp Pub Co.
Munday, R. J., ed. Evidence. 2nd ed. (Butterworths Student Statutes Ser.). 1997. pap. write for info. (*0 406-89105-2*, MEBS2, MICHIE) LEXIS Pub.
Munday, R. J., jt. auth. see Markesinis, Basil S.
Munday, Stephen C. Current Developments in Economics. LC 96-21861. 288p. 1996. pap. 21.95 (*0-312-16339-8*); text 59.95 (*0-312-16338-X*) St Martin.
Munday, Vera, jt. auth. see Munday, Ethel.
Munde, Alan, jt. auth. see Carr, Joe.
Mundel, August B. Ethics in Quality. (Illus.). 232p. 1991. text 75.00 (*0-8247-8513-4*) Dekker.
Mundel, Marvin E. Measuring & Enhancing the Productivity of Service & Government Organizations. 3rd ed. (Illus.). 296p. 1980. pap. text 22.25 (*92-833-1030-6*, 310306) Productivity Inc.
— Measuring the Productivity of Commercial Banks: Algorithms & PC Programs. 100p. 1987. pap. 23.95 (*0-527-91641-2*, 916412) Productivity Inc.
— Measuring Total Productivity in Manufacturing Organization: Algorithms & PC Programs. 155p. 1987. pap. 27.95 (*0-527-91625-0*, 916250) Productivity Inc.
— The White-Collar Knowledge Worker: Measuring & Improving Productivity & Effectiveness. 355p. 1989. pap. text 36.00 (*92-833-1092-6*, 92-833-1092-0) Productivity Inc.
Mundel, Marvin E., ed. Operational Level Productivity Measurement Analysis & Improvement. (Illus.). 213p. 1985. pap. text 15.00 (*92-833-2026-3*, 320263) Productivity Inc.
Mundel, Marvin E. & Danner, David L. BASIC-A Personal Computer Language. 322p. 1986. pap. 14.00 (*92-833-1089-6*, 310890) Productivity Inc.
— Motion & Time Study: Improving Productivity. 7th ed. LC 93-23108. (C). 1994. text 68.20 (*0-13-588369-5*) Prntice Hall Bks.
Mundell, Bryan, jt. ed. see Bacharach, Samuel B.
Mundell, Bryan, jt. ed. see Kuruvilla, Sarosh.
Mundell, E. H. Erle Stanley Gardner: A Checklist. LC 70-97619. (Serif Series of Bibliographies & Checklists: No. 6). 91p. 1969. 17.00 (*0-87338-034-7*) Boulevard.
— Erle Stanley Gardner: A Checklist. LC 70-97619. (Serif Series: Bibliographies & Checklists: No. 6). 104p. reprint ed. pap. 32.30 (*0-8357-5577-0*, 203520400093) Bks Demand.
— A List of the Original Appearances of Dashiell Hammett's Magazine Work. LC 75-97620. (Serif Series: Bibliographies & Checklists: No. 13). 52p. 1968. text 15.00 (*0-87338-033-9*) Boulevard.
Mundell, E. H., compiled by. A List of the Original Appearances of Dashiell Hammett's Magazine Work. LC 75-97620. No. 13. 60p. reprint ed. pap. 25.00 (*0-317-55821-8*, 2029408) Bks Demand.
Mundell, E. H., Jr. & Rausch, G. Jay. The Detective Short Story: A Bibliography & Index. 1974. 15.00 (*0-318-22157-8*) KSU.
Mundell, George H. The Whole Burnt Offering. (Vital Ser.). 1997. pap. 0.75 (*0-87508-521-0*) Chr Lit.
Mundell, Kathleen. Pascha: The Traditions of Easter in Rockland County. (Illus.). 45p. 1984. pap. 5.00 (*0-911183-19-1*) Rockland County Hist.
Mundell Mango, Marlia. Silver Treasure from Early Byzantium: The Kaper Karaon & Related Treasures. LC 86-50138. (Illus.). 125p. (Orig.). 1986. pap. 35.00 (*0-911886-32-X*) Walters Art.
Mundell, Matt. Country Diary. 208p. (C). 1989. 45.00 (*0-903065-33-9*, Pub. by G Wright Pub) St Mut.
Mundell, Matt, jt. auth. see Templeton, John.
***Mundell, Meg.** Sydney. 4th ed. (Illus.). 208p. 2000. pap. 15.95 (*0-86442-724-7*) Lonely Planet.
Mundell, P. Sue, jt. ed. see Martin, Dolores M.
Mundell, Robert, ed. Inflation & Growth in China: Proceedings of a Conference Held in Beijing, China, May 10-12, 1995, Seminar. 1996. pap. 25.00 (*1-55775-542-6*) Intl Monetary.
Mundell, Robert, jt. ed. see Guitian, Manuel.
Mundell, Robert A. The International Monetary System: Conflict & Reform. LC HG3881.M8. (Canadian Trade Committee Publications). 78p. 1965. reprint ed. pap. 30.00 (*0-608-01374-9*, 206211900002) Bks Demand.
***Mundell, Robert A. & Clesse, Armand, eds.** The Euro As a Stabilizer in the International Economic System. 488p. 2000. 120.00 (*0-7923-7755-9*) Kluwer Academic.
Mundell, Robert A. & Swoboda, Alexander K., eds. Monetary Problems of the International Economy. (Midway Reprint Ser.). 1993. pap. text 19.00 (*0-226-55066-4*) U Ch Pr.
Mundell, Susan & DeLario, Karen. Practical Portfolios: Reading, Writing, Math, & Life Skills, Grades 3-6. (Illus.). vii, 149p. 1994. pap. text 22.00 (*1-56308-197-0*) Teacher Ideas Pr.
Munden, Alison. ADHD Handbook: A Guide for Parents & Professionals. 1999. pap. text 17.95 (*1-85302-756-1*) Taylor & Francis.
Munden, D. L. & Dorkin, C. M. Developments in the Clothing Industry. 56p. 1973. 95.00 (*0-7855-7193-0*) St Mut.
Munden, Kenneth W. & Beers, Henry P. The Union: A Guide to Federal Archives Relating to the Civil War. LC 86-8363. 721p. 1986. reprint ed. text 25.00 (*0-911333-46-0*, 100050) National Archives & Recs.
Munder, Barbara, jt. auth. see Barrow, Joe Louis, Jr.
Munder, Carole. Fierce Power Bad Fate. 1987. pap. 15.00 (*0-932526-13-6*) Nexus Pr.
Munderloh, Andre, jt. auth. see Buck, Franziska.
Mundey, Paul. Riding the River: Congregational Outreach & the Currents of the 21st Century. 32p. 1995. pap. 8.00 (*0-9637206-1-9*) LifeQuest IN.
— Unlocking Church Doors: Ten Keys to Positive Change. Miller, Herb, ed. LC 96-42569. (Leadership Insight Ser.). 168p. 1997. pap. 14.95 (*0-687-03087-0*) Abingdon.
Mundey, Paul E., jt. auth. see Dell, Robert W.
Mundfrom, Gerald F. Baptism, a Covenant. (Illus.). 130p. (Orig.). 1985. pap. text 4.00 (*0-9615494-0-8*) Mercy & Truth.
— Depression & What to Do About It. rev. ed. 221p. 1994. pap. 6.00 (*0-9615494-4-0*) Mercy & Truth.
— My Experience with Clinical Depression. rev. ed. Orig. Title: Purged. (Illus.). 191p. 1990. reprint ed. pap. 7.50 (*0-9615494-1-6*) Mercy & Truth.
— The Threat of False Doctrine. 144p. (Orig.). 1988. pap. 5.00 (*0-9615494-2-4*) Mercy & Truth.

M

An Asterisk (*) at the beginning of an entry indicates that the title is appearing for the first time.

Mundhenk, Rosemary J. Victorian Prose: An Anthology. LC 98-46151. 1999. 49.00 (*0-231-11026-X*); pap. text 22.50 (*0-231-11027-8*) Col U Pr.

Mundie, J. H. Emergence Traps for Aquatic Insects. (International Association of Theoretical & Applied Limnology, Communications Ser.: No. 7). (Illus.). 13p. 1956. pap. 15.00 (*3-510-52007-6*, Pub. by E Schweizerbartsche) Balogh.

Mundigo, Axel I. Abortion in the Developing World. 1999. pap. 29.95 (*1-85649-650-3*); text 69.95 (*1-85649-649-X*) St Martin.

***Mundigo, Axel I., et al.** Abortion in the Developing World. LC 99-932010. 498 p. 1999. write for info. (*81-7036-743-3*) S Asia.

Mundill, Robin R. England's Jewish Solution: Experiment & Expulsion, 1262-1290. (Cambridge Studies in Medieval Life & Thought: No. 37). 360p. (C). 1998. text 69.95 (*0-521-58150-8*) Cambridge U Pr.

Mundinger, F., ed. see Stereoencephalotomy Symposium Staff.

Mundis, Hester. Heart Songs for Animal Lovers: Inspiring Stories of Incredible Devotion, Profound Courage, & Enduring Love Between People & Animals. LC 99-16372. 1999. 17.95 (*1-57954-043-0*) Rodale Pr Inc.

— One Hundred One Ways to Avoid Reincarnation: Or Getting It Right the First Time. LC 88-40606. (Illus.). 160p. 1989. pap. 6.95 (*0-89480-383-2*, 1383) Workman Pub.

Mundis, Hester, jt. auth. see Mindell, Earl.

Mundis, Jerrold. Earn What You Deserve: How to Stop Underearning & Start Thriving. 288p. 1996. reprint ed. mass mkt. 6.50 (*0-553-57222-9*) Bantam.

Mundis, Jerrold. How to Get Out of Debt: Mundis,&Jerrold. 1990. audio 12.00 (*1-55994-170-7*, CPN 1857) HarperAudio.

Mundis, Jerrold. How to Get out of Debt, Stay out of Debt, & Live Prosperously. 272p. 1990. mass mkt. 6.99 (*0-553-28396-0*) Bantam.

***Mundis, Jerrold J.** Making Peace with Money. LC 99-18925. 288p. 1999. 14.95 (*0-7407-0040-5*) Andrews & McMeel.

Mundis, Jerrold J. & Leonard, Robert E. King of the Ice Cream Mountain. 1968. 3.50 (*0-87129-437-0*, K14) Dramatic Pub.

Mundkur, B. B. Fungi & Plant Diseases. 196p. 1991. pap. 60.00 (*81-85046-31-X*, Pub. by Scientific Pubs) St Mut.

***Mundlak, Yair.** Agriculture & Economic Growth: Theory & Measurement. LC 99-89905. 2000. text 55.00 (*0-674-00228-8*) HUP.

Mundlak, Yair, jt. auth. see Coeymans, Juan E.

***Mundle, Rob.** Fatal Storm: The Inside Story of the Tragic Sydney-Hobart Race. (Illus.). 304p. 2000. pap. 12.95 (*0-07-136140-5*) McGraw.

Mundle, Rob. Fatal Storm: The Inside Story of the Tragic Sydney to Hobart Race. 251p. 1999. 24.95 (*0-07-135698-3*) McGraw.

Mundle, Sidipto, ed. Public Finance: Policy Issues for India. LC 97-914023. (Oxford India Readings Ser.). 320p. (C). 1998. 29.95 (*0-19-563771-2*) OUP.

Mundo, Philip A. National Politics in a Global Economy: The Domestic Sources of U. S. Trade Policy. LC 99-18788. (Essential Texts in American Government). 288p. (Orig.). 1999. 65.00 (*0-87840-743-X*); pap. 22.95 (*0-87840-744-8*) Georgetown U Pr.

Mundry, E. & Homilius, J. Three Layer Model Curves for Geoelectrical Curves for Geoelectrical Measurements: Schlumberger Array Log Cycle 83,33mm. (ENG & GER., Illus.). 1980. spiral bd. 110.50 (*0-945345-07-0*) Lubrecht & Cramer.

***Mundry, Susan.** Designing Successful Professional Meetings & Conferences in Education: Planning, Implementing & Evaluating. National Institute for Science Education Staff, ed. LC 00-8537. 2000. write for info. (*0-7619-7633-7*) Corwin Pr.

Mundsack, Alan, ed. see Obrecht, Fred.

Mundsack, Allan. How to Prepare for the ELM: California Entry Level Mathematics Test. 2nd ed. LC 96-36104. 224p. 1997. pap. 13.95 (*0-8120-9729-7*) Barron.

Mundt, Astrid. Moglichkeiten und Grenzen des Energiesparens: Eine Analyse am Beispiel der Elektrizitat. (Europaische Hochschulschriften Ser.: Reihe 5, Vol. 2243). (Illus.). 241p. 1998. pap. 39.95 (*3-631-32295-X*) P Lang Pubng.

Mundt, Brian. Jacob's Collection. LC 96-44840. (Publish-a-Book Ser.). (Illus.). (J). (gr. 1-6). 1997. lib. bdg. 22.83 (*0-8172-4433-6*) Raintree Steck-V.

Mundt, C., jt. ed. see Gerbaldo, H.

Mundt, Richard W. & Cyrusa, Lee. Soldat No. 6: Equipping the Waffen SS Panzer Divisions, 1942-45, Vol. 6. LC 88-90959. (Illus.). 152p. 1997. pap. 12.95 (*1-57510-018-5*) Pictorial Hist.

Mundt, Robert J. Historical Dictionary of Cote d'Ivoire (the Ivory Coast) 2nd ed. LC 95-10313. (African Historical Dictionaries Ser.: Vol. 41). 386p. 1995. 63.00 (*0-8108-3015-9*) Scarecrow.

— Historical Dictionary of the Ivory Coast (Cote D'Ivoire) LC 87-12724. (African Historical Dictionaries Ser.: No. 41). (Illus.). 246p. 1987. 31.00 (*0-8108-2029-3*) Scarecrow.

Mundt, William F. & Smith, Michael R. Wisconsin Probate System: Forms & Procedures Handbook. 5th ed. LC 96-46082. 750p. 1996. ring bd. 135.00 (*0-945574-76-2*) State Bar WI.

***Munduruku, Daniel.** Tales of the Amazon: How the Munduruku Indians Live. Springer, Jane, tr. (Illus.). 72p. (J). 2000. 18.95 (*0-88899-392-7*) Grndwd Bks.

Mundus, Frank. Monster Man. 1976. 22.95 (*0-8488-0407-4*); pap. 14.95 (*0-8488-0408-2*) Amereon Ltd.

Mundwiler, Leslie. Michael Ondaatje: World, Image, Imagination. 160p. 1984. pap. 12.95 (*0-88922-216-9*, Pub. by Talonbks) Genl Dist Srvs.

Mundy. Calcium Homeostasis: Hypercal & Hypocalcaemia. 1989. 122.00 (*0-948269-67-7*) CRC Pr.

— Organic & Biological Chemistry. (C). 1993. text 79.50 (*0-03-029013-9*) Harcourt Coll Pubs.

— Story of Music. (Fine Arts Ser.). (J). (gr. 6-9). 1980. lib. bdg. 14.95 (*0-88110-031-5*, Usborne) EDC.

Mundy, A. R. Urodynamic & Reconstructive Surgery: The Practice of Surgery. (Illus.). 348p. 1993. text 260.00 (*0-443-03348-X*) Church.

Mundy, A. R., et al, eds. Urodynamics: Principles, Practice & Application. 2nd ed. (Illus.). 542p. 1994. text 178.00 (*0-443-04081-8*) Church.

Mundy, A. R., jt. auth. see Borzyskowski, M.

Mundy, Barbara E. The Mapping of New Spain: Indigenous Cartography & the Maps of the Relaciones Geograficas. LC 96-15824. (Illus.). 256p. 1996. 40.00 (*0-226-55096-6*) U Ch Pr.

Mundy, Bradford P. & Ellerd, Michael G. Name Reactions & Reagents in Organic Synthesis. LC 88-14915. 560p. 1988. 89.95 (*0-471-83626-5*) Wiley.

— Organic Chemistry - An Alphabetical Guide. 416p. 1996. 44.95 (*0-471-52445-X*) Wiley.

***Mundy, C. E., Jr., ed.** Leading Marines. (Illus.). 124p. 1999. reprint ed. pap. text 25.00 (*0-7881-8271-4*) DIANE Pub.

Mundy, Daniel. On the Banks of the Cimarron. (Illus.). 407p. 1998. pap. write for info. (*0-7541-0487-7*, Pub. by Minerva Pr) Unity Dist.

Mundy, Dave. Duh! Texas - A Case Study in Educational Takeover. LC 98-85514. (Illus.). 165p. 1998. 15.95 (*1-892298-00-7*) Abique.

Mundy, E. F. Mundy: Nicholas Mundy & Descendants Who Settled in NJ in 1665. (Illus.). 160p. 1991. reprint ed. pap. 25.00 (*0-8328-1698-1*); reprint ed. lib. bdg. 35.00 (*0-8328-1697-3*) Higginson Bk Co.

Mundy, E. J. Renaissance into Baroque: Italian Master Drawings by the Zuccari, 1550-1600. (Illus.). 240p. (C). 1990. 95.00 (*0-685-74173-7*) Cambridge U Pr.

Mundy, E. James, jt. auth. see Ourusoff de Fernandez-Gemenez, Elizabeth.

Mundy, Gary, jt. ed. see Acton, Thomas.

Mundy, Gary, jt. ed. see Caffrey, Susan.

Mundy, Godfrey C. Journal of a Tour in India. (C). 1995. reprint ed. 42.00 (*0-614-13257-6*, Pub. by Asian Educ Servs) S Asia.

Mundy, Gregory R. Calcium Homeostasis: Hypercalcemia & Hypocalcemia. 2nd ed. (Illus.). 284p. 1990. text 80.00 (*0-19-520894-3*) OUP.

Mundy, Gregory R. & Martin, T. John, eds. Physiology & Pharmacology of Bone. LC 92-42565. (Handbook of Experimental Pharmacology Ser.: Vol. 107). 1993. 500.00 (*0-387-56293-1*) Spr-Verlag.

***Mundy, Gregory R. & Rubens, Robert.** Cancer & Skeleton. (Illus.). 296p. 2000. 125.00 (*1-85317-756-3*, Pub. by Martin Dunitz) Blackwell Sci.

Mundy, James. Hidden Treasures: Wisconsin Collects Painting & Sculpture. (Illus.). 126p. (Orig.). 1987. pap. 14.00 (*0-944110-04-5*) Milwauk Art Mus.

Mundy, James H. Hard Times, Hard Men: Maine & the Irish, 1830-1860. (Illus.). 210p. 1991. 29.95 (*0-9626389-0-0*) Harp Pubns.

Mundy, Jane. Sydney Wildflower Bushwalks. (Illus.). 96p. pap. 13.95 (*0-86417-335-0*, Pub. by Kangaroo Pr) Seven Hills Bk.

Mundy, Jean. Leisure Education: Theory & Practice. 2nd ed. (Illus.). 270p. (C). 1997. 44.95 (*1-57167-035-1*) Sagamore Pub.

***Mundy, John.** Supplement Europe in the Middle Ages 1150 - 1300 - 3rd ed. 400p. 2000. 79.95 (*0-582-36988-6*) Addison-Wesley.

Mundy, John H. Europe in the High Middle Ages, 1150-1309. 2nd ed. LC 90-42973. (A General History of Europe Ser.). 1991. text. write for info. (*0-582-08016-9*, Pub. by Addison-Wesley) Longman.

— Europe in the High Middle Ages, 1150-1309. 2nd ed. LC 90-42973. (General History of Europe Ser.). (Illus.). 484p. (C). 1995. pap. text 29.40 (*0-582-49395-1*, 78833) Longman.

***Mundy, John H.** Europe in the Middle Ages, 1150-1300. 3rd ed. LC 00-24668. 417p. 1999. pap. 28.60 (*0-582-36987-8*) Addison-Wesley.

— Popular Music on Screen: From Hollywood Musical to Music Video. 1999. 69.95 (*0-7190-4028-0*, Pub. by Manchester Univ Pr); pap. text 19.95 (*0-7190-4029-9*, Pub. by Manchester Univ Pr) St Martin.

Mundy, John H. Repression of Catharism at Tours. pap. text 42.86 (*0-88844-074-X*) Brill Academic Pubs.

Mundy, John H. & Riesenberg, Peter. The Medieval Town. LC 79-9718. (Anvil Ser.). 192p. 1979. reprint ed. pap. 11.50 (*0-88275-906-X*) Krieger.

Mundy, John H., et al. Essays in Medieval Life & Thought. LC 65-25472. 1955. 28.00 (*0-8196-0159-4*) Biblo.

Mundy, Jon. Awaken to Your Own Call: Exploring a Course in Miracles. 192p. (Orig.). 1994. pap. 14.95 (*0-8245-1387-8*) Crossroad NY.

— Listening to Your Inner Guide. 176p. (Orig.). 1995. pap. 13.95 (*0-8245-1498-X*) Crossroad NY.

— The Ten Laws of Happiness. LC 99-193948. 1998. pap. 12.99 (*0-88092-453-5*, 4535) Royal Fireworks.

Mundy, Joseph L., et al, eds. Applications of Invariance in Computer Vision: Second Joint European-U. S. Workshop, Ponta Delgada, Azores, Portugal, October 9-14, 1993. LC 94-3557. (Lecture Notes in Computer Science Ser.: Vol. 825). 1994. 73.95 (*0-387-58240-1*) Spr-Verlag.

Mundy, Joseph L. & Zisserman, Andrew, eds. Geometric Invariance in Computer Vision. (Artificial Intelligence - Bobrow, Brody & Davis Ser.). (Illus.). 560p. 1992. 65.00 (*0-262-13285-0*) MIT Pr.

Mundy, Joseph L., jt. ed. see Kapur, Deepak.

Mundy, Lee G., jt. ed. see Holt, Stephen S.

Mundy, Linus. Complete Guide to Prayer-Walking: A Simple Path to Body-&-Soul Fitness. 144p. 1996. pap. text 13.95 (*0-8245-1546-3*) Crossroad NY.

— Elf-Help for Depression. LC 98-71232. (Elf-Help Bks.). (Illus.). 88p. 1998. pap. 4.95 (*0-87029-315-X*, 20134) Abbey.

— Every-Day Courage Therapy. LC 95-75102. 80p. 1995. pap. 4.95 (*0-87029-274-9*) Abbey.

— Finding Peace of Heart. LC 95-79775. (Wisdom of the Heart Bks.). (Illus.). 78p. 1995. pap. 6.95 (*0-87029-278-1*) Abbey.

— Grief Therapy for Men. LC 97-77160. (Illus.). 88p. 1998. pap. 4.95 (*0-87029-306-0*, 20141) Abbey.

— Grief-Walking: Four Prayerful Steps to Healing after Loss. LC 98-71233. 96p. 1998. pap. 4.95 (*0-87029-316-8*, 20133) Abbey.

— Keep Life Simple Therapy. LC 90-75341. 1993. pap. 4.95 (*0-87029-257-9*) Abbey.

— A Man's Guide to Prayer: New Ideas, Prayers & Meditations from Many Traditions . . . LC 98-7754. 192p. 1998. pap. 13.95 (*0-8245-1762-8*, Crsrd) Crossroad NY.

— Prayer-Walking: A Simple Path to Body & Soul Fitness. LC 93-72446. 55p. (Orig.). 1994. pap. 4.95 (*0-87029-264-1*, 201772) Abbey.

***Mundy, Linus.** PrayerStarters for Dealing with Anger. LC 00-100684. (Prayerstarters Ser.). 72p. 2000. pap. 4.95 (*0-87029-338-9*) Abbey.

Mundy, Linus. Retreat with Benedict & Bernard: Seeking God Alone--Together. 112p. 1998. pap. text 7.95 (*0-86716-301-1*) St Anthony Mess Pr.

***Mundy, Linus.** A Retreat with the Desert Elders. (Retreat with Ser.). 2001. pap. write for info. (*0-86716-371-2*) St Anthony Mess Pr.

Mundy, Linus. Slow-Down Therapy. LC 90-81236. (Illus.). 72p. (Orig.). 1990. pap. 4.95 (*0-87029-229-3*) Abbey.

Mundy, Linus, ed. What Helps the Most . . . When You Lose Someone Close? 101 Insights from People Who Have Been There. LC 96-84550. 88p. (Orig.). 1996. pap. 4.95 (*0-87029-295-1*, 20159) Abbey.

***Mundy, Lisa, et al.** Help Increase the Peace: A Manual for Facilitators. 2nd ed. Wallis, Hope, ed. 166p. 1999. pap., teacher ed. 25.00 (*0-910082-36-7*) Am Fr Serv Comm.

Mundy, Marianne F. Opportunities in Word Processing. (Illus.). 147p. 1985. 13.95 (*0-8442-6200-5*, VGM Career) NTC Contemp Pub Co.

— Opportunities in Word Processing. (Illus.). 147p. 1988. pap. 10.95 (*0-8442-6201-3*, VGM Career) NTC Contemp Pub Co.

— Opportunities in Word Processing Careers. rev. ed. LC 90-50735. (Opportunities In . . . Ser.). 160p. (YA). (gr. 7 up). pap. 12.95 (*0-8442-8165-4*, 297OIWP, VGM Career) NTC Contemp Pub Co.

— Opportunities in Word Processing Careers. rev. ed. (Opportunities in...Ser.). 160p. (YA). (gr. 7 up). 1993. 14.95 (*0-8442-8164-6*, VGM Career) NTC Contemp Pub Co.

Mundy, Martha. Domestic Government: Kinship, Community & Polity in North Yemen. (Society & Culture in the Modern Middle East Ser.). 256p. 1997. text 19.95 (*1-86064-102-4*, Pub. by I B T) St Martin.

***Mundy, Martha & Musallam, Basim, eds.** The Transformation of Nomadic Society in the Arab East. LC 99-45363. (Oriental Publications: Vol. 58). (Illus.). 256p. (C). 2000. write for info. (*0-521-77057-2*) Cambridge U Pr.

***Mundy, Michaelene.** Mad Isn't Bad: A Child's Book about Anger. LC 99-72094. (Elf-Held Books for Kids). (Illus.). 32p. (J). (ps-3). 1999. pap. 5.95 (*0-87029-331-1*, 20106) Abbey.

Mundy, Michaelene. Sad Isn't Bad: A Good-Grief Guidebook for Kids Dealing with Loss. LC 98-72357. (Illus.). 64p. (J). (ps-6). 1998. pap. 5.95 (*0-87029-321-4*) Abbey.

Mundy, Peter, et al. The Vultures of Africa. (Illus.). 450p. 1992. text 105.00 (*0-12-510585-1*) Acad Pr.

Mundy, S. P. A Key to the British & European Freshwater Bryozoans. 1980. 40.00 (*0-900386-39-8*) St Mut.

Mundy, Simon. Elgar. (Illustrated Lives of the Great Composers Ser.). (Illus.). 138p. 1996. 17.95 (*0-7119-0263-1*, OP 46796) Omnibus NY.

— The Illustrated Lives of the Great Composers: Tchaikovsky. (Illus.). 208p. 1998. pap. text 17.95 (*0-7119-6651-6*, OP48021) Omnibus NY.

— Story of Music. (Fine Arts Ser.). (J). (gr. 6-9). 1980. pap. 6.95 (*0-86020-443-X*, Usborne) EDC.

Mundy, Talbot. Avenging Liafail. (Tros of Samothrace Ser.: No. 2). 1978. mass mkt. 2.25 (*0-89083-378-8*, Zebra Kensgtn) Kensgtn Pub Corp.

— Black Light. 288p. 1991. pap. 10.95 (*0-89804-157-0*) Ariel GA.

***Mundy, Talbot.** Caves of Terror. 188p. 2000. pap. 12.99 (*0-89804-180-5*, Pub. by Ariel GA) Alliance Bk Co.

Mundy, Talbot. I Say Sunrise. 1969. pap. 9.95 (*0-87516-068-9*) DeVorss.

— Jimgrim. reprint ed. lib. bdg. 22.95 (*0-89190-488-3*, Rivercity Pr) Amereon Ltd.

— King-of the Khyber Rifles. (Illus.). 1978. 15.00 (*0-937986-14-3*) D M Grant.

— King of the Khyber Rifles. 1976. 27.95 (*0-8488-0837-1*) Amereon Ltd.

— Lud of Lunden, Vol. 1. (Tros of Samothrace Ser.). 1978. mass mkt. 2.25 (*0-89083-372-9*, Zebra Kensgtn) Kensgtn Pub Corp.

***Mundy, Talbot.** Om: The Secret of Ahbor Valley. LC 00-132771. 334p. 2000. reprint ed. write for info. (*1-893766-19-5*) Aeon Pub Co.

Mundy, Talbot. Om - Secret of Ahbor Valley. 1976. reprint ed. 27.95 (*0-8488-1110-0*, Rivercity Pr) Amereon Ltd.

— Om, the Secret of Ahbor Valley. 400p. 1984. pap. 3.95 (*0-88184-045-9*) Carroll & Graf.

— Om, the Secret of Ahbor Valley. 392p. 1980. pap. 15.95 (*0-913004-39-1*) Point Loma Pub.

— Tros of Samothrace. 1995. reprint ed. lib. bdg. 29.95 (*1-56849-584-6*) Buccaneer Bks.

Mundy, Wanda M. & Passmore, Gregory, eds. Curriculum Guide for Nuclear Medicine Technologists. 2nd ed. LC 92-48192. 86p. 1992. 13.95 (*0-932004-42-3*) Soc Nuclear Med.

***Mundy, William L.** Curing Allergies with Visual Imagery. rev. ed. LC 99-76477. 144p. 2000. pap. 14.95 (*1-884820-48-4*) SAFE GOODS.

Muneer, T. & Kambezidis, H. Solar Radiation & Daylight Models for Energy Efficient Design of Buildings. LC 96-51639. 224p. 1997. pap. text 59.95 (*0-7506-2495-7*) Buttrwrth-Heinemann.

***Muneer, Tariq, et al.** Windows in Buildings: Thermal, Acoustic, Visual, & Solar Performance. LC 99-59215. (Illus.). 272p. 2000. 95.00 (*0-7506-4209-2*, Architectural Pr) Buttrwrth-Heinemann.

Munem & Yizze. Precalculus. 6th ed. 1997. student ed. 61.00 (*1-57259-471-3*) W H Freeman.

Munem, M. & Yizze, James. Precalculus: Functions & Graphs - Instructor's Solution Manual. 6th ed. 1997. teacher ed. write for info. (*1-57259-240-0*) Worth.

Munem, M. A. Precalculus. 5th ed. 1989. text 51.95 (*0-87901-418-0*) Worth.

— Precalculus. 6th ed. LC 96-61159. 864p. 1996. text 53.20 (*1-57259-157-9*) Worth.

— Precalculus. 6th ed. 1997. pap. text, student ed. 12.80 (*1-57259-239-7*) Worth.

Munem, M. A. & Foulis, D. J. Calculus. 2nd ed. LC 83-50583. (Illus.). 1048p. 1984. text 72.95 (*0-87901-236-6*); text 40.95 (*0-87901-254-4*) Worth.

— Calculus, 1. 2nd ed. LC 83-50583. (Illus.). 1984. pap. text, student ed. 12.95 (*0-87901-237-4*) Worth.

— Calculus, 2. 2nd ed. LC 83-50583. (Illus.). 1984. pap. text, student ed. 12.95 (*0-87901-253-6*) Worth.

— College Trigonometry with Applications. LC 81-52995. 1982. student ed. 12.95 (*0-87901-175-0*); text 52.95 (*0-87901-171-8*) Worth.

Munem, M. A. & Foulis, David. Algebra & Trigonometry with Applications. 3rd ed. (Illus.). 738p. 1991. text 56.95 (*0-87901-498-9*) Worth.

— Algebra & Trigonometry with Applications. 3rd ed. (Illus.). 544p. 1991. pap. text, student ed. 12.95 (*0-87901-513-6*) Worth.

— College Algebra with Applications. 3rd ed. 510p. 1991. text 55.95 (*0-87901-499-7*) Worth.

— College Algebra with Applications. 3rd ed. 452p. 1991. pap. text, student ed. 12.95 (*0-87901-515-2*) Worth.

Munem, M. A. & Tschirhart, W. Beginning Algebra. 4th ed. 404p. (C). 1987. text 49.95 (*0-87901-378-8*) Worth.

— Beginning Algebra. 4th ed. 328p. (C). 1988. pap. text, student ed. 12.95 (*0-87901-380-X*) Worth.

— College Trigonometry. (Illus.). (C). 1974. student ed. 9.95 (*0-87901-029-0*); text 40.95 (*0-87901-028-2*) Worth.

— Intermediate Algebra. 4th ed. 612p. (C). 1987. text 45.95 (*0-87901-377-X*) Worth.

— Intermediate Algebra. 4th ed. 310p. (C). 1988. pap. text, student ed. 12.95 (*0-87901-379-6*) Worth.

Munem, M. A., jt. auth. see Yizze, James P.

***Munem, Mustafa & West, Carolyn.** Intermediate Algebra: Applications, Graphs & Models. 5th ed. 484p. (C). 1999. per. 73.95 (*0-7872-5862-8*, 41586201) Kendall-Hunt.

— Student Solutions Manual to Accompany Intermediate Algebra: Applications, Graphs, & Models: Applications, Graphs & Models. 5th ed. 254p. (C). 1999. per. 30.95 (*0-7872-5863-6*, 41586301) Kendall-Hunt.

***Munem, Mustafa & Yizze, J.** Precalculus: Functions & Graphs. 6th ed. 716p. (C). 1999. text 80.95 (*0-7872-6044-4*, 41604401) Kendall-Hunt.

***Munem, Mustafa & Yizze, James.** Instructor's Solutions Manual to Accompany Precalculus: Functions & Graphs. 6th ed. 760p. (C). 1999. pap. text. write for info. (*0-7872-6465-2*) Kendall-Hunt.

— Student Solutions Manual to Accompany Precalculus: Functions & Graphs. 6th ed. 226p. (C). 1999. per. 31.95 (*0-7872-6464-4*) Kendall-Hunt.

— Test Manual to Accompany Precalculus: Functions & Graphs. 6th ed. 188p. (C). 1999. pap. text. write for info. (*0-7872-6463-6*) Kendall-Hunt.

Munemasa, A., jt. ed. see Bannai, E.

Munemitsu, Mutsu. Kenkenroku: A Diplomatic Record of the Sino-Japanese War, 1894-95. Berger, Gordon M., ed. & tr. by. 338p. 1995. 64.00 (*0-86008-306-3*, Pub. by U of Tokyo) Col U Pr.

Munenori, Yagyu. The Sword & the Mind. Sato, Hiroaki, tr. from JPN. LC 85-8899. (Illus.). 144p. 1986. 19.95 (*0-87951-209-1*, Pub. by Overlook Pr) Penguin Putnam.

— The Sword & the Mind. Sato, Hiroaki, tr. 144p. 1988. pap. 11.95 (*0-87951-256-3*, Pub. by Overlook Pr) Penguin Books.

Munenori, Yagyu, tr. see Musashi, Miyamoto.

Muneo Saito, et al, eds. Fractionation by Packed-Column SFE & SFC: Principles & Applications. LC 93-44145. 1994. 115.00 (*1-56081-591-4*, Wiley-VCH) Wiley.

Munerlyn, Kubwa E. Faces in Hue: Imagery & Style Collection. Williams, Patricia, ed. 96p. 1996. pap. 10.95 (*1-886493-05-7*) NBC Study Pub.

Muneto, Tatsuo. Dharme Treasures: From Hawaii's Shin Pioneers. 64p. (Orig.). 1997. pap. 7.95 (*0-938474-19-7*) Buddhist Study.

***Munevar, Gonzalo.** Evolution & the Naked Truth: A Darwinian Approach to Philosophy. LC 98-71956. (Avebury Series in Philosophy). 256p. 1998. text 63.95 (*1-84014-344-4*) Ashgate Pub Co.

Munevar, Gonzalo. The Master of Fate. 240p. 2000. 23.95 (*0-930773-55-1*) Black Heron Pr.

— Radical Knowledge: A Philosophical Inquiry into the

An Asterisk (*) at the beginning of an entry indicates that the title is appearing for the first time.

Nature & Limits of Science. LC 81-4258. 135p. (C). 1981. 27.95 (*0-915145-17-0*); pap. 14.95 (*0-915145-16-2*) Hackett Pub.

Munevar, Gonzalo, ed. Beyond Reason: Essays on the Philosophy of Paul Feyerabend. 548p. (C). 1991. lib. bdg. 243.00 (*0-7923-1272-4*, Pub. by Kluwer Academic) Kluwer Academic.

— Spanish Studies in the Philosophy of Science. LC 96-26716. (Boston Studies in the Philosophy of Science: Vol. 186). 376p. (C). 1996. text 147.00 (*0-7923-4147-3*) Kluwer Academic.

Muney, Julia, jt. auth. see Van Liere, Eldon N.

Munez-Ruiz, Angel & Vromans, Herman, eds. Data Acquisition & Measurement Techniques. LC 98-7662. (Illus.). 398p. 1998. 229.00 (*1-57491-068-X*) Interpharm.

Munford, Alan, ed. Management Development: Strategies for Action. 240p. (C). 1991. pap. 95.00 (*0-85292-476-3*, Pub. by IPM Hse) St Mut.

Munford, Christopher. River Night. 50p. (Orig.). 1989. pap. 3.00 (*0-945085-09-5*) Sub Rosa.

— Sermons in Stone. (Illus.). 92p. (Orig.). 1993. pap. 8.95 (*0-913559-22-9*) Birch Brook Pr.

Munford, Clarence J. The Black Ordeal of Slave Trading & Slavery in the French West Indies, 1625-1715, 3 vols., 1. LC 91-22009. 300p. 1991. lib. bdg. 89.95 (*0-7734-9741-2*) E Mellen.

— The Black Ordeal of Slave Trading & Slavery in the French West Indies, 1625-1715, 3 vols., 2. LC 91-22009. 300p. 1991. lib. bdg. 89.95 (*0-7734-9431-6*) E Mellen.

— The Black Ordeal of Slave Trading & Slavery in the French West Indies, 1625-1715, 3 vols., 3. LC 91-22009. 300p. 1991. lib. bdg. 89.95 (*0-7734-9433-2*) E Mellen.

— Race & Reparations: A Black Perspective for the Twenty-First Century. LC 96-10811. 576p. 1996. 79.95 (*0-86543-510-3*); pap. 21.95 (*0-86543-511-1*) Africa World.

Munford, J. Kenneth, ed. see Nash, Wallis.

***Munford, Lois.** Design Climatics No. 3: Learn Overnight How to Interior Decorate Like a Professional. LC 96-19119. 70p. 1998. reprint ed. pap. 9.50 (*0-9668066-0-3*) Jemco Pubns.

Munford, Luther T. Mississippi Appellate Practice. 450p. 1995. 170.00 (*0-9619323-1-7*) On Point Pr.

Munford, Robert. The Plays of Robert Munford. 105p. 1992. pap. 7.95 (*0-929408-06-3*) Amer Eagle Pubns Inc.

Munford, Tony. Victorian Rotherham: A Pictorial History. (Illus.). 80p. (C). 1989. pap. 50.00 (*1-85563-003-6*, Pub. by Quoin Pub Ltd) St Mut.

Munford, William A. Who Was Who in British Librarianship, 1800-1985: A Dictionary of Dates with Notes. LC 87-7220. 103p. reprint ed. pap. 32.00 (*0-608-08892-7*, 206952900004) Bks Demand.

Mungall, Constance & Amer, Elizabeth. Taking Action: Working Together for Positive Change in Your Community. (Reference Ser.). (Illus.). 200p. (Orig.). 1992. pap. 10.95 (*0-88908-532-3*) Self-Counsel Pr.

Mungall, Constance & McLaren, Digby, eds. Planet Under Stress: The Challenge of Global Change. (Illus.). 360p. 1990. pap. text 29.95 (*0-19-540731-8*) OUP.

Mungall, Dennis R., ed. Applied Clinical Pharmacokinetics. fac. ed. LC 83-565. (Illus.). 458p. 1983. pap. 142.00 (*0-7837-7530-X*, 204697400005) Bks Demand.

Mungall, Elizabeth C. & Sheffield, William J. Exotics on the Range: The Texas Example. LC 93-24131. (Louise Lindsey Merrick Natural Environment Ser.: No. 16). (Illus.). 286p. 1994. 49.50 (*0-89096-399-1*) Tex A&M Univ Pr.

Mungazi, Dickson A. The Challenge of Educational Innovation & National Development in Southern Africa. LC 91-38677. (American University Studies: Education: Ser. XIV, Vol. 36). 200p. (C). 1992. text 41.95 (*0-8204-1713-0*) P Lang Pubng.

Colonial Education for Africans: George Stark's Policy in Zimbabwe. LC 91-2273. 176p. 1991. 45.00 (*0-275-94029-2*, C4029, Praeger Pubs) Greenwood.

— Education & Government Control in Zimbabwe: A Study of the Commissions of Inquiry, 1908-1974. LC 89-3655. 154p. 1990. 55.00 (*0-275-93170-6*, C3170, Praeger Pubs) Greenwood.

— Educational Policy & National Character: Africa, Japan, the United States, & the Soviet Union. LC 92-31842. 248p. 1993. 55.00 (*0-275-94423-9*, C4423, Praeger Pubs) Greenwood.

— The Evolution of Educational Theory in the United States. LC 97-43946. 272p. 1999. 59.95 (*0-275-96130-3*, Praeger Pubs) Greenwood.

— The Fall of the Mantle: The Educational Policy of the Rhodesia Front Government & Conflict in Zimbabwe. LC 92-36435. (American University Studies: Regional Studies: Ser. XX, Vol. 7). (Illus.). XXII, 260p. (Orig.). (C). 1993. pap. text 29.95 (*0-8204-2109-X*) P Lang Pubng.

— Gathering under the Mango Tree: Values in Traditional Culture in Africa. LC 93-35796. (American University Studies, Series XXI: Vol. 9). (Illus.). XXV, 314p. (C). 1996. text 64.95 (*0-8204-2336-X*) P Lang Pubng.

***Mungazi, Dickson A.** In the Footsteps of the Masters: Desmond M. Tutu & Abel T. Muzorewa. LC 99-43106. 256p. 2000. write for info. (*0-275-96680-1*, Praeger Pubs) Greenwood.

— The Journey to the Promised Land: The African American Struggle for Development since the Civil War. LC 00-29854. 244p. 2000. 64.00 (*0-275-96824-3*, Praeger Pubs) Greenwood.

Mungazi, Dickson A. The Last British Liberals in Africa: Michael Blundell & Garfield Todd. LC 98-39876. 312p. 1999. 69.50 (*0-275-96283-0*, Praeger Pubs) Greenwood.

— The Last Defenders of the Laager: Ian D. Smith & F. W. De Klerk. LC 97-39772. 304p. 1998. 65.00 (*0-275-96030-7*, Praeger Pubs) Greenwood.

— The Mind of Black Africa. LC 95-34094. 296p. 1996. 65.00 (*0-275-95260-6*, Praeger Pubs); pap. 21.95 (*0-275-95429-3*, Praeger Pubs) Greenwood.

— The Struggle for Social Change in Southern Africa: Visions of Liberty. (Illus.). 180p. (C). 1989. text 85.00 (*0-8448-1594-2*); pap. text 46.95 (*0-8448-1595-0*) Taylor & Francis.

— To Honor the Sacred Trust of Civilization. 320p. 1983. 24.95 (*0-87073-454-7*); pap. 18.95 (*0-87073-455-5*) Schenkman Bks Inc.

— To Honor the Sacred Trust of Civilization: History, Politics, & Education in Southern Africa. LC 83-20084. (Illus.). 333p. 1983. reprint ed. pap. 103.30 (*0-608-05328-7*, 206505500012) Bks Demand.

— Where He Stands: Albert Shanker of the American Federation of Teachers. LC 94-25964. 280p. 1995. 57.95 (*0-275-94929-X*, Praeger Pubs) Greenwood.

Mungazi, Dickson A. & Walker, Kay L., trs. Colonial Agriculture for Africans: Emory Alvord's Policy in Zimbabwe. LC 97-38149. (Society & Politics in Africa Ser.: Vol. 6). (Illus.). XIV, 228p. (C). 1998. text 47.95 (*0-8204-3713-1*) P Lang Pubng.

Mungazi, Dickson A. & Walker, L. Kay. Educational Reform & the Transformation of Southern Africa. LC 96-47620. 240p. 1997. 52.95 (*0-275-95746-2*, Praeger Pubs) Greenwood.

***Mungeam, Frank.** A Guy's Guide to Pregnancy: Preparing for Parenthood Together. LC 97-49131. 156p. 1998. pap. 12.95 (*1-885223-75-7*) Beyond Words Pub.

— A Guy's Guide to Pregnancy: Preparing for Parenthood Together. 144p. 1999. 6.98 (*1-56731-314-0*, MJF Bks) Fine Comms.

Mungello, David E. The Forgotten Christians of Hangzhou. LC 93-36553. (Illus.). 240p. (C). 1994. text 37.00 (*0-8248-1540-8*) UH Pr.

— The Great Encounter of China & the West, 1500-1800. LC 99-12405. 144p. 1999. 22.95 (*0-8476-9439-9*); pap. 12.95 (*0-8476-9440-2*) Rowman.

— Leibniz & Confucianism, the Search for Accord. LC 77-4053. 220p. 1977. reprint ed. pap. 62.70 (*0-608-00528-2*, 2061407) Bks Demand.

***Munger.** Policy Analysis. LC 99-47240. 1999. pap. 22.50 (*0-393-97399-9*) Norton.

Munger, ed. Eighty Readings. 2nd ed. LC 97-218201. 360p. (C). 1997. pap. text 14.66 (*0-321-01648-3*) Addson-Wesley Educ.

Munger, Asahel & Munger, Eliza. Diary of Asahel Munger & Wife: Travel to the Marcus Whitman Mission, May 4, 1839-September 3, 1839. LC 92-19319. 1992. pap. 5.95 (*0-87770-508-9*) Ye Galleon.

Munger, Barry, ed. Caught in the Act: The Photographer in Contemporary Fiction. LC 96-23291. (Illus.). 182p. (Orig.). 1996. pap. 17.95 (*0-943221-27-7*) Timken Pubs.

***Munger, C. G.** Corrosion Prevention by Protective Coatings. (Illus.). 520p. 1999. 97.00 (*1-57590-088-2*, 37507) NACE Intl.

***Munger, David.** Research Online. 3rd ed. 160p. (C). 1999. pap. text 6.67 (*0-321-05802-X*) Addson-Wesley Educ.

***Munger, David, compiled by.** Eighty Readings for College Writers. LC 99-56569. (C). 1999. text. write for info. (*0-321-07668-0*) Addison-Wesley.

— Fifty Readings for College Writers. LC 99-56570. 256p. (C). 2000. pap. text 12.00 (*0-321-07669-9*) Addison-Wesley.

Munger, Donna B. Pennsylvania Land Records: A History & Guide for Research. LC 90-21384. 240p. 1991. 75.00 (*0-8420-2377-1*); pap. 29.95 (*0-8420-2497-2*) Scholarly Res Inc.

Munger, Edwin S. Touched by Africa. 1983. 12.50 (*0-934912-00-9*) Munger Africana Lib.

Munger, Eliza, jt. auth. see Munger, Asahel.

Munger, Elizabeth M. A History of the Trail Creek Region. (Little Bit of History Ser.: Bk. 2). 24p. 1988. 2.00 (*0-935549-11-0*) MI City Hist.

— Michigan City's First Hundred Years. 97p. 1992. pap. 10.00 (*0-935549-16-1*) MI City Hist.

Munger, Evelyn M. & Bowdon, Susan J. The New Beyond Peek-a-Boo & Pat-a-Cake: Activities for Baby's First 24 Months. 3rd ed. LC 93-1421. 256p. 1993. spiral bd. 15.95 (*0-8329-0504-6*) New Win Pub.

Munger, Fredi & Shader, Holly. Skills Drills: A Self-Correcting Math Proficiency Game. (Technical Notes Ser.: Vol. 28). 36p. (Orig.). 1989. pap. 2.00 (*0-932288-81-2*) Ctr Intl Ed U of MA.

Munger, Fredi, jt. auth. see Droegkamp, Janis.

Munger, Guy, ed. see Rogers, Dennis.

Munger, Guy, ed. see Snow, A. C.

Munger, J. P., jt. auth. see Michie Butterworth Editorial Staff.

Munger, James. Two Years in the Pacific & Arctic Oceans & China, Being a Journal of Events Peculiar to a Whaling Voyage. 82p. 1987. 14.95 (*0-87770-401-5*) Ye Galleon.

Munger, James L., jt. auth. see Miller, Erston V.

***Munger, James P.** What's It Worth? 1999 Edition: A Guide to Current Personal Injury Awards & Settlements. 1200p. 1999. 110.00 (*0-327-01390-7*, 6843917) LEXIS Pub.

Munger, James P. What's It Worth, 1998. 1336p. 1998. pap. text 100.00 (*0-327 00185-2*, 68439-16) LEXIS Pub.

Munger, Jeffrey & Zafran, Eric M. The Forsyth Wickes Collection. LC 92-54162. (Illus.). 328p. 1991. text 45.00 (*0-87846-330-5*) Mus Fine Arts Boston.

***Munger, Katy.** Bad to the Bone. 288p. 2000. mass mkt. 5.99 (*0-380-80064-0*) Morrow Avon.

Munger, Katy. Legwork. LC 96-95492. 240p. 1997. mass mkt. 5.50 (*0-380-79136-6*, Avon Bks) Morrow Avon.

— Money to Burn. (Casey Jones Mystery Ser.). 320p. 1999. mass mkt. 5.99 (*0-380-80063-2*, Avon Bks) Morrow Avon.

— Out of Time: A Casey Jones Mystery. LC 97-94934. (Casey Jones Mystery Ser.). 256p. 1998. mass mkt. 5.99 (*0-380-79138-2*, Avon Bks) Morrow Avon.

Munger, Kel. The Fragile Peace You Keep. LC 97-69841. (Minnesota Voices Project Ser.: Vol. 88). 96p. 1998. pap. 12.95 (*0-89823-186-8*) New Rivers Pr.

Munger, Michael C., jt. auth. see Hinich, Melvin.

Munger, Michael C., jt. auth. see Hinich, Melvin J.

Munger, Nancy. Follow the Star. 12p. (J). (ps). bds. 3.99 (*0-310-97554-9*) Zondervan.

— Getting Ready for Christmas. (Christmas Board Bks.). 12p. (J). (ps). 1998. bds. 3.99 (*0-310-97561-1*) Zondervan.

— The "J" Is for Jesus: The Candy Cane Story. (Christmas Board Bks.). 12p. (J). (ps). 1998. bds. 3.99 (*0-310-97553-0*) Zondervan.

— Joy to the World, a Christmas Counting Book. 14p. (J). (ps). 1998. bds. 3.99 (*0-310-97660-X*) Zondervan.

Munger, Ned. Cultures, Chess & Art Vol. 1: A Collector's Odyssey Across Seven Continents: Sub-Saharan Africa. LC 95-81611. (Illus.). x, 120p. 1996. 40.00 (*0-9644046-6-4*) Mundial Pr.

***Munger, Ned.** Cultures, Chess & Art Vol. 3: A Collector's Odyssey Across Seven Continents, Pacific Islands & Asia. Smith, Lisa A., ed. LC 95-81611. (Illus.). xiv, 198p. 2000. 50.00 (*0-9644046-8-0*) Mundial Pr.

Munger, Ned. Cultures, Chess & Art - A Collector's Odyssey Across Seven Continents Vol. 2: The Americas. LC 95-81611. (Illus.). xiv, 224p. 1998. 50.00 (*0-9644046-7-2*) Mundial Pr.

Munger, Prudence & Pilgrim, Donna. Food Allergies, What Do I Eat Now? Coping & Cooking Day to Day. 1998. write for info. (*0-9666006-8-1*) Food Allergy Sol.

Munger, Richard L. Child Mental Health Practice from the Ecological Perspective. 426p. (Orig.). (C). 1991. pap. 39.50 (*0-8191-8319-9*); lib. bdg. 64.50 (*0-8191-8318-0*) U Pr of Amer.

— The Ecology of Troubled Children: Changing Children's Behavior by Changing the Places, Activities, & People in Their Environment. LC 98-10467. 256p. 1997. pap. 24.95 (*1-57129-050-8*) Brookline Bks.

— Rules for Unruly Children: The Parent Discipline Bible. LC 98-93775. (Illus.). ix, 70p. 1998. pap. 7.50 (*0-9668114-0-2*) Child Psych Pr.

Munger, Robert B. Commitment. (Christian Basics Bible Studies). 64p. (Orig.). 1994. pap. 4.99 (*0-8308-2005-1*, 2005) InterVarsity.

— My Heart - Christ's Home. (Horizon Ser.). 1996. pap. 4.99 (*1-56570-033-3*) Meridian MI.

— My Heart, Christ's Home. (Christian Classics Ser.). 1995. pap. 2.99 (*1-56570-014-7*) Meridian MI.

— My Heart-Christ's Home. LC 92-5678. (Stories for Old & Young Ser.). (Illus.). 48p. 1992. reprint ed. 12.99 (*0-8308-1842-1*, 1842) InterVarsity.

Munger, Robert B. & Nystrom, Carolyn. My Heart - Christ's Home: Retold for Children. LC 97-12919. (Illus.). 32p. (J). (gr. 2-6). 1997. 14.99 (*0-8308 1907 X*, 1907) InterVarsity.

Munger, Robert Boyd. My Heart, Christ's Home, 5 vols. rev. ed. 1986. pap. 5.00 (*0-8308-6575-6*) InterVarsity.

Munger, Robert S. Trailing a Bear: Adventures of Fred Bear & Bob Munger. (Illus.). 353p. (Orig.). 1995. lib. bdg. 19.95 (*0-9645143-0-3*) Munger Pub.

Mungin, Horace. Sleepy Willie. Orange, Charlotte, ed. LC 90-82440. 128p. (Orig.). (YA). (gr. 8-12). 1991. pap. 8.95 (*0-936026-24-3*) R&M Pub Co.

***Mungioli, Arnold J.** Christmas Cookies: A Cookbook & Cookie Cutter Set. (Illus.). 2000. pap. 17.99 (*1-58184-100-0*) Somerville Hse.

Mungkandi, Wiwat & Neher, Clark D., eds. U. S. - Thailand Relations in a New International Era, No. 33. (Research Papers & Policy). 350p. (Orig.). 1990. pap. 20.00 (*1-55729-018-0*) IEAS.

Mungkandi, Wiwat, jt. ed. see Jackson, Karl D.

Mungkandi, Wiwat, jt. ed. see Ramsay, Ansil.

Munglani, Rajesh, ed. Scientific Foundations of Chronic Pain Therapy. (Greenwich Medical Media Ser.). (Illus.). 350p. 2002. text 89.50 (*1-900151-83-9*) OUP.

Mungo, Katie, ed. Libraries & Information - Towards a Policy for Schools: Conference Proceedings of the 14th Annual Conference of the IASL. 155p. 1985. pap. 25.00 (*1-890861-05-7*) IASL.

Mungo, Ray. Famous Long Ago. 1990. pap. 14.95 (*0-8065-1204-0*, Citadel Pr) Carol Pub Group.

— The Learning Annex Guide to Getting Successfully Published: From Typewriter to Royalty Checks: All You Need to Know! 256p. 1992. pap. 10.95 (*0-8065-1371-3*, Citadel Pr) Carol Pub Group.

— San Francisco Confidential: Tales of Scandal & Excess from the Town That's Seen Everything. LC 94-12615. (Illus.). 256p. 1994. 19.95 (*1-55972-246-0*) Carol Pub Group.

Mungo, Ray & Yamaguchi, Robert H. No Credit Required: How to Buy a House When You Don't Qualify for a Mortgage. 192p. (Orig.). 1993. mass mkt. 5.99 (*0-451-17564-6*, Sig) NAL.

Mungoshi, Charles. The Setting Sun & the Rolling World: Selected Short Stories. LC 89-42588. 208p. (Orig.). 1989. pap. 12.00 (*0-8070-8321-6*) Beacon Pr.

Mungovan. Competition Law: A Legal Handbook for Business. 104p. 1990. pap. 25.00 (*0-409-89648-9*, MICHIE) LEXIS Pub.

— Contracts: A Legal Handbook for Business. 104p. 1990. pap. 25.00 (*0-409-89659-4*, MICHIE) LEXIS Pub.

Munguia, Juan C. Supervision of Bilingual Programs. Cordasco, Francesco, ed. LC 77-90555. (Bilingual-Bicultural Education in the U. S. Ser.). 1978. lib. bdg. 26.95 (*0-405-11093-6*) Ayer.

Munhall, Edgar. Whistler & Montesquiou: The Butterfly & the Bat. (Illus.). 176p. 1995. 45.00 (*2-08-013577-5*, Pub. by Flammarion) Abbeville Pr.

— Whistler & Montesquiou: The Butterfly & the Bat. (Illus.). Date not set. 45.00 (*0-614-32356-8*) Frick Collection.

Munhall, Edgar, ed. Ange-Laurent de la Live de Jully: A Facsimile Reprint of the Catalogue Historique (1764) & the Catalogue Raisonne des Tableaux (1770) (Reprint Series of Historical Auction Catalogues). (Illus.). 318p. 1988. reprint ed. text 50.00 (*0-317-93171-7*) Acanthus Pr.

Munhall, Edgar, et al. The Frick Collection: A Tour. (Illus.). 128p. 1999. 35.00 (*1-85759-223-9*, Pub. by Scala Books) Antique Collect.

— Whistler & Montesquiou: The Butterfly & the Bat. LC 95-204602. 175 p. 1995. write for info. (*2-08-013578-3*) Flammarion.

Munhall, Edgar, ed. see Davilier, Charles.

Munhall, K. G., jt. auth. see Kelso, J. A.

Munhall, Patricia L. Qualitative Research Proposals & Reports: A Guide. 40p. 1994. 12.95 (*0-88737-606-1*, 19-2609, NLN Pr) Natl League Nurse.

— Revisioning Phenomenology: Nursing & Health Science Research. LC 94-1454. 1994. 28.95 (*0-88737-597-9*) Natl League Nurse.

Munhall, Patricia L., compiled by. En la Experiencia de la Mujer. (SPA.). 1995. write for info. (*0-88737-668-1*, NLN Pr) Natl League Nurse.

Munhall, Patricia L., ed. The Emergence of the Family into the 21st Century. 250p. 1997. 25.95 (*0-88737-745-9*, 14-7459, NLN Pr) Natl League Nurse.

— In Women's Experience, Vol. I. 1994. pap. 25.95 (*0-88737-610-X*) Natl League Nurse.

— In Women's Experience, Vol. II. 1995. pap. 37.95 (*0-88737-647-9*) Natl League Nurse.

Munhall, Patricia L. & Boyd, Carolyn O., eds. Nursing Research: A Qualitative Perspective. 2nd ed. LC 93-20494. 1993. 30.95 (*0-88737-590-1*) Natl League Nurse.

Munhall, Patricia L. & Fitzsimons, Virginia M. The Emergence of Women into the 21st Century. (Women's Issues Ser.). 426p. (Orig.). 1995. pap. 21.95 (*0-88737-662-2*) Natl League Nurse.

***Munhall, Patricia L. & NLN Staff.** Emergence of Family into the 21st Century. (Illus.). 256p. (C). 1999. pap. text 32.50 (*0-7637-1105-5*) JB Pubns.

— Human Understanding. (Illus.). 256p. (C). 2000. pap. text 32.50 (*0-7637-1169-1*) JB Pubns.

— Nursing Research: A Qualitative Perspective. 3rd ed. (Illus.). 288p. (C). 1999. pap. text 32.50 (*0-7637-1135-7*) JB Pubns.

— Qualitative Research Proposals & Reports: A Guide. 2nd ed. (Illus.). 64p. (C). 1999. pap. text 18.75 (*0-7637-1171-3*) JB Pubns.

— Revisioning Phenomenology. 2nd ed. (Illus.). 320p. (C). 2000. pap. text 32.50 (*0-7637-1168-3*) JB Pubns.

Munholland, John K. & Betts, Raymond F., eds. French Colonial Studies-Etudes Coloniales Francaises, Vol. III. LC 76-644752. 118p. (Orig.). (C). 1986. 39.00 (*0-8191-5072-X*); pap. text 17.00 (*0-8191-5073-8*) U Pr of Amer.

Muni, Angirasa. The Angirasa Dictionary of Hindu Religion & Culture. unabridged ed. LC 98-90793. 432 p. 1999. 40.00 (*1-893152-07-3*) Sacred Bks.

— Angirasa Grhyasutra. unabridged ed. LC 98-90794. 265 p. 1999. 33.00 (*1-893152-08-1*) Sacred Bks.

— The Bhagavad-Gita. (Bhagavan - Mahima - The Hindu Scriptures Ser.: Vol. III). 485p. 1999. 33.00 (*1-893152-02-2*) Sacred Bks.

— The Dharmasastra. (Bhagavan - Mahima - The Hindu Scriptures Ser.: Vol. VI). 265p. 1999. 33.00 (*1-893152-05-7*) Sacred Bks.

— The Hindu Festivals & Puja. unabridged ed. LC 98-90792. 344p. 1999. 33.00 (*1-893152-06-5*) Sacred Bks.

— The Hindu Wedding Planner. unabridged ed. (Illus.). 96p. 1999. 15.00 (*1-893152-10-3*) Sacred Bks.

— The Namakarana: Naming of the Child. unabridged ed. LC 98-90795. 66 p. 1999. 5.00 (*1-893152-09-X*) Sacred Bks.

— The Ramayana. (Bhagavan - Mahima - The Hindu Scriptures Ser.: Vol. IV). 656p. 1999. 33.00 (*1-893152-03-0*) Sacred Bks.

— The Satyanarayana - Vrata - Katha. 40p. 1999. 5.00 (*1-893152-11-1*) Sacred Bks.

— Srimad Bhagavata & the Mahabharata. LC 98-90790. (Bhagavan - Mahima - The Hindu Scriptures Ser.: Vol. V). 299p. 1999. 33.00 (*1-893152-04-9*) Sacred Bks.

— The Upanisads. LC 98-90787. (Bhagavan- Mahima- the Hindu Scriptures Ser.: Vol. II). 242p. 1999. 33.00 (*1-893152-01-4*) Sacred Bks.

— The Vedas. unabridged ed. LC 98-90786. (Bhagavan - Mahima - The Hindu Scriptures Ser.: Vol. I). 320p. 1999. 33.00 (*1-893152-00-6*) Sacred Bks.

Muni, Matanga. Brhaddesi of Sri Matanga Muni, Vol. 2. Sharma, Prem L. & Kata, Oren, eds. (C). 1992. 28.50 (*81-208-1032-5*, Pub. by Motilal Bnarsidass) S Asia.

Muni, Narada, ed. see Kripalvananda, Svami.

Muni, P. K., jt. auth. see Padhy, K. S.

Muni, Rajarshi. Awakening the Life Force: The Philosophy & Psychology of Spontaneous Yoga. LC 93-40373. (Illus.). 224p. 1994. pap. 15.00 (*0-87542-581-X*) Llewellyn Pubns.

Muni, S. D. India & Nepal: A Changing Relationship. (C). 1992. 60.00 (*0-7855-0185-1*, Pub. by Ratna Pustak Bhandar) St Mut.

— India & Nepal: Erosion of a Relationship. 308p. 1992. text 30.00 (*81-220-0181-5*, Pub. by Konark Pubs Pvt Ltd) Advent Bks Div.

— Pangs of Proximity: India & Sri Lanka's Ethnic Crisis. LC 93-12317. (Peace Research Institute, Oslo Ser.). (Illus.). 256p. (C). 1993. 33.50 (*0-8039-9112-6*) Sage.

M

An Asterisk (*) at the beginning of an entry indicates that the title is appearing for the first time.

Muni, S. D., ed. Understanding South Asia: Essays in the Memory of Late Professor (Mrs.) Urmila Phadnis. LC 93-908496. (C). 1994. 28.00 (*81-7003-173-7*, Pub. by S Asia Pubs) S Asia.

Muni Shri Nagraj Ji. Agama & Tripitaka Eka Anusilana (A Critical Comparative Study of the Jaina & Buddhist Canonical Literature), Vol. 1: History & Tradition. 900p. 1986. 85.00 (*1-55528-024-2*, Pub. by Today Tomorrow) Scholarly Pubns.

— The Contemporaneity & the Chronology of Mahavira & Buddha. 188p. 1975. 4.00 (*0-88065-163-6*) Scholarly Pubns.

Muniain, J., jt. auth. see Baez, J.

Muniak, Sasha, jt. auth. see Diaz, Ricardo.

Municchi, Anna. Furs for Men. (Twentieth Century-Histories of Fashion Ser.). (Illus.). 143p. 1996. 29.95 (*0-89676-204-1*, Costume & Fashion Pr) QSMG Ltd.

— Ladies in Furs, 1940-1990. (Twentieth Century-Histories of Fashion Ser.). (Illus.). 143p. 1996. 29.95 (*0-89676-207-6*, Costume & Fashion Pr) QSMG Ltd.

— Ladies in Furs, 1900-1940. (Twentieth Century-Histories of Fashion Ser.). (Illus.). 159p. 1996. 29.95 (*0-89676-206-8*, Costume & Fashion Pr) QSMG Ltd.

Munich, Adrienne. Andromeda's Chains: Gender & Interpretation in Victorian Literature & Art. (Illus.). 222p. (C). 1993. pap. 18.00 (*0-231-06873-5*) Col U Pr.

— Queen Victoria's Secrets. LC 95-43737. (Illus.). 246p. 1996. 37.00 (*0-231-10480-4*) Col U Pr.

— Queen Victoria's Secrets. (Illus.). 272p. 1998. pap. 17.50 (*0-231-10481-2*) Col U Pr.

Munich, Adrienne, jt. ed. see Homans, Margaret.

Munich, Adrienne A., jt. ed. see Maynard, John.

Munich, C. Hammer, et al, eds. Transplant International: Proceedings of the 6th ESOT Congress, Rodos, October 25-28, 1993. (Official Journal of the European Society for Organ Transplantation). 705p. 1994. 168.00 (*0-387-57835-8*) Spr-Verlag.

Municio, A. M. & Miras-Portugal, M. T. Cell Signal Transduction, Second Messengers, & Protein Phosphorylation in Health & Disease. (Illus.). 266p. (C). 1994. text 85.00 (*0-306-44814-9*, Kluwer Plenum) Kluwer Academic.

Municipal Analysis Services, Inc., ed. Governments of Kentucky, 1988. (Expert Edition Ser.). 1988. text 325.00 (*1-55507-275-5*) Municipal Analysis.

Municipal Analysis Services, Inc. Staff, ed. Governments of Alabama, 1987. (Governments of Your State Ser.). 1987. text 150.00 (*1-55507-131-7*) Municipal Analysis.

— Governments of Alabama, 1987. (Expert Edition Ser.). 1987. text 325.00 (*1-55507-174-0*) Municipal Analysis.

— Governments of Alabama, 1988. (Governments of Your State Ser.). 1988. text 150.00 (*1-55507-220-8*) Municipal Analysis.

— Governments of Alabama, 1988. (Expert Edition Ser.). 1988. text 325.00 (*1-55507-264-X*) Municipal Analysis.

— Governments of Arkansas, 1987. (Expert Edition Ser.). 1987. text 325.00 (*1-55507-175-9*) Municipal Analysis.

— Governments of Arkansas, 1988. (Governments of Your State Ser.). 1988. text 150.00 (*1-55507-221-6*) Municipal Analysis.

— Governments of Arkansas, 1988. (Expert Edition Ser.). 1988. text 325.00 (*1-55507-265-8*) Municipal Analysis.

— Governments of California, 1987. (Expert Edition Ser.). 1987. text 325.00 (*1-55507-176-7*) Municipal Analysis.

— Governments of California, 1987. (Governments of Your State: Expert Ser.). 1988. text 150.00 (*1-55507-133-3*) Municipal Analysis.

— Governments of California, 1988. (Governments of Your State Ser.). 1988. text 150.00 (*1-55507-222-4*) Municipal Analysis.

— Governments of California, 1988. (Expert Edition Ser.). 1988. text 325.00 (*1-55507-266-6*) Municipal Analysis.

— Governments of Colorado, 1987. (Governments of Your State Ser.). 1987. text 150.00 (*1-55507-134-1*) Municipal Analysis.

— Governments of Colorado, 1987. (Expert Edition Ser.). 1987. text 325.00 (*1-55507-177-5*) Municipal Analysis.

— Governments of Colorado, 1988. (Governments of Your State Ser.). 1988. text 150.00 (*1-55507-223-2*) Municipal Analysis.

— Governments of Colorado, 1988. (Expert Edition Ser.). 1988. text 325.00 (*1-55507-267-4*) Municipal Analysis.

— Governments of Connecticut, 1987. (Governments of Your State Ser.). 1987. text 150.00 (*1-55507-135-X*) Municipal Analysis.

— Governments of Connecticut, 1987. (Expert Edition Ser.). 1987. text 325.00 (*1-55507-178-3*) Municipal Analysis.

— Governments of Connecticut, 1988. (Governments of Your State Ser.). 1988. text 150.00 (*1-55507-224-0*) Municipal Analysis.

— Governments of Connecticut, 1988. (Expert Edition Ser.). 1988. text 325.00 (*1-55507-268-2*) Municipal Analysis.

— Governments of Florida, 1987. (Governments of Your State Ser.). 1987. text 150.00 (*1-55507-136-8*) Municipal Analysis.

— Governments of Florida, 1987. (Expert Edition Ser.). 1987. text 325.00 (*1-55507-179-1*) Municipal Analysis.

— Governments of Florida, 1988. (Governments of Your State Ser.). 1988. text 150.00 (*1-55507-225-9*) Municipal Analysis.

— Governments of Florida, 1988. (Expert Edition Ser.). 1988. text 325.00 (*1-55507-269-0*) Municipal Analysis.

— Governments of Georgia, 1987. (Governments of Your State Ser.). 1987. text 150.00 (*1-55507-137-6*) Municipal Analysis.

— Governments of Georgia, 1987. (Expert Edition Ser.). 1988. text 325.00 (*1-55507-180-5*) Municipal Analysis.

— Governments of Georgia, 1988. (Governments of Your State Ser.). 1988. text 150.00 (*1-55507-226-7*) Municipal Analysis.

— Governments of Georgia, 1988. (Expert Edition Ser.). 1988. text 325.00 (*1-55507-270-4*) Municipal Analysis.

— Governments of Illinois, 1987. (Governments of Your State Ser.). 1987. text 150.00 (*1-55507-138-4*) Municipal Analysis.

— Governments of Illinois, 1987. (Expert Edition Ser.). 1987. text 325.00 (*1-55507-181-3*) Municipal Analysis.

— Governments of Illinois, 1988. (Governments of Your State Ser.). 1988. text 150.00 (*1-55507-227-5*) Municipal Analysis.

— Governments of Illinois, 1988. (Expert Edition Ser.). 1988. text 325.00 (*1-55507-271-2*) Municipal Analysis.

— Governments of Indiana, 1987. (Governments of Your State Ser.). 1987. text 150.00 (*1-55507-139-2*) Municipal Analysis.

— Governments of Indiana, 1987. (Expert Edition Ser.). 1987. text 325.00 (*1-55507-182-1*) Municipal Analysis.

— Governments of Indiana, 1988. (Governments of Your State Ser.). 1988. text 150.00 (*1-55507-228-3*) Municipal Analysis.

— Governments of Indiana, 1988. (Expert Edition Ser.). 1988. text 325.00 (*1-55507-272-0*) Municipal Analysis.

— Governments of Iowa, 1987. (Governments of Your State Ser.). 1987. text 150.00 (*1-55507-140-6*) Municipal Analysis.

— Governments of Iowa, 1987. (Expert Edition Ser.). 1987. text 325.00 (*1-55507-183-X*) Municipal Analysis.

— Governments of Iowa, 1988. (Governments of Your State Ser.). 1988. text 150.00 (*1-55507-229-1*) Municipal Analysis.

— Governments of Iowa, 1988. (Expert Edition Ser.). 1988. text 325.00 (*1-55507-273-9*) Municipal Analysis.

— Governments of Kansas, 1987. (Governments of Your State Ser.). 1987. text 150.00 (*1-55507-141-4*) Municipal Analysis.

— Governments of Kansas, 1987. (Expert Edition Ser.). 1987. text 325.00 (*1-55507-184-8*) Municipal Analysis.

— Governments of Kansas, 1988. (Governments of Your State Ser.). 1988. text 150.00 (*1-55507-230-5*) Municipal Analysis.

— Governments of Kansas, 1988. (Expert Edition Ser.). 1988. text 325.00 (*1-55507-274-7*) Municipal Analysis.

— Governments of Kentucky, 1987. (Expert Edition Ser.). 1987. text 325.00 (*1-55507-185-6*) Municipal Analysis.

— Governments of Kentucky, 1987. (Governments of Your State Ser.). 1987. text 150.00 (*1-55507-142-2*) Municipal Analysis.

— Governments of Kentucky, 1988. (Governments of Your State Ser.). 1988. text 150.00 (*1-55507-231-3*) Municipal Analysis.

— Governments of Louisana, 1987. (Expert Edition Ser.). 1987. text 325.00 (*1-55507-186-4*) Municipal Analysis.

— Governments of Louisiana, 1987. (Governments of Your State Ser.). 1987. text 150.00 (*1-55507-143-0*) Municipal Analysis.

— Governments of Louisiana, 1988. (Governments of Your State Ser.). 1988. text 150.00 (*1-55507-232-1*) Municipal Analysis.

— Governments of Louisiana, 1988. (Expert Edition Ser.). 1988. text 325.00 (*1-55507-276-3*) Municipal Analysis.

— Governments of Maine, 1987. (Governments of Your State Ser.). 1987. text 150.00 (*1-55507-144-9*) Municipal Analysis.

— Governments of Maine, 1987. (Expert Edition Ser.). 1987. text 325.00 (*1-55507-187-2*) Municipal Analysis.

— Governments of Maine, 1988. (Governments of Your State Ser.). 1988. text 150.00 (*1-55507-233-X*) Municipal Analysis.

— Governments of Maine, 1988. (Expert Edition Ser.). 1988. text 325.00 (*1-55507-277-1*) Municipal Analysis.

— Governments of Massachusetts, 1987. (Governments of Your State Ser.). 1987. text 150.00 (*1-55507-145-7*) Municipal Analysis.

— Governments of Massachusetts, 1987: Expert Edition. (Expert Edition 1987 Ser.). 1987. text 325.00 (*1-55507-188-0*) Municipal Analysis.

— Governments of Massachusetts, 1988. (Governments of Your State Ser.). 1988. text 150.00 (*1-55507-234-8*) Municipal Analysis.

— Governments of Massachusetts, 1988. (Expert Edition Ser.). 1988. text 325.00 (*1-55507-278-X*) Municipal Analysis.

— Governments of Michigan, 1987. (Governments of Your State Ser.). 1987. text 150.00 (*1-55507-146-5*) Municipal Analysis.

— Governments of Michigan, 1987. (Expert Edition Ser.). 1987. text 325.00 (*1-55507-189-9*) Municipal Analysis.

— Governments of Michigan, 1988. (Governments of Your State Ser.). 1988. text 150.00 (*1-55507-235-6*) Municipal Analysis.

— Governments of Michigan, 1988. (Expert Edition Ser.). 1988. text 325.00 (*1-55507-279-8*) Municipal Analysis.

— Governments of Minnesota, 1987. (Governments of Your State Ser.). 1987. text 150.00 (*1-55507-147-3*) Municipal Analysis.

— Governments of Minnesota, 1987. (Expert Edition Ser.). 1987. text 325.00 (*1-55507-190-2*) Municipal Analysis.

— Governments of Minnesota, 1988. (Governments of Your State Ser.). 1988. text 150.00 (*1-55507-236-4*) Municipal Analysis.

— Governments of Minnesota, 1988. (Expert Edition Ser.). 1988. text 325.00 (*1-55507-280-1*) Municipal Analysis.

— Governments of Mississippi, 1987. (Governments of Your State Ser.). 1987. text 150.00 (*1-55507-148-1*) Municipal Analysis.

— Governments of Mississippi, 1987. (Expert Edition Ser.). 1987. text 325.00 (*1-55507-191-0*) Municipal Analysis.

— Governments of Mississippi, 1988. (Governments of Your State Ser.). 1988. text 150.00 (*1-55507-237-2*) Municipal Analysis.

— Governments of Mississippi, 1988. (Expert Edition Ser.). 1988. text 325.00 (*1-55507-281-X*) Municipal Analysis.

— Governments of Missouri, 1987. (Governments of Your State Ser.). 1987. text 150.00 (*1-55507-149-X*) Municipal Analysis.

— Governments of Missouri, 1987. (Expert Edition Ser.). 1987. text 325.00 (*1-55507-192-9*) Municipal Analysis.

— Governments of Missouri, 1988. (Governments of Your State Ser.). 1988. text 150.00 (*1-55507-238-0*) Municipal Analysis.

— Governments of Missouri, 1988. (Expert Edition Ser.). 1988. text 325.00 (*1-55507-282-8*) Municipal Analysis.

— Governments of Nebraska, 1987. (Governments of Your State Ser.). 1987. text 150.00 (*1-55507-150-3*) Municipal Analysis.

— Governments of Nebraska, 1987. (Expert Edition Ser.). 1987. text 325.00 (*1-55507-193-7*) Municipal Analysis.

— Governments of Nebraska, 1988. (Governments of Your State Ser.). 1988. text 150.00 (*1-55507-239-9*) Municipal Analysis.

— Governments of Nebraska, 1988. (Expert Edition Ser.). 1988. text 325.00 (*1-55507-283-6*) Municipal Analysis.

— Governments of New Jersey 1987. (Governments of Your State: Expert Ser.). 1987. text 150.00 (*1-55507-151-1*) Municipal Analysis.

— Governments of New Jersey 1987. (Expert Edition Ser.). 1987. text 325.00 (*1-55507-194-5*) Municipal Analysis.

— Governments of New Jersey, 1988. (Governments of Your State Ser.). 1988. text 150.00 (*1-55507-240-2*) Municipal Analysis.

— Governments of New Jersey, 1988. (Expert Edition Ser.). 1988. text 325.00 (*1-55507-284-4*) Municipal Analysis.

— Governments of New York, 1987. (Governments of Your State Ser.). 1987. text 150.00 (*1-55507-152-X*) Municipal Analysis.

— Governments of New York, 1987. (Expert Edition Ser.). 1987. text 325.00 (*1-55507-195-3*) Municipal Analysis.

— Governments of New York, 1988. (Governments of Your State Ser.). 1987. text 150.00 (*1-55507-241-0*) Municipal Analysis.

— Governments of New York, 1988. (Expert Edition Ser.). 1988. text 325.00 (*1-55507-285-2*) Municipal Analysis.

— Governments of North Dakota, 1987. (Governments of Your State Ser.). 1987. text 150.00 (*1-55507-153-8*) Municipal Analysis.

— Governments of North Dakota, 1987. (Expert Edition Ser.). 1987. text 325.00 (*1-55507-196-1*) Municipal Analysis.

— Governments of North Dakota, 1988. (Governments of Your State Ser.). 1988. text 150.00 (*1-55507-242-9*) Municipal Analysis.

— Governments of North Dakota, 1988. (Expert Edition Ser.). 1988. text 325.00 (*1-55507-286-0*) Municipal Analysis.

— Governments of Ohio, 1987. (Governments of Your State Ser.). 1987. text 150.00 (*1-55507-154-6*) Municipal Analysis.

— Governments of Ohio, 1987. (Expert Edition Ser.). 1987. text 325.00 (*1-55507-197-X*) Municipal Analysis.

— Governments of Ohio, 1988. (Governments of Your State Ser.). 1988. text 150.00 (*1-55507-243-7*) Municipal Analysis.

— Governments of Ohio, 1988. (Expert Edition Ser.). 1988. text 325.00 (*1-55507-287-9*) Municipal Analysis.

— Governments of Oklahoma, 1987. (Governments of Your State Ser.). 1987. text 150.00 (*1-55507-155-4*) Municipal Analysis.

— Governments of Oklahoma, 1987. (Expert Edition Ser.). 1987. text 325.00 (*1-55507-198-8*) Municipal Analysis.

— Governments of Oklahoma, 1988. (Governments of Your State Ser.). 1988. text 150.00 (*1-55507-244-5*) Municipal Analysis.

— Governments of Oklahoma, 1988. (Expert Edition Ser.). 1988. text 325.00 (*1-55507-288-7*) Municipal Analysis.

— Governments of Pennsylvania, 1987. (Governments of Your State Ser.). 1987. text 150.00 (*1-55507-156-2*) Municipal Analysis.

— Governments of Pennsylvania, 1987. (Expert Edition Ser.). 1987. text 325.00 (*1-55507-199-6*) Municipal Analysis.

— Governments of Pennsylvania, 1988. (Governments of Your State Ser.). 1988. text 150.00 (*1-55507-245-3*) Municipal Analysis.

— Governments of Pennsylvania, 1988. (Expert Edition Ser.). 1988. text 325.00 (*1-55507-289-5*) Municipal Analysis.

— Governments of South Dakota, 1987. (Governments of Your State Ser.). 1987. text 150.00 (*1-55507-157-0*) Municipal Analysis.

— Governments of South Dakota, 1987. (Expert Edition Ser.). 1987. text 325.00 (*1-55507-200-3*) Municipal Analysis.

— Governments of South Dakota, 1988. (Governments of Your State Ser.). 1988. text 150.00 (*1-55507-246-1*) Municipal Analysis.

— Governments of South Dakota, 1988. (Expert Edition Ser.). 1988. text 325.00 (*1-55507-290-9*) Municipal Analysis.

— Governments of Tennessee, 1987. (Governments of Your State Ser.). 1987. text 150.00 (*1-55507-158-9*) Municipal Analysis.

— Governments of Tennessee, 1987. (Expert Edition Ser.). 1987. text 325.00 (*1-55507-201-1*) Municipal Analysis.

— Governments of Tennessee, 1988. (Governments of Your State Ser.). 1988. text 150.00 (*1-55507-247-X*) Municipal Analysis.

— Governments of Tennessee, 1988. (Expert Edition Ser.). 1988. text 325.00 (*1-55507-291-7*) Municipal Analysis.

— Governments of Texas, 1987. (Governments of Your State Ser.). 1987. text 150.00 (*1-55507-159-7*) Municipal Analysis.

— Governments of Texas, 1987. (Expert Edition Ser.). 1987. text 325.00 (*1-55507-202-X*) Municipal Analysis.

— Governments of Texas, 1988. (Governments of Your State Ser.). 1988. text 150.00 (*1-55507-248-8*) Municipal Analysis.

— Governments of Texas, 1988. (Expert Edition Ser.). 1988. text 325.00 (*1-55507-292-5*) Municipal Analysis.

— Governments of the Carolinas, 1987. (Governments of Your State Ser.). 1987. text 150.00 (*1-55507-165-1*) Municipal Analysis.

— Governments of the Carolinas, 1987. (Expert Edition Ser.). 1987. text 325.00 (*1-55507-208-9*) Municipal Analysis.

— Governments of the Carolinas, 1988. (Governments of Your State Ser.). 1988. text 150.00 (*1-55507-254-2*) Municipal Analysis.

— Governments of the Carolinas, 1988. (Expert Edition Ser.). 1988. text 325.00 (*1-55507-298-4*) Municipal Analysis.

— Governments of the Northeast, 1987. (Governments of Your State Ser.). 1987. text 150.00 (*1-55507-168-6*); text 150.00 (*1-55507-166-X*) Municipal Analysis.

— Governments of the Northeast, 1987. (Expert Edition Ser.). 1987. text 325.00 (*1-55507-211-9*) Municipal Analysis.

— Governments of the Northeast, 1988. (Governments of Your State Ser.). 1988. text 150.00 (*1-55507-257-7*) Municipal Analysis.

— Governments of the Northeast, 1988. (Expert Edition Ser.). 1988. text 325.00 (*1-55507-301-8*) Municipal Analysis.

— Governments of the Northwest, 1987. (Expert Edition Ser.). 1987. text 325.00 (*1-55507-209-7*) Municipal Analysis.

— Governments of the Northwest, 1988. (Governments of Your State Ser.). 1988. text 150.00 (*1-55507-255-0*) Municipal Analysis.

— Governments of the Northwest, 1988. (Expert Edition Ser.). 1988. text 325.00 (*1-55507-299-2*) Municipal Analysis.

— Governments of the West. (Governments of Your State Ser.). 1987. text 150.00 (*1-55507-167-8*) Municipal Analysis.

— Governments of the West, 1987. (Expert Edition Ser.). 1987. text 325.00 (*1-55507-210-0*) Municipal Analysis.

— Governments of the West, 1988. (Governments of Your State Ser.). 1988. text 150.00 (*1-55507-256-9*) Municipal Analysis.

— Governments of the West, 1988. (Expert Edition Ser.). 1988. text 325.00 (*1-55507-300-X*) Municipal Analysis.

— Governments of Vermont, 1987. (Governments of Your State Ser.). 1987. text 150.00 (*1-55507-160-0*) Municipal Analysis.

— Governments of Vermont, 1987. (Expert Edition Ser.). 1987. text 325.00 (*1-55507-203-8*) Municipal Analysis.

— Governments of Vermont, 1988. (Governments of Your State Ser.). 1988. text 150.00 (*1-55507-249-6*) Municipal Analysis.

— Governments of Vermont, 1988. (Expert Edition Ser.). 1988. text 325.00 (*1-55507-293-3*) Municipal Analysis.

— Governments of Virginia, 1987. (Governments of Your State Ser.). 1987. text 150.00 (*1-55507-161-9*) Municipal Analysis.

— Governments of Virginia, 1987. (Expert Edition Ser.). 1987. text 325.00 (*1-55507-204-6*) Municipal Analysis.

— Governments of Virginia, 1988. (Governments of Your State Ser.). 1988. text 150.00 (*1-55507-250-X*) Municipal Analysis.

— Governments of Virginia, 1988. (Expert Edition Ser.). 1988. text 325.00 (*1-55507-294-1*) Municipal Analysis.

— Governments of Washington, 1987. (Governments of Your State Ser.). 1987. text 150.00 (*1-55507-162-7*) Municipal Analysis.

— Governments of Washington, 1987. (Expert Edition Ser.). 1987. text 325.00 (*1-55507-205-4*) Municipal Analysis.

— Governments of Washington, 1988. (Governments of Your State Ser.). 1988. text 150.00 (*1-55507-251-8*) Municipal Analysis.

— Governments of Washington, 1988. (Expert Edition Ser.). 1988. text 325.00 (*1-55507-295-X*) Municipal Analysis.

— Governments of West Virginia, 1987. (Governments of Your State Ser.). 1987. text 150.00 (*1-55507-163-5*) Municipal Analysis.

— Governments of West Virginia, 1987. (Expert Edition Ser.). 1987. text 325.00 (*1-55507-206-2*) Municipal Analysis.

— Governments of West Virginia, 1988. (Governments of Your State Ser.). 1988. text 150.00 (*1-55507-252-6*) Municipal Analysis.

— Governments of West Virginia, 1988. (Expert Edition Ser.). 1988. text 325.00 (*1-55507-296-8*) Municipal Analysis.

— Governments of Wisconsin, 1987. (Governments of Your State Ser.). 1987. text 150.00 (*1-55507-164-3*) Municipal Analysis.

— Governments of Wisconsin, 1987. (Expert Edition Ser.). 1987. text 325.00 (*1-55507-207-0*) Municipal Analysis.

— Governments of Wisconsin, 1988. (Governments of Your State Ser.). 1988. text 150.00 (*1-55507-253-4*) Municipal Analysis.

— Governments of Wisconsin, 1988. (Expert Edition Ser.). 1988. text 325.00 (*1-55507-297-6*) Municipal Analysis.

Municipal Finance Officers Association, Government. State & Local Government Finance & Financial Management: A Compendium of Current Research. LC 78-70328. 690p. 1978. 18.00 (*0-686-84363-0*) Municipal.

Municipal Finance Officers Association Staff. A Capital Improvement Programming Handbook for Small Cities & Other Governmental Units. LC 78-71712. (Illus.). 80p. 1978. 15.00 (*0-686-84280-4*) Municipal.

An Asterisk (*) at the beginning of an entry indicates that the title is appearing for the first time.

— Community Development Block Grant Budgetary & Financial Management. 134p. 1978. 14.95 (*0-686-84366-5*) Municipal.

— A Debt Management Handbook for Small Cities & Other Governmental Units. LC 78-71726. (Debt Administration Ser.). (Illus.). 69p. 1978. 15.00 (*0-686-84294-4*) Municipal.

— Governmental Accounting, Auditing, & Financial Reporting. LC 80-84747. (Illus.). 314p. 1980. 35.00 (*0-686-84252-9*) Municipal.

— Guidelines for the Preparation of a Public Employee Retirement System Comprehensive Annual Financial Report. (Illus.). 66p. 1980. pap. 10.00 (*0-686-84368-1*) Municipal.

— Is Your City Heading for Financial Difficulty? A Guidebook for Small Cities & Other Governmental Units. (Illus.). 43p. 1978. 6.00 (*0-686-84361-4*) Municipal.

— Official Statements for Offerings of Securities by Local Governments - Examples & Guidelines. 64p. 1981. 12.00 (*0-686-84334-7*); 10.00 (*0-686-84335-5*) Municipal.

— State & Local Government Fiscal Almanac 1982-MFOA Membership Directory. 400p. 1982. pap. 50.00 (*0-686-84339-8*) Municipal.

— A Treasury Management Handbook for Small Cities & Other Governmental Units. LC 78-71725. (Illus.). 93p. 1978. 15.00 (*0-686-84374-6*) Municipal.

Municipal Finance Officers Association Staff & Miller, Girard. Systems That Work: Government Financial Manuals, Analyses & Operating Procedures. (Illus.). ix, 273p. write for info. (*0-318-60754-9*) Municipal.

Municipal Finance Officers Association Staff & United States, Bureau of the Census Staff. State Supervision of Local Finance: Proceedings of a Conference, December 4, 5, 6, 1941. 127p. write for info. (*0-318-59326-2*) Municipal.

Municipal Research & Services Center, Washington S & Association of Washington Cities Staff. Handbook for City Officials of Washington Municipal Code Cities. (Illus.). ix, 232p. 1985. pap. write for info. (*0-318-60205-9*) Muni Res WA.

Municipality of Anchorage Department of Economic D. Anchorage Indicators: A Socioeconomic Review. (Orig.). 1989. pap. text 10.00 (*0-685-28889-7*) Municipality Anchorage.

Munier, Bertrand R. Compromise Negotiation. (Theory & Decision Library). 1987. lib. bdg. 161.50 (*90-277-2625-6*) Kluwer Academic.

Munier, Bertrand R., ed. Markets, Risk & Money: Essays in Honor of Maurice Allais. LC 95-36635. (Theory & Decision Library Series B: Vol. 26). 388p. (C). 1995. lib. bdg. 213.50 (*0-7923-2578-8*) Kluwer Academic.

— Models & Experiments in Risk & Rationality. (Theory & Decision Library B). 450p. (C). 1994. lib. bdg. 156.00 (*0-7923-3031-5*) Kluwer Academic.

Munier, Charles. Authorite' Episcopale et Sollicitude Pastorale. (Collected Studies: No. CS341). (FRE.). 142p. 1991. text 119.95 (*0-86078-296-4*, Pub. by Variorum) Ashgate Pub Co.

— Vie Conciliaire et Collections Canoniques en Occident, IVe-XIIe Siecles. (Collected Studies: No. CS265). (FRE.). 318p. (C). 1987. reprint ed. text 115.95 (*0-86078-213-1*, Pub. by Variorum) Ashgate Pub Co.

Munier, Charles, jt. auth. see Benoit, Andre.

Munif, Abd A. Story of a City: A Childhood in Amman. Kawar, Samira, tr. LC 97-154894. 320p. 1998. pap. 15.00 (*0-7043-8023-4*, Pub. by Quartet) Interlink Pub.

Munif, Abdelrahman. Cities of Salt. Theroux, Peter, tr. LC 87-40078. (International Ser.). 464p. (Orig.). 1989. pap. 17.00 (*0-394-75526-X*) Vin Bks.

Muniko, S., et al, eds. Kuria-English Dictionary. 1996. pap. text 22.95 (*3-8258-2951-0*) Transaction Pubs.

Munion, Robert. Apostles, Apostolic People & Churches. 160p. 1999. pap. 8.95 (*1-58169-027-4*) Genesis Comm Inc.

Munir, Edward. Fisheries after Factortame. 104p. 1991. pap. 175.00 (*0-406-00298-3*, U.K., MICHIE) LEXIS Pub.

Munir, Z. A. & Holt, J. B., eds. Combustion & Plasma Synthesis of High-temperature Materials. 501p. 1990. pap. 145.00 (*0-471-23588-1*) Wiley.

Munir, Z. A. & Holt, J. B., eds. Combustion & Plasma Synthesis of High-Temperature Materials: Proceedings of the First International Symposium on Combustion & Plasma Synthesis of High-Temperature Material, October 23-26, 1988, San Francisco, CA. 501p. 1990. 100.00 (*0-89573-756-6*, Wiley-VCH) Wiley.

Munir, Zuhair A., ed. see Symposium on High Temperature Materials Chemistry.

Muniraj, R. Farm Finance for Development. 1987p. (C). 1987. 10.50 (*81-204-0223-5*, Pub. by Oxford IBH) S Asia.

Munirathaam, G., ed. see Swarnalatha.

Munis, G. & Zerzan, John. Unions Against Revolution. 1975. pap. 1.25 (*0-934868-12-3*) Black & Red.

Munishi, G. K., jt. auth. see Mhina, A. K.

Munitz, Milton K. Does Life Have a Meaning? LC 93-29529. 114p. 1993. 26.95 (*0-87975-860-0*) Prometheus Bks.

Munitz, Milton K., ed. Theories of the Universe: From Babylonian Myth to Modern Science. LC 57-6746. 438p. 1965. pap. 17.95 (*0-02-922270-2*) Free Pr.

Munitz, Milton K., jt. ed. see Keifer, Howard.

Munitz, Milton K., jt. ed. see Kiefer, Howard E.

Munitz, Milton K., tr. see Kant, Immanuel.

Muniz Castro, E. English-Spanish, Spanish-English Legal Dictionary. (ENG & SPA.). 613p. 1992. 105.00 (*0-7859-7520-9*, 8476951086) Fr & Eur.

— Spanish-English - English-Spanish Dictionary of Legal Terms. (ENG & SPA.). 613p. 1992. 70.00 (*84-7695-108-6*, Pub. by La Ley) IBD Ltd.

Muniz, Dora Nevares. Derecho de Menores. (SPA.). 128p. (Orig.). (C). 1987. pap. text. write for info. (*0-914939-03-3*) Instituto Desarrollo.

Muniz-Huberman, Angelina. De Magias y Prodigios (Of Magic & Prodigies) (SPA.). 100p. 1987. pap. 7.99 (*968-16-2714-8*, Pub. by Fondo) Continental Bk.

— Enclosed Garden. Miller, Yvette E., ed. Zamora, Lois P., tr. from SPA. LC 87-3643. (Discoveries Ser.). 103p. 1988. pap. 11.50 (*0-935480-29-3*) Lat Am Lit Rev Pr.

Muniz-Huberman, Angelina, ed. La Lengua Florida (The Flowery Language) (SPA.). 303p. 1992. reprint ed. pap. 14.99 (*968-16-3292-3*, Pub. by Fondo) Continental Bk.

Muniz, Humberto G., jt. ed. see Beruff, Jorge R.

Muniz, John. Whispers in the Wind. LC 95-61621. 100p. 1995. pap. text 10.00 (*0-9638455-4-3*) Warwick Hse.

Muniz, John F. Images & Echoes. LC 96-62013. 108p. (Orig.). 1997. pap. 8.95 (*1-890306-00-2*) Warwick Hse.

Muniz, June, jt. auth. see Herbst, Maida R.

Muniz, Mirta. Fidel Castro Reader: Forty Years of the Cuban Revolution. 2000. pap. 21.95 (*1-876175-11-7*) Ocean Pr NJ.

Muniz, Mirta, ed. see Escalante, Fabian.

Muniz, Mirta, ed. see Lechuga, Carlos.

Muniz, Olga M. La Mujer en el Contexto Epistolar Poetico del Siglo de Oro. (Iberica Ser.: Vol. 19). (SPA.). 212p. (C). 1996. text 45.95 (*0-8204-3044-7*) P Lang Pubng.

Muniz, Peter & Chasnoff, Robert. Conflict & Confrontation: A Training Program. 26p. (C). 1981. pap. text 7.00 (*0-943300-01-0*) LABS.

Muniz, Peter, jt. auth. see Chasnoff, Robert.

Muniz, Vicky. Resisting Gentrification & Displacement: Voices of Puerto Rican Women of the Barrio. LC 98-22612. (Latino Communities Ser.). (Illus.). 210p. 1998. 57.00 (*0-8153-3167-3*) Garland.

Muniz, Vik. Making It Real. 1997. pap. text 22.95 (*0-916365-49-2*) Ind Curators.

Munjal, M. L. Acoustics of Ducts & Mufflers. LC 86-32412. 352p. 1987. 180.00 (*0-471-84738-0*) Wiley.

Munk, Arthur W. A Synoptic Approach to the Riddle of Existence: Toward an Adequate World View for a World Civilization. LC 77-818. 264p. 1977. 15.00 (*0-87527-165-0*) Green.

***Munk, Ben.** Frequency Selective Surfaces: Theory & Design. LC 99-39545. 410p. 2000. 125.00 (*0-471-37047-9*) Wiley.

Munk, E. Call of the Torah: Bamidbar. 1993. 20.99 (*0-89906-046-3*); 17.99 (*0-89906-047-1*) Mesorah Pubns.

— Call of the Torah: Bereishis - Genesis. 1994. 20.99 (*0-89906-040-4*); pap. 17.99 (*0-89906-041-2*) Mesorah Pubns.

— Call of the Torah: Shimos - Exodus. 1994. 20.99 (*0-89906-042-0*); pap. 17.99 (*0-89906-043-9*) Mesorah Pubns.

— Call of the Torah: Vayikra. 1992. 20.99 (*0-89906-044-7*); pap. 17.99 (*0-89906-045-5*) Mesorah Pubns.

Munk, Elie. The World of Prayer, 2 vols. pap. 26.95 (*0-87306-170-5*) Feldheim.

— The World of Prayer, 2 vols., Set. 39.95 (*0-87306-080-6*) Feldheim.

Munk, Elie, et al, eds. Shechita: Religious & Historical Research on the Method of Slaughter. (Illus.). 1976. 12.95 (*0-87306-206-X*) Feldheim.

Munk, G. The Canadian Pacific Line. 1990. 75.00 (*0-9516038-5-X*, Pub. by Ship Pictorial Pubng) St Mut.

Munk, K. Virologie in Deutschland: Die Entwicklung Eines Fachgebietes. (Illus.). x, 170p. 1994. 43.50 (*3-8055-6004-4*) S Karger.

Munk, K., et al, eds. Oncogenes in Cancer Diagnostics. (Beitraege Zur Onkologie, Contributions to Oncology Ser.: Vol. 39). (Illus.). viii, 198p. 1990. 68.75 (*3-8055-5231-9*) S Karger.

Munk, K., ed. see Hofschneider, P. H.

Munk, Linda. The Devil's Mousetrap: Redemption & Colonial American Literature. LC 96-41397. (Illus.). 160p. (C). 1997. text 35.00 (*0-19-511494-9*) OUP.

Munk, Michael L. The Wisdom in the Hebrew Alphabet: The Sacred Letters As a Guide to Jewish Deed & Thought. (ArtScroll Mesorah Ser.). (Illus.). 240p. 1983. 22.99 (*0-89906-193-1*); pap. 19.99 (*0-89906-194-X*) Mesorah Pubns.

Munk, Peter L. & Helms, Clyde A., eds. MRI of the Knee. 2nd ed. LC 96-12935. 400p. 1996. text 142.00 (*0-397-51642-8*) Lppncott W & W.

Munk, Petr. Introduction to Macromolecular Science. LC 88-26873. 544p. 1989. 87.95 (*0-471-83212-X*) Wiley.

Munk, Reinier. The Rationale of Halakhic Man: Joseph B. Soloveitchik's Conception of Jewish Thought. LC 97-161875. (Amsterdam Studies in Jewish Thought: Vol. 3). 144p. 1996. lib. bdg. 54.00 (*90-5063-607-1*, Pub. by Gieben) J Benjamins Pubng Co.

Munk, Reinier, ed. see Rotenstreich, Nathan.

Munk, Robert J. & Lovett, Marc. Hospitalwide Education & Training. LC 77-13675. (Illus.). 1977. boxed set 12.00 (*0-87914-045-3*, 549615) Hosp Res & Educ.

Munk, S. Philosophy & Philosophical Authors of the Jews: A Historical Sketch with Explanatory Notes. Kalisch, Isidor, tr. (Reprints in Philosophy Ser.). reprint ed. lib. bdg. 29.50 (*0-697-00012-5*) Irvington.

Munk, Salomon. Melanges Philosophie Juive et Arabe. Katz, Steven, ed. LC 79-7148. (Jewish Philosophy, Mysticism & History of Ideas Ser.). viii, 536p. 1980. reprint ed. lib. bdg. 56.95 (*0-405-12278-0*) Ayer.

Munk, Walter, et al. Ocean Acoustic Tomography. (Monographs on Mechanics). (Illus.). 447p. (C). 1995. text 69.95 (*0-521-47095-1*) Cambridge U Pr.

Munk, William. Euthanasia: Or, Medical Treatment in Aid of an Easy Death. Kastenbaum, Robert J., ed. LC 76-19584. (Death & Dying Ser.). 1979. reprint ed. lib. bdg. 21.95 (*0-405-09580-5*) Ayer.

Munk, Zelda V. Deodorants: Index of New Information & Medical Research Bible. 150p. 1994. 47.50 (*0-7883-0118-7*); pap. 44.50 (*0-7883-0119-5*) ABBE Pubs Assn.

Munkacsi, Bernat, jt. ed. see Kunos, Ignacz.

Munkasey, Michael. The Astrological Thesaurus Vol. 1, Bk. 1: House Keywords. LC 92-34334. (Modern Astrology Library). (Illus.). 490p. 1999. pap. 19.95 (*0-87542-579-8*) Llewellyn Pubns.

Munke, Wolfgang. Mythologie der Chinesischen Antike: Mit Ausblick auf Spatere Entwicklungen. (GER., Illus.). 457p. 1998. 82.95 (*3-631-32776-5*) P Lang Pubng.

Munkelt, Margarete. Buehnenanweisung und Dramaturgie. Hinweise zu Interpretation und Inszenierung in Shakespeare's First Folio und den Quartoversionen. (Bochum Studies in English: No. 12). (GER.). x, 346p. (Orig.). 1981. pap. 37.00 (*90-6032-206-1*) J Benjamins Pubng Co.

***Munker, Reinhold, et al, eds.** Modern Hematology: Biology & Clinical Management. LC 99-49377. (Contemporary Hematology Ser.). 384p. 1999. 79.50 (*0-89603-687-1*) Humana.

Munkholm, Hans J., jt. auth. see Anderson, Douglas R.

***Munki, Eliyahu, tr.** Ohr Hachayim: Commentary on the Tarah, 5 vols. 2066p. 2000. 100.00 (*965-7108-12-8*, Pub. by Urim Pubns) Shalom.

Munkirs, John R. The Transformation of American Capitalism: From Competitive Market Structures to Centralized Private Sector Planning. LC 83-27093. 246p. (gr. 13). 1985. text 50.95 (*0-87332-247-9*) M E Sharpe.

Munkirs, John R. The Transformation of American Capitalism: From Competitive Market Structures to Centralized Private Sector Planning. LC 83-27093. 246p. (gr. 13). 1985. pap. text 40.95 (*0-87332-270-3*) M E Sharpe.

***Munkittrick, Kelly R., et al.** Development of Methods for Effects-Driven Cumulative Effects Assessment Using Fish Populations: Moose River Project. (Illus.). 2000. write for info. (*1-880611-41-4*, SETAC Pr) SETAC.

Munkman, J. Employers Liability (At Common Law) (C). 1985. 480.00 (*0-7855-4177-2*, Pub. by Witherby & Co) St Mut.

Munkman, John. Munkman: Damages for Personal Injuries & Death. 10th ed. 279p. 1996. write for info. (*0-406-05360-X*, MDPI10, MICHIE) LEXIS Pub.

— Munkman: The Technique of Advocacy. 175p. 1991. boxed set 33.00 (*0-406-00264-9*, UK, MICHIE) LEXIS Pub.

Munkman, John, ed. Employer's Liability. 11th ed. 528p. 1990. boxed set 144.00 (*0-406-18100-4*, U.K., MICHIE) LEXIS Pub.

***Munkres.** Topology. 2nd ed. 537p. 1999. 89.33 (*0-13-181629-2*) P-H.

Munkres, James R. Elements of Algebraic Topology. (C). 1984. 54.95 (*0-201-04586-9*) Addison-Wesley.

— Elements of Algebraic Topology. (C). 1993. pap. 55.00 (*0-201-62728-0*) Addison-Wesley.

Munley, Joan. Self Care Deficit Theory of Nursing. 128p. (C). 1984. pap. text. write for info. (*0-910973-03-2*) Arrowhead AZ.

Munman, Robert. Optical Corrections in the Sculpture of Donatello. LC 84-71080. (Transactions Ser.: Vol. 75, Pt. 2). 1985. pap. 18.00 (*0-87169-752-1*, T752-MUR) Am Philos.

— Sienese Renaissance Tomb Monuments. LC 92-85343. (Memoirs Ser.: Vol. 205). (Illus.). 295p. (C). 1993. 20.00 (*0-87169-205-8*, M205-MUR) Am Philos.

Munn, Charles. Becoming the Thinker: Four Steps to Intuition. LC 99-62036. 365p. 1999. 25.00 (*0-7388-0392-8*); pap. 15.00 (*0-7388-0393-6*) Xlibris Corp.

— Paradise Now: Breaking the Trance. LC 99-62035. 365p. 1999. 25.00 (*0-7388-0394-4*); pap. 15.00 (*0-7388-0395-2*) Xlibris Corp.

Munn, Debra D. Big Sky Ghosts: Eerie True Tales of Montana, Vol. 1. LC 93-3176. (Illus.). 146p. 1993. pap. 14.95 (*0-87108-838-X*) Pruett.

— Big Sky Ghosts: Eerie True Tales of Montana, Vol. 2. LC 93-3176. (Illus.). 131p. 1994. pap. 14.95 (*0-87108-839-8*) Pruett.

— Ghosts on the Range: Eerie True Tales of Wyoming. LC 89-39754. 190p. 1989. pap. 14.00 (*0-87108-771-5*) Pruett.

Munn, Debra D., ed. see Krause, Danna J.

***Munn, Felicity.** Travel Smart: Eastern Canada. 3rd ed. (Travel Smart Ser.). (Illus.). 272p. 2000. pap. 16.95 (*1-56261-521-1*, Travel Smart) Avalon Travel.

Munn, Geoffrey C., jt. auth. see Gere, Charlotte.

Munn, Heidi, ed. Culture Shock! Borneo. (Illus.). 250p. 1991. pap. 12.95 (*1-55868-075-6*) Gr Arts Ctr Pub.

Munn, Mark H. Defense of Attica: The Dema Wall & the Boiotian War of 378-375 B.C. (C). 1994. 45.00 (*0-520-07685-0*, Pub. by U CA Pr) Cal Prin Full Svc.

***Munn, Mark Henderson.** The School of History: Athens in the Age of Socrates. LC 99-46451. 510p. 2000. 37.50 (*0-520-21557-5*, Pub. by U CA Pr) Cal Prin Full Svc.

Munn, Michael. Gregory Peck. (Illus.). 240p. 1999. 26.95 (*0-7090-6265-6*, Pub. by R Hale Ltd) Seven Hills Bk.

***Munn, Michael.** Gregory Peck. large type unabridged ed. 304p. 1999. 25.95 (*0-7531-5097-2*, 150972, Pub. by ISIS Lrg Prnt) ISIS Pub.

— Hollywood Connection: The Mafia & the Movie Business - The Explosive Story. 230p. 1999. pap. 13.95 (*1-86105-255-3*) Robson.

Munn, Michael. Hollywood Rogues: The Off-Screen Antics of Hollywood's Hellraisers. large type ed. (Illus.). 283p. 1992. 23.95 (*1-85089-581-3*, Pub. by ISIS Lrg Prnt) Transaction Pubs.

— The Sharon Stone Story. LC 97-69360. (Illus.). 226p. 1998. 27.95 (*1-86105-094-1*, Robson-Parkwest) Parkwest Pubns.

— Stars at War. (Illus.). 294p. 1996. 28.95 (*0-86051-954-6*, Robson-Parkwest) Parkwest Pubns.

***Munn, Michael.** Stars at War. large type unabridged ed. 1999. 25.95 (*1-85089-484-1*, 894841, Pub. by ISIS Lrg Prnt); pap. 19.95 (*0-7531-5071-9*, 150719, Pub. by ISIS Lrg Prnt) ISIS Pub.

Munn, Michael. Trevor Howard. LC 90-41123. (Illus.). 196p. 1990. 19.95 (*0-8128-4006-2*, Scrbrough Hse) Madison Bks UPA.

Munn, Michael. X-Rated: The Paranormal Experiences of the Movie Star Greats. (Illus.). 204p. 1996. 24.95 (*1-86105-017-8*, Robson-Parkwest) Parkwest Pubns.

***Munn, Michael.** X-Rated: The Paranormal Experiences of the Movie Star Greats. 1999. pap. 12.95 (*1-86105-237-5*) Robson.

Munn, Michael, jt. auth. see Sparks, William.

Munn, Michael De, see De Munn, Michael.

Munn, Michael W. Beyond Business As Usual: Practical Lessons in Accessing New Dimensions. LC 98-14677. 184p. 1998. pap. text 18.95 (*0-7506-9926-4*) Buttrwrth-Heinemann.

Munn, Nancy D. The Fame of Gawa: A Symbolic Study of Value Transformation in a Massim (Papua New Guinea) Society. LC 92-9614. (Henry Louis Morgan Lecture Ser.). (Illus.). 352p. 1992. pap. text 18.95 (*0-8223-1270-0*) Duke.

— Walbiri Iconography: Graphic Representation & Cultural Symbolism in a Central Australian Society. LC 86-4320. (Illus.). 244p. (C). 1993. pap. text 12.95 (*0-226-55110-5*) U Ch Pr.

Munn, Pamela & Jonstone, Margaret. Effective Discipline in Primary Schools & Classrooms. 160p. 1992. pap. 29.95 (*1-85396-174-4*, Pub. by P Chapman) Taylor & Francis.

— Effective Discipline in Secondary Schools & Classrooms. 160p. 1992. pap. 29.95 (*1-85396-175-2*, Pub. by P Chapman) Taylor & Francis.

Munn, Pamela, jt. auth. see MacDonald-Clark, Margaret.

Munn, R. E., ed. Boundary Layer Studies & Applications: A Special Issue of Boundary-Layer Meteorology in Honor of Dr. Hans A. Panofsky (1917-1988) (C). 1989. text 260.00 (*0-7923-0277-X*) Kluwer Academic.

— Policy Making in an Era of Global Environmental Change. (Environment & Policy Ser.). 256p. (C). 1996. text 59.00 (*0-7923-3872-3*) Kluwer Academic.

Munn, R. E. & Taylor, P. A. Boundary-Layer Meteorology, 1970-1995: Invited Reviews & Selected Contributions to Recognise Ted Munn's Contribution As Editor over the Past 25 Years - 25th Anniversary Edition. anniversary ed. Garratt, J. R., ed. LC 96-31602. 436p. (C). 1996. text 85.00 (*0-7923-4191-0*) Kluwer Academic.

Munn, R. E., et al. Policy Making in an Era of Global Environmental Change. LC 96-1781. (Environment & Policy Ser.). 1996. write for info. (*0-7923-4072-8*) Kluwer Academic.

Munn, R. W., et al, eds. Electrical & Related Properties of Organic Solids: Proceedings of the NATO Advanced Research Workshop Erpos-7, Electrical & Related Properties of Organic Solids, Polanica Zdroj, Poland, 18-22 June, 1996. (NATO Advanced Science Institutes: Partnership Sub-Series: 3 High Technology). 460p. (C). 1997. text 234.00 (*0-7923-4449-9*) Kluwer Academic.

Munn, R. W. & Beynon, Rob J. Postgraduate Study in the Physical Sciences: A Researcher's Companion. (Illus.). 150p. (Orig.). (C). Date not set. pap. 20.00 (*1-85578-078-X*, Pub. by Portland Pr Ltd) Ashgate Pub Co.

Munn, R. W. & Ironside, C. N., eds. Principles & Applications of Nonlinear Optical Materials. 1993. 101.00 (*0-8493-7109-0*, QC446) CRC Pr.

Munn, Raymond S., ed. Computer Modeling in Corrosion. LC 92-12525. (Special Technical Publication Ser.: Vol. 1154). (Illus.). 300p. 1992. 86.00 (*0-8031-1473-7*, STP1154) ASTM.

Munn, Robert F. Coal Industry in America: Bibliography & Guide to Studies. 2nd ed. LC 77-77913. 351p. 1977. 12.50 (*0-930284-00-3*) West Va U Pr.

— Strip Mining: An Annotated Bibliography. LC 72-96636. 110p. 1973. 10.00 (*0-937058-09-2*) West Va U Pr.

Munn, Robert W., jt. auth. see Hinchliffe, Alan.

Munn, Sheldon A. Freemasons at Gettysburg. (Illus.). 92p. (C). 1993. pap. text 8.95 (*0-939631-68-7*) Thomas Publications.

Munn, Sherrill. Beacon Small-Group Bible Studies, Luke Pt. II, Chaps. 9-24: Lessons on Discipleship. 68p. (Orig.). 1981. pap. 4.99 (*0-8341-0689-2*) Beacon Hill.

Munn, Timothy David. Ontario County: Golden Era of Railroad. (Images of America Ser.). (Illus.). 128p. 1998. pap. 18.99 (*0-7524-1222-1*) Arcadia Publng.

Munn, Vella. Wind Warrior. 352p. 1999. mass mkt. 6.99 (*0-8125-3876-5*, Pub. by Forge NYC) St Martin.

— Wind Warrior. LC 97-29880. 1998. text 23.95 (*0-312-86446-9*) St Martin.

Munn, Vella. Blackfeet Season. LC 98-33241. 1999. 25.95 (*0-312-86734-4*, Pub. by Forge NYC) St Martin.

***Munn, Vella.** Blackfeet Season. 2000. mass mkt. 5.99 (*0-8125-7065-0*, Pub. by Forge NYC) St Martin.

Munn, Vella. Daughter of the Forest. 416p. 1995. mass mkt. 5.99 (*0-8125-3499-9*, Pub. by Forge NYC) St Martin.

***Munn, Vella.** Daughter of the Forest. 2000. pap. 25.95 (*0-312-87530-4*) St Martin.

Munn, Vella. Daughter of the Mountain. 416p. (Orig.). 1994. mass mkt. 5.99 (*0-8125-2325-3*, Pub. by Tor Bks) St Martin.

— The Eagles' Daughter. (Orig.). 1996. mass mkt. write for info. (*0-614-05517-2*) Forge NYC.

— The Man from Forever. (Intimate Moments Ser.). 1996. per. 3.99 (*0-373-07695-9*, 1-07695-9) Silhouette.

***Munn, Vella.** Midnight Sun. LC 99-45471. 1999. 24.95 (*0-7862-2244-1*) Mac Lib Ref.

Munn, Vella. Navajo Nights. 1995. per. 3.50 (*0-373-27058-5*, 1-27058-6) Silhouette.

M

— Precious Love. 288p. 1995. mass mkt. 4.99 (*0-8217-0124-X*, Zebra Kensgtn) Kensgtn Pub Corp.

— Precious Love. large type ed. (Black Satin Romance Ser.). 353p. 1996. 27.99 (*1-86110-014-0*) Ulverscroft.

— The Return of Cord Navarro. 1996. per. 3.99 (*0-373-07749-1*, 1-07749-4) Silhouette.

— The River's Daughter. LC 94-138062. 416p. (Orig.). 1993. mass mkt. 4.99 (*0-8125-1930-2*, Pub. by Tor Bks) St Martin.

— Seminole Song. 1998. mass mkt. 5.99 (*0-8125-3883-8*, Pub. by Forge NYC) St Martin.

— Silver Waves. (American Romance Ser.: No. 444). 1992. per. 3.39 (*0-373-16444-0*, 1-16444-1) Harlequin Bks.

*__Munn, Vella.__ Soul of the Sacred Earth. 400p. 2000. 23.95 (*0-312-86733-6*) Forge NYC.

Munn, Vella. Spirit of The Eagle. (Orig.). 1997. mass mkt. 5.99 (*0-8125-3500-6*, Pub. by Tor Bks) St Martin.

— Spirit of the Eagle. 352p. 1996. 23.95 (*0-312-86096-X*) Forge NYC.

— Winter Legacy. 320p. 1992. mass mkt. 3.99 (*0-8217-3841-0*, Zebra Kensgtn) Kensgtn Pub Corp.

Munn, W. D., et al. Semigroups with Applications: Proceedings of the Conference. 276p. 1992. text 81.00 (*981-02-1121-X*) World Scientific Pub.

Munna, Raymond J. As I See It: Radial Keratotomy Before, During & After Surgery. (Illus.). 110p. 1986. pap. 9.95 (*0-935669-07-8*) A Granite Pubs.

— Franchise Selection: Separating Fact from Fiction. 216p. (Orig.). 1988. pap. 19.95 (*0-935669-12-4*) A Granite Pubs.

— Legal Power for Small Business Owners & Managers. LC 91-8838. 309p. (Orig.). 1991. pap. 19.95 (*0-935669-10-8*) A Granite Pubs.

Munneke, Gary A. Careers in Law. 168p. 1992. 17.95 (*0-8442-8554-4*, VGM Career) NTC Contemp Pub Co.

— Careers in Law. 2nd ed. LC 97-3848. (VGM Professional Careers Ser.). (Illus.). 192p. 1997. 17.95 (*0-8442-4509-7*, 45097, VGM Career); pap. 13.95 (*0-8442-4510-0*, 45100) NTC Contemp Pub Co.

— How to Succeed in Law School. 2nd ed. 280p. 1994. pap. 9.95 (*0-8120-1449-9*) Barron.

— Law Office Management. Date not set. pap. text. write for info. (*0-314-06585-7*) West Pub.

— Law Practice Management: Materials & Cases. (American Casebook Ser.). 634p. (C). 1991. reprint ed. 57.50 (*0-314-83688-8*) West Pub.

— Law Practice Management, Materials & Cases, Teacher's Manual. (American Casebook Ser.). 123p. (C). 1991. pap. text. write for info. (*0-314-00055-0*) West Pub.

— Legal Career Guide: From Law Student to Lawyer. 1993. pap. text 14.95 (*0-89707-763-6*) Amer Bar Assn.

— Opportunities in Law Careers. LC 93-25120. (Opportunities In . . . Ser.). (Illus.). 160p. pap. 11.95 (*0-8442-4087-7*, 40877, VGM Career) NTC Contemp Pub Co.

— Opportunities in Law Careers. (Illus.). 160p. 1989. 13.95 (*0-8442-6174-2*, VGM Career) NTC Contemp Pub Co.

— Opportunities in Law Careers. (Illus.). 160p. 1993. pap. 10.95 (*0-8442-6175-0*, VGM Career) NTC Contemp Pub Co.

— Opportunities in Law Careers. LC 93-25120. (Illus.). 160p. 1994. 14.95 (*0-8442-4086-9*, 40869, VGM Career) NTC Contemp Pub Co.

Munnell, Alicia H. The Economics of Private Pensions. LC 82-4223. (Studies in Social Economics). 240p. 1982. 32.95 (*0-8157-5894-4*); pap. 10.95 (*0-8157-5893-6*) Brookings.

— The Future of Social Security. LC 76-51883. (Studies in Social Economics). 1977. pap. 12.95 (*0-8157-5895-2*) Brookings.

Munnell, Alicia H. & Connolly, Ann M. Pensions for Public Employees. LC 79-89303. 128p. 1979. 7.00 (*0-89068-048-5*) Natl Planning.

Munnell, Alicia H., jt. ed. see Bodie, Zvi.

Munnell, Michael D., ed. American Indian Marriage Record Directory for Ashland County, Wisconsin, 1874-1907. 279p. (Orig.). 1993. pap. 35.00 (*0-9638897-4-5*) Chippewa Heritage.

Munnelly, Tom, jt. ed. see Carolan, Nicholas.

Munner, Robert L. Technologies for Synthetic Environments: Hardware-in-the-Loop Testing II. LC 98-119237. 36p. 1997. pap. 69.00 (*0-8194-2499-4*) SPIE.

Munnich, F. E., jt. ed. see Abshagen, U.

Munnichs, Joep M. Old Age & Finitude: A Contribution to Psychogerontology. Stein, Leon, ed. LC 79-8676. (Growing Old Ser.). 1980. reprint ed. lib. bdg. 18.95 (*0-405-12792-8*) Ayer.

Munnichs, Joep M., et al. Dependency or Interdependency in Old Age. 1976. text 88.00 (*90-247-1895-3*) Kluwer Academic.

Munnick, Adrian R., ed. Catholic Church Records of the Pacific Northwest: St. Ann, Walla Walla & Frenchtown. LC 88-63227. 328p. 1989. 25.00 (*0-8323-0466-2*) Binford Mort.

Munnick, Harriet D. Catholic Church Records of the Pacific Northwest: Oregon City, Salem & Jacksonville. LC 84-70844. (Illus.). 400p. 1984. 25.00 (*0-8323-0429-8*) Binford Mort.

— Catholic Church Records of the Pacific Northwest: St. Paul, Oregon 1839-1898. LC 79-3575. (Illus.). 832p. 1980. 25.00 (*0-8323-0348-8*) Binford Mort.

— Catholic Church Records of the Pacific Northwest: Vancouver & Stellamaris Mission. LC 72-83958. (Illus.). 444p. 1972. 25.00 (*0-8323-0375-5*) Binford Mort.

— Catholic Church Records of the Pacific Northwest Vol. 3: St. Louis, Gervais & Brooks, 7 vols. LC 72-71955. (Illus.). 528p. 1982. 25.00 (*0-8323-0408-5*) Binford Mort.

— Priest's Progress: The Journey of Frances Norbert Blanchet from the Atlantic Ocean to the Pacific in Three Parishes. LC 89-62677. (Illus.). 100p. 1989. 15.00 (*0-8323-0474-3*) Binford Mort.

Munnick, Harriet D., compiled by. Catholic Church Records of the Pacific Northwest: Roseburg & Portland. LC 85-63221. (Illus.). 440p. 1986. 25.00 (*0-8323-0447-6*) Binford Mort.

Munnick, Harriet D. & Beckman, Stephan D., eds. Catholic Church Records of the Pacific Northwest: Grand Ronde. (Illus.). 312p. 1987. 25.00 (*0-8323-0455-7*) Binford Mort.

Munniksma, F. Dictionary of Economics: Oekonomisches Woerterbuch. (ENG & GER.). 764p. 1980. 95.00 (*0-8288-0099-5*, M 15199) Fr & Eur.

— Dictionnaire International du Commerce et de L'Economie: French, English, Esperanto, German, Spanish, Italian, Portuguese, Swedish, Japanese, Chinese. (ENG, ESP, FRE, GER & SPA.). 1990. 75.00 (*0-685-48811-X*, M15696) Fr & Eur.

— International Dictionary of Commerce & Economics: French, English, Esperanto, German, Spanish, Italian, Portuguese, Swedish, Japanese, Chinese. 1991. 75.00 (*0-8288-4041-5*, M15696) Fr & Eur.

Munniksma, F., ed. Dictionnaire International du Commerce et de l'Economie. (FRE.). 1990. write for info. (*0-7859-8704-5*, 7505200259) Fr & Eur.

Munning, K. A., jt. ed. see Taylor, Robert B.

Munnings, Claire, et al. Overnight Float: A Mystery. 288p. 2000. 23.95 (*0-393-03849-1*) Norton.

Munns, Dencie. The Storms of Love. LC 90-7513. 238p. 1990. 15.75 (*0-930950-23-2*); pap. 9.75 (*0-930950-24-0*) Nopoly Pr.

Munns, Donald N., jt. auth. see Singer, Michael J.

*__Munns, Harry.__ Someday Comes. 310p. 1999. pap. 11.95 (*0-9676681-9-0*) Paramax Prods Inc.

Munns, J. Frank, ed. George Tsutakawa & Morris Graves: Paintings, Drawings & Sculpture. (Illus.). 14p. (Orig.). (C). 1978. pap. 10.00 (*1-880269-03-1*) D H Sheehan.

Munns, J. Frank & Lynx, David, eds. The Columbia & Plateau: The Roger J. Bounds Foundation, Inc. Collection Exhibition. (Illus.). 8p. (Orig.). (C). 1990. pap. 4.00 (*1-880269-06-6*) D H Sheehan.

Munns, Jessica. Restoration Politics & Drama: The Plays of Thomas Otway, 1675-1683. LC 95-10377. 272p. 1996. 42.50 (*0-87413-548-6*) U Delaware Pr.

Munns, Jessica & Richards, Penny, eds. The Clothes That Wear Us: Essays on Dressing & Transgressing in Eighteenth-Century Culture. LC 98-47338. (Illus.). 368p. 1999. 49.50 (*0-87413-672-5*) U Delaware Pr.

Munns, Jessica, et al. A Cultural Studies Reader: History, Theory & Practice. LC 95-16009. 704p. (C). 1996. pap. 45.00 (*0-582-21411-4*) Longman.

— A Cultural Studies Reader: History, Theory, Practice. 704p. (C). 1996. text 72.25 (*0-582-21410-6*) Longman.

Munns, Ron R., jt. auth. see Marsh, W. Jeffrey.

Munnsa, Kantilal, jt. auth. see Mouyelo-Katoula, Michel.

Muno, Jean. Glove of Passion, Voice of Blood. Connell, Kim, tr. from FRE. 127p. (Orig.). 1986. pap. 12.00 (*0-937669-22-9*) Owl Creek Pr.

*__Munoa, Phillip B., III.__ Four Powers in Heaven: The Interpretation of Daniel 7 in the Testament of Abraham. (JSP Supplement Ser.: No. 28). 176p. 1998. 52.50 (*1-85075-885-9*, Pub. by Sheffield Acad) CUP Services.

Munonye, John. Obi. (African Writers Ser.). 210p. (C). 1969. pap. 8.95 (*0-435-90045-5*, 90045) Heinemann.

Munoo, Jack. Official Couch Potato Handbook. 100p. 1987. pap. text 6.95 (*0-86719-358-1*) Last Gasp.

Munowitz, M. Coherence & NMR. LC 88-10605. 289p. 1988. 105.00 (*0-471-61523-4*) Wiley.

*__Munowitz, M.__ Principles of Chemistry. LC 98-26497. 1000p. 1999. 104.25 (*0-393-97288-7*) Norton.

Munowitz, Michael. Principles of Chemistry. (C). pap. text. write for info. (*0-393-97550-9*); pap. text, student ed. write for info. (*0-393-97365-4*) Norton.

— Supplementary Exercises Student Version. 2000. pap. write for info. (*0-393-97549-5*) Norton.

Munoz. Islam Modernism & West. 26p. Date not set. text 59.50 (*1-86064-341-8*, Pub. by I B T) St Martin.

— La Musica en Puerto Rico. 1966. 12.95 (*0-87751-012-1*) E Torres & Sons.

— Mystery Title to Come. 2000. pap. 17.25 (*0-07-232616-6*) McGraw.

Munoz, A. Lopez. Programas para Dias Especiales, Vol. I.Tr. of Program for Special Days. (SPA.). 107p. 1986. reprint ed. pap. 5.50 (*0-311-07005-1*) Casa Bautista.

Munoz, A. Lopez. Programas para Dias Especiales, Vol. II.Tr. of Program for Special Days. (SPA.). 64p. 1969. reprint ed. pap. 4.99 (*0-311-07006-X*) Casa Bautista.

Munoz, Alejandra M., ed. Consumer Data Relationships: Relating Consumer, Descriptive, & Lab Data to Better Understand Consumer Responses. 2nd ed. LC 96-52055. (Manual Ser.: No. 30). (Illus.). 110p. 1997. pap. text 43.00 (*0-8031-2073-7*, MNL3) ASTM.

Munoz, Alicia. Complete Idiot's Guide to Learning German on Your Own. 352p. 1997. 16.95 (*0-02-861962-5*) Macmillan Gen Ref.

Munoz, Angel S., ed. El Teatro en Badajoz, 1860-1886. (Fuentes Para la Historia del Teatro en Espana, Series C: Vol. 28). (SPA.). 360p. 1998. 63.00 (*1-85566-055-5*, Pub. by Tamesis Bks Ltd) Boydell & Brewer.

Munoz, Anna, tr. see Maury, Inez.

Munoz, Antonio J. Forgotten Legions: Obscure Combat Formations of the Waffen-SS, 1943-45. (Illus.). 424p. 1991. 59.95 (*0-87364-646-0*) Paladin Pr.

— Hitler's Eastern Legions Vol. I: The Baltic Schutzmannschaft, 1941-1945. (Illus.). 96p. 1998. per. 21.00 (*1-891227-09-2*, Axis Europa Bks) Axis Europa.

— Hitler's Eastern Legions Vol. II: The Osttruppen, 1941-1945. 2nd ed. (Illus.). 56p. 1998. per. 24.00 (*1-891227-10-6*, Axis Europa Bks) Axis Europa.

*__Munoz, Antonio J.__ Iron Fist: A Combat History of the 17.SS Panzergrenadier Division "Gotz von Berlichin-gen" Division, 1943-1945. (Illus.). 82p. 1999. per. 20.00 (*1-891227-29-7*, Axis Europa Bks) Axis Europa.

Munoz, Antonio J. The Kaminski Brigade: A History, 1941-1945. (Illus.). 64p. 1996. pap. 20.00 (*1-891227-02-5*, Axis Europa Bks) Axis Europa.

— Lions of the Desert: Arab Volunteers in the German Army, 1941-1945. 2nd ed. (Illus.). 36p. 1994. pap. 18.00 (*1-891227-03-3*, Axis Europa Bks) Axis Europa.

— Slovenian Axis Forces in World War II, 1941-1945. 2nd expanded rev. ed. Orig. Title: Yugoslav Axis Forces in World War II, Vol. I, Slovenian Volunteers. (Illus.). 84p. 1998. per. 22.00 (*1-891227-12-2*) Axis Europa.

— Slovenian Axis Forces in World War II, 1941-1945. (Illus.). 84p. 1999. per. 22.00 (*1-891227-04-1*, Axis Europa Bks) Axis Europa.

Munoz, Antonio J., ed. The German Police. (Illus.). 442p. 1997. per. 42.00 (*1-891227-11-4*, Axis Europa Bks) Axis Europa.

— Russian Volunteers in Hitler's Army, 1941-1945. (Illus.). 60p. 1996. per. 13.00 (*1-891227-01-7*, Axis Europa Bks) Axis Europa.

Munoz, Antonio J. & Kursiefis, Andris J. The Hungarian Army & Its Military Leadership in World War II. 3rd rev. ed. (Illus.). 88p. 1999. per. 25.00 (*1-891227-28-9*) Axis Europa.

Munoz, Antonio J., ed. see Dobrich, Momcilo.

Munoz, Antonio J., ed. see Kocevar, Monika Kokalj.

Munoz, Antonio J., ed. see Mikulan, Krunoslav.

Munoz, Braulio. Sons of the Wind: The Search for Identity in Spanish American Indian Literature. LC 81-15403. 335p. (Orig.). reprint ed. pap. 103.90 (*0-7837-5678-X*, 205910600005) Bks Demand.

*__Munoz, Braulio.__ A Storyteller: Mario Vargas Llosa Between Civilization & Barbarism. LC 99-38922. 144p. 2000. pap. 17.95 (*0-8476-9751-7*); text 56.95 (*0-8476-9750-9*) Rowman.

Munoz, Carlos. Sixties Chicano Movement: Youth, Identity, Power. 2000. pap. text 20.00 (*1-85984-219-4*, Pub. by Verso) Norton.

*__Munoz, Carlos.__ The Sixties Chicano Movement: Youth, Identity, Power. (Haymarket Ser.). 1999. 60.00 (*1-85984-726-9*, Pub. by Verso) Norton.

Munoz, Carlos. Youth, Identity, Power: The Chicano Movement. (Haymarket Ser.). 320p. (C). 1989. pap. 19.00 (*0-86091-913-7*, Pub. by Verso) Norton.

Munoz-Cobo, J. L. & Difilippo, F. C., eds. Noise & Nonlinear Phenomena in Nuclear Systems. (NATO ASI Series B, Physics: Vol. 192). (Illus.). 482p. 1989. 125.00 (*0-306-43102-5*, Plenum Trade) Perseus Pubng.

Munoz, David G., jt. auth. see Kertesz, Andrew.

Munoz, E. Spanish Dictionary of Uncommon Words - Diccionario de Palabras Olvidadas. (SPA.). 409p. 1992. pap. 30.00 (*0-7859-8922-6*) Fr & Eur.

— Spanish Dictionary of Uncommon Words - Diccionario de Palabras Olvidadas. (SPA.). 409p. 1992. pap. 31.50 (*84-283-1986-3*, Pub. by Paraninfo) IBD Ltd.

Munoz, Elias M. Brand New Memory. LC 98-12855. 224p. 1998. pap. 12.95 (*1-55885-227-1*) Arte Publico.

— Crazy Love. LC 88-6394. 160p. (Orig.). 1989. pap. 9.50 (*0-934770-83-2*) Arte Publico.

— Los Viajes de Orlando Cachumbambe. LC 83-81356. (Coleccion Caniqui). (SPA.). 143p. (Orig.). 1984. pap. 7.95 (*0-89729-332-0*) Ediciones.

— Viajes Fantasticos. 129p. (C). 1994. pap. 20.00 (*0-07-044311-4*) McGraw.

*__Munoz-Furlong, Anne.__ Alexander & His Pals Visit the Main Street School. (J). (gr. k-6). 1999. pap. write for info. (*1-882541-07-3*) Food Allergy.

— Alexander Goes to a Birthday Party. (Illus.). 24p. (J). (gr. k-6). 1999. pap. 5.00 (*1-882541-11-1*) Food Allergy.

— Alexander Goes Trick-or-Treating. (Illus.). 24p. (J). (gr. k-6). 1999. pap. 5.00 (*1-882541-13-8*) Food Allergy.

— Cooking Solutions. 1999. pap. 15.00 (*1-882541-06-5*) Food Allergy.

Munoz-Furlong, Anne. Day Care & Preschool Guide to Managing Food Allergies. 100p. 1997. text 75.00 (*1-882541-04-9*) Food Allergy.

— The Food Allergy News Cookbook. LC 99-204393. 232p. 1998. pap. 14.95 (*1-56561-157-8*) Wiley.

— The Food Allergy News Cookbook. rev. ed. LC 92-97152. 156p. 1996. text 20.00 (*1-882541-00-6*) Food Allergy.

*__Munoz-Furlong, Anne.__ Food Allergy News Cookbook, Vol. 2. 1999. write for info. (*1-882541-10-3*) Food Allergy.

— A Special Day at School. (J). (gr. k-6). 1999. pap. write for info. (*1-882541-08-1*) Food Allergy.

*__Munoz-Furlong, Anne, ed.__ Stories from the Heart: A Collection of Essays from Teens with Food Allergies. 89p. (YA). 2000. spiral bd. 15.00 (*1-882541-17-0*) Food Allergy.

Munoz-Furlong, Anne, jt. auth. see Food Allergy Network Staff.

Munoz-Furlong, Anne, ed. see Sicherer, Scott H.

Munoz-Furlonj, Ann, ed. The School Food Allergy Program. (Illus.). 100p. 1996. 75.00 (*1-882541-03-0*) Food Allergy.

Munoz, Gabriel T. Permanent Work: Poems, 1981-1992. Irby, Patricia L. et al, trs. from SPA. (Baja California Literature in Translation Ser.). 96p. 1993. pap. 12.50 (*1-879691-13-2*) SDSU Press.

Munoz, Gabriela, tr. see Maultsby, Maxie C., Jr.

Munoz, Hector, jt. auth. see Alessio, Luis.

Munoz, Heraldo, ed. Environment & Diplomacy in the Americas. LC 92-4480. 149p. 1992. pap. text 9.95 (*1-55587-390-1*) L Rienner.

— Latin American Views of U. S. Policy: Politics of Latin America. LC 85-19365. (Hoover Institute Ser.). 162p. 1985. 52.95 (*0-275-92048-8*, C2048, Praeger Pubs) Greenwood.

Munoz, Heraldo & Rosenberg, Robin, eds. Difficult Liason: Trade & the Environment in the Americas. LC 93-17922. 304p. (C). 1993. pap. 21.95 (*1-56000-679-X*, Pub. by U Miami N-S Ctr) L Rienner.

Munoz, Heraldo & Tulchin, Joseph S., eds. Latin American Nations in World Politics. 2nd ed. 288p. (C). 1996. pap. 26.00 (*0-8133-0873-9*, Pub. by Westview) HarpC.

Munoz, Heraldo & Vaky, Viron P. The Future of the Organization of American States. LC 93-31243. (Orig.). 1993. pap. 9.95 (*0-87078-348-3*) Century Foundation.

Munoz, Jairo, jt. auth. see Ostwald, Phillip F.

Munoz, James L., jt. auth. see Nordstrown, Kirk.

Munoz, John J. & Bergman, R. K. Bordetella Pertussis: Immunological & Other Biological Activities. LC 76-26453. (Immunology Ser.: No. 4). (Illus.). 249p. reprint ed. pap. 77.20 (*0-7837-0815-7*, 204113000019) Bks Demand.

Munoz, Jose E. Disidentifications: Queers of Color & the Performance of Politics. LC 98-54363. 1999. pap. 19.95 (*0-8166-3015-1*) U of Minn Pr.

*__Munoz, Jose E.__ Disidentifications: Queers of Color & the Performance of Politics. (Cultural Studies of the Americas). 1999. write for info. (*0-8166-3014-3*) U of Minn Pr.

Munoz, Jose E., jt. ed. see Delgado, Celeste F.

Munoz, Juan. Juan Munoz: Segments. (ENG & FRE., Illus.). 77p. 1990. pap. 20.00 (*0-941548-21-X*) Ren Soc U Chi.

— Pepe y la Armadura (Pepe & the Armor) (SPA., Illus.). 120p. (YA). 1994. pap. 5.99 (*968-16-4465-4*, Pub. by Fondo) Continental Bk.

Munoz, Juan & Rothenberg, Susan. Parkett, No. 43. 200p. 1995. pap. 19.50 (*3-907509-93-5*, Pub. by Parkett Verlag AG) Dist Art Pubs.

Munoz, Juan, jt. auth. see Grosh, Margaret E.

Munoz-Knowles, Martha. Servility. LC 94-90479. 1999. 8.95 (*0-533-11248-6*) Vantage.

Munoz, Luis, ed. see Fielding, Henry.

Munoz-Marin, Luis. Mensajes al Pueblo Puertorriqueno: Pronunciados ante las Camaras Legislativas, 1949-1964. LC 80-24258. (Illus.). 358p. 1980. 12.50 (*0-913480-47-9*); pap. 6.95 (*0-913480-48-7*); mass mkt. 4.95 (*0-913480-49-5*) Inter Am U Pr.

Munoz, Mary E., jt. auth. see Pyle, Michael A.

Munoz, Mirta, ed. Elecciones en Cuba: Farsa o Democracia? (SPA.). 172p. 1993. pap. 11.95 (*1-875284-71-0*, Pub. by Ocean Pr NJ) LPC InBook.

Munoz, N., et al, eds. The Epidemiology of Cervical Cancer & Human Papillomavirus. LC 93-179248. (IARC Scientific Publications: No. 119). 306p. 1992. reprint ed. pap. 94.90 (*0-608-04400-8*, 206518100001) Bks Demand.

Munoz, N., ed. see International Agency for Research on Cancer Staff.

Munoz, Olivia, jt. auth. see Lipton, Gladys C.

Munoz, Oscar, ed. Economic Reforms in Chile. 97p. 1992. 8.00 (*0-940602-56-3*) IADB.

— Reformas Economicas en Chile. 105p. 1992. 8.00 (*0-940602-49-0*) IADB.

*__Munoz, Pilar.__ Campo Libre No. 2: La Vida Intima - Workbook. Thacker, Mike, ed. (SPA.). (C). 2000. spiral bd., wbk. ed. 60.00 (*0-85668-690-5*, Pub. by Aris & Phillips) David Brown.

Munoz, Rafael F. Santa Anna: El Dictador Resplandeciente (The Shinning Dictator) (SPA.). 278p. 1984. pap. 8.99 (*968-16-1326-0*, Pub. by Fondo) Continental Bk.

Munoz, Ricardo F., ed. Depression Prevention: Research Directions. 301p. 1987. 76.95 (*0-89116-452-9*) Hemisp Pub.

Munoz, Ricardo F., et al. The Prevention of Depression: Research & Practice. LC 92-49536. (Series in Psychiatry & Neuroscience). (Illus.). 360p. 1993. text 65.00 (*0-8018-4496-7*) Johns Hopkins.

— Social & Psychological Research in Community Settings. LC 79-88107. (Jossey-Bass Social & Behavioral Science Ser.). 416p. reprint ed. pap. 129.00 (*0-8357-6881-3*, 203793300009) Bks Demand.

Munoz, Richard D. RISQ's 1998/99 National Profile Directory of Independent Agents & Brokers. x, 286p. 1998. 250.00 (*0-9667273-0-4*) RISQ Consult Srvc.

Munoz, Rodrigo, jt. auth. see Morrison, James R.

Munoz, Rodrigo A., jt. auth. see Morrison, James.

Munoz, Ronaldo. The God of Christians. 208p. 1994. pap. 30.00 (*0-86012-173-9*, Pub. by Srch Pr) St Mut.

— The God of Christians. Burns, Paul, tr. from SPA. LC 90-25461. (Theology & Liberation Ser.). 208p. 1990. reprint ed. pap. 64.50 (*0-7837-9851-2*, 206058000005) Bks Demand.

Munoz Ryan, Pam. One Hundred Is a Family. LC 93-30914. (Illus.). 32p. (J). (ps-3). 1994. lib. bdg. 13.89 (*1-56282-673-5*, Pub. by Hyprn Child) Little.

— Pinky Baby, Vol. 1. Vol. 1. (Illus.). 32p. (J). (ps-2). 1999. pap. 4.95 (*0-7868-1144-7*, Pub. by Hyperion) Time Warner.

Munoz Seca, Pedro. La Venganza de Don Mendo. (Nueva Austral Ser.: Vol. 30). (SPA.). 1991. pap. text 24.95 (*84-239-1830-0*) Elliots Bks.

Munoz, Silverio. Amanecer en Manhattan. 76p. (Orig.). 1985. pap. text 5.00 (*0-937985-00-7*) Ediciones Arauco.

— Post-Coup Chilean Poetry: A Bilingual Anthology. Acevedo, Mary E. & Paska, Jocelyn, trs. from SPA. LC 86-80932. (Illus.). 88p. 1986. pap. text 7.50 (*0-937985-01-5*) Ediciones Arauco.

— Relatos. (SPA.). 250p. (Orig.). 1991. pap. text 15.00 (*0-937985-06-6*) Ediciones Arauco.

— Tenure-Track: Historia de Profesores. (SPA.). 427p. (Orig.). 1993. pap. 21.50 (*0-937985-07-4*) Ediciones Arauco.

— Vivir en Madrid. (SPA.). 140p. (Orig.). 1991. text 13.50 (*0-937985-05-8*) Ediciones Arauco.

An Asterisk (*) at the beginning of an entry indicates that the title is appearing for the first time.

Munoz, Silverio & Stok, Ana L. Benedictina: Relatos de Silverio Munoz - Dibujos de Ana Luisa Stok. (SPA., Illus.). 122p. (Orig.). 1991. pap. text 12.50 (*0-937985-03-1*) Ediciones Arauco.

Munoz-Smith, Diane, compiled by. The Ancient Schools of Wisdom: A Selection of Teachings from Ramtha. 178p. (Orig.). 1997. pap. 19.95 (*0-9652621-3-8*) Horus Pubng.

— Ramtha - Die Alten Schulen der Weisheit. Orig. Title: The Ancient Schools of Wisdom - A Selection of Teachings from Ramtha. (GER.). 220p. (Orig.). 1997. pap. write for info. (*0-9652621-0-3*) Horus Pubng.

— To Life! A Collection of Prayers from Ramtha. (Illus.). 156p. (Orig.). 1997. pap. 15.95 (*0-9652621-4-6*) Horus Pubng.

Munoz-Smith, Diane, ed. see Ramtha.

Munoz-Timmins, Patricia. Let's Smock It. (Illus.). 64p. 1997. pap. 21.95 (*0-9583873-8-9*, Pub. by Triple T Pubng) Quilters Res.

Munoz, Tisziji. The Beginner's Book Vol. I: The Holy Ground Discourse. 127p. (Orig.). (C). 1981. pap. 15.00 (*0-945174-00-4*) Illum Soc Pubns.

— The Facts of Light, Bk. 1. 25p. (Orig.). (C). 1987. pap. text 10.00 (*0-945174-05-5*) Illum Soc Pubns.

— The Facts of the Process Bk. 1: Free-Master Consciousness. 35p. (Orig.). (C). 1987. pap. text 10.00 (*0-945174-04-7*) Illum Soc Pubns.

— Once Is for Always. (Orig.). 1991. pap. 10.00 (*0-945174-24-1*) Illum Soc Pubns.

— The Song of the Free Self: The Song of Who I Am. 43p. (Orig.). (C). 1981. pap. text 10.00 (*0-945174-03-9*) Illum Soc Pubns.

— Time Mastery: The Beginner's Book, Vol. 5. (Illus.). (Orig.). (C). 1987. pap. 15.00 (*0-945174-02-0*) Illum Soc Pubns.

Munoz, Tizsiji. The Beginners Book Vol. 2: Satsang Talks & Readings. 169p. (Orig.). (C). 1987. pap. text 15.00 (*0-945174-01-2*) Illum Soc Pubns.

Munoz, V. Alberto Ghiraldo: A Chronology. Johnson, W. Scott, tr. (Libertarian & Anarchist Chronology Ser.). 1979. lib. bdg. 59.95 (*0-8490-3033-1*) Gordon Pr.

— Anarchists: A Biographical Encyclopedia. Johnson, Scott, tr. (History of Anarchism Ser.). 1980. lib. bdg. 300.00 (*0-8490-3101-X*) Gordon Pr.

— Anselmo Lorenzo: A Chronology. Johnson, W. Scott, tr. (Libertarian & Anarchist Chronology Ser.). 1979. lib. bdg. 59.95 (*0-8490-3052-8*) Gordon Pr.

— Bakunin: A Chronology. Johnson, W. Scott, tr. (Libertarian & Anarchist Chronology Ser.). 1979. lib. bdg. 59.95 (*0-8490-3025-0*) Gordon Pr.

— E. Armand: A Chronology. Johnson, W. Scott, tr. (Libertarian & Anarchist Chronology Ser.). 1979. lib. bdg. 59.95 (*0-8490-3048-X*) Gordon Pr.

— Eliseo Reclus: A Chronology. Johnson, W. Scott, tr. (Libertarian & Anarchist Chronology Ser.). 1979. lib. bdg. 59.95 (*0-8490-3023-4*) Gordon Pr.

— Federico Urales: A Chronology. (Libertarian & Anarchist Chronology Ser.). 1980. lib. bdg. 59.95 (*0-8490-3089-7*) Gordon Pr.

— Fermin Salvochea: A Chronology. Johnson, W. Scott, tr. (Libertarian & Anarchist Chronology Ser.). 1979. lib. bdg. 59.95 (*0-8490-3039-0*) Gordon Pr.

— Florencio Sanchez: A Chronology. Johnson, W. Scott, tr. (Libertarian & Anarchist Chronology Ser.). 1979. lib. bdg. 59.95 (*0-8490-3041-2*) Gordon Pr.

— Francisco Ferrer: A Chronology. Johnson, W. Scott, tr. (Libertarian & Anarchist Chronology Ser.). 1979. lib. bdg. 59.95 (*0-8490-3044-7*) Gordon Pr.

— Francisco Piy Margall: A Chronology. Johnson, W. Scott, tr. (Libertarian & Anarchist Chronology Ser.). 1979. lib. bdg. 59.95 (*0-8490-3030-7*) Gordon Pr.

— Giovanni Rossi: A Chronology. Johnson, W. Scott, tr. (Libertarian & Anarchist Chronology Ser.). 1979. lib. bdg. 59.95 (*0-8490-3056-0*) Gordon Pr.

— Gustav Landauer: A Chronology. Johnson, W. Scott, tr. (Libertarian & Anarchist Chronology Ser.). 1979. lib. bdg. 59.95 (*0-8490-3029-3*) Gordon Pr.

— Han Ryner: A Chronology. Johnson, W. Scott, tr. (Libertarian & Anarchist Chronology Ser.). 1979. lib. bdg. 59.95 (*0-8490-3024-2*) Gordon Pr.

— Hem Day: A Chronology. Johnson, W. Scott, tr. (Libertarian & Anarchist Chronology Ser.). 1979. lib. bdg. 59.95 (*0-8490-3049-8*) Gordon Pr.

— Henrik Ibsen: A Chronology. Johnson, W. Scott, tr. (Libertarian & Anarchist Chronology Ser.). 1979. lib. bdg. 59.95 (*0-8490-3031-5*) Gordon Pr.

— Johann Most: A Chronology. Johnson, W. Scott, tr. (Libertarian & Anarchist Chronology Ser.). 1979. lib. bdg. 59.95 (*0-8490-3027-7*) Gordon Pr.

— Joseph Ishill: A Chronology. Johnson, W. Scott, tr. (Libertarian & Anarchist Chronology Ser.). 1979. lib. bdg. 59.95 (*0-8490-3035-8*) Gordon Pr.

— Josiah Warren: A Chronology. Johnson, W. Scott, tr. (Libertarian & Anarchist Chronology Ser.). 1979. lib. bdg. 59.95 (*0-8490-3047-1*) Gordon Pr.

— Juan Grave: A Chronology. Johnson, W. Scott, tr. (Libertarian & Anarchist Chronology Ser.). 1979. lib. bdg. 59.95 (*0-8490-3043-9*) Gordon Pr.

— Kropotkin: A Chronology. Johnson, W. Scott, tr. (Libertarian & Anarchist Chronology Ser.). 1979. lib. bdg. 59.95 (*0-8490-3022-6*) Gordon Pr.

— Leo Tolstoy: A Chronology. Johnson, W. Scott, tr. (Libertarian & Anarchist Chronology Ser.). 1979. lib. bdg. 59.95 (*0-8490-3034-X*) Gordon Pr.

— Li Pei Kan & Chinese Anarchism: A Chronology. 1976. 250.00 (*0-87700-242-8*) Revisionist Pr.

— Louis Lecoin: A Chronology. Johnson, W. Scott, tr. (Libertarian & Anarchist Chronology Ser.). 1979. lib. bdg. 59.95 (*0-8490-3051-X*) Gordon Pr.

— Luigi Fabbri: A Chronology. Johnson, W. Scott, tr. (Libertarian & Anarchist Chronology Ser.). 1979. lib. bdg. 59.95 (*0-8490-3040-4*) Gordon Pr.

— Luisa Michel: A Chronology. Johnson, W. Scott, tr. (Libertarian & Anarchist Chronology Ser.). 1979. lib. bdg. 59.95 (*0-8490-3028-5*) Gordon Pr.

— Manuel Gonzalez Prada: A Chronology. Johnson, W. Scott, tr. (Libertarian & Anarchist Chronology Ser.). 1979. lib. bdg. 59.95 (*0-8490-3046-3*) Gordon Pr.

— Maria Lacerda de Moura: A Chronology. Johnson, W. Scott, tr. (Libertarian & Anarchist Chronology Ser.). 1979. lib. bdg. 59.95 (*0-8490-3053-6*) Gordon Pr.

— Max Nettlau Chronology. 1973. 250.00 (*0-87700-179-0*) Revisionist Pr.

— Max Stirner: A Chronology. Johnson, W. Scott, tr. (Libertarian & Anarchist Chronology Ser.). 1979. lib. bdg. 59.95 (*0-8490-3045-5*) Gordon Pr.

— P. J. Proudhon: A Chronology. Johnson, W. Scott, tr. (Libertarian & Anarchist Chronology Ser.). 1979. lib. bdg. 59.95 (*0-8490-3038-2*) Gordon Pr.

— Panait Musoiu: A Chronology. (Libertarian & Anarchist Chronology Ser.). 1980. lib. bdg. 59.95 (*0-8490-3088-9*) Gordon Pr.

— Paul Robin: A Chronology. Johnson, W. Scott, tr. (Libertarian & Anarchist Chronology Ser.). 1979. lib. bdg. 59.95 (*0-8490-3055-2*) Gordon Pr.

— Pedro Vallina: A Chronology. Johnson, W. Scott, tr. (Libertarian & Anarchist Chronology Ser.). 1979. lib. bdg. 59.95 (*0-8490-3057-9*) Gordon Pr.

— Ramon de la Sagra: A Chronology. Johnson, W. Scott, tr. (Libertarian & Anarchist Chronology Ser.). 1979. lib. bdg. 59.95 (*0-8490-3042-0*) Gordon Pr.

— Ricardo Flores Magon: A Chronology. Johnson, W. Scott, tr. (Libertarian & Anarchist Chronology Ser.). 1979. lib. bdg. 59.95 (*0-8490-3050-1*) Gordon Pr.

— Ricardo Mella: A Chronology. Johnson, W. Scott, tr. (Libertarian & Anarchist Chronology Ser.). 1979. lib. bdg. 59.95 (*0-8490-3037-4*) Gordon Pr.

— Robert Owen: A Chronology. Johnson, W. Scott, tr. (Libertarian & Anarchist Chronology Ser.). 1979. lib. bdg. 59.95 (*0-8490-3054-4*) Gordon Pr.

— Rodolfo Gonzalez Pacheco: A Chronology. Johnson, W. Scott, tr. (Libertarian & Anarchist Chronology Ser.). 1979. lib. bdg. 59.95 (*0-8490-3032-3*) Gordon Pr.

— Thoreau: A Chronology. Johnson, W. Scott, tr. (Libertarian & Anarchist Chronology Ser.). 1979. lib. bdg. 59.95 (*0-8490-3021-8*) Gordon Pr.

— Voltairine de Cleyre: A Chronology. Johnson, W. Scott, tr. (Libertarian & Anarchist Chronology Ser.). 1979. lib. bdg. 59.95 (*0-8490-3036-6*) Gordon Pr.

— William Godwin: A Chronology. Johnson, W. Scott, tr. (Libertarian & Anarchist Chronology Ser.). 1979. lib. bdg. 59.95 (*0-8490-3026-9*) Gordon Pr.

Munoz Vasquez, Arturo. Papa Tell Us Another Story.Tr. of Papa Cuentanos Otro Cuento. (ENG & SPA., Illus.). 389p. (Orig.). (C). 1994. pap. 24.95 (*0-927065-14-2*) Marin Chula Vista.

Munoz-Vazquez, Marya & Fernandez-Bauzo, Edwin. El Divorcio en la Sociedad Puertorriquena. LC 88-80390. (Huracan Academia Ser.). (SPA.). 175p. 1988. pap. 7.95 (*0-940238-96-9*) Ediciones Huracan.

Munoz, Victoria I. Where "Something Catches" Work, Love, & Identity in Youth. LC 94-44800. (SUNY Series, Identities in the Classroom). 282p. (C). 1995. text 49.50 (*0-7914-2685-8*); pap. text 16.95 (*0-7914-2686-6*) State U NY Pr.

Munoz, William. Waiting Alligators. LC 98-27339. (Pull Ahead Bks.). 32p. (J). (gr. k-2). 1998. pap. 6.95 (*0-8225-3621-8*, Lerner Publctns) Lerner Pub.

— Waiting Alligators. LC 98-27339. (Pull Ahead Bks.). 32p. (J). (gr. k-2). 1999. 21.27 (*0-8225-3615-3*, Lerner Publctns) Lerner Pub.

Munoz, William, jt. illus. see Patent, Dorothy Hinshaw.

Munqidh, Usamah Ibn, see Ibn Munqidh, Usamah.

Munro. The Collected Short Stories of Saki. (Classics Library). pap. 3.95 (*1-85326-071-1*, 0711WW, Pub. by Wrdsworth Edits) NTC Contemp Pub Co.

Munro. Cotton. 1987. pap. text. write for info. (*0-582-46346-7*, Pub. by Addison-Wesley) Longman.

— MacLeod's Clinical Examination. 9th ed. 1995. pap. text 31.50 (*0-443-04856-8*, W B Saunders Co) Harcrt Hlth Sci Grp.

Munro & Scott. Reproductive Seasonality in Teleosts: Environmental Influence. 264p. 1990. lib. bdg. 219.00 (*0-8493-6875-8*, QL) CRC Pr.

Munro, jt. auth. see Paciorek.

Munro, Ailie, ed. The Democratic Muse: Folk Music Revival in Scotland. 256p. 1990. pap. 48.00 (*1-898218-10-2*) St Mut.

Munro, Alan. Embassy at War. 1996. 32.95 (*1-57488-109-4*) Brasseys.

— An Embassy at War: Politics & Diplomacy Behind the Gulf War. 450p. 1996. 32.95 (*1-85753-148-5*, Pub. by Brasseys) Brasseys.

***Munro, Alan J., et al, eds.** Social Navigation in Information Space. LC 99-25431. xii, 284p. 1999. pap. 89.95 (*1-85233-090-2*, Pub. by Spr-Verlag) Spr-Verlag.

Munro, Alastair, ed. Key Terms in Oncology. (Greenwich Medical Media Ser.). (Illus.). 356p. 1999. pap. text 45.00 (*1-900151-11-1*) OUP.

Munro, Alice. The Beggar Maid: Stories of Flo & Rose. 1991. pap. 12.00 (*0-679-73271-3*) McKay.

— Dance of the Happy Shades & Other Stories. LC 98-5267. 1998. pap. 12.00 (*0-679-78151-X*) Vin Bks.

— Friend of My Youth: Stories. LC 90-50495. 288p. 1991. pap. 12.00 (*0-679-72957-7*) Random.

***Munro, Alice.** The Love of a Good Woman: Stories. LC 98-36721. 352p. 1999. pap. 13.00 (*0-375-70363-2*) Knopf.

Munro, Alice. The Moons of Jupiter: Stories. 233p. 1991. pap. 12.00 (*0-679-73270-5*) Villard Books.

— Open Secrets: Stories. 1995. pap. 13.00 (*0-679-75562-4*) Vin Bks.

***Munro, Alice.** The Progress of Love. 2000. pap. 13.00 (*0-375-72470-2*) Knopf.

Munro, Alice. The Progress of Love. 320p. 1987. pap. 6.95 (*0-14-009879-8*, Penguin Bks) Viking Penguin.

— Selected Stories. LC 96-4145. 544p. 1996. 30.00 (*0-679-44627-3*) Knopf.

— Selected Stories. 1997. pap. 16.00 (*0-679-76674-X*) Random.

***Munro, Alice.** Something I've Been Meaning to Tell You. 2000. pap. write for info. (*0-375-70748-4*) Vin Bks.

Munro, Alistair. Delusional Disorder: Paranoia & Related Illnesses. LC 98-17210. (Illus.). 280p. (C). 1999. text 69.95 (*0-521-58180-X*) Cambridge U Pr.

Munro, Angela, jt. auth. see Graham, Elizabeth.

Munro, Barbara. Statistical Methods for Health Care Research. 3rd ed. LC 96-46123. 464p. 1997. pap. text 38.95 (*0-397-55365-X*) Lppncott W & W.

Munro, Barbara Hazard. Statistical Methods for Health Care Research. 4th ed. 496p. pap. text 39.95 (*0-7817-2175-X*) Lppncott W & W.

Munro, Barry G. Smart Salespeople Sometimes Wear Plaid: Dare to Be Extraordinary in a Mediocre World. LC 93-34369. 304p. 1994. pap. 12.95 (*1-55958-422-X*) Prima Pub.

Munro, Bertha. The Best of Bertha Munro. Wolf, Earl C., ed. 230p. 1986. kivar 11.99 (*0-8341-1140-3*) Beacon Hill.

Munro, Bill. Carbodies. (Illus.). 192p. 1998. 35.95 (*1-86126-127-6*, Pub. by Crolwood) Motorbooks Intl.

***Munro, Bob.** Jane's Gem Combat Aircraft. 1999. pap. 10.00 (*0-00-472279-5*, HarpRes) HarpInfo.

Munro, Charles, ed. see Whiddon, Debra.

Munro, Craig. Inky Stephensen: Wild Man of Letters. (Orig.). 1992. pap. 29.95 (*0-7022-2389-1*, Pub. by Univ Queensland Pr) Intl Spec Bk.

Munro, Craig, ed. The Writer's Press: UQP's First Fifty Years. LC 99-187647. 1998. pap. 9.95 (*0-7022-3005-7*, Pub. by New South Wales Univ Pr) Intl Spec Bk.

Munro, Craig, ed. see Stephensen, P. R.

Munro, D., jt. auth. see Bradley, Raymond S.

Munro, D. G. The Five Republics of Central America. 1976. lib. bdg. 59.95 (*0-8490-1842-0*) Gordon Pr.

Munro, D. R., ed. Boxnet: Equipment Interface Guidelines, Version 2.0. 2nd rev. ed. 322p. 1993. ring bd. 99.00 (*0-89852-323-0*, 0101R183) TAPPI.

Munro, Dana C. A Syllabus of Medieval History, Three Hundred Ninety-Five to Thirteen Hundred. 1980. lib. bdg. 49.95 (*0-8490-3193-1*) Gordon Pr.

Munro, Dana G. Intervention & Dollar Diplomacy in the Caribbean, 1900-1921. LC 80-14089. (Illus.). 553p. 1980. reprint ed. lib. bdg. 85.00 (*0-313-22510-9*, MUIN, Greenwood Pr) Greenwood.

— A Student in Central America, 1914-1916. LC 83-60479. (Publications: No. 51). 75p. 1983. pap. 15.00 (*0-939238-77-2*) Tulane MARI.

— The United States & the Caribbean Republics, 1921-1933. LC 73-16767. 405p. 1974. reprint ed. pap. 125.60 (*0-7837-9397-9*, 206014200004) Bks Demand.

Munro, David, ed. The Oxford Dictionary of the World. LC 95-22546. (Illus.). 698p. 1996. 39.95 (*0-19-866184-3*) OUP.

— The Oxford Dictionary of the World. (Illus.). 704p. 1997. reprint ed. pap. 16.95 (*0-19-860060-7*) OUP.

— World Record of Major Conflict Areas. 600p. 1990. 85.00 (*1-55862-066-4*) St James Pr.

Munro, David, jt. auth. see Jacobs, Peter.

Munro, David, jt. auth. see Wood, Jenny.

Munro, Derek B. & Small, Ernest. Vegetables of Canada. (Illus.). 500p. 1997. 87.50 (*0-660-16708-5*, Pub. by NRC Res Pr) Accents Pubns.

Munro, Donald, et al. Motivation & Culture. LC 96-51882. 256p. (C). 1997. pap. 23.99 (*0-415-91510-4*) Routledge.

— Motivation & Culture. LC 96-51882. 256p. (C). 1997. 75.00 (*0-415-91509-0*) Routledge.

Munro, Donald, jt. ed. see Pieterse, Cosmo.

Munro, Donald J. The Concept of Man in Early China. LC 68-21288. xiv, 224p. 1969. 37.50 (*0-8047-0682-4*) Stanford U Pr.

— The Concept of Man in Early China. LC 68-21288. 272p. 1969. reprint ed. pap. 30.00 (*0-608-04221-8*, 206496500011) Bks Demand.

— Images of Human Nature: A Sung Portrait. LC 88-12661. 334p. 1988. reprint ed. pap. 103.60 (*0-608-07130-7*, 206735600009) Bks Demand.

— The Imperial Style of Inquiry in Twentieth-Century China: The Emergence of New Approaches. LC 96-256. (Michigan Monographs in Chinese Studies: No. 72). 160p. 1996. 50.00 (*0-89264-120-7*) Ctr Chinese Studies.

Munro, Donald J., ed. Individualism & Holism: Studies in Confucian & Taoist Values. LC 84-27417. (Michigan Monographs in Chinese Studies: No. 52). 399p. 1985. pap. text 25.00 (*0-89264-058-8*) Ctr Chinese Studies.

Munro, Douglas P., ed. The Emergency Management Assistance Compact Guidebook & Standard Operating Procedures, 1997. 112p. (C). 1998. pap. text 25.00 (*0-7881-3074-9*) DIANE Pub.

Munro, Eileen. Understanding Social Work: An Empirical Approach. LC 97-31598. 208p. 1998. 70.00 (*0-485-11521-2*, Pub. by Athlone Pr); pap. 25.00 (*0-485-12134-4*, Pub. by Athlone Pr) Humanities.

***Munro, Eleanor.** Originals: American Women Artists. (Illus.). 608p. 2000. pap. text 22.50 (*0-306-80955-9*, Pub. by Da Capo) HarpC.

Munro, Eleanor. Originals: American Women Artists. 1982. pap. 19.00 (*0-671-42812-8*, Touchstone) S&S Trade Pap.

***Munro, Eleanor.** Readings for Remembrance: A Collection for Funerals & Memorial Services. LC 99-39113. 288p. 2000. pap. 13.95 (*0-14-028064-2*, Penguin Bks) Viking Penguin.

Munro, Eleanor, intro. Wedding Readings: Centuries of Writing & Rituals on Love & Marriage. 262p. 1996. pap. 12.95 (*0-14-008879-2*, Viking) Viking Penguin.

Munro, Eleanor, jt. auth. see Merriam, Dena.

***Munro, Eric, ed.** Charged Particle Optics IV. 1999. pap. text 72.00 (*0-8194-3263-6*) SPIE.

Munro, Eric, ed. Charged-Particle Optics II, Vol. 2858. 184p. 1996. 56.00 (*0-8194-2246-0*) SPIE.

— Charged Particle Optics III, Vol. 3155. LC 98-122021. 274p. 1997. 69.00 (*0-8194-2577-X*) SPIE.

Munro-Faure, Lesley, et al. Quality Improvement: Teamwork Solutions from the U. K. & U. S. A. LC 99-178262. 224p. 1998. pap. 27.95 (*0-304-70311-7*) Continuum.

Munro-Faure, Leslie, jt. auth. see Munro-Faure, Malcom.

Munro-Faure, Malcom & Munro-Faure, Leslie. The Success Culture: How to Build an Organization with Vision & Purpose. (Illus.). 256p. 1996. 25.00 (*0-273-62199-8*) F T P-H.

Munro-Foley, Louise. Vampire Cat #01, My Substitute Tracher's Gone Batty! (Vampire Cat Ser.). (J). 1996. 9.70 (*0-606-12032-7*, Pub. by Turtleback) Demco.

— Vampire Cat #02, The Bird Brained Fiasco. (Vampire Cat Ser.). (J). 1996. 9.70 (*0-606-12033-5*, Pub. by Turtleback) Demco.

— Vampire Cat #03. the Phoney-Baloney Professor. (Vampire Cat Ser.). (J). 1996. 9.70 (*0-606-12035-1*, Pub. by Turtleback) Demco.

— Vampire Cat #04, the Catnip Cat-Astrophy. (J). 1997. 9.60 (*0-606-12034-3*, Pub. by Turtleback) Demco.

Munro, George E., jt. ed. see Griffiths, David.

Munro, H. H. "Saki". Sredni Vashtar & Other Stories. unabridged ed. (Thrift Editions Ser.). 96p. (Orig.). 1995. pap. 1.00 (*0-486-28521-9*) Dover.

Munro, H. N. & Danford, D. B. Nutrition, Aging & the Elderly Vol. 6. LC 88-39816. (Human Nutrition Ser.). (Illus.). 414p. 1989. 110.00 (*0-306-43047-9*, Kluwer Plenum) Kluwer Academic.

Munro, Hamish & Schlierf, Gunter, eds. Nutrition of the Elderly. LC 91-40901. (Nestle Nutrition Workshop Ser.: No. 29). (Illus.). 247p. 1992. reprint ed. pap. 76.60 (*0-608-05806-8*, 205977100007) Bks Demand.

Munro-Hay, S. & Jensen, B. Juel. Axumite Coinage. 1995. lib. bdg. 80.00 (*0-907605-63-X*) S J Durst.

Munro-Hay, Stuart. Historical Ethiopia: A Book of Sources & a Guide to Historical Sites. 250p. 1997. 79.95 (*1-56902-069-8*); pap. 24.95 (*1-56902-070-1*) Red Sea Pr.

Munro-Hay, Stuart C. An African Civilization: The Aksumite Kingdom of Northern Ethiopia. 256p. 1991. 75.00 (*0-7486-0106-6*, Pub. by Edinburgh U Pr) Col U Pr.

— Aksum: An African Civilization of Late Antiquity. 288p. 1992. pap. 34.00 (*0-7486-0209-7*, Pub. by Edinburgh U Pr) Col U Pr.

— The Coinage of Aksum. 168p. 1994. 175.00 (*0-9511308-0-3*, Pub. by R C Senior) St Mut.

— Excavations at Aksum: An Account of Research at the Ancient Ethiopian Capital. (Illus.). 400p. 1989. 54.00 (*1-872566-06-5*, Pub. by Brit Inst Estrn Africa) David Brown.

Munro, Hector H., see Saki, pseud.

Munro, Hector H., jt. auth. see Chesny, George T.

Munro, Howard, ed. Greed Is Not Good! Teaching Ethics to Professionals. 100p. 1996. pap. 29.00 (*1-86287-225-2*, Pub. by Federation Pr) Gaunt.

Munro, I. C., et al, eds. Toxicological Risk Assessment: Biological & Statistical Criteria, 2 vols., Vol. II. LC 84-12679. 276p. 1985. 156.00 (*0-8493-5977-5*, RA1199, CRC Reprint) Franklin.

Munro, I. C. & Greaves, N., eds. Synchrotron Radiation Sources & Their Applications: Proceedings of the 30th Scottish Universities' Summer School in Physics, Aberdeen, 1985. (Scottish Universities Summer School in Physics, a NATO Advanced Study Institute Ser.: No. 30). (Illus.). 520p. 1989. 189.00 (*0-905945-13-1*) IOP Pub.

Munro, I. C., jt. auth. see Borodin, Allan.

Munro, I. C., ed. see Krewski, D. & Clayson, D. B.

Munro, Ian R., jt. auth. see Farkas, Leslie G.

Munro, Ion S. Through Fascism to World Power: A History of the Revolution in Italy. 1976. lib. bdg. 50.00 (*0-8490-2748-9*) Gordon Pr.

— Through Fascism to World Power: A History of the Revolution in Italy. LC 73-164618. (Select Bibliographies Reprint Ser.). 1977. reprint ed. 36.95 (*0-8369-5912-4*) Ayer.

Munro, Irmtraut. Untersuchengen zu den Totenbuch-Papyri der 18 Dyn. (GER.). 300p. 1988. lib. bdg. 125.00 (*0-7103-0288-6*) Routledge.

Munro, J. J., ed. see Broke, Arthur.

Munro, J. L., ed. Caribbean Coral Reef Fishery Resources. 2nd ed. (ICLARM Studies & Reviews: No. 7). (Illus.). 276p. 1983. text 37.00 (*971-10-2200-1*, Pub. by ICLARM); pap. text 33.00 (*971-10-2201-X*, Pub. by ICLARM) Intl Spec Bk.

Munro, J. L., et al, eds. Biology, Fisheries, & Culture of Tropical Groupers & Snappers. LC 98-109899. (ICLARM Conference Proceedings Ser.: No. 48). 499p. 1996. pap. 84.95 (*971-8709-62-2*, Pub. by ICLARM) Intl Spec Bk.

Munro, J. L. & Balgos, M. C., eds. Artificial Reefs in the Philippines. (ICLARM Conference Proceedings Ser.: No. 49). 56p. 1995. write for info. (*971-8709-63-0*, Pub. by ICLARM) Intl Spec Bk.

Munro, J. L. & Munro, P. E., eds. The Management of Coral Reef Resource Systems. LC 96-946704. (ICLARM Conference Proceedings Ser.: No. 44). 124p. 1994. per. write for info. (*971-8709-55-X*, Pub. by ICLARM) Intl Spec Bk.

Munro, J. L. & Nash, W. J., eds. A Bibliography of the Giant Clams. (Bibliographies Ser.: No. 5). 26p. 1986. pap. 4.50 (*971-10-2222-2*, Pub. by ICLARM) Intl Spec Bk.

Munro, James. Homeland. large type ed. (General Fiction Ser.). 624p. 1992. 27.99 (*0-7089-8641-2*) Ulverscroft.

Munro, Jane. British Landscape Watercolors: 1750-1850. (Illus.). 160p. 1994. pap. 28.00 (*1-56131-063-8*, NAB) I R Dee.

— Grief Notes & Animal Dreams. LC 96-106107. 80p. 1995. pap. 11.95 (*0-919626-82-3*, Pub. by Brick Bks) Genl Dist Srvs.

Munro, Jane & Fitzwilliam Museum Staff. Shakespeare & the Eighteenth Century LC 98-145244. 23p. 1997. write for info. (*0-904454-45-2*) Fitzwilliam Museum Enterprises Ltd.

Munro, Jane, ed. see Donald, Mary Ellen.

Munro, Jane S. Presence at a Distance: The Educator-Learner Relationship in Distance Education. (Research Monograph: No. 16). 1998. pap. text. write for info. (*1-877780-21-9*) ACSDE.

Munro, Jessie. The Story of Suzanne Aubert. (Illus.). 472p. 1997. pap. 35.95 (*1-86940-155-7*, Pub. by Auckland Univ) Paul & Co Pubs.

Munro, Jill M. Spikenard & Saffron: The Imagery of the Song of Songs. (JSOT Supplement Ser.: No. 203). 166p. 1995. 52.50 (*1-85075-562-0*, Pub. by Sheffield Acad) CUP Services.

***Munro, John.** Assessing & Teaching Phonological Knowledge. 152p. 1998. 49.95 (*0-86431-259-8*, Pub. by Aust Council Educ Res) Stylus Pub VA.

Munro, John, ed. Caton's History of Jason. (EETS, ES Ser.: No. 111). 1972. reprint ed. 40.00 (*0-527-00314-X*) Periodicals Srv.

Munro, John A., Associates, Inc. Staff, ed. see Munro, Robert A.

Munro, John F. & Ford, Michael J., eds. Introduction to Clinical Examination. 6th ed. LC 92-48188. 144p. 1995. pap. text 16.95 (*0-443-04787-1*) Church.

Munro, John H. Bullion Flows & Monetary Policies in England & the Low Countries, 1350-1500. (Collected Studies: No. CS355). 336p. 1992. text 115.95 (*0-86078-312-X*, Pub. by Variorum) Ashgate Pub Co.

— Textiles, Towns & Trades: Essays in the Economic History of Late-Medieval England & the Low Countries. LC 94-4405. (Collected Studies: No. 442). 350p. 1994. 109.95 (*0-86078-404-5*, Pub. by Variorum) Ashgate Pub Co.

Munro, John J., jt. auth. see Furnivall, Frederick J.

Munro, John M. Arthur Symons. Bowman, Sylvia E., ed. LC 68-17234. (Twayne's English Authors Ser.). 174p. (C). 1969. lib. bdg. 20.95 (*0-8290-1721-6*) Irvington.

— James Elroy Flecker. LC 75-46531. (Twayne's English Authors Ser.). 143p. (C). 1976. lib. bdg. 20.95 (*0-8057-6656-1*) Irvington.

— A Mutual Concern: The Story of the American University of Beirut. LC 77-22003. 212p. 1977. 25.00 (*0-88206-014-7*) Caravan Bks.

— Nairn Way: Desert Bus to Baghdad. LC 80-11875. 112p. 1980. 35.00 (*0-88206-035-X*) Caravan Bks.

— The Royal Aquarium: Failure of a Victorian Compromise. 1971. 10.00 (*0-8156-6033-2*, Pub. by Am U Beirut) Syracuse U Pr.

Munro, John M., ed. Decadent Poetry of the Eighteen Nineties. (Illus.). 1967. 11.95 (*0-8156-6018-9*, Pub. by Am U Beirut) Syracuse U Pr.

— Selected Poems of Theo. Marzials. 1973. 10.00 (*0-8156-6040-5*, Pub. by Am U Beirut) Syracuse U Pr.

Munro, John M., jt. ed. see Beckson, Karl.

Munro, Joyce H., jt. auth. see Paciorek, Karen M.

Munro, Joyce H., jt. ed. see Paciorek, Karen M.

Munro, June G. Movement Education: A Program for Young Children Ages 2-7. 2nd ed. (Illus.). 150p. (C). 1995. pap. text 13.95 (*0-685-63072-2*) M D E A.

Munro, Kate & Elder-Woodward, Jim. Independent Living. (Skills for Caring Ser.). (Illus.). 40p. (Orig.). 1992. pap. text 9.95 (*0-443-04533-X*) Church.

Munro, Ken. Amish Justice. 120p. 1996. write for info. (*0-614-13922-8*) Prof Pr NC.

— Creep Frog. (Illus.). 141p. (J). (gr. 3-9). 1998. pap. 5.95 (*1-883294-66-5*) Masthof Pr.

— Doom Buggy. (Illus.). 149p. (J). (gr. 3-9). 1997. pap. 5.95 (*1-883294-48-7*) Masthof Pr.

— Fright Train. (Illus.). 123p. (J). (gr. 3-9). 1997. pap. 5.95 (*1-883294-51-7*) Masthof Pr.

Munro, Kenneth J. The Political Career of Sir Adolphe Chapleau, Premier of Quebec, 1879-1882. LC 92-4338. 244p. 1992. lib. bdg. 89.95 (*0-7734-9494-4*) E Mellen.

Munro-Kua, Anne. Authoritarian Populism in Malaysia. LC 96-15990. 256p. 1997. text 59.95 (*0-312-15826-2*) St Martin.

— Women, Work & Trade Unions. LC 99-25910. (Employment & Work Relations in Context Ser.). 226p. 1999. 75.00 (*0-7201-2328-3*) Continuum.

Munro, Louise. Concepts in Microbiology, a Laboratory Manual. (Illus.). 125p. (Orig.). (C). 1996. lab manual ed. 23.95 (*0-89892-146-5*) Contemp Pub Co of Raleigh.

***Munro, Lyle.** Compassionate Beasts: The Quest for Animal Rights. LC 99-88488. 2000. write for info. (*0-275-96883-9*, Praeger Pubs) Greenwood.

Munro, Mackenzie. Wildflower. 183p. (C). 1990. 90.00 (*0-86439-149-8*, Pub. by Boolarong Pubns) St Mut.

Munro, Malcolm G., jt. auth. see Gomel, Victor.

***Munro, Margaret & Reczuch, Karen.** The Story of Life on Earth. (Illus.). 64p. (ps-3). 2000. 19.95 (*0-88899-401-X*) Grndwd Bks.

Munro, Mary. The Bargain. large type ed. 1991. pap. 16.99 (*0-7089-6982-8*) Ulverscroft.

— A Dream Came True. large type ed. 336p. 1988. 27.99 (*0-7089-1839-5*) Ulverscroft.

— From March to September. large type ed. 1990. 27.99 (*0-7089-2254-6*) Ulverscroft.

— The Honey Pot. large type ed. 368p. 1987. 27.99 (*0-7089-1645-7*) Ulverscroft.

— Second Love. large type ed. 352p. 1986. 27.99 (*0-7089-1464-0*) Ulverscroft.

— Shadow Across the Desert. large type ed. 1989. 27.99 (*0-7089-2094-2*) Ulverscroft.

— The Singing House. large type ed. 336p. 1985. 27.99 (*0-7089-1340-7*) Ulverscroft.

— The Wheel of Life. large type ed. 330p. 1989. 27.99 (*0-7089-1964-2*) Ulverscroft.

— Whispering Sands. large type ed. 400p. 1988. 27.99 (*0-7089-1869-7*) Ulverscroft.

***Munro, Matt.** Jeep. (Illus.). 200p. 2000. 34.95 (*1-86126-319-8*, 130058AE, Pub. by Crolwood) Motorbooks Intl.

Munro, N., ed. Modern Approaches to Control System Design. LC 80-479861. (IEE Control Engineering Ser.: Vol. 9). (Illus.). 431p. reprint ed. pap. 133.70 (*0-608-17791-1*, 203225600079) Bks Demand.

— Symbolic Methods in Control System Analysis & Design. LC 99-169813. (Control Engineering Ser.: No. 56). 420p. 1999. 95.00 (*0-85296-943-0*, CE056) INSPEC Inc.

Munro, Neil. Erchie & Jimmy Swan. 552p. pap. 17.95 (*1-874744-05-X*, Pub. by Birlinn Ltd) Dufour.

— John Splendid: The Tale of a Poor Gentleman & the Little Wars of Lorn. LC 79-8180. reprint ed. 44.50 (*0-404-62072-8*) AMS Pr.

— Para Handy. (Illus.). 432p. pap. 15.95 (*1-874744-02-5*, Pub. by Birlinn Ltd) Dufour.

— STATS Canadian Players Encyclopedia: The Complete Statistical Record of the Canadians Who... 252p. (Orig.). 1996. pap. 17.95 (*1-884064-29-9*) STATS.

Munro, Neil G. Ainu: Creed & Cult. (Kegan Paul Japan Library: Vol. 4). (Illus.). 200p. 1996. 110.00 (*0-7103-0520-6*, Pub. by Kegan Paul Intl) Col U Pr.

Munro, P. E., ed. Genetic Aspects of Conservation & Cultivation of Giant Clams. (ICLARM Conference Proceedings Ser.: No. 39). 47p. 1993. write for info. (*971-8709-36-3*, Pub. by ICLARM) Intl Spec Bk.

Munro, P. E., jt. ed. see Munro, J. L.

Munro, Paciorek. Early Childhood Education. 15th ed. 1994. 12.74 (*1-56134-270-X*) McGraw.

***Munro, Pamela & Lopez, Felipe H.** Di'csyonaary X Tee'n Daii"zh Sah Sann Lu"uc: San Lucas Quiavini Zapotec Dictionary. LC 99-44147. 1999. pap. 35.00 (*0-89551-095-2*) UCLA Chicano Studies.

Munro, Pamela & Willmond, Catherine. Chickasaw: An Analytical Dictionary. LC 94-12872. 608p. 1995. pap. 21.95 (*0-8061-2687-6*) U of Okla Pr.

Munro, Pamela, jt. auth. see Hinton, Leanne.

Munro, Pamela, jt. ed. see Haiman, John.

Munro, Petra. Subject to Fiction: Women Teacher Life History Narratives & Cultural Politics. LC 97-43963. (Feminist Educational Thinking Ser.). 153p. 1998. 85.00 (*0-335-20079-6*); pap. 28.95 (*0-335-20078-8*) OpUniv Pr.

Munro, R. G. Gear Transmission Error. (Technical Papers: Vol. P239.10). (Illus.). 10p. 1967. pap. text 30.00 (*1-55589-306-6*) AGMA.

Munro, Robert, et al. Environmental Protection & Sustainable Development: Legal Principles & Recommendations. LC 87-12232. 1987. lib. bdg. 88.00 (*0-86010-910-0*) Kluwer Academic.

Munro, Robert A. Real Estate Periodicals Index, 1981, Vol. 1. Munro, John A., Associates, Inc. Staff et al, eds. 118p. (Orig.). 1982. pap. text 60.00 (*0-911553-00-2*) Munro Assocs.

— Real Estate Periodicals Index, 1982, Vol. 2. Munro, John A., Associates, Inc. Staff, ed. 135p. (Orig.). 1983. pap. 60.00 (*0-911553-01-0*) Munro Assocs.

Munro, Robert J., jt. auth. see Baldwin, Fletcher N., Jr.

Munro, Robert J., jt. auth. see Taylor, Betty W.

Munro, Roberta, ed. see Hayes, Doven.

Munro, Robin, jt. auth. see Black, George.

Munro, Roderick H. & Young, Lowell S. International Insurance. LC 95-77154. (Illus.). 60p. (C). 1995. pap. text 8.00 (*0-89463-073-3*) Am Inst FCPCU.

Munro, Rolland & Mouritsen, Jan, eds. Accountability: Power, Ethos & the Technologies & Managing. 256p. 1996. mass mkt. 19.99 (*0-412-62560-1*) Chapman & Hall.

Munro, Rolland, jt. auth. see Hetherington, Kevin.

Munro, Rona. Maiden Stone. 96p. 1996. pap. text 14.95 (*1-85459-243-2*, Pub. by N Hern Bks) Theatre Comm.

— Your Turn to Clean the Stair & Fugue. LC 96-134815. 96p. 1996. pap. text 14.95 (*1-85459-248-3*, Pub. by N Hern Bks) Theatre Comm.

Munro, Ross H., jt. auth. see Bernstein, Richard.

Munro, Roxie. Christmastime in New York City. LC 94-16922. (Picture Puffin Ser.). (J). 1994. 11.19 (*0-606-06280-7*, Pub. by Turtleback) Demco.

— Inside-Outside Book of Washington, D. C. (Picture Puffin Ser.). (Illus.). (J). 1993. 10.19 (*0-606-05377-8*, Pub. by Turtleback) Demco.

Munro, Roxie. The Great American Landmarks Adventure. LC 92-31806. (J). 1992. 4.25 (*0-16-038003-0*, 024-005-01105-6) USGPO.

— The Inside-Outside Book of Libraries. LC 96-12111. 40p. (J). 1996. 15.99 (*0-525-45608-2*, Dutton Child) Peng Put Young Read.

Munro, S. Ethiopia. LC 96-192570. (World Bibliographical Ser.). 262p. 1995. lib. bdg. 69.00 (*1-85109-111-4*) ABC-CLIO.

Munro, Sandra H., jt. auth. see Shelley, Mary V.

Munro, Sarah, ed. see Arnold, Emma S.

Munro, Stanley R., ed. from CHI. Genesis of a Revolution: An Anthology of Modern Chinese Short Stories. (Writing in Asia Ser.). 202p. (C). 1979. pap. 7.00 (*0-435-00206-6*, 00206) Heinemann.

Munro, Susan. Music Therapy in Palliative Hospice Care. 112p. (Orig.). (C). 1984. pap. 12.95 (*0-918812-37-2*) MMB Music.

Munro, Vera Gauley. The September Years. (Illus.). 170p. pap. (*0-9695180-6-4*) Shloreline.

Munro, W. H. The History of Bristol: The Story of the New Hope Lands from the Visit of the Northmen to the Present Time. (Illus.). 396p. 1989. reprint ed. lib. bdg. 44.00 (*0-8328-0579-3*) Higginson Bk Co.

Munro, Wilfred H. History of Bristol, R. I. The Story of the Mount Hope Lands. (Illus.). 396p. 1998. reprint ed. pap. 29.00 (*0-7884-0827-5*, M856) Heritage Bk.

Munro, Wilfred H., ed. see Prescott, William H.

Munro, William A. The Moral Economy of the State: Conservation, Community Development & State-Making in Zimbabwe. LC 97-46465. (Monographs in International Studies, Africa: Vol. 68). xxxix, 461p. (C). 1998. pap. text 26.00 (*0-89680-202-7*) Ohio U Pr.

Munro, William B. Crusaders of New France: A Chronicle of the Fleur-de-Lis in the Wilderness. (BCL1 - History - Canada Ser.). 237p. 1991. reprint ed. text 79.00 (*0-7812-6352-2*) Rprt Serv.

— The Invisible Government & Personality in Politics, 2 vols. LC 73-19162. (Politics & People Ser.). 308p. 1974. reprint ed. 23.95 (*0-405-05884-5*) Ayer.

— Makers of the Unwritten Constitution: The Fred Morgan Kirby Lectures Delivered at Lafayette College, 1929. (Fred Morgan Kirby Lectures, Lafayette College, 1929 Ser.). 156p. 1982. reprint ed. 35.00 (*0-8377-0842-7*, Rothman) W S Hein.

Munro, William B., ed. Documents Relating to the Seigniorial Tenure in Canada, 1598-1854, Vol. 3. LC 68-28598. 380p. 1969. reprint ed. lib. bdg. 75.00 (*0-8371-5042-6*, MUDS, Greenwood Pr) Greenwood.

Munro, Winsome. Jesus, Born of a Slave: The Social & Economic Origins of Jesus' Message. LC 97-51518. (Studies in the Bible & Early Christianity: Vol. 37). 712p. 1998. text 139.95 (*0-7734-2440-7*) E Mellen.

Munroe. Maximizing Your Potential. 196p. 1996. 10.99 (*1-56043-182-2*) Destiny Image.

— Seasons of Change. 1997. pap. 9.99 (*1-56229-114-9*) Pneuma Life Pub.

Munroe, Alexandra. Japanese Art after 1945: Scream Against the Sky. LC 94-4557. (Illus.). 416p. 1994. 65.00 (*0-8109-3512-0*, Pub. by Abrams) Time Warner.

— Japanese Art after 1945: Scream Against the Sky. (Illus.). 416p. 1996. pap. 29.95 (*0-8109-2593-1*, Pub. by Abrams) Time Warner.

— Yayoi Kusama: The 1950s & 1960s Paintings, Sculpture, Works on Paper. (Illus.). 40p. (Orig.). 1996. pap. 22.00 (*0-9608210-3-1*) Paula Cooper Gallery.

***Munroe, Alexandra, et al.** Y E S Yoko Ono. (Illus.). 352p. 2000. 60.00 (*0-8109-4587-8*, Pub. by Abrams) Time Warner.

Munroe, Alexandra, jt. auth. see Ulak, James T.

Munroe, Andrew A. Caribbean Stories: Supernatural Tales of Guyana. 145p. (Orig.). 1994. pap. 9.95 (*0-9643010-0-8*) Golden Grove.

— The Obeah Woman May: A Caribbean Novel of Mystery & Magic. 181p. 1998. pap. 12.95 (*0-9643010-1-6*) Golden Grove.

Munroe-Blum, Heather, jt. auth. see Marziali, Elsa.

Munroe, Enid. An Artist in the Garden: A Guide to Creating Small & Natural Gardens. LC 93-30053. 1995. write for info. (*0-8050-2718-1*) H Holt & Co.

Munroe, Eugene. The Moths of America North of Mexico: Fascicle 13.1A-Pyraloidea - Scopariinae, Nymphulinae. Dominick et al, eds. LC 78-149292. (Illus.). 134p. (Orig.). (C). 1972. pap. text 22.00 (*0-900848-53-7*) Wedge Entomological.

— The Moths of America North of Mexico: Fascicle 13.1B-Pyraloidea, Pyralidae: Odontiinae, Glaphyriinae. LC 78-149292. (Illus.). 250p. (Orig.). (C). 1972. pap. text 22.00 (*0-900848-54-5*) Wedge Entomological.

— The Moths of America North of Mexico: Fascicle 13.1C-Pyraloidea, Pyralidae: Evergestinae. LC 78-149292. (Illus.). 304p. (Orig.). (C). 1974. pap. text 44.00 (*0-900848-63-4*) Wedge Entomological.

— The Moths of America North of Mexico: Fascicle 13.2A-Pyraloidea, Pyralidae: Pyraustinae, Pyraustini (Part) LC 78-149292. (Illus.). viii, 78p. (C). 1976. pap. text 38.00 (*0-900848-79-0*) Wedge Entomological.

— The Moths of America North of Mexico: Fascicle 13.2B-Pyraloidea, Pyralidae: Pyraustinae, Pyraustini (Conclusion) LC 78-149292. (Illus.). xviii, 150p. (C). 1976. pap. text 38.00 (*0-900848-96-0*) Wedge Entomological.

Munroe, J. P. Munro: A Sketch of the Munro Clan, Also of William Munro Who, Deported from Scotland, Settled in Lexington, Mass., & Some of His Posterity. 80p. 1992. reprint ed. pap. 16.00 (*0-8328-2693-6*); reprint ed. lib. bdg. 26.00 (*0-8328-2692-8*) Higginson Bk Co.

Munroe, Jeff. Real Friends: Finding Them, Keeping Them. (Life Wise Ser.). 32p. (J). 1997. pap., teacher ed. 7.95 (*1-56212-249-5*, 1210-4018) CRC Pubns.

— Six Unsolved Mysteries: Leader Guide. 58p. (YA). 1997. pap. 8.95 (*1-56212-266-5*, 1210-3075) CRC Pubns.

— Yes, No, Maybe So? Dealing with Doubt. (Life Wise Ser.). 35p. 1996. pap., teacher ed. 7.95 (*1-56212-163-4*, 1210-4012) CRC Pubns.

***Munroe, Jim.** Flyboy Action Figure Comes with Gasmask. LC 99-95357. 256p. (J). 1999. pap. 12.50 (*0-380-81043-3*, Avon Bks) Morrow Avon.

Munroe, John A. History of Delaware. 3rd ed. LC 92-32067. (Illus.). 304p. (C). 1993. 29.50 (*0-87413-493-5*) U Delaware Pr.

Munroe, Kirk. Derrick Sterling: A Story of the Mines. 1993. reprint ed. lib. bdg. 89.00 (*0-7812-5496-5*) Rprt Serv.

***Munroe, Louise.** Essentials for Microbiology Lab. 200p. 1999. pap. text 23.95 (*0-89892-203-8*) Contemp Pub Co of Raleigh.

Munroe, M. International Encyclopaedia of Education, 10 pts. in 5 vols., Set. (C). 1988. 995.00 (*0-7855-0050-2*, Pub. by Print Hse) St Mut.

Munroe, Mary H. & Banja, Judith. The Birthday Book: Birthdates, Birthplaces, & Biographical Source forAmerican Authors & Illustrators of Children's Books. 500p. (C). 1991. text 65.00 (*1-55570-051-9*) Neal-Schuman.

Munroe, Myles. In Pursuit of Purpose. 168p. (Orig.). 1992. pap. 10.99 (*1-56043-103-2*) Destiny Image.

***Munroe, Myles.** Marriage 101: Building a Healthy Relationship with Your Mate. 1999. pap. 5.99 (*1-56229-139-4*) Pneuma Life Pub.

Munroe, Myles. Maximizing Your Potential. 196p. 1996. pap. 10.99 (*1-56043-105-9*) Destiny Image.

— Myles Munroe on Leadership. 1997. pap. 5.99 (*1-56229-115-7*) Pneuma Life Pub.

— Potent Quotes. 76p. (Orig.). 1995. pap. 5.99 (*1-56043-161-X*) Destiny Image.

— Releasing Your Potential. 182p. (Orig.). 1992. pap. 10.99 (*1-56043-072-9*) Destiny Image.

— Releasing Your Potential. 48p. (Orig.). 1993. pap., wbk. ed. 7.99 (*1-56043-093-1*) Destiny Image.

— Sex & Relationships. 1998. pap. 9.99 (*1-56229-125-4*) Pneuma Life Pub.

— Sex 101: Understanding the Real Meaning of Sex. 1998. pap. 5.99 (*1-56229-127-0*) Pneuma Life Pub.

— Single, Married, Separated & Life after Divorce. 140p. (Orig.). 1992. pap. 9.99 (*1-56043-094-X*) Destiny Image.

— Single, Married, Separated & Life after Divorce. 48p. (Orig.). 1993. pap., wbk. ed. 7.99 (*1-56043-115-6*) Destiny Image.

***Munroe, Myles.** Singles 101: Singling Out the Qualites That Make Your Great! 1999. pap. 5.99 (*1-56229-130-0*) Pneuma Life Pub.

Munroe, Myles. Understanding Your Potential. 168p. (Orig.). 1992. pap. 10.99 (*1-56043-046-X*) Destiny Image.

— Understanding Your Potential. 48p. (Orig.). 1992. pap., wbk. ed. 7.99 (*1-56043-092-3*) Destiny Image.

Munroe, Myles E. Becoming a Leader. 1995. pap., wbk. ed. 8.99 (*1-56229-412-1*) Pneuma Life Pub.

— Becoming a Leader: Everyone Can Do It. 1995. pap. 10.99 (*1-56229-401-6*) Pneuma Life Pub.

— Releasing Your Potential. (SPA.). 224p. (Orig.). 1994. pap. 10.99 (*1-56043-108-3*) Destiny Image.

Munroe, R., tr. see Dolci, Danilo.

Munroe, Steven J., jt. auth. see Halter, Steven L.

Munroe, Tapan & Zimmerman, Andrew. The Future of Oil: Managing Risk & Uncertainty. 20p. 1986. pap. 10.00 (*0-918714-12-5*) Intl Res Ctr Energy.

Munroe, Wendy P., et al. Ambulatory Care Clinical Skills Program: Core Module. 464p. 1998. text 219.00 (*1-879907-88-7*) Am Soc Hlth-Syst.

Muns, J. B. Musical Autographs: A Comparative Guide, Suppl. 1. (Illus.). 1992. pap. 15.00 (*1-881858-01-4*) J B Muns.

— Musical Autographs: A Comparative Guide, Suppl. 2. (Illus.). 36p. 1994. pap. 15.00 (*1-881858-02-2*) J B Muns.

Muns, Joaquin, ed. Adjustment, Conditionality, & International Financing. xi, 214p. 1985. reprint ed. pap. 10.00 (*0-939934-28-0*); reprint ed. pap. 10.00 (*0-939934-29-9*) Intl Monetary.

Muns, Ron. The Help Desk Handbook: The Help Desk Institute Guide to Help Desk Operations & Problem Management. Bultema, Patrick et al, eds. (Illus.). (Orig.). (C). pap. write for info. (*1-57125-000-X*) Help Desk Inst.

Munsart, Craig A. American History Through Earth Science. LC 96-49617. 230p. (YA). (gr. 6-12). 1997. pap. text 25.00 (*1-56308-182-2*) Teacher Ideas Pr.

— Investigating Science with Dinosaurs. (Illus.). xiii, 249p. (Orig.). 1993. pap. text 24.50 (*1-56308-008-7*) Teacher Ideas Pr.

Munsart, Craig A. & Izmirian, Christine M. Teaching the Millennium. LC 97-2952. (Illus.). 192p. (J). (gr. 4-8). 1997. pap. 17.95 (*1-55591-284-2*) Fulcrum Pub.

Munsat, Theodore L. Post-Polio Syndrome. (Illus.). 144p. 1990. text 80.00 (*0-409-90153-9*) Buttrwrth-Heinemann.

— Quantification of Neurologic Deficit. (Illus.). 372p. 1989. text 89.95 (*0-409-90152-0*) Buttrwrth-Heinemann.

Munsat, Theodore L., jt. auth. see Mitsumoto, Hiroshi.

Munsat, Theodore L., jt. ed. see Serratrice, Georges.

Munsch, Robert. Aaron's Hair. LC 97-39408. (Illus.). 32p. (J). (ps-2). 1998. 4.99 (*0-590-21103-X*) Scholastic Inc.

— Agu, Agu, Agu.Tr. of Murmel, Murmel, Murmel. (SPA., Illus.). 32p. (YA). (ps-2). 1991. pap. 5.95 (*1-55037-095-2*, Pub. by Annick) Firefly Bks Ltd.

— Agu, Agu, Agu. 2nd ed.Tr. of Murmel, Murmel, Murmel. 1991. 11.15 (*0-606-02296-1*, Pub. by Turtleback) Demco.

— Alligator Baby. LC 97-1419. (Illus.). 32p. (J). (ps-1). 1997. 10.95 (*0-590-21101-3*, Pub. by Scholastic Inc) Penguin Putnam.

— Alligator Baby. (Illus.). (J). 1998. pap. 3.99 (*0-590-34195-2*, Cartwheel) Scholastic Inc.

— Alligator Baby. (Illus.). 32p. (J). (ps-3). 1998. pap. 3.99 (*0-590-88594-4*, Cartwheel) Scholastic Inc.

— Alligator Baby. 1998. 9.19 (*0-606-13117-5*, Pub. by Turtleback) Demco.

— Andrew's Loose Tooth. LC 97-24558. (Illus.). 29p. (J). (ps-1). 1998. 10.95 (*0-590-21102-1*, Pub. by Scholastic Inc) Penguin Putnam.

— Andrew's Loose Tooth. LC 97-24558. (Illus.). 29p. (J). (ps-1). 1999. pap. 4.99 (*0-590-34197-9*, Cartwheel) Scholastic Inc.

An Asterisk (*) at the beginning of an entry indicates that the title is appearing for the first time.

— Angela's Airplane. (Annikin Ser.: Vol. 3). (Illus.). 24p. (J). (ps-1). 1986. pap. 0.99 (*0-920236-75-8*, Pub. by Annick) Firefly Bks Ltd.
— Angela's Airplane. (Illus.). 24p. (J). (gr. k-3). 1988. pap. 5.95 (*1-55037-026-X*, Pub. by Annick); lib. bdg. 15.95 (*1-55037-027-8*, Pub. by Annick) Firefly Bks Ltd.
Munsch, Robert. Angela's Airplane. (Munsch for Kids Ser.). (J). 1988. 11.15 (*0-606-05122-8*, Pub. by Turtleback) Demco.
Munsch, Robert. L' Anniversaire - Moira's Birthday. (Droles D'Histories Ser.). (FRE., Illus.). 24p. (J). (ps up). 1989. pap. 4.95 (*2-89021-114-2*, Pub. by La Courte Ech) Firefly Bks Ltd.
— Au Secours, Maman! - Show & Tell. (Droles D'Histories Ser.). (FRE., Illus.). 24p. (J). (ps up). 1992. pap. 6.95 (*2-89021-183-5*, Pub. by La Courte Ech) Firefly Bks Ltd.
— El Avion de Angela. Langer, Shirley, tr.Tr. of Angela's Airplane. (SPA., Illus.). 32p. (YA). (gr. 1 up). 1991. pap. 5.95 (*1-55037-189-4*, Pub. by Annick) Firefly Bks Ltd.
— L' Avion de Julie. (Droles D'Histories Ser.).Tr. of Angela's Airplane. (FRE., Illus.). 24p. (J). (ps up). 1988. pap. 6.95 (*2-89021-077-4*, Pub. by La Courte Ech) Firefly Bks Ltd.
— Le Bebe - Murmel, Murmel, Murmel. (Droles D'Histories Ser.). (FRE., Illus.). 24p. (J). (ps up). 1983. pap. 6.95 (*2-89021-043-X*, Pub. by La Courte Ech) Firefly Bks Ltd.
— The Boy in the Drawer. (Illus.). 32p. (J). (gr. k-3). 1982. lib. bdg. 15.95 (*0-920236-34-0*, Pub. by Annick) Firefly Bks Ltd.
— The Boy in the Drawer. (Illus.). 32p. (J). (gr. k-3). 1982. pap. 5.95 (*0-920236-36-7*, Pub. by Annick) Firefly Bks Ltd.
— The Boy in the Drawer. (Annikin Ser.: Vol. 5). (Illus.). 32p. (J). (ps-1). 1987. pap. 0.99 (*0-920303-50-1*, Pub. by Annick) Firefly Bks Ltd.
— The Boy in the Drawer. (Munsch for Kids Ser.). 1987. 11.15 (*0-606-00795-4*, Pub. by Turtleback) Demco.
— Los Cochinos.Tr. of Pigs. (SPA., Illus.). 32p. (YA). (gr. k up). 1991. pap. 5.95 (*1-55037-191-6*, Pub. by Annick) Firefly Bks Ltd.
— La Cola de Caballo de Estefania.Tr. of Stephanie's Ponytail. (SPA., Illus.). 32p. (Orig.). (YA). (ps up). 1997. pap. 5.95 (*1-55037-507-5*, Pub. by Annick) Firefly Bks Ltd.
— El Cumpleanos de Moira.Tr. of Moira's Birthday. (SPA., Illus.). 32p. (J). (ps-3). 1992. pap. 5.95 (*1-55037-269-6*, Pub. by Annick) Firefly Bks Ltd.
— The Dark. (Illus.). 32p. (J). (gr. k-3). 1984. pap. 4.95 (*0-920236-85-5*, Pub. by Annick) Firefly Bks Ltd.
— The Dark. (Annikins Ser.: Vol. 5). (Illus.). 24p. (J). (ps-1). 1987. pap. 0.99 (*0-920303-47-1*, Pub. by Annick) Firefly Bks Ltd.
— The Dark. 2nd ed. LC 97-930905. (Illus.). 32p. (J). (ps-1). 1997. lib. bdg. 15.95 (*1-55037-451-6*, Pub. by Annick) Firefly Bks Ltd.
— The Dark. 2nd ed. (J). 1997. 11.15 (*0-606-01337-7*, Pub. by Turtleback) Demco.
— The Dark. 2nd rev. ed. LC 97-930905. (Illus.). 32p. (J). (ps-1). 1997. pap. 5.95 (*1-55037-450-8*, Pub. by Annick) Firefly Bks Ltd.
— David's Father. (Illus.). 32p. (J). (gr. k-3). 1983. lib. bdg. 15.95 (*0-920236-62-6*, Pub. by Annick) Firefly Bks Ltd.
— David's Father. (Munsch for Kids Ser.). (Illus.). 32p. (J). (ps-3). 1983. pap. 5.95 (*0-920236-64-2*, Pub. by Annick) Firefly Bks Ltd.
— David's Father. (Annikins Ser.: Vol. 7). (Illus.). 32p. (J). (ps-2). 1989. pap. 0.99 (*1-55037-011-1*, Pub. by Annick) Firefly Bks Ltd.
— David's Father. (Munsch for Kids Ser.). (J). 1983. 11.15 (*0-606-01343-1*, Pub. by Turtleback) Demco.
— Le Desordre - The Boy in the Drawer. (Droles D'Histories Ser.). (FRE., Illus.). 24p. (J). (ps up). 1984. pap. 6.95 (*2-89021-049-9*, Pub. by La Courte Ech) Firefly Bks Ltd.
— Le Dodo - Mortimer. (Droles D'Histories Ser.). (FRE., Illus.). 24p. (J). (ps up). 1986. pap. 6.95 (*2-89021-055-3*, Pub. by La Courte Ech) Firefly Bks Ltd.
— Droles de Cochons! - Pigs. (Droles D'Histories Ser.). (FRE., Illus.). 24p. (YA). (ps up). 1990. pap. 4.95 (*2-89021-123-1*, Pub. by La Courte Ech) Firefly Bks Ltd.
— La Estacion de los Bomberos.Tr. of Fire Station. (SPA., Illus.). 32p. (J). (ps-2). 1992. pap. 5.95 (*1-55037-268-8*, Pub. by Annick) Firefly Bks Ltd.
— Les Fantasies D'Adele. LC 96-941164. (Droles D'Histoires Ser.). (FRE., Illus.). 24p. (J). 1997. pap. write for info. (*2-89021-284-X*, Pub. by La Courte Ech) Firefly Bks Ltd.
— 50 Below Zero. (Illus.). 24p. (J). (gr. k-3). 1986. pap. 5.95 (*0-920236-91-X*, Pub. by Annick); lib. bdg. 15.95 (*0-920236-86-3*, Pub. by Annick) Firefly Bks Ltd.
Munsch, Robert. 50 Below Zero. (Munsch for Kids Ser.). (J). 1986. 11.15 (*0-606-05098-1*, Pub. by Turtleback) Demco.
Munsch, Robert. The Fire Station. (Annikins Ser.: Vol. 3). (Illus.). 24p. (J). (ps-1). 1986. pap. 0.99 (*0-920236-77-4*, Pub. by Annick) Firefly Bks Ltd.
— The Fire Station. (Illus.). 24p. (J). (gr. k-3). 1991. pap. 5.95 (*1-55037-171-1*, Pub. by Annick); lib. bdg. 15.95 (*1-55037-170-3*, Pub. by Annick) Firefly Bks Ltd.
— Fire Station. (Munsch for Kids Ser.). (J). 1991. 11.15 (*0-606-05288-7*, Pub. by Turtleback) Demco.
— From Far Away. (J). 1995. 10.40 (*0-606-07551-8*) Turtleback.
— Get Me Another One! 32p. 1992. pap. 4.95 (*0-385-25337-0*) Doubleday.
— Get Out of Bed! (Illus.). 32p. (J). (gr. k-1). 1998. 10.95 (*0-590-76977-4*, Pub. by Scholastic Inc) Penguin Putnam.
— Good Families Don't. 32p. 1990. mass mkt. 7.95 (*0-385-25267-6*) Doubleday.
— Le Grenouilles - Frogs. (Droles D'Histories Ser.). (FRE., Illus.). 24p. (J). (ps up). 1994. pap. 6.95 (*2-89021-227-0*, Pub. by La Courte Ech) Firefly Bks Ltd.
— L' Habit De Neige - Thomas' Snowsuit. (Droles D'Histories Ser.). (FRE., Illus.). 24p. (J). (ps up). 1987. pap. 6.95 (*2-89021-070-7*, Pub. by La Courte Ech) Firefly Bks Ltd.
— I Have to Go! (Annikins Ser.: Vol. 5). (Illus.). 24p. (J). (ps-1). 1987. pap. 0.99 (*0-920303-51-X*, Pub. by Annick) Firefly Bks Ltd.
— I Have to Go! (Illus.). 24p. (J). (gr. k-2). 1987. pap. 5.95 (*0-920303-74-9*, Pub. by Annick); lib. bdg. 15.95 (*0-920303-77-3*, Pub. by Annick) Firefly Bks Ltd.
— Jonathan Cleaned Up-Then He Heard a Sound: Or, Blackberry Subway Jam. (Illus.). 32p. (J). (ps-2). 1981. pap. 5.95 (*0-920236-20-0*, Pub. by Annick); lib. bdg. 14.95 (*0-920236-22-7*, Pub. by Annick) Firefly Bks Ltd.
— Jonathan Cleaned Up-Then He Heard a Sound: Or, Blackberry Subway Jam. (Annikins Ser.: Vol. 1). (Illus.). 24p. (J). (ps-2). 1986. pap. 0.99 (*0-920236-21-9*, Pub. by Annick) Firefly Bks Ltd.
Munsch, Robert. Jonathan Cleaned Up-Then He Heard a Sound: Or, Blackberry Subway Jam. (Munsch for Kids Ser.). (J). 1981. 11.15 (*0-606-02255-4*, Pub. by Turtleback) Demco.
Munsch, Robert. Love You Forever. (Illus.). 32p. (J). (gr. 4-10). 1986. 12.95 (*0-920668-36-4*); pap. 4.95 (*0-920668-37-2*) Firefly Bks Ltd.
***Munsch, Robert.** Love You Forever. (Illus.). 32p. 2000. 17.95 (*1-55209-109-0*) Firefly Bks Ltd.
Munsch, Robert. Love You Forever. 1986. 10.15 (*0-606-02470-0*, Pub. by Turtleback) Demco.
— Love You Forever. deluxe ed. (Illus.). 32p. (J). 1995. boxed set 19.95 (*1-895565-66-9*) Firefly Bks Ltd.
— Love You Forever: A Big Book. (Illus.). 32p. (J). (ps-3). 1994. pap. 19.95 (*1-895565-37-5*) Firefly Bks Ltd.
— La Magicienne - Wait & See. (Droles D'Histories Ser.). (FRE., Illus.). 24p. (J). (ps up). 1994. pap. 6.95 (*2-89021-214-9*, Pub. by La Courte Ech) Firefly Bks Ltd.
— Mais, Ou Est Donc Gah-Ning? (FRE., Illus.). 32p. (Orig.). (J). (ps-1). 1994. pap. 4.95 (*1-55037-984-4*, Pub. by Annick) Firefly Bks Ltd.
— Le Metro - Jonathan Cleaned Up. (Droles D'Histories Ser.). (FRE., Illus.). 24p. (J). (ps up). 1991. pap. 6.95 (*2-89021-154-1*, Pub. by La Courte Ech) Firefly Bks Ltd.
— Millicent & the Wind. (Illus.). 32p. (J). (gr. k-3). 1984. lib. bdg. 15.95 (*0-920236-98-7*, Pub. by Annick) Firefly Bks Ltd.
— Millicent & the Wind. (Illus.). 32p. (J). (gr. k-3). 1984. pap. 5.95 (*0-920236-93-6*, Pub. by Annick) Firefly Bks Ltd.
— Millicent & the Wind. (Annikins Ser.: Vol. 7). (Illus.). 32p. (J). (ps-2). 1989. pap. 0.99 (*1-55037-010-3*, Pub. by Annick) Firefly Bks Ltd.
— Millicent & the Wind. (Munsch for Kids Ser.). (J). 1984. 10.15 (*0-606-02788-2*, Pub. by Turtleback) Demco.
***Munsch, Robert.** Mmm, Cookies! LC 99-46966. (Illus.). 32p. (J). (ps-3). 2000. 11.95 (*0-590-89603-2*, Cartwheel) Scholastic Inc.
Munsch, Robert. Moira's Birthday. (Illus.). 32p. (J). (gr. k-3). 1987. pap. 5.95 (*0-920303-83-8*, Pub. by Annick); lib. bdg. 15.95 (*0-920303-85-4*, Pub. by Annick) Firefly Bks Ltd.
— Moira's Birthday. Martchenko, Michael, ed. (Annikins Ser.: Vol. 14). (Illus.). (J). (ps-2). 1995. pap. 0.99 (*1-55037-389-7*, Pub. by Annick) Firefly Bks Ltd.
— Moira's Birthday. (J). 1987. 11.15 (*0-606-05469-3*, Pub. by Turtleback) Demco.
— Mortimer. (Illus.). 24p. (J). (gr. k-3). 1985. lib. bdg. 15.95 (*0-920303-12-9*, Pub. by Annick) Firefly Bks Ltd.
— Mortimer. (Illus.). 24p. (J). (gr. k-3). 1985. pap. 5.95 (*0-920303-11-0*, Pub. by Annick) Firefly Bks Ltd.
— Mortimer. (Annikins Ser.: Vol. 3). (Illus.). 24p. (J). (ps-1). 1986. pap. 0.99 (*0-920236-68-5*, Pub. by Annick) Firefly Bks Ltd.
— Mortimer. (Munsch for Kids Ser.). (J). 1985. 11.15 (*0-606-02845-5*, Pub. by Turtleback) Demco.
— El Muchacho en la Gaveta.Tr. of Boy in the Drawer. (SPA., Illus.). 32p. (YA). (ps-2). 1989. pap. 5.95 (*1-55037-097-9*, Pub. by Annick) Firefly Bks Ltd.
— Mud Puddle. (Annikins Ser.: Vol. 1). (Illus.). 24p. (J). (ps-1). pap. 0.99 (*0-920236-23-5*, Pub. by Annick) Firefly Bks Ltd.
— Mud Puddle. (Illus.). 32p. (J). (ps-2). 1995. lib. bdg. 16.95 (*1-55037-469-9*, Pub. by Annick) Firefly Bks Ltd.
— Mud Puddle. rev. ed. (Illus.). 32p. (J). (ps-2). 1982. pap. 5.95 (*1-55037-468-0*, Pub. by Annick) Firefly Bks Ltd.
— Munschworks: The First Munsch Collection. (Munsch for Kids Ser.). (Illus.). 128p. (J). (ps-2). 1998. text 19.95 (*1-55037-523-7*, Pub. by Annick Pr) Firefly Bks Ltd.
— Munschworks 2: The Second Munsch Treasury. (Illus.). 136p. (J). (ps-2). 1999. text 19.95 (*1-55037-553-9*, Pub. by Annick Pr) Firefly Bks Ltd.
— Murmel, Murmel, Murmel. (Illus.). 32p. (J). (gr. k-2). 1982. lib. bdg. 15.95 (*0-920236-29-4*, Pub. by Annick) Firefly Bks Ltd.
— Murmel, Murmel, Murmel. (Illus.). 32p. (J). (gr. k-3). 1982. pap. 5.95 (*0-920236-31-6*, Pub. by Annick) Firefly Bks Ltd.
— Murmel, Murmel, Murmel. (Munsch for Kids Ser.). (J). 1982. 11.15 (*0-606-02913-3*, Pub. by Turtleback) Demco.
— Ou Es-Tu, Catherine? - Something Good. (Droles D'Histories Ser.). (FRE., Illus.). 24p. (J). (ps up). 1991. pap. 6.95 (*2-89021-155-X*, Pub. by La Courte Ech) Firefly Bks Ltd.
— L' Ouragan - Portus Potter Was Loose! (Droles D'Histories Ser.). (FRE., Illus.). 24p. (J). (ps up). 1993. pap. 6.95 (*2-89021-206-8*, Pub. by La Courte Ech) Firefly Bks Ltd.
— El Papa de David.Tr. of David's Father. (SPA., Illus.). 32p. (YA). (ps up). 1991. pap. 5.95 (*1-55037-096-0*, Pub. by Annick) Firefly Bks Ltd.
— Le Papa de David. (Droles D'Histories Ser.).Tr. of David's Father. (FRE., Illus.). 24p. (J). (ps up). 1990. pap. 4.95 (*2-89021-124-X*, Pub. by La Courte Ech) Firefly Bks Ltd.
— Papa, Reveille-Toi - 50 below Zero. (Droles D'Histories Ser.). (FRE., Illus.). 24p. (J). (ps up). 1987. pap. 6.95 (*2-89021-071-5*, Pub. by La Courte Ech) Firefly Bks Ltd.
— Paper Bag Princess. (Illus.). 32p. (J). (gr. k-3). 1980. pap. 5.95 (*0-920236-16-2*, Pub. by Annick); lib. bdg. 15.95 (*0-920236-82-0*, Pub. by Annick) Firefly Bks Ltd.
— Paper Bag Princess. (Munsch for Kids Ser.). (J). 1980. 11.15 (*0-606-03290-8*, Pub. by Turtleback) Demco.
— The Paper Bag Princess. (Annikins Ser.: Vol. 1). (Illus.). 24p. (J). (ps-1). 1986. pap. 0.99 (*0-920236-25-1*, Pub. by Annick) Firefly Bks Ltd.
— The Paper Bag Princess Doll & Book. (Illus.). 32p. (J). (ps-3). 1995. pap. 19.95 (*1-55037-392-7*, Pub. by Annick) Firefly Bks Ltd.
— Pigs. (Illus.). 32p. (J). (ps-2). 1989. pap. 5.95 (*1-55037-038-3*, Pub. by Annick); lib. bdg. 15.95 (*1-55037-039-1*, Pub. by Annick) Firefly Bks Ltd.
— Pigs. (Annikins Ser.: Vol. 14). (Illus.). (J). (ps-2). 1995. pap. 0.99 (*1-55037-388-9*, Pub. by Annick) Firefly Bks Ltd.
Munsch, Robert. Pigs. (Munsch for Kids Ser.). (J). 1989. 11.15 (*0-606-04299-7*, Pub. by Turtleback) Demco.
Munsch, Robert. Les Pompiers - The Fire Station. (Droles D'Histories Ser.). (FRE., Illus.). 24p. (J). (ps up). 1988. pap. 6.95 (*2-89021-076-6*, Pub. by La Courte Ech) Firefly Bks Ltd.
— La Princesa Vestida con una Bolsa de Papel.Tr. of Paperbag Princess. (SPA., Illus.). 32p. (YA). (ps up). 1991. pap. 5.95 (*1-55037-098-7*, Pub. by Annick) Firefly Bks Ltd.
— La Princess dans un Sac (The Paper Bag Princess) (FRE., Illus.). 32p. (J). 1996. pap. 4.95 (*1-55037-344-7*, Pub. by Annick) Firefly Bks Ltd.
— La Princesse dans un Sac. (Annikins Ser.). (FRE., Illus.). (J). 1996. 0.99 (*1-55037-391-9*, Pub. by Annick) Firefly Bks Ltd.
— Promise Is a Promise. (J). 1988. 11.15 (*0-606-04380-2*, Pub. by Turtleback) Demco.
— Purple, Green & Yellow. (Illus.). 32p. (J). (ps-2). 1992. pap. 5.95 (*1-55037-256-4*, Pub. by Annick); lib. bdg. 15.95 (*1-55037-255-6*, Pub. by Annick) Firefly Bks Ltd.
— Purple, Green & Yellow. 1992. 11.15 (*0-606-02285-6*, Pub. by Turtleback) Demco.
***Munsch, Robert.** Ribbon Rescue. LC 98-30655. (Illus.). 32p. (J). (ps-1). 1999. 11.95 (*0-590-89012-3*) Scholastic Inc.
Munsch, Robert. Show & Tell. (Illus.). 32p. (J). (ps-2). 1991. pap. 5.95 (*1-55037-197-5*, Pub. by Annick); lib. bdg. 15.95 (*1-55037-195-9*, Pub. by Annick) Firefly Bks Ltd.
— Show & Tell. (Munsch for Kids Ser.). (J). 1991. 11.15 (*0-606-05599-1*, Pub. by Turtleback) Demco.
— Siempre Te Querre.Tr. of Love You Forever. (Illus.). 32p. (YA). (gr. k up). 1992. pap. 4.95 (*1-895565-01-4*) Firefly Bks Ltd.
Munsch, Robert. Siempre Te Querre.Tr. of Love You Forever. (SPA.). 1992. 10.15 (*0-606-02298-8*, Pub. by Turtleback) Demco.
Munsch, Robert. Something Good. (Illus.). 24p. (J). (ps-2). 1990. pap. 5.95 (*1-55037-100-2*, Pub. by Annick); lib. bdg. 15.95 (*1-55037-099-5*, Pub. by Annick) Firefly Bks Ltd.
— Something Good. (Annikin Ser.: Vol. 14). (Illus.). (J). (ps-2). 1995. pap. 0.99 (*1-55037-390-0*, Pub. by Annick) Firefly Bks Ltd.
— Something Good. (Munsch for Kids Ser.). (J). 1990. 11.15 (*0-606-05612-2*, Pub. by Turtleback) Demco.
— Stephanie's Ponytail. (Illus.). 24p. (J). (ps-3). 1996. 16.95 (*1-55037-485-0*, Pub. by Annick) Firefly Bks Ltd.
— Stephanie's Ponytail. (Illus.). 24p. (J). (ps-3). 1996. pap. 5.95 (*1-55037-484-2*, Pub. by Annick) Firefly Bks Ltd.
— Stephanie's Ponytail. (J). 1996. 11.15 (*0-606-12819-0*, Pub. by Turtleback) Demco.
— Thomas' Snowsuit. (Illus.). 24p. (J). (gr. k-3). 1985. lib. bdg. 15.95 (*0-920303-32-3*, Pub. by Annick) Firefly Bks Ltd.
— Thomas' Snowsuit. (Illus.). 24p. (J). (ps-2). 1989. pap. 5.95 (*0-920303-33-1*, Pub. by Annick) Firefly Bks Ltd.
Munsch, Robert. Thomas' Snowsuit. (Munsch for Kids Ser.). (J). 1985. 10.15 (*0-606-03487-0*, Pub. by Turtleback) Demco.
Munsch, Robert. Verde, Violeta y Amarillo. LC 94-930412.Tr. of Purple, Green & Yellow. (Illus.). 32p. (YA). (gr. k up). 1994. pap. 5.95 (*1-55037-971-2*, Pub. by Annick) Firefly Bks Ltd.
— Violet, Vert et Jaune: Purple, Green & Yellow in French. (FRE., Illus.). 32p. (J). (ps-2). 1992. pap. 5.95 (*1-55037-272-6*, Pub. by Annick) Firefly Bks Ltd.
— Wait & See. (Illus.). 24p. (J). (ps-2). 1993. pap. 5.95 (*1-55037-334-X*, Pub. by Annick); lib. bdg. 15.95 (*1-55037-335-8*, Pub. by Annick) Firefly Bks Ltd.
Munsch, Robert. Wait & See. (Munsch for Kids Ser.). (J). 1993. 10.15 (*0-606-06079-0*, Pub. by Turtleback) Demco.
Munsch, Robert. We Share Everything! LC 99-13476. (Illus.). 32p. (J). (ps-1). 1999. 11.95 (*0-590-89600-8*, Cartwheel) Scholastic Inc.
— Where Is Gah-Ning? LC 94-225129. (Illus.). 32p. (J). (ps-2). 1994. pap. 4.95 (*1-55037-982-8*, Pub. by Annick); lib. bdg. 14.95 (*1-55037-983-6*, Pub. by Annick) Firefly Bks Ltd.
Munsch, Robert & Askar, Saoussan. From Far Away. (Illus.). 24p. (J). (ps-2). 1995. lib. bdg. 16.95 (*1-55037-397-8*, Pub. by Annick); per. 5.95 (*1-55037-396-X*, Pub. by Annick) Firefly Bks Ltd.
Munsch, Robert & Kusugak, Michael A. A Promise Is a Promise. (Illus.). 32p. (J). (gr. k-3). 1988. pap. 5.95 (*1-55037-008-1*, Pub. by Annick); lib. bdg. 15.95 (*1-55037-009-X*, Pub. by Annick) Firefly Bks Ltd.
— A Promise Is a Promise. 1995. 3.95 (*0-87129-493-1*, P72) Dramatic Pub.
Munsch, Robert & Martchenko, Michael. J'ai Envie... I Have to Go. (Droles D'Histories Ser.). (FRE., Illus.). 24p. (J). (ps up). 1989. pap. 4.95 (*2-89021-115-0*, Pub. by La Courte Ech) Firefly Bks Ltd.
Munsch, Robert, jt. auth. see Annikin.
***Munsch, Robert N.** Aaron's Hair. LC 99-462118. (Illus.). 32p. (J). (ps-1). 2000. pap. 11.95 (*0-439-19258-7*) Scholastic Inc.
— Get Out of Bed! (Illus.). (J). 1999. 10.44 (*0-606-18550-X*) Turtleback.
— Munschworks 3: The Third Munsch Treasury. (Illus.). 144p. (J). (ps-2). 2000. 19.95 (*1-55037-633-0*, Pub. by Annick Pr) Firefly Bks Ltd.
— We Share Everything. (Illus.). 32p. (J). (ps-1). 2000. pap. text 4.99 (*0-590-89601-6*) Scholastic Inc.
***Munsch, Shirley.** Creating the Ultimate Pantry: Quick & Easy. Ybarra, Janice, ed. LC 99-68707. (Illus.). 170p. 2000. 17.95 (*0-9674902-9-4*) Pantree.
Munschauer, John L. Jobs for English Majors & Other Smart People. 3rd ed. LC 91-208. 174p. (Orig.). 1991. pap. 13.95 (*1-56079-050-4*) Petersons.
— World War II Calvacade: An Offer I Couldn't Refuse. (Illus.). 200p. 1996. pap. 18.95 (*0-89745-194-5*) Sunflower U Pr.
***Munscheck, Hedwig.** Die Concordantiae caritatis des Ulrich von Lilienfeld: Untersuchungen zu Inhalt, Quellen und Verbreitung, mit einer Paraphrasierung von Temporale, Sanktorale und Commune. 2000. 63.95 (*3-631-35395-2*) P Lang Pubng.
Munse, W. H. Fatigue of Welded Steel Structures. 1964. 20.00 (*0-318-18646-2*) Welding Res Coun.
Munsell & Clough. Practical Guide for Advanced Writers. 1984. teacher ed. 5.00 (*0-8384-3280-8*) Heinle & Heinle.
Munsell, F. Darrell. The Victorian Controversy Surrounding the Wellington War Memorial: The Archduke of Hyde Park Corner. LC 91-22672. (Illus.). 125p. 1991. lib. bdg. 69.95 (*0-7734-9735-8*) E Mellen.
Munsell, Joel. Origin, Progress & Vicissitudes of the Mohawk & Hudson Railroad. 20p. 1993. reprint ed. lib. bdg. 69.00 (*0-7812-5218-0*) Rprt Serv.
Munsell, Joel, Sons Staff, ed. Index to American Genealogies. 88p. 1987. reprint ed. pap. 10.00 (*0-935207-72-4*) Danbury Hse Bks.
Munsell, W. Keith, jt. auth. see Vanderwerf, Pieter A.
Munsell, W. Keith, jt. auth. see Vanderwerf, Pketer A.
Munsell, W. W., & Co. Staff. History of Morris County, New Jersey 1739-1882. (Illus.). 397p. 1988. reprint ed. 25.00 (*0-614-29777-X*) M C H S.
Munsey, Brenda, ed. Moral Development, Moral Education, & Kohlberg. LC 80-50. 457p. (Orig.). 1980. pap. 24.95 (*0-89135-020-9*) Religious Educ.
Munsey, Terence. Emerald City. LC 98-65102. 300p. 1998. mass mkt. 6.99 (*0-9697066-6-9*) Munsey Music.
— The Flight of the Stoneman's Son. LC 93-93660. (Stoneman Ser.: Bk. 1). (Illus.). 208p. (Orig.). (YA). (gr. 7 up). 1993. reprint ed. mass mkt. 4.99 (*0-9697066-0-X*, 70660) Munsey Music.
— How to Be a Published Author. LC 99-90327. (Illus.). 96p. 1999. mass mkt. 39.95 (*0-9685152-0-7*) Munsey Music.
— The Keeper of Three. LC 93-86550. (Stoneman Ser.: Bk. 2). 230p. (YA). (gr. 7 up). 1995. mass mkt. 4.99 (*0-9697066-1-8*) Munsey Music.
— Labyrinths of Light. LC 95-94007. (Stoneman Ser.: Bk. 3). 248p. (Orig.). 1995. mass mkt. 4.99 (*0-9697066-2-6*) Munsey Music.
— Marks of Stone, Bk. 4. LC 96-94015. (Stoneman Ser.). 312p. (Orig.). (YA). (gr. 7 up). 1996. mass mkt. 5.99 (*0-9697066-3-4*, 70663) Munsey Music.
— Obsession. LC 97-92895. 208p. (Orig.). 1997. mass mkt. 5.99 (*0-9697066-5-0*) Munsey Music.
Munsey, William F., jt. auth. see Sowell, Robert D.
Munshaw, Nancy, jt. ed. see Nagel, Stuart S.
Munshi, A. H. & Javeid, G. N. Systematic Studies in Polygonaceae of Kashmir Himalaya. 215p. (C). 1986. 275.00 (*81-85046-32-8*, Pub. by Scientific) St Mut.
Munshi, Carol. Baby Bunny Sticker Paper Doll. (Illus.). (J). (gr. k-3). 1998. pap. 1.00 (*0-486-27925-1*) Dover.
Munshi, Indra, jt. ed. see Savur, Manorama.
Munshi, J. S. & Dutta, H. M., eds. Fish Morphology: Horizon of New Research. 350p. 1996. text 99.00 (*1-886106-31-2*) Science Pubs.
Munshi, J. S. Datta, see Hughes, G. M. & Datta Munshi, J. S.
Munshi, Jamal. Stock Exchange Automation. LC 94-483. (Financial Sector of the American Economy Ser.). 104p. 1994. text 15.00 (*0-8153-1702-6*) Garland.
Munshi, Javeed. Rectangular Concrete Tanks. 182p. 1995. pap. 30.00 (*0-89312-130-4*, IS003D) Portland Cement.
Munshi, Javeed A., jt. auth. see Fanella, David A.
Munshi, M. Z. & Prasad, P. S. Handbook of Solid State Batteries & Capacitors. 800p. 1995. text 177.00 (*981-02-1794-3*) World Scientific Pub.
Munshi, Usha. An Integrated Approach to Pollution Control. LC 90-43712. (Environment: Problems & Solutions Ser.: Vol. 24). 190p. 1990. text 20.00 (*0-8240-9786-6*) Garland.

M

An Asterisk (*) at the beginning of an entry indicates that the title is appearing for the first time.

Munshower, Frank F. Practical Handbook of Disturbed Land Revegetation. LC 93-21625. 288p. 1993. boxed set 95.00 (*1-56670-026-4*, L1026) Lewis Pubs.

Munshower, Susan S., ed. All the World's a Stage... Art & Pageantry in the Renaissance & Baroque, 2 pts. (Papers in Art History: Vol. VI). (Illus.). 575p. (Orig.). 1990. pap., boxed set 45.00 (*0-915773-05-8*) Penn St Univ Dept Art Hist.

— Projects & Monuments in the Period of the Roman Baroque. LC 83-43269. (Papers in Art History: Vol. I). (Illus.). 168p. (Orig.). 1984. pap. 20.00 (*0-915773-00-7*) Penn St Univ Dept Art Hist.

Munshower, Susan S., jt. ed. see Fleischer, Roland.

Munshower, Susan S., jt. ed. see Hager, Hellmut.

Munshower, Susan S., jt. ed. see Millon, Henry A.

Munshower, Susan S., jt. ed. see Zabel, Craig.

Munshower, Suzanne. Simply Sophisticated: What Every Wordly Person Needs to Know. Towle, Mike, ed. LC 94-42511. (Illus.). 178p. 1994. pap. 12.95 (*1-56530-148-X*) Summit TX.

Munsie, Lynne, jt. auth. see Cairney, Trevor H.

Munsil, Janet. Dinner at Auntie Rose's. (Illus.). 32p. (J). (ps-3). 1984. pap. 4.95 (*0-920236-63-4*, Pub. by Annick) Firefly Bks Ltd.

— Dinner at Auntie Rose's. (Annikins Ser.: Vol. 8). (Illus.). 24p. (J). (ps-2). 1984. pap. 0.99 (*1-55037-047-2*, Pub. by Annick) Firefly Bks Ltd.

— Donde Hay Humo.Tr. of Where There's Smoke. (SPA., Illus.). 32p. (YA). (gr. 1 up). 1994. pap. 5.95 (*1-55037-968-2*, Pub. by Annick) Firefly Bks Ltd.

— Il N'y a Pas de Fumee (Where There's Smoke) (FRE., Illus.). 32p. (J). (ps-2). 1996. pap. 4.95 (*1-55037-311-0*, Pub. by Les Editions) Firefly Bks Ltd.

— Where There's Smoke. (ENG & FRE., Illus.). 24p. (J). (ps-2). 1993. 14.95 (*1-55037-291-2*, Pub. by Annick); pap. 4.95 (*1-55037-290-4*, Pub. by Annick) Firefly Bks Ltd.

Munsing, Stephanie A., ed. Made in America: Printmaking, 1760-1860. LC 73-161317. (Illus.). 59p. (Orig.). 1973. pap. 5.00 (*0-914076-52-3*) Lib Co Phila.

***Munsinger, Shirley.** Kaleidoscope. 1999. pap. write for info. (*1-58235-110-4*) Watermrk Pr.

Munsinger, Lynn. Three Blind Mice. (J). 1995. 19.95 (*0-385-31005-6*) BDD Bks Young Read.

Munsinger, Lynn. A Zooful of Animals. 96p. (J). (ps-8). 1992. 17.95 (*0-395-52278-1*) HM.

Munsinger, Lynn, jt. auth. see Wise, William.

Munsinger, Lynn, jt. illus. see Lester, Helen.

Munske, Horst H. Der Germanische Rechtswortschatz im Bereich der Missetaten, Philologische & Sprachgeographische Untersuchungen: Die Terminologie der Aelteren Westgermanischen Rechtsquellen, Vol. 1. LC 72-76055. (Studia Linguistica Germanica: Vol. 8). 335p. (C). 1973. 96.95 (*3-11-003578-2*) De Gruyter.

— Orthographie Als Sprachkultur. VIII, 336p. 1997. 44.95 (*3-631-31142-7*) P Lang Pubng.

Munslow, Alun. Deconstructing History. LC 97-2974. 288p. (C). 1997. 75.00 (*0-415-13192-8*); pap. 24.99 (*0-415-13193-6*) Routledge.

***Munslow, Alun.** Routledge Companion to Historical Studies. LC 99-27243. 256p. 1999. pap. 19.99 (*0-415-18495-9*) Routledge.

— Routledge Companion to Historical Studies. LC 99-27243. 256p. (C). 2000. text 75.00 (*0-415-18494-0*) Routledge.

Munslow, Alun & Ashton, Owen R., eds. Henry Demarest Lloyd's Critiques of American Capitalism, 1881-1903. LC 95-18559. 268p. 1996. text 89.95 (*0-7734-8916-9*) E Mellen.

Munslow, Barry. Guyana: Microcosm of Sustainable Development Challenges. 130p. 1998. text 51.95 (*1-85972-642-9*, Pub. by Ashgate Pub) Ashgate Pub Co.

— Mozambique: The Revolution & Its Origins. LC 82-16204. 207p. reprint ed. pap. 64.20 (*0-8357-6226-2*, 203446800090) Bks Demand.

— Southern African Annual Review, 1987-88, 2 vols., Set. 1100p. 1989. 170.00 (*0-905450-02-7*, Pub. by H Zell Pubs) Seven Hills Bk.

— Southern African Annual Review, 1987-88, 2 vols., Vol. 1, Country Reviews. 550p. 1990. 85.00 (*0-905450-03-5*, Pub. by H Zell Pubs) Seven Hills Bk.

— Southern African Annual Review, 1987-88, 2 vols., Vol. 2, Regional Review. 550p. 1990. 85.00 (*0-905450-04-3*, Pub. by H Zell Pubs) Seven Hills Bk.

Munslow, Barry, jt. auth. see Ferraz, Bernardo.

Munslow, Barry, ed. see O'Keefe, Phil.

Munslow, Barry, jt. ed. see O'Keefe, Phil.

Munso, J. Diccionario Turistico de Cataluna, Baleares y Andora. deluxe ed. (SPA.). 693p. 1975. 125.00 (*0-8288-5835-7*, S32722) Fr & Eur.

Munson. Contemporary Adulthood. 5th ed. (C). 1994. pap. text, teacher ed. 33.75 (*0-15-501157-X*) Harcourt Coll Pubs.

***Munson.** Fluid Mechanics: Updated Edition. 3rd ed. 1999. text, student ed. 72.00 (*0-471-36023-6*) Wiley.

Munson. Intervention & Reflection. (Philosophy Ser.). 1979. pap. 18.50 (*0-534-00608-6*) Wadsworth Pub.

— Intervention & Reflection. 4th ed. (Philosophy Ser.). 1991. 36.00 (*0-534-16327-0*) Wadsworth Pub.

***Munson & Conway.** Basic Elements of Reasoning. 2000. pap. 13.00 (*0-534-53884-3*) Thomson Learn.

Munson, Anne D. El Nino. 1999. pap. 7.95 (*0-14-012977-4*, Viking) Viking Penguin.

Munson, Barbara J. A Reason for Optimism: Treating Cancer with a Bone Marrow Transplant. LC 96-60273. (Illus.). 110p. (Orig.). 1996. pap. 13.95 (*0-9648754-0-3*) Two Pillars.

Munson, Bruce R. Digital Signal Processing. 512p. (C). 2001. 95.00 (*0-201-51823-6*) Addison-Wesley.

Munson, Bruce R., et al. A Brief Introduction to Fluid Mechanics. LC 96-27443. 512p. 1996. pap. 70.95 (*0-471-13771-5*) Wiley.

Munson, Bruce R., et al. Fundamentals of Fluid Mechanics. 208p. 1997. pap., student ed. 34.95 (*0-471-24011-7*) Wiley.

— Fundamentals of Fluid Mechanics. 3rd ed. LC 97-20666. 896p. 1997. text 103.95 (*0-471-17024-0*) Wiley.

— Fundamentals of Fluid Mechanics. 3rd rev. ed. LC 99-18994. 896p. 1999. 103.95 incl. cd-rom (*0-471-35502-X*) Wiley.

Munson, Carol. Smart Pressure Cooker Cookbook. LC 98-3368. 144p. 1998. 9.95 (*0-8069-9985-3*) Sterling.

Munson, Carlton E. Clinical Social Work Supervision. 2nd ed. 1993. pap. 24.95 (*1-56024-285-X*) Haworth Pr.

— Clinical Social Work Supervision. 2nd ed. LC 92-1462. (Illus.). 478p. 1993. lib. bdg. 59.95 (*1-56024-284-1*) Haworth Pr.

— Family of Origin Applications in Clinical Supervision. LC 84-9017. (Clinical Supervisor Ser.: Vol. 2, No. 2). 86p. (C). 1984. text 29.95 (*0-86656-287-7*) Haworth Pr.

— An Introduction to Clinical Social Work Supervision. LC 83-62. 376p. 1983. text 49.95 (*0-86656-196-X*); pap. text 19.95 (*0-86656-197-8*) Haworth Pr.

***Munson, Carlton E., ed.** The Mental Health Diagnostic Desk Reference: Visual Guides & More for Learning to Use the Diagnostic & Statistical Manual (DSM-IV) LC 99-20779. 396p. 2000. 59.95 (*0-7890-1075-5*, Hawrth Medical); pap. text 24.95 (*0-7890-1076-3*) Haworth Pr.

Munson, Carlton E., ed. Social Work Supervision: Classic Statements & Critical Issues. LC 78-72149. 1979. pap. 22.95 (*0-02-922280-X*) Free Pr.

— Supervising Student Internships in Human Services. LC 83-26393. (Clinical Supervisor Ser.: Vol. 2, No. 1). 84p. 1984. text 29.95 (*0-86656-301-6*) Haworth Pr.

***Munson, Carol.** Smart Clay Pot Cookery. LC 00-28506. (Illus.). 2000. write for info. (*0-8069-7099-5*) Sterling.

Munson, Carol. Smart Soups. LC 98-229850. 144p. 1998. pap. 9.95 (*0-8069-0455-0*) Sterling.

Munson, Carol H. Fast & Lean One-Dish Cuisine: More Than 125 Complete Meals. LC 97-31655. 192p. 1998. pap. text 14.95 (*1-882606-69-8*) Peoples Med Soc.

— Smart Crockery Cooking: Over 100 Delicious Recipes. (Illus.). 144p. 1996. pap. 10.95 (*0-8069-6106-6*) Sterling.

Munson, Carol J. Postcranial Descriptions of Ilaria & Ngapakaldia, Vombatiformes, Marsupialia, & the Phylogeny of the Vombatiforms Based on Postcranial Morphology. (Publications in Zoology: Vol. 125). (C). 1992. pap. 12.00 (*0-520-09772-6*, Pub. by U CA Pr) Cal Prin Full Svc.

Munson, Carol S., jt. auth. see Munson, Noel J.

Munson, Cheryl A., jt. auth. see Sieber, Ellen.

Munson, Danni, ed. Lesbian & Gay Almanac & Events of 1990: Gay Games Edition. (Illus.). 160p. (Orig.). 1989. pap. 9.95 (*0-945043-02-3*) Envoy Enter.

***Munson, Derek.** Enemy Pie. LC 99-50821. (Illus.). (J). 2000. 14.95 (*0-8118-2778-X*) Chronicle Bks.

Munson, Don. Don Munson's WJBC Sesquicentennial Stories: Glimpses of McLean County's 150 Years. (Illus.). 98p. 1980. 1.50 (*0-943788-12-9*) McLean County.

— The Illustrated History of McLean County. Wyckoff, Martin & Koos, Greg, eds. LC 82-14833. (Illus.). 392p. 1982. 29.95 (*0-943788-00-5*) McLean County.

— More of Don Munson's WJBC Sesquicentennial Stories: Glimpses of McLean County's 150 Years. (Illus.). 81p. 1981. 1.50 (*0-943788-13-7*) McLean County.

Munson, Don & Koos, G. WJBC's History You Can See: Fifty Historic Journeys into McLean County's Past. (Illus.). 101p. 1991. 5.00 (*0-943788-11-0*) McLean County.

Munson, Donna P. Belonging to Christ: Basic Biblical Truths for Discipleship. Williamson, Parker T. & Lunceford, Lloyd, eds. (Illus.). 25p. (YA). 1999. pap. text 18.75 (*0-9652602-5-9*) PLC Publns.

Munson, Douglas A. Hostile Witness. 288p. 1992. reprint ed. mass mkt. 4.50 (*1-55817-640-3*, Pinncle Kensgtn) Kensgtn Pub Corp.

Munson, Eric M., ed. see Steiner, H. M.

Munson, Ethan V., et al. Principles of Digital Document Processing: 4th International Workshop, PODDP '98, Saint-Malo, France, March 29-30, 1998: Proceedings, Vol. 148. LC 98-41918. (Lecture Notes in Computer Science Ser.). 1998. pap. 37.00 (*3-540-65086-5*) Spr-Verlag.

Munson, Eve S. & Warren, Catherine A. James Carey: A Critical Reader. LC 97-8082. 1997. pap. 19.95 (*0-8166-2703-7*); text 49.95 (*0-8166-2702-9*) U of Minn Pr.

Munson, Frank M. The Process for Learning, Sharing & Selling. (Illus.). iii, 55p. (Orig.). 1997. pap. 134.95 (*1-891156-01-2*) HSR Pub.

— The Q Factor: The Road to Excellence in Sales & Management. LC 97-74260. (Illus.). iii, 214p. 1997. pap. 13.95 (*1-891156-00-4*) HSR Pub.

Munson, Fred C. Labor Relations in the Lithographic Industry. LC 63-10872. (Wertheim Publications in Industrial Relations). (Illus.). 290p. 1963. 14.95 (*0-674-50850-5*) HUP.

Munson, George A. The Early Years in Smyrna, & Our First Old Home Week. (Illus.). 209p. 1997. reprint ed. lib. bdg. 29.50 (*0-8328-6244-4*) Higginson Bk Co.

— Smyrna: Early Years in Smyrna & Our First Old Home Week, Chenango County, New York. Goerlich, Shirley B., ed. (Illus.). 245p. 1997. reprint ed. vinyl bd. 18.00 (*1-887530-13-4*) RSG Pub.

Munson, Gorham. Aladdin's Lamp: The Wealth of the American People. (Social Credit Ser.). 420p. 1982. lib. bdg. 75.00 (*0-8490-3222-9*) Gordon Pr.

— Awakening Twenties: A Memoir-History of a Literary Period. LC 84-14316. (Illus.). 317p. 1985. 35.00 (*0-8071-1201-1*) La State U Pr.

Munson, Gorham B. Destinations: A Canvass of American Literature since 1900. LC 70-131784. 1971. 7.00 (*0-403-00671-6*) Scholarly.

— Destinations: A Canvass of American Literature since 1900. (BCL1-PS American Literature Ser.). 218p. 1992. reprint ed. lib. bdg. 79.00 (*0-7812-6621-1*) Rprt Serv.

— Robert Frost: A Study in Sensibility & Good Sense. LC 72-10857. (Studies in Poetry: No. 38). 1969. reprint ed. lib. bdg. 75.00 (*0-8383-0788-4*) M S G Haskell Hse.

— Twelve Decisive Battles of the Mind: The Story of Propaganda During the Christian Era, with Abridged Versions of Texts That Have Shaped History. LC 72-167388. (Essay Index Reprint Ser.). 1977. reprint ed. 20.95 (*0-8369-2705-2*) Ayer.

Munson, Henry, Jr. Islam & Revolution in the Middle East. 180p. (C). 1989. reprint ed. pap. 13.00 (*0-300-04604-9*) Yale U Pr.

— Religion & Power in Morocco. LC 92-40202. (Illus.). 256p. 1993. 32.00 (*0-300-05376-2*) Yale U Pr.

Munson, Howard R. Science Activities with Simple Things. (J). (gr. 4-8). 1972. pap. 8.99 (*0-8224-6320-2*) Fearon Teacher Aids.

— Science Experiences with Everyday Things. (J). (gr. 4-8). 1988. pap. 10.99 (*0-8224-6846-8*) Fearon Teacher Aids.

Munson, James D. Alexandria, Virginia Vol. 1: Alexandria Hustings Court Deeds, 1783-1797. 274p. (Orig.). 1990. pap. 20.00 (*1-55613-329-4*) Heritage Bk.

— Alexandria, Virginia Vol. 2: Alexandria Hustings Court Deeds 1797-1801. x, 287p. (Orig.). 1991. pap. 21.50 (*1-55613-448-7*) Heritage Bk.

Munson, James W., ed. Pharmaceutical Analysis: Modern Methods, Pt. B. LC 81-15171. (Drugs & the Pharmaceutical Sciences Ser.: No. 11). 512p. 1984. reprint ed. pap. 158.80 (*0-7837-2772-0*, 204316300002) Bks Demand.

— Pharmaceutical Analysis Pt. A: Modern Methods. LC 81-15171. (Drugs & the Pharmaceutical Sciences Ser.: No. 11, Pt. A). (Illus.). 501p. 1981. reprint ed. pap. 155.40 (*0-608-04432-6*, 204316300001) Bks Demand.

***Munson, Jennifer.** Exercise for Real Life: How to Begin & Maintain an Exercise Program Without Joining (or Buying) a Gym. (Illus.). 86p. 2000. spiral bd. 15.95 (*1-930204-25-6*) Adonai.

Munson, John W. Reminiscences of a Mosby Guerrilla. (Illus.). 277p. 35.00 (*1-56013-012-1*) Olde Soldier Bks.

— Reminscences of a Mosby Guerrilla. 1983. reprint ed. 25.95 (*0-89201-109-2*) Zenger Pub.

Munson, K., jt. auth. see Hooten, Ted.

Munson, Kenneth. Unmanned Aerial Vehicles & Targets. (Illus.). 208p. Date not set. 930.00 (*0-7106-1257-5*) Janes Info Group.

***Munson, Kyle.** Travel Smart: Iowa/Nebraska. (Illus.). 272p. 2000. pap. 15.95 (*1-56261-492-4*, Travel Smart) Avalon Travel.

Munson, Lawrence S. How to Conduct Training Seminars: A Complete Reference Guide for Training Managers. 2nd ed. 1992. 34.95 (*0-07-044201-0*) McGraw.

Munson, Lillian S., jt. auth. see Munson, Voyle L.

Munson, Lulie & Riskin, Karen. In Their Own Words: A Sexual Abuse Workbook for Teenage Girls. (Orig.). 1995. pap. text 10.95 (*0-87868-596-0*) Child Welfare.

***Munson, Lynne.** Exhibitionism: Art in an Era of Intolerance. (Illus.). 256p. 2000. 27.50 (*1-56663-324-9*, Pub. by I R Dee) Natl Bk Netwk.

Munson, M. A. The Munson Record, 1637-1887: A Genealogical & Biographical Account of Captain Thomas Munson (Pioneer of Hartford & New Haven) & His Descendants, 2 vols. in 1. (Illus.). 1263p. 1989. reprint ed. pap. 189.00 (*0-8328-0893-8*); reprint ed. lib. bdg. 197.00 (*0-8328-0892-X*) Higginson Bk Co.

***Munson, Marcia & Stelboum, Judith P., eds.** The Lesbian Polyamory Reader: Open Relationships, Non-Monogamy & Casual Sex. LC 99-10965. 242p. 1999. 49.95 (*0-7890-0660-X*) Haworth Pr.

Munson, Marcia & Stelboum, Judith P., eds. The Lesbian Polyamory Reader: Open Relationships, Non-Monogamy & Casual Sex. LC 99-10965. 274p. 1999. pap. 24.95 (*1-56023-120-3*, Harrington Park) Haworth Pr.

Munson, Michael J., jt. auth. see Tashman, Leonard J.

Munson, Noel J. & Munson, Carol S. Accidental Encounter. unabridged ed. 343p. 1998. mass mkt. 9.50 (*0-9658702-1-9*, 2278) NJM.

— Circle of Distrust. 383p. 1997. mass mkt. 9.50 (*0-9658702-0-0*, 2277) NJM.

Munson, Patrick J. & Harn, Alan D. An Archaeological Survey of the American Bottoms & Adjacent Bluffs, Illinois, 2 pts. (Reports of Investigations: No. 21). (Illus.). 123p. 1971. pap. 3.00 (*0-89792-046-5*) Ill St Museum.

Munson, Paul, ed. Franz Liszt: St. Stanislaus. (Recent Researches in Music of the 19th & Early 20th Centuries Ser.: Vol. RRN26). (Illus.). xiii, 212p. 1998. pap. 75.00 (*0-89579-406-3*) A-R Eds.

Munson, Paul L., et al, eds. Principals of Pharmacology: Basic Concepts & Clinical Applications. LC 94-41659. 1800p. (gr. 13). 1994. text 92.00 (*0-412-04701-2*) Chapman & Hall.

— Vitamins & Hormones, Vol. 38. (Serial Publication Ser.). 1981. text 167.00 (*0-12-709838-0*) Acad Pr.

Munson, Paul L., et al. Principles of Pharmacology: Basic Concepts & Clinical Applications. 2nd ed. (Illus.). 1808p. 1996. text 93.95 (*0-412-12231-6*) OUP.

***Munson, Peggy.** Stricken: Voices from the Hidden Epidemic of Chronic Fatigue Syndrome. 291p. 2000. 59.95 (*0-7890-0894-7*, Hawrth Medical); pap. 24.95 (*0-7890-0895-5*, Hawrth Medical) Haworth Pr.

Munson, R. D. Potassium in Agriculture. (Illus.). 1123p. 1985. 58.00 (*0-89118-086-9*) Am Soc Agron.

Munson, R. W., Jr. Hemerocallis: The Daylily. LC 89-5025. (Illus.). 160p. 1993. pap. 22.95 (*0-88192-240-4*) Timber.

Munson, Robert D. Potassium, Calcium, & Magnesium in the Tropics & Subtropics. Brosheer, J. C., ed. LC 82-11944. (Technical Bulletin Ser.: No. T-23). (Illus.). 70p. (Orig.). 1982. pap. text 4.00 (*0-88090-041-5*) Intl Fertilizer.

Munson, Robert S. Favorite Hobbies & Pastimes: A Sourcebook of Leisure Pursuits. (Illus.). 366p. (Orig.). 1994. pap. 40.00 (*0-8389-0638-9*) ALA.

Munson, Ronald. Intervention & Reflection: Basic Issues in Medical Ethics. 2nd ed. 608p. (C). 1983. pap. write for info. (*0-534-01289-2*) Wadsworth Pub.

— Intervention & Reflection: Basic Issues in Medical Ethics. 3rd ed. 602p. (C). 1987. pap. write for info. (*0-534-08088-X*) Wadsworth Pub.

— Intervention & Reflection: Basic Issues in Medical Ethics. 4th ed. 669p. (C). 1991. mass mkt. 38.25 (*0-534-16326-2*) Wadsworth Pub.

***Munson, Ronald.** Intervention & Reflection: Issues in Medical Ethics. 6th ed. LC 99-19759. (Philosophy Ser.). 891p. 1999. pap. text 70.95 (*0-534-52039-1*) Wadsworth Pub.

Munson, Ronald & Hoffman, Christopher A., selected by. Intervention & Reflection: Basic Issues in Medical Ethics. 5th ed. LC 95-15103. (C). 1995. 45.00 (*0-534-25488-8*) Wadsworth Pub.

Munson, Ronald, jt. auth. see Conway, David A.

Munson, Rosaria V., tr. see Comotti, Giovanni.

Munson, Sammye. Hej Texas, Goodbye Sweden. LC 93-38928. 128p. (J). (gr. 5-6). 1994. 12.95 (*0-89015-948-3*) Sunbelt Media.

— Our Tejano Heroes: Outstanding Mexican-Americans. Eakin, Edwin M., ed. (Illus.). 96p. (J). (gr. 5-6). 1989. 12.95 (*0-89015-691-3*) Sunbelt Media.

***Munson, Sammye.** Today's Tejano Heroes. LC 99-36015. 1999. 15.95 (*1-57168-328-3*, Eakin Pr) Sunbelt Media.

Munson, Sammye. Los Vaqueros: Our First Cowboys. LC 96-50248. (Illus.). 32p. (J). (gr. k-4). 1996. 12.95 (*1-57168-142-6*, Eakin Pr) Sunbelt Media.

Munson, Shirley & Nelson, Jo. Apple-Lovers' Cook Book. LC 89-23639. 120p. (Orig.). 1989. ring bd. 6.95 (*0-914846-43-4*) Golden West Pub.

Munson, Steven C., ed. The State of the Nation: A Conference of the Committee for the Free World. LC 84-23444. 126p. (Orig.). 1985. pap. text 11.50 (*0-8191-4391-X*); lib. bdg. 27.00 (*0-8191-4390-1*) U Pr of Amer.

Munson, Thomas N. The Essential Wisdom of George Santayana. LC 62-10453. 236p. reprint ed. pap. 73.20 (*0-608-10339-X*, 200611600061) Bks Demand.

Munson, Voyle L. & Munson, Lillian S. A Gift of Faith: Elias H. Blackburn. (Illus.). 1991. 27.95 (*0-9617133-2-1*); pap. 17.95 (*0-9617133-1-3*) Basin-Plateau Pr.

Munson, Wayne. All Talk: The Talkshow in Media Culture. LC 92-9389. (Culture & the Moving Image Ser.). 288p. (C). 1993. 49.95 (*0-87722-995-3*) Temple U Pr.

— All Talk: The Talkshow in Media Culture. LC 92-9389. (Culture & the Moving Image Ser.). 232p. (C). 1993. pap. 22.95 (*1-56639-194-6*) Temple U Pr.

Munson, Will. How Lucky Can You Get? How You Can Attract Good Luck by Responding to Everyday Opportunities. Briggs, Charlie, ed. LC 89-81422. 192p. (Orig.). 1990. 12.95 (*0-923485-22-8*); pap. 9.95 (*0-923485-23-6*) Eden Hse.

***Munson-Williams-Proctor Arts Institute Staff, et al.** American Twentieth-Century Watercolors at the Munson-Williams-Proctor Arts Institute. LC 99-89947. 2000. write for info. (*0-915895-22-6*) Munson Williams.

***Munson-Williams-Proctor Institute Staff.** Masterpieces of American Furniture from the Munson-Williams-proctor Institute. 1999. 50.00 (*0-915895-20-X*) Munson Williams.

Munster, Arnold. Classical Thermodynamics. Halberstadt, E. S., tr. LC 71-122348. 401p. reprint ed. pap. 124.40 (*0-608-11837-0*, 202083400019) Bks Demand.

Munster, Ernst F. Staatsmann und Kunstfreund, 1760-1839. (Veroffentlichungen des Landschaftsverbandeshildesheim Ser.: Bd. 1). (GER.). 121p. 1991. write for info. (*3-487-09515-7*) G Olms Pubs.

Munster, Gernot, jt. auth. see Monvay, Istvan.

Munsterberg, Hugo. American Patriotism, & Other Social Studies. LC 68-22934. (Essay Index Reprint Ser.). 1977. 19.95 (*0-8369-0726-4*) Ayer.

— American Problems from the Point of View of a Psychologist. LC 75-84328. (Essay Index Reprint Ser.). 1977. 19.95 (*0-8369-1098-2*) Ayer.

— Chinese Buddhist Bronzes. LC 87-80393. (Illus.). 191p. 1988. reprint ed. lib. bdg. 50.00 (*0-87817-324-2*) Hacker.

— The Japanese Kimono. (Images of Asia Ser.). (Illus.). 80p. 1996. text 17.95 (*0-19-587511-7*) OUP.

— The Japanese Print: A Historical Guide. LC 81-16195. (Illus.). 232p. 1982. 29.95 (*0-8348-0167-1*) Weatherhill.

— On the Witness Stand: Essays on Psychology & Crime. 269p. 1981. reprint ed. 38.00 (*0-8377-0840-0*, Rothman) W S Hein.

— Photoplay: A Psychological Study. LC 79-124021. (Literature of Cinema, Ser. 1). 1970. reprint ed. 14.95 (*0-405-01628-X*) Ayer.

Munsterberg, Hugo. Psychology & Industrial Efficiency. 333p. 90.00 (*1-85506-700-5*) Thoemmes Pr.

Munsterberg, Hugo. Psychology & Industrial Efficiency. LC 73-2979. (Classics in Psychology Ser.). 1974. reprint ed. 23.95 (*0-405-05151-4*) Ayer.

— A Short History of Chinese Art. LC 70-88990. (Illus.). 227p. 1969. reprint ed. lib. bdg. 59.50 (*0-8371-2117-5*, MUCA, Greenwood Pr) Greenwood.

— Symbolism in Ancient Chinese Art. LC 84-82430. (Illus.). 250p. 1986. lib. bdg. 50.00 (*0-87817-303-X*) Hacker.

An Asterisk (*) at the beginning of an entry indicates that the title is appearing for the first time.

— Unspoken Bequest: The Contribution of German Jews to German Culture. (Illus.). 224p. (YA). (gr. 10 up). 1995. 20.00 (*1-878352-10-5*) R Saroff Pub.
— World Ceramics. LC 98-18836. (Illus.). 192p. 1998. 45.00 (*0-670-86741-1*) Viking Penguin.
— Zen & Oriental Art. (Illus.). 158p. 1993. pap. 12.95 (*0-8048-1902-5*) Tuttle Pubng.
Munsterberg, Rudolf. Die Beamtennamen Auf den Griechischen Munzen, Geographisch und Alphabetisch Geordnet. (Subsidia Epigraphica Ser.: Vol. III). (GER.). 338p. 1985. reprint ed. write for info. (*3-487-05059-5*) G Olms Pubs.
Munsterer, Hanns O. The Young Brecht. (Illus.). 220p. 45.00 (*1-870352-73-4*, Pub. by Libris) Paul & Co Pubs.
— The Young Brecht. (Illus.). 220p. 1998. pap. 29.95 (*1-870352-33-5*, Pub. by Libris) Paul & Co Pubs.
Munsterman, G. Thomas. Jury System Management. (Court Management Library: Vol. 2). (Illus.). 200p. (Orig.). 1996. pap. 24.00 (*0-89656-166-6*, R-185) Natl Ctr St Courts.
Munsterman, G. Thomas, et al, eds. Jury Trial Innovations. LC 97-65255. (Illus.). 334p. 1996. pap. 18.00 (*0-89656-174-7*, R-193) Natl Ctr St Courts.
Munsters & the Addams Family Fan Club Staff, ed. The Munsters & the Addams Family Reunion. (Munsters & The Addams Family Television Shows Ser.). (Illus.). 100p. (Orig.). 1997. pap. 30.00 (*0-317-05621-2*) L Wendruck.
Munt, Ian, jt. auth. see Mowforth, Martin.
Munt, Sally. Cultural Studies & the Working Class. LC 99-22404. 1999. 33.95 (*0-304-70549-7*) Continuum.
— Heroic Desire: Lesbian Identity & Cultural Space. LC 97-42268. 200p. 1998. text 55.00 (*0-8147-5606-9*); pap. text 18.50 (*0-8147-5607-7*) NYU Pr.
— Heroic DesireSpace: Lesbian Identities & Cultural. 1997. pap. text. write for info. (*0-304-33454-5*) Continuum.
Munt, Sally, ed. New Lesbian Criticism: Literary & Cultural Readings. (Between Men - Between Women Ser.). 256p. 1992. pap. 18.50 (*0-231-08019-0*); text 57.50 (*0-231-08018-2*) Col U Pr.
Munt, Sally, jt. auth. see Medhurst, Andy.
Munt, Sally R. Murder by the Book? Crime Fiction & Feminism. LC 93-49588. (Narrative Forms & Social Formations Ser.). 200p. (C). 1994. pap. 25.99 (*0-415-10919-1*, B4244) Routledge.
***Muntadas.** On Translation: The Audience. 2000. pap. 15.00 (*90-73362-43-1*) Witte De With CFCA.
Muntaquim, Renee, jt. auth. see Asante, Molefi K.
Muntarbhorn, Vitit. Sexual Exploitation of Children. LC 97-114024. (Human Rights Studies: No. 8). 44p. 25.00 (*92-1-154123-9*, HQ71) UN.
Muntarbhorn, Vitit, ed. The Status of Refugees in Asia. (Illus.). 228p. 1992. text 55.00 (*0-19-825668-X*) OUP.
***Muntean, Joanne.** Fairy Tales for Grownups: Life's Lessons. 33p. 1999. spiral bd. 3.95 (*0-942253-11-6*) PAZ Pub.
***Muntean, Michaela.** Growing up Grouchy: The Story of Oscar the Grouch. (Jellybean Bks.). (Illus.). 24p. (J). (ps). 2000. 2.99 (*0-375-80647-4*, Pub. by Random Bks Yng Read) Random.
— I Want to Be President. (Jellybean Books Just for Preschoolers). (Illus.). 24p. (J). (ps). 2000. 2.99 (*0-375-80550-8*, Pub. by Random Bks Yng Read) Random.
Muntean, Michaela. The Little Engine That Could & the Big Chase. (All Aboard Bks.). (Illus.). 32p. (J). (ps-3). 1988. pap. 2.99 (*0-448-19095-8*, Plat & Munk) Peng Put Young Read.
— Monkey - Little Lamb. (J). 1984. pap. 69.36 (*0-8037-0104-7*, NewStar Pr) NewStar Media.
Munter, Carol, jt. auth. see Hirschmann, Jane R.
Munter, Mary. Business Communication: Strategy & Skill. (Illus.). 448p. 1987. text 49.22 (*0-13-091919-5*) P-H.
***Munter, Mary.** Guide to Managerial Communication: Effective Business Writing & Speaking. 5th ed. LC 99-23920. 198p. 1999. pap. 23.80 (*0-13-013381-7*) P-H.
Munter, Mary. Managerial Communication. 4th ed. LC 97-9000. 1996. pap. text, student ed. 25.00 (*0-13-256447-5*) P-H.
Munter, Pam. Almost Famous: Personal Growth & Other Adventures In & Out of Show Biz. LC 85-13621. (Illus.). 275p. 1985. 16.95 (*0-9614926-0-0*) Westgate Oregon.
Munter, Paul & Ratcliffe, Thomas A. Applying GAAP & GAAS, 2 vols. LC 84-72343. 1985. ring bd. write for info. (*0-8205-1012-2*) Bender.
— A Guide to Financial Statement Disclosures. LC 85-9603. (Illus.). 282p. 1986. 65.00 (*0-89930-032-4*, MUF/, Quorum Bks) Greenwood.
Munter, Preston K. Counseling Students: Lessons from Northfield, Echoes from Fountain Valley. LC 87-35130. 214p. 1988. 52.95 (*0-86569-172-X*, Auburn Hse) Greenwood.
Munter, Robert L. A Dictionary of the Print Trade in Ireland, 1550-1775. LC 88-80279. 351p. reprint ed. pap. 108.90 (*0-7837-5615-1*, 204552200005) Bks Demand.
— The History of the Irish Newspaper, 1685 1760. LC 66-21653. 231p. reprint ed. pap. 65.90 (*0-608-12083-9*, 2024581) Bks Demand.
Munter, Robert L. & Grose, Clyde L. Englishmen Abroad: Being an Account of Their Travels in the Seventeenth Century. LC 87-1547. (Studies in British History: Vol. 3). 496p. 1986. lib. bdg. 109.95 (*0-88946-453-7*) E Mellen.
Munthe, Axel. The Story of San Michele. (Illus.). 351p. 1984. pap. 13.95 (*0-88184-109-9*) Carroll & Graf.
Munthe, Bo F. Traditional Ninjutsu. 112p. 1998. pap. 18.95 (*0-901764-95-7*, 93225, Pub. by P H Crompton) Midpt Trade.
Munthe, Jens. A Guide Book to the Natural Arches of Grand Staircase - Escalante National Monument. (Illus.). 120p. 2001. pap. 9.95 (*1-891858-11-4*, 4014) Arch Hunter Bks.
— Miocene Mammals of the Split Rock Area, Granite Mountains Basin, & Central Wyoming. (UC Publications in Geological Sciences). 1989. pap. 25.00 (*0-520-09706-8*, Pub. by U CA Pr) Cal Prin Full Svc.
Munthe, Kathleen. The Skeleton of the Boraphaginae (Carnivora, Canidae) Morphology & Function. 1990. pap. 20.00 (*0-520-09724-6*, Pub. by U CA Pr) Cal Prin Full Svc.
Munting, Abraham. Fantastic Floral Engravings. Menten, Theodore, ed. (Pictorial Archive Ser.). (Illus.). 120p. 1975. reprint ed. pap. 8.95 (*0-486-23117-8*) Dover.
Munting, Roger. An Economic & Social History of Gambling in Britain & the U. S. A. LC 95-36995. 272p. (C). 1996. text 79.95 (*0-7190-4449-9*, Pub. by Manchester Univ Pr) St Martin.
— Hedges & Hurdles. 144p. 1990. 65.00 (*0-85131-424-4*, Pub. by J A Allen) St Mut.
Munton, Ann. Robert Kroetsch & His Works (Poetry) (Canadian Author Studies). 118p. (C). 1992. pap. 9.95 (*1-55022-072-1*, Pub. by ECW) Genl Dist Srvs.
Munton, Anthony G. Attributions in Action: A Practical Approach to Coding Qualitative Data. 222p. 1999. 75.00 (*0-471-98216-4*) Wiley.
Munton, Don, ed. Hazardous Waste Siting & Democratic Choice: The NIMBY Phenomenon & Approaches to Facility Siting. LC 96-11858. (American Governance & Public Policy Ser.). 416p. (C). 1996. 65.00 (*0-87840-625-5*) Georgetown U Pr.
Munton, Don, ed. see Stairs, Denis.
Munton, R. & Stott, J. R. Refrigeration at Sea. 2nd ed. (Illus.). 238p. 1978. 79.25 (*0-85334-766-2*) Elsevier.
Munton, Tony, jt. auth. see Mooney, Ann.
Munts, Raymond. Bargaining for Health: Labor Unions, Health Insurance & Medical Care. LC 67-13555. 330p. reprint ed. pap. 102.30 (*0-8357-5966-0*, 202371600033) Bks Demand.
Muntz, E. P., et al, eds. Rarefield Gas Dynamics Vol. 2: Physical Phenomena. (PAAS Ser.: Vol. 117). 522p. 1989. 38.00 (*0-930403-54-1*) AIAA.
— Rarefield Gas Dynamics Vol. 3: Theoretical & Computational Techniques. (PAAS Ser.: Vol. 118). 616p. 1989. 38.00 (*0-930403-55-X*) AIAA.
Muntz, E. P., et al. Rarefied Gas Dynamics Vol. 1: Space-Related Studies. Campbell, D. H., ed. (PAAS Ser.: Vol. 116). 570p. 1989. 38.00 (*0-930403-53-3*) AIAA.
Muntz, E. Phillip, jt. auth. see Logan, Wende W.
Muntz, Eugene. Les Arts A la Cour Des Papes Pendant le Fifteenth et le Sixteenth Siecle, 3 vols., Set. (Bibliotheque Des Ecoles Francaises d'Athenes et De Rome Ser.: Nos. 4, 9, 28). 997p. 1983. reprint ed. write for info. (*3-487-07306-4*) G Olms Pubs.
Muntzing, L. Manning. International Instruments for Nuclear Technology Transfer. LC 78-67158. 640p. 1978. 62.00 (*0-89448-016-2*, 690001) Am Nuclear Soc.
Muntzing, L. Manning, ed. Nuclear Power & Its Regulation in the United States, Vol. 7, Pt. 2. (Illus.). 125p. 1981. pap. 36.00 (*0-08-027139-1*, Pergamon Pr) Elsevier.
Muntzing, L. Manning, jt. auth. see Muntzing, William H., II.

Muntzing, William H., II & Muntzing, L. Manning. The Muntzings & Their Related Families: Five Centuries of Ancestors. (Illus.). 224p. 1991. 40.00 (0-9629967-0-X) McClain.
The history of the Muntzing family & their related families (Franz, Hamstead, Cosner, Nine & their connections) covers five centuries. The book contains pictures, copies of translated letters & other items of interest. *Publisher Paid Annotation.*

Munves, James. Andes Rising. LC 98-51319. 192p. 1999. text 21.95 (*0-8112-1407-9*, Pub. by New Directions) Norton.
— The Bees: A Fable for Victims of the Free Market. LC 97-143572. 22p. (Orig.). 1997. pap. 4.95 (*0-9656975-0-9*) Frog Hollow NY.
Munyan, Arthur C., ed. Polar Wandering & Continental Drift. LC 64-6318. (Society of Economic Paleontologists & Mineralogists, Special Publication Ser.: No. 10). 175p. reprint ed. pap. 54.30 (*0-608-12957-7*, 202473600038) Bks Demand.
Munyon, Paul G. A Reassessment of New England Agriculture in the Last Thirty Years of the Nineteenth Century: New Hampshire, a Case History. LC 77-14783. (Dissertations in American Economic History Ser.). 1978. 33.95 (*0-405-11051-0*) Ayer.
***Munyon, Russ.** Twelve Angry Men. LC 99-55869. 224p. (YA). 2000. 17.45 (*0-7377-0314-8*) Greenhaven.
— Twelve Angry Men. LC 99-55869. (Literary Companion Ser.). 224p. (YA). 2000. pap. 17.45 (*0-7377-0313-X*) Greenhaven.
Munz, D., jt. auth. see Fett, T.
Munz, Dietrich & Fett, Theo. Ceramics: Mechanical Properties, Failure Behaviour, Materials Selection. LC 99-10778. (Illus.). xx, 298p. 1999. 89.95 (*3-540-65376-7*) Spr-Verlag.
Munz, Ludwig & Haak, Bob. Rembrandt. (Masters of Art Ser.). (Illus.). 164p. 1984. 24.95 (*0-8109-1594-4*, Pub. by Abrams) Time Warner.
Munz, P. A. Flora of Ecuador No. 89: Tropaeolaceae. (Opera Botanica Series B). 31p. 1973. pap. 15.00 (*1-878762-98-2*, Pub. by Coun Nordic Pubs) Balogh.
— Flora of Ecuador No. 141: Onagraceae. (Opera Botanica Series B). 46p. 1974. pap. 15.00 (*1-878762-99-0*, Pub. by Coun Nordic Pubs) Balogh.
Munz, Peter. Critique of Impure Reason. LC 98-21781. 264p. 1999. 59.95 (*0-275-96384-5*, Praeger Pubs) Greenwood.
— Our Knowledge of the Growth of Knowledge: Popper or Wittgenstein? (International Library of Philosophy). 341p. 1985. 42.50 (*0-7102-0460-4*, Routledge Thoemms) Routledge.
— Philosophical Darwinism: On the Origin of Knowledge by Means of Natural Selection. LC 92-19364. 272p. (C). (gr. 13). 1993. 75.00 (*0-415-08602-7*, B0295) Routledge.
— The Shapes of Time: A New Look at the Philosophy of History. LC 77-2459. 394p. reprint ed. pap. 122.20 (*0-8357-3533-8*, 203466100090) Bks Demand.
Munz, Peter, tr. see Fichtenau, Heinrich.
Munz, Peter, tr. see Garin, Eugenio.
Munz, Philip A. California Desert Wildflowers. (Illus.). (Orig.). 1962. pap. 11.95 (*0-520-00899-5*, Pub. by U CA Pr) Cal Prin Full Svc.
— California Mountain Wildflowers. (Orig.). 1963. pap. 12.95 (*0-520-00901-0*, Pub. by U CA Pr) Cal Prin Full Svc.
— California Spring Wildflowers: From the Base of the Sierra Nevada & Southern Mountains to the Sea. (Orig.). 1961. pap. 12.95 (*0-520-00896-0*, Pub. by U CA Pr) Cal Prin Full Svc.
— A Flora of Southern California. (Illus.). 1974. 70.00 (*0-520-02146-0*, Pub. by U CA Pr) Cal Prin Full Svc.
— Shore Wildflowers of California, Oregon, & Washington. (Illus.). (Orig.). 1965. pap. 11.95 (*0-520-00903-7*, Pub. by U CA Pr) Cal Prin Full Svc.
Munz, Philip A. & Keck, David D. A California Flora & Supplement. 1973. 55.00 (*0-520-02405-2*, Pub. by U CA Pr) Cal Prin Full Svc.
Munz, Rainer & Weiner, Myron, eds. Migrants, Refugees, & Foreign Policy: U. S. & German Policies Toward Countries of Origin. LC 97-2328. (Migration & Refugees: Vol. 2). 384p. 1997. 59.95 (*1-57181-087-0*) Berghahn Bks.
Munz, Rainer, jt. ed. see Fassman, Heinz.
Munz, Rainer, jt. ed. see Schuck, Peter.
Munzberg, Olav. Step Human into This World: Travel Poems. Cohen, Mitch, tr. from GER. LC 90-81862. (Illus.). 125p. (Orig.). 1991. pap. 21.00 (*0-948259-53-1*, Pub. by Forest Bks) Dufour.
Munzel, G Felicitas. Kant's Conception of Moral Character: The "critical" Link of Morality, Anthropology, & Reflect. LC 98-47957. 1999. lib. bdg. 53.00 (*0-226-55133-4*) U Ch Pr.
Munzenrider, Robert F., jt. auth. see Golembiewski, Robert T.
Munzer, Friedrich. Beitrage Zur Quellenkritik der Naturgeschichte Des Plinius. xii, 432p. 1988. write for info. (*3-615-00040-4*) G Olms Pubs.
— Roman Aristocratic Parties & Families. LC 98-36613. 544p. 1999. 68.00 (*0-8018-5990-5*) Johns Hopkins.
Munzer, Stephen R. A Theory of Property. (Cambridge Studies in Philosophy & Law). (Illus.). 501p. (C). 1990. pap. text 33.95 (*0-521-37886-9*) Cambridge U Pr.
Munzert, Alfred W. Poor Richard's Economic Survival Manual. Pepper, Christina A., ed. (Illus.). 272p. (C). 1982. 11.95 (*0-917292-03-0*) H-U Public.
— Self-Scoring I. Q. Test. Elskamp, Karen K., ed. 1977. pap. 1.95 (*0-917292-00-6*) H-U Public.
— Symbol Communication Technique (SCT) A Self-Motivating Method of Learning to Write. rev. ed. Elskamp, Karen K., ed. LC 70-134719. 88p. 1987. pap. 8.95 (*0-917292-04-9*) H-U Public.
— Teacher Handbook for Symbol Communications Technique (SCT) rev. ed. 8p. pap. write for info. (*0-917292-30-8*) H-U Public.
— Test Your I. Q. 3rd ed. 128p. 1994. per. 7.00 (*0-671-87459-4*, Arc) IDG Bks.
— Test Your I. Q. 3rd ed. LC 96-31149. (Illus.). 128p. 1996. 5.99 (*0-517-18287-4*) Random Hse Value.
— Test Your I. Q. 4th ed. LC 97-71466. 128p. 1997. 6.95 (*0-02-861936-6*, Arc) IDG Bks.
***Munzert, Kim K.** Test Yourself IQ: The Easy, Fun Way to Discover Your Intelligence Potential. 5th ed. (Illus.). 128p. 2000. pap. text 6.95 (*0-02-863746-1*, Arco) Macmillan Gen Ref.
Munzmaier, Werner, tr. see Griehl, Manfred.
Muolo, Michael J. Space Handbook: Analyst's Guide, Vol. 2. 392p. 1994. per. 36.00 (*0-16-061357-4*) USGPO.
— Space Handbook: War Fighter's Guide to Space, Vol. 1. 182p. 1993. per. 20.00 (*0-16-061355-8*) USGPO.
Muolo, Paul. Mortgage Industry Directory, 1998 Edition: The Blue Book of the U. S. Mortgage Industry. 1997. 395.00 (*1-57987-021-X*, Natl Mortgage News) Faulkner & Gray.
Muolo, Paul, ed. 1998 Home Equity Lending Directory. 1997. write for info. (*1-57987-039-2*) Faulkner & Gray.
Muolo, Paul, jt. auth. see Pizzo, Stephen.
Muoneke, Romanus O. Art, Rebellion & Redemption: A Reading of the Novels of Chinua Achebe, Vol. 5. LC 92-43155. (American University Studies: African Literature: Ser. XVIII, Vol. 5). X, 176p. (C). 1994. text 37.95 (*0-8204-2049-2*) P Lang Pubng.
***Mupedziswa, Rodrick & Gumbo, P.** Structural Adjustment & Women Informal Sector Traders in Harare, Zimbabwe. LC 99-165859. (Research Report Ser.). 130p. 1999. pap. write for info. (*91-7106-435-4*) Nordisk Afrikainstitutet.
Muppet Workshop Staff, jt. auth. see Henson, Cheryl.
Muppets. Inside Fraggle Rock Story Album & Tape. (J). 1993. 5.98 incl. audio (*0-553-47484-7*) Bantam.
Muqiao, Xue, ed. see Economic Research Centre Staff, et al.
Mur, Frank X., jt. ed. see Moran, Pablo.
Mur, L., jt. ed. see Barica, J.
Mur, L. R., et al. Selection Mechanisms Controlling Biomass Distribution. (Water Science & Technology Ser.: Vol. 32). 222p. 1995. 109.25 (*0-08-042880-0*, Pergamon Pr) Elsevier.
***Mura.** Schaum's Japanese Vocabulary. 2000. 15.98 (*0-07-134219-2*) McGraw.
Mura, David. After We Lost Our Way. LC 97-65568. (Classic Contemporaries Ser.). 81p. 1997. pap. 12.95 (*0-88748-268-6*) Carnegie-Mellon.
— Turning Japanese. 384p. 1992. pap. 14.95 (*0-385-42344-6*, Anchor NY) Doubleday.
— Where the Body Meets the Memory: An Odyssey of Race, Sexuality & Identity. 288p. 1997. pap. 14.95 (*0-385-47184-X*, Anchor NY) Doubleday.
Mura Editors & Kodbov, Tonci. AIDS World in 1999: A Modern Plague That May Destroy the World if We Stay Naive, Passive, Unaware,... (ENG & JPN.). 250p. (Orig.). 1989. pap. write for info. (*0-929602-02-1*) Mura Pub Co.
Mura, John, ed. see Hartford Courant Staff.
Mura, Roberta & Rhemtulla, Akbar. Orderable Groups. LC 76-56702. (Lecture Notes in Pure & Applied Mathematics Ser.: Vol. 27). 175p. reprint ed. pap. 54.30 (*0-608-08967-2*, 206960200005) Bks Demand.
Mura, Toshio. Micromechanics of Defects in Solids. 1982. lib. bdg. 263.50 (*90-247-2560-7*) Kluwer Academic.
— Micromechanics of Defects in Solids. 2nd rev. ed. 1987. pap. text 115.00 (*90-247-3256-5*); lib. bdg. 318.50 (*90-247-3343-X*) Kluwer Academic.
Mura, Toshio, ed. Mathematical Theory of Dislocations. LC 70-88019. 215p. reprint ed. pap. 66.70 (*0-608-30982-6*, 200472200046) Bks Demand.
Mura, Toshio, et al. Variational Methods in Mechanics. (Illus.). 256p. (C). 1992. text 52.95 (*0-19-506830-0*, 230) OUP.
Muraca, Maurizio, ed. Methods in Biliary Research. 336p. 1994. lib. bdg. 210.00 (*0-8493-8701-9*, 8701) CRC Pr.
Murach, Joel. Crash Course - Windows 95 & NT 4.0. LC 98-121020. (Illus.). 53p. 1997. pap. 10.00 (*0-911625-97-6*) M Murach & Assoc.
Murach, Joel, jt. auth. see Prince, Anne.
Murach, Mike. Crash Course - Word 95. LC 98-121021. (Illus.). 83p. 1997. pap. 15.00 (*0-911625-95-X*) M Murach & Assoc.
— Crash Course Word 97. LC 98-121024. (Crash Course Ser.). 1997. pap. text 15.00 (*0-911625-98-4*) M Murach & Assoc.
— Standard COBOL: A Problem-Solving Approach. 2nd ed. LC 74-34184. xii, 433p. 1975. write for info. (*0-574-18401-5*) SRA.
— Word 6 for Windows: How to Use the Mail Merge Feature. LC 95-10340. 71p. 1995. pap. 9.95 (*0-911625-88-7*) M Murach & Assoc.
— Work Like a Pro with Word for Windows 95. LC 96-15269. (Illus.). 369p. (Orig.). 1996. pap. 25.00 (*0-911625-91-7*) M Murach & Assoc.
— Work Like a Pro with Word 6 for Windows. LC 95-32589. 253p. 1995. pap. 20.00 (*0-911625-90-9*) M Murach & Assoc.
Murach, Mike & Noll, Paul. Structured ANS COBOL Pt. 1: A Course for Novices Using 1974 or 1985 ANS COBOL. 2nd ed. LC 86-61654. 438p. 1986. pap. 32.50 (*0-911625-37-2*) M Murach & Assoc.
— Structured ANS COBOL Pt. 2: An Advanced Course Using 1974 or 1985 ANS COBOL. 2nd ed. LC 86-61654. 498p. 1987. pap. 32.50 (*0-911625-38-0*) M Murach & Assoc.
Murad, jt. auth. see Sellers, Larry G.
Murad, Abdal-Hakim, ed. see Al-Haddad, Imam A.
Murad, Anatol. Franz Joseph I of Austria & His Empire. LC 68-17233. (Illus.). 259p. 1968. text 32.50 (*0-8290-0172-7*) Irvington.
— What Keynes Means. 1962. pap. 15.95 (*0-8084-0320-6*, B18) NCUP.
***Murad, Howard.** Expert Healthcare for the Skin. 186p. 1999. 25.95 (*0-8281-1425-0*) Forb Custom Pub.
Murad, Khurram. Desert Chief: The Story of Thumama Ibn. 24p. (J). 1996. pap. 3.50 (*0-614-21000-3*, 197) Kazi Pubns.
— The Long Search. 44p. (J). 1996. pap. 3.50 (*0-614-21023-2*, 733) Kazi Pubns.
— Love at Home. 48p. (J). 1996. pap. 3.50 (*0-614-21025-9*, 738) Kazi Pubns.
— Love Your Brother, Love Your Neighbor. 32p. (J). 1996. pap. 3.50 (*0-614-21026-7*, 740) Kazi Pubns.
— Love Your God. 36p. (J). 1996. pap. 3.50 (*0-614-21027-5*, 741) Kazi Pubns.
— The Persecutor Comes Home. 40p. (J). 1996. pap. 3.50 (*0-614-21038-0*, 951) Kazi Pubns.
— Stories of Broken Idol & the Jewish Rabbi. 28p. (J). 1996. pap. 3.50 (*0-614-21041-0*, 1164) Kazi Pubns.
— Way to the Quran. 145p. 1996. pap. 8.95 (*0-614-21077-1*, 1294) Kazi Pubns.
— The Wise Poet. 24p. 1996. pap. 3.50 (*0-614-21044-5*, 1322) Kazi Pubns.
Murad, Khurram, ed. see Nadwi, A.
Murad, Mounir. Daheshism & the Journey of Life. LC 93-91483. (Illus.). 128p. 1993. 20.00 (*0-9633519-1-5*); pap. 10.00 (*0-9633519-2-3*) Murad Pub.
Murad, Richard D. To the Fallen Angels: Man's Spiritual Heritage, Earthly Missing, & Evolutionary Destiny. LC 94-92105. 104p. 1994. pap. 11.45 (*1-885384-00-9*) Soldier Mystic.
Muradian, Khachik K., jt. auth. see Frolkis, Vladimir V.
Murado, Miguelanxo. A Bestiary of Discontent: Bestiario dos Descontentos. Evans-Corrales, Carys, tr. from SPA. LC 93-32609. (Hispanic Literature Ser.: Vol. 21). (Illus.). 144p. 1993. 69.95 (*0-7734-9338-7*) E Mellen.
***Murahashi, S.** Transition Metal Catalysed Reactions. LC 98-44683. (IUPAC Chemical Data Ser.). (Illus.). 1999. pap. 160.00 (*0-632-05126-4*) Blackwell Sci.

M

An Asterisk (*) at the beginning of an entry indicates that the title is appearing for the first time.

Murai, S., jt. ed. see Singh, R. B.

Murai, Shunji, ed. Toward Global Planning of Sustainable Use of the Earth: Development of Global Eco-Engineering: A Collection of Contributions Based on Lectures Presented at the 8th Toyota Conference, Mikkabi, Shizuoka, Japan, November 8 to 11, 1994. LC 95-18909. 484p. 1995. 210.50 (*0-444-81904-5*) Elsevier.

Murail, Elvire, jt. auth. see Murail, Marie-Aude.

Murail, Marie-Aude. Chanyelin (Changeling) Pieck, Cecilia, tr. (SPA., Illus.). 34p. (J). (gr. 5-6). 1997. pap. 5.99 (*968-16-5461-7*, Pub. by Fondo) Continental Bk.

— Mystere. (Folio - Cadet Bleu Ser.: No. 217). (FRE., Illus.). 64p. (J). (gr. 1-5). 1987. pap. 9.95 (*2-07-031217-8*) Schoenhof.

— Pelirrojita (Little Red Hair) Segovia, Rafael, tr. (SPA., Illus.). 46p. (J). (gr. 3-4). 1997. pap. 5.99 (*968-16-5417-X*, Pub. by Fondo) Continental Bk.

— Uncle Giorgio. (I Love to Read Collection). (Illus.). 46p. (J). (ps-3). 1992. lib. bdg. 12.79 (*0-89565-809-7*) Childs World.

Murail, Marie-Aude & Murail, Elvire. Soui Manga. (SPA., Illus.). (J). (gr. 3-4). 1997. pap. 5.99 (*968-16-5399-8*, Pub. by Fondo) Continental Bk.

Murakami. Secondary Math Network. 240p. 1998. pap. text 24.95 (*0-205-28593-7*) Allyn.

Murakami, H. & Shirahata, S., eds. Animal Cell Technology: Basic & Applied Aspects: Proceedings of the Fourth Annual Meeting of the Japanese Association for Animal Cell Technology, Fukuoka, Japan, 13-15 November 1991. LC 92-23657. 600p. (C). 1992. text 324.50 (*0-7923-1882-X*) Kluwer Academic.

Murakami, Haruki. Dance Dance Dance. Luke, Elmer, ed. Birnbaum, Alfred T., tr. from JPN. LC 93-14098.Tr. of Dansu Dansu Dansu. 352p. 1994. 22.00 (*4-7700-1683-2*) Kodansha.

— Dance Dance Dance.Tr. of Dansu Dansu Dansu. 1995. pap. 14.00 (*0-679-75379-6*) Vin Bks.

— The Hard-Boiled Wonderland & the End of the World. Birnbaum, Alfred T., tr. from JPN. LC 92-56345. 1993. pap. 13.00 (*0-679-74346-4*) Vin Bks.

***Murakami, Haruki.** Norwegian Wood. LC 99-53821. 320p. 2000. pap. 13.00 (*0-375-70402-7*) Vin Bks.

— South of the Border, West of the Sun. 2000. pap. 12.00 (*0-679-76739-8*) Vin Bks.

Murakami, Haruki. South of the Border, West of the Sun: A Novel. Gabriel, Philip, tr. LC 97-49459. 224p. 1999. 22.00 (*0-375-40251-9*) Knopf.

Murakami, Haruki. Underground. write for info. (*0-375-40410-4*) Knopf.

Murakami, Haruki. A Wild Sheep Chase. Birnbaum, Alfred T., tr. 304p. 1990. pap. 12.95 (*0-452-26516-9*, Plume) Dutton Plume.

— The Wind-Up Bird Chronicle. Rubin, Jay, tr. LC 97-2813. 640p. 1997. 25.95 (*0-679-44669-9*) Knopf.

— The Wind-Up Bird Chronicle. 624p. 1998. pap. 14.00 (*0-679-77543-9*) Vin Bks.

Murakami, Hiroki, ed. Trends in Animal Cell Culture Technology: Proceedings of Annual Meeting of the Japanese Association for Animal Cell Technology, 2nd, Tsukuba, Ibaraki, Japan, Nov. 20-22, 1989. 342p. 1990. 95.00 (*3-527-28199-1*, Wiley-VCH) Wiley.

Murakami, Hisayo, ed. Catalogue of Kanagawa Prefecture Magazines: 1945-1949. LC 91-34018. 133p. 1991. 35.00 (*1-880223-00-7*) G W Prange Collect.

***Murakami, Katsumi.** Saijutsu: The Traditional Okinawan Weapon Art. (Illus.). 2000. pap. 19.95 (*0-8048-3244-7*) Tuttle Pubng.

Murakami, Ken, jt. auth. see Engel, Dean.

Murakami, Kisaburo, tr. see Toyofumi, Ogura.

Murakami, Linda K., jt. auth. see Mahoney, Katherine A.

Murakami, M. Melt Processed High Temperature Superconductors. 380p. 1993. text 121.00 (*981-02-1244-5*) World Scientific Pub.

Murakami, M., jt. ed. see Nakajima, S.

Murakami, Mamiko. Love, Hate, & Everything in Between: Put Your Feelings into Words. McCarthy, Ralph F., tr. (Power Japanese Ser.). 144p. 1997. pap. 13.00 (*4-7700-2089-9*) Kodansha.

Murakami, Masahiro. Managing Water for Peace in the Middle East: Alternative Strategies. LC 96-149708. 309p. 1997. pap. write for info. (*92-808-0858-3*, Pub. by UN Univ Pr) Brookings.

Murakami, Naojiro, ed. see MacDonald, Ranald.

Murakami, Paul, jt. auth. see Hanson, Handt.

Murakami, Ryu. Almost Transparent Blue. Shaw, ed. Andrew, Nancy, tr. from JPN. LC 77-75959. 128p. 1992. reprint ed. pap. 11.00 (*0-87011-469-7*) Kodansha.

— Coin Locker Babies. Snyder, Stephen, tr. from JPN. 400p. 1995. 23.00 (*4-7700-1590-9*) Kodansha.

— Coin Locker Babies. Snyder, Stephen, tr. 400p. 1998. pap. 13.00 (*4-7700-2308-1*, Pub. by Kodansha Intl) Kodansha.

— 69. LC 93-28815. 192p. 1995. pap. 10.00 (*4-7700-1951-3*) Kodansha.

Murakami, Sumio, jt. ed. see Fan, Jinghong.

Murakami, T. High Temperature Superconductors: A Special Issue of the Journal Phase Transitions, Section B. 90p. 1989. pap. text 293.00 (*0-677-25820-8*) Gordon & Breach.

Murakami, T., et al. Strategy for Creation. 224p. 1991. 69.95 (*1-85573-061-8*, Pub. by Woodhead Pubng) Am Educ Systs.

Murakami, Takashi & Ewing, R. C., eds. Scientific Basis for Nuclear Waste Management XVIII. (Proceedings from the Eighteenth Symposium on Nuclear Waste Management Ser.: Vol. 353). 1455p. 1995. 30.00 (*1-55899-253-7*) Materials Res.

Murakami, Y. New Developments in Applied Superconductivity. (Progress in High Temperature Superconductivity Ser.: Vol. 15). 828p. (C). 1989. pap. 61.00 (*9971-5-0834-6*); text 161.00 (*9971-5-0816-8*) World Scientific Pub.

— The Rainflow Method in Fatigue. (Illus.). 240p. 1992. text 175.00 (*0-7506-0504-9*) Buttrwrth-Heinemann.

Murakami, Yasusuke. An Anticlassical Political-Economic Analysis: A Vision for the Next Century. Yamamura, Kozo, tr. LC 95-48950. 498p. (C). 1996. text 65.00 (*0-8047-2646-9*) Stanford U Pr.

— An Anticlassical Political-Economic Analysis: A Vision for the Next Century. Yamamura, Kozo, tr. & intro. by. 498p. 1998. pap. 24.95 (*0-8047-3519-0*) Stanford U Pr.

Murakawa, S., jt. auth. see Kiya, F.

Muraki, Eiji & Bock, R. Darrell. Parscale: IRT Based Test Scoring & Item Analysis for Graded Open-Ended Exercises & Performance Tasks. 1993. ring bd. 30.00 (*0-89498-032-7*) Sci Ware.

Murakovic, Antun. Overcome Shyness from Inside & Succeed in Life: New Approach to Shyness Control Without Medication or Boring Treatment. (ENG & JPN.). 200p. (Orig.). 1989. pap. write for info. (*0-929602-01-3*) Mura Pub Co.

Murakushi, Nisabureo. The Transfer of Coal-Mining Technology for Japan to Manchuria & Manpower Problems, Focusing on the Development of the Fushun Coal Mines LC 84-121943. (Hsdp-Je Ser.). 92p. 1981. write for info. (*92-808-0225-9*) UN.

Mural, T. A Real Variable Method for the Cauchy Transform, & Analytic Capacity. (Lecture Notes in Mathematics Ser.: Vol. 1307). viii, 133p. 1988. 31.95 (*0-387-19091-0*) Spr-Verlag.

Muraleedharan, N., jt. auth. see Ananthakrishnan, T. N.

Murali, B. N., jt. auth. see Economides, Michael J.

Murali, K., jt. auth. see Lakshmanan, M.

Muralidhar, B. V., jt. ed. see Jaya Kumar, G. Stanley.

Muralidhar, Rao R. & Ganga, Prasad G. Graphical User Interface (GUI) with X-Windows & Motif. 1994. write for info. (*81-224-0635-1*, Pub. by Wiley Estrn) Franklin.

Muralidhara, H. S., ed. Solid-Liquid Separations: Waste Management & Productivity Enhancement. LC 89-17828. 584p. 1990. 87.50 (*0-935470-54-9*) Battelle.

Muralidharan, S. South Indian Studies. LC 98-915590. viii, 191p. 1998. write for info. (*81-7646-013-3*) BR Pub.

Muralt, Jurgen Von, see Sajhau, Jean-Paul & Von Muralt, Jurgen.

Muramaru, N. Japanese Folktales. (Illus.). 160p. (J). (gr. 4-9). 1993. pap. 11.95 (*4-89684-228-6*, Pub. by Yohan Pubns) Weatherhill.

Muramatsu, Michio. Local Power in the Japanese State. Scheiner, Betsey & White, James, trs. from JPN. LC 96-41515. (Contemporary Japanese Politics Ser.). 206p. 1997. 45.00 (*0-520-07275-8*, Pub. by U CA Pr); pap. 16.00 (*0-520-07276-6*, Pub. by U CA Pr) Cal Prin Full Svc.

Muramatsu, Michio & Naschold, Frieder, eds. State & Administration in Japan & Germany: A Comparative Perspective on Continuity & Change. LC 96-30384. (Studies in Organization: Vol. 75). xiv, 349p. (C). 1996. text 78.95 (*3-11-014462-X*) De Gruyter.

Muramatsu, Mitsuo, jt. ed. see Evans, E. Anthony.

Muramatsu, R. & Dudley, N. A., eds. Production & Industrial Systems: Proceedings of the 4th International Conference on Production Research, Tokyo, 1977. 1340p. 1978. 187.00 (*0-85066-138-2*) Taylor & Francis.

Muramatsu, T. Cell Surface & Differentiation. (Illus.). 160p. (C). 1990. text 69.95 (*0-412-30850-9*, A4750) Chapman & Hall.

Muramatsu, Takashi, ed. Handbook of Endoglycosidases & Glycoamidases. 362p. 1992. lib. bdg. 199.00 (*0-8493-3618-X*, QP 609) CRC Pr.

Muramoto, Naboru. Healing Ourselves. (Illus.). 160p. 1976. pap. 12.50 (*0-380-00900-5*, Avon Bks) Morrow Avon.

***Muran, J. Christopher.** Self-Relations in the Psychotherapy Process. LC 00-40164. 2000. write for info. (*1-55798-733-5*) Am Psychol.

***Muran, J. Christopher & Safran, Jeremy D.** Negotiating the Therapeutic Alliance: A Relational Treatment Guide. LC 99-57055. 264p. 2000. lib. bdg. 32.50 (*1-57230-512-6*, C0512) Guilford Pubns.

Muran, J. Christopher, jt. ed. see Safran, Jeremy D.

Muran, Lois K. Family Tree Questionnaire. 108p. 1997. pap. 14.00 (*0-8063-4554-3*, 9267) Clearfield Co.

Muran, Ruth, jt. auth. see Maran Graphics Staff.

Murano. Understanding Food Science & Technology. (Health Sciences). 2001. pap. 48.00 (*0-534-54486-X*) Wadsworth Pub.

Murano, Elsa, jt. auth. see Hooker, Neal.

Murano, Genesio. Protease Inhibitors of Human Plasma-Biochemistry & Pathophysiology. (Reviews of Hematology: Vol. II). 1985. 69.95 (*0-915340-14-3*) PJD Pubns.

Murano, Genesio, ed. see Bick, Roger L.

Murano, Senchu, tr. see Numata Center Buddhist Translation & Research Staff.

Murano, Vincent. Dead File. 1996. mass mkt. 5.99 (*0-312-95692-4*) Tor Bks.

Murano, Vincent & Hammer, Richard. The Thursday Club: A Novel. Rubenstein, Julie, ed. 288p. 1994. reprint ed. mass mkt. 5.50 (*0-671-73864-X*) PB.

Murano, Vincent & Hoffer, William. Cop Hunter. 320p. 1991. reprint ed. mass mkt. 4.95 (*0-671-66959-1*, Pocket Star Bks) PB.

Muranski, Darlyne. The World of Reptiles: Theme Pack. Schaffer, Donna, ed. (Ranger Rick Science Spectacular Ser.). (Illus.). 16p. (J). (gr. 2-5). 1996. pap. 36.90 (*1-56784-286-0*) Newbridge Educ.

Murant, A. F., jt. ed. see Harrison, B. D.

Murao, Tadahiro, jt. auth. see Welch, Graham.

Muraoka. Macroeconomics 2.0. Date not set. pap. text, student ed. write for info. (*0-314-00840-3*) West Pub.

— Microeconomics 2.0. Date not set. pap. text, student ed. write for info. (*0-314-00838-1*) West Pub.

Muraoka, Kageo & Okamura, Kichiemon. Folk Arts & Crafts of Japan. Stegmaier, Daphne, tr. from JPN. LC 72-78600. (Heibonsha Survey of Japanese Art Ser.: Vol. 26). Orig. Title: Mingei. (Illus.). 168p. 1973. 20.00 (*0-8348-1009-3*) Weatherhill.

***Muraoka, T. & Elwolde, J. F., eds.** Sirach, Scrolls & Sages: Proceedings of a Second International Symposium On The Hebrew Of The Dead Sea Scrolls, Ben Sira & The Mishnah, Held At Leiden University, 15-17 December 1997. LC 99-37993. Vol. 33. (Illus.). Viii, 364p. 1999. text 112.00 (*90-04-11553-6*) Brill Academic Pubs.

Muraoka, T. & Porten, B. A Grammar of Egyptian Aramaic. LC 97-35502. xlix, 393p. 1997. 110.00 (*90-04-10499-2*) Brill Academic Pubs.

Muraoka, T., et al. The Hebrew of the Dead Sea Scrolls & Ben Sira: Proceedings of a Symposium Held at Leiden University, 11-14 December 1995. LC 97-9134. (Studies on the Texts of the Desert of Judah). 1997. 81.00 (*90-04-10820-3*) Brill Academic Pubs.

Muraoka, Takamitsu. Hebrew-Aramaic Index to the Septuagint: Keyed to the Hatch & Redpath Concordance. LC 98-10548. 152p. (C). 1998. pap. 24.99 (*0-8010-2145-6*) Baker Bks.

Muraoka, Tsunetsugu. Studies in Shinto Thought, 10 vols., Set. Brown, Delmer M. & Araki, James T., trs. (Documentary Reference Collections). 293p. 1988. 395.00 (*0-318-35981-2*, CMJ05, Greenwood Pr) Greenwood.

— Studies in Shinto Thought, 10 vols., Vol. 5. Brown, Delmer M. & Araki, James T., trs. LC 88-21311. (Documentary Reference Collections). 293p. 1988. lib. bdg. 49.95 (*0-313-26555-0*, CNJ05, Greenwood Pr) Greenwood.

Murari, B., et al, eds. Smart Power ICs: Technologies & Application. 496p. 1995. 163.95 (*3-540-60332-8*) Spr-Verlag.

Murari, G., jt. ed. see Villa, A.

Murarka. Handbook of Materials for Microelectronics. 900p. text. write for info. (*0-471-29820-4*) Wiley.

Murarka. Solid Waste Disposal & Re-Use in the United States, Vol. I. 200p. 1987. 110.00 (*0-8493-4647-9*, CRC Reprint) Franklin.

— Solid Waste Disposal & Re-Use in the United States, Vol. II. 168p. 1987. 101.00 (*0-8493-4648-7*, CRC Reprint) Franklin.

Murarka, S. P., et al, eds. Advanced Interconnects & Contact Materials & Processes for Future Integrated Circuits Vol. 514: Proceedings Materials Research Society Symposium. LC 98-39943. 560p. 1998. text 81.00 (*1-55899-420-3*) Materials Res.

— Interface Control of Electrical, Chemical, & Mechanical Properties Vol. 318: Materials Research Society Symposium Proceedings. LC 94-7922. 725p. 1994. text 80.00 (*1-55899-217-0*) Materials Res.

Murarka, Shyam P. Metallization: Theory & Practice for VLSI & ULSI. 250p. 1992. text 69.95 (*0-7506-9001-1*) Buttrwrth-Heinemann.

Murarka, Shyam P., ed. Silicides for VLSI Applications. 1983. text 65.00 (*0-12-511220-3*) Acad Pr.

Murarka, Shyam P. & Peckerar, Martin C. Electronic Materials: Science & Technology. 622p. 1989. text 93.00 (*0-12-511120-7*) Acad Pr.

***Murarka, Shyam P., et al.** Copper - Fundamental Mechanisms for Microelectronic Applications: Fundamental Mechanisms & Technological Applications. LC 99-45535. 336p. 2000. text 99.00 (*0-471-25256-5*) Wiley.

Murarka, Shyam P., jt. auth. see Steigerwald, Joseph M.

Muraro, Michelangelo. Paolo da Venezia. LC 77-84667. (Illus.). 1970. 95.00 (*0-271-00098-8*) A Wofsy Fine Arts.

— Venetian Villas. (Art & Architecture Ser.). (Illus.). 512p. 1998. 39.95 (*3-89508-242-2*, 520166) Konemann.

***Muraro, Michelangelo & Marton, Paolo.** Villen in Venetien. (Illus.). 1999. 0.00 (*3-89508-214-7*) Konemann.

Murasaki Shikibu. Diary of Lady Murasaki. LC 96-217268. 160p. 1999. pap. text 6.00 (*0-14-043576-X*) Addson-Wesley Educ.

— Genji Monogatari. Suematsu, Kencho, tr. LC 72-77523. 232p. 1973. reprint ed. pap. 12.95 (*0-8048-1045-1*) Tuttle Pubng.

— The Tale of Genji. Seidensticker, Edward G., tr. from JPN. LC 76-13680. 1978. pap. 29.95 (*0-394-73530-7*) Knopf.

— The Tale of Genji. Seidensticker, Edward G., tr. LC 89-40606. (Vintage Classics Ser.). 256p. 1990. pap. 14.00 (*0-679-72953-4*) Vin Bks.

***Murasaki Shikibu & Waley, Arthur.** The Tale of Genji. LC 00-29542. 2000. pap. write for info. (*0-486-41415-9*) Dover.

Murase, Masatoshi. Dynamics of Cellular Motility. LC 91-19126. (Nonlinear Science: Theory & Applications Ser.). 376p. 1992. 575.00 (*0-471-93576-X*) Wiley.

***Murase, Miyeko, et al.** The Arts of Japan: An International Symposium: Papers Prepared for an International Symposium Organized by the Metropolitan Museum of Art in Conjunction with the Exhibition the Art of Japan from the Mary Griggs Burke Collection. LC 00-27482. (Illus.). 2000. write for info. (*0-87099-951-6*) Metro Mus Art.

— Bridge of Dreams: The Mary Griggs Burke Collection of Japanese Art. LC 99-54465. (Illus.). 650p. 2000. 90.00 (*0-8109-6551-8*, Pub. by Abrams) Time Warner.

Murashima, Kumiko. Katazome: Japanese Paste-Resist Dyeing for Contemporary Use. Rich, Chris, ed. LC 93-34626. (Illus.). 104p. 1994. 19.95 (*0-937274-72-0*) Lark Books.

Murashkevich, A. M. English-Russian Aviation & Space Abbreviations Dictionary. (ENG & RUS.). 622p. 1981. 39.95 (*0-8288-0005-7*, M15483) Fr & Eur.

— Modern English-Russian Aeronautical Dictionary. (ENG & RUS.). 358p. 1993. 95.00 (*0-7859-9079-8*) Fr & Eur.

Murashkevich, A. M. & Novichkov, N. N. English-Russian Dictionary on Advanced Aerospace Systems. unabridged ed. Beregovoy, G. T. & Manucharov, A. A., eds. (ENG & RUS.). 724p. (C). 1993. 39.95 (*0-8285-5064-6*) Firebird NY.

Murashkevich, A. M. & Vladimirov, O. N. English-Russian Aviation & Space Abbreviations Dictionary. (ENG & RUS.). 622p. 1981. 70.00 (*0-7855-7161-2*) St Mut.

Muraski, Michel L., jt. auth. see Zimmerman, Donald E.

Muraskin & Roberts. Visions or Change: Crime & Justice in the 21st Century. 2nd ed. LC 98-19422. 444p. (C). 1998. pap. text 52.00 (*0-13-096239-2*) P-H.

***Muraskin, J.** Morality & Law. 2nd ed. 400p. 2000. pap. 43.00 (*0-13-916958-X*) P-H.

Muraskin, M. Mathematical Aesthetic Principles/ Nonintegrable Systems. 232p. 1995. text 55.00 (*981-02-2200-9*) World Scientific Pub.

Muraskin, Roslyn, ed. Issues in Justice: Exploring Policy Issues in the Criminal Justice System. LC 90-50420. xi, 175p. (C). 1990. text 40.00 (*1-55605-169-7*); pap. text 28.00 (*1-55605-168-9*) Wyndham Hall.

***Muraskin, Roslyn, ed.** Women & Justice. 240p. 1999. pap. text 24.00 (*90-5700-551-4*, Harwood Acad Pubs) Gordon & Breach.

— Women & Justice: Development of International Policy. 240p. 1999. text 40.00 (*90-5700-550-6*, Harwood Acad Pubs) Gordon & Breach.

Muraskin, Roslyn & Alleman, Ted. It's a Crime: Women & Justice. 448p. (C). 1993. pap. text 39.00 (*0-13-962051-6*) P-H.

— It's a Crime: Women in Justice. 2nd ed. LC 99-26309. (Illus.). 488p. (C). 1999. pap. text 35.00 (*0-13-011389-1*) P-H.

Muraskin, William. The Politics of International Health: The Children's Vaccine Initiative & the Struggle to Develop Vaccines for the Third World. LC 97-51725. 288p. (C). 1998. text 65.50 (*0-7914-3999-2*); pap. text 21.95 (*0-7914-4000-1*) State U NY Pr.

Murasov, Jurij, jt. auth. see Drubek Meyer, Natascha.

Murasugi, Kimiko & Stainton, Robert J. Philosophy & Linguistics. LC 99-158487. (Philosophy of Language Ser.). 296p. (C). 1998. text 75.00 (*0-8133-9085-0*, Pub. by Westview) HarpC.

Murasugi, Kunio. Knot Theory & Its Applications. Kurpita, Bohdan, tr. from JPN. LC 96-16329.Tr. of Musubime Riron to Sono Oyo. (Illus.). 341p. 1996. 69.50 (*0-8176-3817-2*) Birkhauser.

— On Closed Three-Braids. LC 74-17176. (Memoirs Ser.: No. 1/151). 114p. 1974. pap. 18.00 (*0-8218-1851-1*, MEMO/1/151) Am Math.

Murasugi, Kunio & Kurpita, Bohdan I. A Study of Braids. LC 99-27052. (Mathematics & Its Applications Ser.). 1999. write for info. (*0-7923-5767-1*) Kluwer Academic.

Murasugi, Kunio & Przytycki, Jozef H. An Index of a Graph with Applications to Knot Theory. LC 93-27284. (Memoirs of the American Mathematical Society Ser.: No. 508). 101p. 1993. pap. 29.00 (*0-8218-2570-4*, MEMO/06/508) Am Math.

Murat, Achille. The United States of North America. 1977. text 23.95 (*0-8369-9231-8*, 9085) Ayer.

***Murat, Carolle Jean.** Natural Pregnancy A-Z. LC 99-45797. (Illus.). 156p. 2000. 19.95 (*1-56170-709-0*, L461) Hay House.

Murat, Ines. Colbert. Cook, Robert F. & Van Asselt, Jeannie, trs. LC 84-2194. (Illus.). 308p. reprint ed. pap. 95.50 (*0-8357-3134-0*, 203939700012) Bks Demand.

Murat, Laure, jt. auth. see Schezen, Roberto.

Murata. Handbook of Optical Fiber & Cables. 2nd ed. (Optical Engineering Ser.: Vol. 53). (Illus.). 552p. 1996. text 170.00 (*0-8247-9719-1*) Dekker.

Murata, Alice. Black Rain. LC 95-79305. (Illus.). 32p. (Orig.). 1996. pap. 7.95 (*1-884242-94-4*) Multicult Pubns.

Murata, H. Development of Optical Fibers in Japan, Vol .2. xii, 156p. 1989. pap. text 107.00 (*2-88124-372-X*) Gordon & Breach.

Murata, K. K. Code Manual for Contain 2.0: Computer Code for Nuclear Reactor Containment Analysis. 956p. 1997. ring bd. 65.00 (*0-16-062873-3*) USGPO.

Murata, Kazuo & Harrison, Alan. How to Make Japanese Management Methods Work Best in the West. 93p. 1991. text 61.95 (*0-566-09085-6*, Pub. by Gower) Ashgate Pub Co.

— How to Make Japanese Management Methods Work in the West. 112p. 1995. pap. 29.95 (*0-566-07675-6*, Pub. by Gower) Ashgate Pub Co.

Murata, Keinosuke, et al. Sakura: Cherry Blossom Paintings by Yoshiko Ishikawa. LC 92-62884. (Illus.). 104p. 1993. pap. text 21.95 (*0-940979-22-5*) Natl Museum Women.

Murata, Kenji. Bosai: A Pocket Color Book. 1997. pap. text 9.95 (*0-87040-997-2*) Japan Pubns USA.

Murata Kyuzo. Four Seasons of Bonsai. McCandless, Kate, tr. 1997. pap. text 19.95 (*4-7700-2120-8*, Pub. by Kodansha Int) OUP.

Murata, Margaret, ed. Marc'Antonio Pasqualini (1614-1691), Vol. 3. (Italian Cantata in the Seventeenth Century Ser.). 300p. 1986. text 25.00 (*0-8240-8877-8*) Garland.

Murata, Michinori. Water & Light: Looking Through Lenses. LC 92-19969. (Illus.). (J). (gr. 1-3). 1993. lib. bdg. 19.93 (*0-8225-2904-1*, Lerner Publctns) Lerner Pub.

Murata, Noboru, jt. auth. see Black, Alexander.

Murata, Noboru, jt. auth. see Black, Alexandra.

M

An Asterisk (*) at the beginning of an entry indicates that the title is appearing for the first time.

Murata, Norio. Stress Responses of Photosynthetic Organisms: Molecular Mechanisms & Molecular Regulations. LC 97-32764. 268p. 1997. 154.50 (*0-444-82884-2*) Elsevier.

Murata, Norio, ed. Research in Photosynthesis: Proceedings of the IXth International Congress on Photosynthesis, Nagoya, Japan, August 30-September 4, 1992, 4 vols. LC 92-39162. 3512p. (C). 1993. text 1516.00 (*0-7923-2073-5*) Kluwer Academic.

Murata, Norio, jt. auth. see Siegenthaler, Paul A.

***Murata, Sachiko.** Chinese Gleams of Sufi Light: Wang Tai-yu's Great Learning of the Pure & Real & Liu Chih's Displaying the Concealment of the Real Realm. With a New Translation of Lawa'ih from the Persian by William C. Chittick. (C). 2000. pap. text 23.95 (*0-7914-4638-7*) State U NY Pr.

— Chinese Gleams of Sufi Light: Wang Tai-yu's Great Learning of the Pure & Real & Liu Chih's Displaying the Concealment of the Real Realm. With a New Translation of Lawa'ih from the Persian by William C. Chittick. (C). 2000. text 71.50 (*0-7914-4637-9*) State U NY Pr.

Murata, Sachiko. The Tao of Islam. 400p. 1996. pap. 22.95 (*0-614-21396-7*, 1215) Kazi Pubns.

— The Tao of Islam: A Sourcebook on Gender Relationships in Islamic Thought. LC 91-2610. 397p. (C). 1992. text 64.50 (*0-7914-0913-9*); pap. text 24.95 (*0-7914-0914-7*) State U NY Pr.

Murata, Sachiko & Chittick, William C. The Vision of Islam: Reflecting on the Hadith of Gabriel. LC 94-16064. (Visions of Reality Ser.). (Illus.). 352p. (Orig.). (C). 1994. pap. text 18.95 (*1-55778-516-3*) Paragon Hse.

Murata, Yasuo. Optimal Control Methods for Linear Discrete-Time Economic Systems. (Illus.). 175p. 1982. 102.95 (*0-387-90709-2*) Spr-Verlag.

Murata, Yoshio, ed. Crop Productivity & Solar Energy Utilization in Various Climates in Japan. LC 76-300339. (JIBP Synthesis Ser.: No. 11). 254p. 1975. reprint ed. pap. 78.80 (*0-608-01591-1*, 206201000001) Bks Demand.

Muratore, Joseph R. Italian-Americans in Rhode Island. (Images of America Ser.). (Illus.). 128p. 1998. pap. 16.99 (*0-7524-0839-9*) Arcadia Publng.

— The Remains of Christopher Columbus. (Illus.). 91p. 1973. pap. 3.00 (*0-686-09021-7*) Muratore.

***Muratore, Marina.** The Bluffer's Guide to Women. (Bluffer's Guides Ser.). 64p. 1999. pap. 5.95 (*1-902825-13-6*) Oval Bks.

Muratore, Mary J. Cornelian Theater: The Metadramatic Dimension. LC 90-70978. 117p. 1990. lib. bdg. 23.95 (*0-917786-84-X*) Summa Pubns.

Muratorio, Blanca. Culture & History in Ecuadorian Upper Amazon: The Life & Times of Grandfather Alonso. (Illus.). 320p. (C). 1991. text 45.00 (*0-8135-1684-6*), pap. text 18.00 (*0-8135-1685-4*) Rutgers U Pr.

Murauchi, Sadanori & Asanuma, Toshioo. Seismic Reflection Profiles in the Western Pacific, 1965-74. LC 80-499022. 232p. 1977. reprint ed. pap. 72.00 (*0-608-01250-5*, 206193800001) Bks Demand.

Murav, Harriet. Holy Foolishness: Dostoevsky's Novels & the Poetics of Cultural Critique. (Illus.). 272p. (C). 1993. 39.50 (*0-8047-2059-2*) Stanford U Pr.

— Russia's Legal Fictions. LC 97-45272. (Law, Meaning, & Violence Ser.). 280p. (C). 1998. text 49.50 (*0-472-10879-4*, 10879) U of Mich Pr.

Muravchick, Stanley. Geroanesthesia: Principles for Management of the Elderly Patient. (Illus.). 320p. (C). (gr. 13). 1996. text 66.95 (*0-8016-7238-4*, 07238) Mosby Inc.

Muravchick, Stanley, ed. Subspecialty Care. LC 97-47123. (Atlas of Anesthesia Ser.: no. 5). (C). 1998. text 135.00 (*0-443-07904-8*) Church.

Muravchik, Joshua. Exporting Democracy: Fulfilling America's Destiny. 192p. 1992. 24.95 (*0-8447-3733-X*, AEI Pr); pap. 12.95 (*0-8447-3734-8*, AEI Pr) Am Enterprise.

— The Imperative of American Leadership: A Challenge to Neo Isolationism. 200p. 1996. 24.95 (*0-8447-3958-8*, AEI Pr) Am Enterprise.

— Nicaragua's Slow March to Communism. 1986. 3.00 (*0-317-90495-7*) Cuban Amer Natl Fndtn.

Murav'Ev, Andrei N. A History of the Church of Russia. LC 76-133816. reprint ed. 49.50 (*0-404-04541-3*) AMS Pr.

***Muraviev, Dimitri, et al.** Ion Exchange. LC 99-51828. (Highlights of Russian Science Ser.). 905p. 2000. 225.00 (*0-8247-0325-1*) Dekker.

Muravina, Nina. Vstrechi s Pasternakom. LC 90-4742. (RUS.). 223p. (Orig.). 1990. pap. 15.00 (*1-55779-036-1*) Hermitage Pubs.

Muravyeva, Irina. Kudriavyi Leitenant. LC 95-25951. (RUS.). 104p. (Orig.). 1995. pap. 9.00 (*1-55779-076-0*) Hermitage Pubs.

***Muravyova, Irina.** The Nomadic Soul. (Glas Ser.: Vol. 22). 240p. 2000. pap. 14.95 (*1-56663-276-5*, Pub. by I R Dee) Natl Bk Netwk.

Murawski, Darlyne. The World of Reptiles. (Ranger Rick Science Spectacular Ser.). (Illus.). 16p. (Orig.). (J). (gr. 2-4). 1996. pap. 16.95 (*1-56784-224-0*) Newbridge Educ.

— The World of Reptiles: Student Book. (Ranger Rick Science Spectacular Ser.). (Illus.). (Orig.). (J). (gr. 2-4). 1996. pap. 3.95 (*1-56784-249-6*) Newbridge Educ.

Murawski, Darlyne, jt. auth. see Cole, Ron.

Murawski, Elisabeth. Moon & Mercury. LC 90-11915. 72p. (Orig.). 1990. pap. 8.00 (*0-931846-37-4*) Wash Writers Pub.

Murawski, Elizabeth. Troubled by an Angel. 30p. (Orig.). 1997. pap. 6.00 (*1-880834-37-5*) Cleveland St Univ Poetry Ctr.

***Murawski, Frank.** Home Networking Structured Wiring Systems: U. S. Markets, Technologies & Competitors: 1999-2003 Analysis & Forecasts. 100p. 1999. pap. text 4900.00 (*1-929904-01-0*) World Info Tech.

Murawski, Frank. U. S. Secondary Telecom Industry - Markets & Opportunities: 1989-1995 Analysis. (Illus.). 320p. 1989. pap. text 2400.00 (*1-878218-24-7*) World Info Tech.

Murawski, Frank, jt. auth. see Bender, Amadee.

Murawski, H., jt. ed. see Dennis, J. G.

Murawski, Hans. Geologisches Woerterbuch. (GER.). 39.95 (*0-7859-8352-X*, 3423030380) Fr & Eur.

— Geology Dictionary: Geologisches Woerterbuch. 9th ed. (GER.). 254p. 1992. pap. 29.95 (*0-8288-1470-8*, M7418) Fr & Eur.

***Murawski, Laura.** How to Draw Cars. LC 00-28040. (Illus.). 2000. write for info. (*0-8239-5548-6*, PowerKids) Rosen Group.

— How to Draw Cats. LC 00-28048. 2000. write for info. (*0-8239-5549-4*, PowerKids) Rosen Group.

— How to Draw Dogs. LC 00-28047. (Illus.). (J). 2000. write for info. (*0-8239-5551-6*, PowerKids) Rosen Group.

— How to Draw Horses. LC 00-28039. 2000. write for info. (*0-8239-5552-4*) Rosen Group.

***Murawski, Thomas A.** Writing Readable Regulations. LC 98-89960. 168p. 1999. spiral bd. 22.50 (*0-89089-849-9*) Carolina Acad Pr.

Muray, Julius J., jt. auth. see Brodie, I.

Muray, Julius J., jt. auth. see Brodie, Ivor.

Muray, Les. An Introduction to the Process Understanding of Science, Society, & the Self: A Philosophy for Modern Man. LC 88-9319. (Symposium Ser.: Vol. 26). 200p. 1988. lib. bdg. 79.95 (*0-88946-336-0*) E Mellen.

Murayama, Milton. All I Asking for Is My Body. LC 88-6967. 120p. 1988. reprint ed. pap. 7.95 (*0-8248-1172-0*, Kolowalu Bk) UH Pr.

— Five Years on a Rock. LC 94-9806. 160p. (C). 1994. 17.95 (*0-8248-1647-1*); pap. 9.95 (*0-8248-1677-3*) UH Pr.

— Plantation Boy. LC 97-33350. 180p. 1998. 24.95 (*0-8248-1965-9*); pap. 14.95 (*0-8248-2007-X*) UH Pr.

Murayama, Yoshimasa. Mesoscopic Systems. 338p. 1999. pap. 99.95 (*3-527-29376-0*, Wiley-VCH) Wiley.

Murbarger, Nell. Ghosts of the Glory Trail. (Illus.). 291p. 1978. 29.95 (*0-913814-68-7*); pap. 14.95 (*0-913814-59-8*) Nevada Pubns.

Murcava, L. O., ed. see Dinneen, Patrick S.

Murch. Intelligent Software Agents. LC 98-43374. 300p. 1998. pap. text 44.99 (*0-13-011021-3*) P-H.

Murch, A. E., tr. see Pavese, Cesare.

Murch, A. E., tr. & intro. see Pavese, Cesare.

Murch, Alma E. Development of the Detective Novel. LC 69-10138. 272p. 1969. reprint ed. lib. bdg. 35.00 (*0 8371 0581-1*, MUDN, Greenwood Pr) Greenwood.

Murch, Alma E., ed. see Dumas, Alexandre.

Murch, Arvin. Black Frenchmen: The Political Integration of the French Antilles. LC 76-170654. 184p. 1971. 18.95 (*0-87073-034-7*) Schenkman Bks Inc.

Murch, Franklin B. Programming Windows in Japanese. (JPN.). (C). 2001. pap. text 34.00 (*0-13-447723-5*) P-H.

Murch, G. E. Atomic Diffusion in Defective Solids. 1980. 36.00 (*0-87849-516-9*, Pub. by Trans T Pub) Enfield Pubs NH.

Murch, G. E., jt. ed. see Chaturverdi, D. K.

Murch, G. E., ed. see Metallurgical Society of AIME Staff.

Murch, Gerald M. Visual & Auditory Perception. LC 74-172349. (Illus.). (C). 1973. pap. write for info. (*0-672-60779-4*, Bobbs) Macmillan.

Murch, Gerald M., ed. Studies in Perception. LC 74-8398. (C). 1976. pap. text. write for info. (*0-672-61189-9*, Bobbs) Macmillan.

Murch, Graeme, ed. Diffusion in Solids: Unsolved Problems. 294p. 1992. text 91.00 (*0-87849-631-9*, Pub. by Trans T Pub) Enfield Pubs NH.

Murch, James. Adventuring for Christ. 360p. pap. 4.99 (*0-89900-236-6*) College Pr Pub.

Murch, Mervyn, jt. auth. see Davis, Gwynn.

Murch, Muriel. Journey in the Middle of the Road: One Woman's Path Through a Midlife Education. Columbus, Marge, ed. LC 96-108474. 200p. 1995. pap. 16.95 (*0-9638327-4-3*) Sibyl Pubns.

Murch, Walter. In the Blink of an Eye: A Perspective on Film Editing. 108p. (Orig.). 1995. pap. 12.95 (*1-879505-23-1*) Silman James Pr.

Murchadha, Diarmaid O. Family Names of County Cork. 338p. 1996. pap. 23.95 (*1-898256-13-6*, Pub. by Collins Press) Irish Bks Media.

Murchie-Beyma, Tia A. An Analytic Profile of Hispanic Organizations of the Washington Area, Vol. O8. 1991. 6.50 (*1-888028-21-1*) GWU Ctr WAS.

— An Annotated Directory of Hispanic Organizations of the Washington Area, Vol. O9. 1991. 6.50 (*1-888028-22-X*) GWU Ctr WAS.

Murchie, Guy. The Seven Mysteries of Life: An Exploration in Science & Philosophy. 1999. pap. 17.00 (*0-395-95791-5*) HM.

— The Soul School: Confessions of a Passenger on Planet Earth. LC 94-18970. (Illus.). 672p. 1994. pap. 14.95 (*1-56474-105-2*) Fithian Pr.

Murchison, Adrianne M. Kalieding on the Road to Happiness. Garvey, Amy, ed. (Illus.). 196p. 1998. pap. 13.95 (*0-9667344-2-4*) Marjun Pubg Co.

Murchison, Bill. Nacogdoches - Past & Present: A Legacy of Texas Pride. Murchison, Cynthia H., ed. LC 86-72139. 100p. (Orig.). 1986. pap. 21.95 (*0-9617381-0-3*) B&C Pub Odessa.

Murchison, Carl. The Case for & Against Psychical Belief. LC 75-7389. (Perspectives in Psychical Research Ser.). (Illus.). 1975. reprint ed. 33.95 (*0-405-07037-3*) Ayer.

— Criminal Intelligence. (Historical Foundations of Forensic Psychiatry & Psychology Ser.). 291p. 1983. reprint ed. lib. bdg. 29.50 (*0-306-76183-1*) Da Capo.

Murchison, Carl, ed. Psychologies of 1930. LC 73-2980. (Classics in Psychology Ser.). 1976. reprint ed. 34.95 (*0-405-05152-2*) Ayer.

Murchison, Claudius T. Resale Price Maintenance. LC 68-56673. (Columbia University. Studies in the Social Sciences: No. 192). reprint ed. 20.00 (*0-404-51192-9*) AMS Pr.

Murchison, Cynthia H., ed. see Murchison, Bill.

Murchison, Keith N. Canadian Success Stories in the Japanese Software Market. (Illus.). 100p. (Orig.). (C). 1995. pap. text 35.00 (*0-7881-2444-7*) DIANE Pub.

Murchison, Kenneth M. Federal Criminal Law Doctrines: The Forgotten Influence of National Prohibition. LC 94-18235. 288p. 1994. text 47.95 (*0-8223-1510-6*) Duke.

Murchison, Marx F. The Taskmaster. 243p. Date not set. mass mkt. 4.99 (*1-55197-113-5*) Picasso Publ.

***Murchison, Shanna.** The Wizard Woman. 204p. 2000. 16.95 (*1-58345-020-3*); pap. 13.95 (*1-58345-018-1*) Domhan Bks.

Murchison, Shanna. The Wizard Woman. LC 98-86290. 325p. 1998. 25.00 (*0-7388-0051-1*); pap. 15.00 (*0-7388-0052-X*) Xlibris Corp.

Murchison, William & Buckley, William F., Jr. There's More to Life Than Politics. rev. ed. LC 98-22732. 300p. 1998. 22.95 (*0-9653208-3-9*) Spence Pub.

Murchland, Bernard. The Dream of Christian Socialism: An Essay on Its European Origins. LC 81-14919. (AEI Studies: No. 343). 88p. reprint ed. pap. 30.00 (*0-7837-1081-X*, 204161100021) Bks Demand.

— Humanism & Capitalism: A Survey of Thought on Morality. LC 83-11785. (AEI Studies: No. 387). 76p. reprint ed. pap. 30.00 (*0-8357-4489-2*, 203734200008) Bks Demand.

***Murchland, Bernard.** Voices of Democracy. LC 00-8863. 232p. 2000. 22.00 (*0-268-04354-X*) U of Notre Dame Pr.

Murchland, Bernard, compiled by. Voices in American Education: Conversations with Fourteen Major Educators & Public Figures. 219p. (Orig.). 1990. pap. 11.95 (*0-911168-77-X*) Prakken.

Murchland, Bernard, ed. Noble Achievements: Ohio Wesleyan from 1942-1992. (Illus.). 316p. 20.00 (*0-9630909-1-7*) OH Wesleyan U.

Murchland, Bernard, ed. Higher Education & the Practice of Democratic Politics: A Political Education Reader. (Kettering Political Education Ser.). 251p. (Orig.). (C). 1991. pap. text. write for info. (*0-923993-01-0*) Kettering Found.

***Murchu, Liam O.** Black Cat in the Window. 216p. 2000. pap. 17.95 (*1-898256-85-3*, Pub. by Collins Press) Irish Bks Media.

Murcia, Eligia. Record Keeping for Small Rural Businesses. (Technical Notes Ser.: No. 26). (Illus.). 25p. (Orig.). pap. text 2.00 (*0-932288-75-8*) Ctr Intl Ed U of MA.

Murcia, Gilbert De, see De Murcia, Gilbert, ed.

Murcia, Marianne C., et al. Teaching Pronunciation: A Reference for Teachers of English As a Second or Foreign Language. LC 96-20132. (C). 1996. audio 16.95 (*0-521-40695-1*) Cambridge U Pr.

Murciano, Carlos. Las Manos en el Agua. (J). (gr. 3-5). 1997. pap. text 7.50 (*84-279-3337-1*) Lectorum Pubns.

— La Nina Que Aprendia los Nombres y Otros Cuentos. (Punto Infantil Ser.). (SPA.). (J). 1989. 10.70 (*0-606-05403-0*, Pub. by Turtleback) Demco.

Murck. Environmental Biology Encarta. 1999. pap. text 66.00 (*0-471-36986-1*) Wiley.

Murck. Environmental Geology: Study Guide. 154p. 1995. pap. text 30.95 (*0-471-31033-6*) Wiley.

Murck. Geology Today with Geoscience Lab: Geoscience Lab 2, 2 vols., Set. 1999. pap. text 121.90 (*0-471-36250-6*) Wiley.

— Home Planet. 155p. (C). 1999. pap., student ed. 32.95 (*0-471-32323-3*) Wiley.

***Murck, Alfreda.** Poetry & Painting in Song China: The Subtle Art of Dissent. LC 99-44492. Vol. 50. (Illus.). 400p. 2000. 60.00 (*0-674-00243-1*) HUP.

***Murck, Barbara W. & Skinner, Brian J.** Geology Today With Cd. LC 98-23728. 608p. 1999. pap. text 81.95 incl. cd-rom (*0-471-16733-9*) Wiley.

Murck, Barbara W., et al. Dangerous Earth: An Introduction to Geologic Hazards. LC 96-23720. 320p. 1996. pap. 65.95 (*0-471-13565-8*) Wiley.

— Environmental Geology. LC 95-37493. 560p. 1995. pap. 83.95 (*0-471-30356-9*) Wiley.

Murck, Barbara Winifred & Skinner, Brian J. Geology Today: Understanding Our Planet. 544p. 1998. pap. text 72.30 (*0-471-33054-X*) Wiley.

Murck, Christian F., jt. ed. see Bush, Susan.

Murcko, Terry, jt. auth. see Peffer, George.

Murcott, Anne. The Nation's Diet: The Social Science of Food Choice. LC 98-11982. 1998. write for info. (*0-582-30285-4*) Addison-Wesley.

Murcott, David J., jt. auth. see Duggan, Andrew.

Murcott, Susan. The First Buddhist Women: Translations & Commentary on the Therigatha. LC 91-10819. 190p. 1992. pap. 15.00 (*0-938077-42-2*) Parallax Pr.

Murcray, David G., ed. Handbook of High Resolution Infrared Laboratory Spectra of Gases of Atmospheric Interest. 288p. 1981. 166.00 (*0-8493-2950-7*, QC879, CRC Reprint) Franklin.

Murcutt, Glenn. Drawings of Glenn Murcutt. 1999. 49.95 (*1-875498-98-2*) Images Aust AT.

Murd, M. A. Intellectual Modernism of Shibli Nu'mani: An Exposition of His Religious & Political Ideas. 1979. pap. 19.95 (*1-56744-060-6*) Kazi Pubns.

Murdaugh, Carolyn L., jt. auth. see Parsons, Mickey L.

Murdaugh, Lee B. Competence Assessment Tools for Health-System Pharmacies. 346p. 1998. spiral bd. 249.00 (*1-879907-85-2*) Am Soc Hlth-Syst.

***Murdaugh, Lee B.** 2000 Update to Competence Assessment Tools for Health-System Pharmacists. 50p. 2000. write for info. (*1-58528-014-3*) Am Soc Hlth-Syst.

Murday, R., jt. ed. see Harrison, M. L.

***Murdick, Robert G.** Business Policy & Strategy: A Guide to Action. 6th ed. LC 00-31085. 2000. write for info. (*1-57444-277-5*) St Lucie Pr.

Murdick, Robert G. MIS: Concepts & Design. 2nd ed. (Illus.). 672p. 1986. text 50.00 (*0-13-586322-8*) P-H.

Murdick, Robert G. & Ross, Joel E. Information Systems for Modern Management. 2nd ed. (Illus.). 640p. 1975. 29.95 (*0-685-03873-4*) P-H.

— Introduction to Management Information Systems. (Illus.). 1977. text 35.40 (*0-13-486233-3*) P-H.

Murdick, Robert G., et al. Information Systems for Modern Management. 3rd ed. (Illus.). 432p. 1984. text 46.00 (*0-13-464736-X*) P-H.

— Services Operations Management. 650p. (C). 1990. text 88.00 (*0-205-12250-7*, H2250-2) Allyn.

— Services Operations Management. 650p. 1990. teacher ed. write for info. (*0-318-66339-2*, H22510) P-H.

Murdick, William. The Portable Business Writer. LC 98-72065. (English Essentials Ser.). vi, 216 p. 1998. pap. text 8.07 (*0-395-90921-X*) HM.

***Murdico, Suzanne J.** Coyote Attacks. (Animal Attacks Ser.). (Illus.). (J). 2000. 19.00 (*0-516-23313-0*) Childrens.

— Coyote Attacks. (High Interest Bks.). (Illus.). 48p. (J). (gr. 4-7). 2000. pap. 6.95 (*0-516-23513-3*) Childrens.

— Coyote Attacks. LC 99-42405. (Animal Attack! Ser.). (Illus.). 2000. pap. write for info. (*0-531-17601-0*) Watts.

Murdico, Suzanne J. Drug Abuse. LC 97-29235. (Preteen Pressures Ser.). (YA). 1998. 24.26 (*0-8172-5027-1*) Raintree Steck-V.

***Murdico, Suzanne J.** Hakeem Olajuwon. LC 97-27930. (Overcoming the Odds Ser.). (Illus.). 48p. (J). (gr. 4-7). 1998. pap. 7.95 (*0-8172-8002-2*) Raintree Steck-V.

Murdico, Suzanne J. Hakeem Olajuwon. LC 97-27930. (Overcoming the Odds Ser.). (J). 1998. lib. bdg. 24.26 (*0-8172-4131-0*) Raintree Steck-V.

***Murdico, Suzanne J.** Mario Lemieux. (Overcoming the Odds Ser.). (Illus.). 48p. (J). (gr. 4-7). 1998. pap. 7.95 (*0-8172-8004-9*) Raintree Steck-V.

Murdico, Suzanne J. Mario Lemieux. LC 97-36691. (Overcoming the Odds Ser.). (J). (gr. 4-6). 1998. 24.26 (*0-8172-4126-4*) Raintree Steck-V.

***Murdico, Suzanne J.** Monica Seles. LC 97-16807. (Overcoming the Odds Ser.). (Illus.). 48p. (J). (gr. 4-7). 1998. pap. 7.95 (*0-8172-8001-4*) Raintree Steck-V.

Murdico, Suzanne J. Monica Seles. LC 97-16807. (Overcoming the Odds Ser.). 1998. 24.26 (*0-8172-4128-0*) Raintree Steck-V.

***Murdico, Suzanne J.** Tiger Attacks. (Animal Attacks Ser.). (Illus.). (J). 2000. 19.00 (*0-516-23319-X*) Childrens.

— Tiger Attacks. (High Interest Bks.). (Illus.). 48p. (J). (gr. 4-7). 2000. pap. 6.95 (*0-516-23519-2*) Childrens.

— Tiger Attacks. LC 99-40448. (Animal Attack! Ser.). (Illus.). 2000. pap. write for info. (*0-531-17607-X*) Watts.

— Volunteering to Help the Environment. (Service-Learning Ser.). (Illus.). (YA). 2000. 19.00 (*0-516-23373-4*) Childrens.

— Volunteering to Help the Environment. LC 99-88962. (Service-Learning Ser.). (Illus.). 48p. (gr. 4-7). 2000. pap. 6.95 (*0-516-23573-7*) Grolier Publishing.

— Wild Dog Attacks. (Animal Attacks Ser.). (Illus.). (J). 2000. 19.00 (*0-516-23316-5*) Childrens.

— Wild Dog Attacks. (High Interest Bks.). (Illus.). 48p. (J). (gr. 4-7). 2000. pap. 6.95 (*0-516-23516-8*) Childrens.

Murdie, Alan. Environmental Law Citizen Action. 176p. (Orig.). 1992. 24.00 (*1-85383-156-5*, Pub. by Escan Pubns) Island Pr.

— Intellectual Property Law. (Questions & Answers Ser.). 300p. 1997. 18.00 (*1-85941-274-2*, Pub. by Cavendish Pubng) Gaunt.

Murdin, L., ed. see Forbes, Eric G.

***Murdin, Lesley.** How Much is Enough? Endings in Psychotherapy in Counselling LC 99-30170. 2000. write for info. (*0-415-18893-8*) Routledge.

Murdin, Lesley & Willmoth, Frances, eds. The Correspondence of John Flamsteed, the First Astronomer Royal, Vol. 2. (Illus.). 1128p. 1997. 300.00 (*0-7503-0391-3*) IOP Pub.

Murdin, Leslie, jt. auth. see Murdin, Paul.

Murdin, P., jt. ed. see Beers, P.

***Murdin, Paul, ed.** Encyclopedia of Astronomy & Astrophysics, 4 vols. (Illus.). 2500p. 2000. 650.00 (*1-56159-268-4*) Groves Dictionaries.

Murdin, Paul & Murdin, Leslie. Supernovae. 256p. 1985. text 32.95 (*0-521-30038-X*) Cambridge U Pr.

Murdoc, Joyce, jt. auth. see Price, Deb.

***Murdocca, Miles.** Principles of Computer Architecture. LC 99-46113. 640p. (C). 1999. 95.00 (*0-201-43664-7*) Addison-Wesley.

Murdocca, Miles J. Principles of Computer Architecture. 656p. (C). 1996. text. write for info. (*0-8053-5460-3*) Benjamin-Cummings.

Murdocca, Sal, jt. auth. see Packard, Edward.

Murdocca, Salvatore. Lucy Takes a Holiday. LC 97-10789. (Illus.). (J). 1998. 15.95 (*1-57255-560-2*) Mondo Pubng.

— Tuttle's Shell. LC 97-51164. (Illus.). 32p. (J). (gr. 1-5). 1999. 15.95 (*1-57255-643-9*) Mondo Pubng.

Murdoch. Basic Behaviour Therapy. 200p. 1991. 38.95 (*0-632-02322-8*) Blackwell Sci.

— British History, 1660-1832: National Identity & Local Culture. LC 98-6883. 224p. 1999. text 55.00 (*0-312-21634-3*) St Martin.

M

An Asterisk (*) at the beginning of an entry indicates that the title is appearing for the first time.

— Clinical Gastroenterology in the Dog & Cat. 1991. write for info. (*0-632-01402-4*) Mosby Inc.

***Murdoch.** Traumatic Brain Injury. 2001. pap. 44.00 (*0-7693-0017-0*) Thomson Learn.

Murdoch & Abram. Governing Growth. 61.95 (*1-84014-929-9*) Ashgate Pub Co.

Murdoch, A. I., jt. ed. see Kosinski, W.

Murdoch, Adrian, ed. see Galdos, Benito P.

Murdoch, Adrian, ed. see Mirbeau, Octave.

Murdoch, Anna. Family Business. 1988. mass mkt. write for info. (*0-449-21678-0*) Ballantine Pub Grp.

Murdoch, Anna. In Her Own Image. large type ed. 432p. 1986. 27.99 (*0-7089-8334-0*, Charnwood) Ulverscroft.

Murdoch, Anna K. Stories from the Motherland. (Illus.). 80p. 1994. 7.00 (*1-86371-228-3*, Pub. by Harper SF) HarpC.

Murdoch, B. E. Dysarthria: A Physiological Approach. Chenery, H. J., ed. (Illus.). 272p. (Orig.). 1998. pap. 47.99 (*1-56593-434-2*, 1103) Singular Publishing.

Murdoch, Beamish. Epitome of the Laws of Nova Scotia, 4 vols. LC 73-26626. 1034p. 1971. reprint ed. lib. bdg. 225.00 (*0-912004-04-5*) Gaunt.

***Murdoch, Brian.** Adam's Grace: Fall & Redemption in Medieval Literature. 240p. 2000. 60.00 (*0-85991-559-X*) Boydell & Brewer.

Murdoch, Brian. Cornish Literature. 184p. (C). 1993. 60.00 (*0-85991-364-3*) Boydell & Brewer.

— The Germanic Hero: Politics & Pragmatism in Early Medieval Poetry. LC 95-49429. 1996. 50.00 (*1-85285-143-0*) Hambledon Press.

Murdoch, Brian, ed. from FRO. The Dedalus Book of Medieval Literature: The Grin of the Gargoyle. 2nd ed. LC 96-145804. 259p. 1999. reprint ed. pap. 14.95 (*1-873982-02-X*) Dedalus.

Murdoch, Brian, tr. see Blumenfeld, Erwin.

Murdoch, Brian, tr. see Farrington, Geoffrey, ed.

Murdoch, Brian O. Im Western Nichts Neues, Remarque: Critical Monographs in English. 68p. 1993. pap. 32.00 (*0-85261-322-9*, Pub. by Univ of Glasgow) St Mut.

Murdoch, Bruce. Speech & Language Disorders in Childhood Cancer. 1999. pap. 47.95 (*1-86156-115-6*) Whurr Pub.

Murdoch, Bruce, ed. Dysarthria: A Physiological Approach to Assessment & Treatment. (Illus.). 376p. 1998. pap. 67.50 (*0-7487-3311-6*, Pub. by S Thornes Pubs) Trans-Atl Phila.

Murdoch, Bruce E., jt. auth. see Sitkin, Lesley A.

Murdoch, Christopher W., et al. Transferring Technologies for the Hardwood Industry: Wetwood Detection, Biocides, Cutting Optimization & Value-Added Wood Products. (Illus.). 70p. (Orig.). (C). 1994. pap. text 50.00 (*0-7881-0547-7*) DIANE Pub.

Murdoch, D. R. Niels Bohr's Philosophy of Physics. (Illus.). 304p. 1989. pap. text 39.95 (*0-521-37927-X*) Cambridge U Pr.

Murdoch, David. Cowboys. (SPA.). 1995. 18.95 (*84-372-3781-5*) Santillana.

***Murdoch, David.** North American Indian. (Eyewitness Books). (Illus.). (J). (gr. 4-7). 2000. 19.99 (*0-7894-6609-0*) DK Pub Inc.

— North American Indian. (Eyewitness Books). (J). (gr. 4-7). 2000. 15.95 (*0-7894-6028-9*) DK Pub Inc.

Murdoch, David & Freed, Stanley A. Los Eyewitness: Indios de Norteamerica. (Eyewitness Books). (SPA., Illus.). 1996. 19.95 (*84-372-3811-0*) Santillana.

Murdoch, David H. The American West: The Invention of a Myth. 200p. 1998. 39.95 (*1-86057-011-9*, Pub. by Welsh Acad); pap. 22.95 (*1-86057-012-7*, Pub. by Welsh Acad) Intl Spec Bk.

***Murdoch, David H.** Cowboy. (Eyewitness Books). (Illus.). (J). (gr. 4-7). 2000. 19.99 (*0-7894-6594-9*) DK Pub Inc.

— Cowboy. (Eyewitness Books). (J). (gr. 4-7). 2000. 15.95 (*0-7894-5854-3*) DK Pub Inc.

Murdoch, David R., jt. auth. see Pollard, Andrew J.

Murdoch, Dorian, tr. see Farrington, Geoffrey, ed.

Murdoch, Dugald, tr. see Descartes, Rene, et al.

Murdoch, Frank. The Quiet Place. (Illus.). 128p. 1990. 45.00 (*0-9625635-0-1*) Sea Quest Pub.

Murdoch, G. M. & Wilson, A. Bennett. Amputation: Surgical Practice & Patient Management. (Illus.). 391p. 1996. text 175.00 (*0-7506-0843-9*) Buttrwrth-Heinemann.

Murdoch, George & Wilson, A. Bennett, Jr. A Primer on Amputations & Artificial Limbs. LC 97-22982. (Illus.). 314p. 1997. text 63.95 (*0-398-06800-3*); pap. text 49.95 (*0-398-06801-1*) C C Thomas.

Murdoch, Heather, jt. auth. see Bozic, Nick.

Murdoch, Iris. An Accidental Man. 448p. 1988. pap. 13.95 (*0-14-003611-3*, Penguin Bks) Viking Penguin.

— The Black Prince. 224p. 1983. pap. 14.95 (*0-14-003934-1*, Penguin Bks) Viking Penguin.

— The Book & the Brotherhood. 624p. 1989. pap. 12.95 (*0-14-010470-4*, Penguin Bks) Viking Penguin.

— Les Cloches. (FRE.). 416p. 1985. pap. 17.95 (*0-7859-4222-X*, 2070376508) Fr & Eur.

— Existentialists & Mystics: Writings on Philosophy & Literature. Conradi, Peter J., ed. LC 97-39579. 546p. 1999. pap. 17.95 (*0-14-026492-2*) Viking Penguin.

— A Fairly Honourable Defeat. 1979. pap. 13.95 (*0-14-003332-7*, Penguin Bks) Viking Penguin.

— The Green Knight. 480p. 1995. pap. 13.95 (*0-14-024337-2*, Penguin Bks) Viking Penguin.

— Jackson's Dilemma. 256p. 1997. pap. 11.95 (*0-14-026189-3*) Viking Penguin.

— Jackson's Dilemma. large type ed. LC 96-8522. 24.95 (*1-56895-340-2*, Compass) Wheeler Pub.

— The Message to the Planet. 640p. 1991. pap. 12.95 (*0-14-012664-3*) Viking Penguin.

— Metaphysics As a Guide to Morals: Philosophical Reflections. 784p. 1994. pap. 15.95 (*0-14-017232-7*, Penguin Bks) Viking Penguin.

— The Nice & the Good. 1978. pap. 13.95 (*0-14-003034-4*, Penguin Bks) Viking Penguin.

— Nuns & Soldiers. 1990. pap. 12.95 (*0-14-005757-9*) Viking Penguin.

***Murdoch, Iris.** The Red & the Green. LC 00-39639. (Illus.). 2000. pap. write for info. (*0-7838-9085-0*, G K Hall & Co) Mac Lib Ref.

Murdoch, Iris. The Sacred & Profane Love Machine. 368p. 1984. pap. 13.95 (*0-14-004111-7*, Penguin Bks) Viking Penguin.

— The Sandcastle. 1978. pap. 13.95 (*0-14-001474-8*, Penguin Bks) Viking Penguin.

— The Sea, the Sea. 1980. pap. 14.95 (*0-14-005199-6*, Penguin Bks) Viking Penguin.

— A Severed Head. 208p. 1976. pap. 12.95 (*0-14-002003-9*, Penguin Bks) Viking Penguin.

***Murdoch, Iris.** Something Special: A Story. (Illus.). 64p. 2000. 15.95 (*0-393-05007-6*) Norton.

Murdoch, Iris. Sous le Filet. (FRE.). 1985. pap. 15.95 (*0-7859-4221-1*) Fr & Eur.

— The Sovereignty of Good. 116p. (C). 1985. pap. 14.99 (*0-415-06593-3*) Routledge.

— Under the Net. 1977. pap. 12.95 (*0-14-001445-4*, Penguin Bks) Viking Penguin.

— Une'Tete Coupee. (FRE.). 316p. 1988. pap. 15.95 (*0-7859-4303-X*, 2070380777) Fr & Eur.

— The Unicorn. 312p. 1987. pap. 17.99 (*0-14-002476-X*, Penguin Bks) Viking Penguin.

Murdoch, J. Review of Caste in India. 110p. 1977. 14.95 (*0-318-36811-0*) Asia Bk Corp.

Murdoch, J. Murray. Portrait of Obedience: The Biography of Robert T. Ketcham. 328p. 1979. pap. 9.99 (*0-87227-070-X*, RBP5076) Reg Baptist.

Murdoch, James. A History of Japan. LC 96-16441. 720p. (C). 1996. 535.00 (*0-415-15076-0*) Routledge.

Murdoch, James E. Stage; or Recollections of Actors & Acting. LC 79-81213. 1972. 24.95 (*0-405-08810-8*) Ayer.

Murdoch, John. The Courtauld Gallery at Somerset House. LC 98-61031. (Illus.). 128p. 1999. pap. 15.95 (*0-500-28091-6*, Pub. by Thames Hudson) Norton.

— Ethnological Results of the Point Barrow Expedition. (Classics of Smithsonian Anthropology Ser.: No. 6). (Illus.). 480p. 1988. reprint ed. pap. text 29.95 (*0-87474-665-5*, MUERP) Smithsonian.

— Hindu & Muhammadan Festivals: Compiled from Wilson, Wilkins, Crooke, Sell, Hughes & Other Writers. (C). 1991. reprint ed. 9.00 (*81-206-0708-2*, Pub. by Asian Educ Servs) S Asia.

— The Mahabharata. 160p. 1986. reprint ed. 14.00 (*0-8364-1762-3*, Pub. by Manohar) S Asia.

Murdoch, John. 17th Century English Miniatures in the Collection of the Victoria & Albert Museum. (Illus.). xx, 375p. 1997. boxed set 207.00 (*0-11-290498-X*, Pub. by Statnry Office) Balogh.

Murdoch, John, ed. The Mahabharata, An English Abridgement with Introduction, Notes & Review. 1987. reprint ed. 12.00 (*0-8364-2042-X*, Pub. by Usha) S Asia.

Murdoch, John, jt. ed. see Mosey, David.

Murdoch, John B., tr. see Sananikone, Oun.

Murdoch, John B., tr. see Wyatt, David K., ed.

Murdoch, John E. Album of Science Vol. 1: Antiquity & the Middle Ages. LC 84-1400. (Illus.). 375p. 1984. 95.00 (*0-684-15496-X*, Scribners Ref) Mac Lib Ref.

Murdoch, Jonathan & Marsden, Terry. Reconstituting Rurality: The Changing Countryside in an Urban Context. (Reconstructing Rural Areas Ser.: No. 2). 192p. 1994. 59.95 (*1-85728-041-5*, Pub. by UCL Pr Ltd) Taylor & Francis.

— Reconstituting Rurality: The Changing Countryside in an Urban Context. (Reconstructing Rural Areas Ser.: No. 2). 192p. 1996. pap. 27.50 (*1-85728-645-6*, Pub. by UCL Pr Ltd) Taylor & Francis.

Murdoch, Joseph, jt. auth. see Tunell, George.

Murdoch, Joseph B. Illumination Engineering: From Edison's Lamp to the Laser. LC 94-30117. (Illus.). 560p. 1995. reprint ed. pap. 54.95 (*1-885750-00-5*, IE-95) Visions Communs.

Murdoch, Joseph S., jt. auth. see Donovan, Richard E.

Murdoch, Kath. Ideas for Environmental Education in the Elementary Classroom: In the Elementary Classroom. LC 94-11803. 194p. 1994. pap. text 17.00 (*0-435-08347-3*, 08347) Heinemann.

Murdoch, Kath, jt. auth. see Hamston, Julie.

Murdoch, Kathleen, jt. auth. see Ray, Stephen.

Murdoch, Kenneth. The Pyramid Piano Tutor. 48p. 1996. pap. 9.95 (*1-85756-275-5*, Pub. by Janus Pubng) Paul & Co Pubs.

Murdoch, Larry & Wilson, David. Alternative Methods for Fluid Delivery & Recovery. (Illus.). 87p. (Orig.). (C). 1995. pap. text 45.00 (*0-7881-1616-9*) DIANE Pub.

Murdoch, Lesley. Discover the Great Barrier Reef Marine Park. 1998. pap. text 9.95 (*0-207-18990-0*) HarpC.

***Murdoch, Marianne.** Ranch Dog: A Tribute to the Working Dog in the American West. (Illus.). 112p. 2000. 12.95 (*1-57223-289-7*) Willow Creek Pr.

***Murdoch, Mary Ruth.** Raising a Christian Daughter in an MTV World. 250p. 2000. pap. 10.99 (*0-87552-373-0*) P & R Pubng.

Murdoch, Nancy & Fassett, Linda. Life: God's Way. 2nd rev. ed. 80p. 1997. wbk. ed. 12.95 (*0-9658737-0-6*) Step Up To Life.

Murdoch, Norman H. Origins of the Salvation Army. LC 94-9334. (Illus.). 256p. (C). 1996. pap. text 16.00 (*0-87049-955-6*) U of Tenn Pr.

Murdoch, Oswald, tr. see Pungier, Jean.

Murdoch, Patricia, jt. auth. see Robinson, Robyn.

Murdoch, Royal. The Disrobing: Sex & Satire. 112p. (Orig.). 1982. pap. 10.00 (*0-917342-96-8*) Gay Sunshine.

— Poet in Despair: A Diary of the Great Depression. LC 73-89987. 1974. write for info. (*0-914290-00-2*) Royal Murdoch.

Murdoch, S., jt. auth. see Johnson, L.

Murdoch, Tessa. Huguenot Artists & Craftsmen in London, 1680-1720. (Illus.). 64p. 1998. pap. 14.95 (*1-898595-25-9*, Pub. by Alpha Pr Ltd) Intl Spec Bk.

Murdoch, Tessa, jt. auth. see Gilbert, Christopher.

Murdoch, Tom, et al. The Streamkeeper's Field Guide: Watershed Inventory & Stream Monitoring Methods. 5th rev. ed. LC 97-144780. (Illus.). 300p. 1996. per. 29.95 (*0-9652109-0-1*) Adopt-A-Stream.

Murdoch, Walter & Drake-Brockman, Henrietta, selected by. Classic Australian Short Stories. 456p. 1998. pap. text 16.95 (*0-19-550619-7*) OUP.

Murdoch, Walter L. Seventy-Two Essays: A Selection. LC 76-90665. (Essay Index Reprint Ser.). 1977. reprint ed. 23.95 (*0-8369-1813-4*) Ayer.

Murdoch, William D. Brahms. LC 74-24161. reprint ed. 37.50 (*0-404-13056-9*) AMS Pr.

— Chopin: His Life. LC 70-136077. (Illus.). 410p. 1971. reprint ed. lib. bdg. 75.00 (*0-8371-5227-5*, MUCH, Greenwood Pr) Greenwood.

Murdoch, William W. The Poverty of Nations: The Political Economy of Hunger & Population. LC 80-16201. (Illus.). 398p. reprint ed. pap. 123.40 (*0-608-08793-9*, 206943200004) Bks Demand.

Murdock. Greatest Secret in the Universe. 1997. pap. text 7.99 (*1-880089-43-2*) Albury Pub.

Murdock & Scutt. Personal Effectiveness. 2nd ed. 288p. 1997. pap. text 34.95 (*0-7506-3393-X*) Buttrwrth-Heinemann.

Murdock, Anna & Jensen, Catharina. Tales of Ye Merrye Woode: A Musical. 57p. (J). (gr. k-6). 1997. pap. 4.00 (*1-57514-285-6*, 4029) Encore Perform Pub.

Murdock, Anna, et al. Castles & Dragons: A Musical. (Elementary School Plays Ser.). (J). 1993. 3.00 (*1-57514-011-X*, 4030) Encore Perform Pub.

Murdock, Babs M. Raymond Floyd Goes to Africa: or There Are No Bears in Africa. (Illus.). 32p. (J). (gr. 1-4). 1993. pap. 6.95 (*0-86543-376-3*) Africa World.

Murdock, Barbara S., ed. Environmental Issues in Primary Care. (Illus.). 76p. (Orig.). (C). 1994. pap. text 40.00 (*0-7881-0819-0*) DIANE Pub.

Murdock, Carol V. Writing Skills. Evento, Susan, ed. (Macmillan Early Skills Program - Conversion Ser.). 64p. 1995. pap. 9.95 (*1-56784-511-8*) Newbridge Educ.

***Murdock, Catherine G.** Domesticating Drink: Women, Men, & Alcohol in America, 1870-1940. LC 98-24285. (Gender Relations in the American Experience Ser.). (Illus.). 244 p. 1998. 38.50 (*0-8018-5940-9*) Johns Hopkins.

Murdock, Clyde. Funny Stuff: Over 300 Clean Jokes You Can Tell Your Grandma. LC 99-193265. 256p. 1998. mass mkt. 1.99 (*1-57748-368-5*) Barbour Pub.

Murdock, Cynthia, et al. Substitute Teacher Handbook: Expectations, Classroom Management & Fill-In Activities. 2nd ed. Smith, Geoffrey G., ed. & illus. by. (J). (gr. k-8). 1997. pap. text 8.95 (*1-890563-02-1*) Subs Tchr Train.

— Substitute Teacher Handbook: Expectations, Classroom Management & Fill-In Activities. 2nd ed. Smith, Geoffrey G., ed. & illus. by. (YA). (gr. 9-12). 1997. pap. text 8.95 (*1-890563-03-X*) Subs Tchr Train.

Murdock, Dick. Bill Knapke - a Railroad Legend: Sketches from the Life of an Oldtime Boomer. Rockefeller, Ruth & Gibbs, Joyce, eds. LC 95-6797. (Illus.). 144p. (Orig.). 1996. pap. 12.95 (*0-932916-18-X*) May-Murdock.

— Lime Point to Lawson's Landing: Outdoors in Marin Sixty-One More Places to Visit. Murdock, Jayne, ed. & photos by by. LC 91-20154. (Illus.). 160p. (Orig.). 1992. pap. 10.95 (*0-932916-15-5*) May-Murdock.

— Smoke in the Canyon: My Steam Days in Dunsmuir. Murdock, Jayne, ed. LC 85-90443. (Illus.). 144p. (Orig.). 1986. pap. 15.95 (*0-932916-10-4*) May-Murdock.

Murdock, Dick, jt. auth. see May, Jayne.

Murdock, Dick, ed. see Murdock, Jayne M.

Murdock, Dick, ed. see Shannon, Wayne.

Murdock, Dick, ed. see Wurm, Ted.

***Murdock, Doris B.** Storm of the Soul. 1998. write for info. (*0-9642338-0-0*) Steppingstone Ent.

Murdock, Eugene C. Ban Johnson: Czar of Baseball, 3. LC 81-20336. (Contributions to the Study of Popular Culture Ser.: No. 3). 294p. 1982. 59.95 (*0-313-23459-0*, MBJ/, Greenwood Pr) Greenwood.

— Mighty Casey: All-American, 7. LC 83-16338. (Contributions to the Study of Popular Culture Ser.: No. 7). 164p. 1984. 45.00 (*0-313-24075-2*, MMC/, Greenwood Pr) Greenwood.

— One Million Men: The Civil War Draft in the North. LC 80-14431. (Illus.). 366p. 1980. reprint ed. lib. bdg. 55.00 (*0-313-22502-8*, MUOM, Greenwood Pr) Greenwood.

— Patriotism Limited, 1862-1865: The Civil War Draft & the Bounty System. LC 67-64665. 296p. reprint ed. pap. 91.80 (*0-8357-9372-9*, 201041300069) Bks Demand.

Murdock, Everett E. Computers Today! 160p. (C). 1995. text 16.68 (*0-697-20403-0*) Bus & Educ Tech.

— DOS - the Easy Way: A Complete Guide to Microsoft's MS-DOS. 350p. (Orig.). (C). 1988. pap. text 18.50 (*0-923178-00-7*) HOT Pr.

— Hypercard: The Easy Way. 2nd ed. 208p. (C). 1992. text 18.12 (*0-697-16563-9*) Bus & Educ Tech.

Murdock, Everett E. & Sudbury, Susan. School & Home Guide to Apple Macintosh Computer. LC 85-530. (Illus.). 204p. 1985. pap. 15.95 (*0-13-793605-2*) P-H.

— School & Home Guide to IBM Compatible Personal Computers. LC 84-24786. 292p. 1985. pap. 18.95 (*0-13-793662-1*) P-H.

— School & Home Guide to the IBM PCjr. (Illus.). 224p. 1985. text 29.00 (*0-13-793654-0*); pap. text 15.95 (*0-13-793647-8*) P-H.

Murdock, George P. Atlas of World Cultures. LC 80-53030. 157p. pap. 48.70 (*0-7837-8551-8*, 204936600011) Bks Demand.

— Outline of World Cultures. 6th rev. ed. LC 83-80510. (HRAF Manuals Ser.). 259p. 1983. pap. 25.00 (*0-87536-664-3*) HRAFP.

— Theories of Illness: A World Survey. LC 80-5257. 142p. 1980. pap. 44.10 (*0-7837-8545-3*, 204936000011) Bks Demand.

Murdock, George P. & O'Leary, Timothy. Ethnographic Bibliography of North America Vol. 4: Eastern United States. LC 75-17091. (Behavior Science Bibliographies Ser.). (Illus.). 293p. reprint ed. pap. 90.90 (*0-7837-1765-2*, 201559200004) Bks Demand.

Murdock, George P. & O'Leary, Timothy J. Ethnographic Bibliography of North America Vol. 2: Arctic & Subarctic. 4th ed. LC 75-17091. (Behavior Science Bibliographies Ser.). (Illus.). 296p. reprint ed. pap. 91.80 (*0-8357-2802-1*, 201559200002) Bks Demand.

Murdock, George P., et al. Outline of Cultural Materials. 5th rev. ed. LC 81-83836. (HRAF Manuals Ser.). 273p. 1982. pap. 25.00 (*0-87536-654-6*) HRAFP.

***Murdock, Graeme.** Calvinism & the Reformed Church in Hungary & Transylvania C. 1600-1660. (Oxford Historical Monographs). 390p. 2000. text 80.00 (*0-19-820859-6*) OUP.

Murdock, Graham, jt. ed. see Golding, Peter.

Murdock, H. David. (Bible Stories Ser.: No. S846-5). (Illus.). (J). (ps-2). pap. 3.95 (*0-7214-5068-7*, Ladybrd) Penguin Putnam.

Murdock, Harold. The Nineteenth of April, 1775: Concord & Lexington. LC 68-58327. (Illus.). 1969. reprint ed. 15.00 (*0-87152-053-2*) Reprint.

Murdock, Hy. Daniel. (Bible Stories Ser.: No. S846-6). (Illus.). (J). (ps-2). pap. 3.95 (*0-7214-5069-5*, Ladybrd) Penguin Putnam.

— Goldilocks & the Three Bears. (First Fairy Tales Ser.: No. S852-3). (Illus.). (J). (ps-2). 1994. pap. 3.95 (*0-7214-5060-1*, Ladybrd) Penguin Putnam.

— Hansel & Gretel. (First Fairy Tales Ser.: No. S852-8). (Illus.). (J). (ps-2). pap. 3.95 (*0-7214-5101-2*, Ladybrd) Penguin Putnam.

— Jack & the Beanstalk. (First Fairy Tales Ser.: No. S852-4). (J). 1989. pap. 3.95 (*0-7214-5061-X*, Ladybrd) Penguin Putnam.

— Joseph. (Bible Stories Ser.: No. S846-4). (Illus.). (J). (ps-2). 3.95 (*0-7214-5067-9*, Ladybrd) Penguin Putnam.

Murdock, J. E. Words from the Heart. 80p. (C). 1991. text 10.95 (*1-56394-001-9*) Wisdom Intl.

Murdock, J. W. & Smith, L. T., eds. ASME Text Booklet, SI Units in Thermodynamics: SI-4. 55p. 1976. 6.50 (*0-317-33430-1*, E00084); 3.25 (*0-317-33431-X*) ASME.

***Murdock, James A., et al.** Perturbations: Theory & Methods. LC 99-36132. (Classics in Applied Mathematics: Vol. 27). xx, 509p. 1999. pap. 53.00 (*0-89871-443-5*, CL27) Soc Indus-Appl Math.

Murdock, James W. Fundamental Fluid Mechanics for the Practicing Engineer. (Mechanical Engineering Ser.: Vol. 82). (Illus.). 440p. 1993. text 137.50 (*0-8247-8808-7*) Dekker.

Murdock, Jayne, ed. see Murdock, Dick.

Murdock, Jayne, ed. see Murdock, Jayne M.

Murdock, Jayne, ed. see Shannon, Wayne.

Murdock, Jayne, ed. see Wurm, Ted.

Murdock, Jayne, ed. & photos by see Murdock, Dick.

Murdock, Jayne M. Brief Infinity: A Love Story in Haiku. Murdock, Dick, ed. LC 80-83998. (Illus.). 64p. (Orig.). 1981. pap. 4.00 (*0-932916-06-6*) May-Murdock.

— I Painted on a Bright Red Mouth: The War Years, 1941-1945. Murdock, Dick, ed. LC 81-90168. (Illus.). 64p. (Orig.). 1981. pap. 5.00 (*0-932916-07-4*) May-Murdock.

— Until Death & After: How to Live with a Dying Intimate. Murdock, Dick & Murdock, Jayne, eds. LC 79-90348. (Illus.). 64p. 1979. pap. 4.00 (*0-932916-05-8*) May-Murdock.

Murdock, Jayne R. Wind Chimes: The Story of a Family. LC 93-33526. (Illus.). 256p. (Orig.). 1993. pap. 14.95 (*0-932916-17-1*) May-Murdock.

Murdock, John E., ed. see International Colloquium on Philosophy, Science Th.

Murdock, Jos. B. Murdock Genealogy: Robert Murdock of Roxbury, MA & Some of His Descendants, with Notes on the Descendants of John Munro of Plymouth; George Murdock of Plainfield, CT; Peter Murdock of Saybrook, CT; William Murdock of Philadelphia & Others. (Illus.). 274p. 1994. reprint ed. pap. 44.00 (*0-8328-4348-2*); reprint ed. lib. bdg. 54.00 (*0-8328-4347-4*) Higginson Bk Co.

Murdock, Katheryn, jt. auth. see Kysilko, David.

***Murdock, Kelly.** Master HTML 4 & Xhtml 1 Visually. (Illus.). 704p. 2000. pap. text 34.99 (*0-7645-3454-8*) IDG Bks.

— 3D Studio Max R3 Bible. LC 99-33676. 1200p. 2000. pap. 49.99 (*0-7645-4621-X*) IDG Bks.

Murdock, Kelly & Couch, Justin. Laura Lemay's Web Workshop: 3D Graphics & VRML 2.0. LC 96-68591. 504p. 1996. 39.99 (*1-57521-143-2*) Sams.

Murdock, Kenneth B. Increase Mather, the Foremost American Puritan. (BCL1 - United States Local History Ser.). 442p. 1991. reprint ed. text 99.00 (*0-7812-6267-4*) Rprt Serv.

— Literature & Theology in Colonial New England. LC 78-104247. 235p. 1970. reprint ed. lib. bdg. 38.50 (*0-8371-3990-2*, MUCN, Greenwood Pr) Greenwood.

Murdock, Kenneth B., ed. see James, Henry.

Murdock, Kenneth B., ed. see Mather, Cotton.

An Asterisk (*) at the beginning of an entry indicates that the title is appearing for the first time.

Murdock, L. J., et al. Concrete Materials & Practice. 6th ed. (Illus.). 480p. 1992. text 120.95 (*0-7131-3653-7*, A7294, Pub. by E A) Routldge.

Murdock, M. S. Vendetta. (Illus.). 1987. mass mkt. 2.95 (*0-445-20520-2*, Pub. by Warner Bks) Little.

***Murdock, Macky.** Last of the Old-Time Texans. 250p. 2000. pap. 17.95 (*1-55622-784-1*, Rep of TX Pr) Wordware Pub.

Murdock, Maureen. Heroine's Journey. LC 89-43513. (Illus.). 160p. 1990. pap. 13.00 (*0-87773-485-2*, Pub. by Shambhala Pubns) Random.

— The Heroine's Journey. LC 97-42875. 1998. pap., wbk. ed. 15.00 (*1-57062-255-8*, Pub. by Shambhala Pubns) Random.

— Spinning Inward: Using Guided Imagery with Children. enl. rev. ed. LC 87-9740. (Illus.). 158p. 1987. pap. 24.95 (*0-87773-422-4*, Pub. by Shambhala Pubns) Random.

Murdock, Mi. Wisdom for Winning. pap. 8.99 (*0-89274-398-0*) Harrison Hse.

Murdock, Michael D. The God-Book. Loy, Joy A., ed. 250p. (Orig.). (YA). 1991. pap. text 4.95 (*1-56394-004-3*) Wisdom Intl.

— The Jesus Book. Loy, Joy A., ed. (Orig.). 1991. pap. text 4.95 (*1-56394-002-7*) Wisdom Intl.

— Jesus Was a Double Diamond Principle. Loy, Joy A., ed. 175p. (Orig.). 1991. pap. text 4.95 (*1-56394-000-0*) Wisdom Intl.

— The Teenager's One Minute Bible. Loy, Joy A., ed. 365p. (Orig.). (YA). 1991. pap. text 5.95 (*1-56394-003-5*) Wisdom Intl.

— The Widow's Topical Bible. Loy, Joy A., ed. 165p. (Orig.). 1991. pap. text 4.95 (*1-56394-005-1*) Wisdom Intl.

Murdock, Michael L. Writing Clearly & Effectively. 2nd ed. 166p. (Orig.). 1981. pap. 7.25 (*0-930124-01-4*) Transemantics.

Murdock, Mike. The Assignment: Powerful Secrets for Discovering Your Destiny. 208p. 1997. pap. 9.99 (*1-880089-94-7*, Pub. by Albury Pub) Appalach Bk Dist.

— Dream Seeds. pap. 8.99 (*0-89274-392-1*) Harrison Hse.

— God Book. 1990. pap. 6.95 (*0-926775-45-6*) Sensible Des.

— The Leadership Secrets of Jesus. 208p. 1997. 14.99 (*1-56292-163-0*) Honor Bks OK.

— Secrets of the Richest Man. 1998. 14.99 (*1-56292-526-1*) Honor Bks OK.

— 31 Reasons Why People Don't Receive Their Financial Harvest. Date not set. 12.00 (*1-56394-057-4*, MM-057) Wisdom Intl.

Murdock, Rick & Fisher, David. Patient Number One: A True Story of How One CEO Took on Cancer & Big Business in the Fight of His Life. LC 99-86763. 320p. 2000. 24.00 (*0-609-60391-4*, Crown) Crown Pub Group.

Murdock, Robert. Bill Freeland. (Illus.). 52p. (Orig.). 1989. pap. 15.00 (*0-944751-02-4*) Maxwells Busn.

Murdock, Robert M. Ceroli Pistoletto. (Illus.). (Orig.). 1969. pap. 1.50 (*0-914782-96-7*) Buffalo Fine-Albrght-Knox.

Murdock, Rosamond L. & Hartley, Mariette. Suffer the Children: A Pediatrician's Reflections on Abuse. LC 91-35371. 220p. 1992. 19.95 (*0-929173-09-0*) Health Press.

***Murdock, Shirley Woodhouse & Gillaspie, James A.** The Longest Flight: Yuma's Quest for the Future. (Illus.). xv, 96p. 1999. pap. 10.00 (*0-9675508-0-7*) Longest Flight.

Murdock, Steve H. & Leistritz, F. Larry. Energy Development in the Western United States: Impact on Rural Areas. LC 79-18478. 363p. 1979. 69.50 (*0-275-90397-4*, C0397, Praeger Pubs) Greenwood.

Murdock, Steve H., et al. The Texas Challenge: Population Change & the Future of Texas. LC 96-23954. 256p. (Orig.). 1996. 19.95 (*0-89096-724-5*) Tex A&M Univ Pr.

Murdock, Steve H., jt. auth. see Albrecht, Don E.

Murdock, Steven, et al. Hazardous Wastes in Rural America: Impacts, Implications & Options for Rural Communities & Waste-Facility Siting in the United States. LC 98-53014. 288p. 1998. 60.00 (*0-8476-9049-0*); pap. 29.50 (*0-8476-9100-4*) Rowman.

Murdock, William D. Chopin: His Life. 1988. reprint ed. lib. bdg. 59.00 (*0-7812-0495-X*) Rprt Serv.

— Chopin: His Life. LC 73-181213. 410p. 1935. reprint ed. 59.00 (*0-403-01625-8*) Scholarly.

Murdy, Edward O., et al. Fishes of Chesapeake Bay. (Illus.). 528p. 1996. 49.95 (*1-56098-638-7*) Smithsonian.

***Murdy, Kay.** From Pharaoh to the Father: A Journey Toward Freedom Through the Lord's Prayer. LC 99-89736. 144p. 2000. pap. 17.95 (*0-89390-500-3*) Resource Pubns.

Murdy, Kay. Ninety Days: Daily Reflections for Lent & Easter. LC 94-33529. 98p. (Orig.). 1995. pap. 8.95 (*0-89390-306-X*) Resource Pubns.

— Season of Emmanuel: Daily Reflections for Advent, Christmas, & Epiphany. LC 96-31499. 160p. (Orig.). 1996. pap. 8.95 (*0-89390-389-2*) Resource Pubns.

Murdy, William H. & Carter, M. E. Brown. Guide to the Plants of Granite Outcrops. LC 99-14453. (Illus.). 120p. 1999. 15.95 (*0-8203-2133-8*) U of Ga Pr.

Murdza, Lydia. A Whisper of Breath. 1998. pap. write for info. (*1-57553-922-5*) Watermrk Pr.

Murdza, Mindy, ed. see Grenevicki, Lawrence.

Murdza, Mindy, ed. see Sims, Ron & Spock, Susan.

Murdza, Peter J., Jr., ed. Immigrants to Liberia, 1865-1904: An Alphabetical Listing. (Liberian Research Working Papers: No. 4). 1975. 15.00 (*0-686-17780-0*) Arden Assocs.

Murdzek, Benjamin P. Emigration in Polish Social & Political Thought, 1870-1914. (East European Monographs: No. 33). 396p. 1977. text 68.00 (*0-914710-26-5*, Pub. by East Eur Monographs) Col U Pr.

Mure, Geoffrey R. Aristotle. LC 75-17199. 282p. 1975. reprint ed. lib. bdg. 38.50 (*0-8371-8298-0*, MUAR, Greenwood Pr) Greenwood.

— An Introduction to Hegel. LC 82-15853. 180p. 1982. reprint ed. lib. bdg. 45.00 (*0-313-23741-7*, MUIH, Greenwood Pr) Greenwood.

— A Study of Hegel's Logic. LC 83-26391. 375p. 1984. reprint ed. lib. bdg. 69.50 (*0-313-24397-2*, MUSH, Greenwood Pr) Greenwood.

Mure, Mary, jt. auth. see Barber, Nicola.

Mure, William. Selections from the Family Papers Preserved at Caldwell, 2 pts. in 3 vols., Set. LC 70-173006. (Maitland Club, Glasgow. Publications: No. 71). reprint ed. 105.00 (*0-404-53091-5*) AMS Pr.

Mureinik, Inez, ed. see Zevin, L. S. & Kimmel, Giora.

Murell, N. Samuel, et al, eds. Chanting down Babylon: The Rastafari Reader. LC 97-25810. 416p. 1998. pap. 29.95 (*1-56639-584-4*); text 69.95 (*1-56639-583-6*) Temple U Pr.

Muren, Nancy L., jt. illus. see Somerville, Sheila.

Murena, Hector E. Ensayos sobre Subversion. (SPA.). 105p. 1963. 2.00 (*0-8477-2413-1*); pap. 1.00 (*0-8477-2414-X*) U of PR Pr.

Murer, Cherilyn G. Case Manager's Sourcebook: A Guide to Designing & Implementing a Centralized Case Management Sourcebook. LC 97-12459. 1997. 60.00 (*0-7863-1221-1*, Irwn Prfssnl) McGraw-Hill Prof.

Murer, Cherilyn G., et al. Post Acute Care Reimbursement Manual. LC 97-36013. 1997. write for info. (*0-7863-1248-3*) McGraw.

Murer, Esther G., tr. see Bjorneboe, Jens.

Murer, Esther Greenleaf, tr. see Bjorneboe, Jens.

Murer, Ewald. Dreams at the End of the Night. 1999. pap. text 12.50 (*80-901257-9-4*) TWISI Pr.

Murer, H., ed. The Molecules of Transport: Carriers. (Journal: Cellular Physiology & Biochemistry: Vol. 4, Nos. 5-6, 1994). (Illus.). 140p. 1994. pap. 75.75 (*3-8055-5972-0*) S Karger.

Murer, Jos. Saemtliche Dramen, 2 vols. Adomatis, Hans-Joachim et al, eds. LC 73-78235. (Ausgaben Deutscher Literatur des XV bis XVIII Jahrhunderts Ser.: Reihe Drama 4). (C). 1974. 634.60 (*3-11-003865-X*) De Gruyter.

Muret, Eduard & Sanders, Daniel. Langenscheidt's Encyclopedic Dictionary of English & German Vol. 1: English-German A-M. (ENG & GER.). 883p. 1992. 195.00 (*0-7859-8385-6*, 3468011202) Fr & Eur.

— Langenscheidt's Encyclopedic Dictionary of English & German Vol. 2: English-German N-Z. (ENG & GER.). 956p. 1992. 195.00 (*0-7859-8386-4*, 3468011229) Fr & Eur.

— Langenscheidt's Encyclopedic Dictionary of English & German Vol. 3: German-English A-K. (ENG & GER.). 973p. 1992. 195.00 (*0-7859-8387-2*, 3468011245) Fr & Eur.

— Langenscheidt's Encyclopedic Dictionary of English & German Vol. 4: German-English L-Z. (ENG & GER.). 1046p. 1992. 195.00 (*0-7859-8388-0*, 3468011261) Fr & Eur.

Muret, M. The Twilight of the White Races. 1976. lib. bdg. 59.95 (*0-8490-2780-2*) Gordon Pr.

Muret-Sanders. Condensed Muret-Sanders English-German Dictionary Vol. .2. 1296p. 1982. 99.00 (*0-88729-007-8*) Langenscheidt.

— Langenscheidt New Muret-Sanders Encyclopedic Dictionary. Incl. Vol. 1, Pt. 1. Muret-Sanders Encyclopedic German Dictionary: A - M. (ENG & GER.). 883p. 1988. 145.00 (*0-88729-001-9*); Vol. 1, Pt. 2. Muret-Sanders Encyclopedic German Dictionary: A - K. (ENG & GER.). 973p. 1988. 145.00 (*0-88729-003-5*); Vol. 2, Pt. 1. Muret-Sanders Encyclopedic German Dictionary: N - Z. (ENG & GER.). 960p. 1988. 145.00 (*0-88729-002-7*); Vol. 2, Pt. 2. Muret-Sanders Encyclopedic German Dictionary. (ENG & GER.). 1048p. 1988. 145.00 (*0-88729-004-3*); write for info. (*0-318-57088-2*) Langenscheidt.

Murfett, Malcolm H. In Jeopardy: The Royal Navy & British Far Eastern Defence Policy 1945-1951. (South-East Asian Historical Monographs). (Illus.). 192p. 1995. text 39.95 (*967-65-3058-1*) OUP.

Murfett, Malcolm H., ed. The First Sea Lords: From Fisher to Mountbatten. LC 94-17009. 328p. 1995. 67.95 (*0-275-94231-7*, Praeger Pubs) Greenwood.

Murfia, Janice. Savory to Sweet Pies & Treats. LC 93-37195. (Creative Cook Ser.). 64p. 1993. 16.95 (*1-56426-651-7*) Cole Group.

Murfin, Andy, jt. auth. see Hawthorne, Nathaniel.

Murfin, J. A. Guide to the Civil War. 1999. mass mkt. 3.95 (*0-446-32886-3*, Pub. by Warner Bks) Little.

Murfin, James V. The Gleam of Bayonets: The Battle of Antietam & Robert E. Lee's Maryland Campaign, Sept 1862. LC 65-11502. (Illus.). 456p. 1982. pap. 17.95 (*0-8071-0990-8*) La State U Pr.

Murfin, James V. & Pavitt, Irene, eds. Sierra Club Guides to the National Parks: The Desert Southwest. rev. ed. LC 95-11448. (Sierra Club Guides to the National Parks Ser.). (Illus.). 400p. 1995. pap. 24.95 (*0-679-76493-3*) Random.

Murfin, James V., jt. auth. see Gibson, William.

Murfin, James V., jt. auth. see National Flag Foundation Staff.

Murfin, Ross. Heart of Darkness. 2nd ed. Date not set. 35.00 (*0-312-15905-6*) St Martin.

Murfin, Ross, ed. see Conrad, Joseph.

Murfin, Ross C. Lord Jim: After the Truth. (Masterwork Studies: No. 88). 160p. (C). 1992. 29.00 (*0-8057-8094-7*, Twyne); pap. 13.95 (*0-8057-8560-4*, Twyne) Mac Lib Ref.

— The Poetry of D. H. Lawrence: Texts & Contexts. LC 82-10940. 281p. reprint ed. pap. 87.20 (*0-7837-4661-X*, 204438600002) Bks Demand.

— Sons & Lovers: A Novel of Division & Desire. (Twayne's Masterworks Ser.: No. 7). 176p. 1987. 23.95 (*0-8057-7967-1*) Macmillan.

— Swinburne, Hardy, Lawrence, & the Burden of Belief. LC 78-3564. 1995. 21.95 (*0-226-55150-4*) U Ch Pr.

— Swinburne, Hardy, Lawrence, & the Burden of Belief. LC 78-3564. 250p. reprint ed. pap. 77.50 (*0-608-09026-3*, 206966100005) Bks Demand.

Murfin, Ross C., ed. Conrad Revisited: Essays for the Eighties. LC 83-17937. 200p. reprint ed. pap. 62.00 (*0-608-09234-7*, 205273800005) Bks Demand.

Murfin, Ross C. & Ray, Supryia M. The Bedford Glossary of Critical & Literary Terms. LC 97-27790. 457p. 1997. pap. text 16.95 (*0-312-11560-1*, PN81) St Martin.

Murfin, Ross C., ed. see Bronte, Emily Jane.

Murfin, Ross C., ed. see Hawthorne, Nathaniel.

Murfin, Ross C., ed. see Shelley, Mary Wollstonecraft.

Murfitt, Janice. First Steps in Cake Decorating: Over 100 Step-By-Step Cake Decorating Techniques & Recipes. (Illus.). 160p. 1996. pap. 19.95 (*1-85238-548-0*, Pub. by New5 Holland) Sterling.

Murfitt, Mary, jt. auth. see Howie, Betsy.

Murfitt, Rex, jt. auth. see Fingerut, Joyce.

Murfree, Mary N. The Amulet. (Notable American Authors Ser.). 1999. reprint ed. lib. bdg. 125.00 (*0-7812-4609-1*) Rprt Serv.

— The Bushwhackers & Other Stories. (Notable American Authors Ser.). 1999. reprint ed. lib. bdg. 125.00 (*0-7812-4604-0*) Rprt Serv.

— Bushwhackers & Other Stories, No. 4. LC 73-90588. (Short Story Index Reprint Ser., Vol. 1). 1977. 20.95 (*0-8369-3071-1*) Ayer.

— The Champion (juvenile) (Notable American Authors Ser.). 1999. lib. bdg. 125.00 (*0-7812-4606-7*) Rprt Serv.

— The Despot of Broomsedge Cove. (Notable American Authors Ser.). 1999. reprint ed. lib. bdg. 125.00 (*0-7812-4597-4*) Rprt Serv.

— Down the Ravine. (Notable American Authors Ser.). 1999. reprint ed. lib. bdg. 125.00 (*0-7812-4593-1*) Rprt Serv.

— The Fair Mississippian. (Notable American Authors Ser.). 1999. reprint ed. lib. bdg. 125.00 (*0-7812-4610-5*) Rprt Serv.

— Frontiersmen. LC 79-116963. (Short Story Index Reprint Ser.). 1977. 24.95 (*0-8369-3467-9*) Ayer.

— The Frontiersmen. (Notable American Authors Ser.). 1999. reprint ed. lib. bdg. 125.00 (*0-7812-4607-5*) Rprt Serv.

— His Vanished Star. (Notable American Authors Ser.). 1999. reprint ed. lib. bdg. 125.00 (*0-7812-4599-0*) Rprt Serv.

— In Stranger People's Country. (Notable American Authors Ser.). 1999. reprint ed. lib. bdg. 125.00 (*0-7812-4598-2*) Rprt Serv.

— In the Clouds. (Notable American Authors Ser.). 1999. reprint ed. lib. bdg. 125.00 (*0-7812-4595-8*) Rprt Serv.

— In the Tennessee Mountains. LC 78-100406. 360p. reprint ed. 111.60 (*0-608-16850-5*, 202756000055) Bks Demand.

— In the Tennessee Mountains. (BCL1-PS American Literature Ser.). 322p. 1992. reprint ed. lib. bdg. 89.00 (*0-7812-6803-6*) Rprt Serv.

— In the Tennessee Mountains. (Notable American Authors Ser.). 1999. reprint ed. lib. bdg. 125.00 (*0-7812-4591-5*) Rprt Serv.

— The Juggler. (Notable American Authors Ser.). 1999. reprint ed. lib. bdg. 125.00 (*0-7812-4602-4*) Rprt Serv.

— The Mystery of Witch-Face Mountain & Other Stories. 1972. reprint ed. lib. bdg. 29.00 (*0-8422-8099-5*) Irvington.

— The Mystery of Witch-Face Mountain & Other Stories. (Notable American Authors Ser.). 1999. reprint ed. lib. bdg. 125.00 (*0-7812-4601-6*) Rprt Serv.

— The Ordeal. (Notable American Authors Ser.). 1999. reprint ed. lib. bdg. 125.00 (*0-7812-4612-1*) Rprt Serv.

— The Phantoms of the Foot-Bridge & Other Stories. (Notable American Authors Ser.). 1999. reprint ed. lib. bdg. 125.00 (*0-7812-4600-8*) Rprt Serv.

— The Phantoms of the Footbridge & Other Stories. (C). 1973. reprint ed. lib. bdg. 32.50 (*0-8422-8100-2*) Irvington.

— The Phantoms of the Footbridge & Other Stories. (C). 1986. reprint ed. pap. text 9.50 (*0-8290-1942-1*) Irvington.

— The Prophet of the Great Smoky Mountains. LC 76-110350. reprint ed. 34.50 (*0-404-04542-1*) AMS Pr.

— The Prophet of the Great Smoky Mountains. (BCL1-PS American Literature Ser.). 308p. 1992. reprint ed. lib. bdg. 89.00 (*0-7812-6804-4*) Rprt Serv.

— The Prophet of the Great Smoky Mountains. (Notable American Authors Ser.). 1999. reprint ed. lib. bdg. 125.00 (*0-7812-4594-X*) Rprt Serv.

— The Raid of the Guerilla & Other Stories. (Notable American Authors Ser.). 1999. reprint ed. lib. bdg. 125.00 (*0-7812-4611-3*) Rprt Serv.

— Raid of the Guerrilla, & Other Stories. LC 71-150556. (Short Story Index Reprint Ser.). (Illus.). 1977. reprint ed. 23.95 (*0-8369-3853-4*) Ayer.

— The Storm Centre. (Notable American Authors Ser.). 1999. reprint ed. lib. bdg. 125.00 (*0-7812-4608-3*) Rprt Serv.

— The Story of Duciehurst. (Notable American Authors Ser.). 1999. reprint ed. lib. bdg. 125.00 (*0-7812-4613-X*) Rprt Serv.

— The Story of Keedon Bluffs. (Notable American Authors Ser.). 1999. reprint ed. lib. bdg. 125.00 (*0-7812-4596-6*) Rprt Serv.

— The Story of Old Fort Loudon. LC 73-104531. (Illus.). 409p. reprint ed. lib. bdg. 39.00 (*0-8398-1269-8*) Irvington.

— The Story of Old Fort Loudon. (C). 1986. reprint ed. pap. text 10.95 (*0-8290-1941-3*) Irvington.

— The Story of Old Fort Loudon. (Notable American Authors Ser.). 1999. reprint ed. lib. bdg. 125.00 (*0-7812-4605-9*) Rprt Serv.

— Where the Battle Was Fought. (Notable American Authors Ser.). 1999. reprint ed. lib. bdg. 125.00 (*0-7812-4592-3*) Rprt Serv.

— Young Mountaineers. LC 70-98588. (Short Story Index Reprint Ser.). 1977. 20.95 (*0-8369-3162-9*) Ayer.

— The Young Mountaineers. (Notable American Authors Ser.). 1999. reprint ed. lib. bdg. 125.00 (*0-7812-4603-2*) Rprt Serv.

Murga Sanz, Vicente. Historia Documental de Puerto Rico: Cedulario Puertorriqueno. (Biblioteca Historica de Puerto Rico Ser.). (SPA.). 456p. 1961. 4.00 (*0-8477-0873-X*) U of PR Pr.

Murgai, Rajeev. Logic Synthesis for Field-Programmable Gate Arrays. (Kluwer International Series in Engineering & Computer Science). 448p. (C). 1995. text 126.50 (*0-7923-9596-4*) Kluwer Academic.

Murgatroyd, Francis D. & Camm, A. John, eds. Atrial Fibrillation for the Clinician. LC 95-176. (Clinical Approaches to Tachyarrhythmias Ser.: Vol. 4). (Illus.). 152p. 1995. 19.00 (*0-87993-614-2*) Futura Pub.

Murgatroyd, Francis D. & Camm, John, eds. Nonpharmacological Management of Atrial Fibrillation. LC 97-4340. (Illus.). 560p. 1997. 120.00 (*0-87993-665-7*) Futura Pub.

***Murgatroyd, P.** Brought Forward: The Amatory Elegies of Johannes Secundus. 2000. 70.00 (*90-04-11603-6*) Brill Academic Pubs.

Murgatroyd, Paul. A Collection of Translations into Latin & Neo-Latin Poetry - Original Compositions. LC 91-31508. 120p. 1991. lib. bdg. 59.95 (*0-7734-9750-1*) E Mellen.

— Melpome: Translations of Selected Greek Lyrics with Notes. 92p. (Orig.). 1989. pap. 15.00 (*90-256-0986-4*, Pub. by AM Hakkert) BookLink Distributors.

Murgatroyd, Paul, ed. Ovid with Love: Selection from the Ars Amatoria, Books I & II. 228p. 1982. pap. text 16.00 (*0-86516-015-5*) Bolchazy-Carducci.

Murgatroyd, Stephen. Counselling & Helping. (Psychology in Action Ser.). 170p. (C). 1986. pap. text 13.95 (*0-901715-41-7*, 9910, Pub. by Brit Psychol Soc) Routledge.

Murgatroyd, Stephen, ed. Helping the Troubled Child: Interprofessional Case Studies. 196p. 1980. pap. 32.95 (*0-335-09818-5*) OpUniv Pr.

Murgatroyd, Stephen & Morgan, Colin. Total Quality Management & the School. LC 92-17386. (Illus.). 221p. 1992. pap. 34.95 (*0-335-15722-X*) OpUniv Pr.

Murgatroyd, Stephen & Woole, Ray. Coping with Crisis: Understanding & Helping People in Need. 180p. 1982. pap. 34.95 (*0-335-09819-3*) OpUniv Pr.

Murgatroyd, Stephen, jt. auth. see Morgan, Colin.

Murgatroyd, Stephen J., jt. auth. see Mills, Albert J.

Murger, Henry. Scenes de la Vie de Boheme. (Folio Ser.: No. 1968). (FRE.). 476p. 1988. pap. 13.95 (*2-07-038055-6*) Schoenhof.

Murgon, Micky. Caring for Green Iguanas: A Complete Authoritative Guide. 64p. 1998. pap. 12.95 (*0-7938-0245-8*, WW079) TFH Pubns.

Murguia, Alejandro. Southern Front. LC 89-7336. 128p. 1990. pap. 11.00 (*0-916950-97-2*) Biling Rev-Pr.

Murguia, Alejandro & Paschke, Barbara, eds. Volcan: Poems from Central America. LC 83-20936. 159p. 1984. pap. 6.95 (*0-87286-153-8*) City Lights.

Murguia, Alejandro, tr. see Murillo, Rosario.

***Murhammer, Martin W. & International Business Machines Corporation Staff.** A Comprehensive Guide to Virtual Private Networks. LC 99-190106. 1998. write for info. (*0-7384-0007-6*) IBM Cary NC.

Murhlhoff, Tim. Shakespeare to U2: How to Know You're in Love. (Life Skills Ser.). (Illus.). 6p. (C). 1995. teacher ed., ring bd. 1.25 (*1-885702-61-2*); student ed., ring bd. 3.25 (*1-885702-60-4*, 742-008s) WSN Pr.

Muri, Donna, ed. see Boloz, Sigmund A.

Muria, Jose M. Breve Historia de Jalisco (Concise History of Jalisco) (Breves Historias de los Estados de Mexico Ser.). (SPA.). 1994. pap. 13.99 (*968-16-4552-9*, Pub. by Fondo) Continental Bk.

Murickan, J. Religion & Power Structure in Rural India: (A Study of Two Fishing Villages in Kerala) Poovar-Sakthikulangara. (C). 1991. 18.00 (*81-7033-117-X*, Pub. by Rawat Pubns) S Asia.

Muricy, Carmen M. The Brazilian Amazon: Institutions & Publications. (Bibliography & Reference Ser.: No. 28). vii, 50p. 1991. pap. 23.50 (*0-685-53178-3*) SALALM.

Murie. Complete Guide to Digital Cameras. 336p. 1999. pap. 39.95 (*0-7906-1175-9*) Prompt Publns.

Murie, Adolph. Mammals of Denali. rev. ed. LC 94-14061. 1994. 9.95 (*0-930931-12-2*) Alaska Natural.

— A Naturalist in Alaska. LC 89-20671. 302p. 1990. reprint ed. pap. 18.95 (*0-8165-1168-3*) U of Ariz Pr.

— Wolves of Mt. McKinley. LC 84-22017. (Illus.). 238p. (Orig.). 1985. reprint ed. pap. 13.95 (*0-295-96203-8*) U of Wash Pr.

Murie, Alan & Wang, Ya P. Housing Policy & Practice in China. LC 96-44855. 256p. 1999. text 79.95 (*0-312-17241-9*) St Martin.

Murie, Alan, jt. auth. see Birrell, Derek.

Murie, Alan, jt. auth. see Forrest, Ray.

Murie, James R. Ceremonies of the Pawnee. Parks, Douglas R., ed. LC 88-28290. (Studies in the Anthropology of North American Indians). (Illus.). xiv, 497p. 1989. reprint ed. text 50.00 (*0-8032-3138-5*) U of Nebr Pr.

Murie, James R., jt. auth. see Fletcher, Alice C.

Murie, Jan O. & Michener, Gail R., eds. The Biology of Ground-Dwelling Squirrels: Annual Cycles, Behavioral Ecology, & Sociality. LC 83-26035. (Illus.). 475p. 1984. reprint ed. pap. 147.30 (*0-7837-8909-2*, 204962000001) Bks Demand.

M

Murie, Margaret & Murie, Olaus. Wapiti Wilderness: The Life of Olaus & Margaret Murie in Jackson Hole, Wyoming. (Illus.). 302p. 1985. pap. 19.95 (*0-87081-155-X*) Univ Pr Colo.

Murie, Margaret E. Grand Teton. LC 83-600157. (Official National Park Handbook Ser.: No. 122). (Illus.). 96p. 1984. pap. 5.50 (*0-912627-19-0*) Natl Park Serv.

— Island Between. LC 76-62991. (Illus.). 228p. 1977. 9.95 (*0-912006-04-8*) U of Alaska Pr.

— Two in the Far North: 35th Anniversary Edition. 5th ed. 1997. pap. 15.95 (*0-88240-489-X*, Alaska NW Bks) Gr Arts Ctr Pub.

Murie, Margaret E., jt. auth. see Schreier, Carl.

Murie, Martin. Losing Solitude. LC 94-77619. 256p. (Orig.). 1996. pap. 14.95 (*0-943972-34-5*) Homestead WY.

— Windswept. 288p. 2000. pap. 14.95 (*0-943972-68-X*) Homestead WY.

Murie, Olaus. Animal Tracks. (Flashguides Ser.). (Illus.). 24p. 1996. pap. 7.95 (*0-395-82997-6*) HM.

Murie, Olaus, jt. auth. see Murie, Margaret.

Murie, Olaus J. Elk of North America. LC 79-83649. (Illus.). 376p. (gr. 7-12). 1990. 15.98 (*0-933160-02-X*); pap. 10.95 (*0-933160-03-8*) Teton Bkshop.

— Fgt. Animal Tracks. 1974. pap. write for info. (*0-395-08037-1*) HM.

— Field Sketches of a Naturalist: Marie Portfolio. (Illus.). 8p. 1986. pap. 9.95 (*0-931895-10-3*) Grand Teton NHA.

— Nature Guide to Jackson Hole. (Illus.). 60p. (Orig.). (gr. 6-12). 1980. pap. 2.95 (*0-933160-05-4*) Teton Bkshop.

Muriedas, Mercedes. Los Anos de Ofun: Recuerdos, Relatos y Anotaciones. LC 92-75279. (Coleccion Caniqui). (SPA., Illus.). 85p. (Orig.). 1993. pap. 9.95 (*0-89729-667-2*) Ediciones.

Muriell, Christopher. An Answer unto the Catholiques Supplication, Presented unto the Kings Maiestie, for a Tolleration of Popish Religion in England...Annexed the Supplication of the Papists. LC 74-28874. (English Experience Ser.: No. 753). 1975. reprint ed. 15.00 (*90-221-0753-1*) Walter J Johnson.

Muriithi, Samuel M. African Crisis: Is There Hope? 220p. (Orig.). (C). 1996. pap. text 29.50 (*0-7618-0245-2*) U Pr of Amer.

— African Development: The Big Debate. LC 96-41720. 144p. 1996. pap. text 24.50 (*0-7618-0547-8*); lib. bdg. 47.50 (*0-7618-0546-X*) U Pr of Amer.

Murillo. Critical Mass. rev. ed. pap. 7.00 (*0-9654598-1-0*, Anthony Douglas) Fresh Fire.

Murillo, L. A. A Critical Introduction to Don Quixote. X, 270p. (C). 1991. pap. 29.95 (*0-8204-0516-7*) P Lang Pubng.

Murillo, Luis. The Noriega Mess: The Drugs, the Canal, & Why America Invaded. (Illus.). 1100p. 1995. 32.00 (*0-923444-02-5*) Video Bks.

Murillo, Mario. I Am the Christian the Devil Warned You About. LC 97-120844. 1997. 15.00 (*0-9654598-0-2*) Fresh Fire.

Murillo, Rosario. Angel in the Deluge. Murguia, Alejandro, tr. from SPA. LC 92-34354. (Pocket Poets Ser.: No. 50). 120p. (Orig.). 1993. pap. 7.95 (*0-87286-274-7*) City Lights.

Murimuth, Adam. Chronica Sui Temporis, Nunc Primum per Decem Annos Aucta, 1303-1346: Cum Eorundem Contunuatione AD 1380 a Quodam Anonymo. (English Historical Society Publications Ser.: Vol. 9). 1972. reprint ed. 30.00 (*0-8115-1534-6*) Periodicals Srv.

Murin, William J. & Pryor, Judith. Delivering Government Services: An Annotated Bibliography. LC 88-23643. (Public Affairs & Administration Ser.). 340p. 1988. text 20.00 (*0-8240-6618-9*) Garland.

Murinde, Victor. Development Banking & Finance. LC 95-83051. 480p. 1996. 91.95 (*1-85628-449-2*, Pub. by Avebry) Ashgate Pub Co.

— Macroeconomic Policy Modelling for Developing Countries. 462p. 1993. 96.95 (*1-85628-448-4*, Pub. by Avebry) Ashgate Pub Co.

Murinde, Victor, jt. auth. see Chanthunya, Charles L.

Murio, Diego A. The Mollification Method & the Numerical Solution of Ill-Posed Problems. 272p. 1993. 130.00 (*0-471-59408-3*) Wiley.

Muris, Timothy J., et al. Strategy, Structure, & Antitrust in the Carbonated Soft Drink Industry. LC 92-34944. 272p. 1993. 65.00 (*0-89930-788-4*, MYJ, Quorum Bks) Greenwood.

Muris, Timothy J., jt. auth. see Beales, J. Howard.

Murison, C., ed. Suetonius: Galba, Otho, Vitellius. (Bristol Latin Texts Ser.). (LAT.). 208p. 1989. pap. 22.95 (*1-85399-120-1*, Pub. by Brist Class Pr) Focus Pub-R Pullins.

Murison, Charles L. Galba, Otho & Vitellius: Careers & Controversies. (GER.). write for info. (*0-318-70630-X*) G Olms Pubs.

— Gallah, Otho & Vitellius: Careers & Controversies. (Spudasmata Ser.: Vol. 52). 179p. 1993. pap. 29.95 (*3-487-09756-7*) G Olms Pubs.

— Rebellion & Reconstruction: Galba to Domitian: An Historical Commentary on Cassius Dio's Roman History Books 64-67 (A. D. 68-96) LC 99-19877. (American Hilological Association Philological Monographs). 291p. 1999. text 45.00 (*0-7885-0547-5*, 400037) OUP.

Murison, David. The Guid Scots Tongue. 64p. (C). 1989. pap. 29.00 (*0-901824-78-X*, Pub. by Mercat Pr Bks) St Mut.

Murison, David, ed. Robert Henryson: Selected Poems. 58p. 1989. 40.00 (*0-85411-010-0*, Pub. by Saltire Soc) St Mut.

Murison, David A., jt. auth. see Grant, William.

Murison, W., ed. see Burke, Edmund.

Murison, William J. The Public Library: Its Origins, Purpose, & Significance. 3rd ed. LC 88-19335. 261p. reprint ed. pap. 81.00 (*0-608-08886-2*, 206952300004) Bks Demand.

Muritala, Adio S. How Can We Tame Them? LC 98-100240. 76p. 1997. pap. 8.95 (*1-85756-299-2*, Pub. by Janus Pubng) Paul & Co Pubs.

Murith, J. Dictionary of Initials of Scientific, Technical & Commercial Organization. 2nd ed. 471p. 1993. 180.00 (*0-7859-8800-9*) Fr & Eur.

— Dictionary of Initials of Scientific, Technical & Commercial Organizations. 2nd ed. 471p. 1993. 200.00 (*2-85206-384-0*) IBD Ltd.

— Dictionary of Scientific, Technical & Economic Abbreviations & Acronyms. 2nd rev. ed. (ENG & FRE.). 949p. 1992. 395.00 (*0-7859-4637-3*) Fr & Eur.

Murith, Jean. Dictionnaire des Sigles Scientifiques, Techniques et Economiques. 2nd ed. (FRE.). 470p. 1987. 250.00 (*0-7859-8071-7*, 2852063840) Fr & Eur.

Murjas, Jolanta, jt. ed. see Butler, W. E.

Murjas, Jolanta, jt. ed. see Butler, William E.

Murjhopadhyay. Handbook on Diseases of Sugar Beet, Vol. I. 208p. 1987. lib. bdg. 170.00 (*0-8493-3131-5*) CRC Pr.

— Handbook on Diseases of Sugar Beet, Vol. II. 192p. 1987. lib. bdg. 170.00 (*0-8493-3132-3*) CRC Pr.

Murji, Karim. Policing Drugs. LC 98-73752. 202p. 1998. text 59.95 (*1-84014-383-5*) Ashgate Pub Co.

Murk, Harri. A Handbook of Estonian Nouns, Adjectives & Verbs. LC 97-69265. (Uralic & Altaic Ser.: Vol. 163). 364p. 1997. 29.50 (*0-933070-42-X*) Res Inst Inner Asian Studies.

Murk-Jansen, Saskia. Brides in the Desert: The Spirituality of the Beguines. LC 98-18340. (Traditions in Christian Spirituality Ser.). 128p. 1998. pap. 13.00 (*1-57075-201-X*) Orbis Bks.

Murkes, Jakob & Carlsson, Claes-Goran. Crossflow Filtration: Theory & Practice. LC 88-20718. (Illus.). 145p. 1988. reprint ed. pap. 45.00 (*0-608-06826-8*, 206702300009) Bks Demand.

***Murkin, Henry R., et al, eds.** Prairie Wetland Ecology: The Contribution of the Marsh Ecology Research Program. (Illus.). 488p. 2000. 79.95 (*0-8138-2752-3*) Iowa St U Pr.

Murko, Carole L. & Carpini, Joseph D. Dodo, the Story. (Illus.). 16p. (J). (gr. k-4). 1998. pap. 4.00 (*0-9669447-0-4*) Dodo.

***Murkoff, Heidi.** What to Expect at a Play Date. (J). 2001. write for info. (*0-694-01330-7*, HarpFestival) HarpC Child Bks.

— What to Expect at Bedtime. LC 99-69938. (What to Expect Kids Ser.). 32p. (J). (ps-k). 2000. 7.99 (*0-694-01325-0*, HarpFestival) HarpC Child Bks.

— What to Expect at Your New School. (What to Expect Kids Ser.). 32p. (J). (ps-k). 2000. 7.99 (*0-694-01326-9*, HarpFestival) HarpC Child Bks.

— What to Expect Kids, No. 9. (J). write for info. (*0-694-01329-3*, HarpFestival) HarpC Child Bks.

— What to Expect When Mommy's Having a Baby. LC 99-68146. (What to Expect Kids Ser.). (Illus.). 32p. (J). (ps-k). 2000. 7.99 (*0-694-01321-8*, HarpFestival) HarpC Child Bks.

— What to Expect When the Babysitter Comes. LC 99-69941. (Illus.). 32p. (J). (ps-k). 2000. pap. 7.99 (*0-694-01323-4*, HarpFestival) HarpC Child Bks.

— What to Expect When the New Baby Comes Home. (What to Expect Kids Ser.). 32p. (J). (ps-k). 2001. 7.99 (*0-694-01327-7*, HarpFestival) HarpC Child Bks.

— What to Expect When You Go to the Dentist. (What to Expect Kids Ser.). 32p. (J). (ps-k). 2000. 7.99 (*0-694-01328-5*, HarpFestival) HarpC Child Bks.

— What to Expect When You Go to the Doctor. LC 99-69943. (What to Expect Kids Ser.). (Illus.). 32p. (J). (ps-k). 2000. 7.99 (*0-694-01324-2*, HarpFestival) HarpC Child Bks.

— What to Expect When You Use the Potty. LC 99-69942. (Illus.). 32p. (J). (ps-k). 2000. pap. 7.99 (*0-694-01322-6*, HarpFestival) HarpC Child Bks.

Murkoff, Heidi E., jt. auth. see Eisenberg, Arlene.

Murkovic, Antun. Blood Transfusion ID Card & Book: For Safer Blood at the Time of AIDS, Hepatitis, VDs, etc. (ENG & JPN.). 120p. (Orig.). 1989. pap. write for info. (*0-929602-00-5*) Mura Pub Co.

***Murkowski, Frank, ed.** Economic Impacts of the Kyoto Protocol: Congressional Hearing. (Illus.). 92p. 2000. pap. text 20.00 (*0-7567-0143-0*) DIANE Pub.

— Nuclear Waste Storage & Disposal Policy: Congressional Hearing. 99p. 2000. pap. text 20.00 (*0-7567-0144-9*) DIANE Pub.

***Murkowski, Frank H., ed.** Climate Change Proposal: Congressional Hearing. (Illus.). 99p. (C). 2000. reprint ed. pap. text 20.00 (*0-7881-8704-X*) DIANE Pub.

— Climate Treaty: Congressional Hearing. (Illus.). 124p. (C). 2000. reprint ed. pap. text 25.00 (*0-7881-8706-6*) DIANE Pub.

Murkowski, Frank H., ed. Nuclear Waste Policy Act of 1997: Hearing Before the Committee on Energy & Natural Resources, U. S. Senate. 119p. (C). 1998. pap. text 25.00 (*0-7881-7297-2*) DIANE Pub.

***Murkowski, Frank H., ed.** Separate Sovereignty or Independence for Puerto Rico: Congressional Hearing. 66p. (C). 2000. reprint ed. pap. text 20.00 (*0-7881-8707-4*) DIANE Pub.

— State of the Petroleum Industry: Congressional Hearing. (Illus.). 120p. (C). 2000. pap. text 30.00 (*0-7567-0041-8*) DIANE Pub.

— U. S. - China Relations: Congressional Hearing. 50p. (C). 2000. reprint ed. pap. text 20.00 (*0-7881-8705-8*) DIANE Pub.

Murkute, S. R. Socio-Cultural Study of Scheduled Tribes: The Pardhans of Maharastra. (Castes & Tribes of India Ser.: Vol. II). 1990. 28.00 (*81-7022-262-1*, Pub. by Concept) S Asia.

Murley, Clare & Murley, Fred. Waterside: A Pictorial Past. (C). 1989. 50.00 (*1-85455-068-3*, Pub. by Ensign Pubns & Print) St Mut.

Murley, Fred, jt. auth. see Murley, Clare.

Murley, John A., et al, eds. Law & Philosophy: The Practice of Theory: Essays in Honor of George Anastaplo, 2 vols., Vols. 1 & 2. LC 91-42908. 617p. (C). 1992. 150.00 (*0-8214-1013-X*) Ohio U Pr.

Murley, John A., jt. ed. see Deutsch, Kenneth L.

Murley, L., ed. Clean Air Around the World. 3rd ed. 502p. 1995. pap. 165.95 (*3-540-58760-8*) Spr-Verlag.

***Murley, Mark.** Across the Threshold: 30 Years of Music & Retrospection. LC 00-32279. 2000. lthr. write for info. (*1-886110-93-X*) Addax Pubng.

***Murley, Mark & Moody Blues.** The Moody Blues, Across the Threshold: Thirty Years of Music & Retrospection. (Illus.). 112p. 2000. 27.95 (*1-886110-99-9*, Pub. by Addax Pubng) Midpt Trade.

Murley, Peter. Gower Handbook of Customer Service. 500p. 1996. text 113.95 (*0-566-07688-8*, Pub. by Gower) Ashgate Pub Co.

Murley, Reginald, et al, eds. Patients or Customers: Are the NHS Reforms Working? (Choice in Welfare Ser.: No. 23). 87p. 1995. pap. 16.95 (*0-255-36360-5*, Pub. by Inst Economic Affairs) Coronet Bks.

Murli, Almerico, ed. Computational Issues in High Performance Software for Nonlinear Optimization. LC 96-50008. 192p. (C). 1997. lib. bdg. 126.50 (*0-7923-9862-9*) Kluwer Academic.

Murli, Almerico, jt. ed. see Messina, Paul C.

Murlin, Bill, ed. see Guthrie, Woody.

Murlis, Helen. Pay at the Crossroads. 128p. 1995. 90.00 (*0-85292-614-6*, Pub. by IPM Hse) St Mut.

Murlis, Helen, jt. auth. see Armstrong, Michael.

Murmann-Kristen, Luise. Das Vegetationsmosaik Im Nordschwarzwaelder Waldebiet. (Dissertationes Botanicae Ser.: Band 104). (GER., Illus.). ix, 316p. 1987. pap. 95.00 (*3-443-64016-8*, Pub. by Gebruder Borntraeger) Balogh.

Murn, Raymond. Mission Possible. 1973. pap. 2.50 (*0-8341-1021-0*) Nazarene.

Murnaghan, Sheila. Mimesis & Indirectiories. 0.00 (*0-691-06844-5*) Princeton U Pr.

Murnaghan, Sheila, jt. auth. see Joshel, Sandra R.

Murname. Rescuing Robinson Crusoe: Reconnecting Schools with the Changing Economy. 1996. 26.00 (*0-02-874066-1*) Free Pr.

Murnane, Lynne, ed. see Carter, Harry.

Murnane, Lynne C., jt. auth. see Powell, Pamela.

Murnane, Lynne C., ed. see IFSTA Committee.

Murnane, Lynne C., ed. see ISFTA Committee.

Murnane, Lynne C., ed. see Walker, Susan S.

Murnane, Mary, jt. auth. see Daniels, Kay.

Murnane, Richard J. & Levy, Frank. Teaching the New Basic Skills: Principles for Educating Children to Thrive in a Changing Economy. 272p. 1996. 23.50 (*0-684-82739-5*) Free Pr.

Murnane, Richard J., et al. Who Will Teach? Policies That Matter. (Illus.). 192p. (C). 1991. 32.00 (*0-674-95192-1*) HUP.

Murnane, Richard J., ed. see National Research Council Staff.

***Murnane, Tim.** The Blue Masked Forest. LC 99-65224. 64p. 2000. pap. 9.95 (*1-58501-021-9*, Pub. by CeShore Pubg) Natl Bk Netwk.

Murnane, William J. Penguin Guide to Ancient Egypt. 2nd ed. LC 97-205405. 1997. pap. 18.95 (*0-14-046952-4*, Penguin Bks) Viking Penguin.

— The Road to Kadesh: A Historical Interpretation of the Battle Reliefs of King Sety I at Karnak. 2nd rev. ed. LC 90-63725. (Studies in Ancient Oriental Civilization: No. 42). (Illus.). 157p. (C). 1990. pap. 25.00 (*0-918986-67-2*) Orient Inst.

Murnane, William J. & Van Siclen, Charles C., III. The Boundary Stelae of Akhenaten. LC 93-7007. (Studies in Egyptology). 1993. write for info. (*0-7103-0464-1*) Routledge.

Murnane, William J., ed. see Nelson, Harold H.

Murner, Thomas. Deutsche Schriften mit den Holzschnitten der Erstdrucke, 9 vols. Schultz, Franz, ed. (C). 1969. reprint ed. 1107.70 (*3-11-000276-0*) De Gruyter.

***Murnigham, Jack & Field, Genevieve, eds.** Full Frontal Fiction: The Best of Nerve.Com. LC 00-30218. 256p. 2000. pap. 14.00 (*0-609-80658-0*, Three Riv Pr) Crown Pub Group.

Murnion, Philip J. The Catholic Priest & the Changing Structure of Pastoral Ministry. 1978. 44.95 (*0-405-10845-1*, 11822) Ayer.

— New Parish Ministers: Laity & Religious on Parish Staffs. (Illus.). (Orig.). 1992. pap. 11.95 (*1-881307-01-8*) Natl Pastoral LC.

***Murnion, Philip J. & DeLambo, David.** Parishes & Parish Ministers: A Study of Parish Lay Ministry. Smith, Karen S., ed. 80p. 1999. pap. 15.95 (*1-881307-21-2*) Natl Pastoral LC.

Murnion, Philip J., et al. Parish Community Profile. (Follow Me! Ser.). 32p. 1997. pap. 9.95 (*1-881307-05-0*, B7050) Natl Pastoral LC.

Muro, ed. Automation Services for Libraries: A Resource Handbook of Marketing & Sales. 3rd ed. (Illus.). 300p. 1996. per. 78.00 (*1-879491-08-7*) Vendor Rltns.

Muro & Kottman. Guidance & Counseling. 1994. teacher ed. 9.06 (*0-697-26388-6*, WCB McGr Hill) McGraw-H Hghr Educ.

Muro, Ernest A. Automation Services for Libraries: A Resource Handbook. 3rd ed. 300p. 1996. per. 78.00 (*1-879491-09-5*) Vendor Rltns.

— Automation Services for Libraries: A Resource Handbook - User Reviews. 2nd ed. 300p. 1996. per. 78.00 (*1-879491-07-9*) Vendor Rltns.

— Automation Services for Libraries: LATINET '91. Lau, Jesus, ed. Allan, Martha, ed. & tr. by. Covitz, Barbara, tr. (Library Management Ser.). (ENG & SPA., Illus.). 347p. 1992. pap. 67.50 (*1-879491-03-6*) Vendor Rltns.

Muro, James J. Creating & Funding Educational Foundations: A Guide for Local School Districts. 272p. (C). 1994. 54.00 (*0-205-15573-1*, Longwood Div) Allyn.

Muro, James J. & Kottman, Terry A. Guidance & Counseling in the Elementary & Middle Schools: A Practical Approach. 528p. (C). 1994. text. write for info. (*0-697-20560-6*) Brown & Benchmark.

Muro, Juan Antonio. Basic Pieces for Guitar Vol. 2: Mel Bay Version. (SPA, ENG & FRE., Illus.). 56p. 1996. 9.95 (*0-7866-1769-1*, 95722) Mel Bay.

Muro, Masaru, tr. see Chomei, Kamono.

Muro, Vincent. Handbook of Financial Analysis for Corporate Managers. rev. ed. 450p. 1998. 89.95 (*0-8144-0399-9*) AMACOM.

Muroga, Saburo. Logic Design & Switching Theory. 636p. (C). 1990. reprint ed. 69.50 (*0-89464-463-7*) Krieger.

Murolo, Priscilla. The Common Ground of Womanhood: Class, Gender & Working Girls' Clubs, 1884-1928. LC 96-45787. 256p. 1996. text 29.95 (*0-252-02107-X*); pap. text 14.95 (*0-252-06629-4*) U of Ill Pr.

Murolo, Priscilla & Chitty, Ben. From the Folks Who Brought You the Weekend: A Short, Illustrated History of Labor in the United States. (Illus.). 1998. 22.95 (*1-56584-444-0*, Pub. by New Press NY) Norton.

Muromcew, Cyril, ed. see Miliukov, P. N., et al.

Muron, A., tr. see Schmirler, Otto.

Muroni, Jean-Marc. Petit Dictionnaire Bantou du Gabon: Francais-Ndjabi, Ndjabi-Francais. (FRE.). 207p. 1989. pap. 55.00 (*0-7859-8014-8*, 2738402658) Fr & Eur.

Murooka, Yoshikatsu & Imanaka, Tadayuki, eds. Recombinant Microbes for Industrial & Agricultural Applications. (Bioprocess Technology Ser.: Vol. 19). (Illus.). 896p. 1993. text 245.00 (*0-8247-9141-X*) Dekker.

Murota, K. Structural Solvability & Controllability. (Algorithms & Combinatorics Ser.: Vol. 3). (Illus.). 295p. 1987. 71.95 (*0-387-17659-4*) Spr-Verlag.

***Murota, Kazuo.** Matrices & Matroids for Systems Analysis. LC 99-52231. (Algorithms & Combinatorics Ser.: Vol. 20). (Illus.). xii, 483p. 2000. 112.00 (*3-540-66024-0*) Spr-Verlag.

Murotsu, Y., jt. auth. see Thoft-Christensen, P.

Murotsu, Yoshisada, et al, eds. 8th International Conference on Adaptive Structure Technology: Proceedings, October 29-31, 1997, Wakayama, Japan. 445p. 1998. 189.95 (*1-56676-656-7*) Technomic.

Murov, Steven L. Handbook of Photochemistry. LC 73-89496. (Illus.). 290p. reprint ed. pap. 89.90 (*0-8357-6137-1*, 203455300090) Bks Demand.

***Murov, Steven L. & Stedjee, Brian.** Experiments & Exercises in Basic Chemistry. 5th ed. 437p. 2000. pap. text. write for info. (*0-471-35862-2*) Wiley.

Murov, Steven L. & Stedjee, Brian. Experiments in Basic Chemistry. 4th ed. 416p. 1996. pap. 49.95 (*0-471-16030-X*) Wiley.

Murov, Steven L., et al. Handbook of Photochemistry. 2nd exp. rev. ed. LC 93-4764. (Illus.). 432p. 1993. text 175.00 (*0-8247-7911-8*) Dekker.

Murowchick, Robert E., ed. China: Ancient Culture, Modern Land. LC 94-13366. (Cradles of Civilization Ser.: Vol. 2). (Illus.). 192p. 1994. write for info. (*0-8061-2683-3*) U of Okla Pr.

***Murph, Roxane C.** The English Civil War Through the Restoration in Fiction: An Annotated Bibliography, 1625-1999, 49. LC 99-58883. (Bibliographies & Indexes in World History Ser.: Vol. 49). 349p. 2000. lib. bdg. 85.00 (*0-313-31425-X*, GR1425, Greenwood Pr) Greenwood.

Murph, Roxane C., compiled by. The Wars of the Roses in Fiction: An Annotated Bibliography, 1440-1994, 41. LC 95-12746. (Bibliographies & Indexes in World History Ser.: Vol. 41). 224p. 1995. lib. bdg. 75.00 (*0-313-29709-6*, Greenwood Pr) Greenwood.

Murphee, Jon T. Divine Paradoxes: A Finite View of an Infinite God. LC 99-168588. 250p. 1998. 16.99 (*0-87509-771-5*) Chr Pubns.

Murphet, Howard. Sai Baba Avatar: A New Journey into Power & Glory. LC 77-83643. 1977. pap. 6.30 (*0-9600958-3-7*) Birth Day.

— Sai Baba, Man of Miracles. LC 90-24107. (Illus.). 224p. 1977. pap. 12.95 (*0-87728-335-4*) Weiser.

— Sai Inner Views & Insights: 30 Years with the Avatar. LC 96-78608. 184p. (Orig.). 1996. pap. 12.00 (*1-887906-00-2*) Leela Pr.

— Walking the Path with Sai Baba. LC 93-12651. Orig. Title: Invitation to Glory. (Illus.). 208p. 1993. pap. 14.95 (*0-87728-781-3*) Weiser.

Murphet, Howard. When Daylight Comes: Biography of Helena Petrouna Blavatsky. LC 74-18958. 1987. pap. 7.50 (*0-8356-0459-4*) Theos Pub Hse.

Murphet, Howard. Where the Road Ends: From Self Through Sai to Self. LC 94-76983. 227p. 1994. reprint ed. pap. 12.00 (*0-9629835-3-5*) Leela Pr.

— Yankee Beacon of Buddhist Light: The Life of Colonel Henry S. Olcott. rev. ed. LC 88-40133. Orig. Title: Hammer on the Mountain. (Illus.). 350p. 1988. reprint ed. pap. 8.75 (*0-8356-0638-4*, Quest) Theos Pub Hse.

***Murphey, Alice.** Kaplan You Can Afford College 2001: The Family Guide to Meeting College Costs. (Illus.). 320p. 2000. pap. 18.00 (*0-684-87348-6*) Kaplan.

Murphey, Brian K. & Smith, Edmund T. Laura Lemay's Web Workshop: Creating Commercial Web Pages. LC 96-68246. 528p. 1996. 39.99 (*1-57521-126-2*) Sams.

An Asterisk (*) at the beginning of an entry indicates that the title is appearing for the first time.

*__Murphey, Cecil.__ My Parents, My Children: Spiritual Help for Caregivers. 244p. 2000. pap. 16.95 (0-664-22246-3) Westminster John Knox.

Murphey, Cecil, jt. auth. see Carson, Ben.

Murphey, Cecil B., jt. auth. see Carson, Ben.

Murphey, Cecil B., jt. auth. see Vaughan, Norman D.

Murphey, Dwight D. The Dispossession of the American Indians - & Other Key Issues in American History. 134p. (Orig.). 1995. pap. 16.00 (1-878465-14-7) Scott-Townsend Pubs.

— Lynching - History & Analysis: A Legal Studies Monograph. (Journal of Social, Political & Economic Studies: No. 24). 1995. pap. text 10.00 (0-930690-53-2) Coun Soc Econ.

Murphey, Edith Van Allen, see Van Allen Murphey, Edith.

Murphey, H. Allen. Problems in Search of Creative Solutions. (Illus.). 112p. 1997. pap. 11.95 (1-880505-52-5, CLC0205) Pieces of Lrning.

Murphey, Joseph C. A Return to the Landscape. Oliphant, Dave, ed. (Illus.). 1979. pap. 5.00 (0-933384-01-7) Prickly Pear.

Murphey-Lenahan, B. J. Colorado Trivia. LC 91-33797. 192p. (Orig.). 1991. pap. 5.95 (1-55853-135-1) Rutledge Hill Pr.

Murphey, M. G., jt. auth. see Flower, E.

Murphey, Mark D., jt. auth. see Kransdorf, Mark.

Murphey, Murray G. Anthony Garvan: Culture, History, & Artifacts - A Memorial Tribute Presented at a Special Meeting of the Library Company of Philadelphia, 25 March, 1992. (Illus.). 20p. 1992. pap. 5.00 (0-914076-87-6) Lib Co Phila.

— Development of Peirce's Philosophy. LC 61-13739. (Illus.). 440p. reprint ed. pap. 136.40 (0-8357-9155-6, 200601300054) Bks Demand.

— The Development of Peirce's Philosophy. LC 93-2777. 448p. (C). 1993. reprint ed. pap. text 19.95 (0-87220-183-X); reprint ed. lib. bdg. 38.95 (0-87220-231-3) Hackett Pub.

— Philosophical Foundations of Historical Knowledge. LC 93-5321. 344p. (C). 1994. text 74.50 (0-7914-1919-3); pap. text 24.95 (0-7914-1920-7) State U NY Pr.

Murphey, Murray G. & Berg, Ivar, eds. Values & Value Theory in Twentieth Century America: Essays in Honor of Elizabeth Flower. LC 87-33675. 308p. (C). 1988. 39.95 (0-87722-557-5) Temple U Pr.

Murphey, Rhoads. East Asia: A New History. LC 96-16976. 450p. (C). 1997. pap. 58.00 (0-673-99350-7) Addson-Wesley Educ.

— Fifty Years of China to Me: Personal Recollections of 1942-1992. LC 93-50528. (Monographs & Occasional Papers) 125p. 1994. pap. 10.00 (0-924304-17-0) Assn Asian Studies.

— A History of Asia. 2nd ed. LC 95-17224. 496p. (C). 1996. text 46.88 (0-673-99407-4) Addson-Wesley Educ.

*__Murphey, Rhoads.__ A History of Asia. 3rd ed. LC 99-22776. 468p. (C). 1999. pap. text 57.00 (0-321-04257-3) Addson-Wesley Educ.

Murphey, Rhoads. Ottoman Warfare, 1500-1700. LC 98-45274. 288p. (C). 1999. text 55.00 (0-8135-2684-1); pap. text 25.00 (0-8135-2685-X) Rutgers U Pr.

— Scope of Geography. 3rd ed. 228p. 1982. pap. 13.95 (0-416-33410-5, NO. 6354) Routledge.

— Survey of Japanese Studies in the United States: The 1990s. LC 96-22246. (Occasional Papers). xx, 328 p. (Orig.). 1996. pap. 15.00 (0-924304-27-8) Assn Asian Studies.

Murphey, Sallyann J. Bean Blossom Dreams. 320p. (Orig.). 1995. mass mkt. 5.99 (0-425-15018-6) Berkley Pub.

— Bean Blossom Dreams: A City Family's Search for a Simple Country Life. large type ed. LC 94-32217. 400p. 1994. pap. 18.95 (0-7838-1127-6, G K Hall Lrg Type) Mac Lib Ref.

*__Murphey, Sallyann J.__ The Metcalfe Family Album: Six Generations of Traditions & Memories. LC 99-89588. (Illus.). 256p. 1999. 29.95 (0-8118-2097-1) Chronicle Bks.

— Recollections: A Scrapbook & Guide for Creating Your Own Family Album. (Illus.). 100p. 2000. 19.95 (0-8118-2745-3) Chronicle Bks.

Murphey, Sallyann J. The Zen of Food: A Philosophy of Nourishment. LC 98-155092. 208p. 1998. pap. 10.95 (0-425-16311-3) Berkley Pub.

Murphey, Wesley. Blacktail Deer Hunting Adventures: A Refreshingly Candid Account Valuable for Hunters Everywhere. LC 94-76671. (Illus.). 176p. 1995. pap. 12.95 (0-9641320-4-4) Lost Creek.

— Conibear Beaver Trapping in Open Water: Master Beaver Trapping Techniques. LC 96-77347. (Illus.). 110p. (Orig.). 1996. pap. 11.00 (0-9641320-3-6) Lost Creek.

Murphree, Dorothy R. The Mask. 1967. pap. 3.50 (0-87129-231-9, M22) Dramatic Pub.

Murphree, Jon T. Miracles of Grace: Inspiring Stories of What God Has Done in Human Lives. 137p. (Orig.). 1996. pap. 7.95 (1-885729-08-1) Toccoa Falls.

— Responsible Evangelism: Relating Theory to Practice. 153p. (Orig.). (C). 1994. pap. 7.95 (1-885729-00-6) Toccoa Falls.

— Road to Sifat. 208p. (Orig.). 1990. pap. text. write for info. (0-932281-06-0) Quill Pubns GA.

Murphree, Julie J., ed. & illus. see Murphree, Pennee.

Murphree, Mabel M., ed. see Tupelo Symphony League Staff.

*__Murphree, Marilyn S.__ Moments with Marilyn. 308p. 1999. pap. 12.95 (0-7392-0313-4, PO3456) Morris Pubng.

Murphree, Pennee. The Adventures of 100Happy Shirt. Murphree, Julie J., ed. & illus. by. 28p. (Orig.). (J). (gr. 1-3). 1995. pap. 10.00 (0-9646188-0-X) Murphree Pr.

Murphree, Wallace A. Numerically Exceptive Logic: A Reduction of the Classical Syllogism. LC 90-23023. (American University Studies: Philosophy: Ser. V, Vol. 112). (Illus.). 222p. (C). 1991. text 32.95 (0-8204-1449-2) P Lang Pubng.

Murphy. Alan Lennox Boyd: A Biography. LC 99-230319. 256p. 1999. text 39.50 (1-86064-406-6) St Martin.

— The Biker Cookbook. 1999. 7.99 (0-517-20565-3) Random Hse Value.

— Blood Brothers. 1999. text. write for info. (0-312-16784-9) St Martin.

— Bloodties. 1988. mass mkt. 3.95 (0-671-64742-3) PB.

— Claris Filemaker Pro 2.1 for Mac: Quick Course. (DF - Computer Applications Ser.). (C). 1996. pap., wbk. ed. 22.95 (0-538-71565-0) S-W Pub.

— College Algebra: Students Solutions Manual. 5th ed. 520p. 1998. pap. text, student ed. 29.33 (0-13-081012-6) P-H.

— Concepts in Federal Taxation: 1998 Edition. 5th ed. 1997. 62.75 (0-314-20553-5) West Pub.

— The Confirmation Process. (C). 2001. text 20.00 (0-205-29007-8, Longwood Div) Allyn.

— Counting to Nine: Analyzing the Supreme Court. (C). 2001. pap. 22.67 (0-205-29008-6, Longwood Div) Allyn.

*__Murphy.__ Curriculum Guide for Middle School. 2000. pap. 12.95 (0-538-72436-6) Thomson Learn.

Murphy. Drug Therapy for Asthma: Research & Clinical Practice. Jenne, John, ed. (Lung Biology in Health & Disease Ser.: Vol. 31). (Illus.). 1152p. 1987. text 295.00 (0-8247-7633-X) Dekker.

— Effective Business Communication. 6th ed. 1991. teacher ed. 27.50 (0-07-044158-8) McGraw.

— Federal Tax 1995. Date not set. pap. text, teacher ed. write for info. (0-314-04393-4) West Pub.

— History Asia & History Atlas Pk. (C). 1998. 53.00 (0-673-78969-1) Addison-Wesley.

— Insights: Readings In Fed Tax. (SWC-Taxation). 1995. mass mkt. 13.75 (0-314-06421-4) West Pub.

— Interoperable & Federated Information Systems. (ITCP-UK Computer Science Ser.). 1997. pap. 35.95 (1-85032-264-3) ITCP.

*__Murphy.__ Jurisprudence. 2000. 53.50 (0-8133-3037-8, Pub. by Westview) HarpC.

Murphy. Microsoft Access 2.0 for Windows: Quick Course. (Quick Course Ser.). 192p. 1995. mass mkt. 15.95 (0-538-64861-9) S-W Pub.

— Microsoft Access 2000: Quicktorial. LC 98-47591. (Computer Applications Ser.). 180p. 1999. pap. 21.95 (0-538-68857-2) S-W Pub.

— Microsoft Excel 5.0 for Macintosh: Quick Course. (DF - Computer Applications Ser.). 1996. mass mkt., wbk. ed. 22.95 (0-538-71575-8) S-W Pub.

— Microsoft Excel 5.0 for Windows: Quick Course. (Quick Course Ser.). 192p. 1995. mass mkt. 15.95 (0-538-64841-4) S-W Pub.

— Microsoft Excel 7.0 for Windows 95: Quick Course. (DF - Computer Applications Ser.). (C). 1996. mass mkt. 22.95 (0-538-71481-6) S-W Pub.

— Microsoft Excel 2000: Quicktorial. LC 98-47588. (Computer Applications Ser.). 1999. pap. 21.95 (0-538-68853-X) S-W Pub.

Murphy. Microsoft Office for Windows: Complete Course. 1995. pap. 42.75 (0-538-64857-0) Thomson Learn.

Murphy. Microsoft Office for Windows 95: Complete Course. (DF - Computer Applications Ser.). (C). 1996. mass mkt. 51.95 (0-538-71478-6) S-W Pub.

— Microsoft PowerPoint 4.0 for Macintosh: Quick Course. (DF - Computer Applications Ser.). 1996. mass mkt. 22.95 (0-538-71580-4) S-W Pub.

— Microsoft PowerPoint 4.0 for Windows: Quick Course. (Quick Course Ser.). 192p. 1995. mass mkt. 15.95 (0-538-64851-1) S-W Pub.

— Microsoft PowerPoint 7.0 for Windows 95: Quick Course. (DF - Computer Applications Ser.). 1996. mass mkt. 22.95 (0-538-71487-5) S-W Pub.

— Microsoft Powerpoint 2000: Quicktorial. LC 98-47590. 174p. 1999. pap. 21.95 (0-538-68861-0) S-W Pub.

— Microsoft Word for Windows 95: Quick Course. (DF - Computer Applications Ser.). 1996. mass mkt. 22.95 (0-538-71469-7) S-W Pub.

— Microsoft Word 6.0 for Macintosh: Quick Course. (DF - Computer Applications Ser.). 1996. mass mkt. 21.95 (0-538-71570-7) S-W Pub.

— Microsoft Word 6.0 for Windows: Quick Course. (DF - Computer Applications Ser.). 1995. mass mkt. 15.95 (0-538-64846-5) S-W Pub.

— Microsoft Word 2000: Quicktorial. LC 98-47587. 227p. 1999. pap. 21.95 (0-538-68849-1) S-W Pub.

Murphy. Microsoft Word 97 for Windows 95: Quicktorial. 1997. 22.95 (0-538-67965-4) Thomson Learn.

Murphy. MS Access 97 for Window 95. (DF - Computer Applications Ser.). 1997. mass mkt. 22.95 (0-538-67973-5) S-W Pub.

*__Murphy.__ MS Office 98. 2000. pap., wbk. ed. 12.95 (0-538-72434-X) Thomson Learn.

Murphy. MS Powerpoint 97 for Window 95: Quicktorial. LC 98-115321. (DF - Computer Applications Ser.). 1997. mass mkt. 22.95 (0-538-67977-8) S-W Pub.

— Multimedia Circuitry: Classroom. 1997. cd-rom 666.67 (0-13-237595-8) P-H.

Murphy. Multimedia Circuits. 1997. cd-rom 37.00 (0-13-861360-5, Prentice Hall) P-H.

Murphy. Multimedia Devices. 208p. 1998. pap. text, student ed. 35.20 (0-13-601907-2) P-H.

*__Murphy.__ Murphy Portrait Of Amer Politi. 3rd ed. 1999. pap. text 21.57 (0-395-88547-7) HM.

— The New York Times Guide to Business Communication Today. LC 99-52892. 1999. pap. text 20.95 (0-324-04161-6) Sth-Wstrn College.

— The New York Times Guide to Business Law. 2000. pap. text 20.95 (0-324-04160-8) Sth-Wstrn College.

— The New York Times Guide to Finance. 2000. pap. text 20.95 (0-324-04158-6) Sth-Wstrn College.

— The New York Times Guide to Marketing. LC 99-49442. 1999. pap. text 20.95 (0-324-04182-9) Sth-Wstrn College.

Murphy. Numerical Analysis Algorithm. 1990. pap. write for info. (0-318-68279-6) P-H.

— Opposites. (J). 1998. 4.99 (0-87628-980-4) Ctr Appl Res.

— Playtime. (Razzle Dazzle Bks.). (Illus.). 12p. (J). (ps-1). 1998. 4.99 (0-689-82056-9) S&S Childrens.

— Portrait of American Politics, 2 vols. LC 93-78690. (C). Date not set. pap., teacher ed., suppl. ed. 27.96 (0-395-68640-7) HM.

— Power in Washington. (C). 1997. pap. text. write for info. (0-15-505379-5) Harcourt Coll Pubs.

Murphy. A Practical Approach to Microsoft Office for Mac: Complete Course. 1997. pap. 53.95 (0-538-67962-X) Thomson Learn.

Murphy. Punishment & Rehabilitation. 4th ed. (Philosophy Ser.). 2001. pap. 26.50 (0-534-52070-7) Wadsworth Pub.

— The St. Martin's Source for Writing Tutors. 64p. 1995. pap. text 10.95 (0-312-11729-9) St Martin.

*__Murphy.__ Secrets of the I Ching. 2000. pap. write for info. (0-13-028455-6) P-H.

Murphy. See What You're Asking! 1992. 58.00 (0-7616-7760-7) Commun Skill.

— Snacktime. (Razzle Dazzle Bks.). (Illus.). 12p. (J). (ps-1). 1998. 4.99 (0-689-82057-7) S&S Childrens.

*__Murphy.__ Sociology & Nature. 2000. pap. 28.00 (0-8133-6661-5, Pub. by Westview) HarpC.

— Sydney. text. write for info. (0-471-48965-4); pap. text. write for info. (0-471-48966-2) Wiley.

— Technical Analysis of the Futures Markets. 1999. 65.00 (0-13-026970-0) P-H.

Murphy. Using Quattro Pro. (C). 1995. pap. text 14.76 (0-395-71402-8) HM.

— Veterinary Virology. 3rd ed. 600p. (C). 1999. text 89.95 (0-12-511340-4) Acad Pr.

*__Murphy & Jennings, Cheryl D.__ The New York Time Guide to Economics. LC 00-21220. 100p. 2000. pap. text 20.95 (0-324-04159-4) Sth-Wstrn College.

Murphy & Laczniak, Gene R. Ethical Marketing Decisions. (C). 1992. pap. text 30.80 (0-205-13627-3) Allyn.

Murphy & Parker. Handbook of EDP Auditing, No. 3314. rev. ed. 1328p. 1991. suppl. ed. 60.25 (0-685-56163-1) Warren Gorham & Lamont.

*__Murphy & Sapir.__ The Last Monarch. (Destroyer Ser.: Bk. 120). 352p. 2000. mass mkt. 5.99 (0-373-63235-5, 1-63235-5, Wrldwide Lib) Harlequin Bks.

Murphy & Sapir. Misfortune Teller. (Destroyer Ser.: No. 115). 1999. per. 5.99 (0-373-63230-4, 1-63230-6, Harlequin) Harlequin Bks.

Murphy & Sapir, Richard. Unite & Conquer. LC 96-2393. (Destroyer Ser.: Vol. 102). 346p. 1996. per. 4.99 (0-373-63217-7, 1-63217-3, Wrldwide Lib) Harlequin Bks.

Murphy & Snell. Forging Heroic Organzation. 1999. pap. text 15.00 (0-7352-0111-0) PH Pr.

Murphy & Sullivan, Michael. Trigonometry Enhanced with Graphs. 320p. 1996. pap. text, student ed. 29.33 (0-13-650953-3) P-H.

Murphy, et al. Captive Management Conservation of Amphibians & Reptiles. LC 94-67894. 408p. 1994. 58.00 (0-916984-33-8) SSAR.

— Disaster Planning Manual: How to Write a Community Disaster Coordination Plan. (Illus.). 300p. 1988. ring bd. 25.00 (0-913724-41-6) Emerg Response Inst.

Murphy, jt. auth. see Glynn.

Murphy, jt. auth. see Jenkins-Murphy, Patricia.

Murphy, jt. auth. see Lunsford, Andrea.

Murphy, jt. auth. see Zitzewitz.

Murphy, ed. see Avienus, Lucius F.

Murphy, A. To Hell & Back. 288p. 1996. reprint ed. 7.98 (1-56731-116-4, MJF Bks) Fine Comms.

Murphy, A., ed. Babel' Four Stories (Chetyre Rasskaza) (Bristol Russian Texts Ser.). (RUS.). 118p. 1993. pap. 18.95 (1-85399-300-X, Pub. by Brist Class Pr) Focus Pub-R Pullins.

Murphy, A. B., ed. Zoshchenko: Stories of the 1920s. (RUS.). 78p. 1991. reprint ed. pap. 16.95 (0-631-14398-X) Blackwell Pubs.

Murphy, Agnes G. Melba: A Biography. LC 74-24162. (Illus.). reprint ed. 37.50 (0-404-13057-7) AMS Pr.

— Melba: A Biography. LC 77-8029. (Music Reprint Ser.). (Illus.). 1977. reprint ed. lib. bdg. 45.00 (0-306-77428-3) Da Capo.

Murphy-Aivazian, Mary K. The Post-Robot Age(1994-?) As More of Us "Get a Life," Work Becomes Personal. 259p. 1995. 29.95 (1-881705-25-0) Antilles Pub.

Murphy, Alan. Bolivia Handbook. (Footprint Handbooks Ser.). (Illus.). 352p. 1997. 21.95 (0-8442-4923-8, 49238, Natl Textbk Co) NTC Contemp Pub Co.

— Ecuador & Galapagos Handbook. LC 96-72523. (Illus.). 416p. 1997. 16.95 (0-8442-4915-7) NTC Contemp Pub Co.

*__Murphy, Alan.__ Footprint Bolivia Handbook. 2nd ed. (Footprint Handbks.). (Illus.). 480p. 2000. pap. 19.95 (0-658-00652-5, 006525) NTC Contemp Pub Co.

— Footprint Ecuador & Galapagos Handbook. 2nd ed. (Footprint Handbooks Ser.). (Illus.). 448p. 1999. pap. 19.95 (0-8442-2129-5, 21295) NTC Contemp Pub Co.

— Peru Handbook. 2nd ed. (Footprint Handbooks Ser.). (Illus.). 512p. 1999. pap. 17.95 (0-8442-2187-2, 21872) NTC Contemp Pub Co.

— Scotland Handbook. (Footprint Handbks.). (Illus.). 650p. 2000. pap. 18.95 (0-658-00370-4, 003704, Passprt Bks) NTC Contemp Pub Co.

Murphy, Alan. Venezuela Handbook. LC 97-78490. (Footprint Handbooks Ser.). 448p. 1998. 21.95 (0-8442-4947-5, 49475, Natl Textbk Co) NTC Contemp Pub Co.

*__Murphy, Alan.__ Venezuela Handbook. 2nd ed. (Footprint Handbooks Ser.). (Illus.). 2000. pap. 19.95 (0-658-00659-2, Passprt Bks) NTC Contemp Pub Co.

Murphy, Albert T. & Fitzsimons, Ruth M. Stuttering & Personality Dynamics: Play Therapy, Projective Therapy, & Counseling. LC 82-8410. 301p. reprint ed. pap. 93.40 (0-608-09264-9, 205406600002) Bks Demand.

Murphy, Albert T., jt. auth. see FitzSimons, Ruth M.

Murphy, Alexander B. The Regional Dynamics of Language Differentiation in Belgium: A Study in Cultural-Political Geography. (Research Papers: No. 227). 1988. pap. text 14.50 (0-89065-132-9) U Ch Pr.

*__Murphy, Alexander B., et al, eds.__ Cultural Encounters with the Environment: Enduring & Evolving Geographic Themes. LC 99-87405. 336p. 2000. pap. 72.00 (0-7425-0105-1) Rowman.

— Cultural Encounters with the Environment: Enduring & Evolving Geographic Themes. LC 99-87405. 336p. 2000. 34.95 (0-7425-0106-X) Rowman.

Murphy, Alexander B., jt. auth. see De Blij, H. J.

*__Murphy, Alexandra R.__ Drawn Into the Light: Jean-Francois Millet. LC 99-11142. (Illus.). 192p. 1999. 45.00 (0-300-07925-7) Yale U Pr.

Murphy, Alexandra R. Winslow Homer in the Clark Collection. LC 86-61315. (Illus.). 76p. (Orig.). 1986. pap. 14.95 (0-931102-19-7) S & F Clark Art.

Murphy, Alexandra R., jt. auth. see Fernandez, Rafael, Jr.

Murphy, Alexandra R., jt. auth. see Museum of Fine Arts, Department of Paintings Staff.

Murphy, Allan, jt. ed. see Katz, Richard W.

Murphy, Amy, ed. see Campbell, C. Blaine.

Murphy, Ana A., jt. auth. see Azziz, Ricardo.

Murphy, Andrew. But the Irish Sea Betwixt Us: Ireland, Colonialism & Renaissance Literature. LC 98-41607. (Irish Literature, History & Culture Ser.). 224p. 1999. 34.95 (0-8131-2086-1) U Pr of Ky.

— Cultural Encounters in the U. S. A. Cross-Cultural Dialogues & Mini-Dramas. 128p. 1994. pap. 9.95 (0-8442-0715-2, Natl Textbk Co) NTC Contemp Pub Co.

Murphy, Andrew. The Renaissance Text: Theory, Editing & Textuality. text. write for info. (0-7190-5398-6, Pub. by Manchester Univ Pr) St Martin.

— The Renaissance Texty: Theory, Editing & Textuality. pap. write for info. (0-7190-5917-8, Pub. by Manchester Univ Pr) St Martin.

Murphy, Andrew. Seamus Heaney. LC 96-217096. (Writers & Their Work Ser.). 95p. (Orig.). 1996. pap. text 17.00 (0-7463-0783-7, Pub. by Northcote House) U Pr of Miss.

Murphy, Andrew, ed. & intro. see Shakespeare, William.

Murphy, Andrew F. Grammar Review for the TOEFL. LC 93-37590. (Test Preparation Ser.). 256p. 1982. pap. 10.95 (0-15-600096-2) Harcourt.

— How to Prepare for the TOEFL. (Test Preparation Ser.). 294p. 1987. pap. 14.95 (0-15-601371-1) Harcourt.

Murphy, Andy. Bloodless. LC 94-72730. 358p. 1996. 24.95 (0-944435-33-5) Glenbridge Pub.

Murphy, Andy & Murphy, Teri. The Husband's Manual: A User's Guide for Husbands or Men Trying Out for the Part. Charles, Rodney & Pasco, Elizabeth, eds. LC 97-61878. 130p. (Orig.). 1996. pap. 12.95 (0-9632336-4-5) SunStar Pr.

— The Husband's Manual: A User's Guide for Husbands or Men Trying Out for the Part. Charles, Rodney & Pasco, Elizabeth, eds. LC 98-60807. 130p. (Orig.). 1998. pap. 12.95 (1-887472-40-1) Sunstar Pubng.

Murphy, Angela C. Whaley & Wong's Essentials of Pediatric Nursing. 5th ed. 328p. (C). (gr. 13). 1996. pap. text, student ed. 19.95 (0-8151-7470-5, 28277) Mosby Inc.

Murphy, Ann & Murphy, John. God's Gift of Life: A Child's First Book about Life. (Illus.). 32p. (Orig.). (J). (gr. 1-3). 1994. pap. text 4.95 (0-8198-3070-4) Pauline Bks.

— God's Gift of Life Parents' Guide. (Illus.). 20p. (Orig.). 1994. pap. 2.75 (0-8198-3071-2) Pauline Bks.

— Sex Education & Successful Parenting. LC 94-4980. 96p. 1996. pap. 4.95 (0-8198-6960-0) Pauline Bks.

Murphy, Ann P. The Parents Answer Book. unabridged ed. Parents Magazine Staff, ed. LC 98-23766. (Illus.). 896p. 1998. text 35.00 (0-307-44060-5, Whitman Coin) St Martin.

Murphy, Anne & Cassidy, Eoin. Neglected Wells: Spirituality & the Arts. LC 97-161612. 144p. 1997. pap. 15.00 (1-85182-294-1, Pub. by Four Cts Pr) Intl Spec Bk.

Murphy, Anne, jt. auth. see Deering, Anne.

Murphy, Anne M. Thomas More. Vardy, Peter, ed. LC 96-52493. (Great Christian Thinkers Ser.). 112p. 1997. reprint ed. pap. 9.00 (0-7648-0117-1, Liguori Triumph) Liguori Pubns.

Murphy, Antoin E. John Law: Economic Theorist & Policy-Maker. LC 96-49939. (Illus.). 404p. (C). 1997. text 75.00 (0-19-828649-X) OUP.

Murphy, Antoin E., ed. Monetary Theory, 1601-1758, 6 vols., Set. LC 95-37515. 2200p. (C). 1997. 980.00 (0-415-12533-2) Routledge.

Murphy, Arthur. The Englishman from Paris. (Augustan Reprints Ser.: No. 137). 1969. reprint ed. 14.50 (0-404-70137-X) AMS Pr.

*__Murphy, Arthur.__ The Faith of a Child: A Step-by-Step Guide to Salvation for Your Child. LC 00-41846. 2000. write for info. (0-8024-5146-2) Moody.

Murphy, Arthur. The Life of Garrick, 2 vols., 1 bk. LC 76-84521. 840p. 1972. 42.95 (0-405-08811-6, Pub. by Blom Pubns) Ayer.

— Lives of Henry Fielding & Samuel Johnson, with Essays from Gray's Inn Journal, 1752-1792. LC 68-24212. 496p. 1968. 95.00 (0-8201-1035-3) Schol Facsimiles.

M

Murphy, Arthur D. & Stepick, Alex. Social Inequality in Oaxaca: A History of Resistance & Change. (Conflicts in Urban & Regional Development Ser.). (Illus.). 300p. (Orig.). (C). 1991. 54.95 (*0-87722-868-X*); pap. 22.95 (*0-87722-869-8*) Temple U Pr.

Murphy, Arthur E. Reason, Reality, & Speculative Philosophy. Singer, Marcus G., ed. & intro. by. LC 96-5988. (Illus.). 330p. 1996. 45.00 (*0-299-15040-2*) U of Wis Pr.

Murphy, Arthur E., ed. see Mead, George Herbert.

Murphy, Arthur W., ed. The Nuclear Power Controversy. LC 76-40017. (American Assembly Guides Ser.). 1976. 9.95 (*0-13-625582-5*); pap. 3.95 (*0-13-625574-4*) Am Assembly.

Murphy, Arthur W., ed. see American Assembly Staff.

Murphy, Ashton. On the Wallaby. (C). 1990. pap. 30.00 (*0-86439-108-0*, Pub. by Boolarong Pubns) St Mut.

Murphy, Audie. To Hell & Back. (Military Classics Ser.). (Illus.). 304p. 1988. 21.95 (*0-8306-4002-9*, 40002) McGraw-Hill Prof.

— To Hell & Back. 284p. 1995. reprint ed. lib. bdg. 24.95 (*1-56849-579-X*) Buccaneer Bks.

Murphy, Austin. Scientific Investment Analysis. LC 99-27823. 504p. 2000. 75.00 (*1-56720-338-8*, Quorum Bks) Greenwood.

— Scientific Investment Analysis. 588p. 1994. 74.95 incl. disk (*0-914061-51-8*) Orchises Pr.

— Sports Illustrated: Best Superbowls. LC 98-85734. (Illus.). 160p. (gr. 3). 1999. 29.95 (*1-883013-41-0*) Time-Life.

***Murphy, Austin.** Sports Illustrated's the Super Bowl. (Illus.). 176p. 2000. pap. 29.95 (*1-892129-93-0*) Total Sprts.

Murphy, B. Greener Pastures on Your Side of the Fence: Better Farming with Voisin Management Intensive Grazing. 4th ed. (Illus.). 379p. 1998. pap. 30.00 (*0-9617807-3-8*) Arriba Pub.

Murphy, B., et al. Basic Principles of Inorganic Chemistry. 160p. 1998. pap. 34.95 (*0-85404-574-0*) Spr-Verlag.

Murphy, B., jt. auth. see Kutten, L. J.

***Murphy, B. D.** Verification of the LWARC Code For Light-Water- Reactor Afterheat Rate Calculations. 15p. 1998. pap. 2.00 (*0-16-062888-1*) USGPO.

Murphy, Barbara. Ace Hits the Big Time. 1995. 9.09 (*0-606-07174-1*, Pub. by Turtleback) Demco.

— Fly Like an Eagle. 1994. 9.09 (*0-606-07524-0*) Turtleback.

— Janey's War. large type ed. 592p. 31.50 (*0-7089-3708-X*) Ulverscroft.

Murphy, Barbara, ed. Nursing Centers: The Time Is Now. 279p. 1995. 20.95 (*0-88737-623-1*, 41-2629, NLN Pr) Natl League Nurse.

Murphy, Barbara, jt. auth. see Hoover, Rosalie.

Murphy, Barbara T. Black Authors & Illustrators of Books for Children & Young Adults: A Biographical Dictionary. 3rd ed. LC 98-42690. (Illus.). 544p. 1998. 65.00 (*0-8153-2004-3*, H2157) Garland.

Murphy, Barry, pref. Portmarnock: A Closer Look. 128p. 1997. pap. 7.95 (*0-86327-100-6*, Pub. by Wolfhound Press) Irish Amer Bk.

Murphy, Beatrice M., ed. Ebony Rhythm. LC 68-57062. (Granger Index Reprint Ser.). 1977. 20.95 (*0-8369-6033-5*) Ayer.

***Murphy, Bernadette.** Sport Readiness. (Illus.). (YA). 1999. pap. 14.95 (*0-673-58914-5*, GoodYrBooks) Addson-Wesley Educ.

***Murphy, Bernice, et al, eds.** On Dialogue: Contempory Australian Art. (Illus.). 216p. 1999. pap. 39.95 (*3-931321-61-4*, Pub. by Jovis Verlags) Dist Art Pubs.

Murphy, Bert. Sun & Shadows Ventures. Appleyard Communications Staff, ed. (Ventures West Ser.: Vol. 1). (Illus.). 150p. (Orig.). 1996. pap. 9.95 (*0-9650298-1-6*, SAW298-9077) MBAR Pubng.

***Murphy, Bert.** Trailing Louis L'Amour from California to Alaska. Appleyard Communication Staff, ed. LC 99-76354. (Illus.). 376p. (Orig.). 2000. pap. write for info. (*0-9650298-2-4*, Pub. by MBAR Pubng) Sunbelt Pubns.

Murphy, Bert. Trailing Louis L'Amour in New Mexico. Appleyard Communications Staff, ed. (Trailing Louis L'Amour Ser.: Vol. 1). (Illus.). 200p. (Orig.). 1996. 19.95 (*0-9650298-0-8*) MBAR Pubng.

Murphy, Betsy, jt. auth. see Connin, Ray.

Murphy, Betty S. & Azoff, Elliot S. Practice & Procedure Before the National Labor Relations Board. 2nd ed. (Corporate Practice Ser.: No. 41). 1989. 95.00 (*1-55871-104-X*) BNA.

Murphy, Beverly B. He Used to Be Somebody: A Journey into Alzheimer's Disease Through the Eyes of a Caregiver. 348p. (Orig.). 1995. pap. 16.95 (*0-943909-14-7*) Gibbs Assocs.

Murphy, Bianca & Dillon, Carolyn. Interviewing in Action: Process & Practice. LC 97-17140. (Social Work Ser.). 320p. 1997. pap. 47.95 (*0-534-34125-X*) Brooks-Cole.

Murphy, Blakely M., ed. Conservation of Oil & Gas: A Legal History, 1948. LC 72-2858. (Use & Abuse of America's Natural Resources Ser.). 776p. 1972. reprint ed. 57.95 (*0-405-04522-0*) Ayer.

Murphy, Bob. Desert Shadows: A True Story of the Charles Manson Family in Death Valley. LC 93-93688. (Illus.). 144p. 1993. pap. 12.95 (*0-930704-29-0*) Sagebrush Pr.

Murphy, Bren Ortega, jt. auth. see Artz, Lee.

Murphy, Brenda. American Realism & American Drama: 1800-1940. (Cambridge Studies in American Literature & Culture: No. 22). 248p. 1987. text 59.95 (*0-521-32711-3*) Cambridge U Pr.

— Clarinet Fingering Chart. (Illus.). 1984. pap. 3.95 (*0-8256-2383-9*, AM35700) Music Sales.

***Murphy, Brenda.** Congressional Theatre: Dramatizing McCarthyism on Stage, Film & Television. LC 99-40314. (Studies in American Theatre & Drama: Vol. 11). (Illus.). 288p. (C). 1999. 54.95 (*0-521-64088-1*) Cambridge U Pr.

Murphy, Brenda. Flute Fingering Chart. (Illus.). 1984. pap. 3.95 (*0-8256-2381-2*, AM35718) Music Sales.

— Miller: "Death of a Salesman" (Plays in Production Ser.). (Illus.). xix, 246 p. (C). 1995. pap. text 18.95 (*0-521-47865-0*) Cambridge U Pr.

— Saxophone Fingering Chart. (Illus.). 1984. pap. 3.95 (*0-8256-2384-7*, AM35742) Music Sales.

— Trumpet Fingering Chart. (Illus.). 1984. pap. 3.95 (*0-8256-2385-5*, AM35759) Music Sales.

***Murphy, Brenda, ed.** The Cambridge Companion to American Women Playwrights. LC 98-36593. (Cambridge Companions to Literature Ser.). (Illus.). 285p. 1999. 64.95 (*0-521-57184-7*); pap. 19.95 (*0-521-57680-6*) Cambridge U Pr.

Murphy, Brenda, ed. Every Musician's Handbook. (Illus.). 64p. 1984. pap. 5.95 (*0-8256-2339-1*, AM37391) Music Sales.

Murphy, Brenda, intro. A Realist in the American Theatre: Selected Drama Criticism of William Dean Howells. LC 92-14195. 256p. (C). 1992. text 34.95 (*0-8214-1036-9*) Ohio U Pr.

Murphy, Brenda, jt. ed. see Monteiro, George.

Murphy, Brenda C. W. & Abbotson, Susan. Understanding Death of a Salesman: A Student Casebook to Issues, Sources & Historical Documents. LC 98-26437. (Literature in Context Ser.). 248p. 1999. 39.95 (*0-313-30402-5*, Greenwood Pr) Greenwood.

***Murphy, Brenda K.** The Launch: A Teacher's Guide to the Code Cards. (Sail Away Ser.). 28p. 1999. pap. text, teacher ed. 8.95 (*1-58504-001-0*) UTW Res Inc.

— The Mate's Log, Level A, Bk. 1. (Sail Away Ser.). 104p. (J). (gr. k-5). 1999. pap. text 16.95 (*1-58504-004-5*) UTW Res Inc.

— The Mate's Log, Level A, Bk. 2. (Sail Away Ser.). 124p. (J). (gr. k-5). 1999. pap. text 16.95 (*1-58504-005-3*) UTW Res Inc.

— The Mate's Log, Level A, Bk. 3. (Sail Away Ser.). 124p. (J). (gr. k-5). 1999. pap. text 16.95 (*1-58504-006-1*) UTW Res Inc.

— The Practice Pack. (Sail Away Ser.). (Illus.). 86p. (J). (ps-5). 1999. pap. text, wbk. ed. 15.95 (*1-58504-002-9*) UTW Res Inc.

— The Practice Pack: A Teacher's Guide. (Sail Away Ser.). 24p. 1999. pap. text 8.95 (*1-58504-003-7*) UTW Res Inc.

Murphy, Brendan. Earth Science Today. (Earth Science Ser.). 1998. pap. 61.25 incl. cd-rom (*0-534-52181-9*) Wadsworth Pub.

— Earth Science Today. (Earth Science Ser.). 1999. pap. 10.50 (*0-534-52184-3*) Wadsworth Pub.

— Earth Science Today with In-Terra Active 2.0 CD-ROM & Infotrac. (Earth Science Ser.). 1998. 54.50 incl. cd-rom (*0-534-52182-7*) Wadsworth Pub.

— Turncoat: The Strange Case of British Traitor Sergeant Harold Cole, "The Worst Traitor of the War" (Illus.). 1987. 19.95 (*0-15-191410-9*) Harcourt.

***Murphy, Brendan & Nance, Damian.** Earth Science Today. (Earth Science Ser.). (C). 2000. text 19.00 (*0-534-76474-6*) Brooks-Cole.

Murphy, Brendan, jt. auth. see Walsh, Gary.

Murphy, Brian. John Chartres: Mystery Man of the Treaty. 190p. 1995. 22.95 (*0-7165-2543-7*, Pub. by Irish Acad Pr) Intl Spec Bk.

— Laura Lemay's Web Workshop. 1996. 39.99 incl. cd-rom (*0-614-20291-4*, SamsNet Software) MCP SW Interactive.

— The New Men: Inside the Vatican's Elite School for American Priests. LC 97-19620. 320p. 1997. 25.95 (*0-399-14328-9*, Grosset-Putnam) Putnam Pub Group.

— New Men: Inside the Vatican's Elite School for American Priests. 320p. 1998. pap. 14.00 (*1-57322-699-8*, Riverhd Trade) Berkley Pub.

— The Other Australia: Experiences of Migration. LC 92-42536. (Illus.). 284p. (C). 1993. text 64.95 (*0-521-44194-3*) Cambridge U Pr.

***Murphy, Brian & Patrikeeff, Felix.** The Russian Civil War: Primary Sources. LC 99-59567. 2000. 65.00 (*0-312-23232-2*) St Martin.

Murphy, Brian, jt. ed. see Charman, Peter.

Murphy, Brian F. & Snay, Cheryl K. Familiar Faces & Places: Recent Paintings by Kiichi Usui. Watson, Debra & Shichi, Asae, eds. (ENG & JPN., Illus.). 40p. (Orig.). 1997. pap. 15.00 (*0-925859-06-0*) Mead Brook Art.

***Murphy, Brian K.** Changing Ourselves, Changing the World. 1999. text 55.00 (*1-85649-706-2*) St Martin.

— Transforming Ourselves, Transforming the World: An Open Conspiracy for Social Change. LC 99-20786. 1999. pap. 19.95 (*1-85649-707-0*) St Martin.

Murphy, Brian R. & Willis, David W., eds. Fisheries Techniques. 2nd ed. LC 96-85438. (Illus.). 732p. (C). 1996. text 86.00 (*1-888569-00-X*, 550.04C) Am Fisheries Soc.

Murphy, Bruce. The Encyclopedia of Murder & Mystery. LC 99-25316. 656p. 1999. text 75.00 (*0-312-21554-1*) St Martin.

***Murphy, Bruce.** Italy for Dummies. (For Dummies Ser.). 544p. 2000. pap. 19.99 (*0-7645-6198-7*) IDG Bks.

— New York City for Dummies. (For Dummies Ser.). 352p. 2000. pap. 15.99 (*0-7645-6160-X*) IDG Bks.

Murphy, Bruce. Sing Sing Sing. 112p. (C). 1990. text 30.00 (*0-8147-5460-0*); pap. text 13.50 (*0-8147-5461-9*) NYU Pr.

Murphy, Bruce, ed. Benet's Reader's Encyclopedia: Fourth Edition. 4th ed. LC 96-217151. 1168p. 1996. 50.00 (*0-06-270110-X*) HarpC.

Murphy, Bruce & de Rosa, Alessandra. The Complete Idiot's Travel Guide to New York City. 2nd ed. (Complete Idiot's Travel Guide Ser.). (Illus.). 320p. 1999. pap. 15.95 (*0-02-863150-1*) Macmillan.

Murphy, Bryan. Experiment with Air. (Science Experiments Ser.). 32p. (J). (gr. 2-5). 1991. lib. bdg. 19.93 (*0-8225-2452-X*, Lerner Publctns) Lerner Pub.

— Experiment with Water. (Science Experiments Ser.). 32p. (J). (gr. 2-5). 1991. lib. bdg. 19.93 (*0-8225-2453-8*, Lerner Publctns) Lerner Pub.

Murphy, C., et al. A Working Method for Physical Chemistry Calculations. 125p. 1997. write for info. (*0-85404-553-8*) Am Chemical.

Murphy, Camay C. Can a Coal Scuttle Fly? LC 96-75870. (Illus.). 32p. (J). (gr. k-3). 1996. 14.00 (*0-938420-55-0*) MD Hist.

Murphy, Carlene U. & Lick, Dale W. Whole Faculty Study Groups: A Powerful Way to Change Schools & Enhance Learning. LC 98-9025. (1-Off Ser.). (Illus.). 216p. 1998. 69.95 (*0-8039-6726-8*); pap. 32.95 (*0-8039-6727-6*) Corwin Pr.

Murphy, Carol. Christopher Columbus. (Famous People Ser.). (Illus.). (J). (gr. k-6). 1991. 13.95 (*0-89868-228-2*); pap. 22.00 (*0-89868-229-0*) ARO Pub.

— Christopher Columbus: Big Big Book. (Famous People Ser.). (Illus.). (J). (gr. k-6). 1991. 22.00 (*0-614-24510-9*) ARO Pub.

— A Deeper Faith. (C). 1958. pap. 4.00 (*0-87574-099-5*) Pendle Hill.

— Martin Luther King, Jr. (Famous People Ser.). (Illus.). (J). (gr. k-6). 1991. 13.95 (*0-89868-230-4*); pap. 22.00 (*0-89868-231-2*) ARO Pub.

Murphy, Carol J. Alienation & Absence in the Novels of Marguerite Duras. LC 82-82426. (French Forum Monographs: No. 37). 172p. (Orig.). 1982. pap. 13.95 (*0-917058-36-4*) French Forum.

— The Allegorical Impulse in the Works of Julien Gracq: History As Rhetorical Enactment in le Rivage des Syrtes & un Balcon en Foret. LC 95-2416. (Studies in the Romance Languages & Literatures: No. 250). 1995. pap. text 34.95 (*0-8078-9254-8*) U of NC Pr.

Murphy, Carol R. The Available Mind. LC 73-94186. (Orig.). 1974. pap. 1.00 (*0-87574-193-2*) Pendle Hill.

Murphy, Carol R. The Examined Life. (C). 1955. pap. 4.00 (*0-87574-085-5*) Pendle Hill.

— The Faith of An Ex-Agnostic. (C). 1949. pap. 4.00 (*0-87574-046-4*) Pendle Hill.

— Four Women: Four Windows on Light. Mather, Eleanore P., ed. LC 81-80220. 26p. 1981. pap. 4.00 (*0-87574-236-X*) Pendle Hill.

— Holy Morality. LC 71-110286. (Orig.). (C). 1970. pap. 4.00 (*0-87574-169-X*) Pendle Hill.

Murphy, Carol R. Man: The Broken Image. LC 68-30960. (Orig.). 1968. pap. 1.00 (*0-87574-158-4*) Pendle Hill.

Murphy, Carol R. Many Religions: One God. LC 66-30689. (Orig.). 1966. pap. 4.00 (*0-87574-150-9*) Pendle Hill.

— Milestone 70. (Orig.). 1989. pap. 4.00 (*0-87574-287-4*) Pendle Hill.

— The Ministry of Counseling. (C). 1952. pap. 4.00 (*0-87574-067-7*) Pendle Hill.

— Nurturing Contemplation. LC 88-62745. (C). 1983. pap. 4.00 (*0-87574-251-3*) Pendle Hill.

Murphy, Carol R. O Inward Traveller. LC 77-91637. 31p. (Orig.). 1977. pap. 1.00 (*0-87574-216-5*) Pendle Hill.

Murphy, Carol R. Religion & Mental Illness. (C). 1955. pap. 4.00 (*0-87574-082-0*) Pendle Hill.

Murphy, Carol R. Revelation & Experience. LC 64-22765. (Orig.). 1964. pap. 1.00 (*0-87574-137-1*) Pendle Hill.

Murphy, Carol R. The Roots of Pendle Hill. LC 78-1768. (Orig.). 1979. pap. 4.00 (*0-87574-223-8*) Pendle Hill.

— The Sound of Silence: Moving with T'ai Chi. LC 75-41548. (Orig.). 1976. pap. 4.00 (*0-87574-205-X*) Pendle Hill.

Murphy, Carol R. The Valley of the Shadow. LC 72-80095. 24p. (Orig.). 1972. pap. 1.00 (*0-87574-184-3*) Pendle Hill.

Murphy, Carol R., ed. see Boulding, Kenneth E. & Mayer, Milton.

Murphy, Carol W. Smashed Potatoes & Other Thanksgiving Disasters. LC 94-15001. 128p. (J). (gr. 3-6). 1994. pap. 2.95 (*0-8167-3518-2*, Rainbow NJ) Troll Communs.

Murphy, Caroline, tr. see Schebera, Jurgen.

Murphy, Carolyn H. Carolina Rocks! The Geology of South Carolina. Tiger Creek Productions Staff, ed. LC 94-20979. (Illus.). 261p. (Orig.). 1995. pap. 19.95 (*0-87844-121-2*) Sandlapper Pub Co.

Murphy, Carolyn S., jt. auth. see Murphy, James O.

***Murphy, Catherine.** Christina Aguilera. (Illus.). (J). 2000. 4.95 (*0-7407-0773-6*) Andrews & McMeel.

Murphy, Catherine. Prince William. LC 98-85422. (Little Bks.). (Illus.). 80p. 1998. 4.95 (*0-8362-7133-5*) Andrews & McMeel.

Murphy, Catherine F., et al. Children's Writer Guide to 1999. (Illus.). 416p. 1999. pap. 19.75 (*1-889715-02-6*) Inst Chldrns Lit.

***Murphy, Catherine Frey, et al.** Children's Writer Guide to 2000. (Illus.). 424p. 2000. pap. 19.75 (*1-889715-03-4*) Inst Chldrns Lit.

Murphy, Charles H. Handbook of Particle Sampling & Analysis Methods. LC 83-18970. 354p. 1984. 80.00 (*0-89573-116-9*, Wiley-VCH) Wiley.

— Yachting Far. LC 97-75684. 80p. 1998. 15.95 (*1-887750-83-5*) Rutledge Bks.

Murphy, Charles M. Wallace Stevens: A Spiritual Poet in a Secular Age. LC 96-51500. 144p. (Orig.). 1997. pap. 9.95 (*0-8091-3708-9*) Paulist Pr.

Murphy, Chester W. Advanced Tennis. 4th ed. 136p. (C). 1988. text. write for info. (*0-697-07274-6*) Brown & Benchmark.

Murphy, Chet. A Parents' Guide to Teaching Kids to Play. LC 81-85622. (Illus.). 144p. (Orig.). 1983. reprint ed. pap. 44.70 (*0-608-07106-4*, 206733300009) Bks Demand.

— Tennis for Thinking Players. 2nd ed. LC 86-110387. (Illus.). 176p. reprint ed. pap. 54.60 (*0-608-20830-2*, 207192900003) Bks Demand.

Murphy, Christina & Law, Joe, eds. Landmark Essays on Writing Centers. (Landmark Essays Ser.: Vol. 9). 272p. (Orig.). (C). 1995. pap. 22.00 (*1-880393-22-0*, Hermagoras) L Erlbaum Assocs.

Murphy, Christina, et al. Writing Centers: An Annotated Bibliography, 17. LC 96-18521. (Bibliographies & Indexes in Education Ser.: Vol. 17). 304p. 1996. lib. bdg. 69.50 (*0-313-29831-9*, Greenwood Pr) Greenwood.

***Murphy, Christine.** Cancer: A Natural Approach. 2000. pap. 10.00 (*1-930051-31-X*) Lantern Books.

***Murphy, Christine, ed.** Allergies & Asthma: A Natural Approach. 96p. 2000. pap. 10.00 (*1-930051-08-5*, Pub. by Booklight Inc) Bks Intl VA.

— Care of the Teeth: A Natural Approach. 96p. 2000. pap. 10.00 (*1-930051-07-7*) Lantern Books.

— Practical Home Care Medicines: A Natural Approach. 96p. 2000. pap. 10.00 (*1-930051-09-3*) Lantern Books.

— Vaccination: A Natural Approach. 96p. 2000. pap. 10.00 (*1-930051-10-7*) Lantern Books.

Murphy, Christopher. Dance for a Diamond. large type ed. 576p. 1988. 27.99 (*0-7089-1775-5*) Ulverscroft.

— I, Said the Sparrow. large type ed. 464p. 1986. 27.99 (*0-7089-1406-3*) Ulverscroft.

— The Jericho Rumble. 1987. 16.95 (*0-8027-0996-6*) Walker & Co.

— The Jericho Rumble. large type ed. 464p. 1985. 27.99 (*0-7089-1286-9*) Ulverscroft.

— Scream at the Sea. large type ed. 432p. 1985. 27.99 (*0-7089-1241-9*) Ulverscroft.

Murphy, Chuck. Alphabet Magic. (J). (ps-k). 1997. 14.95 (*0-614-29100-3*) Litle Simon.

— Black Cat, White Cat: A Pop-Up Opposites Book. (Illus.). 10p. (J). (ps-3). 1998. per. 12.95 (*0-689-81415-1*) S&S Childrens.

***Murphy, Chuck.** Bow Wow: A Pop-Up Book of Shapes. (Pop-Up Bk.). (Illus.). 5p. (J). (ps-3). 1999. per. 12.95 (*0-689-82265-0*) Litle Simon.

Murphy, Chuck. Color Surprises: A Pop-Up Book. (Illus.). 10p. (J). (ps-3). 1997. per. 12.95 (*0-689-81504-2*) Litle Simon.

***Murphy, Chuck.** Easter Basket. (Illus.). 12p. (J). (ps-k). 1999. bds. 4.99 (*0-689-82260-X*) S&S Childrens.

— Easter Egg Hunt. (Razzle Dazzle Bks.). (Illus.). 12p. (J). (ps-k). 1999. bds. 4.99 (*0-689-82259-6*) Litle Simon.

— How Many Hearts? (Razzle Dazzle Bks.). (Illus.). 12p. (J). (ps-k). 1999. bds. 4.99 (*0-689-82257-X*) Litle Simon.

Murphy, Chuck. I Love You. (Illus.). 12p. (J). (ps-k). 1999. bds. 4.99 (*0-689-82258-8*) S&S Trade.

— Jack & the Beanstalk: Three-Dimensional Edition. (Illus.). 12p. (J). (ps-3). 1998. per. 19.95 (*0-689-82207-3*) S&S Childrens.

— Magic Windows ABCs. (Illus.). 14p. (J). (ps-2). 1997. per. 14.95 (*0-689-81286-8*) S&S Childrens.

— My First Book of Animal Sounds. (Lift-the-Flap Concept Bks.). (Illus.). 12p. (J). (ps-k). 1995. 6.95 (*0-590-20301-0*, Cartwheel) Scholastic Inc.

— My First Book of Shapes. LC 93-178664. (Illus.). 12p. (J). (ps-k). 1993. 6.95 (*0-590-46303-9*) Scholastic Inc.

— My First Book of the Alphabet. (Illus.). 12p. (J). 1993. 6.95 (*0-590-46304-7*) Scholastic Inc.

— One-Ten Pop-Up Surprise! LC 95-159624. (Illus.). 10p. (J). (ps-2). 1995. 13.95 (*0-671-89908-2*) Litle Simon.

— Pretend Time. (Razzle Dazzle Bks.). (Illus.). 12p. (J). (ps-1). 1998. 4.99 (*0-689-82055-0*) S&S Childrens.

— Razzle Dazzle Book: Bedtime. (Razzle Dazzle Bks.). (Illus.). 12p. (J). (ps-1). 1998. bds. 4.99 (*0-689-82054-2*) Litle Simon.

— Razzle-Dazzle Colors. LC 97-173747. (Illus.). 12p. (J). (ps-1). 1997. 4.99 (*0-689-81497-6*) S&S Childrens.

— Razzle Dazzle Numbers. LC 97-173748. (Rainbow Book Ser.). (Illus.). 12p. (J). (ps-1). 1997. 4.99 (*0-689-81498-4*) S&S Childrens.

— Razzle Dazzle Opposite. LC 97-173753. (Illus.). 12p. (J). (ps-1). 1997. 4.99 (*0-689-81499-2*) Atheneum Yung Read.

— Razzle Dazzle Shapes. LC 97-173752. (Illus.). 12p. (J). (ps-1). 1997. 4.99 (*0-689-81500-X*) Atheneum Yung Read.

Murphy, Chuck. Big Trucks. (Pop-Out Bks.). (J). (ps-1). 1996. 4.99 (*0-614-15716-1*) Random.

Murphy, Chuck. Jack & the Beanstalk. limited ed. (J). 1998. 100.00 (*0-689-82313-4*) S&S Childrens.

Murphy, Claire. What Does Lucy Like? Big Book. large type ed. (Little Books & Big Bks.). (Illus.). 8p. (J). (ps-1). 1998. pap. text 19.89 (*0-8215-0852-0*) Sadlier.

Murphy, Claire, ed. Olfaction & Taste XII: An International Symposium. LC 98-39456. (Annals of the New York Academy of Sciences Ser.: Vol. 855). 872p. 1999. 160.00 (*1-57331-139-1*); pap. write for info. (*1-57331-140-5*) NY Acad Sci.

Murphy, Claire Rudolf. Caribou Girl. LC 97-40659. (Illus.). 32p. (J). (ps-4). 1998. 16.95 (*1-57098-145-0*) Roberts Rinehart.

Murphy, Claire Rudolf. Gold Star Sister. 1996. 10.09 (*0-606-11400-9*, Pub. by Turtleback) Demco.

Murphy, Claire Rudolf. To the Summit. 208p. 1998. pap. 3.99 (*0-380-79537-X*, Avon Bks) Morrow Avon.

***Murphy, Claire Rudolf.** To the Summit. (J). 1998. 9.09 (*0-606-13853-6*, Pub. by Turtleback) Demco.

Murphy, Claire Rudolf & Haigh, Jane G. Children of the Gold Rush. (Illus.). 96p. (YA). (gr. 3-7). 1999. pap. 14.95 (*1-57098-257-0*, Pub. by Roberts Rinehart) Publishers Group.

An Asterisk (*) at the beginning of an entry indicates that the title is appearing for the first time.

— Gold Rush Women. LC 97-946. (Illus.). 126p. (J). (gr. 7). 1997. pap. 16.95 (*0-88240-484-9*, Alaska NW Bks) Gr Arts Ctr Pub.

***Murphy, Clare M.** Fenians, Nationalists & the Land: A Regional Portrait, 1867-1879. 208p. 1999. 55.00 (*1-85182-501-0*, Pub. by Four Cts Pr) Intl Spec Bk.

Murphy, Clare M., et al, eds. Miscellanea Moreana: Essays for Germain Marc'hadour. (Medieval & Renaissance Texts & Studies: Vol. 61). 608p. 1989. 50.00 (*0-86698-045-8*, MR61) MRTS.

Murphy, Cliona, jt. auth. see Luddy, Maria.

Murphy, Colin R. & Lurie, Ian. The Roof Construction Guide for General Contractors. LC 98-3997. 1998. write for info. (*0-9663701-0-4*) Exterior Res.

***Murphy, Colleen.** Beating Heart Cadaver. 2000. pap. 13.95 (*0-88754-567-X*) Theatre Comm.

Murphy, Corinne. Exploring the Hand Arts: For Juniors, Cadettes, Seniors & Leaders. 112p. (J). (gr. 4-12). 1955. pap. 5.00 (*0-88441-140-0*, 19-994) Girl Scouts USA.

Murphy, Cornelius F. Beyond Feminism: Towards a Dialogue on Difference. LC 93-47404. 203p. (C). 1995. pap. 14.95 (*0-8132-0807-6*) Cath U Pr.

— Cases & Materials on Introduction to Law: Legal Process & Procedure. (American Casebook Ser.). 772p. (C). 1977. 50.50 (*0-314-32845-9*) West Pub.

— Descent into Subjectivity: Rawls, Dworkin & Unger in the Context of Modern Thought. LC 90-6005. 1990. 30.00 (*0-89341-620-7*, Longwood Academic); pap. 14.95 (*0-89341-621-5*, Longwood Academic) Hollowbrook.

Murphy, Cornelius F., Jr. The Search for World Order. 1985. lib. bdg. 100.50 (*90-247-3188-7*) Kluwer Academic.

— Theories of World Governance: A Study in the History of Ideas. LC 99-25222. 1999. pap. 24.95 (*0-8132-0937-4*) Cath U Pr.

Murphy, Craig N., et al. The State of the United Nations, 1992. (Reports & Papers). 92p. (C). 1992. pap. text 10.00 (*1-880660-04-0*) Acad Coun UN Syst.

Murphy, Craig N., jt. auth. see Augelli, Enrico.

Murphy, Cullen. The Word According to Eve: Women & the Bible in Ancient Times & Our Own. LC 98-18015. 278p. 1998. 24.00 (*0-395-70113-9*) HM.

— The Word According to Eve: Women & the Bible in Ancient Times & Our Own. LC 99-40646. 256p. 1999. pap. 14.00 (*0-618-00192-1*, Mariner Bks) HM.

Murphy, Cynthia M. Six Steps to Quality Child Care. 244p. 1995. pap. 19.95 (*1-887931-00-7*); pap., wbk. ed. 15.95 (*1-887931-03-1*) Fam Care Netwrk.

— Six Steps to Quality Elder Care. 244p. 1995. pap. 19.95 (*1-887931-01-5*); pap., wbk. ed. 15.95 (*1-887931-02-3*) Fam Care Netwrk.

Murphy, D. J. Customers & Thieves. 265p. 1986. text 72.95 (*0-566-00882-3*, Pub. by Avebry) Ashgate Pub Co.

— T. J. Ryan: A Political Biography. 1990. pap. 29.95 (*0-7022-2289-5*, Pub. by Univ Queensland Pr) Intl Spec Bk.

Murphy, D. J., ed. The Big Strikes: Queensland 1889-1965. LC 82-23881. (Illus.). 303p. 1983. pap. 18.95 (*0-7022-1721-2*) Intl Spec Bk.

Murphy, Dallas. Apparent Wind. Chelias, Jane, ed. 320p. (Orig.). 1991. mass mkt. 4.99 (*0-671-68554-6*) PB.

— Don't Explain. Grose, Bill, ed. LC 95-8887. 304p. 1996. 22.00 (*0-671-86687-7*, PB Hardcover) PB.

— Don't Explain. 1997. mass mkt. 5.99 (*0-671-86688-5*) PB.

— Fast Forward MBA in Sales & Marketing. LC 96-40005. 288p. 1997. pap. 12.95 (*0-471-16616-2*) Wiley.

— Lover Man. 1988. pap. 4.99 (*0-671-66188-4*) PB.

— Lush Life. 288p. (Orig.). 1993. mass mkt. 4.99 (*0-671-68556-2*) PB.

— Read-Aloud Plays: Pioneers, 1 vol. (Illus.). 64p. 1999. pap. text 9.95 (*0-590-91811-7*) Scholastic Inc.

— Revolutionary War. (Read Aloud Plays Ser.). (J). 2000. 10.95 (*0-590-03325-5*) Scholastic Inc.

Murphy, Dan. The Guadalupe Mountains National Park. Houk, Rose & Peters, Robert, eds. (Illus.). 32p. 1984. pap. 3.00 (*0-916907-00-7*) Carlsbad His.

— Lewis & Clark: Voyage of Discovery. LC 76-57451. (Illus.). 64p. (Orig.). 1977. pap. 7.95 (*0-916122-50-6*) KC Pubns.

— Lewis & Clark: Voyage of Discovery. Morales, Brigitte, tr. (GER., Illus.). 48p. (Orig.). 1997. pap. 8.95 (*0-88714-816-6*) KC Pubns.

— Oregon Trail: Voyage of Discovery. LC 92-70247. (Illus.). 64p. (Orig.). 1992. pap. 7.95 (*0-88714-064-5*) KC Pubns.

— Oregon Trail: Voyage of Discovery. Morales, Brigitte, tr. (GER., Illus.). 48p. (Orig.). 1993. pap. 8.95 (*0-88714-749-6*) KC Pubns.

— Powell, John Wesley: Voyage of Discovery. LC 91-60044. (Illus.). 64p. (Orig.). 1991. pap. 7.95 (*0-88714-059-9*) KC Pubns.

— Santa Fe Trail: Voyage of Discovery. Morales, Brigitte, tr. (GER., Illus.). 48p. (Orig.). 1994. pap. 8.95 (*0-88714-788-7*) KC Pubns.

— Santa Fe Trail: Voyage of Discovery. Marapodi, Carlos, tr. (SPA., Illus.). 48p. (Orig.). 1994. pap. 8.95 (*0-88714-787-9*) KC Pubns.

— Santa Fe Trail: Voyage of Discovery. LC 94-75107. (Illus.). 64p. (Orig.). 1994. pap. 7.95 (*0-88714-086-6*) KC Pubns.

Murphy, Dan, ed. see Dosch, Donald F.

Murphy, Dan J., tr. see Sicardo, Joseph A.

Murphy, Daniel. Christianity & Modern European Literature. LC 97-163982. 576p. 1997. boxed set 65.00 (*1-85182-295-X*, Pub. by Four Cts Pr) Intl Spec Bk.

— Comenius: A Critical Re-Assessment of His Life & Work. 240p. 1995. 45.00 (*0-7165-2537-2*, Pub. by Irish Acad Pr) Intl Spec Bk.

— Imagination & Religion in Anglo-Irish Literature, 1930-80. 228p. 1987. 39.50 (*0-7165-2400-7*, Pub. by Irish Acad Pr) Intl Spec Bk.

— Martin Buber's Philosophy of Education. 240p. 1988. 45.00 (*0-7165-2427-9*, Pub. by Irish Acad Pr) Intl Spec Bk.

— Tolstoy & Education. 304p. 1992. 45.00 (*0-7165-2484-8*, Pub. by Irish Acad Pr) Intl Spec Bk.

***Murphy, Daniel.** Vicente Aleixandre's Stream of Lyric Consciousness. LC 00-34281. 2001. write for info. (*0-8387-5464-3*) Bucknell U Pr.

***Murphy, Daniel J.** Irish Emigrant & Missionary Education: A History. 520p. 2000. 55.00 (*1-85182-522-3*, Pub. by Four Cts Pr) Intl Spec Bk.

Murphy, Daniel J., jt. auth. see Ehrlich, Eugene H.

Murphy, Daniel O. El Morro National Monument. Priehs, T. J., ed. LC 88-63877. (Illus.). 16p. (Orig.). 1989. pap. 3.95 (*0-911408-81-9*) SW Pks Mnmts.

— Salinas Pueblo Missions: Abo, Quarai, & Gran Quivira. Jorgen, Randolph & Foreman, Ronald, eds. LC 91-60459. (Illus.). 64p. 1993. pap. 9.95 (*0-911408-98-3*) SW Pks Mnmts.

Murphy, Danny W., jt. auth. see Dolecheck, Carolyn C.

Murphy, Daryl. Generalities, Truths & Assorted Fables: Aviation Anecdotes & Adventures. Hamilton, Frank et al, eds. (Illus.). 89p. (Orig.). 1995. pap. 14.95 (*1-879825-15-5*) Jones Publish.

Murphy, Daryl E. The Aviation Fact Book. LC 97-221477. 320p. 1998. pap. 24.95 (*0-07-044455-2*) McGraw.

— Flying VFR in Marginal Weather. 3rd ed. (Practical Flying Ser.). (Illus.). 224p. 1991. 28.95 (*0-8306-8699-1*, 3699, TAB-Aero) TAB Bks.

Murphy, David. The Stalker Affair & the Press. 276p. (C). 1990. pap. text 18.95 (*0-04-445412-0*) Routledge.

— The Stalker Affair & the Press. 276p. (C). (gr. 13). 1990. text 52.95 (*0-04-445411-2*) Routledge.

Murphy, David & Carter, David A., eds. Transgenesis Techniques: Principles & Protocols. LC 93-6775. (Methods in Molecular Biology Ser.: Vol. 18). (Illus.). 480p. 1993. 79.50 (*0-89603-245-0*) Humana.

Murphy, David, jt. auth. see Evans, Terry.

Murphy, David, jt. auth. see Franklin, Bob.

Murphy, David B. How You Can Help Save the Rain Forest. (Sound-Off Ser.). 16p. 1998. pap. 2.95 (*0-9646811-5-3*) Stardust PA.

Murphy, David E., et al. Battleground Berlin: CIA vs. KGB in the Cold War. LC 97-16829. (Illus.). 672p. 1997. 30.00 (*0-300-07233-3*) Yale U Pr.

— Battleground Berlin: CIA vs. KGB in the Cold War. (Illus.). 584p. 1999. pap. text 16.95 (*0-300-07871-4*) Yale U Pr.

Murphy, David G. Debates on God & Experience in the Netherlands, 1965-1989. 193p. 1993. 64.95 (*1-883255-09-0*, Cath Scholar Pr) Intl Scholars.

Murphy, David Graham. Debates on God & Experience in the Netherlands, 1965-1989. 193p. 1993. pap. 44.95 (*1-883255-02-3*, Cath Scholar Pr) Intl Scholars.

Murphy, David S. & Goodman, Margaret E. WordPerfect 6.0, Level 1. (Easy Way Ser.). 150p. 1993. pap. 29.95 (*1-57048-340-X*) Trning Express.

Murphy, David S., et al. Personal Computing, Level 1. (Easy Way Ser.). 170p. 1993. pap. 29.95 (*1-57048-000-1*) Trning Express.

— WordPerfect 5.1, Level 1. (Easy Way Ser.). 155p. 1993. pap. 29.95 (*1-57048-040-0*) Trning Express.

— WordPerfect for Windows, Level 1. (Easy Way Ser.). 197p. 1993. pap. 29.95 (*1-57048-100-8*) Trning Express.

Murphy, David T. The Heroic Earth: Geopolitical Thought in Weimar Germany, 1918-1933. LC 96-38231. 1997. 39.00 (*0-87338-564-0*) Kent St U Pr.

Murphy, Dawes, ed. Designing an Effective Compliance Program, 11 vols. (Corporate Compliance Ser.). 1993. 990.00 (*0-685-68839-9*) West Group.

Murphy, Dean A. Fishing Tackle Made in Missouri: History & Identification. 1993. 17.95 (*0-9636800-1-3*) Dammo Pub.

Murphy, Deanna, jt. auth. see O'Rielly, Lily.

Murphy, Deborah A. Pesticide Dangers: And How to Live Without Them. (Sound-Off Ser.). 12p. 1998. pap. 2.50 (*0-9646811-8-8*) Stardust PA.

— Seedsaving Tips: A Starting Guide. (Sound-Off Ser.). 16p. 1996. pap. 2.95 (*0-9646811-1-0*) Stardust PA.

***Murphy, Della M.** Custodial Skills for Adults with Special Needs. (Illus.). 298p. 1998. pap. 36.00 (*0-944352-24-3*) Cleaning Cons.

Murphy, Denis. The Pope's Confessor & Other Stories. 115p. (Orig.). 1985. pap. 8.75 (*971-10-0188-8*, Pub. by New Day Pub) Cellar.

Murphy, Denis, et al. The Premiers of Queensland: Revised Edition of Queensland Political Portraits 1859-1952. rev. ed. 1990. pap. 34.95 (*0-7022-2249-6*, Pub. by Univ Queensland Pr) Intl Spec Bk.

Murphy, Dennis G. The Business Management of Interior Design. (Orig.). (C). 1988. pap. text. write for info. (*0-938614-05-3*) Stratford Hse.

— The Fabric Estimator. (Calculating Wheel for Draperies & Upolstered Furniture Yardage Ser.). (Illus.). 1981. pap. 12.95 (*0-938614-02-9*) Stratford Hse.

— The Materials of Interior Design. Murphy, Gladys N., ed. (Interior Furnishings & Products Ser.). (Illus.). 208p. (Orig.). (C). 1978. 14.00 (*0-938614-00-2*, 211-196) Stratford Hse.

Murphy, Dennis J. Safety & Health for Production Agriculture. LC 92-74464. 256p. 1992. 48.25 (*0-929355-32-6*, M0792) Am Soc Ag Eng.

Murphy, Dennis J., et al. First on the Scene. (Farm Safety Ser.). (Illus.). 45p. 1989. reprint ed. pap. text 6.00 (*0-935817-06-9*, NRAES-12) NRAES.

Murphy, Dennis J., jt. auth. see Arble, William C.

Murphy, Dervla. Cameroon with Egbert. (Illus.). 282p. 1991. 21.95 (*0-87951-415-9*, Pub. by Overlook Pr) Penguin Putnam.

— Cameroon with Egbert. (Illus.). 282p. 1992. pap. 13.95 (*0-87951-476-0*, Pub. by Overlook Pr) Penguin Putnam.

— Cameroon with Egbert. large type ed. 392p. 1995. 24.95 (*1-85089-262-8*, Pub. by ISIS Lrg Prnt) Transaction Pubs.

— Eight Feet in the Andes. 288p. 1989. 22.95 (*0-87951-245-8*, Pub. by Overlook Pr); pap. 13.95 (*0-87951-262-8*, Pub. by Overlook Pr) Penguin Putnam.

— Full Tilt: Ireland to India with a Bicycle. LC 85-13759. 288p. 1987. reprint ed. 22.95 (*0-87951-236-9*, Pub. by Overlook Pr); reprint ed. pap. 13.95 (*0-87951-248-2*, Pub. by Overlook Pr) Penguin Putnam.

Murphy, Dervla. In Ethiopia with a Mule. 1994. pap. 13.95 (*0-00-654798-2*, Pub. by HarpC) Trafalgar.

Murphy, Dervla. Muddling Through in Madagascar. LC 88-22512. (Illus.). 276p. 1989. 22.95 (*0-87951-342-X*, Pub. by Overlook Pr) Penguin Putnam.

— Muddling Through in Madagascar. 276p. 1990. pap. 13.95 (*0-87951-360-8*, Pub. by Overlook Pr) Penguin Putnam.

— On a Shoestring to Coorg: A Travel Memoir of India. LC 89-8830. 272p. 1989. 22.95 (*0-87951-372-1*, Pub. by Overlook Pr) Penguin Putnam.

— On a Shoestring to Coorg: A Travel Memoir of India. LC 89-8830. 272p. 1990. pap. 13.95 (*0-87951-381-0*, Pub. by Overlook Pr) Penguin Putnam.

— A Place Apart. 1980. 15.00 (*0-8159-6516-8*) Devin.

— South from the Limpopo: Travels Through South Africa. LC 99-10486. (Illus.). 432p. 1999. 26.95 (*0-87951-948-7*, Pub. by Overlook Pr) Penguin Putnam.

— Transylvania & Beyond. 256p. 1993. 21.95 (*0-87951-472-8*, Pub. by Overlook Pr) Penguin Putnam.

— Transylvania & Beyond. 256p. 1995. pap. 13.95 (*0-87951-603-8*, Pub. by Overlook Pr) Penguin Putnam.

— Transylvania & Beyond. large type ed. (Charnwood Library). 400p. 1993. 27.99 (*0-7089-8730-3*) Ulverscroft.

— The Ukimwi Road: From Kenya to Zimbabwe. 290p. 1995. 22.95 (*0-87951-556-2*, Pub. by Overlook Pr) Penguin Putnam.

— The Ukimwi Road: From Kenya to Zimbabwe. 290p. 1996. pap. 13.95 (*0-87951-671-2*, Pub. by Overlook Pr) Penguin Putnam.

— The Ukimwi Road: From Kenya to Zimbabwe. large type ed. (Isis Large Print Bks.). 426p. 1995. 24.95 (*1-85695-235-5*, Pub. by ISIS Lrg Prnt) Transaction Pubs.

— The Waiting Land: A Spell in Nepal. LC 85-5736. 216p. 1987. 22.95 (*0-87951-251-2*, Pub. by Overlook Pr) Penguin Putnam.

— The Waiting Land: A Spell in Nepal. 216p. 1989. pap. 13.95 (*0-87951-305-5*, Pub. by Overlook Pr) Penguin Putnam.

Murphy, Dervla. Where the Indus Is Young. 1995. pap. 13.95 (*0-00-654801-6*, Pub. by HarpC) Trafalgar.

Murphy, Desmond. The Death & Rebirth of Religious Life. 243p. 1995. pap. 14.95 (*0-85574-126-0*, Pub. by E J Dwyer) Morehouse Pub.

— A Return to Spirit: After the Mythic Church. LC 97-14140. 264p. 1997. pap. 19.95 (*0-8245-1685-0*) Crossroad NY.

Murphy, Diana, ed. see Maciejunes, Nannette V., et al.

Murphy, Diane, ed. Space News Directory of Worldwide Space, 1997. 200p. (Orig.). 1997. pap. 95.00 (*0-9654543-0-4*) Army Times Pubng.

Murphy, Dolores A. In Red Hats, Beads, & Bags: 1908 Graduates Sharing Their Lives Through Letters. LC 90-80014. (Illus.). 320p. 1990. 18.95 (*0-9625596-0-1*) Cassiopeia Pr.

Murphy, Donal A. The Two Tipperarys: The National & Local Politics - Devolution & Determination - of the Unique 1838 Division into Two Ridings, & the Aftermath. LC 95-132649. (Illus.). 342p. 1994. pap. 29.95 (*0-946327-14-9*, Pub. by Relay Pubns) Irish Bks Media.

Murphy, Donal A., ed. see Houlihan, Elaine B.

Murphy, Donald J. Agriculture in the U. S. A. Today. LC 92-3516. (Illus.). 156p. 1992. pap. text 49.95 (*0-7734-9910-5*) E Mellen.

— Honest Medicine: Shattering the Myths about Aging & Health Care. 336p. 1996. pap. 12.00 (*0-87113-658-9*, Atlntc Mnthly) Grove-Atltic.

***Murphy, Donald R.** Modern Management of Cervical Spine Syndromes. LC 99-35198. 747p. 1999. pap. 95.00 (*0-8385-6386-4*, Apple Lange Med) McGraw.

Murphy, Donald W. Love Vignettes. 2nd ed. LC 97-70957. 84p. 1997. pap. 11.95 (*0-9655599-2-0*) LaRena Pr.

Murphy, Donald w. Love Vignettes. 2nd rev. ed. v, 84p. 1997. 15.95 (*0-9655599-1-2*) LaRena Pr.

Murphy, Donald W. Love Vignettes: Poetry of Love & Light. LC 83-82452. 78p. 1982. 7.95 (*0-9655599-0-4*) LaRena Pr.

Murphy, Donald W. & Interrante, Leonard V., eds. Inorganic Syntheses Vol. 30: Nonmolecular Solids, Vol. 30. LC 39-23015. 328p. 1995. 89.95 (*0-471-30508-1*, Wiley-Interscience) Wiley.

Murphy, Donn B. & Moore, Stephen. Helen Hayes: A Bio-Bibliography, 38. LC 93-83. (Bio-Bibliographies in the Performing Arts Ser.: No. 38). 392p. (gr. 3). 1993. text 55.00 (*0-313-27793-1*, MHV, Greenwood Pr) Greenwood.

Murphy, Donna. Colorado Retirement & Relocation Guide. large type ed. (Retirement & Relocation Guides Ser.). (Illus.). 350p. Date not set. pap. 24.95 (*1-56559-115-1*) HGI-Over Fifty.

Murphy, Donna M. Organize Your Books in 6 Easy Steps: A Workbook for the Sole Proprietor Service-Oriented Business. Maksen, Sue, ed. (Illus.). 152p. 1998. pap. 16.95 (*0-9664848-0-0*) IRIE Pubng.

— The Woman's Guide to Self-Publishing: A Comprehensive Guide to Helping Women Understand & Pursue. LC 99-90428. (Illus.). 208p. 1999. pap. 17.95 (*0-9664848-9-4*) IRIE Pubng.

Murphy, Doris, ed. see Williams, Glenn R.

Murphy, Douglas R. The Story of My Life: Dr. Douglas Roe Murphy, MD-FACS. Erickson, Beverly, ed. LC 98-72288. 150p. 1999. write for info. (*1-885527-16-0*) Feather Fables.

Murphy, Dudley & Edmisten, Rick. Fishing Lure Collectibles. 336p. 1995. 24.95 (*0-89145-541-8*, 3968) Collector Bks.

***Murphy, Dudley & Edmisten, Rick.** Fishing Lure Collectibles: An Identification & Value Guide to the Most Collectible Antique Fishing Lures. 2nd ed. (Illus.). 368p. 2000. 29.95 (*1-57432-196-X*) Collector Bks.

Murphy, E. Jefferson. The Bantu Civilization of Southern Africa. LC 73-17194. (Illus.). 256p. (J). (gr. 7 up). 1974. 14.63 (*0-690-00399-4*) HarpC Child Bks.

Murphy, E. Louise. The History of Winston-Salem State University, 1892-1995. rev. ed. Allen, Simona A. & Turner, William H., eds. LC 92-28011. 1992. write for info. (*0-89865-849-7*) Donning Co.

Murphy, Eamon. Unions in Conflict: A Comparative Study Four South Indian Textile Centres, 1918-1939. 1982. 18.00 (*0-8364-0874-8*) S Asia.

Murphy, Earl F. Energy & Environmental Balance. (Policy Studies). 1980. 96.00 (*0-08-025082-3*, Pergamon Pr) Elsevier.

Murphy, Earline M. & Clark, Deborah M. Laughter among the Tears: Living with Alzheimer's. (Illus.). 200p. 1998. pap. 13.50 (*0-9665468-0-6*) Fly Away Pr.

Murphy, Ed. Handbook for Spiritual Warfare. rev. ed. LC 96-8955. 640p. 1996. 29.99 (*0-7852-1151-9*) Nelson.

***Murphy, Ed.** Handbook for Spiritual Warfare. rev. ed. 640p. 2000. pap. 19.99 (*0-7852-4530-8*) Tommy Nelson.

Murphy, Ed. Manual de Guerra Espiritual.Tr. of Handbook for Spiritual Warfare. (SPA.). 688p. 1995. 19.99 (*0-88113-212-8*) Caribe Betania.

***Murphy, Edmond & Geety, Harry.** Energy Management & Controls. Ambrose, Christine, ed. Orig. Title: Energy Management-Building Controls Systems. (Illus.). 352p. 1999. teacher ed., ring bd. 100.00 (*1-928594-16-6*); student ed., ring bd. 100.00 (*1-928594-15-8*) BOMI Inst.

Murphy, Edmond A. Biostatistics in Medicine. LC 81-48191. (Illus.). 560p. (C). 1982. text 60.00 (*0-8018-2727-2*) Johns Hopkins.

— A Companion to Medical Statistics. LC 84-21806. 288p. (C). 1985. text 47.50 (*0-8018-2612-8*) Johns Hopkins.

— The Logic of Medicine, Vol. 2. 2nd ed. LC 96-20279. 516p. 1997. text 55.00 (*0-8018-5415-6*); pap. text 25.95 (*0-8018-5538-1*) Johns Hopkins.

— Probability in Medicine. LC 78-10611. 320p. 1979. text 47.50 (*0-8018-2135-5*) Johns Hopkins.

— Skepsis, Dogma, & Belief: Uses & Abuses in Medicine. LC 80-8870. 176p. 1981. text 30.00 (*0-8018-2510-5*) Johns Hopkins.

Murphy, Edmond A. & Chase, Gary A. Principles of Genetic Counseling. LC 75-16020. 409p. reprint ed. pap. 126.80 (*0-608-12350-1*, 202426700036) Bks Demand.

Murphy, Edmond A., et al. Underpinnings of Medical Ethics. LC 97-1405. (Illus.). 520p. 1997. text 49.95 (*0-8018-5568-3*) Johns Hopkins.

Murphy, Edmond C., tr. see Favre, Pierre.

***Murphy, Edmund J.** Integrated Optical Circuits & Components: Design & Applications. LC 99-26697. (Optical Engineering Ser.: Vol. 66). (Illus.). 449p. 1999. text 150.00 (*0-8247-7577-5*) Dekker.

Murphy, Edna. ESL: A Handbook for Teachers & Administrators in International Schools. 220p. 1990. 74.95 (*1-85359-090-8*, Pub. by Multilingual Matters) Taylor & Francis.

— Flexible Work. LC 95-21465. 192p. (C). 1996. pap. text 19.95 (*0-13-434184-8*) P-H.

Murphy, Edna, ed. ESL: A Handbook for Teachers & Administrators in International Schools. 192p. 1990. pap. 29.95 (*1-85359-157-2*, Pub. by Multilingual Matters) Taylor & Francis.

Murphy, Edward. Dakto: 173d Airborne Brigade in South Vietnam's Central Highlands, June-November 1967. Grad, Doug, ed. 400p. (Orig.). 1995. mass mkt. 6.99 (*0-671-52268-X*) PB.

Murphy, Edward F. Heroes of WW II. 1991. mass mkt. 5.99 (*0-345-37545-9*) Ballantine Pub Grp.

— Korean War Heroes. LC 91-29472. (Illus.). 336p. 1997. reprint ed. pap. 16.95 (*0-89141-636-6*) Presidio Pr.

***Murphy, Edward F.** Semper Fi Vietnam: From Da Nang to the DMZ Marine Corps Campaigns, 1965-1975. (Illus.). 2000. pap. 19.95 (*0-89141-705-2*) Presidio Pr.

Murphy, Edward F. The Tenth Man. LC 72-4647. (Black Heritage Library Collection). 1977. reprint ed. 29.95 (*0-8369-9114-1*) Ayer.

— Two Thousand Seven Hundred Fifteen One-Line Quotations for Speakers, Writers & Raconteurs. 224p. 1996. 8.99 (*0-517-68236-2*) Random Hse Value.

Murphy, Edward J. & Speidel, Richard E. Studies in Contract Law. 4th ed. (University Casebook Ser.). 1401p. 1991. text 46.50 (*0-88277-875-7*) Foundation Pr.

— Studies in Contract Law, Teaching Notes. 4th ed. (University Casebook Ser.). 150p. (C). 1991. pap. text. write for info. (*0-88277-938-9*) Foundation Pr.

Murphy, Edward J., et al. Studies in Contract Law. 5th ed. LC 97-9348. (University Casebook Ser.). 1083p. 1997. text 42.00 (*1-56662-468-1*) Foundation Pr.

Murphy, Edward J., jt. auth. see Trai Le, Tang T.

Murphy, Edwin. After the Funeral: The Posthumous Adventures of Famous Corpses. LC 94-45464. 256p. 1995. pap. 9.95 (*0-8065-1599-6*, Citadel Pr) Carol Pub Group.

Murphy, Edwin W. The Antiquities of Asia: A Translation, with Commentary, of the Library of History, Book II, by Diodorus Siculus. 117p. 1989. 44.95 (*0-88738-272-X*) Transaction Pubs.

— The Antiquities of Egypt: A Translation, with Notes, of Book I of the Library of History of Diodorus Siculus. 178p. 1989. 44.95 (*0-88738-303-3*) Transaction Pubs.

M

Murphy, Eileen. Healthy Living. (Skills for Caring Ser.). (Illus.). 40p. (Orig.). 1992. pap. text 9.95 (*0-443-04529-1*) Church.

Murphy, Eileen M. The Original Dictionary of Modern Hairstyling for Beauty Salons. (Illus.). 67p. 1981. spiral bd. 12.95 (*0-9609792-0-4*) Eileens Beautique.

Murphy, Elaine. Developing Skills with Tables & Graphs Bk. A: Blackline Masters, Bk. A. text 6.95 (*0-86651-014-1*) Seymour Pubns.

Murphy, Elaine & Alexopoulos, George, eds. Geriatric Psychiatry: Key Research Topics for Clinicians. LC 94-21812. 338p. 1995. 196.00 (*0-471-95168-4*) Wiley.

Murphy, Elaine Cochrane. Dearest Angel: From Vietnam to the Wall. 128p. 1999. pap. 10.00 (*1-892525-02-X*) ACW Press.

Murphy, Elizabeth. The Developing Child: Using Jungian Type to Understand Children. LC 92-29717. 168p. 1992. pap. 13.95 (*0-89106-060-X*, 7390, Davies-Black Pub) Consulting Psychol.

— To Give & Take All. large type ed. 754p. 1992. 27.99 (*0-7505-0099-9*) Ulverscroft.

— A Wise Child. large type ed. (Magna Large Print Ser.). 735p. 1996. 27.99 (*0-7505-0859-0*, Pub. by Mgna Lrg Print) Ulverscroft.

Murphy, Elizabeth C. The Mystery of the African Gray. 64p. 1998. pap. 3.99 (*0-7642-2130-2*) Bethany Hse.

Murphy, Elizabeth R. The Assistant: New Tasks, New Opportunities. LC 81-69370. 191p. reprint ed. pap. 59.30 (*0-8357-5811-7*, 202353200033) Bks Demand.

Murphy, Eloise C. Theodore Roosevelt's Night Ride to the Presidency. (Adirondack Museum Monographs). (Illus.). 36p. 1996. reprint ed. pap. 4.95 (*0-910020-33-7*) Adirondack Mus.

Murphy, Elspeth C. Chalkdust: Prayer Meditations for Teachers. 64p. (gr. 10). 1979. 7.99 (*0-8010-6065-6*) Baker Bks.

— The Mystery of the Birthday Party. LC 97-21121. (Three Cousins Detective Club Ser.: No. 17). 64p. (J). 1997. pap. 3.99 (*1-55661-855-7*) Bethany Hse.

— Mystery of the Copycat Clown. LC 96-45765. (Three Cousins Detective Club Ser.: Vol. 11). (Illus.). 64p. (J). (gr. 2-5). 1996. pap. 3.99 (*1-55661-849-2*) Bethany Hse.

— The Mystery of the Dancing Angels. (Three Cousins Detective Club Ser.: No. 4). 64p. (J). (gr. 2-5). 1995. pap. 3.99 (*1-55661-408-X*) Bethany Hse.

— The Mystery of the Dolphin Detective. LC 95-45258. (Three Cousins Detective Club Ser.: Vol. 8). (Illus.). 64p. (Orig.). (J). (gr. 2-5). 1995. pap. 3.99 (*1-55661-412-8*) Bethany Hse.

— The Mystery of the Eagle Feather. LC 95-45260. (Three Cousins Detective Club Ser.: Vol. 9). (Illus.). 64p. (Orig.). (J). (gr. 4-7). 1995. pap. 3.99 (*1-55661-413-6*) Bethany Hse.

— The Mystery of the Gingerbread House. LC 96-45911. (Three Cousins Detective Club Ser.: Vol. 13). (Illus.). 64p. (J). (gr. 2-5). 1997. pap. 3.99 (*1-55661-851-4*) Bethany Hse.

— Mystery of the Goldfish Pond, Vol. 15. LC 97-4645. (Three Cousins Detective Club Ser.). (Illus.). 64p. (J). (gr. 2-5). 1997. pap. 3.99 (*1-55661-853-0*) Bethany Hse.

— Mystery of the Haunted Lighthouse. (Three Cousins Detective Club Ser.: Vol. 7). (Illus.). 64p. (Orig.). (J). (gr. 2-5). 1995. pap. 3.99 (*1-55661-411-X*) Bethany Hse.

— Mystery of the Haunted Lighthouse/The Mystery of the Dolphin Detective. (Three Cousins Detective Club Ser.). (J). 1997. boxed set 23.99 (*0-7642-8159-3*) Bethany Hse.

— The Mystery of the Hobo's Message. (Three Cousins Detective Club Ser.: No. 5). (Illus.). 64p. (J). (gr. 2-5). 1995. pap. 3.99 (*1-55661-409-8*) Bethany Hse.

— Mystery of the Honeybees' Secret. LC 96-45766. (Three Cousins Detective Club Ser.: Vol. 12). (Illus.). 64p. (J). (gr. 2-5). 1996. pap. 3.99 (*1-55661-850-6*) Bethany Hse.

— The Mystery of the Lost Island. LC 97-21123. (Three Cousins Detective Club Ser.: No. 18). 64p. (J). 1997. pap. 3.99 (*1-55661-856-5*) Bethany Hse.

— The Mystery of the Magi's Treasure. (Three Cousins Detective Club Ser.: No. 6). (Illus.). 64p. (J). (gr. 2-5). 1995. pap. 3.99 (*1-55661-410-1*) Bethany Hse.

— The Mystery of the Sand Castle. LC 97-53761. (Three Cousins Detective Club Ser.). (Illus.). 64p. (J). 1998. pap. 3.99 (*1-55661-858-1*) Bethany Hse.

— Mystery of the Silent Nightingale. LC 94-16718. (Three Cousins Detective Club Ser.: Vol. 1). 64p. (J). (gr. 2-5). 1994. pap. 3.99 (*1-55661-406-3*) Bethany Hse.

— Mystery of the Silly Goose. LC 96-45764. (Three Cousins Detective Club Ser.: Vol. 10). (Illus.). 64p. (J). (gr. 4-7). 1996. pap. 3.99 (*1-55661-848-4*) Bethany Hse.

— Mystery of the Traveling Button. LC 97-21122. (Three Cousins Detective Club Ser.: No. 16). 64p. (J). 1997. pap. 3.99 (*1-55661-854-9*) Bethany Hse.

— The Mystery of the Wedding Cake. LC 97-45440. (Three Cousins Detective Club Ser.). (Illus.). 64p. (J). 1998. pap. 3.99 (*1-55661-857-3*) Bethany Hse.

— Mystery of the White Elephant. LC 94-16719. (Three Cousins Detective Club Ser.). 64p. (J). (ps-3). 1994. pap. 3.99 (*1-55661-405-5*) Bethany Hse.

— Mystery of the White Elephant/The Mystery of the Silent Nightingale. (Three Cousins Detective Club Ser.). (J). 1997. boxed set 23.99 (*0-7642-8158-5*) Bethany Hse.

— Mystery of the Wrong Dog. LC 94-16717. (Three Cousins Detective Club Ser.: Vol. 3). 64p. (J). (gr. 2-5). 1994. pap. 3.99 (*1-55661-407-1*) Bethany Hse.

— The Mystery of the Zoo Camp. LC 96-45912. (Three Cousins Detective Club Ser.: Vol. 14). (Illus.). 64p. (J). (gr. 2-5). 1997. pap. 3.99 (*1-55661-852-2*) Bethany Hse.

— Recess: Prayer Meditations for Teachers. 96p. (Orig.). (gr. 10). 1988. 7.99 (*0-8010-6244-6*) Baker Bks.

Murphy, Elspeth C. & Hanna, Wayne. My First Book about Jesus, 4 bks. Incl. Bk. 3. Jesus Loves Children. 1981. 2.95 (*0-89191-333-5*); (Illus.). 1981. write for info. (*0-318-51433-8*) Chariot Victor.

***Murphy, Elspeth Campbell.** The Mystery of the Attic Lion. (Three Cousins Detective Club Ser.: Vol. 27). (Illus.). 64p. (J). (gr. 2-5). 2000. pap. 3.99 (*0-7642-2135-3*) Bethany Hse.

— The Mystery of the Backdoor Bundle. LC 99-50982. (Three Cousins Detective Club Ser.: Vol. 28). (Illus.). 64p. (J). (gr. 2-5). 2000. pap. 3.99 (*0-7642-2136-1*) Bethany Hse.

Murphy, Elspeth Campbell. Mystery of the Book Fair, Vol.24. LC 99-6449. (Three Cousins Detective Club Ser.). 64p. (J). (gr. 2-5). 1999. pap. text 3.99 (*0-7642-2132-9*) Bethany Hse.

— Mystery of the Butterfly Garden, Vol. 23. LC 99-6448. (Three Cousins Detective Club Ser.). 64p. 1999. pap. text 3.99 (*0-7642-2131-0*) Bethany Hse.

***Murphy, Elspeth Campbell.** Mystery of the Coon Cat. LC 99-6561. (Three Cousins Detective Club Ser.). 64p. (J). 1999. pap. text 3.99 (*0-7642-2133-7*) Bethany Hse.

— Mystery of the Golden Reindeer. (Three Cousins Detective Club Ser.: Vol. 30). (Illus.). 64p. (J). (gr. 2-5). 2000. pap. 3.99 (*0-7642-2138-8*) Bethany Hse.

— Mystery of the Painted Snake. (Three Cousins Detective Club Ser.: Vol. 29). (Illus.). 64p. (J). (gr. 2-5). 2000. pap. 3.99 (*0-7642-2137-X*) Bethany Hse.

— Mystery of the Runaway Scarecrow. LC 99-6565. (Three Cousins Detective Club Ser.). 64p. (J). (gr. 2-5). 1999. pap. text 3.99 (*0-7642-2134-5*) Bethany Hse.

Murphy, Elspeth Campbell. The Mystery of the Sock Monkeys. (Three Cousins Detective Club Ser.: No. 21). (Illus.). 64p. (J). 1998. pap. 3.99 (*1-55661-859-X*) Bethany Hse.

— Three Cousins Detective Club, Vols. 13-18. (Three Cousins Detective Club Ser.). (J). 1997. pap., boxed set 23.99 (*0-7642-8195-X*, 258195) Bethany Hse.

— Three Cousins Detective Club Mix. 1999. boxed set 23.99 (*0-7642-8463-0*) Bethany Hse.

***Murphy, Elspeth Campbell.** Three Cousins Detective Club 25-30. (J). (gr. 4-7). 2000. boxed set 23.99 (*0-7642-8704-4*) Bethany Hse.

***Murphy, Elspeth Campbell & Bernal, Richard.** Fifteen Flamingos. LC 00-8921. (Illus.). (J). 2000. pap. 9.99 (*0-7642-2201-5*) Bethany Hse.

Murphy, Emma, jt. ed. see Niblock, Timothy C.

***Murphy, Emma C.** Economic & Political Change in Tunisia: From Bourguiba to Ben Ali. LC 98-33304. 296p. 1999. text 79.95 (*0-312-22142-8*) St Martin.

Murphy, Emmett C. Leadership IQ: A New Method for Assessing & Improving Your Job Satisfaction & Leadership. LC 96-14172. 288p. 1996. 24.95 (*0-471-14712-5*) Wiley.

— Leadership IQ: The Groundbreaking Program to Develop & Improve Your Leadership Ability. 288p. 1997. pap. 5.99 (*0-471-19327-5*) Wiley.

— The New Murphy's Law: 10 Unconventional Rules for Making Everything Go Right in Your Life & Work. 228p. 1998. 15.95 (*1-886284-19-9*, Pub. by Chandler Hse) Natl Bk Netwk.

Murphy, Emmett C. & Snell, Michael. Forging the Heroic Organization: A Daring Blueprint for Revitalizing American Business. LC 94-34165. 300p. (C). 1994. text 22.95 (*0-13-100793-9*) P-H.

Murphy, Emmy L. Who Made God? (J). (ps-3). 1978. pap. 3.25 (*0-915374-07-2*, 07-2) Rapids Christian.

Murphy, Erin, ed. Angler's Journal. 160p. 1999. pap. 14.95 (*0-87108-899-1*) Pruett.

Murphy, Esther. How to Make a Wedding Cake. 2nd rev. ed. Carnes, Del, ed. (Illus.). 1987. pap. 10.95 (*0-937016-00-4*) Deco-Pr Pub.

— Mrs. Mayo's Book of Creative Foods: A Complete Guide to Fancy Food Decorating Anyone Can Do. rev. ed. Carnes, Del, ed. (Illus.). 176p. (Orig.). 1987. pap. text 6.95 (*0-937016-01-2*) Deco-Pr Pub.

Murphy, F., jt. auth. see Gijlstra, D. J.

Murphy, Frances J. Life Is a Symphony. (Illus.). 36p. (Orig.). 1992. pap. 5.00 (*1-878149-21-0*) Counterpoint Pub.

Murphy, Francesca, ed. see Kolnai, Aurel.

Murphy, Francesca A. Christ the Form of Beauty: A Study in Theology & Literature. 256p. 47.95 (*0-567-09708-0*, Pub. by T & T Clark) Bks Intl VA.

Murphy, Francesco, tr. see Buttiglione, Rocco.

Murphy, Francis. J. Francis Murphy: The Landscape Within. LC 82-80992. (Illus.). 30p. (Orig.). 1982. pap. 3.25 (*0-943651-18-2*) Hudson Riv.

Murphy, Francis, ed. see Whitman, Walt.

Murphy, Francis C. Regulating Flood-Plain Development. LC 59-16022. (University of Chicago, Department of Geography, Research Paper Ser.: No. 56). 216p. reprint ed. pap. 67.00 (*0-7837-0383-X*, 204070300018) Bks Demand.

Murphy, Francis J. Communists & Catholics in France, 1936-1939: The Politics of the Outstretched Hand. (University of Florida Social Sciences Monographs: No. 76). (Illus.). 168p. 1989. pap. 19.95 (*0-8130-0936-7*) U Press Fla.

— Pere Jacques: Resplendent in Victory. LC 98-6863. (Illus.). 214p. 1998. pap. 10.95 (*0-935216-64-2*, RV) ICS Pubns.

Murphy, Francis X. There's Hair Out There: A Chubby's World Adventure. (Chubby's World Adventure Ser.). (Illus.). 24p. (J). (gr. 2-4). 1998. 8.95 (*0-9667642-0-X*, CWA001) Xavier Shott.

***Murphy, Frank.** Ben Franklin & Magic Square. (J). 2001. 9.99 (*0-375-90621-5*) Random.

— Ben Franklin & Magic Square. (J). 2001. mass mkt. 3.99 (*0-375-80621-0*, Pub. by Random Bks Yng Read) Random.

Murphy, Frank. Charlie Harte & His Two-Wheeled Tiger. (Illus.). 96p. 1998. pap. 6.95 (*0-86278-532-4*, Pub. by OBrien Pr) Irish Amer Bk.

— Lockie & Dadge. 192p. (YA). 1997. pap. 6.95 (*0-86278-424-7*, Pub. by OBrien Pr) Irish Amer Bk.

***Murphy, Frank.** The Silence of Great Distance. LC 99-53861. 1999. pap. write for info. (*0-9629243-2-6*) Wind Sprint.

Murphy, Frank & Lizatovic, Josip. Gulliver in Lilliput: A Story Book Color. (Illus.). 32p. (J). 1997. pap. 5.95 (*0-86278-456-5*) Irish Amer Bk.

Murphy, Frank, jt. auth. see Baker, Thomas.

Murphy, Frank J. A Cold Clear Day: The Athletic Biography of Buddy Edelen. LC 91-9113. (Illus.). 200p. (Orig.). 1992. pap. 11.95 (*0-9629243-0-X*) Wind Sprint.

Murphy, Frank L., jt. auth. see Longnecker, David E.

Murphy, Franklin D., jt. auth. see Lawton, Thomas.

Murphy, Franklin D., jt. auth. see Marling, Karal Ann.

Murphy, Franklin D., jt. auth. see Vaughan, William.

Murphy, Fred. Radio-Controlled Action Cars. (Photo-Fact Book). (Illus.). 24p. (Orig.). (J). 1990. pap. 2.50 (*0-942025-87-3*) Kidsbks.

Murphy, Frederick A., et al, eds. Virus Taxonomy: Classification & Nomenclature of Viruses, Sixth Report of the International Committee on Taxonomy of Viruses. (Archives of Virology Ser.: Suppl. No. 10). (Illus.). 595p. 1995. pap. 98.00 (*0-387-82594-0*) Spr-Verlag.

Murphy, Frederick A., jt. auth. see International Committee on Taxonomy of Viruses.

Murphy, Frederick J. Bilingual Homilies for Feast Days & Other Occasions. LC 91-40302. 96p. (Orig.). 1992. pap. 4.95 (*0-8189-0622-7*) Alba.

***Murphy, Frederick J.** Fallen Is Babylon: The Revelation to John. LC 98-9598. 496p. 1998. pap. 30.00 (*1-56338-152-4*) TPI PA.

Murphy, Frederick J. Pseudo-Philo: Rewriting the Bible. LC 92-44041. 336p. 1993. text 65.00 (*0-19-507622-2*) OUP.

— Religious World of Jesus: An Introduction to Second Temple Palestinian Judaism. LC 90-21922. 1991. pap. 24.95 (*0-687-36049-8*) Abingdon.

Murphy, G. Surface Tempering Caused by Grinding. (Technical Papers: Vol. P109.03). (Illus.). 3p. 1953. pap. text 30.00 (*1-55589-223-X*) AGMA.

Murphy, G., ed. Ovid: Metamorphoses XI, Vol. XI. (Bristol Latin Texts Ser.). (LAT.). 144p. 1979. reprint ed. 20.95 (*0-906515-40-8*, Pub. by Brist Class Pr) Focus Pub-R Pullins.

Murphy, G. J. Transport & Distribution. 200p. 1972. pap. 32.00 (*0-8464-1437-6*) Beekman Pubs.

Murphy, G. Ronald. Brecht & the Bible: A Study of Religious Nihilism & Human Weakness in Brecht's Plays. LC 80-20207. (Germanic Languages & Literatures Ser.: No. 96). xi, 107p. 1980. 19.95 (*0-8078-8096-5*) U of NC Pr.

***Murphy, G. Ronald.** The Owl, the Raven & the Dove: The Religious Meaning of the Grimms' Magic Fairy Tales. (Illus.). 224p. 2000. 25.00 (*0-19-513607-1*) OUP.

Murphy, G. Ronald. The Saxon Savior: The Germanic Transformation of the Gospel in the Ninth-Century Heliand. 144p. (C). 1995. pap. text 19.95 (*0-19-509720-3*) OUP.

Murphy, G. Ronald, tr. The Heliand: The Saxon Gospel. 248p. (C). 1992. pap. text 23.95 (*0-19-507376-2*) OUP.

Murphy, G. W., tr. see Schmalenbach, Eugen.

Murphy, Gael, ed. see Lewallen, James E.

Murphy, Gardner & Dale, Laura A. Challenge of Psychical Research: A Primer of Parapsychology, Vol. 26. LC 78-31335. (World Perspectives Ser.: Vol. 26). (Illus.). 297p. 1979. reprint ed. lib. bdg. 65.00 (*0-313-20944-8*, MUCP, Greenwood Pr) Greenwood.

Murphy, Gardner & Kuhlen, Raymond G. Psychological Needs of Adults: A Symposium. LC BF0727.A4M8. (Notes & Essays on Education for Adults Ser.: Vol. 12). 27p. reprint ed. pap. 30.00 (*0-608-30830-7*, 200041000025) Bks Demand.

Murphy, Gene, jt. auth. see Lawson, Robert.

Murphy, Genna & Shauna, Ries. Quality of Life: How To Get It, How To Keep It. LC 98-49836. 204p. 2000. 22.00 (*0-688-16744-6*, Wm Morrow) Morrow Avon.

***Murphy, George.** Poems of Life. 1999. pap. write for info. (*1-58235-202-X*) Watermrk Pr.

Murphy, George, jt. auth. see Zimmerman, Oscar G.

Murphy, George E. It Didn't Happen on My Watch. LC 95-68646. 1995. 19.95 (*1-884570-31-3*) Research Triangle.

— Suicide in Alcoholism. (Monographs in Psychiatry: No. 1). (Illus.). 336p. 1992. text 49.95 (*0-19-507153-0*) OUP.

Murphy, George E., Jr., ed. The Poet's Choice: 100 American Poets' Favorite Poems. 176p. 1980. 12.95 (*0-937504-01-7*); pap. 5.95 (*0-937504-00-9*) Tendril.

Murphy, George E., ed. Tendril, No. 14-15. 256p. 1983. pap. 5.95 (*0-937504-03-3*) Tendril.

— Tendril, No. 16. 182p. 1983. pap. 5.95 (*0-937504-04-1*) Tendril.

— Tendril, No. 17. 212p. 1984. pap. 5.95 (*0-937504-05-X*) Tendril.

— Tendril, Nos. 19-20. 440p. 1985. pap. 10.95 (*0-937504-07-6*) Tendril.

Murphy, George F. Dermatopathology. LC 94-6843. (Illus.). 480p. 1995. text 135.00 (*0-7216-2418-9*, W B Saunders Co) Harcrt Hlth Sci Grp.

Murphy, George F. & Hurtzberg, Arlene. Atlas of Dermatopathology. LC 95-1014. (Illus.). 312p. 1995. text 210.00 (*0-7216-4886-X*, W B Saunders Co) Harcrt Hlth Sci Grp.

Murphy, George J. The Evolution of Canadian Corporate Reporting Practices, 1900-1970. (Foundations of Accounting Ser.: No. 13). 240p. 1988. text 10.00 (*0-8240-6119-5*) Garland.

Murphy, George J., ed. A History of Canadian Accounting Thought & Practice. LC 93-9763. (New Works in Accounting History). 664p. 1993. reprint ed. text 20.00 (*0-8153-1248-2*) Garland.

Murphy, George L., et al. Cosmic Witness: Commentaries on Science-Technology Themes. LC 95-25492. (Orig.). 1996. pap. 18.95 (*0-7880-0724-6*) CSS OH.

Murphy, George M., ed. see AEC Technical Information Center Staff.

Murphy, Gerald. Copper Mandarina: A Memoir. 144p. 1984. 34.00 (*0-7212-0674-3*, Pub. by Regency Pr GBR) St Mut.

Murphy, Gerald P. The American Cancer Society's Informed Decisions: The Complete Book of Cancer Diagnosis, Treatment, & Recovery. 1999. 40.00 (*0-525-93999-7*) NAL.

Murphy, Gerald P., ed. Transplantation in Primates. (Primates in Medicine Ser.: Vol. 7). 1972. 51.50 (*3-8055-1408-5*) S Karger.

Murphy, Gerald P., et al, eds. American Cancer Society Textbook of Clinical Oncology. 2nd ed. LC 95-132. 1995. write for info. (*0-944235-10-7*) Am Cancer NY.

Murphy, Gerald P. & Oelschlager, H., eds. Fosfestrol, Honvanr, St 52r, Honvolr, A Review of New Pharmacokinetic & Clinical Data. (Journal: Urologia Internationalis: Vol. 42, Suppl., 1988). iv, 60p. 1988. 21.00 (*3-8055-4903-2*) S Karger.

Murphy, Gerald P., et al. American Cancer Society's Informed Decisions: The Complete Book of Cancer Diagnosis, Treatment, & Recovery. 1997. 40.00 (*0-614-27855-4*, Viking) Viking Penguin.

Murphy, Gerald P., jt. ed. see McKenna, Robert J., Sr.

Murphy, Gerard. Early Irish Lyrics: 8th-12th Century. 2nd rev. ed. LC 98-159878. 338p. 1998. pap. 39.95 (*1-85182-198-8*, Pub. by Four Cts Pr) Intl Spec Bk.

Murphy, Gerard, tr. The Hypochondriac & Other Plays. 264p. 1998. pap. 18.95 (*1-870259-38-6*) Theatre Comm.

Murphy, Gerard J. C-Algebras & Operator Theory. 296p. (C). 1990. text 65.00 (*0-12-511360-9*) Acad Pr.

Murphy, Geri. Underwater Photography Camera Basics Equipment Care. Shreeves, Karl et al, eds. (Underwater Photography Ser.). (Illus.). 87p. (Orig.). 1989. pap. text 9.95 (*1-878663-03-8*) PADI.

— Underwater Photography Macro. Hurrell, Mary E. et al, eds. (Underwater Photography Ser.). (Illus.). 59p. (Orig.). 1990. pap. text 12.95 (*1-878663-04-6*) PADI.

Murphy, Gerry. The Empty Quarter. 64p. 1995. pap. 12.95 (*1-873790-71-6*) Dufour.

***Murphy, Gerry.** Extracts from the Lost Log Book of Christopher Columbus. LC 99-197283. 72p. 1999. 19.95 (*1-901233-30-8*, Pub. by Dedalus); pap. 12.95 (*1-901233-31-6*, Pub. by Dedalus) Dufour.

Murphy, Gladys N., ed. see Murphy, Dennis G.

Murphy, Glenn W., jt. auth. see Uohara, John K.

Murphy-Gnatz, Mary, jt. contrib. by see Murphy, Nora.

***Murphy, Graham J. & Pitcher, E. W.** The Irish in Popular Literature in the Early American Republic: Paddy Whacking. LC 99-53118. (Studies in British & American Magazines : Vol. 3). 428p. 2000. text 109.95 (*0-7734-7838-8*) E Mellen.

Murphy, Gregory. The Countess. Date not set. pap. 5.95 (*0-8222-1736-8*) Dramatists Play.

Murphy, Gretchen, et al. Electronic Health Records: Changing the Vision. Pfeiffer, Maureen, ed. LC 98-37968. 575p. 1999. text. write for info. (*0-7216-7386-4*, W B Saunders Co) Harcrt Hlth Sci Grp.

Murphy, Harold. I Hate Women: 225 Reasons Why You Should Too. LC 96-53406. (I Hate Ser.). 96p. 1997. pap. 5.95 (*1-57587-054-1*) Crane Hill AL.

Murphy, Harriet. Canetti & Nietzsche: Theories of Humor in Die Blendung. LC 95-52246. (SUNY Series, The Margins of Literature). 444p. (C). 1996. text 65.50 (*0-7914-3133-9*); pap. text 21.95 (*0-7914-3134-7*) State U NY Pr.

***Murphy, Harriet.** Critical Essays on Julian Schutting. LC 00-38053. (Studies in Austrian Literature, Culture & Thought). 2000. write for info. (*1-57241-095-7*) Ariadne CA.

Murphy, Harry J., ed. see California State University at Northridge, Office.

Murphy, Haughton. Murder for Lunch. large type ed. 1990. 27.99 (*0-7089-2225-2*) Ulverscroft.

— Murder Takes a Partner. large type ed. 1990. 27.99 (*0-7089-2158-2*) Ulverscroft.

Murphy, Helen M. & Reilly, James R. Marriages in the Roman Catholic Diocese of Tuam, Ireland, 1821-1829. x, 192p. (Orig.). 1993. pap. text 28.50 (*1-55613-812-1*) Heritage Bk.

Murphy, Henry C. Voyage of Verrazzano. LC 72-126244. (Select Bibliographies Reprint Ser.). 1977. 25.95 (*0-8369-5471-8*) Ayer.

Murphy, Henry C., ed. Anthology of New Netherland or Translations from Early Dutch Poetry of New York. 1972. reprint ed. 15.00 (*0-8422-8101-0*); reprint ed. pap. text 6.50 (*0-8290-0651-6*) Irvington.

Murphy, Henry T., jt. auth. see Kerker, Ann E.

Murphy, Herta A. Effective Business Communications. 7th ed. LC 96-46646. 640p. (C). 1997. pap. 57.50 (*0-07-044398-X*) McGraw.

Murphy, Herta A. & Hildebrandt, Herbert W. Effective Business Communications. 6th ed. 880p. (C). 1991. text 81.00 (*0-07-044157-X*) McGraw.

Murphy, Herta H., jt. auth. see Crosling, G.

Murphy, Higgins. Concepts in Federal Taxation. 8th ed. 2000. pap. text 87.95 (*0-324-02156-9*) Thomson Learn.

Murphy, Hilary Moon, jt. auth. see Wittman, Jason.

Murphy, Hope F. Educating the Independent Mind: The First Hundred Years of Laurel School. (Illus.). 176p. 1998. 39.95 (*0-9664066-0-5*) Laurel Schl.

An Asterisk (*) at the beginning of an entry indicates that the title is appearing for the first time.

M

***Murphy, Jim.** The Memphis Sun. LC PS3563.U738M46 2000. (Wick Poetry Chapbook Ser.). 2000. pap. 4.75 (0-87338-663-9) Kent St U Pr.

Murphy, Jim. Napoleon Lajoic: Modern Baseball's First Superstar, 1988. (Illus.). 88p. 1988. pap. 8.00 (0-910137-31-5) Soc Am Baseball Res.

— Night Terrors. LC 92-27102. 192p. (J). (gr. 7-9). 1993. 13.95 (0-590-45341-6) Scholastic Inc.

— Night Terrors. 192p. (YA). (gr. 7-9). 1994. pap. 3.50 (0-590-45342-4) Scholastic Inc.

— Night Terrors. 1993. 8.60 (0-606-07058-3, Pub. by Turtleback) Demco.

***Murphy, Jim.** Pick-&-Shovel Poet: The Journeys of Pascal D'Angelo. (Illus.). 176p. (J). (gr. 4-7). 2000. 20.00 (0-395-77610-4, Clarion Bks) HM.

Murphy, Jim. Tractors: From Yesterday's Steam Wagons to Today's Turbo-charged Giants. LC 82-48777. (Illus.). 64p. (J). (gr. 3-6). 1984. 11.95 (0-397-32050-7) HarpC Child Bks.

— Two Hundred Years of Bicycles. LC 81-48608. (Illus.). 64p. (J). (gr. 3-6). 1983. lib. bdg. 11.89 (0-397-32008-6) HarpC Child Bks.

— West to a Land of Plenty: The Diary of Teresa Angelino Viscardi, New York to Idaho Territory, 1883. LC 97-23064. (Dear America Ser.). (Illus.). 204p. (YA). (gr. 4-9). 1998. 9.95 (0-590-73888-7) Scholastic Inc.

— A Young Patriot: The American Revolution As Experienced by One Boy. LC 93-38789. (Illus.). 112p. (J). (gr. 4 up). 1996. 16.00 (0-395-60523-7, Clarion Bks) HM.

***Murphy, Jim.** A Young Patriot: The American Revolution As Experienced by One Boy. (J). 1998. 12.05 (0-606-13941-9, Pub. by Turtleback) Demco.

Murphy, Jim. Young Patriot: The American Revolution As Experienced by One Boy. LC 93-603878. (Illus.). 112p. 1998. pap. 6.95 (0-395-90019-0, Clarion Bks) HM.

Murphy, Joan E., ed. Tourette's & Attention Deficit Hyperactivity Disorder: Toughing It Out at Home & at School. 218p. (Orig.). 1995. pap. 18.00 (0-9625194-1-3) Baton Rouge Tourette Grp.

Murphy, Joan E., intro. Toughing Out Tourette's & ADHD-ADD. 240p. (Orig.). 1989. pap. text 12.00 (0-9625194-0-5) Baton Rouge Tourette Grp.

Murphy, Joanne B. Feelings. (Illus.). 24p. (J). (ps-8). 1985. pap. 4.95 (0-88753-129-6) Black Moss.

Murphy, Joel. How to Care for Your Pet Bird: Practical Advice from Dr. Joel Murphy. (Illus.). 336p. (C). 1994. text 65.00 (0-9643838-0-2) Veterinary Connect.

— How to Care for Your Pet Bird Vol. 1: Practical Advice from Dr. Joel Murphy. 336p. (Orig.). 1995. pap. 45.00 (0-9643838-1-0) Veterinary Connect.

Murphy, John. The Additives for Plastics Handbook. LC 96-3458. 550p. 1996. 181.00 (1-85617-281-3) Elsevier.

— A Cheyenne Moon. large type ed. (Western Ser.). 208p. 1994. pap. 16.99 (0-7089-7583-6) Ulverscroft.

— Handbook of Reinforced Plastics. LC 95-112462. 550p. 1994. 173.00 (1-85617-217-1, Pub. by Elsvr Adv Tech) Elsevier.

***Murphy, John.** Imagining the Fifties. 250p. 2000. pap. 29.95 (0-86840-690-2, Pub. by NSW U Pr) Intl Spec Bk.

Murphy, John. Ireland in the Twentieth Century. 2nd ed. 182p. (C). 1992. reprint ed. pap. 17.95 (0-7171-1694-8, Pub. by Gill & MacMill) Irish Bks Media.

— A Little Irish Cookbook. (Little Bks.). (Illus.). 60p. 1996. 7.95 (0-8118-1085-2) Chronicle Bks.

— NT Networking Programming Toolkit. LC 98-31978. (Microsoft Technology Ser.). 256p. 1998. pap. text 49.99 (0-13-081324-9) P-H.

— The Reinforced Plastics Handbook: John Murphy. 2nd ed. LC 98-29947. 1998. 220.50 (1-85617-348-8) Elsevier.

— Solution-Focused Counseling in Middle & High Schools. LC 97-5511. 194p. 1997. pap. text 29.95 (1-55620-170-2, 72640) Am Coun Assn.

***Murphy, John, ed.** Ethic Minorities: Their Families & the Law. 192p. 2000. 45.00 (1-901362-59-0, Pub. by Hart Pub) Intl Spec Bk.

Murphy, John & Stone, Brian, eds. OOIS '95: 1995 International Conference on Object Oriented Information Systems, 18-20 December 1995, Dublin: Proceedings. 366p. 1995. pap. 75.00 (3-540-76010-5) Spr-Verlag.

Murphy, John, jt. auth. see Brazier, Margaret.

Murphy, John, jt. auth. see Longino, Charles.

Murphy, John, jt. auth. see Murphy, Ann.

Murphy, John, jt. ed. see Berdayes, Vicente W.

Murphy, John, jt. ed. see Fletcher, Pauline.

Murphy, John A. The Chancellor Affair. LC 98-96379. (Illus.). 224p. 1998. pap. 17.00 (0-918052-02-5, CA-9801) Brock Publish.

— The College: A History of Queen's/University College, Cork. 469p. 1995. 40.00 (1-85918-056-6, Pub. by Cork Univ) Stylus Pub VA.

— Ireland in the Twentieth Century. 180p. 1975. 9.95 (0-8159-5832-3) Devin.

Murphy, John A., ed. The French Are in the Bay: The Expedition to Bantry Bay 1796. LC 97-189932. 160p. 1997. pap. 12.95 (1-85635-171-8, Pub. by Mercier Pr) Irish Amer Bk.

Murphy, John C. Amphibians & Reptiles of Trinidad & Tobago. LC 95-36455. (Illus.). 304p. 1997. lib. bdg. 72.50 (0-89464-971-X) Krieger.

Murphy, John C. & Henderson, Robert W. Tales of Giant Snakes: A Historical Natural History of Anacondas & Pythons. LC 96-54033. 234p. 1997. 29.50 (0-89464-995-7) Krieger.

Murphy, John D. Azerbaijani Newspaper Reader. (AZE.). 122p. 1993. 46.00 (1-881265-54-4, 3006) Dunwoody Pr.

Murphy, John D. Luganda-English Dictionary. 652p. 1972. 95.00 (0-7859-3733-1, M591) Fr & Eur.

Murphy, John D. & Issa, Abdullahi A. Somali Newspaper Reader. LC 84-72438. iii, 186p. 1984. text 44.00 (0-931745-05-5) Dunwoody Pr.

Murphy, John D. & Rutayuga, John B. Intermediate Swahili Newspaper Reader. LC 84-72435. xix, 259p. 1984. text 45.00 (0-931745-02-0) Dunwoody Pr.

Murphy, John D. & Somay, Metin. Turkish Newspaper Reader. LC 88-70934. 328p. 1988. text 49.00 (0-931745-35-7) Dunwoody Pr.

Murphy, John D., jt. auth. see Gabounia, Ketevan.

Murphy, John D., jt. auth. see Sowhagyalakshmi Vaidyanathan.

Murphy, John D., ed. see Feghali, Habaka J.

Murphy, John E. Clinical Pharmacokinetics Pocket Reference. 400p. 2000. pap. 52.50 (1-879907-98-4) Am Soc Hlth-Syst.

Murphy, John E., intro. Clinical Pharmacokinetics. (Illus.). 383p. (Orig.). 1993. pap. 48.00 (1-879907-31-3) Am Soc Hlth-Syst.

Murphy, John E., jt. ed. see Moore, John A., Jr.

***Murphy, John F., Jr.** Guns of Littleton. 2000. 24.95 (1-56980-161-4) Barricade Bks.

Murphy, John F. Legal Aspects of International Terrorism: Summary Report of an International Conference, No. 19. (Studies in Transnational Legal Policy). 80p. 1980. 4.00 (0-318-13186-2) Am Soc Intl Law.

— Punishing International Terrorists: The Legal Framework for Policy Initiatives. LC 85-15845. 152p. 1985. 45.50 (0-8476-7449-5) Rowman.

— The United Nations & the Control of International Violence: A Legal & Political Analysis. LC 81-69989. 224p. 1983. text 53.00 (0-86598-079-9) Rowman.

Murphy, John F. & Dinnage, James D. The Constitutional Law of the European Union. LC 96-11280. 776p. 1996. teacher ed. 58.95 (0-87084-254-4) Anderson Pub Co.

Murphy, John F., jt. ed. see Dinnage, James D.

Murphy, John J. Agent of Change: Leading a Cultural Revolution. LC 94-61008. 265p. 1994. pap. 14.99 (0-9639013-1-1) Venture Mgmt.

— Agent of Change: Leading a Cultural Revolution. 268p. 1999. pap. write for info. (0-9639013-5-4) Venture Mgmt.

— The Companion Study Guide to Technical Analysis of the Financial Markets. 160p. 1999. pap. 39.95 (0-7352-0065-3) P-H.

— The Eight Disciplines: An Enticing Look into Your Personality. 268p. 1998. pap. 14.99 (0-9639013-4-6) Venture Mgmt.

— Get a Real Life: A Lesson in Personal Empowerment. LC 96-91023. 262p. (Orig.). 1997. pap. 14.99 (0-9639013-3-8) Venture Mgmt.

— Intermarket Technical Analysis: Trading Strategies for the Global Stock, Bond, Commodity & Currency Markets. LC 90-48567. (Finance Editions Ser.). 288p. 1991. 75.00 (0-471-52433-6) Wiley.

— John Murphy on Chart Analysis. 88p. 1999. pap. 19.95 (1-883272-29-7) Traders Lib.

— My Antonia: The Road Home. (Masterwork Studies: No. 31). 136p. (C). 1989. 25.95 (0-8057-7986-8, MWS-31, Twyne); mass mkt. 14.95 (0-8057-8035-1, Twyne) Mac Lib Ref.

— Pulling Together: The Power of Teamwork. LC 93-61170. 200p. (Orig.). 1993. pap. 12.00 (0-9639013-0-3) Venture Mgmt.

— Pulling Together: The Power of Teamwork. LC 96-49713. 192p. (Orig.). 1997. pap. 14.99 (0-922066-92-2) Wynwood.

— Reinvent Yourself: A Lesson in Personal Leadership. LC 95-61979. 188p. (Orig.). 1996. pap. 12.00 (0-9639013-2-X) Venture Mgmt.

— Technical Analysis of the Financial Markets. LC 98-38531. (Illus.). 576p. 1999. 70.00 (0-7352-0066-1) PH Pr.

— Technical Analysis of the Futures Markets: A Comprehensive Guide to Trading Methods & Applications. 570p. (C). 1986. text 59.95 (0-13-898008-X) NY Inst Finance.

— Technical Analysis of the Futures Markets: Study Guide. LC 87-10991. (Illus.). 160p. (Orig.). (C). 1987. pap. text 32.00 (0-13-858747-7) NY Inst Finance.

Murphy, John J., ed. Critical Essays on Willa Cather. (Critical Essays on American Literature Ser.). 344p. (C). 1984. 48.00 (0-8161-8676-6, G K Hall & Co) Mac Lib Ref.

Murphy, John J., et al, eds. Willa Cather: Family, Community, & History. LC 90-85382. (Illus.). xii, 322p. 1990. pap. 5.95 (0-8425-2299-9, Friends of the Library) Brigham.

Murphy, John J. & Duncan, Barry L. Brief Intervention for School Problems: Collaborating for Practical Solutions. LC 96-45265. (School Practitioner Ser.). 1750p. 1997. lib. bdg. 29.00 (1-57230-174-0, 0174) Guilford Pubns.

Murphy, John L. Introduction to Loudspeaker Design. (Illus.). 166p. 1998. pap. 24.95 (0-9663773-2-X, 99-001) True Audio.

— Visual Investor: How to Spot Market Trends. 320p. 1996. 39.95 (0-471-14447-9) Wiley.

Murphy, John M. Confederate Carbines & Musketoons. (Illus.). 224p. 1986. 45.00 (0-9616425-0-5); 125.00 (0-9616425-1-3) J M Murphy.

— Success Without a College Degree: The Secrets of How to Get Ahead & Show Them All. 264p. 1998. pap. 19.95 (0-9662120-0-2) Achiev Dynam.

— Success Without a College Degree: The Secrets of How to Get Ahead & Show Them All. rev. ed. 264p. 1998. pap. 19.95 (0-9662120-1-0) Achiev Dynam.

Murphy, John M. & Madaus, Howard M. Confederate Carbines & Musketoons: Cavalry Small Arms Manufactured in the Southern Confederacy 1861-1865. 2nd rev. ed. (Illus.). 320p. 2000. 69.95 (1-882824-18-0) Graphic Pubs.

— Confederate Rifles & Muskets: Infantry Small Arms Manufactured in the Southern Confederacy 1861-1865. LC 92-75534. 768p. 1996. 119.95 (1-882824-01-6) Graphic Pubs.

Murphy, John M., jt. auth. see Hart, Susannah.

Murphy, John P., ed. Jesuit Latin Poets of the Seventeenth & Eighteenth Centuries: An Anthology of Neo-Latin Poetry. Mertz, James J., tr. LC 88-62698. (ENG & LAT., Illus.). 230p. (Orig.). (C). 1989. pap. 24.00 (0-86516-215-8); text 39.00 (0-86516-214-X) Bolchazy-Carducci.

Murphy, John P., tr. see Cordara, Giulio Cesare.

Murphy, John S. & Hudson, Frederic M. The Joy of Old: A Guide to Successful Elderhood. LC 96-94012. (Illus.). 160p. (Orig.). 1995. pap. 16.95 (1-886851-44-1) Geode Pr.

Murphy, John V. The Dark Angel: Gothic Elements in Shelley's Works. LC 73-8304. 199p. 1975. 32.50 (0-8387-1407-2) Bucknell U Pr.

Murphy, John W. Postmodern Social Analysis & Criticism, 79. LC 88-35774. (Contributions in Sociology Ser.: No. 79). 185p. 1989. 49.95 (0-313-26683-2, MMS/, Greenwood Pr) Greenwood.

Murphy, John W., et al, eds. The Underside of High-Tech: Technology & the Deformation of Human Sensibilities, 59. LC 85-27265. (Contributions in Sociology Ser.: No. 59). 232p. 1986. 62.95 (0-313-24612-2, Greenwood Pr) Greenwood.

Murphy, John W. & Choi, Jung Min. Postmodernism, Unraveling Racism & Democratic Institutions. LC 97-5589. 144p. 1997. 52.95 (0-275-95664-4, Praeger Pubs) Greenwood.

Murphy, John W. & Dison, Jack E., eds. Are Prisons Any Better: Twenty Years of Correctional Reform. (Criminal Justice System Annuals Ser.: Vol. 26). (Illus.). 240p. (C). 1990. 58.00 (0-8039-3569-2); pap. 26.00 (0-8039-3570-6) Sage.

— Are Prisons Any Better? Twenty Years of Correctional Reform. fac. ed. LC 90-8237. (Sage Criminal Justice System Annuals Ser.: No. 26). 178p. 1990. reprint ed. pap. 55.20 (0-608-01004-9, 206186200012) Bks Demand.

Murphy, John W. & Pardeck, John T. The Computerization of Human Service Agencies: A Critical Appraisal. LC 90-22750. 184p. 1991. 49.95 (0-86569-023-5, T023, Auburn Hse) Greenwood.

Murphy, John W. & Pardeck, John T., eds. Technology & Human Productivity: Challenges for the Future. LC 85-23237. 256p. 1986. 62.95 (0-89930-194-0, PTH/, Quorum Bks) Greenwood.

Murphy, John W. & Peck, Dennis L., eds. Open Institutions: The Hope for Democracy. LC 92-20048. 224p. 1992. 57.95 (0-275-94028-4, C4028, Praeger Pubs) Greenwood.

Murphy, John W., jt. auth. see Choi, Jung Min.

Murphy, John W., jt. auth. see Langino, Charles F., Jr.

Murphy, John W., jt. auth. see Vega, William A.

Murphy, Jonathan, tr. see Courtois, Stephane, et al.

Murphy, Jonne. Handbook of Radio Advertising. LC 79-8395. 252p. reprint ed. pap. 78.20 (0-608-15471-7, 202938800060) Bks Demand.

Murphy, Joseph. The Amazing Laws of Cosmic Mind Power. 1989. pap. text 9.95 (0-13-023888-0) P-H.

— Collected Essays of Joseph Murphy. LC 87-70783. (Mentors of New Thought Ser.). 192p. (Orig.). 1987. pap. 9.95 (0-87516-592-3) DeVorss.

— The Cosmic Energizer: Miracle Power of the Universe. 214p. 1996. reprint ed. pap. 12.00 (0-87516-693-8) DeVorss.

— The Cosmic Power Within You. 204p. 1996. 9.98 (1-56731-108-3, MJF Bks) Fine Comms.

— The Cosmic Power Within You. 203p. 1988. pap. text 9.95 (0-13-179128-1) P-H.

— Great Bible Truths for Human Problems. 228p. 1976. pap. 8.00 (0-87516-214-2) DeVorss.

— Handbook of Research on Educational Administration: A Project of the American Educational Research. LC 98-54762. 576p. 1999. text 100.00 (0-7879-4340-1) Jossey-Bass.

— How to Attract Money. 13th ed. 75p. 1975. reprint ed. pap. 4.50 (0-87516-204-5) DeVorss.

— How to Use the Laws of Mind. LC 80-68548. 271p. 1981. pap. 9.50 (0-87516-426-9) DeVorss.

— How to Use Your Healing Power. 158p. 1973. reprint ed. pap. 7.50 (0-87516-186-3) DeVorss.

— Infinite Power for Richer Living. 191p. 1996. reprint ed. pap. 12.00 (0-87516-694-6) DeVorss.

— Living Without Strain. 157p. 1973. pap. 7.50 (0-87516-187-1) DeVorss.

— Maryland Evidence Handbook: 1989 Edition, 1992 Supplement. 1989. text. write for info. (0-87473-499-1, 64905-10, MICHIE) LEXIS Pub.

— Maryland Evidence Handbook: 1991 Cumulative Supplement. 1991. write for info. (0-87473-855-5, 64907-10, MICHIE) LEXIS Pub.

— Miracle Power for Infinite Riches. (C). 1974. pap. text 9.95 (0-13-585612-4, Parker Publishing Co) P-H.

— Pathways to Privatization in Education. LC 97-30771. (Contemporary Studies in Social & Policy Issues in Education). 1998. 73.25 (1-56750-363-2); pap. 24.95 (1-56750-364-0) Ablx Pub.

— Peace Within Yourself. 300p. 1972. pap. 9.00 (0-87516-188-X) DeVorss.

— Power of Your Subconscious Mind. 1963. pap. 5.95 (0-685-03917-X, Reward) P-H.

— The Power of Your Subconscious Mind. 224p. 1982. mass mkt. 6.99 (0-553-27043-5) Bantam.

— The Power of Your Subconscious Mind. 224p. (C). 1988. pap. 10.95 (0-13-687972-1) P-H.

— Pray Your Way Through It. 171p. 1973. pap. 8.50 (0-87516-190-1) DeVorss.

— Prayer Is the Answer. 190p. 1973. pap. 7.50 (0-87516-189-8) DeVorss.

— The Privatization of Schooling: Problems & Possibilities. LC 96-4523. 208p. 1996. pap. 27.95 (0-8039-6394-7); text 61.95 (0-8039-6393-9) Corwin Pr.

— Psychic Perception. LC 94-70459. 241p. 1996. reprint ed. pap. 12.50 (0-87516-670-9) DeVorss.

— Quiet Moments with God. 1958. pap. 5.00 (0-87516-276-2) DeVorss.

— Restructuring Schools: Capturing & Assessing the Phenomena. 144p. (C). 1991. text 36.00 (0-8077-3112-9); pap. text 16.95 (0-8077-3111-0) Tchrs Coll.

***Murphy, Joseph.** Secrets of the I Chang. Irving, Kenneth, ed. LC 99-47862. 240p. 1999. pap. 13.00 (0-7352-0125-0) PH Pr.

Murphy, Joseph. Special Meditations for Health, Wealth & Love. 1952. pap. 4.95 (0-87516-336-X) DeVorss.

Murphy, Joseph. Telepsychics: The Magic Power of Perfect Living. LC 73-6775. 230p. 1988. reprint ed. pap. 11.00 (0-87516-598-2) DeVorss.

Murphy, Joseph. These Truths Can Change Your Life. 280p. 1982. pap. 10.00 (0-87516-476-5) DeVorss.

— Within You Is the Power. LC 77-86026. 1978. pap. 10.00 (0-87516-247-9) DeVorss.

— Write a New Name in the Book of Life. 29p. pap. 1.50 (0-87516-342-4) DeVorss.

— Your Infinite Power to Be Rich. (C). 1968. pap. text 9.95 (0-13-979591-X, Reward) P-H.

Murphy, Joseph, ed. The Educational Reform Movement of the 1980s: Perspectives & Cases. LC 89-63476. 364p. (C). 1990. 38.75 (0-8211-1261-9) McCutchan.

Murphy, Joseph & Beck, Lynn G. School-Based Management As School Reform: Taking Stock. LC 95-7733. (Illus.). 232p. 1995. pap. 27.95 (0-8039-6176-6) Corwin Pr.

— School-Based Management As School Reform: Taking Stock. LC 95-7733. (Illus.). 232p. 1995. 61.95 (0-8039-6175-8) Corwin Pr.

Murphy, Joseph & Forsyth, Patrick B. Educational Administration: A Decade of Reform. (1-Off Ser.). (Illus.). 304p. 1999. 75.95 (0-8039-6608-3); pap. 32.95 (0-8039-6609-1) Corwin Pr.

Murphy, Joseph & Hallinger, Philip. Restructuring Schooling: Learning from Ongoing Efforts. LC 92-39720. 296p. 1993. 65.95 (0-8039-6060-3); pap. 29.95 (0-8039-6061-1) Corwin Pr.

Murphy, Joseph & Hallinger, Philip, eds. Approaches to Administrative Training in Education. LC 86-14579. (SUNY Series, Educational Leadership). 291p. (C). 1987. text 24.50 (0-88706-433-7) State U NY Pr.

Murphy, Joseph & Louis, Karen S., eds. Reshaping the Principalship: Insights from Transformational Reform Efforts. LC 93-44470. 312p. 1994. 69.95 (0-8039-6079-4); pap. 32.95 (0-8039-6080-8) Corwin Pr.

***Murphy, Joseph & McMahan, Ian.** Power of Your Subconscious Mind. rev. expanded ed. (Illus.). 288p. 2000. pap. 13.00 (0-7352-0168-4) PH Pr.

Murphy, Joseph, et al. The Landscape of Leadership Preparation: Reframing the Education of School Administrators. LC 92-16959. 240p. 1992. 61.95 (0-8039-6027-1, 81147); pap. 27.95 (0-8039-6028-X, 81148) Corwin Pr.

Murphy, Joseph, jt. auth. see Beck, Lynn G.

Murphy, Joseph, jt. auth. see Gouldson, Andrew.

Murphy, Joseph E. Bond Tables of Probable Future Prices. unabridged ed. LC 97-224716. 394p. (Orig.). 1997. pap. 19.95 (0-9646292-5-9) Crossgar Pr.

— Bond Tables of Probable Future Returns. unabridged ed. LC 97-223518. 424p. (Orig.). 1997. pap. 19.95 (0-9646292-6-7) Crossgar Pr.

— Bond Tables of Probable Future Yields. LC 97-169279. (Illus.). 452p. (Orig.). 1997. pap. 19.95 (0-9646292-2-4) Crossgar Pr.

***Murphy, Joseph E.** Mauritania in Photographs. (Illus.). 160p. 1999. pap. 25.00 (1-892277-04-2) Crossgar Pr.

Murphy, Joseph E. The Random Character of Corporate Earnings. unabridged ed. LC 98-159234. 386p. (Orig.). 1997. pap. 19.95 (0-9646292-4-0) Crossgar Pr.

— Stock Market Probability: Using Statistics to Predict & Optimize Investment Outcomes, Revised Edition. 2nd rev. ed. LC 94-184784. 1994. text 37.50 (1-55738-564-5, Irwn Prfssnl) McGraw-Hill Prof.

— To the Poles by Ski & Dogsled, 2 vols. in 1. (Illus.). 348p. 1996. pap. 9.95 (0-9646292-1-6) Crossgar Pr.

***Murphy, Joseph E.** The Valuation of Options. 146p. 2000. per. 10.00 (1-892277-06-9) Crossgar Pr.

Murphy, Joseph E. Why the Stock Market Rises: A Statistical Study of Stock Prices. unabridged ed. LC 98-180462. 1998. pap. 19.95 (0-9646292-8-3) Crossgar Pr.

Murphy, Joseph E., jt. ed. see Sigler, Jay A.

Murphy, Joseph F., Jr. Maryland Evidence Handbook. 2nd ed. 1009p. 1993. 90.00 (1-55834-124-2, 64905-11, MICHIE) LEXIS Pub.

***Murphy, Joseph F., Jr.** Maryland Evidence Handbook. 3rd ed. LC 99-64694. 735p. 1999. 120.00 (0-327-01532-2, 6490512) LEXIS Pub.

Murphy, Joseph F. Maryland Evidence Handbook: 1990 Supplement. 1990. write for info. (0-87473-727-3, 64906-10, MICHIE) LEXIS Pub.

Murphy, Joseph H. Murphy's Will Clauses: Annotations & Forms with Tax Effects, 4 vols. 1960. ring bd. 980.00 (0-8205-1441-1) Bender.

An Asterisk (*) at the beginning of an entry indicates that the title is appearing for the first time.

Murphy, Joseph M. Santeria: African Spirits in America. LC 92-8590. 224p. 1993. pap. 16.00 (*0-8070-1021-9*) Beacon Pr.
— Working the Spirit: Ceremonies of the African Diaspora. LC 93-3929. 280p. 1994. pap. 18.00 (*0-8070-1221-1*) Beacon Pr.
Murphy, Joseph P. But, Daddy, Did You See Shoshoni? Pebbles, Rocks, & Steppingstones. 256p. 1991. pap. 17.95 (*0-9631361-0-0*) An Total Pr.
Murphy, Joseph P., jt. auth. see Rumney, Jay.
Murphy, Joseph P., jt. auth. see Sigler, Jay A.
Murphy, Joseph S., II. Deck Officer Study Guide, 5 vols., Set. 1000p. (C). 1990. teacher ed. 85.00 (*0-685-38551-5*); pap. 125.00 (*0-685-38550-7*) Academy Pub.
— Deck Officer Study Guide, 5 vols., Set. 2nd ed. 1000p. (C). 1990. lib. bdg. 85.00 (*0-9625393-0-9*) Academy Pub.
— Deck Officer Study Guide: Deck General, Vol. 1. 2nd ed. 200p. (C). 1990. lib. bdg. write for info. (*0-9625393-1-7*) Academy Pub.
— Deck Officer Study Guide Vol. 2: Navigation General. 2nd ed. 175p. (C). 1990. lib. bdg. write for info. (*0-9625393-2-5*) Academy Pub.
— Deck Officer Study Guide Vol. 3: Deck Safety. 2nd ed. 250p. (C). 1990. lib. bdg. write for info. (*0-9625393-3-3*) Academy Pub.
— Deck Officer Study Guide Vol. 4: Rules of the Road. 2nd ed. 175p. (C). 1990. lib. bdg. write for info. (*0-9625393-4-1*) Academy Pub.
— Deck Officer Study Guide Vol. 5: Navigation Problems. 2nd ed. 300p. (C). 1990. lib. bdg. write for info. (*0-9625393-5-X*) Academy Pub.
Murphy, Joseph S., II, ed. Deck Officer Study Guide. 800p. (C). 1989. teacher ed. 85.00 (*0-685-32261-0*); pap. 125.00 (*0-685-32260-2*) Academy Pub.
Murphy, Judith A. Preparation of Biological Specimens for Scanning Electron Microscopy. Roomans, Godfried M., ed. (Illus.). 352p. (Orig.). (C). 1984. pap. text 32.00 (*0-931288-33-9*) Scanning Microscopy.
Murphy, Judith A., jt. auth. see Burke, Laura J.
Murphy, Judy, jt. ed. see Burke, Laura.
Murphy, Judy, ed. see Zaleski, Karol.
Murphy-Judy, Kathy, tr. see Zumthor, Paul.
Murphy, Julia, jt. auth. see Murphy, Roy.
Murphy, Julien. Feminist Interpretations of Jean-Paul Sartre. LC 98-37145. (Re-Reading the Canon Ser.). 1999. 60.00 (*0-271-01884-4*) Pa St U Pr.
***Murphy, Julien.** Feminist Interpretations of Jean-Paul Sartre. LC 98-37145. (Re-Reading the Canon Ser.). 1999. pap. 19.95 (*0-271-01885-2*) Pa St U Pr.
***Murphy, Julien & Stempinski, Sally.** The Cat Who--Cookbook. LC 99-86496. 2000. 21.95 (*0-425-17674-6*) Berkley Pub.
Murphy, Julien S. The Constructed Body: AIDS, Reproductive Technology, & Ethics. LC 94-30815. 185p. (C). 1995. text 44.50 (*0-7914-2517-7*); pap. text 14.95 (*0-7914-2518-5*) State U NY Pr.
Murphy, K., jt. ed. see Murphy, P.
Murphy, K. J., et al, eds. The Ecology of Loch Lomond. LC 94-34275. (Developments in Hydrobiology Ser.: Vol. 101). 1994. text 191.50 (*0-7923-3168-0*) Kluwer Academic.
Murphy, K. J., jt. auth. see Dickinson, Gordon.
Murphy, Karen H. Halos, Hearts, Horses & Healings. 2nd ed. LC 96-86354. 1998. mass mkt. 14.95 (*1-889131-10-5*) CasAnanda.
***Murphy, Karen H.** Touched by the Light: True Stories about Angels, an Open Heart Nurse & Subtle Energy Therapies. 1999. pap. 14.95 (*0-9663659-2-5*) Spirit Aware.
Murphy, Kathleen. General Chemistry. 2nd ed. 226p. (C). 1995. text, lab manual ed. 37.20 (*0-536-59126-1*) Pearson Custom.
— Teaching Reflectivly about Contemp Issues in Education. 2nd ed. 184p. (C). 1993. pap. 28.40 (*0-536-58389-7*) Pearson Custom.
Murphy, Kathleen, jt. ed. see Alward, Edgar C.
Murphy, Kathleen, jt. ed. see Stygall, Gail.
Murphy, Kathleen A. Pediatric Triage Guidelines. (Illus.). 352p. (C). (gr. 13). 1996. text 35.95 (*0-8151-7333-4*, 27931) Mosby Inc.
Murphy, Kay. Belief Blues. 102p. 1998. pap. 15.00 (*0-916620-88-3*) Portals Pr.
***Murphy, Ken.** Russian Harvest. Turrentine, Jan, ed. 200p. 1999. pap. 10.99 (*1-56309-694-3*) Womans Mission Union.
Murphy, Kenneth. Conceived in Liberty: The Rise & Transformation of Modern Conservatism. 350p. 1994. text 22.95 (*0-02-922317-2*) Free Pr.
— Retreat from the Finland Station: Moral Odysseys in the Breakdown of Communism. 288p. 1992. text 29.95 (*0-02-922315-6*) Free Pr.
Murphy, Kent R. & Pelton, Jeffrey J. ECG Essentials: A Pocket Reference for Systematic Interpretation. (Illus.). 176p. 1991. pap. text 26.00 (*0-86715-222-2*) Quint Pub Co.
Murphy, Kerry, jt. auth. see Consolo-Murphy, Sue.
Murphy, Kevin. Training Your Parrot. (Illus.). 256p. 1983. 23.95 (*0-87666-872-4*, H-1056) TFH Pubns.
Murphy, Kevin & LeVert, Suzanne. Out of the Fog: Treatment Options & Coping Strategies for Adult Attention Deficit Disorder. 320p. (J). 1995. pap. 13.45 (*0-7868-8087-2*, Pub. by Hyperion) Time Warner.
***Murphy, Kevin A.** Dark Tyrants. Achilli, Justin & Hatch, Robert, eds. (Vampire Ser.). 1999. pap. 5.99 (*1-56504-888-1*, 11867, Wrld of Darkness) White Wolf.
Murphy, Kevin C., ed. The Civil War Letters of Joseph K. Taylor of the Thirty-Seventh Massachusetts Volunteer Infantry. LC 98-5740. (Studies in American History: Vol. 20). (Illus.). 248p. 1998. text 89.95 (*0-7734-8449-3*) E Mellen.
Murphy, Kevin D. & Giffen, Sarah L., eds. A Noble & Dignified Stream: The Piscataqua River Region in the Colonial Revival, 1860-1930. 272p. 1992. 50.00 (*0-9631955-0-6*) Old York Hist Soc.
Murphy, Kevin D., et al. Memory & Modernity: Viollet-Le-Duc at Vezelay. LC 98-41262. (Illus.). 596p. 1920. 45.00 (*0-271-01850-X*) Pa St U Pr.
Murphy, Kevin E. Concepts in Federal Taxation: 1995 Edition. LC 93-47062. 766p. 1994. text 63.00 (*0-314-03653-9*) West Pub.
— Concepts in Federal Taxation: 2000 Edition. 7th ed. 1002p. 1999. pap. 77.95 (*0-324-00930-5*) Thomson Learn.
Murphy, Kevin E. & Higgins, Mark. Concepts in Federal Taxation, 1. 6th ed. Crosser, Rick L., ed. 1998. pap. 83.95 (*0-538-88209-3*) Thomson Learn.
Murphy, Kevin George. Emergence. 116p. mass mkt. 4.99 (*1-55197-300-6*) Picasso Publ.
Murphy, Kevin J., jt. auth. see Dickinson, Gordon.
Murphy, Kevin J., ed. see Hallock, Kevin F.
Murphy, Kevin R. Individual Differences & Behavior in Organizations. (Business & Management Ser.). 640p. 1996. 47.95 (*0-7879-0174-1*) Jossey-Bass.
Murphy, Kevin R. & Cleveland, Jeanette. Understanding Performance Appraisal: Social, Organizational, & Goal-Based Perspectives. 500p. 1995. text 58.00 (*0-8039-5474-3*); pap. text 27.95 (*0-8039-5475-1*) Sage.
Murphy, Kevin R. & Davidshofer, Charles O. Psychological Testing: Principles & Applications. 4th ed. LC 97-9966. 602p. 1997. 77.00 (*0-13-263815-0*) P-H.
Murphy, Kevin R. & Myors, Brett. Statistical Power Analysis: A Simple & General Model for Traditional & Modern Hypothesis Tests. LC 97-43919. 200p. 1998. write for info. (*0-8058-2946-6*); pap. write for info. (*0-8058-2947-4*) L Erlbaum Assocs.
Murphy, Kevin R. & Saal, Frank E., eds. Psychology in Organizations: Integrating Science & Practice. 304p. (C). 1990. text 75.00 (*0-8058-0477-3*) L Erlbaum Assocs.
Murphy, Kevin R., jt. auth. see Barkley, Russell A.
Murphy, Kim, ed. see Urroz, Greg & Urroz, Louise.
***Murphy, Klarryse L.** Montana Small Business Start-Up Kit. large type ed. 79p. 1999. 34.95 (*0-9635844-2-1*, Pub. by Lilly & Blair) Sapphire Enter.
Murphy, L. A. Heavensbee. LC 96-75796. (Illus.). 32p. (J). (ps-3). 1996. 15.95 (*0-9641285-4-3*); pap. 6.95 (*0-9641285-7-8*) Little Frnd.
Murphy, L. M., ed. Solar Engineering, 1983. 632p. 1983. pap. text 25.00 (*0-317-02649-6*, H00253) ASME.
Murphy, L. S., et al, eds. Moving up the Yield Curve: Advances & Obstacles. (ASA Special Publications: No. 39). (Illus.). 103p. 1980. pap. 3.85 (*0-89118-064-8*) Am Soc Agron.
Murphy, Lamar R. Enter the Physician: The Transformation of Domestic Medicine, 1760-1860. LC 90-10887. (History of American Science & Technology Ser.). 336p. 1991. text 39.95 (*0-8173-0514-9*) U of Ala Pr.
Murphy, Larry G. Down by the Riverside: Readings in African American Religion. 510p. 1999. pap. text 24.50 (*0-8147-5581-X*) NYU Pr.
***Murphy, Larry G.** Down by the Riverside: Readings in African American Religion. 510p. 1999. text 65.00 (*0-8147-5580-1*) NYU Pr.
Murphy, Larry G., et al, eds. Encyclopedia of African-American Religions. LC 93-7224. (Religious Information Systems Ser.: Vol. 9). 1008p. 1993. text 65.00 (*0-8153-0500-1*, SS721) Garland.
Murphy, Laura, jt. auth. see Murphy, Michael.
Murphy-Lawless, Jo. Reading Birth & Death: A History of Obstetric Thinking. 288p. 1998. 65.00 (*1-85918-176-7*, Pub. by Cork Univ); pap. 20.00 (*1-85918-177-5*, Pub. by Cork Univ) Intl Spec Bk.
— Reading Birth & Death: A History of Obstetric Thinking. LC 99-185712. 352p. 1998. pap. 19.95 (*0-253-21258-8*) Ind U Pr.
— Reading Birth & Death: A History of Obstetric Thinking. LC 99-185712. 352p. 1999. text 39.95 (*0-253-33475-6*) Ind U Pr.
Murphy, Lawrence R. The American University in Cairo, 1919-1986. (Illus.). 256p. 1987. 50.00 (*977-424-156-8*, Pub. by Am Univ Cairo Pr) Col U Pr.
— Philmont: A History of New Mexico's Cimarron Country. 2nd ed. LC 72-76828. (Illus.). 315p. 1976. reprint ed. pap. 97.70 (*0-608-04133-5*, 206486600011) Bks Demand.
Murphy, Lawrence R., ed. Perverts by Official Order: The Campaign Against Homosexuals by the United States Navy. LC 90-4451. (Journal of Homosexuality: No. 1). (Illus.). 340p. 1988. text 49.95 (*0-86656-708-9*) Haworth Pr.
Murphy, Lawrence R., ed. Perverts by Official Order: The Campaign Against Homosexuals by the United States Navy. LC 87-33452. (Journal of Homosexuality Ser.: No. 1). (Illus.). 340p. 1988. pap. text 14.95 (*0-918393-44-2*, Harrington Park) Haworth Pr.
Murphy, Lawrence R., et al, eds. Job Stress Interventions. LC 95-37647. 439p. 1995. pap. text 24.95 (*1-55798-281-3*, 431-8410) Am Psychol.
Murphy, Lawrence R. & Cooper, Cary L. Healthy & Productive Work: An International Perspective. LC 99-55591. 250p. 1999. 54.95 (*0-7484-0839-8*) Taylor & Francis.
Murphy, Lawrence R. & Schoenborn, Theodore F., eds. Stress Management in Work Settings. LC 88-32439. 183p. 1989. 57.95 (*0-275-93271-0*, C3271, Praeger Pubs) Greenwood.
Murphy, Lawrence R., jt. ed. see Rocco, Thomas M.
Murphy, Lawrence R., jt. ed. see Sauter, Steven L.
Murphy, Lawrence R., jt. ed. see Tyler, Ron C.
***Murphy, Lee.** Where Legends Roam. Malkoskie, Mariana, ed. LC 99-75269. (Kodiak Bks.). 288p. 2000. pap. 11.95 (*0-9667704-4-7*) Defining Moments.
Murphy, Leona S. Using the Power of Prayer. 143p. (Orig.). 1987. pap. 5.95 (*0-937580-06-6*) Sumrall Pubng.
Murphy, Leonard J. The History of Urology. (Illus.). 548p. 1972. 91.95 (*0-398-02366-2*) C C Thomas.
Murphy, Lester F. Indiana Medical Malpractice. LC 87-82668. 1991. 115.00 (*0-318-33008-3*) West Group.
— Indiana Medical Malpractice, Suppl. 1992. LC 87-82668. 1991. 55.00 (*0-318-33009-1*) West Group.
***Murphy, Liam B.** Moral Demands in Nonideal Theory. (Oxford Ethics Ser.). 192p. 2000. text 35.00 (*0-19-507976-0*) OUP.
Murphy, Liam D., jt. auth. see Erickson, Paul A.
Murphy, Linda, et al. Basic Math: Concepts & Skills. 1997. teacher ed. 30.02 (*0-256-25742-6*, Irwn McGrw-H) McGrw-H Hghr Educ.
Murphy, Linda J. & Nickerson, Nancy K. Basic College Math. LC 96-17893. 160p. (C). 1996. text 18.90 (*0-256-22015-8*, Irwn McGrw-H) McGrw-H Hghr Educ.
Murphy, Linda L., et al, eds. Tests in Print, 2 vols., No. IV. 1473p. (C). 1994. text 325.00 (*0-910674-53-1*) Buros Inst Mental.
Murphy, Linda L. & Impara, James C., eds. Buros Desk Reference: Assessment of Substance Abuse. (Buros Institute of Mental Measurements Ser.). 350p. 1996. pap. 39.95 (*0-910674-42-6*) Buros Inst Mental.
Murphy, Linda L., jt. ed. see Impara, James C.
Murphy, Linnea S. Mrs. Murphy's Swedish Cook Book. (Illus.). 156p. 1987. 12.98 (*0-9618520-0-3*) J & L Pub.
Murphy, Lisa H. 125 Promotions for Your Restaurant & Bar: Complete Reference Including Guides. LC 93-85256. 182p. 1994. wbk. ed. 20.00 (*1-881908-10-0*) PanPress.
Murphy, Lois. Story Clay. (Illus.). 8p. (J). (gr. 1-8). 1990. pap. write for info. (*0-9672672-0-2*) Dragon Studio.
Murphy, Lois B. On Coping & Change. 17p. (Orig.). pap. 2.50 (*0-918374-19-7*) City Coll Wk.
Murphy, Lois B. & Moriarty, Alice E. Vulnerability, Coping, & Growth: From Infancy to Adolescence. LC 75-2772. 484p. reprint ed. pap. 150.10 (*0-7837-5303-9*, 208031600005) Bks Demand.
Murphy, Lorraine M. The Prize. 192p. (J). (gr. 8). 1993. pap. text 7.95 (*1-883511-02-X*) Veritas Pr CA.
Murphy, Louise S. The Marriage Triangle: Man, Woman & God. 66p. (Orig.). 1984. pap. text 1.95 (*0-937580-40-6*) Sumrall Pubng.
— A Teenager Who Dared Obey God. 97p. (Orig.). (YA). 1985. pap. text 3.95 (*0-937580-44-9*) Sumrall Pubng.
Murphy, Lucy E. & Venet, Wendy H., eds. Midwestern Women: Work, Community, & Leadership at the Crossroads. LC 97-4073. 1997. 39.95 (*0-253-33307-5*); pap. 19.95 (*0-253-21133-6*) Ind U Pr.
***Murphy, Lucy Eldersveld.** A Gathering of Rivers: Indians, Metis & Mining in the Western Great Lakes, 1737-1832. LC 00-27200. (Illus.). 288p. 2000. text 47.50 (*0-8032-3210-1*) U of Nebr Pr.
Murphy, M. Father of the Submarine. (C). 1986. text 140.00 (*0-7855-5303-7*, Pub. by Maritime Bks) St Mut.
Murphy, M., jt. auth. see Harrison, T.
Murphy, M., jt. auth. see Schmid, Michael.
Murphy, M. Gertrude. St. Basil & Monasticism. LC 70-144661. reprint ed. 29.50 (*0-404-04543-X*) AMS Pr.
Murphy, M. J., Jr. & Kuter, D. J. Thrombopoietin: From Molecule to Medicine, Vol. 16, Supplement 2. 259p. 1998. 69.00 (*1-880854-26-0*); pap. 49.00 (*1-880854-24-4*) AlphaMed Pr.
Murphy, Mabel A. When America Was Young. LC 72-38326. (Biography Index Reprint Ser.). (Illus.). 1977. reprint ed. 22.95 (*0-8369-8126-X*) Ayer.
Murphy, Madeline W. Madeline Murphy Speaks. LC 88-63313. (Illus.). 388p. (Orig.). 1988. pap. 15.95 (*0-935132-12-0*) C H Fairfax.
Murphy, Madonna M. Character Education in America's Blue Ribbon Schools: Best Practices for Meeting the Challenge. LC 97-62359. 256p. 1998. pap. text 44.95 (*1-56676-593-5*) Scarecrow.
Murphy Manning, Maryann & Manning, Gary L. Improving Spelling in the Middle Grades. 2nd ed. 48p. 1986. pap. 7.95 (*0-8106-1695-5*) NEA.
***Murphy, Marcia.** The Twins & the Birthday Party. (Illus.). 16p. (J). (ps). 1999. pap. 5.95 (*1-891846-06-X*) Busn Word.
Murphy, Marcy. The Managerial Competencies of Twelve Corporate Librarians: A Validation Study of New Directions in Library & Information Science Education. LC 88-138233. (SLA Research Ser.: No. 2). 43p. reprint ed. pap. 30.00 (*0-7837-6300-X*, 204601500010) Bks Demand.
Murphy, Marcy & Johns, Claude J. Handbook of Library Regulations. LC 76-19994. (Books in Library & Information Science: No. 20). 176p. reprint ed. pap. 54.60 (*0-608-15916-6*, 203086700071) Bks Demand.
Murphy, Marcy, jt. auth. see Jobin, Pamela.
***Murphy, Margaret.** Caging the Tiger. LC 99-11723. 1999. 21.95 (*0-7862-1869-X*) Thorndike Pr.
Murphy, Margaret. The Desire of the Moth. large type ed. 464p. 1998. 29.99 (*0-7089-4017-X*) Ulverscroft.
Murphy, Margaret, ed. see Session, Irie L.
Murphy, Margaret A., jt. ed. see Eisenhauer, Laurel A.
Murphy, Margaret D. The Boston Globe Cookbook: A Collection of Classic New England Recipes. 4th ed. Richardson, Helen W., ed. LC 95-34390. (Illus.). 384p. 1996. pap. 16.95 (*1-56440-736-5*) Globe Pequot.
Murphy, Marge. Monsters. 11p. (J). (gr. 1). 1989. pap. text 2.50 (*1-882225-07-4*) Tott Pubns.
— Work. 9p. (J). (gr. 1). 1988. pap. text 2.50 (*1-882225-08-2*) Tott Pubns.
***Murphy, Margie.** Huachuca Winds. 88p. 1999. pap. write for info. (*0-7392-0438-6*, PO3726) Morris Pubng.
Murphy, Margueritte S. A Tradition of Subversion: The Prose Poem in English from Wilde to Ashbery. LC 91-40282. 264p. (C). 1992. lib. bdg. 32.50 (*0-87023-781-0*) U of Mass Pr.
Murphy, Mariam B., jt. auth. see Powell, Kent.
***Murphy, Marianne & Vickery, Graham.** Strategic Business Services. 240p. 1999. pap. 48.00 (*92-64-17123-1*, 70 1999 04 1 P, Pub. by Org for Econ) OECD.
Murphy, Marie. Authorizing Fictions: Jose Donoso's "Casa de Campo" (Monografias A Ser.: No. A 152). 123p. (C). 1992. 54.00 (*1-85566-020-2*, Pub. by Tamesis Bks Ltd) Boydell & Brewer.
Murphy, Marie A., jt. auth. see Schechter, Leslie F.
Murphy, Marjorie. Blackboard Unions: The AFT & the NEA, 1900-1980. LC 89-46175. (Illus.). 304p. 1991. text 39.95 (*0-8014-2365-1*) Cornell U Pr.
Murphy, Mark. House of Java. (Illus.). 80p. (YA). 1998. pap. 8.95 (*1-56163-202-3*, Comics Lit) NBM.
Murphy, Mark C., jt. auth. see Solomon, Robert C.
Murphy, Marsha A. Secrets of Making A's the Easy Speedlearning Way. LC 92-75555. (Illus.). 300p. 1995. pap. 19.95 (*0-9635508-2-9*) DataQuest VA.
— Secrets of Making A's the Easy SpeedLearning Way: The Learning Kit, Set. LC 92-75555. (Illus.). 300p. (Orig.). 1995. pap. 39.95 incl. audio (*0-9635508-0-2*) DataQuest VA.
Murphy, Martha W. The Bed & Breakfast Cookbook: Great American B & Bs & Their Recipes from All 50 States. LC 91-9701. (Illus.). 288p. 1997. reprint ed. 35.00 (*0-88045-046-0*); reprint ed. pap. 19.95 (*0-88045-047-9*) Stemmer Hse.
— Don Bousquet's Rhode Island Cookbook. (Illus.). 160p. 1998. pap. 14.95 (*1-58066-016-9*, Covered Brdge Pr) Douglas Charles Ltd.
— How to Start & Operate Your Own Bed-&-Breakfast: Down-to-Earth Advice from an Award-Winning B&B Owner. LC 93-37836. (Illus.). 1995. pap. write for info. (*0-8050-2903-6*) H Holt & Co.
— A New England Fish Table: Seafood Recipes & Observations of a Way of Life from a Fisherman's Wife. LC 96-44778. 1995. write for info. (*0-8050-4204-0*) H Holt & Co.
— New England Fish Tales. 1996. pap. 15.95 (*0-8050-4205-9*) St Martin.
Murphy, Martin F. Dominican Sugar Plantations: Production & Foreign Labor Integration. LC 90-44147. 200p. 1991. 62.95 (*0-275-93113-7*, C3113, Praeger Pubs) Greenwood.
Murphy, Martin F. & Margolis, Maxine L., eds. Science, Materialism, & the Study of Culture. (Illus.). 256p. (Orig.). (C). 1995. 49.95 (*0-8130-1413-1*) U Press Fla.
— Science, Materialism, & the Study of Culture. (Illus.). 256p. (Orig.). (C). 1996. pap. 22.95 (*0-8130-1414-X*) U Press Fla.
Murphy, Martin F., jt. ed. see Margolis, Maxine L.
Murphy, Martin F., ed. see Watkins, Daniel P.
Murphy, Martin J., Jr., ed. Blood Cell Growth Factors: Their Present & Future Use in Hematology & Oncology. 225p. (C). 1991. pap. text 89.00 (*1-880854-00-7*) AlphaMed Pr.
— Concise Reviews in Clinical & Experimental Hematology. LC 92-17634. 385p. 1992. 69.00 (*1-880854-01-5*) AlphaMed Pr.
— Polyfunctionality of Hemopoietic Regulators Suppl. 1: The Metcalf Forum, Vol. 12. LC 94-73349. (Illus.). 326p. (C). 1994. text 69.00 (*1-880854-19-8*) AlphaMed Pr.
— Polyfunctionality of Hemopoietic Regulators Suppl. 2: The Metcalf Forum, Vol. 12. LC 94-73349. (Illus.). 326p. (C). 1994. pap. text 49.00 (*1-880854-20-1*) AlphaMed Pr.
Murphy-Martin, Mary. Planning Your Cosmetology Career. LC 93-28878. 108p. (C). 1993. pap. text 13.00 (*0-13-605999-6*) P-H.
***Murphy, Mary.** Caterpillar's Wish. LC 98-28835. (Toddlers Storybook Ser.). (Illus.). 24p. (J). (ps). 2000. pap. text 5.95 (*0-7894-5745-8*, D K Ink) DK Pub Inc.
Murphy, Mary. Empowered for Worship. (C). 1988. 39.00 (*0-85439-123-1*, Pub. by St Paul Pubns) St Mut.
— Here Comes Spring: And Summer & Fall & Winter. LC 98-39001. (Illus.). (J). (ps-k). 1999. 9.95 (*0-7894-3484-9*, D K Ink) DK Pub Inc.
***Murphy, Mary.** Here Comes the Rain. LC 00-20433. (Toddlers Storybook Ser.). (Illus.). (J). (ps-k). 2000. 5.95 (*0-7894-6368-7*) DK Pub Inc.
— I Am an Artist. (Illus.). (J). 2000. 4.95 (*0-618-03401-3*) HM.
— I Feel Happy & Sad & Angry & Glad. LC 99-88536. (Illus.). 32p. (J). (ps-k). 2000. 9.95 (*0-7894-2680-3*, D K Ink) DK Pub Inc.
Murphy, Mary. I Like it When... LC 96-24832. (Illus.). 32p. (J). 1997. 10.95 (*0-15-200039-9*) Harcourt.
***Murphy, Mary.** I Make a Cake. (Illus.). (J). 2000. 4.95 (*0-618-00339-8*) HM.
— If... (Illus.). (J). 2000. 4.95 (*0-618-03399-8*) HM.
— My Puffer Train. LC 98-47803. (Illus.). 32p. (J). 1999. 9.95 (*0-395-97105-5*) HM.
— Please Be Quiet! LC 98-47802. (Illus.). 32p. (J). 1999. 9.95 (*0-395-97113-6*) HM.
Murphy, Mary. Recreating Butte: Men, Women, & Leisure in a Western Mining City, 1914-41. LC 96-9990. (Women in American History Ser.). (Illus.). 320p. 1996. text 39.95 (*0-252-02267-X*); pap. text 18.95 (*0-252-06569-7*) U of Ill Pr.
— Roxie & Bo Together. LC 98-87389. (Illus.). 24p. (J). (ps). 1999. text 12.99 (*0-7636-0870-X*) Candlewick Pr.
***Murphy, Mary.** Some Things Change. LC 00-31946. (Illus.). (J). 2001. write for info. (*0-618-00334-7*) HM.

M

— You Choose. (J). 2000. 4.95 (*0-618-00336-3*) HM.

Murphy, Mary. You Smell . . . & Taste, & Feel, & See, & Hear. LC 97-222210. (Illus.). 32p. (J). (ps-k). 1997. 9.95 (*0-7894-2471-1*) DK Pub Inc.

Murphy, Mary E. Virgin. 352p. (Orig.). 1996. mass mkt. 6.50 (*0-425-15124-7*) Berkley Pub.

Murphy, Mary K., ed. The Advancement President & the Academy: Profiles in Institutional Leadership. LC 97-24098. (Ace/Oryx Series on Higher Education). 216p. (C). 1997. boxed set 34.95 (*1-57356-028-6*) Oryx Pr.

— Building Bridges: Fund Raising for Deans, Faculty, & Development Officers. 131p. 1992. pap. 41.50 (*0-89964-291-8*, 29602) Coun Adv & Supp Ed.

— Cultivating Foundation Support for Education. 210p. 1989. 41.50 (*0-89964-263-2*, 29801) Coun Adv & Supp Ed.

Murphy, Mary-Kate & Knoll, Jean. International Adoption: Sensitive Advice for Prospective Parents. LC 93-41422. 208p. (Orig.). 1994. pap. 12.95 (*1-55652-211-8*) Chicago Review.

Murphy, Mary L. Barnaby: The Struggle of a Word Blind Child. 74p. 1968. pap. 1.95 (*0-85225-535-7*) Ed Solutions.

— Creative Writing: A Log-Book of Teaching 1st Graders. (Illus.). 104p. 1966. 6.35 (*0-87825-254-1*) Ed Solutions.

— Douglas Can't Read. 52p. 1968. pap. 1.95 (*0-85225-531-4*) Ed Solutions.

— To Perceive & to Write. 144p. 1970. pap. 4.35 (*0-85225-536-5*) Ed Solutions.

Murphy, Matthew F. Betraying the Bishops: How the Pastoral Letter on War & Peace Is Being Taught. LC 87-32932. 146p. (C). 1988. pap. text 14.25 (*0-89633-122-9*); lib. bdg. 33.50 (*0-89633-121-0*) Ethics & Public Policy.

Murphy, Maud K., tr. see Warcollier, Rene.

Murphy, Maureen, ed. I Call to the Eye of the Mind: A Memoir by Sara Hyland. 208p. 1997. pap. 26.99 (*1-85594-148-1*, Pub. by Attic Press) Intl Spec Bk.

Murphy, Maureen, ed. see Nicholson.

Murphy, Maureen, ed. see Nicholson, Asenoth.

Murphy, Maureen O. & MacKillop, James, eds. Irish Literature: A Reader. (Irish Studies). 288p. (Orig.). 1987. pap. text 24.95 (*0-8156-2405-0*) Syracuse U Pr.

Murphy, Maureen O., jt. ed. see Ben-Merre, Diana A.

Murphy, Maureen O., jt. ed. see Naylor, Natalie A.

Murphy, May. For the Good of Others. 16.95 (*0-318-03970-2*); pap. 10.95 (*0-318-03971-0*) U Wisc-River Falls Pr.

Murphy, Mel M. The Marriage Mile & Marathon. LC 96-71985. 100p. 1996. pap. text 7.95 (*1-57636-031-8*) SunRise Pbl.

Murphy-Melas, Elizabeth. Watching Bradley Grow: A Story about Premature Birth. LC 95-62127. (Illus.). (J). (ps-3). 1995. pap. 8.95 (*1-56352-282-9*) Longstreet.

Murphy-Melas, Elizabeth, et al. Pennies, Nickels & Dimes. LC 99-18135. (Illus.). 24p. (J). (gr. k-6). 1999. pap. write for info. (*0-929173-32-5*) Health Press.

Murphy Melby, Barbara, jt. auth. see Halvey, John K.

Murphy, Melvin. Barber Shop Talk: The Other Side of Black Men. Hansgen, K. C. & Bailey, Walter, III, eds. LC 96-94702. 228p. 1998. 24.95 (*0-9646799-1-4*) M Murphy.

Murphy, Melvin E. Desire: The Emotional Appetite for Success. Williams, A. et al, eds. LC 95-94334. (Illus.). 136p. 1995. 12.95 (*0-9646799-0-6*) M Murphy.

Murphy, Merilene M. A Book of Cards, 4 vols., Set. (Illus.). (Orig.). 1995. pap. text 19.95 (*0-9644606-5-3*) Telepoetics.

— A Book of Cards, Vol. 2. (Illus.). (Orig.). 1995. pap. text 7.50 (*0-9644606-7-X*) Telepoetics.

— A Book of Cards, Vol. 3. (Illus.). (Orig.). 1995. pap. text 7.50 (*0-9644606-8-8*) Telepoetics.

— A Book of Cards Vol. 1. (Illus.). (Orig.). 1995. pap. text 7.50 (*0-9644606-6-1*) Telepoetics.

— Just People - Just People: Here You Are: A Multimedia Poetic Odyssey. (FRE & SPA., Illus.). 64p. (Orig.). (C). 1995. 19.95 (*0-9644606-1-0*); pap. 9.95 (*0-9644606-2-9*); VHS 19.95 (*0-9644606-4-5*); cd-rom 15.95 (*0-9644606-3-7*) Telepoetics.

— Under Peace Rising. (Series 1A). (Illus.). 64p. 1996. pap. 15.00 (*0-934172-38-2*) WIM Pubns.

Murphy, Merilene M. & Moreta, Andes. A Book of Cards. (Illus.). (Orig.). 1995. pap. text 7.50 (*0-9644606-9-6*) Telepoetics.

Murphy, Michael. The Appalachian Dulcimer Book. LC 75-35427. (Illus.). 110p. 1976. pap. 8.95 (*0-916454-01-0*) Folksay Pr.

— The Appalachian Dulcimer Book. (Illus.). 102p. 1987. pap. 15.95 (*0-8256-2677-3*, AM41278) Music Sales.

***Murphy, Michael.** Every Investor's Guide to High-Tech Stocks & Mutual Funds: Proven Strategies for Picking High-Growth Winners. 3rd ed. LC 99-42585. 320p. 2000. 27.50 (*0-7679-0456-7*) Broadway BDD.

Murphy, Michael. The Future of the Body: Explorations into the Further Evolution of Human Nature. 800p. 1993. pap. 22.95 (*0-87477-730-5*, Tarcher Putnam) Putnam Pub Group.

— Golf in the Kingdom. 202p. 1993. 15.95 (*0-914178-95-4*) Golf Digest.

— Golf in the Kingdom. LC 91-32443. 223p. 1997. pap. 13.95 (*0-14-019549-1*) Penguin Putnam.

— The Kingdom of Shivas Irons. limited ed. (Illus.). 336p. 1997. 250.00 (*0-7679-0017-0*) Broadway BDD.

— The Kingdom of Shivas Irons. (Illus.). 336p. 1998. reprint ed. pap. 14.00 (*0-7679-0019-7*) Broadway BDD.

— My Brother Sam Is Dead - Study Guide. Friedland, Joyce & Kessler, Rikki, eds. (Novel-Ties Ser.). (J). (gr. 6-8). 1993. pap. text 15.95 (*0-88122-119-8*) Lrn Links.

— Popsicle Fish: Tales of Fathering. LC 96-22929. (Illus.). 180p. (Orig.). 1996. pap. 13.95 (*0-929173-23-6*) Health Press.

Murphy, Michael. Small Business Management. 304p. 1996. pap. 43.50 (*0-273-61601-3*) F T P-H.

Murphy, Michael. Working Together in Child Protection: An Exploration of the Multi-Disciplinary Task & System. 224p. 1995. 64.95 (*1-85742-197-3*, Pub. by Arena); pap. 29.95 (*1-85742-198-1*, Pub. by Arena) Ashgate Pub Co.

Murphy, Michael & Donovan, Steven. The Physical & Psychological Effects of Meditation: A Review of Contemporary Meditation Research with a Comprehensive Bibliography, 1931-1988. 187p. (Orig.). (C). 1988. pap. 17.95 (*0-9621232-0-X*) Esalen Inst.

Murphy, Michael & Glynn, John. Finance for Managers. 416p. 2000. pap. 19.99 (*1-86152-085-9*) Thomson Learn.

***Murphy, Michael & Murphy, Laura.** The Natural Waterways of Ireland: A Traveler's Guide to Rental Boating. (Illus.). 2000. pap. 15.00 (*1-56656-381-X*) Interlink Pub.

— Vacation Rentals in Europe: A Guide. 2000. pap. 15.95 (*1-56656-358-5*) Interlink Pub.

Murphy, Michael & Murphy, Laura. The Waterways of Great Britain & Ireland: A Traveller's Guide to Rental Boating. LC 99-39155. 272p. 2000. pap. 15.00 (*1-56656-346-1*) Interlink Pub.

Murphy, Michael & Owen, Michael. CUES Guide to Interpreting the Family & Medical Leave Act of 1993: Answers to Credit Union Specific Questions & an Aid to Policy Development. 63p. (Orig.). 1993. pap. 39.00 (*1-889394-19-X*) Credit Union Execs.

Murphy, Michael & White, Rhea. Psychic Side of Sports. (Illus.). 1978. 10.95 (*0-201-04728-4*) Addison-Wesley.

Murphy, Michael & White, Rhea A. Transcendent Experience in Sports. LC 94-44134. 288p. 1995. pap. 11.95 (*0-14-019492-4*, Arkana) Viking Penguin.

Murphy, Michael, et al. The Physical & Psychological Effects of Meditation: A Review of Contemporary Research with a Comprehensive Bibliography 1931-1996. 2nd ed. LC 96-46701. 1996. write for info. (*0-943951-36-4*) Inst Noetic Sci.

Murphy, Michael, jt. auth. see Leonard, George.

Murphy, Michael, ed. see Chaucer, Geoffrey.

Murphy, Michael, jt. ed. see White, Harry.

Murphy, Michael A. & Matti, Jonathan C. Lower Devonian Conodonts (Hesperius-Kindlei Zones), Central Nevada. LC 82-8638. (University of California Publications in Social Welfare: No. 123). (Illus.). 97p. reprint ed. pap. 30.10 (*0-8357-6863-5*, 203556100095) Bks Demand.

Murphy, Michael A. & Parker, Xenia L. Handbook of EDP Auditing, No. 3314. rev. ed. 1328p. 1989. boxed set 160.00 (*0-7913-0411-6*) Warren Gorham & Lamont.

Murphy, Michael F. The Child Protection Unit: Its History, Function & Effectiveness in the Organization of Child Protection Work. 192p. 1996. text 63.95 (*1-85972-139-7*, Pub. by Avebry) Ashgate Pub Co.

***Murphy, Michael F. & Pamphilon, Derwood H.** Practical Transfusion Medicine. (Illus.). 328p. 2000. 110.00 (*0-632-05114-0*) Blackwell Sci.

Murphy, Michael F., et al. Alzheimer's Disease: Optimizing the Development of the Next Generation of Therapeutic Compounds. (Greenwich Medical Media Ser.). (Illus.). 208p. 1999. text 98.50 (*1-84110-006-4*) OUP.

Murphy, Michael J. Cambridge Newspapers & Opinion, 1780-1850. (Cambridge Town, Gown & County Ser.: Vol. 12). (Illus.). 1977. 21.95 (*0-900891-15-7*) Oleander Pr.

— Field Guide to Common Animal Poisons. LC 96-15732. 472p. 1996. pap. text 34.95 (*0-8138-2934-8*) Iowa St U Pr.

— The Mountain Biking Guide to Vail, Colorado. Giuiland, Mary E., ed. & illus. by. Peterson, Dannette, illus. 72p. (Orig.). 1990. pap. text 8.95 (*0-9626114-0-9*) M Murphy & Assocs.

— Mountain Year. 73p. 1987. pap. 5.95 (*0-685-25951-X*, Pub. by Blackstaff Pr) Dufour.

— Mountain Year. 73p. 1987. pap. 8.95 (*0-85640-382-2*, Pub. by Blackstaff Pr) Dufour.

— Mountain Year: Life on the Slopes of Slieve Gullion. LC 64-25512. 1964. 12.95 (*0-8023-1079-6*) Dufour.

— Poverty in Cambridgeshire. (Cambridge Town, Gown & County Ser.: Vol. 23). (Illus.). 1978. pap. 5.95 (*0-900891-29-7*) Oleander Pr.

Murphy, Michael P. & O'Neil, Luke A., eds. What Is Life? The Next Fifty Years: Speculations on the Future of Biology. 203p. (C). 1995. text 49.95 (*0-521-45509-X*) Cambridge U Pr.

Murphy, Michael P. & O'Neill, Luke A., eds. What Is Life? The Next Fifty Years: Speculations on the Future of Biology. 203p. 1997. pap. 15.95 (*0-521-59939-3*) Cambridge U Pr.

Murphy, Michael R., jt. auth. see Veit, E. Theodore.

Murphy, Michelle. Jackknife & Light. 95p. 1998. pap. 10.00 (*1-880713-11-X*) AVEC Bks.

Murphy, Mike, jt. ed. see Charlton, John.

Murphy-Milano, Susan. Defending Our Lives: Getting Away from Domestic Violence & Staying Safe. LC 96-16417. 256p. 1996. pap. 14.95 (*0-385-48441-0*, Anchor NY) Doubleday.

Murphy, Mildred. Guthrie. Henry Guthrie & John Lane Mason, Their Ancestors, Descendants & Collateral Kin. (Illus.). 179p. 1997. reprint ed. pap. 28.00 (*0-8328-8876-1*); reprint ed. lib. bdg. 38.00 (*0-8328-8875-3*) Higginson Bk Co.

Murphy, Miles. Working Within the System Is Like Milking the Cow: When the Barn Is on Fire. (Illus.). 100p. 1999. pap. write for info. (*0-9669683-0-1*) Inter Drift.

Murphy, Milledge, ed. see Evseeff, David D.

Murphy, Miriam A., et al. A Law Library Move: Planning, Preparation & Execution. LC 97-176940. (Law Library Information Reports: Vol. 18). 1994. pap. 50.00 (*0-87802-097-7*) Glanville.

***Murphy, Miriam B.** A History of Wayne County. LC 98-61322. (Illus.). 1999. write for info. (*0-913738-45-X*) Utah St Hist Soc.

Murphy-Muth, Susan M. Medical Records: Management in a Changing Environment. (Health Care Administration Ser.). 224p. 1987. 65.00 (*0-87189-872-1*) Aspen Pub.

***Murphy, Myles P.** The Life & Times of Archbishop Fulton J. Sheen. LC 99-87648. 2000. pap. 14.95 (*0-8189-0842-4*) Alba.

Murphy, N. Michael. Wisdom of Dying: Practices for Living. LC 99-15432. 256p. 1999. 24.95 (*1-86204-579-8*, Pub. by Element MA) Penguin Putnam.

Murphy, Nancey. Reconciling Theology & Science: A Radical Reformation Perspective. LC 97-931048. 103p. 1997. pap. 14.50 (*0-9698762-4-6*, Pub. by Pandora) Routldge.

Murphy, Nancey, et al, eds. Virtues & Practices in the Christian Tradition: Christian Ethics after MacIntyre. LC 97-41500. 400p. (Orig.). 1997. pap. 25.00 (*1-56338-215-6*) TPI PA.

Murphy, Nancey C. Anglo-American Postmodernity: Philosophical Perspectives on Science, Religion & Ethics. LC 96-37711. 240p. (C). 1997. pap. text 25.00 (*0-8133-2869-1*, Pub. by Westview) HarpC.

— Beyond Liberalism & Fundamentalism: How Modern & Postmodern Philosophy Set the Theological Agenda. Kelber, Werner H., ed. LC 96-24736. (Rockwell Lecture Ser.). 180p. (Orig.). (C). 1996. 20.00 (*1-56338-176-1*) TPI PA.

— Reasoning & Rhetoric in Religion. LC 94-36455. 304p. (Orig.). (C). 1994. pap. 20.00 (*1-56338-098-6*) TPI PA.

— Reasoning & Rhetoric in Religion: Key to the Exercises. LC 94-36455. 24p. 1994. pap. 5.00 (*1-56338-099-4*) TPI PA.

— Theology in the Age of Scientific Reasoning. LC 89-39375. (Cornell Studies in the Philosophy of Religion). 232p. 1993. pap. text 13.95 (*0-8014-8114-7*) Cornell U Pr.

Murphy, Nancy. Earth Science Today. (Earth Science Ser.). 2000. pap. text, lab manual ed. 18.00 (*0-534-37546-4*) Brooks-Cole.

— Earth Science Today. 2nd ed. (Earth Science Ser.). 2000. text, student ed. 13.00 (*0-534-37545-6*) Brooks-Cole.

— Earth Science Today. 2nd ed. 2000. pap. 61.00 (*0-534-37540-5*) Brooks-Cole.

— Nenagh Castle: Chronology & Architecture. (Illus.). 8p. (Orig.). 1996. pap. 2.00 (*0-946327-10-6*, Pub. by Relay Pubns) Irish Bks Media.

— A Trip Through Tipperary Lakeside: From Nenagh to Ballina-Killaloe & from Nenagh to Portumna by the River Shannon's Lough Derg Scenic Routes. (Illus.). 96p. (Orig.). 1996. pap. 23.95 (*0-946327-21-1*, Pub. by Relay Pubns) Irish Bks Media.

— Walk about Nenagh. (Illus.). 139p. (Orig.). 1995. pap. 10.00 (*0-946327-12-2*, Pub. by Relay Pubns) Irish Bks Media.

Murphy, Nancy, jt. auth. see Ellis, George.

Murphy, Nancy, jt. auth. see Luchterhand, Charlene.

Murphy, Niall D. Front Panel: Designing Software for Embedded User Interfaces. 328p. 1998. pap. 49.95 incl. disk (*0-87930-528-2*) C M P Books.

Murphy, Nicola, jt. auth. see Boyarsky, Nicholas.

Murphy, Nicy. The Flip Side: Workin' for the Lord Ain't All That Dull. LC 89-60969. (Illus.). 128p. 1989. pap. 9.95 (*0-88100-062-0*) Natl Writ Pr.

Murphy, Nora. A Hmong Family. LC 96-13533. (J). 1997. lib. bdg. 22.60 (*0-8225-3406-1*, Lerner Publctns) Lerner Pub.

— A Hmong Family. (J). 1997. pap. text 8.95 (*0-8225-9756-X*) Lerner Pub.

— A Hmong Family. (Journey Between Two Worlds Ser.). (Illus.). (J). (gr. 3-6). 1997. pap. 8.95 (*0-614-28837-1*, First Ave Edns) Lerner Pub.

***Murphy, Nora & Murphy-Gnatz, Mary, contrib. by.** Meet African Americans in Minnesota. LC 99-54539. 88p. (J). 2000. 11.95 (*0-87351-380-0*, Borealis Book) Minn Hist.

Murphy, Nora, jt. auth. see Blackburn, Denise A.

Murphy, Norman. True & Faithful Account. (Illus.). 73p. 1995. 25.00 (*0-87008-074-1*) JAS Heineman.

Murphy, O. J., et al. Electrochemistry in Transition: From the 20th to the 21st Century. (Illus.). 702p. (C). 1992. text 140.00 (*0-306-43946-8*, Kluwer Plenum) Kluwer Academic.

Murphy-O'Connor, Jerome. Corinthians. 1989. pap. 24.00 (*0-86217-014-1*, Pub. by Veritas Pubns) St Mut.

— The Ecole Biblique & the New Testament: A Century of Scholarship (1890-1990) (Novum Testamentum et Orbis Antiquus Ser.: Vol. 13). 200p. 1990. text 41.50 (*3-7278-0682-6*, Pub. by Presses Univ Fribourg) Eisenbrauns.

— The Holy Land: An Oxford Archaeological Guide from Earliest Times to 1700. 4th ed. LC 97-11120. (Oxford Archaeological Guides Ser.). (Illus.). 514p. 1998. pap. 18.95 (*0-19-288013-6*) OUP.

— Paul: A Critical Life. LC 97-10250. (Illus.). 432p. 1998. reprint ed. pap. 19.95 (*0-19-285342-2*) OUP.

— St. Paul's Corinth: Texts & Archaeology. LC 83-80110. (Good News Studies: Vol. 6). 192p. 1983. pap. 14.95 (*0-8146-5303-0*) Liturgical Pr.

— The Theology of the Second Letter to the Corinthians. (New Testament Theology Ser.). 178p. (C). 1991. text 54.95 (*0-521-35379-3*); pap. text 16.95 (*0-521-35898-1*) Cambridge U Pr.

Murphy, Oliver F., tr. see Chekhov, Anton.

Murphy, Orville T. Charles Gravier, Comte de Vergennes: French Diplomacy in the Age of Revolution, 1719-1787. LC 81-2281. 607p. (C). 1983. text 74.50 (*0-87395-482-3*); pap. text 24.95 (*0-87395-483-1*) State U NY Pr.

— The Diplomatic Retreat of France & Public Opinion on the Eve of the French Revolution, 1783-1789. LC 96-53231. 1997. 59.95 (*0-8132-0892-0*) Cath U Pr.

Murphy, Owen, jt. auth. see Owen, Lyla H.

Murphy, P. & Murphy, K., eds. What Every Veteran Should Know, 1999: About Veteran's Benefits. 62nd rev. ed. 400p. 1999. 12.00 (*0-9670331-0-1*) Veterans Info.

Murphy, P. J. Reconstructing Beckett: Language & Being in Samuel Beckett's Fiction. 256p. 1990. text 40.00 (*0-8020-5868-X*) U of Toronto Pr.

***Murphy, P. J. & Murphy, Jennifer, eds.** Sentences & Paroles: A Prison Reader. 256p. 1998. pap. 18.00 (*0-921586-63-9*, Pub. by New Star Bks) Genl Dist Srvs.

Murphy, Pam. Winchester - Frederick County, Va. (Illus.). 150p. 1999. 36.95 (*1-890291-11-0*) Platinum Pubng.

Murphy, Pat. By Nature's Design: An Exploratorium Book. Dunham, Judith, ed. LC 92-41313. (Illus.). 120p. 1993. 29.95 (*0-8118-0444-5*); pap. 19.95 (*0-8118-0329-5*) Chronicle Bks.

— The Falling Woman. 288p. 1993. pap. 11.95 (*0-312-85406-4*) Orb NYC.

***Murphy, Pat.** Microsoft Office 98: Macintosh Basics. 2000. pap. 43.95 (*0-538-72431-5*) Thomson Learn.

Murphy, Pat. Nadya. (The Wolf Chronicles). 1996. mass mkt. 6.99 (*0-8125-5188-5*, Pub. by Tor Bks) St Martin.

— Nadya Wolf Chronicles. LC 96-22939. 384p. 1996. 23.95 (*0-312-86226-1*) St Martin.

***Murphy, Pat.** There & Back Again. LC 99-38395. 304p. 1999. 24.95 (*0-312-86644-5*, Pub. by Tor Bks) St Martin.

— There & Back Again. 2000. mass mkt. 6.99 (*0-8125-4172-3*) Tor Bks.

Murphy, Pat. Toss The Feathers: Irish Set Dancing. LC 96-233416. 222p. 1997. pap. 14.95 (*1-85635-115-7*, Pub. by Mercier Pr) Irish Amer Bk.

***Murphy, Pat.** The Wild Angel. 288p. 2000. 23.95 (*0-312-86626-7*, Pub. by Tor Bks) St Martin.

Murphy, Pat & Doherty, Paul. The Color of Nature. (Exploratorium Bks.). (Illus.). 144p. 1996. pap. 22.95 (*0-8118-1357-6*) Chronicle Bks.

Murphy, Pat & Forney, Jeff. Complete Conditioning for Baseball. LC 96-48333. (Illus.). 208p. (Orig.). 1997. pap. 15.95 (*0-87322-886-3*, PMUR0886) Human Kinetics.

Murphy, Pat, et al. The Science Explorer: The Best Family Activities & Experiments from the World's Farovite Hands-On. LC 96-16847. (Exploration-at-Home Bk.: No. 1). (Illus.). 144p. (YA). (gr. 8 up). 1995. pap. 12.95 (*0-8050-4536-8*) H Holt & Co.

— The Science Explorer Out & About: Fantastic Science Experiments Your Family Can Do Anywhere, No. 2. (Exploratorium Science-at-Home Ser.). 144p. 1995. pap. 12.95 (*0-8050-4537-6*) H Holt & Co.

***Murphy, Pat, et al.** Traces of Time: The Beauty of Change in Nature. LC 99-87677. 2000. pap. 19.95 (*0-8118-2857-3*) Chronicle Bks.

***Murphy, Patricia.** Everything You Need to Know about Staying in the Hospital. LC 00-9460. (Need to Know Library). 2000. lib. bdg. write for info. (*0-8239-3325-3*) Rosen Group.

Murphy, Patricia. Making the Connections: Women, Work, & Abuse. LC 92-75487. 280p. 1993. per. 41.95 (*1-878205-65-X*) St Lucie Pr.

— Microsoft Access for Windows 95. (Quicktorial Ser.). (Illus.). 240p. 1996. pap., mass mkt. 21.95 incl. disk (*0-538-71541-3*) S-W Pub.

— Microsoft Access for Windows 95: Quick Course. (Quicktorial Ser.). 1996. mass mkt. 22.95 (*0-538-71494-8*) S-W Pub.

— Microsoft Access 97 for Windows 95. (Quicktorial Ser.). 144p. 1997. pap. text 19.95 (*0-538-68426-7*) S-W Pub.

***Murphy, Patricia.** Microsoft Access 2000, QuickTutorial. LC 98-47591. (Quicktorial Ser.). (Illus.). 144p. 1999. pap. 24.95 (*0-538-68858-0*) Sth-Wstrn College.

Murphy, Patricia. Microsoft Excel 5.0 for Macintosh. (Quicktorial Ser.). (C). 1996. mass mkt. 21.95 (*0-538-71577-4*) S-W Pub.

— Microsoft Excel for Windows 95. (Quicktorial Ser.). (C). 1996. mass mkt. 21.95 (*0-538-71545-6*) S-W Pub.

— Microsoft Excel 97 for Windows 95. (Quicktorial Ser.). 1997. pap. text 19.95 (*0-538-68420-8*) S-W Pub.

***Murphy, Patricia.** Microsoft Excel 2000, Quick Tutorial. LC 98-47588. (Illus.). 176p. 1999. pap. 24.95 (*0-538-68855-6*) Sth-Wstrn College.

Murphy, Patricia. Microsoft Office for Windows: Complete Course. (Quick Course Ser.). 816p. 1995. mass mkt. 53.95 (*0-538-64856-2*) S-W Pub.

***Murphy, Patricia.** Microsoft Office 98 Macintosh Basics. LC 00-26541. (Illus.). 2001. pap. write for info. incl. cd-rom (*0-538-72432-3*) S-W Pub.

Murphy, Patricia. Microsoft PowerPoint for Windows 95. (Quicktorial Ser.). 1996. mass mkt. 21.95 (*0-538-71543-X*) S-W Pub.

Murphy, Patricia. Microsoft PowerPoint 4.0 for Macintosh. (Quicktorial Ser.). (C). 1997. mass mkt. 21.95 (*0-538-71581-2*) S-W Pub.

— Microsoft PowerPoint 2000, QuickTutorial. LC 98-47590. (Illus.). 144p. 1999. pap. 24.95 (*0-538-68862-9*) Sth-Wstrn College.

— Microsoft Word for Windows 95 Quicktorial. (DF - Computer Applications Ser.). 1996. pap. 21.95 (*0-538-71551-0*) S-W Pub.

— Microsoft Word 97 for Windows 95. (Quicktorial Ser.). 1997. pap. text 19.95 (*0-538-67966-2*) S-W Pub.

 An Asterisk (*) at the beginning of an entry indicates that the title is appearing for the first time.

Murphy, Patricia. Microsoft Word 6.0 for Macintosh. (Quicktorial Ser.). (C). 1996. mass mkt. 21.95 (*0-538-71572-3*) S-W Pub.

***Murphy, Patricia.** Microsoft Word 2000, QuickTutorial. LC 98-47587. (Quicktorial Ser.). (Illus.). 192p. 1999. pap. 24.95 (*0-538-68850-5*) Sth-Wstrn College.

Murphy, Patricia. MS PowerPoint 97 for Windows 95. (Quicktorial Ser.). 1997. pap. text 19.95 (*0-538-68427-5*) S-W Pub.

— Trauma & Disability. 2000. write for info. (*1-57444-158-2*) St Lucie Pr.

Murphy, Patricia & Gipps, Caroline, eds. Equity in the Classroom: Towards Effective Pedagogy for Girls & Boys. 208p. 1996. 79.95 (*0-7507-0540-X*, Falmer Pr); pap. 27.95 (*0-7507-0541-8*, Falmer Pr) Taylor & Francis.

Murphy, Patricia, jt. auth. see Gipps, Caroline.

Murphy, Patricia A. A Career & Life Planning Guide for Women Survivors: Making the Connections Workbook. LC 94-73030. 290p. 1995. lib. bdg. 29.95 (*1-57444-021-7*) St Lucie Pr.

Murphy, Patricia B. Learn with Rap Geography. unabridged ed. (Learn with Rap Ser.). (Illus.). 48p. (Orig.). (J). (gr. 2-9). 1995. pap. 19.95 incl. audio (*0-9648725-0-1*) People Are People.

— Learn with Rap Geography. 2nd ed. (Learn with Rap Ser.). (Illus.). 50p. (Orig.). (J). (gr. 2-9). 1996. pap. text 19.95 incl. audio (*0-9648725-1-X*) People Are People.

Murphy, Patricia Beling. Elinor. LC 99-27485. 2000. write for info. (*0-316-91088-0*) Little.

Murphy, Patrick. Biographies: Philadelphia Narratives. (Illus.). 48p. 1999. pap. 14.00 (*0-88454-092-8*) U of Pa Contemp Art.

— Cho Duck-Hyun: After the Fall. (Illus.). 40p. (Orig.). (C). 1995. pap. 12.00 (*0-88454-083-9*) U of Pa Contemp Art.

— An Introduction to Unified Field Astrology. 125p. 1993. pap. 19.95 (*0-9636106-0-0*) Nirvana Pr.

— Terestita Fernandez. (Illus.). 32p. 1999. pap. 18.00 (*0-88454-091-X*) U of Pa Contemp Art.

— Three Stanzas: Miroslaw Balka, Robert Gober & Seamus Heaney. (Illus.). 32p. 1999. pap. 12.00 (*0-88454-090-1*) U of Pa Contemp Art.

Murphy, Patrick, jt. auth. see Bailey, Bill.

Murphy, Patrick, jt. auth. see Barsky, Ivy.

Murphy, Patrick A. Creditors' Rights in Bankruptcy. LC 79-25731. 784p. 1980. text 90.00 (*0-07-044060-3*) Shepards.

Murphy, Patrick C., II, ed. see Murphy, Sara A.

***Murphy, Patrick D.** Farther Afield in the Study of Nature-Oriented Literature. 256p. 2000. 55.00 (*0-8139-1905-3*); pap. 18.50 (*0-8139-1906-1*) U Pr of Va.

Murphy, Patrick D. Literature, Nature, & Other: Ecofeminist Critiques. LC 93-8733. 212p. (C). 1995. text 59.50 (*0-7914-2277-1*); pap. text 19.95 (*0-7914-2278-X*) State U NY Pr.

***Murphy, Patrick D.** A Place for Wayfaring: The Poetry & Prose of Gary Snyder. LC 99-88384. 256p. 2000. pap. 21.95 (*0-87071-479-1*) Oreg St U Pr.

Murphy, Patrick D., ed. Gary Snyder. (Critical Essays on American Literature Ser.). 1990. 48.00 (*0-8161-8900-5*, G K Hall & Co) Mac Lib Ref.

***Murphy, Patrick D., ed.** Literature of Nature: An International Sourcebook. LC 98-233184. 512p. 1998. lib. bdg. 95.00 (*1-57958-010-6*) Fitzroy Dearborn.

Murphy, Patrick D., ed. Staging the Impossible: The Fantastic Mode in Modern Drama, 54. LC 92-10678. (Contributions to the Study of Science Fiction & Fantasy Ser.: No. 54). 256p. 1992. 59.95 (*0-313-27270-0*, MIJ/, Greenwood Pr) Greenwood.

Murphy, Patrick D. & Hyles, Vernon, eds. The Poetic Fantastic: Studies in an Evolving Genre, 40. LC 89-11930. (Contributions to the Study of Science Fiction & Fantasy Ser.: No. 40). 226p. 1989. 59.95 (*0-313-26160-1*, MYT/, Greenwood Pr) Greenwood.

Murphy, Patrick D. & Wu, Dingbo, eds. Science Fiction from China: Eight Stories. LC 89-1866. 217p. 1989. 18.95 (*0-275-93343-1*, C3343, Praeger Pubs) Greenwood.

Murphy, Patrick D., jt. auth. see Gaard, Greta C.

Murphy, Patrick D., jt. ed. see Hoffman, Michael J.

Murphy, Patrick D., jt. ed. see Wu, Dingbo.

Murphy, Patrick E. Eighty Exemplary Ethics Statements. LC 97-28411. xv, 243p. 1998. pap. 18.95 (*0-268-00939-2*) U of Notre Dame Pr.

Murphy, Patrick E., ed. see American Marketing Association Staff.

Murphy, Patrick J. Way Below E. LC 95-126001. 230p. (Orig.). 1994. pap. 14.00 (*1-877727-42-3*) White Pine.

***Murphy, Patrick L.** What Every Veteran Should Know 2000. 2000. pap. 15.00 (*0-9670331-1-X*) Veterans Info.

***Murphy, Patrick T.** Drowning in Hot Water. LC 00-103866. 176p. 2000. 20.00 (*1-892323-94-X*) Vivisphere.

Murphy, Patrick T. Tacita Dean. LC 98-75083. 48 p. 1998. 18.00 (*0 88454-089-8*) U of Pa Contemp Art.

Murphy, Patrick T., intro. Glenn Ligon: Unbecoming. (Illus.). 64p. 1998. pap. 18.00 (*0-88454-086-3*, 810913) U of Pa Contemp Art.

Murphy, Paul. Canary Islands. LC 95-67311. (Illustrated Travel Guides from Thomas Cook Ser.). (Illus.). 192p. 1995. pap. text 12.95 (*0-8442-9070-X*, Passprt Bks) NTC Contemp Pub Co.

— Do You Think You'll Like the Wind? LC 95-168598. 104p. 1995. pap. 14.95 (*1-898256-03-9*) Dufour.

— Frommer's Florida's Best-Loved Driving Tours. 3rd ed. (Illus.). 168p. 1997. pap. 15.95 (*0-02-862236-7*) Macmillan.

— The Meaning of Freedom of Speech, 15. LC 72-133500. (Contributions in American History Ser.: No. 15). 401p. 1972. 39.95 (*0-8371-5176-7*, MCLB, Greenwood Pr) Greenwood.

— The Star Wars Rebel Alliance Sourcebook. (Star Wars Ser.). 144p. 1991. per. 18.00 (*0-87431-178-0*, 40054) West End Games.

— Tenerife. LC 96-68528. (Essential Travel Guides Ser.). (Illus.). 128p. 1997. pap. 7.95 (*0-8442-4813-4*, 48134, Passprt Bks) NTC Contemp Pub Co.

Murphy, Paul, text. Israel. LC 99-222943. 1999. pap. text 8.95 (*2-8315-6307-0*) Berlitz.

— Provence Pocket Guide. rev. ed. LC 99-226248. (Illus.). 144p. 1999. 8.95 (*2-8315-7152-9*) Berlitz.

Murphy, Paul, et al. Focused Quality: Managing for Results. LC 94-17212. 208p. 1994. boxed set 52.95 (*1-884015-18-2*) St Lucie Pr.

Murphy, Paul, jt. auth. see Hicks, Penny.

Murphy, Paul, ed. & tr. see Torres, Jose de.

Murphy, Paul E. Triadic Mysticism. 1986. 23.00 (*0-685-17541-3*, Pub. by Motilal Bnarsidass) S Asia.

— Triadic Mysticism: The Mystic Theology of the Shaivism of Kashmir. 226p. 1986. 23.00 (*81-208-0010-9*, Pub. by Motilal Bnarsidass) S Asia.

Murphy, Paul L. The Constitution in the Twentieth Century. LC 86-70475. (Bicentennial Essays on the Constitution Ser.). 68p. 1985. pap. 7.00 (*0-87229-036-0*) Am Hist Assn.

Murphy, Paul L., ed. The Bill of Rights & the States. (Bill of Rights & American Legal History Ser.). 540p. 1990. reprint ed. 69.00 (*0-8240-5866-6*) Garland.

— Criminal Procedure, 4 vols. (Bill of Rights & American Legal History Ser.). 2768p. 1990. reprint ed. text 80.00 (*0-8240-5865-8*) Garland.

— Free Press, 3 vols. (Bill of Rights & American Legal History Ser.). 2328p. 1990. reprint ed. text 60.00 (*0-8240-5861-5*) Garland.

— Free Speech, 4 vols. (Bill of Rights & American Legal History Ser.). 2544p. 1990. reprint ed. text 80.00 (*0-8240-5860-7*) Garland.

— The Historic Background of the Bill of Rights. (Bill of Rights & American Legal History Ser.). 600p. 1990. reprint ed. text 20.00 (*0-8240-5858-5*) Garland.

— Pre-Nineteen Sixty Developments in the Bill of Rights Area, 2 vols. (Bill of Rights & American Legal History Ser.). 1472p. 1990. reprint ed. text 40.00 (*0-8240-5859-3*) Garland.

— The Right to Privacy & the Ninth Amendment. (Bill of Rights & American Legal History Ser.: Vol. 7). 824p. 1990. reprint ed. text 40.00 (*0-8240-5864-X*) Garland.

— Rights of Assembly, Petition, Arms & Just Compensation. (Bill of Rights & American Legal History Ser.). 764p. 1990. reprint ed. text 20.00 (*0-8240-5863-1*) Garland.

Murphy, Paul R., tr. see Herbert, George.

Murphy Payne, Lauren & Rohling, Claudia. We Can Get Along: A Child's Book of Choices. Espeland, Pamela, ed. LC 96-29528. (Illus.). 36p. (J). (ps-3). 1997. pap. 9.95 (*1-57542-013-9*) Free Spirit Pub.

Murphy, Peter. Evidence & Advocacy. 5th ed. 321p. 1998. pap. 38.00 (*1-85431-767-9*) Gaunt.

— Murphy on Evidence. 5th ed. LC 95-177523. 624p. 1995. pap. 44.00 (*1-85431-373-8*, Pub. by Blackstone Pr) Gaunt.

— Murphy on Evidence. 6th ed. 565p. 1997. pap. 46.00 (*1-85431-682-6*, Pub. by Blackstone Pr) Gaunt.

— A Practical Approach to Evidence. 637p. 1992. pap. 48.00 (*1-85431-223-5*, Pub. by Blackstone Pr) Gaunt.

Murphy, Peter, ed. Blackstone's Criminal Practice, 1998 Edition. 1998. 202.00 (*1-85431-760-1*, Pub. by Blackstone Pr) Gaunt.

— Blackstone's Criminal Practice 1999. 9th ed. 2433p. 1999. 224.00 (*1-85431-916-7*, Pub. by Blackstone Pr) Gaunt.

***Murphy, Peter, ed.** Blackstone's Criminal Practice, 2000. 10th ed. 2684p. 2000. 224.00 (*1-84174-100-0*, Pub. by Blackstone Pr) Gaunt.

Murphy, Peter, ed. Friendship, Vol. 97, No. 1. 200p. 1998. pap. 12.00 (*0-8223-6456-5*) Duke.

Murphy, Peter & Barnard, David. Evidence & Advocacy. 236p. (C). 1986. 110.00 (*0-906322-96-0*, Pub. by Blackstone Pr) St Mut.

— Evidence & Advocacy. 4th ed. LC 96-152448. 288p. 1994. pap. 30.00 (*1-85431-281-2*, Pub. by Blackstone Pr) Gaunt.

Murphy, Peter & Beaumont, John. Evidence: Materials for Discussion. 546p. 1987. pap. 40.00 (*0-906322-97-9*, Pub. by Blackstone Pr) Gaunt.

Murphy, Peter & Koch, Beth H. Math of Astrology. 1996. spiral bd. 14.95 (*0-86690-456-5*, K3590-014) Am Fed Astrologers.

Murphy, Peter, jt. auth. see Broukal, Milada.

Murphy, Peter, jt. ed. see Crozier, Michael.

Murphy, Peter E. Tourism: A Community Approach. 260p. 1986. 42.50 (*0-416-39790-5*, 9612) Routledge.

— Tourism: A Community Approach. 200p. 1995. pap. 26.95 (*0-415-04506-1*, 9613) Thomson Learn.

Murphy, Peter E., ed. Quality Management in Urban Tourism. LC 96-48035. 312p. 1997. 110.00 (*0-471-97099-9*) Wiley.

Murphy, Peter F., ed. Fictions of Masculinity: Crossing Cultures, Crossing Sexualities. LC 93-44104. (C). 1994. text 45.00 (*0-8147-5497-X*); pap. text 19.00 (*0-8147-5498-8*) NYU Pr.

Murphy, Peter J., ed. see Johnsen, Loyd.

Murphy, Peter M. Essays & MCQs in Anaesthesia & Intensive Care. 368p. 1995. pap. text 25.00 (*0-340-62524-4*, Pub. by E A) OUP.

Murphy, Philip. Party Politics & Decolonization: The Conservative Party & British Colonial Policy in Tropical Africa 1951-1964. (Oxford Historical Monographs). 272p. 1995. text 65.00 (*0-19-820505-8*) OUP.

Murphy, Phillip. Prabhupada Saraswati Thakura: Life & Precepts of Srila. Goff, Raoul, ed. (Illus.). 164p. 1997. 60.00 (*0-945475-10-1*, 1046, Pub. by Mandala Pub Grp) Words Distrib.

Murphy, Phyllis, jt. auth. see Michels, Jeanne.

Murphy, Quillian R., ed. Metabolic Aspects of Transport Across Cell Membranes. LC 57-9808. 406p. reprint ed. pap. 125.90 (*0-608-14475-4*, 202114300021) Bks Demand.

Murphy, R. Essential Grammar in Use. 1994. pap. text 17.95 (*0-521-44705-4*) Cambridge U Pr.

Murphy, R. C. Mass Spectrometry of Lipids. (Handbook of Lipid Research Ser.: Vol. 7). (Illus.). 308p. (C). 1993. text 79.50 (*0-306-44361-9*, Kluwer Plenum) Kluwer Academic.

Murphy, R. J., ed. see Vogelsang, Dieter.

Murphy, R. Taggart. The Weight of the Yen. 320p. 1996. 25.00 (*0-393-03832-7*) Norton.

— The Weight of the Yen: How Denials Imperils America's Future & Ruins an Alliance. 352p. 1997. pap. 13.95 (*0-393-31657-2*) Norton.

Murphy, Rae, et al. Brian Mulroney: The Boy from Baie-comeau. 1984. mass mkt. 4.95 (*0-88780-137-4*, Pub. by Formac Publ Co) Formac Dist Ltd.

***Murphy, Ray.** Empire & Victory: A Novel. 224p. 1999. pap. 12.00 (*0-9674823-0-5*, Pub. by R Murphy) AK Pr Dist.

Murphy, Ray. If You Felt Like I Did...You'd Start Running. LC 89-91634. 109p. 1990. pap. write for info. (*0-9626835-1-5*) Stethophonics.

— Siege of Gresham. 1997. pap. text 10.00 (*1-873176-05-8*) AK Pr Dist.

Murphy, Raymond. Basic Grammar in Use: Reference & Practice for Students of English. (Illus.). 234p. (C). 1993. pap. text, student ed. 18.95 (*0-521-42606-5*) Cambridge U Pr.

— Basic Grammar in Use: Reference & Practice for Students of English. (Illus.). 27p. (C). 1993. pap. text, teacher ed. 5.95 (*0-521-42607-3*) Cambridge U Pr.

— English Grammar in Use: A Self Study Reference & Practice Book for Intermediate Students. 2nd ed. 1994. pap. text 18.95 (*0-521-43680-X*) Natural Hist Mus.

— Essential Grammar in Use: With Answers: A Self-Study Reference & Practice Book for Elementary Students of English. 299p. (J). 1997. pap. text 18.95 (*0-521-55928-6*) Cambridge U Pr.

— Grammar in Use: Reference & Practice for Intermediate Students of American English. (Illus.). 288p. (C). 1989. pap. text 19.95 (*0-521-34843-9*) Cambridge U Pr.

— Grammar in Use: Reference & Practice for Intermediate Students of American English. (Illus.). 46p. (C). 1989. pap. text 5.95 (*0-521-35701-2*) Cambridge U Pr.

— Rationality & Nature: A Sociological Inquiry into a Changing Relationship. LC 94-25665. xii, 294p. (C). 1994. pap. 29.00 (*0-8133-2169-7*, Pub. by Westview) HarpC.

— Social Closure: The Theory of Monopolization & Exclusion. 284p. 1988. text 75.00 (*0-19-827268-5*) OUP.

Murphy, Raymond, jt. auth. see Naylor, Helen.

Murphy, Raymond J. Implementing an ISO 9000-Based Quality System. LC 98-35544. 263p. 1998. pap. text 59.00 (*0-86587-638-X*, 638) Gov Insts.

Murphy, Raymond J., jt. auth. see Unger, Darren P.

***Murphy, Reg.** Uncommon Sense: The Achievement of Griffin Bell. LC 99-61755. 304p. 1999. 24.00 (*1-56352-582-8*) Longstreet.

Murphy, Remington. Fear of Vision: A Book of Poems. Probstein, Ian E. & Gluck, Karl, eds. LC 93-70753. 64p. (Orig.). 1993. pap. text 5.00 (*1-882725-01-8*) Arch-Arcada.

Murphy, Rhoda J., jt. auth. see House Beautiful Magazine Editors.

Murphy, Ricardo L., ed. Fiscal Decentralization in Latin America. 250p. (Orig.). 1995. pap. text 18.50 (*0-940602-94-6*) IADB.

Murphy, Richard. Imaginary Worlds: Notes on a New Curriculum. 110p. (Orig.). 1974. pap. 10.95 (*0-915924-00-5*) Tchrs & Writers Coll.

— The Mirror Wall. 64p. 1989. 13.95 (*0-916390-36-5*); pap. 7.95 (*0-916390-35-7*) Wake Forest.

— Modernism, Expressionism & Theories of the Avant-Garde. LC 98-8366. (Literature, Culture, Theory Ser.: No. 32). 260p. (C). 1999. text 57.95 (*0-521-63291-9*); pap. text 19.95 (*0-521-64869-6*) Cambridge U Pr.

— Querini Stampalia Foundation: Venice 1961-3 Carlo Scarpa. (Architecture in Detail Ser.). (Illus.). 60p. (C). 1993. pap. 29.95 (*0-7148-2848-3*, Pub. by Phaidon Press) Phaidon Pr.

Murphy, Richard C. Guestworkers in the German Reich. 1983. text 61.00 (*0-88033-034-1*, 143, Pub. by East Eur Monographs) Col U Pr.

Murphy, Richard T. & Aquinas, Thomas, Saint. An Introduction to the Prophets of Israel. LC 95-19308. 1996. pap. 5.95 (*0-8198-3672-9*) Pauline Bks.

Murphy, Richard W. & Time-Life Books Editors. The Nation Reunited. Flaherty, Thomas, ed. 176p. 1987. lib. bdg. 25.93 (*0-8094-4793-2*) Time-Life.

Murphy, Rick, ed. see Rubenstein, Lona.

***Murphy, Rita.** Black Angels. 2001. mass mkt. (*0-385-32776-5*) BDD Bks Young Read.

— Night Flying. LC 00-20781. (Illus.). (J). 2000. 14.95 (*0-385-32748-X*) Delacorte.

***Murphy, Robert.** British Cinema of the 90s. 264p. 2000. pap. 24.95 (*0-85170-762-9*, Pub. by British Film Inst); lib. bdg. 65.00 (*0-85170-763-7*, Pub. by British Film Inst) Ind U Pr.

Murphy, Robert, Jr. Psychotherapy Based on Human Longing. LC 60-14173. (Orig.). 1960. pap. 4.00 (*0-87574-111-8*) Pendle Hill.

Murphy, Robert. Realism & Tinsel: Cinema & Society in Britain, 1939-1949. LC 91-36369. (Cinema & Society Ser.). (Illus.). 292p. reprint ed. pap. 90.60 (*0-608-20364-5*, 207161700002) Bks Demand.

— Realism & Tinsel: Cinema & Society in Britain, 1989-48. (Cinema & Society Ser.). 288p. 1989. 49.50 (*0-415-02982-1*, A3176) Routledge.

— Sixties British Cinema. (Illus.). 320p. 1992. pap. 25.95 (*0-85170-324-0*, Pub. by British Film Inst); text 59.95 (*0-85170-309-7*, Pub. by British Film Inst) Ind U Pr.

Murphy, Robert, ed. The British Cinema Book. LC 98-111007. (Illus.). 300p. Date not set. write for info. (*0-85170-640-1*, Pub. by British Film Inst); pap. write for info. (*0-85170-641-X*, Pub. by British Film Inst) Ind U Pr.

Murphy, Robert, jt. auth. see Bonvillian, Gary.

Murphy, Robert C. Fish Shape Paumanok. 1976. 16.95 (*0-8488-1111-9*) Amereon Ltd.

— Fish-Shape Paumanok: Nature & Man on Long Island. (Illus.). 88p. 1991. reprint ed. pap. 9.95 (*0-9628492-0-0*) Waterline Bks.

— The Unconscious. 1996. pap. 4.00 (*0-87574-325-0*) Pendle Hill.

Murphy, Robert D. Combat Air Power: Joint Assessment of Air Superiority Can Be Improved. Rodrigues, Louis J., ed. (Illus.). 56p. (C). 1999. pap. text 20.00 (*0-7881-4361-1*) DIANE Pub.

Murphy, Robert D. Diplomat Among Warriors. LC 75-42364. (Illus.). 470p. 1976. reprint ed. lib. bdg. 65.00 (*0-8371-7693-X*, MUDW, Greenwood Pr) Greenwood.

Murphy, Robert F. Body Silent. 1990. pap. 12.95 (*0-393-30702-6*) Norton.

— Cultural & Social Anthropology. 3rd ed. 256p. (C). 1988. pap. text 25.00 (*0-13-195273-0*) P-H.

— The Trumai Indians of Central Brazil. LC 84-45523. (American Ethnological Society Monographs: No. 24). 1988. reprint ed. 22.00 (*0-404-62923-7*) AMS Pr.

Murphy, Robert F., ed. Selected Papers from the "American Anthropologist" 1946-1970. 424p. 1976. pap. 5.00 (*0-685-10030-8*) Am Anthro Assn.

Murphy, Robert F., jt. auth. see Murphy, Yolanda.

Murphy, Robert F., ed. see Steward, Julian.

Murphy, Robert J. & Doring, Denise. Historic Beacon. LC 98-86902. (Images of America Ser.). (Illus.). 128p. 1998. pap. 16.99 (*0-7524-1252-3*) Arcadia Publng.

Murphy, Robert L., jt. auth. see Phair, John P.

Murphy, Robert T. Postal History-Cancellation Study of the U. S. Pacific Islands: Including the Trust Territories. (Illus.). 361p. 1983. 46.00 (*0-933580-11-8*) Am Philatelic Society.

***Murphy, Robin R.** Introduction to AI Robotics. (Intelligent Robotics & Autonomous Agents Ser.). (Illus.). 400p. (C). 2000. 50.00 (*0-262-13383-0*) MIT Pr.

Murphy, Roger & Torrance, Harry. The Changing Face of Educational Assessment. 128p. 1988. pap. 34.95 (*0-335 15826-9*) OpUniv Pr.

Murphy, Roger, et al. Effective Assessment & the Improvement of Education: A Tribute to Desmond Nuttall. 180p. 1995. 85.00 (*0-7507-0374-1*, Falmer Pr) Taylor & Francis.

Murphy, Roland & Huwiler, Elizabeth. Proverbs, Ecclesiastes, Song of Songs & Nibcot 12. LC 98-54757. (New International Biblical Commentary Ser.). 325p. 1999. pap. 11.95 (*1-56563-221-4*) Hendrickson MA.

Murphy, Roland E. The Book of Job: A Short Reading. LC 99-34535. 160p. 1999. pap. 14.95 (*0-8091-3889-1*) Paulist Pr.

— Ecclesiastes. (Biblical Commentary Ser.: Vol. 23A). 29.99 (*0-8499-0222-3*) Word Pub.

***Murphy, Roland E.** The Gift of the Psalms. 2000. pap. 16.95 (*1-56563-474-8*) Hendrickson MA.

Murphy, Roland E. Master of the Sacred Page: Essays & Articles in Honor of Roland E. Murphy, O. Carm., on the Occasion of His Eightieth Birthday. Morrison, Craig E. et al, eds. LC 97-16137. (Illus.). 416p. (Orig.) 1997. pap. 24.00 (*0-9656910-0-4*) Carmelite Inst.

— Proverbs. (Biblical Commentary Ser.: Vol. 22). 450p. 1998. 29.99 (*0-8499-0221-5*) Word Pub.

— The Psalms Are Yours. LC 93-15639. 160p. 1993. pap. 10.95 (*0-8091-3411-X*) Paulist Pr.

— Responses to 101 Questions on the Biblical Torah: Reflections on the Pentateuch. (Responses to 101 Questions Ser.). 144p. 1996. pap. 12.95 (*0-8091-3630-9*, 3630-9) Paulist Pr.

— The Song of Songs. LC 89-16891. (Hermeneia: A Critical & Historical Commentary on the Bible Ser.). 176p. 1990. 43.00 (*0-8006-6024-2*, 1-6024) Augsburg Fortress.

— The Tree of Life: An Exploration of Biblical Wisdom Literature. 2nd ed. LC 96-28479. 248p. 1996. pap. 22.00 (*0-8028-4192-9*) Eerdmans.

— Wisdom, You Are My Sister: Studies in Honor of Roland E. Murphy, O. Carm. on the Occasion of His Eightieth Birthday. Barre, Michael L., ed. LC 97-16060. (Catholic Biblica Quarterly Monograph). 265p. 1997. pap. text. write for info. (*0-915170-28-0*) Catholic Bibl Assn.

***Murphy, Ronald Chase & Murphy, Janice Church.** Irish Famine Immigrants in the State of Vermont, Gravestone Inscriptions. 723p. 2000. pap. 49.95 (*0-8063-4967-0*, Pub. by Clearfield Co) ACCESS Pubs Network.

Murphy, Ronald E. Responses to One Hundred One Questions on the Psalms & Other Writings. LC 94-3739 144p. 1995. pap. 8.95 (*0-8091-3526-4*) Paulist Pr.

Murphy, Rosalie, ed. see Hawthorne, Nathaniel.

Murphy, Roy & Murphy, Julia. The San Gabriel Mountains. (Illus.). 88p. 1985. 25.00 (*0-9615421-0-1*) Big Santa Hist.

Murphy, Roy, et al. Angeles National Forest. (Illus.). 80p. (Orig.). 1991. pap. 9.95 (*0-9615421-4-4*) Big Santa Hist.

Murphy, Sandra. Too Bad It Wasn't a Dream. 180p. 1997. pap. 14.95 (*0-89896-181-5*) Larksdale.

M

An Asterisk (*) at the beginning of an entry indicates that the title is appearing for the first time.

Murphy, Sandra & Smith, Mary A. Writing Portfolios: A Bridge from Teaching to Assessment. (Illus.). 96p. 1995. pap. text 14.00 (*0-88751-044-2*, 00707) Heinemann.

***Murphy, Sandra & Underwood, Terry.** Portfolio Practices: Lessons from Schools, Districts & States. 350p. 2000. pap. text, teacher ed. 38.95 (*1-929024-18-5*, 795) CG Pubs Inc.

Murphy, Sandra, jt. auth. see Ruth, Leo.

Murphy, Santa. To Land a Teaching Job When All Apparent Efforts Have Failed. 87p. 1998. pap. 9.95 (*0-9663061-0-4*) Education Concepts.

Murphy, Sara A. Breaking the Silence: The Little Rock Women's Emergency Committee to Open Our Schools, 1958-1963. Murphy, Patrick C., II, ed. LC 97-2344. 1997. 28.00 (*1-55728-456-3*) U of Ark Pr.

— Breaking the Silence: The Little Rock Women's Emergency Committee to Open Our Schools, 1958-1963. Murphy, Patrick C., II, ed. LC 97-2344. 1997. pap. 20.00 (*1-55728-515-2*) U of Ark Pr.

Murphy, Sara M. RingWrite: Ready Reference Guide on English Mechanics in Writing. 16p. (Orig.). 1997. pap. 6.95 (*0-9658928-2-4*, EMW 02-4) Quannapowitt.

Murphy, Sarah. Connie Many Stories. 160p. 1996. pap. 14.50 (*1-55128-031-0*, Pub. by Mercury Bk) LPC InBook.

— The Deconstruction of Wesley Smithson. pap. 12.95 (*0-920544-94-0*, Pub. by Mercury Bk) LPC InBook.

***Murphy, Scott.** The Inventor's Kit: A Complete Workbook for Filing Patents, Trademarks, & Copyrights. 200p. 2000. pap. 13.95 (*1-57733-064-1*) B Dolphin Pub.

Murphy, Scott B., jt. auth. see Wetzel, Edward D.

Murphy, Seamus. Stone Mad. LC 98-165733. 229p. 1998. pap. 21.00 (*0-85640-617-1*, Pub. by Blackstaff Pr) Dufour.

Murphy, Sean. Astrocytes: Pharmacology & Function. (Illus.). 457p. 1993. text 99.00 (*0-12-511370-6*) Acad Pr.

Murphy, Sean, ed. NO & Nervous System Plasticity: Journal. (Journal Ser.: Vol. 19, No. 3, 1997). (Illus.). 74p. 1997. pap. 40.00 (*3-8055-6525-9*) S Karger.

Murphy, Sean, et al. No Fire, No Thunder: The Threat of Chemical & Biological Weapons. LC 84-20579. 160p. 1984. pap. 10.00 (*0-85345-662-3*, Pub. by Monthly Rev) NYU Pr.

Murphy, Sean D. Humanitarian Intervention: The United Nations in an Evolving World Order. LC 96-32578. (Procedural Aspects of International Law Ser.). 608p. 1996. text 59.95 (*0-8122-3382-4*) U of Pa Pr.

Murphy, Sean P., jt. auth. see Mann, Robert W.

Murphy, Shane M. The Achievement Zone: An 8 Step Guide to Peak Performance in All Areas of Life. 272p. 1997. reprint ed. pap. 14.00 (*0-425-15622-2*) Berkley Pub.

— The Cheers & the Tears: A Healthy Alternative to the Dark Side of Youth Sports Today. LC 98-25525. 230p. 1999. pap. 15.00 (*0-7879-4037-2*) Jossey-Bass.

— Greater Las Vegas/Clark County Street Guide: "Key to the City" (Illus.). 128p. (Orig.). 1996. pap., spiral bd. 18.95 (*0-9656303-0-7*) Metro Maps.

Murphy, Shane M., ed. Sport Psychology Interventions. LC 94-10390. (Illus.). 400p. 1995. text 49.00 (*0-87322-659-3*, BMUR0659) Human Kinetics.

Murphy, Shannon, ed. The Teacher's Handbook of Multicultural Games Children Play. 155p. 1996. teacher ed., per. 21.00 (*0-9630608-9-9*) R Dean Pr.

Murphy, Sharon. The Mailbox Superbook, Grade 1: Your Complete Resource for an Entire Year of First-Grade Success! LC 97-47383. 1997. 29.95 (*1-56234-197-9*) Educ Ctr.

Murphy, Sharon, ed. Celebrate Life! A Guide for Planning All Night Alcohol - Drug-Free Celebrations for Teens. 4th ed. (Illus.). 179p. (Orig.). (YA). (gr. 12 up). 1994. pap. text 25.00 (*0-7881-0865-4*) DIANE Pub.

Murphy, Sharon, et al. Fragile Evidence: A Critique of Reading Assessment. LC 97-42352. 176p. 1998. write for info. (*0-8058-2529-0*); pap. write for info. (*0-8058-2530-4*) L Erlbaum Assocs.

Murphy, Sharon M., jt. auth. see Schilpp, Madelon G.

Murphy, Sheigla & Rosenbaum, Marsha. Pregnant Women on Drugs: Combating Stereotypes & Stigma. LC 98-20130. 192p. (C). 1999. text 49.00 (*0-8135-2602-7*); pap. text 19.00 (*0-8135-2603-5*) Rutgers U Pr.

Murphy, Sheila. Teth. 88p. (Orig.). 1990. pap. 9.00 (*0-925904-05-8*) Chax Pr.

Murphy, Sheila, et al, eds. The Literature of Work: Short Stories, Essays, & Poems by Men & Women of Business. LC 91-67284. 314p. 1991. 24.95 (*1-880708-00-0*) U Phoenix Pr.

Murphy, Sheila, et al. Yefief 5 Vol. 2: Sense: The Constitution of Mercy. (Illus.). 150p. 2000. pap. 24.95 (*1-884434-10-X*) Images For Media.

Murphy, Sheila E. A Clove of Gender. 1995. 13.95 (*1-873012-77-2*) SPD-Small Pr Dist.

— Falling in Love Falling in Love with Your Syntax: Selected & New Poems. LC 98-104317. 209p. (C). 1997. pap. 16.50 (*0-937013-66-8*) Potes Poets.

— Heat a Form of Privacy Like Snow. 64p. 1997. pap. 7.95 (*1-884106-01-3*) Jumping Cholla.

***Murphy, Sheila E.** The Indelible Occasion. 75p. 2000. pap. 11.50 (*1-893541-24-X*, Pub. by Potes Poets) SPD-Small Pr Dist.

Murphy, Sheila E. Tommy & Neil. LC 93-14485. (Illus.). 96p. (Orig.). 1993. 20.00 (*0-933313-17-9*); pap. 12.95 (*0-933313-18-7*) SUN Gemini Pr.

— Tommy & Neil. limited ed. LC 93-14485. (Illus.). 96p. (Orig.). 1993. 30.00 (*0-933313-16-0*) SUN Gemini Pr.

Murphy, Sheila E. & Sollfrey, Stacey. A Rich Timetable & Appendices; Feeling the Roof of a Mouth That Hangs Open, 2 bks. in 1. 1991. pap. 3.00 (*0-935350-30-6*); write for info. (*0-935350-31-4*) Luna Bisonte.

Murphy, Sheila E., et al. Pavement Saw. 40p. 1994. pap. 3.50 (*1-886350-00-0*) Pavement Saw.

Murphy, Sheila E., jt. auth. see Ganick, Peter.

Murphy, Shirley J. Cat in the Dark. LC 98-39206. 272p. 1999. 22.00 (*0-06-105096-2*) HarpC.

— Cat in the Dark. 320p. 1999. mass mkt. 5.99 (*0-06-105947-1*) HarpC.

— Cat Raise the Dead. 304p. 1999. mass mkt. 5.99 (*0-06-105602-2*, HarperPrism) HarpC.

— Cat Under Fire. 256p. 1999. mass mkt. 5.99 (*0-06-105601-4*, HarperPrism) HarpC.

Murphy, Shirley J., ed. see Kelly, H. William.

Murphy, Shirley R. Cat on the Edge RI. 288p. 1999. mass mkt. 5.99 (*0-06-105600-6*, HarperPrism) HarpC.

— The Catsworld Portal. 432p. 1993. mass mkt. 6.99 (*0-451-45275-5*, ROC) NAL.

— The Dragonbards. LC 87-45295. 256p. (YA). (gr. 7 up). 1988. 12.95 (*0-06-024366-X*) HarpC Child Bks.

— The Ivory Lyre. LC 85-45831. 288p. (YA). (gr. 7 up). 1987. 12.95 (*0-06-024362-7*) HarpC Child Bks.

— Wind Child. LC 94-13861. (Illus.). 40p. (J). (gr. k-4). 1999. 15.95 (*0-06-024903-X*); lib. bdg. 15.89 (*0-06-024904-8*) HarpC Child Bks.

Murphy, Shirley R. & Suggs, Welch. Medallion of the Black Hound. LC 88-35825. 192p. (J). (gr. 3-7). 1989. 11.95 (*0-06-024368-6*) HarpC Child Bks.

Murphy, Shirley Rousseau. Cat to the Dogs: A Joe Grey Mystery. LC 99-16854. 256p. 2000. 23.00 (*0-06-105097-0*) HarpC.

— Cat to the Dogs: A Joe Grey Mystery. 304p. 2000. mass mkt. 6.50 (*0-06-105988-9*, Avon Bks) Morrow Avon.

***Murphy, Shirley Rousseau.** Cat to the Dogs: A Joe Grey Mystery. large type ed. LC 00-21593. 2000. 24.95 (*1-57490-264-4*, Beeler LP Bks) T T Beeler.

Murphy, Simon, jt. auth. see Bennett, Paul.

Murphy, Siobhan M., jt. auth. see Birchall, Martin A.

Murphy, Stanley, jt. auth. see Poet's Press-Gyro Publications Staff.

Murphy, Stanley D. & Eddy, John, eds. Current Issues in Higher Education: Research & Reforms. LC 98-34814. 151p. 1998. 49.00 (*0-7618-1218-0*); pap. 29.50 (*0-7618-1219-9*) U Pr of Amer.

Murphy, Stanley D., jt. auth. see Eddy, John.

Murphy, Stephan D. In-Process Measurement & Control. (Manufacturing Engineering & Materials Processing Ser.: Vol. 32). (Illus.). 352p. 1990. text 155.00 (*0-8247-8130-9*) Dekker.

Murphy, Stephanie & Macher, Alan. The Insiders' Guide to Boca Raton & the Palm Beaches. 2nd ed. (Insiders' Guide Travel Ser.). (Illus.). 503p. 1996. pap. 17.99 (*1-57380-007-4*, The Insiders Guide) Falcon Pub Inc.

— The Insiders' Guide to Boca Raton & the Palm Beaches. 3rd rev. ed. (Insiders' Guide Travel Ser.). (Illus.). Date not set. pap. 16.95 (*1-57380-082-1*, The Insiders Guide) Falcon Pub Inc.

Murphy, Stephen. The Carnival Caper: Teenage Mutant Ninja Turtles. (Sound Doodles Ser.). 16p. (J). (ps-2). 1994. write for info. (*1-883366-49-6*) YES Ent.

— The Gift of Immortality: Myths of Power & Humanist Poetics. LC 96-33207. 320p. 1997. 46.50 (*0-8386-3685-3*) Fairleigh Dickinson.

— Het Mysterie Van De Verdwenen Pizza: Teenage Mutant Ninja Turtles. DigiPro Staff, tr. from ENG. (Comes to Life Bks.).Tr. of Mystery of the Missing Pizza. (DUT.). 16p. (J). (ps-2). 1994. write for info. (*1-883366-91-7*) YES Ent.

— I Mostri Sono Tra Noi: Teenage Mutant Ninja Turtles. DigiPro Staff, tr. from ENG. (Comes to Life Bks.).Tr. of Monsters among Us. (ITA.). 16p. (J). (ps-2). 1994. write for info. (*1-883366-97-6*) YES Ent.

— Il Mistero Della Pizza Scomparsa: Teenage Mutant Ninja Turtles. DigiPro Staff, tr. from ENG. (Comes to Life Bks.).Tr. of Mystery of the Missing Pizza. (ITA.). 16p. (J). (ps-2). 1994. write for info. (*1-883366-96-8*) YES Ent.

— Il Mistero Delle Pizze Scomparse: Teenage Mutant Ninja Turtles. DigiPro Staff, tr. from ENG. (Comes to Life Bks.).Tr. of Mystery of the Missing Pizza. (SPA.). 16p. (J). (ps-2). 1994. write for info. (*1-57234-008-8*) YES Ent.

— Monsters among Us: Teenage Mutant Hero Turtles. (Comes to Life Bks.). 16p. (J). (ps-2). 1994. write for info. (*1-883366-76-3*) YES Ent.

— Monsters among Us: Teenage Mutant Ninja Turtles. (Comes to Life Bks.). 16p. (J). (ps-2). 1993. write for info. (*1-883366-09-7*) YES Ent.

— Monstruos Entre Nosotros: Teenage Mutant Ninja Turtles. DigiPro Staff, tr. from ENG. (Comes to Life Bks.).Tr. of Monsters among Us. (SPA.). 16p. (J). (ps-2). 1994. write for info. (*1-57234-009-6*) YES Ent.

— Le Mystere de la Pizza Disparue: Teenage Mutant Ninja Turtles. DigiPro Staff, tr. from ENG. (Comes to Life Bks.).Tr. of Mystery of the Missing Pizza. (FRE.). 16p. (J). (ps-2). 1994. write for info. (*1-883366-66-6*) YES Ent.

— The Mystery of the Missing Pizza: Teenage Mutant Hero Turtles. (Comes to Life Bks.). 16p. (J). (ps-2). 1994. write for info. (*1-883366-75-5*) YES Ent.

— The Mystery of the Missing Pizza: Teenage Mutant Ninja Turtles. (Comes to Life Bks.). 16p. (J). (ps-2). 1993. write for info. (*1-883366-08-9*) YES Ent.

Murphy, Stephen, et al. Developing Natural Supports in the Workplace: A Practitioner's Guide. LC 94-6930. 109p. (Orig.). 1994. pap. 20.00 (*1-883302-06-4*) Trning Res.

Murphy, Stephen T. On Being L. D. Perspectives & Strategies of Young Adults. (Special Education Ser.). 200p. (C). 1992. text 41.00 (*0-8077-3170-6*); pap. text 17.95 (*0-8077-3169-2*) Tchrs Coll.

Murphy, Stephen T. & Rogan, Patricia M. Closing the Shop: Conversion from Sheltered to Integrated Work. 240p. 1995. pap. 27.95 (*1-55766-153-7*) P H Brookes.

Murphy, Stuart, et al. The Fat Firm: Learning to Be a Lean & Mean Corporate Machine. LC 97-19057. (Illus.). 280p. 1997. 18.95 (*0-07-044392-0*) McGraw.

Murphy, Stuart J. Animals on Board: Level 2 - Adding. LC 97-11733. (MathStart Ser.). (Illus.). 40p. (J). (gr. 1-4). 1998. 15.95 (*0-06-027442-5*); lib. bdg. 15.89 (*0-06-027443-3*) HarpC.

— Animals on Board: Level 2: Adding. LC 97-11733. (MathStart Ser.: Level 2). (Illus.). 40p. (J). (gr. 1 up). 1998. pap. 4.95 (*0-06-446716-3*, HarpTrophy) HarpC Child Bks.

***Murphy, Stuart J.** Beep Beep, Vroom Vroom! LC 98-51907. (MathStart 1). (Illus.). 40p. (J). (ps up). 2000. 15.95 (*0-06-028016-6*) HarpC.

— Beep Beep, Vroom Vroom! LC 98-51907. (MathStart Ser.). (Illus.). 40p. (YA). (ps up). 2000. pap. 4.95 (*0-06-446728-7*) HarpC Child Bks.

Murphy, Stuart J. Beep Beep, Vroom Vroom! LC 98-51907. (MathStart Ser.). (Illus.). 40p. (J). (ps-3). 2000. lib. bdg. 15.89 (*0-06-028017-4*) HarpC Child Bks.

***Murphy, Stuart J.** Beep Beep, Vroom Vroom! (Mathstart Ser.). (Illus.). (J). 1998. 10.40 (*0-606-18678-6*) Turtleback.

Murphy, Stuart J. The Best Bug Parade. LC 94-49316. (MathStart Ser.). (Illus.). 40p. (J). (ps-3). 1996. lib. bdg. 15.89 (*0-06-025872-1*) HarpC Child Bks.

— The Best Bug Parade. LC 94-49316. (MathStart Ser.). (Illus.). 40p. (J). (ps up). 1996. 15.95 (*0-06-025871-3*) HarpC Child Bks.

— The Best Bug Parade. annuals LC 94-49316. (MathStart Ser.: Level 1). (Illus.). 40p. (J). (ps-3). 1996. pap. 4.95 (*0-06-446700-7*, HarpTrophy) HarpC Child Bks.

— Best Bug Parade. 1996. 10.15 (*0-606-09597-7*, Pub. by Turtleback) Demco.

— The Best Vacation Ever. LC 95-41191. (MathStart Ser.: Level 1). (Illus.). 40p. (J). (gr. 1 up). 1997. pap. 4.95 (*0-06-446706-6*, HarpTrophy) HarpC Child Bks.

— The Best Vacation Ever. LC 95-41191. (MathStart Ser.: Level 2). (Illus.). 40p. (J). (gr. 1 up). 1997. 14.95 (*0-06-026766-6*); lib. bdg. 15.89 (*0-06-026767-4*) HarpC Child Bks.

— Betcha! LC 96-15486. (MathStart Ser.: Level 1). (Illus.). 32p. (J). (gr. 2 up). 1997. pap. 4.95 (*0-06-446707-4*, HarpTrophy) HarpC Child Bks.

— Betcha! LC 96-15486. (MathStart Ser.: Level 3). (Illus.). 32p. (J). (gr. 2 up). 1997. 14.95 (*0-06-026768-2*); lib. bdg. 15.89 (*0-06-026769-0*) HarperTrade.

Murphy, Stuart J. Captain Invincible & the Space Shapes. 40p. (gr. 1 up). 15.95 (*0-06-028022-0*); 15.89 (*0-06-028023-9*); pap. 4.95 (*0-06-446731-7*) HarpC.

Murphy, Stuart J. Circus Shapes: Level 1: Recognizing Shapes. (Illus.). 32p. (J). 1998. reprint ed. pap. 5.99 (*0-698-11615-1*) HarpC.

— Circus Shapes Level 1: Recognizing Shapes. LC 96-35992. (MathStart Ser.). (Illus.). 40p. (J). (ps-3). 1998. pap. 4.95 (*0-06-446713-9*) HarpC Child Bks.

***Murphy, Stuart J.** Dave's Down-to-Earth Rock Shop. LC 98-32128. 40p. (gr. 2 up). 2000. lib. bdg. 15.89 (*0-06-028019-0*) HarpC Child Bks.

— Dave's Down-to-Earth Rock Shop. LC 98-32128. (Illus.). 40p. (gr. 2-7). 2000. 15.95 (*0-06-028018-2*) HarpC Child Bks.

Murphy, Stuart J. Dave's Down-to-Earth Rock Shop. LC 98-32128. (MathStart Ser.). (Illus.). 40p. (YA). (gr. 2-7). 2000. pap. 4.95 (*0-06-446729-5*) HarpC Child Bks.

***Murphy, Stuart J.** Dave's Down-to-Earth Rock Shop. (Mathstart Ser.). (Illus.). (J). 2000. 10.40 (*0-606-18686-7*) Turtleback.

— Dinosaur Cards. 40p. (gr. 2 up). 15.95 (*0-06-028926-0*); pap. 4.95 (*0-06-446251-X*); lib. bdg. 15.89 (*0-06-028927-9*) HarpC.

Murphy, Stuart J. Divide & Ride. LC 95-26134. (MathStart Ser.: Level 3). (Illus.). 40p. (J). (gr. 2 up). 1997. 14.95 (*0-06-026776-3*); pap. 4.95 (*0-06-446710-4*, HarpTrophy); lib. bdg. 15.89 (*0-06-026777-1*) HarpC Child Bks.

— Elevator Magic. LC 96-5672. (MathStart Ser.: Level 2). (Illus.). 40p. (J). (gr. 1-3). 1997. 14.95 (*0-06-026774-7*) HarpC.

— Elevator Magic. LC 96-5672. (MathStart Ser.: Level 2). (Illus.). 40p. (J). (gr. 1 up). 1997. lib. bdg. 15.89 (*0-06-026775-5*) HarpC.

— Elevator Magic. LC 96-5672. (MathStart Ser.: Level 2). (Illus.). 40p. (J). (gr. 1 up). 1997. pap. 4.95 (*0-06-446709-0*) HarpC Child Bks.

— Every Buddy Counts. LC 95-48840. (MathStart Ser.: Level 1). (Illus.). 40p. (J). (ps up). 1997. 14.95 (*0-06-026772-0*) HarpC Child Bks.

— Every Buddy Counts. LC 95-48840. (MathStart Ser.: Level 1). (Illus.). 40p. (J). (ps up). 1997. pap. 4.95 (*0-06-446708-2*, HarpTrophy); lib. bdg. 15.89 (*0-06-026773-9*) HarpC Child Bks.

— A Fair Bear Share. LC 96-45026. (MathStart Ser.). (Illus.). 40p. (J). (gr. 1-4). 1998. 14.95 (*0-06-027438-7*); pap. 4.95 (*0-06-446714-7*) HarpC.

— A Fair Bear Share. LC 96-45026. (MathStart Ser.). (Illus.). 40p. (J). (gr. 1 up). 1998. lib. bdg. 15.89 (*0-06-027439-5*) HarpC Child Bks.

***Murphy, Stuart J.** Game Time! LC 98-51902. 40p. (J). (gr. 2 up). 2000. pap. 4.95 (*0-06-446732-5*, HarpTrophy) HarpC Child Bks.

— Game Time! LC 98-51902. (Illus.). 40p. (YA). (gr. 2-4). 2000. 15.95 (*0-06-028024-7*) HarpC Child Bks.

— Game Time! LC PZ7.M9563Gam 2000. (Illus.). 40p. (YA). (gr. 2 up). 2000. lib. bdg. 15.89 (*0-06-028025-5*) HarpC Child Bks.

Murphy, Stuart J. Get Up & Go! LC 95-4736. (MathStart Ser.). (Illus.). 40p. (J). (ps-3). 1996. 14.95 (*0-06-025881-0*); pap. 4.95 (*0-06-446704-X*, HarpTrophy); lib. bdg. 15.89 (*0-06-025882-9*) HarpC Child Bks.

— Get Up & Go! (Mathstart Ser.). 1996. 10.15 (*0-606-09598-5*, Pub. by Turtleback) Demco.

— Give Me Half! LC 95-19617. (MathStart Ser.). (Illus.). 40p. (J). (gr. 1 up). 1996. 15.95 (*0-06-025873-X*) HarpC Child Bks.

— Give Me Half! LC 95-19617. (MathStart Ser.). (Illus.). 40p. (J). (ps-3). 1996. pap. 4.95 (*0-06-446701-5*, HarpTrophy); lib. bdg. 15.89 (*0-06-025874-8*) HarpC Child Bks.

— Give Me Half! (Mathstart). 1996. 10.15 (*0-606-09599-3*, Pub. by Turtleback) Demco.

— The Greatest Gymnast of All. LC 97-51273. (MathStart Ser.). (Illus.). 40p. (J). (ps-3). 1998. lib. bdg. 15.89 (*0-06-027609-6*) HarpC.

— The Greatest Gymnast of All. LC 97-51273. (MathStart Ser.). (Illus.). 40p. (J). (ps-3). 1998. 15.95 (*0-06-027608-8*) HarpC.

— The Greatest Gymnast of All: Opposites. LC 97-51273. (MathStart Ser.). (Illus.). 40p. (J). (ps-3). 1998. pap. 4.95 (*0-06-446718-X*) HarpC.

— Henry the Fourth: Level 1: Ordinals. LC 98-4960. (MathStart Ser.). (Illus.). 40p. (YA). (ps-3). 1999. lib. bdg. 15.89 (*0-06-027611-8*) HarpC Child Bks.

— Henry the Fourth: Level 1: Ordinals. LC 98-4960. (MathStart Ser.). (Illus.). 40p. (YA). (ps-3). 1999. 15.95 (*0-06-027610-X*); pap. 4.95 (*0-06-446719-8*, HarpTrophy) HarpC Child Bks.

— Jump, Kangaroo, Jump! Level 3: Fractions. LC 97-45814. (MathStart Ser.). (Illus.). 40p. (YA). (ps-3). 1999. lib. bdg. 15.89 (*0-06-027615-0*) HarpC Child Bks.

— Jump, Kangaroo, Jump! Level 3: Fractions. LC 97-45814. (MathStart Ser.). (Illus.). 40p. (YA). (gr. 2 up). 1999. 15.95 (*0-06-027614-2*) HarpC Child Bks.

— Jump, Kangaroo, Jump! Level 3: Fractions. LC 97-45814. (MathStart Ser.). (Illus.). 40p. (YA). (ps-3). 1999. pap. 4.95 (*0-06-446721-X*, HarpTrophy) HarpC Child Bks.

— Just Enough Carrots. LC 96-19495. (MathStart Ser.: Level 1). (Illus.). 40p. (J). (ps-3). 1997. lib. bdg. 15.89 (*0-06-026779-8*) HarpC.

— Just Enough Carrots. LC 96-19495. (MathStart Ser.: Level 1). (Illus.). 40p. (J). (ps up). 1997. 14.95 (*0-06-026778-X*) HarpC.

— Just Enough Carrots. LC 96-19495. (MathStart Ser.: Level 1). (Illus.). 40p. (J). (ps-3). 1997. pap. 4.95 (*0-06-446711-2*, HarpTrophy) HarpC Child Bks.

— Lemonade for Sale. LC 96-52063. (MathStart Ser.). (Illus.). 40p. (J). (gr. 2-5). 1998. 15.95 (*0-06-027440-9*); pap. 4.95 (*0-06-446715-5*) HarpC.

— Lemonade for Sale. LC 96-52063. (MathStart Ser.). (Illus.). 40p. (J). (gr. 2 up). 1998. lib. bdg. 15.89 (*0-06-027441-7*) HarpC Child Bks.

***Murphy, Stuart J.** Let's Fly a Kite. LC 99-26550. (MathStart Ser.). (Illus.). 40p. (J). (gr. 1-4). 2000. 15.95 (*0-06-028034-4*); lib. bdg. 15.89 (*0-06-028035-2*) HarpC Child Bks.

— Let's Fly a Kite. LC 99-26550. (MathStart Ser.). (Illus.). 40p. (J). (gr. 1 up). 2000. pap. 4.95 (*0-06-446737-6*, HarpTrophy) HarpC Child Bks.

— Missing Mittens. LC 99-41334. (MathStart Ser.). 40p. (J). (ps-2). 2001. pap. 4.95 (*0-06-446733-3*, HarpTrophy) HarpC Child Bks.

— Missing Mittens. LC 99-41334. (MathStart Ser.). 40p. (YA). (ps up). 2001. 15.95 (*0-06-028026-3*); lib. bdg. 15.89 (*0-06-028027-1*) HarpC Child Bks.

— Monster Musical Chairs. LC 99-27902. (MathStart Ser.: Vol. 28). 40p. (J). 2000. lib. bdg. 15.89 (*0-06-028021-2*) HarpC Child Bks.

— Monster Musical Chairs. LC 99-27902. (Illus.). 40p. (J). 2000. pap. 4.95 (*0-06-446730-9*, HarpTrophy) HarpC Child Bks.

— Monster Musical Chairs. 28th ed. LC 99-27902. (MathStart Ser.). (Illus.). 40p. (J). 2000. 15.95 (*0-06-028020-4*) HarpC Child Bks.

Murphy, Stuart J. A Pair of Socks. LC 95-19618. (MathStart Ser.). (Illus.). 40p. (J). (ps-3). 1996. lib. bdg. 15.89 (*0-06-025880-2*) HarpC Child Bks.

— A Pair of Socks. LC 95-19618. (MathStart Ser.: Level 1). (Illus.). 40p. (J). (ps up). 1996. 14.95 (*0-06-025879-9*); pap. 4.95 (*0-06-446703-1*, HarpTrophy) HarpC Child Bks.

Murphy, Stuart J. Pair of Socks. (Mathstart Ser.). 1996. 10.15 (*0-606-09596-9*, Pub. by Turtleback) Demco.

Murphy, Stuart J. The Penny Pot. LC 97-19776. (MathStart Ser.). (Illus.). 40p. (J). (gr. 2-4). 1998. 15.95 (*0-06-027606-1*); lib. bdg. 15.89 (*0-06-027607-X*) HarpC.

— The Penny Pot: Level 3: Counting Coins. LC 97-19776. (MathStart Ser.: Level 3). (Illus.). 40p. (J). (gr. 2-4). 1998. pap. 4.95 (*0-06-446717-1*, HarpTrophy) HarpC Child Bks.

— Pepper's Journal: A Kitten's First Year. LC 98-47523. (Illus.). 40p. (YA). (gr. 1-4). 2000. pap. 4.95 (*0-06-446723-6*) HarpC.

— Pepper's Journal: A Kitten's First Year. LC 98-47523. (MathStart Ser.). (Illus.). 40p. (YA). (gr. 3-7). 2000. lib. bdg. 15.89 (*0-06-027619-3*) HarpC.

— Pepper's Journal: A Kitten's First Year. LC 98-47523. (MathStart Ser. 2). (Illus.). 40p. (YA). (ps-3). 2000. 15.95 (*0-06-027618-5*) HarpC.

***Murphy, Stuart J.** Probably Pistachio. LC 99-27695. (MathStart Ser.). (Illus.). 40p. (J). (gr. 1 up). 2000. lib. bdg. 15.89 (*0-06-028029-8*) HarpC Child Bks.

— Probably Pistachio. LC 99-27695. (MathStart Ser.). 40p. (J). (gr. 1 up). 2001. pap. 4.95 (*0-06-446734-1*, HarpTrophy) HarpC Child Bks.

— Probably Pistachio. LC 99-27695. (MathStart Ser.). (Illus.). 40p. (J). (gr. 1 up). 2001. 15.95 (*0-06-028028-X*) HarpC Child Bks.

Murphy, Stuart J. Rabbit's Pajama Party. LC 98-36617. (MathStart Ser.). (Illus.). 40p. (YA). (ps-3). 1999. 15.95 (*0-06-027616-9*) HarpC Child Bks.

An Asterisk (*) at the beginning of an entry indicates that the title is appearing for the first time.

— Rabbit's Pajama Party. LC 98-36617. (MathStart Ser.). (Illus.). 40p. (YA). (ps up). 1999. lib. bdg. 15.89 (*0-06-027617-7*) HarpC Child Bks.

***Murphy, Stuart J.** Rabbit's Pajama Party. LC 98-36617. (MathStart Ser.). (Illus.). 40p. (YA). (ps up). 1999. pap. 4.95 (*0-06-446722-8*) HarpC Child Bks.

Murphy, Stuart J. Ready, Set, Hop! LC 95-4729. (MathStart Ser.). (Illus.). 40p. (J). (gr. 2 up). 1996. 15.95 (*0-06-025877-2*); pap. 4.95 (*0-06-446702-3*, HarpTrophy) HarpC Child Bks.

— Ready, Set, Hop! (Mathstart). 1996. 10.15 (*0-606-09600-0*, Pub. by Turtleback) Demco.

— Room for Ripley. LC 98-26109. (MathStart Ser.). (Illus.). 40p. (J). (gr. 2-4). 1999. lib. bdg. 15.89 (*0-06-027621-5*) HarpC Child Bks.

— Room for Ripley. LC 98-26109. (MathStart Ser.). (Illus.). 40p. (gr. 2 up). 1999. 15.95 (*0-06-027620-7*) HarpC Child Bks.

***Murphy, Stuart J.** Room for Ripley. LC 98-26109. (MathStart Ser.). (Illus.). 40p. (J). (gr. 2 up). 1999. pap. 4.95 (*0-06-446724-4*) HarpC Child Bks.

— Seaweed Soup. LC 99-87634. 40p. (ps up). pap. 4.95 (*0-06-446736-8*) HarpC.

— Seaweed Soup. LC 99-87634. 40p. 2001. 15.95 (*0-06-028032-8*) HarpC.

— The Shark Swimathon. LC 99-30312. (MathStart Ser.). (Illus.). 40p. (J). (gr. 2 up). 2001. 15.95 (*0-06-028030-1*); pap. 4.95 (*0-06-446735-X*, HarpTrophy) HarpC Child Bks.

— The Shark Swimathon. LC 99-30312. (MathStart Ser.). (Illus.). 40p. (J). (gr. 2 up). 2001. lib. bdg. 15.89 (*0-06-028031-X*) HarpC Child Bks.

Murphy, Stuart J. Spunky Monkeys on Parade. LC 98-6936. (Illus.). 40p. (YA). (gr. 1). 1999. 15.95 (*0-06-028014-X*) HarpC.

— Spunky Monkeys on Parade. LC 98-6936. (Illus.). 40p. (J). (gr. 1-3). 1999. lib. bdg. 15.89 (*0-06-028015-8*) HarpC.

— Spunky Monkeys on Parade. LC 98-6936. (MathStart Ser. 2). (Illus.). 40p. (YA). (ps-3). 1999. pap. 4.95 (*0-06-446727-9*) HarpC.

— Super Sand Castle Saturday. LC 98-3210. (Illus.). 40p. (YA). (ps-3). 1999. lib. bdg. 15.89 (*0-06-027613-4*) HarpC Child Bks.

— Super Sand Castle Saturday: Level 2: Measuring. LC 98-3210. (MathStart Ser.). (Illus.). 40p. (YA). (gr. 1 up). 1999. pap. 4.95 (*0-06-446720-1*) HarpC Child Bks.

— Super Sand Castle Saturday: Level 2: Measuring. LC 98-3210. (Illus.). 40p. (YA). (ps-3). 1999. 15.95 (*0-06-027612-6*) HarpC Child Bks.

— Too Many Kangaroo Things to Do! LC 95-20879. (MathStart Ser.). (Illus.). 40p. (J). (ps-3). 1996. 14.95 (*0-06-025883-7*); lib. bdg. 14.89 (*0-06-025884-5*) HarpC Child Bks.

— Too Many Kangaroo Things to Do! LC 95-20879. (MathStart Ser.: Level 3). (Illus.). 40p. (J). (ps-3). 1996. pap. 4.95 (*0-06-446712-0*, HarpTrophy) HarpC Child Bks.

— Too Many Kangaroo Things to Do! LC 95-20879. (MathStart Ser.). (Illus.). (J). 1996. pap. 5.00 (*0-06-446185-8*) HarpC Child Bks.

— Too Many Kangaroo Things to Do! (Mathstart Ser.). 1996. 10.15 (*0-606-09601-9*, Pub. by Turtleback) Demco.

Murphy, Stuart J. X Marks the Spot. (J). Date not set. pap. write for info. (*0-06-446738-4*, HarpTrophy) HarpC Child Bks.

— X Marks the Spot. 40p. (J). (gr. 2 up). Date not set. 15.95 (*0-06-028036-0*); lib. bdg. 15.89 (*0-06-028037-9*) HarpC Child Bks.

Murphy, Stuart J. & Miller, Ed. Circus Shapes. LC 96-35992. (MathStart Ser.). (Illus.). 40p. (J). (ps-3). 1998. 15.95 (*0-06-027436-0*); lib. bdg. 15.89 (*0-06-027437-9*) HarpC.

Murphy, Susan. I Hate Computers: 225 Reasons Why You Should, Too. LC 97-17537. (I Hate Ser.). 96p. 1997. pap. 5.95 (*1-57587-058-4*) Crane Hill AL.

— I Hate Doctors: 225 Reasons Why You Should, Too. LC 97-17539. (I Hate Ser.). 96p. 1997. pap. 5.95 (*1-57587-055-X*) Crane Hill AL.

— I Hate Getting Old: 225 Reasons Why You Should, Too. (I Hate Ser.). 96p. 1997. pap. 5.95 (*1-57587-060-6*) Crane Hill AL.

— I Hate Lawyers: 225 Reasons Why You Should, Too. LC 97-17540. (I Hate Ser.). 96p. 1997. pap. 5.95 (*1-57587-056-8*) Crane Hill AL.

— I Hate Men: 225 Reasons Why You Should Too. LC 96-53405. (I Hate Ser.). 96p. 1997. pap. 5.95 (*1-57587-053-3*) Crane Hill AL.

— I Hate the IRS: 225 Reasons Why You Should, Too. LC 97-890. (I Hate Ser.). 96p. 1997. pap. 5.95 (*1-57587-059-2*) Crane Hill AL.

— I Hate Thin People: 225 Reasons Why You Should, Too. LC 97-21988. (I Hate Thin Ser.). 96p. 1997. pap. 5.95 (*1-57587-057-6*) Crane Hill AL.

— Mad Dog Mom: Or If all Else Fails, Lower Your Expectations. LC 97-17538. 96p. 1997. pap. 5.95 (*1-57587-064-9*) Crane Hill AL.

***Murphy, Susan.** A Time for Every Purpose. 159p. 2000. pap. 14.00 (*0-7880-1611-3*, Fairway Pr) CSS OH.

Murphy, Susan, jt. auth. see Verlander, Lisette.

Murphy, Susan A. An Etymological Glossary for El Libro del Cauallero Zifar. (American University Studies: Romance Languages & Literature: Ser. II, Vol. 115). (ENG & SPA.). 200p. (C). 1989. text 30.00 (*0-8204-1092-6*) P Lang Pubng.

Murphy, Susan S. Legal Handbook of Texas Nurses. LC 94-27848. 256p. 1995. pap. 17.95 (*0-292-75176-1*); text 35.00 (*0-292-75161-3*) U of Tex Pr.

Murphy, Suzanne. Grandchildren Tend to Be Sticky: A Grandmother's Guide. LC 98-87294. 1998. pap. 6.95 (*1-56664-144-6*) WorldComm.

Murphy, Suzanne M., jt. auth. see Lowman, Dianne K.

Murphy, Sylvia N. Destiny - Hong Kong. LC 97-69232. 128p. 1998. pap. 11.95 (*1-57197-080-0*) Pentland Pr.

Murphy, T. Classic Cocktails. 234p. pap. 6.95 (*0-507-46050-2*, 217) Am Bartenders.

— Tropical Cocktails. 233p. 6.95 (*0-507-46051-0*, 214) Am Bartenders.

***Murphy, T. & Munawar, M., eds.** Aquatic Restoration in Canada. (Ecovision World Monograph Ser.). (Illus.). 224p. 1999. 67.50 (*90-5782-049-8*, Pub. by Backhuys Pubs) Balogh.

Murphy, T., et al. Statistical Methods for Textile Technologists. 107p. 1979. 40.00 (*0-7855-7226-0*) St Mut.

Murphy, T. Wallace, jt. auth. see Ravenscroft, Trevor.

Murphy, Ted. Secrets of Belltown. LC 95-6476. (Belltown Mystery Ser.: No. 1). 144p. (J). (gr. 5-9). 1995. pap. 4.95 (*0-382-39115-2*) Silver Burdett Pr.

Murphy, Ted M. The Secrets of Cain's Castle. LC 96-1436. (Belltown Mystery Ser.: No. 3). 144p. (J). 1996. pap. 4.95 (*0-382-39628-6*) Silver Burdett Pr.

— The Secrets of Cranberry Beach. LC 95-21033. (Belltown Mystery Ser.: No. 2). 144p. (J). 1996. pap. 4.95 (*0-382-39303-1*) Silver Burdett Pr.

— The Secrets of Pilgrim Pond. LC 96-26014. (A Belltown Mystery Ser.: Vol. 4). (J). (gr. 5-8). 1998. pap. 4.95 (*0-382-39776-2*) Silver Burdett Pr.

Murphy, Terence & Hardy, C. Thompson. Hospital-Physician Integration: Strategies for Success. LC 94-27666. 223p. 1994. pap. 57.50 (*1-55648-124-1*, 145159) AHPI.

Murphy, Terence R., jt. auth. see MacDonald, Michael.

Murphy, Teresa A. Ten Hours' Labor: Religion, Reform, & Gender in Early New England. LC 91-55534. 248p. 1992. text 37.50 (*0-8014-2683-9*) Cornell U Pr.

Murphy, Teri, jt. auth. see Murphy, Andy.

Murphy, Terrence & Stortz, Gerald, eds. Creed & Culture: The Place of English-Speaking Catholics in Canadian Society, 1750-1930. (Illus.). 304p. 1993. 55.00 (*0-7735-0954-2*, Pub. by McG-Queens Univ Pr) CUP Services.

Murphy, Terrence, ed. see Crowley, Terry, et al.

Murphy, Terrence V. Tenth Virginia Infantry. (Virginia Regimental Histories Ser.). (Illus.). 186p. 1989. 19.95 (*0-930919-74-2*) H E Howard.

***Murphy, Terri.** Terri Murphy's E-Listing & E-Selling Secrets for the Technologically Clueless. 2nd ed. LC 00-23237. 2000. pap. 24.95 (*0-7931-3548-6*, Real Estate Ed) Dearborn.

Murphy, Terri. Terri Murphy's Listing & Selling Secrets: How to Become a Million Dollar Producer. 168p. 1995. 24.95 (*0-7931-1545-0*, 1907-1601, Real Estate Ed) Dearborn.

Murphy, Terry. Canyon of Crooked Shadows. large type ed. (Linford Western Large Print Ser.). 320p. 1997. pap. 16.99 (*0-7089-5092-2*, Linford) Ulverscroft.

— He Rode with Quantrill. large type ed. (Linford Western Large Print Ser.). 224p. 1997. pap. 16.99 (*0-7089-5048-5*) Ulverscroft.

***Murphy, Terry.** The Hunting Man. large type ed. 216p. 1999. pap. 18.99 (*0-7089-5563-0*, Linford) Ulverscroft.

— Midnight Lynching. large type ed. 256p. pap. 18.99 (*0-7089-5433-2*) Ulverscroft.

Murphy, Terry. Missouri Blood Trail. large type ed. (Linford Western Library). 224p. 1996. pap. 16.99 (*0-7089-7886-X*) Ulverscroft.

***Murphy, Terry.** The Peaks of San Jacinto. large type ed. 232p. 2000. pap. 18.99 (*0-7089-5633-5*, Linford) Ulverscroft.

Murphy, Terry. San Carlos Horse Soldier. large type ed. 288p. 1998. pap. 17.99 (*0-7089-5366-2*, Linford) Ulverscroft.

Murphy, Terry & Klee, Murray. Manual for Better Training Statistics: Conceptual, Measurement & Survey Issues. LC 99-162671. 280p. 1997. pap. 35.00 (*92-64-15566-X*, 91-97-01-1, Pub. by Org for Econ) OECD.

Murphy, Theresa. Love on Turtle Island. large type ed. (Linford Romance Library). 240p. 1998. pap. 17.99 (*0-7089-5236-4*, Linford) Ulverscroft.

***Murphy, Theresa.** The Old Bailey: Eight Hundred Years of Crime, Cruelty & Corruption. 224p. 1999. 35.00 (*1-84018-234-2*, Pub. by Mainstream Pubng) Trafalgar.

Murphy, Therese, jt. ed. see Mills, Elizabeth.

Murphy, Thomas. A Crucial Week in the Life of a Grocer's Assistant: The Fooleen. 84p. 1978. pap. 12.95 (*0-902996-77-0*) Dufour.

— The Gigli Concert. 76p. 1988. pap. 12.95 (*0-904011-52-6*) Dufour.

— The Gioli Concert. pap. 12.95 (*0-902996-76-2*, Pub. by Gallery Pr) Dufour.

— Jubilee History of Lackawanna County, Pennsylvania: Industrial, Religious, Financial, Educations & Cultural Development of County & Subdivisions, 2 vols. (Illus.). 1267p. 1997. reprint ed. lib. bdg. 119.50 (*0-8328-7168-0*) Higginson Bk Co.

— Pastoral Theology: The Pastor in the Various Duties of His Office. unabridged ed. 525p. 1996. 29.95 (*1-889058-01-7*) Old Paths Pubns.

— The Sanctuary Lamp. 54p. 1984. pap. 12.95 (*0-904011-54-2*) Dufour.

Murphy, Thomas, jt. auth. see Christen, William L.

Murphy, Thomas, ed. see Mann, George W.

Murphy, Thomas J. & Snyder, Kenneth. What! I Have to Give a Speech? LC 94-37438. 223p. (Orig.). (J). (gr. 6-9). 1995. pap. 12.95 (*1-883790-10-7*, EDINFO Pr) Grayson Bernard Pubs.

Murphy, Thomas M. Successful Selling for Introverts: Achieving Sales Success Without a Traditional Sales Personality. 1998. pap. 14.95 (*0-9662286-0-X*) T M Murphy.

Murphy, Tim. Drugs & the Law in Ireland. O'Toole, Fintan, ed. (Undercurrents Ser.). 70p. 1996. pap. 7.95 (*1-85918-070-1*, Pub. by Cork Univ) Intl Spec Bk.

Murphy, Tim & Twomey, Patrick, eds. Ireland's Evolving Constitution, 1937-1997: Collected Essays. LC 99-234539. 256p. 1998. 50.00 (*1-901362-16-7*, Pub. by Hart Pub); pap. 30.00 (*1-901362-17-5*, Pub. by Hart Pub) Northwestern U Pr.

Murphy, Timothy. The Deed of Gift. LC 98-14326. 104p. 1998. pap. 12.95 (*1-885266-62-6*) Story Line.

— Getting off Clean. LC 96-31840. 272p. 1997. text 23.95 (*0-312-15132-2*) St Martin.

— Getting off Clean. 336p. 1998. pap. 13.95 (*0-312-18720-3*) St Martin.

— The Oldest Social Science: Configuration of Law & Modernity. LC 97-4164. (Oxford Socio-Legal Studies). 282p. 1997. text 65.00 (*0-19-826559-X*) OUP.

***Murphy, Timothy.** Set the Ploughshare Deep: A Prairie Memoir. LC 99-89156. (Illus.). 144p. 2000. 29.95 (*0-8214-1321-X*, Ohio U Ctr Intl); pap. 19.95 (*0-8214-1322-8*, Ohio U Ctr Intl) Ohio U Pr.

Murphy, Timothy. Weddings. LC 98-32058. (MiniSeries). (Illus.). 192p. 1999. pap. 5.95 (*0-7892-0524-6*) Abbeville Pr.

***Murphy, Timothy, ed.** Reader's Guide to Lesbian & Gay Studies. 1000p. 2000. lib. bdg. 125.00 (*1-57958-142-0*) Fitzroy Dearborn.

Murphy, Timothy F. Ethics in an Epidemic: AIDS, Morality & Culture. LC 94-8248. 1994. 38.00 (*0-520-08636-8*, Pub. by U CA Pr) Cal Prin Full Svc.

— Gay Science: The Ethics of Sexual Orientation Research. LC 97-16308. (Between Men-Between Women Ser.). (Illus.). 320p. 1997. 31.50 (*0-231-10848-6*) Col U Pr.

— Gay Science: The Ethics of Sexual Orientation Research. 1999. pap. 16.50 (*0-231-10849-4*) Col U Pr.

Murphy, Timothy F., ed. Gay Ethics: Controversies in Outing, Civil Rights, & Sexual Science. LC 94-14155. (Journal of Homosexuality Ser.: Vol. 27, Nos. 3-4). (Illus.). 220p. 1994. pap. text 17.95 (*1-56023-056-8*, Harrington Park) Haworth Pr.

— Gay Ethics: Controversies in Outing, Civil Rights & Sexual Science. LC 94-14155. (Journal of Homosexuality Ser.: Vol. 27, Nos. 3-4). (Illus.). 220p. 1994. lib. bdg. 54.95 (*1-56024-671-5*, Harrington Park) Haworth Pr.

Murphy, Timothy F. & Lappe, Marc, eds. Justice & the Human Genome Project. LC 93-18094. 1994. 35.00 (*0-520-08363-6*, Pub. by U CA Pr) Cal Prin Full Svc.

Murphy, Timothy F. & Poirier, Suzanne. Writing AIDS. 1994. pap. 19.50 (*0-231-07865-X*) Col U Pr.

Murphy, Timothy F. & Poirier, Suzanne, eds. Writing AIDS: Gay Literature, Language, & Analysis. LC 92-20373. (Between Men - Between Women Ser.). 352p. (C). 1993. 41.00 (*0-231-07864-1*) Col U Pr.

Murphy, Timothy R. Managing Notorious Trials. 2nd ed. LC 98-67361. 225p. 1998. write for info. (*0-89656-188-7*) Natl Ctr St Courts.

Murphy, Timothy S. Wising up the Marks: The Novels of William S. Burroughs. LC 96-53094. 256p. 1998. 48.00 (*0-520-20950-8*, Pub. by U CA Pr); pap. 17.95 (*0-520-20951-6*, Pub. by U CA Pr) Cal Prin Full Svc.

Murphy, Timothy S., jt. auth. see Stein, Elias M.

***Murphy, Tom.** The Fastest Motocycles on Earth: The History of Land Speed Record Motorcycles. (Illus.). 112p. 2000. pap. 19.95 (*1-884313-17-5*, 130637AE, Pub. by Whitehorse NH) Motorbooks Intl.

Murphy, Tom. The Gigli Concert. (Methuen Modern Plays Ser.). 86p. (Orig.). (C). 1991. pap. write for info. (*0-413-65930-5*, A0591, Methuen Drama) Methn.

— Harley-Davidson Big Twin Performance Handbook. (Illus.). 192p. 1995. pap. text 21.95 (*0-7603-0009-7*) MBI Pubg.

— How to Build Harley-Davidson Horsepower. LC 97-12210. (Illus.). 160p. 1997. pap. 19.95 (*0-7603-0150-6*) MBI Pubg.

— Jack & Bobby. LC 98-7886. (Illus.). 120p. 1998. 19.98 (*1-56799-591-8*, MetroBooks) M Friedman Pub Grp Inc.

— Murphy: Plays One. (Methuen World Dramatists Ser.). 231p. (C). 1992. pap. 14.95 (*0-413-66570-4*, A0660, Methuen Drama) Methn.

— Murphy: Plays Three. 256p. 1994. pap. 15.95 (*0-413-68350-8*, A0692, Methuen Drama) Methn.

— Murphy: Plays Two. LC 93-222005. 241p. (C). 1993. pap. 14.95 (*0-413-67560-2*, A0670, Methuen Drama) Methn.

Murphy, Tom. Murphy's Plays, No. 4. 1997. pap. 14.95 (*0-413-71450-0*) Methn.

— She Stoops to Folly. 2000. pap. 10.95 (*0-413-71400-4*) Methn.

Murphy, Tom. Too Late for Logic. LC 92-231518. (Methuen Modern Plays Ser.). 54p. (C). 1990. pap. 10.95 (*0-413-63220-2*, A0484, Methuen Drama) Methn.

***Murphy, Tom.** The Wake. 1998. pap. 10.95 (*0-413-71410-1*) Methn.

— Web Rules: How the Internet Is Changing the Way Consumers Make Choices. LC 99-86718. 303p. 2000. 25.00 (*0-7931-3613-X*) Dearborn.

Murphy, Tom & Cloud, Barbara. Media Law in Nevada. (State Law Ser.). 74p. (C). 1992. pap. text 10.95 (*0-913507-28-8*) New Forums.

Murphy, Tom, ed. see Hopkins, Tom.

Murphy, Tommy. Elegant Wine Cocktails: One Hundred Eleven Recipes for Delicious Wine Drinks. 256p. 1985. mass mkt. 6.95 (*0-446-38313-9*, Pub. by Warner Bks) Little.

Murphy, Toni & Briggs-Erickson, Carol. Environmental Guide to the Internet. 4th abr. rev. ed. 407p. 1998. pap. 59.00 (*0-86587-643-6*, 643) Gov Insts.

Murphy, Trace. Book of Wisdom. LC 95-13406. 176p. 1995. pap. 6.00 (*0-385-47845-3*) Doubleday.

Murphy, Troy, jt. auth. see Anderson, Kim.

Murphy, V., jt. auth. see Baker, J.

Murphy, Vickie, jt. auth. see Pini, Richard.

Murphy, Victoria. Wyoming: A 20th Century History of Its Citizens, Businesses & Institutions. Parks, Lori, ed. LC 99-73082. (Illus.). 300p. 1999. 39.95 (*1-886483-30-2*, Pub. by Heritge Media) Sunbelt Pubns.

Murphy, Virginia R. Across the Plains in the Donner Party. LC 98-34919. 1998. 14.95 (*0-87770-637-9*); pap. 9.95 (*0-87770-633-6*) Ye Galleon.

— Across the Plains in the Donner Party: 1846-47. Jones, William R., ed. LC 95-40419. (Illus.). 64p. 1980. pap. 6.95 (*0-89646-063-0*) Vistabooks.

— Across the Plains in the Donner Party by Virginia Reed Murphy with Letters by James Reed. Zeinert, Karen, ed. LC 95-52360. (Illus.). xvii, 112p. 1996. lib. bdg. 19.50 (*0-208-02404-2*, Linnet Bks) Shoe String.

Murphy, Vreni, jt. auth. see Baker, Joseph T.

Murphy, Vreni, jt. ed. see Baker, Joseph T.

Murphy, W. Ten Commandments for Children. (J). (ps-3). Date not set. pap. text 1.95 (*0-88271-159-8*) Regina Pr.

Murphy, W. M. & Knecht, D. A., eds. Scientific Basis for Nuclear Waste Management XIX: Materials Research Society Symposium Proceedings, Vol. 412. 937p. 1996. 65.00 (*1-55899-315-0*) Materials Res.

Murphy, W. M., jt. auth. see Ruedi, T. P.

Murphy, W. R., et al. The Effect of Lubricant Traction on Wormgear Efficiency. (Technical Papers: Vol. P254.33). (Illus.). 21p. 1981. pap. text 30.00 (*1-55589-359-7*) AGMA.

Murphy, Walter F. Congress & the Court: A Case Study in the American Political Process. LC 62-9739. 319p. reprint ed. pap. 98.90 (*0-608-09484-6*, 205428500005) Bks Demand.

— Elements of Judicial Strategy. LC 64-24973. 264p. 1973. pap. text 19.00 (*0-226-55370-1*) U Ch Pr.

— Elements of Judicial Strategy. LC 64-24973. 1992. lib. bdg. 17.50 (*0-226-55369-8*) U Ch Pr.

— Roman Enigma. 1981. 13.95 (*0-02-588250-3*) Macmillan.

Murphy, Walter F. & Pritchett, Charles H. Courts, Judges & Politics: An Introduction to the Judicial Process. 4th ed. 560p. (C). 1986. pap. 56.88 (*0-07-554829-1*) McGraw.

Murphy, Walter F., et al. American Constitutional Interpretation. 2nd ed. 1410p. (C). 1995. text 49.95 (*1-56662-240-9*) Foundation Pr.

— American Constitutional Interpretations. LC 86-6240. (University Casebook Ser.). 1262p. 1986. text 40.95 (*0-88277-321-6*) Foundation Pr.

Murphy, Walter L. New Hampshire Civil Jury Instructions. 3rd ed. 456p. 1994. spiral bd. 89.00 (*0-250-40748-5*, MICHIE) LEXIS Pub.

Murphy, Walter L. & Pope, Daniel C. New Hampshire Civil Jury Instructions. 2nd ed. 400p. 1992. ring bd. 75.00 (*1-56257-310-1*, MICHIE) LEXIS Pub.

— New Hampshire Civil Jury Instructions. 2nd ed. 400p. 1993. suppl. ed. 27.00 (*0-685-74472-8*, MICHIE) LEXIS Pub.

Murphy, Walter L. & Pope, Daniel C. New Hampshire Civil Jury Instructions. 3rd ed. 89.00 (*0-250-40766-3*) LEXIS Pub.

— New Hampshire Civil Jury Instructions, Issue 6. 50p. 1999. ring bd. write for info. (*0-327-01695-7*, 8202716) LEXIS Pub.

Murphy, Walter L., jt. auth. see Pope, Daniel C.

Murphy, Warren. American Obsession. 1997. per. 5.50 (*0-373-63224-X*, 1-63224-9, Wrldwide Lib) Harlequin Bks.

— Bamboo Dragon. (Destroyer Ser.: No. 108). 1997. per. 5.50 (*0-373-63223-1*, 1-63223-1, Wrldwide Lib) Harlequin Bks.

— Bay City Blast. (Destroyer Ser.: No. 38). 1990. mass mkt. 3.50 (*1-55817-443-5*, Pinncle Kensgtn) Kensgtn Pub Corp.

— Bottom Line. (Destroyer Ser.: No. 37). 1990. mass mkt. 3.50 (*1-55817-419-2*, Pinncle Kensgtn) Kensgtn Pub Corp.

— The Color of Fear. (Destroyer Ser.). 1995. per. 4.99 (*0-373-63214-2*, 1-63214-0) Harlequin Bks.

— Death Check. (Destroyer Ser.: No. 2). 1988. mass mkt. 3.50 (*1-55817-037-5*, Pinncle Kensgtn) Kensgtn Pub Corp.

— The Destroyer, No. 95. 1999. pap. 4.50 (*0-451-17771-1*, Sig) NAL.

— Feast or Famine. 1997. per. 5.50 (*0-373-63222-3*, 1-63222-3, Wrldwide Lib) Harlequin Bks.

— Honor among Thieves. 448p. 1992. mass mkt. 5.99 (*1-55817-614-4*, Pinncle Kensgtn) Kensgtn Pub Corp.

— Murder Ward. (Destroyer Ser.: No. 15). 1989. mass mkt. 3.50 (*1-55817-197-5*, Pinncle Kensgtn) Kensgtn Pub Corp.

— Never Say Die. (Destroyer Ser.: No. 110). 1998. per. 5.99 (*0-373-63225-8*, 1-63225-6, Wrldwide Lib) Harlequin Bks.

— Prophet of Doom. (Destroyer Ser.: Vol. 111). 1998. per. 5.99 (*0-373-63226-6*, 1-63226-4, Wrldwide Lib) Harlequin Bks.

— Scorched Earth. (Destroyer Ser.: No. 105). 1996. per. 5.50 (*0-373-63220-7*, 1-63220-7, Wrldwide Lib) Harlequin Bks.

— Scorpion's Dance. 1990. mass mkt. 4.95 (*1-55817-333-1*, Pinncle Kensgtn) Kensgtn Pub Corp.

— The Sure Thing. 448p. 1988. mass mkt. 4.50 (*1-55817-129-0*, Pinncle Kensgtn) Kensgtn Pub Corp.

— Trace & Forty-Seven Miles of Rope. (Trace Ser.: No. 2). 1984. pap. 2.95 (*0-317-00847-1*, Sig) NAL.

— White Water. (Destroyer Ser.). 352p. 1997. per. 5.50 (*0-373-63221-5*, 1-63221-5, Wrldwide Lib) Harlequin Bks.

Murphy, Warren & Cochran, Molly. Grandmaster. 1988. pap. 4.95 (*1-55817-458-3*); mass mkt. 4.50 (*1-55817-101-0*, Pinncle Kensgtn) Kensgtn Pub Corp.

— The Temple Dogs. 416p. 1989. 18.95 (0-318-40988-7) NAL.

Murphy, Warren & Sapik, Richard. High Priestess. 1994. per. 4.99 (0-373-63210-X) Harlequin Bks.

Murphy, Warren & Sapir. Angry White Mailmen. (Destroyer Ser.: No. 104). 1996. per. 5.50 (0-373-63219-3, 1-63219-9, Wrldwide Lib) Harlequin Bks.

Murphy, Warren & Sapir, Richard. Deadly Genes. (Destroyer Ser.: No. 117). 1999. per. 5.99 (0-373-63232-0, 1-63232-2, Wrldwide Lib) Harlequin Bks.

— The Empire Dreams. (Destroyer Ser.: No.113). 352p. 1998. per. 5.99 (0-373-63228-2, 1-63228-0, Wrldwide Lib) Harlequin Bks.

— Engines of Destruction. (Destroyer Ser.: No. 103). 1996. per. 5.50 (0-373-63218-5, 1-63218-1, Wrldwide Lib) Harlequin Bks.

***Murphy, Warren & Sapir, Richard.** Fade to Black: The Destroyer. 2000. per. 5.99 (0-373-63234-7) Harlequin Bks.

Murphy, Warren & Sapir, Richard. Failing Marks. (Destroyer Ser.: No. 114). 1999. per. 5.99 (0-373-63229-0) Harlequin Bks.

— The Final Reel. (Destroyer Ser.: Vol. 116). 1999. per. 5.99 (0-373-63231-2, Wrldwide Lib) Harlequin Bks.

— Identity Crisis. 1994. per. 4.99 (0-373-63212-6, 1-63212-4) Harlequin Bks.

— Target of Opportunity. (Destroyer Ser.). 1995. mass mkt. 4.99 (0-373-63213-4, 1-63213-2) Harlequin Bks.

Murphy, Warren & Sapir, Richard, creators. Bidding War. LC 95-22339. (Destroyer Ser.). 347p. 1995. per. 4.99 (0-373-63216-9, 1-63216-5, Wrldwide Lib) Harlequin Bks.

— Last Rites. LC 95-22338. (Destroyer Ser.). 349p. 1995. per. 4.99 (0-373-63215-0, 1-63215-7) Harlequin Bks.

Murphy, Warren, jt. auth. see Cochran, Molly.

Murphy, Weasel. The Professional Gambler's Handbook: Beating the System by Hook & by Crook. LC 97-136647. (Illus.). 208p. 1997. pap. 17.00 (0-87364-915-X) Paladin Pr.

Murphy, Wendy B. Asthma. LC 97-52128. (Medical Library). (Illus.). 128p. (YA). (gr. 7 up). 1998. lib. bdg. 23.90 (0-7613-0364-2) Millbrook Pr.

— Beds & Borders: Traditional & Original Garden Designs. (Illus.). 166p. 1993. pap. 22.95 (0-395-66078-5) HM.

— Healing the Generations: A History of Physical Therapy & the American Physical Therapy Association. (Illus.). 256p. Date not set. 105.00 (0-944641-13-X, APTA-20) Greenwich Pub Group.

***Murphy, Wendy B.** Spare Parts: From Peg Legs to Gene Splices. LC 00-20883. 2000. lib. bdg. write for info. (0-7613-1355-9) TFC Bks NY.

Murphy, Wendy B. & Murphy, Jack. Nuclear Medicine. Garell, Dale C. & Snyder, Solomon H., eds. (Encyclopedia of Health Ser.). (Illus.). 116p. (YA). (gr. 7 up). 1994. lib. bdg. 19.95 (0-7910-0070-2) Chelsea Hse.

Murphy, William A., Jr., et al. Musculoskeletal Disease Test & Syllabus. (Professional Self-Evaluation & Continuing Education Program Ser.: Vol. 37). (Illus.). 900p. 1994. 220.00 (1-55903-036-4) Am Coll Radiology.

Murphy, William D., jt. auth. see Dattilo, John.

Murphy, William E. & Barth, Margaret M., eds. New Developments in Refrigeration for Food Safety & Quality. LC 96-86512. 318p. 1996. pap. 50.50 (0-929355-80-6, P0996) Am Soc Ag Eng.

Murphy, William F. The Tactics of Psychotherapy: An Application of Psychoanalytic Theory to Psychotherapy. LC 65-19462. 1965. 72.50 (0-8236-6360-4) Intl Univs Pr.

Murphy, William F., jt. auth. see Deutsch, Felix.

Murphy, William J. R&D Cooperation among Marketplace Competitors. LC 90-8919. 272p. 1990. 59.95 (0-89930-489-3, MRD/, Quorum Bks) Greenwood.

***Murphy, William James Scott.** Copyrighting America: America's Copyright Guide & Workbook. (Illus.). 126p. 2000. per. 29.95 (0-9661963-2-5) Patacco.

Murphy, William L. A Birder's Guide to Trinidad & Tobago. 2nd ed. LC 95-43230. (Illus.). vi, 160p. (Orig.). 1995. spiral bd. 15.95 (0-941475-02-6) Peregrine Enter.

— Duplin County Wills, Genealogical Abstracts Of, 1730-1860. 280p. 1986. reprint ed. 27.50 (0-89308-597-9, NC 32) Southern Hist Pr.

— Ten-Day Checklist of the Birds of Trinidad & Tobago. 10p. (Orig.). (C). 1994. 3.00 (0-941475-03-4) Peregrine Enter.

— Why? LC 97-132424. (Orig.). 1996. pap. 8.95 (0-533-11764-X) Vantage.

Murphy, William M. Family Secrets: William Butler Yeats & His Relatives. LC 94-19006. (Irish Studies). (Illus.). 464p. 1995. 45.00 (0-8156-0301-0) Syracuse U Pr.

***Murphy, William M.** Urinary Cytopathology. (Illus.). 96p. 2000. 60.00 (0-89189-445-4) Am Soc Clinical.

Murphy, William M. Urological Pathology. 2nd ed. Day, Leslie, ed. LC 96-46546. 656p. 1997. text 195.00 (0-7216-6029-0, W B Saunders Co) Harcrt Hlth Sci Grp.

Murphy, William M., et al, contrib. by. Urological Pathology: Based on the Proceedings of the Sixtieth Annual Anatomic Pathology Slide Seminar of the American Society of Clinical Pathologists: October 27 & 28, 1994, Washington, DC. 112p. 1995. 40.00 (0-89189-393-8) Am Soc Clinical.

Murphy, William M. & Bruckner, D. J., eds. The Idea of the University of Chicago: Selections from the Papers of the First Eight Chief Executives of the University of Chicago from 1891-1975. 1994. 15.00 (0-226-55366-3) U Ch Pr.

Murphy, William M., et al. Tumors of the Urinary Bladder & Related Urinary Structures: Tumors of the Kidney, Bladder & Related Urinary Structures. Farrow, George M., ed. (AFIP Atlas of Tumor Pathology Ser.: Vol. 11). (Illus.). 362p. 1994. pap. text 55.00 (1-881041-15-8) Am Registry Path.

Murphy, William M., jt. auth. see Cullen, Fintan.

Murphy, William T. Managing Audiovisual Records. (Illus.). 51p. (C). 1998. pap. text 25.00 (0-7881-4766-8) DIANE Pub.

Murphy, Yannick. The Sea of Trees. 240p. 1998. pap. 12.00 (0-395-92491-X) HM.

Murphy, Yolanda & Murphy, Robert F. Women of the Forest. 2nd ed. LC 85-14969. 275p. 1985. pap. text 20.00 (0-231-06089-0) Col U Pr.

Murphy, Yolanda, jt. auth. see Fand, Robert.

***Murphy/Nance.** Physical Geology. 2000. pap. 54.00 (0-534-37866-8) Thomson Learn.

Murr, George G. The Lebanese Village: An Old Culture in a New Era. (Illus.). 276p. 1987. 24.95 (0-86685-419-3, LDL4193, Pub. by Librairie du Liban) Intl Bk Ctr.

Murr, Karen, ed. see Harju, Jerry.

Murr, L. Industrial Materials Science & Engineering. (Manufacturing Engineering & Materials Processing Ser.: Vol. 13). (Illus.). 616p. 1984. text 210.00 (0-8247-7174-5) Dekker.

Murr, Lawrence E. Electron & Ion Microscopy & Microanalysis: Principles & Applications. 2nd rev. ed. (Optical Engineering Ser.: Vol. 29). (Illus.). 856p. 1991. text 199.00 (0-8247-8556-8) Dekker.

— Interfacial Phenomena in Metals & Alloys. (Illus.). 390p. (C). 1990. reprint ed. text 91.00 (1-878907-12-3) TechBooks.

— What Every Engineer Should Know about Material & Component Failure, Failure Analysis & Litigation. (What Every Engineer Should Know Ser.: Vol. 20). (Illus.). 176p. 1986. text 65.00 (0-8247-7732-8) Dekker.

Murr, Lawrence E., ed. Materials Science & Engineering for Manufacturing. (Illus.). 375p. (C). 1990. text 89.00 (1-878907-37-9) TechBooks.

— Shock Waves for Industrial Applications. LC 88-27516. (Illus.). 532p. 1989. 129.00 (0-8155-1170-1) Noyes.

Murr, Lawrence E. & Stein, Charles, eds. Frontiers in Materials Science: Distinguished Lectures. LC 75-39870. (Monographs & Textbooks in Material Science: No. 8). (Illus.). 610p. reprint ed. pap. 189.10 (0-7837-0973-0, 204127900019) Bks Demand.

Murr, Lawrence E., et al. Metallurgical & Materials Applications of Shock-Wave & High-Strain-Rate Phenomena: Proceedings of the 1995 International Conference on Metallurgical & Materials Applications of Shock-Wave & High-Strain-Rate Phenomena, El Paso, Texas. LC 95-44209. 952p. 1995. 305.75 (0-444-82010-8) Elsevier.

Murr, Lawrence E., jt. auth. see Staudhammer, Karl P.

Murr, Muhammed A. Dubai Tales. Clark, Peter, tr. from ARA. 160p. (Orig.). 1990. pap. 21.00 (0-948259-86-8, Pub. by Forest Bks) Dufour.

Murr, Naeem. The Boy. LC 97-49150. 176p. 1998. 22.00 (0-395-90106-5) HM.

— The Boy. 224p. 1999. pap. 13.00 (0-395-95790-7, Mariner Bks) HM.

Murra, John V. Research in Economic Anthropology Suppl. 1: The Economic Organization of the Inka State. Isaac, Barry L. & Dalton, George, eds. (Research in Economic Anthropology Ser.: Suppl. 1). 214p. 1980. 78.50 (0-89232-118-0) Jai Pr.

Murra, John V., jt. auth. see Collier, Donald.

Murra, John V., jt. ed. see Urioste, George L.

***Murrah, C. Patrick.** "This Ain't ER" A Heart Surgeon's Struggle to Keep the Faith. LC 00-100651. 250p. 2000. 14.95 (1-885003-49-8, Pub. by R D Reed Pubs) Midpt Trade.

Murrah, David J. Oil, Taxes, & the Cats: A History of the Devitt Family & the Mallet Ranch. LC 93-33654. (Illus.). 247p. 1994. 25.00 (0-89672-332-1) Tex Tech Univ Pr.

Murrah, Judy. Dress Daze: Countless Ideas for Comfortable Dresses. Lowe, Melissa, ed. LC 96-47599. (Illus.). 64p. (Orig.). 1997. pap. 16.95 (1-56477-188-1, B302) Martingale & Co.

— Jazz It Up! 101 Stitching & Embellishing Techniques. LC 98-29410. (Illus.). 128p. 1998. pap. 27.95 (1-56477-245-4, DB373, That Patchwrk Pl) Martingale & Co.

— More Jazz from Judy Murrah: New Shapes & Great Ideas for Wonderful Wearable Art. LC 95-49842. (Illus.). 128p. 1996. pap. 24.95 (1-56477-135-0, B252) Martingale & Co.

Murrant, Jim. The Boating Bible: The Essential Handbook for Every Sailor. (Illus.). 320p. 1991. pap. 29.95 (0-924486-13-9) Sheridan.

Murray. Boys & Girls. (Key Words Readers Ser.: B Series, No. 641-3b). (Illus.). (J). (ps-5). pap. 3.50 (0-7214-0015-9, Ladybrd) Penguin Putnam.

— China Next Superpower: Dilemmas in Change & Continuity. LC 98-6004. 256p. 1998. text 39.95 (0-312-21533-9) St Martin.

— Commercial Law. 2nd ed. (American Casebook Ser.). Date not set. text. write for info. (0-314-06662-4) West Pub.

— Critical Care Assessment. LC 99-21517. 1999. pap. text. write for info. (0-7216-6585-3, W B Saunders Co) Harcrt Hlth Sci Grp.

— Easy to Sound. (Key Words Readers Ser.). (Illus.). (J). (ps-5). 1981. pap. 3.50 (0-7214-0031-0, Ladybrd) Penguin Putnam.

— Extended End-Plate Moment Connections. 43p. 1990. 20.00 (1-56424-029-0, D804) Am Inst Steel Construct.

— Fun at the Farm. (Key Words Readers Ser.: B Series, No. 641-4b). (Illus.). (J). (ps-5). pap. 3.50 (0-7214-0478-2, Ladybrd) Penguin Putnam.

— A Handlist of Howard Carter's Catalogue of Objects in Tutankhamuns Tomb Vol. 1: Tutankhamuns Tomb. 30p. 1963. 30.00 (0-900416-06-8, Pub. by Aris & Phillips) David Brown.

— Harper's Biochemistry. 25th ed. 927p. (C). 1999. pap. 39.95 (0-8385-3684-0, Apple Lange Med) McGraw.

— History of Children's Literature in the U. S. 1997. pap. 12.95 (0-8057-4108-9) Macmillan.

— History of the Bellingham Rotary Club: 1917-1981. (Occasional Papers: No. 16). 1986. pap. 4.95 (0-318-23334-7) WWU CPNS.

— Holy in Christ. 1998. pap. 12.99 (1-85792-144-5, Pub. by Christian Focus) Spring Arbor Dist.

— Humility. (Pocket Ser.). 1992. mass mkt. 3.75 (0-87508-431-1) Chr Lit.

— Looking for the Parade. LC 98-50928. 124p. 1999. 21.00 (0-393-04727-X) Norton.

— Mastering Powerpoint for Windows X. 5th ed. 1996. pap. text 29.99 (0-7821-1923-9) Sybex.

— Medical Microbiology. 3rd ed. LC 97-18902. (Illus.). 736p. (C). (gr. 13). 1997. pap. text 49.00 (0-8151-9035-2, 29126) Mosby Inc.

— Midwives & Safer Motherhood. 1996. mass mkt. 24.00 (0-7234-2122-6) Mosby Inc.

— Ministry of Intercession. 1996. pap. 6.99 (1-85792-145-3, Pub. by Christian Focus) Spring Arbor Dist.

— Modern Critical Theory: A Phenomenological Introduction. 242p. 1975. pap. text 99.50 (90-247-1697-7, Pub. by M Nijhoff) Kluwer Academic.

— Non Disclosure. 1993. 27.95 (0-07-881945-8) McGraw.

— Personal Fitness. Date not set. wbk. ed. write for info. (0-314-09736-8) West Pub.

— Pre Echo. 336p. (C). 1995. pap. text 29.95 (0-13-320714-5) P-H.

— Reindeer & Gold. 1988. pap. 10.95 (1-882008-02-2) WWU CPNS.

***Murray.** South of Eden. 320p. 2000. 23.95 (0-312-86923-1) Forge NYC.

Murray. The Stars Are Waiting. 2001. 16.00 (0-689-80543-8) S&S Childrens.

— Textbook of Respiratory Medicine. 3rd ed. (C). 2000. text. write for info. (0-7216-7711-8, W B Saunders Co) Harcrt Hlth Sci Grp.

— Vietnam: Dawn of a New Market. LC 97-23013. 272p. 1997. text 55.00 (0-312-17390-3) St Martin.

— Write to Learn. 5th ed. (C). 1995. pap. text, teacher ed. 30.00 (0-15-503239-9) Harcourt Coll Pubs.

Murray & Birnbaum. Wall Street Journal. 1987. write for info. (0-318-61167-8) Random.

Murray & Elgers. An Introduction to Using Financial Accounting. 2nd ed. (SWC-Accounting). 1999. pap., student ed. 18.00 (0-324-01518-6) Thomson Learn.

— Using Financial Accounting: An Introduction. 1997. student ed. 17.50 (0-314-20976-X) West Pub.

***Murray & Pappas.** Javascript & HTML 4.0 User Resource. LC 98-39484. 512p. 1998. pap. text 34.99 (0-13-977422-X) P-H.

***Murray & Yang.** Why Were the Japanese Interned? 2000. pap. text 11.95 (0-312-20829-4) St Martin.

***Murray, et al.** Personal Fitness & Wellness. 2001. pap. 35.00 (0-534-56871-8) Thomson Learn.

Murray, jt. auth. see Field, A.

Murray, jt. auth. see Grant Staff.

Murray, jt. auth. see Towell.

Murray, jt. auth. see Wall.

***Murray, Terry A.** An Index to Short Stories in Science Fiction Magazines, 1926-1995. LC 98-53290. 637p. 1999. lib. bdg. 65.00 (0-7864-0691-7) McFarland & Co.

Murray, A. D., ed. John Ludlow: The Autobiography of a Christian Socialist. (Illus.). 354p. 1981. 30.00 (0-7146-3085-3, Pub. by F Cass Pubs) Intl Spec Bk.

Murray, A. T., tr. Private Orations, Vol. IV: 27-40. (Loeb Classical Library: No. 318, 346, 351). 538p. 1936. 18.95 (0-674-99351-9) HUP.

— Private Orations, Vol. V: Nos. 41-49. (Loeb Classical Library: No. 318, 346, 351). 432p. 1939. 18.95 (0-674-99381-0) HUP.

Murray, A. T., tr. see Homer.

Murray, Agnes, tr. see Joy, Janet L.

***Murray, Alan.** The Wealth of Choices: How the New Economy Puts Power in Your Hands & Money in Your Pockets. LC 99-57773. 288p. 2000. 24.95 (0-8129-3266-8) Random.

Murray, Alan F. Applications of Neural Networks. LC 94-43161. 336p. (C). 1994. text 155.00 (0-7923-9442-9) Kluwer Academic.

Murray, Alan F., et al, eds. Pipeline Symposium Vol. 5: Pipeline Symposium. LC 82-70515. (1995 Offshore Mechanics & Arctic Engineering Conference Ser.: Vol. V). 608p. 1995. 180.00 (0-7918-1311-8, H00943) ASME.

Murray, Alan F. & Reekie, H. Martin. Integrated Circuit Design. LC 87-12935. 147p. 1987. 42.00 (0-387-91303-3) Spr-Verlag.

Murray, Alan F. & Tarassenko, Lionel. Analogue Neural VLSI: A Pulse Stream Approach. LC 93-32970. 168p. 1993. mass mkt. 54.95 (0-412-45060-7, Chap & Hall NY) Chapman & Hall.

Murray, Alan F., jt. auth. see Edwards, Peter J.

Murray, Alan I. & Siehl, Caren. Joint Ventures & Other Alliances: Creating a Successful Cooperative Linkage. LC 89-85781. (Illus.). 100p. 1990. pap. 25.00 (0-910586-76-4, 086-90) Finan Exec.

Murray, Alan P. Depreciation. LC 74-172243. (Tax Technique Handbook Ser.). (Illus.). 138p. (Orig.). 1971. pap. 5.00 (0-915506-12-2) Harvard Law Intl Tax.

Murray, Alan S., jt. auth. see Birnbaum, Jeffrey H.

Murray, Alastair. Reconstructing Realism: Between Power Politics & Cosmopolitan Ethics. 224p. 1998. 68.00 (1-85331-196-0, Pub. by Edinburgh U Pr) Col U Pr.

Murray, Albert. The Blue Devils of Nada. 1997. pap. 12.00 (0-679-75859-3) Vin Bks.

— Blue Devils of Nada: A Contemporary American Approach to Aesthetic Statement. 238p. 1996. 23.00 (0-679-44213-8) Pantheon.

— Conversations with Albert Murray. Maguire, Roberta S., ed. LC 97-2626. (Literary Conversations Ser.). 192p. 1997. pap. 17.00 (1-57806-008-7); text 45.00 (1-57806-007-9) U Pr of Miss.

— Good Morning Blues: The Autobiography of Count Basie. (Illus.). 432p. 1995. reprint ed. pap. 15.95 (0-306-80609-6) Da Capo.

— Hero & the Blues. 1996. pap. 9.00 (0-679-76220-5) Random.

— The Omni-Americans: Black Experience & American Culture. (Quality Paperbacks Ser.). 227p. 1990. reprint ed. pap. 13.95 (0-306-80395-X) Da Capo.

— Reflections Behind the Wheel of a Taxi: The Autobiography of a 30-Year Dropout. 258p. (Orig.). 1990. pap. 19.95 (1-877586-01-3) Braimanna Pubs.

— Reflections on Logic, Politics & Reality: A Challenge to the Sacred Consensus of Contemporary American Thinking. 256p. (C). 1989. 24.95 (1-877586-00-5) Braimanna Pubs.

— The Seven League Boots: A Novel. 1997. pap. 13.00 (0-679-75858-5) Knopf.

— The Seven League Boots: A Novel. 369p. 1996. 25.00 (0-679-43986-2) Pantheon.

— South to a Very Old Place. 1992. 20.50 (0-8446-6630-0) Peter Smith.

— South to a Very Old Place. LC 91-50214. 240p. 1991. pap. 11.00 (0-679-73695-6) Vin Bks.

— The Spyglass Tree. LC 92-50077. 1992. pap. 12.00 (0-679-73085-0) Vin Bks.

— Stomping the Blues. (Quality Paperbacks Ser.). (Illus.). 272p. 1989. pap. 16.00 (0-306-80362-3) Da Capo.

— Train Whistle Guitar. LC 98-7128. 208p. 1998. pap. 13.00 (0-375-70336-5) Vin Bks.

Murray, Albert V. The State & the Church in a Free Society. LC 77-27134. (Hibbert Lectures: 1957). reprint ed. 37.50 (0-404-60433-1) AMS Pr.

Murray, Alex, jt. ed. see Fallis, George.

Murray, Alex L. & Wilkinson, Paul F. Integrated Camping & the Retarded, Nos. 949-950. 1976. 12.50 (0-686-20381-X, Sage Prdcls Pr) Sage.

Murray, Alexander. Reason & Society in the Middle Ages. (Illus.). 528p. 1986. pap. 24.95 (0-19-821985-7) OUP.

— Suicide in the Middle Ages: The Violent Against Themselves, Vol. I. LC 97-7806. (Illus.). 510p. 1999. text 49.95 (0-19-820539-2) OUP.

***Murray, Alexander.** Suicide in the Middle Ages Vol. 2: The Curse on Self-Murder. (Illus.). 620p. 2000. text 49.95 (0-19-820731-X) OUP.

***Murray, Alexander, ed.** Sir William Jones, 1746-94: A Commemoration. LC 98-27487. (Illus.). 188p. 1999. text 65.00 (0-19-920190-0) OUP.

Murray, Alexander C. After Rome's Fall: Narrators & Sources of Early Medieval History. LC 99-215973. 400p. 1998. text 55.00 (0-8020-0779-1) U of Toronto Pr.

— Germanic Kinship Structure: Studies in Law & Society in Antiquity & the Early Middle Ages. xii, 256p. pap. text 28.00 (0-88844-065-0) Brill Academic Pubs.

***Murray, Alexander C. & Dutton, Paul E., eds.** From Roman to Merovingian Gaul. (Readings in Medieval Civilizations & Cultures Ser.: Vol. V). 550p. 2000. pap. 26.95 (1-55111-102-0) Broadview Pr.

Murray, Alexander V. The Manual of Mythology: Greek & Roman, Norse & Old German, Hindoo & Egyptian Mythology. Gross, Gina R., ed. (Illus.). 368p. 1993. reprint ed. pap. 12.95 (0-87877-182-4) Newcastle Pub.

Murray, Alice, ed. & intro. see Murray, Raymond L. & Murray, Melba L.

Murray, Alice E. A History of the Commercial & Financial Relations Between England & Ireland from the Period of the Restoration. LC 70-133529. (Select Bibliographies Reprint Ser.). 1977. reprint ed. 28.95 (0-8369-5561-7) Ayer.

Murray, Allison J. No Money, No Honey: A Study of Street Traders & Prostitutes in Jakarta. (Illus.). 190p. (C). 1991. 37.00 (0-19-588991-6) OUP.

***Murray, Anabel.** Sympathetic Strangers. 352p. 1999. 20.99 (1-85389-947-X) Ulverscroft.

***Murray, Andre.** Murder for the Green. LC 00-90507. 2000. 10.95 (0-533-13526-5) Vantage.

Murray, Andrew. Abide in Christ. LC 97-223781. 1992. pap. 9.99 (0-87508-724-8) Chr Lit.

— Abide in Christ. 208p. 1980. mass mkt. 5.99 (0-88368-091-2) Whitaker Hse.

— Abide in Christ. (Andrew Murray Classics Ser.). 176p. 1987. mass mkt. 4.99 (0-310-55152-8, 19015P) Zondervan.

— Absolute Surrender. 144p. 1978. mass mkt. 5.99 (0-87508-398-6, 398) Chr Lit.

— Absolute Surrender. mass mkt. 4.99 (0-8024-0560-6, 72) Moody.

— Absolute Surrender. 139p. 1981. mass mkt. 5.99 (0-88368-093-9) Whitaker Hse.

— Absolute Surrender: A Guide to the Spirit-Filled Life. 142p. 1987. pap. 3.70 (0-310-55132-3, 19013P) Zondervan.

— Aids to Devotion. (Andrew Murray Classics Ser.). 104p. 1987. pap. 4.95 (0-310-55122-6, 19012P) Zondervan.

— Andrew Murray on Prayer. LC 98-27895. (Andrew Murray Anthology Ser.). 657p. 1998. pap. 17.99 (0-88368-528-0) Whitaker Hse.

— Andrew Murray on the Holy Spirit. 203p. 1998. mass mkt. 5.99 (0-88368-306-7) Whitaker Hse.

— The Believer's Absolute Surrender. LC 85-447. 16p. 1985. pap. 7.99 (0-87123-827-6) Bethany Hse.
— The Believer's Daily Renewal. LC 81-6143. 128p. 1981. pap. 6.99 (0-87123-147-6) Bethany Hse.
— The Believer's Full Blessing of Pentecost. LC 84-12301. 112p. 1984. reprint ed. pap. 6.99 (0-87123-597-8) Bethany Hse.
— The Believer's New Covenant. LC 83-21408. 128p. 1984. reprint ed. pap. 7.99 (0-87123-406-8) Bethany Hse.
— The Believer's Prayer Life. rev. ed. LC 83-12254. (Andrew Murray Prayer Library). 144p. 1983. pap. 7.99 (0-87123-277-4) Bethany Hse.
— The Believer's Prayer Life - Chinese Edition. CRM Staff, tr. (CHI.). 187p. 1996. pap. 6.50 (1-56582-033-9) Christ Renew Min.
— The Believer's School of Prayer. rev. ed. LC 82-4401. 28p. 1982. pap. 8.99 (0-87123-195-6) Bethany Hse.
— The Believer's Secret of Holiness. LC 84-2973. 28p. 1984. reprint ed. pap. 8.99 (0-87123-432-7) Bethany Hse.
— The Believer's Secret of Waiting on God. LC 85-32068. 144p. 1986. pap. 7.99 (0-87123-886-1) Bethany Hse.
***Murray, Andrew.** The Best of Andrew Murray on Prayer. (Essential Christian Library Ser.). 392p. 1998. 9.97 (1-57748-344-8) Barbour Pub.
— The Best of Andrew Murray on Prayer. (Christian Classics). 400p. 2000. pap. 4.97 (1-57748-788-5) Barbour Pub.
Murray, Andrew. The Best of Andrew Murray on Prayer: A Daily Devotional Journal. 384p. 1997. 19.97 (1-57748-080-5) Barbour Pub.
— The Blessings of Obedience. Orig. Title: School of Obedience; Believer's Secret of Obedience. 107p. 1984. mass mkt. 4.99 (0-88368-155-2) Whitaker Hse.
— Blood of the Cross. 1992. pap. 6.99 (0-87508-374-9) Chr Lit.
— The Blood of the Cross. 139p. 1981. mass mkt. 5.99 (0-88368-103-X) Whitaker Hse.
— The Blood of the Cross: Understanding the Mystery of Redemption. 96p. 1987. pap. 3.95 (0-310-55112-9, 19011P) Zondervan.
— Confession & Forgiveness. 176p. 1984. reprint ed. pap. 5.95 (0-310-29731-1, 10366P) Zondervan.
— Cross of Christ. 1989. mass mkt. 5.99 (0-310-56122-1) Zondervan.
— Daily Experience with God. LC 99-24257. 153p. 1999. pap. 6.99 (0-88368-570-1) Whitaker Hse.
— The Deeper Christian Life. large type ed. (Large Print Inspirational Ser.). 1987. pap. 8.95 (0-8027-2589-9) Walker & Co.
— The Deeper Christian Life. 112p. 1999. reprint ed. mass mkt. 5.99 (0-88368-298-2) Whitaker Hse.
***Murray, Andrew.** Deeper Christian Life: And Other Writings. (Nelson's Royal Classics Ser.). 2000. 18.99 (0-7852-4524-3) Nelson.
Murray, Andrew. Divine Healing. 1993. pap. 6.99 (0-87508-375-7) Chr Lit.
— Divine Healing. 1980. pap. 2.99 (0-88019-019-1) Schmul Pub Co.
— Divine Healing. 155p. 1982. reprint ed. mass mkt. 5.99 (0-88368-112-9) Whitaker Hse.
— La Escuela de la Obediencia. Orig. Title: The School of Obedience. (SPA.). 112p. 1980. mass mkt. 4.99 (0-8254-1498-9, Edit Portavoz) Kregel.
— An Exciting New Life. Orig. Title: Living the New Life. 255p. 1982. mass mkt. 5.99 (0-88368-413-6) Whitaker Hse.
— Experiencing the Holy Spirit. Orig. Title: In Search of Spiritual Excellence. 133p. 1999. mass mkt. 5.99 (0-88368-452-7) Whitaker Hse.
— Flashpoint: World War III. LC 96-47672. 224p. 1997. 45.00 (0-7453-1073-7, Pub. by Pluto GBR) Stylus Pub VA.
— Flashpoint: World War III. 224p. 1997. pap. 17.95 (0-7453-1072-9, Pub. by Pluto GBR) Stylus Pub VA.
— The Full Blessing of Pentecost. 1979. pap. 5.99 (0-87508-376-5) Chr Lit.
— The Full Blessing of Pentecost. 128p. 1987. pap. 3.95 (0-310-55102-1, 19010P) Zondervan.
— The Geographical Distribution of Mammals. Sterling, Keir B., ed. LC 77-81073. (Biologists & Their World Ser.). (Illus.). 1978. reprint ed. lib. bdg. 59.95 (0-405-10642-4) Ayer.
— God's Best Secrets. LC 93-39325. 384p. 1994. pap. 13.99 (0-8254-3277-4, Kregel Class) Kregel.
— God's Best Secrets. LC 98-47552. 299p. 1999. pap. 12.99 (0-88368-559-0) Whitaker Hse.
— God's Plans for You. LC 97-47202. 143p. 1997. pap. 6.99 (0-88368-512-4) Whitaker Hse.
— God's Power for Today. LC 97-31582. 182p. (Orig.). 1997. pap. 6.99 (0-88368-300-8) Whitaker Hse.
***Murray, Andrew.** God's Promises, Our Benefits. Orig. Title: Covenants & Blessings. 173p. 2000. pap. 6.99 (0-88368-578-7) Whitaker Hse.
Murray, Andrew. God's Will Our Dwelling Place. 168p. 1983. mass mkt. 5.99 (0-88368-119-6) Whitaker Hse.
— Helps to Intercession. 1979. mass mkt. 3.25 (0-87508-377-3) Chr Lit.
— Holiest of All. LC 97-18538. 552p. 1996. pap. 17.99 (0-88368-462-4) Whitaker Hse.
— The Holiest of All: An Exposition of the Epistle to the Hebrews. 576p. 1993. pap. 18.99 (0-8007-5472-7) Revell.
— The Holiest of All: An Exposition of the Epistle to the Hebrews. abr. ed. Ministries, Kenneth C., ed. LC 97-145244. 568p. 1996. pap. 18.95 (0-8010-5763-9, 30-0811) K Copeland Pubns.
— How to Strengthen Your Faith. LC 97-18321. 108p. 1997. pap. 6.99 (0-88368-128-5) Whitaker Hse.
— Humility. LC 98-117049. 1993. mass mkt. 5.99 (0-87508-710-8) Chr Lit.
— Humility. 106p. 1982. mass mkt. 5.99 (0-88368-110-2) Whitaker Hse.
— Humility: The Beauty of Holiness. 75p. 1987. pap. 2.70 (0-310-55092-0, 19009P) Zondervan.
— The Inner Life. 144p. 1984. pap. 4.95 (0-310-29751-6, 10364P) Zondervan.
— Jesus Himself. (Heritage Ser.). 1996. pap. 1.59 (0-87509-663-8) Chr Pubns.
— Life in the Blood. (Vital Ser.). 1997. pap. 0.75 (0-87508-510-5) Chr Lit.
— Like Christ. 240p. 1981. reprint ed. mass mkt. 5.99 (0-88368-099-8) Whitaker Hse.
— The Lord's Table. 1985. mass mkt. 5.99 (0-87508-424-9) Chr Lit.
— The Master's Indwelling. 178p. 1983. mass mkt. 5.99 (0-88368-121-8) Whitaker Hse.
— Mighty Is Your Hand: A Forty-Day Journey in the Company of Andrew Murray. Hazzard, David, ed. LC 93-50653. (Rekindling the Inner Fire Ser.: No. 6). 16p. 1994. pap. 8.99 (1-55661-369-5) Bethany Hse.
— Ministerio de la Oracion Intercesora.Tr. of Ministry of Intercessory Prayer. (SPA.). 176p. (Orig.). 1985. pap. 7.99 (0-88113-207-1) Caribe Betania.
— The Ministry of Intercession. 204p. 1982. mass mkt. 5.99 (0-88368-114-5) Whitaker Hse.
— The Ministry of Intercession: A Plea for More Prayer. 159p. 1987. pap. 3.95 (0-310-55082-3, 19008P) Zondervan.
— The Ministry of Intercessory Prayer. rev. ed. LC 81-18011. 16p. 1981. pap. 7.99 (0-87123-353-3) Bethany Hse.
— Not My Will. Schoolland, Marian M., tr. 1977. pap. 3.95 (0-310-29722-2, 10381P) Zondervan.
— Obtain the Power of God. 104p. 1997. mass mkt. 5.99 (0-88368-501-9) Whitaker Hse.
— Power for Your Life. Orig. Title: Spirit of Christ. 238p. 1984. mass mkt. 5.99 (0-88368-396-2) Whitaker Hse.
— Power of the Blood. 1993. pap. 6.99 (0-87508-381-1) Chr Lit.
— The Power of the Blood of Jesus. 182p. 1993. mass mkt. 5.99 (0-88368-234-6) Whitaker Hse.
— The Power of the Blood of Jesus. 144p. 1987. pap. 6.99 (0-310-29701-X, 10369P) Zondervan.
***Murray, Andrew.** Practice of God's Presence. LC 00-21013. 567p. 2000. pap. 16.99 (0-88368-590-6) Whitaker Hse.
Murray, Andrew. Prayer: A 31-Day Plan to Enrich Your Prayer Life. (Little Library Ser.). 48p. 1995. spiral bd. 0.99 (1-55748-646-8) Barbour Pub.
***Murray, Andrew.** Prayer & the Coming Rivial. 1999. pap. 9.99 (1-84030-053-1) Ambassador Prodns Ltd.
Murray, Andrew. Prayer Guide. Orig. Title: Prayer Topics. 75p. 1992. mass mkt. 5.99 (0-88368-475-6) Whitaker Hse.
— The Prayer Life. pap. 3.99 (0-551-00027-9) Zondervan.
— The Prayer Life: A Guide to the Inner Chamber. 128p. 1987. pap. 3.95 (0-310-55072-6, 19007P) Zondervan.
— Prayer Power. LC 98-43717. Orig. Title: The Prayer Life. 159p. 1999. pap. 6.99 (0-88368-567-1) Whitaker Hse.
— Promise of the Spirit. 1990. pap. 4.99 (0-7208-0748-4) Zondervan.
— Raising Your Children for Christ. 320p. 1997. mass mkt. 7.99 (0-88368-045-9) Whitaker Hse.
— Reaching Your World for Christ. LC 98-100261. 189p. 1997. mass mkt. 5.99 (0-88368-500-0) Whitaker Hse.
— Reign of Love. 1990. pap. 4.99 (0-7208-0751-4, Pub. by M Pickering) Zondervan.
— Revival. 144p. (Orig.). 1990. pap. 7.99 (1-55661-123-4) Bethany Hse.
— Secret of Abiding Presence. rev. ed. (Andrew Murray Secret Ser.: Vol. 1). 90p. 1998. mass mkt. 2.75 (0-87508-792-2, 792) Chr Lit.
— The Secret of Adoration. 65p. pap. text. write for info. (0-614-02760-8) Christ Stewards.
— Secret of Adoration. rev. ed. (Andrew Murray Secret Ser.: Vol. 2). 75p. 1998. mass mkt. 2.75 (0-87508-793-0, 793) Chr Lit.
— Secret of Brotherly Love. rev. ed. LC 99-171906. (Andrew Murray Secret Ser.: Vol. 3). 78p. 1998. mass mkt. 2.75 (0-87508-794-9, 794) Chr Lit.
— Secret of Christ Our Life. rev. ed. LC 99-168798. (Andrew Murray Secret Ser.: Vol. 4). 64p. 1998. mass mkt. 2.75 (0-87508-795-7, 795) Chr Lit.
— Secret of Fellowship. rev. ed. (Andrew Murray Secret Ser.: Vol. 7). 69p. 1998. mass mkt. 2.75 (0-87508-798-1, 798) Chr Lit.
— The Secret of God's Love. Orig. Title: The True Vine. 105p. 1998. mass mkt. 5.99 (0-88368-549-3) Whitaker Hse.
— The Secret of God's Presence. Orig. Title: God's Gift of Perfection. 141p. 1998. pap. 6.99 (0-88368-563-9) Whitaker Hse.
— Secret of Inspiration. rev. ed. (Andrew Murray Secret Ser.: Vol. 8). 80p. 1998. mass mkt. 2.75 (0-87508-799-X, 799) Chr Lit.
— Secret of Intercession. LC 97-195445. 96p. 1995. mass mkt. 5.99 (0-88368-289-3) Whitaker Hse.
— Secret of Intercession. rev. ed. (Andrew Murray Secret Ser.: Vol. 9). 68p. 1998. mass mkt. 2.75 (0-87508-825-2, 825) Chr Lit.
— The Secret of Life & Death, 1969 - 1980. 65p. pap. text. write for info. (0-614-02759-4) Christ Stewards.
— Secret of Power from on High. rev. ed. (Andrew Murray Secret Ser.: Vol. 10). 63p. 1998. mass mkt. 2.75 (0-87508-826-0, 826) Chr Lit.
— The Secret of Spiritual Strength. 92p. 1997. mass mkt. 5.99 (0-88368-305-9) Whitaker Hse.
— Secret of the Cross. rev. ed. LC 98-233824. (Andrew Murray Secret Ser.: Vol. 5). 75p. 1998. mass mkt. 2.75 (0-87508-796-5, 796) Chr Lit.
— The Secret of the Faith Life. 65p. pap. text. write for info. (0-614-02758-6) Christ Stewards.
— Secret of the Faith Life. rev. ed. LC 99-168802. (Andrew Murray Secret Ser.: Vol. 6). 69p. 1998. mass mkt. 2.75 (0-87508-797-3, 797) Chr Lit.
— Secret of the Throne of Grace. rev. ed. LC 99-188250. (Andrew Murray Secret Ser.: Vol. 11). 70p. 1998. mass mkt. 2.75 (0-87508-827-9, 827) Chr Lit.
— Secret of United Prayer. rev. ed. LC 99-188263. (Andrew Murray Secret Ser.: Vol. 12). 70p. 1998. mass mkt. 2.75 (0-87508-828-7, 828) Chr Lit.
— The Spirit of Christ. rev. ed. LC 79-51335. 288p. 1983. pap. 9.99 (0-87123-589-7) Bethany Hse.
— The True Vine. LC 97-206820. (Classics). 112p. 1997. mass mkt. 4.99 (0-8024-6397-5, 397) Moody.
— Trusting the Spirit. (Vital Ser.). 1997. pap. 0.75 (0-87508-517-2) Chr Lit.
***Murray, Andrew.** Two Covenants. 1999. pap. text 5.99 (0-87508-482-6) Chr Lit.
— Waiting on God. 1999. pap. text 5.99 (0-87508-458-3) CLCC.
Murray, Andrew. Waiting on God. 1997. pap. text 8.99 (1-898787-87-5) Emerald House Group Inc.
— Waiting on God. 138p. 1981. mass mkt. 5.99 (0-88368-101-3) Whitaker Hse.
— Waiting on God: Daily Readings on Knowing God. (Andrew Murray Classics Ser.). 110p. 1987. pap. 3.95 (0-310-55142-0, 19014P) Zondervan.
***Murray, Andrew.** With Christ in the School of Prayer. 1998. pap. 9.99 (1-84030-029-9) Ambassador Prodns Ltd.
Murray, Andrew. With Christ in the School of Prayer. 238p. 1981. mass mkt. 5.99 (0-88368-106-4) Whitaker Hse.
— With Christ in the School of Prayer. Chadwick, Harold, ed. LC 99-90643. (Pure Gold Classics Ser.). 1999. pap. 12.99 (0-88270-779-5, Bridge) Bridge-Logos.
— With Christ in the School of Prayer. large type ed. (Large Print Inspirational Ser.). 1987. pap. 9.95 (0-8027-2600-3) Walker & Co.
— With Christ in the School of Prayer. 288p. 1983. reprint ed. pap. 7.99 (0-310-29771-0, 10527P) Zondervan.
— With Wings As Eagles. 95p. 1993. mass mkt. 5.99 (0-88368-262-1) Whitaker Hse.
Murray, Andrew, ed. Wisdom's Way: 101 Tales of Chinese Wit. Lee, Walton, tr. from CHI. LC 96-61429. 168p. (Orig.). 1997. pap. 12.95 (1-886969-36-1, B027/361) YMAA Pubn.
Murray, Andrew & Bryant, Al. Daily Secrets of Christian Living: Devotional Thoughts from the Writings of Andrew Murray. LC 96-22349. 400p. 1996. 13.99 (0-8254-2157-8) Kregel.
Murray, Andrew & Choy, Leona. Key to the Missionary Problem. 1996. pap. 8.99 (0-87508-401-X) Chr Lit.
Murray, Andrew & Finney, Charles G. The Believer's Secret of Spiritual Power. rev. ed. Parkhurst, Louis G., ed. LC 87-16838. 144p. 1987. pap. 7.99 (0-87123-983-3) Bethany Hse.
Murray, Andrew & Hunt, Tim. The Cell Cycle: An Introduction. (Illus.). 264p. (C). 1993. pap. text 29.95 (0-19-509529-4) OUP.
Murray, Andrew & Kinlow, Dennis F. Deeper Christian Life. 112p. 1986. pap. 6.99 (0-310-29791-5, 10365P) Zondervan.
Murray, Andrew & Spurgeon, Charles H. Believer's Secret of Intercession. Parkhurst, Louis G., Jr., ed. & compiled by by. LC 87-34145. 144p. (Orig.). 1988. pap. 7.99 (0-87123-992-2) Bethany Hse.
Murray, Andrew, et al. The Christian Book Lovers' Borrow Book. 1995. pap. text 6.99 (0-87213-994-8) Loizeaux.
— Healing: The Three Great Classics on Divine Healing. Graf, Jonathan L., ed. LC 92-90119. 375p. 1992. 15.99 (0-87509-491-0) Chr Pubns.
Murray, Andrew, ed. see Liu, Qingshan.
Murray, Andrew, ed. see Seabourne, Tom.
Murray, Andrew, ed. see Yang, Jwing-Ming.
Murray, Andrew D., ed. see Katchmer, George A., Jr.
Murray, Andrew D., ed. see Track, Norman S.
***Murray, Angela.** Teach Yourself Business. (Teach Yourself Ser.). 192p. 2000. pap. 9.95 (0-8442-2787-0, Teach Yrslf) NTC Contemp Pub Co.
Murray, Ann, jt. auth. see Mellaart, James.
Murray, Anna. Sarah's Page. 120p. 1998. 14.00 (1-886947-58-9) Sleepng Bear.
Murray, Annabel. Island of Turmoil. large type ed. 1990. lib. bdg. 18.95 (0-263-12349-9) Mac Lib Ref.
— A Man for Christmas. 1993. per. 2.99 (0-373-11613-6, 1-11613-6) Harlequin Bks.
***Murray, Annabel.** A Promise Kept. large type ed. 320p. 2000. pap. 20.99 (1-85389-946-1, Dales) Ulverscroft.
***Murray, Anne, ed.** Great Britain, the United States & the Middle East: Discourse & Dissension. LC 99-71017. 200p. 1999. 21.50 (0-88033-981-0, Pub. by East Eur Monographs) Col U Pr.
Murray, Anne, jt. ed. see Clarke, Don.
Murray, Arthur. Arthur Murray's Dance Secrets. (Ballroom Dance Ser.). 1986. lib. bdg. 79.95 (0-8490-3371-3) Gordon Pr.
— Arthur Murray's Dance Secrets. (Ballroom Dance Ser.). 1985. lib. bdg. 100.00 (0-87700-698-9) Revisionist Pr.
— Down Memory Lane. (Ballroom Dance Ser.). 1986. lib. bdg. 79.95 (0-8490-3370-5) Gordon Pr.
— Down Memory Lane. (Ballroom Dance Ser.). 1985. lib. bdg. 120.00 (0-87700-697-0) Revisionist Pr.
— How to Become a Good Dancer. (Ballroom Dance Ser.). 1986. lib. bdg. 79.95 (0-8490-3369-1) Gordon Pr.
— How to Become a Good Dancer. (Ballroom Dance Ser.). 1985. lib. bdg. 120.00 (0-87700-696-2) Revisionist Pr.
— The Modern Dances. (Ballroom Dance Ser.). 1986. lib. bdg. 79.95 (0-8490-3338-1) Gordon Pr.
— The Modern Dances. (Ballroom Dance Ser.). 1985. lib. bdg. 79.95 (0-87700-695-4) Revisionist Pr.
— Social Dancing. (Ballroom Dance Ser.). 1986. lib. bdg. 79.95 (0-8490-3255-5) Gordon Pr.
— Social Dancing. (Ballroom Dance Ser.). 1985. lib. bdg. 79.95 (0-87700-694-6) Revisionist Pr.
Murray, Arthur, et al. Down Memory Lane: A Pictorial History of Ballroom & Social Dancing. (Ballroom Dance Ser.). 1989. lib. bdg. 79.95 (0-8490-3966-5) Gordon Pr.
Murray, Barbara A. & Murray, Kenneth T. Pitfalls & Potholes: A Checklist for Avoiding Common Mistakes of Beginning Teachers. LC 97-38927. (Checklist Ser.). 56p. (Orig.). 1997. pap. 5.95 (0-8106-2151-7, 2151-7) NEA.
— Survival Guide for the Florida Teacher. 100p. (Orig.). 1995. pap. text 16.95 (0-9644512-1-2) IntraCoast Pub.
Murray, Barbara A., jt. auth. see Murray, Kenneth T.
Murray, Barbara M. Crock-It. 1995. pap. 14.95 (1-57072-042-8) Overmountain Pr.
Murray, Barrie. Electricity Markets: Investment, Performance & Analysis. LC 98-26912. 294p. 1998. 105.00 (0-471-98507-4) Wiley.
Murray, Barry, jt. auth. see Daniels, Paul.
Murray, Bert. The Bon Accord Collection. 52p. Date not set. pap. text 14.95 (1-871931-57-6, TT10056, Pub. by Taigh Teud) Music Sales.
Murray, Beth. Highlights Book of Travel Fun: Crafts & Activities for the Car, Plane, Bus, or Train. LC 94-72625. (Illus.). 32p. (J). (gr. 2-7). 1995. pap. 3.95 (1-56397-405-3) Boyds Mills Pr.
Murray, Beth, ed. Animal Craft Fun: Indoor & Outdoor Animal Crafts Projects. LC 93-70873. (Illus.). 32p. (J). (gr. k-5). 1994. pap. 4.95 (1-56397-314-6) Boyds Mills Pr.
Murray, Betty. Carved in Stone: Heffington Cemetery, Faulkner Co., Arkansas, Vol. 1. Vanaman, Henryetta W., ed. (Illus.). 64p. 1992. 22.95 (1-56869-006-1); pap. 14.95 (1-56869-007-X) Oldbuck Pr.
— Eighteen Sixty U. S. Federal Census, Conway Co., Arkansas. 314p. 1993. 27.95 (1-56869-022-3); pap. 19.95 (1-56869-023-1) Oldbuck Pr.
Murray, Bill. The Old Firm in the New Age: Rangers & Celtic since the Souness Revolution. (Illus.). 192p. 1998. 35.00 (1-85158-984-8, Pub. by Mainstream Pubng) Trafalgar.
***Murray, Bill.** Ready-Made Quizzes. 2nd ed. (Illus.). 192p. 2001. pap. 8.95 (0-7160-2074-2, Pub. by Elliot RW Bks) Midpt Trade.
Murray, Bill. The World's Game: A History of Soccer. LC 95-13742. (Illinois History of Sports Ser.). (Illus.). 224p. 1996. 27.95 (0-252-01748-X) U of Ill Pr.
— World's Game: A History of Soccer. (Illinois History of Sports). 256p. 1998. 15.95 (0-252-06718-5) U of Ill Pr.
***Murray, Bill & Peper, George.** Cinderella Story: My Life in Golf. (Illus.). 224p. 2000. pap. 12.00 (0-7679-0522-9) Broadway BDD.
Murray, Bill & Peper, George. Cinderella Story: My Life in Golf. LC 99-25300. (Illus.). 211p. 1999. 19.95 (0-385-49571-4) Doubleday.
***Murray, Bill & Peper, George.** Cinderella Story: My Life in Golf. large type ed. LC 99-52173. (Illus.). 1999. write for info. (1-56895-789-0) Wheeler Pub.
Murray, Billy. Obedient to the Heavenly Vision. 2nd rev. ed. (Illus.). 280p. 1997. pap. 9.95 (1-889505-07-2) White Wing Pub.
— Obediente a la Vision Celestial.Tr. of Obedient to the Heavenly Vision. (SPA., Illus.). 260p. (Orig.). 1996. pap. 9.95 (1-889505-03-X) White Wing Pub.
Murray, Billy D., Sr. Obedient to the Heavenly Vision. 250p. (Orig.). 1996. pap. 9.95 (0-934942-97-8) White Wing Pub.
Murray, Bob & Fortinberry, Alicia. Maud of Llangibbi. 376p. (Orig.). 1996. pap. 9.95 (1-885610-02-5) European Amer.
Murray, Bob, jt. auth. see Fortinberry, Alicia.
Murray, Bob, ed. see Ati.
Murray Bosrock, Mary. Put Your Best Foot Forward - U. S. A. Vol. VI: A Fearless Guide to Understanding the United States of America. Walker, Catherine A., ed. LC 98-75164. (Put Your Best Foot Forward Ser.: Bk. 6). (Illus.). 475p. 1999. pap. 22.95 (0-9637530-9-6) Int Educ Systs.
***Murray, Brad J.** Perl Tools: A Guide to Streamlining & Automating the Software Development Process Using Perl. (Illus.). 300p. 2000. pap. 39.95 (1-884777-96-1, Pub. by Manning Pubns) IPG Chicago.
Murray, Bruce. Film & the German Left in the Weimar Republic: From Caligari to Kuhle Wampe. (Film Studies). (Illus.). 303p. (C). 1990. pap. 16.95 (0-292-72465-9) U of Tex Pr.
Murray, Bruce A. & Wickham, Christopher J., eds. Framing the Past: The Historiography of German Cinema & Television. LC 91-39848. (Illus.). 384p. (C). 1992. 36.95 (0-8093-1756-7) S Ill U Pr.
Murray, Bruce C. & Burgess, Eric. Flight to Mercury. LC 76-25017. (Illus.). 162p. 1977. text 53.00 (0-231-03996-4) Col U Pr.
Murray, Bruce C., jt. auth. see Davies, Merton.
Murray, C., jt. auth. see Lubbe, G. F.
Murray, C. A. Vectorial Astrometry. (Illus.). 368p. 1983. 44.00 (0-85274-372-6) IOP Pub.
Murray, C. Edgar, ed. What Will the Next Recession Mean to You? rev. ed. (Economic Education Bulletin Ser.: Vol. 38, No. 11). (Illus.). 74p. 1998. pap. 6.00 (0-913610-07-0) Am Inst Econ Res.
Murray, C. H. & Murray, M. S. A Drugless Treatment for Deafness & Partial Deafness: Osteopathic, Somapathic, Naturopathic, Chiropractic & Mechano-Therapic. (Alternative Medicine Ser.). 1991. lib. bdg. 69.95 (0-8490-4263-1) Gordon Pr.
Murray, C. J. The Legend of Story Cazaunoux: A New Orleans Novel. 310p. 1998. pap. 14.95 (1-57502-883-2, PO1996) Morris Pubng.

M

An Asterisk (*) at the beginning of an entry indicates that the title is appearing for the first time.

— The Magic of Isha Swift. 86p. 1998. pap. 13.95 (*1-57502-884-0*, PO2158) Morris Pubng.

Murray, C. J. & Lopez, A. D., eds. Global Comparative Assessments in the Health Sector: Disease Burden, Expenditures & Intervention Packages. LC 96-211984. (Bulletin of WHO Ser.). viii, 196p. 1994. pap. text 18.00 (*92-4-156175-0*, 1150420) World Health.

Murray, Calvin, ed. see Thompson, U. A.

Murray, Carl D. & Dermott, Stanley F. Solar System Dynamics. LC 99-19679. 606p. (C). 2000. pap. 39.95 (*0-521-57597-4*) Cambridge U Pr.

***Murray, Carl D. & Dermott, Stanley F.** Solar System Dynamics. LC 99-19679. (Illus.). 606p. (C). 2000. 90.00 (*0-521-57295-9*) Cambridge U Pr.

Murray, Carol. Women with & Without. (American Dust Ser.: No. 14). 200p. 1984. 10.95 (*0-913218-81-2*) Dustbooks.

Murray, Carol, ed. see Siegel, Jeff.

Murray, Catherine. Recipes of a Lifetime. 1995. pap. 18.95 (*1-878569-33-3*) Badger Bks Inc.

Murray, Catherine T. Grandmothers of Greenbush: Recipes & Memories of the Old Greenbush Neighborhood 1900-1925. LC 96-94510. (Illus.). 168p. 1996. pap. 18.95 (*0-9626346-3-8*) Greenbush Remembered.

— A Taste of Memories from the Old "Bush" Vol. II: Recipes, Memories & Photographs of the Old Greenbush Neighborhood. LC 88-176375. (Illus.). 554p. (Orig.). 1990. spiral bd. 18.50 (*0-9626346-1-1*) Greenbush Remembered.

M

Murray, Catherine T., intro. A Taste of Memories from Columbus Park Vol. III: Recipes, Memories & Photographs of the Old West Side Neighborhood in Kenosha, Wisconsin. LC 91-91350. (Illus.). 535p. (Orig.). 1992. spiral bd. 19.95 (*0-9626346-2-X*) Greenbush Remembered.

Murray, Charles. Does Prison Work? (Choice in Welfare Ser.: No. 38). 55p. 1997. pap. 16.50 (*0-255-36398-2*, Pub. by Inst Economic Affairs) Coronet Bks.

— Hamewith: The Complete Poems of Charles Murray. Shepherd, Nan, ed. (Illus.). 180p. 1982. 15.00 (*0-08-024522-6*, Pergamon Pr); pap. 7.00 (*0-08-024521-8*, Pergamon Pr) Elsevier.

— The Healer's Song: The Authorized Biography of John Lee Hooker. Date not set. write for info. (*0-7868-6071-5*) Hyperion.

— In Pursuit of Happiness & Good Government. LC 94-12169. 1994. pap. 19.95 (*1-55815-297-0*) ICS Pr.

— Losing Ground: American Social Policy, 1950-1980. 10th anniversary ed. LC 94-241150. (Illus.). 352p. 1994. 16.00 (*0-465-04233-3*, Pub. by Basic) HarpC.

— Underclass: The Crisis Deepens. (IEA Health & Welfare Unit Ser.: No. 20). 70p. 1994. pap. 17.95 (*0-255-36355-9*, Pub. by Inst Economic Affairs) Coronet Bks.

***Murray, Charles.** The Underclass Revisited. 43p. 1999. pap. 9.95 (*0-8447-7131-7*, Pub. by Am Enterprise) Pub Resources Inc.

Murray, Charles. What It Means to Be a Libertaria: A Personal Interpretation. 192p. 1997. reprint ed. pap. 12.00 (*0-7679-0039-1*) Broadway BDD.

Murray, Charles, et al. Charles Murray & the Underclass: The Developing Debate. LC 97-173933. (Choice in Welfare Ser.: No. 33). 180p. 1996. pap. 22.50 (*0-255-36391-5*, Pub. by Inst Economic Affairs) Coronet Bks.

Murray, Charles, jt. auth. see Carr, Roy.

Murray, Charles, jt. auth. see Herrnstein, Richard J.

Murray, Charles A. Income Inequality & IQ. LC 98-143726. (AEI Studies in Understanding Economic Inequality). vii, 49 p. 1998. pap. write for info. (*0-8447-7094-9*) Am Enterprise.

— Travels in North America, During the Years 1834-36, Including a Summer with the Pawnees. 2nd ed. LC 68-54845. (American Scene Ser.). 878p. 1974. reprint ed. lib. bdg. 85.00 (*0-306-71021-8*) Da Capo.

***Murray, Charles Fairfax.** Catalogo Dei Libri Posseduti Da Charles Fairfax Murray. 401p. 2000. reprint ed. 85.00 (*1-57898-182-4*) Martino Pubng.

Murray, Charles Fairfax, jt. auth. see Elliott, David B.

Murray, Charles J. Supermen. LC 96-36448. 232p. 1997. 24.95 (*0-471-04885-2*) Wiley.

***Murray, Charles Shaar.** Boogie Man. (Illus.). 544p. 2000. 27.95 (*0-312-26563-8*) St Martin.

Murray, Chas H. & Murray, M. S. A Drugless Treatment for Partial Deafness & Deafness. 39p. 1996. reprint ed. spiral bd. 9.50 (*0-7873-0630-4*) Hlth Research.

Murray, Chris. Butter Thief. (Illus.). 32p. (J). 1991. pap. 9.95 (*0-89213-274-4*, BT) Bhaktivedanta.

— The Butter Thief. 2nd ed. (Illus.). 32p. (J). (gr. k-3). 1999. reprint ed. 14.95 (*1-886069-20-4*, 1216, Pub. by Mandala Pub Grp) Words Distrib.

— Mastering 3D Studio Max R3. 4th ed. 896p. 2000. pap. text 49.99 (*0-7821-2561-1*) Sybex.

Murray, Chris, ed. Dictionary of the Arts: Movements, Terms, People: From Ancient Art to World Music. LC 94-16276. (Illus.). 576p. 1994. 29.95 (*0-8160-3205-X*) Facts on File.

***Murray, Chris, ed.** Encyclopedia of Literary Critics & Criticism, 2 vols. 1332p. 1999. lib. bdg. 285.00 (*1-57958-144-7*) Fitzroy Dearborn.

***Murray, Chris.** Illuminations from the Bhagavad-Gita: Mini Edition. 88p. 2000. pap. 12.95 (*1-886069-32-8*) Mandala Pub Grp.

Murray, Chris, jt. auth. see Murray, Kim.

Murray, Christina. Gender & the New South African Legal Order. 255p. 1994. pap. 34.00 (*0-7021-3316-7*, Pub. by Juta & Co) Gaunt.

Murray, Christina & O'Regan, Catherine. No Place to Rest: Forced Removals & the Law in South Africa. (Contemporary South African Debates Ser.). (Illus.). 256p. 1990. pap. text 15.95 (*0-19-570580-7*, 5164) OUP.

Murray, Christine E., jt. auth. see Grant, Gerald.

***Murray, Christopher.** Sean O'Casey: The Shadow of a Gunman; Juno & the Paycock; The Plough & the Stars. 192p. 2000. pap. 12.00 (*0-571-19780-9*) Faber & Faber.

— Twentieth-Century Irish Drama: Mirror up to Nation. LC 99-89841. (Irish Studies). 278p. 2000. pap. 19.95 (*0-8156-0643-5*) Syracuse U Pr.

Murray, Christopher, ed. see Friel, Brian.

Murray, Christopher, jt. ed. see Hayley, Barbara.

Murray, Christopher, ed. see Robinson, Lennox.

Murray, Christopher J. & Lopez, Alan D. The Global Burden of Disease. LC 96-27266. (Global Burden of Disease & Injury Ser.: No. 1). (Illus.). 900p. 1996. 39.95 (*0-674-35448-6*) HUP.

— Global Epidemiology of Infectious Diseases. (Global Burden of Disease & Injury Ser.). 600p. 1998. 49.95 (*0-674-35446-X*) HUP.

— Global Epidermiology of Noncommunicable Diseases: The Epidemiology & Burdens of Cancers, Cardiovascular Diseases, Diabetes Mellitus, Respiratory Disorders & Other Major Conditions. (Global Burden of Disease & Injury Ser.). 500p. 1998. 49.95 (*0-674-35447-8*) HUP.

Murray, Christopher J. & Lopez, Alan D., eds. Global Health Statistics. LC 96-26652. (Global Burden of Disease & Injury Ser.: No. 2). (Illus.). 1010p. 1996. 39.95 (*0-674-35449-4*) HUP.

— Health Dimensions of Sex & Reproduction: The Global Burden of Sexually Transmitted Diseases, HIV, Maternal Conditions, Perinatal Disorders & Congenital Anomalies. LC 98-30156. (Illus.). 800p. 1998. 39.95 (*0-674-38335-4*) HUP.

Murray, Ciaran. Sharawadgi: The Romantic Return to Nature. LC 98-24897. 470p. 1998. 79.95 (*1-57309-329-7*, Cath Scholar Pr) Intl Scholars.

Murray, Cindy C. Planning a Tradeshow from Z to A Guidebook. Lingham, Gretchen, ed. 24p. (Orig.). 1995. pap. text 14.95 (*0-9645468-0-9*) Staicer & Assocs.

— Planning a Tradeshow from Z to A Worksheets. Lingham, Gretchen, ed. 54p. (Orig.). 1995. 14.95 (*0-9645468-1-7*) Staicer & Assocs.

Murray, Claire. Always Your Friend. 1999. 4.95 (*0-7407-0128-2*) Andrews & McMeel.

***Murray, Claire.** Medieval Forest. 2000. 10.95 (*0-7407-0591-1*) Andrews & McMeel.

Murray, Claire. Nantucket Inspirations. 1997. 39.95 (*0-9652613-0-1*) ANB Internatl.

— Our Nation's Garden. 1999. 10.95 (*0-8362-8743-6*) Andrews & McMeel.

— Seashells. 1999. 10.95 (*0-8362-8192-6*) Andrews & McMeel.

***Murray, Claire.** Thanks, Mom. 2000. pap. 4.95 (*0-7407-1212-8*) Andrews & McMeel.

— Tranquil Pools. 2000. 10.95 (*0-7407-0594-6*) Andrews & McMeel.

***Murray, Claire.** A Book of Days. 1999. 9.95 (*0-7407-0127-4*) Andrews & McMeel.

Murray-Clark, Ian. Night & Day. 1989. 4.95 (*0-945603-02-9*) Dinnerman Bks.

— Windows. 1989. 4.95 (*0-945603-05-3*) Dinnerman Bks.

Murray, Claude C., Jr. Flight Boots to Wooden Shoes. 2nd rev. ed. (Illus.). 67p. 1995. pap. 15.00 (*0-9649119-1-4*) CAVU Pubs.

Murray, Cleitus O. Stories of the Southern Mountains & Swamps. (Illus.). 192p. (Orig.). (YA). 1992. pap. 9.95 (*0-9632132-0-2*) Murray Pubns.

***Murray, Colin.** The Lady & the Vampire. (Illus.). 48p. 1999. pap. 10.95 (*1-56163-237-6*, Eurotica) NBM.

Murray, Colin & Collins1. Celtic Tree Oracle. 28p. 1988. text 29.95 (*0-312-02032-5*) St Martin.

Murray, Colleen O. That Grand, Noble Work: Exploring the Constitution. (Illus.). 1998. teacher ed. 29.95 (*1-55933-232-8*, 4028GD) Know Unltd.

Murray, Coreen. The San Francisco Bay Area: The Nation's Laboratory for New Ideas. Leichner, Nancy M., ed. (Illus.). 180p. 1997. text 49.95 (*0-9634100-4-0*) Wyndham Pubns.

Murray, Corinne, ed. Accessible Art: A Layman's Look at Seattle's Public Art. LC 90-82681. (Illus.). (Orig.). 1990. pap. text 12.95 (*0-9626878-0-4*, 72920) At Your Fingertips.

Murray, Craig. Benjamin Vaughan, Seventeen Fifty-One to Eighteen Thirty-Five: The Life of an Anglo-American Intellectual. 1981. 66.95 (*0-405-14101-7*) Ayer.

Murray, D., et al. Health Care Reform, Regulation, & Innovation in the Medical Device Industry: A Study of Competitiveness in a Vital U. S. Industry. 135p. (Orig.). 1994. pap. text 12.95 (*1-55813-048-9*) Hudson Instit IN.

Murray, D. Duncan, jt. auth. see Burke, David C.

Murray, D. Fred & Murray, Jody L. Caught in a Blizzard: Grandmother & I. LC 98-126000. (Illus.). 208p. 1997. pap. 14.95 (*0-9642685-5-8*) Murray Pubng.

Murray, D. J. Patterns of Decision Making? LC 74-159623. (Decision Making in Britain Ser.). 108p. 1972. write for info. (*0-335-01948-X*) Taylor & Francis.

Murray, D. M. & Wong, T. W. Noodle Words: An Introduction to Chinese & Japanese Characters. LC 79-147179. (Illus.). 96p. (YA). (gr. 9 up). 1971. pap. 8.95 (*0-8048-0948-8*) Tuttle Pubng.

Murray, D. Michael. European Majolica. LC 96-37605. (Illus.). 176p. 1997. pap. 29.95 (*0-7643-0228-0*) Schiffer.

Murray, Dan. None of This Is on the Map. LC 98-138601. write for info. (*0-935252-51-7*) Street Pr.

Murray, Daniel, ed. National Conference on Sanitary Sewer Overflows: Seminar Publication. (Illus.). 588p. (C). 1998. pap. text 50.00 (*0-7881-4890-7*) DIANE Pub.

Murray, Daniel A., jt. auth. see Allen, Will W.

Murray, Dave. House-Training Your VCR: A Help Manual for Humans. 120p. 1992. pap. 9.95 (*0-931011-39-6*) Grapevine Pubns.

Murray, David. Chapters in the History of Bookkeeping, Accountancy & Commercial Arithmetic. Brief, Richard P., ed. LC 77-87281. (Development of Contemporary Accounting Thought Ser.). 1978. reprint ed. lib. bdg. 44.95 (*0-405-10909-1*) Ayer.

***Murray, David.** Indian Giving: Economies of Power in Early Indian-White Exchanges. LC 99-88274. (Native Americans of the Northeast Ser.). 296p. 2000. 50.00 (*1-55849-243-7*); pap. 18.95 (*1-55849-244-5*) U of Mass Pr.

— Inside Solid Works. 2nd ed. 2000. pap. 59.95 (*0-7668-2348-2*) Delmar.

Murray, David. Inside Solidworks (97 & 98) LC 98-25744. 512p. (C). 1998. pap. 63.95 (*1-56690-184-7*) Thomson Learn.

Murray, David. Literary Theory & Poetry: Extending the Canon. LC 90-114975. 216p. 1989. write for info. (*0-7134-5814-3*, Pub. by B T B) U of Pa Pr.

Murray, David. Museums Vol. 1: Their History & Their Use with a Bibliography, 3 vols. in 2. 1999. reprint ed. 150.00 (*1-891396-04-8*) Pober Pub.

— Poems. LC 70-144428. (Bannatyne Club, Edinburgh. Publications: No. 2). reprint ed. 27.50 (*0-404-52702-7*) AMS Pr.

Murray, David, ed. American Cultural Critics. 199p. 1996. pap. 14.95 (*0-85989-404-5*, Pub. by Univ Exeter Pr) Northwestern U Pr.

— Forked Tongues: Speech, Writing & Representation in North American Indian Texts. LC 90-49156. 188p. 1991. 42.00 (*0-253-33942-1*); pap. 15.95 (*0-253-20650-2*, MB-650) Ind U Pr.

— Seed Dispersal. LC 86-72353. 322p. 1987. text 94.00 (*0-12-511900-3*) Acad Pr.

Murray, David & Handler, Richard, eds. Nation, State & Its Sexual Dissidents. 131p. 1996. pap. text 12.00 (*2-88449-242-9*) Gordon & Breach.

Murray, David, jt. auth. see Gigerenzer, Gerd.

Murray, David C., jt. auth. see McIntosh, David M.

Murray, David J. Ethics in Organisations. (Fast Track MBA Ser.). 1997. pap. text 19.95 (*0-7494-1592-4*) Kogan Page Ltd.

Murray, David L. Pragmatism. LC 75-3292. reprint ed. 22.50 (*0-404-59278-3*) AMS Pr.

— Scenes & Silhouettes. LC 68-16959. (Essay Index Reprint Ser.). 1977. reprint ed. 20.95 (*0-8369-0727-2*) Ayer.

Murray, David M. Design & Analysis of Group-Randomized Trials. (Monographs in Epidemiology & Biostatistics: No. 29). (Illus.). 480p. 1998. text 65.00 (*0-19-512036-1*) OUP.

Murray, David N. The Concord & Penacook NH Street Directory. 3rd rev. ed. (Illus.). 125p. 1997. spiral bd. 14.95 (*0-9659149-0-9*) Murray Comns.

Murray, David R., ed. Advanced Methods in Plant Breeding & Biotechnology. (Biotechnology in Agriculture Ser.: No. 4). (Illus.). 384p. 1991. text 120.00 (*0-85198-706-0*) OUP.

Murray, David W. Cooking the Books: Racial & Sexual Politics in the SAT. (Issue Paper #12-94 Ser.). 5p. 1994. pap. text 8.00 (*1-57655-140-7*) Independ Inst.

Murray, David W. & Buxton, Bernard F. Experiments in the Machine Interpretation of Visual Motion. (Artificial Intelligence Ser.). 250p. 1990. 40.00 (*0-262-13263-X*) MIT Pr.

Murray, Denise E. Knowledge Machines. LC 95-6900. (Language in Social Life Ser.). 208p. (C). 1995. pap. text 26.77 (*0-582-07131-3*) Addison-Wesley.

— Knowledge Machines: Language & Information in a Technological Society. LC 95-6900. (Language in Social Life Ser.). 208p. (C). 1995. text 51.95 (*0-582-07132-1*, Pub. by Addison-Wesley) Longman.

Murray, Denise E., ed. Diversity As Resource: Redefining Cultural Literacy. LC 92-61747. 36p. 1992. pap. 22.95 (*0-939791-42-0*) Tchrs Eng Spkrs.

Murray, Dennis, jt. intro. see Williams, William J.

Murray, Dennis F., et al. Using Financial Accounting: An Introduction. LC 96-38399. 650p. 1997. pap. 87.95 (*0-314-06125-8*) West Pub.

Murray, Dennis J. The Guaranteed Fund-Raising System: A Systems Approach to Developing Fund-Raising Plans. 2nd ed. LC 93-74528. 368p. 1994. ring bd. 187.00 (*0-935517-03-0*) Amer Inst Mgnt.

— How to Evaluate Your Fund-Raising Program: A Performance Audit System. LC 84-71530. 215p. 1985. ring bd. 187.00 (*0-935517-00-6*) Amer Inst Mgnt.

Murray, Dennis J., jt. ed. see Keller, Peter A.

Murray, Deryck, jt. auth. see Biddulph, Michael.

Murray, Dian H. Pirates of the South China Coast, 1790-1810. LC 87-10049. (Illus.). 256p. 1987. 39.50 (*0-8047-1376-6*) Stanford U Pr.

Murray, Dian H. & Baoqi, Qin. The Origins of the Tiandihui: The Chinese Triads in Legend & History. xiv, 350p. Date not set. 42.50 (*0-8047-2125-4*) Stanford U Pr.

Murray, Diane H. & Baoqi, Qin. The Origins of the Tiandihui: The Chinese Triads in Legend & History. LC 93-24514. xiv, 350p. 1994. 49.50 (*0-8047-2324-9*) Stanford U Pr.

Murray, Dick. Teaching the Bible to Adults & Youth. rev. ed. LC 93-20102. 176p. 1993. 12.95 (*0-687-41084-3*) Abingdon.

— Teaching the Bible to Adults & Youth: Korean Edition. 176p. 1995. pap. 12.50 (*0-687-00785-2*) Abingdon.

Murray, Donal. The Church Guardian of Freedom. 1989. pap. 25.00 (*0-86217-257-8*, Pub. by Veritas Pubns) St Mut.

— The Future of Faith. 1989. pap. 15.00 (*0-86217-210-1*, Pub. by Veritas Pubns) St Mut.

— On the Road to Emmaus: Eucharist Renewal Today. 1989. pap. 25.00 (*1-85390-111-3*, Pub. by Veritas Pubns) St Mut.

— A Question of Morality: Christian Morality & In Vitro Fertilization. 1989. pap. 22.00 (*0-86217-230-6*, Pub. by Veritas Pubns) St Mut.

Murray, Donald. Crafting a Life in Essay, Story, Poem. LC 96-3819. 165p. 1996. pap. text 20.00 (*0-86709-403-6*, 0403, Pub. by Boynton Cook Pubs) Heinemann.

— A Democracy of Despots. 224p. 1995. pap. 22.95 (*0-7735-1360-4*, Pub. by McG-Queens Univ Pr) CUP Services.

***Murray, Donald.** Writing to Deadline: The Journalist at Work. LC 99-462112. 256p. 1999. pap. 18.95 (*0-325-00225-8*) Heinemann.

Murray, Donald F. Divine Prerogative & Royal Pretension: Pragmatics, Poetics, & Polemics in a Narrative Sequence about David (2 Samuel 5.17-7.29) LC 98-213141. (JSOTS Ser.: Vol. 264). 350p. 1998. 85.00 (*1-85075-930-8*, Pub. by Sheffield Acad) CUP Services.

Murray, Donald M. Expecting the Unexpected: Teaching Myself & Others to Read & Write. LC 88-8490. 276p. (Orig.). (C). 1989. pap. text 22.00 (*0-86709-243-2*, 0243, Pub. by Boynton Cook Pubs) Heinemann.

— Learning by Teaching: Selected Articles on Writing & Teaching. LC 82-20558. 184p. (C). 1982. pap. text 21.50 (*0-86709-025-1*, 0025, Pub. by Boynton Cook Pubs) Heinemann.

— Literature of Tomorrow: An Anthology of Student Fiction, Poetry, & Drama. (C). 1990. teacher ed. write for info. (*0-03-032919-1*) Harcourt Coll Pubs.

— Read to Write. 3rd ed. (Illus.). 608p. (C). 1993. pap. text 39.00 (*0-15-500190-6*) Harcourt.

— Shoptalk: Learning to Write with Writers. LC 89-77216. 208p. (Orig.). (C). 1990. pap. 12.95 (*0-86709-258-0*, 0258, Pub. by Boynton Cook Pubs) Heinemann.

— Write to Learn. 3rd ed. 272p. (C). 1990. teacher ed. write for info. (*0-03-033124-2*) Harcourt Coll Pubs.

— Write to Learn. 4th ed. (Illus.). 240p. (C). 1993. teacher ed. write for info. (*0-15-500204-X*) Harcourt Coll Pubs.

— Write to Learn. 5th ed. (C). 1996. pap. text 35.00 (*0-15-501986-4*) Harcourt Coll Pubs.

— Write to Learn. 6th ed. LC 98-70007. 384p. (C). 1998. pap. text 35.50 (*0-15-505448-1*, Pub. by Harcourt Coll Pubs) Harcourt.

Murray, Donald S. Special Deliverance. 96p. 1990. pap. 21.00 (*1-898218-99-4*) St Mut.

***Murray, Donette.** Kennedy, Macmillan & Nuclear Weapons. LC 99-21772. 256p. 1999. text 65.00 (*0-312-22221-1*) St Martin.

Murray, Donna & Seward, Melea L., eds. Rockhurst Review, 1993: A Fine Arts Journal, Vol. VI. 86p. 1993. pap. 5.00 (*1-886761-05-1*) Rockhurst Col.

***Murray, Donna Huston.** Farewell Performance: A Ginger Barnes Main Line Mystery. 272p. 2000. mass mkt. 5.99 (*0-312-97456-6*, St Martins Paperbacks) St Martin.

Murray, Donna Huston. Final Arrangements. 1996. mass mkt. 5.99 (*0-312-95765-3*, Pub. by Tor Bks) St Martin.

— The Main Line Is Murder. 1995. mass mkt. 5.99 (*0-312-95637-1*) St Martin.

— School of Hard Knocks: A Dead Letter Mystery. (Ginger Barnes Main Line Mysteries Ser.). 288p. 1997. mass mkt. 5.99 (*0-312-96104-9*) St Martin.

— A Score to Settle. 288p. 1999. pap. text 5.99 (*0-312-96951-1*, Thomas Dunne) St Martin.

Murray, Dorothy I. Dear Teddy Bear. 12p. 1994. pap. 5.99 (*0-925037-19-2*) Great Lks Poetry.

— Two Bullies Meet. 12p. 1994. pap. 5.99 (*0-925037-20-6*) Great Lks Poetry.

Murray, Doug. Call to Battle. (Werewolf Ser.). (Illus.). (Orig.). 1996. pap. 5.99 (*1-56504-885-7*, 11304, Wrld of Darkness) White Wolf.

— The 'Nam. (Illus.). 96p. 1999. pap. text 14.95 (*0-7851-0718-5*) Marvel Entrprs.

***Murray, Douglas.** Bosie: A Biography of Alfred Douglas. LC 00-26768. (Illus.). 480p. 2000. 30.00 (*0-7868-6653-5*, Pub. by Hyperion) Time Warner.

Murray, Douglas. Comprehensive Catalog of Large Size Star Notes. (Illus.). 128p. 1996. pap. 25.00 (*0-931960-56-8*) BNR Pr.

— Freedom to Reform: The "Articles Declaratory" of the Church of Scotland, 1921. 121p. 1993. pap. text 25.95 (*0-567-29216-9*, Pub. by T & T Clark) Bks Intl VA.

— Gentle Rain. LC 95-60131. 158p. 1995. pap. 16.95 (*0-9632825-1-4*) Tigermoon Ent.

Murray, Douglas, ed. see Austen, Jane.

Murray, Douglas, jt. ed. see Forrester, Duncan.

Murray, Douglas J. & Viotti, Paul R., eds. The Defense Policies of Nations: A Comparative Study. LC 81-3790. (Illus.). 541p. (Orig.). 1982. reprint ed. pap. 167.80 (*0-8357-7886-X*, 203630500002) Bks Demand.

— The Defense Policies of Nations: A Comparative Study. 2nd ed. LC 89-7947. (Illus.). 716p. (Orig.). 1989. reprint ed. pap. 200.00 (*0-608-04009-6*, 206474500011) Bks Demand.

— The Defense Policies of Nations: A Comparative Study. 3rd ed. LC 93-20958. (Orig.). 1994. text 65.00 (*0-8018-4793-1*); pap. text 29.95 (*0-8018-4794-X*) Johns Hopkins.

Murray, Douglas L. Cultivating Crisis: The Human Cost of Pesticides. 3rd ed. (Illus.). 208p. (C). 1995. pap. 12.95 (*0-292-75169-9*); text 35.00 (*0-292-75168-0*) U of Tex Pr.

Murray, E. B., ed. see Shelley, Percy Bysshe.

Murray, E. B., ed. see Shelley, Percy Bysshe & Shelley, Mary Wollstonecraft.

***Murray, Earl.** Beside Still Water. 2001. text. write for info. (*0-312-86922-3*) St Martin.

Murray, Earl. Gabriela. LC 99-21932. 320p. 1999. text 23.95 (*0-312-86515-5*) Forge Pr.

— Ghosts of the Old West. 256p. 1994. mass mkt. 4.99 (*0-8125-3527-8*, Pub. by Tor Bks) St Martin.

— Ghosts of the Old West. expanded ed. LC 98-20322. 1998. pap. 14.95 (*0-312-86795-6*, Pub. by Tor Bks) St Martin.

An Asterisk (*) at the beginning of an entry indicates that the title is appearing for the first time.

***Murray, Earl.** Hotel Nevada & Other Stories. 224p. 2000. pap. 13.95 (*0-312-87362-X*) St Martin.

Murray, Earl. In the Arms of the Sky. LC 98-19414. 304p. 1998. 22.95 (*0-312-86123-0*, Pub. by Forge NYC) St Martin.

***Murray, Earl.** In the Arms of the Sky. 304p. 2000. mass mkt. 6.99 (*0-8125-5143-5*, Pub. by Forge NYC) St Martin.

Murray, Earl. River at Sundown. 1999. mass mkt. 5.99 (*0-8125-5144-3*, Pub. by Forge NYC) St Martin.

— Savage Whisper. 1998. mass mkt. 5.99 (*0-8125-3886-2*, Pub. by Forge NYC) St Martin.

— Spirit of the Moon. 1998. mass mkt. 5.99 (*0-8125-5093-5*, Pub. by Forge NYC) St Martin.

Murray, Earl P. Flaming Sky. 1996. mass mkt. 5.99 (*0-8125-1320-7*, Pub. by Forge NYC) St Martin.

— Free Flows the River. 416p. 1995. 4.99 (*0-8125-1102-6*, Pub. by Tor Bks) St Martin.

— High Freedom. 480p. 1988. mass mkt. 4.99 (*0-8125-8596-8*, Pub. by Tor Bks) St Martin.

— Mountain Sheriff No. 3: The Canyon Mountain War. 256p. 1988. mass mkt. 2.95 (*0-8217-2413-4*, Zebra Kensgtn) Kensgtn Pub Corp.

— Song of Wovoka. 416p. (Orig.). 1992. pap. 10.99 (*0-8125-2091-2*) Tor Bks.

— Song of Wovoka. 416p. (Orig.). 1993. mass mkt. 4.99 (*0-8125-1318-5*, Pub. by Tor Bks) St Martin.

— Thunder in the Dawn. 416p. 1994. mass mkt. 4.99 (*0-8125-1319-3*, Pub. by Tor Bks) St Martin.

— Whisper on the Water. 1996. mass mkt. 5.99 (*0-8125-3887-0*, Pub. by Forge NYC) St Martin.

Murray, Edmund, et al. Proceedings of the International Churchill Societies 1992-1993. (Oral History Ser.). (Illus.). 152p. (Orig.). 1995. pap. 10.00 (*0-943879-09-4*) Churchill Ctr.

***Murray, Edna.** Faithful Nurse. large type ed. (Dales Romance Ser.). 288p. 1999. pap. 20.99 (*1-85389-907-0*, Dales) Ulverscroft.

Murray, Edward. Varieties of Dramatic Structure: A Study of Theory & Practice. 158p. (Orig.). (C). 1990. pap. text 19.00 (*0-8191-7786-5*); lib. bdg. 38.00 (*0-8191-7785-7*) U Pr of Amer.

Murray, Edward J., ed. Gene Transfer & Expression Protocols. LC 84-15696. (Methods in Molecular Biology Ser.: Vol. 7). (Illus.). 452p. 1991. 89.50 (*0-89603-178-0*) Humana.

Murray, Edward L. Imaginative Thinking & Human Existence. LC 85-27368. 287p. (C). 1986. pap. text 21.50 (*0-8207-0213-7*) Duquesne.

Murray, Edward L., ed. Imagination & Phenomenological Psychology. LC 87-13437. 230p. 1987. text 27.00 (*0-8207-0195-5*) Duquesne.

Murray, Elaine. A Layman's Guide to New Age & Spiritual Terms. LC 92-41892. 208p. (Orig.). 1993. pap. 12.95 (*0-931892-53-8*) B Dolphin Pub.

Murray, Eleanor B. Cherokee County Summer. (Illus.). 48p. (Orig.). (YA). (gr. 9-12). 1981. pap. 3.98 (*1-879313-01-4*) Murrays Leprechaun Bks.

— God's Green Valley: And Its People. (Illus.). 28p. 1983. pap. 2.98 (*1-879313-03-0*) Murrays Leprechaun Bks.

Murray, Eleanor H. Bend Like the Bamboo. (Illus.). 91p. (Orig.). (YA). (gr. 9-12). 1982. pap. 8.95 (*1-879313-02-2*) Murrays Leprechaun Bks.

— Growing up in Aunt Molly's Omaha, 1920-1965: And Facing the World Beyond. (Illus.). 140p. (Orig.). (YA). (gr. 9-12). 1990. pap. 8.95 (*1-879313-00-6*) Murrays Leprechaun Bks.

Murray, Elizabeth. Cultivating Sacred Space: Gardening for the Soul. LC 97-14724. (Illus.). 160p. 1997. boxed set 35.00 (*0-7649-0360-8*, A901) Pomegranate Calif.

— Monet's Gardens at Giverny: A Book of Postcards. 1990. pap. 9.95 (*0-87654-586-X*, A556) Pomegranate Calif.

— Monet's Passion: Ideas, Inspiration & Insights from the Painter's Gardens. LC 89-61640. (Illus.). 144p. 1989. 34.95 (*0-87654-443-X*) Pomegranate Calif.

— Painterly Photography: Awakening the Artist Within. 2nd ed. LC 92-62862. (Illus.). 88p. 1997. boxed set 19.95 (*1-56640-601-3*, A653) Pomegranate Calif.

Murray, Elizabeth & Fell, Derek. Creative Landscaping: Ideas, Designs & Blueprints. LC 94-26765. (Illus.). 160p. 1995. 15.95 (*1-56799-156-4*, Friedman-Fairfax) M Friedman Pub Grp Inc.

Murray, Ellen. Peace & Adventure. (C). 1990. 20.00 (*0-9501351-6-X*, Pub. by Wild Goose Pubns) St Mut.

***Murray, Elsie.** Te-a-o-ga: Annals of a Valley. LC 99-61174. (Pennsylvania History & Legends Ser.). (Illus.). 64p. 1999. pap. 8.95 (*1-889037-18-4*) Wennawoods.

Murray, Elwood, et al. Speech: Science-Art. LC 79-77823. (C). 1969. text. write for info. (*0-672-60863-4*, Bobbs) Macmillan.

Murray, Emily, jt. auth. see Murray, J. B.

Murray, Eugenia B., jt. auth. see Olsen, June L.

Murray, F. W. Astronomy Simply Explained for Beginners. (C). 1987. 45.00 (*0-85174-485-0*) St Mut.

Murray, Fergus, jt. auth. see Knights, David.

Murray, Floyd, ed. see Newspaper Marketing Association Staff.

Murray, Frances. The Belchamber Scandal. large type ed. 5p. 1986. 27.99 (*0-7089-1558-2*) Ulverscroft.

— Payment for the Piper. large type ed. 596p. 1987. 27.99 (*0-7089-1590-6*) Ulverscroft.

***Murray, Francis.** The British Open: A Twentieth-Century History of Golf's Greatest Championship. LC 00-34548. (Illus.). 224p. 2000. 34.95 (*0-8092-9815-5*, Contemporary Bks) NTC Contemp Pub Co.

Murray, Francis J. Introduction to Linear Transformations in Hilbert Space. (Annals of Mathematics Studies). 1941. 25.00 (*0-527-02720-0*) Periodicals Srv.

Murray, Francis J. & Miller, Kenneth S. Existence Theorems for Ordinary Differential Equations. LC 54-10566. 164p. reprint ed. pap. 50.90 (*0-608-30877-3*, 205020600058) Bks Demand.

— Existence Theorems for Ordinary Differential Equations. LC 75-12685. 164p. 1976. reprint ed. 19.50 (*0-88275-320-7*) Krieger.

Murray, Francis X. Where We Agree: Report of the National Coal Policy Project, 2 vols. LC 78-55420. (Special Studies in Natural Resources & Energy Managment). 1978. text 78.00 (*0-89158-175-8*) Westview.

Murray, Frank. Acidophilus & Your Health. LC 98-202883. 48p. 1997. pap. 3.95 (*0-87983-807-8*, 38078K, Keats Publng) NTC Contemp Pub Co.

— Frequently Asked Questions All about Menopause, Phytoestrogens, & Red Clover. (FAQs All about Health Ser.). 1998. mass mkt. 2.99 (*0-89529-909-7*, Avery) Penguin Putnam.

— Ginkgo Biloba. LC 96-24280. (Keats Good Herb Guides Ser.). 64p. (Orig.). 1996. mass mkt. 4.95 (*0-87983-770-5*, Keats Publng) NTC Contemp Pub Co.

— Ginkgo Biloba. (Good Health Guides Ser.). 47p. (Orig.). 1997. pap. 3.95 (*0-87983-601-6*, 36016K, Keats Publng) NTC Contemp Pub Co.

— Happy Feet. 370p. 1990. pap. 11.95 (*0-87983-476-5*, 34765K, Keats Publng) NTC Contemp Pub Co.

***Murray, Frank.** 100 Super Supplements for a Longer Life. 2000. pap. 24.95 (*0-658-00973-7*, Keats Publng) NTC Contemp Pub Co.

Murray, Frank. Remifemin: Herbal Relief for Menopausal Symptoms. (Good Health Guides Ser.). 1996. pap. 3.95 (*0-87983-764-0*, 37640K, Keats Publng) NTC Contemp Pub Co.

Murray, Frank B., ed. Critical Features of Piaget's Theory of the Development of Thought. LC 72-6359. 196p. 1972. pap. text 12.95 (*0-8422-0244-7*) Irvington.

— The Teacher Educator's Handbook: Building a Knowledge Base for the Preparation of Teachers. (Education Ser.). 763p. 1995. text 75.00 (*0-7879-0121-0*) Jossey-Bass.

Murray, Frank B., ed. see Danks, Joseph H. & Pezdek, Kathy.

Murray, Frank B., ed. see Waterhouse, Lynn H., et al.

Murray, Frank S. All Israel Restored. 293p. 1992. 10.00 (*0-910840-21-0*) Kingdom.

— The Sublimity of Faith. LC 81-81770. (Illus.). 952p. 1982. 25.00 (*0-910840-20-2*) Kingdom.

Murray, Frank S., ed. Standard, 20 vols., Vols. 15-35. Incl. Vol. 15. Standard 1963. LC 49-3353. 1963. 3.00 (*0-910840-63-6*); Vol. 16. Standard 1964. 1964. 3.00 (*0-910840-64-4*); Vol. 17. Standard 1965. 1965. 3.00 (*0-910840-65-2*); Vol. 18. Standard 1966. 1966. 3.00 (*0-910840-66-0*); Vol. 19. Standard 1967. 1967. 3.00 (*0-910840-67-9*); Vol. 20. Standard 1968. 1968. 3.00 (*0-910840-68-7*); Vol. 21. Standard 1969. 1969. 3.00 (*0-910840-69-5*); Vol. 22. Standard 1970. 1970. 3.00 (*0-910840-70-9*); Vol. 23. Standard 1971. 1971. 3.00 (*0-910840-71-7*); Vol. 24. Standard 1972. 4p. 1995. pap. 3.00 (*0-910840-72-5*); Vol. 25. Standard 1973. 4p. 1995. pap. 3.00 (*0-910840-73-3*); Vol. 26. Standard 1974. 4p. 1995. pap. 3.00 (*0-910840-74-1*); Vol. 27. Standard 1975. 4p. 1995. pap. 3.00 (*0-910840-75-X*); Vol. 28. Standard 1976. 4p. 1995. pap. 3.00 (*0-910840-76-8*); Vol. 29. Standard 1977. 4p. 1995. pap. 3.00 (*0-910840-77-6*); Vol. 30. Standard 1978. 4p. 1995. pap. 3.00 (*0-910840-78-4*); Vol. 31. Standard 1979. 4p. 1995. pap. 3.00 (*0-910840-79-2*); Vol. 32. Standard 1980. 4p. 1995. pap. 3.00 (*0-910840-80-6*); Vol. 33. Standard 1981. 4p. 1995. pap. 3.00 (*0-910840-81-4*); Vol. 34. Standard 1982. 4p. 1995. pap. 3.00 (*0-910840-82-2*); Vol. 35. Standard 1983. 1995. pap. 3.00 (*0-910840-83-0*); write for info. (*0-318-53986-1*) Kingdom.

Murray, Fred & Murray, Jody L. God Loves Even Cowboys. LC 94-96344. (Illus.). 177p. (Orig.). (J). (gr. 4 up). 1994. pap. 11.95 (*0-9642685-4-X*) F Murray Pubng.

Murray, Frederic W. The Aesthetics of Contemporary Spanish American Social Protest Poetry. LC 90-19948. (Hispanic Literature Ser.: Vol. 9). 224p. 1990. lib. bdg. 89.95 (*0-88946-591-6*) E Mellen.

Murray, Frederick G., jt. auth. see Murray, Janette S.

Murray, Freeman H. Emancipation & the Freed in American Sculpture. LC 70-38016. (Black Heritage Library Collection). 1977. reprint ed. 28.95 (*0-8369-8983-X*) Ayer.

Murray, G., tr. see Wilamowitz & Moellendorff, U.

Murray, G. E. Eisenhower vs. Montgomery: The Continuing Debate. LC 95-42504. 224p. 1996. 62.95 (*0-275-94795-5*, Praeger Pubs) Greenwood.

— Gasoline Dreams. 1978. per. 3.00 (*0-88031-046-4*) Invisible-Red Hill.

— Oils of Evening: Journeys in the Art Trade. Spelius, Carol, ed. 156p. (Orig.). 1995. pap. 12.95 (*0-941363-36-8*) Lake Shore Pub.

— Repairs: Poems. LC 79-5379. (Devins Award Breakthrough Ser.). 96p. 1979. text 18.95 (*0-8262-0290-X*) U of Mo Pr.

— Walking the Blind Dog: Poems by G. E. Murray. 112p. (Orig.). 1992. 10.95 (*0-252-06231-0*) U of Ill Pr.

Murray, G. G. Gobi or Shamo: A Story of Three Songs. Reginald, R. & Melville, Douglas, eds. LC 77-84259. (Lost Race & Adult Fantasy Ser.). 1978. reprint ed. lib. bdg. 34.95 (*0-405-11002-2*) Ayer.

Murray, G. T. Introduction to Engineering Materials: Behavior, Properties, & Selection. LC 93-12660. (Engineering Materials Ser.: Vol. 2). (Illus.). 688p. 1993. text 199.00 (*0-8247-8965-2*) Dekker.

Murray, G. T., ed. Handbook of Materials Selection for Engineering Applications. LC 97-20899. (Mechanical Engineering Ser.: Vol. 113). (Illus.). 632p. 1997. text 170.00 (*0-8247-9910-0*) Dekker.

Murray, Gale B. Toulouse-Lautrec: The Formative Years, 1878-1891. (Clarendon Studies in the History of Art). (Illus.). 332p. 1991. 130.00 (*0-19-817505-1*) OUP.

***Murray, G.E. Patrick.** Victory in Western Europe: From D-day to the Nazi Surrender. LC 99-13506. 128p. 1999. text 14.98 (*1-56799-759-7*) Metro Pr Pubns.

Murray, Gene, jt. auth. see Vivian, John H.

Murray, Geoffrey. Doing Business in China: The Last Great Market. 240p. 1994. pap. 29.95 (*1-873410-29-8*); text 80.00 (*1-873410-28-X*) St Martin.

— Doing Business in China: The Last Great Market. LC 94-13029. 1994. pap. 22.00 (*0-312-11683-7*) St Martin.

— Simple Guide to Vietnam: Customs & Etiquette. (Illus.). 64p. 1997. pap. write for info. (*1-86034-090-3*, Pub. by MAGI1 UK) Midpt Trade.

— Vietnam: Dawn of a New Market. LC 97-23013. 272p. 1997. pap. 20.00 (*0-312-17392-X*) St Martin.

Murray, Geoffrey & Perera, Audrey. Doing Business in Singapore: The Global City-State. LC 95-31701. (Pacific Rim Business Ser.). 288p. 1996. pap. 21.95 (*0-312-12959-9*); text 59.95 (*0-312-12958-0*) St Martin.

Murray, Geoffrey, jt. auth. see Mason, Caroline.

Murray, George, ed. see Marlborough, John C.

Murray, George B., jt. ed. see Fisher, Alden L.

Murray, George W. Sons of Ishmael: A Study of the Egyptian Bedouin. LC 74-15071. reprint ed. 49.50 (*0-404-12115-2*) AMS Pr.

Murray, Gerald F., jt. auth. see Alvarez, Maria D.

Murray, Gerard. John Hume & the SDLP: Impact & Survival in Northern Ireland. LC 98-213903. (New Directions in Irish History Ser.). 342p. 1998. 39.50 (*0-7165-2644-1*, Pub. by Irish Acad Pr) Intl Spec Bk.

Murray, Gerard M. Career Angel: Acting Edition (Female Version) 1945. pap. 13.00 (*0-8222-0183-6*) Dramatists Play.

— Career Angel: Acting Edition (Male Version) 1944. pap. 5.25 (*0-8222-0182-8*) Dramatists Play.

Murray, Germaine F. A Critical Edition of John Beadle's A Journal or Diary of a Thankful Christian. LC 96-2049. (Renaissance Imagination Ser.). (Illus.). 392p. 1996. text 99.00 (*0-8153-1567-8*) Garland.

***Murray, Gerry & White, Amie S.** State of the Document Technologies Market, 1996-2002. 78p. 1998. spiral bd. 30.00 (*0-89258-341-X*, D069) Assn Inform & Image Mgmt.

— State of the Electronic Document Management Market, 1996-2002. 74p. 1998. 30.00 (*0-89258-353-3*, D071) Assn Inform & Image Mgmt.

— State of the Electronic Imaging Market, 1996-2002. 60p. 1998. 30.00 (*0-89258-354-1*, D072) Assn Inform & Image Mgmt.

— State of the Full Text Retrieval Market, 1996-2002. 74p. 1998. 30.00 (*0-89258-355-X*, D073) Assn Inform & Image Mgmt.

— State of the Workflow Market, 1996-2002. 58p. 1998. 30.00 (*0-89258-352-5*, D070) Assn Inform & Image Mgmt.

Murray, Gilbert. Aeschylus, the Creator of Tragedy. LC 77-18893. 242p. 1978. reprint ed. lib. bdg. 35.00 (*0-8371-9919-0*, MUAE, Greenwood Pr) Greenwood.

— Euripides & His Age. LC 79-4184. 132p. 1979. reprint ed. lib. bdg. 35.00 (*0-313-20989-8*, MUEA, Greenwood Pr) Greenwood.

— Five Stages of Greek Religion. LC 76-27675. 276p. 1976. reprint ed. lib. bdg. 35.00 (*0-8371-9080-0*, MUFS, Greenwood Pr) Greenwood.

— Five Stages of Greek Religion: Studies Based on a Course of Lectures Delivered in April 1912 at Columbia University. LC 75-41202. reprint ed. 30.00 (*0-404-14577-9*) AMS Pr.

— From the League to U. N. LC 87-14934. 232p. 1988. reprint ed. lib. bdg. 65.00 (*0-313-26080-X*, MLUN, Greenwood Pr) Greenwood.

— Liberality & Civilization: Lectures Given at the Invitation of the Hibbert Trustees in the Universities of Bristol, Glasgow & Birmingham. LC 77-27139. (Hibbert Lectures). reprint ed. 30.00 (*0-404-60430-7*) AMS Pr.

— Stoic, Christian & Humanist. LC 75-99712. (Essay Index Reprint Ser.). 1977. 19.95 (*0-8369-1363-9*) Ayer.

— Tradition & Progress. LC 68-20323. (Essay Index Reprint Ser.). 1977. 19.95 (*0-8369-0728-0*) Ayer.

— Tradition & Progress. LC 68-20323. (Essay Index Reprint Ser.). 221p. reprint ed. lib. bdg. 19.00 (*0-8290-0490-4*) Irvington.

Murray, Gilbert, tr. The Iphigenia in Tauris of Euripides. 12.00 (*0-8196-2856-5*) Biblo.

Murray, Gilbert, tr. see Aristotle.

Murray, Giles. Instant Business Japanese: Real Life Skills for Real Life Situations. 1997. pap. text 17.00 (*4-7700-2105-4*, Pub. by Kodansha Int) OUP.

— 13 Secrets for Speaking Fluent Japanese. 192p. 1998. pap. text 15.00 (*4-7700-2302-2*, Pub. by Kodansha Intl) Kodansha.

Murray, Glen, ed. Scottish Sea Stories. 1996. pap. 18.95 (*0-7486-6208-1*, Pub. by Polygon) Subterranean Co.

***Murray, Glenn.** Adventure Legend Logbook. 2nd ed. (Illus.). ii, 75p. 1999. 79.95 (*1-58527-021-0*) Legend Pubns NY.

— Antiques Legend Logbook. 2nd ed. (Illus.). ii, 75p. 1999. 79.95 (*1-58527-000-8*) Legend Pubns NY.

— Camping Legend Logbook. 2nd ed. (Illus.). ii, 75p. 1999. 79.95 (*1-58527-001-6*) Legend Pubns NY.

— Contractor Legend Logbook. 2nd ed. (Illus.). ii, 75p. 1999. 79.95 (*1-58527-002-4*) Legend Pubns NY.

— Deep Sea Fishing Legend Logbook. 2nd ed. (Illus.). ii, 75p. 1999. 79.95 (*1-58527-003-2*) Legend Pubns NY.

— Fishing Legend Logbook. 2nd ed. (Illus.). ii, 75p. 1999. 79.95 (*1-58527-004-0*) Legend Pubns NY.

— Fly Fishing Legend Logbook. 2nd ed. (Illus.). ii, 75p. 1999. 79.95 (*1-58527-005-9*) Legend Pubns NY.

— Golf Legend Logbook. 2nd ed. (Illus.). ii, 75p. 1999. 79.95 (*1-58527-007-5*) Legend Pubns NY.

— Home Improvement Legend Logbook. 2nd ed. (Illus.). ii, 75p. 1999. 79.95 (*1-58527-008-3*) Legend Pubns NY.

— Hunting Legend Logbook. 2nd ed. (Illus.). ii, 75p. 1999. 79.95 (*1-58527-009-1*) Legend Pubns NY.

— Legend Logbook. 2nd ed. (Illus.). ii, 75p. 1999. 79.95 (*1-58527-006-7*) Legend Pubns NY.

— Little League Legend Logbook. 2nd ed. (Illus.). ii, 75p. 1999. 79.95 (*1-58527-010-5*) Legend Pubns NY.

— Paintball Legend Logbook. 2nd ed. (Illus.). ii, 75p. 1999. 79.95 (*1-58527-011-3*) Legend Pubns NY.

— Real Estate Sales Legend Logbook. 2nd ed. (Illus.). ii, 75p. 1999. 79.95 (*1-58527-012-1*) Legend Pubns NY.

— Scuba Diving Legend Logbook. 2nd ed. (Illus.). ii, 75p. 1999. 79.95 (*1-58527-013-X*) Legend Pubns NY.

— Skiing Legend Logbook. 2nd ed. (Illus.). ii, 75p. 1999. 79.95 (*1-58527-015-6*) Legend Pubns NY.

— Snowboarding Legend Logbook. 2nd ed. (Illus.). ii, 75p. 1999. 79.95 (*1-58527-016-4*) Legend Pubns NY.

— Softball Legend Logbook. 2nd ed. (Illus.). ii, 75p. 1999. 79.95 (*1-58527-014-8*) Legend Pubns NY.

— Sportsman's Legend Logbook. 2nd ed. (Illus.). ii, 75p. 1999. 79.95 (*1-58527-017-2*) Legend Pubns NY.

— Surf Casting Legend Logbook. 2nd ed. (Illus.). ii, 75p. 1999. 79.95 (*1-58527-018-0*) Legend Pubns NY.

— Travel Legend Logbook. 2nd ed. (Illus.). ii, 75p. 1999. 79.95 (*1-58527-019-9*) Legend Pubns NY.

— Vacation Legend Logbook. 2nd ed. (Illus.). ii, 75p. 1999. 79.95 (*1-58527-020-2*) Legend Pubns NY.

Murray, Glenn E. Collateral Consequences of Criminal Conduct. LC 92-61678. 347p. (Orig.). 1992. pap. 38.00 (*0-942954-53-X*) NYS Bar.

Murray, Gordon, jt. contrib. by see Sloan, Audrey.

Murray, Gordon J. A Teacher's Guide to Eureka! (Creative Art Ser.). 1995. teacher ed. write for info. (*1-887662-00-6*) Kent St Univ.

Murray-Graham, Sylvia A. Living in Eternity: Channeled Wisdom on Life, the Hereafter, & the Reality of It All. 225p. (Orig.). pap. write for info. (*0-9643806-0-9*) CandleLght TX.

Murray, H. M., ed. The Middle English Poem Erthe upon Erthe. (EETS Original Ser.: No. 141). 102p. 1964. reprint ed. 20.00 (*0-19-722141-6*, Pub. by EETS) Boydell & Brewer.

***Murray, Harold.** G. Campbell Morgan: Bible Teacher. (Classic Biographies Ser.). (Illus.). 1999. pap. 10.99 (*1-84030-046-9*) Ambassador Prodns Ltd.

Murray, Harold D. & Leonard, A. B. Handbook of Unionid Mussels in Kansas. (Miscellaneous Publications: No. 28). 184p. 1962. pap. 8.00 (*0-686-79811-2*) U KS Nat Hist Mus.

***Murray, Harold G., Sr.** Mystery Man S. I. X. One Man's Struggle to Become the (666) Beast of Revelation. LC 99-73462. 214p. 1999. pap. 14.95 (*1-890622-94-X*) Leathers Pub.

***Murray, Harry.** Virginia Blue-Ribbon Streams. (Illus.). 96p. 2000. 34.95 (*1-57188-200-6*); pap. 24.95 (*1-57188-159-X*, VABR) F Amato Pubns.

Murray, Harry W. Do Not Neglect Hospitality: The Catholic Worker & the Homeless. 304p. 1991. 37.95 (*0-87722-726-8*) Temple U Pr.

— Fly Fishing for Smallmouth Bass. 1996. pap. text 16.95 (*1-55821-534-4*) Lyons Pr.

— Trout Fishing in the Shenandoah National Park. rev. ed. (Illus.). 124p. (Orig.). 1997. pap. 11.95 (*0-9622555-0-5*) Shenandoah Edinburg.

Murray, Haydn, et al, eds. Kaolin Genesis & Utilization. No. 1. (Special Publication). (Illus.). 341p. (C). 1993. text 25.00 (*1-881208-05-2*) Clay Minerals.

Murray, Heather. Double Lives: Women in the Stories of Katherine Mansfield. 198p. 1990. pap. 19.95 (*0-908569-56-4*, Pub. by Univ Otago Pr) Intl Spec Bk.

— Working in English: History, Institution, Resources. LC 96 173366. (Theory/Culture Ser.). 253p. 1996. text 45.00 (*0-8020-2853-5*) U of Toronto Pr.

— Working in English: History, Institution, Resources. (Theory/Culture Ser.). 288p. 1996. pap. text 16.95 (*0-8020-7350-6*) U of Toronto Pr.

Murray, Helen & Leavens, Donald C. When Your Child Flies Alone: A Guide for Parents. 44p. 1990. pap. text 6.95 (*1-879668-00-9*) Info Finders.

Murray, Henry A. Thematic Apperception Test. LC 43-3797. 20p. 1943. student ed. 54.00 (*0-674-87720-9*); pap. 7.00 (*0-674-87721-7*) HUP.

Murray, Henry A., ed. see Melville, Herman.

Murray, Henry V. & Sluder, Troy B. Fixed Restorative Techniques. enl. rev. ed. Barton, Roger E., ed. LC 88-39479. (Dental Laboratory Technology Manuals Ser.). (Illus.). viii, 364p. 1989. reprint ed. pap. 59.95 (*0-8078-4250-8*) U of NC Pr.

Murray, Hilda, ed. Erthe upon Erthe: All Known Texts. (EETS, OS Ser.: Vol. 141). 1972. reprint ed. 20.00 (*0-8115-3371-9*) Periodicals Srv.

Murray, Holly L. The Anatomy of a Woman. (Illus.). 55p. (Orig.). (C). 1989. pap. 5.95 (*0-9623358-0-0*, TXU 329-044) Pegasus Print.

***Murray, Hugh.** A Directory of York Goldsmiths, Silversmiths & Associated Craftsmen. 180p. 1999. pap. 30.00 (*1-85072-200-5*, Pub. by W Sessions) St Mut.

Murray, Hugh. Dr. Evelyn's York: Illustrations of Bygone York 1891-1935. (Illus.). (C). 1988. 110.00 (*0-900657-85-5*, Pub. by W Sessions) St Mut.

***Murray, Hugh.** Heraldry & the Buildings of York. 1999. pap. 21.00 (*0-9503519-1-1*, Pub. by Yorkshire Architectural) St Mut.

Murray, Hugh. Historical Account of Discoveries & Travels in Asia, from the Earliest Ages to the Present Time, 3 vols. LC 77-153625. reprint ed. lib. bdg. 55.00 (*0-404-09570-4*) AMS Pr.

M

— The History of York Cemetery: The Garden of Death. (C). 1999. pap. text 45.00 (*0-9517737-0-4*, Pub. by W Sessions) St Mut.

— Opportunity of Leisure: The History of the York Railway Institute 1889-1989. (C). 1999. pap. text 21.00 (*0-9514452-0-0*, Pub. by W Sessions) St Mut.

— Photographs & Photographers of York, 1844-1879. (C). 1988. pap. 21.00 (*0-9503519-4-6*, Pub. by W Sessions) St Mut.

*__Murray, Hugh.__ Scarborough, York & Leeds. 1999. pap. text (*0-9519981-3-7*) Yorkshire Architectural.

Murray, Hugh F., compiled by. History of the Town of Orwell, 1806 to 1887. (Illus.). 236p. 1997. reprint ed. lib. bdg. 29.50 (*0-8328-6196-0*) Higginson Bk Co.

Murray, Hwesu S., ed. see Murray, Samuel M.

Murray, I. & Murray, T. The Modern Scottish Novels. 224p. 1984. 19.00 (*0-685-09404-9*, Pergamon Pr); pap. text 15.90 (*0-08-028493-0*, Pergamon Pr) Elsevier.

*__Murray, I. P. & Ell, P. J.__ Nuclear Medicine in Clinical Diagnosis & Treatment. 2nd ed. 1999. 495.00 (*0-443-05861-X*) Church.

Murray, I. P. & Ell, P. J., eds. Nuclear Medicine in Clinical Diagnosis & Treatment, 2 vols. LC 94-34613. (Illus.). 1388p. 1995. text 270.00 (*0-443-04710-3*) Church.

Murray, Iain H. Australian Christian Life from 1788: An Introduction & an Anthology. 347p. 1988. 27.99 (*0-85151-524-X*) Banner of Truth.

— The Forgotten Spurgeon. 256p. 1988. pap. 9.99 (*0-85151-156-2*) Banner of Truth.

— The Invitation System. 1984. pap. 2.99 (*0-85151-171-6*) Banner of Truth.

— Jonathan Edwards: A New Biography. 503p. 1992. pap. 21.99 (*0-85151-704-8*) Banner of Truth.

— The Life of D. M. Lloyd-Jones: The First Forty Years, 1899-1939. (Illus.). 408p. 1983. 35.99 (*0-85151-353-0*) Banner of Truth.

— The Life of D. M. Lloyd-Jones Vol. 2: The Fight of Faith, 1939-1981. 862p. 1990. 39.99 (*0-85151-564-9*) Banner of Truth.

— Pentecost - Today? The Biblical Basis for Understanding Revival. 1998. 19.99 (*0-85151-752-8*) Banner of Truth.

— Pentecost - Today? The Biblical Basis for Understanding Revival. 232p. 1998. 19.99 (*0-9654955-5-8*) Founders Pr.

— The Puritan Hope. 1975. pap. 9.99 (*0-85151-247-X*) Banner of Truth.

— Revival & Revivalism: The Making & Marring of American Evangelicalism 1750-1858. 455p. 1994. 29.99 (*0-85151-660-2*) Banner of Truth.

— Spurgeon un Principe Olvidado. 2nd ed. (SPA.). 156p. 1984. reprint ed. pap. 3.99 (*0-85151-439-1*) Banner of Truth.

— Spurgeon vs. Hyper-Calvinism: The Battle for Gospel Preaching. 164p. 1995. pap. 5.99 (*0-85151-692-0*) Banner of Truth.

Murray, Iain H., ed. Diary of Kenneth Macrae. (Illus.). 535p. 1980. 29.99 (*0-85151-297-6*) Banner of Truth.

Murray, Iain H., ed. see Houghton, S. M.

Murray, Iain H., ed. see Spurgeon, Charles H.

*__Murray, Ian.__ For the Wings of a Dove. 411p. 2000. pap. write for info. (*0-7541-0882-1*, Pub. by Minerva Pr) Unity Dist.

Murray, Ian. Practical Clematis Growing. (Illus.). 64p. 1993. pap. 8.95 (*1-85223-656-6*, Pub. by Crolwood) Trafalgar.

Murray, Ian, ed. The New Penguin Book of Scottish Short Stories. 317p. 2000. pap. 15.95 (*0-14-006411-7*, Pub. by Pnguin Bks Ltd) Trafalgar.

Murray, Ian & Cowe, Ian A., eds. Making Light Work: Advances in Near Infrared Spectroscopy: the 4th International Conference on Near Infrared Spectroscopy, August 19-23, 1991, Aberdeen, Scotland. LC 92-11232. 652p. 1992. 325.00 (*3-527-28498-2*, Wiley-VCH) Wiley.

Murray, Ian, jt. auth. see Miller, Sheila.

Murray, Ian H. The Reformation of the Church: A Collection of Reformed & Puritan Documents on Church Issues. 416p. (C). 1987. reprint ed. 16.99 (*0-85151-118-X*) Banner of Truth.

Murray, Irena, tr. see Tiege, Karel.

Murray, Irena Z. Jana Sterbak: Metamorphosis. (Illus.). 24p. 1997. pap. 7.50 (*0-933519-36-2*) D W Bell Gallery.

— Sources in Iconography in the Blackader-Lauterman Library of Architecture & Art, McGill University: An Annotated Bibliography. (Illus.). 230p. 1997. 49.95 (*0-7735-1452-X*, Pub. by McG-Queens Univ Pr) CUP Services.

Murray, Irene Z., ed. Moshe Safdie: Buildings & Projects, 1967-1992. LC 96-181072. (Illus.). 332p. 1996. pap. 65.00 incl. cd-rom (*0-7735-1510-0*, Pub. by McG-Queens Univ Pr) CUP Services.

*__Murray, Isobel.__ Jessie Kesson: Writing Her Life. 2000. pap. 18.95 (*0-86241-999-9*, Pub. by Canongate Books) Interlink Pub.

Murray, Isobel, ed. see Wilde, Oscar.

Murray, Isobel, ed. & intro. see Wilde, Oscar.

Murray, Isobel M., ed. see Wilde, Oscar.

Murray, Isobel M., ed. & intro. see Wilde, Oscar.

Murray, J. Avifauna of British India & Its Dependencies, Set. 1984. reprint ed. 750.00 (*81-7089-020-9*, Pub. by Intl Bk Distr) St Mut.

— Lord Byron & His Detractors. LC 77-119079. (Studies in Byron: No. 5). 1970. reprint ed. lib. bdg. 75.00 (*0-8383-1075-3*) M S G Haskell Hse.

— Vertebrate Zoology of Sind. 424p. (C). 1988. 275.00 (*81-7089-058-6*, Pub. by Intl Bk Distr) St Mut.

Murray, J., ed. The Cosmic Covenant. (Illus.). 260p. (Orig.). 1990. pap. 68.00 (*0-7220-2750-8*, Pub. by Sheed Ward Ltd) St Mut.

Murray, J., jt. auth. see Watkins, T. F.

Murray, J. A., ed. The Complaynt of Scotlande, Pts. 1 & 2. (EETS, ES Ser.: Nos. 17, 18). 1972. reprint ed. 54.00 (*0-527-00231-3*) Periodicals Srv.

Murray, J. B. & Murray, Emily. And Say What He Is: The Life of a Special Child. LC 75-5810. 304p. 1979. pap. text 5.95 (*0-262-63069-9*) MIT Pr.

Murray, J. C. Excavations in the Medieval Burgh of Aberdeen, 1973-1981. (Illus.). 255p. 1982. pap. 32.00 (*0-903903-02-4*) David Brown.

Murray, J. Clifford. Angiogenesis: Reviews & Protocols. (Methods in Molecular Biology Ser.). 300p. 2000. 89.50 (*0-89603-698-7*) Humana.

Murray, J. D. Asymptotic Analysis. 2nd ed. (Applied Mathematical Sciences Ser.: Vol. 48). Orig. Title: Introduction to Asymptotic Analysis. (Illus.). 160p. 1996. reprint ed. 53.95 (*0-387-90937-0*) Spr-Verlag.

— Mathematical Biology. (Biomathematics Ser.: Vol. 19). (Illus.). 760p. 1989. 64.95 (*0-387-19460-6*) Spr-Verlag.

— Mathematical Biology. 2nd rev. ed. Levin, S. A., ed. (BIOMED Ser.: Vol. 19). (Illus.). xiv, 767p. 1997. 43.95 (*0-387-57204-X*) Spr-Verlag.

— Transgenic Animals in Agriculture. LC 98-30338. 304p. 1999. text 100.00 (*0-85199-293-5*) OUP.

Murray, J. Dennis & Keller, Peter A., eds. Innovations in Rural Community Mental Health. 285p. (Orig.). (C). 1986. pap. text 19.95 (*0-940299-00-3*) Manfld U Rural.

Murray, J. L., intro. Phase Diagrams of Binary Titanium Alloys. (Monograph Series on Alloy Phase Diagrams). (Illus.). 345p. (C). 1987. reprint ed. text 156.00 (*0-87170-248-7*, 57704G) ASM.

Murray, J. Middleton, tr. see Dostoyevsky, Fyodor.

Murray, J. Ross. Influence of Italian Upon English Literature During the Sixteenth & Seventeenth Centuries. LC 70-138743. reprint ed. 29.50 (*0-404-04544-8*) AMS Pr.

Murray, J. S. & Sen, K. Molecular Electrostatic Potentials: Concepts & Applications. 1996. write for info. (*0-614-17931-9*) Elsevier.

Murray, J. S. & Sen, K. D. Molecular Electrostatic Potentials: Concepts & Applications. LC 96-36531. (Theoretical & Computational Chemistry Ser.). 680p. 1996. 372.00 (*0-444-82353-0*) Elsevier.

Murray, J. S., jt. ed. see Politzer, P.

Murray, J. W., ed. see Murray, John W.

Murray, Jack. Accident Investigation in the Private Sector. 110p. 1997. reprint ed. spiral bd. 35.00 (*0-918487-02-1*) Thomas Investigative.

— The Landscapes of Alienation: Ideological Subversion in Kafka, Celine, & Onetti. LC 90-20976. 288p. 1991. 37.50 (*0-8047-1868-7*) Stanford U Pr.

*__Murray, Jack.__ Marketing & Management Maximizer for Your: Investing Practice. (Private Investigation Ser.). (Illus.). 89p. 1999. spiral bd. 38.00 (*1-891247-33-6*) Thomas Investigative.

Murray, Jack & Murray, Jay. Accident Investigation in the Private Sector Vol. II: Introduction to Reconstruction. 2nd ed. (Illus.). 113p. (C). 1997. pap. text 38.00 (*0-918487-06-4*) Thomas Investigative.

Murray, Jacqueline, ed. Conflicted Identities & Multiple Masculinities: Men in the Medieval West. (Medieval Casebooks Ser.: Vol. 25). 328p. 1999. 55.00 (*0-8153-3030-8*) Garland.

Murray, Jacqueline & Eisenbichler, Konrad, eds. Desire & Discipline: Sex & Sexuality in the Postmodern West. 336p. 1996. text 60.00 (*0-8020-0780-5*); pap. text 21.95 (*0-8020-7144-9*) U of Toronto Pr.

Murray, Jacqueline, ed. & tr. see Firenzuola, Agnolo.

Murray, James. Letters of James Murray, Loyalist. (American Biography Ser.). 324p. 1991. reprint ed. lib. bdg. 79.00 (*0-7812-8293-4*) Rprt Serv.

— Morrisville. (Images of America Ser.). 1997. pap. 16.99 (*0-7524-0926-3*) Arcadia Publng.

— Windows NT SNMP: Simple Network Management Protocol. Russell, Debby, ed. 464p. (Orig.). 1998. pap. 34.95 (*1-56592-338-3*) OReilly & Assocs.

Murray, James, jt. ed. see Lennon, Colm.

Murray, James A. Lighten up on God. Heyden, Patricia E., ed. 162p. Date not set. write for info. (*0-9631348-3-3*) Stuart MI.

Murray, James A., ed. Thomas of Erceldoune. (EETS, OS Ser.: No. 61). 1974. reprint ed. 40.00 (*0-527-00055-8*) Periodicals Srv.

Murray, James C. Sold - the Inside Scoop on Selling a House. 192p. 1996. pap. 14.95 (*0-9648287-0-7*) Pyramid Pr GA.

— Spanish Chronicles of the Indies: Sixteenth Century. LC 93-29499. (Twayne's World Authors Series: Spanish Literature: No. 847). 188p. 1994. 25.95 (*0-8057-4306-5*) Macmillan.

Murray, James D. Windows NT Event Logging. Russell, Deborah, ed. (Illus.). 316p. 1998. reprint ed. pap. 34.95 incl. cd-rom (*1-56592-514-9*) OReilly & Assocs.

Murray, James D. & VanRyper, William. Encyclopedia of Graphics File Formats: The Complete Reference on CD-ROM with Links to Internet Resources. 2nd rev. ed. Russell, Deborah, ed. LC 97-140158. 1116p. 1996. pap. 59.95 (*1-56592-161-5*) Thomson Learn.

*__Murray, James L.__ Life Without a Compass: With Revealing Comments about the Decline of the Douglas Aircraft Company. LC 98-73683. (Illus.). 426p. 1998. write for info. (*0-9673924-0-3*) J L Murray.

Murray, James M. Fifty Things You Can Do about Guns. LC 94-17633. 100p. 1994. pap. 7.95 (*1-885003-00-5*) R D Reed Pubs.

Murray, James M., jt. auth. see Hunt, Edwin S.

Murray, James P. Black Comedy: African American Comedians & Their Comic Routines. (Illus.). 224p. 1996. pap. 11.95 (*0-8065-1715-8*, Citadel Pr) Carol Pub Group.

Murray, James W., jt. ed. see Izdar, Erol.

Murray, Jane E. Fear of Filing - Musical. 1995. 5.95 (*0-87129-429-X*, F03) Dramatic Pub.

Murray, Janet H. & Stark, Myra, eds. The Englishwoman's Review of Social & Industrial Questions, 40 vols. 1979. 20.00 (*0-318-52457-0*) Garland.

— The Englishwoman's Review of Social & Industrial Questions, 40 Vols., Set. 1979. lib. bdg. 800.00 (*0-8153-0258-4*) Garland.

Murray, Janet Horowitz. Hamlet on the Holodeck: The Future of Narrative in Cyberspace. LC QA76.76.I59M87. 1997. 23.00 (*0-02-874020-3*) Free Pr.

— Hamlet on the Holodeck: The Future of Narrative in Cyberspace. LC 97-9187. 324p. 1997. 25.00 (*0-684-82723-9*) Free Pr.

— Hamlet on the Holodeck: The Future of Narrative in Cyberspace. LC 98-17955. 336p. 1998. pap. text 15.00 (*0-262-63187-3*) MIT Pr.

Murray, Janette S. & Murray, Frederick G. The Story of Cedar Rapids. (Illus.). 284p. 1995. reprint ed. lib. bdg. 35.00 (*0-8328-4665-1*) Higginson Bk Co.

Murray, Jay, jt. auth. see Murray, Jack.

Murray, Jean, jt. auth. see Darin, Bobby.

Murray, Jean A. Music of the Alaska-Klondike Gold Rush: A Songbook & History. (LanternLight Library: Vol. 3). (Illus.). 440p. 1999. 54.95 (*1-889963-13-5*); spiral bd. 35.95 (*1-889963-14-3*) U of Alaska Pr.

Murray, Jeff. For Big Bucks Only. LC 87-63364. (Hunter's Information Ser.). 216p. 1989. write for info. (*0-914697-17-X*) N Amer Outdoor Grp.

— Moon Struck: Hunting Strategies That Revolve Around the Moon. 174p. 1996. pap. text 14.95 (*0-9646823-0-3*) Fool Moon Pr.

Murray, Jeff & Mcclelland, Mike. How to Win the Walleye Game: Walleye Game. (Illus.). 220p. (Orig.). (C). 1988. write for info. (*0-9622571-0-9*); pap. 17.95 (*0-9622571-3-3*); lib. bdg. write for info. (*0-9622571-1-7*) Fishing Enterprises.

Murray, Jerome. From Uptight to All Right: A Twelve Step Program for Stress Prevention. LC 87-7762. 187p. (Orig.). 1987. pap. 12.95 (*0-942383-06-0*) Manor Hse Pub.

Murray, Jerome T. & Murray, Marilyn J. The Year 2000 Computing Crisis: A Millennium Date Conversion Plan. (Illus.). 320p. 1996. pap. 39.95 incl. cd-rom (*0-07-912945-5*) McGraw.

Murray, Jill. Arrow to the Heart. large type ed. (Linford Romance Library). 1990. pap. 16.99 (*0-7089-6824-4*, Linford) Ulverscroft.

*__Murray, Jill.__ But I Love Him: Protecting Your Teen Daughter from Controlling, Abusive Dating Relationships. 224p. 2000. 25.00 (*0-06-019724-2*, ReganBks) HarperTrade.

Murray, Jill. My Cousin Mandy. large type ed. 1989. 27.99 (*0-7089-2107-8*) Ulverscroft.

— Nurse from Newstone. large type ed. 1991. 27.99 (*0-7089-2522-7*) Ulverscroft.

— Nurse in Izbah. large type ed. (Linford Romance Library). 320p. 1985. pap. 16.99 (*0-7089-6070-7*, Linford) Ulverscroft.

— The Other Margaret. large type ed. 1990. 27.99 (*0-7089-2255-4*) Ulverscroft.

*__Murray, Jim.__ Art of Whisky: A Deluxe Blend of Whiskey Posters from the Public Record Office. 1999. pap. 17.95 (*1-873162-67-7*) PRO Pubns.

— The Art of Whisky: A Deluxe Blend of Whisky Posters from the Public Record Office (U. K.) (Illus.). 80p. 1999. pap. text 25.00 (*0-7881-8123-8*) DIANE Pub.

Murray, Jim. Classic Blended Scotch. (Classic Drinks Ser.). (Illus.). 1999. pap. text 19.95 (*1-85375-297-5*, Pub. by Prion) Trafalgar.

— Classic Bourbon, Tennessee & Rye Whiskey. (Classic Drink Ser.). (Illus.). 192p. 1998. 19.95 (*1-85375-218-5*) Prion.

— Classic Irish Whiskey. (Classic Drink Ser.). (Illus.). 256p. 1997. 19.95 (*1-85375-241-X*) Prion.

— The Complete Guide to Whiskey: Selecting, Comparing & Drinking the World's Great Whiskeys. (Illus.). 208p. (Orig.). 1997. pap. 14.95 (*1-57243-151-2*) Triumph Bks.

*__Murray, Jim.__ The Great Ones. 352p. 1999. 23.95 (*1-883792-56-8*, Pub. by LA Times) Sunbelt Pubns.

Murray, Jim. Jim Murray: Last of the Best. Dwyre, Bill, ed. (Illus.). 334p. 1998. pap. 15.95 (*1-883792-50-9*, Pub. by LA Times) Sunbelt Pubns.

— Jim Murray: The Autobiography. 296p. 1995. 12.95 (*0-02-860430-X*) Macmillan.

— Weight Lifting & Progressive Resistance Exercise. LC GV0511.. 95p. reprint ed. pap. 30.00 (*0-608-13664-6*, 205516700008) Bks Demand.

*__Murray, Jim.__ World Whiskey Guide. (Illus.). 2000. 24.95 (*1-85868-869-8*, Pub. by Carlton Bks Ltd) Natl Bk Netwk.

Murray, Jim. Legends of the Golden Era. (Baseball Legends Ser.). 64p. (J). (gr. 3 up). 1995. 203.80 (*0-7910-3563-8*) Chelsea Hse.

Murray, Jim, intro. Casey Stengel. LC 94-36778. (Baseball Legends Ser.). (Illus.). 64p. (J). (gr. 3 up). 1995. lib. bdg. 15.95 (*0-7910-2172-6*) Chelsea Hse.

— Chipper Jones. LC 99-12001. (Baseball Legends Ser.). (Illus.). 64p. (YA). (gr. 3 up). 1999. 16.95 (*0-7910-5157-9*) Chelsea Hse.

— Early Legends. (Baseball Legends Ser.). (Illus.). 64p. (J). (gr. 3 up). 1997. 134.55 (*0-7910-3561-1*) Chelsea Hse.

— Larry Walker. LC 98-54816. (Baseball Legends Ser.). (Illus.). 64p. (YA). (gr. 3 up). 1999. 16.95 (*0-7910-5159-5*) Chelsea Hse.

— Legends of the 1930s & 1940s. (Baseball Legends Ser.). (Illus.). 64p. (J). (gr. 3 up). 1995. 104.65 (*0-7910-3562-X*) Chelsea Hse.

— Life in the Minor Leagues. LC 99-11980. (Baseball Legends Ser.). (Illus.). 64p. (YA). (gr. 3 up). 1999. 16.95 (*0-7910-5160-9*) Chelsea Hse.

*__Murray, Jim, intro.__ Mark McGwire. LC 98-51065. (Baseball Legends Ser.). (Illus.). 64p. (YA). (gr. 3-7). 1999. 16.95 (*0-7910-5155-2*) Chelsea Hse.

Murray, Jim, intro. Modern Day Legends. (Baseball Legends Ser.). (Illus.). 64p. (J). (gr. 3 up). 1994. 179.40 (*0-7910-3564-6*) Chelsea Hse.

— Randy Johnson. LC 99-18222. (Baseball Legends Ser.). (Illus.). 64p. (YA). (gr. 3-7). 1999. pap. 16.95 (*0-7910-5158-7*) Chelsea Hse.

— Roger Clemens. LC 98-51064. (Baseball Legends Ser.). (Illus.). 64p. (YA). (gr. 3-7). 1999. pap. 16.95 (*0-7910-5156-0*) Chelsea Hse.

*__Murray, Jim, intro.__ Today's Stars. (Illus.). 64p. (gr. 3). 1998. 220.35 (*0-7910-4503-X*) Chelsea Hse.

Murray, Jimm. Comprehensive Study Questions for the EMT-A: Basic Life Support. 151p. 1982. pap. 13.95 (*0-317-58940-7*) P-H.

Murray, Joan. The Best of the Group Of Seven. (Illus.). 96p. 1996. pap. 14.99 (*0-7710-6674-0*) McCland & Stewart.

— Home Truths: A Celebration of Family Life by Canada's Best-Loved Painters. LC 98-110416. (Illus.). 168p. 1998. 40.00 (*1-55013-882-0*) Firefly Bks Ltd.

— The Last Buffalo: The Story of Frederick Arthur Verner, Painter of the Northwest. (Illus.). 192p. 1985. 95.00 (*0-87951-232-6*, Pub. by Overlook Pr) Penguin Putnam.

*__Murray, Joan.__ Looking for the Parade. 144p. 2000. pap. 13.00 (*0-393-32064-2*) Norton.

Murray, Joan. Poems by Joan Murray, 1917-1942. Code, Grant, ed. LC 71-144751. (Yale Series of Younger Poets: No. 45). reprint ed. 18.00 (*0-404-53845-2*) AMS Pr.

*__Murray, Joan.__ Queen of the Mist. 2000. pap. 15.00 (*0-8070-6857-8*) Beacon Pr.

Murray, Joan. Queen of the Mist: The Forgotten Heroine of Niagara. LC 98-42932. 128p. 1999. 20.00 (*0-8070-6852-7*) Beacon Pr.

— The Same Water: Poems. LC 89-33954. (Wesleyan New Poets Ser.). 64p. 1990. pap. 12.95 (*0-8195-1183-8*, Wesleyan Univ Pr) U Pr of New Eng.

— Tom Thomson. Fetherling, Douglas, ed. (New Views on Canadian Artists Ser.). (Illus.). 96p. 1996. pap. 18.95 (*1-55082-155-5*, Pub. by Quarry Pr) LPC InBook.

Murray, Joan, ed. Off the Shelf: A Marketing & Distribution Guide for Independent Literary & Artist Book Publishers. (Illus.). 160p. (Orig.). 1989. pap. 10.95 (*0-9618487-0-7*) Writers & Bks.

Murray, Joan & Abramson, Paul R. Bias in Psychotherapy. 398p. 1983. 69.50 (*0-275-91050-4*, C1050, Praeger Pubs) Greenwood.

Murray, Joan, ed. see Bruce, William B.

Murray, Joan, ed. see Macleod, Pegi N.

Murray, Jocelyn. Africa. (Cultural Atlas for Young People Ser.). (Illus.). 96p. (J). 1990. 19.95 (*0-8160-2209-7*) Facts on File.

— Cultural Atlas of Africa. (Cultural Atlas Ser.). (Illus.). 240p. 1981. 45.00 (*0-87196-558-5*) Facts on File.

— Cultural Atlas of Africa. rev. ed. (Cultural Atlas Ser.). (Illus.). 240p. 1998. 50.00 (*0-8160-3813-9*, Checkmark) Facts on File.

Murray, Jocelyn, ed. see Shank, David A.

Murray, Jody L., jt. auth. see Murray, D. Fred.

Murray, Jody L., jt. auth. see Murray, Fred.

Murray, John. American Nature Writing 1997. 320p. 1997. pap. 15.00 (*0-87156-395-9*, Pub. by Sierra) Random.

*__Murray, John.__ Ancient Law. 14th ed. 415p. 1999. 130.00 (*1-56169-472-X*) Gaunt.

Murray, John. Basic Russian: A Grammar & Workbook. 1999. pap. 21.99 (*0-415-18318-9*) Routledge.

— Cactus Country: An Illustrated Guide. 160p. (Orig.). 1996. pap. 19.95 (*1-57098-076-4*) Roberts Rinehart.

— Christian Baptism. 1974. pap. 5.99 (*0-87552-343-9*) P & R Pubng.

— The Collected Writings of John Murray, 4 vols., Set. 1976. 155.99 (*0-85151-396-4*) Banner of Truth.

— Collected Writings of John Murray Vol. I: Claims of Truth. 374p. 1976. 41.99 (*0-85151-241-0*) Banner of Truth.

— The Collected Writings of John Murray Vol. 2: Lectures in Systematic Theology. 1978. 41.99 (*0-85151-242-9*) Banner of Truth.

— Collected Writings of John Murray Vol. 4: Studies in Theology. 390p. 1983. 41.99 (*0-85151-340-9*) Banner of Truth.

— A Comparative View of the Huttonian & Neptunian Systems of Geology: In Answer to the Illustrations of the Huttonian Theory of the Earth. Albritton, Claude C., Jr., ed. LC 77-6533. (History of Geology Ser.). 1978. reprint ed. lib. bdg. 26.95 (*0-405-10453-7*) Ayer.

— Covenant of Grace: A Biblico-Theological Study. LC 87-29117. 32p. 1987. reprint ed. pap. 2.50 (*0-87552-363-3*) P & R Pubng.

— Divorce. 1961. pap. 5.99 (*0-87552-344-7*) P & R Pubng.

— Imputation of Adam's Sin. LC 59-10078. 1977. pap. 5.99 (*0-87552-341-2*) P & R Pubng.

— Inside Microsoft Windows CE. LC 98-28532. 291p. 29.99 (*1-57231-854-6*) Microsoft.

— The Media Law Dictionary. LC 78-63257. 1978. pap. text 18.50 (*0-8191-0616-X*) U Pr of Amer.

— Old Chestnuts Warmed Up: And Other Favourites. (Illus.). 128p. 1998. 19.95 (*0-7195-5839-5*, Pub. by John Murray) Trafalgar.

— Principles of Conduct: Aspects of Biblical Ethics. 280p. 1957. pap. 15.00 (*0-8028-1144-2*) Eerdmans.

— Redemption Accomplished & Applied. 1955. pap. 12.00 (*0-8028-1143-4*) Eerdmans.

— Romans. rev. ed. 1960. 30.00 (*0-8028-4341-7*) Eerdmans.

— The Russian Press from Brezhnev to Yeltsin: Behind the Paper Curtain. LC 93-49830. (Studies in Communism in Transition). 288p. 1994. 95.00 (*1-85278-885-2*) E Elgar.

— Selections from the Report on the Scientific Results of the

Voyage of H.M.S. Challenger During the Years 1872-76. Egerton, Frank N., 3rd, ed. LC 77-74242. (History of Ecology Ser.). (Illus.). 1978. reprint ed. lib. bdg. 21.95 (*0-405-10411-1*) Ayer.
— X-Stat: Statistical Experiment Design, Data Analysis, & Non-Linear Optimization, Verson 2.0. 2nd ed. 200p. 1992. 715.00 incl. disk (*0-471-52444-1*) Wiley.
Murray, John, ed. American Nature Writing 1995. 1995. pap. 12.00 (*0-87156-438-6*, Pub. by Sierra) Random.
— St. Joseph Daily Prayer Book. (Illus.). 256p. 1998. pap. 4.95 (*0-89942-142-3*, 142/04) Catholic Bk Pub.
Murray, John & Morrison, Catherine. Bi-Lingual Education in the Western Isles, Scotland 1975-81. 1985. 65.00 (*0-86152-036-X*, Pub. by Acair Ltd) St Mut.
Murray, John & Pullar, Laurence. Bathymetrical Survey of the Scottish Fresh Water Lochs, Vol. 1. Egerton, Frank N., 3rd, ed. LC 77-74243. (History of Ecology Ser.). (Illus.). 1978. reprint ed. lib. bdg. 71.95 (*0-405-10412-X*) Ayer.
***Murray, John & Smyth, Sarah.** Basic Russian: A Grammar & Workbook. LC 99-219870. 1999. write for info. (*0-415-18317-0*) Routledge.
— Intermediate Russian: A Grammar & Workbook. LC 00-31058. (ENG & RUS.). 2000. pap. write for info. (*0-415-22103-X*) Routledge.
Murray, John, ed. see Chukhovskaya, Lidiya.
Murray, John, tr. see Pieper, Josef.
Murray, John A. American Nature Writing 1998. 1998. pap. 16.00 (*0-87156-948-5*, Pub. by Sierra) Random.
***Murray, John A.** Cinema Southwest: An Illustrated Guide to the Movies & Their Locations. LC 99-55282. (Illus.). 138p. 2000. pap. 21.95 (*0-87358-747-2*) Northland AZ.
Murray, John A. The Colorado Plateau: A Complete Guide to the National Parks, Monuments of Southern Utah, Northern Arizona, Western Colorado & Northwestern New Mexico. LC 97-31797. (Illus.). 160p. 1998. pap. 16.95 (*0-87358-706-5*) Northland AZ.
— Desert Awakenings. LC 98-3418. (Illus.). 160p. 1998. 29.95 (*1-55971-666-5*) Creat Pub Intl.
— The Gila Wilderness Area: A Hiking Guide. LC 87-35753. (Coyote Bks.). (Illus.). 260p. 1988. pap. 14.95 (*0-8263-1067-2*) U of NM Pr.
— Grizzly Bears: An Illustrated Field Guide. (Illus.). 112p. (Orig.). 1995. pap. 14.95 (*1-57098-029-2*) Roberts Rinehart.
— Nature's New Voices. LC 92-53030. 256p. (Orig.). 1992. pap. 15.95 (*1-55591-117-X*) Fulcrum Pub.
— The River Reader. LC 98-26020. 320p. 1998. 30.00 (*1-55821-699-5*); pap. 17.95 (*1-55821-772-X*) Lyons Pr.
— The Sierra Club Nature Writing Handbook: A Creative Guide. LC 95-5601. 208p. (Orig.). 1995. pap. 14.00 (*0-87156-436-X*, Pub. by Sierra) Random.
Murray, John A., ed. American Nature Writing, 1994. (Orig.). 1995. 21.50 (*0-8446-6858-3*) Peter Smith.
— American Nature Writing, 1994. 288p. (Orig.). 1994. pap. 12.00 (*0-87156-479-3*, Pub. by Sierra) Random.
***Murray, John A., ed.** American Nature Writing, 2000: A Celebration of Women Writers. 240p. 2000. pap. 17.95 (*0-87071-551-8*) Oreg St U Pr.
Murray, John A., ed. The Islands & the Sea: Five Centuries of Nature Writing from the Caribbean. 329p. 1999. reprint ed. pap. text 23.00 (*0-7881-6341-8*) DIANE Pub.
***Murray, John A., ed.** The Mountain Reader: A Nature Conservancy Book. 320p. 2000. 30.00 (*1-58574-022-5*); pap. 17.95 (*1-58574-065-9*) Lyons Pr.
Murray, John A., ed. The Quotable Nature Lover. LC 99-29832. (Nature Conservancy Book Ser.). 1999. 20.00 (*1-55821-942-0*) Lyons Pr.
— The Seacoast Reader. LC 99-12723. (Nature Conservancy Book Ser.). 320p. 1999. 30.00 (*1-55821-781-9*) Lyons Pr.
***Murray, John A., ed.** The Seacoast Reader. LC 99-12723. (Nature Conservancy Book Ser.). 320p. 1999. pap. 17.95 (*1-55821-782-7*) Lyons Pr.
Murray, John A., selected by. American Nature Writing, 1999. (American Nature Writing Ser.). 256p. 1999. pap. 15.95 (*0-87071-550-X*) Oreg St U Pr.
— A Thousand Leagues of Blue: The Sierra Club Book of the Pacific. LC 93-23196. 488p. (Orig.). 1994. pap. 16.00 (*0-87156-452-1*, Pub. by Sierra) Random.
Murray, John A. & O'Driscoll, Aidan. Strategy & Process in Marketing: European Perspective. 505p. 1996. pap. 40.00 (*0-13-182163-6*) P-H.
Murray, John A., jt. ed. see Brown, David E.
Murray, John C. Bridging the Sacred & the Secular: Selected Writings. Hooper, J. Leon, ed. LC 94-9698. (Moral Traditions & Moral Arguments Ser.). 392p. 1994. 55.00 (*0-87840-561-5*) Georgetown U Pr.
— Problem of God: Yesterday & Today. (St. Thomas More Lectures: No. 1). (Orig.). (C). 1965. pap. 12.00 (*0-300-00171-1*, Y138) Yale U Pr.
— Religious Liberty: Catholic Struggles with Pluralism. Hooper, J. Leon, ed. LC 92-17829. (Library of Theological Ethics). 256p. 1993. pap. 19.00 (*0-664-25360-1*) Westminster John Knox.
Murray, John C. & Burghardt, Walter. We Hold These Truths: Catholic Reflections on the American Proposition. LC 60-12876. 350p. 1985. reprint ed. 19.50 (*0-934134-83-9*); reprint ed. pap. 15.95 (*0-934134-50-2*) Sheed & Ward WI.
Murray, John Courtney. Bridging the Sacred & the Secular: Selected Writings of John Courtney Murray. Hooper, Leon J., ed. (Moral Traditions & Moral Arguments Ser.). 392p. (C). 1995. pap. 24.95 (*0-87840-571-2*) Georgetown U Pr.
Murray, John E., Jr. Contracts: Cases & Materials. 4th ed. 1037p. 1991. 51.00 (*0-87473-801-6*, 12177-10, MICHIE) LEXIS Pub.
— Murray on Contracts. 3rd ed. 1202p. 1990. 50.00 (*0-87473-613-7*, MICHIE) LEXIS Pub.
Murray, John E. Murray on Contracts, 1990. 3rd ed. 1990. text 50.00 (*0-87473-656-0*, 12191-10, MICHIE) LEXIS Pub.
Murray, John E. & Flechtner, Harry M. Sales & Leases: Problems & Materials on National & International Transactions. (American Casebook Ser.). 255p. 1994. pap. text. write for info. (*0-314-03487-0*) West Pub.
Murray, John E., Jr. & Fletcher, Harry M. Sales & Leases: Problems & Materials on National & International Transactions. LC 93-11497. (American Casebook Ser.). 399p. 1994. pap. 36.50 (*0-314-02457-3*) West Pub.
***Murray, John Edward, Jr.** Contracts: Cases & Materials, 2000. annuals 5th ed. 2000. text 56.00 (*0-8205-4598-8*) Bender.
Murray, John F. Fallen Warriors: The West Point Class of 1964. LC 96-67866. 160p. 1996. 19.95 (*1-884570-45-3*) Research Triangle.
***Murray, John F.** Intensive Care: A Doctor's Journal. LC 99-56892. 296p. 2000. 27.50 (*0-520-22089-7*, Pub. by U CA Pr) Cal Prin Full Svc.
— Smart Tennis: How to Play & Win the Mental Game. LC 98-40156. 1999. pap. text 18.00 (*0-7879-4380-0*) Jossey-Bass.
Murray, John F., ed. Pulmonary Complications of Systemic Disease. LC 92-18424. (Lung Biology in Health & Disease Ser.: Vol. 59). (Illus.). 708p. 1992. text 250.00 (*0-8247-8707-2*) Dekker.
Murray, John F. & Nadel, Jay A., eds. Textbook of Respiratory Medicine, 2 vols. 2nd ed. LC 92-48497. (Illus.). 2816p. 1994. text 305.00 (*0-7216-3890-2*, W B Saunders Co) Harcrt Hlth Sci Grp.
Murray, John G. A Gentleman Publisher's Commonplace Book. (Illus.). 128p. 1997. 19.95 (*0-7195-5623-6*, Pub. by John Murray) Trafalgar.
Murray, John H., et al. A Guide to TASER Technology: Stunguns, Lies & Videotape. LC 90-62036. (Illus.). 238p. (Orig.). (C). 1997. pap. text 19.95 (*0-9648984-0-3*) Whitewater Pr.
Murray, John J. Amsterdam in the Age of Rembrandt. LC 67-15584. (Centers of Civilization Ser.: No. 21). 203p. reprint ed. 63.00 (*0-8357-9719-8*, 201624200002) Bks Demand.
— Behind a Frowning Providence. 30p. 1990. pap. 2.50 (*0-85151-572-X*) Banner of Truth.
— The Prevention of Dental Disease. 2nd ed. (Illus.). 520p. 1989. 95.00 (*0-19-261807-5*) OUP.
— The Prevention of Dental Disease. 2nd ed. (Illus.). 528p. 1989. pap. 49.95 (*0-19-261806-7*) OUP.
— Senior Citizens on Stage. 1980. pap. 3.00 (*0-686-30558-2*) Eldridge Pub.
— The Tragedye of Solyman & Perseda. LC 91-1465. (Renaissance Imagination Ser.). 168p. 1991. text 20.00 (*0-8153-0457-9*) Garland.
Murray, John J., Jr. Yes, You Can Beat City Hall: Don't Let the Bastards Get You Down. 372p. 1994. 18.95 (*0-89914-039-4*) Third Party Pub.
Murray, John J., ed. Prevention of Oral Disease. 3rd ed. (Illus.). 294p. 1996. pap. text 59.95 (*0-19-262457-1*) OUP.
Murray, John J., ed. see Walpole, Horatio.
Murray, John L. Infaquatics: Teaching Kids to Swim. LC 80-82072. (Illus.). 223p. (Orig.). 1980. reprint ed. pap. 69.20 (*0-608-07107-2*, 206733400009) Bks Demand.
Murray, John L., jt. auth. see Lenz, Heinz W.
Murray, John O. Little Lives of the Great Saints. LC 82-50593. 495p. 1991. reprint ed. pap. 18.00 (*0-89555-190-X*) TAN Bks Pubs.
Murray, John R. The Normal Lung. 2nd ed. (Illus.). 377p. 1986. text 47.00 (*0-7216-6613-2*, W B Saunders Co) Harcrt Hlth Sci Grp.
Murray, John S., et al. Arbitration. (Paralegal). 200p. 1996. pap. text 14.25 (*1-56662-423-1*) Foundation Pr.
— Dispute Resolution: The Role of Lawyers, Notes for Teachers to Processes of. 2nd ed. (University Casebook Ser.). 1996. pap. text. write for info. (*1-56662-389-8*) West Pub.
— Dispute Resolution, Processes of, The Role of Lawyers. (University Casebook Ser.). 761p. 1988. text 38.00 (*0-88277-688-6*) Foundation Pr.
— Mediation, 1996. (Paralegal). 351p. 1996. pap. text 15.00 (*1-56662-429-0*) Foundation Pr.
— Negotiation. (Paralegal). 236p. 1996. pap. text 13.50 (*1-56662-424-X*) Foundation Pr.
— Processes of Dispute Resolution: The Role of Lawyers. 2nd ed. (University Casebook Ser.). 854p. 1996. text 42.95 (*1-56662-330-8*) Foundation Pr.
Murray, John W. Ecology & Palaeoecology of Benthic Foraminifera. 1991. 136.37 (*0-582-05122-3*, Pub. by Addison-Wesley) Longman.
***Murray, John W., Jr.** Exports Guide to Successful Legal Testimony: How to Avoid the Sharks & Come Out Smelling Like a Rose! (Private Investigation Ser.). 1999. pap. 29.95 (*1-891247-34-4*) Thomas Investigative.
Murray, John W. Necessity of Law (1924) 174p. 1998. reprint ed. pap. 17.95 (*0-7661-0591-1*) Kessinger Pub.
— Stratigraphical Atlas of Fossil Foraminifera. 2nd ed. Murray, J. W., ed. 1989. text 159.95 (*0-470-21226-8*) P-H.
***Murray, John Wilson.** Memoirs of a Great Detective. (Other Literature Ser.). 2000. text 36.00 (*1-55246-176-9*) Battered Silicon.
Murray, Jon. Lonely Planet Cape Town. 2nd ed. (Illus.). 160p. 1998. pap. 12.95 (*0-86442-485-X*) Lonely Planet.
— Lonely Planet South Africa Travel Atlas. (Illus.). 80p. 1997. pap. 14.95 (*0-86442-443-4*) Lonely Planet.
Murray, Jon & O'Hair, Madalyn M. All the Questions You Ever Wanted to Ask American Atheists with All the Answers. 2nd ed. 248p. (Orig.). 1986. pap. 14.00 (*0-910309-24-8*, 5356) Am Atheist.
Murray, Jon & Wheeler, Tony. Lonely Planet Papua New Guinea: A Travel Survival Kit. 5th ed. (Illus.). 380p. 1993. pap. 15.95 (*0-86442-190-7*) Lonely Planet.
***Murray, Jon & Williams, Jeff.** South Africa, Lesotho & Swaziland. 4th ed. (Illus.). 672p. 2000. pap. 24.95 (*0-86442-757-3*) Lonely Planet.
Murray, Jon, et al. Lonely Planet South Africa, Lesotho & Swaziland. 3rd ed. (Illus.). 672p. 1997. pap. 21.95 (*0-86442-508-2*) Lonely Planet.
***Murray, Jon, et al.** Victoria. 3rd ed. (Illus.). 450p. 1999. pap. 17.95 (*0-86442-734-4*) Lonely Planet.
Murray, Jon G. Essays on American Atheism, 2 vols., Set. (Orig.). 1986. pap. 19.00 (*0-910309-39-6*, 5351) Am Atheist.
— Essays on American Atheism, Vol. I. 350p. (Orig.). 1986. pap. 10.00 (*0-910309-28-0*, 5349) Am Atheist.
— Essays on American Atheism, Vol. II. 284p. (Orig.). 1986. pap. 10.00 (*0-910309-29-9*, 5350) Am Atheist.
Murray, Joseph. Manual of Dysphagia Assessment in Adults. LC 98-41268. (Illus.). 248p. 1998. pap. 49.95 (*1-56593-871-2*, 1702) Thomson Learn.
— Training for Student Leaders. 384p. (C). 1996. per. 29.95 (*0-8403-9436-5*) Kendall-Hunt.
***Murray, Joseph.** Training for Student Leaders. 384p. (C). 1998. per. 35.95 (*0-7872-4603-4*) Kendall-Hunt.
Murray, Joseph P. Selective English Old-French Glossary As a Basis for Studies in Old French Onomatology & Synonymics. LC 77-128932. (Catholic University of America. Studies in Romance Languages & Literature: No. 40). (ENG & FRE.). reprint ed. 37.50 (*0-404-50340-3*) AMS Pr.
Murray, Judith. Mars. 64p. (Orig.). 1986. write for info. (*0-9617376-0-3*) Murpubco.
Murray, Judith S. Selected Writings of Judith Sargent Murray. Harris, Sharon M., ed. (Women Writers in English 1350-1850 Ser.). 320p. 1995. pap. 21.00 (*0-19-510038-7*); text 55.00 (*0-19-507883-7*) OUP.
Murray, Judy. The Soft Sighs of If. (Illus.). 24p. (Orig.). 1992. pap. 3.00 (*0-926935-75-5*) Runaway Spoon.
Murray, Julia. Master of Herringham. large type ed. 1994. 27.99 (*0-7089-3152-9*) Ulverscroft.
— Wed for a Wager. large type ed. (Linford Romance Large Print Ser.). 368p. 1998. pap. 17.99 (*0-7089-5253-4*, Linford) Ulverscroft.
Murray, Julia K. The Adventuress. large type ed. LC 97-18509. (Nightingale Ser.). 238p. 1997. pap. 17.95 (*0-7838-8219-X*, G K Hall Lrg Type) Mac Lib Ref.
— A Decade of Discovery: Selected Acquisitions, 1970-1980. LC 79-55426. (Illus.). 1979. pap. 18.50 (*0-934686-36-X*) Freer.
— Ma Hezhi & the Illustration of the Book of Odes. (Illus.). 272p. (C). 1993. text 115.00 (*0-521-41787-2*) Cambridge U Pr.
Murray, K. My Husband, Arthur Murray. (Ballroom Dance Ser.). 1985. lib. bdg. 100.00 (*0-87700-693-8*) Revisionist Pr.
Murray, K. M. Caught in the Web of Words: James A. H. Murray & the "Oxford English Dictionary" 1995. pap. 18.00 (*0-300-06310-5*) Yale U Pr.
Murray, Katharine, ed. see Medved, Robert.
Murray, Katherine. Get Your Family on the Internet in a Weekend. LC 98-68394. (In a Weekend Ser.). (Illus.). 309p. 1999. pap. 24.99 incl. cd-rom (*0-7615-1943-2*, Prima Tech) Prima Pub.
— Home but Not Alone: The Parents' Work-at-Home Handbook. LC 97-20392. (Illus.). 400p. (Orig.). 1997. pap. 14.95 (*1-57112-080-7*, PO807) Park Ave.
— Inside Norton Navigator. 1995. pap. 24.95 (*1-55828-467-2*) IDG Bks.
— Lotus Freelance Graphics 96 - Illustrated, Incl. instr. resource kit, test mgr., Web pg. (Illustrated Ser.). (Illus.). 192p. 1996. text. write for info. incl. 3.5 ld (*0-7600-3751-5*) Course Tech.
***Murray, Katherine.** Lotus Notes 5 Fast & Easy. LC 98-65716. (Fast & Easy Ser.). (Illus.). 305p. 1999. pap. 16.99 (*0-7615-1393-0*) Prima Pub.
Murray, Katherine. Mastering PowerPoint 97. 3rd ed. LC 97-69204. 448p. 1997. pap. text 29.99 (*0-7821-2154-3*) Sybex.
— Mastering Powerpoint 2000. (Mastering Ser.). 448p. 1999. pap. 29.99 (*0-7821-2356-2*) Sybex.
— Microsoft Exchange Productivity Guide. LC 96-68065. (Essentials Ser.). 408p. 1996. per. 24.99 (*0-7615-0689-6*) Prima Pub.
— SOS for DOS. 225p. 1993. pap. 12.95 (*1-56884-043-8*) IDG Bks.
— SOS for Windows. 225p. 1993. pap. 12.95 (*1-56884-045-4*) IDG Bks.
— SOS for WordPerfect. LC 93-80871. 225p. 1994. pap. 12.95 (*1-56884-053-5*) IDG Bks.
— The Working Parents' Handbook. (Illus.). 275p. (Orig.). 1996. pap. 14.95 (*1-57112-075-0*, P0750) Park Ave.
Murray, Katherine & Sabotin, Doug. Ten Minute Guide to WordPerfect 5.1. 160p. 1991. 10.95 (*0-672-22808-4*, Alpha Ref) Macmillan Gen Ref.
Murray, Katherine, jt. auth. see Prima Development Staff.
Murray, Katherine, jt. auth. see Sabotin, Kathy M.
Murray, Katherine A., et al. Holocene Human Adaptations in the Missouri Prairie Timberlands. (Illus.). 218p. 1995. pap. 20.00 (*1-56349-076-5*, RS45) AR Archaeol.
Murray, Kathy. Using Microsoft Publisher 2. 2nd ed. LC 94-65329. (Using... Ser.). (Illus.). 350p. (Orig.). 1994. 19.99 (*1-56529-284-7*) Que.
Murray, Keith, jt. auth. see Diviney, Glade.
Murray, Keith A. The Modocs & Their War. LC 59-7488. (Civilization of the American Indian Ser.: Vol. 52). (Illus.). 344p. 1985. pap. 16.95 (*0-8061-1331-6*) U of Okla Pr.
Murray, Keith, Publishing Staff. Memories of Aberdeen a Hundred Years Ago. (C). 1990. reprint ed. 50.00 (*0-7855-5984-1*, Pub. by K Murray Pub) St Mut.
— No State in Earth. (C). 1990. pap. 55.00 (*1-870978-26-9*) St Mut.
Murray, Keith, Publishing Staff & Bold, Alan. The Malfeasance. 1990. pap. text 40.00 (*1-870978-27-7*, Pub. by K Murray Pub) St Mut.
Murray, Ken, ed. see White, Steve & White, Ruth B.
Murray, Kenneth. Footsteps of the Mountain Spirits: Appalachia. (Illus.). 96p. 1992. pap. 14.95 (*0-932807-78-X*) Overmountain Pr.
— Highland Trails: A Guide to Scenic Trails in Northeast Tennessee, Western North Carolina & Southwest Virginia. 3rd rev. ed. (Illus.). 241p. 1997. pap. 17.95 (*1-57072-049-5*) Overmountain Pr.
— Paths of the Ancients . . . Appalachia. (Illus.). 128p. 1993. 22.95 (*0-932807-94-1*) Overmountain Pr.
— The Tennessee Country: A Heritage of Natural Places. (Illus.). 120p. (YA). 1995. 22.95 (*1-57072-032-0*) Overmountain Pr.
— The Tennessee Country: A Heritage of Natural Places. 1995. pap. text 14.95 (*1-57072-034-7*) Overmountain Pr.
Murray, Kenneth T. & Murray, Barbara A. School Law for the Florida Educator. 246p. (C). 1995. pap. text 46.50 (*0-9644512-0-4*) IntraCoast Pub.
Murray, Kenneth T., jt. auth. see Murray, Barbara A.
Murray, Kevin. El Salvador: Peace on Trial. LC 98-130284. (Country Profiles Ser.). (Illus.). 64p. (C). 1997. pap. 9.95 (*0-85598-361-2*, Pub. by Oxfam Pub) Stylus Pub VA.
— Inside El Salvador. 283p. 1995. pap. text 11.95 (*0-911213-53-8*) Interhemisp Res Ctr.
Murray, Kevin, ed. The Judgement of Paris. 192p. (Orig.). pap. 19.95 (*1-86373-055-9*, Pub. by Allen & Unwin Pty) Paul & Co Pubs.
Murray, Kevin R. On Tender Feet & Eagles' Wings. 128p. 1996. pap. 11.98 (*0-88290-587-2*) Horizon Utah.
Murray, Kim & Murray, Chris. Illuminations from the Bhagavad-Gita. 2nd ed. (Illus.). 96p. 1999. reprint ed. 19.95 (*1-886069-21-2*, 1051, Pub. by Mandala Pub Grp) Words Distrib.
***Murray, Kirsty.** What Kids Are Made Of: True Stories of Young Rescuers, Rulers & Rebels. 160p. 2000. pap. 7.95 (*1-55652-414-5*, Pub. by Chicago Review) IPG Chicago.
Murray, Kristy. Man-Eaters & Blood Suckers. (True Stories Ser.). (Illus.). 100p. (J). (gr. 2-3). 1998. pap. 6.95 (*1-86448-630-9*) IPG Chicago.
Murray, Laura J., ed. To Do Good to My Indian Brethren: The Writings of Joseph Johnson, 1751-1776. LC 97-28135. (Native Americans of the Northeast). 344p. 1998. 60.00 (*1-55849-126-0*); pap. 19.95 (*1-55849-127-9*) U of Mass Pr.
Murray, Laura J. & Rice, Keren D., eds. Talking on the Page: Editing Aboriginal Oral Texts. 144p. 1999. text 40.00 (*0-8020-4433-6*); pap. text 14.95 (*0-8020-8230-0*) U of Toronto Pr.
Murray, Laura K. Basic Internet for Busy Librarians: A Quick Course for Catching Up. LC 98-14067. 152p. 1998. 26.00 (*0-8389-0725-3*) ALA.
Murray, Lawrence. The Celluloid Persuasion: Movies & the Liberal Arts. LC 79-16764. 181p. reprint ed. 56.20 (*0-608-16108-X*, 201934600011) Bks Demand.
Murray, Leona E. My World. 1997. pap. write for info. (*1-57553-512-2*) Watermrk Pr.
Murray, Les. The Boys Who Stole the Funeral: A Novel Sequence. LC 91-73731. 80p. 1992. text 20.00 (*0-374-11603-2*) FS&G.
— The Daylight Moon & Other Poems. LC 87-7918. 120p. 1988. 17.95 (*0-89255-125-9*); pap. 9.95 (*0-89255-138-0*) Persea Bks.
— Dog Fox Field: Poems. LC 92-16860. 1993. 19.00 (*0-374-14314-5*) FS&G.
***Murray, Les.** Fredy Neptune. 272p. 2000. pap. 14.00 (*0-374-52676-1*) FS&G.
Murray, Les. Fredy Neptune: A Novel in Verse. LC 98-48911. 208p. 1999. text 25.00 (*0-374-15854-1*) FS&G.
***Murray, Les.** Learning Human: Selected Poems. 240p. 2001. pap. 13.00 (*0-374-52723-7*) FS&G.
Murray, Les. Subhuman Redneck Poems. LC 96-49439. 1997. 18.00 (*0-374-27155-0*) FS&G.
— Subhuman Redneck Poems. 112p. 1998. pap. text 12.00 (*0-374-52538-2*, Noonday) FS&G.
— Translations from the Natural World: Poems. LC 93-11183. 67p. 1994. 21.00 (*0-374-27870-9*) FS&G.
— The Vernacular Republic. 1982. pap. 8.95 (*0-89255-063-5*) Persea Bks.
Murray, Les, ed. Fivefathers: Five Australian Poets of the Pre-Academic Era. 207p. 1995. pap. 18.95 (*1-85754-087-5*, Pub. by Carcanet Pr) Paul & Co Pubs.
***Murray, Les A.** Learning Human. LC 99-42758. 400p. 2000. 35.00 (*0-374-26073-7*) FS&G.
Murray, Les A., ed. The New Oxford Book of Australian Verse. 432p. 1986. 39.95 (*0-19-554618-0*) OUP.
Murray, Linda. High Renaissance & Mannerism: Italy, the North & Spain, 1500-1600. (World of Art Ser.). (Illus.). 288p. 1985. pap. 14.95 (*0-500-20162-5*, Pub. by Thames Hudson) Norton.
— How to Draw Pets. LC 94-47279. (Illus.). (J). 1996. pap. 2.95 (*0-8167-2743-0*) Troll Communs.
— How to Draw Pets. LC 94-47279. (Illus.). (J). 1997. 17.25 (*0-8167-2742-2*) Troll Communs.
Murray, Linda. How to Draw Pets. 1995. 7.70 (*0-606-07678-6*, Pub. by Turtleback) Demco.
Murray, Linda. Michelangelo. (World of Art Ser.). (Illus.). 216p. 1985. pap. 14.95 (*0-500-20174-9*, Pub. by Thames Hudson) Norton.
— Michelangelo. (World of Art Ser.). (Illus.). 216p. 1985. 19.95 (*0-500-18175-6*, Pub. by Thames Hudson) Norton.
Murray, Linda, jt. auth. see Murray, Peter.
Murray, Linda, tr. see Chastel, Andre.
Murray, Lindley. English Grammar. LC 81-9062. (American Linguistics Ser.). 328p. 1982. reprint ed. 50.00 (*0-8201-1369-7*) Schol Facsimiles.

M

An Asterisk (*) at the beginning of an entry indicates that the title is appearing for the first time.

— Narratives of Colored Americans. LC 70-170702. (Black Heritage Library Collection). 1977. reprint ed. 28.95 (*0-8369-8892-2*) Ayer.

Murray, Louann W. Romantic Weekends: Southern California. (Romantic Weekends Ser.). 275p. (Orig.). 1997. pap. 15.95 (*1-55650-774-7*) Hunter NJ.

***Murray, Louisa & Lawrence, Brenda.** Practitioner-Based Enquiry. LC 99-28142. (Social Research & Educational Studies). 1999. write for info. (*0-7507-0771-2*, Falmer Pr) Taylor & Francis.

Murray, Louise G., compiled by. The Dogs of Our Lives: Heartwarming Celebrity Reminiscences of Canine Companions. (Illus.). 256p. 1995. 17.95 (*1-55972-289-4*, Birch Ln Pr) Carol Pub Group.

— The Dogs of Our Lives: Heartwarming Reminiscences of Canine Companions. LC 96-37623. (Illus.). 362p. 1997. pap. 18.95 (*0-8065-1859-6*, Citadel Pr) Carol Pub Group.

Murray, Louise W. A History of Old Tioga Point & Early Athens, Pennsylvania. (Illus.). 656p. 1994. reprint ed. lib. bdg. 65.00 (*0-8328-3878-0*) Higginson Bk Co.

Murray, Lyn. Musician. 384p. 1987. 17.95 (*0-8184-0432-9*) Carol Pub Group.

Murray, Lynne. Large Target: A Josephine Fuller Mystery. mass mkt. write for info. (*0-312-97537-6*) St Martin.

— Large Target: A Josephine Fuller Mystery. LC 99-89839. 272p. 2000. text 23.95 (*0-312-25456-3*, Minotaur) St Martin.

Murray, Lynne. Larger Than Death. LC 97-67282. 300p. 1997. 23.00 (*0-9642949-0-7*) Orloff Pr.

***Murray, Lynne.** Larger Than Death: A Josephine Fuller Mystery. 304p. 2000. mass mkt. 5.99 (*0-312-97277-6*, Minotaur) St Martin.

Murray, Lynne & Cooper, Peter J., eds. Postpartum Depression & Child Development. LC 96-39987. 322p. 1997. lib. bdg. 40.00 (*1-57230-197-X*, 0197) Guilford Pubns.

***Murray, Lynne & Cooper, Peter J., eds.** Postpartum Depression & Child Development. 322p. 1999. pap. text 21.00 (*1-57230-517-7*) Guilford Pubns.

Murray, M. Discovering Dumfriesshire. (Discovering Ser.). 1996. pap. 22.50 (*0-85976-294-7*, Pub. by J Donald) St Mut.

— Modern Philosophy of History: Its Origin & Destination. 137p. 1970. pap. text 57.00 (*90-247-0110-4*, Pub. by M Nijhoff) Kluwer Academic.

Murray, M., jt. auth. see Gilbert, J.

***Murray, M. A.** Legends of Ancient Egypt. LC 99-54804. 96p. 2000. pap. 5.95 (*0-486-41137-0*) Dover.

Murray, M. Mary, jt. auth. see Yesner, Bernice L.

Murray, M. S., jt. auth. see Murray, C. H.

Murray, M. S., jt. auth. see Murray, Chas H.

Murray, Maggie, ed. see Berrner, Karina.

Murray, Maggie P. Changing Styles in Fashion: Who, What, Why. LC 88-82368. (Illus.). 252p. (C). 1988. text 46.00 (*0-87005-585-2*) Fairchild.

Murray, Malcolm G., Jr. Alignment Manual for Horizontal, Flexibly-Coupled Rotating Machines. 3rd ed. LC 83-90158. (Illus.). 200p. (C). 1983. ring bd., vinyl bd. 39.00 (*0-9611896-0-6*) Murray & Garig.

Murray, Marcella M. Goal Performance System: A Complete Guide to Achieving Strategic Goals. 2nd ed. 110p. 1991. student ed. 35.00 (*0-9630252-0-1*) Ctr Human Work.

— Making Positive Change: An Interactive Training Program. 88p. 1993. teacher ed. 2400.00 (*0-9630252-1-X*) Ctr Human Work.

— Stress Recovery & Management: A Guide to Living a Happier & Healthier Life. 100p. 1998. wbk. ed. write for info. (*0-9630252-2-8*) Ctr Human Work.

Murray, Margaret. God of the Witches. (Illus.). 212p. 1970. reprint ed. pap. 12.95 (*0-19-501270-4*) OUP.

Murray, Margaret, tr. see Orff, Carl.

Murray, Margaret A. The Divine King of England: A Study in Anthropology. LC 79-8115. reprint ed. 29.50 (*0-404-18428-6*) AMS Pr.

— Egyptian Religious Poetry. Cranmer-Byng, J. L., ed. LC 79-8714. (Wisdom of the East Ser.). 120p. 1980. reprint ed. lib. bdg. 35.00 (*0-313-21012-8*, MUER, Greenwood Pr) Greenwood.

— Egyptian Sculpture. LC 74-109802. 207p. 1970. reprint ed. lib. bdg. 45.00 (*0-8371-4293-8*, MUEG, Greenwood Pr) Greenwood.

— Egyptian Temples. LC 75-41203. reprint ed. 27.50 (*0-404-14719-4*) AMS Pr.

— Genesis of Religion. 1963. 49.50 (*0-614-00159-5*) Elliots Bks.

Murray, Margaret A., jt. auth. see Lewis, John L.

***Murray, Margaret A. M.** Women Becoming Mathematicians: Creating a Professional Identity in Post-World War II America. LC 99-87169. (Illus.). 529p. 2001. 32.50 (*0-262-13369-5*) MIT Pr.

***Murray, Margaret Cox.** A-Z Children of Maine. (Illus.). 15p. (J). (ps-5). 1999. pap. 6.95 (*0-9665140-1-7*) Rainbw Pr ME.

Murray, Margaret Cox, see Cox Murray, Margaret, ed.

Murray, Margo. Beyond the Myths & Magic of Mentoring: How to Facilitate an Effective Mentoring Program. LC 90-25580. (Management Ser.). 236p. 1991. text 32.95 (*1-55542-333-7*) Jossey-Bass.

Murray, Marian. Circus: From Rome to Ringling. LC 74-171420. (Illus.). 354p. 1973. reprint ed. lib. bdg. 49.75 (*0-8371-6259-9*, MUCI, Greenwood Pr) Greenwood.

Murray, Marilyn J., jt. auth. see Murray, Jerome T.

Murray, Marjorie D. The Stars Are Waiting. LC 97-37123. (Illus.). (J). (ps-k). 1998. lib. bdg. 15.95 (*0-7614-5024-6*) Marshall Cavendish.

Murray, Mark F. International Business. LC 92-46094. (Management Ser.). 1993. 11.25 (*0-87051-132-7*) Am Inst CPA.

— Management Review Guide: A Do-It-Yourself Practice Analysis. 1995. 33.00 (*0-87051-168-8*) Am Inst CPA.

— Violence at Work: How to Safeguard Your Firm. LC 97-19713. 128p. 1997. pap. 37.00 (*0-87051-187-4*, 090430) Am Inst CPA.

Murray, Martin. South Africa: Time of Agony, Time of Destiny: The Upsurge of Popular Protest. 272p. 1987. 39.95 (*0-86091-146-2*); pap. 14.95 (*0-86091-857-2*) Schocken.

***Murray, Martin.** Visions of the New South Africa: Exploring Myth & Memory in Post-Apartheid South Africa. 2000. 30.00 (*1-85984-708-0*, Pub. by Verso) Norton.

Murray, Mary. Artwork of the Mind. Farr, Marcia, ed. LC 95-6445. (Written Language Ser.). 172p. 1995. text 42.50 (*1-881303-63-2*); pap. text 18.95 (*1-881303-64-0*) Hampton Pr NJ.

— Cruel & Unusual Punishment: The U. S. Blockade of Cuba. 117p. 1993. pap. 9.95 (*1-875284-78-8*) Ocean Pr NJ.

— The Law of the Father? Patriarchy in the Transition from Feudalism to Capitalism. LC 94-12147. 176p. (C). 1994. pap. 24.99 (*0-415-04257-7*, B4199) Routledge.

Murray, Mary, jt. auth. see McGlynn, Betty H.

Murray, Mary, jt. auth. see Stone, Joanne.

Murray, Mary B., jt. ed. see Kayser, John.

Murray, Mary E. Sculpture Space: Celebrating 20 Years. (Illus.). 72p. 1995. pap. 15.95 (*0-915895-18-8*) Munson Williams.

Murray, Mary E. & Atkinson, Leslie D. Understanding the Nursing Process: The Next Generation. 5th ed. LC 93-1938. (Illus.). 192p. 1993. pap. text 24.00 (*0-07-105458-8*) McGraw-Hill HPD.

Murray, Mary E., jt. auth. see Atkinson, Leslie D.

Murray, Mary E., jt. auth. see Beesch, Ruth K.

***Murray, Mary J.** Just Mom & Me Having Tea: A New Devotional Bible for Mothers & Daughters. 2001. pap. 9.99 (*0-7369-0426-3*) Harvest Hse.

Murray, Matthew N. Economic Development Incentives & the Tennessee Valley Economy. 95p. (Orig.). (C). 1990. pap. text. write for info. (*0-940191-16-4*) Univ TN Ctr Bus Econ.

— The Father & the Son. 2001. 13.00 (*0-06-093067-5*, Perennial) HarperTrade.

— The Father & the Son: My Father's Journey into the Monastic Life. LC 99-34165. 272p. 1999. 25.00 (*0-06-018782-4*) HarpC.

Murray, Matthew N. & Fox, William F., eds. The Sales Tax in the 21st Century. LC 96-37729. 280p. 1997. 75.00 (*0-275-95827-2*, Praeger Pubs) Greenwood.

Murray, Maxine. Growing up in the Ozarks with Moonshine Whiskey. 32p. 1997. pap. 7.00 (*0-8059-4081-2*) Dorrance.

Murray, Meg M., ed. Face to Face: Fathers, Mothers, Masters, Monsters--Essays for a Nonsexist Future, 36. LC 82-11708. (Contributions in Women's Studies: No. 36). 344p. 1983. 65.00 (*0-313-23044-7*, MFF/, Greenwood Pr) Greenwood.

Murray, Megan, et al. Collecting, Counting, & Measuring: Developing Number Sense. Anderson, Catherine et al, eds. (Investigations in Number, Data, & Space Ser.). (Illus.). 139p. (J). (gr. k). 1997. pap. text 22.95 (*1-57232-928-9*, 47105) Seymour Pubns.

Murray, Megan, jt. auth. see Economopoulos, Karen.

Murray, Melba L., jt. auth. see Murray, Raymond L.

Murray, Melba L., ed. see Murray, Raymond L.

Murray, Melba W. & Hay-Roe, Hugh. Engineered Writing. 2nd ed. 304p. 1986. 25.00 (*0-87814-293-2*) PennWell Bks.

Murray, Melissa, jt. auth. see Mahoney, Mick.

Murray, Melvin L. Fostoria, Ohio Glass II. LC 90-93415. (Illus.). 186p. (Orig.). 1992. pap. 20.00 (*0-9634864-0-3*) M L Murray.

***Murray, Meredith A.** To Live & Die Amongst the Monongahela Hills: The Story of Albert Gallatin & Friendship Hill. (Illus.). 48p. (YA). (gr. 6-12). 1999. pap. 4.95 (*1-888213-34-5*) Eastern National.

***Murray, Merrick & Moseley, Philip.** Beyond the Clinic Survival Skills for Opthalmologists. (Illus.). 224p. 2000. pap. text 40.00 (*0-7506-4487-7*) Buttrwrth-Heinemann.

Murray, Michael. Albert Schweitzer, Musician. 176p. 1994. 59.95 (*1-85928-031-5*, Pub. by Scolar Pr) Ashgate Pub Co.

— Critical Care Medicine: Perioperative Management. 600p. 1996. text 115.00 (*0-397-51637-1*) Lppncott W & W.

— The Encyclopedia of Nutritional Supplements: Essential Guide for Improving Health. LC 96-3804. 576p. 1996. per. 19.95 (*0-7615-0410-9*) Prima Pub.

***Murray, Michael.** FAQs, All about Herpes & Cold Sores. (Illus.). 96p. 2000. mass mkt. 2.99 (*0-89529-964-X*, Avery) Penguin Putnam.

Murray, Michael. French Masters of the Organ. LC 97-41401. 256p. 1998. 30.00 (*0-300-07291-0*) Yale U Pr.

— Glandular Extracts. 47p. 1994. pap. 3.50 (*0-87983-611-3*, 36113K, Keats Publng) NTC Contemp Pub Co.

— Healing Power of Herbs: The Enlightened Person's Guide to the Wonders of Medicinal Plants. (Illus.). 256p. (Orig.). 1992. pap. 12.95 (*1-55958-138-7*) Prima Pub.

— The Saw Palmetto Story. rev. ed. 14p. 1991. reprint ed. pap. 2.95 (*0-9647080-2-7*) Healing Wisdom.

Murray, Michael, ed. Heidegger & Modern Philosophy: Critical Essays. LC 77-21684. (Yale Paperbound Ser.). 397p. reprint ed. pap. 123.10 (*0-7837-3304-6*, 205770600006) Bks Demand.

Murray, Michael & Dunn, Larry. Revitalizing Rural America: A Perspective on Collaboration & Community. 274p. 1996. write for info. (*0-471-96349-6*) Wiley.

— Revitalizing Rural America: A Perspective on Collaboration & Community. 274p. 1996. pap. 70.00 (*0-471-96350-X*) Wiley.

Murray, Michael & Greer, John, eds. Rural Development in Ireland: A Challenge for the 1990s. 278p. 1993. 85.95 (*1-85628-408-5*, Pub. by Avebry) Ashgate Pub Co.

Murray, Michael & Pizzorno, Joseph E. Encyclopedia of Natural Medicine. 640p. (Orig.). 1990. pap. 19.95 (*1-55958-091-7*) Prima Pub.

— Encyclopedia of Natural Medicine, Revised. rev. ed. LC 97-50569. 960p. 1997. per. 24.95 (*0-7615-1157-1*) Prima Pub.

Murray, Michael, jt. auth. see Swan, Anthony V.

Murray, Michael, jt. ed. see Jackson, Linda A.

Murray, Michael D. The Encyclopedia of Television News. LC 98-36705. (Illus.). 336p. 1998. 69.00 (*1-57356-108-8*) Oryx Pr.

— The Political Performers: CBS Broadcasts in the Public Interest. LC 93-30985. 272p. 1994. 59.95 (*0-275-94490-5*, Praeger Pubs) Greenwood.

Murray, Michael D. & Ferri, Anthony J., eds. Teaching Mass Communication: A Guide to Better Instruction. LC 91-28831. 288p. 1992. 59.95 (*0-275-94156-6*, C4156, Praeger Pubs) Greenwood.

Murray, Michael D. & Godfrey, Donald G., eds. Television in America: Local Station History from Across the Nation. 416p. (C). 1996. text 42.95 (*0-8138-2969-0*) Iowa St U Pr.

Murray, Michael J. Critical Care Medicine: Perioperative Management. LC 96-31453. 848p. 1996. text 134.00 (*0-397-51689-4*) Lppncott W & W.

— Washington, D. C.: A Prospice: A Community Study of Political Socialization. LC 78-61328. 300p. text 26.50 (*0-9614642-1-6*) Media Arts.

Murray, Michael J., ed. Reasons for the Hope Within. LC 98-49100. 440p. 1998. pap. 28.00 (*0-8028-4437-5*) Eerdmans.

Murray, Michael J., jt. auth. see Stump, Eleonore.

Murray, Michael K. & Rice, John. Differential Geometry & Statistics. LC 93-12009. 272p. (C). (gr. 13). 1993. ring bd. 73.95 (*0-412-39860-5*, Chap & Hall CRC) CRC Pr.

Murray, Michael K., jt. ed. see Carey, Alan L.

Murray, Michael L. And Economic Justice for All: Welfare Reform for the 21st Century. LC 96-48442. 248p. (C). (gr. 13). 1997. pap. text 31.95 (*1-56324-989-8*) M E Sharpe.

Murray, Michael L. ". . . & Economic Justice for All" Welfare Reform for the 21st Century. LC 96-48442. 248p. (C). (gr. 13). 1997. text 74.95 (*1-56324-988-X*) M E Sharpe.

Murray, Michael P., et al. Recent Recruiting Trends & Their Implications for Models of Enlistment Supply. LC 97-43249. 83p. 1998. pap. 15.00 (*0-8330-2569-4*) Rand Corp.

Murray, Michael T. Arthritis: How You Can Benefit from Diet, Vitamins, Minerals, Herbs, Exercise, & Other Natural Methods. LC 93-50095. (Getting Well Naturally Ser.). 176p. 1994. pap. 9.95 (*1-55958-491-2*) Prima Pub.

— Chronic Candidiasis: How You Can Benefit from Diet - Vitamins - Minerals - Herbs - Exercise & Other Natural Methods. LC 97-13549. (Getting Well Naturally Ser.). 192p. 1997. pap. 11.00 (*0-7615-0821-X*) Prima Pub.

— Chronic Fatigue Syndrome: How You Can Benefit from Diet, Vitamins, Minerals, Herbs, Exercise, & Other Natural Methods. LC 94-7471. (Getting Well Naturally Ser.). 208p. 1994. pap. 11.00 (*1-55958-490-4*) Prima Pub.

— The Complete Book of Juicing: Your Delicious Guide to Healthful Living. (Illus.). 368p. 1992. pap. 12.95 (*1-55958-268-5*) Prima Pub.

— The Complete Book of Juicing: Your Delicious Guide to Healthful Living. 368p. 1997. per. 14.00 (*0-7615-1126-1*) Prima Pub.

— Diabetes & Hypoglycemia. LC 93-36307. (Getting Well Naturally Ser.). 176p. 1994. pap. 9.95 (*1-55958-426-2*) Prima Pub.

***Murray, Michael T.** Dr. Murray's Total Body Tune-Up. 400p. 2000. 25.95 (*0-553-10789-5*, Spectra) Bantam.

Murray, Michael T. 5-HTP: The Natural Way to Overcome Depression, Obesity & Insomnia. 304p. 1999. reprint ed. pap. 11.95 (*0-553-37946-1*) Bantam.

— The Healing Power of Foods: Nutrition Secrets for Vibrant Health & Long Life. LC 93-16251. 448p. (Orig.). 1993. pap. 16.95 (*1-55958-317-7*) Prima Pub.

***Murray, Michael T.** The Healing Power of Foods Cookbook: Over 150 Delicious Meat-Free Recipes for Vibrant Health. 244p. 1999. reprint ed. pap. text 17.00 (*0-7881-6744-8*) DIANE Pub.

Murray, Michael T. The Healing Power of Foods Cookbook: Over 150 Delicious Recipes for Vibrant Health. 256p. (Orig.). 1993. pap. 12.95 (*1-55958-318-5*) Prima Pub.

***Murray, Michael T.** The Healing Power of Herbs: The Enlightened Person's Guide to the Wonders of Medicinal Plants. 2nd expanded rev. ed. (Illus.). 432p. 2000. pap. 15.95 (*1-55958-700-8*) Prima Pub.

— Heart Disease & High Blood Pressure. LC 96-51625. (Getting Well Naturally Ser.). (Illus.). 180p. 1997. pap., per. 11.00 (*0-7615-0658-6*) Prima Pub.

Murray, Michael T. Male Sexual Vitality. LC 93-29270. (Getting Well Naturally Ser.). (Illus.). 160p. 1994. pap. 9.95 (*1-55958-428-9*) Prima Pub.

— Menopause: How You Can Benefit from Diet, Vitamins. LC 93-41651. 192p. 1996. pap. 8.95 (*1-55958-427-0*) Prima Pub.

— Natural Alternatives for Weight Loss. 1996. 20.00 (*0-688-14685-6*, Wm Morrow) Morrow Avon.

— Natural Alternatives for Weight Loss. 176p. 1997. reprint ed. pap. 10.00 (*0-688-15385-2*, Quil) HarperTrade.

— Natural Alternatives (o T C) to Over-The-counter & Prescription Drugs. LC 93-14152. 383p. 1994. 25.00 (*0-688-12358-9*, Wm Morrow) Morrow Avon.

— Natural Alternatives (o T C) to Over-The-counter & Prescription Drugs. 384p. 1999. reprint ed. pap. 13.00 (*0-688-16627-X*, Quil) HarperTrade.

— Natural Alternatives (p Rozac) to Prozac. 240p. 1999. pap. 10.00 (*0-688-16628-8*, Quil) HarperTrade.

— Natural Alternatives (p Rozac) to Prozac. LC 95-47489. 192p. 1996. 20.00 (*0-688-14684-8*, Wm Morrow) Morrow Avon.

Murray, Michael T. Premenstrual Syndrome: How You Can Benefit from Diet, Vitamins. LC 97-5744. (Getting Well Naturally Ser.). 176p. 1997. pap., per. 11.00 (*0-7615-0820-1*) Prima Pub.

— Stomach Ailments & Digestive Disturbances - How You Can Benefit from Diet. LC 97-10373. (Getting Well Naturally Ser.). (Illus.). 256p. 1997. pap., per. 11.00 (*0-7615-0657-8*) Prima Pub.

Murray, Michael T. Stress, Anxiety & Insomnia. LC 94-36752. 192p. 1994. pap. 11.00 (*1-55958-489-0*) Prima Pub.

— Understanding Fats & Oils. 74p. 1997. pap. text 6.95 (*0-9645075-1-X*) Prog Hlth Pub.

Murray, Michael T., jt. auth. see Trillium Health Products Nutritionists Staff.

Murray, Michael T., jt. auth. see Werbach, Melvyn R.

Murray, Michael V., tr. see Giles of Rome.

Murray, Michele. Hymns in the Style of the Masters live Piano. 1997. pap. 9.95 (*0-634-00366-6*) H Leonard.

Murray, Michelle L. Antepartal & Intrapartal Fetal Monitoring. 2nd rev. ed. (Illus.). 538p. 1996. otabind 78.00 (*0-942835-01-8*) Lrning Res Intl.

***Murray, Mike.** Green Solitaire. (Navy Seals Ser.: Vol. 3). 2000. mass mkt. 5.99 (*0-451-20050-0*, Sig) NAL.

— Insurrection Red. (Navy Seals Ser.: 1). 2000. mass mkt. 5.99 (*0-451-19946-4*) NAL.

— Navy Seals, Vol. 2. 2000. 5.99 (*0-451-19971-5*, Sig) NAL.

Murray, Millie. Cairo Hughes. (Livewire Ser.). 128p. (YA). (gr. 7-11). 1997. pap. 6.95 (*0-7043-4936-1*, Pub. by Womens Press) Trafalgar.

— Kiesha. (Livewire Ser.). 160p. (J). (gr. 6-9). pap. 8.95 (*0-7043-4129-8*, Pub. by Womens Press) Trafalgar.

— Lady A: A Teenage DJ. (Livewire Ser.). (YA). (gr. 6-9). pap. 5.95 (*0-7043-4920-5*, Pub. by Womens Press) Trafalgar.

***Murray, Millie.** Sorrelle. 1999. pap. 11.95 (*0-7043-4954-X*, Pub. by Womens Press) Trafalgar.

Murray, Mitch. The Mitch Murray Book of One-Liners for Wedding Speeches & How to Use Them. 128p. (Orig.). 1994. pap. 18.95 (*0-572-01896-7*, Pub. by W Foulsham) Trans-Atl Phila.

***Murray, Mitch.** Mitch Murray's Handbook for the Terrified Speaker. 2000. pap. 14.95 (*0-572-02459-2*) W Foulsham.

— Mitch Murray's One Liners for Business: How to Use Them in Your Speech. 2000. pap. 14.95 (*0-572-02495-9*) Foulsham UK.

Murray, Mitch. One-Liners for Business Speeches. 1998. 29.95 (*0-572-02268-9*, Pub. by W Foulsham) Trans-Atl Phila.

— One-Liners for Speeches on Special Occasions. 1998. 14.95 (*0-572-02388-X*, Pub. by W Foulsham) Trans-Atl Phila.

Murray, Muz. Sharing the Quest. (Illus.). 272p. 1989. pap. 13.95 (*1-85230-087-6*, Pub. by Element MA) Penguin Putnam.

Murray, N. A., jt. auth. see Roberts, I. A.

Murray, N. Patrick. Living Beyond Your Losses: The Healing Journey Through Grief. LC 97-29970. 108p. 1997. pap. 10.95 (*0-8192-1716-6*) Morehouse Pub.

***Murray, N. V., et al, eds.** Automated Reasoning with Analytic Tableaux & Related Methods: Proceedings of the International Conference, TABLEAUX'99, Saratoga Springs, NY, U. S. A., June 7-11, 1999. LC 99-32019. (Lecture Notes in Computer Science Ser.: Vol. 1617). x, 325p. 1999. pap. 56.00 (*3-540-66086-0*) Spr-Verlag.

Murray, Nancy. An Inner Voice for Public Administration. LC 97-5590. 208p. 1997. 55.00 (*0-275-95250-9*, Praeger Pubs) Greenwood.

Murray, Nancy, jt. ed. see Goodsell, Charles T.

Murray, Nancy A. Revision of Cymbopetalum & Porcelia (Annonaceae) Anderson, Christiane, ed. (Systematic Botany Monographs: Vol. 40). (Illus.). 121p. 1993. pap. 16.00 (*0-912861-40-1*) Am Soc Plant.

Murray, Nancy M., ed. see Murray, William J. & Armstrong, Robert.

Murray, Nancy R., jt. auth. see Wall, Jennifer A.

Murray, Nicholas. Bruce Chatwin. (Illus.). 139p. 1993. 30.00 (*1-85411-079-9*, Pub. by Seren Bks) Dufour.

— Bruce Chatwin. (Illus.). 139p. 1993. pap. 15.95 (*1-85411-080-2*, Pub. by Seren Bks) Dufour.

— The Craft of Advice: Essays 1995-1998. 278p. 1999. 29.50 (*0-9655161-1-3*) Nicholas Murray.

— Letters to the Right Rev. John Hughes, Roman Catholic Bishop of New York. Grob, Gerald N., ed. LC 76-46091. (Anti-Movements in America Ser.). 1977. reprint ed. 31.95 (*0-405-09964-9*) Ayer.

— Notes, Historical & Biographical, Concerning Elizabeth-Town: Its Eminent Men, Churches & Ministers. (Illus.). 174p. 1997. reprint ed. lib. bdg. 26.50 (*0-8328-6048-4*) Higginson Bk Co.

— Notes Historical & Biographical, Concerning Elizabeth-Town, New Jersey: Its Eminent Men, Churches & Ministers. xviii, 179p. 1991. reprint ed. pap. 17.50 (*1-55613-392-8*) Heritage Bk.

***Murray, Nicholas.** World Enough & Time: Life of Andrew Marvell. LC 99-88365. (Illus.). 304p. 2000. text 27.95 (*0-312-24277-8*) St Martin.

Murray, Nicholas P. Skimmin' Stones. LC 96-90488. (Orig.). 1997. pap. 12.95 (*0-533-12072-1*) Vantage.

Murray, Nick. Bicycling Around Galena: A Guide to the Backroads. (Illus.). 76p. (Orig.). 1994. pap. write for info. (*0-9644209-0-2*) Omnivore Pr.

An Asterisk (*) at the beginning of an entry indicates that the title is appearing for the first time.

— The Craft of Advice: Essays, 1995-1998. LC 99-90006. 288p. 1999. pap. 29.50 (*0-9669763-0-4*) N Murray Co.

*__Murray, Nick.__ Simple Wealth, Inevitable Wealth: How You & Your Financial Advisor Can Grow Your Fortune in Stock Mutual Funds. 1999. pap. write for info. (*0-9669763-1-2*) N Murray Co.

Murray, Noel W. Introduction to the Theory of Thin-Walled Structures. (Oxford Engineering Science Ser.: No. 13). (Illus.). 465p. 1986. pap. 39.95 (*0-19-856186-5*) OUP.

— When It Comes to the Crunch: The Mechanics of Car Collections. (Series on Engineering Machines). 180p. 1995. text 43.00 (*981-02-2096-0*) World Scientific Pub.

Murray, Oswyn. Early Greece. LC 83-42539. (Illus.). 320p. 1980. pap. 14.95 (*0-8047-1185-2*) Stanford U Pr.

— Early Greece. 2nd ed. LC 93-15040. 376p. 1993. pap. 16.00 (*0-674-22132-X*) HUP.

— Sympotica: A Symposium on the Symposion. (Illus.). 362p. 1995. pap. text 55.00 (*0-19-815004-0*) OUP.

Murray, Oswyn & Price, Simon, eds. The Greek City: From Homer to Alexander. (Illus.). 388p. 1991. reprint ed. pap. text 38.00 (*0-19-814791-0*) OUP.

Murray, Oswyn & Tecusan, Manuela, eds. In Vino Veritas. (Illus.). 318p. 1995. 65.00 (*0-904152-27-8*, Pub. by British Schl Rome) David Brown.

Murray, Oswyn, ed. see Sacks, David.

Murray, Pamela. Fun Bible Trivia: Questions & Answers from the Bible. LC 99-193604. (Young Reader's Activities Bks.). 192p. (J). (gr. 3-7). 1998. pap. 1.39 (*1-57748-185-2*) Barbour Pub.

— The New Success: Redefining, Creating & Surviving Your Own Success. 200p. 1993. pap. 12.95 (*0-9638021-0-0*) Many Waters.

— Remembering Your Destiny: The Twelve Practices. LC 96-79216. 224p. 1997. pap. 14.95 (*1-885221-69-X*) BookPartners.

Murray, Pamela S. Dreams of Development: Colombia's National School of Mines & Its Engineers, 1887-1970. LC 96-16449. (Illus.). 192p. 1997. pap. text 24.95 (*0-8173-0839-3*) U of Ala Pr.

Murray, Patricia. How to Hula. (Illus.). 80p. 1997. pap. 12.95 (*1-56647-099-4*) Mutual Pub HI.

— Let's Learn the Hawaiian Alphabet Coloring & Activity Book. 1988. pap. 2.95 (*0-89610-022-7*) Island Heritage.

— Wings: Student Essays from the Freshman Composition Program at California State University, Northridge, 1995-96. 2nd ed. 88p. (C). 1996. pap. text, per. 9.95 (*0-7872-2060-4*) Kendall-Hunt.

Murray, Patricia, ed. Choosing Childcare: Solving Your Childcare Problems. 1992. 31.00 (*1-85549-062-5*) St Mut.

*__Murray, Patricia, ed.__ Pocket Guide to How to Hula. (Illus.). 88p. 1999. pap. 8.95 (*1-56647-163-X*) Mutual Pub HI.

Murray, Patricia, tr. see Yoshitake, Oka.

Murray, Patricia A. Let's Learn the Hawaiian Alphabet. (Illus.). 24p. (J). (ps). 1987. 10.95 (*0-89610-075-8*) Island Heritage.

— Let's Learn the Hawaiian Alphabet. (Illus.). 24p. (J). (ps). 1988. audio 13.95 (*0-89610-079-0*) Island Heritage.

Murray, Patricia Y. & Covell, Scott F., eds. Living in America: A Popular Culture Reader. LC 97-29734. xxiii, 578p. (C). 1997. pap. text 32.95 (*1-55934-977-8*, 1977) Mayfield Pub.

Murray, Patrick. Mary: A Marian Anthology. 192p. 1989. pap. 22.00 (*0-905092-85-6*, Pub. by Veritas Pubns) St Mut.

*__Murray, Patrick.__ Oracles of God: The Roman Catholic Church & Irish Politics, 1922-37. 2000. 69.95 (*1-900621-27-4*, Pub. by Univ Coll Dublin Pr); pap. 32.95 (*1-900621-28-2*, Pub. by Univ Coll Dublin Pr) Dufour.

Murray, Patrick, ed. Reflections on Commercial Life. 496p. (C). 1997. pap. 25.99 (*0-415-91196-6*) Routledge.

— Reflections on Commercial Life. 496p. (C). 1997. 85.00 (*0-415-91195-8*) Routledge.

Murray, Patrick R. Medical Microbiology. 2nd ed. 768p. 1993. text, teacher ed. 35.00 (*0-7234-2010-6*) Mosby Inc.

*__Murray, Patrick R.__ Medical Microbiology. 4th ed. 2001. pap. text. write for info. (*0-323-01213-2*) Mosby Inc.

Murray, Patrick R. Pocket Guide to Clinical Microbiology. 2nd rev. ed. LC 98-21385. 350p. 1998. pap. 29.95 (*1-55581-137-X*) ASM Pr.

Murray, Patrick R., ed. Manual of Clinical Microbiology. 7th rev. ed. LC 98-46075. (Illus.). 1800p. 1999. 129.95 (*1-55581-126-4*) ASM Pr.

Murray, Patrick T. Friedrich Schiller's Philosophy of Aesthetic Education. LC 92-10126. (Studies in German Language & Literature: Vol. 12). 444p. 1993. lib. bdg. 109.95 (*0-7734-9511-8*) E Mellen.

— Hegel's Philosophy of Mind & Will. LC 91-10314. (Studies in the History of Philosophy: Vol. 21). 145p. 1991. lib. bdg. 69.95 (*0-7734-9773-0*) E Mellen.

Murray, Paul. The Absent Fountain. 72p. (C). 1991. 24.00 (*0-948268-99-9*, Pub. by Dedalus); pap. 25.00 (*0-948268-98-0*, Pub. by Dedalus) St Mut.

— A Fantastic Journey: The Life & Literature of Lafcadio Hearn. LC 97-12758. 408p. (C). 1997. text 34.50 (*0-472-10834-4*, 10834) U of Mich Pr.

— The Mysticism Debate. 1978. pap. 1.00 (*0-8199-0722-7*, Frncscn Herld) Franciscan Pr.

— Rites & Meditations. 55p. 1982. pap. 10.95 (*0-85105-393-9*, Pub. by Smyth) Dufour.

Murray, Pauli. The Autobiography of a Black Activist, Feminist, Lawyer, Priest, & Poet. LC 88-20728. Orig. Title: Song in a Weary Throat; an American Pilgrimage. 464p. 1989. reprint ed. pap. 18.95 (*0-87049-596-8*) U of Tenn Pr.

— Proud Shoes: The Story of an American Family. LC 99-14164. 304p. 1999. pap. 16.00 (*0-8070-7209-5*) Beacon Pr.

Murray, Pauli, jt. auth. see Douglas, Davison M.

Murray, Peggy & Stein, Mary. Child Abuse. 4th rev. ed. (Illus.). 231p. 1997. pap. 44.95 (*1-57801-008-X*) Western Schls.

Murray, Penelope, ed. Plato on Poetry: Ion; Republic 376e-398b9; Republic 595-608b10. (Greek & Latin Classics Ser.). 260p. (C). 1996. pap. text 22.95 (*0-521-34981-8*) Cambridge U Pr.

Murray, Penelope, ed. see Plato.

Murray, Peter. The Architecture of the Italian Renaissance. 256p. 1997. pap. 16.00 (*0-8052-1082-2*) Schocken.

Murray, Peter. Basic Trial Advocacy. 416p. 1995. pap. write for info. (*0-7355-0621-3*, 06213) Panel Pubs.

Murray, Peter. Beavers. (Nature Books Ser.). (Illus.). 32p. (J). (gr. 2-6). 1992. lib. bdg. 22.79 (*0-89565-844-5*) Childs World.

— Beetles. LC 92-29742. (Nature Books Ser.). (Illus.). 32p. (J). (gr. 2-6). 1994. lib. bdg. 22.79 (*1-56766-000-2*) Childs World.

— Black Widows. (Nature Books Ser.). (Illus.). 32p. (J). (gr. 2-6). 1992. lib. bdg. 22.79 (*0-89565-845-3*) Childs World.

— Bravery: The Story of Sitting Bull. LC 95-42267. (Value Biographies Ser.). (Illus.). 32p. (J). (gr. 2-6). 1997. lib. bdg. 21.36 (*1-56766-230-7*) Childs World.

— Cactus. LC 95-5001. (Nature Books Ser.). (Illus.). 32p. (J). (gr. 2-6). 1995. lib. bdg. 22.79 (*1-56766-191-2*) Childs World.

— Curiosity: The Story of Marie Curie. LC 95-42268. (Value Biographies Ser.). (Illus.). 32p. (J). 1997. lib. bdg. 21.36 (*1-56766-229-3*, 62293) Childs World.

— Deserts. (Biomes of Nature Ser.). (Illus.). 32p. (J). (gr. 2-6). 1996. lib. bdg. 22.79 (*1-56766-280-3*) Childs World.

— Dirt, Wonderful Dirt! LC 92-42741. (Umbrella Bks.). (Illus.). (J). (gr. 2-6). Date not set. lib. bdg. 21.36 (*1-56766-079-7*) Childs World.

— Dogs. (Nature Books Ser.). (Illus.). 32p. (J). (gr. 2-6). 1992. lib. bdg. 22.79 (*0-89565-848-8*) Childs World.

— Earthquakes. LC 98-3254. (Illus.). 32p. 1998. lib. bdg. 22.79 (*1-56766-549-7*) Childs World.

— Floods. LC 95-45346. (Forces of Nature Ser.). (Illus.). 32p. (J). (gr. 2-6). 1996. lib. bdg. 22.79 (*1-56766-214-5*) Childs World.

— Frogs. LC 92-32499. (Nature Books Ser.). (Illus.). 32p. (J). (gr. 2-6). 1994. lib. bdg. 22.79 (*1-56766-010-X*) Childs World.

— Gorillas. (Nature Books Ser.). (Illus.). 32p. (J). (gr. 2-6). 1994. lib. bdg. 22.79 (*1-56766-020-7*) Childs World.

— Hurricanes. LC 95-1744. (Forces of Nature Ser.). (Illus.). 32p. (J). (gr. 2-6). 1995. lib. bdg. 22.79 (*1-56766-196-3*) Childs World.

— Hurricanes. LC 98-3256. (Illus.). 32p. 1998. lib. bdg 22.79 (*1-56766-547-0*) Childs World.

— La Lanzadera Espacial. LC 93-17916. (Libro Vision Ser.). (SPA., Illus.). 32p. (J). (gr. 2-6). 1994. lib. bdg. 22.79 (*1-56766-038-X*) Childs World.

— Lightning. (Forces of Nature Ser.). (Illus.). 32p. (J). (gr. 2-6). 1996. lib. bdg. 22.79 (*1-56766-215-3*) Childs World.

— Make a Kite! LC 93-49604. (Umbrella Bks.). (Illus.). 24p. (J). (gr. 2-6). 1998. lib. bdg. 21.36 (*1-56766-083-5*) Childs World.

— Mountains. (Biomes of Nature Ser.). (Illus.). 32p. (J). (gr. 2-6). 1996. lib. bdg. 22.79 (*1-56766-279-X*) Childs World.

— Mushrooms. LC 95-907. (Nature Books Ser.). (Illus.). 32p. (J). (gr. 2-6). 1995. lib. bdg. 22.79 (*1-56766-193-9*) Childs World.

— Orchids. LC 95-906. (Nature Books Ser.). (Illus.). 32p. (J). (gr. 2-6). 1995. lib. bdg. 22.79 (*1-56766-194-7*) Childs World.

— Parrots. LC 92-44265. (Nature Books Ser.). (Illus.). 32p. (J). (gr. 2-6). 1994. lib. bdg. 22.79 (*1-56766-015-0*) Childs World.

— Pigs. LC 97-8363. (Nature Books Ser.). (Illus.). 32p. (J). (gr. 2-6). 1997. lib. bdg. 22.79 (*1-56766-378-8*) Childs World.

— Planet Earth. LC 96-47043. (Our Universe Ser.). (Illus.). 32p. (J). (gr. 2-6). 1997. lib. bdg. 22.79 (*1-56766-387-7*) Childs World.

— The Planets. LC 92-20016. (Umbrella Bks.). (Illus.). 32p. (J). (gr. 2-6). 1993. lib. bdg. 21.36 (*0-89565-975-1*) Childs World.

— Porcupines. LC 93-22833. (Nature Books Ser.). (Illus.). 32p. (J). (gr. 2-6). 1994. lib. bdg. 22.79 (*1-56766-019-3*) Childs World.

— Prairies. LC 96-17569. (Biomes of Nature Ser.). (Illus.). 32p. (J). (gr. 2-6). 1996. lib. bdg. 22.79 (*1-56766-277-3*) Childs World.

— Professor Solomon Snickerdoodle Looks at Air. LC 95-7608. (Umbrella Bks.). (Illus.). 32p. (J). (gr. 2-6). 1997. lib. bdg. 19.93 (*1-56766-082-7*) Childs World.

— Professor Solomon Snickerdoodle Looks at Light. LC 95-10203. (Umbrella Bks.). (Illus.). 32p. (J). (gr. 2-6). 1997. lib. bdg. 19.93 (*1-56766-148-3*) Childs World.

— Rainforests. (Biomes of Nature Ser.). (Illus.). 32p. (J). (gr. 2-6). 1996. lib. bdg. 22.79 (*1-56766-278-1*) Childs World.

— Redwoods. (Nature Books Ser.). (Illus.). 32p. (J). (gr. 2-6). 1996. lib. bdg. 22.79 (*1-56766-216-1*) Childs World.

— Rhinos. (Nature Books Ser.). (Illus.). 32p. (J). (gr. 2-6). 1992. lib. bdg. 22.79 (*0-89565-838-0*) Childs World.

— Roses. LC 95-1747. (Nature Books Ser.). (Illus.). 32p. (J). (gr. 2-6). 1995. lib. bdg. 22.79 (*1-56766-192-0*) Childs World.

— The Sahara. LC 93-25782. (Vision Bks.). (Illus.). 32p. (J). (gr. 2-6). 1994. lib. bdg. 22.79 (*1-56766-023-1*) Childs World.

— Saturn. LC 92-41542. (Vision Bks.). (Illus.). 32p. (J). (gr. 2-6). 1994. lib. bdg. 22.79 (*1-56766-014-2*) Childs World.

— Saturn. LC 96-46674. (Our Universe Ser.). (Illus.). 32p. (J). (gr. 2-4). 1997. lib. bdg. 22.79 (*1-56766-388-5*) Childs World.

— Scorpions. (Nature Books Ser.). (Illus.). 32p. (J). (gr. 2-6). 1996. lib. bdg. 22.79 (*1-56766-217-X*) Childs World.

— Sea Otters. LC 93-42. (Nature Books Ser.). (Illus.). 32p. (J). (gr. 2-6). 1994. lib. bdg. 22.79 (*1-56766-007-X*) Childs World.

— A Sense of Humor: The Story of Mark Twain. LC 98-33758. (Illus.). 32p. (J). 1999. lib. bdg. 21.36 (*1-56766-606-X*) Childs World.

— Sheep. LC 97-5953. (Nature Books Ser.). (Illus.). 32p. (J). (gr. 2-6). 1997. lib. bdg. 22.79 (*1-56766-379-6*) Childs World.

— Silly Science Tricks. LC 92-18903. (Umbrella Bks.). (Illus.). 32p. (J). (gr. 2-6). 1993. lib. bdg. 21.36 (*0-89565-976-X*) Childs World.

— Snails. LC 97-1044. (Nature Books Ser.). (Illus.). 32p. (J). (gr. 2-6). 1997. lib. bdg. 22.79 (*1-56766-382-6*) Childs World.

— Snakes. (Nature Books Ser.). (Illus.). 32p. (J). (gr. 2-6). 1991. lib. bdg. 22.79 (*0-89565-849-6*) Childs World.

— Spiders. (Nature Books Ser.). (Illus.). 32p. (J). (gr. 2-6). 1991. lib. bdg. 22.79 (*0-89565-847-X*) Childs World.

— Tarantulas. (Nature Books Ser.). (Illus.). 32p. (J). (gr. 2-6). 1993. lib. bdg. 22.79 (*1-56766-060-6*) Childs World.

— Tornadoes. LC 98-6138. (Illus.). 32p. 1998. lib. bdg. 22.79 (*1-56766-548-9*) Childs World.

— Volcanoes. LC 95-3515. (Nature Books Ser.). (Illus.). 32p. (J). (gr. 2-6). 1995. lib. bdg. 22.79 (*1-56766-197-1*) Childs World.

— Water Science Tricks. LC 93-1322. (Umbrella Bks.). (Illus.). 32p. (J). (gr. 2-6). 1997. lib. bdg. 19.93 (*1-56766-081-9*) Childs World.

— The World's Greatest Chocolate Chip Cookie. (Umbrella Bks.). (Illus.). 32p. (J). (gr. 2-6). 1993. lib. bdg. 21.36 (*0-89565-892-5*) Childs World.

— The World's Greatest Paper Airplanes. (Umbrella Bks.). (Illus.). 32p. (J). (gr. 2-6). 1993. lib. bdg. 21.36 (*0-89565-963-8*) Childs World.

— You Can Juggle. LC 92-9504. (Umbrella Bks.). (Illus.). 32p. (J). (gr. 2-6). 1993. lib. bdg. 21.36 (*0-89565-966-2*) Childs World.

— Your Bones - An Inside Look at Skeletons. LC 92-7460. (Umbrella Bks.). (Illus.). 32p. (J). (gr. 2-6). 1993. lib. bdg. 21.36 (*0-89565-968-9*) Childs World.

Murray, Peter & Murray, Linda. Art of the Renaissance. LC 84-51305. (World of Art Ser.). (Illus.). 288p. 1985. pap. 14.95 (*0-500-20008-4*, Pub. by Thames Hudson) Norton.

— Diccionario de Artes y Artistas (Dictionary of Arts & Artists)Tr. of Dictionary of Arts & Artists. (SPA.). 600p. 1978. 29.95 (*0 8288-4880-7*, S50013) Fr & Eur.

— The Oxford Companion to Christian Art & Architecture. (Illus.). 608p. 1996. 60.00 (*0-19-866165-7*) OUP.

— The Oxford Companion to Christian Art & Architecture. (Illus.). 624p. 1998. reprint ed. pap. 26.50 (*0-19-860216-2*) OUP.

— Penguin Dictionary of Art & Artists. 7th ed. LC 98-130228. 579p. 1998. pap. 15.95 (*0-14-051300-0*, Penguin Bks) Viking Penguin.

Murray, Peter & Stevens, MaryAnne, eds. Living Bridges: The Inhabited Bridge: Past, Present & Future. LC 97-170710. (Illus.). 160p. 1997. 55.00 (*3-7913-1734-2*, Pub. by Prestel) te Neues.

— New Urban Environments: British Architecture & Its European Context. LC 98-181768. (Illus.). 192p. 1998. 65.00 (*3-7913-1937-X*) te Neues.

Murray, Peter & Trombley, Stephen. Modern Britain. (Illus.). 192p. 1997. 14.95 (*0-7148-3133-6*, Pub. by Phaidon Press) Phaidon Pr.

Murray, Peter, jt. contrib. by see Maxwell, Robert.

Murray, Peter, ed. see Burckhardt, Jacob.

Murray, Peter, tr. see Chastel, Andre.

Murray, Peter B. Shakespeare's Imagined Persons: The Psychology of Role-Playing & Acting. 320p. (C). 1995. pap. text 36.00 (*0-389-21016-1*) B&N Imports.

— Shakespeare's Imagined Persons: The Psychology of Role-Playing & Acting. 320p. (C). 1996. lib. bdg. 57.50 (*0-389-21015-3*) B&N Imports.

*__Murray, Peter D.__ Nietzsche's Affirmative Morality: A Revaluation Based in the Dionysian World-View. LC 99-32855. 320p. 1999. 155.00 (*3-11-016601-1*) De Gruyter.

Murray, Peter L. Basic Trial. 416p. 1995. 28.95 (*0-316-59132-7*, Aspen Law & Bus) Aspen Pub.

Murray, Peter L. & Field, Richard H. Maine Evidence. 3rd ed. 670p. 1994. spiral bd. 115.00 (*1-56257-198-2*, MICHIE) LEXIS Pub.

Murray, Peter L. & Field, Richard H. Maine Evidence: 2000 Edition. 626p. pap. 85.00 (*0-327-12512-8*) LEXIS Pub.

Murray, Peter L. & Levy, Jon D. Maine Family Law, 1997. 2nd ed. LC 97-70182. 636p. 1997. pap. text 75.00 (*1-55834-464-0*, 81640-12, MICHIE) LEXIS Pub.

*__Murray, Phil.__ You Can Always Get What You Want. abr. ed. 1998. mass mkt. 16.85 incl. audio (*1-84032-125-3*, Pub. by HOD2) Ulverscroft.

Murray, Philip, jt. auth. see Cooke, Morris L.

Murray, Philip I. & Fielder, Alistair R. Butterworth-Heinemann Pocket Book of Ophthalmology. LC 96-51441. 128p. 1997. pap. text 22.00 (*0-7506-2371-3*) Buttrwrth-Heinemann.

Murray, Philomena & Holmes, Leslie, eds. Europe: Rethinking the Boundaries. LC 98-19208. 179p. 1998. text 68.95 (*1-84014-003-8*, Pub. by Ashgate Pub) Ashgate Pub Co.

Murray, Philomena, jt. ed. see Holmes, Leslie.

Murray, Placid, ed. see Newman, John Henry.

Murray, Placid, tr. see Holzherr, George.

Murray-Plumer, Sara & Busch, Cindy J. A Hero & a Halo. LC 97-92755. (Illus.). (J). (ps-2). 1997. pap. 8.00 (*0-9661228-0-1*) S Murray-Plumer.

Murray, Polly. The Widening Circle: A Lyme Disease Pioneer Tells Her Story. 336p. 1996. text 23.95 (*0-312-14068-1*) St Martin.

Murray, Priscilla, jt. auth. see Ravindra, Ravi.

Murray, R. Ethical Dilemmas in Health Care: Healing Through Literature. 208p. (Orig.). (C). 1996. pap. text 42.99 (*1-56593-441-5*, 1110) Singular Publishing.

*__Murray, R. A. & Stefan, M. D.__ An Atlas of Schizophrenia. (Encyclopedia of Visual Medicine Ser.). (Illus.). 100p. 2000. 85.00 (*1-85070-074-5*) Prthnon Pub.

Murray, R. Emmett. The Lexicon of Labor: More Than 500 Key Terms, Biographical Sketches, & Historical Insights Concerning Labor in America. LC 98-12783. (Illus.). 192p. 1998. pap. 13.95 (*1-56584-456-4*, Pub. by New Press NY) Norton.

Murray, R. L. Hurrah for the Ould Flag! The True Story of Captain Andrew Cowan & the First New York Independent Battery at Gettysburg. (Illus.). 141p. 1998. pap. 11.95 (*0-9646261-3-6*) R L Murray NY.

— The Redemption of the "Harper's Ferry Cowards" The Story of the 111th & 126th New York Volunteer Regiments at Gettysburg. (Illus.). 178p. 1994. pap. 12.95 (*0-9646261-0-1*) R L Murray NY.

Murray, R. L. & Cobb, G. C. Physics: Concepts & Consequences. (American Nuclear Society Textbook Ser.). 710p. 1970. text 19.00 (*0-13-672501-5*, 350004) Am Nuclear Soc.

Murray, R. M. & Turner, T. H., eds. Lectures on the History of Psychiatry. (Squibb Ser.). 223p. 1990. pap. text 25.00 (*0-88048-601-5*, 8601, Pub. by Royal Coll Psych) Parkwest Pubns.

— Lectures on the History of Psychiatry. LC 91-46193. (Squibb Ser.). 235p. reprint ed. pap. 72.90 (*0-7837-4059-X*, 204400900011) Bks Demand.

Murray, R. Michael. The Golden Age of Walt Disney Records, 1933-1988: Price Guide for Disney Fans & Record Collectors. LC 97-72624. (Illus.). 256p. 1997. pap. 19.95 (*0-930625-70-6*) Krause Pubns.

*__Murray, Rachel.__ The African Commission on Human & Peoples Rights & International Law. 288p. 2000. 54.00 (*1-84113-122-9*, Pub. by Hart Pub) Intl Spec Bk.

Murray, Raymond. Hard Time: Armagh Gaol 1971-1986. LC 99-176455. 128p. 1998. pap. 12.95 (*1-85635-223-4*, Pub. by Mercier Pr) Irish Amer Bk.

*__Murray, Raymond.__ Nuclear Energy: An Introduction to the Concepts, Systems & Applications of Nuclear Processes. 5th ed. 400p. 2000. pap. text 59.95 (*0-7506-7136-X*, Newnes) Buttrwrth-Heinemann.

Murray, Raymond. State Violence: Northern Ireland, 1969-1997. LC 98-235719. 1999. pap. 15.95 (*1-85635-235-8*) Mercier Pr.

Murray, Raymond C. & Tedrow, John C. Forensic Geology. 176p. (C). 1991. text 65.20 (*0-13-327453-5*) P-H.

Murray, Raymond C., jt. ed. see Pray, Lloyd C.

Murray, Raymond L. Grandpa Saw It Happen - WWII: Normandy Beach to Elbe River. Murray, Melba L., ed. (Illus.). 250p. 1993. 19.95 (*0-9640671-0-2*) R L Murray.

— Nuclear Energy. LC 74-8685. 296p. 1975. text 28.00 (*0-685-04008-9*, Pergamon Pr); pap. text 16.50 (*0-685-04009-7*, Pergamon Pr) Elsevier.

— Nuclear Energy: In SI Metric Units. 2nd ed. 1980. text 52.00 (*0-08-024751-2*, Pergamon Pr); pap. text 22.00 (*0-08-024750-4*, Pergamon Pr) Elsevier.

— Understanding Radioactive Waste. 4th ed. Powell, Judith A., ed. LC 94-9995. (Illus.). 220p. 1994. pap. text 12.50 (*0-935470-79-4*) Battelle.

Murray, Raymond L. & Murray, Melba L. How We Uprooted Our Roots & What We Found. Murray, Alice, ed. & intro. by. LC 97-104520. (Illus.). 304p. (Orig.). 1996. per. 25.00 (*0-9640671-2-9*) R L Murray.

Murray, Regina W. The Last One up the Hill: A Biography of Thomas F. Waldron. (Illus.). 150p. 1993. 19.95 (*0-9636918-0-5*) R W Murray.

Murray, Rhea. A Journey to Moriah. Pool, Gary, ed. (Illus.). 160p. 1998. pap. 9.95 (*0-9667237-0-8*) Banta & Pool Litry.

Murray, Richard D., ed. see Society of Photographic Scientists & Engineers Sta.

Murray, Richard M., jt. auth. see Zexiang Li.

Murray, Richard N., jt. auth. see Zimmer, Jim L.

Murray, Richard P. Basic Guide to Understanding Clinical Laboratory Tests. LC 93-77871. 110p. 1993. 14.95 (*1-882657-01-2*) Health Digest.

Murray, Richard W., jt. auth. see Thomas, Robert D.

Murray, Robert. High Cockalorum. 1964. pap. 5.25 (*0-8222-0518-1*) Dramatists Play.

Murray, Robert, jt. auth. see Maughan, Ron J.

Murray, Robert, jt. ed. see Lamb, David R.

Murray, Robert, ed. see McKeag, Douglas B. & Hough, David.

*__Murray, Robert A.__ The People That Anthropologists Do Not Like to Study: (Featuring Negroes with No Known African Origin & Primitive Caucasians) (Illus.). 160p. 2000. pap. write for info. (*0-9676083-0-9*) R Murray.

Murray, Robert D. Thunder over the Door: The Ships, Shores, & Woods of Wisconsin's Door Peninsula. LC 91-16418. (Illus.). (Orig.). 1991. 19.95 (*0-940473-22-4*) Wm Caxton.

Murray, Robert D., et al. The Natural Coumarins: Occurrence, Chemistry & Biochemistry. LC 81-14776. 714p. reprint ed. pap. 200.00 (*0-608-18412-8*, 203042900069) Bks Demand.

Murray, Robert F., jt. auth. see Bowman, James E.

M

Murray, Robert H. Erasmus & Luther: Their Attitude to Toleration. LC 83-45659. (Zodiac Club Ser.). reprint ed. 57.50 (*0-404-19809-0*) AMS Pr.

— Group Movements Throughout the Ages. LC 72-301. (Essay Index Reprint Ser.). 1977. reprint ed. 24.95 (*0-8369-2810-5*) Ayer.

— The Only Way Home. (Illus.). 159p. 1987. 24.00 (*0-9617970-0-2*) Robert H Murray.

Murray, Robert H., jt. auth. see Grant, Harvey D.

Murray, Robert J. & White, Kate. Research for Writers. 152p. (C). 1995. pap. 40.00 (*0-7300-0302-7*, Pub. by Deakin Univ) St Mut.

***Murray, Robert K.** The Harding Era: Warren G. Harding & His Administration. Speirs, Katherine, ed. (Signature Ser.). (Illus.). 626p. 2000. 37.50 (*0-945707-27-4*) Amer Political.

Murray, Robert K. The Harding Era: Warren G. Harding & His Administration. LC 74-91797. 654p. reprint ed. pap. 200.00 (*0-8357-3333-5*, 203955800013) Bks Demand.

Murray, Robert K. & Blessing, Tim H. Greatness in the White House: Rating the Presidents. rev. ed. LC 93-20451. 180p. (C). 1993. pap. 16.95 (*0-271-01090-8*) Pa St U Pr.

Murray, Robert K. & Brucker, Roger W. Trapped! The Story of Floyd Collins. rev. ed. LC 82-40177. (Illus.). 352p. 1999. pap. 19.00 (*0-8131-0153-0*) U Pr of Ky.

Murray, Robert L. The Protogeometric Style: The First Greek Style. (Studies in Mediterranean Archaeology: No. 2). (Illus.). 40p. 1975. pap. 14.95 (*91-85058-65-3*) P Astroms.

Murray, Robert M. Fountain of Guilt: Survivors Guide to the Nuclear Family. 256p. (Orig.). 1996. pap. 11.95 (*1-885610-03-3*) European Amer.

Murray, Robert P. Confessions of a Vermont Realtor: An Optimistic Retrospective. (Illus.). 242p. (Orig.). 1995. pap. 12.60 (*0-9651764-0-1*) Gregg Hill Pub.

Murray, Robert W. C++ Strategies & Tactics. 304p. (C). 1993. pap. text 42.95 (*0-201-56382-7*) Addison-Wesley.

Murray, Robin, et al, eds. The Essentials of Postgraduate Psychiatry. 3rd ed. (Illus.). 868p. 1997. text 125.00 (*0-521-44396-2*) Cambridge U Pr.

— The Essentials of Postgraduate Psychiatry. 3rd ed. LC 96-44256. (Illus.). 868p. (C). 1997. pap. text 59.95 (*0-521-57801-9*) Cambridge U Pr.

Murray, Robin, jt. auth. see Frangou, Sophia.

Murray, Robin, ed. see Royal College of Psychiatrists Staff.

Murray, Robin M., jt. ed. see Keshavan, Matcheri S.

Murray, Roger F. Economic Aspects of Pensions: A Summary Report. (General Ser.: No. 85). 148p. 1968. 38.50 (*0-87014-473-1*) Natl Bur Econ Res.

— Economic Aspects of Pensions: A Summary Report. LC 68-20444. (National Bureau of Economic Research. General Ser.: No. 85). 148p. reprint ed. pap. 45.90 (*0-8357-2602-9*, 201598000006) Bks Demand.

Murray, Roger N. Wordsworth's Style: Figures & Themes in the Lyrical Ballads of 1800. LC 67-13152. 178p. 1967. reprint ed. pap. 55.20 (*0-608-01852-X*, 206250200003) Bks Demand.

Murray, Ronald J., jt. auth. see Hertz, Robert H.

Murray, Ronald O., et al. The Radiology of Skeletal Disorders, 4 vols. 3rd ed. (Illus.). 2368p. 1989. text 520.00 (*0-443-01980-0*) Church.

Murray, Rosalie R., jt. auth. see Murray, William D.

Murray, Rose. Moving to Success: The Astrology of Location. LC 98-43553. (Illus.). 352p. 1999. 12.95 (*1-56718-478-2*, K478) Llewellyn Pubns.

— Quick Chicken. (Illus.). 192p. 1999. pap. 19.95 (*0-7788-0002-4*, Pub. by R Rose Inc) Firefly Bks Ltd.

— When Planets Promise Love: Your Romantic Destiny Through Astrology. 2nd expanded rev. ed. LC 98-31528. (Illus.). 256p. 1999. 12.95 (*1-56718-477-4*, K477) Llewellyn Pubns.

Murray, Royce W. Techniques of Chemistry Molecular Design of Electrode Surfaces. LC 91-25499. (Techniques of Chemistry Ser.: Vol. 22). 448p. 1992. 235.00 (*0-471-55773-0*) Wiley.

Murray, Rupert W. IFOR on IFOR: NATO Peacekeepers in Bosnia-Herzegovina. 1997. pap. 30.00 (*1-901205-00-2*, 205002) Combined Pub.

***Murray, Rupert W.** Road to Peace: NATO & the International Community in Bosnia. 1998. pap. 19.95 (*1-901205-02-9*, 205029) Combined Pub.

Murray, Ruth, et al. Health Assessment & Promotion Strategies Through the Life Span. 6th ed. LC 96-23056. 896p. (C). 1996. pap. text 44.95 (*0-8385-6987-0*, A6987-0) Appleton & Lange.

Murray, Ruth B. & Zentner, Judith P. Health Assessment & Promotion Strategies Through the Life Span. 6th ed. 136p. 1997. teacher ed. write for info. (*0-8385-6990-0*, A6990-4) Appleton & Lange.

Murray, Ruth E. The True Confessions of Charlotte Doyle. LC 90-30624. (Illus.). 224p. (J). (gr. 6-8). 1990. lib. bdg. 17.99 (*0-531-08493-0*) Orchard Bks Watts.

Murray, Ruth E. The True Confessions of Charlotte Doyle. 240p. (YA). (gr. 7 up). 1992. mass mkt. 4.99 (*0-380-71475-2*, Avon Bks) Morrow Avon.

Murray, Ruth E. The True Confessions of Charlotte Doyle. LC 90-30624. 224p. (YA). (gr. 6-8). 1990. 16.95 (*0-531-05893-X*) Orchard Bks Watts.

Murray, Samuel M. Samuel: In Search of the American Dream. unabridged ed. Murray, Hwesu S. & Murray, Vernon Q., eds. 227p. 1996. pap. 10.00 (*0-9653836-0-1*) Gullah Publng.

Murray, Scott. Australia on the Small Screen, 1970-1995: The Complete Guide to Tele-Features & Mini-Series. LC 97-163591. (Illus.). 272p. 1997. pap. text 32.00 (*0-19-553949-4*) OUP.

***Murray, Scott W.** Liberal Diplomacy & German Unification: The Early Career of Robert Morier. LC 99-59653. 304p. 2000. 65.00 (*0-275-96730-1*, C6730, Praeger Pubs) Greenwood.

Murray-Shelley, Richard. Computer Programming for Electrical Engineers. LC 75-20013. 151p. 1975. write for info. (*0-07-084060-1*) McGraw.

Murray, Shirley E., et al. In Every Corner Sing: The Hymns of Shirley Erena Murray. Schrader, Jack, ed. LC 92-73734. 200p. (Orig.). 1992. 14.95 (*0-916642-48-8*, 1051) Hope Pub.

Murray, Shoon. Anchors Against Change: American Opinion Leaders' Beliefs after the Cold War. 224p. (C). 1996. text 47.50 (*0-472-10758-5*, 10758) U of Mich Pr.

***Murray-Slutsky, Carolyn & Paris, Betty B.** Exploring the Spectrum of Autism & Pervasive Developmental Disorders: Intervention Strategies. LC 00-8445. 2000. pap. write for info. (*0-7616-5500-X*, Thrpy Skill Bldrs) Commun Skill.

Murray Smith, Joanna. Honour. 1998. pap. 5.25 (*0-8222-1683-3*) Dramatists Play.

Murray-Smith, Joanna. Honour. rev. ed. 58p. 1997. pap. 16.95 (*0-86819-539-1*, Pub. by Currency Pr) Accents Pubns.

— Redemption. 1997. pap. 14.95 (*0-86819-513-8*, Pub. by Currency Pr) Accents Pubns.

Murray-Smith, Roderick & Johanson, Tor, eds. Multiple Model Approaches to Nonlinear Modelling & Control. LC 97-153224. (Series in Systems & Control). 416p. 1997. 79.95 (*0-7484-0595-X*, Pub. by Tay Francis Ltd) Taylor & Francis.

Murray, Spencer. Pitcairn Island: The 1st 200 Years. LC 92-81932. (Illus.). 192p. 1992. pap. 19.95 (*0-9633229-0-7*) Bounty Sagas.

Murray, Stephen. Beauvis Cathedral: Architecture of Transcendence. LC 88-19952. (Illus.). 276p. 1989. reprint ed. pap. 85.60 (*0-608-07648-1*, 205996500010) Bks Demand.

— Building Troyes Cathedral: The Late Gothic Campaigns. LC 85-45744. (Illus.). 344p. reprint ed. pap. 106.70 (*0-608-09354-8*, 205410000002) Bks Demand.

Murray, Stephen O. American Gay. (Illus.). 332p. (C). 1996. pap. 16.95 (*0-226-55193-8*) U Ch Pr.

— American Gay. LC 95-49388. (Worlds of Desire Ser.). (Illus.). 296p. (C). 1996. lib. bdg. 50.00 (*0-226-55191-1*) U Ch Pr.

— American Sociolinguistics: Theorists & Theory Groups. LC 98-35297. x, 339p. 1998. pap. 29.95 (*1-55619-532-X*) J Benjamins Pubng Co.

— Angkor Life. LC 95-78414. (Illus.). 102p. 1996. pap. 10.95 (*0-942777-15-8*) Floating Lotus.

Murray, Stephen O. Homosexualities. LC 99-87502. (Worlds of Desire Ser.). 1997. 38.00 (*0-226-55194-6*); pap. text 19.95 (*0-226-55195-4*) U Ch Pr.

Murray, Stephen O. Social Theory, Homosexual Realities. 83p. 1984. pap. 8.95 (*0-942777-57-3*) Floating Lotus.

— Theory Groups & the Study of Language in North America: A Social History. LC 93-34835. (Studies in the History of the Language Sciences: No. 69). xv, 598p. 1994. 110.00 (*1-55619-364-5*) J Benjamins Pubng Co.

Murray, Stephen O., ed. Latin American Male Homosexualities. LC 95-4349. 304p. 1995. 45.00 (*0-8263-1646-8*); pap. 24.95 (*0-8263-1658-1*) U of NM Pr.

— Male Homosexuality in Central & South America. 202p. 1987. pap. 10.95 (*0-942777-58-1*) Floating Lotus.

Murray, Stephen O. & Hong, Keelung. Taiwanese Culture, Taiwanese Society: A Critical Review of Social Science Research Done on Taiwan. LC 93-48342. 250p. (Orig.). (C). 1994. pap. text 28.50 (*0-8191-9434-4*); lib. bdg. 49.50 (*0-8191-9433-6*) U Pr of Amer.

Murray, Stephen O. & Roscoe, Will, eds. Islamic Homosexualities: Culture, History, & Literature. LC 96-35677. (Illus.). 390p. (C). 1997. text 55.00 (*0-8147-7467-9*); pap. text 21.00 (*0-8147-7468-7*) NYU Pr.

Murray, Stephen O., jt. ed. see Roscoe, Will.

Murray, Sterling E. Anthologies of Music: An Annotated Index. 2nd ed. LC 92-34086. (Detroit Studies in Music Bibliography: No. 68). 1992. 35.00 (*0-89990-061-5*) Harmonie Park Pr.

Murray, Sterling E., ed. see Rosetti, Antonio.

***Murray, Steve.** AS/400 Associate System Operator Certification Study Guide. 384p. 1999. pap. 119.00 (*1-58347-007-7*) Midrange Comput.

***Murray, Steve & Rochester Community & Technical College Staff.** AS/400 Professional System Operator Certification Study Guide. (Illus.). 544p. 2000. pap., student ed. write for info. (*1-58347-014-X*, IBM) Midrange Comput.

Murray, Steven M. A Guide to the Internet for Churches & Pastors. LC 98-70292. 96p. 1998. pap. 14.95 (*0-88177-244-5*, DR224) Discipleship Res.

Murray, Steven T., tr. see Davidsen, Leif.

Murray, Steven T., tr. see Mankell, Henning.

Murray, Steven T., tr. see Nexo, Martin Anderson.

Murray, Steven T., tr. see Rifbjerg, Klaus.

Murray, Steven T., tr. see Sorensen, Villy.

***Murray Stone, Elaine.** Taming of the Tongue. LC 99-64075. 1999. pap. text 5.99 (*0-88270-777-9*) Bridge-Logos.

Murray, Stuart. All We Have Built: The People of Vermont's Granite Industry. (Illus.). 128p. 21.00 (*1-884592-19-8*) Images from the Past.

— America's Song: The Story of "Yankee Doodle" LC 99-30294. (Illus.). 248p. 1999. 21.00 (*1-884592-18-X*) Images from the Past.

— Church Planting: Laying Foundations. xii, 302p. 1998. reprint ed. pap. 25.00 (*0-85364-825-5*, Pub. by Paternoster Pub) OM Literature.

— Go for the Goal: Techniques & Strategies for the Complete Soccer Player. 192p. 1994. pap. 12.00 (*0-671-88232-5*, Fireside) S&S Trade Pap.

— The Honor of Command: General Burgoyne's Saratoga Campaign June-October 1777. LC 97-25356. (Illus.). 128p. 1998. pap. 14.95 (*1-884592-03-1*) Images from the Past.

— Judith's Dime Novel. LC 97-97220. 192p. 1998. lib. bdg. 18.95 (*0-8034-9290-1*, Avalon Bks) Bouregy.

***Murray, Stuart.** The Last Masterpiece: Frederic Church & Olana. (Illus.). 208p. 2001. 25.00 (*1-884592-27-9*) Images from the Past.

Murray, Stuart. Norman Rockwell at Home in Vermont: The Arlington Years, 1939-1953. LC 96-35007. (Illus.). 96p. 1997. pap. 14.95 (*1-884592-02-3*) Images from the Past.

— Rudyard Kipling in Vermont: Birthplace of The Jungle Books. LC 97-18692. (Illus.). 208p. 1997. 29.00 (*1-884592-04-X*); pap. 18.95 (*1-884592-05-8*) Images from the Past.

— The Shaker Heritage Guidebook: Exploring the Historic Sites, Museums & Collections. LC 93-79992. (Illus.). 261p. (Orig.). 1994. pap. 15.95 (*0-9614876-6-6*) Golden Hl Pr NY.

Murray, Stuart. The Tinman & the Scarecrow. (Illus.). 256p. 25.00 (*1-884592-26-0*) Images from the Past.

Murray, Stuart. Washington's Farewell: The Final Parting With His Officers after Victory in the Revolution. LC 99-43620. (Illus.). 200p. 1999. 21.00 (*1-884592-20-1*) Images from the Past.

***Murray, Stuart.** White Fire. 364p. 2000. 25.00 (*1-884592-25-2*, Pub. by Images from the Past) Koen Bk Distributors.

Murray, Stuart, ed. Not on Any Map: Essays on Postcoloniality & Cultural Nationalism. 192p. 1997. pap. 19.95 (*0-85989-468-1*, Pub. by Univ Exeter Pr) Northwestern U Pr.

Murray, Stuart & McCabe, James. Norman Rockwell's Four Freedoms: Images That Inspired a Nation. LC 93-3545. (Illus.). 176p. 1993. pap. 14.95 (*0-936399-42-2*) Berkshire Hse.

Murray, Stuart, jt. auth. see Keighley, Brian.

Murray, Stuart, jt. auth. see Rockwell, Norman.

Murray, Sue, jt. auth. see Haus, Cari.

Murray, Susan. Birds of Bookhaven. LC 96-95476. 192p. 1997. 18.95 (*0-8034-9227-8*, Avalon Bks) Bouregy.

— Mayhem on Maui. (KC Flanagan Girl Detective Ser.). 1999. pap. 5.99 (*1-55207-022-0*) Genl Dist Srvs.

***Murray, Susan & Davies, Robert.** Outrage in Orlando. 192p. 2000. pap. 5.99 (*1-55207-023-9*) R Davies Pub.

Murray, Susan F. Baby Friendly/Mother Friendly. 1996. mass mkt. 24.00 (*0-7234-2123-4*) Mosby Inc.

Murray, T., jt. auth. see Murray, I.

Murray, T. C. Selected Plays. Cave, Richard Allen, ed. LC 98-40763. (Irish Drama Selections Ser.: No. 10). 274p. 1999. 49.95 (*0-8132-0935-8*); pap. 16.95 (*0-8132-0936-6*) Cath U Pr.

Murray, T. J., jt. ed. see Huth, Edward J.

Murray, T. P. & Horn, R. C. Organic Nitrogen Compounds for Use As Fertilizers. (Technical Bulletin Ser.: No. T-14). 64p. (Orig.). 1979. pap. 4.00 (*0-88090-013-X*) Intl Fertilizer.

Murray, T. S., ed. Modified Essay Questions for the MRCGP Examination. LC 95-34949. 204p. 1995. pap. 29.95 (*0-86542-646-5*) Blackwell Sci.

***Murray, T. Scott.** Adult Literacy in OECD Countries: Technical Report on the First International Adult Literacy Survey. 483p. 1998. pap. 39.00 (*0-16-049372-2*) USGPO.

Murray, Tamela H. Clean Jokes for Kids. (Young Reader's Activities Bks.). 192p. (J). (gr. 3-7). 1998. pap. 1.39 (*1-57748-186-0*) Barbour Pub.

Murray, Tamela H., jt. auth. see Harmon, Dan.

***Murray, Tamela Hancock.** Great Bible Trivia for Kids. (Young Reader's Christian Library). (Illus.). 224p. (J). (gr. 3-7). 2000. pap. 1.39 (*1-57748-655-2*) Barbour Pub.

Murray, Ted, jt. auth. see O'Meara, David.

Murray, Teresa G., Sr. Vocational Guidance in Catholic Secondary Schools: A Study of Developments & Present Status. LC 77-177098. (Columbia University. Teachers College. Contributions to Education Ser.: No. 754). reprint ed. 37.50 (*0-404-55754-6*) AMS Pr.

Murray, Terry. The I. U. Cookbook. 150p. 1993. 18.95 (*1-878208-33-0*); pap. 14.95 (*1-878208-28-4*) Guild Pr IN.

Murray, Terry & McClure, Michael. Moral Panic: Exposing the Religious Right's Agenda on Sexuality. 64p. 1995. pap. 5.95 (*0-304-33327-1*) Bks Intl VA.

Murray, Thelma & McClanahan Book Co., Inc. Staff. Kittens, 12 vols. (Storyshapes Ser.). (Illus.). 24p. (J). 1998. 2.25 (*1-56293-908-4*, McClanahan Book) Learn Horizon.

***Murray, Theresa, ed.** Rehabilitation Sourcebook. (Health Reference Ser.). (Illus.). 1999. lib. bdg. 78.00 (*0-7808-0236-5*) Omnigraphics Inc.

Murray, Thom & Wiley, Linda. Staying Power: How to Get the B. S. Out of College (or the B. A. or the Degree of Your Choice) LC 93-35802. (Practical Guide Ser.: No. 2). 167p. (Orig.). 1994. pap. 18.95 (*0-929398-65-3*) UNTX Pr.

Murray, Thomas. Pitcairn's Island. LC 72-281. (World History Ser.: No. 48). 1972. reprint ed. lib. bdg. 75.00 (*0-8383-1410-4*) M S G Haskell Hse.

— Reclaiming Christian Piety. 1993. pap. 6.95 (*1-55673-548-0*, 7972) CSS OH.

Murray, Thomas B. Par Choix: The Remarkable Life Story of Philippe. LC 93-24253. 192p. (Orig.). 1994. pap. 10.95 (*1-56474-069-2*) Fithian Pr.

Murray, Thomas E. & Murrell, Thomas R. The Language of Sadomasochism: A Glossary & Linguistic Analysis. LC 88-25099. 208p. 1989. lib. bdg. 69.50 (*0-313-26481-3*, MYD/, Greenwood Pr) Greenwood.

Murray, Thomas E. & Ross-Murray, Carmin D., eds. Under Cover of Law: More on the Legality of Surreptitiousrecording. LC 96-7062. (Publications of the American Dialect Society: No. 79). 328p. 1997. pap. text 19.95 (*0-8173-0857-1*) U of Ala Pr.

Murray, Thomas E. & Ross-Murray, Carmin O., eds. Under Cover of Law: More on the Legality of Surreptitious Recording. LC 96-7062. (Publications of the American Dialect Society: No. 79). 80p. 1996. pap. text 12.00 (*0-8173-0825-3*) U of Ala Pr.

Murray, Thomas E., et al. Legal & Ethical Issues in Surreptitious Recording. LC 90-26320. (Publications of American Dialect Society: No. 76). 88p. 1992. pap. text 11.00 (*0-8173-0540-8*) U of Ala Pr.

Murray, Thomas H. Irish Rhode Islanders in the American Revolution. 90p. 1998. pap. 13.00 (*0-7884-0794-5*, M869) Heritage Bk.

— Irish Rhode Islanders in the American Revolution. (Illus.). 90p. 1997. reprint ed. pap. 17.00 (*0-8328-6470-6*) Higginson Bk Co.

— The Worth of a Child. LC 95-46977. 214p. (C). 1996. 29.95 (*0-520-08836-0*, Pub. by U CA Pr) Cal Prin Full Svc.

Murray, Thomas H., ed. The Journal of the American-Irish Historical Society, Vol. 1, 1898. (Illus.). 140p. 1991. reprint ed. pap. 15.00 (*1-55613-432-0*) Heritage Bk.

Murray, Thomas H., et al, eds. Feeling Good & Doing Better: Ethics & Nontherapeutic Drug Use. LC 84-4552. (Contemporary Issues in Biomedicine, Ethics, & Society Ser.). 238p. 1984. 49.50 (*0-89603-061-X*) Humana.

— The Human Genome Project & the Future of Health Care. LC 96-1718. (Medical Ethics Ser.). (Illus.). 264p. 1996. 29.95 (*0-253-33213-3*) Ind U Pr.

Murray, Thomas H. & Caplan, Arthur L., eds. Which Babies Shall Live? Humanistic Dimensions of the Care of Imperiled Newborns. LC 85-18058. (Contemporary Issues in Biomedicine, Ethics, & Society Ser.). 238p. 1985. 49.50 (*0-89603-086-5*) Humana.

Murray, Thomas H. & Mehlman, Maxwell J. Encyclopedia of Ethical, Legal & Policy Issues in Biotechnology, 3 Vols. 2250p. 2000. 750.00 (*0-471-17612-5*) Wiley.

Murray, Thomas J., jt. auth. see Bryson, Reid A.

Murray, Thomas M. & Hymer, David M. Real Property & Commercial Transactions Deadlines Pt. 6: Summer 1992, Action Guide. Stein, Carolyn J., ed. (Meeting Statutory Deadlines Ser.). 78p. 1992. pap. text 47.00 (*0-88124-557-7*, RE-11412) Cont Ed Bar-CA.

Murray, Thomson C. License Plate Book: 1997 Edition. annuals rev. ed. (Annual Ser.). (Illus.). 130p. 1997. pap. 16.95 (*1-886777-01-2*) Inter Directory.

— License Plate Games. 1993. pap. 3.95 (*0-87131-749-4*) M Evans.

***Murray, Thomson C.** The Official License Plate Book: New Edition. (Illus.). 128p. 2000. pap. 16.95 (*1-886777-03-9*, 130115AE, Pub. by Inter Directory) Motorbooks Intl.

Murray, Thomson C. The Official License Plate Book, 1996. (Illus.). 128p. 1996. pap. 12.95 (*0-9629962-8-9*) Inter Directory.

— The Official License Plate Book, 1996: Current Plates of the United States & Canada. (Illus.). 128p. 1996. 16.95 (*0-9629962-9-7*) Inter Directory.

— Road Sign Games. 1993. pap. 3.95 (*0-87131-750-8*) M Evans.

— Truck Games. 1993. pap. 3.95 (*0-87131-748-6*) M Evans.

Murray, Thomson C. & Wiener, Michael C. License Plate Book: How to Read & Decode Plates from All 50 States. 7th ed. (Illus.). 128p. (J). (gr. 2-12). 1992. reprint ed. pap. 12.95 (*0-87131-710-9*) M Evans.

***Murray, Tim.** Encyclopedia of Archaeology: Histories & Discoveries, 3 vols. (Encyclopedia of Archaeology Ser.: Vol. 2). (Illus.). 1800p. 2000. lib. bdg. 275.00 (*1-57607-198-7*) ABC-CLIO.

— Encyclopedia of Archaeology: The Great Archaeologists, 2 vols. LC 99-52159. (Illus.). 950p. 1999. lib. bdg. 150.00 (*1-57607-199-5*) ABC-CLIO.

— Milestones in Archaeology: An Encyclopedia. 2001. lib. bdg. 99.00 (*1-57607-186-3*) ABC-CLIO.

Murray, Tim. Time & Archaeology. LC 99-18440. (One World Archaeology Ser.). 1999. text. write for info. (*0-415-11762-3*) Routledge.

***Murray, Tim, ed.** Archaeology of Aboriginal Australia: A Reader. LC 98-217191. (Illus.). 376p. 1999. pap. 39.95 (*1-86448-066-1*, Pub. by Allen & Unwin Pty) Paul & Co Pubs.

Murray, Tim, ed. The Oxford History of Australia: Aboriginal Australia, Vol. 1. (Illus.). 360p. Date not set. 39.00 (*0-19-554609-1*) OUP.

Murray, Timothy. Drama Trauma: Specters of Race & Sexuality in Performance, Video & Art. LC 97-6184. (Illus.). 320p. (C). 1997. 85.00 (*0-415-15788-9*); pap. 24.99 (*0-415-15789-7*) Routledge.

— Like a Film: Ideological Fantasy on Screen, Camera, & Canvas. LC 93-17147. (Illus.). 272p. (C). 1993. pap. 21.99 (*0-415-07734-6*) Routledge.

— Repossessions: Psychoanalysis & the Phantasms of Early Modern Culture. LC 98-2998. 1998. 54.95 (*0-8166-2960-9*); pap. 21.95 (*0-8166-2961-7*) U of Minn Pr.

Murray, Timothy, ed. Mimesis, Masochism, & Mime: The Politics of Theatricality in Contemporary French Thought. LC 97-601. 328p. (C). 1997. text 52.50 (*0-472-09635-4*, 09635); pap. text 21.95 (*0-472-06635-8*, 06635) U of Mich Pr.

Murray, Timothy D., et al. A Colour Atlas of Diseases of Small Grain Cereal Crops. LC 98-198495. (Illus.). 192p. (C). 1998. text 49.95 (*0-8138-2529-6*) Iowa St U Pr.

An Asterisk (*) at the beginning of an entry indicates that the title is appearing for the first time.

Murray, Tinker D. & Rainey, Don. Fundamentals of Physical Fitness. LC 96-4956. (J). 1996. mass mkt. 39.50 (0-314-08465-7) West Pub.

Murray, Tom. Estimation Exploration. (Illus.). 62p. (J). (gr. 3-8). 1993. pap. text 8.95 (1-882293-02-9, A-1690) Activity Resources.

— Waterfront Supercargo. (Little Bks.). 59p. (Orig.). 1980. pap. 2.25 (0-917300-10-6) Singlejack Bks.

Murray, Toni, ed. see Barth, William.

Murray, Toni, ed. see Lesko, Matthew.

Murray, Toni, ed. see Spencer, Ernest.

Murray, Tracy, Associates Staff, jt. ed. see Walter, Ingo.

Murray, Valton. The Tale of the Old Maypop Tree: A Southern Folktale. rev. ed. LC 96-92600. 45p. 1998. pap. 13.00 (0-9655726-7-6) Proud Two-B Me.

Murray, Van A. Are You on the Menu. (Orig.). 1997. mass mkt. 10.00 (0-9653688-2-3) P & P Ent.

Murray, Venetia. An Elegant Madness: High Society in Regency England. LC 98-31589. (Illus.). 316p. 1999. 29.95 (0-670-88328-X) Viking Penguin.

***Murray, Venetia.** An Elegant Madness: High Society in Regency England. (Illus.). 352p. 2000. pap. 14.95 (0-14-028296-3, Penguin Bks) Viking Penguin.

Murray, Venetia. Shadows from the Past. (C). 1988. 75.00 (1-85219-060-4, Pub. by Bishopsgate Pr Ltd) St Mut.

Murray, Vernon Q., ed. see Murray, Samuel M.

Murray, Victor V., jt. auth. see Cutt, James.

Murray, Victoria Christopher. Collection of Conscious Poetry. LC 98-169369. 123p. 1997. pap. 12.95 (1-881524-11-6) Milligan Bks.

Murray, W. Adventure at the Castle. (Key Words Readers Ser.: B Series, No. 641-10b). (Illus.). (J). (ps-5). pap. 3.50 (0-7214-0022-1, Ladybrd) Penguin Putnam.

— Animals, Birds & Fish. (Sunstart Ser.: No. 747-4). (Illus.). 50p. (J). (ps-5). 3.50 (0-7214-8003-9, Ladybrd) Penguin Putnam.

— The Big House. (Key Words Readers Ser.: B Series, No. 641-8b). (Illus.). (J). (ps-5). pap. 3.50 (0-7214-0544-4, Ladybrd) Penguin Putnam.

— More Sounds to Say. (Key Words Readers Ser.: C Series, No. 641-5c). (Illus.). (J). (ps-5). pap. 3.50 (0-7214-0029-9, Ladybrd) Penguin Putnam.

— Mountain Adventure. (Key Words Readers Ser.: B Series, No. 641-12b). (Illus.). (J). (ps-5). pap. 3.50 (0-7214-0024-8, Ladybrd) Penguin Putnam.

— The Old Firm: Sectarianism, Sport & Society in Scotland. 3rd ed. (Illus.). 304p. (C). 1996. pap. 50.00 (0-85976-121-5, Pub. by J Donald) St Mut.

— On the Beach. (Sunstart Ser.: No. 747-2). (Illus.). 50p. (J). (ps-5). 3.50 (0-7214-8001-2, Ladybrd) Penguin Putnam.

— Open Door to Reading. (Key Words Readers Ser.: C Series, No. 641-12c). (Illus.). (J). (ps-5). pap. 3.50 (0-7214-0036-1, Ladybrd) Penguin Putnam.

— We Like to Help. (Key Words Readers Ser.: B Series, No. 641 6b). (Illus.). (J). (ps-5) pap. 3.50 (0-7214-0542-8, Ladybrd) Penguin Putnam.

Murray, W. Cotter. Irish Fictions. 128p. 1994. pap. 14.95 (0-944266-18-5) Maecenas Pr.

Murray, W. H. Holiday Tales: Christmas in the Adirondacks. LC 96-148471. (Illus.). 118p. 1995. 25.00 (0-925168-02-5) North Country.

— Rob Roy MacGregor: His Life & Times. 288p. 1996. pap. 11.95 (0-86241-538-1, Pub. by Canongate Books) Interlink Pub.

Murray, W. J., jt. ed. see Gilchrist, W.

Murray, W. John. Astor Lectures (1917) 340p. 1998. reprint ed. pap. 27.95 (0-7661-0577-6) Kessinger Pub.

Murray, Wallace J., jt. ed. see Miller, Lucinda G.

Murray, Wayne A., ed. see Valenti, Vince & Jaeger, Jag.

Murray, Wendy, ed. see Tully, Marianne & Scholastic, Inc. Staff.

***Murray, Will.** Nick Fury, Agent of Shield: Empyre. 1999. mass mkt. 6.50 (0-425-16816-6) Berkley Pub.

Murray, Will, jt. auth. see Stockbridge, Grant.

Murray, Will, ed. see Long, Frank B., et al.

Murray, Will, ed. see Smith, Clark A.

Murray, William. Automatic Program Debugging for Intelligent Tutoring Systems. (Research Notes in Artificial Intelligence Ser.). 347p. (C). 1988. pap. text 34.95 (0-934613-98-2) Morgan Kaufmann.

— A Fine Italian Hand: A Shifty Lou Anderson Mystery. LC 95-49582. 256p. 1996. 21.00 (0-87131-797-4) M Evans.

***Murray, William.** Janet, My Mother & Me: A Memoir of Growing Up with Janet Flanner & Natalia Danesi Murray. LC 99-45317. (Illus.). 224p. 2000. 24.00 (0-684-80966-4) S&S Trade.

Murray, William. My Life Without God. enl. rev. ed. LC 92-10586. 1992. mass mkt. 5.99 (1-56507-029-1) Harvest Hse.

***Murray, William.** My Life Without God: The Rest of the Story. 375p. 2000. pap. 11.99 (0-7369-0315-1) Harvest Hse.

Murray, William. Now You See Her, Now You Don't. LC 94-13433. 1995. 22.00 (0-8050-2971-0) H Holt & Co.

— Picture Word Cards. (Read with Me Key Words to Reading Ser.). (J). (ps-2). 1991. pap. 9.95 (0-7214-3232-8, 9113, Ladybrd) Penguin Putnam.

— A Slick Italian Hand. 1995. 22.50 (0-8050-2972-9) H Holt & Co.

— Using Visual Basic. 432p. 1991. pap. 34.95 (0-201-58145-0) Addison-Wesley.

— The Wrong Horse: An Odyssey Through the American Racing Scene. LC 92-15250. 1992. pap. 20.00 (0-671-76774-7) S&S Trade.

Murray, William & Millett, Allan R., eds. Calculations: Net Assessment & the Coming of World War II. 350p. 1992. 40.00 (0-02-921585-4) Free Pr.

***Murray, William & Pappas, Chris.** Visual C++ Templates. (Series on Microsoft Technology). 850p. 1999. pap. 49.99 (0-13-022487-1) P-H.

Murray, William, jt. auth. see Pappas, Chris.

Murray, William D. And You Didn't Think You Had a Prayer. 1993. pap. 8.95 (1-878287-03-6) Type & Temperament.

— Give Yourself the Unfair Advantage: A Serious Practical Guide to Understanding Human Personality That Will Have You Rolling in the Aisles. 1995. pap. 14.95 (1-878287-02-8) Type & Temperament.

— An Introduction to Personality Type Seminar Kit: Based on the Book, "Give Yourself the Unfair Advantage" (Illus.). 185p. 1996. ring bd. 298.00 (1-878287-18-4) Type & Temperament.

— An Introduction to the 4 Temperaments Seminar Kit: Based on the Book, "Give Yourself the Unfair Advantage" (Illus.). 78p. 1996. ring bd. 149.95 (1-878287-19-2) Type & Temperament.

Murray, William D. & Murray, Rosalie R. Introduction to Psychological Type Seminar Kit: An Introduction to Yourself. rev. ed. 145p. 1995. ring bd. 119.95 (1-878287-10-9) Type & Temperament.

— Oppositeness Seminar Kit: How Opposite Personalities Interact. rev. ed. 115p. 1995. ring bd. 119.95 (1-878287-12-5) Type & Temperament.

— Thinkers & Feelers Mini Seminar Kit. rev. ed. (Type & Temperament Seminar Kits Ser.). 83p. 1995. ring bd. 99.95 (1-878287-13-3) Type & Temperament.

— Type & Your Career Seminar Kit: Using Type in Career Selection. rev. ed. 1995. ring bd. 159.95 (1-878287-15-X) Type & Temperament.

— Type Communications Seminar Kit: Using Type to Enhance Organizational & Interpersonal Communication. rev. ed. 130p. 1995. ring bd. 139.95 (1-878287-11-7) Type & Temperament.

— When ENFP & INFJ Interact. (When Types Interact Ser.). 56p. 1987. pap. 9.95 (1-878287-00-1) Type & Temperament.

Murray, William D. & Rigney, Francis J. Fun with Paper Folding & Origami. LC 95-25133. (Game & Puzzle Activity Bks.). 1995. 1.00 (0-486-28810-2) Dover.

Murray, William D. & Walsh, Peter. Type & Team Development Seminar Kit: Using Type to Unleash the Power of Your Team. rev. ed. (Type & Temperament Seminar Kits Ser.). 160p. 1996. ring bd. 159.95 (1-878287-14-1) Type & Temperament.

Murray, William D., et al. The Works - One of Everything: Psychological Type & Temperament Training & Counseling Materials. 124p. 1990. ring bd. 87.50 (1-878287-17-6) Type & Temperament.

Murray, William G., et al. Farm Appraisal & Valuation. 6th ed. LC 83-8408. (Illus.). 304p. 1983. text 41.95 (0-8138-0570-8) Iowa St U Pr.

Murray, William G., jt. ed. see Timmons, John F.

Murray, William H. Adventures in the Wilderness. Verner, William K., ed. LC 72-132972. (Illus.). 332p. 1989. reprint ed. pap. text 16.95 (0-8156-2466-2) Syracuse U Pr.

Murray, William H., 3rd. Borland C++ in Depth. LC 96-165055. 896p. 1996. pap. text 39.95 (0-07-882216-5) McGraw.

Murray, William H. C++ Programmer's Guide. LC 96-121383. 976p. 1995. pap. 39.95 incl. disk (1-56276-361-X, Ziff-Davis Pr) Que.

***Murray, William H.** HTML 4.0 User's Resource. LC 99-207045. 650p. (C). 1998. pap. text 34.99 (0-13-927104-X) P-H.

Murray, William H. Turbo Pascal for Windows Programming: The Complete Guide to Developing Windows Applications. 1994. pap. write for info. (0-201-58118-3) Addison-Wesley.

Murray, William H., 3rd & Pappas, Chris H. Cross-Platform Programming for Windows. 850p. 1995. pap. text 39.95 (0-07-882177-0) McGraw.

***Murray, William H. & Pappas, Chris H.** Introducing Windows 98 Programming. LC 99-24535. (Prentice Hall Series on Microsoft Technologies). (Illus.). 576p. 1999. pap. text 44.99 (0-13-012202-5) P-H.

Murray, William H. & Pappas, Chris H. Mfc Programmg In C++ W/Standard Templte Lib. 550p. (C). 2000. pap. 44.99 (0-13-016111-X) P-H.

Murray, William H., III & Pappas, Chris H. Microsoft C - C++ 7: The Complete Reference. 1008p. 1992. pap. 29.95 (0-07-881664-5) Osborne-McGraw.

— OLE Wizardry: Programming OLE Applications & Custom Controls Using Wizards. 448p. 1995. pap. text 39.95 (0-07-882102-9) Osborne-McGraw.

Murray, William H. & Pappas, Chris H. The Visual Basic 5 Training Guide. LC 97-10938. 1997. 1.95 (0-12-511906-2) Acad Pr.

— Visual Basic Programming with the Windows API. LC 98-9336. 656p. (C). 1998. pap. text 44.95 (0-13-095082-3) P-H.

— Visual Basic 5 Training Guide. (Training Guides Ser.). (Illus.). 532p. (C). 1997. pap., pap. text 49.95 incl. cd-rom (0-12-511905-4) Morgan Kaufmann.

Murray, William H., III & Pappas, Chris H. Visual C++5: The Complete Reference. (Illus.). 1008p. (Orig.). 1997. pap. text 39.99 (0-07-882391-9, Oracle Press) Osborne-McGraw.

Murray, William J. The Church Is Not for Perfect People. 175p. (Orig.). 1987. pap. 6.95 (0-614-13898-1) MFM Publish.

***Murray, William J.** The Church Is Not for Perfect People. 3rd ed. (Orig.). 2000. reprint ed. pap. 9.95 (0-940917-05-X) MFM Publish.

Murray, William J. The Complete Constitution of the United States of America. (Orig.). 1986. pap. 4.95 (0-940917-01-7) MFM Publish.

— Football: A History of the World Game. LC 94-15190. 297p. 1994. 69.95 (1-85928-091-9, Pub. by Scolar Pr) Ashgate Pub Co.

***Murray, William J.** Let Us Pray: A Plea for Prayer in Our Schools. 205p. 1999. reprint ed. text 20.00 (0-7881-6651-4) DIANE Pub.

Murray, William J. Nicaragua: Portrait of a Tragedy. 128p. 1987. pap. 6.95 (0-940917-03-3) MFM Publish.

— The Right-Wing Press in the French Revolution, 1789-1792, No. 44. (Royal Historical Society: Studies in History). 357p. 1986. 75.00 (0-86193-201-3) Boydell & Brewer.

— Uncommon Sense: The Real American Manifesto. LC 94-27822. 383p. (Orig.). 1994. pap. text 6.95 (0-922356-95-5) Amer West Pubs.

***Murray, William J. & Armstrong, Robert.** Stop the Y2K Madness! Murray, Nancy M., ed. (Orig.). 1999. pap. 5.95 (0-940917-04-1) MFM Publish.

Murray, William M. Octavian's Campsite Memorial for the Actian War. LC 89-84932. (Transactions Ser.: Vol. 79, Pt. 4). (Illus.). 161p. 1989. pap. 18.00 (0-87169-794-7, T794-MUW) Am Philos.

Murray, William M., Jr. Thomas W. Martin: A Biography. LC 77-85483. (Illus.). 276p. 1978. 6.50 (0-940824-01-9) S Res Inst.

Murray, William M. & Miller, William R. The Bonded Electrical Resistance Strain Gage. (Illus.). 424p. 1992. text 85.00 (0-19-507209-X) OUP.

Murray, William S. Making of the Balkan States. LC 10-17934. (Columbia University. Studies in the Social Sciences: No. 102). reprint ed. 24.50 (0-404-51102-3) AMS Pr.

Murray, Williamson. Brassey's Mershon American Defense Annual, 1995-96. 272p. 1995. 55.00 (1-57488-037-3); pap. 22.00 (1-57488-038-1) Brasseys.

— Brassey's Mershon American Defense Annual, 1997-98. 368p. Date not set. pap. 27.50 (1-57488-115-9) Brasseys.

— The Change in the European Balance of Power, 1938-1939: The Path to Ruin. LC 83-43085. 515p. 1984. reprint ed. pap. 159.70 (0-7837-9280-8, 206001900004) Bks Demand.

Murray, Williamson. Gulf War Air Power Survey: Operations & Effects & Effectiveness, V. 2. 833p. 1993. per. 49.00 (0-16-042910-2) USGPO.

Murray, Williamson. The Luftwaffe, 1933-45: Strategy for Defeat. 391p. 1983. per. 12.00 (0-16-002160-X) USGPO.

— The Luftwaffe, 1933-45: Strategy for Defeat. (Illus.). 392p. 1996. reprint ed. pap. 22.95 (1-57488-125-6) Brasseys.

Murray, Williamson. Strategy for Defeat: The Luftwaffe, 1933-1945. (Illus.). 391p. pap. 12.00 (1-58566-010-8) Air Univ.

Murray, Williamson. War in the Air: 1914-45. LC 99-495003. (Illus.). 224p. 1999. 29.95 (0-304-35223-3, Pub. by Cassell) Sterling.

Murray, Williamson, ed. The Emerging Strategic Environment: Challenges of the Twenty-First Century. LC 99-39745. 360p. 1999. 59.95 (0-275-96573 2, Praeger Pubs) Greenwood.

Murray, Williamson, et al, eds. The Making of Strategy: Rules, States & War. (Illus.). 696p. (C). 1994. text 54.95 (0-521-45389-5) Cambridge U Pr.

— The Making of Strategy: Rules, States & War. (Illus.). 704p. 1996. pap. text 20.95 (0-521-56627-4) Cambridge U Pr.

Murray, Williamson & Millett, Allan R. Brassey's Mershon American Defense Annual, 1996-97: Current Issues & the Asian Challenge. (Illus.). 320p. 1996. 55.00 (1-57488-096-9); pap. 22.00 (1-57488-098-5) Brasseys.

***Murray, Williamson & Millett, Allan R.** A War to Be Won: Fighting the Second World War, 1937-1945. LC 99-86624. (Illus.). 640p. 2000. pap. text 35.00 (0-674-00163-X) HUP.

Murray, Williamson & Millett, Allan R., eds. Military Innovation in the Interwar Period. 442p. (C). 1996. text 74.95 (0-521-55241-9) Cambridge U Pr.

Murray, Williamson & Thompson, Wayne W. Air War in the Persian Gulf. 1995. 34.95 (1-877853-36-4) Nautical & Aviation.

Murray, Williamson, jt. ed. see Millett, Allan R.

Murray, Winifred. A Socio-Cultural Study of 118 Mexican Families Living in a Low-Rent Public Housing Project in San Antonio, Texas. Cortes, Carlos E., ed. LC 76-1275. (Chicano Heritage Ser.). 1977. reprint ed. lib. bdg. 17.95 (0-405-09515-5) Ayer.

Murray-Wooley, Carolyn & Raitz, Karl B. Rock Fences of the Bluegrass. LC 91-22584. (Illus.). 240p. 1992. 35.00 (0-8131-1762-3) U Pr of Ky.

Murray, Yxta M. Locas: A Novel. 256p. 1998. reprint ed. pap. 12.00 (0-8021-3564-1, Grove) Grove-Atltic.

Murray, Yxta Maya. What It Takes to Get to Vegas. LC 98-50766. 320p. 1999. 24.00 (0-8021-1642-6, Grove) Grove-Atltic.

***Murray, Yxta Maya.** What It Takes to Get to Vegas. 2000. pap. 12.00 (0-8021-3737-7, Grove) Grove-Atltic.

Murre, Jaap, jt. ed. see Broeder, Peter.

Murre, Jacob. Learning & Categorization in Modular Neural Networks. 250p. 1992. pap. 29.95 (0-8058-1338-1); text 49.95 (0-8058-1337-3) L Erlbaum Assocs.

Murrell, Audrey J., et al, eds. Mentoring Dilemmas: Developmental Relationships Within Multicultural Organizations. LC 98-24654. (Applied Social Research Ser.). 280p. 1999. 59.95 (0-8058-2632-7); pap. 29.95 (0-8058-2633-5) L Erlbaum Assocs.

Murrell, Dan & Dwyer, William. Constitutional Law & Liability for Agents, Deputies & Police Officers. LC 92-73633. 192p. 1992. pap. 15.00 (0-89089-521-X) Carolina Acad Pr.

— Constitutional Law & Liability for Public-Sector Police: Airports, Port Authorities, Public Medical Facilities, Public Colleges & Universities. LC 92-71442. 198p. 1992. pap. 15.00 (0-89089-502-3) Carolina Acad Pr.

Murrell, Dan S. Constitutional Law Outline for the Fourth & Fifth Amendments of the United States Constitution. LC 96-83984. 72p. (Orig.). 1996. per. 8.50 (0-89089-868-5) Carolina Acad Pr.

Murrell, Dan S. & Dwyer, William O. Constitutional Law & Liability for Park Law Enforcement Officers. 3rd ed. LC 91-75951. 192p. (C). 1991. pap. text 15.00 (0-89089-474-4) Carolina Acad Pr.

Murrell, G. D. Russia's Transition to Democracy: An Internal Political History. LC 97-123517. 288p. 1996. 69.95 (1-898723-57-5, Pub. by Sussex Acad Pr) Intl Spec Bk.

— Russia's Transition to Democracy: An Internal Political History, 1989-1996 LC 97-123517. xii, 276p. 1997. write for info. (1-898723-58-3) Sussex Acad Pr.

***Murrell, Gary.** Iron Pants: Oregon's Anti-New Deal Governor, Charles Henry Martin. (Illus.). 250p. 2000. pap. 22.95 (0-87422-196-X) Wash St U Pr.

***Murrell, George, et al.** Research in Medicine: Planning a Project, Writing a Thesis. 2nd ed. LC 98-40501. (Studies in the History of Psychology). (Illus.). 105p. (C). 1999. pap. text 21.95 (0-521-62670-6) Cambridge U Pr.

Murrell, Gina, jt. auth. see Sell, Peter.

Murrell, J. C. & Dalton, H. Methane & Methanol Utilizers. (Biotechnology Handbooks Ser.: Vol. 5). (Illus.). 304p. (C). 1992. text 79.50 (0-306-43878-X, Kluwer Plenum) Kluwer Academic.

Murrell, J. C. & Roberts, L. M., eds. Understanding Genetic Engineering. 1989. text 36.95 (0-470-21453-8) P-H.

Murrell, J. Colin & Kelly, Donovan P., eds. Microbiology of Atmospheric Trace Gases: Sources, Sinks & Global Change Processes. LC 95-45667. (NATO ASI Series I: Global Environmental Change: Vol. 39). 306p. 1996. 141.00 (3-540-60612-2) Spr-Verlag.

Murrell, J. N. & Bosanac, S. D. Introduction to the Theory of Atomic & Molecular Collisions. LC 89-9017. 208p. 1989. 325.00 (0-471-92365-6) Wiley.

Murrell, J. N. & Jenkins, A. D. Properties of Liquids & Solutions. 2nd ed. 316p. 1994. pap. 69.95 (0-471-94419-X) Wiley.

Murrell, John. Democracy: A Play. 64p. 1992. pap. 10.95 (0-921368-28-3) Blizzard Publ.

— The Faraway Nearby. 64p. 1996. pap. 10.95 (0-921368-56-9) Blizzard Publ.

***Murrell, John.** The Faraway Nearby: Acting Edition. 49p. 1998. pap. 10.00 (0-929741-44-7) Playsmith.

Murrell, John. Memoir. 124p. 1990. 10.00 (0-317-91357-3) Playsmith.

— The Seagull: A New Version. 57p. (Orig.). 1989. 7.95 (0-317-91355-7) Playsmith.

***Murrell, John.** Uncle Vanya. 76p. 1999. pap. 10.00 (0-929741-46-3) Playsmith.

— Waiting for the Parade. 112p. (Orig.). 1980. pap. 11.95 (0-88922-183-9, Pub. by Talonbks) Genl Dist Srvs.

Murrell, John, tr. from RUS. Uncle Vanya: A New Version. 57p. (Orig.). 1990. 7.95 (0 317-91358-1) Playsmith.

Murrell, John, et al. Heroines. Doolittle, Joyce, ed. LC 92-54101. 192p. 1992. pap. 10.95 (0-88734-624-3); pap. 13.00 (0-88995-081-4, Pub. by Red Deer) Empire Pub Srvs.

Murrell, John N. & Boucher, E. A. Properties of Liquids & Solutions. LC 81-21921. 298p. reprint ed. pap. 92.40 (0-8357-6983-6, 205236000009) Bks Demand.

Murrell, John N. & Harget, A. J. Semi-Empirical Self-Consistent-Field Molecular Orbital Theory of Molecules. LC 71-172470. (Illus.). 190p. reprint ed. pap. 58.90 (0-608-17675-3, 203039200069) Bks Demand.

Murrell, John N. & Jenkins, A. D. Properties of Liquids & Solutions. 2nd ed. LC 93-46721. (Illus.). 315p. 1994. reprint ed. pap. 97.70 (0-608-05294-9, 206583200001) Bks Demand.

Murrell, John N., et al. The Chemical Bond. 2nd ed. LC 85-6383. (Illus.). 345p. reprint ed. pap. 107.00 (0-7837-1875-6, 204207600001) Bks Demand.

— Molecular Potential Energy Functions. LC 84-11821 (Illus.). 205p. 1984. reprint ed. pap. 63.60 (0-608-06822-5, 206701900009) Bks Demand.

— Valence Theory. 2nd ed. LC 70-129161. 444p. reprint ed. pap. 137.70 (0-608-16351-1, 202668800051) Bks Demand.

Murrell, Kathleen B. Moscow Art Nouveau. (Illus.). 160p. 1997. 65.00 (0-85667-488-5, Pub. by P Wilson) Antique Collect.

***Murrell, Kathleen B.** Russia. (Eyewitness Books). (Illus.). (J). (gr. 4-7). 2000. 19.99 (0-7894-6623-6) DK Pub Inc.

— Russia. LC 97-38878. (Illus.). 59p. (YA). (gr. 5 up). 1998. 19.00 (0-679-89118-8) Knopf.

— Russia. LC 97-38878. (Eyewitness Books). (Illus.). 59p. (YA). (gr. 5 up). 1998. lib. bdg. 20.99 (0-679-99118-2) Random.

***Murrell, Kathleen Berto.** Russia. (Eyewitness Books). (J). (gr. 4-7). 2000. 15.95 (0-7894-5880-2) DK Pub Inc.

Murrell, Larry L., jt. ed. see Baker, R. Terry.

Murrell, Patricia H., jt. auth. see Claxton, Charles S.

Murrell, Patricia H., jt. auth. see Davis, Todd M.

Murrell, Peter C., Jr. Like Stone Soup: The Role of the Professional Development School in the Renewal of Urban Schools. 64p. 1998. pap. 24.95 (0-89333-167-8) AACTE.

Murrell, Rachel. Sharpe's Victory: The Story of a Hero's Triumph. (Illus.). 144p. 1998. pap. text 22.95 (1-56649-008-1) Welcome Rain.

Murrell, Robert T. How to Find Anyone Free at Your Local Library: Including Veterans of WWII, Korea, Vietnam, Granada, Panama, Gulf War & Your Former Classmates. 150p. 1998. pap. 30.00 (0-938609-27-0) Graduate Group.

Murrell, Sandra, jt. auth. see Olsen, Paul T.

Murrell, Thomas R., jt. auth. see Murray, Thomas E.

M

Murrell, Virginia. Love Always, Ginner. 200p. 1996. 19.95 (*1-888321-03-2*) Semco Bks.

Murrells, Joseph. Million Selling Records from the 1900s to the 1980s: An Illustrated Directory. (Illus.). 528p. 1985. pap. 9.95 (*0-685-09767-6*, Arco) Macmillan Gen Ref.

***Murren, Doug.** Achieving Your Dreams: The Joseph Factor. 159p. 1999. pap. 9.97 (*1-883906-35-0*) Kingdom Prods.

Murren, Doug. Churches That Heal: Becoming a Church That Mends Broken Hearts & Restores Shattered Lives. LC 99-23968. 256p. 1999. 16.99 (*1-58229-070-9*) Howard Pub LA.

***Murren, Doug.** Leader Shift: How to Avoid Paradigm Shock. (Illus.). 186p. 1999. pap. 9.97 (*1-883906-30-X*) Kingdom Prods.

Murren, Doug. Leadershift. 1994. pap. 16.30 (*0-8307-1691-2*, Regal Bks) Gospel Lght.

Murrer, Barry A., jt. ed. see Abrams, M. J.

***Murrer, Robert L., ed.** Technologies for Synthetic Environments. 494p. 1999. pap. text 92.00 (*0-8194-3171-0*) SPIE.

Murrer, Robert L., ed. Technologies for Synthetic Environments: Hardware-in-the-Loop Testing III. LC 99-160760. (Proceedings of SPIE Ser.: Vol. 3368). 454p. 1998. 89.00 (*0-8194-2817-5*) SPIE.

Murrey, A. Economic Entomology: (Aptera) 433p. 1984. pap. 175.00 (*0-7855-0349-8*, Pub. by Intl Bks & Periodicals) St Mut.

Murrey, Bob, ed. Instant Review Basketball Notebook. LC 97-81339. (U. S. A. Coaches Clinics Ser.: Vol. 8). (Illus.). 292p. 1998. pap. 22.95 (*1-57167-206-0*) Coaches Choice.

— Instant Review Basketball Notebook. LC 97-81339. (U. S. A. Coaches Clinics Ser.: Vol. 1). (Illus.). 290p. 1998. pap. 22.95 (*1-57167-266-4*) Coaches Choice.

— Instant Review Basketball Notebook. (U. S. A. Coaches Clinics Ser.: Vol. 3). (Illus.). 192p. 1998. pap. 22.95 (*1-57167-268-0*) Coaches Choice.

— Instant Review Basketball Notebook. LC 97-81339. (U. S. A. Coaches Clinics Ser.: Vol. 7). (Illus.). 290p. 1998. pap. 22.95 (*1-57167-271-0*) Coaches Choice.

— Instant Review Basketball Notebook. (U. S. A. Coaches Clinics Ser.: Vol. 4). (Illus.). 192p. 1998. pap. 22.95 (*1-57167-269-9*) Coaches Choice.

***Murrey, Bob, ed.** Instant Review Basketball Notebook. (U. S. A. Coaches Clinics Ser.: Vol. 9). (Illus.). 288p. 1998. pap. 22.95 (*1-57167-363-6*) Coaches Choice.

Murrey, Bob, ed. Instant Review Basketball Notebook, Vol. 2. (U. S. A. Coaches Clinics Ser.). (Illus.). 336p. 1999. pap. 22.95 (*1-57167-267-2*) Coaches Choice.

— Instant Review Basketball Notebook, Vol. 5. (U. S. A. Coaches Clinics Ser.). (Illus.). 268p. 1999. pap. 22.95 (*1-57167-375-X*) Coaches Choice.

— Instant Review Basketball Notebook, Vol. 6. Vol. 6. (Illus.). 268p. 1999. pap. 22.95 (*1-57167-270-2*) Coaches Choice.

***Murrey, Bob, ed.** Man-to-Man Defense. 160p. 1999. pap. 16.95 (*1-57167-429-2*) Coaches Choice.

— U. S. A. Coaches Clinic Instant Review Basketball Notebook, Vol. 10. (Illus.). 225p. 2000. pap. 22.95 (*1-57167-440-3*) Coaches Choice.

— U. S. A. Coaches Practice Planning. 160p. 1999. pap. 16.95 (*1-57167-453-5*) Coaches Choice.

***Murrey, Gregory J.** The Forensic Evaluation of Traumatic Brain Injury: A Handbook for Clinicians & Attorneys. LC 00-21760. 2000. write for info. (*0-8493-2035-6*) CRC Pr.

Murrey, Mary. The Inquisitor. LC 97-72088. 196p. (Orig.). 1997. pap. 10.00 (*0-9658298-4-7*) Lapwing Bks.

Murri, Luigi, jt. ed. see Giannitrapani, D.

***Murrieta, Ed & Wakeman, Diana.** Minnie's Tea Party. 18p. (ps-1). 1999. reprint ed. text 10.00 (*0-7881-6632-8*) DIANE Pub.

Murrieta Foundation Staff. Murrieta Hot Springs Vegetarian Cookbook. LC 87-21881. (Illus.). 232p. 1987. pap. 9.95 (*0-913990-54-X*) Book Pub Co.

Murrill, Cynthia A., et al. Primary Care of the Cataract Patient. (Illus.). 267p. (C). 1994. pap. text 110.00 (*0-8385-7899-3*, A7899-6, Apple Lange Med) McGraw.

Murrill, Paul W. Fundamentals of Process Control Theory. LC 80-84764. (Illus.). 253p. reprint ed. pap. 78.50 (*0-7837-1799-7*, 204200000001) Bks Demand.

— Fundamentals of Process Control Theory. 3rd ed. LC 99-27991. 2000. 76.00 (*1-55617-683-X*) ISA.

Murrill, Paul W. & Smith, Cecil L. FORTRAN IV Programming for Engineers & Scientists. 3rd ed. LC 73-1689. (Illus.). 322p. (C). 1985. pap. text 6.95 (*0-06-044684-6*) Addson-Wesley Educ.

— FORTRAN IV Programming for Engineers & Scientists: Solution Manual. 2nd ed. LC 73-1689. (Illus.). 322p. (C). 2001. text 6.95 (*0-06-364697-8*) Addson-Wesley Educ.

— An introduction to FORTRAN IV Programming: A General Approach. LC 73-111936. xi, 276p. 1970. write for info. (*0-7002-2266-9*) ITxtbk.

Murrill, Rupert I. Cranial & Postcranial Skeletal Remains from Easter Island. LC 67-10609. (Illus.). 113p. reprint ed. pap. 35.10 (*0-8357-8854-7*, 203327400085) Bks Demand.

Murrill, W. A. Tropical Polytpores. 1973. reprint ed. 21.00 (*3-7682-0914-8*) Lubrecht & Cramer.

Murrills, Angela. Food City: Vancouver the Delectable Guide to Finding & Enjoying Good Food in Vancouver & the Lower Mainland. (The City Series). (Illus.). 232p. 1998. pap. write for info. (*1-896095-47-X*) Polstar Bk.

Murrin. Mapping Project: Liberty & Equality. 1996. pap. text 14.00 (*0-15-503676-9*, Pub. by Harcourt Coll Pubs) Harcourt.

— Mapping Project: Liberty & Equality. (C). 1996. wbk. ed. 14.00 (*0-15-503581-9*, Pub. by Harcourt Coll Pubs) Harcourt.

Murrin, John M. Beneficiaries of Catastrophe: The English Colonies in America. 2nd expanded rev. ed. (New American History Essays Ser.). 28p. 1997. reprint ed. pap. 5.00 (*0-87229-086-7*) Am Hist Assn.

— Liberty, Equality, Power, Vol. 1. 2nd ed. (C). 1998. pap. text 63.50 (*0-15-508097-0*) Harcourt.

— Liberty, Equality, Power, Vol. 1. 2nd ed. (C). 1998. pap. text, teacher ed. 26.75 (*0-15-508103-9*); pap. text, student ed. 21.00 (*0-15-508099-7*, Pub. by Harcourt Coll Pubs) Harcourt.

— Liberty, Equality, Power, Vol. 2. (C). 1996. pap. text, student ed. 21.00 (*0-15-500583-9*) Harcourt Coll Pubs.

***Murrin, John M.** Liberty, Equality, Power, Vol. 2. 2nd ed. (C). 1998. pap. text 57.50 (*0-15-508098-9*, Pub. by Harcourt Coll Pubs) Harcourt.

Murrin, John M. Liberty, Equality, Power, Vol. 2. 2nd ed. (C). 1998. pap. text, student ed. 21.00 (*0-15-508100-4*, Pub. by Harcourt Coll Pubs) Harcourt.

— Liberty, Equality, Power: A History of the American People. (C). 1995. pap. text, teacher ed. 33.50 (*0-15-500584-7*, Pub. by Harcourt Coll Pubs) Harcourt.

— Liberty, Equality, Power: A History of the American People. (C). 1996. pap. text 441.50 (*0-15-503612-2*) Harcourt Coll Pubs.

— Liberty, Equality, Power: A History of the American People. 2nd ed. LC 98-84610. (C). 1998. text 76.50 (*0-15-508096-2*) Harcourt.

— Liberty, Equality, Power: A History of the American People. 2nd ed. (C). 1998. pap. text 44.50 (*0-15-508104-7*, Pub. by Harcourt Coll Pubs); pap. text 44.50 (*0-15-507151-3*) Harcourt Coll Pubs.

— Liberty, Equality, Power: A History of the American People, No. 1. (C). 1995. pap. text, student ed. 21.00 (*0-15-500582-0*) Harcourt Coll Pubs.

— U. S. History: Domestic Liberty & Equality. (C). 1995. pap. text 8.50 (*0-15-502200-8*) Harcourt Coll Pubs.

— U. S. History Documented: Liberty & Equality, Vol. II. LC 98-103390. (C). 1995. pap. text 8.50 (*0-15-503677-7*) Harcourt Coll Pubs.

Murrin, John M., jt. ed. see Sheridan, Eugene R.

Murrin, Mary R., ed. Religion. LC 89-27949. (New Jersey History Symposium Ser.). 1990. 3.00 (*0-89743-070-0*) NJ Hist Com.

Murrin, Mary R., jt. auth. see York, Hildreth.

Murrin, Michael. History & Warfare in Renaissance Epic. (Illus.). 388p. 1994. 32.50 (*0-226-55403-1*) U Ch Pr.

— History & Welfare in Renaissance Epic. 1997. pap. text 18.95 (*0-226-55405-8*) U Ch Pr.

Murrin, Michael J. The Allegorical Epic: Essays in Its Rise & Decline. LC 79-20832. 288p. 1996. lib. bdg. 28.00 (*0-226-55402-3*) U Ch Pr.

Murrin, Orlando, ed. Dangerous Desserts. LC 98-30233. (Illus.). 176p. 1998. 27.00 (*1-57959-031-4*, SOMA) BB&T Inc.

— Vital Vegetables. LC 99-35529. (Illus.). 160p. 1999. 27.00 (*1-57959-059-4*, SOMA) BB&T Inc.

Murris, Roelef J., jt. ed. see Demaison, Gerard.

Murrison, Todd. Marker Rendering. (Artist's Library). (Illus.). 64p. (Orig.). 1995. pap. 7.95 (*1-56010-127-X*, AL24) W Foster Pub.

Murrmann-Kahl, Michael. Mysterium Trinitatis? Fallstudien Zur Trinitaetslehre In der Evangelischen Dogmatik des 20. Jahrunderts. (Theologische Biblithek Toepelmann Ser.: Vol. 79). (GER.). viii, 376p. (C). 1997. lib. bdg. 134.30 (*3-11-015262-2*) De Gruyter.

— Strukturprobleme Moderner Exegese: Eine Analyse von Rudolf Bultmanns und Leonhard Goppelts "Theologie des Neuen Testaments" (Beitrage zur Rationalen Theologie Ser.: Bd. 5). (GER.). 127p. 1995. 28.95 (*3-631-48342-2*) P Lang Pubng.

Murro, Jonathan. The Divine Image. LC 89-81537. (Illus.). 477p. 1990. 21.95 (*0-917189-08-6*) A R Colton Fnd.

— God-Realization Journal. 337p. 1975. 10.00 (*0-917187-16-4*) A R Colton Fnd.

Murro, Jonathan, jt. auth. see Colton, Ann R.

Murro, Jonathan, jt. auth. see Colton, Ann Ree.

Murro, Jonathon. The Path of Virtue. LC 79-54382. (Illus.). 487p. 1980. 14.95 (*0-917189-00-0*) A R Colton Fnd.

Murroni, Cristina, jt. auth. see Collins, Richard.

Murrow, Bobbi. Natural Acts: A Collection of Poems by Bobbi Murrow. Helfrich, Peter, ed. LC 94-90413. (Illus.). (Orig.). (YA). 1994. pap. 18.00 (*0-938055-00-3*) Emerald People.

Murrow, Edward R. & Bliss, Edward, Jr. In Search of Light: The Broadcasts of Edward R. Murrow, 1938-1961. LC 96-39079. (Illus.). 402p. 1997. reprint ed. pap. 14.95 (*0-306-80762-9*) Da Capo.

Murrow, Gene, jt. auth. see Lang, Serge A.

Murrow, Liza K. Dancing on the Table. MacDonald, Pat, ed. (Illus.). 128p. (J). 1993. reprint ed. pap. 2.99 (*0-671-73829-1*, Minstrel Bks) PB.

— The Ghost of Lost Island. LC 90-47671. 176p. (J). (gr. 4-6). 1991. 15.95 (*0-8234-0874-4*) Holiday.

— The Ghost of Lost Island. (J). 1991. 8.60 (*0-606-05314-X*, Pub. by Turtleback) Demco.

— The Ghost of Lost Island. MacDonald, Patricia, ed. 176p. (J). (gr. 3-6). 1993. reprint ed. pap. 3.50 (*0-671-75368-1*, Minstrel Bks) PB.

— Twelve Days in August. 192p. 1995. reprint ed. mass mkt. 3.99 (*0-380-72353-0*, Avon Bks) Morrow Avon.

— Twelve Days in August: A Novel. LC 92-54489. 160p. (J). (gr. 7-12). 1993. 16.95 (*0-8234-1012-9*) Holiday.

Murrow, Liza Ketchum. Twelve Days in August. (J). 1995. 9.09 (*0-606-08326-X*, Pub. by Turtleback) Demco.

Murry, Calvin. Prisoner on Board the S. S. Beagle. (Prison Writing Ser.). 1983. spiral bd. 5.00 (*0-912678-53-4*, Greenfld Rev Pr) Greenfld Rev Lit.

Murry, Donald A., et al. In Search of Smaller Government: The Case of State Finance in Oklahoma. unabridged ed. Brown, Rosemary, ed. LC 96-71932. (Illus.). 202p. (Orig.). 1996. mass mkt. 30.00 (*1-890100-00-5*) OK Two-Thousand.

Murry, Donald M. The Craft of Revision. 3rd ed. LC 97-70009. 256p. (C). 1997. pap. text 16.50 (*0-15-505446-5*, Pub. by Harcourt Coll Pubs) Harcourt.

Murry, J. M. & Mansfield, Murry, eds. Blue Review May-July, 1913, Nos. 1-3. (Illus.). 220p. 1968. 65.00 (*0-7146-2103-X*, BHA-02103, Pub. by F Cass Pubs) Intl Spec Bk.

Murry, John M. Aspects of Literature. LC 79-128280. (Essay Index Reprint Ser.). 1977. 18.95 (*0-8369-1838-X*) Ayer.

— The Betrayal of Christ by the Churches. 1972. 59.95 (*0-87968-724-X*) Gordon Pr.

— Countries of the Mind: Essays in Literary Criticism, 1st Series. LC 68-22111. (Essay Index Reprint Ser.). 1980. 18.95 (*0-8369-0729-9*) Ayer.

— Countries of the Mind: Essays in Literary Criticism, 2nd Series. LC 68-22112. (Essay Index Reprint Ser.). 1977. 18.95 (*0-8369-0730-2*) Ayer.

— Evolution of an Intellectual. LC 67-28738. (Essay Index Reprint Ser.). 1977. 19.95 (*0-8369-0731-0*) Ayer.

— Heroes of Thought. 368p. 1977. 21.95 (*0-8369-2436-3*) Ayer.

— Keats & Shakespeare: A Study of Keats Poetic Life from 1816-1820. LC 78-15430. 248p. 1978. reprint ed. lib. bdg. 35.00 (*0-313-20581-7*, MUKS, Greenwood Pr) Greenwood.

— Pencillings. LC 70-90666. (Essay Index Reprint Ser.). 1977. 21.95 (*0-8369-1229-2*) Ayer.

— The Problem of Style. LC 80-21463. 133p. 1980. reprint ed. lib. bdg. 49.50 (*0-313-22523-0*, MUPR, Greenwood Pr) Greenwood.

— Reminiscences of D. H. Lawrence. LC 75-157349. (Select Bibliographies Reprint Ser.). 1977. reprint ed. 19.95 (*0-8369-5810-1*) Ayer.

— Selected Criticism, 1916 to 1957. LC 86-18339. 317p. 1986. reprint ed. lib. bdg. 75.00 (*0-313-25219-X*, MUSE, Greenwood Pr) Greenwood.

— Studies in Keats. LC 78-185023. (Studies in Keats: No. 19). 1969. reprint ed. lib. bdg. 75.00 (*0-8383-0671-3*) M S G Haskell Hse.

— Things to Come. LC 70-93364. (Essay Index Reprint Ser.). 1977. 21.95 (*0-8369-1337-X*) Ayer.

— William Blake. LC 71-173845. (Studies in Blake: No. 3). 1971. reprint ed. lib. bdg. 75.00 (*0-8383-1344-2*) M S G Haskell Hse.

Murry, John M., jt. auth. see Mantz, Ruth E.

Murry, Katherine M. Beloved Quixote: The Unknown Life of John Middleton Murry. LC 87-179412. 219p. 1986. write for info. (*0-285-65027-0*) Souvenir Pr Ltd.

***Murry, Terece.** A Measure of Time. 64p. 1999. pap. 7.95 (*1-56167-485-0*, Five Star Spec Ed) Am Literary Pr.

***Murry, Thomas.** Clinical Manual for Swallowing Disorders. (Illus.). 2000. pap. 49.95 (*0-7693-0065-0*) Singular Publishing.

Murry, Thomas, jt. auth. see Robbins, K. Thomas.

Murry, Thomas, jt. ed. see Carrau, Ricardo L.

Murschhauser, Hans, jt. auth. see Benedict, Francis G.

Mursell, Gordon, intro. The Meditations of Guigo I, Prior of the Charterhouse. LC 94-21178. (Cistercian Studies: No. 155). 1994. 25.95 (*0-87907-555-4*); pap. 12.95 (*0-87907-655-0*) Cistercian Pubns.

Mursell, James L. Psychology of Music. 1991. lib. bdg. 45.00 (*0-403-01750-5*) Scholarly.

— The Psychology of Music. LC 77-110274. (Illus.). 389p. 1971. reprint ed. lib. bdg. 69.50 (*0-8371-4500-7*, MUPM, Greenwood Pr) Greenwood.

— Psychology of Music. 1988. reprint ed. lib. bdg. 25.00 (*0-317-90101-X*) Rprt Serv.

Mursell, Norman. Come Dawn, Come Dusk: 50 Years As a Gamekeeper. large type ed. 23.95 (*1-85695-127-8*, Pub. by ISIS Lrg Prnt) Transaction Pubs.

Murshed. Macroeconomics for Open Economies. 1998. pap. 21.99 (*1-86152-457-9*) Thomson Learn.

Murshed, Nabeel A. & Bortolozzi, Flavio, eds. Advances in Document Image Analysis: Proceedings, 1st Brazilian Symposium, BSDIA '97, Curitiba, Brazil, November 2-5, 1997. LC 97-39143. (Lecture Notes in Computer Science Ser.: Vol. 1339). ix, 345p. 1997. pap. 59.00 (*3-540-63791-5*) Spr-Verlag.

Murshed, S. Mansoob. Economic Aspects of North-South Interaction: Analytical Macroeconomic Issues. (Illus.). 208p. 1992. text 85.00 (*0-12-512070-2*) Acad Pr.

Murshed, S. Mansoob & Raffer, Kunibert, eds. Trade, Transfers & Development: Problems & Prospects for the 21st Century. (Illus.). 272p. 1994. 95.00 (*1-85278-796-1*) E Elgar.

Murst, Sarah, jt. tr. see Adams, Jimmy.

Murstein, Bernard I. Paths to Marriage. (Family Studies Text Ser.). (Illus.). 160p. (Orig.). (C). 1986. pap. text 18.95 (*0-8039-2383-X*) Sage.

— Paths to Marriage. LC 86-1884. (Family Studies Text Ser.: Vol. 5). (Illus.). 168p. (Orig.). 1986. reprint ed. pap. 52.10 (*0-608-07685-6*, 206777500010) Bks Demand.

Murtag. Keeping Time. (Sterling Publishing Co. Ser.). 1990. text 25.00 (*0-8273-5394-4*) Delmar.

***Murtagh, Ann-Janine.** Portrait of a Westmeath Tenant Community, 1879-85. LC 99-29356. (Maynooth Studies in Local History). 64p. 2000. pap. 10.95 (*0-7165-2673-5*, Pub. by Irish Acad Pr) Intl Spec Bk.

Murtagh, F., jt. ed. see Heck, Andre.

Murtagh, F. Reed & Schnitzlein, H. Norman. Imaging Anatomy of the Head & Spine: A Photographic Color Atlas of MRI, CT, Gross & Microscopic Anatomy in Axial, Coronal, & Sagittal Planes. 2nd ed. (Illus.). 480p. 1990. 200.00 (*0-683-07622-1*) Lppncott W & W.

Murtagh, Fionn & Heck, Andre. Multivariate Data Analysis. (C). 1986. lib. bdg. 110.00 (*90-277-2425-3*) Kluwer Academic.

— Multivariate Data Analysis. (C). 1987. pap. text 59.50 (*90-277-2426-1*) Kluwer Academic.

— Multivariate Data Analysis. (C). 1988. pap. text 88.00 (*90-277-9154-6*) Kluwer Academic.

Murtagh, Fionn, jt. ed. see Heck, Andre.

Murtagh, J. Worldwide Directory of Distilleries. 900p. 1997. 960.00 (*1-897676-61-1*, Pub. by Univ Nottingham) St Mut.

***Murtagh, James J.** How to Prepare for Real Estate Examinations. 6th ed. LC 99-42815. 480p. 2000. pap. 14.95 (*0-7641-0773-9*) Barron.

— How to Prepare for the Firefighters Exam. 4th ed. LC 99-42815. 448p. 2000. pap. 14.95 (*0-7641-0772-0*) Barron.

Murtagh, John. Cautionary Tales: Authentic Case Histories from Medical Practice. 220p. 1992. text 39.00 (*0-07-452806-8*) McGraw-Hill HPD.

— General Practice. 750p. 1994. text 79.00 (*0-07-452807-6*) McGraw-Hill HPD.

***Murtagh, John.** General Practice. ed. 1999. 69.95 (*0-07-470719-1*, McGrw-H College) McGrw-H Hghr Educ.

Murtagh, John. General Practice. 2nd ed. (Illus.). 1208p. 1999. 125.00 (*0-07-470436-2*) McGraw.

— General Practice: Companion Handbook. (Illus.). 367p. 1996. pap. text 32.00 (*0-07-470275-0*) McGraw-Hill HPD.

— General Practice Companion Handbook. 2nd ed. (Illus.). 450p. 1999. write for info. (*0-07-470722-1*) McGraw-Hill HPD.

— Practice Tips. 2nd ed. (Illus.). 224p. 1995. 49.00 (*0-07-470180-0*) McGraw-Hill HPD.

Murtagh, John H. Patient Education. 2nd ed. LC 97-155548. (Illus.). 200p. 1996. pap. text 49.00 (*0-07-470296-3*) McGraw-Hill HPD.

Murtagh, Peter, jt. auth. see Joyce, Joe.

Murtagh, Steven J. An Analysis of Cost-of-Calls in the Customer Support Industry. Bultema, Patrick et al, eds. (Illus.). 41p. (Orig.). pap. write for info. (*1-57125-018-2*) Help Desk Inst.

— Staffing, Scheduling, & Workforce Planning: A Help Desk Institute White Paper. Bultema, Patrick et al, eds. (Illus.). (Orig.). (C). pap. write for info. (*1-57125-002-6*) Help Desk Inst.

Murtagh, T. N. F., tr. see Ferriares, Gabrielle.

Murtagh, Terence, jt. auth. see Ridpath, Ian.

Murtagh, William J. Keeping Time: The History & Theory of Preservation in America. (Illus.). 240p. 1991. pap. 19.95 (*0-8069-0516-6*, Sterling-Main St) Sterling.

— Keeping Time: The History & Theory of Preservation in America. rev. ed. LC 97-10040. (Illus.). 246p. 1997. pap. 39.95 (*0-471-18240-0*) Wiley.

— Moravian Architecture & Town Planning: Bethlehem, Pennsylvania, & Other Eighteenth-Century American Settlements. LC 97-43397. (Illus.). 160p. (C). 1997. pap. 19.95 (*0-8122-1637-7*) U of Pa Pr.

***Murtaugh.** Critical Care. (Quick Look Veterinary Ser.). 2000. 23.95 (*1-889325-13-9*, Pub. by Fence Crk Pubng) Blackwell Sci.

Murtaugh, Daniel M. Piers Plowman & the Image of God. LC 77-25544. 137p. reprint ed. pap. 42.50 (*0-7837-4909-0*, 204457400004) Bks Demand.

Murtaugh, Frank M. Cavour & the Economic Modernization of the Kingdom of Sardinia. LC 91-28338. (Modern European History Ser.: No. 2). 368p. 1991. text 20.00 (*0-8153-0671-7*) Garland.

Murtaugh, James J. How to Prepare for Fire Fighter Examinations. 3rd ed. LC 94-46425. 1995. pap. 13.95 (*0-8120-9086-1*) Barron.

Murtaugh, Kristen O. Aristo & the Classical Smile. (Studies in Romance Languages: No. 36). 206p. (C). 1981. 12.50 (*0-674-04487-8*) HUP.

Murtaugh, Melinda. Italian Labor in Protest, 1904-1914: Political General Strikes to Protest Eccidi. LC 91-3268. (Modern European History Outstanding Studies & Dissertations). 352p. 1991. text 20.00 (*0-8153-0416-1*) Garland.

Murtaugh, Michael P., jt. ed. see Myers, Michael J.

Murtaza, Mutahhery, jt. auth. see Sadr, Muhammad B.

Murtaza, Niatz. Tracing the Pillage of Sustainability in Eritrea, 1600-Present: Rural Communities & the Creeping Shadows of Hegemony, 197. LC 97-43930. (Contributions in Economics & Economic History Ser.: Vol. 197). 224p. 1998. 59.95 (*0-313-30633-8*, Greenwood Pr) Greenwood.

Murth, D. N., jt. auth. see Osaki, Shunji.

***Murtha, James A.** Decisions Involving Uncertainty: An @RISK Tutorial for the Petroleum Industry. (Illus.). iv, 160p. 2000. pap. 69.95 (*1-893281-02-7*) Palisade Corp.

Murthi, R. K. Historic Assassinations. ix, 158p. 1992. text 25.00 (*81-220-0249-8*, Pub. by Konark Pubs Pvt Ltd) Advent Bks Div.

— Stories of Lord Ganesha. 52p. 1998. pap. 20.00 (*81-209-0839-2*, Pub. by Pitambar Pub) St Mut.

— Tales of Goddness Durga. 1998. pap. 30.00 (*81-209-1033-8*, Pub. by Pitambar Pub) St Mut.

— Tales of Lord Brahma. 1998. pap. 30.00 (*81-209-1032-X*, Pub. by Pitambar Pub) St Mut.

— Tales of Lord Shiva. 1997. pap. 30.00 (*81-209-1016-8*, Pub. by Pitambar Pub) St Mut.

Murthi, R. K., jt. auth. see Sharma, Gautam.

Murthi, V. K. & Sharma, G. Rajiv Gandhi: Challenges & Choices. 1985. 22.95 (*81-7027-089-8*) Asia Bk Corp.

Murthy, A. S. Religion & Society: A Study of Koyas. (C). 1991. text 21.00 (*81-7141-147-9*) S Asia.

Murthy, A. S. & Mohle, R. Henry. Transportation Engineering Basics. LC 93-15229. 52p. 1993. 17.00 (*0-87262-881-7*) Am Soc Civil Eng.

An Asterisk (*) at the beginning of an entry indicates that the title is appearing for the first time.

Murthy, A. V., ed. Studies in South Indian Customs, Vol. 2. (C). 1992. 19.50 (*0-8364-2765-3*, Pub. by New Era Pub) S Asia.

Murthy, Anantha & Kroll, Judith. Bhava. LC 98-906088. xiv, 183 p. 1998. write for info. (*0-14-027649-1*) Viking Penguin.

Murthy, B. Srinivasa. Christian Experiences of a Hindu. 110p. 1998. pap. 19.95 (*0-941910-08-3*) Long Beach Pubns.

— International Relations & Organisation for Law Students. (C). 1991. text 55.00 (*0-89771-501-2*) St Mut.

— Mahatma Gandhi & Christianity. 100p. (Orig.). 1998. pap. 18.95 (*0-941910-06-7*) Long Beach Pubns.

— Mother Teresa & India. LC 82-80522. (Illus.). 144p. (Orig.). 1982. pap. 6.95 (*0-941910-00-8*) Long Beach Pubns.

Murthy, B. Srinivasa, tr. from SAN. The Bhagavad Gita: Translated with Introduction & Notes. 2nd ed. LC 90-82501. 156p. 1998. reprint ed. pap. 11.95 (*0-941910-05-9*) Long Beach Pubns.

Murthy, B. Srinivasa, jt. auth. see Smart, Ninian.

Murthy, C. S., ed. see International Symposium on Process Physics and Modeling in Semiconductor Technology, et al.

***Murthy, C. Silva Ram & Manimaran, G.** Resource Management in Real-Time Systems & Networks. (Illus.). 475p. (C). 2001. 55.00 (*0-262-13376-8*) MIT Pr.

***Murthy, C. Siva Ram, et al.** New Parallel Algorithms for Direct of Linear Equations. LC 99-86570. 200p. 2000. text 69.95 (*0-471-36165-8*) Wiley.

Murthy, D. B. Managing Quality: A Practical Guide to Customer Satisfaction. LC 99-11084. 1999. write for info. (*0-7619-9306-1*) Sage.

Murthy, D. N., jt. ed. see Blischke, Wallace R.

Murthy, D. N. Prabhakar, jt. auth. see Blischke, Wallace R.

Murthy, G. V., jt. ed. see Kadekodi, G. K.

Murthy, H. V. History of India, Pt. 1: For Law Students. 1993. 60.00 (*81-7012-525-1*) St Mut.

Murthy, J. Y., jt. ed. see Kececioglu, I.

Murthy, K. Krishna. Buddhism in Japan. (C). 1989. 34.00 (*81-85067-25-2*, Pub. by Sundeep Prak) S Asia.

— Buddhism in Tibet. (C). 1989. 28.50 (*81-85067-16-3*, Pub. by Sundeep Prak) S Asia.

— Dictionary of Buddhist Literature & Literary Personalities. LC 94-905638. (C). 1994. 34.00 (*81-85067-88-0*, Pub. by Sundeep Prak) S Asia.

— Dictionary of Buddhist Terms & Terminologies. 1991. 37.00 (*81-85067-67-8*, Pub. by Sundeep Prak) S Asia.

— Dictionary of Medical Archaeology. (C). 1996. 40.00 (*81-85067-93-7*, Pub. by Sundeep Prak) S Asia.

— Iconography of Buddhist Deity Heruka. (C). 1988. 20.00 (*81-85067-12-0*, Pub. by Sundeep Prak) S Asia.

— Mirrors of Indian Buddhism. (C). 1991. text 28.50 (*81-85067-72-4*, Pub. by Sundeep Prak) S Asia.

— Sculptures of Vajrayana Buddhism. (C). 1989. 32.50 (*81-85132-06-2*, Pub. by Classics India Pubns) S Asia.

Murthy, K. Krishna & Murthy, P. K. Dictionary of Archeo-Zoology. (C). 1990. 28.00 (*81-202-0287-2*, Pub. by Ajanta) S Asia.

Murthy, Keshava S. National Environmental Policy (NEPA) Process. 224p. 1988. 130.00 (*0-8493-6746-8*, KF3775, CRC Reprint) Franklin.

Murthy, M. K. Nonlinear Hyperbolic Equations & Field Theory. 1992. lib. bdg. 62.95 (*0-582-08766-X*, Pub. by Addison-Wesley) Longman.

Murthy, M. V., et al, eds. Current Research in Heat & Mass Transfer: A Copendiem & Festschrift for Professor Arcot Ramachandran. 283p. 1988. 130.00 (*0-89116-578-9*) Hemisp Pub.

Murthy, Mukunda S., jt. auth. see Ruggles, William S.

Murthy, N. A. & Pandey, D. P. Ayurvedic Cures for Common Diseases. 200p. 1985. 11.95 (*0-318-36354-2*) Asia Bk Corp.

Murthy, N. S. Forts of Andhra Pradesh: From Earliest Times up to 16th Century AD. LC 96-900219. (C). 1996. 140.00 (*81-86050-03-5*, Pub. by Bharat Vidya) S Asia.

Murthy, P. G., jt. auth. see Pavella, M.

Murthy, P. K., jt. auth. see Murthy, K. Krishna.

Murthy, Poolla V. & Wolfendale, Arnold W. Gamma-Ray Astronomy. 2nd ed. LC 92-16465. (Cambridge Astrophysics Ser.: No. 22). (Illus.). 273p. (C). 1993. text 80.00 (*0-521-42081-4*) Cambridge U Pr.

Murthy, S. Laxmana. The Novels of William Styron. 204p. 1988. text 27.50 (*81-85218-03-X*, Pub. by Prestige) Advent Bks Div.

Murthy, S. N. & Curran, E. T., eds. Developments in High-Speed Vehicle Propulsion Systems. (PAAS Ser.: Vol. 137). 537p. 1991. 86.95 (*1-56347-011-X*, V-137) AIAA.

Murthy, S. N. & Paynter, G. C., eds. Numerical Methods for Engine-Airframe Integration. LC 86-10920. (PAAS Ser.: Vol. 102). (Illus.). 544p. 1986. 79.95 (*0-930403-09-6*, V-102) AIAA.

Murthy, S. N., jt. ed. see Borghi, R. P.

Murthy, S. R. Glimpses of Hindu Astrology & Some Aspects of Indology. (C). 1993. 28.00 (*81-7030-383-4*, Pub. by Sri Satguru Pubns) S Asia.

Murthy, S. S., jt. auth. see Mariani, E.

Murthy, Satya M. & Scanlon, Edward F. Injury & Tumor Implantation. LC 93-37851. (Medical Intelligence Unit Ser.). 1993. 99.00 (*1-879702-82-7*) Landes Bioscience.

Murthy, Srikanata K., tr. see Sarngadhara.

Murthy, T. K., ed. Computational Methods in Hypersonic Aerodynamics. LC 91-77003. (Computational Methods in Aerodynamics Ser.). 510p. 1992. 161.00 (*1-56252-083-0*, 1568) Computational Mech MA.

— Dynamics & Control of Structures in Space III. LC 96-83655. (Space Structures Ser.). 696p. 1996. 262.00 (*1-85312-415-X*, 415X) Computational Mech MA.

Murthy, T. K., et al, eds. Computers in Railway Installations, Track, & Signalling. 480p. 1987. 142.95 (*0-387-17933-X*) Spr-Verlag.

— Computers in Railway Management. LC 87-70871. (COMPRAIL Ser.: Vol. 1). 254p. 1987. 66.00 (*0-931215-58-7*) Computational Mech MA.

— Computers in Railway Operations. LC 87-70870. (COMPRAIL Ser.: Vol. 1). 344p. 1987. 84.00 (*0-931215-79-X*) Computational Mech MA.

— Ice Technology. (ITC Ser.: Vol. 1). 1986. 125.00 (*0-931215-27-7*) Computational Mech MA.

— Ice Technology for Polar Operations. LC 90-83758. (ITC Ser.: Vol. 2). 436p. 1990. 146.00 (*0-945824-74-2*) Computational Mech MA.

— Marine & Offshore Computer Applications. LC 88-71664. (CADMO Ser.: Vol. 2). 812p. 1988. 149.00 (*0-945824-05-X*) Computational Mech MA.

— Marine, Offshore & Ice Technology: Proceedings of CADMO 94 & ITC 94. LC 94-72458. (CADMO Ser.: Vol. 4). 416p. 1994. 213.00 (*1-56252-268-X*, 3447) Computational Mech MA.

Murthy, T. K. & Alaez, J. A., eds. Design of Marine & Offshore Structures. 828p. 1992. 305.00 (*1-85312-178-9*) Computational Mech MA.

— Design of Marine & Offshore Structures. LC 92-82811. (CADMO Ser.). 828p. 1992. 305.00 (*1-56252-107-1*, 1789) Computational Mech MA.

Murthy, T. K. & Brebbia, Carlos A., eds. Advances in Computer Technology & Applications in Japan. (Lecture Notes in Engineering Ser.: Vol. 69). (Illus.). xiv, 158p. 1991. pap. 34.00 (*0-387-54072-5*) Spr-Verlag.

— Computers in Design, Construction & Operation of Automobiles. 1987. 72.00 (*0-931215-69-2*) Computational Mech MA.

— Structural Design & Crashworthiness of Automobiles. 1987. 72.00 (*0-931215-21-8*) Computational Mech MA.

— Structural Design & Crashworthiness of Automobiles. 240p. 1987. 81.95 (*0-387-17504-0*) Spr-Verlag.

— Supercomputing in Fluid Flow. LC 90-84998. (Computational Engineering Ser.). 368p. 1992. 195.00 (*0-945824-59-9*) Computational Mech MA.

Murthy, T. K. & Dern, J. C., eds. Marine & Offshore Computer Applications. 810p. 1988. 206.95 (*0-387-50172-X*) Spr-Verlag.

Murthy, T. K. & Fielding, J. P., eds. Computer Applications in Aircraft Design & Operation. 254p. 1987. 72.00 (*0-931215-56-0*) Computational Mech MA.

— Computer Applications in Aircraft Design & Operation. 285p. 1987. 83.00 (*0-387-17749-3*) Spr-Verlag.

Murthy, T. K. & Keramidas, G. A., eds. Computer Aided Design, Manufacture & Operation in the Marine & Offshore Industries. (CADMO Ser.). 659p. 1987. 130.00 (*0-931215-34-X*, 1597) Computational Mech MA.

Murthy, T. K. & Munch, R., eds. Computer Applications in Spacecraft Design & Operation. 198p. 1987. 51.00 (*0 931215-75-7*) Computational Mech MA.

Murthy, T. K. & Ram, Manatha. Law of Adverse Possession. (C). 1988. 100.00 (*0-7855-3533-0*) St Mut.

Murthy, T. K. S., et al, eds. Computers in Railways IV Vol. 1: Railway Design & Management. 600p. 1994. 255.00 (*1-85312-354-4*) Computational Mech MA.

— Computers in Railways IV Vol. 2: Railway Operations. 512p. 1994. 218.00 (*1-85312-359-5*) Computational Mech MA.

— Computers in Railways III Vol. 1: Management. 632p. 1992. 190.00 (*1-85312-207-6*) Computational Mech MA.

— Computers in Railways III Vol. 2: Technology. 498p. 1992. 166.00 (*1-85312-208-4*) Computational Mech MA.

— Marine, Offshore & Ice Technology. 416p. 1994. 213.00 (*1-85312-344-7*) Computational Mech MA.

Murthy, T. K. S. & Brebbia, C. A., eds. Marine Engineering: Design & Operation of Ships & Offshore Structures. 276p. 1994. 157.00 (*1-85312-248-3*) Computational Mech MA.

Murthy, T. S. Maharaj: A Biography of Shriman Tapasviji Maharaj, a Mahatma Who Lived for 185 Years, 1767-1952. rev. ed. 246p. 1986. pap. 8.95 (*0-913922-17-X*) Dawn Horse Pr.

Murthy, T. S., ed. Snake Book of India with Many Plates & Diagrams. (C). 1987. 150.00 (*81-7089-049-7*, Pub. by Intl Bk Distr) St Mut.

Murthy, U. R. Awasthe, A Novel. 1990. 16.00 (*81-7023-298-8*, Pub. by Allied Pubs) S Asia.

— Samskara: A Rite for a Dead Man. Ramnujan, A. K., tr. 168p. 1979. pap. 9.95 (*0-19-561079-2*) OUP.

Murthy, V. A. & Ananthakrishnan, T. N. Studies on Indian Chelonethi. (Oriental Insects Monographs: No. 4). 1977. pap. 55.00 (*1-877711-10-1*) Assoc Pubs FL.

Murthy, V. R., et al, eds. Microwave Materials. vii,257p. 1994. 69.00 (*0-387-58075-1*) Spr-Verlag.

Murthy, V. Rama, jt. ed. see Pollack, H. N.

Murti, Isana & Dayal, Indira. Anjolie Ela Menon: Paintings in Private Collections. (C). 1995. 110.00 (*0-86311-556-X*, Pub. by Ravi Dayal) S Asia.

***Murti, Kamakshi P.** India: The Seductive & Seduced "Other" of German Orientalism. 39. LC 99-44512. (Contributions in Comparative Colonial Studies). 160p. 2000. 55.00 (*0-313-30857-8*) Greenwood.

Murti, Kamakshi P. Die Reinkarnation des Lesers Als Autor: Ein Rezeptionsgeschichtlicher Versuch Uber den Einfluss der Altindischen Literatur auf Deutsche Schriftsteller um 1900. (Quellen und Forschungen zur Sprach und Kulturgeschichte der Germanischen Voelker: NF 96 (220)). vi, 156p. (C). 1990. lib. bdg. 60.00 (*3-11-012371-1*) De Gruyter.

Murti, V., jt. ed. see Pulmano, V. A.

Murtiashaw, Sherer M. Behind Closed Doors: A Consumer's Guide to Psychiatric Hospitals. 128p. 1994. pap. text 9.95 (*0-9639267-9-9*) HRS.

Murton, Bramley J. & Blondel, Phillippe. Handbook of Seafloor Sonar Imagery. LC 96-47603. (Wiley Praxis Ser.). 336p. 1997. 190.00 (*0-471-96217-1*) Wiley.

Murton, Nancy. The Busy Woman's Guide to the Stock Market. 52p. 1994. pap. 7.95 (*0-9641711-0-4*) N Murton.

Murton, Phyllis. How to Get the Teaching Position You Want! 2nd rev. ed. (Illus.). 110p. (Orig.). 1996. pap. 9.95 (*0-9636749-0-0*) Educ Ent.

Murtonen, A. Hebrew in Its West Semitic Setting: A Comparative Survey of Non-Masoretic Hebrew Dialects & Traditions, Pt. I: A Comparative Lexicon, Sect. Bb-E. (Studien in Semitic Languages & Linguistics: Vol. 13-3). x, 516p. 1990. 223.00 (*90-04-08899-7*) Brill Academic Pubs.

— Hebrew in its West Semitic Setting: A Comparative Survey of Non-Masoretic Hebrew Dialects & Traditions. Pt. One: A Comparative Lexicon, Section A: Proper Names. (Studies in Semitic Languages & Linguistics: No. 13). xxxii, 341p. 1986. 145.00 (*90-04-07245-4*) Brill Academic Pubs.

— Hebrew in Its West Semitic Setting: Pt. 2 - Phonetics & Phonology, Pt. 3 - Morphosyntactics. LC 87-32287. (Studies in Semitic Languages & Linguistics: No. 16). (Illus.). 1990. 200.00 (*90-04-09309-5*) Brill Academic Pubs.

***Murtuza, Athar.** Documentation for Business Process Improvement: The New Accounting Manual. 2nd ed. 416p. 2000. text 95.00 (*0-471-37938-7*) Wiley.

Murtuza, Athar. The New Accounting Manual: A Guide to the Documentation Process. LC 94-34136. 384p. 1995. 130.00 (*0-471-30370-4*) Wiley.

— The New Accounting Manual: A Guide to the Documentation Process 1999 Cumulative Supplement. 159p. 1999. pap., suppl. ed. 69.00 (*0-471-29878-6*) Wiley.

Murty, A. S., ed. Toxicity of Pesticides to Fish, Vol. I. 192p. 1986. 111.00 (*0-8493-6058-7*, SH174, CRC Reprint) Franklin.

— Toxicity of Pesticides to Fish, Vol. II. 192p. 1986. 92.00 (*0-8493-6059-5*, SH174, CRC Reprint) Franklin.

Murty, A. V., jt. ed. see Reddy, J. N.

Murty, B. S. The International Law of Propaganda. (C). 1989. lib. bdg. 170.00 (*0-89838-904-6*) Kluwer Academic.

— International Relations & Organisation. (C). 1991. 65.00 (*0-7855-6717-8*) St Mut.

Murty, B. S. & Panda, S. P. Indian Coal Industry & the Coal Miners. 1988. 48.50 (*0-8364-2246-5*) S Asia.

Murty, C. Satyanarayana. Design of Minor Irrigation & Canal Structures. (C). 1991. pap. 16.00 (*81-224-0280-1*) S Asia.

Murty, J. V. Watershed Management in India. 1995. write for info. (*81-224-0566-5*, Pub. by Wiley Estrn) Franklin.

Murty, K. Krishna. Buddha His Nirvana & Mahaparinirvana. (C). 1996. 32.00 (*81-85067-94-5*, Pub. by Sundeep Prak) S Asia.

Murty, K. S. Vedic Hermeneutics. (C). 1993. 14.00 (*81-208-1105-4*, Pub. by Motilal Bnarsidass) S Asia.

Murty, K. Satchidananda. The Quest for Peace. 1986. 17.50 (*81-202-0165-5*, Pub. by Ajanta) S Asia.

Murty, K. Satchidananda & DasGupta, Amit, eds. Divine Peacock: Understanding Contemporary India. (C). 1994. text 24.00 (*81-224-0699-8*) S Asia.

Murty, K. Satchidananda & Vohra, Ashok. Radhakrishnan. (His Life & Ideas Ser.). (C). 1989. 44.00 (*81-202-0253-8*, Pub. by Ajanta) S Asia.

— Radhakrishnan: His Life & Ideas. LC 89-39718. 239p. (C). 1990. pap. text 18.95 (*0-7914-0344-0*) State U NY Pr.

Murty, K. Satya. Handbook of Indian Architecture. 1991. 22.50 (*81-7024-389-0*, Pub. by Ashish Pub Hse) S Asia.

— Textbook of Indian Epigraphy. (C). 1992. text 14.00 (*81-85418-88-8*, Pub. by Low Price) S Asia.

Murty, Katta B. Network Programming. (C). 1992. text 63.80 (*0-13-615493-X*) P-H.

Murty, Katta G. Linear Programming. LC 83-7012. 512p. (C). 1983. text 105.95 (*0-471-09725-X*) Wiley.

— Linear Programming. 231p. (C). 1984. pap. text, suppl. ed. 20.00 (*0-471-89249-1*) Wiley.

— Operations Research: Deterministic Optimization Models. LC 94-19150. 608p. 1994. 58.60 (*0-13-056517-2*) P-H.

Murty, Komanduri S., jt. auth. see Roebuck, Julian B.

Murty, M. N., jt. auth. see Markandya, A.

Murty, M. Ram, ed. Theta Functions. LC 93-15008. (CRM Proceedings & Lecture Notes Ser.: Vol. 1). 174p. 1993. pap. 58.00 (*0-8218-6997-3*, CRMP/1) Am Math.

Murty, M. Ram, jt. auth. see Esmonde, J.

Murty, M. Ram, ed. see Herz, Carl S.

Murty, M. Ram, jt. ed. see Kisilevsky, Hershy.

Murty, Maddipata Narasimha. Economics of Water Pollution: The Indian Experience. LC 99-933480. (Illus.). 312p. 1999. text 35.00 (*0-19-564395-X*) OUP.

Murty, Mantha R. Special Marriage Act. (C). 1990. 138.00 (*0-89771-142-4*) St Mut.

Murty, Maruti R. & Murty, V. Kumar. Non-Vanishing of L-Functions & Applications. LC 97-38038. (Progress in Mathematics Ser.: Vol. 157). (Illus.). x, 196p. 1997. text 47.00 (*3-7643-5801-7*) Birkhauser.

Murty, Maruti R. & Murty, Vijaya K. Non-Vanishing of L-Functions & Applications. LC 97-38038. (Progress in Mathematics Ser.). (Illus.). x, 196p. 1997. pap. write for info. (*0-8176-5801-7*) Birkhauser.

Murty, Ram, jt. ed. see Groves, Michael J.

Murty, Ram, tr. see Levin, L. I.

Murty, Susan A. Research on Social Work & Disasters. Streeter, Calvin L., ed. LC 96-40923. (Journal of Social Service Research: Vol. 22, Nos. 1/2). 160p. (C). 1997. 39.95 (*0-7890-0028-8*); pap. 14.95 (*0-7890-0303-1*) Haworth Pr.

Murty, T. R. Studies in Indian Thought: The Collected Papers of Professor TRV Murti. Coward, Harold, ed. 1983. 25.00 (*0-8364-0866-7*); text 17.00 (*0-8364-0984-1*) S Asia.

Murty, T. S. India-China Boundary: India's Options. 143p. 1987. 24.95 (*0-318-37245-2*) Asia Bk Corp.

Murty, T. S., jt. auth. see Kowalik, Z.

Murty, T. S., jt. ed. see El-Sabh, M. I.

Murty, T. V. Studies in Earth Sciences. 614p. 1971. 25.00 (*0-88065-164-4*) Scholarly Pubns.

Murty, V. Kumar. Introduction to Abelian Varieties. LC 93-14570. (CRM Monograph Ser.: No. 3). 112p. 1993. text 24.00 (*0-8218-6995-7*, CRMM/3) Am Math.

Murty, V. Kumar, ed. Fermat's Last Theorem Vol. 17: Proceedings of the Fields Institute for Research in Mathematical Sciences on Fermat's Last Theorem Held 1993-1994 Toronto, Ontario, Canada, Vol. 17. LC 95-36469. (Canadian Mathematical Society Conference Proceedings Ser.). 265p. 1995. pap. 49.00 (*0-8218-0313-1*, CMSAMS/17) Am Math.

Murty, V. Kumar & Waldschmidt, Michel, eds. Number Theory: Discrete Mathematics & Number Theory, January 3-6, 1996, Tiruchirapalli, India. LC 97-30207. (Contemporary Mathematics Ser.: Vol. 210). 399p. 1997. pap. 69.00 (*0-8218-0606-8*) Am Math.

Murty, V. Kumar, jt. auth. see Murty, Maruti R.

Murty, V. V. & Takeuchi, K. Land & Water Development for Agriculture in the Asia-Pacific Region. (Illus.). 200p. 1996. lib. bdg. 55.00 (*1-886106-60-6*) Science Pubs.

Murty, Vijaya K., jt. auth. see Murty, Maruti R.

Murty, Y. V. & Mollard, F. R., eds. Continuous Casting of Small Cross Sections: Proceedings of a Symposium. LC 81-85418. (Conference Proceedings Ser.). (Illus.). 211p. reprint ed. pap. 65.50 (*0-608-17836-5*, 203259500080) Bks Demand.

Murtz, Harold A. Handguns 2000. 12th ed. LC 88-72115. (Illus.). 352p. 1999. pap. 21.95 (*0-87341-759-3*) Krause Pubns.

Murtz, Harold A., ed. The Gun Digest Book of Exploded Long Gun Drawings. LC 92-81890. (Illus.). 512p. 1993. pap. 20.95 (*0-87349-147-5*, ELD, DBI Bks) Krause Pubns.

— Gun Digest Book of Sporting Clays. 2nd ed. LC 91-71896. (Illus.). 256p. 1999. per. 21.95 (*0-87341-745-3*) Krause Pubns.

— Gun Digest Treasury. 7th ed. LC 61-9610. (Illus.). 320p. 1994. pap. 17.95 (*0-87349-156-4*, GDT7, DBI Bks) Krause Pubns.

— 1999 Guns Illustrated: The Journal for Gun Buffs. 31st ed. LC 69-11342. (Illus.). 352p. 1998. pap. 22.95 (*0-87349-204-8*, GI99) Krause Pubns.

***Murugesan, Sam, et al, eds.** Intelligent Agents in Cyberspace: Papers from the Spring Symposium. (Technical Reports: Vol. SS-99-03). (Illus.). 196p. 1999. spiral bd. 25.00 (*1-57735-081-2*) AAAI Pr.

Murugesan, San, jt. ed. see Gopalakrishnan, B.

Murugiah, R. German-English Dictionary of Economics. (ENG & GER.). 603p. 1993. 195.00 (*0-7859-9571-4*) Fr & Eur.

Murugiah, R. T. German-English Economic Dictionary. 603p. 1993. 195.00 (*3-349-00597-7*) IBD Ltd.

Murugkar, Lata. Dalit Panther Movement in Magarashtra: A Sociological Appraisal. (C). 1990. 32.00 (*0-86132-246-0*, Pub. by Popular Prakashan) S Asia.

Murutes, Harry. Easy Key to German Vocabulary: A Mnemonic List with English Cognates. LC 95-95192. (ENG & GER.). viii, 214p. (Orig.). (C). 1995. pap. text 16.95 (*0-9648579-0-1*) Murutes.

— Easy Key to Spanish Vocabulary: A Mnemonic List with English Cognates. (ENG & SPA.). 90p. 1998. pap. text 9.95 (*0-9648579-1-X*) Murutes.

Murvar, Vatro. Nation & Religion in Central Europe & the Western Balkans - The Muslims in Bosnia, Hercegovina & Sandzak Vol. 1: A Sociological Analysis. 180p. 1990. 30.00 (*0-931633-04-4*); pap. 15.00 (*0-931633-03-2*) Fnd Soc Stdy.

— Submerged Nations: An Introduction to Theory & Bibliography on One Major Case Study. 93p. 1982. pap. 7.50 (*0-931633-01-X*) Fnd Soc Stdy.

— The Vlachs of the Balkans: A Submerged Nation Existing Throughout the Millennia. 155p. 30.00 (*0-931635-02-0*); pap. 16.00 (*0-931635-03-9*) Fnd Soc Stdy.

Murvar, Vatro, ed. Theory of Liberty, Legitimacy & Power: New Directions in the Intellectual & Scientific Legacy of Max Weber. (International Library of Sociology Ser.). 224p. 1985. 39.95 (*0-7102-0355-1*, Routledge Thoemms) Routledge.

Murvar, Vatro, intro. Max Weber Today - An Introduction to a Living Legacy: Selected Bibliography. 159p. 1983. pap. 9.00 (*0-931633-00-1*) Fnd Soc Stdy.

Murvar, Vatro, jt. ed. see Glassman, Ronald M.

Murvin, H. L. Architect's Responsibilities in the Project Delivery Process. 3rd ed. (Illus.). 375p. 1989. pap. 44.50 (*0-9608498-3-1*) H L Murvin.

— Pre-Columbian Architecture, Art, & Artifacts Slide Catalog. 99p. 1988. pap. 3.95 (*0-9608498-2-3*) H L Murvin.

Murvin, Harry J. & Price, Richard L. Micro-Ledger: Financial Accounting Student Workbook Manual & Computer Applications for IBM--Version 2.2. 158p. 1990. pap. text 10.95 (*1-57094-039-8*); pap. text 5.95 (*1-57094-040-1*) S E Warner Sftware.

Murvin, Jimmie W. Paralegal Guide to Automobile Accident Cases, 1. LC 95-23809. (Paralegal Litigation Library). 408p. 1995. boxed set 78.00 (*0-471-00656-4*) Wiley.

Murwin, Susan A. & Payne, Suzzy C. The Quick & Easy Giant Dahlia Quilt on the Sewing Machine: Step-By-Step Instructions & Full Size Templates for Three Quilt Sizes. (Illus.). 80p. (Orig.). 1983. pap. 5.95 (*0-486-24501-2*) Dover.

M

An Asterisk (*) at the beginning of an entry indicates that the title is appearing for the first time.

— Quick & Easy Patchwork on the Sewing Machine: Instructions & Full-Size Templates for 12 Quilts. LC 78-74751. (Illus.). 80p. 1979. pap. 5.95 (0-486-23770-2) Dover.

Muryn, Mary. Water Magic: Healing Bath Recipes for the Body, Spirit & Soul. LC 95-21969. (Illus.). 256p. 1995. pap. 11.00 (0-684-80142-6, Fireside) S&S Trade Pap.

Murzin, Howy, jt. auth. see Schiff, Irwin A.

Mus, David, tr. see Du Bouchet, Andre.

Mus, Paul. Barabudur: Esquisse d'une histoire du bouddhisme fondee sur la critique archeologique des textes, 2 vols. Bolle, Kees W., ed. LC 77-79146. (Mythology Ser.). (FRE.). 1978. reprint ed. lib. bdg. 90.95 (0-405-10555-X) Ayer.

Musa, Adam, ed. Letters & Lectures of Idries Shah. 40p. 1981. pap. 9.00 (0-86304-010-1, Pub. by Octagon Pr) ISHK.

Musa, Al K. Muhammad Ibn, see Muhammad Ibn Musa, Al K.

Musa, John D. Software Reliability: Measurement, Prediction, Application. 621p. (C). 1987. 101.56 (0-07-044093-X) McGraw.

— Software Reliability Engineered Testing. LC 98-25765. (Illus.). 384p. 1998. 65.00 incl. disk (0-07-913271-5) McGraw.

Musa, Mahmoud N., ed. Pharmacokinetics & Therapeutic Monitoring of Psychiatric Drugs. LC 92-48220. (Illus.). 226p. 1993. pap. 36.95 (0-398-06301-X); text 52.95 (0-398-05841-5) C C Thomas.

Musa, Mark. Advent at the Gates: Dante's Comedy. LC 72-21243. 185p. reprint ed. pap. 57.40 (0-8357-5199-6, 205604800044) Bks Demand.

Musa, Mark, tr. Petrarch: The Canzoniere, or Rerum Vulgarium Fragmenta. LC 95-35943. (Illus.). 800p. 1999. pap. 27.95 (0-253-21317-7) Ind U Pr.

Musa, Mark, ed. see Boccaccio, Giovanni.

Musa, Mark, ed. see Dante Alighieri.

Musa, Mark, ed. see Pavese, Cesare.

Musa, Mark, ed. see Petrarca, Francesco.

Musa, Mark, ed. & tr. see Dante Alighieri.

Musa, Mark, tr. see Alighieri, Dante.

Musa, Mark, tr. see Boccaccio, Giovanni.

Musa, Mark, tr. see Dante Alighieri.

Musa, Mark, tr. see Machiavelli, Niccolo.

Musa, Mark, tr. see Pirandello, Luigi.

Musa, Mark, tr. & comment see Dante Alighieri.

Musa, Mark, tr. & comment see Petrarca, Francesco.

Musa, Mark, tr. & intro. see Dante Alighieri.

Musa, Mark, tr. & notes see Dante Alighieri.

Musacchio, Donald J., jt. auth. see Gilson, Robert J.

Musacchio, George. Milton's Adam & Eve: Fallible Perfection. LC 90-49694. (American University Studies: English Language & Literature: Ser. IV, Vol. 118). XII, 216p. (C). 1991. text 37.95 (0-8204-1326-7) P Lang Pubng.

Musacchio, Jacqueline & Van Boxel, Piet. Marriage in Italy, 1300-1650. Dean, Trevor & Lowe, K. J., eds. LC 97-10266. (Illus.). 318p. (C). 1998. text 59.95 (0-521-55402-0) Cambridge U Pr.

Musach, Lita. Selichos: Pocket. 16.99 (0-89906-721-2, SLPH); pap. 13.99 (0-89906-722-0, SLPP) Mesorah Pubns.

Musaeus, J. K. Musaei Lexicon. Bo, Domenico, ed. 96p. 1966. write for info. (0-318-70979-1) G Olms Pubs.

Musafar, Fakir, ed. Body Play: The Book, Vol. I. (Illus.). 132p. (Orig.). 1995. pap. 24.95 (0-9647735-0-3) Insight Books.

***Musah, Abdel-Fatau & Fayemi, Kayode.** Mercenaries: An African Security Dilemma LC 99-34771. 2000. write for info. (0-7453-1476-7, Pub. by Pluto GBR) Stylus Pub VA.

Musah, Abdel Fatau, ed. see Fayemi, Kayode.

Musaiger, A. O. & Harfouche, J. K., contrib. by. Breast-Feeding Patterns: A Review of Studies in the Eastern Mediterranean Region. 2nd rev. ed. (EMRO Technical Publications: No. 4). ix, 231p. 1993. pap. text 9.00 (92-9021-156-3, 1452004) World Health.

Musalem, M. & Vazquez, O. Riosz. Migracion y Etnicidad en Oaxaca. Corbett, J. et al, eds. (Vanderbilt University Publications in Anthropology: No. 43). (SPA.). 176p. (Orig.). 1992. pap. 12.75 (0-935462-34-1) VUPA.

Musallam, Basim, jt. ed. see Mundy, Martha.

Musallam, Musallam A. Iraqi Invasion of Kuwait: Saddam Hussein, His State & International Power Politics. LC 95-79286. 256p. 1996. text 65.00 (1-86064-020-6, Pub. by I B T) St Martin.

Musalo, Karen, et al. Refugee Law & Policy: Cases & Materials. LC 97-11885. 1036p. (C). 1997. boxed set 75.00 (0-89089-870-7) Carolina Acad Pr.

— Refugee Law & Policy: Selected Statutes, Regulations & International Materials. LC 97-77765. 596p. 1998. 75.00 (0-89089-871-5) Carolina Acad Pr.

Musan, Renate. On the Temporal Interpretation of Noun Phrases. rev. ed. LC 97-12397. (Outstanding Dissertations in Linguistics Ser.). 224p. 1997. text 56.00 (0-8153-2886-9) Garland.

Musaph, H. & Mettrop, P. J., eds. The Role of Aggression in Human Pathology. (Psychotherapy & Psychosomatics Ser.: Vol. 20, No. 5). (Illus.). 1972. pap. 15.75 (3-8055-1562-6) S Karger.

Musaph, H., ed. see Congress of International College of Psychosomatic.

Musashi, Miyamoto. A Book of Five Rings. 1985. 42.50 (0-911156-99-2) Bern Porter.

— A Book of Five Rings. Harris, Victor, tr. LC 73-83986. 104p. 1984. pap. 12.95 (0-87951-153-2, Pub. by Overlook Pr) Penguin Putnam.

— Book of Five Rings. 160p. 1992. pap. 10.95 (0-553-35170-2) Bantam.

— Book of Five Rings. 1988. 8.99 (0-517-41528-3) Random Hse Value.

— The Book of Five Rings. Cleary, Thomas & Munenori, Yagyu, trs. from JPN. LC 92-56443. 136p. (Orig.). 1993. pap. 9.00 (0-87773-868-8, Pub. by Shambhala Pubns) Random.

— The Book of Five Rings. Cleary, Thomas, tr. LC 93-36271. (Pocket Classics Ser.). (Orig.). 1994. pap. 7.00 (0-87773-998-6, Pub. by Shambhala Pubns) Random.

***Musashi, Miyamoto.** The Book Of Five Rings. 2000. pap. 11.95 (1-57062-748-7, Pub. by Shambhala Pubns) Random.

Musashi, Miyamoto. The Book of Five Rings: An Illustrated Guide. (Illus.). 192p. (Orig.). 1997. pap. 10.00 (1-889543-04-7) Beachchair Pr.

Musat, V., jt. auth. see Marsh, V.

Musaus. Rubezahl - Marchen. unabridged ed. (World Classic Literature Ser.). (GER.). pap. 5.95 (3-89507-036-X, Pub. by Bookking Intl) Distribks Inc.

Musaus, Johann Karl August, et al. German Romance: Specimens of Its Chief Authors, Musaeus & la Motte Fouque. Carlyle, Thomas, tr. (GERM Ser.: Vol. 61). xvii, 338p. 1992. reprint ed. 55.00 (0-938100-93-9) Camden Hse.

Musavi, Sayyed M. Western Civilization Through Muslim Eyes. Goulding, F. J., tr. from PER. 146p. 1977. 14.95 (0-941722-20-1); pap. 7.95 (0-941722-06-6) Book Dist Ctr.

Musbach, Joan M. & Dewing, Thomas. Colonial Kaleidescope. (Textworks Ser.). (Illus.). ix, 118p. (J). (gr. 4-8). 1995. ring bd. 29.95 (1-58284-016-4, Thoughtful Educ) Silver Strong.

***Musbee de Picardie Staff & Pinette, Matthieu.** From the Sun King to the Royal Twilight: Painting in Eighteenth-Century France from the Musbee de Picardie, Amiens. LC 00-29963. (Illus.). 2000. write for info. (1-885444-13-3) Am Fed Arts.

Musburger, Robert B. Electronic News Gathering: A Guide to ENG. (Electronic Media Guide Ser.). 96p. 1991. pap. text 24.95 (0-240-80079-6, Focal) Buttrwrth-Heinemann.

— Single Camera Video Production. LC 92-13909. (Illus.). 208p. 1992. pap. 24.95 (0-240-80034-6, Focal) Buttrwrth-Heinemann.

— Single-Camera Video Production. 2nd ed. LC 98-7179. (Media Manuals Ser.). (Illus.). 193p. 1999. pap. 24.95 (0-240-80333-7, Focal) Buttrwrth-Heinemann.

Musburger, Robert B., jt. auth. see Kindem, Gorham A.

Musca, Tom, jt. auth. see Menendez, Ramon.

Muscarella, Anthony. Iwo Jima - The Young Heroes. Goodman, Charles, ed. (American Heroes Ser.). (Illus.). 104p. (Orig.). 1989. pap. 9.95 (0-916693-13-9) Castle Bks.

Muscarella, Frank, jt. ed. see Szuchman, Lenore.

Muscarella, Jeffery. 1998 Guide to Intranets in Healthcare: A Comprehensive Guide to New Developments in Networks, Extranets & Electronic Commerce. Koizumi, Luci, ed. (Illus.). 1997. pap. 245.00 (1-57987-032-5) Faulkner & Gray.

Muscarella, Jeffrey W. & Koizumi, Luci, eds. 1999 Guide to Intranets in Health Care. (Illus.). 352p. 1998. pap. 275.00 (1-57987-106-2) Faulkner & Gray.

Muscarella, Len, jt. auth. see Haylock, Christina.

Muscarella, Oscar W. Bronze & Iron: Ancient Near Eastern Artifacts in the Metropolitan Museum of Art. (Illus.). 504p. 1989. 75.00 (0-87099-525-1, 0-8109-6450-3) Metro Mus Art.

— The Catalogue of Ivories from Hasanlu, Iran. Dyson, Robert H., Jr., ed. (University Museum Monographs: Hasanlu Special Studies: Nos. 40 & 2). (Illus.). xi, 231p. (Orig.). (C). 1980. pap. 30.00 (0-934718-33-4) U Museum Pubns.

Muscari, Mary. Lippincott's Review Series: Pediatric Nursing. 3rd ed. 448p. pap. text. write for info. (0-7817-2187-3) Lppncott W & W.

Muscari, Mary, ed. Pediatric Nursing. 2nd ed. LC 95-39932. (Review Ser.). 416p. 1996. pap. text 21.95 (0-397-55195-9) Lppncott W & W.

Muscari, Mary E. Advanced Pediatric Clinical Assessment: Skills & Procedures. 512p. spiral bd. write for info. (0-7817-1879-1) Lppncott W & W.

Muscat, Andrew. The Liability of the Holding Company for the Debts of Its Insolvent Subsidiaries. LC 96-20667. (Illus.). 570p. 1996. text 115.95 (1-85521-844-5, Pub. by Dartmth Pub) Ashgate Pub Co.

Muscat, Collette A. Alone with the One. (Illus.). 100p. (Orig.). 1994. 65.00 (1-883148-00-6) ACMI Pr.

Muscat, Eugene J. & Lorton, Paul, Jr. Information Processing Microcomputer Applications. 2nd ed. 64p. 1990. pap. text 3.96 (0-07-044123-5) McGraw.

Muscat, Glenn, jt. auth. see Carcach, Carlos.

Muscat, Robert J. The Fifth Tiger: A Study of Thai Development Policy. LC 93-25775. 360p. (C). (gr. 13). 1994. text 85.95 (1-56324-323-7, East Gate Bk) M E Sharpe.

Muscat, Robert J. The Fifth Tiger: A Study of Thai Development Policy. LC 93-25775. 360p. (C). (gr. 13). 1994. pap. text 36.95 (1-56324-324-5, East Gate Bk) M E Sharpe.

Muscatelli, Vitantonio. Economic & Political Institutions in Economic Policy. LC 96-28198. 160p. 1997. text 69.95 (0-7190-4993-8) Manchester Univ Pr.

Muscatine. Borzoi College Reader. 7th ed. 1992. teacher ed. 29.37 (0-07-044200-2) McGraw.

Muscatine, Charles. Chaucer & the French Tradition: A Study in Style & Meaning. (C). 1957. pap. 15.95 (0-520-00908-8, Pub. by U CA Pr) Cal Prin Full Svc.

— Medieval Literature, Style, & Culture. LC 97-45297. 288p. 1999. lib. bdg. 39.95 (1-57003-249-1) U of SC Pr.

Muscatine, Charles & Griffith, Marlene. The Borzoi College Reader. 7th ed. (C). 1992. text, student ed. 33.74 (0-07-911261-7) McGraw.

Muscatine, Charles & Griffith, Marlene, eds. The Borzoi College Reader. 7th ed. 864p. (C). 1991. pap. 39.06 (0-07-044166-9) McGraw.

— The Borzoi College Reader. 7th ed. (C). 1992. pap. text, student ed. 10.00 (0-07-044199-5) McGraw.

Muscatine, Doris, et al, eds. University of California Sotheby Book of California Wine. LC 83-47666. (Illus.). 640p. 1984. 32.50 (0-520-05085-1, Pub. by U CA Pr) Cal Prin Full Svc.

Musch, Donald J., jt. auth. see Alexander, Yonah.

Musch, Donald J., jt. ed. see Holbein, James R.

***Muschal-Reinhardt, Rosalie, et al.** Rituals for Women Coping with Breast Cancer. LC BL619.H43R58 2000. (Illus.). 60p. 2000. pap. 12.00 (1-890662-10-0) Prism Coll.

Muschamp, Herbert. Hearts of the City. write for info. (0-375-40406-6) Knopf.

— Man about Town: Frank Lloyd Wright in New York City. (Illus.). 224p. 1985. reprint ed. pap. text 9.95 (0-262-63100-8) MIT Pr.

Muschamp, Herbert, et al. The Once & Future Park. Karasov, Deborah & Waryan, Stephen, eds. LC 92-40464. (Illus.). 64p. (Orig.). 1993. pap. 19.95 (1-878271-76-8) Princeton Arch.

Muschard, Jutta. Relevant Translations: History, Presentation, Criticism, Application. LC 96-10167. (European University Studies, Series XXI: Vol. 163). (Illus.). 253p. 1996. pap. 51.95 (0-8204-3161-3, P306) P Lang Pubng.

***Musche, Brigitte.** Die Liebe in der Altorientalischen Dichtung. Vol. 15. (GER., Illus.). Xiv, 218p. 1999. text 81.50 (90-04-11213-8) Brill Academic Pubs.

Muschell, David. Mixed Emotions. 24p. 1990. pap. 3.50 (0-87129-010-3, M77) Dramatic Pub.

Muschett, F. Douglas, ed. Principles of Sustainable Development. LC 97-116850. (Illus.). 192p. 1996. boxed set 64.95 (1-57444-079-9) St Lucie Pr.

Muschiano, Joe. Election Strategies: How to Find 'Em & Vote 'Em in the 1990's. 218p. mass mkt. 4.99 (1-55197-240-9) Picasso Publ.

Muschik, W. Aspects of Non-Equilibrium Thermodynamics. (Series in Theoretical & Applied Mechanics: Vol. 9). 112p. 1989. text 28.00 (981-02-0087-0) World Scientific Pub.

Muschik, W., ed. Non-Equilibrium Thermodynamics with Application to Solids: Dedicated to the Memory of Professor Theodor Lehmann. (CISM International Centre for Mechanical Sciences Ser.: No. 336). ix, 329p. 1994. 76.95 (0-387-82453-7) Spr-Verlag.

Muschik, W. & Ebeling, W. Statistical Physics & Thermodynamics of Nonlinear Equilibrium Systems. 268p. 1993. text 95.00 (981-02-1134-1) World Scientific Pub.

Muschik, W., jt. ed. see Axelrad, D. R.

***Muschla.** Geometry Teacher's Activities Kit. 2000. spiral bd. 29.95 (0-13-016777-0) P-H.

Muschla, Gary R. English Teacher's Great Books Activities Kit: Sixty Ready-to-Use Activity Packets Featuring Classic, Popular, & Current Literature. LC 93-44779. 336p. 1994. pap. text 27.95 (0-87628-854-9) Ctr Appl Res.

— Reading Workshop Survival Kit: Management Techniques, Reproducible Worksheets, & 100 Mini-Lessons Covering Topics & Skills in Reading. LC 97-17265. (Illus.). 336p. 1998. pap. text 29.95 (0-87628-592-2) Ctr Appl Res.

— Writing Resource Activities Kit: Ready-to-Use Worksheets & Enrichment Lessons for Grades 4-9. LC 88-39425. Vol. 2. 240p. 1989. pap. text 27.95 (0-87628-970-7) Ctr Appl Res.

— The Writing Teacher's Book of Lists: With Ready-to-Use Activities & Worksheets. LC 90-28580. 288p. (C). 1991. pap. text 29.95 (0-13-971169-4, 710302) P-H.

— Writing Workshop Teacher's Survival Kit. LC 92-44853. 272p. 1993. pap. text 28.95 (0-87628-972-3) Ctr Appl Res.

Muschla, Gary R., jt. auth. see Muschla, Judith A.

***Muschla, Judith A.** Math Starters! Five-to-Ten Minute Activities That Make Students Think. LC 98-28657. (Illus.). (YA). (gr. 6-12). 1999. pap. 29.95 (0-87628-566-3) Ctr Appl Res.

Muschla, Judith A. & Muschla, Gary R. Hands-On Math Projects with Real-Life Applications. LC 96-24597. 324p. 1996. pap. text 28.95 (0-87628-384-9) Ctr Appl Res.

— Math Teacher's Book of Lists. LC 94-36753. 432p. (C). 1994. spiral bd. 29.95 (0-13-180357-3) P-H.

— Math Teacher's Book of Lists. LC 94-36753. 432p. (C). 1996. pap., teacher ed. 29.50 (0-13-255910-2) P-H.

Muschler, R. A Manual Flora of Egypt, 2 vols. in one. (Illus.). 1971. reprint ed. 250.00 (3-7682-0678-5) Lubrecht & Cramer.

Muschlitz, Beverly, jt. auth. see Michener, Dorothy.

Muscia, Jorge. El Filete: Popular Art of Buenos Aires. (Illus.). 56p. 1995. pap. 10.95 (1-883675-09-X) J Shaw Studio.

Musciano, Chuck. HTML Definitive Guide. 2nd ed. Loukides, Mike, ed. LC 97-165396. (Illus.). 450p. (Orig.). 1997. pap. 32.95 (1-56592-235-2) Thomson Learn.

Musciano, Chuck & Kennedy, Bill. HTML: The Definitive Guide. 3rd ed. Loukides, Mike, ed. (Illus.). 608p. 1998. pap. 34.95 (1-56592-492-4) OReilly & Assocs.

Musciano, Walter A. Building & Flying Model Airplanes. LC 84-28445. (Illus.). 224p. 1984. pap. 10.95 (0-668-05933-8) Prntice Hall Bks.

— Eagles of the Black Cross. (Illus.). 1965. 27.95 (0-8392-1144-9) Astor-Honor.

— Warbirds of the Sea: A History of Aircraft Carriers & Carrier-Based Aircraft. LC 93-87478. (Illus.). 592p. 1994. 49.95 (0-88740-583-5) Schiffer.

Muscio, Inga. Cunt: A Declaration of Independence. LC 98-31063. 288p. 1998. pap. 14.00 (1-58005-015-8) Seal Pr WA.

Muscle Shoals District Service League Staff. Cooks & Company: A Collection of Recipes from Muscle Shoals District Service League. (Illus.). 320p. 1988. pap. 11.95 (0-9620209-0-7) Muscle Shoals.

***Muscle Shoals District Service Staff.** Art of Cooking. LC 97-76295. (Illus.). 1998. 19.95 (0-9620209-1-5) Muscle Shoals.

Musco, Lydia J. Sugar House Hill. LC 95-78736. (Illus.). 32p. (J). 1995. pap. 8.95 (1-884540-16-3) Haleys.

Muscovitch, Edward, jt. auth. see Chelius, James R.

Muscular Dystrophy Symposium Staff. Muscular Dystrophy, 1976: Proceedings of the Symposium, Jerusalem, 1976. Robin, Gordon C. & Falewski de Leon, George, eds. (Illus.). 1977. 42.75 (3-8055-2680-6) S Karger.

Muscutt, Keith. Warriors of the Clouds: A Lost Civilization of the Upper Amazon of Peru. LC 96-26459. (Illus.). 128p. 1998. 59.95 (0-8263-1979-3); pap. 29.95 (0-8263-1962-9) U of NM Pr.

Muse, Benjamin. American Negro Revolution: From Nonviolence to Black Power, 1963-1967. LC 68-27350. 359p. reprint ed. 111.30 (0-8357-9194-7, 201583100097) Bks Demand.

— Virginia's Massive Resistance. 1990. 16.50 (0-8446-0816-5) Peter Smith.

Muse, Charlotte. The Comfort Teacher. (Flowering Quince Poetry Ser.: No. 5). (Illus.). 24p. (Orig.). 1985. pap. 7.50 (0-940592-17-7) Heyeck Pr.

Muse, Clifford L., ed. see Robinson, Harry G., III & Edwards, Hazel R.

Muse, Daphne, ed. The New Press Guide to Multicultural Resources for Young Readers. (Illus.). 700p. 1997. 60.00 (1-56584-339-8, Pub. by New Press NY) Norton.

— Prejudice: Stories About Hate, Ignorance, Revelation & Transformation. 212p. (J). 1998. pap. 7.95 (0-7868-1310-5, Pub. by Hyperion) Time Warner.

Muse, Eben J. The Land of Nam: The Vietnam War in American Film. LC 94-34912. 288p. 1995. 37.00 (0-8108-2952-5) Scarecrow.

Muse, Ivan. Oral & Nonverbal Expression. (School Leadership Library). (Illus.). 160p. 1996. 29.95 (1-883001-27-7) Eye On Educ.

***Muse, J. Stephen, ed.** Beside Still Waters: Resources for Shepherds in the Market Place. 192p. 2000. pap. 18.00 (1-57312-317-X) Smyth & Helwys.

Muse, Kenneth. Photo One. 2nd ed. (Illus.). 240p. (C). 1987. pap. text 35.20 (0-13-665340-5) P-H.

— The Total Cartoonist. (Illus.). 240p. (C). 1986. 21.00 (0-13-925263-0) P-H.

Muse, Mark, et al. Exercise for the Chronic Pain Patient. 1984. pap. 24.95 (0-932392-19-9) Mouvement Pubns.

Muse, Robert L. The Book of Revelation: An Annotated Bibliography. LC 95-39196. (Books of the Bible: Vol. 02). 394p. 1996. text 75.00 (0-8240-7394-0, H1387) Garland.

Muse, Vance. We Bombed in Burbank: A Joyride to Primetime. 279p. 1994. 22.00 (0-201-62223-8) Addison-Wesley.

— We Were Here. 1997. write for info. (0-679-44204-9) Pantheon.

Muse, Vance, et al. Northern New England. LC 96-40541. (Smithsonian Guide to Historic America Ser.). 294p. 1998. pap. 19.95 (1-55670-635-9) Stewart Tabori & Chang.

Musee en Herbe Staff. Livre de la Tour Eiffel. (Gallimard - Decouverte Cadet Ser.: No. 2). (FRE.). 96p. (J). (gr. 4-9). 1983. 14.95 (2-07-039502-2) Schoenhof.

Museler, Wilhelm. Riding Logic Available. 1985. 20.50 (0-671-76492-6) S&S Trade.

Museley, David & Nichol, Catherine. Aurally Coded English Spelling Dictionary: ACE. 1989. pap. 70.00 (0-7855-1740-5) St Mut.

Musell, R. Mark, jt. auth. see Belasco, Amy.

Musella, Donald F. Selecting School Administrators. LC 83-191790. (Informal Ser.: No. 54). 181p. reprint ed. pap. 56.20 (0-7837-0554-9, 204089500019) Bks Demand.

Musella, Donald F., jt. ed. see Leithwood, Kenneth A.

Musella, Donald F., jt. ed. see Leithwood, Kenneth L.

Musella, Marco & Panico, Carlo, eds. The Money Supply in the Economic Process: A Post Keynesian Perspective, 2 Vols., set. LC 95-32857. (International Library of Critical Writings in Economics Ser.: Vol. 60). 656p. (C). 1996. text 270.00 (1-85898-043-7) E Elgar.

Musella, Marco, jt. auth. see Joss, Bruno.

Musemeche & Ellis. Pete Maravich: Basketball Whiz. 1969. 4.95 (0-685-00420-1) Claitors.

Musen, Mark A. Automated Generation of Model-Based Knowledge-Acquisition Tools. (Research Notes in Artificial Intelligence Ser.). (C). 1989. pap. text 34.95 (1-55860-090-6) Morgan Kaufmann.

Museo del Prado Staff, ed. Museo del Prado Inventario General de Pinturas Vol. 1: La Coleccion Real. (SPA., Illus.). 840p. 1993. 500.00 (84-239-4311-9) Elliots Bks.

— Museo del Prado Inventario General de Pinturas Vol. 2: El Museo de la Trinidad. (SPA., Illus.). 514p. 400.00 (84-239-4312-7) Elliots Bks.

Museo di Castelvecchio (Verona, Italy) Staff, jt. auth. see Filippi, Gian G.

Museo di Palazzo Venezia Staff, et al. Masterpieces of Renaissance & Baroque Sculpture from the Palazzo Venezia, Rome: Georgia Museum of Art, October 5-November 24, 1996. LC 96-36152. (Illus.). 90p. 1996. pap. 25.00 (0-915977-29-X) Georgia Museum of Art.

Muser, Jeanette K. Rocky Hill, Kingstown, & Griggstown. LC 98-87569. (Images of America Ser.). (Illus.). 128p. 1998. pap. 18.99 (0-7524-1204-3) Arcadia Publng.

An Asterisk (*) at the beginning of an entry indicates that the title is appearing for the first time.

Musere, Jonathan. African Proverbs & Proverbial Names. 216p. 1999. pap. text 15.00 (*0-9645969-2-X*) Ariko Pubns.

— African Sleeping Sickness: Political Ecology, Colonialism, & Control in Uganda. LC 90-44199. (Studies in African Health & Medicine: Vol. 5). 224p. 1990. lib. bdg. 89.95 (*0-88946-280-1*) E Mellen.

***Musere, Jonathan.** Southern Californians' Attitudes to Immigrants: Blacks Compared to Other Ethnics. 170p. 2000. pap. text 15.00 (*0-9645969-3-8*) Ariko Pubns.

Musere, Jonathan. Traditional African Names. LC 99-25329. 400p. 1999. 65.00 (*0-8108-3643-2*) Scarecrow.

Musere, Jonathan & Byakutaga, Shirley C. African Names & Naming. LC 98-93629. 155p. 1998. pap. text 12.50 (*0-9645969-0-3*) Ariko Pubns.

Musere, Jonathan & Odhiambo, Christopher. African Ethnics & Personal Names. LC 98-94806. 281p. (C). 1999. pap. text 15.00 (*0-9645969-1-1*) Ariko Pubns.

Muses, Charles. Destiny & Control in Human Systems: Studies in the Interactive Connectedness of Time (Chronotopology) 1984. lib. bdg. 132.00 (*0-89838-156-8*) Kluwer Academic.

Muses, Moses & Wieder, Laurence. The Red Sea Haggadah. 96p. 1995. pap. 10.00 (*1-887478-00-0*, WiseAcre) Red Sea NY.

Museum & Galleries Commission Staff. Manual of Natural History Curatorship. Stansfield, Geoff et al, eds. 306p. 1994. pap. 79.95 (*0-11-290513-7*, HM05137, Pub. by Statnry Office) Balogh.

Museum, Albert, jt. auth. see Museum, Victoria.

Museum Boijmans Van Beuningen Staff. Things. (Illus.). 216p. 1998. 30.00 (*90-6918-188-6*, 810061, Pub. by Boymans Mus) Dist Art Pubs.

Museum Boijmans Van Beuningen Staff, et al. Nineteenth Century Dutch Watercolors & Drawings from the Museum Boijmans Van Beuningen, Rotterdam. LC 98-20287. 1998. 29.95 (*0-88397-129-1*) Art Srvc Intl.

Museum British Press. Assyrians Activity Book. (Illus.). 16p. (gr. 4-7). 1999. pap. text 5.95 (*0-7141-1125-2*) Brimax Bks.

— Make Your Own Viking Ship. 1999. pap. text 6.95 (*0-7141-1786-2*) Brimax Bks.

— Vikings Activity Book. (Illus.). 16p. (gr. 4-7). 1999. pap. text 5.95 (*0-7141-2174-6*) Brimfield Publns.

Museum Curators & PR Associates Staff, ed. see Bright, JoAnn.

Museum Curators, P. R. Assocs. Staff, ed. see Bright, JoAnn.

Museum for East Texas Culture Staff, ed. A Pictorial History of Palestine & Anderson County, Texas. (Illus.). 128p. 1999. 40.00 (*0-9667999-1-7*) Landmark Publ.

Museum of American Folk Art Staff, ed. Patriotic Quilt-Postcards. (Illus.). 1991. pap. text 1.00 (*0-486-26764-4*) Dover.

Museum of Art & Archaeology, University of Missouri, Columbia Staff. The Samuel H. Kress Study Collection at the University of Missouri. Land, Norman E., ed. LC 99-34239. (Illus.). 120p. 1999. pap. 29.95 (*0-8262-1241-7*) U of Mo Pr.

Museum of Art, Rhode Island School Staff. Patterns & Poetry: No-Robes from the Lucy Truman Aldrich Collection at the Museum of Art, Rhode Island School of Design. (Illus.). 192p. 1993. pap. 45.00 (*1-55859-641-0*) Abbeville Pr.

Museum of Arts & Sciences Macon, Georgia Staff. George Bellows: The Personal Side. (Illus.). 56p. (Orig.). 1984. pap. 8.50 (*0-916769-01-1*) Museum Art GA.

Museum of Bad Art Staff, et al. Museum of Bad Art: Art Too Bad to Be Ignored. LC 96-19444. (Illus.). 112p. (Orig.). 1996. pap. 14.95 (*0-8362-2185-0*) Andrews & McMeel.

Museum of Church History & Art Staff, et al. Images of Faith: Art of the Latter-Day Saints. LC 95-16414. (Illus.). 216p. 1995. 49.95 (*0-87579-912-4*) Deseret Bk.

***Museum of Contemporary Art (Los Angeles, Calif.). Giuseppe Panza di Biumo Collection.** Panza: The Legacy of a Collector : the Giuseppe Panza Di Biumo Collection at the Museum of Contemporary Art, Los Angeles. LC 99-47687. 1999. write for info. (*0-914357-73-5*) Los Angeles Mus Contemp.

Museum of Contemporary Art (Los Angeles, Calif.) S, jt. auth. see Butler, Cornelia H.

Museum of Contemporary Art (Los Angeles, Calif.) S, jt. auth. see Schimmel, Paul.

***Museum of Contemporary Art (Los Angeles, Calif) Staff, et al.** The Social Scene: The Ralph M. Parsons Foundation Photography Collection at the Museum of Contemporary Art, Los Angeles. LC 99-86071. 2000. write for info. (*0-914357-74-3*) Los Angeles Mus Contemp.

Museum of Contemporary Art Staff, jt. auth. see Warren, Lynne.

***Museum Of Contemporary Art Staff (Chicago, Ill.).** Sol Lewitt Bands of Color. 1999. pap. text 25.00 (*0-933856-58-X*) MMCAD Systs.

Museum of Fine Arts, Boston & Harvard College Libr. The Artist & the Book in Western Europe & the United States, Eighteen Sixty to Nineteen Sixty. LC 81-81721. (Illus.). 332p. 1982. reprint ed. lib. bdg. 125.00 (*0-87817-277-7*) Hacker.

Museum of Fine Arts, Boston Staff. A Baby Book for You. 64p. 1996. 16.95 (*0-8212-2282-1*, Pub. by Bulfinch Pr) Little.

Museum of Fine Arts Boston Staff. The Scents of Time: Perfume from Ancient Egypt to the 21st Century. (Illus.). 112p. 2000. 35.00 (*0-8212-2635-5*, Pub. by Bulfinch Pr) Little.

Museum of Fine Arts Curatorial Staff. Art for Boston: A Decade of Acquisitions under the Directorship of Jan Fontein. Purvis, Cynthia M., ed. LC 87-61094. (Illus.). 216p. 1987. 17.95 (*0-87846-290-2*); pap. 24.95 (*0-87846-291-0*) Mus Fine Arts Boston.

Museum of Fine Arts, Department of Paintings Staff & Murphy, Alexandra R. European Paintings in the Museum of Fine Arts, Boston: An Illustrated Summary Catalogue. LC 84-60020. (Illus.). 368p. 1985. pap. 28.00 (*0-87846-230-9*) Mus Fine Arts Boston.

***Museum of Fine Arts, Houston Staff, et al.** Masterworks of European Painting in Houston. LC 99-39064. 2000. write for info. (*0-89090-093-0*) Mus Fine TX.

***Museum of Fine Arts Ladies Committee Associates.** Boston Tea Parties. (Illus.). 192p. 2000. pap. 20.00 (*0-87846-559-6*) Mus Fine Arts Boston.

Museum of Fine Arts, Research Laboratory Staff. Applications of Science in Examination of Works of Art: Proceedings of the Museum of Fine Arts, Research Laboratory Seminar, Boston, 1958. LC 78-99280. 1960. 19.95 (*0-405-00070-7*) Ayer.

***Museum of Fine Arts Staff.** Japanese Art In the Museum of Fine Arts. (Illus.). 1999. 100.00 (*0-87846-464-6*) Mus Fine Arts Boston.

Museum of Fine Arts Staff. Mother's Journal: A Book of Days. (Illus.). 128p. 1991. 16.95 (*0-8212-1886-7*, Pub. by Bulfinch Pr) Little.

Museum of Fine Arts Staff, ed. Rembrandt: Experimental Etcher. LC 87-80024. 1988. reprint ed. lib. bdg. 60.00 (*0-87817-320-X*) Hacker.

Museum of Fine Arts Staff, jt. auth. see Camfield, William A.

Museum of Fine Arts Staff, jt. auth. see Warren, David B.

Museum of Fine Arts Staff, jt. auth. see Wilson, Carolyn C.

Museum of History & Technology Staff, jt. auth. see Hoover, Cynthia M.

Museum of International Folk Art (N.M.) Staff, jt. auth. see Kahlenberg, Mary H.

Museum of Modern Art, Film Department Staff, ed. Circulating Film Library Catalog. (Illus.). 304p. (Orig.). 1984. pap. 15.95 (*0-87070-327-7*) Mus of Modern Art.

Museum of Modern Art Library Staff. Annual Bibliography of Modern Art, 1986: Museum of Modern Art Library. 1992. 190.00 (*0-8161-1797-7*, G K Hall & Co) Mac Lib Ref.

— Annual Bibliography of Modern Art, 1987: Museum of Modern Art Library. 1990. 220.00 (*0-8161-1564-8*, G K Hall & Co) Mac Lib Ref.

— Annual Bibliography of Modern Art, 1989: The Museum of Modern Art Library, New York. (Monographs). 700p. (C). 1990. 235.00 (*0-8161-0508-1*, G K Hall & Co) Mac Lib Ref.

— Annual Bibliography of Modern Art, 1990: The Museum of Modern Art, New York. annuals 700p. 1991. 275.00 (*0-8161-0517-0*, G K Hall & Co) Mac Lib Ref.

— Annual Bibliography of Modern Art, 1991. 600p. 1992. 250.00 (*0-8161-0557-X*, G K Hall & Co) Mac Lib Ref.

— Annual Bibliography of Modern Art, 1992. 700p. 1993. 250.00 (*0-8161-0597-9*, Hall Reference) Macmillan.

— Art in Progress: A Survey Prepared for the Fifteenth Anniversary of the Museum of Modern Art, New York Staff. 1981. 35.95 (*0-405-12882-7*) Ayer.

— Bulletin of the Museum of Modern Art, 1933-1963, 7 Vols. LC 38-43. 1967. reprint ed. 35.00 (*0-685-06505-7*) Ayer.

— Bulletin of the Museum of Modern Art, 1933-1963, 7 vols. LC 38-43. 1967. reprint ed. 203.95 (*0-405-01500-3*) Ayer.

— Vincent Van Gogh. Barr, Alfred H., Jr., ed. LC 78-109811. (Illus.). 193p. 1971. reprint ed. lib. bdg. 55.00 (*0-8371-4302-0*, NYVG, Greenwood Pr) Greenwood.

Museum of Modern Art Library Staff & Ritchie, Andrew C. Masters of British Painting, 1800 to 1950. 1981. 24.95 (*0-405-12884-3*) Ayer.

Museum of Modern Art Library Staff, et al. Arp. 1981. 19.95 (*0-405-12886-X*) Ayer.

Museum of Modern Art Oxford Staff. Art from Argentina. 144p. 1994. pap. 95.00 (*0-905836-76-6*, Pub. by Museum Modern Art) St Mut.

— Fisher, Joel. (Illus.). 1977. pap. 30.00 (*0-905836-02-2*, Pub. by Museum Modern Art) St Mut.

— Logan, Andrew: An Artistic Adventure. 1991. pap. 24.00 (*0-905836-73-1*, Pub. by Museum Modern Art) St Mut.

— Soviet Film Posters of the Silent Cinema: Colour Poster of Alexander Ilyich Naumov's "Bella Donna" (Illus.). 1987. pap. 20.00 (*0-905836-59-6*, Pub. by Museum Modern Art) St Mut.

Museum of Modern Art Oxford Staff, ed. Signs of the Times: A Decade of Video, Film & Slide-Tape Installation in Britain 1980-1990. 87p. 1990. pap. 60.00 (*0-905836-72-3*, Pub. by Museum Modern Art) St Mut.

Museum of Modern Art Staff. Annual Bibliography of Modern Art, 1993. 1994. 235.00 (*0-8161-0697-5*, G K Hall & Co) Mac Lib Ref.

— Annual Bibliography of Modern Art, 1994. 1995. 250.00 (*0-7838-2147-6*, G K Hall & Co) Mac Lib Ref.

— Annual Bibliography of Modern Art 1995. 1996. 255.00 (*0-7838-1530-1*, G K Hall & Co) Mac Lib Ref.

— Annual Bibliography of Modern Art, 1996. 1997. 250.00 (*0-7838-2031-3*) Mac Lib Ref.

— Catalog of the Library of the Museum of Modern Art, New York. 1980. 1500.00 (*0-8161-1299-1*, G K Hall & Co) Mac Lib Ref.

***Museum of Modern Art Staff.** The Museum of Modern Art: Highlights of the Collection. (Museum of Modern Art Bks.). 352p. 1999. pap. 18.95 (*0-8109-6201-2*, Pub. by Abrams) Time Warner.

Museum of Modern Art Staff, jt. auth. see Szarkowski, John.

Museum of Natural History, Roger Williams Park Sta. All Things Connected: Native American Creations. 65p. 1995. pap. 14.95 (*0-9646544-0-7*) Mus Nat Hist.

Museum of New Mexico Press Staff. Churches of New Mexico Postcards. 64p. 1994. pap. text 9.95 (*0-89013-269-0*) Museum NM Pr.

— Villages of the Rio Grande Postcards. 64p. 1994. pap. text 9.95 (*0-89013-268-2*) Museum NM Pr.

Museum of Science & Industry Staff. Within the Fairy Castle: Colleen Moore's Doll House at the Museum of Science & Industry, Chica. (Illus.). 128p. 1998. 35.00 (*0-8212-2519-7*, Pub. by Bulfinch Pr) Little.

Museum of Science & Industry Staff, jt. auth. see Nelson, Pamela.

Museum of Television & Radio (New York, N.Y.) Staf. Worlds Without End: The Art & History of the Soap Opera. LC 97-307. (Illus.). 176p. 1997. 29.95 (*0-8109-3997-5*, Pub. by Abrams) Time Warner.

Museum of the American Quilter's Society Staff. Quilts Vol. 2: The Permanent Collection. (Illus.). 80p. 1998. 9.95 (*0-89145-827-1*, 3793) Collector Bks.

Museum of the City of New York Staff & Simmons, Peter. Gotham Comes of Age: New York Through the Lens of the Byron Company, 1892-1942. LC 98-47448. (Illus.). 216p. 1999. pap. 35.00 (*0-7649-0906-1*) Pomegranate Calif.

Museum of the City of New York Staff, jt. auth. see Als, Hilton.

Museum of the City of New York Staff, jt. auth. see McNamara, Brooks.

Museum Practice Program Graduate Students. Margaret Watson Parker: A Collector's Legacy. (Illus.). 30p. 1982. pap. 3.00 (*0-912303-26-3*) Michigan Mus.

Museum Practice Program, Graduate Students Staff. Art a la Carte: Decorative Imagery in Maps, 1600-1900. (Illus.). 22p. 1979. pap. 2.00 (*0-912303-17-4*) Michigan Mus.

Museum Press British. Make Your Own Egyptian Mummy Case. (gr. 4-7). 1999. pap. text 6.95 (*0-7141-1785-4*) Brimax Bks.

— Prehistoric Britain Activity Book. 1999. pap. text 5.95 (*0-7141-1394-8*) Brimax Bks.

— Writing Activity Book. 1999. pap. text 5.95 (*0-7141-1762-5*) Brimax Bks.

Museum Quilts Publications Staff. Beatrix Potter. (Little Brown Notebooks Ser.). 1998. 9.99 (*1-897954-76-X*, Pub. by Mus Quilts Pub) Sterling.

— Black Beauty. (Little Brown Notebooks Ser.). 1998. 9.99 (*1-897954-81-6*, Pub. by Mus Quilts Pub) Sterling.

— Christmas Stories. (Little Brown Notebooks Ser.). 1998. 9.99 (*1-897954-97-2*, Pub. by Mus Quilts Pub) Sterling.

— Emma. (Little Brown Notebooks Ser.). 1998. 9.99 (*1-897954-83-2*, Pub. by Mus Quilts Pub) Sterling.

— Heidi. (Little Brown Notebooks Ser.). 1998. 9.99 (*1-897954-80-8*, Pub. by Mus Quilts Pub) Sterling.

— Jane Eyre. (Little Brown Notebooks Ser.). 1998. 9.99 (*1-897954-82-4*, Pub. by Mus Quilts Pub) Sterling.

— Mark Twain. (Little Brown Notebooks Ser.). 1998. 9.99 (*1-897954-74-3*, Pub. by Mus Quilts Pub) Sterling.

— Secret Garden. (Little Brown Notebooks Ser.). 1998. 9.99 (*1-897954-75-1*, Pub. by Mus Quilts Pub) Sterling.

— Shakespeare's Comedies. (Little Brown Notebooks Ser.). 1998. 9.99 (*1-897954-38-7*, Pub. by Mus Quilts Pub) Sterling.

Museum Quilts Publications Staff, et al. Grimm's Fairy Tales. (Little Brown Notebooks Ser.). 1998. 9.99 (*1-897954-95-6*, Pub. by Mus Quilts Pub) Sterling.

Museum Senior Curators Staff. The Mauritshuis, The Hague. LC 95-166231. (Illus.). 128p. 1994. 30.00 (*1-85759-031-7*) Scala Books.

Museum Store Association Inc. Staff. The Manager's Guide: Basic Guidelines for the New Store Manager. (Illus.). 144p. 1992. spiral bd. 55.00 (*0-9616104-2-5*) Museum Store.

Museum Store Association, Inc. Staff. MSA Data Banque Report, 1990. 215p. (Orig.). 1990. pap. text 50.00 (*0-9616104-1-7*) Museum Store.

— The New Store Workbook: MSA's Guide to Remodeling, Expanding & Opening the Museum Store. (Illus.). 107p. (Orig.). 1994. student ed., spiral bd. 69.95 (*0-9616104-3-3*) Museum Store.

Museum Studies Class of Nineteen Seventy-Eight Sta. Selections from the Frederick Weisman Co. Collection of Southern California. (Illus.). 64p. (Orig.). (C). 1978. pap. text 35.00 (*0-936270-11-X*) CA St U LB Art.

Museum Studies Class Staff. Bryan Hunt: A Decade of Drawings. (Illus.). 61p. 1983. pap. 20.00 (*0-936270-20-9*) CA St U LB Art.

— Doumani House. (Illus.). 11p. 1981. pap. 25.00 (*0-685-42743-9*) CA St U LB Art.

— Vapor Dreams in L.A. Terry Schoonhaven's Empty Stage. (Illus.). 40p. 1982. pap. 20.00 (*0-936270-19-5*) CA St U LB Art.

Museum Studies Class Staff, et al. Arnoldi: Just Bronze. Glenn, Constance W., ed. (Illus.). 56p. (Orig.). (C). 1987. pap. 20.00 (*0-936270-26-8*) CA St U LB Art.

Museum Studies Graduate Certificate Program Staff. In Praise of Nature: The Landscapes of William Wendt. Glenn, Constance W. & Taylor-Winter, Sue, eds. (Illus.). 64p. (Orig.). (C). 1989. pap. text 25.00 (*0-936270-29-2*) CA St U LB Art.

Museum, Victoria & Museum, Albert. Voyages & Visions: Nineteenth-Century, European Images of the Middle East from the Victoria & ALbert Museum. 1995. pap. write for info. (*0-86528-042-8*) SITES.

Museums & Galleries Commission Staff, jt. auth. see Conservation Unit Staff.

Museums at Stony Brook Staff. The Carriage Collection. LC 86-12594. (Illus.). 127p. (Orig.). 1986. pap. 15.00 (*0-943924-09-X*) Mus Stony Brook.

— The Museums at Stony Brook: Highlights of the Collection. LC 82-81912. (Illus.). 72p. (Orig.). 1982. pap. 3.00 (*0-943924-04-9*) Mus Stony Brook.

— Nineteenth Century American Carriages: Their Manufacture, Decoration & Use. LC 87-12282. (Illus.). 112p. (Orig.). 1987. pap. 15.00 (*0-943924-10-3*) Mus Stony Brook.

Museums for a New Century Commission. Museums for a New Century: A Report of the Commission on Museums for a New Century. LC 84-72051. (Illus.). 144p. 1984. pap. 19.00 (*0-931201-08-X*) Am Assn Mus.

***Museveni, Yoweri K.** What Is Africa's Problem? 2000. 47.95 (*0-8166-3277-4*); pap. 18.95 (*0-8166-3278-2*) U of Minn Pr.

Musgrave. Early Modern European Economy. LC 99-12189. 1999. pap. 22.95 (*0-312-22332-3*) St Martin.

***Musgrave.** Early Modern European Economy. LC 99-12189. 1999. text 59.95 (*0-312-22331-5*) St Martin.

Musgrave, Alan E. Commonsense, Science, & Scepticism: A Historical Introduction to the Theory of Knowledge. LC 92-12657. (Illus.). 324p. (C). 1993. pap. text 21.95 (*0-521-43625-7*) Cambridge U Pr.

Musgrave, Alan E., jt. ed. see Currie, Gregory.

Musgrave, Alan E., jt. ed. see Lakatos, Imre.

Musgrave, Anthony. Studies in Political Economy. LC 67-18581. (Reprints of Economic Classics Ser.). viii, 185p. 1968. reprint ed. 35.00 (*0-678-00337-8*) Kelley.

M

Musgrave, Beatrice. Change & Choice: Women & Middle Age. Menell, Zoe, ed. 186p. 1980. 19.95 (*0-685-18790-X*, Pub. by P Owen Ltd) Dufour.

Musgrave, Beatrice & Menell, Zoe, eds. Change & Choice. 1980. text 29.95 (*0-7206-0539-3*) Dufour.

Musgrave, Frank. School & the Social Order. LC 79-40738. 210p. reprint ed. pap. 65.10 (*0-608-17552-8*, 203053200069) Bks Demand.

Musgrave, Gerald L., jt. auth. see Goodman, John C.

Musgrave, James & Anniss, Michael. Relationship Dynamics: Theory & Analysis. (Illus.). 256p. 1996. 25.50 (*0-684-82449-3*) Free Pr.

Musgrave, Jan. Patchwork Projects: With Full Size Patterns & Easy to Follow Step by Step Instructions. 1984. write for info. (*0-914169-00-9*, Patchwrk Orig) Econ America.

Musgrave, Michael. Brahms: A German Requiem. (Cambridge Music Handbooks Ser.). (Illus.). 109p. (C). 1996. pap. text 12.95 (*0-521-40995-0*) Cambridge U Pr.

— Brahms Reader. LC 99-11127. (Illus.). 384p. 1999. 35.00 (*0-300-06804-2*) Yale U Pr.

— The Music of Brahms. (Illus.). 340p. 1994. pap. text 28.00 (*0-19-816401-7*) OUP.

— The Music of Brahms. (Companions to the Great Composers Ser.). (Illus.). 320p. 1985. 39.95 (*0-7100-9776-X*, Routledge Thoemms) Routledge.

— The Musical Life of the Crystal Palace. (Illus.). 286p. (C). 1995. text 59.95 (*0-521-37562-2*) Cambridge U Pr.

Musgrave, Michael, ed. Brahms 2: Biographical, Documentary & Analytical Studies. (Illus.). 264p. 1987. text 69.95 (*0-521-32606-0*) Cambridge U Pr.

— The Cambridge Companion to Brahms. LC 98-3057. (Cambridge Companions to Music Ser.). (Illus.). 348p. (C). 1999. 57.95 (*0-521-48129-5*); pap. 21.95 (*0-521-48581-9*) Cambridge U Pr.

Musgrave, P. W. Curricular Decisions in Their Administrative Contexts. 122p. (C). 1985. 48.00 (*0-7300-0187-3*, Pub. by Deakin Univ) St Mut.

— Socialising Contexts. 200p. 1987. pap. text 21.95 (*0-04-176011-5*) Routledge.

Musgrave, Peggy B. United States Taxation of Foreign Investment Income: Issues & Arguments. LC 68-58098. (Illus.). 186p. (Orig.). 1969. pap. 6.00 (*0-915506-10-6*) Harvard Law Intl Tax.

Musgrave, Percy. Musgrave: Notes on the Ancient Family of Musgrave of Musgrave, Westmorland, England, & Its Various Branches in Cumberland, Yorkshire, Northumberland. (Illus.). 351p. 1993. reprint ed. pap. 49.50 (*0-8328-3724-5*); reprint ed. lib. bdg. 59.50 (*0-8328-3723-7*) Higginson Bk Co.

Musgrave, Peter. Land & Economy in Baroque Italy: The Valpolicella, 1630-1797. LC 92-14244. 1992. 65.00 (*0-7185-1368-1*); text 54.00 (*0-7185-1449-1*) St Martin.

Musgrave, Peter W. From Humanity to Utility: Melbourne University & Public Examinations, 1856-1964. (C). 1992. 95.00 (*0-86431-118-4*, Pub. by Aust Council Educ Res) St Mut.

Musgrave, Richard. Memoirs of the Different Rebellions in Ireland, from the Arrival of the English: Also, a Particular Detail of That Which Broke Out the 23rd of May 1798. (1798 Collection: Vol. 1). 982p. 1995. 49.95 (*0-9643925-0-X*) Round Tower.

Musgrave, Richard A. Fiscal Reform for Colombia: Final Report & Staff Papers of the Colombian Commission on Tax Reform. Gillis, Malcolm, ed. LC 75-148648. (Illus.). 876p. 1971. pap. 15.00 (*0-915506-11-4*) Harvard Law Intl Tax.

— Fiscal Reform in Bolivia: Final Report of the Bolivian Mission on Tax Reform. LC 80-14943. (Illus.). 604p. 1981. pap. text 18.00 (*0-915506-22-X*) Harvard Law Intl Tax.

— Fiscal Systems. LC 80-29652. (Studies in Comparative Economics). (Illus.). 397p. (ps-3). 1981. reprint ed. lib. bdg. 35.00 (*0-313-22431-5*, MUFC, Greenwood Pr) Greenwood.

***Musgrave, Richard A.** Public Finance in a Democratic Society Vol. III: The Foundations of Taxation & Expenditure. 528p. 2000. 120.00 (*1-84064-113-4*) E Elgar.

Musgrave, Richard A. Strengthening the Progressive Income Tax: The Responsible Answer to America's Budget Problem. 1989. 10.00 (*0-944826-07-5*) Economic Policy Inst.

Musgrave, Richard A., ed. Broad-Based Taxes: New Options & Sources. 302p. 1973. 3.00 (*0-87186-238-7*, 238) Comm Econ Dev.

An Asterisk (*) at the beginning of an entry indicates that the title is appearing for the first time.

— Essays in Fiscal Federalism. LC 76-49481. (Brookings Institution, Studies of Government Finance Ser.). (Illus.). 301p. 1977. reprint ed. lib. bdg. 35.00 (*0-8371-9366-4*, MUEFF, Greenwood Pr) Greenwood.

Musgrave, Richard A., jt. auth. see Buchanan, James M.

Musgrave, Ruth & Stein, Mary A. State Wildlife Laws Handbook. LC 93-23418. 840p. 1993. text 94.00 (*0-86587-357-7*) Gov Insts.

Musgrave, Ruth, et al. Federal Wildlife Laws Handbook: With Related Laws. LC 98-36087. 679p. 1998. text 95.00 (*0-86587-557-X*, 557) Gov Insts.

Musgrave, Susan. Dreams Are More Real Than Bathtubs. LC 98-85277. (Illus.). 32p. (J). (gr. k-4). 1999. 14.95 (*1-55143-107-6*) Orca Bk Pubs.

— Forcing the Narcissus. 1994. pap. 12.99 (*0-7710-6659-7*) McCland & Stewart.

— Hag Head. (Illus.). 32p. (J). (ps-3). 1989. 9.95 (*0-7720-1251-2*) Stoddart Publ.

— Things That Keep & Do Not Change. 92p. 2000. 12.95 (*0-7710-6676-7*) McCland & Stewart.

Musgrave, Thomas D. Self-Determination & National Minorities. LC 96-40030. (Oxford Monographs in International Law). 326p. 1997. text 95.00 (*0-19-826058-X*) OUP.

***Musgrave, Thomas D.** Self-Determination & National Minorities. (Oxford Monographs in International Law). 344p. 2000. pap. text 29.95 (*0-19-829898-6*) OUP.

***Musgrave, Toby.** Courtyard Gardens: Imaginative Ideas for Outdoor Living. LC 00-39613. (Illus.). 2001. pap. write for info. (*1-58816-002-5*) Hearst Commns.

— Plant Hunters: Two Hundred Years of Adventure & Discovery Around the World. 2000. pap. 21.95 (*1-84188-001-9*) Seven Dials.

Musgrave, Toby, et al. The Plant Hunters: Two Hundred Years of Adventure & Discovery Around the World. LC 99-178847. 224p. 29.95 (*0-7063-7753-2*, Pub. by WrLock) Sterling.

Musgrove, David. The Bear Hunter, Vol. 1. Hicks, Ed & Montgomery, Theron, eds. 85p. (Orig.). 1996. pap. 7.50 (*0-9653806-0-2*) Al Lit Rev.

Musgrove, Frank & Fielden, Sarah. Ecstacy & Holiness: Counter Culture & the Open Society. (Modern Revivals in Sociology Ser.). 246p. 1994. text 61.95 (*0-7512-0289-4*, Pub. by Gregg Revivals) Ashgate Pub Co.

Musgrove, Gerald L., jt. auth. see Goodman, John C.

Musgrove, James B., jt. auth. see Canadian Bar Association Staff.

Musgrove, Margaret. Ashanti to Zulu: African Traditions. (J). 1976. 10.19 (*0-606-02025-X*, Pub. by Turtleback) Demco.

Musgrove, Margaret W. Ashanti to Zulu: African Traditions. Dillon, Leo, ed. LC 76-6610. (Pied Piper Bks.). (Illus.). 32p. (J). (gr. 4-7). 1976. 18.99 (*0-8037-0357-0*, Dial Yng Read) Peng Put Young Read.

— Ashanti to Zulu: African Traditions. (Illus.). (J). 1992. pap. 5.99 (*0-14-054604-9*, PuffinBks) Peng Put Young Read.

***Musgrove, Margaret Worsham.** Student's Ovid Vol. 26: Selections from the Metamorphoses. (Oklahoma Series in Classical Culture). (Illus.). 224p. 2000. pap. text 16.95 (*0-8061-3220-5*) U of Okla Pr.

Musgrove, Margaret Worsham, jt. auth. see Ovid.

Musgrove, Mary L., jt. ed. see Miller, Juliet V.

Musgrove, Mary R. Beaded Dream Catchers. (Illus.). 4p. 1993. pap. 3.95 (*0-932255-05-1*) Promenade Pub.

Musgrove, Peggy. Pleasing God: A Self-Directed Bible Study for Living the Christian Life. 80p. 1991. pap. text 3.95 (*0-88243-651-1*, 02-0651) Gospel Pub.

— Praying Always: A Self-Directed Bible Study for Christian Service. 80p. 1993. pap. text 3.95 (*0-88243-684-8*, 02-0684) Gospel Pub.

— Women of the Bible. Life Publishers International Staff, tr. (RUS.). 165p. 1999. pap. write for info. (*0-7361-0078-4*) Life Pubs Intl.

Musgrove, Philip. Consumer Behavior in Latin America: Income & Spending of Families in Ten Andean Cities. LC 77-1108. 1978. 36.95 (*0-8157-5914-2*) Brookings.

— United States Household Consumption, Income, & Demographic Changes, 1975-2025. LC 81-86060. (Illus.). 263p. reprint ed. pap. 81.60 (*0-8357-4684-4*, 203763100008) Bks Demand.

Musgrove, Philip, jt. auth. see Grunwald, Joseph.

***Musgrove, Richard W.** History of the Town of Bristol, Grafton Co., 2 vols. (Illus.). 1096p. 1999. reprint ed. lib. bdg. 114.00 (*0-8328-9895-3*) Higginson Bk Co.

Musgrove, S. Shakespeare & Jonson: The Macmillan Brown Lectures. LC 76-38501. reprint ed. 20.00 (*0-404-04545-6*) AMS Pr.

— T. S. Eliot & Walt Whitman. 1972. 200.00 (*0-87968-012-1*) Gordon Pr.

— T. S. Eliot & Walt Whitman. LC 72-100773. (Studies in Comparative Literature: No. 35). (C). 1970. reprint ed. lib. bdg. 49.95 (*0-8383-0332-3*) M S G Haskell Hse.

Musha, T., et al, eds. Noise in Physical Systems & 1-f Fluctuations: Proceedings of the International Conference, ICNF 1991, November 24-27, 1991, Kyoto, Japan. LC 92-52686. 800p. (gr. 12). 1992. 170.00 (*90-5199-083-9*, Pub. by IOS Pr) IOS Press.

Musha, T. & Sawada, Y. Physics of the Living State. LC 93-80960. 289p. (gr. 12). 1994. 70.00 (*90-5199-147-9*, Pub. by IOS Pr) IOS Press.

Mushabac, Jane & Wigan, Angela. A Short & Remarkable History of New York City. LC 99-46888. (Illus.). 128p. 1999. 35.00 (*0-8232-1984-4*, Pub. by Fordham) BookMasters.

***Mushabac, Jane & Wigan, Angela.** A Short & Remarkable History of New York City. LC 99-46888. (Illus.). 128p. 1999. pap. 17.50 (*0-8232-1985-2*, Pub. by Fordham) BookMasters.

Mushaben, Joyce. Persistence of East German Independence. 1999. text. write for info. (*0-312-04787-8*) St Martin.

Mushaben, Joyce Marie. From Post-War to Post-Wall Generations: Changing Attitudes Towards the National Question & NATO in the Federal Republic of Germany. LC 97-31491. 440p. (C). 1997. text 79.00 (*0-8133-1152-7*, Pub. by Westview) HarpC.

Mushaike, Yasuto. Self-Complementary Antennas: Principle of Self-Complementarity for Constant Impedance. LC 95-25745. (Illus.). 150p. 1996. 79.00 (*3-540-76002-4*) Spr-Verlag.

Mushak, Paul. Lead & Public Health Integrated Risk Assessment. (Pharmacology & Toxicology Ser.). 1999. 99.95 (*0-8493-8557-1*, 8557) CRC Pr.

Mushak, Paul & Crocetti, Annemarie F. The Nature & Extent of Lead Poisoning in Children in the U. S. A Report to Congress. (Illus.). 700p. (Orig.). (C). 1999. reprint ed. pap. text 60.00 (*0-7881-3383-7*) DIANE Pub.

Mushakoji Saneatsu. Long Corridor: Selected Poetry of Mushakoji (Surname) Saneatsu. Epp, Robert, tr. from JPN. & intro. by. LC 95-60539. 398p. (C). 1996. text 30.00 (*1-880276-70-4*) Yakusha.

Mushala, Paul S. A Thought, an Intention, a Review & Journal. Mease, Gary, ed. (Illus.). 320p. 1996. pap. 12.95 (*0-9647776-0-6*) Mushala Hse Pub.

Musher, Daniel M., jt. ed. see Schell, Ronald F.

***Mushet, Cindy.** Desserts: Mediterranean Flavors, California Style. (Illus.). 2000. write for info. (*0-684-80054-3*) Scribner.

Mushid, Tazeen M. The Sacred & the Secular: Bengal Muslim Discourses, 1871-1977. (Illus.). 508p. (C). 1996. 39.95 (*0-19-563701-1*) OUP.

Mushin, William W. & Rendell-Baker, Leslie. Origins of Thoracic Anaesthesia. Orig. Title: Principles of Thoracic Anaesthesia. (Illus.). xx, 172p. 1991. reprint ed. write for info. (*0-9614932-2-4*) Wood Lib-Mus.

Mushiru, Hasan. Nationalism & Communal Politics in India. 1979. 18.50 (*0-8364-0198-0*) S Asia.

Mushirul, Hasan. A Nationalist Conscience: M. A. Ansari, the Congress & the Raj. (C). 1987. 25.00 (*81-85054-17-7*, Pub. by Manohar) S Asia.

Mushka Honig, David, tr. see Wallach, Shalom Meir, ed.

Mushka Honig, Sarah, tr. see Wallach, Shalom Meir, ed.

Mushkat, Jerome. Fernando Wood: A Political Biography. LC 90-4486. (Illus.). 334p. 1990. 35.00 (*0-87338-413-X*) Kent St U Pr.

— The Reconstruction of the New York Democracy, 1861-1874. LC 78-16826. 328p. 1981. 33.50 (*0-8386-3002-2*, 3002) Fairleigh Dickinson.

Mushkat, Jerome & Rayback, Joseph G. Martin Van Buren: Law, Politics, & the Shaping of Republican Ideology. LC 97-8710. 272p. 1997. lib. bdg. 35.00 (*0-87580-229-X*) N Ill U Pr.

Mushkat, Marian. Philo-Semitic & Anti-Jewish Attitudes in Post-Holocaust Poland. LC 92-37136. (Symposium Ser.: Vol. 33). 456p. 1992. text 109.95 (*0-7734-9176-7*) E Mellen.

Mushkat, Roda. One Country, Two International Legal Personalities: The Case of Hong Kong. LC 97-160891. 232p. (Orig.). 1997. pap. 42.50 (*962-209-427-9*, Pub. by HK Univ Pr) Coronet Bks.

Mushkatel, Alvin H., jt. auth. see Perry, Ronald W.

Mushkatel, Alvin H., jt. auth. see Statham, E. Robert.

Mushkatel, Alvin H., jt. ed. see Herzik, Eric B.

Mushkatel, Alvin H., jt. ed. see Pijawka, David.

Mushrafi, Mokhdum E. Pakistan & Bangladesh: Political Culture & Political Parties. (C). 1992. 54.00 (*81-85565-17-1*, Pub. by Uppal Pub Hse) S Asia.

Mushrush, George W. & Speight, James G. Petroleum Products: Instability & Incompatibility. 300p. 1995. 95.00 (*1-56032-297-7*) Taylor & Francis.

Mushtaq, Q. & Tan, A. L. A Complete Bibliography of the Works of Seyyed Hossein Nasr: From 1958 Through April 1993. Aminrazavi, Mehdi & Moris, Zailan, eds. (Orig.). 1995. pap. text 14.95 (*0-934905-60-6*) Kazi Pubns.

— Mathematics: The Islamic Legacy. 1995. pap. text 12.95 (*0-934905-59-2*) Kazi Pubns.

Mushtari, K. & Galimov, K. Z. Non-Linear Theory of Thin Elastic Shells. LC 61-62238. 383p. reprint ed. pap. 118.80 (*0-608-31012-3*, 200233300012) Bks Demand.

Mushtukov, V. & Tikhonov, L. Museums of Leningrad. (Illus.). 170p. (C). 1982. 40.00 (*0-7855-5192-1*, Pub. by Collets) St Mut.

Musi, Carla Corradi. Shamanism from East to West. LC 97-179545. (Bibliotheca Shamanistica: No. 4). (Illus.). 114p. 1997. 72.00 (*963-05-7400-4*, Pub. by Akade Kiado) St Mut.

Musi, Pino & Botta, Mario. Mario Botta: Seen by Pino Musi. (Illus.). 342p. 1997. 195.00 (*3-87135-032-X*, Pub. by Daco-Verlag) U of Wash Pr.

Musia, Grzegorz, et al. Poems of Grzegorz Musial: Berliner Tagebuch & Taste of Ash. LC 98-24573. 168p. 1998. 32.50 (*0-8386-3783-3*) Fairleigh Dickinson.

Musial, Diann, jt. auth. see Hammerman, Elizabeth L.

Musial, Mark N., jt. auth. see Musial, Norman T.

Musial, Norman T. & Musial, Mark N. Ohio Estate Planning. (Illus.). x, 277p. (Orig.). 1995. pap. 29.95 (*0-9618030-1-0*) Pam Publishing Co.

Musial, Stan. Stan Musial Plays the Harmonica. 68p. 1994. pap. 8.95 (*0-7866-0138-8*, 95288); pap. 16.95 incl. audio (*0-7866-0536-7*, 95288P) Mel Bay.

Musial, Walter, et al, eds. Wind Energy, 1994, Vol. 15. 288p. 1994. pap. 52.50 (*0-7918-1187-5*) ASME.

Musial, Walter D., et al, eds. Wind Energy, 1995: Proceedings: The Energy & Environmental EXPO '95 - the Energy-Sources Technology Conference & Exhibition (1995: Houston, TX) LC 82-82946. (SED Ser.: Vol. 16). 291p. 1995. pap. 105.00 (*0-7918-1294-4*, H00926) ASME.

Musialowski Ashcraft, Donna, ed. Women's Work: A Survey of Scholarship by & about Women. LC 98-6170. 375p. 1998. pap. 29.95 (*1-56023-909-3*, Harrington Park); lib. bdg. 59.95 (*0-7890-0233-7*, Harrington Park) Haworth Pr.

Music, Bradley, et al, eds. Parasession on Language in Context, Vol. 2. 300p. 1989. pap. 16.00 (*0-914203-33-9*) Chicago Ling.

Music, David H., jt. auth. see Book, Beverley C.

Music, David W. Hymnology: A Collection of Source Readings. LC 96-1827. (Studies in Liturgical Musicology: No. 4). 256p. 1996. 40.00 (*0-8108-3148-1*) Scarecrow.

— Instruments in Church: A Collection of Source Documents. LC 98-41678. (Studies in Liturgical Musicology: No. 7). 240p. 1998. 40.00 (*0-8108-3595-9*) Scarecrow.

— Oliver Holden (1765-1844) Selected Works. (Music of the New American Nation Ser.: Vol. 13). 258p. 1997. text 94.00 (*0-8153-2428-6*) Garland.

***Music, David W. & Price, Milburn.** A Survey of Christian Hymnody. 4th rev. ed. 300p. 1999. pap. text 29.95 (*0-916642-67-4*, 8017) Hope Pub.

Music, David W., ed. see Weldon, John & Congreve, William.

Music, Diane Dalton. Songs That We Sang Together: The Life & Death of an American Family, 3 vols. 1116p. 1999. pap. write for info. (*0-7392-0119-0*, PO3016) Morris Pubng.

— Songs That We Sang Together: The Life & Death of an American Family, Vol. 1. 541p. 1999. pap. write for info. (*0-7392-0118-2*, PO3016) Morris Pubng.

— Songs That We Sang Together: The Life & Death of an American Family, Vol. II. 451p. 1999. pap. text. write for info. (*0-7392-0117-4*, PO3017) Morris Pubng.

— Songs That We Sang Together: The Life & Death of an American Family, Vol. III. 457p. 1999. pap. write for info. (*0-7392-0116-6*, PO3018) Morris Pubng.

Music Education Research Council Staff. Bibliography of Research Studies in Music Education, 1932-48. 119p. 1993. reprint ed. lib. bdg. 69.00 (*0-7812-9685-4*) Rprt Serv.

Music Educators Conference Committee on Standards. Guidelines for Performances of School Music Groups: Expectations & Limitations. (Illus.). 43p. 1994. reprint ed. pap. 12.00 (*0-940796-45-7*) MENC.

Music Educators National Conference (U. S.) Staff, jt. auth. see Price, Harry Edward.

Music Educators National Conference, Music in Gene. Music in General Education. Ernst, Karl D. & Gary, Charles L., eds. LC 65-19741. 231p. 1965. reprint ed. pap. 71.70 (*0-608-04210-2*, 206494800011) Bks Demand.

— Music in the Junior College. LC 71-122451. 62p. 1970. reprint ed. pap. 30.00 (*0-608-04211-0*, 206494900011) Bks Demand.

Music Educators National Conference Staff. The Gifts of Music. LC 95-179615. 184p. 1994. pap. 22.00 (*1-56545-075-2*, 1022) MENC.

— Life in the Music Classroom. 64p. (Orig.). (C). 1992. pap., teacher ed. 11.00 (*1-56545-010-8*, 1021) MENC.

— Perspectives on Implementation: Arts Education Standards for America's Students. Boston, Bruce O., ed. LC 94-227605. 128p. 1994. pap. 19.50 (*1-56545-042-6*, 1622) MENC.

— The School Music Program: A New Vision. LC 94-213092. 48p. (C). 1994. pap. 16.00 (*1-56545-039-6*, 1618) MENC.

— Teacher's Guide for Advocacy. 48p. 1992. pap. 9.50 (*1-56545-016-7*, 1614) MENC.

Music Educators National Conference Staff. Tips: Discipline in the Music Classroom. (TIPS Booklet Ser.). 32p. 1989. pap. 8.50 (*0-940796-60-0*, 1095) MENC.

Music Educators National Conference Staff. Tips: Music Activities in Early Childhood. (TIPS Booklet Ser.). 32p. 1990. pap. 8.50 (*0-940796-76-7*, 1097) MENC.

Music Educators National Conference Staff. Tips: Retirement for Music Educators. Wilson, A. Verne, ed. (TIPS Booklet Ser.). 24p. 1989. pap. 6.00 (*0-940796-59-7*, 1094) MENC.

Music Educators National Conference Staff. Tips: Teaching Music to Special Learners. (TIPS Booklet Ser.). 48p. (C). 1988. pap. 8.50 (*0-940796-56-2*, 1092) MENC.

— Tips: Technology for Music Educators. Boody, Charles G., ed. (TIPS Booklet Ser.). 48p. (C). 1990. pap. 8.50 (*0-940796-72-4*, 1096) MENC.

Music Educators National Conference Staff. What Parents Can Do. (Implementing the Arts Education Standards Ser.). 6p. 1994. pap. 7.75 (*1-56545-061-2*, 4020) MENC.

— What School Administrators Can Do. (Implementing the Arts Education Standards Ser.). 6p. 1994. pap. 7.75 (*1-56545-059-0*, 4018) MENC.

— What School Boards Can Do. (Implementing the Arts Education Standards Ser.). 6p. 1994. pap. 7.75 (*1-56545-058-2*, 4017) MENC.

— What State Education Agencies Can Do. (Implementing the Arts Education Standards Ser.). 6p. (Orig.). (C). 1994. pap. write for info. (*1-56545-060-4*, 4019) MENC.

— What the Arts Community Can Do. (Implementing the Arts Education Standards Ser.). 6p. 1994. pap. 7.75 (*1-56545-062-0*, 4021) MENC.

Music Educators National Conference Staff, compiled by. Kids' Voices: Young People Talk about Music. LC 96-205286. 94p. 1996. pap. 10.00 (*1-56545-098-1*, 1013) MENC.

Music Educators National Conference Staff, jt. auth. see Collins, Irma.

Music Educators National Conference Staff, jt. auth. see Lehman, Paul R.

Music Educators Staff & American String Teachers Association Staff. The Complete String Guide: Standards, Programs, Purchase, & Maintenance. 64p. 1988. 16.50 (*0-940796-38-4*, 1009) MENC.

Music Forum Staff. Music Forum, Vol. 4. 1977. text 65.00 (*0-231-03934-4*) Col U Pr.

Music in Early Childhood Conference Staff. The Young Child & Music: Contemporary Principles in Child Development & Music Education: Proceedings of the Music in Early Childhood Conference, Brigham Young University, June 28-30, 1984, Provo, Utah. Boswell, Jacquelyn, ed. LC 85-226520. (Illus.). 128p. 1985. reprint ed. pap. 39.70 (*0-608-04214-5*, 206495500011) Bks Demand.

Music Library Association Committee, ed. A Survey of Musical Instrument Collections in the United States & Canada. 135p. 1974. 8.50 (*0-318-14925-7*); pap. 6.50 (*0-318-14927-3*) Music Library Assn.

Music Library Association Staff, jt. auth. see Davis, Elizabeth A.

Music Master Staff. Guide to Popular Music, 1996, Vol. 2. 1996. 60.00 (*0-02-864575-8*, Macmillan Ref) Mac Lib Ref.

— Musicmasters Annual Guide to Popular Recordings, 1996, Vol. 1. 1996. 60.00 (*0-02-864515-4*, Schirmer Books) Mac Lib Ref.

***Music Resource Group Staff.** Musician's Atlas 1999: The Ultimate Resource for Working Musicians. (Illus.). 1999. pap. 19.95 (*0-634-00145-0*) H Leonard.

***Music Sales Coporation Staff.** Tori Amos: The Singles. (Illus.). 1999. pap. 24.95 (*0-8256-1753-7*, Amsco Music) Music Sales.

Music Sales Corporation. Irish Tunebook: Part 2. 1997. pap. text 11.95 (*0-946005-15-X*) Dufour.

***Music Sales Corporation.** Wizoo Guide Cubase VST Windows: How to Turn Your Computer in a Digitial Studio with CD-ROM. 1999. pap. 27.90 incl. cd-rom (*3-927954-27-6*) Omnibus NY.

Music Sales Corporation Staff. Bach for Tenoe Sax. 1997. pap. text 9.95 (*0-7119-4226-9*) Music Sales.

***Music Sales Corporation Staff.** Classical Music Fakebook. (Illus.). 1999. pap. 15.95 (*0-7119-4426-1*) Music Sales.

Music Sales Corporation Staff. Complete Christmas Celebration. 1992. pap. 14.95 (*0-8256-9789-1*) Music Sales.

***Music Sales Corporation Staff.** Gig Bag Book of Guitar Care & Repair. 2000. pap. 12.95 (*0-8256-1698-0*) Music Sales.

— Gig Bag Book of Practical Pentatonics. 2000. pap. 12.95 (*0-8256-1700-6*) Music Sales.

— Guitar Chordex. 2000. pap. 9.95 (*0-8256-1754-5*) Music Sales.

Music Sales Corporation Staff. Irish Music by Carolan. 1997. pap. text 11.95 (*0-946005-08-7*) Dufour.

— Irish Tunebook, Pt. 1. 23p. 1997. pap. 8.95 (*0-946005-14-1*) Dufour.

Music Sales Corporation Staff. Paul Simon. (Playtime for Recorder Ser.). 1997. pap. text 7.95 (*0-7119-2848-7*) Music Sales.

Music Sales Corporation Staff. Play Great Chord Riffs in 60 Minutes. (Illus.). 19p. 1998. pap. text 5.95 (*0-7119-5636-7*) Music Sales.

— Scottish Fiddle Tunes. 1997. pap. text 10.95 (*0-946005-29-X*) Dufour.

— Selection's from Moore's Irish Melodies. 1997. pap. text 8.95 (*0-946005-38-9*) Dufour.

— Stone Temple Pilots: Tiny Music: Songs from the Vatican Gift Shop. pap. 19.95 (*0-8256-1547-X*) Omnibus NY.

Music Sales Corporation Staff. Symphonic Themes for Alto Sax. 1997. pap. text 9.95 (*0-7119-4030-4*) Music Sales.

— Symphonic Themes for Clarinet. (That's Easy Ser.). 1997. pap. text 9.95 (*0-7119-4028-2*) Music Sales.

— Symphonic Themes for Trumpet. 1997. pap. text 9.95 (*0-7119-4031-2*) Music Sales.

Music Sales Corporation Staff. Wedding Songbook. 1997. pap. 10.95 (*0-8256-9385-3*) Music Sales.

***Music Sales Corporation Staff, ed.** Harmonica Americana. deluxe ed. 2000. pap. write for info. (*0-930948-20-3*) Cross Harp.

Music Sales Corporation Staff, ed. Symphonic Themes for Flute. (That's Easy! Ser.). 1997. pap. 9.95 (*0-7119-4029-0*) Music Sales.

***Music Sales Corporation Staff & Dick, Arthur.** First Guitar Chords. 40p. 1999. pap. 9.95 incl. audio compact disk (*0-7119-7222-2*) Music Sales.

— First Guitar Riffs. (Illus.). 40p. 1999. pap. 9.95 incl. audio compact disk (*0-7119-7223-0*) Music Sales.

***Music Sales Corporation Staff & Jones, Andy.** First Guitar Scales. (Illus.). 40p. 1999. pap. 9.95 (*0-7119-7224-9*, AM954195) Music Sales.

Music Sales Corporation Staff & Mitchell, Carolyn B. 50 Plus Easy Classical Solos for Alto Sax. 1996. pap. 17.95 (*0-7119-5189-6*, AM932074) Music Sales.

— 50 Plus Easy Classical Solos for Clarinet. 63p. 1996. pap. 17.95 (*0-7119-5187-X*, AM932052) Music Sales.

— 50 Plus Easy Classical Solos for Flute. 1996. pap. 17.95 (*0-7119-5188-8*, AM932063) Music Sales.

— 50 Plus Easy Classical Solos for Tenor Sax. 1996. pap. 17.95 (*0-7119-5285-X*, AM933295) Music Sales.

— 50 Plus Easy Classical Solos for Trumpet. 1996. pap. 17.95 (*0-7119-5190-X*, AM932085) Music Sales.

— 50 Plus Easy Classical Solos for Violin. 1996. pap. 17.95 (*0-7119-5191-8*, AM932096) Music Sales.

Music Sales Publishing Staff. Bob Dylan's Greatest Hits Complete. 168p. pap. 25.95 (*0-8256-1597-6*) Omnibus NY.

— Gig Bag Book of Bass Scales. (Step One Ser.). 1997. pap. text 12.95 (*0-8256-1595-X*, AM942084) Music Sales.

— The Jazz Vocalists. pap. 29.95 (*0-8256-1413-9*) Omnibus NY.

An Asterisk (*) at the beginning of an entry indicates that the title is appearing for the first time.

— The Library of Easiest Book of Piano Classics. 352p. pap. 19.95 (*0-8256-1596-8*) Omnibus NY.

Music Sales Staff. Elvis Costello: Brutal Youth. LC 96-701525. 1997. pap. text 19.95 (*0-7119-4110-6*) Music Sales.

Music Sales Staff. Eric Clapton: A Life in the Blues. LC 96-703597. 352p. 1995. pap. 29.95 (*0-8256-1484-8*, AM 931216) Omnibus NY.

Music Television Video Staff & Heiman, Joe. MTV's Get a Life: A Guide to Jobs, Money & the Real World. LC 96-163557. 224p. 1996. pap. 12.00 (*0-671-00202-3*) PB.

Music Trade Board, U. S. A. Staff. Complete Catalogue of Sheet Music & Musical Works. LC 69-1666. 575p. 1973. reprint ed. lib. bdg. 95.00 (*0-306-71401-9*) Da Capo.

Musical Expeditions Staff. Echoes of the Forests. 1995. audio 16.95 (*1-55961-277-0*, Ellipsis Arts) Relaxtn Co.

Musical Lynn. Cave Man Talk. 6p. (C). 1990. pap. 6.95 (*1-880718-06-5*); pap. text 6.95 (*1-880718-01-4*) Genius New.

— The Early Poems. 5p. (Orig.). (YA). (gr. 12). 1990. pap. 7.95 (*1-880718-05-7*) Genius New.

— Musical Lynn Essays Vol. 1: A Baker's Dozen. 13p. (Orig.). (YA). (gr. 12). 1991. pap. 8.95 (*1-880718-02-2*); pap. text 8.95 (*1-880718-03-0*) Genius New.

— Universal Genius Letter, Vol. I. (Illus.). 22p. (Orig.). (C). 1992. pap. 12.95 (*1-880718-04-9*) Genius New.

Musicant. Empire by Default, Vol. 1. 1950. pap. 15.00 (*0-8050-3501-X*) St Martin.

Musicant, Ivan. Battleship at War. 376p. 1988. mass mkt. 4.95 (*0-380-70487-0*, Avon Bks) Morrow Avon.

***Musicant, Ivan.** Divided Waters: The Naval History of the Civil War. (Illus.). 2000. 9.99 (*0-7858-1210-5*) Bk Sales Inc.

Musicant, Ivan. Empire by Default: The Spanish-American War & the Dawn of the American Century. LC 97-28238. 1995. 35.00 (*0-8050-3500-1*) H Holt & Co.

Musich, Patty. Focus: Orange County '95. Harrison, Dan, ed. (Illus.). 144p. 1994. lib. bdg. 10.95 (*0-942581-12-1*) InfoOutfitters.

— Focus: Orange County '96. 8th rev. ed. Harrison, Dan, ed. (Illus.). 144p. 1996. lib. bdg. 10.95 (*0-942581-16-4*) InfoOutfitters.

— Focus: Orange County '97. Harrison, Dan, ed. (Illus.). 144p. 1996. lib. bdg. 10.95 (*0-942581-18-0*) InfoOutfitters.

— Focus: Riverside County. Harrison, Dan, ed. (Illus.). 128p. 1994. lib. bdg. 9.95 (*0-942581-06-7*) InfoOutfitters.

— Focus: San Diego County '95. Harrison, Dan, ed. (Illus.). 120p. 1994. lib. bdg. 10.95 (*0-942581-13-X*) InfoOutfitters.

Musick. Everyday Object Lessons. LC 98-55278. 2000. pap. 12.99 (*0-310-22652-X*) HarpC.

Musick, David. An Introduction to the Sociology of Juvenile Delinquency. LC 94-14576. 332p. (C). 1995. text 64.50 (*0-7914-2351-4*); pap. text 21.95 (*0-7914-2352-2*) State U NY Pr.

Musick, Jack, jt. auth. see McMillan, Beverly.

Musick, John A., ed. Life in the Slow Lane: Ecology & Conservation of Long-Lived Marine Animals. LC 99-61670. (AFS Symposium Ser.). (Illus.). 280p. 1999. pap. text 47.00 (*1-888569-15-8*, 540.23) Am Fisheries Soc.

Musick, John A., jt. ed. see Lutz, Peter L.

Musick, Judith S. Young, Poor, & Pregnant: The Psychology of Teenage Motherhood. 1995. pap. 16.00 (*0-300-06195-1*) Yale U Pr.

Musick, Judith S. & Weissbourd, Bernice, eds. Infants: Their Social Environments. LC 81-82289. 216p. pap. text 7.00 (*0-912674-76-8*, NAEYC #319) Natl Assn Child Ed.

Musick, Melinda B., ed. see Birchmore, Daniel A.

Musick, Melinda B., ed. see Birchmore, Fred A.

Musick, Michael P. Sixth Virginia Cavalry. (Virginia Regimental Histories Ser.). 177p. 1990. 19.95 (*1-56190-002-8*) H E Howard.

Musick, Nancy, jt. auth. see Johnson, Willie Neal.

Musick Nussbaum, Melissa. The Winter Saints. LC 98-42842. 86p. (J). (ps-5). 1998. pap. 15.00 (*1-56854-246-1*) Liturgy Tr Pubns.

Musick, Phil. Reflections on Roberto. 138p. 1994. pap. 14.95 (*0-9641355-0-7*) Pitts Pirates.

Musick, Ron, jt. ed. see Stolorz, Paul.

Musick, Ruth A. Coffin Hollow & Other Ghost Tales. LC 76-51157. (Illus.). 216p. 1977. pap. 16.00 (*0-8131-1416-0*) U Pr of Ky.

—Green Hills of Magic: West Virginia Folktales from Europe. 320p. 1989. reprint ed. pap. 9.95 (0-87012-475-7) McClain.

During the early 1900s the promise of employment in the great coalfields of northern West Virginia drew numerous immigrants from the poorer countries of Europe. Miners came to the state from Ireland & Spain, the Italian peninsula, the Balkans, Austria, Poland, Russia & Turkey. They brought with them many of the tales & legends of their homelands, which were preserved among themselves & children. From this rich & varied heritage, Dr. Musick has chosen seventy-nine of the best & most representative tales for presentation in this volume. *Publisher Paid Annotation.*

— The Telltale Lilac Bush & Other West Virginia Ghost Tales. LC 64-14000. (Illus.). 208p. 1965. reprint ed. pap. 16.00 (*0-8131-0136-0*) U Pr of Ky.

Musick, Wes. Flame. LC 97-77350. 1997. pap. text, mass mkt. 14.95 (*1-889131-20-2*) CasAnanda.

***Musickant, Claire.** Fibromyalgia: My Journey to Wellness. LC 99-64037. (Illus.). iii, 220p. 1999. pap. 17.95 (*0-89716-931-X*, Peanut Btr Pubng) Elton-Wolf Pub.

Musickant, Claire. Only You Can Do It: A Personal Guide for Career Planning & Job Searching. rev. ed. (Illus.). 1993. pap. text 19.95 (*0-9639752-0-X*) CEM Pubng.

Musico, Giuliana. Hollywood's New Deal. LC 96-34525. (Culture & the Moving Image Ser.). 320p. (C). 1997. 69.95 (*1-56639-495-3*); pap. 22.95 (*1-56639-496-1*) Temple U Pr.

Musiek, Frank E., et al. Neuroaudiology: Case Studies. LC 93-9066. (Illus.). 320p. (Orig.). (C). 1993. pap. text 65.00 (*1-56593-217-X*, 0577) Thomson Learn.

Musiek, Frank E., jt. auth. see Chermak, Gail D.

Musiek, Frank E., jt. auth. see Rintelmann, William F.

Musiela, Merek & Rutkowski, Marek. Martingale Methods in Financial Modeling: Theory & Applications. Karatzas, I. & Yor, M., eds. LC 97-11586. (Applications of Mathematics Ser.: No. 36). 504p. 1997. 79.95 (*3-540-61477-X*) Spr-Verlag.

Musielak, J. Orlicz Spaces & Modular Spaces. (Lecture Notes in Mathematics Ser.: Vol. 1034). 222p. 1983. 35.95 (*0-387-12706-2*) Spr-Verlag.

Musielak, J., ed. see Mathematical Institute of the Polish Academy of Sc & Institute of Mathematics of the Adam Mickiewicz Un.

Musikant, Solomon. Optical Materials: An Introduction to Selection & Application. (Optical Engineering Ser.: Vol. 6). (Illus.). 272p. 1985. text 145.00 (*0-8247-7309-8*) Dekker.

— What Every Engineer Should Know about Ceramics. (What Every Engineer Should Know Ser.: Vol. 28). (Illus.). 224p. 1991. text 59.75 (*0-8247-8498-7*) Dekker.

Musikant, Solomon, ed. Optical Materials Vol. 1: A Series of Advances. (Illus.). 424p. 1990. text 190.00 (*0-8247-8131-7*) Dekker.

Musikas, Claude, jt. ed. see Rydberg, Jan.

Musiker, Naomi & Musiker, Reuben. Historical Dictionary of Greater Johannesburg. LC 98-21819. (Historical Dictionaries of Cities of the World Ser.: No. 7). 544p. 1999. 98.50 (*0-8108-3527-5*) Scarecrow.

Musiker, Naomi, jt. auth. see Musiker, Reuben.

Musiker, Naomi, jt. ed. see Musiker, Reuben.

Musiker, Reuben. South African Bibliography: A Survey of Bibliographies & Bibliographical Work. 3rd ed. 160p. (C). 1996. text 70.00 (*0-7201-2225-2*) Continuum.

Musiker, Reuben & Musiker, Naomi. Conductors & Composers of Popular Orchestral Music: A Biographical & Discographical Sourcebook. LC 97-1714. 360p. 1998. lib. bdg. 75.00 (*0-313-30260-X*, Greenwood Pr) Greenwood.

— Guide to South African Reference Books. 6th ed. LC 96-43885. 192p. 1997. 89.50 (*0-7201-2224-4*) Continuum.

— Southern Africa Bibliography. LC 96-7264. (Area Bibliographies Ser.: No. 11). 1996. 52.00 (*0-8108-3175-9*) Scarecrow.

Musiker, Reuben & Musiker, Naomi, eds. Conductors & Composers of Popular Orchestral Music. 1998. lib. bdg. 85.00 (*1-57958-013-0*) Fitzroy Dearborn.

Musiker, Reuben, jt. auth. see Musiker, Naomi.

Musikwelt, Jahrbuch Der, see Der Musikwelt, Jahrbuch.

Musil, jt. auth. see McKay.

Musil, Alois. Arabia Deserta. LC 77-87085. (American Geographical Society Oriental Explorations & Studies: No. 2). (Illus.). reprint ed. 74.50 (*0-404-60232-0*) AMS Pr.

— Arabia Petraea: Reisebericht, 3 vols. (Illus.). xxxix, 1636p. 1989. reprint ed. write for info. (*0-318-71536-8*) G Olms Pubs.

— Arabia Petraea: Reisebericht, 3 vols., Set. (Illus.). xxxix, 1636p. 1989. reprint ed. write for info. (*3-487-06480-4*) G Olms Pubs.

— Arabia Petraea: Reisebericht, 3 vols., Vol. II. (Illus.). xxxix, 1636p. 1989. reprint ed. write for info. (*0-318-71537-6*) G Olms Pubs.

— Arabia Petraea: Reisebericht, 3 vols., Vol. III. (Illus.). xxxix, 1636p. 1989. reprint ed. write for info. (*0-318-71538-4*) G Olms Pubs.

— The Manners & Customs of the Rwala Bedouins. LC 77-87091. (American Geographical Society Oriental Explorations & Studies: No. 6). reprint ed. 74.50 (*0-404-60236-3*) AMS Pr.

— The Middle Euphrates: A Topographical Itinerary. LC 77-87086. (American Geographical Society Oriental Explorations & Studies: No. 3). reprint ed. 74.50 (*0-404-60233-9*) AMS Pr.

— Northern Arabia, According to the Original Investigations of Alois Musil. LC 77-87092. (American Geographical Society Oriental Explorations & Studies: Map Vol.). reprint ed. 49.50 (*0-404-60237-1*) AMS Pr.

— The Northern Hegaz: A Topographical Itinerary. LC 77-87084. (American Geographical Society Oriental Explorations & Studies: No. 1). reprint ed. 55.00 (*0-404-60231-2*) AMS Pr.

— Northern Negd: A Topographical Itinerary. LC 77-87090. (American Geographical Society Oriental Explorations & Studies: No. 5). reprint ed. 55.00 (*0-404-60235-5*) AMS Pr.

— Palmyrena: A Topographical Itinerary. LC 77-87087. (American Geographical Society Oriental Explorations & Studies: No. 4). reprint ed. 55.00 (*0-404-60234-7*) AMS Pr.

Musil, Caryn M., ed. The Courage to Question. 224p. 1992. 12.00 (*0-911696-55-5*) Assn Am Coll.

— Executive Summary of the Courage to Question. 12p. 1992. pap. 5.00 (*0-911696-59-8*) Assn Am Coll.

— Students at the Center: Feminist Assessment. 80p. 1992. 12.00 (*0-911696-56-3*) Assn Am Coll.

Musil, Caryn M., et al. Diversity in Higher Education: A Work in Progress. LC 95-80686. 69p. 1995. pap. 12.00 (*0-911696-67-9*) Assn Am Coll.

***Musil, Jeri & Suda, Zdenek L., eds.** The Meaning of Liberalism - East & West. LC 00-24117. 288p. (C). 2000. 49.95 (*963-9116-53-X*) Ctrl Europ Univ.

Musil, Jiri, ed. The End of Czechoslovakia. (Central European University Press Bks.). (Illus.). 288p. (C). 1995. pap. 21.95 (*1-85866-020-3*, Pub. by Ctrl Europ Univ) Bks Intl VA.

***Musil, Jiri & Suda, Zdenek L., eds.** Meaning of Liberalism: East & West. LC 00-24117. 2000. pap. text 22.95 (*963-9116-54-8*) Ctrl Europ Univ.

Musil, Robert. Diaries: Robert Musil 1899-1942. Mirsky, Mark, ed. Payne, Philip, tr. from GER. LC 98-36990. 512p. 1998. 40.00 (*0-465-01650-2*, Pub. by Basic) HarpC.

***Musil, Robert.** Diaries: Robert Musil 1899-1942. Mirsky, Mark, ed. Payne, Philip, tr. & selected by by. 563p. 1999. pap. 18.00 (*0-465-01651-0*, Pub. by Basic) HarpC.

— Five Women. Wilkins, Eithne & Kaiser, Ernst, trs. from GER. LC 99-23085. (Verba Mundi Bks.).Tr. of Drei Frauen. 224p. 1999. pap. 14.95 (*1-56792-075-6*) Godine.

Musil, Robert. The Man Without Qualities. 1965. pap. 12.00 (*0-399-50152-5*, Perigee Bks) Berkley Pub.

— Man Without Qualities, Vol. 1. Wilkins, Sophie & Pike, Burton, trs. 1996. pap. 20.00 (*0-679-76787-8*) Vin Bks.

— Man Without Qualities, Vol. 2. Wilkins, Sophie & Pike, Burton, trs. 1996. pap. 24.00 (*0-679-76802-5*) Vin Bks.

— Posthumous Papers of a Living Author. Wortsman, Peter, tr. from GER. LC 87-83298.Tr. of Nachlass zu Lebzeiten. 149p. 1987. pap. 12.00 (*0-941419-01-0*, Eridanos Library) Marsilio Pubs.

— Precision & Soul: Essays & Addresses. Pike, Burton & Luft, David S., eds. & trs. by. xxviii, 329p. 1994. pap. 17.95 (*0-226-55409-0*) U Ch Pr.

— Precision & Soul: Essays & Addresses. Pike, Burton & Luft, David S., eds. & trs. by. LC 90-10828. 330p. 1996. 35.95 (*0-226-55408-2*) U Ch Pr.

— Selected Writings. LC 75-761. (German Library: Vol. 72). 320p. 1986. pap. 19.95 (*0-8264-0304-2*) Continuum.

— Selected Writings. Pike, Burton, ed. LC 77-6952. (German Library: Vol. 72). 320p. 1986. 39.50 (*0-8264-0305-0*) Continuum.

— Die Verwirrungen des Zoglings Torless. (GER.). (C). 1978. 9.95 (*0-8442-2753-6*, X2753-6) NTC Contemp Pub Co.

Musil, Rosemary G. The Ghost of Mr. Penny. (J). 1940. 6.00 (*0-87602-129-1*) Anchorage.

Musin, Oleg, jt. auth. see Oleynik, Igor S.

***Musitano.** The Super 8 Filmmakers Guide. 3rd ed. 224p. 2000. pap. 32.95 (*0-240-51594-3*, Focal) Buttrwrth-Heinemann.

Musk, Bill A. Touching the Soul of Islam. 1998. 16.99 (*1-85424-317-9*) O M Lit.

Musk, Leslie F., et al. Weather Systems. (Cambridge Topics in Geography Ser.). (Illus.). 160p. 1988. pap. text 25.95 (*0-521-27874-0*) Cambridge U Pr.

Musk, Maye. Executive Stamina Vol. I: 21 Days to Change a Habit. Vol. 1. (Illus.). 36p. 1999. pap. 4.95 (*1-893223-00-0*) MMNI.

Muska, Arlene, ed. Vegetarian Creations. (Illus.). 272p. (Orig.). 1992. pap. 17.00 (*0-918224-26-8*) S K Pubns.

Muska, David. Unclogging the Court System Through Juvenile Justice. 18p. 1998. pap. 10.00 (*1-886306-25-7*) Nevada Policy.

Muskas, Tony. Moon Lake. (Illus.). 115p. (Orig.). 1994. pap. 4.75 (*1-884295-05-3*) Ananta Prnting.

Muskat, Beth T. & Neeley, Mary A. The Way It Was: Eighteen Fifty to Nineteen Thirty Photographs of Montgomery & Her Central Alabama Neighbors. LC 85-50334. (Illus.). 185p. 1985. 20.00 (*0-9614653-0-1*) Landmarks Found.

Muskat, Carrie. Barry Bonds. LC 97-1678. (Baseball Legends Ser.). (Illus.). 64p. (J). (gr. 3 up). 1997. 15.95 (*0-7910-4376-2*) Chelsea Hse.

— Bernie Williams. LC 99-53141. (Latinos in Baseball Ser.). 72p. (YA). (gr. 5-10). 2000. lib. bdg. 18.95 (*1-58415-011-4*) M Lane Pubs.

— Mark McGwire. (Baseball Legends Ser.). 1999. pap. 7.95 (*0-7910-5491-8*) Chelsea Hse.

— Moises Alou. LC 98-48046. (Latinos in Baseball Ser.). (Illus.). 64p. (YA). (gr. 5 up). 1999. lib. bdg. 18.95 (*1-883845-86-6*) M Lane Pubs.

***Muskat, Carrie.** Sammy Sosa. (Overcoming Adversity Ser.). (Illus.). 128p. 1999. 19.95 (*0-7910-5300-8*) Chelsea Hse.

Muskat, Carrie. Sammy Sosa. LC 99-19951. (Real-Life Reader Biography Ser.). (Illus.). 32p. (J). (gr. 3-8). 1999. lib. bdg. 15.95 (*1-883845-96-3*) M Lane Pubs.

— Sammy Sosa. LC 98-54377. (Latinos in Baseball Ser.). (Illus.). 72p. (J). (gr. 5-10). 1999. lib. bdg. 18.95 (*1-883845-92-0*) M Lane Pubs.

Muskat, Carrie & Chelsea House Publishing Staff. Frank Thomas. LC 97-5505. (Baseball Legends Ser.). (Illus.). 64p. (J). (gr. 3-7). 1997. 15.95 (*0-7910-4381-9*) Chelsea Hse.

Muskat, Carrie L. Ice Hockey. LC 97-28696. (Composite Guide Ser.). (Illus.). 64p. (YA). (gr. 3 up). 1999. lib. bdg. 7.95 (*0-7910-4727-X*) Chelsea Hse.

— Tennis. LC 97-34276. (Composite Guide Ser.). (Illus.). 64p. (YA). (gr. 3 up). 1999. lib. bdg. 15.95 (*0-7910-4728-8*) Chelsea Hse.

Muskat, Hedda, jt. auth. see Cohen, Amy.

Muske, Carol. Applause. LC 88-29086. (Poetry Ser.). 64p. 1989. text 19.95 (*0-8229-3613-5*) U of Pittsburgh Pr.

— Applause. LC 88-29086. (Poetry Ser.). (Illus.). 64p. 1989. pap. 10.95 (*0-8229-5417-6*) U of Pittsburgh Pr.

— An Octave above Thunder: New & Selected Poems. LC 97-10066. (Poetry Ser.). 200p. 1997. 24.95 (*0-88748-263-5*) Carnegie-Mellon.

— An Octave above Thunder: New & Selected Poems. LC 97-10066. 207p. 1997. pap. 16.95 (*0-14-058794-2*) Viking Penguin.

— Skylight. LC 95-67957. (Classic Contemporaries Ser.). 96p. (C). 1996. pap. 12.95 (*0-88748-229-5*) Carnegie-Mellon.

— Women & Poetry: Truth, Autobiography, & the Shape of the Self. LC 97-6446. 152p. (C). 1997. pap. 13.95 (*0-472-06624-2*, 06624) U of Mich Pr.

— Women & Poetry: Truth, Autobiography, & the Shape of the Self. LC 97-6446. 152p. (C). 1997. text 39.50 (*0-472-09624-9*, 09624) U of Mich Pr.

— Wyndmere. LC 84-19565. (Poetry Ser.). 59p. 1985. pap. 10.95 (*0-8229-5365-X*); text 19.95 (*0-8229-3503-1*) U of Pittsburgh Pr.

Muske, L. E., ed. The Neurobiology of Reproductive Behavior. (Journal: Brains, Behavior & Evolution: Vol. 42, No. 4-5, 1993). (Illus.). 84p. 1993. pap. 42.75 (*3-8055-5852-X*) S Karger.

Muskeg Research Conference Staff. Muskeg & the Northern Environment in Canada. Radforth, N. W. & Brawner, C. O., eds. LC 76-54734. (Illus.). 417p. reprint ed. pap. 129.30 (*0-8357-8238-7*, 203398000088) Bks Demand.

Muskens, George & Gruppelaar, Jacob. Global Telecommunication Networks: Strategic Considerations. (C). 1988. lib. bdg. 130.50 (*90-277-2682-5*) Kluwer Academic.

Muskens, George, jt. ed. see Reichardt, Robert H.

Muskens, Reinhard. Meaning & Partiality. (Studies in Logic, Language & Information: No. 2). 152p. 1995. pap. 22.95 (*1-881526-79-8*) CSLI.

Muskett, John. Site Surveying. 2nd ed. LC 95-1472. 1995. pap. 44.95 (*0-632-03848-9*) Blackwell Sci.

Muskett, Netta. Golden Harvest. large type ed. 544p. 1983. 27.99 (*0-7089-1059-9*) Ulverscroft.

— Love & Deborah. large type ed. 382p. 1982. 27.99 (*0-7089-0776-8*) Ulverscroft.

Muskhelishvili, N. I. Singular Integral Equations: Boundary Problems of Function Theory & Their Application to Mathematical Physics. 2nd ed. 447p. 1992. reprint ed. pap. 14.95 (*0-486-66893-2*) Dover.

Muskie, Edmund S. Exploring Cambodia: Issues & Reality in a Time of Transition. (Illus.). 88p. (C). 1991. pap. 19.95 (*0-944237-33-9*) Ctr National Policy.

Muskie, Edmund S., ed. The U. S. in Space: Issues & Policy Choices for a New Era. 94p. 1988. 19.75 (*0-944237-23-1*) Ctr National Policy.

Muskie, Edmund S., ed. The U. S. in Space: Issues & Policy Choices for a New Era. 94p. 1988. pap. 8.50 (*0-944237-24-X*) Ctr National Policy.

***Muskin, Philip R., ed.** Complementary & Alternative Medicine & Psychiatry. (Review of Psychiatry Ser.: Vol. 19, No. 1). 320p. 2000. pap. 28.50 (*0-88048-174-9*) Am Psychiatric.

Muskoka Pioneer Village Research Committee. Huntsville: More Pictures from the Past. (Illus.). 160p. 1998. pap. 19.95 (*1-55046-231-8*, Pub. by Boston Mills) Genl Dist Srvs.

Muskrat, Bruce, tr. see McKinney, James C.

Musladin, Judith. The New Beagle. 2nd ed. LC 97-39996. 288p. 1998. 27.95 (*0-87605-028-3*) Howell Bks.

Musladin, Judith M. & Lueke, Ada. The New Beagle. (Illus.). 288p. 1990. 25.95 (*0-87605-025-9*) Howell Bks.

Musleah, Rahel. Journey of a Lifetime: The Jewish Life Cycle Book. LC 97-1396. (J). 1997. pap. 5.95 (*0-87441-631-0*) Behrman.

— Why on This Night? A Passover Haggadah for Family Celebration. LC 97-2570. (Illus.). 112p. (J). (gr. 1-5). 2000. pap. 12.99 (*0-689-83313-X*) Aladdin.

— Why on This Night? A Passover Haggadah for Family Celebration. LC 97-2570. (Illus.). 112p. (J). (gr. 1-5). 2000. per. 22.00 (*0-689-81356-2*) S&S Trade.

Musleah, Rahel & Klayman, Michael. Sharing Blessings: Children's Stories for Exploring the Spirit of the Jewish Holidays. LC 96-30047. (Illus.). 64p. (YA). (gr. 1 up). 1997. 18.95 (*1-879045-71-0*) Jewish Lights.

Musleh-ud-Din, Muhammad. Crime & the Islamic Doctrine of Preventive Measures. 1981. 9.95 (*0-935782-65-6*) Kazi Pubns.

— Islamic Education, Its Forms & Features. 1988. 7.50 (*1-56744-094-0*) Kazi Pubns.

— Islamic Jurisprudence & the Rule of Necessity & Need. 1991. 9.95 (*1-56744-097-5*) Kazi Pubns.

Muslehuddin, Mohammad. Insurance & Islamic Law. 1983. pap. 4.95 (*1-56744-058-4*) Kazi Pubns.

Muslehuddin, Muhammad. Philosophy of Islamic Law & the Orientalists. 300p. 1985. 19.95 (*1-56744-353-2*) Kazi Pubns.

— Sociology & Islam. 245p. 1996. pap. 3.50 (*0-614-21524-2*, 1145) Kazi Pubns.

Muslih, Muhammad Y. The Origins of Palestinian Nationalism. (Institute for Palestine Studies). 288p. 1989. pap. text 20.00 (*0-231-06509-4*) Col U Pr.

— Toward Coexistence: An Analysis of the Resolutions of the Palestine National Council. LC 90-81685. (IPS Papers). 56p. (Orig.). (C). 1990. pap. text 3.95 (*0-88728-210-5*) Inst Palestine.

Muslih, Muhammad Y., jt. auth. see Norton, Augustus R.

Muslih-Ud-Din Sadi, Shaikh. Sadi's Scroll of Wisdom: Wisdom of the East (1910) 65p. 1998. reprint ed. pap. 7.95 (*0-7661-0657-8*) Kessinger Pub.

Muslim, M. Sahih Muslim. Siddiqui, Abdul H., tr. 1613p. 1982. 80.00 (*0-318-37192-8*) Asia Bk Corp.

Muslim Students' Association Staff. Contemporary Aspects of Economic Thinking in Islam. 1976. pap. 2.75 (*0-89259-003-3*) Am Trust Pubns.

Muslim Student's Association Staff. The Educational Guide: A Handbook for Foreign Muslim Applicants to U. S. & Canadian Universities. 124p. (Orig.). pap. 4.50 (*0-89259-150-1*) Am Trust Pubns.

M

Muslin, H. L. Lyndon Johnson: The Tragic Self - A Psychohistorical Portrait. LC 91-210. (Illus.). 250p. 1990. 23.95 (*0-306-43563-2*, Plen Insight) Perseus Pubng.

Muslin, Hyman L. The Psychotherapy of the Elderly Self. LC 91-43419. 240p. 1992. text 31.95 (*0-87630-657-1*) Brunner-Mazel.

***Musliner, David & Pell, Barney, eds.** Agents with Adjustable Autonomy: Papers from the AAAI Spring Symposium. (Technical Reports: Vol. SS-99-06). (Illus.). 144p. 1999. spiral bd. 25.00 (*1-57735-102-9*) AAAI Pr.

Musman. Britain Today. Date not set. pap. text. write for info. (*0-582-74930-1*, Pub. by Addison-Wesley) Longman.

— To Catch a Thief. 1970. pap. text. write for info. (*0-582-52738-4*, Pub. by Addison-Wesley) Longman.

Musman, R. Britain Today. 1982. pap. text. write for info. (*0-582-74912-3*, Pub. by Addison-Wesley) Longman.

Musmann, Klaus. Technological Innovations in Libraries, 1860-1960: An Anecdotal History, 73. LC 93-18143. (Contributions in Librarianship & Information Science Ser.: No. 73). 272p. 1993. 65.00 (*0-313-28015-0*, MTV, Greenwood Pr) Greenwood.

Musmanno, Michael A. Proposed Amendments to the Constitution: A Monograph on the Resolutions Introduced in Congress Proposing Amendments to the Constitution of the United States of America, 2nd sess. House. Doc. 551--551. LC 75-35374. (U. S. Government Documents Program Ser.). 253p. 1976. reprint ed. lib. bdg. 65.00 (*0-8371-8610-2*, MUPAC) Greenwood.

Musnick, David & Pierce, Mark. Conditioning for Outdoor Fitness: A Comprehensive Training Guide. LC 99-6365. (Illus.). 320p. 1999. pap. 21.95 (*0-89886-450-X*) Mountaineers.

***Musolf, Karen J.** From Plymouth to Parliament: A Rhetorical History of Nancy Astor's 1919 Campaign. LC 98-41946. 272p. 1998. text 45.00 (*0-312-21364-6*) St Martin.

Musolff, Andreas, et al, eds. Conceiving of Europe: Diversity in Unity. LC 96-1353. 1996. 77.95 (*1-85521-742-2*, Pub. by Dartmth Pub) Ashgate Pub Co.

Muson, Howard. Triumph of the American Spirit: Johnstown, Pennsylvania. (Johnstown Flood Museum Ser.). 1989. 43.00 (*0-8026-0032-8*) Univ Pub Assocs.

Musopole, Augustine C. Being Human in Africa: Toward an African Christian Anthropology. LC 93-14315. (Am. Univ. Studies, XI: Vol. 65). 261p. (Orig.). (C). 1994. text 34.95 (*0-8204-2304-1*) P Lang Pubng.

Muspratt, Sandy, et al, eds. Constructing Critical Literacies: Teaching & Learning Textual Practice. 336p. 1998. pap. 35.00 (*1-86448-433-0*, Pub. by Allen & Unwin Pty) Paul & Co Pubs.

— Constructing Critical Literacies: Teaching & Learning Textual Practice. LC 97-41752. (Language & Social Processes Ser.). 440p. (C). 1998. text 85.00 (*1-57273-102-8*); pap. text 32.50 (*1-57273-103-6*) Hampton Pr NJ.

Muss-Arnolt, William. A Concise Dictionary of the Assyrian Languages, 2 vols., Set. LC 78-72752. (Ancient Mesopotamian Texts & Studies). (AKK.). reprint ed. 97.50 (*0-404-18195-3*) AMS Pr.

Muss-Barnes, Eric. The Gothic Rainbow. LC 96-92869. (Vampire Noctuaries Ser.: Vol. 1). (Illus.). 496p. 1997. pap. 15.00 (*0-9656318-2-6*) Dubh Sith Ink.

Muss, Hyman B., jt. ed. see Foon, Kenneth A.

Mussa, Michael. The Role of Official Intervention. (Occasional Paper Ser.: No. 6). 30p. 1981. pap. 5.00 (*1-56708-005-7*) Grp of Thirty.

***Mussa, Michael & International Monetary Fund Staff.** Exchange Rate Regimes in an Increasingly Integrated World Economy. LC 00-35064. (Occasional Papers). 2000. write for info. (*1-55775-892-1*) Intl Monetary.

Mussa, Michael, jt. auth. see Masson, Paul R.

Mussa, Michael L. Exchange Rates in Theory & in Reality. Riccardi, Margaret B., ed. LC 90-27127. (Essays in International Finance Ser.: No. 179). 46p. 1990. pap. text 10.00 (*0-88165-086-2*) Princeton U Int Finan Econ.

Mussa, Michael L., jt. auth. see Masson, Paul R.

Mussa, Michael L., jt. ed. see Frenkel, Jacob A.

Mussain, Donna. Art for Young Children. Britt, Leslie, ed. LC 96-75148. (Illus.). 80p. (Orig.). (J). (ps-k). 1995. pap. text 9.95 (*0-86530-309-6*, IP 309-6) Incentive Pubns.

Mussalam, Sami. The PLO-The Palestine Liberation Organization: Its Function & Structure. 70p. (Orig.). (C). 1988. pap. 6.95 (*0-915597-72-1*) Amana Bks.

Mussari, Mark. Suzanne De Passe: Motown's Boss Lady. Young, Richard G., ed. LC 91-28541. (Wizards of Business Ser.). (Illus.). 64p. (J). (gr. 4-8). 1992. lib. bdg. 17.26 (*1-56074-026-4*) Garrett Ed Corp.

Mussari, Riccardo, jt. auth. see Caperchione, Eugenio.

Mussati, Ciuliano, ed. Mergers, Markets & Public Policy, Vol. 21. LC 95-31703. (Studies in Industrial Organization). 232p. (C). 1995. lib. bdg. 125.00 (*0-7923-3643-7*) Kluwer Academic.

Mussato, Albertino & Bosoppi, Ivana. Ecerinis - Konkordanz und Frequenzwortlisten. (Alpha-Omega, Reihe B Ser.: Bd. XIV). (GER.). vi, 141p. 1997. write for info. (*3-487-10495-4*) G Olms Pubs.

Mussavian, Massoud, jt. ed. see Dimson, Elroy.

***Musschenga, Albert W. & Van der Steen, Wim J., eds.** Reasoning in Ethics & Law: The Role of Theory Principles & Facts. (Avebury Series in Philosophy). 222p. 1999. text 65.95 (*0-7546-1045-4*, Pub. by Inst Materials) Ashgate Pub Co.

Mussell, Barry D. The Roof Framer's Bible: The Complete Pocket Reference to Roof Framing. 2nd rev. ed. LC 94-96225. (Illus.). 230p. (C). 1996. 18.95 (*0-9643354-1-7*) M E I.

Mussell, Harry & Staples, Richard C., eds. Stress Physiology in Crop Plants. 526p. (C). 1990. reprint ed. lib. bdg. 67.50 (*0-471-03809-1*) Krieger.

Mussell, Kay. Fantasy & Reconciliation: Contemporary Formulas of Women's Romance Fiction, 46. LC 83-12731. (Contributions in Women's Studies: No. 46). 217p. 1984. 57.95 (*0-313-23915-0*, MFR/, Greenwood Pr) Greenwood.

— Women's Gothic & Romantic Fiction: A Reference Guide. LC 80-28683. (American Popular Culture Ser.). 157p. 1981. lib. bdg. 47.95 (*0-313-21402-6*, MGF/, Greenwood Pr) Greenwood.

Mussell, Kay & Tunon, Johanna. North American Romance Writers. LC 98-44836. 296p. 1999. text 39.50 (*0-8108-3604-1*) Scarecrow.

Mussell, Kay, jt. ed. see Brown, Linda K.

Mussell, Kay, ed. see Paradoxa Staff.

Mussell, Michall. New Classic Quilt Designs. LC 99-39939. 112p. 1999. per. 19.95 (*1-57432-735-6*, Am Quilters Soc) Collector Bks.

Musselman, Don, ed. O Ye Jigs & Juleps! (J). 1993. pap. 7.00 (*0-87602-315-4*) Anchorage.

Musselman, Eric P., jt. auth. see Anderson, Christian S.

Musselman, Homer D. Caroline, Light, Parker & Stafford Light Virginia Artillery. (Virginia Regimental Histories Ser.). (Illus.). 144p. 1992. 19.95 (*1-56190-036-2*) H E Howard.

— Forty-Seventh Virginia Infantry. (Virginia Regimental Histories Ser.). (Illus.). 172p. 1991. 19.95 (*1-56190-012-5*) H E Howard.

— Stafford County in the Civil War. (Civil War Battles & Leaders Ser.). (Illus.). 134p. 1995. 19.95 (*1-56190-087-7*) H E Howard.

Musselman, James. Cadillac the Heartbreak of America: Fifteen Years of Consumer Disillusionment. 140p. (Orig.). 1988. pap. 12.95 (*0-9621259-0-3*) Essential Info Inc.

Musselman, L. Parasitic Weeds in Agriculture Striga. LC 86-6139. 328p. 1986. 184.00 (*0-8493-6272-5*, CRC Reprint) Franklin.

Musselman, R. C. The Glacier Lakes Ecosystem Experiments Sites. (Illus.). 100p. 1997. reprint ed. 17.00 (*0-89904-593-6*, Bear Meadows Resrch Grp); reprint ed. pap. 11.00 (*0-89904-594-4*, Bear Meadows Resrch Grp) Crumb Elbow Pub.

Musselman, Vernon A., jt. auth. see Jackson, John H.

Musselwhite, Brian, jt. ed. see Burton, Lesley.

Musselwhite, Caroline & King-DeBaun, Pati. Emergent Literacy Success: Merging Technology & Whole Language for Students with Disabilities. (Illus.). 414p. 1997. pap. text 49.00 (*0-9628290-1-3*) Creative Comm Res Inc.

Musselwhite, Caroline R. Adaptive Play for Special Needs Children: Strategies to Enhance Communication & Learning. LC 90-52761. (Illus.). 249p. (C). 1986. pap. text 29.00 (*0-89079-303-4*, 1751) PRO-ED.

— RAPS: Reading Activities Project for Older Students. (Illus.). 188p. (YA). 1993. 29.00 (*1-884135-50-1*) Mayer-Johnson.

Musselwhite, Charlie, jt. auth. see Duncan, Phil.

Musselwhite, Christopher. Change Style Indicator: Facilitator's Guide. 1998. teacher ed., ring bd. 99.95 (*0-7879-4010-0*, Pfiffr & Co) Jossey-Bass.

— Change Style Indicator: Participant's Guide with Instrument. 1998. ring bd. 12.95 (*0-7879-4009-7*, Pfiffr & Co) Jossey-Bass.

Musselwhite, David. Partings Welded Together: Politics & Desire in the Nineteenth Century English Novel. 304p. 1987. text 57.50 (*0-416-06162-1*); pap. text 14.95 (*0-416-06172-9*) Routledge.

Musselwhite, James C., Jr., jt. auth. see Layton, Bruce D.

Mussen, Eric C. Beekeeping in California. LC 87-71574. (Illus.). 72p. (Orig.). 1987. pap. 3.50 (*0-931876-79-6*, 21422) ANR Pubns CA.

Mussen, Eric C., jt. ed. see Humphrey, Shirley.

Mussen, Paul H. Psychological Development of the Child. 3rd ed. (Foundations of Modern Psychology Ser.). (Illus.). 1979. text 17.95 (*0-13-732420-0*) P-H.

Mussen, Paul H., ed. Annual Review of Psychology, Vol. 22. LC 50-13143. 1971. text 40.00 (*0-8243-0222-2*) Annual Reviews.

— Annual Review of Psychology, Vol. 23. LC 50-13143. 1972. text 40.00 (*0-8243-0223-0*) Annual Reviews.

— Annual Review of Psychology, Vol. 24. LC 50-13143. (Illus.). 1973. text 40.00 (*0-8243-0224-9*) Annual Reviews.

Mussen, Paul H. & Farnsworth, Paul R., eds. Annual Review of Psychology, Vol. 10. LC 50-13143. 1959. 44.00 (*0-8243-0210-9*) Annual Reviews.

Mussen, Paul H. & Markman, Ellen M., eds. Handbook of Child Psychology, 4 vols. 4th ed. Incl. Vol. 3. Cognitive Development. 4th ed. Flavell, John H., ed. LC 83-3468. 942p. 1983. text 94.95 (*0-471-09064-6*); Vol. 4. Handbook of Child Psychology: Socialization, Personality & Social Development. 4th ed. Hetherington, E. Mavis, ed. LC 83-6552. 1043p. 1983. text 94.95 (*0-471-09065-4*); 3819p. 1983. Set text 379.80 (*0-471-05194-2*) Wiley.

Mussen, Paul H., et al. Psychological Development: A Life-Span Approach. LC 78-11977. (C). 1979. text 30.33 (*0-06-044692-7*) Addison-Wesley Educ.

Mussen, Paul H., ed. see Eisenberg, Nancy.

Mussen, William A. Fishing Tackle Source Directory. LC 98-16103. 230p. 1998. pap. 25.00 (*0-7864-0537-6*) McFarland & Co.

***Musser.** Mathematics for Elementary Teachers: A Contemporary Approach, A Guide to Problem Solving. 5th ed. 118p. 1999. pap. 26.95 (*0-471-37803-8*) Wiley.

Musser. Mathematics in Life Society & the World. 1997. pap. text, teacher ed. write for info. (*0-13-259367-X*) Allyn.

Musser, Benjamin F. Franciscan Poets. LC 67-26768. (Essay Index Reprint Ser.). 1977. 19.95 (*0-8369-0732-9*) Ayer.

Musser, Charles. Before the Nickelodeon: Edwin S. Porter & the Edison Manufacturing Company. LC 90-11045. 1990. pap. 40.00 (*0-520-06986-2*, Pub. by U CA Pr) Cal Prin Full Svc.

— Edison Motion Pictures, 1890-1900: An Annotated Filmography. LC 97-75484. (Studies in the History of Film & Television). 720p. 1998. text 75.00 (*1-56098-567-4*) Smithsonian.

— The Emergence of Cinema: The American Screen to 1907. LC 93-40205. 1994. 24.95 (*0-520-08533-7*, Pub. by U CA Pr) Cal Prin Full Svc.

— History of the American Cinema, Vol. 1: The Emergence of Cinema: The American Screen to 1907. Harpole, Charles H. et al, eds. LC 90-48307. 613p. 1990. 85.00 (*0-684-18413-3*, Scribners Ref) Mac Lib Ref.

— Thomas A. Edison & His Kinetographic Motion Pictures. LC 93-96. 1993. 12.95 (*0-9634879-0-6*) Frnds of Edison.

— Thomas A. Edison & His Kinetoscopic Motion Pictures. (Illus.). 70p. (C). 1995. pap. 14.95 (*0-8135-2210-2*) Rutgers U Pr.

Musser, Charles & Nelson, Carol. High-Class Moving Pictures: Lyman H. Howe & the Forgotten Era of Traveling Exhibition, 1880-1920. (Illus.). 351p. 1991. text 49.50 (*0-691-04781-2*, Pub. by Princeton U Pr) Cal Prin Full Svc.

Musser, Charles, ed. see Horak, Jan-Christopher.

Musser, Charles, jt. ed. see Sklar, Robert.

Musser, David. Laser Streak. 49p. 1998. 9.00 (*0-8059-4450-8*) Dorrance.

— Sharing the Vision: How to Become Wealthy, Financially Secure, Well-to-Do. (Illus.). 48p. 1998. 10.00 (*0-8059-4343-9*) Dorrance.

Musser, David R. ADA Generic Library. 1989. 72.95 (*0-387-97133-5*, 3398) Spr-Verlag.

Musser, David R. & Saini, Atul. STL Tutorial & Reference Guide: C++ Programming with Standard Template Library. 432p. (C). 1995. 42.95 (*0-201-63398-1*) Addison-Wesley.

Musser, Donald W. Abingdon Dictionary of Theology. Price, Joseph L., ed. 1997. boxed set 39.95 (*0-687-05325-0*) Abingdon.

Musser, Donald W. & Price, Joseph L., eds. A New Handbook of Christian Theologians. LC 96-12801. 528p. 1996. pap. 29.95 (*0-687-27803-1*) Abingdon.

— A New Handbook of Christian Theology. 544p. (Orig.). 1992. pap. 24.95 (*0-687-27802-3*) Abingdon.

Musser, Doug & Lang, Thomas A. Jujitsu Techniques & Tactics. LC 99-19381. (Martial Arts Ser.). (Illus.). 208p. 1999. pap. 15.95 (*0-88011-830-X*, PMUS0830) Human Kinetics.

Musser, Edward G. Designing Offsite Facilities by Use of Routing Diagrams. fac. ed. LC 83-5608. (Illus.). 78p. (Orig.). 1983. reprint ed. pap. 30.00 (*0-7837-8146-6*, 204795400008) Bks Demand.

Musser, Elizabeth. Two Crosses. 425p. 1996. 11.99 (*1-56476-577-6*, 6-3577, Victor Bks) Chariot Victor.

Musser, Faithe H. My Spiritual Heritage. LC 98-90153. 1998. pap. 8.95 (*0-533-12729-7*) Vantage.

— Wait for True Love. LC 96-90244. (Orig.). 1996. pap. 8.95 (*0-533-11974-X*) Vantage.

Musser, Frederic O. The History of Goucher College, 1930-1985. LC 89-35238. (Goucher College Ser.). (Illus.). 352p. 1990. text 39.95 (*0-8018-3902-5*) Johns Hopkins.

Musser, Gary L. Mathematics for Elementary Teachers: A Contemporary Approach. 4th ed. (Illus.). 1997. teacher ed. 119.90 (*0-471-37478-4*); pap., teacher ed. 119.90 (*0-471-37508-X*) Wiley.

— Mathematics for Elementary Teachers: A Contemporary Approach. 5th ed. 367p. 1999. pap. 26.95 (*0-471-36636-6*) Wiley.

— Mathematics for Elementary Teachers A Contemporary Approach. 5th ed. 408p. 1999. pap. 31.95 (*0-471-36654-4*) Wiley.

Musser, Gary L. & Trimpe, Lynn E. College Geometry: A Problem-Solving Approach with Applications. LC 93-39365. 528p. (C). 1994. 86.00 (*0-02-385450-2*, Macmillan Coll) P-H.

***Musser, Gary L., et al.** Mathematics for Elementary Teachers: A Contemporary Approach. 5th ed. 1056p. 1999. text 87.95 (*0-471-36858-X*) Wiley.

Musser, Guy G., jt. auth. see Robertson, Paul B.

Musser, Joe. The Cereal Tycoon: Henry Parsons Crowell: Founder of Quaker Oats Co. 160p. 1997. pap. 9.97 (*1-885481-28-4*) Quadrus Media.

— Cereal Tycoon: Henry Parsons Crowell Founder of the Quaker Oats Company. 160p. 1997. pap. 9.99 (*0-8024-1623-3*) Moody.

Musser, Joe, et al. Fire on the Hill: The Rochunga Pudaite Story. LC 98-37368. 1998. pap. 9.99 (*0-8423-1891-7*) Tyndale Hse.

Musser, Joe, jt. auth. see Anglin, Patty.

Musser, Joe, jt. auth. see Tada, Joni Eareckson.

***Musser, Kathy.** Rosemary. (Illus.). ii, 18p. 2000. pap. 3.50 (*0-9700720-0-7*) Cloverleaf Herb.

Musser, Kenneth. Cyber Streak. (Illus.). 24p. 1999. pap. 7.00 (*0-8059-4606-3*) Dorrance.

Musser, Linda. Remember Lee: The End Is the Beginning. rev. ed. Johnson, Joy, ed. LC 95-44570. (Illus.). 60p. 1997. pap. 7.95 (*1-56123-020-0*) Centering Corp.

Musser, Paul H. James Nelson Barker, 1784-1858: With a Reprint of His Comedy, Tears & Smiles. LC 73-131785. 1971. 14.00 (*0-403-00672-4*) Scholarly.

— James Nelson Barker, 1784-1858: With a Reprint of His Comedy, Tears & Smiles. LC 71-94313. reprint ed. 29.50 (*0-404-04546-4*) AMS Pr.

— James Nelson Barker, 1784-1858: With a Reprint of His Comedy, Tears & Smiles. (BCL1-PS American Literature Ser.). 230p. 1992. reprint ed. lib. bdg. 79.00 (*0-7812-6673-4*) Rprt Serv.

Musser, Richard, ed. see Smith, Gary M.

Musser, Sandra K. I Would Have Searched Forever. Verica, Thomas, ed. LC 79-64955. 160p. 1992. reprint ed. pap. 11.95 (*0-934896-00-3*) Adopt Aware Pr.

— To Prison with Love: The True Story of Sandy Musser's Indecent Indictment & America's Adoption Travesty. Pesatrice, Terri, ed. (Illus.). 276p. (Orig.). 1995. pap. 14.95 (*0-934896-37-2*) Adopt Aware Pr.

— What Kind of Love Is This? Zimmerman, Steve, ed. LC 82-84236. (Orig.). 1982. pap. 7.95 (*0-934896-43-7*) Adopt Aware Pr.

Musset. La Confession d'un Enfant du Siecle. unabridged ed. (FRE.). pap. 7.95 (*2-87714-231-0*, Pub. by Bookking Intl) Distribks Inc.

— Lorenzaccio. (FRE.). (C). pap. 9.95 (*0-8442-1992-4*, VF1992-4) NTC Contemp Pub Co.

— Lorenzaccio. unabridged ed. (FRE.). pap. 6.95 (*2-87714-193-4*, Pub. by Bookking Intl) Distribks Inc.

Musset, Alfred. Comedies et Proverbes. Gastinel, Francis, ed. (FRE.). 376p. 1957. pap. 28.95 (*0-7859-4694-2*); pap. 28.95 (*0-7859-4695-0*) Fr & Eur.

— Comedies et Proverbes, Vol. 1. Gastinel, Francis, ed. (FRE.). 376p. 1957. pap. 28.95 (*0-7859-4696-9*) Fr & Eur.

— Comedies et Proverbes Vol. 2: On ne Badine pas avec l'Amour, Lorenzaccio. (FRE.). 1985. pap. 8.95 (*0-7859-4699-3*) Fr & Eur.

— Comedies et Proverbes Vol. 3: Le Chandelier, Il ne Faut Jurer de Rein. 2nd ed. (FRE.). 127p. 1985. pap. 8.95 (*0-7859-4700-0*) Fr & Eur.

— Comedies et Proverbes Vol. 4: Louison, on ne Saurait Penser a Tout. (FRE.). 128p. 1985. pap. 8.95 (*0-7859-4698-5*) Fr & Eur.

— Lorenzaccio. (FRE., Illus.). 1964. pap. 10.95 (*0-8288-9647-X*, M2487) Fr & Eur.

— Oeuvres Completes, 3 tomes. Allem, ed. Incl. Tome I. Poesies Completes. 54.95 (*2-07-010387-0*); Tome II. Theatre Complete. deluxe ed. 99.95 (*2-07-011180-6*); Tome III. Oeuvres Completes en Prose. 59.95 (*2-07-010389-7*); (Pleiade Ser.). (FRE.). write for info. (*0-318-52143-1*) Schoenhof.

— Oeuvres Completes, 12 vols., Set. (FRE., Illus.). 300p. 1969. 1995.00 (*0-8288-9648-8*, F69130) Fr & Eur.

— On ne Badine Pas avec l'Amour. (FRE.). 159p. 1992. 49.95 incl. audio (*0-7859-0582-0*); pap. 10.95 (*0-7859-1258-4*, 2038713448) Fr & Eur.

— Premieres Poesies, 1829-1835. Allem, Maurice, ed. (FRE.). 338p. 1958. 29.95 (*0-8288-9649-6*, F69060) Fr & Eur.

— Theatre, Vol. 3. (FRE.). 512p. 1964. 10.95 (*0-8288-9650-X*, FC1473) Fr & Eur.

— Theatre Vol. 2: Avec: Le Quenouille de Barberine, le Chandelier, Il Ne Faut Jurer de Rein, Un Caprice, Il Faut Qu'Une Port Soit Ouverte ou Fermee. Rat, Maurice, ed. (FRE.). 448p. 1964. 10.95 (*0-8288-9651-8*, FC1472) Fr & Eur.

— Theatre, Vol. 1: Avec: Les Marrons de feu, La Nuit Ventienne, La Coup et les Levres, A quoi revent les Jeunes Filles, Andre del Sorto, Les Caprices de Marianne. (FRE.). 448p. 1964. 10.95 (*0-8288-9652-6*, FC1471) Fr & Eur.

Musset, Alfred de. Oeuvres Completes, Vol. 1. Allem, Maurice, ed. (FRE.). 972p. 1933. lib. bdg. 105.00 (*0-7859-3770-6*, 2070103870) Fr & Eur.

— Oeuvres Completes, Vol. 3. Allem, Maurice, ed. (FRE.). 1344p. 1938. lib. bdg. 105.00 (*0-7859-3771-4*, 2070103897) Fr & Eur.

Musset, Alfrede. Les Caprices de Marianne: Ilne Faut Jurer de Rien. unabridged ed. (FRE.). Date not set. reprint ed. pap. 8.95 (*2-03-870125-3*, Pub. by Bookking Intl) Distribks Inc.

Mussett, Alan E., jt. auth. see Brown, Geoffrey C.

***Mussett, Allan E. & Khan, M. Aftab.** Looking into the Earth: An Introduction to Geological Geophysics. LC 00-20382. (Illus.). 608p. (C). 2000. 90.00 (*0-521-78085-3*); pap. 39.95 (*0-521-78574-X*) Cambridge U Pr.

Mussey, Barrows, ed. see Gossage, Howard L.

Mussey, Mary O., jt. auth. see Poor, David M.

Mussey, Robert D., Jr., ed. The First American Furniture Finisher's Manual: A Reprint of "The Cabinetmaker's Guide" of 1827. 160p. 1988. reprint ed. pap. 5.95 (*0-486-25530-1*) Dover.

***Mussi, Margherita, et al, eds.** Hunters of the Golden Age: The Mid-Upper Palaeolithic or Eurasia 30,000-20,000 BP. (Palaeolithic Occupation of Europe Ser.). (Illus.). 420p. 2000. 70.00 (*90-73368-15-4*, Pub. by Leiden Univ Pr) David Brown.

Mussies, G. & Dio Cassius. Dio Chrysostom & the New Testament: Collected Parallels. LC 73-153645. (Studia Ad Corpus Hellenisticum Novi Testamenti Ser.). xii, 257p. 1972. write for info. (*90-04-03405-6*) Brill Academic Pubs.

Mussiett, Salom, ed. Cancionero para Preescolares No. 1: Songbook for Todays Preschooler. (SPA.). 54p. (J). (ps). 1989. pap. 5.50 (*0-311-32226-3*) Casa Bautista.

— Musica para Ocasiones Especiales: Music for Special Occasions. (SPA.). 48p. (Orig.). 1993. pap. 4.50 (*0-311-32219-0*) Casa Bautista.

Mussiett, Salom, tr. see Nelson, Edward W.

Mussiett, Salomon, tr. see Brock, Charles.

Mussig, H. J., jt. auth. see Dabrowski, J.

Mussinan, Cynthia J. & Keelan, Mary E., eds. Sulfur Compounds in Foods. LC 94-20826. (ACS Symposium Ser.: Vol. 564). 304p. 1994. text 85.00 (*0-8412-2943-0*, Pub. by Am Chemical) OUP.

Mussinan, Cynthia J. & Morello, Michael J., eds. Flavor Analysis: Developments in Isolation & Characterization, Vol. 705. LC 98-23312. (ACS Symposium Ser.: No. 705). (Illus.). 402p. 1998. text 115.00 (*0-8412-3578-3*) OUP.

An Asterisk (*) at the beginning of an entry indicates that the title is appearing for the first time.

Mussinan, Cynthia J., jt. ed. see Bills, Donald D.

Mussington, D., et al. Exploring Money Laundering Vulnerabilities Through Emerging Cyberspace Technologies: A Caribbean Exercise. LC 98-222504. 138p. 1998. pap. text 15.00 (*0-8330-2665-8*, MR1005CTI/FinCE) Rand Corp.

Mussini, Gianni, ed. see Prezzolini, Giuseppe.

Mussio, L., et al, eds. Data Acquisition & Analysis for Multimedia GIS, Vol. X. (CISM International Centre for Mechanical Sciences Ser.: Vol. 365). (Illus.). 421p. 1996. pap. 102.00 (*3-211-82806-0*) Spr-Verlag.

***Mussio, Russell.** Central British Columbia, Vol. 6. (Backroad Mapbks.). 1999. pap. text 15.95 (*0-9697877-7-4*) Mussio Ventures.

— Southwestern Alberta. 1998. pap. 15.95 (*0-9697877-9-0*) Mussio Ventures.

***Mussio, Russell & Mussio, Wesley.** Fishing British Columbia: Lower Mainland. 100p. 2000. pap. 15.95 (*0-9685611-0-1*) Mussio Ventures.

Mussio, Russell, jt. auth. see Mussio, Wesley.

***Mussio, Wesley & Mussio, Russell.** Fishing British Columbia: Lower Mainland's Most Comprehensive Fishing Guide. 100p. 2000. pap. 15.95 (*0-9685611-1-X*) Mussio Ventures.

Mussio, Wesley, jt. auth. see Mussio, Russell.

Mussman, Anna, jt. auth. see Clark, Raymond C.

***Mussman, Jay D.** Florida Bar's Fastrain: Purchase/Sale of Residential Property 2nd ed. LC 99-61645. 121p. 1999. write for info. (*1-57976-026-0*) FL Bar Legal Ed.

Mussman, Robert B. The Candle of the Lord. 1992. pap. 5.99 (*0-88019-292-5*) Schmul Pub Co.

Mussmann, Linda. Room - Raum. Schelbert, Tarcisi & Rappolt, Hedwig, trs. from ENG. LC 81-51013. 107p. (Orig.). 1981. pap. 6.00 (*0-939858-00-2*) T S L Pr.

***Musso, Lori Licciardo.** Teaching with Favorite Newbery Books: Engaging Discussion Questions, Vocabulary Builders, Writing. 64p. 1999. pap. 9.95 (*0-590-01975-9*) Scholastic Inc.

Musso, Paul. Fingerstyle Jazz Guitar/Teaching Your Guitar to Walk. 60p. 1995. pap. 17.95 incl. audio compact disk (*0-7866-0314-3*, 95376BCD) Mel Bay.

— Graded Fingerstyle Jazz Guitar Solos. 64p. 1999. pap. 17.95 (*0-7866-3527-4*, 97168BCD) Mel Bay.

Musso, Van A. How to Retire Rich & Stay Rich: A Financial Road Map to Success. LC 94-217881. (Illus.). 224p. (Orig.). 1994. 24.95 (*0-9639484-1-5*); pap. 14.95 (*0-9639484-0-7*) V Musso Ent.

Mussolini, Benito. The Corporate State. 1976. lib. bdg. 59.95 (*0-8490-1675-4*) Gordon Pr.

— My Autobiography. xix, 318p. 1928. 15.25 (*0-8371-4294-6*) Greenwood.

— My Rise & Fall. Ascoli, Max, ed. & tr. by. LC 98-217204. Orig. Title: My Autobiography & the Fall of Mussolini. (Illus.). 590p. 1998. reprint ed. pap. 18.95 (*0-306-80864-1*) Da Capo.

— The Political & Social Doctrine of Fascism. 1976. 250.00 (*0-87968-434-8*) Gordon Pr.

— Talks with Mussolini. Paul, Eden & Paul, Cedar, trs. LC 78-63699. (Studies in Fascism: Ideology & Practice). (Illus.). 256p. reprint ed. 32.00 (*0-404-16968-6*) AMS Pr.

***Musson.** Dysphagia in the Elderly. 2002. pap. 48.50 (*1-56593-858-5*) Thomson Learn.

Musson, A. E. & Robinson, E., eds. Science & Technology in the Industrial Revolution. (Classics in the History & Philosophy of Science Ser.: Vol. 3). xii, 534p. 1969. pap. text 75.00 (*2-88124-382-7*) Gordon & Breach.

Musson, Albert E. Enterprise in Soap & Chemicals: Joseph Crosfield & Sons, Ltd., 1815-1865. LC 68-431. (Illus.). xi, 384p. 1967. 49.50 (*0-678-06763-5*) Kelley.

Musson, Anthony. Public Order & Law Enforcement: The Local Administration of Criminal Justice, 1294-1350. LC 96-6124. (Illus.). 331p. (C). 1996. 90.00 (*0-85115-635-5*) Boydell & Brewer.

Musson, Anthony & Ormrod, W. M. The Evolution of English Justice: Law, Politics, & Society in the Fourteenth Century. LC 98-22634. (British Studies Ser.). x, 249p. 1999. write for info. (*0-333-67671-8*) Macmillan.

— The Evolution of English Justice: Law, Politics, & Society in the Fourteenth Century. LC 98-22634. (British Studies). 264p. 1998. text 59.95 (*0-312-21748-X*) St Martin.

Musson, Cyril D., jt. auth. see Musson, Gloria J.

Musson, Gloria J. & Musson, Cyril D. RAPmetic, the Arithmetic Rap. (Illus.). 48p. (Orig.). (J). (gr. 3 up). 1998. pap. text 3.50 (*0-9619321-0-4*) Sq One Pubns.

— RAPmetic, the Arithmetic Rap. (Illus.). 48p. (Orig.). (J). (gr. 3 up). 1998. audio 6.50 (*0-9619321-1-2*) Sq One Pubns.

Musson, H. E. Trade Union & Social History. 224p. 1974. 37.50 (*0-7146-3031-4*, Pub. by F Cass Pubs) Intl Spec Bk.

Musson, Ian M. & Van den Bergh, Michel. Invariants under Tori of Rings of Differential Operators & Related Topics. LC 98-35281. (Memoirs of the American Mathematical Society Ser.: Vol. 136, No. 650). 85p. 1998. pap. 38.00 (*0-8218-0885-0*) Am Math.

Musson, Jean. Chameleon. large type ed. (Linford Romance Large Print Ser.). 288p. 1998. pap. 17.99 (*0-7089-5246-1*, Linford) Ulverscroft.

— A Distant Dream. large type ed. (Linford Romance Library). 1994. pap. 16.99 (*0-7089-7620-4*, Linford) Ulverscroft.

— Silk Domino. (Rainbow Romances Ser.). 160p. 1993. 14.95 (*0-7090-4924-2*) Parkwest Pubns.

— Silk Domino. large type ed. (Romance Ser.). 1994. pap. 16.99 (*0-7089-7609-3*, Linford) Ulverscroft.

Musson, Jeremy. The English Manor House. 1999. text 60.00 (*1-85410-619-8*) London Brdge.

***Musson, Jeremy & Hall, Michael.** Plasterwork: One Hundred Period Details. (Illus.). 108p. 2000. pap. 24.95 (*1-85410-685-6*, Pub. by Aurum Pr) London Brdge.

Musson, John. Evil - Is It Real? A Theological Analysis. LC 91-34921. (Toronto Studies in Theology: Vol. 61). 168p. 1991. lib. bdg. 79.95 (*0-7734-9654-8*) E Mellen.

Musson, Patricia & Nykor, Lynda M. Mennonite Furniture: The Ontario Tradition in York County. 95p. 1977. 29.95 (*0-88862-148-5*, Pub. by J Lorimer) Formac Dist Ltd.

— Mennonite Furniture: The Ontario Tradition In York County. 95p. 1977. pap. 2.99 (*0-88862-149-3*, Pub. by J Lorimer) Formac Dist Ltd.

Musson, Steve & Gibbons, Maurice. The New Youth Challenge: A Model for Working with Older Children in School-Age Child Care. LC 88-62241. (Illus.). 107p. (Orig.). (C). 1988. pap. text, teacher ed. 12.95 (*0-917505-02-6*) School Age.

Mussorgsky, Modest. Boris Godunov. John, Nicholas, ed. Lloyd-Jones, David, tr. from RUS. (English National Opera Guide Series: Bilingual Libretto, Articles: No. 11). (Illus.). 128p. (Orig.). 1982. pap. 9.95 (*0-7145-3922-8*) Riverrun NY.

— Boris Godunov: Full Score in Three Languages. Lloyd-Jones, David, ed. & tr. by. Hube, Max, tr. (ENG, GER & RUS.). 1206p. 1976. boxed set 180.00 (*0-19-337699-7*) OUP.

— Boris Godunov: Full Score in Three Languages. Lloyd-Jones, David, ed. & tr. by. Hube, Max, tr. (ENG, GER & RUS.). 944p. 1976. pap. 145.00 (*0-19-337700-4*) OUP.

— Coronation Scene from Boris Godounoff: 2 Pianos/4 Hands. 20p. 1995. pap. 4.95 (*0-7935-4296-0*, 50482377) H Leonard.

***Mussorgsky, Modest.** Piano Complete. (Music Scores Ser.). (Illus.). 1998. pap. text 7.98 (*963-8303-77-8*) Kone Music.

Mussorgsky, Modest. Pictures at an Exhibition: Piano 1874 Centennial Edition. 56p. 1986. pap. 9.95 (*0-7935-3889-0*, 50335140) H Leonard.

Mussulman, Joseph A. Dear People . . . Robert Shaw. 270p. 1996. pap. 29.95 (*0-937276-18-9*, HMB206) Hinshaw Mus.

Must, Art, ed. Why We Still Need Public Schools: Church - State Relations & Visions of Democracy. LC 92-4404. 311p. (Orig.). (C). 1992. pap. 18.95 (*0-87975-758-2*) Prometheus Bks.

Must, Dennis. Banjo Grease. LC 98-89657. 192p. 2000. pap. 13.95 (*0-88739-228-8*) Creat Arts Bk.

***Must, Dennis.** Banjo Grease. 2000. 23.50 (*0-88739-325-X*) Creat Arts Bk.

Must, Dennis, ed. Flying Horse, Vol. 2. (Illus.). 100p. (Orig.). 1997. pap. 4.00 (*0-9658480-0-0*) Flying Horse MA.

Mustacchi, Marianna M., ed. see Crenne, Helisenne D.

***Mustacchia, Nick.** Prisoner of War & Peace. LC 98-67436. 192p. 1999. 20.95 (*1-57197-143-2*) Pentland Pr.

Mustachio, Thomas, jt. auth. see Dyches, Richard W.

Mustacich, Suzanne. Nutshell Classics: A Doll's House. 1988. pap. text 40.00 (*0-938735-50-0*) Classic Theatre Schl.

— Nutshell Classics: Cyrano de Bergerac, Set. 1988. pap. text 150.00 (*0-938735-52-7*); pap. text 100.00 (*0-938735-53-5*) Classic Theatre Schl.

Mustafa. Plastics Waste Management: Disposal, Recycling, & Reuse. (Environmental Science & Pollution Ser.: Vol. 5). (Illus.). 432p. 1993. text 180.00 (*0-8247-8920-2*) Dekker.

Mustafa, Saleem. Genetics in Sustainable Fisheries Management. LC 98-38510. 11p. 1998. write for info. (*0-85238-263-4*) Blackwell Sci.

Mustafa, A. S., et al, eds. T-Cell Subsets & Cytokines Interplay in Infectious Diseases. (Illus.). 222p. 1996. 248.00 (*3-8055-6122-9*) S Karger.

Mustafa, Abu H. History of Eastern Arabia. 213p. 1988. 30.00 (*0-86685-022-8*, ABU0228, Pub. by Librairie du Liban) Intl Bk Ctr.

— The Modern History of Kuwait, 1750-1965. 226p. 1983. 35.00 (*0-86685-698-6*, ABU02399) Intl Bk Ctr.

Mustafa, D. & Glover, K. Minimum Entropy H Control. Thoma, M. & Wyner, A., eds. (Lecture Notes in Control & Information Sciences: Vol. 146). (Illus.). ix, 144p. 1990. 37.95 (*0-387-52947-0*) Spr-Verlag.

Mustafa, Fawzia. V. S. Naipaul. (Studies in African & Caribbean Literature: Vol. 4). 267p. (C). 1995. text 59.95 (*0-521-40378-2*); pap. text 19.95 (*0-521-48359-X*) Cambridge U Pr.

Mustafa, Husain. Postal Technology & Management. LC 73-165579. (Illus.). 240p. 1971. 23.50 (*0-912338-01-6*); fiche 9.50 (*0-912338-02-4*) Lomond.

Mustafa, Kemal. Jipemoyo 7. 190p. 1989. write for info. (*951-47-3238-3*, Pub. by Nordic Africa) Transaction Pubs.

***Mustafa, Khateeb S.** Descriptive Grammar of Dakkhini. 2000. 48.50 (*81-215-0886-X*, Pub. by M Manoharial) S Asia.

Mustafa, M. A. Microcomputer Interfacing & Applications. 2nd rev. ed. (Illus.). 432p. 1994. pap. text 59.95 (*0-7506-1752-7*) Buttrwrth-Heinemann.

Mustafa, M. A. & Sharma, Onkar P. Child Labour in India: A Bitter Truth. LC 96-904592. viii, 204 p. 1996. write for info. (*81-7100-842-9*) S Asia.

Mustafa, Mohammad A., et al. Telecommunications Policies for Sub-Saharan Africa. LC 96-37843. (Discussion Papers: No. 353). 90p. 1997. pap. 22.00 (*0-8213-3851-X*, 13851) World Bank.

Mustafa, S. & Chenoy, A. M. Scam: The Cover-Up & Compromise. 1995. write for info. (*81-224-0713-7*, Pub. by Wiley Estrn) Franklin.

Mustafi, C. K. Operations Research Method & Practice. (C). 1988. pap. 20.00 (*81-224-0054-X*) S Asia.

Mustain, Chris, jt. auth. see Werner, Jeffrey.

Mustain, Gene, jt. auth. see Capeci, Jerry.

***Mustaine, Beverly A.** On Lake Worth. (Images of America Ser.). (Illus.). 128p. 1999. pap. 18.99 (*0-7385-0055-0*) Arcadia Publng.

Mustajoki, A. & Nikkila, E. Venajaa Opiskelevan Sanakirja Venaja-Suomi. (FIN & RUS.). 534p. 1982. 49.95 (*0-8288-1076-1*, F 85800) Fr & Eur.

Mustapha, S., jt. auth. see Varopoulos, N.

Mustapha, Samina, ed. see Ghazi, Tasneema.

Mustard, Andrews G. James White & SDA Organization: Historical Development, 1844-1881. (Andrews University Seminary Doctoral Dissertation Ser.: Vol. 12). 328p. 1988. pap. 19.99 (*0-943872-46-4*) Andrews Univ Pr.

***Mustard, David B.** Racial Justice in the United States: A Reference Handbook. 2001. lib. bdg. 45.00 (*1-57607-214-2*) ABC-CLIO.

Mustard, Kirk, ed. see Dunn, Nancy.

Mustard, W. P. Classical Echoes in Tennyson. LC 72-116798. (Studies in Tennyson: No. 27). 1970. reprint ed. lib. bdg. 75.00 (*0-8383-1040-0*) M S G Haskell Hse.

Mustazza, Leonard. The Critical Response to Kurt Vonnegut, 14. LC 94-29147. (Critical Responses in Arts & Letters Ser.). 384p. 1994. lib. bdg. 65.00 (*0-313-28634-5*) Greenwood.

— Forever Pursuing Genesis: The Myth of Eden in the Novels of Kurt Vonnegut. LC 89-46407. 224p. 1991. 37.50 (*0-8387-5176-8*) Bucknell U Pr.

— Ol' Blue Eyes: A Frank Sinatra Encylopedia. LC 97-33017. 480p. 1998. lib. bdg. 59.95 (*0-313-30486-6*, Greenwood Pr) Greenwood.

***Mustazza, Leonard.** Ol'blue Eyes: A Frank Sinatra Encyclopedia. 480p. 1999. pap. 35.00 (*0-275-96758-1*, Praeger Pubs) Greenwood.

Mustazza, Leonard. Sinatra: An Annotated Bibliography, 1939-1998, 74. LC 98-41645. (Music Reference Collection: Vol. 74). 312p. 1999. lib. bdg. 69.50 (*0-313-30829-2*, Greenwood Pr) Greenwood.

— Such Prompt Eloquence: Language As Agency & Character in Milton's Epics. LC 86-48007. 176p. 1988. 32.50 (*0-8387-5121-0*) Bucknell U Pr.

Mustazza, Leonard, ed. Frank Sinatra & Popular Culture: Essays on an American Icon. LC 98-23933. 328p. 1998. 39.95 (*0-275-96495-7*, Praeger Pubs) Greenwood.

Mustazza, Leonard, jt. auth. see Abt, Vicki.

Mustazza, Leonard, jt. ed. see Petkov, Steven.

Muste, A. J. Of Holy Disobedience. 23p. (Orig.). 1964. pap. 1.50 (*0-934676-09-7*) Greenlf Bks.

Muste, A. J. Of Holy Disobedience. LC 52-1568. (Orig.). 1952. pap. 1.00 (*0-87574-064-2*) Pendle Hill.

Muste, A. J. Saints for This Age. LC 62-21962. (Orig.). 1962. pap. 4.00 (*0-87574-124-X*) Pendle Hill.

— War Is the Enemy. (C). 1942. pap. 4.00 (*0-87574-015-4*) Pendle Hill.

— The World Task of Pacifism. (C). 1942. pap. 4.00 (*0-87574-013-8*) Pendle Hill.

Musteikus, Antanas. The Reformation in Lithuania: Religious Fluctuations in the Sixteenth Century. (East European Monographs: No. 246). 125p. 1988. text 40.00 (*0-88033-143-7*, Pub. by East Eur Monographs) Col U Pr.

Mustelier, Evelio, pseud. Kid Tunero: Veinte Anos de Ring...y Fuera. (SPA., Illus.). 119p. (Orig.). 1987. pap. 5.00 (*84-359-0390-7*, Pub. by Editorial Playor) Ediciones.

Mustelin, Tomas. Src Family of Tyrosine Kinases in Leukocytes. (Molecular Biology Intelligence Unit Ser.). 118p. 1994. 99.00 (*1-57059-113-X*, LN9113) Landes Bioscience.

Muster, Bill, jt. auth. see Rand McNally Facts Books Staff.

Muster, John. UNIX Made Easy: The Basics & Beyond! 2nd ed. (Made Easy Ser.). 1061p. 1996. pap. 34.95 (*0-07-882173-8*) McGraw.

— UNIX Programmer's Reference. (Illus.). 288p. (Orig.). 1997. pap. 14.99 (*0-07-882366-8*, Oracle Press) Osborne-McGraw.

Muster, Nori J. Betrayal of the Spirit: My Life Behind the Headlines of the Hare Krishna Movement. 280p. 1996. 24.95 (*0-252-02263-7*); pap. write for info. (*0-252-06566-2*) U of Ill Pr.

Musterd, S., jt. auth. see De Winter, M.

Musterd, Sako & Ostendorf, Wim, eds. Urban Segregation & the Welfare State: Inequality & Exclusion in Western Cities. LC 97-35297. (Illus.). 296p. (C). 1998. 85.00 (*0-415-17059-1*) Routledge.

Musterd, Sako, et al. Multi-Ethinic Metropolis: Patterns & Policies. LC 97-45500. (Geojournal Library: No. 43). 224p. 1997. 110.00 (*0-7923-4854-0*) Kluwer Academic.

Musterman, Jack L., jt. auth. see Eckenfelder, W. W.

***Mustian, Mark.** The Return. LC 99-45716. 304p. 2000. 18.95 (*1-56164-190-1*) Pineapple Pr.

Mustill, Lord & Boyd, Stewart C. Commercial Arbitration. 2nd ed. 836p. 1989. boxed set 220.00 (*0-406-31124-2*, 87246-10, MICHIE) LEXIS Pub.

Mustin, Henry C. Surveying Fiberglass Sailboats: A Step-by-Step Guide for Buyers & Owners. 1993. pap. text 17.95 (*0-87742-347-4*) Intl Marine.

— Surveying Fiberglass Sailboats: A Step by Step Guide for Buyers & Owners. 139p. 1994. pap. 17.95 (*0-07-044248-7*) McGraw.

Musto, David F. The American Disease: Origins of Narcotic Control. LC 72-75204. 368p. reprint ed. pap. 114.10 (*0-8357-8018-X*, 203383800087) Bks Demand.

— The American Disease: Origins of Narcotic Control. 3rd ed. LC 98-24976. 432p. 1999. pap. 17.95 (*0-19-512509-6*) OUP.

Musto, Ken. Breaking into Advertising: Making Your Portfolio Work for You. (Illus.). 144p. 1988. pap. 24.95 (*0-442-26432-1*, VNR) Wiley.

Musto, Michael. Downtown. 1986. 10.95 (*0-317-53541-2*) Vin Bks.

Musto, Ronald G. The Catholic Peace Tradition. LC 86-12494. (Illus.). 396p. (Orig.). reprint ed. pap. 122.80 (*0-7837-9814-8*, 206054300005) Bks Demand.

— Liberation Theologies: A Research Guide. annot. ed. LC 90-29156. 632p. 1991. text 25.00 (*0-8240-3624-7*, SS507) Garland.

Musto, Ronald G., ed. Catholic Peacemakers: A Collection of Readings, 2 vols., Pt. I, Pt. II. fac. ed. LC 92-42658. (Illus.). 1072p. 1996. text 176.00 (*0-8153-0605-9*, H1372) Garland.

— Catholic Peacemakers: A Collection of Readings, 2 vols., Set. LC 92-42658. (Illus.). 864p. 1993. 170.00 (*0-8240-7388-6*) Garland.

— Catholic Peacemakers: A Collection of Readings, 2 vols., Vol. 1: From the Bible to the Crusades. LC 92-42658. (Illus.). 864p. 1993. text 35.00 (*0-8153-0604-0*, H1346) Garland.

Musto, Ronald G., jt. ed. see Harvey, Paul B., Jr.

Musto, Ronald G., jt. ed. see Monfasani, John.

Musto, Ronald G., ed. see Petrarca, Francesco.

Musto, Ronald G., jt. ed. see Porter, Jeanne C.

Musto, Stefan A. & Pinkele, Carl F. Europe at the Crossroads. LC 82-16658. 368p. 1985. 65.00 (*0-275-90147-5*, C0147, Praeger Pubs) Greenwood.

Mustoe. Engineering Math. 1997. pap. write for info. (*0-582-27729-9*) Addison-Wesley.

***Mustoe, L. & Barry, M. D.** Mathematics in Engineering & Science. 768p. 1998. pap. 44.95 (*0-471-97093-X*) Wiley.

Mustoe, L. R. Worked Examples in Advanced Engineering Mathematics. LC 88-2058. (Illus.). 147p. 1988. reprint ed. pap. 45.60 (*0-608-05295-7*, 206583300001) Bks Demand.

***Mustoe, L. R. & Barry, M. D.** Foundation Mathematics. 668p. 1998. pap. 46.50 (*0-471-97092-1*) Wiley.

— Foundation Mathematics. 668p. 1998. 115.00 (*0-471-96948-6*) Wiley.

Mustoe, Leslie R. & Hibberd, Stephen. Mathematical Education of Engineers. (Institute of Mathematics & Its Applications Conference Ser.; New Ser.: No. 57). (Illus.). 406p. (C). 1996. text 120.00 (*0-19-851191-4*) OUP.

Muston, Alexis. The Israel of the Alps: A Complete History of the Waldenses & Their Colonies, 2 vols. Montgomery, John, tr. LC 77-84718. reprint ed. 84.50 (*0-404-16140-5*) AMS Pr.

Mustoo, Terence. Sherlock Holmes in the Deerstalker: Chameleons' Dramascripts. 50p. (Orig.). 1991. pap. 10.00 (*0-86025-886-6*) Players Pr.

Mustrangi, Meika A. & Patton, James L. Phylogeography & Systematics of the Slender Mouse Opossum Marmosops (Marsupialia, Didelphidae) LC 96-36518. 1997. pap. 15.00 (*0-520-09815-3*, Pub. by U CA Pr) Cal Prin Full Svc.

Musu-Boy, R. Dizionario Italiano-Inglese, Inglese-Italiano: Italian-English, English-Italian Dictionary. deluxe ed. (ENG & ITA.). 463p. 1979. 9.95 (*0-8288-4732-0*, M9177) Fr & Eur.

***Musu, Ignazio.** Sustainable Venice: Suggestions for the Future. LC 00-42033. (Economics, Energy & Environment Ser.). (Illus.). 2000. write for info. (*0-7923-6458-9*) Kluwer Academic.

Musu, Ignazio & Siniscalco, Domenico, eds. National Accounts & the Environment. LC 95-38220. (FEEM/Kluwer International Series on Economics, Energy & Environment: Vol. 6). 300p. (C). 1996. lib. bdg. 136.00 (*0-7923-3741-7*) Kluwer Academic.

Musumeci, Diane. Breaking Tradition. LC 96-46729. 160p. (C). 1997. pap. 28.13 (*0-07-044394-7*) McGraw.

— Il Carciofo: Strategie di Lettura e Proposte di Attivia. 200p. (C). 1990. pap. 33.75 (*0-07-557836-0*) McGraw.

Musun, Chris. Peeps & Freaks. LC 85-73404. 446p. (Orig.). 1986. pap. 3.95 (*0-936729-01-5*) Dare Co.

— The White House Sucks. (Orig.). 1986. pap. 8.95 (*0-936729-00-7*) Dare Co.

Musunuru, K. & Hinds, P. W. Cell Cycle Regulators in Cancer. LC 97-22377. (Illus.). x, 162p. 1997. 98.00 (*3-8055-6561-5*) S Karger.

Musurillo, Herbert A. Symbol & Myth in Ancient Poetry. LC 77-2395. 220p. 1977. reprint ed. lib. bdg. 55.00 (*0-8371-9554-3*, MUSM, Greenwood Pr) Greenwood.

Musurillo, Herbertus, ed. Gregorii Nysseni De Vita Moysis. LC 90-15133. (Gregorius Nyssenus Opera Ser.: No. VII,1). (GRE & LAT.). xx, 145p. 1991. reprint ed. 89.50 (*90-04-00747-4*) Brill Academic Pubs.

Musvosvi, Joel N. Vengeance in the Apocalypse. (Andrews University Seminary Doctoral Dissertation Ser.: Vol. 17). 315p. 1993. pap. 19.99 (*0-943872-48-0*) Andrews Univ Pr.

Musyoki, Agnes. An Elementary Swahili Newspaper Reader. LC 85-70271. viii, 201p. 1985. text 45.00 (*0-931745-07-1*) Dunwoody Pr.

Muszynski, Alicja. Cheap Wage Labour: Race & Gender in the Fisheries of British Columbia. LC 97-159439. 328p. 1996. 49.95 (*0-7735-1376-0*, Pub. by McG-Queens Univ Pr) CUP Services.

Muta, T. Foundations of Quantum Chromodynamics: An Introduction to Perturbative Methods in Theories. 424p. 1987. text 97.00 (*9971-950-40-5*); pap. text 44.00 (*9971-950-41-3*) World Scientific Pub.

Muta, T., et al, eds. New Trends in Strong Coupling Gauge Theories. 364p. (C). 1989. text 115.00 (*9971-5-0846-X*) World Scientific Pub.

Muta, T. & Yamawaki, K. Strong Coupling Gauge Theories & Beyond: The 2nd International Workshop. 500p. 1991. text 118.00 (*981-02-0424-8*) World Scientific Pub.

Mutaawe Kasozi, Ferdinand. Self & Social Reality in a Philosophical Anthropology: Inquiring into George Herbert Mead's Socio-Philosophical Anthropology. LC 98-15134. (European University Studies: Series 20, Vol. 560). VII, 277p. (C). 1998. pap. text 48.95 (*0-8204-3585-6*) P Lang Pubng.

M

An Asterisk (*) at the beginning of an entry indicates that the title is appearing for the first time.

*Mutaftschiev, B. Fundamentals & Crystal Growth. (Illus.). 450p. 2000. 106.00 (3-540-66496-3) Spr-Verlag.

Mutaftschiev, B. Interfacial Aspects of Phase Transformation. 1982. text 261.50 (90-277-1440-1) Kluwer Academic.

Mutahaba, Gelase, ed. see Alfani, Mohamed.

Mutahaba, Gelase, jt. ed. see Balogun, M. Jide.

Mutahaba, Gelase R. Reforming Public Administration for Development: Experiences from Eastern Africa. LC 89-24550. (Kumarian Press Library of Management for Development). 200p. reprint ed. pap. 62.00 (0-608-20808-6, 207190700003) Bks Demand.

Mutahabe, Gelase, jt. auth. see Beyene, Asmelash.

Mutahhari, Ayatullah M. Fundamentals of Islamic Thought: God, Man & the Universe. Algar, Hamid, ed. Campbell, R., tr. LC 85-15446. (Contemporary Islamic Thought, Persian Ser.). Orig. Title: Per.. 231p. (Orig.). 1985. pap. 9.95 (0-933782-15-2) Mizan Pr.

— Social & Historical Change: An Islamic Perspective. Algar, Hamid, ed. Campbell, R., tr. from PER. LC 85-28554. (Contemporary Islamic Thought, Persian Ser.). 156p. (C). 1986. 19.95 (0-933782-18-7); pap. 9.95 (0-933782-19-5) Mizan Pr.

Mutahhari, Morteza. The Martyr. Yasin, A., tr. from PER. 28p. pap. 2.00 (0-941722-07-4) Book Dist Ctr.

Mutahhari, Murtada, jt. auth. see Taleqani, Mahmud.

Mutahhari, Murtada, jt. auth. see Talequani, Mahmud.

Mutahhari, Murtaza. Hijab: Islamic Modest Dress. Bakhtiar, Laleh, tr. from PER. 112p. (C). 1993. pap. 9.95 (1-871031-15-X) Abjad Bk.

— Iqbal: Manifestation of the Islamic Spirit. Bakhtiar, Laleh, tr. from PER. 130p. (C). 1993. pap. 12.50 (1-871031-20-6) Abjad Bk.

Mutahhari, Murtaza. The Islamic Modest Dress. 1990. 12.00 (0-685-66737-5) Macmillan.

Mutahhari, Murtaza. Islamic Mysticism (Irfan) An Introduction. Qara'i, Ali Q., tr. 64p. 1989. pap. text 4.50 (1-871031-34-6) Abjad Bk.

— The Universal Prototype: An Islamic Perspective. Bakhtiar, Laleh, tr. from PER. 112p. (Orig.). (C). 1989. pap. 10.00 (1-871031-04-4) Abjad Bk.

Mutahheri, Murtaza. Man & His Destiny. rev. ed. Islamic Seminary Staff, tr. from PER.Tr. of Insan wa Sarnawisht. 124p. (C). 1985. reprint ed. pap. 4.00 (0-941724-39-5) Islamic Seminary.

— Man & Universe: Mugaddamai Bar Jahan Bin'i Islami. rev. ed. Islamic Seminary Staff, tr. from PER. 663p. (C). reprint ed. text 18.00 (0-941724-52-2) Islamic Seminary.

Mutahhery, Murtaza. Master & Mastership: Wila Wa Wilayat. rev. ed. Islamic Seminary Staff & Ansari, M. A., trs. from PER. 131p. (C). 1983. reprint ed. pap. 4.00 (0-941724-15-8) Islamic Seminary.

Mutahhery, Murtaza, et al. Rationality of Islam. rev. ed. Islamic Seminary Staff & Ansari, M. A., trs. from PER. 182p. (C). 1990. reprint ed. pap. 7.00 (0-941724-17-4) Islamic Seminary.

Mutalib, Hussin. Islam & Ethnicity in Malay Politics. (South-East Asian Social Science Monographs). (Illus.). 230p. 1990. 45.00 (0-19-588935-5) OUP.

— Islam in Malaysia: From Revivalism to Islamic State? LC 94-941909. 190p. (Orig.). 1993. pap. 36.00 (9971-69-180-9, Pub. by Sngapore Univ Pr) Coronet Bks.

Mutalik-Desai, A. A., jt. ed. see Kamath, P. M.

Mutalik, Keshav M. Jagannath Dasa: His Life & Works LC 91-904747. ix, 44p. 1990. write for info. (81-7039-194-6) Somaiya Publns.

Mutalik, Keshav M., ed. Songs of Divinity: Songs of the Bards of Karnatak. (C). 1995. 80.00 (81-7154-788-5, Pub. by Popular Prakashan) S Asia.

Mutambara, Arthur G. Decentralized Estimation & Control for Multisensor Systems. LC 97-51553. 256p. 1998. lib. bdg. 79.95 (0-8493-1865-3) CRC Pr.

Mutambara, Arthur G. O. Design & Analysis of Control Systems. LC 99-25429. 832p. 1999. boxed set 79.95 (0-8493-1898-X) CRC Pr.

Mutambirwa, James A. The Rise of Settler Power in Southern Rhodesia (Zimbabwe), 1898-1923. LC 78-75181. 248p. 1970. 34.50 (0-8386-2267-4) Fairleigh Dickinson.

Mutari, Ellen, et al, eds. Gender & Political Economy: Incorporating Diversity into Theory & Policy. LC 96-40285. 260p. (C). (gr. 13). 1997. text 74.95 (1-56324-996-0) M E Sharpe.

Mutari, Ellen, et al, eds. Gender & Political Economy: Incorporating Diversity into Theory & Policy. LC 96-40285. 260p. (C). (gr. 13). 1997. pap. text 32.95 (1-56324-997-9) M E Sharpe.

Mutatkar, R. K. Caste Dimensions in Village. 189p. 1978. 9.95 (0-318-36799-8) Asia Bk Corp.

Mutawakil, G. Business & Law in Saudi Arabia. 220p. (C). 1995. 90.00 (0-907151-18-3, Pub. by IMMEL Pubng) St Mut.

Mutben, Leif & Foundation for European Fiscal Studies Staff. Towards a Dual Income Tax? Scandinavian & Austrian Experiences. LC 99-180622. 89p. 1996. write for info. (90-411-0928-5) Kluwer Law Intl.

Mutch. Mutch Touch. 1991. 14.95 (0-13-608696-9) P-H.

*Mutch, James R. Genealogy of the Mutch Family. fac. ed. 94p. 1999. reprint ed. 28.00 (0-8328-9948-8); reprint ed. pap. 18.00 (0-8328-9949-6) Higginson Bk Co.

Mutch, Robert E. Campaigns, Congress & the Courts: The Making of Federal Campaign Finance Laws. LC 87-30874. 237p. 1988. 57.95 (0-275-92784-9, C2784, Praeger Pubs) Greenwood.

Mutch, Thomas A. Geology of the Moon: A Stratigraphic View. rev. ed. LC 70-38387. 403p. 1972. pap. 125.00 (0-7837-9398-7, 206014300004) Bks Demand.

Mutch, Thomas A., et al. The Geology of Mars. LC 75-30199. (Illus.). 410p. reprint ed. pap. 127.10 (0-7837-1943-4, 204215800001) Bks Demand.

Mutch, William. Tall Trees & Small Woods: How to Grow & Tend Them. (Illus.). 288p. 1998. 40.00 (1-84018-020-X, Pub. by Mainstream Pubng) Trafalgar.

Mutchler, David G. The Deeper Reaches of Love & Fear: The Birth of a New Psychology. 250p. 1989. 18.95 (0-922639-00-0) Lakeshore Counsel.

*Mutchler, John C. The American Directory of Writer's Guidelines: A Compilation for Freelancers from More Than 1,300 Magazine Editors & Book Publishers. 2nd ed. 736p. 1999. pap. 24.95 (1-884956-08-4) Quill Driver.

Mutchnick, Brenda & Casden, Ron. A Noteworthy Tale. LC 97-70933. (Illus.). 32p. (J). (gr. 1-4). 1997. 17.95 (0-8109-1386-0, Pub. by Abrams) Time Warner.

Mutchnick, Robert J. & Berg, Bruce L. Research Methods for the Social Sciences: Practice & Applications. LC 95-11824. 283p. 1995. pap. 35.00 (0-02-385451-0, Macmillan Coll) P-H.

Mutel, C. F. & Donham, K. J. Medical Practice in Rural Communities. (Illus.). 168p. 1983. 58.00 (0-387-91224-X) Spr-Verlag.

Mutel, Cornelia F. Fragile Giants: A Natural History of the Loess Hills. LC 89-35497. (Bur Oak Original Ser.). (Illus.). 304p. 1989. pap. 17.95 (0-87745-257-1) U of Iowa Pr.

— Our Endangered Planet: Tropical Rain Forests. 64p. (J). (gr. 4 up). 1991. lib. bdg. 22.60 (0-8225-2503-8, Lerner Publctns) Lerner Pub.

— Our Endangered Planet: Tropical Rain Forests. (J). (gr. 4 up). 1993. pap. 8.95 (0-8225-9629-6, Lerner Publctns) Lerner Pub.

Mutel, Cornelia F. & Swander, Mary, eds. Land of the Fragile Giants: Landscapes, Environments, & Peoples of the Loess Hills. LC 94-14909. (Bur Oak Original Ser.). (Illus.). 168p. (Orig.). 1994. pap. 24.95 (0-87745-477-9) U of Iowa Pr.

Mutel, Cornelia F., et al. From Grassland to Glacier: The Natural History of Colorado & the Surrounding Region. rev. ed. LC 84-80539. (Illus.). 280p. 1992. pap. 12.95 (1-55566-089-4) Johnson Bks.

Mutel, Cornelia F., jt. auth. see Packard, Stephen.

Mutel, Cornelia F., jt. ed. see Packard, Stephen.

Muten, Burleigh. Grandmothers' Stories: Wise Woman Tales from Many Cultures. (Illus.). 80p. (YA). (gr. 1 up). 1999. 19.95 (1-902283-24-4) Barefoot Bks NY.

— Return of the Great Goddess. LC 97-5529. (Illus.). 192p. 1997. pap. 14.95 (1-55670-608-1) Stewart Tabori & Chang.

Muten, Burleigh, ed. Her Words: An Anthology of Poetry about the Great Goddess. LC 99-23172. 264p. 1999. 22.95 (1-57062-473-9, Pub. by Shambhala Pubns) Random.

Muterthies, Klaus. Esthetic Approach to Metal Ceramic Restorations for the Mandibular Anterior Region. (Illus.). 94p. 1990. text 58.00 (1-85097-016-5) Quint Pub Co.

— Replication of Anterior Teeth in the Four Seasons of Life. (Illus.). 92p. 1991. text 66.00 (1-85097-023-8) Quint Pub Co.

Muth, Annemarie, ed. Death & Dying Sourcebook: Basic Information for the Layperson. LC 99-44810. (Health Reference Ser.). (Illus.). 641p. 1999. lib. bdg. 78.00 (0-7808-0230-6) Omnigraphics Inc.

— Forensic Medicine Sourcebook: Basic Consumer Information for the Layperson about Forensic Midicine. LC 99-26967. (Health Reference Ser.). 574p. 1999. 78.00 (0-7808-0232-2) Omnigraphics Inc.

*Muth, Annemarie S., ed. Allergies Sourcebook: Basic Consumer Health Information about the Causes of Allergies. 2nd ed. (Health Reference Ser.). 650p. 2000. lib. bdg. 78.00 (0-7808-0376-0) Omnigraphics Inc.

— Asthma Sourcebook: Basic Consumer Health Information about Asthma. (Health Reference Ser.). 600p. 2000. lib. bdg. 78.00 (0-7808-0381-7) Omnigraphics Inc.

— Surgery Sourcebook: Basic Consumer Health Information about Major Surgery & Outpatient Surgeries. (Health Reference Ser.). 600p. 2000. lib. bdg. 78.00 (0-7808-0380-9) Omnigraphics Inc.

Muth, Eginhard, ed. see Yeralan, Sencer & Emery, Helen F.

Muth, Hanns P., ed. see Zeidman, Philip.

Muth, James. The Why of Life: Answers Beyond Organized Religion. Westheimer, Mary, ed. LC 94-60596. 112p. (Orig.). 1994. pap. 6.95 (1-885001-02-9) Via Press.

*Muth, John J. Crow, Vol. 2. Vol. 2. (Illus.). 120p. (J). 2000. pap. 10.95 (1-58240-130-6) Image Comics.

Muth, Jon. Swamp Thing: Roots. Roeberg, Shelly, ed. (Illus.). 64p. 1998. pap. 7.95 (1-56389-377-0) DC Comics.

Muth, Jon, jt. auth. see DeMatteis, J. M.

*Muth, Jon J. Vengeance. (Crow Ser.: Vol. 1). (Illus.). 120p. (J). 2000. pap. 10.95 (1-58240-129-2) Image Comics.

*Muth, K. Denise. Teaching & Learning in the Middle Grades. 2nd ed. LC 98-20830. 358p. 1998. 59.00 (0-205-27859-0) P-H.

Muth, K. Denise, ed. Children's Comprehension of Text: Research into Practice. LC 88-34806. 288p. reprint ed. pap. 89.30 (0-7837-5990-8, 204579900008) Bks Demand.

Muth, Marcia. How to Paint & Sell Your Art: A Guide. LC 83-18252. 76p. (Orig.). 1984. pap. 8.95 (0-86534-019-6) Sunstone Pr.

— Indian Pottery of the Southwest: A Selected Bibliography. LC 90-9870. (Illus.). 64p. (Orig.). 1991. pap. 6.95 (0-86534-067-6) Sunstone Pr.

— Is It Safe to Drink the Water? A Guide to Santa Fe. LC 83-9212. 32p. 1983. pap. 2.95 (0-86534-036-6) Sunstone Pr.

— Kachinas: A Selected Bibliography. LC 83-18302. 32p. (Orig.). 1984. pap. 4.95 (0-86534-031-5) Sunstone Pr.

— Sticks & Stones & Other Poems: Poems. 32p. (Orig.). 1994. pap. 4.95 (0-86534-214-8) Sunstone Pr.

— Thin Ice & Other Poems: Poems. LC 85-27958. 48p. (Orig.). 1987. pap. 4.95 (0-86534-081-1) Sunstone Pr.

— Writing & Selling Poetry, Fiction, Articles, Plays & Local History: A Guide. LC 85-490. 96p. (Orig.). 1985. pap. 8.95 (0-86534-048-X) Sunstone Pr.

Muth, Marcia, ed. see Boyce, George A.

Muth, Richard F., jt. auth. see Goodman, A. C.

Muth, Rodney, et al, eds. Harold D. Lasswell: An Annotated Bibliography. 392p. (C). 1990. text 218.00 (0-7923-0018-1) Kluwer Academic.

*Muth, Steve. F2G-1 Super Corsair: A Detailed Photo Essay. (Illus.). 12p. 1999. pap. 7.95 (1-930432-00-3, 1-USN) Peregrine Pubng.

— Me 262A Schwalbe: A Peregrine Photo Essay. (Illus.). 12p. (YA). 2000. pap. 7.95 (1-930432-02-X, 1-Luftwaffe) Peregrine Pubng.

— XF-85 Goblin: A Detailed Photo Essay. (Illus.). 12p. 2000. pap. 7.95 (1-930432-01-1, 1-USAF) Peregrine Pubng.

Muth, Thomas A. State Interest in Cable Communications. Sterling, Christopher H., ed. LC 78-21728. (Dissertations in Broadcasting Ser.). 1980. lib. bdg. 30.95 (0-405-11767-1) Ayer.

*Muth, Timm. Mountain Biking North Carolina. LC 99-55393. (Illus.). 262p. 2000. pap. 16.95 (1-56044-809-1) Falcon Pub Inc.

Muthe, Norma C. Endocrinology: A Nursing Approach. 1981. pap. 13.00 (0-316-59160-2, Little Brwn Med Div) Lppncott W & W.

*Muther, Connie & Bibeau, Anita. My Monarch Journal: Parent-Teacher Edition. (Sharing Nature with Children Book Ser.). (Illus.). 32p. 2000. pap. 7.95 (1-58469-006-2) Dawn CA.

— My Monarch Journal: Student Edition. (Sharing Nature with Children Book Ser.). (Illus.). 32p. (J). 2000. pap., student ed. 7.95 (1-58469-005-4) Dawn CA.

Muther, Richard. Creating Personal Success. LC 86-60274. 1986. 10.00 (0-933684-05-3) Mgmt & Indus Res Pubns.

— German Book Illustration of the Gothic Period & the Early Renaissance (1460-1530) LC 79-186705. (ENG.). xxii, 566p. 1972. write for info. (0-8108-0518-9) Scarecrow.

— Leaders Guide & Casebook for Simplified S. L. P. (Supporting Simplified Systematic Layout Planning Ser.). (Illus.). 130p. (C). 1994. ring bd. 236.00 (0-933684-10-X) Mgmt & Indus Res Pubns.

Muther, Richard & Hales, H. Lee. Systematic Planning of Industrial Facilities, Vol. I. 3rd rev. ed. LC 79-84256. (Illus.). 180p. 1999. pap. 18.00 (0-933684-20-7) Mgmt & Indus Res Pubns.

Muther, Richard & Wheeler, J. D. Simplified Systematic Layout Planning. 3rd ed. (Illus.). 36p. (C). 1994. pap. 12.00 (0-933684-09-6) Mgmt & Indus Res Pubns.

Muther, Richard, et al. Simplified Systematic Handling Analysis. 3rd ed. (Illus.). 24p. (C). 1994. pap. 12.00 (0-933684-11-8) Mgmt & Indus Res Pubns.

— Simplified Systematic Planning of Manufacturing Cells. (Illus.). 24p. 1996. pap. 12.00 (0-933684-13-4) Mgmt & Indus Res Pubns.

Mutherich, F., ed. Drogo-Sakramentar - Le Sacramentaire de Drogon. fac. ed. (Codices Selecti A Ser.: Vol. XLIX). (FRE & GER., Illus.). 260p. 1974. 1130.00 (3-201-00903-2, Pub. by Akademische Druck-und) Balogh.

Mutherich, Florentine & Gaehde, J. E. Carolingian Painting. LC 76-15908. 127p. 1977. pap. 11.95 (0-8076-0852-1) Braziller.

Muthesius, A. & Neret, G. Erotic Art. (J). 1998. 29.99 (3-8228-7764-6, Pub. by Benedikt Taschen) Bks Nippan.

Muthesius, Angelika. Erotic Art. 1998. 19.99 (3-8228-7207-5) Taschen Amer.

*Muthesius, Angelika. Erotismo en el Arte. (SPA., Illus.). 1998. 24.99 (3-8228-7363-2) Benedikt Taschen.

Muthesius, Angelika. Hundertwasser Architektur: Fur ein Natur und Menschengerechteres Bauen. (GER., Illus.). 320p. 1997. 39.99 (3-8228-8594-0) Taschen Amer.

— Hundertwasser's Architecture: Building for Nature & Humankind. (Jumbo Ser.). (Illus.). 1997. 39.99 (3-8228-8564-9) Taschen Amer.

— Jeff Koons. (Big Ser.). 1996. pap. 19.99 (3-8228-9351-X) Taschen Amer.

Muthesius, Hermann. Style-Architecture & Building-Art: Transformations of Architecture in the Nineteenth Century & Its Present Condition. Anderson, Stanford, tr. & intro. by. LC 94-14964. (Texts & Documents Ser.). (Illus.). 142p. 1994. 29.95 (0-89236-282-0, Pub. by J P Getty Trust); pap. 19.95 (0-89236-283-9, Pub. by J P Getty Trust) OUP.

Muthesius, Stefan. Art, Architecture & Design in Poland 966-1990. (Illus.). 108p. 1994. lib. bdg. 29.95 (3-7845-7611-7, Pub. by Langewche) Abaris Bks.

— The English Terraced House. LC 82-50442. (Illus.). 288p. 1982. 65.00 (0-300-02871-7) Yale U Pr.

— Polska - Art, Architecture, Design, 1966-1970. (ENG, FRE, GER & POL.). lib. bdg. 39.95 (3-7845-7612-5, Pub. by Langewche) Abaris Bks.

Muthesius, Stefan & Glendinning, Miles. Tower Block: Modern Public Housing in England, Scotland, Wales, & Northern Ireland. LC 93-26962. (Illus.). 288p. 1993. 75.00 (0-300-05444-0) Yale U Pr.

Muthesius, Stefan, jt. auth. see Dixon, Roger.

Muthiah, S. Splendour of South India. (C). 1992. 20.00 (81-85273-56-1, Pub. by UBS Pubs Dist) S Asia.

*Muthiah, S. Winning Through. 1998. pap. 30.00 (81-86982-99-X, Pub. by Business Pubns) St Mut.

Muthiah, S. Words in Indian English: A Readers Guide. (C). 1991. text 14.00 (81-7223-000-1, Pub. by Indus Pub) S Asia.

Muthien, Yvonne. State & Resistance in South Africa, 1939-1965. (Making of Modern Africa Ser.). 233p. 1994. 82.95 (1-85628-501-4, Pub. by Avebry) Ashgate Pub Co.

Muthien, Yvonne, jt. ed. see Khosa, Meshack.

*Muthmann, Gustav. Reverse English Dictionary. LC 99-11721. xxiv, 482p. 1999. 127.75 (3-11-016362-4) De Gruyter.

Muthmann, Gustav. Reverse English Dictionary: Based on Phonological & Morphological Principles. LC 99-11721. (Topics in English Linguistics Ser.). 1999. write for info. (3-11-016488-4) De Gruyter.

Muthoo, Abhinay. Bargaining Theory with Applications. LC 99-17818. (Illus.). 336p. 1999. 69.95 (0-521-57225-8); pap. 24.95 (0-521-57647-4) Cambridge U Pr.

Muthukumar, M. Polymer Physics: Concepts, Methods & Open Problems. (Lecture Notes in Physics Ser.: Vol. 22). 250p. (C). 1997. text 61.00 (9971-5-0594-0); pap. text 38.00 (9971-5-0595-9) World Scientific Pub.

Muthulakshmi, R. Female Infanticide: Its Causes & Solutions. LC 97-905785. (C). 1997. 22.00 (81-7141-383-8, Pub. by Discovery Pub Hse) S Asia.

Muthumala, D. & Howard, P. S. Health Expenditure Trends in New Zealand, 1980-1994. LC 96-131420. 72 p. 1995. write for info. (0-478-06783-6) Manaaki Whenua.

Muthyala, Ramaiah, ed. Chemistry & Applications of Leuco Dyes. LC 97-11194. (Topics in Applied Chemistry Ser.). (Illus.). 320p. (C). 1997. text 95.00 (0-306-45459-9, Kluwer Plenum) Kluwer Academic.

Muti Al-Hafiz, M. Ulama' Dimashq wa-A'yanuha fi al-Qarn al-Thalith 'Ashar al-Hijri, 2 vols., Set. 1991. 23.95 (1-57547-181-7) Dar Al-Fikr.

— Ulama' Dimashq wa-A'yanuha fi al-Qarn al-Thalith 'Ashar al-Hijri, Vol. 1. 1991. write for info. (1-57547-182-5) Dar Al-Fikr.

— Ulama' Dimashq wa-A'yanuha fi al-Qarn al-Thalith 'Ashar al-Hijri, Vol. 2. 1991. write for info. (1-57547-183-3) Dar Al-Fikr.

Muti Al-Hafiz, M., jt. auth. see Abazah, Nizar.

Mutibwa, Phares. Uganda since Independence. LC 92-53941. 150p. 1992. 49.95 (0-86543-356-9); pap. 16.95 (0-86543-357-7) Africa World.

Mutikainen, Pia K., jt. auth. see Vuorissalo, Timo O.

*Mutimer, David. The Weapons State: Proliferation & the Framing of Security. LC 99-37489. (Critical Security Studies). 222p. 1999. lib. bdg. 49.95 (1-55587-787-7) L Rienner.

Mutin, J. C., jt. ed. see Nonat, A.

Mutis, Alavaro. Summa de Maqroll el Gaviero. 2nd ed. (SPA.). 246p. 1993. 17.99 (968-16-3362-8, Pub. by Fondo) Continental Bk.

Mutis, Alvao. La Muerte del Estratega (Death of a Strategist) 2nd ed. (SPA.). 210p. 1995. reprint ed. 18.99 (968-16-2827-6, Pub. by Fondo) Continental Bk.

Mutis, Alvaro. Caravansary (Caravansary) (SPA.). 64p. 1981. pap. 8.99 (968-16-0846-1, Pub. by Fondo) Continental Bk.

Mutis, Alvaro & Grossman, Edith. The Adventures of Maqroll: Four Novellas. 369p. 24.00 (0-614-32256-1) HarpC.

Mutius, Hans-Georg Von, see Von Mutius, Hans-Georg.

Mutizwa-Mangiza, N. D. & Helmsing, A. H. Rural Development & Planning in Zimbabwe. 491p. 1991. text 101.95 (1-85628-142-6, Pub. by Avebry) Ashgate Pub Co.

*Mutizwa-Mangiza, N. D. & United Nations Centre for Human Settlements Staff. Financing Cities for Sustainable Development: With Specific Reference to East Africa. LC 99-889630. vi, 88p. 1998. write for info. (92-1-131385-6) UN.

Mutizwa-Mangiza, Dorothy. Doctors & the State: The Struggle for Professional Control in Zimbabwe. (Making of Modern Africa Ser.). 274p. 1999. 70.95 (1-84014-914-0, Pub. by Ashgate Pub) Ashgate Pub Co.

Mutka, Norman E. The Degenerates. 175p. (Orig.). 1994. pap. 8.95 (0-9637082-0-1) N E Mutka.

Mutke, Peter H. Selective Awareness: The New Mind-Body Answer to Self Healing. rev. ed. Mikesell, Suzanne, ed. 156p. 1987. pap. 7.95 (0-914629-50-6) Prima Pub.

Mutlak, I., jt. auth. see Elsasser, H. H.

Mutlak, Suheil. In Memory of Kahil Gibran. (ARA.). 1982. 14.95 (0-86685-295-6, Pub. by Librairie du Liban) Intl Bk Ctr.

Mutloatse, Mothobi. Mama Ndiyalila: Stories LC 82-237433. (Staffrider Ser.). 163 p. 1982. write for info. (0-86975-134-4, Pub. by Ravan Pr) Ohio U Pr.

Mutlow, John, ed. Ricardo Legorreta, Architect. LC 96-47059. (Illus.). 240p. 1997. 65.00 (0-8478-2023-8, Pub. by Rizzoli Intl) St Martin.

Mutnick, Alan H., et al, eds. Comprehensive Pharmacy Review Practice Exams. 2nd rev. ed. LC 93-47687. 1994. 19.95 (0-683-06255-7) Lppncott W & W.

Mutnick, Alan H., et al. Comprehensive Pharmacy Review: Practice Exams. (National Medical Series for Independent Study). 175p. 1997. write for info. (0-683-23137-5) Lppncott W & W.

Mutnick, Alan H., jt. auth. see Shargel, Leon.

Mutnick, Alan M., et al. Comprehensive Pharmacy Review: Practice Exams. 3rd ed. LC 98-10428. (Science of Review Ser.). 173p. 1998. pap. 24.95 (0-683-30582-4) Lppncott W & W.

Mutnick, Barbara, ed. see Lenin, Vladimir Il'ich & Trotsky, Leon.

Mutnick, Deborah. Writing in an Alien World: Basic Writing & the Struggle for Equality in Higher Education. LC 95-44181. (Crosscurrents Ser.). 221p. 1995. pap. text 24.50 (0-86709-371-4, 0371, Pub. by Boynton Cook Pubs) Heinemann.

Muto, Albert. The University of California Press: The Early Years, 1893-1953. LC 92-20506. (C). 1993. 35.00 (0-520-07732-6, Pub. by U CA Pr) Cal Prin Full Svc.

An Asterisk (*) at the beginning of an entry indicates that the title is appearing for the first time.

***Muto, Janine.** ClarisWorks for Teachers. LC 98-61240. (Illus.). 273p. 1999. pap. write for info. (*1-57517-121-X*) SkyLght.

Muto, Lisa M. & Bohlmann, Paul A. The Harvard College Guide to Grants. rev. ed. 302p. 1994. pap. 13.00 (*0-943747-14-7*) Harvard OCS.

Muto, Mitsuko. Basic Beadwork for Beginners. (Illus.). 64p. (Orig.). 1996. pap. 16.00 (*0-87040-972-7*) Kodansha.

Muto, Mitsuko, et al. World of Beads. 1998. pap. 16.00 (*4-88996-040-6*, Pub. by Japan JPN) Kodansha.

Muto, Shoichi. American Signs & Facades. Shotenkenchiku-Sha Editorial Staff, ed. (Shop Design Ser.). (Illus.). 172p. 1999. 69.95 (*4-7858-0254-5*, Pub. by Shotenkenchiku-Sha) Bks Nippan.

***Muto, Shoichi.** European Restaurant Design. (Illus.). 208p. 2000. 79.95 (*4-89460-062-5*, Pub. by Puroto Gyarak) Bks Nippan.

Muto, Shoichi. Las Vegas: 16 Hotel & Casinos, 5 Theme Restaurants. LC 98-140734. 1997. 69.95 (*4-7858-0250-2*, Pub. by Shotenkenchiku-Sha) Bks Nippan.

***Muto, Susan.** Catholic Spirituality from A to Z. (Inspirational Dictionary Ser.). 210p. 2000. pap. 11.99 (*1-56955-160-X*) Servant.

Muto, Susan. Dear Master: Letters on Spiritual Direction Inspired by St. John of the Cross: A Companion to "The Living Flame of Love" LC 99-25149. 144p. 1999. pap. 14.95 (*0-7648-0500-2*, Liguori Triumph) Liguori Pubns.

— Late Have I Loved Thee. 1996. 14.95 (*0-8245-1545-5*) Crossroad NY.

Muto, Susan. Womanspirit: Reclaiming the Deep Feminine in Our Human Spirituality. reprint ed. pap. write for info. (*1-880982-14-5*) Epiphany Assn.

***Muto, Susan, contrib. by.** John of the Cross for Today: The Dark Night. 331p. 2000. write for info. (*1-880982-13-7*) Epiphany Assn.

Muto, Susan A. Pathways of Spiritual Living. 2nd ed. LC 84-1564. 191p. 1988. reprint ed. pap. 12.95 (*0-932506-65-8*) St Bedes Pubns.

— A Practical Guide to Spiritual Reading. rev. ed. LC 94-19939. 328p. 1994. reprint ed. pap. 29.95 (*1-879007-09-6*) St Bedes Pubns.

Muto, Susan A., et al, des. A Workbook & Guide for Commitment: Key to Christian Maturity. 1990. pap. 14.95 (*0-8091-3189-7*) Paulist Pr.

Muto, Susan A. & Van Kaam, Adrian. Blessings That Make Us Be. (C). 1988. 39.00 (*0-85439-219-X*, Pub. by St Paul Pubns) St Mut.

— Care for the Caregiver. rev. ed. 42p. 1996. pap. text. write for info. (*1-880982-07-2*) Epiphany Assn.

— The Commandments: Ten Ways to a Happy Life & a Healthy Soul. LC 96-2925. 240p. (Orig.). 1996. pap. 10.99 (*0-89283-953-8*, Charis) Servant.

— Commitment: Key to Christian Maturity. LC 89-9246. 1989. pap., student ed. 8.95 (*0-8091-3069-6*) Paulist Pr.

— Divine Guidance: Seeking to Find & Follow the Will of God. 208p. 1996. pap. 39.95 (*0-85439-498-2*, Pub. by St Paul Pubns) St Mut.

— Harnessing Stress: A Spiritual Quest. (Spirit Life Ser.). 64p. (Orig.). 1993. pap. 3.95 (*1-878718-18-5*, Resurrection Pr) Catholic Bk Pub.

— Healthy & Holy under Stress. (Spirit Life Ser.). 64p. (Orig.). 1993. pap. 3.95 (*1-878718-19-3*, Resurrection Pr) Catholic Bk Pub.

— Late Have I Loved Thee: The Recovery of Intimacy. 144p. 1995. pap. 11.95 (*0-8245-1522-6*) Crossroad NY.

— Practicing the Prayer of Presence. rev. ed. LC 93-83751. 190p. 1993. pap. 8.95 (*1-878718-14-2*, Resurrection Pr) Catholic Bk Pub.

— Stress & the Search for Happiness. (Spirit Life Ser.). 64p. (Orig.). 1993. pap. 3.95 (*1-878718-17-7*, Resurrection Pr) Catholic Bk Pub.

— Words of Wisdom for Our World: The Precautions & Counsels of St. John of the Cross. Kavanaugh, Kieran, tr. & pref. by. LC 94-47484. 80p. (Orig.). 1996. pap. 8.95 (*0-935216-52-9*) ICS Pubns.

Muto, Susan A., et al. Songs for Every Season. LC 88-63860. (Illus.). 55p. 1989. pap. 9.95 (*0-932506-70-4*) St Bedes Pubns.

Muto, Susan A., jt. auth. see Van Kaam, Adrian.

Mutoh, H., et al, eds. Industrial Policies for Pacific Economic Growth. 280p. (C). 1987. text 44.95 (*0-04-330381-1*, Pub. by Allen & Unwin Pty) Paul & Co Pubs.

Mutoh, Y., et al, eds. Medicine & Science in Aquatic Sports. (Medicine & Sport Science Ser.: Vol. 39). (Illus.). xii, 236p. 1994. 215.75 incl. 5.25 hd (*3-8055-5981-X*) S Karger.

***Mutombo, Clement.** La Genese des Unions Bi-Culturelles a Vienne. (Publications Universitaires Europeennes: Vol. 327). 181p. 1998. 37.95 (*3-631-32223-2*, Pub. by P Lang) P Lang Pubng.

Mutombo, Marc. Das Steinschleuderargument und die Wahrheitstheorie. 139p. 1998. 28.95 (*3-631-31910-X*) P Lang Pubng.

Mutrie, Karen, ed. see Turner, Anita Spires.

Mutry, K. Satchidanada. Philosophy in India: Traditions, Teaching & Research. 237p. (C). 1991. reprint ed. 16.00 (*81-208-0002-8*, Pub. by Motilal Bnarsidass) S Asia.

Mutschler, Charles V. & Siegert, Wilmer H. Spokane's Street Railways: An Illustrated History. 208p. (Orig.). 1987. 30.00 (*0-943181-01-1*) IERHS.

Mutschler, Ernst. Woerterbuch der Pharmazie Vol. 2: Pharmakologie. (GER.). 536p. 1985. 75.00 (*0-7859-8487-9*, 3804706673) Fr & Eur.

Mutschler, Ernst & Derendorf, Hartmut. Basic & Applied Principles of Drug Actions. LC 93-36069. 1994. 89.95 (*0-8493-7774-9*) CRC Pr.

Mutschler, Lorraine. What Doesn't Kill You... Definitely Makes You Stronger. 1998. pap. 13.95 (*1-892896-53-2*) Buy Books.

Mutschmann, ed. Sexti Empirici Vol. II: Adversus Dogmaticos. (GRE.). 1984. reprint ed. 49.50 (*3-322-00837-1*, T1801, Pub. by B G Teubner) U of Mich Pr.

Mutschmann, Heinrich. Milton's Eyesight & the Chronology of His Works. LC 75-163458. (Studies in Milton: No. 22). 1971. reprint ed. lib. bdg. 75.00 (*0-8383-1325-6*) M S G Haskell Hse.

— Studies Concerning the Origins of Milton's Paradise Lost. LC 79-163459. (Studies in Milton: No. 22). 1971. reprint ed. lib. bdg. 75.00 (*0-8383-1324-8*) M S G Haskell Hse.

Mutsu, Iso. Kamakura: Fact & Legend. rev. ed. (Illus.). 248p. 1995. pap. 14.95 (*0-8048-1968-8*) Tuttle Pubng.

Mutswairo, Solomon M. Mapondera: Soldier of Zimbabwe. 133p. 1978. pap. 10.00 (*1-57889-046-2*) Passeggiata.

Mutswairo, Solomon T. Chaminuka: Prophet of Zimbabwe. Herdeck, Donald, tr. LC 77-71232. (Illus.). 120p. 1983. 25.00 (*0-89410-002-5*, Three Contnts); pap. 8.95 (*0-89410-003-3*, Three Contnts) L Rienner.

Mutt, Viktor, et al, eds. Neuropeptide Y. LC 89-10128. (Karolinska Institute Nobel Conference Ser.). (Illus.). 377p. 1989. reprint ed. pap. 116.90 (*0-608-00594-0*, 206118100007) Bks Demand.

Mutt, Viktor, jt. ed. see Jorpes, T. E.

***Mutter, John J., Jr.** To Slay a Giant: The Fight to Protect the Wolf River from the Proposed Crandon Copper Mine. LC 00-190291. (Illus.). vii, 269p. 2000. 17.00 (*0-9679770-0-2*) Burstone.

Mutter, Letitia, jt. ed. see Kalb, Mary.

Mutter, Mike. Wesley Goes to School. (Illus.). (J). (ps-2). 1999. pap. 21.00 (*1-85072-186-6*, Pub. by W Sessions) St Mut.

Mutter, R. P., ed. see Fielding, Henry.

Mutter, Scott, photos by. Surrational Images. (Illus.). 96p. (C). 1992. 28.95 (*0-252-01935-0*) U of Ill Pr.

***Mutters, Randall & Soret, Samuel.** Statewide Potential Crop Yield Losses from Ozone Exposure (California) (Illus.). 78p. (C). 2000. reprint ed. pap. text 20.00 (*0-7881-8523-3*) DIANE Pub.

Mutti & Menz, Fredric C. Economics. 11th ed. LC 95-34901. (C). 1997. pap. text, student ed. 36.00 (*0-673-99927-0*) Addson-Wesley Educ.

— Macroeconomics. 11th ed. LC 95-35432. (C). 1997. pap. text, student ed. 33.00 (*0-673-99928-9*) Addson-Wesley Educ.

— Microeconomics. 11th ed. LC 95-34895. (C). 1997. pap. text, student ed. 34.80 (*0-673-99926-2*) Addson-Wesley Educ.

***Mutti, Emiliano, et al.** An Introduction to the Analysis of Ancient Turbidite Basins from an Outcrop Perspective. (Continuing Education Course Notes Ser.: No. 39). (Illus.). 96p. 1999. pap. 35.00 (*0-89181-188-5*, 909) AAPG.

Mutti, Fritz. Breath of New Life: Eight Marks of Spiritual Leadership. LC 98-49922. 64p. 1999. pap. 5.00 (*0-687-07564-5*) Abingdon.

Mutti, Fritz, jt. auth. see Ewers, Duane A.

Mutti, John. Taxes, Subsidies & Competitiveness Internationally. LC 81-86163. (Committee on Changing International Realities Ser.). 76p. 1982. pap. 7.00 (*0-89068-062-0*) Natl Planning.

Mutti, John & Morici, Peter. Changing Patterns of U. S. Industrial Activity & Comparative Advantage. LC 83-62893. (Committee on Changing International Realities Ser.). 72p. 1983. pap. 8.00 (*0-89068-069-8*, NPA 201) Natl Planning.

Mutti, John H., jt. auth. see Gerking, Shelby D.

Mutton, Alice F. Western Europe in Color. (Illus.). 279p. 1972. pap. 12.00 (*0-7137-0555-8*) Transatl Arts.

Muttoni, A., et al. Design of Concrete Structures with Stress Fields. LC 96-48485. 1996. write for info. (*0-8176-5491-7*) Birkhauser.

***Muttukrishna, Shanti & Ledger, William, eds.** Inhibin, Activin & Follistatin in Human Reproductive Physiology. 300p. 2000. 58.00 (*1-86094-205-9*) World Scientific Pub.

Muttukumaru, Anton. The Military History of Ceylon: An Outline. 227p. (C). 1987. 36.00 (*81-7013-046-8*, Pub. by Navarang) S Asia.

Mutunga, jt. auth. see Gibbs.

Muturana, Humberto & Varela, Francisco J. Autopoiesis & Cognition: The Realization of the Living. (Boston Studies in the Philosophy of Science: No. 42). 170p. (C). 1980. pap. text 45.00 (*90-277-1016-3*, D Reidel); lib. bdg. 94.00 (*90-277-1015-5*, D Reidel) Kluwer Academic.

Mutwa, Credo. The Song of the Stars. Larsen, Stephen, ed. LC 95-12499. 224p. 1995. pap. 14.95 (*1-886449-01-5*) Barrytown Ltd.

***Mutwa, Vusamazulu C.** Indaba My Children: African Folktales. LC 98-37776. 720p. 1999. pap. text 18.00 (*0-8021-3604-4*, Grove) Grove-Atltic.

Mutz, Diana C. Impersonal Influence: How Perceptions of Mass Collectives Affect Political Attitudes. LC 98-20488. (Cambridge Studies in Political Psychology & Public Opinion). (Illus.). 288p. (C). 1998. text 54.95 (*0-521-63132-7*); pap. text 19.95 (*0-521-63726-0*) Cambridge U Pr.

Mutz, Diana C., et al, eds. Political Persuasion & Attitude Change. LC 96-10248. 304p. (C). 1996. pap. text 23.95 (*0-472-06555-6*, 06555) U of Mich Pr.

***Mutz, John & Nelson, Katherine.** Fundraising for Dummies. (Illus.). 384p. 2000. pap. 19.99 (*0-7645-5220-1*) IDG Bks.

Mutz, Linda M. Oh! Flower, What Happened to Your Colors? LC 96-78876. 50p. (J). 1996. 29.95 (*1-888024-12-7*) Ahead Desktop.

— Our Destiny: The Child. LC 96-84392. (Illus.). 60p. 1996. 14.95 (*1-888024-06-2*) Ahead Desktop.

— Our Destiny: The Child. LC 96-85822. 80p. 1996. pap. 14.95 (*1-888024-10-0*) Ahead Desktop.

Mutz, Martha. The Bremen Town Musicians: A Folktale Play for Children. (Illus.). 77p. (Orig.). (J). (gr. 1-3). 1996. pap. 16.00 (*1-889397-25-3*, 025) Curiosity Canyon.

— The Gingerbread Man: A Folktale Play for Children. (Illus.). 73p. (Orig.). (J). (gr. k-2). 1996. pap. 16.00 (*1-889397-28-8*, 028) Curiosity Canyon.

— Hansel & Gretel: A Folktale Play for Children. (Illus.). 85p. (Orig.). (J). (gr. 2-3). 1996. pap. 16.00 (*1-889397-29-6*, 029) Curiosity Canyon.

— Henny Penny: A Folktale Play for Children. (Illus.). 77p. (Orig.). (J). (gr. k-3). 1996. pap. 16.00 (*1-889397-24-5*, 024) Curiosity Canyon.

— El Hombrecito de Pan Jengibre (The Gingerbread Man) A Bilingual Folktale Play for Children. Mata, Angelica, tr. from ENG. LC 98-17477. (ENG & SPA., Illus.). 73p. (J). (gr. k-2). 1998. pap. 16.00 (*1-889397-08-3*, 008) Curiosity Canyon.

— Stone Soup: A Folktale Play for Children. (Illus.). 65p. (Orig.). (J). (gr. 1-3). 1997. pap. 16.00 (*1-889397-30-X*, 030) Curiosity Canyon.

— Teaching the Folktale Plays: An Instructional Guide. (Illus.). 57p. (Orig.). 1996. pap. 8.00 (*1-889397-21-0*, 021) Curiosity Canyon.

— The Three Billy Goats Gruff: A Folktale Play for Children. rev. ed. (Illus.). 57p. (Orig.). (J). (gr. k-2). 1996. pap. 16.00 (*1-889397-32-6*) Curiosity Canyon.

Mutz, Martha, et al. Los Tres Chivitos Gruff: A Bilingual Folktale Play for Children. Mata, Angelica, tr. LC 97-32445.Tr. of Three Billy Goats Gruff. (SPA & ENG., Illus.). 57p. (J). (gr. k-2). 1997. pap. 16.00 (*1-889397-03-2*) Curiosity Canyon.

Mutza, Wayne. AH-1 Cobra in Action. LC 98-170327. (Aircraft in Action Ser.: Vol. 168). (Illus.). 50p. 1998. pap. 9.95 (*0-89747-382-5*, 1168) Squad Sig Pubns.

— Air 200: Aircraft of the U. S. Bicentennial. LC 97-67599. 104p. 1998. pap. 19.95 (*0-7643-0388-0*) Schiffer.

— Bent & Battered Rotors, Vol. 3. (Aircraft Specials Ser.). (Illus.). 56p. 1993. pap. 10.95 (*0-89747-306-X*) Squad Sig Pubns.

— C-7 Caribou in Action. (Aircraft in Action Ser.). (Illus.). 50p. 1993. pap. 9.95 (*0-89747-292-6*, 1132) Squad Sig Pubns.

***Mutza, Wayne.** Convair F-102, Delta Dagger. (Illus.). 192p. 2000. pap. 29.95 (*0-7643-1062-3*) Schiffer.

Mutza, Wayne. Grumman Albatross: A History of the Legendary Seaplane. LC 95-71829. (Illus.). 128p. 1996. pap. 19.95 (*0-88740-913-X*) Schiffer.

— H-13 Sioux "Mini" in Action. (Mini in Action Ser.). (Illus.). 50p. 1995. pap. 5.95 (*0-89747-345-0*) Squad Sig Pubns.

— Kaman H-43: An Illustrated History. LC 97-81408. 112p. 1998. pap. 19.95 (*0-7643-0529-8*) Schiffer.

— Lockheed P2V Neptune: An Illustrated History. (Illus.). 176p. 1996. 49.95 (*0-7643-0151-9*) Schiffer.

— UH-1 Huey in Color. (Fighting Colors Ser.). (Illus.). 32p. 1992. pap. 9.95 (*0-89747-279-9*, 6564) Squad Sig Pubns.

Mutzabaugh, Camle A., ed. see Dunn, Jeanette M.

***Mutzabaugh, Grace J.** A Work of His Grace: The Development of the National Institute for Learning Disabilities. (Illus.). 380p. 2000. pap. 24.95 (*0-9678406-0-0*) Nat Inst.

***Mutzebaugh, C. A.** Study Guide. 9th ed. 32p. 1999. 99.50 (*0-88937-223-3*) Hogrefe & Huber Pubs.

— Study Guide: Clinical handbook of psychotropic Drugs. 32p. 1999. 79.50 (*0-88937-210-1*) Hogrefe & Huber Pubs.

Mutzebaugh, Carol A., ed. An AIDS Anthology: Essays, Poems, & Articles for & about Persons with HIV/AIDS. (Illus.). 130p. 1996. pap. write for info. (*1-891814-04-4*) Found Care Mgmt.

Mutzebaugh, Carole A., jt. auth. see Dunn, Jeanette M.

Mutzell, Julius, ed. see Curtius Rufus, Quintus.

Muudee, Maudi H. Hamid Muudee's Oromo Dictionary Vol. I: English-Oromo. LC 94-92137. 1995. 64.95 (*1-887416-01-3*); pap. 49.95 (*1-887416-00-5*) Sagalee Oromoo Pub.

Muus, L. T., et al, eds. Chemically Induced Magnetic Polarization. (Nato Advanced Study Institutes Ser. C: No. 34). 1977. text 155.50 (*90-277-0845-2*) Kluwer Academic.

Muus, L. T. & Atkins, P. W., eds. Electron Spin Relaxation in Liquids. LC 72-181168. (Illus.). 551p. 1972. reprint ed. pap. 170.90 (*0-608-05452-6*, 206592100006) Bks Demand.

***Muus, Philip J., ed.** Exclusion & Inclusion of Refugees in Contemporary Europe. LC 98-216802. (Research in Migration & Ethnic Relations Ser.). 240p. 1999. pap. 20.95 (*90-75719-04-3*, Pub. by Europ Res Centre) Ashgate Pub Co.

Muus, Philip J., et al. Comparative Research on International Migration & International Migration Policy. LC 98-196549. 92 p. 1998. write for info. (*92-828-3225-2*) Intl Pubns Serv.

Muuss, Rolf E. Adolescent Behavior & Society: A Book of Readings. 4th ed. (C). 1990. text 27.25 (*0-07-044164-2*) McGraw.

Muuss, Rolf E., et al. Theories of Adolescence. 6th ed. LC 95-41242. 426p. (C). 1995. pap. 33.13 (*0-07-044267-3*) McGraw.

Muvandi, Ityai, jt. auth. see Duncan, Thomas.

Muvdi, Bichara B. & McNabb, J. W. Engineering Mechanics of Materials. 3rd ed. (Illus.). 704p. 1990. 49.50 (*0-387-97338-9*) Spr-Verlag.

Muvdi, Bichara B., et al. Dynamics for Engineers, Vol. 2. (Illus.). 900p. 1997. 84.95 incl. disk (*0-387-94798-1*) Spr-Verlag.

— Statics for Engineers. LC 96-13159. (Illus.). 928p. 1997. 84.95 incl. disk (*0-387-94779-5*) Spr-Verlag.

Muxworthy, D. T. Programming for Software Sharing. 1983. pap. text 70.50 (*90-277-1547-5*) Kluwer Academic.

Muxworthy, Peter, jt. auth. see Gwynn, David.

Muybridge, Eadweard. Animals in Motion. Brown, Lewis S., ed. (Illus.). 416p. 1957. 29.95 (*0-486-20203-8*) Dover.

— Horses & Other Animals in Motion: Forty-Five Classic Photographic Sequences. (Illus.). 91p. (Orig.). 1985. pap. 9.95 (*0-486-24911-5*) Dover.

— Human Figure in Motion. (Illus.). 390p. 1955. 25.95 (*0-486-20204-6*) Dover.

— The Male & Female Figure in Motion: Sixty Classic Photographic Sequences. (Illus.). vi, 121p. 1984. pap. 10.95 (*0-486-24745-7*) Dover.

— Muybridge's Complete Human & Animal Locomotion: All 781 Plates from the 1887 Animal Locomotion, 3 vols., Set. Incl. Vol. 1. LC 77-1665. 1979. 75.00 (*0-486-23792-3*); Vol. 2. LC 77-1665. 1979. 75.00 (*0-486-23793-1*); Vol. 3. LC 77-1665. 1979. 75.00 (*0-486-23794-X*); (Illus.). 1979. reprint ed. 225.00 (*0-685-01500-9*) Dover.

***Muyebe, Stanslaus C.** The Catholic Missionaries Within & Beyond the Politics of Exclusivity in Colonial Malawi (1901-1945) LC 99-15921. (Studies in the History of Missions: Vol. 18). 220p. 1999. text 89.95 (*0-7734-7985-6*) E Mellen.

Muyerson, George. Rhetoric, Reason, & Society: Rationality As Dialogue. 160p. 1995. text 69.95 (*0-8039-7866-9*); pap. text 26.95 (*0-8039-7867-7*) Sage.

Muyors, Susan, ed. see Wolffe, Mary & Reichardi, Veronica.

Muysken, J., jt. auth. see Heijke, J. A. M.

Muysken, Joan, ed. Measurement & Analysis of Job Vacancies: An International Comparison. LC 94-9578. 304p. 1994. 69.95 (*1-85628-617-7*, Pub. by Avebry) Ashgate Pub Co.

***Muysken, Pieter.** Bilingual Speech: A Typology of Code-Mixing. LC 99-56423. (Illus.). 300p. 2000. write for info. (*0-521-77168-4*) Cambridge U Pr.

Muysken, Pieter & Smith, Norval, eds. Substrata versus Universals in Creole Genesis: Papers from the Amsterdam Creole Workshop, April 1985. LC 86-18856. (Creole Language Library: No. 1). vii, 311p. 1986. 97.00 (*0-915027-90-9*) J Benjamins Pubng Co.

Muysken, Pieter, jt. auth. see Appel, Rene.

Muysken, Pieter, jt. auth. see Lefebvre, Claire.

Muysken, Pieter, jt. ed. see Van Riemsdyk, H.

Muyskens. Bravo. 3rd ed. (College French Ser.). (C). 1998. pap., teacher ed. 30.95 (*0-8384-8172-8*) Heinle & Heinle.

***Muyskens.** Bravo. 3rd ed. 2000. pap. 44.75 (*0-8384-1191-6*) Heinle & Heinle.

Muyskens. Bravo 3e-workbook/lab Manual Answer Key. 3rd ed. (Secondary French). (C). 1998. pap., lab manual ed. 4.00 (*0-8384-0077-9*, Newbury) Heinle & Heinle.

— Rendez Vous. 4th ed. 1994. teacher ed. 62.50 (*0-07-044338-6*) McGraw.

***Muyskens.** Rendez-Vous. 5th ed. 248p. 1998. pap. 23.44 (*0-07-044439-0*) McGraw.

Muyskens, jt. auth. see Aausc.

Muyskens, Dirk. Cleaning Compounds: Highlighting Additives to Surfactants in These Compounds. (Illus.). 179p. 1993. 2650.00 (*1-56965-003-9*, C-174) BCC.

Muyskens, James L. The Sufficiency of Hope: Conceptual Foundations of Religion. LC 79-18714. (Philosophical Monographs: Third Annual Ser.: 3rd Annual Ser.). 186p. 1979. 27.95 (*0-87722-162-6*) Temple U Pr.

Muyskens, Judith A. Bravo! 2nd ed. (College French Ser.). (FRE.). (C). 1993. mass mkt., teacher ed. 41.95 (*0-8384-4416-4*); mass mkt., teacher ed. 13.95 (*0-8384-4419-9*) Heinle & Heinle.

— Bravo! 2nd ed. (College French Ser.). (C). 1993. mass mkt., suppl. ed. 36.95 (*0-8384-4423-7*) Heinle & Heinle.

— Bravo! 2nd ed. (College French Ser.). (FRE.). (C). 1993. student ed., suppl. ed. 13.95 incl. audio (*0-8384-4417-2*) Heinle & Heinle.

Muyskens, Judith A. & Harlow. Bravo! 2nd ed. (College French Ser.). (C). 1993. suppl. ed., wbk. ed. 74.00 incl. audio (*0-8384-9685-7*) Heinle & Heinle.

— Bravo! Communication et Grammaire. (C). 1989. pap. 25.25 (*0-8384-1719-1*) Heinle & Heinle.

— Bravo! Communication et Grammaire. (C). 1989. text, mass mkt. 35.50 incl. audio (*0-8384-1885-6*) Heinle & Heinle.

— Bravo! Communication et Grammaire. (C). 1989. mass mkt., student ed. 34.00 (*0-8384-1720-5*); audio 22.95 (*0-8384-1724-8*) Heinle & Heinle.

Muyskens, Judith A., et al. Bravo! 3rd ed. LC 97-49675. (FRE.). (C). 1998. pap. 55.95 (*0-8384-7988-X*) Heinle & Heinle.

— Bravo! Communication et Grammaire. 2nd ed. LC 92-38753. (C). 1993. pap., student ed. 32.95 (*0-8384-4418-0*) Heinle & Heinle.

— Bravo! Communication et Grammaire. 2nd ed. LC 92-38753. (C). 1993. mass mkt. 35.95 (*0-8384-4422-9*) Heinle & Heinle.

— Bravo! Communication et Grammaire. 2nd ed. LC 92-38753. (C). 1993. 41.95 (*0-8384-4427-X*) Heinle & Heinle.

— Rendez-Vous: An Invitation to French. 3rd ed. 1990. teacher ed. 23.75 incl. reel tape (*0-07-540877-5*) McGraw.

— Rendez-Vous: An Invitation to French. 4th ed. LC 93-35951. 1994. text 19.68 (*0-07-044342-4*) McGraw.

— Rendez-Vous: An Invitation to French. 4th ed. LC 93-35951. (C). 1994. pap. text, wbk. ed. 18.25 (*0-07-044339-4*) McGraw.

— Rendez-Vous: An Invitation to French. 4th ed. LC 93-35951. (C). 1994. pap. text, lab manual ed. 18.25 (*0-07-044340-8*) McGraw.

M

— Vis-a-Vis: Beginning French. 608p. (C). 1996. text, student ed. 68.13 incl. audio (0-07-912278-7) McGraw.
Muyskens, Judity A., jt. auth. see Amon, Evelyne.
Muzafarov, Victory, tr. see Antonevich, Anatolij.
Muzaffar, Chandra, jt. auth. see Sivaraksa, Sulak.
Muzaffaruddin, Syed. Comparative Study of Islam & Other Religions. 125p. (Orig.). 1987. pap. 9.95 (1-56744-254-4) Kazi Pubns.
Muzaffer Ozak, Sheikh. Love Is the Wine: Talks of a Sufi Master in America. 2nd ed. LC 98-83050. 1999. pap. 9.95 (0-89314-425-8) Philos Res.
***Muzaurrieta, Jose M.** Manual Del Perfecto Sinverguenza. Madrigal, Jose A. & Montaner, Carlos A., eds. LC 99-65162. (Coleccion Cuba y Sus Jueces). (SPA., Illus.). 94p. 1999. pap. 9.95 (0-89729-907-8) Ediciones.
Muzbek, Laszo, ed. Hemostasis & Cancer. 280p. 1987. 159.00 (0-8493-5754-3, RC262, CRC Reprint) Franklin.
Muzeul National De Art, et al. Old Masters Brought to Light: European Paintings from the National Museum of Art of Romania. LC 96-54293. 1997. pap. 19.95 (0-88397-122-4) Art Srvc Intl.

M

Muzi. Child Development Through Time & Transition. LC 99-54949. 616p. 2000. pap. 72.00 (0-13-131681-8) P-H.
— Psychology Every Day. (C). 2000. text. write for info. (0-15-507352-4); pap. text, student ed. write for info. (0-15-507354-0) Harcourt Coll Pubs.
Muzi, ed. The Experience of Parenting. LC 99-32340. 480p. (C). 1999. 62.00 (0-321-01160-0, Prentice Hall) P-H.
Muzi, Malinda. Psychology: Biographical Approach. 680p. (C). 1997. text 64.00 (0-536-00131-6) Pearson Custom.
Muzik, Katy. At Home in the Coral Reef. LC 92-70577. (Illus.). 32p. (J). (ps-3). 1992. pap. 6.95 (0-88106-486-6) Charlesbridge Pub.
— At Home in the Coral Reef. Dworkin Wright, Elena, ed. LC 92-70577. (Illus.). 32p. (J). (ps-3). 1992. 15.95 (0-88106-487-4) Charlesbridge Pub.
— At Home in the Coral Reef. 1992. 12.15 (0-606-07212-8, Pub. by Turtleback) Demco.
— Dentro Del Arrecife De Coral. 1993. 12.15 (0-606-07430-9, Pub. by Turtleback) Demco.
— Dentro del Arrecife de Coral (At Home in the Coral Reef) LC 93-70040. (Illus.). 32p. (J). (ps-3). 1993. pap. 6.95 (0-88106-422-X) Charlesbridge Pub.
Muzikowski, Joseph, jt. auth. see Demery, Angela.
Muzinga. The C Language Book for Beginners: And a Good Reference for Professionals. (Illus.). 200p. (C). 1996. pap. 29.95 (1-882938-03-8) AmaZulu Pr.
— The Computer Book for Beginners: Level I. 190p. 1992. pap. 24.95 (1-882938-02-X); lib. bdg. 29.95 (1-882938-00-3) AmaZulu Pr.
— The Computer Book for Beginners: Level I. deluxe ed. 190p. 1992. 65.95 (1-882938-01-1) AmaZulu Pr.
Muzinic, Jason M., ed. see Lassila, Dennis R. & Kilpatrick, Bob.
Muzj, Maria G. Transfiguration: Introduction to the Contemplation of Icons. Whitehead, Kenneth D., tr. LC 91-2341. (Illus.). 184p. 1991. 19.95 (0-8198-7350-0) Pauline Bks.
Muzny, Charles C. The Vietnamese in Oklahoma City: A Study of Ethnic Change. LC 88-35115. (Immigrant Communities & Ethnic Minorities in the U. S. & Canada Ser.: No. 37). 1989. 45.00 (0-404-19447-8) AMS Pr.
Muzoleski, Pamela, ed. see Keane, Stephen.
Muzoleski, Pamela, ed. see Mediresky, J. Laszlo.
Muzorewa, Gwinyai H. An African Theology of Mission. LC 89-78555. (Studies in History of Missions: Vol. 5). (Illus.). 224p. 1990. lib. bdg. 89.95 (0-88946-073-6) E Mellen.
***Muzorewa, Gwinyai H.** The Origins & Development of African Theology. 160p. (Orig.). 2000. pap. 18.00 (1-57910-339-1) Wipf & Stock.
Muzorewa, Gwinyai H. The Origins & Development of African Theology. LC 84-14769. 160p. (Orig.). reprint ed. pap. 49.60 (0-8357-4068-4, 203675800005) Bks Demand.
Muzum Myers, Janet. Strange Stuff: True Stories of Odd Places & Things. LC 98-52389. (Illus.). vii, 104p. (J). (gr. 4-9). 1999. 19.50 (0-208-02405-0, Linnet Bks) Shoe String.
Muzycka, Daniel F., jt. ed. see Birley, Sue.
Muzyka, Brian C., jt. auth. see Glick, Michael.
Muzyka, Daniel F., et al, eds. Research at the Marketing - Entrepreneurship Interface, 1993. 1993. 19.95 (1-884058-05-1) U Ill Chicago.
— Research at the Marketing - Entrepreneurship Interface, 1995. (Orig.). 1995. pap. 19.95 (1-884058-07-8) U Ill Chicago.
Muzyka, Daniel F., jt. auth. see Birley, Sue.
Muzzarelli, R., et al. Chitin in Nature & Technology. LC 85-28088. (Illus.). 594p. (C). 1986. text 155.00 (0-306-42211-5, Kluwer Plenum) Kluwer Academic.
Muzzarelli, R. A. A., jt. ed. see Jolles, P.
Muzzarelli, Riccardo A. Chitin. LC 76-52421. 365p. 1977. 158.00 (0-08-020367-1, Pub. by Pergamon Repr) Franklin.
— Natural Chelating Polymers. 260p. 1973. 124.00 (0-08-017235-0, Pub. by Pergamon Repr) Franklin.
Muzzarelli, Riccardo A., jt. auth. see Jollaes, Pierre.
Muzzey, David S. The Spiritual Franciscans. 1972. 59.95 (0-8490-1113-2) Gordon Pr.
Muzzio, John. Astrological Life Scripts: Mythological Archtypes in the Natal Horoscope. 190p. 1986. pap. 7.95 (0-930706-17-X) Seek-It Pubns.
Muzzio, Juan C., ed. see Henrard, J. & Ferraz-Mello, Sylvio.
Muzzy, Kirk. The Monster Tots: Opening Day at Loretta's Day Care Center. LC 98-68212. (Illus.). (J). (ps-5). 1999. 14.95 (1-880015-31-5) Petra Pub.
Muzzy, Ruth & Hughes, Kent. The Christian Wedding Planner. rev. ed. 351p. 1991. pap. 16.99 (0-8423-0456-8) Tyndale Hse.
Mvula, Enoch T. Tukumba Pounding Songs: A Device for Resolving Familial Conifict. (Graduate Student Term Papers). 19p. 1984. pap. text 2.00 (0-941934-45-4) Indiana Africa.
Mwadilifu, Mwalimu I. A Bibliographical & Pictorial Curriculum Guide to Egypt: From Abu Simbel to the Egyptian Museum of Antiquities. LC 89-81781. (Monograph Ser.: No. 5). 64p. 1989. 4.95 (0-938818-20-1, Alkebulan Hist Res Soc) ECA Assoc.
— European Scholars on the African Origins of the Africans of Antiquity. LC 91-93121. (Monograph Ser.: No. 6). 85p. 1991. 11.95 (0-938818-47-3) ECA Assoc.
— How to Plan African Heritage Book Fairs. 1993. 11.95 (0-938818-84-8) ECA Assoc.
— Selected Speeches, Sermons & Writings of Adam Clayton Powell Jr., 1935-1971. LC 89-81785. 150p. pap. 10.95 (0-938818-17-1) ECA Assoc.
Mwadilifu, Mwalimu I., ed. Who's Who in African Heritage Book Publishing, 1989-90. 2nd ed. LC 89-647142. 300p. 1990. 24.95 (0-938818-16-3) ECA Assoc.
— Who's Who in African Heritage Book Publishing, 1990-1991. 3rd ed. LC 89-647142. 1990. 25.95 (0-938818-51-1) ECA Assoc.
— Who's Who in African Heritage Book Publishing, 1991-1992. 4th ed. LC 89-647142. 325p. 1992. spiral bd. 34.95 (0-938818-95-3) ECA Assoc.
Mwadilifu, Mwalimu I. & Alexander, E. Curtis. Black History & the Mental Health Question: Reflections for Praxis. (African Heritage Education & Research Studies). 100p. (Orig.). (C). 1996. pap. 6.95 (0-938818-72-4) ECA Assoc.
Mwaipaya, Paul A. The Foundation of Hume's Philosophy. LC 99-71886. (Avebury Series in Philosophy). 148p. 1999. text 61.95 (1-84014-957-4, Pub. by Ashgate Pub) Ashgate Pub Co.
***Mwakikagile, Godfrey.** Economic Development in Africa. LC 99-41866. 267p. 1999. 59.00 (1-56072-708-X) Nova Sci Pubs.
Mwale, Genevieve & Burnard, Philip. Women & AIDS in Rural Africa: Rural Women's Views of AIDS in Zambia. 135p. 1992. 66.95 (1-85628-396-8, Pub. by Avebry) Ashgate Pub Co.
Mwalimu. A Mixed Medicine Bag: Original Folk-Tales from a Black Wampanaog Culture, the Red Book, Vol. 2. Nurse, Shirley et al, eds. (YA). 1999. pap. 7.00 (0-9662428-1-5) Talking Drum Pr.
— A Mixed Medicine Bag Vol. 4: Original Folk-Tales from a Black Wampanaoag Culture, the Gold Book. Nurse, Shirley & Brown, Katherine, eds. 49p. (YA). 1998. pap. 8.00 (0-9662428-0-7) Talking Drum Pr.
Mwamula-Lubandi, E. D. Clan Theory in African Development Studies: Reconsidering African Development Promotive Bases. 240p. (C). 1992. lib. bdg. 52.50 (0-8191-8427-6) U Pr of Amer.
Mwan, Geoffrey, jt. auth. see Handa, Jadish.
Mwangi, John M., tr. see Wright, Michelle D.
Mwangi, Meja. Cockroach Dance. 1990. pap. 9.95 (0-582-64276-0) Longman.
— The Cockroach Dance. (Longman African Writers Ser.). (C). 1995. pap. text 10.66 (0-582-26433-2) Addison-Wesley.
— Cockroach Dance Longman. (C). 1995. pap. 16.80 (0-582-00392-X, 76410) Longman.
— Going down River Road. (African Writers Ser.). 215p. (C). 1976. pap. 8.95 (0-435-90176-1, 90176) Heinemann.
— Striving for the Wind. (African Writers Ser.). 199p. (C). 1992. pap. 8.95 (0-435-90979-7, 90979) Heinemann.
Mwangudza, Johnson A. Mijikenda. (Kenya People Ser.). (Illus.). 37p. (YA). (gr. 6-9). 1991. pap. write for info. (0-237-50490-1) EVN1 UK.
Mwaniki, Nyaga. Pastoral Societies & Resistance to Change: A Re-evaluation. (Graduate Student Papers Competition: No. 3). 40p. (Orig.). 1980. pap. text 2.00 (0-941934-32-2) Indiana Africa.
Mwansa, Michelle. Stolen Kisses. (Heartbeats Ser.). 112p. (YA). (gr. 7 up). 1995. pap. 5.95 (0-7910-2929-8) Chelsea Hse.
Mwansasu, Bismarck U. & Pratt, Cranford, eds. Towards Socialism in Tanzania. LC 78-10350. (Illus.). 253p. reprint ed. pap. 78.50 (0-8357-3662-8, 203638900003) Bks Demand.
Mwansasu, Bismarck U., jt. ed. see Pratt, Cranford.
Mwaria, Cheryl B., ed. see McLaren, Joseph.
***Mwaria, Cheryl Benoit, et al.** African Visions: Literary Images, Political Chnage, & Social Struggle in Contemporary Africa, 197. LC 99-43520. 296p. 2000. 65.00 (0-313-31045-9) Greenwood.
Mwaura, Muroki. Management of Organizations in Africa: A Handbook & Reference. Waiguchu, J. Muruku & Tiagha, Edward, eds. LC 98-4975. 432p. 1999. 79.50 (1-56720-188-1, Quorum Bks) Greenwood.
Mwps Engineers Staff. Farm & Home Concrete, MWPS-35. LC 89-14021. (Illus.). 44p. 1989. pap. 6.00 (0-89373-079-3, MWPS-35) MidWest Plan Serv.
— House Planning Handbook. 2nd ed. LC 88-9305. (Illus.). 84p. 1988. pap. 7.00 (0-89373-073-4, MWPS-16) MidWest Plan Serv.
MWPS Engineers Staff. Mechanical Ventilating Systems for Livestock Housing. LC 89-77073. (Illus.). 70p. 1990. pap. 6.00 (0-89373-075-0, MWPS-32) MidWest Plan Serv.
MWPS Staff, ed. see Midwest Plan Service Engineers Staff.
Myachina, E. N. The Swahili Language: A Descriptive Language. (Languages of Asia & Africa Ser.). 96p. (Orig.). (C). 1981. pap. 19.95 (0-7100-0849-X, Routledge Thoemms) Routledge.
***Myal, Mick.** Alternative Engines, Vol. II. 304p. 2000. pap. 45.00 (0-9643613-3-7) Fiesta Pubng.
Myal, Suzanne. Tucson's Mexican Restaurants: Repasts, Recipes & Remembrances. Elizabeth Shaw Association Staff, ed. (Illus.). 184p. 1997. pap. 14.95 (0-9643613-1-0) Fiesta Pubng.
***Myal, Suzanne.** Tucson's Mexican Restaurants: Repasts, Recipes & Remembrances. LC 99-16544. 1999. pap. 14.95 (0-8165-2039-9) U of Ariz Pr.
— Tucson's Mexican Restaurants: Repasts, Recipes & Remembrances. (Illus.). 184p. 1999. pap. 14.95 (0-8165-2019-4) U of Ariz Pr.
Myal, Suzanne, jt. auth. see Grossman, Carolyn.
Myall, Carolynne & Carter, Ruth C., eds. Portraits in Cataloging & Classification: Theorists, Educators, & Practitioners of the Late Twentieth Century, Vol. 25. LC 98-18930. 344p. 1998. 59.95 (0-7890-0543-3) Haworth Pr.
Myall, Carolynne, jt. auth. see Chambers, Sydney.
Myamlin, Viktor & Pleskov, Yurii V. Electrochemistry of Semiconductors. LC 66-12887. 452p. reprint ed. pap. 140.20 (0-608-13248-9, 205579000038) Bks Demand.
Myanmar Language Commission, ed. Myanmar - English Dictionary. 672p. 1997. reprint ed. 94.00 (1-881265-47-1) Dunwoody Pr.
Myanmar Pitaka Associates Staff, ed. Twenty-five Suttas from Uparipannasa: Suttanta Pitaka. Majjhima Nikaya Medium Length Discourses of the Buddha. (C). 1991. 23.00 (81-7030-294-3) S Asia.
Myant, Martin R. Socialism & Democracy in Czechoslovakia, 1945-1948. LC 80-41951. (Soviet & East European Studies). 312p. reprint ed. pap. 89.00 (0-608-15771-6, 2031697) Bks Demand.
— Successful Transformations? The Creation of Market Economies in Eastern Germany & the Czech Republic. LC 96-23168. (Studies of Communism in Transition). 288p. 1996. 90.00 (1-85898-495-5) E Elgar.
— Transforming Socialist Economies: The Case of Poland & Czechoslovakia. LC 93-2692. (Studies of Communism in Transition). 320p. 1993. 95.00 (1-85278-786-4) E Elgar.
Myant, Martin R., ed. Industrial Competitiveness in East-Central Europe. LC 98-51382. 232p. 1999. 85.00 (1-84064-019-7) E Elgar.
Myant, Martin R., jt. ed. see Waller, Michael.
Myasnikov, A. Atherosclerosis & Thrombosis. (Illus.). 229p. 1967. 25.00 (0-8464-1078-8) Beekman Pubs.
Myasnikova, L. & Marikhin, V. A., eds. Orientational Phenomena in Polymers. (Progress in Colloid & Polymer Science Ser.). 142p. 1994. 83.95 (0-387-91453-6) Spr-Verlag.
Myasoedova. Physical Chemistry of Non-Aqueous Solutions of Cellulose & Its Derivatives. LC 99-40221. 2000. 120.00 (0-471-95924-3) Wiley.
***Myatt, Carl.** Traveler's Companion Guide to Hawaii. 2nd ed. (Illus.). 320p. 2000. pap. text 23.95 (0-7627-0608-2) Globe Pequot.
Myatt, Frederick. British Sieges of the Peninsular War. (Illus.). 192p. (C). 1997. 34.95 (0-946771-59-6, Pub. by Spellmnt Pubs) St Mut.
Myatt, G., jt. auth. see Cashmore, R. J.
Myatt, John. Effective Skippering: A Comprehensive Guide to Yacht Mastery. (Illus.). 256p. 1992. 29.95 (0-924486-32-5) Sheridan.
— Simple Boat Electrics: Keep the Juice Flowing. (Illus.). 95p. 1998. pap. 16.95 (1-898660-25-5) Motorbooks Intl.
Myatt, Robert L., Jr., jt. auth. see Muller, Edward J.
Mycak, Sonia. In Search of the Split Subject: Psychoanalysis, Phenomenology & the Novels of Margaret Atwood. 300p. 1996. pap. 19.95 (1-55022-269-4, Pub. by ECW) Genl Dist Srvs.
Mycek, Mary. Illustrated Reviews: Pharmacology. 2nd ed. LC 96-9180. (Illus.). 480p. 1996. pap. text 29.95 (0-397-51567-7) Lppncott W & W.
***Mycek, Mary.** Pharmacology. 2nd ed. (Illustrated Reviews Ser.). (Illus.). 1999. pap. 32.95 (0-7817-2413-9, Lippnctt) Lppncott W & W.
Mycielski, Jan, et al, eds. Structures in Logic & Computer Science: A Selection of Essays in Honor of A. Ehrenfeucht, Vol. 126. LC 97-27558. (Lecture Notes in Computer Science Ser.: Vol. 1261). x, 371p. 1997. pap. write for info. (3-540-63246-8) Spr-Verlag.
Mycoff, David, tr. see Maurus, Rhabanus.
Mycoskie, Pam. Butter Busters. 1993. pap. 19.95 (0-9633507-0-6) Butter Busters.
— Butter Busters. 1994. mass mkt. 19.99 (0-446-75008-5, Pub. by Warner Bks) Little.
— Butter Busters. 7th ed. 496p. 1994. mass mkt. 19.99 (0-446-67040-5, Pub. by Warner Bks) Little.
— I'm Listening. 1995. mass mkt. 16.99 (0-446-75010-7, Pub. by Warner Bks) Little.
— I'm Listening! The Butter Busters Cookbook Companion. 592p. (Orig.). 1995. mass mkt. 16.99 (0-446-67189-4, Pub. by Warner Bks) Little.
Mycroft, Alan, ed. Static Analysis: Second International Symposium, SAS '95, Glasgow, U. K. September 1995. LC 95-38035. (Lecture Notes in Computer Science Ser.: No. 983). 423p. 1995. 68.00 (3-540-60360-3) Spr-Verlag.
Mycue, Alfredo J., ed. see Mycue, David J.
Mycue, David J. Road Makers: Marks in Time along the Rio Grande: Hidalgo County & Nuevo Santander. Mycue, Alfredo J., ed. (Took South Texas Regional History Ser.: No. 1). (Illus.). 120p. 2000. pap. 15.00 (1-879457-09-1) Norton Coker Pr.
***Mycue, Edward.** The Assault on Summer, Vol. 4. (Illus.). 160p. 2000. pap. 22.00 (1-879457-63-6) Norton Coker Pr.
Mycue, Edward. Damage Within the Community. (Illus.). 72p. 1973. pap. 6.00 (0-915572-11-7) Panjandrum.
***Mycue, Edward.** Life in a Peaceful New World. (Illus.). 64p. 1999. pap. 13.00 (1-879457-64-4) Norton Coker Pr.
Mycue, Edward. Life Is Built from the Inside Out: Meditation on the Pronoun "It" (Illus.). 50p. 1999. pap. 10.00 (1-879457-61-X) Norton Coker Pr.
— Night Boats. rev. ed. (Illus.). 64p. (Orig.). 1999. pap. 10.00 (1-879457-38-5) Norton Coker Pr.
— Rainbow Behind Irene. (Illus.). 40p. 2000. pap. 10.00 (1-879457-83-0, Minotaur Editions) Norton Coker Pr.
— Speculum: Dies Irae. (Illus.). 40p. 2000. pap. 8.00 (1-879457-60-1) Norton Coker Pr.
Mycue, Edward & Gove, Jim. Split. (Took Modern Poetry in English Ser.: No. 40). (Illus.). 28p. (Orig.). 1993. pap. 4.00 (1-879457-35-0) Norton Coker Pr.
Mycue, Edward, et al. The Whispering Surgeon. 2nd ed. Uphoff, Joseph A., Jr., ed. (Illus.). 32p. 1986. pap. text 2.00 (0-943123-01-1) Arjuna Lib Pr.
Mycue, Edward, ed. see Albert, Gwendolyn.
Mycue, Edward, ed. see Albert, Gwen & Sparling, Kent.
Mycue, Edward, ed. see Bellm, Dan.
Mycue, Edward, ed. see Blevins, Richard W.
Mycue, Edward, ed. see Bove, Robert.
Mycue, Edward, ed. see Bunch, Richard A.
Mycue, Edward, ed. see Bunse, Lois.
Mycue, Edward, ed. see Cannarozzi, Sam.
Mycue, Edward, ed. see Erickson, Ann.
Mycue, Edward, ed. see Farnsworth, Vincent.
Mycue, Edward, ed. see Foley, Jack.
Mycue, Edward, ed. see Ford, Betsy.
Mycue, Edward, ed. see Foster, Edward.
Mycue, Edward, ed. see Gallegos, Frances.
Mycue, Edward, ed. see Gigiorno, Geri.
Mycue, Edward, ed. see Gove, Chris M.
Mycue, Edward, ed. see Gove, Jim.
Mycue, Edward, ed. see Hamill, Tom.
Mycue, Edward, ed. see Hill, Crag.
Mycue, Edward, ed. see Hill, Owen.
Mycue, Edward, ed. see Hurst, Elizabeth.
Mycue, Edward, ed. see Jameson, Carol.
Mycue, Edward, ed. see Jensen, Dale.
Mycue, Edward, ed. see Johnson, Honor.
Mycue, Edward, ed. see Johnson, Wayne.
Mycue, Edward, ed. see Kennelly, Laura B.
Mycue, Edward, ed. see King, Martha.
Mycue, Edward, ed. see Leigh, Julianne.
Mycue, Edward, ed. see Mann, Jules.
Mycue, Edward, ed. see McPherson, D. Jayne.
Mycue, Edward, ed. see Neville, Mark.
Mycue, Edward, ed. see Powell, Douglas A.
Mycue, Edward, ed. see Powell, Douglas A., et al.
Mycue, Edward, ed. see Retecki, Richard.
Mycue, Edward, ed. see Selawsky, John.
Mycue, Edward, ed. see Stedman, Judy.
Mycue, Edward, ed. see Sventitsky, Helen.
Mycue, Edward, ed. see Talcott, William.
Mycue, Edward, ed. see Taylor, Ruth.
Mydal, Gunnar. An American Dilemma Vol. 1: The Negro Problem & Modern Democracy. 920p. (C). 1996. pap. text 29.95 (1-56000-856-3) Transaction Pubs.
Mydans, Shelly. Thomas. lib. bdg. 27.95 (0-8488-2105-X) Amereon Ltd.
Myddelton. Accounting & Financial Decisions. 1992. pap. text. write for info. (0-582-04091-4, Pub. by Addison-Wesley) Longman.
Myddelton, D. R. Accountants Without Standards: Compulsion or Evolution in Company Accounting. (IEA Hobart Paper Ser.: No. 128). 77p. 1995. pap. 19.95 (0-255-36372-9, Pub. by Inst Economic Affairs) Coronet Bks.
Myddelton, David R. The Essence of Financial Management. LC 94-35311. (Essence of Management Ser.). 196p. (C). 1995. pap. text 19.95 (0-13-284787-6) P-H.
***Myddelton, David R.** Managing Business Finance. LC 99-89251. 2000. pap. write for info. (0-273-64645-1) F T P-H.
Myddelton, David R., jt. auth. see Reid, Walter.
Myddleton. Accounting & Decision Making. 1985. pap. text. write for info. (0-582-35476-5, Pub. by Addison-Wesley) Longman.
Mydlarz, Anna, jt. auth. see Hutton, Donald B.
***Mydlo, Jack H., ed.** Renal Cancer. 400p. 2000. 99.50 (0-89603-828-9) Humana.
Mydosh, John A. Spin Glasses: An Experimental Introduction. 280p. 1993. 99.95 (0-7484-0038-9) Taylor & Francis.
Myeers. Theology of the Letter to Hebrews. 1992. pap. write for info. (0-521-35778-0) Cambridge U Pr.
Myeller, Ingo & Ruggeri, Tommaso. Rational Extended Thermodynamics. 2nd ed. Truesdell, C., ed. LC 97-31936. (Springer Tracts in Natural Philosophy Ser.: Vol. 37). (Illus.). 400p. 1998. 69.95 (0-387-98373-2) Spr-Verlag.
Myer. Assessment for Crisis Intervention. (Counseling Ser.). 2000. pap. text 22.00 (0-534-36232-X) Brooks-Cole.
Myer, Bruce. The Dybbuk. 48p. (Orig.). 1990. 7.95 (0-317-91356-5) Playsmith.
Myer, Charles M., et al, eds. The Pediatric Airway: An Interdisciplinary Approach. (Illus.). 400p. 1994. text 79.00 (0-397-51415-8) Lppncott W & W.
Myer, Charles M., III, jt. auth. see Handler, Steven D.
Myer, Charles M., 3rd, jt. ed. see Cotton, Robin T.
Myer, Dillon S. Uprooted Americans: The Japanese Americans & the War Relocation Authority During World War II. LC 76-125169. (Illus.). 390p. reprint ed. pap. 120.90 (0-608-15587-X, 202965600062) Bks Demand.
Myer, Donna. Answers to Your Mushroom Questions Plus Recipes. LC 77-87780. (Illus.). 1977. pap. 3.95 (0-9601516-1-3) Mushroom Cave.
Myer, Edwin C., jt. auth. see Pellock, John M.

Myer, G. Cathy's Story. 1997. pap. 2.99 (*1-85792-287-5*, Pub. by Christian Focus) Spring Arbor Dist.

*Myer, Hanna, ed. Reference Encyclopaedia India 2001. 1999. 158.00 (*0-8364-5984-9*) S Asia.

Myer, Isaac. Qabbalah: The Philosophical Writings of Solomon Ben Yehudah Ibn Gabirol. 1975. 250.00 (*0-8490-0922-7*) Gordon Pr.

Myer, John. Silverlock, Bk. 5. LC 83-1039. 544p. (Orig.). (J). (gr. 3-5). 1984. mass mkt. 6.99 (*0-441-76674-9*) Ace Bks.

Myer, L. R., et al, eds. Fractured & Jointed Rock Masses: Proceedings of the Conference on Fractured & Joint Rock Masses, Lake Tahoe, California, Held June 3-5, 1992. (Illus.). 786p. (C). 1996. text 155.00 (*90-5410-591-7*, Pub. by A A Balkema) Ashgate Pub Co.

Myer, Laura. Ecology: Christian Reflections. 48p. (Orig.). 1994. pap. 2.95 (*0-88028-152-9*, 1273) Forward Movement.

Myer, Lois. Happy Hours with Henry. 52p. (J). (gr. 1-4). 1982. pap. 1.90 (*0-7399-0177-X*, 2931) Rod & Staff.

Myer, Peter. Art: Do It! LC 96-142696. 256p. (C). 1996. pap. text 61.95 (*0-7872-0228-2*) Kendall-Hunt.

Myer, Phillip C. Creative Paint Finishes for Furniture. (Illus.). 144p. 1996. 27.99 (*0-89134-636-8*, North Lght Bks) F & W Pubns Inc.

— Creative Paint Finishes for the Home. (Illus.). 144p. 1992. 27.99 (*0-89134-433-0*, 30426, North Lght Bks) F & W Pubns Inc.

— Painting & Decorating Boxes. LC 96-50004. (Creative Finishes Ser.). (Illus.). 112p. 1997. pap. 23.99 (*0-89134-768-2*, North Lght Bks) F & W Pubns Inc.

— Painting & Decorating Cabinets & Chests. LC 98-19914. (Creative Finishes Ser.). (Illus.). 112p. 1998. pap. 23.99 (*0-89134-804-2*, North Lght Bks) F & W Pubns Inc.

— Painting & Decorating Frames. LC 97-53121. (Creative Finishes Ser.). (Illus.). 112p. 1998. pap. 23.99 (*0-89134-803-4*, North Lght Bks) F & W Pubns Inc.

— Painting & Decorating Tables. LC 97-3071. (Creative Finishes Ser.). (Illus.). 112p. 1997. pap. 23.99 (*0-89134-769-0*, North Lght Bks) F & W Pubns Inc.

— Painting Styles Mix Media Painting Techniques. (Designer Ser.). (Illus.). 32p. 1986. pap. 8.95 (*0-917121-15-5*, 50-102) M F Weber Co.

Myer, Ruth. A-Worming We Did Go. (Illus.). 1968. pap. 8.00 (*0-9600102-1-1*) Shields.

— ABCs of the Earthworm Business. (Orig.). 1969. pap. 8.00 (*0-9600102-2-X*) Shields.

— A Farm Girl in the Great Depression. 2nd rev. ed. 190p. 1998. pap. 19.95 (*0-9666196-0-9*) BUSCA.

— Thirty-One Days of Praise: Prayer Journal Edition. 176p. 1996. 12.99 (*0-88070-898-0*, Multnomah Bks) Multnomah Pubs.

Myer, Ruth & Myers, Warren. 31 Days of Prayer Journal. LC 97-20963. 176p. 1997. 12.99 (*1-57673-099-9*, Multnomah Bks) Multnomah Pubs.

Myer, Ruth, jt. auth. see Myers, Warren.

Myer, Suzzanne N. & Enslin, Teresa K. Nutrition in Kitchen: A Cookbook. (Illus.). (Orig.). 1988. pap. 7.95 (*0-317-91385-9*) Cooking Concepts.

Myer, Valerie G. Jane Austen. LC 81-459683. 153p. 1980. write for info. (*0-216-90844-2*) Penguin Books.

— Jane Austen: Obstinate Heart. LC 97-5679. (Illus.). 288p. 1997. 25.45 (*1-55970-387-3*, Pub. by Arcade Pub Inc) Time Warner.

— Jane Austen: Obstinate Heart. LC 97-5679. (Illus.). 288p. 1998. pap. 13.45 (*1-55970-435-7*, Pub. by Arcade Pub Inc) Time Warner.

— Margaret Drabble: A Reader's Guide. LC 91-10737. (Critical Studies of Key Texts). 224p. 1991. text 29.95 (*0-312-06104-8*) St Martin.

— Ten Great English Novelists. LC 89-77771. 160p. 1990. text 39.95 (*0-312-03564-0*) St Martin.

Myer, Valerie G., ed. Samuel Richardson: Passion & Prudence. LC 86-10809. 224p. 1986. 50.00 (*0 389 20650-4*, N8208) B&N Imports.

Myer, Walter. To Tame a Tyrant. LC 97-60975. 224p. 1997. pap. 14.99 (*1-57921-034-1*) WinePress Pub.

Myerberg, Cynthia, jt. auth. see Mori, Joyce.

Myerburg, Robert J., ed. Sudden Cardiac Death. (Journal: Cardiology: Vol. 74, Suppl. 2, 1987). (Illus.). iv, 72p. 1987. pap. 23.50 (*3-8055-4629-7*) S Karger.

Myerhoff, Barbara. Number Our Days. 318p. 1980. pap. 12.00 (*0-671-25430-8*, Touchstone) S&S Trade Pap.

Myerhoff, Barbara G. Peyote Hunt: The Sacred Journey of the Huichol Indians. LC 73-16923. (Symbol, Myth & Ritual Ser.). (Illus.). 288p. 1976. pap. text 12.95 (*0-8014-9137-1*) Cornell U Pr.

Myerhoff, Barbara G. & Simic, Andrei, eds. Life's Career; Aging: Cultural Variations on Growing Old. (Cross-Cultural Research & Methodology Ser.: Vol. 4). 252p. 1979. pap. 23.95 (*0-8039-6000-X*) Sage.

Myerley, Scott H. British Military Spectacle: From the Napoleonic Wars Through the Crimea. LC 96-17260. (Illus.). 336p. 1996. 35.00 (*0-674-08249-4*) HUP.

Myerovich, Marcy. Rabbits: Look & Learn. (Illus.). 64p. pap. 6.95 (*0-7938-0171-0*, KD-004S) TFH Pubns.

Myers. Absent & Accounted For. pap. 7.95 (*0-89480-123-6*) Workman Pub.

Myers. Beyond the Water's Edge. 1990. pap. 39.95 (*0-87901-439-3*) Worth

— Cluttering: A Clinical Perspective. 148p. 1995. reprint ed. pap. 29.95 (*1-56593-543-8*, 0488) Thomson Learn.

— Compensation Management. 832p. 1989. 75.00 (*0-685-67123-2*, 5109) CCH INC.

— Computer Programming Basics. 1990. text 59.92 (*0-395-52433-4*) HM.

Myers. Computer Programming in BASIC, 001. 1985. text 64.56 (*0-395-36082-X*) HM.

— Contemporary Art & Music. 6th ed. (Illus.). 502p. 1997. pap. 47.00 (*0-536-00576-1*) P-H.

Myers. Experimental Psychology. (Psychology Ser.). 1980. mass mkt. 29.00 (*0-534-25795-X*); mass mkt., teacher ed. 3.75 (*0-534-25796-8*) Brooks-Cole.

— Exploring Psychology. 1990. 11.00 (*0-87901-443-1*) Worth.

— Exploring Psychology. 1990. text 38.95 (*0-87901-485-7*) Worth.

— Exploring Psychology. 2nd ed. 1992. text 37.40 (*0-87901-578-0*) Worth.

— Exploring Psychology. 2nd ed. 1992. pap. text, student ed. 10.60 (*0-87901-605-1*) Worth.

— Exploring Psychology. 4th ed. 1998. teacher ed. write for info. incl. cd-rom (*1-57259-734-8*) Worth.

— Exploring Social Psychology. 2nd ed. LC 99-15842. 464p. 1999. pap. 33.13 (*0-07-234487-3*) McGraw.

— Helpmate. 1998. per. 4.50 (*0-373-87036-1*, Harlequin) Harlequin Bks.

— Human Resources Management Principles & Practice. 2nd ed. 1120p. 1992. 74.50 (*0-685-67136-4*, 4821) CCH INC.

— Index to Record Review, 1978 to 1983, Supplement 1. 1990. suppl. ed. 185.00 (*0-8161-1565-6*, G K Hall & Co) Mac Lib Ref.

— Irm Dynamics Of Human Communic. 6th ed. 1992. 17.81 (*0-07-044232-0*) McGraw.

— Lingua Facts: Dimes y Directes en Espanol. 272p. 1998. pap. text 36.95 (*0-536-01694-1*) Pearson Custom.

— Marketing Research. (General Business & Business Education Ser.). 1996. pap. 13.00 (*0-8273-6252-8*) Delmar.

— Math Electronics. Date not set. pap. text, student ed. write for info. (*0-314-02809-9*) West Pub.

— Object Oriented C++ 2nd ed. 1999. teacher ed. 24.95 (*0-07-023928-2*) McGraw.

*Myers. PPM for Environmental Technology. (Business Math). (C). 2000. pap. 14.25 (*0-7668-0222-1*) Delmar.

Myers. Precalculus: A Quantitative Reasoning Approach. 2nd ed. 466p. (C). 1998. per. 69.95 (*0-7872-5252-2*, 41525201) Kendall-Hunt.

— Presentation Mgr Social Psych. 6th ed. 1998. 15.00 (*0-07-290223-X*) McGraw.

*Myers. Psychology. 6th ed. 2000. pap. text, student ed. write for info. (*1-57259-958-8*) Worth.

— Psychology Plus for Instructors. 5th ed. 1998. 4.95 (*1-57259-748-8*) Worth.

Myers. Safe at Home. 1982. pap. 3.95 (*0-915936-10-0*) Armstrong Pub.

— School Store: Experience in Entrepreneurship. (General Business & Business Education Ser.). 1995. pap. 13.00 (*0-8273-6254-4*) Delmar.

*Myers. Social Psychology. 6th ed. 252p. 1998. pap., student ed. 22.50 (*0-07-290218-3*) McGrw-H Hghr Educ.

Myers. Social Security. 2nd ed. (C). 1981. 44.95 (*0-256-02585-1*, Irwn Prfssnl) McGraw-Hill Prof.

— Stop Violence in the Workplace: A Guide to Understanding & Prevention. 264p. 1995. pap. 39.00 (*0-8080-0059-4*, 5073) CCH INC.

— Stories Latin America. 144p. 1987. pap. text 19.67 (*0-13-850223-4*) P-H.

— Surface Plotter. (Mathematics Ser.). 1991. pap. 14.95 (*0-534-13725-3*) Brooks-Cole.

— Surface Plotter. (Mathematics Ser.). 1991. 53.95 (*0-534-13719-9*); 53.95 (*0-534-13716-4*) Brooks-Cole.

Myers & Dolson. Missouri Corporate Forms, Issue No. 9. 200p. 1998. ring bd. write for info. (*0-327-00626-9*, 8191314) LEXIS Pub.

*Myers & Hansen. Experimental Psychology. 5th ed. (C). 2001. text 62.50 (*0-534-56008-3*) Wadsworth Pub.

*Myers, et al. Pathophysiology for the Emt. (C). 2002. pap. 25.50 (*0-7668-2548-5*) Delmar.

Myers, jt. auth. see Beare, Patricia G.

Myers, jt. ed. see Rose.

Myers, Marc. How to Make Luck: 7 Secrets Lucky People Use to Succeed. LC 98-47882. 224p. 1998. pap. 14.95 (*1-58063-058-8*, Pub. by Renaissance) St Martin.

Myers, A., et al. Petroleum & Marine Technology Information Guide: A Bibliographic Sourcebook & Directory of Services. 4th ed. LC 95-24320. (Illus.). 405p. (C). 1993. 325.00 (*0-419-18210-1*, E & FN Spon) Routledge.

Myers, A. R. Crown, Household & Parliament in Fifteenth-Century England. Clough, Cecil H., ed. 400p. 1985. 60.00 (*0-907628-63-X*) Hambledon Press.

— London in the Age of Chaucer. LC 73-177342. (Centers of Civilization Ser.: Vol. 31). (Illus.). 256p. 1988. reprint ed. pap. 9.95 (*0-8061-2111-4*) U of Okla Pr.

Myers, A. R., ed. English Historical Documents, 1327-1485, Vol. 4. (Illus.). 1313p. (C). 1996. 265.00 (*0-415-14369-1*, D2253) Routledge.

Myers, Alan. Myers' Literary Guide: The North East. LC 95-211452. 192p. (Orig.). pap. 17.95 incl. Apple II (*1-85754-199-5*, Pub. by Carcanet Pr) Paul & Co Pubs.

Myers, Alan, jt. auth. see Astley, Neil.

Myers, Alan, ed. & tr. see Dostoyevsky, Fyodor.

Myers, Alan, tr. see Brodsky, Joseph.

Myers, Alan, tr. see Bykau, Vasil.

Myers, Alan, tr. see Dombrovsky, Yury.

Myers, Alan, tr. see Dostoyevsky, Fyodor.

Myers, Alan, tr. see Pushkin, Aleksandr.

Myers, Albert. Blueprint for Success: The Complete Guide to Starting a Business after Fifty. 1991. pap. 12.95 (*0-87877-166-2*) Newcastle Pub.

Myers, Albert C. Hannah Logan's Courtship. 1993. reprint ed. lib. bdg. 89.00 (*0-7812-5497-3*) Rprt Serv.

— Immigration of the Irish Quakers into Pennsylvania, 1682-1750. LC 99-158507. (Illus.). 503p. 1998. pap. 35.50 (*0-7884-1021-0*, M917) Heritage Bk.

— Narratives of Early Pennsylvania, West New Jersey & Delaware, 1630-1707. (Illus.). xvi, 476p. 1989. reprint ed. pap. 25.00 (*1-55613-176-3*) Heritage Bk.

— Quaker Arrivals at Philadelphia, 1682-1750: Being a List of Certificates of Removal Received at Philadelphia Monthly Meeting of Friends. LC 70-77321. 131p. 1999. reprint ed. pap. 16.50 (*0-8063-0253-4*) Clearfield Co.

Myers, Albert C., ed. William Penn's Own Account of Lenni Lenape or Delaware Indians. (Illus.). 96p. 1986. pap. 7.95 (*0-912608-13-7*) Mid Atlantic.

Myers, Albert C., ed. see Wister, Sally.

Myers, Alfred S. Letters for All Occasions. 272p. (Orig.). 1996. mass mkt. 6.50 (*0-06-109283-5*, Harp PBks) HarpC.

— Letters for All Occasions: Revised edition. rev. ed. Ferrari, Lynn, ed. LC 92-34472. (Illus.). 208p. (Orig.). 1993. pap. 13.00 (*0-06-273177-7*) HarperTrade.

Myers, Alice & Wight, Sarah, eds. No Angels: Women Who Commit Violence. (Illus.). 256p. 1995. pap. text 17.50 (*0-04-440957-5*) NYU Pr.

Myers, Allan, et al. The Gaming Table: Chip, Check & Token Collectors Guide. 2nd rev. ed. (Illus.). xv, 425p. 1998. per. 35.00 (*0-9632002-1-6*) KMW Pub.

*Myers, Allen. Strawberry Mansion: Jewish Community. (Images of America Ser.). 128p. 1999. pap. 18.99 (*0-7385-0234-0*) Arcadia Publng.

Myers, Allen C., ed. Eerdmans' Bible Dictionary. 1104p. 1996. pap. 27.50 (*0-8028-4250-X*) Eerdmans.

Myers, Allen R. NMS Medicine. 4th ed. 775p. pap. text 30.00 (*0-7817-2144-X*) Lppncott W & W.

Myers, Allen R., ed. Medicine. 3rd ed. LC 96-13091. (National Medical Ser.). 752p. 1997. pap. 30.00 (*0-683-18105-X*) Lppncott W & W.

Myers, Alonzo F. A Teacher-Training Program for Ohio. LC 70-177049. (Columbia University. Teachers College. Contributions to Education Ser.: No. 266). reprint ed. 37.50 (*0-404-55266-8*) AMS Pr.

Myers, Amy. Murder at Plum's. 224p. (Orig.). 1993. mass mkt. 4.50 (*0-380-76586-1*, Avon Bks) Morrow Avon.

— Murder at Plum's. large type ed. (General Ser.). 432p. (Orig.). 1993. pap. 11.50 (*0-7089-2847-1*) Ulverscroft.

— Murder at the Masque. 256p. 1993. mass mkt. 4.99 (*0-380-76584-5*, Avon Bks) Morrow Avon.

*Myers, Amy. Murder at the Music Hall. 1999. pap. 11.00 (*0-7472-4843-5*, Pub. by Headline Bk Pub) Trafalgar.

Myers, Amy. Murder in Pug's Parlour. 256p. (Orig.). 1992. mass mkt. 4.50 (*0-380-76587-X*, Avon Bks) Morrow Avon.

— Murder in Pug's Parlour. large type ed. 432p. (Orig.). 1993. pap. 27.99 (*0-7089-2732-7*) Ulverscroft.

— Murder in the Limelight. 224p. 1992. mass mkt. 4.50 (*0-380-76585-3*, Avon Bks) Morrow Avon.

— Murder in the Limelight. large type ed. (General Ser.). 1993. 27.99 (*0-7089-2435-2*) Ulverscroft.

*Myers, Amy. Murder in the Motor Stable. 1999. pap. 11.00 (*0-7472-4844-3*, Pub. by Headline Bk Pub) Trafalgar.

— Murder in the Queen's Boudoir. unabridged ed. 2000. 26.00 (*0-7278-5561-1*) Severn Hse.

Myers, Amy. Murder in the Smokehouse: An Auguste Didier Whodunit. LC 97-12327. 1997. 23.95 (*0-312-15598-0*) St Martin.

— Murder with Majesty. 288p. 1999. 25.00 (*0-7278-5415-1*, Pub. by Severn Hse) Chivers N Amer.

Myers, Amy, ed. see Hofstrand, Richard K. & Dobbertin, Richard F.

Myers, Andrew, jt. auth. see Braganza, Ashley.

Myers, Andrew B., ed. see Irving, Washington.

*Myers, Anita M. Program Evaluation for Exercise Leaders. LC 99-33757. (Illus.). 168p. 1999. pap. 28.00 (*0-88011-709-5*) Human Kinetics.

*Myers, Anna. Captain's Command. LC 99-15213. 144p. (YA). (gr. 5-9). 1999. 15.95 (*0-8027-8706-1*) Walker & Co.

— Ethan Between Us. (Illus.). (J). 2000. 13.30 (*0-606-18742-1*) Turtleback.

Myers, Anna. Ethan Between Us. LC 98-10697. 160p. (YA). (gr. 6-9). 1998. 15.95 (*0-8027-8670-7*) Walker & Co.

*Myers, Anna. Ethan Between Us. 160p. (YA). (gr. 7 up). 2000. pap. 7.95 (*0-8027 7581 5*) Walker & Co.

Myers, Anna. Fire in the Hills. LC 97-50526. (Puffin Bks.). 176p. (J). (gr. 7-12). 1998. pap. 4.99 (*0-14-130074-4*, PuffinBks) Peng Put Young Read.

— Fire in the Hills. (Puffin Novel Ser.). 1998. 10.09 (*0-606-13385-2*, Pub. by Turtleback) Demco.

— Fire in the Hills. 192p. (YA). (gr. 7 up). 1996. 15.95 (*0-8027-8421-6*) Walker & Co.

— Graveyard Girl. LC 93-615. 128p. (J). (gr. 4-7). 1995. 14.95 (*0-8027-8260-4*) Walker & Co.

— The Keeping Room. LC 97-2964. 144p. (J). (gr. 3-7). 1997. 15.95 (*0-8027-8641-3*) Walker & Co.

— Red Dirt Jessie. LC 97-15220. (Illus.). 128p. (J). (gr. 3-7). 1997. pap. 4.50 (*0-14-038734-X*, PuffinBks) Peng Put Young Read.

— Red Dirt Jessie. 1997. 9.60 (*0-606-12796-8*, Pub. by Turtleback) Demco.

— Red Dirt Jessie. 107p. (YA). 1992. 13.95 (*0-8027-8172-1*) Walker & Co.

— Rosie's Tiger. LC 94-50814. 128p. (J). 1994. 14.95 (*0-8027-8305-8*) Walker & Co.

— Spotting the Leopard. (J). 1997. 9.09 (*0-606-13087-X*, Pub. by Turtleback) Demco.

— Spotting the Leopard. LC 96-13697. 1996. 15.95 (*0-8027-8459-3*) Walker & Co.

*Myers, Anna. When the Bough Breaks. (YA). (gr. 7 up). 2000. write for info. (*0-8027-8725-8*) Walker & Co.

Myers, Anne. Experimental Psychology. 2nd ed. LC 86-10728. (Psychology Ser.). 386p. (C). 1986. mass mkt. 48.50 (*0-534-06618-6*) Brooks-Cole.

Myers, Anne & Hansen, Christine. Experimental Psychology. 3rd ed. Date not set. teacher ed. write for info. (*0-534-16760-8*) Brooks-Cole.

— Experimental Psychology. 4th ed. LC 96-5045. (Psychology Ser.). 567p. (C). 1996. mass mkt. 87.95 (*0-534-33979-4*) Brooks-Cole.

— Experimental Psychology. 4th ed. 1997. teacher ed. write for info. (*0-534-34345-7*) Brooks-Cole.

— Experimental Psychology: Study Guide. 4th ed. (C). 1996. mass mkt., student ed., wbk. ed. 17.25 (*0-534-34346-5*) Brooks-Cole.

Myers, Anne B. & Rizzo, Thomas R., eds. Laser Techniques in Chemistry. (Techniques of Chemistry Ser.: Vol. 23). 448p. 1995. 139.00 (*0-471-59769-4*) Wiley.

Myers, Antoinette & Hansen, Christine. Experimental Psychology. 3rd ed. 448p. (C). 1993. text 47.50 (*0-534-16758-6*) Brooks-Cole.

Myers, Art. Winged Victory: Altered Images; Transcending Breast Cancer. LC 96-68207. (Illus.). 56p. (Orig.). 1996. pap. 24.95 (*1-889169-00-5*) Photo Gallery.

Myers, Arthur. Communicating with Animals. LC 96-44650. 256p. 1997. pap. 14.95 (*0-8092-3149-2*, 314920, Contemporary Bks) NTC Contemp Pub Co.

— Drugs & Emotions. LC 96-26581. (Drug Abuse Prevention Library). (Illus.). 64p. (YA). (gr. 7-12). 1996. lib. bdg. 17.95 (*0-8239-2283-9*, D2283-9) Rosen Group.

— Drugs & Peer Pressure. LC 94-37885. (Drug Abuse Prevention Library). (Illus.). 64p. (YA). (gr. 7-12). 1995. lib. bdg. 17.95 (*0-8239-2066-6*) Rosen Group.

— The Ghosthunter's Guide. LC 92-10505. 336p. 1993. pap. 15.95 (*0-8092-4288-5*, 428850, Contemporary Bks) NTC Contemp Pub Co.

— Ghostly American Places. LC 94-44788. 320p. 1995. 8.99 (*0-517-12391-6*) Random Hse Value.

— The Ghostly Gazetteer. 320p. (Orig.). 1990. pap. 16.95 (*0-8092-4204-4*, 420440, Contemporary Bks) NTC Contemp Pub Co.

— The Ghostly Register. LC 86-13416. (Illus.). 256p. (Orig.). 1986. pap. 16.95 (*0-8092-5081-0*, 508100, Contemporary Bks) NTC Contemp Pub Co.

— Little Giant Book of True Ghost Stories: 84 Scary Tales. LC 98-151818. (Illus.). 352p. (J). 1998. 6.95 (*0-8069-0555-7*) Sterling.

— The Pawnee. large type ed. (First Bks.). (Illus.). 64p. (J). (gr. 5-8). 1994. pap. 6.95 (*0-531-15702-4*) Watts.

Myers, Avanelle W. House of Myers. 76p. 1992. pap. 4.00 (0-87012-620-2) McClain.

Myers, B., et al. Effluent Irrigated Plantations: Design & Management. (Illus.). 24p. 1996. pap. 14.95 (*0-643-05824-9*, Pub. by CSIRO) Accents Pubns.

Myers, B. A. All the Right Places. (Orig.). 1997. mass mkt. 6.50 (*1-56333-482-8*, Badboy) Masquerade.

Myers, Barbara K. Young Children & Spirituality. LC 96-45442. 132p. (C). 1996. 65.00 (*0-415-91654-2*); pap. 18.99 (*0-415-91655-0*) Routledge.

Myers, Barbara K. & Myers, William R. Engaging in Transcendence: The Church's Ministry & Covenant with Young Children. LC 92-22223. 192p. (Orig.). 1992. pap. 14.95 (*0-8298-0932-5*) Pilgrim OH.

Myers, Barton, intro. Barton Myers Associates, Inc. LC 95-169721. (Master Architect Ser.: Vol. 3). (Illus.). 256p. 1994. 69.95 (*1-875498-15-X*, Pub. by Images Aust AT) Bks Nippan.

*Myers, Ben, ed. Ben Myers' Best American Beers: An Enthusiast's Guide to the Most Distinctive Craft Brews of the US & Canada. (Illus.). 416p. 1999. pap. 9.99 (*1-84100-137-6*) Quadrillion Media.

Myers, Ben, jt. auth. see Lees, Graham.

Myers, Bernard L. History of Art. 1988. 29.98 (*0-671-07208-0*) S&S Trade.

Myers, Bernice. Because of a Sneeze. (Whole-Language Big Bks.). (Illus.). 16p. (Orig.). (J). (ps-2). 1994. pap. 16.95 (*1-56784-059-0*) Newbridge Educ.

— Company's Coming. (Whole-Language Big Bks.). (Illus.). 16p. (Orig.). (J). (ps-2). 1994. pap. 16.95 (*1-56784-064-7*) Newbridge Educ.

— Ding-a-Ling-a-Ling. (Whole-Language Big Bks.). 16p. (J). (ps-2). 1992. pap. 16.95 (*1-56784-055-8*) Newbridge Educ.

— Iti-Tiriti-Ti! Palacios, Argentina, tr. (Spanish Whole Language Big Bks.).Tr. of Root-a-Toot-Toot. (SPA., Illus.). 16p. (Orig.). (J). (ps-2). 1994. pap. 16.95 (*1-56784-090-6*) Newbridge Educ.

— Off to Grandpa's. (Whole-Language Big Bks.). (Illus.). 16p. (Orig.). (J). (ps-2). 1994. pap. 16.95 (*1-56784-068-X*) Newbridge Educ.

— Por un Estornudo. Palacios, Argentina, tr. (Spanish Whole Language Big Bks.).Tr. of Because of a Sneeze. (SPA., Illus.). 16p. (Orig.). (J). (ps-2). 1993. pap. 16.95 (*1-56784-091-4*) Newbridge Educ.

— Root-a-Toot-Toot. (Whole-Language Big Bks.). (Illus.). 16p. (Orig.). (J). (ps-2). 1994. pap. 16.95 (*1-56784-066-3*) Newbridge Educ.

— Sidney Rella & the Glass Sneaker. (J). (gr. 3). 1995. 8.60 (*0-395-73226-3*) HM.

— Sidney Rella & the Glass Sneaker. large type ed. 54p. (J). (gr. 3). 13.50 (*0-614-20619-7*, L-38214-00 APHB) Am Printing Hse.

— A Ver Al Abuelito. Palachos, Argentina, tr. (Spanish Whole Language Big Bks.).Tr. of Off to Grandpa's. (SPA., Illus.). 16p. (Orig.). (J). (ps-2). 1994. pap. 14.95 (*1-56784-095-7*) Newbridge Educ.

Myers, Betty, jt. auth. see Mager, Gerald M.

*Myers, Beverly J. Max of Palm Beach. (J). (gr. k-3). 2000. pap. 5.95 (*0-533-13107-3*) Vantage.

Myers, Bill. Baseball for Breakfast: The Story of a Boy Who Hated to Wait. LC 99-12182. (Illus.). 32p. (J). (gr. 1-3). 1999. 14.99 (*0-8499-5871-7*) Tommy Nelson.

— Blood of Heaven. 304p. 1996. pap. 12.99 (*0-310-20119-5*) Zondervan.

— Blood of Heaven, Vol. 1. LC 99-21872. 1999. 25.95 (*0-7862-1958-0*) Thorndike Pr.

— Bloodhounds Inc. 1998. pap., boxed set 23.99 (*0-7642-8389-8*) Bethany Hse.

— Case of the Missing Minds, Vol. 6. LC 99-6474. (Bloodhounds, Inc. Ser.). 128p. (J). (gr. 3-8). 1999. pap. text 5.99 (*1-55661-490-X*) Bethany Hse.

— The Curse. (Forbidden Doors Ser.: No. 7). (J). 1997. pap. 5.99 (*0-8423-5966-4*) Tyndale Hse.

— Dark Side of the Supernatural World: The Hidden Dangers in Today's Fascination with the Paranormal. LC 99-6637. 1999. pap. 12.99 (*0-7642-2151-5*) Bethany Hse.

— The Deceived. LC 94-60550. (Forbidden Doors Ser.: Vol. 2). 176p. (YA). (gr. 8-12). 1994. pap. 5.99 (*0-8423-1352-4*) Tyndale Hse.

***Myers, Bill.** Eli. 2000. pap. 12.99 (*0-310-21803-9*) Zondervan.

Myers, Bill. The Encounter. (Forbidden Doors Ser.: Vol. 6). 1995. pap. 5.99 (*0-8423-5957-5*) Tyndale Hse.

***Myers, Bill.** Fangs for the Memories. LC 99-6408. 128p. 1999. pap. text 5.99 (*1-55661-489-6*) Bethany Hse.

— Fire of Heaven. LC 99-15207. 304p. 2000. pap. 12.99 (*0-310-21738-5*) Zondervan.

Myers, Bill. Forbidden: The Ancients, Vol. 10. LC 98-170606. 1998. pap. 4.99 (*0-8423-5971-0*) Tyndale Hse.

— Forbidden: The Scream, Vol. 9. LC 98-170604. 1999. pap. 4.99 (*0-8423-5970-2*) Tyndale Hse.

M

— The Ghost of KRZY. LC 97-21042. (Bloodhounds, Inc. Ser.: No. 1). 128p. (J). (gr. 3-8). 1997. pap. 5.99 (*1-55661-890-5*) Bethany Hse.

— The Guardian: Someone-Or Something-Is Watching over Julie. (Forbidden Doors Ser.: Vol. 5). 170p. 1995. pap. 5.99 (*0-8423-5956-7*) Tyndale Hse.

— Hot Topics, Tough Questions. 144p. (YA). 1987. pap. 5.99 (*0-89693-517-5*, 6-2517, Victor Bks) Chariot Victor.

— Hot Topics, Tough Questions: Honest Answers to Your Hardest Questions. LC 96-45770. (Illus.). 144p. (YA). (gr. 8-12). 1996. pap. 7.99 (*1-55661-870-0*) Bethany Hse.

***Myers, Bill.** I Want My Mummy. (Bloodhounds, Inc. Ser.: Vol. 8). (Illus.). 128p. (J). (gr. 3-8). 2000. pap. 5.99 (*1-55661-492-6*) Bethany Hse.

Myers, Bill. Invasion of the UFOs. 144p. 1998. pap. 5.99 (*1-55661-893-X*) Bethany Hse.

— Last Leaf. 12.99 (*0-310-23091-8*) Zondervan.

— My Life As a Bigfoot Breath Mint. LC 96-32349. (Incredible Worlds of Wally McDoogle Ser.: No. 12). 128p. (J). (gr. 3-7). 1997. pap. 5.99 (*0-8499-3876-7*) Tommy Nelson.

— My Life As a Blundering Ballerina. LC 97-34366. (Incredible Worlds of Wally McDoogle Ser.: No. 13). 128p. (Orig.). (J). (gr. 3-7). 1997. pap. 5.99 (*0-8499-4022-2*) Tommy Nelson.

— My Life As a Broken Bungee Cord. (Incredible Worlds of Wally McDoogle Ser.: No. 3). 128p. (J). (gr. 3-7). 1993. pap. 5.99 (*0-8499-3404-4*) Tommy Nelson.

***Myers, Bill.** My Life as a Busted-Up Basketball Backboard. LC 00-25058. (Incredible Worlds of Wally McDoogle Ser.: No. 18). 128p. (J). (gr. 3-7). 2000. pap. 5.99 (*0-8499-4027-3*) Tommy Nelson.

Myers, Bill. My Life As a Human Hairball. LC 98-7219. (Incredible Worlds of Wally McDoogle Ser.: No. 15). (J). (gr. 3-7). 1998. 5.99 (*0-8499-4024-9*) Tommy Nelson.

— My Life As a Human Hockey Puck. (Incredible Worlds of Wally McDoogle Ser.: No. 7). 128p. (J). (gr. 3-7). 1994. pap. 5.99 (*0-8499-3601-2*) Tommy Nelson.

***Myers, Bill.** My Life as a Mixed-Up Millennium Bug. LC 99-35244. (Incredible Worlds of Wally McDoogle Ser.: No. 17). 128p. (J). (gr. 3-7). 1999. 5.99 (*0-8499-4026-5*) Tommy Nelson.

Myers, Bill. My Life As a Screaming Skydiver. LC 98-11458. (Incredible Worlds of Wally McDoogle Ser.: No. 14). (Illus.). 128p. (J). (gr. 3-7). 1998. 5.99 (*0-8499-4023-0*) Tommy Nelson.

— My Life As a Smashed Burrito. (Incredible Worlds of Wally McDoogle Ser.: No. 1). 128p. (J). (gr. 3-7). 1993. pap. 5.99 (*0-8499-3402-8*) Tommy Nelson.

— My Life As a Smashed Burrito. (Incredible Worlds of Wally McDoogle Ser.: No. 1). (J). (gr. 3-7). 1999. pap. 1.99 (*0-8499-7508-5*) Tommy Nelson.

— My Life As a Toasted Time Traveler. (Incredible Worlds of Wally McDoogle Ser.: No. 10). 128p. (Orig.). (J). (gr. 3-7). 1996. pap. 5.99 (*0-8499-3867-8*) Tommy Nelson.

— My Life As a Torpedo Test Target. (Incredible Worlds of Wally McDoogle Ser.: No. 6). 128p. (J). (gr. 3-7). 1994. pap. 5.99 (*0-8499-3538-5*) Tommy Nelson.

— My Life as a Walrus Whoopee Cushion. LC 99-13459. (Incredible Worlds of Wally McDoogle Ser.: No. 16). 116p. (J). (gr. 3-7). 1999. pap. text 5.99 (*0-8499-4025-7*) Tommy Nelson.

— My Life As Alien Monster Bait. (Incredible Worlds of Wally McDoogle Ser.: No. 2). 128p. (J). (gr. 3-7). 1993. pap. 5.99 (*0-8499-3403-6*) Tommy Nelson.

— My Life As an Afterthought Astronaut. LC 94-45373. (Incredible Worlds of Wally McDoogle Ser.: No. 8). 128p. (J). (gr. 3-7). 1989. pap. 55.99 (*0-8499-3602-0*) Tommy Nelson.

— My Life As Crocodile Junk Food. (Incredible Worlds of Wally McDoogle Ser.: No. 4). 128p. (J). (gr. 3-7). 1993. pap. 5.99 (*0-8499-3405-2*) Tommy Nelson.

— My Life as Dinosaur Dental Floss. (Incredible Worlds of Wally McDoogle Ser.: No. 5). 128p. (J). (gr. 3-7). 1994. pap. 5.99 (*0-8499-3537-7*) Tommy Nelson.

— My Life As Polluted Pond Scum. LC 96-8256. (Incredible Worlds of Wally McDoogle Ser.: No. 11). 128p. (Orig.). (J). (gr. 3-7). 1996. pap. 5.99 (*0-8499-3875-9*) Tommy Nelson.

— My Life As Reindeer Road Kill. (Incredible Worlds of Wally McDoogle Ser.: No. 9). 128p. (J). (gr. 3-7). 1995. pap. 5.99 (*0-8499-3866-X*) Tommy Nelson.

— The Mystery of the Invisible Knight. LC 97-21043. (Bloodhounds, Inc. Ser.: No. 2). 128p. (J). (gr. 3-8). 1997. pap. 5.99 (*1-55661-891-3*) Bethany Hse.

***Myers, Bill.** Phantom of the Haunted Church. LC 97-45451. (Bloodhounds, Inc. Ser.). (Illus.). 124p. (J). (gr. 4-8). 1998. pap. 5.99 (*1-55661-892-1*) Bethany Hse.

— The Secret of the Ghostly Hot Rod. (Bloodhounds, Inc. Ser.: Vol. 7). (Illus.). 128p. (J). (gr. 3-5). 2000. pap. 5.99 (*1-55661-491-8*) Bethany Hse.

— Skate Expectations: Skate Expectations/In the Nick of Time/Twister & Shout. (Illus.). 2000. pap. 6.99 (*0-8423-3667-2*) Tyndale Hse.

Myers, Bill. The Society. LC 94-7014. (Forbidden Doors Ser.: Vol. 1). 1994. pap. 5.99 (*0-8423-5922-2*) Tyndale Hse.

— The Spell: It's Time for Revenge. (Forbidden Doors Ser.: Vol. 3). 1995. pap. 5.99 (*0-8423-5927-3*) Tyndale Hse.

— The Tablet. LC 92-34301. (Journeys to Fahrah Ser.: Vol. 4). (Illus.). 144p. (Orig.). (J). (gr. 3 up). 1992. pap. 5.99 (*1-55661-299-0*) Bethany Hse.

— Take Me Out of the Ball Game. (McGee & Me! Ser.: Vol. 8). 92p. (J). 1990. pap. 5.99 (*0-8423-4113-7*) Tyndale Hse.

***Myers, Bill.** Take Me Out of the Ball Game: Three Books in One. (McGee & Me! Ser). (Illus.). 240p. (J). (gr. 4-7). 2000. pap. text 6.99 (*0-8423-3666-4*) Tyndale Hse.

Myers, Bill. Threshold. LC 98-56120. 1999. pap. text 22.95 (*0-7862-1824-X*) Mac Lib Ref.

— Threshold. LC 97-20587. 304p. 1997. pap. 12.99 (*0-310-20120-9*) Zondervan.

— T'was the Fight Before Christmas. (McGee & Me! Ser: Vol. 9). (J). 1990. pap. 5.99 (*0-8423-4114-5*) Tyndale Hse.

— The Undead. (Forbidden Doors Ser.: No. 8). (J). 1997. pap. 5.99 (*0-8423-5967-2*) Tyndale Hse.

Myers, Bill & Johnson, Ken. Skate Expectations. (McGee & Me! Ser.: Vol. 4). (J). (gr. 3-7). 1989. pap. 5.99 (*0-8423-4165-X*) Tyndale Hse.

***Myers, Bill & Ross, Michael.** Faith Encounter: Experience the Ultimate with Jesus. LC 99-21700. 160p. 1999. pap. 8.99 (*0-7369-0158-2*) Harvest Hse.

Myers, Bill & West, Robert. In the Nick of Time. LC 93-16107. (McGee & Me Ser.: Vol. 10). (Illus.). (J). (gr. 3-7). 1993. pap. 5.99 (*0-8423-4122-6*) Tyndale Hse.

Myers, Bill & West, Robert E. Beauty in the Least. LC 93-14026. (McGee & Me! Ser.: Vol. 12). (J). 1993. 5.99 (*0-8423-4124-2*) Tyndale Hse.

Myers, Bob. Kill the Fine Young Dreamers. LC 98-73372. (Illus.). viii, 328p. 1998. 23.75 (*0-9665812-1-0*); pap. 15.65 (*0-9665812-0-2*) Abiding Mystery Pr.

— Parenting Teenagers. 152p. 1996. pap. 19.95 (*1-85302-366-3*, Pub. by Jessica Kingsley) Taylor & Francis.

— Raising Responsible Teenagers. LC 96-3424. 256p. 1996. pap. 24.95 (*1-85302-429-5*, Pub. by Jessica Kingsley) Taylor & Francis.

— The Spirit in Politics. 208p. 1996. pap. 9.95 (*1-881571-09-2*) Letters Etcetera.

Myers, Brad A., ed. Languages for Developing User Interfaces. LC 92-3677. (Illus.). 480p. (C). 1992. text 72.00 (*0-86720-450-8*) AK Peters.

Myers-Breslin, Linda, ed. Administrative Problem-Solving for Writing Programs & Writing Centers: Scenarios in Effective Program Management. LC 99-12806. 301p. 1999. pap. 29.95 (*0-8141-0051-1*) NCTE.

Myers, Brian. Han Sorya & North Korean Literature: The Failure of Socialist Realism in the DPRK. (Cornell East Asia Ser.: No. 69). 224p. (C). 1994. 18.70 (*0-939657-84-8*); pap. 11.90 (*0-939657-69-4*) Cornell East Asia Pgm.

***Myers, Brian.** MCSE Exam 70-217: Implementing & Administering a Microsoft Windows 2000 Directory Services Information. 600p. 2000. pap. 39.99 (*0-7897-2382-4*) Que.

Myers, Bruce. Walker County, Alabama Census of 1850. fac. ed. 75p. 1980. spiral bd. 15.00 (*0-944619-22-3*) Gregath Pub Co.

— Walker County, Alabama Early Records, 1830 & 1840 Census. fac. ed. 24p. 1980. spiral bd. 15.00 (*0-944619-21-5*) Gregath Pub Co.

— Walker County Alabama, 1880 Census. fac. ed. 85p. 1999. spiral bd. 20.00 (*0-944619-24-X*) Gregath Pub Co.

— Walker County Alabama, 1860 Census. fac. ed. 68p. 1980. spiral bd. 15.00 (*0-944619-23-1*) Gregath Pub Co.

— Walker County Cemeteries. vii, 143p. 1980. pap. 20.00 (*0-944619-20-7*) Gregath Pub Co.

— Wilson County Alabama, 1880 Census. fac. ed. 114p. 1980. spiral bd. 20.00 (*0-944619-25-8*) Gregath Pub Co.

— Winston County, Alabama, 1870 Census. fac. ed. 50p. 1980. spiral bd. 15.00 (*0-944619-26-6*) Gregath Pub Co.

Myers, Bryant L. The Changing Shape of World Mission. 52p. 1993. pap. 5.95 (*0-912552-83-2*) MARC.

— The New Context of World Mission. LC 97-173725. 60p. 1996. pap. 8.95 (*1-887983-00-7*) MARC.

— Walking with the Poor: Principles & Practice of Transformational Development. LC 99-26625. 288p. 1999. pap. 22.00 (*1-57075-275-3*) Orbis Bks.

Myers, C. Roger, jt. ed. see Wright, Mary J.

Myers, Calvin P. Mammography Quality Control: The Why & How Book. (Illus.). 41p. 1997. pap. text 19.95 (*0-944838-83-9*) Med Physics Pub.

Myers, Candice E., jt. auth. see Myers, Stanley E.

Myers, Carol, jt. auth. see Myers, Dwight.

Myers, Carol A. & Weiner, Ronald G. Coping with Tax Reform. LC 87-406325. 51p. reprint ed. pap. 30.00 (*0-7837-6626-2*, 204620800011) Bks Demand.

Myers, Catherine. Delay Learning in Artificial Neural Networks. LC 92-19237. (Neural Computing Ser.). 1992. write for info. (*0-442-31627-5*) Chapman & Hall.

Myers, Catherine E. Delay Learning in Artificial Neural Networks. (ITCP-UK Computer Science Ser.). (C). 1992. mass mkt. 46.50 (*0-412-45050-X*) Chapman & Hall.

Myers, Catherine E., jt. auth. see Gluck, Mark A.

Myers, Celia. Stoma Care Nursing: A Patient-Centered Approach. 240p. 1995. pap. 45.00 (*1-56593-597-7*, 1222) Singular Publishing.

Myers, Charles. Memoirs of a Hunter. (American Autobiography Ser.). 309p. 1995. reprint ed. lib. bdg. 89.00 (*0-7812-8599-2*) Rprt Serv.

Myers, Charles A. The Role of the Private Sector in Manpower Development. LC 72-152912. (Policy Studies in Employment & Welfare: No. 13). 111p. reprint ed. pap. 34.50 (*0-608-11898-2*, 202313400032) Bks Demand.

Myers, Charles A., ed. Wages, Prices, Profits & Productivity. LC 59-12574. 1959. 4.00 (*0-936904-07-0*) Am Assembly.

Myers, Charles B. The Professional Educator. (Education Ser.). 1995. student ed. 17.50 (*0-534-20575-5*) Wadsworth Pub.

Myers, Charles B. & Myers, Lynn K. The Professional Educator: A NEW Introduction to Teaching & Schools. rev. ed. LC 94-23321. 634p. 1995. 88.95 (*0-534-20574-7*) Wadsworth Pub.

Myers, Charles B. & Simpson, Douglas J. Re-Creating Schools: Places Where Everyone Learns & Likes It. LC 97-21224. 200p. 1997. 55.95 (*0-8039-6425-0*); pap. 24.95 (*0-8039-6426-9*) Corwin Pr.

Myers, Charles E. A Connecticut Yankee in Penn's Woods: The Life & Times of Thomas Bennet. LC 93-60796. (Illus.). 220p. (Orig.). 1993. pap. 14.95 (*0-912975-03-2*) Upshur Pr.

Myers, Charles E., ed. Arctic Science, Engineering, & Education: Directory of Awards: Fiscal Year 1996. (Illus.). 98p. (C). 1998. pap. text 25.00 (*0-7881-7539-4*) DIANE Pub.

***Myers, Charles E., Jr., et al.** Eating Your Way to Better Health: The Prostate Forum Nutrition Guide. 2000. 25.00 (*0-9676129-0-X*) Rivanna Health.

Myers, Charles F. Missouri Corporate Forms: Practice. 1993. disk 95.00 (*0-614-03773-5*, MICHIE) LEXIS Pub.

Myers, Charles F. & Dolson, Edward M. Missouri Corporate Forms, 2 vols. 1993. suppl. ed. 89.00 (*0-685-74599-6*, MICHIE) LEXIS Pub.

— Missouri Corporate Forms, 2 vols., Set. 1100p. 1994. spiral bd. 239.00 (*0-87189-067-4*, 81905-10, MICHIE) LEXIS Pub.

Myers, Charles S. Industrial Psychology. Stein, Leon, ed. LC 77-70519. (Illus.). 1977. reprint ed. lib. bdg. 19.95 (*0-405-10188-0*) Ayer.

Myers, Ched. Binding the Strong Man: A Political Reading of Mark's Story of Jesus. LC 88-39205. 512p. 1988. pap. 21.00 (*0-88344-620-0*, 620-0) Orbis Bks.

— Who Will Roll Away This Stone? Discipleship Queries for First World Christians. LC 94-4445. 425p. (Orig.). 1994. pap. 22.00 (*0-88344-947-1*) Orbis Bks.

Myers, Ched & Aldridge, Robert. Resisting the Serpent: Palau's Struggle for Self-Determination. (Illus.). 211p. (Orig.). 1990. pap. 9.95 (*1-879175-05-3*) Fortkamp.

Myers, Ched, et al. Say to This Mountain: Mark's Story of Discipleship. Lattea, Karen, ed. LC 96-33153. 256p. 1996. pap. 15.00 (*1-57075-100-5*) Orbis Bks.

***Myers, Christopher.** Sparrows. 32p. (J). 2001. 15.99 (*0-7868-0652-4*, Pub. by Disney Pr) Time Warner.

Myers, Christopher A. Black Cat. LC 98-28609. (Illus.). 40p. (J). (gr. k-3). 1999. 15.95 (*0-590-03375-1*) Scholastic Inc.

***Myers, Christopher A.** Wings. LC 99-87389. (Illus.). 40p. (YA). (gr. 2 up). 2000. 16.95 (*0-590-03377-8*) Scholastic Inc.

Myers, Christopher A., jt. auth. see Myers, Lynne B.

Myers, Christopher A., jt. auth. see Myers, Walter Dean.

Myers, Clyde R., ed. see Myers, Gary.

Myers, Coco, jt. auth. see Carlton, Susan.

Myers, Colin, ed. Professional Awareness in Software Engineering: Or Should a Software Engineer Wear a Suit? LC 94-45888. 1995. write for info. (*0-07-707837-3*) McGraw.

Myers, Colin, et al. The Responsible Software Engineer: Selected Readings in IT Professionalism. LC 96-9538. (Illus.). 360p. 1996. 64.95 (*3-540-76041-5*) Spr-Verlag.

Myers, Constance A. The Prophet's Army: Trotskyists in America, 1928-1941, 56. LC 76-15330. (Contributions in American History Ser.: No. 56). 281p. 1977. 59.95 (*0-8371-9030-4*, MPA/, Greenwood Pr) Greenwood.

Myers-Cooke, Brodee. Gardens for Pleasure. 1998. 20.00 (*0-207-18901-3*) HarpC.

***Myers, Courtney.** Ronan Keating. (Illus.). 48p. 1999. write for info. (*0-7119-7659-7*) Omnibus NY.

Myers, Courtney. Unofficial & Unauthorised Spice Talk! The Queens of Pop in Their Own Words, 1 vol. (Illus.). 31p. 1999. pap. 9.95 (*0-7119-7559-0*) Music Sales.

Myers, Cynthia L., jt. ed. see Madden, Carolyn G.

Myers, D. A., et al. Geology of the Late Paleozoic Horseshoe Atoll in West Texas. (Publication Ser.: PUB 5607). (Illus.). 113p. 1956. pap. 2.00 (*0-686-29360-6*) Bur Econ Geology.

Myers, D. G. The Elephants Teach: Creative Writing since 1880. LC 95-15224. (Studies in Writing & Culture). 224p. (C). 1995. pap. text 33.40 (*0-13-324013-4*) P-H.

Myers, D. J. Remembering Pearl Harbor. pap. 9.95 (*0-681-02821-1*) Booklines Hawaii.

Myers, Dale K. Computer Animation: Expert Advice on Breaking into the Business. 140p. 1999. pap. 19.95 (*0-9662709-6-7*) Oak Cliff.

— With Malice: Lee Harvey Oswald & the Murder of Officer J. D. Tippit. LC 98-91213. (Illus.). 704p. 1998. 35.00 (*0-9662709-7-5*) Oak Cliff.

Myers, Dan A. Golden Rules for Parenting: A Child Psychiatrist Discovers the Bible. LC 98-28246. 144p. 1998. pap. 10.95 (*0-8091-3777-1*) Paulist Pr.

Myers, Danielle, jt. auth. see Myers, Jeff.

***Myers, Danny C.** The Man Who Squeezed the Buffalo off the Nickel. (Illus.). ii, 24p. 1999. pap. 5.00 (*0-9700701-0-1*) D C Myers.

Myers, Darlene. Computer Science Resources: A Guide to Professional Literature. LC 81-559. 346p. 1981. pap. 59.50 (*0-313-25774-4*, Greenwood Pr) Greenwood.

Myers, Dave, jt. auth. see Forman, Jeffrey W.

Myers, David. Exploring Psychology. 544p. 1995. text 39.80 (*1-57259-083-1*) Worth.

Myers, David. Exploring Psychology. 3rd ed. 544p. 1995. pap. text 36.00 (*1-57259-069-6*) Worth.

Myers, David, ed. Storms in a Japanese Teacup: Satiric Tales. LC 97-194335. (Illus.). 138p. 1996. pap. 16.95 (*1-875998-14-4*) Central Queensland.

Myers, David & Jeeves, Malcolm. Psychology Through the Eyes of Faith. 240p. 1987. pap. 14.00 (*0-06-065557-7*, Pub. by Harper SF) HarpC.

Myers, David & PC World Editors. LOGO for IBM Personal Computers. 1985. pap. 16.95 (*0-671-49284-5*) S&S Trade.

Myers, David, et al. Easton Archer's Almanac. LC 97-67133. (Illus.). 286p. 1997. pap. 10.00 (*1-890497-00-2*) Rocky Pt.

Myers, David, jt. auth. see Plemmons, Patrick.

Myers, David, jt. ed. see Ishido, Kotaku.

Myers, David A., et al. Cases & Materials on Copyright & Other Aspects of Entertainment Litigation-Including Unfair Competition, Defamation & Privacy. 4th ed. (American Casebook Ser.). (Illus.). 1177p. (C). 1991. text 56.00 (*0-314-83541-5*) West Pub.

Myers, David B. Marx & Nietzsche: The Record of an Encounter-the Reminiscences & Transcripts of a Nineteenth Century Journalist. (Illus.). 186p. (Orig.). (C). 1986. pap. text 21.00 (*0-8191-5102-5*) U Pr of Amer.

— New Soviet Thinking & U. S. Nuclear Policy. 304p. 1990. 49.95 (*0-87722-710-1*) Temple U Pr.

Myers, David E. Heartful Parenting: Connected Parenting & Emotional Intelligence. LC 96-23796. 208p. 1997. 14.95 (*0-933025-51-3*) Blue Bird Pub.

***Myers, David G.** The American Paradox: Spiritual Hunger in an Age of Plenty. LC 99-88870. (Illus.). 400p. 2000. 29.95 (*0-300-08111-1*) Yale U Pr.

Myers, David G. Exploring Psychology. 4th ed. (Illus.). (C). 1998. text 43.00 (*1-57259-656-2*); pap. text 38.00 (*1-57259-416-0*); pap. text, student ed. 14.00 (*1-57259-676-7*) Worth.

***Myers, David G.** Exploring Psychology. 4th ed. 1999. 55.95 (*1-57259-866-2*) Worth.

Myers, David G. Exploring Social Psychology. LC 93-17347. (Series in Social Psychology). (C). 1993. pap., student ed. 15.63 (*0-07-044303-3*) McGraw.

— Exploring Social Psychology. LC 93-17347. (Series in Social Psychology). 352p. (C). 1994. pap. 33.13 (*0-07-044296-7*) McGraw.

— Faculty Guide for Discovering Psychology Telecourse. 3rd ed. 1996. teacher ed. write for info. (*1-57259-191-9*) Worth.

— The Inflated Self: Human Illusions & the Biblical Call to Hope. 176p. 1984. 5.95 (*0-8164-2326-1*) Harper SF.

— Psychology. 693p. 1986. text 34.95 (*0-87901-311-7*) Worth.

— Psychology. 2nd ed. xxvi, 623p. (C). 1988. text 57.95 (*0-87901-400-8*) Worth.

— Psychology. 3rd ed. 636p. 1991. text 57.95 (*0-87901-506-3*) Worth.

— Psychology. 3rd ed. 636p. 1991. pap. text, student ed. 13.95 (*0-87901-507-1*) Worth.

— Psychology. 5th ed. (Illus.). (C). 1997. text 52.40 (*1-57259-590-6*) Worth.

— Psychology, 1995. 4th ed. 1994. text 50.80 (*0-87901-644-2*) Worth.

— Psychology, 1995. 4th ed. 1994. pap. text, student ed. 12.40 (*0-87901-645-0*) Worth.

— Pursuit of Happiness Co. 336p. 1993. reprint ed. pap. 13.50 (*0-380-71522-8*, Avon Bks) Morrow Avon.

***Myers, David G.** A Quiet World: Living with Hearing Loss. (Illus.). 176p. 2000. 18.50 (*0-300-08439-0*) Yale U Pr.

Myers, David G. Social Psychology. 5th ed. (C). 1995. pap., student ed. 23.75 (*0-07-044360-2*); text 57.74 (*0-07-044377-7*) McGraw.

— Social Psychology. 6th ed. LC 98-14877. 1998. 71.50 (*0-07-290217-5*) McGraw.

— Study Guide for Discovering Psychology Telecourse to Accompany Psychology. 5th ed. (C). 1997. pap. text 12.80 (*1-57259-546-9*) Worth.

— Study Guide to Accompany Psychology. 5th ed. (C). 1997. pap. text 12.80 (*1-57259-208-7*) Worth.

Myers, David G. & Scientific American Staff. Psychology & Scientific American Mysteries of the Mind Magazine. 5th ed. (Illus.). (C). 1997. text 52.40 (*1-57259-206-0*) Worth.

Myers, David J. Venezuela's Pursuit of Caribbean Basin Interests: Implications for United States National Security. LC 83-19144. 1985. pap. text 4.00 (*0-8330-0527-8*, R-2994-AF) Rand Corp.

Myers, David J., jt. ed. see Martz, John D.

Myers, David L., jt. auth. see Wilcox, Howard J.

Myers, David L., jt. auth. see Wilcox, Howard L.

Myers, David N. & Rowe, William V. From Ghetto to Emancipation: Historical & Contemporary Reconsiderations of the Jewish Community. LC 97-40037. 1997. 24.95 (*0-940866-72-2*); pap. write for info. (*0-940866-73-0*) U Scranton Pr.

An Asterisk (*) at the beginning of an entry indicates that the title is appearing for the first time.

Myers, David N. & Ruderman, David B., eds. The Jewish Past Revisited: Reflections on Modern Jewish Historians. LC 97-36811. (Studies in Jewish Culture & Society). 256p. 1998. 27.50 (*0-300-07216-3*) Yale U Pr.

Myers, Dawn. Angels, Angels Everywhere. LC 94-26038. 128p. (Orig.). (J). 1994. pap. 3.99 (*0-380-77935-8*, Avon Bks) Morrow Avon.

Myers, Dennis & Lamb, Annette. Hypercard (Mac) Authoring Tool 2.0. Schach, Mickey, ed. 800p. 1993. pap. text 49.95 incl. mac hd (*0-89262-362-4*) Career Pub.

Myers, Denys P. Gaslighting in America: A Pictorial Survey, 1815-1910. (Illus.). 288p. 1990. pap. 16.95 (*0-486-26482-3*) Dover.

— Origin & Conclusion of the Paris Pact. LC 75-147608. (Library of War & Peace; Kellogg Pact & the Outlawry of War). 1975. lib. bdg. 46.00 (*0-8240-0368-3*) Garland.

Myers, Desaix. The Nuclear Power Debate. 153p. 1977. 25.95 (*0-275-56440-1*) Greenwood.

Myers, Desaix B., et al. U. S. Business in South Africa: The Economic, Political, & Moral Issues. LC 79-3638. 389p. reprint ed. pap. 111.50 (*0-608-18469-1*, 2056713) Bks Demand.

— U. S. Business in South Africa: The Economic, Political, & Moral Issues. LC 79-3638. 391p. 1980. reprint ed. pap. 121.30 (*0-608-10380-2*, 205671300081) Bks Demand.

Myers, Diana, ed. see Brodsky, Joseph, et al.

Myers, Diana K. & Bean, Susan S. From the Land of the Thunder Dragon: Textile Arts of Bhutan. (Illus.). 248p. 1994. pap. 29.95 (*0-906026-33-4*) Peabody Essex Mus.

Myers, Diana K. & Bean, Susan S., eds. From the Land of the Thunder Dragon: Textile Arts of Bhutan. (Illus.). 248p. 1995. 44.95 (*0-906026-31-8*, Pub. by Serindia) Weatherhill.

Myers, Diana K., et al. Temple Household Horseback: Rugs of the Tibetan Plateau. LC 84-52139. (Illus.). 112p. 1984. pap. 27.50 (*0-87405-024-3*) Textile Mus.

***Myers, Dolores H.** The Greatest of These Is Love. 365p. 1999. pap. 14.95 (*0-9653831-1-3*) BHse Publng.

Myers, Donald. U. S. Master Human Resources Guide. 800p. 1998. pap. 75.00 (*0-8080-0274-0*) CCH INC.

Myers, Donald A., jt. auth. see Baltz, Elmer H.

***Myers, Donald F.** Your War, My War: A Marine in Vietnam. LC 99-74221. (Illus.). 400p. 2000. pap. 23.95 (*1-57197-187-4*) Pentland Pr.

Myers, Donald J. & Richman, Michael B. ERISA Class Exemptions. 2nd ed. LC 96-37679. 1263p. 1997. pap., suppl. ed. 165.00 (*1-57018-050-4*, 9114-PR9) BNA Books.

— ERISA Class Exemptions: 1998 Supplement. 178p. 1999. pap. 55.00 (*1-57018-114-4*, 1114-PR9) BNA Books.

Myers, Donald W. Establishing & Building Employee Assistance Programs. LC 83-21168. (Illus.). 335p. 1984. 65.00 (*0-89930-044-8*, MYF/, Quorum Bks) Greenwood.

***Myers, Donald W.** U. S. Master Human Resources Guide, 2000. 1200p. 1999. pap. 79.95 (*0-8080-0389-5*) CCH INC.

Myers, Donald W., ed. Employee Problem Prevention & Counseling: A Guide for Professionals. LC 84-26499. 338p. 1985. 65.00 (*0-89930-084-7*, MEM/, Quorum Bks) Greenwood.

Myers, Doris T. C. S. Lewis in Context. 264p. 1998. pap. 16.00 (*0-87338-617-5*) Kent St U Pr.

— C. S. Lewis in Context. LC 94-7537. 264p. 1994. reprint ed. pap. 81.90 (*0-608-07357-1*, 206758500009) Bks Demand.

Myers, Doug. Essential Cubs. LC 99-11603. 384p. 1999. pap. 16.95 (*0-8092-2610-3*, 261030, Contemporary Bks) NTC Contemp Pub Co.

***Myers, Doug.** Louisville Slugger Presents Batting Around: A Comprehensive Collection of Hitting Achievements, Anecdotes & Analyses. LC 99 86838. (Illus.). 400p. 2000. pap. 19.95 (*0-8092-2519-0*, Contemporary Bks) NTC Contemp Pub Co.

***Myers, Doug & Gola, Mark.** The Louisville Slugger Complete Book of Pitching. LC 99-46713. 224p. 2000. pap. 17.95 (*0-8092-2668-5*, 266850, Contemporary Bks) NTC Contemp Pub Co.

***Myers, Douglas G.** Mister Zoo: The Life & Legacy of Dr. Charles Schroeder. LC 99-61695. (Illus.). 304p. 1999. 28.00 (*0-911461-15-9*) Zoological Soc.

Myers, Dowell. Analysis with Local Census Data: Portraits of Change. (Illus.). 369p. 1992. pap. text 54.95 (*0-12-512308-6*) Acad Pr.

Myers, Dowell, ed. Housing Demography: Linking Demographic Structure & Housing Markets. LC 90-50094. (Social Demography Ser.). 320p. (C). 1991. pap. text 19.95 (*0-299-12554-8*) U of Wis Pr.

Myers, Drew. Surfaces, Interfaces, & Colloids: Principles & Applications. 433p. 1991. 49.50 (*1-56081-033-5*, Wiley-VCH) Wiley.

— Surfaces, Interfaces, & Colloids: Principles & Applications. 2nd ed. LC 98-38906. 501p. (C). 1999. 94.95 (*0-471-33060-4*) Wiley.

— Surfactant Science & Technology. 2nd ed. 360p. 1992. 49.50 (*1-56081-586-8*, Wiley-VCH) Wiley.

Myers, Drew. Surfactant Science & Technology. 2nd ed. 352p. 1992. 79.95 (*0-471-18841-7*, Wiley-VCH) Wiley.

Myers, Dwight & Myers, Carol. Literary New Mexico: Essays from Book Talk. LC 97-38390. 1998. 70.00 (*1-58096-001-4*) Ancient City Pr.

Myers, E. & Dodge, A. J. Preserving the Dead. 1997. reprint ed. pap. 9.95 (*0-917914-24-4*) Lindsay Pubns.

Myers, E. J. Let's Get Rid of Social Security: How Americans Can Take Charge of Their Own Future. LC 95-47520. 273p. 1996. 26.95 (*1-57392-015-0*) Prometheus Bks.

Myers, E. J., jt. auth. see Mudd, G. C.

Myers, E. M. Head & Neck Oncology: Diagnosis, Treatment, & Rehabilitation. 1991. 115.00 (*0-316-59317-6*, Little Brwn Med Div) Lppncott W & W.

Myers, E. R., et al, eds. Ferroelectric Thin Films III. (Symposium Proceedings Ser.: Vol. 310). 499p. 1993. text 81.00 (*1-55899-206-5*) Materials Res.

Myers, E. R. & Kingon, A. I., eds. Ferroelectric Thin Films. (MRS Symposium Proceedings Ser.: Vol. 200). 341p. 1990. text 17.50 (*1-55899-089-5*) Materials Res.

Myers, Edith. The Mysteries of the Rosary. (Illus.). 41p. 1977. reprint ed. 3.00 (*0-912414-13-8*) Stella Maris Bks.

***Myers, Edward.** The Adventures of Forri the Baker. 83p. (J). (gr. 3-6). 1999. pap. 6.00 (*0-9674477-0-4*, M-9900-01) Montemayor Pr.

Myers, Edward. The Chosen Few: Surviving the Nuclear Holocaust. LC 82-72604. 180p. (Orig.). 1982. pap. 7.95 (*0-89708-107-2*) And Bks.

— Climb or Die. (J). 1997. lib. bdg. 14.49 (*0-7868-2350-X*, Pub. by Hyperion) Little.

— Climb or Die. LC 93-44861. 192p. (J). (gr. 5-9). 1994. 14.95 (*0-7868-0026-7*, Pub. by Hyprn Child) Time Warner.

— Climb or Die. 192p. (J). 1996. pap. 4.95 (*0-7868-1181-1*, Pub. by Hyprn Child) Time Warner.

— Climb or Die. LC 93-44861. 192p. (J). (gr. 5-9). 1996. pap. 4.95 (*0-7868-1129-3*, Pub. by Hyprn Ppbks) Little.

— Climb or Die. LC 93-44861. (J). 1996. 10.05 (*0-606-10162-4*, Pub. by Turtleback) Demco.

— Hostage. LC 95-38160. 208p. (J). (gr. 3-7). 1996. 15.95 (*0-7868-0115-8*, Pub. by Hyprn Child) Time Warner.

— Hostage. LC 95-38160. 192p. (J). (gr. 5-9). 1997. reprint ed. pap. 4.95 (*0-7868-1207-9*, Pub. by Hyprn Ppbks) Little.

— When Parents Die. LC 96-28999. 1997. pap. 12.95 (*0-14-026231-8*) Viking Penguin.

Myers, Edward & Myers, Jane E. Spirit Writer Asks. 2nd rev. ed. (Illus.). xii, 235p. (Orig.). 1996. pap. 26.50 (*0-9651038-1-1*) Cntry Pr.

Myers, Edward, jt. auth. see Koman, Aleta.

Myers, Edward C. Children of the Thunderbird. 160p. 1994. pap. 9.95 (*0-88839-264-8*) Hancock House.

Myers, Edward P. After These Things I Saw: A Study of Revelation. LC 97-19160. 1997. 21.99 (*0-89900-786-4*) College Pr Pub.

— Hostage! 1997. 10.05 (*0-606-13491-3*, Pub. by Turtleback) Demco.

— If I Had One More Sermon to Preach. 1986. pap. 8.25 (*0-89137-328-4*) Quality Pubns.

— Letters from the Lord of Heaven: The Seven Churches of Asia (Revelation 2-3) (Small Group Studies). 90p. 1996. pap. 5.99 (*0-89900-705-8*, T96-705-8) College Pr Pub.

— A Study of Angels: Systematic Bible Doctrines. rev. ed. 112p. (Orig.). 1993. pap. 9.99 (*1-878990-00-4*) Howard Pub LA.

Myers, Edwards, jt. auth. see Turner, J. J.

Myers, Elaine, ed. Grandma's Keepsakes: A Scrapbook of Love. (Illus.). 16p. 1997. 8.59 (*0-944943-93-4*) Current Inc.

— Keepsake Scrapbook. 16p. 1997. 8.59 (*0-944943-94-2*) Current Inc.

Myers, Elaine M., ed. The Soup Collection. 1995. write for info. (*0-944943-55-1*, 25272-8) Current Inc.

Myers, Elizabeth L. The Upper Places: Nazareth, Gnadenthal & Christian's Spring. 10p. (Orig.). 1978. reprint ed. pap. text 3.00 (*1-877701-04-1*) NCH&GS.

***Myers, Eric.** Uncle Mame: The Life of Patrick Dennis. 2000. 24.95 (*0-312-24655-2*) St Martin.

Myers, Esther. Yoga & You: Energizing & Relaxing Yoga for New & Experienced Students. 208p. 1997. pap. 22.00 (*0-394-22404-3*) Beginner.

— Yoga & You: Energizing & Relaxing Yoga for New & Experienced Teachers. LC 96-36916. (Illus.). 256p. 1997. pap. 17.95 (*1-57062-320-1*, Pub. by Shambhala Pubns) Random.

Myers, Esther S. Roses in December. (Illus.). 164p. 1979. 13.00 (*0-931068-01-0*) Purcells.

Myers, Eugene N. Advances in Otolaryngology. 2001. text 85.95 (*0-323-00938-7*) Harcourt.

— Advances in Otolaryngology. 2002. text 85.95 (*0-323-00939-5*) Harcourt.

— Advances in Otolaryngology. 2000. text 85.95 (*0-323-00937-9*) Harcrt Hlth Sci Grp.

— Advances in Otolaryngology, 12. (Illus.). 344p. 1998. text 89.00 (*0-8151-9821-3*, 25056) Mosby Inc.

— Advances in Otolaryngology, 13. (Illus.). 248p. 1999. text 89.00 (*0-8151-9822-1*, 25057) Mosby Inc.

— Operative Otolaryngology, 2 vols., Set. McGrew, Larry, ed. LC 96-16724. (Illus.). 1408p. 1997. text 365.00 (*0-7216-3841-4*, W B Saunders Co) Harcrt Hlth Sci Grp.

Myers, Eugene N., ed. Advances in Otolaryngology - Head & Neck Surgery, Vol. 7, 1993. LC 88-654898. 333p. 1993. reprint ed. pap. 103.30 (*0-608-02413-9*, 206305500007) Bks Demand.

Myers, Eugene N., et al, eds. Tracheotomy. (Illus.). 318p. 1985. text 49.95 (*0-443-08381-9*) Church.

Myers, Eugene N. & Suen, James Y., eds. Cancer of the Head & Neck. 2nd ed. (Illus.). 1132p. 1989. text 209.00 (*0-443-08597-8*) Church.

Myers, Eugene N., et al. Tracheotomy: Airway Management, Communication, & Swallowing. LC 98-7965. (Illus.). 320p. 1998. pap. 109.95 (*1-56593-990-5*, 1962) Thomson Learn.

Myers, Eugene N., jt. auth. see Suen, James Y.

Myers, Eugene N., jt. ed. see Suen, James Y.

Myers, Eunice, jt. ed. see Adamson, Ginette.

Myers, F. J., jt. auth. see Harring, H. K.

Myers, F. M. The Comanches. 1976. 39.50 (*0-934085-00-5*, J M C & Co) Amereon Ltd.

Myers, F. W. Essays, Classical & Modern, 2 Vols. LC 72-13467. (Essay Index Reprint Ser.). 1977. reprint ed. 30.95 (*0-8369-8170-7*) Ayer.

Myers, Florence L., jt. auth. see Wall, Meryl J.

Myers, Frank. Soldiering in Dakota among the Indians in 1865. LC 77-160983. (Select Bibliographies Reprint Ser.). 1977. reprint ed. 15.95 (*0-8369-5851-9*) Ayer.

***Myers, Fred.** The Cumberland River Cruise Guide. 2nd ed. (Illus.). 95p. (Orig.). 1999. pap. 14.95 (*0-9632005-7-7*) F Myers.

— The Tenn-Tom Nitty-Gritty Cruise Guide. 3rd ed. (Illus.). 103p. (Orig.). 1999. pap. 16.95 (*0-9632005-8-5*) F Myers.

Myers, Fred. The Tennessee River Cruise Guide. 3rd ed. (Illus.). 197p. 1998. pap. 18.95 (*0-9632005-6-9*) F Myers.

Myers, Fred R. Pintupi Country, Pintupi Self: Sentiment, Place & Politics among Western Desert Aborigines. (Illus.). 334p. 1991. pap. 16.95 (*0-520-07411-4*, Pub. by U CA Pr) Cal Prin Full Svc.

Myers, Fred R., jt. ed. see Marcus, George E.

Myers, Frederic W. Human Personality & Its Survival of Bodily Death, 2 vols. LC 75-7391. (Perspectives in Psychical Research Ser.). 1975. reprint ed. 132.95 (*0-405-07038-1*) Ayer.

— The Subliminal Consciousness. LC 75-37305. (Occult Ser.). 1976. reprint ed. 58.95 (*0-405-07952-4*) Ayer.

Myers, G. & Hirschberg, D., eds. Combinatorial Pattern Matching: Proceedings of the 7th Annual Symposium, CPM 96, Laguna Beach, California, June 10-12, 1996. LC 96-8355. (Lecture Notes in Computer Science Ser.: Vol. 107). 392p. 1996. pap. 62.00 (*3-540-61258-0*) Spr-Verlag.

***Myers, G. A.** Hugs from Heaven: The Christmas Story: Sayings, Scriptures & Stories from the Bible Revealing God's Love. LC 99-47422. 128p. 1999. 10.99 (*1-58229-082-2*) Howard Pub LA.

Myers, G. A. Hugs from Heaven on Angel Wings: Sayings, Scriptures & Stories from the Bible Revealing God's Love. LC 98-36851. (Illus.). 128p. 1998. 10.99 (*1-878990-90-X*) Howard Pub LA.

***Myers, G. A. & Weiss, LeAnn.** Celebrating Friendship: Sayings, Scriptures & Stories from the Bible Revealing God. (Hugs from Heaven Ser.). (Illus.). 128p. 2000. 10.99 (*1-58229-130-6*) Howard Pub LA.

Myers, Gail E. & Myers, Michele T. The Dynamics of Human Communication: A Laboratory Approach. 6th ed. 480p. (C). 1991. 45.94 (*0-07-044231-2*) McGraw.

Myers, Gary. Lifetime Possessions. LC 98-161467. 36p. 1997. 5.00 (*1-890044-07-5*) Riverstone PA.

— Pancakes & Coffee: A Canoe Trek Through the Alaskan Wilderness. unabridged ed. Marvin, Janice K. & Myers, Clyde R., eds. 167p. 2000. pap. 8.95 (*0-9668176-1-3*, 1002) Myers Pubg.

— Sinew Man, 1. 1998. pap. 7.95 (*0-9668176-0-5*) Myers Pubg.

***Myers, Gary.** Smart Mom's Baby-Sitting Co-op Handbook: Sanity Coming Soon to a Family Near You. 144p. 2000. pap. 14.95 (*0-9678748-0-7*) Tukwila.

Myers, Gary C., Jr., jt. auth. see Gessow, Alfred.

Myers, Gary E. Do You Hear That Beat? Wisconsin Pop/Rock in the 50s & 60s. LC 94-96410. (Illus.). 385p. 1994. pap. 27.90 (*0-9643073-9-1*) Hummngbrd Pub.

Myers, Gary L. The Caterpillar's Reunion. (Illus.). 64p. 1997. 8.95 (*0-9649123-1-7*) Crosswrks Pub.

— The Caterpillar's Reward. (Illus.). 64p. 1997. 8.95 (*0-9649123-0-9*) Crosswrks Pub.

Myers, Gene. Children & Animals: Social Development & Our Connections to Other Species. LC 97-26350. (Lives in Context Ser.). 1997. text 69.00 (*0-8133-3171-4*, Pub. by Westview) HarpC.

— LeaderTrip: A Lesson in Organizational Transformation. Beauchemin, Tim et al, eds. (Illus.). 320p. (Orig.). 1993. text 47.77 (*1-884332-00-5*); pap. text 27.77 (*1-884332-01-3*) Netwrk Pr TX.

Myers, Gene, ed. see Cotsonitis, Nicholas J.

Myers, Gene, ed. see Otto, Helen T.

Myers, Geoffrey, tr. see Giono, Jean.

Myers, Geoffrey M., et al, eds. Les Chetifs. LC 79-2565. (Old French Crusade Cycle Ser.: Vol. V). 416p. 1981. text 39.50 (*0-8173-0023-6*) U of Ala Pr.

Myers, George, Jr. Bodies of Water. (Ohio Writers Ser.: No. 7). (Illus.). 40p. (Orig.). 1987. pap. 4.95 (*0-933087-09-8*) Bottom Dog Pr.

— Nairobi. LC 77-99271. 1978. pap. 3.00 (*0-917976-01-0*, White Ewe Pr) Thunder Baas Pr.

Myers, George. Piranhas. 128p. 11.95 (*0-87666-771-X*, M539) TFH Pubns.

Myers, George D. Air Brakes/Air Systems. (Illus.). iv, 22p. 1997. spiral bd. 7.00 (*1-892365-00-6*) Epic Conver.

— Ask George: 222 Bus Conversion Questions. LC 98-94886. (Illus.). ix, 122p. 1999. spiral bd. 19.50 (*1-892365-05-7*) Epic Conver.

— Designing Electrical Layouts for Coach Conversions. LC 98-92743. (Illus.). xvi, 284p. 1998. pap., spiral bd. 39.50 (*1-892365-03-0*) Epic Conver.

— Fiberglass on Plywood Tanks. (Illus.). iii, 18p. 1997. spiral bd. 6.00 (*1-892365-02-2*) Epic Conver.

— Low Cost Conversions. iii, 27p. 1997. spiral bd. 5.00 (*1-892365-01-4*) Epic Conver.

Myers, George D. & Myers, Suzanne. Bus Conversion Sources. LC 99-220178. ix, 68p. 1999. spiral bd. 9.50 (*1-892365-07-3*) Epic Conver.

***Myers, George D. & Myers, Suzanne D.** Bus Conversion Sources. 2nd ed. 108p. 2000. 9.50 (*1-892365-08-1*) Epic Conver.

Myers, Gerald. Viral Regulatory Structures. LC 98-11770. 1997. pap. 35.00 (*0-201-32822-4*) Addison-Wesley.

Myers, Gerald, jt. auth. see Irani, K. S.

Myers, Gerald, jt. ed. see Rosenberg, Alan.

Myers, Gerald E. Insurance Manual for Libraries. LC 77-24524. 78p. reprint ed. pap. 30.00 (*0-608-17144-1*, 202735900055) Bks Demand.

Myers, Gerald E., ed. see James, William.

Myers, Gerald E., jt. ed. see Rosenberg, Alan.

Myers, Ginger S. Hanover Harmonies: The Musical Heritage of Hanover, PA. LC 99-173704. (Illus.). 112p. 1998. pap. 14.95 (*0-9664263-0-4*) Pudlee Pubng.

Myers, Glen E. Analytical Methods in Conduction Heat Transfer. 2nd ed. (Illus.). xx, 409p. (C). 1998. 49.00 (*0-9666065-0-7*) AMCHT.

Myers, Glenford J. Advances in Computer Architecture. LC 77-19001. (Illus.). 332p. 1978. pap. 103.00 (*0-7837-3529-4*, 205786500008) Bks Demand.

— The Art of Software Testing. LC 78-12923. (Business Data Processing Ser.). 192p. 1979. 99.95 (*0-471-04328-1*, Wiley-Interscience) Wiley.

— Software Reliability: Principles & Practices. (Business Data Processing Ser.). 360p. 1976. 69.95 (*0-471-62765-8*, Wiley-Interscience) Wiley.

***Myers, Glenn.** The Arab World. (Briefings Ser.). (Illus.). 64p. 1998. reprint ed. pap. 6.99 (*1-85078-287-3*, Pub. by O M Pubng) OM Literature.

— Children in Crisis. (Briefings Ser.). (Illus.). 64p. 1998. reprint ed. pap. 6.99 (*1-85078-270-9*, Pub. by O M Pubng) OM Literature.

— The Poorest of the Poor? The Peoples of the West African Sahel. (Briefings Ser.). (Illus.). 64p. 1998. reprint ed. pap. 6.99 (*1-85078-299-7*, Pub. by O M Pubng) OM Literature.

— The Rim of Fire: Indonesia & the Malay-Speaking Muslim World. (Briefings Ser.). (Illus.). 64p. 1998. reprint ed. pap. 6.99 (*1-85078-298-9*, Pub. by O M Pubng) OM Literature.

Myers, Glenn. World Christian Starter Kit. rev. ed. 126p. 1992. reprint ed. pap. text 4.99 (*0-9630908-5-2*) O M Lit.

Myers, Gloria E. A Municipal Mother: Portland's Lola Greene Baldwin, America's First Policewoman. LC 95-16780. 240p. 1995. text 26.95 (*0-87071-386-8*) Oreg St U Pr.

Myers, Gordon. I Sing - Therefore, I Am. xii, 421p. 1998. pap. 22.50 (*1-878617-25-7*) Leyerle Pubns.

— Singing Teachers Wear Many Hats. (Illus.). 86p. (Orig.). (C). 1992. pap. 8.00 (*1-878617-02-8*) Leyerle Pubns.

— Twenty-Four Songs of Early Americans - For Church: A Thanksgiving Celebration. (Orig.). (C). 1994. pap. 12.95 (*1-878617-06-0*) Leyerle Pubns.

Myers, Gordon B. & Wolfson, William Q. Corticotropin: Its Pharmacologic Effects in Man & Practical Therapeutic Utilization. LC 55-7773. (Illus.). 83p. reprint ed. pap. 30.00 (*0-7837-3823-4*, 204364300010) Bks Demand.

Myers Gorrie, Trula, et al. Clinical Manual for Foundations of Maternal-Newborn Nursing. 2nd ed. Connor, Maura, ed. (Illus.). 510p. (C). 1998. pap. text 21.50 (*0-7216-7466-6*, W B Saunders Co) Harcrt Hlth Sci Grp.

Myers, Greg. Ad Worlds: Brands, Media, Audiences. LC 98-20774. (Arnold Publications). (Illus.). 264p. 1998. pap. text 19.95 (*0-340-70007-6*) OUP.

— Words in Ads. (Illus.). 232p. 1995. pap. text 18.95 (*0-340-61444-7*, B4707, Pub. by E A) OUP.

— Writing Biology: Texts in the Social Construction of Scientific Knowledge. LC 89-40263. (Science & Literature Ser.). (Illus.). 320p. reprint ed. pap. 99.20 (*0-608-09918-X*, 206925600003) Bks Demand.

Myers, Gregory. Lavrsky (Troitsky) Kondakar Vol. 1: The Medieval (Late Twelfth Century) Russian Musical Code. (CHU, ENG & GRE., Illus.). 264p. 1998. 249.00 (*954-580-006-2*, Pub. by Heron Pr) Intl Scholars.

Myers, Gregory W. Land & Power: The Impact of the Land Use Act in Southwest Nigeria. (Research Paper Ser.: Vol. 108). (Illus.). xv, 145p. (C). 1991. pap. 7.00 (*0-934519-18-8*, RP108) U of Wis Land.

Myers, Gregory W. & West, Harry G. Land Tenure Security & State Farm Divestiture in Mozambique: Case Studies in Nhamatanda, Manica & Montepuez Districts. (Research Paper Ser.: Vol. 110). (Illus.). xvi, 87p. (C). 1993. pap. 7.00 (*0-934519-21-8*, RP110) U of Wis Land.

Myers, Gregory W., et al. Security, Conflict, & Reintegration in Mozambique: Case Studies of Land Access in the Postwar Period. (Research Paper Ser.: Vol. 119). (Illus.). xvi, 152p. (C). 1994. pap. 12.00 (*0-934519-30-7*, RP119) U of Wis Land.

Myers Gross, Pati. Home Safety. Marger, Carol, ed. LC 98-68650. (Adventures in the Roo World - Young Roo Ser.: Vol. 4). (Illus.). 24p. (Orig.). (J). (ps-2). 1999. pap. 4.95 (*0-9652579-4-0*) Roo Publns.

Myers, Gustavus. The Ending of Hereditary American Fortunes. LC 68-20528. (Reprints of Economic Classics Ser.). vi, 395p. 1969. reprint ed. 49.50 (*0-678-00454-4*) Kelley.

— The History of American Idealism. LC 74-26126. (Labor Movement in Fiction & Non-Fiction Ser.). reprint ed. 45.00 (*0-404-58506-X*) AMS Pr.

Myers, Gustavus. A History of Canadian Wealth. 354p. 1975. 24.95 (*0-88862-017-9*, Pub. by J Lorimer); pap. 14.95 (*0-88862-016-0*, Pub. by J Lorimer) Formac Dist Ltd.

Myers, Gustavus. History of Canadian Wealth. LC 68-9159. 1968. reprint ed. 20.00 (*0-87266-024-9*) Argosy.

— History of Public Franchises in New York City: Manhattan, Bronx, March, 1900. LC 73-19163. (Politics & People Ser.). 136p. 1974. reprint ed. 13.95 (*0-405-05885-3*) Ayer.

— History of the Great American Fortunes, Vol. I. 296p. text 70.00 (*0-88286-068-2*) C H Kerr.

***Myers, Guy L.** Touched by the Great Physician. LC 99-63454. 128p. 1999. pap. 10.95 (*1-57921-192-5*, Pub. by WinePress Pub) BookWorld.

M

An Asterisk (*) at the beginning of an entry indicates that the title is appearing for the first time.

Myers, H. Ann. 50 Ways to Leave Your Love Handles: Your Guide to Healthier Eating & More Enjoyable Exercise in 50 Quick Tips. large type ed. (Think Fit Ser.). (Illus.). 60p. (Orig.). 1995. reprint ed. pap. 4.95 (*1-887011-02-1*); reprint ed. pap. 19.95 incl. audio (*1-887011-03-X*) Fresh Aer Hlth.

Myers, H. D. Brandi. LC 93-86270. 1994. pap. 12.95 (*1-885487-03-7*) Brownell & Carroll.

Myers, H. M. Fluorides & Dental Fluorosis. (Monographs in Oral Science: Vol. 7). (Illus.). 1978. 34.00 (*3-8055-1412-3*) S Karger.

Myers, H. M., compiled by. Reprinted Selected Top Articles Published, 1977, No. 1. (Karger Highlights, Oral Science One Ser.). 1979. 13.25 (*3-8055-3028-5*) S Karger.

Myers, H. M., ed. New Biotechnology in Oral Research. (Illus.). x, 170p. 1989. 128.00 (*3-8055-4916-4*) S Karger.

Myers, H. M., ed. see Levy, Barnet M., et al.

Myers, H. P. Introductory Solid State Physics. 2nd ed. LC 97-196471. 576p. 1997. 89.95 (*0-7484-0659-X*, Pub. by Tay Francis Ltd); pap. 39.95 (*0-7484-0660-3*, Pub. by Tay Francis Ltd) Taylor & Francis.

Myers, Harris. William Henry Pyne & His Microcosm. (Illus.). 288p. 1996. 53.95 (*0-7509-1232-4*, Pub. by Sutton Pub Ltd) Intl Pubs Mktg.

M

Myers, Hector F., et al, compiled by. Black Child Development in America, 1927-1977: An Annotated Bibliography. LC 78-20028. 470p. 1979. lib. bdg. 49.95 (*0-313-20719-4*, FBC/, Greenwood Pr) Greenwood.

Myers, Hector F., et al, compiled by. Research in Black Child Development: Doctoral Dissertation Abstracts, 1927-1979. LC 81-13425. (Illus.). 737p. 1982. lib. bdg. 59.95 (*0-313-22631-8*, FRC/, Greenwood Pr) Greenwood.

Myers, Hector F., et al, eds. Ethnic Minority Perspectives on Clinical Training & Services in Psychology. 194p. 1991. pap. 14.95 (*1-55798-120-5*) Am Psychol.

Myers, Helen. Music of Hindu Trinidad: Songs from the India Diaspora. LC 97-25692. (Illus.). 480p. 1998. pap. text 39.00 (*0-226-55453-8*); lib. bdg. 85.00 (*0-226-55451-1*) U Ch Pr.

Myers, Helen & Sadie, Stanley, eds. Ethnomusicology. (Grove Handbooks in Music Ser.). (Illus.). 300p. 1992. 35.00 (*0-393-03377-5*) Norton.

— Ethnomusicology: Historical & Regional Studies. (Illus.). 400p. 1993. 40.00 (*0-393-03378-3*) Norton.

Myers, Helen, jt. auth. see Nettl, Bruno.

Myers, Helen R. After That Night... 1996. per. 3.99 (*0-373-24066-X*, 1-24066-2) Silhouette.

— Baby in a Basket. (Romance Ser.). 1996. per. 3.25 (*0-373-19169-3*, 1-19169-1) Silhouette.

— Beloved Mercenary. 1998. per. 4.25 (*0-373-24162-3*, 1-24162-9) Silhouette.

— Come Sundown. (Mira Bks.). 1998. per. 5.99 (*1-55166-436-4*, 1-66436-6, Mira Bks) Harlequin Bks.

— Confidentially Yours. (Men at Work Ser.: Vol. 6). 1998. mass mkt. 4.50 (*0-373-81018-0*, 1-81018-3) Harlequin Bks.

— A Father's Promise. (Silhouette Romance Ser.). 1994. per. 2.75 (*0-373-19002-6*, 5-19002-0) Harlequin Bks.

— A Fine Arrangement. (Family Continuity Program Ser.: No. 5). 1999. mass mkt. 4.50 (*0-373-82153-0*, 1-82153-7) Harlequin Bks.

— Forbidden Passion. large type ed. LC 93-20047. 234p. 1993. lib. bdg. 16.95 (*1-56054-683-2*) Thorndike Pr.

— Jake. (Desire Ser.). 1993. per. 2.99 (*0-373-05797-0*, 5-05797-1) Silhouette.

— Just a Memory Away. LC 96-7348. (Desire Ser.). 184p. 1996. per. 3.50 (*0-373-05990-6*, 1-05990-6) Silhouette.

— The Law Is No Lady. (Montana Mavericks Ser.). 1995. per. 3.99 (*0-373-50172-2*, 1-50172-5) Harlequin Bks.

— Lost. 2000. per. 5.99 (*1-55166-572-7*, Mira Bks) Harlequin Bks.

— The Merry Matchmakers. 1995. per. 2.99 (*0-373-19121-9*, 1-19121-2) Silhouette.

— More Than You Know. (Mira Bks.). 400p. 1999. mass mkt. 5.99 (*1-55166-504-2*, Mira Bks) Harlequin Bks.

— Night Mist. (Shadows Ser.: No. 6). 1993. per. 3.50 (*0-373-27006-2*) Silhouette.

— The Officer & the Renegade. 1997. per. 3.50 (*0-373-76102-3*, 1-76102-2) Silhouette.

— The Rebel & the Hero. (Desire Ser.). 1995. per. 3.25 (*0-373-05941-8*, 1-05941-9) Silhouette.

— Three Little Chaperones. (Romance Ser.: No. 861). 1992. per. 2.69 (*0-373-08861-2*, 5-08861-2) Silhouette.

— Through My Eyes. large type ed. 214p. 1992. reprint ed. lib. bdg. 18.95 (*1-56054-308-6*) Thorndike Pr.

— To Wed at Christmas: (Under the Mistletoe) (Romance Ser.). 1994. per. 2.75 (*0-373-19049-2*, 1-19049-5) Silhouette.

— Watching for Willa. (Shadows Ser.). 1995. mass mkt. 3.50 (*0-373-27049-6*, 1-27049-5) Silhouette.

*Myers, Helen R. Whispers in the Wood. 2000. mass mkt. 4.50 (*0-373-82217-0*, 1-82217-0) Harlequin Bks.

Myers, Helen R. Whispers in the Woods. (Shadows Ser.). 1994. mass mkt. 3.50 (*0-373-27023-2*, 5-27023-6) Silhouette.

Myers, Henry, jt. auth. see Holbik, Karel.

Myers, Henry S., Jr. Fundamentally Speaking. LC 77-3072. 128p. (Orig.). 1977. pap. 9.95 (*0-89407-007-X*) Strawberry Hill.

Myers, Iris, ed. see Collier, R. B.

Myers, Irma. Destiny. 404p. (Orig.). 1993. pap. 16.95 (*1-880365-29-4*) Prof Pr NC.

Myers, Isabel B. Murder Yet to Come. LC 93-49476. 256p. 1994. reprint ed. 16.00 (*0-935652-22-1*) Ctr Applications Psych.

Myers, Isabel B. & Myers, Peter B. Gifts Differing: Understanding Personality Type. 3rd ed. LC 93-13087. 248p. 1995. reprint ed. pap. 16.95 (*0-89106-074-X*, 7270, Davies-Black Pub) Consulting Psychol.

Myers, J. Arthur. Captain of All These Men of Death: Tuberculosis Historical Highlights. 300p. 1977. 14.80 (*0-87527-160-X*) Green.

— Masters of Medicine: An Historical Sketch of the College of Medical Sciences of the University of Minnesota, 1888-1966. LC 68-8890. (Illus.). 942p. 1968. 22.50 (*0-87527-058-1*); pap. 17.50 (*0-87527-140-5*) Green.

Myers, J. E., jt. auth. see Bennett, C. O.

Myers, J. Gordon. People & Change: Planning for Action. (Illus.). 60p. 1997. pap. 19.95 (*1-884731-15-5*, 06200) Oriel Inc.

Myers, J. Martin. Cures by Psychotherapy: What Effects Change? LC 83-21195. 159p. 1984. 45.00 (*0-275-91445-3*, C1445, Praeger Pubs) Greenwood.

Myers, J. P., Jr., et al, eds. Constructivity in Computer Science: Summer Symposium, San Antonio, TX, June 19-22, 1991, Proceedings. LC 92-19519. (Lecture Notes in Computer Science Ser.: Vol. 613). x, 247p. 1992. 47.00 (*0-387-55631-0*); pap. 43.00 (*3-540-55631-1*) Spr-Verlag.

Myers, J. Wilson, et al, eds. An Aerial Atlas of Ancient Crete. LC 91-20649. (Centennial Bk.). (C). 1992. 135.00 (*0-520-07382-7*, Pub. by U CA Pr) Cal Prin Full Svc.

Myers, Jack. Adbashing: Surviving the Attacks on Advertising. 325p. (Orig.). (C). 1993. pap. text 17.95 (*0-9635864-0-8*) Amer Media Coun.

Myers, Jack. Blindsided. 80p. 1993. pap. 12.95 (*0-87923-956-5*) Godine.

Myers, Jack. Can Birds Get Lost? And Other Questions about Animals. LC 90-85911. (Illus.). 64p. (J). (gr. 1-7). 1994. pap. 7.95 (*1-56397-401-0*) Boyds Mills Pr.

— Do Cats Really Have Nine Lives? And Other Questions about Your World. LC 91-77713. (Illus.). 64p. (J). (gr. 1-7). 1994. pap. 7.95 (*1-56397-215-8*) Boyds Mills Pr.

— Highlights Book of Science Questions That Children Ask. LC 94-79501. (Illus.). 256p. (J). (gr. 1-5). 1995. 10.95 (*1-56397-478-9*) Boyds Mills Pr.

— How Do We Dream? And Other Questions about Your Body. LC 91-77601. (Illus.). 64p. (J). (gr. 1-7). 1994. pap. 7.95 (*1-56397-400-2*) Boyds Mills Pr.

— I'm Amazed That You're Still Singing. LC 81-8452. 69p. 1981. text 9.95 (*0-934332-35-5*); pap. text 4.25 (*0-934332-34-7*) LEpervier Pr.

— On the Trail of the Komodo Dragon: And Other Explorations of Science in Action. LC 98-73073. (Illus.). 64p. (J). (gr. 4-7). 1999. 17.95 (*1-56397-761-3*) Boyds Mills Pr.

— One on One: Poems. LC 98-74999. v, 90p. 1999. pap. 14.95 (*0-9669419-0-X*) Autumn Hse Pr.

— Reconnecting with Customers: How Advertisers Are Building Brands & Profits in the Relationship Age & How You Can Do It Too! (Illus.). 250p. 1998. 27.95 (*1-888232-48-X*, Pub. by Spurge ink) Natl Bk Netwk.

*Myers, Jack. What Happened to the Mammoths? And Other Explorations of Science in Action. LC 99-65422. (Illus.). 64p. (J). (gr. 4-7). 2000. 17.95 (*1-56397-801-6*) Boyds Mills Pr.

Myers, Jack & Weingarten, Roger, eds. New American Poets of the 80's. 480p. 1984. pap. 12.95 (*0-931694-35-3*) Wampeter Pr.

— New American Poets of the 90's. 464p. 1991. pap. 19.95 (*0-87923-907-7*) Godine.

Myers, Jack & Wojahn, David, eds. A Profile of Twentieth-Century American Poetry. LC 90-37757. 336p. (C). 1991. text 18.95 (*0-8093-1349-9*) S Ill U Pr.

Myers, Jack, jt. ed. see Elliott, Mark.

Myers, Jack D., ed. see Ryan, Will G.

Myers, Jacob M. Esdras One & Two, Vol. 42. 1974. 18.00 (*0-385-00426-5*) Doubleday.

Myers, Jacob M., ed. Chronicles One. LC 65-17226. (Anchor Bible Ser.: Vol. 12). 336p. 1965. 32.00 (*0-385-01259-4*, Anchor NY) Doubleday.

— Chronicles Two. (Anchor Bible Ser.: Vol. 13). 312p. 1965. 18.00 (*0-385-03757-0*, Anchor NY) Doubleday.

— Ezra & Nehemiah. LC 65-23788. (Anchor Bible Ser.: Vol. 14). 1965. 29.00 (*0-385-04695-2*, Anchor NY) Doubleday.

Myers, James C. Science & Technology of Building Seals, Sealants, Glazing & Waterproofing, Vol. 6. (STP 1286 Ser.). (Illus.). 163p. 1996. pap. text 47.00 (*0-8031-2044-3*, STP1286) ASTM.

Myers, James C., ed. Science & Technology of Building Seals, Sealants, Glazing & Waterproofing, Vol. 3. (Special Technical Publication: No. 1254). (Illus.). 106p. 1994. text 59.00 (*0-8031-1993-3*, STP1254) ASTM.

Myers, James E. The Great American Liar: A Treasury of Tall Tales. 375p. (Orig.). 1987. pap. 9.95 (*0-942936-13-2*) Lincoln-Herndon Pr.

— Jones. LC 82-81241. 216p. 1982. 12.95 (*0-942936-03-5*) Lincoln-Herndon Pr.

— A Treasury of Farm & Ranch Humor. (Illus.). 325p. 1989. pap. 10.95 (*0-942936-15-9*) Lincoln-Herndon Pr.

— A Treasury of Victorious Women's Humor. (Illus.). 340p. 1999. pap. 12.95 (*0-942936-35-3*, Pub. by Lincoln-Herndon Pr) Distributors.

Myers, James E., contrib. by. A Treasury of Musical Humor. LC 98-68114. (Illus.). 300p. 1998. pap. 12.95 (*0-942936-34-5*) Lincoln-Herndon Pr.

Myers, James E., ed. America's Phunniest Phellow - Josh Billings. 275p. 1985. 14.95 (*0-942936-05-1*); pap. 7.95 (*0-942936-07-8*) Lincoln-Herndon Pr.

— Grandpa's Rib Ticklers & Knee-Slappers. 1984. 15.95 (*0-942936-02-7*); pap. 8.95 (*0-942936-01-9*) Lincoln-Herndon Pr.

— A Treasury of Business Humor. (Orig.). 1996. pap. 12.95 (*0-942936-28-0*) Lincoln-Herndon Pr.

Myers, James E., Sr., ed. A Treasury of Cocktail Humor. 300p. 1995. pap. 10.95 (*0-942936-27-2*) Lincoln-Herndon Pr.

Myers, James E., ed. A Treasury of Hunting & Fishing Humor. (Illus.). 320p. 1990. pap. 10.95 (*0-942936-19-1*) Lincoln-Herndon Pr.

— A Treasury of Husband & Wife Humor. 350p. (Orig.). 1993. pap. 10.95 (*0-942936-22-1*) Lincoln-Herndon Pr.

— A Treasury of Medical Humor. 350p. (Orig.). 1992. pap. 10.95 (*0-942936-21-3*) Lincoln-Herndon Pr.

— A Treasury of Mom, Pop & Kids' Humor. (Illus.). 225p. (Orig.). 1997. pap. 10.95 (*0-942936-29-9*) Lincoln-Herndon Pr.

Myers, James E., Sr., ed. A Treasury of Religious Humor. (Illus.). 300p. 1994. pap. 10.95 (*0-942936-24-8*) Lincoln-Herndon Pr.

Myers, James E., ed. A Treasury of Senior Humor. 350p. (Orig.). 1992. pap. 10.95 (*0-942936-20-5*) Lincoln-Herndon Pr.

Myers, James E., et al, eds. A Treasury of Military Humor. (Illus.). 350p. (Orig.). 1989. pap. 10.95 (*0-942936-16-7*) Lincoln-Herndon Pr.

Myers, James E., jt. auth. see Lehmann, Arthur C.

Myers, James E., ed. see Benton, Frank.

Myers, James E., jt. ed. see Lehmann, Arthur C.

Myers, James E., ed. see Whiting, Robert R.

Myers, James G. Mastering Psychology: A Computer Assisted Laboratory Manual. 2nd ed. (Illus.). 278p. (C). 1994. reprint ed. pap. text 32.00 (*1-879972-00-X*, NW Innovations) Chemeketa Coll.

*Myers, James H. Measuring Customer Satisfaction: Hot Buttons & Other Measurement Issues LC 99-32740. 1999. write for info. (*0-87757-276-3*) Am Mktg.

Myers, James H., ed. Pediatric Heart Surgeon & Facility Directory: Profiles of Individual Surgeons & Congenital Heart Programs. LC 97-68297. (Illus.). 128p. 1997. pap. 40.00 (*0-9658918-0-1*) CHASER.

Myers, James J. Massachusetts Construction Law. LC 98-65213. xxi, 698 p. 1998. 95.00 (*1-55834-882-4*) LEXIS Pub.

Myers, James J., jt. auth. see Cushman, Robert F.

Myers, James L. Resurrection of Doctor Buzz. LC 97-90553. 1997. pap. 14.95 (*0-533-12426-3*) Vantage.

Myers, James M. The Bureau of Motion Pictures & Its Influence on Film Content During World War II: The Reasons for Its Failure. LC 98-27519. 244p. 1998. text 89.95 (*0-7734-8304-7*) E Mellen.

Myers, James P., Jr. Writing Irish: Interviews with Irish Writers from the Irish Literary Supplement. LC 99-20928. (Irish Studies). 216p. 1999. 29.95 (*0-8156-0598-6*) Syracuse U Pr.

Myers, James P., Jr., ed. see Davies, John.

Myers, James T. Enemies Without Guns: The Catholic Church in China. LC 90-23647. (Illus.). 334p. (C). 1991. 19.95 (*0-943852-90-0*) Prof World Peace.

Myers, James T., et al, eds. Chinese Politics, Documents & Analysis: The Death of Mao (1976) to the Fall of Hua Kuo-feng (1980), Vol. 3. LC 85-22466. Vol. 3. 1995. text 69.95 (*1-57003-062-6*) U of SC Pr.

— Chinese Politics, Documents & Analysis: The Fall of Hua Kuo-feng (1980) to the Twelfth Party Congress (1982), Vol. 4. LC 85-22466. Vol. 4. 4p. 1996. text 69.95 (*1-57003-063-4*) U of SC Pr.

Myers, James T., et al. Chinese Politics, Documents & Analysis Vol. 2: Ninth Party Congress (1969) to the Death of Mao (1976) LC 85-2466. 467p. (C). 1989. text 69.95 (*0-87249-601-5*) U of SC Pr.

Myers, James T., jt. auth. see Lin, Bih-Jaw.

Myers, James T., jt. ed. see Lin, Bih-Jaw.

Myers, Jane E. Empowerment for Later Life. 1990. pap. write for info. (*1-56109-029-8*) CAPS Inc.

Myers, Jane E., ed. Developing & Directing Counselor Education Laboratories: Proceedings of an ACES National Conference Think Tank. LC 94-3946. 216p. 1994. pap. text 33.95 (*1-55620-137-0*, 72583) Am Coun Assn.

Myers, Jane E. & Brown, Jill S. The Student Body: A Survival Guide to College Eating & Weight Control. 90p. (C). 1993. pap. 11.95 (*0-9635449-1-8*) Two-J Bks.

Myers, Jane E. & Riker, Harold C. Retirement Counseling: A Handbook for Action. (Death Education, Aging & Health Care Ser.). 1989. 66.95 (*0-89116-628-9*) Hemisp Pub.

Myers, Jane E. & Schwiebert, Valerie L. Competencies for Gerontological Counseling. 241p. 1996. pap. text 25.95 (*1-55620-149-4*, 72620) Am Coun Assn.

Myers, Jane E., et al. Stuart Davis: Graphic Work & Related Paintings with a Catalogue Raisonne of the Prints. LC 86-70931. (Illus.). 100p. 1986. pap. 2.50 (*0-88360-055-2*) Amon Carter.

Myers, Jane E., jt. auth. see Myers, Edward.

Myers, Jane E., jt. ed. see Schwiebert, Valerie L.

Myers, Janet L. Productive Bankers & Profitable Banks: The Grand Slam of Banking. LC 91-61867. (Illus.). 176p. 1992. 49.95 (*1-880023-44-X*) Dearborn Busn Pr.

Myers, Jay A. Fighters of Fate. LC 79-84329. (Essay Index Reprint Ser.). 1977. 21.95 (*0-8369-1099-0*) Ayer.

— Tuberculosis: A Half-Century of Study & Conquest. LC 75-96989. (Illus.). 378p. 1970. 17.50 (*0-87527-059-X*) Green.

Myers, Jean M., jt. auth. see Myers, Joseph A.

Myers, Jeff. Playpen to Podium: Giving Your Child the Communication Advantage in Every Area of Life. 230p. (Orig.). 1997. pap. 12.95 (*1-56857-068-6*, 1799) Noble Pub Assocs.

Myers, Jeff & Myers, Danielle. Of Knights & Fair Maidens: A Radical New Way to Develop Old-Fashioned Relationships. LC 95-95345. 104p. (Orig.). 1996. pap. 8.95 (*0-9650538-0-6*, B-002) Heartlnd Edu Consul.

Myers, Jeffrey C. Geostatistical Error Management: Quantifying Uncertainty for Environmental Sampling & Mapping. (Industrial Engineering Ser.). 571p. 1997. 99.00 (*0-471-28556-0*, VNR) Wiley.

Myers, Jeffrey C. Geostatistical Error Management (GEM) Quantifying Uncertainty for Environmental Problems. LC 96-37272. (Industrial Engineering Ser.). (GER.). 592p. 1997. text 79.95 (*0-442-01429-5*, VNR) Wiley.

Myers, Jeffrey R. Shakespeare's Mannerist Canon: Ut Picturas Poemata. (Literature & the Visual Arts: Ser.: Vol. 2). (Illus.). XIV, 224p. (C). 1989. text 52.00 (*0-8204-0891-3*) P Lang Pubng.

Myers, Jeffrey T. Unfinished "Errand into the Wilderness" Tendenzen und Schwerpunkte der Homiletik in Den U. S. A., 1960-1985. (Europaische Hochschulschriften Ser.: Reihe 23, Bd. 581). (GER., Illus.). 242p. 1996. 44.95 (*3-631-30273-8*) P Lang Pubng.

Myers, Jeffrey W. Automated Defibrillation for Professional & Lay Rescuers. LC 98-31919. (Illus.). 145p. (C). 1999. pap. text 15.95 (*0-8036-0454-8*) Thomson Learn.

Myers, Jerome L. & Well, Arnold D. Research Design & Statistical Analysis. LC 95-8542. 728p. 1995. reprint ed. 49.95 (*0-8058-2067-1*) L Erlbaum Assocs.

Myers, Jim. Afraid of the Dark: What Whites & Blacks Need to Know about Each Other. LC 99-47760. 224p. 2000. 22.95 (*1-55652-342-4*, Pub. by Chicago Review) IPG Chicago.

Myers, John. The Eucharist: Sacrifice of Love. (Queen of Apostles Ser.: Vol. XIII). 17p. 1995. 0.65 (*1-56036-025-9*, 49744) AMI Pr.

— Personal Housekeeping. 12p. 1997. pap., wbk. ed. 4.95 (*0-929690-38-9*) Herit Pubs AZ.

Myers, John & Monson, Luetta. Involving Families in Middle Level Education. 48p. (C). 1992. pap. text 10.00 (*1-56090-065-2*) Natl Middle Schl.

Myers, John, et al. Interviewing Young Children about Body Touch & Handling. 236p. 1996. pap. text 14.00 (*0-226-77401-5*) U Ch Pr.

Myers, John, jt. auth. see Church, David.

Myers, John, jt. auth. see Digby, Christine.

Myers, John, jt. auth. see Koprowicz, Constance L.

Myers, John, ed. see Finnerty, Margaret.

Myers, John, ed. see King, Jean B.

Myers, John A., Jr. A Manual of Usage. 1986. teacher ed. 6.96 (*0-88334-076-3*, 75752); student ed. 7.50 (*0-8013-0088-6*, 75752) Longman.

Myers, John B. Legal Issues in Child Abuse & Neglect Practice. (Interpersonal Violence: the Practice Ser.: Vol. 1). (Illus.). 184p. (C). 1992. 48.00 (*0-8039-4231-1*); pap. 21.50 (*0-8039-4232-X*) Sage.

Myers, John D. Solar Applications in Industry & Commerce. (Illus.). 432p. (C). 1984. text 43.00 (*0-13-822404-8*) P-H.

Myers, John E. The Backlash: Child Protection under Fire. 176p. 1994. 42.00 (*0-8039-5403-4*); pap. 19.50 (*0-8039-5404-2*) Sage.

— Evidence in Child Abuse & Neglect Cases, 2 vols., Vol. 2. 3rd ed. LC 97-25136. (Trial Practice Library Ser.). 1272p. 1997. boxed set 265.00 (*0-471-16749-5*) Wiley.

— Legal Issues in Child Abuse & Neglect Practice. 2nd ed. LC 98-9022. (Interpersonal Violence Ser.). 1998. 68.50 (*0-7619-1665-2*); pap. 31.95 (*0-7619-1666-0*) Sage.

— A Mother's Nightmare - Incest: A Practical Legal Guide for Parents & Professionals. LC 97-4759. 256p. 1997. 49.95 (*0-7619-1057-3*); pap. 22.95 (*0-7619-1058-1*) Sage.

— The Way of the Pipa: Structure & Imagery in Chinese Lute Music. LC 91-33965. (World Music Ser.). (Illus.). 152p. 1992. lib. bdg. 35.00 (*0-87338-455-5*) Kent St U Pr.

Myers, John L. & Blanc, Tara. 6 Keys to Success Through Customer Service. rev. ed. 56p. 1999. pap. 7.95 (*0-929690-44-3*) Herit Pubs AZ.

*Myers, John L. & Blanc, Tara A. 6 Claves para Lograr el Exito Mediante el Servicio al Cliente.Tr. of 6 Keys to Success through Customer Service. (SPA.). 1999. 7.95 (*0-929690-45-1*) Herit Pubs AZ.

Myers, John M. The Alamo. LC 48-5208. (Illus.). 240p. 1973. reprint ed. pap. 10.95 (*0-8032-5779-1*, Bison Books) U of Nebr Pr.

— Bravos of the West. LC 95-16895. (Illus.). xi, 467p. 1995. pap. 15.00 (*0-8032-8222-2*, Bison Books) U of Nebr Pr.

— Doc Holliday. LC 55-5528. 224p. 1973. reprint ed. pap. 9.95 (*0-8032-5781-3*, Bison Books) U of Nebr Pr.

— The Saga of Hugh Glass: Pirate, Pawnee, & Mountain Man. LC 75-38613. vii, 237p. 1976. reprint ed. pap. 10.95 (*0-8032-5834-8*, Bison Books) U of Nebr Pr.

— Silverlock. (Orig.). 1993. reprint ed. lib. bdg. 18.95 (*0-89968-409-2*, Lghtyr Pr) Buccaneer Bks.

— Tombstone's Early Years. LC 94-41319. (Illus.). 266p. 1995. pap. 12.00 (*0-8032-8215-X*, Bison Books) U of Nebr Pr.

Myers, John M., anno. The Westerners: A Roundup of Pioneer Reminiscences. annot. ed. LC 97-1510. xvii, 258p. 1997. pap. 13.00 (*0-8032-8236-2*, Bison Books) U of Nebr Pr.

Myers, Jonathan. Helping Your Child to Read: How to Prepare the Child of Today for the World of Tomorrow. (Family Reference Ser.). 144p. 1996. pap. 19.95 (*1-85703-192-X*, Pub. by How To Bks) Trans-Atl Phila.

— Profits Without Panic: Investment Psychology for Personal Wealth. LC 99-11373. (Illus.). 312p. 1999. 25.00 (*1-85788-217-2*) Nicholas Brealey.

Myers, Jonathan N. Essentials of Cardiopulmonary Exercise Testing. LC 96-1015. (Illus.). 192p. 1996. text 30.00 (*0-87322-636-4*, BMYE0636) Human Kinetics.

Myers, Jonathan N., jt. auth. see Froelicher, Victor F.

Myers, Joseph, ed. see Myers, Raquelle.

Myers, Joseph A. & Myers, Jean M. Nine Lives: The Reincarnation Story. rev. ed. 220p. 1994. pap. 14.95 (*0-913911-08-9*) Akashic Pr.

An Asterisk (*) at the beginning of an entry indicates that the title is appearing for the first time.

Myers, Joseph A., ed. & frwd. see American Indian Lawyer Training Program, Inc., Sta.

Myers, Joseph R. Edward Bellamy Writes Again. LC 97-93135. x, 257p. 1997. pap. 11.95 (*0-9657458-0-5*, 1001) Asaph Commun.

***Myers, Judith L.** Quick Medication Administration Reference. 3rd ed. LC 99-174426. (Illus.). 80p. 1998. write for info. (*1-55664-481-7*) Mosby Inc.

Myers, Judith L., jt. auth. see Beare, Patricia G.

Myers, Judith L., jt. ed. see Beare, Patricia G.

Myers, Julie. Dream Builder. (Superromance Ser.). 1993. per. 3.39 (*0-373-70535-2*, 1-70535-9) Harlequin Bks.

Myers, K. H. & Danner, R. P. Prediction Methods for Organo-Metallic Compounds: Supplements. (Design Institute for Physical Property Data Ser.). 186p. 1991. spiral bd. 45.00 (*0-8169-0560-6*) Am Inst Chem Eng.

Myers, K. Sara. Ovid's Causes: Cosmogony & Aetiology in the Metamorphoses. 224p. 1994. text 47.50 (*0-472-10459-4*, 10459) U of Mich Pr.

Myers, Karen. Harmonious Companions, Vol. 1: Being a Compendium of One Hundred Dramatic, Romantic, Convivial, Sporting, Seasonal, Martial & Celebratory Songs. LC 92-85278. (Illus.). 272p. (Orig.). 1993. pap. 19.95 (*0-9635384-7-0*) Perkunas Pr.

Myers, Karen, ed. see Lyncheski, Stephanie.

Myers, Karen K., ed. see Fisher, Gail.

***Myers, Kate.** Whatever Happened to Equal Opportunities in Schools? LC 99-23609. 1999. pap. 26.95 (*0-335-20303-5*) OpUniv Pr.

Myers, Kate, ed. School Improvement in Practice: Schools Make a Difference. LC 95-23592. 1996. 79.95 (*0-7507-0439-X*, Falmer Pr); pap. 27.95 (*0-7507-0440-3*, Falmer Pr) Taylor & Francis.

Myers, Kate, jt. ed. see Stoll, Louise.

Myers, Kath V. So . . . How Does the Rope Get up There Anyway? An Expert Guide to Rock Climbing Watch. LC 97-31304. (Illus.). 96p. (Orig.). 1997. pap. 10.00 (*1-879415-17-8*) Mtn n Air Bks.

Myers, Katherine. The Lehi Tree: A Novel. 188p. 1996. pap. text 7.95 (*1-57636-026-1*) SunRise Pbl.

Myers, Kathy. Understains: The Sense & Seduction of Advertising. (Comedia Bks.). 160p. 1988. pap. text 13.95 (*0-906890-98-5*, Pub. by Comedia) Routldge.

Myers, Keith. Sugahtown. 136p. (Orig.). 1995. pap. 9.95 (*0-9641196-5-X*) Champion Bks.

Myers, Keith, jt. ed. see Emery, Dominic.

Myers, Ken. All God's Children & Blue Suede Shoes: Christians & Popular Culture. LC 87-71899. (Turning Point Christian Worldview Ser.). 224p. 1989. pap. 14.99 (*0-89107-538-0*) Crossway Bks.

Myers, Kenneth A., ed. see Berger, Peter L., et al.

Myers, Kenneth D. False Security: Greed & Deception in America's Multibillion-Dollar Insurance Industry. LC 94-40533. 288p. (C). 1995. 25.95 (*0-87975-928-3*) Prometheus Bks.

Myers, Kenneth H. Marketing Policy Determination by a Major Firm in a Capital Goods Industry. LC 75-41773. (Companies & Men: Business Enterprises in America Ser.). 1976. 47.95 (*0-405-08087-5*) Ayer.

***Myers, Kenneth N.** Manager's Guide to Contingency Planning for Disasters: Protecting Vital Facilities & Critical Operations. 2nd ed. LC 99-38841. 234p. 1999. 39.95 (*0-471-35838-X*) Wiley.

Myers, Kevin J., ed. Sports Marketplace Directory, 1999. 1600p. 1998. pap. 199.00 (*1-883219-91-4*) Franklin Covey.

Myers, Kirk. When Old Town Was Young: The Early Decades of Old Pasadena. 24p. 1994. pap. 6.95 (*0-9642429-0-7*) K Myers.

Myers, Kristen A., et al, eds. Feminist Foundations: Toward Transforming Sociology. LC 98-8933. (Gender & Society Readers Ser.). 439p. 1997. 59.00 (*0-7619-0785-8*); pap. 26.00 (*0-7619-0786-6*) Sage.

Myers, Kurtz, compiled by. Index to Record Reviews, 5 vols. 2000p. 1978. 485.00 (*0-8161-0087-X*, G K Hall & Co) Mac Lib Ref.

Myers, L. Becoming an Effective Tutor. Gerould, Phil, ed. LC 89-82096. (Fifty-Minute Ser.). 89p. (Orig.). 1990. pap. 10.95 (*1-56052-028-0*) Crisp Pubns.

— Create a Computer Bulletin Board System. 1991. 30.50 (*0-8306-6225-1*) McGraw-Hill Prof.

Myers, L. Rex. Daviess County, Indiana, Vol. II. LC 88-50352. 456p. 1991. 45.00 (*1-56311-003-2*) Turner Pub KY.

— Daviess County, Indiana History. LC 88-50352. 336p. 1988. 50.00 (*0-938021-66-4*) Turner Pub KY.

Myers, Larry. Training with Cerutty. LC 77-85323. (Illus.). 176p. 1978. pap. 6.95 (*0-89037-081-8*) Anderson World.

Myers, Larry T. Stories from Latin America: An ESL-EFL Reader. (Illus.). 96p. (C). 1987. pap. text. write for info. (*0-318-61593-2*) P-H.

Myers, Laura G., jt. auth. see Landau, Lois.

Myers, Laurie. Earthquake in the Third Grade. LC 92-26609. 64p. (J). 1993. 15.00 (*0-395-65360-6*, Clarion Bks) HM.

— Earthquake in the Third Grade. LC 92-26609. (Illus.). 64p. (J). (gr. 2-4). 1998. pap. 5.95 (*0-395-92866-4*, Clarion Bks) HM.

— Guinea Pigs Don't Talk. LC 93-39642. (Illus.). 96p. (YA). 1994. 13.95 (*0-395-68967-8*, Clarion Bks) HM.

— Guniea Pigs Don't Talk. LC 93-39642. (Illus.). 96p. (J). (gr. 2-5). 1998. pap. 5.95 (*0-395-92865-6*, Clarion Bks) HM.

***Myers, Laurie.** Seaman's Tale. 2001. text 15.95 (*0-8050-6368-4*) St Martin.

— Surviving Brick Johnson. LC 00-24309. (Illus.). 80p. (gr. 4-7). 2000. 15.00 (*0-395-98031-3*, Clarion Bks) HM.

Myers, Lawrence E., jt. ed. see Schaffers, Kathleen I.

Myers, Lawrence W. Improvised Radio Jamming Techniques: Electronic Guerrilla Warfare. (Illus.). 256p. 1989. pap. 19.95 (*0-87364-520-0*) Paladin Pr.

— Spycomm: Covert Communication Techniques of the Underground. LC 98-143737. (Illus.). 256p. 1991. pap. 22.95 (*0-87364-643-6*) Paladin Pr.

Myers, Lena. Black Male Socialization. LC 98-34238. (Contemporary Studies in Sociology: Vol. 16). 1998. 78.50 (*0-7623-0453-7*) Jai Pr.

Myers, Leo O. Debtor-Creditor Relations: Manual & Forms. LC 86-7179. 734p. 1986. text 95.00 (*0-07-044266-5*) Shepards.

***Myers, Leon E., et al.** Precalculus: A Quantitative Reasoning Approach. 2nd ed. 466p. (C). 1999. per. 69.95 (*0-7872-6281-1*, 41628102) Kendall-Hunt.

Myers, Leon E., jt. auth. see Hugine, Andrew, Jr.

Myers, Leopold H. Clio. 1971. reprint ed. 29.00 (*0-403-00673-2*) Scholarly.

— Orissers. 1971. reprint ed. 59.00 (*0-403-01125-6*) Scholarly.

Myers, Leora. Menopause & Beyond: A Fitness Plan for Life. Kath, Laura, ed. (Illus.). 208p. (Orig.). 1995. reprint ed. pap. 12.95 (*0-9647666-0-4*) Adelaide Pr.

Myers, Linda, ed. Approaches to Computer Writing Classrooms: Learning from Practical Experience. LC 92-32896. (SUNY Series, Literacy, Culture, & Learning: Theory & Practice). (Illus.). 225p. (C). 1993. text 64.50 (*0-7914-1567-8*); pap. text 21.95 (*0-7914-1568-6*) State U NY Pr.

Myers, Linda J. Understanding of Afrocentric World View: Introduction to an Optimal Psychology. 128p. 1995. per. 20.95 (*0-8403-8342-8*) Kendall-Hunt.

Myers, Loicy, jt. auth. see Tatam, Robert D.

Myers, Lois, jt. auth. see Pelton, Charles L.

Myers, Lois E. Letters by Lamplight: A Woman's View of Everyday Life in South Texas, 1873-1883. LC 90-85476. (Illus.). 240p. 1991. 23.95 (*0-918954-53-3*) Baylor Univ Pr.

— Letters by Lamplight: A Woman's View of Everyday Life in South Texas, 1873-1883. LC 90-85476. (Illus.). 240p. 1999. pap. 14.95 (*0-918954-69-X*) Baylor Univ Pr.

Myers, Lois M. & Landau, Laura G. Too Many Tomatoes, Squash, Beans, & Other Good Things: A Cookbook for When Your Garden Explodes. large type ed. LC 97-8469. (Spec-Hall Ser.). 412p. 1997. lib. bdg. 25.95 (*0-7838-8210-6*, G K Hall Lrg Type) Mac Lib Ref.

Myers, Lora, jt. auth. see Gardner, Janet.

Myers, Loretta, jt. auth. see Krek, Lydia T.

Myers, Loretta C. The Socialization of Neophyte Nurses. Kalisch, Philip & Kalisch, Beatrice, eds. LC 82-7014. (Studies in Nursing Management: No. 1). (Illus.). 156p. 1982. reprint ed. pap. 48.40 (*0-8357-1339-3*, 207002200063) Bks Demand.

Myers, Lorraine F., jt. auth. see Brown, Stuart E.

Myers, Lorraine F., jt. auth. see Brown, Stuart E., Jr.

***Myers, Lowell.** Echoes from the Lengthening Shadows. 274p. 1999. pap. 11.00 (*0-7392-0400-9*, PO3631) Morris Pubng.

Myers, Lowell K. Bread upon the Waters: History - Nostalgia - Folklore - Adventure. 200p. (Orig.). 1996. pap. write for info. (*1-57502-108-0*) Morris Pubng.

Myers, Lynn & Midence, Kenny, eds. Adherence to Treatment in Medical Conditions. 517p. 1998. text 71.00 (*90-5702-264-8*, Harwood Acad Pubs); pap. text 28.00 (*90-5702-265-6*, Harwood Acad Pubs) Gordon & Breach.

Myers, Lynn K., jt. auth. see Myers, Charles B.

Myers, Lynn R., jt. auth. see Terry, George D.

Myers, Lynne B. & Myers, Christopher A. Galapagos: Islands of Change. LC 94-26173. (Illus.). 48p. (J). (gr. 3-7). 1995. 16.95 (*0-7868-0074-7*, Pub. by Hyprn Child) Time Warner.

— Galapagos: Islands of Change. LC 94-26173. (Illus.). 48p. (J). (gr. 4-7). 1995. lib. bdg. 16.89 (*0-7868-2061-6*, Pub. by Hyprn Child) Little.

— Turnip Soup. LC 93-11744. (Illus.). 32p. (J). (ps-3). 1994. 13.95 (*1-56282-445-7*, Pub. by Hyprn Child); lib. bdg. 13.89 (*1-56282-446-5*, Pub. by Hyprn Child) Little.

Myers, M., ed. Harriet E. P. Spofford: An Anthology in Memoriam (1835-1921) LC 96-86092. 184p. (Orig.). 1996. pap. text 24.95 (*1-879183-32-3*) Bristol Banner.

— Memorable Poetry, 1999: People, Animals & Events to be Remembered in Our Hearts. LC 99-90109. 85p. 1999. pap. 24.95 (*1-879183-22-6*) Bristol Banner.

— Paul Laurence Dunbar: An Anthology in Memoriam (1872-1906) LC 97-71073. 168p. (Orig.). 1997. pap. text 16.95 (*1-879183-34-X*) Bristol Banner.

— Richard Henry Wilde: An Anthology in Memoriam (1789-1847) LC 97-75063. 167p. 1997. pap. 16.95 (*1-879183-35-8*) Bristol Banner.

Myers, M., ed. see Scott, Helen E.

Myers, M. A., ed. Ann Eliza Bleecker: An Anthology in Memoriam (1752-1783) LC 93-71851. 251p. (Orig.). 1993. pap. text 24.95 (*1-879183-21-8*) Bristol Banner.

— Celia Thaxter: An Anthology in Memoriam (1835-1894) LC 93-74631. (Orig.). 1994. pap. 24.95 (*1-879183-23-4*) Bristol Banner.

— Charles Warren Stoddard: An Anthology in Memioriam (1843-1909) 160p. (Orig.). 1993. pap. text 24.95 (*1-879183-18-8*) Bristol Banner.

— Eugene Field: An Anthology in Memoriam (1850-1895) LC 94-73734. 184p. (Orig.). 1995. pap. text 24.95 (*1-879183-25-0*) Bristol Banner.

— Henry C. Bunner: An Anthology in Memoriam (1855-1896) LC 96-83789. 183p. (Orig.). 1996. pap. text 24.95 (*1-879183-31-5*) Bristol Banner.

— Lydia Sigourney: An Anthology in Memoriam, 1791-1865. LC 95-79334. 160p. (Orig.). 1995. pap. 24.95 (*1-879183-27-7*) Bristol Banner.

— Memorable Poetry, 1998: People, Animals, & Events to be Remembered in Our Hearts. LC 97-75064. 120p. 1998. pap. text 15.95 (*1-879183-37-4*) Bristol Banner.

— Sara Jane Clarke Lippincott: An Anthology in Memoriam (1823-1904) LC 97-75065. 108p. 1998. pap. text 15.95 (*1-879183-36-6*) Bristol Banner.

— Sorin of Notre Dame: A Centennial Celebration in Poetry on the Anniversary of the Death of Edward Sorin, C. S. C. 1814-1893. LC 91-75432. 211p. (Orig.). 1991. pap. text 14.95 (*1-879183-07-2*) Bristol Banner.

Myers, M. Bert, jt. ed. see Grabb, William C.

Myers, M. J., jt. auth. see Peters, A. M.

Myers, M. Scott. Poems for Free Spirits: Candid Views of Sacred Cows. (Illus.). 168p. 1996. pap. 10.00 (*0-9639930-3-8*) Choctaw Pubng.

— Rhymes of the Ancient Manager: Leadership in the New Age. LC 94-70151. (Illus.). 192p. (Orig.). 1994. 19.95 (*0-9639930-0-3*); pap. 14.95 (*0-9639930-1-1*) Choctaw Pubng.

Myers, M. Scott & Howard, Jennifer. Countering Sexual Harassment: A Handbook for Self Defense. (Illus.). 192p. 1995. 18.00 (*0-9639930-2-X*) Choctaw Pubng.

Myers, Marcia J. & Jirjees, Jassim M. The Accuracy of Telephone Reference-Information Services in Academic Libraries: Two Studies. LC 82-10785. 282p. 1983. 26.50 (*0-8108-1584-2*) Scarecrow.

Myers, Margaret. Blowing Her Own Trumpet: European Ladies' Orchestras & Other Women Musicians in Sweden, 1870-1950. (Goteborg Univ. Dept. of Musicology Ser.: No. 30). 411p. (Orig.). 1993. pap. 99.50 (*91-85974-22-6*) Coronet Bks.

— Monetary Proposals for Social Reform. LC 71-110574. 1970. reprint ed. 20.00 (*0-404-04548-0*) AMS Pr.

Myers, Margaret & Scarborough, Mayra, eds. Women in Librarianship: Melvil's Rib Symposium. (Issues in Library & Information Sciences Ser.: No. 2). 1975. pap. text 15.00 (*0-8135-0807-X*) Rutgers U SICLS.

Myers, Margaret, jt. auth. see Heim, Kathleen M.

Myers, Margaret E. Myersville, Md., Lutheran Baptisms. Russell, Donna V., ed. (Illus.). 70p. 1986. pap. 11.00 (*0-914385-04-6*) Catoctin Pr.

Myers, Margaret G. A Financial History of the United States. LC 70-104900. (Illus.). 463p. reprint ed. pap. 143.60 (*0-608-30004-7*, 201988800015) Bks Demand.

Myers, Marie L. Shortcuts to Beginning Reading: A How-To Manual. LC 96-9173. 184p. 1996. pap. 16.50 (*0-8108-3213-5*) Scarecrow.

Myers, Marilyn. Economic Planning & Political Process Altering Urban Open Space: Selected References with a Case Study. (CPL Bibliographies Ser.: No. 56). 72p. 1981. 10.00 (*0-86602-056-X*, Sage Prdcls Pr) Sage.

Myers, Marilyn, jt. auth. see Myers, Richard.

***Myers, Martha A.** Race, Labor, & Punishment in the New South. LC 98-20124. (History of Crime & Criminal Justice Ser.). (Illus.). 335p. 1998. text 55.00 (*0-8142-0797-9*, MYERAC) Ohio St U Pr.

Myers, Martha A. Race, Labor & Punishment in the New South. LC 98-20124. (History of Crime & Criminal Justice Ser.). (Illus.). 464p. 1998. pap. text 24.95 (*0-8142-5001-7*, MYERAX) Ohio St U Pr.

Myers, Mary, jt. ed. see Heron, Alastair.

Myers, Mary D., jt. auth. see Fettus, Sharon H.

Myers, Mary L. French Architectural & Ornament Drawings of the Eighteenth Century. (Illus.). 256p. 1991. pap. 30.00 (*0-87099-626-6*) Metro Mus Art.

Myers, Mary R. Costly Pleasures. 416p. 1985. mass mkt. 3.95 (*0-345-31759-9*, Ballantine) Ballantine Pub Grp.

— Ice Hot. 1986. pap. write for info. (*0-345-32988-0*) Macmillan.

Myers, MaryAnn. Favored to Win. 460p. 2000. pap. 16.95 (*0-9668780-2-7*) Lighthouse Lit.

***Myers, MaryAnn.** Maple Dale, 1. LC 98-94135. 1999. pap. text 12.95 (*0-9668780-1-9*) Lighthouse Lit.

Myers, Maryanne. Random: The Nefarious Realm. 214p. 1999. pap. 14.95 (*0-7414-0065-0*) Buy Books.

Myers, Marye, ed. see Grieco, Joseph.

Myers, Max A. & LaChat, Michael R., eds. Studies in the Theological Ethics of Ernst Troeltsch. LC 90-33012. (Toronto Studies in Theology: Vol. 49). 264p. 1991. lib. bdg. 89.95 (*0-88946-923-7*) E Mellen.

Myers, Max H., ed. see American Joint Committee on Cancer.

Myers, Melinda. Bird-Lovers Garden. (Illus.). 128p. 2000. text 25.00 (*1-56799-727-9*, Friedman-Fairfax) M Friedman Pub Grp Inc.

— The Garden Book for Wisconsin. (Illus.). 446p. 1999. pap. 19.95 (*1-888608-53-6*) Cool Springs Pr.

***Myers, Melinda.** Month by Month Gardening in Wisconsin. (Illus.). 320p. 2000. pap. 18.95 (*1-888608-26-9*) Cool Springs Pr.

— My Wisconsin Garden: A Gardener's Journal. (Illus.). 128p. 2000. spiral bd. 19.95 (*1-930604-05-X*) Cool Springs Pr.

***Myers, Melody.** Stephen Crane: An Anthology in Memoriam (1871-1900) LC 00-190014. 80p. 2000. pap. 24.95 (*1-879183-43-9*) Bristol Banner.

Myers, Melody, ed. Elizabeth Drew Barstow Stoddard: An Anthology in Memoriam (1823-1902) LC 98-86961. 150p. 1998. pap. 15.95 (*1-879183-38-2*) Bristol Banner.

— Robert Charles Sands: An Anthology in Memoriam (1799-1832) LC 98-89628. 150p. 1999. pap. 15.95 (*1-879183-39-0*) Bristol Banner.

***Myers, Melody, ed.** Thomas MacKellar: An Anthology in Memoriam (1812-1899) LC 99-91039. 96p. 1999. pap. 24.95 (*1-879183-40-4*) Bristol Banner.

Myers, Melvin L., et al, eds. Papers & Proceedings of the Surgeon General's Conference on Agricultural Safety & Health. (Illus.). 645p. (Orig.). (C). 1994. pap. text 75.00 (*0-7881-1225-2*) DIANE Pub.

Myers, Michael. Fuer den Buerger: The Role of Christian Schubart's Deutsche Chronik in the Development of a Political Public Sphere. LC 89-37984. (German Life & Civilization Ser.: Vol. 6). VIII, 302p. (C). 1990. text 46.50 (*0-8204-1168-X*) P Lang Pubng.

***Myers, Michael & Meyers, Michael.** The A+ Certification Exam Guide. LC 98-7472. (Illus.). 600p. 1998. 54.99 incl. cd-rom (*0-07-913765-2*) McGraw.

Myers, Michael F. How's Your Marriage? A Book for Men & Women. 240p. 1998. 24.95 (*0-88048-695-3*, 8695) Am Psychiatric.

— Men & Divorce. LC 88-35101. 286p. 1989. lib. bdg. 35.00 (*0-89862-386-3*) Guilford Pubns.

Myers, Michael J. & Murtaugh, Michael P., eds. Cytokines in Animal Health & Disease. LC 95-13663. (Illus.). 480p. 1995. text 199.00 (*0-8247-9435-4*) Dekker.

Myers, Michael R. It's Time to Remember America! Connecting the Past with the Present. 225p. 1999. pap. 10.99 (*0-88965-149-3*, Pub. by Horizon Books) Chr Pubns.

Myers, Michael W. Let the Cow Wander: Modeling the Metaphors in Veda & Vedanta. LC 95-16070. (Monographs of the Society for Asian & Comparative Philosophy: No. 14). 144p. 1995. pap. text 12.00 (*0-8248-1753-2*) UH Pr.

Myers, Michele T., jt. auth. see Myers, Gail E.

Myers, Mildred D. Miss Emily: Emily Howland, Teacher of Freed Slaves, Suffragist & Friend of Susan B. Anthony & Harriet Tubman. LC 98-60582. (Illus.). 240p. 1998. pap. 12.95 (*1-881539-20-2*) Tabby Hse Bks.

Myers, Mildred S. Writing Skills for Bankers. (Illus.). 1992. student ed. 49.00 (*0-685-62688-1*) Am Bankers.

Myers, Miles. Changing Our Minds: Negotiating English & Literacy. LC 95-35855. 357p. 1995. pap. 28.95 (*0-8141-3304-5*) NCTE.

Myers, Miles & Spalding, Elizabeth, eds. Assessing Student Performance. LC 96-47771. (Standards Exemplar Ser.). 134p. (J). (gr. k-5). 1997. 15.95 (*0-8141-4698-8*) NCTE.

— Assessing Student Performance. LC 96-47771. (Standards Exemplar Ser.). (Illus.). 115p. (YA). (gr. 6-8). 1997. 15.95 (*0-8141-4700-3*) NCTE.

— Assessing Student Performance: Grades 9-12. LC 96-47771. (Standards Exemplar Ser.). 117p. (YA). (gr. 9-12). 1997. 15.95 (*0-8141-4701-1*) NCTE.

Myers, Milton L. The Soul of Modern Economic Man: Ideas of Self-Interest, Thomas Hobbes to Adam Smith. LC 82-23790. 160p. 1983. lib. bdg. 17.50 (*0-226-55448-1*) U Ch Pr.

— The Soul of Modern Economic Man: Ideas of Self-Interest, Thomas Hobbes to Adam Smith. LC 82-23790. 160p. 1992. pap. text 7.95 (*0-226-55450-3*) U Ch Pr.

Myers, Minor, jt. auth. see Thackray, Arnold W.

Myers, Minor, jt. auth. see Thorp, Willard.

Myers, Mitzi & Knoepflmacher, U. C., eds. Children's Literature No. 25: Special Issue on Cross Writing Child & Adult. (Illus.). 288p. 1997. 50.00 (*0-300-07000-4*); pap. 18.00 (*0-300-07001-2*) Yale U Pr.

Myers-Moro, Pamela. Thai Music & Musicians in Contemporary Bangkok. LC 93-32327. (Center for Southeast Asia Studies: No. 34). 271p. 1993. pap. text 22.50 (*0-944613-20-9*) UC Berkeley Ctrs SE Asia.

Myers, N., ed. Tropical Forests & Climate. 272p. (C). 1992. text 179.50 (*0-7923-1688-6*) Kluwer Academic.

Myers, N. A. & Angerpointner, T. A., eds. Paediatric Thoracic Surgery. (Progress in Pediatric Surgery Ser.: Vol. 27). (Illus.). 272p. 1991. 185.00 (*0-387-52525-4*) Spr-Verlag.

Myers, Nancy. Mathematics for Electronics. Pullins, ed. LC 92-25704. 450p. (C). 1993. mass mkt. 37.25 (*0-314-01266-4*) West Pub.

Myers, Nancy, intro. Evelyn Madsen Miles: a Teacher's Perspective of Austin, Nevada: 1932-1936. (Illus.). 86p. 1983. lib. bdg. 34.50 (*1-56475-232-1*); fiche. write for info. (*1-56475-233-X*) U NV Oral Hist.

Myers, Nancy C. Nancy Landon Kassebaum: A Senate Profile. LC 97-47240. (Contemporary Profiles & Policy Series for the Younger Reader). 70p. (YA). (gr. 8 up). 1998. 20.00 (*0-934272-47-6*); pap. 12.95 (*0-934272-46-8*) J G Burke Pub.

Myers, Nancy J., jt. ed. see Lopez, George A.

Myers, Nathan. Crafting C++ Libraries. (C). Date not set. pap. 44.95 (*0-201-32568-3*) Addison-Wesley.

Myers, Neil. All That, So Simple. LC 78-71637. 72p. 1980. pap. 12.95 (*0-911198-56-3*) Purdue U Pr.

— The Blade of Manjusri. 64p. 1989. pap. 15.00 (*0-9620634-1-X*) Sun Moon Bear Pr.

— The Blade of Manjusri. deluxe limited ed. 64p. 1989. 40.00 (*0-9620634-2-8*) Sun Moon Bear Pr.

Myers, Nicholas G. My Memoirs of World War Two. Harris, Paul N., ed. (Illus.). 144p. (Orig.). 1988. pap. 8.95 (*0-915180-31-6*) Harrowood Bks.

Myers, Norma. Reconstructing the Past: Blacks in Britain, c. 1780-1830. LC 96-6900. (Slave & Post-Slave Societies & Cultures Ser.). 200p. 1996. 49.50 (*0-7146-4575-3*, Pub. by F Cass Pubs); pap. 22.50 (*0-7146-4130-8*, Pub. by F Cass Pubs) Intl Spec Bk.

Myers, Norma & Scobey, Joan. Gifts from the Kitchen. LC 79-8914. 320p. 1980. reprint ed. pap. 9.95 (*0-672-52631-X*, Bobbs) Macmillan.

Myers, Norman. Not Far Afield: U. S. Interests & the Global Environment. LC 87-50723. 84p. 1987. pap. text 10.00 (*0-915825-24-4*) World Resources Inst.

— Population, Resources & Environment: The Critical Challenges. 154p. 1991. pap. 24.75 (*0-89714-101-6*, E.91.III.I.1) UN.

— The Primary Source: Tropical Forests & Our Future. 2nd ed. (Illus.). 448p. 1992. pap. 12.95 (*0-393-30828-6*) Norton.

— The Sinking Ark: A New Look at the Problem of Disappearing Species. LC 79-40232. 1979. 145.00 (*0-08-024501-3*, Pub. by Pergamon Repr) Franklin.

— Ultimate Security: The Environmental Basis of Political Instability. 319p. (C). 1996. reprint ed. pap. 17.95 (*1-55963-499-5*) Island Pr.

An Asterisk (*) at the beginning of an entry indicates that the title is appearing for the first time.

M

Myers, Norman, ed. Gaia, an Atlas of Planet Management. rev. ed. LC 92-18126. 256p. 1992. pap. 23.00 (*0-385-42626-7*) Doubleday.

Myers, Norman, ed. The Gaia Atlas of Planet Management. 288p. 1994. pap. 16.99 (*1-85675-061-2*, Pub. by Oxfam Pub) Stylus Pub VA.

Myers, Norman, ed. Rainforests. LC 92-46131. (Illustrated Library of the Earth Ser.). 1994. 35.00 (*0-87596-597-0*) Rodale Pr Inc.

Myers, Norman & Kent, Jennifer. Environmental Exodus: An Emergent Crisis in the Global Arena. (Illus.). 214p. (Orig.). 1995. pap. 18.00 (*0-9623610-2-X*) Climate Inst.

***Myers, Norman & Kent, Jennifer.** Perverse Subsidies: How Misused Tax Dollars Harm the Environment & the Economy. (Illus.). 240p. 2000. 40.00 (*1-55963-834-6*, Shearwater Bks); pap. 20.00 (*1-55963-835-4*, Shearwater Bks) Island Pr.

Myers, Patricia, jt. ed. see Cleaver, Richard.

Myers, Patricia, ed. see Marenzio, Luca.

Myers, Patricia A. A Glossary for Radiologic Technologists. LC 80-20917. 194p. 1981. 59.95 (*0-275-91351-1*, C1351, Praeger Pubs) Greenwood.

Myers, Patricia I. & Hammill, Donald D. Learning Disabilities: Basic Concepts, Assessment Practices, & Instructional Strategies. 4th ed. LC 89-29044. (Illus.). 593p. (Orig.). 1990. text 43.00 (*0-89079-225-9*, 1499) PRO-ED.

Myers, Patrick R. Succession Between International Organizations. LC 92-2353. (Publication of the Graduate Institute of International Studies, Geneva). 200p. 1993. 89.95 (*0-7103-0457-9*, B0088) Routledge.

Myers, Patty Barthell. Cargill/Cargile/Cargal of the South & Southwest: Descendants of Cornelius Cargill of Virginia, John Cargile of Virginia & North Carolina, John Cargile of Virginia & Georgia, Andrew J. & John Cargal of South Carolina & Georgia. LC 97-65627. (Illus.). write for info. (*0-89725-296-9*, Penobscot Pr) Picton Pr.

Myers, Paul. Leonard Bernstein. LC 99-182081. (Twentieth Century Composers Ser.). (Illus.). 240p. 1998. pap. 19.95 (*0-7148-3701-6*, Pub. by Phaidon Press) Phaidon Pr.

Myers, Paul, jt. auth. see Ross, Jim.

Myers, Paul, jt. ed. see Ross, Jim.

Myers, Paul S. Knowledge Management & Organizational Design. LC 96-1840. (Resources for the Knowledge-Based Economy Ser.). 224p. 1996. pap. 21.95 (*0-7506-9749-0*) Buttrwrth-Heinemann.

Myers, Paul W. Lawrence County, PA Soldiers. 91p. 1988. pap. text 9.00 (*0-933227-86-8*, 314) Closson Pr.
— Mercer County, PA Soldiers. 78p. 1988. pap. text 8.50 (*0-933227-84-1*, 315) Closson Pr.
— Pennsylvania Soldiers of the Revolutionary War. 30p. 1987. per. 5.00 (*0-933227-64-7*, 485) Closson Pr.
— Revolutionary War Veterans Who Settled in Butler County, Pennsylvania. 30p. 1987. per. 5.00 (*0-933227-69-8*, 206) Closson Pr.
— Venango County, PA Soldiers. 73p. 1988. pap. text 8.50 (*0-933227-83-3*, 317) Closson Pr.
— Washington County Frontier Rangers. 1988. pap. text 7.00 (*0-933227-85-X*, 318) Closson Pr.
— Westmoreland County, PA in the American Revolution. 263p. 1989. per. 24.00 (*1-55856-001-7*, 515) Closson Pr.

Myers-Pelton, Lois, jt. auth. see Pelton, Charles L.

Myers, Penelope S. Right Hemisphere Damage: Disorders of Communication & Cognition. LC 98-22184. (Illus.). 360p. 1998. pap. 62.95 (*1-56593-224-2*, 0584) Thomson Learn.

***Myers, Pennie & Nance, Don W.** Bouncing Back: Increasing Your Personal & Professional Resiliency: An Independent Study Course for Health Care Professionals. 71p. 1999. 40.00 (*0-9620723-9-7*) MAS.

Myers, Pennie & Nance, Don W. Making the Connection: Keys to Quality Customer Service in Health Care. 60p. 1997. spiral bd., wbk. ed. 29.00 (*0-9620723-7-0*) MAS.
— Tactful Toughness Workbook. 1994. spiral bd. 25.00 (*0-9620723-5-4*) MAS.
— Taking Care of Residents: A Customer Service Approach. 60p. 1997. reprint ed. spiral bd., wbk. ed. 29.00 (*0-9620723-6-2*) MAS.
— The Upset Book: A Guide for Dealing with Upset People. (Illus.). 222p. (Orig.). 1986. pap. 8.95 (*0-937647-01-2*) Academic Pubns.
— The Upset Book: How to Deal with Upset People. rev. ed. 218p. (Orig.). 1991. pap. 12.95 (*0-9620723-4-6*) MAS.
— The Upset Workbook: Client Service Edition for Insurance Companies & Agencies. 118p. 1989. student ed. 59.00 (*0-9620723-1-1*) MAS.
— The Upset Workbook: Health Care Edition. 118p. 1989. 59.00 (*0-9620723-2-X*) MAS.
— The Upset Workbook: Insurance Claims Edition. 132p. (Orig.). 1988. student ed. 59.00 (*0-9620723-0-3*) MAS.
— The Upset Workbook: Patient Representative Edition. 130p. 1990. 59.00 (*0-9620723-3-8*) MAS.

Myers, Pennie & Nance, Dori W. Tactful Toughness: An Independent Study Course for Court Clerks. 37p. 1998. spiral bd., wbk. ed. 25.00 (*0-9620723-8-9*) MAS.

Myers, Peter B., jt. auth. see Myers, Isabel B.

Myers, Peter C. The ADA & You: A Guide for Deaf & Hard of Hearing People. (Illus.). viii, 69p. 1992. pap. 19.00 (*1-893891-01-1*) Gallaudet U Contin Ed.
— Our Only Star & Compass: Locke & the Struggle for Political Rationality. LC 98-36862. 288p. 1998. 23.95 (*0-8476-9099-7*); pap. 63.00 (*0-8476-9098-9*) Rowman.

***Myers, Peter J.** United States History LC 99-189509. (Fearon Foundations Ser.). 746 p. 1999. write for info. (*0-8359-2258-8*) Globe Fearon.

***Myers, Peter L. & Salt, Norman L.** Addiction Counselors Training & Development. (Illus.). 320p. (C). 1999. text 35.00 (*0-7637-0795-3*) Jones & Bartlett.

***Myers, Philip.** Aboveground Storage Tank Inspection Guide. (Professional Engineering Ser.). (Illus.). 640p. 2000. 89.95 (*0-07-135726-2*) McGraw-Hill Prof.

Myers, Philip. Patterns of Reproduction of 4 Species of Vespertilionid Bats in Paraguay. LC 76-3878. (University of California Publications in Social Welfare: No. 107). (Illus.). 71p. reprint ed. pap. 30.00 (*0-608-18308-3*, 203157800075) Bks Demand.

Myers, Philip E. Aboveground Storage Tanks. LC 96-51117. 690p. 1997. 94.95 (*0-07-044272-X*) McGraw.

Myers-Phinney, Linda, jt. auth. see Morrow, Lynn.

Myers, Phyllis, jt. auth. see Gruber, Samuel.

Myers, Poochie. Knit Like Crazy. 62p. 1993. student ed. 19.95 (*1-881571-04-1*) Letters Etcetera.

Myers, R. B. & Cantino, E. C. The Gamma Particle: A Study of Cell-Organelle Interactions in the Development of the Water Mold Blastocladiella Emersonii. (Monographs in Developmental Biology: Vol. 8). 150p. 1974. 58.50 (*3-8055-1735-1*) S Karger.

Myers, R. C., jt. ed. see Burgess, C. P.

Myers, R. David, intro. Toward a History of the New Left: Essays from Within the Movement. LC 89-25472. 210p. 1989. 50.00 (*0-926019-23-6*) Carlson Pub.

Myers, R. E. Character Matters. (Illus.). 144p. 1999. pap. text 12.95 (*0-673-58644-8*) Addson-Wesley Educ.
— Cognitive Connections: Multiple Ways of Thinking with Math, Grades 4-8. (Illus.). 176p. 1996. pap., teacher ed. 32.00 (*1-56976-035-7*) Zephyr Pr AZ.

Myers, R. E. & Torrance, E. P. Wondering: Invitations to Think about the Future for Primary Grades. (Orig.). 1984. pap. 14.95 (*0-936386-22-3*) Creative Learning.

Myers, R. H., Tenants, jt. auth. see Menorah Park Center for the Aging Residents Staff.

Myers, Ralph G. Mabuhay: Sentimental Journey World War II Experience. (Illus.). 62p. (Orig.). (C). 1989. pap. 7.95 (*0-962557l-0-2*) R E Myers.

Myers, Ramon H. China's Economic Revolution & It's Implications for Sino-U. S. Relations. LC 95-44401. (Essays in Public Policy Ser.: No. 63). 1995. pap. 5.00 (*0-8179-5682-4*) Hoover Inst Pr.
— The Chinese Peasant Economy: Agricultural Development in Hopei & Shantung, 1890-1949. LC 79-115189. (Harvard East Asian Ser.: No. 47). 410p. reprint ed. pap. 127.10 (*0-608-10275-X*, 200549800054) Bks Demand.
— Thoughts on U. S. Foreign Policy Toward the People's Republic of China. LC 94-5583. (Essays in Public Policy Ser.: No. 47). 1994. pap. text 5.00 (*0-8179-5522-4*) Hoover Inst Pr.

Myers, Ramon H., ed. Last Chance in Manchuria: The Diary of Chang Kia-ngau. Zen, Dolores, tr. (Publication Series: Archival Documentaries: No. 379). 350p. 1989. text 36.95 (*0-8179-8791-6*) Hoover Inst Pr.
— Two Societies in Opposition: The Republic of China & the People's Republic of China after Forty Years. (Publication Ser.: No. 401). 370p. (C). 1991. text 38.95 (*0-8179-9091-7*); pap. text 25.95 (*0-8179-9092-5*) Hoover Inst Pr.

Myers, Ramon H., ed. A Unique Relationship: The United & the Republic of China under the Taiwan Relations Act. (Publication Ser.: No. 387). 370p. 1989. 25.95 (*0-8179-8871-8*); pap. 15.95 (*0-8179-8872-6*) Hoover Inst Pr.

Myers, Ramon H., ed. The Wealth of Nations in the Twentieth Century: The Policies & Institutional Determinants of Economic Development. LC 96-35432. (Publication Ser.: No. 437). 1996. pap. 24.95 (*0-8179-9452-1*) Hoover Inst Pr.

Myers, Ramon H. & Metzger, Thomas A., eds. Greater China & U.S. Foreign Policy: The Choice Between Confrontation & Mutual Respect. (Publication Ser.: No. 433). 130p. 1996. pap. 16.95 (*0-8179-9412-2*) Hoover Inst Pr.

Myers, Ramon H. & Peattie, Mark R., eds. The Japanese Colonial Empire, 1895-1945. LC 83-42571. (Illus.). 560p. 1983. pap. text 26.95 (*0-691-10222-8*, Pub. by Princeton U Pr) Cal Prin Full Svc.

Myers, Ramon H., jt. auth. see Chao, Linda.

Myers, Ramon H., jt. auth. see Kuo, Tai-chun.

Myers, Ramon H., jt. ed. see Chang, Sidney H.

Myers, Ramon H., jt. ed. see Hollerman, Leon.

Myers, Ramon H., jt. ed. see Mo, Jongryn.

Myers, Raquelle. The Significant Ties Exception to the Indian Child Welfare Act: Judicial Decision-Making or Incorporating Bias into Law? Thorington, Nancy & Myers, Joseph, eds. (Illus.). 46p. 1998. pap. 10.00 (*1-893299-00-7*) Natl Indian Just.

Myers, Rawley. Daily Reflections with Jesus. (Illus.). 96p. (Orig.). 1995. pap. 3.95 (*0-89942-734-0*, 740/04) Catholic Bk Pub.
— Daily Reflections with the Saints. (Illus.). 1986. pap. 3.95 (*0-89942-880-0*, 880/04) Catholic Bk Pub.
— Embraced by Mary: Marian Devotions & Prayers Throughout the Year. LC 96-70436. 224p. 1997. pap. 9.95 (*0-87973-604-6*) Our Sunday Visitor.
— The Saints Show Us Christ: Daily Readings on the Spiritual Life. LC 95-75665. 364p. (Orig.). 1996. pap. 14.95 (*0-89870-542-8*) Ignatius Pr.

Myers, Rawley, ed. Daily Reflections with Mary. (Illus.). 95p. 1988. pap. 3.95 (*0-89942-372-8*, 372-04) Catholic Bk Pub.

Myers, Raymond E. The Zollie Tree: General Felix K. Zollicoffer & the Battle of Mill Springs. rev. ed. LC 97-6054. (Filson Club Publications, Second Ser.: No. 2). (Illus.). 200p. 1998. reprint ed. 29.95 (*0-9601072-6-6*) Filson Club.

Myers, Raymond H. & Milton, J. Susan. A First Course in the Theory of Linear Statistical Models. 352p. (C). 1991. text 72.95 (*0-534-91645-7*) Wadsworth Pub.

Myers, Raymond H. & Montgomery, Douglas C. Response Surface Methodology: Process & Product Optimization Using Designed Experiments. LC 94-45548. (Series in Probability & Mathematical Statistics). 728p. 1995. 89.95 (*0-471-58100-3*) Wiley.

Myers, Raymond R. & Long, J. S., eds. Characterization of Coatings Pt. 1: Physical Techniques. LC TP0156.. (Treatise on Coatings Ser.: No. 2). 680p. reprint ed. pap. 200.00 (*0-608-30337-2*, 205532100017) Bks Demand.
— Characterization of Coatings Pt. 2: Physical Techniques. LC 67-21701. (Treatise on Coatings Ser.: No. 2). (Illus.). 677p. reprint ed. pap. 200.00 (*0-7837-4303-3*, 204399400002) Bks Demand.
— Film Forming Compositions, Pt. 2. LC 67-21701. (Treatise on Coatings Ser.: Vol. 1). 446p. pap. 138.30 (*0-7837-0016-4*, 202709700002) Bks Demand.
— Film Forming Compositions Pt. 3. LC 67-21701. (Treatise on Coatings Ser.: No. 1). 606p. reprint ed. pap. 187.90 (*0-608-16928-5*, 202709700003) Bks Demand.
— Formulations, Pt. 1. LC 67-21701. (Treatise on Coatings Ser.: No. 4). (Illus.). 607p. reprint ed. pap. 188.20 (*0-8357-6119-3*, 203455400001) Bks Demand.
— Pigments, Pt. 1. LC 67-21701. (Treatise on Coatings Ser.: No. 3). (Illus.). 590p. reprint ed. pap. 182.90 (*0-7837-0885-8*, 204119100001) Bks Demand.
— Treatise on Coatings, Vol. 2, Part 1. LC 67-21701. reprint ed. pap. 160.00 (*0-608-16884-X*, 2026411) Bks Demand.

Myers, Renee, ed. see Myers, Terry.

Myers, Rex C. & Ashby, Norma B. Symbols of Montana. (Illus.). 32p. (Orig.). 1989. reprint ed. pap. 5.00 (*0-917298-26-8*, 4537) MT Hist Soc.

Myers, Reyburn W., jt. auth. see Marcum, Richard.

Myers, Reyburn W., jt. auth. see Wills, Donald H.

Myers, Richard. William Morris Tiles. (Illus.). 152p. 1996. 80.00 (*0-903685-43-4*, Pub. by R Dennis) Antique Collect.

Myers, Richard & Myers, Marilyn. Best Guide to Florida Golf. 2nd ed. 150p. 1993. pap. 14.95 (*0-9631786-1-X*) SwainMyer Pubn.

Myers, Richard, jt. auth. see Benjamin, Hugh.

Myers, Richard, jt. auth. see Malcolmson, Patrick.

Myers, Richard, jt. auth. see Yorgason, Brenton G.

Myers, Richard B. The Best of the Peter Island Morning Sun: Excerpts from Peter Island Resort's Daily Newspaper. LC 94-37959. 128p. (Orig.). 1995. pap. 12.95 (*0-9639905-2-7*) Two Thous-Three Assocs.
— Tennis for Humans: A Simple Blueprint for Winning. LC 96-54275. 128p. (Orig.). 1997. pap. 13.95 (*0-9639905-8-6*) Two Thous-Three Assocs.
— Visiting the Virgin Islands with the Kids: A Complete Guide to Enjoyable Travel with Kids in the British & U. S. Virgin Islands. LC 96-2165. (Illus.). 128p. (Orig.). 1996. pap. 13.95 (*0-9639905-6-X*) Two Thous-Three Assocs.

Myers, Richard B., jt. auth. see Acheson, Pamela.

Myers, Richard D., ed. The Cowboy Humor of Alfred Henry Lewis. 350p. 1987. pap. 9.95 (*0-942936-12-4*) Lincoln-Herndon Pr.

Myers, Richard L. Immunology. 3rd ed. 1999. pap. text, lab manual ed. 24.00 (*0-697-28600-2*) McGraw.
— Immunology: A Laboratory Manual. 2nd ed. 128p. (C). 1994. text. write for info. (*0-697-11313-2*, WCB McGr Hill) McGrw-H Hghr Educ.

Myers, Richmond E. Northampton County in the American Revolution. (Publications of the Northampton County Historical & Genealogical Society: No. 6). (Illus.). vi, 90p. 1976. 10.00 (*1-877701-12-2*) NCH&GS.

Myers, Robert. Indexation of Pension & Other Benefits. (C). 1978. 12.50 (*0-256-02118-X*, Irwn McGrw-H) McGrw-H Hghr Educ.
— The Professional Wrestling Trivia Book. 2nd ed. Caso, Adolph, ed. LC 99-12748. (Illus.). 140p. 1999. pap. 9.95 (*0-8283-2045-4*) Branden Bks.
— Solstice Points. 1988. pap. write for info. (*0-87500-022-3*) RKM Pub Co.
— Take It to Heart: Your Complete Guide to Preventing & Treating Heart Disease. (Illus.). 160p. 1997. pap. 16.95 (*1-55022-339-9*, Pub. by ECW) Genl Dist Srvs.
— The Twelve Who Survive: Strengthening Programmes of Early Childhood Development in the Third World. 2nd ed. LC 95-31582. 496p. 1995. 14.95 (*0-929816-99-4*, R1055) High-Scope.

Myers, Robert, jt. auth. see Lieske, Ewald.

Myers, Robert, ed. see Coryell, Janet.

Myers, Robert A. Dominica. LC 88-150889. (World Bibliographical Ser.: No. 82). 218p. 1987. lib. bdg. 55.00 (*1-85109-031-2*) ABC-CLIO.
— Ghana. LC 92-146703. (World Bibliographical Ser.). 466p. 1991. lib. bdg. 108.50 (*1-85109-135-1*) ABC-CLIO.

Myers, Robert A., ed. Nigeria. (World Bibliographical Ser.: No. 100). (Illus.). 496p. 1989. lib. bdg. 80.00 (*1-85109-083-5*, Pub. by Clio Pr) ABC-CLIO.

Myers, Robert C. Historical Sketches of Berrien County. House, Jan H., ed. (Illus.). 71p. 1988. pap. 7.95 (*0-9660808-1-5*) Berrien Cnty.
— Historical Sketches of Berrien County, Vol. 2. House, Jan H., ed. (Illus.). 74p. 1989. pap. 7.95 (*0-9660808-2-3*) Berrien Cnty.

***Myers, Robert C.** Millennial Visions & Earthly Pursuits: The Israelite House of David. LC 99-492276. (Illus.). 31p. 1999. pap. 8.95 (*0-9660808-9-0*) Berrien Cnty.

Myers, Robert E. The Intersection of Science Fiction & Philosophy: Critical Studies, 4. LC 82-25162. (Contributions to the Study of Science Fiction & Fantasy Ser.: No. 4). (Illus.). 262p. 1983. 55.00 (*0-313-22493-5*, MYS/, Greenwood Pr) Greenwood.
— Mind Sparklers Bk. 1: Fireworks for Igniting Creativity in Young Minds. (Illus.). 94p. 1997. pap. 17.95 (*1-882664-32-9*) Prufrock Pr.
— Mind Sparklers Bk. 2: Fireworks for Igniting Creativity in Young Minds. (Illus.). 1998. pap. 17.95 (*1-882664-33-7*) Prufrock Pr.

Myers, Robert E. & Torrance, E. Paul. What Next? Futuristic Scenarios for Creative Problem Solving. LC 94-3990. 1994. 29.00 (*1-56976-001-2*) Zephyr Pr AZ.

Myers, Robert F. Micronesian Reef Fishes: A Practical Guide to the Identification of the Coral Reef Fishes of the Tropical Central & Western Pacific. (Illus.). iv, 288p. 1989. text 49.95 (*0-9621564-1-8*); pap. text 35.95 (*0-9621564-0-X*) Coral Graphics.
— Micronesian Reef Fishes: A Practical Guide to the Identification of the Coral Reef Fishes of the Tropical Central & Western Pacific. 2nd ed. (Illus.). 442p. 1991. 46.00 (*0-9621564-3-4*); pap. 33.50 (*0-9621564-2-6*) Coral Graphics.

***Myers, Robert H.** Self-governance & Cooperation. LC 99-12991. 192p. 2000. text 45.00 (*0-19-823839-8*) OUP.

Myers, Robert J. 100 Most Asked Questions about Your Social Security Benefits. Todd, Victor, ed. LC 94-67720. 136p. 1994. pap. 2.95 (*0-9648635-1-0*) Srs Coalition.
— Social Security. 4th ed. LC 92-30848. (Pension Research Council Publications). (Illus.). 968p. (C). 1993. text 62.95 (*0-8122-3191-0*) U of Pa Pr.
— Speaking Truth to Power. (Eleventh Morgenthau Memorial Lectures). 23p. 1991. pap. 4.00 (*0-87641-116-2*) Carnegie Ethics & Intl Affairs.

***Myers, Robert J.** U. S. Foreign Policy in the Twenty-First Century: The Relevance of Realism. LC 98-50300. (Political Traditions in Foreign Policy Ser.). 184p. 1999. 24.95 (*0-8071-2345-5*) La State U Pr.

Myers, Robert J., ed. Religion & the State: The Struggle for Legitimacy & Power. LC 85-72100. (Annals of the American Academy of Political & Social Science Ser.: Vol. 483). 1986. text 26.00 (*0-8039-2538-7*); pap. text 17.00 (*0-8039-2539-5*) Sage.

Myers, Robert J., et al. 1995 Mercer Guide to Social Security & Medicare Special Edition. 23rd rev. ed. (Illus.). 184p. 1995. pap. 7.95 (*1-880754-95-9*) W M Mercer.

Myers, Robert J., jt. auth. see Detlefs, Dale.

Myers, Robert J., jt. ed. see Sung-joo, Han.

Myers, Robert J., jt. ed. see Thompson, Kenneth.

Myers, Robert M. The Children of Pride: Selected Letter of the Family of the Rev. Dr. Charles Colcock Jones 1860-1868 with the Addition of Several Presviously Unpublished Letters. LC 83-10377. 688p. 1987. reprint ed. pap. 22.00 (*0-300-04053-9*, Y-675) Yale U Pr.
— From Beowulf to Virginia Woolf: An Astounding & Wholly Unauthorized History of English Literature. 2nd ed. LC 84-5974. (Illus.). 112p. 1984. pap. 7.95 (*0-252-01150-3*) U of Ill Pr.
— Handel's Messiah, a Touchstone of Taste: Music Book Index. 338p. 1993. reprint ed. lib. bdg. 89.00 (*0-7812-9600-5*) Rprt Serv.
— Quintet: A Five-Play Cycle Drawn from The Children of Pride. 256p. 1991. text 29.95 (*0-252-01751-X*) U of Ill Pr.
— Reluctant Expatriate: The Life of Harold Frederic, 59. LC 94-39267. (Contributions to the Study of World Literature Ser.: Vol. 59). 224p. 1995. 55.00 (*0-313-29256-6*, Greenwood Pr) Greenwood.

Myers, Robin. A Dictionary of Literature in the English Language, 2 vols. LC 68-18529. 1978. 670.00 (*0-08-016143-X*, Pub. by Pergamon Repr); 906.00 (*0-08-023684-7*, Pub. by Pergamon Repr) Franklin.

Myers, Robin & Harris, M. Antiquaries, Book Collectors & the Circles of Learning. LC 96-2914. (Publishing Pathways Ser.). 1996. 39.95 (*1-884718-24-8*) Oak Knoll.
— Fakes & Frauds: Varieties of Deception in Print & Manuscript. LC 96-43066. 1996. 35.00 (*1-884718-31-0*) Oak Knoll.

Myers, Robin & Harris, Michael, eds. Aspects of Printing from 1600. (Illus.). 186p. 1987. 28.00 (*0-902692-36-4*) Oak Knoll.
— Censorship & the Control of Print in England & France, 1600-1910. 154p. 1992. 30.00 (*1-873040-16-4*) Oak Knoll.
— Maps & Prints: Aspects of the English Booktrade. (Publishing History Occasional Ser.). (Illus.). 130p. 1984. pap. write for info. (*0-902692-33-X*) Chadwyck-Healey.
— Medicine, Mortality & the Book Trade. LC 99-47430. (Publishing Pathways Ser.). 170p. 1998. 39.95 (*1-884718-81-7*, No. 53864RB) Oak Knoll.
— A Millennium of the Book: Production, Design & Illustration in Manuscript & Print 900-1900. LC 94-30712. (Publishing Pathways Ser.: No. 8). (Illus.). 192p. 1995. 30.00 (*1-884718-07-8*) Oak Knoll.
— Pioneers in Bibliography. LC 96-43082. 117p. 1996. 30.00 (*1-884718-30-2*) Oak Knoll.
— Serials & Their Readers, 1620-1914. 192p. 1993. 30.00 (*0-938768-48-4*) Oak Knoll.
— Spreading the Word: Distribution Networks of Print 1550-1850. 254p. 1990. 30.00 (*0-906795-87-7*) Oak Knoll.
— Stationers' Company & the Book Trade, 1550-1990. LC 97-40367. 234p. 1997. 39.95 (*1-884718-45-0*, 50315) Oak Knoll.
— Stationers' Company Archive: An Account of the Records, 1554-1984. 413p. 1990. 60.00 (*0-906795-71-0*) Oak Knoll.

***Myers, Robin & Harris, Michael.** Journeys Through the Market: Travel, Travellers & the Book Trade. (Publishing Pathways Ser.). 164p. 2000. 39.95 (*1-58456-014-2*) Oak Knoll.

Myers, Roger, compiled by. Guide to Archival Materials of the Center for Creative Photography. 136p. 25.00 (*0-938262-13-0*) Ctr Creat Photog.

Myers, Rollie J., jt. auth. see Mahan, Bruce M.

An Asterisk (*) at the beginning of an entry indicates that the title is appearing for the first time.

Myers, Rollo H. Debussy: Music Book Index. 125p. 1993. reprint ed. lib. bdg. 89.00 (*0-7812-9592-0*) Rprt Serv.
— Erik Satie. (Orig.). 1988. reprint ed. lib. bdg. 75.00 (*0-7812-0772-X*) Rprt Serv.
— Erik Satie. LC 73-181217. 150p. (Orig.). 1948. reprint ed. 59.00 (*0-403-01628-2*) Scholarly.
— Music in the Modern World; Music Book Index. 211p. 1993. reprint ed. lib. bdg. 79.00 (*0-7812-9576-9*) Rprt Serv.
— Ravel: His Life & Works. LC 73-2340. (Illus.). 239p. 1973. reprint ed. lib. bdg. 65.00 (*0-8371-6841-4*, MYRA, Greenwood Pr) Greenwood.
Myers, Rollo H., ed. Strauss-Rolland Correspondence. 1987. pap. 11.95 (*0-7145-0503-X*) Riverrun NY.
Myers, Ronald L. & Ewel, John J., eds. Ecosystems of Florida. 765p. (C). 1990. 49.95 (*0-8130-1012-8*); pap. 34.95 (*0-8130-1022-5*) U Press Fla.
Myers, Rose S. Saunders Manual of Physical Therapy Practice. LC 94-452. (Illus.). 1072p. 1995. text 87.00 (*0-7216-3671-3*, W B Saunders Co) Harcrt Hlth Sci Grp.
Myers, Roy E. Microcomputer Graphics. (Illus.). 304p. 1984. pap. text. write for info. (*0-318-56714-8*) Addison-Wesley.
— Microcomputer Graphics for the IBM PC. 1438p. 1984. pap. 14.95 (*0-201-05158-3*); Apple II. write for info. (*0-201-05312-8*) Addison-Wesley.
Myers, Roy E., jt. auth. see Finley, Clarence W., Jr.
Myers, Roy J. & Myers, Stephanie E. The Rescue of Robby Robo. LC 93-79744. (The Robby Robo Ser.: No. 1). (Illus.). 20p. (Orig.). (J). (gr. k-6). 1995. pap. write for info. (*1-884108-00-8*) R J Myers Pub.
***Myers, Ruth.** The Perfect Love: Intensely Personal, Overflowing, & Never Ending... 320p. 1999. pap. 12.95 (*1-57856-255-4*) Waterbrook Pr.
— The Perfect Love: Intensely Personal, Overflowing, Never Ending... LC 98-229107. 320p. 1998. 19.95 (*1-57856-002-0*); pap., student ed. 6.95 (*1-57856-083-7*) Waterbrook Pr.
— The Satisfied Heart: 31 Days of Experiencing God's Love. 128p. 1999. 12.95 (*1-57856-278-3*) Waterbrook Pr.
Myers, Ruth. 31 Days of Praise: Enjoying God Anew. 160p. 1998. 9.99 (*1-57673-334-3*) Multnomah Pubs.
***Myers, S.** EPAC 98: 6th European Particle Accelerator Conference; Stockholm, 22-26 June 1998. 1998. write for info. (*0-7503-0600-9*); write for info. (*0-7503-0601-7*) IOP Pub.
Myers, S. Fifth European Particle Accelerator Conference: Sitges, Barcelona, 10 to 14 June, 1996. LC 96-48490. 1996. write for info. (*0-7503-0387-5*) Institute of Personal Magnetism.
— Myers' History of West Virginia, 2 vols., Set. 1993. reprint ed. lib. bdg. 105.00 (*0-8328-3087-9*) Higginson Bk Co.
Myers, S., jt. auth. see European Particle Accelerator Conference Staff.
Myers, S., jt. auth. see European Particle Accelerator Staff.
Myers, Samuel L., Sr., ed. Desegregation in Higher Education. LC 88-39407. (Illus.). 98p. (Orig.). (C). 1989. pap. text 13.50 (*0-8191-7291-X*) U Pr of Amer.
Myers, Samuel L., Jr. & Simms, Margaret C., eds. The Economics of Race & Crime. 220p. (Orig.). 1988. pap. 21.95 (*0-88738-755-1*) Transaction Pubs.
Myers, Samuel L., Jr., jt. auth. see Darity, William A., Jr.
Myers, Samuel L., jt. auth. see Darity, William A.
Myers, Sandra T. Practice with Spreadsheets. 254p. (C). 1997. pap. text 32.00 (*0-13-456682-3*) P-H.
Myers, Sarah E. & Lind, Mary B. Recipes from the Old Mill: Baking with Whole Grains. LC 95-35567. (Illus.). 252p. 1995. pap. 13.95 (*1-56148-176-9*) Good Bks PA.
Myers, Sarah K. Language Shift among Migrants to Lima, Peru. LC 73-78730. (University of Chicago, Department of Geography, Research Paper Ser.: No. 147). 219p. 1973. reprint ed. pap. 67.90 (*0-608-02278-0*, 206291900004) Bks Demand.
Myers-Scotton, Carol. Dueling Languages: Grammatical Structure in Codeswitching. (Illus.). 300p. 1997. reprint ed. pap. text 29.95 (*0-19-823712-X*) OUP.
— Social Motivations for Codeswitching: Evidence from Africa. (Oxford Studies in Language Contact). (Illus.). 192p. 1995. pap. text 22.00 (*0-19-823923-8*) OUP.
Myers-Scotton, Carol, ed. Codes & Consequences: Choosing Lignuistic Varieties. LC 98-7061. (Illus.). 232p. 1998. pap. text 24.95 (*0-19-511523-6*) OUP.
— Codes & Consequences: Choosing Linguistic Varieties. LC 98-7061. (Illus.). 232p. 1998. text 55.00 (*0-19-511522-8*) OUP.
Myers, Selma & Filner, Barbara. Resolving Conflict Across Cultures: Talking It Out to Mediation. 90p. 1997. 21.95 (*1-883998-19-0*) Amherst Educ.
Myers, Selma & Lambert, Joanna. Diversity Icebreakers: A Guide for Diversity Training. 56p. 1994. pap. text 55.00 (*1-883998-11-5*) Amherst Educ.
Myers, Selma & Lambert, Jonamay. Customer Relations & the Diversity Challenge: A Trainer's Guide. 55p. 1995. 69.95 (*1-883998-16-6*) Amherst Educ.
— More Diversity Icebreakers: A Trainer's Guide. 77p. 1996. 55.00 (*1-883998-18-2*) Amherst Educ.
Myers, Selma, jt. auth. see Lambert, Jonamay.
Myers, Selma G. & Harris, Anthony W. Tools for Valuing Diversity: A Practical Guide to Techniques to Capitalize in Team Diversity. (Workplace Diversity Ser.). (Illus.). 120p. 1995. pap. 12.95 (*1-883553-70-9*) R Chang Assocs.
Myers-Shaffer, Christina. How to Prepare for SAT II: Literature. 1996. pap. 12.95 (*0-8120-9165-5*) Barron.
***Myers-Shaffer, Christina.** How to Prepare for Sat II: Literature. 2nd ed. LC 99-31976. 384p. 2000. 13.95 (*0-7641-0769-0*) Barron.
Myers, Sherrill M., jt. auth. see Beckley, Robert M.
Myers, Sherrill M., jt. auth. see O'Connor, Sara.
***Myers, Shirley E.** How to Make a Book Report: Grades 6-8. (Illus.). 48p. 1999. pap., teacher ed. 7.95 (*1-57690-487-3*, TCM 2487) Tchr Create Mat.
Myers, Shirley E. Language Arts: Activities. (Illus.). 144p. (J). 1997. pap., teacher ed. 14.95 (*1-57690-349-4*, TCM2349) Tchr Create Mat.
Myers, Sloan. The Stand up Communicator: A Guide to Powerful Presentations. (Illus.). 108p. 1999. pap. 29.95 (*0-9672830-0-0*) M2 Assocs.
Myers, Sondra, jt. auth. see Rittner, Carol.
Myers, Sophia. Beginning from the Middle: A Collection of Fiction, Poetry, & Essays by the Kansas City Writers' Group. 128p. (Orig.). 1994. pap. 9.95 (*0-9644170-0-6*) Whispering Prairie.
***Myers, Stacy Erin.** Maremaid: A Pony's Tale. (Illus.). 32p. (J). (ps-3). 2000. 15.95 (*1-929845-11-1*) DeFranco Ent.
Myers, Stanley E. RPG IV Programming on the AS-400. LC 97-28296. 738p. (C). 1997. pap. 79.00 (*0-13-460411-3*) P-H.
— RPG II, RPG III & RPG-400 with Business. 2nd ed. 896p. 1991. pap. 77.00 (*0-13-783077-7*, 260301) P-H.
Myers, Stanley E. & Myers, Candice E. RPG-400 Programming on the AS-400. LC 94-25819. 752p. (C). 1995. pap. 77.00 (*0-13-096736-X*) P-H.
Myers, Stephan, jt. auth. see Dunn, Barbara.
Myers, Stephanie E., jt. auth. see Myers, Roy J.
Myers, Stephen & McLaren, Tim. MCSE Study Guide: Windows 95 & Networking Essentials. LC 96-24486. 900p. 1996. student ed. 75.00 (*1-56205-568-2*) New Riders Pub.
Myers, Stephen W. Yeat's Book of the Nineties: Poetry, Politics, & Rhetoric. LC 92-17894. (American University Studies: English Language & Literature: Ser. IV, Vol. 150). XX, 186p. (C). 1993. text 35.95 (*0-8204-1957-5*) P Lang Pubng.
Myers, Steve, jt. auth. see Sanders, Pete.
Myers, Steve, jt. auth. see Saunders, Pete.
Myers, Stewart C., jt. auth. see Brealey, Richard.
Myers, Stewart C., jt. auth. see Brealey, Richard A.
Myers, Stuart. Between the Worlds: Witchcraft & the Tree of Life: a Program of Spiritual Development. LC 95-41367. (Illus.). 256p. 1995. pap. 17.95 (*1-56718-480-4*) Llewellyn Pubns.
Myers, Susan, ed. see Baker, Terry L.
Myers, Suzanne, jt. auth. see Myers, George D.
Myers, Suzanne D., jt. auth. see Myers, George D.
Myers, Sylvia H. The Bluestocking Circle: Women, Friendship, & the Life of the Mind in Eighteenth-Century England. (Illus.). 360p. (C). 1990. 75.00 (*0-19-811767-1*) OUP.
Myers, Talarico. The Social Contexts of Criminal Sentencing. LC 87-4771. (Research in Criminology Ser.). 245p. 1987. 126.00 (*0-387-96483-5*) Spr-Verlag.
Myers, Tamar. Baroque & Desperate: A Den of Antiquity Mystery. (Den of Antiquity Mystery Ser.). 256p. 1999. mass mkt. 5.99 (*0-380-80225-2*, Avon Bks) Morrow Avon.
— Eat, Drink & Be Wary: With Recipes. (Penndutch Mysteries Ser.). 272p. 1998. mass mkt. 5.99 (*0-451-19231-1*, Sig) NAL.
***Myers, Tamar.** Estate of Mind. 320p. 1999. mass mkt. 6.50 (*0-380-80227-9*, Avon Bks) Morrow Avon.
Myers, Tamar. Gilt By Association. LC 96-96487. 256p. 1996. mass mkt. 6.50 (*0-380-78237-5*, Avon Bks) Morrow Avon.
***Myers, Tamar.** Hand That Rocks the Ladle. (Pennsylvania Dutch Mystery with Recipes Ser.). 261p. 2000. mass mkt. 5.99 (*0-451-19755-0*, Sig) NAL.
Myers, Tamar. Just Plain Pickled. 1997. mass mkt. 5.99 (*0-451-19293-1*, Sig) NAL.
— Larceny & Old Lace. 224p. (Orig.). 1996. mass mkt. 5.99 (*0-380-78239-1*, Avon Bks) Morrow Avon.
— Ming & I. LC 97-93174. 256p. 1997. mass mkt. 5.99 (*0-380-79255-9*, Avon Bks) Morrow Avon.
— No Use Dying over Spilled Milk: A Pennsylvania-Dutch Mystery with Recipes. 272p. 1997. mass mkt. 5.99 (*0-451-18854-3*, Sig) NAL.
— Parsley, Sage, Rosemary & Crime. 1996. mass mkt. 5.99 (*0-451-18297-9*, Sig) NAL.
***Myers, Tamar.** A Penny Urned. 288p. 2000. mass mkt. 6.50 (*0-380-81189-8*, Avon Bks) Morrow Avon.
Myers, Tamar. Play It Again Spam. 262p. 1999. mass mkt. 5.99 (*0-451-19754-2*, Sig) NAL.
— So Faux, So Good. LC 97-94765. (Den Of Antiquity Ser.). 256p. 1998. mass mkt. 6.50 (*0-380-79254-0*, Avon Bks) Morrow Avon.
— Too Many Crooks Spoil the Broth. 256p. 1995. mass mkt. 5.99 (*0-451-18296-0*, Sig) NAL.
Myers, Ted. Faith & Survival: Ethiopian Jewish Life, 1983-1992. LC 92-60746. (Illus.). 8p. (Orig.). 1992. pap. 2.50 (*0-943376-51-3*) Magnes Mus.
Myers, Terence M. Business Owner's Tax Savings & Financing Deskbook, 1999 ed. 1998. pap. text 79.00 (*0-15-606620-3*) Harcourt.
***Myers, Terence M.** 2000 Business Owner's Tax & Finance Deskbook. 700p. (C). 1999. pap. text 89.00 (*0-15-607009-X*) Harcourt.
***Myers, Terry.** Take Control of Your Game: A Learning Guide for Simple & Consistent Golf. Myers, Renee, ed. LC 00-190340. (Illus.). viii, 172p. 2000. 17.95 (*0-9679153-0-9*) T Myers.
Myers, Terry, et al, eds. Reasoning & Discourse Processes. (Cognitive Science Ser.). 312p. 1986. text 160.00 (*0-12-512320-5*) Acad Pr.
***Myers, Terry M.** Business Owner's Complete Tax & Employment Advisor 2000. LC 00-265497. 400p. 1999. pap. 79.00 (*0-15-606832-X*) Harcourt.
***Myers, Terry R.** Standing Still & Walking in Los Angeles. Coleman, Candy, ed. (Illus.). 20p. 1999. pap. 10.00 (*1-880154-32-3*) Gagosian Gallery.
***Myers, Terry R. & Overby, Robert.** Robert Overby: Parallel, 1969-1978. LC 00-8917. 2000. write for info. (*0-943739-22-5*) F S Wight Art.
Myers, Theresa F., jt. auth. see Moran, Mary Y.
Myers, Theresa F., jt. compiled by see Marquis, Bernie.
Myers, Theresa F., ed. see Heffernan, Anne E.
Myers, Theresa F., jt. text see Tschanz, Mary K.
Myers, Thomas, ed. see Calvin, John.
Myers, Thomas, ed. see Lawrence, Carl.
Myers, Thomas G. Census Index - Bucks County, Pennsylvania, 1900. LC 93-80295. 183p. (Orig.). 1993. spiral bd. 13.00 (*0-9637799-1-5*) T G Myers.
— 1920 Census Index: Bucks County, PA. LC 93-91749. 190p. 1993. spiral bd. 13.00 (*0-9637799-0-7*) T G Myers.
***Myers, Thomas G.** Solliday/Sallade Family of Bucks County, PA. Kurtzman, Ralph H., Jr., ed. (Illus.). 599p. 1999. 49.99 (*0-9637799-2-3*, Pub. by T G Myers) Kurtzman.
— Solliday/Sollade Family of Bucks County, PA - Clockmakers' Edition. Kurtzman, Ralph H., Jr., ed. (Illus.). 100p. 1999. pap. 14.50 (*0-9637799-3-1*, Pub. by T G Myers) Kurtzman.
Myers, Thomas M., et al. Fateful Journey: Injury & Death on Colorado River Trips. (Illus.). 192p. pap. 19.95 (*1-884546-02-1*) Red Lake Bks.
Myers, Thurman. So! You Want to Know Why Your Here? 177p. (Orig.). 1997. 12.95 (*0-9659572-9-2*) Blue Owl.
Myers-Tierney, Linda. The Impact of Web Technologies on Electronic Document Management & Delivery. 52p. 1997. 150.00 (*0-89258-339-8*, D068) Assn Inform & Image Mgmt.
Myers, Tim. Let's Call Him Lau-Wili-Wili-Humu-Humu-Nukunuku-Nukunuku-Apuaa-Oioi. LC 93-72767. (Illus.). 24p. (J). (ps-3). 1993. pap. 6.95 (*1-880188-66-X*) Bess Pr.

Myers, Tom. Moccasin Trails of the French & Indian War the Eastern Frontier, 1743-1758, Vol. 1. 280p. 1995. pap. 9.95 (*0-87012-532-X*) McClain.
A century & a half passed while three groups of people, the Indians, French & English fought for the vast, fertile land known by the Europeans as the New World. Immigrants were landing daily on the shores of the eastern seaboard from England, Scotland & Ireland. The people from these countries were migrating to America to escape tyranny, persecution & overcrowding. Josh Parker was a man caught up in these times. He was a friend to the Indians but had to fight for his family & livelihood. As he did this, others followed. A nation that we now enjoy, was born. Purchase with SHADOWS IN THE FOREST for $20 for both titles. *Publisher Paid Annotation.*

— Professional JAVA Script Objects. 450p. 1998. pap. text 49.99 (*1-86100-189-4*, Pub. by Wrox Press) Wrox Pr Inc.
***Myers, Tom & Nakhimovsky, Alexander.** Professional Java XML Programming with Servlets & JSP. 400p. 1999. pap. 49.99 (*1-86100-285-8*) Wrox Pr Inc.

Myers, Tom E. Shadows of the Forest, Vol. II. 272p. 1997. pap. 11.95 (*0-87012-582-6*) McClain.
SHADOWS OF THE FOREST, Volume II is the continuing saga of Josh & Libby Parker & the next generation as they pioneer the eastern frontier. Volume II follows MOCCASIN TRAILS OF THE FRENCH & INDIAN. Join BUCKTAIL'S & JOSH'S children as they grow & learn with struggles & triumphs. Purchase with MOCCASIN TRAILS for $20 for both. *Publisher Paid Annotation.*

Myers, Tona Pearce, ed. The Soul of Creativity: Insights into the Creative Process. LC 98-53426. 224p. 1999. pap. 14.00 (*1-57731-077-2*) New Wrld Lib.
Myers, Valerie L. Respond to the Rhythms of Change: Using Biblical Principles. 1997. pap. text 12.95 (*1-880560-69-0*) DaBaR Srvs.
Myers, Virginia. The Dad Next Door, Bk. 71. 1999. per. 4.50 (*0-373-87071-X*, 1-87071-6) Harlequin Bks.
Myers, W. D., et al. Radioactive Nuclear Beam. 644p. (C). 1990. text 144.00 (*981-02-0101-X*) World Scientific Pub.
Myers, W. D., jt. auth. see Hasse, R. W.
Myers, W. David. Poor, Sinning Folk: Confession & Conscience in Counter-Reformation Germany. LC 95-46885. (Illus.). 224p. (C). 1996. text 37.50 (*0-8014-3081-X*) Cornell U Pr.
Myers, W. E., jt. auth. see Bequele, Assefa.
***Myers, W T. D. & Gardner, Douglas W.** Legal Research Guides of Texas Tech University. LC 98-87658. Vol. 32. x, 84p. 1998. 42.00 (*1-57588-451-8*, 311820) W S Hein.
Myers-Walls, Judith. Families as Educators for Global Citizenship. 59.95 (*1-85972-356-X*) Ashgate Pub Co.
Myers-Walls, Judith, jt. auth. see Fry-Miller, Kathleen.
Myers, Walter Dean. African Princess: The Life of Sarah Bonetta Forbes. LC 98-7217. (Illus.). 160p. (YA). (gr. 4-7). 1999. 15.95 (*0-590-48669-1*) Scholastic Inc.
— Amistad: A Long Road to Freedom. LC 98-9283. (Illus.). 94p. 1998. 16.99 (*0-525-45970-7*) NAL.
— Amistad Affair. 1999. pap. 5.99 (*0-14-130004-3*) Viking Penguin.
— Angel to Angel: A Mother's Gift of Love. LC 97-17498. (Illus.). 40p. (J). (gr. 4 up). 1998. 15.95 (*0-06-027721-1*) HarpC.
— Angel to Angel: A Mother's Gift of Love. LC 97-17498. (Illus.). 40p. (J). (ps-3). 1998. lib. bdg. 15.89 (*0-06-027722-X*) HarpC.
***Myers, Walter Dean.** Angel to Angel: A Mother's Gift of Love. LC 97-17498. (Illus.). 40p. (J). (ps-3). 2000. pap. 5.95 (*0-06-446242-0*, HarpTrophy) HarpC Child Bks.
— Angel to Angel: A Mother's Gift of Love. (Illus.). (J). 2000. 11.40 (*0-606-18673-5*) Turtleback.
— At Her Majesty's Request: An African Princess in Victorian England. (Illus.). write for info. (*0-439-07762-1*) Scholastic Inc.
— The Blues of Flats Brown. LC 99-16695. (Illus.). 32p. (J). 2000. 16.95 (*0-8234-1480-9*) Holiday.
Myers, Walter Dean. Brown Angels: An Album of Pictures & Verse. LC 92-36792. (Illus.). 40p. (J). (ps-3). 1993. 16.95 (*0-06-022917-9*) HarpC Child Bks.
— Brown Angels: An Album of Pictures & Verse. LC 92-36792. (Illus.). 40p. (J). (gr. k up). 1996. pap. 5.95 (*0-06-443455-9*, HarpTrophy) HarpC Child Bks.
Myers, Walter Dean. Brown Angels: An Album of Pictures & Verse. LC 92-36792. 1993. 11.15 (*0-606-09106-8*, Pub. by Turtleback) Demco.
Myers, Walter Dean. Brown Angels: An Album of Pictures & Verse. large type ed. (J). 1995. 22.00 (*0-614-09549-2*, L-32493-00) Am Printing Hse.
— Crystal. (Illus.). (J). 1990. mass mkt. 5.95 (*0-440-80157-5*) BDD Bks Young Read.
— Darnell Rock Reporting. (Illus.). 144p. (J). (gr. 5). 1996. pap. 4.50 (*0-440-41157-2*) Dell.
— Darnell Rock Reporting. (J). 1996. 9.09 (*0-606-09182-3*, Pub. by Turtleback) Demco.
— Darnell Rock Reporting. (YA). (gr. 5 up). reprint ed. pap. 3.99 (*0-614-15578-9*, YB BDD) BDD Bks Young Read.
***Myers, Walter Dean.** Dragon Takes a Wife. (Illus.). (J). 2000. 11.44 (*0-606-18871-1*) Turtleback.
— Dragon Takes a Wife. rev. ed. (Illus.). 32p. (ps-3). 2000. pap. text 5.99 (*0-590-46694-1*) Scholastic Inc.
— Fallen Angels. 1999. 12.25 (*0-8335-3180-8*) Econo-Clad Bks.
Myers, Walter Dean. Fallen Angels. 320p. (J). (gr. 7-9). 1988. 14.95 (*0-590-40942-5*) Scholastic Inc.
— Fallen Angels. LC 87-23236. 320p. (J). (gr. 7-12). 1989. pap. 4.99 (*0-590-40943-3*) Scholastic Inc.
— Fallen Angels. (J). 1988. 10.09 (*0-606-04220-2*, Pub. by Turtleback) Demco.
— Fast Sam, Cool Clyde & Stuff. (J). (gr. 5-9). 1988. pap. 4.99 (*0-14-032613-8*, PuffinBks) Peng Put Young Read.
— Fast Sam, Cool Clyde & Stuff. (J). 1995. 18.75 (*0-8446-6798-6*) Peter Smith.
— Fast Sam, Cool Clyde & Stuff. (J). 1975. 10.09 (*0-606-03575-3*, Pub. by Turtleback) Demco.
Myers, Walter Dean. The Gifts We Bring, 5. 96p. (gr. 3-7). 14.95 (*0-06-027809-9*) HarpC Child Bks.
— The Gifts We Bring, No. 1. 96p. (J). (gr. 3-7). 2001. 14.95 (*0-06-027805-6*) HarpC Child Bks.
— The Gifts We Bring, No. 2. 96p. (J). (gr. 3-7). 2002. 14.95 (*0-06-027806-4*) HarpC Child Bks.
— The Gifts We Bring, No. 6. 96p. (J). (gr. 3-7). 14.95 (*0-06-027810-2*) HarpC Child Bks.
Myers, Walter Dean. Glorious Angels: A Celebration of Children. 1997. 12.15 (*0-606-11393-2*, Pub. by Turtleback) Demco.
— Glorious Angels: A Celebration of Children. LC 94-49699. (Trophy Bk.). 48p. (J). (ps-3). 1997. reprint ed. pap. 6.95 (*0-06-446726-0*, HarpTrophy) HarpC Child Bks.
— The Glory Field. LC 93-43520. 288p. (J). (gr. 7-9). 1994. 14.95 (*0-590-45897-3*) Scholastic Inc.
— The Glory Field. 288p. (J). (gr. 7-12). 1996. pap. 4.99 (*0-590-45898-1*) Scholastic Inc.
— The Glory Field. (J). 1994. 10.09 (*0-606-08527-0*, Pub. by Turtleback) Demco.
***Myers, Walter Dean.** The Greatest: Muhammad Ali. (Illus.). 224p. (YA). (gr. 5 up). 2000. 16.95 (*0-590-54342-3*) Scholastic Inc.
— Handbook for Boys. 240p. 15.95 (*0-06-029146-X*) HarpC.
— Handbook for Boys. 240p. lib. bdg. 15.89 (*0-06-029147-8*); mass mkt. 5.95 (*0-06-440930-9*) HarpC.
Myers, Walter Dean. Harlem: A Poem. LC 96-8108. (Illus.). 32p. (J). (gr. 1-4). 1997. 16.95 (*0-590-54340-7*) Scholastic Inc.
— Harlem: A Poem. LC 96-8108. (J). 1997. write for info. (*0-590-54341-5*) Scholastic Inc.
Myers, Walter Dean. Harlem: A Poem. 1997. 27.00 incl. audio (*0-8045-6852-9*) Spoken Arts.
Myers, Walter Dean. Hoops. 192p. (YA). (gr. 7 up). 1983. mass mkt. 4.99 (*0-440-93884-8*, LLL BDD) BDD Bks Young Read.
— Hoops. (J). 1981. 9.60 (*0-606-03053-0*, Pub. by Turtleback) Demco.
— How Mr. Monkey Saw the Whole World. (Illus.). 32p. (J). (ps-3). 1997. pap. 5.99 (*0-440-41415-6*) BDD Bks Young Read.
Myers, Walter Dean. How Mr. Monkey Saw the Whole World. 1997. 11.19 (*0-606-13495-6*, Pub. by Turtleback) Demco.
Myers, Walter Dean. The Journal of Joshua Loper: A Black Cowboy, The Chisholm Trail, 1871. LC 98-18661. (My Name Is America Ser.). (Illus.). 158p. (J). (gr. 4-9). 1999. 10.95 (*0-590-02691 7*) Scholastic Inc.
— The Journal of Scott Pendeleton Collins: A World War II Soldier, Normandy, France 1944. LC 99-13615. (My Name Is America Ser.). (Illus.). 140p. (J). (gr. 4-9). 1999. 10.95 (*0-439-05013-8*) Scholastic Inc.
— The Legend of Tarik. 192p. (J). (gr. 7-9). 1991. pap. 3.50 (*0-590-44426-3*) Scholastic Inc.
— Un Lugar en las Sombras.Tr. of Somewhere in the Darkness. (SPA.). 176p. (J). (gr. 7-9). 1994. pap. 3.50 (*0-590-47701-3*) Scholastic Inc.

M

— Un Lugar Entre Las Sombras. (Mariposa Scholastica en Espanol Ser.). 1994. 8.60 (*0-606-06834-1*, Pub. by Turtleback) Demco.

— Malcolm X: A Fire Burning Brightly. LC 99-21527. (Illus.). 40p. (J). (gr. k-3). 2000. 15.95 (*0-06-027707-6*) HarpC.

***Myers, Walter Dean.** Malcolm X: A Fire Burning Brightly. LC 99-21527. (Illus.). 40p. (J). (gr. k-3). 2000. lib. bdg. 15.89 (*0-06-027708-4*) HarpC Child Bks.

Myers, Walter Dean. Malcolm X: By Any Means Necessary. 224p. (J). (gr. 7-9). 1993. 13.95 (*0-590-46484-1*) Scholastic Inc.

— Malcolm X: By Any Means Necessary. LC 92-13480. 224p. (J). (gr. 5 up). 1994. pap. 4.50 (*0-590-48109-6*) Scholastic Inc.

— Malcolm X: By Any Means Necessary. (Illus.). 224p. (J). 1998. pap. 5.99 (*0-590-29912-3*) Scholastic Inc.

— Malcolm X: By Any Means Necessary. 1999. pap. 5.99 (*0-590-98759-3*) Scholastic Inc.

— Malcolm X: By Any Means Necessary. (YA). (gr. 5-8). 1999. mass mkt. 4.99 (*0-590-66221-X*) Scholastic Inc.

— Malcolm X: By Any Means Necessary: A Biography. (J). 1993. 9.60 (*0-606-05919-9*, Pub. by Turtleback) Demco.

Myers, Walter Dean. Martin Luther King Biography. 32p. (gr. k-3). 15.89 (*0-06-027704-1*) HarpC.

Myers, Walter Dean. Me, Mop & the Moondance Kid. (J). 1995. pap. 4.99 (*0-440-91071-4*) BDD Bks Young Read.

— Me, Mop & the Moondance Kid. (J). 1996. pap. 4.99 (*0-440-91093-5*) BDD Bks Young Read.

— Me, Mop & the Moondance Kid. Foresmann, Scoot, ed. 160p. (J). 1994. pap. 3.50 (*0-440-91005-6*) Dell.

— Me, Mop, & the Moondance Kid. (J). 1988. 9.60 (*0-606-04745-X*, Pub. by Turtleback) Demco.

— Me, Mop & the Moondance Kid. large type ed. (Illus.). 1995. pap. 41.50 (*0-614-09601-4*, L-34842-00) Am Printing Hse.

— Me, Mop & the Moondance Kid. LC 88-6503. 160p. (J). (gr. 4-7). 1990. reprint ed. pap. 4.99 (*0-440-40396-0*) Dell.

— Monster. LC 98-40958. (Illus.). 288p. (J). (gr. 7-12). 1999. 15.95 (*0-06-028077-8*) HarpC Child Bks.

— Monster. LC 98-40958. (Illus.). 288p. (YA). (gr. 7 up). 1999. lib. bdg. 15.89 (*0-06-028078-6*) HarpC Child Bks.

— Mop, Moondance, & the Nagasaki Knights. (J). (gr. 6). 1995. 9.28 (*0-395-73269-7*) HM.

— Mop, Moondance, & the Nagasaki Knights. large type ed. 174p. 43.50 (*0-614-20605-7*, L-38204-00 APHB) Am Printing Hse.

— Motown & Didi: A Love Story. 176p. (YA). (gr. k-12). 1987. mass mkt. 4.99 (*0-440-95762-1*, LLL BDD) BDD Bks Young Read.

Myers, Walter Dean. Motown & Didi: A Love Story. (Laurel-Leaf Contemporary Fiction Ser.). (J). 1987. 9.60 (*0-606-03623-7*, Pub. by Turtleback) Demco.

Myers, Walter Dean. The Mouse Rap. LC 89-36419. 192p. (J). (gr. 5-9). 1990. lib. bdg. 14.89 (*0-06-024344-9*) HarpC Child Bks.

— The Mouse Rap. Bacha, Andy, ed. & contrib. by by. LC 89-36419. (Trophy Bk.). 192p. (YA). (gr. 5-9). 1992. pap. 4.95 (*0-06-440356-4*, HarpTrophy) HarpC Child Bks.

— Mouse Rap. 1992. 9.60 (*0-606-01077-7*, Pub. by Turtleback) Demco.

Myers, Walter Dean. Muhammad Ali Biography. 40p. 15.95 (*0-06-029131-1*); pap. 5.95 (*0-06-443718-3*); lib. bdg. 15.89 (*0-06-029132-X*) HarpC.

— Now Is Your Time! The African-American Struggle for Freedom. LC 91-314. (Trophy Nonfiction Bk.). (Illus.). 320p. (YA). (gr. 6 up). 1992. pap. 11.95 (*0-06-446120-3*, HarpTrophy) HarpC Child Bks.

Myers, Walter Dean. Now Is Your Time! The African-American Struggle for Freedom. 1991. 16.05 (*0-606-01107-2*, Pub. by Turtleback) Demco.

***Myers, Walter Dean.** 145th Street Stories. LC 99-36097. 176p. (gr. 7-12). 2000. 15.95 (*0-385-32137-6*) Delacorte.

Myers, Walter Dean. One More River to Cross: An African American Photograph Album. LC 95-3839. (Illus.). 192p. 1995. 40.00 (*0-15-200089-5*) Harcourt.

Myers, Walter Dean. Outside Shot. (J). 1987. 9.09 (*0-606-03069-7*, Pub. by Turtleback) Demco.

Myers, Walter Dean. The Outside Shot. 192p. (YA). (gr. k-12). 1986. reprint ed. mass mkt. 4.50 (*0-440-96784-8*, LLL BDD) BDD Bks Young Read.

— Patrol. (Illus.). 40p. (J). (gr. 3-7). 15.95 (*0-06-028363-7*); lib. bdg. 15.89 (*0-06-028364-5*) HarpC.

— The Righteous Revenge of Artemis Bonner. LC 91-42401. (Trophy Bk.). (Illus.). 144p. (YA). (gr. 5-9). 1994. pap. 4.95 (*0-06-440462-5*, HarpTrophy) HarpC Child Bks.

Myers, Walter Dean. The Righteous Revenge of Artemis Bonner. (YA). 1994. 10.05 (*0-606-06698-5*, Pub. by Turtleback) Demco.

Myers, Walter Dean. Scorpions. LC 85-45815. 160p. (J). (gr. 7-12). 1988. 15.95 (*0-06-024364-3*) HarpC Child Bks.

— Scorpions. LC 85-45815. 224p. (J). (gr. 7 up). 1988. lib. bdg. 15.89 (*0-06-024365-1*) HarpC Child Bks.

— Scorpions. LC 85-45815. (Trophy Bk.). 224p. (YA). (gr. 7-12). 1990. pap. 5.95 (*0-06-447066-0*, HarpTrophy) HarpC Child Bks.

— Scorpions. LC 85-45815. (Trophy Bk.). 224p. (J). (gr. 12 up). 1996. pap. 5.95 (*0-06-440623-7*, HarpTrophy) HarpC Child Bks.

— Scorpions. 1990. 10.05 (*0-606-09833-X*, Pub. by Turtleback) Demco.

— Scorpions. (J). 1990. 9.60 (*0-606-04533-3*, Pub. by Turtleback) Demco.

Myers, Walter Dean. Scorpions, Class Set. unabridged ed. (J). 1997. 105.30 incl. audio (*0-7887-2585-8*, 46431) Recorded Bks.

— Scorpions, Homework Set. unabridged ed. (J). 1997. 48.20 incl. audio (*0-7887-1599-2*, 40630) Recorded Bks.

Myers, Walter Dean. Shadow of the Red Moon. LC 94-42298. (Illus.). 288p. (J). (gr. 4 up). 1995. 14.95 (*0-590-45895-7*, Scholastic Hardcover) Scholastic Inc.

— Shadow of the Red Moon. LC 94-42298. 192p. (J). (gr. 4-7). 1997. mass mkt. 4.50 (*0-590-45896-5*) Scholastic Inc.

— Shadow of the Red Moon. (Point Fantasy Ser.). (J). 1997. 9.60 (*0-606-11831-4*, Pub. by Turtleback) Demco.

— Slam! (J). 1996. 15.95 (*0-614-25384-5*) Scholastic Inc.

— Slam! LC 95-46647. 240p. (YA). (gr. 7-12). 1996. 15.95 (*0-590-48667-5*); pap. 4.99 (*0-590-48668-3*, Pub. by Scholastic Inc) Penguin Putnam.

***Myers, Walter Dean.** Smiffy Blue: Ace Crime Detective. 1999. mass mkt. 3.99 (*0-590-67666-0*) Scholastic Inc.

Myers, Walter Dean. Smiffy Blue, Ace Crime Detective: The Case of the Missing Ruby & Other Stories. (Illus.). (J). (gr. 3-6). 1996. 14.95 (*0-614-15761-7*) Scholastic Inc.

— Somewhere in the Darkness. LC 91-19295. 176p. (J). (gr. 7 up). 1992. 14.95 (*0-590-42411-4*, Scholastic Hardcover) Scholastic Inc.

— Somewhere in the Darkness. 176p. (YA). (gr. 7 up). 1993. pap. 3.50 (*0-590-42412-2*) Scholastic Inc.

Myers, Walter Dean. Somewhere in the Darkness. LC 91-19295. 176p. (YA). (gr. 5-9). 1997. pap. text 3.99 (*0-590-34186-3*) Scholastic Inc.

Myers, Walter Dean. Somewhere in the Darkness. LC 91-19295. 1992. 9.09 (*0-606-11861-6*, Pub. by Turtleback) Demco.

— Somewhere in the Darkness. (Point Ser.). (J). 1992. 9.09 (*0-606-05613-0*, Pub. by Turtleback) Demco.

— The Story of the Three Kingdoms. LC 94-2685. (Illus.). 32p. (J). (gr. k-3). 1997. pap. 6.95 (*0-06-443475-3*, HarpTrophy) HarpC Child Bks.

— Sweet Illusions. 146p. (Orig.). (YA). 1987. pap. 8.95 (*0-915924-15-3*) Tchrs & Writers Coll.

— Tales of a Dead King. 93rd ed. 1993. pap. text 15.40 (*0-15-300375-8*, Harcourt Child Bks) Harcourt.

— Toussaint L'Ouverture: The Fight for Haiti's Freedom. LC 95-30046. (Illus.). 40p. (J). (gr. 3-7). 1996. mass mkt. 16.00 (*0-689-80126-2*) S&S Bks Yung.

— Won't Know Till I Get There. LC 87-7340. (J). (gr. 3 up). 1988. pap. 4.99 (*0-14-032612-X*, PuffinBks) Peng Put Young Read.

***Myers, Walter Dean.** Won't Know Till I Get There. (J). (gr. 4-8). 2000. 19.00 (*0-8446-7149-5*) Peter Smith.

Myers, Walter Dean. Won't Know Till I Get There. LC 81-71128. (J). 1982. 10.09 (*0-606-03681-4*, Pub. by Turtleback) Demco.

— The Young Landlords. (ALA Notable Bk.). 208p. (J). (gr. 5-9). 1989. pap. 4.99 (*0-14-034244-3*, PuffinBks) Peng Put Young Read.

— The Young Landlords. (J). (gr. 6-10). 1992. 18.75 (*0-8446-6569-X*) Peter Smith.

— The Young Landlords. (J). 1979. 10.09 (*0-606-04432-9*, Pub. by Turtleback) Demco.

— Young Martin's Promise. Hayley, Alex, ed. LC 92-18070. (Stories of America Ser.). (Illus.). 32p. (J). (gr. 2-5). 1992. lib. bdg. 22.83 (*0-8114-7210-8*) Raintree Steck-V.

— Young Martin's Promise. Haley, Alex, ed. LC 92-18070. (Stories of America Ser.). (Illus.). 32p. (J). (gr. 4-7). 1993. pap. 4.95 (*0-8114-8050-X*) Raintree Steck-V.

***Myers, Walter Dean & Myers, Christopher A.** Monster. LC 98-40958. (Illus.). 288p. (YA). (gr. 7 up). 1999. 5.95 (*0-06-440731-4*) HarpC Child Bks.

Myers, Walter Dean, et al. Turning Points: When Everything Changes. LC 98-131202. (Target Ser.). 160p. (Orig.). (J). (ps-1). 1996. pap. text 11.95 (*0-8167-4275-8*) Troll Communs.

Myers, Walter L. The Later Realism: A Study of Characterization in the British Novel. LC 73-2801. (Select Bibliographies Reprint Ser). 1977. reprint ed. 20.95 (*0-8369-7166-3*) Ayer.

Myers, Ware, jt. auth. see Putnam, Lawrence H.

***Myers, Warren.** Discovering God's Will. 2000. pap. 10.00 (*1-57683-178-7*) NavPress.

Myers, Warren. How to Have a Quiet Time. 1991. pap. 2.50 (*0-89109-568-3*) NavPress.

Myers, Warren & Myer, Ruth. Como Tener un Tiempo de Quietud. (Serie Realidades - Realities Ser.).Tr. of How to Have a Quiet Time. (SPA.). 93p. 1994. 1.99 (*1-56063-918-0*, 498134) Editorial Unilit.

— 31 Days of Prayer: Moving God's Mighty Hand. 212p. 1999. 9.99 (*1-57673-385-8*) Multnomah Pubs.

Myers, Warren, jt. auth. see Myer, Ruth.

Myers, Wayne A. Dynamic Therapy of the Older Patient. LC 83-25772. 270p. 1984. 45.00 (*0-87668-623-4*) Aronson.

Myers, William. Milton & Freewill: An Essay in Criticism & Philosophy. 256p. 1987. 65.00 (*0-7099-4620-1*) Routledge.

— The Presence of Persons: Essays on the Literature & Thought of the Nineteenth Century. LC 98-23626. (Nineteenth Century Ser.). 256p. 1998. text 78.95 (*1-84014-645-1*, PR453.M94, Pub. by Ashgate Pub) Ashgate Pub Co.

Myers, William, ed. see Farquhar, George.

Myers, William A. Replacing the Warrior: Cultural Ideals & Militarism. LC 85-81253. 32p. (Orig.). 1985. pap. 1.00 (*0-87574-263-7*) Pendle Hill.

Myers, William C. Environmental Legislation: The Increasing Costs of Regulatory Compliance to the City of Columbus (Ohio) (Illus.). 150p. (Orig.). (C). 1995. pap. text 30.00 (*0-7881-1657-6*) DIANE Pub.

Myers, William E., ed. Protecting Working Children. LC 91-13767. 192p. (C). 1991. text 62.50 (*1-85649-006-8*, Pub. by Zed Books); text 22.50 (*1-85649-007-6*, Pub. by Zed Books) St Martin.

Myers, William F. The Brightness of His Presence: Theological Dissertation. LC 82-90351. 64p. 1982. 6.95 (*0-87948-049-1*) Beatty.

Myers, William H. God's Yes Was Louder Than My No: Rethinking the African American Call to Ministry. 300p. (Orig.). (C). 1994. 49.95 (*0-86543-426-3*); pap. 16.95 (*0-86543-427-1*) Africa World.

Myers, William R. Black & White Styles of Youth Ministry: Two Congregations in America. LC 90-43961. 202p. (Orig.). 1990. pap. 13.95 (*0-8298-0868-X*) Pilgrim OH.

***Myers, William R.** Research in Ministry: A Primer for the Doctor of Ministry Program. 3rd ed. LC 99-67033. (Studies in Ministry & Parish Life). xvi, 89p. 2000. pap. 12.00 (*0-913552-63-1*) Exploration Pr.

Myers, William R., ed. Becoming & Belonging: A Practical Design for Confirmation. LC 93-23349. 184p. 1993. pap. 12.95 (*0-8298-0942-2*) Pilgrim OH.

Myers, William R., jt. auth. see Modley, Rudolf.

Myers, William R., jt. auth. see Myers, Barbara K.

Myers, William S., ed. Woodrow Wilson: Some Princeton Memories - George McLean Harper, Robert K. Root, Edward S. Corwin et al. LC 47-266. 101p. 1946. reprint ed. pap. 31.40 (*0-7837-9399-5*, 206014400004) Bks Demand.

Myers, William S. & Newton, Walter H. Hoover Administration: A Documented Narrative. LC 79-145202. 1971. reprint ed. 69.00 (*0-403-01126-4*) Scholarly.

Myers, William T., jt. ed. see Browning, Douglas.

Myers, Yock. The Brain, Head, Neck & Spine with Mr. Correlations: A Teaching File. (Illus.). 608p. 2001. text 99.00 (*0-8151-9000-X*, 29915) Mosby Inc.

Myerscough, Philip R. & Ford, Michael J. Talking with Patients: Keys to Good Communication. 3rd ed. (Oxford Medical Publications). (Illus.). 258p. (C). 1996. pap. text 39.50 (*0-19-262570-5*) OUP.

Myerscough, Thomas R. A Photographic Study Guide for Oriental Rugs. LC 84-90640. 1983. 45.00 (*0-318-04446-3*) Persian Rug Ctr.

Myerson. Foot & Ankle Disorders. LC 99-11880. 1999. text 295.00 (*0-7216-7155-1*) Harcourt.

— Handbook of Industrial Crystalization. 2nd ed. 448p. 2000. text 99.00 (*0-7506-7012-6*, Newnes) Buttrwrth-Heinemann.

Myerson, Abraham. The Inheritance of Mental Diseases. LC 75-16724. (Classics in Psychiatry Ser.). 1976. reprint ed. 28.95 (*0-405-07448-4*) Ayer.

— The Nervous Housewife. LC 72-2616. (American Women Ser.: Images & Realities). 278p. 1974. reprint ed. 21.95 (*0-405-04470-4*) Ayer.

— Speaking of Man. Grob, Gerald N., ed. LC 78-22577. (Historical Issues in Mental Health Ser.). 1980. reprint ed. lib. bdg. 23.95 (*0-405-11929-1*) Ayer.

Myerson, Allan S. Handbook of Industrial Crystallization. LC 92-14704. (Series in Chemical Engineering). 300p. 1992. text 130.00 (*0-7506-9155-7*) Buttrwrth-Heinemann.

Myerson, Allan S., ed. Molecular Modeling Applications in Crystallization. LC 98-44694. (Illus.). 300p. (C). (up). 1999. text 110.00 (*0-521-55297-4*) Cambridge U Pr.

Myerson, Allan S., et al, eds. Crystal Growth of Organic Materials. LC 96-1348. (ACAS Conference Proceedings Ser.). (Illus.). 320p. 1996. text 125.00 (*0-8412-3382-9*, Pub. by Am Chemical) OUP.

Myerson, Allan S. & Toyokura, Ken, eds. Crystallization As a Separations Process. LC 90-1162. (Symposium Ser.: No. 438). (Illus.). 405p. 1990. 99.95 (*0-8412-1864-1*) Am Chemical.

***Myerson, Daniel.** Blood & Splendor: The Lives of Five Tyrants, from Nero to Saddam Hussein. 304p. 2000. pap. 14.00 (*0-380-80489-1*) Morrow Avon.

Myerson, George. The Argumentative Imagination: Wordsworth, Dryden, Religious Dialogues. 208p. 1992. text 89.95 (*0-7190-3676-3*, Pub. by Manchester Univ Pr) St Martin.

Myerson, George & Rydin, Yvonne. The Language of Environment: A New Rhetoric. LC 96-219744. 256p. 1996. 65.00 (*1-85728-330-9*) U of Wash Pr.

— The Language of Environment: A New Rhetoric. LC 96-219744. 256p. 1997. pap. 24.95 (*1-85728-331-7*) U of Wash Pr.

Myerson, Jeremy. Beware Wet Paint: Designs by Alan Fletcher. LC 96-144039. (Illus.). 266p. 1995. 55.00 (*0-7148-3354-1*, Pub. by Phaidon Press) Phaidon Pr.

— Gordon Russell - Designer of Furniture, 1892-1992. 144p. (C). 1992. text 115.00 (*0-85072-306-X*) St Mut.

— International Interiors 5, Vol. 5. (Illus.). 256p. 1996. 65.00 (*1-85669-071-7*, Pub. by Law King Ltd) Trafalgar.

***Myerson, Jeremy.** International Interiors 7. (Illus.). 240p. 2000. 65.00 (*1-85669-183-7*, Pub. by L King Pubng) Antique Collect.

Myerson, Jeremy. International Lighting Design. (Illus.). 192p. 1996. 50.00 (*1-85669-086-5*, Pub. by L King Pubng) Bks Nippan.

— Makepeace: A Spirit of Adventure in Craft & Design. (Illus.). 192p. 1995. 45.00 (*0-7892-0067-8*, Cross Riv Pr) Abbeville Pr.

— New Public Architecture. (Illus.). 240p. 1996. 65.00 (*1-85669-083-0*, Pub. by L King Pubng) Bks Nippan.

Myerson, Jeremy, ed. Design for Change: The Architecture of DEGW. (Illus.). 190p. 1998. pap. 45.00 (*3-7643-5738-X*, Pub. by Birkhauser) Princeton Arch.

Myerson, Jeremy & Ross, Philip. The Creative Office. (Illus.). 240p. 1999. 65.00 (*1-58423-008-8*) Gingko Press.

Myerson, Jeremy, jt. auth. see Turner, Gavin.

Myerson, Joel. Critical Essays on Henry David Thoreau's Walden. (Critical Essays Ser.). 240p. 1988. 48.00 (*0-8161-8885-8*, G K Hall & Co) Mac Lib Ref.

— Emily Dickinson: A Descriptive Bibliography. LC 83-21678. (Series in Bibliography). (Illus.). 226p. 1984. 100.00 (*0-8229-3491-4*) U of Pittsburgh Pr.

— Margaret Fuller: A Descriptive Bibliography. LC 78-4203. (Series in Bibliography). (Illus.). 178p. 1978. 100.00 (*0-8229-3381-0*) U of Pittsburgh Pr.

— New England Transcendentalists & the DIAL: A History of the Magazine & Its Contributors. LC 78-66814. 400p. 1970. 45.00 (*0-8386-2294-1*) Fairleigh Dickinson.

— Ralph Waldo Emerson: A Descriptive Bibliography. LC 81-11502. (Series in Bibliography). (Illus.). 830p. 1982. 110.00 (*0-8229-3452-3*) U of Pittsburgh Pr.

— Studies in the American Renaissance, 1995, Vol. 19. (Illus.). 400p. (C). 1995. text 50.00 (*0-8139-1631-3*) U Pr of Va.

***Myerson, Joel.** Transcendentalism: A Reader. 688p. 2000. pap. 29.95 (*0-19-512213-5*); text 65.00 (*0-19-512212-7*) OUP.

Myerson, Joel. Walt Whitman: A Descriptive Bibliography. LC 92-25927. (Series in Bibliography). (Illus.). 1128p. (C). 1993. text 250.00 (*0-8229-3739-5*) U of Pittsburgh Pr.

***Myerson, Joel, compiled by.** Margaret Fuller: An Annotated Bibliography of Criticism, 1983-1995, 27. LC 97-49188. (Bibliographies & Indexes in Women's Studies: Vol. 27). 160p. 1998. lib. bdg. 69.50 (*0-313-29577-8*, Greenwood Pr) Greenwood.

Myerson, Joel, ed. The American Renaissance in New England. LC 77-82803. (Dictionary of Literary Biography Ser.: Vol. 1). (Illus.). 240p. 1978. text 155.00 (*0-8103-0913-0*) Gale.

— Antebellum Writers in New York & the South, Vol. 3. LC 79-15481. (Dictionary of Literary Biography Ser.: Vol 3.). (Illus.). 400p. 1979. text 155.00 (*0-8103-0915-7*) Gale.

Myerson, Joel, ed. The Cambridge Companion to Henry David Thoreau. (Cambridge Companions to Literature Ser.). 248p. (C). 1995. text 64.95 (*0-521-44037-8*); pap. text 18.95 (*0-521-44594-9*) Cambridge U Pr.

— Emerson & Thoreau: The Contemporary Reviews. (American Critical Archives Ser.). (Illus.). 480p. (C). 1992. text 110.00 (*0-521-38336-6*) Cambridge U Pr.

— Emerson Centenary Essays. LC 81-18516. 230p. 1982. 21.95 (*0-8093-1023-6*) S Ill U Pr.

— A Historical Guide to Ralph Waldo Emerson. LC 99-13122. (Historical Guides to American Authors Ser.). (Illus.). 336p. 2000. pap. 16.95 (*0-19-512094-9*); text 35.00 (*0-19-512093-0*) OUP.

— Studies in the American Renaissance, 1983. (Illus.). x, 417p. 1983. text 50.00 (*0-8139-0997-X*) U Pr of Va.

— Studies in the American Renaissance, 1985. (Illus.). x, 410p. 1985. text 50.00 (*0-8139-1060-9*) U Pr of Va.

— Studies in the American Renaissance, 1984. (Illus.). vii, 458p. (C). 1984. text 50.00 (*0-8139-1021-8*) U Pr of Va.

— Studies in the American Renaissance, 1986. (Illus.). x, 450p. 1986. text 50.00 (*0-8139-1106-0*) U Pr of Va.

— Studies in the American Renaissance, 1988. (Illus.). 475p. 1989. text 50.00 (*0-8139-1164-8*) U Pr of Va.

— Studies in the American Renaissance, 1987. (Illus.). x, 416p. 1987. text 50.00 (*0-8139-1114-1*) U Pr of Va.

— Studies in the American Renaissance, 1989. (Illus.). 400p. 1990. text 50.00 (*0-8139-1230-X*) U Pr of Va.

— Studies in the American Renaissance, 1996. (Illus.). 400p. 1996. text 50.00 (*0-8139-1663-1*) U Pr of Va.

— Studies in the American Renaissance, 1991. 15th ed. (Illus.). 436p. (C). 1992. text 50.00 (*0-8139-1337-3*) U Pr of Va.

— Studies in the American Renaissance, 1992, Vol. 16. (Illus.). 350p. (C). 1992. text 50.00 (*0-8139-1389-6*) U Pr of Va.

— Studies in the American Renaissance, 1993, Vol. 17. 400p. 1993. text 50.00 (*0-8139-1453-1*) U Pr of Va.

— Studies in the American Renaissance, 1994, Vol. 18. 1994. text 50.00 (*0-8139-1534-1*) U Pr of Va.

— The Transcendentalists: A Review of Research & Criticism. LC 83-19442. (Reviews of Research Ser.: No. 7). xix, 534p. 1984. pap. 25.00 (*0-87352-261-3*, Z540P) Modern Lang.

***Myerson, Joel, ed.** Whitman in His Own Time: A Biographical Chronicle of His Life, Drawn from Recollections, Memoirs & Interviews by Friends & Associates. expanded ed. (Illus.). 366p. 2000. pap. text 19.95 (*0-87745-728-X*) U of Iowa Pr.

Myerson, Joel, ed. Whitman in His Own Time: A Biographical Chronicle of His Life, Drawn from Recollections, Memoirs, Interviews by His Friends & Associates. (Writers in Their Own Time Ser.). (Illus.). 1991. lib. bdg. 65.00 (*1-55888-424-6*) Omnigraphics Inc.

Myerson, Joel, jt. auth. see Burkholder, Robert E.

Myerson, Joel, jt. contrib. by see Burkholder, Robert E.

Myerson, Joel, ed. see Alcott, Louisa May.

Myerson, Joel, ed. see Bruccoli, Matthew J.

Myerson, Joel, ed. see Emerson, Ralph Waldo.

Myerson, Joel, ed. see Whitman, Walt.

***Myerson, Julie.** Laura Blundy. 272p. 2000. 23.95 (*1-57322-168-6*) Putnam Pub Group.

Myerson, Julie. Me And The Fat Man. LC 98-37747. 224p. 1999. 23.95 (*0-88001-649-3*) HarpC.

Myerson, Kathleen, et al. Introduction to Data Processing. 1978. text 12.00 (*0-89433-036-5*); pap. text 9.95 (*0-89433-035-7*); 15.00 (*0-89433-037-3*) Petrocelli.

Myerson, Marian. Risk Management Processes for Software Engineering Models. LC 96-35955. 226p. 1996. 29.00 (*0-89006-635-3*) Artech Hse.

Myerson, Mark. Foot & Ankle Trauma & Reconstruction. (Illus.). 480p. 1997. text 99.00 (*0-07-044328-9*) McGraw.

Myerson, Melbourne Z. Potpourri of Land & Sea. 192p. 1998. pap. 12.50 (*0-9665757-0-9*) Ponder Pubns.

Myerson, Michael, jt. auth. see Abt, John.

An Asterisk (*) at the beginning of an entry indicates that the title is appearing for the first time.

Myerson, Paul G. Childhood Dialogues & the Lifting of Repression: Character Structure & Psychoanalytic Technique. 192p. (C). 1991. 32.00 (*0-300-04928-5*) Yale U Pr.

Myerson, Richard J. Is Selling for You? It's a Great Job & Somebody's Got to Do It. 112p. (Orig.). 1992. pap. 12.95 (*0-9631841-9-9*) Pine Pubns.

Myerson, Roger B. Game Theory: Analysis of Conflict. (Illus.). 576p. 1991. 52.00 (*0-674-34115-5*, MYEGAM) HUP.

— Game Theory: Analysis of Conflict. (Illus.). 584p. 1997. reprint ed. pap. 24.95 (*0-674-34116-3*) HUP.

Myes, M., ed. John Trumbull: An Anthology in Memoriam (1756-1843) LC 93-70706. 109p. (Orig.). 1993. pap. 24.95 (*1-879183-19-6*) Bristol Banner.

Myette, Willie. Complete Adventures in Jazz. (Illus.). 60p. (J). (gr. k-12). 1998. pap. text 29.95 (*1-891679-04-X*, COM) Jazzkids.

— First Adventures in Jazz. 2nd rev. ed. (Adventures in Jazz Ser.). (Illus.). 36p. (J). (ps-12). 1996. pap. text 10.00 (*1-891679-00-7*, FAJ) Jazzkids.

— More Adventures in Jazz. (Adventures in Jazz Ser.). (Illus.). 36p. (J). (gr. k-12). 1997. pap. text 10.00 (*1-891679-02-3*, MAJ) Jazzkids.

Myfois, Kevin, ed. see Pemberton, Kermit.

Mygak, Joe, jt. auth. see Mavlin, George J.

Mygind, Holger. Deafmutism. 1976. 300.00 (*0-8490-0008-4*) Gordon Pr.

Mygind, Niels & Naclerio, Robert M., eds. Allergic & Non-Allergic Rhinitis: Clinical Aspects. (Illus.). 200p. 1993. text 57.95 (*0-7216-5146-1*, W B Saunders Co) Harcrt Hlth Sci Grp.

Mygind, Niels, et al. Essential Allergy. 2nd rev. ed. LC 95-14201. (Essentials Ser.). 496p. 1996. 64.95 (*0-632-03645-1*) Blackwell Sci.

— Instant Allergy. LC 96-44629. (Illus.). 184p. 1997. pap. text 29.95 (*0-632-04232-X*) Blackwell Sci.

Myhammad, Maulana. Manual of Hadith. 1987. 10.95 (*0-913321-15-X*) Ahmadiyya Anjuman.

Myhra, jt. ed. see Riviere.

***Myhra, David.** Bachem BA 349 Natter: X-Plane of the 3rd Reich. (Illus.). 128p. 2000. pap. 14.95 (*0-7643-1032-1*) Schiffer.

— Focke-Wulf Ta 183. LC 99-61083. (Illus.). 64p. 1999. pap. 9.95 (*0-7643-0907-2*) Schiffer.

Myhra, David. Heinkel He 162. (Illus.). 96p. 1999. pap. 14.95 (*0-7643-0955-2*) Schiffer.

— The Horten Brothers & Their All-Wing Aircraft. LC 97-68960. (Illus.). 320p. 1998. 59.95 (*0-7643-0441-0*) Schiffer.

***Myhra, David.** Horten Ho 9. LC 99-61379. (Illus.). 80p. 1999. pap. 12.95 (*1-7643-0916-1*) Schiffer.

— Messerschmitt Me 209. (Illus.). 112p. 2000. pap. 14.95 (*0-7643-1107-7*) Schiffer.

Myhra, David. Messerschmitt Me 263. (Illus.). 64p. 1999. pap. 9.95 (*0-7643-0909-9*) Schiffer.

— Messerschmitt P.1101. LC 99-61085. (Illus.). 64p. 1999. pap. 9.95 (*0-7643-0908-0*) Schiffer.

— Secret Aircraft Designs of the Third Reich. LC 97-81279. 352p. 1998. 59.95 (*0-7643-0564-6*) Schiffer.

***Myhra, David.** Tank TA 154. (Illus.). 124p. 2000. pap. 14.95 (*0-7643-1111-5*) Schiffer.

Myhre, David, jt. ed. see Cornelius, Wayne A.

Myhre, Dick, intro. Lives in Focus: Profiles of Struggle & Strength. 112p. (Orig.). 1988. pap. 2.95 (*0-939159-15-5*) Cityhill Pub.

Myhre, Helen & Vold, Mona. Farm Recipes & Other Secrets from the Norske Nook: The Midwest's Number One Roadside Cafe. LC 92-12628. 320p. 1993. 24.00 (*0-517-58550-2*, Crown) Crown Pub Group.

Myhre, M., ed. see McManus, Dorothy.

Myhrman, David V. Sumerian Administrative Documents Dated in the Reigns of the Kings of the Second Dynasty of the Ur from the Temple Archives of Nippur Preserved in Philadelphia. LC 11-1230. (University of Pennsylvania, Babylonian Expedition, Series A: Cuneiform Texts: Vol. 3, Pt. 1). 242p. reprint ed. pap. 75.10 (*0-608-14325-1*, 205201300027) Bks Demand.

Myhrman, Matts & MacDonald, S. O. Build it with Bales - Version Two: A Step-by-Step Guide to Straw-Bale Construction. 2nd rev. ed. (Illus.). 148p. 1997. pap. 29.95 (*0-9642821-1-9*, Pub. by Out OBale) Chelsea Green Pub.

Myin, Erik, jt. auth. see Goguen, Joseph A.

Myint, H., jt. auth. see Lal, Deepak.

Myint-U, T. Ordinary Differential Equations. 296p. 1977. 45.75 (*0-444-00233-2*) P-H.

Myint-U, T. & Debnath, L. Partial Differential Equations for Scientists & Engineers. 3rd ed. 620p. 1987. 45.75 (*0-444-01173-0*) P-H.

Myintu. Partial Differential Equations in Science. 3rd ed. 1987. 60.80 (*0-13-051665-1*) P-H.

Myka, Frank P. Decline of Indigenous Populations: The Case of the Andaman Islanders. (C). 1993. 18.00 (*81-7033-208-7*, Pub. by Rawat Pubns) S Asia.

Mykian, M. Numerology Made Easy. 1979. pap. 10.00 (*0-87980-376-2*) Wilshire.

Mykkeltveit, S., jt. auth. see Husebye, Eystein S.

Mykland, Robert. Palm Programming: Ground Up. 1999. write for info. (*0-07-212150-5*) McGraw.

***Mykland, Robert.** Palm Programming from the Ground Up. (From the Ground Up Ser.). 608p. 1999. pap. 34.99 incl. cd-rom (*0-07-212152-1*) Osborne-McGraw.

Myklebust, Helmer R. Conscience: Knowing Right from Wrong. LC 97-28399. (Augustana College Press Monograph Ser.: Vol. 7). 120p. 1997. pap. 10.95 (*0-931170-65-6*) Ctr Western Studies.

— Understanding Ourselves as Adults: The Meaning of Emotional Maturity. 180p. 1999. pap. 10.95 (*0-931170-64-8*) Ctr Western Studies.

Myklebust, Helmer R. Understanding Ourselves as Adults: The Meaning of Emotional Maturity. LC 93-37825. 1994. pap. write for info. (*0-89876-198-0*) Gardner Pr.

Myklebust, Helmer R., jt. auth. see Johnson, Doris J.

Myklebust, Joel B., et al, eds. Neural Stimulation, 2 vols. 1985. 124.95 (*0-318-58963-X*, RC350, CRC Reprint) Franklin.

— Neural Stimulation, 2 vols., Vol. I. 168p. 1985. 100.00 (*0-8493-5253-3*, RC350, CRC Reprint) Franklin.

— Neural Stimulation, 2 vols., Vol. II. 176p. 1985. 101.00 (*0-8493-5254-1*, RC350, CRC Reprint) Franklin.

Myklestad, J. Meyer & Soras, H. Norwegian-English, English-Norwegian Dictionary, Norwegian-English Dictionary. (ENG & NOR.). 42.50 (*0-87557-054-2*) Saphrograph.

Myklevoll, Martinus. Martinus Myklevolls Sjfartsminner. (NOR.). (Orig.). 1989. pap. 8.95 (*0-9621657-0-0*) Jest Pubns.

Mykoff, M. H., et al, eds. The Living Nach - Sacred Writings, Vol. III. Rubin, Gaviel et al, trs. (Living Nach Ser.). (Illus.). 943p. 1999. 38.00 (*1-885220-22-7*) Moznaim.

Mykoff, Moshe, ed. see Kramer, Chaim.

Mykoff, Moshe, ed. see Nachman & Nathan.

Mykoff, Moshe, ed. see Rabbi Nachman of Breslov.

Mykoff, Moshe, ed. see Rebbe Nachman of Breslov.

Mykoff, Moshe, ed. see Starret, Yehoshua & Kramer, Chaim.

Mykoff, Moshe, ed. & tr. see Nachman.

Mykoff, Moshe, ed. & tr. see Rabbe Nachman.

Mykoff, Moshe, ed. & tr. see Rabbi Nachman of Breslov.

Mykoff, Moshe, tr. see Yerushalmi, Shmuel.

Mykoff, Moshe, tr. & intro. see Rabbi Nachman of Breslov.

Mykowski, Michelle. Explore God's Desert. Ring, Laura, ed. LC 98-61291. (Shaped Paperbacks Ser.). (Illus.). 24p. (J). (ps-1). 1999. pap. 2.99 (*0-7847-0898-3*, 03788) Standard Pub.

— Explore God's Forest. Ring, Laura, ed. (Shaped Paperbacks Ser.). (Illus.). 24p. (J). (ps-1). 1999. pap. 2.99 (*0-7847-0900-9*, 03790) Standard Pub.

— Explore God's Jungle. Ring, Laura, ed. LC 98-61292. (Shaped Paperbacks Ser.). (Illus.). 24p. (J). (ps-1). 1999. pap. 2.99 (*0-7847-0899-1*, 03789) Standard Pub.

— Explore God's Ocean. Ring, Laura, ed. LC 98-61293. (Shaped Paperbacks Ser.). (Illus.). 24p. (J). (ps-1). 1999. pap. 2.99 (*0-7847-0897-5*, 03787) Standard Pub.

Mykrantz, John R. Garden Design Kit: Flowering Perennials. (Illus.). 20p. 1993. student ed. 24.95 (*1-880301-02-4*) Gardeners.

— Garden Planning Kit: Vegetable Garden Planner. (Illus.). 7p. 1993. student ed. 24.95 (*1-880301-00-8*) Gardeners.

Mykytiuk, Stefan, ed. see Vilenkin, N. Y.

Mykytyns. Micro Mainframe Connection. 1985. text. write for info. (*0-442-26419-4*, VNR) Wiley.

Myladil, Thomas. St. John of the Cross & the Baghavad Gita. 320p. pap. 19.95 (*0-940121-53-0*, Pub. by Cross Cultural Pubns) BookWorld.
This is a work on St. John of the Cross, one of the great Christian spiritual masters & the Bhagavadgita, the best known text from the Hindu scriptures. The focus of the work is renunciation & love, the central themes in spiritual & mystical writings of all times. Thomas Myladil, a member of the Discalaced Carmelite Order, teaches courses in Hinduism at Rutgers. The State University of New Jersey. *Publisher Paid Annotation.*

Myland, Jan C., jt. auth. see Oldham, Keith B.

Mylander, Charles, jt. auth. see Anderson, N.

Mylander, Charles, jt. auth. see Anderson, Neil T.

Mylander, Maureen, jt. auth. see Adams, Patch.

Mylar, Barry. Don't Give Me Any of That C.R.A.P. 32p. 1996. pap. 4.99 (*0-9627099-5-6*) Zephyr Pub Corp.

Mylar, Isaac L. Early Days at the Mission San Juan Bautista: Portrayal of an Historic California Town by an Early Settler. (Illus.). 204p. 1994. pap. 9.95 (*1-884995-02-0*) Word Dancer.

***Myldner, Tomasz.** Java for C Programers. LC 99-89910. 500p. 2000. pap. 35.00 (*0-201-70279-7*) Addison-Wesley.

***Mylenbusch, Diane.** Getting a Loan. (Cliffs Notes Ser.). 128p. 1999. pap. text 8.99 (*0-7645-8543-6*) IDG Bks.

Myler, Harley R. Fundamentals of Engineering Programming with C & Fortran. LC 97-43343. (Illus.). 224p. (C). 1998. 69.95 (*0-521-62063-5*); pap. text 27.95 (*0-521-62950-0*) Cambridge U Pr.

— Fundamentals of Machine Vision. LC 98-31172. 133p. 1998. 42.00 (*0-8194-3049-8*) SPIE.

— Pocket Handbook of Image Processing Algorithms in C. 303p. (C). 1993. 30.00 (*0-13-642240-3*) P-H.

***Myler, P.** Gentleman Jim Corbett: The Truth Behind a Boxing Legend. LC 99-197475. 1999. 29.95 (*1-86105-212-X*) Robson Bks.

***Myler, Patrick.** A Century of Boxing Greats: Inside the Ring with the Hundred Best Boxers. 394p. 2000. pap. 14.95 (*1-86105-258-8*) Robson.

Myler, Patrick. A Century of Boxing Greats: Inside the Ring with the 100 Best Boxers. LC 97-75450. (Illus.). 394p. 1998. 29.95 (*1-86105-134-4*, Pub. by Robson Bks) Parkwest Pubns.

Myler, Randal. The Adventures of Huckleberry Finn. 1990. pap. 5.25 (*0-87129-141-X*, A50) Dramatic Pub.

Myler, Terry. Drawing Made Easy. 48p. 1995. pap. 8.95 (*0-947962-94-8*, Pub. by Anvil Books Ltd) Dufour.

— Drawing Made Very Easy. 32p. 1998. pap. 7.95 (*1-901737-00-4*) Dufour.

Myler, Terry, jt. auth. see Arrigan, Mary.

Myler, Terry, jt. auth. see Flynn, Mary.

Myler, Terry, jt. auth. see Hickey, Tony.

Myler, Terry, jt. auth. see McMahon, Kate.

Myler, Terry, jt. auth. see Regan, Peter.

Myler, Terry, jt. auth. see Webb, Sarah.

***Myler, Thomas.** Boxing's Greatest Upsets: Fights That Shook the World. 180p. 1999. text 25.95 (*1-86105-202-2*) Robson.

Myles, Anita. Doris Lessing: A Novelist with Organic Sensibility. 1990. text 22.50 (*81-7045-068-3*, Pub. by Assoc Pub Hse) Advent Bks Div.

Myles, Brenda & Simpson, Richard L. Asperger Syndrome: A Guide for Educators & Parents. LC 97-17269. 1997. 38.89 (*0-89079-727-7*) PRO-ED.

Myles, Brenda, jt. auth. see Simpson, Richard L.

Myles, Bruce. Night Witches: The Amazing Story of Russia's Women Pilots in WWII. 3rd ed. (Illus.). 272p. 1997. reprint ed. pap. 13.00 (*0-89733-288-1*) Academy Chi Pubs.

Myles, Carolyn, jt. auth. see Day, Anne L.

Myles, Colette G., ed. The Butterflies Carried Him Home & Other Indian Tales. LC 80-70506. (Illus.). 73p. 1981. 4.95 (*0-9605468-1-2*) Artmans Pr.

Myles, Douglas. Krakken. 374p. mass mkt. 4.99 (*1-55197-228-X*) Picasso Publ.

Myles, Eileen. Bread & Water. 208p. (Orig.). 1987. pap. 5.95 (*0-937815-02-0*) Hanuman Bks.

— Chelsea Girls. LC 94-9895. 276p. 1997. 25.00 (*0-87685-933-3*); pap. 14.00 (*0-87685-932-5*) Black Sparrow.

***Myles, Eileen.** Cool for You. 2000. pap. 14.00 (*1-887128-59-X*) Soft Skull Pr.

Myles, Eileen. Maxfield Parrish: Early & New Poems. LC 95-8852. 229p. (Orig.). (C). 1995. 25.00 (*0-87685-975-9*); pap. 14.00 (*0-87685-974-0*) Black Sparrow.

— Maxfield Parrish: Early & New Poems, signed ed. deluxe ed. LC 95-8852. 229p. (Orig.). (C). 1995. 35.00 (*0-87685-976-7*) Black Sparrow.

— Not Me. 202p. 1991. pap. 6.00 (*0-936756-67-5*) Autonomedia.

— School of Fish. LC 97-11773. 200p. (Orig.). 1997. 25.00 (*1-57423-032-8*); pap. 14.00 (*1-57423-031-X*) Black Sparrow.

— School of Fish. deluxe limited ed. LC 97-11773. 200p. (Orig.). 1997. 35.00 (*1-57423-033-6*) Black Sparrow.

Myles, Eileen & Kotz, Liz. The New Fuck You: Adventures in Lesbian Reading. 1995. pap. 8.00 (*1-57027-057-0*) Autonomedia.

Myles, Elizabeth & MacFarlane, Bert. Viagra, Sex & Romance: The Women Who Take It Reveal Their Erotic Tales. Choueke, Esmond, ed. 168p. 1999. pap. 12.95 (*0-9659583-1-0*) Boca Pubns.

Myles, Florence, jt. auth. see Mitchell, Rosamond.

Myles, Gareth D. Public Economics. LC 94-44774. 560p. (C). 1995. pap. text 26.95 (*0-521-49769-8*) Cambridge U Pr.

Myles, Glenn. Down & Country. LC 74-82249. (Bebop Drawing Club Book Ser.). (Illus.). 58p. 1974. pap. 4.95 (*0-9605468-0-4*) Artmans Pr.

Myles, Glenn, ed. see Lehman, Yvette K.

Myles, Janet. L. N. Cottingham (1787-1857) Architect of the Gothic Revival. (Illus.). 176p. 1995. 35.00 (*0-85331-678-3*, Pub. by Lund Humphries) Antique Collect.

Myles, Jeanette. Change of Heart. large type ed. (Linford Romance Library). 1991. pap. 16.99 (*0-7089-7057-5*) Ulverscroft.

— Dreams of Yesterday. (Rainbow Romances Ser.). 160p. 1993. 14.95 (*0-7090-4903-X*) Parkwest Pubns.

— Images of Clover. large type ed. (Linford Romance Library). 272p. 1992. pap. 16.99 (*0-7089-7288-8*) Ulverscroft.

Myles, John. Old Age in the Welfare State: The Political Economy of Public Pensions LC 83-24923. (Little Brown Series on Gerontology Ser.). xii, 140 p. 1984. write for info. (*0-316-59367-2*) Little.

Myles, John & Quadgano, Jill, eds. States, Labor Markets & the Future of Old Age Policy. 340p. 1991. 69.95 (*0-87722-790-X*) Temple U Pr.

Myles, John, jt. auth. see Clement, Wallace.

Myles, Paul, jt. auth. see Gin, Tony.

Myles, Robert. Chaucerian Realism. LC 94-5852. (Chaucer Studies: Vol. XX). 167p. (C). 1994. 75.00 (*0-85991-409-7*, DS Brewer) Boydell & Brewer.

Myles, W. C. Transition to Manhood: Through Rites of Passage. Cook, Edward, tr. (Illus.). 165p. (C). 1993. pap. write for info. (*0-9638582-0-3*) Stud Ninety.

Mylet, Trish. Fun Phonics, Children, Today's Joy!, 20 vols., Set. 2nd rev. ed. (Illus.). 476p. (J). (ps-3). 1996. pap. text 39.95 (*0-945590-96-2*) Sizzy Bks.

Mylin, Barbara K., jt. ed. see Fulton, Eleanore J.

Mylin, Deborah, ed. Body Language: New Moon Talks about Growing Up. (Illus.). 24p. 1999. 8.95 (*0-9652777-3-9*) New Moon MN.

Mylius, K. Worterbuch Sanskrit to German. 5th ed. (GER & SAN.). 583p. 1997. 150.00 (*0-320-00462-7*) Fr & Eur.

Mylius, Klaus. Sanskrit-German Dictionary (Woerterbuch Sanskrit-Deutsch) 3rd ed. (GER & SAN.). 583p. 1987. 150.00 (*0-8288-1157-1*, F60923) Fr & Eur.

— Woerterbuch Deutsch-Sanskrit. 2nd ed. (GER & SAN.). 322p. 1992. 135.00 (*0-7859-8305-8*, 3324003377) Fr & Eur.

— Woerterbuch Sanskrit-Deutsch. 4th ed. (GER & SAN.). 583p. 1992. 150.00 (*0-7859-8300-7*, 3324002451) Fr & Eur.

Myller, E. & Muller, E. E. IGFs in the Nervous System (Insulin-Like Growth Factors in the Nervous System: Proceedings. LC 97-41301. 130p. 1997. pap. 49.00 (*3-540-75042-8*) Spr-Verlag.

Myller-Olm, Markus. Modular Compiler Verification: A Refinement-Algebraic Approach Advocating Stepwise Abstraction, Vol. 128. Goos, G. et al, eds. LC 97-13428. (Lecture Notes in Computer Science Ser.: Vol. 1283). xv, 250p. 1997. pap. 49.00 (*3-540-63406-1*) Spr-Verlag.

Myller, Rolf. How Big Is a Foot? 48p. (J). 1991. pap. 3.99 (*0-440-40495-9*) Dell.

— How Big Is a Foot? (J). 1992. pap. 7.95 (*0-440-80332-2*) Dell.

Myller, Rolf. How Big is a Foot? 1990. 9.19 (*0-606-04940-1*, Pub. by Turtleback) Demco.

Myller, Werner E., et al, eds. Molecular Evolution: Evidence for Monophyly of Metazoa. LC 97-27728. (Progress in Molecular & Subcellular Biology Ser.: Vol. 19). (Illus.). 198p. 1998. 119.00 (*3-540-63229-8*) Spr-Verlag.

Mylls, Robert. Information Engineering: Case, Practices & Techniques. (New Dimensions in Engineering Ser.). 440p. 1993. 110.00 (*0-471-58711-7*) Wiley.

Myllylae, G., jt. ed. see Lane, T. A.

Myllymaki, Theodora & Akerson, James. Comprehensive Guide to Cosmetic Sources. 225p. 1992. pap. 26.95 (*1-56253-102-6*) Thomson Learn.

***Myllyntaus, Timo & Saikku, Mikko, eds.** Encountering the Past in Nature: Essays in Environmental History. (Series in Ecology & History). 184p. (C). 2000. text 39.95 (*0-8214-1357-0*); pap. text 16.95 (*0-8214-1358-9*) Ohio U Pr.

M

Myine, Alexander. Vitae Dunkeldensis Ecclesiae Episcoporum, a Prima Sedis Foundatione, ad Annum MDXV Ab Alexandro Myln, Eiusdem Ecclesiae Canonica Conscriptae, Repr. Of 1823 Ed. Thomson, Thomas, ed. LC 78-173008. 20.00 (*0-404-52701-9*) AMS Pr.

Mylnikov, V., et al. Photoconducting Polymers & Metal-Containing Polymers. (Advances in Polymer Science Ser.: Vol. 115). (Illus.). 145p. 1994. 114.95 (*0-387-57476-X*) Spr-Verlag.

Mylonas, Anastassios D. Perception of Police Power: A Study in Four Cities. (N. Y. U. Criminal Law Education & Research Center, Monograph Ser.: Vol. 8). (Illus.). x, 131p. 1974. reprint ed. pap. 19.50 (*0-8377-0418-9*, Rothman) W S Hein.

Mylonas, George E. Mycenae & the Mycenaean Age. LC 65-17154. (Illus.). 340p. reprint ed. pap. 105.40 (*0-8357-6229-7*, 203428500089) Bks Demand.

Mylopoulos, John, et al, eds. Advanced Information Systems Engineering. LC 96-8634. xi, 582p. 1996. pap. 87.00 (*3-540-61292-0*) Spr-Verlag.

Mylopoulos, John & Brodie, Michael, eds. Readings in Artificial Intelligence & Databases. 650p. (C). 1988. pap. text 48.95 (*0-934613-53-2*) Morgan Kaufmann.

Mylopoulos, John, jt. ed. see Brodie, M. L.

Mylott, Thomas R., III. Computer Law for Computer Professionals. write for info. (*0-318-58179-5*) P-H.

— Computer Outsourcing: Managing the Transition of Information Systems. LC 94-42556. 385p. 1995. 24.95 (*0-13-127614-X*) P-H.

Mylroie, jt. auth. see Carew.

Mylroie, John E., ed. Proceedings of the 4th Symposium on the Geology of the Bahamas. (Illus.). 381p. (Orig.). (C). 1989. pap. text 20.00 (*0-935909-31-1*) Bahamian.

Mylroie, John E. & Carew, James L. A Field Trip Guide Book of Lighthouse Cave, San Salvador Island, Bahamas. (Illus.). 10p. (Orig.). (C). 1994. pap. text 4.00 (*0-935909-48-6*) Bahamian.

Mylroie, John E., jt. auth. see Carew, James L.

Mylroie, Laurie. The Future of Iraq. LC 91-4277. (Policy Papers: No. 24). 68p. 1991. pap. 8.00 (*0-944029-10-8*) Wash Inst NEP.

***Mylroie, Laurie.** Study of Revenge: Saddam Hussein's Unfinished War Against America. 300p. 2000. pap. 24.95 (*0-8447-4127-2*, Pub. by Am Enterprise) Pub Resources Inc.

Mymer, Stephen, jt. ed. see Kay, Geoffrey.

Mynard, D. C. Excavation of Two Medieval Sites at Milton Keynes. (Milton Keynes Archaeological Reports). (Illus.). 192p. 1994. pap. 32.50 (*0-949003-15-8*) David Brown.

Mynard, D. C. & Zeepvat, R. J. Great Linford. (Milton Keynes Archaeological Reports). (Illus.). 394p. 1992. pap. 54.00 (*0-949003-08-5*) David Brown.

Mynard, D. C., jt. auth. see Croft, R. A.

Mynatt, jt. auth. see Doherty.

Mynatt, Clifford R. & Doherty, Michael E. Understanding Human Behavior. LC 98-7068. 448p. 1998. write for info. (*0-205-29082-5*) Allyn.

— Understanding Human Behavior. LC 98-7068. 430p. (C). 1998. pap. text 47.00 (*0-205-14000-9*) Allyn.

Mynatt, Daniel S. The Sub Loco Notes in the Torah of Biblia Hebraica Stuttgartensia. LC 95-6988. (Dissertation Ser.: No. 2). 288p. 1995. pap. 18.95 (*0-941037-33-9*, BIBAL Press) D & F Scott.

Mynatt, Elizabeth B., ed. see Brown, Alma C.

Mynatt, Margaret, jt. auth. see Kapp, Yvonne.

***Mynbaev, Djafar K.** Fiber Optics Communications Technology. 528p. 2000. 93.00 (*0-13-962069-9*, Prentice Hall) P-H.

Myneni, R. B. & Ross, J., eds. Photon-Vegetation Interactions: Applications in Optical Remote Sensing & Plant Ecology. (Illus.). 560p. 1991. 262.95 (*0-387-52108-9*) Spr-Verlag.

Mynne, Hugh. The Faerie Way: A Healing Journey to Other Worlds. LC 96-16408. (Celtic Wisdom Ser.). (Illus.). 152p. (Orig.). 1999. pap. 12.95 (*1-56718-483-9*) Llewellyn Pubns.

Mynors, R. A. B., ed. & tr. see William of Malmesbury.

Mynors, Roger A. Opera. (Oxford Classical Texts Ser.). 468p. 1969. text 21.00 (*0-19-814653-1*) OUP.

Mynors, Roger A., ed. Epistularum Libri Decem. (Classical Texts Ser.). 386p. 1963. text 35.00 (*0-19-814643-4*) OUP.
— Georgics. 440p. 1994. reprint ed. pap. text 35.00 (*0-19-814978-6*) OUP.
— XII Panegyrici Latini. (Oxford Classical Texts Ser.). 312p. 1964. text 45.00 (*0-19-814647-7*) OUP.
Mynors, Roger A. & Thomson, R. M. Catalogue of the Manuscripts of Hereford Cathedral Library. (Illus.). 272p. (C). 1993. 215.00 (*0-85991-390-2*) Boydell & Brewer.
Mynors, Roger A., ed. see Catullus, Gaius Valerius.
Mynors, Roger A., ed. & tr. see Bede.
Mynors, Roger A., ed. & tr. see Erasmus, Desiderius.
Mynors, Roger A., tr. see Bietenholz, Peter G., ed.
Mynors, Roger A., tr. see Bietenholz, Peter G., et al.
Mynors, Roger A., tr. see Erasmus, Desiderius.
Mynors, Roger A., tr. & anno. see Erasmus, Desiderius.
Mynster, jt. auth. see Benfield.
Mynter, Jen. Mountain Bike America: Vermont: An Atlas of Vermont's Greatest Off-Road Bicycle Rides. (Illus.). 192p. 2000. pap. 14.95 (*1-882997-07-7*, Pub. by Beachway Pr) Globe Pequot.
Mynton, Henry. The Pachinko Woman. LC 99-18700. 400p. 1999. 25.00 (*0-688-16170-7*, Wm Morrow) Morrow Avon.
***Myntti, Cynthia.** Paris Along The Nile; Architecture In Cairo From The Belle Epoque. 1999. 39.95 (*977-424-510-5*, Pub. by Am Univ Cairo Pr) Col U Pr.
Myo-Bong, Master & Hye-Am Choi. Gateway to Patriarchal Son (Zen) Venerable Master Hye-Am's Dharma Talks. LC 86-50754. (CHI & KOR.). 524p. (Orig.). 1986. 14.95 (*0-938647-01-6*) Western Son Acad.
Myoken, Hajime. Optimal Stabilization Policies of Dynamic Economic Systems under Decentralized Information & Control-Regulation Structures. (Collection des Theses de la Faculte des Sciences Economiques et Sociales de l'Universite de Geneve). (Illus.). XIV, 293p. 1990. pap. 55.00 (*3-261-04261-3*) P Lang Pubng.
Myokyo-Ni. Zen Way. 117p. 1995. pap. 12.95 (*0-8048-3076-2*) Tuttle Pubng.
Myong-Won Cho, Litt D. Landscape, Peoplescape & Self-Escape. (C). 1989. pap. text 49.00 (*1-85821-032-1*, Pub. by Pentland Pr) St Mut.
Myopia International Conference Staff. Proceedings of the Myopia International Conference, 3rd, Copenhagen, 1980. Fledelius, H. C. et al, eds. (Documenta Ophthalmologica Proceedings Ser.: No. 28). 266p. 1981. text 191.50 (*90-6193-725-6*) Kluwer Academic.
Myors, Brett, jt. auth. see Murphy, Kevin R.
Myotis, Gille, jt. auth. see Gekko, Alexander.
Myra, Anne & Benjamin, Goodman. Decadence in Thirteenth Century Provencial & Hebrew Poetry. (Medieval & Renaissance Monograph: No. VIII). 249p. (Orig.). 1987. pap. 10.00 (*0-941107-01-9*) MARC Pub Co.
Myra, Harold. Easter Bunny, Are You for Real? LC 97-32656. (Illus.). 32p. (J). (ps-2). 1998. 7.99 (*0-8499-1493-0*) Tommy Nelson.
— Halloween, Is It for Real? LC 97-20393. (Illus.). 32p. (J). (ps-3). 1997. pap. 7.99 (*0-8499-1494-9*) Tommy Nelson.
— Santa, Are You for Real? LC 97-25497. (Illus.). 32p. (J). (ps-3). 1997. 5.95 (*0-8499-1492-2*) Tommy Nelson.
Myra, Lawrence. Analisis De La Mano. (SPA.). 1997. pap. text 15.98 (*968-13-0018-1*) Libros Fronteras.
Myrad, Ferid, et al, eds. Advances in Pharmacology: DNA Topoisomerases, Vol. 29B. (Illus.). 315p. 1994. text 84.00 (*0-12-032930-1*) Acad Pr.
Myrad, Ferid, et al, eds. Advances in Pharmacology Vol. 29A: DNA Topoisomerases. (Illus.). 320p. 1994. text. write for info. (*0-12-032929-8*) Acad Pr.
Myrada Organization: India Staff & International Institute of Rural Reconstruction Staff. Resource Management in Rainfed Drylands: An Information Kit. LC 98-915190. 356 p. 1997. write for info. (*0-942717-71-6*) Intl Inst Rural.
Myradal, Gunnar. An American Dilemma Vol. 1 & 2: The Negro Problem & Modern Democracy, 2 vols., Set. 1896p. (C). 1996. pap. text 49.95 (*1-56000-858-X*) Transaction Pubs.
Myran, Gunder, et al. Community College Leadership in the New Century: Learning to Improve Learning. 92p. 1995. pap. 24.00 (*0-87117-281-X*, 1381) Comm Coll Pr Am Assn Comm Coll.
Myrand, D., jt. auth. see Shah, H. N.
***Myranda, Rafaheal C.** Puerto Rico: Independence Is A Necessity: Rafael Cancel Miranda on the Fight Against U. S. Colonial Rule. LC 99-187953. 36p. 1998. pap. 3.00 (*0-87348-895-4*) Pathfinder NY.
Myrberg, Mats. Towards an Ergonomic Theory of Text Design & Composition. (Upsala Studies in Education: No. 5). 175p. (Orig.). 1978. pap. 29.50 (*91-554-0762-5*) Coronet Bks.
Myrdal, Alva & Sorsa, Kalevi. Steps Towards European Nuclear Disarmament: Two Papers for the Rome Consultation on Nuclear Disarmament. 79p. (Orig.). 1981. pap. 18.95 (*0-85124-304-5*, Pub. by Spkesman) Coronet Bks.
Myrdal, Alva, et al. America's Role in International Social Welfare. 1990. 16.50 (*0-8446-1320-7*) Peter Smith.
— Dynamics of European Nuclear Disarmament. 1982. 40.00 (*0-85124-320-7*, Pub. by Spkesman); pap. 15.95 (*0-85124-321-5*, Pub. by Spkesman) Dufour.
Myrdal, Gunnar. An American Dilemma Vol. 2: The Negro Problem & Modern Democracy. LC 95-31355. 976p. (C). 1996. pap. text 29.95 (*1-56000-857-1*) Transaction Pubs.
— Beyond the Welfare State: Economic Planning & Its International Implications. LC 82-15819. 287p. 1982. reprint ed. lib. bdg. 38.50 (*0-313-23697-6*, MYBW, Greenwood Pr) Greenwood.
***Myrdal, Gunnar.** The Essential Myrdal. 2000. 45.00 (*1-56584-600-1*, Pub. by New Press NY) Norton.
— The Essential Myrdal. Appelqvist, Orjan & Andersson, Stellan, eds. 2000. pap. 21.95 (*1-56584-601-X*, Pub. by New Press NY) Norton.
Myrdal, Gunnar. Monetary Equilibrium. LC 65-23216. (Reprints of Economic Classics Ser.). xi, 214p. 1965. reprint ed. 35.00 (*0-678-00092-1*) Kelley.
— Objectivity in Social Research. LC H 0062.M9. 125p. 1983. reprint ed. pap. 38.80 (*0-7837-8198-9*, 204790300008) Bks Demand.
— The Political Element in the Development of Economic Theory. 311p. (C). 1990. pap. 24.95 (*0-88738-827-2*) Transaction Pubs.
Myrdal, Jam. When Our Tomorrows Sang: From Forgotten Years. Swandon, Christine, tr. from SWE. Orig. Title: Nar Morgondagarna Sjong. 2000. 22.95 (*0-941702-52-9*, 52-9) Lake View Pr.
Myrdal, Jan. Another World. LC 93-41239. 1994. 19.95 (*1-884468-00-4*) Ravenswood Bks.
— Childhood. Swanson, Christine, tr. LC 91-26744. (SWE.). 192p. 1991. 22.95 (*0-941702-29-4*) Lake View Pr.
— Confessions of a Disloyal European. 216p. 1990. 25.00 (*0-941702-27-8*); pap. 14.95 (*0-941702-26-X*) Lake View Pr.
— India Waits. Bernstein, Alan, tr. from SWE. LC 86-20069. (Illus.). 364p. (Orig.). 1986. 35.00 (*0-941702-06-5*) Lake View Pr.
— 12 Going on 13: An Autobiographical Novel. Swanson, Christine, tr. from SWE. LC 95-35488. 200p. 1995. 19.95 (*1-884468-01-2*, 01-2) Ravenswood Bks.
Myrdal, Jan & Kessle, Gun. Albania Defiant. LC 74-21469. 249p. reprint ed. pap. 77.20 (*0-8357-5294-1*, 203076400070) Bks Demand.
Myreng, Svein. Plum Poems. LC 99-24382. (Illus.). 80p. (Orig.). 1998. pap. 10.00 (*1-888375-06-X*) Parallax Pr.
Myrent, Glenn, et al. Henri Langlois, First Citizen of Cinema. LC 94-27336. (Filmmakers Ser.). (Illus.). 300p. 1995. 33.00 (*0-8057-4522-X*, Twyne); pap. 22.00 (*0-8057-4521-1*, Twyne) Mac Lib Ref.
Myrer, Anton. A Green Desire. 720p. 1983. pap. 3.95 (*0-380-61580-0*, Avon Bks) Morrow Avon.
— The Last Convertible. 1993. reprint ed. lib. bdg. 37.95 (*1-56849-240-5*) Buccaneer Bks.
— Once an Eagle. 1976. 49.95 (*0-8488-1438-X*) Amereon Ltd.
***Myrer, Anton.** Once an Eagle. 960p. 2000. 25.00 (*0-06-019696-3*) HarpC.
Myrer, Anton. The Tiger Waits: A Novel. LC 72-10355. 378 P.p. (J). 1973. write for info. (*0-393-08672-0*) Norton.
Myrer, Joseph. Musculoskeletal Functional Human Anatomy. 176p. (C). 1996. pap. text, spiral bd. 36.95 (*0-7872-1912-6*, 41191201) Kendall-Hunt.
Myres, John L. Handbook of the Cesnola Collection of Antiquities from Cyprus. LC 77-168425. (Metropolitan Museum of Art Publications in Reprint). (Illus.). 656p. 1974. reprint ed. 60.95 (*0-405-02263-8*) Ayer.
— The Political Ideas of the Greeks. 436p. 1927. 25.00 (*0-8196-1163-8*) Biblo.
— Political Ideas of the Greeks. LC 71-137278. reprint ed. 22.50 (*0-404-04549-9*) AMS Pr.
Myres, John L., ed. see Pitt-Rivers, Augustus H.
Myres, John N. The English Settlements. (Oxford History of England Ser.: Vol. IB). (Illus.). 288p. 1986. text 45.00 (*0-19-821719-6*) OUP.
— The English Settlements. (Oxford History of England Ser.: Vol. 18). (Illus.). 284p. 1989. reprint ed. pap. 19.95 (*0-19-282235-7*) OUP.
Myres, John N., jt. auth. see Collingwood, R. G.
Myres, John N., jt. auth. see Green, Barbara.
Myres, Sandra L. Native Americans of Texas. (Texas History Ser.). (Illus.). 46p. 1981. pap. text 9.95 (*0-89641-083-8*) American Pr.
— Westering Women & the Frontier Experience. LC 82-6956. (Histories of the American Frontier Ser.). (Illus.). 365p. 1982. pap. 16.95 (*0-8263-0626-8*) U of NM Pr.
Myres, Sandra L., ed. Ho for California! Women's Overland Diaries from the Huntington Library. LC 79-28115. (Illus.). 320p. 1999. pap. 14.95 (*0-87328-119-5*, Pub. by Huntington Lib) A Schwartz & Co.
Myres, Sandra L., ed. see Alexander, Eveline M.
Myres, Sandra L., ed. see Van Zandt, K. M.
Myrfors, Jesper. Castle Skye. (Pandevelopment Ser.). 128p. 1993. pap. 11.95 (*1-880992-14-0*) Wizards Coast.
— The Compleat Necromancer. (Pandevelopment Ser.). 72p. 1994. pap. 10.95 (*1-880992-18-3*) Wizards Coast.
***Myrhe, Robert.** CCNA Certification: Routing Basics for Cisco Certified Network Associates Exam 640-407. LC 99-55011. (Illus.). 544p. 1999. pap. text 49.99 (*0-13-086185-5*) P-H.
Myrianthopoulos, Ntinos C., ed. External Ear Malformations: Epidemiology, Genetics & Natural History. LC 79-2501. (Alan R. Liss Ser.: Vol. 15, No. 9). 1979. 22.00 (*0-685-03287-6*) March of Dimes.
Myrianthopoulos, Ntinos C. & Bergsma, Daniel, eds. Recent Advances in the Developmental Biology of Central Nervous System Malformations. LC 79-4947. (Alan R. Liss Ser.: Vol. 15, No. 3). 1979. 19.00 (*0-685-03296-5*) March of Dimes.
Myrick, Cynthia. Easy Bible Study: A Step-by-Step Guide to Understanding God's Word. (Illus.). 68p. 1999. pap. 12.99 (*0-9671679-2-2*) Almost Home.
Myrick, David F. Montecito & Santa Barbara, Vol. 2. LC 87-30188. (Illus.). 320p. (YA). (gr. 11). 1991. 54.95 (*0-87046-100-1*) Pentrex Media.
— New Mexico's Railroads: A Historical Survey. rev. ed. LC 89-27309. (Illus.). 276p. 1990. pap. 18.95 (*0-8263-1185-7*) U of NM Pr.
Myrick-Harris, Clarissa, et al. Mainstreaming African-American Studies: A Resource Guide for Middle & High School Teachers. 240p. (Orig.). 1990. pap. text. write for info. (*1-878531-02-6*) Black Res Ctr.
Myrick-Harris, Clarissa, jt. ed. see Harris, Norman.
***Myrick, Leland.** The Sweet Collection. (Illus.). 128p. 2000. per. 12.95 (*0-9701288-0-0*) Adept Bks.
Myrick, Linda S., jt. auth. see Myrick, Robert D.
Myrick, N., ed. Heritage Seventy Six. (Illus.). 117p. (C). 1976. 5.00 (*0-686-81380-4*) Ridgefield Bicen Com.
***Myrick, Paula & Scribner, Jay Paredes, eds.** Case Studies of the Superintendency. LC 99-55522. 175p. 2000. text 36.50 (*0-8108-3752-8*) Scarecrow.
Myrick, Richard. Deer Isle Sketches. (Illus.). 72p. (Orig.). 1990. pap. 9.50 (*0-9625851-0-6*) R Myrick.
Myrick, Robert D. Developmental Guidance & Counseling: A Practical Approach. 3rd ed. LC 96-61505. 390p. (C). 1997. text 34.95 (*0-932796-76-1*) Ed Media Corp.
Myrick, Robert D. & Bowman, Robert P. Becoming a Friendly Helper: A Handbook for Student Facilitators. Sorenson, Don L., ed. LC 81-82899. (Illus.). 120p. (Orig.). (gr. 5-6). 1981. pap. 5.95 (*0-932796-08-7*) Ed Media Corp.
— Children Helping Children: Teaching Students to Become Friendly Helpers. Sorenson, Don L., ed. LC 81-82900. (Illus.). 280p. 1991. pap. text 10.95 (*0-932796-09-5*) Ed Media Corp.
***Myrick, Robert D. & Erney, Tom.** Caring & Sharing: Becoming a Peer Facilitator. 2nd rev. ed. LC 00-100766. (Illus.). 256p. (YA). (gr. 8-12). 2000. pap. text 10.95 (*0-932796-99-0*) Ed Media Corp.
Myrick, Robert D. & Erney, Tom. Youth Helping Youth: A Handbook for Training Peer Facilitators. Sorenson, Don L., ed. LC 78-70544. (Illus.). 224p. 1985. pap. text 8.95 (*0-932796-02-8*) Ed Media Corp.
Myrick, Robert D. & Folk, Betsy E. Peervention: Training Peer Facilitators for Prevention Education. LC 90-86235. (Illus.). 210p. 1991. pap. text 14.95 (*0-932796-35-4*) Ed Media Corp.
— The Power of Peervention: A Manual for the Trainers of Peer Facilitators. LC 90-86234. (Illus.). 226p. (C). 1991. teacher ed., spiral bd. 39.95 (*0-932796-36-2*) Ed Media Corp.
Myrick, Robert D. & Myrick, Linda S. The Teacher Advisor Program: An Innovative Approach to School Guidance. 117p. 1990. pap. 16.95 (*1-56109-003-4*) CAPS Inc.
Myrick, Robert D. & Sorenson, Don L. Helping Skills for Middle School Students. LC 92-70820. (Illus.). 160p. (Orig.). (J). (gr. 6-8). 1992. pap. text 7.95 (*0-932796-40-0*) Ed Media Corp.
— Peer Helping: A Practical Guide. 2nd rev. ed. LC 97-60266. (Illus.). 160p. 1997. pap. text 9.95 (*0-932796-81-8*) Ed Media Corp.
— Teaching Helping Skills to Middle School Students: Program Leader's Guide. LC 92-70804. (Illus.). 128p. (Orig.). (J). (gr. 6-8). 1992. pap., teacher ed. 8.95 (*0-932796-41-9*) Ed Media Corp.
Myrick, Robert D., jt. auth. see Sabella, Russell A.
Myrick, Roger, ed. AIDS, Communication, & Empowerment: Gay Male Identity & the Politics of Public Health Messages. LC 95-45914. 141p. (C). 1996. 34.95 (*1-56023-884-4*, Haworth Pastrl) Haworth Pr.
Myrick, Roger, ed. AIDS, Communication, & Empowerment: Gay Male Identity & the Politics of Public Health Messages. LC 95-45914. 141p. (C). 1997. pap. 19.95 (*1-56023-907-7*, Haworth Pastrl) Haworth Pr.
Myrick, Sue. Challenging the Status Quo. 256p. 2001. 16.99 (*0-7852-7483-9*) Nelson.
Myrick, Susan. White Columns in Hollywood: Reports from the GWTW Sets. LC 82-18881. (Illus.). 345p. 1982. pap. 14.95 (*0-86554-245-7*, MUP/P037) Mercer Univ Pr.
Myring, Lynn. First Guide to the Universe. (Explainers Ser.). 72p. (J). (gr. 2-4). 1982. 12.95 (*0-86020-611-4*, Usborne) EDC.
— Lasers. (Introductions Ser.). (Illus.). 48p. (YA). (gr. 6-12). 1984. pap. 7.95 (*0-86020-722-6*) EDC.
Myring, Lynn. Rockets & Spaceflight. (Explainers Ser.). (Illus.). 24p. (J). (gr. 2-4). 1982. pap. 4.95 (*0-86020-584-3*, Usborne) EDC.
Myring, Lynn. Sun, Moon & Planets. (Explainers Ser.). (Illus.). 24p. (J). (gr. 2-4). 1982. pap. 4.50 (*0-86020-580-0*, Usborne) EDC.
Myriveles, Strates. Life in the Tomb. Bien, Peter, tr. from GER. LC 86-40519. 352p. 1987. reprint ed. pap. 109.20 (*0-608-02321-3*, 206296200004) Bks Demand.
Myrman, M. B., jt. auth. see Collin, P. H.
Myrna, J. Adam & Myrna, John W. Winning the Workplace Race: Get Promoted First. Survive the Downsizing. (Short Attention Span Library: Vol. 8). 140p. 1998. pap. 5.95 (*1-891660-01-2*) Quick Study.
Myrna, John W. One Hundred Quick Tips for Business Success. Taylor, Don, ed. 112p. (Orig.). 1994. pap. 3.95 (*0-9637314-1-6*) Quick Study.
Myrna, John W., jt. auth. see Myrna, J. Adam.
Myron, Monique, jt. auth. see Truax, Pamela.
Myron, Robert. Art History. (Barron's EZ-101 Study Keys Ser.). 144p. 1991. pap. 5.95 (*0-8120-4595-5*) Barron.
Myron, Robert, jt. auth. see Watson, Clarissa H.
***Myrone, Martin.** Representing Britain, 1500-2000: 100 Works from Tate Collections. (Illus.). 144p. 2000. pap. 24.95 (*1-85437-321-8*) U of Wash Pr.
Myrone, Martin & Peltz, Lucy, eds. Producing the Past: Aspects of Antiquarian Culture & Practice (1700-1850) LC 98-53016. (Illus.). 298p. 1999. text 86.95 (*1-84014-275-8*) Ashgate Pub Co.
Myrowitz, Catherine H. Finding a Home for the Soul: Interviews with Converts to Judaism. LC 94-32903. 424p. 1995. pap. 35.00 (*1-56821-322-0*) Aronson.
Myrsiades, Kostas. Others Must Dance for the Lord Dionysus Now: A Poetic Memoir. LC 93-85993. (Illus.). 72p. (Orig.). 1993. pap. text 10.00 (*0-918618-55-X*) Pella Pub.
Myrsiades, Kostas, ed. Approaches to Teaching Homer's Iliad & Odyssey. LC 86-31167. (Approaches to Teaching World Literature Ser.: No. 13). x, 158p. 1987. pap. 18.00 (*0-87352-500-0*, AP13P); lib. bdg. 37.50 (*0-87352-499-3*, AP13C) Modern Lang.
Myrsiades, Kostas & McGuire, Jerry, eds. Order & Partialities: Theory, Pedagogy & the "Postcolonial" LC 94-41282. (SUNY Series, Interruptions). 415p. (C). 1995. pap. text 19.95 (*0-7914-2640-8*) State U NY Pr.
— Order & Partialities: Theory, Pedagogy & the "Postcolonial" LC 94-41282. (SUNY Series, Interruptions). 415p. (C). 1995. text 59.50 (*0-7914-2639-4*) State U NY Pr.
Myrsiades, Kostas & Myrsiades, Linda, eds. Karagiozis: Three Classic Plays. LC 99-70136. 240p. 1999. pap. 15.00 (*0-918618-73-8*) Pella Pub.
Myrsiades, Kostas & Myrsiades, Linda S. Karagiozis: Culture & Comedy in Greek Puppet Theater. LC 92-9927. (Illus.). 248p. (C). 1992. text 35.00 (*0-8131-1795-X*) U Pr of Ky.
Myrsiades, Kostas & Myrsiades, Linda S., eds. Margins in the Classroom: Teaching Literature. LC 93-8692. (Pedagogy & Cultural Practices Ser.: Vol. 2). 1994. pap. 17.95 (*0-8166-2320-1*); text 44.95 (*0-8166-2319-8*) U of Minn Pr.
Myrsiades, Kostas, jt. auth. see Myrsiades, Linda S.
Myrsiades, Kostas, ed. & tr. see Ritsos, Yannis.
Myrsiades, Kostas, tr. see Papatsonis, Takis.
Myrsiades, Kostas, tr. see Ritsos, Yannis.
Myrsiades, Linda, jt. ed. see Mrysiades, Kostas.
Myrsiades, Linda, jt. ed. see Myrsiades, Kostas.
Myrsiades, Linda S. & Myrsiades, Kostas. Cultural Representation in Historical Resistance: Complexity & Construction in Greek Guerrilla Theater. LC 98-49143. (Illus.). 376p. 1999. 52.50 (*0-8387-5407-4*) Bucknell U Pr.
Myrsiades, Linda S., jt. auth. see Myrsiades, Kostas.
Myrsiades, Linda S., jt. ed. see Myrsiades, Kostas.
***Myrsidaes, Kostas & Myrsides, Linda, eds.** Un-Disciplining Literature: Literature, Law & Culture. (Counterpoints). 1999. 29.95 (*0-8204-4541-X*) P Lang Pubng.
Myrsides, Linda, jt. ed. see Myrsidaes, Kostas.
Myrtek, Michael, jt. ed. see Fahrenberg, Jochen.
Myrus, Joyce. Master of Moonlight. 384p. 1995. mass mkt. 4.99 (*0-8217-4900-5*, Pinncle Kensgtn) Kensgtn Pub Corp.
Myrvaagnes, Eric, et al. Foundations of Problem Solving. (Illus.). 415p. (C). 1997. pap. text 30.00 (*1-878437-77-1*) Pac Crest Soft.
— Foundations of Quantitative Reasoning. (Illus.). 400p. (Orig.). (C). 1997. pap. text 40.00 (*1-878437-08-9*) Pac Crest Soft.
Myrvang, June C. & Myrvang, Steve. The Home Design Handbook: The Essential Planning Guide for Building, Buying, or Remodeling a Home. (Illus.). 256p. (Orig.). 1995. pap. 14.95 (*0-8050-1833-6*, Owl) H Holt & Co.
Myrvang, Steve, jt. auth. see Myrvang, June C.
Myrvik, Quentin N. & Weiser, Russell S. Fundamentals of Medical Bacteriology & Mycology. 2nd ed. LC 87-2866. 611p. reprint ed. pap. 189.50 (*0-7837-2733-X*, 204311300006) Bks Demand.
Myrvik, Quentin N., jt. auth. see Kucera, Louis S.
Mysak, Joe. The Handbook for Mini-Bond Issuers. LC 97-52168. (Professional Library). (Illus.). 256p. 1998. 40.00 (*1-57660-023-8*, Pub. by Bloomberg NJ) Norton.
Mysak, Susan, ed. see Greeley, Patricia.
Myscofski, Carol A. When Men Walk Dry: Portuguese Messianism in Brazil. LC 88-24015. (American Academy of Religion Academy Ser.). 211p. 1989. pap. 15.95 (*1-55540-257-7*, 01-01-61) OUP.
Mysell, Bella, tr. see Yablokoff, Herman.
Mysels, Karol J., jt. ed. see Fort, Tomlinson.
Mysen, B. O. Structure & Properties of Silicate Melts. (Developments in Geochemistry Ser.: Vol. 4). 354p. 1988. 150.00 (*0-444-42959-X*) Elsevier.
Mysen, B. O., ed. Magmatic Processes: Physicochemical Principles. LC 86-83155. (Special Publication: No. 1). 490p. 1987. 65.00 (*0-941809-00-5*) Geochemical Soc.
— Phase Diagrams for Ceramists Vol. VIII: High-Pressure Systems. 416p. 1990. 150.00 (*0-944904-23-8*, PH08) Am Ceramic.
Myshanick. Today's Technician: Medium/Heavy Engine Repair. (Automotive Technology Ser.). 1998. pap., teacher ed. 16.50 (*0-8273-7222-1*) Delmar.
— Today's Technician: Medium/Heavy Engine Repair. (Automotive Technology Ser.). 2000. pap. 57.95 (*0-8273-7221-3*) Delmar.
— Today's Technician: Medium/Heavy Engine Repair IRK. (Automotive Technology Ser.). 1998. 99.99 (*0-8273-7223-X*) Delmar.
Myshaniuk. Today's Technician: Medium/Heavy Truck AC & Refrigeration. (Automotive Technology Ser.). 1999. teacher ed. 16.00 (*0-8273-7255-8*) Delmar.
— Today's Technician: Medium/Heavy Truck Air Conditioning & Refrigeration. (Automotive Technology Ser.). 1999. pap. 56.00 (*0-8273-7254-X*) Delmar.
— Today's Technician: Medium/Heavy Truck Air Conditioning & Refrigeration IRK. (Automotive Technology Ser.). 1999. 99.99 (*0-8273-7256-6*) Delmar.
Myshkis, A. & Kolmanovski, Vladimir B. Applied Theory of Functional Differential Equations. LC 92-35413. (Mathematics & Its Applications. Soviet Ser.: Vol. 85). 1992. text 152.50 (*0-7923-2013-1*) Kluwer Academic.
Myshkis, A. D., et al, eds. Low-Gravity Fluid Mechanics: Mathematical Theory of Capillary Phenomena. Wadhwa, R. S., tr. from RUS. (Illus.). 610p. 1987. 175.95 (*0-387-16189-9*) Spr-Verlag.

An Asterisk (*) at the beginning of an entry indicates that the title is appearing for the first time.

Myshkis, A. D. & Kolmanovskfi, Vladimir B. Introduction to the Theory & Applications of Functional Differential Equations. LC 98-49064. (Mathematics & Its Applications Ser.). 12p. 1999. write for info. (*0-7923-5504-0*) Kluwer Academic.

Mysina, S. D., jt. auth. see Knorre, D. K.

Myslenski, Skip, jt. auth. see Henson, Lou.

Myslik, Constance S. Gathering the Soul. Date not set. write for info. (*0-913660-27-2*); pap. write for info. (*0-913660-29-9*) Magic Cir Pr CT.

***Myslik, Constance Simpson.** Gathering the Soul. LC 99-90693. 1999. 24.00 (*0-7388-0472-X*); pap. 18.00 (*0-7388-0473-8*) Xlibris Corp.

Myslivecek, Josef. Josef Myslivecek: Three Violin Concertos. White, Chappell, ed. (Recent Researches in Music of the Classic Era Ser.: Vol. RRC41). xiv, 136p. 1994. pap. 50.00 (*0-89579-290-7*) A-R Eds.

Myslivecek, Milan. Erbovnik: 1152 Cost-of-Arms in Color. (CZE.). 1993. 52.00 (*0-614-02657-1*) Szwede Slavic.

***Mysliwiec, Karol.** The Twilight of Ancient Egypt: First Millennium, B. C. E. 2000. 55.00 (*0-8014-3716-4*) Cornell U Pr.

— The Twilight of Ancient Egypt: First Millennium, B. C. E. Lorton, David, tr. from GER. LC 00-34039. (Illus.). 2000. pap. 24.95 (*0-8014-8630-0*) Cornell U Pr.

Mysliwski, Wieslaw. The Palace. Phillips, Ursula, tr. from POL. 208p. 1991. 32.00 (*0-7206-0790-6*, Pub. by P Owen Ltd) Dufour.

Myslobodsky, Michael S., ed. The Mythomanias: The Nature of Deception & Self-Deception. LC 96-13605. 416p. 1996. text 79.95 (*0-8058-1919-3*) L Erlbaum Assocs.

Myslowski, Tadeusz. Tadeusz Myslowski Towards Organic Geometry, 1972-1994: 163 Selected Photographic Images on Japanese Paper. (Illus.). 176p. 1994. text 75.00 (*0-9640648-0-4*) I Hockman Fine.

Mysnyk, Mark, et al. Winning Wrestling Moves. LC 93-42161. (Illus.). 208p. 1994. pap. 19.95 (*0-87322-482-5*, PMYS0482) Human Kinetics.

Myss, Caroline. Anatomy of the Spirit: The Seven Stages of Power & Healing. LC 96-220328. 320p. 1996. 25.00 (*0-517-70391-2*) Harmony Bks.

— Anatomy of the Spirit: The Seven Stages of Power & Healing. 352p. 1997. pap. 14.00 (*0-609-80014-0*) Random Hse Value.

— Energy Anatomy, Set. unabridged ed. 1996. pap. 59.95 incl. audio (*1-56455-379-5*, F041) Sounds True.

— Invisible Acts of Power. 2003. 17.00 (*0-517-70793-4*, Crown) Crown Pub Group.

— Sacred Contract. 1997. 25.00 (*0-517-70392-0*) Random Hse Value.

— Why People Don't Heal & How They Can. LC 97-22798. 1997. 25.00 (*0-609-60090-7*) Harmony Bks.

— Why People Don't Heal & How They Can. 288p. 1998. pap. 14.00 (*0-609-80224-0*) Harmony Bks.

Myss, Caroline, jt. auth. see Shealy, C. Norman.

Mysse, Janet W. Cabbage Soup: Knitting Patterns for Soft-Sculptured Dolls. (Illus.). pap., spiral bd. 4.95 (*0-9623098-0-X*) Janknits.

— Knitting for All Seasons: A Collection of Thirty Knit Classics, Bk. I. (Illus.). (Orig.). pap., spiral bd. 4.95 (*0-9623098-2-6*) Janknits.

— Knitting for All Seasons: A Collection of Thirty Knit Classics, Bk. II. (Illus.). (Orig.). pap., spiral bd. 4.95 (*0-9623098-3-4*) Janknits.

— Knitting for All Seasons: A Collection of Thirty Knit Classics, Bk. II. Hay, Richard, ed. (Illus.). (Orig.). 1989. pap. 9.95 (*0-685-29410-2*) Janknits.

— Knitting for All Seasons: A Collection of Thirty Knit Classics, Bk. III. (Illus.). (Orig.). pap., spiral bd. 4.95 (*0-9623098-4-2*) Janknits.

— Knitting for All Seasons: A Collection of Thirty Knit Classics, Bk. IV. (Illus.). (Orig.). pap., spiral bd. 4.95 (*0-9623098-5-0*) Janknits.

Myst, H. D. Secrets of My Past. LC 99-63917. 250p. 1999. pap. 6.99 (*1-893181-20-0*) Le Gesse Stevens.

Mystery, James I. The Promises of Infinity. rev. ed. LC 97-94735. (Illus.). 454p. (YA). (gr. 8 up). Date not set. 24.95 (*0-9661550-0-9*, Tomorrow) INEDIN.

Mystery Scene Editors. The Fine Art of Murder: The Mystery Reader's Indispensable Companion. (Illus.). 208p. 1993. pap. 15.95 (*0-88184-972-3*) Carroll & Graf.

Mystery Scene Magazine Editors, ed. The Year's Twenty-Five Finest Crime & Mystery Stories, Vol. 1. annuals 352p. 1994. pap. 12.95 (*0-7867-0018-1*) Carroll & Graf.

— The Year's Twenty-Five Finest Crime & Mystery Stories, Vol. 3. annuals 3rd ed. 352p. 1994. 20.00 (*0-7867-0141-2*) Carroll & Graf.

Mystery Scene Magazine Staff. Mystery's Most Wanted: Staff of Mystery Scene. 1997. mass mkt. 5.99 (*0-312-96476-5*) St Martin.

Mystery Science Theater 3000 Writers & Performers. The Mystery Science Theater 3000: Amazing Colossal Episode Guide. 208p. 1996. pap. 17.95 (*0-553-37783-3*) Bantam.

Mystery Writers of America Staff, jt. auth. see Turow, Scott.

Mystic Jhamom Publishers Staff, ed. Is Man a Free Agent? Illustrations Booklet: Supplement. (Conversations with a Mystic Ser.: No. 1). 12p. 1985. pap. 1.75 (*0-933961-02-2*) Mystic Jhamom.

Mystic Jhamon Publishers Staff, ed. Free Agent Horoscope Charts: Supplement. (Conversations with a Mystic Ser.: No. 1). 12p. 1985. pap. 1.25 (*0-933961-03-0*) Mystic Jhamom.

— Is Man a Free Agent? (Conversations with a Mystic Ser.: No. 1). (Illus.). 128p. (J). (gr. 6 up). 1985. pap. 9.95 (*0-933961-01-4*) Mystic Jhamom.

— Jhamom's Story of Creation. (Conversations with a Mystic Ser.: No. 3). (Illus.). 136p. 1986. pap. 9.95 (*0-933961-07-3*) Mystic Jhamom.

— Jhamom's Story of Creation Illustration Booklet: Supplement. (Conversations with a Mystic Ser.: No. 3). (Illus.). 16p. 1986. pap. 2.00 (*0-933961-08-1*) Mystic Jhamom.

— The Phenomena of Life. (Conversations with a Mystic Ser.: No. 4). (Illus.). 1986. pap. write for info. (*0-933961-09-X*) Mystic Jhamom.

— The Phenomena of Life Illustrations Booklet: Supplement. (Conversations with a Mystic Ser.: No. 4). (Illus.). 24p. 1986. pap. write for info. (*0-933961-10-3*) Mystic Jhamom.

— Why? Psychic Development & How! (Conversations with a Mystic Ser.: No. 2). (Illus.). 176p. 1985. pap. 11.75 (*0-933961-05-7*) Mystic Jhamom.

— Why? Psychic Development & How! Illustration Booklet, Supplement. (Conversations with a Mystic Ser.: No. 2). (Illus.). 12p. 1985. pap. 1.75 (*0-933961-06-5*) Mystic Jhamom.

Mystic Seaport Museum Staff. All Seasons Cookbook. (Illus.). 1994. pap. 15.95 (*0-939510-06-5*) Mystic Sea Mus.

— Global Feast Cookbook: Recipes from Around the World. LC 94-71298. (Illus.). 254p. 1994. pap. 15.95 (*0-939510-25-1*) Mystic Sea Mus.

Mystrom, Fred & Mystrom, Mardi. Special Places: For the Discerning Traveler. 7th rev. ed. Jones, Alex, ed. (Illus.). 208p. (Orig.). 1997. pap. 18.95 (*0-936777-04-4*) Special Pl.

Mystrom, Mardi, jt. auth. see Mystrom, Fred.

Myszka. Machines & Mechanisms. 1999. pap. text, student ed. write for info. (*0-13-973322-1*) P-H.

Myszka, David. Machines & Mechanisms: Applied Kinematic Analysis. LC 98-20255. 482p. 1998. 93.00 (*0-13-597915-3*) P-H.

Myszkowski, Eugene. The Remington-Lee Rifle. (Illus.). 104p. (Orig.). 1994. pap. 22.95 (*1-880677-04-0*) Excalibur AZ.

***Myszkowski, Eugene.** The Winchester-Lee Rifle. (Illus.). 96p. (Orig.). 1999. pap. 22.95 (*1-880677-15-6*) Excalibur AZ.

Mytelka, Lynn K., ed. Strategic Partnerships: States, Firms & International Competition. LC 90-49475. 1991. 45.00 (*0-8386-3445-1*) Fairleigh Dickinson.

***Mytelka, Lynn Krieger, ed.** Competition, Innovation & Competitiveness in Developing Countries. (Development Centre Studies). 216p. 1999. pap. 42.00 (*92-64-17091-X*, 41 1999 07 1 P, Pub. by Org for Econ) OECD.

Mythen, John. Claude M. Sing Around: Fighting Against Multiple Sclerosis. 1990. pap. 14.95 (*0-9694457-0-9*) Gordon Soules Bk.

Mytum, Harold & Waugh, K., eds. Rescue Archaeology - What's Next? 127p. 1987. 9.00 (*0-946722-05-6*, Pub. by U York Dept Archaeol) David Brown.

Myung, H. C., ed. Hadronic Mechanics & Nonpotential Interactions - 5, Pt. II: Physics. 421p. (C). 1992. text 225.00 (*1-56072-043-3*) Nova Sci Pubs.

— Hadronic Mechanics & Nonpotential Interactions - 5, Pt. 1: Mathematics. 293p. (C). 1992. text 195.00 (*1-56072-035-2*) Nova Sci Pubs.

Myung, H. C., et al, eds. Applications of Lie-Admissible Algebras in Physics, Vol. 2. 595p. 1978. reprint ed. pap. text 55.00 (*0-911767-04-5*) Hadronic Pr Inc.

Myung, H. C., jt. ed. see Gonzalez, Santos.

Myung Hun Kang. The Korean Business Conglomerate: Chaebol Then & Now. LC 96-33946. (Korea Research Monographs: No. 21). 1996. pap. 20.00 (*1-55729-051-2*) IEAS.

Myung, Hyo C. Lie Algebras & Flexible Lie-Admissible Algebras. (Monographs in Mathematics). 351p. (Orig.). (C). 1983. pap. text 50.00 (*0-911767-00-2*) Hadronic Pr Inc.

— Malcev-Admissible Algebras. (Progress in Mathematics Ser.: Vol. 64). 376p. 1986. 84.00 (*0-8176-3345-6*) Birkhauser.

Myung, Hyo C., jt. auth. see Elduque, Alberto.

Myung Ki Kim. The Korean War & International Law. 280p. 1991. 31.95 (*0-941690-44-X*, Paige Pr) Regina Bks.

Myung Mi Kim. Dura. (New American Poetry Ser.: No. 28). 108p. (Orig.). 1998. pap. 11.95 (*1-55713-292-5*) Sun & Moon CA.

Myung, Yoon S. Intestinal Parasites & Worms in Adults & Children: Index of New Information. 1998. 47.50 (*0-7883-1844-6*); pap. 44.50 (*0-7883-1845-4*) ABBE Pubs Assn.

Myzk, William R. The History & Origins of the Virginia Gold Cup. Woolfe, Raymond, Jr., ed. LC 88-9993. (Illus.). 300p. (C). 1988. 485.00 (*0-929129-00-8*) Piedmont VA.

MZ Media Group, Inc. Staff. Agora Services Guide. 14.95 (*1-885313-01-2*) MZ Group.

— Top One Hundred Guide. 1994. 14.95 (*1-885313-00-4*) MZ Group.

Mzamane, Mbulelo. The Children of Soweto. (C). 1995. pap. 14.20 (*0-582-01680-0*) Addison-Wesley.

— Mzala. (Writers Ser.). 185p. 1995. reprint ed. pap. text 12.95 (*0-86975-465-3*, Pub. by Ravan Pr) Ohio U Pr.

Mzamane, Mbulelo V., jt. auth. see Ball, Howard.

Mzamane, Mbulelo-Vizikhungo. Children of the Diaspora & Other Stories of Exile. 145p. 1998. pap. 12.95 (*0-86543-691-6*) Africa World.

***Mzamane, Mbulelo-Vizikhungo.** Children of the Diaspora & Other Stories of Exile. 145p. 1998. 29.95 (*0-86543-690-8*) Africa World.

Mzimela, Sipo E. Marching to Slavery: South Africa's Descent into Communism. Wheeler, Dennis, ed. 258p. (Orig.). (C). 1993. pap. 12.50 (*0-9626646-8-5*) Soundview Pubns.

N

N. E. Thing Enterprises Staff. Garfield's Magic Eye.Tr. of Garfield, l'Oeil Magique. (FRE., Illus.). 32p. (J). pap. 9.99 (*0-590-16004-4*) Scholastic Inc.

— Magic Eye.Tr. of Oeil Magique. (FRE., Illus.). (J). pap. 7.99 (*0-590-24505-8*) Scholastic Inc.

— Magic Eye: A New Bag of Tricks. (Illus.). 32p. 1995. 12.95 (*0-8362-0768-8*) Andrews & McMeel.

— Magic Eye Gallery: A Showing of 88 Images. (Illus.). 96p. 1995. 12.95 (*0-8362-7044-4*) Andrews & McMeel.

— Magic Eye Poster Book: A Book of Posters. 1994. pap. 12.95 (*0-8362-3203-8*) Andrews & McMeel.

— Magic Eye III, Vol. III.Tr. of Oeil Magique III. (FRE., Illus.). (J). pap. 7.99 (*0-590-24610-0*) Scholastic Inc.

N. F. R. Crafts Staff. Can De-Industrialization Seriously Damage Your Wealth? A Review of Why Growth Rates Differ & How to Improve Economic Performance. (IEA Hobart Paper Ser.: No. 120). 92p. 1993. pap. 26.50 (*0-255-36316-8*, Pub. by Inst Economic Affairs) Coronet Bks.

N. J. Self-Help Clearinghouse Staff, et al, eds. The Self-Help Group Directory. 15th rev. ed. 600p. 1998. pap. 25.00 (*0-9634322-8-1*) St Clares Hlth.

N. K. C. A. In't Veld Staff, jt. auth. see Altes, A. Korthals.

'N Sync. 'N Sync: The Official Book. LC 99-165768. 96p. (J). 1998. pap. 9.95 (*0-440-41636-1*) BDD Bks Young Read.

N T C Contemporary Publishing Company Staff. The Literature of Africa. 1998. pap. 17.44 (*0-8442-1202-4*) NTC Contemp Pub Co.

— Literature of Greece & Rome. 1998. 21.19 (*0-8442-1191-5*) NTC Contemp Pub Co.

— The Literature of Spain & the Americas. 1998. 21.99 (*0-8442-1198-2*); pap. 17.44 (*0-8442-1199-0*) NTC Contemp Pub Co.

***N T C Contemporary Publishing Company Staff.** Literture of Africa. 1998. 17.44 (*0-8442-1328-4*) NTC Contemp Pub Co.

N T C Contemporary Publishing Company Staff. Liturature of Greece & Rome. 1998. pap. 17.44 (*0-8442-1192-3*) NTC Contemp Pub Co.

N T C Contemporary Publishing Staff, ed. Edges of Reality: Confronting the Uncanny. LC 98-43951. 1998. write for info. (*0-8442-0502-8*) NTC Contemp Pub Co.

N::olleat, Leo M., ed. Handbook of Food Analysis, Vol. 2. (Food Science & Technology Ser.: Vol. 77). (Illus.). 2040p. 1996. text 450.00 (*0-8247-9683-7*) Dekker.

Na. Buffy the Vampire Slayer: The Postcards, 1. (J). 1999. per. 8.00 (*0-671-03640-8*) PB.

— A Place Among the Stars: The Women of the Star Trek Voyager. (Star Trek Ser.). 1998. pap. 8.00 (*0-671-03455-3*) PB.

Na, ed. see Shin, Laura.

***Na Allah, Abdul Rasheed.** Almajiri. LC 99-31451. (HAU.). 1999. write for info. (*0-86543-788-2*) Africa World.

Na, T. Y. & Seshadri, R. Group Invariance in Engineering Boundary Value Problems. LC 95-5333. (Illus.). 225p. 1985. 54.00 (*0-387-96128-3*) Spr-Verlag.

Na, Tsung, jt. auth. see Aziz, A.

NAACP Legal Defense & Educational Fund Staff. Death Row U. S. A. Reporter: 1975-1988 & 1989-1997 Supplements. LC 89-81793. 1990. ring bd. 395.00 (*0-89941-708-6*, 306050) W S Hein.

NAACP Staff. The Crisis - a Record of the Darker Races 1910-60: Journal of the National Association for the Advancement of Colored People, 50 vols, Set. LC 70-84750. 1985.50 (*0-405-01001-X*) Ayer.

Naadimuthu, Govindsami, jt. auth. see Bronson, Richard.

***Naaeye, Robert.** Signals from Outer Space: The Chandra X-Ray Observatory. (Space Explorer Ser.). (Illus.). (J). 2000. pap. 8.95 (*0-7398-2225-X*) Raintree Steck-V.

— Signals from Space: The Chandra X-Ray Observatory. (Space Explorer Ser.). (Illus.). (J). 2000. 28.54 (*0-7398-2215-2*) Raintree Steck-V.

Naake, John T. Slavonic Fairy Tales: From the Russian, Polish, Serbian & Bohemian. 1972. 59.95 (*0-8490-1062-4*) Gordon Pr.

Naallah, Abdul-Rasheed. Ogoni's Agonies: Ken Saro-Wiwa & the Crisis in Nigeria. LC 98-22493. 350p. 1998. 79.95 (*0-86543-646-0*); pap. 21.95 (*0-86543-647-9*) Africa World.

Naaman, A. E. & Reinhardt, H. W., eds. High Performance Fiber Reinforced Cement Composites: Proceedings of the International Workshop, No. 2. (Rilem Proceedings Ser.: Vol. 31). (Illus.). 528p. (C). 1996. 160.00 (*0-419-21180-2*, E & FN Spon) Routledge.

Naaman, A. E., et al. High Early Strength Fiber-Reinforced Concrete. 297p. (Orig.). (C). 1993. pap. text 15.00 (*0-309-05618-7*, SHRP-C-366) SHRP.

Naaman, A. E., jt. ed. see Reinhart, H. W.

***Naaman, Antoine E.** Ferrocement & Laminated Cementitious Composites. (Illus.). 372p. 1999. text 75.00 (*0-9674939-0-0*) Techno Pr.

Naaman, Antoine E. Prestressed Concrete: Analysis & Design. (Illus.). 736p. (C). 1982. text 73.00 (*0-07-045761-1*) McGraw.

— Prestressed Concrete Analysis & Design. (C). 1983. pap. text, teacher ed. 27.50 (*0-07-045762-X*) McGraw.

Naaman, Antoine Y., jt. auth. see Flaubert, Gustave.

Naaman, Fred & Huntz, Hellen. America Today. LC 99-60671. 96p. 1999. pap. 9.95 (*1-56167-490-7*, Five Star Spec Ed) Am Literary Pr.

Na'aman, N. Borders & Districts in Biblical Historiography. (Jerusalem Biblical Studies: Vol. 4). 275p. 1986. pap. text 28.00 (*965-242-005-0*, Pub. by Simor Ltd) Eisenbrauns.

Naaman, R. & Vager, Z., eds. The Structure of Small Molecules & Ions. (Illus.). 354p. 1988. 95.00 (*0-306-43016-9*, Plenum Trade) Perseus Pubng.

Naar, M. D. Law of Suffrage & Elections: Being a Compendium of Cases & Decisions Showing the Origin of the Elective Franchise & Defining Citizenship & Legal Residence, Together with the Clauses of the State Constitutions Prescribing the Qualifications for Suffrage & the Law Governing the Conduct of Elections in the States - With an Appendix Containing the Provisions of the United States Constitution & Revised Statutes Regulation. (Illus.). xii, 317p. 1985. reprint ed. 42.00 (*0-8377-0910-5*, Rothman) W S Hein.

Naar, Maria E. Colloquial Portugese. (Trubner's Colloquial Manuals Ser.). 192p. 1983. pap. 14.95 (*0-7100-7450-6*, Routledge Thoemms) Routledge.

Naar, Ray. A Primer of Group Psychotherapy. LC 81-4244. 215p. 1982. 35.95 (*0-89885-027-4*, Kluwer Acad Hman Sci); pap. 22.95 (*0-89885-289-7*, Kluwer Acad Hman Sci) Kluwer Academic.

Naas. Great Time Pieces of World. LC 97-76961. 1998. 49.95 (*0-8478-2093-9*, Pub. by Rizzoli Intl) St Martin.

Naas, Jayni, jt. auth. see Carey, Frank.

Naas, Lucille, jt. ed. see McAllister, Donald.

Naas, Michael. Turning: From Persuasion to Philosophy. LC 93-20211. (Philosophy & Literary Theory Ser.). 344p. (C). 1995. text 55.00 (*0-391-03821-4*) Humanities.

Naas, Michael, tr. see Derrida, Jacques.

Naas, Michael, tr. see Lyotard, Jean-Francois & Gruber, Eberhard.

Naastepad, C. W. Budget Deficit & Macroeconomic Performance: A Real-Financial College Model for India. LC 99-932756. (Illus.). 343p. 1999. text 32.00 (*0-19-564849-8*) OUP.

Naastepad, C. W. & Storm, Servaas, eds. The State & the Economic Process. LC 95-42421. (Belgian-Dutch Post-Keynesian Association for Post-Keynesian Economics Ser.). (Illus.). 288p. 1996. 90.00 (*1-85898-168-9*) E Elgar.

***Naatanen, R., ed.** Mismatch Negativity. (Audiology & Neuro-Otology Ser.: 5). (Illus.). 150p. 2000. pap. 39.25 (*3-8055-7100-3*) S Karger.

Naatanen, Risto. Attention & Brain Function. 494p. 1992. text 89.95 (*0-8058-0984-8*) L Erlbaum Assocs.

Naatanen, Risto, jt. ed. see Csepe, Valeria.

Naats, I. E. & Zuev, Vladimir E. Inverse Problems of Lidar Sensing of the Atmosphere. (Optical Sciences Ser.: Vol. 29). (Illus.). 260p. 1983. 80.95 (*0-387-10913-7*) Spr-Verlag.

NAB Staff. Careers in Radio. rev. ed. (Illus.). 32p. (Orig.). 1991. student ed. 3.50 (*0-89324-106-7*) Natl Assn Broadcasters.

— NAB Guide for Broadcast Station Chief Operators. 82p. 1991. 60.00 (*0-89324-105-9*) Natl Assn Broadcasters.

— NAB Guide to Advanced Television Systems, 1991. 2nd ed. (Illus.). 150p. (Orig.). 1991. 60.00 (*0-89324-111-3*) Natl Assn Broadcasters.

Nabar, Vrinda. Endless Female Hungers: A Study of Kamala Das. LC 93-910374. (C). 1994. write for info. (*81-207-1282-X*) Sterling Pubs.

Nabarro, F. R., ed. Dislocations & Disclinations. (Dislocations in Solids Ser.: Vol. 9). 424p. 1992. 260.50 (*0-444-89560-4*) Elsevier.

Nabarro, F. R. & Duesbery, M. S., eds. L12 Ordered Alloys. (Part of Disclotions in Solis Ser.: Vol. 10). 632p. 1996. 284.50 (*0-444-82370-0*) Elsevier.

Nabarro, F. R. & Filmer, H. Physics of Creep & Creep-Resistant Alloys. LC 95-215798. 200p. 1993. 110.00 (*0-85066-852-2*) Taylor & Francis.

Nabarro Nathanson Pensions Department Members & Quarrell, John. Nabarro Nathanson: Pensions Law. 1997. pap. write for info. (*0-406-04933-5*, NNPL, MICHIE) LEXIS Pub.

Nabasa, J., et al. Participatory Rural Appraisal Practical Experiences. 1995. pap. 25.00 (*0-85954-392-7*, Pub. by Nat Res Inst) St Mut.

Nabauns, Leroy. Love Blossom. McCann, Yvette D., ed. 136p. (Orig.). 1997. pap. 14.00 (*0-9660263-2-2*) Vol Pr.

Nabb, Magdalen. The Enchanted Horse. LC 93-18423. (Illus.). 96p. (J). (gr. 3-6). 1993. 15.95 (*0-531-06805-6*) Orchard Bks Watts.

— The Enchanted Horse. LC 95-3785. (J). (gr. 3-6). 1995. 9.05 (*0-606-09239-0*, Pub. by Turtleback) Demco.

Nabban, Gary P. Cultures of Habitat: On Nature, Culture & Story. 352p. 1998. reprint ed. pap. 15.00 (*1-887178-96-1*, Pub. by Counterpt DC) HarpC.

Nabbes, Thomas. Works of Thomas Nabbes, 2 vols. Bullen, Arthur H., ed. LC 68-24818. 1972. reprint ed. 36.95 (*0-405-08812-4*) Ayer.

Nabe, jt. auth. see Corr, Charles A.

Nabe, Clyde M. Mystery & Religion: Newman's Epistemology of Religion. 76p. (Orig.). (C). 1988. pap. text 13.00 (*0-8191-6712-6*) U Pr of Amer.

Naber, Gregory L. The Geometry of Minkowski Spacetime: An Introduction to the Mathematics of the Special Theory of Relativity. LC 92-12652. (Applied Mathematical Sciences Ser.: Vol. 92). (Illus.). 280p. 1992. 65.95 (*0-387-97848-8*) Spr-Verlag.

— Spacetime & Singularities: An Introduction. (London Mathematical Society Student Texts Ser.: No. 10). (Illus.). 192p. 1989. pap. text 25.95 (*0-521-33612-0*) Cambridge U Pr.

— Topology, Geometry & Gauge Fields. Foundations. LC 96-49166. (Texts in Applied Mathematics Ser.: Vol. 25). (Illus.). 416p. 1997. 49.95 (*0-387-94946-1*) Spr-Verlag.

***Naber, Gregory L.** Topology, Geometry & Gauge Fields: Interactions. LC 99-52753. (Applied Mathematical Sciences Ser.: Vol. 141). (Illus.). 461p. 2000. 59.95 (*0-387-98947-1*) Spr-Verlag.

Naber, John, ed. Awaken the Olympian Within: Stories from America's Greatest Olympic Motivators. (Illus.). 192p. 1998. pap. 19.95 (*1-882180-98-4*) Griffin CA.

N

An Asterisk (*) at the beginning of an entry indicates that the title is appearing for the first time.

Naber, Robert J., jt. ed. see Hearn, Gregory K.

Nabet, Bahram & Pinter, Robert B. Sensory Neural Networks: Lateral Inhibition. 200p. 1991. lib. bdg. 89.95 (0-8493-4278-3, QA) CRC Pr.

Nabet, Bahram, jt. auth. see Pinter, Robert B.

Nabeya, K., ed. see Fifth World Congress of the International Society.

Nabhan. Gathering the Desert. LC 85-13933. (Illus.). 209p. 1985. pap. 18.95 (0-8165-1014-8) U of Ariz Pr.

Nabhan, David. Predicting the Next Great Quake. (Illus.). 68p. (Orig.). 1996. pap. 6.95 (0-9654681-0-0) Red Lion Pub.

Nabhan, Gary P. Desert Legends: Storying the Sonoran Borderlands. (J). 1995. 45.00 (0-8050-3100-6) H Holt & Co.

— The Desert Smells Like Rain: A Naturalist in Papago Indian Country. LC 81-81505. 158p. 1987. pap. 12.00 (0-86547-050-2) N Point Pr.

— Enduring Seeds: Native American Agriculture & Wild Plant Conservation. 230p. 1991. pap. 14.00 (0-86547-344-7) N Point Pr.

— Saguaro: A View of Saguaro National Monument & the Tucson Basin. Priehs, T. J. & Dodson, Carolyn, eds. LC 86-61422. (Illus.). 76p. (Orig.). 1986. pap. 4.95 (0-911408-69-X) SW Pks Mnmts.

— Songbirds, Truffles & Wolves: An American Naturalist in Italy. 256p. 1994. reprint ed. pap. 12.95 (0-14-023972-3, Penguin Bks) Viking Penguin.

Nabhan, Gary P., ed. Counting Sheep: Twenty Ways of Seeing Desert Bighorn. LC 93-12477. (Southwest Center Ser.). 261p. 1994. pap. 17.95 (0-8165-1398-8) U of Ariz Pr.

Nabhan, Gary P. & Carr, John L., eds. Ironwood: An Ecological & Cultural Keystone of the Sonoran Desert. LC 94-70016. 92p. 1995. pap. 10.00 (1-881173-07-0, Pub. by Conser Intl) U Ch Pr.

Nabhan, Gary P., jt. auth. see Buchmann, Stephen L.

Nabhan, Gary P., jt. auth. see Trimble, Stephen A.

Nabhan, Martin. Men in the Middle. (Basketball Heroes Ser.). 48p. (J). (gr. 3-8). 1992. lib. bdg. 15.95 (0-86593-158-5) Rourke Corp.

Nabhan, Martin, et al. World Partners, 6 bks. (Illus.). 384p. (YA). (gr. 7 up). 1990. lib. bdg. 95.58 (0-86593-087-2); lib. bdg. 77.70 (0-685-36361-9) Rourke Corp.

Nabhi, N. Exporter's Manual, 1991. (C). 1990. 75.00 (0-89771-312-5) St Mut.

— Labour Laws: One Should Know, 1991. (C). 1990. 55.00 (0-89771-309-5) St Mut.

— Manual for One Hundred Percent Export Units, Free Trade & Export Processing Zones, 1991. (C). 1990. 110.00 (0-89771-311-7) St Mut.

Nabholtz, John R. My Reader, My Fellow-Labourer: A Study of English Romantic Prose. LC 85-20118. 144p. 1986. text 24.95 (0-8262-0491-0) U of Mo Pr.

Nabholtz, John R., ed. see Hazlitt, William C.

Nabholz, A., jt. ed. see Folsch, D. W.

Nabi, Ijaz, et al. The Agrarian Economy of Pakistan: Issues & Policies. (Illus.). 350p. 1987. pap. text 19.95 (0-19-577349-7) OUP.

Nabi, Ijaz, jt. ed. see Lele, Uma.

Nabi, Malik B. The Quranic Phenomenon. Kirkari, Abu B., tr. from FRE. LC 82-70460. (Illus.). 187p. (Orig.). 1982. pap. 7.00 (0-89259-023-8) Am Trust Pubns.

Nabighian, Misac N., ed. Electromagnetic Methods in Applied Geophysics Vol. 1: Theory. LC 87-6330. (Investigations in Geophysics Ser.: No. 2). (Illus.). 528p. 1988. pap. 47.00 (0-931830-51-6, 103A) Soc Expl Geophys.

— Electromagnetic Methods in Applied Geophysics Vol. 2: Applications. LC 87-6330. (Investigations in Geophysics Ser.: No. 3). (Illus.). 992p. (C). 1991. pap. 82.00 (1-56080-022-4, 104A) Soc Expl Geophys.

Nabiulin, M. K. Stationary Motions & Stability of Flexible Satellites, Vol. 4. LC 95-32737. (Advanced Series in Mathematical Science & Engineering). 1995. write for info. (1-885978-03-0) Wrld Fed Pubs.

***Nabli, Mustapha K.** Financial Integration, Vulnerabilities to Crisis & EU Accession in Five Central European Countries. LC 99-28651. (Technical Papers). 1999. pap. 22.00 (0-8213-4506-0) World Bank.

Nablo, S. Progress in Radiation Processing: Proceedings of the International Meeting, 5th, San Diego, California, October 24-26, 1984. 916p. 1985. pap. 205.00 (0-08-032620-X, Pub. by PPL) Elsevier.

Nablow, Ralph A. The Addisonian Tradition in France: Passion & Objectivity in Social Observation. LC 89-45404. (Illus.). 280p. 1990. 42.50 (0-8386-3379-X) Fairleigh Dickinson.

Nabney, Peter. Marketing Opportunities in Ireland. 246p. 1985. 450.00 (0-903706-75-X, Pub. by Euromonitor PLC) St Mut.

Nabokov, Dmitri & Bruccoli, Matthew J., eds. The Nabokov Letters. 1989. 29.95 (0-685-26632-X) Harcourt.

Nabokov, Dmitri, ed. see Nabokov, Vladimir.

Nabokov, Dmitri, tr. see Lermontov, Mikhail.

Nabokov, Dmitri, tr. see Nabokov, Vladimir.

Nabokov, Dominique. New York Living Rooms. LC 98-16619. (Illus.). 1998. text 29.95 (0-87951-875-8, Pub. by Overlook Pr) Penguin Putnam.

***Nabokov, Isabelle.** Religion Against the Self: An Ethnography of Tamil Rituals. LC 99-34727. 256p. 2000. 45.00 (0-19-511364-0) OUP.

— Religion against the Self: An Ethnography of Tamil Rituals. LC 99-34727. 256p. 2000. pap. 25.00 (0-19-511365-9) OUP.

Nabokov, P. Who Spirits This Place? LC 90-55770. 20.00 (0-06-250646-3); pap. 10.00 (0-06-250722-2, Perennial) HarperTrade.

Nabokov, Peter. Indian Running: Native American History & Tradition. 2nd ed. LC 87-71658. (Illus.). 208p. 1987. reprint ed. pap. 15.95 (0-941270-41-6) Ancient City Pr.

***Nabokov, Peter.** Native American Testimony: A Chronicle of Indian-White Relations from Prophecy to the Present, 1492-2000. rev. ed. (Illus.). 512p. 1999. pap. 16.95 (0-14-028159-2, Penguin Bks) Viking Penguin.

Nabokov, Peter. Two Leggings: The Making of a Crow Warrior. LC 82-6979. (Illus.). xxx, 242p. 1982. reprint ed. pap. 11.95 (0-8032-8351-2, Bison Books) U of Nebr Pr.

Nabokov, Peter & Easton, Robert. Native American Architecture. (Illus.). 432p. 1988. 65.00 (0-19-503781-2) OUP.

— Native American Architecture. (Illus.). 432p. 1990. pap. 35.00 (0-19-506665-0) OUP.

Nabokov, Vladimir. Ada: Ardor. 1989. pap. 10.95 (0-685-26529-3) Vin Bks.

— Ada: Ardor: A Family Chronicle. 608p. 1990. pap. 16.00 (0-679-72522-9) Vin Bks.

— The Annotated Lolita. Appel, Alfred, Jr., ed. LC 90-50264. 544p. 1991. pap. 19.00 (0-679-72729-9) Vin Bks.

— Bend Sinister. LC 89-40559. (Vintage International Ser.). 256p. 1990. pap. 14.00 (0-679-72727-2) Vin Bks.

— Blednyi Ogon' (RUS.). 1983. 27.50 (0-88233-602-9) Ardis Pubs.

— Blednyi Ogon' (RUS.). 1983. pap. 15.00 (0-88233-603-7) Ardis Pubs.

— The Defense: A Novel. LC 89-40546. (Vintage International Ser.). 256p. 1990. pap. 13.00 (0-679-72722-1) Vin Bks.

— Despair: A Novel. (International Ser.). 212p. 1989. pap. 13.00 (0-679-72343-9) Vin Bks.

— The Enchanter. LC 90-55704. 128p. 1991. pap. 12.00 (0-679-72886-4) Vin Bks.

— Eugene Onegin: A Commentary. (Bollingen Ser.: No. LXXII). 1152p. (C). 1964. pap. text 37.50 (0-691-01904-5, Pub. by Princeton U Pr) Cal Prin Full Svc.

— The Eye. Nabokov, Dmitri, tr. LC 90-50265. (Vintage International Ser.). 128p. 1990. pap. 11.00 (0-679-72723-X) Vin Bks.

— The Gift: A Novel. Scammell, Michael, tr. 366p. 1991. pap. 14.00 (0-679-72725-6) Knopf.

— Glory. LC 91-50488. (Vintage International Ser.). 224p. 1991. pap. 14.00 (0-679-72724-8) Vin Bks.

— Le Guetteur. (FRE.). 1984. pap. 10.95 (0-7859-4209-2) Fr & Eur.

— Invitation to a Beheading. Nabokov, Dmitri, tr. 1989. pap. 12.00 (0-679-72531-8) Vin Bks.

— Invitations au Supplice. (FRE.). 1980. pap. 10.95 (0-7859-4129-0) Fr & Eur.

— King, Queen, Knave. (International Ser.). 1989. pap. 13.00 (0-679-72340-4) Vin Bks.

— Laughter in the Dark. 1989. pap. 8.95 (0-07-045848-0) McGraw.

— Laughter in the Dark. (Vintage International Ser.). 1989. pap. 13.00 (0-679-72450-8) Vin Bks.

— Laughter in the Dark. LC 91-18665. (New Directions Classics Ser.: Vol. 729). 296p. 1991. reprint ed. pap. 11.95 (0-8112-1186-X, NDP729, Pub. by New Directions) Penguin Books.

— Lectures on Literature. LC 79-3690. 416p. 1982. pap. 15.00 (0-15-649589-9, Harvest Bks) Harcourt.

— Lectures on Literature: British, French & German Writers. Bowers, Fredson, ed. LC 79-3690. 416p. 1980. 19.95 (0-15-149597-1) Harcourt.

— Lectures on Russian Literature. Bowers, Fredson, ed. LC 81-47315. (Illus.). 352p. 1982. pap. 14.00 (0-15-649591-0, Harvest Bks) Harcourt.

— Lectures on Ulysses: A Facsimile of the Manuscript. limited ed. 1980. 85.00 (0-89723-027-2) Bruccoli.

— Lolita. LC 92-52931. 368p. 1993. 17.00 (0-679-41043-0) Everymns Lib.

— Lolita. (FRE.). 1973. pap. 13.95 (0-7859-4075-8) Fr & Eur.

— Lolita. (International Ser.). 336p. 1989. pap. 13.00 (0-679-72316-1) Vin Bks.

— Lolita. 1996. pap. text 12.00 (0-676-51419-7) Vin Bks.

— Lolita. adapted ed. 1983. pap. 5.25 (0-8222-0683-8) Dramatists Play.

— Lolita. large type ed. 483p. 1997. 24.95 (0-7838-8080-4, G K Hall Lrg Type) Mac Lib Ref.

— Lolita. 300p. 1991. reprint ed. lib. bdg. 22.95 (0-89966-860-7) Buccaneer Bks.

— Lolita: A Screenplay. LC 96-30305. 1997. pap. 12.00 (0-679-77255-3) McKay.

***Nabokov, Vladimir.** Lolita: Mason,&James. abr. ed. 1998. audio 12.00 (0-694-52015-2, Caedmon) HarperAudio.

Nabokov, Vladimir. Look at the Harlequins! LC 89-40553. (Vintage International Ser.). 272p. 1990. pap. 14.00 (0-679-72728-0) Vin Bks.

— The Man from the U. S. S. R. & Other Plays. Nabokov, Dmitri, tr. 342p. 1986. 75.60 (0-317-40746-5) St Mut.

— Mary: A Novel. Glenny, Michael, tr. (Vintage International Ser.). 1989. pap. 12.00 (0-679-72620-9) Vin Bks.

— Nabokov's Butterflies: Unpublished & Uncollected Writings. Boyd, Brian & Pyle, Robert M., eds. Nabokov, Dmitri, tr. LC 98-42846. (Illus.). 800p. 2000. 45.00 (0-8070-8540-5) Beacon Pr.

— Nabokov's Butterflies: Unpublished & Uncollected Writings. limited ed. Boyd, Brian et al, eds. Nabokov, Dmitri, tr. from RUS. LC 98-42846. (Illus.). 800p. 1999. boxed set 150.00 (0-8070-8542-1) Beacon Pr.

— Nabokov's Dozen: A Collection of Thirteen Stories. LC 82-45237. (Short Story Index Reprint Ser.). 1977. 27.82 (0-8369-3078-9) Ayer.

— Nikolai Gogol. LC 44-8135. 1961. pap. 9.95 (0-8112-0120-1, NDP78, Pub. by New Directions) Norton.

— Novels & Memoirs, 1941-1951: The Real Life of Sebastian Knight; Bend Sinister; Speak, Memory. Boyd, Brian, ed. LC 96-15257. (Illus.). 710p. 1996. 35.00 (1-883011-18-3, Pub. by Library of America) Penguin Putnam.

— Novels, 1955-1962: Lolita; Pnin; Pale Fire; Lolita: A Screenplay. Boyd, Brian, ed. LC 96-15256. 925p. 1996. 35.00 (1-883011-19-1, Pub. by Library of America) Penguin Putnam.

— Novels, 1969-1974: Ada, or Ardor; Transparent Things; Look at the Harlequins! Boyd, Brian, ed. LC 96-15255. 824p. 1996. 35.00 (1-883011-20-5, Pub. by Library of America) Penguin Putnam.

— Pale Fire. 1992. 17.00 (0-679-41077-5) McKay.

— Pale Fire: A Novel. (International Ser.). 1989. pap. 13.00 (0-679-72342-0) Vin Bks.

— Pnin. Barabtarlo, G., tr. from ENG. (RUS.). 175p. 1983. 25.00 (0-88233-737-8); pap. 12.50 (0-88233-738-6) Ardis Pubs.

— Pnin. (International Ser.). 1989. pap. 11.00 (0-679-72341-2) Vin Bks.

— Pnin. LC 82-1208. 192p. 1982. reprint ed. 16.00 (0-8376-0465-6) Bentley Pubs.

— The Real Life of Sebastian Knight. LC 59-9489. 1959. 16.00 (0-8112-0327-1, Pub. by New Directions) Norton.

— The Real Life of Sebastian Knight. LC 59-9489. 1977. pap. 9.95 (0-8112-0644-0, NDP432, Pub. by New Directions) Norton.

— The Real Life of Sebastian Knight. 1992. pap. 13.00 (0-679-72726-4) Vin Bks.

— Roi, Dame, Valet. (FRE.). 1975. pap. 11.95 (0-7859-4045-6) Fr & Eur.

— A Russian Beauty. 1976. 22.95 (0-8488-0838-X) Amereon Ltd.

— A Russian Beauty & Other Stories. 1998. lib. bdg. 24.95 (1-56723-143-8) Yestermorrow.

— Sobranie Sochinenii Vol. 10: Lolita. (Collected Works: 10). (RUS.). 312p. 1989. 25.00 (0-88233-535-9) Ardis Pubs.

— Speak, Memory: An Autobiography Revisited. LC 98-49237. 268p. 1999. 17.00 (0-375-40553-4) Everymns Lib.

— Speak, Memory: An Autobiography Revisited. (International Ser.). 1989. pap. 14.00 (0-679-72339-0) Random.

— The Stories of Vladimir Nabokov. Nabokov, Dmitri, ed. 640p. 1995. 40.00 (0-394-58615-8) Random.

— The Stories of Vladimir Nabokov. LC 95-23466. 663p. 1996. pap. 18.00 (0-679-72997-6) Random.

— Strong Opinions. (Vintage International Ser.). 1990. pap. 15.00 (0-679-72609-8) Vin Bks.

— Transparent Things. (Vintage International Ser.). 1989. pap. 11.00 (0-679-72541-5) Vin Bks.

— V. D. Nabokov & the Russian Provisional Government, 1917. Medlin, Virgil D. & Parsons, Steven L., eds. LC 75-18177. 196p. reprint ed. pap. 60.80 (0-8357-8363-4, 203382300087) Bks Demand.

Nabokov, Vladimir, tr. from RUS. The Song of Igor's Campaign. 135p. 1989. reprint ed. pap. 9.95 (0-87501-061-X) Ardis Pubs.

Nabokov, Vladimir, ed. see Kafka, Franz.

Nabokov, Vladimir, tr. see Carroll, Lewis, pseud.

Nabokov, Vladimir, tr. see Lermontov, Mikhail.

Nabokov, Vladimir, tr. see Pushkin, Aleksandr.

Nabors Baker, Carolyn. Caught in a Higher Love: Inspiring Stories of Women in the Bible. LC 98-18641. 190p. 1998. pap. 9.99 (0-8054-1198-4) Broadman.

***Nabours, Robert E., et al.** Electrical Injuries: Engineering, Medical & Legal Aspects. LC 99-51916. 693p. 2000. 99.00 (0-913875-95-3, 0993-N) Lawyers & Judges.

Nabseth, Lars & Ray, G. F., eds. The Diffusion of New Industrial Processes: An International Study. LC 73-88309. (National Institute of Economic & Social Research Occasional Papers: No. 29). 346p. reprint ed. pap. 98.70 (0-608-13033-8, 2024504) Bks Demand.

Nabuco, Carolina. The Life of Joaquim Nabuco. Hilton, Ronald, ed. LC 50-8549. 398p. 1950. reprint ed. pap. 30.00 (0-608-08257-0, 202508400042) Bks Demand.

Nabwire, Constance. Cooking the African Way. (Illus.). 48p. (YA). (gr. 5 up). 1990. pap. 5.95 (0-8225-9564-8, Lerner Publctns) Lerner Pub.

Nabwire, Constance, jt. auth. see Montgomery, Bertha V.

Naby, Eden, jt. auth. see Magnus, Ralph H.

Nacca, Rick, ed. see Finch, John.

Naccache, Paul H., ed. G Proteins & Calcium Signaling. 160p. 1989. lib. bdg. 159.00 (0-8493-4572-3, QP55) CRC Pr.

***Naccarelli, Gerald V., et al, eds.** EPSAP II: Electrophysiology Self-Assessment Program. LC 99-67738. 595p. 2000. pap. 645.00 (1-58397-007-X) Am Coll Cardiology.

NACE Committee T-6A Staff. Coatings & Linings for Immersion Service, TPC 2. rev. ed. (Illus.). 305p. 1998. pap. 98.00 (1-877914-84-3, 25020) NACE Intl.

Nace, Edgar P. Achievement & Addiction: A Guide to the Treatment of Professionals. LC 95-2834. 272p. 1995. text 34.95 (0-87630-753-5) Brunner-Mazel.

***NACE Research Committee, ed.** Proceedings of the Corrosion - 2000 Research Topical Symposium. (Illus.). 150p. 2000. pap. 45.00 (1-57590-090-4, 37406) NACE Intl.

— Proceedings of the Corrosion/99 Research Topical Symposium. (Illus.). 150p. 1999. pap. 35.00 (1-57590-068-8, 37405) NACE Intl.

NACE Research Committee Staff, ed. Proceedings of the Corrosion 98 Research Topical Symposia. (Illus.). 100p. 1998. pap. 36.00 (1-57590-040-8, 37403) NACE Intl.

— Proceedings of the Corrosion 97 Research Topical Symposia. 1997. pap. 50.00 (1-57590-028-9, 37402) NACE Intl.

NACE Staff. Atmospheric Corrosion of Control Equipment, Pub. No. 38. (Illus.). 77p. 1993. pap. 91.00 (1-877914-52-5) NACE Intl.

— The Development of Controlled Hydrodynamic Techniques for Corrosion Testing. (MTI Publication: No. T-3). (Illus.). 188p. 1992. 25.00 (1-877914-43-6) NACE Intl.

— Guidelines for Assessing Fire & Explosion Damage, Pub. No. 30. (Illus.). 142p. 1990. pap. 74.00 (1-877914-16-9) NACE Intl.

— Guidelines for the Mothballing of Process Plants, Pub. No. 34. LC 89-63607. (MTI Publicattion: No. 34). 128p. 1989. pap. 53.00 (1-877914-00-2) NACE Intl.

— Hydrodynamic Modeling of Corrosion of Carbon Steels & Cast Irons in Sulfuric Acid. (MTI Publication: No. T-2). (Illus.). 272p. 1992. 30.00 (1-877914-40-1) NACE Intl.

— Inspection Guidelines for Pressure Vessels & Piping Vol. 1: New Fabrication, Pub. No. 40. (Illus.). 136p. 1994. 115.00 (1-877914-64-9) NACE Intl.

— Thermal Spray Coating Applications in the Chemical Process Industries, Pub. No. 42. (Illus.). 252p. 1994. 56.00 (1-877914-59-2) NACE Intl.

Nace, Ted, jt. auth. see Felici, James.

Nace, Vaughn M., ed. Nonionic Surfactants: Polyoxyalkylerie Block Copolymers. (Surfactant Science Ser.: Vol. 60). (Illus.). 280p. 1996. text 150.00 (0-8247-9700-0) Dekker.

Nacelewicz, Barbara. Jesus Our Guide: Activity Book. Puccetti, Patricia I., ed. (Faith & Life Ser.). (Illus.). 144p. (J). (gr. 4). 1987. pap. text 3.95 (0-89870-154-6) Ignatius Pr.

Nacfaire, H., ed. Grid-Connected Wind Turbines: Proceedings of a Contractors' Meeting on Wind Demonstration Projects, Organized by the Commision of the European Communities, Directorate-General for Energy, Alghero, Italy, 11-12 June 1987. 128p. 1988. mass mkt. 62.50 (1-85166-185-9) Elsevier.

Nachaef. Chemical Elements: The Exciting Story of Their Discovery & of the Great Scientists Who Found Them. 1997. pap. 18.95 (1-899618-11-2, Pub. by Tarquin Pubns) Parkwest Pubns.

Nachalo, Sophia & Vochek, Yarostan. Letters of Insurgents. 1976. pap. 7.50 (0-934868-13-1) Black & Red.

Nachamie, Lois. So Glad We Waited! A Hand-Holding Guide for Over-35 Parents. LC 99-58221. 224p. 2000. pap. 14.00 (0-609-80346-8, FAM036000, Three Riv Pr) Crown Pub Group.

***Nachamkin, Irving & Blaser, Martin J., eds.** Campylobacter. 2nd ed. (Illus.). 520p. 2000. 89.95 (1-55581-165-5) ASM Pr.

Nachazel, Greg. Deer Camp Dictionary: Hunting Terms of EnDeerment. LC 97-118818. (Illus.). 96p. (Orig.). 1996. pap. 8.95 (0-9649401-4-0) Rhodes & Easton.

Nachazel, Karel. Estimation Theory in Hydrology & Water Systems. LC 92-9199. (Developments in Water Science Ser.: Vol. 42).Tr. of Teorie Odhadu V Hydrologii A Ve Vodnim Hospodarstvi. 270p. 1993. 218.00 (0-444-98726-6) Elsevier.

Nachbar, C. M. American Language Today, Checklist 1. 1989. write for info. (0-07-045751-4) McGraw.

— American Language Today, Checklist 2. 1989. write for info. (0-07-045753-0) McGraw.

— American Language Today, Checklist 5. 1989. write for info. (0-07-045755-7) McGraw.

— American Language Today, Level 3. 1989. write for info. (0-07-045783-2) McGraw.

— American Language Today, Level 4. 1989. write for info. (0-07-045784-0) McGraw.

— American Language Today, Level 5. 1989. write for info. (0-07-045785-9) McGraw.

Nachbar, Jack & Lause, Kevin, eds. Popular Culture: An Introductory Text. LC 92-73539. (Illus.). 502p. (C). 1992. pap. 23.95 (0-87972-572-9) Bowling Green Univ Popular Press.

Nachbin, A. Modelling of Water Waves in Shallow Channels. LC 92-75036. (Topics in Engineering Ser.: Vol. 13). 160p. 1993. 95.00 (1-56252-062-8, 1355) Computational Mech MA.

Nachbin, Leopoldo. Elements of Approximation Theory. LC 76-48. 131p. reprint ed. pap. 40.70 (0-8357-8869-5, AU0037000085) Bks Demand.

— Holomorphic Functions, Domains of Holomorphy & Local Properties. LC 78-134642. (North-Holland Mathematics Studies: Vol. 1). 130p. reprint ed. pap. 40.30 (0-608-15994-8, AU0036800083) Bks Demand.

— Introduction to Functional Analysis, Banach Spaces, & Differential Calculus. LC 80-24382. (Monographs & Textbooks in Pure & Applied Mathematics: No. 60). 182p. reprint ed. pap. 56.50 (0-7837-5886-3, 204560600006) Bks Demand.

— Topology & Order. Bechtolsheim, Lulu, tr. from POR. LC 76-59. (Illus.). 128p. reprint ed. pap. 39.70 (0-8357-7057-5, AU0036900085) Bks Demand.

— Topology & Order. LC 76-59. 128p. 1976. reprint ed. 15.00 (0-88275-387-8) Krieger.

— Topology in Spaces of Holomorphic Mappings. LC 68-29710. (Ergebnisse der Mathematik und Ihrer Grenzgebiete Ser.: Vol. 47). 1969. 64.95 (0-387-04470-1) Spr-Verlag.

***Nachef, Antoine E.** Mary's Pope: John Paul II, Mary & the Church since Vatican II. LC 00-33883. 220p. 2000. write for info. (1-58051-077-9) Sheed & Ward WI.

— The Mystery of the Trinity in the Theological Thought of Pope John Paul II. LC 99-17572. (American University Studies, VII: Vol. 211). 289p. 1999. text 33.00 (0-8204-4524-X) P Lang Pubng.

Nachel, Marty. Beer Across America: A Regional Guide to Brewpubs & Microbreweries. (Illus.). 192p. 1995. pap. 14.95 (0-88266-902-8, Storey Pub) Storey Bks.

— Homebrewing for Dummies. LC 97-80303. (For Dummies Ser.). (Illus.). 432p. 1997. pap. 19.99 (0-7645-5046-2) IDG Bks.

An Asterisk (*) at the beginning of an entry indicates that the title is appearing for the first time.

Nachel, Marty & Ettlinger, Steve. Beer for Dummies. (For Dummies Ser.). 360p. 1996. pap. 19.99 (*1-56884-865-X*) IDG Bks.

Nachel, Marty, jt. auth. see Johnson, Steve.

Nachemson. Back Pain. 1993. write for info. (*0-397-51202-3*) Lppncott W & W.

Nachemson, Alf L. & Jonsson, Egon. Neck & Back Pain: The Scientific Evidence of Causes, Diagnosis, & Treatment. 544p. text 89.00 (*0-7817-2760-X*) Lppncott W & W.

Nachfolger, Adolph H. Ulex Auction Sale Catalog. 173p. 1981. reprint ed. 5.00 (*1-889172-10-3*) Numismatic Intl.

Nachi-Fujikoshi, ed. Training for TPM: A Manufacturing Success Story. LC 90-40276. (Illus.). 274p. 1990. 50.00 (*0-915299-34-8*) Productivity Inc.

Nachman. Likutey Moharan Vol. 4: Lessons 23-32. Mykoff, Moshe, ed. & tr. by. from HEB. Bergman, Ozer, ed. (Illus.). 520p. 1992. 20.00 (*0-930213-79-3*) Breslov Res Inst.

— Likutey Moharan Vol. 10: Lessons 109-194. Mykoff, Moshe, ed. & tr. by. from HEB. Bergman, Ozer, ed. (Illus.). 480p. 1992. 20.00 (*0-930213-85-8*) Breslov Res Inst.

— Le Tikoun Haklali. rev. ed. Dimermanas, Alon, ed. & tr. by. (FRE.). 115p. 1989. pap. text 7.00 (*0-930213-34-3*) Breslov Res Inst.

Nachman & Nathan. Mayim. Mykoff, Moshe, ed. 64p. (Orig.). 1987. pap. 3.00 (*0-930213-28-9*) Breslov Res Inst.

Nachman, Gerald. Raised on Radio: In Quest of the Lone Ranger, Jack Benny, Amos 'n' Andy, the Shadow, Mary Noble, & the Great Gildersleeve. LC 98-10355. (Illus.). 535p. 1998. 28.50 (*0-375-40287-X*) Pantheon.

***Nachman, Gerald.** Raised on Radio: In Quest of the Lone Ranger, Jack Benny, Amos 'n' Andy, the Shadow, Mary Noble, & the Great Gildersleeve. LC 99-86212. 544p. 2000. pap. text 18.95 (*0-520-22303-9*, Pub. by U CA Pr) Cal Prin Full Svc.

Nachman, Jerry. Psychological Crime Thriller. (*0-679-41275-1*) Random.

Nachman, Joseph F. & Lundin, C. E., eds. Rare Earth Research, Vol. 1. xvi, 354p. 1962. text 516.00 (*0-677-10490-1*) Gordon & Breach.

Nachman, Louis J. Fundamental Mathematics. LC 77-17239. 677p. reprint ed. pap. 200.00 (*0-608-10685-2*, 205129700093) Bks Demand.

Nachman of Breslov. Advice. Greenbaum, Avraham, tr. from HEB. LC 83-70202.Tr. of Likutey Etzot. 384p. 1983. 17.00 (*0-930213-04-1*) Breslov Res Inst.

— Les Contes. Regnot, Franz, tr. from YID.Tr. of Sippurey Ma'asioth. (FRE.). 180p. (Orig.). 1981. pap. 7.00 (*0-930213-22-X*) Breslov Res Inst.

— The Fixer. Succot, Miriam & Succot, Eliyah, trs. from HEB. (Illus.). (J). (gr. 3-12). 1977. pap. 2.50 (*0-917246-04-7*) Maimes.

— The Gems of Rabbi Nachman. Rosenfeld, Tzvi A., ed. Kaplan, Aryeh, tr. from HEB. (Illus.). 186p. (Orig.). 1980. pap. 3.00 (*0-930213-10-6*) Breslov Res Inst.

— Hitbodedouth: Ou La Porte du Ciel. (FRE.). 110p. (Orig.). 1982. pap. 2.00 (*0-930213-27-0*) Breslov Res Inst.

— Rabbi Nachman's Stories. Kaplan, Aryeh, tr. from HEB. LC 83-70201.Tr. of Sippurey Ma'asioth. 552p. 1983. 21.00 (*0-930213-02-5*) Breslov Res Inst.

— Rabbi Nachman's Stories: Skazocnniji Histori Rabbi Nechman iz Bratzlav. Avni, Baruch, tr. from HEB.Tr. of Sippurey Maasiot. (Illus.). 332p. (Orig.). (C). 1987. pap. 10.00 (*0-930213-29-7*) Breslov Res Inst.

— Rabbi Nachman's Tikkun: The Comprehensive Remedy. Greenbaum, Avraham, tr. from HEB. 256p. 1984. 13.00 (*0-930213-06-8*) Breslov Res Inst.

— Rabbi Nachman's Wisdom. Rosenfeld, Zvi A., ed. Kaplan, Aryeh, tr. from HEB.Tr. of Shevachay HaRan-Sichos HaRan. (Illus.). 510p. 1984. reprint ed. 16.00 (*0-930213-00-9*) Breslov Res Inst.

Nachman of Breslov & Nathan of Breslov. Ayeh? (Where)? Greenbaum, Avraham, tr. from HEB. 64p. (Orig.). 1985. pap. 3.00 (*0-930213-12-2*) Breslov Res Inst.

— Azamra (I Will Sing) Greenbaum, Avraham, tr. from HEB. 64p. (Orig.). 1984. pap. 3.00 (*0-930213-11-4*) Breslov Res Inst.

— Courage!Tr. of Meshivat Nefesh. 119p. (Orig.). 1983. pap. 3.00 (*0-930213-23-8*) Breslov Res Inst.

— Outpouring of the Soul. Kaplan, Aryeh, tr. from HEB.Tr. of Hishtap'kuth HaNefesh. 96p. (Orig.). 1980. reprint ed. pap. 4.00 (*0-930213-14-9*) Breslov Res Inst.

— Restore My Soul. Greenbaum, Avraham, tr. from HEB.Tr. of Meshivat Nefesh. 128p. (Orig.). 1980. pap. 4.00 (*0-930213-13-0*) Breslov Res Inst.

Nachman, Patricia. You & Your Only Child: The Joys, Myths & Challenges of Raising an Only Child. LC 88-45065. 256p. 1998. pap. 12.00 (*0-06-092896-4*, Perennial) HarperTrade.

Nachman, Patricia & Thompson, Andrea. You & Your Only Child: The Joys, Myths, & Challenges of Raising an Only Child. LC 96-32531. 256p. 1997. 22.00 (*0-06-017331-9*) HarpC.

Nachman, Rebbe. Azamra. Dimermanas, Alon, ed. & tr. by. from ENG. (FRE.). 64p. 1989. pap. text 3.00 (*0-930213-33-5*) Breslov Res Inst.

Nachman, Resi. Seven Poems. 1971. reprint ed. pap. 1.00 (*0-918230-01-2*) Barnstable.

Nachmani, Amikam. Great Power Discord in Palestine: The Anglo-American Committee of Inquiry into the Problems of European Jewry & Palestine, 1945-1946. (Illus.). 296p. 1986. 49.50 (*0-7146-3298-8*, Pub. by F Cass Pubs) Intl Spec Bk.

— International Intervention in the Greek Civil War: The United Nations Special Committee on the Balkans, 1947-1952. LC 89-26544. 216p. 1990. 55.00 (*0-275-93367-9*, C3367, Greenwood Pr) Greenwood.

— Israel, Turkey, Greece: Uneasy Relations in the East Mediterranean. 1987. 39.50 (*0-7146-3321-6*, Pub. by F Cass Pubs) Intl Spec Bk.

Nachmanovitch, Stephen. Free Play: The Power of Improvisation in Life & the Arts. (Illus.). 224p. 1991. pap. 12.95 (*0-87477-631-7*, Tarcher Putnam) Putnam Pub Group.

Nachmanson, Eva, ed. see Kemp-Slaughter, James.

Nachmias. Bureaucratic Government. 2nd ed. 2000. pap. text. write for info. (*0-312-00501-6*) St Martin.

— Research Methods. 4th ed. 1991. pap. text 41.00 (*0-312-03652-3*) St Martin.

— Research Methods. 5th ed. 2000. pap. text 46.60 (*0-312-13774-5*) St Martin.

***Nachmias.** Research Methods in Social Science. 6th ed. 1999. pap. text, student ed. write for info. (*1-57259-908-1*) Worth.

Nachmias. Research Methods in Social Science. 6th ed. LC 99-46162. 2000. pap. text. write for info. (*1-57259-794-1*) Worth.

— Research Methods in the Social Sciences. 5th ed. 224p. 1995. pap., student ed. 16.95 (*0-312-10160-0*); pap. text, teacher ed. 10.00 (*0-312-10161-9*) St Martin.

Nachmias, Chara F. & Nachmias, David. Research Methods in the Social Sciences. 4th ed. LC 90-63540. 592p. (C). 1991. text. write for info. (*0-312-06275-3*); pap. text, teacher ed. 1.50 (*0-312-06758-5*) St Martin.

Nachmias, Chava & Rodeghier, Mark. Social Statistics for a Diverse Society. LC 96-45371. (Pine Forge Press Series on Research Methods & Statistics). 1997. pap. write for info. (*0-8039-9026-X*) Pine Forge.

Nachmias, David, jt. auth. see Nachmias, Chara F.

Nachmias, Nitza. Transfer of Arms, Leverage, & Peace in the Middle East, 83. LC 88-17777. (Contributions in Military Studies Ser.: No. 83). 208p. 1988. 55.00 (*0-313-26300-0*, NAT/, Greenwood Pr) Greenwood.

Nachmias, Nitza, jt. ed. see Belgrad, Eric A.

Nachod, E. C., tr. see Steudel, Ralf.

Nachowitz, Todd. Alternative Directory of Nongovernmental Organizations in South Asia. rev. ed. (Foreign & Comparative Studies Program, South Asian Ser.: No. 14). 1990. pap. text 15.00 (*0-915984-41-5*) Syracuse U Foreign Comp.

Nachowitz, Todd, ed. An Alternative Directory of Non-Governmental Organizations in South Asia. LC 89-83678. (Orig.). (C). 1989. pap. 15.00 (*0-9622716-0-8*) Fourth Wrld Pr.

Nachshoni. Studies, 5 vols. 119.99 (*0-89906-945-2*, STSH) Mesorah Pubns.

Nachshoni, Yehuda. Studies in the Weekly Parashah, Vol. I: Bereishis, Vol. I. Himelstein, Shmuel, tr. from HEB. (ArtScroll Judaica Classics Ser.). 320p. 1988. 22.99 (*0-89906-933-9*); pap. 19.99 (*0-89906-934-7*) Mesorah Pubns.

— Studies in the Weekly Parashah, Vol. II: Sh'mos, Vol. II. Himelstein, Shmuel, tr. from HEB. (ArtScroll Judaica Classics Ser.). 296p. 1988. 22.99 (*0-89906-935-5*); pap. 19.99 (*0-89906-936-3*) Mesorah Pubns.

— Studies in the Weekly Parashah, Vol. III: Vayikra, Vol. III. Himelstein, Shmuel, tr. from HEB. (ArtScroll Judaica Classics Ser.). 278p. 1989. 22.99 (*0-89906-937-1*); pap. 19.99 (*0-89906-938-X*) Mesorah Pubns.

— Studies in the Weekly Parashah, Vol. IV: Bamidbar, Vol. IV. Blumberg, Raphael, tr. from HEB. (ArtScroll Judaica Classics Ser.). 296p. 1989. 22.99 (*0-89906-939-8*); pap. 19.99 (*0-89906-940-1*) Mesorah Pubns.

— Studies in the Weekly Parashah, Vol. V: Devarim, Vol. V. Himelstein, Shmuel, tr. from HEB. (ArtScroll Judaica Classics Ser.). 256p. 1989. 22.99 (*0-89906-941-X*); pap. 19.99 (*0-89906-942-8*) Mesorah Pubns.

Nachsin, Wilma, jt. auth. see Harris, Mary.

Nacht, Michael. The Age of Vulnerability: Threats to the Nuclear Stalemate. LC 84-45849. 209p. 1985. 14.95 (*0-8157-5964-9*); pap. 14.95 (*0-8157-5963-0*) Brookings.

— The War in Vietnam: The Influence of Concepts on Policy. (CISA Working Papers: No. 26). 28p. (Orig.). 1980. pap. 15.00 (*0-86682-025-6*) Ctr Intl Relations.

Nacht, Michael, jt. auth. see Goodwin, Craufurd D.

Nachtegael, Mike, jt. auth. see Kerre, Etienne E.

Nachtigal, Chester & Martin, Marvin D. Instrumentation & Control: Fundamentals & Applications. LC 90-30083. 912p. 1990. 250.00 (*0-471-88045-0*) Wiley.

Nachtigal, Paul, jt. auth. see Haas, Toni.

Nachtigall, D., ed. see Fischer, Hans E.

Nachtigall, Lila & Heilman, Joan R. Estrogen. 2nd ed. LC 95-6222. 208p. 1995. pap. 12.00 (*0-06-092602-3*, Perennial) HarperTrade.

Nachtigall, Lila, et al. What Every Woman Should Know: Staying Healthy after 40. 1996. pap. write for info. (*0-446-67214-9*) Warner Bks.

Nachtigall, Lila, jt. auth. see Wren, Barry.

***Nachtigall, Lila E.** Estrogen. 3rd ed. LC 99-44799. 240p. 2000. pap. 12.00 (*0-06-095556-2*, HarpRes) HarpInfo.

Nachtigall, P. E. & Moore, P. W. Animal Sonar: Processes & Performance. LC 88-28886. (NATO ASI Ser.: Vol. 156). (Illus.). 878p. (C). 1988. text 195.00 (*0-306-43031-2*, Kluwer Plenum) Kluwer Academic.

Nachtigall, Werner. Exploring with the Microscope: A Book of Discovery & Learning. LC 94-23844. (ENG & GER., Illus.). 160p. (YA). (gr. 7-12). 1995. 19.95 (*0-8069-0866-1*) Sterling.

— Exploring with the Microscope: A Book of Discovery & Learning. (Illus.). 160p. (J). 1997. pap. 14.95 (*0-8069-0867-X*) Sterling.

— Temperature Relations in Animals & Man. (BIONA Report Ser.: No. 4). 229p. 1986. pap. 19.00 (*0-89574-226-8*, Pub. by Gustav Fischer) Balogh.

Nachtigall, Werner, ed. Biona Report Five - Bat Flight. 1987. pap. text 40.00 (*0-89574-239-X*, Wiley-VCH) Wiley.

— The Flying Honeybee: Aspects of Energetics. (BIONA Report Ser.: No. 6). (ENG & GER.). 148p. 1989. pap. text 20.00 (*0-89574-289-6*, Pub. by Gustav Fischer) Balogh.

Nachtman, Elliot & Kalpakjian, Serope. Lubricants & Lubrication in Metalworking Operations. (Manufacturing Engineering & Materials Processing Ser.: Vol. 14). (Illus.). 288p. 1985. text 150.00 (*0-8247-7401-9*) Dekker.

Nachtman, Nancy. Where Have All the Roses Gone? An Eclectic Collection of Poems by Leslie Rivers. 33p. 1998. pap. write for info. (*0-9671052-0-X*) L Rivers.

Nachtmann, Francis W. Exercises in French Phonics. 79p. (C). 1981. reprint ed. pap. text 5.95 (*0-87563-215-7*) Stipes.

Nachtmann, O. Elementary Particle Physics. (Texts & Monographs in Physics). (Illus.). 592p. 1989. 98.00 (*0-387-50496-6*, 2466); 59.95 (*0-387-51647-6*) Spr-Verlag.

Nachtmann, Rita. How I Spent My Life's Vacation - A Drama with Music. 85p. 1998. pap. 5.95 (*0-87129-832-5*, H75) Dramatic Pub.

Nachtscheim, Daniel. Urological Oncology. (Vademecum Ser.). 2000. spiral bd. 45.00 (*1-57059-571-2*) Landes Bioscience.

Nachtsheim, Mary L. On the Way: The Journey of the Idaho Benedictine Sisters. LC 97-98877. 344p. 1998. pap. 14.95 (*0-9658209-0-4*) Idaho Corp of Benedctne.

***Nachtwey, James.** Inferno. 428p. 1999. 95.00 (*0-7148-3815-2*) Phaidon Pr.

Nachtwey, James, et al, photos by. Aperture: Dark Days: Mystery, Murder, Mayhem. (Aperture Ser.: Vol. 147). (Illus.). 80p. 1997. pap. 27.95 (*0-89381-698-1*) Aperture.

Nachtwey, James, photos by. Stern Portfolio: Civil Wars. (Illus.). 96p. 1998. pap. 19.95 (*3-570-12021-X*) te Neues.

Nachtwey, Jutta, jt. auth. see Gerdes, Claudia.

Nachum, Lilach. The Origins of the International Competitiveness of Firms: The Impact of Location & Ownership in the Professional Service Industries. LC 98-42883. (New Horizons in International Business Ser.). 256p. 1999. 85.00 (*1-84064-012-X*) E Elgar.

Nachum, Lilach, jt. auth. see Aharoni, Yair.

Nacianceno, Natividad T. & Waterman, Floyd T. The Trail of Education in Two Cities Omaha & Manila. 100p. (Orig.). 1985. pap. 6.00 (*1-55719-057-7*) U NE CPAR.

Nacianceno, Natividad T., jt. auth. see Waterman, Floyd T.

Nack, William. Secretariat: The Making of a Champion. (Quality Paperbacks Ser.).Tr. of Big Red of Meadow Farm. (Illus.). 342p. 1988. reprint ed. pap. 13.95 (*0-306-80317-8*) Da Capo.

— Secretariat Making of a Champ. 1989. pap. text 10.95 (*0-306-88317-1*) Da Capo.

Nackaerts, Kris. Heparan Sulfate Proteoglycans in Malignant Cells. (Acta Biomedica Lovaniensia Ser.). (Illus.). 127p. 1998. pap. 45.00 (*90-6186 891-2*, Pub. by Leuven Univ) Coronet Bks.

Nacke, Judith P. Grayson County, Kentucky 1810-1840 Census & 1815, 1825 & 1834 Tax Lists. 83p. 1986. pap. 11.00 (*1-889221-05-8*) Ancestral Trails.

Nacke, Judy & Cote, Thelma D. Ten-Year Index (1976-1985) to Ancestral News. 96p. 1987. pap. 12.00 (*1-889221-35-X*) Ancestral Trails.

Nackenoff, Carol. The Fictional Republic: Horatio Alger & American Political Discourse. (Illus.). 384p. 1994. text 34.95 (*0-19-507923-X*) OUP.

Nackerud, Larry G. The Central American Refugee Issue in Brownsville, Texas: Seeking Understanding of Public Policy Formulation from Within a Community Setting. LC 93-24044. 236p. 1993. text 89.95 (*0-7734-2240-4*) E Mellen.

Nackley, Jeffrey V. Primer on Workers' Compensation. 2nd ed. 200p. 1989. trans. 45.00 (*0-87179-596-5*, 0596) BNA Books.

Nackman, Lee R., jt. auth. see Barton, John J.

NACLA Staff, ed. Haiti: Dangerous Crossroads. 256p. 1995. 35.00 (*0-89608-506-6*); pap. 15.00 (*0-89608-505-8*) South End Pr.

Naclerio, Frank A. Insurance Wise: A Guide to Homeowners & Automobile Insurance. (Illus.). 72p. 1996. pap. 11.95 (*0-8059-3946-6*) Dorrance.

***Naclerio, Robert M. & Durham, Steven R., eds.** Rhinitis. LC 98-39370. (Lung Biology in Health & Disease Ser.). (Illus.). 558p. 1998. text 195.00 (*0-8247-0189-5*) Dekker.

Naclerio, Robert M., jt. ed. see Mygind, Niels.

Naclerio, Ron, jt. auth. see Valenti, John.

NACM Staff. Statutory Supplement. 2nd ed. LC 98-207861. 1998. pap. 69.95 (*1-888505-04-4*) NACM.

Nacos, Brigitte, jt. auth. see Edinger, Lewis.

Nacos, Brigitte L. The Press, Presidents, & Crises. 288p. 1990. text 44.00 (*0-231-07064-0*) Col U Pr.

— Terrorism & the Media: From the Iran Hostage Crisis to the Oklahoma City Bombing. 214p. 1996. pap. 18.50 (*0-231-10015-9*) Col U Pr.

— Terrorism & the Media: From the Iran Hostage Crisis to the World Trade Center Bombing. LC 94-4602. 224p. 1994. 38.50 (*0-231-10014-0*) Col U Pr.

***Nacos, Brigitte L., et al, eds.** Decisionmaking in a Glass House: Mass Media, Public Opinion, & American & European Foreign Policy in the 21st Century. 384p. 2000. 79.00 (*0-8476-9826-2*); pap. 26.95 (*0-8476-9827-0*) Rowman.

***Nacpil, Emerito P.** Jesus' Strategy for Social Transformation. LC 99-31490. 1999. pap. text 15.00 (*0-687-07136-4*) Abingdon.

Nacpil, Emerito P., ed. see All-Asia Consultation on Theological Education for.

Nacson, Leon. Dream Journal. (Illus.). 156p. 1999. 16.95 (*1-56170-590-X*, L444) Hay House.

Nacson, Leon. Interpreting Dreams A-Z. LC 98-37433. (Illus.). 156p. 1999. text 19.95 (*1-56170-576-4*, L442) Hay House.

***Nacson, Leon.** Interpreting Dreams A-Z. (Illus.). 156p. 2001. pap. 11.95 (*1-56170-789-9*, L484) Hay House.

Nacson, Leon, jt. auth. see Wilde, Stuart.

Nacson, Leon, ed. see Chopra, Deepak.

Nacubo, jt. auth. see Case.

***Nacy, Michele J.** Members of the Regiment: Army Officers' Wives on the Western Frontier, 1865-1890, 187. LC 99-45564. (Contributions in American History Ser.). 144p. 2000. write for info. (*0-313-30998-1*) Greenwood.

Naczk, Marion, jt. auth. see Shahidi, Fereidoon.

NADA Official Used Car Guide Co. Staff. N. A. D. A. Retail Consumer Edition. Weaver, Lynn A., ed. 320p. 1992. pap. 9.95 (*1-881406-00-8*) NADA VA.

Nada-Yolanda. Angels & Man. LC 73-90881. 138p. 1974. 15.00 (*0-912322-03-9*) Mark-Age.

— Evolution of Man: Two Hundred Six Million Years on Earth. 2nd ed. LC 88-61526. 161p. 1988. 15.00 (*0-912322-06-3*) Mark-Age.

— MAPP to Aquarius: Mark Age Period & Program. LC 85-62167. (Illus.). 351p. 1985. 20.00 (*0-912322-05-5*); pap. 15.00 (*0-912322-53-5*) Mark-Age.

— Visitors from Other Planets. LC 73-90880. 334p. 1974. 15.00 (*0-912322-04-7*) Mark-Age.

Nada-Yolanda, et al. Facts of Life: In the Beginning. LC 98-86286. (Illus.). 170p. 1998. pap. 15.00 (*0-912322-56-X*) Mark-Age.

Nadakavukaren, Anne. Our Global Environment: A Health Perspective. 4th rev. ed. (Illus.). 711p. (C). 1995. pap. text 32.95 (*0-88133-831-1*) Waveland Pr.

***Nadakavukaren, Anne.** Our Global Environment: A Health Perspective. 5th ed. (Illus.). 697p. (C). 2000. pap. 34.95 (*1-57766-098-6*) Waveland Pr.

Nadakavukaren, Anne. Study Guide to Accompany Our Global Environment: A Health Perspective. 4th rev. ed. 196p. (C). 1995. pap. text 11.50 (*0-88133-832-X*) Waveland Pr.

***Nadakavukaren, Anne.** Study Guide to Accompany Our Global Environment: A Health Perspective. 5th ed. 187p. (C). 2000. pap., student ed. 11.95 (*1-57766-122-2*) Waveland Pr.

***Nadal, David A.** Easy Classics for Guitar. 2000. pap. 10.95 (*0-486-41177-X*) Dover.

— Guitar Classics: Works By Albeniz, Bach, Dowland, Granados, Scarlatti, Sor & Other Great Composers. (Illus.). 1999. pap. 12.95 (*0-486-40633-4*) Dover.

Nadal, Ehrman S. Virginian Village, & Other Papers. LC 68-20324. (Essay Index Reprint Ser.). 1977. 20.95 (*0-8369-0733-7*) Ayer.

Nadal, Jean-Pierre, jt. ed. see Grassberger, Peter.

Nadal, R. M., tr. see Calderon de la Barca, Pedro.

Nadal, Rafael M. Lorca's the Public: A Study of His Unfinished Play el Publico & of Love & Death in the Work of Federico Garcia Lorca. 247p. (C). 1981. pap. 9.95 (*0-7145-2752-1*) M Boyars Pubs.

Nadan, Corinne J. & Blue, Rose. Jerry Rice. LC 94-4596. (Football Legends Ser.). (Illus.). 96p. (J). (gr. 3 up). 1994. lib. bdg. 15.95 (*0-7910-2456-3*) Chelsea Hse.

Nadan, Corrine J., jt. auth. see Blue, Rose.

Nadaner, Dan, jt. ed. see Egan, Kieran.

Nadar, Gaspard F. Quand J'etais Photographie. Sobieszek, Robert A. & Bunnell, Peter C., eds. LC 76-24657. (Sources of Modern Photography Ser.). (FRE.). 1979. reprint ed. lib. bdg. 18.95 (*0-405-09636-4*) Ayer.

Nadarajah, Devapoopathy. Love in Sanskrit & Tamil Literature: A Study of Characters & Nature. (C). 1995. 26.00 (*81-208-1215-8*, Pub. by Motilal Bnarsidass) S Asia.

***Nadarajah, M.** Culture, Gender & Ecology: Beyond Workerism. LC 99-938117. 1999. 18.75 (*81-7033-515-9*, Pub. by Rawat Pubns) S Asia.

Nadarajan, R., jt. auth. see Krishna, Reddy G.

Nadaraya, E. A. Nonparametric Estimation of Probability Densities & Regression Curves. (C). 1988. text 185.00 (*90-277-2757-0*) Kluwer Academic.

Nadas, John. Journey Toward Energy. 260p. (Orig.). 1995. pap. 11.95 (*0-9644756-0-X*) J Nadas.

Nadas, Peter. A Book of Memories: A Novel. 720p. 1998. pap. 14.95 (*0-14-027567-3*) Viking Penguin.

— The End of a Family Story. LC 98-7887. 224p. 1998. 23.00 (*0-374-14832-5*) FS&G.

***Nadas, Peter.** End of a Family Story. 256p. 2000. pap. 12.95 (*0-14-029179-2*) Viking Penguin.

— Love. Goldstein, Imre, tr. from HUN. LC 00-27908. 128p. 2000. 20.00 (*0-374-19228-6*) FS&G.

Nadas, Peter. A Lovely Tale of Photography. 120p. 1999. pap. 14.50 (*80-902171-6-8*, Pub. by Twisted Spoon) SPD-Small Pr Dist.

Nadas, Peter & Goldshtain, Imri. A Book of Memories: A Novel. Sanders, Ivan, tr. LC 96-50236. 706p. 1997. text 35.00 (*0-374-11543-5*) FS&G.

Nadasdy, Dean, jt. auth. see Schroeder, Theodore W.

***Nadathur, Gopalan.** Principles & Practice of Declarative Programming: International Conference, PPDP '99, Paris, France, September 29-October 1, 1999, Proceedings. Goos, G. et al, eds. LC 99-47356. (Lecture Notes in Computer Science Ser.: Vol. 1702). x, 434p. 1999. pap. 69.00 (*3-540-66540-4*) Spr-Verlag.

Nadaus, R. O. Dictionary Jarogt des Cibistes (CB Slang) (FRE.). 91p. 1997. 35.00 (*0-320-00479-1*) Fr & Eur.

Nadaus, Roland. Dictionnaire Initiatique de l'Orant. (FRE.). 1993. write for info. (*0-7859-8190-X*, 2-87744-154-7) Fr & Eur.

Nadawi, Abul H. Islam & the World. Kidwai, Mohammad A., tr. from ARA.Tr. of Madha Khasira al-Alam bi-Inhtat al-Muslimin. 218p. (Orig.). 1977. pap. 5.95 (*0-939830-04-3*, Pub. by IIFSO KW) New Era Publns MI.

N

An Asterisk (*) at the beginning of an entry indicates that the title is appearing for the first time.

Naddaf, Gerard. L' Origine et l'Evolution du Concept Crec de Phusis. LC 92-43280. (FRE.). 616p. 1993. text 129.95 (0-7734-9937-7) E Mellen.

Nade, Sydney, jt. auth. see Warren, Grace.

Nadeau, Alyce. Making & Selling Herbal Crafts: Tips, Techniques, Projects. (Illus.). 128p. 1996. pap. 14.95 (0-8069-3176-0) Sterling.

Nadeau, Alyce P. Observations of an Uppity Woman: Poems & Word Pictures. LC 99-10423. 64p. 1999. pap. 10.00 (1-887905-15-4) Pkway Pubs.

Nadeau, Claude H., ed. see North American Society for the Psychology of Sport & Physical Activity Staff.

*Nadeau-Dostie, Benoit. Design for at-Speed Test, Diagnosis & Measurement. LC 99-46022. (Frontiers in Electronic Testing Ser.). 2000. write for info. (0-7923-8669-8) Kluwer Academic.

NaDeau, E. G., jt. auth. see Thompson, David J.

Nadeau, Ellyn. A Garden of Memories: A Written Remembrance. (Illus.). 192p. 1999. 19.95 (0-9672261-0-4) Grief Recovery.

Nadeau, Gene A. Highway to Paradise: A Pictorial History of the Roadway to Mount Rainier. (Illus.). 148p. (Orig.). 1983. pap. 14.95 (0-9613891-0-9) Nadeau Pub.

Nadeau, Hugues W., jt. auth. see Black, Bernard.

Nadeau, Janice W. Families Making Sense of Death. LC 97-21080. (Understanding Families Ser.: Vol. 10). 331p. 1997. 52.00 (0-7619-0265-1); pap. 24.95 (0-7619-0266-X) Sage.

Nadeau, Jean-Pau, jt. auth. see Center, Candy.

Nadeau, Kathleen, et al. Understanding Girls with AD/HD. LC 99-22182. (Illus.). 1999. pap. 19.95 (0-9660366-5-4) Advantage Books.

Nadeau, Kathleen G. ADD in the Workplace: Choices, Changes, & Challenges. LC 97-1312. 248p. 1997. pap. 23.95 (0-87630-847-7) Brunner-Mazel.

— Adventures in Fast Forward: Life, Love, & Work for the ADD Adult. 224p. 1996. pap. 18.95 (0-87630-800-0) Brunner-Mazel.

— Help4ADD@HighSchool. unabridged ed. LC 98-8578. (Illus.). 148p. (YA). (gr. 9-12). 1998. pap. 19.95 (0-9660366-1-1) Advantage Books.

— Survival Guide for College Students with ADD or LD. LC 94-15724. (Illus.). 64p. 1994. pap. 9.95 (0-945354-63-0) Am Psychol.

Nadeau, Kathleen G., ed. A Comprehensive Guide to Attention Deficit Disorder in Adults: Research, Diagnosis, & Treatment. 432p. 1995. 39.95 (0-87630-760-8) Brunner-Mazel.

Nadeau, Kathleen G. & Dixon, Ellen B. Learning to Slow down & Pay Attention: A Book for Kids about ADD. 2nd ed. (Illus.). 80p. (J). (gr. 1-5). Date not set. pap. 10.95 (1-55798-456-5) Am Psychol.

Nadeau, Kathleen G., et al. Succeeding in the Workplace: Attention Deficit Disorder & Learning Disabilities in the Workplace: a Guide for Success. 154p. (Orig.). 1994. pap. text 25.00 (1-883560-03-9) JKL Communs.

Nadeau, Lyn, jt. auth. see Molino, Virginia.

Nadeau, Lynn. Haggadah: The Promised Land. 3rd ed. (Illus.). 32p. (Orig.). 1997. pap. 8.00 (0-9646074-9-2) Anagogala.

Nadeau, M. & Levesque, D. English-French Lexicon of Childhood Problems: Lexique Anglais-Francais de l'Enfant en Difficulte. (ENG & FRE.). 454p. 1982. pap. 35.00 (0-8288-0938-0, M8670) Fr & Eur.

Nadeau, Maurice. The History of Surrealism. Howard, Richard, tr. from FRE. LC 88-39354. (Paperbacks in AA History Ser.). (Illus.). 376p. 1989. reprint ed. pap. 20.50 (0-674-40345-2) HUP.

Nadeau, Michael. Byte Guide to CD ROM. 1994. pap., pap. text 39.95 incl. cd-rom (0-07-881982-2) Osborne-McGraw.

— Byte Guide to CD-ROM. 2nd ed. LC 96-175240. (Byte Ser.). 496p. 1995. pap. text 39.95 incl. cd-rom (0-07-882104-5) Osborne-McGraw.

Nadeau, R., jt. auth. see Kafatos, M.

Nadeau, Ray. Building a Better Vocabulary: By Studying Words in Context. LC 97-27589. 208p. (C). 1997. pap. 24.50 (0-7618-0857-4) U Pr of Amer.

Nadeau, Ray E. Expand Your Vocabulary: The Dynamic In-Context Way. LC 96-31236. 272p. 1996. pap. text 26.50 (0-7618-0462-5) U Pr of Amer.

Nadeau, Ray E., et al. Speaking Effectively in Public Settings: A Modern Rhetoric with a Traditional Base. 296p. (Orig.). (C). 1993. pap. text 27.50 (0-8191-9122-1) U Pr of Amer.

Nadeau, Remi. Fort Laramie & the Sioux. 3rd rev. ed. LC 97-66337. 370p. 1997. pap. 15.95 (0-9627104-6-6) Crest Pubs.

— Ghost Towns & Mining Camps of California: A History & Guide. 4th rev. ed. LC 98-74517. (Illus.). 335p. (Orig.). 1999. pap. 15.95 (0-9627104-8-2) Crest Pubs.

— The Silver Seekers: They Tamed California's Last Frontier. LC 98-73976. (Illus.). 350p. (Orig.). 1998. pap. 17.95 (0-9627104-7-4) Crest Pubs.

— Stalin, Churchill, & Roosevelt Divide Europe, Vol. 3. LC 90-7413. 272p. 1990. 65.00 (0-275-93450-0, C3450, Praeger Pubs) Greenwood.

— The Water Seekers. 3rd rev. ed. (Illus.). 286p. 1997. pap. 14.95 (0-9627104-5-8) Crest Pubs.

Nadeau, Richard. Adirondack Journal-Book. (Illus.). 48p. 1992. mass mkt. 4.95 (1-881857-00-X) Moose Riv Trading.

— Historical Post Cards of the Adirondacks, Vol. 2. 24p. 1995. mass mkt. 9.95 (1-881857-05-0) Moose Riv Trading.

Nadeau, Richard P. Historical Post Cards of the Adirondacks, Vol. I. 24p. 1993. pap. text 9.95 (1-881857-04-2) Moose Riv Trading.

— Outdoor Journal-Book. 48p. 1994. pap. text 4.95 (1-881857-02-6) Moose Riv Trading.

Nadeau, Robert & Kafatos, Menas. The Non-Local Universe: The New Physics & Matters of the Mind. LC 99-17062. (Illus.). 256p. 1999. 27.50 (0-19-513256-4) OUP.

Nadeau, Robert, jt. auth. see Kafatos, Minas C.

Nadeau, Robert L. Nature Talks Back: Surviving in the Nuclear Age. LC 84-3574. (Illus.). 128p. (Orig.). 1984. pap. 6.00 (0-914061-01-1) Orchises Pr.

— Readings from the New Book on Nature: Physics & Metaphysics in the Modern Novel. LC 81-2625. 224p. 1981. lib. bdg. 30.00 (0-87023-331-9) U of Mass Pr.

— S/He Brain: Science, Sexual Politics, & the Myths of Feminism. LC 96-3211. 184p. 1996. 19.95 (0-275-95593-1, Praeger Pubs) Greenwood.

Nadeau, Roch, jt. auth. see Bizier, Richard.

Nadeau, Stephen E., et al, eds. Aphasia & Language: Theory to Practice. (Science & Practice of Neuropsychology Ser.). 446p. Date not set. lib. bdg. 65.00 (1-57230-581-9, C0581) Guilford Pubns.

Nadeau, Tom. Seven Lean Years: America's New High-Tech Underclass. 130p. 1999. spiral bd. 8.95 (0-9671089-0-X) T Nadeau.

— Showdown at the Bouzy Rouge: People vs. PG&E. LC 98-130243. (Illus.). 128p. (Orig.). 1998. pap. 12.50 (0-933994-17-6) Comstock Bon.

Nadeau, Tom, jt. auth. see Stein, Peter.

Nadeen, Satyam. From Onions to Pearls. LC 98-49527. 220p. 1999. pap. 12.95 (1-56170-587-X) Hay House.

— From Onions to Pearls: A Journal of Awakening & Deliverance. LC 97-172722. (Illus.). iii, 199p. (Orig.). 1996. pap. 12.95 (0-9653850-0-0) New Freedom Pr.

— From Seekers to Finders. LC 99-47549. 176p. 2000. pap. 12.95 (1-56170-588-8, 596) Hay House.

Nadejda Gorodetzky. St. Tikhon of Zadonsk: Inspirer of Dostoevsky. LC 76-49919. 320p. 1977. pap. 11.95 (0-913836-32-X) St Vladimirs.

Nadel, Alan. Containment Culture: American Narratives, Postmodernism, & the Atomic Age. LC 95-16631. (New Americanists Ser.). 336p. 1995. text 54.95 (0-8223-1701-X); pap. text 17.95 (0-8223-1699-4) Duke.

— Flatlining on the Field of Dreams: Cultural Narratives in the Films of President Reagan's America. LC 96-49062. (Illus.). 224p. (C). 1997. text 48.00 (0-8135-2439-3); pap. text 17.95 (0-8135-2440-7) Rutgers U Pr.

— Invisible Criticism: Ralph Ellison & the American Canon. LC 87-25071. 197p. 1988. reprint ed. pap. text 13.95 (0-87745-321-7) U of Iowa Pr.

Nadel, Alan, ed. May All Your Fences Have Gates: Essays on the Drama of August Wilson. LC 93-34628. (Illus.). 282p. 1993. pap. text 16.95 (0-87745-439-6) U of Iowa Pr.

Nadel, Eric. The Texas Rangers: The Authorized History. LC 97-9629. (Illus.). 256p. 1997. 36.95 (0-87833-139-5); 75.00 (0-87833-140-9) Taylor Pub.

Nadel, Harold, ed. see Anderson, Alex.

Nadel, Harold, ed. see McClun, Diana & Nownes, Laura.

Nadel, Harold, ed. see McDowell, Ruth B.

Nadel, Harold, ed. see Montano, Judith B.

Nadel, Harold, ed. see Peters, Margaret.

Nadel, Harold, ed. see Porcella, Yvonne.

Nadel, Harold, ed. see Wolfrom, Joen.

Nadel, Ira. Leonard Cohen: A Life in Art. large type ed. (Illus.). 190p. 1996. pap. 15.95 (1-55022-267-8, Pub. by ECW) Genl Dist Srvs.

Nadel, Ira, ed. see Adams, Henry B.

Nadel, Ira B. Joyce & the Jews: Culture & Text. Bowen, Zack, ed. & frwd. by. (Florida James Joyce Ser.). 304p. (Orig.). (C). 1996. pap. 19.95 (0-8130-1425-5) U Press Fla.

— Joyce & the Jews: Culture & Texts. LC 88-50767. 302p. 1989. text 34.95 (0-87745-221-0) U of Iowa Pr.

— Leonard Cohen: A Life in Art. LC 94-232066. (Illus.). 160p. 1994. pap. 9.95 (1-55022-210-4, Pub. by ECW) LPC InBook.

— Various Positions: A Life of Leonard Cohen. 1996. 26.00 (0-679-44235-9) Random.

Nadel, Ira B., ed. The Cambridge Companion to Ezra Pound. LC 98-12923. (Cambridge Companions to Literature Ser.). 350p. (C). 1999. 54.95 (0-521-43117-4); pap. 19.95 (0-521-64920-X) Cambridge U Pr.

Nadel, Ira B., et al, eds. Victorian Novelists Before 1885. LC 83-8848. (Dictionary of Literary Biography Ser.: Vol. 21). 432p. 1983. text 155.00 (0-8103-1701-X) Gale.

Nadel, Ira B. & Fredeman, William E., eds. Victorian Novelists after 1885. (Dictionary of Literary Biography Ser.: Vol. 18). (Illus.). 410p. 1983. text 155.00 (0-8103-1143-7) Gale.

Nadel, Ira B., ed. see Bulwer Lytton, Edward & Swinburne, Algernon Charles.

Nadel, Ira B., jt. ed. see Fredeman, William E.

Nadel, Ira B., jt. ed. see Neuman, Shirley.

Nadel, Ira B., ed. see Pound, Ezra.

Nadel, Jack. How to Succeed in Business Without Lying, Cheating or Stealing. Peters, Sally, ed. 168p. (Orig.). 1993. pap. 7.00 (0-671-79543-0) PB.

— Louisiana Estate Planning, Will Drafting, & Estate Administration. 1994. disk 75.00 (0-614-03737-9, MICHIE) LEXIS Pub.

— There's No Business Like Your Business: How to Turn Your Knowledge into Personal Profit. 240p. (Orig.). 1996. pap. 14.95 (1-887697-03-9) Two Roads Pubng.

Nadel, Jack, jt. auth. see Cohn, Beverly.

Nadel, Jacqueline & Butterworth, George, eds. Imitation in Infancy. LC 99-213860. (Cambridge Studies in Cognitive & Perceptual Development: No. 1). (Illus.). 304p. (C). 1999. text 59.95 (0-521-58033-1) Cambridge U Pr.

Nadel, Jay A., ed. Physiology & Pharmacology of the Airways. LC 80-16046. (Lung Biology in Health & Disease Ser.: No. 15). (Illus.). 371p. reprint ed. pap. 115.10 (0-7837-0863-7, 204117100019) Bks Demand.

Nadel, Jay A., jt. ed. see Murray, John F.

Nadel, Jay A., jt. ed. see Olivieri, D.

Nadel, Jennifer. Sara Thornton. (Illus.). 256p. 1994. pap. 15.95 (0-575-05581-2, Pub. by V Gollancz) Trafalgar.

Nadel, Joel & Wright, J. R. Special Men & Special Missions: Inside American Special Operations Forces, 1945 to the Present. LC 93-41727. (Illus.). 256p. 1994. 29.95 (1-85367-159-2, 5593) Stackpole.

Nadel, Laurie. The Kremlin Coup. (YA). 1992. pap. 4.80 (0-395-62468-1) HM.

— The Kremlin Coup. LC 91-36892. (Illus.). 64p. (J). (gr. 5-8). 1992. pap. 6.95 (1-878841-94-7); lib. bdg. 23.40 (1-56294-170-4) Millbrook Pr.

Nadel, Laurie, et al. The Sixth Sense. 304p. 1992. reprint ed. mass mkt. 4.99 (0-380-71503-1, Avon Bks) Morrow Avon.

Nadel, Lynn. 1991 Lectures in Complex Systems. (C). 1992. 54.00 (0-201-57834-4) Addison-Wesley.

Nadel, Lynn, ed. The Psychobiology of Down Syndrome. (Issues in the Biology of Language & Cognition Ser.). 496p. 1988. 44.00 (0-262-14043-8, Bradford Bks) MIT Pr.

Nadel, Lynn & Cooper, Lynn A., eds. Neural Connections, Mental Computation. (Illus.). 368p. 1992. reprint ed. pap. text 27.50 (0-262-64029-5, Bradford Bks) MIT Pr.

Nadel, Lynn & Epstein, Charles J., eds. Down Syndrome & Alzheimer Disease. 334p. 1992. 208.50 (0-471-58841-5) Wiley.

Nadel, Lynn & Rosenthal, Donna M., eds. Down Syndrome: Living & Learning in the Community. 312p. 1995. 79.95 (0-471-02192-X); pap. 24.95 (0-471-02201-2) Wiley.

Nadel, Lynn & Stein, Daniel L. 1993 Lectures in Complex Systems. 639p. (C). 1995. 61.00 (0-201-48368-8) Addison-Wesley.

Nadel, Lynn, jt. ed. see Lane, Richard D.

Nadel, Maria, jt. auth. see Diaz, Jose M.

Nadel, Maria F., jt. auth. see Diaz, Jose M.

Nadel, Mark V., ed. Consumer Protection Policy. (Orig.). (C). 1983. pap. 15.00 (0-918592-60-7) Pol Studies.

Nadel, Max. How to Prepare for the Advanced Placement Test: English. 6th ed. LC 96-51482. 464p. 1997. pap. text 12.95 (0-8120-9727-0) Barron.

Nadel, Semen N. Contemporary Capitalism & the Middle Classes. LC 82-1046. 448p. reprint ed. pap. 127.70 (0-7837-0586-7, 2040930) Bks Demand.

Nadel, Siegfried F. Black Byzantium: The Kingdom of Nupe in Nigeria. 1976. lib. bdg. 59.95 (0-8490-1510-3) Gordon Pr.

— The Nuba: An Anthropological Study of the Hill Tribes in Kordofan. LC 76-44768. reprint ed. 67.50 (0-404-15957-5) AMS Pr.

Nadel, Stanley. Little Germany: Ethnicity, Religion & Class in New York City, 1845-80. LC 89-20684. (Illus.). 264p. 1990. text 37.50 (0-252-01677-7) U of Ill Pr.

Nadel, Steven J., jt. auth. see Hill, Russell J.

Nadel, Steven M., et al. Energy Efficient Motor Systems: A Handbook on Technology, Program, & Policy Opportunities. (Illus.). 379p. (C). 1997. pap. 31.00 (0-918249-10-4) Am Coun Energy.

Nadelhaft, Jerome J. The Disorders of War: The Revolution in South Carolina. 310p. 1981. reprint ed. 27.50 (0-89101-048-3); reprint ed. pap. 12.95 (0-89101-049-1) U Maine Pr.

Nadelhaft, Matthew, jt. ed. see Long, Kristi S.

Nadelhaft, Ruth, ed. see Conrad, Joseph.

Nadell, et al. The Macmillan Reader. 5th ed. LC 98-21422. 762p. 1998. pap. 37.00 (0-205-28216-4) Allyn.

— The Macmillan Writer: Rhetoric, Reader & Handbook. 4th ed. LC 99-22375. 718p. 1999. pap. 47.00 (0-205-29854-0, Longwood Div) Allyn.

— Macmillan Writer Brief. 4th ed. 653p. 1999. pap. text 44.00 (0-205-29855-9, Longwood Div) Allyn.

Nadell, Judith, et al. The Macmillan Reader. 3rd ed. (Illus.). 768p. (C). 1992. teacher ed. write for info. (0-318-69337-2) Macmillan.

— Vocabulary Basics. 265p. (C). 1997. pap. text 7.90 (0-944210-40-6) Townsend NJ.

Nadell, Judith, jt. auth. see Langan, John.

Nadell, Pamela S. Conservative Judaism in America: A Biographical Dictionary & Sourcebook. LC 87-31782. (Jewish Denominations in America Ser.). 436p. 1988. lib. bdg. 85.00 (0-313-24205-4, NCJ, Greenwood Pr) Greenwood.

— Women Who Would Be Rabbis: A History of Women's Ordination, 1889-1985. LC 98-7321. 320p. 1998. 30.00 (0-8070-3648-X) Beacon Pr.

— Women Who Would Be Rabbis: A History of Women's Ordination, 1889-1985. LC 98-7321. 320p. 1999. pap. 18.00 (0-8070-3649-8) Beacon Pr.

Nadelman, Barry M. & Solomon, Lewis D. Estate Planning: Complete Guide & Workbook. 450p. 1996. ring bd., wbk. ed. 139.00 (1-886035-06-7) Pro Tax & Business.

Nadelman, Cynthia, intro. Elie Nadelman. (Illus.). 36p. 1996. pap. 25.00 (1-58821-050-2) Salander OReilly.

*Nadelman, Cynthia & Forcade, Dominique, texts. Jeff Novatt. (Illus.). 22p. 1998. pap. 10.00 (1-58821-055-3) Salander OReilly.

Nadelmann, Ethan A. Conflict of Laws. 1972. pap. text 80.00 (90-247-1212-2, Pub. by M Nijhoff) Kluwer Academic.

— Cops Across Borders: The Internationalization of U. S. Criminal Law Enforcement. LC 93-1305. 558p. 1993. pap. 18.95 (0-271-01095-9) Pa St U Pr.

— Cops without Borders: International Law Enforcement. 1994. 24.95 (0-02-922421-7) S&S Trade.

Nadelson, Carol C. Encyclopedia of Psychological Disorders, 8 vols. (Encyclopedia of Psychological Disorders Ser.). 1998. 160.65 (0-7910-4902-7) Chelsea Hse.

— Life Out of Focus: Alzheimer's Disease & Dementia. LC 98-26537. (Encyclopedia of Psychological Disorders Ser.). 144p. 1999. 24.95 (0-7910-4896-9) Chelsea Hse.

Nadelson, Carol C., et al, eds. The Woman Patient Vol. 2: Concepts of Femininity & the Life Cycle. LC 82-5326. (Women in Context Ser.). 216p. 1982. 45.00 (0-306-40846-5, Plenum Trade) Perseus Pubng.

Nadelson, Carol C. & Marcotte, David B., eds. Treatment Interventions In Human Sexuality. LC 83-4078. (Critical Issues in Psychiatry Ser.). 502p. 1983. 89.50 (0-306-41082-6, Plenum Trade) Perseus Pubng.

Nadelson, Carol C. & Polonsky, Derek C., eds. Marriage & Divorce, a Contemporary Perspective. LC 83-1567. (Guilford Family Therapy Ser.). (Illus.). 285p. 1984. reprint ed. pap. 88.40 (0-608-07577-9, 205989100010) Bks Demand.

Nadelson, Carol C. & Reinburg, Claire E., eds. Child Abuse & Neglect: Examining the Psychological Components. LC 98-53702. (Encyclopedia of Psychological Disorders Ser.). 144p. (YA). (gr. 7 up). 1999. lib. bdg. 24.95 (0-7910-4955-8) Chelsea Hse.

*Nadelson, Carol C. & Reinburg, Claire E., eds. Cutting the Pain Away: Understanding Self-Mutilation. LC 99-19764. (Encyclopedia of Psychological Disorders Ser.). (Illus.). 144p. (YA). (gr. 7 up). 1999. lib. bdg. 24.95 (0-7910-4951-5) Chelsea Hse.

Nadelson, Carol C. & Reinburg, Claire E., eds. Drowning Our Sorrows: Psychological Effects of Alcohol Abuse. LC 99-11418. 144p. (YA). (gr. 7 up). 1999. lib. bdg. 24.95 (0-7910-4954-X) Chelsea Hse.

— Psychological Disorders Related to Designer Drugs. LC 99-13437. (Encyclopedia of Psychological Disorders Ser.). (Illus.). 144p. (YA). (gr. 7 up). 1999. lib. bdg. 24.95 (0-7910-4957-4) Chelsea Hse.

*Nadelson, Carol C. & Reinburg, Claire E., eds. Sibling Rivalry: Relational Disorders Between Brothers & Sisters. LC 98-56102. (Encyclopedia of Psychological Disorders Ser.). (Illus.). 144p. (YA). (gr. 7 up). 1999. lib. bdg. 24.95 (0-7910-4952-3) Chelsea Hse.

— Smoke Screen: Psychological Disorders Related to Nicotine Use. LC 99-13338. (Encyclopedia of Psychological Disorders Ser.). (Illus.). 144p. (YA). (gr. 7 up). 1999. lib. bdg. 24.95 (0-7910-4958-2) Chelsea Hse.

Nadelson, Carol C., ed. see Connelly, Elizabeth Russell.

Nadelson, Carol C., ed. see Connelly, Elizabeth Russell & Connolly, Beth.

Nadelson, Carol C., ed. see Harmon, Dan.

Nadelson, Carol C., ed. see Harmon, Daniel E.

Nadelson, Carol C., ed. see Holmes, Ann.

Nadelson, Carol C., ed. see Holmes, Ann E.

Nadelson, Carol C., ed. see Holmes, Ann & Harmon, Dan.

Nadelson, Carol C., ed. see Holmes, Ann & Reinburg, Claire E.

Nadelson, Carol C., jt. ed. see Mak, Felice L.

Nadelson, Carol C., jt. ed. see Notman, Malkah T.

*Nadelson, Mark & Hagan, Thomas. C++ Objects for Making UNIX & WinNT Talk. 512p. 2000. pap. 49.95 incl. cd-rom (1-929629-07-9, Pub. by C M P Books) Publishers Group.

Nadelson, Mark & Hagan, Thomas. Making UNIX & Windows NT Talk: Object-Oriented Inter-Platform Communications. 512p. 1999. pap. 44.95 incl. disk (0-87930-584-3) C M P Books.

*Nadelson, Reggie. Bloody London. LC 99-45941. 272p. 2000. text 24.95 (0-312-24372-3, Minotaur) St Martin.

— Hot Poppies. large type ed. 384p. 1999. 31.99 (0-7089-4077-3) Ulverscroft.

Nadelson, Reggie. Hot Poppies: An Artie Cohen Mystery. LC 98-50724. 256p. 1998. text 22.95 (0-312-19986-4) St Martin.

— Red Hot Blues. LC 97-46498. Orig. Title: Red Mercury Blues. 272p. 1998. text 22.95 (0-312-18166-3) St Martin.

Nadelstern, Paula. Color Design in Patchwork: With Plastic Templates for 10 Pairs of Blocks. (Needlecraft Ser.). (Illus.). 32p. (Orig.). 1991. pap. 5.95 (0-486-26736-9) Dover.

— Kaleidoscopes & Quilts. Jonsson, Lee, ed. LC 96-17491. (Illus.). 144p. (Orig.). 1996. pap. 24.95 (1-57120-018-5, 10142) C & T Pub.

Nadelstern, Paula. Star Quilt-Stickers: 25 Sensitive Designs. (Illus.). (J). 1993. pap. 1.00 (0-486-27484-5) Dover.

Naden, C. J. I Can Read About All Kinds of Giants. LC 78-65833. (Illus.). (J). (gr. 2-4). 1997. pap. 2.95 (0-89375-201-0) Troll Communs.

— I Can Read About Creepy Crawly Creatures. LC 78-68469. (Illus.). (J). (gr. 3-6). 1979. pap. 2.95 (0-89375-207-X) Troll Communs.

— I Can Read About Motorcycles. LC 78-74657. (Illus.). (J). (gr. 3-6). 1997. pap. 2.95 (0-89375-212-6) Troll Communs.

— I Can Read About Racing Cars. LC 78-74658. (Illus.). (J). (gr. 3-6). 1997. pap. 2.95 (0-89375-216-9) Troll Communs.

— I Can Read about Sharks. LC 95-5942. (Illus.). 48p. (J). (gr. k-3). 1996. pap. 4.95 (0-8167-3647-2) Troll Communs.

— I Can Read About Sharks. LC 78-73736. (Illus.). (J). (gr. 2-6). 1997. pap. 2.95 (0-89375-218-5) Troll Communs.

— John Henry, the Steeldriving Man. LC 79-66317. (Illus.). 48p. (J). (gr. 3-6). 1980. pap. 3.95 (0-89375-303-3); lib. bdg. 15.85 (0-89375-304-1) Troll Communs.

Naden, C. J., adapted by. Pegasus, the Winged Horse. LC 80-50069. (Illus.). 32p. (J). (gr. 4-8). 1980. lib. bdg. 18.60 (0-89375-361-0) Troll Communs.

— Pegasus, the Winged Horse. LC 80-50069. (Illus.). 32p. (J). (gr. 4-8). 1997. pap. 3.95 (0-89375-365-3) Troll Communs.

An Asterisk (*) at the beginning of an entry indicates that the title is appearing for the first time.

***Naden, Corinne & Blue, Rose.** Chancellorsville to Appomattox: Battles of 1863 to 1865. LC 99-15597. (House Divided Ser.). (Illus.). 112p. (YA). (gr. 6-8). 2000. 28.54 (*0-8172-5582-6*) Raintree Steck-V.

Naden, Corinne J. John Muir: Saving the Wilderness. (J). (gr. 4-7). 1992. pap. 4.80 (*0-395-63569-1*) HM.

— John Muir: Saving the Wilderness. (Gateway Greens Ser.). 1994. 12.15 (*0-606-12363-6*, Pub. by Turtleback) Demco.

— Ronald McNair. (Black Americans of Achievement Ser.). (J). 1991. 14.15 (*0-606-08082-1*) Turtleback.

— Ronald McNair: Astronaut. Huggins, Nathan I., ed. (Black Americans of Achievement Ser.). (Illus.). 124p. (YA). (gr. 5 up). 1993. pap. 8.95 (*0-7910-1158-5*) Chelsea Hse.

***Naden, Corinne J. & Blue, Rose.** Belle Starr & the Old West. LC 00-8437. (Notorious Americans & Their Times Ser.). (Illus.). 112p. 2000. 19.95 (*1-56711-223-4*) Blackbirch.

— The Bloodiest Days: The Battles of 1861 & 1862. LC 99-15599. (House Divided Ser.). (Illus.). 112p. (YA). (gr. 6-8). 1999. 28.54 (*0-8172-5581-8*) Raintree Steck-V.

— Christa McAuliffe: Teacher in Space. (Gateway Biographies Ser.). (Illus.). 48p. (J). (gr. 2-4). 1991. lib. bdg. 20.90 (*1-56294-046-5*) Millbrook Pr.

— Civil War Ends: Assassination, Reconstruction & the Aftermath. LC 99-15598. (House Divided Ser.). (Illus.). 112p. (YA). (gr. 6-8). 1999. 28.54 (*0-8172-5583-4*) Raintree Steck-V.

Naden, Corinne J. & Blue, Rose. Heroes Don't Just Happen: Biographies of Overcoming Bias & Building Character in Politics. LC 98-221227. 88p. 1997. 8.95 (*1-56256-437-4*) Peoples Pub Grp.

— John Muir: Saving the Wilderness. LC 91-18106. (Gateway Biographies Ser.). (Illus.). 48p. (J). (gr. 2-4). 1992. pap. 5.95 (*1-56294-797-4*); lib. bdg. 19.90 (*1-56294-110-0*) Millbrook Pr.

***Naden, Corinne J. & Blue, Rose.** Why Fight? The Causes of the American Civil War. LC 99-20910. (Civil War Ser.). (Illus.). 112p. (YA). (gr. 6-8). 1999. 28.54 (*0-8172-5580-X*) Raintree Steck-V.

Naden, Corinne J., jt. auth. see Blue, Rose.

Naden, Corinne J., jt. auth. see Gillespie, John T.

Naden, Corinne J., jt. auth. see Huggins, Nathan I.

Naden, Corinne J., jt. ed. see Gillespie, John T.

Naden, Corrine J. Christa McAuliffe: Teacher in Space. (Gateway Biography Ser.). (J). 1994. 14.15 (*0-606-12220-6*, Pub. by Turtleback) Demco.

Naden, Corrine J. & Blue, Rose. Christa McAuliffe: Teacher in Space. (Gateway Biographies Ser.). 48p. (J). (gr. 2-4). 1992. pap. 4.80 (*1-878841-58-0*) Millbrook Pr.

Naden, D., jt. ed. see Streat, M.

Nadenicek, Daniel J. What Do We Expect to Learn from Our History? The First Symposium on History in Landscape Architecture. Pennypacker, Eliza, ed. (Illus.). 156p. (Orig.). 1996. pap. write for info. (*1-888901-00-4*) PSU Ctr for SILH.

Nader, Edith. Cooking Without No-No's. 200p. 1994. pap. 14.95 (*0-9643513-0-7*) E G Nader.

Nader, Helen. Liberty in Absolutist Spain: The Habsburg Sale of Towns, 1516-1700. (Johns Hopkins University Studies in Historical & Political Science). 400p. (C). 1993. reprint ed. pap. text 19.95 (*0-8018-4731-1*) Johns Hopkins.

— The Mendoza Family in the Spanish Renaissance, 1350-1550. LC 79-9945. 291p. reprint ed. pap. 90.30 (*0-8357-7949-1*, 205702400002) Bks Demand.

— Rights of Discovery: Christopher Columbus's Final Appeal to King Fernando. 94p. 1992. 25.00 (*0-916617-41-6*) J C Brown.

Nader, Helen & Formisano, Luciano, eds. Book of Privileges Issued to Christopher Columbus by King Fernando & Queen Isabel, 1492-1502. (Repertorium Columbianum Ser.: Vol. 2). (Illus.). 434p. 1995. 55.00 (*0-520-08897-2*, Pub. by U CA Pr) Cal Prin Full Svc.

Nader, Iyad A. Kangaroo Rats: Intraspecific Variation in Dipodomys Spectabilis Merriam & Dipodomys Deserti Stephens. LC 78-9317. (Illinois Biological Monographs: No. 49). 128p. reprint ed. pap. 39.70 (*0-8357-9686-8*, 201900400010) Bks Demand.

Nader, Jonah. Prentice Hall Illustrated Dictionary of Computing. 2nd ed. LC 94-47617. 650p. (C). 1995. pap. text 24.95 (*0-13-205725-5*) P-H.

Nader, Jonar. Prentice Hall's Illustrated Dictionary of Computing. LC 92-19637. 544p. (C). 1992. pap. text 24.95 (*0-13-719998-8*) P-H.

***Nader, Jonar C.** How to Lose Friends & Infuriate People: Leadership in the Networked World. 384p. 2000. 20.00 (*0-9577165-4-0*, Pub. by PLUTONIUM) Publishers Group.

Nader, Jonar C. Prentice Hall's Illustrated Dictionary of Computing. 3rd ed. LC 98-4713. (Illus.). 792p. (C). 1998. pap. 34.95 incl. cd-rom (*0-13-095104-8*) P-H.

Nader, Laura. Harmony Ideology: Justice & Control in a Zapotec Mountain Village. LC 89-78333. 366p. 1990. 47.50 (*0-8047-1809-1*); pap. 17.95 (*0-8047-1810-5*) Stanford U Pr.

***Nader, Laura.** Honoring Differences: Cultural Issues in the Treatment of Trauma & Loss. (Series in Trauma & Loss). 1999. pap. text 29.95 (*0-87630-935-X*) Brunner-Mazel.

Nader, Laura, ed. Law in Culture & Society. LC 96-34175. 460p. 1997. pap. 19.95 (*0-520-20833-1*, Pub. by U CA Pr) Cal Prin Full Svc.

— Naked Science: Anthropological Inquiry into Boundaries, Power & Knowledge. LC 95-23650. 333p. (C). 1996. pap. 23.99 (*0-415-91465-5*) Routledge.

Nader, Nathra, jt. auth. see Nader, Rose B.

Nader, R. & Smith, W. J. No Contest. 464p. 1998. pap. 13.00 (*0-375-75258-7*) Random.

Nader, Ralph. Canada Firsts. 1992. pap. 14.99 (*0-7710-6713-5*) McCland & Stewart.

***Nader, Ralph.** Cutting Corporate Welfare. LC 00-20219. (Open Media Pamphlet Ser.: Vol. 18). 96p. 2000. pap. 7.95 (*1-58322-033-X*, Pub. by Seven Stories) Publishers Group.

— The Ralph Nader Reader. 640p. 2000. 35.95 (*1-58322-046-1*); pap. 19.95 (*1-58322-057-7*, Pub. by Seven Stories) Publishers Group.

Nader, Ralph & Ditlow, Clarence. The Lemon Book. 4th rev. ed. LC 96-39310. 396p. (Orig.). pap. 16.95 (*1-55921-196-2*) Moyer Bell.

Nader, Ralph & Smith, Wesley J. Collision Course: The Truth About Airline Safety. LC 93-8266. 1993. 21.95 (*0-8306-4271-4*) McGraw-Hill Prof.

— No Contest: How the Power Lawyers Are Perverting Justice in America. (Illus.). 336p. 1996. 25.95 (*0-679-42972-7*) Random.

Nader, Ralph, et al. Case Against "Free Trade" GATT, NAFTA, & the Globalization of Corporate Power. 230p. (Orig.). 1993. pap. 10.00 (*1-55643-169-4*) North Atlantic.

— Who's Poisoning America? Corporate Polluters & Their Victims in the Chemical Age. LC 80-29608. xiv, 369 p. 1981. write for info. (*0-87156-280-4*) Sierra.

Nader, Ralph, jt. auth. see Vaughn, Robert G.

Nader, Rose B. & Nader, Nathra. It Happened in the Kitchen: Recipes for Food & Thought. LC 91-70432. 180p. (Orig.). 1991. pap. 9.00 (*0-936758-29-5*) Ctr Responsive Law.

Nader, Sam. The River of Years: Looking Back on My Life As a Methodist Minister. 208p. (Orig.). 1995. pap. 9.95 (*0-925854-14-X*) Defiant Pr.

***Nadesan, Dilley.** The Person & Personality of the Holy Spirit. 120p. 1999. pap. write for info. (*0-7392-0480-7*, PO3818) Morris Pubng.

— The Prophetic Cry of Wisdom. 1999. pap. write for info. (*0-7392-0481-5*, PO3820) Morris Pubng.

Nadezhin, D. K., jt. auth. see Imshennik, V. S.

Nadgorny, Boris E., jt. auth. see Cahn, Sidney B.

Nadi, Aldo. The Living Sword: A Fencer's Autobiography. Lobo, Lance C., ed. LC 94-77796. (Illus.). 416p. 1995. pap. 17.95 (*1-884528-20-1*) Laureate Pr.

— On Fencing. LC 93-80473. (Illus.). 300p. 1994. reprint ed. pap. 19.95 (*1-884528-04-X*) Laureate Pr.

Nadich, Judah. The Legends of the Rabbis Vol. 1: Jewish Legends of the Second Commonwealth. LC 94-208. 512p. 1994. pap. 25.00 (*1-56821-130-9*) Aronson.

— The Legends of the Rabbis Vol. 2: The First Generation after the Destruction of the Temple & Jerusalem. LC 94-209. 264p. 1994. pap. 20.00 (*1-56821-131-7*) Aronson.

— Rabbi Akiba & His Contemporaries. LC 97-2410. 256p. 1998. pap. 30.00 (*0-7657-5975-6*) Aronson.

Nadich, Judah, ed. The Legends of the Rabbis, 2 vol. set. LC 94-1942. 776p. 1994. pap. 45.00 (*1-56821-129-5*) Aronson.

Nadien, Margot B. & Denmark, Florence. Females & Autonomy: A Life-Span Perspective. LC 98-12181. 176p. 1998. pap. text 41.00 (*0-205-19856-2*) Allyn.

Nadin. Dictionary of European Spatial. text 93.00 (*0-471-98534-1*); pap. text 34.00 (*0-471-98535-X*) Wiley.

***Nadin, Elvita.** Jewish: Does It Make a Difference? 284p. 2000. 23.00 (*0-8246-0420-2*) Jonathan David.

Nadin, Mihai. The Civilization of Illiteracy. LC 97-194223. 881p. 1998. 79.00 (*3-931828-38-7*, Pub. by Dresden Univ Pr) Paul & Co Pubs.

Nadin, Mihai & Zakia, Richard D. Creating Effective Advertising: Using Semiotics. LC 94-4481. 268p. 1994. 39.95 (*0-913069-46-9*) Consultant Pr.

Nadin, Peter, et al. Peter Nadin: Recent Work & Notes on Six Series. limited ed. (Illus.). 72p. (Orig.). 1992. pap. 24.95 (*0-685-63223-7*) Yale Ctr Brit Art.

Nadin, Val. Breaking the Blue Line: A Dying Declaration. LC 97-91349. 1998. pap. 12.95 (*0-533-12628-2*) Vantage.

Nadin, Vincent & Doak, Joe. Town Planning Responses to City Change. 252p. 1991. text 77.95 (*1-85628-161-2*, Pub. by Avebry) Ashgate Pub Co.

Nadin, Vincent, jt. auth. see Cullingworth, J. B.

Nadin, Vincent, jt. ed. see Hill, L.

Nadine. Halfway to Hell. 83p. (Orig.). 1996. pap. 20.00 (*0-9656427-0-4*) Nadines.

— Rape Hurts. (Orig.). Date not set. pap. write for info. (*0-9656427-1-2*) Nadines.

Nadir, Shams. The Astrolabe of the Sea. Dickson, C., tr. from FRE. 160p. (Orig.). 1996. pap. 9.95 (*0-87286-314-X*) City Lights.

Nadiri, M. Ishaq & Rosen, Sherwin. Disequilibrium Model of Demand for Factors of Production. (General Ser.: No. 99). 226p. 1974. 58.80 (*0-87014-261-5*) Natl Bur Econ Res.

Nadiri, M. Ishaq, jt. ed. see Labys, Walter C.

Nadji, Mehrzad, ed. Federal Power: Issues Related to the Divestiture of Federal Hydropower Resources. (Illus.). 114p. (C). 1999. pap. text 30.00 (*0-7881-7637-4*) DIANE Pub.

Nadji, Mehrzad, jt. auth. see Harris, Curtis C., Jr.

Nadkarni, K. M., ed. Dr. K. M. Nadkarni's Indian Materia Medica. (C). 1988. 70.00 (*0-8364-2337-2*, Pub. by Popular Prakashan) S Asia.

— Indian Materia Medica, 2 vols., Set. 1989. 74.00 (*0-8364-2572-3*, Pub. by Popular Prakashan) S Asia.

Nadkarni, M. G. Basic Ergodic Theory. 2nd ed. LC 98-31194. 1998. 44.50 (*0-8176-5816-5*) Birkhauser.

— Basic Ergodic Theory. 2nd ed. LC 98-31194. (Birkhauser Advanced Texts Ser.). 160p. 1999. 44.50 (*3-7643-5816-5*) Birkhauser.

— Spectral Theory of Dynamical Systems. LC 98-31195. 1998. 59.50 (*0-8176-5817-3*) Birkhauser.

— Spectral Theory of Dynamical Systems. LC 98-31195. (Birkhauser Advanced Texts Ser.). 192p. 1999. 59.50 (*3-7643-5817-3*) Birkhauser.

Nadkarni, M. V. Marketable Surplus & Market Dependence: A Study of a Millet Region. 176p. 1980. 24.95 (*0-940500-80-9*, Pub. by Allied Pubs) Asia Bk Corp.

Nadkarni, M. V., et al, eds. India - The Emerging Challenges: Essays in Honour of Professor V. K. R. V. Rad. 400p. (C). 1991. 38.00 (*0-8039-9665-9*) Sage.

Nadkarni, M. V., et al. The Political Economy of Forest Use & Management. 184p. (C). 1989. text 22.50 (*0-8039-9591-1*) Sage.

Nadkarni, M. V., jt. ed. see Bharadwaj, R.

Nadkarni, Mahan. Bhimsen Joshi: A Biography. LC 94-905427. (C). 1995. 22.50 (*81-7223-126-1*, Pub. by Indus Pub) S Asia.

Nadkarni, Nalini M. & Wheelwright, Nathaniel T., eds. Monteverde: Ecology & Conservation of a Tropical Cloud Forest. LC 98-26919. (Illus.). 608p. 2000. pap. 75.00 (*0-19-513310-2*) OUP.

— Monteverde: Ecology & Conservation of a Tropical Cloud Forest. LC 98-26919. (Illus.). 608p. 2000. text 130.00 (*0-19-509560-X*) OUP.

Nadkarni, Nalini M., jt. ed. see Lowman, Margaret D.

***Nadkarni, R. A.** Guide for Analysis of Test Methods of Petroleum Products & Lubricants. LC 00-30620. (Manual Ser.). 2000. write for info. (*0-8031-2087-7*) ASTM.

Nadkarni, R. A., ed. Analysis of Petroleum Products & Lubricants. LC 91-10488. (Special Technical Publication Ser.: No. STP 1109). (Illus.). 165p. 1991. text 55.00 (*0-8031-1416-8*, STP1109) ASTM.

Nadkarnia, M. V. Marketable Surplus & Market Dependence in a Millet Region. 176p. 1980. 24.95 (*0-318-37333-5*) Asia Bk Corp.

Nadleigh, Dana L. The Adventures of Sammy Starfish: The English Channel Episode. (Illus.). (J). (gr. k-3). 1999. pap. 5.95 (*0-533-12911-7*) Vantage.

Nadler, ed. Continuum Theory: An Introduction. (Pure & Applied Mathematics Ser.: Vol. 158). (Illus.). 352p. 1992. text 175.00 (*0-8247-8659-9*) Dekker.

Nadler & Hibino. Creative Solution Finding. LC 94-19879. 512p. 1995. 24.95 (*1-55958-567-6*) Prima Pub.

Nadler, jt. auth. see Shovel.

***Nadler, Allan.** Faith of Mithnagdim: The Rabbinic Responses to Hasidic Rapture. 1999. pap. text 17.95 (*0-8018-6182-9*) Johns Hopkins.

Nadler, Allan. The Faith of the Mithnagdim: Rabbinic Responses to Hasidic Rapture. LC 96-6608. (Jewish Studies). 264p. 1997. text 35.00 (*0-8018-5560-8*) Johns Hopkins.

Nadler, Beth. George of the Jungle Junior Novel. LC 96-71633. 96p. (J). (gr. 3-7). 1997. pap. 4.95 (*0-7868-4131-1*, Pub. by Disney Pr) Time Warner.

Nadler, Beth. Jack. (J). 1996. pap. 4.95 (*0-7868-1193-5*, Pub. by Hyprn Child) Little.

Nadler, Beth. Jack: Junior Novelization. LC 96-76655. 96p. (J). (gr. 5-9). 1996. pap. 4.95 (*0-7868-1155-2*, Pub. by Hyprn Ppbks) Little.

— The Magic School Bus Inside Ralphie: A Book about Germs. Duchesne, Lucie, tr. (Magic School Bus Ser.). (FRE., Illus.). 32p. (J). (gr. k-2). pap. 5.99 (*0-590-24658-5*) Scholastic Inc.

— The Magic School Bus Inside Ralphie: A Book about Germs. LC 94-44655. (Magic School Bus Ser.). (Illus.). 32p. (J). (ps-3). 1995. pap. 2.99 (*0-590-40025-8*) Scholastic Inc.

— The Magic School Bus Inside Ralphie: A Book about Germs. (Magic School Bus Ser.). (Illus.). (J). (gr. k-2). 1995. 8.19 (*0-606-07824-X*, Pub. by Turtleback) Demco.

Nadler, Bob. The Illustrated B&W Darkroom Book. LC 79-9933. (Illus.). 176p. 1979. 21.95 (*0-933596-01-4*) F-Twenty-Two.

Nadler, Burton J. Naked at the Interview: Tips & Quizzes to Prepare You for Your First Real Job. 230p. 1994. pap. 10.95 (*0-471-59449-0*) Wiley.

Nadler, David, et al. Competing by Design: The Power of Organizational Architecture. LC 96-41167. (Illus.). 256p. 1997. 27.50 (*0-19-509917-6*) OUP.

Nadler, David A. Champions of Change: How CEO's & their COmpanies Are Mastering the Skills of Radical Change. LC 97-25973. 368p. 1998. mass mkt. 25.50 (*0-7879-0947-5*) Jossey-Bass.

— Executive Teams. LC 97-30446. 352p. 1997. 29.95 (*0-7879-1023-6*) Jossey-Bass.

— Feedback & Organization Development: Using Data-Based Methods. (Illus.). 203p. (C). 1977. pap. text 40.00 (*0-201-05006-4*) Addison-Wesley.

Nadler, David A., et al, eds. The Management of Organizations: Strategies, Tactics, Analyses. 600p. 1989. 54.95 (*0-88730-380-3*, HarpBusn) HarpInfo.

Nadler, David A., et al. Organizational Architecture: Designs for Changing Organizations. LC 92-4071. (Management Ser.). 304p. 1992. text 34.95 (*1-55542-443-0*) Jossey-Bass.

Nadler, Dru, jt. auth. see Hare, Deborah.

Nadler, Ellis. The Busy World Word Book. LC 97-44876. (J). 1998. write for info. (*0-7894-3111-4*) DK Pub Inc.

Nadler, Gerald & Hibino, Shozo. Breakthrough Thinking: The Seven Principles of Creative Problem Solving. 2nd rev. ed. LC 93-23559. 432p. 1994. 24.95 (*1-55958-421-1*) Prima Pub.

— Breakthrough Thinking: Why We Must Change the Way We Solve Problems. 1989. 24.95 (*1-55958-004-6*) Prima Pub.

Nadler, Gerald, et al. Creative Solution Finding: The Triumph of Full Spectrum Creativity over Conventional Thinking. LC 94-19879. 498p. 1999. pap. 18.00 (*0-7615-1714-6*) Prima Pub.

Nadler, Holly M. Haunted Island: True Ghost Stories from Martha's Vineyard. LC 94-72609. (Illus.). 144p. (Orig.). 1994. pap. 10.95 (*0-89272-353-X*) Down East.

Nadler, James & Guarnieri, Donald. Netware Answers: Certified Tech Support. (Certified Tech Support Ser.). 240p. 1994. pap. 16.95 (*0-07-882044-8*) McGraw.

Nadler, L. Designing Training Programs: The Critical Events Model. 1982. 25.95 (*0-201-05168-0*) Addison-Wesley.

Nadler, Lawrence B., et al, eds. Advances in Gender & Communication Research. LC 87-13350. 428p. (Orig.). 1987. pap. text 34.00 (*0-8191-6478-X*) U Pr of Amer.

Nadler, Leonard. Corporate Human Resources Development: A Management Tool. 217p. 16.95 (*0-318-13267-2*, NACB); 13.50 (*0-318-13268-0*) Am Soc Train & Devel.

— Employee Training in Japan. LC 65-22294. (Illus.). 49p. (C). 1965. text 10.00 (*0-87657-117-8*) Ed & Training.

— Human Resource Development: The Perspective of Business & Industry. 42p. 1983. 4.25 (*0-318-22128-4*, IN259) Ctr Educ Trng Employ.

Nadler, Leonard & Nadler, Zeace. The Comprehensive Guide to Successful Conferences & Meetings: Detailed Instructions & Step-by-Step Checklists. LC 87-45412. (Management Ser.). 466p. 1987. text 51.95 (*1-55542-051-6*) Jossey-Bass.

— Designing Training Programs: The Critical Events Model. 2nd ed. LC 94-637. 280p. 1994. pap. 32.50 (*0-88415-100-X*, 5100) Gulf Pub.

— Developing Human Resources: Concepts & a Model. 3rd ed. LC 88-46096. (Management Ser.). 328p. 1989. text 36.95 (*1-55542-155-5*) Jossey-Bass.

— Every Manager's Guide to Human Resource Development. LC 91-36300. (Management Ser.). 187p. 1992. text 30.95 (*1-55542-421-X*) Jossey-Bass.

— Living Judaism Around the World. LC 97-65959. 264p. (Orig.). 1997. pap. 15.95 (*1-57197-065-7*) Pentland Pr.

Nadler, Leonard & Wiggs, Garland D. Managing Human Resource Development: A Practical Guide. LC 86-7339. (Management Ser.). 213p. 1986. text 30.95 (*1-55542-006-0*) Jossey-Bass.

Nadler, M. P., et al, eds. Glare & Contrast Sensitivity for Clinicians. (Illus.). 248p. 1989. 122.00 (*0-387-97009-6*) Spr-Verlag.

Nadler, Marcus, jt. auth. see Bogen, Jules I.

Nadler, Marcus, jt. auth. see Madden, John T.

Nadler, Marcus, ed. see Conant, Charles A.

Nadler, Morton & Smith, Eric P. Pattern Recognition Engineering. LC 92-10636. 608p. 1993. 120.00 (*0-471-62293-1*) Wiley.

Nadler, Myra, ed. How to Start an Audiovisual Collection. LC 78-1993. 1978. 24.00 (*0-8108-1124-3*) Scarecrow.

Nadler, Paul S. The Financial Battlefield: Reports from the Front Lines. 550p. 1998. 29.95 (*0-9667943-0-3*) Comm Finan.

Nadler, R. D., et al. The Neglected Ape. (Illus.). 312p. (C). 1996. 102.00 (*0-306-45213-8*, Plenum Trade) Perseus Pubng.

Nadler, Reldan S., jt. auth. see Luckner, John L.

Nadler, Sam B. Hyperspaces of Sets: A Text with Research Questions. LC 78-9013. (Monographs & Textbooks in Pure & Applied Mathematics: No. 49). 727p. reprint ed. pap. 200.00 (*0-608-20001-8*, 207127800010) Bks Demand.

Nadler, Sam B., Jr. & Quinn, J. Embeddability & Structure Properties of Real Curves. LC 72-4343. (Memoirs Ser.: No. 1/125). 74p. 1972. pap. 17.00 (*0-8218-1825-2*, MEMO/1/125) Am Math.

Nadler, Sam B., jt. auth. see Illanes, Alejandro.

Nadler, Sheryl. Cypress & Sand: Florida Poems. (Illus.). 40p. 1998. pap. 6.00 (*0-9662606-0-0*) S Nadler.

— Poems for the Ladies. (Illus.). 40p. 1998. pap. 6.00 (*0-9662606-1-9*) S Nadler.

Nadler, Steven. Spinoza: A Life. LC 98-36034. (Illus.). 350p. (C). 1999. 34.95 (*0-521-55210-9*) Cambridge U Pr.

***Nadler, Steven, ed.** The Cambridge Companion to Malebranche. (Cambridge Companions to Philosophy Ser.). 352p. (C). 2000. 54.95 (*0-521-62212-3*); pap. 19.95 (*0-521-62729-X*) Cambridge U Pr.

Nadler, Steven, ed. Causation in Early Modern Philosophy: Cartesianism, Occasionalism, & Preestablished Harmony. 232p. (C). 1993. 35.00 (*0-271-00863-6*) Pa St U Pr.

Nadler, Steven, ed. see Malebranche, Nicolas.

Nadler, Susan. Good Girls Gone Bad: American Women in Crime. LC 86-29155. 288p. 1987. 17.95 (*0-88191-048-1*) Freundlich.

Nadler, Zeace, jt. auth. see Nadler, Leonard.

Nadoff, Yisroel. Yom Tov in Halachah. 1997. 13.95 (*0-87306-817-3*) Feldheim.

Nadol, J. B., Jr., jt. auth. see Wilson, W. R.

Nadol, Joseph B., Jr., ed. Meniere's Disease. LC 89-19868. (Illus.). 568p. 1989. lib. bdg. 163.00 (*90-6299-052-5*, Pub. by Kugler) Kugler Pubns.

Nadol, Joseph B., Jr. & Schuknecht, Harold F., eds. Surgery of the Ear & Temporal Bone. (Illus.). 494p. 1992. text 204.00 (*0-88167-803-1*, 2287) Lppncott W & W.

— Surgery of the Ear & Temporal Bone. (Illus.). 494p. 1993. sl. 315.00 (*0-88167-935-6*) Lppncott W & W.

Nadolny & Young. Regulatory Management & Compliance Audit Deskbook. 2nd ed. 550p. 1992. 195.00 (*1-55738-364-2*, Irwn Prfssnl) McGraw-Hill Prof.

Nadolny, et al. Bank Internal Audit: Conducting the Internal Audit Program, Vol. II. 1995. 155.00 (*0-7863-0770-6*, Irwn Prfssnl) McGraw-Hill Prof.

Nadolny, Nancy Z. & Young, John G. The Regulatory Management Compliance Audit Deskbook. 1995. 155.00 (*0-7863-0752-8*, Irwn Prfssnl) McGraw-Hill Prof.

Nadolny, Paul R., jt. auth. see Rosenberg, Marc L.

Nadolny, Sten. Discovery of Slowness. 336p. 1997. pap. 11.95 (*0-14-026584-8*) Viking Penguin.

— The God of Impertinence. Mitchell, Breon, tr. LC 96-52431. 224p. 1998. pap. 12.95 (*0-14-025452-8*) Viking Penguin.

N

— Road to Emancipation. 1999. pap. 29.95 (0-670-86754-3) Viking Penguin.
Nadon & Brumbach Staff. Industrial Electricity. 6th ed. LC 98-21852. 672p. 1998. text 53.95 (0-7668-0101-2) Delmar.
— Industrial Electricity: Instructor's Guide. 6th ed. 128p. 1998. teacher ed. 17.95 (0-7668-0102-0) Delmar.
Nadon, John M. & Gelmine, Bert J. Industrial Electricity. 4th ed. 1989. pap., teacher ed. 13.00 (0-8273-3569-5) Delmar.
Nadon, John M., et al. Industrial Electricity. 5th ed. LC 93-20198. 658p. 1993. mass mkt. 42.25 (0-8273-6074-6) Delmar.
— Industrial Electricity: Instructor's Guide. 5th ed. 111p. 1994. 16.50 (0-8273-6075-4) Delmar.
Nadotti, Maria, jt. ed. see Bruno, Giuliana.
Nadramia, Peggy, ed. Narcopolis & Other Poems. (Illus.). 64p. (Orig.). (C). 1989. pap. 4.00 (0-9623286-1-8) Hells Kitchen.
Nadrchal, J. & De Groot, Roy A. Computational Physics: Proceedings of the Computational Physica 1992 Europhysics Conference. 540p. 1993. text 121.00 (981-02-1245-3) World Scientific Pub.
Nadvi, S. Arab Navigation. 1988. 15.95 (0-935782-39-7) Kazi Pubns.
— A Geographical History of the Qur'an. 1991. 14.50 (1-56744-020-7) Kazi Pubns.
— Glory of Iqbal. 1992. 19.95 (1-56744-025-8) Kazi Pubns.
— Heroic Deeds of Muslim Women. 1991. pap. 3.50 (1-56744-037-1) Kazi Pubns.
— Religion & Civilization. 1993. 4.00 (0-933511-34-5) Kazi Pubns.
— Vocabulary of the Quran. 846p. 1996. 22.50 (0-614-21076-3, 1289) Kazi Pubns.
— Western Civilization, Islam & Muslims. 1997. 18.50 (0-933511-87-6) Kazi Pubns.
Nadvi, S. & Nadwi, Abul H. Four Pillars of Islam. 132p. 1979. 16.95 (1-56744-015-0) Kazi Pubns.
Nadvis, S. The Arabs Must Win. 30p. 1996. pap. 2.50 (0-614-21479-3, 66) Kazi Pubns.
Nadvis, S., et al. Saviors of the Islamic Spirit, Set, Nos. I & II. 820p. (C). 1995. text 39.95 (0-934905-65-7) Kazi Pubns.
Nadwi, A. Learn the Language of the Holy Qur'an. 4th rev. ed. Ghazi, Abidullah et al, eds. 430p. 1987. 18.00 (1-56316-009-9) Iqra Intl Ed Fdtn.
— Muslims in the West: The Message & the Mission. Murad, Khurram, ed. 191p. (Orig.). 1983. pap. 6.95 (0-86037-130-1) New Era Publns MI.
Nadwi, Abul H., jt. auth. see Nadvi, S.
Nadworny, Laura. The Memory Keeper. LC 99-90365. xiii, 201p. (YA). (gr. 10 up). 1999. pap. 12.00 (0-9659078-0-5) dARCY LIAT.
Nadzhafov, M., ed. see Kerimov, Liatif.
Nadzieja, Tadeusz, jt. ed. see Biler, Piotr.
Nadzo, Nancy R., jt. auth. see Nadzo, Stefan C.
Nadzo, Stefan C. Being Who You Are. LC 82-84415. 140p. 1983. pap. 6.95 (0-937226-02-5) Laugh Cat.
— In the Beginning: The Eden Conspiracy Unveiled. LC 89-83895. 100p. 1989. pap. 10.95 (0-937226-06-8) Laugh Cat.
— Take off Your Shoes. 120p. 1981. pap. 4.57 (0-318-57336-9) Coleman Pub.
— Take off Your Shoes: A Guide to the Nature of Reality. LC 81-66185. 140p. (Orig.). 1981. pap. 5.95 (0-937226-01-7) Laugh Cat.
— There Is a Way. 129p. 1981. pap. 4.75 (0-318-57337-7) Coleman Pub.
— There Is a Way: Meditations for a Seeker. LC 80-66831. (Illus.). 129p. (Orig.). 1980. pap. 5.95 (0-937226-00-9) Laugh Cat.
Nadzo, Stefan C. & Nadzo, Nancy R. Hear the Wind, See the Wind. LC 87-82954. 113p. (Orig.). 1987. pap. 8.50 (0-937226-03-3) Laugh Cat.
Nae, Randolph. Decapitated Head of a Dog: Baroque Outhouse. 64p. (Orig.). 1991. pap. 7.00 (0-916397-16-5) Manic D Pr.
Naeb, Yuli, tr. see Lehman, Yvette K.
Naeem, Ahmad. Philosophy in Pakistan. LC 97-26581. (Cultural Heritage & Contemporary Change Series IIA). 1997. pap. 17.50 (1-56518-108-5) Coun Res Values.
Naeem, Muhammad. Muslim Military History: A Preliminary Bibliography. (Orig.). 1992. pap. 12.00 (1-56744-460-1) Kazi Pubns.
Naef, Adam. The Barbury Hall Murders: A Mystery Set in the England of Jane Austen. LC 96-28397. 216p. (Orig.). 1997. pap. 12.95 (0-9633494-8-1) Picardy Pr.
Naef, Weston. In Focus - Alfred Stieglitz: Photographs from the J. Paul Getty Museum. LC 95-22818. (In Focus Ser.). (Illus.). 144p. (Orig.). 1995. pap. 16.95 (0-89236-303-7, Pub. by J P Getty Trust) OUP.
Naef, Weston J. The J. Paul Getty Museum Handbook of the Photographs Collection. LC 94-22516. (Illus.). 256p. 1995. pap. 15.95 (0-89236-316-9, Pub. by J P Getty Trust) OUP.
Naef, Weston J., et al. Pioneers of Landscape Photography: Gustave LeGray & Carleton E. Watkins. (Illus.). 128p. 1993. 45.00 (0-89236-299-5, Pub. by J P Getty Trust) OUP.
Naegele. Experiments in Physical Science. 2nd ed. 1997. 9.74 (0-07-365492-2) McGraw.
Naegele, Bede. Minute Meditations for Each Day. (Spiritual Life Ser.). 1982. vinyl bd. 6.25 (0-89942-190-3, 190/09) Catholic Bk Pub.
Naegele, Gerhard, jt. auth. see Walker, Alan.
Naegele, John A., ed. Air Pollution Damage to Vegetation: A Symposium Sponsored by the Division of Agricultural & Food Chemistry at the 161st Meeting of the American Chemical Society, Los Angeles, CA, March 31-April 1, 1971. LC 73-85001. (Advances in Chemistry Ser.: No. 122). (Illus.). 151p. 1973. reprint ed. pap. 46.90 (0-608-06779-2, 206697600009) Bks Demand.
Naegele, Thomas A. & Glime, Janice P. Edible & Medicinal Plants of the Great Lakes Region. 2nd rev. ed. LC 96-12137. (Illus.). 482p. (Orig.). 1996. pap. 18.95 (0-923568-37-9) Wilderness Adventure Bks.
Naegele, Timothy D. A Tapestry of Life. (Illus.). 1400p. 1990. write for info. (0-9625131-7-2) Sotweed Pr.
Naegeli, Bruce A., jt. auth. see Gara, Otto G.
Naegeli, Hanspeter. Mechanisms of DNA Damage Recognition in Mammalian Cells. LC 97-6442. (Molecular Biology Intelligence Unit Ser.). 1997. 99.00 (1-57059-438-4) Landes Bioscience.
Naegeli, K. Die Neuren Algensysteme & Versuch zur Begruendung eines Eigenen Systems der Algen & Florideen. (Illus.). 1970. reprint ed. 77.00 (90-6123-204-X) Lubrecht & Cramer.
Naegelin, Lanny. Getting Started in Oral Interpretation. 96p. (YA). (gr. 7-12). 1993. teacher ed. 10.60 (0-8442-5404-5, Natl Textbk Co) NTC Contemp Pub Co.
— Getting Started in Oral Interpretation. 144p. (YA). (gr. 7-12). 1995. pap. text 13.25 (0-8442-5403-7, Natl Textbk Co) NTC Contemp Pub Co.
***Naeger, Bill, et al.** Ste Genevieve: A Leisurely Stroll Through History. rev. ed. (Illus.). xiii, 226p. 1999. 39.95 (0-9676039-0-0) Merchant St.
Naegle, Madeline, ed. Substance Abuse Education for Nursing: A Model Curriculum, 3 vols. 1992. pap. write for info. (0-685-56350-2) Natl League Nurse.
— Substance Abuse Education for Nursing: A Model Curriculum, 3 vols., Vol. I. 624p. 1992. pap. 16.50 (0-88737-523-5) Natl League Nurse.
— Substance Abuse Education for Nursing: A Model Curriculum, 3 vols., Vol. II. 688p. 1992. pap. 20.95 (0-88737-545-6) Natl League Nurse.
— Substance Abuse Education for Nursing: A Model Curriculum, 3 vols., Vol. III. 544p. 1992. pap. 20.95 (0-88737-546-4) Natl League Nurse.
Naehring, Douglas, jt. auth. see Emerson, Howard.
Naeim. Design of Seismic Isolated Structures: From Theory to Practice. LC 98-51588. 304p. 1999. text 79.95 incl. cd-rom (0-471-14921-7) Wiley.
Naeim, Faramarz. Pathology of Bone Marrow. LC 91-35311. (Illus.). 376p. 1992. 175.00 (0-89640-209-6) Igaku-Shoin.
— Pathology of Bone Marrow. 2nd ed. LC 97-42119. 1998. 149.00 (0-683-30336-8) Lppncott W & W.
Naeim, Farzad & Anderson, James C. Classification & Evaluation of Earthquake Records for Design. (Illus.). 288p. (Orig.). (C). 1994. pap. text 75.00 (0-7881-0877-8) DIANE Pub.
Naeim, Farzed, ed. The Seismic Design Handbook. (Illus.). 576p. 1989. text 95.00 (0-442-26922-6) Chapman & Hall.
Naenna, Patricia C. Costume & Culture: Vanishing Textiles of Some of the Tai Groups in Laos P. D. R. (Illus.). 48p. 1992. pap. text 20.00 (0-8248-1454-1, Pub. by P C Naenna) UH Pr.
Naerebout, F. G. Attractive Performances: Ancient Greek Dance: Three Preliminary Studies. LC 97-218251. xx, 452p. 1997. lib. bdg. 107.00 (90-5063-307-2, Pub. by Gieben) J Benjamins Pubng Co.
Naerssen, A. X. Van, see Van Naerssen, A. X., ed.
Naerssen, Margaret Van, see Van Naerssen, Margaret.
Naert, I. The Influence of Prosthetic Design & Implant Type on Tissue Reactions Around Oral Implants. No. 40. 148p. 1991. pap. 49.50 (90-6186-442-9, Pub. by Leuven Univ) Coronet Bks.
Naert, I. E. Passive Fit of Implant Supported Superstructures: Fiction or Reality? (Illus.). 113p. 1995. pap. 62.50 (90-6186-716-9, Pub. by Leuven Univ) Coronet Bks.
Naert, Ignace, et al, eds. Osseointegration in Oral Rehabilitation: An Introductory Textbook. (Illus.). 211p. (Orig.). 1993. pap. text 45.00 (1-85097-030-0, B8807) Quint Pub Co.
Naert, P. A. & Leeflang, P. S. Building Implementable Marketing Models. 1978. pap. text 48.50 (90-207-0674-8, Pub. by Kluwer Academic) Kluwer Academic.
Naes, Tomrod & Risvik, Einar, eds. Multivariate Analysis of Data in Sensory Science. (Data Handling in Science & Technology Ser.: Vol. 16). 364p. 1996. text 225.50 (0-444-89956-1) Elsevier.
Naes, Tormod, jt. auth. see Martens, Harold.
Naeser, Margaret A. Outline Guide to Chinese Herbal Patent Medicines in Pill Form - with Sample Pictures of the Boxes: An Introduction to Chinese Herbal Medicines. 2nd ed. LC 90-80264. (Illus.). 372p. (Orig.). 1990. pap. 34.95 (0-9625651-1-3) Boston Chinese Med.
Naeser, Margaret A. & Xiu-Bing Wei. Laser Acupuncture, an Introductory Textbook for Treatment of Pain, Paralysis, Spasticity & Other Disorders: Clinical & Research Uses of Laser Acupuncture from Around the World. (Illus.). 218p. 1994. spiral bd. 44.95 (0-9625651-2-1) Boston Chinese Med.
Naeser, N. D. & McCullogh, T. H., eds. Thermal History of Sedimentary Basins: Methods & Case Histories. (Illus.). 320p. 1988. 112.95 (0-387-96702-8) Spr-Verlag.
Naeseth, Henriette C. The Swedish Theatre of Chicago, 1868-1950. LC 51-14886. (Augustana College Library Publications: No. 22). 390p. 1951. 4.95 (0-910182-17-5) Augustana Coll.
— The Swedish Theatre of Chicago, 1869-1950. LC 51-14886. (Augustana Historical Society Publications: Vol. 12). 390p. 1951. 4.00 (0-910184-12-7) Augustana.
Naess, A., ed. see Krenk, S.
Naess, Arne. Ecology, Community & Lifestyle: Outline of an Ecosophy. Rothenberg, David, tr. (Illus.). 237p. (C). 1990. pap. text 27.95 (0-521-34873-0) Cambridge U Pr.
***Naess, Atle.** Doubting Thomas: A Novel about Caravaggio. Born, Anne, tr. from NOR. 2000. 29.95 (0-7206-1082-6, Pub. by P Owen Ltd) Dufour.
Naess, Harald S., ed. A History of Norwegian Literature. LC 92-20990. (Histories of Scandinavian Literature Ser.: Vol. 2). (Illus.). xviii, 435p. (C). 1993. text 60.00 (0-8032-3317-5) U of Nebr Pr.
Naess, Harald S. & Stafford, Kate. On Both Sides of the Ocean: The Memoirs of Per Hagen. Lovoll, Odd Sverre, ed. (Travel & Description Ser.). (Illus.). 70p. 1984. 12.00 (0-87732-069-1) Norwegian-Am Hist Assn.
Naess, Harald S., jt. ed. see McFarlane, James.
***Naess, Robert O.** Optics for Technology Students. 2000. teacher ed. write for info. (0-13-018880-8) P-H.
— Optics for Technology Students. LC 99-89482. (Illus.). 384p. 2000. 88.00 (0-13-011294-1) P-H.
Naess, Tor. A New Generation Floating Production Facility. 1989. 150.00 (90-6314-505-5, Pub. by Lorne & MacLean Marine) St Mut.
— A New Generation Floating Production Facility. (C). 1989. 110.00 (0-89771-732-5, Pub. by Lorne & MacLean Marine) St Mut.
Naess, Tor, jt. ed. see Andenaes, Olav.
Naessens, Gaston, et al. Do No Harm: The Scientific, Ethical, Legal & Spiritual Revelation of Somatidian Orthobiology & 714X. LC 95-24978. 1995. write for info. (0-09-647030-5) Writers & Res.
Naeth, Marie-Luise. Chinas Weg in die Weltpolitik: Die Nationalen und Aussenpolitischen Konzeptionen Sun Yat-Sens, Chiang Kaisheks und Mao Tse-Tungs. (Beitraege zur Auswaertigen und Internationalen Politik Ser.: Vol. 7). (C). 1976. pap. 93.85 (3-11-004737-3) De Gruyter.
Naether, Carl. Pigeons. (Illus.). 96p. 1989. 9.95 (0-87666-837-6, KW-148) TFH Pubns.
Naeve, Milo M. Identifying American Furniture: A Pictorial Guide to Styles & Terms Colonial to Contemporary. 3rd ed. LC 97-33729. (American Association for State & Local History Book Ser.). 112p. 1998. pap. 14.95 (0-7619-8961-7) AltaMira Pr.
— Identifying American Furniture: A Pictorial Guide to Styles & Terms: Colonial to Contemporary. 3rd ed. (Illus.). 112p. 1998. pap. 14.95 (0-393-31844-3) Norton.
— John Lewis Krimmel: An Artist in Federal America. LC 83-40480. (Illus.). 208p. 1988. 85.00 (0-87413-232-0) U Delaware Pr.
Naeve, Milo M., ed. Winterthur Portfolio, No. 3. (Winterthur Bk.: Vol. 3). (Illus.). 232p. 1978. lib. bdg. 24.00 (0-226-92127-1) U Ch Pr.
Naeve, Peter, jt. ed. see Buning, Herbert.
Naeve, Robert A. Maintaining a Drug-Free Workplace: The Management Primer on the Major Legal Issues Surrounding Drugs & Alcohol in the Workplace. Johnson, Margaret L., ed. 199p. (Orig.). 1990. pap. 38.00 (0-932823-03-3) Am Somerset.
***Naf, Franz.** Das Monochord: Versuchsinstrument zur quantitativen Erklarung von Tonsystemen. 1999. 29.95 (3-906763-30-7, Pub. by P Lang) P Lang Pubng.
NAF Legal Clearinghouse Staff. The First Amendment Book: A Guide for Abortion Providers & Their Attorneys. rev. ed. 1992. pap. text 15.00 (0-9601326-9-4) Natl Abort Fed.
Nafaile, Carlos E. Rangel, see Rangel Nafaile, Carlos E.
***Naff.** To Look Like America. 2000. pap. 49.00 (0-8133-6762-X, Pub. by Westview) HarpC.
Naff, Alixa. Becoming American: The Early Arab Immigrant Experience. LC 92-33848. 392p. 1993. pap. 18.95 (0-8093-1896-2) S Ill U Pr.
Naff, Clayton. About Face: How I Stumbled onto Japan's Social Revolution. Turner, Philip, ed. 352p. 1996. pap. 14.00 (1-56836-131-9) Kodansha.
Naff, Cynthia D., jt. auth. see Baxter, Pat J.
***Naff, Katherine C.** To Look Like America: Dismantling Barriers for Women & Minorities in the Federal Civil Service. 250p. 2000. pap. 25.00 (0-8133-6763-8) Westview.
***Naff, Monza.** Exultation: A Poem Cycle in Celebration of the Seasons. (Illus.). 40p. 1999. pap. 12.95 (0-9673025-1-X) Wyatt-MacKenzie Pubg.
— Healing the Womanheart. 151p. 1999. pap. 14.95 (0-9673025-0-1) Wyatt-MacKenzie Pubg.
Naff, Thomas. Paths to the Middle East: 10 Scholars Look Back. LC 93-14597. 360p. (C). 1993. pap. text 21.95 (0-7914-1884-7) State U NY Pr.
— Paths to the Middle East: 10 Scholars Look Back. LC 93-14597. 360p. (C). 1993. text 64.50 (0-7914-1883-9) State U NY Pr.
Naff, Thomas, ed. The Middle East Challenge, 1980-1985. LC 81-5651. 192p. (Orig.). 1981. pap. 17.95 (0-8093-1042-2) S Ill U Pr.
Naff, William E., tr. see Shimazaki Toson.
Naffah, Aunele, ed. see De LaFayette, Jean M.
Naffah, Aurele, ed. see De LaFayette, Jean M.
Naffah, Aurele, ed. see De Lafayette, Jean M.
Naffah, Aurele, ed. see De LaFayette, Jean M.
Naffah, N., jt. auth. see Ellis, C.
Naffine. Law & the Sexes: Explorations in Feminist Jurisprudence. 184p. pap. 19.95 (0-04-442210-5, Pub. by Allen & Unwin Pty) Paul & Co Pubs.
Naffine, Ngaire. Female Crime: The Construction of Women in Criminology. LC 87-14372. 1988. text 44.95 (0-04-302004-6, Pub. by Allen & Unwin Pty); pap. text 18.95 (0-04-330393-5, Pub. by Allen & Unwin Pty) Paul & Co Pubs.
— Feminism & Criminology. 210p. 1997. pap. 24.95 (1-86448-248-6, Pub. by Allen & Unwin Pty) Paul & Co Pubs.
— Feminism & Criminology. LC 96-9483. 256p. (C). 1997. 49.95 (1-56639-507-0); pap. 16.95 (1-56639-508-9) Temple U Pr.
Naffine, Ngaire, ed. Gender Crime & Feminism. (International Library of Criminology, Criminal Justice & Penology). (Illus.). 512p. 1995. text 203.95 (1-85521-543-8, Pub. by Dartmth Pub) Ashgate Pub Co.
Naffine, Ngaire & Owens, Rosemary, eds. Sexing the Subject of Law. LC 97-146742. 299p. 1997. pap. 55.00 (0-455-21469-7, 14605, Pub. by LawBk Co) Gaunt.
Nafi. Economic & Social Development in Quatar. 1992. text 55.00 (0-86187-389-0, Pub. by P P Pubs) Cassell & Continuum.
Nafi, Basheer M. Arabism, Islamism & the Palestine Question: A Political Study. 300p. 1998. 45.00 (0-86372-235-0, Pub. by Garnet-Ithaca) LPC InBook.
Naficie, Said. French-Persian Dictionary: Dictionnaire Francais-Persan, 2 vols., Set. (FRE & PER.). 2300p. 1985. 150.00 (0-8288-1123-7, F126574) Fr & Eur.
Naficy, Hamid. Home, Exile, Homeland. LC 98-5993. (AFI Film Readers Ser.). (Illus.). 256p. (C). 1998. 75.00 (0-415-91946-0); pap. 19.99 (0-415-91947-9) Routledge.
— The Making of Exile Cultures: Iranian Television in Los Angeles. LC 93-13428. 302p. 1993. pap. 19.95 (0-8166-2087-3); text 49.95 (0-8166-2084-9) U of Minn Pr.
Naficy, Hamid, compiled by. Iran Media Index. 1. LC 84-6572. (Bibliographies & Indexes in World History Ser.: No. 1). 264p. 1984. lib. bdg. 69.50 (0-313-23895-2, NIR/, Greenwood Pr) Greenwood.
Naficy, Hamid, ed. Discourse of the Other: Postcoloniality, Positionality, & Subjectivity. 275p. 1991. pap. text 14.00 (3-7186-0536-8, Harwood Acad Pubs) Gordon & Breach.
Naficy, Hamid & Gabriel, Teshome, eds. Otherness & the Media: The Ethnography of the Imagined & the Imaged, Vol. 3. 256p. 1993. pap. text 12.00 (3-7186-0569-4) Gordon & Breach.
***Naficy, Majid.** Muddy Shoes. (Illus.). 86p. 1999. pap. 8.00 (1-892184-01-X, Pub. by Beyond Baroque) SPD-Small Pr Dist.
Naficy, Majid, ed. Modernism & Ideology in Persian Literature: A Return to Nature in the Poetry of Nima Yushij. LC 97-29537. 144p. (C). 1997. 27.50 (0-7618-0862-0) U Pr of Amer.
Naficy, Mariam. The Fast Track: The Insider's Guide to Winning Jobs in Management Consulting, Investment Banking, & Securities Trading. LC 97-20959. (Illus.). 368p. (Orig.). 1997. pap. 16.95 (0-7679-0040-5) Broadway BDD.
NAFSA, Association of International Educators (Was, jt. auth. see Feagles, Shelley M.
NAFSA, Association of International Educators (Was, jt. auth. see Thullen, Manfred.
NAFSA: Association of International Educators (Was, jt. auth. see Hoffa, William.
Naftali, Joel, jt. auth. see Naftali, Lee.
Naftali, Lee & Naftali, Joel. You're Certifiable: The Alternative Career Guide to More than 700 Certificate Programs, Trade Schools, & Job Opportunities. LC 98-55504. 384p. 1999. pap. 13.00 (0-684-84996-8, Fireside) S&S Trade Pap.
Naftali, Lee, jt. auth. see Ross, Joel.
Naftali, Tim. X2: A History of American Counterespionage. 352p. Date not set. pap. write for info. (0-465-09282-9) Basic.
***Naftali, Tim.** X2: A History of American Counterespionage. 352p. 1998. 24.00 (0-465-09281-0, Pub. by Basic) HarpC.
Naftali, Timothy. The Presidential Recordings, 3 vol. set. 150.00 (0-393-04954-X) Norton.
Naftali, Timothy, jt. auth. see Fursenko, Aleksandr.
Naftali, Timothy J., jt. auth. see Doran, Cahrles F.
Naftalin, Ethan S. Federal Spill Reporting Requirements: A Reference Guide. LC 94-199238. 175p. 1994. pap. text 89.00 (0-86587-371-2) Gov Insts.
— Waste Generator's Compliance Manual. LC 96-181098. 452p. 1996. pap. text 89.00 (0-86587-507-3) Gov Insts.
Naftalin, Ethan S., jt. auth. see Turnbull, Bruce H.
Naftalin, Maurice, et al, eds. FME '94: Industrial Benefit of Formal Methods: Proceedings of the Second International Symposium of Formal Methods Europe, Barcelona, Spain, October 24-28, 1994. xi, 723p. 1994. 102.95 (3-540-58555-9) Spr-Verlag.
Naftalin, Maurice, ed. see International Symposium of Formal Methods Europe.
Naftchi, N. E., ed. Spinal Cord Injury. LC 81-8573. (Illus.). 306p. 1982. text 45.00 (0-88331-202-6) R B Luce.
Naftolin, Frederick & Stubblefield, Phillip G., eds. Dilatation of the Uterine Cervix: Connective Tissue Biology & Clinical Management. fac. ed. LC 78-19621. 406p. pap. 125.90 (0-7837-7509-1, 204699600005) Bks Demand.
***Nafus, Roland L.** Navy Island: Historic Treasure of the Niagara Heritage - Archaeology - Folklore. (Illus.). 168p. 1998. pap. 14.95 (0-941967-21-2) Old Fort Niagara Assn.
Nafy-al-Nazzam. Encyclopedie De l'Islam, 2 vols., Set. 1903p. 1993. pap. 95.00 (0-7859-6440-1, 9004097589) Fr & Eur.
Nafzawi, Umar ibn Muhammad. The Perfumed Garden. Burton, Richard F., tr. (Illus.). 96p. 1992. pap. 19.95 (0-89281-443-8, Park St Pr) Inner Tradit.
— The Perfumed Garden. Burton, Richard F., tr. from ARA. LC 98-37553. 224p. 1999. mass mkt. 5.95 (0-451-52659-7, Sig Classics) NAL.
Nafzger, Carl A. The Traits of a Winner: The Formula for Developing Thoroughbred Racehorses. LC 94-35092. 1994. 29.95 (0-929346-32-7) R Meerdink Co Ltd.
Nafziger, E. Wayne. The Debt Crisis in Africa. LC 92-23735. 288p. 1993. text 42.50 (0-8018-4476-2) Johns Hopkins.
— Economics in Developing Countries. 3rd ed. LC 96-22745. 630p. 1996. 98.00 (0-13-339995-8) P-H.

An Asterisk (*) at the beginning of an entry indicates that the title is appearing for the first time.

— Fathers, Sons, & Daughters: Industrial Entrepreneurs, During India's Liberalization. LC 98-52216. (Industrial Development & the Social Fabric Ser.: Vol. 15). 1999. 73.25 (*0-7623-0440-5*) Jai Pr.

— Learning from the Japanese: Japan's Pre-War Development & the Third World. LC 94-27010. (Japan in the Modern World Ser.). 238p. (C). (gr. 13). 1994. text 70.95 (*1-56324-485-3*, East Gate Bk); pap. text 34.95 (*1-56324-486-1*, East Gate Bk) M E Sharpe.

— Poverty & Wealth: Comparing Afro-Asian Development. (Contemporary Studies in Economic & Financial Analysis: Vol. 75). 1994. 78.50 (*1-55938-761-0*) Jai Pr.

***Nafziger, E. Wayne, et al, eds.** War, Hunger & Displacement Vol. 1: The Origins of Humanitarian Emergencies. (Wider Studies in Development Economics). 368p. 2000. text 74.00 (*0-19-829739-4*) OUP.

— War, Hunger & Displacement Vol. 2: The Origins of Humanitarian Emergencies. (Wider Studies in Development Economics). 512p. 2000. text 85.00 (*0-19-829740-8*) OUP.

Nafziger, Elfrieda T. A Man of His Word: A Biography of John A. Toews. (Illus.). 200p. (Orig.). 1992. pap. 11.50 (*1-895432-18-9*) Kindred Prods.

Nafziger, G. F. The Wurttemberg Army, 1792-1815. 2nd rev. ed. (Illus.). 1991. pap. 21.95 (*1-58545-001-4*) Nafziger Collection.

Nafziger, George. Napolean at Dresden: The Battles of August 1813. (Ancient Empires Ser.). (Illus.). 48p. (Orig.). 1991. 38.00 (*0-9626655-4-1*, Pub. by Emperors Pr) Combined Pub.

— Napoleon at Leipzig: The Battle of Nations 1813. (Illus.). 368p. 1997. 38.00 (*1-883476-10-0*, Pub. by Emperors Pr) Combined Pub.

Nafziger, George F. The Afrika Korps, an Organizational History, 1941-1943. 128p. 1997. pap. 19.95 (*1-58545-025-1*) Nafziger Collection.

***Nafziger, George F.** The American Army in World War II: 1st - 40th Infantry Divisions, 4, Vol. 1. 124p. 2000. pap. 19.95 (*1-58545-055-3*) Nafziger Collection.

— The American Army in World War II - Independent Armored, Mechanized Calvary, Artillery, Anti-Aircraft & Engineer Battalions, 4, Vol. 3. 82p. 2000. pap. 19.95 (*1-58545-057-X*) Nafziger Collection.

— The American Army in World War II Vol. 4: Armored Divisions, 4 vols. 104p. 2000. pap. 19.95 (*1-58545-058-8*) Nafziger Collection.

— The American Army in World War II - 41st-104th Infantry & Airborne Divisions, 4 vols., Vol. 2. 118p. 2000. pap. 19.95 (*1-58545-056-1*) Nafziger Collection.

Nafziger, George F. The Armies of Brunswick, Hanover, Hesse-Cassel & the Hanseatic Cities. 2nd ed. (Illus.). 1991. pap. 19.95 (*1-58545-000-6*) Nafziger Collection.

— The Armies of Germany & the Confederation of the Rhine (1806-1815) Anhalt, Saxe-Gotha, Saxe-Hildburghausen, Saxe-Meinigen, Coburg, Frankfurt Primate, Hasse-Darmstadt, Nassau, Mecklenburg-Schwerin & Strelitz, 2 vols. 2nd ed. (Illus.). 1991. pap. 19.95 (*1-58545-002-2*) Nafziger Collection.

— The Armies of Spain & Portugal, 1808-1815. (Illus.). 93p. 1993. pap. 19.95 (*1-58545-007-3*) Nafziger Collection.

— The Armies of the Kingdom of Bavaria & the Grand Duchy of Wurzburg, 1792-1815. 102p. 1993. pap. 19.95 (*1-58545-003-0*) Nafziger Collection.

— The Armies of Westphalia & Cleves-Berg, 1805-1815. (Illus.). 80p. 1993. pap. 19.95 (*1-58545-005-7*) Nafziger Collection.

— Bulgarian Order of Battle in World War II: An Organizational History of the Bulgarian Army in World War II. 75p. 1995. pap. 19.95 (*1-58545-020-0*) Nafziger Collection.

— Foreigners in Field Gray Vol. 7: Russians, Corats & Italians in the Wehrmacht. 85p. 1995. pap. 19.95 (*1-58545-024-3*) Nafziger Collection.

— German Order of Battle: Panzers & Artillary in World War II. LC 98-47381. 1999. 59.95 (*1-85367-359-5*) Stackpole.

***Nafziger, George F.** The German Order of Battle Infantry in World War II. 2000. 59.95 (*1-85367-393-5*) Greenhill Bks.

— The Growth & Organization of the Chinese Army from 1895 to 1945. 100p. 1999. pap. 19.95 (*1-58545-047-2*) Nafziger Collection.

Nafziger, George F. Imperial Bayonets: Tactics of the Napoleonic Battery, Battalion, & Brigade As Found in Contemporary Regulations. LC 96-32212. 240p. 1996. 44.95 (*1-85367-250-5*) Stackpole.

— The Imperail Russian Army - 1763-1815 Vol. 1: Infantry, Engineers, & Opolchenie. (Illus.). 107p. 1996. pap. 19.95 (*1-58545-013-8*) Nafziger Collection.

— The Imperial Russian Army - 1763-1815 Vol. 2: Cavalry, Cossacks, Guard & Artillery. (Illus.). 103p. 1996. pap. 19.95 (*1-58545-014-6*) Nafziger Collection.

— Italian Order of Battle in World War II, an Organizational History of the Italian Army in WWII Vol. 2: Infantry Division. 95p. 1996. pap. 19.95 (*1-58545-022-7*) Nafziger Collection.

— Italian Order of Battle in World War II, an Organizational History of the Italian Army in WWII Vol. 3: Black Shirt, Mountain Assault & Landing Divisions, Corps Troops & the 1944 Liberation Army. 78p. 1996. pap. 19.95 (*1-58545-023-5*) Nafziger Collection.

— Napoleon's Invasion of Russia. 704p. 1998. pap. 24.95 (*0-89141-661-7*) Presidio Pr.

— The Prussian Army During the Napoleonic Wars Vol. 1: Infantry. 122p. 1996. pap. 19.95 (*1-58545-015-4*) Nafziger Collection.

— The Prussian Army During the Napoleonic Wars Vol. 2: Guard & Landwehr. (Illus.). 69p. 1996. pap. 19.95 (*1-58545-016-2*) Nafziger Collection.

— The Prussian Army During the Napoleonic Wars Vol. 3: Cavalry & Artillery. 107p. 1996. pap. 19.95 (*1-58545-017-0*) Nafziger Collection.

— Royal, Republican, Imperail. A History of the French Army from 1792-1815 Vol. 5: Regiments Horse de Ligne (Foreign Regiments) 133p. 1997. pap. 19.95 (*1-58545-012-X*) Nafziger Collection.

— Royal, Republican, Imperial. A History of the French Army from 1792-1815 Vol. 1: The Infantry. (Illus.). 98p. 1997. pap. 19.95 (*1-58545-008-1*) Nafziger Collection.

— Royal, Republican, Imperial. A History of the French Army from 1792-1815 Vol. 2: The Infantry. (Illus.). 103p. 1997. pap. 19.95 (*1-58545-009-X*) Nafziger Collection.

— Royal, Republican, Imperial. A History of the French Army from 1792-1815 Vol. 3: The Cavalry, Artillery & Train. (Illus.). 127p. 1997. pap. 19.95 (*1-58545-010-3*) Nafziger Collection.

— Royal, Republican, Imperial. A History of the French Army from 1792-1815 Vol. 4: The Imperial Guard. 141p. 1997. pap. 19.95 (*1-58545-011-1*) Nafziger Collection.

— Rumanian Order of Battle in World War II, an Organizational History of the Romanian Army in World War II. 90p. 1995. pap. 19.95 (*1-58545-019-7*) Nafziger Collection.

Nafziger, George F. & Gilbert, M. The Armies of Germany & the Confederation of the Rhine (1806-1815) Baden, Lippe, Reuss, Schwarzburg & Waldeck, 2 vols. (Illus.). 1993. pap. 19.95 (*1-58545-004-9*) Nafziger Collection.

***Nafziger, George F. & Gioannini, Marco.** The Defense of the Napoleonic Kingdom of Northern Italy, 1813-14. 2001. write for info. (*0-275-96797-2*) Greenwood.

Nafziger, George F., et al. Poles & Saxons of the Napoleonic Wars. (Illus.). 266p. 1991. 35.00 (*0-9626655-3-3*, Pub. by Emperors Pr) Combined Pub.

Nafziger, James A. International Sports Law. 246p. 1988. lib. bdg. 55.00 (*0-941320-52-9*) Transnatl Pubs.

Nafziger, L. Cherries! Cherries! Cherries! (Illus.). 176p. 1997. spiral bd. 5.95 (*1-57166-089-5*) Hearts N Tummies.

— Citrus! Citrus! Citrus! (Illus.). 176p. 1997. spiral bd. 5.95 (*1-57166-085-2*) Hearts N Tummies.

Nafziger, Ralph O., compiled by. International News & the Press: An Annotated Bibliography. LC 72-4675. (International Propaganda & Communications Ser.). 223p. 1980. reprint ed. 17.95 (*0-405-04759-2*) Ayer.

Nag, A. Management Refresher. 1993. 30.00 (*0-7069-6818-2*, Pub. by Vikas) S Asia.

Nag, B. R. Electron Transport in Compound Semiconductors. (Solid-State Sciences Ser.: Vol. 11). (Illus.). 470p. 1980. 56.00 (*3-540-09845-3*) Spr-Verlag.

— Theory of Electrical Transport in Semi-Conductors. 238p. 1972. 110.00 (*0-08-016802-7*, Pub. by Pergamon Repr) Franklin.

Nag, Chitta R. Mizo Society in Transition. (C). 28.00 (*0-7069-6963-4*, Pub. by Vikas) S Asia.

Nag, Chitta Ranjan. Mizo Polity & Political Modernisation: Pre-Colonial & Colonial Institutions. LC 98-903446. 1998. 20.00 (*81-259-0451-4*, Pub. by Vikas) S Asia.

***Nag, Chitta Ranjan.** Post-Colonial Mizo Politics, 1947-1998. 1999. 30.00 (*81-259-0800-5*, Pub. by Vikas) S Asia.

Nag, Moni. Factors Affecting Human Fertility in Nonindustrial Societies: A Cross-Cultural Study. LC 68-22204. (Yale University Publications in Anthropology Reprints Ser.: No. 66). 227p. 1968. pap. 20.00 (*0-87536-514-0*) HRAFP.

— Sexual Behaviour & AIDS in India. LC 96-902172. (C). 1997. 24.00 (*81-259-0125-6*, Pub. by Vikas) S Asia.

Nag, Moni, ed. Population & Social Organization. (World Anthropology Ser.). x, 368p. 1975. 35.40 (*90-279-7589-2*) Mouton.

Nag, N. K. Elements of Mathematics. 1985. 100.00 (*0-7855-0729-9*, Pub. by Current Dist) St Mut.

Nag, Prithvish. Population, Settlement & Development in Zambia. 1990. 34.00 (*81-7022-268-0*, Pub. by Concept) S Asia.

Nag, Prithvish, ed. Thematic Cartography & Remote Sensing. (C). 1992. 38.00 (*81-7022-410-1*, Pub. by Concept) S Asia.

Nag, Prithvish, et al. Geography & Environment. LC 97-904789. 1997. write for info. (*81-7022-605-8*) Concept.

Nag, Raj T. & DiCosmo, F. A Monograph of Herknessia & Mastigospoella with Notes on Associated Teleomorphs. (Bibliotheca Mycologica Ser.: Vol. 80). (Illus.). 160p. 1981. text 40.00 (*3-7682-1300-5*) Lubrecht & Cramer.

Nag, Sajal. India & North-east India: Mind, Politics & the Process of Integration, 1946-1950. LC 98-915278. 125p. 1998. write for info. (*81-86030-76-X*) Regency Pubns.

Nag, Subir, ed. Principles & Practice of Brachytherapy. LC 96-46939. (Illus.). 752p. 1997. 160.00 (*0-87993-654-1*) Futura Pub.

Nagabhushanam, R. & Thompson, M. F., eds. Fouling Organisms of the Indian Ocean: Biology & Control Technology. (Illus.). 548p. (C). 1997. text 120.00 (*90-5410-739-1*, Pub. by A A Balkema) Ashgate Pub Co.

Nagabhushanam, R., jt. ed. see Fingerman, Milton.

Nagabhushanam, Rachakonda & Russell, F. E. The Venomous & Poisonous Marine Invertebrates of the Indian Ocean. (Illus.). 270p. 1996. lib. bdg. 89.00 (*1-886106-56-8*) Science Pubs.

Nagabhushanam, Rachakonda, jt. auth. see Thompson, Mary.

Nagabhushanam, Rachakonda, jt. ed. see Fingerman, Milton.

Nagabodhi. The Mindfulness of Breathing. 36p. (Orig.). 1995. pap. write for info. (*0-904766-99-3*) Windhorse Pubns.

— The Practice of Loving Kindness. 32p. (Orig.). 1995. pap. 3.95 (*0-904766-51-9*) Windhorse Pubns.

Nagae, T., ed. Nuclear Physics at Intermediate Energy. 484p. (C). 1989. text 151.00 (*981-02-0000-5*) World Scientific Pub.

Nagaev, Robert F. Mechanical Processes with Repeated Attenuated Impacts. Kremer, Eugueni B., ed. & tr. by. 250p. 1998. 48.00 (*981-02-3504-6*) World Scientific Pub.

Nagahara, Yoshiaki S. Strategic Concepts of Go. 1972. pap. 13.95 (*4-87187-006-5*, G6) Ishi Pr Intl.

Nagahara, Yoshiaki S., jt. auth. see Haruyama Isamu, Eight-Dan.

Nagai, Althea K., et al. Giving for Social Change: Foundations, Public Policy & the American Political Agenda. LC 93-25060. 240p. 1994. 62.95 (*0-275-94697-5*, C4697, Praeger Pubs) Greenwood.

Nagai, Gayle A., jt. auth. see Johnson, Betty S.

Nagai, H. & Kamiya, K., eds. Intracranial Pressure IX: Proceedings of the Ninth International Symposium on Intracranial Pressure Held in Nagoya, Japan 16-19, 1994. 685p. 1995. 171.00 (*0-387-70146-X*) Spr-Verlag.

Nagai, Jeanette & George-Olsen, Becky. Thank You for Calling. large type ed. Drolet, Cindy, ed. 98p. 1995. spiral bd., wbk. ed. 59.00 incl. audio (*1-883315-12-3*, 4032) Imaginart Intl.

Nagai, Jun, jt. auth. see Adachi, Hideo.

Nagai, K. & Mattaj, I., eds. RNA-Protein Interactions: Frontiers in Molecular Biology. (Illus.). 290p. 1995. text 105.00 (*0-19-963505-6*); pap. text 55.00 (*0-19-963504-8*) OUP.

Nagai, K. & Wachi, M., eds. Animal Cell Technology. LC 98-150745. 416p. 1998. text 234.00 (*0-7923-4835-4*) Kluwer Academic.

Nagai Kafu, pseud. During the Rains & Flowers in the Shade: Two Novellas. Dunlop, Lane, tr. LC 93-24945. xviii, 223p. 1994. 39.50 (*0-8047-2259-5*); pap. 13.95 (*0-8047-2260-9*) Stanford U Pr.

Nagai, Katsuya. Central Regulation of Energy Metabolism. 208p. 1992. lib. bdg. 129.00 (*0-8493-6657-7*, QP356) CRC Pr.

Nagai, M., ed. Brain Tumor Research & Therapy. (Illus.). 454p. 1996. 174.00 (*4-431-70164-8*) Spr-Verlag.

Nagai, Michio, ed. see Conference on Development in the Non-Western World.

Nagai, Mona, tr. see Tanaka, Yukiko & Hanson, Elizabeth, eds.

Nagai, Nobuo, ed. Linear Circuits, Systems & Signal Processing: Advanced Theory & Applications. (Electrical Engineering & Electronics Ser.: Vol. 62). (Illus.). 456p. 1989. text 160.00 (*0-8247-8185-6*) Dekker.

Nagai, Noriko, jt. ed. see Mazuka, Reiko.

Nagai Sokichi, see Nagai Kafu, pseud.

Nagai, Takashi. The Bells of Nagasaki. Johnston, William, tr. 118p. 1994. pap. 11.00 (*4-7700-1845-2*) Kodansha.

Nagaich, Sangeeta. Changing Status of Women in India. 1998. 38.00 (*81-7488-558-7*) Anmol.

Nagaitis, Carl, jt. auth. see Mantle, Philip.

Nagaki, Dick A., et al, eds. Synthesis & Properties of Advanced Catalytic Materials. (MRS Symposium Proceedings Ser.: Vol. 368). 394p. 1995. 77.00 (*1-55899-270-7*) Materials Res.

Nagakura, Mieko, jt. ed. see Lowrie, Jean E.

Nagakura, S., ed. Functionality of Molecular Systems Vol. 1: From Molecules to Molecular Systems. (Illus.). xvi, 336p. 1997. 149.00 (*4-431-70159-1*) Spr-Verlag.

***Nagakura, Saburo, et al.** Dynamic Spin Chemistry: Magnetic Controls & Spin Dynamics of Chemical Reactions. 297p. 1999. 125.00 (*0-471-32836-7*) Wiley.

Nagal, Robert F. Judicial Power & American Character: Censoring Ourselves in an Anxious Age. LC 93-41891. 208p. 1994. text 55.00 (*0-19-508901-4*) OUP.

Nagamachi, Mitsuo, jt. ed. see Helander, Martin.

Nagamatsu, Ernest T., ed. see Friedman, Dave.

Nagamine, S. Essence of Okinawan Karate Do. 1976. 29.95 (*0-685-83525-1*) Wehman.

Nagamine, Shoshin. The Essence of Okinawan Karate-do. LC 75-28717. (Illus.). 278p. 1998. pap. 19.95 (*0-8048-1163-6*) Tuttle Pubng.

— Essence of Okinawan Karate-Do. (Illus.). 280p. 1998. pap. 19.95 (*0-8048-2110-0*) Tuttle Pubng.

— Tales of Okinawa's Great Masters. McCarthy, Patrick, tr. from JPN. (Illus.). 192p. 1998. 24.95 (*0-8048-2089-9*, Periplus Eds) Tuttle Pubng.

***Nagan, Greg.** The Five-Minute Iliad & Other Instant Classics: Great Books for the Short Attention Span. LC 00-22750. (Illus.). 224p. 2000. pap. 12.00 (*0-684-86767-2*, Fireside) S&S Trade Pap.

Nagan, Robert, jt. ed. see Arregui, Maurice E.

Nagano, M. & Takahara, F., eds. Astrophysical Aspects of the Most Energetic Cosmic Rays. 516p. (C). 1991. text 118.00 (*981-02-0686-0*) World Scientific Pub.

Nagano, Makoto, et al, eds. The Adapted Heart. LC 94-19637. (Illus.). 542p. 1994. reprint ed. pap. 168.10 (*0-608-05871-8*, 205983800007) Bks Demand.

— The Cardiomyopathic Heart. LC 93-4656. (Illus.). 493p. 1994. reprint ed. pap. 152.90 (*0-608-05820-3*, 205978500007) Bks Demand.

— Cardiovascular Disease in Diabetes. (Developments in Cardiovascular Medicine Ser.). 416p. (C). 1992. text 187.00 (*0-7923-1554-5*) Kluwer Academic.

Nagano, Makoto & Dhalla, Naranjan S., eds. The Diabetic Heart. LC 90-9173. (Illus.). 558p. 1991. reprint ed. pap. 173.00 (*0-608-05870-X*, 205983700007) Bks Demand.

Nagano, Tadashi. Homotopy Invariants in Differential Geometry. LC 52-42839. (Memoirs Ser.: No. 1/100). 41p. 1992. pap. 16.00 (*0-8218-1800-7*, MEMO/1/100) Am Math.

Nagao, Gadjin M. Madhyamika & Yogacara: A Study of Mahayana Philosophies. Kawamura, Leslie S., ed. LC 89-4278. (SUNY Series in Buddhist Studies). 318p. 1991. text 21.50 (*0-7914-0186-3*) State U NY Pr.

***Nagao, Gajin & Silk, Jonathan A.** Wisdom, Compassion & the Search for Understanding: The Buddhist Studies Legacy of Gadjin M. Nagao. LC 00-33780. (Studies in the Buddhist Traditions). (Illus.). 2000. write for info. (*0-8248-2086-X*) UH Pr.

Nagao, Makoto & Matsuyama, Takashi, eds. A Structural Analysis of Complex Aerial Photographs. (Advanced Applications in Pattern Recognition Ser.). 224p. 1980. 75.00 (*0-306-40571-7*, Plenum Trade) Perseus Pubng.

Nagao, Masanori. Impressions of Edentulous Patients. (Dental Technique Ser.: No. 4). (Illus.). 51p. 1995. per. 30.00 (*1-56386-028-7*, Ishiyaku EuroAmerica) Med Dent Media.

***Nagao, Tadahiko & Saiteo, Isamu.** Kokology: The Game of Self-Discovery. LC 00-36575. 2000. pap. 10.00 (*0-684-87148-3*, Fireside) S&S Trade Pap.

Nagao, Yoshimi, ed. Coastlines of Japan 2. LC 93-2250. (Coastlines of the World Ser.). 352p. 1993. 31.00 (*0-87262-957-0*) Am Soc Civil Eng.

Nagao, Yoshimi & Magoon, Orville T., eds. Coastlines of Japan. (Coastlines of the World Ser.). 472p. 1991. pap. text 47.00 (*0-87262-838-8*) Am Soc Civil Eng.

Nagaoka, Megumi, jt. ed. see Owens, Jessie A.

Nagaoka, Y. & Fukuyama, H., eds. Anderson Localization, Kyoto, Japan, 1981: Proceedings. (Solid-State Sciences Ser.: Vol. 39). (Illus.). 225p. 1982. 61.00 (*0-387-11518-8*) Spr-Verlag.

***Nagaosa, N.** Quantum Field Theory in Condensed Matter Physics. Heusler, S., tr. from JPN. LC 99-35358. (Texts & Monographs in Physics). (Illus.). x, 208p. 1999. 54.00 (*3-540-65537-9*) Spr-Verlag.

— Quantum Field Theory in Strongly Correlated Electronic Systems. Heusler, S., tr. from JPN. LC 99-16714. (Texts & Monographs in Physics). (Illus.). x, 170p. 1999. 59.95 (*3-540-65981-1*) Spr-Verlag.

***Nagar.** Iconography of Jaina Deities. 1999. 285.00 (*81-7646-055-9*, Pub. by BR Pub) S Asia.

Nagar, A., ed. Fracture & Damage. (AD Ser.: Vol. 27). 148p. 1992. 45.00 (*0-7918-1074-7*, G00718) ASME.

Nagar, A. & Kuo, A. Y., eds. Fatigue & Fracture of Aerospace Structural Materials. LC 93-73600. 225p. pap. 60.00 (*0-7918-1049-6*) ASME.

Nagar, A. & Mall, S., eds. Fatigue & Fracture at Elevated Temperatures Vol. 50: Proceedings of the ASME International Mechanical Engineering Congress & Exposition, 1995, San Francisco, CA. LC 95-81264. (1995 ASME International Mechanical Engineering Congress & Exposition Ser.: AD-Vol. 50). 264p. 1995. 88.00 (*0-7918-1731-8*, H01013) ASME.

Nagar, A., jt. ed. see Basu, P. K.

Nagar, Amritial. Face Behind Seven Veils: English Translation of Famous Hindi Novel Saat Ghunghat Wala Mukhada. (New World Literature Ser.: No. 55). (C). 1992. 5.00 (*81-7018-712-5*, Pub. by BR Pub) S Asia.

Nagar, D. K., jt. auth. see Gupta, A. K.

Nagar, Munari L. & Lee, K. M., eds. Laukikanyayanjali: A Handful of Popular Maxims Current in Sanskrit Literature. rev. ed. LC 97-51342. (Universal Laws of Interpretation Ser.: Vol. 3). (ENG & SAN.). 361p. 1998. pap. 45.00 (*0-943913-28-4*) Intl Lib Ctr.

Nagar, Munari L., ed. see Udasina, Raghunatha V.

Nagar, Murari L. Indo-American Library Cooperation, 2 pts. Nagar, Sarla D., ed. LC 91-32130. (Spectrum of Alpha: America's Library Promotional Heritage in Asia). 89p. (Orig.). 1991. pap. 20.00 (*0-943913-22-5*) Intl Lib Ctr.

— Shri Sayajirao Gaikwad, Maharaja of Baroda: The Prime Promoter of Public Libraries. Nagar, Sarla D., ed. LC 92-2528. (Spectrum of Alpha: America's Library Promotional Heritage in Asia: No. 5). 72p. (Orig.). 1992. pap. 18.00 (*0-943913-24-1*) Intl Lib Ctr.

Nagar, Rajeev. Windows NT File System Internals. LC 97-208501. (Illus.). (Orig.). 1997. pap. 49.95 (*1-56592-249-2*) OReilly & Assocs.

Nagar, Sarla D. Gandharan Sculpture: A Catalogue of the Collection in the Museum of Art & Archaeology, University of Missouri-Columbia. (Illus.). 72p. (Orig.). 1981. pap. 6.00 (*0-910501-02-5*) U of Missouri Mus Art Arch.

Nagar, Sarla D., ed. see Nagar, Murari L.

Nagar, Sasla D., ed. see Udasina, Raghunatha V.

Nagar, Shanti L. Cult of Vinayaka. (Illus.). 270p. (C). 1992. 59.00 (*81-7076-044-5*, Pub. by Intellect Pub Hse) Nataraj Bks.

— Hanuman in Art, Culture, Thought & Literature. (Illus.). xxviii, 417p. 1995. 133.00 (*0-614-07911-X*, Pub. by Intellect Pub Hse) Nataraj Bks.

— Indian Gods & Goddesses. LC 98-909938. 1998. write for info. (*81-7646-032-X*) Asia Bk Corp.

— Indian Monoliths. (Illus.). xv, 142p. (C). 1992. 39.00 (*81-7076-043-7*, Pub. by Intellect Pub Hse) Nataraj Bks.

— Mahishasuramardini in Indian Art. (C). 1988. 74.00 (*81-85179-09-3*, Pub. by Aditya Prakashan) S Asia.

— Siva in Art, Literature & Thought. LC 94-907470. (C). 1995. 125.00 (*81-7387-019-5*, Pub. by Indus Pub) S Asia.

— Temples of Himachal Pradesh. (C). 1990. 120.00 (*81-85179-48-4*, Pub. by Aditya Prakashan) S Asia.

— Varaha in Indian Art, Culture & Literature. (C). 1993. 60.00 (*81-7305-030-9*, Pub. by Aryan Bks Intl) S Asia.

***Nagar, Shanti Lal, tr.** Madhava Kandali Ramayana, Pt. 1. 2000. 68.50 (*81-215-0936-X*, Pub. by M Manoharial) S Asia.

Nagar, Shanti Lal, see Lal Nagar, Shanti.

Nagara, Susumu. Japanese Pidgin English in Hawaii: A Bilingual Description. LC 70-184352. (Oceanic Linguistics Special Publication Ser.: No. 9). 341p. reprint ed. pap. 105.80 (*0-608-18712-7*, 202703100053) Bks Demand.

N

Nagaraj, T. S. Principles of Testing Soils, Rock, & Concrete. LC 92-25238. 708p. 1993. 299.50 (*0-444-88911-6*) Elsevier.

Nagaraj, T. S. & Srinivasa, B. R. Analysis & Prediction of Soil Behaviour. 1994. write for info. (*81-224-0633-5*, Pub. by Wiley Estrn) Franklin.

Nagaraja, H. N., et al, eds. Statistical Theory & Applications: Papers in Honor of Herbert A. David, Vol. XVII. (Illus.). 334p. 1995. 72.95 (*0-387-94591-1*) Spr-Verlag.

Nagarajan, ed. Glycopeptide Antibiotics. LC 94-585. (Drugs & the Pharmaceutical Sciences Ser.: Vol. 63). (Illus.). 448p. 1994. text 199.00 (*0-8247-9193-2*) Dekker.

Nagarajan, Nadia G. Jewish Tales from Eastern Europe. LC 99-18833. 256p. 1999. 30.00 (*0-7657-6086-X*) Aronson.

Nagarajan, B. S., jt. auth. see Sumangala, M.

Nagarajan, Nilakantan. Testbank to Accompany Systems Analysis & Design: An Organizational Approach, by R. McLeod. 176p. (C). 1994. pap. text 43.50 (*0-03-076683-4*) Dryden Pr.

Nagarajan, R., jt. auth. see Isaacs, H. P.

Nagarajan, Radhakrishnan, jt. ed. see Kwong, Norman S.

Nagarajan, S. & Viswanathan, S. Shakespeare in India. 128p. 1987. 18.95 (*0-685-21573-3*) Asia Bk Corp.

Nagarajan, S., jt. auth. see Shakespeare, William.

***Nagarajan, V. & Okut-Uma, Rogers W.** Environmental Assessment of Development Projects. 259p. 2000. pap. 45.00 (*0-85092-556-8*, Pub. by Comm Sec) Stylus Pub VA.

Nagarathna, R., et al. Yoga for Common Ailments. (Illus.). 96p. (Orig.). 1991. pap. 13.95 (*0-671-70528-8*, Fireside) S&S Trade Pap.

Nagaratnam, Nataraj, et al. Java Networking & AWT API SuperBible. (Illus.). 960p. 1996. 59.99 (*1-57169-031-X*) Sams.

Nagaratnam, R. Criminal Procedure: Principles & Precedents. (C). 1990. 150.00 (*0-89771-164-5*) St Mut.

Nagarjuna. The Fundamental Wisdom of the Middle Way: Nagarjuna's Mulamadhyamakakarika. Garfield, Jay L., tr. & comment by. 400p. 1995. pap. 16.95 (*0-19-509336-4*) OUP.

— She-rab Dong-bu, or Prajnya Danda: A Metrical Translation in Tibetan of a Sanskirt Ethical Work. Campbell, W. L., ed. LC 78-70103. reprint ed. 27.50 (*0-404-17354-3*) AMS Pr.

Nagarkar, Kiran. Seven Sixes Are Forty-Three. (Asian Writers Ser.). 177p. 1995. pap. 10.95 (*0-435-95088-6*, 95088) Heinemann.

Nagarkatte, Umesh, jt. auth. see Berebom, Joshua.

Nagasaka, Francis G., ed. Japanese Studies in the Philosophy of Science. LC 97-37661. (Boston Studies in the Philosophy of Science). 224p. 1998. lib. bdg. write for info. (*0-7923-4781-1*) Kluwer Academic.

Nagasaka, Kenji. Analytic Number Theory & Related Topics: Proceedings of the Conference. 190p. 1993. text 53.00 (*981-02-1499-5*) World Scientific Pub.

Nagasaka, Kenji, et al, eds. Prospects of Mathematical Science. 284p. (C). 1988. pap. 40.00 (*9971-5-0465-0*); text 98.00 (*9971-5-0454-5*) World Scientific Pub.

Nagasaki, Eizo. Mathematics Program in Japan to Upper Secondary School. 49p. 1997. pap. 5.50 (*0-16-063631-0*) USGPO.

Nagasako, Kou, et al. Atlas of Gastroenterologic Endoscopy: By High-Resolution Video-Endoscope. 164p. 150.00 (*4-260-14346-8*) Lppncott W & W.

Nagasawa, Hiroshi, ed. Prolactin Lesions in Breasts, Uterus, Prostate. 272p. 1988. 138.00 (*0-8493-6836-7*, RC280, CRC Reprint) Franklin.

Nagasawa, Hiroshi & Abe, K., eds. Hormone-Related Tumors. 380p. 1981. 94.95 (*0-387-10925-0*) Spr-Verlag.

Nagasawa, Hiroshi, et al. One-Dimensional Conductors. (Solid-State Sciences Ser.: Vol. 72). (Illus.). 270p. 1988. 79.95 (*0-387-18154-7*) Spr-Verlag.

Nagasawa, Hiroshi, jt. ed. see Mori, Takao.

Nagasawa, Kimiko & Condon, Camy. Eating Cheap in Japan: The Gaijin Gourmet's Guide to Ordering in Non-Tourist Restaurants. (Illus.). 104p. (Orig.). 1972. pap. 9.95 (*4-07-971548-X*, Pub. by Shufunomoto Co Ltd) Tuttle Pubng.

Nagasawa, Masao. Schrodinger Equations & Diffusion Theory. LC 93-1170. xii, 319p. 1993. 115.00 (*0-8176-2875-4*) Birkhauser.

***Nagasawa, Masao.** Stochastic Processes in Quantum Physics. LC 99-59188. (Monographs in Mathematics Ser.: Vol. 94). 624p. 2000. 124.00 (*3-7643-6208-1*) Birkhauser.

Nagasawa, Richard. Summer Wind: The Story of an Immigrant Chinese Politician. LC 86-50080. 19.95 (*0-87026-063-4*) Westernlore.

Nagase, Hideaki, jt. auth. see Woessner, Fred.

Nagase, Michihiro, tr. see Kumano-Go, Hitoshi.

Nagashima, Hiroyuki & Baba, Yoshikazu. Introduction to Chaos: Analysis & Mathematics of the Phenomenon. LC 98-39253. 1998. 90.00 (*0-7503-0507-X*) IOP Pub.

***Nagashima, Hiroyuki & Baba, Yoshikazu.** Introduction to Chaos: Analysis & Mathematics of the Phenomenon. LC 98-39253. viii, 168p. 1999. pap. 27.00 (*0-7503-0508-8*) IOP Pub.

Nagashima, Kei, jt. auth. see Waranabe, Masahiro.

Nagashima, Kei, jt. auth. see Watanabe, Masahiro.

Nagashima, Soichiro. One Hundred Management Charts. 2nd ed. 344p. 1987. reprint ed. text 38.00 (*92-833-1043-8*); reprint ed. pap. text 32.75 (*92-833-1044-6*) Productivity Inc.

Nagashima, Yoichi. Objective Description of the Self: The Literary Theory of Iwano Homei. LC 98-153773. 240p. 1997. 29.95 (*87-7288-611-0*, Pub. by Aarhus Univ Pr) David Brown.

Nagaswamy, R. Masterpieces of Early South Indian Bronzes. 172p. 1983. 52.95 (*0-940500-90-6*, Pub. by Natl Museum) Asia Bk Corp.

Nagata, D. K. Legacy of Injustice: Exploring the Cross-Generational Impact of the Japanese American Internment. (Critical Issues in Social Justice Ser.). (Illus.). 298p. (C). 1993. 45.00 (*0-306-44425-9*, Plenum Trade) Perseus Pubng.

Nagata, Hiromi, tr. see Kodaira, Kunihiko.

Nagata, J. Modern General Topology. 3rd rev. ed. (Mathematical Library: Vol. 33). 522p. 1985. 228.00 (*0-444-87655-3*, North Holland) Elsevier.

Nagata, J., jt. ed. see Morita, K.

Nagata, Judith A. Continuity & Change among the Old Order Amish of Illinois. LC 87-45783. (Immigrant Communities & Ethnic Minorities in the U. S. & Canada Ser.: No. 18). 1988. 59.50 (*0-404-19428-1*) AMS Pr.

Nagata, Katsutaro, et al. Comprehensive Medicine: An Oriental & Occidental Overview of Biopsychosocial Medicine. LC 98-71383. (Illus.). 220p. 1998. lib. bdg. 52.00 (*0-934314-02-0*) Intl Found Biosocial Dev.

***Nagata, Kazuhiro & Handa, H.** Real-Time Analysis of Biomolecular Interactions: Applications of Biacore. LC 00-38756. 2000. write for info. (*4-431-70289-X*) Spr-Verlag.

Nagata, Linda. Vast. 416p. 1998. mass mkt. 5.99 (*0-553-57630-5*, Spectra) Bantam.

Nagata, M. Polynomial Rings & Affine Spaces. LC 78-8264. (CBMS Regional Conference Series in Mathematics: No. 37). 33p. 1978. reprint ed. pap. 17.00 (*0-8218-1687-X*, CBMS/37) Am Math.

Nagata, M. & Peng, T. A., eds. Algebraic Geometry. 152p. (C). 1988. text 59.00 (*9971-5-0604-1*) World Scientific Pub.

Nagata, Masayoshi. Field Theory. LC 76-11106. (Pure & Applied Mathematics Ser.: Vol. 40). 280p. reprint ed. pap. 86.80 (*0-608-08968-0*, 206960300005) Bks Demand.

— Theory of Commutative Fields. LC 93-6503. (Translations of Mathematical Monographs: Vol. 125). 249p. 1993. text 49.00 (*0-8218-4572-1*, MMONO/125) Am Math.

Nagata, Seiji. Hokusai: Genius Of The Japanese Ukiyo-e. (Illus.). 96p. 1999. pap. 25.00 (*4-7700-2479-7*, Pub. by Kodansha Intl) Kodansha.

Nagata, Wayne, jt. ed. see Langford, William F.

Nagata, Yoshimi. Stone Cats. LC 93-18223.Tr. of Ishikoro No Dobutsutachi. (Illus.). 48p. 1993. 14.95 (*0-8348-0279-1*) Weatherhill.

Nagata, Yuriko. Japanese Internment. 1996. pap. 24.95 (*0-614-25004-8*, Pub. by Univ Queensland Pr) Intl Spec Bk.

Nagataki, Shigenobu, ed. Chernobyl Update & in the Future. LC 94-35040. (International Congress Ser.: No. 1074). 292p. 1994. 178.50 (*0-444-81953-3*) Elsevier.

Nagataki, Shigenobu, et al, eds. Prevention of Type One Diabetes & Autoimmune Thyroid Disease. (Current Clinical Practice Ser.: Vol. 49). 158p. 1988. 65.75 (*0-685-20122-8*) Elsevier.

Nagataki, Shigenobu & Yamashita, Shunichi, eds. Radiation & Human Health Proposal from Nagasaki: Proceedings of the Nagasaki Symposium '95, 50th Anniversary Meeting of the Atomic Bombing in Nagasaki, Nagasaki, Japan, 19 September 1995. (International Congress Ser.: No. 1103). 306p. 1996. text 176.00 (*0-444-82287-9*, Excerpta Medica) Elsevier.

Nagatani, Keizo. Macroeconomic Dynamics. LC 80-28883. (Illus.). 272p. 1981. text 85.00 (*0-521-23515-4*) Cambridge U Pr.

— Political Macroeconomics. (Illus.). 288p. 1990. text 75.00 (*0-19-828642-2*) OUP.

Nagatani, Keizo & Edgington, David W., eds. Japan & the West: The Perception Gap. LC 97-77894. 198p. 1998. text 59.95 (*1-85972-528-7*, Pub. by Ashgate Pub) Ashgate Pub Co.

Nagatani, T., tr. see Bloom, Alfed.

Nagatani, T., tr. see Tabrah, Ruth M., ed.

Nagatomi, Masatoshi, et al, eds. Sanskrit & Indian Studies: Essays in Honour of Daniel H. H. Ingalls. (Studies in Classical India: No. 2). 278p. 1980. text 126.50 (*90-277-0991-2*, D Reidel) Kluwer Academic.

Nagatomo, Kazuhiko. Talk Japanese Gambatte! Hirowatari, Taro & Hulbert, Paul, eds. 1995. audio 25.00 (*4-7700-1933-5*) Kodansha.

— Talk Japanese Gambatte! (Illus.). 156p. 1995. pap. 19.00 (*4-7700-1932-7*) Kodansha.

Nagatomo, Kazuhiko & Steinburg, Miho. Do-It-Yourself Japanese Through Comics. (Illus.). 156p. 1995. pap. 15.00 (*4-7700-1935-1*) Kodansha.

Nagatomo, Shigenori. Attunement Through the Body. LC 91-39372. (SUNY Series, The Body in Culture, History, & Religion). 305p. (C). 1992. text 64.50 (*0-7914-1231-8*); pap. text 21.95 (*0-7914-1232-6*) State U NY Pr.

— A Philosophical Foundation of Miki Kiyoshi's Concept of Humanism. LC 94-39460. (Studies in Asian Thought & Religion: Vol. 15). 130p. 1995. text 69.95 (*0-7734-9145-7*) E Mellen.

Nagatomo, Shigenori, tr. see Motoyama, Hiroshi.

Nagatomo, Shigenori, tr. see Yuasa, Yasuo.

Nagatsu, T., et al, eds. Basic, Clinical & Therapeutic Aspects of Alzheimer's & Parkinson's Disease, Vol. 1. (Advances in Behavioral Biology Ser.: Vol. 38A). (Illus.). 830p. (C). 1990. text 210.00 (*0-306-43680-9*, Kluwer Plenum) Kluwer Academic.

— Basic, Clinical & Therapeutic Aspects of Alzheimer's & Parkinson's Diseases, Vol. 2. (Advances in Behavioral Biology Ser.: Vol. 38B). (Illus.). 638p. (C). 1990. text 186.00 (*0-306-43681-7*, Kluwer Plenum) Kluwer Academic.

Nagayama, Kokan. Connoisseur's Book of Japanese Swords. 1998. 65.00 (*4-7700-2071-6*, Pub. by Kodansha Intl) Kodansha.

Nagda, Ann W. Bamboo Valley: A Story of a Chinese Bamboo Forest. LC 97-8677. (Habitat Ser.). (Illus.). 32p. (J). (gr. 1-4). 1997. 15.95 (*1-56899-491-5*); 19.95 incl. audio (*1-56899-493-1*, BC7006); pap. 5.95 (*1-56899-492-3*) Soundprints.

— Bamboo Valley: A Story of a Chinese Bamboo Forest, Incl. toy. (Habitat Ser.). (Illus.). 36p. (J). (gr. 1-4). 1997. 35.95 incl. audio (*1-56899-494-X*); 26.95 (*1-56899-498-2*); pap. 16.95 (*1-56899-495-8*); pap. 19.95 incl. audio (*1-56899-496-6*) Soundprints.

— Canopy Crossing: A Story of an Atlantic Rainforest. (Illus.). 36p. (J). (gr. 1-4). 1997. 15.95 (*1-56899-449-4*); 19.95 incl. audio (*1-56899-452-4*, BC7004); pap. 5.95 (*1-56899-450-8*) Soundprints.

— Canopy Crossing: A Story of an Atlantic Rainforest, Incl. toy. (Illus.). 36p. (J). (gr. 1-4). 1997. 26.95 (*1-56899-451-6*); 31.95 incl. audio (*1-56899-453-2*); pap. 16.95 (*1-56899-454-0*); pap. 19.95 incl. audio (*1-56899-456-7*) Soundprints.

— Tiger Territory: A Story of the Chitwan Valley. LC 98-42571. (Habitat Ser.: Vol. 11). (Illus.). 36p. (J). (gr. 1-4). 1999. 15.95 (*1-56899-720-5*); 19.95 incl. audio (*1-56899-722-1*, BC7011); pap. 5.95 (*1-56899-721-3*); pap. 10.95 incl. audio (*1-56899-723-X*) Soundprints.

— Tiger Territory: A Story of the Chitwan Valley, Incl. toy. (Habitat Ser.: Vol. 11). (Illus.). 36p. (J). (gr. 1-4). 1999. 26.95 (*1-56899-724-8*); 31.95 incl. audio (*1-56899-726-4*); pap. 16.95 (*1-56899-725-6*); pap. 19.95 incl. audio (*1-56899-727-2*) Soundprints.

***Nagda, Ann Whitehead.** So You Want to be a Snake Charmer. 2002. text 15.95 (*0-8050-6499-0*) St Martin.

— Tiger Math. LC 99-46686. (Illus.). 32p. (gr. 2-5). 2000. text 15.95 (*0-8050-6248-3*) St Martin.

— World above the Clouds: A Story of a Himalayan Ecosystem. (Habitat Ser.: Vol. 18). (Illus.). 36p. (J). (gr. 1-4). 2000. 15.95 (*1-56899-878-3*); 26.95 (*1-56899-882-1*); pap. 5.95 (*1-56899-879-1*); pap. 16.95 (*1-56899-883-X*) Soundprints.

Nagda, Niren L., ed. Modeling of Indoor Air Quality & Exposure. LC 93-31561. (Special Technical Publication Ser.: No. 1205). (Illus.). 310p. 1993. 65.00 (*0-8031-1875-9*, STP1205) ASTM.

— Radon: Prevalence, Measurements, Health Risks, & Control. LC 94-11665. (ASTM Manual Ser.: MNL 15). (Illus.). 170p. 1994. text 59.00 (*0-8031-2057-5*, MNL15) ASTM.

Nagda, Niren L. & Harper, J. P., eds. Design & Protocol for Monitoring Indoor Air Quality. LC 88-37486. (Special Technical Publication Ser.: No. STP 1002). (Illus.). 310p. 1989. text 53.00 (*0-8031-1176-2*, STP1002) ASTM.

Nagdi, Khairi. Rubbers As an Engineering Material: Guidelines for Users. 322p. 1992. 98.00 (*1-56990-067-1*) Hanser-Gardner.

Nagdi, P. M., et al, eds. Non-Linear Elasticity & Theoretical Mechanics: In Honour of A. E. Green. (Illus.). 286p. 1994. text 85.00 (*0-19-853486-8*) OUP.

Nagdy, jt. auth. see Gray.

Nageak, J., jt. as told by see Nashaknik, H.

Nagel. Bulgaria 2nd ed. 527p. 1985. 39.95 (*2-8263-0560-3*, NTC Business Bks) NTC Contemp Pub Co.

— Egypt. Date not set. 49.95 (*2-8263-0020-2*) NTC Contemp Pub Co.

— Nagel's Guide to Sweden. 1991. 39.95 (*0-8442-9782-8*, Passprt Bks) NTC Contemp Pub Co.

***Nagel.** 2001 Electronic Commerce Assurance. 1350p. 2000. pap. text 159.00 (*0-15-607201-7*) Harcourt Legal.

***Nagel, Karl D.** 2000 Miller Electronic Commerce Assurance Services. 1999. pap. text 149.00 (*0-15-606973-3*) Harcourt.

***Nagel, Karl D. & Gray, Glen L.** Electronic Commerce Assurance Services 2000: Electronic Workpapers & Reference Guide. 1378p. 2000. pap. 149.00 incl. cd-rom (*0-15-606974-1*) Harcourt Legal.

Nagel, Alexander. Mermaids. 1996. write for info. (*0-8212-2264-3*) Little.

***Nagel, Alexander & Buonarroti, Michelangelo.** Michelangelo & the Reform of Art. LC 99-55668. 2000. write for info. (*0-521-66292-3*) Cambridge U Pr.

Nagel, Alexander & Stout, Edgar L., eds. The Madison Symposium on Complex Analysis: (Proceedings of the Symposium on Complex Analysis Held June 2-7, 1991 at the University of Wisconsin-Madison) LC 92-23702. (Contemporary Mathematics Ser.: Vol. 137). 478p. 1992. pap. 49.00 (*0-8218-5147-0*, CONM/137) Am Math.

Nagel, David C., jt. ed. see Wiener, Earl L.

Nagel, Ed. Cheez! Uncle Sam. 1978. 8.95 (*0-9603096-0-8*) Santa Fe Comm Sch.

Nagel, Edward A. Heat Merchants. 1999. 23.50 (*0-88739-276-8*) Creat Arts Bk.

— No Entry. LC 94-37598. 184p. 1995. 20.00 (*1-56858-025-8*) FWEW.

Nagel, Ernest. The Structure of Science. LC 60-15504. 640p. (C). 1979. reprint ed. pap. text 19.95 (*0-915144-71-9*); reprint ed. lib. bdg. 39.95 (*0-915144-72-7*) Hackett Pub.

— Teleology Revisited & Other Essays in the Philosophy & History of Science. LC 78-1437. 368p. 1982. pap. text 23.00 (*0-231-04505-0*) Col U Pr.

Nagel, Ernest & Newman, James R. Godel's Proof. LC 58-5610. (C). 1958. pap. text 11.50 (*0-8147-0325-9*) NYU Pr.

Nagel, Ernest, jt. auth. see Cohen, Morris R.

Nagel, Ernest, ed. see Wesleyan Conference on Induction Staff.

Nagel, Fritz. Fritz: The World War I Memoirs of a German Lieutenant. 2nd ed. Baumgartner, Richard A., ed. (Illus.). 160p. (Orig.). 1995. 22.95 (*1-885033-15-X*) Blue Acorn Pr.

Nagel, G. A., et al, eds. Plasmapheresis in Immunology & Oncology: Beitraege zur Onkologie. Contributions to Oncology, Vol. 10. (Illus.). viii, 266p. 1982. pap. 50.50 (*3-8055-3467-1*) S Karger.

Nagel, G. A., jt. ed. see Burkert, H.

Nagel, Gordon. The Structure of Experience: Kant's System of Principles. LC 82-24814. 296p. 1994. 27.50 (*0-226-56766-4*) U Ch Pr.

Nagel, Greta. The Tao of Parenting: The Ageless Wisdom of Taoism & the Art of Raising Children. LC 98-19436. 304p. 1998. pap. 11.95 (*0-452-28005-2*, Plume) Dutton Plume.

Nagel, Greta, told to. The Tao of Teaching: The Special Meaning of the Tao Te Ching As Related to the Art of Teaching. 1998. pap. 12.95 (*0-452-28095-8*) NAL.

***Nagel, Greta K.** Effective Grouping for Literacy Instruction: Knowledge, Power, & Affection. 160p. 2000. pap. 22.00 (*0-205-30920-8*) S&S Trade.

Nagel, Greta K. The Tao of Teaching: The Special Meaning of the Tao Te Ching As Related to the Art of Teaching. LC 94-71108. 240p. 1994. pap. 12.95 (*1-55611-415-X*, Pub. by D I Fine) Penguin Putnam.

Nagel, Gwen L. & Nagel, James. Essays on Hamlin Garland: A Reference Guide. limited ed. LC 77-7392. 1982. lib. bdg. 40.00 (*0-614-24927-9*, G K Hall Lrg Type) Mac Lib Ref.

Nagel, H. H., jt. ed. see Orban, Guy A.

Nagel, Harry L., jt. auth. see Bosworth, Bruce.

Nagel, Helmut. Karl der Grosse Und die Theologischen Herausforderungen Seiner Zeit: Zur Wechselwirkung Zwischen Theologie Und Politik Im Zeitalter Des Grossen Frankenherrschers. (Illus.). 261p. 1998. 45.95 (*3-631-34028-1*) P Lang Pubng.

Nagel, Hildegard, et al, trs. from GER. The Place of Creation Vol. 3: Essays of Erich Neumann. 280p. 1989. text 65.00 (*0-691-09965-0*, Pub. by Princeton U Pr) Cal Prin Full Svc.

Nagel, Hildegard, tr. see Jung, Emma.

Nagel, Ivan. Autonomy & Mercy: Reflections on Mozart's Operas. Faber, Marion, tr. LC 90-22827. 149p. 1974. 29.00 (*0-674-05477-6*, NAGAUT) HUP.

Nagel, Jack H. The Descriptive Analysis of Power. LC 74-14087. 214p. reprint ed. pap. 66.40 (*0-8357-8092-9*, 203383900087) Bks Demand.

Nagel, James. Stephen Crane & Literary Impressionism. LC 80-16051. 200p. (C). 1980. 35.00 (*0-271-00267-0*) Pa St U Pr.

Nagel, James, ed. American Fiction: Historical & Critical Essays. LC 77-88848. 216p. 1977. text 30.00 (*0-8057-9006-3*) NE U Pr.

— Critical Essays on Ernest Hemingway's The Sun Also Rises. LC 94-34994. (Critical Essays on American Literature Ser.). 1995. 47.00 (*0-8161-7312-5*, Twyne) Mac Lib Ref.

— Ernest Hemingway: The Oak Park Legacy. 248p. 1996. pap. text 19.95 (*0-8173-0842-3*) U of Ala Pr.

— Ernest Hemingway: The Writer in Context. LC 83-40268. 264p. reprint ed. pap. 81.90 (*0-608-20457-9*, 207171000002) Bks Demand.

Nagel, James & Quirk, Tom, eds. The Portable American Realism Reader. LC 97-12448. 1997. pap. 14.95 (*0-14-026830-8*) Viking Penguin.

Nagel, James, jt. auth. see Nagel, Gwen L.

Nagel, James, ed. see Pizer, Donald.

Nagel, James, ed. see Von Kurowsky, Agnes & Hemingway, Ernest.

***Nagel, Jeanne.** Careers in Television. LC 00-9849. (Careers Ser.). 2000. lib. bdg. write for info. (*0-8239-3187-0*) Rosen Group.

Nagel, Jeff. The Blind Date Survival Guide: A Practical & Funny (Well, Practically Funny) Step-by-Step Guide to Meeting the Person of Your Dreams. (Illus.). 128p. (Orig.). 1988. pap. 5.95 (*0-923032-00-2*) Blockbuster Pubns Inc.

Nagel, Joane. American Indian Ethnic Renewal: Red Power & the Resurgence of Identity & Culture. (Illus.). 320p. 1997. reprint ed. pap. 19.95 (*0-19-512063-9*) OUP.

Nagel, John D. Introduction to Comparative Politics: Challenges of Conflict & Change in a New Era. 5th rev. ed. LC 97-22360. (Illus.). 456p. (C). 1998. pap. text 40.95 (*0-8304-1475-4*) Thomson Learn.

Nagel, Judith Kurka, see Kurka Nagel, Judith.

Nagel, K. H. Der Bau der Thiersee- und Karwendelmulde (Tirol) (Geotektonische Forschungen Ser.: Vol. 48). (GER.). ii, 136p. 1975. 55.00 (*3-510-50014-8*, Pub. by E Schweizerbartsche) Balogh.

Nagel, Karen. Two Crazy Pigs. (Hello, Reader! Ser.). (J). 1992. 8.70 (*0-606-01970-7*, Pub. by Turtleback) Demco.

Nagel, Karen B. The Lunch Line. LC 96-14354. (Hello Math Reader Ser.: Level 3). (Illus.). 32p. (J). (gr. 1-4). 1996. 3.50 (*0-590-60246-2*, Cartwheel) Scholastic Inc.

Nagel, Karen B. Two Crazy Pigs. LC 91-18860. (Illus.). 32p. (J). (ps-3). 1992. pap. 3.50 (*0-590-44972-9*, Cartwheel) Scholastic Inc.

***Nagel, Karen B. & Croll, Carolyn.** Snow? Let's Go! LC 99-30154. (My First Hello Reader Ser.). (Illus.). 32p. (J). (ps-1). 2000. 3.99 (*0-439-09906-4*) Scholastic Inc.

Nagel, Karen Berman. The Lunch Line. (Hello Math Reader Ser.). (J). 1996. 8.70 (*0-606-11584-6*, Pub. by Turtleback) Demco.

Nagel, Kurt. Lexikon EDV und Rechnungswesen. (GER.). 1977. 59.95 (*0-8288-5493-9*, M7203) Fr & Eur.

Nagel, Mechtild, jt. auth. see Light, Andrew.

Nagel, Michael. Emancipation des Juden im Roman oder Tendenz zur Isolierung? Das Deutsch-Judische Jugendbuch in der Diskussion Zwischen Aufklarung, Reform und Orthodoxie (1780-1860) (Haskala Ser.: Bd. 19). (GER.). viii, 458p. 1999. 80.00 (*3-487-10878-X*, Pub. by G Olms Verlag) Lubrecht & Cramer.

Nagel, Molli E. Two Hundred Fifty Reasons to Quit Smoking. Bacci, Andrea, ed. 78p. (Orig.). (C). 1994. pap. 8.95 (*1-56550-021-0*) Vis Bks Intl.

Nagel, Muska. Elements. 135p. (Orig.). 1990. pap. 10.95 (*0-913006-44-0*) Puckerbrush.

— Letter to the Interior. Hunting, Constance, ed. 80p. (Orig.). 1996. pap. 10.95 (0-913006-63-7) Puckerbrush.

— Things That Surround Us. Hunting, Constance, ed. 68p. (Orig.). 1987. pap. 8.95 (0-913006-39-4) Puckerbrush.

— A Voice . . . Translations of Paul Celan. Hunting, Constance, ed. 180p. 1998. pap. 12.95 (0-913006-67-X) Puckerbrush.

Nagel, Muska, tr. see Bobrowski, Johannes.

Nagel, Myra B. Deliver Us from Evil: What the Bible Says about Satan. LC 98-50323. 112p. 1999. pap. 12.95 (0-8298-1319-5) Pilgrim OH.

— Journey to the Cross: Lenten Reflections for Individuals & Groups. LC 96-44148. 104p. (Orig.). 1996. pap. 8.95 (0-8298-1140-0) Pilgrim OH.

— Talking with Your Child about Prayer. LC 89-39927. (Growing Together Ser.). (Orig.). 1990. pap. 2.25 (0-8298-0845-0) Pilgrim OH.

Nagel, Nancy G. Learning Through Real-World Problem Solving: The Power of Integrative Teaching. LC 95-35442. (Illus.). 184p. 1996. 55.95 (0-8039-6359-9); pap. 24.95 (0-8039-6360-2) Corwin Pr.

Nagel, Paul C. Adams Women: Abigail & Louisa Adams, Their Sisters & Daughters. 1999. pap. text 14.95 (0-674-00410-8) HUP.

— Descent from Glory: 4 Generations of the John Adams Family. LC 99-202717. 1999. pap. text 16.95 (0-674-19829-8) HUP.

— John Quincy Adams: A Public Life, a Private Life. 1999. pap. text 16.95 (0-674-47940-8) HUP.

— John Quincy Adams: A Public Life, a Private Life. LC 96-49640. (Illus.). 464p. 1997. 30.00 (0-679-40444-9) Knopf.

— Missouri: A History. LC 88-27761. xiv, 210p. 1988. pap. 9.95 (0-7006-0386-7) U Pr of KS.

— One Nation Indivisible: The Union in American Thought, 1776 to 1861. LC 80-36682. 328p. 1980. reprint ed. lib. bdg. 35.00 (0-313-22656-3, NAON, Greenwood Pr) Greenwood.

Nagel, R., ed. One Parameter Semigroups of Positive Operators. (Lecture Notes in Mathematics Ser.: Vol. 1184). x, 460p. 1986. 57.30 (0-387-16454-5) Spr-Verlag.

Nagel, R., jt. auth. see Engel, K. J.

Nagel, R. L. Genetically Abnormal Red Cells, 2 vols., Set. 1988. reprint ed. 217.00 (0-8493-6825-1, CRC Reprint) Franklin.

***Nagel, Rob.** Body by Design, 2 vols. LC 99-14642. 410p. (J). 1999. text 63.00 (0-7876-3897-8) Gale.

Nagel, Rob. Body by Design: From the Digestive to the Skeleton LC 99-14642. 1999. write for info. (0-7876-3899-4) Visible Ink Pr.

***Nagel, Rob.** Dangerous Planet: The Science of Natural Disasters, 3 vols. DesChenes, Betz, ed. LC 98-54422. 600p. (J). 1998. text 84.00 (0-7876-2848-4, 00158652, UXL) Gale.

Nagel, Rob. Endangered Species. LC 98-34259. 1998. 84.00 (0-7876-1876-4, UXL); 84.00 (0-7876-1878-0, UXL); pap. 84.00 (0-7876-1877-2, UXL) Gale.

***Nagel, Rob, ed.** Endangered Species, 3 vols. LC 98-34259. 576p. 1998. text 84.00 (0-7876-1875-6, UXL) Gale.

Nagel, Rob & Betz Des Chenes. Dangerous Planet: The Science of Natural Disasters. LC 98-54422. 1999. write for info. (0-7876-2851-4, UXL) Gale.

Nagel, Rob & Commire, Anne, eds. World Leaders: People Who Shaped the World. LC 94-20544. 480p. 1994. text 69.00 (0-8103-9768-4, UXL) Gale.

Nagel, Rob & Rose, Sharon, eds. Hispanic American Biography, 2 vols. LC 95-158001. (Hispanic American Reference Library: Vol. 2, Pt. 2). 238p. 1995. text 67.00 (0-8103-9828-1) Gale.

Nagel, Robert F. Constitutional Cultures: The Mentality & Consequences of Judicial Review. 1989. pap. 15.95 (0-520-08278-8, Pub. by U CA Pr) Cal Prin Full Svc.

— Judicial Power & American Character: Censoring Ourselves in an Anxious Age. 208p. 1996. pap. 19.95 (0-19-510662-8) OUP.

Nagel, Roger N. & Dove, Rick. 21st Century Manufacturing Enterprise Strategy Vol. I: An Industry-Led View. (Illus.). 58p. (C). 1998. reprint ed. pap. text 20.00 (0-7881-7458-4) DIANE Pub.

— 21st Century Manufacturing Enterprise Strategy Vol. II: Infrastructure. (Illus.). 126p. (C). 1998. pap. text 25.00 (0-7881-7459-2) DIANE Pub.

Nagel, Ronald L., ed. Genetically Abnormal Red Cells, 2 vols., Vol. I. 192p. 1988. 105.00 (0-8493-6826-X, RC647, CRC Reprint) Franklin.

— Genetically Abnormal Red Cells, 2 vols., Vol. II. 208p. 1988. 113.00 (0-8493-6827-8, RC647, CRC Reprint) Franklin.

***Nagel, Stephan.** Brahmas Geheime Schopfung: Die Indische Reformbewegung der Brahma Kumaris/Quellen, Lehre, Raja Yoga. (Theion. Jahrbuch fur Religionskultur Ser.). XII, 439p. 1999. 52.95 (3-631-35484-3) P Lang Pubng.

Nagel, Steve, ed. see Pellowski, Anne.

Nagel, Stuart. Research in Public Policy Analysis & Management, Vol. 9. 1998. 78.50 (0-7623-0508-8) Jai Pr.

***Nagel, Stuart, ed.** Policy Analysis Methods. 267p. 1999. 49.00 (1-56072-657-1) Nova Sci Pubs.

Nagel, Stuart & Lazin, Fred. Policy Studies & Developing Nations Vol. 6: The Policy Implementation in Developing Nations, No. 6. (Policy Studies & Developing Nations: Vol.'6). 1999. 78.50 (0-7623-0221-6) Jai Pr.

Nagel, Stuart S. Causation, Prediction & Legal Analysis. LC 86-8142. 298p. 1986. 55.00 (0-89930-180-0, NCP/, Quorum Bks) Greenwood.

— Computer-Aided Judicial Analysis: Predicting, Prescribing, & Administering. LC 91-33090. 392p. 1992. 85.00 (0-89930-670-5, NJP/, Quorum Bks) Greenwood.

— Contemporary Public Policy Analysis. LC 82-21787. (Illus.). 192p. 1984. pap. 59.60 (0-608-05144-6, 206570500005) Bks Demand.

— Creativity & Public Policy: Generating Super-Optimum Solutions. LC 98-35235. (Policy Studies Organization). 200p. 1999. 69.95 (1-84014-018-6) Ashgate Pub Co.

***Nagel, Stuart S.** Critical Issues in Cross-national Public Administration: Privatization, Democratization, Decentralization. LC 99-40350. 272p. 2000. write for info. (1-56720-299-3, Quorum Bks) Greenwood.

Nagel, Stuart S. Decision-Aiding Software & Legal Decision-Making: A Guide to Skills & Applications Throughout the Law. LC 88-39911. 269p. 1989. 72.95 (0-89930-382-X, NLD, Quorum Bks) Greenwood.

— Evaluative & Explanatory Legal Reasoning. LC 91-32381. 232p. 1992. 65.00 (0-89930-445-1, NEE/, Quorum Bks) Greenwood.

***Nagel, Stuart S.** Handbook of Global International Policy. LC 00-24053. (Public Administration & Public Policy Ser.). 2000. write for info. (0-8247-0346-4) Dekker.

Nagel, Stuart S. Higher Goals for America: Doing Better Than the Best. LC 88-31498. (Illus.). 246p. (Orig.). (C). 1989. pap. text 22.50 (0-8191-7307-X); lib. bdg. 45.00 (0-8191-7306-1) U Pr of Amer.

— Law, Policy & Optimizing Analysis. LC 86-8140. 347p. 1986. 65.00 (0-89930-181-9, NLP/, Quorum Bks) Greenwood.

— Legal Scholarship, Microcomputers, & Super-Optimized Decision-Making. LC 92-44684. 232p. 1993. 67.95 (0-89930-444-3, NLA, Quorum Bks) Greenwood.

— Microcomputers As Decision Aids in Law Practice. LC 86-16873. 394p. 1987. 79.50 (0-89930-197-5, NLU/, Quorum Bks) Greenwood.

***Nagel, Stuart S.** National Development: Being More Effective & More Efficient. LC 99-43344. 200p. 2000. write for info. (1-84014-024-0) Ashgate Pub Co.

Nagel, Stuart S. Policy-Analysis Methods & Super-Optimum Solutions. 227p. 1994. lib. bdg. 95.00 (1-56072-135-9) Nova Sci Pubs.

— Policy Evaluation: Making Optimum Decisions. LC 81-12123. 329p. 1982. 49.95 (0-275-90866-6, C0866, Praeger Pubs) Greenwood.

— The Policy Process. LC 99-26784. 1999. 49.00 (1-56072-650-4) Nova Sci Pubs.

— Policy Process & Super-Optimum Solutions. 274p. 1994. lib. bdg. 95.00 (1-56072-134-0) Nova Sci Pubs.

— Policy Studies: Integration & Evaluation. LC 88-4148. 320p. 1989. pap. 22.95 (0-275-93007-6, B3007, Praeger Pubs) Greenwood.

— Policy Studies: Integration & Evaluation, 216. LC 88-3122. (Contributions in Political Science Ser.: No. 216). 320p. 1988. 65.00 (0-313-26256-X, NSP/, Greenwood Pr) Greenwood.

— Policy Within & Across Developing Nations. LC 97-27228. (Policy Studies Organization). (Illus.). 200p. 1997. text 72.95 (1-84014-019-4, Pub. by Ashgate Pub) Ashgate Pub Co.

— Professional Developments in Policy Studies, 297. LC 91-38209. (Contributions in Political Science Ser.: No. 297). 288p. 1993. 69.50 (0-313-28429-6, NPV, Greenwood Pr) Greenwood.

— Public Policy: Goals, Means & Methods. 546p. (C). 1983. teacher ed. write for info. (0-318-57732-1) St Martin.

— Public Policy: Goals, Means & Methods. 480p. (C). 1990. reprint ed. pap. text 39.00 (0-8191-7912-4) U Pr of Amer.

— Public Policy Evaluation: Making Super-Optimum Decisions. LC 97-27227. (Policy Studies Organization). (Illus.). 361p. 1997. text 89.95 (1-84014-017-8, Pub. by Ashgate Pub) Ashgate Pub Co.

***Nagel, Stuart S.** The Substance of Public Policy. LC 99-25734. 1999. 49.00 (1-56072-649-0) Nova Sci Pubs.

Nagel, Stuart S. Super-Optimum Solutions & Win-Win Policy: Basic Concepts & Principles. LC 96-54284. 256p. 1997. 67.95 (1-56720-118-0, Quorum Bks) Greenwood.

Nagel, Stuart S., ed. Advances in Developmental Policy Studies, Vol. 1. 1996. 73.25 (1-55938-560-X) Jai Pr.

— Africa, Development & Public Policy. LC 93-26989. 1994. text 75.00 (0-312-10383-2) St Martin.

— Asia, Development & Public Policy. LC 93-31946. (Policy Studies Organization). 1994. text 75.00 (0-312-10649-1) St Martin.

— Basic Facilities & Institutions in Policy Studies. (C). 1972. pap. 15.00 (0-918592-01-1) Pol Studies.

— Basic Issues & References in Policy Studies. (C). 1972. pap. 15.00 (0-918592-00-3) Pol Studies.

— Computer-Aided Decision Analysis: Theory & Applications. LC 92-38003. 304p. 1993. 79.50 (0-89930-771-X, NCK/, Quorum Bks) Greenwood.

— East Europe, Development & Public Policy. LC 93-31947. (Policy Studies Organization). 1994. text 75.00 (0-312-10648-3) St Martin.

— Encyclopedia of Policy Studies. 2nd expanded rev. ed. LC 93-44894. (Public Administration & Public Policy Ser.: Vol. 53). (Illus.). 984p. 1994. text 215.00 (0-8247-9142-8) Dekker.

— Environmental Policy & Political Science Fields. (C). 1973. pap. 15.00 (0-918592-03-8) Pol Studies.

— Evaluation Analysis with Microcomputers, Suppl. 2. (Research in Public Policy Analysis & Management Ser.). 480p. 1989. 109.25 (1-55938-018-7) Jai Pr.

***Nagel, Stuart S., ed.** Handbook of Global Economic Policy. LC 00-21482. (Public Administration & Public Policy Ser.). 572p. 2000. 195.00 (0-8247-0328-6) Dekker.

Nagel, Stuart S., ed. Improving Policy Analysis. LC 79-23019. (Sage Focus Editions Ser.: Vol. 16). 264p. 1980. reprint ed. pap. 81.90 (0-608-03376-6, 205964000008) Bks Demand.

— India Development & Public Policy. LC 97-37211. (Policy Studies Organization). 200p. 1998. text 69.95 (1-84014-022-4, Pub. by Ashgate Pub) Ashgate Pub Co.

— Interdisciplinary Approaches to Policy Studies. (C). 1973. pap. 15.00 (0-918592-04-6) Pol Studies.

— Law & Social Change. LC 73-89941. (Sage Contemporary Social Science Issues Ser.: Vol. 3). 118p. 1974. reprint ed. pap. 36.60 (0-608-03377-4, 205964100008) Bks Demand.

— Law, Decision-Making, & Microcomputers: A Cross-National Perspective. LC 90-8918. 376p. 1991. 80.00 (0-89930-503-2, NLM/, Quorum Bks) Greenwood.

— Policy Studies & the Social Sciences. (Organization Ser.). 329p. 1975. pap. 15.00 (0-317-35632-1) Pol Studies.

— Policy Studies & the Social Sciences. LC 77-82859. 315p. 1979. reprint ed. pap. text 21.95 (0-87855-641-9) Transaction Pubs.

— Policy Studies Around the World. 1973. pap. 15.00 (0-918592-02-X) Pol Studies.

— Policy Studies in America & Elsewhere. (Organization Ser.). 229p. 1975. 15.00 (0-317-35633-X) Pol Studies.

— Policy Studies in Developing Nations, Vol. 2: Political Reform & Developing Nations. 363p. 1995. 78.50 (1-55938-106-X) Jai Pr.

— Policy Studies in Developing Nations Vol. 3: Public Budgeting & Financial Administration in Developing Nations. 1996. 78.50 (1-55938-190-6) Jai Pr.

— Policy Studies Review Annual, Vol. 1. 704p. 1977. text 69.95 (0-8039-0848-2) Transaction Pubs.

— Public Administration & Decision-Aiding Software: Improving Procedure & Substance, 23. LC 90-36737. (New Directions in Information Management Ser.: No. 23). 280p. 1990. 65.00 (0-313-27518-1, NPA, Greenwood Pr) Greenwood.

— Public Policy Studies: Basic Concepts & Methods, 10 vols. 1986. 732.50 (0-89232-370-1) Jai Pr.

— Research in Law & Policy Studies, Vol. 2. 277p. 1988. 73.25 (0-89232-662-X) Jai Pr.

— Research in Law & Policy Studies, Vol. 4. 348p. 1995. 73.25 (1-55938-112-4) Jai Pr.

— Research in Law & Policy Studies, Vol. 5. Date not set. 73.25 (0-7623-0041-8) Jai Pr.

— Research in Public Policy Analysis & Management, Vol. 3. 270p. 1986. 78.50 (0-89232-533-X) Jai Pr.

— Research in Public Policy Analysis & Management, Vol. 4. 299p. 1987. 78.50 (0-89232-663-8) Jai Pr.

— Research in Public Policy Analysis & Management, Vol. 6. 1995. 78.50 (1-55938-389-5) Jai Pr.

— Research in Public Policy Analysis & Management, Vol. 7. 285p. 1995. 78.50 (1-55938-841-2) Jai Pr.

— Research in Public Policy Analysis & Management, Vol. 8. 1998. 78.50 (0-7623-0044-2) Jai Pr.

***Nagel, Stuart S., ed.** Resolving Developmental Policy Controversies. LC 99-51428. 257p. 1999. text 59.00 (1-56072-739-X) Nova Sci Pubs.

Nagel, Stuart S., ed. Resolving International Disputes Through Win-Win or SOS Solutions. (Advances in Developmental Policy Studies: Vol. 2). Date not set. 73.25 (0-7623-0192-9) Jai Pr.

— The Rights of the Accused in Law & Action. LC 72-84052. (Sage Criminal Justice System Annuals Ser.: No. 1). 320p. reprint ed. pap. 99.20 (0-8357-8500-9, 202193600026) Bks Demand.

***Nagel, Stuart S., ed.** Super-Optimizing Examples: Across Public Policy. LC 99-51430. 256p. 1999. text 49.00 (1-56072-746-2) Nova Sci Pubs.

— Teaching Public Administration & Public Policy. LC 99-51429. 279p. (C). 1999. text 34.00 (1-56072-738-1) Nova Sci Pubs.

— Training Public Administrators Around the World. LC 99-45494. 185p. 2000. write for info. (1-56720-298-5, Quorum Bks) Greenwood.

Nagel, Stuart S. & Bievenue, Lisa A. Social Science, Law, & Public Policy. 344p. (C). 1992. pap. text 32.50 (0-8191-8429-2); lib. bdg. 57.50 (0-8191-8428-4) U Pr of Amer.

— Teach Yourself Decision-Aiding Software. LC 92-11135. 318p. (Orig.). (C). 1992. lib. bdg. 47.50 (0-8191-8738-0) U Pr of Amer.

Nagel, Stuart S. & Crecine, John P., eds. Basic Theory, Methods & Perspectives, Vol. 1. (Research in Public Policy Analysis & Management Ser.). 309p. 1981. 78.55 (0-89232-044-3) Jai Pr.

— The New Educational Programs in Public Policy: The 1st Decade. (Research in Public Policy Analysis & Management Ser.: Suppl. No. 1). 225p. 1983. 73.25 (0-89232-244-6) Jai Pr.

— Policy & Applied Research, Vol. 2. (Research in Public Policy Analysis & Management Ser.). 382p. 1981. 78.50 (0-89232-210-1) Jai Pr.

Nagel, Stuart S. & Dunn, William N., eds. Policy Theory & Evaluation Concepts, Knowledge, Causes & Norms, 258. LC 89-25784. (Contributions in Political Science Ser.: No. 258). 256p. 1990. 75.00 (0-313-27356-1, NPT/, Greenwood Pr) Greenwood.

Nagel, Stuart S. & Mills, Miriam. Developing Nations & Super-Optimum Policy Analysis. (Political Science). 275p. 1999. text 45.95 (0-8304-1274-3) Thomson Learn.

Nagel, Stuart S. & Mills, Miriam K. Multi-Criteria Methods in Alternative Dispute Resolution: With Microcomputer Software Applications. LC 90-8416. 288p. 1990. 77.50 (0-89930-520-2, NMC, Quorum Bks) Greenwood.

Nagel, Stuart S. & Mills, Miriam K., eds. Public Policy in China, 318. LC 92-37519. (Contributions in Political Science Ser.: No. 318). 176p. 1993. 62.95 (0-313-28848-8, GM8848) Greenwood.

— Systematic Analysis in Dispute Resolution. LC 90-22125. 304p. 1991. 75.00 (0-89930-623-3, NSA, Quorum Bks) Greenwood.

Nagel, Stuart S. & Munshaw, Nancy, eds. Policy Studies Personnel Directory. 1979. pap. 15.00 (0-918592-33-X) Pol Studies.

***Nagel, Stuart S. & Nam, Julian.** Promoting Democracy: Via Political & Social Policy. LC 00-34800. 144p. 2000. 60.00 (0-7391-0165-X) Lxngtn Bks.

— Promoting Peace: Via Legal & International Policy. LC 00-34801. 256p. 2000. 60.00 (0-7391-0164-1) Lxngtn Bks.

— Promoting Prosperity: Via Economic & Technology Policy. LC 00-34795. 176p. 2000. 60.00 (0-7391-0163-3) Lxngtn Bks.

Nagel, Stuart S. & Neef, Marian. Operations Research Methods. LC 76-25693. (Quantitative Applications in the Social Sciences Ser.: Vol. 2). 76p. 1976. pap. 10.95 (0-8039-0651-X) Sage.

— Policy Studies Directory. 1976. pap. 15.00 (0-918592-18-6) Pol Studies.

— Political Science Utilization Directory. 1975. pap. 15.00 (0-918592-19-4) Pol Studies.

Nagel, Stuart S. & Neef, Marian, eds. Policy Grants Directory. 1977. pap. 15.00 (0-918592-25-9) Pol Studies.

— Policy Research Centers Directory. 1978. pap. 15.00 (0-918592-30-5) Pol Studies.

Nagel, Stuart S., jt. ed. see Calista, Donald J.

Nagel, Stuart S., jt. ed. see Clarke, Duncan L.

Nagel, Stuart S., jt. ed. see Dunn, William.

Nagel, Stuart S., jt. ed. see Edward, George C.

Nagel, Stuart S., jt. ed. see Eyestone, Robert.

Nagel, Stuart S., jt. ed. see Garson, G. David.

Nagel, Stuart S., jt. ed. see Holzer, Marc.

Nagel, Stuart S., ed. see Jones, L. R. & Bixler, Glenn C.

Nagel, Stuart S., jt. ed. see Judd, Dennis R.

Nagel, Stuart S., jt. ed. see Mills, Miriam K.

Nagel, Stuart S., jt. ed. see Rogers, Harrell R., Jr.

Nagel, Susan. The Influence of the Novels of Jean Giraudoux on the Hispanic Language Novels of the 1920s-1930s. LC 90-55650. 152p. 1991. 32.50 (0-8387-5201-2) Bucknell U Pr.

Nagel, Suzanne R., ed. see Materials Research Society Staff.

Nagel, Thomas. Equality & Partiality. 208p. 1991. text 45.00 (0-19-506967-6) OUP.

— Equality & Partiality. 208p. 1995. pap. text 17.95 (0-19-509839-0) OUP.

— The Last Word. 160p. 1997. 22.00 (0-19-510834-5) OUP.

— Mortal Questions. (Canto Book Ser.). (Illus.). 229p. (C). 1991. pap. 12.95 (0-521-40676-5) Cambridge U Pr.

— Other Minds: Critical Essays, 1969-1994. 240p. 1995. text 35.00 (0-19-509008-X) OUP.

— Other Minds: Critical Essays 1969-1994. 229p. 1999. pap. 17.95 (0-19-513246-7) OUP.

— The Possibility of Altruism. LC 78-4323. 150p. 1979. pap. text 13.95 (0-691-02002-7, Pub. by Princeton U Pr) Cal Prin Full Svc.

— The View from Nowhere. 256p. 1989. reprint ed. pap. text 18.95 (0-19-505644-2) OUP.

— What Does It All Mean? A Very Short Introduction to Philosophy. 112p. 1987. text 25.00 (0-19-505292-7); pap. text 14.95 (0-19-505216-1) OUP.

Nagel, Thomas, ed. Experimental & Theoretical Studies of Consciousness - Symposium No. 174. (CIBA Foundation Symposium Ser.: No. 174). 326p. 1993. 135.00 (0-471-93866-1) Wiley.

Nagel, Thomas & Scanlon, Thomas. Rights & Wrongs of Abortion. (Philosophy & Public Affairs Reader Ser.). 127p. 1960. pap. text 12.95 (0-691-01979-7, Pub. by Princeton U Pr) Cal Prin Full Svc.

***Nagel, Tilman.** The History of Islamic Theology: From Muhammad to the Present. Lewis, Bernard & Hamori, Andras, eds. Thornton, Thomas, tr. from GER. LC 99-49828. (Princeton Series on the Middle East).Tr. of Geschichle der Islamischen Theologie. 420p. (C). 1999. text 89.95 (1-55876-202-7) Wiener Pubs Inc.

— The History of Islamic Theology: From Muhammad to the Present. Thornton, Thomas, tr. from GER. LC 99-49828 (Princeton Series on the Middle East).Tr. of Geschichle der Islamischen Theologie. 420p. 1999. pap. text 28.95 (1-55876-203-5) Wiener Pubs Inc.

Nagel, Walter H. & Ndyajunwoha, Gaston Z. Export Marketing Handbook. LC 87-38186. 149p. 1988. 52.95 (0-275-92949-3, C2949, Praeger Pubs) Greenwood.

Nagel, Walter H., et al. Leading U. S. Supreme Court Tax Cases: Official Syllabi, Notes, & Indices. LC 94-41031. 1994. write for info. (1-55871-312-3) Tax Mgmt.

Nagele, Rainer. Echoes of Translation: Reading Between Texts. LC 96-47331. 120p. 1997. text 29.95 (0-8018-5545-4) Johns Hopkins.

— Reading after Freud: Essays on Goethe, Holderlin, Habermas, Nietzsche, Brecht, Celan, & Freud. LC 86-20730. 216p. 1987. text 57.50 (0-231-06286-9) Col U Pr.

— Theater, Theory, Speculation: Walter Benjamin & the Scenes of Modernity. LC 90-45358. 208p. 1991. text 42.00 (0-8018-4123-2) Johns Hopkins.

Nagele, Rainer, ed. Benjamin's Ground: New Readings of Walter Benjamin. LC 88-14300. (Culture of Jewish Modernity Ser.: No. 17). 190p. reprint ed. pap. 58.90 (0-608-10538-4, 2071158) Bks Demand.

Nageleisen, John A. Charity for the Suffering Souls. LC 82-83797. 375p. 1994. reprint ed. pap. 16.50 (0-89555-200-0) TAN Bks Pubs.

Nagelfell, Karl. North American Indian Chiefs. 64p. 1995. 16.95 (1-57215-055-6) World Pubns.

Nagelhout. Review of Nurse Anesthesiology. LC 99-19474. 1999. pap. text 49.95 (0-7216-7531-X, W B Saunders Co) Harcrt Hlth Sci Grp.

Nagelhout, John J. & Zaglaniczny, Karen L. Handbook of Nurse Anesthesia. Connor, Maura, ed. LC 96-20547. (Illus.). 445p. 1997. pap. text 36.95 (0-7216-6694-9, W B Saunders Co) Harcrt Hlth Sci Grp.

— Nurse Anesthesia: Clinical Textbook. Connor, Maura, ed. (Illus.). 1375p. 1996. pap. text 130.00 (*0-7216-6479-2*, W B Saunders Co) Harcrt Hlth Sci Grp.

Nagell, Trygve. Introduction to Number Theory. 309p. 1981. 19.95 (*0-8284-0163-2*) Chelsea Pub.

Nagelschmidt, Joseph S., ed. The Public Affairs Handbook. LC 82-6710. 319p. reprint ed. pap. 98.90 (*0-608-12449-4*, 205575000036) Bks Demand.

***Nagelson, Betsy.** Fit over 40 for Dummies. (Illus.). 384p. 2000. pap. 19.99 (*0-7645-5305-4*) IDG Bks.

Nagem, Monique F., tr. see Chawaf, Chantal.

Nagem, Monique F., tr. see Rolin, Dominique.

Nagenda, John. The Seasons of Thomas Tebo. (African Writers Ser.). 156p. (Orig.). (C). 1986. pap. 8.95 (*0-435-90824-3*, 90824) Heinemann.

Nagendra, K. N., jt. ed. see Stenflo, Jan O.

***Nagendran, T.** A Moral Guide for the Teenagers of the Next Millennium. 35p. 1999. pap. 9.95 (*0-7414-0116-9*) Buy Books.

Nagengast, Bernard, jt. auth. see Kamin, John V.

Nager, George T. Pathology of the Ear & Temporal Bone. LC 93-27739. (Illus.). 1408p. 1993. 295.00 (*0-683-63049-0*) Lppncott W & W.

Nager, Larry. Memphis Beat. LC 97-47305. 1998. text 23.95 (*0-312-15587-5*) St Martin.

Nager, Nancy & Shapiro, Edna K., eds. Revisiting a Progressive Pedagogy: The Developmental-Interaction Approach. LC 99-39477. (C). 2000. pap. text 22.95 (*0-7914-4468-6*) State U NY Pr.

— Revisiting a Progressive Pedagogy: The Developmental-Interaction Approach. LC 99-39477. (C). 2000. text 68.50 (*0-7914-4467-8*) State U NY Pr.

Nager, Norman R. & Allen, T. Harrell. Public Relations: Management by Objectives. (Illus.). 416p. (C). 1991. reprint ed. pap. text 26.50 (*0-8191-8330-X*) U Pr of Amer.

Nager, Norman R. & Truitt, Richard H. Strategic Public Relations Counseling: Models from the Counselors Academy. 392p. (C). 1991. reprint ed. pap. 34.50 (*0-8191-8331-8*) U Pr of Amer.

Nager, Sandra, ed. see Millinary Institute Staff.

Nagera, Humberto. Early Childhood Disturbances, the Infantile Neurosis, & the Adult Disturbances. LC 66-17526. (Psychoanalytic Study of the Child Monographs: No. 2). 96p. 1966. 27.50 (*0-8236-1520-0*) Intl Univs Pr.

— Obsessional Neuroses: Developmental Psychopathology. LC 84-45012. 240p. 1993. pap. 40.00 (*1-56821-151-1*) Aronson.

— Vincent Van Gogh. (Illus.). 182p. 1990. pap. 24.95 (*0-8236-8326-5*, BN 26741) Intl Univs Pr.

Nagera, Humberto, ed. Basic Psychoanalytic Concepts on Metapsychology, Conflicts, Anxiety & Other Subjects. 240p. 1990. reprint ed. pap. text 28.00 (*0-9507146-6-6*, Pub. by H Karnac Bks Ltd) Other Pr LLC.

— Basic Psychoanalytic Concepts on the Libido Theory. 194p. 1990. reprint ed. pap. text 26.00 (*0-9507146-3-1*, Pub. by H Karnac Bks Ltd) Other Pr LLC.

— Basic Psychoanalytic Concepts on the Theory of Dreams, Vol. II. 121p. 1990. reprint ed. pap. text 25.00 (*0-9507146-4-X*, Pub. by H Karnac Bks Ltd) Other Pr LLC.

— Basic Psychoanalytic Concepts on the Theory of Instincts. 212p. 1990. reprint ed. pap. text 25.00 (*0-9507146-5-8*, Pub. by H Karnac Bks Ltd) Other Pr LLC.

Nagesh Kumar. Foreign Direct Investment & Technology Transfer: Globalization & the Developing World. LC 98-11117. (Intech Series in New Technology & Development). (Illus.). 248p. (C). 1998. 90.00 (*0-415-19111-4*) Routledge.

Nagesh Kumar & Siddharthan, N. S. Technology, Market Structure, & Internationalization: Issues & Policies for Developing Countries. LC 97-7415. 176p. (C). 1997. 75.00 (*0-415-16925-9*) Routledge.

Nageswara Rao, N. Studies in Urban Public Sector, India. 1985. 30.00 (*0-8364-1386-5*, Pub. by Ashish Pub Hse) S Asia.

Nageswara Rao, R. C., jt. auth. see Wright, G. C.

Naggar. Dictionnaire des Photographes. rev. ed. (FRE.). 567p. 1982. 175.00 (*0-8288-7909-5*, 8185243077) Fr & Eur.

Naggar, Carole & Ritchin, Fred. Mexico Through Foreign Eyes: Visto por Ojos Extranjeros, 1850-1990. (Illus.). 320p. 1996. pap. 35.00 (*0-393-31491-X*, Norton Paperbks) Norton.

Naggar, David. Beyond Blind Faith: A Thinking Person's Guide to Meaning & Inner Peace. 1999. pap. text 10.95 (*1-57746-560-1*) DaJe Pubng.

***Naggar, David.** The Music Business (Explained in Plain English) What Every Artist & Songwriter Should Know to Avoid Getting Ripped Off! 2nd ed. 136p. 2000. pap. 12.95 (*1-57746-570-9*, Pub. by DaJe Pubng) SCB Distributors.

Naggar, David & Brandstetter, Jeffrey D. The Music Business (Explained in Plain English) What Every Artist & Songwriter Should Know to Avoid Getting Ripped Off! 122p. 1995. pap. 12.95 (*0-9648709-0-8*) DaJe Pubng.

Naggar, Said El, see El Naggar, Said, ed.

Nagi, B. S. Child Marriage in India: A Study of Its Differential Patterns in Rajasthan. (C). 1993. 12.50 (*81-7099-460-8*, Pub. by Mittal Pubs Dist) S Asia.

Nagi Condo. Condos Managing Diversity. (C). Date not set. pap. 24.76 (*0-395-76930-2*) HM.

— Managing Diversity. (C). Date not set. pap. 11.96 (*0-395-76931-0*) HM.

Nagi, Dennis L. The Albanian-American Odyssey: A Pilot Study of the Albanian Community of Boston, Massachusetts. LC 87-45791. (Immigrant Communities & Ethnic Minorities in the U. S. & Canada Ser.: No. 26). 1988. 37.50 (*0-404-19436-2*) AMS Pr.

Nagi, Dinesh K., jt. auth. see Burr, William A.

Nagi, Mohamad, et al. Optimization of Highway Concrete Technology. 275p. (C). 1994. pap. text 15.00 (*0-309-05751-5*, SHRP-C-373) SHRP.

Nagi, R. ASEAN: The Association of South-East Asian Nations 20 Years. (C). 1988. 28.50 (*81-7095-008-2*, Pub. by Lancer India) S Asia.

— Big Powers & South-East Asian Security. xiv, 220p. 1986. 12.50 (*0-685-67632-3*, Pub. by Lancer India) Nataraj Bks.

Nagi, Saad Z. Child Maltreatment in the United States: A Challenge to Social Institutions. LC 77-22121. 1977. text 52.50 (*0-231-04394-5*) Col U Pr.

Nagin, Paul A., jt. auth. see Impagliazzo, John.

Naginski, Isabelle H. George Sand: Writing for Her Life. LC 90-42140. 280p. (C). 1991. text 40.00 (*0-8135-1640-4*) Rutgers U Pr.

— George Sand: Writing for Her Life. 280p. (C). 1994. reprint ed. pap. text 19.00 (*0-8135-1674-9*) Rutgers U Pr.

Nagirnev & Poutanban, J. Astrophysics & Space Physics Reviews Vol. 9, Pt. 1: Single Compton Scattering, Vol. 9. (Astrophysics & Space Physics Reviews Ser.). 80p. 1994. pap. text 129.00 (*3-7186-5497-0*) Gordon & Breach.

Nagl, A., et al. Nuclear Pion Photoproduction. (Tracts in Modern Physics Ser.: Vol. 120). viii, 174p. 1991. 107.95 (*0-387-50671-3*) Spr-Verlag.

Nagl-Docekal, Herta, jt. auth. see Klinger, Cornelia.

Nagl, M., ed. Building Tightly Integrated Software Development Environments Vol. IX: The IPSEN Approach. LC 96-37808. (Lecture Notes in Computer Science Ser.: Vol. 1170). 709p. 1996. pap. 106.00 (*3-540-61985-2*) Spr-Verlag.

— Graph-Theoretic Concepts in Computer Science. (Lecture Notes in Computer Science Ser.: Vol. 411). vii, 374p. 1990. 38.60 (*0-387-52292-1*) Spr-Verlag.

— Graph-Theoretic Concepts in Computer Science: Twenty-First International Workshop, WG'95, Aachen, Germany, June 20-22, 1995. Proceedings. (Lecture Notes in Computer Science Ser.: Vol.107). 403p. 1995. 68.00 (*3-540-60618-1*) Spr-Verlag.

Nagla, B. K. Development & Transformation: Themes & Variations in Indian Society. (C). 1993. 36.00 (*81-7033-189-7*, Pub. by Rawat Pubns) S Asia.

— Women Crime & Law. (C). 1991. 14.00 (*0-685-66147-4*, Pub. by Rawat Pubns) S Asia.

Nagle. College Writing. 1999. 17.70 (*0-07-431522-6*) McGraw.

— Differential Equations. 5th ed. LC 99-17732. 752p. (C). 1999. 96.00 (*0-201-33868-8*) Addison-Wesley.

***Nagle.** Differential Equations & Boundary Value Problems. 3rd ed. LC 99-14104. 928p. (C). 1999. 103.00 (*0-201-33867-X*) Addison-Wesley.

Nagle, Ami. Dollars & Sense: A Guide to Spending on Children & Families in Illinois. (C). 1995. pap. 15.00 (*1-886008-01-9*) Voices IL Chdrn.

— Illinois Kids Count: Learning Begins at Birth. (Illus.). 56p. 1998. pap. 15.00 (*1-886008-05-1*) Voices IL Chdrn.

Nagle, Ami & Jacobs, Victoria. Illinois Kids Count 1995: Building the Future. 65p. (C). pap. 15.00 (*1-886008-02-7*) Voices IL Chdrn.

Nagle, Ami & Richards, Katie. Illinois Kids Count: Rise to the Challenge. (Illus.). 65p. (Orig.). 1997. pap. 15.00 (*1-886008-03-5*) Voices IL Chdrn.

Nagle, Ami, et al. Illinois Kids Count, 1994: Raising the Grade. (Orig.). 1994. pap. 15.00 (*1-886008-00-0*) Voices IL Chdrn.

Nagle, Barbara T., jt. auth. see Hitner, Henry.

Nagle, Bernard A. & Pascarella, Perry. Leveraging People & Profit: The Hard Work of Soft Management. LC 97-14579. 224p. 1997. pap. text 17.95 (*0-7506-9961-2*) Buttrwrth-Heinemann.

Nagle, Betty R. Ovid Fasti, Vol. V. (Latin Commentaries Ser.). 96p. (Orig.). (C). 1996. pap. text 6.00 (*0-929524-86-1*) Bryn Mawr Commentaries.

— Ovid's Fasti: Roman Holidays. LC 94-21660. Orig. Title: Fasti. (ENG.). 224p. 1995. pap. 8.95 (*0-253-20933-1*) Ind U Pr.

Nagle, Betty R., tr. & notes see Ovid.

Nagle, D. Brendan. The Ancient World: A Social & Cultural History. 4th ed. LC 98-18331. 450p. (C). 1998. pap. 48.00 (*0-13-080741-9*) P-H.

Nagle, D. Brendan, jt. ed. see Burstein, Stanley M.

Nagle, Elizabeth N. Legacy of Grace. LC 85-96921. 1986. 10.00 (*0-87212-191-7*) Libra.

Nagle, Evelyn M. Winning with Astrology. 18p. 1988. 6.00 (*0-86690-358-5*, N2834-014) Am Fed Astrologers.

Nagle, Francis J., et al. Living Fit. 300p. (C). 1988. pap. text 23.75 (*0-8053-8180-5*) Benjamin-Cummings.

***Nagle, Garrett.** South Africa. LC 98-52756. (Country Studies Ser.). 1999. 27.07 (*1-57572-896-6*) Heinemann Lib.

***Nagle, Garrett & Spencer, Kris.** Geographical Enquiries: Skills & Techniques for Geography. 2nd ed. (Illus.). 128p. 2000. pap. 22.50 (*0-7487-5318-4*, Pub. by S Thornes Pubs) Trans-Atl Phila.

Nagle, Geraldine. The Arts: World Themes. 368p. (C). 1993. text. write for info. (*0-697-12048-1*) Brown & Benchmark.

Nagle, J. F. Collins, the Courts & the Colony: Law & Society in Colonial New South Wales 1788-1796. LC 96-148219. 337p. 1996. pap. 34.95 (*0-86840-127-7*, Pub. by New South Wales Univ Pr) Intl Spec Bk.

Nagle, Jack. Power Pattern Offenses for Winning Basketball. LC 85-32072. 192p. (C). 1986. 27.95 (*0-13-687708-7*, Parker Publishing Co) P-H.

Nagle, James F. A History of Government Contracting. 575p. 1992. pap. 35.00 (*0-935165-21-5*) GWU Gov Contracts.

***Nagle, James F.** How to Review Federal Government Solicitations & Contracts & Research Federal Contract Law. LC 00-32756. 2000. write for info. (*1-57073-799-1*) Amer Bar Assn.

Nagle, James F. Recovering Attorneys & Consultants Fees: Special Guidance in Terminations for Convenience for Contractors. large type ed. 23p. 1995. pap. 41.50 (*1-56726-061-6*) Mgmt Concepts.

Nagle, James J. Genitourinary Surgery. (Perioperative Nursing Ser.). (Illus.). 400p. (C). (gr. 13). 1997. text 54.95 (*0-8151-7029-7*, 27474) Mosby Inc.

Nagle, Jill. Claiming the Virgin. LC 96-48791. 240p. (C). 1997. pap. 19.99 (*0-415-91567-8*) Routledge.

— Claiming the Virgin. LC 96-48791. 240p. (C). 1997. 75.00 (*0-415-91566-X*) Routledge.

Nagle, Jill, ed. Whore & Other Feminists. LC 96-36045. 256p. (C). 1997. 80.00 (*0-415-91821-9*) Routledge.

— Whores & Other Feminists. LC 96-36045. 256p. 1997. pap. 19.99 (*0-415-91822-7*) Routledge.

Nagle, Joan G. Handbook for Preparing Engineering Documents: From Concept to Completion. 392p. 1995. 49.95 (*0-7803-1165-5*, PC4515); pap. 39.95 (*0-7803-1097-7*, PP4515) Inst Electrical.

Nagle, John. Sheet Metalwork. LC 79-730773. 1977. student ed. 7.00 (*0-8064-0231-8*, 507) Bergwall.

— Woodworking Hand Tools Explained. LC 78-730852. 1979. student ed. 7.00 (*0-8064-0263-6*, 703) Bergwall.

Nagle, John C. The Meaning of the Prohibition on Taking An Endangered Species. LC 99-161327. (Briefly--Perspectives on Legislation, Regulation, & Litigation Ser.). 33p. 1998. write for info. (*0-937299-74-X*) Natl Legal Ctr Pub Interest.

Nagle, John D. Confessions from the Left: On the Pain, Necessity, & Joys of Political Renewal. (Major Concepts in Politics & Political Theory Ser.: Vol. 15). IX, 318p. (C). 1998. pap. text 29.95 (*0-8204-3913-4*) P Lang Pubng.

— The National Democratic Party: Right Radicalism in the Federal Republic of Germany. LC 78-101340. 231p. reprint ed. pap. 71.70 (*0-608-15846-1*, 203144300074) Bks Demand.

Nagle-Lechman, Barbara A. Conflict & Resolution. LC 97-20103. 150p. 1997. pap. text 30.95 (*1-56706-478-7*) Aspen Law.

Nagle, P. G. Glorieta Pass. LC 98-23447. 384p. 1999. 24.95 (*0-312-86548-1*, Pub. by Forge NYC) St Martin.

***Nagle, P. G.** Glorietta Pass. 512p. 2000. mass mkt. 6.99 (*0-8125-4049-2*, Pub. by Forge NYC) St Martin.

— The Guns for Valverde. pap. 15.95 (*0-312-87602-5*) St Martin.

— The Guns of Valverde. 384p. 2000. 25.95 (*0-312-86549-X*) Forge NYC.

Nagle, P. Michael. Guide to Annual Meeting, Special Meetings, & Elections. (GAP Reports: Vol. 21). (C). 1992. pap. 17.50 (*0-944715-22-2*) CAI.

— Guide to Annual Meetings, Special Meetings & Elections No. 21: GAP Reports. 2nd ed. 52p. (C). 1996. pap. 17.50 (*0-944715-53-2*) CAI.

Nagle, P. Michael, jt. auth. see Schenk, Anita H.

Nagle, R. Kent. Differential Equations. 3rd rev. ed. 750p. (C). 1994. teacher ed. 23.66 (*0-8053-5057-8*) Addison-Wesley.

— Fundamentals of Differential Equations. 3rd rev. ed. Moller, Lisa, ed. 750p. (C). 1993. text 83.44 (*0-8053-5056-X*) Addison-Wesley.

— Fundamentals of Differential Equations. 4th ed. (C). 1995. text. write for info. (*0-201-46151-X*) Addison-Wesley.

— Fundamentals of Differential Equations. 4th ed. 416p. (C). 1996. pap. text, student ed. 25.00 (*0-201-80877-3*) Addison-Wesley.

***Nagle, R. Kent.** Fundamentals of Differential Equations. 5th ed. (C). 1999. 5.25 hd. write for info. (*0-201-70439-0*) Addison-Wesley.

Nagle, R. Kent. Fundamentals of Differential Equations Utility Software. 4th ed. 1996. 31.00 (*0-201-82688-7*) Addison-Wesley.

— Fundamentals of Differential Equations with Linear Algebra. (C). 1996. text. write for info. (*0-201-54234-X*) Addison-Wesley.

Nagle, R. Kent & Saff, Edward B. Fundamentals of Differential Equations. 2nd ed. (Illus.). 820p. (C). 1989. text 60.25 (*0-8053-0254-9*); pap. text 10.75 (*0-8053-0256-5*) Addison-Wesley.

— Fundamentals of Differential Equations. 4th ed. LC 95-9799. 704p. (C). 1995. text 92.00 (*0-201-80875-7*) Addison-Wesley.

— Fundamentals of Differential Equations & Boundary Value Problems. 2nd ed. LC 95-10162. 912p. (C). 1995. text 92.00 (*0-201-80879-X*) Addison-Wesley.

— Fundamentals of Differential Equations with Boundary Value Problems. (Illus.). 864p. (C). 1992. write for info. (*0-318-69246-5*) Addison-Wesley.

Nagle, S. D., jt. auth. see Colclaser, R. A.

Nagle, Ted & Zinovich, Jordan. The Prospector: North of Sixty. 1989. pap. 14.95 (*0-919433-67-7*) Lone Pine.

Nagle, Thomas T. The Strategy & Tactics of Pricing: A Guide to Profitable Decision Making (CollegeVersion) 2nd ed. LC 94-15812. 400p. (C). 1994. 66.67 (*0-13-669060-2*) P-H.

Nagle, Thomas T., jt. auth. see Holden, Reed K.

Nagle, Timothy E. & Pfeiffer, Heather D., eds. Conceptual Structures - Theory & Implementation: Proceedings of the Seventh Annual Workshop, Las Cruces, New Mexico, U. S. A., July 1992. LC 93-39736. (Lecture Notes in Computer Science, Lecture Notes in Artificial Intelligence Ser.: Vol. 754). 1993. 54.00 (*0-387-57454-9*) Spr-Verlag.

Nagle, Troy, jt. auth. see Phillips, Charles L.

Naglee, David I. From Everlasting to Everlasting: John Wesley on Eternity & Time, 2 vols., 1. LC 90-47316. (American University Studies: Theology & Religion: Ser. VII, Vols. 65 & 66). 651p. (C). 1992. text 103.80 (*0-8204-1113-2*) P Lang Pubng.

— Sons of Eli. (Illus.). 400p. 1993. pap. 14.95 (*0-938991-82-5*) Colonial Pr AL.

Nagler, A. M. Theatre Festivals of the Medici, 1539-1637. LC 76-8447. (Music Reprint Ser.). 190p. 1976. reprint ed. lib. bdg. 32.50 (*0-306-70779-9*) Da Capo.

Nagler, Adam, jt. auth. see Nagler, Mark.

Nagler, Alois M. The Medieval Religious Stage: Shapes & Phantoms. Schoolfield, George C., tr. LC 75-43328. (Illus.). 120p. reprint ed. pap. 37.20 (*0-8357-8220-4*, 203384000087) Bks Demand.

— Source Book in Theatrical History. Orig. Title: Sources of Theatrical History. (Illus.). 611p. 1959. pap. 12.95 (*0-486-20515-0*) Dover.

Nagler, Barney, jt. auth. see Brenner, Teddy.

Nagler, Eric P. Learning C++ A Hands-On Approach. Mixter, ed. LC 93-16017. 650p. (C). 1994. pap. text 41.50 (*0-314-02464-6*) West Pub.

— Learning C++ A Hands-On Approach. 2nd ed. LC 96-20162. 550p. (C). 1999. mass mkt. 55.95 (*0-314-20039-8*) West Pub.

Nagler, Gillian, jt. ed. see Lafo, Rachel Rosenfield.

Nagler, Harris M., jt. auth. see Thomas, Anthony J., Jr.

Nagler, Harris M., jt. ed. see Whitehead, E. Douglas.

Nagler, Jorg, jt. ed. see Forster, Stig.

Nagler, Jorg, jt. ed. see Hoerder, Dirk.

Nagler, Mark, ed. Perspectives on Disability: Text & Readings on Disability. 2nd ed. 460p. (C). 1993. text 45.00 (*0-9627640-3-5*) Hlth Mrkts Res.

Nagler, Mark & Nagler, Adam. What's Stopping You? Living Successfully with a Disability. 1999. pap. text 15.95 (*0-7737-6027-X*) Genl Dist Srvs.

— Yes You Can! A Guide for Parents with Disabilities. LC 99-182837. 224p. 1997. pap. 13.95 (*0-7737-5866-6*) Stoddart Publ.

***Nagler, Michael.** The Steps of Nonviolence. Deats, Richard, ed. (Illus.). 36p. 1999. pap. 4.50 (*0-911810-83-8*, Fellwship Pubns) Fellowship of Recon.

Nagler, Michael & Swanson, William, eds. Stolen Moments: Stories of Men, Women & Desire. LC 95-69093. 325p. (Orig.). (C). 1998. pap. 14.50 (*0-88739-112-5*) Creat Arts Bk.

***Nagler, Michael N.** Is There No Other Way? The Search for a Nonviolent Future. (Illus.). 448p. 2000. pap. 19.95 (*1-893163-16-4*) Berkeley Hills.

Nagler, Monte. How to Improve Your Photographic Vision. Farrar, Bev, ed. 1988. pap. 14.95 (*0-9620829-1-0*) Suburb Comns.

— How to Improve Your Photographic Vision. limited ed. Farrar, Bev, ed. 1988. 250.00 (*0-9620829-0-2*) Suburb Comns.

Nagler, Norbert. Fruhkatholizismus: Zur Methodologie Einer Kritischen Debatte. (Regensburger Studien Zur Theologie Ser.: Bd. 43). (GER.). X, 209p. 1994. 35.95 (*3-631-46634-X*) P Lang Pubng.

Nagler, Richard. Oakland Rhapsody: The Secret Soul of an American Downtown. (Illus.). 112p. (Orig.). (C). 1995. 35.00 (*1-55643-197-X*); pap. 22.95 (*1-55643-196-1*) North Atlantic.

Naglieri, Jack A. The Essentials of CAS Assessment. LC 98-40739. (Essentials of Psychological Assessment Ser.). 205p. 1999. pap. 29.95 (*0-471-29015-7*) Wiley.

Naglin. Family Fraud. 1998. 26.00 (*0-684-81226-6*) S&S Trade.

Nagodawithana, Tilak W. Savory Flavors. (Illus.). 480p. (C). 1995. write for info. (*0-9646172-3-4*) Esteekay Assocs.

Nagodawithana, Tilak W. & Reed, Gerald, eds. Commercial Fermentations & Nutritional Needs of Their Microorganisms. 500p. (C). 1998. write for info. (*0-9646172-1-8*) Esteekay Assocs.

Nagodawithana, Tilak W., jt. ed. see Reed, Gerald.

Nagorny, G. W. & Stutchfield, R. A. Gear Noise - The Generation of Rotational Harmonic Frequencies in Marine Propulsion Gears. (Technical Papers: Vol. P299.06A). (Illus.). 41p. 1981. pap. text 30.00 (*1-55589-384-8*) AGMA.

Nagorsen, D. W. & Peterson, R. L. Mammal Collectors' Manual. (Illus.). 80p. pap. 16.57 (*0-88854-255-0*) Brill Academic Pubs.

Nagorsen, David W. Opossums, Shrews, & Moles of British Columbia. LC 97-124283. (Royal British Columbia Museum Handbook Ser.). (Illus.). 176p. 1996. pap. 24.95 (*0-7748-0563-3*) U of Wash Pr.

Nagorsen, David W. & Brigham, R. Mark. Bats of British Columbia. LC 94-153386. (Mammals of British Columbia Ser.: Vol. 1). (Illus.). 176p. 1993. pap. 19.95 (*0-7748-0482-3*) U of Wash Pr.

***Nagorski, E.** Face Painting. (Golden Bks.). (Illus.). 24p. (ps-3). 2000. pap. 7.99 (*0-307-30477-9*) Gldn Bks Pub Co.

***Nagorski, Eva.** Poky's Bathtime Adventure. (Illus.). (J). 2000. 7.99 (*0-307-12199-2*) Gldn Bks Pub Co.

Nagourney, Adam, jt. auth. see Clendinen, Dudley.

Nagpal, Arvind, jt. auth. see Kasturi, Rajeev.

Nagpal, B. N., jt. auth. see Sharma, V. P.

Nagpal, Kavita, jt. auth. see Thiyam, Ratan.

Nagpal, R. & Sell, H. Assessment of Subjective Well-Being: The Subjective Well-Being Inventory (SUBI) (SEARO Regional Health Papers: No. 24). v, 37p. 1993. pap. text 6.30 (*92-9022-193-3*, 1580024) World Health.

— Subjective Well-Being. (SEARO Regional Health Papers: No. 7). 161p. 1985. pap. text 10.00 (*92-9022-176-3*, 1580007) World Health.

Nagpal, R. C. Modern Hindu Law. (HIN.). 815p. 1984. 225.00 (*0-7855-1365-5*) St Mut.

N

An Asterisk (*) at the beginning of an entry indicates that the title is appearing for the first time.

Nagpal, Tanvi & Foltz, Camilla, eds. Choosing Our Future: Visions of a Sustainable World. LC 95-16459. 181p. 1995. 25.00 (*1-56973-028-8*) World Resources Inst.

Nagpal, Tanvi, jt. ed. see Shah, Jitendra J.

Nagpaul, Hans. Modernization & Urbanization in India. 1996. 34.00 (*0-614-25276-8*, Pub. by Rawat Pubns) S Asia.

Nagrin, Daniel. Dance & the Specific Image: Improvisation. (Illus.). 256p. (C). 1993. pap. 19.95 (*0-8229-5520-2*); text 49.95 (*0-8229-3776-X*) U of Pittsburgh Pr.

— How to Dance Forever: Surviving Against the Odds. Williams, Jennifer, ed. LC 88-1421. (Illus.). 320p. 1988. pap. 14.95 (*0-688-07479-0*, Quil) HarperTrade.

— The Six Questions: Acting Techniques for Dance Performance. LC 96-51277. (Illus.). 221p. 1997. pap. 19.95 (*0-8229-5624-1*); text 45.00 (*0-8229-3974-6*) U of Pittsburgh Pr.

Nagrodskaia, E. The Wrath of Dionysus: A Novel. McReynolds, Louise, ed. & tr. by. from RUS. LC 97-445. 1997. pap. 14.95 (*0-253-21132-8*) Ind U Pr.

Nagrodskaia, Evdokia. Wrath of Dionysus. 1997. pap. text 14.95 (*0-253-22132-3*) Ind U Pr.

— The Wrath of Dionysus: A Novel. McReynolds, Louise, ed. & tr. by. from RUS. LC 97-445. 1997. 29.95 (*0-253-33304-0*) Ind U Pr.

Nagtegaal, Luc. Riding the Dutch Tiger: The Dutch East Indies Company & the Northeast Coast of Java, 1680-1743. (KITLV Verhandelingen Ser.: No. 171). (Illus.). 257p. (Orig.). 1996. pap. 37.00 (*90-6718-103-X*, Pub. by KITLV Pr) Cellar.

Naguib, Mohammed. Egypt's Destiny: A Personal Statement by Mohammed Naguib. LC 84-1516. 256p. 1984. reprint ed. lib. bdg. 65.00 (*0-313-24433-2*, NAED/, Greenwood Pr) Greenwood.

Nagumo, Mitio. Collected Papers. Yamaguti, Masaya et al, eds. LC 93-9561. (ENG, FRE & GER.). 1993. 159.00 (*0-387-70112-5*) Spr-Verlag.

Nagurney, Anna. Network Economics: A Variational Inequality Approach. LC 92-36524. (Advances in Computational Economics Ser.). 384p. (C). 1992. lib. bdg. 148.50 (*0-7923-9293-0*) Kluwer Academic.

— Network Economics: A Variational Inequality Approach. LC 98-45144. 5p. 1999. 150.00 (*0-7923-8350-8*) Kluwer Academic.

Nagurney, Anna & Siokos, Stavros. Financial Networks: Statics & Dynamics. LC 97-26140. (Advances in Spatial Science Ser.). 1997. text. write for info. (*3-540-63116-X*) Spr-Verlag.

Nagurney, Anna & Zhang, Ding. Projected Dynamical Systems & Variational Inequalities with Applications. (International Series in Operations Research & Management Science: Vol. 2). 320p. (C). 1995. lib. bdg. 121.00 (*0-7923-9637-5*) Kluwer Academic.

Nagurny, Kyle, ed. see Junior League of Harrisburg Staff.

Nagurny, Kyle D. The Pennsylvania Heritage Cookbook: A Cook's Tour of Keystone Cultures, Customs, & Celebrations. LC 97-32175. (PA Traveler's Guide Ser.). (Illus.). 224p. 1998. pap. 16.95 (*0-8117-2496-4*) Stackpole.

Nagus, John. Tense: New Work by Leslie Bellavance. (Illus.). 15p. (Orig.). 1994. pap. 5.00 (*0-944110-41-X*) Milwauk Art Mus.

Nagy. Principles of Cost Accounting. 10th ed. (AB - Accounting Principles Ser.). (C). 1995. pap. 49.95 (*0-538-84403-5*) S-W Pub.

— Principles of Cost Accounting, Study Guide & Working Papers. 10th ed. (AB - Accounting Principles Ser.). (C). 1995. pap. 27.95 (*0-538-84404-3*) S-W Pub.

Nagy, et al. Adulteration of Fruit Juice Beverages. Rhodes, Martha E., ed. (Food Science & Technology Ser.: Vol. 30). (Illus.). 568p. 1988. text 225.00 (*0-8247-7912-6*) Dekker.

Nagy, Agnes N. Agnes Nemes Nagy on Poetry, a Hungarian Perspective. Ferencz, Gyozo & Hobbs, John, eds. Hamori, Monika, tr. from HUN. LC 98-22550. 196p. 1998. text 77.95 (*0-7734-8355-1*) E Mellen.

Nagy, Alexander G., jt. ed. see Cuesta, Miguel A.

Nagy, Allen & Nagy, Geraldine F. How to Raise Your Child's Emotional Intelligence: 101 Ways to Bring Out the Best in Your Children & Yourself. (Illus.). 198p. 1999. pap. 12.95 (*0-9664287-0-6*) Heartfelt Pubns.

Nagy, Andrew F., jt. auth. see Schunk, Robert W.

Nagy, Angela F. Dining Out in Hungary. 84p. 1999. 21.00 (*963-13-3891-6*, Pub. by Corvina Bks) St Mut.

***Nagy, Balazs.** Autobiography of Charles IV of Luxemburg, Holy Roman Emperor & King of Bohemia. Knoll, Paul W. & Schaer, Frank, trs. (Central European Medieval Texts Ser.: Vol. 2). 300p. (C). 2000. 49.95 (*963-9116-32-7*) Ctrl Europ Univ.

***Nagy, Balazs & Sebok, Marcell, eds.** The Man of Many Devices, Who Wandered Full Many Ways: Festschrift in Honor of Janos M. Bak. 600p. (C). 1999. 69.95 (*963-9116-67-X*) Ctrl Europ Univ.

Nagy, Bernard S. La Magie du Subconscient. 222p. 1985. 18.50 (*2-920083-08-2*) Edns Roseau.

***Nagy, Beth & Nagy, Bridget.** Rhino Wings. large type ed. (Illus.). 36p. (J). (ps-5). 1999. 19.00 (*0-9679868-0-X*) Purple Rhino.

Nagy, Bridget, jt. auth. see Nagy, Beth.

Nagy, Caroline S. Introduction to Dialogue, for Flute & Keyboard (Harpsichord) (Contemporary Instrumental Ser.: No. 9). 8p. 1995. pap. text 10.00 (*1-56571-123-8*) PRB Prods.

Nagy, Doreen E. Popular Medicine in Seventeenth-Century England. LC 88-70523. 140p. (C). 1988. 26.95 (*0-87972-435-8*); pap. 13.95 (*0-87972-436-6*) Bowling Green Univ Popular Press.

Nagy, Edit. Working in Underground Offices. (Illus.). 193p. 1998. pap. 46.50 (*91-22-01798-4*, Pub. by Almqvist Wiksell) Coronet Bks.

Nagy, Elizabeth. English-Hungarian Technical Dictionary. 5th ed. (ENG & HUN.). 791p. 1980. 65.00 (*0-8288-0674-8*, M 8433) Fr & Eur.

— English-Hungarian Technical Dictionary. 7th ed. (ENG & HUN.). 1990. 63.00 (*0-7859-8957-9*) Fr & Eur.

— English-Hungarian Technical Dictionary. 7th ed. 789p. 1990. 50.00 (*963-05-5709-6*) IBD Ltd.

— Hungarian English Technical Dictionary. (ENG & HUN.). 752p. 1993. 85.00 (*0-7859-7153-X*) Fr & Eur.

— Hungarian-English Technical Dictionary. 6th ed. (ENG & HUN.). 1990. 63.00 (*0-7859-8963-3*) Fr & Eur.

— Hungarian-English Technical Dictionary. 6th ed. 752p. 1990. 50.50 (*963-05-5708-8*) IBD Ltd.

Nagy, Elizabeth & Klaar, J. German-Hungarian Technical Dictionary. 1392p. 1992. 120.00 (*963-05-5981-1*, Pub. by Akade Kiado) St Mut.

Nagy, Elizabeth & Klar, J. Hungarian-German Technical Dictionary. 1300p. 1992. 120.00 (*963-05-5982-X*, Pub. by Akade Kiado) St Mut.

Nagy, Elizabeth & Klar, J., eds. English-Hungarian Technical Dictionary. (ENG & HUN.). 792p. 1980. 70.00 (*0-7855-7264-3*) St Mut.

Nagy, Ellen M. Women in Germanics, 1850-1950. (Studies in Modern German Literature: Vol. 86). (Illus.). X, 186p. (C). 1998. text 43.95 (*0-8204-3659-3*) P Lang Pubng.

Nagy, F. & Klar, J. Hungarian-German Technical Dictionary. 4th ed. (GER & HUN.). 1300p. 1987. 125.00 (*0-8288-2147-X*, M8438) Fr & Eur.

Nagy-Farkas, David. Easter Eggs: Software Surprises. LC 97-10457. 1997. 16.95 (*1-55755-326-2*) Abacus MI.

Nagy, Gabor O. Abriss Einer Funktionellen Semantik. (Janua Linguarum, Series Minor: No. 137). 1973. 61.55 (*90-279-2519-4*) Mouton.

Nagy, George L. English-Hungarian Dictionary of Idioms. 708p. 1996. 30.00 (*963-05-7381-4*, Pub. by Akade Kiado) Intl Spec Bk.

Nagy, Geraldine F., jt. auth. see Nagy, Allen.

Nagy, Gloria. Marriage. 432p. 1996. mass mkt. 5.99 (*1-57566-098-9*, Knsington) Kensgtn Pub Corp.

Nagy, Gregory. The Best of the Achaeans: Concepts of the Hero in Archaic Greek Poetry. LC 79-9907. 416p. 1981. pap. 16.95 (*0-8018-2388-9*) Johns Hopkins.

— The Best of the Achaeans: Concepts of the Hero in Archaic Greek Poetry. rev. ed. LC 98-22262. 420p. 1998. 18.95 (*0-8018-6015-6*) Johns Hopkins.

— Comparative Studies in Greek & Indic Meter. LC 73-90339. (Studies in Comparative Literature: No. 33). 360p. 1974. 34.00 (*0-674-15275-1*) HUP.

— Greek Dialects & the Transformation of an Indo-European Process. LC 69-12730. (Loeb Classical Monographs). 214p. reprint ed. 66.40 (*0-8357-9160-2*, 201673200005) Bks Demand.

— Greek Mythology & Poetics. LC 89-17447. (Myth & Poetics Ser.). 384p. 1992. pap. text 17.95 (*0-8014-8048-5*) Cornell U Pr.

— Homeric Questions. (C). 1996. pap. 12.95 (*0-292-75562-7*); text 30.00 (*0-292-75561-9*) U of Tex Pr.

— Pindar's Homer: The Lyric Possession of an Epic Past. LC 89-19938. 552p. 1990. text 50.00 (*0-8018-3932-7*) Johns Hopkins.

— Poetry As Performance: Homer & Beyond. 264p. (C). 1996. pap. text 19.95 (*0-521-55848-4*) Cambridge U Pr.

Nagy, Gregory, jt. auth. see Householder, Fred W.

Nagy, Gregory, jt. ed. see Figueira, Thomas J.

Nagy, I. Introduction to Chemical Process Instrumentation. (Process Measurement & Control Ser.: Vol. 3). 428p. 1992. 253.75 (*0-444-98712-6*) Elsevier.

Nagy, I. & Kertai, A. Technical Dictionary of Water Management. 516p. (C). 1988. 100.00 (*0-569-09157-8*, Pub. by Collets) St Mut.

Nagy, Imre & Kiraly, Bela K., eds. A Magyar Nep Vedelmeben: Vitairatok es beszedek, 1955-1956. xix, 265p. (Orig.). 1984. pap. 10.00 (*0-930888-27-8*, Pub. by Dialogues Europeennes) Puski-Corvin.

Nagy, Jean. Brown Bagging It: A Guide to Fresh Food Cooking in the Wilderness. (Illus.). 1976. pap. 2.50 (*0-917296-00-1*) Marty-Nagy.

Nagy, Jill, jt. auth. see Lee, Harry O.

Nagy, Jill, ed. see Lee, Harry O., et al.

Nagy, John. Steelhead Guide: Fly Fishing Techniques & Strategies for Lake Erie Steelhead. LC 98-72333. (Illus.). 150p. 1998. pap. 19.95 (*0-9665172-0-2*) Great Lakes.

***Nagy, John.** Steelhead Guide: Fly Fishing Techniques & Strategies for Lake Erie Steelhead. (Illus.). 192p. 2000. pap. 24.95 (*0-9665172-1-0*) Great Lakes.

Nagy, John & Verakis. Development & Control of Dust Explosions. (Occupational Safety & Health Ser.: Vol. 8). (Illus.). 296p. 1983. text 140.00 (*0-8247-7004-8*) Dekker.

Nagy, Joseph F. Conversing with Angels & Ancients: The Literary Myths of Medieval Ireland. LC 97-2192. 376p. 1996. text 49.95 (*0-8014-3300-2*); pap. text 22.50 (*0-8014-8368-9*) Cornell U Pr.

***Nagy, Joseph Falaky.** Handbook of Celtic Mythology. 2001. lib. bdg. 55.00 (*1-57607-227-4*) ABC-CLIO.

Nagy, K. R. & Blum, A. E., eds. Scanning Probe Microscopy of Clay Minerals. (CMS Workshop Lectures: Vol. 7). (Illus.). 256p. (Orig.). (C). 1994. pap. text 23.00 (*1-881208-08-7*) Clay Minerals.

Nagy, Karoly, ed. see Bibo, Istvan.

Nagy, Kenneth A. & Peterson, Charles C. Scaling of Water Flux Rate in Animals. LC 88-10791. (University of California Publications in Zoology: No. 120). 186p. 1988. pap. 57.70 (*0-7837-7496-6*, 204921800010) Bks Demand.

Nagy, Krisztina. Dog Days: An Opposites Book. 10p. 1999. 9.95 (*1-58117-053-X*) Intervisual Bks.

***Nagy, Krisztina.** Fuzzy Bear: A Getting Dressed Book. large type ed. (Illus.). 10p. (J). 2000. 16.95 (*1-58117-050-5*, Piggy Toes Pr) Intervisual Bks.

— Sleepy Bear: A Bedtime Book. (Illus.). (J). 2000. 16.95 (*1-58117-052-1*, Piggy Toes Pr) Intervisual Bks.

Nagy, Lajos, jt. auth. see Blanpain, Roger.

Nagy, Laszlo. Bibliography of Hungarian Legal Literature 1945-1980. 429p. (C). 1988. 114.00 (*963-05-4339-7*, Pub. by Akade Kiado) St Mut.

— First European Regional Congress of Labour Law & Social Security: Proceedings, Szeged, Hungary, 19-21 September 1984, 2 vols., Set. (ENG, FRE & GER.). 1020p. (C). 1987. 225.00 (*963-05-4756-2*, Pub. by Akade Kiado) St Mut.

— The Socialist Collective Agreement. 257p. (C). 1984. 70.00 (*963-05-3368-5*, Pub. by Akade Kiado) St Mut.

Nagy, Laszlo, jt. auth. see Molnar, Miklos.

Nagy, Laszlo, jt. auth. see Molnar, Niklos.

Nagy, Marilyn. Philosophical Issues in the Psychology of C. G. Jung. LC 89-26319. 252p. (C). 1991. text 21.50 (*0-7914-0451-X*) State U NY Pr.

Nagy, Moses M. Christopher Columbus in World Literature: An Annotated Bibliography. LC 93-24541. (Reference Library of the Humanities: Vol. 1629). (Illus.). 378p. 1994. text 20.00 (*0-8153-0927-9*, H1629) Garland.

— A Journey into History: Essays on Hungarian Literature. LC 89-27320. (American University Studies: General Literature: Ser. IXX, Vol. 25). 240p. 1990. text 44.50 (*0-8204-1201-5*) P Lang Pubng.

Nagy, P. English-Hungarian Banking & Finance Directory. (ENG & HUN.). 649p. 1993. 150.00 (*0-7859-8883-1*) Fr & Eur.

***Nagy, P.** Phyllis Nagy Plays. 2000. pap. 14.95 (*0-413-72370-4*) Methn.

Nagy, P. & Tarjan, G. Elsevier's Dictionary of Microelectronics in English, German, French, Spanish & Japanese. (ENG, FRE, GER, JPN & SPA.). 944p. 1988. 350.00 (*0-8288-0314-5*, M1655) Fr & Eur.

Nagy, P. & Tarjan, G., eds. Elsevier's Dictionary of Microelectronics: In English, German, French, Spanish, & Japanese. 956p. 1988. 286.25 (*0-444-42659-0*) Elsevier.

Nagy, P. & Trutz, S. English-Hungarian Banking & Finance Dictionary. 900p. 1993. 90.00 (*963-05-6593-5*, Pub. by Akade Kiado) St Mut.

Nagy, Paul. Satisfactions. 1977. pap. 5.00 (*0-918406-08-0*) Future Pr.

Nagy, Phyllis. Butterfly Kiss. 96p. 1994. pap. 12.95 (*1-85459-251-3*, Pub. by N Hern Bks) Theatre Comm.

— Neverland. LC 97-150384. 1996. pap. 11.95 (*0-413-70140-9*, Methuen Drama) Methn.

— Trip's Cinch. 1995. 3.50 (*0-87129-512-1*, T39) Dramatic Pub.

— Weldon Rising & Disappeared. 1996. pap. 15.95 (*0-413-70150-6*, Methuen Drama) Methn.

***Nagy, Piroska Mohacsi.** The Meltdown of the Russian State: The Deformation & Collapse of the State in Russia. 160p. 2000. 65.00 (*1-85898-820-9*) E Elgar.

Nagy, Rebecca M., et al, eds. Sepphoris in Galilee: Crosscurrents of Culture. LC 96-69214. (Illus.). 275p. 1996. 29.95 (*0-88259-971-2*) NCMA.

Nagy, Silvia. Historia de la Cancion Folklorica en los Andes. (American University Studies: Romance Languages & Literature: Ser. II, Vol. 73). 210p. (C). 1989. text 32.95 (*0-8204-0597-3*) P Lang Pubng.

Nagy, Steven, et al, eds. Fruit Juice Processing Technology. LC 92-38443. (Illus.). 713p. (C). 1993. text 148.00 (*0-9631397-1-1*) AgScience.

— Fruits of Tropical & Subtropical Origin: Composition, Properties & Uses. LC 89-92429. (Illus.). 391p. (C). 1990. text 70.00 (*0-944961-00-2*) AgScience.

Nagy, Steven & Attaway, John A., eds. Citrus Nutrition & Quality: Based on a Symposium Sponsored by the Division of Agricultural & Food Chemistry at the 179th Meeting of the American Chemical Society, Houston, TX, March 26, 1980. LC 80 22562. (ACS Symposium Ser.: No. 143). 464p. reprint ed. pap. 143.90 (*0-8357-2530-8*, 205240900014) Bks Demand.

Nagy, Steven & Wade, Robert L., eds. Methods to Detect Adulteration of Fruit Juice Beverages, 1 of 3 vols., Vol. 1. LC 94-40210. (Illus.). 452p. (C). 1995. text 84.00 (*0-9631397-3-8*) AgScience.

***Nagy-Talavera, Nicolas M.** The Green Shirts & Others: A History of Fascism in Hungary & Romania. (Illus.). 432p. 2000. 49.95 (*973-9432-11-5*, Pub. by Ctr Romanian Studies) Intl Spec Bk.

***Nagy, Thomas F.** Ethics in Plain English: An Illustrative Casebook for Psychologists. LC 99-30351. 261p. 1999. pap. 24.95 (*1-55798-604-5*, 431-2090) Am Psychol.

Nagy, William E. Teaching Vocabulary to Improve Reading Comprehension. 52p. 1988. pap. 8.25 (*0-87207-151-0*) Intl Reading.

— Teaching Vocabulary to Improve Reading Comprehension. 42p. 1998. pap. 7.95 (*0-8141-5238-4*) NCTE.

Nagy, Z. L. Iron & Steel Production: Technical Dictionary of. 686p. (C). 1987. 125.00 (*0-89771-921-2*, Pub. by Collets) St Mut.

— The Liberal Opposition in Hungary, 1919-1945. (Studia Historica Academiae Scientiarum Hungaricae: No. 185). 143p. (C). 1983. 30.00 (*963-05-2998-X*, Pub. by Akade Kiado) St Mut.

Nagy-Zekmi, Silvia. Paralelismos Transatlanticos: Postcolonialismo y Narrativa Feminina en America Latina y Africa del Norte. (SPA.). 140p. 1996. pap. 25.00 (*1-888135-02-6*) Ediciones Inti.

Nagy, Zoltan, ed. Electrochemical Synthesis of Inorganic Compounds: A Bibliography. LC 85-3642. 488p. 1985. 125.00 (*0-306-41938-6*, Plenum Trade) Perseus Pubng.

Nagybakay, Peter. Summoning Tablets of Guilds in Hungary. 114p. 1999. 25.00 (*963-13-1066-3*, Pub. by Corvina Bks) St Mut.

Nagylaki, T. Introduction to Theoretical Population Genetics. Levin, S. A., ed. (Biomathematics Ser.: Vol. 21). (Illus.). 384p. 1992. 86.95 (*0-387-53344-3*) Spr-Verlag.

— Selection in One-&-Two-Locus Systems. (Lecture Notes in Biomathematics Ser.: Vol. 15). 1977. 35.95 (*0-387-08247-6*) Spr-Verlag.

Nagyszalanczy, Sandor. The Art of Fine Tools. LC 98-6562. (Illus.). 231p. 1998. 37.00 (*1-56158-263-8*, 070380) Taunton.

***Nagyszalanczy, Sandor.** The Art of Fine Tools. (Illus.). 240p. 2000. reprint ed. pap. 24.95 (*1-56158-361-8*) Taunton.

Nagyszalanczy, Sandor. Fixing & Avoiding Woodworking Mistakes. LC 95-19283. (Illus.). 208p. 1995. pap. 19.95 (*1-56158-097-X*, 70229) Taunton.

***Nagyszalanczy, Sandor.** Setting up Shop: The Practical Guide to Designing & Building Your Dream Shop. LC 99-86701. (Illus.). 224p. 2000. 39.95 incl. cd-rom (*1-56158-360-X*) Taunton.

Nagyszalanczy, Sandor. The Wood Sanding Book: A Guide to Abrasives, Machines & Methods. LC 97-12591. (Illus.). 224p. 1997. pap. 19.95 (*1-56158-175-5*, 70302) Taunton.

— Woodshop Dust Control. LC 96-10487. (Illus.). 208p. 1996. pap. 19.95 (*1-56158-116-X*, 70246) Taunton.

— Woodshop, Jigs & Fixtures. LC 94-15224. (Illus.). 240p. (Orig.). 1994. pap. 22.95 (*1-56158-073-2*) Taunton.

Nahabedian, Cynthia A., jt. ed. see Lattimore, Pamela K.

Nahai, Foad, jt. auth. see Mathes, Stephen J.

***Nahai, Gina B.** Cry of the Peacock. 352p. 2000. reprint ed. 13.95 (*0-7434-0337-1*) PB.

Nahal, Chaman. The Bhagavad-Fita. 64p. (C). 1997. pap. 20.00 (*81-209-0032-4*, Pub. by Pitambar Pub) St Mut.

— The Bhagavad-Gita. 64p. (C). 1989. 60.00 (*81-209-0733-7*, Pub. by Pitambar Pub) St Mut.

— Learning Computers, Bk. II. 1997. pap. 30.00 (*81-209-0753-1*, Pub. by Pitambar Pub) St Mut.

— The Narrative Pattern in Ernest Hemingway's Fiction. 245p. 1975. 27.50 (*0-8386-7795-9*) Fairleigh Dickinson.

— The New Literatures in English. 225p. 1986. 24.00 (*81-7023-056-X*, Pub. by Allied Pubs) S Asia.

— Sunrise in Fiji. (C). 1988. 21.00 (*0-8364-2367-4*, Pub. by Allied Pubs) S Asia.

***Naham, Andrew.** Flying Machine. (Eyewitness Books). (Illus.). (J). (gr. 4-7). 2000. 19.99 (*0-7894-6571-X*) DK Pub Inc.

— Flying Machine. (Eyewitness Books). (J). (gr. 4-7). 2000. 15.95 (*0-7894-5766-0*) DK Pub Inc.

Nahar, Chand. Jainism: Precepts & Practice, 2 vols., Set. (C). 1988. 105.00 (*81-85066-18-3*) S Asia.

Nahar, Umed R., jt. auth. see Lal, Sheo K.

Naharo, Master, jt. auth. see Liaites, Bill.

Nahas, Dominique & Perreault, John. Public Mind: Les Levine's Media Sculpture & Mass Ad Campaigns. Piche, Thomas E., ed. LC 90-84035. (Illus.). 128p. (Orig.). 1990. text. write for info. (*0-914407-14-7*) Everson Mus.

Nahas, Gabriel G. Cannabis: Physiopathology, Epidemiology, Detection, Proceedings of the Second International Symposium, Paris, April 8-9, 1992. Latour, Colette, ed. 432p. 1992. boxed set 156.95 (*0-8493-8310-2*, QP801) CRC Pr.

— Cocaine: The Great White Plague. 320p. 1989. 19.95 (*0-8397-1700-8*) Eriksson.

— Handbook of Toxicology of Controlled Substances. 1995. write for info. (*0-8493-7939-3*) CRC Pr.

— Keep off the Grass. 5th rev. ed. LC 90-3658. (Illus.). 400p. 1990. reprint ed. pap. 12.95 (*0-8397-4384-X*) Eriksson.

— A Manual on Drug Dependence. (Illus.). 268p. (Orig.). 1992. pap. 12.95 (*0-929240-46-4*) EMIS.

— Marihuana in Science & Medicine. LC 84-11697. 326p. 1984. reprint ed. pap. 101.10 (*0-608-03433-9*, 206413400008) Bks Demand.

Nahas, Gabriel G., et al, eds. Marihuana & Medicine. LC 99-13481. 848p. 1999. 135.00 (*0-89603-593-X*) Humana.

Nahas, Gabriel G. & Burks, T. F., eds. Drugs of Abuse & the Decade of the Brain. LC 96-78413. 320p. (YA). (gr. 12). 1996. 79.50 (*90-5199-305-6*, 305-6) IOS Press.

Nahas, Gabriel G. & Latour, C. Physiopathology of Illicit Drugs: Cannabis, Cocaine, Opiates. (Advances in the Biosciences Ser.: Vol. 80). 346p. 1991. 181.50 (*0-08-041146-0*, Pergamon Pr) Elsevier.

Nahas, Gabriel G., ed. see International Congress of Pharmacology Staff.

Nahas, Richard, jt. auth. see Supica, Jim.

Nahas, Violetta, jt. auth. see Nash, Erica.

Nahata, Milap C. & Hipple, Thomas F. Pediatric Drug Formulations. 3rd ed. LC 97-22898. xvi, 118p. (Orig.). 1997. pap. text 31.95 (*0-929375-19-X*) H W Bks.

Nahata, Milap C., jt. auth. see Bates, Richard D.

Nahavandi, Afsaneh. The Art & Science of Leadership. 500p. (C). 1996. pap. text 55.00 (*0-13-381534-X*) P-H.

***Nahavandi, Afsaneh.** The Art & Science of Leadership. 2nd ed. LC 99-27537. 259p. 1999. pap. 55.00 (*0-13-085459-X*) P-H.

Nahavandi, Afsaneh & Malekzadeh, Ali R. Organizational Behavior: The Person-Organization Fit. LC 98-21488. 609p. 1998. 96.00 (*0-13-285982-3*) P-H.

— Organizational Culture in the Management of Mergers. LC 92-44685. 200p. 1993. 55.00 (*0-89930-669-1*, NAU, Quorum Bks) Greenwood.

Nahaylo, Bohdan. The Ukrainian Resurgence: From Dependence to Independence. LC 99-475861. (Illus.). 454p. 1997. pap. text 24.95 (*0-8020-7977-6*) U of Toronto Pr.

Nahaylo, Bohdan & Swoboda, Victor. Soviet Disunion: A History of the Nationalities Problem in the USSR. 448p. 1990. 35.00 (*0-02-922401-2*) Free Pr.

N

***NAHB Labor Safety Staff.** Construction Safety Program Manual: A Guide for Home Builders & Contractors. LC 99-47330. 122p. 1999. pap. write for info. (*0-86718-508-2*) Home Builder.

NAHB Research Center, Inc. Staff. A Builder's Guide to Residential HVAC Systems. LC 96-36821. (Illus.). 64p. (Orig.). 1997. pap. 27.50 (*0-86718-423-X*) Home Builder.

NAHB Research Center, Inc. Staff, jt. auth. see Caldeira, Edward.

NAHB Research Center Staff. Building with Alternatives to Lumber & Plywood. LC 93-41672. 72p. (Orig.). 1994. pap. 7.50 (*0-86718-392-6*) Home Builder.

— Residential Concrete. 2nd rev. ed. LC 93-36745. (Illus.). 96p. 1994. pap. 22.00 (*0-86718-389-6*) Home Builder.

NAHB Research Foundation Staff. Off Center Spliced Floor Joists, Vol. 4. (Research Report Ser.). 58p. 1982. pap. 9.00 (*0-86718-143-5*) Home Builder.

— Performance of Nominal Five-Eighths Inch Plywood Over Joists Spaced 24 Inches on Center, Vol. 1. (Research Report Ser.). 11p. 1981. pap. 5.50 (*0-86718-114-1*) Home Builder.

— Plywood Headers for Residential Construction, Vol. 5. (Research Report Ser.). 48p. 1983. pap. 8.00 (*0-86718-200-8*) Home Builder.

— Stress & Deflection Reduction in 2x4 Studs Spaced 24 Inches on Center Resulting from the Addition of Interior & Exterior Surfaces, Vol. 3. (Research Report Ser.). 46p. 1981. pap. 6.50 (*0-86718-117-6*) Home Builder.

NAHBB Staff. Home Based Business Occupational Handbook. LC 96-135350. 128p. 1996. pap. text, per. 21.95 (*0-7872-1685-2*) Kendall-Hunt.

Nahed, Nicola. Al Aalam Fi Kitab. Diyraney, Saleam, ed.Tr. of World in a Book. (ARA., Illus.). 1119p. (J). (gr. 2-7). 1992. 146.99 (*1-58311-011-9*) Eastern Corp.

— Al Jism Albachari. Diyraney, Saleam, ed. (Silsilat Alouloum Al Mousawara (Illustrated Science) Ser.: No. 1).Tr. of Human Body. (ARA., Illus.). 60p. (J). (gr. 2-7). 1986. pap. 12.50 (*1-58311-054-2*) Eastern Corp.

— Alinsan Walnabat. Diyraney, Saleam, ed. (Silsilat Alouloum Al Mousawara (Illustrated Science) Ser.: No. 6).Tr. of Man & Vegetation. (ARA., Illus.). 60p. (J). (gr. 2-7). 1986. pap. 12.50 (*1-58311-059-3*) Eastern Corp.

— Aljaw Waltayran. Diyraney, Saleam, ed. (Silsilat Alouloum Al Mousawara (Illustrated Science) Ser.: No. 3).Tr. of Atmosphere & Aviation. (ARA., Illus.). 60p. (J). (gr. 2-7). 1986. pap. 12.50 (*1-57311-256-9*) Eastern Corp.

— Alkilaa Walhousoun. Diyraney, Saleam, ed. (Silsilat Alouloum Al Mousawara (Illustrated Science) Ser.: No. 7).Tr. of Fortressess. (ARA., Illus.). 60p. (J). (gr. 2-7). 1986. pap. 12.50 (*1-58311-060-7*) Eastern Corp.

— Almazareh Walhoukoul. Diyraney, Saleam, ed. (Silsilat Alouloum Al Mousawara (Illustrated Science) Ser.: No. 5).Tr. of Farms & Prairies. (ARA., Illus.). 60p. (J). (gr. 2-7). 1986. pap. 12.50 (*1-58311-058-5*) Eastern Corp.

— Altabiaa Walmanakn. Diyraney, Saleam, ed. (Silsilat Alouloum Al Mousawara (Illustrated Science) Ser.: No. 4).Tr. of Nature & Weather. (ARA., Illus.). 60p. (J). (gr. 2-7). 1986. pap. 12.50 (*1-58311-057-7*) Eastern Corp.

— Assila WA Ajwiba. Diyraney, Saleam, ed.Tr. of Question & Answers Encyclopedia. (ARA., Illus.). 1200p. (J). (gr. 2-5). 1991. 439.00 (*1-58311-003-8*) Eastern Corp.

— Ghizaouna. Diyraney, Saleam, ed. (Silsilat Alouloum Al Mousawara (Illustrated Science) Ser.: No. 2).Tr. of Nutrition. (ARA., Illus.). 60p. (J). (gr. 2-7). 1986. pap. 12.50 (*1-58311-055-0*) Eastern Corp.

— Hayawanat Istiwaiya. Diyraney, Saleam, ed. (Silsilat Alouloum Al Mousawara (Illustrated Science) Ser.: No. 8).Tr. of Tropical & Equatorial Animals. (ARA., Illus.). 60p. (J). (gr. 2-7). 1986. pap. 12.50 (*1-58311-061-5*) Eastern Corp.

— Mawsouat Al Mawsouaa. Diyraney, Saleam, ed.Tr. of Encyclopedia of Encyclopedias. (ARA., Illus.). 3864p. 1985. 985.00 (*1-58311-000-3*) Eastern Corp.

— Silsilat Tasliyati, Vol. 1. Diyraney, Saleam, ed.Tr. of Child Fun Series Workbook. (ARA., Illus.). 8p. (J). (ps-1). 1992. pap. 4.75 (*1-58311-046-1*) Eastern Corp.

— Silsilat Tasliyati, Vol. 2. Diyraney, Saleam, ed.Tr. of Child Fun Series Workbook. (ARA., Illus.). 8p. 1992. pap. 4.75 (*1-58311-047-X*) Eastern Corp.

— Silsilat Tasliyati, Vol. 3. Diyraney, Saleam, ed.Tr. of Child Fun Series Workbook. (ARA., Illus.). 8p. (J). (ps-1). 1992. pap. 4.75 (*1-58311-048-8*) Eastern Corp.

— Silsilat Tasliyati, Vol. 4. Diyraney, Saleam, ed.Tr. of Child Fun Series Workbook. (ARA., Illus.). 8p. (J). (ps-1). 1992. pap. 4.75 (*1-58311-049-6*) Eastern Corp.

— Silsilat Tasliyati, Vol. 5. Diyraney, Saleam, ed.Tr. of Child Fun Series Workbook. (ARA., Illus.). 8p. (J). (ps-1). 1992. 4.75 (*1-58311-050-X*) Eastern Corp.

— Silsilat Tasliyati, Vol. 6. Diyraney, Saleam, ed.Tr. of Child Fun Series Workbook. (ARA., Illus.). 8p. (J). (ps-1). 1992. pap. 4.75 (*1-58311-051-8*) Eastern Corp.

— Silsilat Tasliyati, Vol. 7. Diyraney, Saleam, ed.Tr. of Child Fun Series Workbook. (ARA., Illus.). 8p. (J). (ps-1). 1992. pap. 4.75 (*1-58311-052-6*) Eastern Corp.

— Silsilat Tasliyati, Vol. 8. Diyraney, Saleam, ed.Tr. of Child Fun Series Workbook. (ARA., Illus.). 8p. (J). (ps-1). 1992. pap. 4.75 (*1-58311-053-4*) Eastern Corp.

Naheed, Qamar. D. H. Lawrence: Treatment of Nature in Early Novels. viii, 117p. 1998. 14.00 (*81-7024-951-1*, Pub. by Ashish Pub Hse) Nataraj Bks.

Nahem, Joseph. Psychology & Psychiatry Today: A Marxist View. LC 81-680. 264p. reprint ed. pap. 81.90 (*0-7837-0580-8*, 204092400019) Bks Demand.

Naher, S. & Mehlhorn, Kurt. LEDA: A Platform for Combinatorial & Geometric Computing. LC 99-24952. (Illus.). 500p. (C). 1999. text 80.00 (*0-521-56329-1*) Cambridge U Pr.

Nahfouz, Naguib. Maramar (Novel in Arabic) (ARA.). 141p. 1980. pap. 8.95 (*0-86685-159-3*, LDL538) Intl Bk Ctr.

Nahikian, Howard M. Modern Algebra for Biologists. LC 64-13948. 248p. reprint ed. 76.90 (*0-8357-9650-7*, 201576000097) Bks Demand.

***Nahikian-Nelms, Marcia & Anderson.** Medical Nutrition Therapy: A Case Study Approach. 2001. pap. 38.00 (*0-534-52410-9*) Thomson Learn.

Nahin, P. J. Time Machines: Time Travel in Physics, Metaphysics, & Science Fiction. 2nd ed. LC 98-25145. (Illus.). xxxii, 628 p. 1998. pap. 29.95 (*0-387-98571-9*) Spr-Verlag.

***Nahin, Paul J.** Duelling Idiots & Other Probability Puzzlers. LC 99-87353. (Illus.). 256p. 2000. 24.95 (*0-691-00979-1*) Princeton U Pr.

— An Imaginary Tale: The Story of (The Square Root of Minus One) LC 97-52082. 274p. 1998. 24.95 (*0-691-02795-1*, Pub. by Princeton U Pr) Cal Prin Full Svc.

Nahin, Paul J. Oliver Heaviside: Sage in Solitude. LC 87-26044. 344p. 1988. 39.95 (*0-87942-238-6*, PCO2279) Inst Electrical.

— Science of Radio. 1995. pap. 21.95 (*1-56396-347-7*) Spr-Verlag.

— Time Machines: Time Travel in Physics, Metaphysics, & Science Fiction. LC 92-75255. 1993. 40.00 (*0-88318-935-6*) Spr-Verlag.

— Time Machines: Time Travel in Physics, Metaphysics, & Science Fiction. LC 92-75255. (Illus.). 408p. 1997. pap. text 15.95 (*1-56396-371-X*) Spr-Verlag.

— Time Travel. LC 96-30080. (Science Fiction Writing Ser.). (Illus.). 208p. 1997. pap. 16.99 (*0-89879-748-9*, Wrtrs Digest Bks) F & W Pubns Inc.

Nahirny, Vladimir. The Russian Intelligentsia: From Torment to Silence. LC 82-4796. 192p. 1982. 34.95 (*0-87855-463-7*) Transaction Pubs.

Nahkosteen, J. A., jt. ed. see Allegra, G.

Nahl, Diane, jt. auth. see James, Leon.

Nahler, Gerhard. Dictionary of Pharmaceutical Medicine. LC 94-11648. 1994. 31.95 (*0-387-82557-6*) Spr-Verlag.

— Dictionary of Pharmaceutical Medicine: English-German, German-English. (ENG & GER.). 177p. 1994. 69.95 (*0-7859-9985-X*) Fr & Eur.

Nahler, Gerhard R., jt. ed. see Brunier, Dominique P.

Nahm, Andrew C. Historical Dictionary of the Republic of Korea. LC 93-3033. (Asian Historical Dictionaries Ser.: No. 11). (Illus.). 336p. 1993. 50.00 (*0-8108-2603-8*) Scarecrow.

— I Love Korea! Jones, B. J. & Lee, Gi-eun, eds. (Illus.). 86p. (J). (gr. 1-5). 1994. 23.95 (*0-930878-87-6*) Hollym Intl.

— Korea - Tradition & Transformation: A History of the Korean People. 2nd ed. LC 86-81681. 583p. 1996. 52.95 (*1-56591-070-2*) Hollym Intl.

— A Panorama of Five Thousand Years: Korean History. 2nd rev. ed. (Illus.). 123p. 1997. reprint ed. 27.95 (*0-930878-23-X*) Hollym Intl.

Nahm, Andrew C., jt. ed. see Koo, John H.

Nahm, Milton C., jt. auth. see Clarke, F. P.

Nahm, Monica. Saga of the Italian Peninsula: People & Places. (Illus.). 400p. 1999. pap. 32.95 (*1-57197-171-8*) Pentland Pr.

Nahm, W. Conformally Invariant Quantum Field Theories in Two Dimensions. (Advanced Series in Mathematical Physics: Vol. 6). 250p. 1997. text 61.00 (*9971-5-0649-1*); pap. text 40.00 (*9971-5-0650-5*) World Scientific Pub.

Nahm, W., et al. Topological Methods in Quantum Field Theories. 184p. 1991. pap. 28.00 (*981-02-0497-3*); text 68.00 (*981-02-0496-5*) World Scientific Pub.

Nahm, W., jt. ed. see Chau, Ling-Lie.

***Nahmad, Claire.** The Cat Herbal: Simple Green Remedies for Your Cat. 2000. pap. 13.95 (*0-285-63509-3*, Pub. by Souvenir Pr Ltd) IPG Chicago.

Nahmad, Claire. Earth Magic: A Wisewoman's Guide to Herbal, Astrological, & Other Folk Wisdom. (Illus.). 207p. (Orig.). 1993. pap. 12.95 (*0-89281-424-1*) Inner Tradit.

— Fairy Spells: Seeing & Communicating with the Fairies. (Illus.). 64p. 1998. 12.95 (*0-285-63470-4*) IPG Chicago.

Nahmad, H. M., jt. auth. see Haywood, J. A.

***Nahman, Eftyhia.** Yannina. (Library of Holocaust Testimonies). (Illus.). 192p. 2000. pap. 19.50 (*0-85303-387-0*) Intl Spec Bk.

Nahman, N. Stanley, jt. ed. see Mandal, Anil K.

Nahmias. Production Operations Analysis. 4th ed. 2000. 70.74 (*0-07-231265-3*) McGraw.

Nahmias-Radovici, Nadia. A Youthful Love: Jane Austen & Tom Lefroy? LC 96-143334. 1995. write for info. (*0-86303-681-3*) Merlin Bks.

Nahmias, Steven. Production & Operations Analysis. (C). 1992. 57.00 (*0-256-05550-5*, Irwn McGrw-H) McGrw-H Hghr Educ.

— Production & Operations Analysis. 2nd ed. LC 92-23790. 800p. (C). 1992. text 74.65 (*0-256-10664-9*, Irwn McGrw-H) McGrw-H Hghr Educ.

— Production & Operations Analysis. 3rd ed. LC 96-28689. 864p. (C). 1996. text 74.65 (*0-256-19508-0*, Irwn McGrw-H) McGrw-H Hghr Educ.

Nahmod, Sheldon H. Civil Rights & Civil Liberties Litigation: The Law of Section 1983. 4th ed. LC 98-106664. 1997. write for info. (*0-8366-1216-7*) West Group.

Nahmod, Sheldon H., ed. A Section 1983 Civil Rights Anthology. LC 93-19309. 303p. 1993. pap. 29.95 (*0-87084-135-1*) Anderson Pub Co.

Nahmod, Sheldon H., et al. Constitutional Torts Casebook. LC 94-43425. 448p. 1995. 56.95 (*0-87084-903-4*) Anderson Pub Co.

Nahoa Lucas, Paul F. A Dictionary of Hawaiian Legal Land-Terms. LC 95-12500. 1995. pap. text 25.00 (*0-8248-1636-6*) UH Pr.

Nahohai, Milford & Phelps, Elisa. Dialogues with Zuni Potters. (Illus.). 100p. (Orig.). 1995. 45.00 (*0-9641401-2-8*); pap. 19.95 (*0-9641401-3-6*) Zuni Ashiwi.

Nahon, Daniel. Introduction to the Petrology of Soils & Chemical Weathering. LC 90-40173. (Basic Topics in Geology Ser.). 336p. 1991. 150.00 (*0-471-50861-6*) Wiley.

Nahon, Marco. Birkenau: The Camp of Death. Bowman, Steven, ed. Bowers, Jacqueline H., tr. from FRE. LC 89-4661. (Judaic Studies). 169p. 1989. reprint ed. pap. 52.40 (*0-608-03806-7*, 206465700009) Bks Demand.

Nahorski, S. R., ed. Transmembrane Signalling, Intracellular Messengers & Implications for Drug Development. LC 89-24919. 264p. 1990. 305.00 (*0-471-92432-6*) Wiley.

Nahorski, Z., et al. Optimization of Discrete Time Systems: The Upper Boundary Approach. (Lecture Notes in Control & Information Sciences: Vol. 51). 137p. 1983. 18.95 (*0-387-12258-3*) Spr-Verlag.

Nahory, Robert E., jt. auth. see Harbison, James P.

Nahoun, Joel D., jt. auth. see Vellani, Karim H.

Nahouraii, E., ed. Assessment of Software Tools & Technologies: Proceedings of the Fifth International Symposium on Assessment of Software Tools & Technologies, Pittsburgh, Pennsylvania, 1997. LC 97-71758. 300p. 1997. pap. 115.00 (*0-8186-7940-9*) IEEE Comp Soc.

Nahra, Nancy, jt. auth. see Randall, Willard S.

Nahrstedt, Klara, jt. auth. see Steinmetz, Ralf.

Nahser, F. Byron. Learning to Read the Signs: Reclaiming Pragmatism in Business. LC 96-39571. 224p. 1997. pap. text 17.95 (*0-7506-9901-9*) Buttrwrth-Heinemann.

Nahser, F. Byron & Mehrtens, Susan E. Executive Summary What's Really Going On? A Pragmatic Method for Achieving Success Through Self-Doubt. 33p. 1993. pap. text 5.00 (*1-884670-00-8*) The Nashser Agency.

Nahshon, Edna. Yiddish Proletarian Theatre: The Art & Politics of the Artef, 1925-1940, 85. LC 98-15599. (Contributions in Drama & Theatre Studies: Vol. 85). 288p. 1998. 59.95 (*0-313-29063-6*, Greenwood Pr) Greenwood.

Nahum, Alan & Melvin, John, eds. Accidental Injury: Biomechanics & Prevention. LC 92-2381. 1997. text 121.95 (*0-387-97881-X*) Spr-Verlag.

***Nahum, Alan M. & Melvin, John W.** Accidental Injury: Biomechanics & Prevention. 2nd ed. LC 00-24950. (Illus.). 872p. 2000. 165.00 (*0-387-98820-3*) Spr-Verlag.

Nahum, Andrew. Alec Issigonis. 100p. (C). 1988. pap. text 50.00 (*0-85072-172-5*) St Mut.

Nahum, Fasil. Constitution for a Nation of Nations: The Ethiopian Prospect. LC 97-9251. 1997. pap. 19.95 (*1-56902-051-5*) Red Sea Pr.

— Constitution for a Nation of Nations: The Ethiopian Prospect. LC 97-9251. 1997. write for info. (*1-56902-050-7*) Red Sea Pr.

Nahum, Katherine, jt. auth. see Conley, Alston.

Nahum, Lucien. Shadow Eighty-One. large type ed. 1981. 27.99 (*0-7089-0556-0*) Ulverscroft.

Nahum-Valensi, Maya. Mom's Sore Throat. (I Love to Read Collection). (Illus.). 48p. (J). (ps-3). 1992. lib. bdg. 12.79 (*0-89565-807-0*) Childs World.

Nahumck, Nadia C. & Nahumck, Nicholas. Isadora Duncan: The Dances Choreographed in Labanotation. LC 93-43279. 532p. 1994. 165.00 (*0-940979-23-3*) Natl Museum Women.

Nahumck, Nicholas, jt. auth. see Nahumck, Nadia C.

Nahvi, Mahmood S. & Zadeh, Loftia A. Circuits, Systems & Information. 203p. 1991. 40.00 (*0-9627451-0-3*) TSI Pr.

Nahvi, Mahmood S., jt. auth. see Edminister, Joseph A.

Nahvi, Reza & Sodersrand, Michael A. Electric Circuits Fundamentals. (Illus.). 947p. (C). 1995. pap. text, student ed. 31.95 (*0-03-098252-9*) OUP.

Nai-Shan, Ch'eng. The Banker. Dean, Britten, tr. & intro. by. 459p. 1993. pap. 19.95 (*0-8351-2492-4*) China Bks.

— The Blue House. 400p. (Orig.). 1989. pap. 8.95 (*0-8351-2065-1*) China Bks.

Nai, Xia. Jade & Silk of Han China. Li, Chu-tsing, tr. LC 83-50538. (Franklin D. Murphy Lectures: No. 3). (Illus.). 88p. 1983. 12.00 (*0-913689-10-6*) Spencer Muse Art.

Naiad Press Authors Staff. The Romantic Naiad. Forrest, Katherine V. & Grier, Barbara, eds. 352p. 1993. pap. 14.95 (*1-56280-054-X*) Naiad Pr.

***Naiad Press Staff.** The Very Thought of You: Erotic Love Stories. Grier, Barbara & Cassidy, Christine, eds. LC 98-48236. 304p. 1999. pap. 14.95 (*1-56280-250-X*) Naiad Pr.

Naib, Zuher M. Cytopathology. 4th ed. LC 95-2408. 752p. 1995. 99.95 (*0-316-59674-4*, Little Brwn Med Div) Lppncott W & W.

***Naiboo, Phyllis, compiled by.** African Millenium Diary. (Illus.). 144p. 1999. 36.95 (*0-620-25035-6*, Pub. by Skotaville Pubs) Intl Spec Bk.

NAIC Staff, ed. Official NAIC Annual Statement Blanks - Title, 1994. 86p. (C). 1994. ring bd. 50.00 (*0-89382-269-8*) Nat Assn Insurance.

Naidenow, W. T., jt. ed. see Golemansky, V. G.

Naidich, David P. & Zerhouni, Elias A. Computed Tomography & Magnetic Resonance of the Thorax. 3rd ed. LC 98-36942. 772p. 1998. text 145.00 (*0-7817-1660-8*) Lppncott W & W.

Naidich, David P., et al. Computed Tomography & Magnetic Resonance of the Thorax. 2nd ed. (Illus.). 624p. 1991. text 153.00 (*0-88167-567-9*) Lppncott W & W.

***Naidich, Yu I, et al.** Strength of the Diamond-Metal Interface & Soldering of Diamonds. 180p. 1999. boxed set 76.00 (*1-898326-49-5*, Pub. by CISP) Balogh.

Naiditch, David. Rendezvous with ADA 95. 2nd ed. 608p. 1995. pap. 59.99 (*0-471-01276-9*) Wiley.

Naiditch, P. G. A. E. Housman at University College, London: The Election of 1892. LC 88-21007. 1998. pap. 73.00 (*90-04-08848-2*) Brill Academic Pubs.

— Problems in the Life & Writings of A. E. Housman. 264p. (C). 1995. 40.00 (*0-9647634-1-9*) Krown & Spellman.

Naidoo. Chain of Fire. 1995. pap. text. write for info. (*0-582-25403-5*, Pub. by Addison-Wesley) Longman.

— Practising Health Promotion. (C). 1998. pap. text 35.00 (*0-7020-2122-9*, W B Saunders Co) Harcrt Hlth Sci Grp.

Naidoo, Beverley. Chain of Fire. LC 89-27551. (Illus.). 256p. (J). (gr. 6 up). 1990. 14.00 (*0-397-32426-X*) HarpC Child Bks.

— Chain of Fire. LC 89-27551. (Trophy Bk.). 256p. (J). (gr. 7 up). 1993. pap. 4.95 (*0-06-440468-4*, HarpTrophy) HarpC Child Bks.

— Chain of Fire. 1993. 10.05 (*0-606-02551-0*, Pub. by Turtleback) Demco.

— Journey to Jo'burg: A South African Story. LC 85-45508. (Illus.). 96p. (J). (gr. 7 up). 1986. lib. bdg. 15.89 (*0-397-32169-4*) HarpC Child Bks.

— Journey to Jo'burg: A South African Story. LC 85-45508. (J). 1986. 10.15 (*0-606-03834-5*, Pub. by Turtleback) Demco.

— Journey to Jo'burg: A South African Story. LC 85-45508. (Trophy Bk.). (Illus.). 96p. (J). (gr. 4-7). 1988. reprint ed. pap. 4.95 (*0-06-440237-1*, HarpTrophy) HarpC Child Bks.

— No Turning Back: A Novel of South Africa. LC 96-28980. 208p. (J). (gr. 3-7). 1997. lib. bdg. 15.89 (*0-06-027506-5*, HarpTrophy) HarpC Child Bks.

— No Turning Back: A Novel of South Africa. LC 96-28980. 208p. (J). (gr. 3-7). 1999. pap. 4.95 (*0-06-440749-7*, HarpTrophy) HarpC Child Bks.

Naidoo, Beverly. Journey to Jo'burg: A South African Story. (Longman Literature Ser.). 1995. pap. text. write for info. (*0-582-25402-7*, Pub. by Addison-Wesley) Longman.

Naidoo, Jennie & Wills, Jane. Health Promotion: Foundations for Practice. (Illus.). 314p. 1995. pap. text 29.50 (*0-7020-1680-2*, Pub. by W B Saunders) Saunders.

***Naidoo, Jennie & Wills, Jane.** Health Promotion: Foundations for Practice. 2nd ed. LC 99-17031. 2000. text. write for info. (*0-7020-2448-1*, Pub. by W B Saunders) Saunders.

Naidoo, Kumi, ed. see CIVICUS Staff.

Naidoo, P., jt. auth. see Savage, M. B.

Naidoo, Sandhya, jt. auth. see Haynes, Corinne.

Naidoo, Sandhya, jt. auth. see Pringle, M.

Naidoo, Thillayvel. Arya Samaj Movement in South Africa. (C). 1992. 18.00 (*81-208-0769-3*, Pub. by Motilal Bnarsidass) S Asia.

***Naidu, A. S.** Lactoferrin: Natural - Multifunctional - Antimicrobial. 184p. 2000. per. 69.95 (*0-8493-0909-3*) CRC Pr.

— Natural Food Antimicrobial Systems. LC 00-36053. 832p. 2000. boxed set 149.95 (*0-8493-2047-X*) CRC Pr.

Naidu, C. M. Nationalism in South India: Its Economic & Social Background, 1885-1918. 216p. (C). 1988. 31.00 (*81-7099-043-2*, Pub. by Mittal Pubs Dist) S Asia.

— Salt Satyagraha in Coastal Andhra. 238p. 1986. 13.50 (*0-8364-2033-0*, Pub. by Mittal Pubs Dist) S Asia.

Naidu, D. S. Singular Perturbation Methodology in Control Systems. (Control Engineering Ser.: No. 34). 1987. 95.00 (*0-86341-107-X*, CE034) INSPEC Inc.

Naidu, D. S. & Rao, A. K. Singular Perturbation Analysis of Discrete Control Systems. (Lecture Notes in Mathematics Ser.: Vol. 1154). 195p. 1985. 37.95 (*0-387-15981-9*) Spr-Verlag.

Naidu, D. Subbaram. Aeroassisted Orbital Transfer: Guidance & Control Strategies. LC 93-38670. 1993. 51.95 (*0-387-19819-9*) Spr-Verlag.

Naidu, D. Suran. The Congress Party in Transition. (C). 1991. 22.50 (*81-85135-64-9*, Pub. by Natl Bk Orgn) S Asia.

Naidu, Leela. New Housewife's First Cookbook. (C). 1992. pap. 16.00 (*81-85846-00-6*, Pub. by UBS Pubs Dist) S Asia.

Naidu, Motukuru S., jt. auth. see Kamaraju, V.

Naidu, Prabhakar S. Modern Spectrum Analysis of Time Series. 416p. 1995. boxed set 84.95 (*0-8493-2464-5*, 2464) CRC Pr.

***Naidu, Prabhakar S.** Sensor Array Signal Processing. LC 00-30409. (Illus.). 2000. pap. write for info. (*0-8493-1195-0*) CRC Pr.

Naidu, Prabhakar S. & Mathew, M. P. Analysis of Geophysical Potential Fields: A Digital Signal Processing Approach. LC 98-10235. (Advances in Exploration Geophysics Ser.). 298p. 1998. 195.50 (*0-444-82801-X*) Elsevier.

Naidu, Ratna. Old Cities, New Predicaments: A Study of Hyderabad. 178p. 1991. text 27.50 (*0-8039-9658-6*) Sage.

Naidu, Ravendra. Australian Sodic Soils: Distribution, Properties & Management. LC 96-137486. 1995. pap. text 120.00 (*0-643-05537-1*, Pub. by CSIRO) Accents Pubns.

Naidu, Ravendra, et al, eds. Contaminants & the Soil Environment in the Australasia-Pacific Region: Proceedings of the First Australasia-Pacific Conference on Contaminants & Soil Environment in the Australasia-Pacific Region, Held in Adelaide, Australia February 20 -24, 1996. 738p. (C). 1996. text 257.50 (*0-7923-3900-2*) Kluwer Academic.

Naidu, Ravendra, jt. ed. see Sumner, Malcolm E.

***Naidu, Vayu.** Stories from India. LC 99-48318. (Multicultural Stories Ser.). 2000. write for info. (*0-7398-2035-4*) Raintree Steck-V.

— Stories from India. (Multicultural Stories Ser.). (Illus.). 48p. (J). (ps-3). 2000. lib. bdg. 25.69 (*0-7398-1335-8*) Raintree Steck-V.

An Asterisk (*) at the beginning of an entry indicates that the title is appearing for the first time.

Naidus, Beverly. One Size Does Not Fit All. LC 93-30780. 1993. reprint ed. 35.00 (*1-883930-01-4*); reprint ed. pap. 15.00 (*1-883930-00-6*) AIGIS Pubns.

Naier, Jeffrey. New York International Chess: Tournament, 1984. 1985. 17.50 (*0-911971-11-4*) Effect Pub.

Naierman, Naomi, ed. see Fitzgerald, Helen.

Naifeh, Steven & Smith, Gregory W. The Best Lawyers in America, 1999-2000. 8th ed. Gibbons, Michael W., ed. 1500p. 1998. lib. bdg. 150.00 (*0-913391-20-4*) Woodward-White.

— Jackson Pollock: An American Saga. (Illus.). 1989. reprint ed. pap. 27.95 (*0-913391-19-0*) Woodward-White.

***Naifeh, Steven & Smith, Gregory White, eds.** The Best Lawyers in America, 2001-2002. 800p. 2000. write for info. (*0-913391-22-0*) Woodward-White.

— The Best Lawyers in America, 2001-2002, Vol. II. 800p. 2000. write for info. (*0-913391-23-9*) Woodward-White.

Naifeh, Steven W. A Stranger in the Family. 1996. mass mkt. 7.99 (*0-451-40622-2*, Onyx) NAL.

Naifeh, Steven W., jt. auth. see Smith, Gregory W.

Naigeon, Jacques A. La Militaire Philosophe. 200p. 1978. reprint ed. write for info. (*3-487-06568-1*) G Olms Pubs.

Naijrass, Brian & Altomare, Mary. The Natural Step for Business: Wealth, Ecology, & the Evolutionary Corporation. (Illus.). 222p. 1999. pap. 16.95 (*0-86571-384-7*, Pub. by New Soc Pubs) Consort Bk Sales.

Naik, A. Am I Normal? 1995. pap. text 7.95 (*0-340-63438-3*, Pub. by Hodder & Stought Ltd) Trafalgar.

— Wise Guide to Drugs. 1997. mass mkt. 8.95 (*0-340-69973-6*, Pub. by Hodder & Stought Ltd) Trafalgar.

— Wise Guides: Sex. 1998. mass mkt. 8.95 (*0-340-71042-X*, Pub. by Hodder & Stought Ltd) Trafalgar.

Naik, D. N., jt. auth. see Khattree, R.

Naik, Dayanand N., jt. auth. see Khatree, Ravinda.

Naik, Dayanand N., jt. auth. see Khatree, Ravindra.

Naik, Dayanand N., jt. auth. see Khattree, Ravindra.

Naik, Dilip. Internet Standards & Protocols. LC 98-22927. 512p. 1997. pap. text 29.99 (*1-57231-692-6*) Microsoft.

Naik, J. A. Death or Resurrection: A Story of the Hindus. (C). 1995. 14.00 (*0-8364-2909-5*, Pub. by Ajanta) S Asia.

— The Opposition in India & the Future of Democracy. 236p. 1988. 35.00 (*0-7855-1198-9*) St Mut.

— Russia's Policy Towards India: From Stalin to Yeltsin. 219p. 1995. pap. 150.00 (*81-85880-79-4*, Pub. by Print Hse) St Mut.

Naik, J. P. Education Commission & After. (Illus.). viii, 335p. 1997. 26.00 (*81-7024-905-8*, Pub. by APH Pubng) Nataraj Bks.

Naik, M. K. Dimensions of Indian English Literature. v, 208p. 1984. text 20.00 (*0-86590-230-5*) Apt Bks.

— A History of Indian English Literature. 1982. 11.00 (*0-8364-1595-7*, Pub. by National Sahitya Akademi) S Asia.

— A History of Indian English Literature. 1998. 11.00 (*81-7201-840-1*, Pub. by Rabindra Bhawn) S Asia.

Naik, M. K., ed. Perspectives on Indian Fiction in English. 1985. 20.00 (*0-8364-1412-8*, Pub. by Abhinav) S Asia.

Naik, M. K. & Mokashi-Punekar, S. Perspectives on Indian Drama in English. 1977. text 7.50 (*0-19-560825-9*) OUP.

Naik, Niranjan. Woven Fabric Composites. LC 93-60363. 200p. 1993. pap. 99.95 (*0-87762-990-0*) Technomic.

Naik, Ranjit. Fundamentals of Financial Analysis. (Euromoney/DC Gardner Self-Study Workbook Ser.). 1997. pap. 295.00 (*1-85564-615-3*, Pub. by Euromoney) Am Educ Systs.

Naik, Sandra, jt. auth. see Pennington, G. W.

Naik, Shailaja D. Folk Embroidery & Traditional Handloom Weaving. LC 97-906372. (Illus.). xiv, 208p. 1997. 29.00 (*81-7024-877-9*, Pub. by APH Pubng) Nataraj Bks.

— Traditional Embroideries of India. (C). 1996. 28.00 (*81-7024-731-4*, Pub. by Ashish Pub Hse) S Asia.

Naik, T. B. Impact of Education on the Bhils. 337p. 1977. 14.95 (*0-318-36824-2*) Asia Bk Corp.

Naik, Tarun R., ed. Temperature Effect on Concrete - STP 858. LC 84-70335. (Illus.). 180p. 1985. text 28.00 (*0-8031-0435-9*, STP858) ASTM.

Naik, Vijay K. Multiprocessing: Trade-Offs in Computation & Communication. LC 93-17930. (International Series in Engineering & Computer Science, VLSI, Computer Architecture, & Digital Screen Processing: Vol. 236). 224p. (C). 1993. text 131.50 (*0-7923-9370-8*) Kluwer Academic.

Naikar, Basavaraj S. Shakespeare's Last Plays. 1993. text 30.00 (*81-85231-10-9*, Pub. by Creative Pubs) Advent Bks Div.

Nail, Gene, ed. see Minns, Michael L.

Nail, James D. Whose Tracks Are These? A Clue Book of Familiar Forest Animals. LC 94-65087. (Illus.). 32p. (J). (gr. k-4). 1994. 13.95 (*1-879373-89-0*) Roberts Rinehart.

— Whose Tracks Are These? A Clue Book of Familiar Forest Animals. 2nd ed. LC 94-65087. (Illus.). 32p. (J). (gr. 1-5). 1996. reprint ed. pap. 7.95 (*1-57098-078-0*) Roberts Rinehart.

Nail, Simonne & Caillot, Simonne. How to Get Your Child to Read. LC 81-71138. (Illus.). 122p. 1982. pap. 9.00 (*0-942010-00-0*) Famous Pr Pub.

Nailen, Richard L. Managing Controls: The Complete Book of Motor Control Application & Maintenance. (Illus.). 130p. 1993. text 49.95 (*0-943876-06-0*) Barks Pubns.

Nailen, Richard L. Managing Motors: The Complete Book of Electric Motor Application & Maintenance. 2nd rev. ed. (Illus.). 464p. 1996. text 74.95 (*0-943876-09-5*) Barks Pubns.

Nailen, Richard L. & Haight, James S. Beertown Blazes. 2nd rev. ed. 1982. 20.00 (*0-932476-01-5*) Renaiss Bks.

Naillen, A. Van Der, see Ruhnau, Helena E. & Van Der Naillen, A.

Nails, Debra. Agora, Academy & the Conduct of Philosophy. LC 95-9150. (Philosophical Studies: Vol. 63). 284p. (C). 1995. lib. bdg. 130.00 (*0-7923-3543-0*, Pub. by Kluwer Academic) Kluwer Academic.

Nails, Debra, jt. ed. see Shimony, Abner.

***Nails-Pierce, Rebecca.** No Weapons Formed Against Me. 288p. 1999. pap. 12.95 (*0-9673149-4-1*) Treasured Spirit.

Naim, A. E. & Stehli, F. G. The Ocean Basins & Margins Vol. 7A: The Pacific Ocean. (Illus.). 748p. (C). 1985. 135.00 (*0-306-37777-2*, Plenum Trade) Perseus Pubng.

Naim, A. E., et al. The Ocean Basins & Margins Vol. 7B: The Pacific Ocean. (Illus.). 656p. (C). 1988. 135.00 (*0-306-37778-0*, Plenum Trade) Perseus Pubng.

Naim, A. E., et al. The Ocean Basins & Margins Vol. 8: The Tethys Ocean, Vol 8. (Illus.). 517p. (C). 1996. 150.00 (*0-306-45156-5*, Plenum Trade) Perseus Pubng.

Naim, Moises. Latin America's Journey to the Market: From Macroeconomic Shocks to Institutional Therapy. LC 94-42487. (Occasional Papers: No. 62). 1994. pap. 9.95 (*1-55815-457-4*) ICS Pr.

— Paper Tigers & Minotaurs: The Politics of Venezuela's Economic Reforms. LC 92-35295. 1992. 24.95 (*0-87003-025-6*); pap. 8.95 (*0-87003-026-4*) Carnegie Endow.

Naim, Moises & Tulchin, Joseph S., eds. Competition, Deregulation & Modernization in Latin America: Policy Perspectives. LC 99-11102. 285p. 1999. lib. bdg. 55.00 (*1-55587-818-0*) L Rienner.

Naim, Moises, jt. ed. see Edwards, Sebastian.

Naim, Patrick, jt. auth. see Davalo, Eric.

Naim, Rob. What Is Meditation? Buddhism for Everyone. LC 98-4305. 112p. 1999. 16.00 (*1-57062-421-6*, Pub. by Shambhala Pubns) Random.

Naima. Annals of the Turkish Empire from 1591 to 1659 of the Christian Era. Fraser, Charles, tr. LC 73-6294. (Middle East Ser.). 1973. reprint ed. 33.95 (*0-405-05352-5*) Ayer.

Naiman. Understand Statistics. 3rd ed. 1983. 26.87 (*0-07-045864-2*) McGraw.

Naiman, Arnold & Rosenfeld, Robert. Understanding Statistics. 4th ed. (C). 1996. pap. text, student ed. 26.88 (*0-07-045996-7*) McGraw.

Naiman, Arnold, et al. Understanding Statistics. 4th ed. LC 95-39801. 416p. (C). 1995. pap. 61.88 (*0-07-045915-0*) McGraw.

Naiman, Arthur, jt. auth. see Zepezauer, Mark.

Naiman, Arthur, ed. & compiled by see Chomsky, Noam.

Naiman, Doris. Curriculum for Multiply Handicapped Deaf Students. 196p. (C). 1982. pap. 4.95 (*0-913072-47-8*) Natl Assn Deaf.

Naiman, Eric. Sex in Public: The Incarnation of Early Soviet Ideology. LC 96-43642. 328p. 1997. text 39.50 (*0-691-02626-2*, Pub. by Princeton U Pr) Cal Prin Full Svc.

— Sex in Public: The Incarnation of Early Soviet Ideology. LC 96-43642. (Illus.). 307p. 1999. pap. 21.95 (*0-691-02625-4*, Pub. by Princeton U Pr) Cal Prin Full Svc.

Naiman, Ingrid. Cancer, Vol. IV. 2nd ed. (Astrology of Healing Ser.). (Illus.). 216p. 1997. reprint ed. 35.00 (*1-882834-04-6*) Seventh Ray.

— Cancer Salves: A Botanical Approach to Treatment. 3rd rev. ed. (Illus.). 220p. 1997. 30.00 (*1-882834-11-9*) Seventh Ray.

— Cancer Salves: A Botanical Approach to Treatment. 3rd rev. ed. (Illus.). 272p. 1999. pap. text 27.50 (*1-882834-15-1*) Seventh Ray.

***Naiman, Ingrid.** Cancer Salves: A Botanical Approach to Treatment. 3rd rev. ed. (Illus.). 272p. 1999. 45.00 (*1-882834-16-X*) Seventh Ray.

Naiman, Ingrid. The Elements Vol. II: Symptoms of Disease. 7th ed. (Astrology of Healing Ser.). (Illus.). 183p. 1997. reprint ed. pap. 35.00 (*1-882834-02-X*) Seventh Ray.

— Immunity. 3rd rev. ed. (Astrology of Healing Ser.: Vol. V). 72p. 1997. pap. 20.00 (*1-882834-05-4*) Seventh Ray.

— Lunar Consciousness. 2nd ed. 120p. Date not set. pap. 25.00 (*1-882834-00-3*) Seventh Ray.

— Stress Vol. I: The Cause of Disease. 5th ed. (Astrology of Healing Ser.). (Illus.). 274p. 1997. reprint ed. pap. 35.00 (*1-882834-01-1*) Seventh Ray.

Naiman, Neil, et al. The Good Language Learner. LC 95-25384. (Modern Languages in Practice Ser.: Vol. 4). 230p. 1995. pap. 29.95 (*1-85359-313-3*, Pub. by Multilingual Matters) Taylor & Francis.

Naiman, R. J. & Bilby, R. E., eds. River Ecology & Management: Lessons from the Pacific Coastal Region. (Illus.). 540p. 1998. pap. text 39.95 (*0-387-98324-4*) Spr-Verlag.

Naiman, Rina. A Family for Christmas. (Intimate Moments Ser.: No. 828). 1997. per. 3.99 (*0-373-07828-5*, 1-07828-6) Harlequin Bks.

Naiman, Robert J., ed. Watershed Management: Balancing Sustainability & Environmental Change. (Illus.). 542p. 1992. 79.00 (*0-387-97790-2*) Spr-Verlag.

— Watershed Management: Balancing Sustainability & Environmental Change. (Illus.). 560p. 1995. 42.95 (*0-387-94232-7*) Spr-Verlag.

Naiman, Robert J. & Bilby, Robert E., eds. River Ecology & Management: Lessons from the Pacific Coastal Ecoregion. LC 97-44766. (Illus.). 896p. 1998. text 189.00 (*0-387-98323-6*) Spr-Verlag.

Naiman, Robert J. & Decamps, H., eds. The Ecology & Management of Aquatic-Terrestrial Ecotones. (Man & the Biosphere Ser.: Vol. 4). (Illus.). 316p. 1990. 65.00 (*1-85070-271-3*) Prthnon Pub.

Naiman, Robert J., et al. The Freshwater Imperative: A Research Agenda. LC 94-39852. 200p. 1995. text 38.00 (*1-55963-406-5*) Island Pr.

— The Freshwater Imperative: A Research Agenda. LC 94-39852. 200p. (C). 1995. pap. text 25.00 (*1-55963-407-3*) Island Pr.

— Pacific Salmon & Their Ecosystems: Status & Future Options. LC 96-38439. (Illus.). 512p. 1997. write for info. (*0-412-98691-4*) Kluwer Academic.

Naiman, Robert J., jt. auth. see Soltz, David L.

Naimark, Dana W., jt. ed. see McGuire, Therese J.

Naimark, George M. Communications on Communication. 3rd ed. 135p. 1987. 19.95 (*0-911204-03-2*) Rajah.

Naimark, M. A. Theory of Group Representations. (Illus.). 576p. 1982. 149.95 (*0-387-90602-9*) Spr-Verlag.

Naimark, M. A., jt. auth. see Swinfen, A.

***Naimark, Norman & Gibianskii, Leonid, eds.** Establishment of Communist Regimes in Eastern Europe, 1944-1949. 328p. 1998. pap. text 30.00 (*0-8133-3534-5*, Pub. by Westview) HarpC.

***Naimark, Norman M.** Fires of Hatred: Ethnic Cleansing in Twentieth-Century Europe. 256p. 2001. 24.95 (*0-674-00313-6*) HUP.

Naimark, Norman M. A History of the "Proletariat" The Emergence of Marxism in the Kingdom of Poland, 1870-1887. (East European Monographs: No. 54). 329p. 1979. text 72.50 (*0-914710-50-8*, Pub. by East Eur Monographs) Col U Pr.

— The Russians in Germany: A History of the Soviet Zone of Occupation, 1945-1949. LC 95-7725. (Illus.). 608p. (C). 1995. 37.95 (*0-674-78405-7*) Belknap Pr.

— The Russians in Germany: A History of the Soviet Zone of Occupation, 1945-1949. 624p. 1997. pap. text 18.50 (*0-674-78406-5*) HUP.

— Terrorists & Social Democrats: The Russian Revolutionary Movement under Alexander III. (Russian Research Center Studies: No. 82). 328p. 1983. 43.00 (*0-674-87464-1*) HUP.

Naimark, Norman M., jt. ed. see Holloway, David.

Naime, A. K. The Flowering Plants of Western India. 401p. (C). 1976. text 160.00 (*0-89771-608-6*, Pub. by Intl Bk Distr) St Mut.

Naimer, Lucille. The Zen of Cooking. 209p. 1996. 23.95 (*0-87951-594-5*, Pub. by Overlook Pr) Penguin Putnam.

Naimipour, Kamarss, jt. auth. see Neapolitan, Richard E.

Naimipour, Kumarss, jt. auth. see Neapolitan, Richard E.

Naimy, Mikhail. El Libro de Mirdad. (SPA.). 248p. pap. 15.00 (*84-404-1600-8*) Rosycross Pr.

Naimy, Nadeem N. The Lebanese Prophets of New York. 112p. 1986. text 19.95 (*0-8156-6073-1*, Pub. by Am U Beirut) Syracuse U Pr.

— Mikhail Naimy: An Introduction. 1967. pap. 15.95 (*0-8156-6028-6*, Pub. by Am U Beirut) Syracuse U Pr.

Naine, D. T. Sundiata: An Epic of Old Mali. (C). 1965. pap. text 11.95 (*0-582-26475-8*, Pub. by Addison-Wesley) Longman.

Naipaul, Shiva. North of South: An African Journey. LC 97-106091. 352p. 1997. pap. 12.95 (*0-14-018826-6*, Penguin Bks) Viking Penguin.

***Naipaul, V. S.** Among Believers: An Islamic Journey. 2000. 27.50 (*0-8446-7130-4*) Peter Smith.

Naipaul, V. S. Among the Believers: An Islamic Journey. LC 82-40048. 448p. 1982. pap. 16.00 (*0-394-71195-5*) Vin Bks.

— An Area of Darkness. 1993. 24.75 (*0-8446-6680-7*) Peter Smith.

— A Bend in the River. LC 99-24655. 1999. 26.95 (*0-7838-8616-0*, G K Hall Lrg Type) Mac Lib Ref.

Naipaul, V. S. A Bend in the River. 1989. 7.95 (*0-07-558711-4*) McGraw.

Naipaul, V. S. A Bend in the River. LC 96-52567. 1997. 16.50 (*0-679-60267-4*) Modern Lib NY.

— A Bend in the River. 1992. 24.50 (*0-8446-6631-9*) Peter Smith.

— A Bend in the River. (International Ser.). 1989. pap. 13.00 (*0-679-72202-5*) Vin Bks.

***Naipaul, V. S.** Between Father & Son: Family Letters. Aitken, Gillon, ed. LC 99-31089. 352p. 2000. 26.00 (*0-375-40730-8*) Knopf.

Naipaul, V. S. Beyond Belief. 432p. 1999. pap. 15.00 (*0-375-70648-8*) Knopf.

— Beyond Belief. 368p. 1998. 27.95 (*0-375-50118-5*) Random.

— The Enigma of Arrival: A Novel. LC 87-45937. 368p. 1988. reprint ed. pap. 15.00 (*0-394-75760-2*) Vin Bks.

— Guerrillas. 1975. 24.50 (*0-8446-6910-5*) Peter Smith.

— Guerrillas. LC 90-50147. (Vintage International Ser.). 256p. 1990. pap. 12.00 (*0-679-73174-1*) Random.

— A House for Mr. Biswas. 592p. 1995. 20.00 (*0-679-44458-0*) Knopf.

— In a Free State. 1984. pap. 10.00 (*0-394-72205-1*) Vin Bks.

— Miguel Street. (Caribbean Writers Ser.). 172p. (C). 1974. pap. 7.95 (*0-435-98645-7*, 98645) Heinemann.

— Miguel Street. 288p. 1977. pap. 11.95 (*0-14-003302-5*, Penguin Bks) Viking Penguin.

Naipaul, V. S. The Mystic Masseur. (Caribbean Writers Ser.). 214p. (C). 1971. pap. 8.95 (*0-435-98646-5*, 98646) Heinemann.

— Reading & Writing: A Personal Account. LC 99-49615. 80p. 2000. 16.95 (*0-940322-38-2*) NY Rev Bks.

Naipaul, V. S. A Turn in the South. 1989. 18.45 (*0-07-546835-2*) McGraw.

— A Turn in the South. 1990. pap. 14.00 (*0-679-72488-5*) Vin Bks.

— A Way in the World. 1994. 25.00 (*0-8446-6909-1*) Peter Smith.

— A Way in the World. 1995. pap. 14.00 (*0-679-76166-7*) Random.

Nair. Methodologies in Nucleoside Synthesis. 250p. 1998. 1.00 (*0-12-513810-5*) Acad Pr.

Nair, Adoor. Slavery in Kerala. 1986. 18.00 (*0-8364-1914-6*, Pub. by Mittal Pubs Dist) S Asia.

***Nair, Anita.** The Better Man. LC 00-27420. 288p. 2000. text 24.00 (*0-312-25311-7*, Picador USA) St Martin.

Nair, B. R., ed. see ASME-CSME Montreal Pressure Vessel & Piping Confer.

Nair, C. G. Krishnadas, see Krishnadas Nair, C. G.

Nair, C. N., jt. auth. see Reese, A. C.

Nair, C. Sankaran. Gandhi & Anarchy. (C). 1995. reprint ed. 28.50 (*0-614-07150-X*, Pub. by Motilal Bnarsidass) S Asia.

Nair, Garyth. Voice - Tradition & Technology: A State-of-the-Art Studio. LC 99-16180. (Illus.). 406p. 1999. pap. 63.95 (*0-7693-0028-6*, 2030) Thomson Learn.

Nair, Gopinathan M. Mental Science 101. 1997. pap. 12.95 (*0-7880-0926-5*, Fairway Pr) CSS OH.

Nair, Gwyneth, et al, eds. Highley. (C). 1989. 39.00 (*0-947712-13-5*, Pub. by S A Baldwin) St Mut.

Nair, Indira, tr. see Novozhilov, K. V., ed.

Nair, Janaki. Miners & Millhands: Work, Culture & Politics in Princely Mysore. LC 98-12773. 308p. (C). 1998. 44.95 (*0-7619-9251-0*) Sage.

Nair, Janaki, jt. ed. see John, Mery.

Nair, K. M. & Bhalla, A. S., eds. Advances in Dielectric Ceramic Materials. (Ceramic Transactions Ser.: Vol. 88). (Illus.). 481p. 1998. 95.00 (*1-57498-033-5*, CT088) Am Ceramic.

***Nair, K. M. & Bhalla, A. S., eds.** Dielectric Ceramic Materials. (Ceramic Transactions Ser.: Vol. 100). 26p. 1999. text 95.00 (*1-57498-066-1*, CT100) Am Ceramic.

Nair, K. M. & Shukla, V. N., eds. Hybrid Microelectronic Materials. (Ceramic Transactions Ser.: No. 68). (Illus.). 296p. 1996. 95.00 (*1-57498-013-0*, CT068) Am Ceramic.

Nair, K. N., et al. Ecology or Economics in Cardamom Development. (C). 1989. 14.00 (*81-204-0426-2*, Pub. by Oxford IBH) S Asia.

Nair, K. N., jt. ed. see Doornbos, Martin.

Nair, Ken. Discovering the Heart of a Man. rev. ed. 227p. 1992. pap. 8.95 (*0-9635458-0-9*) K Nair.

— Discovering the Mind of a Woman. 123p. 1982. pap. 6.95 (*0-937929-00-X*) K Nair.

— Discovering the Mind of a Woman. 224p. 1995. 14.99 (*0-7852-7811-7*) Nelson.

Nair, Keshavan. Beyond Winning. LC 87-62803. 105p. (Orig.). 1988. 14.95 (*0-945150-19-9*); pap. 9.95 (*0-945150-22-9*) Paradox AZ.

— Higher Standard of Leadership: Lessons from the Life of Gandhi. LC 94-26927. 174p. 1997. pap. 16.95 (*1-57675-011-6*) Berrett-Koehler.

Nair, Kusum. Blossoms in the Dust: The Human Element in Indian Development. LC 78-66080. (Midway Reprint Ser.). (Illus.). 200p. reprint ed. pap. 62.00 (*0-608-09485-4*, 205428600005) Bks Demand.

Nair, Kusum. In Defense of the Irrational Peasant: Indian Agriculture after the Green Revolution. LC 78-26707. 1996. 20.50 (*0-226-56798-2*) U Ch Pr.

Nair, Kusum. In Defense of the Irrational Peasant: Indian Agriculture after the Green Revolution. LC 78-26707. 176p. reprint ed. pap. 54.60 (*0-608-09486-2*, 205428700005) Bks Demand.

Nair, M. B. Politics in Bangladesh: A Study of Awami League, 1949-1958. 1990. 40.00 (*81-85119-79-1*, Pub. by Northern Bk Ctr) S Asia.

Nair, M. C., et al, eds. Advances in Mushroom Biotechnology: The National Symposium on Mushroom 1991 at Thiruvanantapuram, Kerala. 1991. pap. 105.00 (*81-7233-080-4*, Pub. by Scientific Pubs) St Mut.

Nair, M. K., et al, eds. Advances in Coconut Research & Development: Proceedings of the International Symposium on Coconut Research & Development. 776p. (C). 1994. text 130.00 (*1-881570-27-4*) Science Pubs.

Nair, Mohan. Activity-Based Information Systems: A Executive's Guide to Implementation. LC 99-17670. (Cost Management Ser.). 240p. 1999. 65.00 incl. cd-rom (*0-471-32431-0*) Wiley.

Nair, Murali D. & Brody, Ralph. Community Service: The Art of Volunteering & Service Learning. 2000th ed. 115p. pap. 18.00 (*0-911541-46-2*) Gregory Pub.

Nair, Murali D., jt. auth. see Brody, Ralph.

Nair, P. K. Advances in Palynology. 500p. (C). 1981. text 400.00 (*0-89771-603-5*, Pub. by Intl Bk Distr) St Mut.

— Advances in Pollen Spore Research, Vol. XII. 170p. 1984. 30.00 (*1-55528-061-7*, Pub. by Today Tomorrow) Scholarly Pubns.

— Essentials of Palynology. 150p. (C). 1991. text 160.00 (*0-7855-6589-2*, Pub. by Intl Bk Distr) St Mut.

— Essentials of Palynology. 129p. 1985. 19.00 (*1-55528-030-7*, Pub. by Today Tomorrow) Scholarly Pubns.

— Plantation & Agri-Horticultural Resources of Kerala. (Aspects of Plant Sciences Ser.: Vol. 7). 120p. 1984. 19.00 (*1-55528-165-6*, Pub. by Today Tomorrow) Scholarly Pubns.

— Progress in Palynology: Cumulation of Journal of Palynology, 2 vols. in 4 pts., Vols. 1-20. 3500p. 1986. 300.00 (*1-55528-077-3*, Pub. by Today Tomorrow) Scholarly Pubns.

Nair, P. K., ed. Advances in Pollen Spore Research, Vol. 1. 167p. 1975. 19.00 (*0-88065-165-2*) Scholarly Pubns.

— Advances in Pollen Spore Research, Vol. II. 160p. 1977. 19.00 (*0-88065-166-0*) Scholarly Pubns.

— Advances in Pollen Spore Research, Vol. IV. 160p. 1979. 12.00 (*0-88065-168-7*) Scholarly Pubns.

— Advances in Pollen Spore Research, Vols. V - VII. 160p. 1980. 45.00 (*0-88065-169-5*) Scholarly Pubns.

— Agroforestry Systems in the Tropics. (Forestry Sciences Ser.). (C). 1989. text 320.50 (*90-247-3790-7*) Kluwer Academic.

— Aspects of Plant Sciences, Vol. I. 210p. 1976. 15.00 (*0-88065-170-9*) Scholarly Pubns.

N

— Aspects of Plant Sciences, Vol. II. 164p. 1979. 15.00 (0-88065-171-7) Scholarly Pubns.
— Cytological Research Monographs. (Glimpses in Plant Research Ser.: Vol. VIII). (Illus.). 250p. 1988. 69.00 (1-55528-164-8, Pub. by Today Tomorrow) Scholarly Pubns.
— Glimpses in Plant Research, Vol. VII. 202p. 1986. 39.00 (1-55528-104-4, Pub. by Today Tomorrow) Scholarly Pubns.
— Glimpses in Plant Research, Vol. VIII. (Illus.). 250p. 1988. 69.00 (0-685-24663-9, Pub. by Today Tomorrow) Scholarly Pubns.
— Pollen Morphology of Angiosperms: A Historical & Phylogenetic Study. 200p. (C). 1991. text 200.00 (0-89771-607-8, Pub. by Intl Bk Distr) St Mut.
Nair, P. K., et al, eds. Agroforestry Education & Training: Present & Future. (Forestry Sciences Ser.). (C). 1990. text 98.50 (0-7923-0864-6) Kluwer Academic.
Nair, P. K. & Achar, K. Prabhakar. A Textbook of Cell Biology. 224p. 1990. text 25.00 (81-220-0123-8, Pub. by Konark Pubs Pvt Ltd) Advent Bks Div.
— A Textbook of Genetics & Evolution. (Illus.). 356p. 1990. text 30.00 (81-220-0127-0, Pub. by Konark Pubs Pvt Ltd) Advent Bks Div.
Nair, P. K. & Kothari, Sushma. Studies in the Pollen Morphology of Indian Heteromerae. (Advances in Pollen Spore Research Ser.: Vol. 13). xii, 90p. 1985. 15.00 (1-55528-055-2) Scholarly Pubns.
Nair, P. K. & Lawrence, R. Pollen Morphology of Indian Compositae. (Advances in Pollen Spore Research Ser.: Vol. XIV). (Illus.). 176p. 1985. 25.00 (1-55528-043-9) Scholarly Pubns.
Nair, P. K., jt. auth. see Yunus, Durdana.
Nair, P. K., ed. see Katiyar, Kamlesh.
Nair, P. K., jt. ed. see Khoshoo, T. N.
Nair, P. K., ed. see Srivastava, D.
Nair, P. P. & Kritchevsky, David, eds. The Bile Acids: Chemistry, Physiology & Metabolism. Incl. Chemistry. LC 71-138520. 384p. 1971. 65.00 (0-306-37131-6, Kluwer Plenum); Physiology & Metabolism. LC 71-138520. 330p. 1973. 65.00 (0-306-37132-4, Kluwer Plenum); Vol. 3. Pathophysiology. LC 71-138520. 242p. 1976. 55.00 (0-306-37133-2, Kluwer Plenum); LC 71-138520. write for info. (0-318-55308-2, Plenum Trade) Perseus Pubng.
Nair, P. Ramachandran. An Introduction to Agroforestry. LC 92-46550. 1993. lib. bdg. 222.00 (0-7923-2134-0) Kluwer Academic.
Nair, P. S., jt. auth. see Mordeson, J. N.
Nair, P. Thankappan. British Beginnings in Bengal. (C). 1991. text 54.00 (81-85094-36-5, Pub. by Punthi Pus) S Asia.
— Calcutta in the Eighteenth Century. 1984. 22.50 (0-8364-1232-X, Pub. by Mukhopadhyaya) S Asia.
— Calcutta in the Seventeenth Century. 1986. 38.00 (0-8364-1619-8) S Asia.
— A History of Calcutta's Streets: A Tercentenary History of Calcutta. 992p. 1987. 72.00 (0-8364-1934-0) S Asia.
— Indian National Songs & Symbols. (C). 1987. 16.50 (0-8364-2128-0) S Asia.
Nair, P. Thankappan, ed. Bruton's Visit of Lord Jagannath 350 Years Ago: British Beginnings in Orissa. 1986. 14.00 (0-8364-1610-4, Pub. by Minerva) S Asia.
Nair, Premchand S., jt. auth. see Mordeson, John N.
Nair, R. D., jt. auth. see Rittenberg, Larry.
Nair, R. V. Taxonomy of Angiosperms. (Illus.). 403p. 1997. 69.00 (81-7024-809-4, Pub. by APH Pubng) Nataraj Bks.
***Nair, S.** Thoughts to Live By. 1998. pap. 100.00 (81-86982-18-3, Pub. by Business Pubns) St Mut.
— Thoughts to Manage By. 1998. pap. 125.00 (81-86982-19-1, Pub. by Business Pubns) St Mut.
Nair, S. K. Review of Models Used for Determining Consequences of UF6 Release: Development of Model Evaluation Criteria. 50p. 1997. pap. 4.50 (0-16-054784-9) USGPO.
— Review of Models Used for Determining Consequences of UF6 Release: Model Evaluation Report. 214p. 1997. per. 21.00 (0-16-062869-5) USGPO.
Nair, S. S. & Mistry, S. I., eds. Fluid Power Systems & Technology, 1998; Proceedings: ASME International Mechanical Engineering Congress & Exposition (1998: Anaheim, CA) 229p. 1998. pap. 100.00 (0-7918-1593-5) ASME Pr.
Nair, Sadanandan K. & White, Shirley A., eds. Perspectives on Development Communication. LC 93-25691. 256p. 1994. text 36.00 (0-8039-9132-0); pap. text 16.50 (0-8039-9133-9) Sage.
Nair, Sami, et al, eds. Perspectives on Europe. (Contemporary European Affairs Ser.: No. JCEA 4). 272p. 1992. pap. 27.25 (0-08-041923-2, Pergamon Pr) Elsevier.
Nair, Satish S. & Chandran, Ram S. Fluid Power Systems & Technology: Proceedings, ASME International Mechanical Engineering Congress & Exposition, 1996. LC 96-78676. (FPST Ser.: Vol. 3). 131p. 1996. pap. 72.00 (0-7918-1534-X, TJ843) ASME.
Nair, Satish S., jt. ed. see Chandran, Ram S.
Nair, Shanti. Islam in Malaysian Foreign Policy. LC 98-107788. (Politics in Asia Ser.). 320p. (C). 1997. 90.00 (0-415-10341-X) Routledge.
Nair, Shanti V. & Jakus, Karl. High Temperature Mechanical Behavior of Ceramic Composites. 371p. 1995. text 185.00 (0-7506-9399-1) Buttrwrth-Heinemann.
Nair, Sobha B. Social Security & the Weaker Sections. 1990. 17.50 (81-85199-38-8, Pub. by Renaiss Publng Hse) S Asia.
Nair, Sreekantan S. On Certain Priority Queues. LC 78-132638. 171p. 1969. 22.00 (0-403-04521-5) Scholarly.
Nair, Supriya. Caliban's Curse: George Lamming & the Revisioning of History. LC 96-10322. 184p. (C). 1996. text 37.50 (0-472-10717-8, 10717) U of Mich Pr.
Nair, V. Balakrishnan. Social Development & Demographic Changes in South India: Focus on Kerala. LC 94-904657. 216p. 1994. pap. 150.00 (81-85880-50-6, Pub. by Print Hse) St Mut.
Nair, V. Sankaran. How Students Wrought for Freedom: A Collection of Documents. (C). 1993. 24.00 (81-7099-269-9, Pub. by Mittal Pubs Dist) S Asia.
— Role of Students in Freedom Movement: With Special Reference to Madras Presidency. 248p. 1991. text 30.00 (81-220-0197-1, Pub. by Konark Pubs Pvt Ltd) Advent Bks Div.
Nairn, A. E., jt. auth. see Alsharhan, A. S.
Nairn, Alan E. & Moullade, M., eds. The Phanerozoic Geology of the World Vol. IB: The Paleozoic. 704p. 1995. 293.25 (0-444-82090-6) Elsevier.
Nairn, Alan E. & Stehli, Francis G., eds. The Ocean Basins & Margins. Incl. Vol. 1, The South Atlantic. LC 72-83046. 600p. 1973. (0-306-37771-3, Kluwer Plenum); Vol. 2, The North Atlantic. LC 72-83046. 662p. 1974. (0-306-37772-1, Kluwer Plenum); Vol. 3, The Gulf of Mexico & The Caribbean. LC 72-83046. 722p. 1975. (0-306-37773-X, Kluwer Plenum); Vol. 4A, The Eastern Mediterranean. LC 72-83046. 520p. 1977. (0-306-37774-8, Kluwer Plenum); Vol. 4B, The Western Mediterranean. LC 72-83046. 462p. 1978. (0-306-37779-9, Kluwer Plenum); Vol. 5, The Arctic Ocean. LC 72-83046. 686p. 1981. (0-306-37775-6, Kluwer Plenum); LC 72-83046. (Illus.). 125.00 (0-685-04080-1, Plenum Trade) Perseus Pubng.
— The Ocean Basins & Margins Vol. 6: The Indian Ocean. LC 72-83046. 794p. 1982. 125.00 (0-306-37776-4, Plenum Trade) Perseus Pubng.
Nairn, Alan E., jt. auth. see Moullade, M.
Nairn, Alan E., jt. ed. see Moullade, M.
***Nairn, Allan.** Our Kind of Guys The United States & the Indonesian Military. 1999. 20.00 (1-85984-735-8, Pub. by Verso) Norton.
Nairn, Allan & Associates Staff, ed. The Reign of ETS: The Corporation That Makes up Minds. LC 80-107761. (Ralph Nader Report on the Educational Testing Service Ser.). 554p. (Orig.). 1980. pap. 30.00 (0-936486-00-7) R Nader.
Nairn, Angus C., jt. ed. see Shenolikar, Shirish.
Nairn, C., jt. auth. see Pevsner, Nikolaus.
Nairn, G., jt. auth. see Nairn, J. A.
Nairn, J. A. & Nairn, G. Greek Through Reading. (GRE.). 384p. 1988. pap. 27.95 (1-85399-037-X, Pub. by Brist Class Pr) Focus Pub-R Pullins.
Nairn, Nick. Nick Nairn's Island Harvest. 1999. pap. text 26.95 (1-884656-10-2) W One Hund Seventy Five.
Nairn, Richard & Crowley, Miriam. Wild Wicklow: Nature in the Garden of Ireland. LC 98-230753. (Illus.). 272p. 1998. 29.95 (1-86059-048-9, Pub. by Town Hse) Roberts Rinehart.
Nairn, Rob. Diamond Mind: A Psychology of Meditation. LC 99-23691. 112p. 1999. 16.95 (1-57062-536-0, Pub. by Shambhala Pubns) Random.
Nairn, Ronald C. International Aid to Thailand: The New Colonialism? 1966. 59.50 (0-685-45681-1) Elliots Bks.
Nairn, Thom, jt. ed. see Crawford, Robert.
***Nairn, Tom.** After Britain: New Labour & the Return of Scotland. 324p. 2000. 24.95 (1-86207-293-0, Pub. by Granta) Midpt Trade.
Nairn, Tom. Enchanted Glass: Britain & Its Monarchy. 1989. pap. 12.95 (0-09-172955-6, Pub. by Hutchnson) Trafalgar.
— Faces of Nationalism: Janus Revisited. 1998. pap. 20.00 (1-85984-194-5, Pub. by Verso) Norton.
— Faces of Nationalism: Janus Revisited. (C). 1998. 50.00 (1-85984-823-0, Pub. by Verso) Norton.
Nairn, Tom, jt. auth. see Quattrochi, Angelo.
Nairne, Alexander K. History of Konkan. (C). 1988. reprint ed. 17.00 (81-206-0275-7, Pub. by Asian Educ Servs) S Asia.
Nairne, Carolina O. The Life & Songs of the Baroness Nairne, with a Memoir & Poems of Caroline Oliphant the Younger. LC 70-144571. (Illus.). reprint ed. 42.50 (0-404-08577-6) AMS Pr.
Nairne, James S. Psychology: The Adaptive Mind. 1996. pap., teacher ed. write for info. (0-534-34373-2) Brooks-Cole.
— Psychology: The Adaptive Mind. LC 96-28954. (Psychology Ser.). 659p. (C). 1996. mass mkt. 52.50 (0-534-20682-4) Brooks-Cole.
***Nairne, James S.** Psychology: The Adaptive Mind. 2nd ed. LC 99-16382. (Psychology Ser.). 750p. 1999. mass mkt. 79.95 (0-534-35766-0) Brooks-Cole.
Nairne, Kathy & Smith, Gerrilyn. Dealing with Drepression. 2nd ed. 257p. 1997. pap. 13.95 (0-7043-4443-2, Pub. by Womens Press) Trafalgar.
Nairon, Kevin. Building a Robot: A Straightforward Approach. (Illus.). 152p. 1993. 19.95 (0-9635636-1-0) Humanform Robot.
Naisawald, L. VanLoan. Grape & Canister, the Story of the Field Artillery of the Army of the Potomac. 593p. 35.00 (1-56013-007-5) Olde Soldier Bks.
— In Some Foreign Field: Four British Graves & Submarine Warfare on the North Carolina Outer Banks. LC 98-130102. (Illus.). x, 99p. (YA). (gr. 8-12). 1997. pap. 12.00 (0-86526-272-1) NC Archives.
Naisawald, L.Vanloan. Grape & Canister: The Story of the Field Artillery of the Army of the Potomac, 1861-1865. 2nd ed. LC 99-38769. 1999. 34.95 (0-8117-0702-4) Stackpole.
***Naisbett.** Megatrends Asia. 1999. pap. 9.98 (0-671-04442-7) PB.
Naisbitt. The Year Ahead. 1999. mass mkt. write for info. (0-446-38343-0, Pub. by Warner Bks) Little.
Naisbitt Group Staff. Small Business in America: The Year 2000 & Beyond. (Illus.). 20p. (Orig.). 1986. pap. 6.00 (0-940791-00-5) NFIB Found.
Naisbitt Group Staff & Naisbitt, John. The Year Ahead, 1987: 1987. (Orig.). 1999. mass mkt. 6.95 (0-446-38342-2, Pub. by Warner Bks) Little.
Naisbitt, John. Global Paradox. 400p. 1995. mass mkt. 6.50 (0-380-72489-8, Avon Bks) Morrow Avon.
Naisbitt, John. Megatrends Asia: Eight Asian Megatrends That Are Reshaping Our World. 1997. per. 12.00 (0-684-82706-9, Touchstone) S&S Trade Pap.
Naisbitt, John, et al, contrib. by. The Hospitality & Leisure Architecture of Wimberly Allison Tong & Goo. rev. ed. (Illus.). 192p. 1997. pap. write for info. (1-56496-506-6) Rockport Vitae Pub.
Naisbitt, John & Aburdene, Patricia. Megatrends 2000. 448p. 1991. mass mkt. 6.99 (0-380-70437-4, Avon Bks) Morrow Avon.
Naisbitt, John, et al. High Tech/High Touch: Technology & Our Search for Meaning. LC 99-37766. 290p. 1999. 25.00 (0-7679-0383-8) Bantam.
Naisbitt, John, jt. auth. see Aburdene, Patricia.
Naisbitt, John, jt. auth. see Naisbitt Group Staff.
Naish, Camille. A Genetic Approach to Structures in the Work of Jean Genet. LC 78-7059. (Studies in Romance Languages: No. 34). 219p. 1978. 14.00 (0-674-34581-9) HUP.
Naish, Camille, tr. see Des Rosieres, Alain.
Naish, Camille, tr. see Le Brun, Annie.
Naish, Camille, tr. see Levi, Giovanni & Schmitt, Jean C., eds.
Naish, Camille, tr. see Levi, Giovanni & Schmitt, Jean-Claude, eds.
Naish, Camille, tr. see Tillard, Francoise.
Naish, Camille, tr. see Vermeil, Jean.
Naish, Francesca & Roberts, Janette. Healthy Parents, Better Babies: A Couple's Guide to Pre-Conception Health Care. LC 98-55113. Orig. Title: Natural Way to Better Babies. 1999. pap. 18.95 (0-89594-955-5) Crossing Pr.
Naish, G. P., ed. Nelson's Letters to His Wife & Other Documents. 1989. 80.00 (0-7855-1148-2) St Mut.
Naish, John. A Physician's Eye. LC 97-4009. (Mellen Lives Ser.: Vol. 6). (Illus.). 172p. 1997. text 79.95 (0-7734-8662-3) E Mellen.
Naish, John M. The Interwoven Lives of George Vancouver, Archibald Menzies, Joseph Whidbey, & Peter Puget. LC 95-43268. 1996. write for info. (0-7734-8857-X) E Mellen.
Naish, L. Negation & Control in Prology. (Lecture Notes in Computer Science Ser.: Vol. 238). ix, 119p. 1988. 26.00 (0-387-16815-X) Spr-Verlag.
Naish, Lee, ed. Logic Programming: Proceedings of the Fourteenth International Conference. (Logic Programming Ser.). (Illus.). 448p. (Orig.). 1997. pap. text 85.00 (0-262-64035-X) MIT Pr.
Naish, Nora. The Butterfly Box. 256p. 1995. pap. 8.99 (0-7493-2128-8) Buttrwrth-Heinemann.
— The Butterfly Box. large type ed. (Large Print Ser.). 464p. 1996. 27.99 (0-7089-3557-5) Ulverscroft.
— The Magistrate's Tale. 1996. pap. 9.99 (0-7493-2415-5) Buttrwrth-Heinemann.
— Sunday Lunch. 1995. pap. 8.99 (0-7493-2133-4) Buttrwrth-Heinemann.
— Sunday Lunch. large type ed. 1995. 27.99 (0-7089-3277-0) Ulverscroft.
***Naish, Nora.** A Time to Learn. large type unabridged ed. 361p. 1999. 25.95 (0-7531-5972-4, 159724, Pub. by ISIS Lrg Prnt) ISIS Pub.
Naish, Paul & Bishop, Peter. Designing Asics. 1988. text 41.95 (0-470-21375-2) P-H.
Naish, Peter L., ed. What Is Hypnosis? Current Theories & Research. 224p. 1987. 113.00 (0-335-15338-0); pap. 38.95 (0-335-15337-2) OpUniv Pr.
Naismith, Archibald. 1200 Bosquejos Biblicos. (SPA.). 271p. 1996. 12.99 (0-89922-492-X, C014-492X) Caribe Betania.
Naismith, Archibald, ed. Twelve Hundred Notes, Quotes, & Anecdotes. 237p. 1987. pap. 12.99 (0-310-55311-3, 190210P) Zondervan.
Naismith, Helen. One Hundred American Festivals & Their Foods. 232p. 1990. write for info. (0-87651-989-3) Southern U Pr.
— Walking Cape Ann. (Illus.). 254p. (Orig.). 1994. pap. 11.95 (0-938459-08-2) Ten Pound Isl Bk.
Naismith, Helen, compiled by. One Hundred Famous American Festivals & Their Foods. LC 75-30398. (Illus.). 1979. pap. 12.95 (0-933718-30-6) Browning Pubns.
Naismith, James. Basketball: Its Origin & Development. LC 95-44893. (Illus.). xxi, 191p. 1996. pap. 10.00 (0-8032-8370-9, Bison Books) U of Nebr Pr.
— Basketball's Origins: Creative Problem-Solving in the Gilded Age. Cheney, Robert B. et al, eds. (Illus.). (YA). (gr. 7 up). 1976. reprint ed. pap. 1.95 (0-912934-03-4) Bear.
Naismith, Robert J. The Story of Scotland's Towns. (Illus.). 200p. (C). 1996. 45.00 (0-85976-257-2, Pub. by J Donald) St Mut.
Naison, Mark. Communists in Harlem During the Depression. LC 84-48112. 384p. 1985. pap. 9.95 (0-8021-5183-3, Grove) Grove-Atltic.
— Communists in Harlem During the Depression. LC 82-10848. (Blacks in the New World Ser.). 384p. 1983. text 34.95 (0-252-00644-5) U of Ill Pr.
Naithani, B. D. Flora of Chamoli, Vols. 1 & 2. (C). 1988. text 50.00 (0-7855-7054-3, Pub. by Scientific); text 50.00 (0-7855-7055-1, Pub. by Scientific) St Mut.
Naithani, H. B. Flowering Plants of India, Nepal & Bhutan. (C). 1990. 252.00 (0-7855-0180-0, Pub. by Ratna Pustak Bhandar) St Mut.
— Forest Flora of Goa. LC 98-901748. 666p. 1997. pap. 375.00 (81-7089-242-2, Pub. by Intl Bk Distr) St Mut.
***Naithani, H. B.** Valley of Flowers with More Than 100 Colour Plates. 1998. pap. 130.00 (0-7855-7663-0) St Mut.
Naithani, H. B., jt. auth. see Negi, S. S.
Naito, Akira. Katsura: A Princely Retreat. Terry, Charles S., tr. (Illus.). 182p. 1994. 150.00 (4-7700-0542-3) Kodansha.
Naito, H., ed. Nutrition & Heart Disease. (Monographs of the American College of Nutrition: Vol. 5). 365p. 1982. text 37.50 (0-88331-168-2) R B Luce.
Naito, Hideharu. Dinosaur Carton Craft. (Illus.). 68p. (Orig.). 1992. pap. 10.95 (0-87040-911-5) Japan Pubns USA.
Naito, Hiromi & Paine, Stefani H. Sockeye Salmon: A Pictorial Tribute. 120p. 1995. pap. 19.95 (0-89886-458-5) Mountaineers.
Naito, T., jt. auth. see Ninomiya, I.
Naitoh, Hideharu. Animal Carton Craft. (Illus.). 70p. (Orig.). 1993. pap. 13.00 (0-87040-919-0) Japan Pubns USA.
Naitonal Tooling & Machining Assn. Staff, ed. see Foster, Lowell.
Naj, Amal. Peppers: A Story of Hot Pursuits. LC 92-50625. 1993. pap. 12.00 (0-679-74427-4) Vin Bks.
Najafi, S. I. & Armenise, Mario N., eds. Integrated Optics Devices Vol. 2997: Potential for Commercialization. LC 98-114651. 370p. 1997. 89.00 (0-8194-2408-0) SPIE.
Najafi, S. I., jt. ed. see Hubert-Pfalzgraf, Liliane G.
Najafi, S. Iraj. Selected Papers on Sol-Gel for Photonics. LC 98-6654. (Milestone Ser.). 1998. 110.00 (0-8194-2939-2) SPIE.
Najafi, S. Iraj, ed. Glass Integrated Optics & Optical Fiber Devices. LC 94-11385. (Critical Reviews of Optical Science & Technology Ser.: Vol. CR53). 1994. 40.00 (0-8194-1386-0); pap. 40.00 (0-8194-1385-2) SPIE.
— Introduction to Glass Integrated Optics. (Optoelectronics Library). 208p. 1992. text 10.00 (0-89006-547-0) Artech Hse.
Najafi, S. Iraj, jt. auth. see Andrews, Mark P.
Najafi, S. Iraj, jt. ed. see Righini, Giancarlo C.
Najar, Qasim. The Army of Lions. (Illus.). 190p. (YA). (gr. 6-11). 1998. mass mkt. write for info. (1-889720-15-1, Pub. by Amirah Pubng) Intl Bks & Tapes.
— Ibrahim's Search. (Illus.). 30p. (J). (gr. 1-4). 1998. pap. write for info. (1-889720-20-8, Pub. by Amirah Pubng) Intl Bks & Tapes.
Najar, Qasim M. Burhaan Khan: Six Tales about Growing Up. (Illus.). 80p. (J). (gr. 3-5). 1996. mass mkt. write for info. (1-889720-03-8, Pub. by Amirah Pubng) Intl Bks & Tapes.
Najar, Qasim M. & Baig, Samina. Finders Keepers & Other Stories. (Illus.). 102p. (J). (gr. 3-5). 1996. mass mkt. write for info. (1-889720-08-9, Pub. by Amirah Pubng) Intl Bks & Tapes.
***Najarian.** How I Trade Options. (Trading Advantage Ser.). 288p. 2000. 29.95 (0-471-31278-9) Wiley.
Najarian, Carolann S. A Call from Home: Armenia & Karabagh - My Journal. (Illus.). 306p. 1999. 22.95 (0-9664985-0-X) Arpen Pr.
Najarian, Haig H. Sex Lives of Animals Without Backbones. LC 75-4447. 125p. (Orig.). 1976. lib. bdg. 9.50 (0-684-14613-4) Krieger.
Najarian, John S. & Simmons, Richard L. Transplantation. LC 73-135689. (Illus.). 811p. reprint ed. 200.00 (0-8357-9424-5, 201456600092) Bks Demand.
Najarian, John S., et al. Manual of Vascular Access, Organ Donation, & Transplantation. (Comprehensive Manuals of Surgical Specialties Ser.). (Illus.). 355p. 1984. 207.00 (0-387-90965-6) Spr-Verlag.
Najarian, Peter. Daughters of Memory. LC 85-63859. (Illus.). 176p. (Orig.). 1986. pap. 8.95 (0-933944-13-6) City Miner Bks.
— The Great American Loneliness. LC 99-18076. (Illus.). 200p. 1999. pap. 17.95 (1-886434-09-3) Blue Crane Bks.
— Voyages. LC 79-23722. 1980. 8.95 (0-933706-12-X); pap. 4.95 (0-933706-13-8) Ararat Pr.
— Wash Me on Home Mama. 86p. (Orig.). 1978. pap. 9.95 (0-917658-10-8) BPW & P.
Najavits, Joseph. How to Trash Our Young via Public Education: A Practical Guide. LC 93-86162. 182p. 1993. pap. 12.95 (0-9638307-5-9) Open Vistas.
***Najda, Ruth.** Building Sustainable Homes Packet: A Key Stage 3 Packet Aimed at Design & Technology Teachers, Set. 36p. 2000. 22.00 incl. VHS (1-85339-513-7, Pub. by Intermed Tech) Stylus Pub VA.
Najder, Zdzislaw. Conrad in Perspective: Essays on Art & Fidelity. LC 96-37923. 252p. (C). 1997. text 59.95 (0-521-57321-1) Cambridge U Pr.
Najean, Y., et al, eds. Safety Problems Related to Chloramphenicol & Thiamphenicol. LC 80-5838. (Monographs of the Mairo Negri Institute for Pharmacological Research, Milan). (Illus.). 128p. 1981. reprint ed. pap. 36.50 (0-7837-9562-9, 2060311) Bks Demand.
Najem, R., jt. auth. see Wedemeyer, C.
Najemy, John M. Between Friends: Discourses of Power & Desire in the Machiavelli-Vettori Letters of 1513-1515. LC 93-9737. 392p. 1993. text 49.50 (0-691-03262-9, Pub. by Princeton U Pr) Cal Prin Full Svc.
— Corporation & Consensus in Florentine Electoral Politics 1280 to 1400. LC 81-16481. 358p. reprint ed. pap. 111.00 (0-8357-4407-8, 203722700008) Bks Demand.
Najera, Manuel G. Cuentos Completos y Otras Narraciones (Complete Stories & Other Narrations) (SPA.). 477p. 1958. 10.99 (968-16-1443-7, Pub. by Fondo) Continental Bk.

An Asterisk (*) at the beginning of an entry indicates that the title is appearing for the first time.

Najera-Ramirez, Olga. La Fiesta de los Tastoanes: Critical Encounters at a Mexican Festival. (SPA., Illus.). 187p. 1998. pap. 18.95 (*0-8263-1998-X*) U of NM Pr.
— La Fiesta de los Tastoanes: Critical Encounters in Mexican Festival Performance. LC 97-4615. (Illus.). 187p. 1997. 50.00 (*0-8263-1795-2*) U of NM Pr.
Najera, Rick. The Pain of the Macho: And Other Plays. unabridged ed. Landes, William-Alan, ed. LC 96-39820. 152p. 1997. pap. 13.00 (*1-55885-190-9*, Pub. by Arte Publico) Empire Pub Srvs.
***Najibi, Neda.** The Ground I Walk On. (Illus.). 128p. (J). 1999. pap. 14.95 (*0-9672640-0-6*, 1966) Peace By Piece.
Najim, F., jt. auth. see Amerasekera, A.
Najim, K. & Dufour, E., eds. Advanced Control of Chemical Processes (ADCHEM '91) Selected Papers from the IFAC Symposium, Toulouse, France, 14-16 October 1991. LC 92-2270. (IFAC Symposia Ser.). 312p. 1992. 124.25 (*0-08-041267-X*, Pergamon Pr) Elsevier.
Najim, K., jt. auth. see Poznyak, Alexander S.
Najim, Kaddour. Control of Liquid-Liquid Extraction Columns, Vol. 4. Hughes, Richard, ed. (Topics in Chemical Engineering Ser.: Vol. 5). xii, 260p. 1988. text 171.00 (*2-88124-703-2*) Gordon & Breach.
Najim, Kaddour, ed. Process Modeling & Control in Chemical Engineering. (Chemical Industries Ser.: Vol. 38). (Illus.). 504p. 1989. text 210.00 (*0-8247-8204-6*) Dekker.
Najim, Kaddour & Poznyak, Alexandr S. Learning Automata: Theory Applications. LC 94-19346. 238p. 1994. text 107.50 (*0-08-042024-9*, Pergamon Pr) Elsevier.
Najim, Michel & Frazier, T. L. Understanding the Orthodox Liturgy: A Guide for Participating in the Liturgy of St. John Chrysostom. (Illus.). 178p. 1995. per. 12.50 (*1-879038-25-0*, Fellowshp of St John) Oakwood Pubns.
Najimy, Kathy & Gaffney, Mo. Parallel Lives. 1993. pap. 5.25 (*0-8222-1308-7*) Dramatists Play.
Najita, Joyce M., ed. Arbitration 1996 at the Crossroads: Proceedings of the 49th Annual Meeting of the National Academy of Arbitrators, Toronto, Ontario, Canada, 1996. 392p. 1997. 40.00 (*1-57018-066-0*, 1066) BNA Books.
— Arbitration, 1995: New Challenges & Expanding Responsibilities: Proceedings Annual Meeting National Academy of Arbitrators, San Francisco, CA, 1995. 343p. 1996. 40.00 (*1-57018-024-5*, 70999) BNA Books.
Najita, Joyce M., ed. see Nicolau, George, et al.
Najita, Joyce M., jt. ed. see Stern, James L.
Najita, Tetsuo. Hara Kei in the Politics of Compromise, 1905-1915. LC 67-27090. (Harvard East Asian Ser.: No. 31). 338p. reprint ed. pap. 104.80 (*0-7837-2302-4*, 205739000004) Bks Demand.
— Japan: The Intellectual Foundations of Modern Japanese Politics. LC 79-23710. 160p. 1980. reprint ed. pap. text 11.95 (*0-226-56803-2*, P883) U Ch Pr.
— Visions of Virtue in Tokugawa Japan: The Kaitokudo Merchant Academy of Osaka. LC 86-19825. 344p. (C). 1993. lib. bdg. 37.50 (*0-226-56804-0*) U Ch Pr.
— Visions of Virtue in Tokugawa Japan: The Kaitokudo Merchant Academy of Osaka. LC 86-19825. 344p. (C). 1995. pap. text 18.95 (*0-226-56805-9*) U Ch Pr.
— Visions of Virtue in Tokugawa Japan: The Kaitokudo Merchant Academy of Osaka. LC 97-15881. 344p. 1997. pap. text 26.00 (*0-8248-1991-8*) UH Pr.
Najita, Tetsuo, ed. Tokugawa Political Writings. (Cambridge Texts in Modern Politics Ser.). 229p. (C). 1998. text 59.95 (*0-521-56186-8*); pap. text 18.95 (*0-521-56717-3*) Cambridge U Pr.
Najita, Tetsuo & Koschmann, J. Victor, eds. Conflict in Modern Japanese History: The Neglected Tradition. LC 82-47605. 467p. 1982. reprint ed. pap. 144.80 (*0-608-03751-6*, 206457500009) Bks Demand.
Najita, Tetsuo, ed. see Scheiner, Irwin.
Najjar. Law Dictionary French-Arabic: Dictionnaire Juridique. (ARA & FRE.). 1983. 40.00 (*0-86685-303-0*) Intl Bk Ctr.
Najjar, A. Majid. Khilafat al Insan Bayna al Wahy wa al 'Aql: Bahth fi Jadaliyat al Nass wa al 'Aql wa al Waqi' - (Man's Vicegenerency Between Revelation & Reason) 2nd ed. LC 91-38923. (Silsilat al Manhajiyah al Islamiyah Ser.: No. 5). (ARA.). 141p. 1993. pap. 5.00 (*1-56564-001-2*) IIIT VA.
Najjar, Abdallah E., ed. see Najjar, Abdallah M.
Najjar, Abdallah M. The Druze. Najjar, Abdallah E., ed. Massey, Fred I., tr. from ARA. & intro. by. (Illus.). 215p. 1973. write for info. (*0-9600800-1-5*) A E Najjar.
Najjar, Abdul Majid al, see Majid al Najjar, Abdul.
Najjar, Ibrahim. Legal Dictionary: Dictionnaire Juridique. (ARA & FRE.). 292p. 1983. 75.00 (*0-8288-0971-2*, F48378) Fr & Eur.
Najjar, Matthew F. Clinical Chemistry Profile Data for Hispanics, 1982-84. LC 92-48934. (Vital & Health Statistics Ser.: Series 11, No. 241). 1992. write for info. (*0-8406-0467-X*) Natl Ctr Health Stats.
Najjar, Victor A. The Biological Effects of Glutamic Acid & Its Derivatives. 1982. text 278.00 (*90-6193-841-4*) Kluwer Academic.
— Immunologically Active Peptides. 1982. text 176.50 (*90-6193-842-2*) Kluwer Academic.
Najjar, Victor A., ed. Enzyme Induction & Modulation. 1983. text 208.00 (*0-89838-583-0*) Kluwer Academic.
Najjar, Victor A. & Lorand, Laszlo, eds. Transglutaminase. (Developments in Molecular & Cellular BioChemistry Ser.). 1984. text 141.00 (*0-89838-593-8*) Kluwer Academic.
Najlis, Elena. Lengua Abipona, 2 vols., Set. 1966. 60.00 (*0-7859-0703-3*, S-33069) Fr & Eur.
Najm, Ramzi. The Pharaoh's Falcon. Thomson, G. G., ed. LC 97-66343. (ARA & ENG., Illus.). 60p. (Orig.). (C). 1997. pap. text 18.95 (*1-887003-47-9*) Dancng Jester.
Najm, Yussof A. A Dictionary of Medicinal Plants. (ARA, FRE & LAT., Illus.). 170p. 1994. 35.00 (*0-86685-658-7*, LDL6587, Pub. by Librairie du Liban) Intl Bk Ctr.
Najmabadi, Afsaneh. Land Reform & Social Change in Iran. LC 87-31630. 256p. reprint ed. pap. 79.40 (*0-7837-6870-2*, 204670000003) Bks Demand.
— The Story of the Daughters of Quchan: Gender & National Memory in Iranian History. LC 98-26381. (Modern Intellectual & Political History of the Middle East Ser.). 1998. pap. 29.95 (*0-8156-2791-2*) Syracuse U Pr.
Najmabadi, Afsaneh, ed. Women's Autobiographies in Contemporary Iran. (Middle Eastern Monographs: No. 26). 64p. 1991. pap. 9.95 (*0-685-38745-3*, NAJWOM) HUP.
Najmabadi, Farrokh & Lall, Sanjaya. Developing Industrial Technology: Lessons for Policy & Practice. (World Bank Operations Evaluation Study Ser.). 136p. 1995. pap. 22.00 (*0-8213-3398-4*, 13398) World Bank.
Najmaldin, A. S., et al, eds. Endoscopic Surgery in Children. LC 99-10448. (Illus.). 250p. 1999. 129.00 (*3-540-64073-8*) Spr-Verlag.
Najmaldin, Azad & Guillou, Pierre J. A Guide to Laparoscopic Surgery. LC 98-5987. (Illus.). 169p. 1998. pap. 47.95 (*0-86542-649-X*) Blackwell Sci.
Najman, A., et al, eds. The Inhibitors of Hematopoiesis. (Colloquim Ser.: No. 162). 364p. (Orig.). 1987. pap. 65.00 (*2-85598-340-1*) S M P F Inc.
Najman, Dragoljub, jt. auth. see D'Orville, Hans.
***Najman, Jake & Western, John, eds.** A Sociology of Australian Society: Introductory Readings. 3rd ed. 650p. 2000. pap. 46.95 (*0-7329-5695-1*, Pub. by Macmill Educ) Paul & Co Pubs.
Najmee, S. A. Islamic Legal Theory & the Orientalists. 1994. pap. 25.00 (*1-56744-101-7*) Kazi Pubns.
Najock, ed. Anonyma. (GRE.). 1975. 18.95 (*3-322-00201-2*, T1008, Pub. by B G Teubner) U of Mich Pr.
Najock, Dietmar. Pars Quarta Vol. I: Tabulae: Tabulae in Epistulas et Orationes. (Alpha-Omega, Reihe A Ser.: Bd. L, 4.1). (GER.). xlv, 894p. 1996. write for info. (*3-487-10131-9*) G Olms Pubs.
Najock, Dietmar, jt. auth. see Rosumek, Peter.
Najock, Dietmar, ed. see Felix, Menucius.
Najock, Dietmar, jt. ed. see Fischer, Klaus-Dietrich.
Najock, Dietmar, jt. ed. see Morgenroth, Hermann.
Najock, Dietmar, ed. see Plinius Secundus, C.
Najock, Dietmar, jt. ed. see Rapsch, Jurgen.
Najock, Dietmar, jt. ed. see Rosumek, Peter.
Najock, Dietmar, ed. see Secundus, C. Plinius.
Najock, Dietmar, ed. see Secundus, Plinius C.
Najvar, Daniel. Avoid the Abyss: Embrace the Cross. viii, 82p. 1997. pap. write for info. (*1-928541-05-4*) Mobius.
— Beyond the Surface: A Dictionary & Daily Planner for Continuous Improvement, Vols. 1, 2 & 3. xxv, 2190p. Date not set. pap. write for info. (*1-928541-21-6*) Mobius.
— Beyond the Surface: A Dictionary & Daily Planner for Continuous Improvement, Vols. 1-12. xi, 730p. 1994. pap. write for info. (*1-928541-12-7*) Mobius.
— Beyond the Surface: A Dictionary & Daily Planner for Continuous Improvement, Vols. 13-24. v, 730p. 1994. pap. write for info. (*1-928541-13-5*) Mobius.
— Beyond the Surface: A Dictionary & Daily Planner for Continuous Improvement, Vols. 25-36. ix, 730p. 1994. pap. write for info. (*1-928541-14-3*) Mobius.
— By the Grace of God - And Free Will. iv, 82p. 1999. pap. write for info. (*1-928541-18-6*) Mobius.
— Faith Seeks Understanding: Seven Miles to Emmaus. (Seven Miles to Emmaus Ser.: Vol. 3). (Illus.). xiii, 128p. 1995. pap. write for info. (*1-928541-08-9*) Mobius.
— Faith Seeks Understanding: Seven Miles to Emmaus & the Catechism of the Catholic Church. (Seven Miles to Emmaus Ser.: Vol. 2). (Illus.). viii, 330p. 1995. pap. write for info. (*1-928541-07-0*) Mobius.
— From My Father's House. viii, 114p. 1994. pap. write for info. (*1-928541-03-8*) Mobius.
— In Courage Meant for Salvation. v, 365p. 1999. pap. write for info. (*1-928541-17-8*) Mobius.
— Jacob's Well: Mystery of the Manger. vii, 365p. 1994. pap. write for info. (*1-928541-01-1*) Mobius.
— Knock, Knock. iv, 365p. 1995. pap. write for info. (*1-928541-00-3*) Mobius.
— Reign Drops: A Poetic Devotional. v, 76p. 1995. pap. write for info. (*1-928541-02-X*) Mobius.
— Seven Miles to Emmaus, Vols. 1, 2 & 3. (Illus.). xxxi, 670p. 1996. pap. write for info. (*1-928541-19-4*) Mobius.
— Seven Miles to Emmaus: A Thematic Walk with Jesus - The Unrecognized Truth. x, 212p. 1996. pap., wbk. ed. write for info. (*1-928541-06-2*) Mobius.
— Seven Miles to Emmaus: Inspirational Reflections Beyond the Surface, 3 vols. Cranley, Paul, ed. xxvii, 2190p. 1994. pap. write for info. (*1-928541-20-8*) Mobius.
— Seven Miles to Emmaus: Inspirational Reflections Beyond the Surface, Vols. 1-12. Cranley, Paul, ed. vii, 730p. 1994. pap. write for info. (*1-928541-09-7*) Mobius.
— Seven Miles to Emmaus: Inspirational Reflections Beyond the Surface, Vols. 13-24. Cranley, Paul, ed. xi, 730p. 1994. pap. write for info. (*1-928541-10-0*) Mobius.
— Seven Miles to Emmaus: Inspirational Reflections Beyond the Surface, Vols. 25-36. Cranley, Paul, ed. ix, 730p. 1994. pap. write for info. (*1-928541-11-9*) Mobius.
— Sources of Sayings: S. O. S. vi, 117p. 1996. pap. write for info. (*1-928541-04-6*) Mobius.
— What Nature Teaches: Why Is the Owl So Wise? 18p. (J). (gr. 1-6). 1996. pap. write for info. (*1-928541-15-1*) Mobius.
— What's Right for Organizational Success: How to Succeed by Really Trying. iv, 137p. 1994. pap. write for info. (*1-928541-16-X*) Mobius.
Naka, Norio. Predicting Outcomes in United States-Japan Trade Negotiations. LC 95-24916. 296p. 1996. 65.00 (*1-56720-005-2*) Greenwood.
***Nakabayashi, Nobuo & Pashley, David H.** Hybridization of Dental Hard Tissues. (Illus.). 135p. 2000. pap. 40.00 (*4-87417-575-9*, Pub. by QPC) Quint Pub Co.
Nakache, Stephanie, tr. see Liebes, Yehuda.
Nakadate, Neil. Understanding Jane Smiley. LC 98-40224. (Understanding Contemporary American Literature Ser.). 192p. 1999. 29.95 (*1-57003-251-3*) U of SC Pr.
Nakadate, Neil, ed. Robert Penn Warren: Critical Perspectives. LC 79-57569. 336p. 1981. 35.00 (*0-8131-1425-X*) U Pr of Ky.
Nakae, Kiyose. Jiu Jitsu Complete. 10.95 (*0-685-21995-X*); pap. 6.95 (*0-686-66565-1*) Wehman.
Nakae, Kiyose & Yeager, Charles. Jiu Jitsu Complete. (Illus.). 176p. 1995. pap. 12.00 (*0-8065-0418-8*, Citadel Pr) Carol Pub Group.
Nakagaki, M., jt. ed. see Drioli, E.
Nakagaki, Nobuo. Diagram Graphics 2. (Illus.). 224p. 1995. 69.95 (*4-938586-74-6*, Pub. by PIE Bks) Bks Nippan.
Nakagami, Kenji. The Cape: And Other Stories from the Japanese Ghetto. Zimmerman, Eve, tr. from JPN. LC 99-12378. 192p. 1999. pap. 12.95 (*1-880656-39-6*, Pub. by Stone Bridge Pr) Consort Bk Sales.
— Snakelust. Rankin, Andrew, tr. from JPN. 144p. 1999. 25.00 (*4-7700-2354-5*, Pub. by Kodansha Intl) Kodansha.
Nakagawa, Allen S. LIMS: Implementation Management. 180p. 1994. 73.00 (*0-85186-824-X*, R6824) CRC Pr.
Nakagawa, Dai & Matsunaka, Ryoji, eds. Funding Transport Systems: A Comparision among Developed Countries. LC 98-135017. 200p. 1997. 81.50 (*0-08-043071-6*, Pergamon Pr) Elsevier.
Nakagawa, George. Seki-nin (Duty Bound) 1989. 19.95 (*0-930046-10-2*) CSUF Oral Hist.
Nakagawa, Go, jt. auth. see Hata, Hiroyuki.
Nakagawa, Hidemi, jt. ed. see Osada, Yoshihito.
Nakagawa, Jin. Orders of a Quartic Field, Vol. 122, No. 583. LC 96-12849. (Memoirs of the American Mathematical Society Ser.). 75p. 1996. pap. 34.00 (*0-8218-0472-3*, MEMO/122/583) Am Math.
Nakagawa, Kathryn, jt. auth. see Lewis, Dan A.
Nakagawa, Keiichiro, ed. see International Conference on Business History Staff.
***Nakagawa, Kerry Yo.** Through a Diamond: 100 Years of Japanese American Baseball LC 99-36520. 2000. write for info. (*0-945213-39-5*) Rudi Pub.
Nakagawa, Masao. Chaos & Fractals in Engineering. 960p. 1999. 86.00 (*981-02-3833-9*) World Scientific Pub.
Nakagawa, T., jt. auth. see Akaike, H.
Nakagawa, Yasuzo. Japanese Radar & Related Weapons of World War II. 137p. 1998. pap. 26.80 (*0-89412-271-1*, M-27) Aegean Park Pr.
Nakagawara, Michio, jt. ed. see Kariya, Tetsuhiko.
Nakagoshi, N. & Golley, Frank B., eds. Coniferous Forest Ecology, from an International Perspective. (Illus.). 182p. 1991. pap. 50.00 (*90-5103-065-7*, Pub. by SPB Acad Pub) Balogh.
Nakahara, David, jt. auth. see Carradine, David.
Nakahara, David, ed. see Eng, Paul.
Nakahara, H. & Suga, Shoichi, eds. Mechanisms & Phylogeny of Mineralization in Biological Systems: Biomineralization '90. (Illus.). 528p. 1991. 141.95 (*0-387-70068-4*) Spr-Verlag.
Nakahara, M. Geometry, Topology & Physics. (Graduate Student Series in Physics). (Illus.). 520p. (C). 1990. 209.00 (*0-85274-094-8*); pap. 64.00 (*0-85274-095-6*) IOP Pub.
***Nakahara, M.** Geometry, Topology & Physics. (Graduate Student Series in Physics). 1999. 190.00 (*0-7503-0605-X*) IOP Pub.
— Geometry, Topology & Physics. 2nd ed. (Graduate Student Series in Physics). 1999. pap. text 64.00 (*0-7503-0606-8*) IOP Pub.
Nakahara, Yasuo. Complete Japanese Joinery. (Illus.). 428p. 1995. pap. text 29.95 (*0-88179-121-0*) Hartley & Marks.
Nakahira, Masahiko. Street Fighter II: Cammy. (Illus.). 208p. 1997. pap. text 15.95 (*1-56931-212-5*, Viz Comics) Viz Commns Inc.
Nakai, Carlos. Art of Native American Flute. (Illus.). 1997. pap. 19.95 (*0-7866-2898-7*) Mel Bay.
Nakai, Kate W. Shogunal Politics: Arai Hakuseki & the Premises of Tokugawa Rule. LC 87-30517. (East Asian Monographs: No. 134). 400p. 1987. 32.50 (*0-674-80653-0*) HUP.
Nakai, Kate W., tr. & intro. see Kikue, Yamakawa.
Nakai, M., jt. auth. see Sario, Leo.
***Nakai, Sadao, et al, eds.** High-Power Lasers in Civil Engineering & Architecture. 2000. pap. text 84.00 (*0-8194-3485-X*) SPIE.
Nakai, Sadao & Miley, George H. Laser Interaction & Related Plasma Phenomena: 12th International Conference, 2 vols. Incl. Vol. 1. (Illus.). 784p. 1996. Not sold separately (*1-56396-623-9*, AIP Pr); Vol. 2. (Illus.). 672p. 1996. Not sold separately (*1-56396-624-7*, AIP Pr); (AIP Press Conference Proceedings Ser.: No. 369). 150.00 (*1-56396-445-7*, CP 369, AIP Pr) Spr-Verlag.
Nakai, Shuryo, et al, eds. Food Proteins: Properties & Characterization. (Food Science & Technology Ser.). (Illus.). xii, 544p. 1995. 160.00 (*1-56081-691-0*, Wiley-VCH) Wiley.
Nakai, Shuryo & Li-Chan, Eunice. Hydrophobic Interaction in Food Systems. 224p. 1988. 118.00 (*0-8493-6044-7*, QP551, CRC Reprint) Franklin.
Nakai, Shuryo & Modler, H. W., eds. Food Proteins: Properties & Characterization. 560p. 1996. 205.00 (*0-471-18614-7*, Wiley-VCH) Wiley.
Nakai, Shuryo & Modler, H. Wayne, eds. Food Proteins: Processing Applications, Vol. 2. LC 99-10842. 390p. 1999. 99.95 (*0-471-29785-2*) Wiley.
— Food Proteins: Properties & Characterization. (Food Science & Technology Ser.). (Illus.). 500p. 1996. 160.00 (*1-56081-918-9*, Wiley-VCH) Wiley.
Nakai, Shuryo, jt. ed. see Sim, J. S.
Nakaike, Toshiyuki. Enumeratio Pteridophytarum Japonicarum: Filicales. LC 76-454911. 389p. 1975. reprint ed. pap. 120.60 (*0-608-01253-X*, 206194100001) Bks Demand.
Nakaike, Toshiyuki, jt. auth. see Kurata, Satoru.
Nakaike, Toshiyuki, jt. ed. see Kurata, Satoru.
Nakajima. Introduction to Bioprogressive Therapy. (Illus.). 166p. 1987. text 80.00 (*1-85097-007-6*) Quint Pub Co.
Nakajima, A., jt. ed. see Tsuruta, T.
Nakajima, Caroline. Connecting Cultures & Literature. Miriani, Patricia, ed. (Curriculum Connections Ser.). (Illus.). 144p. (gr. k-3). 1992. student ed. 14.95 (*1-55734-347-0*) Tchr Create Mat.
— In the Year of the Boar & Jackie Robinson: A Literature Unit. (Literature Units Ser.). (Illus.). 48p. (Orig.). 1992. student ed. 7.95 (*1-55734-417-5*) Tchr Create Mat.
— Journey to Topaz: A Literature Unit. (Literature Units Ser.). (Illus.). 48p. (Orig.). 1993. pap., student ed. 7.95 (*1-55734-430-2*) Tchr Create Mat.
— Roald Dahl: Favorite Authors. (Favorite Authors Ser.). (Illus.). 1994. 11.95 (*1-55734-453-1*) Tchr Create Mat.
— Tuck Everlasting: A Literature Unit. Miriani, Patricia, ed. (Illus.). 48p. (Orig.). 1992. pap., student ed. 7.95 (*1-55734-408-6*) Tchr Create Mat.
Nakajima, F. Sanseido's New Concise Japanese-English Dictionary. (ENG & JPN.). 1362p. 1985. 49.95 (*0-8288-0465-6*, M9989) Fr & Eur.
Nakajima, H. & Ogawa, H. Compact Disc Technology. 228p. (gr. 12). 1992. 60.00 (*90-5199-066-9*, Pub. by IOS Pr) IOS Press.
Nakajima, Heizo, ed. Current English Linguistics in Japan. LC 91-22180. (Trends in Linguistics, State-of-the-Art Reports: No. 16). vi, 544p. (C). 1991. lib. bdg. 198.50 (*3-11-011781-9*, 151-91) Mouton.
***Nakajima, Hiraku.** Lectures on Hilbert Schemes of Points on Surfaces. LC 99-39163. (University Lecture Ser.). 132p. 1999. 21.00 (*0-8218-1956-9*) Am Math.
Nakajima, John M., jt. auth. see Francis, Carolyn B.
Nakajima-Okana, Kimiko, jt. auth. see Young, John.
Nakajima, R. & Yuasa, T., eds. The IOTA Programming System. (Lecture Notes in Computer Science Ser.: Vol. 160). 217p. 1983. 28.00 (*0-387-12693-7*) Spr-Verlag.
Nakajima, S. The Physics of Elementary Excitations. (Solid-State Sciences Ser.: Vol. 12). (Illus.). 340p. 1980. 82.95 (*0-387-09921-2*) Spr-Verlag.
Nakajima, S., ed. The Science of Superconductivity & New Materials. 348p. (C). 1989. text 86.00 (*9971-5-0885-0*) World Scientific Pub.
Nakajima, S. & Murakami, M., eds. Advances in Superconductivity IX: Proceedings of the 9th International Symposium on Superconductivity. (Illus.). 1550p. 1997. 239.00 (*4-431-70198-2*) Spr-Verlag.
Nakajima, Seiichi. Introduccion Al TPM (Mantenimiento Productivo Total) (SPA., Illus.). (Orig.). pap. 45.00 (*84-87022-10-3*) Productivity Inc.
— Introduction to TPM: Total Productive Maintenance. LC 88-61394. (Illus.). 149p. 1988. 45.00 (*0-915299-23-2*) Productivity Inc.
— Programa de Desarrollo del TPM. (SPA., Illus.). 428p. (Orig.). 1991. pap. 65.00 (*84-87022-82-0*) Productivity Inc.
Nakajima, T. & Yamaguchi, T., eds. Multimodality Therapy for Gastric Cancer. LC 99-27919. (Illus.). xii, 288p. 1999. 169.00 (*4-431-70255-5*) Spr-Verlag.
Nakajima, Teruo & Ono, Taketoshi, eds. Emotion, Memory & Behavior: Studies on Human & Nonhuman Primates. (Taniguchi Symposia on Brain Sciences Ser.: No. 18). 252p. 1996. 95.00 (*0-614-29961-6*, JS7777H3Y) CRC Pr.
— Taniguchi Symposia on Brain Sciences No. 18: Emotion, Memory & Behavior: Studies on Human & Nonhuman Primates. (Taniguchi Symposia on Brain Sciences Ser.: No. 18). 1995. 99.95 (*0-8493-7777-3*, JS7777) CRC Pr.
Nakajima, Tsuyoshi, ed. Fluorine-Carbon & Fluorine-Carbon Materials: Chemistry, Physics, & Applications. LC 94-24904. (Illus.). 416p. 1994. text 195.00 (*0-8247-9286-6*) Dekker.
Nakajima, Tsuyoshi & Watanabe, Nobuatsu. Graphite Fluorides & Carbon-Fluorine Compounds. (Illus.). 168p. 1990. 145.00 (*0-8493-5605-9*, QD181, CRC Reprint) Franklin.
***Nakajima, Tsuyoshi, et al.** Advanced Inorganic Fluorides: Synthesis, Characterization, & Applications. LC 99-32125. 1999. write for info. (*0-444-72002-2*) Elsevier.
Nakakuki, Teruo, ed. Oligosaccharides: Production, Properties & Applications, Vol. 3. (Japanese Technology Reviews Ser.). 235p. 1993. pap. text 101.00 (*2-88124-890-X*) Gordon & Breach.
Nakamoto, Kazuo. Infared & Raman Spectra of Inorganic & Coordination Compounds Pt. B: Applications in Coordination, Organometallic & Bioinorganic Chemistry, Pt. B. 5th ed. LC 96-33456. 400p. 1997. 79.95 (*0-471-16392-9*) Wiley.
Nakamoto, Kazuo. Infrared & Raman Spectra of Inorganic & Coordination Compounds, 2 vols., Vol. 2. 5th ed. LC 96-33456. 771p. 1997. 145.00 (*0-471-19406-9*) Wiley.
Nakamoto, Kazuo. Infrared & Raman Spectra of Inorganic & Coordination Compounds Pt. A: Theory & Applications in Inorganic Chemistry, Pt. A. 5th ed. LC 96-33456. 408p. 1997. 79.95 (*0-471-16394-5*, C100) Wiley.
Nakamoto, Kazuo, jt. ed. see Ferraro, John R.
Nakamoto, Steve. Men Are Like Fish: What Every Woman Needs to Know about Catching a Man. LC 99-60652. (Illus.). 192p. 2000. pap. 14.95 (*0-9670893-0-1*, Pub. by JAVA Bks) ACCESS Pubs Network.

N

Nakamura. Bonsai Miniatures: Quick & Easy. (Illus.). 62p. 1992. pap. text 5.95 (*4-07-975322-5*) Shufu no Tomo-Sha.

— Classroom Management: Motivation, Communication & Discipline. LC 99-46273. (Education). 1999. pap. text 60.95 (*0-534-56727-4*) Thomson Learn.

Nakamura. Health in America: A Multicultural Perspective. LC 98-26179. 272p. 1998. pap. text 37.00 (*0-205-29012-4*) Allyn.

— Japanese-English-Japanese Glossary of Social Welfare & Related Sciences. (ENG & JPN.). 246p. 1981. 49.95 (*0-8288-2364-2*, M 10061) Fr & Eur.

***Nakamura, Akira.** Fiber Science & Technology. LC 00-30061. (Illus.). 284p. 2000. text 69.50 (*1-57808-134-3*) Science Pubs.

Nakamura, Akira, et al, eds. Parallel Image Analysis: Second International Conference, ICPIA '92, Ube, Japan, December 1992: Proceedings. LC 92-39674. (Lecture Notes in Computer Science Ser.: Vol. 654). 1992. 52.95 (*0-387-56346-6*) Spr-Verlag.

Nakamura, Akira, jt. auth. see Kamachi, Mikiharu.

Nakamura, Akira, jt. auth. see Kamchi, Mikiharu.

Nakamura, Alice O., jt. ed. see Diewert, W. Erwin.

Nakamura, Eiji. Quick & Easy Flying Origami. (Illus.). 60p. 1993. pap. 17.00 (*0-87040-925-5*) Japan Pubns USA.

Nakamura, George, ed. Arizona Visitor's Guide for Japanese, Vol. 1. (JPN.). 104p. 1991. pap. 7.50 (*0-9629581-0-7*) ACE Japan.

***Nakamura, Gisaku.** Inverse Problems & Related Topics. LC 99-462330. (Research Notes in Mathematics Ser.). 248p. 2000. per. 69.95 (*1-58488-191-7*) CRC Pr.

Nakamura, H., jt. auth. see Kato, H.

Nakamura, Hajima. History of Early Vedanta Philosophy, Pt. 2. 1990. 32.50 (*81-208-0651-4*, Pub. by Motilal Bnarsidass) S Asia.

Nakamura, Hajime. Buddhism in Comparative Light. 2nd rev. ed. 182p. 1986. reprint ed. 14.00 (*81-208-0184-9*, Pub. by Motilal Bnarsidass) S Asia.

— A Comparative History of Ideas. 580p. 1986. lib. bdg. 65.00 (*0-7103-0122-7*) Routledge.

— A Comparative History of Ideas. 572p. 1993. pap. 29.95 (*0-7103-0384-X*, A4717) Routledge.

— Comparative History of Ideas. (C). 1986. text 30.00 (*81-208-1004-X*, Pub. by Motilal Bnarsidass) S Asia.

— Gotama Buddha. LC 77-8589. 1977. 12.95 (*0-914910-05-1*); pap. 10.95 (*0-914910-06-X*) Buddhist Bks.

— A History of the Development of Japanese Thought: From 1592 to 1868. 300p. 1999. 110.00 (*0-7103-0650-4*, Pub. by Kegan Paul Intl) Col U Pr.

— The Ways of Thinking of Eastern Peoples, 10 vols. (Documentary Reference Collections). 1988. 395.00 (*0-318-35983-9*, CMJ/, Greenwood Pr) Greenwood.

— The Ways of Thinking of Eastern Peoples, 10 vols., Vol. 1. LC 88-21947. (Documentary Reference Collections). 657p. 1988. lib. bdg. 69.50 (*0-313-26556-9*, CMJ01, Greenwood Pr) Greenwood.

— Ways of Thinking of Eastern Peoples: India, China, Tibet, Japan. LC 96-41818. 1997. 42.50 (*0-7103-0571-0*, Pub. by Kegan Paul Intl) Col U Pr.

— Ways of Thinking of Eastern Peoples: India, China, Tibet, Japan. rev. ed. Wiener, Philip P., ed. 732p. (C). 1981. pap. text 20.00 (*0-8248-0078-8*) UH Pr.

— Ways of Thinking of Eastern Peoples: India, Tibet, China, Japan. 1991. 27.00 (*81-208-0764-2*, Pub. by Motilal Bnarsidass) S Asia.

Nakamura, Hiroshi. Spirulina: Food for a Hungry World; A Pioneer's Story in Aquaculture. Hills, Christopher, ed. Wargo, Robert, tr. from JPN. LC 82-4816. (Illus.). 224p. (Orig.). 1982. pap. 15.95 (*0-916438-47-3*) Dr Hills Technol.

Nakamura, Hiroshi. Treadmill: A Documentary Novel. 220p. 1996. pap. 16.95 (*0-88962-595-6*) Mosaic.

Nakamura, Hiroshi, jt. auth. see Hills, Christopher.

Nakamura, I., et al. Emerging Nuclear Energy Systems - Icenes 1993: Proceedings of the Seventh International Conference. 580p. 1994. text 122.00 (*981-02-1719-6*) World Scientific Pub.

Nakamura, Joyce. Contemporary Authors, Vol. 19. (Autobiography Ser.). 350p. 1994. text 150.00 (*0-8103-4516-1*, 002902) Gale.

— Contemporary Authors, Vol. 20. (Autobiography Ser.). 350p. 1994. text 150.00 (*0-8103-4517-X*, 002903) Gale.

— Contemporary Authors Autobiography Series, Vol. 22. 350p. 1995. text 150.00 (*0-8103-4519-6*) Gale.

Nakamura, Joyce. An Inter-Industry Translog Model of Prices & Technical Change for the West German Economy. (Lecture Notes in Economics & Mathematical Systems Ser.: Vol. 221). 290p. 1983. 41.00 (*0-387-12709-7*) Spr-Verlag.

— Major Authors & Illustrated Children, Vol. 5. 1992. write for info. (*0-8103-8495-7*, 101444) Gale.

— Major Authors & Illustrators Children & Young Adults Supplement. LC 99-159523. 652p. 1997. 95.00 (*0-7876-1704-0*) Gale.

— Mathematica: Operation Research. (C). 1995. pap. text. write for info. (*0-201-42731-1*) Addison-Wesley.

Nakamura, Joyce. SATA Autobiography Series, Vol. 14. 300p. 1992. text 108.00 (*0-8103-4463-7*) Gale.

— SATA Autobiography Series, Vol. 15. 300p. 1992. text 108.00 (*0-8103-4464-5*) Gale.

— SATA Autobiography Series, Vol. 18. 300p. 1994. text 108.00 (*0-8103-4467-X*) Gale.

— SATA Autobiography Series, Vol. 19. 300p. 1994. text 108.00 (*0-8103-4468-8*) Gale.

Nakamura, Joyce, ed. Contemporary Authors, Vol. 12. LC 84-647879. (Autobiography Ser.). (Illus.). 400p. 1990. text 150.00 (*0-8103-4511-0*) Gale.

— Contemporary Authors Autobiography Series, Vol. 21. 400p. 1995. text 150.00 (*0-8103-4518-8*) Gale.

— Contemporary Authors Autobiography Series, Vol. 23. 350p. 1996. text 150.00 (*0-8103-9330-1*) Gale.

— Contemporary Authors Autobiography Series, Vol. 24. 350p. 1996. text 150.00 (*0-8103-9331-X*) Gale.

— Something about the Author, Vol. 6. (Autobiography Ser.). 300p. 1988. text 108.00 (*0-8103-4455-6*) Gale.

— Something about the Author, Vol. 7. (Autobiography Ser.). 300p. 1988. text 108.00 (*0-8103-4456-4*) Gale.

— Something about the Author, Vol. 8. (Autobiography Ser.). 300p. 1989. text 108.00 (*0-8103-4457-2*) Gale.

— Something about the Author, Vol. 9. (Autobiography Ser.). 400p. 1989. text 108.00 (*0-8103-4458-0*) Gale.

— Something about the Author, Vol. 10. LC 86-641293. (Autobiography Ser.). (Illus.). 384p. 1990. text 108.00 (*0-8103-4459-9*, 002713) Gale.

— Something about the Author, Vol. 20. (Autobiography Ser.: Vol. 2). 300p. 1995. text 108.00 (*0-8103-4469-6*) Gale.

Nakamura, Joyce, et al. Papers on the Archaeology of the Mojave Desert, Vol. 32, Pt. 2. (Archives of California Prehistory Ser.: Vol. 32). (Illus.). 125p. (Orig.). (C). 1991. pap. text 13.75 (*1-55567-072-5*) Coyote Press.

Nakamura, Joyce, jt. ed. see Collier, Laurie.

Nakamura, Joyce, jt. ed. see Gottfries, C. G.

Nakamura, Kaicho T. One Day-One Lifetime: An Illustrated Guide to the Spirit, Practice, & Philosophy of Seido Karate Meditation. (Illus.). 210p. 1995. 25.00 (*0-8048-3064-9*) Tuttle Pubng.

NaKamura, Kaiko, tr. see Chijiiwa, Hideaki.

Nakamura, Kajito, tr. see Al-Ghazali, Muhammad.

Nakamura, Katsuhiro. Quantum Versus Chaos: Questions Emerging from Mesoscopic Cosmos. LC 97-13936. (Fundamental Theories of Physics Ser.). 1997. text 107.00 (*0-7923-4557-6*) Kluwer Academic.

***Nakamura, Kiharu.** Secrets of the Geisha. 2001. write for info. (*0-06-019704-8*, HarpCollins) HarperTrade.

Nakamura, Koichiro & Child, C. Allan. Pycnogonida from Waters Adjacent to Japan. LC 91-1984. (Smithsonian Contributions to Zoology Ser.: No. 512). 80p. reprint ed. pap. 30.00 (*0-7837-0268-X*, 204057700017) Bks Demand.

— Shallow-Water Pycnogonida from the Izu Peninsula, Japan. LC 83-10183. (Smithsonian Contributions to Zoology Ser.: No. 386). 76p. reprint ed. pap. 30.00 (*0-608-14272-7*, 202220200025) Bks Demand.

Nakamura, Kojito, tr. & pref. see Al-Ghazali.

Nakamura, Kyoko M., tr. Miraculous Stories from the Japanese Buddhist Tradition: The Nihon Ryoiki of the Monk Kyokai. 344p. (C). 1997. text 49.00 (*0-7007-0449-3*, Pub. by Curzon Pr Ltd) UH Pr.

Nakamura, M. & Vanhoutte, Paul M., eds. Coronary Circulation in Physiological & Pathophysiological States. (Illus.). xiii, 178p. 1991. 69.00 (*0-387-70053-6*) Spr-Verlag.

Nakamura, Majime. Indian Buddhism: A Survey with Bibliographical Notes. 1996. reprint ed. 56.00 (*81-208-0272-1*, Pub. by Motilal Bnarsidass) S Asia.

Nakamura, Margaret, jt. auth. see Osborne, Larry N.

Nakamura, Matazo. Kabuki - Backstage, Onstage. Oshima, Mark, tr. (Illus.). 164p. 1990. 18.95 (*0-87011-985-0*) Kodansha.

Nakamura, Mie, et al, eds. Corporate Profile Graphics. Herbert, Sue, tr. LC 96-124906. (Illus.). 224p. 1995. 69.95 (*4-938586-73-8*, Pub. by PIE Bks) Bks Nippan.

Nakamura, Moritaka, et al, eds. 1998 3rd Annual Symposium on Plasma Process-Induced Damage. annuals LC 98-65928. (Illus.). 1998. pap. 65.00 (*0-9651577-2-5*) Nrthrn CA Chapter.

Nakamura, N., jt. auth. see Chihara, H.

Nakamura, Norio, et al, eds. Recent Advances in Neurotraumatology. LC 92-48234. 1993. 1174.00 (*0-387-70115-X*) Spr-Verlag.

Nakamura, Norio, jt. auth. see Chihara, K.

Nakamura, R., et al, eds. Wrist Disorders: Current Concepts & Challenges. LC 92-29763. 1993. 221.00 (*0-387-70102-8*) Spr-Verlag.

Nakamura, Raymond M. The Power of Positive Coaching. LC 96-4186. 1996. pap. 33.75 (*0-7637-0031-2*) Jones & Bartlett.

Nakamura, Robert M., contrib. by. Agglutination Analyses: Antibody Characteristics, Methodology, Limitations, & Clinical Validation; Approved Guideline (1993) 1993. 75.00 (*1-56238-195-4*, D13-A) NCCLS.

— Blood Collection on Filter Paper for Neonatal Screening Programs: Approved Standard (1992) 2nd ed. 1992. 75.00 (*1-56238-157-1*, LA4-A2) NCCLS.

— Glossary & Guidelines for Immunodiagnostic Procedures, Reagents & Reference Materials: Approved Guideline (1992) 1992. 75.00 (*1-56238-140-7*, D11-A2) NCCLS.

— Immunoprecipitin Analyses: Procedures for Evaluating the Performance of Materials; Approved Guideline 1993. 1993. 75.00 (*1-56238-194-6*, D12-A2) NCCLS.

— Primary Reference Preparations Used to Standardize Calibration of Immunochemical Assays for Serum Prostate Specific Antigen (PSA) Approved Guideline (1996) 1996. 75.00 (*1-56238-263-2*, I/LA19-A) NCCLS.

— Quality Assurance for the Indirect Immunofluorescence Test for Autoantibodies to Nuclear Antigen (IF-ANA) Tentative Guideline (1993) 1993. 75.00 (*1-56238-187-3*, I/LA2-T) NCCLS.

Nakamura, Robert M., et al, eds. Immunochemical Assays & Biosensor Technology for the 1990s. (Illus.). 421p. 1992. text 51.00 (*1-55581-040-3*) ASM Pr.

Nakamura, Robert M. & Folds, James D. Clinical Diagnostic Immunology: Protocols in Quality Assurance & Standardization. LC 98-21394. (Illus.). 512p. 1998. 110.00 (*0-86542-518-3*) Blackwell Sci.

Nakamura, Robert M., jt. auth. see Wu, James T.

Nakamura, Robert M., jt. auth. see Yoshitsugi, Hokama.

Nakamura, Robert T., jt. auth. see Church, Thomas W.

Nakamura, Sadao. The Color Source Book for Graphic Designers. (Illus.). 116p. (Orig.). (C). 1992. pap. 19.95 (*4-8381-0110-4*, Pub. by Mitsumura Suiko Shoin) Weatherhill.

Nakamura, Sharon M., et al. Sourcebook of Apraxia Remediation Activities. 160p. 1990. pap. text 32.00 (*0-930951-47-6*) Acad Comm.

Nakamura, Shigehiro. Go-Go Tools: Five Essential Activities for Leading Small Groups. LC 98-17033. (Illus.). 110p. 1998. pap. 25.00 (*1-56327-200-8*) Productivity Inc.

— The New Standardization: Keystone of Continuous Improvement in Manufacturing. Talbot, Bruce, tr. from JPN. (Illus.). 286p. 1993. 50.00 (*1-56327-039-0*) Productivity Inc.

Nakamura, Shoichiro. Computational Methods in Engineering & Science. LC 85-9737. 472p. 1986. reprint ed. lib. bdg. 52.95 (*0-89874-867-4*) Krieger.

— Numerical Analysis & Graphic Visualization with MATLAB. LC 95-32597. 496p. (C). 1995. 90.00 (*0-13-051518-3*) P-H.

— Numerical Methods Software: Computational Software Library (CSL) 178p. (Orig.). (C). 1990. pap. text 35.00 (*0-9626943-8-X*) Compu Methods.

Nakamura, Shoichiro & Carswell, Peter. Scientific Computer Graphics in C. (C). 1998. text 34.50 (*0-13-795790-4*) P-H.

***Nakamura, Shuji & Chichibu, Shigefusa F.** Introduction to Nitride Semiconductor Blue Lasers & Light Emitting Diodes LC 99-16708. 1999. write for info. (*0-7484-0836-3*, Pub. by Tay Francis Ltd) Taylor & Francis.

Nakamura, Shuji & Fasol, Gerhard. The Blue Laser Diode: Gan Based Light Emitters & Lasers. LC 97-3755. 343p. 1997. 69.95 (*3-540-61590-3*) Spr-Verlag.

Nakamura, T. & Nosay, G. Decorative Hand-Guards for Japanese Swords. (Legends in Japanese Ser.). (Illus.). 100p. 1983. pap. 17.50 (*0-87556-578-6*) Saifer.

Nakamura, T., jt. ed. see Sato, H.

Nakamura, Tadashi. Karate: Technique & Spirit. (Illus.). 168p. 1986. 24.95 (*4-07-974179-0*, Pub. by Shufunomoto Co Ltd) Tuttle Pubng.

Nakamura, Takafusa. A History of Showa Japan, 1926-1989. 520p. 1998. text 60.00 (*0-86008-521-X*, Pub. by U of Tokyo) Col U Pr.

— The Postwar Japanese Economy: Its Development & Structure. 300p. 1995. pap. 34.00 (*0-86008-514-7*, Pub. by U of Tokyo) Col U Pr.

— The Postwar Japanese Economy: Its Development & Structure. LC HC0462.9.N31. 291p. 1981. reprint ed. pap. 90.30 (*0-608-01254-8*, 206194200001) Bks Demand.

Nakamura, Tomoko, tr. see Shohno, Naomi.

Nakamura, Toshikazu & Matsumoto, Kunio, eds. Growth Factors: Cell Growth, Morphogenesis & Transformation. LC 94-7003. (Gann Monographs on Cancer Research: No. 42). 1994. 94.95 (*0-8493-7775-7*) CRC Pr.

Nakamura, Toshio, ed. Cesar Pelli. (ENG & JPN., Illus.). 232p. 1985. 150.00 (*0-685-63203-2*); pap. 100.00 (*0-685-63204-0*) Elliots Bks.

Nakamura, Tsuneo. Dolphins. LC 96-37202. 1997. pap. 10.95 (*0-8118-1621-4*) Chronicle Bks.

***Nakamura, Y. & Sessle, B. J., eds.** Neurobiology of Mastication. (International Congress Ser.: Vol. 1186). 540p. 1999. 200.50 (*0-444-50113-4*, Excerpta Medica) Elsevier.

Nakamura, Y. & Taketani, Y., eds. New Aspects of Pathophysiology & Treatment of Polycycstic Ovary Syndrome: Journal: Hormone Research, Vol. 33. (Illus.). vi, 50p. 1990. 24.50 (*3-8055-5262-9*) S Karger.

Nakamura, Yoshikatsu, et al. Kodansha's Pocket Romanized Japanese-English Dictionary. LC 93-30096. (ENG & JPN.). 480p. 1994. pap. 12.00 (*4-7700-1800-2*) Kodansha.

Nakamura, Yoshikatsu, jt. auth. see Yoshida, Masatoshi.

Nakamura, Zentaro, jt. auth. see Senju, Shizuo.

Nakane, Chie. Garo & Khasi: A Comparative Study in Matrilineal Systems. 1967. pap. text 30.80 (*3-10-800106-X*) Mouton.

— Japanese Society. LC 71-100021. (Center for Japanese & Korean Studies, UC Berkeley: No. 4). (C). 1970. pap. 15.95 (*0-520-02154-1*, Pub. by U CA Pr) Cal Prin Full Svc.

Nakane, Chie & Oishi, Shinsaburo. Tokugawa Japan: The Social & Economic Antecedents of Modern Japan. Totman, Conrad, tr. 248p. 1992. pap. 19.50 (*0-86008-490-6*, Pub. by U of Tokyo) Col U Pr.

Nakane, Hisao. Building a Continuous Improvement Culture . . . from the Bottom Up! 1997. pap. text 10.00 (*1-886769-03-6*) Gold Leaf Pr.

Nakane, Hisao & Darga, Rita. Continuous Improvement Culture: To the Next Generation. LC 98-139132. (Illus.). 112p. (Orig.). 1997. pap. 12.95 (*1-886769-14-1*) Gld Leaf Pr.

Nakane, Kazuko, jt. auth. see Lippard, Lucy R.

Nakane, Kinsaku. Kyoto Gardens: A Pocket Color Book. 1997. pap. text 9.95 (*0-87040-996-4*) Japan Pubns USA.

Nakanhara, Mikio, tr. see Tsuneto, T.

Nakanishi, Akira. Writing Systems of the World: Alphabets, Syllabaries, Pictograms. LC 79-64826. (Illus.). 122p. 1980. pap. 16.95 (*0-8048-1654-9*) Tuttle Pubng.

Nakanishi, Doanld T., et al, eds. Discrimination & Prejudice: An Annotated Bibliography. LC 92-11244. 312p. 1992. 89.95 (*0-942259-03-3*) Westerfield Enter.

***Nakanishi, Don T. & Wu, Ellen D.** Distinguished Asian American Political & Governmental Leaders. (Illus.). 344p. 2001. boxed set 69.95 (*1-57356-325-0*) Oryx Pr.

Nakanishi, Donald T., et al, eds. Discrimination & Prejudice: An Annotated Bibliography. LC 92-11244. 312p. 1992. pap. 59.95 (*0-942259-02-5*) Westerfield Enter.

Nakanishi, Donald T. & Lai, James S., eds. Political Roster: National Asian Pacific American Political Roster & Resource Guide, No. 8. 8th rev. ed. 322p. 1998. pap. 15.00 (*0-934052-30-1*) UCLA Asian Am Studies Ctr.

Nakanishi, Donald T. & Nishida, Tina Y., eds. The Asian American Educational Experience: A Sourcebook for Teachers & Students. LC 94-16361. 288p. (C). 1994. pap. 19.99 (*0-415-90872-8*, B3003) Routledge.

— The Asian American Educational Experience: A Sourcebook for Teachers & Students. LC 94-16361. 288p. (C). (gr. 13). 1995. 65.00 (*0-415-90871-X*, B2999) Routledge.

***Nakanishi, Keoji, et al.** The Biology-Chemistry Interface: A Tribute to Koji Nakanishi. LC 99-35166. (Illus.). 496p. 1999. text 195.00 (*0-8247-7116-8*) Dekker.

Nakanishi, Koji. Changing Trends in Structural Natural Products Chemistry: Selected Papers of Koji Nakanishi. (Series on 20th Century Chemistry). 600p. 1998. text 109.00 (*981-02-1827-3*) World Scientific Pub.

— One Dimensional & Two Dimensional NMR Spectra by Modern Pulse Techniques. (Illus.). 336p. 1990. pap. text 38.50 (*0-935702-63-6*) Univ Sci Bks.

— A Wandering Natural Products Chemist. Seeman, Jeffrey I., ed. LC 90-45062. (Profiles, Pathways, & Dreams Ser.). (Illus.). 200p. 1991. text 36.00 (*0-8412-1775-0*, Pub. by Am Chemical) OUP.

Nakanishi, Koji & Harada, Nobuyuki. Circular Dichroic Spectroscopy: Exciton Coupling in Organic Stereochemistry. LC 81-51270. (Illus.). 460p. (C). 1984. text 46.50 (*0-935702-09-1*) Univ Sci Bks.

Nakanishi, Koji & Solomon, Philippa H. Infrared Absorption Spectroscopy. 2nd ed. LC 76-27393. 1977. pap. 36.95 (*0-8162-6251-9*) Holden-Day.

Nakanishi, Koji, et al. Circular Dichroism: Principles & Applications. LC 93-39221. 1994. 125.00 (*1-56081-618-X*, Wiley-VCH) Wiley.

— Circular Dichroism: Principles & Applications. 2nd ed. LC 99-49620. 864p. 2000. 195.00 (*0-471-33003-5*) Wiley.

— Natural Products Chemistry, Vol. III. LC 74-6431. (Illus.). 700p. 1984. 90.00 (*0-935702-14-8*) Univ Sci Bks.

Nakanishi, Koji, jt. ed. see Barton, Derek H.

Nakanishi, Kunio, ed. Switching Phenomena in High-Voltage Circuit Breakers. (Electrical Engineering & Electronics Ser.: Vol. 75). (Illus.). 296p. 1991. text 155.00 (*0-8247-8543-6*) Dekker.

Nakanishi, N. Graph Theory & Feynman Integrals, Vol. 11. (Mathematics & Its Applications Ser.). xii, 224p. 1971. text 245.00 (*0-677-02950-0*) Gordon & Breach.

Nakanishi, N., jt. auth. see Ojima, Iwao.

Nakanishi, S., et al, eds. Gene Targeting & New Developments in Neurobiology: Proceedings of the 19th International Symposium in Brain Science of the Taniguchi Foundation, Nara, March 1996. (Taniguchi Symposia on Brain Sciences Ser.: Vol. 19). (Illus.). x, 254p. 1996. 237.50 (*3-8055-6401-5*) S Karger.

Nakanishi, T., ed. Long Term Clinical Care of Parkinson's Disease: Journal: European Neurology, Vol. 30, Suppl. 1, 1990. vi, 42p. 1990. pap. text 21.00 (*3-8055-5161-4*) S Karger.

— Long Term Clinical Care of Parkinson's Disease: 3rd Symposium, Tokyo, April 1988. (Journal: European Neurology: Vol. 29, Suppl. 1, 1988). 38p. 1989. pap. 19.25 (*3-8055-4969-5*) S Karger.

— Long Term Clinical Care of Parkinson's Disease, Tokyo, April 1987: Second Symposium. (Journal: European Neurology: Vol. 28, Suppl. 1, 1988). vi, 42p. 1988. pap. 15.00 (*3-8055-4833-8*) S Karger.

— Long Term Clinical Care of Parkinson's Disease, 5th Symposium, Tokyo, April 1990. (Journal: European Neurology: Vol. 31, Suppl. 1, 1991). (Illus.). iv, 60p. 1991. pap. 28.00 (*3-8055-5401-X*) S Karger.

— Long-Time Clinical Care of Parkinson's Disease, Symposium, Tokyo, April 1986: Journal: European Neurology, Vol. 26, Suppl. 1, 1987. (Illus.). iv, 56p. 1987. pap. 18.50 (*3-8055-4590-8*) S Karger.

— Sixth Symposium on a Long Term Clinical Care of Parkinson's Disease, Tokyo, October 1991. (Journal: European Neurology: Vol. 32, Suppl. 1, 1992). (Illus.). vi, 54p. 1992. pap. 26.25 (*3-8055-5664-0*) S Karger.

Nakanishi, Teruyuki, jt. ed. see Iwama, George K.

Nakanishik, K. 3rd Annual Japanese Symposium on Molecular Simulation. 172p. 1991. pap. text 516.00 (*2-88124-811-X*) Gordon & Breach.

Nakano, Daniel Ken. Projective Modules over Lie Algebras of Cartan Type. LC 92-12518. (Memoirs Ser.: No. 470). 84p. 1992. pap. 24.00 (*0-8218-2530-5*, MEMO/98/470) Am Math.

Nakano, Dokuotei. Easy Origami. LC 93-86669. 1994. 11.19 (*0-606-06345-5*, Pub. by Turtleback) Demco.

Nakano, Dokuotei. Origami Classroom, Vol. I. (Illus.). 24p. 1993. pap. 12.95 (*0-87040-912-3*) Japan Pubns USA.

— Origami Classroom, Vol. 2. (Illus.). 24p. 1994. boxed set 12.95 (*0-87040-938-7*) Japan Pubns USA.

Nakano, Hidegoreo. Linear Lattices. 2nd abr. ed. LC 66-24169. 157p. reprint ed. pap. 48.70 (*0-7837-3774-2*, 204359200010) Bks Demand.

Nakano, Hidegoro. Uniform Spaces & Transformation Groups. LC 68-13935. 269p. reprint ed. pap. 83.40 (*0-7837-3776-9*, 204359500010) Bks Demand.

Nakano, Hiroshi, jt. auth. see Hayashi, Susumu.

Nakano, Hiroshige, ed. see International Symposium on Etiopathogenesis & Trea.

Nakano, Imaharu & Hirano, Asao, eds. Amyotrophic Lateral Sclerosis: Progress & Perspectives in Basic Research & Clinical Application: Proceedings of the 11th Tokyo Metropolitan Institute for Neuroscience (TMIN) International Symposium, Tokyo, October 25-27, 1995. LC 96-7789. (International Congress Ser.: No. 1104). 420p. 1996. 200.75 (*0-444-82286-0*) Elsevier.

An Asterisk (*) at the beginning of an entry indicates that the title is appearing for the first time.

Nakano, Jiro. Kanda Home: Biography of Shigefusa & Sue Kanda. (Illus.). 128p. (C). 1996. pap. text 14.00 (*0-8248-1812-1*) Iao Congreg Church.

Nakano, Jiro, ed. from JPN. Outcry from the Inferno, Atomic Bomb Tanka Anthology. LC 95-23262. (Bamboo Ridge Ser.: Nos. 67-68). 104p. 1995. pap. 10.00 (*0-910043-38-8*) Bamboo Ridge Pr.

Nakano, Jiro & Hallett, Brien, eds. Heiwa: Peace Poetry in English & Japanese. LC 95-42220. (ENG & JPN.). 176p. (C). 1996. pap. text 17.00 (*0-8248-1813-X*) U HI MIFP.

Nakano, Jiro, ed. & tr. see Soga, Keiho, et al.

Nakano, Kay, ed. & tr. see Soga, Keiho, et al.

Nakano, Kenneth K. & Tsushima, William T. Effective Medical Testifying: A Courtroom Handbook for Physicians. LC 97-34806. 227p. 1997. pap. text 34.95 (*0-7506-9986-8*) Buttrwrth-Heinemann.

Nakano, Kii, tr. see Natsume Soseki, pseud.

Nakano, Leatrice, jt. auth. see Nakano, Takeo U.

Nakano, M & Koyama, K., eds. Electrorheological Fluids, Magnetorheological Suspensions & Their Application: Proceedings of the 6th Int'l Conference Yonezawa, Japan 22 - 25 July 1997. 890p. 148.00 (*981-02-3750-2*) World Scientific Pub.

Nakano, Mei T. Japanese American Women: Three Generations, 1890-1990. LC 89-91580. (Illus.). 256p. (Orig.). 1998. reprint ed. pap. 14.95 (*0-942610-06-7*) Mina Pr.

— Riko Rabbit. LC 82-81737. (J). (gr. 2-5). 1982. pap. 5.95 (*0-942610-00-8*) Mina Pr.

Nakano, Michio, tr. see Kyozo, Takagi.

Nakano, T. & Goldhaber, Samuel Z. Pulmonary Embolism. LC 99-24991. viii, 192p. 1999. 132.00 (*4-431-70238-5*) Spr-Verlag.

Nakano, T. & Hartshorne, D. J., eds. Regulation of the Contractile Cycle in Smooth Muscle. 239p. 1995. 133.00 (*3-540-70149-4*) Spr-Verlag.

— Regulation of the Contractile Cycle in Smooth Muscle. 1996. 133.00 (*0-387-70149-4*); 133.00 (*4-431-70149-4*) Spr-Verlag.

Nakano, Takeo U. & Nakano, Leatrice. Within a Barbed Wire Fence: A Japanese Man's Account of His Internment in Canada. (Illus.). 126p. 1980. mass mkt. 3.95 (*0-88780-102-1*, Pub. by Formac Publ Co) Formac Dist Ltd.

Nakano, Takeshi & Koriyama, Naoshi, eds. We Wrote These Poems: A Collection of Poems by Mentally Retarded Children at Nomura Gakuen, Japan. (Illus.). 143p. 1997. pap. 14.95 (*4-590-00670-7*, Pub. by Hokuseido Pr) Book East.

Nakano, Tomio. Ordinance Power of the Japanese Emperor. LC 71-173009. reprint ed. 31.50 (*0-404-04650-9*) AMS Pr.

Nakano, Yoshiko, jt. ed. see Knight, Alan.

Nakano, Yuichi, ed. Cholesteatoma & Mastoid Surgery: Proceedings of the Fourth International Conference, Nigata, Japan, September 8-12, 1993. LC 93-41769. (Illus.). 1993. lib. bdg. 228.50 (*90-6299-102-5*, Pub. by Kugler) Kugler Pubns.

Nakanose, Shigeyuki. Josiah's Passover: Sociology & the Liberating Bible. LC 93-18286. (Bible & Liberation Ser.). 208p. (Orig.). reprint ed. pap. 64.50 (*0-608-20258-4*, 207151700012) Bks Demand.

Nakao, Seigo. Random House Japanese Dictionary. 1996. pap. write for info. (*0-679-74668-4*) Random Ref & Info.

— Random House Japanese-English English-Japanese Dictionary. (JPN.). 600p. 1995. 22.00 (*0-679-44149-2*) Random Ref & Info.

— Random House Japanese-English English-Japanese Dictionary. 1997. pap. 12.95 (*0-679-78001-7*) Random Ref & Info.

— Random House Japanese-English, English-Japanese Dictionary. (JPN & ENG.). (Orig.). 1996. mass mkt. 6.99 (*0-345-40548-X*) Ballantine Pub Grp.

Nakao, Shigeo. The Political Economy of Japanese Money. 215p. 1995. 48.00 (*0-86008-507-4*, Pub. by U of Tokyo) Col U Pr.

Nakarada, Radmila & Oberg, Jan, eds. Surviving Together: The Olaf Palme Lectures on Common Security, 1988. 214p. 1989. text 61.95 (*1-85521-067-3*, Pub. by Dartmth Pub) Ashgate Pub Co.

Nakarai, Toyozo W. The Study of the Impact of Buddhism Upon Japanese Life As Revealed in the Order of Kokin-Shu. 1972. 59.95 (*0-8490-1156-6*) Gordon Pr.

Nakari, Risto, jt. auth. see Kalliola, Satu.

Nakari, Risto, jt. ed. see Kalliola, Satu.

Nakas, James P., jt. ed. see Mitchell, Myron J.

Nakasa, Nat, jt. auth. see Patel, Essop.

Nakase, A., jt. ed. see Tsuchida, T.

Nakash, Yitzhak. The Shiis of Iraq. LC 93-31786. 340p. 1994. text 45.00 (*0-691-03431-1*, Pub. by Princeton U Pr) Cal Prin Full Svc.

— The Shi'is of Iraq. 312p. 1998. 27.00 (*0-7881-5462-1*) DIANE Pub.

Nakashima, Cynthia L., jt. ed. see Williams-Leon, Teresa.

Nakashima, George. The Soul of a Tree: A Master Woodworker's Reflections. LC 81-80655. 224p. 1988. pap. 45.00 (*0-87011-903-6*) Kodansha.

Nakashima, Hideyuki, ed. see Pacific Rim International Workshop on Multi-Agents Staff.

Nakashima, Lex, ed. see Wyman, Vicky.

Nakashima, S., ed. see Matsunami, H.

Nakashima, Signe E. The Cardinal Mine: A Ghost of the Past. 120p. 1995. pap. text 9.95 (*0-9646928-0-5*) S E Nakashima.

Nakashima, T. & Kojiro, M. Hepatocellular Carcinoma. (Illus.). 280p. 1987. 312.00 (*0-387-70018-8*) Spr-Verlag.

Nakashima, Tsutomu, jt. ed. see Yanagita, Noriyuki.

Nakasian, Samuel. America's Adopted Son: The Remarkable Story of an Orphaned Immigrant Boy. LC 96-47365. 394p. 1997. 18.95 (*1-880404-12-5*) Bkwrights.

Nakasone, Edwin M. The Nisei Soldier: Historical Essays on World War II. 96p. (C). 1997. pap. text 8.50 (*0-9660111-3-9*) J Press.

— The Nisei Soldier: Historical Essays on World War II & the Korean War. 2nd rev. ed. LC 98-75578. (Illus.). 206p. (Orig.). 1999. pap. 19.95 (*0-9660111-5-5*, Pub. by J Press) Baker & Taylor.

Nakasone, Henry Y. & Paull, Robert E. Tropical Fruits. LC 97-44048. (Crop Production Science in Horticulture Ser.: No. 7). (Illus.). 472p. 1998. text 55.00 (*0-85199-254-4*) OUP.

Nakasone, Karen K. Cultural Studies & Identification of Wood-Inhabiting Corticiaceae & Selected Hymenomycetes from North America. (Mycologia Memoir Ser.: No. 15). (Illus.). 412p. 1990. 89.00 (*3-443-76005-8*, Pub. by Gebruder Borntraeger) Balogh.

Nakasone, Riri. Shiki: Four Seasons in the Eden. (ENG & JPN., Illus.). 20p. 1988. pap. 25.00 (*0-944290-02-7*) Light Speed.

Nakasone, Ronald Y. Ethics of Enlightenment: Essays & Sermons in Search for a Buddhist Ethic. (Illus.). 200p. (Orig.). 1990. 30.00 (*0-9623086-0-9*); pap. 12.00 (*0-9623086-1-7*) Dharma Cloud Pubs.

Nakasone, Ronald Y., ed. Reflections on the Okinawan Experience: Essays Commemorating 100 Years of Okinawan Immigration. LC 96-84002. (Illus.). 135p. 1996. 28.00 (*0-9623086-3-3*); pap. 14.00 (*0-9623086-4-1*) Dharma Cloud Pubs.

Nakasone, Yasuhiro. Beyond the Horizon of the Pacific. (CISA Working Papers: No. 63). 21p. (Orig.). 1988. pap. 15.00 (*0-86682-080-9*) Ctr Intl Relations.

Nakata, Atsuko. Origami: Balloon, Airplane, No. 2. (Illus.). 16p. 1986. pap. 4.95 (*0-89346-273-X*) Heian Intl.

— Origami: Coaster, Birdmobile, No. 7. (Illus.). 16p. 1986. pap. 4.95 (*0-89346-278-0*) Heian Intl.

— Origami: Flower, Rocket, No. 3. (Illus.). 16p. 1986. pap. 4.95 (*0-89346-274-8*) Heian Intl.

— Origami: Fox, Ladybug, Crown, No. 6. (Illus.). 16p. 1986. pap. 4.95 (*0-89346-277-2*) Heian Intl.

— Origami: House, Hat, Organ, No. 1. (Illus.). 16p. 1986. pap. 4.95 (*0-89346-272-1*) Heian Intl.

— Origami: Purse, Tulip, Umbrella, No. 8. (Illus.). 16p. 1986. pap. 4.95 (*0-89346-279-9*) Heian Intl.

— Origami: Rabbit, Dog, Whale, No. 4. (Illus.). 16p. 1986. pap. 4.95 (*0-89346-275-6*) Heian Intl.

Nakata, I., et al, eds. Software Science & Engineering: Selected Papers from the Kyoto Symposia. (Computer Science Ser.: Vol. 31). 256p. (C). 1991. text 74.00 (*981-02-0776-X*) World Scientific Pub.

Nakata, M. & Wei, Stephen H. Occlusal Guidance in Pediatric Dentistry. (Illus.). 100p. 1988. 30.00 (*0-912791-63-2*, Ishiyaku EuroAmerica) Med Dent Media.

Nakata, R. Let's Go: Student's Book 2. (Illus.). 80p. 1993. pap. text 9.25 (*0-19-434397-9*) OUP.

Nakata, Ritsuko. Let's Go. (Illus.). 64p. 1992. pap. text, wbk. ed. 5.95 (*0-19-434395-2*) OUP.

— Let's Go Picture Dictionary. (Illus.). 110p. 1999. 12.50 (*0-19-435865-8*) OUP.

— Let's Go Starter. (Illus.). 64p. 1998. pap. text, student ed. 9.25 (*0-19-435290-0*) OUP.

— Let's Go Starter. (Illus.). 80p. 1998. pap. text, teacher ed. 16.95 (*0-19-435292-7*) OUP.

Nakata, Ritsuko & Frazier, Karen. Let's Go, Bk. 3. 3rd ed. (Illus.). 80p. 1994. pap. text, student ed. 9.25 (*0-19-434401-0*) OUP.

— Let's Go, Bk. 3. 3rd ed. (Illus.). 78p. 1994. pap. text, wbk. ed. 5.95 (*0-19-434403-7*) OUP.

— Let's Go, Bk. 3. 3rd ed. (Illus.). 114p. 1994. pap. text, teacher ed. 16.95 (*0-19-434402-9*) OUP.

— Let's Go, Vol. 6. (Illus.). 116p. 1997. teacher ed., spiral bd. 16.95 (*0-19-434675-7*) OUP.

— Let's Go: Level 4 Student Book. 4th ed. (Illus.). 80p. 1994. pap. text, student ed. 9.25 (*0-19-434405-3*) OUP.

— Let's Go: Level 4 Teacher's Book. 4th ed. (Illus.). 110p. 1995. pap. text, teacher ed. 16.95 (*0-19-434406-1*) OUP.

— Let's Go: Level 4 Workbook. 4th ed. (Illus.). 78p. 1995. pap. text, wbk. ed. 5.95 (*0-19-434407-X*) OUP.

— Let's Go: Student Cards 4. 1994. student ed. 11.95 (*0-19-434537-8*) OUP.

— Let's Go: Teacher's Cards 4. 1994. teacher ed. 49.95 (*0-19-434493-2*) OUP.

— Let's Go Level 3: Teacher's Cards 3. 1994. teacher ed. 11.95 (*0-19-434536-X*) OUP.

— Let's Go Level 3: Teacher's Cards 3. 1994. student ed. 49.95 (*0-19-434492-4*) OUP.

Nakatani, Alan I., ed. see American Chemical Society, Division of Polymeric M.

Nakatani, Iwao. Japanese Firm in Transition. 102p. 1988. 21.75 (*92-833-1097-7*); pap. 17.25 (*92-833-1098-5*) Productivity Inc.

Nakatani, Robert, jt. ed. see Tom, Janette.

Nakato, Tatsuaki & Ettema, Robert, eds. Issues & Directions in Hydraulics: Proceedings of an Iowa Hydraulics Colloquium, Iowa City, Iowa, U. S. A., 22-24 May, 1995. (Illus.). xxvii, 495p. (C). 1996. text 142.00 (*90-5410-810-X*, Pub. by A A Balkema) Ashgate Pub Co.

Nakato, Tatsuaki & Ogden, Fred L., eds. John F. Kennedy Student Paper Competition & Specialty Seminar Summaries: Proceedings of the John F. Kennedy Student Paper Competition & Specialty Seminar Summaries: The 27th Congress of the International Association for Hydraulic Research: San Francisco, California, August 10-15, 1997. LC 97-17972. (Water for a Changing Global Community Ser.). 120p. 1997. 16.00 (*0-7844-0275-2*) Am Soc Civil Eng.

Nakauchi, Isao, jt. auth. see Drucker, Peter F.

Nakawa, Keiko, jt. ed. see Chatani, Masahiro.

Nakawatari, Harutaka. The Sea & I. Matsui, Susan, tr. (Illus.). 32p. (J). (ps-3). 1994. pap. 5.95 (*0-374-46454-5*, Sunburst Bks) FS&G.

— Sea & I. (J). 1992. 10.40 (*0-606-08140-2*) Turtleback.

Nakayama, Akira. PC-Aided Numerical Heat Transfer & Convective Flow. LC 95-7112. 320p. 1995. boxed set 139.95 (*0-8493-7656-4*, 7656) CRC Pr.

Nakayama, B. Mishoryu: Shinka Style. 1996. pap. 10.95 (*4-07-973323-2*) Shufu No.

Nakayama, Don K., et al, eds. Critical Care of the Surgical Newborn. LC 97-16497. (Illus.). 624p. 1997. 150.00 (*0-87993-653-3*) Futura Pub.

Nakayama, F. S. & Bucks, D. A. Trickle Irrigation for Crop Production. (Developments in Agricultural Engineering Ser.: Vol. 9). 383p. 1986. 153.25 (*0-444-42615-9*) Elsevier.

Nakayama, Grey, ed. see Simms, Darrell D.

Nakayama, J. The Chemistry of 2-Alkoxy-1,3-Benzodithioles & 1,3-Benzodithiolium Salts, Reactions & Synthetic Applications, Vol. 4. 35p. 1985. pap. text 43.00 (*3-7186-0288-1*) Gordon & Breach.

Nakayama, Masatoshi. Best Karate, Vol. 10. LC 77-74829. (Illus.). 1988. pap. 17.00 (*0-87011-734-3*) Kodansha.

— Best Karate: Bassai Sho, Kanku Sho Chintei. LC 77-74829. (Best Karate Ser.: Vol. 9). (Illus.). 144p. 1986. pap. 17.00 (*0-87011-680-0*) Kodansha.

— Best Karate: Comprehensive. LC 77-74829. (Best Karate Ser.: Vol. 1). (Illus.). 144p. 1977. pap. 15.00 (*0-87011-317-8*) Kodansha.

— Best Karate: Fundamentals. LC 77-74829. (Best Karate Ser.: Vol. 2). (Illus.). 144p. 1978. pap. 15.00 (*0-87011-324-0*) Kodansha.

— Best Karate: Kata: Bassai & Kanku. LC 77-74829. (Best Karate Ser.: Vol. 6). (Illus.). 144p. (Orig.). 1980. pap. 17.00 (*0-87011-383-6*) Kodansha.

— Best Karate: Kata: Gankaku, Jion. LC 77-74829. (Best Karate Ser.: Vol. 8). (Illus.). 144p. (Orig.). 1981. pap. 17.00 (*0-87011-402-6*) Kodansha.

— Best Karate: Kata: Heian & Tekki. LC 77-74829. (Best Karate Ser.: Vol. 5). 144p. 1979. pap. 17.00 (*0-87011-379-8*) Kodansha.

— Best Karate: Kata: Jutte, Hangetsu, Empi. LC 77-74829. (Best Karate Ser.: Vol. 7). (Illus.). 144p. 1981. pap. 17.00 (*0-87011-390-9*) Kodansha.

— Best Karate: Kumite 1. LC 77-74829. (Best Karate Ser.: Vol. 3). (Illus.). 144p. 1978. pap. 17.00 (*0-87011-332-1*) Kodansha.

— Best Karate Vol. 11: Gojushiho Dai, Gojushiho Sho, Meikyo. LC 77-74829. (Best Karate Ser.). (Illus.). 144p. 1990. pap. 17.00 (*0-87011-758-0*) Kodansha.

— Dynamic Karate. Kauz, Herman, tr. LC 66-28954. (Illus.). 308p. 1966. 35.00 (*0-87011-037-3*) Kodansha.

— Dynamic Karate. LC 66-28954. (Illus.). 308p. 1987. pap. 28.00 (*0-87011-788-2*) Kodansha.

— Dynamic Karate. (Illus.). 1966. 22.95 (*0-685-21935-6*) Wehman.

Nakayama, Nobu. Hawaiian Light: The Tao of the Islands. (Illus.). 108p. 1997. pap. 24.95 (*1-56931-219-2*, Cadence Bks) Viz Commns Inc.

Nakayama, S. Mishoryu: Love & Flowers. 1996. pap. 10.95 (*4-07-973317-8*) Shufu No.

— Mishoryu: Scandinavian Glass. 1996. pap. 10.95 (*4-07-973300-3*) Shufu No.

Nakayama, Shigeki, jt. ed. see Fukui, Kiichi.

Nakayama, Shigeru. History of Japanese Astronomy: Chinese Background & Western Impact. LC 68-21980. (Harvard-Yenching Institute Monographs: No. 18). (Illus.). 324p. 1969. 22.50 (*0-674-39725-8*) HUP.

— Science, Technology & Society in Postwar Japan. (Japanese Studies). 296p. 1992. 89.95 (*0-7103-0428-5*, A6701) Routledge.

Nakayama, Shignobu, jt. auth. see Inaba, Kazuya.

Nakayama, Thomas K. & Martin, Judith N. Whiteness: The Communication of Social Identity. LC 98-19674. 314p. 1998. 52.00 (*0-7619-0862-5*); pap. 24.95 (*0-7619-0863-3*) Sage.

Nakayama, Thomas K., jt. auth. see Martin, Judith N.

Nakayama, Wataru. Japanese Electronics Industry. LC 99-28223. 152p. 1999. per. 44.95 (*1-58488-026-0*) CRC Pr.

Nakayama, Wataru & Yang, Kwang-Tzu, eds. Computers & Computing in Heat Transfer Science & Engineering. LC 92-38379. 496p. 1992. 217.95 (*0-8493-9935-1*, TJ260) CRC Pr.

Nakayama, Yasuki & Boucher, Robert. Fluid Mechanics. LC 99-182817. 244p. 1999. pap. 44.95 (*0-470-23629-9*) Wiley.

Nakayama, Yasuki & Tanida, Yoshimichi, eds. Atlas of Visualization, Vol. II. (Illus.). 256p. 1996. boxed set 104.95 (*0-8493-2656-7*) CRC Pr.

Nakayama, Yasuki, jt. ed. see Visualization Society of Japan.

Nakayama, Yoshihiro, jt. ed. see Gray, John E.

Nakayama, Yukio. Japan: Funny Side Up. Date not set. pap. 11.95 (*4-89684-204-9*) Weatherhill.

Nakazato, Nariaki. Agrarian System in Eastern Bengal C 1870-1910. LC 94-900283. (C). 1994. 27.50 (*81-7074-145-9*, Pub. by KP Bagchi) S Asia.

Nakazawa, Akira, jt. auth. see Haga, Michio.

Nakazawa, Hiromu. Principles of Precision Engineering. LC 93-43452. (Illus.). 280p. (C). 1994. text 115.00 (*0-19-856266-7*) OUP.

Nakazawa, K., jt. auth. see Ide, Y.

Nakazawa, Keiji. Barefoot Gen Vol. 1: A Cartoon Story of Hiroshima. 284p. 1990. 12.95 (*0-86719-450-2*) Last Gasp.

Nakazawa, Keiji & Spiegelman, Art. Barefoot Gen: Out of the Ashes. 288p. 1994. pap. 12.95 (*0-86719-453-7*) Last Gasp.

Nakazawa, Keiko. Pop-Up Best Greeting Cards. (Illus.). 92p. (Orig.). 1995. pap. 17.00 (*0-87040-964-6*) Japan Pubns USA.

Nakazawa, Keiko, jt. auth. see Chatani, Masahiro.

Nakazawa, S., jt. ed. see Fujita, R.

Nakazawa, Teruko, et al, eds. Molecular Biology of Pseudomonads. LC 96-18032. 526p. 1996. 98.00 (*1-55581-104-3*) ASM Pr.

Nakazawa, Tomoe. One & Two Color Graphics. LC 98-127380. (Illus.). 224p. 1997. 59.95 (*4-89444-040-7*, Pub. by PIE Bks) Bks Nippan.

— Successful Direct Mail Design. LC 98-102377. (Illus.). 224p. 1997. 75.00 (*4-89444-051-2*, Pub. by PIE Bks) Bks Nippan.

Nakell, Barry & Hardy, Kenneth A. The Arbitrariness of the Death Penalty. LC 86-5931. 1986. lib. bdg. 59.95 (*0-87722-443-9*) Temple U Pr.

Nakell, Martin. The Library of Thomas Rivka. LC 97-14755. (New American Fiction Ser.: No. 40). 86p. (Orig.). 1997. pap. 11.95 (*1-55713-089-2*) Sun & Moon CA.

***Nakell, Martin.** Two Fields That Face & Mirror Each Other. 380p. 2000. pap. 16.95 (*1-892295-97-0*) Green Integer.

Nakhaeizadeh, G. & Taylor, C. C., eds. Machine Learning & Statistics: The Interface. LC 96-4668. (Sixth-Generation Computer Technologies Ser.). 343p. 1996. 105.00 (*0-471-14890-3*) Wiley.

Nakhimovsky, Alexander & Nakhimovsky, Alice. Witness to History: The Photographs of Yevgeny Khaidel. LC 97-73708. (Illus.). 96p. 1997. 60.00 (*0-89381-738-4*) Aperture.

Nakhimovsky, Alexander, jt. auth. see Myers, Tom.

Nakhimovsky, Alexander D. & Leed, Richard L. Advanced Russian. 2nd rev. ed. 262p. (C). 1987. pap. text 19.95 (*0-89357-178-4*) Slavica.

Nakhimovsky, Alexander D., et al. Beginning Russian. 2nd rev. ed. (RUS., Illus.). xii, 283p. (Orig.). (C). 1991. pap. text 19.95 (*0-89357-221-7*) Slavica.

Nakhimovsky, Alice, jt. auth. see Nakhimovsky, Alexander.

Nakhimovsky, Alice S. Russian-Jewish Literature & Identity: Jabotinsky, Babel, Grossman, Galich, Roziner, Markish. LC 90-15804. (Jewish Studies). 240p. 1991. text 42.00 (*0-8018-4205-0*) Johns Hopkins.

N

Nakhjavani, Bahiyyih. Four on an Island. 144p. 1983. 13.50 (*0-85398-173-6*); pap. 7.25 (*0-85398-174-4*) G Ronald Pub.

***Nakhjavani, Bahiyyih.** The Saddlebag. 272p. 2000. 22.00 (*0-8070-8342-9*) Beacon Pr.

Nakhjavani, Bahiyyih. When We Grow Up. 120p. 1979. 11.50 (*0-85398-085-3*); pap. 6.00 (*0-85398-086-1*) G Ronald Pub.

Nakhla, Fayek & Jackson, Grace. Picking up the Pieces: Two Accounts of a Psychoanalytic Journey. LC 93-1304. 192p. 1993. 23.00 (*0-300-05653-2*) Yale U Pr.

Nakhla, M. S., ed. Modeling & Simulation of High Speed VLSI Interconnects. 108p. (C). 1994. text 106.00 (*0-7923-9441-0*) Kluwer Academic.

Nakhleh, Emile A. The Gulf Cooperation Council: Policies, Problems & Prospects. LC 86-8186. 147p. 1986. 57.95 (*0-275-92152-2*, C2152, Praeger Pubs) Greenwood.

— Persian Gulf & American Policy. LC 82-13125. 151p. 1982. 45.00 (*0-275-90867-4*, C0867, Praeger Pubs) Greenwood.

— The West Bank & Gaza: Toward the Making of a Palestinian State. LC 79-536. (AEI Studies: No. 232). (Illus.). 73p. reprint ed. pap. 30.00 (*0-8357-4544-9*, 203744200008) Bks Demand.

Nakhleh, Emile A., ed. A Palestinian Agenda for the West Bank & Gaza. LC 80-15596. (AEI Studies: No. 277). 143p. reprint ed. pap. 44.40 (*0-8357-4520-1*, 203737900008) Bks Demand.

Nakhleh, Issa. Encyclopedia of the Palestine Problem, Set, Vols. I & II. (Illus.). 1131p. 1991. 69.99 (*0-685-50253-8*) Morning NY.

— The True History of the Land of Canaan. 112p. 1989. pap. 4.00 (*0-9622881-1-X*) Morning NY.

Nakhleh, Khalil. Palestinian Dilemma: Nationalist Consciousness & University Education in Israel. (Monographs: No. 10). 134p. (Orig.). 1979. pap. text 6.00 (*0-937694-04-5*) Assn Arab-Amer U Grads.

— The Two Galilees. (Occasional Papers: No. 7). 27p. 1982. pap. text 1.00 (*0-937694-57-6*) Assn Arab-Amer U Grads.

Nakhre, Amrot. Social Psychology of Nonviolent Action: A Study of Three Satyagrahas. 1982. 15.00 (*0-8364-0897-7*, Pub. by Chanakya) S Asia.

Nakhshabi, Ziya'u'd-din. The Cleveland Museum of Art's Tuti-Nama: Tales of a Parrot. Simsar, Muhammed A., tr. LC 76-55714. (Illus.). 362p. 1978. 35.00 (*0-910386-29-3*) Cleveland Mus Art.

Nakicenovic, N. & Grubler, A., eds. Diffusion of Technologies & Social Behavior. (Illus.). xxvi, 605p. 1991. 191.95 (*0-387-53846-1*) Spr-Verlag.

Nakicenovic, Nebojsa, et al, eds. Global Energy Perspectives. (Illus.). 250p. (C). 1998. 69.95 (*0-521-64200-0*); pap. 27.95 (*0-521-64569-7*) Cambridge U Pr.

Nakielny, Richard, jt. ed. see Chapman, Stephen.

Nakken, Craig. The Addictive Personality: Understanding the Addictive Process & Compulsive Behavior. rev. ed. 130p. pap. 11.95 (*1-56838-129-8*) Hazelden.

***Nakken, Craig.** Reclaim Your Family from Addiction: How Couples & Families Recover Love & Meaning. 208p. 2000. pap. 14.00 (*1-56838-519-6*) Hazelden.

Nakken, Craig & Twerski. Addictive Thinking & the Addictive Personality, 2 bks. in 1. 288p. 1999. 7.98 (*1-56731-331-0*, MJF Bks) Fine Comms.

Nakken, Han, et al, eds. Research on Intervention in Special Education. LC 92-7742. 452p. 1992. lib. bdg. 109.95 (*0-7734-9514-2*) E Mellen.

Nakken, Jane. Enabling Change-When Your Child Returns from Treatment. 24p. 1985. pap. 2.00 (*0-89486-264-2*, 1271B) Hazelden.

— Kiss: Step 2. wbk. ed. 4.25 (*0-89486-459-9*, 5381 B) Hazelden.

— Step Two for Young Adults. (Step Pamphlets for Young Adults Ser.). 20p. (Orig.). 1986. pap. 3.25 (*0-89486-351-7*) Hazelden.

— Straight Back Home: To the Young Person Leaving Treatment. 16p. (Orig.). 1984. pap. 1.75 (*0-89486-250-2*, 1401B) Hazelden.

Nakken, Jane & Van Dyke, Della. Kiss: Step 1. wbk. ed. 4.25 (*0-89486-458-0*, 5380 B) Hazelden.

Nakken, Jane, jt. auth. see Van Dyke, Della.

Nakkula, Michael J. Matters of Interpretation: Mutual Transformation in the Counseling Relationship. LC 97-29503. 1997. 39.00 (*0-7879-0957-2*) Jossey-Bass.

Nakladal, Bretislav, jt. auth. see Kliment, Charles K.

Nakoa, Sarah, jt. tr. see Mookini, Esther T.

Nakon, Robert. Chemical Problem Solving Using Dimensional Analysis. 3rd ed. 416p. (C). 1990. pap. text 46.00 (*0-13-131392-4*) P-H.

Nakoryakov, V. E., et al, eds. Wave Propagation in Gas-Liquid Media. 2nd ed. LC 93-15417. 240p. 1993. boxed set 189.95 (*0-8493-9906-8*, QC153) CRC Pr.

Nakos. Linear Algebra. LC 97-47341. (Mathematics Ser.). 666p. 1998. mass mkt. 88.95 (*0-534-95526-6*) PWS Pubs.

— Linear Algebra. (Mathematics Ser.). 1998. pap., student ed. 28.95 (*0-534-95529-0*) PWS Pubs.

Nakos, Dorothy. Dictionary of Medical Imaging: French-English, English-French. (ENG & FRE.). 108p. 1995. 49.95 (*0-7859-9752-0*) Fr & Eur.

Nakosteen, Mehdi K. The History & Philosophy of Education. LC 65-12757. (Illus.). 758p. reprint ed. pap. 200.00 (*0-608-30497-2*, 202224400025) Bks Demand.

— History of Islamic Origins of Western Education. 362p. (C). 1964. 30.00 (*0-936347-32-5*) IBEX.

— Sufism & Human Destiny & Sufi Thought in Persian Literature. 236p. 1977. 25.00 (*0-936347-17-1*) IBEX.

Nakosteen, Mehdi K., ed. Return Ties of Existence.Tr. of Tarjiband. (ENG & PER.). 50p. 1975. lib. bdg. 20.00 (*0-936347-46-5*) IBEX.

Nakosteen, Mehdi K. & Zakani, Obeyd E. A Tale of Cats & Mice of Obeyd of Zakan. (ENG & PER., Illus.). 65p. 1988. 20.00 (*0-936347-41-4*) IBEX.

Nakosteen, Mehdi K., tr. see Khawju of Kirman.

Nakosteen, Mehdi K., tr. & intro. see Oryan, Baba T.

Nakosteen, Mehdi K., tr. & intro. see Sa'di.

Nakou & Pantelakis. Child in the World of Tomorrow: The Next Generation. 420p. 1996. 79.00 (*0-08-042568-2*, Pergamon Pr) Elsevier.

Nakra, Onita. Children & Learning Difficulties. 261p. 1996. pap. 110.00 (*81-7023-472-7*, Pub. by Print Hse) St Mut.

Nakuina, Emma M. Nanaue the Shark Man & Other Hawaiian Shark Stories. Kawaharada, Dennis, ed. LC 93-83814. 96p. (Orig.). 1994. pap. 7.95 (*0-9623102-4-7*) Kalamaku Pr.

Nal-Dutton Staff. Movie-A-Day. 736p. 1999. 10.95 (*0-525-94503-2*) NAL.

Nal-Dutton Staff, ed. Animal Treasury. 1999. 19.99 (*0-525-45419-5*) NAL.

— The Call of the Wild Wind. 1999. pap. 5.99 (*0-451-40616-8*, Onyx) NAL.

— Can of Worms. 1999. pap. 9.99 (*0-525-45416-0*) NAL.

— 50 Ways to Cope with Diabetes. 1996. pap. 4.99 (*0-451-18585-4*, Sig) NAL.

— Flatten Your Stomach: Men's Edition. 1992. pap. 2.99 (*0-451-82243-9*) NAL.

— Flatten Your Stomach: Women's Edition. 1992. pap. 2.99 (*0-451-82244-7*) NAL.

— How to Win the Lottery. 1999. pap. 2.99 (*0-451-18588-9*, Sig) NAL.

— Masters of Art. 1999. pap. 22.50 (*0-525-45838-7*) NAL.

— Medical-Surgical Supplies Market in Freestanding Outpatient Healthcare Delivery Centers. (Marketing Research Reports). 1987. 1975.00 (*0-86621-863-7*, A1684) NAL.

— Ocean Black. 1993. pap. 4.50 (*0-8217-4329-5*) NAL.

— Strands of Strands. 1999. pap. 5.99 (*0-451-45573-8*, ROC) NAL.

— Unused. 1999. pap. 5.50 (*0-451-45582-7*, ROC) NAL.

— Young African American. 1999. pap. 19.95 (*0-525-45275-3*) NAL.

Nala. Manual for the Legal Assistant. 2nd ed. Date not set. pap. text, teacher ed. 21.50 (*0-314-92995-9*) West Pub.

NALA Staff. NALA Manual for Legal Assistants. 3rd ed. LC 98-23892. (Paralegal Ser.). 425p. 1998. pap., student ed. 77.95 (*0-7668-0393-7*) Delmar.

Nalanda, C., tr. The Rain of Wisdom: The Essence of the Ocean of True Meaning. 416p. 39.95 (*1-57062-491-7*, Pub. by Shambhala Pubns) Random.

Nalanda Translation Committee, jt. auth. see Trungpa, Chogyam.

***Nalapat, M.D.** Indutva. 296p. 1999. 24.00 (*81-241-0575-8*, Pub. by Har-Anand Pubns) Nataraj Bks.

Nalbandian, John, jt. auth. see Klingner, Donald E.

Nalbandov, Andrew V. Advances in Neuroendocrinology. LC 63-7252. 537p. reprint ed. pap. 166.50 (*0-8357-5174-0*, 202226000026) Bks Demand.

Nalbantian, Haig. Incentives, Cooperation & Risk Sharing: Economic & Psychological Perspectives on Employment Contracts. 256p. (C). 1988. text 68.50 (*0-8476-7464-9*) Rowman.

Nalbantian, Suzanne. Aesthetic Autobiography: From Life to Art in Marcel Proust, James Joyce, Virginia Woolf, & Anais Nin. LC 94-9925. 240p. 1994. text 39.95 (*0-312-12170-9*) St Martin.

— Aesthetic Autobiography. 240p. 1997. pap. 18.95 (*0-312-17289-3*) St Martin.

— Anais Nin: Literary Perspectives. LC 96-3084. 301p. 1997. pap. 17.95 (*0-312-16524-2*); text 49.95 (*0-312-16523-4*) St Martin.

— Seeds of Decadence in the Late Nineteenth-Century Novel. 1984. pap. 15.95 (*0-333-47400-7*, Pub. by Macmillan) St Martin.

— The Symbol of the Soul from Holderlin to Yeats: A Study in Metonymy. LC 76-25550. 159p. reprint ed. pap. 49.30 (*0-8357-4574-0*, 203748300008) Bks Demand.

Nalbantoglu, Gulsum B. & Thai, Wong C., eds. Postcolonial Space(s) LC 97-10109. (Illus.). 128p. (Orig.). 1997. pap. 19.95 (*1-56898-075-2*) Princeton Arch.

NALCO Chemical Company Staff. The NALCO Guide to Boiler Failure Analysis. 293p. 1991. 59.00 (*0-07-045873-1*) McGraw.

— The NALCO Water Handbook. 2nd ed. 1120p. 1988. 85.50 (*0-07-045872-3*) McGraw.

NALCO Chemical Company Staff, et al. The NALCO Guide to Cooling-Water System Failure Analysis. LC 92-22428. 420p. 1993. 60.00 (*0-07-028400-8*) McGraw.

Nalco-Exxon Energy Chemicals, L.P. Staff, jt. auth. see Peyton, Kim.

Naldi, Gino J. Constitutional Rights in Namibia. 109p. 1995. pap. 46.00 (*0-7021-3380-9*, Pub. by Juta & Co) Gaunt.

— Documents of the Organization of African Unity. 256p. 1992. 130.00 (*0-7201-2136-1*) Continuum.

— The Organization of African Unity: An Analysis of Its Role. 328p. 1989. text 130.00 (*0-7201-2006-3*) Continuum.

— The Organization of African Unity: An Analysis of Its Role 2nd ed. LC 99-15336. 2000. 99.95 (*0-7201-2243-0*) Mansell Pub.

Naldrett, Anthony J., et al. Geology & Metallogeny of Copper Deposits. (Illus.). 620p. 1986. 171.95 (*0-387-16101-5*) Spr-Verlag.

Nalebuff, Barry J., jt. auth. see Dixit, Avinash K.

Nalecz, M., ed. Control Aspects of Biomedical Engineering. (IFAC Publication). (Illus.). 334p. 1987. 72.00 (*0-08-032553-X*, Pergamon Pr) Elsevier.

Naleid, James C. Celebrating a Century As the Genuine Article: The Story of Oshkosh B'Gosh. Robbins, Ceila D., ed. (Illus.). 60p. 1995. write for info. (*0-944641-10-5*) Greenwich Pub Group.

Nalepa, B. H., jt. auth. see Blendon, E. G.

Nalepa, Thomas F. & Schloesser, Don, eds. Zebra Mussels: Biology, Impacts, & Control. 832p. 1992. lib. bdg. 95.00 (*0-87371-696-5*, L696) Lewis Pubs.

Naletov, Igor. Alternatives to Positivism: Criticism of Bourgeois Ideology & Revisionism. 470p. 1984. 30.00 (*0-7855-2977-2*) St Mut.

Nalevanko, Eileen M., jt. auth. see Wedl, Janice.

***Nalewaja, John D., et al, eds.** Pesticide Formulations & Application Systems, Vol. 18. (STP Ser.: No. 1347). 338p. 1998. pap. text 88.00 (*0-8031-2491-0*, STP1347) ASTM.

Nalewajski, R. F., ed. Topics in Current Chemistry Vol. 180: Density Functional Theory I. xiv, 252p. 1996. 149.50 (*3-540-61091-X*) Spr-Verlag.

— Topics in Current Chemistry Vol. 181: Density Functional Theory II. xiv, 206p. 1996. 146.00 (*3-540-61092-8*) Spr-Verlag.

— Topics in Current Chemistry Vol. 182: Density Functional Theory III. xiv, 175p. 1996. 125.00 (*3-540-61132-0*) Spr-Verlag.

— Topics in Current Chemistry Vol. 183: Density Functional Theory IV. xiv, 205p. 1996. 139.50 (*3-540-61131-2*) Spr-Verlag.

Nalewajski, R. F. & Korchowiec, J. Charge Sensitivity Approach to Electronic Structure & Chemical Reactivity. (Advanced Series in Physical Chemistry). 300p. 1997. text 78.00 (*981-02-2245-9*) World Scientific Pub.

Naliboff, Jane. Kids Will Be Kids: Excellent, Tried-&-True Reasons for Thinking Twice about Having Children. LC 96-54257. (Illus.). 192p. (Orig.). 1997. pap. 9.95 (*1-888952-31-8*) Cumberland Hse.

Nalibow, Kenneth L. Genus versus Sexus: Professional Titles, Working Titles & Surnames for Women in Contemporary Standard Polish-Slavonic Languages & Literatures. (European University Studies: Ser. 16, Vol. 2). 139p. 1973. pap. 38.00 (*3-261-00892-X*) P Lang Pubng.

Nalin, David R. Medieval Sculpture from Eastern India: Selections from the Nalin Collection. Casey, Jane A., ed. (Illus.). 108p. (Orig.). 1985. pap. 45.00 (*0-9614416-0-7*) Nalini Intl Pubs.

Nalivkin, Dmitrii V. Geology of the U. S. S. R. Rast, N. & Westoll, T. S., eds. LC 75-317194. 905p. reprint ed. pap. 200.00 (*0-608-16888-2*, 205613800050) Bks Demand.

***Nalkowska, Zofia.** Medallions. Kuprel, Diana, tr. from POL. LC 99-48758. 80p. 1999. 39.95 (*0-8101-1742-8*); pap. 12.95 (*0-8101-1743-6*) Northwestern U Pr.

Nall, Barry T. & Dill, Ken A., eds. Conformations & Forces in Protein Folding. LC 91-7369. (AAAS Miscellaneous Publications: No. 91-05S). (Illus.). 234p. (Orig.). reprint ed. pap. 72.60 (*0-7837-6740-4*, 204636800011) Bks Demand.

Nall, Bruce N. Model Railroading's Guide to Model Photography. Lee, Randall B., ed. (Illus.). 64p. 1993. pap. 8.95 (*0-9612692-8-6*) Rocky Mntn Pub Co.

Nall, C. Van, jt. auth. see Kerckhove, Michael C.

Nall, Jasper R. Freeborn Slave: Diary of a Black Man in the South. 112p. 1996. 14.95 (*1-881548-28-7*) Crane Hill AL.

***Nall, Jasper Rastus.** Freeborn Slave: Diary of a Black Man in the South. (Illus.). 112p. 2000. pap. 10.95 (*1-57587-165-3*, Pub. by Crane Hill AL) Blair.

Nall, Joy & Nall, Thomas, Jr. The Candy Cane Story. LC 97-7644. (Illus.). 32p. (J). (gr. k-5). 1998. reprint ed. 11.95 (*0-9651185-3-3*) B & D Gleasner.

Nall, Lexie, jt. auth. see Farber, Eugene M.

Nall, Lexie, jt. auth. see Jacobs, Paul H.

Nall, Lexie, jt. ed. see Jacobs, Paul H.

Nall, S. E., jt. auth. see Day, P. D.

Nall, Thomas, Jr., jt. auth. see Nall, Joy.

Nall, Van C., jt. auth. see Kerckhove, Michael C.

Nalla, Mahesh & Newman, Graeme. A Primer in Private Security. LC 89-26994. (Special Edge Supplementary Text Ser.). 170p. 1990. pap. text 22.50 (*0-911577-18-1*, Criminal Justice) Willow Tree NY.

***Nallanj, Gofalchari.** Discovery of the Soul. 2000. pap. 9.50 (*0-9672833-2-9*) Think Club.

Nallari, Raj, jt. auth. see Mills, Cadman A.

Nalle, Sara T. God in la Mancha: Religious Reform & the People of Cuenca, 1500-1650. LC 92-2625. (Johns Hopkins University Studies in Historical & Political Science: Series 110, Vol. 2). (Illus.). 324p. reprint ed. pap. 100.50 (*0-608-06172-7*, 206650500008) Bks Demand.

Nalley, Kathleen, ed. see Goodwin, Ben.

Nalls, Elaine, tr. see McIntosh, Noel & Oliveras, Elizabeth, eds.

Nalls, Patricia & Maine, Cathleen M. The AIDS Drug Assistance Program (ADAP) A Resource Guide for Women Living with HIV/AIDS. 36p. 1996. pap. 5.00 (*1-877966-38-X*) Ctr Women Policy.

Nalluri, C., jt. auth. see Featherstone, R. E.

Nally Gallagher, Joan. Buying Power. (Internet Investigations Ser.). (Illus.). 24p. 1999. pap. text, teacher ed. 8.95 (*1-58108-027-1*) Pencil Point.

— Famous Mathematician Women. (Internet Investigations Ser.). (Illus.). 24p. 1999. pap. text, teacher ed. 8.95 (*1-58108-029-8*) Pencil Point.

Nally Gallegher, Joan. Great Disasters. (Internet Investigations Ser.). (Illus.). 24p. Date not set. pap. text, teacher ed. 8.95 (*1-58108-022-0*) Pencil Point.

— Playing the Stock Market. (Internet Investigations Ser.). (Illus.). 24p. 1999. pap. text, teacher ed. 8.95 (*1-58108-031-X*) Pencil Point.

— Understanding the Stock Market. (Internet Investigations Ser.). (Illus.). 24p. 1998. pap. text, teacher ed. 8.95 (*1-58108-025-5*) Pencil Point.

— Weather. (Internet Investigations Ser.). (Illus.). 24p. 1999. pap. text, teacher ed. 8.95 (*1-58108-026-3*) Pencil Point.

Nally, Joseph R. How Great a Salvation. 178p. 1997. pap. 12.95 (*1-57502-537-X*, PO1577) Morris Pubng.

Nally, Susan & Lee, Liz. How to Feel Most Excellent! About Who You Are (& Really Enjoy It) LC 93-48685. (Spending Prime Time with God Ser.). (J). (gr. 5-7). 1994. pap. 8.99 (*0-8054-4008-9*, 4240-08) Broadman.

— How to Stay Way Cool! When Things Are Tough (& Really Like It) (Spending Prime Time with God Ser.). 208p. (J). (gr. 5-7). 1994. pap. 8.99 (*0-8054-4010-0*, 4240-10) Broadman.

NALP Foundation Staff. Keeping the Keepers: Strategies for Associate Retention in Times of Attrition. 112p. 1998. pap. 275.00 (*1-55733-015-8*) NALP.

NALP Staff. Beyond L. A. Law: Stories of People Who've Done Fascinating Things with a Law Degree. 224p. 1997. pap. text 17.95 (*0-15-900182-X*) Harcourt Legal.

— National Directory of Legal Employers. 1352p. 1996. pap. 49.95 (*0-15-900179-X*) Harcourt Legal.

NALP Staff. National Directory of Legal Employers. 2nd ed. 1352p. 1997. pap. text 49.95 (*0-15-900225-7*) Harcourt Legal.

Nalsa Inc. Flashpoints SAT Survival Kit. (Illus.). 918p. (YA). (gr. 10-12). 1996. boxed set 69.95 (*1-889417-01-7*, FP Set) NALSA.

Nalsa Incorporated Staff. Archiflash. 3rd rev. ed. (Illus.). 1152p. 1998. 89.95 (*1-889417-04-1*, 04-1) NALSA.

Nalty. Electrotherapy Clinical Procedures. 356p. 1999. 42.00 (*0-07-134317-2*) McGraw.

***Nalty.** The Vietnam War: The History of America's Conflict in Southeast Asia. (Illus.). 1998. pap. 16.95 (*1-84065-003-6*, Pub. by Salamander) Combined Pub.

Nalty, Bernard C. Air War: World War II Chronicles. LC 99-18049. 128p. 1999. text 14.98 (*1-56799-758-9*) M Friedman Pub Grp Inc.

***Nalty, Bernard C.** The American Soldier in World War II. (Illus.). 176p. 2000. 24.95 (*0-7603-0969-8*, 130748AP, Pub. by MBI Pub) Motorbooks Intl.

Nalty, Bernard C. Cape Gloucester: The Green Inferno. 36p. 1994. pap. 2.75 (*0-16-045697-5*) USGPO.

— Cape Gloucester: The Green Inferno. (Illus.). 33p. (C). 1996. reprint ed. pap. text 20.00 (*0-7881-3534-1*) DIANE Pub.

***Nalty, Bernard C.** D-Day: Operation Overload from Its Planning to the Liberation of Paris. (Classic Conflicts Ser.). (Illus.). 1999. pap. 16.95 (*1-84065-095-8*) Salamander.

Nalty, Bernard C. Flying Aces: Heroic Dogfights of World War II. LC 99-35932. 1999. text 35.00 (*1-56799-815-1*, Friedman-Fairfax) M Friedman Pub Grp Inc.

— The Right to Fight: African-American Marines in World War II. (Illus.). 29p. 1996. reprint ed. pap. text 20.00 (*0-7881-3531-7*) DIANE Pub.

— Strength for the Fight: A History of Black Americans in the Military. 1989. pap. 16.95 (*0-02-922411-X*) Free Pr.

***Nalty, Bernard C.** War in the Pacific: Pearl Harbor Tokyo Bay. LC 99-41907. 304p. 1999. pap. write for info. (*0-8061-3199-3*) U of Okla Pr.

— War in the Pacific: The Story of the Bitter Struggle in the Pacific Theatre of World War II. (Classic Conflicts Ser.). (Illus.). 1999. pap. 16.95 (*1-84065-094-X*) Salamander.

***Nalty, Bernard C., ed.** American Soldier in World War Two. (Illus.). 2000. 29.95 (*1-84065-189-X*, Pub. by Salamander) Combined Pub.

— War in the Pacific: Pearl Harbor to Tokyo Bay. (Illus.). 2000. 34.95 (*1-84065-150-4*, Pub. by Salamander) Combined Pub.

— Winged Shield, Winged Sword: A History of the United States Air Force, 2 vols. (Illus.). 1192p. 1997. 77.00 (*0-16-049009-X*) AFH & MP.

Nalty, Bernard C., et al, eds. Wrecks, Rescues & Investigations: Selected Documents of the U. S. Coast Guard & Its Predecessors. LC 78-12312. (Illus.). 473p. 1978. lib. bdg. 85.00 (*0-8420-2130-2*) Scholarly Res Inc.

Nalty, Bernard C. & MacGregor, Morris J., eds. Blacks in the Military: Essential Documents. LC 80-54664. 367p. 1981. lib. bdg. 50.00 (*0-8420-2183-3*) Scholarly Res Inc.

Nalty, Bernard C., et al. With Courage: The U.S. Army Air Forces in World War II. Beck, Alfred M., ed. LC 94-4716. (General Histories Ser.). 1995. 31.00 (*0-16-036396-9*, 008-070-00663-4) USGPO.

Nalty, Bernard C., jt. auth. see Thompson, Wayne.

Nalty, Lily N., jt. auth. see Quattlebaum, Patricia D.

Nalty, Theresa. Physical Therapy Licensure Examination Guide: Pretest Self-Assessment & Review. 208p. 1999. pap. write for info. (*0-07-134723-2*) McGraw-Hill HPD.

Nalubega, Maimuna, jt. auth. see Kansiime, Frank.

Nalven, Gail. Plant Safety. LC 96-24177. (Practical Engineering Perspectives ;). 272p. 1996. 85.00 (*0-8169-0709-9*, Q-1) Am Inst Chem Eng.

Nalven, Gail, ed. Distillation & Other Industrial Separations. LC 97-149. (Practical Engineering Perspectives Ser.). 285p. 1997. 85.00 (*0-8169-0712-9*, Q-4) Am Inst Chem Eng.

— Environment: Air, Water & Soil. LC 96-41927. (Practical Engineering Perspectives). 1997. 85.00 (*0-8169-0713-7*, Q-5) Am Inst Chem Eng.

— Environmental Management & Pollution Prevention. LC 96-41208. (Practical Engineering Perspectives Ser.). 148p. 1997. 85.00 (*0-8169-0711-0*, Q-3) Am Inst Chem Eng.

— Plant Operations & Optimization. LC 96-24176. (Practical Engineering Perspectives Ser.). 372p. 1996. 85.00 (*0-8169-0710-2*, Q-2) Am Inst Chem Eng.

Nalven, Nancy. The Famous Mister Ed: The Unbridled Truth about America's Favorite Talking Horse. 1991. mass mkt. 9.99 (*0-446-39296-0*, Pub. by Warner Bks) Little.

Nalwa. Handbook of Low & High Dielectric Constant Materials & Their Applications, 2 vols. (Illus.). 1100p. (C). 1999. 550.00 (*0-12-513905-5*, Pub. by Acad Pr) Harcourt.

— Low & High Dielectric Constant Materials & Their Applications. LC 98-43222. 750p. (C). 1999. write for info. (*0-12-513906-3*); write for info. (*0-12-513907-1*) Acad Pr.

Nalwa, Hari S. Ferroelectric Polymers. (Plastics Engineering Ser.: vol. 28). (Illus.). 920p. 1995. text 250.00 (*0-8247-9468-0*) Dekker.

— Handbook of Organic Conductive Molecules & Polymers, Vol. 1, Charge-Transfer Salts, Fullerenes & Photoconductors, Vol. 1, Charge-Transfer Salts, Fullerenes and Phot. LC 96-30337. 828p. 1997. 352.50 (*0-471-96593-6*) Wiley.

— Handbook of Organic Conductive Molecules & Polymers, Vol. 2, Conductive Polymers, Vol. 2, Conductive Polymers. LC 96-30337. 888p. 1997. 352.50 (*0-471-96594-4*) Wiley.

— Handbook of Organic Conductive Molecules & Polymers, Vol. 3, Conductive Polymers, Vol. 3, Conductive Polymers. LC 96-30337. 890p. 1997. 352.50 (*0-471-96595-2*) Wiley.

— Handbook of Organic Conductive Molecules & Polymers, 4 Vol. Set, 4 vols., Vol. 4. LC 96-30337. 3334p. 1997. 1410.00 (*0-471-96275-9*) Wiley.

Nalwa, Hari S. & Miyata, Seizo, eds. Nonlinear Optics of Organic Molecules & Polymeric Materials. LC 96-20281. (Illus.). 896p. 1996. boxed set 199.95 (*0-8493-8923-2*) CRC Pr.

Nalwa, Hari S., jt. ed. see Miyata, Seizo.

Nalwa, Hari Singh. Handbook of Nanostructured Materials & Nanotechnology, 5 vols., Set. LC 98-43220. 3608p. 1999. 1500.00 (*0-12-513760-5*) Acad Pr.

Nam, Charles. Our Population: Thinking About. lib. bdg. 28.90 (*0-8027-6753-2*) Walker & Co.

Nam, Charles B. Nationality Groups & Social Stratification: A Study of the Socioeconomic Status & Mobility of Selected European Nationality Groups in America. Cordasco, Francesco, ed. LC 80-882. (American Ethnic Groups Ser.). 1981. lib. bdg. 30.95 (*0-405-13443-6*) Ayer.

— Our Population: The Changing Face of America. LC 87-21601. 1988. pap. 5.95 (*0-8027-6754-0*) Walker & Co.

— Understanding Population Change. LC 93-71269. 471p. (C). 1994. boxed set 50.00 (*0-87581-377-1*, UPC) F E Peacock Pubs.

Nam, Charles B., et al, eds. International Handbook on Internal Migration. LC 89-7487. 453p. 1990. lib. bdg. 105.00 (*0-313-25858-9*, NIH/, Greenwood Pr) Greenwood.

Nam, Charles B., jt. auth. see Folger, John K.

Nam, Inja & Schmidt, Arno. The Art of Garnishing. 128p. 1993. 39.95 (*0-471-28474-2*, VNR) Wiley.

Nam, Inja & Schmidt, Arno B. The Art of Garnishing. LC 93-7905. (Illus.). 1994. text 32.95 (*0-442-01084-2*, VNR) Wiley.

— The Book of Hors d'Oeuvres & Canapes. 1996. 49.95 (*0-614-95794-X*, VNR) Wiley.

Nam, Inja, jt. auth. see Schmidt, Arno.

Nam, Jee-Sun. Classification Syntaxique des Constructions Adjectivales en Coreen. (Lingvisticae Investigationes Supplementa Ser.: Vol. 21). xxvi, 560p. 1996. lib. bdg. 99.00 (*1-55619-751-9*) J Benjamins Pubng Co.

Nam, Julian, jt. auth. see Nagel, Stuart S.

Nam, Ngoc N. Nguoi Viet Dau Tu Luat Thue Vu 1986 Cua Hoa Ky (The Vietnamese & the Tax Reform Act of 1986) 135p. (Orig.). 1987. pap. 8.00 (*0-9614634-1-4*) N N Nguyen.

— Nguoi Viet Dau Tu (The Vietnamese Investor) 267p. (Orig.). 1985. pap. 15.00 (*0-9614634-0-6*) N N Nguyen.

***Nam, Park & Chunghwa, Kay.** Korean Basic Course Level 2 with 16 Cassettes. (Multilingual Books Intensive Cassette Foreign Language Ser.). 560p. 1999. pap. text 230.00 (*1-58214-039-1*) Mltilingl Bks.

Nam, Park B., jt. auth. see Miller, Dan.

Nam, Park Bok. Fundamentals of Pa Kua Chang. 1998. pap. text. write for info. (*1-883175-05-4*) High View Pubns.

Nam-Sung Song. Thematic Relations & Transitivity in English, Japanese, & Korean. LC 93-29693. (Center for Korean Studies Monograph: No. 17). 1994. pap. text 15.00 (*0-8248-1580-7*) Ctr Korean Studies.

Nama, H. S. Cestods, Parasites of Indian Animals. (C). 1990. text 150.00 (*81-85046-97-2*, Pub. by Scientific Pubs) St Mut.

Nama, P. G., et al. Breast Self Examination & You. 1995. pap. 6.00 (*0-318-37463-3*) Budlong.

Nama, Prabharathie G., jt. auth. see Tetzleff, Judith.

Namachchivaya, N. S., jt. ed. see Paidoussis, M. P.

Naman, Anne A. The Jew in the Victorian Novel: Some Relationships Between Prejudice & Art. LC 79-8634. (Studies in the Nineteenth Century: No. 1). 1980. 34.50 (*0-404-18023-X*) AMS Pr.

Namanny, Dorothy C., jt. auth. see Dupree, Garland C.

Namara, Martha. An Nan Galateeffadha (Oromo Language Hymnal) 282p. 1997. spiral bd. 12.00 (*1-886513-05-8*) Kirk Hse Pubs.

Namartha-nirnaya of Kaundabhatta. The Meaning of Nouns: Semantic Theory in Classical & Medieval India. LC 92-17009. (Studies of Classical India: Vol. 13). 308p. (C). 1992. lib. bdg. 273.50 (*0-7923-1847-1*, Pub. by Kluwer Academic) Kluwer Academic.

***Namaste, Viviane K.** Invisible Lives. 1998. lib. bdg. 50.00 (*0-226-56809-1*) U Ch Pr.

— Invisible Lives: The Erasure of Transsexual & Transgendered People in the Cultural & Institutional World. LC 00-24155. 1998. pap. text 18.00 (*0-226-56810-5*) U Ch Pr.

Namazi, Abby. Dreams, Stockmarket & Casinos. (Illus.). (Orig.). 1996. pap. 12.95 (*0-9651150-0-3*) Namazi.

***Namazi, Kevan H. & Chefetz, Paul K., eds.** Assisted Living: Current Issues in Facility Management & Resident Care. 288p. 2000. 65.00 (*0-86569-301-3*, Auburn Hse) Greenwood.

Namazi, N. M., ed. Signal & Image Processing. 520p. 1995. 170.00 (*0-88986-185-4*, 237) Acta Pr.

Namazi, N. M. & Matthews, K., eds. Signal & Image Processing. LC 97-18517. (Illus.). 364p. 1996. pap. 118.00 (*0-88986-215-X*) Acta Pr.

— Signal & Image Processing & Applications. LC 97-18540. (Illus.). 263p. 1996. pap. 90.00 (*0-88986-203-6*) Acta Pr.

Namba, M., ed. see Seventh International Symposium Staff.

Namba, Makoto. Geometry of Projective Algebraic Curves. LC 84-17636. (Monographs & Textbooks in Pure & Applied Mathematics: Vol. 88). (Illus.). 427p. reprint ed. pap. 132.40 (*0-608-08969-9*, 206960400005) Bks Demand.

Namba, S., et al, eds. Science & Technology of Mesoscopic Structures. LC 92-30098. 1993. write for info. (*4-431-70090-0*); write for info. (*3-540-70090-0*); 218.95 (*0-387-70090-0*) Spr-Verlag.

— Science & Technology of Microfabrication. (MRS Symposium Proceedings Ser.: Vol. 76). 1987. text 17.50 (*0-931837-42-1*) Materials Res.

Namban, Akahige. Chrysanthemum, Rose, & the Samurai. 202p. 1989. mass mkt. 7.95 (*0-929654-06-4*, Pub. by Blue Moon Bks) Publishers Group.

***Namban, Akahige.** Women of the Mountain, Warriors of the Town. 224p. 2000. mass mkt. 7.95 (*1-56201-174-X*, Pub. by Blue Moon Bks) Publishers Group.

Nambiar, A. C. Handloom Industry in India. (Illus.). xvii, 169p. (C). 1996. 28.00 (*81-7024-770-5*, Pub. by Ashish Pub Hse) S Asia.

— Rural Poverty: Problems & Prospects. (Illus.). xiv, 134p. (C). 1992. 18.00 (*81-7024-510-9*, Pub. by Ashish Pub Hse) Nataraj Bks.

Nambiar, E. K., jt. auth. see Bowen, Glyn D.

Nambiar, R. G., et al. Complementarity in Trade & Production: Intra-South Potentials. LC 94-23401. (Indo-Dutch Studies on Development Alternatives: Vol. 15). 180p. 1995. 25.00 (*0-8039-9206-8*) Sage.

Nambiar, Sita. The Ritual of Teyyam & Bhutaradhana. (C). 1996. 58.00 (*81-7013-149-9*, Pub. by Navarang) S Asia.

Nambisan, K. M. Design Elements of Landscape Gardening. (C). 1992. 36.00 (*81-204-0683-4*, Pub. by Oxford IBH) S Asia.

***Nambisan, Kavery.** Mango-coloured Fish. LC 98-917645. 1998. write for info. (*0-14-027814-1*) Penguin Books.

Namboodiri, Krishnan. Demographic Analysis: A Stochastic Approach. 370p. 1990. text 69.95 (*0-12-513830-X*) Acad Pr.

— Matrix Algebra: An Introduction. (Quantitative Applications in the Social Sciences Ser.: Vol. 38). 96p. (Orig.). (C). 1984. pap. text 10.95 (*0-8039-2052-0*) Sage.

— Methods for Macrosociological Research. (Illus.). 293p. 1994. text 79.95 (*0-12-513345-6*) Acad Pr.

— A Primer of Population Dynamics. (Plenum Series on Demographic Methods & Population Analysis). (Illus.). 349p. (C). 1996. text 59.00 (*0-306-45338-X*, Kluwer Plenum) Kluwer Academic.

Namboodiri, Krishnan & Corwin, Ronald G. The Logic & Method of Macro Sociology: An Input-Output Approach to Organizational Networks. LC 93-20302. 192p. 1993. 62.95 (*0-275-94529-4*, C4529, Praeger Pubs) Greenwood.

Namboodiri, Krishnan & Suchindran, C. M., eds. Life Table Techniques & Their Applications. (Studies in Population). 1987. text 75.00 (*0-12-513930-6*) Acad Pr.

Namboodiri, M. N., jt. auth. see Nebbia, G.

Namboodiri, M. N., tr. see Jnanamritananda, Swami.

Namboodiri, M. N., tr. see Menon, T. V.

Namboodiri, P. K., et al. Intervention in the Indian Ocean. 361p. 1982. 35.95 (*0-940500-81-7*, Pub. by ABC Pub Hse) Asia Bk Corp.

Namboodiripad, E. M. Kerala: Society & Politics - An Historical Survey. 1985. 10.00 (*0-8364-1495-0*) S Asia.

Nambooripad, K. S. Structure of Regular Semigroups, No. 1. LC 79-21160. (Memoirs of the American Mathematical Society Ser.: No. 224). 132p. reprint ed. pap. 41.00 (*0-7837-7001-4*, 204681400004) Bks Demand.

— Structure of Regular Semigroups - I. K. S. Nambooripad. LC 79-21160. (Memoirs Ser.: No. 22/224). 117p. 1985. reprint ed. pap. 18.00 (*0-8218-2224-1*, MEMO/22/224) Am Math.

Nambu, John, tr. see Transnational College of LEX Staff.

Nambu, Y. Quarks: Frontiers in Elementary Particle Physics. 240p. 1985. text 47.00 (*9971-966-65-4*); pap. text 14.00 (*9971-966-66-2*) World Scientific Pub.

Nambudiri, P. P. Aryans in South India. (C). 1992. 32.00 (*81-210-0266-4*, Pub. by Inter-India Pubns) S Asia.

***Nambudripad, Devi S.** Despidase de las Enfermedades! (Say Goodbye to Illness) (SPA.). xvii, 273p. 1999. pap. 21.00 (*0-9658242-6-8*) Delta Pubs.

— Naet Guide Book: The Companion to "Say Good-Bye to Illness" 4th ed. 1999. pap. 12.00 (*0-9658242-3-3*) Delta Pubs.

— Say Good-Bye to ADD & ADHD. (Say Good-Bye to... Ser.). 1999. pap. 18.00 (*0-9658242-4-1*) Delta Pubs.

— Say Good-Bye to Allergy-Related Autism. (Say Good-Bye to... Ser.). 1999. pap. 18.00 (*0-9658242-5-X*) Delta Pubs.

— Say Goodbye to Illness. 2nd ed. (Say Goodbye Ser.). (Illus.). xxxiv, 521p. 1999. pap. 24.00 (*0-9658242-1-7*) Delta Pubs.

Nambudripad, Devi S. You Can Reprogram Your Brain to Perfect Health: Unsolved Health Problems Solved. (Illus.). 140p. (Orig.). 1990. pap. 47.60 (*0-685-29804-3*) Singer Pub.

Nambuthiri, R. R., jt. ed. see Tamma, K. K.

Name, Willard G. Van, see Van Name, Willard G.

Namee, J. William Van, see Van Namee, J. William.

Namekata, Tsukasa & Du V Florey, Charles, eds. Health Effects of Air Pollution & the Japanese Compensation Law. LC 87-14548. 188p. 1987. text 37.50 (*0-935470-38-7*) Battelle.

Nameroff, Rochelle. Body Prints. LC 73-155607. 54p. 1972. 2.95 (*0-87886-022-3*, Greenfld Rev Pr) Greenfld Rev Lit.

Nameroff, Steven, jt. auth. see O'Brien, Stephen K.

***Namerov, Jeremy.** Dandelion Dreams & others Poems. (Illus.). 224p. 1999. pap. 8.95 (*0-9641235-1-7*) Dormer Window.

Namerow. Neurorehabilitation. Date not set. text. write for info. (*0-7216-5646-3*, W B Saunders Co) Harcrt Hlth Sci Grp.

Names, Larry. Green Bay Packers Facts & Trivia. 5th ed. 1997. pap. text 12.99 (*0-938313-30-4*) E B Houchin.

Names, Larry D. Bury My Heart at Wrigley Field. (History of the Chicago Cubs When the Cubs Were the White Sox Ser.: Bk. 1). (Illus.). 240p. 1996. pap. 12.99 (*0-939995-05-0*); text 20.00 (*0-939995-04-2*) Angel Pr WI.

— Chicago White Sox Facts & Trivia. (Illus.). 160p. (Orig.). 1996. pap. 9.99 (*0-938313-15-0*) E B Houchin.

— The History of the Green Bay Packers: The Lambeau Years, Bk. I, Pt. 1. (Illus.). 256p. 1987. 16.95 (*0-939995-00-X*) Angel Pr WI.

— The History of the Green Bay Packers Pt. 4 of 4: The Shameful Years. LC 95-78491. (Illus.). 250p. 1995. 18.00 (*0-939995-03-4*) Angel Pr WI.

— History of the Green Bay Packers Vol. III: Lambeau Years, Pt. 3. 1996. 18.95 (*0-939995-02-6*) Angel Pr WI.

— The History of the Green Bay Packers, Part II: The Lambeau Years. (Illus.). 272p. 1989. 18.95 (*0-939995-01-8*) Angel Pr WI.

— Ironclads: Man-of-War. 384p. (Orig.). 1995. mass mkt. 5.99 (*0-380-77619-7*, Avon Bks) Morrow Avon.

Names, Larry D., ed. see Hollatz, Tom.

Namestka. Wonders of Technology, Level 1. (Tech & Industrial Education Ser.). 1992. pap., teacher ed. 108.95 (*0-8273-4704-9*); pap., suppl. ed. 11.95 (*0-8273-4701-4*) Delmar.

— Wonders of Technology, Level 2. (Tech & Industrial Education Ser.). 1992. pap., teacher ed. 108.95 (*0-8273-4705-7*); pap., suppl. ed. 11.95 (*0-8273-4702-2*) Delmar.

— Wonders of Technology, Level 3. (Tech & Industrial Education Ser.). 1992. pap., teacher ed. 108.95 (*0-8273-4706-5*); pap., suppl. ed. 11.95 (*0-8273-4703-0*) Delmar.

Namestka, Keith B. & Moyer, Philip D. Mountain Lake Diving: California-Nevada. (Illus.). 1998. pap. text 14.95 (*0-9666143-0-5*) Enviro-tech Dist.

***Namey, Laura.** City Sights. Wise, Noreen, ed. (Book-a-Day Collection). (Illus.). 32p. (YA). (ps up). 2000. pap. 5.95 (*1-58584-374-1*) Huckleberry CT.

Namias, Jerome. Thirty-Day Forecasting: A Review of a Ten-Year Experiment. (Meteorological Monograph: Vol. 2, No. 6). (Illus.). 83p. (Orig.). 1953. pap. 17.00 (*0-933876-01-7*) Am Meteorological.

Namias, June. First Generation: In the Words of Twentieth-Century American Immigrants. 2nd ed. (Illus.). 304p. 1992. pap. text 17.95 (*0-252-06170-5*) U of Ill Pr.

— White Captives: Gender & Ethnicity on the American Frontier. LC 92-31235. (Illus.). xxii, 378p. (C). 1993. pap. text 19.95 (*0-8078-4408-X*) U of NC Pr.

Namias, June, ed. & anno. see Wakefield, Sarah F.

Namias, June, ed. & intro. see Seaver, James E.

***Namie, Gary & Namie, Ruth.** The Bully at Work: What You Can Do to Stop the Hurt & Reclaim Your Dignity on the Job. 304p. 2000. pap. 49.95 (*1-57071-534-3*) Sourcebks.

Namie, Ruth, jt. auth. see Namie, Gary.

Namier, Lewis B. Conflicts. LC 73-90667. (Essay Index Reprint Ser.). 1977. 20.95 (*0-8369-1230-6*) Ayer.

— Crossroads of Power. LC 77-119604. (Essay Index Reprint Ser.). 1977. 18.95 (*0-8369-1690-5*) Ayer.

— Eighteen Forty-Eight: Raleigh Lectures on History, 1944. 138p. 1992. pap. text 16.95 (*0-19-726111-6*) OUP.

— Europe in Decay Nineteen Thirty-Six to Nineteen Forty. 1990. 16.50 (*0-8446-1322-3*) Peter Smith.

— In the Margin of History. LC 69-18934. (Essay Index Reprint Ser.). 1977. 20.95 (*0-8369-0050-2*) Ayer.

— Skyscrapers, & Other Essays. LC 68-22113. (Essay Index Reprint Ser.). 1977. 18.95 (*0-8369-0734-5*) Ayer.

— Vanished Supremacies, Vol. 1. Collected Es. LC 73-119603. (Select Bibliographies Reprint Ser.). 1977. 15.95 (*0-8369-5195-6*) Ayer.

Namikawa, A. Cleavage Lines of the Skin. (Bibliotheca Anatomica Ser.: No. 27). (Illus.). viii, 140p. 1986. 77.50 (*3-8055-4202-X*) S Karger.

Namiki, Mikio. Quantum Physics, Chaos Theory & Cosmology. LC 96-31759. 1996. 65.00 (*1-56396-544-5*) Spr-Verlag.

Namiki, Mikio, et al. Stochastic Quantization. Beiglbock, W. et al, eds. LC 92-17584. (Lecture Notes in Physics, New Series, Monographs: Vol. M9). (Illus.). x, 217p. 1992. 58.95 (*0-387-55563-3*) Spr-Verlag.

Namikoshi, Ti. Shiatsu Therapy: Theory & Practice. pap. 18.95 (*0-685-70705-9*) Wehman.

Namikoshi, Tokujiro. Shiatsu: Japanese Finger Pressure Therapy. LC 68-19983. (Illus.). 84p. 1994. pap. 12.00 (*0-87040-169-6*) Japan Pubns USA.

Namikoshi, Toru. The Complete Book of Shiatsu Therapy: Health & Vitality at Your Fingertips. LC 79-1963. (Illus.). 256p. 1994. pap. 22.00 (*0-87040-461-X*) Japan Pubns USA.

— Shiatsu Way to Health: Relaxation & Relief at a Touch. McCandless, Susan K., tr. LC 87-81676. (Illus.). 160p. 1988. pap. 25.00 (*0-87011-796-3*) Kodansha.

***Namikoshi, Toru.** Touch & Stretch: Shiatsu for Everyone. 2000. pap. 16.95 (*4-8170-9004-9*, Pub. by Japan JPN) Kodansha.

Namio, Jody, ed. see Backaus, Balbir.

Namioka, Aki, jt. ed. see Schuler, Douglas.

Namioka, Isaac. Partially Ordered Linear Topological Spaces. fac. ed. LC 52-42839. (American Mathematical Society, Memoirs Ser.: No. 24). 56p. 1957. reprint ed. pap. 30.00 (*0-608-01005-7*, 206186300012) Bks Demand.

— Partially Ordered Linear Topological Spaces. LC 52-42389. (Memoirs Ser.: No. 1/24). 50p. 1990. reprint ed. pap. 22.00 (*0-8218-1224-6*, MEMO/1/24) Am Math.

Namioka, Lensey. April & the Dragon Lady. LC 93-27958. 224p. (YA). (gr. 7 up). 1994. 10.95 (*0-15-276644-8*, Harcourt Child Bks) Harcourt.

Namioka, Lensey. April & the Dragon Lady. LC 93-27958. 1994. 10.10 (*0-606-06182-7*, Pub. by Turtleback) Demco.

Namioka, Lensey. April & the Dragon Lady P. LC 93-27958. (Illus.). 224p. (YA). (gr. 7 up). 1994. pap. 6.00 (*0-15-200886-1*, Harcourt Child Bks) Harcourt.

— The Coming of the Bear. LC 91-17331. 192p. (YA). (gr. 7 up). 1992. 14.00 (*0-06-020288-2*) HarpC Child Bks.

— Den of the White Fox. LC 96-34840. 1997. pap. 6.00 (*0-15-201283-4*) Harcourt.

— Den of the White Fox. LC 96-34840. 224p. 1997. 14.00 (*0-15-201282-6*) Harcourt.

— Den of the White Fox. LC 96-34840. 1997. 11.10 (*0-606-11250-2*, Pub. by Turtleback) Demco.

— Island of Ogres. LC 88-22058. 208p. (YA). (gr. 7 up). 1989. 13.95 (*0-06-024372-4*) HarpC Child Bks.

— The Laziest Boy in the World. LC 97-9053. (Illus.). (J). (ps-3). 1998. 16.95 (*0-8234-1330-6*) Holiday.

— Ties That Bind, Ties That Break. LC 98-27877. 160p. (YA). (gr. 7 up). 1999. 15.95 (*0-385-32666-1*) BDD Bks Young Read.

***Namioka, Lensey.** Ties That Bind, Ties That Break. 2000. mass mkt. 4.99 (*0-440-41599-3*, LE) Dell.

Namioka, Lensey. Yang the Eldest & His Odd Jobs. LC 99-36935. 144p. (J). (gr. 3-7). 1999. 15.95 (*0-316-59011-8*) Little.

— Yang the Second. LC 97-38616. (Illus.). 144p. (J). (gr. 4-6). 1998. 15.95 (*0-316-59731-7*) Little.

***Namioka, Lensey.** Yang the Second & Her Secret Admirers. (Illus.). 144p. (J). (gr. 4-7). 2000. pap. 4.50 (*0-440-41641-8*, Yearling) BDD Bks Young Read.

Namioka, Lensey. Yang the Third & Her Impossible Family. (Illus.). 144p. (J). (gr. 4-7). 1996. pap. 4.50 (*0-440-41231-5*, YB BDD) BDD Bks Young Read.

— Yang the Third & Her Impossible Family. LC 94-30110. (J). 1996. 9.09 (*0-606-10096-2*, Pub. by Turtleback) Demco.

— Yang the Youngest & His Terrible Ear. 144p. (J). (gr. 4-7). 1994. pap. 4.50 (*0-440-40917-9*) Dell.

— Yang the Youngest & His Terrible Ear. (Illus.). (YA). (gr. 4 up). 1995. 9.00 (*0-395-73239-5*) HM.

— Yang the Youngest & His Terrible Ear. (J). 1992. 9.09 (*0-606-06107-X*, Pub. by Turtleback) Demco.

— Yang the Youngest & His Terrible Ear. large type ed. (Illus.). 164p. (YA). (gr. 4 up). 41.00 (*0-614-20631-6*, L-38184-00 APHB) Am Printing Hse.

***Namioka, Lensey & Soyabe, Aki.** The Hungriest Boy in the World. LC 00-25142. (Illus.). (J). 2001. write for info. (*0-8234-1542-2*) Holiday.

Namjestnik, Kenneth J. Trust Audit Manual: Fiduciary Audit Practices, Policies & Regulations. rev. ed. 250p. (C). 1995. per. 65.00 (*1-55738-782-6*, Irwn Prfssnl) McGraw-Hill Prof.

Namjoshi, Suniti. Feminist Fables. 132p. 1994. pap. 12.95 (*1-875559-19-1*, Pub. by SpiniFex Pr) LPC InBook.

— St. Suniti & the Dragon. 1999. pap. 12.95 (*1-875559-18-3*, Pub. by SpiniFex Pr) LPC InBook.

Namka, Lynne. How to Let Go of Your Mad Baggage. (Illus.). 48p. 1996. pap. 11.95 (*0-9642167-1-X*) Talk Trust & Feel.

— The Mad Family Gets Their Mads Out: Fifty Things Your Family Can Say & Do to Express Anger Constructively. LC 94-60804. (Illus.). 48p. (Orig.). 1994. pap. 10.95 (*0-9642167-0-1*) Talk Trust & Feel.

***Namkhainyambuu, Ts.** Bounty from the Sheep: Autobiography of a Herdsman. 170p. 2000. 65.00 (*1-874267-45-6*, Pub. by White Horse Pr) Paul & Co Pubs.

Namkoong, G., et al. A Philosophy of Strategy for Breeding Tropical Forest Trees. 1980. 60.00 (*0-85074-034-7*) St Mut.

— Tree Breeding: Principles & Strategies. (Monographs on Theoretical & Applied Genetics: Vol. 11). (Illus.). 190p. 1988. 141.00 (*0-387-96747-8*) Spr-Verlag.

Namkung, Ju, ed. Phonological Inventories of Tibeto-Burman Languages. (STEDT Monograph Ser.: Vol. 3). 507p. 1996. pap. text 35.00 (*0-944613-28-4*) UC Berkeley Ctrs SE Asia.

Namm. Human Anatomy & Physiology. 2nd ed. 1992. teacher ed. 36.87 (*0-07-011011-5*) McGraw.

Namm, Diane. First Love. LC 94-14502. (Kisses Ser.: No. 1). (Illus.). 224p. (YA). (gr. 6 up). 1997. pap. 3.50 (*0-8167-3440-2*) Troll Communs.

— Good-Bye Kiss. LC 94-16883. (Kisses Ser.: No. 2). (Illus.). 224p. (YA). (gr. 6 up). 1997. pap. 3.50 (*0-8167-3441-0*) Troll Communs.

— Little Bear. (My First Reader Ser.). (Illus.). 28p. (J). (ps-2). 1990. pap. 3.95 (*0-516-45356-4*) Childrens.

— Never Tell Ben. (Love Stories Ser.). 192p. (YA). (gr. 7-12). 1996. mass mkt. 3.99 (*0-553-57045-5*) Bantam.

— Senior Kisses. LC 94-25436. (Kisses Ser.: No. 3). 224p. (YA). (gr. 6 up). 1997. pap. 3.50 (*0-8167-3442-9*, WestWind) Troll Communs.

Nammacher, Scott A., jt. auth. see Altman, Edward I.

Namnucci, Maurizio. Hortus Botanicus. LC 95-199757. 1994. pap. text 14.95 (*3-89322-562-5*) Dr Cantz sche Druckerei GmbH.

N

Namoo, So. The Third God. 208p. 1998. 19.95 (*1-58244-009-3*) Rutledge Bks.

Namoodiri, Neelakantan, ed. see Amritaswarupananda, Swami.

Namorato, Cono, jt. auth. see Mortimer, Maxwell.

Namorato, Michael V. The Catholic Church in Mississippi, 1911-1984: A History. LC 97-53288. (Contributions to the Study of Religion: Vol. 54). 352p. 1998. 59.95 (*0-313-30719-9*, Greenwood Pr) Greenwood.

— Rexford G. Tugwell: A Biography. LC 88-2397. 202p. 1988. 57.95 (*0-275-92961-2*, C2961, Praeger Pubs) Greenwood.

Namorato, Michael V., ed. The Diary of Rexford G. Tugwell: The New Deal, 1932-1935. 136. LC 92-1166. (Contributions in Economics & Economic History Ser.: No. 136). 544p. 1992. 69.50 (*0-313-28017-7*, NDY/, Greenwood Pr) Greenwood.

Namos, Larry D. Bury My Heart at Wrigley Field: When the Cubs Were the White Sox. (History of the Chicago Cubs Ser.: Pt. 1). (Illus.). 280p. 1989. 18.95 (*0-9621684-0-8*) G K Scott Pub.

Namovicz-Peat, Susan & Darby, Mary, eds. St. Anthony's Integrated Health Care Directory. 2nd ed. 600p. (C). Date not set. 595.00 (*1-56329-319-6*) St Anthony Pub.

***Namovicz-Peat, Susan & Swann, James P., eds.** 1999 Directory of Health Care Management Companies. 2nd rev. ed. 564p. 1999. pap. 294.00 (*0-929156-68-4*) Atlantic Info Services Inc.

Namovicz-Peat, Susan, jt. ed. see Melville, Beth.

Namoyo, Veronica. A Memory for Wonders: A True Story. LC 92-74110. 189p. (Orig.). 1993. pap. 9.95 (*0-89870-430-8*) Ignatius Pr.

Namson, Jay S., jt. ed. see Davis, Thomas L.

Namson, Jay S., jt. ed. see Davis, T.

Namsrai, Khavtgain. Nonlocal Quantum Theory & Stochastic Quantum Mechanics. 1985. text 274.00 (*90-277-2001-0*) Kluwer Academic.

Namuth, Hans. Pollock Painting. Rose, Barbara, ed. LC 79-57621. (Illus.). 112p. 1980. 95.00 (*0-9601068-6-3*); pap. 65.00 (*0-9601068-5-5*) Agrinde Pubns.

— Twenty-Five Artists. Bujese, Arlene, ed. 108p. 1982. lib. bdg. 75.00 (*0-313-27081-3*, U7081, Greenwood Pr) Greenwood.

Namy, Verna. Baba Ali & His Magical Pajamas. 48p. 1998. pap. 7.95 (*0-944581-15-3*) Earth Star.

— Baba Ali & His Magical Pajamas. LC 98-74329. (Illus.). 38p. (J). (ps-12). 1998. pap. 7.95 (*0-944851-15-0*) Earth Star.

***Namy, Verna.** The Passage from Dark into Light: An Experience in the Grief Process. LC 99-63383. (Illus.). 56p. 1999. pap. 9.95 (*0-944851-16-9*) Earth Star.

Nan Deventer, Cyrus C. Clarke: Ancestors & Descendants of Rev. Henry Clarke & His Wife Catherine Pendleton, of Madison County, New York. (Illus.). 128p. 1997. reprint ed. pap. 19.00 (*0-8328-7966-5*); reprint ed. lib. bdg. 29.00 (*0-8328-7965-7*) Higginson Bk Co.

Nan, Huai-Chin. Tao & Longevity: Mind-Body Transformation. Chu, Wen Kuan, tr. LC 82-60164. (Illus.). 160p. (Orig.). 1984. pap. 9.95 (*0-87728-542-X*) Weiser.

— To Realize Enlightenment: Practice of the Cultivation Path. LC 94-12741. 320p. (Orig.). 1994. pap. 14.95 (*0-87728-802-X*) Weiser.

Nan Huai-Chin. Working Toward Enlightenment: The Cultivation of Practice. LC 93-13536. 304p. (Orig.). 1993. pap. 14.95 (*0-87728-776-7*) Weiser.

An Asterisk (*) at the beginning of an entry indicates that the title is appearing for the first time.

Nan, Mistress. My Private Life: Real Experiences of a Dominant Woman. Bean, Joseph, ed. LC 94-69814. 196p. (Orig.). 1995. pap. 14.95 (*1-881943-11-9*) Daedalus Pub.

Nan, Yue & Shi, Yang. The Dead Suffered Too: The Excavation of a Ming Tomb. Tingquan, Zhang, tr. (Illus.). 281p. 1996. 7.95 (*7-5071-0298-X*, Pub. by Panda Bks) China Bks.

Nana. Afrika, It's People, & Our History. 1997. pap. 18.00 (*1-56411-167-9*) Untd Bros & Sis.

Nana, Burt, jt. auth. see Bennis, Warren G.

Nanajivako, Bhikkhu. Schopenhauer & Buddhism. 94p. 1988. 3.75 (*955-24-0047-3*, Pub. by Buddhist Pub Soc) Vipassana Res Pubns.

Nanamoli, Bhikkha, tr. see Buddhaghosa, Bhadantacariya.

Nanamoli, Bhikkhu. The Life of Buddha: According to Pali Canon. 400p. 1992. 19.20 (*955-24-0063-5*, Pub. by Buddhist Pub Soc) Vipassana Res Pubns.

— Mindfulness of Breathing. 126p. 1982. 4.20 (*955-24-0167-4*, Pub. by Buddhist Pub Soc) Vipassana Res Pubns.

— A Pali-English Glossary of Buddhist Technical Terms. LC 94-904965. 176p. 1994. 9.60 (*955-24-0086-4*, Pub. by Buddhist Pub Soc) Vipassana Res Pubns.

— The Practice of Loving Kindness. 28p. 1987. 1.50 (*955-24-0005-8*, Pub. by Buddhist Pub Soc) Vipassana Res Pubns.

Nanamoli, Bhikkhu, tr. The Buddha's Words on Kamma. 48p. 1993. 3.75 (*955-24-0073-2*, Pub. by Buddhist Pub Soc) Vipassana Res Pubns.

— The Discourse on Right View: Sammaditthi Sutta (MN 9) 80p. 1991. 5.25 (*955-24-0079-1*, Pub. by Buddhist Pub Soc) Vipassana Res Pubns.

— The Lion's Roar: Sihanada Suttas (MN 11 & 12) 48p. 1993. 3.75 (*955-24-0115-1*, Pub. by Buddhist Pub Soc) Vipassana Res Pubns.

Nanamoli, Bhikkhu & Bodhi, Bhikkhu, trs. from PLI. The Middle Length Discourses of the Buddha: A New Translation of the Majjhima Nikaya. LC 37-636. (Teachings of the Buddha Ser.). 1424p. (C). 1995. 60.00 (*0-86171-072-X*) Wisdom MA.

Nanamoli, Bhikkhu, jt. auth. see Thera, Nyanaponika.

Nanamoli, Bhikkhu, tr. see Buddhaghosa, Acaeiya.

Nanamoli, Ven, tr. from PLI. The Guide. (C). 1962. 41.90 (*0-86013-024-X*) Wisdom MA.

— The Minor Readings & the Illustrator of Ultimate Meaning. (C). 1960. 37.00 (*0-86013-023-1*, Pub. by Pali Text) Elsevier.

— The Path of Discrimination. (C). 1982. 61.00 (*0-86013-074-6*, Pub. by Pali Text) Elsevier.

Nanamoli, Ven., tr. from PLI. Pitaka Disclosure. (C). 1964. 48.00 (*0-86013-026-6*, Pub. by Pali Text) Elsevier.

Nanananda, Bhikkhu. Concept & Reality in Early Buddhist Thought. 170p. 1997. 7.80 (*955-24-0136-4*, Pub. by Buddhist Pub Soc) Vipassana Res Pubns.

— The Magic of the Mind: An Exposition of the Kalakarama Sutta. 90p. 1997. 7.20 (*955-24-0135-6*, Pub. by Buddhist Pub Soc) Vipassana Res Pubns.

Nananukool, Surasak, et al. Productivity Improvement Through QC Circles in Service Industry. (Productivity Ser.: No. 21). (Illus.). 27p. 1987. pap. text 7.50 (*92-833-1711-4*, 317114) Productivity Inc.

Nanao, Jun. Contemplating Your Bellybutton. Stinchecum, Amanda M., tr. from JPN. (Illus.). 32p. (J). (ps-k). 1995. 11.95 (*0-916291-60-X*) Kane-Miller Bk.

Nanarama Mahathera, Matara S. Seven Contemplations of Insight. 165p. 1997. write for info. (*955-24-0124-0*, Pub. by Buddhist Pub Soc) Vipassana Res Pubns.

— The Seven Stages of Purification & the Insight Knowledges. 80p. 1993. 6.00 (*955-24-0059-7*, Pub. by Buddhist Pub Soc) Vipassana Res Pubns.

Nanassy, Louis C. & Fancher, C. General Business & Economic Understandings. 4th ed. 1973. text 25.00 (*0-13-348946-9*); student ed. 8.96 (*0-13-348953-1*); student ed. 8.96 (*0-13-348961-2*) P-H.

Nanassy, Louis C., et al. Principles & Trends in Business Education. LC 76-57995. 1977. text. write for info. (*0-672-97092-9*) Macmillan.

Nanassy, Louis C., jt. auth. see Selden, William.

Nanatsuki, Kyoichi. Samurai Shodown. (Illus.). 192p. 1997. pap. text 15.95 (*1-56931-213-3*, Viz Comics) Viz Commns Inc.

Nanavati, Manilal B. & Vakil, Chandulal N. Group Prejudices in India: A Symposium. LC 79-98783. 223p. 1970. reprint ed. lib. bdg. 65.00 (*0-8371-3132-4*, NAGP, Greenwood Pr) Greenwood.

Nanavaty, Mahesh. Silk Production, Processing & Marketing. (C). 1990. 52.00 (*81-224-0282-8*) S Asia.

Nanayakkara, R. Standards Specifications for the CDM Regulations Health & Safety File. 1997. pap. 40.00 (*0-86022-442-2*, Pub. by Build Servs Info Assn) St Mut.

Nanayakkara, R. & Smith, M. H. Operating & Maintenance Audits. 67p. 1997. pap. 80.00 (*0-86022-477-5*, Pub. by Build Servs Info Assn) St Mut.

Nanayakkara, R., jt. auth. see BSRIA Staff.

Nanayakkara, Vesak. Return to Kandy. LC 93-911135. (C). 1994. 58.00 (*81-7013-121-9*, Pub. by Navarang) S Asia.

Nanayon, Upasika K. An Unentangled Knowing: Lessons in Training the Mind. 176p. 1996. 12.00 (*955-24-0145-3*, Pub. by Buddhist Pub Soc) Vipassana Res Pubns.

Nanby, Jeremy. The Cosmic Serpent: DNA & the Origins of Knowledge. LC 97-36344. (Illus.). 272p. 1999. reprint ed. pap. 12.95 (*0-87477-964-2*, Tarcher Putnam) Putnam Pub Group.

Nancarrow, Loren & Taylor, Janet. Dead Snails Leave No Trails: Natural Pest Control for Home & Garden. LC 96-12460. (Illus.). 160p. (Orig.). 1996. pap. 11.95 (*0-89815-852-4*) Ten Speed Pr.

Nancarrow, Loren & Taylor, Janet H. The Worm Book: The Complete Guide to Worms in Your Garden. LC 97-48841. Orig. Title: Long Slim Slimy Ones, Short Fat Juicy Ones - Complete Guide to Worms in Your Garden. (Illus.). 150p. 1998. pap. 11.95 (*0-89815-994-6*) Ten Speed Pr.

***Nancarrow, Loren & Taylor, Janet Hogan.** Dead Daisies Make Me Crazy: Garden Solutions Without Chemical Pollution. LC 99-89595. 160p. 2000. pap. 11.95 (*1-58008-156-8*) Ten Speed Pr.

Nancarrow, Paula R., et al, compiled by. Word Processors & the Writing Process: An Annotated Bibliography. LC 83-22749. 146p. 1984. lib. bdg. 45.00 (*0-313-23995-9*, NAW/, Greenwood Pr) Greenwood.

Nance, Barry. Introduction to Networking. 2nd ed. (Illus.). 521p. 1993. 35.00 (*1-56529-297-9*) Que.

— Introduction to Networking. 4th ed. LC 96-72212. 408p. 1997. 29.99 (*0-7897-1158-3*) Que.

— Networking Windows for Workgroups. 320p. 1993. pap. 22.95 (*0-471-59583-7*) Wiley.

Nance, Barry & Cady, Dorothy. Introduction to Networking. LC 96-69866. (Illus.). 676p. (C). 1997. pap. text 84.00 (*1-57576-559-4*) Que Educ & Trng.

Nance, Barry & Halliday, Caroline M. Using OS - 2 2.1 Special Edition. (Illus.). 944p. 1993. 29.95 (*1-56529-118-2*) Que.

Nance, C. Roger. The Archaeology of la Calsada: A Rockshelter in the Sierra Madre Oriental, Mexico. LC 91-41040. (Texas Archaeology & Ethnography Ser.). (Illus.). 256p. 1992. text 35.00 (*0-292-70427-5*) U of Tex Pr.

Nance, Cheryl. Modern Real Estate Practice in Texas. 9th ed. LC 97-32354. 528p. 1998. pap. text 44.95 (*0-7931-2689-4*, 1510-0609, Real Estate Ed) Dearborn.

***Nance, Cheryl P.** Modern Real Estate Practice in Texas. 10th ed. LC 99-53864. 2000. pap. 44.95 (*0-7931-3483-8*) Dearborn.

Nance, Dale A. Law & Justice: Cases & Readings on the American Legal System. LC 94-71947. 744p. (C). 1994. boxed set 60.00 (*0-89089-600-3*) Carolina Acad Pr.

— Law & Justice: Cases & Readings on the American Legal System. 2nd ed. LC 98-89275. xix, 708p. 1999. 75.00 (*0-89089-865-0*) Carolina Acad Pr.

Nance, Damian, jt. auth. see Murphy, Brendan.

Nance, Don W. How Therapists ACT: Combining Major Approaches to Psychotherapy & the Adaptive Counseling & Therapy Model. 232p. 1995. 69.95 (*1-56032-410-4*); pap. 29.95 (*1-56032-390-6*) Taylor & Francis.

Nance, Don W., jt. auth. see Myers, Pennie.

Nance, Dori W., jt. auth. see Myers, Pennie.

Nance, Douglas W. Chapter Disk. (Computer Science Ser.). (C). 1993. pap. write for info. (*0-314-00444-0*) West Pub.

— Fundamentals of PASCAL. 2nd ed. 1990. mass mkt. 46.75 (*0-314-66501-3*) West Pub.

— Fundamentals of PASCAL: Understanding Programming & Problem Solving. 3rd ed. LC 96-49164. 1997. mass mkt. 65.95 (*0-314-20554-3*) West Pub.

— Introduction to Computer Science. 2nd ed. Date not set. pap. text, teacher ed. write for info. (*0-314-00707-5*) West Pub.

— Mac Chapter Disk. (Computer Science Ser.). (C). 1993. pap. write for info. (*0-314-00445-9*) West Pub.

— Pascal: Introduction to Programming & Problem Solving. (Illus.). 639p. (YA). (gr. 9-12). 1986. reprint ed. mass mkt. 38.50 (*0-314-93206-2*) West Pub.

— Pascal: Understanding Programming & Problem Solving. 2nd alternate ed. Westby, ed. 596p. (C). 1992. reprint ed. pap. text 50.75 (*0-314-93304-2*) West Pub.

— Pascal: Understanding Programming & Problem Solving. 3rd ed. Westby, ed. 716p. (C). 1992. pap. text 49.50 (*0-314-90877-3*) West Pub.

— Pascal: Understanding Programming & Problem Solving. 3rd alternate ed. LC 94-37681. 728p. (C). 1995. mass mkt. 71.95 (*0-314-04361-6*) West Pub.

— Understanding Turbo Pascal: Programming & Problem Solving. Westby, ed. LC 93-28875. 650p. (C). 1993. mass mkt. 50.75 (*0-314-02812-9*) West Pub.

Nance, Douglas W. & Naps, Thomas L. Introduction to Computer Science: Programming, Problem Solving & Data Structures. LC 88-33775. xxiv, 1044p. 1989. write for info. (*0-314-48131-1*) West Pub.

— Introduction to Computer Science: Programming, Problem Solving & Data Structures. 2nd ed. Westby, ed. 900p. (C). 1992. text 65.25 (*0-314-93306-9*) West Pub.

— Introduction to Computer Science: Programming, Problem Solving & Data Structures. 3rd ed. LC 94-44474. 1362p. (C). 1995. mass mkt. 91.95 (*0-314-04556-2*) West Pub.

Nance, Douglas W., jt. auth. see Lambert.

Nance, Douglas W., jt. auth. see Lambert, Kenneth.

Nance, Douglas W., jt. auth. see Lambert, Kenneth A.

Nance, Douglas W., jt. auth. see Naps, Thomas L.

Nance, E. Paul, et al. Emergency Radiology of the Pelvis & Lower Extremities, Vol. 17. (Advanced Exercises in Diagnostic Radiology Ser.). (Illus.). 176p. 1983. pap. text 53.00 (*0-7216-6653-1*, W B Saunders Co) Harcrt Hlth Sci Grp.

Nance, Frank. Blossoms from the Desert. 94p. (Orig.). 1981. pap. 5.00 (*0-9615739-0-2*) F Nance.

— Footprints in the Grass. 159p. (Orig.). 1990. pap. text 6.00 (*0-9615739-2-9*) F Nance.

— Warm Memories. 106p. (Orig.). 1985. pap. text 5.00 (*0-9615739-1-0*) F Nance.

Nance, Harold W., jt. auth. see Crossan, Richard M.

Nance, Harold W., jt. auth. see Heyel, Carl.

Nance, Herschel G. Contracting to Build Your Home: A Guidebook. Smith, James C., Jr., ed. LC 91-32694. 160p. (Orig.). 1992. pap. 12.95 (*0-86534-160-5*) Sunstone Pr.

Nance, James B. Intermediate Logic. (Illus.). 164p. (Orig.). (YA). (gr. 9). 1996. pap. text 25.00 (*1-885767-13-7*) Canon Pr ID.

Nance, James B. Intermediate Logic: For Christian Private & Home Schools, Answer Key. (Mars Hill Textbook Ser.). 70p. 1996. spiral bd. 6.50 (*1-885767-57-9*) Canon Pr ID.

— Intermediate Logic: Tests. 27p. (YA). (gr. 7-12). 1998. spiral bd. 10.00 (*1-930443-02-1*, C172, Pub. by Logos Schl) Veritas Pr PA.

— Introductory Logic: Tests. 3rd rev. ed. 24p. (YA). (gr. 7-12). 1998. 10.00 (*1-930443-00-5*, C162, Pub. by Logos Schl) Veritas Pr PA.

Nance, James B., jt. auth. see Wilson, Douglas J.

***Nance, Jean Wertz.** Cinematic Wilmington: Making Movies on the Cape Fear Coast. (Illus.). viii, 240p. 2000. pap. 17.00 (*0-9702179-2-7*) Tidal Pr NC.

Nance, Joanne L. Charlotte County, Virginia, 1816-1850: Marriage Bonds & Ministers' Returns (with Additions to Marriages, 1764-1815) LC 87-81976. 176p. 1987. per. 22.00 (*0-944334-00-8*) N W Lapin.

Nance, Joanne L., compiled by. Charlotte County, Virginia, 1765-1771, Deed Bks. 1 & 2. LC 90-6208. (Illus.). viii, 102p. 1990. per. 18.00 (*0-944334-01-6*) N W Lapin.

***Nance, John J.** Blackout. LC 99-48843. 430p. 2000. 23.95 (*0-399-14594-X*) Putnam Pub Group.

— Blackout. large type ed. (Americana Ser.). 737p. 2000. 29.95 (*0-7862-2509-2*) Thorndike Pr.

Nance, John J. Final Approach. 1992. mass mkt. 5.99 (*0-449-45257-3*, Crest) Fawcett.

— Final Approach. 1992. mass mkt. 5.99 (*0-449-22035-4*) Fawcett.

— Final Approach. 1994. mass mkt. 5.99 (*0-449-45450-9*) Fawcett.

— Final Approach. 1996. pap. 5.99 (*0-449-45631-5*) Fawcett.

— The Land & People of the Philippines. LC 76-30543. (Portraits of the Nations Ser.). (J). (gr. 5-9). 1977. lib. bdg. 12.89 (*0-397-31656-9*) HarpC Child Bks.

— The Last Hostage. LC 97-44861. 384p. 1998. 23.95 (*0-385-49055-0*) Doubleday.

— The Last Hostage. large type ed. LC 98-22082. (Compass Press Large Print Book Ser.). 1998. 26.95 (*1-56895-606-1*, Compass) Wheeler Pub.

***Nance, John J.** The Last Hostage, Vol. 1. 419p. 1998. 6.99 (*0-312-96639-3*, Pub. by Tor Bks) St Martin.

Nance, John J. Medusa's Child. 1997. mass mkt. 6.99 (*0-312-96245-2*, St Martins Paperbacks) St Martin.

— On Shaky Ground. 448p. 1989. mass mkt. 4.95 (*0-380-70743-8*, Avon Bks) Morrow Avon.

— Pandora's Clock. 1996. mass mkt. 6.99 (*0-312-96034-4*) St Martin.

Nance, John J. Pandora's Clock. abr. ed. 1995. write for info. incl. audio (*0-7871-0534-1*, Pub. by NewStar Media) Lndmrk Audiobks.

Nance, John J. Pandora's Clock. large type ed. 630p. 1996. 25.95 (*0-7838-1577-8*, G K Hall Lrg Type) Mac Lib Ref.

— Phoenix Rising. 1995. mass mkt. 6.99 (*0-449-18290-8*, GM) Fawcett.

***Nance, John J.** El Reloj de Pandora. 1998. pap. 11.95 (*84-08-02190-7*) Planeta.

Nance, John J. Scorpion Strike. 1994. mass mkt. 5.99 (*0-449-22221-7*, Crest) Fawcett.

Nance, Joseph M. After San Jacinto: The Texas-Mexican Frontier, 1836-1841. LC 62-9789. (Illus.). 681p. reprint ed. pap. 200.00 (*0-8357-5246-1*, 202790800057) Bks Demand.

Nance, Joseph M. & McDonald, Archie P. Dare-Devils All: The Texan Mier Expedition, 1842-1844. LC 97-32637. 1997. 59.95 (*1-57168-214-7*, Eakin Pr) Sunbelt Media.

Nance, Kathleen. More Than Magic. 400p. 1999. mass mkt. 5.99 (*0-505-52299-3*) Dorchester Pub Co.

***Nance, Kathleen.** The Trickster. (Time of Your Life Ser.). 400p. 2000. mass mkt. 5.99 (*0-505-52382-5*, Love Spell) Dorchester Pub Co.

Nance, Kathleen. Wishes Come True. 384p. (Orig.). 1998. mass mkt. 5.50 (*0-505-52248-9*, Love Spell) Dorchester Pub Co.

Nance, Kimberly A. & Rivera, Isidro J. Aprendizaje: Tecnicas de Composicion. (SPA.). (C). 1996. text, teacher ed. 40.76 (*0-669-33174-0*); pap. text 39.56 (*0-669-33173-2*) HM.

Nance, Kimi. How to Use Microsoft Access '97 - CD. Paulsen & Associates Staff & Macoff & Associates Staff, eds. (Illus.). 103p. 1998. pap. 225.00 incl. cd-rom (*1-56562-097-6*) OneOnOne Comp Trng.

— How to Use Microsoft PowerPoint, '97. Young, Natalie B., ed. (Illus.). 103p. 1997. pap. 225.00 (*1-56562-090-9*) OneOnOne Comp Trng.

— How to Use PowerPoint, '97 CD. Paulsen & Associates Staff & Macoff & Associates Staff, eds. (Illus.). 109p. 1998. pap. 225.00 (*1-56562-098-4*) OneOnOne Comp Trng.

— How to Use WordPerfect 7 for Windows. Menges, Patricia A., ed. (Illus.). 102p. 1996. pap. 225.00 (*1-56562-085-2*) OneOnOne Comp Trng.

Nance, Kimi, ed. see Wolf, Charles.

Nance, Kimi, ed. see Young, Natalie B.

Nance, Martha A. Living with Ataxia: An Information & Resource Guide. LC 96-72598. Date not set. pap. text 10.00 (*0-943218-09-8*) Natl Ataxia Found.

Nance, Paul J. The Nance Museum - A Journey into Traditional Saudi Arabia. Nawwab, Ismail I. & Norberg, Robert N., eds. (Illus.). 208p. 1999. 39.95 (*0-9671454-5-7*) Nance Mus.

Nance, R. Damian & Thompson, Margaret D., eds. Avalonian & Related Peri-Gondwanan Terranes of the Circum-North Atlantic. (Special Papers: No. 304). (Illus.). 1996. pap. 95.00 (*0-8137-2304-3*) Geol Soc.

***Nance, R. Morton.** Classic Sailing-Ship Models in Photographs. LC 00-34534. (Illus.). 2000. pap. write for info. (*0-486-41249-0*) Dover.

Nance, R. Morton. Cornish-English - English-Cornish Dictionary. (COR & ENG.). 409p. (C). 1990. reprint ed. 48.50 (*1-85022-055-7*, Pub. by Dyllansow Truran) IBD Ltd.

Nance, Sandra J., jt. ed. see Reid, Marion E.

Nance, Sandra T., ed. Alloimmunity: 1993 & Beyond. 212p. 1993. text 9.00 (*1-56395-025-1*) Am Assn Blood.

— Blood Supply: Risks, Perceptions & Prospects for the Future. (Illus.). 197p. (C). 1994. text 30.00 (*1-56395-033-2*) Am Assn Blood.

Nance, Scott. Making of Quantum Leap. 208p. 1996. 5.50 (*0-06-105438-0*, HarperPrism) HarpC.

Nance, Stephen W. Sing to the Lord: A Survey of Christian Hymnody. LC 95-32679. 201p. (Orig.). 1996. pap. 16.95 (*0-942597-89-3*, Ragged Edge) White Mane Pub.

Nance, T. El Escudero de Dios.Tr. of God's Armorbearer. 4.50 (*0-7899-0459-4*, 495025) Editorial Unilit.

Nance, Terry. God's Armor Bearer. 80p. 1999. pap. 5.99 (*0-89274-723-4*, HH723) Dake Pub.

— God's Armor Bearer, Bk. 2. 80p. 1999. pap. 5.99 (*0-89274-733-1*, HH-733) Dake Pub.

Nance, Virginia L. & McMahon, Kay E. Golf. 7th ed. 144p. (C). 1993. text. write for info. (*0-697-12656-0*) Brown & Benchmark.

— Golf. 8th ed. LC 96-80372. 144p. (C). 1997. text. write for info. (*0-697-34538-6*, WCB McGr Hill) McGrw-H Hghr Educ.

Nance, William De, see De Nance, William.

Nancollas, G. H., et al. Biological Mineralization & Demineralization: Report on the Dahlemn Workshop Berlin 1981. (Dahlem Workshop Reports: Vol. 23). (Illus.). 420p. 1982. 42.95 (*0-387-11521-8*) Spr-Verlag.

Nancoo, Stephen E., et al, eds. Promoting Quality & Participation (Rewards & Recognition) (Quality & Participation Ser.). 51p. 30.00 (*0-614-04830-3*, KSA 7) Assn Qual & Part.

Nancy, Ashis. Alternative Sciences: Creativity & Authenticity in Two Indian Scientists. 168p. 1995. text 19.95 (*0-19-563198-6*) OUP.

Nancy, Daughter of Helen. To Whom It May Concern: Many Are Called. LC 98-73838. 224p. 1998. pap. 14.95 (*1-57502-944-8*, PO2598) Morris Pubng.

Nancy, E. Once I Was a Child & There Was Much Pain . . . A Glimpse into the Soul of an Incest Survivor. LC 88-28281. (Illus.). 104p. (Orig.). 1989. pap. 6.95 (*0-9603628-7-8*) Frog in Well.

Nancy, Jean L. & Maffesoli, Michel. Techno: An Artistic & Political Laboratory of the Present. (Illus.). 128p. 1998. pap. 23.50 (*2-906571-76-8*, Pub. by Editions Dis Voir) Dist Art Pubs.

Nancy, Jean-Luc. The Birth to Presence. 440p. (C). 1993. pap. 16.95 (*0-8047-2189-0*) Stanford U Pr.

— The Birth to Presence. Holmes, Brian et al, trs. from FRE. LC 92-30596. 440p. 1993. 49.50 (*0-8047-2060-6*) Stanford U Pr.

— The Experience of Freedom. McDonald, Bridget, tr. from FRE. LC 93-16348. (Meridian: Crossing Aesthetics Ser.).Tr. of Experience de la Liberte. 248p. 1993. 39.50 (*0-8047-2175-0*) Stanford U Pr.

— The Gravity of Thought. Francois, Raffoul & Recco, Gregory, trs. LC 96-8808. (Philosophy & Literary Theory Ser.). 108p. (C). 1997. text 39.95 (*0-391-03985-7*) Humanities.

— The Gravity of Thought. LC 99-10397. (Philosophy & Literary Theory Ser.). 1999. write for info. (*1-57392-566-7*, Humanity Bks) Prometheus Bks.

— The Inoperative Community, Vol. 76. (Theory & History of Literature Ser.). 217p. (Orig.). 1991. pap. 16.95 (*0-8166-1924-7*); text 39.95 (*0-8166-1923-9*) U of Minn Pr.

— The Muses. Kamuf, Peggy, tr. LC 96-10880. (Meridian: Crossing Aesthetics Ser.). 1996. 39.50 (*0-8047-2780-5*) Stanford U Pr.

Nancy, Jean-Luc & Lacoue-Labarthe, Philippe. Retreating the Political. LC 97-187874. (Warwick Studies in European Philosophy Ser.). 232p. (C). 1997. 80.00 (*0-415-15162-7*) Routledge.

— The Title of the Letter: A Reading of Lacan. Pettigrew, David & Raffoul, Francois, trs. from FRE. LC 91-15114. (SUNY Series in Contemporary Continental Philosophy). 151p. 1992. text 16.50 (*0-7914-0961-9*) State U NY Pr.

Nancy, Jean-Luc & Lacoue-Labarthe, Phillippe. Retreating the Political. LC 97-187874. (Warwick Studies in European Philosophy Ser.). 232p. (C). 1997. pap. 25.99 (*0-415-15163-5*) Routledge.

Nancy, Jean-Luc, jt. auth. see Lacoue-Labarthe, Philippe.

***Nancy, Ted L.** Chock Full of Nut. LC 00-29688. 224p. 2000. text 16.95 (*0-312-26155-1*) St Martin.

— Letters from a Nut. LC 96-47610. 192p. 1999. 15.00 (*0-380-97354-5*, Avon Bks) Morrow Avon.

Nancy, Ted L. More Letters from a Nut. (Illus.). 208p. 1998. 18.00 (*0-553-10958-8*) Bantam.

Nand, Nitya & Kumar, Kamlesh. The Holy Himalaya: A Geographical Interpretation of Garwal. 1989. 86.00 (*81-7035-055-7*, Pub. by Daya Pub Hse) S Asia.

Nand, Sucha, jt. auth. see Schumacher, Harold R.

Nanda. Cultural Anthropology. 1982. pap. write for info. (*0-534-26246-5*) Wadsworth Pub.

— Cultural Anthropology. 2nd ed. (Anthropology Ser.). 1983. pap., teacher ed. write for info. (*0-534-02750-4*) Wadsworth Pub.

— Cultural Anthropology. 2nd ed. (Anthropology Ser.). 1984. mass mkt. 18.75 (*0-534-02749-0*) Wadsworth Pub.

— Cultural Anthropology. 3rd ed. 1986. pap. write for info. (*0-534-07249-6*) Wadsworth Pub.

N

An Asterisk (*) at the beginning of an entry indicates that the title is appearing for the first time.

— Cultural Anthropology. 4th ed. (Anthropology Ser.). 1990. mass mkt., teacher ed. write for info. (*0-534-13957-4*) Wadsworth Pub.

— The Hijras of India. 2nd ed. LC 98-41187. (Anthropology Ser.). (C). 1998. pap. 28.95 (*0-534-50903-7*) Wadsworth Pub.

***Nanda, et al.** Anthropology. 2001. pap. 51.00 (*0-534-57969-8*) Thomson Learn.

Nanda, B. R. Gandhi: Pan-Islamism, Imperialism, & Nationalism. (Illus.). 450p. 1990. text 21.00 (*0-19-562299-5*) OUP.

— Gandhi & His Critics. (Oxford India Paperbacks Ser.). 188p. 1994. reprint ed. pap. text 9.95 (*0-19-563363-6*) OUP.

— Gokhale: The Indian Moderates & the British Raj. (Oxford India Paperbacks Ser.). (Illus.). 542p. 1998. pap. 19.95 (*0-19-564751-3*) OUP.

— In Gandhi's Footsteps: The Life & Times of Jamnalal Bajaj. (Illus.). 428p. (C). 1990. 32.00 (*0-19-562550-1*) OUP.

— Jawaharlal Nehru: Rebel & Statesman. (Illus.). 322p. 1995. text 27.00 (*0-19-563684-8*) OUP.

— Jawaharlal Nehru: Rebel & Statesman. (Illus.). 322p. 1998. reprint ed. pap. text 11.95 (*0-19-564586-3*) OUP.

— Mahatma Gandhi: A Biography. 541p. 1989. 34.95 (*0-318-36657-6*) Asia Bk Corp.

— Mahatma Gandhi: A Biography: Complete. unabridged ed. (Oxford India Paperbacks Ser.). (Illus.). 542p. (C). 1996. pap. 18.95 (*0-19-563855-7*) OUP.

— Mahatma Gandhi, 125 Years: Remembering Gandhi, Understanding Gandhi, Relevance of Gandhi. LC 95-903287. (C). 1995. 56.00 (*81-224-0723-4*, Pub. by Wiley Estrn) Franklin.

Nanda, B. R., ed. Indian Women: From Purdah to Modernity. 175p. 1990. text 27.50 (*81-7027-146-0*, Pub. by Radiant Pubs) S Asia.

— Science & Technology in India. 1978. 9.00 (*0-8364-0170-0*) S Asia.

— Selected Works of Govind Ballabh Pant, Vol. 2. 422p. 1994. 26.00 (*0-19-563463-2*) OUP.

— Selected Works of Govind Ballabh Pant, Vol. 3. 426p. 1995. 26.00 (*0-19-563464-0*) OUP.

Nanda, B. R., ed. Socialism in India. 1991. 17.00 (*0-7069-5795-4*, Pub. by Vikas) S Asia.

Nanda, B. R., ed. see Pant, G. B.

Nanda, B. R., ed. see Pant, Govind B.

Nanda, B. R., ed. see Pant, Govind Ballabh.

Nanda, B. S., et al. Aging Pigment: Current Research, Vol. 1. 191p. 1974. text 28.50 (*0-8422-7197-X*) Irvington.

Nanda, Bal R. Gokhale: The Indian Moderates & the British Raj. LC 77-72129. 540p. reprint ed. pap. 167.40 (*0-7837-1415-7*, 204176900023) Bks Demand.

Nanda, Basant. Instant PowerBuilder 5 Objects. LC 96-60556. 400p. 1996. pap. 39.95 incl. cd-rom (*1-86100-006-5*) Wrox Pr Inc.

Nanda, Bikram N. & Islamia, Jamia M. Contours of Continuity & Change: The Story of the Bonda Highlanders. LC 94-31771. 228p. 1995. text 39.95 (*0-8039-9193-2*) Sage.

Nanda, Gulshan. Mahorun Badlai Gayun (Gujerati) large type ed. (Charnwood Large Print Ser.). 1990. 27.99 (*0-7089-2271-6*, Charnwood) Ulverscroft.

Nanda, J. N. Development of the Resources of the Sea: India. (C). 1988. 22.00 (*81-7022-220-6*, Pub. by Concept) S Asia.

Nanda, Jai. What's That From? The Ultimate Quiz Book of Memorable Movie Lines since 1969. 208p. 1996. pap. 9.95 (*0-312-14145-9*) St Martin.

***Nanda, Jata S., ed.** Rice Breeding & Genetics: Research Priorities & Challenges. (Illus.). 370p. 2000. text 75.00 (*1-57808-086-X*) Science Pubs.

Nanda, K. K. Conquering Kashmir-A Pakistani Obsession. LC 94-905413. (C). 1995. 36.00 (*81-7095-045-7*, Pub. by Lancer India) S Asia.

Nanda-Nandana, Sri. The Secret Teachings of the Vedas: The Ancient Knowledge of the East. LC 86-51209. 320p. (Orig.). 1987. pap. 14.95 (*0-9617410-0-7*) World Relief.

Nanda, Navin C. Doppler Echocardiography. 2nd ed. (Illus.). 466p. 1993. text 129.00 (*0-8121-1588-0*) Lppncott W & W.

Nanda, Navin C., ed. Advances in Echo Imaging Using Contrast Enhancement. LC 92-46545. 408p. (C). 1993. text 178.50 (*0-7923-2137-5*) Kluwer Academic.

— Atlas of Color Doppler Echocardiography. LC 88-8994. (Illus.). 544p. 1989. 149.00 (*0-8121-1078-1*) Lppncott W & W.

Nanda, Navin C., et al, eds. Advances in Echo Imaging Using Contrast Enhancement. 2nd ed. LC 97-190483. 698p. 1997. text 155.00 (*0-7923-4355-7*) Kluwer Academic.

Nanda, Navin C. & Domanski, Michael J. Atlas of Transesophageal Echocardiography. LC 97-33648. 521p. 1998. 165.00 (*0-683-06320-0*) Lppncott W & W.

Nanda, Neeru. Forest for Whom? Destruction & Restoration in the U. P. Himalaya. LC 99-932765. 231p. 1999. write for info. (*81-241-0322-4*, Pub. by Har-Anand Pubns) S Asia.

Nanda, Rajni. Early History of Gold in India. (C). 1992. 27.00 (*81-215-0548-8*, Pub. by M Manoharial) Coronet Bks.

Nanda, Ravi. Evolution of National Strategy of India. 1987. 27.00 (*81-7095-000-7*, Pub. by Lancer India) S Asia.

***Nanda, Ravi.** Kargil: A Wake-Up Call. LC 99-940154. 1999. 29.50 (*81-7095-074-0*, Pub. by Lancer India) S Asia.

Nanda, Ravi. National Security: Perspective Policy & Planning. (C). 1991. text 32.00 (*81-7095-026-0*, Pub. by Lancer International) S Asia.

Nanda, Ravindra. Biomechanics in Clinical Orthodontics. McGrew, Larry, ed. 368p. 1996. text 130.00 (*0-7216-2784-6*, W B Saunders Co) Harcrt Hlth Sci Grp.

Nanda, Ravindra & Burstone, Charles J., eds. Retention & Stability in Orthodontics. (Illus.). 176p. 1993. text 79.00 (*0-7216-4342-6*, W B Saunders Co) Harcrt Hlth Sci Grp.

Nanda, Sanjiv, jt. ed. see Goodman, David J.

Nanda, Serena. Cultural Anthropology. 3rd ed. 431p. (C). 1986. mass mkt. 28.00 (*0-534-07248-8*) Wadsworth Pub.

— Cultural Anthropology. 4th ed. 457p. (C). 1990. mass mkt. 34.00 (*0-534-13956-6*) Wadsworth Pub.

— Cultural Anthropology. 5th ed. LC 93-5967. 506p. 1993. mass mkt. 43.25 (*0-534-21438-X*) Wadsworth Pub.

— Cultural Anthropology. 6th ed. 1998. student ed. 15.25 (*0-534-50638-0*) Brooks-Cole.

— Cultural Anthropology. 6th ed. LC 97-29363. (C). 1997. 70.95 (*0-534-50637-2*) Wadsworth Pub.

***Nanda, Serena.** Gender Diversity: Crosscultural Variations. 127p. (C). 1999. pap. 9.95 (*1-57766-074-9*) Waveland Pr.

Nanda, Serena. Neither Man nor Woman: The Hijras of India. 170p. (C). 1989. mass mkt. 19.25 (*0-534-12204-3*) Wadsworth Pub.

***Nanda, Serena & Warms, Richard L.** Cultural Anthropology. 7th ed. (Anthropology Ser.). 2001. 50.50 (*0-534-55739-2*) Wadsworth Pub.

Nanda, Serena, jt. auth. see Norgren, Jill.

NANDA Staff. NANDA Nursing Diagnoses: Definitions & Classifications 1997-1998. 120p. (C). 1996. pap. 11.00 (*0-9637042-3-0*) N Am Nursing.

Nanda, Ved P. International Environmental Law & Policy. 469p. 1995. lib. bdg. 95.00 (*0-941320-59-6*) Transnatl Pubs.

— The Law of Transnational Business Transactions, 3 vols., Set. LC 81-2392. (International Business & Law Ser.). 1981. ring bd. 375.00 (*0-87632-342-5*) West Group.

***Nanda, Ved P.** Nuclear Weapons & the World Court. LC 98-20697. 1998. 95.00 (*1-57105-051-5*) Transnatl Pubs.

Nanda, Ved P., ed. Hindu Law & Legal Theory. LC 96-43414. (International Library of Essays in Law & Legal Theory). 500p. (C). 1997. lib. bdg. 150.00 (*0-8147-5772-3*) NYU Pr.

— Refugee Law & Policy: International & U. S. Responses, 9. LC 89-11901. (Studies in Human Rights: No. 9). 238p. 1989. 62.95 (*0-313-26870-3*, NRP/, Greenwood Pr) Greenwood.

Nanda, Ved P., et al, eds. World Debt & the Human Condition: Structural Adjustments & the Right to Development, 14. LC 92-9329. (Studies in Human Rights: No. 14). 272p. 1992. 65.00 (*0-313-28531-4*, NWD, Greenwood Pr) Greenwood.

Nanda, Ved P. & Pansius, David K. Litigation of International Disputes in U. S. Courts. LC 86-13667. (International Business & Law Ser.). 1986. ring bd. 145.00 (*0-87632-509-6*) West Group.

Nanda, Ved P., et al. Breach & Adaptation of International Contracts: An Introduction to Lex Mercatoria. 240p. 1992. boxed set 105.00 (*0-88063-750-1*, MICHIE) LEXIS Pub.

Nanda, Ved P., jt. auth. see Evan, William M.

Nanda, Ved P., jt. ed. see Sheperd, George W.

Nandakumar, Prema. The Mother of Sri Aurobindo Ashram. (National Biography Ser.). 1979. pap. 2.25 (*0-89744-198-2*) Auromere.

Nandan, Anshu P. Nicobarese of Great Nicobar: An Ethnography. 1993. 14.00 (*81-212-0403-8*, Pub. by Gian Publng Hse) S Asia.

Nandan, Deoki. Hindu Law: Marriage & Divorce. (C). 1989. 325.00 (*0-7855-3687-6*) St Mut.

Nandan, Deoki, ed. see Monir, M.

Nandan, Yash, compiled by. The Durkheimian School: A Systematic & Comprehensive Bibliography. LC 77-112. 457p. 1977. lib. bdg. 65.00 (*0-8371-9532-2*, NAD/, Greenwood Pr) Greenwood.

Nandell, Bob. A Certain Longing: The Photography of Bob Nandell. LC 94-72899. (Illus.). 96p. (Orig.). 1994. pap. 10.00 (*1-883477-01-8*) Lone Oak MN.

Nandgopal, Choodamani. Dance & Music in the Temple Architecture. 1990. 135.00 (*81-7186-000-1*, Pub. by Agam) S Asia.

Nandi, Asoke K. Blind Estimation Using Higher-Order Statistics LC 98-55181. 1999. write for info. (*0-7923-8442-3*) Kluwer Academic.

Nandi, Asoke K., jt. auth. see Azzouz, Elsayed.

Nandi, Jean. Playing with the Elements of Music: A Guide to Music Theory. LC 88-92717. (Illus.). 153p. (Orig.). (C). 1989. pap. 22.95 (*0-9622023-1-2*) Bon Gout Pub.

— Skill & Style on the Harpsichord: A Reference Manual for the Developing Harpsichordist. LC 88-92719. (Illus.). 147p. (Orig.). (C). 1990. pap. 22.95 (*0-9622023-2-0*) Bon Gout Pub.

Nandi, Jean & Anderson, Rica, eds. Recollections of Judy Greenwood. (Illus.). 92p. (Orig.). 1990. pap. 10.00 (*0-9622023-3-9*) Bon Gout Pub.

Nandi, Jean & Jenkins, Leonie. Starting on the Harpsichord: A First Book for the Beginner. LC 88-92718. (Illus.). 212p. (Orig.). (C). 1989. pap. 22.95 (*0-9622023-0-4*) Bon Gout Pub.

Nandi, N. Civil Ready Referencer, 2 vols. 4th ed. (C). 1989. 250.00 (*0-7855-6135-8*) St Mut.

Nandi, Proshanta K. & Shahidullah, Shahid M. Globalization & the Evolving World Society. LC 98-34821. (International Studies in Sociology & Social Anthropology). 1998. pap. 47.50 (*90-04-11247-2*) Brill Academic Pubs.

Nandi, Ramendra N. Social Roots of Religion in Ancient India. 218p. (C). 1987. 22.00 (*81-7074-009-6*) S Asia.

***Nandi, S.** International Money & Capital. 1998. pap. 250.00 (*81-86982-77-9*, Pub. by Business Pubns) St Mut.

***Nandi, Sukumar.** Growth Financial Cycles & Bank Efficiency: A Study of the Indian Money Market. LC 99-931185. 1998. pap. 248.00 (*81-86982-52-3*, Pub. by Business Pubns) St Mut.

Nandimath, S. C. A Handbook of Virasaivism. 1979. 9.95 (*0-89684-053-0*, Pub. by Motilal Bnarsidass) S Asia.

Nandris, Grigore. Old Church Slavonic Grammar: Handbook of Old Church Slavonic, Pt. 1. LC 88-3481. (London East European Ser.). (C). 1965. pap. 39.95 (*0-485-17520-7*, Pub. by Athlone Pr) Humanities.

Nandu. The Mobile Scheduled Castes: Rise of a New Middle Class. (C). 1988. 27.50 (*81-7075-007-5*, Pub. by Hindustan) S Asia.

***Nandy, Ashis.** The Ambiguous Journey to the City: The Village & Other Odd Ruins of the Self in the Indian Imagination. 156p. 2000. text 16.95 (*0-19-565242-8*) OUP.

Nandy, Ashis. Exiled at Home: Comprising at the Edge of Psychology, the Intimate Enemy & Creating a Nationality. LC 98-902993. (Illus.). 506p. 1998. text 24.95 (*0-19-564177-9*) OUP.

— The Illegitimacy of Nationalism: Rabindrath Tagore & the Politics of Self. 106p. 1994. pap. text 9.95 (*0-19-563298-2*) OUP.

— The Intimate Enemy: Loss & Recovery of Self under Colonialism. 142p. 1989. pap. text 8.95 (*0-19-562237-5*) OUP.

— Return from Exile: Comprising Alternative Sciences, the Illegitimacy of Nationalism, & the Savage Freud. LC 99-933486. 560p. 1999. text 23.95 (*0-19-564178-7*) OUP.

— The Savage Freud & Other Essays on Possible & Retrievable Selves. LC 94-46626. (Studies in Culture - Power - History). 284p. 1995. text 49.50 (*0-691-04411-2*, Pub. by Princeton U Pr); pap. text 17.95 (*0-691-04410-4*, Pub. by Princeton U Pr) Cal Prin Full Svc.

***Nandy, Ashis.** The Secret Politics of Our Desires: Innocence, Culpability & Indian Popular Cinema. LC 98-909293. 1998. write for info. (*0-19-563936-7*) OUP.

Nandy, Ashis. The Secret Politics of Our Desires: Nation, Culture, & Gender in Indian Popular Cinema. LC 97-24677. 1997. text 22.50 (*1-85649-516-7*) Humanities.

— The Secret Politics of Our Desires: Nation, Culture & Gender in Indian Popular Cinema. LC 97-24677. 240p. 2000. text 62.50 (*1-85649-515-9*, Pub. by Zed Books) St Martin.

***Nandy, Ashis.** The Tao of Cricket: On Games of Destiny & the Destiny of Games. 176p. 2000. pap. 9.95 (*0-19-565321-1*) OUP.

Nandy, Ashis. Traditions, Tyranny & Utopias: Essays in the Politics of Awareness. (Oxford India Paperbacks Ser.). 188p. 1993. pap. text 8.95 (*0-19-563067-X*) OUP.

Nandy, Ashis, ed. Science, Hegemony & Violence: A Requiem for Modernity. (Oxford India Paperbacks Ser.). (Illus.). 309p. 1990. reprint ed. pap. text 12.95 (*0-19-562580-3*) OUP.

Nandy, Ashis, et al. Creating a Nationality: The Ramjanmabhumi Movement & Fear of the Self. (Oxford India Paperbacks Ser.). (Illus.). 228p. 1998. reprint ed. pap. text 11.95 (*0-19-564271-6*) OUP.

Nandy, Ashis, jt. auth. see Pai Panandiker, V. A.

Nandy, Ashis, jt. ed. see Sheth, D. L.

Nanes, Allan, jt. auth. see Alexander, Yonah.

Nanetti, Rafaella Y. Growth & Territorial Policies: The Italian Model of Social Capitalism. 220p. 1992. 47.50 (*0-86187-651-2*) St Martin.

Nanetti, Rafaella Y. & Leonardi, Robert, eds. Italian Politics Vol. 2: A Review. 220p. 1988. text 42.50 (*0-86187-955-4*, Pub. by P P Pubs) Cassell & Continuum.

Nanetti, Rafaella Y., jt. auth. see La Cava, Gloria.

Nanetti, Rafaella Y., jt. ed. see Leonardi, Robert.

Nanetti, Raffaella, jt. auth. see Leonardi, Robert.

Nanetti, Raffaella Y., jt. auth. see Leonardi, Robert.

Nancz-Falcon, Guillermo, ed. The Rosemonde E. & Emile Kuntz Collection: A Catalogue of the Manuscripts & Printed Ephemera. LC 81-13168. 1981. pap. 20.00 (*0-9603212-3-3*) Tulane Univ.

Nanez-Falcon, Guillermo, ed. The Favrot Family Papers: Sixteen Ninety - Seventeen Eighty-Two, 2 vols., Vol. 2. LC 88-590. (FRE & SPA., Illus.). xliv, 286p. 1988. 15.00 (*0-87409-002-4*) Tulane Univ.

— The Favrot Family Papers: Sixteen Ninety - Seventeen Eighty-Two, 2 vols., Vol. 3. LC 88-590. (FRE & SPA., Illus.). xlii, 328p. 1988. 15.00 (*0-87409-003-2*) Tulane Univ.

Nanez, Lilia, jt. auth. see Benavides, Dalia.

Nanfara, Frank. CNC Workshop. LC 99-12091. 350p. (C). 1999. pap. text 52.00 (*0-201-33145-4*) Addison-Wesley.

Nanfara, Frank, et al. The CNC Workbook: Computer Numerical Control Programming Made Easy. LC 94-4362. (Illus.). 350p. (C). 1995. pap. 55.00 (*0-201-65600-0*) Addison-Wesley.

Nanfeldt, Suzan. Plus Style: The Plus-Size Guide to Looking Great. (Illus.). 384p. (Orig.). 1996. pap. 19.95 (*0-452-27596-2*, Plume) Dutton Plume.

Nanfeldt, Suzan, ed. see Schuller, Catherine.

Nanfito, Jacqueline C. El Sueno: Cartographies of Knowledge & the Self. LC 99-13325. (Wor(l)ds of Change Ser.: Vol. 46). 176p. 2000. text 44.95 (*0-8204-4419-7*) P Lang Pubng.

Nanfito, Kenneth L., ed. see Foster, Monica M.

Nangia, Sudesh, jt. ed. see Sundram, K. V.

Nangini, Mary A. My Ontario Beautiful. LC 94-5676. 64p. 1995. pap. 14.95 (*0-7734-2726-0*, Mellen Poetry Pr) E Mellen.

Nangle, Clint. Some Things Harvard Never Taught Me. LC 92-97522. 160p. (Orig.). 1993. pap. 14.95 (*0-9635615-2-9*) Blue Horiz Pr.

Nangle, Hilary, ed. see Leocha, Charles.

Nangoli, Musamaali. The African Cause: Speech to Mother Africa. 2nd rev. ed. (African Heritage Educational Bks.). (Illus.). 55p. 1987. pap. 4.95 (*0-940385-04-X*) Holly-Star Bks.

— How to Stop Wishing You Were Rich & Actually Become Rich Through Amway. LC 86-72152. 64p. (Orig.). 1986. pap. 4.95 (*0-940385-00-7*) Holly-Star Bks.

— No More Lies about Africa: Here's the Truth from an African. LC 86-72151. 210p. (Orig.). (C). 1987. 16.95 (*0-940385-01-5*); pap. 9.95 (*0-940385-03-1*) Holly-Star Bks.

Nani, Daniel. Dictionary of Vitamins: Dictionnaire des Vitamines. (ENG & SPA.). 1986. 24.95 (*0-8288-1820-7*, M2330) Fr & Eur.

— Dictionnaire des Vitamines. (FRE.). 155p. 1993. pap. 12.95 (*0-7859-7985-9*, 2732841870) Fr & Eur.

Nania, Georges A. Computers Dictionary: Dictionnaire D'Informatique. (ENG, FRE, ITA, POR & SPA.). 1000p. 1983. 150.00 (*0-8288-3917-4*) Fr & Eur.

— Dictionary of Computer Science Terminology: English-Spanish-French. 2nd ed. (ENG, FRE & SPA.). 1990. 64.00 (*0-7859-8949-8*) Fr & Eur.

— Dictionary of Computer Science Terminology: English-Spanish-French. 2nd ed. (ENG, FRE & SPA.). 783p. (C). 1990. 65.00 (*84-283-1413-6*, Pub. by Paraninfo) IBD Ltd.

— Dictionnaire d'Informatique. (ENG, FRE, ITA, POR & SPA.). 1000p. 1983. 150.00 (*0-8288-0272-6*, M 14464) Fr & Eur.

— Spanish, English & French Computers Dictionaries: Diccionario de Informatica. (ENG, FRE & SPA.). 783p. 1985. 95.00 (*0-8288-0271-8*, S16405) Fr & Eur.

Naniewicz, Z. & Panagiotopoulos, P. D. Mathematical Theory of Hemivariational Inequalities & Applications. LC 94-35419. (Pure & Applied Mathematics Ser.: Vol. 188). (Illus.). 296p. 1994. text 145.00 (*0-8247-9330-7*) Dekker.

Nanino, Giovanni M. Giovanni Maria Nanino: Fourteen Liturgical Works. Schuller, Richard J., ed. (Recent Researches in Music of the Renaissance Ser.: Vol. RRR5). (Illus.). xi, 84p. 1969. pap. 35.00 (*0-89579-014-9*) A-R Eds.

Nanji, Azim. The Muslim Almanac I. LC 95-17324. 581p. 1995. 105.00 (*0-8103-8924-X*) Gale.

— The Nizari Ismaili Tradition in the Indo-Pakistan Subcontinent. LC 78-12990. (Monographs in Islamic Religion & Theology). 232p. 1979. 35.00 (*0-88206-020-1*) Caravan Bks.

Nanji, Azim, ed. Mapping Islamic Studies: Genealogy, Continuity & Change. LC 97-15820. (Religion & Reason Ser.). 270p. 1997. text 132.00 (*3-11-014187-6*) Mouton.

Nanji, Shenaaz & Shaker, Shahd. The Old Fisherman of Lamu. 1996. pap. 6.95 (*0-920661-53-X*, Pub. by TSAR Pubns) LPC InBook.

Nanjiani, Max. Fluorescein Angiography: Technique, Interpretation, & Application. (Illus.). 144p. 1992. 79.50 (*0-19-261932 2*) OUP.

Nanjing Hydraulic Research Institute Staff, ed. Coastal & Port Engineering in Developing Countries 1987: Proceedings, 2 vols. 2250p. (C). 1987. pap. 50.00 (*7-5027-0052-8*, Pub. by Trans T Pub) Enfield Pubs NH.

Nanjing Institute of Geology & Palaeontology, Acad, ed. Palaeontologia Cathayana, Vol. 6. 454p. 1996. 80.00 (*7-03-002816-3*, Pub. by Sci Pr) Lubrecht & Cramer.

Nanjio, Bunyiu, compiled by. A Short History of the Twelve Japanese Buddhist Sects. LC 78-70104. reprint ed. 37.50 (*0-404-17355-1*) AMS Pr.

Nanjio, Bunyiu, tr. from JPN. Short History of the Twelve Buddhist Sects. LC 78-52924. (Studies in Japanese History & Civilization). 173p. 1979. reprint ed. lib. bdg. 62.50 (*0-313-26989-0*, U6989, Greenwood Pr) Greenwood.

Nankervis, Kathryn, jt. auth. see Mills, Daniel S.

***Nankivell-Aston, Sally.** Science Experiments with Color. (Science Experiments Ser.). (Illus.). (YA). 2000. pap. 6.95 (*0-531-15442-4*) Watts.

— Science Experiments with Electricity. (Science Experiments Ser.). (Illus.). (YA). 2000. pap. 6.95 (*0-531-15443-2*) Watts.

— Science Experiments with Forces. (Science Experiments Ser.). (Illus.). (YA). 2000. pap. 6.95 (*0-531-15444-0*) Watts.

— Science Experiments with Light. (Science Experiments Ser.). (Illus.). (J). 2000. pap. 6.95 (*0-531-15429-7*) Watts.

— Science Experiments with Magnets. (Science Experiments Ser.). (Illus.). (J). 2000. pap. 6.95 (*0-531-15430-0*) Watts.

— Science Experiments with Simple Machines. (Science Experiments Ser.). (Illus.). (YA). 2000. pap. 6.95 (*0-531-15445-9*) Watts.

— Science Experiments with Sound. LC 99-38246. 2000. 20.00 (*0-531-14578-6*) Watts.

— Science Experiments with Water. (Science Experiments Ser.). (Illus.). (J). 2000. pap. 6.95 (*0-531-15432-7*) Watts.

***Nankivell-Aston, Sally & Jackson, Dorothy.** Science Experiments with Color. LC 99-88992. (Illus.). 2000. 20.00 (*0-531-14581-6*) Watts.

— Science Experiments with Electricity. LC 99-86438. 2000. 20.00 (*0-531-14580-8*) Watts.

— Science Experiments with Light LC 99-38289. 2000. 20.00 (*0-531-14577-8*) Watts.

— Science Experiments with Magnets. LC 99-38328. (Illus.). 2000. 20.00 (*0-531-14576-X*) Watts.

— Science Experiments with Sound LC 99-38246. 2000. pap. 6.95 (*0-531-15431-9*) Watts.

***Nankivell-Aston, Sally & Jackson, Dorothy M.** Science Experiments with Water LC 99-33475. 2000. 20.00 (*0-531-14575-1*) Watts.

N

Nankivell, Owen. Economics, Society & Values. 272p. 1995. 77.95 (*1-85628-866-8*, Pub. by Avebry) Ashgate Pub Co.

Nanko, Carmen. Campus Ministry: Identity, Mission & Praxis. LC 97-206420. 75p. 1997. pap. write for info. (*1-55833-186-7*) Natl Cath Educ.

Nanko, Heroki & Cote, Wilfred A. Bark Structure: Hardwoods Grown on Southern Pine Sites. 1980. pap. 29.95 (*0-8156-2234-1*) Syracuse U Pr.

Nann, Hermann, ed. Nuclear Structure at High Spin, Excitation, & Momentum Transfer. LC 86-70837. (AIP Conference Proceedings Ser.: No. 142). 488p. 1986. lib. bdg. 70.00 (*0-88318-341-2*) Am Inst Physics.

Nann, Hermann & Stephenson, Edward J., eds. Particle Production near Threshold. (AIP Conference Proceedings Ser.: No. 221). (Illus.). 488p. 1991. 95.00 (*0-88318-829-5*) Am Inst Physics.

Nann, Lizzie. Brush, Brush Bunny. 1997. 4.99 (*0-679-86970-0*, Pub. by Random Bks Yng Read) Random.

— Comb! Comb! Puppy. 1997. 4.99 (*0-679-86971-9*, Pub. by Random Bks Yng Read) Random.

Nann, Richard C. Uprooting & Surviving: Adaptation & Resettlement of Migrant Families. 1982. text 106.00 (*90-277-1339-1*) Kluwer Academic.

Nann, Richard C., et al, eds. Mental Health, Cultural Values & Social Development. 1983. text 226.00 (*90-277-1622-6*) Kluwer Academic.

Nann, Richard C., jt. auth. see Leung, Joe C.

Nann Winter, Deborah Du, see Wessells, Michael & Du Nann Winter, Deborah, eds.

Nannemann, John, Jr. Flashers Offical Gamebook. (Illus.). 128p. (Orig.). pap. 14.99 (*0-9655129-8-3*) Roadwary Designs.

Nannen, Sadie. Grandma Sadie's Poem. 1998. pap. write for info. (*1-57553-923-3*) Watermrk Pr.

Nannenga-Bremekamp, N. E. A Guide to Temperate Myxomycetes. Feest, A. & Burggraaf, Y., trs. (Illus.). 409p. 1991. 90.00 (*0-948737-12-3*, Pub. by Biopress) Balogh.

Nannery, Diane S., jt. auth. see Swirsky, Joan.

Nannes, Caspar H. Politics in the American Drama. LC 60-50101. 272p. reprint ed. pap. 84.40 (*0-608-17236-7*, 202949500061) Bks Demand.

N

Nannestad, Elizabeth. If He's a Good Dog, He'll Swim: If He's a Good Dog, He'll Swim. 64p. 1996. pap. 12.95 (*1-86940-146-8*, Pub. by Auckland Univ) Paul & Co Pubs.

Nannestad, Peter. Danish Design or British Disease? Danish Economic Crisis Policy 1974-1979 in Comparative Perspective. (Acta Jutlandica Ser.: Vol. 67:2). (Illus.). 288p. (Orig.). (C). 1992. pap. 23.00 (*87-7288-399-5*, Pub. by Aarhus Univ Pr) David Brown.

— Reactive Voting in Danish General Elections, 1971-1979: A Revisionist Interpretation. (Illus.). 207p. (Orig.). (C). 1989. pap. 23.00 (*87-7288-243-3*, Pub. by Aarhus Univ Pr) David Brown.

Nanney, Donald C. Environmental Risks in Real Estate Transanctions: A Practical Guide. 520p. 1994. pap. 75.00 (*0-471-12593-8*) Wiley.

— Environmental Risks in Real Estate Transanctions: A Practical Guide. 2nd ed. 429p. 1992. 79.95 (*0-7816-0255-6*, P7420) Exec Ent Pubns.

— John Dos Passos Revisited. LC 98-34787. 1998. 32.00 (*0-8057-3971-8*, Twyne) Mac Lib Ref.

Nanney, J. Louis & Cable, John L. Beginning Algebra. 512p. (C). 1991. text, student ed. 18.75 (*0-697-12086-4*, WCB McGr Hill) McGrw-H Hghr Educ.

— Beginning Algebra. (Illus.). 491p. (C). 1991. text 50.00 (*0-697-11652-2*) Quant Syst.

— Developing Skills in Algebra: A Lecture Worksheet. 5th ed. (Illus.). 438p. (C). 1991. text, student ed. 50.00 (*0-697-08585-6*) Quant Syst.

— Developing Skills in Algebra Vol. I: A Lecture Worktext. 4th ed. 264p. (C). 1987. text 38.13 (*0-697-06768-8*, WCB McGr Hill) McGrw-H Hghr Educ.

— Developing Skills in Algebra Vol. I: A Lecture Worktext, 2. 4th ed. 264p. 1987. text 42.50 (*0-697-06767-X*, WCB McGr Hill) McGrw-H Hghr Educ.

— Elementary Algebra. 496p. 1984. text 42.50 (*0-697-05826-3*, WCB McGr Hill) McGrw-H Hghr Educ.

— Intermediate Algebra. 688p. (C). 1991. text, teacher ed. 18.75 (*0-697-12078-3*, WCB McGr Hill) McGrw-H Hghr Educ.

— Intermediate Algebra. 3rd ed. (Illus.). 668p. (C). 1990. text 50.00 (*0-697-11653-0*) Quant Syst.

— Prealgebra College Preparatory Mathematics: College Preparatory Mathematics. (Illus.). 431p. (C). 1989. text 48.75 (*0-697-06428-X*) Quant Syst.

— Preparation for Algebra. (Illus.). 530p. (C). 1992. text 50.00 (*0-697-12801-6*) Quant Syst.

Nanney, J. Louis & Noll, Rhona S. Developing Skills in Algebra: A Lecture Worktext. 5th ed. 140p. (C). 1991. text, student ed. 17.50 (*0-697-14159-4*, WCB McGr Hill) McGrw-H Hghr Educ.

Nanney, J. Louis & Shaffer, Richard D. Arithmetic: A Review. LC 75-93297. 316p. reprint ed. pap. 98.00 (*0-8357-5736-6*, 202321300032) Bks Demand.

Nanney, James S. Army Air Forces Medical Services in World War 2. (Illus.). 41p. 1998. pap. 4.25 (*0-16-049742-6*) USGPO.

Nanni, jt. auth. see Bergstein, Mary.

Nanni, Antonio, ed. Fibre Reinforcing Plastic for Concrete Structures: Properties & Applications. LC 93-25585. (Developments in Civil Engineering Ser.: Vol. 42). 458p. 1993. 231.50 (*0-444-89689-9*) Elsevier.

***Nanni, Luciano & Federici, Corrado.** Communication: The Power of Location - Essays on Adespotic Aesthetics. LC 99-30292. (Semiotics & the Human Sciences Ser.: Vol. 19). 208p. 2000. text 48.95 (*0-8204-4544-4*) P Lang Pubng.

Nanni, Lyn, jt. auth. see Hemperly, Ilona.

Nanni, Teresa, ed. see Frenzel, Burkhard.

Nannipieri, Paolo, jt. ed. see Alef, Kassem.

Nanny, Mark A., et al, eds. Nuclear Magnetic Resonance Spectroscopy in Environment Chemistry. LC 95-47215. (Topics in Enviornmental Chemistry). (Illus.). 344p. 1997. text 70.00 (*0-19-509751-3*) OUP.

***Nanny, Max & Fischer, Olga, eds.** Form Miming Meaning: Iconicity in Language & Literature. LC 99-10763. xxxvi, 443p. 1999. 120.00 (*1-55619-533-8*) J Benjamins Pubng.

Nano, Gail, ed. see Picard, Dennis D.

Nanopoulos, D. V., ed. Astroparticle Physics. 500p. (C). 1991. pap. 46.00 (*981-02-0583-X*); text 128.00 (*981-02-0582-1*) World Scientific Pub.

Nanopoulos, D. V., jt. auth. see Lopez, J. L.

***Nanos, Linda.** Minor Respondent. 313p. 1999. pap. 16.95 (*0-9674090-0-4*) B & Nanos.

Nanos, Mark D. The Mystery of Romans: The Jewish Context of Paul's Letter. LC 95-47643. 424p. 1996. pap. 29.00 (*0-8006-2937-X*, 1-2937, Fortress Pr) Augsburg Fortress.

Nansen, Fridtjof. Adventure, & Other Papers. LC 67-23251. (Essay Index Reprint Ser.). 1977. 15.95 (*0-8369-0735-3*) Ayer.

— Armenia & the Near East. LC 76-25120. (Middle East in the 20th Century Ser.). 1976. reprint ed. lib. bdg. 37.50 (*0-306-70760-8*) Da Capo.

— Eskimo Life. LC 74-5856. (Illus.). reprint ed. 57.50 (*0-404-11664-7*) AMS Pr.

— Farthest North: The Incredible Three Year Voyage to the Frozen Latitudes of the North. Krakauer, Jon, ed. LC 99-29282. (Modern Library Exploration Ser.). 608p. 1999. pap. 14.95 (*0-375-75472-5*) Modern Lib NY.

— In Northern Mists: Arctic Exploration in Early Times, 2 vols. Chater, Arthur G., tr. LC 75-94314. (Illus.). reprint ed. 94.50 (*0-404-01955-2*) AMS Pr.

— Through Siberia: The Land of the Future. Chater, A. G., tr. from NOR. LC 73-115568. (Russia Observed Ser.). (Illus.). 1971. reprint ed. 39.95 (*0-405-03087-8*) Ayer.

Nansen, Fridtjof, ed. Norwegian North Polar Expedition, 1893-96: Scientific Results, 6 Vols. LC 68-55206. (Illus.). 1971. reprint ed. lib. bdg. 495.00 (*0-8371-3852-3*, NANO) Greenwood.

— Norwegian North Polar Expedition, 1893-96: Scientific Results, 6 Vols, Vol. 1. LC 68-55206. (Illus.). 1971. reprint ed. lib. bdg. 95.00 (*0-8371-3877-9*, NANP) Greenwood.

— Norwegian North Polar Expedition, 1893-96: Scientific Results, 6 Vols, Vol. 2. LC 68-55206. (Illus.). 1971. reprint ed. lib. bdg. 95.00 (*0-8371-3881-7*, NANQ) Greenwood.

— Norwegian North Polar Expedition, 1893-96: Scientific Results, 6 Vols, Vol. 3. LC 68-55206. (Illus.). 1971. reprint ed. lib. bdg. 95.00 (*0-8371-3882-5*, NANR) Greenwood.

— Norwegian North Polar Expedition, 1893-96: Scientific Results, 6 Vols, Vol. 4. LC 68-55206. (Illus.). 1971. reprint ed. lib. bdg. 95.00 (*0-8371-3883-3*, NANS) Greenwood.

— Norwegian North Polar Expedition, 1893-96: Scientific Results, 6 Vols, Vol. 5. LC 68-55206. (Illus.). 1971. reprint ed. lib. bdg. 95.00 (*0-8371-3884-1*, NANT) Greenwood.

— Norwegian North Polar Expedition, 1893-96: Scientific Results, 6 Vols, Vol. 6. LC 68-55206. (Illus.). 1971. reprint ed. lib. bdg. 95.00 (*0-8371-3885-X*, NANU) Greenwood.

Nansen, P., et al, eds. Epidemiology & Control of Nematodiasis in Cattle: Current Topics in Veterinary Medicine & Animal Science, No. 9. 616p. 1981. text 249.00 (*90-247-2502-X*) Kluwer Academic.

Nansen, Ralph. Sun Power: The Global Solution for the Coming Energy Crisis. 252p. 1996. pap. 14.95 (*0-9647021-1-8*) Ocean Pr WA.

Nanstad, Randy K., et al, eds. Effects of Radiation on Materials: 18th International Symposium. (Illus.). 1150p. 1999. text 149.00 (*0-8031-2614-X*, STP1325) ASTM.

Nantambu, Kwame. Decoding European Geo-Politics: Afrocentric Perspectives. expanded ed. 128p. (Orig.). (C). 1994. pap. 11.95 (*0-9613067-2-6*) Imhotep.

— Egypt & Afrocentric Geopolitics: Essays on European Supremacy. 255p. (Orig.). 1996. pap. 14.95 (*0-9613067-8-5*) Imhotep.

Nantell, Judith. The Poetry of Francisco Brines: The Deconstructive Effects of Language. LC 93-30378. 1995. 29.50 (*0-8387-5277-2*) Bucknell U Pr.

Nanteuil, Luc De, see De Nanteuil, Luc.

Nanthawan Bunyapraphatsexon Staff, jt. auth. see Farnsworth, Norman R.

Nantier, Terry, tr. see Pratt, Hugo.

Nanton, Isabel & Simpson, Mary. Adventuring in British Columbia. LC 91-10193. (Adventure Travel Guide Ser.). (Illus.). 368p. 1992. reprint ed. pap. 15.00 (*0-87156-674-5*, Pub. by Sierra) Random.

— Adventuring in British Columbia: Exploring the Great Wilderness Areas of Western Canada from the Rocky Mountains to the Pacific Slope. 2nd rev. ed. (Illus.). 384p. 1996. pap. 16.00 (*0-87156-875-6*, Pub. by Sierra) Random.

***Nantuna, Leonido Corpuz.** The King is Coming. LC 98-91007. 2000. 10.95 (*0-533-13020-4*) Vantage.

Nantz, Karen S., jt. auth. see Hartman, Diane B.

Nantz, Kathryn, jt. auth. see Miners, Laurence.

Nanus, Burt. The Vision Retreat: A Participant's Workbook. (Business & Management Ser.). 80p. 1995. 13.95 (*0-7879-0176-8*) Jossey-Bass.

— Vision Retreat Complete Package. 1995. 64.95 (*0-7879-0188-1*) S&S Trade.

— Vision Retreat Package 5 Workbooks 1 Guide. 1995. 49.95 (*0-7879-0186-5*) S&S Trade.

— Visionary Leadership: Creating a Compelling Sense of Direction for Your Organization. LC 92-18435. (Management Ser.). 263p. 1992. 30.50 (*1-55542-460-0*) Jossey-Bass.

— Visionary Leadership: Creating a Compelling Sense of Direction for Your Organization. LC 92-18435. (Management Ser.). 267p. 1995. mass mkt. 18.50 (*0-7879-0114-8*) Jossey-Bass.

***Nanus, Burt & Dobbs, Stephen M.** Leaders Who Make a Difference: Essential Strategies for Meeting the Nonprofit Challenge. LC 99-6757. 304p. 1999. 26.00 (*0-7879-4665-6*) Jossey-Bass.

Nanus, Burt, et al. Perspectives on Leadership. 137p. 1995. pap. 35.00 (*0-614-10808-X*) APPA VA.

Nanus, Burt, jt. auth. see Bennis, Warren G.

Nanushkid, Fran. Grandma Beatrice Brings Spring to Minsk. (J). 1999. write for info. (*0-7868-0175-1*) Hyperion.

— Grandma Beatrice Brings Spring to Minsk. (J). Date not set. lib. bdg. write for info. (*0-7868-2147-7*) Hyprn Child.

Nanvutty, Piloo. Gathas of Zarathustra: Hymns in Praise of Wisdom, 1. 1999. 14.95 (*1-890206-11-3*) Grantha.

Nanxe, Aline de. Diccionario del Amor. (SPA.). 122p. 1969. pap. 9.95 (*0-8288-6572-8*, S-50136) Fr & Eur.

Nanyang Business School Staff. Business Opportunities in India. LC 97-126140. (Nanyang Business Report Ser.). 230p. (C). 1996. pap. text 29.95 (*0-13-267899-3*) P-H.

— Business Opportunities in Sichuan Province, China. LC 97-126139. (Nanyang Business Report Ser.). 180p. (C). 1996. pap. text 29.95 (*0-13-267881-0*) P-H.

— Business Opportunities in the Philippines. LC 97-126838. (Nanyang Business Report Ser.). 290p. (C). 1996. pap. text 29.95 (*0-13-267915-9*) P-H.

Nanyenya-Takirambudde, Peter. Technology Transfer & International Law. LC 79-23571. 177p. 1980. 36.95 (*0-275-90529-2*, C0529, Praeger Pubs) Greenwood.

Nanzig, Thomas P. Third Virginia Cavalry. (Virginia Regimental Histories Ser.). (Illus.). 142p. 1989. 19.95 (*0-930919-85-8*) H E Howard.

Nao, T. Van. Forest Fire Prevention & Control. 1982. text 153.00 (*90-247-3050-3*) Kluwer Academic.

***Naoas, John.** Transformation. LC 98-68349. 248p. 1999. 19.95 (*0-9644756-1-8*) J Nadas.

Naock, Ruth. How to Play the Piano. LC 86-51471. 83p. 1988. 34.95 incl. VHS (*0-942229-02-9*); spiral bd. 5.95 (*0-942229-01-0*) Video Album.

Naoi, M. & Parvez, S. H., eds. Tyrosine Hydroxylase: A Tribute to Toshiharu Nagatsu. x, 312p. 1993. 147.50 (*90-6764-154-5*) Coronet Bks.

Naokes, Jeremy, ed. Nazism, 1919-1945 - A Documentary Reader Vol. 4: The German Home Front in World War II. 640p. 1998. pap. text 24.95 (*0-85989-311-1*, Pub. by Univ Exeter Pr) Northwestern U Pr.

***Naomi, Miss.** Visions of Erotica. (Illus.). 176p. 1999. 49.95 (*0-7643-1025-9*) Schiffer.

Naor, Bezalel. Lights of Prophecy: Orot Ha-Nevuah. 96p. (Orig.). (C). 1990. pap. 4.95 (*1-879016-00-1*) UOJC Amer.

***Naor, Bezalel.** Post-Sabbatian Sabbatianism: Study of an Underground Messianic Movement. (Illus.). 224p. 1999. pap. 24.95 (*0-9674512-1-3*) Orot Inc.

Naor, Bezalel, ed. Orot: A Multidisciplinary Journal of Judaism. v, 119p. 1991. 17.95 (*0-9674512-0-5*) Orot Inc.

Naor, Bezalel, tr. Of Societies Perfect & Imperfect: Selected Readings from Eyn Ayah, Rav Kook's Commentary to Eyn Yaakov (Legends of the Talmud) LC 95-37358. 1995. 17.50 (*0-87203-144-6*) Hermon.

Naor, Bezalel, tr. & intro. see Kook, Abraham I.

Naor, Chaya, tr. see Shavit, Yaacov.

Naor, David, et al, eds. Immunosuppression & Human Malignancy. LC 89-7474. (Contemporary Immunology Ser.). 288p. 1990. 99.50 (*0-89603-149-7*) Humana.

Naor, Mordechai. Israel: Book of the 20th Century. (Illus.). 618p. 1998. 29.95 (*3-89508-595-2*, 520357) Konemann.

Naor, Z., et al, eds. Leukotrienes & Prostanoids in Health & Disease. (New Trends in Lipid Mediators Research Ser.: Vol. 3). (Illus.). x, 346p. 1989. 278.50 (*3-8055-5011-1*) S Karger.

Naoroji, Dadabhai. Poverty & Un-British Rule in India. 1990. reprint ed. 20.00 (*81-85395-87-X*, Pub. by Low Price) S Asia.

Naosherwan, Anzar, ed. The Ancient One: A Disciple's Memoirs of Meher Baba. (Illus.). 280p. (Orig.). 1985. 16.95 (*0-685-10268-8*); pap. 12.00 (*0-685-10269-6*) Beloved Bks.

Naoum, Phokion. Nitroglycerine & Nitroglycerine Explosives. Symmes, E. M., tr. (World Wide Chemical Translation Ser.: No. 1). 512p. (C). 1928. reprint ed. 18.00 (*0-913022-46-2*) Angriff Pr.

NAPA Staff. Basic Heavy Truck Systems. (IT-Automotive Technology Ser.). 288p. 1996. 29.40 (*0-8273-7881-5*) Delmar.

Napaljarri, Peggy R. & Cataldi, Lee. Walpiri Dreamings & Histories. 1994. pap. 22.95 (*0-7619-8992-7*) Sage.

Napaljarri, Peggy R. & Cataldi, Lee. Walpiri Dreamings & Histories: Newly Recorded Stories from the Aboriginal Elders of Central Australia. (Sacred Literature Ser.). (Illus.). 226p. 1995. 32.95 (*0-7619-8991-9*) AltaMira Pr.

Napaljarri, Peggy R & Cataldi, Lee, trs. from ENG. Warlpiri Dreamings & Other Narratives: Yimikirli. LC 93-34863. (Sacred Literature Ser.). 224p. 1994. 20.00 (*0-06-066125-9*) Harper SF.

Napalkov, N. P., et al, eds. Perinatal & Multigeneration Carcinogenesis. (IARC Scientific Publications: No. 96). (Illus.). 462p. 1989. pap. 110.00 (*92-832-1196-0*) OUP.

Napalkov, N. P. & Eckhardt, S. Cancer Control in the Countries of the Council of Mutual Economic Assistance. 741p. (C). 1982. 105.00 (*963-05-3036-8*, Pub. by Akade Kiado) St Mut.

— Cancer Control in the Countries of the Council of Mutual Economic Assistance. 742p. 1982. 177.00 (*0-569-08718-X*) St Mut.

Napalkov, N. P., ed. see International Agency for Research on Cancer Staff.

Naparstek, Arthur J., et al. Neighborhood Networks for Humane Mental Health Care. 238p. 1982. 42.50 (*0-306-41051-6*, Plenum Trade) Perseus Pubng.

Naparstek, Belleruth. Diabetes. 1993. audio 12.00 (*1-57042-008-4*, Pub. by Warner Bks) Little.

— Grief. 1993. audio 12.00 (*1-57042-009-2*, Pub. by Warner Bks) Little.

— Staying Well with Guided Imagery. 1995. pap. write for info. (*0-446-67159-2*); mass mkt. 12.99 (*0-446-67134-7*, Pub. by Warner Bks) Little.

— Your Sixth Sense: Activating Your Psychic Potential. LC 96-30248. 1997. 22.00 (*0-06-251359-1*, Pub. by Harper SF) HarpC.

— Your Sixth Sense: Activating Your Psychic Potential. LC 96-30248. 256p. 1998. pap. 13.00 (*0-06-251360-5*, Pub. by Harper SF) HarpC.

Naparstek, Belleruth. Your Sixth Sense: Activating Your Psychic Potential. unabridged ed. 1997. audio 18.00 (*0-694-51806-9*, CPN 2646) HarperAudio.

Napheys, George H., jt. auth. see Brinton, D. G.

Naphy, William G. Documents on Continental Reform. LC 96-7157. 200p. 1996. text 49.95 (*0-312-16129-8*) St Martin.

Napier. Mastering & Using Lotus 1-2-3 R3.4. 1994. 35.75 (*0-87709-306-7*) Course Tech.

— Mastering & Using Microsoft Word 6, Windows 3.1. 1996. 23.95 (*0-7600-4090-7*) Course Tech.

— Mastering & Using Microsoft Word 97 to Create Web Pages. (C). 1998. pap. 14.95 (*0-7600-7347-3*) S-W Pub.

— Mastering & Using Wordperfect 6.0. 1994. teacher ed. 35.75 (*0-87709-427-6*) Course Tech.

— Microsoft Access 2000. LC 99-235883. 1999. pap. 31.95 (*0-538-42610-1*); pap. 12.95 (*0-538-42623-3*) S-W Pub.

— Microsoft Excel 2000. 1999. pap. 39.95 (*0-538-42613-6*) S-W Pub.

— MicroSoft Excel 2000. (School Transfer from CT). 1999. pap., wbk. ed. 12.95 (*0-538-42624-1*) S-W Pub.

— Microsoft Office 2000. (School Transfer from CT). 1999. pap., wbk. ed. 12.95 (*0-538-42621-7*) S-W Pub.

— Microsoft Office 9X. LC 99-218729. 2000. pap. 38.95 (*0-538-42604-7*) S-W Pub.

— Microsoft Powerpoint 2000. LC 99-230371. 1999. pap. 37.95 (*0-538-42616-0*); pap., wbk. ed. 12.95 (*0-538-42625-X*) S-W Pub.

— Microsoft Word 2000. (School Transfer from CT). 1999. pap., wbk. ed. 12.95 (*0-538-42622-5*) S-W Pub.

Napier & Judd. Mastering & Using Corel Word Perfect 8. (C). 1998. pap. text 56.95 (*0-7600-5780-X*) Course Tech.

— Mastering & Using the Internet for Office Professional: Netscape V. (C). 1997. pap. 17.95 (*0-7600-5013-9*) Course Tech.

— Mastering & Using the Internet for Office Professional Using Netscape Communicator. (C). 1997. pap. text 22.95 (*0-7600-5779-6*) Course Tech.

Napier, A. David. Foreign Bodies: Performance, Art & Symbolic Anthropology. (C). 1992. 48.00 (*0-520-06583-2*, Pub. by U CA Pr) Cal Prin Full Svc.

— Foreign Bodies: Performance, Art & Symbolic Anthropology. LC 90-34530. (Illus.). 223p. (C). 1996. pap. 16.95 (*0-520-20517-0*, Pub. by U CA Pr) Cal Prin Full Svc.

— Masks, Transformation, & Paradox. 1986. pap. 18.95 (*0-520-04533-5*, Pub. by U CA Pr) Cal Prin Full Svc.

Napier, A. Kam, jt. auth. see Chenoweth, Candace A.

Napier, A. S., jt. ed. see Ker, William P.

Napier, Al. Mastering & Using the Internet for Office Professionals Using Microsoft Internet Explorer 4.0. (Mastering & Using Ser.). 1997. pap. 22.95 (*0-7600-7184-5*) Course Tech.

Napier, Al & Judd, Philip. Mastering & Using Microsoft Access 97. (Illustrated Ser.). (Illus.). 208p. (C). 1997. pap. 30.95 (*0-7600-5061-9*) Course Tech.

— Mastering & Using Microsoft Excel 7 for Windows 95. 536p. (C). 1996. pap. 44.95 (*0-7600-4598-4*) Course Tech.

— Mastering & Using Microsoft Excel 7 for Windows 95. 536p. 1997. teacher ed. write for info. (*0-7600-4600-X*) Course Tech.

— Mastering & Using Microsoft Office for Windows 95: Professional Edition. 880p. (C). 1996. pap. 59.95 (*0-7600-4440-6*) Course Tech.

— Mastering & Using Microsoft Office for Windows 95 Professional Edition. 1997. teacher ed. write for info. (*0-7600-4594-1*) Course Tech.

— Mastering & Using Microsoft Word 7 for Windows 95. 656p. (C). 1996. pap. 56.95 (*0-7600-4595-X*) Course Tech.

— Mastering & Using Microsoft Word 7 for Windows 95. 656p. 1997. teacher ed. write for info. (*0-7600-4597-6*) Course Tech.

— Mastering Microsoft Excel 5 for Windows 3.1. 256p. 1996. pap. 23.95 (*0-7600-4091-5*) Course Tech.

— Mastering Microsoft Excel 5 for Windows 3.1. 256p. 1996. teacher ed. write for info. (*0-7895-0599-1*) Course Tech.

Napier, Albert H. & Judd, Philip J. Mastering & Using WordPerfect 6.1 for Windows. 1995. mass mkt., teacher ed. 50.50 (*0-7895-0600-9*) Course Tech.

Napier, Alexander, ed. see Barrow, Isaac.

Napier, Arthur. Wulfstan. viii, 367p. 1967. write for info. (*3-296-25100-6*, Pub. by Weidmann) Lubrecht & Cramer.

Napier, Arthur S., ed. The Crawford Collection of Early Charters & Documents Now in the Bodleian Library. (Anecdota Oxoniensia Ser.: No. 7). 1988. reprint ed. 59.50 (*0-404-63957-7*) AMS Pr.

An Asterisk (*) at the beginning of an entry indicates that the title is appearing for the first time.

— History of the Holy Rood-Tree. (EETS, OS Ser.: No. 103). 1969. reprint ed. 45.00 (*0-527-00104-X*) Periodicals Srv.

— Old English Glosses, Chiefly Unpublished. (Anecdota Oxoniensia Ser.: No. 11). 1988. reprint ed. 76.50 (*0-404-63961-5*) AMS Pr.

— Old English Glosses, Chiefly Unpublished. (Anecdota Oxoniensia Ser.: Vol. IV, Pt. XI). xxxix, 302p. 1969. reprint ed. 50.70 (*0-685-66495-3*, 05102254) G Olms Pubs.

Napier, Augustus Y. Weight Watchers Fat Sorter. 1995. pap. 3.00 (*0-671-50126-7*) S&S Trade.

Napier, Augustus Y. & Whitaker, Carl A. The Family Crucible: The Intense Experience of Family Therapy. LC 74-1872. 320p. 1988. pap. 14.00 (*0-06-091489-0*, PL-1489, Perennial) HarperTrade.

Napier, C., jt. auth. see Zambon, S.

Napier, Charles J. Colonization: Particularly in South Australia, with Some Remarks on Small Farms & Overpopulation. LC 68-56551. (Reprints of Economic Classics Ser.). xxxii, 269p. 1969. reprint ed. 45.00 (*0-678-00575-3*) Kelley.

Napier, Charles J., comment. Life in Napoleon's Army: The Memoirs of Captain Elzear Blaze. (Napoleonic Library: Vol. 28). (Illus.). 208p. 1995. 35.00 (*1-85367-196-7*, Pub. by Greenhill Bks) Stackpole.

Napier, Christopher, ed. Environmental Conflict Resolution. 1998. 130.00 (*1-874698-66-X*) Gaunt.

Napier, Claude, tr. see Haslund, Henning.

Napier, Edward. The English Teachers. 5.95 (*0-8222-1723-6*) Dramatists Play.

Napier, Elizabeth R. The Failure of Gothic: Problems of Disjunction in an Eighteenth-Century Literary Form. 184p. 1987. text 65.00 (*0-19-812860-6*) OUP.

Napier, Elizabeth R., tr. see Marinetti, Filippo Tommaso.

Napier, Gerald. The Sapper VCs: The Story of Valour in the Royal Engineers & Its Associated Corps. 280p. 1998. 70.00 (*0-11-772835-7*, Pub. by Statnry Office) Balogh.

Napier, H. Albert. Mastering & Using Lotus, Release 4.0 for Windows. 640p. (C). 1994. pap. 44.95 (*0-87709-169-2*) Course Tech.

— Mastering & Using the Internet for Office Professionals: Netscape Navigator Software Version, Internet Explorer Version. 96p. 1997. write for info. incl. disk (*0-7600-5015-5*) Course Tech.

— Mastering & Using Wordperfect 6.1 with Windows. (DF - Computer Applications Ser.). 648p. 1995. mass mkt. 46.95 (*0-7895-0404-9*) Course Tech.

— Master/Users Manual for WordPerfect 5.1 for DOS. (DF - Computer Applications Ser.). 1995. text, suppl. ed. 37.95 (*0-7895-0067-1*) S-W Pub.

Napier, H. Albert & Judd, Philip. Mastering & Using Lotus for DOS, Release 4.0. (C). 1995. mass mkt., teacher ed. 50.50 (*0-87709-549-3*) Course Tech.

— Mastering & Using Lotus 1-2-3 for Windows, Release 4.0. (C). 1995. mass mkt., teacher ed. 50.50 (*0-87709-534-5*) Course Tech.

— Mastering & Using Lotus 1-2-3, Release 5.0 for Windows. 1995. mass mkt., teacher ed. 50.50 (*0-7895-0596-7*) Course Tech.

Napier, H. Albert & Judd, Philip J. Mastering & Using Corel WordPerfect 7. 640p. 1997. teacher ed. write for info. (*0-7600-5005-8*) Course Tech.

— Mastering & Using Corel WordPerfect 7. 640p. (C). 1997. pap. 56.95 (*0-7600-5004-X*) Course Tech.

***Napier, H. Albert & Judd, Philip J.** Mastering & Using Microsoft Access 2000. (Office 2000 Ser.). 448p. 1999. pap. 34.95 (*0-538-42611-X*) Sth-Wstrn College.

Napier, H. Albert & Judd, Philip J. Mastering & Using Microsoft Excel Version 5.0. (C). 1995. mass mkt., teacher ed. 31.50 (*0-87709-309-1*) Course Tech.

***Napier, H. Albert & Judd, Philip J.** Mastering & Using Microsoft Excel 2000. LC 99-230211. (Office 2000 Ser.). 560p. 1999. pap. 42.95 (*0-538-42615-2*) Sth-Wstrn College.

Napier, H. Albert & Judd, Philip J. Mastering & Using Microsoft Excel 97. 512p. (C). 1997. pap. 44.95 (*0-7600-5024-4*) Course Tech.

— Mastering & Using Microsoft Excel 97. 10th ed. 512p. (C). 1997. mass mkt., teacher ed. 1.00 (*0-7600-5025-2*) Course Tech.

***Napier, H. Albert & Judd, Philip J.** Mastering & Using Microsoft Office 2000. LC 99-218729. (Office 2000 Ser.). 896p. 1999. pap. 54.95 (*0-538-42605-5*) Sth-Wstrn College.

Napier, H. Albert & Judd, Philip J. Mastering & Using Microsoft Office 97: Professional Edition. 1024p. 1997. teacher ed. write for info. (*0-7600-5021-X*) Course Tech.

— Mastering & Using Microsoft Office 97: Professional Edition. 1024p. (C). 1997. pap. 59.95 (*0-7600-5020-1*) Course Tech.

***Napier, H. Albert & Judd, Philip J.** Mastering & Using Microsoft Powerpoint 2000. (Office 2000 Ser.). 480p. 1999. pap. 39.95 (*0-538-42617-9*) Sth-Wstrn College.

Napier, H. Albert & Judd, Philip J. Mastering & Using Microsoft Word for Windows 6.0. LC 94-23822. 664p. 1995. 46.95 (*0-7895-0010-8*) Course Tech.

***Napier, H. Albert & Judd, Philip J.** Mastering & Using Microsoft Word 2000. (Office 2000 Ser.). 784p. 1999. pap. 54.95 (*0-538-42608-X*) Sth-Wstrn College.

— Mastering & Using Microsoft Word 2000: Advanced Course. LC 99-233542. 304p. 1999. pap. 25.95 (*0-538-42814-7*) Sth-Wstrn College.

— Mastering & Using Microsoft Word 2000: Beginning Course. 304p. 1999. pap. 25.95 (*0-538-42812-0*) Sth-Wstrn College.

— Mastering & Using Microsoft Word 2000: Intermediate Course. 304p. 1999. pap. 25.95 (*0-538-42813-9*) Sth-Wstrn College.

Napier, H. Albert & Judd, Philip J. Mastering & Using Microsoft Word 6.0 for Windows. 1995. mass mkt., teacher ed. 31.50 (*0-7895-0011-6*) Course Tech.

— Mastering & Using Microsoft Word 97. 704p. (C). 1997. pap. 56.95 (*0-7600-5022-8*) Course Tech.

— Mastering & Using Microsoft Word 97. 10th ed. 704p. (C). 1997. mass mkt., teacher ed. 1.00 (*0-7600-5023-6*) Course Tech.

— Mastering & Using WordPerfect 6.0 for Windows. LC 94-14819. 751p. (C). 1994. mass mkt. 46.95 (*0-87709-536-1*) Course Tech.

Napier, H. Albert & Judd, Phillip J. Mastering & Using Lotus for DOS, Release 4.0. 656p. (C). 1995. pap., mass mkt. 43.95 incl. disk (*0-87709-548-5*) Course Tech.

— Mastering & Using Lotus 1-2-3, Release 5.0 for Windows. 640p. 1995. pap. 30.00 incl. disk (*0-7895-0039-6*) Course Tech.

— Mastering & Using the Microsoft Office (Windows 3.1) Professional Edition. 704p. 1996. pap., mass mkt. 36.75 incl. disk (*0-7895-0361-1*) Course Tech.

Napier, H. Albert, et al. Mastering & Using Microsoft PowerPoint 97 for Business Presentations. 320p. (C). 1997. pap. 41.95 (*0-7600-5026-0*) Course Tech.

— Mastering & Using Microsoft PowerPoint 97 for Business Presentations. 10th ed. 320p. (C). 1997. mass mkt., teacher ed. 1.00 (*0-7600-5027-9*) Course Tech.

Napier, J. A. Blood Transfusion Therapy: A Problem Oriented Approach. 498p. 1996. 275.00 (*0-471-95378-4*) Wiley.

Napier, J. R. & Napier, P. H. The Natural History of the Primates. (Illus.). 200p. 1994. pap. text 21.00 (*0-262-64033-3*) MIT Pr.

Napier, Jesse, ed. see Rick-Burge, L. Cortney.

Napier, John. Charismatic Challenge: Four Key Questions. 256p. 1995. pap. text 14.95 (*1-881576-62-0*) Providence Hse.

— De Arte Logistica Joannis Naperi Merchistonii, Baronis Libri Qui Supersunt. LC 76-173010. (Maitland Club, Glasgow. Publications: No. 47). reprint ed. 37.50 (*0-404-52773-6*) AMS Pr.

— Hands. rev. ed. Tuttle, Russell H., ed. LC 92-14513. (Science Library). (Illus.). 194p. (C). 1993. pap. 14.95 (*0-691-02547-9*, Pub. by Princeton U Pr) Cal Prin Full Svc.

— Rabdology. Richardson, William F., tr. from GAE. (Charles Babbage Institute Reprint Series for the History of Computing). 138p. 1990. 40.00 (*0-262-14046-2*) MIT Pr.

Napier, John H. The Air Force Officer's Guide. 29th ed. LC 86-644873. (Illus.). 424p. 1992. pap. 19.95 (*0-8117-3020-4*) Stackpole.

Napier, John H., 3rd. The Air Force Officer's Guide. 30th ed. (Illus.). 376p. 1995. pap. 19.95 (*0-8117-2410-7*) Stackpole.

Napier, Judd. Mastering & Using in Workplace. (C). 1997. text 7.95 (*0-7600-5072-4*) Course Tech.

— Mastering & Using Microsoft Frontpage 2000. 2000. pap. 28.95 (*0-538-43151-2*) Sth-Wstrn College.

— Microsoft Word 2000. LC 99-232324. 2000. ring bd. 37.95 (*0-538-42607-1*) S-W Pub.

Napier, Kristine. Power Nutrition for Your Chronic Illness. LC 98-5192. 320p. 1999. 19.95 (*0-02-862059-3*) Macmillan.

Napier, Kristine M. Eat to Heal: The Phytochemical Diet & Nutrition Plan. 288p. 1998. mass mkt. 5.99 (*0-446-60475-5*, Pub. by Warner Bks) Little.

— How Nutrition Works. (How It Works Ser.). (Illus.). 169p. (Orig.). 1995. pap. 19.95 (*1-56276-254-0*, Ziff-Davis Pr) Que.

Napier, Kristine M., jt. auth. see Foreyt, John P.

Napier, L. A., ed. Brassey's Armed Services Careers Yearbook, 1987-88. 344p. 1986. 57.75 (*0-08-033598-5*, T120, K122, Pergamon Pr) Elsevier.

***Napier, Linda.** Tender Medicine: Touching the Heart, Healing the Hurt. 234p. 2000. pap. 12.95 (*0-9679300-0-6*) Wing & Pray.

Napier, Mark, ed. Memorials of Montrose & His Times, 2 vols. LC 73-173012. (Maitland Club, Glasgow. Publications: No. 66). reprint ed. 85.00 (*0-404-53075-3*) AMS Pr.

Napier, Mark, ed. see Spottiswood, John.

Napier, Michael & Wheat, Kay. Recovering Damages for Psychiatric Injury. 208p. 1995. 19.95 (*1-85431-352-5*, Pub. by Blackstone Pr) Gaunt.

Napier, Miles. The Racing Men of TV. 128p. 1990. pap. 21.00 (*0-85131-301-9*, Pub. by J A Allen) St Mut.

Napier, Miles, ed. Treasures of the Bloodstock Breeder's Review. 700p. 1990. 100.00 (*0-85131-502-X*, Pub. by J A Allen) St Mut.

Napier, Nancy J. Getting Through the Day: Strategies for Adults Hurt As Children. 304p. 1994. pap. 14.00 (*0-393-31242-9*) Norton.

— Recreating Your Self: Building Self-Esteem Through Imaging & Self-Hypnosis. 1996. pap. 12.95 (*0-393-31243-7*) Norton.

— Sacred Practices for Conscious Living. LC 96-44656. 240p. 1997. 25.00 (*0-393-04052-6*) Norton.

Napier, Nancy K. & Taylor, Sully. Western Women Working in Japan: Breaking Corporate Barriers. LC 95-9841. 256p. 1995. 65.00 (*0-89930-901-1*, Quorum Bks) Greenwood.

Napier, Nancy K., jt. ed. see Ofsanko, Frank J.

Napier, P. H., jt. auth. see Napier, J. R.

Napier, Priscilla. Barbarian Eye: Lord Napier in China-The Prelude to Hong Kong. (Illus.). 250p. 1995. 32.95 (*1-85753-116-7*, Pub. by Brasseys) Brasseys.

Napier, Rod & Gershenfeld, Matti K. Advanced Games for Trainers: Paradigm-Busting Experiential Learning Activities. 300p. 1999. ring bd. 119.95 (*0-07-045997-5*) McGraw.

Napier, Rodney & Gershenfeld, Matti K. Groups, Theory & Experience 6th ed. LC 98-72066. xxii, 568p. 1999. text 51.57 (*0-395-90417-X*) HM.

Napier, Rodney, et al. High Impact Tools & Activities for Strategic Planning: Creative Techniques for Facilitating Your Organization's Planning Process. LC 97-42111. 424p. 1998. 149.00 (*0-07-913726-1*) McGraw.

Napier, Rodney W. Groups, 5 vols. 5th ed. (C). 1992. text 64.36 (*0-395-63869-0*) HM.

Napier, Rodney W., jt. auth. see Gershenfeld, Matti K.

Napier, Susan. La Amante del Novio: Mistress of the Groom. (Bianca Ser.: Vol. 459).Tr. of Groom's Lover. (SPA.). 1998. per. 3.50 (*0-373-33459-1*, 1-33459-8) Harlequin Bks.

— The Cruellest Lie. (Presents Ser.). 1994. per. 2.99 (*0-373-11674-8*, 1-11674-8) Harlequin Bks.

— Deal of a Lifetime. (Presents Ser.: No. 460). 1992. per. 2.89 (*0-373-11460-5*, 1-11460-2) Harlequin Bks.

— Deal of a Lifetime. large type ed. 1991. reprint ed. lib. bdg. 18.95 (*0-263-12687-0*) Mac Lib Ref.

— Escape from the Wasteland: Romanticism & Realism in the Fiction of Mishima Yukio & Oe Kenzaburo. 258p. 1996. pap. text 20.00 (*0-674-26181-X*) HUP.

— The Fantastic in Modern Japanese Literature: Subversion of Modernity. 272p. (C). 1995. 85.00 (*0-415-12457-3*) Routledge.

— The Fantastic in Modern Japanese Literature: Subversion of Modernity. (Nissan Institute/Routledge Japanese Studies Ser.). 272p. (C). 1996. pap. 25.99 (*0-415-12458-1*) Routledge.

— The Hawk & the Lamb Presents Plus. (Presents Ser.). 1994. per. 2.99 (*0-373-11616-0*, 1-11616-9) Harlequin Bks.

— Honeymoon Baby: (Do Not Disturb) (Presents Ser.: Vol. 1985). 1998. per. 3.75 (*0-373-11985-2*, 1-11985-8) Harlequin Bks.

— Honeymoon Baby: (Do Not Disturb) 1999. 21.95 (*0-263-15850-0*, G K Hall & Co) Mac Lib Ref.

— In Bed with the Boss. 1999. per. 3.75 (*0-373-12009-5*, Harlequin) Harlequin Bks.

— In Bed with the Boss. 1999. 21.95 (*0-263-16060-2*, G K Hall & Co) Mac Lib Ref.

— A Lesson in Seduction. (Presents Ser.). 1997. per. 3.50 (*0-373-11870-8*, 1-11870-2) Harlequin Bks.

— Lesson in Seduction. large type ed. (Harlequin Romance Ser.). 1997. 20.95 (*0-263-15069-0*) Thorndike Pr.

***Napier, Susan.** The Mistress Deception: Presents Passion. (Presents Ser.: Bk. 2111). 2000. per. 3.99 (*0-373-12111-3*, 1-12111-0) Harlequin Bks.

Napier, Susan. Mistress of the Groom. 1997. per. 3.50 (*0-373-11918-6*, 1-11918-6) Harlequin Bks.

— No Reprieve. large type ed. 1991. reprint ed. lib. bdg. 18.95 (*0-263-12624-2*) Mac Lib Ref.

— Phantom Lover. (Presents Ser.). 1994. per. 2.99 (*0-373-11707-8*, 1-11707-6) Harlequin Bks.

— Phantom Lover. large type ed. (Harlequin Ser.). 1995. lib. bdg. 18.95 (*0-263-13938-7*) Thorndike Pr.

— Reckless Conduct. 1996. per. 3.50 (*0-373-11847-3*, 1-11847-0) Harlequin Bks.

— Reckless Conduct. large type ed. 288p. 1997. 20.95 (*0-263-14800-9*) Thorndike Pr.

***Napier, Susan.** Revenge Affair. large type ed. (Thorndike Harlequin Romance Ser.). 2000. 22.95 (*0-263-16355-5*) Mills & Boon.

— The Revenge Affair: Sweet Revenge/Seduction. (Presents Ser.: No. 2062). 1999. per. 3.75 (*0-373-12062-1*, 1-12062-5) Harlequin Bks.

Napier, Susan. Una Rubia Muy Especial - A Very Special Blonde Girl, Vol. 421. (Harlequin Bianca Ser.).Tr. of A Very Special Blonde Girl. (SPA.). 1997. per. 3.50 (*0-373-33421-4*, 1-33421-8) Harlequin Bks.

— Savage Courtship. LC 95-6876. (Presents Ser.). 186p. 1995. per. 3.25 (*0-373-11744-2*, 1-11744-9) Harlequin Bks.

— Savage Courtship. large type ed. (Harlequin Romance Ser.). 283p. 1995. lib. bdg. 18.95 (*0-263-14102-0*) Mac Lib Ref.

— Secret Admirer. (Presents Ser.). 1993. pap. 2.89 (*0-373-11554-7*, 1-11554-2) Harlequin Bks.

***Napier, Susan.** Secret Seduction. (Presents Ser.: Bk. 2135). 2000. mass mkt. 3.99 (*0-373-12135-0*, 1-12135-9) Harlequin Bks.

Napier, Susan. Seduccion Salvaje (Savage Courtship) (Harlequin Bianca - Harlequin Presents Ser.: Vol. 359).Tr. of Savage Courtship. (ENG & SPA.). 1996. per. 3.50 (*0-373-33359-5*) Harlequin Bks.

— The Sister Swap. LC 95-22371. (Presents Ser.). 189p. 1996. per. 3.25 (*0-373-11788-4*, 1-11788-6) Harlequin Bks.

— The Sister Swap. (Promo Ser.). 1999. per. 4.50 (*0-373-21987-3*, 1-21987-2) Harlequin Bks.

— The Sister Swap. large type ed. (Harlequin Romance Ser.). 1995. 19.95 (*0-263-14287-6*) Mac Lib Ref.

— Tempt Me Not. (Presents Ser.). 1993. pap. 2.89 (*0-373-11531-8*, 1-11531-0) Harlequin Bks.

— True Enchanter. large type ed. (Magna Large Print Ser.). 1994. 27.99 (*0-7505-0745-4*, Pub. by Mgna Lrg Print) Ulverscroft.

— Viejos Suenos. (Harlequin Bianca Ser.: No. 369). 1996. per. 3.50 (*0-373-33369-2*, 1-33369-9) Harlequin Bks.

— Winter of Dreams. large type ed. 1993. reprint ed. lib. bdg. 18.95 (*0-263-13199-8*) Mac Lib Ref.

Napier, Susan, jt. auth. see Lee, Miranda.

Napier, Susan J. Escape from the Wasteland: Romanticism & Realism in the Fiction of Mishima Yukio & Oe Kenzaburo. (Harvard-Yenching Institute Monographs: No. 33). 250p. (C). 1991. 28.00 (*0-674-26180-1*) HUP.

Napier, T. C., et al. The Basal Forebrain: Anatomy to Function. (Advances in Experimental Medicine & Biology Ser.: Vol. 295). (Illus.). 504p. (C). 1991. text 174.00 (*0-306-43932-8*, Kluwer Plenum) Kluwer Academic.

***Napier, Ted L.** Soil & Water Conservation Policies: Successes & Failures. LC 99-47523. 656p. 1999. boxed set 69.95 (*0-8493-0005-3*) CRC Pr.

Napier, Ted L., et al, eds. Adopting Conservation on the Farm: An International Perspective of the Socioeconomics of Soil & Water Conservation. LC 94-29289. 530p. 1994. pap. text 40.00 (*0-935734-31-7*) Soil & Water Conserv.

— Water Resources Research: Problems & Potentials for Agriculture & Rural Communities. LC 83-4821. 247p. 1983. 7.00 (*0-935734-10-4*) Soil & Water Conserv.

Napier, Ted L., pref. Implementing the Conservation Title of the Food Security Act of 1985. 355p. 1990. 18.00 (*0-935734-22-8*) Soil & Water Conserv.

Napier, Ted L., jt. ed. see Lovejoy, Stephen B.

Napier, William. History of the War in the Peninsula & in the South of France, 5 vols. LC 77-118946. (Illus.). reprint ed. 345.00 (*0-404-04660-6*) AMS Pr.

Napier, Winston. African American Literary Theory: A Reader. 2000. pap. 24.95 (*0-8147-5810-X*) NYU Pr.

***Napier, Winston, ed.** African American Literary Theory: A Reader. 576p. 1999. text 75.00 (*0-8147-5809-6*) NYU Pr.

Napierala, Susanna. Water Birth: A Midwife's Perspective. LC 93-49703. (Illus.). 256p. 1994. pap. 16.95 (*0-89789-285-2*, Bergin & Garvey) Greenwood.

Napieralski, Andrzej, et al, eds. Mixed Design of Integrated Circuits & Systems. LC 97-48316. 256p. 1998. lib. bdg. 110.00 (*0-7923-8116-5*) Kluwer Academic.

***Napierkowski, Marie Rose & Ciccarelli, Sheryl, eds.** Novels for Students. 5th ed. 350p. 1999. text 60.00 (*0-7876-2115-3*) Gale.

***Napierkowski, Marie Rose & Stanley, Deborah A., eds.** Novels for Students. 6th ed. 350p. 1999. text 60.00 (*0-7876-2116-1*) Gale.

Napiewocki, John, jt. auth. see Langabeer, James R., II.

Napiorkowski, Andrzej. Schrift - Tradition - Kirche: Glaubensquelle in Matthias Joseph Scheebens Theologischer Erkenntnislehre. (Regensburger Studien Zur Theologie Ser.: Bd. 49). (GER.). 295p. 1996. 54.95 (*3-631-30330-0*) P Lang Pubng.

Napler, Susan. Mistress of the Groom. large type ed. (Harlequin Romance Ser.). 288p. 1998. 20.95 (*0-263-15403-3*) Thorndike Pr.

***Naples, Gary J.** Beyond the Numbers: Managing the Assets of an Automobile Parts Business. LC 99-53230. 2000. write for info. (*0-7680-0122-6*) Soc Auto Engineers.

Naples, Gary J. By the Numbers: Principles of Automotive Parts Management. 224p. 1994. 29.00 (*1-56091-520-X*, R140) Soc Auto Engineers.

Naples-Marco Philharmonic League Staff. Naples-Marco Philharmonic League Cookbook: Fantastic Foods of the Philharmonic. 324p. (Orig.). 1989. pap. text 12.50 (*0-685-29164-2*) Naples Marco.

Naples, Marge. A Step-by-Step Book about Siamese Cats. (Step-by-Step Ser.). (Illus.). 64p. (YA). (gr. 9-12). 1988. pap. 5.95 (*0-86622-473-4*, SK-021) TFH Pubns.

Naples, Marie, ed. see Johnson, Lois M. & Stinnett, Hester.

Naples, Mary A., ed. see Williamson, Marianne.

Naples, Michael J. Effective Frequency: The Relationship Between Frequency & Advertising Effectiveness. 152p. 1994. pap. 14.95 (*0-8442-3132-0*, NTC Business Bks) NTC Contemp Pub Co.

Naples, Michele I., jt. auth. see Aslanbeigui, Nahid.

Naples, Nancy, ed. Community Activism & Feminist Politics: Organizing Across Race, Class & Gender. LC 97-26531. 368p. (C). 1997. pap. 24.99 (*0-415-91630-5*) Routledge.

Naples, Nancy A. Grassroots Warriors: Activist Mothering, Community Work, & the War on Poverty. LC 97-35178. (Perspectives on Gender Ser.). 256p. (C). 1998. 65.00 (*0-415-91024-2*) Routledge.

— Grassroots Warriors: Activist Mothering, Community Work & the War on Poverty. LC 97-35178. (Perspectives on Gender Ser.). 256p. (C). 1998. pap. 18.99 (*0-415-91025-0*) Routledge.

Naples, Nancy A., ed. Community Activism & Feminist Politics: Organizing Across Race, Class & Gender. LC 97-26531. 368p. (C). 1997. 80.00 (*0-415-91629-1*) Routledge.

Napodano, Rudolph J. Values in Medical Practice: A Statement of Philosophy for Physicians & Model for Teaching a Healing Science. LC 85-19742. 144p. 1986. 32.95 (*0-89885-268-4*, Kluwer Acad Hman Sci) Kluwer Academic.

Napolean. Norbert Nipkin: Teacher's Resource Package. 1995. pap. text, teacher ed. 8.95 (*0-929141-44-X*) Napoleon Publ.

— Norbert Nipkin & the Magic Riddle Stone: Teacher's Resource Package. (Illus.). 1995. pap. text, teacher ed. 8.95 (*0-929141-45-8*) Napoleon Publ.

— Strawberry Jam: Teacher's Resource Package. 1995. pap., teacher ed. 8.95 (*0-929141-47-4*) Napoleon Publ.

Napoleani, Claudio. Diccionario de Economia Politica, Vol. 1. 3rd ed. (SPA.). 832p. 1988. 95.00 (*0-7859-6193-3*, 8471891646) Fr & Eur.

— Diccionario de Economia Politica, Vol. 2. 3rd ed. (SPA.). 836p. 1988. 95.00 (*0-7859-6194-1*, 8471891654) Fr & Eur.

Napoleon, 3rd. The Second Empire & Its Downfall. Wilson, Herbert, tr. LC 74-126266. (Select Bibliographies Reprint Ser.). 1977. reprint ed. 18.95 (*0-8369-5464-5*) Ayer.

N

Napoleon, Davi. Chelsea on the Edge: The Adventures of an American Theater. LC 91-8660. (Illus.). 317p. 1991. reprint ed. pap. 98.30 (*0-608-06868-3*, 206707500009) Bks Demand.

Napoleon First. Correspondance de Napoleon Ier, Supplement: Lettres Curieuses Omises par le Comite de Publication, Rectifications. LC 77-173013. 1975. reprint ed. 96.00 (*0-404-07148-1*) AMS Pr.

Napoleon Hill Foundation Staff. Piense Y Hagase Rico. 1997. pap. 13.98 (*970-05-0381-X*) Grijalbo Edit.

Napoleon I. Correspondance de Napoleon Ier; Publiee, 32 vols., 26. Incl. Set. 3060.00 (*0-404-07400-6*); 1. 95.65 (*0-404-07401-4*); 2. 95.65 (*0-404-07402-2*); 3. 95.65 (*0-404-07403-0*); 4. 95.65 (*0-404-07404-9*); 5. 95.65 (*0-404-07405-7*); 6. 95.65 (*0-404-07406-5*); 7. 95.65 (*0-404-07407-3*); 8. 95.65 (*0-404-07408-1*); 9. 95.65 (*0-404-07409-X*); 10. 95.65 (*0-404-07410-3*); 11. 95.65 (*0-404-07411-1*); 12. 95.65 (*0-404-07412-X*); 13. 95.65 (*0-404-07413-8*); 14. 95.65 (*0-404-07414-6*); 15. 95.65 (*0-404-07415-4*); 16. 95.65 (*0-404-07416-2*); 17. 95.65 (*0-404-07417-0*); 18. 95.65 (*0-404-07418-9*); 19. 95.65 (*0-404-07419-7*); 20. 95.65 (*0-404-07420-0*); 21. 95.65 (*0-404-07421-9*); 22. 95.65 (*0-404-07422-7*); 23. 95.65 (*0-404-07423-5*); 24. 95.65 (*0-404-07424-3*); 25. 95.65 (*0-404-07425-1*); reprint ed. 95.65 (*0-404-07426-X*) AMS Pr.

— Correspondance de Napoleon Ier; Publiee, Vol. 27. reprint ed. 95.65 (*0-404-07427-8*) AMS Pr.

— Correspondance de Napoleon Ier; Publiee, Vol. 28. reprint ed. 95.65 (*0-404-07428-6*) AMS Pr.

— Correspondance de Napoleon Ier; Publiee, Vol. 29. reprint ed. 95.65 (*0-404-07429-4*) AMS Pr.

— Correspondance de Napoleon Ier; Publiee, Vol. 30. reprint ed. 95.65 (*0-404-07430-8*) AMS Pr.

— Correspondance de Napoleon Ier; Publiee, Vol. 31. reprint ed. 95.65 (*0-404-07431-6*) AMS Pr.

— Correspondance de Napoleon Ier; Publiee, Vol. 32. reprint ed. 95.65 (*0-404-07432-4*) AMS Pr.

Napoleon, Kawika. 'Ai'ai. Wilson, William & Cleeland, Hokulani, eds. (HAW., Illus.). 35p. (J). (gr. 3-5). 1993. pap. 6.95 incl. audio (*0-9645646-9-6*) Aha Punana Leo.

***Napoleon, Kawika.** 'O Lepeamoa. (HAW., Illus.). 25p. (J). (gr. 2-3). 1999. pap. 6.95 incl. audio (*1-58191-057-6*) Aha Punana Leo.

***Napoleon, Kawika & Wilson, William H.** No Ma'ikoha a Me Ka Wauke. (HAW., Illus.). 29p. (J). (gr. 1-3). 1999. pap. 6.95 incl. audio (*1-58191-062-2*) Aha Punana Leo.

Napoleon, Landon J. ZigZag. LC 98-42408. 273p. 1999. 24.00 (*0-8050-6048-0*) H Holt & Co.

— ZigZag: A Novel. Date not set. pap. 12.00 (*0-8050-6047-2*, Owl) H Holt & Co.

Napoleon Third. Oeuvres de Napoleon III, 5 vols., Set. LC 74-173015. reprint ed. 150.00 (*0-404-07380-8*) AMS Pr.

Napoleone, Angelo, ed. see Di Terlizzi, Maurizio.

Napoleone, Mary A., et al. Spirits & Seasons. (Illus.). 83p. 1982. pap. 3.95 (*0-9610038-0-4*) Heatherdown Pr.

Napoleoni, Claudio. Diccionario de Economia Politica, 2 vols. 3rd ed. (SPA.). 1668p. 1988. 175.00 (*0-7859-3361-1*) Fr & Eur.

Napoles Fajardo, Juan C. Cucalambe: Seleccion de las Mejores Decimas Cubanas del Cucalambe. 4th rev. ed. LC 84-80491. (Coleccion Clasicos Cubanos Ser.: Vol. 12). (SPA., Illus.). 176p. 1999. pap. 13.00 (*0-89729-878-0*) Ediciones.

Napoles, V. Corporative Identity Design. 1988. pap. 32.95 (*0-442-26844-0*, VNR) Wiley.

Napoles, Veronica. Corporate Identity Design. 144p. 1987. pap. 34.95 (*0-471-28947-7*, VNR) Wiley.

Napoli, Dede & Reynolds, Bill. The Starving Students' Cookbook. 144p. (Orig.). 1984. mass mkt. 6.95 (*0-446-38145-4*, Pub. by Warner Bks) Little.

Napoli, Donna J. Albert. LC 97-7089. (Illus.). (J). 2000. 16.00 (*0-15-201572-8*) Harcourt.

— Changing Tunes. LC 98-10034. 130p. (J). (gr. 3-6). 1998. 15.99 (*0-525-45861-1*, Dutton Child) Peng Put Young Read.

— Jimmy, the Pickpocket of the Palace. LC 94-26089. (Illus.). 166p. (J). (gr. 2-5). 1995. 14.99 (*0-525-45357-1*, Dutton Child) Peng Put Young Read.

— Jimmy, the Pickpocket of the Palace. (Illus.). 176p. (J). (gr. 3-7). 1997. pap. 3.99 (*0-14-038037-X*, PuffinBks) Peng Put Young Read.

— Linguistics: An Introduction. (Illus.). 592p. (C). 1996. pap. text 44.95 (*0-19-509175-2*) OUP.

— The Magic Circle. (Illus.). 128p. (YA). (gr. 7 up). 1995. pap. 4.99 (*0-14-037439-6*, PuffinBks) Peng Put Young Read.

— One Leap Forward. LC 99-23980. (Aladdin Angelwings Ser.: No. 4). (Illus.). 96p. (J). (gr. 2-5). 1999. pap. 3.99 (*0-689-82986-8*) Aladdin.

— Predication Theory: A Case-Study for Indexing Theory. (Cambridge Studies in Linguistics: No. 50). (Illus.). 384p. 1989. text 95.00 (*0-521-35298-3*); pap. text 35.95 (*0-521-36820-0*) Cambridge U Pr.

— Syntax: Theory & Problems. (Illus.). 616p. (C). 1993. pap. text 45.95 (*0-19-507946-9*) OUP.

Napoli, Donna J., ed. Elements of Tone, Stress, & Intonation. LC 78-4961. 179p. 1978. reprint ed. pap. 55.50 (*0-608-00687-4*, 205254400009) Bks Demand.

Napoli, Donna J. & Kegl, J., eds. Bridges Between Psychology & Linguistics: A Swarthmore Festschrift for Lila Gleitman. 312p. (C). 1991. text 59.95 (*0-8058-0783-7*) L Erlbaum Assocs.

Napoli, Donna J. & Rando, Emily N. Syntactic Argumentation Vol. 1: Text. LC 79-17605. 430p. reprint ed. pap. 133.30 (*0-7837-6334-4*, 204604700001) Bks Demand.

— Syntactic Argumentation Vol. 2: Teacher's Guide. LC 79-17605. 45p. pap., teacher ed. 30.00 (*0-7837-6335-2*, 204604700002) Bks Demand.

Napoli, Donna J. & Rando, Emily N., eds. Lingua Franca: An Anthology of Poetry by Linguists. ii, 157p. (Orig.). 1990. pap. 24.00 (*0-933104-29-4*) Jupiter Pr.

Napoli, Donna Jo. April Flowers. LC 99-87894. (Aladdin Angelwings Ser.: No. 7). (Illus.). 80p. (J). (gr. 2-5). 2000. per. 3.99 (*0-689-83207-9*) Aladdin.

***Napoli, Donna Jo.** April Flowers. (Illus.). (J). 2000. 9.34 (*0-606-17910-0*) Turtleback.

— Changing Tunes. (Illus.). 144p. (YA). (gr. 3-7). 2000. pap. 4.99 (*0-14-130811-7*, PuffinBks) Peng Put Young Read.

— Changing Tunes. (Illus.). (J). 2000. 10.34 (*0-606-18394-9*) Turtleback.

— Crazy Jack. LC 99-12243. 134p. (YA). (gr. 7-12). 1999. 15.95 (*0-385-32627-0*) Delacorte.

— Flamingo Dream. (J). 2001. 15.95 (*0-688-16796-9*, Grenwillow Bks); lib. bdg. 15.89 (*0-688-17863-4*, Grenwillow Bks) HarpC Child Bks.

— For the Love of Venice. 256p. (J). (gr. 7-12). 2000. mass mkt. 4.50 (*0-440-41411-3*, LLL BDD) BDD Bks Young Read.

Napoli, Donna Jo. For the Love of Venice. LC 97-31624. 240p. (YA). (gr. 7-12). 1998. 15.95 (*0-385-32531-2*) Delacorte.

***Napoli, Donna Jo.** For the Love of Venice. (Illus.). (J). 2000. 9.85 (*0-606-17998-4*) Turtleback.

— Friends Everywhere. LC 98-52882. (Angelwings Ser.: No. 1). (Illus.). 74p. (J). (gr. 2-5). 1999. pap. 3.99 (*0-689-82694-X*) S&S Childrens.

— Friends Everywhere. (Illus.). (J). 1999. 9.34 (*0-606-17904-6*) Turtleback.

Napoli, Donna Jo. Give & Take. (Angelwings Ser.: Vol. 5). (Illus.). 80p. (J). (gr. 2-5). 2000. per. 3.99 (*0-689-83205-2*) Aladdin.

***Napoli, Donna Jo.** Give & Take. (Illus.). (J). 2000. 9.34 (*0-606-17908-9*) Turtleback.

— Know-It-All: A Back-to-School Special. (Angelwings Ser.: Vol. 11). (Illus.). 80p. (J). (gr. 2-5). 2000. pap. 3.99 (*0-689-83572-8*) Aladdin.

— Lies & Lemons. LC 99-87417. (Angelwings Ser.: Vol. 9). 80p. (J). (gr. 4-7). 2000. pap. 3.99 (*0-689-83209-5*) Aladdin.

— Lion. LC 99-89923. (J). 2000. write for info. (*0-689-83589-2*) Atheneum Yung Read.

Napoli, Donna Jo. Little Creatures. LC 98-49675. (Angelwings Ser.: No. 2). (Illus.). 96p. (J). (gr. 2-4). 1999. per. 3.99 (*0-689-82695-8*) Aladdin.

***Napoli, Donna Jo.** Little Creatures. (Illus.). (J). 1999. 9.34 (*0-606-17905-4*) Turtleback.

Napoli, Donna Jo. Magic Circle. 1995. 9.60 (*0-606-07818-5*, Pub. by Turtleback) Demco.

***Napoli, Donna Jo.** New Voices. (Angelwings Ser.: Vol. 12). (Illus.). 80p. (J). (gr. 2-5). 2000. pap. 3.99 (*0-689-83573-6*) Aladdin.

Napoli, Donna Jo. No Fair. LC 99-38627. (Aladdin Angelwings Ser.: (gr. 4-6). 2000. pap. 3.99 (*0-689-83206-0*) Aladdin.

***Napoli, Donna Jo.** No Fair! (Illus.). (J). 2000. 9.34 (*0-606-17909-7*) Turtleback.

Napoli, Donna Jo. On Guard. 128p. (YA). (gr. 3-7). 1999. pap. 4.99 (*0-14-130118-X*, PuffinBks) Peng Put Young Read.

***Napoli, Donna Jo.** On Her Own. LC 99-27370. (Aladdin Angelwings Ser.: No. 3). Orig. Title: Room to Grow. 96p. (J). (gr. 2-5). 1999. per. 3.99 (*0-689-82985-X*) Aladdin.

— On Her Own. Orig. Title: Room to Grow. (Illus.). (J). 1999. 9.34 (*0-606-17906-2*) Turtleback.

— One Leap Forward. (Illus.). (J). 1999. 9.34 (*0-606-17907-0*) Turtleback.

— Playing Games. LC 99-87418. (Angelwings Ser.: No. 8). (Illus.). 80p. (J). (gr. 2-5). 2000. pap. 3.99 (*0-689-83208-7*) Aladdin.

Napoli, Donna Jo. The Prince of the Pond: Otherwise Known as De Fawg Pin. LC 91-40340. (Illus.). 112p. (J). (gr. 2-5). 1992. 15.99 (*0-525-44976-0*, Dutton Child) Peng Put Young Read.

— The Prince of the Pond: Otherwise Known as De Fawg Pin. (Illus.). 160p. (J). (gr. 3-7). 1994. pap. 4.99 (*0-14-037151-6*, PuffinBks) Peng Put Young Read.

Napoli, Donna Jo. The Prince of the Pond: Otherwise Known as De Fawg Pin. 1994. 9.60 (*0-606-07071-0*, Pub. by Turtleback) Demco.

— Running Away. LC 99-87419. (Angelwings Ser.: Vol. 10). 80p. (gr. 4-7). 2000. per. 3.99 (*0-689-83210-9*) Aladdin.

— Shark Shock. (J). 1996. 9.09 (*0-606-11837-3*, Pub. by Turtleback) Demco.

— Shelley Shock. (Illus.). 160p. (J). (gr. 3-7). 2000. 14.99 (*0-525-46452-2*, Dutton Child) Peng Put Young Read.

Napoli, Donna Jo. Sirena. LC 97-48391. 256p. (YA). (gr. 7-12). 1998. 15.95 (*0-590-38388-4*, Pub. by Scholastic) Scholastic Inc.

***Napoli, Donna Jo.** Sirena. 224p. (YA). 2000. pap. 4.99 (*0-590-38389-2*) Scholastic Inc.

— Soccer Shock. 1993. 10.09 (*0-606-06008-1*, Pub. by Turtleback) Demco.

Napoli, Donna Jo. Song of the Magdalene: A Novel. LC 96-7066. 256p. (J). (gr. 7 up). 1996. 15.95 (*0-590-93705-7*) Scholastic Inc.

— Song of the Magdalene: A Novel. (YA). (gr. 7 up). 1998. mass mkt. 4.99 (*0-590-93706-5*, Point) Scholastic Inc.

— Song of the Magdalene: A Novel. (J). 1998. 10.09 (*0-606-13789-0*, Pub. by Turtleback) Demco.

— Stones in Water. LC 97-14253. 154p. (YA). (gr. 5-9). 1997. 15.99 (*0-525-45842-5*, Dutton Child) Peng Put Young Read.

— Trouble on the Tracks. LC 96-27934. (J). 1996. pap. write for info. (*0-590-13472-8*) Scholastic Inc.

— Trouble on the Tracks. LC 96-27934. 160p. (gr. 4-7). 1997. 14.95 (*0-590-13447-7*) Scholastic Inc.

— Zel. 240p. (J). (gr. 5-9). 1998. pap. 4.99 (*0-14-130116-3*, PuffinBks) Peng Put Young Read.

Napoli, Donna Jo & Tchen, Richard. Spinners. LC 98-54640. 192p. (gr. 7 up). 1999. 15.99 (*0-525-46065-9*, Dutton Child) Peng Put Young Read.

***Napoli, Giuseppe & Elmo, Francis, trs.** Flights to the New Earth. LC 00-102023. 112p. 2000. pap. write for info. (*0-936707-06-2*) Action Life Pubns.

Napoli, Giuseppe, tr. see de Llover, Claudia Cordova & Eisenthal, Zitta Waleska, eds.

Napoli, Joseph. A Dying Cadence: Memories of a Sicilian Childhood. (Illus.). 108p. 1986. 15.00 (*0-9617151-0-3*) Marna Pr.

***Napoli, Joseph.** New York Student Supplement for Litigation. LC 99-52329. 1999. pap. text 21.95 (*0-7355-1285-X*) Panel Pubs.

Napoli, Joseph. Threnody & Other Memories: 17 Chronicles. 350p. (Orig.). 1995. pap. 20.00 (*1-886166-02-1*) Marna Pr.

Napoli, Maryann. Health Facts: A Critical Evaluation of the Major Problems, Treatments & Alternatives Facing Medical Consumers. LC 81-2127. 400p. 1984. 22.95 (*0-87951-132-X*, Pub. by Overlook Pr); pap. 8.95 (*0-87951-196-6*, Pub. by Overlook Pr) Penguin Putnam.

Napoli, Maryann, ed. The Cntr. for Med. Consumers Ult. Med. Answerbook. 464p. 1997. reprint ed. pap. 12.00 (*0-688-15124-8*, Quil) HarperTrade.

Napoli, Tony. The Dark Curtain. LC 95-76737. (Ten-Minute Thrillers Ser.). 32p. (YA). (gr. 6-12). 1995. pap. 2.95 (*0-7854-1064-3*, 40802) Am Guidance.

— The Dark Curtain Readalong. (Ten-Minute Thrillers Ser.). 32p. (YA). (gr. 6-12). 1995. pap. 12.95 incl. audio (*0-7854-1075-9*, 40804) Am Guidance.

Napoli, Tony, ed. Stephen Crane: Great American Short Stories II. LC 94-75023. (Classic Short Stories Ser.). (Illus.). 80p. 1994. pap. 5.95 (*0-7854-0583-6*, 40022) Am Guidance.

Napoli, Vincent & Jenrette, Mardee S. The Teaching/Learning Enterprise: Miami-Dade Community College's Blueprint for Change. 216p. (C). 1994. text 33.95 (*0-9627042-8-8*) Anker Pub.

Napoli, Vincent & Mendoza, Manuel G. Systems of Society: An Introduction to Social Science. 6th ed. (C). 1995. text, teacher ed. 2.66 (*0-669-39320-7*); pap. text 52.36 (*0-669-39319-3*) HM Trade Div.

Napoli, Vincent, et al. Adjustment & Growth in a Changing World. 4th ed. Marshall, ed. 514p. (C). 1992. mass mkt. 38.25 (*0-314-93372-7*) West Pub.

— Adjustment & Growth In A Changing World. 5th ed. LC 94-32602. (Psychology). 575p. (C). 1995. mass mkt. 42.00 (*0-314-04557-0*) West Pub.

Napoliello, Mike. Pop Poems & Selections. 120p. pap. text 4.50 (*0-9640052-0-4*) US Mrkting.

— Suicide Poems. 58p. (Orig.). pap. text 4.50 (*0-9640052-1-2*) US Mrkting.

Napolit. Spacelab to Space Station. (Earth Oriented Applications of Space Technology). 1985. pap. 73.00 (*0-08-032539-4*, Pergamon Pr) Elsevier.

***Napolitan, Richard.** Wall Township. (Images of America Ser.). (Illus.). (Orig.). 1999. pap. 18.99 (*0-7385-0162-X*) Arcadia Publng.

Napolitano, Andrew P. Recent Case Law Developments in New Jersey Civil Practice, 1996-97. LC 98-219852. 100 p. 1996. write for info. (*1-57625-028-8*) Amer Law Media.

Napolitano, Annamaria & Devine, Maria T. Manuale Di Grammatica Italiana. (C). 1979. pap. text 29.50 (*0-915838-98-2*) Anma Libri.

Napolitano, Carole S. & Henderson, Lida J. Leadership Odyssey: A Self-Development Guide to New Skills for New Times. LC 97-17810. 288p. 1997. pap. 28.95 (*0-7879-1011-2*) Jossey-Bass.

Napolitano, George, ed. TV Wrestlers Presents No. 37: Raw vs. Nitro. 1999. pap. 4.99 (*0-934551-63-4*) Starlog Grp Inc.

Napolitano, George & Benson, Michael, eds. Starlog's Premiere Wrestling Presents No. 3: Ringside Wrestling Scrapbook. 1999. pap. 3.99 (*0-934551-75-8*) Starlog Grp Inc.

— Starlog's Premiere Wrestling Presents No. 4: Ringside Wrestling Photo Album. 1999. pap. 3.99 (*0-934551-76-6*) Starlog Grp Inc.

— Superstar Wrestlers No. 1: Ultimate Wrestling. 1998. pap. 4.99 (*0-934551-70-7*) Starlog Grp Inc.

— TV Wrestlers Presents No. 6: Beauties of Wrestling. 1999. pap. 4.99 (*0-934551-61-8*) Starlog Grp Inc.

— TV Wrestlers Presents No. 38: Bad Dudes. 1999. pap. 4.99 (*0-934551-64-2*) Starlog Grp Inc.

Napolitano, Lisa & Pusateri, Mike. Unlocking Profits: The Strategic Advantage of Key Account Management. Conlon, Ginger, ed. (Illus.). (Orig.). 1997. pap. 14.95 (*0-9657422-0-2*) SAMA.

Napolitano, Louise. An American Story: Pietro DiDonato's Christ in Concrete. LC 93-36534. (Studies in Southern Italian & Italian American Culture: Vol. 4). 164p. (C). 1995. pap. text 29.95 (*0-8204-2094-8*) P Lang Pubng.

Napolitano, Luigi G. Microgravity Sciences & Processes. 1983. pap. 37.00 (*0-08-029985-7*, Pergamon Pr) Elsevier.

— Space: Mankind's Fourth Environment, Vol. II. 1983. pap. 75.00 (*0-08-029986-5*, Pergamon Pr) Elsevier.

Napolitano, Luigi G., ed. Space Developments for the Future of Mankind II: Proceedings of the Thirtieth International Astronautical Congress, Munich, FRG. September 16-23 1979. 228p. 1980. pap. 58.00 (*0-08-026159-0*, Pergamon Pr) Elsevier.

— Space Two Thousand - Activities to Be Performed for the Next Decade: Selected Papers from the 33rd IAF Congress, Paris, France, 27 September - 2 October 1982. 150p. 1983. pap. 91.00 (*0-08-031106-7*, Pergamon Pr) Elsevier.

Napolitano, Luigi G., et al, eds. Astronautical Research: International Astronautical Congress. Incl. Proceedings, 1975 - Space & Energy. 1976. write for info. (*0-318-55138-1*, Pub. by Pergamon Repr) Franklin.

Napolitano, Luigi G., jt. auth. see International Astronautical Congress Staff.

Napolitano, Luigi G., ed. see Congress of the International Astronautical Federa.

Napolitano, M., et al, eds. Thirteenth International Conference on Numerical Methods in Fluid Dynamics: Proceedings of the Conference Held at the Consiglio Nazionale Delle Ricerche, Rome, Italy, 6-10 July 1992. (Lecture Notes in Physics Ser.: Vol. 414). xiv, 541p. 1993. 101.95 (*0-387-56394-6*) Spr-Verlag.

Napolitano, Maida. Using Modeling to Solve Warehousing Problems: A Collection of Decision-Making Tools for Warehouse Planning & Design. Coleman, Rita, ed. (Illus.). 132p. 1998. pap. 54.00 (*1-892663-00-7*) WERC.

Napolitano, Maida & Gross & Associates Staff. Time, Space & Cost Guide to Better Warehouse Design. LC 94-69586. 106p. 1994. pap. 49.95 (*0-915910-38-1*) Distrib Ctr Mgmt.

Napolitano, Valentina, tr. see Archetti, Eduardo P.

Napora, Joe. To Recognize This Dying. Gogol, John M. & Davies, Robert A., eds. (Poetry Chapbook Ser.). 48p. (Orig.). 1987. pap. 10.00 (*0-932191-09-6*) Mr Cogito Pr.

Napora, Joe, jt. auth. see Jaffe, Maggie.

Napora, Paul E. The Teachings of Oscar Camille, 2 vols., Vol. 1. LC 96-8154. 160p. 1996. pap. 12.95 (*0-931892-36-8*) B Dolphin Pub.

— The Teachings of Oscar Camille, 2 vols., Vol. 2. LC 96-8154. 144p. 1996. pap. 12.95 (*0-931892-37-6*) B Dolphin Pub.

— The Teachings of Oscar Camille, Vols. 1 & 2. Costa, Gwen, ed. LC 91-32254. 1992. 21.95 (*0-87949-354-2*); 21.95 (*0-87949-362-3*) Ashley Bks.

Napp, Ann C. & Wolf, Kenneth E. The Competitive Edge for Audiologists Negotiating with Managed Care Organizations. LC 98-176669. 1997. 38.00 incl. audio (*1-58041-005-7*, 0112072) Am Speech Lang Hearing.

Napp-Zinn, Klaus. Anatomie des Blattes: Blattanatomie der Gymnospermen. (Handbuch der Pflanzenanatomie Encyclopedia of Plant Anatomy - Traite d' Anatomie Vegetale Ser.: Band VIII, Teil 1). (GER., Illus.). xiv, 369p. 1966. 71.00 (*3-443-39012-9*, Pub. by Gebruder Borntraeger) Balogh.

— Anatomie des Blattes Lieferung 1: Blattanatomie der Angiospermen: Entwicklungsgeschichtliche und Topographische Anatomie des Angiospermenblattes. (Handbuch der Pflanzenanatomie Encyclopedia of Plant Anatomy - Traite d' Anatomie Vegetale Ser.: Band VIII, Teil 2A). (GER., Illus.). xvi, 764p. 1973. 148.00 (*3-443-14007-6*, Pub. by Gebruder Borntraeger) Balogh.

— Anatomie des Blattes Lieferung 2: Blattanatomie der Angiospermen: Entwicklungsgeschichtliche und Topographische Anatomie des Angiospermenblattes. (Handbuch der Pflanzenanatomie Encyclopedia of Plant Anatomy - Traite d' Anatomie Vegetale Ser.: Band VIII, Teil 2A). (GER., Illus.). viii, 660p. 1974. 126.00 (*3-443-14008-4*, Pub. by Gebruder Borntraeger) Balogh.

— Anatomie des Blattes - Blattanatomie der Angiospermen Lieferung 1: Experimentelle und Oekologisch. (Handbuch der Pflanzenanatomie Encyclopedia of Plant Anatomy - Traite d' Anatomie Vegetale Ser.: Band VIII, Teil 2B). (GER., Illus.). xvi, 519p. 1984. 116.00 (*3-443-14014-9*, Pub. by Gebruder Borntraeger) Balogh.

— Anatomie des Blattes - Blattanatomie der Angiospermen Lieferung 2: Experimentelle und Oekologisch Anatomie des Angiospermenblattes. (Handbuch der Pflanzenanatomie Encyclopedia of Plant Anatomy - Traite d' Anatomie Vegetale Ser.: Band VIII, Teil 2B). (GER., Illus.). xii, 910p. 1988. 203.00 (*3-443-14015-7*, Pub. by Gebruder Borntraeger) Balogh.

Nappa, Amy. Legacy of Virtue: A Devotional for Mothers. LC 99-212484. 1999. 14.99 (*1-57748-493-2*) Barbour Pub.

Nappa, Amy, jt. auth. see Nappa, Mike.

Nappa, Mike. Heart Like His: Discovering the Heart of Jesus in the Fruit of the Spirit. 256p. 1999. 4.97 (*1-57748-504-1*) Barbour Pub.

— True Stories of Answered Prayer: God's Response to Famous & Everyday People. LC 99-22980. 1999. 9.99 (*0-8423-5178-7*) Tyndale Hse.

***Nappa, Mike.** True Stories of Answered Prayer: God's Response to Famous & Everyday People. large type ed. (Inspirational Ser.). 2000. 25.95 (*0-7838-9017-6*, G K Hall Lrg Type) Mac Lib Ref.

Nappa, Mike. True Stories of Transformed Lives: How Famous & Everyday People Met Jesus. LC 99-23255. 1999. 9.99 (*0-8423-5179-5*) Tyndale Hse.

— What I Wish My Youth Leader Knew about Youth Ministry. Reeves, Dale, ed. LC 98-45041. (Empowered Youth Products Ser.). 208p. 1999. pap. 14.99 (*0-7847-0911-4*, 23331) Standard Pub.

***Nappa, Mike.** Zachary's Zoo. (J). 2000. 7.99 (*0-310-23208-2*, Zondervan Childrens Bks) Zondervan.

Nappa, Mike, ed. Clip-Art Cartoons for Churches. LC 97-202552. (Illus.). 176p. 1995. pap. 16.99 (*1-55945-791-0*) Group Pub.

Nappa, Mike & Lessard, Paul N., eds. Super Plays for Worship & Special Occasions: For Youth & Adults. LC 94-27700. (Illus.). 140p. (YA). 1994. pap. 14.99 (*1-55945-254-4*) Group Pub.

Nappa, Mike & Nappa, Amy. Fifty-Two Fun Family Devotions: Exploring & Discovering God's Word. LC 93-47945. 1994. pap. 8.99 (*0-8066-2698-4*, 9-2698, Augsburg) Augsburg Fortress.

— 52 Fun Family Prayer Adventures: Creative Ways to Pray Together. LC 95-49167. 96p. 1996. pap. 8.99 (*0-8066-2841-3*, 9-2841, Augsburg) Augsburg Fortress.

N

— Imagine That! 365 Ways to Build a Creative Christian Family. LC 98-10850. 128p. 1998. pap. 9.99 (*0-8066-3618-1*, 9-3618) Augsburg Fortress.

***Nappa, Mike & Nappa, Amy.** A Mind Like His: Developing the Character of Christ. 272p. 2000. 4.97 (*1-57748-835-0*) Barbour Pub.

Nappa, Mike & Wakefield, Norm. Legacy of Joy: A Devotional for Fathers. 224p. 1998. 14.99 (*1-57748-379-0*) Barbour Pub.

Nappa, Mike, jt. auth. see Nappa, Tony.

Nappa, Mike, ed. see Yount, Christine.

***Nappa, Tony & Nappa, Mike.** Lunch Box Laughs: Over 75 Tear-Out Jokes to Make Your Child Giggle. Caldwell, Lise, ed. (Illus.). 160p. (J). (gr. 1-6). 2000. pap. 5.99 (*0-7847-1064-3*) Standard Pub.

— Lunch Box Promises. 160p. (J). (gr. 1-6). 2000. pap. 6.99 (*0-7847-1181-X*, 04326) Standard Pub.

— Lunch Box Trivia: Over Seventy-five Tear-Out Fun Facts about the Bible & Other Cool Stuff. 160p. (J). (gr. 1-6). 2000. pap. 6.99 (*0-7847-1180-1*, 04325) Standard Pub.

***Nappen, Evan F.** Nappen on New Jersey Gun Law. (Illus.). 400p. 1999. pap. 24.95 (*0-9670660-2-6*) Gun Writes Pr Inc.

***Nappen, Evan F. & Nappen, Louis F.** The Declaration. LC 99-94232. (Illus.). 220p. 1999. 14.92 (*0-9670660-1-8*) Gun Writes Pr Inc.

Nappen, Louis F., jt. auth. see Nappen, Evan F.

Napper, Elizabeth, ed. see Dalai Lama XIV.

Napper, Elizabeth S. Dependent-Arising & Emptiness: A Tibetan Buddhist Interpretation of Madhyamika Philosophy Emphasizing the Compatability of Emptiness & Convential Phenomena. LC 89-40013. (Advanced Book - Blue Ser.). (Illus.). 846p. (Orig.). 1989. 37.50 (*0-86171-057-6*) Wisdom MA.

Napper, Elizabeth S., jt. auth. see Magee, William A.

Napper, Elizabeth S., ed. see Hopkins, Jeffrey.

Napper, Elizabeth S., ed. see Rinbochay, Lati.

Napper, Lewis. Winsock 2.O. LC 97-76684. 576p. 1995. pap. 39.99 (*0-7645-8049-3*) IDG Bks.

***Napper, Lewis W.** Arrest This Book: Offer Void Where Prohibited by Law Subject to Change Without Notice. (Illus.). 2001. pap. write for info. (*0-9679525-0-6*) Shillelagh Pubng.

Nappholz, Carol, tr. from PRO. Unsung Women: The Anonymous Female Voice in Troubadour Poetry. LC 93-37317. (Studies in the Humanities: Literature-Politics-Society: Vol. 13). 140p. (C). 1994. text 39.95 (*0-8204-2376-9*) P Lang Pubng.

Nappi, Carmine. La Structure des Exportations du Quebec. LC 79-1097. (Accent Quebec Ser.). 74p. 1978. reprint ed. pap. 30.00 (*0-608-01369-2*, 206210900002) Bks Demand.

Nappi, Giuseppe, et al, eds. Headache & Depression: Serotonin Pathways As a Common Clue. LC 91-42003. (Illus.). 340p. 1991. reprint ed. pap. 105.40 (*0-608-05809-2*, 205977400007) Bks Demand.

— Neurodegenerative Disorders: The Role Played by Endotoxins & Xenobiotics. LC 88-18437. 344p. 1988. reprint ed. pap. 106.70 (*0-608-00304-2*, 206102100007) Bks Demand.

— Stress & the Aging Brain: Integrative Mechanisms. LC 90-8692. (Aging Ser.: Vol. 37). 239p. 1990. reprint ed. pap. 74.10 (*0-608-03434-7*, 206413500008) Bks Demand.

Nappi, Giuseppe & Gerber, W. D., eds. Update on Non-Narcotic Analgesic Research: Fiuggi, Italy, October 2-3, 1992. LC 93-11312. 1993. write for info. (*0-8176-2917-3*) Birkhauser.

Naprawa, Andrew, ed. see Lesko, Matthew.

Naprstek, J., jt. auth. see Fryba, Ladislav.

Naps & Pothering. Data Structures & Algorithm Analysis. 350p. spiral bd., lab manual ed. 21.95 (*0-314-06730-2*) PWS Pubs.

Naps, Thomas L. Introduction to Computer Science, Vol. 2. 3rd ed. Date not set. pap. text, teacher ed. write for info. (*0-314-07138-5*) West Pub.

— Programme Design. Date not set. pap. text, teacher ed., lab manual ed. write for info. (*0-314-01818-2*) West Pub.

Naps, Thomas L. & Nance, Douglas W. Introduction to Computer Science: Programming, Problem Solving & Data Structures, Alternate. 3rd alternate ed. LC 94-44472. 1242p. (C). 1995. mass mkt. 91.95 (*0-314-04565-1*) West Pub.

— Introduction to Computer Science: Programming, Problem Solving & Data Structures, 2nd Alternate Edition. Westby, ed. 900p. (C). 1992. text 65.25 (*0-314-93307-7*) West Pub.

Naps, Thomas L. & Pothering, George J. Introduction to Data Structures & Algorithm Analysis with Pascal. 2nd ed. Westby, ed. 679p. (C). 1992. text 57.50 (*0-314-93305-0*) West Pub.

Naps, Thomas L. & Singh, Bhagat. Advanced Programming & Data Structures with Pascal. 493p. (C). 1988. text 52.00 (*0-314-62540-2*) West Pub.

Naps, Thomas L., et al. Introduction to Computer Science: Programming, Problem Solving & Data Structures. LC 88-33762. xxiv, 940 p. 1989. write for info. (*0-314-48132-X*) West Pub.

Naps, Thomas L., jt. auth. see Lambert, Kenneth A.

Naps, Thomas L., jt. auth. see Nance, Douglas W.

Naps, Thomas L., jt. auth. see Pascal.

Naps, Thomas L., jt. auth. see Pothering, George J.

Naps, Thomas L., jt. auth. see Statsky, William P.

***Napsha, Cheryl.** Cher. (Women of Achievement Ser.). 2000. 19.95 (*0-7910-5907-3*) Chelsea Hse.

— Cher. (Women of Achievement Ser.). (Illus.). 2001. pap. 9.95 (*0-7910-5908-1*) Chelsea Hse.

Naptke, H. G. & Cempel, Czes A. Model-Aided Diagnosis of Mechanical Systems: Fundamentals, Detection, Localization, & Assessment. LC 96-25712. 1996. write for info. (*0-387-61065-0*) Spr-Verlag.

Napton, L. Kyle. Archeological Overview of Yosemite National Park, California. (National Park Service, Western Archaeological & Conservation Center Publications in Anthropology). (Illus.). 520p. (C). 1978. reprint ed. pap. text 53.75 (*1-55567-417-8*) Coyote Press.

***Napton, L. Kyle & Greathouse, E. A.** Archaeological Investigations at the CDF Hurley Fire Station Site CA-FRE-002240, Fresno County, California, No. 23. (California Department of Forestry & Fire Protection Ser.). (Illus.). 196p. (C). 1999. pap. text 6.25 (*1-55567-842-4*) Coyote Press.

Napton, L. Kyle & Greathouse, Elizabeth A. The Altaville Schoolhouse: Community & State Cooperation in Local Historical Resource Preservation. (California Department of Forestry Archaeological Reports: Vol. 19). (Illus.). 135p. (C). 1997. pap. text 6.25 (*1-55567-654-5*) Coyote Press.

Napton, Robert, jt. auth. see Liefeld, Rob.

Napuk, Kerry. The Strategy-Led Business. rev. ed. LC 96-12410. 1996. pap. write for info. (*0-07-709285-6*) McGraw.

Naqash, Nasir A. SAARC: Challenges & Opportunities. ix, 175p. (C). 1994. 20.00 (*81-7024-611-3*, Pub. by APH Pubng) Nataraj Bks.

Naqash, Nasir A., jt. auth. see Wani, Gull M.

Naqavi, S. Ali Mohammad, jt. ed. see Waseem, Shah Mohammad.

Naqshi, A. R. An Introduction to Botanical Nomenclature. 96p. 1993. pap. 60.00 (*81-7233-051-0*, Pub. by Scientific Pubs) St Mut.

Naquet, Vidal. Cleisthenes the Athenian. (Illus.). 1996. pap. 19.95 (*1-57392-333-8*) Prometheus Bks.

Naqui, Shaz, jt. auth. see Crane, Randy.

Naquin, Susan. Millenarian Rebellion in China: The Eight Trigrams Uprising of 1813. LC 75-18180. (Yale Historical Publications: Miscellany: No. 108). (Illus.). 398p. reprint ed. pap. 123.40 (*0-8357-8224-7*, 203384100087) Bks Demand.

***Naquin, Susan.** Peking: Temples, Public Space, & Urban Identities, 1400-1900. LC 99-32294. (Illus.). 935p. 2000. 80.00 (*0-520-21991-0*, Pub. by U CA Pr) Cal Prin Full Svc.

Naquin, Susan & Rawski, Evelyn S. Chinese Society in the Eighteenth Century. 270p. (C). 1989. reprint ed. pap. 19.00 (*0-300-04602-2*) Yale U Pr.

Naquin, Susan & Yu, Chun-Fang, eds. Pilgrims & Sacred Sites in China. LC 91-20671. (Studies on China: Vol. 15). 456p. (C). 1992. 60.00 (*0-520-07567-6*, Pub. by U CA Pr) Cal Prin Full Svc.

Naqvi, Akbar. Image & Identity: Fifty Years of Painting & Sculpture in Pakistan. LC 99-188770. (Illus.). 912p. 1999. text 75.00 (*0-19-577803-0*) OUP.

Naqvi, Farzana. Energy, Economy & Equity Interactions in a CGE Model for Pakistan. LC 97-74460. (Illus.). 312p. 1997. text 78.95 (*1-85972-169-9*, Pub. by Avebry) Ashgate Pub Co.

Naqvi, Haider, jt. auth. see Nawab, Syed N.

Naqvi, Maniza. Mass Transit. LC 98-930644. 208p. 1998. 12.95 (*0-19-577900-2*) OUP.

***Naqvi, Maniza.** On Air. 164p. 2000. pap. 10.95 (*0-19-579397-8*) OUP.

Naqvi, N. H. & Blaufox, D. The History of Blood Pressure Management. LC 98-16126. (Illus.). 170p. 1998. 65.00 (*1-85070-013-3*) Prthnon Pub.

Naqvi, S. M., ed. Precambrian Continental Crust & Its Economic Resources: Developments in Precambrian Geology, No. 13. 690p. 1990. 201.25 (*0-444-88310-X*) Elsevier.

Naqvi, Syed N. Ethics & Economics: An Islamic Synthesis. 176p. (Orig.). 1981. 17.25 (*0-86037-079-8*); pap. 9.95 (*0-86037-080-1*) New Era Publns MI.

— Islam, Economics, & Society. LC 93-2443. 220p. 1994. 56.50 (*0-7103-0470-6*) Routledge.

Naqvi, Syed N., et al. External Shocks & Domestic Adjustment: Pakistan's Case (1970-1990) LC 97-210569. (UGC Series in Economics). 142p. 1997. 21.00 (*0-19-577691-7*) OUP.

Naqvi, Tahira, tr. from URD. Attar of Roses & Other Stories from Pakistan. LC 97-15869. 145p. 1997. 25.00 (*0-89410-808-5*, Three Contnts); pap. 15.95 (*0-89410-809-3*, Three Contnts) L Rienner.

Naqvi, Tahira, jt. auth. see Allouache, Merzak.

Naqvi, Tahira, tr. see Chughtai, Ismat.

Naqvi, Tahira, tr. see Mastur, Khadija.

Naqvi, Tehseen. Master Your PC Visually with Minimal Reading. LC 97-90013. (Orig.). 1997. pap. 12.95 (*0-533-12268-6*) Vantage.

Nar, Narayan D., jt. ed. see Kesavan, K. V.

Nara, Andrew R., et al. Blood Pressure. Pramik-Holdaway, Mary J., ed. (Biophysical Measurement Ser.). 109p. (Orig.). (C). 1989. 28.00 (*0-9627449-0-5*) SpaceLabs.

Nara, I. S. Safarnama & Zafarnama. 327p. 1986. 25.00 (*0-8364-1793-3*, Pub. by Minerva) S Asia.

Nara, Robert O. & Kemppainen, Rudolph C. Building the One Hundred Thousand Dollar Dental Practice. LC 81-8550. 268p. 1981. 41.50 (*0-13-086256-8*, Busn) P-H.

Nara, Robert O. & Mariner, Steven A. How to Become Dentally Self-Sufficient. LC 79-90865. 1979. pap. write for info. (*0-933420-01-3*) Oramedics Intl.

— Money - By the Mouthful! LC 79-91111. 1979. pap. write for info. (*0-933420-00-5*) Oramedics Intl.

— The One Hundred Eighty Degree Theory: How to Become Mentally Self-Sufficient. LC 79-90866. 194p. 1979. pap. write for info. (*0-933420-02-1*) Oramedics Intl.

Narabayashi, H., ed. see International Symposium on Stereoencephalotomy Resesearch Staff.

Narabayashi, Hirotaro, et al, eds. Parkinson's Disease: From Basic Research to Treatment. LC RC0321.A276. (Advances in Neurology Ser.: No. 60). (Illus.). 799p. 1993. reprint ed. pap. 200.00 (*0-608-05812-2*, 205977700007) Bks Demand.

Narada. The Bhakti Sutras of Narada. Sinha, Nandalal, tr. & intro. by. LC 73-3792. (Sacred Books of the Hindus: No. 7, Pt. 1). reprint ed. 17.50 (*0-404-57807-1*) AMS Pr.

— Narada Bhakti Sutras: The Gospel of Divine Love. Tyagisananda, Swami, tr. 287p. 1949. pap. 4.95 (*81-7120-329-9*) Vedanta Pr.

— Narada's Way of Divine Love: The Bhakti Sutras. Prabhavananda, Swami, tr. from SAN. LC 75-161488. 177p. 1971. pap. 4.95 (*81-7120-506-2*) Vedanta Pr.

Narada Media Staff. A Guide to Odin's Rune Cards: Commentary by Cheryl Barnes. Maris, Mariann & Aufderheide, Anne, eds. LC 95-68996. (Illus.). 64p. (Orig.). 1995. pap. 6.98 (*0-934245-35-5*) Narada Prodns.

— A Guide to Odin's Rune Cards Book & Card Set: Commentary by Cheryl Barnes. Maris, Mariann & Aufderheide, Anne, eds. (Illus.). 64p. 1995. pap. 20.98 (*0-934245-36-3*) Narada Prodns.

Narada, Ven U. Guide to Conditional Relations: Being a Guide to Pages 1-12 of "Conditional Relations" Patthana, Pt. 1. (Pali Text Society Ser.). 321p. (C). 1979. 41.90 (*0-7100-0280-7*, Routledge Thoemms) Routledge.

Narada, Ven U., tr. from PLI. Conditional Relations, 2 vols., 1. (C). 1981. 63.50 (*0-86013-028-2*, Pub. by Pali Text) Elsevier.

— Conditional Relations, 2 vols., 2. (C). 1981. 75.90 (*0-86013-264-1*, Pub. by Pali Text) Elsevier.

— Conditional Relations, 2 vols., Set. (C). 1981. 133.90 (*0-86013-257-9*, Pub. by Pali Text) Elsevier.

— Discourse on Elements. (C). 1962. 28.50 (*0-86013-025-8*, Pub. by Pali Text) Elsevier.

Naraghi, Ehsan. From Palace to Prison: Inside the Iranian Revolution. Mobasser, Nilou, tr. from FRE. LC 93-13873.Tr. of Des Palais du Chah aux Prisons de la Revolution. 304p. 1994. text 28.95 (*1-56663-033-9*) I R Dee.

Naraghi, Fred, ed. Spine Secrets. (Secrets Ser.). (Illus.). 350p. 2000. text 39.00 (*1-56053-358-7*) Hanley & Belfus.

Naragon, Steve, ed. & tr. see Kant, Immanuel.

Narahashi, Keiko. I Have a Friend. LC 86-27628. (Illus.). 32p. (J). (ps-3). 1987. 16.00 (*0-689-50432-2*) McElderry Bks.

— I Have a Friend. LC 86-27628. (Illus.). 32p. (J). (ps-1). 1998. per. 5.99 (*0-689-82032-1*) S&S Childrens.

Narahashi, Keiko. Is That Josie? LC 93-81163. (Illus.). 32p. (J). (ps-3). 1994. pap. 14.95 (*0-689-50606-6*) McElderry Bks.

— Two Girls Can! LC 98-45301. Orig. Title: Friends. (Illus.). 32p. (ps-3). 2000. 16.00 (*0-689-82618-4*) McElderry Bks.

Narahashi, T. Ion Channels, Vol. 1. (Illus.). 348p. (C). 1988. text 110.00 (*0 306 42655-2*, Kluwer Plenum) Kluwer Academic.

— Ion Channels, Vol. 2. LC 88-647703. (Illus.). 302p. (C). 1990. text 110.00 (*0-306-43352-4*, Kluwer Plenum) Kluwer Academic.

— Ion Channels, Vol. 3. (Illus.). 366p. (C). 1992. text 110.00 (*0-306-44166-7*, Kluwer Plenum) Kluwer Academic.

Narahashi, T. & Chambers, J. E. Insecticide Action: From Molecule to Organism. LC 89-26592. (Illus.). 284p. (C). 1989. text 110.00 (*0-306-43406-7*, Kluwer Plenum) Kluwer Academic.

Narahashi, Toshio, ed. Cellular & Molecular Neurotoxicology. LC 84-17681. (Illus.). 320p. 1984. reprint ed. pap. 99.20 (*0-608-00653-X*, 206124100007) Bks Demand.

Narahashi, Toshio, ed. Ion Channels, Vol. 4. (Illus.). 476p. (C). 1996. text 132.00 (*0-306-45224-3*, Kluwer Plenum) Kluwer Academic.

Narahashi, Toshio & Conn, P. Michael, eds. Methods in Neurosciences Vol. 19: Ion Channels of Excitable Cells. (Illus.). 387p. 1994. text 104.00 (*0-12-185287-3*) Acad Pr.

Narain, A., et al, eds. Fluids Engineering Division: Proceedings, ASME International Mechanical Engineering Congress & Exposition, Dallas, TX, 1997. LC 97-76714. (FED Ser.: Vol. 244). 524p. 1997. pap. 170.00 (*0-7918-1838-1*, TA357) ASME Pr.

Narain, A. K. Studies in Buddhist Art of South Asia. (Illus.). 140p. 1986. 48.00 (*0-8364-1852-2*, Pub. by Usha) S Asia.

Narain, Brij. Indian Economic Life Past & Present. 1990. reprint ed. 22.00 (*81-85395-81-0*, Pub. by BR Pub) S Asia.

Narain, Dharm. Studies on Indian Agriculture. Raj, K. N. et al, eds. 264p. 1990. 17.95 (*0-19-562106-9*) OUP.

Narain, Igbal & Atal, Yogesh. Social Sciences & the Government: The Asian Scene. (C). 1987. 20.00 (*81-7062-032-5*, Pub. by Lancer India) S Asia.

Narain, Iqbal. Literature, Social Consciousness & Polity. Lutze, L., ed. (C). 1987. 17.00 (*81-85054-21-5*, Pub. by Manohar) S Asia.

— Pages from a Vice-Chancellor's Diary. 1990. 21.50 (*81-7001-080-2*, Pub. by Chanakya) S Asia.

— Political Dimensions of Development. (C). 1994. 18.50 (*81-7033-253-2*, Pub. by Rawat Pubns) S Asia.

Narain, Iqbal & Mathur, P. C. Politics in Changing India. (C). 1994. text 34.00 (*81-7033-227-3*, Pub. by Rawat Pubns) S Asia.

Narain, K. An Outline of Madhva Philosophy. 241p. 1986. 39.95 (*0-318-37015-8*) Asia Bk Corp.

Narain, K. S., jt. auth. see Gava, E.

***Narain, Kirti.** Press, Politics & Society: Uttar Pradesh, 1885-1914. LC 98-905069. 1998. 20.00 (*81-7304-223-3*, Pub. by Manohar) S Asia.

Narain, Lakshimi, jt. auth. see Ball, Andrew.

Narain, Lakshmi, jt. auth. see Ball, Andrew.

Narain, Laxmi. Parliament & Public Enterprise in India. 1979. text 20.00 (*0-685-14088-1*) Coronet Bks.

Narain, N. V., jt. ed. see Chakravarty, S. R.

***Narain, Partap.** Subedar to Field Marshal. LC 99-931519. 1999. 44.00 (*81-7049-072-3*, Pub. by Manas Pubns) S Asia.

Narain, R. B. Buddhist Remains in Afghanistan. 68p. 1991. 12.00 (*0-685-62631-8*, Pub. by Kala Prakashan) Nataraj Bks.

Narain, Sanjai, jt. auth. see Rothenberg, Jeff.

Narain, Udai. Reagan's Nuclear Terrorism. 1985. 18.50 (*0-8364-1312-1*, Pub. by Deep & Deep Pubns) S Asia.

Narain, Virendra, jt. ed. see Chakravarty, S. R.

Naraine, Bishnu, jt. auth. see Miller, Don.

Naraine, Gayatri & Strano, Anthony. Living Values: A Guidebook. (Illus.). 110p. (Orig.). (C). 1995. pap. text. write for info. (*1-886872-09-0*) Brahma Kumaris.

— Living Values Statements. Gill-Kozul, Carol, ed. (Illus.). 85p. 1995. pap. text. write for info. (*1-886872-01-5*) Brahma Kumaris.

Naral Foundation Staff. Choices: Women Speak Out about Abortion. 1998. pap. 14.95 (*0-9662262-0-8*) Nat Abort & Repro.

Narang, A. S. Democracy, Development & Distortion: Punjab Politics in National Perspective. 1986. 22.00 (*0-8364-1537-X*, Pub. by Gitanjali Prakashan) S Asia.

— Punjab Accord & Elections Retrospect & Prospect. 1986. pap. 8.50 (*0-8364-1796-8*, Pub. by Minerva) S Asia.

Narang, C. L. History of Punjabi: Literature. 210p. 1987. 26.50 (*0-8364-2076-4*, Pub. by Usha) S Asia.

Narang, Gopi C. Rajinder Singh Bedi: Selected Short Stories. (C). 1989. 12.50 (*0-8364-2620-7*, Pub. by Indian Pubs) S Asia.

— Urdu: Readings in Literary Urdu Prose. LC 70-2757. 396p. reprint ed. pap. 122.80 (*0-608-11005-1*, 200465700045) Bks Demand.

Narang, Harish, jt. auth. see Mehta, Gurleena.

Narang, Harish, ed. see Rahman, Tariq.

Narang, P. K., jt. auth. see Cutler, N. R.

Narang, Rajanini, ed. see Barber, Ezekiel.

Narang, S. K. & Sharma, S. L. A Text Book of Physical Education & Sports. 188p. 1996. pap. 60.00 (*81-209-0975-5*, Pub. by Pitambar Pub) St Mut.

Narang, S. Karl, et al, eds. Applications of Genetics to Arthropods of Biological Control Significance. LC 00-976. 224p. 1994. lib. bdg. 125.00 (*0-8493-2607-9*) CRC Pr.

Narang, Saloni. The Coloured Bangles & Other Stories. LC 83-50208. 78p. (C). 1984. 17.00 (*0-89410-403-9*, Three Contnts); pap. 8.00 (*0-89410-404-7*, Three Contnts) L Rienner.

— Khadi & the Bullet. 1991. text 30.00 (*0-7069-5603-6*, Pub. by Vikas) S Asia.

Narang, Sandhya. Coping with Role Conflicts: Employed Married Women. 156p. 1996. pap. 113.00 (*81-85880-96-4*, Pub. by Print Hse) St Mut.

Narang, Satya P., ed. Modern Evaluation of the Mahabharata: Sharma Felicitation Volume. LC 95-900349. (C). 1995. 54.00 (*81-7081-291-7*, Pub. by Nag Pubs) S Asia.

Narang, Satya P., jt. ed. see Kulshreshtha, Sushma.

Narang, Satyapal, jt. auth. see Kulshreshtha, Sushma.

Narang, V. P. & Batra, Vijay K. Ayakar Vidhi ke Tatva (Elements of Income Tax Law in Hindi) 852p. 1980. 90.00 (*0-7855-1359-0*) St Mut.

— Elements of Income Tax Law. 817p. 1979. 75.00 (*0-7855-1361-2*) St Mut.

Naranjo. Mud Woman: Poems from the Clay. LC 91-16611. (Sun Tracks Ser.: Vol. 20). (Illus.). 127p. (Orig.). 1992. pap. 17.95 (*0-8165-1281-7*) U of Ariz Pr.

Naranjo, C. A. & Sellers, Edward M., eds. Novel Pharmacological Interventions for Alcoholism. (Illus.). xv, 378p. 1991. 82.95 (*0-387-97741-4*) Spr-Verlag.

Naranjo, Carmen. There Never Was a Once upon a Time. Miller, Yvette E., ed. Britt, Linda, tr. from SPA. & intro. by. LC 89-12822. (Illus.). 94p. 1989. pap. 11.50 (*0-935480-41-2*) Lat Am Lit Rev Pr.

Naranjo, Claudio. Character & Neurosis: An Integrative View. LC 94-21263. 352p. (Orig.). 1994. pap. 21.95 (*0-89556-066-6*) Gateways Bks & Tapes.

— The Divine Child & the Hero: Inner Meaning in Children's Literature. (Illus.). 168p. 1997. pap. 15.95 (*0-89556-109-3*) Gateways Bks & Tapes.

— The End of Patriarchy: And the Dawning of a Tri-Une Society. LC 94-77707. 156p. 1998. pap. 14.95 (*1-56937-065-6*) Amber Lotus.

— Enneatypes in Psychotherapy. LC 94-77115. 160p. (Orig.). 1995. pap. 14.95 (*0-934252-47-5*, Pub. by Hohm Pr) SCB Distributors.

— Gestalt Therapy: The Attitude & Practice of an Atheoretical Experientialism. 352p. 1993. 29.95 (*0-89556-090-9*) Gateways Bks & Tapes.

— Transformation Through Insight: Enneatypes in Clinical Practice. LC 97-1010. (Illus.). 544p. (Orig.). 1997. pap. 24.95 (*0-934252-73-4*, Pub. by Hohm Pr) SCB Distributors.

Naranjo, Efren. Lucha Obrera de Cuba. LC 91-75690. (Coleccion Cuba y sus Jueces). (SPA.). 80p. (Orig.). 1992. pap. 9.95 (*0-89729-621-4*) Ediciones.

Naranjo-Morse, Nora. Mud Woman: Poems from the Clay. LC 91-16611. (Sun Tracks Ser.: Vol. 20). (Illus.). 127p. (Orig.). 1992. 38.50 (*0-8165-1248-5*) U of Ariz Pr.

Naranjo, N. Venezuela & Its Ruler. 1976. lib. bdg. 59.95 (*0-8490-2794-2*) Gordon Pr.

Naranjo, Tito. A Day with a Pueblo. LC 98-54143. (Day with Ser.). 48p. (J). (gr. 5-7). 1999. 22.60 (*0-8225-1919-4*, Runestone Pr) Lerner Pub.

Narasaiah, P. V. Sericulture in India. (C). 1992. 34.00 (*81-7024-508-7*, Pub. by Ashish Pub Hse) S Asia.

N

*__Narasaiah, P. V. & Raju.__ Rural Development & Anti-Poverty Programme. 1999. 32.00 (*81-7141-470-2*, Pub. by Discovery Pub Hse) S Asia.

Narashima, R., jt. ed. see Liepmann, Hans W.

*__Narashima, Tomo.__ Spider: A Larger Than Life 3-D Book. (Giant Look at Little Bugs Ser.). (Illus.). (J). 2000. 9.95 (*1-58117-097-1*, Piggy Toes Pr) Intervisual Bks.

Narasimha, N. S. & Babaji, Ramananda. The Way of Vaisnava Sages: A Medieval Story of South Indian Sadhus. LC 86-28251. (Sanskrit Notes of Visnu-vijay Swami Ser.). 422p. (Orig.). 1987. lib. bdg. 59.50 (*0-8191-6060-1*) U Pr of Amer.

Narasimhacharya. History of Kannada Literature: Readership Lectures. 1988. reprint ed. 8.00 (*81-206-0303-6*, Pub. by Asian Educ Servs) S Asia.

Narasimhaiah, C. D. Indian Critical Scene: Controversial Essays. 1990. 36.00 (*81-7018-599-8*, Pub. by BR Pub) S Asia.

*__Narasimhaiah, C. D.__ Swan & the Eagle: Essays on Indian English Literature. 3rd ed. 1999. pap. 16.00 (*81-7094-338-8*, Pub. by Vision) S Asia.

*__Narasimham, R. K.__ Human Rights & Social Justice. 1999. 52.00 (*81-7169-570-1*, Pub. by Commonwealth) S Asia.

Narasimham, Raji, jt. auth. see Sertha, Reajei.

Narasimhamurty, T. S. Photoelastic & Electro-Optic Properties of Crystals. LC 79-409. (Illus.). 544p. 1981. 110.00 (*0-306-31101-1*, Plenum Trade) Perseus Pubng.

Narasimhan. Poems to Shiva. 19.00 (*0-06-066080-5*) HarpC.

— Poems to Vishnu the Lord. 20.00 (*0-06-066079-1*) HarpC.

— Sea Principles of Continuum Mechanics. 584p. 1994. pap. text 189.95 (*0-471-12131-2*) Wiley.

Narasimhan, C. R. Rajagopalachari: A Biography. 260p. 1992. 35.00 (*81-7027-156-8*, Pub. by Radiant Pubs) S Asia.

Narasimhan, C. V. United Nations: An Inside View. 1995. 32.00 (*0-7069-9682-8*, Pub. by Vikas) S Asia.

*__Narasimhan, C. V., et al.__ The Mahabharata: An English Version Based on Selected Verses. LC 98-148375. (Illus.). 1998. text 16.50 (*0-231-02624-2*) Col U Pr.

Narasimhan, Chakravarthi V. Mahabharata: An English Version Based on Selected Verses. rev. ed. LC 98-148375. 254p. 1997. pap. 18.50 (*0-231-11055-3*) Col U Pr.

Narasimhan, K. S., jt. ed. see Cadle, Terry.

*__Narasimhan, M. Jeersannidi.__ Paradox Trilogies, Vol. 1. 1998. pap. write for info. (*0-7541-0509-1*, Pub. by Minerva Pr) Unity Dist.

Narasimhan, Murali K., jt. ed. see Yallup, Kevin.

Narasimhan, Mysore N. Principles of Continuum Mechanics. 584p. 1992. 139.00 (*0-471-54000-5*) Wiley.

Narasimhan, Raghavan. Analysis of Real & Complex Manifolds. 2nd rev. ed. (North-Holland Mathematical Library: Vol. 25). 246p. 1986. 137.00 (*0-444-87776-2*, North Holland) Elsevier.

— Compact Riemann Surfaces. LC 92-19717. (Lectures in Mathematics ETH Zurich). v, 120p. 1992. pap. 32.50 (*3-7643-2742-1*) Birkhauser.

— Compact Riemann Surfaces. LC 92-19717. (Lectures in Mathematics ETH Zurich Ser.). v, 120p. 1996. 32.50 (*0-8176-2742-1*) Birkhauser.

— Several Complex Variables. LC 75-166949. (Chicago Lectures in Mathematics). 184p. (Orig.). 1974. pap. text 22.00 (*0-226-56817-2*) U Ch Pr.

— Several Complex Variables. LC 75-166949. (Chicago Lectures in Mathematics). (Orig.). 1992. lib. bdg. 7.00 (*0-226-56816-4*) U Ch Pr.

Narasimhan, Raghavan, ed. A Perspective in Theoretical Computer Science. 456p. (C). 1989. pap. 37.00 (*9971-5-0926-1*); text 113.00 (*9971-5-0925-3*) World Scientific Pub.

Narasimhan, Raji. The Sky Changes: A Novel. 1991. 8.00 (*81-7018-664-1*, Pub. by BR Pub) S Asia.

Narasimhan, Ram, jt. auth. see Carter, Joseph R.

Narasimhan, Ram, jt. auth. see Melnyk, Steven.

Narasimhan, Ram, jt. auth. see Melnyk, Steven A.

Narasimhan, Rangaswamy. Language Behaviour: Acquisition & Evolutionary History. LC 97-45132. (Language & Development Ser.). 219p. 1998. write for info. (*0-7619-9232-4*) Sage.

Narasimhan, Sakuntala. Empowering Women: An Alternative Strategy from Rural India LC 99-17497. 1999. 0.00 (*0-7619-9341-X*) Sage.

Narasimhan, Seetharama L., et al. Production Planning & Inventory Control. 2nd ed. LC 94-22418. 752p. (C). 1994. text 74.20 (*0-13-186214-6*) P-H.

*__Narasimhan, Shankar & Jordache, Cornelius.__ Data Reconciliation & Gross Error Detection: An Intelligent Use of Process Data. LC 99-44868. 406p. 1999. 95.00 (*0-88415-255-3*) Gulf Pub.

Narasimhan, T. N., ed. Recent Trends in Hydrogeology. LC 82-2872. (Geological Society of America, Special Paper: No. 189). (Illus.). 456p. reprint ed. pap. 141.40 (*0-7837-1850-0*, 204205000001) Bks Demand.

Narasin, Rochelle M., jt. auth. see Yang, Sunny.

Narasinga, Rao. Kisamwar Glossary of Kannada Words. (ENG & KAN.). 1985. 24.95 (*0-8288-1768-5*, M7860) Fr & Eur.

Narasingha, P. Sil. Swami Vivekananda: A Reassessment. LC 96-29425. (Illus.). 256p. 1997. 41.50 (*0-945636-97-0*) Susquehanna U Pr.

Narasingha, Swami B. G. The Authorized Sri Caitanya-Saraswata Parampara. (Illus.). 248p. 1999. 14.95 (*1-886069-05-0*, Pub. by Mandala Pub Grp) Bookpeople.

Narasingha, Swami B. G., ed. Sri Gayatri Mantrartha Dipika: Illuminations on the Essential Meaning of Gayatri Mantra. (Illus.). 210p. 1999. 14.95 (*1-886069-00-X*, Pub. by Mandala Pub Grp) Bookpeople.

Narasu, P. Lakshmi. The Essence of Buddhism. 212p. 1986. reprint ed. 15.00 (*0-8364-1748-8*, Pub. by Manohar) S Asia.

— A Study of Caste. (C). 1988. reprint ed. 15.00 (*81-206-0411-3*, Pub. by Asian Educ Servs) S Asia.

Naravane, M. S. Forts of Maharashtra. LC 95-904814. (Illus.). xx, 508p. (C). 1995. 99.00 (*81-7024-696-2*, Pub. by Ashish Pub Hse) Nataraj Bks.

— The Maritime & Coastal Forts of India. LC 97-906960. (Illus.). xvi, 196p. (C). 1998. 39.00 (*81-7024-910-4*, Pub. by APH Pubng) Nataraj Bks.

Naravane, Vishwanath S. A Cultural History of Modern India. (C). 1991. 23.00 (*81-85119-92-9*, Pub. by Northern Bk Ctr) S Asia.

Naravane, Vishwanath S. Sarojini Naidu: An Introduction to Her Life, Work & Poetry. 1996. reprint ed. 14.00 (*81-250-0931-0*, Pub. by Orient Longman Ltd) S Asia.

*__Naray, Peter.__ Russia & the World Trade Organization. LC 00-33290. 2000. write for info. (*0-312-23773-1*) St Martin.

Naray-Szabo, Gabor, et al. Applied Quantum Chemistry. (C). 1987. text 294.00 (*90-277-1901-2*) Kluwer Academic.

Naray-Szabo, Gabor, jt. ed. see Simon, K.

Narayan, Anand, et al. Study of Effect of Machining Parameters on Performance of Worm Gears. (Technical Papers: Vol. 95FTM14). (Illus.). 9p. 1995. pap. text 30.00 (*1-55589-663-4*) AGMA.

Narayan, B. K. Mohammad the Prophet of Islam. 205p. 1978. 29.95 (*0-318-37191-X*) Asia Bk Corp.

— Saint Shah Waris Ali & Sai Baba. (C). 1995. 14.00 (*0-7069-8755-1*, Pub. by Vikas) S Asia.

Narayan, B. K. & Sawhney, Rajeev. Dialogues of Kabir. 1998. 16.00 (*81-259-0651-7*, Pub. by Vikas) S Asia.

— Dialogues of the Sufi Mystic Bawa Muhaiyaddeen. LC 98-915425. 203 p. 1999. 32.00 (*81-259-0612-6*, Pub. by Vikas); pap. 15.00 (*81-259-0686-X*, Pub. by Vikas) S Asia.

Narayan, C. Giri. Group Invariance in Statistical Inference. LC 97-125954. 250p. 1996. text 48.00 (*981-02-1875-3*) World Scientific Pub.

Narayan Das, Ram. Sterling Dictionary of Anthropology. (C). 1997. pap. write for info. (*81-7359-068-0*) Sterling Pubs.

Narayan, Deepa. The Contribution of People's Participation: Evidence from 121 Rural Water Supply Projects. LC 94-34109. (Environmentally Sustainable Development Occasional Papers: No. 1). 116p. 1995. pap. 22.00 (*0-8213-3043-8*, 13043) World Bank.

— Participatory Evaluation: Tools for Managing Change in Water & Sanitation. LC 93-4478. (Technical Papers: No. 207). 136p. 1993. pap. 22.00 (*0-8213-2477-2*, 12477) World Bank.

— Toward Participatory Research. LC 95-45755. (Technical Papers: No. 307). 276p. 1996. pap. 22.00 (*0-8213-3473-5*) World Bank.

— Voices of the Poor: Poverty & Social Capital in Tanzania. LC 97-34898. (Environmentally & Socially Sustainable Development Studies & Monographs: No. 20). 96p. 1997. pap. 22.00 (*0-8213-4061-1*, 14061) World Bank.

Narayan, Deepa & Ebbe, Katrinka. Design of Social Funds: Participation, Demand-Orientation, & Local Organizational Capacity. LC 97-18345. (Discussion Paper Ser.: No. 375). 85p. 1997. pap. 22.00 (*0-8213-4019-0*, 14019) World Bank.

*__Narayan, Deepa & Petesch, Patti L., eds.__ Voices of the Poor: From Many Lands. (World Bank Publications). 300p. 2000. 25.00 (*0-19-521603-2*, 61603) OUP.

Narayan, Deepa & Srinivasan, Lyra. Participatory Development Tool Kit: Materials to Facilitate Community Empowerment. 1994. pap. 40.00 (*0-8213 2687-2*, 12687) World Bank.

*__Narayan, Deepa & Walton, Michael, eds.__ Voices of the Poor Vol. 1: Can Anyone Hear Us? (A World Bank Publication). 360p. 2000. 25.00 (*0-19-521601-6*, 61601) OUP.

*__Narayan, Deepa, et al.__ Voices of the Poor: Crying Out for Change. (World Bank Publications). 200p. 2000. 15.00 (*0-19-521602-4*, 61602) OUP.

Narayan, Deepa, jt. auth. see Rietbergen-McCracken, Jennifer.

Narayan, Giddu. As the River Joins the Ocean: Reflections about J. Krishnamurti. Narsipur, Chandramouli, ed. & notes by. LC 98-71018. (Illus.). 96p. 1998. per. 14.95 (*0-9649247-5-7*) Edwin Hse.

Narayan, J. P. Towards Total Revolution: Writings of Jayaprakash Narayan, 4 vols., Set. (C). 1978. 34.00 (*0-8364-2547-2*, Pub. by Popular Prakashan) S Asia.

Narayan, Jagdish, et al, eds. High Temperature Superconductors - Fundamental Properties & Novel Materials Processing Vol. 169: Materials Research Society Symposium Proceedings. 1321p. 1990. text 17.50 (*1-55899-057-7*) Materials Res.

Narayan, Kirin. Earth into Gold: Himalayan Foothill Folktales told by Urmila Devi Sood. LC 96-27891. (Illus.). 288p. 1997. pap. 15.95 (*0-19-510349-1*); text 55.00 (*0-19-510348-3*) OUP.

— Love, Stars & All That. Rosenman, Jane, ed. 320p. 1995. pap. 10.00 (*0-671-79396-9*) PB.

— Storytellers, Saints, & Scoundrels: Folk Narrative in Hindu Religious Teaching. LC 89-31363. (Publications of the American Folklore Society, Bibliographical & Special Ser.). (Illus.). 296p. (C). 1989. pap. text 16.50 (*0-8122-1269-X*) U of Pa Pr.

Narayan, M. R. Tigers of Lanka: From Boys to Guerrillas. LC 94-906525. (C). 1995. reprint ed. 36.00 (*81-220-0386-9*, Pub. by Konark Pubs) S Asia.

Narayan, Mary C., et al. Telephone Triage for Home Care. LC 97-37808. 350p. Date not set. 149.00 (*0-8342-0978-0*, S478) Aspen Pub.

Narayan, P. B., jt. auth. see Brar, A. S.

Narayan, Perin. The New Dalda Cook Book. (Illus.). 200p. 1978. 11.95 (*0-7069-0377-3*) Asia Bk Corp.

Narayan, R. K. The Bachelor of Arts. 268p. 1980. pap. 15.00 (*0-226-56833-4*) U Ch Pr.

— Critical Perspectives. McLeod, A. L., ed. (C). 1994. write for info. (*81-207-1623-X*) Sterling Pubs.

— The Dark Room. LC 80-39930. 214p. (C). 1981. pap. 10.95 (*0-226-56837-7*) U Ch Pr.

— The English Teacher. LC 80-16374. 184p. 1980. pap. 15.00 (*0-226-56835-0*) U Ch Pr.

— The Financial Expert. LC 81-3020. 224p. (C). 1981. pap. 13.00 (*0-226-56841-5*) U Ch Pr.

— The Financial Expert. LC 81-3020. 224p. (C). 1995. lib. bdg. 18.00 (*0-226-56840-7*) U Ch Pr.

— Gods, Demons & Others. LC 92-43997. (Illus.). 252p. (Orig.). (C). 1993. pap. 15.00 (*0-226-56825-3*) U Ch Pr.

— Grandmother's Tale And Selected Stories. LC 98-3489. 320p. 1999. reprint ed. pap. 16.00 (*0-88001-624-8*) HarpC.

— The Guide. 224p. 1992. pap. 12.95 (*0-14-018547-X*, Penguin Classics) Viking Penguin.

Narayan, R. K. Indian Thought: A Miscellany. LC 97-904971. 1997. write for info. (*0-14-026951-7*) Penguin Books.

Narayan, R. K. The Mahabharata. (C). 1989. reprint ed. 8.00 (*81-7094-001-X*, Pub. by Vision) S Asia.

*__Narayan, R. K.__ The Mahabharata: A Shortened Modern Prose Version of the Indian Epic. LC 00-33776. 2000. pap. write for info. (*0-226-56822-9*) U Ch Pr.

Narayan, R. K. Malgudi Days. 256p. 1995. pap. 11.95 (*0-14-018543-7*, Penguin Classics) Viking Penguin.

— Malgudi Days II. 1999. pap. write for info. (*0-670-80632-3*) Viking Penguin.

— The Man-Eater of Malgudi. 176p. 1993. pap. 16.99 (*0-14-018548-8*, Penguin Classics) Viking Penguin.

— Mr. Sampath: The Printer of Malgudi. LC 80-27352. 220p. (C). 1981. pap. 10.95 (*0-226-56839-3*) U Ch Pr.

— My Days: A Memoir. LC 98-14082. 192p. 1999. reprint ed. 14.00 (*0-88001-625-6*) HarpC.

— The Ramayana. 190p. (C). 1998. pap. 9.95 (*0-14-018700-6*) Addson-Wesley Educ.

— Swami & Friends. LC 80-16119. 192p. 1980. pap. 14.00 (*0-226-56831-8*) U Ch Pr.

— Swami & Friends. LC 80-16119. 192p. 1994. lib. bdg. 13.00 (*0-226-56829-6*) U Ch Pr.

— A Tiger for Malgudi. 160p. 1994. pap. 10.95 (*0-14-018545-3*, Penguin Classics) Viking Penguin.

— Under the Banyan Tree. 208p. 1993. pap. 10.95 (*0-14-018544-5*, Penguin Classics) Viking Penguin.

— Waiting for the Mahatma. LC 81-3075. 256p. (C). 1981. reprint ed. pap. 12.95 (*0-226-56828-8*) U Ch Pr.

— Waiting for the Mahatma. LC 81-3075. 256p. (C). 1996. reprint ed. lib. bdg. 18.00 (*0-226-56826-1*) U Ch Pr.

Narayan, Raj K., et al, eds. Neurotrauma. (Illus.). 1728p. 1996. text 245.00 (*0-07-045662-3*) McGraw-Hill HPD.

Narayan, S. Anthropological & Archaeological Research & Development LC 98-915992. 199 p. 1999. write for info. (*81-212-0619-7*) Gian Publng Hse.

Narayan, S., ed. Buddhism in World Peace. 1990. 21.50 (*81-210-0251-6*, Pub. by Inter-India Pubns) S Asia.

— Jharkhand Movement: Origin & Evolution. (Tribal Studies of India Series T: No. 157). (C). 1992. 23.50 (*81-210-0290-7*, Pub. by Inter-India Pubns) S Asia.

Narayan, Uma. Dislocating Cultures: Third World Feminism & the Politics of Knowledge. LC 97-12405. (Thinking Gender Ser.). 176p. 1997. pap. 17.99 (*0-415-91419-1*) Routledge.

— Dislocating Cultures: Third World Feminism & the Politics of Knowledge. LC 97-12405. (Thinking Gender Ser.). 176p. (C). 1997. 70.00 (*0-415-91418-3*) Routledge.

Narayan, Uma & Bartkowiak, Julia, eds. Having & Raising Children: Unconventional Families, Hard Choices, & the Social Good. LC 98-39336. 232p. 1999. 47.50 (*0-271-01886-0*); pap. 17.95 (*0-271-01887-9*) Pa St U Pr.

*__Narayan, Uma & Harding, Sandra.__ Decentering the Center: Philosophy for a Multicultural, Postcolonial & Feminist World. LC 99-53662. (Hypatia Book Ser.). 336p. 2000. pap. 16.95 (*0-253-21384-3*); lib. bdg. 39.95 (*0-253-33737-2*) Ind U Pr.

Narayan, Uma, jt. auth. see Shanley, Mary L.

Narayan, Vijay. Venereal Diseases: A Social Dilemma. (Illus.). 345p. (C). 1985. 32.95 (*0-317-66157-4*) Asia Bk Corp.

Narayana. Animal Fables of India. Hutchins, Francis G., tr. from SAN. & afterword by by. LC 85-71820. (Illus.). 269p. 1985. 26.00 (*0-935100-03-2*); pap. 12.00 (*0-935100-04-0*) Amarta Pr.

Narayana, Asha, jt. auth. see Singer, Daniel R.

Narayana, C. S. Contemporary Studies in Organizational Behaviour. (Dynamic Organisational Behaviour Ser.). (C). 1991. 34.00 (*81-7141-117-7*) S Asia.

Narayana, Dhruva, et al. Analog Computer Simulation of the Runoff Characteristics of an Urban Watershed. LC 77-141023. 88p. 1969. 19.00 (*0-403-04522-3*) Scholarly.

Narayana, N. S. S., ed. see Srinivasan, T. N.

Narayana, P. S. Commentaries on Indian Easements Act, 1882. (C). 1988. 100.00 (*0-7855-4786-X*) St Mut.

— The Consumer Protection Act. (C). 1990. 100.00 (*0-89771-193-9*) St Mut.

Narayana, P. S., ed. Law of Specific Relief. (C). 1990. 100.00 (*0-89771-240-4*) St Mut.

Narayana, P. S., jt. auth. see Rao, V. S.

*__Narayana Prasad.__ Prasna Upanisad: With the Original Text in Sanskrit & Roman Transliteration. LC 99-936802. 1999. pap. 14.00 (*81-246-0129-1*, Pub. by D K Printwrld) S Asia.

*__Narayana, Rao Nannapaneni, abr.__ Elements of Engineering Electromagnetics. 5th ed. LC 98-52162. 788p. 1999. 100.00 (*0-13-013201-2*, Prentice Hall) P-H.

Narayana Reddy, G. Women & Child Development: Some Contemporary Issues. (C). 1987. 22.00 (*0-317-68214-8*, Pub. by Chugh Pubns) S Asia.

Narayanan. Concrete Structures. (C). 1994. 86.95 (*0-582-06450-3*, Pub. by Addison-Wesley) Longman.

Narayanan, A. Sampath, jt. auth. see Bartold, P. Mark.

Narayanan, Ajit. On Being a Machine: Formal Aspects of Artificial Intelligence, Vol. 1. 192p. 1988. text 41.95 (*0-470-21235-7*) P-H.

Narayanan, Ajit & Sharkey, Noel E. An Introduction to LISP. LC 85-21847. (Artificial Intelligence Ser.). 277p. 1985. pap. text 29.95 (*0-470-20244-0*) P-H.

Narayanan, Ajit, jt. auth. see Asady, Raad A.

Narayanan, Gomathi. The Sahibs & the Natives. 174p. 1986. 18.50 (*81-7001-016-0*, Pub. by Chanakya) S Asia.

Narayanan, H. Submodular Functions & Electrical Networks. LC 97-4313. (Annals of Discrete Mathematics Ser.). 680p. 1997. 164.00 (*0-444-82523-1*) Elsevier.

Narayanan, Leila. Ethnicity in Urban Context. (C). 1989. 32.00 (*81-7033-071-8*, Pub. by Rawat Pubns) S Asia.

Narayanan, R., ed. Composite Steel Structures: Proceedings of the International Conference on Steel Aluminium Structures Cardiff, U. K., 8-10 July, 1987. 178p. 1987. mass mkt. 77.95 (*1-85166-122-0*) Elsevier.

— Steel-Framed Structures: Stability & Strength. 352p. 1985. mass mkt. 151.50 (*0-85334-329-2*) Elsevier.

— Steel Structures - Advances, Design & Construction: Proceedings of the International Conference on Steel & Aluminum Structures, Cardiff, U. K., 8-10 July, 1987. 860p. 1987. mass mkt. 257.95 (*1-85166-120-4*) Elsevier.

— Structural Connections: Stability & Strength. (Illus.). 269p. 1985. mass mkt. 164.95 (*1-85166-288-X*) Elsevier.

— Structures Subjected to Repeated Loading: Stability & Strength. 286p. 1991. mass mkt. 166.50 (*1-85166-567-6*) Elsevier.

Narayanan, R. & Roberts, T., eds. Structures Subjected to Dynamic Loading: Stability & Strength. 342p. 1991. mass mkt. 156.50 (*1-85166-582-X*) Elsevier.

*__Narayanan, R. S. & Beeby, A. W.__ Introduction to Design for Civil Engineers. LC 00-44548. (Illus.). 2000. pap. write for info. (*0-419-23550-7*, E & FN Spon) Routledge.

Narayanan, R. S., jt. auth. see Beeby, A. W.

Narayanan, Ram M. & Kalshoven, James E., eds. Advances in Laser Remote Sensing for Terrestrial & Hydrographic Applications. (Proceedings of SPIE Ser.: Vol. 3382). 188p. 1998. 59.00 (*0-8194-2831-0*) SPIE.

— Advances in Laser Remote Sensing for Terrestrial & Oceanographic Applications. LC 98-111059. 33p. 1997. pap. 69.00 (*0-8194-2474-9*) SPIE.

Narayanan, Ranga, jt. ed. see Shyy, Wei.

*__Narayanan, S. Naru & Liu, Juhne.__ Enterprise Java Developer's Guide. LC 99-14561. (Developer's Guide Ser.). (Illus.). 500p. 1999. pap. 49.99 incl. cd-rom (*0-07-134673-2*) McGraw.

Narayanan, Sampat, jt. auth. see Asopa, V. N.

Narayanan, Sampat, jt. ed. see Vatsyayan, Kapila.

Narayanan, T. K. Nyayasara of Bhasarvajna: A Critical Study. (C). 1992. text 20.00 (*81-7099-391-1*, Pub. by Mittal Pubs Dist) S Asia.

Narayanan, Usha. Sweet & Sour: Burmese Short Stories. LC 98-915881. xvi, 173 p. 1999. write for info. (*81-207-2141-1*) Sterling Pubs.

*__Narayanan, V. K.__ Managing Technology & Innovation for Competitive Advantage. 528p. 2000. 80.00 (*0-13-030506-5*) P-H.

Narayanan, V. K. & Nath, Raghu. Organization Theory: A Strategic Approach. LC 92 31180. 608p. (C). 1993. text 71.35 (*0-256-08778-4*, Irwn McGrw-H) McGrw-H Hghr Educ.

Narayanan, V. N. Tryst with Terror. (C). 1996. 20.00 (*81-202-0470-0*, Pub. by Ajanta) S Asia.

Narayanan, Vasudha. The Vernacular Veda: Revelation, Recitation, & Ritual. LC 93-44400. 260p. (C). 1994. text 42.95 (*0-87249-965-0*) U of SC Pr.

Narayanan, Vasudha & Creel, Austin B., eds. Monastic Life in the Christian & Hindu Traditions: A Comparative Study. LC 90-30951. (Studies in Comparative Religion: Vol. 3). (Illus.). 608p. 1990. lib. bdg. 129.95 (*0-88946-502-9*) E Mellen.

Narayanan, Vasudha, jt. auth. see Carman, John.

Narayanan, Vijay K., jt. auth. see Titus, James G.

Narayanananda, Swami. The Primal Power in Man: The Kundalini Shakti. 155p. 1996. reprint ed. spiral bd. 15.00 (*0-7873-0631-2*) Hlth Research.

Narayanasamy, P. Plant Pathogen Detection & Disease Diagnosis. LC 97-23414. (Books in Soils, Plants & the Environment: Vol. 59). (Illus.). 344p. 1997. text 145.00 (*0-8247-0040-6*) Dekker.

*__Narayanasamy, Punitha.__ Poverty & Food Security of Small Farm Households in South India: Impact of Various Policy Instruments. 280p. 1999. pap. 29.95 (*3-8258-2968-5*, Pub. by CE24) Transaction Pubs.

Narayanaswami, P. P., jt. auth. see Gaskill, Herbert S.

Narayanaswamy, M. Commentary on Law Relating to Insecticides in India. (C). 1988. 175.00 (*0-7855-4792-4*) St Mut.

Narayani, Lucy L., jt. auth. see Sivananda Yoga Center Staff.

Narazaki. Ukiyo-E Masterpieces in European Collections Vol. 7: Musee Guimet II, Paris, Vol. 7. LC 87-81680. 286p. 1991. 300.00 (*0-87011-878-1*) Kodansha.

Narazaki, Muneshige. Sharaku: Masterworks of Ukiyo-E. Abiko, Bonnie F., tr. (Illus.). 96p. 1995. 40.00 (*4-7700-1910-6*) Kodansha.

— Ukiyo-E Masterpieces in European Collections Vol. 6: Musee Guimet I, Paris, Vol. 6. (UKIYO-E Ser.). (Illus.). 280p. 1990. 300.00 (*0-87011-877-3*) Kodansha.

An Asterisk (*) at the beginning of an entry indicates that the title is appearing for the first time.

— Ukiyo-E Masterpieces in European Collections Vol. 8: Bibliotheque Nationale, Paris, Vol. 8. (UKIYO-E Ser.). (Illus.). 284p. 1990. 300.00 *(0-87011-879-X)* Kodansha.

Narazaki, Muneshige, contrib. by. Ukiyo-E Masterpieces in European Collections: Museum fur Ostasiatische Kunst, Berlin, Vol. 12. LC 87-81680. (Illus.). 260p. 1988. 300.00 *(0-87011-882-X)* Kodansha.

— Ukiyo-E Masterpieces in European Collections: Victor & Albert Museum, I, Vol. 4. LC 87-81680. (Illus.). 280p. 1989. 300.00 *(0-87011-875-7)* Kodansha.

— Ukiyo-E Masterpieces in European Collections Vol. 9: Musees Royaux d'Art et D'Histoire, Vol. 9. (Illus.). 272p. 1989. 300.00 *(0-87011-880-3)* Kodansha.

Narazaki, Muneshige, ed. Ukiyo-E Masterpieces in European Collections Vol. 3: British Museum III. LC 87-81680. (Illus.). 278p. 1989. 300.00 *(0-87011-874-9)* Kodansha.

— Ukiyo-E Masterpieces in European Collections Vol. 11: Museo d'Arte Orientale, Genoa II, Vol. 11. 260p. 1989. 300.00 *(0-87011-881-1)* Kodansha.

Narbeth, Colin, ed. Admiral Seymour's Expedition & Taku Forts, 1900. 88p. (C). 1987. 60.00 *(0-902633-69-4*, Pub. by Picton) St Mut.

Narbikova, Valeri I. Day Equals Night. Graham, Seth, tr. 195p. 1998. 32.00 *(0-87501-174-8)* Ardis Pubs.

— In the Here & There. Gessen, Masha, tr. from ENG. LC 97-6324. 200p. 1998. 32.00 *(0-87501-154-3)* Ardis Pubs.

***Narbikova, Valeria.** Day Equals Night. Graham, Seth, tr. 160p. 1999. 32.00 *(0-87501-117-9)* Ardis Pubs.

Narbo, Don. Flying Saucers: Opposing Viewpoints. LC 95-30344. (Great Mysteries Ser.). (Illus.). 112p. (J). (gr. 5-12). 1996. lib. bdg. 22.45 *(1-56510-351-3)* Greenhaven.

Narboni, Jean, ed. see Godard, Jean-Luc.

Narcejac, Thomas. The Living & the Dead. Boileau, Pierre, ed. 20.95 *(0-8488-0175-X)* Amereon Ltd.

Narcejac, Thomas, jt. auth. see Boileau, Pierre.

Narcisco, John, jt. auth. see Burkett, David.

Narcisi & Montanari. Conflict of Laws in Italy. LC 97-4505. 1997. 41.00 *(90-411-0999-4)* Kluwer Law Intl.

Narciso, John & Burkett, David. Relating Redefined: Discovering the New Language for Living. rev. ed. LC 94-225652. (Illus.). 127p. (C). 1994. pap. text 17.95 *(1-879797-01-1)* Redman Wright.

Narciss, Georg. Knaurs Woerterbuch der Medizin. 2nd ed. (GER.). 574p. 1988. 59.95 *(0-7859-8358-9*, 3426263610) Fr & Eur.

Narconon International Staff, jt. auth. see Hernandez, Robert.

Narcowich, Francis J. & Fulling, Stephen A. Wigner Distribution Functions. (Discourses in Mathematics & Its Applications Ser.). iii, 45p. (Orig.). 1994. pap. 6.00 *(0-9630728-1-1)* TX A&M Dept Math.

Narcowich, Francis J., jt. ed. see Fulling, S. A.

Nard, M. Le, see De Hertogh, A. & Le Nard, M., eds.

Nardantonio, Dennis N. Sound Studio Production Techniques. (Illus.). 288p. 1989. 28.95 *(0-8306-9250-9)*; pap. 19.95 *(0-8306-3250-6)* McGraw-Hill Prof.

Nardelli, G. F., jt. ed. see Maradudin, A. A.

Narden, Joyce C. Imaginative Activities for Today's Students. 29p. 1991. spiral bd. 4.05 *(0-939507-16-1*, B307) Amer Classical.

Nardi, Adriano & Meucci, Antonella. The Children's World Pictorial Atlas of the World. (Illus.). 48p. (J). (gr. 2 up). 1998. 11.95 *(0-7641-5062-6)* Barron.

Nardi, Annette M. Mother Bear's Christmas Dilemma. 2nd ed. LC 97-226312. (Illus.). 24p. (Orig.). (J). (ps-3). 1996. per. 7.95 *(0-9648150-0-1)* TRI-CAR Pubns.

Nardi, Bonnie A. A Small Matter of Programming: Perspectives on End User Computing. LC 93-9124. (Illus.). 178p. 1993. 31.50 *(0-262-14053-5)* MIT Pr.

Nardi, Bonnie A., ed. Context & Consciousness: Activity Theory & Human-Computer Interaction. LC 95-10974. (Illus.). 414p. (C). 1995. 48.50 *(0-262-14058-6)* MIT Pr.

Nardi, Bonnie A. & O'Day, Vicki. Information Ecologies: Using Technology with Heart. LC 98-29318. (Illus.). 208p. 1999. 27.50 *(0-262-14066-7)* MIT Pr.

***Nardi, Bonnie A. & O'Day, Vicki.** Information Ecologies: Using Technology with Heart. (Illus.). 246p. 2000. reprint ed. pap. 15.95 *(0-262-64042-2)* MIT Pr.

***Nardi, Dario.** Character & Personality Type: Discovering Your Uniqueness for Career & Relationship Success. (Understanding Yourself & Others Ser.). (Illus.). 76p. 1999. 11.95 *(0-9664624-6-7)* Telos Pubns.

Nardi, Dario, jt. auth. see Berens, Linda V.

Nardi, G. L., jt. auth. see Cordiano, C.

Nardi, Jim. Close Encounters with Insects & Spiders. LC 87-26284. (Illus.). 204p. (Orig.). 1988. 21.95 *(0-8138-1978-4)* Iowa St U Pr.

***Nardi, Katy, ed.** National Needs in Ionizing Radiation Measurements & Standards: Second Report. (Illus.). 106p. (C). 2000. reprint ed. pap. text 35.00 *(0-7881-8517-9)* DIANE Pub.

Nardi, Ken. Why Dogs Bite: How to Prevent My Dog from Becoming a Biter. Gile, Dave, ed. (Illus.). 26p. 1998. pap. 3.95 *(0-9664819-0-9)* Nardi.

Nardi, Peter. Gay Men's Friendships: Invincible Communities. LC 98-49657. 216p. 1999. pap. 15.00 *(0-226-56849-0)*; lib. bdg. 36.00 *(0-226-56843-1)* U Ch Pr.

Nardi, Peter, et al, eds. Growing up Before Stonewall: Life Stories of Some Gay Men. LC 93-20939. (Illus.). 240p. (C). (gr. 13). 1994. 75.00 *(0-415-10151-4)*; pap. 22.99 *(0-415-10152-2)* Routledge.

Nardi, Peter M., ed. Men's Frendships. (Research on Men & Masculinities Ser.: Vol. 2). (Illus.). 320p. 1992. 58.00 *(0-8039-3773-3)*; pap. 26.00 *(0-8039-3774-1)* Sage.

Nardi, Peter M. & Schneider, Beth E. Social Perspectives in Lesbian & Gay Studies: A Reader. LC 97-2918. (Illus.). 640p. (C). 1998. 85.00 *(0-415-16708-6)*; pap. 27.99 *(0-415-16709-4)* Routledge.

Nardi, R. V., jt. auth. see Cocchetto, David M.

Nardi, Thomas. Karate & Judo. (J). 1997. pap. text 5.95 *(0-8172-6854-5)* Raintree Steck-V.

***Nardi, William A.** How to Solve Algebra Word Problems. 3rd ed. (Illus.). 192p. 2000. pap. text 10.95 *(0-02-863744-5*, Arco) Macmillan Gen Ref.

Nardin, Jane. He Knew She Was Right: The Independent Woman in the Novels of Anthony Trollope. LC 88-15785. (Ad Feminam Ser.). 254p. (C). 1989. text 31.95 *(0-8093-1484-3)* S Ill U Pr.

— Those Elegant Decorums: The Concept of Propriety in Jane Austen's Novels. LC 73-4821. 168p. (C). 1973. text 29.50 *(0-87395-236-7)* State U NY Pr.

— Trollope & Vicorian Moral Philosophy. LC 95-33251. 179p. 1996. 34.95 *(0-8214-1139-X)* Ohio U Pr.

Nardin, Terry. Ethics of War & Peace: Religious & Secular Perspectives. 296p. 1996. pap. text 17.95 *(0-691-05840-7*, Pub. by Princeton U Pr) Cal Prin Full Svc.

Nardin, Terry & Mapel, David R., eds. Traditions of International Ethics. (Studies in International Relations: No. 17). 342p. (C). 1993. pap. text 22.95 *(0-521-45757-2)* Cambridge U Pr.

Nardin, Terry, jt. auth. see Mapel, David.

Nardine, Arlene. In Search of the Yellow Submarine. 222p. 1985. pap. write for info. *(0-88144-065-5)* Christian Pub.

Nardinelli, Clark. Child Labor & the Industrial Revolution. LC 89-46001. 207p. 1990. pap. 64.20 *(0-608-05037-7*, 205969800004) Bks Demand.

Nardini, Gloria. Che Bella Figura! The Power of Performance in an Italian Ladies' Club in Chicago. LC 99-19064. (SUNY Series in Speech Communication & SUNY Series in Italian - American Studies). 164p. (C). 1999. text 59.50 *(0-7914-4091-5)*; pap. text 19.95 *(0-7914-4092-3)* State U NY Pr.

Nardini, Jerry, ed. see Olsen, Brad.

Nardini, Robert F. Asbestos: An Annotated Bibliography. (CompuBibs Ser.: No. 14). 1986. pap. 15.00 *(0-914791-13-3)* Vantage Info.

Nardini, William, ed. see Caldwell, Robert G.

Nardo, Anna K. The Ludic Self in Seventeenth-Century English Literature. LC 90-44797. (SUNY Series, the Margins of Literature). 263p. (C). 1991. pap. text 21.95 *(0-7914-0722-5)* State U NY Pr.

— Milton's Sonnets & the Ideal Community. LC 79-17221. 227p. reprint ed. pap. 70.40 *(0-7837-1824-1*, 204202400001) Bks Demand.

Nardo, Don. The Age of Augustus. LC 96-14183. (World History Ser.). (Illus.). (J). (gr. 4-12). 1996. lib. bdg. 22.45 *(1-56006-306-8)* Lucent Bks.

***Nardo, Don.** Ancient Greece. LC 99-86966. 2000. lib. bdg. write for info. *(0-7377-0425-X)* Greenhaven.

Nardo, Don. Ancient Greece. LC 93-6904. (World History Ser.). 112p. (J). (gr. 6-9). 1994. lib. bdg. 22.45 *(1-56006-229-0)* Lucent Bks.

***Nardo, Don.** The Ancient Greeks. LC 00-8760. (Lost Civilizations Ser.). (J). 2000. write for info. *(1-56006-705-5)* Lucent Bks.

— The Ancient Romans. LC 00-8650. (Lost Civilizations Ser.). (Illus.). (J). 2000. write for info. *(1-56006-706-3)* Lucent Bks.

Nardo, Don. Anxiety & Phobias. (Encyclopedia of Health Ser.). (Illus.). 116p. (YA). (gr. 7 up). 1992. lib. bdg. 19.95 *(0-7910-0041-9)* Chelsea Hse.

— The Assyrian Empire. LC 97-50166. (World History Ser.). (Illus.). 96p. (YA). (gr. 7 up). 1998. lib. bdg. 22.45 *(1-56006-313-0)* Lucent Bks.

— The Battle of Marathon: Battles of the Ancient World. LC 95-11710. (Battle Ser.). (Illus.). 112p. (J). (gr. 7-9). 1996. lib. bdg. 26.20 *(1-56006-412-9)* Lucent Bks.

— The Battle of Zama: Battles of the Ancient World. LC 95-11760. (Battle Ser.). (Illus.). 112p. (YA). (gr. 5-12). 1996. lib. bdg. 26.20 *(1-56006-420-X)* Lucent Bks.

***Nardo, Don.** The Black Death. LC 98-44752. (Turning Points in World History Ser.). 288p. (gr. 7-12). 1999. lib. bdg. 27.45 *(1-56510-995-3)* Greenhaven.

— The Black Death. LC 98-44752. (Turning Points in World History Ser.). 220p. 1999. pap. 17.45 *(1-56510-994-5)* Greenhaven.

Nardo, Don. Braving the New World: From the Arrival of the Enslaved Africans to the American Revolution (1619-1784) LC 94-2963. 128p. (J). (gr. 5 up). 1994. pap. 8.95 *(0-7910-2685-X)* Chelsea Hse.

— Braving the New World: From the Arrival of the Enslaved Africans to the American Revolution (1619-1784) LC 94-2963. 128p. (YA). (gr. 5 up). 1994. lib. bdg. 19.95 *(0-7910-2259-5)* Chelsea Hse.

— Caesar's Conquest of Gaul. LC 95-16225. (World History Ser.). (Illus.). 112p. (YA). (gr. 7 up). 1996. lib. bdg. 22.45 *(1-56006-301-7)* Lucent Bks.

— Charles Darwin. LC 99-19093. (People Who Made History Ser.). 144p. (YA). (gr. 9-12). 2000. lib. bdg. 27.45 *(0-7377-0081-5)* Greenhaven.

— Charles Darwin. LC 99-19093. (People Who Made History Ser.). (Illus.). 144p. (YA). (gr. 9-12). 2000. pap. 17.45 *(0-7377-0080-7)* Greenhaven.

***Nardo, Don.** Cleopatra. LC 99-85743. (People Who Made History Ser.). 2000. pap. write for info. *(0-7377-0322-9)* Greenhaven.

Nardo, Don. The Collapse of the Roman Republic. LC 97-10492. (World History Ser.). (Illus.). (YA). (gr. 4-12). 1997. lib. bdg. 22.45 *(1-56006-456-0)* Lucent Bks.

— The Declaration of Independence: A Model for Individual Rights. LC 98-7338. (Words That Changed History Ser.). (Illus.). (YA). (gr. 4-7). 1998. lib. bdg. 23.70 *(1-56006-368-8)* Lucent Bks.

***Nardo, Don.** The Decline & Fall of Ancient Greece. LC 99-36891. (Turning Points in World History Ser.). 288p. 2000. pap. 13.96 *(0-7377-0240-0)* Greenhaven.

— The Decline & Fall of Ancient Greece. LC 99-36891. (Turning Points in World History Ser.). 288p. (YA). 2000. 17.45 *(0-7377-0241-9)* Greenhaven.

Nardo, Don. The Decline & Fall of the Roman Empire. LC 97-49334. (World History Ser.). (Illus.). 112p. (YA). (gr. 7 up). 1998. lib. bdg. 22.45 *(1-56006-314-9)* Lucent Bks.

— Democracy. LC 93-4912. (Overview Ser.). (J). (gr. 5-8). 1994. lib. bdg. 22.45 *(1-56006-147-2)* Lucent Bks.

— Dinosaurs: Unearthing the Secrets of Ancient Beasts. (Encyclopedia of Discovery & Invention Ser.). (Illus.). 96p. (J). (gr. 5-8). 1994. lib. bdg. 23.70 *(1-56006-253-3)* Lucent Bks.

— Eating Disorders. LC 91-15563. (Overview Ser.). (Illus.). 112p. (YA). (gr. 5-8). 1991. lib. bdg. 22.45 *(1-56006-129-4)* Lucent Bks.

***Nardo, Don.** Egyptian Mythology. LC 00-8513. (Mythology Ser.). (YA). 2000. write for info. *(0-7660-1407-X)* Enslow Pubs.

— France LC 99-12685. 2000. 32.00 *(0-516-21052-1)* Childrens.

Nardo, Don. Franklin D. Roosevelt. LC 94-37511. (Great Achievers Ser.). 1995. pap. 10.01 *(0-7910-2407-5)* Chelsea Hse.

— Franklin D. Roosevelt. LC 94-37511. (Great Achievers Ser.). (Illus.). 120p. (YA). (gr. 5 up). 1996. lib. bdg. 19.95 *(0-7910-2406-7)* Chelsea Hse.

— The French Revolution. LC 98-16604. (Turning Points in World History Ser.). 223p. (YA). (gr. 9-12). 1998. pap. 17.45 *(1-56510-933-3)* Greenhaven.

***Nardo, Don.** Games of Ancient Rome. LC 99-33783. (Way People Live Ser.). (Illus.). 112p. (YA). (gr. 6-9). 2000. lib. bdg. 23.70 *(1-56006-655-5)* Lucent Bks.

— The Great Depression. LC 99-28801. (Turning Points in World History Ser.). 288p. (YA). (gr. 9-12). 2000. pap. 17.45 *(0-7377-0230-3)*; lib. bdg. 27.45 *(0-7377-0231-1)* Greenhaven.

— Greece. LC 99-41295. (Overview Ser.). (Illus.). 144p. (YA). (gr. 6-9). 2000. lib. bdg. 23.70 *(1-56006-587-7)* Lucent Bks.

Nardo, Don. Greek & Roman Mythology. LC 97-7481. (World History Ser.). (Illus.). 112p. (YA). (gr. 4-12). 1997. lib. bdg. 22.45 *(1-56006-308-4)* Lucent Bks.

— Greek & Roman Science. LC 97-22336. (World History Ser.). (Illus.). 128p. (YA). (gr. 4-12). 1997. lib. bdg. 22.45 *(1-56006-317-3)* Lucent Bks.

***Nardo, Don.** Greek & Roman Sport. LC 98-39636. (World History Ser.). (Illus.). 128p. (YA). 1999. lib. bdg. 23.70 *(1-56006-436-6)* Lucent Bks.

Nardo, Don. Greek & Roman Theatre: World History Ser. LC 94-6459. (Illus.). 128p. (YA). (gr. 5 up). 1995. lib. bdg. 22.45 *(1-56006-249-5)* Lucent Bks.

— Greek Drama. LC 99-29775. (Literary Companion Ser.). 144p. (YA). (gr. 9-12). 2000. 27.95 *(0-7377-0207-9)* Greenhaven.

***Nardo, Don.** Greek Drama. LC 99-29775. (Literary Companion Ser.). 144p. (YA). (gr. 9-12). 2000. pap. 17.45 *(0-7377-0206-0)* Greenhaven.

Nardo, Don. Julius Caesar. LC 96-14186. (Importance of Ser.). (Illus.). (J). (gr. 4-12). 1996. lib. bdg. 22.45 *(1-56006-083-2)* Lucent Bks.

— Life in Ancient Athens. LC 99-24576. (Way People Live Ser.). (Illus.). 112p. (YA). (gr. 6-9). 2000. lib. bdg. 23.70 *(1-56006-494-3)* Lucent Bks.

— Life in Ancient Greece. LC 95-30504. (Way People Live Ser.). (Illus.). 112p. (J). (gr. 5-12). 1996. lib. bdg. 22.45 *(1-56006-327-0)* Lucent Bks.

— Life in Ancient Rome. LC 96-14184. (Way People Live Ser.). (Illus.). 112p. (YA). 1996. lib. bdg. 22.45 *(1-56006-335-1)* Lucent Bks.

— Life of a Roman Slave. LC 97-46715. (Way People Live Ser.). (YA). (gr. 7 up). 1998. lib. bdg. 22.45 *(1-56006-388-2)* Lucent Bks.

***Nardo, Don.** The Life of a Roman Soldier. LC 00-9161. (Way People Live Ser.). 2000. write for info. *(1-56006-679-2)* Lucent Bks.

Nardo, Don. The Medieval Castle. LC 97-34638. (Building History Ser.). (Illus.). 96p. (YA). (gr. 4-12). 1997. lib. bdg. 22.45 *(1-56006-430-7)* Lucent Bks.

— The Mexican-American War. LC 99-14263. (World History Ser.). (Illus.). 128p. (YA). (gr. 4-12). 1999. lib. bdg. 23.70 *(1-56006-495-1)* Lucent Bks.

— Modern Japan. (World History Ser.). (Illus.). 112p. (J). (gr. 5-9). 1995. lib. bdg. 22.45 *(1-56006-281-9*, 2819) Lucent Bks.

***Nardo, Don.** North American Indian Wars. LC 98-47353. (Turning Points in World History Ser.). 220p. 1999. pap. 17.45 *(1-56510-958-9)* Greenhaven.

Nardo, Don. North American Indian Wars. LC 98-47353. (Turning Points in World History Ser.). 221p. (YA). (gr. 9 up). 1999. lib. bdg. 27.45 *(1-56510-959-7)* Greenhaven.

***Nardo, Don.** Origin of Species: Darwin's Theory of Evolution. LC 00-9681. (Words That Changed History Ser.). 2001. lib. bdg. write for info. *(1-56006-801-9)* Lucent Bks.

Nardo, Don. Ozone. LC 91-6275. (Overview Ser.). (Illus.). 112p. (YA). (gr. 5-8). 1991. lib. bdg. 22.45 *(1-56006-101-4)* Lucent Bks.

— The Parthenon of Ancient Greece. LC 98-4279. (Building History Ser.). (Illus.). 96p. (YA). (gr. 5 up). 1998. lib. bdg. 23.70 *(1-56006-431-5)* Lucent Bks.

— The Persian Empire. LC 97-3081. (World History Ser.). (Illus.). (J). (gr. 4-12). 1997. lib. bdg. 22.45 *(1-56006-320-3)* Lucent Bks.

— The Persian Gulf War. LC 91-23064. (America's Wars Ser.). (Illus.). 112p. (J). (gr. 5-8). 1991. lib. bdg. 26.20 *(1-56006-411-0)* Lucent Bks.

***Nardo, Don.** Philip II & Alexander the Great Unify Greece in World History. LC 99-37004. (In World History Ser.). (Illus.). 112p. (gr. 5 up). 2000. lib. bdg. 20.95 *(0-7660-1399-5)* Enslow Pubs.

Nardo, Don. Population. LC 90-23525. (Overview Ser.). (Illus.). 112p. (YA). (gr. 5-8). 1991. lib. bdg. 22.45 *(1-56006-123-5)* Lucent Bks.

— The Punic Wars. LC 95-11713. (World History Ser.). (Illus.). 112p. (YA). (gr. 7 up). 1996. lib. bdg. 22.45 *(1-56006-417-X)* Lucent Bks.

— Readings on "Frankenstein" LC 99-29029. (Literary Companion Ser.). 224p. (YA). (gr. 9-12). 2000. pap. 17.45 *(0-7377-0182-X)* Greenhaven.

***Nardo, Don.** Readings on "Frankenstein" LC 99-29029. (Literary Companion Ser.). 127p. (YA). (gr. 9-12). 2000. lib. bdg. 27.45 *(0-7377-0183-8)* Greenhaven.

— Readings on Medea. LC 00-26429. (Literary Companion to World Literature Ser.). 2000. pap. write for info. *(0-7377-0403-9)* Greenhaven.

— Readings on "Othello" LC 99-29219. (Literary Companion Ser.). 224p. (YA). (gr. 9-12). 2000. pap. 17.45 *(0-7377-0186-2)*; lib. bdg. 27.45 *(0-7377-0187-0)* Greenhaven.

— The Rise of Christianity. LC 00-9243. (World History Ser.). 2001. write for info. *(1-56006-808-6)* Lucent Bks.

Nardo, Don. The Roman Colosseum. LC 97-2839. (Building History Ser.). (Illus.). (YA). (gr. 4-12). 1997. lib. bdg. 22.45 *(1-56006-429-3)* Lucent Bks.

***Nardo, Don.** The Roman Empire. LC 00-25740. (Turning Points in World History Ser.). 2000. pap. write for info. *(0-7377-0372-5)* Greenhaven.

— Roman Roads & Aqueducts. LC 00-9155. (Building History Ser.). (Illus.). 2000. write for info. *(1-56006-721-7)* Lucent Bks.

— Rulers of Ancient Rome. LC 98-3841. (History Makers Ser.). (Illus.). 144p. (YA). (gr. 4-12). 1998. lib. bdg. 23.70 *(1-56006-356-4)* Lucent Bks.

— Scientists of Ancient Greece. LC 98-3842. (History Makers Ser.). (Illus.). 144p. (YA). (gr. 4-12). 1998. lib. bdg. 23.70 *(1-56006-362-9)* Lucent Bks.

Nardo, Don. The Scopes Trial. (Famous Trials Ser.). (Illus.). (YA). 1996. lib. bdg. 22.45 *(1-56006-268-1)* Lucent Bks.

— Teen Sexuality. LC 96-8696. (Overview Ser.). (Illus.). (YA). (gr. 4-12). 1996. lib. bdg. 22.45 *(1-56006-189-8)* Lucent Bks.

— Thomas Jefferson. LC 92-43913. (Importance of Ser.). (Illus.). 112p. (J). (gr. 5-8). 1993. lib. bdg. 22.45 *(1-56006-037-9)* Lucent Bks.

— The Trial of Joan of Arc. LC 97-9871. (Famous Trials Ser.). (Illus.). (YA). 1997. lib. bdg. 22.45 *(1-56006-466-8)* Lucent Bks.

— The Trial of Socrates. LC 96-20407. (Famous Trials Ser.). (Illus.). (YA). 1996. lib. bdg. 22.45 *(1-56006-267-3)* Lucent Bks.

— The U. S. Congress. LC 93-41137. (Overview Ser.). (Illus.). (YA). (gr. 5-8). 1994. lib. bdg. 22.45 *(1-56006-155-3)* Lucent Bks.

— The U. S. Presidency. (Overview Ser.). (Illus.). (YA). (gr. 5-8). 1995. lib. bdg. 22.45 *(1-56006-157-X)* Lucent Bks.

— Vitamins & Minerals. (Encyclopedia of Health Ser.). (Illus.). 116p. (YA). (gr. 7 up). 1994. lib. bdg. 19.95 *(0-7910-0032-X)* Chelsea Hse.

***Nardo, Don.** Walt Disney. LC 99-16772. (Importance of...Ser.). (Illus.). 128p. (YA). (gr. 6-9). 2000. lib. bdg. 23.70 *(1-56006-605-9)* Lucent Bks.

— The War Against Iraq. LC 00-9318. 2001. write for info. *(1-56006-715-2)* Lucent Bks.

— The War of 1812. LC 99-14587. (World History Ser.). (Illus.). 128p. (YA). (gr. 8 up). 2000. lib. bdg. 23.70 *(1-56006-581-8)* Lucent Bks.

— Women Leaders of Nations. LC 98-35810. (History Makers Ser.). (Illus.). 144p. (YA). (gr. 4-12). 1998. lib. bdg. 23.70 *(1-56006-397-1)* Lucent Bks.

— Women of Ancient Greece. LC 99-53699. (World History Ser.). 128p. (J). (gr. 4-12). 2000. 18.96 *(1-56006-646-6)* Lucent Bks.

Nardo, Don, ed. The American Revolution. LC 97-49627. (Opposing Viewpoints Digests Ser.). 143p. (YA). (gr. 8 up). 1998. pap. 17.96 *(1-56510-754-3)*; lib. bdg. 22.45 *(1-56510-755-1)* Greenhaven.

— The Bill of Rights. LC 97-27519. (Opposing Viewpoints Digests Ser.). (YA). (gr. 4-12). 1997. pap. 13.70 *(1-56510-740-3)* Greenhaven.

— The Fall of the Roman Empire. LC 97-25205. (Opposing Viewpoints Digests Ser.). (YA). (gr. 4-12). 1997. pap. 13.70 *(1-56510-738-1)*; lib. bdg. 22.45 *(1-56510-739-X)* Greenhaven.

— The French Reformation. LC 98-16604. (Turning Points in World History Ser.). 223p. (YA). (gr. 9-12). 1998. lib. bdg. 27.45 *(1-56510-934-1)* Greenhaven.

— The Great Depression. LC 97-31173. (Opposing Viewpoints Digests Ser.). 128p. (YA). (gr. 7 up). 1997. pap. 13.70 *(1-56510-742-X)*; lib. bdg. 22.45 *(1-56510-743-8)* Greenhaven.

— Julius Caesar. LC 98-29762. (Literary Companion Ser.). 176p. (YA). (gr. 9-12). 1998. pap. 17.45 *(1-56510-852-3)*; lib. bdg. 27.45 *(1-56510-853-1)* Greenhaven.

— Readings on Antigone. LC 98-51924. (Literary Companion Ser.). 224p. 1999. lib. bdg. 27.45 *(1-56510-969-4)* Greenhaven.

— Readings on Antigone. LC 98-51924. (Literary Companion Ser.). 127p. 1999. pap. 17.45 *(1-56510-968-6)* Greenhaven.

— Readings on Homer. LC 97-9458. (Literary Companion Ser.). 176p. 1997. pap. 16.20 *(1-56510-638-5)* Greenhaven.

— Readings on Homer. LC 97-9458. (Literary Companion Ser.). 176p. (YA). (gr. 9-12). 1997. lib. bdg. 26.20 *(1-56510-639-3)* Greenhaven.

— Readings on Romeo & Juliet. LC 97-10491. (Literary Companion Ser.). (YA). (gr. 9-12). 1997. pap. 16.20 *(1-56510-646-6)*; lib. bdg. 26.20 *(1-56510-647-4)* Greenhaven.

N

An Asterisk (*) at the beginning of an entry indicates that the title is appearing for the first time.

— The Rise of Christianity. LC 98-17499. (Turning Points in World History Ser.). (YA). (gr. 9-12). 1998. lib. bdg. 27.45 (*1-56510-963-5*) Greenhaven.

*__Nardo, Don, ed.__ The Rise of Christianity. LC 98-17499. (Turning Points in World History Ser.). (YA). (gr. 9-12). 1998. pap. 17.45 (*1-56510-962-7*) Greenhaven.

Nardo, Don, ed. The Rise of Nazi Germany. LC 98-8404. (Turning Points in World History Ser.). (YA). (gr. 9-12). 1998. lib. bdg. 27.45 (*1-56510-965-1*) Greenhaven.

*__Nardo, Don, ed.__ The Rise of Nazi Germany. LC 98-8404. (Turning Points in World History Ser.). (YA). (gr. 9-12). 1998. pap. 17.45 (*1-56510-964-3*) Greenhaven.

Nardo, Don, ed. Sophocles. LC 96-18327. (Literary Companion Ser.). 1996. pap. 13.96 (*1-56510-581-8*) Greenhaven.

— A Tale of Two Cities. LC 97-5019. (Literary Companion Ser.). (YA). (gr. 9-12). 1997. pap. 16.20 (*1-56510-648-2*); lib. bdg. 26.20 (*1-56510-649-0*) Greenhaven.

*__Nardo, Don, et al.__ Leaders of Ancient Greece. LC 99-18176. (History Makers Ser.). (Illus.). 128p. (YA). (gr. 4-12). 1999. lib. bdg. 23.70 (*1-56006-543-5*) Lucent Bks.

Nardo, Don, ed. see Shakespeare, William.

Nardo, Don, jt. ed. see Siebold, Tom.

Nardo, Paolo Di, see Claycomb, William C. & Di Nardo, Paolo, eds.

Nardocchio, Elaine F., ed. Reader Response to Literature: The Empirical Dimension. LC 92-35778. (Approaches to Semiotics Ser.: No. 108). xiv, 313p. (C). 1993. lib. bdg. 129.25 (*3-11-012764-4*) Mouton.

Nardon, J. David. Bridge & Structure Estimating. LC 95-23949. 698p. 1996. 85.00 (*0-07-045669-0*) McGraw.

Nardone, Giorgio. Brief Strategic Solution-Oriented Therapy of Phobic & Obsessive Disorders. LC 95-52096. 1996. 45.00 (*1-56821-804-4*) Aronson.

*__Nardone, Giorgio.__ Brief Strategic Therapy (A1) 2000. write for info. (*0-7657-0280-0*) Aronson.

Nardone, M. A., ed. Accounting. 428p. (C). 1990. pap. 50.00 (*1-85352-582-0*, Pub. by HLT Pubns); pap. 50.00 (*1-85352-020-9*, Pub. by HLT Pubns) St Mut.

— Solicitors' Accounts. 204p. (C). 1990. pap. 65.00 (*1-85352-897-8*, Pub. by HLT Pubns) St Mut.

*__Nardone, Mary S.__ Direct Digital Control Systems. LC 99-12053. viii, 252 p. 1999. write for info. (*0-412-14821-8*) Chapman & Hall.

Nardone, Nancy K., jt. ed. see Frankel, Walter A.

Nardone, Richard M. The Story of the Christian Year. 1991. pap. 9.95 (*0-8091-3277-X*) Paulist Pr.

Nardozzi, Charlie & National Gardening Association Editors, The. Vegetable Gardening for Dummies. 2nd ed. LC 98-89728. (For Dummies Ser.). (Illus.). 384p. 1999. pap. 16.99 (*0-7645-5129-9*) IDG Bks.

Narducci, L. M., et al, eds. Lasers & Quantum Optics. (CIF Ser.: Vol. 13). 420p. (C). 1990. text 138.00 (*9971-5-0952-0*) World Scientific Pub.

Narducci, L. M. & Abraham, N. B. Laser Physics & Laser Instabilities. 320p. (C). 1988. text 71.00 (*9971-5-0062-0*); pap. text 37.00 (*9971-5-0063-9*) World Scientific Pub.

Narducci, L. M., jt. ed. see Machado, M. A.

Nardulli. Democracy Practice. 2000. pap. text. write for info. (*0-312-18783-1*) St Martin.

— University of Illinois. 1997. pap. text, lab manual ed. 13.95 (*0-312-17070-X*) St Martin.

Nardulli, Peter F., ed. The Constitution & American Political Development: An Institutional Perspective. 344p. 1992. text 39.95 (*0-252-01787-0*); pap. text 17.95 (*0-252-06174-8*) U of Ill Pr.

— Diversity, Conflict, & State Politics: Regionalism in Illinois. LC 88-18719. 352p. 1989. text 34.95 (*0-252-01576 2*); pap. text 19.95 (*0-252-06036-9*) U of Ill Pr.

Narduzzi, James L. Mental Health among Elderly Native Americans. LC 93-34972. (Studies on the Elderly in America). 248p. 1993. text 30.00 (*0-8153-1568-6*) Garland.

NAREA Staff. Appraisal Guide & Instructions for Completing the New Condominium Form. 20p. (Orig.). 1995. pap. 25.00 (*0-614-23696-7*) Todd Pub.

— Residential Appraiser's Handbook. 158p. (Orig.). 1995. pap. 29.50 (*0-614-23692-4*) Todd Pub.

Narell, Irena. History's Choice: A Writer's Journey from Poland to America. Browning, Peter, ed. 160p. (Orig.). 1996. pap. 11.95 (*0-934764-03-4*) Akiba Pr.

— Joshua: Fighter for Bar Kochba. LC 78-55959. (J). (gr. 6-12). 1978. pap. 5.95 (*0-934764-01-8*) Akiba Pr.

— Our City: The Jews of San Francisco. 1981. 25.00 (*0-317-61576-9*) Akiba Pr.

Naremore, James. Acting in the Cinema. 316p. 1988. pap. 16.95 (*0-520-07194-8*, Pub. by U CA Pr) Cal Prin Full Svc.

— Acting in the Cinema. (C). 1988. 45.00 (*0-520-06228-0*, Pub. by U CA Pr) Cal Prin Full Svc.

*__Naremore, James.__ Film Adaptation. LC 99-45923. (Depth of Field Ser.). (Illus.). 304p. (C). 2000. pap. text 20.00 (*0-8135-2814-3*) Rutgers U Pr.

Naremore, James. The Films of Vincente Minnelli. LC 92-39912. (Cambridge Film Classics Ser.). (Illus.). 214p. (C). 1993. text 54.95 (*0-521-38366-8*); pap. text 14.95 (*0-521-38770-1*) Cambridge U Pr.

— The Magic World of Orson Welles. LC 89-42895. (Illus.). 328p. 1989. reprint ed. pap. 14.95 (*0-87074-299-X*) SMU Press.

— More Than Night: Film Noir in Its Contexts. LC 97-33090. 342p. 1998. 45.00 (*0-520-21293-2*, Pub. by U CA Pr); pap. 19.95 (*0-520-21294-0*, Pub. by U CA Pr) Cal Prin Full Svc.

*__Naremore, James, ed.__ Film Adaptation. LC 99-45923. (Depth of Field Ser.). (Illus.). 304p. (C). 2000. text 52.00 (*0-8135-2813-5*) Rutgers U Pr.

Naremore, James, ed. Treasure of Sierra Madre. LC 78-53298. (Screenplay Ser.). (Illus.). 206p. 1979. pap. 9.95 (*0-299-07684-9*) U of Wis Pr.

Naremore, James & Brantlinger, Patrick, eds. Modernity & Mass Culture. LC 90-41881. (Illus.). 288p. 1991. 39.95 (*0-253-33968-5*); pap. 15.95 (*0-253-20627-8*, MB-627) Ind U Pr.

Naremore, James, ed. see Hitchcock, Alfred.

*__Naremore, Rita C.__ Assessment & Treatment Resource Manual for School-Age Language Disorders. (Illus.). 2000. pap. 49.95 (*0-7693-0056-1*) Singular Publishing.

Naremore, Rita C. Language Intervention with School-Aged Children: Conversation Narrative, & Text. (Illus.). 292p. (Orig.). (C). 1994. pap. text 49.95 (*1-56593-222-6*, 0582) Thomson Learn.

Naremore, Rita C. & Hooper, Robert. Children Learning Language. LC 97-6678. 240p. 1997. 39.95 (*1-56593-856-9*, 1674) Thomson Learn.

*__Narena, Tammy.__ This Great Love to Cherish. (Illus.). 64p. 1999. pap. 12.50 (*1-929319-00-2*) Sean & I Pubg.

*__Narendran, Paliath & Rusinowitch, M., eds.__ Rewriting Techniques & Applications: Proceedings, 10th International Conference, RTA'99, Trento, Italy, July 2-4, 1999. LC 99-34032. (Lecture Notes in Computer Science Ser.: Vol. 1631). xi, 397p. 1999. pap. 69.00 (*3-540-66201-4*) Spr-Verlag.

Narens, Louis. Abstract Measurement Theory. 344p. 1985. 45.00 (*0-262-14037-3*) MIT Pr.

Narey, Wayne, ed. Medieval Dramatic Continuity in Shakespeare's Plays. 288p. 2001. pap. 28.95 (*0-8143-2602-1*) Wayne St U Pr.

Narez, Jesus. Materiales Arqueologicos de Tlapacoya. 149p. 1990. pap. 9.00 (*968-6487-18-2*, IN030) UPLAAP.

*__NarFreitag, Burkhard.__ Transactions & Change in Logic Databases: International Seminar on Logic Database & the Meaning of Change, Vol.147. LC 98-32082. (Lecture Notes in Computer Science Ser.). 1998. 67.00 (*3-540-65305-8*) Spr-Verlag.

Nargolkar, Vasant, ed. & tr. see Bhave, Vinoba.

Nariai, K. & Matsui, Y. Fundamentals of Practical Aberration Theory - Fundamental Knowledge & Techniques. 192p. 1993. text 61.00 (*981-02-1349-2*) World Scientific Pub.

Narici, Lawrence, et al. Functional Analysis & Valuation Theory. (Pure & Applied Mathematics Ser.: Vol. 5). (Illus.). 200p. 1971. text 135.00 (*0-8247-1484-9*) Dekker.

Narici, Lawrence, jt. auth. see Bachman, George.

Narici, Lawrencel & Beckenstein, Edward. Topological Vector Spaces. (Pure & Applied Mathematics Ser.: Vol. 95). (Illus.). 432p. 1985. text 175.00 (*0-8247-7315-2*) Dekker.

Narikawa, Hirotoshi & Takimoto, Teruko. Purr-fect Shiatsu: Tender Touches for the 90s Cat. (Illus.). 96p. (Orig.). 1993. pap. 9.95 (*1-881267-07-5*) Intercultural.

Nariman, Gushtaspshah K. Literary History of Sanskrit Buddhism. LC 78-70106. reprint ed. 37.50 (*0-404-17356-X*) AMS Pr.

Nariman, Gushtaspshah K., tr. see Harshadeva.

Nariman, Heidi N. Soap Operas for Social Change: Toward a Methodology for Entertainment-Education Television. LC 92-36547. (Media & Society Ser.). 184p. 1993. 49.95 (*0-275-94389-5*, C4389, Praeger Pubs) Greenwood.

Nariman, J. K. Literary History of Sanskrit Buddhism: From Winternitz, Sylvain Levi, Huber. (C). 1992. reprint ed. text 16.00 (*81-208-0795-2*, Pub. by Motilal Bnarsidass) S Asia.

Narine. Psychology: The Adaptive Mind. (Psychology Ser.). 1996. pap., student ed. 17.25 (*0-534-33853-4*) Brooks-Cole.

Narine, Dalton, ed. see Douglas, Bobb.

*__Narins, Brigham, ed.__ World of Health. LC 99-31918. (Illus.). 1424p. 2000. 99.00 (*0-7876-3649-5*) Gale.

Narins, Brigham, et al, eds. Contemporary Literary Criticism. (Contemporary Literary Criticism Ser.: Vol. 94). 500p. 1996. text 150.00 (*0-7876-0767-3*) Gale.

*__Narins, Brigham & Stanley, Deborah A.__ Contemporary Literary Criticism, Vol. 108. 500p. 1998. text 150.00 (*0-7876-2031-9*) Gale.

Narins, Brigham & Stanley, Deborah A., eds. Contemporary Literary Criticism. (Contemporary Literary Criticism Ser.: Vol. 90). 525p. 1996. text 150.00 (*0-8103-9268-2*) Gale.

— Contemporary Literary Criticism, Vol. 92. 500p. 1996. text 150.00 (*0-8103-9270-4*) Gale.

— Contemporary Literary Criticism, Vol. 93. 500p. 1996. text 150.00 (*0-8103-9271-2*) Gale.

— Contemporary Literary Criticism Vol. 91: Yearbook, 1995. 540p. 1996. text 150.00 (*0-8103-9269-0*) Gale.

Narison, S. QCD Spectral Sum Rules. (Lecture Notes in Physics Ser.: Vol. 26). 544p. 1990. text 48.00 (*9971-5-0653-X*) World Scientific Pub.

Narison, S., ed. Non-Perturbative Methods: Proceedings of the Workshop at Montpellier, France, July 9-13, 1985. 480p. 1986. text 137.00 (*9971-5-0012-4*) World Scientific Pub.

Narita, S., jt. ed. see Motus, L.

Narita, Shigehira, et al. Kodansha Japanese-English Dictionary. 1250p. 1984. pap. 45.95 (*0-87011-671-1*) Kodansha.

*__Naritoku, D., ed.__ Vagus Nerve Stimulation. 2000. write for info. (*0-444-50191-6*, Excerpta Medica) Elsevier.

*__Narizny, Susan & Hill, Susan.__ The Pacific Northwest Plant Locator, 2000-2001. 350p. 2000. pap. 19.95 (*0-9674907-1-5*) Black-Eyed.

— The Pacific Northwest Plant Locator, 1999-2000. 280p. 1999. pap. 19.99 (*0-9674907-0-7*) Black-Eyed.

Narke, Rob. Succeed. LC 83-71420. (Illus.). 336p. (Orig.). 1983. pap. 7.95 (*0-9611336-0-0*) Dreaming.

Narkiewicz-Laine, Christian K. Distant Fires: A Collection of Poems. LC 98-115014. 1997. write for info. (*0-935119-08-6*) Metro Pr Pubns.

Narkiewicz, Olga A. Eastern Europe Nineteen Sixty-Eight to Nineteen Eighty-Four. LC 85-22985. 288p. (C). 1986. 57.00 (*0-389-20607-5*, N8166) B&N Imports.

— Eurocommunism, 1968-1986: A Select Bibliography. 200p. 1987. text 110.00 (*0-7201-1801-8*) Continuum.

Narkiewicz, Robert D. The Outplacement of Older Psychiatric Patients into the Community. LC 91-37479. (Studies on the Elderly in America). 96p. 1992. text 20.00 (*0-8153-0520-6*) Garland.

*__Narkiewicz, W.__ The Development of Prime Number Theory: From Euclid to Hardy & Littlewood. (Monographs in Mathematics). xii, 448p. 2000. 94.00 (*3-540-66289-8*) Spr-Verlag.

Narkiewicz, Wladyslaw. Elementary & Analytic Theory of Algebraic Numbers. 850p. 1990. 136.95 (*0-387-51250-0*, 3310) Spr-Verlag.

— Number Theory. Kanemitsu, S., tr. 371p. 1984. text 54.00 (*9971-950-13-8*); pap. text 30.00 (*9971-950-26-X*) World Scientific Pub.

— Polynomial Mappings. LC 95-18957. (Lecture Notes in Mathematics Ser.: Vol. 1600). 1995. write for info. (*0-387-59435-3*) Spr-Verlag.

— Polynomial Mappings. Dold, A. & Takens, F., eds. (Lecture Notes in Mathematics Ser.: Vol. 1600). vii, 130p. 1995. pap. 29.95 (*3-540-59435-3*) Spr-Verlag.

— Uniform Distribution of Sequences of Integers in Residue Classes. (Lecture Notes in Mathematics Ser.: Vol. 1087). vii, 125p. 1984. 29.95 (*0-387-13872-2*) Spr-Verlag.

Narkis, M. & Rosenzweig, N., eds. Polymer Powder Technology. LC 95-3061. 644p. 1995. 305.00 (*0-471-93872-6*) Wiley.

Narkiss, Bezalel. The Golden Haggadah. (Illus.). 64p. (Orig.). 1997. pap. 16.95 (*0-87654-481-2*) Pomegranate Calif.

Narkiss, Bezalel, intro. Journal of Jewish Art, 2 vols., Set, Vols. III-IV. (Illus.). 143p. (Orig.). (C). 1977. pap. 22.95 (*0-935982-32-9*, JJA-03) Spertus Coll.

— Journal of Jewish Art, Vol. V. 115p. (Orig.). (C). 1978. pap. 22.95 (*0-935982-33-7*) Spertus Coll.

Narkiss, Uzi. The Liberation of Jerusalem. 2nd ed. 285p. 1992. text 34.50 (*0-85303-209-2*, Pub. by M Vallentine & Co) Intl Spec Bk.

— Soldier of Jerusalem. Kett, Martin, tr. from HEB. LC 97-21946. (Illus.). 250p. 1997. 39.50 (*0-7146-4800-0*, Pub. by F Cass Pubs); pap. 22.50 (*0-7146-4372-6*, Pub. by F Cass Pubs) Intl Spec Bk.

— Soldier of Jerusalem. (Illus.). 1998. 47.50 (*0-85303-348-X*, Pub. by M Vallentine & Co) Intl Spec Bk.

— Soldier of Jerusalem. (Illus.). 268p. 1999. pap. 22.50 (*0-85303-349-8*, Pub. by M Vallentine & Co) Intl Spec Bk.

Narla, V. R. Gods, Goblins & Men. 1979. 12.00 (*0-8364-0559-5*, Pub. by Minerva) S Asia.

Narlikar, A. V., ed. Studies of High Temperature Superconductors, Vol. 1. (Illus.). 382p. 1989. text 175.00 (*0-941743-54-3*) Nova Sci Pubs.

— Studies of High Temperature Superconductors, Vol. 5. (Illus.). 413p. (C). 1990. text 175.00 (*0-941743-87-X*) Nova Sci Pubs.

— Studies of High Temperature Superconductors, Vol. 6. (Illus.). 413p. (C). 1990. text 175.00 (*0-941743-88-8*) Nova Sci Pubs.

— Studies of High Temperature Superconductors, Vol. 7. 398p. (C). 1991. text 175.00 (*1-56072-007-7*) Nova Sci Pubs.

— Studies of High Temperature Superconductors, Vol. 8. 414p. (C). 1991. text 175.00 (*1-56072-019 0*) Nova Sci Pubs.

— Studies of High Temperature Superconductors, Vol. 9. 331p. 1992. 175.00 (*1-56072-061-1*) Nova Sci Pubs.

— Studies of High Temperature Superconductors, Vol. 11. (Illus.). 467p. 1993. lib. bdg. 165.00 (*1-56072-132-4*) Nova Sci Pubs.

— Studies of High Temperature Superconductors: Advances in Research & Applications, Vol. 2. (Illus.). 370p. 1989. text 175.00 (*0-941743-55-1*) Nova Sci Pubs.

— Studies of High Temperature Superconductors: Advances in Research & Applications, Vol. 3. (Illus.). 413p. 1989. text 175.00 (*0-941743-56-X*) Nova Sci Pubs.

— Studies of High Temperature Superconductors: Advances in Research & Applications, Vol. 4. (Illus.). 402p. 1989. text 175.00 (*0-941743-57-8*) Nova Sci Pubs.

— Studies of High Temperature Superconductors: Advances in Research & Applications, Vol. 10. 345p. (C). 1992. lib. bdg. 175.00 (*1-56072-087-5*) Nova Sci Pubs.

— Studies of High Temperature Superconductors Vol. 12: High Tc Squids & Related Studies. (Illus.). 212p. (C). 1994. lib. bdg. 175.00 (*1-56072-184-7*) Nova Sci Pubs.

— Studies of High Temperature Superconductors Vol. 13: HTSC Thin Films. (Illus.). 323p. (C). 1994. lib. bdg. 175.00 (*1-56072-183-9*) Nova Sci Pubs.

— Studies of High Temperature Superconductors Vol. 14: Field Penetration & Magnetization of High Temperature Superconductors. (Illus.). 445p. (C). 1994. lib. bdg. 175.00 (*1-56072-182-0*) Nova Sci Pubs.

*__Narlikar, Anant.__ Microstructures & Related Studies of High Temperature Superconductors II. LC 99-56622. (Studies of High Temperature Superconductors: Vol. 30). 187p. 2000. lib. bdg. 97.00 (*1-56072-771-3*) Nova Sci Pubs.

— PseudoGAP in High Temperature Superconductors. LC 99-22946. (Studies of High Temperature Superconductors: Vol. 27). 286p. 1999. lib. bdg. 89.00 (*1-56072-684-9*) Nova Sci Pubs.

*__Narlikar, Anant, contrib. by.__ Studies of High Temperature Superconductors. LC 99-48784. (Studies of High Temperature Superconductors: Vol 29). 246p. 1999. lib. bdg. 93.00 (*1-56072-735-7*) Nova Sci Pubs.

*__Narlikar, Anant, ed.__ A. C. Losses & Flux Pinning in High Temperature Superconductors Vol. 32: Studies of High Temperature Superconductors. 249p. 2000. lib. bdg. 98.00 (*1-56072-789-6*) Nova Sci Pubs.

— Chemistry & Related Aspects of High Temperature Superconductors. (Studies of High Temperature Superconductors: Vol. 25). 1998. text 93.00 (*1-56072-539-7*) Nova Sci Pubs.

Narlikar, Anant, ed. Conductor Development of High Temperature Superconductors. (Studies of High Temperature Superconductors). 292p. (C). 1997. lib. bdg. 145.00 (*1-56072-419-6*) Nova Sci Pubs.

— Critical Current, Flux Pinning & Optical Studies of High-Temperature Superconductors, Vol. 22. (Studies of High Temperature Superconductors). 278p. (C). 1997. lib. bdg. 145.00 (*1-56072-420-X*) Nova Sci Pubs.

— Electron Microscopy & Channeling Studies of High Temperature Superconductors. (Studies of High Temperature Superconductors: Vol. 15). (Illus.). 302p. (C). 1995. lib. bdg. 165.00 (*1-56072-219-3*) Nova Sci Pubs.

*__Narlikar, Anant, ed.__ Flux Pinning in High Temperature Superconductors Vol. 31: Studies of High Temperature Superconductors. 258p. 2000. lib. bdg. 98.00 (*1-56072-790-X*) Nova Sci Pubs.

Narlikar, Anant, ed. Micro Structural Studies of High TC Superconductors & More on Quaternary Borocarbides. LC 99-22945. (Studies of High Temperature Superconductors: Vol. 28). 287p. 1999. lib. bdg. 93.00 (*1-56072-685-7*) Nova Sci Pubs.

Narlikar, Anant, ed. Microwave Studies of High Temp Superconductors. (Studies of High Temperature Superconductors: Vol. 17, Pt. I). 262p. 1996. text 175.00 (*1-56072-380-7*) Nova Sci Pubs.

Narlikar, Anant, ed. Quaternary Borocarbide Superconductors & Hg-Based High Tc Superconductors Vol. 26: Studies of High Temperature Superconductors. (Advances in Research & Applications Ser.). 279p. 1998. 97.00 (*1-56072-628-8*) Nova Sci Pubs.

— Studies of High Temperature Superconductors: Hg-Based High Tc Superconductors, Vol. 23, Pt. 1. 287p. 1997. lib. bdg. 135.00 (*1-56072-472-2*) Nova Sci Pubs.

— Studies of High Temperature Superconductors: Hg-Based High Tc Superconductors, Vol. 24, Pt. 2. LC 98-108085. 244p. 1997. 135.00 (*1-56072-524-9*) Nova Sci Pubs.

— Studies of High Temperature Superconductors Vol. 18: Microwave Studies of High Temperature Superconductors, Pt. 2. 265p. 1996. 145.00 (*1-56072-381-5*, QC611) Nova Sci Pubs.

— Synthesis, High Pressure Effects & Some Miscellaneous Aspects. (Studies of High Temperature Superconductors: Vol. 16). 307p. 1995. 175.00 (*1-56072-251-7*) Nova Sci Pubs.

— Thermal Properties & Some Miscellaneous Aspects of High Temperature Superconductors. (Studies of High Temperature Superconductors: Vol. 19). (Illus.). 262p. (C). 1996. lib. bdg. 145.00 (*1-56072-393-9*) Nova Sci Pubs.

— Tunnelling Studies of High Temperature Superconductors. (Studies of High Temperature Superconductors: Vol. 20). 239p. (C). 1996. lib. bdg. 145.00 (*1-56072-394-7*) Nova Sci Pubs.

Narlikar, Jayant V. From Black Cloud to Black Hole. 2nd ed. 180p. 1995. text 53.00 (*981-02-2032-4*); pap. text 28.00 (*981-02-2033-2*) World Scientific Pub.

— From Black Clouds to Black Holes. LC 85-3334. 160p. 1985. text 52.00 (*9971-978-13-X*); pap. text 23.00 (*9971-978-15-6*) World Scientific Pub.

— Introduction to Cosmology. (Illus.). 484p. 1983. 55.00 (*0-86720-015-4*) Jones & Bartlett.

— Introduction to Cosmology. 2nd ed. (Illus.). 431p. (C). 1993. text 85.00 (*0-521-41250-1*) Cambridge U Pr.

— The Lighter Side of Gravity. LC 81-19496. (Illus.). 194p. (C). 1982. pap. text 11.20 (*0-7167-1344-6*) W H Freeman.

— The Lighter Side of Gravity. 2nd ed. (Illus.). 229p. (C). 1996. pap. 17.95 (*0-521-56565-0*); text 44.95 (*0-521-55009-2*) Cambridge U Pr.

— Seven Wonders of the Cosmos. LC 98-35561. (Illus.). 334p. (C). 1999. write for info. (*0-521-63087-8*) Cambridge U Pr.

*__Narlikar, Jayant V.__ Seven Wonders of the Cosmos. LC 98-35561. (Illus.). 334p. (C). 1999. pap. write for info. (*0-521-63898-4*) Cambridge U Pr.

Narlikar, Jayant V. & Padmanabhan, T. Gravity, Gauge Theories & Quantum Cosmology. 1986. text 247.50 (*90-277-1948-9*) Kluwer Academic.

Narlikar, Jayant V., jt. auth. see Hoyle, Fred.

Narlikar, Jayant V., jt. auth. see Kembhavi, Ajit K.

Narlikar, Jayant V., jt. ed. see Vatsyayan, Kapila.

Narlock, Lori, ed. see Diamond, Wendy.

NARMIC-AFSC Staff, ed. see Lamperti, John.

Narmour, Eugene. The Analysis & Cognition of Basic Melodic Structures: The Implication-Realization Model. LC 90-35357. (Illus.). 480p. 1990. lib. bdg. 66.00 (*0-226-56845-8*) U Ch Pr.

— The Analysis & Cognition of Melodic Complexity: The Implication-Realization Model. LC 91-37919. (Illus.). 444p. 1992. 57.50 (*0-226-56842-3*) U Ch Pr.

— Beyond Schenkerism: The Need for Alternatives in Music Analysis. LC 76-25632. xii, 238p. 1992. pap. 7.50 (*0-226-56848-2*, P893) U Ch Pr.

Narmour, Eugene & Solie, Ruth A., eds. Explorations in Music, the Arts, & Ideas: Essays in Honor of Leonard B. Meyer. LC 87-32858. (Festschrift Ser.: No. 7). (Illus.). 470p. 1989. lib. bdg. 54.00 (*0-918728-94-0*) Pendragon NY.

Narney, Dean. The Christmas Tree That Ate My Mother. 96p. (J). (gr. 3-7). 1992. 3.50 (*0-590-44881-1*, Apple Paperbacks) Scholastic Inc.

Naro, Anthony J., tr. see Camara, J. Mattoso, Jr.

N

Naro, Anthony J., tr. & compiled by see Camara, Joaquim M.

Naro, Nancy P., tr. see De Jesus, Carolina M.

*__Naro, Nancy Priscilla.__ A Slave's Place, a Master's World: Fashioning Dependency in Rural Brazil. LC 99-43275. (Black Atlantic Ser.). 256p. 2000. write for info. (*0-304-70550-0*) Continuum.

Narode, Ronald, et al. Teaching Thinking Skills: Science. 48p. 1987. pap. 7.95 (*0-8106-0202-4*) NEA.

Naroditsky, V., jt. ed. see Lam, Lui.

Narodny, Ivan. American Artists. LC 74-93365. (Essay Index Reprint Ser.). 1977. 20.95 (*0-8369-1311-6*) Ayer.

Narogin, Mudrooroo. Dalwurra the Black Bittern. pap. 10.95 (*0-86422-068-5*, Pub. by Univ of West Aust Pr) Intl Spec Bk.

Naroll, Raoul. The Moral Order: An Introduction to the Human Situation. LC 82-19204. 498p. reprint ed. pap. 154.40 (*0-7837-1129-8*, 204165900022) Bks Demand.

Naroll, Raoul, et al. Worldwide Theory Testing. LC 76-48559. (HRAF Manuals Ser.). 139p. 1976. pap. 10.00 (*0-87536-662-7*) HRAFP.

Naroola, Gurmeet. QS-9000 Registration & Implementation. LC 96-32729. (Quality & Reliability Ser.: Vol. 49). (Illus.). 288p. 1996. text 49.75 (*0-8247-9808-2*) Dekker.

Naroola, Gurmeet & Mac Connell, Robert. How to Achieve ISO 9000 Registration Economically & Efficiently. (Quality & Reliability Ser.: Vol. 48). (Illus.). 216p. 1996. text 49.75 (*0-8247-9758-2*) Dekker.

Narr, Tony, jt. auth. see Plotkin, Martha R.

Narramore, Bruce S. No Condemnation: Rethinking Guilt Motivation in Counseling, Preaching & Parenting. 208p. 1984. pap. 16.99 (*0-310-30401-6*, 11244P) Zondervan.

— An Ounce of Prevention: A Parent's Guide to Moral & Spiritual Growth in Children. 160p. 1973. pap. 5.95 (*0-310-30301-X*, 11035P) Zondervan.

— Parenting with Love & Limits. 312p. 1987. pap. 8.95 (*0-310-30541-1*, 11246P) Zondervan.

— Why Children Misbehave: A Guide To Positive Parenting. 248p. 1987. pap. 7.95 (*0-310-30501-2*, 11247P) Zondervan.

Narramore, Bruce S. & Carter, John. The Integration of Psychology & Theology: An Introduction. (Rosemead Ser.). 139p. (Orig.). 1979. mass mkt. 14.99 (*0-310-30341-9*, 11190P) Zondervan.

Narramore, Clyde M. The Compact Encyclopedia of Psychological Problems. LC 83-12265. 400p. 1984. 11.95 (*0-310-29880-6*, 12265) Zondervan.

— Counseling Youth. 128p. (Orig.). 1973. pap. 5.95 (*0-310-29891-1*, 12229P) Zondervan.

— Enciclopedia de Problemas Psicologicos.Tr. of Encyclopedia of Psychological Problems. (SPA.). 256p. 1987. pap. 7.99 (*1-56063-000-0*, 497701) Editorial Unilit.

— Psicologia de la Felicidad.Tr. of This Way to Happiness. (SPA.). 92p. 1989. pap. write for info. (*0-614-27125-8*) Editorial Unilit.

— Psicologia de la Felicidad.Tr. of This Way to Happiness. (SPA.). 1990. 3.99 (*0-945792-82-4*, 497702) Editorial Unilit.

— Psychology of Counseling. 303p. 1960. 16.99 (*0-310-29930-6*, 10409) Zondervan.

— This Way to Happiness: Meeting Your Basic Emotional Needs Leads to Lasting Happiness. 2nd rev. ed. 176p. 1997. pap. text. write for info. (*0-9658067-0-7*) C Narramore.

Narramore, Kathy & Hill, Alice. Kindred Spirits: Developing Godly Friendship. 144p. (Orig.). 1985. pap. 5.95 (*0-310-30531-4*, 11245P) Zondervan.

Narramore, Robert E., jt. auth. see Nolen, Ben M.

Narre, Anne. All Magic in Your Hand. 84p. 1993. pap. 6.88 (*1-887404-01-5*) A Griffin Pr.

Narrett, David E. Inheritance & Family Life in Colonial New York City. LC 92-7680. 264p. 1992. text 45.00 (*0-8014-2517-4*) Cornell U Pr.

Narrett, David E. & Goldberg, Joyce S., eds. Essays on Liberty & Federalism: The Shaping of the U. S. Constitution. LC 88-2105. (Walter Prescott Webb Memorial Lectures: No. 22). 152p. 1988. 18.95 (*0-89096-341-X*) Tex A&M Univ Pr.

Narrett, David E., jt. ed. see Cawthon, Elisabeth A.

Narrett, Eugene. Henry Schwartz. (Illus.). 28p. 1990. 10.00 (*0-934358-26-5*) Fuller Mus Art.

Narrin, JaneAnne. One Degree Beyond: A Reiki Journey into Energy Medicine: Your 21-Day Step-by-Step Guide to Relax, Open & Celebrate. 2nd rev. ed. (Illus.). 320p. (Orig.). 1998. pap. 18.95 (*0-9658545-4-X*) Little Whte Buffalo.

Winner, National book award. Coalition of Visionary Retailer's Visionary Award, 1st runner up, Best Alternative Health Book of 1999. Widely acclaimed book by JaneAnne Narrin, celebrated seminar leader & popular speaker about owning your own power. Details ways to touch in with the energy medicine "available at your very fingertips" through Reiki (simple hands-on technique.) Looks at the practical relationship between Reiki & modern scientific theory. Uses tools of self-inquiry, stories & a great workbook section to engage readers. Excellent reference section for research in energy medicine, Reiki teachers, success stories & more. The "Put Reiki to Work in Your Life" book perfect for anyone interested in learning about Reiki for the first time or for advanced practitioners. Says Whole Life Times: "Interested in learning more about Reiki, stress management, relaxation, alternative medicine? This book will teach you these things & more ...." Awareness Magazine says: "What a pleasure to find a book on Reiki that brings healing, even by reading it. ...." Available through Ingram, Baker & Taylor, Bookpeople & online at Amazon.com, barnesandnoble.com, or through Little White Buffalo Publishing Cottage, Inc.PMB204, 12345 Lake City Way, NE, Seattle, WA 98125, 425-771-2744
Publisher Paid Annotation.

— A Quantum Breeze: Meditations in Postmodern Time. Boylan, John, ed. (Illus.). 102p. 2000. 14.95 (*0-9658545-0-7*, Pub. by Little Whte Buffalo) New Leaf Dist.

Narrod, Ruth. Hudson. LC 97-61996. (Illus.). 80p. (J). (gr. 3-5). 1997. pap. 4.99 (*0-9660780-0-4*) Themis Pub.

Narrow, Barbara W. & Buschl, Kay. Fundamentals of Nursing Practice. 2nd ed. 1024p. 1989. 14.95 (*0-8273-4322-1*) Delmar.

Narrowe, Judith. Under One Roof: On Becoming a Turk in Sweden. 266p. 1998. pap. 49.50 (*91-7153-748-1*, Pub. by Almqvist Wiksell) Coronet Bks.

Nars, K., ed. Excellence in Debt Management. 178p. 1996. 245.00 (*1-85564-572-6*, Pub. by Euromoney) Am Educ Systs.

Narsavage, Robert J., Jr., jt. auth. see Kimbler, Frank S.

Narsimhachary, M., jt. auth. see Smith, H. Daniel.

Narsimhan, Ganesan, et al. COFE 1995: Advances in Food Engineering: Proceedings of the 4th Conference of Food Engineering. LC 97-27028. 1997. write for info. (*0-931682-64-9*) Purdue U Pubns.

Narsipur, Chandramouli, ed. & notes see Narayan, Giddu.

Nart, Inigo, tr. see Robbins, Harold.

Nartoomid, Simeon, jt. auth. see Shamayyim, Maia C.

Nartoomid, Simeon, ed. see Shamayyim, Maia C.

Nartov, P. S., ed. Disk Soil-Working Implements. Sivaramakrishnan, M. M., tr. from RUS. 156p. (C). 1985. text 123.00 (*90-6191-443-4*, Pub. by A A Balkema) Ashgate Pub Co.

*__Nartsupha, Chatthip.__ Thai Village Economy in the Past. 2000. pap. 17.50 (*974-7551-09-8*) U of Wash Pr.

NARUC Staff Subcommittee on Water. Model Record-Keeping Manual for Small Water Companies. 95p. 1978. 5.00 (*0-317-01666-0*) NARUC.

Narula. Design Analysis Compare Exper. 1997. 14.95 (*0-07-045944-4*) McGraw.

Narula, Chaitanya K. Ceramic Precursor Technology & Its Applications. (Illus.). 350p. 1995. text 150.00 (*0-8247-9310-2*) Dekker.

Narula, Karen S. Voyage of the Emerald Buddha. (Images of Asia Ser.). (Illus.). 120p. 1994. text 16.95 (*967-65-3057-3*) OUP.

Narula, Rajneesh, jt. auth. see Dunning, John H.

Narula, Rajneesh, jt. ed. see Dunning, John H.

Narula, Rajneesh, jt. ed. see Van Hoesel, Roger.

*__Narula, Satwant K. & Coffman, Robert L.__ New Cytokines as Potential Drugs. LC 99-47593. (Progress in Inflammation Research Ser.). 2000. write for info. (*0-8176-5883-1*) Birkhauser.

Narula, Uma & Pearce, W. Barnett. Development As Communication: A Perspective on India. LC 85-2088. 240p. 1986. text 21.95 (*0-8093-1223-9*) S Ill U Pr.

Narula, Uma & Pearce, W. Barnett, eds. Cultures, Politics & Research Programs: An International Assessment of Practical Problems in Field Research. 264p. (C). 1990. text 59.95 (*0-8058-0134-0*) L Erlbaum Assocs.

Narula, Uma, jt. auth. see Hanson, Jarice.

Narumov, B. P., jt. auth. see Sadikov, A. V.

*__Narus, Don.__ Apparent Suicide: A Noah Wharton Mystery. LC 99-91665. 2000. 25.00 (*0-7388-1176-9*); pap. 18.00 (*0-7388-1177-7*) Xlibris Corp.

Narus, James, jt. auth. see Anderson, James.

*__Naruse, S. & Watari, H., eds.__ Ultrafast Magnetic Resonance Imaging in Medicine. (International Congress Ser.). 376p. 1999. 152.50 (*0-444-50280-7*, Excerpta Medica) Elsevier.

Narvaez, Concha L. Las Cabritas de Martin (Martin's Little Goats) (SPA., Illus.). 40p. (J). (gr. 1-3). 1994. 12.99 (*968-16-4445-X*, Pub. by Fondo) Continental Bk.

Narvaez, Darcia F., jt. ed. see Rest, James R.

Narvaez, Leon O. La Soledad de un Sacerdote (The Lonely Priest) (SPA.). 1995. write for info. (*0-945792-31-X*) Editorial Unilit.

Narvaez, Leon O., ed. see Narvaez, Ricardo A.

Narvaez, Peter, ed. The Good People: New Fairylore Essays. LC 97-25305. (Illus.). 536p. (C). 1997. pap. text 21.00 (*0-8131-0939-6*) U Pr of Ky.

Narvaez, Peter & Laba, Martin, eds. Media Sense: The Folklore-Popular Culture Continuum. LC 86-70527. 168p. 1986. 18.95 (*0-87972-343-2*) Bowling Green Univ Popular Press.

Narvaez, Ricardo A. Morfologia Flexional del Espanol. Narvaez, Leon O., ed. LC 85-1208. (Illus.). 184p. (Orig.). (C). 1985. pap. text 13.95 (*0-930795-00-8*) Editorial AI.

Narveson, Eric J. The Historical Process: Critical Thinking & Historical Methodology. 143p. (C). 1998. pap. text. write for info. (*0-9650663-2-0*) BEK Publns.

— Sondenos in War: The Story of the Sondeno Family of Turlock, California in World War II. (Illus.). 110p. (Orig.). 1996. pap. 11.95 (*0-9650663-0-4*, 1021) BEK Publns.

Narveson, Jan. Moral Matters. 256p. 1993. pap. 16.95 (*1-55111-011-3*) Broadview Pr.

— Moral Matters. 2nd ed. 300p. 1999. pap. 19.95 (*1-55111-212-4*) Broadview Pr.

— Morality & Utility. LC 66-29908. 313p. reprint ed. pap. 97.10 (*0-608-10130-3*, 200388900037) Bks Demand.

Narveson, Jan, ed. Moral Issues. 462p. 1983. pap. text 28.95 (*0-19-540426-2*) OUP.

Narveson, Jan, jt. auth. see Friedman, Marilyn.

Narwal, S. S. & Tauro, P. Allelopathy in Agriculture & Forestry: International Conference on Allelopathy, Symposium 1994, New Delhi. LC 94-906771. 310p. 1994. pap. 120.00 (*81-7233-085-5*, Pub. by Scientific Pubs) St Mut.

— Proceedings of International Conference on Allelopathy, Vols. 1 & 2. LC 96-906254. 1994. pap. 440.00 (*81-7233-132-0*, Pub. by Scientific Pubs) St Mut.

— Proceedings of the International Conference on Allelopathy in Sustainable Agriculture, Forestry & Environmental, Vol. 1. 1999. pap. 250.00 (*81-7233-130-4*, Pub. by Scientific Pubs) St Mut.

— Proceedings of the International Conference on Allelopathy in Sustainable Agriculture, Forestry & Environmental, Vol. 2. 1999. pap. 255.00 (*81-7233-131-2*, Pub. by Scientific Pubs) St Mut.

Narwal, S. S., et al. Neem in Sustainable Agriculture International Symposium on Allelopathy in Sustainable Agriculture, Forestry & Environment New Delhi 1994. LC 97-913999. 1997. pap. 135.00 (*81-7233-167-3*, Pub. by Scientific Pubs) St Mut.

*__Narwal, Shamsher S.__ Allelopathy Update, 2 vols. LC 99-43493. 1999. write for info. (*1-57808-065-7*) Science Pubs.

*__Narwal, Shamsher S., ed.__ Allelopathy Update: International Status - Basic & Applied Aspects, 2 vols., 1. (Illus.). 694p. 1999. text 140.00 (*1-57808-063-0*) Science Pubs.

Narwal, Shamsher S., jt. auth. see International Congress on Allelopathy in Ecological Agriculture & Forestry Staff.

Narwekar, Sanjit, compiled by. Directory of Indian Film-Makers & Films. LC 93-44642. 576p. 1994. lib. bdg. 89.50 (*0-313-29284-1*, Greenwood Pr) Greenwood.

Nary, Rhoda, jt. auth. see McMakin, Jacqueline.

Naryanana Reddy, G. Rural Elite & Community Work. 1986. 31.00 (*81-85076-03-0*, Pub. by Chugh Pubns) S Asia.

Narzakian, Garine, tr. see Narzakian, Sarkis.

Narzakian, Sarkis. Memoirs of Sarkis Narzakian. Narzakian, Garine, tr. from ARM. LC 95-77088. (Gomidas Institute Memoir Ser.: Vol. 2). (Illus.). x, 247p. 1995. pap. 25.00 (*1-884630-00-6*, Pub. by Gomidas Inst) Whitehurst & Clark.

Narzarieff, S. Early Erotic Photography. (Illus.). 1994. pap. 24.99 (*3-8228-9453-2*) Taschen Amer.

Nas, Peter J., ed. Urban Symbolism. LC 93-16885. (Studies in Human Society: No. 8). (Illus.). vi, 394p. 1993. pap. 99.00 (*90-04-09855-0*) Brill Academic Pubs.

Nas, Tevfik F. Cost-Benefit Analysis: Theory & Application. LC 95-41788. 220p. 1996. 42.00 (*0-8039-7132-X*); pap. 19.95 (*0-8039-7133-8*) Sage.

Nas, Tevfik F. & Odekon, Mehmet, eds. Economics & Politics of Turkish Liberalization. LC 91-60583. (Illus.). 200p. 1992. 38.50 (*0-934223-19-X*) Lehigh Univ Pr.

— Liberalization & the Turkish Economy. 86. LC 88-9755. (Contributions in Economics & Economic History Ser.: No. 86). 231p. 1988. 59.95 (*0-313-26031-1*, NLZ/, Greenwood Pr) Greenwood.

NASA-Genesis Space Photo Staff, photos by. Journey into Space. LC 98-87332. (Illus.). (J). (gr. 2-5). 1999. 17.99 (*0-7636-0869-6*) Candlewick Pr.

NASA, Jet Propulsion Lab Staff. Space Images. LC 81-84668. (Illus.). 100p. 1982. 27.95 (*0-912810-37-8*); pap. 15.95 (*0-912810-36-X*) Lustrum Pr.

NASA Johnson Space Center Staff & Gose, W. Journal of the Geochemical Society & Meteorcritical Society, 3 vols., Suppl. 5. LC 74-23095. 1974. 1428.00 (*0-08-018318-2*, Pub. by Pergamon Repr) Franklin.

NASA Public Affairs Staff. The Kennedy Space Center Story. rev. ed. (Illus.). 208p. (Orig.). 1991. pap. text 8.95 (*0-9610648-5-4*) Graphic Hse.

— NASA Kennedy Space Center's Spaceport U. S. A. Tour Book. Delavega, tr. (FRE, GER, ITA & SPA., Illus.). 48p. (Orig.). 1991. reprint ed. pap. 5.00 (*0-9610648-6-2*) Graphic Hse.

NASA Staff. Laser Gyroscopes: April 86 - April 90. 1990. 85.00 (*0-614-18520-3*, 135P24) Info Gatekeepers.

— Laser Gyroscopes: April 86 - May 89. 1989. 85.00 (*0-614-18517-3*, 135P13) Info Gatekeepers.

NASA Staff & MSFC Staff. Standards for Epoxies Used in Microelectronics. 115p. 1990. reprint ed. pap. 58.00 (*0-938648-17-9*) T-C Pr CA.

NASA/Goddard Space Flight Center Staff. High Energy Solar Physics. (AIP Press Conference Proceedings Ser.: No. 374). (Illus.). 560p. 1996. 140.00 (*1-56396-542-9*, CP 374, AIP Pr) Spr-Verlag.

Nasacu Group Staff & Wells, Marna R. National Index of Recognized & Unrecognized Alternative & Non-Traditional Colleges & Universities in the United States: The Best & Worst Non-Traditional & Alternative Schools in America. 3rd ed. (Non-Traditional Higher Education in the U. S. Ser.). (Illus.). 164p. 1991. pap. 30.00 (*0-939877-32-5*) ACUPAE.

Nasa'i, Ahmad S. Kitab al 'Ilm: (The Book of Knowledge) Hamadah, Faruq, ed. LC 92-31589. (Silsilat Taysir al Turath al Islami Ser.: No. 4). (ARA.). 222p. (Orig.). 1993. pap. 7.75 (*1-56564-005-5*) IIIT VA.

Nasar. 22 Rules of Day Trading Online. 1999. pap. 21.95 (*0-07-135463-8*) McGraw.

Nasar, Al-Din. Tales of Nasr-ed-Din Khoja. Barnham, Henry D., tr. from TUR. LC 77-87632. 1977. reprint ed. 32.50 (*0-404-16457-9*) AMS Pr.

*__Nasar, Jack L.__ Design by Competition: Making Design Competition Work. LC 98-44685. (Environment & Behavior Ser.). (Illus.). 224p. (C). 1999. text 49.95 (*0-521-44449-7*) Cambridge U Pr.

Nasar, Jack L. The Evaluative Image of the City. LC 97-21151. 208p. 1997. 38.95 (*0-8039-5447-6*, 54476); pap. 18.95 (*0-8039-5448-4*, 54484) Sage.

Nasar, Jack L., ed. Environmental Aesthetics: Theory, Research & Application. (Illus.). 557p. (C). 1992. pap. text 31.95 (*0-521-42916-1*) Cambridge U Pr.

*__Nasar, Jack L. & Presiser, Wolfgang F. E., eds.__ Directions in Person-Environment Research & Practice. LC 98-73756. (Ethnoscapes Ser.). 379p. 1999. 78.95 (*1-84014-178-6*, Pub. by Ashgate Pub) Ashgate Pub Co.

Nasar, Syed A. Electric Energy Systems. rev. ed. LC 95-34198. Orig. Title: Electric Energy Conversion & Transmission. 416p. 1995. 110.00 (*0-02-386111-8*, Macmillan Coll) P-H.

Nasar, Syed A. Electric Machines & Power Systems. LC 94-32717. (Electrical & Computer Engineering, Power & Energy Ser.: Vol. 1). 512p. (C). 1994. 66.88 (*0-07-045958-4*) McGraw.

— Permanent Magnet, Reluctance & Self-Synchronous Motors. 288p. 1993. boxed set 120.00 (*0-8493-9313-2*, TK2787) CRC Pr.

— Schaum's Outline of Basic Electrical Engineering. 2nd ed. Cathey, Jimmy J., ed. LC 96-47056. (Schaum's Outline Ser.). (C). 1997. pap. 15.95 (*0-07-011355-6*) McGraw.

— Schaum's Outline of Electric Machines & Electromechanics. 2nd ed. LC 97-23529. (Schaum's Outline Ser.). (Illus.). 224p. (C). 1997. pap. 15.95 (*0-07-045994-0*) McGraw.

— Solutions Manual for Electric Power Systems. 1999. ring bd. write for info. (*0-8493-2295-2*) CRC Pr.

— Vector Control of AC Drives. 256p. 1992. boxed set 136.95 (*0-8493-4408-5*, TK2791) CRC Pr.

Nasar, Syed A. & Boldea, Ion. Electric Machines: Dynamics & Control. 240p. 1992. lib. bdg. 129.00 (*0-8493-9312-4*, TK2781) CRC Pr.

Nasar, Syed A. & Paul, Clayton R. Essential Engineering Equations. 176p. 1991. boxed set 47.95 (*0-8493-4263-5*, TA330) CRC Pr.

Nasar, Syed A. & Trutt, F.C. Electric Power System. LC 98-38265. 1998. 74.95 (*0-8493-1666-9*) CRC Pr.

Nasar, Syed A., jt. auth. see Boldea, I.

Nasar, Syed A., jt. auth. see Boldea, Ion.

Nasar, Syed A., jt. auth. see Cathey, J. J.

Nasar, Syed A., jt. auth. see Paul, Clayton R.

Nasar, Sylvia. A Beautiful Mind: A Biography of John Forbes Nash, Jr., Winner of the Nobel Prize for Economics, 1994. LC 98-2795. (Illus.). 448p. 1998. 25.00 (*0-684-81906-6*) S&S Trade.

— A Beautiful Mind: A Biography of John Forbes Nash, Jr., Winner of the Nobel Prize for Economics, 1994. (Illus.). 464p. 1999. per. 14.00 (*0-684-85370-1*) S&S Trade Pap.

Nasatir, A. P., ed. Before Lewis & Clark: Documents Illustrating the History of the Missouri, 1785-1804, Vol. 1. LC 89-25080. 397p. 1990. reprint ed. pap. 123.10 (*0-608-02784-7*, 206385100001) Bks Demand.

Nasatir, Abraham P. Borderland in Retreat: From Spanish Louisiana to the Far Southwest. LC 75-21183. 187p. reprint ed. pap. 58.00 (*0-8357-7351-5*, 203100500073) Bks Demand.

Nasatir, Abraham P. & Monell, Gary E. British Activities in California & the Pacific Coast of North America to 1860: An Archival Calendar Guide. 1224p. 1990. 175.00 (*0-916304-85-X*) SDSU Press.

Nasatir, Abraham P., jt. auth. see Din, Gilbert C.

Nasatir, Abraham P., ed. see Douglas, Walter B.

*__Nasaw, David.__ The Chief: The Life of William Randolph Hearst. LC 99-462122. (Illus.). 688p. 2000. 35.00 (*0-395-82759-0*) HM.

Nasaw, David. Children of the City: At Work & at Play. (Illus.). 251p. 1986. pap. text 12.95 (*0-19-504015-5*) OUP.

— Going Out: The Rise & Fall of Public Amusements. 1999. pap. text 16.95 (*0-674-35622-5*) HUP.

— Schooled to Order: A Social History of Public Schooling in the United States. 302p. 1981. pap. text 13.95 (*0 19 502892-9*) OUP.

*__Nasaw, Jonathan.__ The Girls He Adored. 2001. 24.95 (*0-671-78726-8*, PB Hardcover) PB.

Nasaw, Jonathan. Shadows. 1998. mass mkt. 6.99 (*0-451-18659-1*, Sig) NAL.

— The World on Blood. 1999. audio 16.95 (*0-14-086268-4*) Viking Penguin.

Nasaw, Jonathan Lewis. Shakedown Street. 1995. 9.09 (*0-606-08151-8*) Turtleback.

NASBE School-to-Work Study Group Staff. Framework for the Future: Creating a School-to-Work System for Learning, Livelihood, & Life. 2nd ed. 31p. 1995. pap. 10.00 (*1-58434-021-5*) NASBE.

NASBE Staff. The National Youth Summit on HIV Prevention & Education: Summary Report & Recommendations. 2nd ed. 43p. 1995. pap. 10.00 (*1-58434-013-4*) NASBE.

NASBE Study Group on Education Accountability Staff. Public Accountability for Student Success: Standards for Education Accountability Systems. 55p. 1998. pap. 12.00 (*1-58434-038-X*) NASBE.

NASBE Study Group on Education Governance Staff. A Motion to Reconsider: Education Governance at a Crossroads. 2nd ed. 56p. 1996. pap. 12.00 (*1-58434-022-3*) NASBE.

NASBE Study Group on Funding Education in the 21st Century Staff. Financing Student Success: Beyond Equity & Adequacy. 2nd ed. 32p. 1997. pap. 10.00 (*1-58434-019-3*) NASBE.

NASBE Study Group on School Infrastructure Staff. Building Our Future: Making School Facilities Ready for the 21st Century. 2nd ed. 28p. 1996. pap. 10.00 (*1-58434-023-1*) NASBE.

NASBE Study Group on Special Education Staff. Winners All: A Call for Inclusive Schools. 2nd ed. 44p. 1992. pap. 10.00 (*1-58434-004-5*) NASBE.

N

An Asterisk (*) at the beginning of an entry indicates that the title is appearing for the first time.

NASBE Study Group on State Board Linkages with Higher Education Staff. Learning for a Lifetime: The Report of the NASBE Study Group on State Board Linkages with Higher Education. 2nd ed. 32p. 1994. pap. 7.50 (*1-58434-024-X*) NASBE.

NASBE Study Group on Statewide Assessment Systems Staff. The Full Measure: The Report of the NASBE Study Group on Statewide Assessment Systems. 2nd ed. 44p. 1997. pap. 12.00 (*1-58434-010-X*) NASBE.

NASBE Study Group on Teacher Development, Supply, & Demand Staff. The Numbers Game: Ensuring Quantity & Quality in the Teaching Work Force. 48p. 1998. pap. 12.00 (*1-58434-039-8*) NASBE.

NASBE Study Group on Violence & Its Impact on Schools & Learning Staff. Schools Without Fear: The Report of the NASBE Study Group on Violence & Its Impact on Schools & Learning. 2nd ed. 32p. 1994. pap. 9.00 (*1-58434-011-8*) NASBE.

NASBE Task Force on Early Childhood Education Staff. Right from the Start. 2nd ed. 55p. 1998. pap. 8.50 (*1-58434-000-2*) NASBE.

Nasby, David P., jt. auth. see Denton, Bob C.

***Nasca.** Introduction to Cancer Epidemiology. 2000. 59.00 (*0-8342-1776-7*) Aspen Pub.

Nasca, Phillip C. Cancer: Epidemiology & Prevention in Public Health Practice. 350p. Date not set. 71.00 (*0-8342-0769-9*) Aspen Pub.

Nasca, Robert A. Testing Fluid Power Components. (Illus.). 448p. 1990. 49.95 (*0-8311-3002-4*) Indus Pr.

NASCAR (Association) Staff. Nascar Thunder of Amer. LC 97-50245. 2000. lthr. 75.00 (*0-06-105075-X*) HarpC.

***NASCAR Staff.** Hammer Down. 128p. (YA). 1999. mass mkt. 3.99 (*0-06-105965-X*) HarpC.

Nascar Staff. NASCAR Cooks: The Tabasco/NASCAR 50th Anniversary Cookbook. LC 97-11208. (Illus.). 96p. 1998. 17.95 (*0-06-105066-0*) HarpC.

NASCAR Staff. NASCAR Encyclopedia. 2000. 40.00 (*0-06-105076-8*) HarpC.

— Official NASCAR Busch Series Handbook. LC 99-11063. (Illus.). 128p. 1999. pap. 19.95 (*0-06-107332-6*) HarpC.

— The Official NASCAR Handbook: Everything You Want to Know about the NASCAR Winston Cup Series. LC 98-6580. (NASCAR/Winston Cup Stock Car Racing Ser.). (Illus.). 192p. 1998. pap. 19.95 (*0-06-107318-0*) HarpC.

Nascar Staff. Official NASCAR Trivia: The Ultimate Challenge for NASCAR Fans. LC 98-16564. 192p. 1998. pap. 9.95 (*0-06-107304-0*) HarpC.

***NASCAR Staff.** Race Week: A Week in the Life of the Daytona 500. 192p. 2000. 50.00 (*0-06-105077-6*) HarpC.

NASCAR Staff & Vedral, Joyce L. Nascar: The Thunder of America. 50th anniversary ed. LC 97-50245. (Illus.). 200p. 1998. 45.00 (*0-06-105060-1*) HarpC.

Nascentes, A. Dicionario de Sinonimos. 3rd ed.Tr. of Dictionary of Synonyms. (POR.). 485p. 1981. 22.50 (*0-8288-1995-5*, M14429) Fr & Eur.

Nascenzi, Joseph P. Bygone New England... (Illus.). 160p. 2000. pap. 14.95 (*1-58066-027-4*) Douglas Charles Ltd.

Nascher, Ignatz L. Geriatrics: The Diseases of Old Age & Their Treatment. Kastenbaum, Robert J., ed. LC 78-22212. (Aging & Old Age Ser.). (Illus.). 1979. reprint ed. lib. bdg. 40.95 (*0-405-11825-2*) Ayer.

Naschold, Frieder. New Frontiers in Public Sector Management: Trends & Issues in State & Local Government in Europe. Watt, Andrew, tr. (De Gruyter Studies in Organization: No. 69). xiv, 329p. (C). 1996. text 79.95 (*3-11-015016-6*) De Gruyter.

Naschold, Frieder & De Vroom, Bert, eds. Regulating Employment & Welfare: Company & National Policies of Labour Force Participation at the End of Worklife in Industrial Countries. LC 93-35001. (Studies in Organization: No. 53). x, 496p. (C). 1993. lib. bdg. 94.95 (*3-11-013513-2*) De Gruyter.

Naschold, Frieder & Von Otter, Casten. Public Sector Transformation: Rethinking Markets & Hierarchies in Government. LC 96-291. (Dialogues on Work & Innovation Ser.: Vol. 1). vi, 176p. 1996. pap. 47.95 (*1-55619-825-6*) J Benjamins Pubng Co.

Naschold, Frieder, jt. ed. see Muramatsu, Michio.

***Naschy, Paul.** Paul Naschy: Memoirs of a Wolfman. 256p. 2000. pap. 20.00 (*1-887664-38-6*, Pub. by Midnght Marquee Pr) Koen Bk Distributors.

— Paul Naschy: Memoirs of a Wolfman. (Illus.). 256p. 2000. 55.00 (*1-887664-37-8*, Pub. by Midnght Marquee Pr) Koen Bk Distributors.

Nascimbene, Bruno. Nationality Laws in the European Union = Le Droit de la Nationalitbe Dans l'Union Europbeenne. LC 97-123863. xv, 771p. 1996. write for info. (*88-14-06139-4*) Giuffre.

Nascimbene, Yan. Ocean Deep. LC 98-50011. (J). 1999. 23.95 (*1-56846-161-5*, Creative Eds) Creative Co.

— Reader's Journal. (Illus.). 144p. 1998. pap. 17.95 (*1-55670-808-4*) Stewart Tabori & Chang.

Nascimbene, Yan. Wine: A Record Keeping Journal. 160p. 1996. spiral bd. 17.95 (*1-55670-515-8*) Stewart Tabori & Chang.

Nascimento, Abdias D. Orixas: Os Deuses Vivos da Africa. 170p. 1997. 79.95 (*85-85853-01-8*) Temple U Pr.

Nascimento, Amos, ed. A Matter of Discourse: Community & Communication in Contemporary Philosophies. LC 97-77554. (Avebury Series in Philosophy). 248p. 1998. text 67.95 (*1-85972-681-X*, Pub. by Ashgate Pub) Ashgate Pub Co.

Nascimento, Elisa L., tr. see Do Nascimento, Abdias.

Nascimento, M. A. Molecular Modeling - the Chemistry of the 21st Century. 172p. 1994. text 81.00 (*981-02-1620-3*) World Scientific Pub.

NASCU Staff, ed. see De Lafayette, Jean M.

***NASDIJJ.** The Blood Runs Like a River Through My Dreams: A Memoir. 224p. 2000. 23.00 (*0-618-04892-8*) HM.

NASDTEC Staff. NASDTEC Manual on Certification & Preparation of Educational Personnel in the U. S. 456p. 1995. pap. text, per. 74.95 (*0-7872-1681-X*) Kendall-Hunt.

— The NASDTEC Manual on the Preparation & Certification of Educational Personnel, 1998-1999. 4th ed. 456p. 1997. spiral bd. 74.95 (*0-7872-4537-2*); per. 74.95 (*0-7872-4536-4*) Kendall-Hunt.

Nase, Eckart. Oskar Pfisters Analytische Seelsorge: Theorie & Praxis des Ersten Pastoralpsychologen, Dargestellt an Zwei Fallstudien. (Arbeiten zur Praktischen Theologie Ser.: Bd. 3). (GER., Illus.). xviii, 622p. (C). 1993. lib. bdg. 167.70 (*3-11-013235-4*) De Gruyter.

Naseef, A., ed. Today's Problems, Tomorrow's Solutions: The Future Structure of Muslim Societies. 190p. 1988. text 95.00 (*0-7201-1991-X*) Continuum.

***Naseef, Fatima Umar.** Women in Islam: A Discourse in Rights & Obligations. 1999. 28.00 (*81-207-2181-0*, Pub. by Sterling Pubs) S Asia.

Naseef, Robert A. Ordinary Parents, Exceptional Children. LC 96-49752. 256p. 1997. 21.95 (*1-55972-377-7*, Birch Ln Pr) Carol Pub Group.

***Naser, Fadwa Kassis.** No Choice: Autobiography of an Arabian-American Lady. LC 99-90816. 1999. 25.00 (*0-7388-0516-5*); pap. 18.00 (*0-7388-0517-3*) Xlibris Corp.

Naser, Joseph, ed. Expert Systems Applications for the Electric Power Industry, 2 vols., Set. 1450p. 1990. 258.00 (*1-56032-102-4*) Hemisp Pub.

Naser, Najih & Naser, Saleh A. Clinical Chemistry Laboratory Manual. (Illus.). 360p. (C). 1998. wbk. ed. write for info. (*0-8151-2581-X*) Mosby Inc.

Naser, Saleh A., jt. auth. see Naser, Najih.

Nasgaard, Roald & Spalding, Jeffrey, contrib. by. Concealing/Revealing: Voices from the Canadian Foothills. (Illus.). 56p. 1997. pap. 17.50 (*1-889282-03-0*) FSU Mus Fine Arts.

Nasgowitz, David, jt. auth. see Oriental Institute Staff.

Nash. American People: Ben Franklin, Vol. 2. 4th ed. (C). 1998. 62.34 (*0-201-43783-X*) Addison-Wesley.

***Nash.** The American People Brief 3E SVE: Creating a Nation & Society. 3rd abr. ed. LC 99-29223. 907p. (C). 1999. pap. 39.67 (*0-321-00564-3*) Addison-Wesley.

— The American People Brief 3E SVE: Creating a Nation & Society, Vol. 1. 3rd abr. ed. LC 99-29223. Vol. 1. 483p. (C). 1999. pap. text 35.00 (*0-321-00566-X*) Addison-Wesley.

— The American People Brief 3E SVE: Creating a Nation & Society, Vol. 2. 3rd abr. ed. LC 99-29223. Vol. 2. 472p. (C). 1999. pap. text 35.00 (*0-321-00568-6*) Addison-Wesley.

Nash. Cases in Managerial Accounting. 1995. pap. 35.95 (*0-87393-413-X*) Dame Pubns.

Nash. Creating a Nation & a Society: Since 1865, 2. 2nd ed. 1997. suppl. ed. write for info. (*0-201-38939-8*) Addison-Wesley.

Nash. Good Intentions Aside. 250p. 1990. 29.95 (*0-07-103259-2*) McGraw.

— Military & Industrial Complexes. 2000. 25.00 (*0-465-04594-4*) HarpC.

— The Private Side of American History, Vol. 1. 5th ed. (C). 1999. pap. text 31.00 (*0-15-505541-0*, Pub. by Harcourt Coll Pubs) Harcourt.

— Recent Developments in Transport Economics. De Rus, ed. 328p. 1997. 78.95 (*1-85972-500-7*, Pub. by Ashgate Pub) Ashgate Pub Co.

— Red, White & Black. 4th ed. LC 99-27631. 362p. 1999. pap. text 34.40 (*0-13-956756-9*) P-H.

Nash. Republicanism in Modern Britain. 54.95 (*1-85928-374-8*) Ashgate Pub Co.

Nash. Retracing the Past: Readings in the History of the American People. 4th ed. LC 99-20996. 233p. (C). 1999. pap. text 37.00 (*0-321-04849-0*) Addison-Wesley.

— Retracing the Past: Readings in the History of the American People, Vol. 2. 4th ed. LC 99-20996. 236p. 1999. pap. text 37.00 (*0-321-04850-4*) Addison-Wesley.

— Social Psychology. Date not set. pap. text, teacher ed. write for info. (*0-314-87237-X*) West Pub.

— Universal Difference: Feminism & the Decidability of "Women" LC 97-28032. 256p. 1997. text 65.00 (*0-312-21004-3*) St Martin.

Nash, ed. Retracing the Past, Vol. 1. 4th ed. LC 97-10816. (C). 1999. text. write for info. (*0-673-98573-3*) Addison-Wesley.

— Retracing the Past, Vol. 2. 4th ed. (C). 1998. text. write for info. (*0-673-98574-1*) Addison-Wesley.

Nash & Bartell. Cases in Corporate Financial Planning & Control. 1997. pap. 35.95 (*0-87393-629-9*) Dame Pubns.

Nash, Kimberleigh. Cultural Competence: A Guide for Human Service Agencies. 1999. pap. text 12.95 (*0-87868-753-X*, CWLA Pr) Child Welfare.

Nash, Alan E. Population & Public Policy. (C). 1996. pap. text 29.95 (*0-8133-7893-1*) Westview.

Nash, Alan E., ed. Human Rights & the Protection of Refugees under International Law. 338p. 1989. 29.95 (*0-88645-080-2*, Pub. by Inst Res Pub) Ashgate Pub Co.

Nash, Alice. Collector's Handbook. (Illus.). 40p. (Orig.). 1982. pap. 5.00 (*0-911431-00-4*) Harmon-Meek Gal.

Nash, Alissa. Markita. LC 95-128561. 1997. pap. text 7.95 (*0-913543-39-X*) African Am Imag.

Nash, Allan. Managerial Compensation. (Studies in Productivity: Highlights of the Literature Ser.: Vol. 15). 56p. 1980. pap. 55.00 (*0-89361-022-4*) Work in Amer.

— Managerial Compensation, Vol. 15. LC 80-21044. (Work in America Institute Studies in Productivity). 1982. pap. 35.00 (*0-685-05448-9*, Pergamon Pr) Elsevier.

Nash, Amy K. North Korea: Major World Nations. LC 97-21857. (Major World Nations Ser.). (Illus.). 144p. (YA). (gr. 5 up). 1999. lib. bdg. 19.95 (*0-7910-4746-6*) Chelsea Hse.

Nash, Andrea, et al. Talking Shop: A Curriculum Sourcebook for Participatory Adult ESL. Keenan, Fran, ed. (Language in Education Ser.). (Illus.). 70p. (Orig.). 1992. pap. text 10.50 (*0-937354-78-3*) Delta Systems.

Nash, Andrew, ed. see Newman, John Henry.

Nash, Andy. Growing up Adventist: A Fond Look Back at the Church that Taught Me Faith, Love & Laughter. LC 96-50202. 1997. pap. 6.97 (*0-8163-1365-2*) Pacific Pr Pub Assn.

Nash, Ann E., tr. see Bouyer, Louis.

Nash, Anne. Prize of Fear. large type ed. (General Ser.). 336p. (Orig.). 1993. 27.99 (*0-7089-2848-X*) Ulverscroft.

Nash, Anne E., tr. from FRE. The Complete Works of Elizabeth of the Trinity, Vol. 2. LC 84-3748. 400p. (Orig.). 1995. pap. 12.95 (*0-935216-54-5*) ICS Pubns.

Nash, Arnold S., ed. Protestant Thought in the Twentieth Century: Whence & Whither? LC 78-5860. 296p. 1978. reprint ed. lib. bdg. 65.00 (*0-313-20484-5*, NAPT, Greenwood Pr) Greenwood.

Nash, Artemis D. Soft Tissue Sarcomas: Histological Diagnosis. LC 88-26490. (Biopsy Interpretation Ser.). 285p. 1989. reprint ed. pap. 88.40 (*0-7837-8354-X*, 204914400010) Bks Demand.

Nash, Barbara. From Acupressure to Zen: An Encyclopedia of Natural Therapies. 266p. 1998. pap. text 16.00 (*0-7881-5698-5*) DIANE Pub.

Nash, Bartleby. Mother Nature's Greatest Hits: The Top 40 Wonders of the Animal World. (Illus.). 132p. (Orig.). (J). 1991. pap. 5.95 (*0-9626072-7-4*) Living Planet Pr.

Nash, Bob. On My Way: Fragments of My Life As an Artist. (Illus.). 64p. (Orig.). 1996. pap. 10.00 (*0-931104-42-4*) SunInk Pubn.

Nash, Bradley D., et al. Organizing & Staffing the Presidency, Vol. III. (Proceedings Ser.). (Orig.). 1980. 11.00 (*0-938204-01-7*) Ctr Study Presidency.

Nash, Bruce. The Baseball Hall of Shame. 1989. per. 9.00 (*0-671-68766-2*) PB.

— The Fishing Hall of Shame. 256p. 1991. pap. 13.95 (*0-440-50318-3*) Dell.

— Runner's Weight Control Book. 1982. pap. 9.95 (*0-02-499640-8*, Macmillan Coll) P-H.

— Runner's Weight Control Book. 1984. 9.95 (*0-02-499650-5*, Macmillan Coll) P-H.

— Spooky Kids: Strange But True Tales. 1994. 8.05 (*0-606-06762-0*, Pub. by Turtleback) Demco.

Nash, Bruce. Totally Haunted Kids: True Ghost Stories. 1995. 8.05 (*0-606-06819-8*, Pub. by Turtleback) Demco.

Nash, Bruce & Zullo, Allan. Amazing but True Cat Tales. (Illus.). 96p. (Orig.). 1993. pap. 7.95 (*0-8362-8034-2*) Andrews & McMeel.

— Amazing but True Fishing Stories. LC 92-34622. 96p. 1993. pap. 7.95 (*0-8362-8022-9*) Andrews & McMeel.

— Amazing but True Golf Facts. 96p. 1992. pap. 7.95 (*0-8362-7994-8*) Andrews & McMeel.

— The Baseball Hall of Shame: Young Fans' Edition, No. 1. Clancy, Lisa, ed. 160p. (YA). (gr. 5 up). 1990. per. 2.99 (*0-671-69354-9*, Archway) PB.

— Baseball Hall of Shame 2: Young Fans' Edition, No. 2. Clancy, Lisa, ed. 144p. (Orig.). (YA). (gr. 5 up). 1991. per. 2.99 (*0-671-73533-0*, Archway) PB.

— The Baseball Hall of Shame's Funtastic Trivia & Sticker Book. (Illus.). 24p. (J). (gr. 1 up). 1992. pap. 3.95 (*0-671-74439-9*) Litle Simon.

— Baseball Hall of Shame's Warped Record Book. (Hall of Shame Ser.). 288p. (Orig.). 1991. pap. 9.95 (*0-02-029485-9*) Macmillan.

— Basketball Hall of Shame. Grad, Doug, ed. 192p. (Orig.). 1991. pap. 10.00 (*0-671-69414-6*) PB.

— The Football Hall of Shame. (Orig.). 1991. per. 8.95 (*0-671-74551-4*) PB.

— The Football Hall of Shame, Vol. 2. Vezeris, Olga, ed. 192p. (Orig.). 1990. per. 7.95 (*0-671-69413-8*) PB.

— The Football Hall of Shame: Young Fans' Edition, No. 1. (Illus.). 144p. (J). (gr. 5 up). 1990. mass mkt. 2.95 (*0-671-72922-5*, Archway) PB.

— The Football Hall of Shame Two: Young Fans' Edition, No. 2. Clancy, Lisa, ed. 160p. (Orig.). (YA). (gr. 5 up). 1991. pap. 2.99 (*0-671-73534-9*, Archway) PB.

— Freebies for Cat Lovers. (Illus.). 128p. 1986. pap. 5.95 (*0-668-06267-3*) P-H.

— The Golf Hall of Shame. 224p. 1991. per. 12.00 (*0-671-74583-2*) PB.

— Golf's Most Outrageous Quotes: An Official BGA Book. (Illus.). 96p. 1995. pap. 7.95 (*0-8362-1789-6*) Andrews & McMeel.

— The Greatest Sports Stories Never Told. LC 92-15352. (Illus.). 96p. (J). (gr. 2-6). 1993. mass mkt. 8.95 (*0-671-75938-8*) S&S Trade.

— The Hole Truth: Inside the Ropes of the PGA Tour. (Illus.). 192p. 1995. pap. 8.95 (*0-8362-7029-0*) Andrews & McMeel.

— The Insider's Guide to Baseball Autographs. LC 93-49371. (Illus.). 128p. (J). 1994. 7.95 (*0-8362-8050-4*) Andrews & McMeel.

— Spooky Kids: Strange but True Tales. LC 93-44029. (Illus.). 128p. (J). (gr. 1-6). 1996. pap. 3.95 (*0-8167-3447-X*) Troll Communs.

— The Sports Hall of Fame. 1987. write for info. (*0-318-62709-4*) PB.

— The Sports Hall of Shame: Young Fans Edition. MacDonald, Patricia, ed. 176p. (YA). (gr. 5 up). 1990. reprint ed. mass mkt. 2.95 (*0-671-69355-7*, Archway) PB.

— The Sports Hall of Shame's Funtastic Trivia & Sticker Book. (Illus.). 24p. (J). (gr. 1 up). 1992. pap. 3.95 (*0-671-74438-0*) Litle Simon.

— Totally Haunted Kids: True Ghost Stories. LC 94-18862. 128p. (J). (gr. 3-5). 1996. pap. 3.95 (*0-8167-3538-7*) Troll Communs.

Nash, Bruce & Zullo, Allan, eds. Lawyer's Wit & Wisdom: Quotations on the Legal Profession, in Brief. LC 94-73880. (Quote Bks.). (Illus.). 224p. 1995. 14.95 (*1-56138-650-2*) Running Pr.

Nash, Bruce, et al. Amazing but True Dog Tales. LC 94-25535. 128p. 1994. pap. 6.95 (*0-8362-8066-0*) Andrews & McMeel.

— The Golf Nut's Book of Amazing Feats & Records. 192p. 1994. pap. 12.95 (*0-8092-3790-3*, 379030, Contemporary Bks) NTC Contemp Pub Co.

— Haunted Kids: True Ghost Stories. LC 93-14489. (Illus.). (J). (gr. 4-9). 1993. pap. 3.50 (*0-8167-3266-3*) Troll Communs.

Nash, Bruce M. Baseball Hall of Shame. 2nd ed. 1991. 8.09 (*0-606-02053-5*, Pub. by Turtleback) Demco.

Nash, C. A., jt. auth. see Fowkes, A. S.

Nash, C. E., ed. Production of Aquatic Animals: Crustaceans, Molluscs, Amphibians & Reptiles. (World Animal Science Ser.: Vol. C4). 244p. 1991. 203.25 (*0-444-88312-6*) Elsevier.

Nash, C. E. & Novotny, A. J., eds. Production of Aquatic Animals: Fishes. (World Animal Science Ser.: Vol. C8). 422p. 1995. 259.25 (*0-444-81950-9*) Elsevier.

Nash, C. Robert, jt. auth. see Nash, T. M.

Nash, Carol R. AIDS: Choices for Life. LC 97-1255. (Issues in Focus Ser.). (Illus.). 112p. (YA). (gr. 6 up). 1997. lib. bdg. 20.95 (*0-89490-903-7*) Enslow Pubs.

— The Fight for Women's Right to Vote in American History. LC 97-18043. (In American History Ser.). 128p. (YA). (gr. 5 up). 1998. lib. bdg. 20.95 (*0-89490-986-X*) Enslow Pubs.

— Sexual Harassment: What Teens Should Know. LC 95-43806. (Issues in Focus Ser.). (Illus.). 112p. (YA). (gr. 6 up). 1996. lib. bdg. 20.95 (*0-89490-735-2*) Enslow Pubs.

Nash, Charles. Differential Topology & Quantum Field Theory. (Illus.). 386p. 1992. reprint ed. pap. text 63.00 (*0-12-514076-2*) Acad Pr.

Nash, Charles & Sen, Siddharta. Topology & Geometry for Physicists. 311p. 1988. reprint ed. pap. text 58.00 (*0-12-514081-9*) Acad Pr.

Nash, Charles E. Biographical Sketches of Gen. Pat Cleburne & T. C. Hindman. (Illus.). 300p. 1977. reprint ed. 25.00 (*0-89029-039-3*) Morningside Bkshop.

— History of Augusta Maine, First Settlements & Early Days As a Town, Including the Diary of Mrs. Martha Moore Ballard (1785-1812) (Illus.). 612p. 1997. reprint ed. lib. bdg. 64.00 (*0-8328-7099-4*) Higginson Bk Co.

Nash, Christopher. World Games: The Tradition of Anti-realist Revolt. 440p. 1988. text 42.50 (*0-416-34710-X*) Routledge.

— World PostModern Fiction. LC 92-39356. (C). 1993. pap. text 34.50 (*0-582-20910-2*, 79761) Longman.

Nash, Christopher, jt. ed. see Nash, Cristopher.

Nash, Christopher A. The Economics of Public Transport. LC 81-215543. (Modern Economics Ser.). (Illus.). 206p. reprint ed. pap. 63.90 (*0-8357-6588-1*, 203598300097) Bks Demand.

Nash, Claude, III, ed. see Sim.

Nash, Claude H. & Underkoffler, Leland A., eds. Developments in Industrial Microbiology: Proceedings of 1983 Annual Meeting, Vol. 25. LC 83-83097. 800p. 1984. 38.95 (*0-318-01836-5*) Society Indust Microb.

Nash, Clayton. Brazos Station. large type ed. 256p. pap. 18.99 (*0-7089-5434-0*) Ulverscroft.

Nash, Clayton. Dakota Wolf. large type ed. (Linford Western Library Ser.). 256p. 1997. pap. 16.99 (*0-7089-5150-3*) Ulverscroft.

***Nash, Clayton.** Die Like a Man. 240p. 2000. 18.99 (*0-7089-5684-X*) Ulverscroft.

— Hell's Doorway. large type ed. 240p. 2000. 20.99 (*1-84137-021-5*, Pub. by Mgna Lrg Print) Ulverscroft.

Nash, Clayton. Long-Riding Man. large type ed. (Linford Western Large Print Ser.). 256p. 1998. pap. 17.99 (*0-7089-5272-0*, Linford) Ulverscroft.

Nash, Colin E. Aquaculture Sector Planning & Management. 288p. 1995. 89.95 (*0-85238-227-8*) Blackwell Sci.

Nash, Colin E., jt. auth. see Insull, David.

Nash, Constance & Oakey, Virginia. Screen-Writer's Handbook. LC 77-76031. 160p. 1978. pap. 12.50 (*0-06-463454-X*, EH 454) HarpC.

Nash, Corbin. Take Your Victory! 42p. (Orig.). 1996. pap. 5.00 (*0-9649747-0-3*) Chrstian Outreach.

Nash, Corbin N. The Trying of Your Faith. 48p. 1998. pap. 5.00 (*0-9649747-2-X*) Chrstian Outreach.

— Who Are You! Knowing Your True Identity in Christ. 48p. 1997. pap. 5.00 (*0-9649747-1-1*) Chrstian Outreach.

Nash, Crabtree, & Dunn, et al. History Besieged. 336p. 1998. pap. 15.00 (*0-679-76750-9*) Vin Bks.

Nash, Cristopher & Nash, Christopher, eds. Narrative in Culture: Storytelling in the Sciences, Philosophy & Literature. LC 94-18539. (Warwick Studies in Philosophy & Literature). 256p. (C). 1994. pap. 24.99 (*0-415-10344-4*, B4640) Routledge.

Nash-Cummings, Nancy, jt. auth. see Adams, Anne B.

Nash, Daphne. Coinage of the Celtic World. (Illus.). 153p. 1987. lib. bdg. 45.00 (*0-900652-85-3*) S J Durst.

***Nash, Dave.** KDE Bible. (Bible Ser.). (Illus.). 900p. 2000. pap. text 39.99 (*0-7645-4692-9*) IDG Bks.

Nash, David. Secularism, Art & Freedom. 224p. 1992. text 54.00 (*0-7185-1417-3*, Pub. by Leicester U Pr) Cassell & Continuum.

— Secularism, Art & Freedom, Vol. 1. (C). 1994. pap. text 19.00 (*0-7185-2084-X*) Bks Intl VA.

Nash, David, jt. auth. see Pchiluk, William.

Nash, David, jt. auth. see Pochiluk, William.

Nash, David, ed. see Pochiluk, William.

Nash, David, jt. ed. see Seltzer, Jonathan.

***Nash, David B.** Connecting with the New Healthcare Consumer: Defining Your Strategy. LC 99-59088. 1999. 60.00 (*0-07-134672-4*) McGraw.

An Asterisk (*) at the beginning of an entry indicates that the title is appearing for the first time.

Nash, David B., ed. The Cardiologist's Managed Care Manual. (Illus.). 250p. (Orig.). 1997. spiral bd. 54.95 (*1-890045-03-9*) T L C Med Pub.
— Future Practice Alternatives in Medicine. 2nd ed. LC 93-14635. (Illus.). 432p. 1993. pap. 24.50 (*0-89640-236-3*) Igaku-Shoin.
— The Health Care Administrator's Managed Care Manual. (Illus.). 250p. (Orig.). 1997. spiral bd. 54.95 (*1-890045-05-5*) T L C Med Pub.
— The Oncologists Managed Care Manual. (Illus.). 250p. (Orig.). 1997. spiral bd. 54.95 (*1-890045-02-0*) T L C Med Pub.
— The Pharmacist's Managed Care Manual. (Illus.). 250p. (Orig.). 1997. spiral bd. 54.95 (*1-890045-04-7*) T L C Med Pub.
— The Physician's Guide to Managed Care. 272p. 1994. 67.00 (*0-8342-0393-6*, 20393) Aspen Pub.
Nash, David B. & Carroll, Patricia, eds. The Nurse's Managed Care Manual. (Illus.). 260p. (Orig.). 1997. spiral bd. 54.95 (*1-890045-01-2*) T L C Med Pub.
Nash, David B., jt. auth. see Majumdar, Shyamal K.
Nash, David B., jt. auth. see Markson, Leona E.
Nash, David B., jt. ed. see Goldfield, Norbert.
Nash, David B., jt. ed. see Johnson, Nelda E.
Nash, David B., jt. ed. see Todd, Warren E.
Nash, David S. Blasphemy in Modern Britain: 1789 to the Present. LC 98-24459. 304p. 1998. text 78.95 (*1-85928-023-4*, KD8073.N37, Pub. by Ashgate Pub) Ashgate Pub Co.
Nash, Dennison. Anthropology of Tourism. LC 96-218409. (Tourism Social Science Ser.). 240p. 1995. text 65.00 (*0-08-042398-1*, Pergamon Pr) Elsevier.
— Little Anthropology. 3rd ed. LC 98-30166. 210p. 1998. pap. text 27.20 (*0-13-906736-1*) P-H.
Nash, Derek, jt. auth. see Nash, Susan.
Nash, Diane & Treffinger, Donald J. The Mentor Kit: A Step-by-Step Guide to Creating An Effective Mentor Program in Your School. 76p. 1993. pap. 24.95 (*1-882664-06-X*) Prufrock Pr.
Nash, Dominie. Warp Painting: A Manual for Weavers. (Illus.). 32p. (Orig.). 1990. pap. 7.95 (*0-9623468-2-9*) Stellar Pub Hse.
***Nash, Douglas.** Orchids. (Illus.). 2000. 19.98 (*1-57145-265-6*, Thunder Bay) Advantage Pubs.
Nash, Douglas. The Politics of Space: Architecture, Painting & Theater in Postmodern Germany, Vol. 107. LC 94-36388. (American University Studies Germanic Languages & Literature Ser.: Ser. I). X, 232p. (C). 1996. 44.95 (*0-8204-2599-0*) P Lang Pubng.
Nash, E. New York's 50 Best Skyscrapers. LC 97-29334. 128p. 1997. pap. text 12.00 (*1-885492-47-2*) City & Co.
Nash, E., et al. Human Behavior: Guidelines for Health Professionals. 4th ed. 621p. 1994. reprint ed. pap. text 66.00 (*0-7021-2337-4*, Pub. by Juta & Co) Intl Spec Bk.
Nash, E. B. Leaders in Homoeopathic Therapeutics. 1981. 8.95 (*0-685-76565-2*) Formur Intl.
Nash, Edward L. Allahu Akbar. (Illus.). 500p. (Orig.). 1988. 29.95 (*0-918266-21-1*); pap. 15.00 (*0-918266-20-3*) Smyrna.
— Database Marketing: The Ultimate Marketing Tool. 336p. 1993. 44.95 (*0-07-046063-9*) McGraw.
***Nash, Edward L.** Direct Marketing. 4th ed. (Illus.). 600p. 2000. 54.95 (*0-07-135287-2*) McGraw.
— Direct Marketing: Strategy, Planning, Execution. 3rd ed. 480p. 1994. 44.95 (*0-07-046032-9*) McGraw.
Nash, Elizabeth. The Luminous Ones: A History of the Great Actresses. LC 91-19225. (American University Studies: Theatre Arts: Ser. XXVI, Vol. 10). 224p. 1992. 43.95 (*0-8204-1577-4*) P Lang Pubng.
— Pieces of Rainbow. LC 93-33450. (American University Studies, XX, Fine Arts: Vol. 22). 136p. (C). 1994. text 34.95 (*0-8204-2413-7*) P Lang Pubng.
— Plaisirs D'Amour: An Erotic Guide to the Senses. LC 94-23173. 192p. 1995. pap. 20.00 (*0-06-251149-1*, Pub. by Harper SF) HarpC.
Nash, Eric. Manhattan Skyscrapers. LC 98-50603. (Illus.). 1999. 45.00 (*1-56898-181-3*) Princeton Arch.
Nash, Eric Peter. Ansel Adams the Spirit of Wild Things. 1998. 16.98 (*1-880908-37-9*) Todtri Prods.
— Frank Lloyd Wright: Force of Nature, 1. 1998. pap. text 10.98 (*1-880908-50-6*) Todtri Prods.
Nash, Erica & Nahas, Violetta. Understanding the ECG: A Guide for Nurses. (An Arnold Publication). 208p. 1996. pap. text 19.50 (*0-17-008927-4*, Pub. by E A) OUP.
Nash, Florence. Crossing Water. 48p. (Orig.). 1996. pap. 9.43 (*0-9654797-0-6*) Gravity Pr NC.
Nash, Franklin R. Estimating Device Reliability: Assessment of Credibility. LC 92-34878. (International Series in Engineering & Computer Science, VLSI, Computer Architecture, & Digital Screen Processing: Vol. 206). 1992. text 105.00 (*0-7923-9304-X*) Kluwer Academic.
Nash, Fred. Meta-Imperialism: A Study in Political Science. (Avebury Series in Philosophy). 544p. 1994. 104.95 (*1-85628-694-0*, Pub. by Avebury) Ashgate Pub Co.
***Nash, Gary B.** American Odyssey: The United States in the Twentieth Century LC 99-202488. 1010 p. 1999. write for info. (*0-02-822154-0*) Glencoe.
— American Odyssey: The United States in the Twentieth Century. LC 99 202488. 1999. teacher ed. write for info. (*0-02-822158-3*) Glencoe.
Nash, Gary B. The American People. (C). 2000. pap. text. write for info. (*0-321-06679-0*) Addson-Wesley Educ.
— American People. 3rd ed. 240p. (C). 1999. pap. text, student ed. 20.00 (*0-321-06379-1*); pap. text, student ed. 20.00 (*0-321-06380-5*) Addson-Wesley.
***Nash, Gary B.** The American People. 4th ed. 1200p. (C). 1998. text 75.00 (*0-321-04490-8*) Addson-Wesley.
— American People. 4th ed. (C). 1998. text. write for info. (*0-321-02579-2*); text. write for info. (*0-321-03810-X*) Addson-Wesley Educ.
Nash, Gary B. The American People, Vol. 1. 4th ed. (C). 1999. pap. text. write for info. (*0-321-03669-7*) Addison-Wesley Educ.
***Nash, Gary B.** American People, Vol. 2. 5th ed. (C). 2000. text. write for info. (*0-321-07634-6*) Addison-Wesley.
— The American People: Brief Edition. 4th ed. (C). 1999. pap. write for info. (*0-321-03673-5*) Addison-Wesley.
Nash, Gary B. American People Brief Edition. 4th ed. (C). 1999. lib. bdg. write for info. (*0-321-03671-9*) Addison-Wesley.
— America's Hidden Mestizo History. 1996. pap. write for info. (*0-8050-4954-1*) H Holt & Co.
— Forbidden Love. LC 98-12154. (Illus.). (YA). (gr. 9 up). 1998. 18.95 (*0-8050-4953-3*, Bks Young Read) H Holt & Co.
— Forging Freedom: The Formation of Philadelphia's Black Community, 1720-1840. 368p. 1991. pap. 19.50 (*0-674-30933-2*, NASFOX) HUP.
— From These Beginnings, Vol. 2. 4th ed. (C). 1997. pap. 27.50 (*0-06-044747-8*) Addson-Wesley Educ.
— Quakers & Politics: Pennsylvania, 1681-1726. rev. ed. 384p. 1993. pap. text 18.95 (*1-55553-166-0*) NE U Pr.
— Race & Revolution. 224p. 1990. pap. 15.95 (*0-945612-21-4*); text 29.95 (*0-945612-11-7*) Madison Hse.
— The Urban Crucible: The Northern Seaports & the Origins of the American Revolution. (Illus.). 300p. 1986. pap. 17.95 (*0-674-93059-2*) HUP.
***Nash, Gary B., ed.** American People. 4th ed. (C). 1998. text. write for info. (*0-321-02581-4*) Addson-Wesley Educ.
Nash, Gary B., ed. The American People, Vol. 1. 4th ed. Vol. 1. 573p. (C). 1997. pap. 60.00 (*0-673-98576-8*) Addison-Wesley.
Nash, Gary B. & Alfers. American People Telecourse, Vol. 2. (C). 1992. pap., student ed. 24.33 (*0-06-500726-3*) HarpC.
Nash, Gary B. & Schultz. Retracing the Past, 2 vols., Vol. 1. 3rd ed. 288p. (C). 1997. pap. 36.00 (*0-06-501060-4*) Addson-Wesley Educ.
Nash, Gary B. & Schultz, Ronald. Retracing the Past, 2 vols. 3rd ed. (C). 1997. pap. 36.00 (*0-06-501061-2*) Addson-Wesley Educ.
Nash, Gary B. & Soderlund, Jean R. Freedom by Degrees: Emancipation in Pennsylvania & Its Aftermath. (Illus.). 272p. 1991. text 49.95 (*0-19-504583-1*) OUP.
Nash, Gary B., et al. The American People. 3rd ed. (C). 1997. pap. 72.00 (*0-06-501055-8*) Addson-Wesley Educ.
— The American People: Creating a Nation & a Society. 4th abr. ed. LC 96-52439. 1050p. (C). 1997. 78.00 (*0-673-98575-X*) Longman.
— Private Side of American History: Readings in Everyday Life, Vol. 1: To 1877. 4th ed. 459p. (C). 1987. pap. text 37.00 (*0-15-571960-2*, Pub. by Harcourt Coll Pubs) Harcourt.
Nash, Gary B., jt. ed. see Crabtree, Charlotte A.
Nash, Gary B., jt. ed. see Sweet, David G.
Nash, Geoffrey. The Arab Writer in English: Arab Themes in Metropolitan Language, 1908-1958. LC 97-39709. Orig. Title: Arab Writers Who Write in English. 224p. 1998. 59.95 (*1-898723-84-2*, Pub. by Sussex Acad Pr) Intl Spec Bk.
— The Phoenix & the Ashes. 160p. 1985. pap. 8.25 (*0-85398-199-X*) G Ronald Pub.
Nash, George. Do-It-Yourself Housebuilding: The Complete Handbook. LC 94-2371. (Illus.). 704p. 1995. pap. 24.95 (*0-8069-0424-0*) Sterling.
— Finishing Details. 1997. write for info. (*0-8069-8102-4*) Sterling.
— Old Houses: A Rebuilder's Manual. (Illus.). 1979. pap. 12.95 (*0-686-96841-7*) P-H.
***Nash, George.** Renovating Old Houses. 1999. 29.50 (*0-8446-6994-6*) Peter Smith.
Nash, George. Renovating Old Houses. LC 95-44407. (Illus.). 352p. 1996. reprint ed. pap. 19.95 (*1-56158-128-3*, 070258) Taunton.
— Wooden Fences. LC 97-18619. (Illus.). 240p. 1997. 29.95 (*1-56158-151-8*, 070280) Taunton.
— Wooden Fences. (Illus.). 1999. pap. 22.95 (*1-56158-292-1*) Taunton.
Nash, George H. The Conservative Intellectual Movement in America Since 1945. LC 98-70719. 1998. pap. 16.95 (*1-882926-20-X*) ISI Books.
— The Conservative Intellectual Movement in America since 1945. 2nd ed. LC 96-75872. 467p. 1996. 24.95 (*1-882926-12-9*) ISI Books.
— Herbert Hoover & Stanford University. (Publication Ser.: No. 369). 224p. 1988. 24.95 (*0-8179-8691-X*); pap. text 18.95 (*0-8179-8692-8*) Hoover Inst Pr.
— The Life of Herbert Hoover: Master of Emergencies, 1917-1918, Vol. 3. (Illus.). 704p. 1996. 45.00 (*0-393-03841-6*) Norton.
— The Life of Herbert Hoover: The Humanitarian, 1914-1917, Vol. 2. (Illus.). 1988. 25.00 (*0-393-02550-0*) Norton.
Nash, Gerald D. A. P. Giannini & the Bank of America. LC 92-54131. (Oklahoma Western Biographies Ser.: Vol. 5). (Illus.). 174p. 1992. 26.95 (*0-8061-2461-X*) U of Okla Pr.
— The American West Transformed: The Impact of the Second World War. LC 89-24957. (Illus.). xii, 320p. 1990. reprint ed. pap. 12.50 (*0-8032-8360-1*, Bison Books) U of Nebr Pr.
— Creating the West: Historical Interpretations, 1890-1990. LC 91-8584. (Calvin P. Horn Lectures in Western History & Culture). (Illus.). 318p. 1991. pap. 18.95 (*0-8263-1267-5*) U of NM Pr.
— The Crucial Era: The Great Depression & World War II, 1929-1945. 2nd ed. (Illus.). 213p. (C). 1998. reprint ed. pap. text 12.95 (*1-57766-022-6*) Waveland Pr.
— The Federal Landscape: An Economic History of the Twentieth-Century West. LC 99-6027. (Modern American West Ser.). 224p. 1999. pap. 17.95 (*0-8165-1988-9*) U of Ariz Pr.
— The Federal Landscape: An Economic History of the Twentieth-Century West. LC 99-6027. (The Modern American West Ser.). (Illus.). 224p. 1999. 40.00 (*0-8165-1863-7*) U of Ariz Pr.
— State Government & Economic Development. Bruchey, Stuart, ed. LC 78-56676. (Management of Public Lands in the U. S. Ser.). 1979. reprint ed. lib. bdg. 31.95 (*0-405-11346-3*) Ayer.
— World War II & the West: Reshaping the Economy. LC 89-4935. 326p. 1990. reprint ed. pap. 101.10 (*0-608-03474-6*, 206418400008) Bks Demand.
Nash, Gerald D., ed. see Davies, Richard O.
Nash, Gerald Q., et al. The Vital Records of Hudson, NH, 1734-1985. LC 98-152423. 596p. 1998. pap. 39.50 (*0-7884-0799-6*, N074) Heritage Bk.
Nash, Gerald R. Why God Allows Trials & Disappointments. (Uplook Ser.). 31p. 1972. pap. 0.99 (*0-8163-0082-8*, 23618-2) Pacific Pr Pub Assn.
Nash, Gilbert. Humphreys Families in America: (Dorchester & Weymouth Families) (Illus.). 275p. 1992. reprint ed. pap. 39.00 (*0-8328-2389-9*); reprint ed. lib. bdg. 49.00 (*0-8328-2388-0*) Higginson Bk Co.
Nash, Grace C. Creative Approaches to Child Development with Music, Language & Movement: Incorporating the Philosophies & Techniques of Orff, Kodaly, & Laban. LC 73-93672. (Illus.). 176p. 1974. pap. text 28.95 (*0-88284-014-2*, 1405) Alfred Pub.
Nash, Grace C. & Rapley, Janice. Holidays & Special Days. Feldstein, Sandy et al, eds. (Illus.). 260p. (J). (gr. k-6). 1988. teacher ed. 31.95 (*0-88284-368-0*, 3517) Alfred Pub.
— Holidays & Special Days. Feldstein, Sandy et al, eds. (Illus.). 136p. (J). (gr. k-6). 1988. student ed. 9.95 (*0-88284-369-9*, 3516) Alfred Pub.
— Music in the Making. 160p. 1990. pap. 27.95 (*0-88284-448-2*, 3557) Alfred Pub.
Nash, Grace C., et al. Do It My Way: A Handbook for Building Creative Teaching Experiences. 184p. 1977. pap. text 24.95 (*0-88284-055-X*, 1442) Alfred Pub.
***Nash, Harold W.** Our Aging Brain: Changing & Growing. Nash, Timothy A., ed. LC 98-92099. (Illus.). 162p. 1999. pap. 15.00 (*0-9666162-0-0*) Ontarolina.
Nash, Helen. Aquatic Plants. 1998. 29.95 (*0-676-57283-9*) Random.
— Challenging Cryptograms. LC 93-39591. 128p. 1994. pap. 5.95 (*0-8069-0594-8*) Sterling.
— The Complete Pond Builder: Creating a Beautiful Water Garden. (Illus.). 144p. 1997. pap. 17.95 (*0-8069-3867-6*) Sterling.
***Nash, Helen.** Helen Nash's Kosher Kitchen. 2000. write for info. (*0-7657-6154-8*) Aronson.
Nash, Helen. Kosher Cuisine. LC 95-15218. 360p. 1995. reprint ed. pap. 30.00 (*1-56821-611-4*) Aronson.
— The Living Pond: Water Gardens with Fish & Other Creatures. (Illus.). 2000. 24.95 (*0-8069-0705-3*) Sterling.
— Low-Maintenance Water Gardens. (Illus.). 128p. 1998. pap. 17.95 (*0-8069-4283-5*) Sterling.
— Low Maintenance Water Gardens. Date not set. pap. 17.95 (*0-676-57331-2*) Random.
— The Pond Doctor: Planning & Maintaining a Healthy Water Garden. (Illus.). 160p. (Orig.). 1995. pap. 17.95 (*0-8069-0687-1*) Sterling.
— Pond Planting: Practical Designs for Water Gardens. 2000. write for info. (*0-8069-9757-5*) Sterling.
***Nash, Helen.** Water Gardening Basics. (Illus.). 2000. pap. 14.95 (*0-8069-5575-9*) Sterling.
Nash, Helen. Water Gardening Basics: Pond Primer. LC 99-11932. 1999. 21.95 (*0-8069-5747-6*) Sterling.
Nash, Helen & Hughes, Eamonn. Waterfalls, Fountains, Pools & Streams: Designing & Building Water Features for Your Garden. (Illus.). 128p. 1999. pap. 17.95 (*0-8069-9666-8*) Sterling.
Nash, Helen & Masterson, Dorothy. Humorous Cryptograms. LC 95-12624. 128p. 1995. pap. 5.95 (*0-8069-3982-6*) Sterling.
Nash, Helen & Speichert, C. Greg. Water Gardening in Containers: Small Ponds Indoors & Out. LC 96-11986. (Illus.). 128p. 1996. 24.95 (*0-8069-8197-0*) Sterling.
***Nash, Helen & Stroupe, Steve.** Plants for Water Gardens: The Complete Guide to Aquatic Plants. (Illus.). 224p. 1999. pap. 19.95 (*0-8069-9980-2*) Sterling.
Nash-Hoff, Michele. For-Profit Incubators: An Industry Survey Report. 100p. 1998. pap. 26.00 (*1-887183-45-0*) NBIA.
Nash, Howard P., Jr. Andrew Johnson: Congress & Reconstruction. LC 72-248. 170p. 1972. 18.00 (*0-8386-1129-X*) Fairleigh Dickinson.
— Stormy Petrel: The Life & Times of General Benjamin F. Butler, 1818-1893. LC 71-81498. 335p. 1975. 35.00 (*0-8386-7383-X*) Fairleigh Dickinson.
Nash, Hugh O., Jr. Electrical Systems for Health Care Facilities. (Management & Compliance Ser.: Vol. 7). (Illus.). 144p. 1992. ring bd. 110.00 (*0-87258-608-1*, 055206) Am Hospital.
Nash, Ian & Walshe, John. Overcoming Exclusion Through Adult Learning. 180p. 1999. pap. 29.00 (*92-64-17026-X*, 96 1999 03 1 P, Pub. by Org for Econ) OECD.
Nash, Ilana, jt. auth. see Farah, David.
***Nash, Ira S. & Fuster, Valentin.** Efficacy of Myocardial Infarction Therapy: An Evaluation of Clinical Trials Evidence. LC 99-10224. (Illus.). 520p. 1999. text 195.00 (*0-8247-1932-8*) Dekker.
Nash, Irwin. Diccionario Practico De Herramientas y Maquinaria.Tr. of Dictionary of Tools & Machinery. (SPA.). 204p. (Orig.). 1996. pap. 7.95 (*0-9645504-0-7*) Albacore Pr.
Nash, J. M. The Age of Rembrandt & Vermeer: Dutch Painting in The Seventeenth Century. LC 72-172647. 271p. 1972. write for info. (*0-7148-1528-4*) Phaidon Pr.
Nash, J. M., ed. see American Society of Mechanical Engineers Staff.
Nash, J. R. & Ross, Stanley R. MPG Consumer Annual 1988 (Films of 1987) (Illus.). 320p. (Orig.). 1997. pap. 19.95 (*0-933997-17-5*) CineBks.
Nash, Jacqueline A. & Kinkaid, Joann. Stenotype Theory for the Professional Scopist. Ritter, Beverly L. & Rhyne, Patricia J., eds. (Realtime Machine Shorthand Ser.). 218p. (Orig.). (C). 1995. pap. text 25.00 (*0-938643-64-9*) Stenotype Educ.
Nash, James A. Loving Nature: Ecological Integrity & Christian Responsibility. 1991. pap. 16.95 (*0-687-22824-7*) Abingdon.
Nash, James H. & Nash, Mary F. A Nash-Allen Genealogy: Zachariah H. Nash, Lawson Allen, & Their Descendants. LC 83-62562. (Illus.). 1984. 22.00 (*0-9612498-0-3*) J H Nash.
Nash, Jane C. Veiled Images: Titian's Mythological Paintings for Philip II. LC 83-45949. (Illus.). 120p. 1986. 35.00 (*0-87982-511-1*) Art Alliance.
Nash, Jay R. Bloodletters & Badmen: A Narrative Encyclopedia of American Criminals from the Pilgrims to the Present. expanded rev. ed. LC 94-49585. (Illus.). 704p. 1995. pap. 19.95 (*0-87131-777-X*) M Evans.
— Bloodletters I. 1989. mass mkt. 4.95 (*0-446-35574-7*, Pub. by Warner Bks) Little.
— Citizen Hoover: A Critical Study of the Life & Times of J. Edgar Hoover & His FBI. LC 72-76266. (Illus.). 304p. 1972. text 29.95 (*0-911012-60-5*) Burnham Inc.
— Dictionary of Crime: Criminal Injustice, Criminology & Law Enforcement. 433p. 1994. 39.95 (*1-56924-873-7*) Marlowe & Co.
— The Dillinger Dossier. LC 83-72087. (Illus.). 312p. 1983. pap. 25.00 (*0-913204-16-1*) December Pr.
— Encyclopedia of Western Lawmen. 572p. 1994. 49.95 (*1-56924-897-4*) Marlowe & Co.
— Encyclopedia of Western Lawmen & Outlaws. LC 94-15032. (Illus.). 581p. 1994. reprint ed. pap. 25.95 (*0-306-80591-X*) Da Capo.
— Jay Robert Nash's Crime Chronology: A Worldwide Record, 1900-1983. LC 83-14046. (Illus.). 230p. reprint ed. pap. 71.30 (*0-7837-5344-6*, 204508700005) Bks Demand.
— On All Fronts. LC 74-81911. (Illus.). 147p. 1974. pap. 15.00 (*0-913204-03-X*) December Pr.
— Spies: A Narrative Encyclopedia of Dirty Tricks & Double Dealing from Biblical Times to Today. (Illus.). 640p. (Orig.). 1997. pap. 24.95 (*0-87131-790-7*) M Evans.
— World Encyclopedia of Organized Crime. 624p. 1994. 49.95 (*1-56924-898-2*) Marlowe & Co.
— World Encyclopedia of Organized Crime. (Illus.). 634p. 1993. reprint ed. pap. 27.50 (*0-306-80535-9*) Da Capo.
— World Encyclopedia of 20th Century Murder. 693p. 1994. 49.95 (*1-56924-872-9*) Marlowe & Co.
Nash, Jay R., et al, eds. The Motion Picture Guide: Annual 1990. The Films of 1989. 700p. 1990. write for info. (*3-598-10934-2*) K G Saur Verlag.
— The Motion Picture Guide: Annual 1991 - The Films of 1990. 720p. 1991. write for info. (*3-598-11067-7*) K G Saur Verlag.
— The Motion Picture Guide: Annual 1993 - The Films of 1992. ix, 635p. 1993. write for info. (*3-598-11168-1*) K G Saur Verlag.
— The Motion Picture Guide: Annual 1995 - The Films of 1994. 650p. 1995. write for info. (*3-598-11268-8*) K G Saur Verlag.
— The Motion Picture Guide: Annual 1996 - The Films of 1995. 600p. 1996. write for info. (*3-598-11330-7*) K G Saur Verlag.
— The Motion Picture Guide: Annual 1997 - The Films of 1996. 600p. 1997. write for info. (*3-598-11354-4*) K G Saur Verlag.
— The Motion Picture Guide Annual, 1999. 600p. 1999. 179.95 (*0-933997-43-4*, Pub. by CineBks) Whitehurst & Clark.
— The Motion Picture Guide 1998: The Films of 1997. annuals 600p. 1998. 180.00 (*3-598-11386-2*) K G Saur Verlag.
Nash, Jay R. & Ross, Stanley R. The Motion Picture Guide, 12 vols., Set. LC 85-71145. (Complete Film Resource Center Ser.). 1987. 600.00 (*0-933997-00-0*) CineBooks.
— The Motion Picture Guide Index, 2 vols. LC 85-71145. 3170p. 1987. 100.00 (*0-933997-11-6*) CineBks.
Nash, Jay R. & Ross, Stanley R., eds. The Motion Picture Guide 1988 Annual: The Films of 1987. (Illus.). 799p. 1997. 99.50 (*0-933997-16-7*) CineBks.
— The Motion Picture Guide 1989 Annual: The Films of 1988. (Films of 1988 Ser.). (Illus.). 665p. 1997. 99.50 (*0-933997-20-5*) CineBks.
— The Motion Picture Guide 1987 Annual: The Films of 1986. (Illus.). 726p. 1997. 99.50 (*0-933997-15-9*) CineBks.
— The Motion Picture Guide 1986 Annual: The Films of 1985. (Illus.). 450p. 1997. 99.50 (*0-933997-14-0*) CineBks.
— The Motion Picture Guide 1990 Annual: The Films of 1989. (Illus.). 480p. 1997. 99.50 (*0-933997-29-9*) CineBks.
Nash, Jay Robert. Terrorism in the 20th Century: A Narrative Encyclopedia from the Anarchists, Through the Weather. LC 98-22532. 468p. 1998. pap. 24.95 (*0-87131-855-5*) M Evans.
***Nash, Jean.** A Love Through All Time. 392p. 1999. pap. 9.95 (*1-893896-03-X*) Ima Jinn.
Nash, Jeffery E., jt. auth. see Higgins, Paul C.
Nash, Jeffrey E. Social Psychology: Society & Self. (Illus.). 425p. (C). 1985. text 52.00 (*0-314-85281-6*) West Pub.

N

Nash, Jeffrey E. & Calonico, James M. Institutions in Modern Society: Meanings, Forms, & Character. 1993p. 1990. text 38.95 (*0-930390-07-5*); pap. text 22.95 (*0-930390-06-7*) Gen Hall.

— The Meaning of Social Interaction: An Introduction to Social Psychology. LC 96-75605. 376p. (Orig.). 1996. text 39.95 (*1-882289-30-7*); pap. text 25.95 (*1-882289-29-3*) Gen Hall.

Nash, Jerry C. The Love Aesthetics of Maurice Sceve: Poetry & Struggle. (Cambridge Studies in French: No. 34). 217p. (C). 1991. text 64.95 (*0-521-39412-0*) Cambridge U Pr.

Nash, Jerry C., ed. Pre-Pleiade Poetry. LC 84-81851. (French Forum Monographs: No. 57). 148p. (Orig.). 1985. pap. 12.95 (*0-917058-57-7*) French Forum.

— A Sceve Celebration: Delie, 1544-1994. LC 94-214962. (Stanford French & Italian Studies: No. 77). 200p. 1993. pap. 56.50 (*0-915838-93-1*) Anma Libri.

Nash, Jerry C., jt. ed. see Bowen, Barbara C.

Nash, Jerry C., jt. ed. see Lacy, Norris J.

Nash, Jesse W. The Myth of Warmth. LC 93-72178. 78p. (Orig.). 1994. pap. 12.95 (*0-9625762-4-7*) Art Review Pr.

— Vietnamese Catholicism. LC 93-56459. (Illus.). xix, 184p. (Orig.). (C). 1994. pap. 9.95 (*0-9625762-1-2*) Art Review Pr.

Nash, Jesse W. & Nguyen, Elizabeth T. The L. S. A. T. Study Companion: Logical Reasoning. LC 93-72179. 200p. (Orig.). (C). 1994. pap. 14.95 (*0-9625762-3-9*) Art Review Pr.

Nash, Jesse W. & Nguyen, Elizabeth T., eds. Romance, Gender, & Religion in a Vietnamese-American Community: Tales of God & Beautiful Women. LC 94-16411. 192p. 1995. text 79.95 (*0-7734-9087-6*) E Mellen.

Nash, John. Vermeer. (Illus.). 128p. 1991. 25.00 (*1-870248-62-7*) Scala Books.

— Views of the Royal Pavilion. (Illus.). 128p. 1992. 9.98 (*1-55859-340-3*, Cross Riv Pr) Abbeville Pr.

Nash, John & Takacs, Wendy. Trade Policy Reform: Lessons & Implications. LC 98-10663. (Regional & Sectoral Study Ser.). 372p. 1998. pap. 30.00 (*0-8213-3983-4*, 13983) World Bank.

Nash, John, jt. auth. see Csaki, Csaba.

Nash, John, ed. see Graham, Mary & McGee, Michelle.

Nash, John, jt. ed. see Thomas, Vinod.

Nash, John, ed. see Williams, Douglas W.

Nash, John C. Compact Numerical Methods for Computers: Linear Algebra & Function Minimisation. 2nd ed. (Illus.). 292p. 1990. 154.00 (*0-85274-318-1*); pap. 47.00 (*0-85274-319-X*) IOP Pub.

Nash, John D., jt. auth. see Csaki, Csaba.

Nash, John F. Essays on Game Theory. LC 96-26478. 112p. 1996. 45.00 (*1-85898-426-2*) E Elgar.

***Nash, Jonell.** Essence Brings You Great Cooking. 2001. pap. 20.00 (*0-06-095813-8*) HarpC.

— Essence Brings You Great Cooking. LC 93-25624. (Illus.). 480p. 1999. 29.95 (*1-56743-033-3*, Amistad) HarperTrade.

Nash, Jonell. Low-Fat Soul. LC 97-97059. 224p. 1997. pap. 14.00 (*0-345-41363-6*) Ballantine Pub Grp.

***Nash, Joyce.** Steps Thru Life. 1999. pap. write for info. (*1-58235-095-7*) Watermrk Pr.

***Nash, Joyce D.** Binge No More: Your Guide to Overcoming Disordered Eating. 224p. 1999. pap. 14.95 (*1-57224-174-8*) New Harbinger.

Nash, Joyce D. The New Maximize Your Body Potential: Lifetime Skills for Weight Management. 2nd ed. LC 96-39862. (Illus.). 475p. 1997. pap. text 24.95 (*0-923521-36-4*) Bull Pub.

— Taking Charge of Your Smoking. 124p. (Orig.). 1981. student ed. 14.95 (*0-915950-50-2*) Bull Pub.

Nash, June. I Spent My Life in the Mines: The Story of Juan Rojas, Bolivian Tin Miner. (Illus.). 416p. 1992. text 64.50 (*0-231-07936-2*); pap. text 23.00 (*0-231-07937-0*) Col U Pr.

— We Eat the Mines & the Mines Eat Us: Dependency & Exploitation in Bolivian Tin Mines. (Illus.). 384p. 1993. pap. 22.50 (*0-231-08051-4*); text 57.50 (*0-231-08050-6*) Col U Pr.

Nash, June, et al, eds. Ideology & Social Change in Latin America. vi, 306p. 1977. text 102.00 (*0-677-04170-5*) Gordon & Breach.

— Popular Participation in Social Change: Cooperatives, Collectives, & Nationalized Industry. (World Anthropology Ser.). xviii, 622p. 1976. 73.10 (*90-279-7849-2*) Mouton.

Nash, June & Safa, Helen I., eds. Women & Change in Latin America: New Directions in Sex & Class. LC 85-18563. (Illus.). 384p. 1985. 47.95 (*0-89789-069-8*, Bergin & Garvey); pap. 19.95 (*0-89789-070-1*, Bergin & Garvey) Greenwood.

Nash, June C., ed. Crafts in the World Market: The Impact of Global Exchange on Middle American Artisans. LC 91-21308. (SUNY Series in the Anthropology of Work). 264p. (C). 1993. text 19.50 (*0-7914-1061-7*) State U NY Pr.

Nash, K. L. & Choppin, G. R. Separations of F Elements: Proceedings of an ACS Symposium of f Elements Separations Held in San Diego, California, March 13-17, 1994. (Illus.). 286p. (C). 1995. text 114.00 (*0-306-45070-4*, Kluwer Plenum) Kluwer Academic.

Nash, Kate. Contemporary Political Sociology: Globalization, Politics & Power. LC 99-16133. 304p. 1999. text 59.95 (*0-631-20660-4*) Blackwell Pubs.

***Nash, Kate.** Contemporary Political Sociology: Globalization, Politics & Power. LC 99-16133. 304p. 1999. pap. text 27.95 (*0-631-20661-2*) Blackwell Pubs.

Nash, Kate, ed. Readings in Contemporary Political Sociology. LC 99-16940. 448p. 1999. text 64.95 (*0-631-21363-5*) Blackwell Pubs.

***Nash, Kate, ed.** Readings in Contemporary Political Sociology. LC 99-16940. 448p. 1999. pap. text 32.95 (*0-631-21364-3*) Blackwell Pubs.

***Nash, Kate & Scott, Alan, eds.** The Blackwell Companion to Political Sociology. 2000. 99.95 (*0-631-21050-4*) Blackwell Pubs.

Nash, Kermit B., ed. Psychosocial Aspects of Sickle Cell Disease: Past, Present, & Future Directions of Research. LC 94-12367. (Journal of Health & Social Policy: Vol. 5, Nos. 3 & 4). (Illus.). 282p. 1994. 49.95 (*1-56024-578-6*) Haworth Pr.

***Nash, Kevin.** New Illustrated Encyclopedia of Motorcycles. (Illus.). 2000. 24.99 (*0-7858-1163-X*) Bk Sales Inc.

Nash, Kimberley. Creative Writing Level 1: Teach-a-Script. 61p. (YA). (gr. 3 up). 1998. spiral bd. 12.95 (*0-9653723-1-6*) Resurrection Res.

***Nash, Kimberley.** How to Write Essays & Research Reports: A 25 Week Journaling Workbook, Grades 5-7, Level A. (Illus.). 162p. (YA). (gr. 3-12). 1999. wbk. ed. 19.95 (*0-9653723-6-7*) Resurrection Res.

Nash, Kimberley. Joy: Halloween. (Illus.). 104p. (YA). (gr. 2-10). 1996. pap. 6.95 (*0-9653723-0-8*) Resurrection Res.

***Nash, Kimberley.** Lab Reports: How to Write Lab Reports for Science Fairs & Classroom Experiments. (Illus.). 82p. (YA). (gr. 3-12). 1999. spiral bd., wbk. ed. 14.95 (*0-9653723-3-2*) Resurrection Res.

— More Lab Reports: For Grades 3-6. (Illus.). 58p. (J). (gr. 3-6). 1999. spiral bd., wbk. ed. 6.95 (*0-9653723-4-0*) Resurrection Res.

— More Lab Reports: For Grades 7-12. (Illus.). 89p. (YA). (gr. 7-12). 1999. spiral bd., wbk. ed. 8.95 (*0-9653723-5-9*) Resurrection Res.

Nash, Kitty. Irish Blessings: With Legends, Poems & Greetings. 96p. 1996. 5.99 (*0-517-39989-X*) Random Hse Value.

Nash, Knowlton. Cue the Elephant! Backstage Tales at the CBC. (Illus.). 326p. 1997. pap. text 15.95 (*0-7710-6735-6*) McCland & Stewart.

— Microphone Wars: A History of Triumph & Betrayal at CBC. (Illus.). 584p. 1996. pap. text 24.99 (*0-7710-6715-1*) McCland & Stewart.

— The Microphone Wars: A History of Triumph & Betrayal at the CBC. (Illus.). 528p. 1994. 35.00 (*0-7710-6712-7*) McCland & Stewart.

— Trivia Pursuit: How Showbiz Values are Corrupting the News. LC 98-225373. 224p. 1999. 26.99 (*0-7710-6752-6*) McCland & Stewart.

***Nash, Knowlton.** Trivia Pursuit: How Showbiz Values Are Corrupting the News. rev. ed. 240p. 2000. pap. 18.95 (*0-7710-6761-5*) McCland & Stewart.

Nash, Laura L. The Aggelia in Pindar. LC 89-25937. (Harvard Dissertations in the Classics Ser.). 264p. 1990. reprint ed. text 25.00 (*0-8240-3307-8*) Garland.

— Good Intentions Aside: A Manager's Guide to Resolving Ethical Problems. LC 93-14788. 288p. 1993. reprint ed. pap. 15.95 (*0-87584-429-4*) Harvard Busn.

Nash, Laura L., jt. ed. see Heuberger, Frank W.

Nash, Lee. North Cove Yacht Harbor. Brady, Maxine, ed. (Illus.). 50p. write for info. (*0-318-64708-7*) Watermark Assocs.

Nash, Lee, ed. Understanding Herbert Hoover: Ten Perspectives. (Publication Ser.: No. 354). 196p. 1988. 21.95 (*0-8179-8541-7*) Hoover Inst Pr.

Nash, Leonard K. The Atomic-Molecular Theory. LC 50-12355. (Harvard Case Histories in Experimental Science Ser.: Case 4). 163p. reprint ed. pap. 50.60 (*0-8357-5857-5*, 200642600059) Bks Demand.

— ChemThermo: A Statistical Approach to Thermodynamics. (C). 1972. pap. text. write for info. (*0-201-05237-7*) Addison-Wesley.

— Elements of Statistical Thermodynamics. 2nd ed. 1974. pap. text 16.25 (*0-201-05229-6*) Addison-Wesley.

Nash, Linda J. The Shorter Road to Success. LC 96-92278. 192p. (Orig.). 1996. pap. 10.00 (*0-9636702-1-2*) PRISM MO.

Nash, Linda J. & Kampen, Martha G. Surviving in the Jungle: What You Really Need to Know to Market Your Business Without Losing Your Shirt. (Illus.). 153p. (Orig.). 1993. pap. 12.95 (*0-9636702-0-4*) PRISM MO.

Nash, Liz, tr. see Filippini, Serge.

Nash, Liz, tr. see Germain, Sylvie.

Nash, M., et al. Better Baby Care: A Book for Family Day Care Providers. rev. ed. 164p. 1993. pap. text 15.95 (*1-884093-03-5*) Chldrns Fnd.

— Mejor Cuidado Infantil: Un Libro Para Proveedoras de Cuidado Para Ninos En el Hogar. (SPA.). 184p. 1993. pap. text 19.95 (*1-884093-04-3*) Chldrns Fnd.

Nash, M. A., pseud. How to Save a Fortune Using Refunds & Coupons. 32p. (Orig.). 1997. pap. 7.95 (*0-934650-03-9*) Sunnyside.

***Nash, Madeleine.** El Nino. 2001. write for info. (*0-446-52481-6*) Warner Bks.

Nash, Manning. The Cauldron of Ethnicity in the Modern World. LC 88-29522. 150p. 1989. pap. text 9.95 (*0-226-56867-9*) U Ch Pr.

— The Cauldron of Ethnicity in the Modern World. LC 88-29522. 150p. 1996. lib. bdg. 30.00 (*0-226-56866-0*) U Ch Pr.

— Golden Road to Modernity. 1993. reprint ed. pap. text 2.95 (*0-226-56860-1*, P548) U Ch Pr.

— Machine Age Maya: The Industrialization of a Guatemalan Community. LC 67-20810. 1992. pap. text 3.95 (*0-226-56863-6*, P262) U Ch Pr.

Nash, Manning, ed. Essays on Economic Development & Cultural Change: In Honor of Bert F. Hoselitz. 466p. 1996. pap. text 18.00 (*0-226-56865-2*) U Ch Pr.

Nash, Manning, jt. ed. see Wauchope, Robert.

***Nash, Marcus & Loomis, Scott B.** Pushing the Limits: A Nordic Skiiing Saga. (Illus.). 142p. 1999. pap. 14.95 (*0-914339-89-3*) P E Randall Pub.

Nash, Margaret. Class 1 Spells Trouble. 96p. (J). (gr. 3-6). 1993. pap. 7.95 (*0-14-034224-9*, Pub. by Pnguin Bks Ltd) Trafalgar.

— Secret in the Mist. 2000. pap. 6.95 (*1-86233-057-3*) Levinson Bks.

Nash, Margaret. Secret in the Mist. LC 99-202825. 1999. 14.95 (*1-899607-98-6*) Sterling.

***Nash, Marilyn.** Secrets of Hollywood Heydays: Stars Fitness Diet. (Illus.). 143p. 2000. spiral bd. 24.95 (*0-9675668-1-9*) M Nash.

Nash-Marshall, Siobhan. Joan of Arc: A Spiritual Biography. LC 99-38952. 1999. 19.95 (*0-8245-2350-4*) Crossroad NY.

***Nash-Marshall, Siobhan.** Participation & the Good: A Study of Boethian Metaphysics. LC 99-50966. 320p. 2000. pap. 49.95 (*0-8245-1852-7*, Pub. by Crossroad NY) Natl Bk Netwk.

Nash, Mary. Defying Male Civilization: Women in the Spanish Civil War. LC 95-18301. (Women & Modern Revolution Ser.). (Illus.). 261p. (Orig.). (C). 1996. text 32.00 (*0-912869-15-1*); pap. text 22.50 (*0-912869-16-X*) Arden Pr.

Nash, Mary F., jt. auth. see Nash, James H.

Nash, Mary H. Skulls Are Forever: A Book of Secret Truths. (Illus.). (Orig.). 1986. pap. 12.95 (*0-9618893-0-6*) Ichthys VA.

Nash, Michael. Computers, Automation, & Cybernetics at the Hagley Museum & Library. (Illus.). 99p. (Orig.). 1989. pap. 5.00 (*0-914650-27-0*) Hagley Museum.

— Managing Organizational Performance. LC 82-49040. (Management Ser.). 380p. 1983. text 45.95 (*0-87589-561-1*) Jossey-Bass.

— Runner's World Weight Control Book. (Runner's World Instructional Ser.). (Illus.). 200p. (Orig.). 1981. spiral bd. 11.95 (*0-89037-087-7*) Anderson World.

Nash, Michael, et al. Pennsylvania Power & Light Company: A Guide to the Records. 226p. 1985. 10.00 (*0-914650-22-X*) Hagley Museum.

Nash, Michael, jt. auth. see Fromm, Erika.

Nash, Michael H. Conflict & Accommodation: Coal Miners, Steel Workers & Socialism, 1890 to 1920, 11. LC 81-6691. (Contributions in Labor History Ser.: No. 11). (Illus.). 197p. 1982. 52.95 (*0-313-22838-8*, NCO/, Greenwood Pr) Greenwood.

Nash, Michael M. Managing Organizational Performance. LC 82-49049. (Joint Publication in the Jossey-Bass Management Series & the Jossey-Bass Social & Behavioral Science Ser.). 382p. 1983. reprint ed. pap. 118.50 (*0-7837-2545-0*, 204270400006) Bks Demand.

Nash, Michael R., jt. ed. see Fromm, Erika.

Nash, Mike. Police, Probation & Protecting the Public. LC 99-205096. 228p. 1999. pap. 34.00 (*1-85431-735-0*, Pub. by Blackstone Pr) Gaunt.

Nash, Mildred J. Beyond Their Dreams. LC 89-37565. 100p. (Orig.). 1989. pap. 5.95 (*0-936015-16-0*) Pocahontas Pr.

Nash, N. Richard. Rouge Atomique. 1955. pap. 3.25 (*0-8222-0972-1*) Dramatists Play.

— Selected Plays. unabridged ed. 525p. 1996. 27.95 (*1-888825-01-4*) Greenhse & Kirby.

— Selected Plays, Vol. 1. unabridged ed. 525p. 1996. pap. 12.95 (*1-888825-02-2*) Greenhse & Kirby.

— The Young & Fair. 1948. pap. 5.25 (*0-8222-1289-7*) Dramatists Play.

Nash, Nancy, jt. auth. see Malmstrom, Karin.

Nash, Newlyn. Beach of Dreams. large type ed. (Linford Romance Library). 288p. 1989. pap. 16.99 (*0-7089-6665-9*, Linford) Ulverscroft.

— Dance of Destiny. large type ed. (Linford Romance Library). 1990. pap. 16.99 (*0-7089-6825-2*) Ulverscroft.

— Magic of Love. large type ed. (Linford Romance Library). 1989. pap. 16.99 (*0-7089-6784-1*, Linford) Ulverscroft.

— The Pearl. large type ed. 1990. pap. 16.99 (*0-7089-6885-6*, Linford) Ulverscroft.

Nash, Ogden. The Adventures of Isabel. 32p. (J). (gr. k-3). 1994. pap. 5.95 (*0-316-59883-6*) Little.

Nash, Ogden. Adventures of Isabel. 1991. 11.15 (*0-606-06163-0*, Pub. by Turtleback) Demco.

Nash, Ogden. Custard the Dragon & the Wicked Knight. (Illus.). 32p. (J). (ps-3). 1999. pap. 5.95 (*0-316-59905-0*) Little.

— I Wouldn't Have Missed It: Selected Poems of Ogden Nash. Eberstadt, Isabel, ed. LC 75-14008. 407p. (gr. 8). 1975. 33.00 (*0-316-59830-5*) Little.

— I'm a Stranger Here Myself. (Orig.). 1994. lib. bdg. 21.95 (*1-56849-468-8*) Buccaneer Bks.

— Ogden Nash's Zoo. LC 86-23173. (Illus.). 84p. 1986. 10.95 (*0-941434-95-8*) Stewart Tabori & Chang.

— The Pocket Book of Ogden Nash. 1976. 19.95 (*0-8488-1439-8*) Amereon Ltd.

— The Pocket Book of Ogden Nash. 197p. 1990. mass mkt. 5.50 (*0-671-72789-3*) PB.

— The Pocket Book of Ogden Nash. 200p. 1991. reprint ed. lib. bdg. 18.95 (*0-89966-867-4*) Buccaneer Bks.

— Selected Poems of Ogden Nash. 704p. 1995. 14.98 (*1-884822-30-4*) Blck Dog & Leventhal.

— The Tale of Custard the Dragon. 1998. 11.15 (*0-606-13833-1*, Pub. by Turtleback) Demco.

— The Tale of the Custard Dragon. (Illus.). 32p. (J). (gr. k-3). 1998. pap. 5.95 (*0-316-59031-2*) Little.

Nash, Ogden, ed. The Moon Is Shining Bright As Day. LC 53-7143. (Illus.). 192p. (YA). (gr. 7 up). 1953. 12.95 (*0-397-30244-4*) HarpC Child Bks.

Nash, Ogden & Lee, Katie. Under Water with Ogden Nash. LC 96-51448. 64p. (gr. 8). 1997. 16.95 (*0-8212-2404-2*) Little.

Nash, Ogden, jt. auth. see Lear, Edward.

Nash, Ogden, jt. auth. see Stuart, David.

Nash, Padder. Coup de Grass. large type ed. (Linford Mystery Library). 304p. 1996. pap. 16.99 (*0-7089-7854-1*, Linford) Ulverscroft.

— Grass. large type ed. 1991. pap. 16.99 (*0-7089-7026-5*) Ulverscroft.

— Grass & Supergrass. large type ed. (Linford Romance Library). 1989. pap. 16.99 (*0-7089-6756-6*) Ulverscroft.

— Grass' Fancy. large type ed. (Linford Mystery Library). 304p. 1993. pap. 16.99 (*0-7089-7346-9*) Ulverscroft.

— Grass in Idleness. large type ed. (Linford Mystery Library). 304p. 1994. pap. 16.99 (*0-7089-7484-8*, Linford) Ulverscroft.

— Grass Makes Hay. large type ed. (Mystery Ser.). 304p. 1994. pap. 16.99 (*0-7089-7558-5*) Ulverscroft.

— Sheep Grass. large type ed. (Linford Mystery Library). 1996. pap. 16.99 (*0-7089-7863-0*, Linford) Ulverscroft.

— Wayward Seeds of Grass. large type ed. (Linford Mystery Library). 1991. pap. 16.99 (*0-7089-7131-8*) Ulverscroft.

Nash, Paul. Authority & Freedom in Education: An Introduction to the Philosophy of Education. LC 66-17624. 352p. reprint ed. pap. 109.20 (*0-8357-5900-8*, 201261400082) Bks Demand.

— Models of Man: Explorations in the Western Educational Tradition. LC 83-8369. 484p. 1983. reprint ed. text 53.50 (*0-89874-634-5*) Krieger.

— Super Structures. Harris, Peter, ed. LC 89-12009. (Illus.). 32p. (J). (gr. 2-4). 1989. lib. bdg. 13.26 (*0-944483-37-2*) Garrett Ed Corp.

Nash, Paul, jt. auth. see Flavell, A. J.

Nash, Paul, jt. auth. see Tilling, Mike.

Nash, Paul J. Land Hermit Crabs. (Illus.). 32p. 1976. pap. 1.79 (*0-87666-907-0*, A-325) TFH Pubns.

Nash, Paul W. The Gilded Fly: Short Stories. (Illus.). 40p. 1993. 35.00 (*0-930126-42-4*) Typographeum.

Nash, Peggy N. & Nash, R. Mr. McCamey-- Claude W. Brown: Life of a West Texas Oil Man. LC 94-37570. 120p. 1995. 15.96 (*0-89015-976-9*, Eakin Pr) Sunbelt Media.

Nash, Peter. Systems Modelling & Optimisation. (Control Engineering Ser.: No. 16). 224p. 1981. boxed set 75.00 (*0-906048-63-X*, CE016) INSPEC Inc.

Nash, Peter, ed. Phase Diagrams of Binary Nickel Alloys. (Monograph Series on Alloy Phase Diagrams). (Illus.). 394p. (C). 1991. text 326.00 (*0-87170-365-3*, 57712G) ASM.

Nash, Peter, jt. auth. see Anderson, Edward J.

Nash, Petra, jt. auth. see Edmonds, Janet.

Nash, Philip. The Other Missiles of October: Eisenhower, Kennedy & the Jupiters, 1957-1963. LC 96-43691. 232p. (gr. 13). 1997. pap. 19.95 (*0-8078-4647-3*); lib. bdg. 49.95 (*0-8078-2339-2*) U of NC Pr.

Nash, Philip, et al, eds. Applications of Thermodynamics in the Synthesis & Processing of Materials: Symposium on Applications of Thermodynamics in the Synthesis & Processing of Materials (1994: Rosemont, IL) (Illus.). 512p. 1995. 20.00 (*0-87339-291-4*, 2914) Minerals Metals.

Nash, Poppy. Living with Disfigurement: Psychological Implications of Being Born with a Cleft Palate. (CEDR Ser.). 304p. 1995. 79.95 (*1-85628-967-2*, Pub. by Avebry) Ashgate Pub Co.

Nash-Price, Barbara. Inside Story: Official Real Estate Manual. 3rd ed. LC 97-1583. (Illus.). 266p. 1997. pap. 25.40 (*0-13-281164-2*) P-H.

— Inside Story: Real Estate Agent Manual, Vol. 1. (Illus.). 264p. (Orig.). 1994. pap., student ed. 29.95 (*0-9634419-0-6*) Nash-Price Pubs.

— Life Awareness Manual. (Illus.). 98p. (Orig.). 1995. pap. 8.95 (*0-9634419-1-4*) Nash-Price Pubs.

***Nash-Price, Barbara.** Real Estate Field Manual: Selling Guide. 4th ed. 336p. 2000. pap. 26.67 (*0-13-015596-9*, Prentice Hall) P-H.

Nash, R. Studies in Medieval Indian Architecture. LC 94-906612. 172p. 1995. pap. 375.00 (*81-85880-56-5*, Pub. by Print Hse) St Mut.

Nash, R., ed. Environment & Americans: The Problem of Priorities. LC 79-4177. (American Problem Studies). 126p. 1979. reprint ed. pap. text 9.50 (*0-88275-936-1*) Krieger.

Nash, R., jt. auth. see Nash, Peggy N.

Nash, Ralph, jt. auth. see Tasso, Torquato.

Nash, Ralph, tr. see Sannazaro, Jacopo.

Nash, Ralph, tr. see Tasso, Torquato.

Nash, Ralph, tr. & intro. see Sannazaro, Jacopo.

Nash, Ralph C. Government Contract Changes & Supplement. 2nd ed. (Illus.). 600p. 1989. 175.00 (*0-317-03297-6*) Fed Pubns Inc.

Nash, Ralph C., Jr. & Cibinic, John, Jr. Competitive Negotiation: The Source Selection Process. LC 93-44517. 952p. 1993. boxed set 90.00 (*0-935165-25-8*) GWU Gov Contracts.

— Federal Procurement Law Vol. 1: Contract Formation, Vol. 1. 3rd ed. 938p. 1977. boxed set 50.00 (*0-935165-00-2*) GWU Gov Contracts.

Nash, Ralph C., Jr. & Rawicz, Leonard. Intellectual Property in Government Contracts, 3 vols., Set. 2nd ed. 1141p. 1995. pap., per. 120.00 (*0-935165-40-1*) GWU Gov Contracts.

— Intellectual Property in Government Contracts, Vol. 1: Intellectual Property Rights. 443p. 1995. per. 45.00 (*0-935165-43-6*) GWU Gov Contracts.

— Intellectual Property in Government Contracts, Vol. 2: Technical Data & the Freedom of Info Act. 2nd ed. 479p. 1995. pap., per. 45.00 (*0-935165-44-4*) GWU Gov Contracts.

— Intellectual Property in Government Contracts, Vol. 3: Computer Software & Remedies. 2nd ed. 219p. 1995. per. 45.00 (*0-935165-45-2*) GWU Gov Contracts.

Nash, Ralph C., Jr. & Schooner, Steven L. Desktop Set: Acronyms & Abbreviations in Government Contracting & the Government Contracts Reference Book: A Comprehensive Guide to the Language of Procurement, 2 vols., Set. Phillips, Joan N., ed. 626p. (Orig.). 1993. pap., per. 55.00 (*0-935165-23-1*) GWU Gov Contracts.

— The Government Contracts Reference Book: A Comprehensive Guide to the Language of Procurement. 350p. 1992. pap., per. 40.00 (*0-935165-19-3*) GWU Gov Contracts.

Nash, Ralph C., et al. Intellectual Property in Government Contracts. 3rd ed. LC 98-164017. 1997. write for info. (*0-935165-61-4*); write for info. (*0-935165-62-2*); write for info. (*0-935165-63-0*) GWU Gov Contracts.

Nash, Ralph C., Jr., jt. auth. see Cibinic, John, Jr.

Nash, Ralph G. & Leslie, Anne R., eds. Groundwater Residue Sampling Design. LC 91-15752. (ACS Symposium Ser.: No. 465). (Illus.). 395p. 1991. text 95.00 (*0-8412-2091-3*, Pub. by Am Chemical) OUP.

Nash, Ray. American Penmanship, 1800-1850. (Illus.). 315p. 1969. 35.00 (*1-884718-72-8*, 7237) Oak Knoll.

— American Penmanship Eighteen Hundred to Eighteen Fifty: A History of Writing & a Bibliography of Copybooks from Jenkins to Spencer. LC 78-106556. 303p. 1969. 27.50 (*0-912296-10-0*) Am Antiquarian.

Nash, Ray, et al. Education in the Graphic Arts. 1969. 5.00 (*0-89073-025-3*, 115) Boston Public Lib.

Nash, Renea D. Coping As a Biracial-Biethnic Teen. LC 94-22140. (YA). (gr. 7-12). 1995. lib. bdg. 17.95 (*0-8239-1838-6*) Rosen Group.

— Everything You Need to Know about Being a Biracial/Biethnic Teen. LC 94-34644. (Need to Know Library). (Illus.). 64p. (YA). (gr. 7-12). 1995. lib. bdg. 17.95 (*0-8239-1871-8*) Rosen Group.

Nash, Richard N. John Craige's "Mathematical Principles of Christian Theology" LC 89-39678. (Journal of the History of Philosophy Monograph Ser.). 156p. (C). 1991. pap. 17.95 (*0-8093-1662-5*) S Ill U Pr.

— Lengthen Your Smile: A Year's Supply of Stories for Latter-Day Saints. LC 96-19527. 1996. pap. 9.95 (*1-57345-046-4*) Deseret Bk.

Nash, Robert. Faith, Hype & Clarity: Teaching about Religion in American Schools & Colleges. (Advances in Contemporary Educational Thought Ser.). 224p. 1999. text 51.00 (*0-8077-3806-9*); pap. text 23.95 (*0-8077-3805-0*) Tchrs Coll.

Nash, Robert A., jt. auth. see Berky, Ira A.

Nash, Robert J. Answering the "Virtuecrats" A Moral Conversation on Character Education. LC 97-23123. (Advances in Contemporary Educational Thought Ser.). 1997. 48.00 (*0-8077-3670-8*); pap. 22.95 (*0-8077-3669-4*) Tchrs Coll.

— "Real World" Ethics: Frameworks for Educators & Human Service Professionals. LC 96-21591. (Professional Ethics in Education Ser.: Vol. 8). 192p. (C). 1996. text 46.00 (*0-8077-3557-4*); pap. text 21.95 (*0-8077-3556-6*) Tchrs Coll.

Nash, Robert N. An 8-Track Church in a CD World: The Modern Church in a Postmodern World. LC 97-11347. 144p. 1997. 17.00 (*1-57312-095-2*) Smyth & Helwys.

Nash, Robert N., Jr., jt. auth. see Sheely, Steven M.

Nash, Rod. In Germany: Textbook. 12.95 (*0-8219-0907-X*) EMC-Paradigm.

— In Germany: Workbook. 8.95 (*0-8219-0908-8*) EMC-Paradigm.

— In Germany: Workbook, teacher's edition. 9.95 (*0-8219-0909-6*) EMC-Paradigm.

Nash, Rod & Osthecker, Sonja. In Deutschland: Textbook. 17.95 (*0-8219-1081-7*) EMC-Paradigm.

Nash, Roderick. American Environmentalism: Reading in Conservation History. 3rd ed. 398p. (C). 1989. pap. 31.88 (*0-07-046059-0*) McGraw.

— The Big Drops: Ten Legendary Rapids of the American West. rev. ed. LC 89-63129. 240p. 1989. reprint ed. pap. 10.95 (*1-55566-051-7*) Johnson Bks.

— From These Beginnings: A Biographical Approach to American History, Vol. 1. 6th ed. LC 99-16632. Vol. 1. 289p. (C). 1999. pap. text 37.00 (*0-321-00295-4*) Addison-Wesley.

***Nash, Roderick.** From These Beginnings: A Biographical Approach to American History, Vol. 2. 6th ed. LC 99-16632. Vol. 2. 353p. (C). 1999. pap. text 37.00 (*0-321-00315-2*) Addison-Wesley.

Nash, Roderick. The Nervous Generation: American Thought, 1917-1930. 185p. 1990. pap. text 12.95 (*0-929587-21-9*, Elephant Paperbacks) I R Dee.

— The Rights of Nature: A History of Environmental Ethics. (History of American Thought & Culture Ser.). 320p. (C). 1989. pap. text 19.95 (*0-299-11844-4*) U of Wis Pr.

— Wilderness & the American Mind. 3rd rev. ed. LC 82-4874. 380p. 1982. pap. 16.00 (*0-300-02910-1*, Y-440) Yale U Pr.

Nash, Roger. Night Flying. 83p. 1990. pap. 7.95 (*0-86492-116-0*, Pub. by Goose Ln Edits) Genl Dist Srvs.

— Settlement in a School of Whales & Other Poems. (C). 1989. 45.00 (*0-907839-26-6*, Pub. by Brynmill Pr Ltd) St Mut.

Nash, Ronald H. Christian Faith & Historical Understanding. 176p. (C). 1984. pap. 12.95 (*0-310-45121-3*, 12379P) Zondervan.

— Christianity & the Hellenistic World. (CFUC Ser.). 1984. pap. 14.95 (*0-310-45210-4*, 12383P) Zondervan.

— Faith & Reason: Searching for a Rational Faith. 464p. 1988. 24.99 (*0-310-29400-2*, 12385) Zondervan.

— Faith & Reason: Searching for a Rational Faith. 296p. 1994. pap. 19.99 (*0-310-29401-0*) Zondervan.

— Freedom, Justice, & the State. LC 80-8145. 243p. 1980. pap. text 22.00 (*0-8191-1196-1*) U Pr of Amer.

— The Gospel & the Greeks: Did the New Testament Borrow from Pagan Thought? LC 91-40299. Orig. Title: Christianity & the Hellenistic World Ser.. 318p. (C). 1992. pap. 14.99 (*0-945241-09-7*) Probe Bks.

— Life's Ultimate Questions. LC 99-26079. 464p. 1999. 29.99 (*0-310-22364-4*) HarpC.

— The Light of the Mind: St. Augustine's Theory of Knowledge. LC 69-19765. 159p. reprint ed. 49.30 (*0-8357-9790-2*, 201609900098) Bks Demand.

— Poverty & Wealth: Why Socialism Doesn't Work. LC 92-14204. 224p. (C). 1992. reprint ed. pap. 14.99 (*0-945241-16-X*) Probe Bks.

— When a Baby Dies. LC 98-39673. 1999. pap. 9.99 (*0-310-22556-6*) Zondervan.

— The Word of God & the Mind of Man. 137p. 1992. reprint ed. pap. 9.99 (*0-87552-354-4*) P & R Pubng.

— The Word of God & the Mind of Man: The Crisis of Revealed Truth in Contemporary Theology. 176p. (Orig.). 1982. pap. 10.95 (*0-310-45131-0*, 12380P) Zondervan.

— Worldviews in Conflict: Choosing Christianity in the World of Ideas. 224p. 1992. pap. 12.99 (*0-310-57771-3*) Zondervan.

Nash, Ronald H. & Baldwin, J. F. The Summit Ministries Guide to Choosing a College. 1995. pap. write for info. (*0-936163-34-8*) Summit Pr CO.

Nash, Ronald H. & Taber, Ron. The Case for School Choice: How to Improve Our Schools. 98p. (Orig.). 1995. pap. 2.00 (*0-9647998-0-4*) Triune Pr.

Nash, Rose. Comparing English & Spanish: Patterns in Phonology & Orthography. (C). 1977. pap. text 10.95 (*0-88345-297-9*, 18448); audio 25.00 (*0-685-79303-6*, 58449) Prentice ESL.

— Multilingual Lexicon of Linguistics & Philology: English, Russian, German, French. (Miami Linguistic Ser.). 52.50 (*0-685-36678-2*) Fr & Eur.

— NTC's Dictionary of Spanish Cognates: Thematically Organized. (SPA.). 320p. 1999. pap. 15.95 (*0-8442-7962-5*) NTC Contemp Pub Co.

— NTC's Dictionary of Spanish Cognates Thematically Arranged. LC 97-16771. (SPA & ENG., Illus.). 320p. 1997. 19.95 (*0-8442-7961-7*, 79617) NTC Contemp Pub Co.

— Turkish Intonation: An Instrumental Study. LC 71-120351. (Janua Linguarum, Series Practica: No. 114). (Illus.). 190p. (Orig.). 1973. pap. text 55.40 (*90-279-2369-8*) Mouton.

Nash, Rose, ed. Readings in Spanish-English Contrastive Linguistics, Vol. I. LC 73-85939. 249p. 1973. pap. 4.50 (*0-913480-20-7*) Inter Am U Pr.

Nash, Rose & Alleyne, M. Lexique Multiligue de la Linguistique et de la Philogie: Anglais-Russe-Allemand-Francais. (ENG, FRE, GER & RUS.). 416p. 1968. pap. 99.50 (*0-8288-6654-6*, M-6422) Fr & Eur.

Nash, Rose & Belaval, Domitila, eds. Readings in Contrastive Spanish Linguistics, Vol II. LC 73-85939. 265p. 1980. pap. 7.95 (*0-913480-41-X*) Inter Am U Pr.

— Readings in Spanish-English Contrastive Linguistics, Vol. III. LC 73-85939. 270p. (C). 1982. pap. text 9.95 (*0-913480-42-8*) Inter Am U Pr.

***Nash, Rose & National Textbook Company Staff.** Dictionary of Russian Cognates. LC 99-39590. (AFR.). 2000. 18.95 (*0-8442-0459-5*) NTC Contemp Pub Co.

Nash, Roy. Conquest of Brazil. LC 67-29550. 1926. 30.00 (*0-8196-0207-8*) Biblo.

Nash, S. Nash Family: or Records of the Descendants of Thomas Nash of New Haven, Connecticut, 1640. (Illus.). 304p. 1989. reprint ed. pap. 45.50 (*0-8328-0897-0*); reprint ed. lib. bdg. 53.50 (*0-8328-0896-2*) Higginson Bk Co.

Nash, Scott, ed. Interpreting Ephesians for Preaching & Teaching. LC 96-20829. (Kerygma & Church Ser.). 144p. 1996. pap. 12.00 (*1-57312-042-1*) Smyth & Helwys.

— Interpreting Galatians for Teaching & Preaching. (Kerygma & Church Ser.). 192p. 1994. pap. 14.00 (*1-880837-87-0*) Smyth & Helwys.

— The Sermon on the Mount: Studies & Sermons. LC 92-42137. (Kerygma & Church Ser.). 192p. 1992. pap. 12.00 (*1-880837-06-4*) Smyth & Helwys.

Nash, Scott, jt. auth. see Crunk, Tony.

Nash, Scott, jt. auth. see GeBraad, Doug.

Nash, Scott, jt. auth. see Martin, David.

Nash, Seymour C., jt. auth. see Meyer, Sylvan.

***Nash, Sibylla. DreamCity. LC 00-191182. 224p. (Orig.). 2000. pap. 14.95 (*0-9701706-0-2*) Tribeca Hse.**
This debut novel captures a year in the life of an East Coast transplant, Adrianna Whittaker, as she struggles in Hollywood chasing her dreams of becoming a star. She's a Gen X'er on the cusp of 30 & she's searching for self-realization but will settle for a paycheck. The supporting case of characters includes her family which borders on dysfuntional, annoying colorful friends & neighbors. Filled with humor & raw emotion this poignant story unfolds through the pages of Adrianna's diary as she shares her devastating losses, her triumphs & heartbreaking struggle of a friend's drug addiction. It's bittersweet coming-of-age story for grownups as the main character battles life's daily dramas & the everyday madness associated with trying to fine one's place in the world. Contact the publisher directly for ordering information. *Publisher Paid Annotation.*

Nash, Stanley D. Prostitution in Great Britain, 1485-1901: An Annotated Bibliography. LC 94-331. 267p. 1994. 34.50 (*0-8108-2734-4*) Scarecrow.

***Nash, Stephen E.** It's about Time: A History of Archaeological Dating in North America. LC 99-46316. 296p. 2000. 45.00 (*0-87480-621-6*) U of Utah Pr.

Nash, Stephen Edward. Time, Trees & Prehistory: Tree-Ring Dating & the Development of North American Archaeology, 1914 to 1950. LC 98-56281. (Illus.). 294p. 1999. 29.95 (*0-87480-589-9*) U of Utah Pr.

Nash, Stephen G., et al, eds. The Impact of Emerging Technologies on Computer Science & Operations Research. LC 94-41217. (Operations Research - Computer Science Interface Ser.). 328p. (C). 1995. lib. bdg. 112.00 (*0-7923-9542-5*) Kluwer Academic.

Nash, Stephen G. & Sofer, Ariela. Linear & Nonlinear Programming. (Series in Industrial Engineering & Management Science). (Illus.). 692p. (C). 1995. 90.63 (*0-07-046065-5*) McGraw.

Nash, Stephen J. Cost, Uncertainty, & Welfare: Frank Knight's Theory of Imperfect Competition. 205p. 1998. text 59.95 (*1-84014-585-4*, Pub. by Ashgate Pub) Ashgate Pub Co.

Nash, Steve. Blue Ridge 2020: An Owner's Manual. LC 98-20106. (Illus.). 232p. 1999. pap. 19.95 (*0-8078-4759-3*) U of NC Pr.

Nash, Steven A. Arneson & Politics: A Commemorative Exhibition. LC 93-73198. (Illus.). 56p. 1995. pap. 14.95 (*0-88401-077-5*) Fine Arts Mus.

— Ben Nicholson: Fifty Years of His Art. LC 78-62949. (Illus.). 1978. 14.00 (*0-914782-21-5*) Buffalo Fine-Albrght-Knox.

Nash, Steven A., ed. Facing Eden: 100 Years of Landscape Art in the Bay Area. (Illus.). 250p. 1995. 60.00 (*0-520-20362-3*, Pub. by U CA Pr); pap. 34.95 (*0-520-20363-1*, Pub. by U CA Pr) Cal Prin Full Svc.

— Picasso & the War Years, 1937-1945. LC 98-60335. (Illus.). 256p. 1998. 50.00 (*0-500-09274-5*, Pub. by Thames Hudson) Norton.

Nash, Steven A., et al, eds. Naum Gabo: 60 Years of Constructivism. (Illus.). 272p. 1986. 60.00 (*3-7913-0742-8*, Pub. by Prestel) te Neues.

Nash, Steven A. & Albright-Knox Art Gallery Staff. Painting & Sculpture from Antiquity to Nineteen Forty-Two. LC 77-79651. (Illus.). 1979. pap. 25.00 (*0-914782-17-7*) Buffalo Fine-Albrght-Knox.

***Nash, Steven A. & Gopnik, Adam.** Wayne Thiebaud: A Paintings Retrospective. LC 99-67631. (Illus.). 192p. 2000. 45.00 (*0-500-09292-3*, Pub. by Thames Hudson) Norton.

***Nash, Steven A., et al.** Masterworks of European Painting in the California Palace of the Legion of Honor. LC 99-65341. (Illus.). 144p. 1999. 50.00 (*1-55595-182-1*, Pub. by Hudson Hills) Natl Bk Netwk.

Nash, Steven A., jt. auth. see Eitner, Lorenz E.

Nash, Sunny. Bigmama Didn't Shop at Woolworth's. LC 96-14743. (Wardlaw Book Ser.). (Illus.). 208p. (C). 1997. 19.95 (*0-89096-716-4*) Tex A&M Univ Pr.

***Nash, Susan.** Dating, Mating & Relating: The Complete Guide to Finding & Keeping Your Ideal Partner. (Illus.). 208p. 2000. pap. 24.95 (*1-85703-590-9*, Pub. by How To Bks) Midpt Trade.

***Nash, Susan & Nash, Derek.** Exceeding Customer Expectations: Find Out What Your Customers Want - And Give Them Even More. (Pathways Ser.). (Illus.). 208p. 2000. pap. 24.50 (*1-85703-564-X*, Pub. by How To Bks) Midpt Trade.

Nash, Susan A. Turning Team Performance Inside Out: Team Types & Temperament for High-Impact Results. LC 99-33220. 312p. 1999. 29.95 (*0-89106-136-3*, Davies-Black Pub) Consulting Psychol.

Nash, Susan S. The Airport Is My Etude. 32p. 1996. pap. 5.00 (*0-945926-42-1*, Pub. by Paradigm RI) SPD-Small Pr Dist.

— Catfishes & Jackals. LC 98-118737. 96p. (C). 1997. pap. 12.00 (*0-937013-67-6*) Potes Poets.

— Channel-Surfing the Apocalypse: A Day in the Life of the Fin-de-Millennium Mind. LC 95-77362. (Illus.). 189p. 1996. pap. 11.95 (*1-880713-06-3*, Pub. by AVEC Bks) SPD-Small Pr Dist.

— Dealing with Date Rape: True Stories from Survivors. 160p. (Orig.). 1996. pap. 12.00 (*0-9641837-1-4*) Texture Pr.

— A Half-Dozen Eclairs. 60p. pap. 10.00 (*0-9641837-3-0*) Texture Pr.

— Liquid Babylon. 55p. pap. 8.00 (*1-884438-07-5*) Epiphany AR.

— Liquid Babylon. limited ed. 54p. 1994. 18.00 (*0-937013-50-1*) Potes Poets.

— Mind Noir & el Siglo de Oro. 20p. (Orig.). 1995. pap. 5.00 (*0-9535350-5-3*) Luna Bisonte.

— A Paleontologist's Notebook. (Illus.). 96p. 1995. pap. 9.00 (*1-880516-16-0*) Left Hand Bks.

— Pornography. (Chapbook Ser.). 24p. 1992. pap. 5.00 (*0-945112-15-7*) Generator Pr.

Nash, Susan S., ed. Texture: Journal of Writing & Art, No. 6. 200p. (Orig.). 1995. pap. 10.00 (*0-9641837-2-2*) Texture Pr.

Nash, Susan Smith, see Smith Nash, Susan.

Nash, Susie. Between France & Flanders: Manuscript Illumination in Aiens in the Fifteenth Century. (British Library Studies in Medieval Culture). (Illus.). 304p. 1996. text 90.00 (*0-8020-4114-0*) U of Toronto Pr.

Nash, Suzanne. Les Contemplations of Victor Hugo: An Allegory of the Creative Process. LC 76-3273. 239p. reprint ed. pap. 74.10 (*0-8357-6188-6*, 203429700089) Bks Demand.

— Paul Valery's Album de Vers Anciens: A Past Transfigured. LC 82-47606. 339p. reprint ed. pap. 105.10 (*0-7837-1934-5*, 204214900001) Bks Demand.

Nash, Suzanne, ed. Home & Its Dislocations in Nineteenth-Century France. LC 92-31575. (SUNY Series, The Margins of Literature). 345p. (C). 1993. pap. text 21.95 (*0-7914-1550-3*) State U NY Pr.

— Home & Its Dislocations in Nineteenth-Century France. LC 92-31575. (SUNY Series, The Margins of Literature). 345p. (C). 1993. text 64.50 (*0-7914-1549-X*) State U NY Pr.

Nash, T. A., ed. The Diary of an Unprofessional Soldier. 204p. 1991. 45.00 (*0-948251-50-6*, Pub. by Picton) St Mut.

Nash, T. H., III, ed. see Herzig, Rolf & Urech, Martin.

Nash, T. M. & Nash, C. Robert. Quick Reference Guide to WordStar. (Opposing Viewpoints Sources Ser.). 82p. 1985. student ed. 19.95 (*0-934569-99-1*) Nash Group.

Nash, Theodore E. Love & Vengeance: or Little Viola's Victory. LC 78-173016. reprint ed. 27.50 (*0-404-00095-9*) AMS Pr.

Nash, Thomas. Pierce Penilesse. (BCL1-PR English Literature Ser.). 137p. 1992. reprint ed. lib. bdg. 69.00 (*0-7812-7217-3*) Rprt Serv.

Nash, Thomas, jt. auth. see Marlowe, Christopher.

Nash, Thomas H., III, ed. Lichen Biology. (Illus.). 315p. (C). 1996. text 74.95 (*0-521-45368-2*); pap. text 27.95 (*0-521-45974-5*) Cambridge U Pr.

Nash, Thomas H., III, et al, eds. Lichens, Bryophytes & Air Quality. (Bibliotheca Lichenologica: Vol. 30). (GER., Illus.). 297p. 1988. 53.00 (*3-443-58009-2*, Pub. by Gebruder Borntraeger) Balogh.

Nash, Thomas H., III, et al. A Revision of the Lichen Genus Xanthoparmelia in South America. (Bibliotheca Lichenologica: Vol. 56). (GER., Illus.). 157p. 1995. pap. 48.00 (*3-443-58035-1*, Pub. by Gebruder Borntraeger) Balogh.

Nash, Tim, jt. auth. see Akers, Michelle.

Nash, Tim, ed. see Dorrance, Anson.

Nash, Tim, ed. see Gregg, Lauren.

Nash, Timothy A., ed. see Nash, Harold W.

Nash, Tom. The Christian Communicator's Handbook. 240p. 1995. 16.99 (*1-56476-384-6*, 6-3384, Victor Bks) Chariot Victor.

Nash, Tony. Farewell Mum & Dad: The Diary of a London Evacuee. 114p. 1991. pap. 4.50 (*0-9630676-0-5*) T Nash.

Nash, Valery. The Narrows. (CSU Poetry Ser.: No. VII). 62p. (Orig.). 1980. pap. 3.50 (*0-914946-16-1*) Cleveland St Univ Poetry Ctr.

— October Swimmer. (Chapbook Ser.: No. 2). 40p. (Orig.). 1996. pap. 8.95 (*0-9649463-1-9*) Folly Cove.

Nash, W. G. Bricklaying. (Illus.). 128p. (Orig.). 1991. pap. 24.00 (*0-7487-1292-5*, Pub. by S Thornes Pubs) Trans-Atl Phila.

Nash, W. J. A Bibliography of Trouchus (Trochus Niloticus L.) (Bibliographies Ser.: No. 7). 1987. pap. 3.00 (*971-10-2232-X*, Pub. by ICLARM) Intl Spec Bk.

Nash, W. J., jt. ed. see Munro, J. L.

Nash, Wallis. Oregon: There & Back in 1877. Munford, J. Kenneth, ed. LC 76-9770. (Illus.). 348p. 1976. reprint ed. 19.95 (*0-87071-077-X*) Oreg St U Pr.

Nash, Walter. Jargon: Its Uses & Abuses. LC 92-36120. (Language Library). 1993. 31.95 (*0-631-18063-X*) Blackwell Pubs.

— Language & Creative Illusion. LC 97-46988. (English Language Ser). 1998. text 67.07 (*0-582-29163-1*) Addison-Wesley.

— Language & Creative Illusion. LC 97-46988. (English Language Ser.). 1998. pap. text 26.05 (*0-582-29164-X*) Longman.

— Language in Popular Fiction. (Interface Ser.). 256p. (C). 1990. pap. text 16.95 (*0-415-02944-9*, A4187) Routledge.

— Language of Humour. (English Language Ser.). (C). 1985. pap. text 18.95 (*0-582-29127-5*, 71754) Longman.

Nash, Walter, ed. The Writing Scholar: Language & Conventions of Academic Disclosure. (Written Communication Annual Ser.: Vol. 3). (Illus.). 320p. (C). 1990. 62.00 (*0-8039-3692-3*) Sage.

— The Writing Scholar: Studies in Academic Discourse. LC 86-655578. (Written Communication Annual Ser.: Vol. 3). (Illus.). 239p. reprint ed. pap. 74.10 (*0-608-09806-X*, 206997500001) Bks Demand.

Nash, Walter & Stacey, David. Creating. LC 96-44575. (English Language Ser.). 1997. pap. 26.78 (*0-582-24486-2*) Longman.

Nash, Walter, jt. auth. see Carter, Ronald.

Nash, Walter F. Under the Skin of the Road. 1993. pap. 9.00 (*0-9639407-0-8*) W F Nash.

Nash, Wanda. At Ease with Stress. LC 91-65006. 224p. (Orig.). 1991. pap. 9.95 (*0-89622-482-1*, C55) Twenty-Third.

— People Need Stillness. pap. write for info. (*0-232-51971-4*) S Asia.

Nash, William A. Hydrostatically Loaded Structures: The Structural Mechanics, Analysis, & Design of Powered Submersibles. 184p. 1995. 157.00 (*0-08-037876-5*, Pergamon Pr) Elsevier.

— Schaum's Outline of Strength of Materials. 3rd ed. 464p. (C). 1994. pap. 14.95 (*0-07-045903-7*) McGraw.

— Schaum's Strength of Materials. 4th ed. LC 98-28410. (Schaum's Outline Ser.). 432p. 1998. pap. 15.95 (*0-07-046617-3*) McGraw.

— Statics & Mechanics of Materials: Including 400 Solved Problems. 288p. (C). 1992. pap. 15.95 (*0-07-045896-0*) McGraw.

Nash-Williams, A. H. Advanced Latin Prose Composition. 172p. 1992. pap. 20.95 (*1-85399-351-4*, Pub. by Brist Class Pr) Focus Pub-R Pullins.

— Legenda. 88p. (C). 1982. pap. text 39.00 (*0-900269-18-9*, Pub. by Old Vicarage) St Mut.

Nashabe, Hisham. Muslim Educational Institutions. 183p. 1989. 16.95 (*0-86685-470-3*, LDL4703, Pub. by Librairie du Liban) Intl Bk Ctr.

Nashaknik, H. & Nageak, J., as told by. Anulhuyuk. (ESK.). 56p. 1973. pap. 4.00 (*0-933769-38-5*) Alaska Native.

N

Nashashibi, Adib Y., et al. Measurement & Modeling Millimeter-Wave Response from Soil Surfaces. LC QC0973.. (University of Michigan Reports: No. 029721-2-T). 60p. reprint ed. pap. 30.00 (*0-7837-6779-X*, 204660900003) Bks Demand.

Nashashibi, Karim. The Fiscal Dimensions of Adjustment in Low-Income Countries. (Occasional Papers: No. 95). vi, 59p. 1992. pap. 15.00 (*1-55775-229-X*) Intl Monetary.

Nashashibi, Karim, jt. auth. see Hansen, Bent.

Nashashibi, Karim A. & International Monetary Fund Staff. Algeria: Stabilization & Transition to the Market. LC 98-194079. (Occasional Papers). vii, 86 p. 1998. write for info. (*1-55775-691-0*) Intl Monetary.

Nashashibi, Salwa Mikdadi, ed. Rythm & Form: Visual Reflections on Arabic Poetry. (Illus.). 67p. 1997. pap. 15.00 (*0-9659490-0-1*) Cultural & Visual.

Nashashibi, Salwa Mikdadi, et al. Forces of Change: Artists of the Arab World. 146p. 1994. 39.95 (*0-940979-27-6*) Natl Museum Women.

— Forces of Change: Artists of the Arab World. LC 93-47447. 146p. 1994. pap. 29.95 (*0-940979-26-8*) Natl Museum Women.

Nashat, Guity, ed. Middle Eastern History. (Selected Reading Lists & Course Outlines from Leading American Colleges & Universities Ser.). 300p. (Orig.). 1988. pap. 16.95 (*0-910129-70-3*) Wiener Pubs Inc.

Nashat, Guity & Tucker, Judith E. Women in the Middle East. LC 99-11042. (Restoring Women to History Ser.). (Illus.). 144p. 1999. pap. 11.95 (*0-253-21264-2*) Ind U Pr.

***Nashat, Guity & Tucker, Judith E.** Women in the Middle East: Restoring Women to History. LC 99-11042. (Restoring Women to History Ser.). (Illus.). 160p. 1999. 29.95 (*0-253-33478-0*) Ind U Pr.

Nashe, Thomas. A Concordance to the Works of Thomas Nashe, 2 vols., Set. Ule, Louis, ed. (Alpha-Omega Series C. English Authors: Vol. 4). 1000p. write for info. incl. 3.5 hd (*3-487-09704-4*) G Olms Pubs.

— The Unfortunate Traveller & Other Works. Steane, J. B., ed. & intro. by. (English Library). 512p. 1972. pap. 13.95 (*0-14-043067-9*, Penguin Classics) Viking Penguin.

Nashed, Fred. Time-Saver Details for Exterior Wall Designs. LC 95-34805. 288p. 1995. 74.95 (*0-07-046082-5*) McGraw.

— Time-Saving Techniques for Architectural Construction Drawings. (Architecture Ser.). 242p. 1992. 64.95 (*0-471-28455-6*, VNR) Wiley.

Nashed, Fred. Time-Saving Techniques for Architectural Construction Drawings. LC 92-18922. 1993. text 54.95 (*0-442-00951-8*, VNR) Wiley.

Nashed, Z., ed. see Morozov, V. A.

Nashelsky, Louis. Introduction to Digital Computer Technology. 3rd ed. LC 82-13377. 536p. (C). 1983. text 45.95 (*0-471-09646-6*, VT30); pap. text 9.50 (*0-471-89528-8*) P-H.

Nashelsky, Louis & Boylestad, Robert L. IBM-PC-XT: BASIC Programming & Applications. (Illus.). 304p. 1986. pap. 22.50 (*0-13-448325-1*); student ed. write for info. incl. disk (*0-318-57914-6*) P-H.

Nashelsky, Louis, jt. auth. see Boylestad, Robert.

Nasheri, Hebieh. Betrayal of Due Process: A Comparative Assessment of Plea Bargaining in the United States & Canada. LC 98-16031. 212p. (C). 1998. 49.00 (*0-7618-1108-7*); pap. 32.50 (*0-7618-1109-5*) U Pr of Amer.

Nasheri, Hedi & Kratcoski, Peter C. A Guide to a Successful Legal Internship. LC 96-83678. 176p. (C). 1996. pap. 22.95 (*0-87084-329-X*) Anderson Pub Co.

Nashie, M. S. El, see Aref, Hassan & El Nashie, M. S., eds.

Nashif, Ahid D., et al. Vibration Damping. LC 84-17247. 480p. 1985. 150.00 (*0-471-86772-1*, Wiley-Interscience) Wiley.

Nashif, Taysir N. Nuclear Weapons in Israel. viii, 124p. 1996. 15.00 (*81-7024-753-5*, Pub. by Ashish Pub Hse) Nataraj Bks.

***Nashif, Tim.** Eternity; The Ultimate Experience: Follow up Assimilation Manual. 2000. pap. text 39.99 (*1-886849-68-4*) City Bible Pub.

— Turning Points, 1. 2000. pap. text, teacher ed. 29.99 (*1-886849-59-5*); pap. text, student ed. 6.99 (*1-886849-56-0*) City Bible Pub.

***Nashimoto, K., et al, eds.** Thin Films for Optical Waveguide Devices & Materials for Optical Limiting Vol. 597: Materials Research Society Symposium Proceedings. 2000. text 93.00 (*1-55899-505-6*) Materials Res.

Nashman, Honey W., jt. auth. see Hoare, Carol H.

Nashoba, Nuchi. Ben Nighthorse Campbell, Senator & Artist. (Illus.). (J). (gr. 1-4). 1995. pap. 4.95 (*0-8136-5763-6*); lib. bdg. 10.60 (*0-8136-5757-1*) Modern Curr.

Nashold, Blaine S., Jr. & Ovelmen-Levitt, Janice, eds. Deafferentation Pain Syndromes: Pathophysiology & Treatment. LC 91-21919. (Advances in Pain Research & Therapy Ser.: Vol. 19). (Illus.). 367p. reprint ed. pap. 113.80 (*0-608-09763-2*, 206993600007) Bks Demand.

Nashold, Blaine S., Jr., ed. see Ovelmen-Levitt, Janice.

Nashone. Grandmother Stories of the Northwest: Northwestern Indian Tales. (Illus.). 58p. (J). (gr. 5-12). 1987. pap. 6.95 (*0-940113-06-6*) Sierra Oaks Pub.

— Where Indians Live: American Indian Houses. (Illus.). 38p. (Orig.). (J). (gr. k-6). 1989. pap. 6.95 (*0-940113-16-3*) Sierra Oaks Pub.

Nashua History Committee Staff. The Nashua Experience: History in the Making. LC 78-980. 1978. 15.95 (*0-914016-50-4*); pap. 8.95 (*0-914016-51-2*) Phoenix Pub.

Nashville State Technical Institute Staff. Supplemental Readings for DSR 0853. 36p. 1998. pap. text 5.20 (*0-536-01358-6*) Pearson Custom.

Nasi, Franco, ed. see Paolini, Marco & Vacis, Gabriele.

Nasib al-Mahamid, Ahmad. Al-Hubb bayn al-'Abd wa-al-Rabb. 1995. 4.95 (*1-57547-213-9*); pap. 6.95 (*1-57547-214-7*) Dar Al-Fikr.

Nasibova, Aida. Art Treasures of the Moscow Kremlin. (Illus.). 238p. (C). 1988. text 300.00 (*0-7855-5862-4*, Pub. by Collets) St Mut.

— Faceted Chamber in the Moscow Kremlin. (Illus.). 228p. (C). 1978. text 130.00 (*0-7855-5864-0*, Pub. by Collets) St Mut.

Nasibova, Aida & Mendeleyev, William. Art Treasures of the Moscow Kremlin. 200p. 1984. 275.00 (*0-7855-1769-3*, Pub. by Collets) St Mut.

***Nasica, Eric.** Finance, Investment & Economic Fluctuations: An Analysis in the Tradition of Hyman P. Minsky. LC 99-87210. 240p. 2000. 90.00 (*1-85898-896-9*) E Elgar.

Nasim, Anjum. Financing Pakistan's Development in the 1990s. (Illus.). 662p. 1993. text 45.00 (*0-19-577459-0*) OUP.

Nasim, Anwar, et al, eds. Molecular Biology of the Fission Yeast. (Cell Biology Ser.). 545p. 1989. text 157.00 (*0-12-514085-1*) Acad Pr.

Nasio, Juan-David. Five Lessons on the Psychoanalytic Theory of Jacques Lacan. Pettigrew, David & Raffoul, Francois, trs. from FRE. LC 97-35886. (SUNY Series in Psychoanalysis & Culture). 192p. (C). 1998. text 59.50 (*0-7914-3831-7*); pap. text 19.95 (*0-7914-3832-5*) State U NY Pr.

— Hysteria from Freud to Lacan: The Splendid Child of Psychoanalysis. LC 98-39631. (Lacanian Clinical Field Ser.). Orig. Title: Hysteria: The Splendid Child of Psychoanalysis. (Illus.). 176p. 1998. reprint ed. pap. 17.95 (*1-892746-02-6*, 46026) Other Pr LLC.

Nasipuri, D. Stereochemistry of Organic Compounds: Principles & Applications. 2nd ed. 1994. write for info. (*81-224-0570-3*, Pub. by Wiley Estrn) Franklin.

Nasir, Jamal J. The Islamic Law of Personal Status. 2nd ed. 1986. lib. bdg. 219.00 (*0-86010-826-0*) G & T Inc.

— Status of Women under Islam. LC 94-39478. (Arab & Islamic Laws Ser.). 1995. lib. bdg. 86.00 (*1-85966-084-3*) Kluwer Academic.

Nasir, Jamal J., ed. The Status of Women under Islamic Law: And under Modern Arab Islamic Legislation. (C). 1990. lib. bdg. 71.00 (*1-85333-281-X*, Pub. by Graham & Trotman) Kluwer Academic.

Nasir, Jamil. Distance Haze. 320p. 2000. mass mkt. 5.99 (*0-553-57995-9*) Bantam Dell.

— Tower of Dreams. 240p. 1999. mass mkt. 5.99 (*0-553-58089-2*, Spectra) Bantam.

***Nasir, S.** Economics & Management of Maintenance Planning. 1998. pap. 348.00 (*81-86982-31-0*, Pub. by Business Pubns) St Mut.

— Storage & Material Handling Equipment Requirement Factors. 1998. pap. 248.00 (*81-86982-32-9*, Pub. by Business Pubns) St Mut.

Nasir, Tamir T., tr. see Saudi, Mona.

Nasir, Tania Tamari, jt. auth. see Saudi, Mona.

Nasiruddin, Al-Amir. Ar-Rafed: Arabic-Arabic Dictionary. 1971. 19.95 (*0-86685-101-1*) Intl Bk Ctr.

Nasiruddin, Emir. Characteristics & Peculiarities of the Arabic Language. (ARA.). 308p. 1968. 29.95 (*0-86685-056-2*, LDL0562, Pub. by Librairie du Liban) Intl Bk Ctr.

Nasisse, Andy & Wahlam, Maude. Baking in the Sun: Visionary Images from the South. (Illus.). 136p. (Orig.). 1987. pap. 30.00 (*0-936819-03-0*) USL Art Museum.

Nasits, Mary, et al. Stanley the Fly. (Illus.). 24p. (J). (gr. k-3). 1999. spiral bd. 14.00 (*0-8059-4570-9*) Dorrance.

Nasjleti, Maria, jt. auth. see James, Beverly.

***Naskar, Kumudranjan & Mandal, Rathindranath.** Ecology & Biodiversity of Indian Mangroves, 2 vols. LC 99-936264. (Illus.). 1999. 275.00 (*81-7035-190-1*, Pub. by Daya Pub Hse) S Asia.

Naskar, Satyendranath. Foreign Impact on Indian Life & Culture. 1996. 38.00 (*81-7017-298-5*, Pub. by Abhinav) S Asia.

Naske, Claus M. Bob Bartlett of Alaska...a Life in Politics. LC 79-65321. (Illus.). 247p. 1979. 12.95 (*0-912006-05-6*) U of Alaska Pr.

— Paving Alaska's Trails: The Work of the Alaska Road Commission. LC 86-15850. (Illus.). 354p. (Orig.). (C). 1986. lib. bdg. 62.00 (*0-8191-5576-4*) U Pr of Amer.

Naske, Claus M. & Slotnick, Herman E. Alaska: A History of the 49th State. LC 87-40215. (Illus.). 368p. 1994. pap. 18.95 (*0-8061-2573-X*) U of Okla Pr.

***Naskrecki, Piotr.** Katidids of Costa Rica: Systematics & Bioacoustics of Cone-Head Katydids. (Publications on Orthopteran Diversity: Vol. 1). (Illus.). 164p. 2000. 25.00 (*1-929014-01-5*) Orthopterists.

Naskrecki, Piotr & Colwell, Robert K. Systematics & Host Plant Affiliations of Humingbird Flower Mites of The Genera Tropicoseius Baker & Yunker & Rhinoseius Baker & Yunker. (Monographs, Thomas Say Publications in Entomology Ser.). (Illus.). 184p. 1998. pap. 35.00 (*0-938522-67-1*) Entomol Soc.

Naslain, R., jt. ed. see Evans, A. G.

Nasledov, Dmitrii N. & Goryunova, N. A., eds. Soviet Research in New Semiconductor Materials. Tybulewicz, A., tr. LC 65-11956. 126p. reprint ed. pap. 39.10 (*0-608-10299-7*, 202066800018) Bks Demand.

***Naslund, Sena Jeter.** Ahab's Wife: Or, the Star Gazer. 688p. 2000. pap. 15.00 (*0-688-17785-9*, Perennial) HarperTrade.

Naslund, Sena Jeter. Ahab's Wife: Or, the Star Gazer. LC 99-22135. (Illus.). 688p. 1999. 28.00 (*0-688-17187-7*, Wm Morrow) Morrow Avon.

***Naslund, Alan.** Silk Weather. 72p. (Orig.). 1999. pap. 10.00 (*0-9652520-3-5*) Fleur-de-lis Pr.

Naslund, Sena J. The Disobedience of Water. LC PS3564.A827D57 1996. 224p. 1999. 21.95 (*1-56792-071-3*) Godine.

***Naslund, Sena J.** The Disobedience of Water: Stories & Novellas. 224p. 2000. pap. 13.00 (*0-688-17845-6*) Morrow Avon.

Naslund, Sena J. Sherlock in Love. 240p. 1993. 21.95 (*0-87923-977-8*) Godine.

***Naslund, Sena J.** Sherlock in Love. 2001. write for info. (*0-688-17844-8*, Perennial) HarperTrade.

Naslund, Willard E. NATO Airpower: Organizing for Uncertainty. LC 93-38717. 1994. pap. 9.00 (*0-8330-1474-9*, MR-215-AF) Rand Corp.

Nasman, jt. auth. see Bertoline.

Nasman, Leonard O. Beginning Cadkey Light. 240p. (Orig.). pap. text 29.95 (*1-880544-12-1*, Pub. by Micro Educ) Tech Ed Concepts.

— Beginning Cadkey 6. (Illus.). 440p. (C). 1993. pap. 36.95 (*1-880544-18-0*, CAD6-1, Pub. by Micro Educ) Tech Ed Concepts.

— Beginning DataCAD. LC 91-66358. 165p. (C). 1991. pap. 29.95 (*1-880544-00-8*, Pub. by Micro Educ) Tech Ed Concepts.

— The Cadkey 97 Project Book: A Quick Guide to the Power of Cadkey. 2nd ed. 402p. 1998. pap. 39.95 (*1-880544-68-7*, Pub. by Micro Educ) Tech Ed Concepts.

— The Cadkey Seven Workbook. (Illus.). 110p. 1994. student ed. 19.95 (*1-880544-49-0*, CAD7-1, Pub. by Micro Educ) Tech Ed Concepts.

— Cadkey 107: The Complete Cadkey 7 Textbook. (Illus.). 330p. 1995. pap. text 43.95 (*1-880544-51-2*, CAD7-2, Pub. by Micro Educ) Tech Ed Concepts.

— The Cadkey 98 Project Book: A Quick Guide to the Power of Cadkey 98. deluxe ed. (Illus.). 512p. (C). 1999. pap. 54.95 (*1-880544-71-7*, Pub. by Micro Educ) Tech Ed Concepts.

— The DataCAD 8 Project Book: A Quick Guide for DataCAD 8 for Windows. (Illus.). 218p. 1998. pap. 34.95 (*1-880544-69-5*, Pub. by Micro Educ) Tech Ed Concepts.

— An Introduction to DataCAD 5. (Illus.). 302p. (C). 1994. pap. 34.95 (*1-880544-34-2*, DCAD5-1, Pub. by Micro Educ) Tech Ed Concepts.

— El Libro de Datacad 5 en Espanol. Herrera, Raul, tr. (SPA., Illus.). 120p. 1994. student ed. 15.95 (*1-880544-37-7*, DCAD5-2, Pub. by Micro Educ) Tech Ed Concepts.

— The Mastercam 4 Design Workbook. (Illus.). 100p. 1994. student ed. 24.95 (*1-880544-48-2*, Pub. by Micro Educ) Tech Ed Concepts.

— The Renderize Live Project Book: Photorealistic Rendering for DataCAD 8. 90p. 1998. pap. 29.95 (*1-880544-70-9*, Pub. by Micro Educ) Tech Ed Concepts.

Nasman, Leonard O., et al. Fundamentals of Graphics Communication: 1994 ANSI Update & Glossary. (C). 1996. text 51.95 (*0-256-24274-7*, Irwn McGrw-H) McGrw-H Hghr Educ.

— Technical Graphics Communication & Autocad. (C). 1995. text 98.20 (*0-256-19305-3*, Irwn McGrw-H) McGrw-H Hghr Educ.

Nasmith, David. Institutes of English Adjective Law: Procedure in Court - Embracing an Outline of the Law of Evidence & Measure of Damages. xxi, 355p. 1980. reprint ed. 48.00 (*0-8377-0904-0*, Rothman) W S Hein.

— Institutes of English Private Law: Embracing an Outline of the Substantive Branch of the Law of Persons & Things, 2 vols., Set. 720p. 1980. reprint ed. 85.00 (*0-8377-0903-2*, Rothman) W S Hein.

— Institutes of English Public Law: Embracing an Outline of General Jurisprudence, the Development of the British Constitution, Public International Law & the Public Municipal Law of England. vi, 455p. 1980. reprint ed. lib. bdg. 35.00 (*0-8377-0905-9*, Rothman) W S Hein.

Nasmyth, Peter. Georgia: In the Mountains of Poetry. LC 98-17593. 352p. 1998. text 45.00 (*0-312-21524-X*) St Martin.

Nasmyth, Spike, jt. auth. see Nasmyth, Virginia.

Nasmyth, Virginia & Nasmyth, Spike. Hanoi Release John Nasmyth. Behar, June, ed. (Illus.). 345p. 1984. 9.95 (*0-9613991-0-4*) V Parr Pub.

Naso. Stirling Machine. write for info. (*0-471-87725-5*) Wiley.

Naso, P. Ovidius. Heroidenbrief Der XII: Medea an Jason. Heinze, Theodor, ed. & intro. by. (Mnemosyne Ser.: No. 170). xii, 292p. 1997. 111.50 (*90-04-10800-9*, NLG 175) Brill Academic Pubs.

Nason, Arthur H. Heralds & Heraldry in Ben Jonson's Plays, Masques & Entertainments. LC 68-59042. 173p. (C). 1968. reprint ed. 50.00 (*0-87752-076-3*) Gordian.

— James Shirley, Dramatist. LC 67-23860. (Illus.). 1972. reprint ed. 30.95 (*0-405-08813-2*, Pub. by Blom Pubns) Ayer.

Nason, Beverly A., ed. see W.E.N. Screenwriters & Assoc. Staff & Nason, Willie E.

Nason-Clark, Nancy. The Battered Wife: How Christians Confront Family Violence. LC 97-23724. 1997. pap. 22.95 (*0-664-25692-9*) Westminster John Knox.

Nason, Elias. A Gazateer of the State of Massachusetts. (Illus.). 809p. 1998. reprint ed. pap. 51.50 (*0-7884-1043-1*, 75) Heritage Bk.

— Gazetteer of the State of Massachusetts, with Numerous Illustrations on Wood & Steel. (Illus.). 576p. 1998. reprint ed. lib. bdg. 55.00 (*0-8328-7114-1*) Higginson Bk Co.

— A History of the Town of Dunstable, Mass., from Its Earliest Settlement to the Year 1873. (Illus.). 316p. 1989. reprint ed. lib. bdg. 37.00 (*0-8328-0824-5*, MA0045) Higginson Bk Co.

— Howe Family Gathering, Harmony Grove, S. Framingham, Massachusetts, 1871. 46p. 1994. reprint ed. pap. 9.00 (*0-8328-4128-5*) Higginson Bk Co.

Nason, Emma H. Old Hallowell on the Kennebec, Maine. (Illus.). 359p. 1997. reprint ed. lib. bdg. 42.00 (*0-8328-5849-8*) Higginson Bk Co.

Nason, James D., jt. auth. see Marshall, Mac.

Nason, Jerry, et al. Famous American Athletes of Today, Seventh Series. LC 70-93348. (Essay Index Reprint Ser.). 1977. reprint ed. 30.95 (*0-8369-2250-6*) Ayer.

Nason, John W. Foundation Trusteeship: Service in the Public Interest. LC 88-38128. 173p. (Orig.). 1989. pap. 19.95 (*0-87954-285-3*) Foundation Ctr.

— The Nature of Trusteeship. 136p. 1982. 16.00 (*0-318-17378-6*) Assn Gov Bds.

— The Nature of Trusteeship: The Role & Responsibilities of College & University Boards. LC 83-174535. 102p. 1982. 9.95 (*0-318-03585-5*) Assn Gov Bds.

— Presidential Assessment. 86p. 1980. 18.00 (*0-318-17382-4*) Assn Gov Bds.

— Presidential Search. 92p. 1982. 18.00 (*0-318-17380-8*) Assn Gov Bds.

— Trustees & the Future of Foundations. LC 77-76677. 112p. 1977. pap. 12.00 (*0-913892-00-9*) Coun Found.

Nason, Kelly, jt. auth. see Laughlin, Brenda.

Nason, Richard. A Modern Dunciad. LC 77-92992. 114p. 1978. pap. 15.00 (*0-912292-49-0*) Smith.

— Old Soldiers. LC 88-90815. (Illus.). 68p. 1988. pap. 10.00 (*0-912292-80-6*) Smith.

Nason, Richard W. Two Radicals: Unpublished Essays on Jean Genet & Ezra Pound Plus Selected Reviews on Sundry Subjects. LC 92-75617. 112p. 1993. pap. 25.00 (*0-9635297-5-7*) Black Spruce.

— The Wedding at Touisset. LC 75-538. (Illus.). 56p. 1975. pap. 10.00 (*0-912292-37-7*) Smith.

Nason, Tema. Full Moon. LC 93-25035. 39p. (Orig.). 1993. pap. 7.95 (*0-9619111-5-8*) Chicory Blue.

Nason, Thelma C. A Stranger Here, Myself. Hunting, Constance, ed. 1980. pap. 3.50 (*0-913006-11-4*) Puckerbrush.

Nason, Tim. Days with Cedar Whitewater. LC 96-79365. (Cranberry Manifesto Ser.: Bk. 1). (Illus.). 56p. (Orig.). 1997. pap. 14.95 (*0-9635297-1-4*) Black Spruce.

Nason, Willie E., jt. auth. see W.E.N. Screenwriters & Assoc. Staff.

NASPE Staff. Moving into the Future: National Standards for Physical Education: A Guide to Content & Assessment. 3rd ed. 125p. (Orig.). (C). (gr. 13). 1995. text 22.00 (*0-8151-7338-5*, 304-10083) AAHPERD.

— National Standards for Athletic Coaches: Quality Coaches, Quality Sports. 128p. (Orig.). 1995. pap. 22.00 (*0-7872-1282-2*, 304-10084) Kendall-Hunt.

Nasper, Ellen, jt. auth. see Degen, Kathleen.

Naspitz, Charles K., jt. ed. see Tinkelman, David G.

Nasr, Constantine. The Bible in the Liturgy. 75p. spiral bd. 9.95 (*1-880321-01-7*) Theosis Pub.

Nasr, Hatem N., ed. Automatic Object Recognition. (Institute Ser.: Vol. IS07). 254p. 1991. 20.00 (*0-8194-0467-5*) SPIE.

— Automatic Object Recognition. 734p. 1991. 65.00 (*0-8194-0769-0*); pap. 50.00 (*0-8194-0770-4*) SPIE.

— Selected Papers on Model-Based Vision. LC 92-42878. (Milestone Ser.: Vol. MS 72). 1993. pap. 45.00 (*0-8194-1165-5*) SPIE.

— Selected Papers on Model-Based Vision. LC 92-42878. (Milestone Ser.: Vol. MS 72/HC). 1993. 55.00 (*0-8194-1164-7*) SPIE.

Nasr, Isam & Cordero, Marco. Medical Spanish: An Instant Translator. (SPA., Illus.). 394p. 1996. pap. text 20.95 (*0-7216-6052-5*, W B Saunders Co) Harcrt Hlth Sci Grp.

Nasr, Isam & Cordero, Marco. Medical Spanish in Pediatrics: An Instant Translator. 380p. Date not set. pap. text. write for info. (*0-7216-8447-5*, W B Saunders Co) Harcrt Hlth Sci Grp.

***Nasr, Jimmy & Mahler, Roger.** Designing Secure Database Driven Web Sites. 400p. 2000. pap. text 44.99 (*0-13-085458-1*) P-H.

Nasr, Kameel. Bicycle Touring International: The Complete Book on Adventure Cycling. LC 92-75117. (Illus.). 288p. 1996. 18.95 (*0-933201-53-2*) MBI Pubg.

Nasr, Kameel. Cycling the Mediterranean: Bicycle Touring in Spain, France, Italy, Greece & Beyond. LC 95-76303. (Active Travel Ser.). (Illus.). 224p. (Orig.). 1996. pap. 5.98 (*0-933201-74-5*, Bicycle Bks) MBI Pubg.

Nasr, Kameel B. Arab & Israeli Terrorism: The Causes & Effects of Political Violence, 1936-1993. LC 96-38464. 269p. 1996. lib. bdg. 42.50 (*0-7864-0280-6*) McFarland & Co.

Nasr, Louise H. Geothermal Loan Guaranty Program & Its Impact on Exploration & Development. 207p. 1979. pap. 1.00 (*0-918062-05-5*) Colo Sch Mines.

Nasr, Mohammed. Arabic Standard Atlas Book. (ARA.). 1983. pap. 14.95 (*0-86685-164-X*) Intl Bk Ctr.

Nasr, Raja T. Applied English Phonology: For ESL/EFL Teacher. LC 96-48662. 124p. 1997. 42.50 (*0-7618-0640-7*); pap. 21.50 (*0-7618-0641-5*) U Pr of Amer.

— Colloquial Arabic: An Oral Approach. (ARA.). 195p. 1968. 17.95 (*0-86685-044-9*, LDL449, Pub. by Librairie du Liban) Intl Bk Ctr.

— Communicate in Colloquial Arabic. (ARA.). 146p. 1989. pap. 12.00 (*0-86685-457-6*, LDL4576, Pub. by Librairie du Liban) Intl Bk Ctr.

— English-Colloquial Arabic Dictionary. (ARA & ENG.). 285p. pap. 7.95 (*0-86685-079-1*, LDL0791, Pub. by Librairie du Liban) Intl Bk Ctr.

— A First English Dictionary: For ESL Students. 276p. 1994. lib. bdg. 47.50 (*0-8191-9730-0*) U Pr of Amer.

— A First English Dictionary: For ESL Students. 276p. (C). 1994. pap. text 21.95 (*0-8191-9731-9*) U Pr of Amer.

— Intermediate Colloquial Arabic. (ARA.). 289p. 1974. 18.95 (*0-86685-046-5*, LDL0465, Pub. by Librairie du Liban) Intl Bk Ctr.

An Asterisk (*) at the beginning of an entry indicates that the title is appearing for the first time.

*Nasser, David S. A Call to Die: A 40 Day Journey of Fasting from the World & Feasting on God. (Illus.). 304p. 2000. 20.00 (*1-888237-30-9*) Baxter Pr.

Nasser, Essam. Fundamentals of Gaseous Ionization & Plasma Electronics. LC 77-125275. (Wiley Series in Plasma Physics). 470p. reprint ed. pap. 145.70 (*0-608-10057-9*, 205518400011) Bks Demand.

Nasser, Fred N. & Giuliani, Emilio R. Clinical Two-Dimensional Echocardiography. LC 82-20215. (Illus.). 274p. reprint ed. pap. 85.00 (*0-8357-7625-5*, 205694800096) Bks Demand.

Nasser, Kazem A. Dictionary of English Idioms: Comprehensive. (ARA & ENG.). 1997. 35.00 (*0-86685-686-2*) Intl Bk Ctr.

Nasser, Martin & Vivier, Frank. Mindset for the New Generation Organization. (Illus.). 169p. (C). 1993. pap. text 41.45 (*0-7021-2879-1*, Pub. by Juta & Co) Intl Spec Bk.

Nasser, Mervat. Culture & Weight Consciousness. LC 96-43021. 154p. (C). 1997. 60.00 (*0-415-16152-5*); pap. 22.99 (*0-415-16153-3*) Routledge.

Nasser, Nemat S. Theoretical Foundation for Large-Scale Computations for Nonlinear Material Behavior. 1984. text 206.50 (*90-247-3092-9*) Kluwer Academic.

Nasset, William J. Inventor's Rights: Petition to Congress. Brooks, Liz, ed. (Illus.). 40p. 1994. pap. 5.00 (*1-889285-50-1*) Little Inventor.

— This Little Inventor Went to the Patent Office: Phase I & Phase II (Under One Cover) 2nd ed. Brooks, Liz, ed. (Illus.). 107p. 1996. lib. bdg. 59.90 (*1-889285-00-5*) Little Inventor.

Nassib, Selim & Tisdall, Caroline. Beirut: Frontline Story. (Illus.). 160p. 1983. pap. 6.95 (*0-86543-000-4*) Africa World.

Nassif, Janet Z. Handbook of Health Careers: A Guide to Employment Opportunities. LC 79-23027. 354p. 1980. 49.95 (*0-87705-489-4*, Kluwer Acad Hman Sci) Kluwer Academic.

*Nassif, Janet Zhun. Caring for Cancer Patients: A Handbook for the Home Care Aide. 3rd rev. ed. iii, 120p. 1999. pap. write for info. (*1-930304-01-3*) Home Care Univ.

Nassif, R. E. & Thaddeus, J. D., eds. Education for Health Manpower in the Middle East. 1967. pap. 12.95 (*0-8156-6006-5*, Pub. by Am U Beirut) Syracuse U Pr.

*Nassif, Tony. Jesus, Politics & the Church. 2000. pap. 12.99 (*0-9654133-2-2*) Elijah Prod.

Nassif, Tony. Jesus, Politics, & the Church: The Mind of Christ on Christians in Politics. LC 97-167769. 240p. 1996. 19.99 (*1-883893-55-0*) WinePress Pub.

Nassimbene, Raymond, jt. auth. see Carmichael, Fitzhugh L.

Nassirova, Firangiz, tr. see Afkhami, Mahnaz & Vaziri, Haleh.

Nassis, George, jt. auth. see Rainis, Kenneth G.

Nassivera, John. The Colour of Love. 53p. 1997. pap. 10.00 (*0-929741-47-1*) Playsmith.

— Making a Killing: A New Play. LC 87-460823. 88 p. 1986. write for info. (*0-573-60847-4*) S French Trade.

Nasson, Bill. Abraham Esau's War: A Black South African War in the Cape, 1899-1902. (African Studies: No. 68). (Illus.). 271p. (C). 1991. text 74.95 (*0-521-38512-1*) Cambridge U Pr.

*Nasson, Bill. The South African War, 1899-1902. (Illus.). 320p. 1999. text 75.00 (*0-340-74154-6*); pap. text 24.95 (*0-340-61427-7*) OUP.

Nassour, Ellis. Honky Tonk Angel: The Intimate Story of Patsy Cline. 1994. mass mkt. 5.99 (*0-312-95158-2*) St Martin.

NASSP Curiculum Council Staff. Rethinking Reform: The Principal's Dilemma. 80p. (Orig.). 1986. pap. 9.00 (*0-88210-193-5*) Natl Assn Principals.

NASSP Middle Level Council Staff. Developing a Mission Statement for the Middle Level School. 40p. (Orig.). 1987. pap. text 7.00 (*0-88210-204-4*) Natl Assn Principals.

NASSP Staff. GED Study Skills Workshop Kit. (Orig.). 1986. pap. 16.50 (*0-88210-199-4*) Natl Assn Principals.

Nassr, Donald. In the Shadows of the Cross. 410p. 1994. 24.95 (*0-9642463-0-9*) ICAM Pub Co.

— The Scroll. 368p. 1997. 24.95 (*0-9642463-2-5*) ICAM Pub Co.

— The Scroll. unabridged ed. 368p. Date not set. pap. 24.95 (*0-9642463-3-3*) ICAM Pub Co.

Nasstrom, Britt-Mari. Freyja: The Great Goddess of the North. (Lund Studies in History of Religions: No. 5). 244p. 1995. pap. 47.50 (*91-22-01694-5*) Coronet Bks.

*Nasstrom, Kathryn L. Everybody's Grandmother & Nobody's Fool: Frances Freeborn Pauley & the Struggle for Social Justice. LC 99-59993. 256p. 2000. 26.00 (*0-8014-3782-2*) Cornell U Pr.

Nassutti, Colette P. Turning Sales over to the Pros: Fourteen CPA Firms Share Their Experiences. LC 96-14161. 1996. write for info. (*0-87051-178-5*) Am Inst CPA.

Nassutti, Colette P., ed. The Marketing Advantage: How to Get & Keep the Clients You Want. LC 93-47895. 1993. 85.00 (*0-87051-146-7*) Am Inst CPA.

Nast, D. J. Handbook for Civil Technicians. 300p. (C). 1996. pap. text 24.95 (*0-89641-299-7*) American Pr.

Nast, Heidi J. & Pile, Steve. Places Through the Body. LC 97-37994. (Illus.). 448p. (C). 1998. 85.00 (*0-415-17904-1*) Routledge.

— Places Through the Body. LC 97-37994. 344p. (C). 1998. pap. 27.99 (*0-415-17905-X*) Routledge.

Nast, Jo A., jt. auth. see Coggeshall, John M.

Nast, Lenora H., et al, eds. Baltimore: A Living Renaissance. LC 82-80490. (Illus.). 336p. 1982. 12.95 (*0-942460-00-6*) Hist Balt Soc.

Nast, Matthias. Die Stummen Verkaufer Lebensmittelverpackungen Im Zeitalter der Konsumgesellschaft: Umwelthistorische Untersuchung Uber die Entwicklung der Warenpackung und den Wandel der Einkaufsgewohnheiten (1950er Bis 1990er Jahre) (Europaische Hochschulschriften Ser.: Reihe 3, Bd. 759). (GER.). 376p. 1997. 55.95 (*3-906759-12-1*, Pub. by P Lang) P Lang Pubng.

Nast, Thomas. Thomas Nast Christmas. (Illus.). (J). 1985. pap. 4.95 (*0-486-25004-0*) Dover.

Nast, Thomas. Thomas Nast's Christmas Drawings. (Illus.). 96p. 1978. pap. 6.95 (*0-486-23660-9*) Dover.

Nasta, Cynthia V. Peter & His Pick-Up Truck: A Southwestern Children's Tale. LC 89-80351. (Illus.). 24p. (J). (ps-8). 1989. pap. 6.95 (*0-9622064-0-7*) Little Buckaroo.

— Peter & His Pick-up Truck: An Arizona Children's Tale. LC 89-80352. (Illus.). 24p. (J). (ps-8). 1989. pap. 6.95 (*0-9622064-2-3*); lib. bdg. 6.95 (*0-9622064-1-5*) Little Buckaroo.

Nasta, Phyllis. Aaron Goes to the Shelter: A Story about Abuse, Placement & Protective Services. LC 93-61181. (ENG & SPA., Illus.). 29p. (Orig.). (J). (gr. k-6). 1994. pap. 6.95 (*1-880702-01-0*) Whole Child.

Nasta, Susheila, ed. Critical Perspectives on Sam Selvon. LC 81-51645. (Critical Perspectives Ser.). 280p. 1988. 35.00 (*0-89410-238-9*, Three Contnts); pap. 16.95 (*0-89410-239-7*, Three Contnts) L Rienner.

— Motherlands: Black Women's Writings from Africa, the Caribbean, & South Asia. LC 91-30110. 365p. 1992. text 45.00 (*0-8135-1781-8*); pap. text 17.95 (*0-8135-1782-6*) Rutgers U Pr.

*Nasta, Susheila, ed. Reading the 'New' Literatures. (English Association Ser.). 160p. 2000. 45.00 (*0-85991-601-4*) Boydell & Brewer.

Nasta, Tony. How to Design the Vocational Curriculum: A Practical Guide for Schools & Colleges. LC 94-27668. 160p. 1994. pap. 25.00 (*0-7494-1112-0*, Kogan Pg Educ) Stylus Pub VA.

*Nastal, David T. Children's Choir Basics. (Basics Ser.). 1999. pap. 11.95 (*1-56929-032-6*, Pastoral Press) OR Catholic.

Nastase, Ilie. The Net. Schwartz, Ros, tr. 1988. pap. 3.95 (*0-317-70084-7*) St Martin.

Nastasescu, Constantin & Van Oystaeyen, Freddy. Dimensions of Ring Theory. 1987. text 188.50 (*90-277-2461-X*) Kluwer Academic.

Nastasi, Bonnie K. & Dezolt, Denise M. School Interventions for Children of Alcoholics. LC 94-853. (School Practitioner Ser.). 275p. 1994. lib. bdg. 31.00 (*0-89862-367-7*) Guilford Pubns.

Nastasi, M. A., et al, eds. Beam-Solid Interactions: Fundamentals & Applications. (Materials Research Society Symposium Proceedings Ser.: Vol. 279). 909p. 1993. text 30.00 (*1-55899-174-3*) Materials Res.

Nastasi, Michael A., et al, eds. Handbook of Modern Ion Beam Materials Analysis: Materials Research Society-Handbook. (Illus.). 700p. 1995. 200.00 (*1-55899-254-5*, IBH) Materials Res.

Nastasi, Michael A., et al. Ion-Solid Interactions: Fundamentals & Applications. (Solid State Science Ser.). (Illus.). 568p. (C). 1996. text 119.95 (*0-521-37376-X*) Cambridge U Pr.

Nastasi, Michael A., jt. auth. see Maggiora, Carl J.

Nastasi, Michael A., ed. see NATO Advanced Study Institute on Mechanical Proper.

Naster, P., et al, eds. A Survey of Numismatic Research, 1966-71, 3 vols. 1133p. 1973. 20.00 (*0-89722-069-2*) Am Numismatic.

Nastick, Sharon. Mr. Radagast Makes an Unexpected Journey. LC 80-8107. (Illus.). 96p. (J). (gr. 3-7). 1981. 10.95 (*0-690-04050-4*); lib. bdg. 11.89 (*0-690-04051-2*) HarpC Child Bks.

Nastiuk, Virginia. Split/Divided Skirts: Secrets to Great Fit. (Illus.). 10p. (Orig.). 1997. pap. 4.95 (*0-942003-39-X*) Personal Pattern.

— Your Perfect Pattern: Custom Fit by Jinni. (Illus.). 22p. (Orig.). 1997. lib. bdg. 4.95 (*0-942003-42-X*) Personal Pattern.

Nastiuk, Virginia M. Personal Patterns by Jinni: A Manual for Flat Pattern Design, Vol. 2. (Illus.). 347p. 1988. lib. bdg. 39.95 (*0-942003-07-1*) Personal Pattern.

— Personal Patterns by Jinni: A Manual for Perfect Patternmaking, 2 vols., Vol. 1. (Illus.). 281p. 1987. reprint ed. lib. bdg. 36.95 (*0-942003-01-2*) Personal Pattern.

— Personal Patterns by Jinni: Fitting Problems & Their Corrections. (Illus.). 101p. 1987. pap. 14.95 (*0-942003-15-2*); lib. bdg. 14.95 (*0-942003-16-0*) Personal Pattern.

— Personal Patterns by Jinni: Introduction to Design. (Illus.). 110p. 1987. pap. 7.90 (*0-942003-20-9*) Personal Pattern.

— Personal Patterns by Jinni: Pants - Fit & Design. (Illus.). 100p. 1987. pap. 14.95 (*0-942003-25-X*); lib. bdg. 14.95 (*0-942003-27-6*) Personal Pattern.

— Personal Patterns by Jinni: Skirts - Fit & Design. (Illus.). 110p. 1987. pap. 7.90 (*0-942003-30-6*) Personal Pattern.

Nasty, Mack. Take No Prisoners: Destroying Enemies with Dirty & Malicious Tricks. LC 90-62143. 128p. 1990. pap. 12.95 (*1-55950-043-3*, 19169) Loompanics.

Nasu, Eisho, jt. ed. see Tanaka, Kenneth K.

Nasu, K. Relaxations of Excited States & Photo-Induced Structural Phase Transitions: Proceedings of the 19th Taniguchi Symposium, Kashikojima, Japan, July 18-23, 1996, Vol. 124. LC 96-29968. (Springer Series in Solid-State Sciences). 1997. 109.00 (*3-540-62473-2*) Spr-Verlag.

Nasu, Kiyoshi. From the Darkness to the Light. LC 98-90588. 1999. pap. 12.95 (*0-533-12848-X*) Vantage.

Nasu, Masakazu. Textile Systems for Endomorphisms & Automorphisms of the Shift. LC 94-43210. (Memoirs Ser.: Vol. 546). 215p. 1995. pap. 43.00 (*0-8218-2606-9*, MEMO/114/546) Am Math.

Nasu, Masamoto. Children of the Paper Crane: The Story of Sadako Sasaki & Her Struggle with the A-Bomb Disease. Yoshida, Kyoko et al, trs. from JPN. LC 91-9130. 232p. (C). (gr. 13). 1991. 53.95 (*0-87332-715-2*, East Gate Bk) M E Sharpe.

— Children of the Paper Crane: The Story of Sadako Sasaki & Her Struggle with the A-Bomb Disease. Baldwin, Elizabeth W. & Leeper, Steven L., trs. from JPN. LC 91-9130. 232p. (C). (gr. 13). 1994. pap. 26.95 (*0-87332-716-0*, East Gate Bk) M E Sharpe.

Nasu, Masamotot. Children of the Paper Crane: The Story of Sadako Sasaki & Her Struggle with the A-Bomb. Baldwin, Elizabeth W. et al, trs. LC 96-2047. 232p. (C). 1996. pap. 20.95 (*1-56324-801-8*, N Castle) M E Sharpe.

Nasu, N., et al, eds. Formation of Active Fault Margins. 1986. text 468.00 (*90-277-2302-8*) Kluwer Academic.

Nasu, N. & Honjo, S., eds. New Directions of Oceanographic Research & Development. LC 92-32507. 1993. write for info. (*4-431-70113-3*) Spr-Verlag.

— New Directions of Oceanographic Research & Development. (Illus.). 232p. 1993. 158.95 (*0-387-70113-3*) Spr-Verlag.

Nasu, Shiroshi. Aspects of Japanese Agriculture: A Preliminary Survey. LC 75-30073. (Institute of Pacific Relations Ser.). reprint ed. 32.50 (*0-404-59575-8*) AMS Pr.

Nasurf. Surface Engineering to Combat Wear & Corrosion. 34p. 1997. pap. 50.00 (*1-86125-043-6*) Institute of Management Consultants.

*Nasuti, Harry P. Defining the Sacred Songs: Genre, Tradition & the Post-Critical Interpretation of the Psalms. (Journal for the Study of the Old Testament Supplement Ser.: No. 218). 231p. 1999. 57.50 (*1-84127-028-8*, Pub. by Sheffield Acad) CUP Services.

Nasuti, James F. & Rotwitt, Jeffrey B. The Pennsylvania Corporation: Legal Aspects of Organization & Operation. 2nd ed. (Corporate Practice Ser.: No. 30). 1995. pap. 95.00 (*1-55871-313-1*) BNA.

Nasuti, Mike, jt. auth. see Freeman, Stan.

Nasution, Anwar & World Institute for Development Economics Research Staff. The Banking System & Monetary Aggregates Following Financial Sector Reforms: Lessons from Indonesia. LC 97-185079. (Research for Action Ser.). ix, 50p. 1996. write for info. (*952-9520-41-7*) UN.

NASW Legislative Affairs Department Staff. Social Worker's Guide to the Family Support Act of 1988. 30p. 1989. pap. 6.95 (*0-87101-173-5*) Natl Assn Soc Wkrs.

NASW Press Staff. An Author's Guide to Social Work Journals. 4th ed. LC 96-49622. 378p. (C). 1997. pap. text 35.95 (*0-87101-271-5*) Natl Assn Soc Wkrs.

NASW Press Staff, jt. auth. see Mattaini, Mark A.

NASW Professional Symposium on Social Work Staff. Social Work in a Turbulent World: Seventh NASW Symposium: Selected Papers, Seventh NASW Professional Symposium on Social Work, November 18-21, 1981, Philadelphia, PA. Dinerman, Miriam, ed. LC 83-8216. 220p. reprint ed. pap. 68.20 (*0-7837-6548-7*, 204568500007) Bks Demand.

NASW Staff, ed. Social Work Speaks: NASW Policy Statements. 3rd ed. LC 94-187940. 304p. (C). 1994. pap. text 31.95 (*0-87101-234-0*, 2340) Natl Assn Soc Wkrs.

Nat. Author Catalog of the Peruvian Collection of the National Library of Peru. 1992. 865.00 (*0-7838-1012-1*, G K Hall & Co) Mac Lib Ref.

Nat, Arnold Vander, see Moser, Paul K. & Vander Nat, Arnold.

NATA Board of Certification Staff. Role Delineation Study of the Entry-Level Athletic Trainer Certification Examination. 3rd ed. 62p. (C). 1994. pap. text 27.95 (*0-8036-6504-0*) Davis Co.

— Study Guide for the Nata Board of Certification, Inc. Entry-Level Athletic Trainer Certification Examination. 2nd ed. (Illus.). 146p. (C). 1993. pap. text, student ed. 33.95 (*0-8036-6501-6*) Davis Co.

Natachee, Allan, tr. see Beier, Ulli, ed.

Nataf, Daniel. Democratization & Social Settlements: The Politics of Change in Contemporary Portugal. LC 94-33690. 289p. (C). 1995. text 64.50 (*0-7914-2589-4*); pap. text 21.95 (*0-7914-2590-8*) State U NY Pr.

Nataf, Zachary I. Lesbians Talk Transgender. Date not set. pap. 8.95 (*1-85727-008-8*, Pub. by Scarlet Pr) LPC InBook.

Natal, Thomas. The Birdcatcher. rev. ed. LC 97-65913. Orig. Title: Reign of the Madman: The Birdcatcher. 342p. 1997. text 39.99 (*0-936978-50-3*); pap. text 24.99 (*0-936978-03-1*) Pheasant Run.

Natale, C. Di. Sensors & Microsystems: Proceedings of the 3rd Italian Conference Genova, Italy, 11-13 February. 400p. 1999. 88.00 (*981-02-3759-6*) World Scientific Pub.

Natale, C. D. & Davide, F., eds. Artificial & Natural Perception: Proceedings of the 2nd Italian Conference on Sensors & Microsystems Rome, Italy 3-5 February, 1997. LC 98-202086. 390p. 1998. 84.00 (*981-02-3299-3*) World Scientific Pub.

Natale, Frank. Trance Dance: The Dance of Life. LC 95-12177. 128p. 1995. pap. 22.95 incl. audio compact disk (*1-85230-702-1*, Pub. by Element MA) Penguin Putnam.

Natale, Joseph, Jr. The New Home & Warranty Inspection Handbook. 40p. 1997. pap. 19.95 (*0-9659999-0-4*) ARCC.

Natale, Leo. When Soul & Spirit Agree: Anchoring the Soul to the Spirit to Achieve Ultimate Success & Prosperity. 115p. (Orig.). 1994. pap. 7.99 (*0-88270-683-7*) Bridge-Logos.

Natale, Luigi, ed. see American Society of Civil Engineers Staff.

*Natale, Robert. Fast Stocks, Fast Money: How to Invest in New Issues & Quickly Growing Small Companies. (Illus.). 416p. 2000. 21.95 (*0-07-045980-0*) McGraw.

Natale, Samjuel M., et al, eds. Business Education & Training Vol. IV: A Value-Laden Process: Corporate Structures, Business, & the Management of Values. (Illus.). 350p. 1998. pap. 39.50 (*0-7618-1003-X*) U Pr of Amer.

Natale, Samuel M. Ethics & Morals in Business. 2nd ed. LC 87-9424. 209p. 1987. pap. 21.95 (*0-89135-063-2*) Religious Educ.

— Loneliness & Spiritual Growth. LC 86-10012. 171p. (Orig.). 1986. pap. 16.95 (*0-89135-055-1*) Religious Educ.

*Natale, Samuel M., ed. Business Education & Training - A Value-Laden Process Vol. VI: On the Threshold of the Millennium. (Management of Values Ser.: Vol. VI). 336p. 2000. 64.00 (*0-7618-1648-8*); pap. 39.50 (*0-7618-1649-6*) U Pr of Amer.

— Business Education & Training - A Value-Laden Process Vol. VII: New Wine in Old Bottles. (Management of Values Ser.: Vol. VII). 352p. 2000. 64.00 (*0-7618-1650-X*); pap. 39.50 (*0-7618-1651-8*) U Pr of Amer.

Natale, Samuel M., ed. Psychotherapy & the Lonely Patient. LC 86-12108. (Psychotherapy Patient Ser.: Vol. 2, No. 3). 120p. (C). 1986. text 3.95 (*0-86656-517-5*) Haworth Pr.

— Psychotherapy & the Lonely Patient. LC 86-12101. (Psychotherapy Patient Ser.: Vol. 2, No. 3). 120p. 1986. reprint ed. pap. 29.95 (*0-918393-26-4*, Harrington Park) Haworth Pr.

Natale, Samuel M., et al, eds. Business Education & Training Vol. IV: A Value-Laden Process: Corporate Structures, Business, & the Management of Values. (Illus.). 350p. 1998. 64.00 (*0-7618-1002-1*) U Pr of Amer.

— Business Education & Training Vol. V: A Value-Laden Process: The Management of Values: Organizational & Educational Issues. (Illus.). 400p. (C). 1998. 67.00 (*0-7618-1004-8*); pap. 42.50 (*0-7618-1005-6*) U Pr of Amer.

Natale, Samuel M. & Fenton, Mark B., eds. Business Educaiton & Training Vol. II: A Value-Laden Process: The Developing Professional: Maintaining Values in "Practical" Training. LC 96-41779. (Illus.). 314p. 1996. 62.50 (*0-7618-0570-2*); pap. 38.50 (*0-7618-0571-0*) U Pr of Amer.

— Business Education & Training Vol. I: A Value-Laden Process: Education & Value Conflict. LC 96-41779. (Illus.). 298p. 1996. 59.50 (*0-7618-0568-0*); pap. 38.50 (*0-7618-0569-9*) U Pr of Amer.

Natale, Samuel M. & Wilson, John B., eds. The Ethical Contexts for Business Conflicts, Vol. 1. LC 89-22762. (Ethical Conflict Ser.). (Illus.). 202p. (Orig.). 1990. pap. text 23.00 (*0-8191-7598-6*) U Pr of Amer.

Natale, Samuel M., jt. auth. see Wilson, John B.

Natale, Samuel M., ed. see Fenton, Mark B.

Natali, Alan. Woody's Boys: 20 Famous Buckeyes Talk Amongst Themselves. LC 95-70158. (Illus.). 528p. 1995. 35.00 (*1-882203-04-6*) Orange Frazer.

*Natali, Antonio. Andrea Del Sarto. (Illus.). 220p. 1999. 125.00 (*0-7892-0531-9*) Abbeville Pr.

*Natali, Carlo. The Wisdom of Aristotle. Parks, Gerald, tr. (C). 2001. pap. text 20.95 (*0-7914-4896-7*) State U NY Pr.

— The Wisdom of Aristotle. Parks, Gerald, tr. (C). 2001. text 62.50 (*0-7914-4895-9*) State U NY Pr.

Natali, Enrico & Sandrof, Mark. American Landscapes: 1968-1990. (Illus.). 104p. (Orig.). 1991. pap. 29.00 (*0-945149-02-6*) Panopticon Pr.

Natali, Louis M., Jr. In Re: Grooten. 54p. 1991. pap. 22.95 (*1-55681-278-7*) Natl Inst Trial Ad.

Natali, Louis M., jt. auth. see Bocchino, Anthony J.

Natali, Patricia, jt. auth. see Chambers.

Natali, Patricia, jt. auth. see Chambers, Kate.

Natalia. The Victorious Queen of the World: The Spiritual Diary of Sr. Natalia of Hungary. Foglein, Stephen, tr. 159p. 1992. pap. 7.50 (*1-884722-01-6*) Two Hrts Bks.

*Natalicchi, Giorgio. Behind European Integration. 288p. 2000. pap. 22.95 (*0-8476-9909-9*) Rowman.

Natalie, jt. auth. see Young, Loy.

Natalie, Andrea. Stonewall Riots. (Stonewall Riots Cartoons Ser.). (Illus.). 74p. (Orig.). 1990. pap. 4.95 (*0-9628027-0-0*, VA 154-987) A Natalie Pub.

— Stonewall Riots. (Illus.). 76p. (Orig.). 1990. reprint ed. pap. 4.95 (*0-9628027-1-9*, VA154987) A Natalie Pub.

Natalino, Ronzitti. Rescuing Nationals Abroad Through Military Coercion & Intervention on Grounds of Humanity. 1985. lib. bdg. 109.50 (*90-247-3135-6*) Kluwer Academic.

Natalizio, Michael G. History Buff's Crosswords Plus American Government & Economics: 135 Crossword Puzzle, Word Search & Word Match Activities Dealing with American Government & Economics from the Constitution to the Theories of Capitalism. LC 98-92805. (Illus.). vi, 300p. 1998. pap. 28.95 (*1-891769-20-0*, Educ Express) Nataco Pubg.

— History Buff's Crosswords Plus United States History: 200 Crossword Puzzle, Word Search & Word Match Activities Dealing with U. S. History from the Early American Indians to the 1990s. LC 97-95341. (Illus.). vi,500p. 1998. pap. 36.00 (*1-891769-08-1*, Educ Express) Nataco Pubg.

— History Buff's Crosswords Plus World History Book I: 145 Crossword Puzzle, Word Search & Word Match Activities Dealing with World History from the Antiquities to the Age of Feudalism. LC 98-93689. (Illus.). vi, 338p. 1998. pap. 28.95 (*1-891769-27-8*, Educ Express) Nataco Pubg.

— History Buff's Crosswords Plus World History Book II: 145 Crossword Puzzle, Word Search & Word Match

Activities Dealing with World History from the Middle Ages to the Late 1800s. (Illus.). vi, 340p. 1999. pap. 28.95 (*1-891769-30-8*, Educ Express) Nataco Pubg.
Natambu, Kofi. The Melody Never Stops. 72p. (Orig.). 1991. pap. 10.00 (*0-9622474-3-X*) Past Tents Pr.
***Natansohn, Almeria, ed.** Azobenzene: Containing Materials. 176p. 1999. 75.00 (*3-527-29805-3*) Wiley.
Natanson, Jan. Learning through Play. LC 98-128644. (Illus.). 128p. 1998. pap. 19.95 (*0-7063-7623-4*) Sterling.
Natanson, Maurice A. A Critique of Jean-Paul Sartre's Ontology. 150p. 1973. reprint ed. pap. text 75.50 (*90-247-1490-7*, Pub. by M Nijhoff) Kluwer Academic.
— A Critique of Jean-Paul Sartre's Ontology. LC 72-8367. (Studies in Philosophy: No. 40). 136p. 1972. reprint ed. lib. bdg. 75.00 (*0-8383-1412-0*) M S G Haskell Hse.
— Edmund Husserl: Philosopher of Infinite Tasks. (Studies in Phenomenology & Existential Philosophy). 227p. 1973. 39.95 (*0-8101-0425-3*); pap. 22.95 (*0-8101-0456-3*) Northwestern U Pr.
— The Erotic Bird: Phenomenology in Literature. LC 97-19372. 208p. 1998. text 35.00 (*0-691-01219-9*, Pub. by Princeton U Pr) Cal Prin Full Svc.
Natanson, Maurice A., ed. Phenomenology & the Social Sciences, I. LC 79-91001. (Studies in Phenomenology & Existential Philosophy). 1066p. (C). 1973. pap. 19.95 (*0-8101-0616-7*) Northwestern U Pr.
Natanson, Nicholas. The Black Image in the New Deal: The Politics of FSA Photography. LC 91-14344. (Illus.). 320p. (C). 1992. pap. 18.95 (*0-87049-724-3*); text 45.00 (*0-87049-723-5*) U of Tenn Pr.
Natarajan, A. T., jt. ed. see Obe, G.
Natarajan, B., tr. see Tirumulav.
Natarajan, Balas K. Machine Learning: A Theoretical Approach. 250p. 1991. text 46.95 (*1-55860-148-1*) Morgan Kaufmann.
Natarajan, C., tr. see Shul'man, S. G., ed.
Natarajan, G., jt. auth. see Viswanath, D. S.
Natarajan, K. & Raman, N. South Indian Agaricales, Preliminary Study of Some Dark Spored Species. (Bibliotheca Mycologica Ser.: No. 89). (Illus.). 204p. 1983. text 80.00 (*3-7682-1344-7*) Lubrecht & Cramer.
Natarajan, N., jt. ed. see Vajpeyi, Dhirendra K.
Natarajan, Nalini, ed. Handbook of Twentieth-Century Literatures of India. LC 95-20938. 448p. 1996. lib. bdg. 89.50 (*0-313-28778-3*, Greenwood Pr) Greenwood.
Natarajan, Sundaram. Theory & Design of Linear Active Networks. 464p. 1987. write for info. (*0-317-53615-X*) Macmillan.
Natarajan, Swaminathan, ed. Imprecise & Approximate Computation. LC 95-15532. (Kluwer International Series in Engineering & Computer Science). 200p. (C). 1995. text 103.00 (*0-7923-9579-4*) Kluwer Academic.
Natarjan, Uttara. Hazlitt & the Reach of Sense: Criticism, Morals, & the Metaphysics of Power. (Oxford English Monographs). 224p. 1999. text 72.00 (*0-19-818437-9*) OUP.
***Nataro, James P., et al, eds.** Persistent Bacterial Infections. (Illus.). 500p. 2000. 115.95 (*1-55581-159-0*) ASM Pr.
Natches, Gilbert. Northern Paiute Verbs. fac. ed. (University of California Publications in American Archaeology & Ethnology: Vol. 20: 14). 18p. (C). 1923. reprint ed. pap. text 2.19 (*1-55567-250-7*) Coyote Press.
Natchev, Alexi. Tom, Babette & Simon: Three Tales of Transformation. LC 94-35195. 112p. (J). (gr. 3-7). 1997. mass mkt. 4.50 (*0-380-72770-6*, Avon Bks) Morrow Avon.
Natchez, Gladys. Personality Patterns & Oral Reading: A Study of Overt Behavior in the Reading Situation As It Reveals Reactions of Dependence, Aggression, & Withdrawal in Children. LC 60-6043. 112p. reprint ed. pap. 34.80 (*0-608-11175-9*, 205032200061) Bks Demand.
Natella, Arthur A., Jr. Anacronismos De la Nueva Literatura Latinoamericana. LC 89-83446. (SPA.). 64p. (Orig.). 1991. pap. 10.00 (*0-89729-527-7*) Ediciones.
Natella, Arthur A., jt. ed. see McKinniss, Candace B.
Natelson, B. H. Tomorrow's Doctors: The Path to Successful Practice in the 1990's. LC 89-26563. (Illus.). 302p. (C). 1990. 19.95 (*0-306-43195-5*, Plen Insight) Perseus Pubng.
Natelson, Benjamin H. Facing & Fighting Fatigue: A Practical Approach. LC 97-30094. 203p. 1998. pap. 15.00 (*0-300-07401-8*) Yale U Pr.
***Natelson, Benjamin H.** Facing & Fighting Fatigue: A Practical Approach. LC 97-30094. 208p. 1998. 30.00 (*0-300-06848-4*) Yale U Pr.
Natelson, Ethan A., jt. ed. see Natelson, Samuel.
Natelson, Jonathan D., jt. auth. see Cumpiano, William R.
Natelson, Nina, ed. Future Medical Research Without the Use of Animals: Facing the Challenge - May 15-16, 1990, Tel Aviv, Israel. (Illus.). (Orig.). 1991. pap. write for info. (*0-9631596-0-7*) CFH Animals IS.
Natelson, Robert G. Children of the Night. 1994. 75.00 (*0-316-59888-7*) Little.
— Deeds, Set. 633p. 1993. 125.00 (*0-316-59885-2*, Aspen Law & Bus) Aspen Pub.
— Deeds: 1994. 1994. suppl. ed. 75.00 (*0-316-59886-0*, Aspen Law & Bus) Aspen Pub.
— Law of Property Owners Associations. 784p. 1989. 125.00 (*0-316-59865-8*, Aspen Law & Bus) Aspen Pub.
— Modern Deeds. 1995. suppl. ed. 80.00 (*0-316-59933-6*, Aspen Law & Bus) Aspen Pub.
— Modern Law of Deeds to Real Property. 640p. 1992. 125.00 (*0-316-59876-3*, Aspen Law & Bus) Aspen Pub.
— Property Ownership, 1995. 1995. suppl. ed. 80.00 (*0-316-59932-8*, Aspen Law & Bus) Aspen Pub.
— Property Ownership Set. 779p. 1990. 125.00 (*0-316-59871-2*) Little.
— State Fiscal Policy & Economic Growth in the Rocky Mountain West. (Issue Paper #6-98 Ser.). 14p. 1998. pap. text 8.00 (*1-57655-168-7*) Independ Inst.
— Tax & Spending Limits for Montana? Criteria for Assessing Current Proposals. (Issues Paper #10-94 Ser.). 30p. 1994. pap. text 8.00 (*1-57655-138-5*) Independ Inst.
— Tax & Spending Limits for Montana? Criteria for Assessing Current Proposals. (issue Papers: No. 10-94). 30p. 1994. pap. text 8.00 (*1-57655-056-7*) Independ Inst.
Natelson, Samuel & Natelson, Ethan A., eds. Principles of Applied Clinical Chemistry: Chemical Background & Medical Applications, 2 vols. Incl. Erythrocyte Chemical Composition, Normal & Aberrant Metabolism. LC 75-4798. 584p. 1978. 79.50 (*0-306-35232-X*, Kluwer Plenum); Maintenance of Fluid & Electrolyte Balance. LC 75-4798. 394p. 1975. 55.00 (*0-306-35231-1*, Kluwer Plenum); LC 75-4798. (Illus.). write for info. (*0-318-55335-X*, Plenum Trade) Perseus Pubng.
Natelson, Samuel, et al. Amniotic Fluid: Physiology, Biochemistry, & Clinical Chemistry. LC 74-4444. (Current Topics in Clinical Chemistry Ser.: Vol. 1). 406p. reprint ed. pap. 125.90 (*0-8357-5415-4*, 205509300008) Bks Demand.
Natelson, Stephen E. Die Ganze Mispoche: An Account of the Author's Family Notes, Oujevolk, Rosenfeld, Natelson, Winick, Bershansky, Movitz, Siegel, Brody, Burden, Melnick, Notkin, Tkotch, Schulman & Kuznitz Are Some of the Families Included. 280p. 1995. write for info. (*0-9645349-0-8*) S E Natelson.
Nateman, D. S. Introduction to Art. 320p. (C). 1993. pap. 9.95 (*0-07-045912-6*) McGraw.
Natenberg, Sheldon. Option Volatility & Pricing: Advanced Trading Strategies & Techniques. rev. ed. 350p. 1994. text 50.00 (*1-55738-486-X*, Irwn Prfssnl) McGraw-Hill Prof.
***Natenshon, Abigail.** When Your Child Has an Eating Disorder: A Step-by-Step Workbook for Parents & Other Caregivers. 224p. 1999. pap. 22.00 (*0-7879-4578-1*) Jossey-Bass.
Natera, Maria, et al. The California Latino-Chicano High School Dropout Prevention Project, 4 vol. set. (Illus.). 1220p. (YA). (gr. 9-12). 1996. ring bd. write for info. (*1-889621-00-5*) Hispnc Ed & Media.
Naterop, Eric & Wolffers, Ivan, eds. Health & Health Care in Transition: The Example of Vietnam. (Primary Health Care Publications: No. 10). 114p. 1996. pap. 17.00 (*90-5383-406-0*, Pub. by VUB Univ Pr) Paul & Co Pubs.
Natesa, Sastri P. & Kingscote, Georgiana H. Folklore of Southern India or Tales of the Sun. 320p. 1986. 17.50 (*0-8364-1711-9*, Pub. by Usha) S Asia.
— Tales of the Sun: Folklore of Southern India. LC 78-67728. (Folktale Ser.). reprint ed. 28.00 (*0-404-16137-5*) AMS Pr.
Natesa, Sastri S. Folklore in Southern India, 3 vols. in 1. LC 78-63212. (Folktale Ser.). reprint ed. 26.50 (*0-404-16148-0*) AMS Pr.
Natesa, Sastri S. & Cardew, A. G. Indian Folk Tales. LC 78-63218. (Folktale Ser.). reprint ed. 38.50 (*0-404-16149-9*) AMS Pr.
Natesan, K., ed. see Metallurgical Society of AIME Staff.
Natesh, R., ed. see American Society for Metals Staff.
Natesh, S., et al. Biotechnology in Agriculture. 1987. 47.50 (*81-204-0241-3*, Pub. by Oxford IBH) S Asia.
Natesh, S., ed. see Ramachandran, S.
NATFACS Staff. It's about Time - Recipes, Realities, Reflections. LC 98-68074. 1998. 19.95 (*0-9666613-0-3*) Natl Assn Tchr Fam.
Nath & Thind, S. K. Staff. Unrolithiasis Research. (C). 1989. 34.00 (*81-7024-244-4*, Pub. by Ashish Pub Hse) S Asia.
Nath, Aman. Arts & Crafts of Rajasthan. (Illus.). 228p. 1997. 45.00 (*0-944142-06-0*) Grantha.
— Jaipur: The Last Destination. LC 95-62321. (Illus.). 224p. 1996. 75.00 (*1-86064-042-7*, Pub. by I B T) St Martin.
— Jaipur: The Last Destination. (Illus.). 224p. 1996. 70.00 (*0-614-96972-7*) St Martin.
Nath, Aman & Wacziarg, Francis. Arts & Crafts of Rajasthan. (Illus.). 229p. 1994. 45.00 (*81-85822-23-9*, Pub. by Mapin Pubng) Antique Collect.
Nath, Bholeshwar. Cases & Materials on Code of Civil Procedure. (C). 1990. write for info. (*0-7855-2611-0*) St Mut.
— Cases & Materials on Criminal Procedure Code, 1987: With Supplement 1989. 3rd ed. (C). 1989. 275.00 (*0-7855-4700-2*) St Mut.
— Cases & Materials on Law of Evidence. 578p. 1983. 240.00 (*0-7855-1355-8*) St Mut.
— Cases & Materials on Law of Evidence. 2nd ed. (C). 1991. 95.00 (*0-7855-5568-4*) St Mut.
— Cases & Materials on Transfer of Property Act, 1882: 1987 Edition. (C). 1987. 195.00 (*0-7855-4689-8*) St Mut.
— Civil Referencer. 1733p. (C). 1989. 370.00 (*0-7855-5150-6*); 175.00 (*0-7855-5253-7*) St Mut.
— Commentaries on Mental Health Act, 1987. (C). 1989. 60.00 (*0-7855-3517-9*) St Mut.
— Commentaries on Mental Health Act, 1987: With Supplement. (C). 1991. 70.00 (*0-7855-5487-4*) St Mut.
Nath, Bholeshwar, et al, eds. Environmental Management Vol. 1: The Compartmental Approach. (Illus.). 340p. 1994. pap. 45.00 (*90-5487-033-8*) Paul & Co Pubs.
— Environmental Management Vol. 2: The Ecosystems Approach. (Illus.). 252p. 1994. pap. 45.00 (*90-5487-034-6*) Paul & Co Pubs.
— Environmental Management Vol. 3: Instruments for Implementation. 295p. 1994. pap. 45.00 (*90-5487-035-4*) Paul & Co Pubs.
— Sustainable Development. LC 96-165886. 365p. 1996. 29.00 (*90-5487-115-6*, Pub. by VUB Univ Pr) Paul & Co Pubs.
Nath, Bholeshwar & Chakravarti, S. Cases & Materials on Code of Civil Procedure. 4th ed. (C). 1991. 100.00 (*0-7855-5634-6*) St Mut.
Nath, Bholeshwar & Malik, P. L. Cases & Materials on Criminal Procedure Code. (C). 1991. 285.00 (*0-89771-778-3*, Pub. by Eastern Book) St Mut.
— Cases & Materials on Criminal Procedure Code. 1199p. 1984. reprint ed. 390.00 (*0-7855-1357-4*) St Mut.
— Cases & Materials on Criminal Procedure Code. 3rd ed. (C). 1990. suppl. ed. 275.00 (*0-7855-5106-9*) St Mut.
Nath, Bholeshwar, jt. auth. see Malik, P. L.
***Nath, Birbal.** Kashmir: The Nuclear Flashpoint. 1998. 44.00 (*81-7049-097-9*, Pub. by Manas Pubns) S Asia.
Nath, D. Smith. Apocalypses. 40p. 1994. pap. 5.95 (*1-886134-02-2*) Miraculous Fngerprnt.
— Seeking. 50p. 1994. pap. 5.95 (*1-886134-01-4*) Miraculous Fngerprnt.
— She, the Tale of a Sail. 30p. (J). (gr. k-2). pap. 5.95 (*1-886134-03-0*) Miraculous Fngerprnt.
***Nath, Joginder, et al.** CentiGrad: A Celebration of the First 100 Graduates of the Genetics & Developmental Biology Program. LC 98-60709. 1998. write for info. (*0-937058-44-0*) West Va U Pr.
Nath Kanungo, Rabindra. Entrepreneurship & Innovation: Models for Development. LC 98-37838. (OBS for Social Transformation Ser.). 1998. 45.00 (*0-7619-9284-7*); pap. write for info. (*0-7619-9285-5*) Sage.
Nath, Lala B., tr. see Puranas, Brahmandapurana.
Nath, Malik A. Phonology & Morphology of Panjabi. LC 95-910300. 388p. (C). 1995. 49.50 (*81-215-0644-1*, Pub. by M Manoharial) Coronet Bks.
— Reflections of an Industrialist: From Mudhouse to Millionaire. 187p. (C). 1992. text 25.00 (*0-7069-6026-2*, Pub. by Vikas) S Asia.
Nath, Marie-Luise, ed. The Republic of China on Taiwan in International Politics. LC 98-11550. (Saabrucker Politikwissenschaft Ser.: Vol. 23). (Illus.). 148p. (C). 1998. pap. text 22.95 (*0-8204-3257-1*) P Lang Pubng.
Nath, Marie-Luise, ed. see Ladany, Laszlo.
Nath, N., et al, eds. Cases & Materials on Criminal Procedure Code: With Supplement. 3rd ed. (C). 1990. text 275.00 (*0-89771-502-0*) St Mut.
Nath, N. C., ed. Transfer of Technology in Indian Agriculture: Experience of Agricultural Universities. (C). 1992. 18.00 (*81-85182-70-1*, Pub. by Indus Pub) S Asia.
Nath, P. Fisheries of Eastern India Vol. 1: (Arunachal Pradesh) 350p. (C). 1991. text 350.00 (*0-89771-609-4*, Pub. by Intl Bk Distr) St Mut.
— Supersymmetry & Unification of Fundamental Interaction (Susy 93) Proceedings of the International Workshop. 644p. 1993. text 121.00 (*981-02-1593-2*) World Scientific Pub.
Nath, P., ed. Particles, Strings & Cosmology (PASCOS '98) Proceedings of the 6th International Symposium Boston, U. S. A., 22-29 March 1998. LC 98-51619. 950p. 1999. 128.00 (*981-02-3612-3*) World Scientific Pub.
Nath, P., et al. Physics from Planck Scale to Electroweak Scale. 508p. 1995. text 124.00 (*981-02-2184-3*) World Scientific Pub.
Nath, Pandit Shambhu, see Shambhu Nath, Pandit.
Nath, Pashupati & Nath, Siddha. Environmental Pollution, Conservation & Planning, 2 vols., Set. 1990. 78.50 (*81-85076-86-3*) S Asia.
Nath, Pathikonda Viswambara. Tat Tvam Asi: The Universal Massage in the Bhagavadgeitea. LC 98-906124. 828p. 1998. pap. 400.00 (*81-208-1585-8*, Pub. by Motilal Bnarsidass) St Mut.
Nath, Pran & Reucroff, Stephen, eds. Particles, Strings & Cosmology: Proceedings of the Second International Symposium, Northeastern Univ., Boston, 25-30 March 1991. 800p. 1992. text 121.00 (*981-02-0971-1*) World Scientific Pub.
Nath, Pran & Reucroft, Stephen, eds. Particles, Strings & Cosmology - 90: Proceedings of the First International Symposium on Particles, Strings & Cosmology, Boston, U. S. A., March 27-31, 1990. 716p. 1991. pap. 55.00 (*981-02-0393-4*); text 167.00 (*981-02-0392-6*) World Scientific Pub.
Nath, Pran, et al. Applied N Equals One Supergravity. (ICIP Lecture Series in Theoretical Physics Lectures: Vol. 1). 116p. 1984. text 36.00 (*9971-966-48-4*); pap. text 15.00 (*9971-966-49-2*) World Scientific Pub.
Nath, R. The Art of Khajuraho. 1980. 90.00 (*0-8364-0608-7*, Pub. by Abhinav) S Asia.
— Environmental Pollution of Cadmium Biological, Physiological & Health Effects. 166p. (C). 1986. 150.00 (*81-85017-24-7*, Pub. by Interprint) St Mut.
— History of Decorative Art in Mughal Architecture. 1986. reprint ed. 16.50 (*81-208-0077-X*, Pub. by Motilal Bnarsidass) S Asia.
— History of Mughal Architecture, Vol. III. (C). 1994. 155.00 (*81-7017-159-8*, Pub. by Abhinav) S Asia.
— History of Mughal Architecture Vol. 3: The Transitional Phase of Colour & Design. (C). 1994. 140.00 (*81-7017-297-7*, Pub. by Abhinav) S Asia.
— History of Mughal Architecture, Vol. 2: Akbar. 1986. 125.00 (*0-8364-1628-7*, Pub. by Abhinav) S Asia.
— History of Sultanate Architecture. 1978. 44.00 (*0-8364-0176-X*) S Asia.
— India As Seen by Babur: Ad 1504-1530. LC 96-900868. 118p. 1996. pap. 200.00 (*81-7533-000-7*, Pub. by Print Hse) St Mut.
— Medieval Indian History & Architecture. LC 95-906159. (Illus.). xvi, 331p. 1995. 64.00 (*81-7024-697-0*, Pub. by Ashish Pub Hse) Nataraj Bks.
— Mughal Sculpture: Study of Stone Sculptures of Birds, Beasts, Mythical Animals, Human Beings & Deities in Mughal Architecture. LC 97-914268. (Illus.). xx, 218p. 1997. 67.00 (*81-7024-870-1*, Pub. by APH Pubng) Nataraj Bks.
— Some Aspects of Mughal Architecture. LC 76-902803. 1976. 38.50 (*0-88386-825-3*) S Asia.
— Tajmahal & Its Incarnation. 232p. 1985. 49.95 (*0-318-36975-3*) Asia Bk Corp.
Nath, R., ed. Electrical & Optical Behaviour of Solids. (C). 1989. 72.50 (*81-7099-097-1*, Pub. by Mittal Pubs Dist) S Asia.
Nath, R., et al. Molecular Aspects of Idiopathic Urolithiasis. (Illus.). 176p. 1984. pap. 59.00 (*0-08-031697-2*, Pergamon Pr) Elsevier.
Nath, Raghu, ed. Comparative Management: A Regional View. LC 87-17459. 328p. 1987. text 32.00 (*0-88730-136-3*, HarpBusn) HarpInfo.
— Comparative Management: A Regional View. 344p. 1988. pap. 18.95 (*0-88730-367-6*, HarpBusn) HarpInfo.
Nath, Raghu, jt. auth. see Narayanan, V. K.
Nath, Rajendra. Military Leadership in India: Vedic Period to Indo-Pak Wars. 1990. 72.50 (*81-7095-018-X*, Pub. by Lancer India) S Asia.
Nath, Ravinder, et al. Intravascular Brachytherapy Physics No. 66: Report of the AAPM Radiation Therapy Committee TG #60. (Report Number 66 Ser.). 33p. 1999. pap. text 10.00 (*1-888340-23-1*) AAPM.
Nath, Robert G. The Unofficial Guide to Dealing with the IRS. (Unofficial Guides Ser.). (Illus.). 492p. 1999. pap. 15.95 (*0-02-862683-4*, Pub. by Macmillan) S&S Trade.
Nath, S. K. A Reappraisal of Welfare Economics. LC 70-80108. vii, 247p. 1969. 35.00 (*0-678-06507-1*) Kelley.
Nath, Sanjiva K. & Kahn, Philippe. The Power of Turbo Pascal. 320p. 1986. pap. 19.95 (*0-89303-791-5*); disk 39.95 (*0-89303-794-X*) P-H.
Nath, Sankar Kumar, jt. auth. see Patra, Hari Pada.
Nath, Shaileshwar. Terrorism in India. 350p. 1980. 25.95 (*0-940500-27-2*) Asia Bk Corp.
Nath, Shambhu. Speaking of Yoga: A Practical Guide to Better Living. (C). 1995. pap. write for info. (*81-207-1794-5*) Sterling Pubs.
Nath, Siddha, jt. auth. see Nath, Pashupati.
Nath, Tribhuvan & Gupta, Madan M. On the Yeti Trail: The Search for the Elusive Snowman. (C). 1995. 7.00 (*81-86112-29-4*, Pub. by UBS Pubs Dist) S Asia.
Nath, Vijay. Dana: Gift System in Ancient India: A Socio-Economic Perspective. 1988. 33.50 (*81-215-0054-0*, Pub. by M Manoharial) Coronet Bks.
Nathal, M. V., et al, eds. Structural Intermetallics, 1997: International Symposium on Structural Intermetallics, Champion, Penn. LC 97-71555. (Illus.). 975p. 1997. 230.00 (*0-87339-375-9*, 3759) Minerals Metals.
Nathan. Practical Approach to Assessment of Liability & Damages in Tort. 1986. 148.00 (*9971-70-051-4*, MICHIE) LEXIS Pub.
— Le Sagesse de Rebbe Nachman. Dimermanas, Alon, ed. & tr. by. from HEB. (FRE.). 334p. 1989. text 15.00 (*0-930213-31-9*); pap. text 13.00 (*0-930213-32-7*) Breslov Res Inst.
— Tefilin: A Chassidic Discourse. Greenbaum, Avraham, ed. & tr. by. from HEB. (Illus.). 96p. 1989. pap. text 10.00 (*0-930213-38-6*) Breslov Res Inst.
Nathan, ed. U. S. Foreign Policy & World Order. 5th ed. (C). 2000. text. write for info. (*0-321-01107-4*) Addison-Wesley.
Nathan & Neff. Louisiana Estate Planning, Will Drafting, & Estate Administration, 3 vols. LC 98-87232. 2000p. 1998. ring bd. 340.00 (*0-327-00260-3*, 81329-11) LEXIS Pub.
Nathan, jt. auth. see Nachman.
Nathan, jt. auth. see Septien, Al.
Nathan, A. & Baltes, H. Microtransducer CAD: Physical & Computational Aspects. Selberherr, S., ed. LC 99-23861. (Computational Microelectronics Ser.). (Illus.). 300p. 1998. 189.00 (*3-211-83103-7*) Spr-Verlag.
Nathan, A. W., jt. auth. see Timmis, A. D.
Nathan Adelson Hospice Staff. Best Bets: Las Vegas Cooking at Its Best. LC 93-72353. (Illus.). 1993. pap. write for info. (*0-87197-383-9*) Favorite Recipes.
Nathan, Amy. Everything You Need to Know about Conflict Resolution. (Need to Know Library). (Illus.). 64p. (gr. 7-12). 1996. lib. bdg. 17.95 (*0-8239-2058-5*) Rosen Group.
— Fruit. (Illus.). 144p. 1988. 29.95 (*0-87701-556-2*); pap. 16.95 (*0-87701-444-2*) Chronicle Bks.
— The Kids' Allowance Book. LC 97-49314. (Illus.). 128p. (J). (gr. 4-7). 1998. 15.95 (*0-8027-8651-0*); pap. 8.95 (*0-8027-7532-2*) Walker & Co.
— Surviving Homework: Tips from Teens. (Illus.). 80p. (J). (gr. 5-9). 1996. lib. bdg. 23.90 (*1-56294-185-2*) Millbrook Pr.
— Surviving Homework: Tips That Really Work! (Illus.). 80p. (J). (gr. 4-8). 1998. pap. 8.95 (*0-7613-0137-2*) Millbrook Pr.
***Nathan, Amy.** The Young Musician's Survival Guide: Tips from Teens & Pros. (Illus.). 122p. (YA). 2000. pap. 9.95 (*0-19-512612-2*); text 18.95 (*0-19-512611-4*) OUP.
Nathan, Andrew. China's Transition. LC 97-24417. (Illus.). 336p. 1997. 28.50 (*0-231-11022-7*) Col U Pr.
— China's Transition. 1999. pap. 16.50 (*0-231-11023-5*) Col U Pr.
Nathan, Andrew J. China's Crisis: Dilemmas of Reform & Prospects for Democracy. 1990. pap. 19.00 (*0-231-07285-6*) Col U Pr.
— Chinese Democracy. 313p. (C). 1986. pap. 16.95 (*0-520-05933-6*, Pub. by U CA Pr) Cal Prin Full Svc.
— History of the China International Famine Relief Commission. LC 65-5839. (East Asian Monographs: No. 17). 114p. 1965. pap. 20.00 (*0-674-40200-6*) HUP.
— Peking Politics, 1918-1923: Factionalism & the Failure of Constitutionalism. LC 98-2892. (Michigan Monographs in Chinese Studies). 320p. 1998. 50.00 (*0-89264-131-2*) Ctr Chinese Studies.

N

An Asterisk (*) at the beginning of an entry indicates that the title is appearing for the first time.

Nathan, Andrew J., et al, eds. Dilemmas of Reform in Jiang Zemin's China. LC 99-19294. 250p. 1999. lib. bdg. 52.00 (*1-55587-851-2*) L Rienner.

Nathan, Andrew J. & Ross, Robert S. The Great Wall & the Empty Fortress: China's Search for Security. LC 97-6385. (Illus.). 352p. 1997. 27.50 (*0-393-04076-3*) Norton.

— The Great Wall & the Empty Fortress: China's Search for Security. 288p. 1998. pap. 13.95 (*0-393-31784-6*) Norton.

Nathan, Andrew J., jt. auth. see Edwards, Randle.

Nathan, Ann A. & Mirviss, Suzanne. Therapy Techniques Using the Creative Arts. LC 98-6514. 300p. 1998. pap. text 25.00 (*1-882883-30-6*, 346) Idyll Arbor.

Nathan Associates, Inc. Staff. Replacing the Federal Income Tax with a Consumption-Based Tax System. (Orig.). 1996. pap. 40.00 (*0-614-30166-1*) Nat Retail Fed.

Nathan, Barbara. Gambling Times Guide to Basketball Handicapping. 253p. 1984. pap. 5.95 (*0-89746-023-5*) Gambling Times.

Nathan, Barry R., jt. auth. see Decker, Phillip J.

***Nathan, Bevis.** Touch & Emotion in Manual Therapy. LC 99-37127. 1999. write for info. (*0-443-05657-9*, W B Saunders Co) Harcrt Hlth Sci Grp.

Nathan, Breda. Footballics Anonymous LC 99-175784. 123p. 1998. write for info. (*1-86059-068-3*, Pub. by Town Hse) Roberts Rinehart.

Nathan, Bruce. Business Law Monographs Vol. G-5: Protecting Corporate Creditors under the Bankruptcy Code. text 82.00 (*0-8205-2076-4*) Bender.

Nathan, Carl F. Plague Prevention & Politics in Manchuria, 1910-1931. LC 67-8500. (East Asian Monographs: No. 23). (Illus.). 111p. 1967. pap. 12.00 (*0-674-67050-7*) HUP.

Nathan, Cheryl & McCourt, Lisa. The Long & Short of It. (Illus.). 32p. (J). (ps-3). 1999. pap. 5.95 (*0-8167-5609-0*) BrdgeWater.

Nathan, David. The Soulful Divas. LC 98-45684. (Illus.). 320p. 1999. 24.95 (*0-8230-8425-6*) Watsn-Guptill.

Nathan, David G. Genes, Blood & Courage: A Boy Called Immortal Sword. LC 95-6080. (Illus.). 288p. (C). 1995. 24.95 (*0-674-34473-1*) Belknap Pr.

— Genes, Blood & Courage: A Boy Called Immortal Sword. 1995. write for info. (*0-614-15009-4*) HUP.

Nathan, David G. & Orkin, Stuart H. Nathan & Oski's Hematology of Infancy & Childhood. 5th ed. Lampert, Richard, ed. LC 96-41120. (Illus.). 2096p. 1997. text 295.00 (*0-7216-5951-9*, W B Saunders Co) Harcrt Hlth Sci Grp.

***Nathan, David H.** The McFarland Baseball Quotations Dictionary. 304p. 2000. 45.00 (*0-7864-0888-X*) McFarland & Co.

Nathan, David H., compiled by. Baseball Quotations: The Wisdom & Wisecracks of Players, Managers, Owners, Umpires, Announcers, Writers & Fans on the Great American Pastime. LC 90-53512. 231p. 1991. lib. bdg. 29.95 (*0-89950-562-7*) McFarland & Co.

Nathan, Debbie & Snedeker, Mike. Satan's Silence. 366p. 1996. pap. 14.00 (*0-465-07181-3*) HarpC.

Nathan, Debbie, tr. see Crosthwaite, Luis H.

Nathan, Dev, ed. From Tribe to Caste. LC 98-901487. 462p. 1997. 34.00 (*81-85952-43-4*, Pub. by Indian Inst) Nataraj Bks.

***Nathan, Dev & Kelkar, Govind.** Collective Villages in the Chinese Market. 68p. 2000. reprint ed. pap. text 25.00 (*0-7881-8597-7*) DIANE Pub.

Nathan, Dev, jt. auth. see Kelkar, Govind.

Nathan, Emma. What Do You Call a Baby Crab? And Other Baby Ocean Creatures. LC 99-20528. (What Do You Call a... Ser.). (Illus.). 24p. (J). (gr. 3-5). 1999. lib. bdg. 15.95 (*1-56711-365-6*) Blackbirch.

— What Do You Call a Baby Rhino? And Other Baby Mammals. LC 99-20250. (What Do You Call a... Ser.). (Illus.). 24p. (J). (gr. 3-5). 1999. lib. bdg. 15.95 (*1-56711-364-8*) Blackbirch.

— What Do You Call a Baby Scorpion? And Other Baby Spiders & Insects. LC 99-20242. (What Do You Call a... Ser.). (Illus.). 24p. (J). (gr. 3-5). 1999. lib. bdg. 15.95 (*1-56711-361-3*) Blackbirch.

— What Do You Call a Baby Swan? And Other Baby Birds. LC 99-14386. (What Do You Call a... Ser.). (Illus.). 24p. (J). (gr. 3-5). 1999. lib. bdg. 15.95 (*1-56711-362-1*) Blackbirch.

— What Do You Call a Baby Turtle? And Other Baby Reptiles & Amphibians. LC 99-25282. (What Do You Call a... Ser.). (Illus.). 24p. (J). (gr. 3-5). 1999. lib. bdg. 15.95 (*1-56711-366-4*) Blackbirch.

***Nathan, Emma.** What Do You Call a Group of Alligators? And Other Reptile & Amphibian Groups. LC 00-9057. (What Do You Call a... Ser.). (Illus.). 24p. (J). (gr. 4-7). 2000. pap. 15.95 (*1-56711-358-3*) Blackbirch.

— What Do You Call a Group of Butterflies? And Other Insects. LC 00-8229. (What Do You Call a... Ser.). 24p. (J). 2000. 15.95 (*1-56711-359-1*) Blackbirch.

— What Do You Call a Group of Hippos? And Other Mammals. LC 00-8228. (What Do You Call a... Ser.). 24p. (J). (gr. 4-7). 2000. 15.95 (*1-56711-356-7*) Blackbirch.

— What Do You Call a Group of Turkeys? And Other Birds. LC 00-8223. (What Do You Call a... Ser.). (J). 2000. 15.95 (*1-56711-357-5*) Blackbirch.

— What Do You Call a Squirrel Home? And Other Animal Homes. LC 00-9009. (What Do You Call a... Ser.). (Illus.). 24p. 2000. 15.95 (*1-56711-354-0*) Blackbirch.

***Nathan, Geoffrey S.** The Family in Late Antiquity: The Rise of Christianity & the Endurance of Tradition. LC 99-30699. 304p. 2000. 75.00 (*0-415-16665-9*) Routledge.

Nathan, Geoffrey S. & Winters, Margaret E., eds. Papers from the First Conference on the Uses of Phonology, Held at Southern Illinois University, Carbondale, Illinois. (Occasional Papers on Linguistics: No. 12). 126p. 1984. reprint ed. pap. text 13.75 (*1-55567-485-2*) Coyote Press.

Nathan, George J. Art of the Night. LC 75-120099. 296p. 1975. 25.00 (*0-8386-7965-X*) Fairleigh Dickinson.

— Autobiography of an Attitude. LC 76-145204. 1971. reprint ed. 39.00 (*0-403-00758-5*) Scholarly.

— Bottoms Up. LC 70-148843. (Select Bibliographies Reprint Ser.). 1977. 15.95 (*0-8369-5657-5*) Ayer.

— Critic & the Drama. LC 75-120099. 152p. 1975. 20.00 (*0-8386-7964-1*) Fairleigh Dickinson.

— Entertainment of a Nation. LC 75-120099. 290p. 1975. 26.50 (*0-8386-7887-4*) Fairleigh Dickinson.

— Materia Critica. LC 75-120099. 242p. 1975. 24.50 (*0-8386-7966-8*) Fairleigh Dickinson.

— Mr. George Jean Nathan Presents. LC 75-120099. 310p. 1975. 25.00 (*0-8386-7967-6*) Fairleigh Dickinson.

— Mister George Jean Nathan Presents. LC 70-145205. 1971. reprint ed. 18.00 (*0-403-03648-8*) Scholarly.

— Morning after the First Night. LC 75-120099. 282p. 1975. 25.00 (*0-8386-7779-7*) Fairleigh Dickinson.

— My Very Dear Sean: George Jean Nathan on Sean O'Casey, Letters & Articles. Angelin, Patricia & Lowery, Robert, eds. LC 82-48549. 192p. 1985. 32.50 (*0-8386-3166-5*) Fairleigh Dickinson.

— Passing Judgments. LC 71-86774. (Essay Index Reprint Ser.). 1977. 18.95 (*0-8369-1150-4*) Ayer.

— Passing Judgments: The Theatre World of George Jean Nathan. LC 75-120099. 271p. 1975. 25.00 (*0-8386-7722-3*) Fairleigh Dickinson.

— Popular Theatre. LC 75-120099. 236p. 1975. 25.00 (*0-8386-7945-5*) Fairleigh Dickinson.

— The Theater Book of the Year, 1947-1948. 350p. 1970. 29.50 (*0-8386-1176-1*) Fairleigh Dickinson.

— The Theatre Book of the Year, 1942-1943. LC 75-120099. (Illus.). 350p. 1975. 29.50 (*0-8386-7946-3*) Fairleigh Dickinson.

— The Theatre Book of the Year, 1943-1944. LC 75-120099. 350p. 1975. 29.50 (*0-8386-7962-5*) Fairleigh Dickinson.

— The Theatre Book of the Year, 1944-1945. LC 75-120099. 350p. 1975. 29.50 (*0-8386-7961-7*) Fairleigh Dickinson.

— The Theatre Book of the Year, 1945-1946. LC 75-120099. (Theatre World of George Jean Nathan Ser.). 350p. 1974. 29.50 (*0-8386-1174-5*) Fairleigh Dickinson.

— The Theatre Book of the Year, 1946-1947. LC 75-120099. (Theatre World of George Jean Nathan Ser.). 350p. 1975. 29.50 (*0-8386-1175-3*) Fairleigh Dickinson.

— Theatre of the Moment. LC 75-120099. (Theatre World of George Jean Nathan Ser.). 310p. 1975. 25.00 (*0-8386-7775-4*) Fairleigh Dickinson.

— The World in Falseface. LC 75-120099. 326p. 1975. 29.50 (*0-8386-7963-3*) Fairleigh Dickinson.

— The World of George Jean Nathan: Selected Essays & Reviews. Angoff, Charles, ed. LC 97-28486. 520p. 1998. pap. 24.95 (*1-55783-313-3*) Applause Theatre Bk Pubs.

Nathan, George J. & Mencken, H. L. The American Credo: A Contribution Toward Interpretation of the National Mind. enl. rev. ed. (BCL1 - U. S. History Ser.). 266p. 1991. reprint ed. lib. bdg. 79.00 (*0-7812-6016-7*) Rprt Serv.

Nathan, George J. & Mencken, H. L., eds. The American Mercury: Facsimile Edition of Vol. One: The Original Issues of Jan., Feb., March & April, 1924. 600p. 1984. reprint ed. lib. bdg. 50.00 (*0-89345-050-2*, Freedeeds Libr) Garber Comm.

Nathan Hale Institute Staff, ed. see McNamara, Francis J.

Nathan Hale Institute Staff, ed. see Sulc, Lawrence B.

Nathan, Hans, ed. see Billings, William.

Nathan, Hans, ed. see Weill, Kurt & Milhaud, Darius.

Nathan, Harold D. Chemistry Quick Review. (Cliffs Quick Reviews Ser.). (Illus.). 174p. (C). 1993. pap. text 7.95 (*0-8220-5318-7*, Cliff) IDG Bks.

Nathan, Harriet. Critical Choices in Interviews: Conduct, Use & Research Role. LC 86-10523. 156p. reprint ed. pap. 48.40 (*0-608-20122-7*, 207139400011) Bks Demand.

Nathan, Harriet & Scott, Stanley, eds. Emerging Issues in Public Policy: Research Reports & Essays, 1960-1965. LC 73-8712. 184p. reprint ed. pap. 57.10 (*0-7837-2126-9*, 204240800004) Bks Demand.

— Emerging Issues in Public Policy: Research Reports & Essays, 1966-1972. LC 73-8711. 218p. reprint ed. pap. 67.60 (*0-7837-2127-7*, 204240900004) Bks Demand.

— Emerging Issues in Public Policy: Research Reports & Essays, 1973-1976. LC 77-6469. 178p. reprint ed. pap. 55.20 (*0-7837-2128-5*, 204241000004) Bks Demand.

— Politics, Government, & Related Policy Issues, 1977-1982. LC 83-26374. (Emerging Issues in Public Policy: Research Reports & Essays). 45p. reprint ed. pap. 30.00 (*0-7837-2129-3*, 204241100004) Bks Demand.

Nathan, Harriet, jt. auth. see Kreinberg, Nancy.

Nathan, Harriet, ed. see Kroeger, Louis J.

Nathan, Harvey K., jt. auth. see Lage, Gustavo A.

Nathan, Henry, ed. see Cunningham, Merce & Lesschaeve, Jacqueline.

***Nathan, Ian, ed.** Empire Classic Movie Scenes. (Illus.). 144p. 2000. 24.95 (*0-233-99601-X*, Pub. by Andre Deutsch) Trafalgar.

Nathan, Isaac. Memoirs of Madame Malibran De Beriot. LC 80-2291. reprint ed. 32.50 (*0-404-18860-5*) AMS Pr.

***Nathan, James A.** Anatomy of the Cuban Missile Crisis. LC 00-25115. (Greenwood Press Guides to Historic Events of the Twentieth Century Ser.). 208p. 2000. 40.00 (*0-313-29973-0*, GR9973, Greenwood Pr) Greenwood.

Nathan, James A., ed. The Cuban Missile Crisis Revisited. 304p. 1993. pap. 17.95 (*0-312-09725-5*) St Martin.

Nathan, James A. & Oliver, James K. Foreign Policy Making & the American Political System. 3rd ed. LC 94-7530. 1994. text 45.00 (*0-8018-4771-0*); pap. text 16.95 (*0-8018-4772-9*) Johns Hopkins.

— Foreign Policy Making in the American Political System. 2nd ed. (C). 1987. pap. text 24.00 (*0-673-39467-0*) Addson-Wesley Educ.

— The Future of United States Naval Power. LC 78-9512. 255p. reprint ed. pap. 79.10 (*0-608-17033-X*, 205624700056) Bks Demand.

— US Foreign Policy World. 4th ed. 512p. (C). 1997. pap. text 69.00 (*0-673-39689-4*) Addson-Wesley Educ.

Nathan, Jay, jt. auth. see Ellis, Dennis.

Nathan, Jean, ed. Ohio Marriage Records in County Courts Through 1820: And Index. 1996. 65.00 (*0-935057-88-9*) OH Genealogical.

Nathan, Joan. The Children's Jewish Holiday Kitchen. (Illus.). 176p. (J). 1995. 24.00 (*0-8052-4130-2*) Schocken.

— The Children's Jewish Holiday Kitchen: 70 Fun Recipes for You & Your Kids. LC 95-5981. (Illus.). 176p. 2000. 14.95 (*0-8052-1056-3*) Schocken.

***Nathan, Joan.** The Foods of Modern Israel. LC 00-44354. (Illus.). 2001. write for info. (*0-679-45107-2*) Knopf.

Nathan, Joan. Jewish Cook in America. 1997. pap. 18.00 (*0-679-76578-6*) Random.

— Jewish Cooking in America: Expanded Edition. exp. ed. LC 98-27952. (Illus.). 496p. 1998. 35.00 (*0-375-40276-4*) Random.

— The Jewish Holiday Baker. LC 97-9775. 1997. 23.00 (*0-8052-4142-6*) Schocken.

— The Jewish Holiday Baker. 224p. 1999. pap. 16.95 (*0-8052-1117-9*) Schocken.

— The Jewish Holiday Kitchen: 250 Recipes from Around the World to Make Your Celebrations Special. LC 98-216821. 416p. 1998. pap. 19.95 (*0-8052-1109-8*) Schocken.

***Nathan, Joe.** Charter Schools: Creating Hope & Opportunity for American Education. LC 99-188904. 1999. pap. text 18.00 (*0-7879-4454-8*) Jossey-Bass.

Nathan, Joe. Free to Teach: Achieving Equity & Excellence in Schools. 204p. 1984. 7.95 (*0-86683-859-7*) Harper SF.

Nathan, Joe, ed. Public Schools by Choice: Expanding Opportunities for Parents, Students & Teachers. LC 89-80266. 266p. (Orig.). 1989. pap. 9.00 (*0-9622302-0-0*) Inst Learn Teach.

Nathan, Joel. Australia: Treasure Island. 1998. 24.95 (*1-86436-279-0*, Pub. by New5 Holland) Sterling.

— What to Do When They Say "It's Cancer" A Survivor's Guide, 1. 1999. pap. text 16.95 (*1-86448-635-X*, Pub. by Allen & Unwin Pty) IPG Chicago.

***Nathan, John.** Mishima: A Biography. (Illus.). 352p. 2000. pap. text 17.00 (*0-306-80977-X*) Da Capo.

Nathan, John. Mishima: A Biography. LC 74-12184. xx, 300 p. 1974. write for info. (*0-316-59844-5*) Little.

— Sony. LC 99-29810. 288p. 1999. 26.00 (*0-395-89327-5*) HM.

Nathan, John, tr. see Mishima, Yukio, pseud.

Nathan, John, tr. see Oe, Kenzaburo.

Nathan, Julian. Back to Basics Audio. LC 99-162320. 344p. 1998. pap. text 39.95 (*0-7506-9967-1*, Newnes) Buttrwrth-Heinemann.

Nathan, Kurt, jt. auth. see Strom, Steven.

Nathan, Laura E., jt. auth. see Kiecolt, K. Jill.

Nathan, Leonard. Diary of a Left-Handed Birdwatcher. LC 96-75788. 128p. 1996. 18.95 (*1-55597-250-0*) Graywolf.

— Diary of a Left-Handed Birdwatcher. LC 97-21766. 1998. pap. 10.00 (*0-15-600538-7*, Harvest Bks) Harcourt.

— The Poets Work: An Introduction to Czeslaw Milosz. 1991. pap. 15.00 (*0-674-68970-4*) HUP.

— The Potato Eaters. LC 98-12926. 96p. 1999. pap. 12.95 (*0-914061-75-5*) Orchises Pr.

— Returning Your Call: Poems. LC 75-3485. (Contemporary Poets Ser.). 76p. 1975. text 21.95 (*0-691-06296-X*, Pub. by Princeton U Pr) Cal Prin Full Svc.

— The Teachings of Grandfather Fox. LC 76-57990. 49p. 1976. 3.50 (*0-87886-079-7*, Greenfld Rev Pr) Greenfld Rev Lit.

Nathan, Leonard & Larson, James, trs. from SWE. Songs of Something Else: Selected Poems of Gunnar Ekelof. LC 81-47915. (Lockert Library of Poetry in Translation). 344p. 1982. pap. 12.95 (*0-691-01389-6*, Pub. by Princeton U Pr) Cal Prin Full Svc.

Nathan, Leonard & Quinn, Arthur. The Poet's Work: An Introduction to Czeslaw Milosz. (C). 1991. pap. 9.95 (*0-685-48477-7*) HUP.

Nathan, Leonard, tr. see Sen, Ramprasad.

Nathan, Leonard, tr. see Swir, Anna.

Nathan, Leonard E. The Tragic Drama of William Butler Yeats: Figures in a Dance. LC 65-16513. 319p. reprint ed. pap. 98.90 (*0-8357-4570-8*, 203748000008) Bks Demand.

Nathan, Marilyn. The Headteacher's Survival Guide. (Management & Leadership in Education Ser.). 192p. 1995. pap. 29.95 (*0-7494-1707-2*, Kogan Pg Educ) Stylus Pub VA.

***Nathan, Marilyn.** The Headteacher's Survival Guide. 2nd ed. 208p. 2000. pap. 32.50 (*0-7494-3179-2*, Pub. by Kogan Page Ltd) Stylus Pub VA.

Nathan, Marlene. Living by the Spirit. LC 99-173518. 96p. 1998. pap. 6.50 (*1-57683-084-5*) NavPress.

Nathan, Marvin R. San Francisco's International Expositions, a Bibliography, Including Listings for the Mechanics' Institute Exhibitions. LC 95-78357. (Illus.). 128p. 1995. text 25.95 (*0-9647514-0-2*); pap. text 11.95 (*0-9647514-1-0*) Lawthorne Pr.

Nathan, Maud. Once upon a Time & Today. LC 74-3964. (Women in America Ser.). (Illus.). 360p. 1974. reprint ed. 31.95 (*0-405-06113-7*) Ayer.

— Once upon a Time & Today. (American Biography Ser.). 327p. 1991. reprint ed. lib. bdg. 79.00 (*0-7812-8294-2*) Rprt Serv.

Nathan, Max, Jr. & Neff, Carole C. Louisiana Estate Planning, Will Drafting, & Estate Administration, 3 vols. 1994. suppl. ed. 85.00 (*0-685-74479-5*, MICHIE) LEXIS Pub.

***Nathan, Max, Jr. & Neff, Carole C.** Louisiana Estate Planning, Will Drafting & Estate Administration, Issue 1. 2nd ed. 100p. 1999. spiral bd. write for info. (*0-327-01525-X*, 8133621) LEXIS Pub.

Nathan, Max, Jr. & Neff, Carole C. Louisiana Estate Planning, Will Drafting, & Estate Administration, 3 vols., Set. 1800p. 1992. spiral bd. 255.00 (*1-56257-952-5*, 813310-10, MICHIE) LEXIS Pub.

Nathan, Michael & Galloway, Jeff. Runners Log Two Thousand. (Illus.). 80p. (Orig.). 1988. spiral bd. write for info. (*0-318-63185-7*) Nathan & Co.

Nathan, N. M. Will & World: Metaphysics. 192p. 1992. text 60.00 (*0-19-823954-8*) OUP.

Nathan, Norma. Boston's Most Eligible Bachelors, 1989. (Illus.). 200p. (Orig.). 1988. pap. 8.95 (*0-9621200-0-6*) N Nathan.

Nathan, Norman. Prince William B. The Philosophical Conceptions of William Blake. LC 75-331669. (Studies in English Literature ; V. 100). 164 p. 1975. write for info. (*90-279-3071-6*) Mouton.

— Prince William B. The Philosophical Conceptions of William Blake. (Studies in English Literature: No. 100). 164p. 1975. pap. text 35.40 (*90-279-3117-8*) Mouton.

Nathan of Breslov, jt. auth. see Nachman of Breslov.

Nathan, Otto. Nazi War Finance & Banking. (Occasional Papers). 100p. 1944. reprint ed. 27.60 (*0-87014-335-2*) Natl Bur Econ Res.

Nathan, P. E., jt. ed. see Marlatt, G. Alan.

***Nathan, Paul.** Count Your Enemies. 2000. per. 5.99 (*0-373-26348-1*) Harlequin Bks.

Nathan, Paul. Count Your Enemies: A Bert Swain Mystery. LC 96-41920. (Bert Swain Mystery Ser.). 224p. 1997. 21.95 (*0-8027-3296-8*) Walker & Co.

— No Good Deed. LC 94-10137. 202p. 1995. 22.00 (*1-877946-56-7*) Permanent Pr.

— Protocol for Murder. LC 93-27529. 176p. 1994. 22.00 (*1-877946-46-X*); pap. 16.00 (*1-877946-64-8*) Permanent Pr.

Nathan, Paul D., tr. see Simpson, Lesley B., ed.

Nathan, Paul S., tr. see Gor'kii, Maksim.

Nathan, Paul S., tr. see Gorky, Maxim.

Nathan, Peter E. The Nervous System. 4th ed. 320p. 1997. pap. 45.00 (*1-56593-828-3*, 1620) Singular Publishing.

Nathan, Peter E. & Gorman, Jack M. A Guide to Treatments That Work: A Review of the Outcome Studies on Psychotherapies & Drugs. LC 97-36492. (Illus.). 624p. 1997. text 75.00 (*0-19-510227-4*) OUP.

Nathan, Peter E., et al. Treating Mental Disorders: A Guide to What Works. LC 98-49355. 240p. 1999. 27.50 (*0-19-510228-2*) OUP.

Nathan, Peter E., ed. see Behrman, Debra L.

Nathan, Peter E., jt. ed. see Hay, William H.

Nathan, Peter E., ed. see Segalla, Rosemary A.

Nathan, Peter E., ed. see Weissbourd, Katherine.

Nathan, R. K. A Practical Approach to Evidence in Malaysia & Singapore. 500p. 1993. 160.00 (*0-409-99646-7*, SI, MICHIE) LEXIS Pub.

— Quantum of Damages. 455p. 1991. boxed set 160.00 (*0-409-99598-3*, SI, MICHIE) LEXIS Pub.

Nathan, Rabbi. Tzaddik. Greenbaum, Avraham, tr. from HEB. Orig. Title: Chayey Moharan. 1988. 18.00 (*0-930213-17-3*) Breslov Res Inst.

Nathan, Rhoda B., ed. Critical Essays on Katherine Mansfield. LC 93-2963. (Critical Essays on British Literature Ser.). 300p. 1993. 48.00 (*0-8161-8868-8*, Hall Reference) Macmillan.

— Nineteenth-Century Women Writers of the English-Speaking World, 69. LC 85-27250. (Contributions in Women's Studies: No. 69). 299p. 1986. 57.95 (*0-313-25170-3*, NWW/, Greenwood Pr) Greenwood.

Nathan, Rich & Wilson, Ken. Empowered Evangelicals: Bringing Together the Best of the Evangelical & Charismatic Worlds. 190p. 1995. pap. 10.99 (*0-89283-929-5*, Vine Bks) Servant.

Nathan, Richard A., ed. Fuels from Sugar Crops: Systems Study for Sugarcane, Sweet Sorghum, & Sugar Beets. LC 78-19127. (DOE Critical Review Ser.). 151p. 1978. pap. 11.75 (*0-87079-111-7*, TID-22781); fiche 9.00 (*0-87079-212-1*, TID-22781) DOE.

Nathan, Richard P. Social Sciences in Government: The Role of Policy Researchers. LC 99-87567. (Illus.). 200p. 1999. pap. 16.95 (*0-914341-66-9*, Pub. by Nelson Rockefeller Inst Govt) Brookings.

— Social Sciences in Government: The Role of Policy Researchers. 2nd rev. ed. LC 99-87567. (Illus.). 200p. 1999. 38.95 (*0-914341-65-0*, Pub. by Nelson Rockefeller Inst Govt) Brookings.

— Turning Promises into Performance: The Management Challenge of Implementing Workfare. LC 92-42821. 160p. (C). 1993. pap. 18.50 (*0-231-07963-X*); text 57.50 (*0-231-07962-1*) Col U Pr.

Nathan, Richard P. & Adams, Charles F., Jr. Revenue Sharing: The Second Round. LC 76-51884. 286p. reprint ed. pap. 88.70 (*0-608-12718-3*, 202539100043) Bks Demand.

Nathan, Richard P. & Webman, Jerry A. The Urban Development Action Grant Program. 125p. 1980. pap. text 21.95 (*0-938882-01-5*) Transaction Pubs.

Nathan, Richard P., et al. The Consequences of Cuts: The Effects of the Reagan Domestic Program on State & Local Governments. LC 83-60542. (Illus.). 221p. (Orig.). 1983. pap. 7.95 (*0-938882-06-6*) Woodrow Wilson Schl.

An Asterisk (*) at the beginning of an entry indicates that the title is appearing for the first time.

— Monitoring Revenue Sharing. LC 74-28124. 416p. reprint ed. pap. 129.00 (*0-608-12214-9*, 202539200043) Bks Demand.

— Public Service Employment: A Field Evaluation. LC 81-4596. 121p. 1981. pap. 12.95 (*0-8157-5987-8*) Brookings.

— Reagan & the States. LC 87-45529. 392p. 1987. reprint ed. pap. 121.60 (*0-7837-9400-2*, 206014500004) Bks Demand.

Nathan, Richard P., jt. ed. see DiIulio, John J., Jr.

Nathan, Richard P., ed. see Heller, Walter, et al.

Nathan, Richard P., jt. ed. see Schill, Michael H.

Nathan, Robert. The Barly Fields. 1976. 33.95 (*0-8488-0099-0*) Amereon Ltd.

— The Enchanted Voyage. LC 86-22753. 187p. 1987. reprint ed. lib. bdg. 55.00 (*0-313-25270-X*, NAEN, Greenwood Pr) Greenwood.

— Portrait of Jennie. 1976. 19.95 (*0-8488-1096-1*) Amereon Ltd.

— Portrait of Jennie. 10.00 (*0-89064-051-3*) NAVH.

— Portrait of Jennie. 293p. (J). 1981. reprint ed. lib. bdg. 21.95 (*0-89966-356-7*); reprint ed. lib. bdg. 16.95 (*0-89967-030-X*, Harmony Rain) Buccaneer Bks.

***Nathan, Robert.** Portrait of Jennie. 1998. reprint ed. pap. 14.00 (*1-892391-03-1*) Tachyon Pubns.

Nathan, Robert. Sir Henry. LC 79-12787. vi, 187p. 1979. reprint ed. pap. 21.00 (*0-89370-236-6*) Millefleurs.

Nathan, Robert & Hill, Linda. Career Counselling in Practice. (Counselling in Practice Ser.). (Illus.). 160p. (C). 1992. 49.95 (*0-8039-8695-5*); pap. 21.50 (*0-8039-8696-3*) Sage.

Nathan, Robert L. The Dreamtime. LC 74-21584. 280p. 1975. 22.50 (*0-87951-028-5*, Pub. by Overlook Pr) Penguin Putnam.

Nathan, Robert S. The White Tiger. 432p. 1988. mass mkt. 4.95 (*0-446-35206-3*, Pub. by Warner Bks) Little.

Nathan, Ronald G. The Doctor's Guide to Instant Stress Relief. 288p. 1989. mass mkt. 5.99 (*0-345-35622-5*) Ballantine Pub Grp.

Nathan, Ronald G. & Stuart, Marian R. Coping with the Stressed-out People in Your Life. 288p. (Orig.). 1994. pap. 10.00 (*0-345-38186-6*) Ballantine Pub Grp.

Nathan, Ruth, et al. Classroom Strategies That Work: An Elementary Teacher's Guide to Process Writing. LC 88-17602. (Illus.). 162p. (Orig.). (C). (gr. k). 1988. pap. text 24.00 (*0-435-08479-8*, 08479) Heinemann.

Nathan, Ruth, et al. Leap into Literacy Teacher Manual. write for info. (*1-58605-016-8*) Knowledge Kids.

Nathan, Ruth, et al. Write on Track: A Handbook for Young Writers, Thinkers & Learners. (Illus.). 400p. (J). (gr. k-3). 1996. text 19.33 (*0-669-40880-8*); pap. text 15.33 (*0-669-40881-6*) Great Source.

Nathan, S. S., jt. ed. see Gupta, B. M.

Nathan Staff. Anglais Banque. (ENG & FRE.). 141p. 1992. 18.95 (*0 7859-0971-0*, 2098866011) Fr & Eur.

— Anglais Hotellerie. (ENG & FRE.). 125p. 1992. 18.95 (*0-7859-0972-9*, 2098866046) Fr & Eur.

— Anglais Restauration. (ENG & FRE.). 125p. 1992. 18.95 (*0-7859-0973-7*, 2098866070) Fr & Eur.

Nathan, Theodore R. Hotelmanship: A Guide to Hospitality Industry Marketing & Management. LC 81-7051. 264p. 1981. 49.50 (*0-685-05973-1*, Inst Busn Plan) P-H.

Nathan-Wlodarski, Anne, jt. auth. see Wlodarski, Robert.

Nathanael, Ardella. Dance of the Soul: Peter Deunov's Pan-E4-Rhythmy. unabridged ed. LC 99-174469. (Illus.). 152p. 1998. per. 17.95 (*1-889280-22-4*) Esoteric Publng.

Nathanail, Paul. Greek Dictionary: Greek-English & English-Greek Pocket Dictionary. (ENG & GRE.). 1985. pap. 16.95 (*0-7100-0625-X*) Routledge.

***Nathane, Yvonne Grays.** Working in the Dark. 256p. 2000. pap. 12.00 (*0-9675636-0-7*) VK Pr.

Nathaniel, Isabel. The Dominion of Lights: Poems. LC 96-3724. 61p. (Orig.). 1996. pap. 9.95 (*0-914278-69-X*) Copper Beech.

Nathaniel, Paul. National Textbook Company's New College Greek & English Dictionary. (GRE & ENG., Illus.). 560p. 1994. 29.95 (*0-8442-8473-4*, 84734, Natl Textbk Co) NTC Contemp Pub Co.

***Nathanielsz.** Gift of Health. 2000. 25.00 (*0-06-019763-3*); pap. 14.00 (*0-06-095705-0*) HarpC.

Nathanielsz, Peter W. Life Before Birth: The Challenges of Fetal Development. 250p. 1996. pap. 13.95 (*0-7167-3025-1*) W H Freeman.

— Life Before Birth & a Time to Be Born. LC 92-26052. (Illus.). 250p. 1992. 25.00 (*0-916859-55-X*) Promethean Pr.

— Life in the Womb: The Origin of Health & Disease. LC 98-51356. (Illus.). 363p. 1999. 27.50 (*0-916859-56-8*) Promethean Pr.

— Origins of Health & Disease, Vol. 1. Date not set. pap. text. write for info. (*0-7167-2999-7*); pap. text. write for info. (*0-7167-3024-3*) W H Freeman.

Nathanielsz, Peter W., jt. ed. see Beard, Richard W.

***Nathans, Sari.** SAP R/3 for the Informix DBA. LC 99-49912. 304p. 1999. pap. text 49.99 (*0-13-022554-1*) P-H.

Nathans, Sydney. Daniel Webster & Jacksonian Democracy. LC 72-10779. (Johns Hopkins University Studies in Historical & Political Science: Series 91, No. 1). 263p. reprint ed. pap. 81.60 (*0-608-17920-5*, 202789900057) Bks Demand.

— The Quest for Progress: The Way We Lived in North Carolina 1870-1920. LC 82-20133. 120p. 1983. reprint ed. pap. 37.20 (*0-608-00293-3*, 205932100008) Bks Demand.

Nathans, Sydney, ed. see Clayton, Thomas H.

Nathans, Sydney, ed. see Fenn, Elizabeth & Wood, Peter H.

Nathans, Sydney, ed. see Watson, Harry L.

Nathanson. Basic Environmental Technology. 3rd ed. LC 99-32662. (Illus.). 522p. 1999. 81.00 (*0-13-082626-X*) P-H.

— Should We Consent to Be Governed? 2nd ed. (Philosophy Ser.). 2000. pap. text 18.75 (*0-534-57416-5*) Brooks-Cole.

Nathanson, A. Thomas Simon, His Life & Work. (Illus.). 1975. lib. bdg. 16.00 (*0-932106-34-X*) S J Durst.

***Nathanson, Amy.** Thomas on the Moon. 24p. (J). 2001. mass mkt. 2.99 (*0-375-81147-8*, Pub. by Random Bks Yng Read) Random.

Nathanson, Bernard N. The Hand of God: A Journey from Death to Life by the Abortion Doctor Who Changed His Mind. LC 95-26848. 208p. 1996. 24.95 (*0-89526-463-3*) Regnery Pub.

Nathanson, Bernard N. & Ostling, Richard N. Aborting America. 320p. (C). 1981. reprint ed. pap. 6.95 (*0-919225-00-4*) Life Cycle Bks.

Nathanson, Carol, jt. auth. see Rosenberg, Barry A.

Nathanson, Constance A. Dangerous Passage: The Social Control of Sexuality in Women's Adolescence. LC 90-20580. (Health, Society, & Policy Ser.). 350p. 1991. 59.95 (*0-87722-824-8*) Temple U Pr.

Nathanson, Donald L. Shame & Pride: Affect, Sex & the Birth of the Self. 496p. 1994. pap. 16.95 (*0-393-31109-0*) Norton.

Nathanson, Donald L., ed. Knowing Feeling. 448p. 1996. 45.00 (*0-393-70214-6*) Norton.

— The Many Faces of Shame. LC 86-31937. 370p. 1987. lib. bdg. 47.00 (*0-89862-705-2*) Guilford Pubns.

Nathanson, E. M. & Bank, Aaron. Knight's Cross: A Novel. LC 92-35891. 1993. 19.95 (*1-55972-168-5*, Birch Ln Pr) Carol Pub Group.

— Knight's Cross: A Novel. 448p. 1995. mass mkt. 5.99 (*0-8439-3724-6*) Dorchester Pub Co.

***Nathanson, Fred E.** Radar Design Principles. 2nd ed. (Illus.). 746p. 1999. reprint ed. text 74.95 (*1-891121-09-X*) SciTech Pub.

Nathanson, Ilene L. & Tirrito, Terry T. Gerontological Social Work: Theory into Practice. LC 97-23144. (Illus.). 176p. 1998. 37.95 (*0-8261-9890-2*) Springer Pub.

Nathanson, Irwin D. How to Start & Operate Your Own Profitable Consulting Business: The Successful Consultant's Course. (Illus.). 294p. 1990. 79.00 (*1-878614-02-9*) Worldwide Mktg.

***Nathanson, Jeanne H.** Pocket Condition of Education. 28p. 1999. pap. 2.00 (*0-16-050214-4*) USGPO.

Nathanson, Jerry A. Basic Environmental Technology: Water Supply, Waste Disposal, Pollution Control. LC 86-1682. 479p. 1986. text 44.50 (*0-471-81886-0*) P-H.

Nathanson, Jerry A. & Kissam, Philip C. Surveying Practice. 4th ed. 608p. 1987. text 52.72 (*0-07-034903-7*) Glencoe.

Nathanson, Jerry A. & Kobabian, J. W., eds. Cyclic Nucleotides Part I: Biochemistry. (Handbook of Experimental Pharmacology Ser.: Vol. 58, Pt. I). (Illus.). 736p. 1982. 344.00 (*0-387-10786-X*) Spr-Verlag.

Nathanson, L., et al. Small Group Problem Solving: An Aid to Organizational Effectiveness. 1981. pap. write for info. (*0-201-05203-2*) Addison-Wesley.

Nathanson, Larry, ed. Basic & Clinical Aspects of Malignant Melanoma. 240p. (C). 1987. text 152.00 (*0-89838-856-2*) Kluwer Academic.

— Current Research & Clinical Management of Melanoma, Alk. paper. LC 93-9325. (Cancer Treatment & Research Ser.: Vol. 65). 400p. (C). 1993. text 291.50 (*0-7923-2152-9*) Kluwer Academic.

— Malignant Melanoma: Biology, Diagnosis, & Therapy. (Cancer Treatment & Research Ser.). (C). 1988. text 150.00 (*0-89838-384-6*) Kluwer Academic.

— Management of Advanced Melanoma. (Contemporary Issues in Clinical Oncology Ser.: Vol. 6). (Illus.). 272p. 1986. text 41.50 (*0-685-17326-7*) Church.

— Management of Advanced Melanoma. fac. ed. LC 86-17154. (Contemporary Issues in Clinical Oncology Ser.: No. 6). (Illus.). 286p. 1986. reprint ed. pap. 88.70 (*0-7837-7901-1*, 204765700008) Bks Demand.

— Melanoma Research: Genetics, Growth Factors, Metastases & Antigens. (Cancer Treatment & Research Ser.). (C). 1991. text 172.50 (*0-7923-0895-6*) Kluwer Academic.

Nathanson, Laura W. Horse Does Jumping. Date not set. 13.95 (*0-399-21568-9*) Putnam Pub Group.

— The Portable Pediatrician for Parents. LC 93-24395. (Illus.). 544p. 1994. pap. 23.00 (*0-06-273176-9*, Harper Ref) HarpC.

— The Portable Pediatrician's Guide to Kids: Your Child's Physical & Behavioral Development from... LC 96-8801. 352p. 1996. pap. 21.00 (*0-06-273347-8*) HarpC.

Nathanson, Leonard. The Strategy of Truth: A Study of Sir Thomas Browne. LC 67-18216. 253p. reprint ed. pap. 78.50 (*0-608-30619-3*, 202013500016) Bks Demand.

Nathanson, Linda S., jt. auth. see Thayer, Stevan J.

Nathanson, Linda Sue, jt. auth. see Thayer, Stevan J.

Nathanson, Martha D. Home Health Care Answer Book: Legal Issues for Providers. 272p. 1995. text 77.00 (*0-8342-0575-0*, 20575) Aspen Pub.

Nathanson, Martha Dale, see Dale Nathanson, Martha.

Nathanson, Melvyn B. Additive Number Theory: Inverse Problems & the Geometry of Sumsets. LC 96-12929. (Graduate Texts in Mathematics Ser.: Vol. 165). 293p. 1996. 49.95 (*0-387-94655-1*) Spr-Verlag.

— Additive Number Theory: The Classical Bases. LC 96-11745. (Graduate Texts in Mathematics Ser.: Vol. 164). 342p. 1996. 49.95 (*0-387-94656-X*) Spr-Verlag.

***Nathanson, Melvyn B.** Elementary Methods in Number Theory. Axler, S. et al, eds. LC 99-42812. (Graduate Texts in Mathematics Ser.: Vol. 195). 400p. 1999. 49.95 (*0-387-98912-9*) Spr-Verlag.

Nathanson, Melvyn B., et al, eds. Number Theory: New York Seminar, 1989-1900. (Illus.). viii, 275p. 1991. 40.95 (*0-387-97670-1*) Spr-Verlag.

Nathanson, Melvyn B., et al. Number Theory. (Lecture Notes in Mathematics Ser.: Vol. 1135). v, 283p. 1985. 42.95 (*0-387-15649-6*) Spr-Verlag.

Nathanson, Melvyn B., ed. & tr. see Freiman, Grigori.

Nathanson, Melvyn B., tr. see Karatsuba, Anatoly A.

Nathanson, Nabarro. Doing Business in Poland. 2nd ed. LC 95-232771. (International Business Ser.). 1997. pap. 30.00 (*0-7494-1473-1*) Kogan Page Ltd.

Nathanson, Neal & Gordis, Leon, eds. Epidemiologic Reviews, Vol. 3, 1981. LC 79-7564. (Illus.). 259p. 1981. reprint ed. pap. 80.30 (*0-608-04006-1*, 206474300003) Bks Demand.

— Epidemiologic Reviews, Vol. 4, 1982. LC 79-7564. (Illus.). 223p. 1982. reprint ed. pap. 69.20 (*0-608-04007-X*, 206474300004) Bks Demand.

Nathanson, Neal M. Viral Pathogenesis. LC 96-23106. 1,040p. 1996. text 170.00 (*0-7817-0297-6*) Lppncott W & W.

Nathanson, Neil M. & Harden, T. Kendall, eds. G Proteins & Signal Transduction. (Society of General Physiologists Ser.). 211p. 1990. pap. 50.00 (*0-87470-046-9*) Rockefeller.

Nathanson, Paul. Over the Rainbow: The Wizard of Oz As a Secular Myth of America. LC 90-10163. (McGill Studies in the History of Religions). (Illus.). 432p. (C). 1991. pap. text 21.95 (*0-7914-0710-1*) State U NY Pr.

— Over the Rainbow: The Wizard of Oz As a Secular Myth of America. LC 90-10163. (McGill Studies in the History of Religions). (Illus.). 432p. (C). 1992. text 64.50 (*0-7914-0709-8*) State U NY Pr.

Nathanson, Richard. Can You Afford to Grow Old: How to Address the Risks of Needing Long Term Care. LC 98-91229. 106p. 1998. pap. write for info. (*1-57502-735-6*, PO2048) Morris Pubng.

Nathanson, Stephen. Economic Justice. LC 97-5286. 144p. 1997. pap. text 24.80 (*0-13-741844-2*) P-H.

— An Eye for an Eye: The Morality of Punishing by Death. LC 87-9579. (C). 1987. text 52.50 (*0-8476-7561-0*) Rowman.

— Eye for an Eye: The Morality of Punishing by Death. 176p. 1992. pap. 14.95 (*0-8476-7725-7*) Rowman.

— Patriotism, Morality, & Peace. LC 92-32412. (Studies in Social & Political Philosophy). 1993. 59.00 (*0-8476-7799-0*); pap. 23.95 (*0-8476-7800-8*) Rowman.

Nathanson, Tenney. Whitman's Presence: Body, Voice & Writing in Leaves of Grass. (C). 1994. pap. text 18.50 (*0-8147-5779-0*) NYU Pr.

***Nathanson, William S. & Cipriane, John L., Jr.** Connecticut Closing Practice: A Lawyer's Guide to Residential Real Estate Closings (with Forms) 184p. 2000. ring bd. 125.00 (*1-878698-60-5*) Atlantic Law.

Nathe, Sarah K., jt. ed. see Arnold, Christopher.

Nathenson, Michael B., jt. ed. see Henderson, Euan S.

Nather, Wolfgang. Effective Observation of Random Fields. 184p. (C). 1985. 60.00 (*0-7855-4989-7*, Pub. by Collets) St Mut.

Nather, Wolfgang, jt. auth. see Bandemer, Hans.

Natiello, Loretta, ed. see Foley, Raymond P.

Natilus International Staff & Westcott, Wayne L. Building Strength & Stamina: New Nautilus Training for Total Fitness. LC 96-15784. (Illus.). 248p. (Orig.). 1996. pap. 16.95 (*0-88011-550-5*, PWES0550) Human Kinetics.

Nation, Allan. Grass Farmers. (Illus.). 192p. (C). 1993. pap. 23.50 (*0-9632460-1-1*) Green Park.

— Knowledge Rich Ranching. 336p. 2000. pap. text 32.00 (*0-9632460-6-2*) Green Park.

— Paddock Shift: Changing Views on Grassland Farming. LC 97-12623. 192p. (Orig.). 1997. pap. text 25.95 (*0-9632460-5-4*) Green Park.

— Pasture Profits with Stocker Cattle. rev. ed. LC 97-41057. (Illus.). 224p. (C). 1998. pap. 24.95 (*0-9632460-7-0*) Green Park.

— Quality Pasture: How to Create It, Manage It & Profit from It. (Illus.). (C). 1995. pap. 32.50 (*0-9632460-3-8*) Green Park.

Nation, Craig. Turkey Between East & West: New Challenges for a Rising Regional Power. Mastny, Vojtech, ed. LC 97-19972. 296p. (C). 1997. pap. 27.00 (*0-8133-3412-8*, Pub. by Westview) HarpC.

Nation, Daryl. Teaching & Learning Vocabulary. 275p. (J). 1990. mass mkt. 26.95 (*0-8384-2863-0*) Heinle & Heinle.

Nation, Daryl, jt. auth. see Evans, Terry.

Nation, Daryl, jt. ed. see Evans, Terry.

Nation, Earl F., ed. Men & Books. (Illus.). x, 67p. 1987. reprint ed. 20.00 (*0-937543-01-2*) Sacrum Pr.

Nation, Edna. Caring Enough to Discipline: A Guide for Parents & Teachers. 128p. (Orig.). 1987. pap. 5.95 (*0-9614669-3-6*) Edna Nation.

— Emotional Healing: Helps for the Hurting. 128p. (Orig.). 1993. pap. 8.00 (*0-9614669-4-4*) Edna Nation.

— More Than a Fig Leaf: A Guide for Christian Clothing, Clarification of Women's Clothing, Men's Clothing & the Distinction Between the Two. 128p. (Orig.). 1986. pap. 5.95 (*0-9614669-2-8*) Edna Nation.

— Spenser Leslie Wise Vol. 5: A Biographical Sketch of a Pioneer Pentecostal Preacher. unabridged ed. Wallace, Mary & Bernard, David, eds. 164p. 1988. pap. 6.99 (*0-9614669-5-2*) Edna Nation.

Nation, Edna & Lamb, Joyce. Joyce: "Roaring Rorie", Ward of the State, Victim of Divorce, Alcoholism, & Neglect. (Illus.). 128p. (Orig.). 1985. pap. 5.95 (*0-9614669-0-1*) Edna Nation.

Nation, J. D. & Eaton, J. G., eds. Stratigraphy, Depositional Environments & Sedimentary Tectonics of the Western Margin, Cretaceous Western Seaway. (Special Papers: No. 260). (Illus.). 240p. 1991. pap. 21.00 (*0-8137-2260-8*) Geol Soc.

Nation, Jack R. Research Methods. LC 96-41289. 448p. (C). 1996. 79.00 (*0-02-386132-0*, Macmillan Coll) P-H.

Nation, Jack R., jt. auth. see LeUnes, Arnold.

Nation, Joseph E., ed. The De-Escalation of Nuclear Crises. LC 91-20553. 210p. 1992. text 59.95 (*0-312-05245-6*) St Martin.

Nation, Lindsay, jt. auth. see Johnson, Susan.

Nation Magazine Staff. View of the Nation, 1955-1959. Christman, Henry M., ed. LC 79-111853. (Essay Index Reprint Ser.). 1977. 21.95 (*0-8369-1620-4*) Ayer.

Nation Muzzle Loading Rifle Association Staff. Muzzle Blasts: Early Years Plus Vol. I & II, 1939-41. LC 74-11637. 352p. 1974. pap. 20.00 (*0-87387-069-7*) Shumway.

Nation, Nyle N. The Pine Nut Chronicle: The History & Adventures of Mining in Douglas County, Nevada. 300p. 1991. pap. 12.95 (*0-9630420-0-9*) Triple N Ent.

— The Pine Nut Chronicle: The History & Adventures of Mining in Douglas County Nevada. 2nd ed. Parkhurst, Sue, ed. 250p. 1992. reprint ed. pap. 12.95 (*0-9630420-1-7*) Triple N Ent.

Nation of Islam Staff. The Secret Relationship Between Blacks & Jews, Vol. 1. 334p. 1991. pap. text 19.95 (*0-9636877-0-0*) Hist Res Dept.

Nation, Paul, ed. New Ways in Teaching Vocabulary. 218p. 1994. pap. 22.95 (*0-939791-51-X*) Tchrs Eng Spkrs.

Nation, R. Craig. Black Earth, Red Star: A History of Soviet Security Policy, 1917-1991. LC 92-3717. (Illus.). 360p. 1993. text 42.50 (*0-8014-2725-8*); pap. text 16.95 (*0-8014-8007-8*) Cornell U Pr.

— War on War: Lenin, the Zimmerwald Left, & the Origins of Communist Internationalism. LC 89-35744. 304p. 1989. text 54.95 (*0-8223-0944-0*) Duke.

Nation, Richard D., jt. auth. see Aufmann, Richard N.

***Nation, Winona Morris.** If I Still Hold Earth As Dear. LC 99-93932. 2000. pap. 12.00 (*0-533-13192-8*) Vantage.

National Academic Recognition Information Center S. International Guide to Qualifications in Education. 3rd ed. LC 91-27610. 880p. 1996. 200.00 (*0-7201-2085-3*) Weidner & Sons.

National Academic Recognition Information Center S, ed. International Guide to Qualifications in Education. 4th ed. LC 95-18218. 896p. 1995. 200.00 (*0-7201-2217-1*) Continuum.

National Academies Policy Advisory Group (Great Britain) Staff & British Academy Staff. Energy & the Environment in the 21st Century. LC 96-141602. v, 104p. 1995. write for info. (*0-85403-498-6*) Royal Soc London.

National Academy of Arbitrators, Meeting (13th, 1960, Washington, D. C.) Staff. Challenges to Arbitration: Proceedings of the Thirteenth Annual Meeting National Academy of Arbitrators, Washington, DC, January 27-29, 1960. McKelvey, Jean T., ed. LC 55-57413. 196p. reprint ed. pap. 60.80 (*0-608-00757-9*, 206155100010) Bks Demand.

National Academy of Arbitrators, Meeting (31st: 19. Truth, Lie Detectors, & Other Problems in Labor Arbitration: Proceedings of the Thirty-First Annual Meeting, National Academy of Arbitrators, New Orleans, LA, April 4-7, 1978. Stern, James L. & Dennis, Barbara D., eds. LC 78-21950. 490p. 1979. reprint ed. pap. 151.90 (*0-608-00740-4*, 206152700010) Bks Demand.

National Academy of Arbitrators, Meeting (32nd: 1979: Dearborn, MI) Staff. Arbitration of Subcontracting & Wage Incentive Disputes: Proceedings of the Thirty-Second Annual Meeting, National Academy of Arbitrators, Dearborn, MI, May 9-12, 1979. Stern, James L. & Dennis, Barbara D., eds. LC 79-24133. 316p. reprint ed. pap. 98.00 (*0-608-00741-2*, 206152800010) Bks Demand.

National Academy of Arbitrators, Meeting (33rd, 1980, Los Angeles, CA) Staff. Decisional Thinking of Arbitrators & Judges: Proceedings of the 33rd Annual Meeting, National Academy of Arbitrators, Los Angeles, CA, June 10-13, 1980. Stern, James L. & Dennis, Barbara D., eds. LC 81-3900. 502p. reprint ed. pap. 155.70 (*0-608-00742-0*, 206152900010) Bks Demand.

National Academy of Arbitrators, Meeting (36th: 1983: Quebec) Staff. Arbitration, Promise & Performance: Proceedings of the Thirty-Sixth Annual Meeting, National Academy of Arbitrators, Quebec City, May 24-27, 1983. Stern, James L. & Dennis, Barbara D., eds. LC 83-18926. 304p. reprint ed. pap. 94.30 (*0-608-00743-9*, 206153200010) Bks Demand.

National Academy of Arbitrators Meeting Staff. Arbitration & the Law: Proceedings of the Twelfth Annual Meeting, National Academy of Arbitrators, Detroit, MI, January 29-31, 1959. LC 59-12890. 222p. reprint ed. pap. 68.90 (*0-608-00756-0*, 206155000010) Bks Demand.

— Arbitration 1984: Absenteeism, Recent Law, Panels, & Published Decisions: Proceedings of the Thirty-Seventh Annual Meeting, National Academy of Arbitrators, Chicago, IL, May 22-25, 1984. Gershenfeld, Walter J., ed. LC 84-23224. 313p. 1985. reprint ed. pap. 97.10 (*0-608-00744-7*, 206153300010) Bks Demand.

— Arbitration 1985: Law & Practice: Proceedings of the Thirty-Eighth Annual Meeting, National Academy of Arbitrators, Seattle, WA, May 27-31, 1985. Gershenfeld, Walter J., ed. LC 85-29987. 323p. 1986. reprint ed. pap. 100.20 (*0-608-00745-5*, 206153400010) Bks Demand.

— Arbitration 1988: Emerging Issues for the 1990s: Proceedings of the Forty-First Annual Meeting, National Academy of Arbitrators, Vancouver, BC, May 30-June 3, 1988. Gruenberg, Gladys W., ed. LC KF3424.A2N36. 399p. 1989. reprint ed. pap. 123.70 (*0-608-00746-3*, 206153700010) Bks Demand.

— Arbitration 1989: The Arbitrator's Discretion During & after the Hearing: Proceedings of the Forty-Second Annual Meeting, National Academy of Arbitrators,

N

Chicago, IL, May 28-June 3, 1989. Gruenberg, Gladys W., ed. LC KF3424.A2N36. 301p. 1990. reprint ed. pap. 93.40 (*0-608-00747-1*, 206153800010) Bks Demand.

— Arbitration 1990: New Perspectives on Old Issues: Proceedings of the Forty-Third Annual Meeting, National Academy of Arbitrators, San Diego, CA, May 27-June 2, 1990. Gruenberg, Gladys W., ed. LC 91-211776. 320p. 1991. reprint ed. pap. 99.20 (*0-608-00748-X*, 206153900010) Bks Demand.

National Academy of Arbitrators Staff. Arbitration & Social Change: Proceedings of the Twenty-Second Annual Meeting, National Academy of Arbitrators, Colorado Springs, CO, January 29-31, 1969. Somers, Gerald G., ed. LC 55-57413. 245p. reprint ed. pap. 76.00 (*0-608-05985-4*, 205971600008) Bks Demand.

— Arbitration Today: Proceedings of the 8th Annual Meeting, Boston Massachusetts, January 27-28, 1955. McKelvey, Jean T., ed. LC HD5504.A3. 219p. reprint ed. pap. 67.90 (*0-8357-5709-9*, 202678800052) Bks Demand.

— Critical Issues in Labor Arbitration: Proceedings of the Tenth Annual Meeting. McKelvey, Jean T., ed. LC HD5481.N32. (National Academy of Arbitrators: Proceedings of the Annual Meeting Ser.: No. 10). 227p. reprint ed. pap. 70.40 (*0-608-18376-8*, 205617500054) Bks Demand.

— Management Rights & the Arbitration Process: Proceedings of the Ninth Annual Meeting. McKelvey, Jean T., ed. LC HD548l.N32. (National Academy of Arbitrators: Proceedings of the Annual Meeting Ser.: Vol. 9). 245p. reprint ed. pap. 76.00 (*0-608-16811-4*, 205617600054) Bks Demand.

National Academy of Early Childhood Programs Staff. Guide to Accreditation. LC 85-60990. 226p. pap. text 37.00 (*0-912674-93-8*, NAEYC #916) Natl Assn Child Ed.

National Academy of Engineering & the Institute of. New Medical Devices: Invention, Development & Use. 204p. 1988. 34.50 (*0-309-03847-2*); pap. 24.50 (*0-309-03846-4*) Natl Acad Pr.

National Academy of Engineering, Committee on Engi. Forces Shaping the U. S. Academic Engineering Research Enterprise. 144p. (Orig.). (C). 1995. pap. text 29.00 (*0-309-05284-X*) Natl Acad Pr.

— National Interests in an Age of Global Technology. Lee, Thomas H. & Reid, Proctor R., eds. (Prospering in a Global Economy Ser.). 176p. 1991. pap. 29.95 (*0-309-04329-8*) Natl Acad Pr.

National Academy of Engineering, Pharmaceutical Pa. The Competitive Status of the U. S. Pharmaceutical Industry. LC 83-50568. 102p. 1983. pap. text 12.95 (*0-309-03396-9*) Natl Acad Pr.

National Academy of Engineering Staff. Application of Technology to Improve Productivity in the Service Sector of the National Economy: Summary Report & Recommendations Based on a Symposium & Workshops Held on the Occasion of the Eighth Annual Meeting, November 1 & 2, 1971, at the National Academy of Engineering. LC 72-83855. 376p. reprint ed. pap. 116.60 (*0-8357-7695-6*, 203604700002) Bks Demand.

— The Competitive Status of the U. S. Auto Industry: A Study of the Influences of Technology in Determining International Industrial Competitive Advantage. LC 82-12506. 217p. 1982. pap. 67.30 (*0-7837-7450-8*, 204917200010) Bks Demand.

— Cutting Edge Technologies. 192p. 1984. pap. text 18.95 (*0-309-03489-2*) Natl Acad Pr.

— Design & Analysis of Integrated Manufacturing Systems. 248p. 1988. text 29.50 (*0-309-03844-8*) Natl Acad Pr.

— Education for the Manufacturing World of the Future. 136p. 1985. pap. text 16.75 (*0-309-03584-8*) Natl Acad Pr.

— Engineering & the Advancement of Human Welfare: Ten Outstanding Achievements, 1964-1989. 48p. 1989. pap. text 8.95 (*0-309-04185-6*) Natl Acad Pr.

— Engineering Within Ecological Constraints. Schulze, Peter, ed. 204p. (Orig.). (C). 1996. text 37.95 (*0-309-05198-3*) Natl Acad Pr.

— Foreign Participation in U. S. Research & Development: Asset or Liability? Reid, Proctor P. & Schriesheim, Alan, eds. (Prospering in a Global Economy Ser.). 204p. (Orig.). (C). 1996. pap. text 29.95 (*0-309-05095-2*) Natl Acad Pr.

— Frontiers of Engineering: Reports on Leading-Edge Engineering from the 1997 NAE Symposium on Frontiers of Engineering. LC 98-84374. 125p. (C). 1998. pap. 35.00 (*0-309-05983-6*) Natl Acad Pr.

***National Academy of Engineering Staff.** Frontiers of Engineering: Reports on Leading Edge Engineering from the 1999 NAE Symposium. 138p. 2000. pap. 31.00 (*0-309-06933-5*) Natl Acad Pr.

National Academy of Engineering Staff. The Future of Aerospace. 88p. (Orig.). (C). 1993. pap. text 23.00 (*0-309-04881-8*) Natl Acad Pr.

— Globalization of Technology: International Perspectives. 224p. 1988. pap. text 22.50 (*0-309-03842-1*) Natl Acad Pr.

— The Greening of Industrial Ecosystems. Allenby, Braden R. et al, eds. 272p. (Orig.). (C). 1994. text 34.95 (*0-309-04937-7*) Natl Acad Pr.

— Hazards: Technology & Fairness. (Series on Technology & Social Priorities). 240p. 1986. pap. text 24.95 (*0-309-03644-5*) Natl Acad Pr.

— Improving Aircraft Safety. 118p. 1980. pap. text 12.95 (*0-309-03091-9*) Natl Acad Pr.

— Keeping Pace with Science & Engineering: Case Studies in Environmental Regulation. Uman, Myron F., ed. LC 93-5530. 296p. 1993. text 39.95 (*0-309-04938-5*) Natl Acad Pr.

— Lasers: Invention to Application. Whinnery, John R., ed. 144p. 1987. pap. text 14.95 (*0-309-03776-X*) Natl Acad Pr.

— Managing Innovation: Cases from the Services Industries. 224p. (C). 1988. text 32.50 (*0-309-03926-6*) Natl Acad Pr.

— Managing Innovation: Cases from the Services Industries. 224p. (C). 1988. pap. text 22.50 (*0-309-03891-X*) Natl Acad Pr.

— Mastering a New Role: Shaping Technology Policy for National Economic Performance. (Prospering in a Global Economy Ser.). 144p. 1993. pap. text 22.95 (*0-309-04646-7*) Natl Acad Pr.

— Measures of Environmental Performance & Ecosystem Condition. Schulze, Peter, ed. LC 98-43781. 180p. 1998. text 32.95 (*0-309-05441-9*) Natl Acad Pr.

— Memorial Tributes: National Academy of Engineering. 320p. 35.00 (*0-309-05575-X*) Natl Acad Pr.

— Memorial Tributes: National Academy of Engineering, Vol. 1. 303p. 1979. text 24.95 (*0-309-02889-2*) Natl Acad Pr.

— Memorial Tributes: National Academy of Engineering, Vol. 2. 318p. 1984. text 24.95 (*0-309-03482-5*) Natl Acad Pr.

— Memorial Tributes: National Academy of Engineering, Vol. 3. 388p. 1989. text 27.95 (*0-309-03939-8*) Natl Acad Pr.

— Memorial Tributes: National Academy of Engineering, Vol. 4. 356p. (C). 1991. text 42.00 (*0-309-04349-2*) Natl Acad Pr.

— Memorial Tributes: National Academy of Engineering, Vol. 5. 312p. (C). 1992. text 36.00 (*0-309-04689-0*) Natl Acad Pr.

— Memorial Tributes: National Academy of Engineering, Vol. 6. 280p. 1993. text 41.00 (*0-309-04847-8*) Natl Acad Pr.

— Memorial Tributes: National Academy of Engineering, Vol. 7. 256p. 1994. text 46.00 (*0-309-05146-0*) Natl Acad Pr.

— Product Liability & Innovation: Managing Risk in an Uncertain Environment. Hunziker, Janet R. & Jones, Trevor O., eds. 216p. (C). 1994. text 37.95 (*0-309-05130-4*) Natl Acad Pr.

— Revolution in the U. S. Information Infrastructure. 88p. 1995. pap. text 12.00 (*0-309-05287-4*) Natl Acad Pr.

— Risk & Innovation: The Role & Importance of Small, High-Tech Companies in the U. S. Economy. 104p. (Orig.). 1995. pap. text 20.00 (*0-309-05376-5*) Natl Acad Pr.

— Technology & Economics. 140p. 1991. pap. text 19.00 (*0-309-04397-2*) Natl Acad Pr.

— Technology & Environment. Ausubel, Jesse H. & Slodevich, Hedy E., eds. 236p. (C). 1991. pap. text 25.95 (*0-309-04426-X*) Natl Acad Pr.

— Technology in Services: Policies for Growth, Trade, & Employment. Guile, Bruce R. & Quinn, James B., eds. 256p. 1988. pap. 24.95 (*0-309-03887-1*) Natl Acad Pr.

National Academy of Engineering Staff & National Research Council Staff. People & Technology in the Workplace. 336p. 1991. text 29.95 (*0-309-04583-5*) Natl Acad Pr.

National Academy of Engineering Staff, et al. Science & Technology in the Academic Enterprise: Status, Trends, & Issues. 120p. 1989. pap. text 15.00 (*0-309-04175-9*) Natl Acad Pr.

***National Academy of Psychology Staff, et al.** Perspectives on Psychology & Social Development: Proceedings of the VII & VIII Congress of the National Academy of Psychology, India LC 98-915277. (Advances in Psychological Research in India Ser.). xi, 442 p. 1999. write for info. (*81-7022-768-2*, Pub. by Concept) S Asia.

National Academy of Public Administration Staff, et al. Building Stronger Communities & Regions: Can the Federal Government Help? LC 98-230067. 75p. 1998. pap. 20.00 (*1-57744-065-X*) Nat Acad Public Admin.

National Academy of Science (U. S.) Staff. High Schools & the Changing Workplace: The Employer's View: Report of the Panel on Secondary School Education for the Changing Workplace. LC 84-60887. 64p. reprint ed. pap. 30.00 (*0-8357-7711-1*, 203606700002) Bks Demand.

— Rapid Population Growth Vol. 1: Consequences & Policy Implications. LC 71-30348. 119p. reprint ed. pap. 36.90 (*0-608-06202-2*, 206653400001) Bks Demand.

***National Academy of Science Staff.** Biographical Memoirs, Vol. 76. 382p. 1999. 79.00 (*0-309-06434-1*) Natl Acad Pr.

— Biographical Memoirs, Vol. 77. 362p. 1999. 79.00 (*0-309-06644-1*) Natl Acad Pr.

National Academy of Science Staff. Planetary Sciences: American & Soviet Research - Proceedings from the U. S.-U. S. S. R. Workshop on Planetary Sciences. Donahue, T. M. et al, eds. 304p. 1991. pap. text 29.00 (*0-309-04333-6*) Natl Acad Pr.

***National Academy of Science Staff.** Review of the Hanford Thyroid Disease Study Draft Final Report. 228p. 2000. pap. 46.50 (*0-309-06883-5*) Natl Acad Pr.

National Academy of Science Staff, et al. Capitalizing on Investments in Science & Technology. 128p. 1999. pap. 38.00 (*0-309-06291-8*, Joseph Henry Pr) Natl Acad Pr.

***National Academy of Science Staff, et al.** Observations on the President's Fiscal Year 2000 Federal Science & Technology Budget. 24p. 1999. pap. 12.00 (*0-309-06487-2*) Natl Acad Pr.

National Academy of Science Staff, et al. Policy Implications of Greenhouse Warming: Mitigation, Adaptation, & the Science Base. 944p. (C). 1992. text 89.95 (*0-309-04386-7*) Natl Acad Pr.

National Academy of Sciences. Biotechnology in China. 110p. 1989. pap. text 15.00 (*0-309-04132-5*) Natl Acad Pr.

National Academy of Sciences (U. S.) Staff. Corporate Restructuring & Industrial Research & Development. LC 89-63979. 160p. 1990. reprint ed. pap. 49.60 (*0-608-02447-3*, 206309000004) Bks Demand.

National Academy of Sciences (U. S.) Staff, jt. auth. see United States Congress, Senate Committee on Foreign Relations.

National Academy of Sciences (U.S.), Institute of. Aging & Medical Education: Report of a Study. LC 81-600911. (Publication IOM Ser.: No. 78-04). 82p. reprint ed. pap. 30.00 (*0-8357-7691-3*, 203604200002) Bks Demand.

National Academy of Sciences, Committee on Linking. Linking Trade & Technology Policies: An International Comparison of the Policies of Industrialized Nations. Moore, Gordon E. & Harris, Martha C., eds. LC 92-29614. (Prospering in a Global Economy Ser.). 176p. (C). 1992. pap. text 26.00 (*0-309-04645-9*) Natl Acad Pr.

National Academy of Sciences, Institute of Medicin, et al. Careers in Science & Engineering: A Student Planning Guide to Graduate School & Beyond. 160p. (Orig.). 1996. pap. 11.95 (*0-309-05393-5*) Natl Acad Pr.

National Academy of Sciences, International Affair. Challenges for the 1990s for Arms Control & International Security. 86p. 1989. pap. text 15.00 (*0-309-04084-1*) Natl Acad Pr.

National Academy of Sciences, National Academy of. Responsible Science Vol. II: Background Papers & Resource Documents. 288p. 1993. pap. text 35.00 (*0-309-04788-9*) Natl Acad Pr.

National Academy of Sciences, Office of the Home S. Biographical Memoirs, Vol. 65. 500p. 1994. text 59.00 (*0-309-05037-5*) Natl Acad Pr.

— Biotechnology in China. 116p. 1989. 15.00 (*0-309-03988-6*) Natl Acad Pr.

National Academy of Sciences Panel on Decisionmaki, et al. Major Award Decisionmaking at the National Science Foundation. LC 94-66065. 174p. (Orig.). (C). 1994. pap. text 35.00 (*0-309-05029-4*) Natl Acad Pr.

National Academy of Sciences Staff. Biographical Memoirs, Vol. 44. xii, 370p. 1974. text 29.50 (*0-309-02238-X*) Natl Acad Pr.

— Biographical Memoirs, Vol. 45. vii, 465p. 1974. text 29.50 (*0-309-02239-8*) Natl Acad Pr.

— Biographical Memoirs, Vol. 46. 435p. 1975. 29.50 (*0-309-02240-1*) Natl Acad Pr.

— Biographical Memoirs, Vol. 47. 551p. 1975. text 29.50 (*0-309-02245-2*) Natl Acad Pr.

— Biographical Memoirs, Vol. 50. 416p. 1979. text 29.50 (*0-309-02549-4*) Natl Acad Pr.

— Biographical Memoirs, Vol. 51. 418p. 1980. text 29.50 (*0-309-02888-4*) Natl Acad Pr.

— Biographical Memoirs, Vol. 53. 400p. 1982. text 29.50 (*0-309-03287-3*) Natl Acad Pr.

— Biographical Memoirs, Vol. 54. 448p. 1983. text 29.50 (*0-309-03391-8*) Natl Acad Pr.

— Biographical Memoirs, Vol. 55. LC 05-26629. 636p. reprint ed. pap. 197.20 (*0-7837-2594-9*, 204275700055) Bks Demand.

— Biographical Memoirs, Vol. 56. 640p. 1987. text 29.50 (*0-309-03693-3*) Natl Acad Pr.

— Biographical Memoirs, Vol. 57. (Illus.). 560p. 1987. text 29.50 (*0-309-03729-8*) Natl Acad Pr.

— Biographical Memoirs, Vol. 58. 556p. 1989. text 29.50 (*0-309-03938-X*) Natl Acad Pr.

— Biographical Memoirs, Vol. 59. 500p. (C). 1990. text 29.50 (*0-309-04198-8*) Natl Acad Pr.

— Biographical Memoirs, Vol. 67. Office of Home Secretary Staff, ed. 404p. 1995. text 79.00 (*0-309-05238-6*) Natl Acad Pr.

— Biographical Memoirs, Vol. 72. 392p. 1997. text 79.00 (*0-309-05788-4*) Natl Acad Pr.

— Biographical Memoirs: 1991, Vol. 60. LC 05-26629. 429p. reprint ed. pap. 133.00 (*0-7837-3573-1*, 204343200060) Bks Demand.

— Chemical Ecology: The Chemistry of Biotic Interaction. Eisner, Thomas & Meinwald, Jerrold, eds. LC 95-18685. 1995. text 49.95 (*0-309-05281-5*) Natl Acad Pr.

— Ecological Risks: Perspectives from Poland & the United States. Grodzinski, Wladyslaw et al, eds. 428p. 1990. pap. text 35.00 (*0-309-04293-3*) Natl Acad Pr.

— The Future of the U. S.-Soviet Nuclear Relationship. 76p. 1991. pap. 9.95 (*0-309-04582-7*) Natl Acad Pr.

— The Future of U. S. Nuclear Weapons Policy. LC 97-68120. 100p. 1997. pap. 15.00 (*0-309-06367-1*) Natl Acad Pr.

— Information Technology & the Transformation of Undergraduate Education. 200p. 1999. text 34.95 (*0-309-06572-0*) Natl Acad Pr.

— National Academy of Sciences: The First Hundred Years, 1863-1963. 694p. 1978. text 39.95 (*0-309-02518-4*) Natl Acad Pr.

— National Science & Technology Strategies in a Global Context: Report of an International Symposium. 54p. 1998. pap. text 15.00 (*0-309-06132-6*) Natl Acad Pr.

— A Positron Named Priscilla: Scientific Discovery at the Frontier. Bartusiak, Marcia et al, eds. 360p. (C). 1994. 29.95 (*0-309-04893-1*) Natl Acad Pr.

— Reykjavik & Beyond: Deep Reductions in Strategic Nuclear Arsenals & the Future Direction of Arms Control. 80p. 1988. pap. text 12.95 (*0-309-03799-9*) Natl Acad Pr.

— Science & Creationism: A View from the National Academy of Sciences. 28p. (C). 1984. pap. 5.00 (*0-309-03440-X*) Natl Acad Pr.

— Science & Creationism: A View from the National Academy of Sciences. 2nd ed. LC 99-6259. 32p. (C). 1998. pap. text 7.95 (*0-309-06406-6*) Natl Acad Pr.

— Science & Judgement in Risk Assessment: Student Edition. 352p. 1996. pap. text, student ed. 36.95 (*1-56032-589-5*) Taylor & Francis.

— Scientific Communication & National Security. 188p. (C). 1982. pap. text 19.95 (*0-309-03332-2*) Natl Acad Pr.

— Tempo & Mode in Evolution: Genetics & Paleontology 50 Years After Simpson. Fitch, Walter & Ayala, Francisco J., eds. (Orig.). (C). 1995. text 49.95 (*0-309-05191-6*) Natl Acad Pr.

National Academy of Sciences Staff & Leo A. Orleans for the Committee on Scholarly Comm. Chinese Students in America: Policies, Issues & Numbers. 156p. 1988. pap. text 14.95 (*0-309-03886-3*) Natl Acad Pr.

National Academy of Sciences Staff & True, Frederick W. A History of the First Half-Century of the National Academy of Sciences, 1863-1913, Vol. 1. 1980. 26.95 (*0-405-12698-0*) Ayer.

— A History of the First Half-Century of the National Academy of Sciences, 1863-1913, Vol. 2. 1980. 26.95 (*0-405-12699-9*) Ayer.

National Academy of Sciences Staff & Vedral, Joyce L. Teaching about Evolution & the Nature of Science. LC 98-16100. 150p. 1997. pap. 19.95 (*0-309-06364-7*) Natl Acad Pr.

National Academy of Sciences Staff, et al. Adviser, Teacher, Role Model, Friend: On Being a Mentor to Students in Science & Engineering. LC 97-220701. 96p. 1997. pap. 9.95 (*0-309-06363-9*) Natl Acad Pr.

***National Academy of Sciences Staff, et al.** Balancing Scientific Openness & National Security Controls at the Nuclear Weapons Laboratories. 40p. 1999. pap. 12.00 (*0-309-06833-9*) Natl Acad Pr.

National Academy of Sciences Staff, et al. Balancing the National Interest: U. S. National Security Export Controls & Global Economic Competition. 368p. 1987. text 29.95 (*0-309-03738-7*) Natl Acad Pr.

— Evaluating Federal Research Programs: Research & the Government Performance & Results Act. 96p. 1999. pap. text 18.00 (*0-309-06430-9*) Natl Acad Pr.

— Fateful Choices: The Future of the U. S. Academic Research Enterprise. 72p. 1992. pap. 19.00 (*0-309-04643-2*) Natl Acad Pr.

— The Myrna Mack Case: An Update. LC 98-231770. 16p. (C). 1998. pap. text 10.00 (*0-309-06077-X*) Natl Acad Pr.

— Nature & Human Society: The Quest for a Sustainable World. Raven, Peter H. & Williams, Tania, eds. LC 99-50565. (Illus.). 500p. 1999. 42.00 (*0-309-06555-0*) Natl Acad Pr.

— Observations on the President's Fiscal Year, 1999 Federal Science & Technology Budget. LC 99-165073. 32p. 1998. pap. text 10.00 (*0-309-06127-X*) Natl Acad Pr.

— On Being a Scientist: Responsible Conduct in Research. 2nd rev. ed. 40p. (C). 1995. pap. text 5.00 (*0-309-05196-7*) Natl Acad Pr.

— Science & Technology Leadership in America Government: Ensuring the Best Presidential Appointments. 104p. (C). 1992. pap. text 12.95 (*0-309-04727-7*) Natl Acad Pr.

National Academy of Sciences Staff, jt. auth. see Greenwood, Addison.

National Academy of Sciences Staff, jt. auth. see Institute of Medicine Staff.

National Academy of Sciences Staff, jt. auth. see National Research Council Staff.

National Academy of Sciences Staff, jt. auth. see Science, Engineering Committee.

National Academy of Sciences, U. S. Committee on I. Nuclear Arms Control: Background & Issues. LC 84-62287. 378p. 1985. pap. text 24.95 (*0-309-03491-4*) Natl Acad Pr.

National Academy of Social Insurance (U.S.) Staff & Diamond, Peter A. Issues in Privatizing Social Security: Report of an Expert Panel of the National Academy of Social Insurance. LC 99-19902. (Illus.). 208p. 1999. 25.00 (*0-262-04177-4*) MIT Pr.

National Academy of the Avant Garde Staff. Proceedings of the National Academy of the Avant Garde. Korn, Henry J., ed. 1975. pap. 5.00 (*0-915066-62-9*) Assembling Pr.

National Academy Press Staff. Future Role of Pesticides. 296p. 1999. 44.95 (*0-309-06526-7*, Joseph Henry Pr) Natl Acad Pr.

— Making the Surface Transportation System More Secure: A Research & Development Strategy to Improve the Surface Transportation System. 1999. 44.95 (*0-309-06529-1*) Natl Acad Pr.

***National Academy Press Staff.** Separation Technologies for the Industries of the Future. LC 98-83160. xiii, 113p. 1999. pap. 35.00 (*0-309-06377-9*) Natl Acad Pr.

— Work-Related Musculoskeletal Disorders: Report, Workshop Summary & Workshop Papers. LC 99-61013. 240p. 1999. pap. 47.00 (*0-309-06397-3*, Joseph Henry Pr) Natl Acad Pr.

National Academy Press Staff, contrib. by. Guide for the Care & Use of Laboratory Animals. rev. ed. 140p. 1996. pap. text 9.95 (*0-309-05377-3*) Natl Acad Pr.

— WIC Nutrition Risk Criteria: A Scientific Assessment. 377p. (Orig.). 1996. pap. text 39.00 (*0-309-05385-4*) Natl Acad Pr.

National Accounts Review Committee. The National Economic Accounts of the United States: Review, Appraisal, & Recommendations. (General Ser.: No. 64). 206p. 1958. reprint ed. 53.60 (*0-87014-063-9*) Natl Bur Econ Res.

National Action Committee on the Status of Women, contrib. by. The NAC Voters' Guide: The National Action Committee on the Status of Women. LC 97-184794. (Illus.). 158p. 1997. pap. 9.95 (*1-55028-552-1*, Pub. by J Lorimer) Formac Dist Ltd.

National Adult Day Services Association (U.S.) Sta, et al. Standards & Guidelines for Adult Day Services. 3rd ed. LC 97-31313. 1997. write for info. (*0-910883-86-6*) Natl Coun Aging.

An Asterisk (*) at the beginning of an entry indicates that the title is appearing for the first time.

National Advertising Company Staff. America's Advertisers: Who They Are, Where They Are, How They Have Developed, & What They Are Doing at the Present Time. LC 75-22830. (America in Two Centuries Ser.). 1976. reprint ed. 65.95 (*0-405-07702-5*) Ayer.

National Advisory Committee on Adult Religious Edu. Catechism of the Catholic Church: An Access Guide for Adult Discussion Groups. 15p. (Orig.). 1995. pap. 2.95 (*1-55586-050-8*) US Catholic.

National Advisory Committee on Criminal Justice St. Disorders & Terrorism: Report of the Task Force on Disorders & Terrorism, 1976. LC 77-601645. 1978. reprint ed. lib. bdg. 58.00 (*0-89941-530-X*, 200420) W S Hein.

National Advisory Council on Bilingual Education. Bilingual Education. Cordasco, Francesco, ed. LC 77-90411. (Bilingual-Bicultural Education in the U. S. Ser.). 1978. reprint ed. lib. bdg. 19.95 (*0-405-11080-4*) Ayer.

National Aeronautics & Space Adm., NASA History Of & Gawdiak, Ihor Y., contrib. by. Astronautics & Aeronautics, 1986-1990: A Chronology. LC 97-20215. 1997. per. 21.00 (*0-16-049134-7*) USGPO.

National Aeronautics & Space Administration, Lyndo. NASA FAR Supplement. 1995. ring bd. 167.00 (*1-56726-075-6*) Mgmt Concepts.

National Air & Space Museum Library Staff, ed. The International Handbook of Aerospace Awards & Trophies. LC 77-25053. (Illus.). 252p. 1978. pap. text 32.00 (*0-87474-670-1*, NAAH) Smithsonian.

National Air & Space Museum Staff. Aircraft of the National Air & Space Musuem. 5th ed. LC 97-46804. 1998. pap. 11.95 (*1-56098-449-X*) Smithsonian.

National Air & Space Museum Staff & Harwit, Martin O. Treasures of the National Air & Space Museum. LC 94-41496. (Tiny Folios Ser.). (Illus.). 320p. 1996. pap. 11.95 (*1-55859-822-7*) Abbeville Pr.

National Air & Space Museum Staff & Smithsonian Institution Staff. Aerospace Periodical Index: 1973 to 1982. 1983. 124.80 (*0-8161-0428-X*, G K Hall & Co) Mac Lib Ref.

National Alliance for Business Staff. Basic Skills for Job Performance: PICs & Workplace Literacy. 38p. 1991. pap. 5.95 (*0-88713-652-4*) Nat Alliance.

National Alliance of Business Staff. Job Performance Learning: High Performance Workforce Training Systems. 41p. 1993. pap. 7.95 (*0-88713-656-7*) Nat Alliance.

National Anti-Vivi Section Society Staff. Personal Care for People Who Care. 9th ed. 204p. 1998. pap. 6.95 (*1-888635-01-0*) Nat Anti-Vivisect.

National Anti-Vivisection Society Staff. Personal Care for People Who Care. 8th ed. Orig. Title: Personal Care with Principle. (Illus.). 200p. (Orig.). 1996. pap. 4.95 (*1-888635-00-2*) Nat Anti-Vivisect.

***National Anti-Vivisection Society Staff.** Personal Care for People Who Care. 10th ed. Orig. Title: Personal Care with Principle. (Orig.). 2000. pap. 9.50 (*1-888635-02-9*) Nat Anti-Vivisect.

National Apartment Association Staff, jt. auth. see Urban Land Institute Staff.

National Aquarium Staff. Living in Water: An Aquatic Science Curriculum for Grades 5-7. 3rd ed. LC 98-129711. 420p. (C). 1997. per. 23.95 (*0-7872-4366-3*) Kendall-Hunt.

National Archives & Records Administration Staff. Black Studies: A Select Catalog of National Archives Microfilm Publications. LC 83-15134. 97p. (Orig.). 1984. pap. text 3.50 (*0-911333-08-8*, 200011) National Archives & Recs.

— Federal Population Censuses, 1790 to 1890. rev. ed. 96p. 1997. reprint ed. pap. 3.50 (*0-911333-63-0*, 200032) National Archives & Recs.

— Gerald R. Ford. (Presidential Perspectives from the National Archives Ser.). (Illus.). 32p. 1994. pap. 3.50 (*1-880875-04-7*, 200020) National Archives & Recs.

— Guide to Cartographic Records in the National Archives. LC 76-611061. (Illus.). 444p. 1971. 25.00 (*0-911333-19-3*, 100005) National Archives & Recs.

— A Guide to Civil War Maps in the National Archives. rev. ed. LC 86-5132. (Illus.). 140p. 1986. text 30.00 (*0-911333-36-3*, 100040) National Archives & Recs.

— Milestone Documents in the National Archives. rev. ed. LC 93-23047. Orig. Title: The Written Word Endures. (Illus.). 112p. 1995. pap. 12.00 (*0-911333-98-3*, 100006) National Archives & Recs.

— Military Service Records: A Select Catalog of National Archives Microfilm Publications. 330p. 1985. pap. text 3.50 (*0-911333-07-X*, 200028) National Archives & Recs.

— National Archives Microfilm Resources for Research: A Comprehensive Catalog. rev. ed. LC 85-15242. 136p. 1996. pap. 5.00 (*0-911333-34-7*, 200033) National Archives & Recs.

National Archives & Records Administration Staff, contrib. by. United States Government Manual, 1997-98. (Illus.). 867p. 1997. per. 40.00 (*0-16-049122-3*) USGPO.

National Archives & Records Administration Staff, jt. auth. see West, Jean.

National Archives of Canada Staff. Treasures of the National Archives. (Illus.). 368p. 1992. text 50.00 (*0-8020-5022-0*) U of Toronto Pr.

National Archives of Canada Staff, jt. auth. see Cottam, S. Barry.

National Archives of Finland, Norway & Sweden Staf, ed. Guide to the Sources for the History of Nations, 3rd Series, Vol. 3: Sources of the History of North Africa, Asia & Oceania in Scandinavia, Pt. 2: Sources of the History of North Africa, Asia & Oceania in Finland, Norway & Sweden. 233p. 1981. lib. bdg. 95.00 (*3-598-21475-8*) K G Saur Verlag.

National Archives of Hungary Staff, jt. ed. see International Council on Archives Staff.

National Archives Staff. Teaching with Documents, Vol. 1. LC 89-12602. (Illus.). 225p. (C). 1989. pap. 15.00 (*0-911333-79-7*, 200047) National Archives & Recs.

***National Archives Staff, contrib. by.** NSA Cryptologic Documents. (Cryptographic Ser.). vi, 134p. 1999. pap. 26.80 (*0-89412-277-0*, C-83) Aegean Park Pr.

National Archives Staff, ed. Federal Population Census, 1910. LC 72-610891. 44p. (Orig.). 1982. pap. text 3.50 (*0-911333-15-0*, 200009) National Archives & Recs.

— Federal Population Census, 1920. LC 91-3417. (Orig.). 1992. pap. text 3.50 (*0-911333-86-X*) National Archives & Recs.

National Archives Staff, ed. see Kennedy, John F.

National Art Education Association Staff, ed. see Lowenfeld, Viktor.

National Assembly on Foreign Language & Internatio. Toward Education with a Global Perspective: A Report. LC LC1090.N3. 19p. 1980. reprint ed. pap. 30.00 (*0-608-01794-9*, 206244700003) Bks Demand.

National Assessment Institute Staff. Handbook for Safe Food Service Management. 2nd ed. LC 97-10103. (n). 200p. 1997. pap. 49.00 (*0-13-236118-3*) P-H.

National Association Colonial Dames of America Sta. The Register Book for the Parish Prince Frederick Winyaw: Anno Domini 1713. (Illus.). 270p. 1982. reprint ed. 25.00 (*0-89308-299-6*) Southern Hist Pr.

National Association for Chicano Studies Staff & Garcia, J., eds. The Chicano Struggle: Analysis of Past & Present Efforts. LC 84-70569. 213p. 1984. pap. 20.00 (*0-916950-50-6*) Biling Rev-Pr.

National Association for Equal Opportunity in High. A Resource Guide on Blacks in Higher Education. 66p. (Orig.). (C). 1988. pap. text 10.50 (*0-8191-6949-8*) NAEOHE.

***National Association for Law Placement Staff.** National Directory of Legal Employers: 22,000 Great Job Openings for Law Students & Law Schools. 1999. pap. 39.95 (*0-15-900434-9*) Harcourt Legal.

***National Association for Law Staff.** National Directory of Legal Employers: 22,000 Great Job Openings for Law Students & Law Schools. (Illus.). 2000. pap. 39.95 (*0-15-900454-3*) Harcourt.

National Association for Preservation & Perpetuati, ed. More Best-Loved Stories Told at the National Storytelling Festival. 224p. 1992. 24.95 (*1-879991-09-8*); pap. 14.95 (*1-879991-08-X*) Natl Storytlng Network.

National Association for Sport & Physical Education Staff, jt. auth. see Mohnsen, Bonnie S.

National Association for Teaching of the Deaf Staf. A Second Reader for Deaf Children. 1973. 59.95 (*0-8490-1009-8*) Gordon Pr.

National Association for the Advancement of Colore. Thirty Years of Lynching in the United States, 1889-1918. LC 73-94142. (American Negro: His History & Literature. Series 3). 1970. reprint ed. 18.95 (*0-405-01932-7*) Ayer.

— Thirty Years of Lynching in the United States, 1889-1918. LC 72-89046. (Illus.). 105p. 1970. reprint ed. lib. bdg. 35.00 (*0-8371-1950-2*, LYU&, Greenwood Pr) Greenwood.

National Association for the Education of Young Ch, jt. auth. see Hannigan, Irene L.

National Association for the Education of Young Children, jt. auth. see Schickedanz, Judith A.

National Association for the Practice of Anthropology Staff, jt. auth. see Sabloff, Paula L. W.

National Association for the Prevention of Addicti. Developments in the Field of Drug Abuse: Proceedings. Senay, Edward C., ed. 1130p. 1975. 79.95 (*0-87073-388-5*) Transaction Pubs.

National Association for the Promotion of Social S. Trades' Societies & Strikes: Report of the Committee on Trades' Societies Presented at the 4th Annual Meeting, Glasgow, Sept. 1860. LC 67-20514. (Reprints of Economic Classics Ser.). xxi, 651p. 1968. reprint ed. 65.00 (*0-678-00347-5*) Kelley.

National Association of Baptist Professors of Reli & Leschert, Dale F. Hermeneutical Foundations of Hebrews: A Study in the Validity of the Epistle's Interpretation of Some Core Citations from the Psalms. (NABPR Dissertation Ser.: No. 10). 1995. write for info. (*0-7734-2860-7*) E Mellen.

National Association of Bond Lawyers Staff. Federal Taxation of Municipal Bonds: Statutes, Regulations, Rulings. Israel, Perry E. et al, eds. LC 93-35553. 6518p. 1993. 825.00 incl. disk (*0-13-300302-7*) Aspen Law.

National Association of Bond Lawyers Staff, et al, eds. Federal Taxation of Municipal Bonds: 1996 Deskbook. rev. ed. 2598p. 1996. pap., per. 145.00 (*1-56706-299-7*, 62997) Aspen Law.

National Association of Broadcasters Staff. Advertising Revenues Per Television Household: A Market by Market Analysis. 51p. (Orig.). 1993. pap. 100.00 (*0-89324-209-8*) Natl Assn Broadcasters.

— Broadcasting Bibliography. rev. ed. Hill, Suan M., ed. 74p. 1989. 10.00 (*0-89324-076-1*) Natl Assn Broadcasters.

— Careers in Television. 32p. (Orig.). 1991. pap. 3.50 (*0-89324-117-2*) Natl Assn Broadcasters.

— Digital Audio Broadcasting: Status Report & Outlook. 69p. (Orig.). 1990. pap. 45.00 (*0-89324-098-2*) Natl Assn Broadcasters.

— The NAB Guide to AM & FM Radio Performance Measurements. 50p. (Orig.). 1990. pap. 60.00 (*0-685-47799-1*) Natl Assn Broadcasters.

— Radio Employee Compensation, '90. 82p. (Orig.). 1990. pap. 100.00 (*0-89324-093-1*) Natl Assn Broadcasters.

— Radio Financial Report, 1993. 225p. (Orig.). 1993. pap. 225.00 (*0-89324-200-4*) Natl Assn Broadcasters.

— Satellites & Broadcasting, 1990: U. S. Domestic & International Market Directions & Issues. 42p. (Orig.). 1989. 60.00 (*0-89324-075-3*) Natl Assn Broadcasters.

— Trends in Radio Station Sales, 1991-1993. 160p. (Orig.). 1993. pap. 225.00 (*0-89324-201-2*) Natl Assn Broadcasters.

— TV Financial Report, 1993. 235p. (Orig.). 1993. pap. 225.00 (*0-89324-148-2*) Natl Assn Broadcasters.

— TV Market Analysis, 1990. 135p. (Orig.). 1990. pap. 400.00 (*0-89324-096-6*) Natl Assn Broadcasters.

National Association of Church Personnel Administr. Working in the Catholic Church: An Attitudinal Survey. LC 93-19042. 184p. (Orig.). 1993. pap. 14.95 (*1-55612-568-2*) Sheed & Ward WI.

National Association of College & University Busin. Annual NACUBO Endowment Study: Executive Summary. 358p. 1994. 28.00 (*0-685-59359-2*) NACUBO.

— Annual NACUBO Endowment Study: NAIS Endowment Study. 358p. 1994. 30.00 (*0-685-59360-6*) NACUBO.

— Annual NACUBO Endowment Study: 1995. 358p. 1996. 85.00 (*0-685-59358-4*) NACUBO.

— NACUBO Executive Briefing Series, 6 papers. McDonald, Deirdre & Reeder, Jefferson, eds. 1991. 37.50 (*0-915164-62-0*); 37.50 (*0-915164-65-5*); 37.50 (*0-915164-66-3*); 37.50 (*0-915164-67-1*) NACUBO.

— Nonpension Postretirement Benefits: Strategies for Colleges & Universities. Reeder, Jefferson, ed. 173p. 1992. 42.95 (*0-915164-80-9*) NACUBO.

***National Association of College & University Busin, contrib. by.** Administering Food Service Contracts: Handbook for Contract Administrators in College & University Food Services. unabridged ed. 120p. 1999. pap. 40.00 (*0-9674161-0-8*) Natl Coll Univ Food.

National Association of College & University Busin & National Association of College & University Busin. NACUBO Annual Membership Directory. 415p. 1996. 115.00 (*0-685-48508-0*) NACUBO.

National Association of College & University Busin, jt. auth. see National Association of College & University Busin.

National Association of Collegiate Director of Ath. The National Directory of College Athletics (Men's Edition), 1988-1989. 1988. pap. 15.00 (*0-318-41469-4*) R Franks Ranch.

— The National Directory of College Athletics, 1988-1989: Women's Edition. 1988. pap. 11.00 (*0-318-41470-8*) R Franks Ranch.

National Association of Corrosion Engineers Staff, jt. auth. see American Society for Testing & Materials Staff.

National Association of Elementary School Principa. Best Ideas for Reading from America's Blue Ribbon Schools: What Award-Winning Elementary & Middle School Principals Do. LC 98-40125. 152p. 1998. pap. 32.95 (*0-8039-6773-X*) Corwin Pr.

— Best Ideas from America's Blue Ribbon Schools: What Award-Winning Elementary & Middle School Principals Do. 120p. 1994. pap. 18.95 (*0-8039-6177-4*) Corwin Pr.

— Best Ideas from America's Blue Ribbon Schools Vol. 2: What Award-Winning Elementary & Middle School Principals Do. 160p. 1995. pap. 22.95 (*0-8039-6272-X*) Corwin Pr.

National Association of Elementary School Principals (U.S.). Best Ideas for Reading from America's Blue Ribbon Schools: What Award-Winning Elementary & Middle School Principals Do. LC 98-40125. 152p. 1998. 51.95 (*0-8039-6772-1*) Corwin Pr.

National Association of Emergency Medical Technici. Prehospital Trauma Life Support. 4th ed. LC 98-27270. (Illus.). 384p. (gr. 13). 1998. pap. text 36.95 (*0-8151-4569-1*, 30219) Mosby Inc.

***National Association of Emergency Technicians Staff.** Prehospital Trauma Life Support. 4th ed. 1998. teacher ed. write for info. (*0-323-00300-1*) Mosby Inc.

National Association of EMS Physicians Executive S. EMS Medical Directors' Handbook. 2nd ed. (Illus.). 512p. (gr. 13). 1994. pap. text 46.95 (*0-8016-6580-9*, 06580) Mosby Inc.

National Association of EMS Physicians Staff. Quality Assurance in Prehospital Care. Swor, Robert A. et al, eds. LC 92-49237. (Illus.). 272p. (gr. 13). 1992. pap. text 19.95 (*0-8016-6579-5*, 06579) Mosby Inc.

National Association of EMT's Pre-Hospital Life Su, et al. Pre-Hospital Trauma Life Support. rev. ed. Butman, Alexander M. et al, eds. 358p. 1990. reprint ed. pap. text 22.50 (*0-940432-07-2*) Educ Direction.

National Association of Federal Credit Unions Staff, jt. auth. see Braun, Robert E.

National Association of Federal Credit Unions Staff, jt. auth. see Hyland, Christiane Gigi.

National Association of Federal Credits Unions Staff, jt. auth. see Pedersen, Aksel G.

National Association of Home Builders, Legal Depar. Contracts & Liability for Builders & Remodelers. (Illus.). 119p. 1993. pap. 25.00 (*0-86718-376-4*) Home Builder.

National Association of Home Builders NAHB Staff. Wood Frame House Construction. 280p. 1991. mass mkt. 25.75 (*0-8273-4739-1*) Delmar.

National Association of Home Builders, Remodelors. Quality Standards for the Professional Remodeler. rev. ed. LC 90-24100. 81p. 1991. reprint ed. 18.00 (*0-86718-359-4*) Home Builder.

National Association of Home Builders Research Fou. NAHB Thermal Performance Guidelines. 16p. 1983. pap. 8.00 (*0-86718-192-3*) Home Builder.

National Association of Home Builders Staff. Accounting & Financial Management. 68p. 1985. pap. 27.50 (*0-86718-232-6*) Home Builder.

— Developer's Guide to Clean Air Act Regulations. LC 98-45859. 1999. write for info. (*0-86718-456-6*) Home Builder.

— Financing for Small Builders & Developers. LC 95-32637. (Illus.). 80p. 1995. pap. 19.25 (*0-86718-408-6*) Home Builder.

— The Future of Home Building: 1992-1994 & Beyond. 212p. 1992. pap. 42.00 (*0-86718-468-X*) Home Builder.

— Impact Fee Handbook. 3rd ed. LC 96-37759. (Illus.). 176p. 1996. pap. text 33.00 (*0-86718-431-0*) Home Builder.

***National Association of Home Builders Staff.** Producing Affordable Housing: Partnerships for Profit. LC 99-42067. (Illus.). 1999. write for info. (*0-86718-486-8*) Home Builder.

National Association of Home Builders Staff. Profile of the New Home Buyer, 1991: Based on 1990 Home Buyers. 150p. 1991. pap. 65.00 (*0-86718-467-1*) Home Builder.

— Seniors Housing: A Development & Management Handbook. LC 87-62642. (Illus.). 121p. 1987. pap. 40.00 (*0-86718-275-X*) Home Builder.

National Association of Home Builders Staff & Ratzlaff, Patricia. The New Home Buyer's Workbook. Tuttle, John, ed. 32p. 1995. student ed. 25.00 (*0-86718-402-7*) Home Builder.

National Association of Home Builders Staff, jt. auth. see Mitchell, Jan.

National Association of Insurance Commissioners St. 1985 Proceedings of the National Association of Insurance Commissioners, Vol. II. Miller, Karen P., ed. 772p. 1985. 175.00 (*0-89382-165-9*) Nat Assn Insurance.

National Association of Insurance Commissioners St, ed. Model Laws, Regulations & Guidelines, 4 vols., Set. rev. ed. 1992. ring bd. 250.00 (*0-9601244-1-1*) Nat Assn Insurance.

National Association of Legal Assistants, Inc. Sta. CLA Study Guide & Mock Examination. LC 97-148083. 250p. (C). 1994. pap., student ed., suppl. ed. 18.25 (*0-314-04630-5*) West Pub.

— Manual for Legal Assistants. 529p. 1979. 18.95 (*0-318-15095-6*) Natl Assn Legal Secys.

— MANUAL FOR LEGAL ASSISTANTS 2E. 2nd ed. Hannan, ed. (Paralegal). 397p. (C). 1991. mass mkt. 53.50 (*0-314-80780-2*) West Pub.

National Association of Legal Assistants, Inc. Sta & Koerselman, Virginia. CLA Review Manual: A Practical Guide to CLA Exam Preparation. Hannan, ed. LC 93-8171. 700p. (C). 1993. pap. text 68.50 (*0-314-01349-0*) West Pub.

National Association of Legal Secretaries (NALS) S. Career Legal Secretary. 770p. 1993. reprint ed. text 30.50 (*0-314-32237-X*) West Pub.

— Manual for the Lawyer's Assistant. 2nd ed. 1118p. 1991. reprint ed. text 32.95 (*0-314-41162-3*) West Pub.

National Association of Legal Secretaries (NALS) S, et al. The Career Legal Secretary. 4th ed. LC 97-25678. 777p. (C). 1997. 35.50 (*0-314-21448-8*) West Pub.

National Association of Legal Secretaries Staff, et al. NALS - Probate Handbook for the Lawyer's Assistant. 403p. (C). 1993. pap. text. write for info. (*0-314-02351-8*) West Pub.

National Association of Legal Secretary Staff & Aoki, Kaye. NALS - The Career Legal Secretary. 3rd ed. 864p. 1993. text 31.50 (*0-314-02353-4*) West Pub.

National Association of Parliamentarians Staff. Thirty-Six Programs for Unit Study & Workshop Leaders: Compiled from NAP Training Guides. 198p. (Orig.). 1995. pap. 25.00 (*1-884048-12-9*) Natl Assn Parliamentarians.

National Association of Professional Pet Sitters S. Why You Should Use a Pet Sitter: A Guide to Using Professional Pet Sitting Services. 12p. (Orig.). 1995. pap. text 5.00 (*0-938369-21-0*) Greeting Card Assn.

***National Association of Purchasing Management.** Purchasing & Supply Yearbook. LC 99-57984. (Illus.). 540p. 2000. 89.95 (*0-07-135860-9*, McGrw-H College) McGrw-H Hghr Educ.

National Association of Rainbow Division Veterans. 42nd Rainbow Infantry Division. LC 87-50364. 128p. 1987. 34.95 (*0-938021-13-3*) Turner Pub KY.

National Association of Realtors, Economics & Rese. SIOR Industrial Real Estate Market Survey: 1986 Review - 1987 Forecast. 240p. 1987. pap. 50.00 (*0-939623-06-4*) Soc Industrial Realtors.

National Association of Realtors Staff. Real Estate Index, 2 vols. 1987. 169.00 (*0-938785-00-1*) Natl Assoc Realtors.

— Real Estate Index, 2 vols., Vol. I: Author-Title. 1987. 99.00 (*0-938785-01-X*) Natl Assoc Realtors.

— Real Estate Index, 2 vols., Vol. II: Subject. 1987. 99.00 (*0-938785-02-8*) Natl Assoc Realtors.

— Real Estate Index - Supplement, Vol. 3. LC 86-23878. 1800p. 1988. 49.50 (*0-938785-04-4*) Natl Assoc Realtors.

— Real Estate Index, 1991. 1992. 15.00 (*0-685-63292-X*) Natl Assoc Realtors.

National Association of Realtors Staff & Society of Industrial & Office Realtors Staff. Guide to Industrial & Office Real Estate Markets. 1988. per. 35.00 (*0-939623-20-X*) Soc Industrial Realtors.

National Association of Realtors Staff, jt. auth. see Society of Industrial Realtors Staff.

National Association of Retired Federal Employees. Open Season Guide: Federal Health Benefits & Premiums, 1993. Brown, Gordon F., ed. 152p. (Orig.). 1992. pap. 9.95 (*0-9631168-2-7*) Natl Ret Fed Emps.

National Association of Review Appraisers & Mortga. Establishing an Appraisal Quality Control Program. LC 89-50439. 97p. 1989. pap. text 65.00 (*0-935988-38-6*, 357) Todd Pub.

N

An Asterisk (*) at the beginning of an entry indicates that the title is appearing for the first time.

National Association of Review Appraisers & Mortga & Arnold, Fayette F., III. Reviewing Condominium Projects. LC 80-53455. (Illus.). 156p. 1981. 21.50 (*0-935988-21-1*) Todd Pub.

National Association of Review Appraisers Staff & Everhart, Marion E. Land Classification for Land Uses, Management & Valuation. LC 82-74565. (Illus.). 220p. 1983. 19.50 (*0-935988-23-8*, 311) Todd Pub.

National Association of Safety & Health Profession. Handbook of Emergency Response & Toxic Chemical Releases. Cheremisinoff, Nicholas P., ed. (Illus.). 316p. 1992. 24.95 (*0-925760-57-9*) SciTech Pubs.

National Association of School Psychologists. Helping Children Grow Up in the 90's: A Resource Book for Parents & Teachers. 400p. 1992. pap. text 35.00 (*0-932955-07-X*) Natl Assn Schl Psych.

— Professional Conduct Manual. 2nd ed. 1992. pap. text 12.00 (*0-932955-12-6*) Natl Assn Schl Psych.

National Association of Secondary School Principal. How Fares the Ninth Grade? A Day in the Life of a 9th Grader. Koerner, Thomas F., ed. (Orig.). 1985. pap. 12.00 (*0-88210-167-6*) Natl Assn Principals.

— The School-College Connection: Relationships & Standards. LC LB2350.S36. 89p. reprint ed. pap. 30.00 (*0-8357-4664-X*, 203760400008) Bks Demand.

— Student Learning Styles & Brain Behavior: Programs, Instrumentation, Research. LC 83-110391. (Illus.). 240p. reprint ed. pap. 74.40 (*0-8357-5551-7*, 203517000093) Bks Demand.

National Association of Securities Dealers Staff. The NASDAQ Handbook: A Complete Reference for Investors, Registered Reps., Researchers & Analysts. rev. ed. 525p. 1992. text 40.00 (*1-55738-403-7*, Irwn Prfssnl) McGraw-Hill Prof.

National Association of Social Workers Staff. Changing Services for Changing Clients. LC 69-18878. 139p. reprint ed. pap. 43.10 (*0-608-15257-9*, 205220500059) Bks Demand.

— Contemporary Developments in Social Work Research Methodology. LC HV0011.C7183. 61p. reprint ed. pap. 30.00 (*0-7837-6546-0*, 204568300007) Bks Demand.

— Impaired Social Worker Program: Resource Book. LC 87-24011. 43p. reprint ed. pap. 30.00 (*0-7837-6544-4*, 204568100007) Bks Demand.

— Social Group Work with Older People. Stein, Leon, ed. LC 79-8684. (Growing Old Ser.). 1980. reprint ed. lib. bdg. 18.95 (*0-405-12801-0*) Ayer.

***National Association of Social Workers Staff.** Social Work Speaks: National Association of Social Workers Policy Statements, 2000-2003. 5th ed. LC 00-28749. 2000. write for info. (*0-87101-318-5*) Natl Assn Soc Wkrs.

National Association of Social Workers Staff, jt. auth. see Freeman, Edith M.

National Association of Social Workers Staff, jt. auth. see Middleman, Ruth R.

National Association of State Budget Officers Staff. Budget Stability. 42p. (Orig.). Date not set. pap. 20.00 (*1-887253-02-5*) NASBD.

— 1995 State Expenditure Report. annuals (Illus.). 133p. 1996. pap. 35.00 (*1-887253-04-1*) NASBD.

— 1994 State Expenditure Report. (Illus.). 127p. (Orig.). 1995. pap. text 35.00 (*1-887253-01-7*) NASBD.

— Workforce Policies: State Activity & Innovations. 132p. (Orig.). 1995. pap. text 25.00 (*1-887253-00-9*) NASBD.

National Association of State Budget Officers Staff, jt. auth. see National Governors' Association Staff.

National Association of State Development Agencies. Directory of Incentives for Business Investment & Development in the United States: A State-by-State Guideline. 3rd ed. LC 86-157140. (Illus.). 790p. (C). 1991. pap. text 75.00 (*0-87766-501-X*) Urban Inst.

National Association of State Textbook Administrat, et al. Manufacturing Standards & Specifications for Textbooks. 1976. write for info. (*0-318-55921-8*) Textbk Specif.

National Association of Stove Manufacturers Staff, compiled by. Names of Stoves, Ranges, & Furnaces, 1876. 74p. 1992. reprint ed. pap. 12.50 (*0-9612204-1-4*) Autonomy Hse.

National Association of the Deaf Staff. Legal Rights: The Guide for Deaf & Hard of Hearing People. 4th rev. ed. LC 91-44372. (Illus.). 282p. 1992. pap. 19.95 (*1-56368-000-9*) Gallaudet Univ Pr.

National Association of Towns & Townships Staff. Accidents Will Happen: A Small Town Guide to Planning for Hazardous Materials Response. (Illus.). 64p. (Orig.). 1990. pap. 19.95 (*0-925532-03-7*) Natl Ctr Small Commun.

— Getting Out from Under: Underground Storage Tank Alternatives for Small Towns. (Illus.). 80p. (Orig.). 1991. pap. text 19.95 (*0-925532-07-X*) Natl Ctr Small Commun.

— Growing Our Own Jobs: A Small Town Guide to Creating Jobs Through Agricultural Diversification. (Illus.). 55p. (Orig.). 1988. pap. text 19.95 (*0-925532-05-3*) Natl Ctr Small Commun.

— Harvesting Hometown Jobs: A Small Town Guide to Recycling. (Illus.). 35p. (Orig.). 1985. pap. text 24.95 (*0-925532-04-5*) Natl Ctr Small Commun.

— Innovative Grassroots Financing: A Small Town Guide to Raising Funds & Cutting Costs. (Illus.). 64p. (Orig.). 1990. pap. text 19.95 (*0-925532-06-1*) Natl Ctr Small Commun.

— Treat It Right: A Local Official's Guide to Small Town Wastewater Treatment. (Illus.). 64p. (Orig.). 1989. pap. 19.95 (*0-925532-02-9*) Natl Ctr Small Commun.

— Why Waste a Second Chance? A Small Town Guide to Recycling. (Illus.). 48p. (Orig.). 1989. pap. text 19.95 (*0-925532-00-2*) Natl Ctr Small Commun.

National Association of Underwater Instructors Sta. Advanced Diving: Technology & Techniques. (Illus.). 304p. (gr. 13). 1994. pap. text 35.95 (*0-8151-6286-3*, 25366) Mosby Inc.

— Adventures in Scuba Diving: A Text for the Beginning Diver. (Illus.). 240p. (C). (gr. 13). 1994. pap. text 25.95 (*0-8151-6277-4*, 25356) Mosby Inc.

— NAUI Diving Log Book. 1973. 8.95 (*0-916974-05-7*, 80034) NAUI.

— NAUI Training Record. 1973. 8.95 (*0-916974-06-5*, 80010) NAUI.

National Association Of Underwater Instructors Sta. Scuba Rescue: Skills & Techniques. (Illus.). 208p. (gr. 13). 1995. pap. text 7.25 (*0-8151-6289-8*, 25369) Mosby Inc.

National Association of Unemployment Insurance Appellate Boards. Handbook for a Sufficient Hearing Record. 180p. 1996. pap. 15.00 (*0-9675816-1-3*, Pub. by NAUIAB) Natl Judicial Coll.

— Telephone Hearings Handbook. 150p. 1995. pap. 15.00 (*0-9675816-0-5*, Pub. by NAUIAB) Natl Judicial Coll.

***National Athletic Trainers' Association Staff.** Proceedings: National Athletic Trainers' Association, 1999 Athletic Training. 112p. (C). 1999. pap. text 12.00 (*1-55642-414-0*) SLACK Inc.

— Proceedings: National Athletic Trainers' Association 51st Annual Meeting. 332p. 2000. pap. 15.00 (*0-7360-3333-5*) Human Kinetics.

National Athletic Trainers' Association Staff. Proceedings of the National Athletic Trainers' Association 48th Annual Meeting & Clinical Symposia. 276p. 1997. pap. 20.00 (*0-88011-826-1*) Human Kinetics.

National Audubon Society, jt. see Smith, C. Lavett.

National Audubon Society Staff. Audubon Life-List Journal. (Illus.). 256p. 1999. 30.00 (*1-57965-133-X*, 85133) Artisan.

— Audubon Society Wildflowers. Borneman, John, ed. LC 96-1543. 1999. 20.00 (*0-517-20026-0*) Random.

— Audubon's Birds of America. (Illus.). 435p. 1989. lthr. 35000.00 (*0-89659-425-4*) Abbeville Pr.

— Audubon's Birds of America. 7 vols. deluxe ed. (Illus.). 435p. 1989. bond lthr. 35000.00 (*0-89659-427-0*) Abbeville Pr.

— The National Audubon Society: Speaking for Nature: A Century of Conservation. Line, Les, ed. (Illus.). 240p. 1999. 60.00 (*0-88363-799-5*, Pub. by H L Levin) Publishers Group.

— National Audubon Society Field Guide to the Mid-Atlantic States. LC 98-38191. (Illus.). 448p. 1999. 19.95 (*0-679-44682-6*) Knopf.

— National Audubon Society Field Guide to the Rocky Mountain States. LC 98-38192. (Illus.). 448p. 1999. 19.95 (*0-679-44681-8*) Knopf.

— National Audubon Society Field Guide to the Southeastern States: Alabama, Arkansas, Georgia, Kentucky, Lousiana, Mississippi, North Carolina, South Carolina & Tennessee. LC 99-27921. 1999. 19.95 (*0-679-44683-4*) Knopf.

— National Audubon Society Field Guide to the Southwestern States: Arizona, New Mexico, Nevada & Utah. LC 99-27920. 1999. 19.95 (*0-679-44680-X*) Knopf.

— National Audubon Society First Field Guides: Weather. LC 98-2938. (Audubon Society First Field Guide Ser.). (Illus.). 160p. (J). (gr. 3-7). 1998. pap. 10.95 (*0-590-05488-0*) Scholastic Inc.

— National Audubon Society Interactive CD-Rom Guide to North American Birds. 1996. cd-rom 56.95 (*0-679-76016-4*) Knopf.

National Audubon Society Staff, ed. Sibley Guide to Birds. (Audubon Society Nature Guides Ser.). (Illus.). 544p. 2000. 35.00 (*0-679-45122-6*) Knopf.

National Audubon Society Staff & Croxton Collaborative, Architects Staff. Audubon House: Building the Environmentally Responsible, Energy-Efficient Office. (Sustainable Design Ser.). (Illus.). 240p. 1994. 29.95 (*0-471-02496-1*) Wiley.

National Audubon Society Staff & Grassy, John. Mammals. LC 98-2939. (Audubon Society First Field Guide Ser.). (Illus.). 160p. (YA). (gr. 3-7). 1998. 17.95 (*0-590-05471-6*, Pub. by Scholastic Inc); vinyl bd. 10.95 (*0-590-05489-9*, Pub. by Scholastic Inc) Penguin Putnam.

National Audubon Society Staff & Kahl, Jonathan D. Weather. LC 98-2938. (Audubon Society First Field Guide Ser.). (Illus.). 160p. (YA). (gr. 3-7). 1998. 17.95 (*0-590-05469-4*, Pub. by Scholastic Inc) Penguin Putnam.

National Audubon Society Staff, jt. auth. see Alden, Peter.

National Audubon Society Staff, jt. auth. see Cassie, Brian.

National Audubon Society Staff, jt. auth. see Hood, Susan.

National Audubon Society Staff, jt. auth. see Ricciuti, Edward R.

National Audubon Society Staff, jt. auth. see Smith, C. Lavett.

National Audubon Society Staff, jt. auth. see Weidensaul, Scott.

National Audubon Society Staff, jt. auth. see Wilsdon, Christina.

National Aviation Weather Services Committee & National Research Council Staff. Aviation Weather Services: A Call for Federal Leadership & Action. LC 95-72006. 120p. 1995. pap. 30.00 (*0-309-05380-3*) Natl Acad Pr.

National Ballet School Staff. The Ballet Book: The Young Performer's Guide to Classical Dance. (Illus.). 144p. (YA). (gr. 3-8). 1999. lib. bdg. 19.95 (*1-55209-352-2*) Firefly Bks Ltd.

***National Bankruptcy Review Commission (U. S.).** Bankruptcy: The Next Twenty Years: National Bankruptcy Review Commission Final Report. LC 00-21683. 2000. reprint ed. 150.00 (*1-57588-626-X*) W S Hein.

National Basketball Association Staff. Official NBA Finals Retrospective 1999, Vol. 1. 1999. pap. 19.95 (*0-8129-3309-5*, Times Bks) Crown Pub Group.

***National Basketball Association Staff.** Official NBA Basketball Encyclopedia. (Illus.). 992p. 2000. 50.00 (*0-385-50130-7*) Doubleday.

National Board for Prices & Incomes Staff. Pay & Productivity in the Water Supply Industry. LC 79-560507. (Great Britain, Parliament, Papers by Command). vi, 87 p. 1970. write for info. (*0-10-144340-4*) U Pr of Amer.

National Board for Professional Teaching Standards, jt. auth. see Division of Early Childhood, Council on Exceptiona.

National Board of Employment, Education & Training. The Land Still Speaks: A Review of Aboriginal & Torres Strait Islander Language Maintenance & Development Needs & Activities. 290p. 1996. pap. 24.95 (*0-644-45945-X*, Pub. by Aust Gov Pub) Accents Pubns.

National Board of the Changing Relations Project S & Bach, Robert L. Changing Relations: Newcomers & Established Residents in U. S. Communities : A Report to the ford Foundation by the National Board of the Changing Relations Project. LC 92-46770. 1993. write for info. (*0-916584-48-8*) Ford Found.

National Book Foundation Staff. National Book Awards: 48 Years of Literary Excellence, Winners & Finalists, 1950-1997. 2nd ed. 1998. pap. 10.00 (*1-889099-24-4*) Natl Bk Fnd.

National Book League (Great Britain) Staff, jt. auth. see Ray, Colin H.

National Book Trust Staff, jt. auth. see Hoffman, Haya.

National Broiler Staff. The Chicken Cookbook. 1997. mass mkt. 4.99 (*0-553-85185-3*) Bantam.

— Chicken Cookbook. rev. ed. 1995. pap. 5.99 (*0-440-22177-3*) Bantam.

National Broiler Staff. The Chicken Cookbook. 4th ed. 128p. 1997. mass mkt. 1.11 (*0-553-57908-8*) Bantam.

National Building Agency Staff. Common Building Defects: Diagnosis & Remedy. LC 87-54040. (Illus.). 197p. 1992. pap. 61.10 (*0-608-05246-9*, 206578300001) Bks Demand.

National Building Museum Staff & Thomas, Bernice L. America's 5 & 10 Cent Stores: The Kress Legacy. LC 97-4171. (Illus.). 200p. 1997. pap. 21.95 (*0-471-18195-1*) Wiley.

National Bureau of Economic Research, Bureau of th. Seasonal Analysis of Economic Time Series. Zellner, Arnold, ed. LC 78-606108. (Economic Research Report Ser.: No. ER-1). 498p. reprint ed. pap. 154.40 (*0-608-15353-2*, 205636900061) Bks Demand.

National Bureau of Economic Research Conference on. The Economics of Physician & Patient Behavior. Fuchs, Victor R. & Newhouse, Joseph P., eds. LC RA0410.53.N3. (Journal of Human Resources Ser.: Vol. 13, Supplement). 262p. reprint ed. pap. 81.30 (*0-608-15349-4*, 205636700061) Bks Demand.

National Bureau of Economic Research Staff. The Measurement & Behavior of Unemployment: A Conference of the Universities-National Bureau Committee for Economic Research. LC 57-5442. (National Bureau of Economic Research Ser.: Vol. 8). (Illus.). 615p. reprint ed. pap. 190.70 (*0-608-11576-2*, 201964100013) Bks Demand.

— Measurement & Interpretation of Job Vacancies. (Other Conferences Ser.: No. 5). 603p. 1966. reprint ed. 156.80 (*0-87014-471-5*) Natl Bur Econ Res.

— NBER Macroeconomics Annual, 1986. Fischer, Stanley, ed. LC 87-642897. 417p. reprint ed. pap. 129.30 (*0-8357-7930-0*, 205233000002) Bks Demand.

— Transportation Economics. (Universities-National Bureau Conference Ser.: No. 17). 482p. 1965. 124.80 (*0-87014-308-5*) Natl Bur Econ Res.

— Transportation Economics: A Conference of the Universities-National Bureau Committee for Economic Research. LC 65-11221. (National Bureau of Economic Research. Special Conference Ser.: No. 17). (Illus.). 480p. reprint ed. pap. 148.80 (*0-8357-7584-4*, 205690500096) Bks Demand.

National Bureau of Economic Research Staff, jt. auth. see Feenstra, Robert C.

National Bureau of Standards, Cryogenics Division. Grain Boundary Segregation in Copper & Copper Alloys. 59p. 1975. 8.85 (*0-317-34529-X*, 237) Intl Copper.

National Bureau of Standards Staff. Diffusion Rate Data & Mass Transport Phenomena for Cooper Systems. (INCRA Monographs). 322p. 1977. 20.00 (*0-317-42799-7*) Intl Copper.

— Low Temperature Mechanical Properties of Copper & Selected Copper Alloys. 165p. 1967. 24.75 (*0-317-34537-0*, 50) Intl Copper.

National Bureau Special Staff, jt. auth. see Committee on Recent Economic Changes of the Presid.

National Business Employment Staff, ed. see Tye, Joe.

National Business Employment Weekly Staff. National Business Employment Weekly's Guide to Self-Employment. LC 95-51321. 266p. 1996. pap. 12.95 (*0-471-10918-5*) Wiley.

***National Business Employment Weekly Staff & Besson, Taunee S.** Resumes. 3rd ed. LC 98-53411. (National Business Employment Weekly Premier Guides Ser.). (Illus.). 320p. 1999. pap. 12.95 (*0-471-32259-8*) Wiley.

***National Business Employment Weekly Staff & Hirsch, Arlene S.** National Business Employment Weekly Guide to Interviewing. 3rd ed. LC 98-33164. (National Business Employment Weekly Premier Guides Ser.). (Illus.). 240p. 1999. pap. 12.95 (*0-471-32257-1*) Wiley.

National Business Employment Weekly Staff & Hirsch, Arlene S. National Business Employment Weekly Interviewing. 288p. 1997. pap. 5.99 (*0-471-19118-3*) Wiley.

National Business Employment Weekly Staff & Tye, Joe. Personal Best: 1001 Great Ideas for Achieving Success in Your Career. LC 96-20398. 320p. 1996. pap. 12.95 (*0-471-14888-1*) Wiley.

National Cambridge Society Staff. Colors in Cambridge. (Illus.). 128p. 1997. 19.95 (*0-89145-270-2*, 1523) Collector Bks.

National Campaign for Freedom of Expression. The NCFE Handbook to Understanding, Preparing for & Responding to Challenges to Freedom of Artistic Expression. Publishing Resources Staff, ed. LC 98-67316. (Illus.). 50p. 1998. pap. 15.00 (*0-9666029-0-0*) Natl Free Expr.

***National Campaign to Prevent Teen Pregnancy Staff.** Evaluating Abstinence - Only Interventions. 21p. 1998. pap. 10.00 (*1-58671-020-6*) Natl Cpgn Teen Preg.

— Not Just for Girls: Involving Boys & Men in Teen Pregnancy Prevention. 35p. 1997. pap. 15.00 (*1-58671-021-4*) Natl Cpgn Teen Preg.

— Snapshots from the Front Line: Lessons about Teen Pregnancy Prevention from States & Communities. (Illus.). 16p. 1997. pap. 5.00 (*1-58671-025-7*) Natl Cpgn Teen Preg.

— Snapshots from the Front Line II: Lessons from Programs That Involve Parents & Other Adults in Preventing Teen Pregnancy. (Illus.). 22p. 1998. pap. 5.00 (*1-58671-026-5*) Natl Cpgn Teen Preg.

— Start Early, Stay Late: Linking Youth Development & Teen Pregnancy Prevention. (Illus.). 25p. 1998. pap. 5.00 (*1-58671-018-4*) Natl Cpgn Teen Preg.

— Where Are the Adults? The Attitudes of Parents, Teachers, Clergy, Coaches & Youth Workers on Teen Pregnancy: A Focus Group Report. 58p. 1998. pap. 10.00 (*1-58671-014-1*) Natl Cpgn Teen Preg.

— While the Adults Are Arguing, the Teens Are Getting Pregnant: Overcoming Conflict in Teen Pregnancy Prevention. 32p. 1998. pap. 10.00 (*1-58671-019-2*) Natl Cpgn Teen Preg.

***National Campaign to Prevent Teen Pregnancy Staff, ed.** Voices Carry: Teens Speak Out on Sex & Teen Pregnancy. (Illus.). 35p. (YA). 2000. pap. 5.00 (*1-58671-030-3*) Natl Cpgn Teen Preg.

***National Campaign to Prevent Teen Pregnancy Staff, et al.** Trends in Sexual Activity & Contraceptive Use among Teens. 25p. (C). 1999. pap. 5.00 (*1-58671-029-X*) Natl Cpgn Teen Preg.

National Cancer Foundation, Inc. Staff, jt. auth. see Cancer Care, Inc. Staff.

***National Cancer Policy Board Staff, et al.** Ensuring Quality Cancer Care. Hewitt, Maria E. & Simone, Joseph V., eds. LC 99-6488. 256p. 1999. pap. 34.95 (*0-309-06480-5*, Joseph Henry Pr) Natl Acad Pr.

National Cargo Bureau, Inc. Staff. General Information for Grain Loading. 2nd ed. Boyle, Edward, ed. (Illus.). 114p. 1994. pap. text 7.50 (*0-9627009-1-6*) Natl Cargo Bureau.

National Catholic Development Conference Staff. Bibliography of Fund Raising & Philanthropy. 2nd ed. LC 82-81523. 76p. 1982. 22.50 (*0-9603196-1-1*) Natl Cath Dev.

National Catholic Education Association Staff & National Conference of Catechetical Leadership, &. Those Who Hear You, Hear Me: A Resource for Bishops & Diocesan Education-Catechetical Leaders. 44p. (Orig.). 1995. pap. text 5.95 (*1-55586-051-6*) US Catholic.

National Cattlemens Beef Association & Nat. Pork C. The Guide to Identifying Meat Cuts. rev. ed. (Illus.). 56p. 1998. pap. write for info. (*0-88700-020-7*) Natl Live Stock.

National Center Construction Staff. Instrumentation Level 1: Perfect Bound Without Core, Trainee Guide. (C). 1996. pap. text 50.00 (*0-13-245366-5*) P-H.

— Instrumentation Level 3: Trainee Guide. (C). 1996. pap. text 80.00 (*0-13-245531-5*) P-H.

— Instrumentation Level 4: Trainee Guide. (C). 1996. per. 80.00 (*0-13-245556-0*) P-H.

— Millwright: Trainee Guide, Level 4. (C). 1996. per. 80.00 (*0-13-245812-8*) P-H.

National Center for Children in Poverty Staff. Child Welfare Reform. 58p. (Orig.). 1991. pap. text 8.00 (*0-926582-06-2*) NCCP.

National Center for Construction & Research Staff. Glazier: Trainee Guide, Level 2. (Wheels of Learning Ser.). (C). 1996. student ed., ring bd. 55.00 (*0-13-265018-5*) P-H.

— Glazier: Trainee Guide, Level 3. (Trainee Ser.). (C). 1996. student ed., ring bd. 55.00 (*0-13-265026-6*) P-H.

National Center for Construction Education & Reseach Staff. Carpentry: Instructor's Guide, Level 2. (Wheels of Learning Ser.). (C). 1996. teacher ed., ring bd. 80.00 (*0-13-265091-6*) P-H.

— Carpentry: Instructor's Guide, Level 3. (Wheels of Learning Ser.). (C). 1996. teacher ed., ring bd. 80.00 (*0-13-265109-2*) P-H.

— Carpentry: Trainee Guide, Level 4. (Wheels of Learning Ser.). (C). 1996. student ed., ring bd. 80.00 (*0-13-264821-0*) P-H.

— Core Curriculum. (Wheels of Learning Ser.). (C). 1996. pap. text, teacher ed. 50.00 (*0-13-530247-1*) P-H.

— Core Curriculum Basic Construction Skill: Instructor's Guide. (Wheels of Learning Ser.). (C). 1996. teacher ed., ring bd. 50.00 (*0-13-265125-4*) P-H.

— Electrical, Level 3. (Wheels of Learning Ser.). (C). 1996. pap. text, teacher ed. 80.00 (*0-13-530502-0*) P-H.

— Exploring Careers in Construction. 94p. (C). 1998. pap. text 12.00 (*0-13-910159-4*, Macmillan Coll) P-H.

— Glazier, Level 1. (Wheels Ser.). (C). 1996. teacher ed., ring bd. 75.00 (*0-13-265190-4*) P-H.

An Asterisk (*) at the beginning of an entry indicates that the title is appearing for the first time.

N

— The National Home & Hospice Care Survey: 1992 Summary. LC 94-1779. (Vital & Health Statistics Ser.: Series 13, No. 117). 110p. 7.00 (*0-614-02910-4*, 017-022-01271-5) Natl Ctr Health Stats.
— National Hospital Discharge Survey: Annual Summary, 1992. LC 94-1779. (Vital & Health Statistics Ser.: Series 13, No. 119). 63p. 4.75 (*0-614-02912-0*, 017-022-01274-0) Natl Ctr Health Stats.
— National Medical Ambulatory Medical Care Survey, 1991: Summary. LC 94-1777. (Vital & Health Statistics Ser.: Series 13, No. 116). 110p. 6.50 (*0-614-02909-0*, 017-022-01288-3) Natl Ctr Health Stats.
— Plan & Operation of the 3rd National Health & Nutrition Examination Survey, 1988-94. LC 94-1308. (Vital & Health Statistics Ser.: Series 1, No. 32). 407p. 25.00 (*0-614-02899-X*, 017-022-01260-0) Natl Ctr Health Stats.

National Center For Health Statistics Staff. Prenatal Care in the United States, 1980-94. LC 96-9472. (Vital & Health Statistics Ser.: Series 21, No. 54). 1996. write for info. (*0-8406-0518-8*) Natl Ctr Health Stats.

National Center for Health Statistics Staff. State Definitions & Reporting Requirements for Live Births, Fetal Deaths & Induced Termination of Pregnancy. LC 97-29256. 1997. write for info. (*0-8406-0534-X*, (PHS) 98-1119) Natl Ctr Health Stats.

***National Center for Health Statistics Staff.** Trends in Pregnancies & Pregnancy Rates by Outcome: Estimates for the United States, 1976-96. LC 99-88898. (Vital & Health Statistics Ser.). 1999. pap. write for info. (*0-8406-0561-7*) Natl Ctr Health Stats.

National Center for Health Statistics Staff. United States Decennial Life Tables for 1989-91, Vol. 1. LC 97-29284. 1997. write for info. (*0-8406-0533-1*) Natl Ctr Health Stats.
— Vital & Health Statistics: Proceedings of the International Collaborative Effort on Automating Mortality Statistics. LC 98-25577. (DHHS Publications). 1998. write for info. (*0-8406-0548-X*) Natl Ctr Health Stats.
— Vital Statistics of the United States, 1989: Mortality, Parts A & B, Vol. II. LC 93-1101. (Vital Statistics of the United States Ser.). 730p. 48.00 (*0-614-02950-3*, 017-022-01234-1) Natl Ctr Health Stats.
— Vital Statistics of the United States, 1989: Natality, Vol. I. LC 93-1100. (Vital Statistics of the United States Ser.). 508p. 43.00 (*0-614-02949-X*, 017-022-01233-2) Natl Ctr Health Stats.
— Vital Statistics of the United States, 1990 Life Tables, Vol. I. LC 94-1104. 20p. 2.25 (*0-614-02951-1*, 017-022-01266-9) Natl Ctr Health Stats.

National Center for Health Statistics Staff & National Survey of Family Growth Staff. Surgical Sterilization in the United States: Prevalence & Characteristics, 1965-95. LC 98-22554. (DHHS Publication Statistics Ser.). 1998. 4.00 (*0-8406-0547-1*) Natl Ctr Health Stats.

National Center for Health Statistics Staff, jt. auth. see Anderson, Robert N.

National Center for Health Statistics Staff, jt. auth. see Botman, Steven.

National Center for Health Statistics Staff, jt. auth. see Rosenberg, Harry M.

National Center for History in the Schools Staff, et al. National Standards for History. LC 97-152950. ix, 225p. 1996. write for info. (*0-9633218-4-6*) Natl Ctr Hist.

***National Center for Nonprofit Boards Staff.** Chief Executive Compensation: A Guide for Nonprofit Boards. 20p. 1999. pap. text 16.00 (*0-925299-96-0*) Natl Ctr Nonprofit.

National Center for Pastoral Leadership Staff. Covenant for Renewal: A Pastoral Vision for Ministry in the 21st Century. 48p. 1996. pap. 6.95 (*0-8245-1644-3*) Crossroad NY.

National Center for Research in Vocational Educati. Accept Responsibility Module, Connections: School & Work Transitions - Work Skills-Work Maturity Skills. 1987. write for info. (*0-318-67156-5*, SP100CB12) Ctr Educ Trng Employ.
— Adult Career Guidance, Options: Expanding Educational Services for Adults. 1987. 12.95 (*0-317-03853-2*, SP500FA) Ctr Educ Trng Employ.
— Aid Professional Growth Module, Competency-Based Career Guidance (CBCG) - Category D: Operating. 1985. 7.95 (*0-317-03854-0*, CG100D02) Ctr Educ Trng Employ.
— Apply for Jobs Module, Connections: School & Work Transitions - Work Skills-Job Search Skills. 1987. write for info. (*0-318-67157-3*, SP100CB04) Ctr Educ Trng Employ.
— Apprenticeship in Employment & Training Programs: An Action Planning Guidebook. 83p. 1983. 6.75 (*0-318-22035-0*, RD221) Ctr Educ Trng Employ.
— Basics: Bridging Vocational & Academic Skills. 1987. 198.00 (*0-318-35278-8*, SP 300) Ctr Educ Trng Employ.
— The Bridger's Guide, Basics: Bridging Vocational & Academic Skills. 1987. 75.00 (*0-317-03855-9*, SP300A) Ctr Educ Trng Employ.
— Build a Guidance Program Planning Model Module, Competency-Based Career Guidance (CBCG) - Category A: Guidance Program Planning. 1985. 7.95 (*0-317-03856-7*, CG100A05) Ctr Educ Trng Employ.
— Career Passport Leader's Guide, Connections: School & Work Transitions - Career Passports. 1987. 9.50 (*0-317-03857-5*, SP100DA) Ctr Educ Trng Employ.
— Career Passport Student Workbook, Connections: School & Work Transitions - Career Passport. 1987. write for info. (*0-318-67158-1*, SP100DB) Ctr Educ Trng Employ.
— Career Portfolio, Connections: School & Work Transitions - Employment File. 1987. write for info. (*0-318-67159-X*, SP100EA02) Ctr Educ Trng Employ.
— Case Studies of Programs Serving Adults, Options: Expanding Educational Services for Adults. 1987. 39.95 (*0-317-03858-3*, SP500G) Ctr Educ Trng Employ.
— Certificates of Completion, PACE: A Program for Acquiring Competence in Entrepreneurship, 3 levels. rev. ed. 1983. 20.00 (*0-317-03859-1*) Ctr Educ Trng Employ.
— Certificates of Completion, PACE Level 1: A Program for Acquiring Competence in Entrepreneurship, 3 levels. rev. ed. 1983. 5.00 (*0-317-06025-2*, RD240EA) Ctr Educ Trng Employ.
— Certificates of Completion, PACE Level 2: A Program for Acquiring Competence in Entrepreneurship, 3 levels. rev. ed. 1983. 5.00 (*0-317-06026-0*, RD240EB) Ctr Educ Trng Employ.
— Certificates of Completion, PACE Level 3: A Program for Acquiring Competence in Entrepreneurship, 3 levels. rev. ed. 1983. 5.00 (*0-317-06027-9*, RD240C) Ctr Educ Trng Employ.
— Choosing the Type of Ownership Module, PACE: A Program for Acquiring Competence in Entrepreneurship, 3 levels. rev. ed. 1983. 2.50 (*0-317-06028-7*) Ctr Educ Trng Employ.
— Choosing the Type of Ownership Module, PACE Level 1: A Program for Acquiring Competence in Entrepreneurship, 3 levels. rev. ed. 1983. 2.50 (*0-317-06029-5*, RD240AB5) Ctr Educ Trng Employ.
— Choosing the Type of Ownership Module, PACE Level 2: A Program for Acquiring Competence in Entrepreneurship, 3 levels. rev. ed. 1983. 2.50 (*0-317-06030-9*, RD240BB5) Ctr Educ Trng Employ.
— Choosing the Type of Ownership Module, PACE Level 3: A Program for Acquiring Competence in Entrepreneurship, 3 levels. rev. ed. 1983. 2.50 (*0-317-06031-7*, RD240CB5) Ctr Educ Trng Employ.
— Collaborate with the Community Module, Competency-Based Career Guidance (CBCG) - Category A: Guidance Program Planning. 1985. 7.95 (*0-317-03860-5*, CG100A03) Ctr Educ Trng Employ.
— Communicate & Use Evaluation-Based Decisions Module, Competency-Based Career Guidance (CBCG) - Category E: Evaluating. 1985. 6.95 (*0-317-03861-3*, CG100E02) Ctr Educ Trng Employ.
— Communicate Effectively Module, Connections: School & Work Transitions - Work Skills-Work Maturity Skills. 1987. write for info. (*0-318-67160-3*, SP100CB11) Ctr Educ Trng Employ.
— A Compendium of What Works for Vocational Educators in Dropout Prevention. 1988. 11.50 (*0-317-03862-1*, SP700DP03) Ctr Educ Trng Employ.
— Competency-Based Career Guidance (CBCG) Modules. 1985. 245.00 (*0-317-03863-X*, CG100) Ctr Educ Trng Employ.
— Complying with Government Regulations Module, PACE: A Program for Acquiring Competence in Entrepreneurship, 3 levels. rev. ed. 1983. 2.50 (*0-317-06032-5*); 2.50 (*0-317-06033-3*, RD240AB10); 2.50 (*0-317-06034-1*, RD240BB10); 2.50 (*0-317-06035-X*, RD240CB10) Ctr Educ Trng Employ.
— Conduct Computerized Guidance Module, Competency-Based Career Guidance (CBCG) - Category C: Implementing. 1985. 6.95 (*0-317-03864-8*, CG100C03) Ctr Educ Trng Employ.
— Conduct Placement & Referral Activities Module, Competency-Based Career Guidance (CBCG) - Category C: Implementing. 1985. 7.95 (*0-317-03866-4*, CG100C10) Ctr Educ Trng Employ.
— Conduct Staff Development Activities Module, Competency-Based Guidance (CBCG) - Category C: Implementing. 1985. 6.95 (*0-317-03865-6*, CG100B04) Ctr Educ Trng Employ.
— Connections: School & Work Transitions. 1987. 350.00 (*0-318-35279-6*, SP 100PR) Ctr Educ Trng Employ.
— The Connector's Guide, Connections: School & Work Transitions. 1987. 39.95 (*0-317-03867-2*, SP100AA) Ctr Educ Trng Employ.
— Cooperate with Others Module, Connections: School & Work Transitions - Work Skills-Work Maturity Skills. 1987. write for info. (*0-318-67161-1*, SP100CB13) Ctr Educ Trng Employ.
— Coordinate Career Resource Centers Module, Competency-Based Career Guidance (CBCG) - Category C: Implementing. 1985. 7.95 (*0-317-03868-0*, CG100C05) Ctr Educ Trng Employ.
— Counsel Individuals & Groups Module, Competency-Based Career Guidance (CBCG) - Category C: Implementing. 1985. 7.95 (*0-317-03869-9*, CG100C01) Ctr Educ Trng Employ.
— Create & Use an Individual Career Development Plan Module, Competency-Based Career Guidance (CBCG) - Category C: Implementing. 1985. 6.95 (*0-317-03870-2*, CG100C12) Ctr Educ Trng Employ.
— Credentials for Employment, Connections: School & Work Transitions - Employment File. 1987. write for info. (*0-318-67162-X*, SP100EA01) Ctr Educ Trng Employ.
— Dealing with Legal Issues Module, PACE: A Program for Acquiring Competence in Entrepreneurship, 3 levels. rev. ed. 1983. 2.50 (*0-317-06036-8*); 2.50 (*0-317-06037-6*, RD240AB9); 2.50 (*0-317-06038-4*, RD240BB9); 2.50 (*0-318-67163-8*, RD240CB9) Ctr Educ Trng Employ.
— Determine Client & Environment Needs Module, Competency-Based Career Guidance (CBCG) - Category A: Guidance Program Planning. 1985. 7.95 (*0-317-03871-0*, CG100A06) Ctr Educ Trng Employ.
— Determining Your Potential As an Entrepreneur Module, PACE: A Program for Acquiring Competence in Entrepreneurship, 3 levels. rev. ed. 1983. 2.50 (*0-318-67164-6*, RD240AB2); 2.50 (*0-317-06041-4*, RD240BB2); 2.50 (*0-317-06042-2*, RD240CB2); write for info. (*0-318-67165-4*, RD240AB2) Ctr Educ Trng Employ.
— Develop a Work Experience Program Module, Competency-Based Career Guidance (CBCG) - Category C: Implementing. 1985. 6.95 (*0-317-03873-7*, CG100C07) Ctr Educ Trng Employ.
— Develop Ethical & Legal Standards Module, Competency-Based Career Guidance (CBCG) - Category C: Implementing. 1985. 6.95 (*0-317-04751-5*, CG100C19) Ctr Educ Trng Employ.
— Developing a Curriculum in Response to Change, Options: Expanding Educational Services for Adults. 1987. 39.95 (*0-317-03874-5*, SP500E) Ctr Educ Trng Employ.
— Developing the Business Plan Module, PACE: A Program for Acquiring Competence in Entrepreneurship, 3 levels. rev. ed. 1983. 2.50 (*0-317-06043-0*, RD240AB3); 2.50 (*0-317-06044-9*, RD240BB3); 2.50 (*0-317-06045-7*, 2D240CB3) Ctr Educ Trng Employ.
— Dignity in the Workplace: A Labor Studies Curriculum Guide for Vocational Educators' Connections: School & Work Transitions - Coordinator's Resources. 1987. 18.50 (*0-317-03875-3*, SP100AC01) Ctr Educ Trng Employ.
— Dignity in the Workplace: A Student's Guide to Labor Unions, Connections: School & Work Transitions - Coordinator's Resources. 1987. 7.75 (*0-317-03876-1*, SP100AC02) Ctr Educ Trng Employ.
— Educator's Guide, Options: Expanding Educational Services for Adults. 1987. 5.25 (*0-317-03877-X*, SP500A) Ctr Educ Trng Employ.
— The Employer's Choice, Connections: School & Work Transitions, Set. 1987. 84.00 (*0-317-03879-6*, SP100BX) Ctr Educ Trng Employ.
— Employer's Choice Resource Manual, Connections: School & Work Transitions. 1987. 25.50 (*0-317-03880-X*, SP100BA01) Ctr Educ Trng Employ.
— Enhance Understanding of Individuals with Disabilities Module, Competency-Based Career Guidance (CBCG) - Category C: Implementing. 1985. 6.95 (*0-317-03881-8*, CG100C14) Ctr Educ Trng Employ.
— Ensure Program Operations Module, Competency-Based Career Guidance (CBCG) - Category D: Operating. 1985. 6.95 (*0-317-03882-6*, CG100D01) Ctr Educ Trng Employ.
— Es Tu Vida...Toma Control: It's Your Life...Take Charge Student Workbook, Dropout Prevention. (SPA.). 1988. write for info. (*0-318-67166-2*, SP700TC02) Ctr Educ Trng Employ.
— Establish a Career Development Theory Module, Competency-Based Career Guidance (CBCG) - Category A: Guidance Program Planning. 1985. 7.95 (*0-317-04752-3*, CG100A04) Ctr Educ Trng Employ.
— Evaluate Guidance Activities Module, Competency-Based Career Guidance (CBCG) - Category E: Evaluating. 1985. 7.95 (*0-317-04611-X*, CG100E01) Ctr Educ Trng Employ.
— Exhibit Positive Work Attitudes Module, Connections: School & Work Transitions - Work Skills-Work Maturity Skills. 1987. write for info. (*0-318-67167-0*, SP100CB08) Ctr Educ Trng Employ.
— Facilitate Follow-up & Follow-Through Module, Competency-Based Career Guidance (CBCG) - Category C: Implementing. 1985. 8.95 (*0-317-03885-0*, CG100C11) Ctr Educ Trng Employ.
— Financing the Business Module, PACE Level 1: A Program for Acquiring Competence in Entrepreneurship, 3 levels. rev. ed. 1983. 2.50 (*0-318-67168-9*, RD240AB8) Ctr Educ Trng Employ.
— Financing the Business Module, PACE Level 2: A Program for Acquiring Competence in Entrepreneurship, 3 levels. rev. ed. 1983. 2.50 (*0-318-67169-7*, RD240BB8) Ctr Educ Trng Employ.
— Financing the Business Module, PACE Level 3: A Program for Acquiring Competence in Entrepreneurship, 3 levels. rev. ed. 1983. 2.50 (*0-318-67170-0*, RD240CB8) Ctr Educ Trng Employ.
— Handle Job Offers Module, Connections: School & Work - Work Skills-Job Search Skills. 1987. write for info. (*0-318-67171-9*, SP100CB06) Ctr Educ Trng Employ.
— Help Ethnic Minorities with Career Guidance Module, Competency-Based Career Guidance (CBCG) - Category C: Implementing. 1985. 7.95 (*0-317-04612-8*, CG100C15) Ctr Educ Trng Employ.
— Helping Process Overview Guidebook, Dropout Prevention. 1988. 6.50 (*0-317-03888-5*, SP700HP01) Ctr Educ Trng Employ.
— The Helping Process Professional Set, Dropout Prevention. 1988. 39.50 (*0-317-03887-7*, SP700HP) Ctr Educ Trng Employ.
— Identify & Plan for Guidance Program Change Module, Competency-Based Career Guidance (CBCG) - Category A: Guidance Program Planning. 1985. write for info. (*0-318-67172-7*) Ctr Educ Trng Employ.
— Implementation Guide: Basics: Bridging Vocational & Academic Skills - The Bridger's Guide. 1987. 10.95 (*0-317-03890-7*, SP300AA) Ctr Educ Trng Employ.
— Improve Public Relations & Community Involvement Module, Competency-Based Career Guidance (CBCG) - Category B: Supporting. 1985. 6.95 (*0-317-03891-5*, CB100B03) Ctr Educ Trng Employ.
— Influence Legislation Module, Competency-Based Career Guidance (CBCG) - Category B: Supporting. 1985. 19.95 (*0-317-03893-1*, CG100B01) Ctr Educ Trng Employ.
— Infuse Curriculum Plus Based Guidance Module, Competency-Based Career Guidance (CBCG) - Category C: Implementing. 1985. 7.95 (*0-317-03894-X*, CG100C04) Ctr Educ Trng Employ.
— Instructional Materials Development, Basics: Bridging Vocational & Academic Skills - Instructional Program Development. 1987. 13.95 (*0-317-04613-6*, SP300DA) Ctr Educ Trng Employ.
— Instructional Program Development, Basics: Bridging Vocational & Academic Skills. 1987. 50.00 (*0-317-03895-8*, SP300D) Ctr Educ Trng Employ.
— Instructor Guide, PACE Level 1: A Program for Acquiring Competence in Entrepreneurship, 3 levels. rev. ed. 1983. 14.50 (*0-317-06049-X*, RD240AA) Ctr Educ Trng Employ.
— Instructor Guide, PACE Level 2: A Program for Acquiring Competence in Entrepreneurship, 3 levels. rev. ed. 1983. 14.50 (*0-317-06050-3*, RD240BA) Ctr Educ Trng Employ.
— Instructor Guide, PACE Level 3: A Program for Acquiring Competence in Entrepreneurship, 3 levels. rev. ed. 1983. 14.50 (*0-317-06051-1*, RD240CA) Ctr Educ Trng Employ.
— Interview for Jobs Module, Connections: School & Work Transitions - Work Skills-Job Search Skills. 1987. write for info. (*0-318-67173-5*, SP100CB05) Ctr Educ Trng Employ.
— Introduction to Connections, Connections: School & Work Transitions. 1987. 25.00 (*0-317-03897-4*, SP100AB) Ctr Educ Trng Employ.
— It's Your Life . . . Take Charge Professional Set, Dropout Prevention. 1988. 49.50 (*0-317-03898-2*, SP700TC) Ctr Educ Trng Employ.
— It's Your Life . . . Take Charge Student Workbook, Dropout Prevention. 1988. write for info. (*0-318-67174-3*, SP700C01) Ctr Educ Trng Employ.
— Job Placement in Employment & Training Programs: An Action Planning Guidebook. 121p. 1983. 9.00 (*0-318-22136-5*, RD218) Ctr Educ Trng Employ.
— Keeping the Business Records Module, PACE Level 1: A Program for Acquiring Competence in Entrepreneurship, 3 levels. rev. ed. 1983. 2.50 (*0-317-06052-X*, RD240AB15) Ctr Educ Trng Employ.
— Keeping the Business Records Module, PACE Level 2: A Program for Acquiring Competence in Entrepreneurship, 3 levels. rev. ed. 1983. 2.50 (*0-317-06053-8*, RD240BB15) Ctr Educ Trng Employ.
— Keeping the Business Records Module, PACE Level 3: A Program for Acquiring Competence in Entrepreneurship, 3 levels. rev. ed. 1983. 2.50 (*0-317-06054-6*, RD240CB15) Ctr Educ Trng Employ.
— Linking with Employers, Options: Expanding Educational Services for Adults. 1987. 39.95 (*0-317-03900-8*, SP500D) Ctr Educ Trng Employ.
— Literacy Enhancement for Adults, Options: Expanding Educational Services for Adults. 1987. 9.50 (*0-317-03901-6*, SP500FB) Ctr Educ Trng Employ.
— Locating the Business Module, PACE Level 1: A Program for Acquiring Competence in Entrepreneurship, 3 levels. rev. ed. 1983. 2.50 (*0-318-67175-1*, RD240AB7) Ctr Educ Trng Employ.
— Locating the Business Module, PACE Level I: A Program for Acquiring Competence in Entrepreneurship, 3 levels. rev. ed. 1983. write for info. (*0-318-67176-X*, RD240AB7) Ctr Educ Trng Employ.
— Locating the Business Module, PACE Level 2: A Program for Acquiring Competence in Entrepreneurship, 3 levels. rev. ed. 1983. 2.50 (*0-317-06056-2*, RD240BB7) Ctr Educ Trng Employ.
— Locating the Business Module, PACE Level 3: A Program for Acquiring Competence in Entrepreneurship, 3 levels. rev. ed. 1983. 2.50 (*0-317-06057-0*, RD240CB7) Ctr Educ Trng Employ.
— Managing Customer Credit & Collections Module, PACE: A Program for Acquiring Competence in Entrepreneurship, Level 1. rev. ed. 1983. 2.50 (*0-317-06061-9*, RD240AB17) Ctr Educ Trng Employ.
— Managing Customer Credit & Collections Module, PACE: A Program for Acquiring Competence in Entrepreneurship, Level 2. rev. ed. 1983. 2.50 (*0-317-06062-7*, RD240BB17) Ctr Educ Trng Employ.
— Managing Customer Credit & Collections Module, PACE: A Program for Acquiring Competence in Entrepreneurship, Level 3. rev. ed. 1983. 2.50 (*0-318-67177-8*, RD240CB17) Ctr Educ Trng Employ.
— Managing Human Resources Module, PACE Level 1: A Program for Acquiring Competence in Entrepreneurship, 3 levels. rev. ed. 1983. 2.50 (*0-317-06067-8*, RD240AB12) Ctr Educ Trng Employ.
— Managing Human Resources Module, PACE Level 2: A Program for Acquiring Competence in Entrepreneurship, 3 levels. rev. ed. 1983. 2.50 (*0-317-06068-6*, RD240BB12) Ctr Educ Trng Employ.
— Managing Human Resources Module, PACE Level 3: A Program for Acquiring Competence in Entrepreneurship, 3 levels. rev. ed. 1983. 2.50 (*0-317-06069-4*, RD240CB12) Ctr Educ Trng Employ.
— Managing Sales Efforts Module, PACE Level 1: A Program for Acquiring Competence in Entrepreneurship, 3 levels. rev. ed. 1983. 2.50 (*0-318-67178-6*, RD240AB14) Ctr Educ Trng Employ.
— Managing Sales Efforts Module, PACE Level 2: A Program for Acquiring Competence in Entrepreneurship, 3 levels. rev. ed. 1983. 2.50 (*0-317-06071-6*, RD240BB14) Ctr Educ Trng Employ.
— Managing Sales Efforts Module, PACE Level 3: A Program for Acquiring Competence in Entrepreneurship, 3 levels. rev. ed. 1983. 2.50 (*0-317-06072-4*, RD240CB14) Ctr Educ Trng Employ.
— Managing the Business Module, PACE Level 1: A Program for Acquiring Competence in Entrepreneurship, 3 levels. rev. ed. 1983. 2.50 (*0-317-06058-9*, RD240AB11) Ctr Educ Trng Employ.
— Managing the Business Module, PACE Level 2: A Program for Acquiring Competence in Entrepreneurship, 3 levels. rev. ed. 1983. 2.50 (*0-317-06059-7*, RD240BB11) Ctr Educ Trng Employ.
— Managing the Business Module, PACE Level 3: A Program for Acquiring Competence in Entrepreneurship, 3 levels. rev. ed. 1983. 2.50 (*0-317-06060-0*, RD240CB11) Ctr Educ Trng Employ.

N

An Asterisk (*) at the beginning of an entry indicates that the title is appearing for the first time.

— Managing the Finance Module, PACE Level 1: A Program for Acquiring Competence in Entrepreneurship, 3 levels. rev. ed. 1983. 2.50 (*0-317-06064-3*, RD240AB16) Ctr Educ Trng Employ.

— Managing the Finance Module, PACE Level 2: A Program for Acquiring Competence in Entrepreneurship, 3 levels. rev. ed. 1983. 2.50 (*0-317-06065-1*, RD240BB16) Ctr Educ Trng Employ.

— Managing the Finance Module, PACE Level 3: A Program for Acquiring Competence in Entrepreneurship, 3 levels. rev. ed. 1983. 2.50 (*0-317-06066-X*, RD240CB16) Ctr Educ Trng Employ.

— Math on the Job: Graphic Designer. (Orig.). 1987. pap. text 14.95 (*0-923325-88-3*) Conover Co.

— Meet Initial Guidance Needs of Older Adults Module, Competency-Based Career Guidance (CBCG) - Category C: Implementing. 1985. 7.95 (*0-317-03902-4*, CG100C16) Ctr Educ Trng Employ.

— Obtaining Technical Assistance Module, PACE Level 1: A Program for Acquiring Competence in Entrepreneurship, 3 levels. rev. ed. 1983. 2.50 (*0-317-06073-2*, RD240AB4) Ctr Educ Trng Employ.

— Obtaining Technical Assistance Module, PACE Level 2: A Program for Acquiring Competence in Entrepreneurship, 3 levels. rev. ed. 1983. 2.50 (*0-317-06074-0*, RD240BB4) Ctr Educ Trng Employ.

— Obtaining Technical Assistance Module, PACE Level 3: A Program for Acquiring Competence in Entrepreneurship, 3 levels. rev. ed. 1983. 2.50 (*0-317-06075-9*, RD240CB4) Ctr Educ Trng Employ.

— On the Job Student Book, Connections: School & Work Transitions - Employer's Choice. 1987. 7.25 (*0-317-04614-4*, SP100BB02) Ctr Educ Trng Employ.

— Options: Expanding Educational Services for Adults. 1987. 174.00 (*0-318-35280-X*, SP 500) Ctr Educ Trng Employ.

— Organize Guidance Program Development Team Module, Competency-Based Career Guidance (CBCG) - Category A: Guidance Program Planning. 1985. 7.95 (*0-317-04753-1*, CG100A02) Ctr Educ Trng Employ.

— Orientation to Options: Expanding Educational Services for Adults. 1987. 25.00 (*0-317-03905-9*, SP500BVHS) Ctr Educ Trng Employ.

— Orientation to the World of Work Module, Connections: School & Work Transitions - Work Skills. 1987. write for info. (*0-318-67179-4*, SP100CB01) Ctr Educ Trng Employ.

— Planning the Marketing Strategy Module, PACE Level 1: A Program for Acquiring Competence in Entrepreneurship, 3 levels. rev. ed. 1983. 2.50 (*0-317-06076-7*, RD240AB6) Ctr Educ Trng Employ.

— Planning the Marketing Strategy Module, PACE Level 2: A Program for Acquiring Competence in Entrepreneurship, 3 levels. rev. ed. 1983. 2.50 (*0-317-06077-5*, RD240BB6) Ctr Educ Trng Employ.

— Planning the Marketing Strategy Module, PACE Level 3: A Program for Acquiring Competence in Entrepreneurship, 3 levels. rev. ed. 1983. 2.50 (*0-318-67180-8*, RD240CB6) Ctr Educ Trng Employ.

— Practice Ethical Behavior Module, Connections: School & Work Transitions - Work Skills-Work Maturity Skills. 1987. write for info. (*0-318-67182-4*, SP100CB10) Ctr Educ Trng Employ.

— Practice Good Work Habits Module, Connections: School & Work Transitions - Work Skills-Work Maturity Skills. 1987. write for info. (*0-318-67181-6*, SP100CB09) Ctr Educ Trng Employ.

— Prepare for the Job Search Module, Connections: School & Work Transitions - Work Skills-Job Search Skills. 1987. write for info. (*0-318-67183-2*, SP100CB02) Ctr Educ Trng Employ.

— Present a Positive Image Module, Connections: School & Work Transitions - Work Skills-Work Maturity Skills. 1987. write for info. (*0-318-67184-0*, SP100CB07) Ctr Educ Trng Employ.

— Primer of Exemplary Strategies, Basics: Bridging Vocational & Academic Skills - The Bridger's Guide. 1987. 11.95 (*0-317-03906-7*, SP300AB) Ctr Educ Trng Employ.

— Priorities That Count Student Book, Connections: School & Work Transitions - Employer's Choice. 1987. 4.00 (*0-317-03907-5*, SP100BB01) Ctr Educ Trng Employ.

— Promote Equity & Client Advocacy Module, Competency-Based Career Guidance (CBCG) - Category C: Implementing. 1985. 6.95 (*0-317-03908-3*, CG100C17) Ctr Educ Trng Employ.

— Promoting the Business Module, PACE Level 1: A Program for Acquiring Competence in Entrepreneurship, 3 levels. rev. ed. 1983. 2.50 (*0-318-67185-9*, RD240AB13); write for info. (*0-318-67186-7*, RD240AB13) Ctr Educ Trng Employ.

— Promoting the Business Module, PACE Level 2: A Program for Acquiring Competence in Entrepreneurship, 3 levels. rev. ed. 1983. 2.50 (*0-317-06080-5*, RD240BB13) Ctr Educ Trng Employ.

— Promoting the Business Module, PACE Level 3: A Program for Acquiring Competence in Entrepreneurship, 3 levels. rev. ed. 1983. 2.50 (*0-317-06081-3*, RD240CB13) Ctr Educ Trng Employ.

— Protecting the Business Module, PACE Level 1: A Program for Acquiring Competence in Entrepreneurship, 3 levels. rev. ed. 1983. 2.50 (*0-317-06082-1*, RD240CB18) Ctr Educ Trng Employ.

— Protecting the Business Module, PACE Level 2: A Program for Acquiring Competence in Entrepreneurship, 3 levels. rev. ed. 1983. 2.50 (*0-317-06083-X*, RD240BB18) Ctr Educ Trng Employ.

— Protecting the Business Module, PACE Level 3: A Program for Acquiring Competence in Entrepreneurship, 3 levels. rev. ed. 1983. 2.50 (*0-317-06084-8*, RD240CB18) Ctr Educ Trng Employ.

— Provide Career Guidance to Girls & Women Module, Competency-Based Career Guidance (CBCG) - Category C: Implementing. 1985. 7.95 (*0-317-03910-5*, CG100C13) Ctr Educ Trng Employ.

— Provide for Employability Skill Development Module, Competency-Based Career Guidance (CBCG) - Category C: Implementing. 1985. 7.95 (*0-317-03911-3*, CG100C08) Ctr Educ Trng Employ.

— Provide for the Basic Skills Module, Competency-Based Career Guidance (CBCG) - Category C: Implementing. 1985. 7.95 (*0-317-03909-1*, CG100C09) Ctr Educ Trng Employ.

— Publicity Kit, Options: Expanding Educational Services for Adults. 1987. 29.95 (*0-317-03912-1*, SP500C) Ctr Educ Trng Employ.

— Questions Frequently Asked about Vocational Education. 33p. 1987. 4.75 (*0-318-23416-5*, SN 57) Ctr Educ Trng Employ.

— Resource Guide, PACE: A Program for Acquiring Competence in Entrepreneurship. rev. ed. 1983. 7.95 (*0-318-67187-5*, RD240D) Ctr Educ Trng Employ.

— Search for Available Jobs Module, Connections: School & Work Transitions - Work Skills-Job Search Skills. 1987. write for info. (*0-318-67188-3*, SP100CB03) Ctr Educ Trng Employ.

— Special Services for Adult Learners, Options: Expanding Educational Sources for Adults. 1987. 29.50 (*0-317-04616-0*, SP500F) Ctr Educ Trng Employ.

— Student's Choice Student Workbook, Dropout Prevention. 1988. write for info. (*0-318-67189-1*, SP700SC01) Ctr Educ Trng Employ.

— Supplemental Instructional Resources, Basics: Bridging Vocational & Academic Skill - Instructional Program Development. 1987. 7.95 (*0-317-03915-6*, SP300DB) Ctr Educ Trng Employ.

— Technique for Individualization: The Academic Development Plan, Basics: Bridging Vocational & Academic Skills - Targeting Teaching Techniques. 1987. 9.95 (*0-317-03918-0*, SP300EE) Ctr Educ Trng Employ.

— Technique for Management: Time for Learning, Basics: Bridging Vocational & Academic Skills - Targeted Teaching Techniques. 1987. 7.50 (*0-317-03919-9*, SP300EB) Ctr Educ Trng Employ.

— Technique for Remediation: Peer Tutoring with Audiocassette, Basics: Bridging Vocational & Academic Skills - Targeted Teaching Techniques. 1987. 13.95 (*0-317-03920-2*, SP300EC) Ctr Educ Trng Employ.

— Techniques of Joint Effort: The Vocational Academic Approach with Audiocassette, Basics: Bridging Vocational & Academic Skills - Targeted Teaching Techniques. 1987. 13.95 (*0-317-03916-4*, SP300EA) Ctr Educ Trng Employ.

— Tutor Clients Module, Competency-Based Career Guidance (CBCG) - Category C: Implementing. 1985. 7.95 (*0-317-03921-0*, CG100C02) Ctr Educ Trng Employ.

— Understanding the Nature of Small Business Module, PACE: A Program for Acquiring Competence in Entrepreneurship, 3 levels. rev. ed. 1983. write for info. (*0-318-67190-5*, RD240AB1) Ctr Educ Trng Employ.

— Understanding the Nature of Small Business Module, PACE Level 1: A Program for Acquiring Competence in Entrepreneurship, 3 levels. rev. ed. 1983. 6.50 (*0-317-06086-4*, RD240AB1) Ctr Educ Trng Employ.

— Understanding the Nature of Small Business Module, PACE Level 2: A Program for Acquiring Competence in Entrepreneurship, 3 levels. rev. ed. 1983. 6.50 (*0-317-06087-2*, RD240BB1) Ctr Educ Trng Employ.

— Understanding the Nature of Small Business Module, PACE Level 3: A Program for Acquiring Competence in Entrepreneurship, 3 levels. rev. ed. 1983. 6.50 (*0-318-67191-3*, RD240CB1) Ctr Educ Trng Employ.

— Use & Comply with Administrative Mechanisms Module, Competency-Based Career Guidance (CBCG) - Category B: Supporting. 1985. 7.95 (*0-317-03922-9*, CB100B05) Ctr Educ Trng Employ.

— Work Skills Instructor Guide, Connections: School & Work Transitions. 1987. 4.75 (*0-317-03924-5*, SP100CA02) Ctr Educ Trng Employ.

— Work Skills Modules, Connections: School & Work Transitions - Work Skills. 1987. 39.00 (*0-317-03925-3*, SP100CA03) Ctr Educ Trng Employ.

— Work Skills Resource Manual, Connections: School & Work Transitions - Work Skills. 1987. 29.95 (*0-317-03926-1*, SP100CA01) Ctr Educ Trng Employ.

National Center for Research in Vocational Educati, et al. Improving Perkins II Performance Measures & Standards: Lessons Learned from Early Implementers in Four States. LC 94-41826. 91p. 1995. pap. text 15.00 (*0-8330-1613-X*, MR-526-NCRVE/UB) Rand Corp.

National Center for Small Communities Staff. The Americans with Disabilities Act: A Compliance Workbook for Small Communities. LC 92-17025. 1992. 19.95 (*0-925532-08-8*) Natl Ctr Small Commun.

— Tapping Your Own Resources: A Decision-Maker's Guide for Small Town Drinking Water. 1993. 19.95 (*0-925532-09-6*) Natl Ctr Small Commun.

National Center for State Courts. Bias in the Court! Focusing on the Behavior of Judges, Lawyers, & Court Staff in Court Interactions. LC 97-69654. 1997. write for info. (*0-89656-176-3*) Natl Ctr St Courts.

— Judicial Mentoring: Starting, Organizing, & Sustaining a Program for Mentoring Persons of Color to the Bench. LC 97-69656. 1997. write for info. (*0-89656-179-8*) Natl Ctr St Courts.

National Center for State Courts, jt. auth. see Richardson, John G.

National Center for State Courts Staff. Guidelines for State Court Decision Making in the Life-Sustaining Medical Treatment. 2nd rev. ed. 250p. 1993. pap. text. write for info. (*0-314-02226-0*) West Pub.

National Center for the Early Childhood Work Force Staff, jt. auth. see Bellm, Dan.

National Center for the Study Staff. The Annual Review of Adult Learning & Literacy, 2000. 384p. 1999. text 34.95 (*0-7879-4741-5*) Jossey-Bass.

National Center Staff. Competing in World-Class Manufacturing: Deloitte & Touche Special Edition, America's 21st Century Challenge. 448p. 1990. text. write for info. (*1-55623-516-X*, Irwn Prfssnl) McGraw-Hill Prof.

National Centre for Development Studies Staff, jt. ed. see Asia Pacific Press Staff.

National Cervical Screening Programme Staff. National Cervical Screening Programme Policy LC 97-153727. 47p. 1996. write for info. (*0-478-09451-5*, Pub. by Manaaki Whenua) Balogh.

National Child Labor Committee. Proceedings of the National Child Labor Committee, 1905, Vol. 1. Bremner, Robert H., ed. LC 74-1699. (Children & Youth Ser.). 1974. 36.95 (*0-405-05976-0*) Ayer.

National Childbirth Trust Staff & Loader, Anne, compiled by. Pregnancy & Parenthood. (Illus.). 1980. 16.95 (*0-19-217684-6*); pap. 8.95 (*0-19-286006-2*) OUP.

National Children's Bureau Staff & Pilling, Doria. Escape from Disadvantage. 250p. 1990. 69.95 (*1-85000-678-4*, Falmer Pr); pap. 34.95 (*1-85000-679-2*, Falmer Pr) Taylor & Francis.

National Civic League Staff. Handbook for Council Members. 5th ed. LC 76-9624. 40p. 1992. 10.00 (*0-916450-51-1*) Nat Civic League.

— Healthy Communities Directory. 1994. 20.00 (*0-916450-50-3*) Nat Civic League.

— Healthy Communities Resource Guide. 1994. 20.00 (*0-916450-49-X*) Nat Civic League.

***National Civil Engineering Education Congress Staff, et al.** Forming Civil Engineering's Future: 1999 National Civil Engineering Education Congress: October 16-20, 1999, Charlotte, North Carolina. LC 99-44186. 192p. 1999. 32.00 (*0-7844-0455-0*) Am Soc Civil Eng.

National Clearinghouse on Licensure, Enforcement, & Council of State Governments Staff. Antitrust, Competition Policy & State Professional Regulation: A Manual for Regulators. Zeitlin, Kim A., ed. LC 85-622991. 48p. 1985. 15.00 (*0-87292-059-3*, C-32) Coun State Govts.

National Cloak & Suit Co. Staff. Women's Fashions of the Early 1900s: An Unabridged Republication of "New York Fashions, 1909", Vol. 900. unabridged ed. LC 92-21805. (Illus.). 128p. 1992. reprint ed. pap. text 11.95 (*0-486-27276-1*) Dover.

National Coalition for Cancer Survivorship Staff. A Cancer Survivor's Almanac: Charting Your Journey. 352p. 1996. pap. 18.95 (*0-471-34669-1*) Wiley.

— A Cancer Survivor's Almanac: Charting Your Journey. 2nd rev. ed. Hoffman, Barbara, ed. 354p. 1996. pap. 18.95 (*1-56561-104-7*) Wiley.

National Coalition for Music Education Staff, ed. Building Support for School Music: A Practical Guide. 80p. 1991. 10.50 (*0-940796-97-X*, 1004) MENC.

National Coalition for the Homeless Staff. Homelessness in America. Baumohl, Jim, ed. LC 96-30244. (Illus.). 320p. 1996. boxed set 44.50 (*0-89774-869-7*) Oryx Pr.

National Coalition of Advocates for Students Staff. Criteria for Evaluating an AIDS Curriculum. rev. ed. 23p. 1992. reprint ed. pap. 4.00 (*1-880002-02-7*) Natl Coal Advocates.

National College of Chiropractic Staff. Manual of Chiropractic Diagnosis & Therapeutics. 500p. 1993. pap. 39.95 (*0-8016-6468-3*) Mosby Inc.

National College of Juvenile and Family Law Staff. Glossary of Selected Legal Terms for Juvenile Justice Personnel. 10p. 1978. 3.00 (*0-318-36218-X*) Natl Juv & Family Ct Judges.

***National Collegiate Athletic Association Staff.** NCAA Basketball: The Official 2000 Men's College Basketball Records Book. 1999. pap. 17.95 (*1-57243-311-6*) Triumph Bks.

National Collegiate Athletic Association Staff. NCAA Basketball's Finest: All-Time Great Men's Players & Coaches. 1998. pap. 15.95 (*1-57243-316-7*) Triumph Bks.

***National Collegiate Athletic Association Staff.** NCAA Final Four: The Official 2000 Final Four Records Book. (Illus.). 204p. 1999. pap. text 15.95 (*1-57243-313-2*) Triumph Bks.

— Official Rules of NCAA Basketball: 2000. (Illus.). 194p. 1999. pap. 9.95 (*1-57243-333-7*) Triumph Bks.

National Comission of Inquire of Child Abuse. Childhood Matters: Report of the National Commission of Inquiry into the Prevention of Child Abuse. LC 97-213264. 1996. 85.00 (*0-11-321997-0*, Pub. by Statnry Office) Bernan Associates.

National Comm. on Correctional Health Care Staff & Anno, B. Jay. Prison Health Care: Guidelines for the Management of an Adequate Delivery System, 1992. 350p. 1991. 55.00 (*0-929561-04-X*) NCCHC.

National Commission for Cooperative Education Staf. Directory of College Cooperative Education Programs. LC 96-33008. 232p. 1996. pap. 49.95 (*0-89774-998-7*) Oryx Pr.

National Commission of Family Foster Care Staff, compiled by. A Blueprint for Fostering Infants, Children, & Youths in the 1990s. 155p. 1991. pap. 7.50 (*0-87868-441-7*) Child Welfare.

National Commission on Allied Health Education Sta. The Future of Allied Health Education. LC 79-9666. (Jossey-Bass Series in Higher Education). 314p. reprint ed. pap. 97.40 (*0-8357-4955-X*, 203788700009) Bks Demand.

National Commission on Community Health Services. Health Is a Community Affair: Report. LC 66-27415. (Illus.). 266p. 1966. pap. 15.00 (*0-674-38451-2*) HUP.

National Commission on Crime & Justice Staff. A Call to Action: An Analysis & Overview of the United States Criminal Justice System, with Recommendations. Thurston, Linda M., ed. LC 91-68516. 102p. (Orig.). 1993. pap. 8.00 (*0-88378-067-4*) Third World.

National Commission on Economic Growth & Tax Reform (U.S.) Staff. Report of the National Commission on Economic Growth & Tax Reform: Hearing Before the Committee on Finance, United States Senate, One Hundred Fourth Congress, Second Session, January 31, 1996. LC 98-158319. (S. Hrg. Ser.). iv, 169 p. 1997. write for info. (*0-16-056147-7*) USGPO.

National Commission on Excellence in Education. Meeting the Challenge of a Nation at Risk. LC 84-50559. (Illus.). 128p. (Orig.). 1984. pap. 9.95 (*0-917191-04-8*) USA Res.

National Commission on Law Observance & Enforcemen. Report on the Police, Vol. 14. LC 77-154578. (Police in America Ser.). 1971. reprint ed. 13.95 (*0-405-03376-1*) Ayer.

National Commission on Music Education Staff. Growing up Complete: The Imperative for Music Education. (Illus.). 56p. 1991. pap. 10.50 (*0-940796-89-9*) MENC.

National Commission on Music Education (U. S.) Staff. Growing up Complete: The Imperative for Music Education: The Report of the National Commission on Music Education. LC 91-228588. (Illus.). 60p. reprint ed. pap. 30.00 (*0-608-20176-6*, 207143400012) Bks Demand.

National Commission on Resources for Youth. You're the Tutor. 66p. 1970. pap. 2.00 (*0-912041-03-X*) Natl Comm Res Youth.

National Commission on Secondary Vocational Educat. The Unfinished Agenda. 35p. 1985. 4.75 (*0-318-22226-4*, IN289) Ctr Educ Trng Employ.

National Commission on the Environment Staff. Choosing a Sustainable Future: The Report of the National Commission on the Environment. LC 92-35267. (Illus.). 190p. (C). 1992. pap. text 20.00 (*1-55963-232-1*) Island Pr.

National Commission on the Insanity Defense, (U. S & National Mental Health Association (U. S.) Staff. Myths & Realities: A Report of the National Commission on the Insanity Defense. LC 83-60609. (Illus.). 50p. 1983. 3.95 (*0-317-00680-0*, PE0902SH) Natl Mental Health.

— Myths & Realities: Hearing Transcript of the National Commission on the Insanity Defense. LC 83-60608. 214p. 1983. 9.95 (*0-317-00681-9*, PE0903SH) Natl Mental Health.

National Commission on the Role of the School & the Community in Improving Adolescent Health. Code Blue: Uniting for Healthier Youth. 2nd ed. 52p. 1990. pap. 6.00 (*1-58434-015-0*) NASBE.

National Commisssion on Excellence in Education. A Nation at Risk: The Full Account. 2nd ed. U. S. A. Research, Inc., Staff, ed. (Illus.). 128p. (Orig.). (C). 1994. pap. 12.95 (*0-917191-02-1*) USA Res.

National Committee Against Discrimination in Housi. Fair Housing & Exclusionary Land Use: Historical Overview, A Summary of Litigation & a Comment with Research Bibliography. LC 74-13552. (Urban Land Institute Research Reports: No. 23). 80p. reprint ed. pap. 30.00 (*0-608-12221-1*, 202388400034) Bks Demand.

National Committee for Clinical Laboratory Standar. Additives to Blood Collection Devices: Heparin: Tentative Standard (1988), Vol. 8. rev. ed. 1988. 75.00 (*1-56238-053-2*, H24-T) NCCLS.

— Assessing the Quality of Radioimmunoassay Systems: Approved Guideline, Vol. 5. 2nd ed. 1994. 75.00 (*1-56238-073-7*, LA1-A2) NCCLS.

— Citrate Agar Electrophoresis for Confirming the Identification of Variant Hemoglobins: Tentative Guideline, Vol. 8. 1988. 75.00 (*1-56238-052-4*, H23-T) NCCLS.

— Definitions of Quantities & Conventions Related to Blood pH & Gas Analysis (1994) 2nd ed. (Tentative Standard Ser.: Vol. 2). 1994. 75.00 (*1-56238-138-5*, C12-A) NCCLS.

— Devices for Collection of Skin Puncture Blood Specimens: Approved Guideline (1990), Vol. 5. 2nd ed. 1990. 75.00 (*1-56238-109-1*, H14-A2) NCCLS.

— Enzyme & Fluorescence Immunoassays: Tentative Guideline (1996), Vol. 6. 1986. 75.00 (*1-56238-067-2*, D14-T) NCCLS.

— Evacuated Tubes for Blood Specimen Collection. 3rd ed. (Approved Standard Ser.). 1991. 75.00 (*1-56238-107-5*, H1-A3) NCCLS.

— Histochemical Method for Leukocyte Alkaline Phosphatase: Proposed Standard (1984), Vol. 4. 1984. 75.00 (*1-56238-051-6*, H22-P) NCCLS.

— Internal Quality Control Testing: Principles & Definitions (1991) (Approved Guideline Ser.: Vol. 7). 1991. 75.00 (*1-56238-112-1*, C24-A) NCCLS.

— Methods for the Human Erythrocyte Sedimentation Rate (E. S. R.) Test: Approved Standard. 3rd ed. 1993. 75.00 (*1-56238-034-6*, H2-A3) NCCLS.

— Percutaneous Collection of Arterial Blood for Laboratory Analysis: Approved Standard, 1992, Vol. 5. 2nd ed. 1992. 100.00 (*1-56238-130-X*, H11-A2) NCCLS.

— Performance Characteristics for Devices Measuring PO2 & PCO2 in Blood Samples: Approved Standard, Vol. 9. 1992. 75.00 (*1-56238-135-0*, C21-A) NCCLS.

— Preparation & Testing of Reagent Water in the Clinical Laboratory. 3rd ed. (Approved Guideline Ser.: Vol. 8). 1991. 75.00 (*1-56238-127-X*, C3-A2) NCCLS.

— Procedures for the Handling & Processing of Blood Specimens: Approved Guideline, Vol. 4. 1990. 85.00 (*1-56238-110-5*, H18-A) NCCLS.

N

An Asterisk (*) at the beginning of an entry indicates that the title is appearing for the first time.

— Quantitative Measurement of Fetal Hemoglobin by the Alkali Denaturation Method: Approved Guideline, Vol. 6. 1989. 75.00 (*1-56238-043-5*, H13-A) NCCLS.

— Reference Leukocyte Differential Count (Proportional) & Evaluation of Instrumental Methods: Approved Standard, Vol. 4. 1992. 85.00 (*1-56238-131-8*, H20-A) NCCLS.

— Specimen Handling & Use of Rubella Serology Tests in the Clinical Laboratory: Proposed Guideline, Vol. 4. 1984. 75.00 (*1-56238-070-2*, I/LA7-P) NCCLS.

— User Precision Performance of Clinical Chemistry Devices: Tentative Guideline, Vol. 4. 2nd ed. 1992. 85.00 (*1-56238-145-8*, EP5-T2) NCCLS.

National Committee for Mental Health. State Hospitals in the Depression. Grob, Gerald N., ed. LC 78-22579. (Historical Issues in Mental Health Ser.). 1980. reprint ed. lib. bdg. 17.95 (*0-405-11931-3*) Ayer.

National Committee of Japanese Historians Staff, ed. Historical Studies in Japan (Seven) 1983-1987. vi, 350p. 1991. pap. 87.00 (*90-04-09292-7*) Brill Academic Pubs.

National Committee on Pay Equity. The Wage Gap: Women Have Made Slow, Steady Progress in the Labor Market since 1979 but the Wage Gap Has Not Narrowed Significantly. (Briefing Papers: No. 1). 7p. 1989. pap. 4.00 (*0-685-29940-6*) Inst Womens Policy Rsch.

National Committee on Pay Equity & Institute for Women's Policy Research Staff. OPM Comparable Worth - Pay Equity Study Overstates Women's Progress in Federal Workforce. 10p. 1987. pap. 5.00 (*0-685-29950-3*) Inst Womens Policy Rsch.

National Committee on Uniform Traffic Laws & Ordin. Uniform Vehicle Code & Model Traffic Ordinance, 1992. (Orig.). 1992. pap. 22.00 (*0-317-05952-1*) Natl Comm Traffic.

National Committee to Save America's Cultural Coll. Caring for Your Collections: Preserving & Protecting Your Art & Other Collectibles. (Illus.). 208p. 1992. 39.95 (*0-8109-3174-5*, Pub. by Abrams) Time Warner.

National Communications Forum Staff. Proceedings of the National Communications Forum, Vol. 44, 1990. fac. ed. LC 86-642827. (Illus.). 1058p. 1990. reprint ed. pap. 200.00 (*0-7837-7723-X*, 202917300044) Bks Demand.

— Proceedings of the National Communications Forum, Vol. 45, 1991. fac. ed. LC 86-642827. (Illus.). 783p. 1991. reprint ed. pap. 200.00 (*0-7837-7724-8*, 202917300045) Bks Demand.

— Proceedings of the National Communications Forum, 1984, Vol. 38. LC 45-8478. 714p. reprint ed. pap. 200.00 (*0-608-15244-7*, 202917300038) Bks Demand.

National Communications System Technology & Standards Division. Telecommunications: Glossary of Telecommunications Terms. 480p. 1997. pap. text 69.00 (*0-86587-580-4*) Gov Insts.

National Compassionate Friends Chapters, jt. auth. see Wisler, Alice J.

National Conditions Investigation Group Staff & Chinese Academy of Sciences Staff, eds. Survival & Development. 200p. 1996. 30.00 (*7-03-002853-8*, Pub. by Sci Pr) Lubrecht & Cramer.

National Conference & Workshop Staff. Proceedings of the 1st National Conference & Workshop, Environmental Stress Screening of Electronic Hardware, March 1979. LC 62-38584. 1979. pap. text 65.00 (*0-915414-59-7*) IEST.

National Conference for Community & Justice Staff. Intergroup Relations in the United States: Programs & Organizations. LC 98-67499. 128p. 1998. pap. 14.95 (*0-9665452-1-4*) Natl Conference.

National Conference of Catechetical Leadership, &, jt. auth. see National Catholic Education Association Staff.

National Conference of Catholic Bishops. Called & Gifted: The American Catholic Laity: Reflections of the American Bishops Commemorating the Fifteenth Anniversary of the Issuance of the "Decree on the Apostolate of the Laity" 4p. 1980. pap. 0.75 (*1-55586-727-8*) US Catholic.

— Called to Be Peacemakers & Apostles of Hope. Rabil, Dick, tr. (Illus.). 72p. (Orig.). 1995. pap. 8.95 (*1-55586-053-2*) US Catholic.

— The Challenge of Peace: God's Promise & Our Response. 152p. (Orig.). 1983. pap. 3.95 (*1-55586-863-0*) US Catholic.

— Una Decada Despues de "Justicia Economica Para Todos" Normas Perecederas, Contexto Diferente, Nuevos Retos. Herrera, Marina, tr. (SPA.). 17p. (Orig.). 1995. pap. text 0.75 (*1-57455-041-1*) US Catholic.

— A Decade after "Economic Justice for All" Continuing Principles, Changing Context, New Challenges. 17p. (Orig.). 1995. pap. text 0.75 (*1-57455-040-3*) US Catholic.

— Encounters with Faith: A Handbook for Observance of the Fifth Centenary of Evangelization in the Americas. 88p. (Orig.). (C). 1991. pap. 8.95 (*1-55586-416-3*) US Catholic.

— Environment & Art in Catholic Worship. 38p. 1993. pap. 8.00 (*0-929650-65-4*, EADOC) Liturgy Tr Pubns.

— Families at the Center: A Handbook for Parish Ministry with a Family Perspective. 52p. (Orig.). 1990. pap. 3.95 (*1-55586-337-X*) US Catholic.

— The Hispanic Presence in the New Evangelization in the United States. (ENG & SPA., Illus.). 56p. (Orig.). 1996. pap. text 5.95 (*1-55586-460-0*) US Catholic.

— Liturgy Documentary Series 5: General Instruction of the Liturgy of the Hours. 78p. (Orig.). (C). 1983. pap. 5.95 (*1-55586-898-3*) US Catholic.

— Missal: The Order of Mass in English. Johnson, Kevin O., ed. LC 96-72375. 50p. 1997. pap. 4.00 (*0-9653660-2-2*) Pangaeus Pr.

— A Pastoral Statement for Catholics on Biblical Fundamentalism English & Spanish. Herrera, Marina, tr. (ENG & SPA.). 20p. (Orig.). 1987. pap. 1.95 (*1-55586-161-X*) US Catholic.

— The Promise & Peril of Genetic Screening. (Science & the Catholic Church Ser.). 6p. (Orig.). (C). 1997. pap. 1.00 (*1-57455-076-4*) US Catholic.

— Rite of Christian Initiation of Adults. International Commission on English in the Liturgy, ed.Tr. of Ordo Initationis Christianae Adulorum. 404p. 1988. 23.95 (*0-89942-355-8*, 355-22) Catholic Bk Pub.

— Science & the Catholic Church. 6p. (Orig.). 1995. pap., mass mkt. 1.00 (*1-55586-085-0*) US Catholic.

— Shorter Christian Prayer. 670p. 1988. vinyl bd. 11.25 (*0-89942-408-2*, 408/10) Catholic Bk Pub.

— Sowing Weapons of War: A Pastoral Reflection on the Arms Trade & Landmines. 9p. 1995. pap. text 1.50 (*1-57455-028-4*) US Catholic.

— Statement on School-Based Clinics. (Orig.). 1987. pap. 0.95 (*1-55586-196-2*) US Catholic.

— Strengthening the Bonds of Peace: Parish Resource Packet. 52p. (Orig.). 1996. pap. text 9.95 (*1-57455-018-7*) US Catholic.

National Conference of Catholic Bishops & United States Catholic Conference Administrative B. Prayers for the Beginning of Life. 16p. (Orig.). 1989. pap. 1.95 (*1-55586-297-7*) US Catholic.

— Prayers of the Lenten & Easter Seasons. 63p. (Orig.). 1989. pap. 2.95 (*1-55586-301-9*) US Catholic.

National Conference of Catholic Bishops & United States Catholic Conference Staff. Catholic Household Blessings & Prayers. 444p. 1989. pap. 14.95 (*1-55586-292-6*) US Catholic.

National Conference of Catholic Bishops, jt. auth. see Bishop's Committee on Marriage & Family Staff.

National Conference of Catholic Bishops, jt. auth. see Secretariat for Black Catholics Staff.

National Conference of Catholic Bishops Staff. Complementary Norms. 56p. (Orig.). (C). 1991. pap. 3.95 (*1-55586-433-3*) US Catholic.

— Heritage & Hope: Evangelization in the United States. Herrera, Marina, tr. (ENG & SPA.). 108p. (Orig.). (C). 1990. pap. 5.95 (*1-55586-386-8*) US Catholic.

— Norms for Priests & Their Third Age. 6p. (Orig.). 1988. pap. 0.50 (*1-55586-207-1*) US Catholic.

— Together, a New People: Pastoral Statement on Migrants & Refugees. 32p. (Orig.). 1987. pap. 3.95 (*1-55586-147-4*) US Catholic.

— United in Service: Reflections on the Presbyteral Council. 20p. (Orig.). (C). 1992. pap. 1.95 (*1-55586-482-1*) US Catholic.

National Conference of Catholic Bishops Staff, jt. auth. see Bishops' Committee on Priestly Life & Ministry Sta.

National Conference of Catholic Bishops Staff, jt. auth. see Bishops' Committee on Vocations Staff.

National Conference of Catholic Bishops Staff, ed. see Bishops' Committee on the Laity Staff.

National Conference of Charities & Correction Staf. History of Child Saving in the United States. LC 70-108228. (Criminology, Law Enforcement, & Social Problems Ser.: No. 111). 1971. reprint ed. 28.00 (*0-87585-111-8*) Patterson Smith.

National Conference of CUSL Staff. National Conference of Commissioners on Uniform State Laws Handbooks, 10 vols., Set. LC 06-25307. 1982. lib. bdg. 422.50 (*0-89941-317-X*, 302830) W S Hein.

National Conference of Social Work Staff. Social Work in the Current Scene, 1950: Selected Papers of the National Conference of Social Work, 77th. LC 72-3382. (Essay Index Reprint Ser.). 1977. reprint ed. 25.95 (*0-8369-2915-2*) Ayer.

National Conference of Standards Laboratories, Accredited Standards Committee on General Requirements for Calibration Laboratories. U. S. Guide to the Expression of Uncertainty in Measurement: ANSI-NCSL Z540-2-1997. 2nd unabridged ed. (Illus.). 101p. 1997. reprint ed. 25.00 (*1-58464-005-7*) Natl Conf Stds Labs.

National Conference of Standards Laboratories Glossary Committee. NCSL Glossary of Metrology Terms. unabridged ed. 56p. 1994. 10.00 (*1-58464-001-4*) Natl Conf Stds Labs.

***National Conference of Standards Laboratories in Healthcare Metrology Committee.** Calibration Control Systems for the Biomedical & Pharmaceutical Industry: RP-6. (RP Ser.: No. 6). 17p. 1999. reprint ed. text 15.00 (*1-58464-014-6*) Natl Conf Stds Labs.

National Conference of Standards Laboratories Laboratories Standards Committee. Laboratory Design: Recommended Practice RP-7. 2nd ed. (RP Ser.: No. 7). (Illus.). 181p. 1993. reprint ed. 20.00 (*1-58464-015-4*) Natl Conf Stds Labs.

National Conference of Standards Laboratories, Utilities Committee. Computer Systems in Metrology: Recommended Practice RP-13. (RP Ser.). (Illus.). 12p. 1996. reprint ed. 15.00 (*1-58464-021-9*) Natl Conf Stds Labs.

National Conference of State Legislatures Education, jt. auth. see Trolin, Brenda.

National Conference of State Legislatures Staff. Issues Outlook, 1993: A Survey of State Legislative Priorities. 44p. 1992. pap. text 30.00 (*1-55516-990-2*, 9350) Natl Conf State Legis.

— Lead Poisoning Prevention: Directory of State Contacts, 1995-1996. 193p. 1996. 20.00 (*1-55516-430-7*, 4648) Natl Conf State Legis.

National Conference of State Legislatures Staff & Farquhar, Doug. Lead Poisoning Prevention: A Guide for Legislators. 48p. 1996. 65.00 (*1-55516-496-X*, 4638) Natl Conf State Legis.

National Conference of State Legislatures Staff & Neal, Tommy. Lawmaking & the Legislative Process: Committees, Connections, & Compromises. LC 96-20568. (Illus.). 160p. 1996. pap. 26.50 (*0-89774-944-8*) Oryx Pr.

National Conference of State Legislatures Staff, et al. Early Childhood Care & Education: An Investment That Works. 2nd rev. ed. LC 97-208884. 120p. 1997. 25.00 (*1-55516-650-4*, 6137) Natl Conf State Legis.

National Conference of State Legislatures Staff, jt. auth. see Education Commission of the States Staff.

National Conference of State Legislatures Staff, jt. auth. see Education Partners (Project) Staff.

National Conference of State Legislatures Staff, jt. auth. see Mackey, Scott R.

National Conference of State Legislatures Staff, jt. auth. see May, Annelise.

National Conference of State Legislatures Staff, jt. auth. see Morandi, Larry B.

National Conference of State Staff, jt. auth. see Snell, Ronald K.

National Conference on Bail & Criminal Justice Sta. Proceedings & Interim Report of the National Conference on Bail & Criminal Justice, May 27-29, 1964 & May 1964-April 1965. Fogelson, Robert M., ed. LC 74-3839. (Criminal Justice in America Ser.). 1974. reprint ed. 33.95 (*0-405-06156-0*) Ayer.

***National Conference on Communications, et al.** Communications '98: Proceedings of the National Conference on Communications, Indian Institute of Science, Bangalore, January 29-31, 1998. LC 99-939751. (Illus.). 1998. write for info. (*0-07-463021-0*) McGrw-H Hghr Educ.

***National Conference on Community Systems-Building and Services Integration, et al, contrib. by.** Many Streams Make a River: Proceedings of National Conference on Community Systems Building & Services Integration, September 14-15, 1997. LC 98-68316. (Illus.). 96p. 1998. pap. write for info. (*1-57285-055-8*) Nat Ctr Educ.

National Conference on Intermodalism Staff. Intermodalism: Making the Case, Making It Happen. LC 96-199729. 254p. 1996. pap. 45.00 (*0-309-06211-X*, CP011) Natl Res Coun.

National Conference on Motion Pictures Staff & Motion Picture Producers & Distributors of America. The Community & the Motion Picture: Report of the National Conference on Motion Pictures, New York, 1929. LC 77-160242. (Moving Pictures Ser.). 96p. 1971. reprint ed. lib. bdg. 19.95 (*0-89198-043-1*) Ozer.

National Conference on Object Oriented Technology Staff, et al. Proceedings of the 1997 National Conference on Object Oriented Technology (NCOOT '97), August 22-24, 1997. LC 97-914243. x, 125 p. 1997. write for info. (*81-7023-630-4*) Allied Pubs.

National Conference on Regulatory Reform Staff. Buying a Better Environment: Cost-Effective Regulation Through Permit Trading: The Proceedings of a National Conference on Regulatory Reform, Transferable Permits & Enhancement of Environmental Quality, Madison, WI, June 23-25, 1982. Joeres, Erhard F. & David, Martin H., eds. LC 83-47673. (Land Economics Monographs: Vol. 6). (Illus.). 294p. reprint ed. pap. 91.20 (*0-608-20445-5*, 207169800002) Bks Demand.

National Conference on Setting an Intermodal Transportation Research Framework, et al. National Conference on Setting An Intermodal Transportation Research Framework, Washington, D.c., March 4-5, 1996. LC 97-203582. (Conference Proceedings / Transportation Research Board Ser.). 97 p. 1997. 27.00 (*0-309-05968-2*, CP012) Natl Acad Pr.

National Conference on Technology & Education Staf. Technology & Education: Policy, Implementation, Evaluation-Proceedings of the National Conference on Technology & Education, January 26-28, 1981. 340p. 1981. lib. bdg. 20.00 (*0-318-03015-2*) Inst Educ Lead.

National Conference on the Diabetic Foot Staff. The Foot in Diabetes: Proceedings of the First National Conference on the Diabetic Foot, Malvern, May 1986. Connor, H. et al, eds. LC 86-32514. (Wiley-Medical Publication). 182p. reprint ed. pap. 56.50 (*0-8357-6982-8*, 205235900009) Bks Demand.

National Conference on the Future of Social Work R. Future of Social Work Research: Selected Papers - National Conference, October 15-18, 1978, San Antonio, TX. Fanshel, David, ed. LC 79-92733. 208p. reprint ed. pap. 64.50 (*0-7837-6534-7*, 204567000007) Bks Demand.

National Conference on the Psychological Aspects o. Rehabilitation Psychology: Proceedings. Neff, Walter S., ed. LC 75-183150. 337p. reprint ed. pap. 104.50 (*0-7837-0492-5*, 204081600018) Bks Demand.

National Conference on Thermal Spray, Second, Long. Second National Conference on Thermal Spray: 31 October-2 November, 1984, Hyatt Regency Long Beach, Long Beach, California. LC 85-71832. (Illus.). 152p. pap. 47.20 (*0-7837-1864-0*, 204206500001) Bks Demand.

***National Conference Standards Laboratories Staff, ed.** 1999 NCSL Workshop & Symposium Proceedings: Metrology - At the Threshold of the Century Are We Ready? (Illus.). 1097p. 1999. text 50.00 (*1-58464-029-4*) Natl Conf Stds Labs.

National Conference State Legislature Fiscal Dept. Critical Issues in State-Local Fiscal Policy: Sorting Out State & Local Responsibilities. LC 97-221392. 16p. 1997. 15.00 (*1-55516-559-1*, 5335) Natl Conf State Legis.

National Congress on Pressure Vessels & Piping Sta. Dynamics of Fluid-Structure Systems in the Energy Industry: Presented at the Third National Congress on Pressure Vessel & Piping, San Francisco, California, June 25-29, 1979. Au-Yang, M. K. & Brown, S. J., eds. LC 79-51763. (PVP Ser.: No. 39). 234p. reprint ed. pap. 72.60 (*0-8357-6997-6*, 203905000010) Bks Demand.

— Lifeline Earthquake Engineering - Buried Pipelines, Seismic Risk, & Instrumentation: Presented at the Third National Congress on Pressure Vessels & Piping, San Francisco, California, June 25-29, 1979. Ariman, Teoman et al, eds. LC 79-50126. (PVP Ser.: No. 34). (Illus.). 291p. reprint ed. pap. 90.30 (*0-8357-2870-6*, 203910600011) Bks Demand.

— Safety Relief Valves: Prepared at the Third National Congress on Pressure Vessels & Piping, San Francisco, CA, June 24-29, 1979. Haupt, R. W. & Meyer, R. A., eds. LC 79-50127. (PVP Ser.: No. 33), (Illus.). 200p. reprint ed. pap. 62.00 (*0-8357-3523-0*, 205681300089) Bks Demand.

National Congress on Pressure Vessels & Piping Staff. Flow Induced Vibrations: Presented at the 3rd National Congress on Pressure Vessel & Piping Technology, San Francisco, CA, June 25-29, 1979. Chen, Shoei-Sheng & Bernstein, Martin D., eds. LC 79-50128. 158p. reprint ed. pap. 49.00 (*0-608-30911-7*, 202111600020) Bks Demand.

— Pressure Vessels & Piping: Verification & Qualification of Inelastic Analysis Computer Programs, Proceedings of the National Congress on Pressure Vessels & Piping, 2nd, San Francisco, 1975. Corum, J. M. & Wright, W. B., eds. LC 75-8090. (Illus.). 117p. reprint ed. pap. 36.30 (*0-608-30361-5*, 201681300005) Bks Demand.

National Consortium for Environmental Education &. EE Toolbox Slide Resource Kit. 20p. 1994. ring bd. 49.95 (*1-884782-01-9*) Natl Consort EET.

— Getting Started: A Guide to Bringing Environmental Education into Your Classroom. (EEToolbox-Workshop Resource Manual Ser.). 140p. 1994. 9.95 (*1-884782-00-0*) Natl Consort EET.

National Consortium for Physical Education & Recre. Adapted Physical Education National Standards: National Consortium for Physical Education & Recreation for Individuals with Disabilities (U. S.) Kelly, Luke E., ed. LC 95-3492. 224p. (Orig.). 1995. pap. text 26.00 (*0-87322-962-2*, BNCP0962) Human Kinetics.

National Consultancy Congress Staff, et al. Financing & Management of Infrastructure Projects: Papers Presented at the 2nd National Consultancy Congress, 15-16 January, 1999, New Delhi. LC 99-932055. xi, 173p. 1999. write for info. (*81-7023-863-3*) Allied Pubs.

National Consumer Council Staff. The Consumer & the State: Getting Value for Public Money, 2 vols. LC 81-465348. 1979. pap. write for info. (*0-905653-24-6*) Natl Consumer Coun.

— Shades of Green: Consumers' Attitudes to Green Shopping. LC 97-175711. 24 p. 1996. write for info. (*1-899581-75-8*) Natl Consumer Coun.

National Consumer Law Center, Inc. Staff. Consumer Law Training Manual & Repossession Materials. 262p. 1986. 18.50 (*0-685-23172-0*, 41,264) NCLS Inc.

***National Consumer Law Center, Inc. Staff.** Credit Discrimination. 2nd ed. LC 98-68302. (Consumer Credit & Sales Legal Practice Ser.). 464p. 1998. pap. 80.00 (*1-881793-73-7*) Nat Consumer Law.

National Consumer Law Center, Inc. Staff. Fair Credit Reporting Act. 4th ed. LC 98-68301. (Consumer Credit & Sales Legal Practice Ser.). 784p. 1998. pap. 100.00 (*1-881793-74-5*) Nat Consumer Law.

— The Regulation of Rural Electric Cooperatives. LC 93-84977. (Utility Law Practice Ser.). 208p. 1993. pap. 60.00 (*1-881793-08-7*) Nat Consumer Law.

— Repossessions & Foreclosures. 4th ed. LC 99-68476. (Consumer Credit & Sales Legal Practice Ser.). 896p. 1999. pap. 100.00 (*1-881793-88-5*) Nat Consumer Law.

— Tenants' Rights to Utility Service, 1993. LC 93-86927. (Utility Law Practice Ser.). 180p. 1994. pap. 60.00 (*1-881793-19-2*) Nat Consumer Law.

— Truth in Lending. 4th ed. LC 99-68928. (Consumer Credit & Sales Legal Practice Ser.). 920p. 1999. pap. 110.00 (*1-881793-89-3*) Nat Consumer Law.

— Truth in Lending Case Summaries. 3rd ed. 350p. (Orig.). 1983. pap. 15.00 (*0-941077-04-7*, 22,250) NCLS Inc.

National Consumer Law Center Staff. Consumer Credit Law Manual. LC 98-23760. 1998. 155.00 (*0-8205-3045-X*); 155.00 (*0-8205-4010-2*) Bender.

— Consumer Warranty Law. (Consumer Credit & Sales Legal Practice Ser.). 784p. 1997. pap. 90.00 (*1-881793-62-1*) Nat Consumer Law.

National Council, Committee on Geodosy Staff. Airborne Geophysics & Precise Positioning: Scientific Issues & Future Directions. 128p. (Orig.). (C). 1995. pap. text 30.00 (*0-309-05183-5*) Natl Acad Pr.

National Council, Committee on Oceanic Carbon. Applications of Analytical Chemistry to Oceanic Carbon Cycle Studies. 96p. (Orig.). (C). 1993. pap. text 26.00 (*0-309-04928-8*) Natl Acad Pr.

National Council for Accreditation in Teacher Education Staff. A Guide to College Programs in Teacher Preparation. LC 99-11026. (Orig.). 1999. pap. 24.95 (*0-7879-4693-1*) Jossey-Bass.

National Council for Civil Liberties (Great Britain) Staff, jt. auth. see Foley, Conor.

National Council for International Health (U.S.) S, jt. auth. see Levinger, Beryl.

National Council for Research on Women Staff, ed. see Phillips, Lynn.

National Council for the Social Studies Staff. Curriculum Standards for Social Studies Expectations of Excellence. LC 94-68635. (Orig.). 1994. pap. 15.00 (*0-87986-065-0*) Nat Coun Soc Studies.

— Evaluation in Social Studies. Berg, Harry D., ed. LC 31-6192. (Yearbook Ser.: 35). 265p. reprint ed. pap. 82.20 (*0-608-11954-7*, 202318900032) Bks Demand.

An Asterisk (*) at the beginning of an entry indicates that the title is appearing for the first time.

National Council for Vocational Qualifications Sta. British Qualifications. 744p. 1989. pap. 74.95 (*0-8464-1407-4*); text 74.95 (*0-8464-1406-6*) Beekman Pubs.

National Council of American Soviet Friendship Sta. Science in Soviet Russia. LC 74-25151. (History, Philosophy & Sociology of Science Ser.). 1975. reprint ed. 18.95 (*0-405-06635-X*) Ayer.

***National Council of Applied Economic Research.** India: Human Development Report a Profile of Indian States in the 1990s. (Illus.). 384p. 2000. pap. text 29.95 (*0-19-564762-9*) OUP.

***National Council of Examines Staff.** Principles & Practice of Engineering (PE) Sample Problems & Solutions in Electrical Engineering. 1998. pap. 41.75 (*0-7803-4596-7*) Inst Electrical.

National Council of Instructors in Landscape Archi. Specialization in Landscape Architectural Education: Proceedings NCILA, 1975, Texas A & M, July 10-12. LC SB0469.23.C6. 98p. pap. 30.40 (*0-8357-3042-5*, 203929700012) Bks Demand.

National Council of Jewish Women, Omaha Section St. The Kitchen Connection. Kutler, Sandy & Polikov, Sheila, eds. (Illus.). (Orig.). 1983. pap. 11.95 (*0-9612406-0-1*) Omaha Sec Nat.

National Council of Jewish Women Staff. Abortion: Challenges Ahead. (Illus.). 25p. (Orig.). 1985. pap. text 5.00 (*0-941840-19-0*) NCJW.

— Caring for Older Adults: A Handbook. 1993. 4.00 (*0-614-06653-0*) NCJW.

— Choosing Family Child Care: A Handbook for Parents. (Illus.). 21p. 1990. 3.00 (*0-685-62941-4*) NCJW.

— Como Elegir Una Casa Particular Donde Le Cuiden a Su Nino: Manual Para Padres. (Illus.). 21p. 1992. 3.00 (*0-685-62942-2*) NCJW.

— Domestic Violence Program Guide: "A Family Affair" 14p. (Orig.). 1983. pap. text 3.00 (*0-941840-12-3*) NCJW.

— Employers & Family Day Care. (Illus.). 50p. 1991. 10.00 (*0-685-62940-6*) NCJW.

— An Employers Guide to Eldercare: Institute on Aging, Work, & Health. 1991. 4.00 (*0-614-06654-9*) NCJW.

— The Hard Questions in Family Day Care: National Issues & Exemplary Programs. 122p. 1991. 18.95 (*0-685-62943-0*) NCJW.

— Juvenile Waiver. (Illus.). (Orig.). 1985. pap. text 3.50 (*0-941840-22-0*) NCJW.

— A Marketing Kit for Family Day Care Providers. 1990. 10.00 (*0-614-06656-5*) NCJW.

— Options for the 90's: Employer Support for Child Care. 22p. 1991. 10.00 (*0-685-62939-2*) NCJW.

— The Partnership Guide: Strategies for Supporting Family Day Care in Your Community. 49p. 1991. 15.00 (*0-685-62944-9*) NCJW.

— Working with Employers & Other Community Partners. 1992. 10.00 (*0-614-06655-7*) NCJW.

National Council of Juvenile & Family Court Judges. Judicial Review of Children in Placement Deskbook. 195p. 1981. 20.00 (*0-318-21318-4*) Natl Juv & Family Ct Judges.

National Council of Juvenile Court Judges Staff. Guides for Juvenile Court Judges. 145p. 1963. 1.50 (*0-318-15366-1*) Natl Coun Crime.

National Council of Negro Women Staff. Black Family Reunion Cookbook: Recipes & Food Memories. LC 92-41128. (Illus.). 224p. 1993. per. 12.00 (*0-671-79629-1*) S&S Trade.

— Celebrating Our Mothers' Kitchens: Words of Wisdom & Treasured Recipes. Wimmer, Glen, ed. LC 94-18488. (Illus.). 224p. 1994. 15.95 (*1-879958-23-6*, Tradery) Wimmer Cos.

National Council of Negro Women Staff, ed. see Thurman, Sue Bailey.

National Council of Professors of Educational Administration Staff, jt. auth. see Jenlink, Patrick M.

National Council of Staff, Program & Organizationa. Community Colleges, the Future & SPOD (Staff, Program & Organizational Development) Brass, Richard J., ed. LC 84-61248. 162p. (Orig.). 1984. pap. 18.95 (*0-913507-01-6*) New Forums.

National Council of Teachers of English. English for Today, Bk. 5: Life in English Speaking Countries, Vol. 5. 1967. text, student ed. 1.95 (*0-07-046108-2*) McGraw.

— English for Today, Book 5: Our Changing Culture. 2nd ed. (gr. 10-12). 1975. text, student ed. 12.72 (*0-07-045816-2*) McGraw.

National Council of Teachers of English, Comparati. Yearbook of Comparative & General Literature, No. 32, 1983. LC PN0851.Y4. 160p. pap. 49.60 (*0-608-14589-0*, 202482100032) Bks Demand.

— Yearbook of Comparative & General Literature, 1982, No. 31. LC PN0851.Y4. 167p. reprint ed. pap. 51.80 (*0-608-14268-9*, 202220400025) Bks Demand.

— Yearbook of Comparative & General Literature, 1984, No. 33. LC PN0851.Y4. 128p. pap. 39.70 (*0-608-16758-4*, 202624300049) Bks Demand.

— Yearbook of Comparative & General Literature, 1993 Vol. 41, Vol. 4. LC PN0851.Y4. 245p. 1993. reprint ed. pap. 76.00 (*0-608-01625-X*, 206221000002) Bks Demand.

— Yearbook of Comparative & General Literature, 1994 Vol. 42, Vol. 4. LC PN0851.Y4. 188p. 1994. reprint ed. pap. 58.30 (*0-608-01626-8*, 206221100002) Bks Demand.

National Council of Teachers of English Staff. English for Today. 2nd ed. Incl. Bk. 1. At Home & at School. 1973. text 13.60 (*0-07-045802-2*); Bk. 2. World We Live In. 1973. text 13.60 (*0-07-045806-5*); Bk. 3. Way We Live. 1973. text 13.60 (*0-07-045810-3*); write for info. (*0-318-54193-9*) McGraw.

— English for Today Bk. IV Vol. 4: Our Changing World, Vol. 4. 1966. text, student ed. 1.95 (*0-07-046106-6*) McGraw.

— English for Today [0016]ol. 4: Book 3-A, Vol. 4. 2nd ed. 1977. text 1.50 (*0-07-045955-X*) McGraw.

— English for Today Vol. 1: Book 1-A. 2nd ed. 1977. text 1.50 (*0-07-045951-7*) McGraw.

— English for Today Vol. 1: Book 1-B. 2nd ed. 1977. text 1.50 (*0-07-045952-5*) McGraw.

— English for Today Vol. 2: Book 2-A, Vol. 2. 2nd ed. 1977. text 1.50 (*0-07-045953-3*) McGraw.

— English for Today Vol. 3: Book 2-B, Vol. 3. 2nd ed. 1977. text 1.50 (*0-07-045954-1*) McGraw.

— English for Today Vol. 5: Book 3-B, Vol. 5. 2nd ed. 1977. text 1.50 (*0-07-045956-8*) McGraw.

— Pathways to English, Bk. 1. 1984. pap. text, wbk. ed. 5.37 (*0-07-046605-X*) McGraw.

— Pathways to English, Bk. 1. 3rd ed. 1984. text, teacher ed. 14.95 (*0-07-046591-6*) McGraw.

— Pathways to English, Bk. 2. 3rd ed. 1984. text, wbk. ed. 5.37 (*0-07-046616-5*) McGraw.

— Pathways to English, Bk. 2. 3rd ed. 1984. text 93.92 (*0-07-046619-X*) McGraw.

— Pathways to English, Bk. 2. 3rd ed. 1984. text, teacher ed. 14.95 (*0-07-046592-4*) McGraw.

— Pathways to English, Bk. 3. 3rd ed. 1984. text, teacher ed. 14.95 (*0-07-046593-2*); pap. text, wbk. ed. 5.37 (*0-07-046626-2*) McGraw.

— Pathways to English, Bk. 4. 3rd ed. 1984. text, teacher ed. 14.95 (*0-07-046633-5*); pap. text, wbk. ed. 5.37 (*0-07-046610-6*) McGraw.

— Pathways to English, Bk. 4. 3rd ed. 1984. text 93.92 (*0-07-046611-4*) McGraw.

— Pathways to English, Bk. 5. 3rd ed. 1984. text 8.51 (*0-07-046635-1*); pap. text, wbk. ed. 5.37 (*0-07-046620-3*) McGraw.

— Pathways to English, Bk. 5. 3rd ed. 1984. text 93.92 (*0-07-046621-1*) McGraw.

— Pathways to English, Bk. 5. 3rd ed. 1984. text, teacher ed. 14.95 (*0-07-046636-X*) McGraw.

— Pathways to English, Bk. 6. 3rd ed. 1984. text 8.51 (*0-07-046638-6*); text, teacher ed. 14.95 (*0-07-046639-4*) McGraw.

— Pathways to English, Bk. 6. 3rd ed. 1984. pap. text, wbk. ed. 5.37 (*0-07-046630-0*) McGraw.

National Council of Teachers of English Staff. Pathways to English, Vol. 1. 3rd ed. 192p. 1983. 8.51 (*0-07-046581-9*) McGraw.

National Council of Teachers of English Staff. Pathways to English, Vol. 2. 3rd ed. 1984. text 8.51 (*0-07-046582-7*) McGraw.

— Practicing What We Know: Informed Reading Instruction. Weaver, Constance, ed. LC 98-10262. 587p. 1998. pap. 26.95 (*0-8141-3675-5*) NCTE.

— Reading in an Age of Mass Communication: Report of the Committee on Reading at the Secondary School & College Levels. Gray, William S., ed. LC 70-167390. (Essay Index Reprint Ser.). 1977. reprint ed. 13.95 (*0-8369-2481-3*) Ayer.

— Teaching Reading & Literature. LC 96-17940. (Standards Consensus Ser.). 93p. (J). (gr. 4-6). 1996. 12.95 (*0-8141-5189-2*) NCTE.

— Teaching Reading & Literature in the Early Elementary Grades. LC 96-54826. (Standards Consensus Ser.). 108p. 1997. 12.95 (*0-8141-5193-0*) NCTE.

— Those Who Do, Can: Teachers Writing, Writers Teaching. Root, Robert L., Jr. & Steinberg, Michael, eds. LC 96-22113. 264p. 1996. pap. 26.95 (*0-8141-1860-7*) NCTE.

National Council of Teachers of English Staff, jt. auth. see Durst, Russel K.

National Council of Teachers of English Staff, jt. auth. see Freedman, Sarah W.

National Council of Teachers of English Staff, jt. auth. see International Reading Association Staff.

National Council of Teachers of English Staff, jt. auth. see NCTE Elementary Section Steering Committee.

National Council of Teachers of English Staff, jt. auth. see Oglan, Gerald R.

National Council of Teachers of English Staff, jt. auth. see Tinberg, Howard B.

National Council of Teachers of Mathematics Staff. Assessment Standards for School Mathematics. LC 95-17267. (Illus.). 112p. 1995. pap. 19.75 (*0-87353-419-0*) NCTM.

— Cumulative Index: The Arithmetic Teacher, 1954-1973. LC 56-37587. 124p. 1974. pap. 12.00 (*0-87353-027-6*) NCTM.

— Cumulative Index: The Mathematics Teacher, 1966-1975. LC 42-24844. 90p. 1977. pap. 10.00 (*0-87353-029-2*) NCTM.

— Enrichment Mathematics for High School. LC 63-14060. (National Council of Teachers of Mathematics Yearbook Ser.: 28th). 398p. reprint ed. pap. 123.40 (*0-608-16671-5*, 202706000053) Bks Demand.

— Enrichment Mathematics for the Grades. LC 63-14059. (National Council of Teachers of Mathematics Yearbook Ser.: 27th). 378p. reprint ed. pap. 117.20 (*0-608-16644-8*, 202705600053) Bks Demand.

— Evaluation in Mathematics. LC 61-11906. (National Council of Teachers of Mathematics Yearbook Ser.: 26th). 222p. reprint ed. pap. 68.90 (*0-608-16634-0*, 202705500053) Bks Demand.

— The Growth of Mathematical Ideas, Grades K-12. LC 60-1738. (National Council of Teachers of Mathematics Yearbook Ser.: 24th). 517p. reprint ed. pap. 160.30 (*0-608-16618-9*, 202705300053) Bks Demand.

— Historical Topics for the Mathematics Classroom. rev. ed. LC 89-12208. (Illus.). 542p. 1989. pap. 35.95 (*0-87353-281-3*) NCTM.

— A History of Mathematics Education in the United States & Canada. LC 71-105864. (National Council of Teachers of Mathematics Yearbook Ser.: No. 32). 577p. reprint ed. pap. 178.90 (*0-608-09207-X*, 205271100003) Bks Demand.

— Instruction in Arithmetic. LC 60-7488. (National Council of Teachers of Mathematics Yearbook Ser.: 25th). 372p. reprint ed. pap. 115.40 (*0-608-16626-X*, 202705400053) Bks Demand.

— Instructional Aids in Mathematics. LC 76-189323. (National Council of Teachers of Mathematics Yearbook Ser.: 34th). 460p. reprint ed. pap. 142.60 (*0-608-16663-4*, 202705900053) Bks Demand.

— The Learning of Mathematics: Its Theory & Practice. LC QA0001.N3. (National Council of Teachers of Mathematics Yearbook Ser.: 21st). 365p. reprint ed. pap. 113.20 (*0-608-16588-3*, 202705200053) Bks Demand.

***National Council of Teachers of Mathematics Staff.** Principles & Standards for School Mathematics. LC 00-32109. 2000. write for info. (*0-87353-480-8*) NCTM.

National Council of Teachers of Mathematics Staff. The Teaching of Secondary School Mathematics. LC 27-7119. (National Council of Teachers of Mathematics Yearbook Ser.: 33rd). 441p. reprint ed. pap. 136.80 (*0-608-16656-1*, 202705800053) Bks Demand.

National Council of Teachers of Mathematics Staff, jt. auth. see Moses, Barbara.

National Council of the Churches of Christ in the United States of America Staff, jt. auth. see Rumer, Patricia.

National Council of Young Israel NCYI Staff. Words of Torah: A Collection of Divrei Torah by Young Israel Rabbis. LC 98-10687. 1998. 50.00 (*0-7657-6004-5*) Aronson.

National Council on Aging Staff. Myth & Reality of Aging, 1974. LC 79-84576. 1979. write for info. (*0-89138-971-7*) ICPSR.

National Council on Compensation Insurance Staff. The National Council Workmen's Compensation Unit Statistical Plan Manual. (Illus.). 1983. write for info. (*0-318-58248-1*) Natl Comp Ins.

National Council on Crime & Delinquency Staff. Community Crime Prevention: An Annotated Bibliography. 1983. 4.50 (*0-318-02049-1*) Natl Coun Crime.

— Executive Summary of the National Evaluation of Delinquency Prevention: Final Report. 1980. 1.50 (*0-318-02056-4*) Natl Coun Crime.

National Council on Crime & Delinquency Staff & O'Leary, Vincent. Correctional Policy Inventory. 1970. ring bd. 4.10 (*0-318-02051-3*) Natl Coun Crime.

— Frames of Reference in Sentencing & Parole Inventory. 1977. ring bd. 4.10 (*0-318-02052-1*) Natl Coun Crime.

National Council on Governmental Accounting Staff. Governmental Accounting & Financial Reporting Principles. LC 79-87496. (NCGA Statement: No. 1). (Illus.). 49p. 1979. pap. 10.00 (*0-686-84258-8*) Municipal.

National Council on Public History Staff. The Records of Government. LC 87-3384. 192p. 1987. reprint ed. lib. bdg. 22.50 (*0-89464-231-6*) Krieger.

National Council on Radiation Protection & Measure. Acceptability of Risk from Radiation - Application to Human Space Flight: Application to Human Space Flight: Held May 29, 1996, Arlington, Virginia. LC 97-10709. (Symposium Proceedings Ser.: Vol. 3). 200p. 1997. pap. 30.00 (*0-929600-56-8*) NCRP Pubns.

— Carbon-14 in the Environment. LC 84-29586. (Report Ser.: No. 81). 112p. 1985. pap. text 35.00 (*0-913392-73-1*) NCRP Pubns.

— Deposition, Retention & Dosimetry of Inhaled Radioactive Substances: Recommendations of the National Council on Radiation Protection & Measurements. LC 96-37944. (NCRP Reports: Vol. 125). (Orig.). 1997. pap. 40.00 (*0-929600-54-1*) NCRP Pubns.

— Evaluating the Reliability of Biokinetic & Dosimetric Models & Parameters Used to Assess Individual Doses for Risk Assessment Purposes. LC 98-4408. (NCRP Commentaries Ser.: Vol. 15). 119p. 1998. pap. 30.00 (*0-929600-58-4*) NCRP Pubns.

— Operational Radiation Safety Program: Recommendations of the National Council on Radiation Protection & Measurements. LC 98-4407. (NCRP Reports: Vol. 127). 1998. pap. 30.00 (*0-929600-59-2*) NCRP Pubns.

***National Council on Radiation Protection & Measure.** Radiation Protection in Medicine: Comtemporary Issues: Program: Thirty-Fifth Annual Meeting, April 7-8, 1999, Crystal Forum Crystal City Marriott, Arlington, VA. LC 99-13821. (NCRP Annual Meeting Proceedings Ser.). 1999. 65.00 (*0-929600-62-2*) NCRP Pubns.

National Council on Radiation Protection & Measure. Radionuclide Exposure of the Embryo/Fetus. LC 98-27800. (NCRP Reports: No. 128). 1998. pap. 35.00 (*0-929600-60-6*) NCRP Pubns.

National Council on Radiation Protection & Measure & Boice, John D. Implications of New Data on Radiation Cancer Risk: Proceedings of the Thirty-Second Annual Meeting, 3-4 April 1996, As Presented at the Crystal City Marriott, Arlington, Va. LC 97-3044. (Proceedings Ser.: Vol. 18). (Illus.). 314p. (Orig.). 1997. pap. 45.00 (*0-929600-55-X*) NCRP Pubns.

National Council on Radiation Protection & Measure & Till, John E. Environmental Dose Reconstruction & Risk Implications: Proceedings of the Thirty-First Annual Meeting 12-13 April 1995, As Presented at the Crystal City Marriott, Arlington, VA. LC 96-34921. (Annual Meeting Proceedings Ser.: No. 17). 373p. 1996. pap. 50.00 (*0-929600-53-3*) NCRP Pubns.

National Council on the Aging, Inc. Staff. Respite Resource Guide. 40p. 1990. pap. 8.00 (*0-910883-51-3*, 2040) Natl Coun Aging.

National Council on the Aging Staff, ed. see Alvarez, Ronald A. & Kline, Susan C.

National Council on the Aging Staff, ed. see Hettlinger, Richard F. & Worth, Grace.

National Council on the Handicapped Staff. On the Threshold of Independence: Progress on Legislative Recommendations Toward Independence. 100p. (Orig.). 1988. write for info. (*0-936825-01-4*) Nat Coun Handicapped.

***National Craft Association Staff.** The Complete Idiot's Guide to Making Money with Your Hobby. (Complete Idiot's Guide Ser.). 384p. 2000. pap. 18.95 (*0-02-863825-5*, Alpha Ref) Macmillan Gen Ref.

National Crime Prevention Council Staff. Making a Difference: Young People in Community Crime Prevention. LC 85-61344. (Illus.). 132p. (Orig.). 1985. pap. 11.95 (*0-934513-00-7*, M2B) Natl Crime DC.

National Crime Prevention Institute Staff. Understanding Crime Prevention. (Illus.). 207p. (C). 1986. 34.95 (*0-409-90075-3*) Buttrwrth-Heinemann.

***National Crime Prevention Institute Staff, ed.** Understanding Crime Prevention. 2nd ed. 208p. 2000. pap. 29.95 (*0-7506-7220-X*) Buttrwrth-Heinemann.

National Crime Prevention Institute Staff & Crowe, Timothy D. Crime Prevention Through Environmental Design. 258p. 1991. 49.95 (*0-7506-9058-5*) Buttrwrth-Heinemann.

National Crime Prevention Institute Staff & D'Addario, Francis J. Loss Prevention Through Crime Analysis. (Illus.). 96p. 1989. pap. 27.95 (*0-409-90191-1*) Buttrwrth-Heinemann.

National Curriculum Editors. The English Book: A Perma-Bound Teach & Use Handbook for the Secondary Level. Snodgrass, Mary E., ed. (Illus.). 252p. 1991. lib. bdg. 15.30 (*0-7804-1950-2*, 089669) Perma-Bound.

National Curriculum Publishing Editors. Great American English Handbook. rev. ed. Snodgrass, Mary E., ed. (Illus.). 235p. 1988. reprint ed. lib. bdg. 15.30 (*0-8000-2426-5*, 122550) Perma-Bound.

National Defence Staff, ed. The Canadian Military Experience, 1867-1995: A Bibliography. 3rd ed. LC 96-980424. (FRE & ENG.). 151p. 1997. pap. 17.95 (*0-660-60164-8*, Pub. by Canadian Govt Pub) Accents Pubns.

National Defense Research Institute (U. S.) Staff. Sexual Orientation & U. S. Military Personnel Policy: Options & Assessment. 546p. 1993. pap. text 16.00 (*0-8330-1441-2*, MR-323-OSD) Rand Corp.

National Defense University Staff. Essays, 1998. LC 98-39455. 1998. write for info. (*1-57906-014-5*) Natl Defense.

***National Defense University Staff.** Essays 1999. LC 99-36786. 1999. write for info. (*1-57906-050-1*) Natl Defense.

National Democratic Institute for International Af. An Assessment of the elections in Cameroon October 11, 1992. (ENG & FRE.). 260p. 1993. pap. 9.95 (*1-880134-19-5*) Natl Demo Inst.

— An Assessment of the Senegalese Electoral Code. (ENG & FRE.). 140p. 1991. pap. 6.00 (*1-880134-07-1*) Natl Demo Inst.

— Coordinating Observers for Niger's 1993 Elections. (ENG & FRE.). 170p. 1993. pap. 10.95 (*1-880134-22-5*) Natl Demo Inst.

— Democracies in Regions of Crisis: Botswana, Costa Rica & Israel. LC 90-60684. 145p. 1990. pap. 7.95 (*1-880134-03-9*) Natl Demo Inst.

— An Evaluation of the Elections in Ethiopia, June 21, 1992. 160p. 1992. pap. 9.95 (*1-880134-18-7*) Natl Demo Inst.

— The June 1990 Elections in Bulgaria. 117p. 1990. pap. 6.00 (*1-880134-00-4*) Natl Demo Inst.

— The May 1990 in Romania. 133p. 1991. pap. 6.00 (*1-880134-05-5*) Natl Demo Inst.

— The May 7, 1989 Panamanian Elections. 126p. 1989. pap. 6.00 (*1-880134-01-2*) Natl Demo Inst.

— Nation Building: The U. N. & Namibia. 130p. 1990. pap. 6.95 (*1-880134-06-3*) Natl Demo Inst.

— The National Elections in Paraguay, 1993. 200p. pap. 10.95 (*1-880134-24-1*) Natl Demo Inst.

— NDI Handbook How Domestic Organizations Monitor Elections: An A to Z Guide. 160p. 1995. pap. 14.95 (*1-880134-17-9*) Natl Demo Inst.

— The 1989 Paraguayan Elections: A Foundation for Democratic Change. 68p. 1989. pap. 6.00 (*1-880134-02-0*) Natl Demo Inst.

— The 1990 General Elections in Guatemala. 114p. 1991. pap. 10.95 (*1-880134-11-X*) Natl Demo Inst.

— The 1990 General Elections in Haiti. 123p. (Orig.). 1991. pap. 10.95 (*1-880134-08-X*) Natl Demo Inst.

— The 1993 Elections in Senegal. LC 94-38717. (ENG & FRE.). 250p. pap. 10.95 (*1-880134-21-7*) Natl Demo Inst.

— The October, 1990 Elections in Pakistan. 236p. 1991. pap. 10.00 (*1-880134-04-7*) Natl Demo Inst.

— Promoting Participation in Yemen's 1993 Elections. LC 94-4307. 150p. 1994. pap. 8.95 (*1-880134-23-3*) Natl Demo Inst.

— Reforming the Philippine Electoral Process: Developments, 1986-88. 86p. 1991. pap. 8.95 (*1-880134-10-1*) Natl Demo Inst.

— Voting for Greater Pluralism: The May 26, 1991 Municipal Elections in Paraguay. 97p. 1992. pap. 8.95 (*1-880134-13-6*) Natl Demo Inst.

National Democratic Institute for International Af & Carter Center of Emory University Staff. The October 31st, 1991 Presidential & Legislative Elections in Zambia. 167p. 1992. pap. 9.95 (*1-880134-14-4*) Natl Demo Inst.

National Democratic Institute for International Af & International Republican Institute Staff. The October 13th, 1991 Legislative & Municipal Elections in Bulgaria. 136p. 1992. pap. 9.95 (*1-880134-12-8*) Natl Demo Inst.

N

***National DMDA Staff.** Restoring Intimacy: The Patient's Guide to Maintaining Relationships During Depression. 144p. 1999. pap. 12.95 (*0-9673893-0-5*, Pub. by Nat Dprsv & Mnc-Dprsv) ACCESS Pubs Network.

National Drug Abuse Conference Inc. Staff. Critical Concerns in the Field of Drug Abuse: Proceedings of the National Drug Abuse Conference, 3rd, New York, 1976. LC 78-12871. 1464p. reprint ed. pap. 200.00 (*0-608-16846-7*, 202708500054) Bks Demand.

National Drug Abuse Conference, 2nd, 1975, New Orl. Drug Abuse: Modern Trends, Issues, & Perspectives: Proceedings of the Second National Drug Abuse Conference, Inc., New Orleans, Louisiana, 1975. Kaufman, Edward et al, eds. LC 78-4091. 1254p. reprint ed. pap. 200.00 (*0-608-16879-3*, 202708900054) Bks Demand.

***National Economic United.** Fertility & Family Surveys in Countries of the Ece Region: Standard Country Report, Finland. 10g. 87p. 1998. pap. 25.00 (*92-1-100770-4*) UN.

National Editorial Board, New & Letters Staff. American Civilization on Trial: Black Masses As Vanguard. 4th ed. (Illus.). 48p. 1983. pap. 2.00 (*0-914441-03-5*) News & Letters.

National Education Association, Committee on Secon. Report of the Committee on Secondary School Studies, Appointed at the Meeting of the National Education Association. LC 70-89222. (American Education: Its Men, Institutions, & Ideas. Series 1). 1978. reprint ed. 21.95 (*0-405-01403-1*) Ayer.

National Education Association of the United State. A Teacher Survey NEA Report: Computers in the Classroom. LC LB1028.5.T38. 98p. reprint ed. pap. 30.40 (*0-608-15298-6*, 202954300061) Bks Demand.

National Education Association of the United State, jt. auth. see Hiraoka, Leona.

National Education Association of the United States Staff, jt. auth. see Stiggins, Richard J.

National Education Association Staff. Appropriate Inclusion & Paragraphs. 1996. pap. 12.50 (*0-8106-1875-3*) NEA.

— Assessing Learning in Classroom. 1995. pap. 8.69 (*0-8106-1868-0*) NEA.

— Building Parent Partnerships. 1996. pap. text, teacher ed. 16.25 (*0-8106-2911-9*) NEA.

— Copyright Primer for Librarian. (Illus.). 1998. pap. 27.50 (*0-8106-1870-2*) NEA.

N

National Education Association Staff. How Letters Make Words. 1983. pap. 1.95 (*0-380-82685-2*, Avon Bks) Morrow Avon.

— Learning to Add. 1983. pap. 1.95 (*0-380-82719-0*, Avon Bks) Morrow Avon.

— Learning to Subtract. 1983. pap. 1.95 (*0-380-82735-2*, Avon Bks) Morrow Avon.

National Education Association Staff. Multicultural Resource Guide. (Illus.). 1997. pap. 23.75 (*0-8106-2005-7*) NEA.

— Providing Safe Health Care. 1996. pap. 13.75 (*0-8106-1876-1*) NEA.

National Education Association Staff. Shapes & Patterns. 1983. pap. 1.95 (*0-380-82701-8*, Avon Bks) Morrow Avon.

National Education Association Staff. Working Together to Improve Schools. pap. 13.75 (*0-8106-6518-2*) NEA.

National Education Associaton of the United States Staff, jt. auth. see NEA Professional Library Association Staff.

National Education Task Force Staff. Foundations for Spiritual Education. 208p. 1995. pap. 9.95 (*0-87743-245-7*) Bahai.

***National Educational Computing Conference 1999 Staff.** NECC 99 Conference Proceedings. (Illus.). 317p. 1999. spiral bd. 25.00 (*1-56484-151-0*) Intl Society Tech Educ.

National Educational Systems Inc. Staff. Diccionario Escolar, Sinonimos y Antonimos. (SPA., Illus.). 128p. (J). (gr. 3-12). 1998. pap. write for info. (*1-893493-02-4*) Natl Educ Systs.

National Effective Transfer Consortium Staff. Enhancing Transfer Effectiveness: A Model for the 1990s. 1990. pap. 10.00 (*0-87117-250-X*, 1314) Comm Coll Pr Am Assn Comm Coll.

National Election Studies, Center for Political St & Miller, Warren E. American National Election Study, 1978. 2nd ed. LC 79-91223. 1979. write for info. (*0-89138-963-6*) ICPSR.

— American National Election Study, 1978, I. 2nd ed. LC 79-91223. 1979. write for info. (*0-89138-957-1*) ICPSR.

— American National Election Study, 1978, II. 2nd ed. LC 79-91223. 1979. write for info. (*0-89138-958-X*) ICPSR.

— American National Election Study, 1980, 5 vols. LC 82-82378. 1982. write for info. (*0-89138-921-0*); write for info. (*0-89138-922-9*); write for info. (*0-89138-916-4*); write for info. (*0-89138-923-7*); write for info. (*0-89138-924-5*) ICPSR.

— American National Election Study, 1980, 5 vols., Set. LC 82-82378. 1982. write for info. (*0-89138-925-3*, ICPSR 7763) ICPSR.

— American National Election Study, 1984: Appendix: Notes & Questionnaire. 2nd ed. LC 86-80606. (American National Election Studies). 529p. 1986. write for info. (*0-89138-887-7*) ICPSR.

— American National Election Study, 1984: Pre & Post-Election Survey. 2nd ed. LC 86-80607. (American National Election Studies). 642p. 1986. write for info. (*0-89138-886-9*) ICPSR.

— American National Election Study, 1986: Appendices. 2nd ed. LC 87-83560. (American National Election Studies). 1988. write for info. (*0-89138-880-X*) ICPSR.

National Election Studies Center for Political Stu & Miller, Warren E. American National Election Study, 1986: Post-Election Survey. 2nd ed. LC 87-83559. (American National Election Studies). 439p. 1988. write for info. (*0-89138-879-6*) ICPSR.

National Election Studies Staff & Miller, Warren E. American National Election Study, 1982, 2 vols. LC 85-117505. 1983. write for info. (*0-89138-902-4*); write for info. (*0-89138-900-8*) ICPSR.

— American National Election Study, 1982, 2 vols., Set. LC 85-117505. 1983. write for info. (*0-89138-899-0*) ICPSR.

— American National Election Study, 1988: Pre- & Post-Election Survey & Appendix. 2nd ed. LC 89-82313. 724p. 1990. write for info. (*0-89138-872-9*); write for info. (*0-89138-871-0*) ICPSR.

National Election Studies Staff, et al. American National Election Study, 1990: Post-Election Survey. 2nd ed. LC 92-70528. (American National Election Studies). 772p. 1992. write for info. (*0-89138-865-6*) ICPSR.

— American National Election Study, 1992 Vol. 1: Pre- & Post-Election Survey (Enhanced with 1990 & 1991 Data): Introduction & 1990 Codebook Variables. LC 93-80826. 544p. 1993. write for info. (*0-89138-858-3*) ICPSR.

— American National Election Study, 1992 Vol. 2: Pre- & Post-Election Survey (Enhanced with 1990 & 1991 Data): 1991 & 1992 Codebook Variables. LC 93-80826. 696p. 1993. write for info. (*0-89138-859-1*) ICPSR.

— American National Election Study, 1992 Vol. 3: Pre- & Post-Election Survey (Enhanced with 1990 & 1991 Data): Appendix, Notes, Frequency Addendum, & Questionnnaires. LC 93-80826. 632p. 1993. write for info. (*0-89138-860-5*) ICPSR.

National Electric Safety Code, ANSI C2 Staff. NESC Interpretations Second Interim Collection, 1991-1993. (Illus.). 68p. (Orig.). 1990. pap. 35.00 (*1-55937-025-4*) IEEE Standards.

National Electronic Packaging & Production Confere. National Electronic Packaging & Production Conference, 1984 West: Proceedings of the Technical Program, Anaheim CA, February 28, 29, & March 1, 1984. LC TK7872.. 529p. 1984. reprint ed. pap. 164.00 (*0-608-11869-9*, 202306000031) Bks Demand.

— National Electronic Packaging & Production Conference, 1985 East: Proceedings of the Technical Program, Boston, MA, June 19-21, 1985. LC TK7872.. 541p. 1985. reprint ed. pap. 167.80 (*0-608-16876-9*, 202768700056) Bks Demand.

— National Electronic Packaging & Production Conference, 1985 West: Proceedings of the Technical Program, Anaheim CA, February 26-28, 1985. LC TK7872.. 973p. 1985. reprint ed. pap. 200.00 (*0-608-13005-2*, 202509000042) Bks Demand.

— National Electronic Packaging & Production Conference, 1986 East: Proceedings of the Technical Program, Boston, MA, June 10-12, 1986. LC TK7872.. 452p. 1986. reprint ed. pap. 140.20 (*0-608-15440-7*, 202936600060) Bks Demand.

— National Electronic Packaging & Production Conference, 1986 West: Proceedings of the Technical Program, Anaheim, CA, February 25-27, 1986, 2 vols., 1. LC TK7872.. 536p. 1986. reprint ed. pap. 166.20 (*0-608-16870-X*, 202768600001) Bks Demand.

— National Electronic Packaging & Production Conference, 1986 West: Proceedings of the Technical Program, Anaheim, CA, February 25-27, 1986, 2 vols., 2. LC TK7872.. 486p. 1986. reprint ed. pap. 150.70 (*0-608-16871-8*, 202768600002) Bks Demand.

— National Electronic Packaging & Production Conference, 1987 West: Proceedings of the Technical Program, February 24-26, 1987, 2 vols., 1. LC TK7872.. (Illus.). 596p. 1987. pap. 184.80 (*0-608-17396-7*, 203023700001) Bks Demand.

— National Electronic Packaging & Production Conference, 1987 West: Proceedings of the Technical Program, February 24-26, 1987, 2 vols., 2. LC TK7872.. (Illus.). 487p. 1987. pap. 151.00 (*0-608-17397-5*, 203023700002) Bks Demand.

— National Electronic Packaging & Production Conference, 1988 East: Proceedings of the Technical Program, June 13-16, 1988, Boston, MA. LC TK7872.. (Illus.). 515p. 1988. reprint ed. pap. 159.70 (*0-608-18186-2*, 203291400081) Bks Demand.

— National Electronic Packaging & Production Conference, 1988 West: Proceedings of the Technical Program, February 22-25, 1988. LC TK7872.. 947p. reprint ed. pap. 200.00 (*0-608-18184-6*, 203291100081) Bks Demand.

— National Electronic Packaging & Production Conference, 1989 West: Proceedings of the Technical Program; NEPCON West '89, Anaheim, CA, March 6-9, 1989, Vol. 1. LC TK7870.N3. (Illus.). 978p. 1989. reprint ed. pap. 200.00 (*0-8357-6738-8*, 203539400001) Bks Demand.

— National Electronic Packaging & Production Conference, 1989 West: Proceedings of the Technical Program; NEPCON West '89, Anaheim, CA, March 6-9, 1989, Vol. 2. LC TK7870.N3. (Illus.). 1010p. 1989. reprint ed. pap. 200.00 (*0-8357-6739-6*, 203539400002) Bks Demand.

— National Electronic Packaging & Production Conference, 1990 Vol. 1: Proceedings of the Technical Program, Anaheim, CA, February 26-March 1, 1990. LC TK7870.N33. 984p. 1990. 200.00 (*0-7837-0145-4*, 204043500001) Bks Demand.

— National Electronic Packaging & Production Conference, 1990 East: Proceedings of the Technical Program, Boston, MA, June 11-14, 1990. LC TK7870.N33. 1056p. 1990. pap. 200.00 (*0-7837-0148-9*, 204043700016) Bks Demand.

— National Electronic Packaging & Production Conference, 1990 West Vol. 2: Proceedings of the Technical Program, Anaheim, CA, February 26-March 1, 1990. LC TK7870.N33. 929p. 1990. 200.00 (*0-7837-0146-2*, 204043500002) Bks Demand.

— National Electronic Packaging & Production Conference, 1991 West: Proceedings of the Technical Program, Anaheim CA, February 24-28, 1991, Vol. 1. LC TK7870.N33. 782p. 1991. pap. 200.00 (*0-7837-0149-7*, 204043800001) Bks Demand.

— National Electronic Packaging & Production Conference, 1991 West: Proceedings of the Technical Program, Anaheim CA, February 24-28, 1991, Vol. 2. LC TK7870.N33. 705p. 1991. pap. 200.00 (*0-7837-0150-0*, 204043800002) Bks Demand.

— National Electronic Packaging & Production Conference, 1991 West: Proceedings of the Technical Program, Anaheim CA, February 24-28, 1991, Vol. 3. LC TK7870.N33. 923p. 1991. pap. 200.00 (*0-7837-0151-9*, 204043800003) Bks Demand.

— National Electronic Packaging & Production Conference, 1992 East: Proceedings of the Technical Program, Boston, MA, June 15-18, 1992. LC TK7874.N35. 467p. 1992. reprint ed. pap. 144.80 (*0-7837-2688-0*, 204306600006) Bks Demand.

— National Electronic Packaging & Production Conference, 1992 West: Proceedings of the Technical Program, Anaheim CA, February 23-27, 1992, Vol. 1. LC TK7874.N35. (Illus.). 464p. 1992. reprint ed. pap. 143.90 (*0-7837-3073-X*, 204306500001) Bks Demand.

— National Electronic Packaging & Production Conference, 1992 West: Proceedings of the Technical Program, Anaheim CA, February 23-27, 1992, Vol. 2. LC TK7874.N35. (Illus.). 663p. 1992. reprint ed. pap. 200.00 (*0-7837-3074-8*, 204306500002) Bks Demand.

— National Electronic Packaging & Production Conference, 1992 West: Proceedings of the Technical Program, Anaheim CA, February 23-27, 1992, Vol. 3. LC TK7874.N35. (Illus.). 805p. 1992. reprint ed. pap. 200.00 (*0-7837-3075-6*, 204306500003) Bks Demand.

— National Electronic Packaging & Production Conference, 1993 East: Proceedings of the Technical Program, Bayside Exposition Center, Boston, Massachusetts, June 14-17, 1993. LC TK7874.N35. (Illus.). 600p. 1993. reprint ed. pap. 186.00 (*0-7837-7035-9*, 204685000004) Bks Demand.

— National Electronic Packaging & Production Conference, 1993 West: Proceedings of the Technical Program, Anaheim CA, February 7-11, 1993, Vol. 1. LC TK7874.N35. (Illus.). 562p. 1993. reprint ed. pap. 174.30 (*0-7837-7036-7*, 204685100001) Bks Demand.

— National Electronic Packaging & Production Conference, 1993 West: Proceedings of the Technical Program, Anaheim CA, February 7-11, 1993, Vol. 2. LC TK7874.N35. (Illus.). 579p. 1993. reprint ed. pap. 179.50 (*0-7837-7037-5*, 204685100002) Bks Demand.

— National Electronic Packaging & Production Conference, 1993 West: Proceedings of the Technical Program, Anaheim CA, 1993, Vol. 3. LC TK7874.N35. (Illus.). 974p. 1993. reprint ed. pap. 200.00 (*0-7837-7038-3*, 204685100003) Bks Demand.

— National Electronic Packaging & Production Conference, 1994 West: Proceedings of the Technical Program, Anaheim CA, February 27-March 4, 1994, Vol. 1. LC TK7874.N35. (Illus.). 840p. 1994. reprint ed. pap. 200.00 (*0-7837-7039-1*, 204685200001) Bks Demand.

— National Electronic Packaging & Production Conference, 1994 West: Proceedings of the Technical Program, Anaheim CA, February 27-March 4, 1994, Vol. 2. LC TK7874.N35. (Illus.). 852p. 1994. reprint ed. pap. 200.00 (*0-7837-7040-5*, 204685200002) Bks Demand.

— National Electronic Packaging & Production Conference, 1994 West: Proceedings of the Technical Program, Anaheim CA, February 27-March 4, 1994, Vol. 3. LC TK7874.N35. 878p. 1993. reprint ed. pap. 200.00 (*0-7837-7041-3*, 204685200003) Bks Demand.

National Electronics Conference Staff. National Electronics Conference: Proceedings: Regency Hyatt O'Hare, Chicago, Illinois, October 6-8, 1975, Vol. 30. Tranter, William H., ed. LC TK0005.M37. 369p. reprint ed. pap. 114.40 (*0-608-16741-X*, 202680600030) Bks Demand.

— National Electronics Conference: Proceedings: The Conrad Hilton Hotel, Chicago, Illinois, December 8-10, 1969, Vol. 25. LC TK0005.N37. 972p. reprint ed. pap. 200.00 (*0-608-16728-2*, 202680500025) Bks Demand.

National Elevator Industry, Inc. Safety Committee, jt. auth. see Elevator World, Inc. Staff.

National Emergency Nurses' Association Staff. Standards for Emergency Nursing Practice. 2nd ed. 104p. (C). (gr. 13). 1993. pap. text 22.00 (*0-8016-8094-8*, 08094) Mosby Inc.

National Employment Law Project Staff, jt. auth. see Hernandez, Theresa.

National Employment Screening Services Staff. The National Employment Screening Directory, 1987: A Guide to Background Investigations. (National Employment Screening Directory Ser.). (Illus.). 320p. 1987. pap. 95.00 (*0-941233-14-6*) Source Okla.

National Endowment for Financial Education Academi. The Financial Planner's Desk Reference: A Glossary of Terms. LC 96-190933. (Illus.). 238p. (Orig.). (C). 1994. pap. 29.95 (*1-884383-01-7*) Natl Endowment.

National Engineering Consortium Staff. Annual Review of Communications, Vol. 46. fac. ed. LC 86-642827. 1132p. pap. 200.00 (*0-7837-8644-1*, 204785200046) Bks Demand.

National Environment on Health Staff. Fundamental Toxicology & Risk Assessment. 259p. 1991. lib. bdg. 495.00 (*0-87371-641-8*) Lewis Pubs.

***National Environmental Health Association Staff.** Body Art: A Model Code & Comprehensive Guidebook. (Illus.). 1999. pap. text 99.00 (*0-944111-01-7*) Natl Environ Health.

— NEHA Body Art Code & Guidelines. 22p. 1998. pap. text 45.00 (*0-944111-00-9*) Natl Environ Health.

National Environmental Policy Institute Staff. Reinventing the Vehicle for Environmental Management: Summer 1995 - First Phase Report. 122p. 1995. 20.00 (*0-614-16679-9*) Nat Environ Policy.

National Environmental Satellite, Data & Informati & Satellite Applications Lab Staff. Polar Orbiter Satellite Imagery Interpretation. (NWA Publication: No. 2-88). 42p. (C). 1988. pap. text 84.00 incl. sl. (*1-883563-06-2*) Natl Weather.

— Satellite Imagery Indicators of Turbulence. (NWA Publication: No. 1-91). 17p. (C). 1991. pap. text 84.00 incl. sl. (*1-883563-08-9*) Natl Weather.

— Winds of the World as Seen in Satellite Imagery. (NWA Publication: No. 1-90). 21p. 1990. pap. text 84.00 incl. sl. (*1-883563-07-0*) Natl Weather.

National Epidermolysis Bullosa Registry U.S. Staff, jt. auth. see Fine, Jo-David.

National Evaluation Systems Inc. Staff. Official TASP Test Study Guide. 1992. pap. 12.00 (*0-89056-007-2*) Natl Eval Systs.

— Tasp: The Official Tasp Test Study Guide. (Illus.). 713p. 1993. pap. 12.00 (*0-89056-010-2*, NE6010) Natl Eval Systs.

National Executive Committee - Socialist Labor Par, jt. auth. see De Leon, Daniel.

National Family Caregivers Association Staff. The Resourceful Caregiver: Helping Family Caregivers Help Themselves. 168p. (C). (gr. 13). 1996. pap. text 12.95 (*0-8151-5556-5*, 30587) Mosby Inc.

National Federation for Catholic Youth Ministry Staff. From Age to Age: The Challenge of Worship with Adolescents. (SPA & ENG.). 56p. (YA). pap. 9.95 (*0-88489-510-6*) St Marys.

National Federation for Catholic Youth Ministry Staff. Youth Ministry in Rural & Small Town Settings: A Planning Resource. 40p. 1998. pap. 9.95 (*0-88489-511-4*) St Marys.

National Federation for Constitutional Liberties Staff. National Action Conference for Civil Rights: April 19-20, 1942. 40p. 1996. pap. 10.00 (*0-88092-196-X*, 196X, Kav Bks) Royal Fireworks.

National Federation for Teaching Entrepreneurship, jt. auth. see Mariotti, Steve.

National Federation Interscholastic Coaches Educat, jt. auth. see American Sport Education Program Staff.

National Federation of Independent Business Staff, jt. auth. see Insurance Research Council, Inc. Staff.

***National Fire Protection Agency Staff.** National Electrical Code 1999. (Illus.). 1998. pap. 51.50 (*0-87765-433-6*) Natl Fire Prot.

— National Electrical Code 1999. 775p. (C). 1998. pap. 51.50 (*0-87765-432-8*) Thomson Learn.

National Fire Protection Agency Staff. National Electrical Code: 1999 Handbook. 3rd ed. Earley, Mark W., ed. LC 77-93950. (Electrical Trades Ser). (Illus.). 1074p. (C). 1999. pap. 98.50 (*0-87765-437-9*, 70HB99) Thomson Learn.

National Fire Protection Assoc. Staff. National Code. 1996. (McGuffey Editions Ser.). 917p. 1995. pap. 54.95 (*0-442-02223-9*, VNR) Wiley.

National Fire Protection Association Staff. Fire Protection Guide on Hazardous Materials. 10th ed. LC 78-59832. 550p. 1997. pap. 97.25 (*0-87765-130-2*, HAZ-94) Natl Fire Prot.

— Portable Fire Extinguishers. 56p. 1998. 26.00 (*0-317-63040-7*, 10-98) Natl Fire Prot.

National Fire Protection Association Staff & Society of Fire Protection Engineers Staff. SFPE Handbook of Fire Protection Engineering. 2nd ed. LC 95-68247. 1995. 196.25 (*0-87765-354-2*) Natl Fire Prot.

National Fire Protection Association Staff, jt. auth. see Foley, Stephen N.

National Fire Service Incident Management System Committee. Model Procedures Guide for Structural Firefighting. (Illus.). 72p. 1993. pap. text 14.00 (*0-87939-108-1*) IFSTA.

— Structural Collapse & US&R Operations. (Illus.). 174p. 1998. pap. text 25.00 (*0-87939-158-8*) IFSTA.

National Fire Service Incident Management System Committee & Model Procedures Committee. Model Procedures Guide for Emergency Medical Incidents. Wieder, Michael A., ed. (Illus.). 116p. 1997. pap. text 21.00 (*0-87939-137-5*, 36005) IFSTA.

— Model Procedures Guide for High-Rise Firefighting. Wieder, Michael A., ed. (Illus.). 144p. 1997. pap. text 23.00 (*0-87939-136-7*, 36004) IFSTA.

National Flag Foundation Staff & Murfin, James V. National Park & America's Wit. (Illus.). 432p. 1992. 19.95 (*0-317-91090-6*, 34526) Interp Mktg Prods.

National Flag Foundation Staff, jt. auth. see Allegheny Trails Council, Boy Scouts of America.

National Flight Nurses Association Staff, jt. auth. see Holleran, Renee S.

National Fluid Power Association Staff. National Fluid Power Association Directory & Member Guide, 1997-98. 208p. 1997. 100.00 (*0-942220-39-0*) Natl Fluid Power.

National Fluid Power Association Staff, ed. Modern Water Hydraulics - Your Choice for the Future. 16p. 1995. pap. 3.00 (*0-942220-33-1*) Natl Fluid Power.

— Proceedings of the Forty-Seventh National Conference on Fluid Power. 378p. 1996. pap. 60.00 (*0-942220-36-6*) Natl Fluid Power.

— Proceedings of the Forty-Seventh National Conference on Fluid Power, Vol. II. 480p. 1996. pap. 60.00 (*0-942220-37-4*) Natl Fluid Power.

— Your Guide to Cost Reduction Through Pneumatics Automation. (Illus.). 64p. (Orig.). (C). 1990. pap. 3.00 (*0-942220-23-4*) Natl Fluid Power.

— Your Guide to the Electronic Control of Fluid Power. (Illus.). 64p. (Orig.). 1992. pap. 5.00 (*0-942220-28-5*) Natl Fluid Power.

An Asterisk (*) at the beginning of an entry indicates that the title is appearing for the first time.

National Football League Staff. Best Shots: The Greatest NFL Photography of the Century. LC 99-23273. 160p. 1999. 30.00 (*0-7894-4639-1*) DK Pub Inc.

***National Football League Staff.** Make the Right Call! Football. 3rd ed. 1999. pap. 14.95 (*1-57243-342-6*) Triumph Bks.

National Football League Staff. The Official NFL 1998 Record & Fact Book. (Illus.). 480p. 1998. pap. 15.95 (*0-7611-1319-3*, 11319) Workman Pub.

— Official Rules of the NFL. rev. ed. (Official Rules Ser.). (Illus.). 202p. 1996. pap. 8.95 (*1-57243-142-3*) Triumph Bks.

***National Football League Staff.** Official Rules of the NFL: 2000. 995p. 1999. pap. 9.95 (*1-57243-334-5*) Triumph Bks.

— Official Rules of the NFL 2001. (Illus.). 2000. pap. 9.95 (*1-57243-401-5*) Triumph Bks.

— Official Rules of the NHL 2001. (Illus.). 2000. pap. 9.95 (*1-57243-399-X*) Triumph Bks.

National Foreign Assessment Center Staff. Directory of Soviet Research Organization. LC 79-121624. 300p. reprint ed. pap. 93.00 (*0-8357-2914-1*, 203915300011) Bks Demand.

National Forensic Center Staff. Forensic Services Directory, 1981. 800p. 1981. text 52.50 (*0-685-05353-9*) West Pub.

National Forum for School Science Staff. The Science Curriculum: The Report of the 1986 National Forum for School Science. LC Q 0181.A1. (This Year in School Science Ser.: No. 1986). 285p. reprint ed. pap. 88.40 (*0-8357-2823-4*, 203905900011) Bks Demand.

— Science Teaching: The Report of the 1985 National Forum for School Science. Champagne, Audrey B. & Hornig, Leslie E., eds. LC Q 0181.A1.N2. (AAAS Publication: No. 86-6). 250p. reprint ed. pap. 77.50 (*0-7837-0060-1*, 204030700016) Bks Demand.

— Students & Science Learning: Papers from the 1987 National Forum for School Science. Champagne, Audrey B. & Hornig, Leslie E., eds. LC Q 0181.A1.N2. (AAAS Publication: No. 87-29). 181p. reprint ed. pap. 56.20 (*0-8357-2824-2*, 203906000011) Bks Demand.

National Forum on Health in Canada Staff. What Determines Health? Summaries of a Series of Papers on the Determinants of Health 2nd ed. LC 98-180356. 130p. 1996. write for info. (*0-662-25077-X*, Pub. by Can7 Govern Pub) Intl Spec Bk.

National Forum on the Future of Children & Family. Effective Services for Young Children: Report of a Workshop. fac. ed. Schorr, Lisbeth B. et al, eds. LC 91-62826. 126p. 1991. pap. 39.10 (*0-7837-7560-1*, 204731300007) Bks Demand.

National Forum on Water Management Policy Staff. Water Resouces Administration in the United States: Policy, Practice, & Emerging Issues: Selected Papers from the American Water Resources Association National Forum on Water Management Policy, June 28-July 1, 1992, Washington, DC. Reuss, Martin, ed. LC 93-7668. (Illus.). 326p. 1993. reprint ed. pap. 101.10 (*0-7837-9226-3*, 204997700004) Bks Demand.

National Foundation for Ileitis & Colitis Staff. The Crohn's Disease & Ulcerative Colitis Fact Book. Banks, Peter A. et al, eds. (Illus.). 208p. 1983. 18.95 (*0-684-17967-9*, Scribners Ref) Mac Lib Ref.

National Foundation for Transplants Staff. Recipes for Life. (Illus.). 168p. 1997. pap. 15.00 (*0-9669993-0-4*) Natl Fndt Transp.

National Foundation for UC & WC Staff. Employer's Workers' Compensation Cost Control Handbook. LC 95-69015. 52p. (Orig.). 1997. pap. text 30.00 (*0-9646875-1-8*) NFUCWC.

National Fuel Efficiency Service Ltd. Staff. Boiler Operators Handbook. 2nd ed. (C). 1990. lib. bdg. 53.00 (*1-85333-285-2*) G & T Inc.

National Gallery (Great Britain) Staff & Egerton, Judy. The British School. LC 97-76288. (National Gallery Catalogues Ser.). 456 p. 1998. write for info. (*1-85709-170-1*) Nat Gallery Pubns.

National Gallery London Staff. The Christmas Story from the New Testament: Illustrations from Paintings in the National Gallery in London. LC 92-11580. (Illus.). 32p. (J). (gr. 3 up). 1992. per. 17.00 (*0-671-79364-0*) S&S Bks Yung.

***National Gallery London Staff.** Perspective. (Eyewitness Books). 64p. (J). (gr. 4-7). 2000. 15.95 (*0-7894-5585-4*, D K Ink) DK Pub Inc.

National Gallery of Art (U. S.) Staff. National Gallery of Art, Washington. rev. ed. LC 95-1028. (Illus.). 696p. 1995. pap. 39.98 (*0-8109-8148-3*, Pub. by Abrams) Time Warner.

National Gallery of Art (U. S.) Staff, et al. The Mark J. Millard Architectural Collection. LC 93-4308. 1993. write for info. (*0-89468-265-2*) Natl Gallery Art.

National Gallery of Art (U. S.) Staff, jt. auth. see Boyer, Patricia E.

National Gallery of Art (U. S.) Staff, jt. auth. see Cikovsky, Nicolai.

National Gallery of Art Staff. The Artist's Workshop. Lukehart, Peter M., ed. LC 72-600309. (Studies in the History of Art: Vol. 38, No. 22). (Illus.). 195p. reprint ed. pap. 60.50 (*0-608-10439-6*, 207107300038) Bks Demand.

— Claude Lorrain, 1600-1682: A Symposium. Askew, Pamela, ed. LC 85-141863. (Studies in the History of Art: Vol. 14, No. 3). (Illus.). 90p. reprint ed. pap. 30.00 (*0-608-10432-9*, 207106600014) Bks Demand.

***National Gallery of Art Staff.** Collecting for the Nation: A Decade of Acquisitions. LC 00-33936. (Illus.). 2000. write for info. (*0-89468-281-4*) Natl Gallery Art.

National Gallery of Art Staff. Eius Virtutis Studiosi: Classical & Postclassical Studies in Memory of Frank Edward Brown (1908-1988) Scott, Russell T. & Scott, Ann R., eds. LC 94-120148. (Studies in the History of Art: Vol. 43, No. 23). (Illus.). 501p. reprint ed. pap. 155.40 (*0-608-10442-6*, 207107600043) Bks Demand.

— El Greco: Italy & Spain. Brown, Jonathan & Pita Andrade, Jose M., eds. LC 72-600309. (Studies in the History of Art: Vol. 13, No. 2). (Illus.). 189p. reprint ed. pap. 58.60 (*0-608-10431-0*, 207106500013) Bks Demand.

— Figures of Thought: El Greco As Interpreter of History, Tradition & Ideas. Brown, Jonathan, ed. LC 82-6317. (Studies in the History of Art: Vol. 11). (Illus.). 100p. reprint ed. pap. 31.00 (*0-608-10429-9*, 207106300011) Bks Demand.

— Flowers of Youth: Images of Children from the National Gallery of Art. LC 96-5906. 96p. 1996. 19.95 (*0-8212-2321-6*, Pub. by Bulfinch Pr) Little.

— Interpretation of Architectural Sculpture in Greece & Rome. LC 97-179027. (Studies in the History of Art Ser.). 1997. 40.00 (*0-89468-255-5*) Natl Gallery Art.

— Macedonia & Greece in Late Classical & Early Hellenistic Times. Barr-Sharrar, Beryl & Borza, Eugene N., eds. LC 82-150109. (Studies in the History of Art: Vol. 10, No. 1). (Illus.). 266p. reprint ed. pap. 82.50 (*0-608-10428-0*, 207106200010) Bks Demand.

— Raphael before Rome. Beck, James, ed. LC 86-174215. (Studies in the History of Art: Vol. 17, No. 5). (Illus.). 213p. reprint ed. pap. 66.10 (*0-608-10434-5*, 207106800017) Bks Demand.

— Retaining the Original: Multiple Originals, Copies & Reproductions. Preciado, Kathleen, ed. LC 72-600309. (Studies in the History of Art: Vol. 20, No. 7). (Illus.). 179p. reprint ed. pap. 55.50 (*0-608-10436-1*, 207107000020) Bks Demand.

— Stained Glass Before 1700 in American Collections: Mid-Atlantic & Southeastern Seaboard States: Corpus Vitrearum Checklist II. LC 84-22794. (Studies in the History of Art: Vol. 23, No. I). (Illus.). 201p. reprint ed. pap. 62.40 (*0-608-10437-X*, 207107100023) Bks Demand.

— Stained Glass Before 1700 in American Collections: New England & New York: Corpus Vitrearum Checklist I. Caviness, Madeline H. et al, eds. LC 84-22794. (Studies in the History of Art: Vol. 15, No. I). (Illus.). 218p. reprint ed. pap. 67.60 (*0-608-10433-7*, 207106700015) Bks Demand.

— Stained Glass Before 1700 in American Collections: Silver-Stained Roundels & Unipartite Panels, Corpus Vitrearum Checklist IV. Beaven, Marilyn, ed. LC 72-600309. (Studies in the History of Art: Vol. 39, No. I). (Illus.). 276p. reprint ed. pap. 85.60 (*0-608-10440-X*, 2071074) Bks Demand.

— Studies in the History of Art, Vol. 9. LC 72-600309. (Illus.). 89p. reprint ed. pap. 30.00 (*0-608-10427-2*, 207106100009) Bks Demand.

— Studies in the History of Art, Vol. 12. LC 72-600309. (Illus.). 108p. reprint ed. pap. 33.50 (*0-608-10430-2*, 207106400012) Bks Demand.

— Studies in the History of Art, Vol. 24. Sweeney, Jane, ed. LC 72-600309. (Illus.). 178p. reprint ed. pap. 55.20 (*0-608-10438-8*, 207107200024) Bks Demand.

— Studies in the History of Art, 1974, Vol. 6. LC 72-600309. (Illus.). 212p. reprint ed. pap. 65.80 (*0-608-10424-8*, 207105800006) Bks Demand.

— Studies in the History of Art, 1975, Vol. 7. LC 72-600309. (Illus.). 92p. reprint ed. pap. 30.00 (*0-608-10425-6*, 207105900007) Bks Demand.

National Gallery of Art Staff, et al. James McNeill Whistler: A Reexamination. Fine, Ruth E., ed. LC 72-600309. (Studies in the History of Art: Vol. 19, No. 6). (Illus.). 102p. reprint ed. pap. 31.70 (*0-608-10435-3*, 207106900019) Bks Demand.

— Studies in the History of Art, Vol. 8. LC 72-600309. (Illus.). 91p. reprint ed. pap. 30.00 (*0-608-10426-4*, 207106000008) Bks Demand.

National Gallery of Art Staff, jt. auth. see Callahan, Harry.

National Gallery of Art Staff, jt. auth. see Farrell, Kate.

National Gallery of Art Staff, jt. auth. see Wheelock, Arthur K.

National Gallery of Art U. S. Staff, jt. auth. see Wheelock, Arthur K.

National Gallery of Australia Staff. Don't Leave Me This Way: Art in the Age of AIDS. LC 94-61764. (Australian National Gallery Ser.). (Illus.). 256p. 1995. pap. 19.95 (*0-500-97420-9*, Pub. by Thames Hudson) Norton.

***National Gallery of Australia Staff.** National Gallery of Australia: An Introduction to the Collection. LC 00-272597. 1998. write for info. (*0-642-13093-0*, Pub. by Natl Gallery) U of Wash Pr.

National Gallery of Canada, Ottawa Staff. Catalogue of the Library of the National Gallery of Canada: First Supplement, 6 vols., Set. (Library Reference Ser.). 1981. 915.00 (*0-8161-0291-0*, G K Hall & Co) Mac Lib Ref.

National Gallery of Canada Staff. Catalogue of the Library of the National Gallery of Canada, 8 vols., Set. 1973. 905.00 (*0-8161-1043-3*, G K Hall & Co) Mac Lib Ref.

National Gallery of Canada Staff, jt. auth. see Newlands, Anne.

National Gallery of Ireland Staff. Little Book of Irish Verse. (Illus.). 60p. 1993. 7.95 (*0-8118-0508-5*) Chronicle Bks.

National Gallery of London Staff. Costume in Art. (Illus.). 144p. 1999. pap. 14.95 (*0-8230-0333-7*) Watsn-Guptill.

— Heaven in Art. (Illus.). 144p. 1999. pap. 14.95 (*0-8230-0334-5*) Watsn-Guptill.

— People in Art. (Illus.). 144p. 1999. pap. 14.95 (*0-8230-0335-3*) Watsn-Guptill.

— Places in Art. (Illus.). 144p. 1999. pap. 14.95 (*0-8230-0336-1*) Watsn-Guptill.

National Gallery Staff. The National Gallery. (Academy Architecture Ser.). (Illus.). 96p. 1986. pap. 19.95 (*0-312-55953-4*) St Martin.

National Gallery, Washington, D.C. Staff. Jesus of Nazareth: Illustrated with Painting from the National Gallery in Washington. LC 93-35867. (Illus.). 40p. (J). 1994. 16.00 (*0-671-88651-7*) S&S Bks Yung.

National Gardening Association Editors, ed. Landscaping for Dummies: A Reference for the Rest of Us! LC SB473.G56 1999. (For Dummies Ser.). (Illus.). 384p. 1999. pap. 16.99 (*0-7645-5128-0*) IDG Bks.

National Gardening Association Editors & Glattstein, Judy. Flowering Bulbs for Dummies. LC SB425.G585 1998. (For Dummies Ser.). (Illus.). 384p. 1998. pap. 16.99 (*0-7645-5103-5*) IDG Bks.

National Gardening Association Editors & Hodgson, Larry. Houseplants for Dummies. LC 98-86178. (For Dummies Ser.). (Illus.). 392p. 1998. pap. 16.99 (*0-7645-5102-7*) IDG Bks.

***National Gardening Association Editors & Marken, Bill.** Annuals for Dummies. LC 97-81233. (For Dummies Ser.). (Illus.). 384p. 1998. pap. 16.99 (*0-7645-5056-X*) IDG Bks.

National Gardening Association Editors & Walheim, Lance. Lawn Care for Dummies. LC 97-81232. (For Dummies Ser.). (Illus.). 376p. 1998. pap. 16.99 (*0-7645-5077-2*) IDG Bks.

National Gardening Association Editors, jt. auth. see MacCoskey, Michael.

National Gardening Association Editors, ed. see Beckstrom, Robert J.

National Gardening Association Editors, ed. see MacCaskey, Michael.

National Gardening Association Editors, ed. see Marken, Bill.

National Gardening Association Editors, ed. see Tatroe, Marcia.

National Gardening Association Editors, ed. see Walheim, Lance.

National Gardening Association Editors, The, jt. auth. see Nardozzi, Charlie.

National Gardening Association Staff. Cucumbers, Melons & Squash. LC 86-40341. 88p. 1987. pap. 4.95 (*0-317-56629-6*) Villard Books.

— The Dictionary of Horticulture. (Illus.). 848p. 1996. pap. 19.95 (*0-14-017882-1*, Viking) Viking Penguin.

— Eggplant, Okra & Peppers. LC 86-40342. 1987. pap. 4.95 (*0-317-56626-1*) Villard Books.

— Gardening: The Complete Guide to Growing America's Favorite Fruits & Vegetables. (Illus.). 432p. 1986. 34.95 (*0-201-10866-6*); pap. 19.18 (*0-201-10855-0*) Addison-Wesley.

— Lettuce & Greens. LC 86-40343. 1987. pap. 4.95 (*0-317-56625-3*) Villard Books.

— NGA Garden Library, Set. Incl. Beans. 36p. 1980. pap. 3.50 (*0-915873-08-7*, 1-1010C); Cauliflower, Broccoli, & Cabbage. 36p. 1980. pap. 3.50 (*0-915873-14-1*, 1-1010H); Corn. 36p. pap. 3.50 (*0-915873-16-8*, 1-1010J); Cucumbers, Melons & Squash. 36p. 1980. pap. 3.50 (*0-915873-12-5*, 1-1010F); Eggplant, Okra & Peppers. 36p. 1980. pap. 3.50 (*0-915873-15-X*, 1-1010I); Lettuce & Greens. 36p. pap. 3.50 (*0-915873-11-7*, 1-1010E); Onions. 36p. 1980. pap. 3.50 (*0-915873-07-9*, 1-1010A); Peas & Peanuts. 36p. 1980. pap. 3.50 (*0-915873-17-6*, 1-1010K); Potatoes. pap. 3.50 (*0-915873-13-3*, 1-1010G); Root Crops. 36p. 1980. pap. 3.50 (*0-915873-10-9*, 1-1010D); Tomatoes. 36p. 1980. pap. 2.50 (*0-915873-09-5*, 1-1010B); 32p. Set pap. 29.50 (*0-915873-18-4*, 1-1009C) Natl Gardening Assn.

— Tomatoes. 1987. pap. 4.95 (*0-317-56624-5*) Villard Books.

National Gardening Association Staff & Buczacki, Stefan T. Gardeners' Questions Answered. LC 86-15759. 160p. 1987. 19.95 (*0-317-56609-1*) Villard Books.

***National Gardening Association Staff, et al.** Herb Gardening for Dummies. 384p. 2000. pap. 16.99 (*0-7645-5200-7*) IDG Bks.

National Gardening Association Staff, jt. auth. see Walheim, Lance.

National Gardening Association Staff, jt. auth. see Whitman, Ann.

National Gardens Scheme Staff. Gardens of England & Wales Open for Charity. 1999. annuals (Illus.). 385p. 1999. pap. 12.95 (*0-900558-31-8*) Seven Hills Bk.

— Gardens of England & Wales, 1997: Open for Charity. (Illus.). 385p. (Orig.). 1997. pap. 6.95 (*0-900558-29-6*, Pub. by Portfolio) Seven Hills Bk.

National Gardens Scheme Staff, ed. Gardens of Scotland. 1999. pap. text. write for info. (*0-901549-13-4*) Natl Gardens.

National Garment Cutter Staff. Garment Patterns: 1889. Kliot, Jules & Kliot, Kaethe, eds. (Illus.). 144p. 1996. pap. 16.00 (*0-916896-74-9*, LA36) Lacis Pubns.

National Geographic Editors. National Geographic: The Photographs. (Illus.). 1994. pap. 46.95 (*0-87044-987-7*) Natl Geog.

— National Geographic Guide to the Civil War: National Battlefield Parks. (Illus.). 160p. 1993. per. 12.00 (*0-87044-878-1*) Natl Geog.

National Geographic Magazine Staff. Cultural & Geographical Exploration: Chronicles from National Geographic. 1998. 19.95 (*0-7910-5096-3*) Chelsea Hse.

National Geographic Society. Inside Out: The Best of National Geographic Diagrams & Cutaways. LC 98-4636. 128p. 1998. 25.00 (*0-7922-7371-0*) Natl Geog.

— National Geographic Atlas of the World. 7th ed. LC 99-27026. (Illus.). 280p. 1999. per. 125.00 (*0-7922-7528-4*) Natl Geog.

— National Geographic Traveler France. LC 98-54974. 400p. 1999. per. 27.95 (*0-7922-7426-1*, Pub. by Natl Geog) S&S Trade.

***National Geographic Society.** South Central States: Regional Map & Travel Planner; Including Arkansas, Oklahoma, Louisiana and. (National Geographic Close-Up Maps Ser.). 1998. pap. 7.95 (*1-57262-420-5*) MapQuest.

***National Geographic Society & Baker, Christopher P.** Costa Rica: A Century of Travel Experience in Every Guide. (Illus.). 2000. pap. 22.95 (*0-7922-7946-8*) Natl Geog.

National Geographic Society (U. S.) Staff. Incredible Voyage: Exploring the Human Body. LC 98-4635. 352 p. :p. 1998. write for info. (*0-7922-7149-1*) Natl Geog.

***National Geographic Society (U. S.) Staff.** National Geographic Animal Encyclopedia. LC 99-48020. 2000. write for info. (*0-7922-7180-7*) Natl Geog.

National Geographic Society (U. S.) Staff. National Geographic Atlas of the World. 2nd rev. ed. LC 95-19579. 1995. pap. text. write for info. (*0-7922-3036-1*) Natl Geog.

***National Geographic Society (U. S.) Staff.** National Geographic Expeditions Atlas. LC 99-86883. 2000. write for info. (*0-7922-7617-5*) Natl Geog.

National Geographic Society (U. S.) Staff. National Geographic Guide to America's Hidden Corners deluxe ed. LC 98-4637. 384 p. 1998. write for info. (*0-7922-7210-2*) Natl Geog.

— National Geographic's Last Wild Places. LC 96-22973. 1997. 35.00 (*0-7922-3500-2*) Natl Geog.

— Photographs Then & Now. LC 98-23421. 1998. 50.00 (*0-7922-7203-X*) Natl Geog.

***National Geographic Society (U. S.) Staff.** Rediscovering Ancient Egypt. LC 99-24269. (J). 1999. 19.95 (*0-7910-5445-4*) Chelsea Hse.

National Geographic Society (U. S.) Staff. Restless Earth. LC 97-8115. 1997. write for info. (*0-7922-7121-1*); denim. write for info. (*0-7922-7006-1*) Natl Geog.

— Wild Animals of North America. LC 98-2798. 1998. 35.50 (*0-7922-7062-2*); 41.95 (*0-7922-7066-5*) Natl Geog.

— The Wonders of the World. LC 98-11976. 1998. 29.95 (*0-7922-7201-3*) Natl Geog.

National Geographic Society (U. S.) Staff, jt. auth. see Browler, Kenneth.

National Geographic Society (U. S.) Staff, jt. auth. see Fagan, Brian M.

National Geographic Society (U. S.) Staff, jt. auth. see Howell, Catherine H.

National Geographic Society (U. S.) Staff, jt. auth. see Vesilind, Priit.

National Geographic Society (U. S.), Staff, jt. auth. see Watkins, T. H.

National Geographic Society Book Division Staff. The Builders: Marvels of Engineering. Newhouse, Elizabeth L., ed. LC 92-30615. (Illus.). 288p. 1992. 41.95 (*0-87044-837-4*) Natl Geog.

— The Builders: Marvels of Engineering. Newhouse, Elizabeth L., ed. LC 92-30615. (Illus.). 288p. 1994. 40.00 (*0-87044-836-6*) Natl Geog.

— Crossing America: National Geographic's Guide to the Interstates. LC 94-16464. 1995. pap. 21.95 (*0-87044-985-0*) Natl Geog.

— Exploring Canada's Spectacular National Parks. LC 95-24289. 200p. 1995. 16.00 (*0-7922-2735-2*) Natl Geog.

— National Geographic's Guide to Scenic Highways & Byways. LC 95-16166. (Illus.). 352p. 1996. per. 21.95 (*0-7922-2950-9*) Natl Geog.

— National Geographic's Guide to Scenic Highways & Byways. deluxe ed. LC 95-16166. (Illus.). 1995. write for info. (*0-7922-2951-7*) Natl Geog.

— National Parks of North America. LC 95-10989. 336p. 1996. 40.00 (*0-7922-2954-1*) Natl Geog.

— National Parks of North America. deluxe ed. LC 96-34242. (Illus.). 336p. 1995. write for info. (*0-7922-2955-X*) Natl Geog.

National Geographic Society, Book Division Staff. Raging Forces: Earth in Upheaval. deluxe ed. LC 95-36295. 1995. write for info. (*0-7922-2965-7*) Natl Geog.

National Geographic Society Book Division Staff. Whales, Dolphins & Porpoises. deluxe ed. 232p. 1995. 50.00 (*0-7922-2953-3*) Natl Geog.

— Wild Animals of North America. deluxe rev. ed. 406p. 1995. write for info. (*0-7922-2960-6*) Natl Geog.

— Wonders of the Ancient World: National Geographic Atlas of Archaeology. deluxe ed. LC 94-16650. 1994. pap. 46.95 (*0-87044-983-4*) Natl Geog.

National Geographic Society Editorial Staff, jt. auth. see Aikman, Lonnelle.

National Geographic Society Staff. Along a Rocky Shore. (Kids Want to Know Ser.). (Illus.). 32p. (J). (ps-3). 1996. pap. text 4.95 (*0-7922-3611-4*, Pub. by Natl Geog) S&S Trade.

National Geographic Society Staff. Amazing Monkeys: A National Geographic Pop-Up Book. (Pop-Up Bks.). (Illus.). 10p. (J). (gr. k-3). 1991. 16.00 (*0-87044-596-0*, Pub. by Natl Geog) S&S Trade.

National Geographic Society Staff. Animal Architects. Crump, Donald J., ed. LC 87-12198. (Books for World Explorers Series 8: No. 4). (Illus.). 104p. (J). (gr. 3-8). 1994. 12.50 (*0-87044-612-6*) Natl Geog.

National Geographic Society Staff. Animal Clowns. (Kids Want to Know Ser.). 32p. (J). (gr. k-3). 1996. pap. 4.95 (*0-7922-3409-X*, Pub. by Natl Geog) S&S Trade.

National Geographic Society Staff. Animals in Summer. (Kids Want to Know Ser.). (Illus.). 32p. 1997. pap. text 4.95 (*0-7922-3613-0*) Natl Geog.

National Geographic Society Staff. Animals in Winter. (Kids Want to Know Ser.). (Illus.). 32p. (J). (ps-3). pap. 4.95 (*0-7922-3601-7*, Pub. by Natl Geog) Publishers Group.

N

An Asterisk (*) at the beginning of an entry indicates that the title is appearing for the first time.

— Animals Showing Off: A National Geographic Pop-Up Book. (Pop-Up Bks.). (Illus.). 12p. (YA). (ps up). 16.00 (*0-87044-724-6*, Pub. by Natl Geog) Publishers Group.

National Geographic Society Staff. Atlas of North America: Space Age Portrait of a Continent. (Illus.). 264p. 1988. 39.95 (*0-87044-605-3*) Natl Geog.

— Beyond the Horizon. LC 99-198614. (Destinations Ser.). 200p. 1998. per. 15.00 (*0-7922-7361-3*) Natl Geog.

— Books for Young Explorers, 4 vols., set 8. (Illus.). (J). (ps-3). 1981. lib. bdg. 16.95 (*0-87044-405-0*); lib. bdg. 13.95 (*0-87044-410-7*) Natl Geog.

— Books for Young Explorers, 4 vols, set 9. (YA). (gr. 6 up). 1982. lib. bdg. 16.95 (*0-87044-966-4*) Natl Geog.

— The Builders. 288p. 1998. per. 23.00 (*0-7922-7351-6*, Pub. by Natl Geog) S&S Trade.

— Close-Up: U. S. A. Florida: Regional Map & Travel Planner. 1998. pap. text 7.95 (*1-57262-424-8*, Ntl Geog Maps) MapQuest.

— Creatures of the Desert World: A National Geographic Pop-Up Book. (Pop-Up Bks.). (Illus.). 12p. (J). (gr. k-3). 1991. 16.00 (*0-87044-687-8*, Pub. by Natl Geog) S&S Trade.

— Crossing America: Nationa Geographic's Guide to the Interstates. 2nd ed. LC 99-19616. 352p. 1999. pap. 24.95 (*0-7922-7474-1*) Natl Geog.

— Destination Rain Forest. (J). Date not set. 14.95 incl. VHS (*0-7922-2701-8*, 51667) Natl Geog.

National Geographic Society Staff. Dinosaur Babies: A National Geographic Pop-Up Book. (Pop-Up Bks.). (Illus.). 10p. (YA). (ps up). 16.00 (*0-87044-841-2*, Pub. by Natl Geog) Publishers Group.

National Geographic Society Staff. Experiences in the Grand Canyon. LC 99-24929. (Cultural & Geographical Exploration Ser.). 144p. (gr. 7-12). 1999. 19.95 (*0-7910-5442-X*) Chelsea Hse.

— Great Journeys of the World. LC 99-198522. (Destinations Ser.). 1998. pap. 15.00 (*0-7922-7358-3*) Natl Geog.

— Hawaii & the Islands of the Pacific. LC 99-28850. (Cultural & Geographical Exploration Ser.). 144p. 1999. 19.95 (*0-7910-5443-8*) Chelsea Hse.

— Historical Atlas of the United States. rev. ed. LC 93-32201. (Illus.). 289p. 1994. 100.00 (*0-87044-970-2*) Natl Geog.

National Geographic Society Staff. How Animals Care for Their Babies. (Kids Want to Know Ser.). (Illus.). 32p. (J). (gr. k-3). 1996. pr. 4.95 (*0-7922-3407-3*, Pub. by Natl Geog) S&S Trade.

— How Animals Talk. (Kids Want to Know Ser.). (Illus.). 32p. (J). (ps-3). pap. 4.95 (*0-7922-3406-5*, Pub. by Natl Geog) Publishers Group.

— How Animals Talk. (Illus.). (J). 1987. 10.40 (*0-606-18342-6*) Turtleback.

National Geographic Society Staff. Incredible Voyage. LC 98-4635. (Illus.). 352p. (YA). (gr. 6 up). 1998. 35.00 (*0-7922-7148-3*) Natl Geog.

— Indian Tribes of the Americas. LC 99-28194. (Cultural & Geographical Exploration Ser.). 144p. 1999. 19.95 (*0-7910-5447-0*) Chelsea Hse.

— Islands Lost in Time. LC 96-54853. 1997. write for info. (*0-7922-4231-9*) Natl Geog.

— Islands Lost in Time. LC 99-198644. (Destinations Ser.). 1998. pap. 15.00 (*0-7922-7360-5*) Natl Geog.

— Journey into China. 5th ed. LC 82-14132. (Illus.). 518p. 1984. lib. bdg. 23.95 (*0-87044-461-1*) Natl Geog.

— Lighthouses: Beacons of the Sea. LC 99-26494. (Cultural & Geographical Exploration Ser.). (Illus.). 144p. 1999. 19.95 (*0-7910-5444-6*) Chelsea Hse.

National Geographic Society Staff. Lion Cubs & Their World: A National Geographic Pop-Up Book. (Pop-Up Bks.). (Illus.). 10p. (YA). (gr. k up). 1991. 16.00 (*0-87044-871-4*, Pub. by Natl Geog) S&S Trade.

— Lions, Tigers & Leopards: The Big Cats. (Kids Want to Know Ser.). (Illus.). 32p. (J). (ps-3). pap. 4.95 (*0-7922-3603-3*, Pub. by Natl Geog) Publishers Group.

— Mid-Atlantic States: Regional Map & Travel Panner; Including West Virginia, Virginia, Maryland. 1998. pap. 7.95 (*1-57262-425-6*) MapQuest.

National Geographic Society Staff. National Geographic Atlas of the World. 2nd ed. LC 95-19579. 1995. 100.00 (*0-7922-3038-8*) Natl Geog.

— National Geographic Atlas of the World. 6th deluxe rev. ed. LC 92-27845. (Special Publications Series 26). (Illus.). 412p. 1993. 100.00 (*0-87044-835-8*) Natl Geog.

***National Geographic Society Staff.** National Geographic Beginner's World Atlas: A First Atlas For Beginning Explorers. LC 99-34652. (Illus.). 64p. (J). (gr. k-3). 1999. per. 17.95 (*0-7922-7502-0*) Natl Geog.

— National Geographic Book of Mammals. (Illus.). 608p. (YA). (gr. 5 up). 1998. per. 34.45 (*0-7922-7141-6*, Pub. by Natl Geog) Publishers Group.

National Geographic Society Staff. The National Geographic Desk Reference: A Geographical Reference with Hundreds of Photographs, Maps, Charts & Graphs. LC 99-23549. (Illus.). 1999. write for info. (*0-7922-7083-5*) Natl Geog.

— National Geographic Driving Guide to America. 1999. pap. 14.95 (*0-7922-7422-9*); pap. 14.95 (*0-7922-7423-7*); per. 14.95 (*0-7922-7421-0*, Pub. by Natl Geog) S&S Trade.

National Geographic Society Staff. National Geographic Europe: Continent Maps. 1997. pap. 9.95 (*1-57262-150-8*); pap. 14.95 (*1-57262-151-6*) MapQuest.

— National Geographic Expeditions Atlas. LC 99-86883. (Illus.). 304p. 2000. per. 39.50 (*0-7922-7616-7*, Pub. by Natl Geog) S&S Trade.

National Geographic Society Staff. National Geographic Eyewitness to the 20th Century. deluxe ed. LC 98-22756. 1998. write for info. (*0-7922-7025-8*) Natl Geog.

— National Geographic Guide to America's Hidden Corners. LC 98-4637. (Illus.). 384p. 1999. pap. 25.00 (*0-7922-7211-0*) Natl Geog.

— National Geographic Guide to Birdwatching Sites. LC 98-53023. 320p. 1999. pap. 21.00 (*0-7922-7374-5*) Natl Geog.

***National Geographic Society Staff.** National Geographic Italy: Country & Region Map. 1998. pap. 13.95 (*1-57262-368-3*) MapQuest.

— National Geographic Japan: Country & Region Maps: County & Region Maps. 1998. pap. 27.95 (*1-57262-369-1*) MapQuest.

— National Geographic Photographs: The Milestones: A Visual Legacy of the World. LC 99-29397. (Illus.). 1999. write for info. (*0-7922-7521-7*) Natl Geog.

National Geographic Society Staff. National Geographic Picture Atlas of Our Fifty States. Sedeen, Margaret, ed. LC 91-28084. (Illus.). 264p. 1994. 25.00 (*0-87044-859-5*) Natl Geog.

— National Geographic Picture Atlas of Our World. rev. ed. LC 93-4514. (Illus.). 256p. 1993. lib. bdg. write for info. (*0-87044-964-8*) Natl Geog.

— National Geographic Picture Atlas of Our World. rev. ed. LC 93-4514. (Illus.). 256p. 1994. 25.00 (*0-87044-960-5*) Natl Geog.

— National Geographic Traveler Britian. LC 99-11700. 400p. 1999. pap. 27.95 (*0-7922-7425-3*) Natl Geog.

— National Geographic Traveler Canada. LC 99-10549. 1999. pap. 27.95 (*0-7922-7427-X*) Natl Geog.

— National Geographic Traveler London. LC 99-12613. 272p. 1999. pap. 22.95 (*0-7922-7428-8*, Pub. by Natl Geog) S&S Trade.

***National Geographic Society Staff.** National Geographic United States Atlas for Young Explorers: A Complete Reference Guide to the United States. (Illus.). 176p. (J). (gr. 2-6). 1999. 24.95 (*0-7922-7115-7*) Natl Geog.

— National Geographic United States Physical. (Reference Maps Ser.). 1998. pap. 12.95 (*1-57262-329-2*) MapQuest.

— National Geographic United States Political. (Reference Maps Ser.). 1997. pap. 12.95 (*1-57262-249-0*) MapQuest.

— National Geographic United States Political. 1998. pap. 9.95 (*1-57262-374-8*) MapQuest.

National Geographic Society Staff. National Geographic World Atlas for Young Explorers: A Complete World Reference for Adventurous Minds. LC 98-18366. (National Geographic Ser.). (Illus.). 176p. (J). (gr. 3-7). 1998. per. 24.95 (*0-7922-7341-9*) Natl Geog.

***National Geographic Society Staff.** National Geographic World Physical/Ocean Floor. 1998. pap. 59.95 (*1-57262-332-2*) MapQuest.

— National Geographic World Physical/Ocean Floor. 1998. pap. 34.95 (*1-57262-278-4*) MapQuest.

— National Geographic World Political. (Reference Maps Ser.). 1998. pap. 9.95 (*1-57262-373-X*) MapQuest.

— National Geographic World Satellite. 1998. pap. 15.95 (*1-57262-377-2*); pap. 25.95 (*1-57262-378-0*) MapQuest.

National Geographic Society Staff. National Geographic's Driving Guides to America. LC 96-29758. 1997. write for info. (*0-7922-3428-6*) Natl Geog.

— National Geographic's Guide to the State Parks of the United States. LC 97-14297. 1997. write for info. (*0-7922-7050-9*); pap. write for info. (*0-7922-7051-7*) Natl Geog.

— National Geographic's Guide to the State Parks of the United States. LC 97-14297. 384p. 1998. 30.00 (*0-7922-7024-X*) Natl Geog.

— New York. LC 99-11701. (National Geographic Traveler Ser.). 272p. 1999. pap. 22.95 (*0-7922-7430-X*, Pub. by Natl Geog) S&S Trade.

***National Geographic Society Staff.** Northwest: Regional Map & Travel Planner, Including Washington, Oregon, Idaho, Montana & Wyoming. 1998. pap. 7.95 (*1-57262-416-7*) MapQuest.

National Geographic Society Staff. Orbit: NASA Astronauts Photograph the Earth. LC 96-24428. 1996. write for info. (*0-7922-3715-3*) Natl Geog.

— Orbit: NASA Astronauts Photograph the Earth. (Illus.). 224p. 1996. 40.00 (*0-7922-3714-5*) Natl Geog.

National Geographic Society Staff. Our Amazing Animal Friends. (Kids Want to Know Ser.). (Illus.). 32p. (J). (ps-3). pap. 4.95 (*0-7922-3408-1*, Pub. by Natl Geog) Publishers Group.

National Geographic Society Staff. Our Inviting Eastern Parklands. LC 94-19638. 200p. 1994. 16.00 (*0-87044-978-8*) Natl Geog.

— Paris. LC 99-11168. (National Geographic Traveler Ser.). (Illus.). 272p. 1999. per. 22.95 (*0-7922-7429-6*, Pub. by Natl Geog) S&S Trade.

— Penguins & Polar Bears. (Illus.). 32p. (J). 1996. pap. text 4.95 (*0-7922-3604-1*) Natl Geog.

National Geographic Society Staff. Saving Our Animal Friends. (Kids Want to Know Ser.). (Illus.). 32p. (J). (ps-3). 1996. pr. 4.95 (*0-7922-3602-5*, Pub. by Natl Geog) S&S Trade.

— U. S. Scenic Drives. (Illus.). 1999. pap. 6.99 (*1-57262-491-4*) MapQuest.

— Whales: Mighty Giants of the Sea. (Pop-Up Bks.). (Illus.). 12p. (J). (gr. k-3). 1996. pr. 16.00 (*0-87044-810-2*, Pub. by Natl Geog) S&S Trade.

National Geographic Society Staff. What Is It? (Illus.). 26p. Date not set. 3.00 (*0-7922-1969-4*) Natl Geog.

— Wild Shores of Australia. 200p. 1998. pap. 15.00 (*0-7922-7362-1*) Natl Geog.

***National Geographic Society Staff.** Wisconsin, Michigan & the Great Lakes: Regional Map & Travel Planner. (National Geographic Close-Up Maps Ser.). 1998. pap. 7.95 (*1-57262-421-3*) MapQuest.

National Geographic Society Staff, ed. Books for Young Explorers, 4 vols, Set 2. (J). (ps-3). 1973. lib. bdg. 16.95 (*0-87044-305-4*) Natl Geog.

— Books for Young Explorers, 4 vols., Set 3. (Illus.). (J). (ps-3). 1974. 13.95 (*0-87044-157-4*); lib. bdg. 16.95 (*0-87044-310-0*) Natl Geog.

— Books for Young Explorers, 4 vols., Set 4. (J). lib. bdg. 16.95 (*0-87044-175-2*) Natl Geog.

— Books for Young Explorers, 4 vols., Set 5. (J). lib. bdg. 16.95 (*0-87044-205-8*) Natl Geog.

— Books for Young Explorers, 4 vols., Set 6. (J). 13.95 (*0-87044-245-7*); lib. bdg. 16.95 (*0-87044-250-3*) Natl Geog.

— Books for Young Explorers, 4 vols, Set 7. (Illus.). (J). (gr. 4-8). 1978. lib. bdg. 16.95 (*0-87044-270-8*) Natl Geog.

— Books for Young Explorers, Set 15. (J). (gr. k-4). 1988. 16.95 (*0-87044-737-8*); lib. bdg. 21.95 (*0-87044-742-4*) Natl Geog.

— The Incredible Incas & Their Timeless Land. LC 74-28805. (Special Publications Series 10: No. 2). (Illus.). 200p. 1975. 12.95 (*0-87044-177-9*); lib. bdg. 12.95 (*0-87044-182-5*) Natl Geog.

— National Geographic Atlas of the World, Series 26. 6th rev. ed. (Special Publications). (Illus.). 1990. 65.00 (*0-87044-834-X*) Natl Geog.

— Primitive Worlds: People Lost in Time. LC 73-830. (Special Publications Series 8: No. 2). 1973. 8.95 (*0-87044-127-2*) Natl Geog.

National Geographic Society Staff & Winston, Peggy D. Explore a Tropical Forest: A National Geographic Pop-Up Book. (Pop-Up Bks.). (Illus.). 12p. (J). (gr. k-3). 1996. 16.00 (*0-87044-757-2*, Pub. by Natl Geog) S&S Trade.

National Geographic Society Staff, jt. auth. see Grove, Noel.

National Geographic Society Staff, jt. auth. see Heacox, Kim.

National Geographic Society Staff, jt. auth. see Martin, Glen.

National Geographic Society Staff, jt. auth. see McCauley, Jane R.

National Geographic Society Staff, jt. auth. see Stuart, Gene S.

National Geographic Society Staff, ed. see Aikman, Lonnelle.

National Geographic Society Staff, ed. see McCarry, John.

***National Geographic Society, U. S. Staff.** Enduring Treasures: National Parks of the World. LC 00-41841. (Illus.). 2000. write for info. (*0-7922-7865-8*) Natl Geog.

National Geographic Society U. S. Staff. Exploring the Rivers of North America. LC 99-25185. 1999. write for info. (*0-7922-7847-X*) Natl Geog.

National Geographic Society U. S. Staff, et al. New England. LC 96-24771. (National Geographic's Driving Guides to America Ser.). 160p. 1997. per. 14.95 (*0-7922-3424-3*) Natl Geog.

National Geographic Society, U. S. Staff, jt. auth. see White, Mel.

National Geographic Staff. The American Road, an Atlas & Travel Planner. (Illus.). 256p. 1998. 39.95 (*1-57262-328-4*, N3020) MapQuest.

— At the Zoo: A National Geographic Action Book. (Pop-Up Bks.). (Illus.). 10p. (YA). (ps up). 1993. 16.00 (*0-87044-872-2*, Pub. by Natl Geog) Publishers Group.

— Bass Master. LC 98-30572. 1998. 19.95 (*0-7922-7376-1*) Natl Geog.

***National Geographic Staff.** Bass Master Shaw Grigsby: Notes on Fishing & Life. 192p. 2000. 12.00 (*0-7922-7613-2*) Natl Geog.

National Geographic Staff. Cat Shots. LC 98-26393. (National Geographic Action Bk.). 108p. 1998. per. 25.00 (*0-7922-7398-2*) Natl Geog.

***National Geographic Staff.** Dolphins. LC 99-86772. 228p. 2000. per. 34.50 (*0-7922-7594-2*, Pub. by Natl Geog) S&S Trade.

— Equal Justice under Law - The Supreme Court in American Life. 151p. 1975. pap. text. write for info. (*1-56986-027-0*, CON-75-151) Federal Bar.

National Geographic Staff. Everyday Life in Bible Times. (Story of Man Ser.). pap. write for info. (*0-87044-131-0*) Natl Geog.

— Eye of the Beholder: The Photography of James L. Stanfield. LC 98-25669. (Illus.). 168p. 1998. 40.00 (*0-7922-7379-6*) Natl Geog.

***National Geographic Staff.** Forces of Change: A New View of Nature. LC 99-87996. 256p. 2000. 40.00 (*0-7922-7596-9*) Natl Geog.

National Geographic Staff. From the Field. 456p. 1998. pap. 15.00 (*0-7922-7394-X*) Natl Geog.

— Guide to the Lewis & Clark. LC 98-20061. 1998. pap. 14.00 (*0-7922-7154-8*) Natl Geog.

***National Geographic Staff.** Italy. (National Geographic Traveler Ser.). 400p. 2000. 27.95 (*0-7922-7562-4*) Natl Geog.

National Geographic Staff. Lewis & Clark. LC 98-20061. 256p. 1998. per. 35.00 (*0-7922-7084-3*) Natl Geog.

— National Geographic: The Photographs. (Illus.). 400p. 1994. per. 50.00 (*0-87044-986-9*) Natl Geog.

— National Geographic Atlas of the World. (n). (Illus.). 90p. 1997. per. 25.00 (*0-7922-7120-3*) Natl Geog.

***National Geographic Staff.** National Geographic Eyewitness to the 20th Century. LC 98-22756. (Destinations Ser.). (Illus.). 400p. (YA). (gr. 5-8). 1998. per. 40.00 (*0-7922-7049-5*) Natl Geog.

— National Geographic Family Adventure Vacations: Animal Encounters Cultural Explorations & Learning Escapes in the US & Coastline Evolution of the Upper Adriatic Sea Due to Sea Level Rise & Natural Anthropogenic Land Subsidence. LC 99-462106. 320p. 2000. per. 25.00 (*0-7922-7590-X*) Natl Geog.

— National Geographic Guide to 100 Easy Hikes: Washington DC, Virginia, Maryland, Delaware. LC 99-462358. 224p. 2000. per. 15.00 (*0-7922-7588-8*, Pub. by Natl Geog) S&S Trade.

— National Geographic Guide to Small Town Escapes. LC 00-35144. (Illus.). 352p. 2000. per. 25.00 (*0-7922-7589-6*, Pub. by Natl Geog) S&S Trade.

National Geographic Staff. National Geographic Guide to Watching Wildlife. LC 97-46750. 1998. pap. 25.00 (*0-7922-7130-0*) Natl Geog.

***National Geographic Staff.** National Geographic Photographs: Then & Now. 1998. 50.00 (*0-676-57897-7*) Random.

National Geographic Staff. National Geographic Road Atlas & Travel Planner. (Illus.). 124p. 1998. pap. 6.95 (*1-57262-414-0*, N3012) MapQuest.

— National Geographics Birder's Journal. 464p. 1999. per. 14.95 (*0-7922-7456-3*, Pub. by Natl Geog) S&S Trade.

***National Geographic Staff.** Nature's Medicine: Plants That Heal. LC 99-89037. 400p. 2000. per. 34.50 (*0-7922-7586-1*, Pub. by Natl Geog) S&S Trade.

— Northern Rockies. LC 99-85986. (National Geographic Guide to America's Outdoors). (Illus.). 288p. 2000. per. 24.00 (*0-7922-7741-4*, Pub. by Natl Geog) S&S Trade.

National Geographic Staff. Park Profile: America's Hid. 1997. pap. 12.95 (*0-7922-7033-9*) Natl Geog.

National Geographic Staff. Park Profile: Grand Canyon. 200p. 1997. per. 15.00 (*0-7922-7032-0*, Pub. by Natl Geog) S&S Trade.

National Geographic Staff. Perfume. LC 98-23082. 176p. 1998. per. 34.50 (*0-7922-7378-8*) Natl Geog.

***National Geographic Staff.** Photographs Then & Now. Bendavid-Val, Leah, ed. LC 98-23421. (Illus.). 304p. (YA). (gr. 5 up). 1998. per. 50.00 (*0-7922-7202-1*) Natl Geog.

National Geographic Staff. Pile of Puppies. (J). (ps). 1993. 4.50 (*0-7922-1834-5*) Natl Geog.

— Restless Earth: Nature's Aw. LC 97-8115. 288p. 1997. per. 35.00 (*0-7922-7026-6*) Natl Geog.

***National Geographic Staff.** Rome. (National Geographic Traveler Ser.). 272p. 2000. per. 22.95 (*0-7922-7566-7*) Natl Geog.

— San Francisco. (National Geographic Traveler Ser.). 272p. 2000. per. 22.95 (*0-7922-7565-9*) Natl Geog.

National Geographic Staff. Satellite Atlas of the World. (Illus.). 224p. 1998. 0.50 (*0-7922-7216-1*) Natl Geog.

— Wonders of the World. 232p. 1999. 35.00 (*0-7922-7200-5*) Natl Geog.

— The Year of the Tiger. LC 98-26376. 160p. 1998. per. 40.00 (*0-7922-7377-X*, Pub. by Natl Geog) S&S Trade.

— Yosemite: An American Treasure. (National Geographic Park Profiles Ser.). 200p. 1997. per. 15.00 (*0-7922-7030-4*, Pub. by Natl Geog) S&S Trade.

National Geographic Staff, ed. National Geographic Driving Guide - California. 1998. pap. 14.95 (*0-7922-7365-6*) Natl Geog.

— National Geographic Driving Guide - Canada. 160p. 1998. per. 14.95 (*0-7922-7366-4*) Natl Geog.

— National Geographic Driving Guide - Florida. 160p. 1998. per. 14.95 (*0-7922-7368-0*) Natl Geog.

— National Geographic Driving Guide - New York. 1998. pap. 14.95 (*0-7922-7369-9*) Natl Geog.

— National Geographic Driving Guide to Pacific Northwest. 160p. 1998. per. 14.95 (*0-7922-7367-2*) Natl Geog.

— National Geographic Guide to State Parks. 384p. 1998. per. 24.00 (*0-7922-7364-8*) Natl Geog.

— National Geographic Park Profiles: Canada's National Parks. 200p. 1998. per. 15.00 (*0-7922-7355-9*) Natl Geog.

***National Geographic Staff & Ferguson, Gary.** New England. (National Geographic Guide to America's Outdoors). (Illus.). 288p. 2000. per. 24.00 (*0-7922-7742-2*) Natl Geog.

National Geographic Staff & Hamm, Jack. Robed in Light. 111p. (Orig.). 1989. pap. write for info. (*0-614-29607-2*) R A Lectures.

National Geographic Staff & Klerein, Tom. Weather: A Naitonal Geographic Pop-Up Book. LC 94-25394. (Pop-Up Bks.). (Illus.). 12p. (J). (ps-3). 1991. 16.00 (*0-7922-2782-4*, Pub. by Natl Geog) S&S Trade.

National Geographic Staff & Newhouse, Elizabeth L. National Geographic's Guide to the National Parks of the United States. LC 97-168279. (Illus.). 448p. 1997. per. 24.00 (*0-7922-7016-9*) Natl Geog.

National Geographical Society Staff, ed. Books for Young Explorers, 4 vols., Set 1. Incl. Dinosaurs. LC 72-91418. 1972. Dogs Working for People. 1972. Lion Cubs. 1972. Treasures in the Sea. 1972. (J). (ps-3). 1972. Set lib. bdg. 16.95 (*0-87044-300-3*) Natl Geog.

National Gerontologic Nurses Association Staff. NGNA Care Curriculum for Gerontological Nurses & Associates. (Illus.). 768p. (C). (gr. 13). 1995. pap. text 46.95 (*0-8151-6424-6*, 24848) Mosby Inc.

National Glass Association Staff. Auto Glass Customer Service Representative Study Guide. (Illus.). 174p. 1996. pap. 189.90 (*1-56393-015-3*) National Glass Assn.

— Auto Glass Customer Service Representative Study Guide: Instructor's Edition. (Illus.). 208p. 1996. pap. 339.90 (*1-56393-014-5*) National Glass Assn.

— Auto Glass Repair Technician Reference Manual. (Illus.). 176p. 1999. pap. 69.90 (*1-56393-019-6*) National Glass Assn.

— Auto Glass Technician Training Manual. 2nd rev. ed. (Illus.). 332p. 1998. pap. 89.90 (*1-56393-000-5*) National Glass Assn.

— Basic Guide to Glass & Glazing: Level I. 1993. pap. text 69.90 (*1-56393-004-8*) National Glass Assn.

— Custom Mirrors: Fabrication & Installation. (Illus.). 180p. 1998. pap. 69.90 (*1-56393-016-1*) National Glass Assn.

An Asterisk (*) at the beginning of an entry indicates that the title is appearing for the first time.

— Design & Construction Considerations of a Glass & Metal Framing System: Video & Guidebook. (Illus.). 20p. 1998. pap. 69.90 (*1-56393-020-X*) National Glass Assn.

— Fundamentals of Auto Glass Adhesives: An Introductory Guide. LC 97-106886. 40p. 1996. pap. text 39.90 (*1-56393-011-0*) National Glass Assn.

— Guide to Glass & Glazing Requirements of the Model Building Codes. LC 96-205092. (Illus.). 52p. (Orig.). (C). 1996. pap. text 49.90 (*1-56393-012-9*) National Glass Assn.

— Guide to Manufacturers Auto Glass Adhesives: A Comprehensive Guide to Auto Glass Adhesives. 200p. 1997. pap. 139.90 (*1-56393-013-7*) National Glass Assn.

National Golf Foundation Staff. Golf Course Directory, 2 vols. 1160p. 1999. pap. 199.00 (*1-57701-079-5*, 99GR112) Natl Golf.

— The NGF's Golf Course Directory. 1147p. 1999. 199.00 (*1-57701-105-8*) Natl Golf.

National Golf Foundation Staff. 2000 NGF Directory of Golf: The People & Businesses in Golf. rev. ed. 400p. (Orig.). 2000. pap. 60.00 (*1-57701-049-3*) Natl Golf. This publication covers the entire golf industry & lists more than 6,000 golf-related businesses & 10,000 executives. The 2000 Directory of Golf is organized into three distinct reference sections: The "Business to Business section lists over 6,000 companies alphabetically & includes such information as mail, e-mail & web addresses, phone, fax & 800 numbers, key personnel & their titles, plus the products & services offered. by each company. "The Industry Executive" section lists 10,000 golf industry executives alphabetically along with their company affiliation & telephone number. "The Product & Service Index" section organizes companies alphabetically into one of over 100+ golf product or service groupings & further defines the specific type of product or service. The Directory also includes a calendar of major golf industry events scheduled in 2000. Currently in its fourth edition, the 2000 Directory of Golf has become the definitive source for accurate & up-to-the-minute information. *Publisher Paid Annotation.

National Golf Foundation Staff. Women in Golf. 34p. 1998. pap. 50.00 (*1-57701-083-3*) Natl Golf.

National Golf Foundation Staff, ed. Golf Practice Range & Learning Center Directory. 160p. 1999. pap. 99.00 (*1 57701 080-9*, 99GR113) Natl Golf.

— Off-Course Golf Retail Store Directory. 88p. 1998. pap. 99.00 (*1-57701-081-7*, 99GR114) Natl Golf.

— Par 3 & Executive Course Directory. 168p. 1999. pap. 99.00 (*1-57701-082-5*, 99GR115) Natl Golf.

National Governors' Assoc. Staff, ed. see Forcella, Domenic.

National Governors' Association Staff. Community Service: A Resource Guide for States. Glass, Karen, ed. 40p. (Orig.). 1989. pap. text 10.00 (*1-55877-053-4*) Natl Governor.

— Directory of Governors of the American States, Commonwealths, & Territories, 1989. 68p. (Orig.). 1989. pap. text 8.95 (*1-55877-034-8*) Natl Governor.

— Directory of Governors of the American States, Commonwealths, & Territories, 1990. Miller, Mark, ed. 76p. (Orig.). 1990. pap. text 8.95 (*1-55877-073-9*) Natl Governor.

— Governors' Staff Directory, 1989. 75p. (Orig.). 1989. pap. text 7.50 (*1-55877-035-6*) Natl Governor.

— Health Issues in Rural America. (New Alliances for Rural America Ser.). 120p. (Orig.). 1988. pap. text 6.00 (*1-55877-015-1*) Natl Governor.

— Policy Positions, 1988-89. (Policy Positions Ser.). 280p. (Orig.). 1988. pap. text 15.00 (*1-55877-023-2*) Natl Governor.

— Policy Positions, 1989-90. Miller, Mark, ed. 316p. (Orig.). 1989. pap. text 15.00 (*1-55877-064-X*) Natl Governor.

— Results in Education, 1988. (Time for Results Ser.). (Orig.). 1988. pap. text 12.50 (*1-55877-013-5*) Natl Governor.

National Governors' Association Staff & National Association of State Budget Officers Staff. Fiscal Survey of the States - October 1988. 50p. (Orig.). 1988. pap. text 20.00 (*1-55877-024-0*) Natl Governor.

National Graves Association of Ireland Staff. The Last Post. MacCiarnain, Seamus & Conlon, Vincent, eds. (Illus.). 234p. 1986. 10.00 (*0-9616291-0-X*) Natl Graves Assn.

National Guitar Workshop Staff, jt. auth. see Hamburger, David.

National Guitar Workshop Staff, ed. see York, Andrew.

National Health - Education Consortium Staff. Florida's Youth, Florida's Future. 20p. 1993. 12.00 (*0 937846-52-X*) Inst Educ Lead.

— Texas' Youth, Texas' Future. 20p. 1993. 12.00 (*0-937846-50-3*) Inst Educ Lead.

National Health & Education Consortium Staff. Putting Children First: State-Level Collaboration Between Education & Health. 50p. 1995. 10.00 (*0-937846-43-0*) Inst Educ Lead.

— Starting Young: School-Based Health Centers at the Elementary Level. 50p. 1995. 10.00 (*0-937846-42-2*) Inst Educ Lead.

National Health & Nutrition Examination Survey Sta, ed. see Russell, Louise B., et al.

National Health Bureau of America Staff. Perfect Health Vol. II: How to Be Young at 60 & Live to Be 100. 55p. 1996. reprint ed. spiral bd. 11.00 (*0-7873-0633-9*) Hlth Research.

***National Health Council Staff.** Standards of Accounting & Financial Reporting for Voluntary Health. 4th ed. 144p. 1998. text 75.00 (*0-7872-5422-3*, 41542201) Kendall-Hunt.

National Health Law Program Staff, jt. auth. see Michigan Legal Services Staff.

National Health Lawyers Association Staff. Health Law Practice Guide, 3 vols. King, Marylou, ed. LC 93-17568. (Health Law Ser.). 1993. 450.00 (*0-87632-912-1*) West Group.

National Health Lawyers Association Staff, et al. Medicare Fraud & Abuse: Understanding the Law. LC 86-61317. 300p. 1986. 36.00 (*0-918945-01-1*) Am Hlth Lawyers.

National Health Service Estates Staff. Firecode: Alarm Protection Systems. (Fire Publications: No. 82). 39p. 1996. pap. 70.00 (*0-11-322045-6*) Statnry Office.

— Firecode: Fire Precautions in New Hospitals. rev. ed. (Fire Publications: No. 81). 83p. 1996. pap. 70.00 (*0-11-322249-1*) Statnry Office.

— Firecode: Fire Precautions in Patient Hotels. (Fire Publications: No. 7). 21p. 1995. pap. 40.00 (*0-11-321769-2*) Statnry Office.

— Firecode: Fire Risk Assessment in Nucleus Hospitals. (Fire Publications). 80p. 1997. pap. 70.00 (*0-11-322059-6*) Statnry Office.

— Firecode: Laboratories on Hospital Premises. (Fire Publications: No. 10). 20p. 1996. pap. 40.00 (*0-11-322038-3*) Statnry Office.

— Firecode: NHS Healthcare Fire Statistics. (Fire Publications: No. 9, 1994/95). 37p. 1996. pap. 60.00 (*0-11-322244-0*) Statnry Office.

National Health Service States Staff. Firecode: Fire Safety in Healthcare Premises - General Fire Precautions. (Fire Publications: No. 83). 62p. 1994. pap. 40.00 (*0-11-321725-0*) Statnry Office.

National Heart, Lung & Blood Institute Staff, jt. auth. see NIH Staff.

National Heat Transfer Conference Staff. Basic Aspects of Two Phase Flow & Heat Transfer: Presented at the 22nd National Heat Transfer Conference & Exhibition, Niagara Falls, New York, August 5-8, 1984. Dhir, V. K. & Schrock, V. E., eds. LC 84-71692. (HTD Ser.: Vol. 34). 189p. pap. 58.60 (*0-7837-0205-1*, 204050100017) Bks Demand.

— Condensation Heat Transfer: Presented at the 18th National Heat Transfer Conference, San Diego, CA, August 6-8, 1979. Marto, Paul J. & Kroeger, P. G., eds. LC 79-53410. 124p. reprint ed. pap. 38.50 (*0-608-15926-3*, 203088700071) Bks Demand.

— Experimental & Analytical Modeling of LWR Safety Experiments: Presented at the 19th National Heat Transfer Conference, Orlando, Florida, July 27-30, 1980. Hochreiter, L. E. & Sozzi, G. L., eds. LC 80-66050. (HTD Ser.: Vol. 7). (Illus.). 144p. reprint ed. pap. 44.70 (*0-8357-2836-6*, 203907200010) Bks Demand.

— Fouling in Heat Exchange Equipment: Presented At the 20th ASME-AICHE Heat Transfer Conference, Milwaukee, WI, August 2-5, 1981, (Sponsored by the Heat Transfer Equipment (K-10) Committee of the ASME Heat Transfer Division) Chenoweth, James M. & Impagliazzo, Mike, eds. LC 81-65617. (HTD Ser.: Vol. 17). 110p. reprint ed. pap. 34.10 (*0-608-16196-9*, 205615900052) Bks Demand.

— Fundamentals of Natural Convection - Electronic Equipment Cooling: Presented at the 22nd National Heat Transfer Conference & Exhibition, Niagara Falls, New York, August 5-8, 1984. Witte, L. C. & Saxena, L. S., eds. LC 84-71690. (HTD Ser.: Vol. 32). 103p. pap. 32.00 (*0-7837-0204-3*, 204050000017) Bks Demand.

— Natural Convection in Enclosures: Presented at the 19th National Heat Transfer Conference, Orlando, Florida, July 27-30, 1980. Torrance, K. E. & Catton, I., eds. LC 80-65786. (HTD Ser.: Vol. 8). (Illus.). 128p. reprint ed. pap. 39.70 (*0-8357-2814-5*, 203905300010) Bks Demand.

— Nonequilibrium Interfacial Transport Processes: Presented at the 18th National Heat Transfer Conference, San Diego, California, August 6-8, 1979. Chen, J. C. & Bankoff, S. G., eds. LC 79-53412. (Illus.). 95p. reprint ed. pap. 30.00 (*0-8357-2868-4*, 203910400011) Bks Demand.

— Thermal-Hydraulics in Nuclear Power Technology: Presented at the 20th National Heat Transfer Conference, Milwaukee, Wisconsin, August 2-5, 1981. Sun, K. H. et al, eds. LC 81-65616. (HTD Ser.: Vol. 15). (Illus.). 92p. reprint ed. pap. 30.00 (*0-8357-2815-3*, 203905400010) Bks Demand.

National Helpers Network Staff. The Helper Program: Making It Happen. rev. ed. 1998. spiral bd. 15.00 (*1-891455-10-9*) Natl Helpers.

— Learning Helpers: A Guide to Training & Reflection. rev. ed. (Illus.). x, 70p. 1998. ring bd. 55.00 (*1-891455-01-X*) Natl Helpers.

— The Partners Program: A Guide for Teachers & Program Leaders. (Illus.). 85p. 1991. spiral bd. 30.00 (*1-891455-02-8*) Natl Helpers.

— Reflection: The Key to Service Learning. 2nd rev. ed. LC 98-229061. 1998. spiral bd. 30.00 (*1-891455-12-5*) Natl Helpers.

— Sharing & Learning: Partners' Service Across the Curriculum. (Illus.). vi, 98p. 1997. spiral bd. 40.00 (*1-891455-05-2*) Natl Helpers.

— Student Evaluators: A Guide to Implementation. (Illus.). vi, 20p. 1994. spiral bd. 30.00 (*1-891455-06-0*) Natl Helpers.

— Take Action! Exploring with 6-10 Year Olds. (Illus.). x, 61p. (J). (gr. 5-8). 1995. ring bd. 25.00 (*1-891455-08-7*) Natl Helpers.

— Take Action! Exploring with 3-5 Year Olds. (Illus.). 37p. (J). (gr. 5-8). 1995. ring bd. 25.00 (*1-891455-07-9*) Natl Helpers.

— Teaching & Learning: Helpers' Service Across the Curriculum. vii, 103p. 1995. ring bd. 35.00 (*1-891455-09-5*) Natl Helpers.

— Youth to Youth: Training Guidelines for Young Adult-Led Service Programs. 83p. 1997. spiral bd. 25.00 (*1-891455-11-7*) Natl Helpers.

National Helpers Network Staff, jt. auth. see Gill, Tom.

National Herbart Society Staff. National Herbart Society Yearbooks One to Five, 1895-1899, 5 vols., Set. LC 70-89209. (American Education: Its Men, Institutions & Ideas, Ser. 1). 1978. reprint ed. 47.95 (*0-405-01448-1*) Ayer.

National Heritage Preservation Institute Staff, et al. Caring for Your Historic House. LC 97-33266. 1998. lib. bdg. 16.00 (*0-8109-2779-9*, Pub. by Abrams) Time Warner.

— Caring for Your Historic House. LC 97-33266. (Illus.). 256p. 1998. lib. bdg. 39.95 (*0-8109-4087-6*, Pub. by Abrams) Time Warner.

National Hispanic Staff. Modulo II (Bilingue) (Module II (Bilingual)) Programa de Capacitacion para Misioneros(as) Laicos(as) y Pastores (Lay Missioner & Pastor-Mentor Training Program) (ENG & SPA.). 312p. 1997. pap. 16.95 (*0-88177-240-2*, DR240) Discipleship Res.

National Hispanic Women's Health Initiative Staff & Delgado, Jane L. Salud! (SPA) Guia para la salud integral de la mujer Latina:Cuerpo, Mente y Espiritu. LC 97-23270. (SPA., Illus.). 432p. 1997. pap. 20.00 (*0-06-095261-X*, Perennial) HarperTrade.

National History Standards Task Force Staff. National Standards for United States History: Exploring the American Experience. (National History STandards Project Ser.). (Illus.). 310p. (Orig.). (C). 1994. pap. text 24.95 (*0-9633218-1-1*) Natl Ctr Hist.

— National Standards for World History: Exploring Paths to the Present. (National History STandards Project Ser.). (Illus.). 310p. (Orig.). (C). 1994. pap. text 24.95 (*0-9633218-2-X*) Natl Ctr Hist.

National Hockey League Staff. Hockey Rules in Pictures. (Sports Rules in Pictures Ser.). (Illus.). 96p. 1992. pap. 8.95 (*0-399-51772-3*, Perigee Bks) Berkley Pub.

— Official Rules of the NHL. rev. ed. (Official Rules Ser.). (Illus.). 201p. (Orig.). 1996. pap. 8.95 (*1-57243-141-5*) Triumph Bks.

***National Hockey League Staff.** Official Rules of the NHL: 2000. LC 96-30000. 160p. 1999. pap. 9.95 (*1-57243-335-3*) Triumph Bks.

National Hospice Organization. Developing a Hospice Ethics Committee. LC 99-163803. 78p. 1998. 11.85 (*0-931207-53-3*) Natl Hospice.

— Hospice Care - A Physician's Guide. 2nd ed. LC 98-196850. 96p. 1998. pap. 5.95 (*0-931207-54-1*) Natl Hospice.

National Hospice Organization AIDS Resource Commit. Resource Manual for Providing Hospice Care to People Living with AIDS. 109p. (Orig.). 1996. pap., per. 11.85 (*0-931207-44-4*) Natl Hospice.

National Hospice Organization, Alternative Care Ta. Alternative Care Programs in Hospice. 29p. 1991. 10.50 (*0-931207-11-8*) Natl Hospice.

National Hospice Organization, Commercial Reimburs. Commercial Reimbursement Insurance Monograph. 10p. 1991. 7.35 (*0-931207-25-8*) Natl Hospice.

— Managed Care Monograph. 37p. 1993. 10.50 (*0-931207-21-5*) Natl Hospice.

National Hospice Organization, Ethics Committee. Discontinuation of Hospice Care: Ethical Issues. 15p. 1993. 15.75 (*0-931207-22-3*) Natl Hospice.

National Hospice Organization Ethics Committee. Hospice Code of Ethics. 7p. (Orig.). 1995. pap. 8.30 (*0-931207-43-6*, 713024) Natl Hospice.

National Hospice Organization Ethics Committee, ed. Proactive Responses to the Assisted Suicide/Euthanasia Debate. 96p. (Orig.). 1996. pap., per. 11.85 (*0-931207-45-2*, 713438) Natl Hospice.

National Hospice Organization Medical Guidelines T, jt. auth. see National Hospice Organization Standards & Accredit.

National Hospice Organization Staff. Hospice Bereavement Bibliography. 48p. 1993. 15.75 (*0-931207-26-6*) Natl Hospice.

— Hospice Bibliography. 185p. 1993. 26.25 (*0-931207-29-0*) Natl Hospice.

— Hospice Legislation: 1977-1994. 252p. (C). 1995. ring bd. 60.00 (*0-931207-34-7*) Natl Hospice.

— Hospice Operations Manual: 1997 Edition. 528p. 1997. ring bd. 130.00 (*0-7872-1830-8*) Kendall-Hunt.

— Hospice Services Guidelines & Definitions. Brandt, Katherine, ed. 8p. (Orig.). 1995. pap. 7.35 (*0-931207-31-2*) Natl Hospice.

— 1993 Hospice Personnel Compensation Study. 21p. 1993. 105.00 (*0-931207-13-4*) Natl Hospice.

— Standards of a Hospice Program of Care. 40p. 1993. ring bd. 31.50 (*0-931207-20-7*) Natl Hospice.

— Volunteer Training Curriculum. Bates, Ira J. & Brandt, Katherine E., eds. 147p. 1990. ring bd. 45.00 (*0-931207-06-1*) Natl Hospice.

National Hospice Organization, Standards & Accredi. Quality Assurance: A Primer for Hospice Programs. 38p. 1989. 10.50 (*0-931207-17-7*) Natl Hospice.

National Hospice Organization Standards & Accredit & National Hospice Organization Medical Guidelines T. Medical Guidelines for Determining Prognosis in Selected Non-Cancer Diseases. 2nd ed. 58p. (Orig.). 1996. pap. 11.85 (*0-931207-50-9*, 713008) Natl Hospice.

National Hospice Organization, 1991 Ethics Committ. Do-Not Resuscitate (DNR) Decisions in the Context of Hospice Care. 32p. 1992. 10.50 (*0-931207-19-3*) Natl Hospice.

National Housing Law Project Staff. Housing Law Bulletin, Vol. 26. Date not set. write for info. (*0-614-14614-3*) Natl Housing Law.

— HUD Housing Programs: Tenants' Rights. (Orig.). 1996. pap., suppl. ed. 95.00 (*0-614-14612-7*) Natl Housing Law.

— HUD Housing Programs: Tenants' Rights. 2nd rev. ed. LC 97-112641. 650p. (Orig.). 1994. pap. 165.00 (*0-9606098-6-5*) Natl Housing Law.

— Outline of New Developments since the Writing of HUD Housing Programs: Tenants Rights, 1985 Supplement. 42p. 1987. pap. 4.50 (*0-685-23181-X*, 41,125) NCLS Inc.

— RHCDS (FmHA) Housing Programs: Tenants' & Homeowners' Rights. 2nd rev. ed. LC 97-112411. 600p. 1995. pap. 95.00 (*0-9606098-7-3*) Natl Housing Law.

National Housing Law Project Staff & Johnson, Sara E. Preserving HUD-Assisted Housing for Use by Low-Income Tenants: An Advocate's Guide. 484p. (Orig.). 1985. pap. 25.00 (*0-941077-05-5*, 38,900) NCLS Inc.

National Housing Law Project Staff, et al. Housing for All: Keeping the Promise. 24p. (Orig.). 1995. pap. 10.00 (*0-614-14613-5*) Natl Housing Law.

***National HRD Network (India)., et al.** Leading Change Through Human Resources: Towards a Globally Competitive India: Papers Presented at the 6th National Conference of the National HRD Network, New Delhi, February 1998 LC 98-904232. xvi, 346 p. 1998. (*0-07-463437-2*) McGraw.

***National Immigration Forum Staff.** Immigration Policy Handbook. 76p. 2000. pap. 40.00 (*0-9645220-4-7*) Nat Immig Forum.

National Immigration Project (U.S.) Staff, et al. Immigration Law & the Family. LC 94-23089. 1994. ring bd. 115.00 (*0-87632-223-2*) West Group.

National Immigration Project of the National Lawye. Immigration Act of 1990 Handbook: The Complete Guide to the 1990 Ace, 1992. 1992. pap. 79.50 (*0-87632-822-2*) West Group.

National Imperial Glass Collector's Society Staff. Imperial Glass Encyclopedia Vol. I: A - Cane, 1. Measell, James, ed. (Illus.). 208p. 1995. pap. 34.95 (*1-57080-007-3*) Antique Pubns.

— Imperial Glass Encyclopedia Vol. I: A Cane. Measell, James, ed. (Illus.). 208p. 1995. 44.95 (*1-57080-008-1*) Antique Pubns.

National Incinerator Conference Staff. Resource Recovery Through Incineration: Proceedings; Papers Presented at 1974 National Incinerator Conference, Miami, Florida, May 12-15, 1974. LC 70-124402. 380p. reprint ed. pap. 117.80 (*0-608-14522-7*, 201686600007) Bks Demand.

National Indian Traders Association Staff. American Indian & Alaska Native Traders Directory. 140p. 1990. pap. 21.45 (*0-935151-16-8*) Arrowstar Pub.

National Industrial Conference Board, Inc. Staff. Trade Association: Their Economic Significance & Legal Status. 2nd rev. ed. LC 25-12032. xiv, 388p. 1982. reprint ed. lib. bdg. 48.50 (*0-89941-164-9*, 302310) W S Hein.

— The Work of the International Labor Organization. 1983. reprint ed. lib. bdg. 40.00 (*0-89941-211-4*, 303010) W S Hein.

National Industrial Conference Board Staff. The Banking Situation in the United States. Bruchey, Stuart, ed. LC 80-1188. (Rise of Commercial Banking Ser.). (Illus.). 1981. reprint ed. lib. bdg. 18.95 (*0-405-13671-4*) Ayer.

National Industrial Council Staff & Du Preez, B. G., eds. Main Agreement of the National Industrial Council for the Motor Industry. 1989. ring bd. write for info. (*0-7021-2263-7*, Pub. by Juta & Co) Gaunt.

National Industrial Council Staff & Levy, David, eds. Consolidated Agreements of the National Industrial Council for the Iron, Steel, Engineering & Metallurgical Industry. 1987. ring bd. 67.50 (*0-7021-1920-2*, Pub. by Juta & Co) Gaunt.

National Information Center for Educational Media. Audiocassette & CD Finder: A Subject Guide to Educational & Literary Materials on Audiocassette & CD. 3rd ed. 1400p. 1993. 125.00 (*0-937548-14-6*) Natl Info Ctr NM.

— Index to AV Producers & Distributors. 10th ed. LC 82-60346. 1996. pap. 89.00 (*0-937548-13-8*) Natl Info Ctr NM.

— Index to AV Producers & Distributors. 10th ed. LC 82-60346. (NILEM Ser.). 626p. 1997. pap. 89.00 (*0-937548-30-8*) Plexus Pub.

— NICEM Thesaurus. LC 98-72499. 300p. 1998. pap. 59.95 (*0-89320-200-2*) Natl Info Ctr NM.

National Information Standards Organization Staff. American National Standard for Computerized Book Ordering: Abstract: Approved October 10, 1992 by the American National Standards Institute. LC 93-16162. (National Information Standards Ser.). 1993. pap. 40.00 (*0-88738-931-7*) Transaction Pubs.

— ANSI/NISO/ISO 12083 Electronic Manuscript Preparation & Markup. LC 95-33008. (National Information Standards Ser.). 200p. 1995. 125.00 (*1-880124-20-3*) NISO.

— Codes for the Representation of Languages for Information Interchange Z39.53 - 1994. LC 94-36086. (National Information Standards Ser.). 12p. 1994. 45.00 (*1-880124-10-6*) NISO.

— Codes for the Representation of Names of Countries: ANSI-NISO-ISO 3166. 76p. (C). 1993. pap. 50.00 (*0-88738-937-6*) Transaction Pubs.

N

National Information Standards Organization Staff. Computer Software Description, Z39.67-1993. LC 93-45764. (National Information Standards Ser.: No. 1041-5653). 22p. 1994. 45.00 (*1-880124-05-X*) NISO.

— Data Elements for Binding Library Materials, Z39.76-1996. LC 96-43632. (National Information Standards Ser.). 48p. 1997. pap. 49.00 (*1-880124-29-7*) NISO.

National Information Standards Organization Staff. Durable Hardcover Binding for Books, Z39.66-1992 (R1998) rev. ed. LC 95-41629. (National Information Standards Ser.). (Illus.). 22p. 1995. reprint ed. 40.00 (*1-880124-18-1*, 1041-5653) NISO.

***National Information Standards Organization Staff.** Environmental Conditions for Exhibiting Library & Archival Materials, Z39.79-2000. 36p. 2000. 49.00 (*1-880124-44-0*) NISO.

National Information Standards Organization Staff. Extended Latin Alphabet Coded Character Set for Bibliographic Use (ANSEL) Z39.47-1993 (R1998) LC 92-7411. (National Information Standards Ser.). 277p. 1993. pap. 45.00 (*1-880124-02-5*) NISO.

***National Information Standards Organization Staff.** Eye-Legible Information on Microfilm Leaders & Trailers & on Containers of Processed Microfilm on Open Reels, Z39.62-2000. 15p. 2000. 45.00 (*1-880124-48-3*) NISO.

National Information Standards Organization Staff. Guidelines for Abstracts, Z39.14-1997. LC 97-10459. (National Information Standards Ser.). 24p. 1997. pap. 45.00 (*1-880124-31-9*) NISO.

— Guidelines for Indexes & Related Information Retrieval Devices, TR02-1997. LC 97-31018. (Niso Technical Reports). 54p. 1997. pap. 55.00 (*1-880124-36-X*) NISO.

***National Information Standards Organization Staff.** Guidelines for Information about Preservation Products, Z39.77-2000. 48p. 2000. 49.00 (*1-880124-49-1*) NISO.

National Information Standards Organization Staff. Guidelines for the Construction, Format, & Management of Monolingual Thesauri, Z39.19-1993 (R1998) LC 93-42543. (National Information Standards Ser.). 84p. 1994. 55.00 (*1-880124-04-1*) NISO.

— Guides to Accompany Microform Sets, Z39.74-1996. LC 96-15296. (National Information Standards Ser.). 20p. 1996. pap. 40.00 (*1-880124-26-2*) NISO.

— Information Interchange Format, Z39.2-1994. LC 94-9641. (National Information Standards Ser.). 12p. 1994. 45.00 (*1-880124-08-4*) NISO.

— Information on Microfiche Headers, Z39.32-1996. LC 96-15295. (National Information Standards Ser.). 20p. 1996. pap. 39.00 (*1-880124-25-4*) NISO.

— Information Retrieval: Application Service Definition & Protocol Specification, Z39.50-1995. rev. ed. LC 95-39670. (National Information Standards Ser.). 180p. 1995. pap. 99.00 (*1-880124-22-X*) NISO.

— Interlibrary Loan Data Elements, Z39.63-1989. rev. ed. LC 95-41631. (National Information Standards Ser.). 62p. 1995. reprint ed. 55.00 (*1-880124-17-3*, 1041-5653) NISO.

— International Standard Serial Numbering. 16p. 1992. reprint ed. pap. 20.00 (*0-88738-992-9*, Z39.9) Transaction Pubs.

— International Standard Serial Numbering (ISSN), Z39.9-1992. rev. ed. LC 95-41630. (National Information Standards Ser.). 19p. 1995. reprint ed. 40.00 (*1-880124-12-2*, 1041-5653) NISO.

***National Information Standards Organization Staff.** Library Binding, Z39.78-2000. LC 99-88934. 40p. 2000. 59.00 (*1-880124-43-2*) NISO.

National Information Standards Organization Staff. Library Statistics, Z39.7-1995. LC 97-27081. (National Information Standards Ser.). 1997. pap. 45.00 (*1-880124-27-0*) NISO.

— 1998 Holdings Statements for Bibliographic Items, Z39.71-1999. LC 99-10693. 50p. 1999. 55.00 (*1-880124-39-4*) NISO.

— Permanence of Paper for Publications & Documents in Libraries & Archives, Z39.48, 1992 (R1997) LC 93-148. (National Information Standards Ser.). 10p. 1993. 40.00 (*1-880124-00-9*) NISO.

— Printed Information of Spines, Z39.41-1997. LC 98-37801. 24p. 1998. 40.00 (*1-880124-32-7*) NISO.

— Printed Information on Spines, Z39.41-1990. 1991. 20.00 (*0-88738-944-9*) Transaction Pubs.

— Proof Corrections: Z39.22-1989. rev. ed. (National Information Standards Ser.). 38p. 1991. pap. 45.00 (*0-88738-949-X*) Transaction Pubs.

— Scientific & Technical Reports: Elements, Organization, & Design, Z39.18-1995. LC 95-22240. (National Information Standards Ser.). 44p. 1995. 59.00 (*1-880124-24-6*) NISO.

— Serial Item & Contribution Identifier, 1991. 1992. 40.00 (*0-88738-943-0*, Z39.56) Transaction Pubs.

— Serial Item & Contribution Identifier (SICI), Z39.56-1996. LC 96-43631. (National Information Standards Ser.). 36p. 1996. pap. 49.00 (*1-880124-28-9*) NISO.

— Single-Tier Steel Bracket Library Shelving, Z39.73-1994. LC 94-45135. (National Information Standards Ser.). 10p. 1995. pap. 49.00 (*1-880124-09-2*) NISO.

— Standard Address Number (SAN) for the Publishing Industry, Z39.43-1993. rev. ed. LC 95-39985. (National Information Standards Ser.). 19p. 1995. reprint ed. 40.00 (*1-880124-14-9*, 1041-5653) NISO.

— Standard Technical Report Number Format & Creation, Z39.23-1997. LC 96-53246. (National Information Standards Ser.). 12p. 1997. 40.00 (*1-880124-30-0*) NISO.

***National Information Standards Organization Staff.** Syntax for the Digital Object Identifier, Z39.84-2000. LC 99-40445. (National Information Standards Ser.). 24p. 2000. 39.00 (*1-880124-47-5*) NISO.

National Information Standards Organization Staff. Volume & File Structure of CD-ROM for Information Exchange: ANSI-NISO-ISO 9660. LC 93-3113. 64p. (C). 1993. pap. 48.00 (*0-88738-936-8*) Transaction Pubs.

National Information Standards Organization Staff & Wilson, William K. Environmental Guidelines for the Storage of Paper Records, (TR01-1995) LC 95-23518. (NISO Technical Report: Vol. 1). 40p. 1995. 39.00 (*1-880124-21-1*) NISO.

National Insecurity Council Staff. It's a Conspiracy! 252p. 1992. pap. 9.95 (*1-879682-10-9*) Bathroom Reader.

National Inst. for Social Work Staff. The Swing Directory of Social Welfare Information Networks. (C). 1988. 35.00 (*0-7855-4021-0*, Pub. by Natl Inst Soc Work) St Mut.

National Inst. of Construction Law, I Staff. Construction & Design Law Digest, August 1998. 90p. 1998. pap. write for info. (*0-327-00337-5*, 5017515) LEXIS Pub.

National Institue for Social Work Staff, ed. Personal Social Services Council: At Home in a Boarding House. 1981. 30.00 (*0-7855-0839-2*, Pub. by Natl Inst Soc Work) St Mut.

National Institute for Constitution Law, Inc. Staf. Construction & Design Law Digest, September, 1998. 95p. 1998. pap. write for info. (*0-327-00485-1*, 5017615) LEXIS Pub.

National Institute for Construction & Design Law Staff. Construction & Design Law Digest: 1998 Bound, Vol. 1. 608p. 1999. write for info. (*0-327-01129-7*, 6491210) LEXIS Pub.

— Construction & Design Law Digest: 1998 Bound, Vol. 2. 625p. 1999. write for info. (*0-327-01130-0*, 6491310) LEXIS Pub.

— Construction & Design Law Digest: 1998 Bound Volume, 2 vols. 1200p. 1999. write for info. (*0-327-00989-6*, 6491110) LEXIS Pub.

— Construction & Design Law Digest Vols. 1 & 2: 1998 Bound Volume, 2 vols., Set. 625p. 1999. write for info. (*0-327-01131-9*) LEXIS Pub.

— Construction & Design Law Digest, April 1999. 116p. 1999. pap. write for info. (*0-327-01143-2*, 5017116) LEXIS Pub.

— Construction & Design Law Digest, March 1999. 116p. 1999. pap. write for info. (*0-327-01142-4*, 5017016) LEXIS Pub.

— Construction & Design Law Digest, May 1999. 100p. 1999. pap. write for info. (*0-327-01144-0*, 5017216) LEXIS Pub.

National Institute for Construction & Design Law Staff. Construction & Design Law Digest, December 1998. 98p. (Orig.). 1999. pap. write for info. (*0-327-00902-0*, 5017915) LEXIS Pub.

National Institute for Explication Staff. Children of Conflict: Nicaragua. Barker, Barry, ed. (Illus.). 1989. 17.00 (*0-317-93725-1*) W T Swengros.

National Institute for Exploration Members. Egypt Images of Adventure. Nichols, Tim et al, eds. (Illus.). 132p. 1988. 24.95 (*0-942529-01-4*) Viewfinder Pubns.

National Institute for Science Education Staff, ed. see Mundry, Susan.

National Institute for Social Work Staff. The Barclay Report: Social Workers, Their Role & Tasks. Report of an Independent Working Party. (C). 1982. 60.00 (*0-7855-5896-9*, Pub. by Natl Inst Soc Work) St Mut.

— Residential Care for Elderly People: Using Research to Improve Practice. (C). 1988. text 45.00 (*0-902789-49-X*, Pub. by Natl Inst Soc Work) St Mut.

National Institute for Social Work Staff, ed. 1924-1983: Commentary by a Social Servant. 1984. 35.00 (*0-7855-0829-5*, Pub. by Natl Inst Soc Work) St Mut.

— PSSC, the Case History of an Advisory Non-Governmental Organisation, 1973-1980. 1981. 15.00 (*0-7855-0994-1*) St Mut.

National Institute for Social Work Staff, jt. auth. see Douglas, Robin.

National Institute for Social Work Staff, ed. see Epstein, Laura.

National Institute for Social Work Staff, ed. see Payne, Chris & Scott, Tony.

National Institute for the Control of Pharmaceutic, ed. Colour Atlas of Chinese Traditional Drugs, Vol. 1. (Illus.). 300p. 1987. text 110.00 (*0-945345-09-7*, Pub. by Sci Pr) Lubrecht & Cramer.

National Institute for Trial Advocacy Staff, jt. auth. see Cooley, John W.

National Institute for Work & Learning. Getting a Job in the Computer Age. LC 86-776. 101p. (Orig.). 1986. pap. 3.95 (*0-87866-440-8*) Petersons.

National Institute of Business Management Staff. Three Hundred Sixty Most Guarded Secrets of Executive Success. 381p. 1990. write for info. (*1-880024-00-4*) Natl Inst Busn.

National Institute of Construction Law Inc. Construction & Design Law Digest. 1998. pap. write for info. (*0-327-00113-5*, 50171-15) LEXIS Pub.

National Institute of Construction Law Inc. & Boggs, Patton. Construction & Design Law Digest. 550.00 (*0-327-01929-8*) LEXIS Pub.

National Institute of Construction Law, Inc. Edito. Construction & Design Law Digest. 125.00 (*0-87215-979-5*, MICHIE); 110.00 (*0-87473-271-9*, MICHIE); 110.00 (*0-87473-491-6*, MICHIE); 110.00 (*0-87473-655-2*, MICHIE) LEXIS Pub.

— Construction & Design Law Digest. annuals 100.00 (*0-87473-363-4*, MICHIE) LEXIS Pub.

— Construction & Design Law Digest. 1990. ring bd. 150.00 (*0-685-57944-1*, MICHIE) LEXIS Pub.

— Construction & Design Law Digest: June, 1998. 100p. 1998. pap. write for info. (*0-327-00241-7*, 50173-15) LEXIS Pub.

— Construction & Design Law Digest, May 1998. 1998. pap. write for info. (*0-327-00183-6*, 50172-15) LEXIS Pub.

National Institute of Economic & Social Research Staff. The United Kingdom Economy. 4th ed. LC 80-500945. (Studies in the British Economy). iv, 119p. 1976. 6.95 (*0-435-84581-0*) Heinemann.

National Institute of Economic & Social Research Staff, et al. United Kingdom Economy. 2nd ed. LC 77-361447. (Studies in British Economy Ser.). ix, 132 p. 1976. 1.25 (*0-435-84567-5*) Heinemann.

National Institute of Economic & Social Research Staff, et al. The United Kingdom Economy. 3rd ed. LC 79-306195. viii, 137p. 1977. 1.25 (*0-435-84575-6*) Heinemann.

National Institute of Educational Planning and Administration (India) Staff, jt. auth. see Mehta, Arun C.

National Institute of Hydrology (India) Staff, jt. auth. see Goyal, V. C.

National Institute of Mental Health (U. S.) Staff. The Neuroscience of Mental Health. LC 84-601129. 94p. reprint ed. pap. 30.00 (*0-8357-7855-X*, 203623200002) Bks Demand.

National Institute of Mental Health Staff. The Mental Health of the Child: Program Reports. Segal, Julius, ed. 1973. 19.95 (*0-405-03149-1*) Ayer.

National Institute of Public Health & Environmenta, jt. auth. see Scenario Committee on Aging Staff.

National Institute of Public Health & the Environm. Scanning the Global Environment: A Framework & Methodology for Integrating Environmental Reporting & Assessment. 68p. 20.00 (*92-807-1491-0*) UN.

***National Institute of Senior Centers Staff.** The National Institute of Senior Centers' Senior Center Self-Assessment & National Accreditation Manual. 159p. 1999. ring bd. 125.00 (*0-910883-94-7*) Natl Coun Aging.

National Institute of Standards & Technology Staff, jt. auth. see Chase, M. W.

National Institute of Standards & Technology Staff, jt. ed. see Stricklett, K. L.

National Institute on Drug Abuse, Institute of Med. Development of Medications for the Treatment of Opiate & Cocaine Addictions: Issues for the Government & Private Sector. Fulco, Carolyn E. et al, eds. 272p. (Orig.). (C). 1995. pap. text 37.00 (*0-309-05244-0*) Natl Acad Pr.

National Institute on Drug Abuse Staff, et al. Creative Parenting Made Easier: From Infant to Teenager to Adulthood. Royal, Travis W., ed. LC 97-94195. (Illus.). 200p. 1999. pap. 14.95 (*0-9659730-0-X*) Missy Merch.

National Institute on Student Achievement Curriculum Staff. The Educational System in the United States: Case Study Findings. LC 99-187423. xxi, 219 p. 1999. write for info. (*0-16-049929-1*) USGPO.

National Institutes of Child Health & Human Development Staff, et al, eds. The Psychological Development of Low-Birthweight Children. (Advances in Applied Developmental Psychology Ser.: Vol. 6). 505p. (C). 1992. text 83.50 (*0-89391-855-5*) Ablx Pub.

***National Institutes of Mental Health (U.S.) & Library of Congress.** The Adaptable Brain: Papers Presented at a Symposium Cosponsored by the National Institute of Mental Health & the Library of Congress. Levy-Reiner, Sherry, ed. LC 98-41659. (Decade of the Brain Ser.: Vol. 2). (Illus.). 84p. 1998. pap. 12.00 (*0-8444-0971-5*) Lib Congress.

***National Instruments Staff.** Labview Version 5.0. 1999. pap. text, student ed. 85.33 (*0-201-36184-1*) Addison-Wesley.

***National Insurance Law Service.** Illinois Related Regulations. LC 98-67494. 1998. write for info. (*0-89246-505-0*) NILS Pub.

National Insurance Law Service, jt. auth. see Illinois.

National Insurance Law Service, jt. auth. see Oregon. Insurance Division.

National Issues Forum Institute Staff. Boundaries of Free Speech: Deciding How Free Is Too Free. abr. ed. 32p. 1991. 3.25 (*0-8403-6927-1*) Kendall-Hunt.

— The Boundaries of Free Speech: How Free Is Too Free? 32p. 1996. 3.25 (*0-8403-6924-7*) Kendall-Hunt.

— Criminal Violence: What Direction Now for the War on Crime? 32p. 1995. 3.25 (*0-8403-7435-6*) Kendall-Hunt.

— The Day Care Dilemma: Who Should Be Responsible for the Children. 48p. 1989. 3.25 (*0-8403-5264-6*) Kendall-Hunt.

— The Day Care Dilemma: Who Should Be Responsible for the Children. 48p. 1989. teacher ed., per. 15.00 (*0-8403-5266-2*) Kendall-Hunt.

— The Drug Crisis: Public Strategies for Breaking the Habit. 80p. 1989. teacher ed. 15.00 (*0-8403-5272-7*) Kendall-Hunt.

— Energy Options: Finding a Solution to the Power Predicament. 32p. 1996. 3.25 (*0-8403-6923-9*) Kendall-Hunt.

— The Environment at Risk: Responding to Growing Dangers. abr. ed. 32p. 1992. 3.25 (*0-8403-5268-9*) Kendall-Hunt.

— The Four Trillion Dollar Debt: Tough Choices about Soaring Federal Deficits. 36p. 1993. 3.25 (*0-8403-8653-2*) Kendall-Hunt.

— The Four Trillion Dollar Debt: Tough Choices about Soaring Federal Deficits. abr. ed. 32p. 1993. 3.25 (*0-8403-8654-0*) Kendall-Hunt.

— Growing up at Risk. abr. ed. 32p. (C). 1990. 3.25 (*0-8403-6029-0*) Kendall-Hunt.

— The Health Care Cost Explosion. 32p. 1993. 3.25 (*0-8403-8656-7*) Kendall-Hunt.

— The Health Care Cost Explosion. abr. ed. 32p. 1993. 3.25 (*0-8403-8657-5*) Kendall-Hunt.

— The Health Care Crisis: Containing Costs, Expanding Coverage. abr. ed. 32p. 1992. 3.25 (*0-8403-7433-X*) Kendall-Hunt.

— The Health Crisis: Containing Costs, Expanding Coverage. 32p. 1992. 3.25 (*0-8403-7432-1*) Kendall-Hunt.

— The Poverty Puzzle: What Should Be Done to Help the Poor? abr. ed. 32p. 1995. 3.25 (*0-8403-8652-4*) Kendall-Hunt.

— Prescription for Prosperity: Four Paths to Economic Renewal. 32p. 1992. 3.25 (*0-8403-7438-0*) Kendall-Hunt.

— The Public Debt: Breaking the Habit of Deficit Spending. abr. ed. 32p. 1988. 3.25 (*0-8403-4794-4*) Kendall-Hunt.

***National Issues Forums Staff.** Jobs: Preparing a Workforce for the 21st Century (Regular) LC 99-182100. 28p. 1998. pap. text 3.60 (*0-7872-4881-9*, 41488101) Kendall-Hunt.

National Issues Institute Staff. Admission Decisions. abr. ed. (Abridged Ser.). 76p. 1995. 49.50 (*0-7872-0501-X*) Kendall-Hunt.

— Admission Decisions: Should Immigration Be Restricted? 32p. 1994. 3.25 (*0-8403-9446-2*) Kendall-Hunt.

— Admission Decisions: Should Immigration be Restricted? abr. ed. 32p. 1994. 3.25 (*0-8403-9447-0*) Kendall-Hunt.

— Contested Values. abr. ed. 32p. 1994. 3.25 (*0-8403-9891-3*) Kendall-Hunt.

— Contested Values. abr. ed. (Abridged Ser.). 76p. 1995. 49.50 (*0-7872-0502-8*) Kendall-Hunt.

— Education: How Do We Get the Results We Want? 32p. 1992. 3.50 incl. disk (*0-8403-8138-7*) Kendall-Hunt.

— Education (Issues in Brief Package) 12p. 1992. boxed set 10.00 (*0-8403-8139-5*) Kendall-Hunt.

— Juvenile Violence. abr. ed. (Abridged Ser.). 76p. 1995. 49.50 (*0-7872-0500-1*) Kendall-Hunt.

— People & Politics: Who Should Govern? 48p. 1993. 3.25 incl. disk (*0-8403-8091-7*) Kendall-Hunt.

— Politics in the Twenty-First Century. 48p. 1993. 4.00 incl. disk (*0-8403-8393-2*) Kendall-Hunt.

National Japanese American Historical Society Staf. Japanese American Oral History Guide. 46p. 1992. pap. text 6.50 (*1-881506-01-0*) Natl Japnse Am HS.

National Jewish Center for Learning & Leadership S. Sacred Times. (Illus.). 132p. 1992. write for info. (*0-9633329-0-2*) Natl Jew Ctr Lrn & Ldership.

National Jewish Welfare Board Staff. Bibliography of Jewish Instrumental Music. 60p. 1993. reprint ed. lib. bdg. 69.00 (*0-7812-9686-2*) Rprt Serv.

— Bibliography of Jewish Vocal Music. 66p. 1993. reprint ed. lib. bdg. 69.00 (*0-7812-9687-0*) Rprt Serv.

National Joint Committee for the Communication Nee, jt. auth. see McCarthy, Claire F.

National Joint Committee on Learning Disabilities. Collective Perspectives on Issues Affecting Learning Disabilities: Position Papers & Statements. LC 94-215805. 110p. 1994. pap. text 8.00 (*0-89079-534-7*, 6779) PRO-ED.

***National Joint Committee on Learning Disabilities.** Collective Perspectives on Issues Affecting Learning Disabilities: Position Papers & Statements. 2nd ed. LC 00-32337. 2000. write for info. (*0-89079-845-1*) PRO-ED.

National Judicial College Staff. Americans with Disabilities Act - An Instructional Guide for Judges & Court Administrators. 448p. 1994. ring bd. 50.00 (*0-614-06248-9*) Natl Judicial Coll.

— Planning - Conducting a Course: "Managing Trials Effectively" 273p. 1994. ring bd. 35.00 (*0-614-06247-0*) Natl Judicial Coll.

National Judicial College Staff & ABA-JAD National Conference of State Trial Judges. Capital Cases Benchbook. 383p. 1994. ring bd. 35.00 (*0-614-06244-6*) Natl Judicial Coll.

— The Judge's Book. 2nd ed. 437p. 1994. 39.95 (*0-614-06246-2*) Natl Judicial Coll.

National Jury Project Staff. Jurywork: Systematic Techniques, 2 vols., Set. 2nd ed. LC 82-22635. 1983. ring bd. 230.00 (*0-87632-322-0*) West Group.

National Kitchen & Bath Assoc. Staff. Bathroom Basics. (Training Primer for K&B Specialists Ser.). (Illus.). 363p. (Orig.). 1996. pap. text 50.00 (*1-887127-14-3*, 7003) Natl Kit Bath.

National Kitchen & Bath Association Staff. Bathroom Industry Manual Vol. 1: Building Materials, Construction & Estimating. (Illus.). 263p. (Orig.). 1997. pap. text 50.00 (*1-887127-22-4*, 5081) Natl Kit Bath.

— Bathroom Industry Technical Manual Vol. 2: Bathroom Mechanical Systems. (Illus.). 144p. (Orig.). 1997. pap. text 50.00 (*1-887127-23-2*, 5082) Natl Kit Bath.

— Bathroom Industry Technical Manual Vol. 3: Bathroom Equipment & Materials. (Illus.). 200p. (Orig.). 1997. pap. text 50.00 (*1-887127-24-0*, 5083) Natl Kit Bath.

— Bathroom Industry Technical Manual Vol. 4: Bathroom Planning Standards & Safety Criteria. (Illus.). 340p. 1997. pap. text 50.00 (*1-887127-25-9*, 5084) Natl Kit Bath.

— Bathroom Industry Technical Manual Vol. 5: Design Principles for Bathroom Planning. (Illus.). 85p. (Orig.). 1997. pap. text 50.00 (*1-887127-26-7*, 5085) Natl Kit Bath.

— Bathroom Industry Technical Manual Vol. 6: Drawing & Presentation Standards for Bathroom Professional. (Illus.). 229p. (Orig.). 1997. pap. text 50.00 (*1-887127-27-5*, 5086) Natl Kit Bath.

— The Essential Bathroom Design Guide. LC 96-47467. 752p. 1996. 120.00 (*0-471-12673-X*) Wiley.

— The Essential Kitchen Design Guide. LC 96-33745. 752p. 1996. 120.00 (*0-471-12672-1*) Wiley.

National Kitchen & Bath Association Staff. The Essential Kitchen Design Guide: The Essential Bathroom Design Guide Set. 1472p. 1997. 200.00 (*0-471-16272-8*) Wiley.

N

An Asterisk (*) at the beginning of an entry indicates that the title is appearing for the first time.

N

An Asterisk (*) at the beginning of an entry indicates that the title is appearing for the first time.

— Central & Western Pacific Ocean & Indian Ocean. (Tide Tables 1999 Ser.). 1998. pap. text 25.95 (*0-07-047187-8*) Intl Marine.
— Europe & West Coast of Africa: Including the Mediterranean Sea. (Tide Tables 1999 Ser.). 1998. pap. text 25.95 (*0-07-047184-3*) Intl Marine.
— Pacific Coast of North America & Asia. (Tide Tables 1999 Ser.). 1998. pap. text 13.95 (*0-07-047188-6*) Intl Marine.
— West Coast of North & South America: Including the Hawaiian Islands. (Tide Tables 1999 Ser.). 1998. pap. text 13.95 (*0-07-047233-5*) Intl Marine.
National Oceanic & Atmospheric Administration Staf. Aeronautical Chart Users Guide: #ASA-CUG. (Government Reprints Ser.). (Illus.). 104p. (C). 1994. pap. 12.95 (*1-56027-192-2*, ASA-CUG) ASA Inc.
— Central & Western Pacific Ocean & Indian Ocean: Tide Tables 1997. 424p. 1996. pap. text 25.95 (*0-07-047082-0*) McGraw.
— Europe & West Coast of Africa, Including the Mediterranean Sea: Tide Tables 1997. 224p. 1996. pap. text 25.95 (*0-07-047083-9*) McGraw.
— Tidal Current Tables, 1997: Atlantic Coast of North America. 216p. 1996. pap. text 13.95 (*0-07-047084-7*) McGraw.
— Tide Tables, 1997: East Coast of North & South America. 320p. 1996. pap. text 14.95 (*0-07-047087-1*) McGraw.
National Oceanic & Atmospheric Administration Staf, jt. auth. see Federal Aviation Administration Staff.
National Office Products Association Staff. Marketing Your Product to the Federal Government: An Introduction to GSA Schedule Contracts. (Illus.). 183p. write for info. (*0-318-62124-X*) Bus Prod Indust.
National Opinion Research Center Staff. General Social Survey 1976. 1977. write for info. (*0-89138-158-9*) ICPSR.
National Organization for Rare Disorders Staff. The Complete Directory for People with Rare Disorders, 1998/99. (Illus.). 726p. 1998. 190.00 (*1-891482-03-3*); pap. 165.00 (*0-939300-98-2*) Grey Hse Pub.
National Organization of Social Security Claimants. Social Security Practice Guide, 5 vols. 1984. ring bd. 870.00 (*0-8205-1637-6*) Bender.
National Outdoor Leadership School Staff. The NOLS Cookery: Experience the Art of Outdoor Cooking. LC 88-60635. 112p. 1991. pap. 8.95 (*0-8117-3083-2*) Stackpole.
National Outdoor Leadership School U. S. Staff, jt. auth. see Powers, Phil.
National P. R. Task Force on Educational Policy St. Toward a Language Policy for Puerto Ricans in the U. S. An Agenda for a Community in Movement. 21p. 1982. pap. 3.00 (*1-878483-16-1*) Hunter Coll CEP.
National Paideia Center Staff, jt. auth. see Roberts, Terry.
National Palace Museum of Taipai Staff. Snuff Bottles in the National Palace Museum. (Illus.). 382p. 1991. 85.00 (*957-562-061-5*) Heian Intl.
National Palace Museum Staff, compiled by. Kuan Ware, Sung Dynasty. (Illus.). 198p. 85.00 (*957-562-073-9*) Heian Intl.
National Park Foundation Staff. Complete GD AM PK 1986. 1986. pap. 7.95 (*0-685-14507-7*) Viking Penguin.
National Park Foundation Staff & Everglades National Park Interpretive Staff. Exploring the Waters of Our National Parks: The Everglades. (Illus.). 48p. 1997. 9.95 (*1-888631-03-1*) Watercourse.
National Park Foundational Staff, jt. auth. see Chambers, S. Allen.
National Park Handbook Staff. The Forts Of Old San Juan: San Juan National Historic Site, Puerto Rico. LC 96-21604. (Official National Park Handbook Ser.: Vol. 151). 1996. pap. 5.50 (*0-912627-62-X*) Natl Park Serv.
National Park Service Staff. Acadia Motorist Guide. rev. ed. (Illus.). 32p. 1996. pap. 0.95 (*0-915992-91-4*) Eastern National.
— Castillo de San Marcos: A Guide to Castillo de San Marcos National Monument. LC 92-40413. (Official National Park Handbook Ser.: No. 149). (Illus.). 64p. 1994. pap. 6.00 (*0-912627-59-X*) Natl Park Serv.
— Charlestown Navy Yard: Boston National Historical Park, Massachusetts. LC 95-12868. (Official National Park Handbook Ser.: Vol. 152). (Illus.). 1995. pap. 4.75 (*0-912627-60-3*) Natl Park Serv.
— Chesapeake & Ohio Canal. LC 88-25305. (Official National Park Handbook Ser.: No. 142). (Illus.). 1991. pap. 6.50 (*0-912627-43-3*, 024-005-01076-9) Natl Park Serv.
— Congress Hall: Capitol of the U. S. 1790-1800. LC 90-13556. (Official National Park Handbook Ser.: No. 147). (Illus.). 49p. 1991. pap. 2.00 (*0-912627-42-5*, 024-005-01074-2) Natl Park Serv.
— Craters of the Moon National Monument, Idaho. LC 89-13670. (Official National Park Handbook Ser.: No. 139). (Illus.). 64p. 1991. pap. 3.00 (*0-912627-44-1*, 024-005-01077-7) Natl Park Serv.
— First Mothers: The Stories of the Women Whose Sons Became President of the United States. 58p. 1990. pap. 3.00 (*0-915992-49-3*) Eastern National.
— Fort Vancouver National Historical Site, Washington: Master Plan. (Illus.). 50p. 1995. 11.00 (*0-89904-400-X*, Silhouette Imprints); pap. 8.00 (*0-89904-401-8*, Silhouette Imprints) Crumb Elbow Pub.
— National Parks for the Twenty-First Century: The Vail Agenda. LC 92-60471. (Illus.). 160p. (Orig.). 1991. pap. 14.95 (*0-9603410-7-2*) Natl Pk Found.
— North Cascades. (Official National Park Handbook Ser.: No. 131). (Illus.). 112p. 1986. pap. 7.50 (*0-912627-31-X*) Natl Park Serv.
— Respectful Rehabilitation: Answers to Your Questions about Old Buildings. LC 96-21906. (Illus.). 200p. 1995. pap. 14.95 (*0-471-14419-3*) Wiley.
— Saving the Neighborhood: You Can Fight Developers & Win. (Illus.). 428p. (Orig.). 1995. pap. 16.95 (*0-471-14420-7*) Wiley.
— Sequoia & Kings Canyon: A Guide to Sequoia & Kings Canyon National Parks, California. LC 91-37844. (Official National Park Handbook Ser.: No. 145). (Illus.). 128p. 1992. pap. 5.00 (*0-912627-47-6*, 024-005-01095-9) Natl Park Serv.
— Washington, D. C. LC 87-600287. (Official National Park Handbook Ser.: No. 102). (Illus.). 176p. 1988. pap. 7.00 (*0-912627-36-0*) Natl Park Serv.
— Yosemite. LC 88-17932. (Official National Park Handbook Ser.: No. 138). (Illus.). 144p. 1989. pap. 9.00 (*0-912627-37-9*) Natl Park Serv.
National Park Service Staff & Mobium Corporation Staff. Apostle Islands. LC 87-600289. (Official National Park Handbook Ser.: No. 141). (Illus.). 64p. 1988. pap. 5.50 (*0-912627-35-2*) Natl Park Serv.
National Park Service Staff & Preservation Press Staff. National Register of Historic Places 1966 to 1994. 2nd ed. (Illus.). 926p. 1995. pap. 98.00 (*0-471-14403-7*) Wiley.
National Park Service Staff, ed. see Hayden, Elizabeth W.
National Park Service, U.S. Department of the Inte & Burns, John A. Recording Historic Structures. (Illus.). 270p. 1989. pap. 19.95 (*1-55835-021-7*) AIA Press.
National Parking Association Staff & Urban Land Institute Staff. The Dimensions of Parking. 3rd ed. LC 93-61039. 207p. 1993. pap. 34.95 (*0-87420-744-4*, D85) Urban Land.
National Parks & Conservation Association Staff. Guide to National Parks in the Heartland. LC 99-23821. (NPCA National Park Guide Ser.). (Illus.). 96p. 2000. pap. text 11.95 (*0-7627-0571-X*) Globe Pequot.
— Guide to National Parks in the Pacific Northwest. LC 99-29268. (NPCA National Park Guide Ser.). (Illus.). 96p. 2000. pap. text 11.95 (*0-7627-0574-4*) Globe Pequot.
— Guide to National Parks in the Pacific Region. LC 99-23822. (NPCA National Park Guide Ser.). (Illus.). 96p. 2000. pap. text 11.95 (*0-7627-0573-6*) Globe Pequot.
— Guide to National Parks in the Rocky Mountain Region. LC 99-31036. (NPCA National Park Guide Ser.). (Illus.). 96p. 2000. pap. text 11.95 (*0-7627-0575-2*) Globe Pequot.
— Guide to National Parks in the Southeast Region. LC 99-15690. (NPCA National Park Guide Ser.). (Illus.). 96p. 2000. pap. text 11.95 (*0-7627-0576-0*) Globe Pequot.
— Guide to National Parks in the Southwest Region. LC 99-42904. (NPCA National Park Guide Ser.). (Illus.). 96p. 2000. pap. text 11.95 (*0-7627-0577-9*) Globe Pequot.
— Investing in Park Futures - The National Park System Plan: Executive Summary: A Blueprint for Tomorrow. 44p. (C). 1988. pap. 9.95 (*0-940091-20-8*) Natl Parks & Cons.
— Investing in Park Futures - The National Park System Plan Vol. I: To Preserve Unimpaired: The Challenge of Protecting Park Resources; a Blueprint for Tomorrow. (C). 1988. pap. 9.95 (*0-940091-21-6*) Natl Parks & Cons.
— Investing in Park Futures - The National Park System Plan Vol. III: Parks & People: A Natural Relationship; a Blueprint for Tomorrow. (C). 1988. pap. 8.50 (*0-940091-23-2*) Natl Parks & Cons.
— Investing in Park Futures - The National Park System Plan Vol. VI: Planning & Public Involvement: Constituency Building for the Parks; a Blueprint for Tomorrow. (C). 1988. pap. 4.50 (*0-940091-26-7*) Natl Parks & Cons.
— Investing in Park Futures - The National Park System Plan Vol. VII: Land Acquisition: Completing the Parks; a Blueprint for Tomorrow. (C). 1988. pap. 4.95 (*0-940091-27-5*) Natl Parks & Cons.
— The National Park Activist Guide: A Manual for Citizen Action. 1993. write for info. (*0-318-72303-4*) Natl Parks & Cons.
— National Parks in Crisis. 17p. 1993. write for info. (*0-318-72304-2*) Natl Parks & Cons.
***National Parks & Conservation Association Staff & Butcher, Russell D.** Guide to National Parks in the Northeast Region. LC 99-16309. (NPCA National Park Guide Ser.). (Illus.). 103p. 1999. pap. text 11.95 (*0-7627-0572-8*) Globe Pequot.
National Parks & Conservation Association Staff & Dunbar, David. Yellowstone: National Park. LC 94-18570. (Tiny Folios Ser.). (Illus.). 328p. 1996. pap. 11.95 (*1-55859-825-1*) Abbeville Pr.
National Parks & Conservation Association Staff & Levin, Ted. Everglades. LC 94-46988. (Tiny Folios Ser.). (Illus.). 328p. 1996. pap. 11.95 (*1-55859-827-8*) Abbeville Pr.
National Parks Service - Cordova Historical Societ. Cordova to Kennecott, Alaska. Spude, Robert et al, eds. (Illus.). 52p. (C). 1995. reprint ed. pap. 10.00 (*0-9623320-0-3*) Cordova Historical.
***National Parks Service Staff.** Pioneers of American Landscape Design. LC 00-36155. (Illus.). 352p. 2000. 59.95 (*0-07-134420-9*) McGraw-Hill Prof.
National Parks Service Staff. Vicksburg. LC 86-749. (Official National Park Handbook Ser.: No. 137). 1986. pap. 6.50 (*0-912627-32-8*) Natl Park Serv.
National Passive Solar Conference Staff. Proceedings of the National Passive Solar Conference, 3rd, San Jose, 1979. Miller, Harry et al, eds. 1979. pap. text 80.00 (*0-89553-015-5*) Am Solar Energy.
— Proceedings of the National Passive Solar Conference, 5th, Amherst, 1980, 2 vols., Set. Hayes, John & Snyder, Rachel, eds. (Illus.). 1980. pap. text 60.00 (*0-89553-025-2*) Am Solar Energy.
National Pastoral Life Center Staff. Vatican Two, Act Two: Families, Participant's Guide. 64p. (Orig.). 1990. pap. 3.95 (*0-8146-1972-X*) Liturgical Pr.
— Vatican Two, Act Two: Living in God's World, Convener's Guide. 74p. (Orig.). 1990. pap. 6.95 (*0-8146-1971-1*) Liturgical Pr.
— Vatican Two, Act Two: Living in God's World, Participant's Guide. 61p. 1990. pap. 3.95 (*0-8146-1970-3*) Liturgical Pr.
National Phonograph Company Staff. Edison Phonograph Monthly, 1903-1916. Moore, Wendell, ed. Incl. Vol. 1, 1903. 190p. 15.95 (*0-934281-50-5*); Vol. 2, 1904. 194p. 15.95 (*0-934281-51-3*); Vol. 3, 1905. 190p. 15.95 (*0-934281-52-1*); Vol. 4, 1906. 222p. 15.95 (*0-934281-53-X*); Vol. 5, 1907. 226p. 15.95 (*0-934281-54-8*); Vol. 6, 1908. 308p. 17.95 (*0-934281-55-6*); Vol. 7, 1909. 334p. 17.95 (*0-934281-56-4*); Vol. 8, 1910. 309p. 19.95 (*0-934281-57-2*); (Illus.). reprint ed. write for info. (*0-318-59213-4*) W Moore Pub.
— Edison Phonograph Monthly, 1903-1916, Vol.9. Moore, Wendell, ed. 309p. 1911. 25.00 (*0-934281-58-0*) W Moore Pub.
National Plan Service, Inc. Staff. Country Rustic Home Plans. (Illus.). 32p. (Orig.). reprint ed. pap. 3.95 (*0-934039-03-8*, A48) Hme Dsgn Altntves.
National Plan Service Inc. Staff. One & One-Half & Two Story Home Plans. (Illus.). 32p. reprint ed. pap. 3.95 (*0-934039-05-4*, A55) Hme Dsgn Altntves.
National Plan Service, Inc. Staff, ed. Affordable Ranch Homes. (Illus.). 32p. (Orig.). reprint ed. pap. 3.95 (*0-934039-04-6*, A42) Hme Dsgn Altntves.
— America's Best Project Plans, No. A100. (Ucando Ser.). (Illus.). 64p. 1990. pap., per. 4.95 (*0-934039-30-5*) Hme Dsgn Altntves.
— The Best Small Home Plans. (Illus.). 32p. (Orig.). reprint ed. pap. 3.95 (*0-934039-06-2*, A49) Hme Dsgn Altntves.
— Better Living Home Plans. (Illus.). 32p. reprint ed. pap. 3.95 (*0-934039-19-4*, A36) Hme Dsgn Altntves.
— Build Your Own Garage Manual. (Illus.). 88p. 1987. pap. 12.95 (*0-934039-26-7*, A270) Hme Dsgn Altntves.
— Classic Designs. (Illus.). 32p. reprint ed. pap. 3.95 (*0-934039-24-0*, A35) Hme Dsgn Altntves.
— Consumer Approved Home Designs, No. A132. (Illus.). 88p. 1990. pap., per. 5.95 (*0-934039-29-1*) Hme Dsgn Altntves.
— Contemporary Home Plans. (Illus.). 32p. reprint ed. pap. 3.95 (*0-934039-21-6*, A47) Hme Dsgn Altntves.
— Duplex-Townhouse Plans. rev. ed. (Illus.). 32p. (Orig.). reprint ed. pap. 3.95 (*0-934039-08-9*, A51) Hme Dsgn Altntves.
— Early American Colonial Homes. rev. ed. (Illus.). 32p. reprint ed. pap. 3.95 (*0-934039-12-7*, A39) Hme Dsgn Altntves.
— Energy Saving Home Plans. (Illus.). 32p. (Orig.). reprint ed. pap. 3.95 (*0-934039-07-0*, A56) Hme Dsgn Altntves.
— Energy Saving New Home Plans, Bk. 2. (Illus.). 32p. reprint ed. pap. 4.95 (*0-934039-15-1*, A103) Hme Dsgn Altntves.
— Garage Plans. rev. ed. (Illus.). 20p. reprint ed. pap. 3.95 (*0-934039-23-2*, A57) Hme Dsgn Altntves.
— Home Designs for Narrow Lots, No. A-131. (Illus.). 88p. (Orig.). 1986. per. 5.95 (*0-934039-01-1*, A-131) Hme Dsgn Altntves.
— Multi-Level . . . Hillside Home Plans. (Illus.). 32p. reprint ed. pap. 3.95 (*0-934039-16-X*, A41) Hme Dsgn Altntves.
— A Portfolio of Best Selling House Plans. (Illus.). 32p. reprint ed. pap. 3.95 (*0-934039-22-4*, A34) Hme Dsgn Altntves.
— Practical Contemporary Home Plans. (Illus.). 32p. (Orig.). reprint ed. pap. 3.95 (*0-934039-09-7*, A52) Hme Dsgn Altntves.
— Selected Small Homes . . . Keyed to the Times. rev. ed. (Illus.). 32p. reprint ed. pap. 3.95 (*0-934039-11-9*, A37) Hme Dsgn Altntves.
— Tudor Homes & Other Popular Designs. (Illus.). 32p. (Orig.). 1987. pap. 3.95 (*0-934039-02-X*, A70) Hme Dsgn Altntves.
— Vacation Homes. (Illus.). 32p. reprint ed. pap. 3.95 (*0-934039-14-3*, A50) Hme Dsgn Altntves.
National Plan Service Staff, ed. Quality Home Designs. (Illus.). 32p. reprint ed. 4.95 (*0-934039-34-8*, A103) Hme Dsgn Altntves.
— Sunbelt Designs: Outdoor Living . . . Indoors. (Illus.). (Orig.). 1988. pap. 3.95 (*0-934039-27-5*, A72) Hme Dsgn Altntves.
— Transitional Home Designs, No. A104. (Illus.). 32p. reprint ed. 4.95 (*0-934039-35-6*) Hme Dsgn Altntves.
— Victorian & Country Home Designs, No. A102. (Illus.). 32p. reprint ed. 4.95 (*0-934039-33-X*) Hme Dsgn Altntves.
National Plan Service Staff, ed. see Bynre, Randy.
National Plan Service Staff, ed. see Byrne, Randy.
National Planning Association, Center for Economic. Basic Maps of the U. S. Economy, Nineteen Sixty-Seven to Nineteen Ninety. 304p. 1979. 25.00 (*0-686-28102-0*) Natl Planning.
National Planning Association Committee of New Eng, ed. The Economic State of New England: Report of the Committee of New England of the National Planning Association. 738p. 1954. 100.00 (*0-317-27450-3*) Elliots Bks.
National Planning Association Staff. The Creole Petrolum Corporation in Venezuela. Bruchey, Stuart & Bruchey, Eleanor, eds. LC 76-5019. (American Business Abroad Ser.). 1976. reprint ed. lib. bdg. 19.95 (*0-405-09286-5*) Ayer.
— The Firestone Operations in Liberia. Bruchey, Stuart & Bruchey, Eleanor, eds. LC 76-5020. (American Business Abroad Ser.). (Illus.). 1976. reprint ed. 17.95 (*0-405-09287-3*) Ayer.
— The General Electric Company in Brazil. Bruchey, Stuart & Bruchey, Eleanor, eds. LC 76-5021. (American Business Abroad Ser.). (Illus.). 1976. reprint ed. 19.95 (*0-405-09288-1*) Ayer.
— Stanvac in Indonesia. Bruchey, Stuart & Bruchey, Eleanor, eds. LC 76-5022. (American Business Abroad Ser.). (Illus.). 1976. reprint ed. 19.95 (*0-405-09289-X*) Ayer.
— The United Fruit Company in Latin America. Bruchey, Stuart & Bruchey, Eleanor, eds. LC 76-5023. (American Business Abroad Ser.). (Illus.). 1976. reprint ed. 31.95 (*0-405-09290-3*) Ayer.
National Police Chiefs & Sheriffs Information Bure. 1991-1992 National Directory of Law Enforcement Administrators, Vol. XXVII. 552p. 1991. 49.00 (*1-880245-01-9*) SPAN Pub.
National Police Convention Staff. Official Proceedings of the National Police Convention. LC 70-154579. (Police in America Ser.). 1971. reprint ed. 13.95 (*0-405-03379-6*) Ayer.
National Policy Association (U.S.), jt. auth. see Auerbach, James A.
National Policy Association (U.S.). Committee on New American Realities, jt. auth. see Cappelli, Peter.
National Portrait Gallery (Australia) Staff, jt. auth. see Clark, Julia.
National Portrait Gallery, Smithsonian Institution, et al. Arnold Newman's Americans. (Illus.). 160p. 1992. reprint ed. pap. 35.00 (*0-8212-1901-4*, Pub. by Bulfinch Pr) Little.
National Portrait Gallery Staff. George C. Marshall: Soldier of Peace. LC 97-34989. (Illus.). 104p. 1997. pap. 29.95 (*0-8018-5814-3*) Johns Hopkins.
— Pre-Raphaelite Circle. LC 99-215291. (Character Sketches Ser.). 1997. 11.95 (*1-85514-231-7*, Pub. by Lund Humphries) Antique Collect.
National Portrait Gallery Staff & National Museum of American History Staff. Red Hot & Blue. (Illus.). 80p. 1997. pap. 19.95 (*0-7893-0045-1*) St Martin.
National Powder Metallurgy Conference, Chicago IL. National Powder Metallurgy Conference Proceedings, 1972. LC TN0695.N3. (Progress in Powder Metallurgy Ser.: No. 28). (Illus.). 322p. reprint ed. pap. 99.90 (*0-7837-1741-5*, 205727200024) Bks Demand.
National Powder Metallurgy Conference Staff. National Powder Metallurgy Conference Proceedings, 1974. Smith, Gaylord D., ed. LC TN0695.N3. (Progress in Powder Metallurgy Ser.: No. 31). 312p. reprint ed. pap. 96.80 (*0-8357-6991-7*, 205707500009) Bks Demand.
— National Powder Metallurgy Conference Proceedings, 1975. Halter, Richard F., ed. LC TN0695.N3. (Progress in Powder Metallurgy Ser.: No. 30). 213p. reprint ed. pap. 66.10 (*0-8357-6990-9*, 205707400009) Bks Demand.
— National Powder Metallurgy Conference Proceedings, 1977: Sponsored by the Metal Powder Industries Federation & the American Powder Metallurgy Institute, May 24-25, 1977, Detroit Plaza Hotel, Detroit, Michigan. Mocarski, Stanley & Pietrocini, Thomas W., eds. LC TN0695.N3. (Progress in Powder Metallurgy Ser.: No. 33). 283p. reprint ed. pap. 87.80 (*0-7837-3165-5*, 204281300006) Bks Demand.
— National Powder Metallurgy Conference Proceedings, 1978: April 24-26, 1978, Los Angeles, CA & the 1979 National Powder Metallurgy Conference, June 4-6, 1979, Cincinnati, OH. Hoffman, James et al, eds. LC TN0695.N3. (Progress in Powder Metallurgy Ser.: Vol. 34-35). (Illus.). 439p. reprint ed. pap. 136.10 (*0-7837-1556-0*, 204184900024) Bks Demand.
— National Powder Metallurgy Conference Proceedings, 1982: Sponsored by the Metal Powder Industries Federation & the American Powder Metallurgy Institute, May 24-27, 1982, Westin Bonaventure Hotel, Montreal, Quebec, Canada. Bewley, James G. & McGee, Sherwood W., eds. LC TN0695.N3. (Progress in Powder Metallurgy Ser.: No. 38). 283p. reprint ed. pap. 87.80 (*0-7837-3164-7*, 204281400006) Bks Demand.
***National Press Photographers Association Staff.** The Best of Photojournalism, 2000. 192p. 2000. 25.00 (*0-9701104-0-5*) Ntl Pr Photo.
National Press Photographers Association Staff & University of Missouri School of Journalism Staff. The Best of Photojournalism No. 21: Newspaper & Magazine Pictures of the Year. (Illus.). 240p. pap. 27.95 (*1-56138-772-X*) Running Pr.
National Prison Association Staff. Proceedings of the Annual Congress of the National Prison Association of the United States. LC 77-154586. (Police in America Ser.). 1971. reprint ed. 16.95 (*0-405-03377-X*) Ayer.
***National Psoriasis Foundation Staff.** The Best of It Works for Me, 1991-1999. (Illus.). 120p. 2000. pap. 7.00 (*0-9700982-0-0*) Nat Psoriasis.
National PTA Staff. The PTA Story: A Century of Commitment to Children. 200p. 1997. 34.95 (*0-88109-001-8*) Natl PTA.
National Public Radio Staff, jt. auth. see Numrich, Carol.
National Publishing Register Staff. Directory of Corporate Affiliations 1999, 5 Vols. 1999. 1059.00 (*0-87217-382-8*) Natl Register.
National Quantum Electronics Conference (4th: 1979. Laser Advances & Applications: Proceedings of the Fourth National Quantum Electronics Conference, Heriot-Watt University, Edinburgh, September, 1979. LC 80-40119. (Illus.). 300p. reprint ed. pap. 93.00 (*0-608-17597-8*, 203044500069) Bks Demand.
— Quantum Electronics & Electo-Optics: Proceedings of the Fifth National Quantum Electronics Conference, Hull University, Hull, September 1981. Knight, Peter, ed. LC 82-24778. (Illus.). 477p. reprint ed. pap. 147.90 (*0-8357-4315-2*, 203711400007) Bks Demand.

N

An Asterisk (*) at the beginning of an entry indicates that the title is appearing for the first time.

National Quarantine & Sanitary Convention Staff. Proceedings of the National Quarantine & Sanitary Convention, 1st-4th: Original Anthology. Rosenkrantz, Barbara G., ed. LC 76-40668. (Public Health in America Ser.). 1977. reprint ed. lib. bdg. 89.95 (*0-405-09877-4*) Ayer.

National Quotation Bureau Editorial Staff. National Quotation Bureau Stock Summary. annuals (Orig.). 120.00 (*1-57447-000-0*) Nat Quot Bur.

National Quotation Bureau Staff. National Quotation Bureau Bond Summary. annuals (Orig.). 115.00 (*1-57447-001-9*) Nat Quot Bur.

National R&S Committee on High School Choirs Staff. Guide for the Beginning Choral Director. (Monograph Ser.: No. 1). 41p. 1972. 5.00 (*0-614-05588-1*) Am Choral Dirs.

National Radio Science Conference Staff, et al. Proceadings [SIC] of the Fifteenth National Radio Science Conference, NRSC '98, Cairo, Egypt, February 24-26, 1998. LC 98-226158. 1998. pap. write for info. (*0-7803-4310-7*) Inst Electrical.

National Recreation & Park Association Staff. Aging & Leisure. LC GV0184.A3. (Illus.). 136p. reprint ed. pap. 42.20 (*0-7837-1547-1*, 204183500024) Bks Demand.

— Demand for Recreation in America. LC GV0191.4.D45. (Quest for Quality Ser.: No. 1). 39p. reprint ed. pap. 30.00 (*0-7837-1537-4*, 204181900024) Bks Demand.

National Recreation & Park Association Staff & Weir, Lebert H. Europe at Play: A Study of Recreation & Leisure. 63.95 (*0-405-19033-6*) Ayer.

National Register of Historic Places Staff. African American Historic Places. Savage, Beth L. et al, eds. LC 94-33218. (Illus.). 624p. (Orig.). 1995. pap. 25.95 (*0-471-14345-6*) Wiley.

National Register Publishing Co. Staff. Corporate Finance Sourcebook 1999. 1998. 575.00 (*0-87217-924-9*) Natl Register.

— 1999 Official Museum Directory. 1998. 286.25 (*0-87217-908-7*) Natl Register.

— Official Catholic Directory 1998, Set, 2 vols. 1998. 225.00 (*0-87217-963-X*) Natl Register.

— Official Museum Directory 1999, Set, 2 vols. 1998. 229.00 (*0-87217-961-3*) Natl Register.

— Standard Directory of Adveritsers, October Supplement 1998. 1998. write for info. (*0-87217-272-4*) Natl Register.

— Standard Directory of Advertisers, 1999. Date not set. 575.00 (*0-87217-270-8*) Natl Register.

— Standard Directory of Advertisers, 1999 Vol. 2: Geographical Edition. 1999. 625.00 (*0-87217-290-2*) Natl Register.

— Standard Directory Of Advertisers Set, 1999 Ed. 1998. pap. text 748.75 (*0-87217-288-0*) Natl Register.

— Standard Directory of Advertisers, 2000 Vol. 1: Business Classifications Edition. 1999. 823.75 (*0-87217-295-3*) Natl Register.

— Standard Directory of Advertisers, 2000 Vol. 2: Geographical Edition. 1999. 823.75 (*0-87217-294-5*) Natl Register.

— Standard Directory of Avdertisers, July Supplement 1998. 1998. write for info. (*0-87217-271-6*) Natl Register.

National Register Publishing Editorial Staff. America's Corporate Finance Directory, 1998. 1610p. 1997. 575.00 (*0-87217-917-6*) Natl Register.

— Co-op Advertising Programs Sourcebook, Spring 1998: The Comprehensive Guide to Programs for - Media Companies, Ad Agencies, Manufacturers & Retailers. 1030p. 1998. pap. 418.50 (*0-87217-874-9*) Natl Register.

— Co-op Advertising Programs Sourcebook Fall, 1996: The Comprehensive Guide to Programs for: Media Companies, Ad Agencies, Manufacturers & Retailers. 1999. 499.00 (*0-87217-877-3*) Natl Register.

— Co-op Advertising Programs Sourcebook Spring, 1996: The Comprehensive Guide to Programs for: Media Companies, Ad Agencies, Manufacturers & Retailers. 1999. 499.00 (*0-87217-876-5*) Natl Register.

— Direct Marketing Market Place 1999. 1150p. 1998. 239.95 (*0-87217-332-1*); 239.95 (*0-87217-333-X*) Natl Register.

— Standard Directory of Advertisers: Indexes. 1023p. 1998. write for info. (*0-87217-285-6*) Natl Register.

***National Register Publishing Editorial Staff.** Standard Directory of Advertisers: Indexes. 1999. 625.00 (*0-87217-293-7*) Natl Register.

National Register Publishing Editorial Staff. Standard Directory of Advertisers, 1998: Geographic Edition. 1810p. 1998. 575.00 (*0-87217-282-1*) Natl Register.

— Standard Directory of Advertising Agencies 1995. 2000. write for info. (*0-87217-296-1*) Natl Register.

— Standard Directory of Advertising, July 1998: The Agency Red Book. 1690p. 1997. pap. 575.00 (*0-87217-352-6*) Natl Register.

***National Register Publishing Editorial Staff.** Standard Directory of International Advertisers & Agencies: The International Red Book. 1999. 1395.00 (*0-87217-292-9*) Natl Register.

National Register Publishing Editorial Staff. Standard Directory of International Advertisers & Agencies, January 1998: The International Red Book. 1274p. 1998. pap. 495.00 (*0-87217-149-3*) Natl Register.

National Register Publishing Editorial Staff, ed. America's Corporate Finance Directory 1999. 1540p. 1998. 650.00 (*0-87217-918-4*) Natl Register.

— Co-op Advertising Programs Sourcebook 1999: Fall. 1028p. 1997. pap. 479.00 (*0-87217-875-7*) Natl Register.

— Co-op Advertising Programs Sourcebook 1999: Spring. 1999. 479.00 Natl Register.

— Directory of Corporate Affiliations: Who Owns Whom, 5 vols. Incl. International Public & Private Companies. 2016p. 1997. pap. (*0-87217-207-4*); Master Index II. 2194p. 1997. pap. (*0-87217-210-4*); U. S. Private Companies. 1446p. 1997. pap. (*0-87217-206-6*); U. S. Public Companies. 2296p. 1997. pap. (*0-87217-208-2*); Vol. I. Master Index I. 1920p. 1997. pap. (*0-87217-209-0*); 998.00 (*0-87217-211-2*) Natl Register.

— Directory of Corporate Affiliations 1998, 5 vols. Incl. Directory of Corporate Affiliations: International Public & Private Companies. 2016p. 1998. pap. (*0-87217-213-9*); Directory of Corporate Affiliations: Master Index. 1932p. 1998. pap. (*0-87217-215-5*); Directory of Corporate Affiliations: U. S. Private Companies. 1436p. 1998. pap. (*0-87217-212-0*); Directory of Corporate Affiliations: U. S. Public Companies. 2214p. 1998. pap. (*0-87217-214-7*); Vol. 2. Directory of Corporate Affiliations: Master Index. 2192p. 1998. pap. (*0-87217-216-3*); 1998. 1039.95 (*0-87217-217-1*) Natl Register.

***National Register Publishing Editorial Staff, ed.** The Official Catholic Directory. 1999. pap. 289.24 (*0-87217-987-7*) Natl Register.

National Register Publishing Editorial Staff, ed. Standard Directort Advertising Agencies 1999, Set, 3 vols. 1999. 1029.00 (*0-87217-321-6*) Natl Register.

— Standard Directory of Advertisers, 1999 Vol. 1: Business Classifications Edition. 1999. 625.00 (*0-87217-286-4*) Natl Register.

— Standard Directory of Advertisers 1999: Geographical Edition. 1999. 599.00 Natl Register.

— Standard Directory of Advertising Agencies, January 1998: The Agency Red Book. 1728p. 1998. pap. 575.00 (*0-87217-299-6*) Natl Register.

— Standard Directory of Advertising Agencies 1999: Without Supplement. 1999. 599.00 (*0-87217-297-X*) Natl Register.

— Standard Directory of Advertising Agencies 1999: Without Supplement. 1999. 599.00 Natl Register.

— Standard Directory of International Advertisers & Agencies 1999. 1999. 539.00 (*0-87217-291-0*) Natl Register.

***National Register Publishing Editors, ed.** American Art Directory: 1999-2000. 1999. 229.00 (*0-87217-133-7*) Natl Register.

— America's Corporate Finance Directory 2000. 1999. 675.00 (*0-87217-919-2*) Natl Register.

— Offical Museum Directory 2000, vols., 2, Set. 30th ed. 1999. 245.00 (*0-87217-911-7*) Natl Register.

***National Register Publishing Staff.** The Corporate Finance Sourcebook 2000: The Guide to Major Capital Investment Sources & Related Financial Services. (Illus.). 1999. pap. text 748.75 (*0-87217-923-0*) Natl Register.

— Standard Directory of Advertising Agencies 1999: Without Supplements. 1999. 625.00 (*0-87217-298-8*) Natl Register.

***National Register Publishing Staff, ed.** America's Corporate Finance Directory 2001. 2000. write for info. (*0-87217-920-6*) Natl Register.

— Co-op Advertising Programs Sourcebook: Fall 2000. 2000. 549.00 (*0-87217-879-X*) Natl Register.

— Co-op Advertising Programs Sourcebook: Spring 2000, Set, 2 vols. 2000. 549.00 (*0-87217-880-3*) Natl Register.

— The Corporate Finance Sourcebook 2001: The Guide to Major Capital Investment Sources & Related Financial Services. 2000. write for info. (*0-87217-922-2*) Natl Register.

— Direct Marketing Market Place 2000. 1999. 269.00 (*0-87217-334-8*) Natl Register.

— Direct Marketing Market Place 2001. 2000. write for info. (*0-87217-343-7*) Natl Register.

— Directory of Corporate Affiliations 2000, Set, 5 vols. 2000. 1159.00 (*0-87217-388-7*) Natl Register.

— The Official Catholic Directory Supplement 2000. 2000. write for info. (*0-87217-374-7*) Natl Register.

— The Official Catholic Directory 2000, Set, 2 vols. 2000. 259.00 (*0-87217-400-X*) Natl Register.

— Standard Directory of Advertisers. (Illus.). 2000. pap. 659.00 (*0-87217-338-0*) Natl Register.

— Standard Directory of Advertisers 2000. (Illus.). 1999. pap. 659.00 (*0-87217-339-9*) Natl Register.

— Standard Directory of Advertising Agencies 2000: Without Supplements. 2000. 659.00 (*0-87217-342-9*) Natl Register.

National Register Staff. Standard Directory of Advertisers, 1997: Business Classification Edition. 3050p. 1997. 549.95 (*0-87217-267-8*) Natl Register.

National Register Staff, ed. Standard Directory of Advertisers 1999: Geographical Edition. 1999. 599.00 (*0-87217-287-2*) Natl Register.

National Renewable Energy Laboratory Staff, compiled by. Proceedings of the DOE-NREL 1997 Hydrogen Program Review (May 21-23) (Hydrogen Fuel Information Ser.: No. VI). (Illus.). 565p. 1997. lib. bdg. 255.00 (*0-89934-331-7*, BT975) Bus Tech Bks.

— Proceedings of the 1995 DOE-NREL Hydrogen Program Review (April 18-21, 1995), Vols. A & B. (Hydrogen Fuel Information Ser.: Vol. II). (Illus.). 880p. 1996. lib. bdg. 385.00 (*0-89934-294-9*, BT954) Bus Tech Bks.

— Proceedings of the 1996 DOE-NREL 1996 DOE-NREL Hydrogen Program Review. (Hydrogen Fuel Information Ser.: No. III, Pts. A & B). (Illus.). 885p. 1997. lib. bdg. 405.00 (*0-89934-326-0*, BT968) Bus Tech Bks.

National Renewable Energy Laboratory Staff, ed. see Cawthon, Thomas.

National Research Bureau Staff. The 1997 Shopping Center Directory & Top Contacts, 5 vols. 37th ed. 5800p. (Orig.). 1996. pap. 765.00 (*1-886257-19-1*) Natl Res Bur.

National Research Conference on Smoking Behavior (. Studies & Issues in Smoking Behavior. Zagona, Salvatore V., ed. LC 67-26650. 277p. reprint ed. pap. 85.90 (*0-608-17780-6*, 203148900074) Bks Demand.

National Research Coucil Staff. Harnessing Light: Exploiting Optical Science & Engineering for the 21st Century. LC 98-86525. 175p. (C). 1998. pap. text 42.00 (*0-309-05991-7*) Natl Acad Pr.

National Research Council. The Impacts of Natural Disasters: A Framework for Loss Estimation. 80p. 1999. pap. 18.00 (*0-309-06394-9*) Natl Acad Pr.

***National Research Council.** Incorporating Science, Economics & Sociology in Developing Sanitary & Phytosanitary Standards in International Trade: Proceedings of a Conference. 290p. 2000. pap. 57.00 (*0-309-07090-2*) Natl Acad Pr.

— Nutrient Requirements of Beef Cattle: Update 2000. 248p. 1996. pap. 34.95 (*0-309-06934-3*) Natl Acad Pr.

National Research Council. Privacy Issues in Biomedical & Clinical Research: Privacy Issues in Biomedical & Clinical Research Proceedings of Forum on November 1, 1997, National Academy of Sciences, Washington, D. C. LC 99-183451. (Compass Ser.). ix, 48 p. 1998. write for info. (*0-309-06328-0*) Natl Acad Pr.

***National Research Council.** Vision 21: Fossil Fuel Options for the Future. 158p. 2000. pap. 34.50 (*0-309-06979-3*) Natl Acad Pr.

***National Research Council & Institute of Medicine Staff.** Adolescent Development & the Biology of Puberty: Summary of a Workshop on New Research. Kipke, Michele D., ed. 44p. 1999. pap. 12.00 (*0-309-06582-8*) Natl Acad Pr.

National Research Council (U. S.), Committee on Effect on Smaller Crews on Maritime Safety Staff. Crew Size & Maritime Safety. LC 90-48577. 184p. reprint ed. pap. 57.10 (*0-608-02333-7*, 206297400004) Bks Demand.

National Research Council (U. S.), Committee on Mandatory Retirement in Higher Education Staff. Ending Mandatory Retirement for Tenured Faculty: The Consequences for Higher Education. Hammond, P. Brett & Morgan, Harriet P., eds. LC 91-61424. 167p. reprint ed. pap. 51.80 (*0-608-02334-5*, 206297500004) Bks Demand.

National Research Council (U. S.), Advisory Board. Hospital Patient Feeding Systems: Proceedings of a Symposium Held at Radisson South Hotel, Minneapolis, MN, October 19-21, 1981. LC 82-61132. (Illus.). 373p. reprint ed. pap. 115.70 (*0-8357-6811-2*, 203549400095) Bks Demand.

National Research Council (U. S.), Astronomy Surve. Challenges to Astronomy & Astrophysics: Working Documents of the Astronomy Survey Committee. LC 83-60509. (Illus.). 296p. reprint ed. pap. 91.80 (*0-8357-6810-4*, 203549300095) Bks Demand.

National Research Council (U. S.), Carbon Dioxide. Changing Climate. LC 83-62680. (Illus.). 520p. reprint ed. pap. 161.20 (*0-8357-6592-X*, 203598700097) Bks Demand.

National Research Council (U. S.), Committee on Bi. Biologic Markers of Air-Pollution Stress & Damage in Forests. LC 89-62584. 377p. reprint ed. pap. 116.90 (*0-7837-0345-7*, 204066400018) Bks Demand.

— Cognitive Testing Methodology: Proceedings of a Workshop Held on June 11-12, 1984. LC UC0713.N37. 214p. reprint ed. pap. 66.40 (*0-8357-7688-3*, 203603900002) Bks Demand.

— Directory of Atomic, Molecular, & Optical Scientists. LC 86-62825. 191p. reprint ed. pap. 59.30 (*0-8357-6812-0*, 203549500095) Bks Demand.

— Disposal of Offshore Platforms. LC TA0654.D57. 99p. reprint ed. pap. 30.70 (*0-8357-7692-1*, 203604300002) Bks Demand.

— Evaluation of Methodologies for Estimating Vulnerability to Electromagnetic Pulse Effects: A Report. LC QC0793.3.E45. 111p. reprint ed. pap. 34.50 (*0-8357-7705-7*, 203606000002) Bks Demand.

— Feasibility of Assessment of Health Risks from Vapor-Phase Organic Chemicals in Gasoline & Diesel Exhaust. LC TD0886.5.F43. 67p. reprint ed. pap. 30.00 (*0-8357-7707-3*, 203606300002) Bks Demand.

— Human Resource Practices for Implementing Advanced Manufacturing Technology. LC HD0045.H85. 83p. reprint ed. pap. 30.00 (*0-8357-7696-4*, 203604800002) Bks Demand.

— Lead: Airborne Lead in Perspective. LC 71-186214. (Its Biologic Effects of Atmospheric Pollutants Ser.). 344p. reprint ed. pap. 106.70 (*0-8357-7700-6*, 203605300002) Bks Demand.

— Nutrition Services in Perinatal Care. LC RG0559.N86. 82p. reprint ed. pap. 30.00 (*0-8357-7702-2*, 203605600002) Bks Demand.

— Ocean Disposal Systems for Sewage Sludge & Effluent. LC 84-61848. 136p. reprint ed. pap. 42.20 (*0-8357-2695-9*, 204023200015) Bks Demand.

— Protection Against Trichothecene Mycotoxins. LC 83-62917. (Illus.). 239p. reprint ed. pap. 74.10 (*0-8357-6813-9*, 203549600095) Bks Demand.

— The Role of Manufacturing Technology in Trade Adjustment Strategies. LC HF1421.N5. 64p. reprint ed. pap. 30.00 (*0-8357-7685-9*, 203603500002) Bks Demand.

National Research Council (U. S.), Committee on Nutrition in Medical Education Staff. Nutrition Education in U. S. Medical Schools. LC 85-61572. 151p. 1985. reprint ed. pap. 46.90 (*0-608-02335-3*, 206297600004) Bks Demand.

National Research Council (U. S.), Committee on Risk Perception & Communication Staff. Improving Risk Communication: Working Papers. LC 89-9464. 58p. reprint ed. pap. 30.00 (*0-8357-7686-7*, 203603600002) Bks Demand.

National Research Council (U. S.), Committee on the Atmospheric Effect of Nuclear Explosion Staff. The Effects on the Atmosphere of a Major Nuclear Exchange. LC 84-62739. 202p. reprint ed. pap. 62.70 (*0-608-02341-8*, 206298200004) Bks Demand.

National Research Council (U. S.) Continuing Educa. Continuing Education of Engineers. LC 85-62019. (Engineering Education & Practice in the United States Ser.). 102p. 1985. pap. 31.70 (*0-7837-7451-6*, 204917300010) Bks Demand.

National Research Council (U. S.), Geophysics Stud. Climate in Earth History. LC 82-18857. (Studies in Geophysics). 212p. reprint ed. pap. 65.80 (*0-7837-0349-X*, 204066800018) Bks Demand.

National Research Council (U. S.), Marine Board St. Criteria for the Depths of Dredged Navigational Channels. LC TC0187.C7. 177p. reprint ed. pap. 54.90 (*0-8357-7710-3*, 203606600002) Bks Demand.

— Marine Salvage in the United States. LC VK1491.M36. 159p. reprint ed. pap. 49.30 (*0-8357-7706-5*, 203606100002) Bks Demand.

— Toward More Productive Naval Shipbuilding. LC VM0299.N37. 214p. reprint ed. pap. 66.40 (*0-8357-7704-9*, 203605800002) Bks Demand.

National Research Council (U. S.), Panel on Altern. Alcohol & Public Policy: Beyond the Shadow of Prohibition. Moore, Mark H. & Gerstein, Dean R., eds. LC 81-11217. 477p. reprint ed. pap. 147.90 (*0-7837-0351-1*, 204067000018) Bks Demand.

— Development During Middle Childhood: The Years from Six to Twelve. Collins, W. Andrew, ed. LC 84-11457. 448p. reprint ed. pap. 138.90 (*0-7837-0350-3*, 204066900018) Bks Demand.

— Engineering Graduate Education & Research. LC 85-71643. 131p. reprint ed. pap. 40.70 (*0-7837-0348-1*, 204066700018) Bks Demand.

— Improving Energy Demand Analysis. Stern, Paul C., ed. LC 84-60902. (Illus.). 134p. reprint ed. pap. 41.60 (*0-8357-6809-0*, 203549200095) Bks Demand.

— Quality Criteria for Water Reuse. LC 82-61430. (Illus.). 153p. reprint ed. pap. 47.50 (*0-8357-6815-5*, 203549800095) Bks Demand.

— Technology & Employment Effects: Interim Report. LC HD6331.2.U6T. 160p. reprint ed. pap. 49.60 (*0-8357-7687-5*, 203603800002) Bks Demand.

— Toward the Prevention of Alcohol Problems: Government, Business, & Community Action. Gerstein, Dean R., ed. LC 84-16543. 188p. reprint ed. pap. 58.30 (*0-8357-6816-3*, 203549900095) Bks Demand.

National Research Council (U. S.) Panel on Earthqu. Estimating Losses From Future Earthquakes. LC TH1095.N54. 249p. reprint ed. pap. 77.20 (*0-8357-7697-2*, 203604900002) Bks Demand.

National Research Council (U. S.), Panel on Immigration Statistics Staff. Immigration Statistics: A Story of Neglect. 2nd ed. Levine, Daniel B. et al, eds. LC 85-61694. 336p. 1985. reprint ed. pap. 104.20 (*0-608-02449-X*, 206309200004) Bks Demand.

National Research Council (U. S.) Staff. Alternatives for Ground Water Cleanup. LC 94-29573. (Illus.). 333p. reprint ed. pap. 103.30 (*0-608-06201-4*, 206653300008) Bks Demand.

— Assigning Economic Value to Natural Resources. LC 94-69496. (Illus.). 195p. reprint ed. pap. 60.50 (*0-608-06194-8*, 206652600008) Bks Demand.

— Causes & Effects of Stratospheric Ozone Reduction, an Update: A Report. LC 82-81229. 351p. reprint ed. pap. 108.90 (*0-8357-3446-3*, 203970600013) Bks Demand.

— Charting a Course into the Digital Era: Guidance for NOAA's Nautical Charting Mission/Committee on Nautical Charts & Information, Marine Board Commission on Engineering & Technical Systems, Mapping Science Committee Commission on Geosciences, Environment, & Resources, National Research Council. LC 94-66559. (Illus.). 149p. 1994. reprint ed. pap. 46.20 (*0-608-02962-9*, 206342700006) Bks Demand.

— Drinking Water & Health, Vol. 1. LC 77-89284. 948p. reprint ed. pap. 200.00 (*0-8357-2696-7*, 204023300001) Bks Demand.

— Drinking Water & Health, Vol. 4. LC 77-89284. 311p. reprint ed. pap. 96.50 (*0-8357-3448-X*, 203970800004) Bks Demand.

— Engineering Technology Education. LC 85-62838. 59p. reprint ed. pap. 30.00 (*0-8357-3447-1*, 203970700013) Bks Demand.

— Environmental Management Technology-Development Program at the Department of Energy: 1995 Review. LC 96-649683. (Illus.). 145p. reprint ed. pap. 45.00 (*0-608-06197-2*, 206652900008) Bks Demand.

— Environmental Science in the Coastal Zone: Issues for Further Research/Commission on Geosciences, Environment, & Resources. LC 93-85862. (Illus.). 180p. 1994. reprint ed. pap. 55.80 (*0-608-02964-5*, 206342900006) Bks Demand.

***National Research Council (U. S.) Staff.** Genetically Modified Pest-Protected Plants: Science & Regulation. LC 00-9457. 2000. write for info. (*0-309-06930-0*) Natl Acad Pr.

National Research Council (U. S.) Staff. Health Risks of Radon & Other Internally Deposited Alphaemitters/ Committee on the Biological Effects of Ionizing Radiations, Board on Radiation Effects Research, Commission on Life Sciences, National Research Council. LC 87-31280. (BEIR Ser.: No. 4). (Illus.). 619p. 1988. reprint ed. pap. 191.90 (*0-608-02960-2*, 206342500006) Bks Demand.

***National Research Council (U. S.) Staff.** Industrial Environmental Performance Metrics: Challenges & Opportunities. LC 99-6298. 280p. 1999. pap. 54.95 (*0-309-06242-X*, Joseph Henry Pr) Natl Acad Pr.

N

An Asterisk (*) at the beginning of an entry indicates that the title is appearing for the first time.

National Research Council (U. S.) Staff. International Competition in Advanced Technology: Decisions for America. A Consensus Statement Prepared by the Panel on Advanced Technology Competition & the Industrialized Allies, Office of International Affairs, National Research Council. LC 83-60712. (Illus.). 79p. 1983. reprint ed. pap. 30.00 (*0-608-02961-0*, 206342600006) Bks Demand.

— Laboratory Animal Housing: Proceedings of a Symposium Held at Hunt Valley, Maryland, September 22-23, 1976. LC 78-12545. 228p. reprint ed. pap. 70.70 (*0-8357-3450-1*, 203971100013) Bks Demand.

— Measuring & Improving Infrastructure Performance. LC 95-68207. (Studies in Infrastructure Technology & Policy). 132p. reprint ed. pap. 41.00 (*0-608-06196-4*, 206652800008) Bks Demand.

— Models for Biomedical Research: A New Perspective. LC 85-60945. 192p. reprint ed. pap. 59.60 (*0-8357-3451-X*, 203971200013) Bks Demand.

***National Research Council (U. S.) Staff.** Oil Spill Risks from Tank Vessel Lightering LC 98-75577. xii, 125 p. 1998. write for info. (*0-309-06190-3*) Natl Acad Pr.

National Research Council (U. S.) Staff. Precision Agriculture in the 21st Century: Geospatial & Information Technologies in Crop Management. LC 97-45268. 1997. 39.95 (*0-309-05893-7*) Natl Acad Sci.

— Rethinking the Ozone Problem in Urban & Regional Air Pollution. LC 91-68142. (Illus.). 524p. reprint ed. pap. 162.50 (*0-608-06192-1*, 206652400008) Bks Demand.

— Review of the National Automated Highway System Research Program, Vol. 253. LC 98-15309. (Special Report Ser.). 1998. write for info. (*0-309-06221-7*) Natl Acad Pr.

— Risking the Future Vol. 1: Adolescent Sexuality, Pregnancy, & Childbearing. LC 86-31181. 351p. reprint ed. pap. 108.90 (*0-608-06199-9*, 206653100001) Bks Demand.

National Research Council (U. S.) Staff. Roadway Markings & Traffic Control in Work Zones. LC 86-31240. (Transportation Research Record Ser.). 42p. 1986. 7.20 (*0-309-04106-6*) Transport Res Bd.

National Research Council (U. S.) Staff. Space Technology for the New Century LC 98-128343. x, 46 p. 1998. write for info. (*0-309-05987-9*) Natl Acad Pr.

— Transportation for a Sustainable Environment, Vol. 251. LC 97-19443. (Special Report Ser.). 1997. write for info. (*0-309-05969-0*) Natl Acad Pr.

— Ward Valley: An Examination of Seven Issues in Earth Sciences & Ecology. LC 95-69191. (Illus.). 252p. 1995. reprint ed. pap. 78.20 (*0-608-06193-X*, 206652500008) Bks Demand.

— Water Transfers in the West: Efficiency, Equity, & the Environment. LC 92-5740. (Illus.). 330p. 1992. reprint ed. pap. 102.30 (*0-608-06195-6*, 206652700008) Bks Demand.

***National Research Council (U. S.) Staff & United States Staff.** Upgrading the Space Shuttle LC 99-60001. (Compass Ser.). x, 72 p. 1999. write for info. (*0-309-06382-5*) Natl Acad Pr.

National Research Council (U. S.) Staff, jt. auth. see Frank Wilson & Associates Staff.

National Research Council (U. S.) Staff, jt. auth. see Research & Technology Coordinating Committee (U. S.

National Research Council (U. S.), Steering Commit. Oil in the Sea: Inputs, Fates, & Effects. LC 85-60541. 621p. reprint ed. pap. 192.60 (*0-7837-0347-3*, 204066600018) Bks Demand.

National Research Council (U. S.) Transportation Research Board Staff & Research & Technology Coordinating Committee (U. S. Highway Research: Current Programs & Future Directions. LC 94-42203. (Special Report, Transportation Research Board, National Research Council: Vol. 244). 1994. write for info. (*0-309-06054-0*) Transport Res Bd.

National Research Council (U. S.), Working Group o. Human Factors Aspects of Simulation. Jones, Edward R. et al, eds. LC QA0076.9.C65. 165p. reprint ed. pap. 51.20 (*0-8357-7698-0*, 203605000002) Bks Demand.

National Research Council (U.S.). Policy Options for Intermodal Freight Transportation LC 98-16533. (Special Report Ser.). viii, 315p. 1998. write for info. (*0-309-06451-1*) Natl Acad Pr.

National Research Council (U.S.) Committee of the. Atmosphere-Biosphere Interactions: Toward a Better Understanding of the Ecological Consequences of Fossil Fuel Combustion: a Report. LC 81-84469. 279p. 1981. reprint ed. pap. 86.50 (*0-608-02339-6*, 206298000004) Bks Demand.

National Research Council (US) Panel of Plasma Pro. Plasma Processing of Materials: Scientific Opportunities & Technological Challenges. fac. ed. LC 91-66812. (Illus.). 87p. 1991. pap. 30.00 (*0-7837-7559-8*, 204731200007) Bks Demand.

National Research Council (U.S.) Panel on Spatial. Criminal Careers & "Career Criminals", Vol. 1. Blumstein, Alfred et al, eds. LC 86-18282. 474p. 1986. reprint ed. pap. 147.00 (*0-608-02336-1*, 206297700001) Bks Demand.

— Spatial Statistics & Digital Image Analysis. LC 90-63215. 245p. 1991. reprint ed. pap. 76.00 (*0-608-02340-X*, 206298100004) Bks Demand.

National Research Council, Academy Industry Progra. Europe 1992: The Implication of Market Integration for R&D-Intensive Firms. 180p. 1991. pap. text 18.00 (*0-309-04332-8*) Natl Acad Pr.

National Research Council, Agricultural Board Staf. Pest Control Strategies for the Future. 383p. reprint ed. pap. 118.80 (*0-608-13709-X*, 2055289) Bks Demand.

National Research Council, Agricultural Board Staff. Pest Control Strategies for the Future. LC SB0950.N29. 383p. 1972. reprint ed. pap. 118.80 (*0-608-09962-7*, 205528900013) Bks Demand.

National Research Council, Astronomy & Astrophysic. The Decade of Discovery in Astronomy & Astrophysics. 200p. (C). 1991. pap. text 24.95 (*0-309-04381-6*) Natl Acad Pr.

— Working Papers: Astronomy & Astrophysics Panel Reports. 356p. (C). 1991. pap. text 35.00 (*0-309-04383-2*) Natl Acad Pr.

National Research Council, Board on Agriculture St. Agriculture & the Undergraduate. 296p. (C). 1992. pap. text 33.00 (*0-309-04682-3*) Natl Acad Pr.

— Investing in Research: A Proposal to Strengthen the Agricultural, Food & Environmental System. 168p. 1989. pap. text 20.00 (*0-309-04127-9*) Natl Acad Pr.

— Investing in the National Research Initiative: An Update of the Competitive Grants Program in the U. S. Department of Agriculture (15) 80p. (Orig.). (C). 1994. pap. text 20.00 (*0-309-05235-1*) Natl Acad Pr.

— Nutrient Requirements of Fish. LC 93-39031. (Nutrient Requirements of Domestic Animals Ser.). 124p. (C). 1993. pap. text 24.95 (*0-309-04891-5*) Natl Acad Pr.

— Sustainable Agriculture & the Environment in the Humid Tropics. LC 92-36869. 720p. (C). 1993. text 49.95 (*0-309-04749-8*) Natl Acad Pr.

National Research Council, Board on Atmospheric Sc. Ozone Depletion, Greenhouse Gases, & Climate Change: Proceedings of a Joint Symposium. fac. ed. LC 88-31544. (Illus.). 136p. 1989. pap. 38.80 (*0-7837-7565-2*, 2036997) Bks Demand.

National Research Council, Board on Global Change. Solar Influences on Global Change. 180p. (Orig.). (C). 1994. pap. text 25.00 (*0-309-05148-7*) Natl Acad Pr.

National Research Council, Board on Infrastructure. Financing Tomorrow's Infrastructure - Challenges & Issues: Proceedings of a Colloquium. LC 96-69107. 114p. (Orig.). 1996. pap. text 29.00 (*0-309-05543-1*) Natl Acad Pr.

National Research Council, Board on Mathematical S. Large-Scale Structures in Acoustics & Electromagnetics: Proceedings of a Symposium. (Orig.). 1996. pap. text 29.00 (*0-309-05337-4*) Natl Acad Pr.

National Research Council, Board on Science & Tech. Lost Crops of Africa Vol. I: Grains, Vol. I: Grains. LC 93-86876. 408p. (Orig.). (C). 1996. pap. 24.95 (*0-309-04990-3*) Natl Acad Pr.

National Research Council, Building Research Board. Committing to the Cost of Ownership: Maintenance & Repair of Public Buildings. (Special Reports: No. 60). 53p. (Orig.). 1990. pap. text 30.00 (*0-917084-07-1*) Am Public Works.

National Research Council Canada Staff. 5th International Symposium on Bacterial Polyhydroxyalkanoates. Eggink, Gerrit et al, eds. 185p. 1997. 81.50 (*0-660-17083-3*) NRC Res Pr.

National Research Council Canada Staff, jt. auth. see Schmid, F.

National Research Council, Climate Research Commit. GOALS (Global Ocean-Atmosphere-Land System) for Predicting Seasonal-to-Interannual Climate: A Program of Observation, Modeling & Analysis. 116p. (Orig.). (C). 1994. pap. text 27.00 (*0-309-05180-0*) Natl Acad Pr.

— Natural Climate Variability on Decade-to-Century Time Scales. LC 96-67828. 700p. (Orig.). 1996. text 59.00 (*0-309-05449-4*) Natl Acad Pr.

National Research Council, Comm. on Engineering & & Committee on Alternative Chemical Demilitarization. Alternative Technologies for the Destruction of Chemical Agents & Munitions. 342p. (Orig.). 1993. pap. text 42.00 (*0-309-04946-6*) Natl Acad Pr.

National Research Council, Commission of Behaviora. The Transition to Democracy: Proceedings of a Workshop. 104p. 1991. pap. text 19.00 (*0-309-04441-3*) Natl Acad Pr.

National Research Council, Commission on Behaviora & National Research Council Staff. Population & Land Use in Developing Countries: Report of a Workshop. 172p. (Orig.). (C). 1993. pap. text 26.50 (*0-309-04838-9*) Natl Acad Pr.

National Research Council, Commission on Engineeri. Learning to Change: Opportunities to Improve the Performance of Smaller Manufacturers. 152p. (C). 1993. pap. text 26.00 (*0-309-04982-2*) Natl Acad Pr.

National Research Council, Commission on Geoscienc. National Geomagnetic Initiative. 264p. (Orig.). (C). 1993. pap. text 28.00 (*0-309-04977-6*) Natl Acad Pr.

— Radioactive Waste Repository Licensing: Synopsis of a Symposium. 112p. (C). 1992. pap. text 19.00 (*0-309-04691-2*) Natl Acad Pr.

National Research Council, Commission on Life Scie. A Biological Survey for the Nation. 224p. (Orig.). (C). 1993. pap. text 26.00 (*0-309-04984-9*) Natl Acad Pr.

National Research Council, Commission on Physical. Assessing the Nation's Earthquakes: The Health & Future of Regional Seismograph Networks. 80p. 1991. pap. text 15.00 (*0-309-04291-7*) Natl Acad Pr.

— Atomic, Molecular, & Optical Science: An Investment in the Future. (Physics in a New Era Ser.). 224p. (Orig.). (C). 1994. pap. text 30.00 (*0-309-05032-4*) Natl Acad Pr.

— A Census That Mirrors America: Interim Report. ix, 97p. (C). 1993. pap. text 29.00 (*0-309-04979-2*) Natl Acad Pr.

— Information Technology in the Service Society: A 21st Century Lever. LC 94-142322. 288p. (Orig.). (C). 1993. pap. text 29.00 (*0-309-04876-1*) Natl Acad Pr.

— Margins: A Research Initiative for Interdisciplinary Studies of the Processes Attending Lithospheric Extension & Convergence. 296p. 1990. pap. text 30.00 (*0-309-04188-0*) Natl Acad Pr.

— Mathematical Research in Materials Science: Opportunities & Perspectives. 144p. (Orig.). (C). 1993. pap. text 23.00 (*0-309-04930-X*) Natl Acad Pr.

— Potential Applications of Concentrated Solar Energy: Proceedings of a Workshop. 164p. 1991. pap. 20.00 (*0-309-04577-0*) Natl Acad Pr.

— Research-Doctorate Programs in the United States: Continuity & Change. Goldberger, Marvin et al, eds. LC 95-35154. 768p. (Orig.). (C). 1995. text 59.95 (*0-309-05094-4*) Natl Acad Pr.

National Research Council Committee for the Future. Shopping for Safety: Providing Consumer Automotive Safety Information. LC 96-11131. (Special Report Transportation Research Board, National Research Council Ser.: No. 248). 160p. 1996. pap. 20.00 (*0-309-06209-8*) Transport Res Bd.

National Research Council, Committee for the Study. The Internationalization of U. S. Manufacturing: Causes & Consequences. 180p. 1990. pap. text 15.00 (*0-309-04331-X*) Natl Acad Pr.

National Research Council, Committee on Alternative Chemical Demilitarization Technologies. Alternative Technologies for the Destruction of Chemical Agents & Munitions. LC 93-84706. (Illus.). 341p. reprint ed. pap. 105.80 (*0-608-10444-2*, 207107800008) Bks Demand.

National Research Council Committee on Coatings fo. Coatings for High-Temperature Structural Materials: Trends & Opportunities. LC 96-68712. 102p. (Orig.). 1996. pap. text 29.00 (*0-309-05381-1*) Natl Acad Pr.

National Research Council Committee on Environment. Research to Protect, Restore, & Manage the Environment. 256p. (Orig.). (C). 1993. pap. text 28.00 (*0-309-04929-6*) Natl Acad Pr.

National Research Council, Committee on Haze in Na. Protecting Visibility in National Parks & Wilderness Areas. 316p. (Orig.). (C). 1993. pap. text 38.00 (*0-309-04844-3*) Natl Acad Pr.

National Research Council, Committee on Hypersonic. Hypersonic Technology for Military Application. 94p. 1990. pap. text 15.00 (*0-309-04229-1*) Natl Acad Pr.

National Research Council, Committee on Natural Di. Saragosa, Texas, Tornado, May 22, 1987: An Evaluation of the Warning System. (Natural Disaster Studies: Vol. 2). 76p. 1991. pap. text 19.00 (*0-309-04435-9*) Natl Acad Pr.

National Research Council Committee on Next-Genera. Counterfeit Deterrent Features for the Next-Generation Currency Design. 144p. (Orig.). (C). 1994. pap. text 29.00 (*0-309-05028-6*) Natl Acad Pr.

National Research Council Committee on Psychiatric. The Problem of Mental Disorder. Grob, Gerald N., ed. LC 78-22580. (Historical Issues in Mental Health Ser.). 1980. reprint ed. lib. bdg. 30.95 (*0-405-11932-1*) Ayer.

National Research Council, Committee on Vision Sta. Advances in Photoreception: Proceedings of a Symposium on Frontiers of Visual Science. 160p. 1990. pap. text 16.00 (*0-309-04240-2*) Natl Acad Pr.

— Beach Nourishment & Protection. 334p. 1995. text 44.95 (*0-309-05290-4*) Natl Acad Pr.

— The Bering Sea Ecosystem. 320p. (Orig.). 1996. pap. text 35.00 (*0-309-05345-5*) Natl Acad Pr.

— Biosafety in the Laboratory: Prudent Practices for Handling & Disposal of Infectious Materials. 244p. 1989. 39.95 (*0-309-03975-4*) Natl Acad Pr.

— Contraception & Reproduction: Health Consequences for Women & Children in the Developing World. 120p. 1989. pap. text 15.00 (*0-309-04094-9*) Natl Acad Pr.

— Contraceptive Use & Controlled Fertility: Health Issues for Women & Children. 172p. 1989. pap. text 18.00 (*0-309-04096-5*) Natl Acad Pr.

— Disasters & the Mass Media: Proceedings of the Committee on Disasters & the Mass Media Workshop, February 1979. LC 79-27615. (Illus.). 315p. reprint ed. pap. 97.70 (*0-8357-4270-9*, 203706600002) Bks Demand.

— Distributed Decision Making: Report of a Workshop. 74p. (C). 1990. pap. text 15.00 (*0-309-04199-6*) Natl Acad Pr.

— Dogs. LC 94-960. (Laboratory Animal Management Ser.). 152p. (Orig.). (C). 1994. pap. text 24.95 (*0-309-04744-7*) Natl Acad Pr.

— The Evaluation of Forensic DNA Evidence. rev. ed. 270p. 1996. text 37.95 (*0-309-05395-1*) Natl Acad Pr.

— Freshwater Ecosystems: Revitalizing Educational Programs in Limnology. 384p. 1996. text 49.95 (*0-309-05443-5*) Natl Acad Pr.

— High-Stakes Aviation: U. S. - Japan Technology Linkages in Transport Aircraft. LC 94-65759. 152p. (Orig.). (C). 1994. pap. text 27.00 (*0-309-05045-6*) Natl Acad Pr.

— Hurricane Hugo, Puerto Rico, the Virgin Islands, & Charleston, South Carolina, Sept. 17-22, 1989. (Natural Disaster Studies). 296p. 1994. pap. text 39.00 (*0-309-04475-8*) Natl Acad Pr.

— Improving Fish Stock Assessments. 200p. (C). 1997. text 36.00 (*0-309-05725-6*) Natl Acad Pr.

— Myopia: Prevalence & Progression. 126p. 1989. pap. text 15.00 (*0-309-04081-7*) Natl Acad Pr.

— The New Year's Eve Flood on Oahu, Hawaii: December 31, 1987-January 1, 1988. (Natural Disaster Studies: Vol. 1). 88p. 1990. pap. text 19.00 (*0-309-04433-2*) Natl Acad Pr.

— Nutrient Requirements of Goats: Angora, Dairy, & Meat Goats in Temperate & Tropical Countries. (Nutrient Requirements of Domestic Animals Ser.). 84p. (C). 1981. pap. text 24.95 (*0-309-03185-0*) Natl Acad Pr.

— Purposeful Jettison of Petroleum Cargo. 216p. (Orig.). (C). 1994. pap. text 33.00 (*0-309-05081-2*) Natl Acad Pr.

— Research Strategies for the U. S. Global Change Research Program. 294p. 1990. pap. text 28.00 (*0-309-04348-4*) Natl Acad Pr.

— Structural Adhesives with Emphasis on Aerospace Applications: A Report of the Ad Hoc Committee on Structural Adhesives for Aerospace Use, National Materials Advisory Board, National Research Council. LC 75-17033. (Treatise on Adhesion & Adhesives Ser.: Vol. 4). 264p. reprint ed. pap. 81.90 (*0-608-17070-4*, 202712200054) Bks Demand.

— Tanker Spills: Prevention by Design. 384p. 1991. text 39.95 (*0-309-04377-8*) Natl Acad Pr.

— Treatise on Marine Ecology & Paleoecology. Hedgpeth, Joel W., ed. LC 57-4669. (Geological Society of America, Memoir Ser.: No. 67, Vol. 1). 1352p. pap. 200.00 (*0-608-15637-X*, 203178400077) Bks Demand.

National Research Council Committee on Women in Sc. Women Scientists & Engineers Employed in Industry: Why So Few? 144p. (Orig.). (C). 1993. pap. text 29.00 (*0-309-04991-1*) Natl Acad Pr.

National Research Council, Committee to Review the. An Assessment of Atlantic Bluefin Tuna. 166p. (Orig.). (C). 1994. pap. text 29.00 (*0-309-05181-9*) Natl Acad Pr.

National Research Council, Computer Science & Tech. Keeping the U. S. Computer & Communications Industry Competitive: Converence of Computing, Communications, & Entertainment. 90p. (Orig.). (C). 1995. pap. text 25.00 (*0-309-05089-8*) Natl Acad Pr.

— Keeping the U. S. Computer Industry Competitive: Defining the Agenda. 127p. 1990. pap. text 15.00 (*0-309-04176-7*) Natl Acad Pr.

— Keeping the U. S. Computer Industry Competitive: Systems Integration. 106p. 1991. pap. text 19.00 (*0-309-04544-4*) Natl Acad Pr.

National Research Council, Ecology Panel Staff. Assessment of the U. S. Outer Continental Shelf Environmental Studies Program, Vol. 2: Ecology. 162p. 1992. pap. text 21.00 (*0-309-04598-3*) Natl Acad Pr.

National Research Council, Engineering Research Bo. Directions in Engineering Research: An Assessment of Opportunities & Needs. 364p. 1987. pap. text 34.95 (*0-309-03747-6*) Natl Acad Pr.

National Research Council, Geophysics Study Commit. Material Fluxes on the Surface of the Earth. LC 94-20773. (Studies in Geophysics). 192p. (C). 1994. text 39.95 (*0-309-04745-5*) Natl Acad Pr.

National Research Council Glen Canyon Environmenta. River Resource Management in the Grand Canyon. 226p. (Orig.). 1996. pap. text 35.00 (*0-309-05448-6*) Natl Acad Pr.

National Research Council, Hazardous Biological Substances Staff. Biosafety in the Laboratory: Prudent Practices for the Handling & Disposal of Infectious Materials. LC 89-13004. (Illus.). 236p. 1989. reprint ed. pap. 73.20 (*0-608-04256-0*, 206501100012) Bks Demand.

National Research Council, Institute of Medicine. Under the Influence? Drugs & the American Workforce. Normand, Jacques et al, eds. 336p. (C). 1993. text 39.95 (*0-309-04885-0*) Natl Acad Pr.

National Research Council, International Affairs O. Saline Agriculture: Salt-Tolerant Plants for Developing Countries. 152p. 1990. pap. text 15.00 (*0-309-04189-9*) Natl Acad Pr.

National Research Council, Manufacturing Studies B. Toward a New Era in U. S. Manufacturing: The Need for a National Vision. LC 86-50832. (Illus.). 190p. reprint ed. pap. 58.90 (*0-8357-4222-9*, 203700700007) Bks Demand.

National Research Council, Mapping Science Committ. Promoting the National Spatial Data Infrastructure Through Partnerships. LC 94-66772. 113p. (Orig.). (C). 1995. pap. text 24.00 (*0-309-05141-X*) Natl Acad Pr.

National Research Council, Materials for High-Temp. Materials for High-Temperature Semiconductor Devices. 136p. (Orig.). (C). 1995. pap. text 34.00 (*0-309-05335-8*) Natl Acad Pr.

National Research Council, Mathematical Sciences E. Everybody Counts: A Report to the Nation on the Future of Mathematics Education. 128p. 1989. pap. text 8.95 (*0-309-03977-0*) Natl Acad Pr.

— Measuring What Counts: A Conceptual Guide for Mathematics Assessment. 236p. 1993. pap. text 17.95 (*0-309-04981-4*) Natl Acad Pr.

— Measuring What Counts: A Policy Brief. 32p. 1993. pap. text 3.95 (*0-309-04986-5*) Natl Acad Pr.

National Research Council, Microwave Proccessing o. Microwave Processing of Materials. LC 94-66560. (Publication NMAB Ser.: No. 473). (Illus.). 166p. 1994. reprint ed. pap. 51.50 (*0-608-04259-5*, 206501400012) Bks Demand.

National Research Council New Materials for Advanc. New Materials for Next-Generation Commercial Transports. 98p. (Orig.). 1996. pap. text 29.00 (*0-309-05390-0*) Natl Acad Pr.

National Research Council, NII 2000 Steering Commi. The Unpredictable Certainty: Information Infrastructure Through 2000. LC 96-67383. 250p. (Orig.). 1996. pap. 24.95 (*0-309-05432-X*) Natl Acad Pr.

***National Research Council Ocean Staff, ed.** Tidal Current Tables Atlantic Coast of North America 2001. (Tidal Current Tables Ser.). (Illus.). 2000. pap. 13.95 (*0-07-136458-7*) McGraw.

— Tidal Current Tables Pacific Coast of North America & Asia 2001. (Illus.). 2000. pap. 13.95 (*0-07-136459-5*) McGraw.

National Research Council of Canada, Associate Com. Muskeg Engineering Handbook. MacFarlane, Ivan C., ed. LC 78-447167. (Canadian Building Ser.: No. 3). 320p. reprint ed. pap. 99.20 (*0-608-16673-1*, 205611400050) Bks Demand.

National Research Council, Office of International. Dual-Use Technologies & Export Administration in the Post-Cold War Era. LC 93-65016. 232p. (Orig.). (C). 1994. pap. text 33.00 (*0-309-05031-6*) Natl Acad Pr.

— U. S. - Japan Technology Linkages in Biotechnology: Challenges for the 1990's. 106p. (C). 1992. pap. text 19.00 (*0-309-04699-8*) Natl Acad Pr.

N

An Asterisk (*) at the beginning of an entry indicates that the title is appearing for the first time.

National Research Council, Office of the Home Secr. Biographical Memoirs, Vol. 61. 512p. (C). 1992. text 59.00 (*0-309-04746-3*) Natl Acad Pr.

— Biographical Memoirs, Vol. 64. 500p. 1994. text 59.00 (*0-309-04978-4*) Natl Acad Pr.

National Research Council, Panel on Aerosol Radiat. A Plan for a Research Program on Aerosol Radiative Forcing & Climate Change. 180p. (Orig.). 1996. pap. text 34.00 (*0-309-05429-X*) Natl Acad Pr.

National Research Council, Panel on Child Care Pol. Caring for America's Children. Meadows, Anne, ed. 48p. 1991. pap. text 6.50 (*0-309-04580-0*) Natl Acad Pr.

National Research Council, Panel on Confidentialit. Private Lives & Public Policies: Confidentiality & Accessibility of Government Statistics. Jabine, Thomas B. et al, eds. LC 93-31312. 288p. (C). 1993. text 34.95 (*0-309-04743-9*) Natl Acad Pr.

National Research Council, Panel on Dosimetric Ass. Comparative Dosimetry of Radon in Homes & Mines. 256p. 1991. text 29.95 (*0-309-04484-7*) Natl Acad Pr.

National Research Council, Panel on Effects of Pas. Effects of Past Global Change on Life. (Studies in Geophysics). 272p. (C). 1994. text 49.95 (*0-309-05127-4*) Natl Acad Pr.

National Research Council, Panel on Employer Polic. Work & Family: Policies for a Changing Workforce. Ferber, Marianne A. & O'Farrell, M. Brigid, eds. 268p. 1990. 29.95 (*0-309-04277-1*) Natl Acad Pr.

National Research Council, Panel on International. Following the Money: U. S. Finance in the World Economy. Kester, Anne Y., ed. LC 95-32043. 224p. 1994. text 34.95 (*0-309-04883-4*) Natl Acad Pr.

National Research Council, Panel on Monitoring the. The Social Impact of AIDS in the United States. 336p. 1993. 39.95 (*0-309-04628-9*) Natl Acad Pr.

National Research Council, Panel on Needle Exchang & Institute of Medicine Staff. Proceedings-Workshop on Needle Exchange & Bleach Distribution Programs. 320p. (Orig.). (C). 1994. pap. text 39.00 (*0-309-05084-7*) Natl Acad Pr.

National Research Council, Panel on Opportunities. Plasma Science: From Fundamental Research to Technological Applications. (Physics in a New Era Ser.). 224p. (Orig.). (C). 1995. pap. text 35.00 (*0-309-05231-9*) Natl Acad Pr.

National Research Council, Panel on Organizational. Organizational Linkages: Understanding the Productivity Paradox. Harris, Douglas H., ed. 320p. (Orig.). 1994. text 44.95 (*0-309-04934-2*) Natl Acad Pr.

National Research Council, Panel on Planning for S. The Bridge Builders: African Experiences with Information & Communication Technology. LC 96-68711. 304p. (Orig.). (C). 1996. pap. text 39.00 (*0-309-05483-4*) Natl Acad Pr.

National Research Council, Panel on Poverty & Fami. Measuring Poverty: A New Approach. Michael, Robert T. & Citro, Constance F., eds. 536p. (C). 1995. text 44.95 (*0-309-05128-2*) Natl Acad Pr.

National Research Council, Panel on Research on Ch. Understanding Child Abuse & Neglect. LC 93-29640. 408p. (C). 1993. text 44.95 (*0-309-04889-3*) Natl Acad Pr.

National Research Council, Panel on Review & Evalu. Review & Evaluation of Alternative Chemical Disposal Technologies. LC 96-61747. 272p. (Orig.). (C). 1996. pap. text 45.00 (*0-309-05525-3*) Natl Acad Pr.

National Research Council, Panel on Small Spacecra. Technology for Small Spacecraft. 156p. (Orig.). (C). 1994. pap. text 27.00 (*0-309-05075-8*) Natl Acad Pr.

National Research Council, Panel on Statistical Me. Statistical Software Engineering. 84p. (Orig.). 1996. pap. text 29.00 (*0-309-05344-7*) Natl Acad Pr.

National Research Council, Panel on the Understand. Understanding & Preventing Violence Vol. 2: Biobehavioral Influences. Reiss, Albert J., Jr. et al, eds. 560p. (Orig.). (C). 1994. pap. text 45.00 (*0-309-04649-1*) Natl Acad Pr.

— Understanding & Preventing Violence Vol. 3: Social Influences. Reiss, Albert J., Jr. & Roth, Jeffrey A., eds. 592p. (Orig.). (C). 1994. pap. text 45.00 (*0-309-05080-4*) Natl Acad Pr.

— Understanding & Preventing Violence Vol. 4: Consequences & Control. Reiss, Albert J., Jr. et al, eds. 408p. (Orig.). (C). 1994. pap. text 39.00 (*0-309-05079-0*) Natl Acad Pr.

National Research Council, Panel on Violence Again. Understanding Violence Against Women. Crowell, Nancy A. & Burgess, Ann W., eds. LC 96-17335. 240p. 1996. 29.95 (*0-309-05425-7*) Natl Acad Pr.

National Research Council, Panel to Evaluate the S. The Future of the Survey of Income & Program Participation. Citro, Constance F. & Kalton, Graham, eds. LC 92-62584. 298p. (Orig.). 1993. pap. text 38.00 (*0-309-04795-1*) Natl Acad Pr.

National Research Council, Physics Survey Committe. Scientific Interfaces & Technological Applications. LC 85-32039. (Physics Through the 1990's Ser.). 284p. reprint ed. pap. 88.10 (*0-7837-3570-7*, 204342800009) Bks Demand.

National Research Council Polymer Science & Engine. Polymer Science & Engineering: The Shifting Research Frontiers. 192p. (C). 1994. text 34.95 (*0-309-04998-9*) Natl Acad Pr.

National Research Council Protection & Management. Upstream: Salmon & Society in the Pacific Northwest. 472p. 1996. 44.95 (*0-309-05325-0*) Natl Acad Pr.

National Research Council, Rediscovering Geography. Rediscovering Geography: New Relevance for Science & Society. LC 97-4630. 300p. (Orig.). (C). 1997. text 34.95 (*0-309-05199-1*) Natl Acad Pr.

National Research Council, Remedial Action Priorit. Ranking Hazardous-Waste Sites for Remedial Action. LC 94-66574. (Illus.). 312p. 1994. reprint ed. pap. 96.80 (*0-608-04258-7*, 206501300012) Bks Demand.

National Research Council, Renaissance Committee S. Realizing the Information Future: The Internet & Beyond. 320p. (Orig.). (C). 1994. pap. 24.95 (*0-309-05044-8*) Natl Acad Pr.

National Research Council, Roundtable on Head Star & Institute of Medicine Staff. Beyond the Blueprint: Directions for Research on Head Start Families. Phillips, Deborah A. & Cabrera, Natasha J., eds. 104p. (Orig.). 1996. pap. text 17.00 (*0-309-05485-0*) Natl Acad Pr.

National Research Council, Safe Drinking Water Com. Drinking Water & Health, Vol. 5. 157p. 1983. pap. text 18.95 (*0-309-03381-0*) Natl Acad Pr.

— Drinking Water & Health, Vol. 6. 457p. 1986. pap. text 39.95 (*0-309-03687-9*) Natl Acad Pr.

— Drinking Water & Health: Selected Issues in Risk Assessment, Vol. 9. 284p. 1989. pap. text 29.95 (*0-309-03897-9*) Natl Acad Pr.

— Drinking Water & Health, Vol. 7: Disinfectants & Disinfectant By-Products. 212p. 1987. pap. text 19.95 (*0-309-03741-7*) Natl Acad Pr.

— Drinking Water & Health, Vol. 8: Pharmacokinetics in Risk Assessment. 512p. 1987. pap. text 43.50 (*0-309-03775-1*) Natl Acad Pr.

National Research Council, Safety of Marine Pipeli. Improving the Safety of Marine Pipelines. 156p. (Orig.). (C). 1994. pap. text 32.00 (*0-309-05047-2*) Natl Acad Pr.

National Research Council, Science & Technology fo. Food Aid Projections for the Decade of the 1990s. 194p. 1989. pap. text 20.00 (*0-309-04268-2*) Natl Acad Pr.

National Research Council, Socioeconomics Panel St. Assessment of the U. S. Outer Continental Shelf Environmental Studies Program, No. 3: Social & Economic Studies. LC 89-63847. 164p. (Orig.). (C). 1993. pap. text 30.00 (*0-309-04835-4*) Natl Acad Pr.

National Research Council, Solar-Terrestrial Resea. A Space Physics Paradox: Why Has Increased Funding Been Accompanied by Decreased Effectiveness in the Conduct of Space Physics Research? 112p. (Orig.). (C). 1994. pap. text 29.00 (*0-309-05177-0*) Natl Acad Pr.

National Research Council Staff. Acid Deposition: Atmospheric Processes in Eastern North America. LC 83-61851. (Review of Current Scientific Understanding Ser.). 391p. reprint ed. pap. 121.30 (*0-7837-5038-2*, 204471400004) Bks Demand.

— Acid Deposition: Long-Term Trends. 520p. (Orig.). 1986. pap. text 34.95 (*0-309-03647-X*) Natl Acad Pr.

— Active Tectonics: Impact on Society. 280p. 1986. text 29.95 (*0-309-03638-0*) Natl Acad Pr.

— Ada & Beyond: Software Policies for the Department of Defense. LC 96-71960. 116p. (Orig.). 1997. pap. 29.00 (*0-309-05597-0*, Joseph Henry Pr) Natl Acad Pr.

— Adequacy of Climate Observing Systems. 66p. 1999. pap. 18.00 (*0-309-06390-6*) Natl Acad Pr.

— Adolescent Decision Making: Implications for Prevention Programs: Summary of a Workshop. Fischhoff, Baruch et al, eds. 32p. 1999. pap. 12.00 (*0-309-06479-1*) Natl Acad Pr.

***National Research Council Staff.** Advanced Engineering Environments Phase 1: Achieving the Vision. 58p. 1999. pap. 18.00 (*0-309-06541-0*) Natl Acad Pr.

National Research Council Staff. Advanced Power Sources for Space Missions. 156p. 1989. pap. text 23.50 (*0-309-03999-1*) Natl Acad Pr.

— Advanced Technology for Human Support in Space. LC 97-68305. 150p. 1997. pap. text 35.00 (*0-309-05744-2*) Natl Acad Pr.

***National Research Council Staff.** Advanced Technology Program: Challenges & Opportunities. Wessner, Charles W., ed. 140p. 1999. pap. 31.50 (*0-309-06775-8*) Natl Acad Pr.

National Research Council Staff. Aeronautical Technologies for the Twenty-First Century. (Illus.). 314p. (Orig.). (C). 1992. pap. text 38.00 (*0-309-04732-3*) Natl Acad Pr.

— The Aging Population in the Twenty-First Century: Statistics for Health Policy. 340p. 1988. pap. text 27.95 (*0-309-03881-2*) Natl Acad Pr.

— Agricultural Biotechnology: Strategies for National Competitiveness. LC 87-12181. 221p. reprint ed. pap. 68.60 (*0-7837-2776-3*, 204316700006) Bks Demand.

— Agricultural Crop Issues & Policies. (Managing Global Genetic Resources Ser.). 480p. (C). 1994. text 49.95 (*0-309-04430-8*) Natl Acad Pr.

— Agriculture's Role in K-12 Education: Proceedings of a Forum on the National Science Education Standards. LC 98-84942. 56p. 1998. pap. text 15.00 (*0-309-06048-6*) Natl Acad Pr.

— Airline Passenger Security Screening: New Technologies & Implementation Issues. LC 96-69048. 88p. (Orig.). 1996. pap. text 28.00 (*0-309-05439-7*) Natl Acad Pr.

— The Airliner Cabin Environment: Air Quality & Safety. 318p. 1986. pap. text 29.95 (*0-309-03690-9*) Natl Acad Pr.

— Animals as Sentinels of Environmental Health Hazards. 176p. 1991. pap. text 17.50 (*0-309-04046-9*) Natl Acad Pr.

— Antarctic Treaty System: An Assessment. 456p. (Orig.). 1986. text 45.95 (*0-309-03640-2*) Natl Acad Pr.

— Applying Advanced Information Systems to Ports & Waterways Management. 66p. 1999. pap. 18.00 (*0-309-06380-9*) Natl Acad Pr.

— Arsenic in Drinking Water. 330p. 1999. pap. 50.00 (*0-309-06333-7*, Joseph Henry Pr) Natl Acad Pr.

— Assessing Knowledge of Retirement Behavior. Hanushek, Eric A. & Maritato, Nancy, eds. LC 96-69361. 288p. (Orig.). 1996. pap. text 47.00 (*0-309-05547-4*) Natl Acad Pr.

— Assessing the Value of Research in the Chemical Sciences. LC 98-86063. 196p. 1998. pap. text 35.00 (*0-309-06139-3*) Natl Acad Pr.

— Assessment of Exposure-Response Functions for Rocket-Emission Toxicants. LC 98-86245. 228p. 1998. pap. text 39.00 (*0-309-06144-X*) Natl Acad Pr.

— Assessment of Hydrologic & Hydrometeorological Operations & Services. (Toward a New National Weather Service Ser.). 62p. (C). 1996. pap. text 15.00 (*0-309-05634-9*) Natl Acad Pr.

— Assessment of Research Needs for Wind Turbine Rotor Materials Technology. 120p. (C). 1991. pap. text 19.00 (*0-309-04479-0*) Natl Acad Pr.

***National Research Council Staff.** The Assessment of Science Meets the Science of Assessment: Summary of a Workshop. 48p. 1999. pap. 12.00 (*0-309-06546-1*) Natl Acad Pr.

— Assessment of Technologies Deployed to Improve Aviation Security. 86p. 1999. pap. 18.00 (*0-309-06787-1*) Natl Acad Pr.

National Research Council Staff. An Assessment of the Advanced Weather Interactive Processing System: Operational Test & Evaluation of the First System Build. LC 98-103405. 52p. (C). 1997. pap. text 15.00 (*0-309-05995-X*) Natl Acad Pr.

— An Assessment of the International Science & Technology Center: Redirecting Expertise in Weapons of Mass Destruction in the Former Soviet Union. LC 97-107281. 60p. (Orig.). 1996. pap. text 15.00 (*0-309-05678-0*, Joseph Henry Pr) Natl Acad Pr.

— Assessment of the Possible Health Effects of the Ground Wave Emergency Network. 180p. (Orig.). (C). 1993. pap. text 33.00 (*0-309-04777-3*) Natl Acad Pr.

— Assessment of the U. S. Army Chemical & Biological Defense Command Report 1: Technical Assessment of the Man-in-Simulant Test Program. LC 97-226254. 86p. (C). 1997. pap. text 15.00 (*0-309-05940-2*) Natl Acad Pr.

— Assessment of the U. S. Army Natick Research, Development & Engineering Center. LC 98-138591. 202p. (C). 1997. pap. text 36.00 (*0-309-05978-X*) Natl Acad Pr.

— Assessment of the U. S. Outer Continental Shelf Environmental Studies Program, Vol. 1: Physical Oceanography. LC 89-63847. 153p. reprint ed. pap. 47.50 (*0-7837-5037-4*, 204471300001) Bks Demand.

— Assessment of Two Cost-Effectiveness Studies on Cocaine Control Policy. Manski, Charles F. et al, eds. 64p. 1999. pap. 18.00 (*0-309-06477-5*) Natl Acad Pr.

— Astronomy & Astrophysics. (Space Science in the Twenty-First Century Series: Imperatives for the Decades 1995 to 2015). 84p. 1988. pap. text 14.95 (*0-309-03875-8*) Natl Acad Pr.

— Atmospheric Effects of Aviation: A Review of NASA's Subsonic Assessment Project. 54p. (C). 1999. pap. text 12.00 (*0-309-06425-2*) Natl Acad Pr.

— The Atmospheric Effects of Stratospheric Aircraft Project: An Interim Review of Science & Progress. 68p. 1998. pap. text 15.00 (*0-309-06095-8*) Natl Acad Pr.

— The Atmospheric Sciences Entering the Twenty-First Century. LC 98-40083. 450p. (C). 1998. text 47.95 (*0-309-06415-5*) Natl Acad Pr.

— Atomic, Molecular, & Optical Physics. (Physics Through the 1990's Ser.). 200p. 1986. pap. text 24.50 (*0-309-03575-9*) Natl Acad Pr.

— Barrier Technologies for Environmental Mangement: Summary of a Workshop. LC 96-72353. 188p. (Orig.). 1997. pap. 36.00 (*0-309-05685-3*, Joseph Henry Pr) Natl Acad Pr.

— Beam Technologies for Integrated Processing. 106p. 1992. pap. text 19.00 (*0-309-04635-1*) Natl Acad Pr.

— Behavioral & Social Science: Fifty Years of Discovery. 312p. 1986. text 29.50 (*0-309-03588-0*) Natl Acad Pr.

— The Behavioral & Social Sciences: Achievements & Opportunities. Gerstein, Dean R. et al, eds. 304p. 1988. text 29.50 (*0-309-03749-2*) Natl Acad Pr.

***National Research Council Staff.** Being Fluent with Information Technology. LC 99-63379. 128p. 1999. pap. 28.00 (*0-309-06399-X*) Natl Acad Pr.

National Research Council Staff. Bereavement: Reactions, Consequences, & Care. 312p. 1984. pap. 29.95 (*0-309-03438-8*) Natl Acad Pr.

— Biobased Industrial Products: Research & Commercialization Priorities. LC 99-50917. 162p. (C). 1999. pap. 35.00 (*0-309-05392-7*) Natl Acad Pr.

— Biodiversity Conservation in Transboundary Protected Areas. Breymeyer, Alicja & Noble, Reginald, eds. LC 96-69773. 288p. (Orig.). 1996. pap. text 35.00 (*0-309-05576-8*) Natl Acad Pr.

— Biographical Memoirs, Vol. 62. 512p. (C). 1993. text 59.00 (*0-309-04782-X*) Natl Acad Pr.

— Biographical Memoirs, Vol. 70. 448p. (C). 1996. text 79.00 (*0-309-05541-5*) Natl Acad Pr.

— Biographical Memoirs, Vol. 71. 394p. (C). 1997. text 79.00 (*0-309-05738-8*) Natl Acad Pr.

— Biologic Markers in Immunotoxicology. 224p. (C). 1992. pap. text 37.95 (*0-309-04389-1*) Natl Acad Pr.

— Biologic Markers in Reproductive Toxicology. 420p. 1989. pap. text 32.95 (*0-309-03979-7*) Natl Acad Pr.

— Biologic Markers in Urinary Toxicology. Subcommittee on Biologic Markers in Urinary Toxico, ed. LC 94-69722. 210p. (Orig.). (C). 1995. pap. text 34.00 (*0-309-05228-9*) Natl Acad Pr.

— Biologic Markers of Pulmonary Toxicology. 196p. 1989. text 34.95 (*0-309-03992-4*); pap. text 24.95 (*0-309-03990-8*) Natl Acad Pr.

— Black & Smokeless Powders: Finding the Bombs & Catching the Bombers. LC 98-87764. 100p. (C). 1998. pap. text 30.00 (*0-309-06246-2*) Natl Acad Pr.

— Boundary Layer Dynamics. LC 97-212240. 50p. (C). 1997. pap. text 10.00 (*0-309-05742-6*) Natl Acad Pr.

— Breaking the Mold: Forging a Common Defense Manufacturing Vision. 94p. (Orig.). (C). 1993. pap. text 24.00 (*0-309-04789-7*) Natl Acad Pr.

National Research Council Staff. Bridging Boundaries Through Regional Marine Research. 128p. pap. 29.25 (*0-309-06832-0*) Natl Acad Pr.

National Research Council Staff. Brucellosis in the Greater Yellowstone Area. 328p. (C). 1998. pap. text 29.00 (*0-309-05989-5*) Natl Acad Pr.

— Building a Diverse Workforce: Scientists & Engineers in the Office of Naval Research. 160p. (C). 1997. pap. text 29.50 (*0-309-05849-X*) Natl Acad Pr.

— Building a Foundation for Sound Environmental Decisions. LC 97-67451. 104p. 1997. pap. text 29.00 (*0-309-05795-7*) Natl Acad Pr.

— Building an Effective Environmental Management Science Program: Final Assessment. 184p. 1997. pap. 35.00 (*0-309-05730-2*, Joseph Henry Pr) Natl Acad Pr.

— Building for Tomorrow: Global Enterprise & the U. S. Construction Industry. 120p. 1988. pap. text 14.95 (*0-309-03937-1*) Natl Acad Pr.

— Building Ocean Science Partnerships: The United States & Mexico Working Together. 292p. 1999. pap. 45.00 (*0-309-05881-3*) Natl Acad Pr.

— Capacity of U. S. Climate Modeling Efforts to Support Climate Change Assessment Activities. LC 99-184680. 78p. 1999. pap. text 18.00 (*0-309-06375-2*) Natl Acad Pr.

***National Research Council Staff.** Carbon Filtration for Reducing Emissions from Chemical Agent Incineration. 102p. 1999. pap. 25.00 (*0-309-06595-X*) Natl Acad Pr.

National Research Council Staff. Carcinogens & Anti-Carcinogens in the Human Diet: A Comparison of Naturally Occurring & Synthetic Substances... 436p. (Orig.). 1996. pap. text 44.95 (*0-309-05391-9*) Natl Acad Pr.

— The Case for Human Factors in Industry & Government: Report of a Workshop. Rouse, William et al, eds. LC 97-221351. 50p. (C). 1997. pap. text 10.00 (*0-309-05894-5*) Natl Acad Pr.

— Catalysis Looks to the Future. 96p. 1991. pap. text 19.00 (*0-309-04584-3*) Natl Acad Pr.

— Causes & Effects of Stratospheric Ozone Reduction: An Update. 339p. (C). 1982. pap. text 29.95 (*0-309-03248-2*) Natl Acad Pr.

— The Changing Nature of Telecommunications & Information Infrastructure. 240p. (Orig.). (C). 1995. pap. text 27.00 (*0-309-05091-X*) Natl Acad Pr.

— The Changing Nature of Work: Implications for Occupational Analysis. LC 99-6682. 376p. 1999. 49.95 (*0-309-06525-9*, Joseph Henry Pr) Natl Acad Pr.

— Chimpanzees in Research: Strategies for Their Ethical Care, Management, & Use. LC 97-208778. 108p. (C). 1997. pap. text 21.75 (*0-309-05891-0*) Natl Acad Pr.

— Clean Ships, Clean Ports, Clean Oceans: Controlling Garbage & Plastic Wastes at Sea. 384p. (C). 1995. text 42.95 (*0-309-05137-1*) Natl Acad Pr.

— Climate, Climatic Change & Water Supply. (Studies in Geophysics). 132p. 1977. pap. text 14.95 (*0-309-02625-3*) Natl Acad Pr.

— Climbing the Ladder: An Update on the Status of Doctoral Women Scientists & Engineers. 112p. (C). 1983. pap. text 14.95 (*0-309-03341-1*) Natl Acad Pr.

— Coal: Energy for the Future. 304p. (Orig.). (C). 1995. text 44.95 (*0-309-05232-7*) Natl Acad Pr.

— Coastal Meteorology: A Review of the State of the Science. 112p. (C). 1992. pap. text 24.00 (*0-309-04687-4*) Natl Acad Pr.

— Commercial Aviation Security: Integrating People & Equipment to Improve Threat Detection. 180p. 1999. text 36.95 (*0-309-07153-4*) Natl Acad Pr.

— Commercial Multimedia Technologies for Twenty-First Century Army Battlefields: A Technology Management Strategy. LC 95-72007. 104p. 1995. pap. text 29.00 (*0-309-05378-1*) Natl Acad Pr.

— Commercialization of New Materials for a Global Economy. 80p. (C). 1993. pap. text 25.00 (*0-309-04734-X*) Natl Acad Pr.

***National Research Council Staff.** Committee on Military Nutrition Research: Activity Report 1994-1999. 304p. 1999. pap. 59.25 (*0-309-06585-2*) Natl Acad Pr.

National Research Council Staff. A Common Destiny: Blacks & American Society. Jaynes, Gerald D. & Williams, Robin M., Jr., eds. 624p. 1990. 22.95 (*0-309-03998-3*) Natl Acad Pr.

— The Community Development Quota Program in Alaska. 228p. 1999. pap. 49.00 (*0-309-06082-6*) Natl Acad Pr.

— Companion Guide to Infectious Diseases of Mice & Rats. 108p. 1991. pap. text 16.00 (*0-309-04283-6*) Natl Acad Pr.

— Comparable Worth: New Directions for Research. 192p. 1985. pap. text 19.95 (*0-309-03534-1*) Natl Acad Pr.

— Competition in the Electric Industry: Emerging Issues, Opportunities, & Risks for Facility Operators. LC 97-106979. 98p. (Orig.). 1996. pap. text 15.00 (*0-309-05681-0*, Joseph Henry Pr) Natl Acad Pr.

— The Competitive Edge: Research Priorities for U. S. Manufacturing. 184p. 1991. pap. text 24.95 (*0-309-04784-6*) Natl Acad Pr.

— The Competitive Status of the U. S. Civil Aviation Manufacturing Industry. 168p. 1985. pap. text 19.95 (*0-309-03399-3*) Natl Acad Pr.

— The Competitiveness of the U. S. Minerals & Metals Industries. 160p. 1990. pap. text 22.95 (*0-309-04245-3*) Natl Acad Pr.

— Complex Mixtures: Methods for In Vivo Toxicity Testing. 240p. 1988. text 35.00 (*0-309-03778-6*) Natl Acad Pr.

— Computer Chips & Paper Clips: Technology & Women's Employment, Vol I. Tilly, Louise A. et al, eds. 216p. 1986. pap. text 19.95 (*0-309-03688-7*) Natl Acad Pr.

— Computer Chips & Paper Clips Vol. 2: Technology &

N

An Asterisk (*) at the beginning of an entry indicates that the title is appearing for the first time.

Women's Employment, Case Studies & Policy Perspectives. Tilly, Louise A. et al, eds. (Case Studies & Policy Perspectives). 456p. 1987. pap. text 34.95 (*0-309-03727-1*) Natl Acad Pr.
— Computer Science & Artificial Intelligence. 32p. (C). 1997. pap. text 10.00 (*0-309-05831-7*) Natl Acad Pr.
— Computing & Communications in the Extreme: Research for Crisis Management & Other Applications. LC 96-60885. 176p. (Orig.). (C). 1996. pap. text 29.00 (*0-309-05540-7*) Natl Acad Pr.
— Computing Professionals: Changing Needs for the 1990's. 1993. pap. text 19.00 (*0-309-04790-0*) Natl Acad Pr.
— Computing the Future: A Broader Agenda for Computer Science & Engineering. 288p. (C). 1992. pap. 24.95 (*0-309-04740-4*) Natl Acad Pr.
— Condensed-Matter Physics. (Physics Through the 1990's Ser.). 328p. 1986. pap. text 31.50 (*0-309-03577-5*) Natl Acad Pr.
— Configuration Management & Performance Verification of Explosives-Detection Systems. LC 99-181538. 71p. 1998. pap. text 15.00 (*0-309-06196-2*) Natl Acad Pr.
— Confronting Climate Change: Strategies for Energy Research & Development. 144p. (C). 1990. pap. text 17.95 (*0-309-04347-6*) Natl Acad Pr.
— Conserving Biodiversity: A Research Agenda for Development Agencies. 140p. (C). 1992. pap. text 19.00 (*0-309-04683-1*) Natl Acad Pr.
— Considerations in Contact Lens Use under Adverse Conditions: Proceedings of a Symposium. Flattau, Pamela E., ed. 178p. (C). 1991. pap. text 23.00 (*0-309-04438-3*) Natl Acad Pr.
— Containing the Threat from Illegal Bombings: An Integrated National Strategy for Marking, Tagging, Rendering Inert & Licening Explosives & Their Precursors. 275p. (C). 1998. pap. text 39.00 (*0-309-05990-9*) Natl Acad Pr.
— Containing the Threat from Illegal Bombings: An Integrated National Strategy for Marking, Tagging, Rendering Inert, & Licensing Explosives & Their Precursors. LC 98-19665. 1998. pap. text 39.00 (*0-309-06126-1*) Natl Acad Pr.
— Contaminated Marine Sediments: Assessment & Remediation. 508p. 1989. pap. text 35.00 (*0-309-04095-7*) Natl Acad Pr.
— Contaminated Sediments in Ports & Waterways: Clean-Up Strategies & Technologies. LC 96-52050. 320p. (C). 1996. text 42.95 (*0-309-05493-1*) Natl Acad Pr.
***National Research Council Staff.** Cooperative Stewardship: Managing the Nation's Multidisciplinary User Facilities. 86p. 1999. pap. 18.00 (*0-309-06831-2*) Natl Acad Pr.
National Research Council Staff. Criminal Careers & "Career Criminals", Vol II. Blumstein, Alfred et al, eds. 404p. 1986. text 49.95 (*0-309-03683-6*) Natl Acad Pr.
— Currency Features for Visually Impaired People. 144p. (Orig.). (C). 1995. pap. text 27.00 (*0-309-05194-0*) Natl Acad Pr.
— Data Priorities for Population & Health in Developing Countries: Summary of a Workshop. LC 97-104354. 40p. (C). 1996. pap. text 10.00 (*0-309-05626-8*) Natl Acad Pr.
— Database Needs for Modeling & Simulation of Plasma Processing. (Illus.). 74p. (Orig.). 1996. pap. text 15.00 (*0-309-05591-1*, Joseph Henry Pr) Natl Acad Pr.
— Decade-to-Century-Scale Climate Variability & Change: A Science Strategy. 175p. (C). 1998. pap. text 39.00 (*0-309-06098-2*) Natl Acad Pr.
***National Research Council Staff.** Decision Making in the U. S. Department of Energy's Environmental Management Office of Science & Technology. 230p. 1999. pap. 46.75 (*0-309-06347-7*) Natl Acad Pr.
National Research Council Staff. Defense Manufacturing in 2010 & Beyond: Meeting the Changing Needs of National Defense. 150p. 1999. text 35.00 (*0-309-06376-0*) Natl Acad Pr.
— Defining a Decade: Envisioning CSTB's Second 10 Years. LC 98-102975. 116p. (C). 1997. pap. text 23.00 (*0-309-05933-X*) Natl Acad Pr.
— Democratization in Africa: African Views, African Voices. Kpundeh, Sahr J., ed. (Project on Democratization Ser.). 94p. (Orig.). (C). 1992. pap. text 27.00 (*0-309-04797-8*) Natl Acad Pr.
— Demographic Effects of Economic Reversals in Sub-Saharan Africa. (Population Dynamics of Sub-Saharan Africa Ser.). 208p. (Orig.). (C). 1993. pap. text 33.00 (*0-309-04898-2*) Natl Acad Pr.
— The Demography of Forced Migration: Summary of a Workshop. Reed, Holly et al, eds. LC 98-190466. 34p. 1998. pap. text 10.00 (*0-309-06141-5*) Natl Acad Pr.
— Designing an Agricultural Genome Program: Proceedings of Forum on April 26, 1997. LC 99-173792. 32p. (C). 1998. pap. text 10.00 (*0-309-06039-7*) Natl Acad Pr.
— Designing Foods: Animal Product Options in the Marketplace. 384p. 1988. 39.95 (*0-309-03798-0*); pap. text 29.95 (*0-309-03795-6*) Natl Acad Pr.
***National Research Council Staff.** Designing Mathematics or Science Curriculum Programs: A Guide for Using Mathematics & Science Education Standard. 70p. 1999. pap. 12.95 (*0-309-06527-5*) Natl Acad Pr.
National Research Council Staff. Detection of Explosives for Commercial Aviation Security. 108p. (Orig.). (C). 1993. pap. text 28.00 (*0-309-04945-8*) Natl Acad Pr.
— Developing a Digital National Library for Undergraduate Science, Mathematics, Engineering, & Technology Education: Report of a Workshop. LC 97-45304. 190p. (C). 1997. pap. text 31.00 (*0-309-05977-1*) Natl Acad Pr.
— Diet, Nutrition, & Cancer. 496p. 1982. pap. text 29.95 (*0-309-03280-6*) Natl Acad Pr.
— The Digital Dilemma: The Future of Intellectual Property in the Information Infrastructure. 240p. 2000. pap. 42.95 (*0-309-06499-6*, Pub. by Natl Acad Pr) World Scientific Pub.
— Digital Instrumentation & Control Systems in Nuclear Power Plants: Safety & Reliability Issues. 128p. (Orig.). 1997. pap. text 36.00 (*0-309-05732-9*, Joseph Henry Pr) Natl Acad Pr.
— Disability Evaluation Study Design: First Interinm Report. 43p. (C). 1997. pap. text 10.00 (*0-309-05889-9*) Natl Acad Pr.
— Dispelling the Manufacturing Myth: American Factories Can Compete in the Global Marketplace. LC 92-21775. 126p. 1992. reprint ed. pap. 39.10 (*0-608-03813-X*, 206466300009) Bks Demand.
***National Research Council Staff.** Disposition of High-Level Radioactive Waste Through Geological Isolation: Development, Current Status & Technical & Policy. 44p. 1999. pap. 12.00 (*0-309-06778-2*) Natl Acad Pr.
— Distributed Geolibraries: Spatial Information Resources, Summary of a Workshop. 136p. 1999. pap. 30.50 (*0-309-06540-2*) Natl Acad Pr.
National Research Council Staff. District Heating & Cooling in the United States: Prospects & Issues. 168p. 1985. pap. text 19.95 (*0-309-03537-6*) Natl Acad Pr.
— Double-Hull Tanker Legislation: An Assessment of the Oil Pollution Act of 1990. LC 97-81450. 200p. 1997. pap. 45.00 (*0-309-06370-1*) Natl Acad Pr.
***National Research Council Staff.** Downstream: Adaptive Management of Glen Canyon Dam & the Colorado River. 242p. 1999. pap. 48.75 (*0-309-06579-8*) Natl Acad Pr.
National Research Council Staff. Drilling & Excavation Technologies for the Future. 176p. (Orig.). (C). 1994. pap. text 27.00 (*0-309-05076-6*) Natl Acad Pr.
— Earthquake Engineering for Concrete Dams: Design, Performance, & Research Needs. 158p. 1991. pap. text 19.00 (*0-309-04336-0*) Natl Acad Pr.
— The Earth's Electrical Environment. (Studies in Geophysics). 263p. 1986. text 28.95 (*0-309-03680-1*) Natl Acad Pr.
— Ecological Knowledge & Environmental Problem Solving: Concepts & Case Studies. 400p. 1986. pap. text 29.95 (*0-309-03645-3*) Natl Acad Pr.
— Education & Training for Civilian Aviation Careers. 176p. (Orig.). 1997. pap. text 37.00 (*0-309-05648-9*, Joseph Henry Pr) Natl Acad Pr.
— Education & Training in the Care & Use of Laboratory Animals: A Guide for Developing Institutional Programs. 152p. (C). 1991. pap. text 11.95 (*0-309-04382-4*) Natl Acad Pr.
— The Effect of Genetic Variance on Nutritional Requirements of Animals: Proceedings of a Symposium, University of Maryland, College Park, Maryland, July 31, 1974. LC 75-10567. 129p. reprint ed. pap. 40.00 (*0-7837-1638-9*, 204193100024) Bks Demand.
— Effectiveness of the United States Advanced Battery Consortium As a Government-Industry Partnership. LC 98-86227. 90p. 1998. pap. text 15.00 (*0-309-06143-1*) Natl Acad Pr.
— Effects of Health Programs on Child Mortality in Sub-Saharan Africa. Ewbank, Douglas C. & Gribble, James N., eds. (Population Dynamics of Sub-Saharan Africa Ser.). 208p. (Orig.). (C). 1993. pap. text 33.00 (*0-309-04941-5*) Natl Acad Pr.
— Electricity in Economic Growth. 165p. (Orig.). 1986. pap. text 19.95 (*0-309-03677-1*) Natl Acad Pr.
— Electrometallurgical Techniques for DOE Spent Fuel Treatment: Spring 1988 Status Report on Argonne National Laboratory's R&D Activity. 78p. (C). 1998. pap. text 15.00 (*0-309-06284-5*) Natl Acad Pr.
— Electronic Commerce for the Procurement of Construction & Architect-Engineer Services: Implementing the Federal Acquisition Streamlining Act. LC 97-226193. 60p. (C). 1997. pap. text 15.00 (*0-309-05932-1*) Natl Acad Pr.
— Elementary-Particle Physics. (Physics Through the 1990's Ser.). 248p. 1986. pap. text 24.50 (*0-309-03576-7*) Natl Acad Pr.
— Elementary Particle Physics: Revealing the Secrets of Energy & Matter. 108p. (C). 1998. pap. text 35.00 (*0-309-06037-0*) Natl Acad Pr.
***National Research Council Staff.** Embedding Questions: The Pursuit of a Common Measure in Uncommon Tests. Koretz, Daniel M. et al, eds. 96p. 1999. pap. 18.00 (*0-309-06789-8*) Natl Acad Pr.
— Emerging Global Water & Energy Initiatives: An Integrated Perspective. 32p. 1999. pap. 12.00 (*0-309-06643-3*) Natl Acad Pr.
— Emerging Needs & Opportunities for Human Factors Research. Nickerson, Raymond & Committee on Human Factors, eds. 336p. (Orig.). (C). 1995. pap. text 39.00 (*0-309-05276-9*) Natl Acad Pr.
National Research Council Staff. Enabling Technologies for Unified Life-Cycle Engineering of Structural Components. 112p. 1991. pap. text 19.00 (*0-309-04492-8*) Natl Acad Pr.
— An End State Methodology for Identifying Technology Needs for Environmental Management: With an Example from the Handford Site Tanks. LC 99-205002. 106p. 1999. pap. 25.75 (*0-309-06183-0*) Natl Acad Pr.
— An End State Methodology for Identifying Technology Needs for Environmental Management, with an Example from the Hanford Site Tanks. 100p. 1999. pap. text 22.75 (*0-309-06344-2*) Natl Acad Pr.
— Energy-Efficient Technologies for the Dismounted Soldier. LC 97-80862. 232p. (Orig.). 1997. pap. text 42.00 (*0-309-05934-8*) Natl Acad Pr.
— Engineering Education: Designing an Adaptive System. 96p. 1995. pap. text 27.00 (*0-309-05278-5*) Natl Acad Pr.
— Engineering Education & Practice in the United States: Foundations of Our Techno-Economic Future. LC 85-60423. (Illus.). 150p. reprint ed. pap. 46.50 (*0-7837-5355-1*, 204511700005) Bks Demand.
— Engineering Employment Characteristics. (Engineering Education & Practice in the United States Ser.). 94p. 1985. pap. text 12.50 (*0-309-03586-4*) Natl Acad Pr.
— Engineering in Society. (Engineering Education & Practice in the United States Ser.). 132p. 1985. pap. text 15.95 (*0-309-03592-9*) Natl Acad Pr.
— Engineering Infrastructure Diagramming & Modeling. (Engineering Education & Practice in the United States Ser.). 156p. (Orig.). 1986. pap. text 15.95 (*0-309-03639-9*) Natl Acad Pr.
***National Research Council Staff.** Engineering Tasks for the New Century: Japanese & U. S. Perspectives. 96p. 1999. pap. 18.00 (*0-309-06588-7*) Natl Acad Pr.
National Research Council Staff. Engineering Undergraduate Education. (Engineering Education & Practice in the United States Ser.). 104p. (Orig.). 1986. pap. text 12.50 (*0-309-03642-9*) Natl Acad Pr.
***National Research Council Staff.** Enhancing Access to NEXRAD Data - A Critical National Resource. 28p. 1999. pap. 12.00 (*0-309-06636-0*) Natl Acad Pr.
National Research Council Staff. Enhancing Organizational Performance. Druckman, Daniel et al, eds. LC 97-1782. 304p. 1997. 39.95 (*0-309-05397-8*) Natl Acad Pr.
— Environmental Epidemiology Vol. 1: Public Health & Hazardous Wastes. 296p. 1992. text 29.95 (*0-309-04496-0*) Natl Acad Pr.
— Environmental Information for Outer Continental Shelf Oil & Gas Decisions in Alaska. 270p. (Orig.). (C). 1994. pap. text 49.00 (*0-309-05036-7*) Natl Acad Pr.
— Environmental Management Systems & ISO 14001 Federal Facilities Council Report, No. 138. 48p. 1999. pap. 12.00 (*0-309-06442-2*) Natl Acad Pr.
— Environmental Neurotoxicology. 168p. 1992. pap. text 24.95 (*0-309-04531-2*) Natl Acad Pr.
— Environmental Tobacco Smoke: Measuring Exposures & Assessing Health Effects. LC 86-28622. 351p. reprint ed. pap. 108.90 (*0-7837-1299-5*, 204144000020) Bks Demand.
— Equity & Adequacy Issues in School Finance. 400p. 1998. text 34.95 (*0-309-06563-1*) Natl Acad Pr.
— Equivalency & Linkage of Education Tests: Interim Report. Feuer, Michael J. et al, eds. LC 99-173074. (The Compass Ser.). vii, 38p. 1998. pap. text 10.00 (*0-309-06177-6*) Natl Acad Pr.
— Estimating Probabilities of Extreme Floods: Methods & Recommended Research. LC 87-34839. 157p. reprint ed. pap. 48.70 (*0-8357-4268-7*, 203706400002) Bks Demand.
— Evaluating AIDS Prevention Programs. expanded ed. Coyle, Susan L. et al, eds. 392p. (Orig.). (C). 1991. pap. 39.95 (*0-309-04281-X*) Natl Acad Pr.
***National Research Council Staff.** Evaluating Food Assistance Programs in an Era of Welfare Reform: Summary of a Workshop. Evanson, Elizabeth et al, eds. 72p. 1999. pap. 18.00 (*0-309-06494-5*) Natl Acad Pr.
National Research Council Staff. Evaluating Human Genetic Diversity. LC 97-81059. 108p. (C). 1998. pap. text 36.00 (*0-309-05931-3*) Natl Acad Pr.
— Evaluating the Biological Potential in Samples Returned from Planetary Satellites & Small Solar System Bodies: Framework for Decision Making. LC 98-85797. 116p. (C). 1998. pap. text 37.00 (*0-309-06136-9*) Natl Acad Pr.
***National Research Council Staff.** Evaluating Welfare Reform: A Framework & Review of Current Work, Interim Report. 160p. 1999. pap. 31.50 (*0-309-06649-2*) Natl Acad Pr.
National Research Council Staff. Evaluation of Guidelines for Exposure to Technologically Enhanced Naturally Occuring Radioactive Materials. 270p. 1999. pap. text 42.00 (*0-309-06297-7*) Natl Acad Pr.
— Evaluation of "Redesigning the National Assessment of Educational Progress" LC 97-118484. 36p. (C). 1997. pap. text 10.00 (*0-309-05587-3*) Natl Acad Pr.
— An Evaluation of the U. S. Navy's Extremely-Low-Frequency Submarine Communications Ecological Monitoring Program. LC 96-70733. 240p. (Orig.). 1997. pap. text 39.00 (*0-309-05590-3*) Natl Acad Pr.
— Evaluation of the U.S. Department of Energy's Alternatives for the Removal & Disposition of Molten Salt Reactor Experiment Flouride Salts. 148p. (Orig.). 1997. pap. 29.00 (*0-309-05684-5*, Joseph Henry Pr) Natl Acad Pr.
***National Research Council Staff.** Evaluation of the Voluntary National Tests, Year 2: Final Report. Wise, Lauress L. et al, eds. 110p. 1999. pap. 26.25 (*0-309-06788-X*) Natl Acad Pr.
National Research Council Staff. Every Child a Scientist: Achieving Scientific Literacy for All. 32p. 1997. pap. text 10.00 (*0-309-05986-0*) Natl Acad Pr.
— The Evolution of Untethered Communications. LC 97-80464. 108p. (C). 1997. pap. text 34.00 (*0-309-05946-1*) Natl Acad Pr.
— Expanding the Vision of Sensor Materials. 146p. (Orig.). (C). 1994. pap. text 35.00 (*0-309-05175-4*) Natl Acad Pr.
— Exploring the Trans-Neptune Solar System. 70p. (C). 1998. pap. text 15.00 (*0-309-06041-9*) Natl Acad Pr.
— Factors Affecting Contraceptive Use in Sub-Saharan Africa. (Population Dynamics of Sub-Saharan Africa Ser.). 272p. (Orig.). (C). 1993. pap. text 35.00 (*0-309-04944-X*) Natl Acad Pr.
— Federal Facilities Beyond the 1990's: Ensuring Quality in an Era of Limited Resources, Summary of a Symposium. LC 97-165092. 180p. (C). 1997. pap. text 32.50 (*0-309-05746-9*) Natl Acad Pr.
— Female Engineering Faculty at U. S. Institutions: A Databook. 150p. (C). 1998. pap. text 36.00 (*0-309-06092-3*) Natl Acad Pr.
— The Field of Solar Physics: Review & Recommendations for Ground-Based Solar Research. 72p. 1989. pap. text 15.00 (*0-309-04082-5*) Natl Acad Pr.
— Film Badge Dosimetry in Atmospheric Nuclear Tests. 244p. 1989. pap. text 22.00 (*0-309-04079-5*) Natl Acad Pr.
— Finding the Forest in the Trees: The Challenge of Combining Diverse Environmental Data. Pilot Study on Database Interfaces Committee & U. S. National Committee for CODATA, eds. 144p. (Orig.). (C). 1995. pap. text 25.00 (*0-309-05082-0*) Natl Acad Pr.
***National Research Council Staff.** Finding the Path: Issues of Access to Research Resources. 58p. 1999. pap. 18.00 (*0-309-06625-5*) Natl Acad Pr.
National Research Council Staff. Fire Suppression Substitutes & Alternatives to Halon for U. S. Navy Applications. LC 97-200932. 110p. (C). 1997. pap. text 22.00 (*0-309-05782-5*) Natl Acad Pr.
— Flood Risk Management & the American River Basin: An Evaluation. Committee on Flood Control Alternatives in America, ed. 256p. (Orig.). (C). 1995. pap. text 29.00 (*0-309-05334-X*) Natl Acad Pr.
— Forested Landscapes in Perspective: Prospects & Opportunities for Sustainable Management of America's Nonfederal Forests. LC 98-9017. 230p. (C). 1997. 39.95 (*0-309-05641-1*, Joseph Henry Pr) Natl Acad Pr.
— Forestry Research: A Mandate for Change. 96p. 1990. pap. text 14.95 (*0-309-04248-8*) Natl Acad Pr.
— Forests of the Pacific Northwest. 350p. 1998. 44.95 (*0-309-05328-5*) Natl Acad Pr.
— Fostering Flexibility in the Engineering Work Force. 180p. (C). 1990. pap. text 17.00 (*0-309-04276-3*) Natl Acad Pr.
— Fostering Research on the Economic & Social Impacts of Information Technology. LC 98-86542. 228p. (C). 1998. pap. text 35.00 (*0-309-06032-X*) Natl Acad Pr.
— Four-Dimensional Model Assimilation of Data: A Strategy for the Earth System Sciences. 88p. 1991. pap. text 19.00 (*0-309-04536-3*) Natl Acad Pr.
— Fourth Dimension in Building: Strategies for Avoiding Obsolescence. 114p. (Orig.). (C). 1993. pap. text 28.00 (*0-309-04842-7*) Natl Acad Pr.
— From Earth to Orbit: An Assessment of Transportation Options. 104p. (C). 1992. pap. text 19.00 (*0-309-04726-9*) Natl Acad Pr.
— From Monsoons to Microbes: Understanding the Ocean's Role in Human Health. LC 99-6094. 220p. 1999. 34.95 (*0-309-06569-0*) Natl Acad Pr.
— Frontiers in Chemical Engineering: Research Needs & Opportunities. 232p. 1988. pap. text 29.95 (*0-309-03793-X*) Natl Acad Pr.
— Fundamental Physics & Chemistry. (Space Science in the Twenty-First Century Series: Imperatives for the Decades 1995 to 2015). 108p. 1988. pap. text 14.95 (*0-309-03841-3*) Natl Acad Pr.
— Funding a Revolution: Government Support for Computing Research. LC 98-88131. 320p. 1999. pap. text 44.00 (*0-309-06278-0*) Natl Acad Pr.
— The Funding of Young Investigators in the Biological & Biomedical Sciences. 128p. (Orig.). (C). 1994. pap. text 24.00 (*0-309-05077-4*) Natl Acad Pr.
***National Research Council Staff.** Future Biotechnology Research on the International Space Station. 88p. 2000. pap. 18.00 (*0-309-06975-0*) Natl Acad Pr.
National Research Council Staff. Future Directions for the National Science Foundation's Arctic Natural Sciences Program. LC 99-181634. 80p. 1998. pap. text 15.00 (*0-309-06193-8*) Natl Acad Pr.
— Future Materials Science Research on the International Space Station. LC 98-100499. 72p. (C). 1997. pap. text 15.00 (*0-309-05979-8*) Natl Acad Pr.
— The Future of Air Traffic Control: Human Operators & Automation. Wickens, Christopher D. et al, eds. LC 97-45303. 336p. (C). 1998. text 44.95 (*0-309-06412-0*) Natl Acad Pr.
— The Future of Statistical Software: Proceedings of a Forum. 100p. 1991. pap. text 19.00 (*0-309-04599-1*) Natl Acad Pr.
— Future of the National Weather Service Cooperative Observer Network: Toward a New National Weather Service. LC 98-86724. (Toward a New National Weather Service Ser.). 78p. 1998. pap. text 15.00 (*0-309-06146-6*) Natl Acad Pr.
— Genetic Engineering of Plants: Agricultural Research Opportunities & Policy Concerns. 96p. 1984. pap. text 12.95 (*0-309-03434-5*) Natl Acad Pr.
— Geodesy in the Year 2000. 186p. 1990. pap. text 20.00 (*0-309-04145-7*) Natl Acad Pr.
***National Research Council Staff.** The GEWEX Global Water Vapor Project (GVaP) - U. S. Opportunities. 28p. 1999. pap. 12.00 (*0-309-06642-5*) Natl Acad Pr.
National Research Council Staff. Glass As a Waste Form & Vitrification Technology: Summary of an International Workshop. LC 97-141965. 176p. (C). 1997. pap. text 32.00 (*0-309-05682-9*) Natl Acad Pr.
— Global Change & Our Common Future: Papers from a Forum. 244p. 1989. pap. text 24.00 (*0-309-04089-2*) Natl Acad Pr.
— Global Dimensions of Intellectual Property Rights in Science & Technology. Wallerstein, Mitchel B. et al, eds. 450p. (C). 1993. text 49.95 (*0-309-04833-8*) Natl Acad Pr.
— Global Economy, Global Technology, Global Corporations. LC 98-209484. 74p. 1998. pap. text 21.50 (*0-309-05847-3*) Natl Acad Pr.
— Global Energy & Water Cycle (GWEX) Continental-Scale International Project: A Review of Programs & Opportunities. LC 98-85699. 100p. 1998. pap. text 27.00 (*0-309-06081-8*) Natl Acad Pr.
— Global Environmental Change: Research Pathways for the Next Decade. LC 99-6463. 616p. (C). 1999. text 89.95 (*0-309-06420-1*) Natl Acad Pr.
— Global Environmental Change: Research Pathways for the Next Decade, Overview. LC 98-86191. 82p. 1998. pap. text 15.00 (*0-309-06138-5*) Natl Acad Pr.

N

An Asterisk (*) at the beginning of an entry indicates that the title is appearing for the first time.

— Global ocean science: Integrated Approach for Ocean Research. 200p. 1998. text 39.95 (*0-309-06564-X*) Natl Acad Pr.

***National Research Council Staff.** Global Perspectives for Local Action: Using TIMSS to Improve U. S. Mathematics & Science Education. 150p. 1999. pap. 19.95 (*0-309-06530-5*, Joseph Henry Pr) Natl Acad Pr.

National Research Council Staff. The Global Positioning System: A Shared National Asset. 284p. 1995. pap. text 42.00 (*0-309-05283-1*) Natl Acad Pr.

— Global Tropospheric Chemistry: A Plan for Action. 194p. 1984. pap. text 24.95 (*0-309-03481-7*) Natl Acad Pr.

— Governance & Opportunity in Metropolitan America: Governmental Arrangements & Individual Life Chances in Urban America. Altshuler, Alan et al, eds. LC 99-6607. 360p. (C). 1999. 49.95 (*0-309-06553-4*) Natl Acad Pr.

— Government/Industry Forum on Capital Facilities & Core Competencies: Summary Report. 50p. (C). 1998. pap. text 10.00 (*0-309-06244-6*) Natl Acad Pr.

— Grasslands & Grassland Sciences in Northern China. 230p. (C). 1992. pap. text 31.00 (*0-309-04684-X*) Natl Acad Pr.

— Gravitation, Cosmology & Cosmic-Ray Physics. (Physics Through the 1990's Ser.). 192p. 1986. pap. text 24.50 (*0-309-03579-1*) Natl Acad Pr.

***National Research Council Staff.** Gravitational Physics: Exploring the Structure of Space & Time. 126p. 1999. pap. 35.00 (*0-309-06635-2*) Natl Acad Pr.

National Research Council Staff. Ground Water at Yucca Mountain: How High Can It Rise? 242p. (Orig.). (C). 1992. pap. text 34.00 (*0-309-04748-X*) Natl Acad Pr.

— Ground Water Vulnerability Assessment: Predicting Relative Contamination Potential under Conditions of Uncertainty. 224p. 1993. text 34.95 (*0-309-04799-4*) Natl Acad Pr.

***National Research Council Staff.** Groundwater & Soil Cleanup: Improving Management of Persistent Contaminants. 304p. 1999. 52.00 (*0-309-06549-6*) Natl Acad Pr.

— Hardrock Mining on Federal Lands. 260p. 1999. pap. 33.00 (*0-309-06596-8*) Natl Acad Pr.

— Harnessing Science & Technology for America's Economic Future: National & Regional Priorities. LC 99-63564. 176p. 1999. pap. 29.00 (*0-309-06538-0*) Natl Acad Pr.

National Research Council Staff. Hazardous Waste Site Management: Water Quality Issues. 224p. 1988. pap. text 27.95 (*0-309-03790-5*) Natl Acad Pr.

— Haze in the Grand Canyon: An Evaluation of the Winter Haze Intensive Tracer Experiment. 108p. 1991. pap. text 17.00 (*0-309-04341-7*) Natl Acad Pr.

— Headline News, Science Views. Jarmut, David, ed. 248p. 1991. 24.95 (*0-309-04480-4*) Natl Acad Pr.

— Headline News, Science Views. Jarmul, David, ed. 248p. 1991. pap. 14.95 (*0-309-04384-0*) Natl Acad Pr.

— Headline News, Science Views II. Jarmul, David, ed. 256p. 1993. pap. 19.95 (*0-309-04834-6*) Natl Acad Pr.

— Health Effects of Exposure to Low Levels of Ionizing Radiation: Beir V. 436p. 1990. pap. text 39.95 (*0-309-03995-9*) Natl Acad Pr.

— Health Effects of Exposure to Radon: BEIR VI. 350p. 1998. text 54.95 (*0-309-05645-4*, Joseph Henry Pr) Natl Acad Pr.

— Health Effects of Exposure to Radon: Time for Reassessment? 114p. (Orig.). (C). 1994. pap. text 24.00 (*0-309-05087-1*) Natl Acad Pr.

— Health Effects of Ingested Fluoride. 206p. (Orig.). (C). 1993. pap. text 35.00 (*0-309-04975-X*) Natl Acad Pr.

— Health Performance Measurement in the Public Sector: Principles & Policies for Implementing an Information Network. Perrin, Edward B. et al, eds. LC 99-6159. 192p. 1999. pap. 32.00 (*0-309-06436-8*, Joseph Henry Pr) Natl Acad Pr.

— Hierarchical Structures in Biology as a Guide for New Materials Technology. 144p. (Orig.). (C). 1994. pap. text 38.00 (*0-309-04638-6*) Natl Acad Pr.

— High Performance Synthetic Fibers for Composites. 148p. 1991. pap. text 19.00 (*0-309-04337-9*) Natl Acad Pr.

— High Stakes: Testing for Tracking, Promotion & Graduation. Heubert, Jay P. & Hauser, Robert M., eds. LC 98-40215. 352p. 1999. text 39.95 (*0-309-06280-2*) Natl Acad Pr.

— Hormonally Active Agents in the Environment. 452p. (C). 2000. 59.95 (*0-309-06419-8*) Natl Acad Pr.

— How People Learn: Brain, Mind, Experience & School. Bransford, John B. et al, eds. LC 98-40290. 280p. 1999. 39.95 (*0-309-06557-7*) Natl Acad Pr.

***National Research Council Staff.** How People Learn: Bridging Research & Practice. Donovan, M. Suzanne et al, eds. 88p. 1999. pap. 18.00 (*0-309-06536-4*) Natl Acad Pr.

National Research Council Staff. Human Dimensions of Climate Variability. Stern, Paul C. & Easterling, William F., eds. 192p. 1999. text 39.95 (*0-309-06573-9*) Natl Acad Pr.

***National Research Council Staff.** Human Dimensions of Global Environmental Change: Research Pathways for the Next Decade. 100p. 1999. pap. 18.00 (*0-309-06592-5*) Natl Acad Pr.

National Research Council Staff. The Human Exploration of Space. LC 98-195220. 174p. 1997. pap. text 31.75 (*0-309-06034-6*) Natl Acad Pr.

— Human Exposure Assessment for Airborne Pollutants: Advances & Opportunities. LC 90-63324. (Illus.). 337p. 1991. pap. 104.50 (*0-608-04830-5*, 206548700004) Bks Demand.

— Human Factors Research Needs for an Aging Population. 110p. 1990. pap. text 15.00 (*0-309-04178-3*) Natl Acad Pr.

— Human Factors Specialists' Education & Utilization: Results of a Survey. Van Cott, Harold P. & Huey, Beverly M., eds. 144p. 1992. pap. text 19.00 (*0-309-04693-9*) Natl Acad Pr.

— Humanities Doctorates in the United States: 1995 Profile. 100p. (C). 1997. pap. text 15.00 (*0-309-05844-9*) Natl Acad Pr.

***National Research Council Staff.** Hydrologic Science Priorities for the U. S. Global Change Research Program: An Initial Assessment. 46p. 1999. pap. 12.00 (*0-309-06648-4*) Natl Acad Pr.

National Research Council Staff. Hydrologic Sciences: Taking Stock & Looking Ahead. LC 98-84689. 180p. 1998. pap. text 35.00 (*0-309-06076-1*) Natl Acad Pr.

— Hypersonic Technology for Military Application. LC 90-60076. (Illus.). 118p. reprint ed. pap. 36.60 (*0-8357-4265-2*, 203706100002) Bks Demand.

***National Research Council Staff.** Identifying Future Drinking Water Contaminants. 276p. 1999. pap. 45.00 (*0-309-06432-5*) Natl Acad Pr.

National Research Council Staff. Immunodeficient Rodents: A Guide to Their Immunobiology, Husbandry, & Use. 260p. 1989. text 29.95 (*0-309-03796-4*) Natl Acad Pr.

***National Research Council Staff.** Impact of Advances in Computing & Communications Technologies on Chemical Science & Technology: Report of a Workshop. 236p. 1999. pap. write for info. (*0-309-06577-1*) Natl Acad Pr.

National Research Council Staff. Implementation Challenges for High-Temperature Composites. (Fifth Lecture International Science Lecture Ser.). 34p. (C). 1996. pap. text 10.00 (*0-309-05830-9*) Natl Acad Pr.

— Improved Fire- & Smoke-Resistant Materials for Commercial Aircraft Interiors: A Proceedings. Committee on Fire- & Smoke-Resistant Materials for, ed. 258p. (Orig.). (C). 1995. pap. text 45.00 (*0-309-05336-6*) Natl Acad Pr.

***National Research Council Staff.** Improving American River Flood Frequency Analyses. 132p. 1999. pap. 30.00 (*0-309-06433-3*) Natl Acad Pr.

National Research Council Staff. Improving America's Schools: The Role of Incentives. Hanushek, Eric A. & Jorgenson, Dale, eds. LC 96-44606. 280p. 1996. text 49.95 (*0-309-05436-2*) Natl Acad Pr.

— Improving Data on America's Aging Population: Summary of a Workshop. Carr, Deborah et al, eds. LC 97-105542. 64p. (C). 1996. pap. text 15.00 (*0-309-05633-0*) Natl Acad Pr.

— Improving Engineering Design: Designing for Competitive Advantage. 120p. 1991. pap. text 19.00 (*0-309-04478-2*) Natl Acad Pr.

— Improving Indicators of the Quality of Science & Mathematics Education in Grades 1-12. Raizen, Senta A. & Murnane, Richard J., eds. 232p. 1988. pap. text 22.95 (*0-309-03740-9*) Natl Acad Pr.

***National Research Council Staff.** Improving Intergroup Relations Among Youth: Summary of a Research Workshop. 94p. 2000. 59.95 (*0-309-06792-8*) Natl Acad Pr.

— Improving Operations & Long-Term Safety of the Waste Isolation Pilot Plants: Interim Report. 56p. 2000. pap. 18.00 (*0-309-06928-9*) Natl Acad Pr.

— Improving Project Management in the Department of Energy. 150p. 1999. pap. 33.00 (*0-309-06626-3*) Natl Acad Pr.

National Research Council Staff. Improving Risk Communication. 352p. (C). 1989. pap. text 29.95 (*0-309-03943-6*) Natl Acad Pr.

***National Research Council Staff.** Improving Student Learning: A Strategic Plan for Education Research & Its Utilization. LC 99-6599. 92p. 1999. pap. 18.00 (*0-309-06489-9*, Joseph Henry Pr) Natl Acad Pr.

National Research Council Staff. Improving Student Learning in Mathematics & Science: The Role of National Standards in State Policy. LC 97-215255. 56p. (C). 1997. pap. text 10.00 (*0-309-05888-0*) Natl Acad Pr.

***National Research Council Staff.** Improving Surface Transportation Security: A Research & Development Strategy. 96p. 1999. pap. 18.00 (*0-309-06776-6*) Natl Acad Pr.

National Research Council Staff. Improving Teacher Preparation & Credentialing Consistent with the National Science Education Standards: Report of a Symposium. LC 97-151612. 90p. (C). 1997. pap. text 15.00 (*0-309-05692-6*) Natl Acad Pr.

— Improving the Continued Airworthiness of Civil Aircraft: A Strategy for the FAA's Aircraft Certification Service. LC 99-181005. 86p. 1998. pap. text 15.00 (*0-309-06185-7*) Natl Acad Pr.

— Improving the Environment: An Evaluation of the DOE's Environmental Management Program. LC 95-73219. 226p. 1996. pap. text 29.00 (*0-309-05440-0*) Natl Acad Pr.

— Improving Theory & Research on Quality Enhancement in Organizations: Report of a Workshop. LC 99-164033. 32p. (C). 1997. pap. text 10.00 (*0-309-05937-2*) Natl Acad Pr.

— In Our Own Backyard: Principles for Effective Improvement of the Nation's Infrastructure. Grant, Albert A. & Lemer, Andrew C., eds. (Studies in Infrastructure Technology & Policy). 128p. (Orig.). (C). 1994. text 25.00 (*0-309-04878-8*) Natl Acad Pr.

— In Situ Bioremediation: When Does It Work? LC 93-5531. 224p. 1993. text 29.95 (*0-309-04896-6*) Natl Acad Pr.

— Industrial Research & Innovation Indicators: Report of a Workshop. LC 98-116461. 62p. (C). 1997. pap. text 15.00 (*0-309-05994-1*) Natl Acad Pr.

***National Research Council Staff.** Industrial Technology Assessments: An Evaluation of the Research Program of the Office of Industry. 70p. 1999. pap. 18.00 (*0-309-06631-X*) Natl Acad Pr.

National Research Council Staff. Infectious Diseases of Mice & Rats. 410p. 1998. reprint ed. text 49.95 (*0-309-06332-9*) Natl Acad Pr.

— Infectious Diseases of Mice & Rats, Set. 415p. 1991. text 65.00 (*0-309-03794-8*) Natl Acad Pr.

— Information Technology for Manufacturing: A Research Agenda. 192p. (Orig.). (C). 1995. pap. text 28.00 (*0-309-05179-7*) Natl Acad Pr.

— Innovations in Ground Water & Soil Cleanup. LC 97-21190. 275p. 1997. 39.95 (*0-309-06358-2*) Natl Acad Pr.

— Inspection & Other Strategies for Assuring Quality in Government Construction. Ledbetter, William B. & Lemer, Andrew C., eds. 84p. 1991. pap. text 19.00 (*0-309-04547-9*) Natl Acad Pr.

— An Interim Assessment of the AEAP's Emissions Characterization & Near-Field Interactions Elements. LC 97-220273. 28p. (C). 1997. pap. text 10.00 (*0-309-05846-5*) Natl Acad Pr.

— Interim Review of the Subsonic Assessment Project: Management, Science, & Goals. LC 97-220037. 44p. (C). 1997. pap. text 10.00 (*0-309-05845-7*) Natl Acad Pr.

— Intermetallic Alloy Development: A Program Evaluation. LC 97-162620. 68p. (C). 1997. pap. text 15.00 (*0-309-05727-2*) Natl Acad Pr.

— An International Directory of Building Research Organizations. 112p. 1988. pap. text 29.95 (*0-309-04027-2*) Natl Acad Pr.

— International Friction & Cooperation in High-Technology Development & Trade: Papers & Proceedings. Wessner, Charles W., ed. LC 97-211790. 394p. (C). 1997. pap. text 64.75 (*0-309-05729-9*) Natl Acad Pr.

— International Network of Global Fiducial Stations: Science & Implementation Issues. 144p. 1991. pap. text 19.00 (*0-309-04543-6*) Natl Acad Pr.

— Investing in Research Infrastructure in the Behavioral & Social Sciences. LC 99-181009. 36p. 1998. pap. text 10.00 (*0-309-06248-9*) Natl Acad Pr.

— Issues in Marine & Intermodal Transportation. LC 93-5129. (Transportation Research Record Ser.: No. 1383). 94p. pap. text 25.00 (*0-309-05453-2*) Transport Res Bd.

— Issues in Potable Reuse: The Viability of Augmenting Drinking Water Supplies with Reclaimed Water. LC 98-19686. 200p. (C). 1998. text 44.95 (*0-309-06416-3*) Natl Acad Pr.

— Issues in Risk Assessment. LC 92-61838. 374p. (Orig.). (C). 1993. pap. text 46.50 (*0-309-04786-2*) Natl Acad Pr.

— Japan's Growing Technological Capability: Implications for the U. S. Economy. Arrison, Thomas S. et al, eds. 244p. (Orig.). (C). 1992. pap. text 30.00 (*0-309-04780-3*) Natl Acad Pr.

— Land Use Planning & Oil & Gas Leasing on Onshore Federal Lands. 180p. 1989. pap. text 25.00 (*0-309-04144-9*) Natl Acad Pr.

— Learning about Assessment, Learning Through Assessment. Driscoll, Mark & Bryant, Deborah, eds. LC 99-173534. 60p. 1998. pap. text 15.00 (*0-309-06133-4*) Natl Acad Pr.

— Learning from TIMSS: Results of the Third International Mathematics & Science Study, Summary of a Symposium. Beatty, Alexandra, ed. LC 98-121443. 56p. (C). 1997. pap. text 15.00 (*0-309-05975-5*) Natl Acad Pr.

— Learning, Remembering, Believing: Enhancing Human Performance. Druckman, Daniel & Bjork, Robert A., eds. 416p. (C). 1994. 39.95 (*0-309-04993-8*) Natl Acad Pr.

— Lessons Learned from the Clementine Mission. LC 97-196894. 38p. (C). 1997. pap. text 10.00 (*0-309-05839-2*) Natl Acad Pr.

— Life Sciences. (Space in the 21st Century Ser.). 160p. 1988. pap. text 19.95 (*0-309-03880-4*) Natl Acad Pr.

— Linking Science & Technology to Society's Environmental Goals. LC 96-47176. 544p. 1996. text 69.95 (*0-309-05578-4*) Natl Acad Pr.

— Liquid Crystalline Polymers. (Illus.). 122p. (Orig.). (C). 1990. pap. text 17.00 (*0-309-04231-3*) Natl Acad Pr.

— Live Fire Testing of the F-22. 142p. (Orig.). (C). 1995. pap. text 35.00 (*0-309-05333-1*) Natl Acad Pr.

— Livestock. (Managing Global Genetic Resources Ser.). 296p. (C). 1993. text 34.95 (*0-309-04394-8*) Natl Acad Pr.

— Living on a Restless Earth: The Challenge of Earthquake Science. (Illus.). 276p. 1998. text 49.95 (*0-309-06562-3*) Natl Acad Pr.

— Local Fiscal Effects of Illegal Immigration: Report of a Workshop. Edmonston, Barry & Lee, Ronald, eds. LC 97-102935. 40p. (C). 1996. pap. text 10.00 (*0-309-05592-X*) Natl Acad Pr.

— Longitudinal Surveys of Children. West, Kirsten K. et al, eds. LC 98-87275. 128p. (C). 1998. pap. text 24.75 (*0-309-06192-X*) Natl Acad Pr.

— Low-Frequency Sound & Marine Mammals: Current Knowledge & Research Needs. LC 93-61700. (Illus.). 93p. 1994. pap. 30.00 (*0-608-04831-3*, 206548800004) Bks Demand.

— Maintaining U. S. Leadership in Aeronautics: Breakthrough Technologies to Meet Future Air & Space Transportation Needs & Goals. LC 98-226157. 148p. 1998. pap. text 27.75 (*0-309-06226-8*) Natl Acad Pr.

— Making Money Matter: Financing America's Schools. Ladd, Helen F. & Hansen, Janet S., eds. 368p. 1999. 49.95 (*0-309-06528-3*, Joseph Henry Pr) Natl Acad Pr.

— Management of Technology: The Hidden Competitive Advantage. LC HD0045.T36. 51p. reprint ed. pap. 30.00 (*0-8357-6917-8*, 203797600009) Bks Demand.

— Managing Wastewater in Coastal Urban Areas. LC 93-1845. 496p. (Orig.). (C). 1993. text 49.95 (*0-309-04826-5*) Natl Acad Pr.

— Managing Water Resources in the West under Conditions of Climate Uncertainty: A Proceedings. 358p. (C). 1991. pap. text 39.00 (*0-309-04677-7*) Natl Acad Pr.

— Manufacturing Process Controls for the Industries of the Future. LC 99-177575. (Compass Ser.). 72p. 1998. pap. text 15.00 (*0-309-06184-9*) Natl Acad Pr.

— The March 5, 1987 Ecuador Earthquake: Mass Wasting & Socioeconomic Effects. (Natural Disaster Studies: Vol. 5). 184p. 1991. pap. text 19.00 (*0-309-04444-8*) Natl Acad Pr.

— Marine Structures Research Recommendations: Recommendations for the Interagency Ship Structure Committee's 1998-1999 Research Program. 108p. (C). 1997. pap. text 21.75 (*0-309-05786-8*) Natl Acad Pr.

— Materials for High-Density Electronic Packaging & Interconnection. 156p. (C). 1990. pap. text 19.00 (*0-309-04233-X*) Natl Acad Pr.

— Materials Research Agenda for the Automobile & Aircraft Industries. 83p. 1993. pap. text 25.00 (*0-309-04985-7*) Natl Acad Pr.

***National Research Council Staff.** Materials Science & Engineering: Forging Stronger Links to Users. 124p. 1999. pap. 29.00 (*0-309-06826-6*) Natl Acad Pr.

National Research Council Staff. Mathematical Challenges from Theoretical/Computational Chemistry. 144p. 1995. pap. text 25.00 (*0-309-05097-9*) Natl Acad Pr.

— Mathematics & Physics of Emerging Biomedical Imaging. 260p. (Orig.). 1996. pap. text 29.00 (*0-309-05387-0*) Natl Acad Pr.

— Mathematics & Science Education Around the World: What Can We Learn from the Survey of Mathematics & Science Opportunities (SMSO) & the Third International Mathematics & Science Study (TIMSS) LC 97-105406. 32p. (C). 1996. pap. text 10.00 (*0-309-05631-4*) Natl Acad Pr.

***National Research Council Staff.** Mathematics Education in the Middle Grades: Teaching to Meet the Needs of Middle Grades Learners & to Maintain High Expectations : Proceedings of a National Convocation & Action Conferences. LC 99-50765. 270p. 1999. pap. 29.00 (*0-309-06797-9*) Natl Acad Pr.

National Research Council Staff. Maximizing U. S. Interests in Science & Technology Relations with Japan. 148p. (C). 1997. pap. text 28.00 (*0-309-05884-8*) Natl Acad Pr.

***National Research Council Staff.** Measuring a Changing Nation: Modern Methods for the 2000 Census. LC 99-213866. 124p. 1999. pap. 28.75 (*0-309-06444-9*) Natl Acad Pr.

National Research Council Staff. Measuring & Understanding Coastal Processes. 130p. 1989. pap. text 15.00 (*0-309-04129-5*) Natl Acad Pr.

***National Research Council Staff.** Measuring Health Performance in the Public Sector: A Summary of Two Reports. 48p. 1999. pap. 12.00 (*0-309-06583-6*) Natl Acad Pr.

National Research Council Staff. Measuring the Government Sector of the U. S. Economic Accounts. Slater, Courtenay M. & David, Martin H., eds. 40p. 1998. pap. text 10.00 (*0-309-06135-0*) Natl Acad Pr.

***National Research Council Staff.** Measuring the Science & Engineering Enterprise: Priorities for the Division of Science Resources Studies. 160p. 2000. pap. 34.75 (*0-309-06892-4*) Natl Acad Pr.

National Research Council Staff. Meeting Megacity Challenges: A Role for Innovation & Technology. 150p. (Orig.). (C). 1998. pap. 30.00 (*0-309-05538-5*) Natl Acad Pr.

***National Research Council Staff.** Meeting Research & Education Needs in Coastal Engineering. 74p. 1999. pap. 18.00 (*0-309-06381-7*) Natl Acad Pr.

National Research Council Staff. Meeting the Nation's Needs for Biomedical & Behavioral Scientists. 174p. (Orig.). (C). 1994. pap. text 27.00 (*0-309-05086-3*) Natl Acad Pr.

— Meeting vs. Energy Resource Needs: The Energy Resources Program of the U. S. Geological Survey. 85p. (C). 1998. pap. text 15.00 (*0-309-06283-7*) Natl Acad Pr.

— The Meteorological Buoy & Coastal Marine Automated Network for the United States. LC 98-85592. (Compass Ser.). xii, 97 p. 1998. pap. text 15.00 (*0-309-06088-5*) Natl Acad Pr.

***National Research Council Staff.** Methyl Bromide Risk Characterization in California. 112p. 2000. pap. 26.75 (*0-309-07087-2*) Natl Acad Pr.

— Mexico City's Water Supply: Improving the Outlook for Sustainability. 256p. 1995. pap. text 30.00 (*0-309-05245-9*) Natl Acad Pr.

— Microbial & Phenotypic Definition of Rats & Mice: Proceedings of the 1998 U. S. - Japan Conference. 110p. 1999. pap. 26.25 (*0-309-06591-7*) Natl Acad Pr.

National Research Council Staff. Microelectromechanical Systems: Advanced Materials & Fabrication Methods. 76p. (C). 1997. pap. text 15.00 (*0-309-05980-1*) Natl Acad Pr.

— Minding the Helm: Marine Navigation & Piloting. 528p. (C). 1994. text 54.95 (*0-309-04829-X*) Natl Acad Pr.

— Modeling & Simulation: Linking Entertainment & Defense. LC 97-68732. 175p. 1997. pap. text 29.00 (*0-309-05842-2*) Natl Acad Pr.

— Modeling Human Organizational Behavior: Application to Military Simulations. Pew, Richard W. & Mavor, Anne S., eds. LC 98-19705. 424p. 1998. pap. text 47.00 (*0-309-06096-6*) Natl Acad Pr.

***National Research Council Staff.** Monoclonal Antibody Production. 74p. 1999. pap. 18.00 (*0-309-06447-3*) Natl Acad Pr.

National Research Council Staff. More Than Screen Deep: Toward Every-Citizen Interfaces to the Nation's Information Infrastructure. LC 97-21211. 275p. 1997. pap. 29.95 (*0-309-06357-4*) Natl Acad Pr.

N

— Moving Beyond Myths: Revitalizing Undergraduate Mathematics. 80p. 1991. pap. text 7.95 (*0-309-04489-8*) Natl Acad Pr.

National Research Council Staff. Myths & Tradeoffs: The Role of Tests in Undergraduate Admissions. Beatty, Alexandra et al, eds. 58p. 1999. pap. 18.00 (*0-309-06597-6*) Natl Acad Pr.

National Research Council Staff. The National Energy Modeling System. LC 93-205713. 164p. 1992. pap. text 19.00 (*0-309-04634-3*) Natl Acad Pr.

— National Science Education Standards. 272p. 1995. pap. 19.95 (*0-309-05326-9*) Natl Acad Pr.

— The Nature & Role of Algebra in the K - 14 Curriculum: Proceedings of a National Symposium. LC 99-179839. 206p. (C). 1998. pap. text 36.75 (*0-309-06147-4*) Natl Acad Pr.

— Nature's Numbers: Expanding the National Economic Accounts to Include the Environment. Nordhaus, William D. & Kokkelenberg, Edward C., eds. LC 99-6236. 262p. 1999. text 44.95 (*0-309-07151-8*) Natl Acad Pr.

— Naval Expeditionary Logistics: Enabling Operational Maneuver from the Sea. 110p. (C). 1999. pap. text 26.25 (*0-309-06429-5*) Natl Acad Pr.

— Neem: A Tree for Solving Problems. 152p. (C). 1992. pap. text 23.00 (*0-309-04686-6*) Natl Acad Pr.

— New Directions in Water Resources Planning for the U. S. Army Corps of Engineers. 120p. (C). 1999. pap. text 39.00 (*0-309-06097-4*) Natl Acad Pr.

— A New Era for Irrigation. 225p. 1996. text 39.95 (*0-309-05331-5*) Natl Acad Pr.

— New Horizons in Electrochemical Science & Technology. 164p. 1987. pap. text 17.95 (*0-309-03735-2*) Natl Acad Pr.

— A New Science Strategy for Space Astronomy & Astrophysics. LC 97-193223. 92p. (C). 1997. pap. text 15.00 (*0-309-05827-9*) Natl Acad Pr.

— New Strategies for America's Watersheds. LC 98-58156. 328p. (C). 1999. text 49.00 (*0-309-06417-1*) Natl Acad Pr.

— New Strategies for New Challenges: Corporate Innovation in the United States & Japan. 54p. 1999. pap. 18.00 (*0-309-05848-1*) Natl Acad Pr.

N

— New Vistas in Transatlantic Science & Technology Cooperation. Wessner, Charles W., ed. 178p. 1999. pap. 38.00 (*0-309-06197-0*) Natl Acad Pr.

National Research Council Staff. 1999 Assessment of the Office of Naval Research's Air & Surface Weapons Technology Program. 46p. 1999. pap. 12.00 (*0-309-06632-8*) Natl Acad Pr.

National Research Council Staff. NOAA's Arctic Research Initiative: Proceedings of a Workshop. LC 98-138586. 190p. (C). 1997. pap. text 34.00 (*0-309-05992-5*) Natl Acad Pr.

— Nonconventional Concrete Technologies: Renewal of the Highway Infrastructure. LC 97-170982. 124p. (C). 1997. pap. text 24.25 (*0-309-05687-X*) Natl Acad Pr.

— Nonlinear Science. LC 97-220788. 50p. 1997. pap. text 10.00 (*0-309-05843-0*) Natl Acad Pr.

— Nuclear Physics: The Core of Matter, the Fuel of Stars. LC 98-89539. 222p. (C). 1999. pap. 42.00 (*0-309-06276-4*) Natl Acad Pr.

— Nuclear Power: Technical & Institutional Options for the Future. 234p. (C). 1992. pap. text 27.00 (*0-309-04395-6*) Natl Acad Pr.

— Nuclear Wastes: Technologies for Separations, Transmutation. 592p. (Orig.). (C). 1996. text 79.95 (*0-309-05226-2*) Natl Acad Pr.

— The Nuclear Weapons Complex: Management for Health, Safety & the Environment. 156p. 1989. pap. text 19.00 (*0-309-04179-1*) Natl Acad Pr.

— Nutrient Adequacy: Assessment Using Food Consumption Surveys. 160p. 1986. pap. text 19.95 (*0-309-03634-8*) Natl Acad Pr.

— Nutrient Requirements of Beef Cattle. 7th rev. ed. (Nutrient Requirements of Domestic Animals Ser.). 250p. 1996. pap. text 29.95 (*0-309-05426-5*) Natl Acad Pr.

National Research Council, Staff. Nutrient Requirements of Dairy Cattle: Update 1989. 6th rev. ed. 168p. 1989. pap. text 19.95 (*0-309-03826-X*) Natl Acad Pr.

National Research Council Staff. Nutrient Requirements of Dogs, 1985. rev. ed. 88p. 1985. reprint ed. pap. text 24.95 (*0-309-03496-5*) Natl Acad Pr.

— Nutrient Requirements of Horses, Set. 5th rev. ed. 112p. 1989. pap. text 24.95 (*0-309-03989-4*) Natl Acad Pr.

— Nutrient Requirements of Laboratory Animals. 4th rev. ed. (Nutrient Requirements of Domestic Animals Ser.). 176p. (C). 1995. pap. text 29.95 (*0-309-05126-6*) Natl Acad Pr.

— Nutrient Requirements of Laboratory Animals: Rat, Mouse, Gerbil, Guinea Pig, Hamster, Vole, Fish. 3rd rev. ed. LC 78-15118. (Nutrient Requirements of Domestic Animals Ser.: No. 10). (Illus.). 104p. reprint ed. pap. 32.30 (*0-7837-5983-5*, 204579000007) Bks Demand.

— Nutrient Requirements of Mink & Foxes. 2nd rev. ed. LC 82-14486. (Nutrient Requirements of Domestic Animals Ser.: Vol. 7). 80p. 1982. reprint ed. pap. 30.00 (*0-608-03814-8*, 206466400009) Bks Demand.

— Nutrient Requirements of Non-Human Primates. LC 78-60949. (Nutrient Requirements of Domestic Animals Ser.: No. 14). 93p. reprint ed. pap. 30.00 (*0-7837-2778-X*, 204316900006) Bks Demand.

— Nutrient Requirements of Sheep. 6th rev. ed. (Nutrient Requirements of Domestic Animals Ser.). 112p. 1985. pap. text 19.95 (*0-309-03596-1*) Natl Acad Pr.

— Nutrient Requirements of Swine. 10th rev. ed. LC 98-9007. 210p. (C). 1998. pap. text 39.95 (*0-309-05993-3*) Natl Acad Pr.

— Nutrient Requirements of Swine, 1988. 9th rev. ed. 104p. 1988. pap. text 14.95 (*0-309-03779-4*) Natl Acad Pr.

— Nutritional Energetics of Domestic Animals & Glossary of Energy Terms. 2nd rev. ed. LC 80-28912. 60p. (Orig.). reprint ed. pap. 30.00 (*0-8357-4998-3*, 203793100009) Bks Demand.

— Oceanography in the Next Decade: Building New Partnerships. LC 92-34458. 216p. (C). 1992. pap. text 39.95 (*0-309-04794-3*) Natl Acad Pr.

— Office Workstations in the Home. LC 85-3022. 168p. 1985. pap. text 19.95 (*0-309-03483-3*) Natl Acad Pr.

— On the Shoulders of Giants: New Approaches to Numeracy. Steen, Lynn A., ed. 144p. 1990. 17.95 (*0-309-04234-8*) Natl Acad Pr.

— On Time to the Doctorate: A Study of the Lengthening Time to Completion for Doctorates in Science & Engineering. 163p. 1990. pap. text 19.00 (*0-309-04085-X*) Natl Acad Pr.

— Opportunities & Priorities in Arctic Geoscience. 80p. 1991. pap. text 19.00 (*0-309-04485-5*) Natl Acad Pr.

— Opportunities in Biology. LC 89-13098. (Illus.). 468p. reprint ed. pap. 145.10 (*0-7837-5356-X*, 204511800005) Bks Demand.

— Opportunities in Chemistry. 334p. (C). 1985. text 34.95 (*0-309-03633-X*) Natl Acad Pr.

— Orbital Debris: A Technical Assessment. 224p. (C). 1995. text 39.95 (*0-309-05125-8*) Natl Acad Pr.

National Research Council Staff. Our Common Journey: A Transition Toward Sustainability. 360p. 1999. pap. 60.00 (*0-309-06783-9*) Natl Acad Pr.

National Research Council Staff. Our Seabed Frontier: Challenges & Choices. 150p. 1989. pap. text 17.00 (*0-309-04126-0*) Natl Acad Pr.

— Overview. (Space Science in the Twenty-First Century Series: Imperatives for the Decades 1995 to 2015). 108p. 1988. pap. text 14.95 (*0-309-03838-3*) Natl Acad Pr.

— Ozone Depletion, Greenhouse Gases, & Climate Change: Proceedings of a Joint Symposium by the Board of Atmospheric Sciences & Climate & the Committee on Global Change. LC 88-31544. (Illus.). 136p. reprint ed. pap. 42.20 (*0-8357-4215-6*, 203699700003) Bks Demand.

— Partners on the Frontier: The Future of U. S.-Russian Cooperation in Science & Technology. LC 98-84557. 35p. (C). 1998. pap. text 10.00 (*0-309-06042-7*) Natl Acad Pr.

— Path to the Ph. D. Measuring Graduate Attrition in the Sciences & Humanities. LC 96-67827. 90p. (Orig.). 1997. pap. text 29.00 (*0-309-05482-6*) Natl Acad Pr.

— Pathological Gambling. LC 99-6598. 300p. 1999. 27.95 (*0-309-06571-2*) Natl Acad Pr.

— Pay Equity: Empirical Inquiries. Michael, Robert T. et al, eds. 272p. 1989. pap. text 27.95 (*0-309-03978-9*) Natl Acad Pr.

— Pay Now or Pay Later: Controlling Cost of Ownership from Design Throughout the Service Life of Public Buildings. 72p. (C). 1991. pap. text 19.00 (*0-309-04481-2*) Natl Acad Pr.

— Peer Review in Environmental Technology Programs. LC 99-191406. 126p. (C). 1999. pap. text 29.00 (*0-309-06338-8*) Natl Acad Pr.

— Peer Review in the Department of Energy - Office of Science & Technology: Interim Report. 68p. (C). 1997. pap. text 15.00 (*0-309-05943-7*) Natl Acad Pr.

— People & Pixels: Linking Remote Sensing & Social Science. LC 98-8945. 1998. pap. 30.00 (*0-309-06408-2*) Natl Acad Pr.

— Performance Assessment in the Workplace Vol. I: Technical Issues. Wigdor, Alexandra K. & Green, Bert F., Jr., eds. 344p. 1991. text 45.00 (*0-309-04539-8*) Natl Acad Pr.

National Research Council Staff. Perspectives on Biodiversity: Valuing Its Role in an Everchanging World. 168p. 1999. pap. 37.00 (*0-309-06581-X*) Natl Acad Pr.

— The Pervasive Role of Science, Technology & Health in Foreign Policy: Imperatives for the Department of State. 124p. 1999. pap. 29.00 (*0-309-06785-5*) Natl Acad Pr.

National Research Council Staff. Pesticides in the Diets of Infants & Children. LC 93-14961. 408p. 1993. pap. text 47.95 (*0-309-04875-3*) Natl Acad Pr.

— Photonics: Maintaining Competitiveness in the Information Era. 112p. 1988. pap. text 14.95 (*0-309-03940-1*) Natl Acad Pr.

— Planetary & Lunar Exploration. (Space Science in the Twenty-First Century Ser.). 128p. (C). 1988. pap. text 14.95 (*0-309-03885-5*) Natl Acad Pr.

— Plant Biology Research & Training for the 21st Century. 80p. (C). 1992. pap. text 19.00 (*0-309-04679-3*) Natl Acad Pr.

— Plasmas & Fluids. (Physics Through the 1990's Ser.). 336p. 1986. pap. text 31.50 (*0-309-03548-1*) Natl Acad Pr.

— Policy Issues in Aerospace Offsets: Report of a Workshop. Wessner, Charles W. & Wolff, Alan W., eds. LC 97-220794. 44p. (C). 1997. pap. text 10.00 (*0-309-05840-6*) Natl Acad Pr.

— Population Dynamics of Kenya. Brass, William & Jolly, Carole L., eds. (Population Dynamics of Sub-Saharan Africa Ser.). 200p. (Orig.). (C). 1993. pap. text 33.00 (*0-309-04943-1*) Natl Acad Pr.

— Population Dynamics of Senegal. Pison, Gilles et al, eds. LC 95-68873. (Population Dynamics of Sub-Saharan Africa Ser.). 272p. (Orig.). (C). 1995. pap. text 35.00 (*0-309-05280-7*) Natl Acad Pr.

— Population Growth & Economic Development: Policy Questions. 120p. (Orig.). (C). 1986. pap. text 24.95 (*0-309-03641-0*) Natl Acad Pr.

— Post-Cold War Conflict Deterrence. 244p. (Orig.). 1997. pap. 47.00 (*0-309-05639-X*, Joseph Henry Pr) Natl Acad Pr.

— Potential Applications of Concentrated Solar Photons. 90p. 1991. pap. text 19.00 (*0-309-04576-2*) Natl Acad Pr.

National Research Council Staff. The Practicality of Pulsed Fast Neutron Transmission Spectroscopy for Aviation Security. 58p. 1999. pap. 18.00 (*0-309-06449-X*) Natl Acad Pr.

National Research Council Staff. Precollege Science & Mathematics Teachers: Monitoring Supply, Demand, & Quality. 266p. 1990. pap. text 25.00 (*0-309-04197-X*) Natl Acad Pr.

— Preparing for the 2000 Census: Interim Report II. LC 97-214302. 104p. (C). 1997. pap. text 21.25 (*0-309-05880-5*) Natl Acad Pr.

— Preparing for the Workplace: Charting a Course for Federal Postsecondary Training Policy. Hansen, Janet S., ed. LC 93-37934. 224p. (C). 1993. text 34.95 (*0-309-04935-0*) Natl Acad Pr.

— Preservation of Historical Records. 108p. 1986. text 17.95 (*0-309-03681-X*) Natl Acad Pr.

— Preserving Scientific Data on Our Physical Universe: A New Strategy for Archiving the Nation's Scientific Information Resources. LC 94-68991. 80p. 1995. pap. text 25.00 (*0-309-05186-X*) Natl Acad Pr.

— Preserving Strength While Meeting Challenges: Summary Report of a Workshop on Actions for the Mathematical Sciences. LC 97-216317. 92p. (C). 1997. pap. text 15.00 (*0-309-05883-X*) Natl Acad Pr.

— Preventing & Mitigating AIDS in Sub-Saharan Africa: Research & Data Priorities for the Social & Behavioral Science. Cohen, Barney & Trussell, James, eds. LC 96-11347. 368p. (Orig.). 1996. pap. text 39.00 (*0-309-05480-X*) Natl Acad Pr.

— Preventing Drug Abuse: What Do We Know? Gerstein, Dean R. & Green, Lawrence W., eds. 176p. 1993. text 32.95 (*0-309-04627-0*) Natl Acad Pr.

— Preventing Reading Difficulties in Young Children. Snow, Catherine E. et al, eds. LC 98-9031. 350p. (C). 1998. text 35.95 (*0-309-06418-X*) Natl Acad Pr.

— Priorities for Coastal Ecosystem Science. 116p. (Orig.). (C). 1995. pap. text 29.00 (*0-309-05096-0*) Natl Acad Pr.

— Probability & Algorithms. 188p. (Orig.). (C). 1992. pap. text 26.00 (*0-309-04776-5*) Natl Acad Pr.

— The Proceedings: Fifth International Conference on Numerical Ship Hydrodynamics, No. 5. 744p. (C). 1990. text 50.00 (*0-309-04241-0*) Natl Acad Pr.

— Productive Agriculture & a Quality Environment. LC S 0601.N28. 335p. reprint ed. pap. 103.90 (*0-608-13707-3*, 205529000013) Bks Demand.

— Proliferation Concerns: Assessing U.S. Efforts to Help Contain Nuclear & Other Dangerous Materials & Technologies in the Former Soviet Union. 160p. (Orig.). 1997. pap. 36.00 (*0-309-05741-8*, Joseph Henry Pr) Natl Acad Pr.

National Research Council Staff. Protecting Nuclear Weapons Material in Russia. 64p. 1999. pap. 18.00 (*0-309-06547-X*) Natl Acad Pr.

National Research Council Staff. Protecting the Space Shuttle from Meteoroids & Orbital Debris. 70p. (C). Date not set. pap. text 15.00 (*0-309-05988-7*) Natl Acad Pr.

— Providing National Statistics on Health & Social Welfare Programs in an Era of Change: Summary of a Workshop. Citro, Constance F. et al, eds. LC 98-207848. 72p. 1998. pap. text 15.00 (*0-309-06040-0*) Natl Acad Pr.

— Prudent Practices in the Laboratory: Handling & Disposal of Chemicals. 448p. (C). 1995. text 69.95 (*0-309-05229-7*) Natl Acad Pr.

— The Psychological Well-Being of Nonhuman Primates. LC 98-40103. 130p. (Orig.). (C). 1998. 35.00 (*0-309-05233-5*) Natl Acad Pr.

— Putting Biotechnology to Work: Bioprocess Engineering. LC 92-61717. 132p. (Orig.). (C). 1992. pap. text 24.00 (*0-309-04785-4*) Natl Acad Pr.

National Research Council Staff. A Question of Balance: Private Rights & the Public Interest in Scientific. 158p. 1999. pap. 29.00 (*0-309-06825-8*) Natl Acad Pr.

National Research Council Staff. Racial & Ethnic Differences in the Health of Older Americans. Martin, Linda G. & Soldo, Beth J., eds. LC 97-33731. 450p. (Orig.). (C). 1997. pap. 42.00 (*0-309-05489-3*) Natl Acad Pr.

National Research Council Staff. Radiation & the International Space Station: Recommendations to Reduce Risk. 92p. 2000. pap. 25.25 (*0-309-06885-1*) Natl Acad Pr.

National Research Council Staff. Radiation-Dose Reconstruction for Epidemiologic Uses. 140p. (C). 1995. text 34.95 (*0-309-05099-5*) Natl Acad Pr.

— Radiological Assessments for the Resettlement of Rongelap in the Republic of the Marshall Islands. 124p. (Orig.). (C). 1994. pap. text 37.00 (*0-309-05049-9*) Natl Acad Pr.

National Research Council Staff. Realizing the Potential of C4I: Fundamental Challenges. 298p. 1999. pap. 42.00 (*0-309-06485-6*, Joseph Henry Pr) Natl Acad Pr.

National Research Council Staff. A Reassessment of the Marine Salvage Posture of the United States. LC 94-68622. 144p. (Orig.). (C). 1994. pap. text 33.00 (*0-309-05149-5*) Natl Acad Pr.

— Recapitalizing the Navy: A Strategy for Managing the Infrastructure. LC 99-182093. 146p. 1999. pap. text 32.50 (*0-309-06335-3*) Natl Acad Pr.

— Recognition & Alleviation of Pain & Distress in Laboratory Animals. 160p. 1992. text 29.95 (*0-309-04275-5*) Natl Acad Pr.

— Recommendations for the Disposal of Chemical Agents & Munitions. 220p. (Orig.). (C). 1994. pap. text 34.00 (*0-309-05046-4*) Natl Acad Pr.

National Research Council Staff. Reconciling Observations of Global Temperature Change. 104p. 2000. pap. 25.25 (*0-309-06891-6*) Natl Acad Pr.

National Research Council Staff. Recruitment, Retention, & Utiliation of Federal Scientists & Engineers. 192p. 1990. pap. text 17.00 (*0-309-04330-1*) Natl Acad Pr.

— Reducing Hazardous Waste Generation: An Evaluation & a Call for Action. 76p. 1985. pap. text 9.95 (*0-309-03498-1*) Natl Acad Pr.

— Reducing the Costs of Space Science Research Missions: Proceedings of a Workshop. LC 97-220849. 84p. (C). 1997. pap. text 15.00 (*0-309-05829-5*) Natl Acad Pr.

National Research Council Staff. Reducing the Logistics Burden for the Army after Next: Doing More with Less. 224p. 1999. pap. 45.75 (*0-309-06378-7*) Natl Acad Pr.

National Research Council Staff. Regulating Pesticides in Food: The Delaney Paradox. LC 87-61095. (Illus.). 288p. reprint ed. pap. 89.30 (*0-7837-5984-3*, 204579100007) Bks Demand.

— Renewing U. S. Mathematics: A Plan for the 1990s. 148p. (C). 1990. pap. text 15.00 (*0-309-04228-3*) Natl Acad Pr.

— Report of the Observer Panel for the U. S. - Japan Earthquake: Policy Symposium. LC 97-141593. 72p. (C). 1997. pap. text 15.00 (*0-309-05691-8*) Natl Acad Pr.

National Research Council Staff. Reporting District-Level NAEP Data: Summary of a Workshop. DeVito, Pasquale J. & Koenig, Judith A., eds. 66p. 2000. pap. 18.00 (*0-309-06893-2*) Natl Acad Pr.

National Research Council Staff. Representing Human Behavior in Military Simulations: Interim Report. Pew, Richard W. & Mavor, Anne S., eds. 62p. (C). 1997. pap. text 15.00 (*0-309-05747-7*) Natl Acad Pr.

National Research Council Staff. Research Agenda for Test Methods & Models to Simulate the Accelerated Aging of Infrastructure Materials: Report of a Workshop. 160p. 1999. pap. 34.75 (*0-309-06384-1*) Natl Acad Pr.

National Research Council Staff. Research & Education Reform: Roles for the Office of Educational Research & Improvement. Atkinson, R. C. & Jackson, G. B., eds. 204p. (C). 1992. pap. text 29.00 (*0-309-04729-3*) Natl Acad Pr.

— Research Directions in Computational Mechanics: A Series. 144p. (C). 1991. pap. text 19.00 (*0-309-04648-3*) Natl Acad Pr.

— Research Management & Peer Review Practices in the U.S. Environmental Protection Agency. 150p. 1998. pap. text 34.00 (*0-309-06552-6*) Natl Acad Pr.

National Research Council Staff. Research on Power-Frequency Fields Completed under the Energy Policy Act of 1992. 112p. 1999. pap. 26.75 (*0-309-06543-7*) Natl Acad Pr.

National Research Council Staff. Research Opportunities for Materials with Ultrafine Microstuctures. 130p. 1990. pap. text 19.00 (*0-309-04183-X*) Natl Acad Pr.

— Research Priorities for Airborne Particulate Matter: Immediate Priorities & a Long-Range Research Portfolio. LC 98-85286. 216p. 1998. pap. text 35.00 (*0-309-06094-X*) Natl Acad Pr.

National Research Council Staff. Research Priorities for Airborne Particulate Matter Vol. II: Evaluating Research Progress & Updating the Portfolio. 128p. 1999. pap. 28.00 (*0-309-06638-7*) Natl Acad Pr.

National Research Council Staff. Research Required to Support Comprehensive Nuclear Test Ban Treaty Monitoring. LC 97-68150. 150p. (C). 1997. pap. text 39.00 (*0-309-05826-0*) Natl Acad Pr.

National Research Council Staff. Research Teams & Partnerships: Trends in the Chemical Sciences, Report of a Workshop. 158p. 2000. pap. 34.50 (*0-309-06827-4*) Natl Acad Pr.

National Research Council Staff. Reshaping School Mathematics: A Philosophy & Framework for Curriculum. 72p. 1990. pap. text 7.95 (*0-309-04187-2*) Natl Acad Pr.

— Reshaping the Graduate Education of Scientists & Engineers. LC 95-69122. 220p. 1995. pap. text 29.00 (*0-309-05285-8*) Natl Acad Pr.

— Responding to Changes in Sea Level: Engineering Implications. LC 87-21965. 160p. 1987. pap. text 24.95 (*0-309-03781-6*) Natl Acad Pr.

— Restoring & Protecting Marine Habitat: The Role of Engineering & Technology. 212p. (Orig.). (C). 1994. pap. text 27.00 (*0-309-04843-5*) Natl Acad Pr.

National Research Council Staff. Review & Evaluation of Alternative Technologies for Demilitarization of Assembled Chemical Weapons. 266p. 1999. pap. 52.75 (*0-309-06639-5*) Natl Acad Pr.

National Research Council Staff. Review & Recommendations: The Uses of Microsimulation Modeling, Vol. 1: Review & Recommendations. (Improving Information for Social Policy Decisions Ser.: Vol. 1). 360p. (C). 1991. pap. text 35.00 (*0-309-04541-X*) Natl Acad Pr.

— A Review of Decontamination & Recommissioning Technology Development Programs at the Department of Energy. LC 99-207392. 75p. (C). 1998. pap. text 15.00 (*0-309-06281-0*) Natl Acad Pr.

National Research Council Staff. Review of EPA's Environmental Monitoring & Assessment Program: Overall Evaluation. 178p. 1995. pap. text 35.00 (*0-309-05286-6*) Natl Acad Pr.

— A Review of NASA's 'Atmospheric Effects of Stratospheric Aircraft' Project. 60p. 1999. pap. 18.00 (*0-309-06589-5*) Natl Acad Pr.

National Research Council Staff. Review of NASA's Distributed Active Archive Centers. 156p. 1999. pap. 49.00 (*0-309-06331-0*) Natl Acad Pr.

— Review of New York State Low-Level Radioactive Waste Siting Process. LC 96-69080. 306p. (Orig.). 1996. pap. text 35.00 (*0-309-05539-3*) Natl Acad Pr.

An Asterisk (*) at the beginning of an entry indicates that the title is appearing for the first time.

— Review of Northeast Fishery Stock Assessments. LC 98-84912. 160p. 1998. pap. text 42.00 (*0-309-06030-3*) Natl Acad Pr.

— Review of Recommendations for Probabilistic Seismic Hazard Analysis: Guidance on Uncertainty & Use of Experts. LC 97-106769. 84p. (C). 1996. pap. text 15.00 (*0-309-05632-2*) Natl Acad Pr.

— A Review of the Department of Energy Classification: Policy & Practice. LC 95-70717. 128p. (Orig.). (C). 1995. pap. text 29.00 (*0-309-05338-2*) Natl Acad Pr.

— Review of the Department of Energy's Inertial Confinement Fusion Program: The National Ignition Facility. 64p. (C). 1997. pap. text 15.00 (*0-309-05778-7*) Natl Acad Pr.

***National Research Council Staff.** Review of the Draft Plan for the Modernization & Associated Restructuring Demonstration. (Toward a New National Weather Service Ser.). 30p. 1999. pap. 12.00 (*0-309-06482-1*) Natl Acad Pr.

— Review of the Need for a Large-Scale Test Facility for Research on the Effects of Extreme Winds on Structures. 48p. 1999. pap. 12.00 (*0-309-06483-X*) Natl Acad Pr.

National Research Council Staff. Review of the Prince William Sound, Alaska, Risk Assessment Study. 78p. 1998. pap. text 15.00 (*0-309-06078-8*) Natl Acad Pr.

— Review of the Research & Development Plan for the Office of Advanced Automotive Technologies. LC 98-177353. 80p. 1998. pap. text 15.00 (*0-309-05997-6*) Natl Acad Pr.

— Review of the Research Program of the New Partnership for a New Generation of Vehicles: Third Report. LC 97-66882. 156p. 1997. pap. 32.00 (*0-309-05776-0*) Natl Acad Pr.

***National Research Council Staff.** Review of the Research Program of the Partnership for a New Generation of Vehicles: Fifth Report. LC 99-62352. 124p. 1999. pap. 32.00 (*0-309-06443-0*, Joseph Henry Pr) Natl Acad Pr.

National Research Council Staff. Review of the Research Program of the Partnership for a New Generation of Vehicles: Fourth Report. LC 98-84940. 136p. 1998. pap. text 32.00 (*0-309-06087-7*) Natl Acad Pr.

***National Research Council Staff.** Review of the Research Strategy for Biomass-Derived Transportation Fuels. 60p. 1999. pap. 18.00 (*0-309-06779-0*) Natl Acad Pr.

— A Review of the Sandia Science & Technology Park Initiative. Wessner, Charles W., ed. 122p. 1999. pap. 28.25 (*0-309-06199-7*) Natl Acad Pr.

National Research Council Staff. Review of the Systemization of the Tooele Chemical Agent Disposal Facility. LC 96-67977. 134p. (Orig.). 1996. pap. text 34.00 (*0-309-05486-9*) Natl Acad Pr.

***National Research Council Staff.** Review of the U. S. Army's Health Risk Assessments for Oral Exposure to Six Chemical-Warfare Agents. 1999. pap. 60.00 (*0-309-06598-4*) Natl Acad Pr.

— Review of the U. S. Department of Energy Office of Fossil Energy's Research Plan for Fine Particulates. 58p. 1999. pap. 18.00 (*0-309-06782-0*) Natl Acad Pr.

National Research Council Staff. Risk Assessment & Management at Desert Chemical Depot & the Tooele Chemical Agent Disposal Facility. LC 97-226624. (Compass Ser.). 96p. (C). 1997. pap. text 15.00 (*0-309-05841-4*) Natl Acad Pr.

— Risk Assessment in the Federal Government: Managing the Process. 191p. (C). 1983. pap. text 27.95 (*0-309-03349-7*) Natl Acad Pr.

— Risk Assessment of Exposure to Radon in Drinking Water. LC 99-6134. 296p. 1999. pap. text 49.95 (*0-309-06292-6*) Natl Acad Pr.

— Rock Fractures & Fluid Flow: Contemporary Understanding & Applications. 568p. (C). 1996. text 74.95 (*0-309-04996-2*) Natl Acad Pr.

— Rodents. (Laboratory Animal Management Ser.). 190p. (Orig.). (C). 1996. pap. text 24.95 (*0-309-04936-9*) Natl Acad Pr.

— The Role of Chromium in Animal Nutrition. LC 97-80669. 100p. 1997. pap. 23.00 (*0-309-06354-X*) Natl Acad Pr.

***National Research Council Staff.** The Role of Diffusion Processes in Fertility Change in Developing Countries. 42p. 1999. pap. 12.00 (*0-309-06478-3*) Natl Acad Pr.

National Research Council Staff. The Role of Public Agencies in Fostering New Technology & Innovation in Building. Lemer, Andrew C. & Dibner, David R., eds. LC 92-62883. 142p. (Orig.). 1993. pap. text 28.00 (*0-309-04783-8*) Natl Acad Pr.

— The Role of Scientists in the Professional Development of Science Teachers. 238p. (C). 1996. text 37.95 (*0-309-04999-7*) Natl Acad Pr.

— Safe Water from Every Tap: Improving Water Service to Small Communities. LC 96-70443. 230p. (Orig.). (C). 1996. pap. text 39.95 (*0-309-05527-X*) Natl Acad Pr.

— A Safer Future: Reducing the Impacts of Natural Disasters. 76p. 1991. pap. text 12.95 (*0-309-04546-0*) Natl Acad Pr.

— Safety in the Underground Construction & Operation of the Exploratory Studies Facility at Yucca Mountain. 176p. 1995. pap. text 34.00 (*0-309-05243-2*) Natl Acad Pr.

— Safety of Dams: Flood & Earthquake Criteria. 320p. 1985. pap. text 29.95 (*0-309-03532-5*) Natl Acad Pr.

— Safety of Tourist Submersibles. 162p. 1991. pap. text 19.00 (*0-309-04232-1*) Natl Acad Pr.

— Satellite Gravity & the Geosphere: Contributions to the Study of the Solid Earth & Its Fluid Envelopes. LC 97-67450. 126p. 1997. pap. text 39.00 (*0-309-05792-2*) Natl Acad Pr.

— Scaling Up: A Research Agenda for Software Engineering. 100p. 1989. pap. text 15.00 (*0-309-04131-7*) Natl Acad Pr.

— Science & Engineering Programs: On Target for Women? Matyas, Marsha L. & Dix, Linda S., eds. LC 92-61248. (Illus.). 240p. (Orig.). (C). 1992. pap. text 29.00 (*0-309-04778-1*) Natl Acad Pr.

— Science & Stewardship in the Antarctic. 127p. (Orig.). (C). 1993. pap. text 25.00 (*0-309-04947-4*) Natl Acad Pr.

***National Research Council Staff.** Science for Decisionmaking: Coastal & Marine Geology at the U. S. Geological Survey. 124p. 1999. pap. 28.75 (*0-309-06584-4*) Natl Acad Pr.

National Research Council Staff. Science Management in the Human Exploration of Space. LC 97-229226. 48p. (C). 1997. pap. text 10.00 (*0-309-05887-2*) Natl Acad Pr.

— Science Teaching Reconsidered: A Handbook. LC 97-4492. 104p. (Orig.). (C). 1997. pap. text 14.00 (*0-309-05498-2*) Natl Acad Pr.

— The Scientific Bases for the Preservation of the Mariana Crow. 104p. (Orig.). 1997. pap. text 29.00 (*0-309-05581-4*) Natl Acad Pr.

***National Research Council Staff.** A Scientific Rationale for Mobility in Planetary Environments. 67p. 1999. pap. 18.00 (*0-309-06437-6*) Natl Acad Pr.

National Research Council Staff. A Scientific Strategy for U. S. Participation in the GOALS (Global Ocean-Atmosphere-Land System) Component of the Clivar (Climate Variability & Predictability Programme) 73p. 1998. pap. text 15.00 (*0-309-06145-8*) Natl Acad Pr.

— Sea-Level Change. (Studies in Geophysics). 256p. 1990. text 29.95 (*0-309-04039-6*) Natl Acad Pr.

— The Search for Life's Origins: Progress & Future Directions in Planetary Biology & Chemical Evolution. 160p. 1990. pap. text 16.00 (*0-309-04246-1*) Natl Acad Pr.

***National Research Council Staff.** Securing America's Industrial Strength. 126p. 1999. pap. 29.00 (*0-309-06448-1*) Natl Acad Pr.

National Research Council Staff. Seeing into the Earth: Noninvasive Charaterization of the Shallow Subsurface. 148p. 2000. 37.95 (*0-309-06359-0*) Natl Acad Pr.

— Seismic Signals from Mining Operations & the Comprehensive Test Ban Treaty: Comments on a Draft Report by a Department of Energy Working Group. LC 99-172835. 68p. 1998. pap. text 15.00 (*0-309-06178-4*) Natl Acad Pr.

— Seismological Research Requirements for a Comprehensive Test-Ban Monitoring System. LC 95-70295. 94p. 1995. pap. text 29.00 (*0-309-05332-3*) Natl Acad Pr.

— Selecting Instructional Materials: A Guide for K-12 Science. Singer, Maxine & Tuomi, Jan, eds. LC 99-50481. 136p. 1999. pap. 18.95 (*0-309-06533-X*, Joseph Henry Pr) Natl Acad Pr.

— Setting Priorities among Drinking Water Contaminants. LC 98-88191. 120p. 1998. pap. text 35.00 (*0-309-06293-4*) Natl Acad Pr.

— Setting Priorities for Land Conservation. 150p. (Orig.). (C). 1993. pap. text 39.95 (*0-309-04836-2*) Natl Acad Pr.

— Sharing the Fish: Toward a National Policy on Individual Fishing Quotas. LC 98-58045. 436p. 1999. 59.95 (*0-309-06330-2*) Natl Acad Pr.

— Shipbuilding Technology & Education. 160p. (Orig.). 1996. pap. text 29.00 (*0-309-05382-X*) Natl Acad Pr.

— Shiphandling Simulation: Application to Waterway Design. Webster, William C., ed. 172p. 1992. pap. text 19.00 (*0-309-04338-7*) Natl Acad Pr.

— Simulated Voyages: Using Simulation Technology to Train & License Mariners. 304p. (Orig.). 1996. pap. text 38.00 (*0-309-05383-8*) Natl Acad Pr.

***National Research Council Staff.** Size Limits of Very Small Microorganisms: Proceedings of a Workshop. 164p. 1999. pap. 35.50 (*0-309-06634-4*) Natl Acad Pr.

National Research Council Staff. Small-Area Estimates of School-Age Children in Poverty: Interim Report 1, Evaluation of 1993 County Estimates for Title I Allocations. LC 97-68115. 96p. (C). 1997. pap. text 15.00 (*0-309-05832-5*) Natl Acad Pr.

— Small-Area Estimates of School-Age Children in Poverty: Interim Report 2. LC 98-194377. 186p. 1998. pap. text 33.50 (*0-309-06045-1*) Natl Acad Pr.

***National Research Council Staff.** The Small Business Innovation Research Program: Challenges & Opportunities. Wessner, Charles W., ed. 186p. 1999. pap. 39.25 (*0-309-06198-9*) Natl Acad Pr.

National Research Council Staff. Snow Avalanche Hazards & Mitigation in the United States. 96p. 1990. pap. text 15.00 (*0-309-04335-2*) Natl Acad Pr.

— Social & Economic Aspects of Radioactive Waste Disposal: Considerations for Institutional Management. 175p. 1984. pap. text 19.95 (*0-309-03444-2*) Natl Acad Pr.

— Social Dynamics of Adolescent Fertility in Sub-Saharan Africa. Bledsoe, Caroline H. & Cohen, Barney, eds. (Population Dynamics of Sub-Saharan Africa Ser.). 224p. (Orig.). (C). 1993. pap. text 33.00 (*0-309-04897-4*) Natl Acad Pr.

— Soil & Water Quality: An Agenda for Agriculture. 442p. (C). 1993. text 54.95 (*0-309-04933-4*) Natl Acad Pr.

— Soil Conservation Vol. 1: An Assessment of the National Resources Inventory. 112p. 1986. pap. text 14.95 (*0-309-03649-6*) Natl Acad Pr.

— Soil Conservation Vol. 2: An Assessment of the National Resources Inventory. 314p. 1986. pap. text 24.95 (*0-309-03675-5*) Natl Acad Pr.

— Solar & Space Physics. (Space Science in the Twenty-First Century Series: Imperatives for the Decades 1995 to 2015). 150p. 1988. pap. text 17.95 (*0-309-03848-0*) Natl Acad Pr.

— Solid-Earth Sciences & Society. 368p. 1993. text 49.95 (*0-309-04739-0*) Natl Acad Pr.

— Soviet-American Dialogue in the Social Sciences: Research Workshops on Interdependence among Nations. 84p. (C). 1990. pap. text 15.00 (*0-309-04289-5*) Natl Acad Pr.

— Spacecraft Maximum Allowable Concentrations for Selected Airborne Contaminants, Vol. 2. LC 95-73151. 408p. 1996. pap. text 35.00 (*0-309-05478-8*) Natl Acad Pr.

— Spacecraft Maximum Allowable Concentrations for Selected Airborne Contaminants, Vol. 3. 362p. (C). 1997. pap. text 45.00 (*0-309-05629-2*, Joseph Henry Pr) Natl Acad Pr.

— Standards, Conformity Assessment, & Trade: Into the 21st Century. 238p. (Orig.). (C). 1995. pap. text 37.95 (*0-309-05236-X*) Natl Acad Pr.

— Star 21: Strategic Technologies for the Army in the Twenty-First Century. 334p. 1992. text 34.95 (*0-309-04629-7*) Natl Acad Pr.

***National Research Council Staff.** The State of Development of Waste Forms for Mixed Wastes: U. S. Department of Energy's Office of Environmental Management. 140p. 1999. pap. 31.50 (*0-309-06431-7*) Natl Acad Pr.

National Research Council Staff. Statistics on U. S. Immigration: An Assessment of Data Needs for Future Research. Edmonston, Barry, ed. LC 96-69271. 100p. (Orig.). 1996. pap. text 24.00 (*0-309-05275-0*) Natl Acad Pr.

***National Research Council Staff.** Statistics, Testing & Defense Acquisition: Background Papers. Cohen, Michael L. et al, eds. 1999. pap. 38.25 (*0-309-06627-1*) Natl Acad Pr.

National Research Council Staff. Statistics, Testing, & Defense Acquisition: New Approaches & Methodological Improvements. Cohen, Michael L. et al, eds. LC 98-9065. 250p. (C). 1998. pap. 39.00 (*0-309-06551-8*) Natl Acad Pr.

— Status & Applications of Diamond & Diamond-Like Materials: An Emerging Technology. 114p. 1990. pap. text 15.00 (*0-309-04196-1*) Natl Acad Pr.

— Stemming the Tide: Controlling Introductions of Nonindigenous Species by Ships' Ballast Water. 160p. (C). 1996. text 39.95 (*0-309-05537-7*) Natl Acad Pr.

— Stewardship of Federal Facilities: A Proactive Strategy for Managing the Nation's Public Assets. LC 98-87971. 128p. 1998. pap. text 33.00 (*0-309-06189-X*) Natl Acad Pr.

— A Strategy for Research in Space Biology & Medicine into the Next Century. LC 98-86544. 296p. 1998. pap. text 49.00 (*0-309-06047-8*) Natl Acad Pr.

— Strategy for the Detection & Study of Other Planetary Systems & Extrasolar Planetary Materials: 1990-2000. 96p. 1990. pap. text 15.00 (*0-309-04193-7*) Natl Acad Pr.

***National Research Council Staff.** Strengthening the Linkages Between the Sciences & the Mathematical Sciences. 138p. 2000. pap. 31.00 (*0-309-06947-5*) Natl Acad Pr.

— Submarine Exposure Guidance Levels for Selected Hydrofluorocarbons: HFC-236fa, HFC-23 & HFC-404a. 98p. 2000. pap. 18.00 (*0-309-07084-8*) Natl Acad Pr.

— Summary of a Workshop on Information Technology Research for Crisis Management. 104p. 1999. pap. 25.25 (*0-309-06790-1*) Natl Acad Pr.

National Research Council Staff. Supply Chain Integration: New Roles for Small & Medium-Sized Manufacturers. 230p. 1999. 35.95 (*0-309-06570-4*) Natl Acad Pr.

— Support Organizations for the Engineering Community. (Engineering Education & Practice in the United States Ser.). 80p. 1986. pap. text 10.50 (*0-309-03629-1*) Natl Acad Pr.

— Supporting Research & Data Analysis in NASA's Science Programs: Engines for Innovation & Synthesis. LC 98-232302. 118p. 1998. pap. text 23.25 (*0-309-06275-6*) Natl Acad Pr.

— Sustaining Marine Fisheries. LC 98-58059. xvi, 164p. (C). 1999. text 42.95 (*0-309-05526-1*) Natl Acad Pr.

— Systems Analysis & Systems Engineering in Environmental Remediation Programs at the Department of Energy Hanford Site. LC 99-178110. 62p. 1998. pap. text 15.00 (*0-309-06181-4*) Natl Acad Pr.

— Tactical Display for Soldiers: Human Factors Considerations. LC 96-39712. 246p. (Orig.). 1997. pap. text 45.00 (*0-309-05638-1*, Joseph Henry Pr) Natl Acad Pr.

— Taking Stock: What Have We Learned about Making Education Standards Internationally Competitive? Summary of a Workshop. Beatty, Alexandra, ed. LC 98-142450. 48p. (C). 1997. pap. text 10.00 (*0-309-05944-5*) Natl Acad Pr.

— Teacher Supply, Demand, & Quality: Policy Issues, Models, & Data Bases. Boe, Erling E. & Gifford, Dorothy M., eds. LC 92-50735. 344p. (C). 1992. pap. text 44.00 (*0-309-04792-7*) Natl Acad Pr.

National Research Council Staff. Technical Bases for Yucca Mountain Standards. Committee on Technical Bases for Yucca Mountain St, ed. 222p. (Orig.). (C). 1995. pap. text 39.00 (*0-309-05289-0*) Natl Acad Pr.

— Technology-Based Pilot Programs: Improving Future U. S. Military Reserve Forces. 94p. 1999. pap. 18.00 (*0-309-06576-3*) Natl Acad Pr.

National Research Council Staff. Technology for the United States Navy & Marine Corps, 2000-2035 Vol. 2: Becoming a 21st Century Force: Technology. 160p. 1998. pap. text 58.50 (*0-309-05897-X*) Natl Acad Pr.

— Technology for the United States Navy & Marine Corps, 2000-2035 Vol. 5: Becoming a 21st Century Force: Weapons. 160p. 1998. pap. text 52.00 (*0-309-05925-9*) Natl Acad Pr.

***National Research Council Staff.** Testing, Teaching & Learning: A Guide for States & School Districts. 200p. 1999. pap. 19.96 (*0-309-06534-8*, Joseph Henry Pr) Natl Acad Pr.

— Tests & Teaching Quality: Interim Report. 50p. 2000. pap. 12.00 (*0-309-06946-7*) Natl Acad Pr.

— Time-Use Measurement & Research: Report of a Workshop. 128p. 2000. pap. 29.75 (*0-309-07092-9*) Natl Acad Pr.

National Research Council Staff. Tinnitus: Facts, Theories, & Treatments. 150p. (C). 1982. pap. text 14.95 (*0-309-03328-4*) Natl Acad Pr.

***National Research Council Staff.** Tooele Chemical Agent Disposal Facility: Update on National Research Council Recommendations. 94p. 1999. pap. 18.00 (*0-309-06882-7*) Natl Acad Pr.

National Research Council Staff. Toward a Coordinated Spatial Data Infrastructure for the Nation. 192p. (Orig.). (C). 1993. pap. text 24.00 (*0-309-04899-0*) Natl Acad Pr.

— Toward an Earth Science Enterprise Federation: Results from a Workshop. LC 99-178268. 68p. 1998. pap. text 15.00 (*0-309-06134-2*) Natl Acad Pr.

— Toward Infrastructure Improvement: An Agenda for Research. Gould, James P. & Lemer, Andrew C., eds. LC 94-67335. (Studies in Infrastructure Technology & Policy). 144p. (Orig.). (C). 1994. pap. text 30.00 (*0-309-05144-4*) Natl Acad Pr.

— Toward Sustainability: Soil & Water Research Priorities for Developing Countries. 76p. 1991. pap. text 9.95 (*0-309-04641-6*) Natl Acad Pr.

***National Research Council Staff.** Toxicity of Military Smokes & Obscurants, Vol. 2. 132p. 1999. pap. 30.00 (*0-309-06329-9*) Natl Acad Pr.

— Toxicity of Military Smokes & Obscurants, Vol. 3. 108p. 1999. pap. 26.00 (*0-309-06599-2*) Natl Acad Pr.

National Research Council Staff. Toxicity Testing: Strategies to Determine Needs & Priorities. 382p. 1984. pap. text 34.95 (*0-309-03433-7*) Natl Acad Pr.

— Toxicologic Assessment of the Army's Zinc Cadmium Sulfide Disperion Tests: Answers to Commonly Asked Questions. 28p. (C). 1997. pap. text 10.00 (*0-309-05799-X*) Natl Acad Pr.

— Toxicological & Performance Aspects of Oxygenated Motor Vehicle Fuels. LC 96-69352. 176p. (Orig.). 1996. pap. text 35.00 (*0-309-05545-8*) Natl Acad Pr.

***National Research Council Staff.** Transforming Undergraduate Education in Science, Mathematics, Engineering & Technology. LC 99-6151. 126p. 1999. pap. 24.00 (*0-309-06294-2*, Joseph Henry Pr) Natl Acad Pr.

National Research Council Staff. Transitions in Work & Learning: Implications for Assessment. Lesgold, Alan et al, eds. 296p. (C). 1997. pap. text 42.00 (*0-309-06365-5*) Natl Acad Pr.

***National Research Council Staff.** Transnational Organized Crime. Reuter, Peter & Petrie, Carol, eds. 76p. 1999. pap. 18.00 (*0-309-06575-5*) Natl Acad Pr.

National Research Council Staff. Trends & Challenges in Aerospace Offsets. Wessner, Charles W., ed. LC 98-89552. 248p. 1999. pap. 45.00 (*0-309-06080-X*) Natl Acad Pr.

— Trends in the Early Careers of Life Scientists. LC 98-87338. 120p. (C). 1998. pap. text 39.00 (*0-309-06180-6*) Natl Acad Pr.

— Trust in Cyberspace. LC 98-58061. 352p. 1999. 54.00 (*0-309-06558-5*) Natl Acad Pr.

— Twenty-First Symposium on Naval Hydrodynamics. 1102p. (C). 1997. text 171.00 (*0-309-05879-1*) Natl Acad Pr.

— U. S.-Europe Collaboration in Space Science. LC 98-179956. 108p. (C). 1998. pap. text 36.00 (*0-309-05984-4*) Natl Acad Pr.

— The U. S. Global Change Research Program: An Assessment in the FY 1991 Plans. 128p. 1990. pap. text 15.00 (*0-309-04328-X*) Natl Acad Pr.

— U. S. Industry in 2000: Studies in Competitive Performance. Mowery, David C., ed. LC 99 6102. 424p. 1999. 65.00 (*0-309-06179-2*, Joseph Henry Pr) Natl Acad Pr.

— The U. S. National Plant Germplasm System. 196p. 1990. text 19.95 (*0-309-04390-5*) Natl Acad Pr.

— U. S. Nuclear Engineering Education: Status & Prospects. 180p. (C). 1990. pap. text 19.00 (*0-309-04280-1*) Natl Acad Pr.

***National Research Council Staff.** U. S. Research Institutes in the Mathematical Sciences: Assessment & Perspectives. 42p. 1999. pap. 12.00 (*0-309-06492-9*) Natl Acad Pr.

National Research Council Staff. Undersea Vehicles & National Needs. LC 96-71679. 116p. (Orig.). 1996. pap. text 39.00 (*0-309-05384-6*) Natl Acad Pr.

— Understanding Agriculture: New Directions for Education. 80p. 1988. pap. text 16.95 (*0-309-03936-3*) Natl Acad Pr.

— Understanding & Preventing Violence. Reiss, Albert J., Jr. & Roth, Jeffrey A., eds. 480p. 1996. pap. text 24.95 (*0-309-05476-1*) Natl Acad Pr.

— Understanding Marine Biodiversity. LC 94-44420. 180p. (Orig.). (C). 1995. text 29.95 (*0-309-05225-4*) Natl Acad Pr.

— Understanding Risk: Informing Decisions in a Democratic Society. Stern, Paul C. & Fireberg, Harvey V., eds. 350p. 1996. text 39.95 (*0-309-05396-X*) Natl Acad Pr.

— Underutilized Resources As Animal Feedstuffs. LC 83-13311. 273p. reprint ed. pap. 84.70 (*0-7837-2779-8*, 204317000006) Bks Demand.

— Undiscovered Oil & Gas Resources: An Evaluation of the Department of the Interior's 1989 Assessment Procedures. 192p. 1991. pap. text 23.00 (*0-309-04533-9*) Natl Acad Pr.

— The United States Antarctic Research Report to the

N

Scientific Committee on Antarctic Research (SCAR), No. 32, 1990. 104p. 1991. pap. text 19.00 (0-309-04626-2) Natl Acad Pr.
— The Unpredictable Certainty: White Papers. 632p. 1998. pap. text 67.00 (0-309-06036-2) Natl Acad Pr.
— Urban Policy in a Changing Federal System. 278p. 1985. pap. text 24.95 (0-309-03591-0) Natl Acad Pr.
— The Use of Drugs in Food Animals: Benefits & Risks. LC 98-58111. xxi, 253p. 1998. 34.95 (0-309-05434-6) Natl Acad Pr.
— The Use of Multi-State Life Tables in Estimating Places for Biomedical & Behavioral Scientists: A Technical Paper. LC 98-102273. 42p. (C). 1997. pap. text 10.00 (0-309-05794-9) Natl Acad Pr.
— Use of Reclaimed Water & Sludge in Food Crop Production. LC 96-67381. 192p. (Orig.). 1996. pap. text 29.00 (0-309-05479-6) Natl Acad Pr.
— Use of Underground Facilities to Protect Critical Infrastructures: Summary of a Workshop. Little, Richard G. et al, eds. LC 99-181641. 64p. 1998. pap. text 15.00 (0-309-06288-8) Natl Acad Pr.
— Uses of Risk Analysis to Achieve Balanced Safety in Building Design an Operations. McDowell, Bruce D. & Lemers, Andrew C., eds. (Studies in Management of Building Technicians). 84p. (C). 1992. pap. text 19.00 (0-309-04680-7) Natl Acad Pr.
— Using Oil Spill Dispersants on the Sea. 352p. (C). 1989. text 29.95 (0-309-03889-8) Natl Acad Pr.
— Using Oil Spill Dispersants on the Sea. LC 88-38879. 351p. 1989. reprint ed. pap. 108.90 (0-608-02776-6, 206384300007) Bks Demand.
— Vetiver Grass: A Thin Green Line Against Erosion. LC 92-50175. 188p. (Orig.). (C). 1993. pap. text 12.00 (0-309-04269-0) Natl Acad Pr.
— Video Displays, Work, & Vision. 273p. 1983. pap. text 19.95 (0-309-03388-8) Natl Acad Pr.
— Virtual Reality: Scientific & Technological Challenges. Mavor, Anne S. & Durlach, Nathaniel I., eds. 556p. (C). 1994. text 59.95 (0-309-05135-5) Natl Acad Pr.
— Visionary Manufacturing Challenges for 2020. LC 98-40274. 176p. 1998. text 34.95 (0-309-06182-2) Natl Acad Pr.
— Waste Incineration & Public Health. 315p. 1998. 44.95 (0-309-06371-X) Natl Acad Pr.
— Water Chemicals Codex. 73p. (C). 1982. pap. text 12.95 (0-309-03338-1) Natl Acad Pr.
— Water for the Future: The West Bank & Gaza Strip, Israel, & Jordon. LC 97-80489. 200p. (C). 1998. pap. text 35.00 (0-309-06421-X) Natl Acad Pr.
*National Research Council Staff. Watershed Management for Portable Water Supply: Assessing the New York City Strategy. 564p. 2000. pap. 56.00 (0-309-06777-4) Natl Acad Pr.
National Research Council Staff. Welfare, the Family & Reproductive Behavior: Report of a Meeting. Haaga, Jojn & Moffitt, Robert A., eds. LC 98-120996. 34p. 1997. pap. text 10.00 (0-309-06025-7) Natl Acad Pr.
— Welfare, the Family, & Reproductive Behavior: Research Perspectives. Moffitt, Robert A., ed. LC 98-9099. 256p. 1998. pap. text 37.00 (0-309-06125-3) Natl Acad Pr.
— Wetlands: Characteristics & Boundaries. 328p. (Orig.). (C). 1995. text 37.95 (0-309-05134-7) Natl Acad Pr.
— Wolves, Bears, & Their Prey in Alaska: Biological & Social Challenges in Wildlife Management. LC 97-75390. 224p. (C). 1997. pap. text 37.00 (0-309-06405-8) Natl Acad Pr.
— Women's Work, Men's Work: Sex Segregation on the Job. 186p. (Orig.). (C). 1986. pap. text 29.95 (0-309-03429-9) Natl Acad Pr.
— Wood in Our Future: The Role of Life-Cycle Analysis. LC 97-66726. 144p. 1997. pap. 34.00 (0-309-05745-0) Natl Acad Pr.
— Work-Related Musculoskeletal Disorders: A Review of the Evidence. 42p. 1998. pap. text 10.00 (0-309-06327-2) Natl Acad Pr.
— Workload Transition: Implications for Individual & Team Performance. Huey, Beverly M. & Wickens, Christopher D., eds. 304p. (Orig.). (C). 1993. pap. text 36.00 (0-309-04796-X) Natl Acad Pr.
— Youth Development & Neighborhood Influences: Challenges & Opportunities. Chalk, Rosemary & Phillips, Deborah A., eds. 40p. (Orig.). 1996. pap. text 10.00 (0-309-05649-7, Joseph Henry Pr) Natl Acad Pr.
National Research Council Staff, ed. Improving Productivity in U. S. Marine Container Terminals. 205p. 1986. pap. text 32.50 (0-309-03694-1) Natl Acad Pr.
***National Research Council Staff, ed.** Juvenile Crime, Juvenile Justice. (Illus.). 220p. 2000. 29.95 (0-309-06842-8) Natl Acad Pr.
National Research Council Staff, ed. Losing Generations: Adolescents in High-Risk Settings. 288p. (Orig.). (C). 1993. pap. 19.95 (0-309-05234-3) Natl Acad Pr.
— Mathematical Science, Technology & Economic Competition. 128p. (C). 1991. pap. text 22.00 (0-309-04483-9) Natl Acad Pr.
National Research Council Staff & Alberts, Betty. Starting Out Right: A Guide to Promoting Children's Reading Success. Burns, M. Susan, ed. LC 98-25492. (Illus.). 182p. 1998. pap. 14.95 (0-309-06410-4) Natl Acad Pr.
National Research Council Staff & Blumstein, Alfred. Research on Sentencing: The Search for Reform, 2 vols., Vol. 1. LC 83-4048. 315p. (C). 1983. pap. text 52.75 (0-309-03347-0) Natl Acad Pr.
***National Research Council Staff & Commission on Engineering Staff.** Integrated Design of Alternative Technologies for Bulk-Only Chemical Agent Disposal Facilities. 58p. 2000. pap. 18.00 (0-309-06945-9) Natl Acad Pr.
***National Research Council Staff & Commission on Physical Science Staff.** Networking Health: Prescriptions for the Internet. 388p. 2000. write for info. (0-309-06843-6, Pub. by Natl Acad Pr) World Scientific Pub.
National Research Council Staff & Committee on Academic Careers for Experimental Com. Academic Careers for Experimental Computer Scientists & Engineers. LC 93-84437. 152p. (Orig.). (C). 1993. pap. text 27.00 (0-309-04931-8) Natl Acad Pr.
National Research Council Staff & Harvard University, John F. Kennedy School of Gove. Violence in Urban America: Mobilizing a Response. 118p. (Orig.). (C). 1994. pap. text 12.95 (0-309-05039-1) Natl Acad Pr.
National Research Council Staff & Institute of Medicine Staff. Exposure of the American People to Iodine-131 from Nevada Nuclear-Bomb Tests: Review of the National Cancer Institute Report & Public Health Implications of Exposure. LC 98-83277. 288p. (C). 1999. pap. 35.00 (0-309-06175-X) Natl Acad Pr.
— From Generation to Generation: The Healthy & Well-Being of Children in Immigrant Families. Hernandez, Donald & Charney, Evan, eds. LC 98-25472. 230p. 1998. text 47.95 (0-309-06561-5) Natl Acad Pr.
— Measuring Functional Capacity & Work Requirements: Summary of a Workshop. LC 99-184679. 124p. (C). 1999. pap. text 28.75 (0-309-06385-X) Natl Acad Pr.
— New Findings on Welfare & Children's Development: Summary of a Research Briefing. Phillips, Deborah & Bridgman, Anne, eds. LC 97-145038. 32p. (Orig.). 1997. pap. text 10.00 (0-309-05689-6, Joseph Henry Pr) Natl Acad Pr.
— Productive Roles in an Older Society. (America's Aging Ser.). 168p. 1986. pap. text 19.95 (0-309-03637-2) Natl Acad Pr.
***National Research Council Staff & Institute of Medicine Staff.** Risks & Opportunities: Synthesis of Studies on Adolescence. Kipke, Michele D., ed. 96p. 1999. pap. 18.00 (0-309-06791-X) Natl Acad Pr.
— Spacecraft Maximum Allowable Concentrations for Selected Airborne Contaminants, Vol. 4. 2000. pap. 73.25 (0-309-06795-2) Natl Acad Pr.
National Research Council Staff & Institute of Medicine Staff. Systems of Accountability: Implementing Children's Health Insurance Programs. LC 99-188101. 40p. 1998. pap. text 10.00 (0-309-06149-0) Natl Acad Pr.
— Taking Action to Reduce Tobacco Use. LC 98-195008. 42p. 1998. pap. text 10.00 (0-309-06038-9) Natl Acad Pr.
— Toward a National Health Care Survey: A Data System for the 21st Century. Wonderlich, Gooloo S., ed. 204p. (C). 1992. pap. text 27.00 (0-309-04692-0) Natl Acad Pr.
National Research Council Staff & Levenson, Milton. Research Reactor Aluminum Spent Fuel: Treatment Options for Disposal. LC 98-84670. 240p. 1998. pap. text 39.00 (0-309-06049-4) Natl Acad Pr.
National Research Council Staff & National Academy of Sciences Staff. Supercomputers: Directions in Technology & Applications. 112p. 1989. pap. text 17.00 (0-309-04088-4) Natl Acad Pr.
National Research Council Staff & North Carolina Board of Science Staff. Collaboratories - Improving Research Capabilities in Chemical & Biomedical Sciences: Proceedings of a Multi-Site Electronic Workshop. 58p. 1999. pap. 18.00 (0-309-06340-X) Natl Acad Pr.
***National Research Council Staff & Ocean Studies Board Staff.** 50 Years of Ocean Discovery: National Science Foundation 1950-2000. (Illus.). 276p. 2000. 45.00 (0-309-06398-1) Natl Acad Pr.
National Research Council Staff & Panel on Reactor-Related Options for Dispositioin. Management & Disposition of Excess Weapons Plutonium: Reactor-Related Options. 436p. (Orig.). (C). 1995. pap. text 45.00 (0-309-05145-2) Natl Acad Pr.
***National Research Council Staff & Shannon, Ann.** Keeping Score. 96p. 1999. pap. 18.00 (0-309-06535-6) Natl Acad Pr.
National Research Council Staff & Vedral, Joyce L. Computer-Aided Materials Selection During Structural Design. 84p. 1995. pap. text 29.00 (0-309-05193-2) Natl Acad Pr.
National Research Council Staff, et al. The Academic Research Enterprise Within the Industrialized Nations: Comparative Perspectives. 124p. (C). 1990. pap. text 15.00 (0-309-04249-6) Natl Acad Pr.
— Dolphins & the Tuna Industry. LC 92-10603. 192p. 1992. pap. text 22.95 (0-309-04735-8) Natl Acad Pr.
***National Research Council Staff, et al.** Early Childhood Intervention: Views from the Field: Report of a Workshop. 64p. 2000. pap. 18.00 (0-309-07039-2) Natl Acad Pr.
National Research Council Staff, et al. Information Technology & the Conduct of Research: The User's View. 88p. 1989. pap. text 12.95 (0-309-03888-X) Natl Acad Pr.
National Research Council Staff, et al. Integrating Federal Statistics on Children: Report of a Workshop. 224p. (Orig.). (C). 1995. pap. text 25.00 (0-309-05249-1) Natl Acad Pr.
— Laboratory Design, Construction & Renovation: Participants, Process & Product. 170p. 2000. pap. 35.00 (0-309-06633-6) Natl Acad Pr.
National Research Council Staff, et al. Marshaling Technology for Development: Proceedings of a Symposium. LC 95-71477. 264p. (Orig.). (C). 1995. pap. text 35.00 (0-309-05349-8) Natl Acad Pr.
***National Research Council Staff, et al.** Review of the Research Program of the Partnership for a New Generation of Vehicles: Sixth Report. 132p. 2000. pap. 32.00 (0-309-07094-5) Natl Acad Pr.
National Research Council Staff, et al. Science & the National Parks. LC 92-26303. (Illus.). 136p. (C). 1992. pap. text 19.95 (0-309-04781-1) Natl Acad Pr.
— Sowing Seeds of Change: Informing Public Policy in the Economic Research Service of USDA. LC 99-6262. 176p. 1999. pap. text 32.00 (0-309-07152-6) Natl Acad Pr.
***National Research Council Staff, et al.** Strategies to Protect the Health of Deployed U. S. Forces: Detecting, Characterizing & Documenting Exposures. 272p. 2000. pap. 73.25 (0-309-06875-4) Natl Acad Pr.
— Surviving Supply Chain Integration: Strategies for Small Manufacturers. LC 00-8199. 166p. 2000. pap. 35.95 (0-309-06878-9) Natl Acad Pr.
National Research Council Staff, jt. auth. see Aging of U. S. Air Force Aircraft Committee.
National Research Council Staff, jt. auth. see Board on Agriculture Staff.
National Research Council Staff, jt. auth. see Commission on Physical Sciences, Mathematics, & Ap.
National Research Council Staff, jt. auth. see Committe for Review of Oversight Mechanisms for Sp.
National Research Council Staff, jt. auth. see Hernandez, Donald J.
National Research Council Staff, jt. auth. see Institute of Medicine Staff.
National Research Council Staff, jt. auth. see Low-Altitude Wind Shear & Its Hazard to Aviation C.
National Research Council Staff, jt. auth. see Mathematical Sciences Education Board Staff.
National Research Council Staff, jt. auth. see National Academy of Engineering Staff.
National Research Council Staff, jt. auth. see National Aviation Weather Services Committee.
National Research Council Staff, jt. auth. see National Research Council, Commission on Behaviora.
National Research Council Staff, jt. auth. see National Weather Service Staff.
National Research Council Staff, jt. auth. see Ocean Studies Board Staff.
National Research Council Staff, jt. auth. see Panel on Foreign Trade Statistics Staff.
National Research Council Staff, jt. auth. see Transportation Research Board Staff.
National Research Council Staff, jt. ed. see Broderick, Renae F.
National Research Council Staff, ed. see Pimentel, George C. & Coonrod, Janice A.
***National Research Council Staff (U. S.).** Entry & Competition in the U. S. Airline Industry: Issues & Opportunities. LC 99-40166. (Special Report Ser.). 1999. write for info. (0-309-07069-4) Transport Res Bd.
National Research Council Staff (U. S.). Rethinking Urban Policy: Urban Development in an Advanced Economy. Hanson, Royce, ed. LC 83-19422. 231p. reprint ed. pap. 71.70 (0-7837-3738-6, 204343000009) Bks Demand.
National Research Council Staff (U.S.). Policy Options for Intermodal Freight Transportation, Vol. 252. LC 98-16533. (Special Reports). 1998. write for info. (0-309-06220-9) Natl Acad Pr.
National Research Council, Subcommittee on Metabol, jt. auth. see Institute of Medicine Staff.
National Research Council, Subcommittee on Metabolism Staff. Manual of Standardized Methods for Veterinary Microbiology. Cottral, George E., ed. LC 77-90900. 733p. reprint ed. pap. 200.00 (0-608-08087-X, 206904600002) Bks Demand.
— Metabolic Modifiers: Effects on the Nutrient Requirements of Food-Producing Animals. 96p. (Orig.). (C). 1994. pap. text 27.95 (0-309-04997-0) Natl Acad Pr.
National Research Council, Technology & Telecommun. Research Recommendations to Facilitate Distributed Work. 84p. (Orig.). (C). 1994. pap. text 25.00 (0-309-05185-1) Natl Acad Pr.
National Research Council, Transportation Research. Geometric Design of Interchanges. LC 92-45821. (Transportation Research Record Ser.: No. 1375). write for info. (0-309-05419-2) Transport Res Bd.
— Intermodal Transportation Education & Training: Proceedings of a Conference, Washington, D. C., November 2-5, 1997. LC 98-210008. (Conference Proceedings Ser.). vi, 113p. 1998. 26.00 (0-309-06453-8, CP017) Natl Acad Pr.
— Safety Research: Heavy Vehicles, Information Systems, & Crash Studies & Methods. LC 92-45740. (Transportation Research Record Ser.: No. 1377). 1993. write for info. (0-309-05417-6) Transport Res Bd.
National Research Council U. S. Committee on a Nat. Monitoring Human Tissues for Toxic Substances. 2nd ed. LC 91-61252. 223p. 1991. reprint ed. pap. 69.20 (0-608-02444-9, 206308700004) Bks Demand.
National Research Council, U. S. Geodynamics Commi. Mount Rainier: Active Cascade Volcano. 128p. (Orig.). (C). 1994. pap. text 29.00 (0-309-05083-9) Natl Acad Pr.
National Research Council, U. S. National Committe. Behavioral Measures of Neurotoxicity. Russell, Roger W. et al, eds. 452p. 1990. text 42.50 (0-309-04047-7) Natl Acad Pr.
National Research Council U. S. Staff. Asbestiform Fibers: Nonoccupational Health Risks. LC 84-60249. 352p. reprint ed. pap. 109.20 (0-7837-2041-6, 204230800003) Bks Demand.
— The Competitive Status of the U. S. Steel Industry: A Study of the Influences of Technology in Determining International Industrial Competitive Advantage. LC 84-63017. 172p. reprint ed. pap. 53.40 (0-7837-2038-6, 204230600003) Bks Demand.
— Diet, Nutrition, & Cancer: Directions for Research. LC 83-61699. 86p. reprint ed. pap. 30.00 (0-7837-2039-4, 204230500003) Bks Demand.
— Drinking Water & Health. 1980, Vol. 3. LC 77-89284. 427p. pap. 132.40 (0-7837-1075-5, 204160400003) Bks Demand.
— Frontiers in Chemical Engineering: Research Needs & Opportunities. fac. ed. LC 88-4120. (Illus.). 231p. 1994. pap. 71.70 (0-7837-7561-X, 204731400007) Bks Demand.
— Improving Risk Communication. fac. ed. LC 89-9464. (Illus.). 352p. 1994. pap. 109.20 (0-7837-7564-4, 204731700007) Bks Demand.
— Managing Speed: Methods for Setting & Enforcing Speed Limits, Vol. 254. LC 98-40323. (Special Report National Research Council, Transportation Research Board). 1998. write for info. (0-309-06502-X) Natl Acad Pr.
***National Research Council U. S. Staff.** Natural Attenuation for Groundwater Remediation. LC 00-8896. 2000. pap. write for info. (0-309-06932-7) Natl Acad Pr.
National Research Council U. S. Staff. New Directions for Biosciences Research in Agriculture: High-Reward Opportunities. LC 85-60580. 136p. reprint ed. pap. 42.20 (0-7837-2037-8, 204230400003) Bks Demand.
— Nutrient Requirements of Rabbits. 2nd fac. rev. ed. LC 77-6318. 36p. 1977. pap. 30.00 (0-7837-7562-8, 204731500007) Bks Demand.
— Pesticide Resistance: Strategies & Tactics for Management. fac. ed. LC 85-25919. 482p. 1986. pap. 149.50 (0-7837-7558-X, 204731100007) Bks Demand.
— Poultry Inspection: The Basis for a Risk-Assessment Approach. LC 87-60910. 177p. reprint ed. pap. 54.90 (0-7837-2042-4, 204230900003) Bks Demand.
National Research Council, U. S. Staff. Quantitative Modeling of Human Performance in Complex, Dynamic Systems. Baron, Sheldon et al, eds. LC 89-63540. 108p. reprint ed. pap. 33.50 (0-7837-1298-7, 204143900020) Bks Demand.
National Research Council U. S. Staff. Surface Coal Mining Effects on Ground Water Recharge. fac. ed. LC 90-60773. (Illus.). 169p. 1990. pap. 52.40 (0-7837-7567-9, 204732000007) Bks Demand.
— What Is America Eating? Proceedings of a Symposium. LC 85-62945. 183p. reprint ed. pap. 56.80 (0-7837-2088-2, 204236400004) Bks Demand.
— Women in Science & Engineering: Increasing Their Numbers in the 1990s; a Statement on Policy & Strategy. fac. ed. LC 91-66811. (Illus.). 164p. 1991. pap. 50.90 (0-7837-7563-6, 204731600007) Bks Demand.
National Research Council, Unit Manufacturing Comm. Unit Manufacturing Processes: Issues & Opportunities in Research. 228p. (Orig.). (C). 1995. pap. text 39.00 (0-309-05192-4) Natl Acad Pr.
National Research Council U.S. Staff. Fairness in Employment Testing: Validity Generalization, Minority Issues, & the General Aptitude Test Battery. fac. ed. Hartigan, John A. & Wigdor, Alexandra K., eds. LC 89-32841. (Illus.). 368p. 1989. pap. 114.10 (0-7837-7569-5, 204732200007) Bks Demand.
National Research Council, Waste Isolation Pilot P. The Waste Isolation Pilot Plant: A Potential Solution for the Disposal of Transuranic Waste. LC 96-68944. 175p. (Orig.). (C). 1996. pap. text 40.00 (0-309-05491-5) Natl Acad Pr.
National Research Council, Water Science & Technol. Sustaining Our Water Resources. 128p. (Orig.). (C). 1993. pap. text 25.00 (0-309-04948-2) Natl Acad Pr.
National Research Council's Geotechnical Board, ed. Practical Lessons from the Loma Prieta Earthquake. (Illus.). 274p. (C). 1994. 25.00 (0-309-05030-8, LP-93) Natl Acad Pr.
National Research Staff. Evolving the High Performance Computing & Communications Initiative to Support the Nation's Information Infrastructure. 136p. 1995. pap. text 25.00 (0-309-05277-7) Natl Acad Pr.
***National Research Staff, ed.** Clean Coastal Waters: Understanding & Reducing the Effects of Nutrient Pollution. LC 00-9621. (Illus.). 2000. write for info. (0-309-06948-3) Natl Acad Pr.
National Resesrch Council Staff, jt. ed. see Poterba, James.
National Resources Committee. Our Cities: Their Role in the National Economy. LC 73-11923. (Metropolitan America Ser.). (Illus.). 108p. 1974. reprint ed. 18.95 (0-405-05406-8) Ayer.
National Resources Defense Council Staff, et al. Hazardous Waste Surface Impoundments: The Nation's Most Serious & Neglected Threat to Groundwater. 49p. 1983. 5.00 (0-318-20476-2) Natl Resources Defense Coun.
National Restaurant Assn. Educational Foundation S. Managing Foodservice Facilities & Equipment: Student Manual. 80p. (Orig.). 1990. pap. text. write for info. (0-915452-50-2) Educ Found.
National Restaurant Association, Educational Found. Sirviendo Alimentos Sanos: Una Guia Para Empleados de la Industria Gastronomica. (ServSafe Ser.).Tr. of Serving Safe Food. (SPA., Illus.). 52p. (Orig.). (C). 1990. pap. text 5.95 (0-915452-55-3) Educ Found.
National Retail Federation Staff. User Guide: NRF Color & Size Codes. 111p. 1997. pap. 235.00 (0-9645599-0-0) Nat Retail Fed.
National Retailing Conference (1994: Richmond, VA). Retailing: Theories & Practices for Today & Tomorrow: Proceedings of the Fourth Triennial National Retailing Conference Presented by the Academy of Marketing Science & the American Collegiate Retailing Association, Richmond, VA, October 22-24, 1994. King, Robert L., ed. LC HF5429.N37. (Special Conference Ser.: Vol. 7). 189p. 1994. reprint ed. pap. 58.60 (0-608-00731-5, 206150700009) Bks Demand.
National Rivers Authority Staff. Contaminated Land & the Water Environment. (Water Quality Ser.: No. 15). 66p. 1994. pap. 15.00 (0-11-886521-8, HM65218, Pub. by Statnry Office) Bernan Associates.
— Discharge Consents & Compliance - NRA's Approach to

N

An Asterisk (*) at the beginning of an entry indicates that the title is appearing for the first time.

Control of Discharges to Water. (Water Quality Ser.: No. 17). 76p. 1994. pap. 15.00 (*0-11-886513-7*, HM65137, Pub. by Statnry Office) Bernan Associates.
— Toxic Blue-Green Algae. (Water Quality Ser.: No. 2). 120p. 1990. pap. 30.00 (*0-11-885804-1*, HM58041, Pub. by Statnry Office) Balogh.

National Rural Electric Cooperative Staff, jt. auth. see Plexus Research Staff.

National Rural Electric Cooperative Association, jt. auth. see Dorsett, William S.

National Rural Electric Cooperative Association St, jt. auth. see Moncreif, William A.

National Rural Electric Cooperative Association St, jt. auth. see Stanley Consultants Staff.

National Rural Electric Cooperative Association Staff, jt. auth. see Burns & McDonnell Engineering Company Staff.

National Rural Electric Cooperative Association Staff, jt. auth. see Plexus Research Inc. Staff.

National Rural Electric Cooperative Association Staff, jt. auth. see Ulteig Engineers, Inc. Staff.

National Safety Council Staff. Accident Facts: 1995 Edition. LC 91-60648. (Illus.). 160p. reprint ed. pap. 49.60 (*0-608-08712-2*, 206928000003) Bks Demand.
— Accident Facts: 1996 Edition. LC 91-60648. (Illus.). 160p. reprint ed. pap. 49.60 (*0-608-08713-0*, 206928100003) Bks Demand.
— Accident Facts, 1984. LC HB1323.A2. 97p. pap. 30.10 (*0-8357-5037-X*, 202501000040) Bks Demand.
— Accident Facts, 1985. LC HB1323.A2. 98p. pap. 30.40 (*0-8357-5036-1*, 202671100051) Bks Demand.
— Accident Facts, 1987. LC HA0217.A4. (Illus.). 109p. reprint ed. pap. 33.80 (*0-8357-5038-8*, 203311300083) Bks Demand.
— Accident Facts, 1988. (Illus.). 107p. reprint ed. pap. 30.50 (*0-8357-6875-9*, 2035573) Bks Demand.
— Accident Facts, 1989. LC HA0217.A4. (Illus.). 107p. reprint ed. pap. 33.20 (*0-7837-1098-4*, 204163000021) Bks Demand.
— Accident Facts, 1990. LC HA0217.A4. 112p. reprint ed. pap. 34.80 (*0-7837-6436-7*, 204643600012) Bks Demand.
— Accident Facts, 1991. LC 91-60648. 112p. reprint ed. pap. 34.80 (*0-7837-6437-5*, 204643700012) Bks Demand.
— Accident Facts, 1992. LC 91-60648. (Illus.). 112p. 1992. reprint ed. pap. 34.80 (*0-7837-9215-8*, 204996500004) Bks Demand.
— Accident Facts, 1993 Edition. LC 91-60648. 126p. 1993. reprint ed. pap. 39.10 (*0-608-02390-6*, 206303100004) Bks Demand.
— Accident Facts, 1994 Edition. LC 91-60648. (Illus.). 128p. 1994. pap. 39.70 (*0-608-04841-0*, 206549800004) Bks Demand.
— Accident Prevention Manual for Business & Industry Vol. 1: Administration & Programs. 10th ed. LC 91-66437. (Occupational Safety & Health Ser.). (Illus.). 575p. 1992. reprint ed. pap. 178.30 (*0-608-07545-0*, 206775800001) Bks Demand.
— Accident Prevention Manual for Business & Industry Vol. 2: Engineering & Technology. 10th ed. LC 91-66437. (Occupational Safety & Health Ser.). (Illus.). 800p. 1992. reprint ed. pap. 200.00 (*0-608-07540-X*, 206775800002) Bks Demand.
— Accident Prevention Manual for Industrial Operations. LC 47-40. 544p. 1946. reprint ed. pap. 168.70 (*0-8357-5040-X*, 202920800059) Bks Demand.
— Accident Prevention Manual for Industrial Operations. 7th ed. LC 74-79025. 1533p. 1974. reprint ed. pap. 200.00 (*0-8357-5039-6*, 202031500016) Bks Demand.
— Accident Prevention Manual for Industrial Operations, Vol. 1. 9th ed. LC 86-63578. (Occupational Safety & Health Ser.). (Illus.). 541p. 1988. reprint ed. pap. 167.80 (*0-7837-3071-3*, 204263200001) Bks Demand.
— Accident Prevention Manual for Industrial Operations, Vol. 1, Administration & Programs. 8th ed. McElroy, Frank E., ed. LC 80-81376. 761p. 1980. pap. 200.00 (*0-8357-5044-2*, 203204200001) Bks Demand.
— Accident Prevention Manual for Industrial Operations, Vol. 2. LC 86-63578. (Occupational Safety & Health Ser.). (Illus.). 512p. 1988. reprint ed. pap. 158.80 (*0-7837-3072-1*, 204263200002) Bks Demand.
— Accident Prevention Manual for Industrial Operations, Vol. 2, Engineering & Technology. 8th ed. McElroy, Frank E., ed. LC 80-81376. 768p. 1980. pap. 200.00 (*0-8357-5043-4*, 2032042) Bks Demand.
— Automated External Defibrillation. LC 98-140463. (Emergency Care Ser.). 64p. 1997. pap. 7.50 (*0-7637-0422-9*) Jones & Bartlett.
— Automatic External Defibrillation: Instructor's Resource Manual. 1998. pap. 10.00 (*0-7637-0720-1*) Jones & Bartlett.

***National Safety Council Staff.** Aviation Ground Operation Safety Handbook. 5th ed. LC 00-31040. 2000. write for info. (*0-87912-214-5*) Natl Safety Coun.

National Safety Council Staff. Bloodborne Pathogens. 2nd ed. LC 96-47085. (Emergency Care Ser.). 80p. 1996. pap. 20.00 (*0-7637-0229-3*) Jones & Bartlett.
— Bloodborne Pathogens: Four Color Edition. LC 93-26138. 1994. pap. 17.50 (*0-86720-818-X*) Jones & Bartlett.
— Bloodborne Pathogens: Instructor's Resource Manual. 2nd ed. 1998. pap. 10.00 (*0-7637-0732-5*) Jones & Bartlett.
— Bloodborne Pathogens: Interactive Training. (Emergency Care Ser.). 32p. 1998. pap. 11.25 (*0-7637-0519-5*) Jones & Bartlett.
— Bloodborne Pathogens: Teaching Package. 2nd ed. (Emergency Care Ser.). 1998. teacher ed., ring bd. 395.00 (*0-7637-0528-4*) Jones & Bartlett.
— Bloodborne Pathogens - Academic. LC 92-49476. 80p. 1992. pap. text 15.00 (*0-86720-771-X*); sl. 195.00 (*0-86720-773-6*) Jones & Bartlett.
— Bloodborne Pathogens - Academic. LC 92-49476. 64p. 1992. pap., teacher ed. 15.00 (*0-86720-772-8*) Jones & Bartlett.
— Bloodborne Pathogens - Academic. LC 92-49476. 80p. 1993. teacher ed., ring bd. 395.00 (*0-86720-798-1*) Jones & Bartlett.
— Bloodborne Pathogens (Smithkline) 1993. pap. 12.50 (*0-86720-793-0*) Jones & Bartlett.
— Bloodborne Pathogens Teaching Package. 1992. ring bd. 395.00 (*0-86720-774-4*) Jones & Bartlett.
— CPR: 1992 Guidelines. 2nd ed. (Emergency Care Ser.). 120p. (C). 1993. pap. text, teacher ed. 15.00 (*0-86720-811-2*) Jones & Bartlett.
— CPR for the Professional Rescuer. LC 97-42361. (Emergency Care Ser.). 120p. 1998. pap. 15.00 (*0-7637-0420-2*) Jones & Bartlett.
— CPR for the Professional Rescuer: Instructor's Resource Manual. 1998. pap. write for info. (*0-7637-0753-8*) Jones & Bartlett.
— CPR Instructor's Manual. 2nd ed. (Emergency Care Ser.). 144p. 1997. pap., teacher ed. 10.00 (*0-7637-0582-9*) Jones & Bartlett.
— CPR Manual. 2nd ed. LC 96-33450. (Emergency Care Ser.). 96p. 1997. pap. 13.75 (*0-7637-0213-7*) Jones & Bartlett.

National Safety Council Staff. CPR Manual: SOS Version. (Illus.). 31p. (C). 1995. pap. text 1.22 (*0-7637-0037-1*) Jones & Bartlett.

National Safety Council Staff. CPR Manual: 1992 Guidelines. LC 92-40649. 128p. 1992. pap. text 13.75 (*0-86720-784-1*) Jones & Bartlett.

***National Safety Council Staff.** CPR Review Manual. (Illus.). 32p. (C). 1998. pap. text 5.30 (*0-7637-0894-1*) JB Pubns.

National Safety Council Staff. CPR Review Manual. LC 93-46698. (Emergency Care Ser.). (C). 1994. pap. text 3.75 (*0-86720-849-X*) Jones & Bartlett.
— CPR Teaching Package. 2nd ed. (Emergency Care Ser.). 1997. 395.00 (*0-7637-0560-8*) Jones & Bartlett.
— CPR Teaching Package: 1992 Guidelines, Set. 1993. pap. 395.00 (*0-86720-815-5*) Jones & Bartlett.
— Early Heart Attack Care. (Emergency Care Ser.). 1998. pap. 1.25 (*0-7637-0421-0*) Jones & Bartlett.

National Safety Council Staff. Emergency First Aid Guide. (Illus.). 32p. (C). 1996. pap. text 200.00 (*0-86720-543-1*) JB Pubns.

National Safety Council Staff. Essentials of First Aid & CPR. LC 94-10092. 192p. 1994. pap. 21.25 (*0-86720-979-8*) Jones & Bartlett.
— First Aid. (Emergency Care Ser.). 176p. (C). 1993. pap. 19.95 (*0-86720-755-8*) Jones & Bartlett.
— First Aid. (Emergency Care Ser.). 176p. (C). 1993. pap., teacher ed. 15.00 (*0-86720-781-7*); teacher ed., boxed set 395.00 (*0-86720-780-9*) Jones & Bartlett.
— First Aid. 2nd ed. LC 97-20507. (Emergency Care Ser.). 140p. 1997. pap. 21.25 (*0-7637-0418-0*) Jones & Bartlett.
— First Aid: Instructor's Resource Manual. 2nd ed. 1998. pap. 10.00 (*0-7637-0715-5*) Jones & Bartlett.
— First Aid - CPR Infants & Children: Instructor's Manual. 2nd ed. (Emergency Care Ser.). 128p. (C). 1994. pap. text 15.00 (*0-86720-838-4*) Jones & Bartlett.

***National Safety Council Staff.** First Aid & CPR. (Illus.). 104p. (C). 1998. pap. text, teacher ed. 15.00 (*0-7637-0947-6*) JB Pubns.

National Safety Council Staff. First Aid & CPR. 288p. 1991. pap., teacher ed. 10.00 (*0-86720-195-9*) Jones & Bartlett.
— First Aid & CPR. 2nd ed. LC 92-42883. 1993. pap., teacher ed. 10.00 (*0-86720-791-4*) Jones & Bartlett.
— First Aid & CPR. 2nd ed. LC 92-42883. 1993. teacher ed. 795.00 (*0-86720-802-3*) Jones & Bartlett.
— First Aid & CPR. 3rd ed. 1996. teacher ed., ring bd. 795.00 incl. VHS, sl. (*0-7637-0197-1*) Jones & Bartlett.
— First Aid & CPR, Level 1. 96p. 1990. pap. 7.50 (*0-86720-154-1*); pap., teacher ed. 11.00 (*0-86720-157-6*) Jones & Bartlett.
— First Aid & CPR, Set. 96p. 1990. teacher ed. 650.00 (*0-86720-161-4*) Jones & Bartlett.
— First Aid & CPR: Academic Version. 288p. 1991. pap. 30.00 (*0-86720-193-2*) Jones & Bartlett.
— First Aid & CPR: Academic Version. 288p. 1991. teacher ed., boxed set 795.00 (*0-86720-194-0*) Jones & Bartlett.
— First Aid & CPR: Academic Version. 2nd ed. LC 92-42883. 1993. pap. text 33.75 (*0-86720-785-X*) Jones & Bartlett.
— First Aid & CPR: Infants & Children. 2nd ed. 208p. 1994. pap. 23.75 (*0-86720-835-X*) Jones & Bartlett.
— First Aid & CPR: Infants & Children, Instructor's Resource Manual. 3rd ed. 250p. 1998. pap. 26.25 (*0-7637-0764-3*) Jones & Bartlett.
— First Aid & CPR: Interactive First Aid: A Scenario Based Approach. 3rd ed. 1997. pap. 495.00 (*0-7637-0254-4*) Jones & Bartlett.
— First Aid & CPR: Level 2. 2nd ed. 192p. 1994. pap. 12.00 (*0-86720-825-2*) Jones & Bartlett.
— First Aid & CPR: Level 3. 2nd ed. LC 93-23167. 288p. 1994. pap. 21.00 (*0-86720-824-4*) Jones & Bartlett.
— First Aid & CPR: Test Bank. 2nd ed. LC 92-42883. 1994. pap., teacher ed. 50.00 (*0-86720-801-5*) Jones & Bartlett.

***National Safety Council Staff.** First Aid & CPR Web Enhanced. 3rd ed. (Illus.). 468p. (C). 1998. pap. text 40.00 (*0-7637-0833-X*) JB Pubns.

National Safety Council Staff. First Aid & CPR Advanced. (Emergency Care Ser.). 488p. 1997. pap. 33.75 (*0-7637-0530-6*) Jones & Bartlett.
— First Aid & CPR Essentials. 2nd ed. (Emergency Care Ser.). 160p. 1997. pap. 21.25 (*0-7637-0434-2*) Jones & Bartlett.
— First Aid & CPR for Infants & Children. (First Aid Ser.). 224p. (C). 1992. pap. text 22.50 (*0-86720-249-1*) Jones & Bartlett.
— First Aid & CPR for Infants & Children. (First Aid Ser.). 200p. (C). 1992. pap., teacher ed. 15.00 (*0-86720-759-0*); sl. 150.00 (*0-86720-761-2*) Jones & Bartlett.
— First Aid & CPR for Infants & Children. (First Aid Ser.). 224p. (C). 1993. teacher ed., ring bd. 450.00 (*0-86720-800-7*) Jones & Bartlett.
— First Aid & CPR for Infants & Children, First Aid. (First Aid Ser.). 224p. (C). 1991. VHS 325.00 (*0-86720-273-4*) Jones & Bartlett.
— First Aid & CPR Standard. 3rd ed. LC 96-47633. (Emergency Care Ser.). 160p. 1997. pap. 11.25 (*0-7637-0329-X*) Jones & Bartlett.

National Safety Council Staff. First Aid & CPR Standard: SOS Version. (Illus.). 96p. (C). 1995. pap. text 3.65 (*0-7637-0039-8*) Jones & Bartlett.

National Safety Council Staff. First Aid & CPR Standard: SOS Version. (Emergency Care Ser.). 160p. 1997. pap. 18.75 (*0-7637-0555-1*) Jones & Bartlett.
— First Aid Children: Quick Parent Guide. (Emergency Care Ser.). 32p. (C). 1996. pap. text 10.00 (*0-86720-546-6*) Jones & Bartlett.
— First Aid CPR: Academic. 3rd ed. (Emergency Care Ser.). 152p. 1996. pap., teacher ed. 15.00 (*0-7637-0200-5*) Jones & Bartlett.
— First Aid CPR: Test Bank. 3rd ed. (Emergency Care Ser.). 272p. 1996. pap. 50.00 (*0-7637-0199-8*) Jones & Bartlett.

National Safety Council Staff. First Aid CPR Infant Child. 2nd ed. (Illus.). 196p. (C). 1996. pap. text 22.50 (*0-86720-833-3*) JB Pubns.

National Safety Council Staff. First Aid CPR Infant Child. 3rd ed. LC 97-41585. (Emergency Care Ser.). 212p. 1997. pap. 26.25 (*0-7637-0633-7*) Jones & Bartlett.
— First Aid CPR Standard. (Emergency Care Ser.). 136p. 1997. pap., teacher ed. 15.00 (*0-7637-0520-9*) Jones & Bartlett.
— First Aid CPR Transition Kit. (Emergency Care Ser.). 1997. boxed set 295.00 (*0-7637-0553-5*) Jones & Bartlett.
— First Aid Guide. 2nd ed. 64p. (Orig.). 1993. pap. text 200.00 (*0-86720-803-1*) Jones & Bartlett.
— First Aid Guide, Certification Cards. (Illus.). 1p. (Orig.). 1991. pap. 10.00 (*0-86720-234-3*) Jones & Bartlett.
— First Aid Handbook. (Emergency Care Ser.). Date not set. pap. 65.70 (*0-86720-946-1*) Jones & Bartlett.
— First Aid Handbook. (Illus.). 208p. 1994. 14.95 (*0-86720-943-7*) Jones & Bartlett.
— First Aid Handbook. LC 94-21032. (Illus.). 208p. 1995. pap. 10.95 (*0-86720-846-5*) Jones & Bartlett.
— First Aid Pocket Guide. 132p. Date not set. pap. 47.70 (*0-86720-538-5*) Jones & Bartlett.
— First Aid Quick. (Emergency Care Ser.). 32p. (C). 1996. pap. text 10.00 (*0-86720-545-8*) Jones & Bartlett.
— Fundamentals of Industrial Hygiene. 2nd ed. Olishifski, Julian B., ed. LC 78-58307. (N.S.C. Occupational Safety & Health Ser.). 1297p. reprint ed. pap. 200.00 (*0-608-17741-5*, 203204300077) Bks Demand.
— Good Samaritan: Helping in an Emergency. LC 95-41959. 1996. pap. 99.95 (*0-86720-544-X*) Jones & Bartlett.
— Guards Illustrated: Ideas for Mechanical Safety. 3rd ed. LC 69-21916. 125p. reprint ed. pap. 35.70 (*0-608-13960-2*, 2025014) Bks Demand.
— Guards Illustrated: Ideas for Mechanical Safety. 4th ed. LC 80-83322. 93p. reprint ed. pap. 30.00 (*0-608-16289-2*, 202666600051) Bks Demand.
— Heartsaver Facts: First Aid, AED, CPR Training System. LC 98-43210. 1998. write for info. (*0-7637-0954-9*) Jones & Bartlett.
— Infant & Child CPR. (Emergency Care Ser.). 64p. 1997. pap. 22.50 (*0-7637-0211-0*) Jones & Bartlett.
— Infant & Child CPR. (Emergency Care Ser.). 96p. 1997. pap., teacher ed. 10.00 (*0-7637-0583-7*) Jones & Bartlett.
— Infants & Children Teaching Package. 1992. ring bd. 450.00 (*0-86720-760-4*) Jones & Bartlett.
— Instructor Recertification Kit. (Emergency Care Ser.). 1997. 19.95 (*0-7637-0554-3*) Jones & Bartlett.
— Interactive First Aid Workbook. (Emergency Care Ser.). 80p. 1996. pap. 11.25 (*0-7637-0358-3*) Jones & Bartlett.

National Safety Council Staff. Learn to Swim: Exploration Journeys. (Illus.). 176p. (C). 1996. pap. text 10.00 (*0-7637-0221-8*) Jones & Bartlett.

National Safety Council Staff. Meat Industry Safety Guidelines. 2nd ed. LC 78-52082. (Illus.). 112p. reprint ed. pap. 34.80 (*0-7837-0579-4*, 204092300019) Bks Demand.
— National Safety Council - First Aid - CPR I-III: Instructor's Manual. 2nd ed. 216p. 1993. pap. text 15.00 (*0-86720-795-7*) Jones & Bartlett.

***National Safety Council Staff.** NSC- First Aid & CPR Standard Web Enhanced. 2nd ed. (Illus.). 160p. (C). 1998. pap. text 5.70 (*0-7637-0897-6*) JB Pubns.

National Safety Council Staff. NSC First Aid & CPR: Advanced. 3rd ed. LC 96-21029. 1996. pap. 35.75 (*0-7637-0183-1*) Jones & Bartlett.
— Oxygen Administration. LC 94-215136. 60p. 1994. pap. 15.00 (*0-86720-983-6*); pap., teacher ed. 15.00 (*0-86720-986-0*) Jones & Bartlett.
— Oxygen Administration Teaching Package. (Emergency Care Ser.). 1994. 395.00 (*0-86720-925-9*) Jones & Bartlett.
— Parent Handbook for Water Exploration. (Emergency Care Ser.). 16p. Date not set. pap. 2.50 (*0-86720-537-7*) Jones & Bartlett.
— Power Press & Safety Manual. 2nd ed. LC TJ1450.N27. 96p. reprint ed. pap. 30.00 (*0-608-13917-3*, 202501100040) Bks Demand.
— Power Press Safety Manual. 3rd ed. LC 79-63712. (Illus.). 107p. reprint ed. pap. 33.20 (*0-8357-6425-7*, 20357930097) Bks Demand.
— Primeros Auxilios y RCP. (Emergency Care Ser.). 96p. (C). 1994. pap. text 12.50 (*0-86720-847-3*) Jones & Bartlett.
— Product Safety: Management Guidelines. LC 88-61858. (Illus.). 199p. (Orig.). 1989. reprint ed. pap. 61.70 (*0-608-01653-5*, 206230500002) Bks Demand.
— Product Safety Management Guidelines. 2nd ed. LC 96-42201. 189p. 1996. 43.95 (*0-87912-193-9*, 17655-0000) Natl Safety Coun.
— Safeguarding Concepts Illustrated. 5th ed. LC 86-61185. (Illus.). 94p. reprint ed. pap. 30.00 (*0-7837-5569-4*, 204534600005) Bks Demand.
— Scuba Diving First Aid. LC 94-48302. (Emergency Care Ser.). 65p. 1995. pap. 13.75 (*0-86720-944-5*) Jones & Bartlett.
— Stress Management. LC 94-16818. 72p. 1994. pap. 16.25 (*0-86720-980-1*) Jones & Bartlett.
— Stress Management: Instructor's Resource Manual. 1994. pap. 12.00 (*0-86720-999-2*) Jones & Bartlett.
— Stress Management Teaching Package. (Emergency Care Ser.). 1995. 395.00 (*0-86720-938-0*) Jones & Bartlett.
— Supervisors' Safety Manual. 9th ed. LC 97-8993. 416p. 1997. 99.95 (*0-87912-197-1*, 15143-0000) Natl Safety Coun.
— Swimming Challenge: Instructor's Manual. (Emergency Care Ser.). 48p. 1995. pap., teacher ed. 10.00 (*0-86720-534-2*) Jones & Bartlett.
— Water Exploration: Instructor's Manual. (Emergency Care Ser.). 78p. 1995. pap., teacher ed. 10.00 (*0-86720-536-9*) Jones & Bartlett.

National Safety Council Staff. Wilderness First Aid. (Illus.). 360p. (C). 1997. pap. text 19.95 (*0-7637-0722-8*) Jones & Bartlett.

National Safety Council Staff & Ellis & Associates Staff. Learn to Swim: Instructor's Manual. (Emergency Care Ser.). 100p. (C). 1993. pap. text 15.00 (*0-86720-809-0*) Jones & Bartlett.

National Safety Council Staff & Thygerson, Alton L. CPR Manual. (First Aid Ser.). (C). 1991. VHS 195.00 (*0-86720-159-2*) Jones & Bartlett.
— CPR Manual. (First Aid Ser.). (C). 1991. 10.00 (*0-86720-233-5*) Jones & Bartlett.
— CPR Manual. (First Aid Ser.). (C). 1992. pap. text 12.50 (*0-86720-192-4*) Jones & Bartlett.
— First Aid Pocket Guide. LC 94-21045. (Emergency Care Ser.). 128p. 1995. pap. 7.95 (*0-86720-843-0*) Jones & Bartlett.

National Safety Council Staff & Wilderness Medical Society Staff. Wilderness First Aid. LC 97-31077. 360p. 1997. pap. 19.95 (*0-7637-0407-5*) Jones & Bartlett.

National Safety Council Staff, et al. Nursing Assessment - Bloodborne Valuepack. (Nursing-Health Science Ser.). (C). 1993. text 57.50 (*0-86720-690-X*) Jones & Bartlett.

National Safety Council Staff, jt. auth. see AAOS Staff.

National Safety Council Staff, jt. auth. see Swartz, George.

National SAMPE Symposium & Exhibition Staff. Advancing Technology in Materials & Processes: National SAMPE Symposium & Exhibition, 30th, Disneyland Hotel, Anaheim, California, March 19-21, 1985. LC TA0401.3.S6. (Science of Advanced Materials & Process Enginnering Ser.: No. 30). 1699p. reprint ed. pap. 200.00 (*0-7837-1283-9*, 204142400020) Bks Demand.
— Material & Process Applications - Land, Sea, Air Space, 26th, National SAMPE Symposium & Exhibition. LC 81-183027. (Science of Advanced Materials & Process Enginnering Ser.: No. 26). 893p. reprint ed. pap. 200.00 (*0-7837-1279-0*, 204142000020) Bks Demand.
— Materials & Processes - Continuing Innovations: National SAMPE Symposium & Exhibition, 28th, Disneyland Hotel, Anaheim, California, April 12-14, 1983. LC 83-177138. (Science of Advanced Materials & Process Enginnering Ser.: No. 28). 1571p. reprint ed. pap. 200.00 (*0-7837-1281-2*, 204142200020) Bks Demand.
— Materials Overview for 1982: National SAMPE Symposium & Exhibition, 27th, Town & Country Hotel, San Diego, California, May 4-6, 1982. LC 82-179801. (Science of Advanced Materials & Process Enginnering Ser.: No. 27). 1080p. reprint ed. pap. 200.00 (*0-7837-1280-4*, 204142100020) Bks Demand.
— The 1980s, Payoff Decade for Advanced Materials: 25th National SAMPE Symposium & Exhibition, Town & Country Hotel, San Diego, California, May 6-8, 1980. LC 80-133416. (Science of Advanced Materials & Process Enginnering Ser.: No. 25). 790p. reprint ed. pap. 200.00 (*0-7837-1278-2*, 204141900020) Bks Demand.
— Selective Application of Materials for Products & Energy: 23rd National SAMPE Symposium & Exhibition, Disneyland Hotel, Anaheim, California, May 2-4, 1978. LC 78-105428. (Science of Advanced Materials & Process Enginnering Ser.: No. 23). 1260p. reprint ed. pap. 200.00 (*0-7837-1277-4*, 204141800020) Bks Demand.
— Technology Vectors: National SAMPE Symposium & Exhibition, 29th, MGM Grand Hotel, Reno, Nevada, April 3-5, 1984. LC 84-215021. (Science of Advanced Materials & Process Enginnering Ser.: No. 29). 1638p. reprint ed. pap. 200.00 (*0-7837-1282-0*, 204142300020) Bks Demand.

National SAMPE Technical Conference Staff. Bicentennial of Materials: National SAMPE Technical Conference, 8th, Sea-Tac Motor Inn, Seattle, Washington, October 12-14, 1976. LC 76-381464. (National SAMPE Technical Conference Ser.: No. 8). 518p. reprint ed. pap. 160.60 (*0-7837-1288-X*, 204142900020) Bks Demand.
— Hi-Tech Review, 1984: National SAMPE Technical Conference, 16th, Clarion Four Seasons Motor Inn, Albuquerque, New Mexico, October 9-11, 1984. LC

N

84-251355. (National SAMPE Technical Conference Ser.: No. 16). 792p. reprint ed. pap. 200.00 (*0-7837-1292-8*, 204143300020) Bks Demand.

— Material & Process Advances '82: National SAMPE Technical Conference, 14th, Sheraton Hotel, Atlanta, Georgia, October 12-14, 1982. LC 82-232953. (National SAMPE Technical Conference Ser.: No. 14). 584p. reprint ed. pap. 181.10 (*0-7837-1290-1*, 204143100020) Bks Demand.

— Materials on the Move: The Sixth National SAMPE Technical Conference, Dayton, OH, October 8-10, 1974. LC 74-194771. (National SAMPE Technical Conference Ser.: No. 6). 477p. reprint ed. pap. 147.90 (*0-7837-1286-3*, 204142700020) Bks Demand.

— Materials Review, '75: National SAMPE Technical Conference, 7th, Hilton Inn, Albuquerque, New Mexico, October 14-16, 1975. LC 75-332485. (National SAMPE Technical Conference Ser.: No. 7). 548p. reprint ed. pap. 169.90 (*0-7837-1287-1*, 204142800020) Bks Demand.

— Technology Transfer: National SAMPE Technical Conference, 13th, Mount Airy Lodge, Mount Pocono, Pennsylvania, October 13-15, 1981. LC 82-103085. (National SAMPE Technical Conference Ser.: No. 13). 711p. reprint ed. pap. 200.00 (*0-7837-1289-8*, 204143000020) Bks Demand.

— Twenty-Twenty Vision in Materials for 2000: National SAMPE Technical Conference, 15th, Marriott Inn, Cincinnati, Ohio, October 4-6, 1983. LC 83-231242. (National SAMPE Technical Conference Ser.: No. 15). 795p. reprint ed. pap. 200.00 (*0-7837-1291-X*, 204143200020) Bks Demand.

National School Boards Association Staff. Violence in the Schools: How America's Schools Are Safeguarding Our Children. (NSBA Best Practices Ser.). 115p. (Orig.). 1993. pap. 15.00 (*0-88364-180-1*, 04-111) Natl Sch Boards.

National School Public Relations Association Staff. Evaluating Your PR Investment. 1986. 17.95 (*0-87545-048-2*, 411-13364) Natl Sch PR.

— School PR: The Complete Book. 1986. 29.95 (*0-87545-051-2*, 411-13346) Natl Sch PR.

National School Services (Wheeling, Ill.), jt. auth. see Markert, Kathleen O'Donnell.

National School Services Staff. Assessing & Improving Student Achievement: Guidebook. (C). 1994. 25.00 (*0-932957-97-8*) Natl School.

— Assessing & Improving Student Achievement: Training Manual. (C). 1994. 95.00 (*0-932957-85-4*) Natl School.

— Coaching & Supervising Teachers. (C). 1991. teacher ed. 85.00 (*0-932957-80-3*) Natl School.

— Coaching & Supervising Teachers: Guidebook. (C). 1991. 25.00 (*0-932957-59-5*) Natl School.

— Curriculum Development & Alignment. (C). 1993. teacher ed. 95.00 (*0-932957-82-X*) Natl School.

— Curriculum Development & Alignment: Guidebook. (C). 25.00 (*0-932957-95-1*) Natl School.

— Desarrollo y Alineacion del Curriculo: Guia. (SPA.). (C). 1994. teacher ed. 125.00 (*0-932957-83-8*) Natl School.

— Desarrollo y Alineacion del Curriculo: Guia. (SPA.). (C). 1994. student ed. 25.00 (*0-932957-71-4*) Natl School.

— Dirigiendo y Supervisando a los Maestros: Guia - Guidebook. (SPA.). (C). 1992. teacher ed. 125.00 (*0-932957-81-1*) Natl School.

— Dirigiendo y Supervisando a los Maestros: Guia - Guidebook. (SPA.). (C). 1992. student ed. 25.00 (*0-932957-68-4*) Natl School.

— Estrategias Practicas para el Mejoramiento de la Escuela: Guia - Guidebook. (SPA.). (C). 1994. 25.00 (*0-932957-69-2*) Natl School.

— Estrategias Practicas para el Mejoramiento de la Escuela - Teacher Manual. (SPA.). (C). 1992. teacher ed. 125.00 (*0-932957-57-9*) Natl School.

— Helen's Helpful Homework Hints: Training Guide. (Illus.). 1995. 10.95 (*0-932957-02-1*) Natl School.

— Management System for Teachers. 290p. (C). 1988. 95.00 (*0-932957-88-9*); teacher ed. 110.00 (*0-932957-87-0*) Natl School.

— Management System for Teachers: Guidebook. (C). 1996. 25.00 (*0-932957-78-1*) Natl School.

— Practical Strategies for School Improvement. (C). 1991. teacher ed. 95.00 (*0-932957-56-0*) Natl School.

— Practical Strategies for School Improvement: Guidebook. (C). 25.00 (*0-932957-58-7*) Natl School.

— Programa para el Mejoramiento del Aprovechamiento del Estudiante: Guia - Guidebook. (SPA.). (C). 1994. student ed. 25.00 (*0-932957-67-6*) Natl School.

— Programa para el Mejoramiento del Aprovechamiento del Estudiante - Training Manual. (SPA.). (C). 1993. teacher ed. 125.00 (*0-932957-74-9*) Natl School.

— Sistema de Manejo Para Maestros: Guia - Guidebook. (SPA.). (C). 1994. student ed. 25.00 (*0-932957-70-6*) Natl School.

— Sistema de Manejo Para Maestros: Leaders Manual. (SPA.). (C). 1991. teacher ed. 125.00 (*0-932957-79-X*) Natl School.

National School Services Staff, jt. auth. see Mulvey, Joanne.

National Science Foundation (U. S.) Staff, jt. auth. see Weiss, Benjamin.

National Science Foundation Staff, et al. Geographic Information Systems & Their Application in Geotechnical Earthquake Engineering: Proceedings of a Workshop Sponsored by the National Science Foundation Through the Earthquake Hazard Mitigation Program & the Geomechanical, Geotechnical, & Geo-Environmental Systems Program. Frost, J. David & Chameau, Jean-Lou A., eds. LC 93-5432. 132p. 1993. 20.00 (*0-87262-973-2*) Am Soc Civil Eng.

National Science Resource Center Staff. Islands Lost in Time. LC 96-54853. 1997. write for info. (*0-7922-3651-3*) Random.

National Science Resource Center Staff. National Geographic Atlas of the World. 2nd rev. ed. LC 95-19579. 1995. text. write for info. (*0-7922-3040-X*) Natl Geog.

National Science Resource Center Staff. Soils Student Notebook. (Science & Technology for Children Ser.). (Illus.). 21p. (J). (gr. 2). 1996. pap. text, student ed., wbk. ed. write for info. (*0-89278-738-4*, 97-1603) Carolina Biological.

— Soils Teacher's Guide. (Science & Technology for Children Ser.). (Illus.). 215p. 1996. pap. text, teacher ed. write for info. (*0-89278-737-6*, 97-1602) Carolina Biological.

National Science Resource Center Staff. The White House: An Historical Guide. 20th ed. LC 98-60939. 160p. 1999. 6.50 (*0-912308-75-3*); pap. 5.00 (*0-912308-74-5*) White House Hist.

National Science Resource Center Staff, jt. auth. see Langone, John.

National Science Resources Center (U.S.) Staff, et al. Changes: Complete Unit. LC 98-125169. (Science & Technology for Children Ser.). vii, 199 p. (J). (gr. 2). 1997. pap. text. write for info. (*0-89278-628-0*) Carolina Biological.

National Science Resources Center Staff. Animal Studies Student Activity Book. (Science & Technology for Children Ser.). (Illus.). 60p. (J). (gr. 4). 1997. pap. text, student ed. write for info. (*0-89278-650-7*, 97-2403) Carolina Biological.

— Animal Studies Teacher's Guide. (Science & Technology for Children Ser.). (Illus.). 232p. 1997. pap. text, teacher ed. write for info. (*0-89278-649-3*, 97-2402) Carolina Biological.

National Science Resources Center Staff. Balancing & Weighing: Complete Unit. (Science & Technology for Children Ser.). (Illus.). (J). (gr. 2 up). 1995. pap. text. write for info. (*0-89278-728-7*) Carolina Biological.

— Balancing & Weighing Student Notebook. (Science & Technology for Children Ser.). (Illus.). 17p. (J). (gr. 2). 1995. pap. text, student ed. write for info. (*0-89278-730-9*) Carolina Biological.

— Balancing & Weighing Teacher's Guide. (Science & Technology for Children Ser.). (Illus.). 159p. (J). (gr. 2). 1995. pap. text, teacher ed. write for info. (*0-89278-729-5*) Carolina Biological.

National Science Resources Center Staff. Changes Student Notebook. (Science & Technology for Children Ser.). (Illus.). 24p. (J). (gr. 2). 1997. pap. text, student ed., wbk. ed. write for info. (*0-89278-630-2*, 97-1803) Carolina Biological.

— Changes Teacher's Guide. (Science & Technology for Children Ser.). (Illus.). 210p. 1997. pap. text, teacher ed. write for info. (*0-89278-629-9*, 97-1802) Carolina Biological.

National Science Resources Center Staff. Chemical Tests: Complete Unit. (Science & Technology for Children Ser.). (Illus.). (J). (gr. 3). 1994. pap. text. write for info. (*0-89278-703-1*) Carolina Biological.

— Chemical Tests Student Activity Book. (Science & Technology for Children Ser.). (Illus.). 74p. (J). (gr. 3). 1994. pap. text, student ed. write for info. (*0-89278-705-8*) Carolina Biological.

— Chemical Tests Teacher's Guide. (Science & Technology for Children Ser.). (Illus.). 207p. (J). (gr. 3). 1994. pap. text, teacher ed. write for info. (*0-89278-704-X*) Carolina Biological.

National Science Resources Center Staff. Comparing & Measuring Student Notebook. (Science & Technology for Children Ser.). (Illus.). 17p. (J). (gr. 1). 1996. pap. text, student ed., wbk. ed. write for info. (*0-89278-610-8*, 97-1303) Carolina Biological.

— Comparing & Measuring Teacher's Guide. (Science & Technology for Children Ser.). (Illus.). 148p. 1996. pap. text, teacher ed. write for info. (*0-89278-609-4*, 97-1302) Carolina Biological.

— Ecosystems Student Activity Book. (Science & Technology for Children Ser.). (Illus.). 80p. (J). (gr. 5). 1996. pap. text, student ed. write for info. (*0-89278-734-1*, 97-2803) Carolina Biological.

— Ecosystems Teacher's Guide. (Science & Technology for Children Ser.). (Illus.). 238p. 1996. pap. text, teacher ed. write for info. (*0-89278-733-3*, 97-2802) Carolina Biological.

National Science Resources Center Staff. Electric Circuits: Complete Unit. (Science & Technology for Children Ser.). (Illus.). (J). (gr. 4). 1991. pap. text. write for info. (*0-89278-660-4*) Carolina Biological.

— Electric Circuits Student Activity Book. (Science & Technology for Children Ser.). (Illus.). 51p. (J). (gr. 4). 1991. pap. text, student ed. write for info. (*0-89278-662-0*) Carolina Biological.

— Electric Circuits Teacher's Guide. (Science & Technology for Children Ser.). (Illus.). 119p. (J). (gr. 4). 1991. pap. text, teacher ed. write for info. (*0-89278-661-2*) Carolina Biological.

— Experiments with Plants: Complete Unit. (Science & Technology for Children Ser.). (Illus.). (J). (gr. 6). 1992. pap. text. write for info. (*0-89278-679-5*) Carolina Biological.

— Experiments with Plants Student Activity Book. (Science & Technology for Children Ser.). (Illus.). 74p. (J). (gr. 6). 1992. pap. text, student ed. write for info. (*0-89278-681-7*) Carolina Biological.

— Experiments with Plants Teacher's Guide. (Science & Technology for Children Ser.). (Illus.). 147p. 1992. pap. text, teacher ed. write for info. (*0-89278-680-9*) Carolina Biological.

— Floating & Sinking: Complete Unit, Complete Unit. (Science & Technology for Children Ser.). (Illus.). (J). (gr. 5). 1995. pap. text. write for info. (*0-89278-725-2*) Carolina Biological.

— Floating & Sinking: Student Activity Book. (Science & Technology for Children Ser.). (Illus.). 56p. (Orig.). (J). (gr. 5). 1995. pap. text, student ed. write for info. (*0-89278-727-9*) Carolina Biological.

— Floating & Sinking Teacher's Guide. (Science & Technology for Children Ser.). (Illus.). 167p. (J). (gr. 5). 1995. pap. text, teacher ed. write for info. (*0-89278-726-0*) Carolina Biological.

— Food Chemistry: Complete Unit. (Science & Technology for Children Ser.). (Illus.). (J). (gr. 5). 1994. pap. text. write for info. (*0-89278-709-0*) Carolina Biological.

— Food Chemistry Student Activity Book. (Science & Technology for Children Ser.). (Illus.). 85p. (J). (gr. 5). 1994. pap. text, student ed. write for info. (*0-89278-711-2*) Carolina Biological.

— Food Chemistry Teacher's Guide. (Science & Technology for Children Ser.). (Illus.). 183p. (J). (gr. 5). 1994. pap. text, teacher ed. write for info. (*0-89278-710-4*) Carolina Biological.

National Science Resources Center Staff. Land & Water Student Activity Book. (Science & Technology for Children Ser.). (Illus.). 87p. (J). (gr. 4). 1997. pap. text, student ed. write for info. (*0-89278-740-6*, 97-2303) Carolina Biological.

— Land & Water Teacher's Guide. (Science & Technology for Children Ser.). (Illus.). 232p. 1997. pap. text, teacher ed. write for info. (*0-89278-739-2*, 97-2302) Carolina Biological.

National Science Resources Center Staff. The Life Cycle of Butterflies: Complete Unit. (Science & Technology for Children Ser.). (Illus.). (J). (gr. 2). 1992. pap. write for info. (*0-89278-616-7*) Carolina Biological.

— The Life Cycle of Butterflies Student Notebook. (Science & Technology for Children Ser.). (Illus.). 20p. (J). (gr. 2). 1992. pap. text, student ed. write for info. (*0-89278-618-3*) Carolina Biological.

— The Life Cycle of Butterflies Teacher's Guide. (Science & Technology for Children Ser.). (Illus.). 124p. 1992. pap. text, teacher ed. write for info. (*0-89278-617-5*) Carolina Biological.

— Magnets & Motors: Complete Unit. (Science & Technology for Children Ser.). (Illus.). (Orig.). (YA). (gr. 6 up). 1991. pap. text. write for info. (*0-89278-691-4*) Carolina Biological.

— Magnets & Motors Student Activity Book. (Science & Technology for Children Ser.). (Illus.). 61p. (YA). (gr. 6 up). 1991. pap. text, student ed. write for info. (*0-89278-693-0*) Carolina Biological.

— Magnets & Motors Teacher's Guide. (Science & Technology for Children Ser.). (Illus.). 136p. (YA). (gr. 6 up). 1991. pap. text, teacher ed. write for info. (*0-89278-692-2*) Carolina Biological.

— Measuring Time: Complete Unit. (Science & Technology for Children Ser.). (Illus.). (Orig.). (YA). (gr. 6 up). 1994. pap. text. write for info. (*0-89278-706-6*) Carolina Biological.

— Measuring Time Student Activity Book. (Science & Technology for Children Ser.). (Illus.). 65p. (YA). (gr. 6 up). 1994. pap. text, student ed. write for info. (*0-89278-708-2*) Carolina Biological.

— Measuring Time Teacher's Guide. (Science & Technology for Children Ser.). 179p. (YA). (gr. 6 up). 1994. pap. text, teacher ed. write for info. (*0-89278-707-4*) Carolina Biological.

— Microworlds: Complete Unit. (Science & Technology for Children Ser.). (Illus.). (J). (gr. 5). 1991. pap. text, student ed. write for info. (*0-89278-664-7*) Carolina Biological.

— Microworlds Student Activity Book. (Science & Technology for Children Ser.). (Illus.). 61p. (J). (gr. 5). 1991. pap. text, student ed. write for info. (*0-89278-666-3*) Carolina Biological.

— Microworlds Teacher's Guide. (Science & Technology for Children Ser.). (Illus.). 123p. (J). (gr. 5). 1991. pap. text, teacher ed. write for info. (*0-89278-665-5*) Carolina Biological.

National Science Resources Center Staff. Motion & Design Student Activity Book. (Science & Technology for Children Ser.). (Illus.). 69p. (J). (gr. 4). 1997. pap. text, student ed. write for info. (*0-89278-677-9*, 97-3003) Carolina Biological.

— Motion & Design Teacher's Guide. (Science & Technology for Children Ser.). (Illus.). 205p. 1997. pap. text, teacher ed. write for info. (*0-89278-676-0*, 97-3002) Carolina Biological.

— Organisms Student Notebook. (Science & Technology for Children Ser.). (Illus.). 18p. (J). (gr. 1). 1996. pap. text, student ed., wbk. ed. write for info. (*0-89278-736-8*, 97-1103) Carolina Biological.

— Organisms Teacher's Guide. (Science & Technology for Children Ser.). (Illus.). 243p. 1996. pap. text. write for info. (*0-89278-735-X*, 97-1102) Carolina Biological.

National Science Resources Center Staff. Plant Growth & Development: Complete Unit. (Science & Technology for Children Ser.). (Illus.). (Orig.). (J). (gr. 3). 1991. pap. text. write for info. (*0-89278-632-9*) Carolina Biological.

— Plant Growth & Development Student Activity Book. (Science & Technology for Children Ser.). (Illus.). 50p. (J). (gr. 3). 1991. pap. text, student ed. write for info. (*0-89278-634-5*) Carolina Biological.

— Plant Growth & Development Teacher's Guide. (Science & Technology for Children Ser.). (Illus.). 142p. (J). (gr. 3). 1991. pap. text, teacher ed. write for info. (*0-89278-633-7*) Carolina Biological.

National Science Resources Center Staff. Rocks & Minerals Student Activity Book. (Science & Technology for Children Ser.). (Illus.). 63p. (J). (gr. 3). 1997. pap. text, student ed. write for info. (*0-89278-747-3*, 97-2003) Carolina Biological.

— Rocks & Minerals Teacher's Guide. LC 98-181828. (Science & Technology for Children Ser.). (Illus.). 163p. 1997. pap. text, teacher ed. write for info. (*0-89278-746-5*, 97-2002) Carolina Biological.

— Solids & Liquids Student Notebook. (Science & Technology for Children Ser.). (Illus.). 16p. (J). (gr. 1). 1996. pap. text, student ed., wbk. ed. write for info. (*0-89278-614-0*, 97-1403) Carolina Biological.

— Solids & Liquids Teacher's Guide. (Science & Technology for Children Ser.). (Illus.). 176p. 1996. pap. text, teacher ed. write for info. (*0-89278-613-2*, 97-1402) Carolina Biological.

— Sound Student Activity Book. (Science & Technology for Children Ser.). (Illus.). 67p. (J). (gr. 3). 1997. pap. text, student ed. write for info. (*0-89278-745-7*, 97-2203) Carolina Biological.

National Science Resources Center Staff. Sound Teacher's Guide. LC 98-181833. (Science & Technology for Children Ser.). vii, 138 p. 1997. pap. text, teacher ed. write for info. (*0-89278-744-9*) Carolina Biological.

National Science Resources Center Staff. The Technology of Paper Student Activity Book. LC 97-221756. (Science & Technology for Children Ser.). (Illus.). 88p. (J). (gr. 6 up). 1997. pap. text, student ed. write for info. (*0-89278-685-X*, 97-3303) Carolina Biological.

— The Technology of Paper Teacher's Guide. LC 97-221767. (Science & Technology for Children Ser.). (Illus.). 263p. 1997. pap. text, teacher ed. write for info. (*0-89278-684-1*, 97-3302) Carolina Biological.

National Science Resources Center Staff. Weather Student Notebook. (Science & Technology for Children Ser.). (Illus.). 16p. (J). (gr. 1). 1995. pap. text, student ed. write for info. (*0-89278-714-7*) Carolina Biological.

— Weather Teacher's Guide. (Science & Technology for Children Ser.). (Illus.). 188p. (J). (gr. 1). 1995. pap. text, teacher ed. write for info. (*0-89278-713-9*) Carolina Biological.

National Science Resources Center Staff. Weather: Complete Unit. (Science & Technology for Children Ser.). (J). (gr. 1). 1995. pap. write for info. (*0-89278-712-0*) Carolina Biological.

National Science Resources Center Staff, et al. Resources for Teaching Middle School Science. LC 98-12987. 496p. 1998. pap. 24.95 (*0-309-05781-7*) Natl Acad Pr.

***National Security Agency Staff.** U.S. Military Intelligence Personnel, 1944-1945. (Intelligence Series: I-18). iv, 118p. (C). 2000. pap. 28.80 (*0-89412-285-1*) Aegean Park Pr.

***National Security Agency Staff, contrib. by.** Vatican Code Systems. 80p. 1999. pap. 28.80 (*0-89412-280-0*, C-86) Aegean Park Pr.

National Security Archive Staff. Iran: The Making of U. S. Policy, 1977-1980, Guide & Index, 2 vols., Vols. 1 & 2. Hooglund, Eric et al, eds. (Making of U. S. Policy Ser.). (Illus.). (C). 1990. write for info. (*0-89887-068-2*) Chadwyck-Healey.

National Security Archive Staff. U. S. Nuclear Non-Proliferation, 1945-1991: Guide & Index, 2 vols. Chadwyck-Healey Staff et al, eds. (Making of U. S. Policy Ser.). (Illus.). 1992. write for info. (*0-89887-094-1*) Chadwyck-Healey.

National Security Archive Staff & Chadwyck-Healey Staff. Afghanistan: The Making of U. S. Policy, 1973-1990, Guide & Index, 2 vols. Galster, Steve, ed. (Making of U. S. Policy Ser.). (Illus.). 1991. write for info. (*0-89887-075-5*) Chadwyck-Healey.

— The Berlin Crisis, 1958-1962: Guide & Index, 2 vols., Set. Chang, Laurence, ed. (Making of U. S. Policy Ser.). (Illus.). 1992. write for info. (*0-89887-096-8*) Chadwyck-Healey.

— Cuban Missile Crisis, 1962: The Making of U. S. Policy, 1962, Guide & Index, 2 vols. Chang, Laurence et al, eds. (Making of U. S. Policy Ser.). (Illus.). (C). 1990. write for info. (*0-89887-071-2*) Chadwyck-Healey.

— El Salvador: The Making of U. S. Policy, 1977-1984, 2 vols. Di Vinenzo, Janet et al, eds. (Making of U. S. Policy Ser.). (Illus.). (C). 1989. write for info. (*0-89887-062-3*) Chadwyck-Healey.

— Nicaragua: The Making of U. S. Policy, 1978-1990, Guide & Index, 2 vols., Set. Kornbluh, Deter, ed. (Making of U. S. Policy Ser.). (Illus.). 1991. write for info. (*0-89887-088-7*) Chadwyck-Healey.

— The Philippines: U. S. Policy During the Marcos Years, 1965-1986, Guide & Index, 3 vols. Nelson, Craig et al, eds. (Making of U. S. Policy Ser.). (Illus.). 1990. write for info. (*0-89887-077-1*) Chadwyck-Healey.

— South Africa: The Making of U. S. Policy, 1962-1989, Guide & Index, 2 vols. Mokoena, Kenneth, ed. (Making of U. S. Policy Ser.). (Illus.). 1992. write for info. (*0-89887-073-9*) Chadwyck-Healey.

— The U. S. Intelligence Community: Organizations, Operations & Management, 1947-1989, Guide & Index. Richelson, Jeffrey T., ed. (Making of U. S. Policy Ser.). 1990. (*0-89887-083-6*) Chadwyck-Healey.

— U. S. Military Uses of Space, 1945-1991: Guide & Index, Set. Richelson, Jeffrey T., ed. (Making of U. S. Policy Ser.). (Illus.). 1992. write for info. (*0-89887-092-5*) Chadwyck-Healey.

National Security Council (U.S.) Staff, et al. Minutes of Meetings of the National Security Council: With Special Advisory Reports LC 86-892100. 3 p. 1982. write for info. (*0-89093-462-2*) U Pubns Amer.

— Minutes of Meetings of the National Security Council, 3rd Supplement. 3rd ed. LC 96-32873. 1996. suppl. ed. 965.00 (*1-55655-600-4*) U Pubns Amer.

National Security Council (U.S.) Staff, jt. auth. see Kesaris, Paul.

***National Seminars Staff.** How to Manage Conflict: Turn All Conflicts into Win-Win Outcomes. 3rd ed. LC 99-51920. 128p. 1999. pap. 10.99 (*1-56414-440-2*) Career Pr Inc.

— Powerful Planning Skills: Envisioning the Future & Making It Happen. LC 99-56825. 128p. 1999. pap. 10.99 (*1-56414-441-0*) Career Pr Inc.

An Asterisk (*) at the beginning of an entry indicates that the title is appearing for the first time.

N

— Discovering Deserts. LC 98-39956. (Ranger Rick's Naturescope Ser.: Vol. 1). (Illus.). 96p. (J). (gr. 1-7). 1999. lib. bdg. 19.95 (*0-7910-4880-2*) Chelsea Hse.

— Discovering Deserts. (J). (gr. k-8). 1991. pap. 7.95 (*0-945051-34-4*, 75005) Natl Wildlife.

— Diving into Oceans. (Ranger Rick's Naturescope Ser.). (Illus.). 96p. (J). (gr. 1-7). 1999. lib. bdg. 19.95 (*0-7910-4832-2*) Chelsea Hse.

— Diving into Oceans. (J). (gr. k-8). 1991. pap. 7.95 (*0-945051-36-0*, 75042) Natl Wildlife.

— Endangered Species. (J). (gr. k-8). 1991. pap. 7.95 (*0-945051-37-9*, 75033) Natl Wildlife.

— Endangered Species: Wild & Rare. LC 97-28733. (Ranger Rick's Naturescope Ser.). (Illus.). 96p. (J). (gr. 1-7). 1999. lib. bdg. 19.95 (*0-7910-4833-0*) Chelsea Hse.

— Endangered Species Wild & Rare. LC 97-10378. (Ranger Rick's NatureScope Ser.). (Illus.). 96p. (J). (gr. k-8). 1997. pap. 12.95 (*0-07-046508-8*) McGraw.

— Geology: The Active Earth. LC 97-30689. (Ranger Rick's Naturescope Ser.). (Illus.). 96p. (J). (gr. 1-7). 1999. lib. bdg. 19.95 (*0-7910-4834-9*) Chelsea Hse.

— Geology: The Active Earth. (J). (gr. k-8). 1991. pap. 7.95 (*0-945051-38-7*, 75032) Natl Wildlife.

— Geology: The Active Earth. 2nd ed. (Ranger Rick's NatureScope Ser.). (Illus.). 96p. (J). (gr. 1-4). 1998. pap. 12.95 (*0-07-046511-8*) McGraw.

— Incredible Insects. LC 98-39957. (Ranger Rick's Naturescope Ser.: Vol. 1). (Illus.). 96p. (J). (gr. 1-7). 1999. lib. bdg. 19.95 (*0-7910-4881-0*) Chelsea Hse.

— Incredible Insects. LC 97-36216. (Ranger Rick's Naturescope Ser.). 96p. (J). (gr. k-3). 1998. pap. 12.95 (*0-07-047102-9*) McGraw.

— Incredible Insects. (J). (gr. k-8). 1991. pap. 7.95 (*0-945051-39-5*, 75001) Natl Wildlife.

— Let's Hear It for Herps. (J). (gr. k-8). 1991. pap. 7.95 (*0-945051-42-5*, 75034) Natl Wildlife.

— Let's Hear It for Herps! All about Reptiles & Amphibians. LC 97-51602. (Ranger Rick's Naturescope Ser.). (Illus.). 96p. (J). (gr. 1-7). 1999. lib. bdg. 19.95 (*0-7910-4835-7*) Chelsea Hse.

— 1999 Conservation Directory. 44th ed. Gordon, Rue E., ed. 544p. 1999. pap. 61.00 (*1-55821-920-X*) Lyons Pr.

*__National Wildlife Federation Staff.__ Pollution: Problems & Solutions. LC 98-39954. (Ranger Rick's Naturescope Ser.: Vol. 1). (Illus.). 96p. (J). (gr. 1-7). 1999. lib. bdg. 19.95 (*0-7910-4882-9*) Chelsea Hse.

National Wildlife Federation Staff. Pollution: Problems & Solutions. LC 97-36214. (Ranger Rick's Naturescope Ser.). 96p. 1998. pap. 12.95 (*0-07-047105-3*) McGraw.

— Pollution: Problems & Solutions. (J). (gr. k-8). 1991. pap. 7.95 (*0-945051-40-9*, 75045) Natl Wildlife.

— Rain Forests: Tropical Treasures. LC 97-34033. (Ranger Rick's Naturescope Ser.). (Illus.). 96p. (J). (gr. 1-7). 1999. lib. bdg. 19.95 (*0-7910-4836-5*) Chelsea Hse.

— Rain Forests: Tropical Treasures. (J). (gr. k-8). 1991. pap. 7.95 (*0-945051-41-7*, 75044) Natl Wildlife.

— Rain Forests Tropical Treasures. 2nd ed. LC 97-10376. (Ranger Rick's NatureScope Ser.). (Illus.). 96p. (J). (gr. k-8). 1997. pap. 12.95 (*0-07-046510-X*) McGraw.

— Trees Are Terrific. (J). (gr. k-8). 1991. pap. 7.95 (*0-945051-43-3*, 75021) Natl Wildlife.

— Trees Are Terrific! LC 98-39955. (Ranger Rick's Naturescope Ser.: Vol. 1). (Illus.). 96p. (J). (gr. 1-7). 1999. lib. bdg. 19.95 (*0-7910-4883-7*) Chelsea Hse.

— Trees Are Terrific! LC 97-36212. (Ranger Rick's Naturescope Ser.). (Illus.). 96p. (J). 1998. pap. 12.95 (*0-07-047101-0*) McGraw.

*__National Wildlife Federation Staff.__ 2001 Conservation Directory: A Guide to Worldwide Environmental Organizations. 2000. pap. 70.00 (*1-58574-114-0*) Lyons Pr.

National Wildlife Federation Staff. Wading into Wetlands. LC 97-28938. (Ranger Rick's Naturescope Ser.). (Illus.). 96p. (J). (gr. 1-7). 1999. lib. bdg. 19.95 (*0-7910-4837-3*) Chelsea Hse.

— Wading into Wetlands. (J). (gr. k-8). 1991. pap. 7.95 (*0-945051-44-1*, 75025) Natl Wildlife.

— Wading into Wetlands. 2nd ed. LC 97-10377. (Ranger Rick's NatureScope Ser.). (Illus.). 90p. (J). (gr. k-8). 1997. pap. 12.95 (*0-07-046507-X*) McGraw.

— Wild about Weather. (Ranger Rick's Naturescope Ser.). (Illus.). 96p. (J). (gr. 1-7). 1999. lib. bdg. 19.95 (*0-7910-4838-1*) Chelsea Hse.

— Wild about Weather. (J). (gr. k-8). 1991. pap. 7.95 (*0-945051-45-X*, 75003) Natl Wildlife.

— Wild & Crafty. LC 98-39164. (Ranger Rick's Naturescope Ser.: Vol. 1). (Illus.). 96p. (J). (gr. 1-7). 1999. lib. bdg. 19.95 (*0-7910-4884-5*) Chelsea Hse.

— Wild & Crafty. LC 97-36213. (Ranger Rick's Naturescope Ser.). 96p. 1998. pap. 12.95 (*0-07-047112-6*) McGraw.

— Wild & Crafty. (J). (gr. k-8). 1991. pap. 7.95 (*0-945051-46-8*, 75043) Natl Wildlife.

National Wildlife Federation Staff, jt. auth. see Halpin, Anne.

National Women's Advisory Board on Sailing Staff. Women's Sailing Resource. 1994. pap. 3.00 (*0-914747-04-5*) Offshore Sail Schl.

National Women's History Project Staff, jt. auth. see Bernikow, Louise.

National Writers Union Staff. Byline: An Insider's Guide to Chicago-Area Print Media. 184p. 1994. pap. 14.95 (*0-9637796-0-5*) Nat Writ Union.

*__National Writers Union Staff.__ National Writer's Union Freelance Writer's Guide. 2nd ed. 2000. pap. 24.95 (*0-9644208-1-3*, Pub. by Natl Writ Union) F & W Pubns Inc.

National Writers Union Staff. National Writers Union Guide to Freelance Rates & Standard Practice. 200p. 1995. pap. 19.95 (*0-9644208-0-5*) Natl Writ Union.

National Zoological Park Staff, et al. Culture: The Missing Element in Conservation & Development. LC 98-11541. 160p. 1998. per. 18.95 (*0-7872-4761-8*) Kendall-Hunt.

Nations, Howard & Kilpatrick, John. Texas Workers' Compensation Law, 4 vols. 1990. write for info. (*0-8205-1735-6*, 735) Bender.

Nations, J. Dale & Stump, Edmund. Geology of Arizona. 2nd ed. 272p. (C). 1996. pap. text, per. 42.95 (*0-7872-2525-8*, 41252501) Kendall-Hunt.

*__Nations, James D., et al, eds.__ Thirteen Ways of Looking at a Tropical Forest: Guatemala's Maya Biosphere Reserve. LC 98-72972. 108 p. 1999. write for info. (*1-881173-27-5*) Conser Intl.

Nations Population Fund Staff. Fertility & Family Surveys in Countries of the ECE Region: Standard County Report, the Netherlands. (Economics Studies: No. 10C). 94p. 1997. pap. 25.00 (*92-1-100758-5*) UN.

Nations Unies, Commission des Sciences et de la Te, ed. L'Autre Developpement: L'Egalite des Sexes dans la Science et la Technologie. LC 96-980107. (FRE.). 400p. 1996. pap. 24.00 (*0-88936-791-4*, Pub. by IDRC Bks) Stylus Pub VA.

Natishan, P. M., et al, eds. Critical Factors in Localized Corrosion, Vol. II. LC 95-61588. (Proceedings Ser.: Vol. 95-15). (Illus.). 456p. 1996. 64.00 (*1-56677-110-2*) Electrochem Soc.

— Passivity & It's Breakdown. LC 98-218261. (Proceedings Ser.: Vol. 97-26). 1038p. 1998. 99.00 (*1-56677-179-X*) Electrochem Soc.

Natiuk, Robert. Your Destiny: Your Life & Work Become One. rev. ed. 96p. 1994. pap. 8.00 (*1-884667-07-4*) Prime Concepts Grp.

Nativ, Ronit. Hydrogeology & Hydrochemistry of the Ogallala Aquifer, Southern High Plains, Texas Panhandle & Eastern New Mexico. (Reports of Investigations: RI 177). (Illus.). 64p. 1988. pap. 3.00 (*0-317-03112-0*) Bur Econ Geology.

Native American Cooperative Staff & Synder, Fred, eds. Native American Directory: Alaska, Canada & U. S. (Illus.). 880p. 1996. reprint ed. pap. 59.95 (*0-9610334-5-2*); reprint ed. lib. bdg. 125.00 (*0-9610334-3-6*) Natl Native.

Native Women's Circle Staff. Into the Moon: Heart, Mind, Body, Soul. 128p. 1996. pap. 11.95 (*1-896705-04-9*) Sister Vis Pr.

Natividad, Irene, jt. ed. see Gall, Susan B.

Natividad, Josephine C. My Oneness with God. Gabrawy, M., tr. LC 89-90122. (ARA., Illus.). 160p. (Orig.). 1989. pap. 4.95 (*0-685-25931-5*) J C Natividad.

Natividad, Oscar, tr. see Carlson, Daniel J.

Natke, H. G., ed. Application of System Identification in Engineering. (CISM International Centre for Mechanical Sciences Ser.: Vol. 296). (Illus.). 583p. 1988. 91.95 (*0-387-82052-3*) Spr-Verlag.

Natke, H. G. & Cempel, Czes A. Model-Aided Diagnosis of Mechanical Systems: Fundamentals, Detection, Localization, & Assessment. LC 96-25712. 330p. 1996. 129.50 (*3-540-61065-0*) Spr-Verlag.

Natke, H. G., ed. see Ben-Haim, Yakov.

Natkiel, Richard, jt. auth. see Ferrell, Robert H.

Natkin, Robert. Subject Matter & Abstraction in Exile. (Illus.). 56p. 1993. pap. 9.95 (*1-870626-58-3*, Pub. by Claridge Pr) Paul & Co Pubs.

Natl. Academy of Engineering Staff. Fourth Annual Symposium on Frontiers of Engineering. LC 99-60544. 160p. (C). 1999. pap. text 30.50 (*0-309-06287-X*) Natl Acad Pr.

— Frontiers of Engineering: Reports on Leading Edge Engineering from the 1996 NAE Symposium on Frontiers of Engineering. LC 97-65474. 136p. (Orig.). 1997. pap. 35.00 (*0-309-05726-4*, Joseph Henry Pr) Natl Acad Pr.

Natl Clearinghouse on Disability & Exch. Staff, jt. auth. see Mobility International U. S. A. Staff.

Natl. Inst. for Social Work Staff. The Barclay Report: Social Workers, Their Role & Tasks. (C). 1987. 65.00 (*0-7855-3743-0*, Pub. by Natl Inst Soc Work) St Mut.

Nat'l Institute for Construction & Design Law. Construction & Design Law Digest, January 1999. 98p. 1999. pap. write for info. (*0-327-01052-5*, 5018015) LEXIS Pub.

Natl. Lubricating Grease Inst. Staff. Guia para Grasas Lubricantes. 4th rev. ed. Ehrlich, Mel, ed.Tr. of NLGI Lubricating Grease Guide. (SPA., Illus.). 148p. 1997. pap. 36.00 (*0-614-28586-0*) Natl Lubrica Grease.

— NLGI Lubricating Grease Guide. 4th rev. ed. Ehrlich, Mel, ed. (Illus.). 148p. 1996. pap. 26.00 (*0-9613935-1-3*) Natl Lubrica Grease.

Natl. Recreation & Park Ethnic Minority Soc. Staff. Colors of Recreation. Hope, Barbara, ed. LC 96-70408. (Illus.). 110p. 1996. 35.00 (*0-9627161-3-8*) QLP CA.

Natl. Research Council Staff. Aviation Safety & Pilot Control: Understanding & Preventing Unfavorable Pilot-Vehicle Interactions. LC 97-65884. 220p. (Orig.). 1997. pap. 37.00 (*0-309-05688-8*, Joseph Henry Pr) Natl Acad Pr.

— Condensed-Matter & Materials Physics: Basic Research for Tomorrow's Technology. LC 99-62179. 324p. (C). 1999. pap. text 52.00 (*0-309-06349-3*, Joseph Henry Pr) Natl Acad Pr.

Natland, James, jt. ed. see Taylor, Brian.

Natland, Manley L., et al. A System of Stages for Correlation of Magallanes Basin Sediments. LC 74-75964. (Geological Society of America, Memoir Ser.: No. 139). 202p. reprint ed. pap. 62.70 (*0-608-13872-X*, 202373500033) Bks Demand.

Natlis, Elena Bruno, see Bruno Natlis, Elena.

*__NATO Advanced Research Workshop on Biogeochemical Cycling & Sediment Ecology Staff, et al.__ Biochemical Cycling & Sediment Ecology. LC 99-29598. (NATO ASI Ser.). 1999. write for info. (*0-7923-5770-1*) Kluwer Academic.

*__NATO Advanced Research Workshop on Ferromagnetic Nano-Crystalline & Thin Film Magnetooptical & Microwave Materials Staff, et al.__ Nano-Crystalline & Thin Film Mangnetic Oxides: Proceedings of the NATO Advanced Research Workshop on Ferromagnetic Nano-Crystalline & Thin Film Magnetooptical & Microwave Materials, Sozopol, Bulgaria Sept. 27 - Oct. 3, 1998. LC 99-37366. (NATO Science Ser. 3). 1999. write for info. (*0-7923-5872-4*) Kluwer Academic.

*__NATO Advanced Research Workshop on Implementing Ecological Integrity: Restoring Regional & Global Environmental & Human Health Staff & Crabbae, P.__ Implementing Ecological Integrity: Restoring Regional & Global Enivronmental & Human Health. LC 00-30179. (NATO Science Ser.). 2000. write for info. (*0-7923-6351-5*) Kluwer Academic.

NATO Advanced Research Workshop on Mathematics Education. Learning from Computers - Mathematics Education & Technology: Proceedings of the NATO Advanced Research Workshop on Mathematics Education & Technology, Held in Villard-de-Lans, Grenoble, France, May 6-11, 1993. Keitel, Christine & Ruthven, Kenneth, eds. LC 93-34948. (NATO ASI Series F: Computer & Systems Sciences, Special Programme AET: Vol. 121). 1993. 93.95 (*0-387-57277-5*) Spr-Verlag.

NATO Advanced Research Workshop on Prediction of I. Prediction of Interannual Climate Variations. Shukla, J., ed. LC 93-18453. (ASI Series 1, Global Environmental Change: Vol. 6). 1993. 174.95 (*0-387-54591-3*) Spr-Verlag.

NATO Advanced Research Workshop on Recent Research. Recent Research Advances in the Fluid Mechanics of Turbulent Jets & Plumes. Do Castelo, Viana, ed. LC 94-684. (NATO Advanced Study Institutes Series E, Applied Sciences: Vol. 255). 1994. text 301.50 (*0-7923-2699-7*) Kluwer Academic.

*__NATO Advanced Research Workshop on RNA: Biochemistry & Biotechnology Staff.__ RNA Biochemistry & Biotechnology: Proceedings of NATO Advanced Research Workshop on RNA, Biochemistry & Biotechnology, Held in Poznan, Poland, on October 10-17, 1998. Barciszewski, Jan & Clark, Brian F., eds. LC 99-38089. (NATO ASI Ser.: Vol. 70). 386p. 1999. 174.00 (*0-7923-5861-9*) Kluwer Academic.

NATO Advanced Research Workshop on Software for Pa. Software for Parallel Computation: Proceedings of the NATO Advanced Research Workshop on Software for Parallel Computation, Held at Cetraro, Cosenza, Italy, June 22-26, 1992. Kowalik, Janusz S. & Grandinetti, Lucio, eds. LC 93-16443. (NATO ASI Series F: Computer & Systems Sciences, Special Programme AET: Vol. 106). 1993. 100.95 (*0-387-56451-9*) Spr-Verlag.

NATO Advanced Research Workshop on the Future. The Future of the Defence Firm - New Challenges, New Directions: Proceedings of the NATO Advanced Research Workshop on the Future of the Defence Firm, Hecla Island, Manitoba, Canada, 21-23 May 1992. Latham, Andrew & Hooper, Nicholas, eds. LC 94-23942. (NATO ASI Series D: Behavioral Sciences: No. 79). 1995. write for info. (*0-7923-3268-7*) Spr-Verlag.

*__NATO Advanced Research Workshop on Unconventional Optical Elements for Information Storage Processing Staff & Marom, E.__ Unconventional Optical Elements for Information Storage, Processing & Communications. LC 00-21744. (NATO ASI Ser.). 2000. write for info. (*0-7923-6190-3*) Kluwer Academic.

NATO Advanced Study Institute (1974: Newcastle upo. The Physics & Chemistry of Minerals & Rocks. Strens, R. G., ed. LC 75-6930. (Illus.). 715p. reprint ed. pap. 200.00 (*0-608-17618-4*, 203047100069) Bks Demand.

NATO Advanced Study Institute (1975: University of. The Early History of the Earth: Based on the Proceedings of a NATO Advanced Study Institute Held at the University of Leicester, April 5-11, 1975. Windley, Brian F., ed. LC 75-26610. 629p. reprint ed. pap. 195.00 (*0-608-15412-1*, 202926600059) Bks Demand.

NATO Advanced Study Institute in Information Scien. Information Science Search for Identity: Proceedings of the 1972 NATO Advanced Study Institute in Information Science Held at Seven Springs, Champion, Pennsylvania, August 12-20, 1972. Debons, Anthony, ed. LC 73-85383. (Books in Library & Information Science: Vol. 7). 511p. reprint ed. pap. 158.50 (*0-608-16578-6*, 202780900054) Bks Demand.

NATO Advanced Study Institute on Materials Science of Carbides & Nitrides Staff, et al. Materials Science of Carbides, Nitrides & Borides: Proceedings of the NATO Advanced Study Institute on Materials Science of Carbides, Nitrides & Borides, St. Petersburg, Russia, August 12-22, 1998. LC 99-25783. (NATO Science Ser.). 1999. write for info. (*0-7923-5706-X*) Kluwer Academic.

NATO Advanced Study Institute on Chemical Separation Technologies and Related Methods: Applications Problems, et al. Chemical Separation Technologies & Related Methods of Nuclear Waste Management: Applications, Problems, & Research Needs. LC 99-13872. (Nato Science Series. Partnership Sub-Series Environmental Security, 2). 1999. write for info. (*0-7923-5638-1*) Kluwer Academic.

NATO Advanced Study Institute on Diffuse Waves in Complex Media Staff & Fouque, Jean-Pierre. Diffuse Waves in Complex Media: Proceedings of the Nato Advanced Study Institute on Diffuse Waves in Complex Media, Les Houches, France, March 17-27, 1998. LC 99-21105. (NATO ASI Series, Series C., Mathematical & Physical Sciences). 1999. write for info. (*0-7923-5679-9*) Kluwer Academic.

*__NATO Advanced Study Institute on Ionic Polymerizations & Related Processes Staff, et al.__ Ionic Polymerizations & Related Processes LC 99-15696. (NATO ASI Ser.). 1999. write for info. (*0-7923-5811-2*) Kluwer Academic.

NATO Advanced Study Institute on Mechanical Proper. Mechanical Properties & Deformation Behavior of Materials Having Ultra-Fine Microstructures: Proceedings of the NATO Advanced Study Institute, Porto Novo, Portugal, June 28 - July 10, 1992. Nastasi, Michael A. et al, eds. LC 93-12427. (NATO Advanced Study Institutes Series E, Applied Sciences: No. 233). 640p. (C). 1993. text 353.00 (*0-7923-2195-2*) Kluwer Academic.

NATO Advanced Study Institute on Mobile Particulat. Mobile Particulate Systems: Proceedings of the NATO Advanced Study Institute, Cargese, Corsica, France, July 4-15, 1994. Guazzelli, Elisabeth, ed. LC 95-9886. (NATO Advanced Science Institutes Series C: Vol. 287). 408p. (C). 1995. text 217.50 (*0-7923-3437-X*) Kluwer Academic.

NATO Advanced Study Institute on Modern Aspects of. Modern Aspects of Small-Angle Scattering: Proceedings of the NATO Advanced Study Institute on Modern Aspects of Small-Angle Scattering, Como, Italy, May 12-22, 1993. Brumberger, H., ed. LC 94-40632. (NATO ASI, Series C). 480p. (C). 1994. text 285.00 (*0-7923-3251-2*) Kluwer Academic.

NATO Advanced Study Institute on Probability Theory. Probability & Phase Transition: Proceedings of the NATO Advanced Study Institute on Probability Theory of Spatial Disorder & Phase Transition, Cambridge, U. K., July 4-16, 1993. Grimmett, Geoffrey, ed. LC 94-669. (NATO Advanced Study Institutes Series C, Mathematical & Physical Sciences: Vol. 420). 340p. (C). 1994. text 183.00 (*0-7923-2720-9*) Kluwer Academic.

NATO Advanced Study Institute on Solar Physics Sta. Solar Physics: The Proceedings of NATO Advanced Study Institute on Solar Physics Held at Lagonissi, Athens, Greece, September 1965. fac. ed. Xanthakis, John N., ed. LC 67-29173. (Illus.). 551p. pap. 170.90 (*0-7837-7365-X*, 204717400005) Bks Demand.

NATO Advanced Study Institute on Synthesis & Analysis. Synthesis & Analysis Methods for Safety & Reliability Studies. Apostolakis, G. et al, eds. LC 79-21315. (Illus.). 473p. reprint ed. pap. 146.70 (*0-608-05467-4*, 206593600006) Bks Demand.

NATO Advanced Study Institute on the Gamma Ray Sky. The Gamma Ray Sky with Compton GRO & SIGMA: Proceedings of the NATO ASI, Les Houches, France, January 25 - February 4, 1994. Vedrenne, G. et al, eds. LC 95-9888. (NATO Advanced Science Institutes Series C: Vol. 401). 436p. (C). 1995. text 217.50 (*0-7923-3440-X*) Kluwer Academic.

NATO Advanced Study Institute on the Origin of the. The Origin of the Solar System. Dermott, S. F., ed. LC 77-7547. (Illus.). 686p. reprint ed. pap. 200.00 (*0-608-17678-8*, 203039500069) Bks Demand.

*__NATO Advanced Study Institute on Theoretical & Observational Cosmology Staff & Rey, Marc L.__ Theoretical & Observational Cosmology: Proceedings of the NATO Advanced Study Institute on Theoretical & Observational Cosmology, Cargese, France, August 17-29, 1998. LC 99-42394. (NATO Science Ser.). 396p. 1999. write for info. (*0-7923-5945-3*) Kluwer Academic.

NATO Advanced Study Institute Staff. Algae & Man. Jackson, Daniel F., ed. LC 63-21218. (Illus.). 444p. 1964. reprint ed. pap. 137.70 (*0-608-05418-6*, 206588700006) Bks Demand.

— Atmospheric Effects on Radar Target Identification & Imaging: Proceedings of the NATO Advanced Study Institute, Goslar, 1975. Jeske, H., ed. (Mathematical & Physical Sciences Ser.: No. 27). 1976. lib. bdg. 141.50 (*90-277-0769-3*) Kluwer Academic.

— Bifurcation Phenomena in Mathematical Physics & Related Topics: Proceedings of the NATO Advanced Study Institute, Cargese, Corsica, June 24 - July, 1979. Bardos, Claude & Bessis, Daniel, eds. (NATO Advanced Study Institutes Series C, Mathematical & Physical Sciences: No. 54). 608p. 1980. text 255.50 (*90-277-1086-4*) Kluwer Academic.

— Charged & Reactive Polymers: Proceedings of the NATO Advanced Study Institute, Forges-les-Eaux, June 18-28, 1972, Vol. 1. Selegny, Eric et al, eds. LC 73-91435. 300p. 1974. text 261.50 (*90-277-0434-1*) Kluwer Academic.

— Chemical Spectroscopy & Photochemistry in the Vacuum: Proceedings of the NATO Advanced Study Institute, 1973. Sandorfy, Camille et al, eds. LC 73-91209. (NATO Advanced Study Institutes Ser.: No. C-8). 1974. text 226.00 (*90-277-0418-X*) Kluwer Academic.

— Combinatorial Programming: Methods & Application, Proceedings of the NATO Advanced Study Institute, Versailles, France, September 2-13, 1974. Roy, B., ed. (NATO Advanced Study Institutes Ser.: No. C19). 221p. 1975. pap. text 58.00 (*90-277-0506-2*, D Reidel) Kluwer Academic.

— Combinatorics: Proceedings of the NATO Advanced Study Institute, Breukelen, the Netherlands, 1974, C16. Hall, M., Jr. & Van Lint, J. H., eds. LC 75-8819. (NATO Advanced Study Institute Ser.: No. C-16). 480p. 1975. text 155.50 (*90-277-0593-3*) Kluwer Academic.

— Computational Techniques in Quantum Chemistry & Molecular Physics: Proceedings of the NATO Advanced Study Institute, C15, Ramsau, Germany, 1974. Diercksen, G. H., ed. LC 75-9913. 568p. 1975. text 206.50 (*90-277-0588-7*) Kluwer Academic.

— Cytopharmacology of Secretion: Proceedings of the NATO Advanced Study Institute, Venice & Milan, June 16-23, 1973. fac. ed. Ceccarelli, B. et al, eds. LC 74-76090. (Advances in Cytopharmacology Ser.: No. 2). (Illus.). 398p. pap. 123.40 (*0-7837-7287-4*, 204701900005) Bks Demand.

An Asterisk (*) at the beginning of an entry indicates that the title is appearing for the first time.

— Earthquake Displacement Fields & the Rotation of the Earth: Proceedings of the NATO Advanced Study Institute Conference, Department of Geophysics, University of Western Ontario, London, Canada, June 22-28, 1969. Mansinha, L. et al, eds. LC 72-118130. (Astrophysics & Space Science Library: No. 20). 308p. 1970. text 126.50 (*90-277-0159-8*) Kluwer Academic.

— Electrode Processes in Solid State Ionics: Proceedings. Kleitz, M. & Dupuy, J., eds. LC 75-44113. 1975. text 208.00 (*90-277-0679-4*) Kluwer Academic.

— Electronic States of Inorganic Compounds - New Experimental Techniques: Proceedings of the NATO Advanced Study Institute, Inorganic Laboratory, St. John's College, Oxford, September 8-18, 1974. Day, P., ed. LC 75-17752. (NATO Advanced Study Institute Ser: No. C20). 541p. 1975. text 206.50 (*90-277-0627-1*) Kluwer Academic.

— Far-Infrared Properties of Solids: Proceedings. Mitra, S. S. & Nudelman, S., eds. LC 78-122627. (Optical Physics & Engineering Ser.). (Illus.). 613p. 1970. reprint ed. pap. 190.10 (*0-608-05483-6*, 206595200006) Bks Demand.

— Geodynamics of Iceland & the North Atlantic Area: Proceedings of the NATO Advanced Study Institute, University of Iceland, Reykjavik, Iceland, July 1-7, 1974. Kristjansson, L., ed. LC 74-27848. (NATO Advanced Study Institute Ser.: No. C11). 323p. 1974. text 126.50 (*90-277-0505-4*) Kluwer Academic.

— Geometric Methods in System Theory: Proceedings of the NATO Advanced Study Institute, 1973. Mayne, D. Q. & Brockett, R. W., eds. LC 73-91206. (NATO Advanced Study Institutes Ser.: No. C-3). 1973. text 126.50 (*90-277-0415-5*) Kluwer Academic.

— Group Theory in Non-Linear Problems: Lectures in Mathematical Physics at the NATO Advanced Study Institute, Istanbul, Turkey, August, 1972. Barut, Asim O., ed. LC 73-91202. (NATO Advanced Study Institutes Ser.: No. C-7). 1974. text 164.50 (*90-277-0412-0*) Kluwer Academic.

— Interstellar Medium: Proceedings of the NATO Advanced Study Institute, Schliersee, Germany, April, 1973. Pinkau, K., ed. LC 73-91208. (NATO Advanced Study Institutes Ser.: No. C-6). 1974. lib. bdg. 100.50 (*90-277-0417-1*) Kluwer Academic.

— The Lives of the Neutron Stars: Proceedings of the NATO Advanced Study Institute on the Lives of the Neutron Stars (1993: Kemer, Turkey) Van Paradijs, Jan et al, eds. LC 94-40636. (NATO ASI Ser.: Vol. 450). 576p. (C). 1994. text 357.00 (*0-7923-3246-6*) Kluwer Academic.

— Long-Time Predictions in Dynamics: Proceedings of the NATO Advanced Study Institute held in Cortina d'Ampezzo, Italy, August 3-16, 1975. Szebehely, Victor G. & Tapley, Byron D., eds. LC 76-7373. (NATO Advanced Study Institutes Ser.: No. 26). 1975. lib. bdg. 112.00 (*90-277-0692-1*) Kluwer Academic.

— Modern Aspects of Mass Spectrometry: Proceedings of the NATO Advanced Study Institute on Mass Spectrometry, 2nd, 1966. Reed, Rowland I., ed. LC 68-16994. 401p. reprint ed. pap. 124.40 (*0-608-09938-4*, 202070300018) Bks Demand.

— Modern Topics in Micro Wave Propagation & Air-Sea Interaction: Proceedings of the NATO Advanced Study Institute, Sorrento, Italy, June, 1973. Zancla, A., ed. LC 73-91210. (NATO ASI Series C: No. 5). 1973. text 195.00 (*90-277-0419-8*) Kluwer Academic.

— New Advances in Distributed Computer Systems: Proceedings of the NATO Advanced Study Institute, Bonas, France, June 15-26, 1981. Beauchamp, Kenneth G., ed. x, 417p. 1982. text 281.50 (*90-277-1379-0*) Kluwer Academic.

— Numerical Solution of Partial Differential Equations: Proceedings of the NATO Advanced Study Institute, Kjeller, Norway, August, 1973. Gram, J., ed. LC 73-91204. (NATO Advanced Study Institutes Ser.: No. C-2). 1973. text 162.50 (*90-277-0413-9*) Kluwer Academic.

— The Physics of Non-Thermal Radio Sources: Proceedings of the NATO Advanced Study Institute, Urbino, 1975. Setti, Giancarlo, ed. (Mathematical & Physical Sciences Ser.: No. 28). 1976. lib. bdg. 88.00 (*90-277-0753-7*) Kluwer Academic.

— Physics of the Solar Corona: Proceedings of the NATO Advanced Study Institute on Physics of the Solar Corona, Cavouri-Vouliagmeni, Athens, 1970. Macris, C. J., ed. LC 76-154741. (Astrophysics & Space Science Library: No. 27). 345p. 1971. text 178.50 (*90-277-0204-7*) Kluwer Academic.

— Reactions on Polymers: Proceedings of the NATO Advanced Study Institute, No. C-4, Troy, N. Y., July, 1973. Moore, James A., ed. LC 73-91207. 1973. text 171.00 (*90-277-0416-3*) Kluwer Academic.

— Recent Advances in Dynamical Astronomy: Proceedings of the NATO Advanced Study Institute in Dynamical Astronomy, Cortina D'ampezzo, August, 1972. Tapley, Byron D. & Szebehely, Victor G., eds. LC 73-83571. (Astrophysics & Space Science Library: No. 39). 490p. 1973. text 255.50 (*90-277-0348-5*) Kluwer Academic.

— Scattering Theory in Mathematical Physics: Proceedings of the NATO Advanced Study Institute, Denver, Colorado, June, 1973. LaVita, J. A. & Marchand, J. P., eds. LC 73-91205. 1974. text 148.50 (*90-277-0414-7*) Kluwer Academic.

— Semiclassical Methods in Molecular Scattering & Spectroscopy: Proceedings of the NATO Advanced Study Institute, Cambridge, England, September, 1979. Child, M. S., ed. (NATO Advanced Study Institutes Series C, Mathematical & Physical Sciences: No. 53). 344p. 1980. text 135.00 (*90-277-1082-1*) Kluwer Academic.

— Studies in Mathematical Physics: Lectures in Mathematical Physics at the NATO Advanced Study Institute, Istanbul, Turkey, August, 1970, Vol. 1. Barut, Asim O., ed. LC 73-88587. (NATO Advanced Study Institutes Ser.: No. C-1). 1973. text 126.50 (*90-277-0405-8*) Kluwer Academic.

— The Theory & Application of Differential Games: Proceedings of the NATO Advanced Study Institute, University of Warwick, Coventry England, August 27 - September 6, 1974. Grote, J. D., ed. LC 74-34041. (NATO Advanced Study Institutes Ser.: No. C13). 310p. 1975. lib. bdg. 104.50 (*90-277-0581-X*) Kluwer Academic.

NATO Advanced Study Institute Staff & Holtet, Jan A. ELF-VLF Radio Wave Propagation: Proceedings of the NATO Advanced Study Institute, Spatind, Norway, April 17-27, 1974. LC 74-83870. 450p. 1974. text 171.00 (*90-277-0503-8*) Kluwer Academic.

NATO Advanced Study Institute Staff & Ribeiro, F. Ramoa. Zeolites: Proceedings: Science & Technology, NATO Advanced Study Institute on Zeolites, Portugal, 1983. 1984. text 289.00 (*90-247-2935-1*) Kluwer Academic.

NATO Advanced Study Institute Staff & Simbo, C. Hamiltonian Systems with Three or More Degrees of Freedom: Proceedings of the NATO Advanced Study Institute Held in S'agaro (spain) from June 19 to 30, 1995. LC 99-25781. (NATO ASI Series, Series C, Mathematical & Physical Sciences). 1999. write for info. (*0-7923-5710-8*) Kluwer Academic.

NATO ASI & AMS Summer Seminar in Applied Mathemati. Geometrical Methods for the Theory of Linear Systems: Proceedings of the NATO ASI & AMS Summer Seminar in Applied Mathematics held at Harvard University, Cambridge, MA, June 18-29, 1979. Byrnes, Christopher I. & Martin, Clyde F., eds. (NATO ASI Series C, Mathematical & Physical Sciences: No. 62). 313p. 1980. text 135.00 (*90-277-1154-2*) Kluwer Academic.

NATO Defense College Staff, ed. Co-Operative Security Arrangements in Europe. (Euro-Atlantic Security Studies: Vol. 5). 153p. 1997. pap. 35.95 (*3-631-31894-4*) P Lang Pubng.

— Military Assistance to the Civil Authorities in Democracies: Case Studies & Perspectives. LC 96-38060. (Euro-Atlantic Security Studies: Vol. 4). 145p. 1996. pap. 35.95 (*3-631-30485-4*) P Lang Pubng.

NATO Defense College Staff, ed. see Lupiy, Bohdan.

NATO Economic Directorate Staff, ed. Cmea: Energy, 1980-1990. (NATO Colloquim Publications). 337p. 1982. 45.00 (*0-89250-341-6*) Orient Res Partners.

***NATO International Scientific Exchange Programmes Advanced Study Institute Staff, et al.** Oxygen Ion & Mixed Conductors & Their Technological Applications: Proceedings from the NATO International Scientific Exchange Programmes Advanced Study Institute, Erice, Sicily, Italy, 15-30 July, 1997. LC 00-26058. (NATO Science Ser.). 2000. write for info. (*0-7923-6253-5*) Kluwer Academic.

NATO Science Committee Conference on Catalysis Sta. Catalysis, Progress in Research: Proceedings. Basolo, Fred & Burwell, Robert L., Jr., eds. LC 73-81490. (Illus.). 209p. reprint ed. pap. 64.80 (*0-608-05468-2*, 206593700006) Bks Demand.

NATO Scientific Affairs Organization Staff. Tumor Biology: Regulation of Cell Growth, Differentiation & Genetics in Cancer. Tsiftoglou, Asterios S., ed. LC 96-32244. (NATO ASI Ser.; Cell Biology). 331p. 1996. 149.50 (*3-540-61492-3*) Spr-Verlag.

NATO Staff. Atmospheric Nuclear Tests: Environmental & Human Consequences. Shapiro, Charles S., ed. LC 97-38993. (NATO ASI Ser.: Vol. 35). 294p. 1998. 130.00 (*3-540-63804-0*) Spr-Verlag.

— Economic Reforms in Eastern Europe. 1981. pap. write for info. (*0-08-026800-5*, Pergamon Pr) Elsevier.

— Nuclear Tests: Long-Term Consequences in the Semipalatinsk/Altai Region. Shapiro, Charles S. et al, eds. LC 97-39008. (NATO ASI Ser.: Vol. 36). 202p. 1998. 110.00 (*3-540-63805-9*) Spr-Verlag.

— The Stratosphere & Its Role in the Climate System. Brasseur, Guy P., ed. LC 97-36268. (NATO ASI Ser.: Series I, Global Environmental Change: Vol. 54). xx, 368p. 1997. text 368.00 (*3-540-63474-6*) Spr-Verlag.

NATO Study Institute Staff & Thoft-Christensen, P. Continuum Mechanics Aspects of Geodynamics & Rock Fracture Mechanics: Proceedings of the NATO Study Institute, Reykjavik, Iceland, August 11-20, 1974. LC 74-34161. (NATO Advanced Study Institutes Ser.: No. C12). 273p. 1974. text 106.00 (*90-277-0504-6*) Kluwer Academic.

Natoli, Charles M. Nietzsche & Pascal on Christianity. LC 83-49020. (American University Studies: Philosophy: Ser. V, Vol. 3). 197p. (Orig.). (C). 1985. pap. text 24.25 (*0-8204-0071-8*) P Lang Pubng.

Natoli, Joseph P. Hauntings: Popular Film & American Culture 1990-1992. LC 94-5027. (SUNY Series in Postmodern Culture). 238p. (C). 1994. pap. text 16.95 (*0-7914-2154-6*) State U NY Pr.

— Hauntings: Popular Film & American Culture 1990-1992. LC 94-5027. (SUNY Series in Postmodern Culture). 238p. (C). 1994. text 49.50 (*0-7914-2153-8*) State U NY Pr.

***Natoli, Joseph P.** Postmodern Journeys: Film & Culture 1996-1998. LC 00-20339. (C). 2000. text 57.50 (*0-7914-4771-5*) State U NY Pr.

— Postmodern Journeys: Film & Culture, 1996-1998. LC 00-20339. 2000. pap. 18.95 (*0-7914-4772-3*) State U NY Pr.

Natoli, Joseph P. A Primer to Postmodernity. LC 97-7779. 224p. 1997. text 57.95 (*1-57718-060-7*); pap. text 21.95 (*1-57718-061-5*) Blackwell Pubs.

— Speeding to the Millennium: Film & Culture, 1993-1995. LC 97-26977. (SUNY Series in Postmodern Culture). 288p. (C). 1998. text 65.50 (*0-7914-3727-2*); pap. text 21.95 (*0-7914-3728-0*) State U NY Pr.

Natoli, Joseph P., ed. Literary Theory's Future(s) LC 88-31742. 352p. 1989. text 34.95 (*0-252-01599-1*); pap. text 14.95 (*0-252-06049-0*) U of Ill Pr.

— Tracing Literary Theory. LC 86-24982. 400p. 1987. pap. 14.95 (*0-252-01384-0*) U of Ill Pr.

Natoli, Joseph P. & Hutcheon, Linda, eds. A Postmodern Reader. LC 92-39294. 584p. (C). 1993. pap. text 21.95 (*0-7914-1638-0*) State U NY Pr.

— A Postmodern Reader. LC 92-39294. 584p. (C). 1993. text 59.50 (*0-7914-1637-2*) State U NY Pr.

Natoli, Joseph P. & Rusch, Frederik L., compiled by. Psychocriticism: An Annotated Bibliography, 1. LC 84-4689. (Bibliographies & Indexes in World Literature Ser.: No. 1). 267p. 1984. lib. bdg. 59.95 (*0-313-23641-0*, NPL/, Greenwood Pr) Greenwood.

Natoli, Marie D. American Prince, American Pauper: The Contemporary Vice-Presidency in Perspective, 134. LC 84-28965. (Contributions in Political Science Ser.: No. 134). 204p. 1985. 49.95 (*0-313-24750-1*, NAR/, Greenwood Pr) Greenwood.

Natoli, Salvatore J., ed. Strengthening Geography in the Social Studies. LC 88-61299. (Bulletin Ser.: No. 8). (Illus.). 127p. 1994. reprint ed. pap. 9.95 (*0-87986-056-1*, BU810088) Nat Coun Soc Studies.

Natoli, Salvatore J., ed. see Roseman, Curtis C.

Natoli, Salvatore J., ed. see Salter, Christopher & Lloyd, William.

Natonek, Emerico, jt. ed. see Stein, Matthew R.

Natori, M., et al, eds. Proceedings of the Fourth International Conference on Adaptive Structures. 686p. 1994. 79.95 (*1-56676-161-1*, 761611) Technomic.

— Proceedings of the Third International Conference on Adaptive Structures. LC 93-60100. 735p. 1993. text 79.95 (*1-56676-028-3*) Technomic.

Natori, Yoshihiro, jt. auth. see Rhoton, Albert L., Jr.

***Natorp, Hans-Jorg.** Die Rechtslage der DDR-Naturschutzgebiete in Mecklenburg-Vorpommern Nach Dem Einigungsvertrag. (Europaische Hochschulschriften Ser: Bd. 2763). 257p. 1999. 45.95 (*3-631-35617-X*) P Lang Pubng.

Natorp, Paul. Die Ethica des Demokritos. vi, 198p. 1970. reprint ed. write for info. (*0-318-70980-5*) G Olms Pubs.

— Forschungen Zur Geschichte Des Erkenntnisproblems Im Altertum. Protagoras, Demokrit, Epikuruund die Skepsis. viii, 316p. 1990. reprint ed. write for info. (*3-487-01087-9*) G Olms Pubs.

***Natov, Nikolay.** Foreign Investments in Bulgaria. LC 00-21883. 276p. 2000. 87.45 (*90-411-1278-2*) Kluwer Law Intl.

Natov, Roni. Leon Garfield. (Twayne's English Authors Ser.: No. 505). 176p. 1994. 22.95 (*0-8057-7042-9*, Twyne) Mac Lib Ref.

Natow. Eating Out Nutrition Guide. 1998. mass mkt. 6.99 (*0-671-89471-4*) PB.

— The Food Shopping Counter. LC 99-236278. 1999. mass mkt. 6.99 (*0-671-00452-2*) S&S Trade.

Natow, Annette. Pocket Fat Counter. 2nd ed. 1998. per. 2.99 (*0-671-00450-6*, Pocket Books) PB.

***Natow, Annette & Heslin, Jo-Ann.** Calcium Counts. 96p. 2000. per. 3.50 (*0-671-04272-6*) PB.

— The Fat Counter. 5th rev. ed. 736p. 2000. per. 6.99 (*0-671-02565-1*, Pocket Books) PB.

Natow, Annette & Heslin, Jo-Ann. The Mini Baby Counter. 208p. 1999. per. 3.99 (*0-671-02563-5*) PB.

— The Most Complete Food Counter. LC 99-17169. 448p. 1999. per. 16.00 (*0-671-02561-9*, PB Trade Paper) PB.

Natow, Annette B. The Anti-Oxidant Counter. LC 97-122165. 1994. mass mkt. 5.99 (*0-671-78320-3*) PB.

— The Cholesterol Counter. 5th rev. ed. 704p. 1998. per. 6.99 (*0-671-00451-4*) PB.

— Cholesterol Counter News Week. 1989. per. 4.95 (*0-671-68274-1*) PB.

— Fast Food Nutrition Counter. 288p. 1994. per. 5.99 (*0-671-89475-7*) PB.

— The Fat Counter. 3rd rev. ed. 1995. mass mkt. 6.99 (*0-671-78335-1*) PB.

— The Fat Counter. 4th ed. 1998. per. 6.99 (*0-671-55500-5*, Pocket Books) PB.

— The Supermarket Nutrition Counter. 2nd ed. (Orig.). 1997. per. 6.99 (*0-671-89473-0*) PB.

Natow, Annette B. & Helsin, Jo-Ann. The Protein Counter. 576p. 1997. per. 6.99 (*0-671-00381-X*, Pocket Books) PB.

Natow, Annette B. & Heslin, Jo-Ann. The Calorie Counter. 1997. per. 6.99 (*0-671-89474-9*) PB.

***Natow, Annette B. & Heslin, Jo-Ann.** The Calorie Counter. 2nd rev. ed. 624p. 2000. per. 6.99 (*0-671-02564-3*, Pocket Books) PB.

Natow, Annette B. & Heslin, Jo-Ann. The Carbohydrate, Fiber & Sugar Counter. 1999. per. 6.99 (*0-671-03648-3*) PB.

— Carbohydrate Fiber & Sugar Counter. 1999. per. 6.99 (*0-671-02562-7*) S&S Trade.

— The Cholesterol Counter. 4th ed. 1996. mass mkt. 6.99 (*0-671-89472-2*) S&S Trade.

— The Diabetes Carbohydrate & Calorie Counter. Peters, Sally, ed. 265p. 1991. per. 6.50 (*0-671-69565-7*) PB.

— The Pocket Fat Counter. 1996. pap. 2.99 (*0-671-53260-X*, PB Trade Paper) PB.

— The Supermarket Nutrition Counter. Rubinstein, Julie, ed. 608p. (Orig.). 1995. mass mkt. 5.99 (*0-671-78328-9*) PB.

Natow, Annette B. & Heslin, Joann. Count on a Healthy Pregnancy. Peters, Sally, ed. LC 93-133759. 304p. 1999. per. 6.99 (*0-671-69563-0*, Pocket Star Bks) PB.

Natow, Annette B. & Heslin, JoAnn. The Fat Attack Plan. Zion, Claire, ed. 400p. 1991. reprint ed. per. 6.99 (*0-671-73426-1*) PB.

Natow, Annette B. & Hesun, Jo-Ann. The Cholesterol Counter. 3rd rev. ed. Peters, Sally, ed. 592p. 1993. mass mkt. 5.99 (*0-671-75173-5*) PB.

Natow, Annette B. & Hesun, JoAnn. Sodium Counter. Peters, Sally, ed. 576p. (Orig.). 1993. pap. text 5.99 (*0-671-69566-5*) PB.

Natowitz, J. B., ed. Nuclear Dynamics & Nuclear Disassembly. 552p. (C). 1989. text 151.00 (*9971-5-0945-8*) World Scientific Pub.

Natriello, Gary. Schooling Disadvantaged Children: Racing Against Catastrophe. 272p. (C). 1990. pap. text 19.95 (*0-8077-3014-9*) Tchrs Coll.

Natriello, Gary, contrib. by. The New Regents High School Graduation Requirements: Curricular & Instructional Implications & Estimates of Resources Necessary to Meet the New Standards. 86p. 1998. 15.00 (*0-88156-252-1*) Comm Serv Soc NY.

Natriello, Gary, ed. School Dropouts: Patterns & Policies. enl. ed. 192p. 1986. reprint ed. pap. 17.95 (*0-8077-2835-7*) Tchrs Coll.

— School Dropouts: Patterns & Policies. LC 86-22978. 191p. 1987. reprint ed. pap. 59.30 (*0-608-01657-8*, 206230900002) Bks Demand.

Natriuretic Hormone Symposium Staff. Regulation of Body Fluid Volumes by the Kidney: Proceedings of the Natriuretic Hormone Symposium, Czechoslovakia, June, 1969. Cort, J. H. & Lichardus, B., eds. (Illus.). 192p. 1970. 59.25 (*3-8055-0772-0*) S Karger.

Natsios, Andrew S. Stay the Course: European Unity & Atlantic Solidarity, 171. LC 96-54065. (Washington Papers: Vol. 171). 128p. 1997. 52.95 (*0-275-95932-5*, Praeger Pubs); pap. 15.95 (*0-275-95933-3*, Praeger Pubs) Greenwood.

— U. S. Foreign Policy & the Four Horsemen of the Apocalypse: Humanitarian Relief in Complex Emergencies, 170. LC 96-52721. 216p. 1997. 57.95 (*0-275-95920-1*); pap. 18.95 (*0-275-95921-X*) Greenwood.

Natsolim. Gniezniks, Polonian Pioneers. LC 83-60206. (Illus.). 304p. (Orig.). 1984. pap. text 15.00 (*0-918020-06-9*) Masspac Pub.

Natsoulas, John, ed. see De Paoli, Geri & Resler, Nancy D.

Natsoulas, John, ed. see Foley, Jack, et al.

Natsoulas, John, ed. see Nixon, Bruce & Hopps, Walter.

***Natsuishi, Ban'ya.** A Future Waterfall: 100 Haiku from the Japanese. Kacian, Jim et al, trs. 72p. 1999. pap. 12.00 (*1-893959-04-X*) Red Moon Pr.

Natsume Kinnosuke, see Natsume Soseki, pseud.

Natsume Soseki, pseud. And Then: Natsume Soseki's Novel Sorekara. Field, Norma M., tr. from JPN. LC 97-21881. (Michigan Classics in Japanese Studies: Vol. 17). viii, 280p. 1997. reprint ed. pap. 15.95 (*0-939512-82-3*) U MI Japan.

— Botchan. Shaw, ed. Turney, Alan, tr. from JPN. LC 71-174215. (Illus.). 173p. 1992. reprint ed. pap. 10.00 (*0-87011-367-4*) Kodansha.

— Botchan. Saski, Umeji, tr. LC 68-11794. 192p. 1968. reprint ed. pap. 9.95 (*0-8048-1620-4*) Tuttle Pubng.

— Grass on the Wayside. McClellan, Edwin, tr. & intro. by. LC 90-1363. (Michigan Classics in Japanese Studies: No. 2). xii, 169p. 1990. reprint ed. pap. text 8.95 (*0-939512-45-9*) U MI Japan.

— I Am a Cat. Ito, Aiko & Wilson, Graeme, trs. LC 78-182064. 220p. 1972. reprint ed. pap. 12.95 (*0-8048-1621-2*) Tuttle Pubng.

— I Am a Cat, Bk. II. Ito, Aiko & Wilson, Graeme, trs. from JPN. LC 78-182064. 268p. 1979. pap. 12.95 (*0-8048-1280-2*) Tuttle Pubng.

— I Am a Cat, Vol. 3. Ito, Aiko & Wilson, Graeme, trs. 270p. 1993. pap. 12.95 (*0-8048-1860-6*) Tuttle Pubng.

— Kokoro. McClellan, Edwin, tr. LC 85-7574. 248p. 1996. pap. 14.95 (*0-89526-715-2*, Gateway Editions) Regnery Pub.

— Kokoro & Selected Essays. McClellan, Edwin & Rubin, Jay, trs. from JPN. (Library of Japan). 375p. 1992. 29.95 (*0-8191-8248-6*) Madison Bks UPA.

— Light & Darkness. 397p. 1971. 33.00 (*0-7206-0400-1*, Pub. by P Owen Ltd) Dufour.

— The Miner. Rubin, Jay, tr. from JPN. LC 87-26711. 200p. 1988. 32.50 (*0-8047-1460-6*) Stanford U Pr.

— The Tower of London. Milward, Peter & Nakano, Kii, trs. LC 93-109654. (Illus.). 80p. 1997. pap. 9.95 (*1-873047-90-8*, Pub. by In Print Pub) Weatherhill.

— The Wayfarer. Beongcheon Yu, tr. from JPN. & intro. by. LC 66-26974. 326p. reprint ed. pap. 101.10 (*0-7837-3625-8*, 204349100009) Bks Demand.

Natsuyama, H. H. & Kalaba, Robert E. Integral equations via imbedding methods. LC 74-13228. 1974. write for info. (*0-201-04106-5*) Addison-Wesley.

Natsuyama, H. H., et al. Multiple Scattering Processes: Inverse & Direct. LC 75-22363. 1975. write for info. (*0-201-04104-9*) Addison-Wesley.

Natsuyama, H. H., et al. Terrestrial Radiative Transfer: Modeling, Computation, & Data Analysis. (Illus.). xxii, 282p. 1998. pap. 99.95 (*4-431-70206-7*) Spr-Verlag.

Natt, Ted. 3-Minute Dieting: The Holistic Approach to Permanent Weight Loss. (Illus.). 248p. (Orig.). 1996. pap., spiral bd. 29.97 (*0-9654658-0-2*) Light Inc.

Natta, G. & Danusso, F. Contributions of G. Natta & His School to Polymer Chemistry, 2 vols., Set. LC 63-10026. (Stereoregular Polymers & Stereospecific Polymerizations Ser.). 1967. 408.00 (*0-08-010156-9*, Pub. by Pergamon Repr) Franklin.

***Nattel, Lilian.** The River Midnight: A Novel. 416p. 1999. per. 14.00 (*0-684-85304-3*) S&S Trade Pap.

Nattel, Lilian. The River Midnight: A Novel. LC 98-27773. 416p. 1999. 24.50 (*0-684-85303-5*) Scribner.

Natter, Elizabeth U., jt. auth. see Harker, Donald F.

***Natter, Irving.** Natter's New York City Education Bluebook, 1999-2000. 58p. 1999. pap. 4.50 (*0-936143-14-2*) Natter Pub.

Natter, Tobias G., jt. ed. see Frodl, Gerbert.

N

Natter, Wolfgang, et al, eds. Objectivity & Its Other. 214p. 1995. pap. text 18.95 (*0-89862-545-9*) Guilford Pubns.

Natter, Wolfgang, jt. auth. see Schatzki, Theodore R.

Natter, Wolfgang, jt. ed. see Schatzki, Theodore R.

***Natter, Wolfgang G.** Literature at War, 1914-1940: Representing the Time of Greatness in Germany. LC 98-39029. (Illus.). 280p. 1999. 35.00 (*0-300-05558-7*) Yale U Pr.

Natterson, Joseph M. Beyond Countertransference: The Therapist's Subjectivity in the Therapeutic Process. LC 90-14542. 256p. 1991. 50.00 (*0-87668-558-0*) Aronson.

— The Dream in Clinical Practice. LC 80-65142. 520p. 1993. pap. 50.00 (*1-56821-091-4*) Aronson.

Natterson, Joseph M., ed. The Dream in Clinical Practice. LC 80-65142. 498p. 1980. 40.00 (*0-87668-402-9*) Aronson.

Natterson, Joseph M. & Friedman, Raymond J. A Primer of Clinical Intersubjectivity. LC 94-43799. 184p. 1995. pap. 35.00 (*1-56821-446-4*) Aronson.

Natterstad, Jerry, jt. auth. see Levenson, Leah.

Natterstad, Jerry H. Francis Stuart. (Irish Writers Ser.). 88p. 1975. 8.50 (*0-8387-7895-X*); pap. 1.95 (*0-8387-7979-4*) Bucknell U Pr.

Natterstad, Jerry H., jt. auth. see Levenson, Leah.

Natti, Jouko, jt. auth. see Julkumen, Raija.

Natti, Lee K., ed. Cape Ann: A Photographic Portrait. (Pilot Press-Twin Lights Ser.). (Illus.). 128p. 1999. 24.95 (*1-885435-07-X*, PilotPress Pubs) Twin Lights.

Natti, Susanna, jt. auth. see Adler, David A.

Nattier, Jan. Once upon a Future Time: Studies in a Buddhist Prophecy of Decline. LC 91-42549. (Nanzan Studies in Asian Religions: Vol. 1). 352p. (C). 1992. text 50.00 (*0-89581-925-2*); pap. text 25.00 (*0-89581-926-0*) Asian Humanities.

Nattiez, Jean-Jacques. Proust As Musician. Puffett, Derrick, tr. 136p. (C). 1989. text 49.95 (*0-521-36349-7*) Cambridge U Pr.

— Wagner Androgyne. (Princeton Studies in Opera). 380p. 1993. pap. text 18.95 (*0-691-04832-0*, Pub. by Princeton U Pr) Cal Prin Full Svc.

Nattiez, Jean-Jacques, ed. see Boulez, Pierre.

Nattinger, J. R. & De Carrico, J. Lexical Phrases & Language Teaching. (Illus.). 236p. 1992. pap. text 21.95 (*0-19-437164-6*) OUP.

Nattkemper, Jean, ed. see Haggerty, Brian A.

Nattrass, Leonora. William Cobbett: The Politics of Style. (Cambridge Studies in Romanticism: No. 11). 263p. (C). 1995. text 64.95 (*0-521-46036-0*) Cambridge U Pr.

Nattrass, Leonora, ed. William Cobbett: Selected Writings, 6 vols. LC 98-26512. (Pickering Masters Ser.: Vol. 6). 2500p. 1998. text 695.00 (*1-85196-375-8*, Pub. by Pickering & Chatto) Ashgate Pub Co.

Nattrass, Malcolm. Malin's Clinical Diabetes. 2nd ed. (Illus.). 432p. 1996. text 75.00 (*0-412-30860-6*, Pub. by E A) OUP.

Natu, Bal. Conversations with the Awakener. 113p. 1991. pap. 10.00 (*1-880619-00-8*) Sheriar Found.

— Glimpses of the God-Man, Meher Baba (1943-1948), Vol. 1. LC 76-57047. 431p. 1997. pap. 10.95 (*0-915828-12-X*) Sufism Reoriented.

— Glimpses of the God-Man, Meher Baba: (March 1954-April 1955), Vol. VI. 264p. (Orig.). 1995. pap. 12.00 (*1-880619-05-9*) Sheriar Found.

— Glimpses of the God-Man, Meher Baba Vol. IV: February - December, 1953. LC 79-913293. (Illus.). 218p. (Orig.). 1984. pap. 10.00 (*0-913078-52-2*) Sheriar Pr.

***Natu, Bal.** Intimate Conversations with the Awakener. 100p. 1998. pap. 12.00 (*1-880619-22-9*) Sheriar Found.

Natu, Bal. More Conversations with the Awakener. 100p. (Orig.). 1993. pap. 10.00 (*1-880619-07-5*) Sheriar Found.

— The Samadhi: Star of Infinity. LC 97-68256. (Illus.). 129p. 1997. pap. 12.00 (*1-880619-19-9*) Sheriar Found.

Natu, Bal, ed. see Baba, Meher.

Natuf. Dictionary of the Occult. (Reference Library). 256p. 1997. pap. 6.95 (*1-85326-333-8*, 3338WW, Pub. by Wrdsworth Edits) NTC Contemp Pub Co.

Natural & Ajjan, Diana L. Asthma & Allergies: The Natural Way of Healing. 400p. 1995. mass mkt. 5.99 (*0-440-21662-1*) Dell.

— Stress, Anxiety, & Depression: The Natural Way of Healing. LC 95-157966. 304p. 1995. mass mkt. 5.99 (*0-440-21659-1*) Dell.

Natural & Digeronimo, Theresa. Chronic Pain: The Natural Way of Healing. 352p. 1995. mass mkt. 5.99 (*0-440-21658-3*) Dell.

Natural & Papas, Diana L. Women's Health: The Natural Way of Healing. 400p. 1995. mass mkt. 5.50 (*0-440-21661-3*) Dell.

***Natural Area Preservation Division Staff.** Along the Huron: The Natural Communities of the Huron River Corridor in Ann Arbor, Michigan. 136p. 1999. pap. 15.95 (*0-472-08651-0*, 08651) U of Mich Pr.

Natural Fibers Information Center Staff. History of Cotton in Texas. 50p. (Orig.). 1989. pap. 5.00 (*0-87755-317-3*) Bureau Busn TX.

Natural Fibers Research & Information Center Staff. Natural Fibers Fact Book, 1998. (Illus.). 50p. 1995. pap. 15.00 (*0-87755-329-7*) Bureau Busn TX.

Natural Health Magazine Editors & Jacobi, Dana. The Natural Health Cookbook: More than 150 Recipes to Sustain & Heal the Body. LC 95-8. 272p. 1995. 24.00 (*0-684-80398-4*) S&S Trade.

Natural Health Magazine Editors & Mayeell, Mark. The Natural Health First-Aid Guide: The Definitive Handbook of Natural Remedies for Treating Minor Emergencies. LC 93-11906. 558p. 1994. pap. 14.00 (*0-671-79273-3*) PB.

Natural Health Magazine Editors & Mayell, Mark. 52 Simple Steps to Natural Health: A Week-by-Week Guide to More Healthful Living. Zion, Claire, ed. 448p. 1995. per. 14.00 (*0-671-88061-6*) PB.

Natural History Museum (London), General Library S, jt. auth. see Thackeray, John C.

Natural History Museum Staff. Rocks & Minerals. LC 87-26514. (Eyewitness Books). (Illus.). 64p. (J). (gr. 5 up). 1988. 19.00 (*0-394-89621-1*, Pub. by Knopf Bks Yng Read) Random.

— Rocks & Minerals. LC 87-26514. (Eyewitness Books). (Illus.). 64p. (J). (gr. 5 up). 1988. lib. bdg. 20.99 (*0-394-99621-6*, Pub. by Knopf Bks Yng Read) Random.

Natural Resource, Agriculture & Engineering Service Conference Staff, ed. Apple Harvesting, Hangling & Storage: Proceedings from the Harvesting, Handling & Storage Workshop, Cornell University, Ithaca, New York, August 14, 1997. (NRAES Ser.: Vol. 112). 84p. 1997. pap. text 15.00 (*0-935817-61-1*, NRAES-112) NRAES.

— Expansion Strategies for Dairy Farms: Facilities & Financial Planning, Notebook for the Expansion Strategies for Dairy Farms National Conference, Ellicott City, Maryland, December 8 & 9, 1994. abr. ed. (NRAES Ser.: Vol. 77). (Illus.). 490p. 1994. ring bd. 50.00 (*0-935817-63-8*, NRAES-77) NRAES.

— Farm Machinery Days for Small & Part-Time Farmers: Proceedings from Farm Machinery Days for Small & Part-Time Farmers, Dauphin, Pennsylvania, April 6, 1990. (NRAES Ser.: Vol. 45). (Illus.). 55p. 1990. pap. text 10.00 (*0-935817-15-8*, NRAES-45) NRAES.

— Managing Nutrients & Pathogens from Animal Agriculture: Proceedings from "Managing Nutrients & Pathogens from Animal Agriculture, a Conference for Nutrient Management Consultants, Extension Educators & Producer Advisors," Camp Hill, Pennsylvania, March 28-30, 2000. LC 00-20869. (Illus.). 508p. 2000. pap. text 30.00 (*0-935817-54-9*, NRAES-130) NRAES.

— Nutrient Management Software: Proceedings from the Nutrient Management Software Workshop, December 11, 1996. (NRAES Ser.: Vol. 100). 60p. 1996. pap. text 11.00 (*0-935817-16-6*, NRAES-100) NRAES.

Natural Resource, Agriculture & Engineering Service Conference Staff, jt. auth. see Dairy Feeding Systems Management Components Staff.

***Natural Resource, Agriculture Staff.** Alternatives to Insecticides for Managing Vegetable Insects: Proceedings of a Farmer/Scientist Conference, December 6 & 7, 1998, New Haven, Connecticut. Stoner, Kimberly A., ed. LC 99-52323. (Illus.). 80p. 1999. pap. text 8.00 (*0-935817-49-2*, NRAES-138) NRAES.

***Natural Resource, Agriculture Staff, ed.** Dairy Housing & Equipment Systems: Managing & Planning for Profitability: Proceedings from the Conference "Dairy Housing & Equipment Systems: Managing & Planning for Profitability," Radisson Penn Harris Hotel & Convention Center, Camp Hill, Pennsylvania, Feb. 1-3,2000. LC 99-55356. (Illus.). 456p. 2000. pap. text 30.00 (*0-935817-52-2*, NRAES-129) NRAES.

Natural Resource, Agriculture Staff, jt. auth. see McEvoy, Thomas J.

Natural Resources Canada-Canadian Permanent Commit, ed. Concise Gazeteer of Canada. 2nd ed. LC 97-228859. (FRE & ENG., Illus.). 636p. 1997. pap. 39.95 (*0-660-60185-0*, Pub. by Canadian Govt Pub) Accents Pubns.

Natural Resources Defense Council Staff. Ebb Tide for Pollution: Actions for Cleaning up Coastal Waters. 1989. 7.00 (*0-317-01843-4*) Natl Resources Defense Coun.

— For Our Kids' Sake: How to Protect Your Child Against Pesticides in Foods. 90p. 1989. 7.95 (*0-317-01840-X*) Natl Resources Defense Coun.

Natural Resources Defense Council Staff & Edgerton, Lynne T. The Rising Tide: Global Warming & World Sea Levels. LC 90-5376. 136p. 1991. text 38.00 (*1-55963-068-X*); pap. text 22.00 (*1-55963-067-1*) Island Pr.

Natural Resources Defense Council Staff, jt. auth. see Garland, Ann W.

Natural Science Centers Conference Staff. Natural Science Centers Conference, 1974, Nashville, Tennessee: Proceedings. Gardner, John F., ed. (Illus.). (Orig.). 1975. 5.00 (*0-916544-04-4*) Natural Sci Youth.

Natural Science for Youth Foundation Staff, ed. Changing Emphasis in Environmental Education: Proceedings of the Natural Science Centers Conference 1972-Jacksonville Florida. (Illus.). (Orig.). 1973. 5.00 (*0-916544-02-8*) Natural Sci Youth.

Natural Trust (Great Britain) Staff. Westbury Court Garden, Gloucestershire. LC 78-326435. 28 p. 1975. write for info. (*0-7078-0033-1*) Natl Trust.

Naturalization Staff & President's Commission on Immigration. Whom We Shall Welcome. LC 73-146270. (Civil Liberties in American History Ser.). 1971. reprint ed. lib. bdg. 45.00 (*0-306-70145-6*) Da Capo.

Nature Conservancy Council Staff. Uncommon Wealth: Essays on Virginia Wild Places. Riordan, Robert M., ed. LC 99-30128. (Illus.). 216p. 1999. 19.95 (*1-56044-915-2*) Falcon Pub Inc.

Nature Conservancy of Washington Staff. Preserving Washington's Wild Lands: A Guide to the Nature Conservancy's Preserves in Washington. LC 92-85124. 96p. (Orig.). 1992. pap. 14.95 (*0-89886-350-3*) Mountaineers.

Nature Conservancy of Wisconsin Staff. The Places We Save: A Guide to the Nature Conservancy's Preserves in Wisconsin. LC 96-46823. (Illus.). 128p. (Orig.). 1997. pap. 16.95 (*1-55971-597-9*, NorthWord Pr) Creat Pub Intl.

Nature Conservancy Staff. Parks in Peril Source Book. Mansour, Jane A., ed. 131p. 1995. pap. 15.00 (*1-886765-01-4*) Nature VA.

Nature Guild Study Editors. Master Flower Finder. 224p. 1986. mass mkt. 3.95 (*0-446-32934-7*, Pub. by Warner Bks) Little.

Nature Institute Staff, jt. auth. see Day, Marlena.

Nature's Images Staff, jt. auth. see Berman, Ruth.

Naturman, Louis, ed. Polymer-Plastics Technology & Engineering, Vol. 2. LC 73-9411. (Illus.). 270p. reprint ed. pap. 83.70 (*0-608-18026-2*, 202900600002) Bks Demand.

— Polymer-Plastics Technology & Engineering, Vol. 3. LC 73-94111. (Illus.). 268p. reprint ed. pap. 83.10 (*0-608-18027-0*, 202900700003) Bks Demand.

Natvig, Jacob B., et al, eds. Amyloid & Amyloidosis 1991. (C). 1991. text 405.00 (*0-7923-1089-6*) Kluwer Academic.

***Natvig, Jacob B. & Turner, Malcolm W.** Immunology Nomenclature: The Immunologist, Supplement 1, 1998. LC 98-73937. 158p. 1998. pap. 29.50 (*0-88937-208-X*) Hogrefe & Huber Pubs.

Natwar-Singh, K. Profiles & Letters LC 97-913667. xii, 244p. 1998. write for info. (*81-207-2066-0*) Sterling Pub.

Natzke, John R. & Volakis, John L. Diffraction by Parallel Resistive Half Plane Structures. LC QC0385.. (University of Michigan Reports: No. 390968-2-T). 36p. reprint ed. pap. 30.00 (*0-7837-4622-9*, 204434500002) Bks Demand.

Natzmer, Oldwig, jt. auth. see Rauss, Erhard.

***Nau, Arlo J.** Impact of Context on Content in Matthew. 2000. pap. text 29.95 (*0-7880-1467-6*) CSS.

Nau, B. S. Fluid Sealing. 1992. text 316.50 (*0-7923-1669-X*) Kluwer Academic.

Nau, B. S., ed. Fluid Sealing. 450p. 1989. 214.95 (*0-387-51383-3*) Spr-Verlag.

— Fluid Sealing: Proceedings of the 11th International Conference, Cannes, France, 8-10 April, 1987, Organized by BHRA, The Fluid Engineering Center, Cranfield, England. 795p. 1987. 169.25 (*1-85166-100-X*) Elsevier.

Nau, Bernard, jt. auth. see Muller, Heinz Konrad.

Nau, Douglas S. CRIS Case Studies for the 90s. (YA). (gr. 9-12). 1994. 18.00 (*1-881678-54-7*) CSEE.

— The New CRIS Case Studies. 57p. (J). (gr. 5-12). 1982. pap. 17.50 (*1-881678-03-2*) CSEE.

Nau, Erika S., jt. auth. see Turner Publishing Co. Staff.

Nau, H. Pharmacokinetics/Teratogenesis. 280p. 1987. 157.00 (*0-8493-6873-1*, CRC Reprint) Franklin.

— Pharmacokinetics/Teratogenesis, Vol. II. 248p. 1987. 141.00 (*0-8493-6874-X*, CRC Reprint) Franklin.

Nau, H. & Scott, W. M., Jr. Pharmacokinetics in Teratogenesis, 2 vols., Set. 1987. reprint ed. 298.00 (*0-8493-6872-3*, CRC Reprint) Franklin.

***Nau, Heinz & Blaner, William S., eds.** Retinoids: The Biochemical & Molecular Basis of Vitamin A & Retinoid Action. LC 99-35527. (Handbook of Experimental Pharmacology Ser.: Vol. 139). (Illus.). 650p. 1999. 432.00 (*3-540-65892-0*) Spr-Verlag.

Nau, Henry R. National Politics & International Technology: Nuclear Reactor Development in Western Europe. LC 73-19344. 304p. 1974. reprint ed. pap. 94.30 (*0-608-04059-2*, 206479500011) Bks Demand.

— Trade & Security: U. S. Policies at Cross-Purposes. 100p. 1995. pap. 9.95 (*0-8447-7038-8*) Am Enterprise.

— Trade & Security: U. S. Policies at Cross-Purposes. 128p. 1995. 29.95 (*0-8447-7056-6*, AEI Pr) Am Enterprise.

Nau, Henry R., ed. Domestic Trade Politics & the Uruguay Round. 240p. 1988. pap. text 19.00 (*0-231-06823-9*) Col U Pr.

— Domestic Trade Politics & the Uruguay Round. LC 88-25762. 234p. reprint ed. pap. 72.60 (*0-7837-0424-0*, 204074700018) Bks Demand.

Nau, Henry R. & Quigley, Kevin F., eds. The Allies & East-West Economic Relations: Past Conflicts & Present Choices. 42p. 1989. pap. 4.00 (*0-87641-306-8*) Carnegie Ethics & Intl Affairs.

***Nau, Jim.** Ball Culture Guide: The Encyclopedia of Seed Germination. 3rd ed. LC 98-43750. 248p. 1999. pap. 49.95 (*1-883052-19-X*) Ball Pub.

Nau, Jim. Ball Perennial Manual: Propagation & Production. LC 95-20481. (Illus.). 512p. 1996. text 64.95 (*1-883052-10-6*, B027) Ball Pub.

Nau, Paul & Berthod, Rene. Pope or Church? Essays on the Infallibility of the Ordinary Magisterium. 72p. 1998. pap. 5.45 (*0-935952-90-X*) Angelus Pr.

Nau, Robert, et al, eds. Economic & Environmental Risk & Uncertainty: New Models & Methods. LC 97-8443. (Theory & Decision Library. Mathematical & Statistical Methods). 1997. lib. bdg. 130.50 (*0-7923-4556-8*) Kluwer Academic.

Nauck, Anja, tr. see Storm, Theodor.

Nauck, August. Tragicae Dictionis Index, Spectans ad Tragicorum Graecorum Fragmenta. xxxii, 738p. 1962. reprint ed. write for info. (*0-318-70981-3*); reprint ed. write for info. (*0-318-72057-4*) G Olms Pubs.

— Tragicorum Graecorum Fragmenta. xxvi, 1048p. 1983. reprint ed. write for info. (*3-487-00622-7*); reprint ed. suppl. ed. write for info. (*0-318-70982-1*) G Olms Pubs.

Nauck, Detlef, et al. Foundations of Neuro-Fuzzy Sys. LC 97-30674. 316p. 1997. 94.95 (*0-471-97151-0*) Wiley.

Nauck, Kurt, jt. auth. see Sutton, Allan.

Naudain, Barbara, ed. see Fourth Pacific Islands Conference of Leaders Staff.

Naudain, Barbara, jt. ed. see Halapua, Sitiveni.

Naudascher, Eduard. Flow-Induced Vibrations: An Engineering Guide. (Hydraulic Structures Design Manual Ser.: Vol. 7). (Illus.). 450p. (C). 1994. text 136.00 (*90-5410-131-8*, Pub. by A A Balkema) Ashgate Pub Co.

— Hydrodynamic Forces. (Hydraulic Structures Design Manual Ser.: No. 3). (Illus.). 307p. (C). 1990. text 116.00 (*90-6191-993-2*, Pub. by A A Balkema) Ashgate Pub Co.

Naudascher, Edward, ed. see IUTAM-IAHR Symposium Staff.

Naude. Trauma Secrets. LC 98-27476. 1998. 38.00 (*1-56053-256-4*) Hanley & Belfus.

Naude, Alain, ed. see Wright-Hubbard, Elizabeth.

Naude, Alain, tr. see Hahnemann, Samuel.

Naude, Gabriel. Considerations Politiques Sur Les Coups d'Etat. (GER.). 115p. 1993. reprint ed. write for info. incl. 3.5 hd (*3-487-09628-5*) G Olms Pubs.

— Considerations Politiques Sur les Coups d'Etat. 115p. reprint ed. write for info. incl. 3.5 hd (*0-318-71380-2*) G Olms Pubs.

Naude, Peter & Turnbull, Peter W. Network Dynamics in International Marketing. LC 98-8167. (International Business & Management Ser.). xix, 321 p. 1998. 88.50 (*0-08-043358-8*) Elsevier.

Naude, Piet. The Zionist Christian Church in South Africa: A Case-Study in Oral Theology. LC 94-39459. 164p. 1995. text 79.95 (*0-7734-9147-3*) E Mellen.

Naude, Virginia N., ed. Sculptural Monuments in an Outdoor Environment: A Conference Held at the Penn. Academy of the Fine Arts. 2nd ed. (Illus.). 116p. (Orig.). 1986. reprint ed. pap. 14.95 (*0-943836-04-2*) Penn Acad Art.

Naudet, Jean-Jaques, ed. see Cady, Barbara.

Naudin, Jean-Bernard, photos by. Matisse: A Way of Life in the South of France. (Illus.). 192p. 1998. 40.00 (*0-8478-2088-2*, Pub. by Rizzoli Intl) St Martin.

Naudin, Jean-Bernard, et al. Renoir's Table: The Art of Living & Dining with One of the World's Greatest Impressionist Painters. LC 94-7792. (Illus.). 192p. 1994. 35.00 (*0-671-89845-0*) S&S Trade.

Nauen, Elinor. American Guys. LC 96-40202. 1997. 20.00 (*1-882413-41-5*); pap. 12.00 (*1-882413-40-7*) Hanging Loose.

Nauen, Elinor, ed. Diamonds Are a Girl's Best Friend: Women Writers on Baseball. 295p. 1998. text 23.00 (*0-7881-5577-6*) DIANE Pub.

— Diamonds Are a Girl's Best Friend: Women Writers on Baseball. 295p. 1995. pap. 12.95 (*0-571-19853-8*) Faber & Faber.

Nauen, F. G. Revolution, Idealism & Human Freedom: Schelling, Holderlin & Hegel & the Crisis of Early German Idealism. (International Archives of the History of Ideas Ser.: No. 45). 113p. 1971. lib. bdg. 66.50 (*90-247-5117-9*) Kluwer Academic.

Nauen, Lindsay B., ed. Guide to the Wisconsin Jewish Archives at the State Historical Society of Wisconsin. LC 74-16073. (Guides to Historical Resources Ser.). 28p. 1974. pap. 1.00 (*0-87020-145-X*) State Hist Soc Wis.

Nauenberg, M., jt. ed. see Dalitz, R. H.

Nauenberg, Michael, jt. auth. see Dalitz, R. H.

Nauer, Barbara. Jimmy Swaggart - Dead Man Rising: On Black Light As a Weapon in the Culture Wars. LC 97-77986. 527p. (Orig.). 1997. mass mkt. 19.95 (*0-9657943-0-X*) Glory Arts.

Nauerby, Tom. No Nation Is an Island: Language, Culture, & National Identity in the Faroe Islands. LC 97-111483. (North Atlantic Studies: Vol. 3). (Illus.). 237p. (C). 1996. 27.00 (*87-983424-5-2*, Pub. by Aarhus Univ Pr) David Brown.

Nauert, Charles G., Jr. The Age of Renaissance & Reformation. LC 81-40034. 330p. 1982. reprint ed. pap. text 23.50 (*0-8191-1862-1*) U Pr of Amer.

Nauert, Charles G. Agrippa & the Crisis of Renaissance Thought. LC 65-63002. (Illinois, University, Illinois Studies in the Social Sciences Ser.: Vol. 55). 382p. reprint ed. pap. 118.50 (*0-8357-5273-9*, 201902700010) Bks Demand.

— Humanism & the Culture of Renaissance Europe. (New Approaches to European History Ser.: Vol. 7). (Illus.). 247p. (C). 1995. text 54.95 (*0-521-40364-2*); pap. text 16.95 (*0-521-40724-9*) Cambridge U Pr.

Nauert, Peter W., jt. auth. see Callaghan, Ed.

Nauerth, Claudia. Agnellus von Ravenna. (Munchener Beitrage zur Mediavistik und Renaissance-Forschung Ser.: Bd. 15). (GER.). x, 129p. 1974. 24.80 (*3-615-00152-4*, Pub. by Weidmann) Lubrecht & Cramer.

Nauerth, Thomas. Untersuchungen zur Komposition der Jakoberzahlungen: Auf der Suche Nach der Endgestalt des Genesisbuches. (Beitrage zur Erforschung des Alten Testaments & Antiken Judentums Ser.: Bd. 27). (GER.). 318p. 1996. 57.95 (*3-631-30220-7*) P Lang Pubng.

Naufftus, William F., ed. see Layman, Bruccoli-Clark.

Naughtie, James, jt. auth. see Brown, Gordon.

Naughtin, Gerry & Laidler, Terry. When I Grow Too Old to Dream: Coping with Alzheimer's Disease. 1992. 13.00 (*1-86371-075-2*) Harper SF.

Naughton. Blood on the Rock. 250p. 13.95 (*0-06-024513-1*); lib. bdg. 13.89 (*0-06-024514-X*) HarpC Child Bks.

Naughton. Late Night on Watling Street. Date not set. pap. text. write for info. (*0-582-23367-4*, Pub. by Addison-Wesley) Longman.

Naughton, Abbey L., ed. see Jacobs, Russell F.

Naughton, Barry. Growing Out of the Plan: Chinese Economic Reform, 1978-1993. (Illus.). 391p. (C). 1995. text 59.95 (*0-521-47055-2*) Cambridge U Pr.

— Growing Out of the Plan: Chinese Economic Reform, 1978-1993. 384p. 1996. pap. text 21.95 (*0-521-57462-5*) Cambridge U Pr.

Naughton, Barry, ed. The China Circle: Economics & Technology in the PRC, Taiwan, & Hong Kong. LC 97-21095. 316p. 1997. 49.95 (*0-8157-5998-3*); pap. 19.95 (*0-8157-5999-1*) Brookings.

Naughton, Barry, jt. ed. see McMillan, John.

An Asterisk (*) at the beginning of an entry indicates that the title is appearing for the first time.

Naughton, Bill. Alfie. 192p. 1995. pap. write for info. (*0-85031-794-0*) Allison & Busby.

Naughton, Bill. Goalkeeper's Revenge & Other Stories. 128p. 1968. pap. 7.95 (*0-14-030348-0*, Pub. by Pnguin Bks Ltd) Trafalgar.

Naughton, Bill. Neither Use nor Ornament: A Memoir of Bolton, 1920s. 206p. 1996. 45.00 (*1-85224-303-1*, Pub. by Bloodaxe Bks); pap. 19.95 (*1-85224-304-X*, Pub. by Bloodaxe Bks) Dufour.

— On the Pig's Back: An Autobiographical Excursion. 266p. 1991. 21.95 (*1-85089-530-9*, Pub. by ISIS Lrg Prnt) Transaction Pubs.

Naughton, Emma & Smith, Turner. Beset by Contradictions: Islamization, Legal Reform & Human Rights in Sudan. Black, George, ed. 98p. (Orig.). 1996. pap. 12.00 (*0-934143-80-3*) Lawyers Comm Human.

Naughton, Gabriel. Chardin. LC 96-165899. (Color Library). (Illus.). 128p. (Orig.). (C). 1996. pap. 14.95 (*0-7148-3336-3*, Pub. by Phaidon Press) Phaidon Pr.

Naughton, J., tr. see Holub, Miroslav.

Naughton, J. D. Colloquial Czech: The Complete Course for Beginners. 2nd ed. LC 98-16728. (Colloquials Ser.). (CZE.). 368p. (C). 1999. pap. 18.99 (*0-415-16134-7*); audio 27.99 (*0-415-16135-5*) Routledge.

Naughton, James. Colloquial Czech. (Colloquials Ser.). 244p. 1988. pap. 16.95 (*0-7102-0857-X*, 08575, Routledge Thoemms) Routledge.

Naughton, James. Colloquial Czech. (Colloquials Ser.). 1988. pap. 15.95 incl. audio (*0-7102-1104-X*, 1104x, Routledge Thoemms) Routledge.

Naughton, James. Colloquial Czech, Set. (Colloquials Ser.). 320p. 1988. 34.99 incl. audio (*0-415-00076-9*, A2567, Routledge Thoemms) Routledge.

— Colloquial Czech: Complete Beginner's Course. 2nd ed. (Colloquials Ser.). (CZE.). 368p. (C). (gr. 13). 1999. spiral bd. 37.99 (*0-415-16136-3*) Routledge.

— Colloquial Slovak. (Illus.). 304p. 1997. pap. 24.99 (*0-415-11540-X*) Routledge.

— Colloquial Slovak. (Illus.). 288p. 1997. 27.99 incl. audio (*0-415-11542-6*) Routledge.

Naughton, Jeffrey F. & Weikum, Gerhard, eds. Parallel & Distributed Information Systems. LC 97-44658. 116p. 1998. text 107.50 (*0-7923-8087-8*) Kluwer Academic.

Naughton, Jim. MY BRO STEALING 2ND. LC 88-22035. (Trophy Keypoint Bk.). 288p. (YA). (gr. 7 up). 1991. mass mkt. 3.95 (*0-06-447017-2*, HarpTrophy) HarpC Child Bks.

Naughton, Jim. Taking to the Air: The Rise of Michael Jordan. 288p. 1993. mass mkt. 4.99 (*0-446-36401-0*, Pub. by Warner Bks) Little.

***Naughton, John.** Brief History of the Future: From Radio Days to Internet Years in a Lifetime. LC 00-26265. (Illus.). 320p. 2000. 29.95 (*1-58567-032-4*, Pub. by Overlook Pr) Penguin Putnam.

Naughton, John. Movies: A Crash Course. (Illus.). 144p. 1998. 14.95 (*0-8230-0977-7*) Watsn-Guptill.

Naughton, John T. The Poetics of Yves Bonnefoy. LC 87-5097. (Illus.). x, 224p. 1984. 24.00 (*0-226-56947-0*) U Ch Pr.

Naughton, John T., ed. see Bonnefoy, Yves.

Naughton, John T., ed. & tr. see Bonnefoy, Yves.

Naughton, John T., tr. see Bonnefoy, Yves.

Naughton, Lee. Sand Through My Fingers. large type ed. 1990. 27.99 (*0-7089-2129-9*) Ulverscroft.

Naughton, Michael J. The Good Stewards: Practical Applications of the Papal Social Vision of Work. 163p. (Orig.). (C). 1992. pap. text 24.50 (*0-8191-8599-X*); lib. bdg. 48.00 (*0-8191-8598-1*) U Pr of Amer.

Naughton, Patrick. The Java Handbook. 424p. 1996. pap. 27.95 (*0-07-882199-1*) McGraw.

— Java 1.1: The Complete Reference. 2nd ed. LC 98-123671. 1040p. 1999. pap. text 39.99 (*0-07-882436-2*) Osborne-McGraw.

Naughton, Patrick & Schildt, Herb. Java 2: The Complete Reference. 3rd ed. 1108p. 1999. pap. 39.99 (*0-07-211976-4*) McGraw.

Naughton, Patrick & Schildt, Herbert. Java the Complete Reference. LC 97-129811. 800p. 1996. pap. text 39.95 (*0-07-882231-9*) Osborne-McGraw.

Naughton, Renee, jt. ed. see Graef, Robert.

Naughton, Sean. Nine Hundred Words of Wisdom: The Real Truth about 900. DeMarco, Barbara, ed. (Orig.). 1993. student ed. 99.00 (*0-9638246-1-9*); pap. 198.00 (*0-9638246-0-0*); audio 98.00 (*0-9638246-2-7*) Future Freedom.

Naughton, T. Raymond, jt. auth. see Goebel, Julius L.

Naughton, W. P., jt. auth. see Dooley, R. B.

Naugle, D., ed. Ordering Disorder: Prospect & Retrospect in Condensed Matter Physics. (AIP Conference Proceedings Ser.: No. 286). (Illus.). 352p. 1993. text 125.00 (*1-56396-255-1*, AIP Pr) Spr-Verlag.

Naugle, Helen H., ed. see Johnson, Samuel.

Naugle, John M., jt. auth. see Fothergill, Augusta B.

Naugle, June. The Great American Swindle. Burns, Luisa E., ed. LC 95-72088. (Illus.). 530p. (Orig.). 1996. 34.95 (*0-9649069-0-2*); pap. 24.95 (*0-9649069-1-0*) Randolph IN.

Naugle, Matthew. Illustrated TCP/IP. LC 98-8271. (Illustrated Network Ser.). (Illus.). 512p. 1998. pap. text 39.99 incl. disk (*0-471-19656-8*) Wiley.

Naugle, Matthew G. Illustrated Network Book. 528p. 1994. pap. 46.95 (*0-442-01826-6*, VNR) Wiley.

Naugle, Matthew G. The Illustrated Network Book: A Graphic Guide to Understanding Computer Networks. 528p. 1994. pap. 46.95 (*0-471-28624-9*, VNR) Wiley.

Naugle, Matthew G. The Illustrated Network Book: A Graphic Guide to Understanding Computer Networks. (Illus.). 512p. 1994. pap. 42.95 (*0-442-01790-1*, VNR) Wiley.

— Local Area Networking. 400p. 1991. 39.00 (*0-07-046455-3*) McGraw.

— Network Protocol Handbook: Signature Edition. 2nd ed. LC 98-20249. (Computer Communications Ser.). 650p. 1998. pap. 59.95 (*0-07-046603-3*) McGraw.

Naugle, Richard I., et al. Introduction to Clinical Neuropsychology: A Casebook. LC 97-6565. (Illus.). 320p. 1998. text 38.00 (*0-89079-714-5*, 8339) PRO-ED.

Naugle, Ronald C., jt. auth. see Olson, James C.

Naugle, Ronald C., jt. ed. see Crews, Patricia C.

Naugle, Thomas C., Jr., et al, eds. Diagnosis & Management of Oculoplastic & Orbital Disorders: Proceedings of the 43rd Annual Symposium, New Orleans, LA, February 18-20, 1994. LC 95-46564. 1995. 103.00 (*90-6299-132-7*) Kugler Pubns.

Naugolnykh, K. A. & Ostrovsky, L. A. Nonlinear Acoustics. (Research Trends in Physics Ser.). (Illus.). 336p. 1994. boxed set 94.95 (*1-56396-338-8*) Spr-Verlag.

— Nonlinear Wave Processes in Acoustics. LC 98-2925. (Cambridge Texts in Applied Mathematics Ser.: No. 9). (Illus.). 308p. (C). 1998. text 74.95 (*0-521-39080-X*); pap. text 29.95 (*0-521-39984-X*) Cambridge U Pr.

Nauhaus, Gerd. The Marriage Diaries of Robert & Clara Schumann: From Their Wedding Day to the Russia Trip. Ostwald, Peter F., tr. from GER. & pref. by. (Illus.). 256p. 1993. text 35.00 (*1-55553-171-7*) NE U Pr.

NAUI Staff. Entry Scuba Experience & Passport Manual. (Illus.). 12p. 1997. pap. text 1.50 (*1-57743-013-1*, 11002) NAUI.

— Libro Detext. (Illus.). 188p. 1994. pap. 24.95 (*0-916974-56-1*, 11003) NAUI.

Naujok, Michael. This Is Boat Interior Construction. (Illus.). 138p. 1993. pap. 29.95 (*0-7136-4954-2*) Sheridan.

Naul, Roland, ed. Contemporary Studies in the National Olympic Games Movement. LC 97-44537. (Sport Sciences International Ser.: Vol. 2). (Illus.). VIII, 219p. (C). 1997. pap. text 34.95 (*0-8204-3544-9*) P Lang Pubng.

Nault, L. R. & Rodriguez, J. G., eds. The Leafhoppers & Planthoppers. LC 85-5383. 500p. 1985. 220.00 (*0-471-80611-0*, Wiley-Interscience) Wiley.

Naum, Gellu. Ekzakto de L'Ombro, L' Vlad, Sasha, tr. from RUM. (ESP.). 20p. 1995. pap. 3.00 (*1-882251-11-3*) Eldonejo Bero.

***Naum, Gellu.** My Tired Father. Brook, James, tr. (Green Integer Bks.: No. 19). 80p. 1999. pap. 8.95 (*1-892295-07-5*, Pub. by Green Integer) SPD-Small Pr Dist.

Naum, Gellu. Patro Mia Laca - L'Avantago de l'Vertebroj. Vlad, Sasha & Onet, Ionel, trs. from RUM. (ESP., Illus.). 44p. (Orig.). 1996. pap. 7.05 (*1-882251-15-6*) Eldonejo Bero.

— Zenobia. 220p. 1995. pap. 14.95 (*0-8101-1255-8*) Northwestern U Pr.

— Zenobia. Brook, James & Vlad, Sasha, trs. from RUM. LC 95-10848. (Writings from an Unbound Europe). 220p. 1995. text 39.95 (*0-8101-1254-X*) Northwestern U Pr.

Nauman, Ann & Dearman, Marvene. Making Every Minute Count: Time Management for Librarians. (Illus.). 100p. (C). 1991. 19.50 (*0-931315-06-9*) Lib Learn Res.

Nauman, Ann K. Biographical Handbook of Education: Five Hundred Contributions to the Field. 238p. 1985. pap. text 19.95 (*0-8290-0722-9*) Irvington.

***Nauman, Ann K.** The Career of Dona Ines de Suarez the First European Woman in Chile. LC 00-29188. 204p. 2000. text 89.95 (*0-7734-7739-X*) E Mellen.

Nauman, Anne. The Junior Partner: Edith Loring Fullerton, Long Island Pioneer. LC 97-68114. (Illus.). xii, 207p. 1997. pap. 24.00 (*0-9637126-2-4*) Scrub Oak Pr.

Nauman, Anne, ed. Gardener of Eden: The Wit & Wisdom of Hal B. Fullerton. LC 97-62436. (Illus.). x, 209p. 1998. pap. 24.00 (*0-9637126-3-2*) Scrub Oak Pr.

Nauman, Bruce. Interviews, 1967-1988. (Illus.). 200p. 1996. text 18.00 (*90-5705-017-X*) Gordon & Breach.

Nauman, Chuck, jt. auth. see Strain, Dave.

Nauman, E. Bruce. Chemical Reactor Design. LC 91-45050. 456p. (C). 1992. reprint ed. lib. bdg. 67.95 (*0-89464-707-5*) Krieger.

Nauman, E. Bruce & Buffham, B. A. Mixing in Continuous Flow Systems. LC 82-24858. (Wiley-Interscience Publications). (Illus.). 299p. 1983. reprint ed. pap. 92.70 (*0-7837-2369-5*, 204005500006) Bks Demand.

Nauman, E. Burce. Introductory Systems Analysis for Process Engineers. (Chemical Engineering Ser.). 264p. 1990. text 59.95 (*0-409-90254-3*) Buttrwrth-Heinemann.

***Nauman, Eileen.** Homeopathy 911. 2000. pap. 14.00 (*1-57566-694-4*, Knsington) Kensgtn Pub Corp.

Nauman, Eileen. Medical Astrology. 3rd rev. ed. 357p. (Orig.). 1996. pap. 29.95 (*0-9634662-4-0*) Blue Turtle.

— Poisons That Heal. 270p. 1995. pap. 14.95 (*0-929385-62-4*) Light Tech Pubng.

Nauman, Eileen & Gent, Ruth. Colored Stones & Their Meaning. 26p. 1988. pap. 4.95 (*0-9634662-1-6*) Blue Turtle.

Nauman, Jim & Cabrillo National Monument Foundation Staff. An Account of the Voyage of Juan Rodriguez Cabrillo. LC 99-10798. 1999. write for info. (*0-941032-07-8*) Cabrillo Natl Monumnt.

Nauman, St. Joel & Wagoner, James D. Electronic Music Technique. 1984. text. write for info. (*0-582-28281-0*) Macmillan.

Naumani, Shibli. Umar the Great, 2. 1993. 14.50 (*0-933511-80-9*) Kazi Pubns.

Naumann, Bernd, et al, eds. Language & Earth: Elective Affinities Between the Emerging Sciences of Linguistics & Geology. LC 91-35106. (Studies in the History of the Language Sciences: No. 66). xvi, 445p. 1992. 118.00 (*1-55619-361-0*) J Benjamins Pubng Co.

Naumann, Cynthia E., ed. see Cutburth, Ronald W.

Naumann, David, jt. auth. see Davis, Gordon B.

Naumann, Earl. Creating Customer Value: The Path to Sustainable Competitive Advantage. LC 94-159. (C). 1994. pap. 32.95 (*0-538-83847-7*) S-W Pub.

— Love At First Sight. 2001. pap. 18.95 (*1-57071-623-4*, Casablanca) Sourcebks.

Naumann, Earl & Giel, Kathleen. Customer Satisfaction Measurement & Management. 457p. 1995. 37.00 (*0-87389-427-8*) ASQ Qual Pr.

— Customer Satisfaction Measurement & Management: Using the Voice of the Customer. (SB - Marketing Education Ser.). 457p. 1995. text 32.95 (*0-538-84439-6*) S-W Pub.

Naumann, Einar. Einfuehrung in die Bodenkunde der Seen. (Binnengewaesser Ser.: Band IX). (GER., Illus.). ix, 126p. 1930. 21.00 (*3-510-40709-1*, Pub. by E Schweizerbartsche) Balogh.

— Grundlinien der Experimentellen Planktonforschung. (Binnengewaesser Ser.: Band VI). (GER., Illus.). ix, 100p. 1929. 15.00 (*3-510-40706-7*, Pub. by E Schweizerbartsche) Balogh.

— Grundzuege der Regionalen Limnologie. (Binnengewaesser Ser.: Band XI). (GER., Illus.). xiv, 176p. 1932. 25.00 (*3-510-40711-3*, Pub. by E Schweizerbartsche) Balogh.

Naumann, Emil. History of Music to the Middle Ages, Vol. II. (Illus.). 300p. 1998. reprint ed. pap. 35.00 (*0-87556-823-8*) Saifer.

***Naumann, Francis M.** Apropos of Marcel: Making Art After Marcel Duchamp in the Age of Mechanical Reproduction. (Illus.). 45p. 1999. pap. 40.00 (*0-9674819-0-2*) C Marcus Galry.

Naumann, Francis M. Beatrice Wood: A Centennial Tribute. (Illus.). 168p. 1997. pap. write for info. (*1-890385-00-X*, 4000) American Craft.

— New York Dada, 1915-23. LC 93-34280. (Illus.). 256p. 1994. 60.00 (*0-8109-3676-3*, Pub. by Abrams) Time Warner.

Naumann, Francis M. & Duchamp, Marcel. Marcel Duchamp: The Art of Making Art in the Age of Mechanical Reproduction. LC 99-29063. (Illus.). 336p. 2000. 70.00 (*0-8109-6334-5*, Pub. by Abrams) Time Warner.

Naumann, Francis M. & Venn, Beth. Making Mischief: Dada Invades New York. (Illus.). 256p. 1996. 49.50 (*0-8109-6821-5*, Pub. by Abrams) Time Warner.

Naumann, Francis M., et al. Making Mischief: Dada Invades New York. LC 96-9890. 1996. write for info. (*0-87427-105-3*) Whitney Mus.

Naumann, Francis M., jt. auth. see Moeller, Achim.

Naumann, Francis M., ed. see De Zayas, Marius.

Naumann, Francis M., ed. see De Zayas, Marous.

Naumann, Francis M., ed. see Duchamp, Marcel.

Naumann, Francis M., jt. ed. see Kuenzli, Rudolf E.

Naumann, Gottfried O. & Apple, D. J. Pathology of the Eye. (Illus.). xxxv, 998p. 1986. 460.00 (*0-387-96044-9*) Spr-Verlag.

Naumann, Hans H. Differential Diagnosis in Otorhinolaryngology: Symptoms, Syndromes, & Interdisciplinary Issues. LC 93-26903.Tr. of Differentialdiagnostik in der Hals-Nasen Ohren-Heilkunde. 1993. 89.00 (*0-86577-507-9*) Thieme Med Pubs.

Naumann, Ian, ed. Systematic & Applied Entomology: An Introduction. 496p. 1994. pap. 49.95 (*0-522-84518-5*, Pub. by Melbourne Univ Pr) Paul & Co Pubs.

Naumann, K. Chemistry of Plant Protection Vol. 4: Synthetic Pyrethroid Insecticides, Structures & Properties. Bowers, W. S. et al, eds. (Illus.). xvi, 241p. 1990. 185.95 (*0-387-51313-2*) Spr-Verlag.

— Chemistry of Plant Protection Vol. 5: Synthetic Pyrethroid Insecticides, Chemistry & Patents. Bowers, W. S. et al, eds. (Illus.). 412p. 1990. 318.95 (*0-387-51314-0*) Spr-Verlag.

Naumann, Klaus, jt. ed. see Heer, Hannes.

Naumann, Lillian W. & Volker, Virginia S. Laboratory & Lecture Guide to Human Anatomy. 5th ed. 160p. (C). 1996. spiral bd. 23.04 (*0-7872-2006-X*) Kendall-Hunt.

Naumann, Nelly. Die Einheimische Religion Japans. (GER.). xi, 264p. 1994. 114.50 (*90-04-10178-0*) Brill Academic Pubs.

Naumann, Otto, ed. The Illustrated Bartsch Vol. 6: Netherlandish Artists. 1980. lib. bdg. 149.00 (*0-89835-006-9*) Abaris Bks.

— The Illustrated Bartsch Vol. 7: Netherlandish Artists. 1978. lib. bdg. 149.00 (*0-89835-007-7*) Abaris Bks.

Naumann, Victoria, jt. auth. see Bassett, Mark.

Naumburg, Margaret. Dynamically Oriented Art Therapy: Its Principles & Practice. (Illus.). 168p. (C). 1987. reprint ed. 38.95 (*0-9613309-1-0*) Magnolia St Pub.

— An Introduction to Art Therapy: Studies of the "Free" Art Expression of Behavior Problem Children & Adolescents As a Means of Diagnosis & Therapy. rev. ed. LC 73-78074. (Illus.). 240p. 1973. pap. text 18.95 (*0-8077-2425-4*) Tchrs Coll.

Naumenko, Evgenii V. Central Regulation of the Pituitary-Adrenal Complex. LC 73-17250. (Studies in Soviet Science). 205p. reprint ed. pap. 63.60 (*0-608-13735-9*, 202068600018) Bks Demand.

Naumenko, Maria. The Life of Saint Seraphim Wonderworker of Sarov.Tr. of Zhitie Prepodobnovo Seraphima, Sarovskovo Chudotvortsa. (Illus.). 22p. (Orig.). (J). (gr. 5-10). 1992. pap. 3.00 (*0-88465-049-9*) Holy Trinity.

— The Life of Saint Seraphim Wonderworker of Sarov: (Zhitie Prepodobnovo Serpahima, Sarovskovo Chudotvortsa) (RUS., Illus.). 22p. (Orig.). (J). (gr. 5-10). 1992. pap. 3.00 (*0-88465-052-9*) Holy Trinity.

Naumer, Janet N. & Thurman, Glenda B. The Works for Library & Media Center Management: DOS & Windows Edition. LC 97-19924. (Illus.). xxii, 178p. (Orig.). 1998. pap. 34.00 (*1-56308-543-7*) Libs Unl.

Naumes, Margaret J., jt. auth. see Naumes, William.

Naumes, William & Naumes, Margaret J. The Art & Craft of Case Writing LC 99-6230. 1999. write for info. (*0-7619-1725-X*) Sage.

Naumkin, Pavel I. & Shishmarev, Ilia A. Nonlinear Nonlocal Equations in the Theory of Waves. LC 93-8452. (Translations of Mathematical Monographs: Vol. 133).Tr. of Nelineinye Nelokalnye Uravneniia v Teorii Voln. 289p. 1994. text 149.00 (*0-8218-4573-X*, MMONO/133) Am Math.

Naumkin, Vitaly V. Central Asia & Transcaucasia: Ethnicity & Conflict, 339. LC 93-31624. (Contributions in Political Science Ser.: No. 339). 256p. 1994. 65.00 (*0-313-29154-3*, Greenwood Pr) Greenwood.

Naumoff, Lawrence. From Portfolio of American Business. (Illus.). 36p. 1981. pap. 2.95 (*0-933974-03-5*) Bull City.

— The Night of the Weeping Women. LC 97-20028. 256p. 1997. pap. 11.00 (*0-15-600364-3*) Harcourt.

— A Plan for Women. LC 97-10951. 288p. 1997. 23.00 (*0-15-100231-2*) Harcourt.

— A Plan for Women. 259p. (C). 1999. pap. 13.00 (*0-15-600452-6*, Harvest Bks) Harcourt.

— Rootie Kazootie. 288p. 1996. pap. 12.00 (*0-15-600336-8*) Harcourt.

— Silk Hope, N. C. 368p. 1995. pap. 12.00 (*0-15-600207-8*) Harcourt.

— Silk Hope, N. C. A Novel. 1994. 21.95 (*0-15-188900-7*) Harcourt.

— Taller Women: A Cautionary Tale. LC 91-131. 1992. 21.95 (*0-15-187991-5*) Harcourt.

— Taller Women: A Cautionary Tale. (Harvest American Writing Ser.). 304p. 1994. pap. 10.95 (*0-15-688162-4*) Harcourt.

Naumoff, Olga. About the Splendid Macedonians: A Coloring Book & Much, Much More. (Illus.). 64p. (J). 1982. pap. 4.95 (*0-941983-00-5*) Splendid Assocs.

Naumov, A. D., et al, eds. Interactions & Adaptation Strategies of Marine Organisms: Proceedings of the 31st European Marine Biology Symposium, Held in St. Petersburg, Russia, 9-13 September, 1996, Vol. 121. LC 97-44044. (Developments in Hydrobiology Ser.). 190p. 1998. text 130.50 (*0-7923-4927-X*) Kluwer Academic.

Naumov, B. Nonlinear Control Systems. 1990. 80.00 (*0-8493-7127-9*, QA402) CRC Pr.

Naumov, N. P. The Ecology of Animals. Levine, Norman D., ed. Plous, Frederick K., Jr., tr. from RUS. LC 71-170965. (RUS., Illus.). 661p. reprint ed. 200.00 (*0-8357-9670-1*, 201492600094) Bks Demand.

Naumov, Oleg V. & Lih, Lars T., eds. Stalin's Letters to Molotov, 1925-1936. Fitzpatrick, Catherine A., tr. from RUS. LC 94-44050. (Annals of Communism Ser.). (Illus.). 308p. 1995. 35.00 (*0-300-06211-7*) Yale U Pr.

Naumov, Oleg V., jt. auth. see Getty, J. Arch.

Naumova, T. N. Apomixis in Angiosperms: Nucellar & Integumentary Embryony. Mershchikova, I., tr. 160p. 1992. lib. bdg. 169.00 (*0-8493-4570-7*, QK826) CRC Pr.

Naumovich, Epshtein M. Ottsovstvo. LC 92-17804. (RUS.). 160p. (Orig.). 1992. pap. 12.00 (*1-55779-045-0*) Hermitage Pubs.

Naunheimer, H., jt. auth. see Lechner, G.

Naunin, D. H., ed. see Bausiere, R., et al.

Naunin, D. H., ed. see Buxbaum, A. & Schierau, K.

Naunton. Think First: Self Study Guide. Date not set. pap. text. write for info. (*0-582-55984-7*, Pub. by Addison-Wesley) Longman.

Naunton, Robert. Fragmenta Regalia: 1630. Arber, Edward, ed. 272p. 1984. pap. 17.50 (*0-87556-577-8*) Saifer.

— Fragmenta Regalia, or, Observations on Queen Elizabeth, Her Times & Favorites. Cerovski, John S., ed. LC 82-49310. (Illus.). 120p. 1985. 26.50 (*0-918016-71-1*) Folger Bks.

Naunyn, Bernhard. Memories, Thoughts & Convictions. LC 94-2999. (Resources in Medical History Ser.).Tr. of Erinnerungen, Gedanken und Meinungen. 1994. 30.00 (*0-88135-059-1*, Sci Hist) Watson Pub Intl.

Naur, Maja. Political Mobilization & Industry in Libya. (Illus.). 268p. (Orig.). 1986. pap. text 52.50 (*87-500-2648-8*) Coronet Bks.

Naur, Peter. Computing: A Human Activity. (Illus.). 656p. (C). 1992. pap. text 32.95 (*0-201-58069-1*) Addison-Wesley.

— Knowing & the Mystique of Logic & Rules: Including True Statements in Knowing & Action "Computer Modelling of Human Knowing Activity" Coherent Description As the Core of Scholarship & Science. LC 95-34299. (Studies in Cognitive Systems COGS: Vol. 18). 380p. (C). 1995. lib. bdg. 154.50 (*0-7923-3680-1*, Pub. by Kluwer Academic) Kluwer Academic.

Nauratil, Marcia J. The Alienated Librarian, 20. LC 88-34797. (New Directions in Information Management Ser.: No. 20). 139p. 1989. 49.95 (*0-313-25996-8*, NLL/, Greenwood Pr) Greenwood.

— Public Libraries & Nontraditional Clienteles: The Politics of Special Services. LC 84-19342. (New Directions in Librarianship Ser.: No. 8). 180p. 1985. 47.95 (*0-313-23819-7*, NAP/, Greenwood Pr) Greenwood.

Nauright, John. Sport, Cultures, & Identities in South Africa. LC 97-20139. (Sport & Nation Ser.). 224p. 1998. 85.00 (*0-7185-0049-0*); pap. 27.95 (*0-7185-0072-5*) Bks Intl VA.

Nauright, John & Chandler, Timothy J., eds. Making Men: Rugby & Masculine Identity. LC 95-35435. (Illus.). 260p. 1996. 52.50 (*0-7146-4637-7*, Pub. by F Cass Pubs); pap. 26.50 (*0-7146-4156-1*, Pub. by F Cass Pubs) Intl Spec Bk.

Nauright, John, jt. auth. see Mangan, J. A.

Nauright, John, jt. ed. see Chandler, Timothy J. L.

N

Naurocki, Jerzy, et al. Real-Time Systems Education III: Proceedings, IEEE Real-Time Systems Education Workshop (3rd: 1998: Poznan, Poland) LC 99-60761. 162p. 1999. pap. 105.00 (*0-7695-0134-6*) IEEE Comp Soc.

Nauroth, Holger. The Luftwaffe from the North Cape to Tobruk, 1939-1945: An Illustrated History. LC 91-61441. (Illus.). 236p. 1991. 29.95 (*0-88740-361-1*) Schiffer.

Nauroth, Holger & Held, Werner. German Fighters in World War Two: The Night Fighters. LC 91-61123. (Illus.). 232p. 1991. 29.95 (*0-88740-356-5*) Schiffer.

— The Messerschmitt Bf110 - Over All Fronts, 1939-1945. LC 90-62987. (Illus.). 248p. 1991. 29.95 (*0-88740-286-0*) Schiffer.

Nauroy, J. F., ed. see CLAROM Staff & Le Tirant, Pierre.

***Naus, D. J.** Investigation of Tendon Sheathing Filler Migration into Concrete. 84p. 1998. pap. 14.00 (*0-16-062900-4*) USGPO.

Naus, Joseph I. Data Quality Control & Editing. LC 74-19804. (Statistics, Textbooks & Monographs: Vol. 10). 216p. reprint ed. pap. 67.00 (*0-608-16847-5*, 202708600054) Bks Demand.

Naus, Joseph I., jt. auth. see Neff, Norman D.

Nauser, Markus, jt. ed. see Steiner, Dieter.

Nauta, Bram. Analog CMOS Filters for Very High Frequencies. LC 92-27778. (International Series in Engineering & Computer Science, VLSI, Computer Architecture, & Digital Screen Processing). (C). 1992. text 109.00 (*0-7923-9272-8*) Kluwer Academic.

Nauta, Doede. The Meaning of Information. LC 79-173382. (Approaches to Semiotics Ser.: No. 20). (Illus.). 314p. 1972. text 66.15 (*90-279-1996-8*) Mouton.

Nauta, Lodi W., jt. auth. see Hoenen, Maarten J.

***Nauta, Ruurd R.** Poetry for Patrons: Literary Communication in the Age of Domitian. 375p. 2000. 98.00 (*90-04-10885-8*) Brill Academic Pubs.

Nauta Staff. Diccionario de la Lengua Espanola: Dictionary of the Spanish Language, 2 vols., Set. (SPA.). 704p. 1978. 195.00 (*0-8288-4887-4*, S50030) Fr & Eur.

— Diccionario Enciclopedico Areas, 10 vols., Set. (SPA.). 4140p. 1990. 1495.00 (*0-7859-5843-6*, 8427813597) Fr & Eur.

— Diccionario Enciclopedico Areas, Vol. 2. (SPA.). 424p. 1990. 150.00 (*0-7859-5844-4*, 8427813619) Fr & Eur.

— Diccionario Enciclopedico Areas, Vol. 3. (SPA.). 404p. 1990. 150.00 (*0-7859-5845-2*, 8427813627) Fr & Eur.

— Diccionario Enciclopedico Areas, Vol. 4. (SPA.). 424p. 1990. 150.00 (*0-7859-5846-0*, 8427813635) Fr & Eur.

— Diccionario Enciclopedico Areas, Vol. 5. (SPA.). 416p. 1990. 150.00 (*0-7859-5847-9*, 8427813643) Fr & Eur.

— Diccionario Enciclopedico Areas, Vol. 6. (SPA.). 416p. 1990. 150.00 (*0-7859-5848-7*, 8427813651) Fr & Eur.

— Diccionario Enciclopedico Areas, Vol. 7. 416p. 1990. 150.00 (*0-7859-6457-6*) Fr & Eur.

— Diccionario Enciclopedico Areas, Vol. 8. (SPA.). 408p. 1990. 150.00 (*0-7859-5849-5*, 8427813678) Fr & Eur.

— Diccionario Enciclopedico Areas, Vol. 9. (SPA.). 408p. 1990. 150.00 (*0-7859-5850-9*, 8427813686) Fr & Eur.

— Diccionario Enciclopedico Areas, Vol. 10. (SPA.). 404p. 1990. 150.00 (*0-7859-5851-7*, 8427813694) Fr & Eur.

— Enciclopedia de la Tecnica y de la Mecanica, 8 vols., Set. 5th ed. (SPA.). 2920p. 1975. 595.00 (*0-8288-5866-7*, S14237) Fr & Eur.

— Enciclopedia de los Animales. (SPA.). 400p. 1976. 75.00 (*0-8288-5661-3*, S50536) Fr & Eur.

— Enciclopedia General, 10 vols., Set. (SPA.). 4092p. 1978. 750.00 (*0-8288-5225-1*, S50465) Fr & Eur.

— Enciclopedia Medica Familiar, 2 vols., Set. 5th ed. (SPA.). 448p. 1979. pap. 75.00 (*0-8288-4742-8*, S50532) Fr & Eur.

— Enciclopedia Universal Nauta, 10 vols., Set. 10th ed. (SPA.). 2144p. 1978. 795.00 (*0-8288-5230-8*, S12303) Fr & Eur.

— Mi Primera Enciclopedia, 2 vols., Set. 7th ed. (SPA.). 420p. (J). 1978. 65.00 (*0-8288-5254-5*, S26910) Fr & Eur.

— Multidiccionario. (SPA.). 544p. 1979. 38.95 (*0-8288-4825-4*, S50514) Fr & Eur.

Nauta, Stephen, jt. auth. see Esh, Janice.

Nauta, Walle J. Neuroanatomy: Selected Papers of Walle J. H. Nauta. LC 93-10358. (Contemporary Neuroscientists Ser.). (Illus.). 614p. 1993. 109.00 (*0-8176-3539-4*) Birkhauser.

Nautical Almanac Office of the U. S. Naval Observatory Staff, jt. auth. see Her Majesty's Nautical Almanac Office, Rutherford Appleton Laboratory Staff.

***Nautical Almanac Office Staff.** NAVPAC & Compact Data, 2001-2005: Astro-Navigation Methods & Software for the PC. 125p. 2000. pap. 80.00 incl. cd-rom (*0-11-887311-3*, Pub. by Statnry Office) Balogh.

— Planetary & Lunar Co-ordinates, 2001-2020. 70p. 2000. pap. 40.00 incl. cd-rom (*0-11-887312-1*, Pub. by Statnry Office) Balogh.

Nautilus Publishing, Inc. Staff. Fishing Vessels of the United States, 1993: A Complete Directory of All Vessels over 85 Feet. Udbye, Andreas & Angelsen, Jan E., eds. (Illus.). 360p. (Orig.). 1992. pap. 29.95 (*0-9634338-0-6*) Nautilus Pub.

— Fishing Vessels of the United States, 1994: 1,400 Vessels - 850 Photos, a Complete Directory of All Vessels over 79 Feet Registered Length. Udbye, Andreas, ed. (Illus.). 448p. (Orig.). 1994. pap. 29.95 (*0-9634338-1-4*) Nautilus Pub.

Nautilus Publishing Staff. Fishing Vessels of the U. S. 1995-96 Edition. Udbye, Andreas, ed. (Illus.). 436p. (Orig.). 1995. pap. 29.95 (*0-9634338-3-0*) Nautilus Pub.

Nautiyal, Annpurna, jt. ed. see Nautiyal, R. R.

Nautiyal, D. P. Narayan Datt Tiwari: Life Story. LC 95-900085. (C). 1994. write for info. (*81-207-1655-8*) Sterling Pubs.

Nautiyal, K. P. Proto-Historic India. (C). 1989. 76.00 (*0-8364-2481-6*, Pub. by Agam) S Asia.

Nautiyal, R. R. & Nautiyal, Annpurna, eds. Uttarakhand in Turmoil. 150p. 1996. pap. 125.00 (*81-7533-024-4*, Pub. by Print Hse) St Mut.

***Nautrup, Cordula Poulsen & Tobias, Ralf.** Atlas & Textbook of Diagnostic Ultrasonography of the Dog & Cat. Cartee, Robert E., ed. (Illus.). 400p. (C). 1999. pap. text 149.00 (*1-884254-49-7*) Vet Lrn Syst.

Nauts, Charles, jt. auth. see Bridewell, David A.

***Nav Press Staff.** Nuestra Esperanza en Cristo.Tr. of Our Hope in Christ. (SPA.). 48p. (YA). 2000. pap. 3.99 (*0-311-13662-1*, Edit Mundo) Casa Bautista.

Nava. Educating Americans in a Multiethnic Society. 3rd ed. 1995. pap. text 21.50 (*0-07-046474-X*) McGraw.

Nava, Alejandro. La Inquieta Superficie Terrestre. (Ciencia para Todos Ser.). (SPA.). pap. 6.99 (*968-16-3467-5*, Pub. by Fondo) Continental Bk.

— Terremotos. (Ciencia para Todos Ser.). (SPA.). pap. 6.99 (*968-16-4847-1*, Pub. by Fondo) Continental Bk.

Nava, Andrea, et al. Arrhythmogenic Right Ventricular Cardiomyopathy Dysplasia. LC 97-37685. (International Congress Ser.). 506p. 1997. write for info. (*0-444-82447-2*) Elsevier.

Nava, Jean. Exploring the Castle: The Study Guide for Learning-Life in the Castle. (More Than Conquerors Ser.). (Illus.). 101p. 1999. spiral bd. 9.95 (*0-9659952-3-2*) Kingdom Pr.

— Laboring-Life in the Outpost. LC 98-92088. (More Than Conquerors Ser.: Vol. 2). (Illus.). 490p. (J). (gr. 4 up). 1998. pap. 12.95 (*0-9659952-1-6*) Kingdom Pr.

***Nava, Jean.** Leading-Life at the Battlefront. (More Than Conquerors Ser.: Vol. 3). (Illus.). 454p. 1999. pap. 12.95 (*0-9659952-4-0*) Kingdom Pr.

Nava, Jean. Learning-Life in the Castle: An Allegory of the Christian Way. LC 97-94200. (More Than Conquerors Ser.: Vol. 1). (Illus.). 1997. pap. 11.95 (*0-9659952-0-8*) Kingdom Pr.

Nava, Kathryn, tr. see Minnaar, Phillip.

Nava, Mica. Changing Cultures: Feminism, Youth & Consumerism. (Theory, Culture & Society Ser.). 256p. (C). 1992. text 55.00 (*0-8039-8607-6*); pap. text 21.95 (*0-8039-8608-4*) Sage.

Nava, Mica, et al, eds. Buy This Book: Studies in Advertising & Consumption. LC 96-15071. 368p. (C). 1997. 80.00 (*0-415-14131-1*); pap. 24.99 (*0-415-14132-X*) Routledge.

Nava, Mica & O'Shea, Alan, eds. Modern Times: Reflections on a Century of English Modernity. LC 95-16372. 288p. (C). 1996. 80.00 (*0-415-06932-7*); pap. 25.99 (*0-415-06933-5*) Routledge.

Nava, Michael. The Burning Plain. 416p. 1999. mass mkt. 5.99 (*0-553-58085-X*) Bantam.

— Created Equal: Why Gay Rights Matter to America. 1995. pap. 8.95 (*0-312-11764-7*, Stonewall Inn) St Martin.

— Death of Friends. 256p. 1998. reprint ed. mass mkt. 5.99 (*0-553-57763-8*) Bantam.

— Goldenboy. LC 96-21334. 224p. 1996. reprint ed. pap. 10.00 (*1-55583-366-7*) Alyson Pubns.

— How Town. (Los Angeles Mysteries Ser.). 240p. 1991. mass mkt. 4.99 (*0-345-36987-4*) Ballantine Pub Grp.

— The Little Death. 165p. 1997. reprint ed. pap. 9.95 (*1-55583-388-8*) Alyson Pubns.

Nava, Michael, ed. Finale: Short Stories of Mystery & Suspense. LC 89-85942. 207p. 1997. reprint ed. pap. 10.95 (*1-55583-395-0*) Alyson Pubns.

Nava, Simonetta, jt. auth. see Pedrocco, Filippo.

Nava, Yolanda. It's All in the Frijoles: One Hundred Famous Latinos Share Real Life Stories, Timed Tested Dichos, Favorite Folktales & Inspiring Words of Wisdom. 336p. 2000. per. 13.00 (*0-684-84900-3*) S&S Trade.

***Nava, Yolanda.** It's All in the Frijoles: 100 Famous Latinos Share Real-Life Stories, Time-Tested Dichos, Favorite Folk Tales & Inspiring Words of Wisdom. (Illus.). (J). 2000. 18.35 (*0-606-18894-0*) Turtleback.

***Navabi, Zainalabedin.** Verilog Digital System Design: Analysis & Design of Digital Systems. LC 99-25563. (Professional Engineering Ser.). 500p. 1999. 75.00 (*0-07-047164-9*) McGraw.

Navabi, Zainalabedin. VHDL: Analysis & Modeling of Digital Systems. (C). 1993. text 56.25 (*0-07-046472-3*) McGraw.

— VHDL: Analysis & Modeling of Digital Systems. 2nd ed. LC 97-31667. (Illus.). 500p. 1997. text 60.00 (*0-07-046479-0*) McGraw-Hill Prof.

Navabpour, Reza. Iran. LC 88-144739. (World Bibliographical Ser.: No. 81). 328p. 1988. lib. bdg. 65.00 (*1-85109-036-3*) ABC-CLIO.

Navailles, Louisette, ed. see Poisson, Raymond.

Navajas, Gonzalo. Mimesis y Cultura en la Ficcion: Teoria de la Novela. (Monagrafias A Ser.: No. 115). (SPA.). 214p. (C). 1985. 58.00 (*0-7293-0212-1*, Pub. by Tamesis Bks Ltd) Boydell & Brewer.

***Navajata.** A Divine Life in a Divine Body. 263p. 1998. pap. 10.95 (*81-7060-119-3*, Pub. by SAA) E-W Cultural Ctr.

Navajo-Ayora, Jose L. Mi Mayor Legado. (SPA.). 1998. pap. 5.99 (*0-8297-0987-8*) Vida Pubs.

Navajo School of Indian Basketry Staff. Indian Basket Weaving. (Illus.). 104p. 1971. reprint ed. pap. 5.95 (*0-486-22616-6*) Dover.

Naval Education & Training Command Staff. Construction & Home Repair Techniques Simply Explained: Woodworking, Scaffolding, Leveling & Grading, Concrete, Masonry, Flooring & Roofing, Exterior & Interior Finishing, Plastering, Stuccoing, Tiling, Etc. LC 99-30931. (Illus.). 569p. 1999. pap. text 18.95 (*0-486-40481-1*) Dover.

Naval Historical Center (U. S.) Staff, jt. auth. see Carlisle, Rodney P.

Naval Observatory Library Staff. Catalog of the Naval Observatory Library, Washington, D.C. 1977. 750.00 (*0-8161-1515-X*, G K Hall & Co) Mac Lib Ref.

***Naval Studies Board Staff, et al.** An Assessment of Undersea Weapons Science & Technology. 70p. 2000. pap. 18.00 (*0-309-06926-2*) Natl Acad Pr.

Naval War College Press Staff, ed. see Laning, Harris.

Naval War College Staff. Sound Military Decision. Hatendorf, John B. & Hughes, Wayne P., Jr., eds. LC 91-45244. (Classics of Sea Power Ser.). (Illus.). 243p. 1992. 39.95 (*1-55750-752-X*) Naval Inst Pr.

Naval War College, Strategy & Force Planning Faculty Staff, jt. auth. see Lloyd, Richmond M.

Navantes, S. The Imitation of St. Therese of the Child Jesus. Grace, Mary, tr. LC 79-1132. 227p. reprint ed. pap. 70.40 (*0-608-13432-5*, 202257200028) Bks Demand.

Navaratham, V., jt. auth. see Spencer, Christopher.

Navaratna-Bandara, Abeysinghe M. The Management of Ethnic Seccessionist Conflict: The Big Neighbor Syndrome. (Illus.). 208p. 1995. text 79.95 (*1-85521-698-1*, Pub. by Dartmth Pub) Ashgate Pub Co.

— Unraveling the Asian Miracle: Explorations in Development Strategies, Geopolitics & Regionalism. Lele, Jayant & Ofori-Yeboah, Kwasi, eds. 248p. 1996. text 79.95 (*1-85521-740-6*, Pub. by Dartmth Pub) Ashgate Pub Co.

***Navaratnam, Ramon V.** Healing the Wounded Tiger: How the Turmoil Is Reshaping Malaysia LC 98-944987. 151 p. 1999. write for info. (*967-978-674-9*, Pub. by Pelanduk) Weatherhill.

Navaratnam, Ramon V. Strengthening the Malaysian Economy: Policy Changes & Reforms. LC 98-944489. 190 p. 1998. write for info. (*967-978-642-0*) Pelanduk.

Navard, Jean. Scientifically Yours, French & English, 2 vols. (ENG & FRE.). 502p. 1995. 125.00 (*0-320-00031-1*) Fr & Eur.

Navaretta, Cynthia. American Women Artists: Works on Paper & an American Album. LC 85-62160. (Women/Art Ser.). (Illus.). 45p. 1985. pap. 7.00 (*0-9602476-5-3*) Midmarch Arts.

— Guide to Women's Art Organizations & Directory for the Arts. rev. ed. LC 82-80588. (Directories Ser.). (Illus.). 1982. pap. text 8.50 (*0-9602476-3-7*) Midmarch Arts.

— Whole Arts Directory. LC 87-62289. (Directories Ser.). (Illus.). 172p. (Orig.). 1989. pap. 12.95 (*0-9602476-7-X*) Midmarch Arts.

Navaretta, Cynthia & Marxer, Donna. Artists Colonies, Retreats & Study Centers. rev. ed. LC 95-75216. (Directories Ser.). 46p. 1999. pap. text 6.50 (*1-877675-17-2*) Midmarch Arts.

Navaretta, Cynthia, jt. ed. see Moore, S.

Navarette, Susan J. The Shape of Fear: Horror & the Fin de Siecle Culture of Decadence. LC 97-34081. (Illus.). 272p. 1997. 37.95 (*0-8131-2013-6*) U Pr of Ky.

Navaretti, G. Barba, et al, eds. Creation & Transfer of Knowledge: Institutions & Incentives. LC 98-27171. (Illus.). vi, 313p. 1998. 95.00 (*3-540-64426-1*) Spr-Verlag.

Navaretti, Giorgio B., et al, eds. Labour, Poverty, & Development. (Queen Elizabeth House Series in Development Studies). (Illus.). 287p. 1999. text 78.00 (*0-19-829353-4*) OUP.

***Navaretti, Peter Y. & Turnbull, Jeffrey, eds.** The Griffins in Australia & India: The Complete Works & Projects of Walter Burley Griffin & Marion Mahony Griffin. (Illus.). 320p. 1999. 95.00 (*0-522-84830-3*, Pub. by Melbourne Univ Pr) Paul & Co Pubs.

***Navari, Cornelia.** Internationalism & the State in the Twentieth Century. LC 99-42565. 256p. 2000. pap. text 22.99 (*0-415-09748-7*) Routledge.

— Internationalism & the State in the Twentieth Century. LC 99-42565. 256p. (C). 2000. text. write for info. (*0-415-09747-9*) Routledge.

Navari, Cornelia, ed. see Schneider, Margaret M.

Navaro, Anna, tr. see Swart, Susan.

***Navarra.** Seton Hall University (CH) (Images of America Ser.). 128p. 1999. pap. 18.99 (*0-7385-0062-3*) Arcadia Publng.

Navarra, A. Beyond el Nino: Decadal & Interdecadal Climate Variability. LC 99-18126. 374p. 1999. 119.00 (*3-540-63662-5*) Spr-Verlag.

Navarra, A., jt. ed. see Storch, H. V.

Navarra, Anthony. Cobweb to a Star & Other Poems. (Illus.). 176p. (Orig.). 1988. pap. text 8.95 (*0-9612678-2-8*) Abbott Pr.

— Whisperings on the Porch: A Collection of Haiku. (Illus.). 128p. (Orig.). 1992. pap. 6.95 (*0-9632041-3-0*) Japan Am Comm.

Navarra, Antonio, ed. see Von Storch, Hans.

Navarra, Ignazio, ed. Atre e Storie a Sciacca, Celtabellotta, e Burgio del XV el XVII Secolo: Italian Stories & Art.Tr. of Art & Stories of Sciacca, Caltebelotta & Burgio from the XVth to XVIIth Centuries. xvi, 144p. 1986. pap. 15.00 (*0-89304-554-3*) Cross-Cultrl NY.

Navarra, Tova. Howell & Farmingdale. LC 97-112633. (Images of America Ser.). 128p. 1996. pap. 16.99 (*0-7524-0283-8*) Arcadia Publng.

— The New Jersey Shore a Vanishing Splendor. LC 84-9337. (Illus.). 112p. 1985. pap. 9.95 (*0-8453-4793-4*, Cornwall Bks) Assoc Univ Prs.

— On My Own: Helping Kids Help Themselves. (Illus.). 128p. (J). (gr. 2-8). 1993. pap. 9.95 (*0-8120-1563-0*) Barron.

— On My Own: Helping Kids Help Themselves. 1993. 14.15 (*0-606-05521-5*, Pub. by Turtleback) Demco.

— Toward Painless Writing: A Guide for Health Professionals. LC 98-12762. 128p. 1998. pap. text 19.95 (*1-55642-293-8*, 42938) SLACK Inc.

— Wisdom for Caregivers. LC 95-19269. 176p. 1995. pap. 12.00 (*1-55642-288-1*) SLACK Inc.

Navarra, Tova & Ferrer, Margaret. An Insider's Guide to Home Health Care. LC 96-3195. 208p. 1996. pap. 28.00 (*1-55642-287-3*, 42873) SLACK Inc.

Navarra, Tova & Lipkowitz, Myron. Allegeries A-Z. LC 93-33379. 368p. 1994. 40.00 (*0-8160-2824-9*) Facts on File.

Navarra, Tova & Lipowitz, Myron A. Encyclopedia of Vitamins, Minerals, & Supplements. LC 95-12645. 304p. 1995. 35.00 (*0-8160-3183-5*) Facts on File.

— Encyclopedia of Vitamins, Minerals, & Supplements. LC 95-12645. 304p. 1997. pap. 17.95 (*0-8160-3241-6*) Facts on File.

***Navarra, Tova & Lundrigan, Margaret.** Staten Island, Vol. II. (Images of America Ser.). 128p. 1999. pap. 18.99 (*0-7385-0203-0*) Arcadia Publng.

Navarra, Tova, et al. Therapeutic Communication: A Guide to Effective Interpersonal Skills for Health Care Professionals. LC 88-43159. 158p. 1990. pap. 23.00 (*1-55642-075-7*) SLACK Inc.

Navarra, Tova, jt. auth. see Lipkowitz, Myron A.

Navarra, Tova, jt. auth. see Lundrigan, Margaret.

***Navarre.** Instrumental Music Teacher's Survival Kit. 2000. spiral bd. 32.95 (*0-13-017821-7*) P-H.

Navarre, Marguerite de. L' Heptameron. Francois, ed. (Coll. Prestige). 27.95 (*0-685-34187-9*); pap. 14.95 (*0-685-34186-0*) Fr & Eur.

— The Heptameron. Chilton, Paul A., tr. & intro. by. (Classics Ser.). 544p. 1984. pap. 14.95 (*0-14-044355-X*, Penguin Classics) Viking Penguin.

— Oeuvres Choisies, 2 vols. Clive, H. P., ed. Incl. Vol. 1. Poemes. LC 68-12125. (FRE.). 1968. pap. text 6.95 Vol. 2. Theatre et Nouvelles. LC 68-12125. (FRE.). 1968. pap. text 6.95 (*0-89197-323-0*); LC 68-12125. (Medieval French Literature Ser.). (FRE.). 1968. pap. text. write for info. (*0-318-53720-6*) Irvington.

Navarre, Monty, jt. ed. see Miller, Newton W.

Navarre, Yves. Cronus' Children. Girven, Howard, tr. from FRE. 320p. 1990. pap. 14.95 (*0-7145-4014-5*) Riverrun NY.

— Our Share of Time. Di Bernardi, Dominic & Domke, Noelle, trs. from FRE. LC 86-72136. Orig. Title: Le Temps Uoulu. 240p. 1988. reprint ed. pap. 12.50 (*0-916583-28-7*) Dalkey Arch.

— Sweet Tooth. Watson, Donald, tr. from FRE. 1980. 14.95 (*0-7145-3522-2*) Riverrun NY.

— Swimming Pools at War. Watson, Donald, tr. from FRE. 168p. (Orig.). 1982. pap. 8.95 (*0-913745-00-6*) Ubu Repertory.

Navarrete, Carlos & Lujan, Luis. El Gran Monticulo de la Culebra en el Valle de Guatemala. 106p. 1986. pap. 4.57 (*968-837-714-7*, UN018) UPLAAP.

Navarrete, Carlos, jt. ed. see Serra, Mari C.

Navarrete, Ignacio. Orphans of Petrarch: Poetry & Theory in the Spanish Renaissance. LC 93-4559. (Publications of the Center for Medieval & Renaissance Studies: Vol. 25). 1994. 48.00 (*0-520-08373-3*, Pub. by U CA Pr) Cal Prin Full Svc.

Navarrete, Pablo F. Planning, Estimating & Control of Chemical Construction Projects. LC 95-124. (Cost Engineering Ser.: Vol. 23). (Illus.). 344p. 1995. text 135.00 (*0-8247-9359-5*) Dekker.

Navarrette, Francis G. American Politics. 288p. (C). 1996. pap. text 40.95 (*0-7872-1712-3*, 41171201) Kendall-Hunt.

— Pak: Pragmatics of California Government. 288p. (C). 1995. pap. text 30.95 (*0-7872-1344-6*, 41134401) Kendall-Hunt.

— Pak: Pragmatics of Government. 416p. (C). 1995. pap. text 38.95 (*0-7872-1294-6*, 41129401) Kendall-Hunt.

Navarria, F. L. & Pelfer, P. G. The Standard Model & Just Beyond. 520p. 1993. text 121.00 (*981-02-1319-0*) World Scientific Pub.

Navarria, F. L., et al. Experimental Apparatus for High Energy Physics & Astrophysics. 564p. 1991. text 151.00 (*981-02-0465-5*) World Scientific Pub.

Navarro. Mechanics & Physics of Aerating Grain. 1995. 284.00 (*0-8493-4542-1*, CRC Reprint) Franklin.

***Navarro.** Power of Microeconomics. 1999. cd-rom 21.56 (*0-07-228314-9*) McGraw.

Navarro, Adolfo. El Dominio del Aire. (Ciencia para Todos Ser.). (SPA.). pap. 6.99 (*968-16-4373-9*, Pub. by Fondo) Continental Bk.

Navarro, Ann. Effective Web Design. (No Experience Required Ser.). 1998. pap. text 34.99 (*0-7821-2196-9*) Sybex.

— Effective Web Design - Master the Essentials. LC 97-80781. 624p. 1998. pap. text 34.99 (*0-7821-2278-7*) Sybex.

— Mastering XML. 4th ed. (Mastering Ser.). 832p. 1999. pap. text 39.99 (*0-7821-2266-3*) Sybex.

***Navarro, Ann.** XHTML by Example. 500p. 2000. pap. text 29.99 (*0-7897-2385-9*) Que.

Navarro, Armando. The Cristal Experiment: A Chicano Struggle for Community Control. LC 98-17431. (Illus.). 424p. (Orig.). 1998. pap. 22.95 (*0-299-15824-1*); text 59.95 (*0-299-15820-9*) U of Wis Pr.

— The Demographics of California's Latinos: Maps & Statistics. 19p. 1988. pap. 8.50 (*1-883638-09-7*) Rose Inst.

— Environmentally Safe Drilling Practices. 250p. 1995. 79.95 (*0-87814-437-4*) PennWell Bks.

— Mexican American Youth Organization: Avant-Garde of the Chicano Movement in Texas. (Illus.). (C). 1995. pap. 16.95 (*0-292-75557-0*); text 40.00 (*0-292-75556-2*) U of Tex Pr.

— La Raza Unida Party: A Chicano Challenge to the U. S. Two-Party Dictatorship. (Illus.). 344p. 2000. 83.50 (*1-56639-770-7*) Temple U Pr.

An Asterisk (*) at the beginning of an entry indicates that the title is appearing for the first time.

Navarro, Armando. La Raza Unida Party: A Chicano Challenge to the U. S. Two-Party Dictatorship. (Asian American History & Culture Ser.). (Illus.). 344p. (C). 2000. pap. 27.95 (*1-56639-771-5*) Temple U Pr.

Navarro, Carlos F. Categories. (Start Smart Ser.). (J). (gr. k-2). 1990. student ed. 4.50 (*1-878396-02-1*) Start Smart Bks.

— Early Geometry. (Start Smart Ser.). (Illus.). 64p. (Orig.). (J). (gr. 2-3). 1990. pap. text 6.50 (*1-878396-04-8*) Start Smart Bks.

— Early Reading Through Phonics, Vol. I. Kurfehs, Judith, ed. (Start Smart Ser.). (Illus.). 64p. 1989. student ed. 4.50 (*0-685-30107-9*) Start Smart Bks.

— Early Reading Through Phonics, Vol. II. Kurfehs, Judith, ed. (Start Smart Ser.). (Illus.). 64p. 1989. student ed. 3.50 (*0-685-30104-4*) Start Smart Bks.

— Prefixes & Suffixes. Navarro, Judith, ed. (Start Smart Ser.). 80p. 1990. student ed. 7.50 (*0-685-35594-2*) Start Smart Bks.

— Thinking with Words. Navarro, Judith, ed. (Start Smart Ser.). 64p. 1990. student ed. 6.50 (*1-878396-05-6*) Start Smart Bks.

— Verbal Correspondences. (Start Smart Ser.). (J). (gr. k-2). 1990. student ed. 4.50 (*1-878396-00-5*) Start Smart Bks.

— Word Games to Learn By: Categories. Navarro, Judith, ed. (Start Smart Ser.). (Illus.). 32p. 1989. student ed. 3.50 (*0-685-30103-6*) Start Smart Bks.

— Word Games to Learn By: Distinctions. Navarro, Judith, ed. (Start Smart Ser.). 32p. 1989. student ed. 3.50 (*0-685-30105-2*) Start Smart Bks.

— Word Games to Learn By: Verbal Correspondences. Navarro, Judith, ed. (Start Smart Ser.). 32p. 1989. student ed. 3.50 (*0-685-30106-0*) Start Smart Bks.

Navarro, Christina, ed. see Thompson, Sherrie.

***Navarro, Christine Schmertz.** Teaching Activities Manual for the Catholic Youth Bible. LC 99-50758. 432p. 2000. 24.95 (*0-88489-560-2*) St Marys.

Navarro, Concha L. El Gran Amor de Una Gallina.Tr. of Hen's Great Love. (SPA., Illus.). 86p. (J). (gr. 2-4). 1997. 7.50 (*84-207-7556-8*, Pub. by SM Ediciones) IBD Ltd.

Navarro, Concha L. El Gran Amor De Una Gallina. 1997. 7.95 (*84-207-6970-3*) Anaya Pubs.

Navarro, Dagnino J. Vocabulario Maritimo Ingles-Espanol y Espanol-Ingles. 5th ed. (ENG & SPA.). 151p. 1976. pap. 19.95 (*0-8288-5766-0*, S12239) Fr & Eur.

***Navarro, Dave.** Spread: A Year in the Life of Dave Navarro. 256p. 2000. 29.95 (*0-06-039368-8*, ReganBks) HarperTrade.

— Strip. 2000. pap. 16.00 (*0-06-098853-3*) HarpC.

Navarro, Dorian S., et al. Infant-Tell. (Knight & Dey Ser.). 225p. (Orig.). 1984. pap. 4.50 (*0-932079-00-8*) TimeFare.

Navarro, Gilbert & Shea, Mary E. Good Days Action Planning Guide, 1994. (Yearly Datebook Ser.). 175p. (C). 1993. ring bd. 25.00 (*0-9626626-3-1*) Twin Stars.

— Good Days Action Planning Guide, 1995. 160p. (Orig.). (C). 1994. pap., ring bd. 25.00 (*0-9626626-4-X*) Twin Stars.

Navarro, Gilbert, jt. auth. see Shea, Mary.

Navarro, Gilbert, jt. auth. see Shea, Mary E.

Navarro, Grabriel. Characters & Blocks of Finite Groups. LC 98-29339. (London Mathematical Society Lecture Note Ser.: No. 250). 304p. (C). 1998. pap. 39.95 (*0-521-59513-4*) Cambridge U Pr.

Navarro, J. & Schmitz, J., eds. Paediatric Gastroenterology. Barefoot, Brian, tr. (Illus.). 572p. 1992. 165.00 (*0-19-261771-0*) OUP.

Navarro, J. M. De, see De Navarro, J. M.

Navarro, J. Nelson. Marine Diatoms Associated with Mangrove Prop Roots in the Indian River, Florida, U. S. A. (Bibliotheca Phycologica Ser.: Vol. 61). (Illus.). 151p. (Orig.). 1982. pap. text 35.00 (*3-7682-1337-4*) Lubrecht & Cramer.

Navarro, Jesus, et al, eds. Microscopic Quantum Many-Body Theories & Their Applications: Proceedings of a European Summer School, Held at Valencia, Spain, 8-19 September 1997. LC 98-23302. (Lecture Notes in Physics Ser.: Vol. 510). xiii, 379p. 1998. 86.00 (*3-540-64471-7*) Spr-Verlag.

Navarro, Jose A. Defending Mexican Valor in Texas: Jose Antonio Navarro's Historical Writings, 1853-1857. McDonald, David R. & Matovina, Timothy M., eds. LC 95-38156. (Illus.). 128p. 1995. 24.95 (*1-880510-31-6*) State House Pr.

Navarro, Jose A., jt. auth. see Matovina, Timothy M.

Navarro, Jose L. Blue Day on Main Street. LC 73-88742. 1973. pap. 3.95 (*0-88412-063-5*) TQS Pubns.

Navarro, Jose M. & Navarro, Ramil A. Mastering Spanish Vocabulary: A Thematic Approach. (Mastering Vocabulary Ser). 368p. 1995. pap. 8.95 (*0-8120-9110-8*) Barron.

Navarro, Juan C., ed. Community Organizations in Latin America. 160p. 1994. pap. text 18.50 (*0-940602-75-X*) IADB.

Navarro, Judith, ed. see Navarro, Carlos F.

Navarro, Julio A. & Chang, Kai. Integrated Active Antennas & Spatial Power Combining. LC 95-46168. (Wiley Series in Microwave & Optical Engineering). 368p. 1996. 93.50 (*0-471-04984-0*) Wiley.

***Navarro, Laura.** Don Sabino, el Murcielago de la Ciudad: Don Sabino the City Bat. (Illus.). 48p. 1999. pap. 8.95 (*0-292-75569-4*) U of Tex Pr.

Navarro, Laura. Marcelo el Murcielago (Marcelo the Bat) LC 97-202990. (ENG & SPA.). (Illus.). 40p. (J). (gr. k-3). 1997. 8.95 (*0-292-75567-8*) Bat Conserv.

— Valentin, a Special Bat. 48p. (J). (gr. k-3). pap. 8.95 (*0-292-70874-2*) U of Tex Pr.

Navarro, M. Pilar. Decorating Ceramics: A Guide to the History, Materials, Equipment & Techniques of... (Illus.). 144p. 1996. pap. text 29.95 (*0-8230-3910-2*) Watsn-Guptill.

Navarro, Marysa, et al. Women in Latin America & the Caribbean. LC 99-10085. (Restoring Women to History Ser.). (Illus.). 144p. 1999. text 29.95 (*0-253-33479-9*) Ind U Pr.

***Navarro, Marysa, et al.** Women in Latin America & the Caribbean. LC 99-10085. (Restoring Women to History Ser.). (Illus.). 144p. 1999. pap. 11.95 (*0-253-21307-X*) Ind U Pr.

Navarro, Nick & Sadler, Jeff. The Cuban Cop: The True Story of One Tough Cop ... & His Rise from an Undercover Narc to a Celebrated Sheriff. (Illus.). 320p. 1997. 24.95 (*1-890819-01-8*) TransMedia FL.

Navarro, Peter. The Policy Game: How Special Interests & Ideologues Are Stealing America. 360p. (C). 1986. 18.95 (*0-669-14112-7*) Free Pr.

— San Diego Confidential: A Candidate's Odyssey. LC 98-96458. (Illus.). 241p. 1999. pap. 9.95 (*0-9665688-7-7*) Q T Pr.

Navarro, R. Lacasa & De Bustamante, I. Diaz. Spanish-English - English-Spanish Dictionary of Law, Economics & Politics. 4th ed. 761p. 1991. 130.00 (*84-7130-306-X*, Pub. by Edit De Derecho) IBD Ltd.

Navarro, Ramil A., jt. auth. see Navarro, Jose M.

***Navarro, Ramon Gil.** The Gold Rush Diary of Ramon Gil Navarro. Reher, David & Ferreyra, Maria, eds. LC 00-20988. (Illus.). 360p. 2000. 45.00 (*0-8032-3343-4*) U of Nebr Pr.

***Navarro, Robert.** Managed Care Pharmacy Practice. LC 99-29131. 656p. 1999. write for info. (*0-8342-1205-6*) Aspen Pub.

Navarro, Robert & Wertheimer, Albert I. Managing the Pharmacy Benefit LC 96-164710. xxii, 376 p. 1996. write for info. (*0-9651745-0-6*) Emron.

Navarro, Robert, jt. ed. see Wertheimer, Albert I.

Navarro Rojas, Oscar, jt. ed. see Garfield, Donald.

***Navarro, S. D.** The Valedictorian & Other Stories. 2000. pap. write for info. (*0-927534-97-5*) Biling Rev-Pr.

***Navarro, Shlomo.** The Mechanics & Physics of Modern Grain Aeration Management. 288p. 1999. 139.00 (*0-8493-1355-4*) CRC Pr.

Navarro, Vicente. Crisis, Health & Medicine: A Social Critique. 300p. 1986. 32.50 (*0-422-60580-8*, 1006, Pub. by Tavistock); pap. 13.95 (*0-422-60170-5*, 9760, Pub. by Tavistock) Routldge.

— Dangerous to Your Health: The Crisis of Medical Care in the United States. (Cornerstone Bks.)..144p. 1993. pap. text 13.00 (*0-85345-865-0*, Pub. by Monthly Rev) NYU Pr.

— The Politics of Health Policy: The U. S. Reforms, 1980-1993. LC 93-40683. 260p. 1994. pap. 29.95 (*1-55786-318-0*) Blackwell Pubs.

Navarro, Vicente, ed. Health & Medical Care in the U. S. A Critical Analysis. LC 77-80380. (Policy, Politics, Health & Medicine Ser.: Vol. 1). 162p. 1977. pap. 22.00 (*0-89503-000-4*) Baywood Pub.

— Imperialism, Health, & Medicine. LC 80-67832. (Policy, Politics, Health & Medicine Ser.: Vol. 3). 285p. (C). 1981. pap. text 28.00 (*0-89503-019-5*) Baywood Pub.

— Why the United States Does Not Have a National Health Program. (Policy, Politics, Health & Medicine Ser.). 266p. 1992. pap. text 30.00 (*0-89503-105-1*) Baywood Pub.

Navarro, Vicente & Berman, Daniel, eds. Health & Work under Capitalism: An International Perspective. (Policy, Politics, Health & Medicine Ser.: Vol. 5). 311p. 1983. pap. text 28.00 (*0-89503-035-7*) Baywood Pub.

Navarro, Yvonne. Aliens: Music of the Spears. 288p. 1996. mass mkt. 4.99 (*0-553-57492-5*, Spectra) Bantam.

***Navarro, Yvonne.** DeadTimes. 254p. 2000. pap. 24.99 (*0-9672029-5-7*) Darktales Pubns.

Navarro, Yvonne. First Name Reverse Dictionary: Given Names Listed by Meaning. LC 92-50314. 217p. 1993. lib. bdg. 35.00 (*0-89950-748-4*) McFarland & Co.

***Navarro, Yvonne.** Paleo. (Buffy the Vampire Slayer Ser.: Vol. 11). 272p. (gr. 8-12). 2000. 6.99 (*0-7434-0034-8*) PB.

Navarro, Yvonne. Red Shadows. 512p. 1998. mass mkt. 6.50 (*0-553-57749-2*) Bantam.

— Species II. 352p. 1998. mass mkt. 6.99 (*0-8125-7075-8*, Pub. by Tor Bks) St Martin.

***Navarro, Yvonne.** That's Not My Name. 432p. 2000. mass mkt. 6.50 (*0-553-57750-6*) Bantam.

Navarro, Yvonne. The Willow File, Vol. 1. (Buffy the Vampire Slayer Ser.: No. 13). (Illus.). 196p. (YA). (gr. 7-12). 1999. mass mkt. 4.99 (*0-671-03918-0*) PB.

***Navarro, Yvonne.** Willow Files. (Illus.). (J). 1999. 10.34 (*0-606-18367-1*) Turtleback.

Navas, Deborah. Murdered by His Wife. LC 99-15160. (Illus.). 193p. 1999. 25.00 (*1-55849-227-5*) U of Mass Pr.

— Things We Lost, Gave Away, Bought High & Sold Low: Stories. LC 92-53612. 152p. 1992. 16.95 (*0-87074-336-8*) SMU Press.

Navas, Gerardo. La Dialectica del Desarrollo Nacional: El Caso de Puerto Rico. LC 77-5824. (Planning Ser.: No. G-3). (SPA.). 1978. 6.40 (*0-8477-2436-0*) U of PR Pr.

Navas, Gerardo, ed. Crisis, Planificacion y el Desarrollo Social-Nacional. LC 77-22995. (Planning Ser.: No. S-3). 327p. 1978. pap. 6.00 (*0-8477-2437-9*) U of PR Pr.

— Geography & Planning, No. 1. 67p. 1977. pap. text 2.80 (*0-8477-2433-6*) U of PR Pr.

***Navas, Jim.** Super Socket 7: Building Faster & Cheaper PCs. 250p. 1999. 29.99 (*0-7897-2137-6*) Que.

Navas, R. Jose, tr. see Casey, Bill & McMullin, Rian E.

Navas Robleto, Jose J. Como Tomar Decisiones y Solucionar Problemas Racionalmente. (SPA.). 380p. 1997. pap. write for info. (*1-881713-07-5*) Pubns Puertorriquenas.

— Conceptos y Teorias del Aprendizaje. (SPA.). 162p. 1996. pap. write for info. (*0-929441-86-9*) Pubns Puertorriquenas.

Navas, Ruiz R., ed. see Hartzenbusch, Juan E.

Navascues, Palacio P. Monasterios de Espana. 5th ed. (Illus.). 334p. 1988. 295.00 (*84-239-5271-1*) Elliots Bks.

***Navasky, Victor & Vanden Heuvel, Katrina, eds.** The Best of the Nation, 1990-2000: Selections from the Independent Magazine of Politics & Culture. LC 00-21769. 420p. 2000. pap. 19.95 (*1-56025-267-7*, Thunders Mouth) Avalon NY.

Navasky, Victor, jt. auth. see Cerf, Christopher B.

Navatana, ed. see Jwala, pseud & Smith, Roul.

Navathe, jt. auth. see Elmasri.

Navathe, Shamkant B., jt. auth. see Elmasri, Ramez A.

Navathe, Shankrant B., jt. auth. see Elmasri, Ramez A.

Navato Senior High Archaeology Club Staff. Report on the Excavation of Marin-374. (Illus.). 49p. (C). 1967. reprint ed. pap. text 5.31 (*1-55567-411-9*) Coyote Press.

Navazelskis, Ina. Leonid Brezhnev. (World Leaders Past & Present Ser.). (Illus.). 120p. (YA). (gr. 5 up). 1987. lib. bdg. 19.95 (*0-87754-513-8*) Chelsea Hse.

Navch, Z. & Lieberman, A. S. Landscape Ecology. (Environmental Management Ser.). (Illus.). xxviii, 356p. 1989. pap. 49.00 (*0-387-97169-6*) Spr-Verlag.

Nave, Brenda C., jt. auth. see Nave, Carl R.

Nave, Carl R. & Nave, Brenda C. Physics for the Health Sciences. 3rd ed. (Illus.). 1985. pap., teacher ed. write for info. (*0-7216-2043-4*, W B Saunders Co) Harcrt Hlth Sci Grp.

— Physics for the Health Sciences. 3rd ed. (Illus.). 432p. (C). 1985. pap. text 46.00 (*0-7216-1309-8*, Pub. by SCP) Harcourt.

Nave, Eric, jt. auth. see Rusbridger, James.

Nave, James. The Road. LC 96-77134. (Illus.). 84p. 1998. pap. 12.95 (*1-885221-52-5*) BookPartners.

Nave, Jean R. The Quest for Success Rediscovering American Business Values. Orig. Title: Quest ...in Search of Values. 104p. 1987. pap. 9.95 (*0-930115-08-2*) Windemere Pr.

— Women . . . The World's Greatest Salesmen! 96p. (Orig.). 1984. pap. 6.95 (*0-930115-00-7*) Windemere Pr.

Nave, Karen, et al. Educationally Disabling Syndromes, Diseases & Disorders of Exceptional Children: Causes, Characteristics & Resources. 630p. (C). per. 63.95 (*0-7872-6627-2*) Kendall-Hunt.

Nave, Mark J. Power Line Filter Design for Switched-Mode Power Supplies. (Illus.). 224p. 1991. text 54.95 (*0-442-00453-2*, VNR) Wiley.

Nave, Orville J. Nave's Topical Bible. enl. rev. ed. 1114p. 1969. 29.99 (*0-310-33710-0*, 12246) Zondervan.

— Nave's Topical Bible Condensed. mass mkt. 5.99 (*0-8024-0030-2*, 224) Moody.

Nave, Patricia S., ed. see Hackman, Porter L., et al.

Nave, Yolanda. Breaking Up: From Heartache to Happiness in 48 Pages. LC 84-40680. (Illus.). 48p. (Orig.). 1985. pap. 3.95 (*0-89480-839-7*, 839) Workman Pub.

***Nave, Yolanda.** 64 Ways to Beat the Blues. LC 99-41385. (Illus.). 96p. 1999. pap. 6.95 (*0-7611-0596-4*) Workman Pub.

Nave, Yolanda. Welcome to Our Company: Your Office Manual. LC 88-40251. (Illus.). 96p. 1988. pap. 6.95 (*0-89480-608-4*, 1608) Workman Pub.

Naveau, Jacques. International Air Transport in a Changing World. (C). 1989. lib. bdg. 114.00 (*90-247-3727-3*) Kluwer Academic.

***Naveaux, Ralph & Wilkie, Rachel.** Escape to Frenchtown: A Narrative of the War of 1812 at the River Raisin. vii, 109p. (YA). (gr. 7-12). 2000. 10.00 (*0-615-11452-0*) Monro Cty Hist.

***Naveen, Ron.** Waiting to Fly: My Escapades with the Penguins of Antarctica. 384p. 2000. reprint ed. pap. 14.00 (*0-688-17573-2*, Wm Morrow) Morrow Avon.

— Waiting to Fly: My Escapades with the Penguins of Antarctica. LC 98-28539. (Illus.). 320p. 1999. 26.00 (*0-688-15894-3*, Wm Morrow) Morrow Avon.

Naveh, Eyal J. Crown of Thorns: Political Martyrdom in American from Abraham Lincoln to Martin Luther King, Jr. 248p. (C). 1992. pap. text 19.00 (*0-8147-5776-6*) NYU Pr.

Naveh, Joseph. Early History of the Alphabet: An Introduction to West Semitic Epigraphy & Palaeography. 2nd ed. ix, 213p. (C). 1987. text 25.00 (*965-223-436-2*, Pub. by Magnes Pr) Eisenbrauns.

Naveh, Joseph & Shaked, S. Amulets & Magic Bowls: Aramaic Incantations of Late Antiquity. 2nd ed. LC 99-201169. (Illus.). 300p. 1987. text 28.00 (*965-223-531-8*, Pub. by Magnes Pr) Eisenbrauns.

Naveh, Joseph, jt. auth. see Eph'al, Israel.

Naveh, Joseph, jt. auth. see Shaked, S.

Naveh, Shimon. In Pursuit of Military Excellence: The Evolution of Operational Theory. LC 97-14835. (Cummings Center Ser.: Vol. 7). 424p. (C). 1997. reprint ed. text 59.50 (*0-7146-4727-6*, Pub. by F Cass Pubs); reprint ed. pap. text 29.50 (*0-7146-4277-0*, Pub. by F Cass Pubs) Intl Spec Bk.

Naveh, Zev & Lieberman, A. S. Landscape Ecology: Theory & Application. (Environmental Management Ser.). (Illus.). 335p. 1983. 59.50 (*0-387-90849-8*) Spr-Verlag.

— Landscape Ecology: Theory & Application. 2nd ed. (Illus.). 400p. 1993. pap. write for info. (*3-540-94059-6*) Spr-Verlag.

— Landscape Technology: Theory & Application. 2nd rev. ed. (Illus.). 472p. 1994. reprint ed. 60.95 (*0-387-94059-6*) Spr-Verlag.

Naveh, Zev, jt. ed. see Bakshi, Trilochan S.

Naveira, A. M., ed. Differential Geometry. (Lecture Notes in Mathematics Ser.: Vol. 1045). viii, 194p. 1984. 35.95 (*0-387-12882-4*) Spr-Verlag.

Naveira, A. M., et al, eds. Differential Geometry, Pensacola 1985. (Lecture Notes in Mathematics Ser.: Vol. 1209). 306p. 1986. pap. 39.30 (*0-387-16801-X*) Spr-Verlag.

Navel, Georges. Travaux. (FRE.). 1979. pap. 10.95 (*0-7859-4127-4*) Fr & Eur.

Navellier. Louis Navellier Modern Portrait Theory. 1996. text 27.95 (*0-07-046482-0*) McGraw.

Navenec, Carole-Lynne Le, see Le Navenec, Carole-Lynne.

Naversen, Kenneth. Beautiful America's California Victorians. LC 98-4295. (Illus.). 80p. 1998. pap. 15.95 (*0-89802-700-4*) Beautiful Am.

***Naversen, Kenneth.** Beautiful America's Northwest Victorians. 80p. 2000. 22.95 (*0-89802-727-6*); pap. 15.95 (*0-89802-726-8*) Beautiful Am.

Naversen, Kenneth. Beautiful America's Orange County. LC 95-30269. (Illus.). 80p. 1995. 19.95 (*0-89802-663-6*); pap. 12.95 (*0-89802-662-8*) Beautiful Am.

— California Victorians. 80p. 1998. 22.95 (*0-89802-701-2*) Beautiful Am.

Naversen, Kenneth, photos by. Beautiful America's San Diego. LC 92-42559. (Illus.). 80p. 1993. 19.95 (*0-89802-629-6*); pap. 12.95 (*0-89802-632-6*) Beautiful Am.

Naves, Elaine K. Journey to Vaja: Reconstructing the World of a Hungarian-Jewish Family. (Illus.). 304p. 1996. 49.95 (*0-7735-1511-9*, Pub. by McG-Queens Univ Pr); pap. 19.95 (*0-7735-1534-8*, Pub. by McG-Queens Univ Pr) CUP Services.

— The Writers of Montreal. (Illus.). 192p. (Orig.). 1993. pap. 16.00 (*1-55065-045-9*, Pub. by Vehicule Pr) Genl Dist Srvs.

Naves, Elaine Kalman, jt. auth. see Demchinsky, Bryan.

***Naves, Mario, text.** John Dubrow: Paintings. (Illus.). 20p. 1998. pap. 20.00 (*1-58821-017-0*) Salander OReilly.

Naves, Raymond, ed. see Voltaire.

Naveson, Jan, jt. ed. see Sanders, John T.

NAVI Staff. Beginning with Christ. rev. ed. 1980. pap. 12.00 (*0-89109-159-9*) NavPress.

Navia, Jose B. Environmental & Water Law in the South. 334p. 1994. pap. 39.95 (*90-6224-907-8*) LPC InBook.

Navia, Luis E. The Adventure of Philosophy. LC 99-14838. 176p. 1999. pap. 19.95 (*0-275-96547-3*, Greenwood Pr) Greenwood.

— The Adventure of Philosophy, 71. LC 99-14838. (Contributions in Philosophy Ser.: No. 71). 176p. 1999. 55.00 (*0-313-30976-0*, GM976, Greenwood Pr) Greenwood.

— Classical Cynicism: A Critical Study, 58. LC 96-22007. (Contributions in Philosophy Ser.: No. 58). 240p. 1996. 67.95 (*0-313-30015-1*, Greenwood Pr) Greenwood.

— Diogenes of Sinope: The Man in the Tub, 67. LC 98-15322. (Contributions in Philosophy Ser.: Vol. 67). 224p. 1998. 59.95 (*0-313-30672-9*, Greenwood Pr) Greenwood.

— The Philosophy of Cynicism: An Annotated Bibliography, 4. LC 95-16465. (Bibliographies & Indexes in Philosophy Ser.: No. 4). 232p. 1995. lib. bdg. 69.50 (*0-313-29249-3*, Greenwood Pr) Greenwood.

— The Presocratic Philosophers: An Annotated Bibliography. LC 93-16207. 752p. 1993. text 120.00 (*0-8240-9776-9*, SS704) Garland.

— Socrates: The Man & His Philosphy. (Illus.). 376p. (Orig.). 1985. pap. text 25.50 (*0-8191-4855-5*) U Pr of Amer.

— Socratic Testimonies. (Illus.). 380p. (Orig.). 1987. pap. text 31.00 (*0-8191-6115-2*) U Pr of Amer.

Navia, Luis E. & Kelly, Eugene W., eds. Ethics & the Search for Values. LC 80-82123. 530p. (C). 1980. pap. 24.95 (*0-87975-139-8*) Prometheus Bks.

Navia, Luis E., jt. auth. see Kelly, Eugene W.

Navias, Martin S. Going Ballistic: The Build-up of Missiles in the Middle East. (Illus.). 270p. 1993. 45.00 (*1-85753-020-9*, Pub. by Brasseys) Brasseys.

— Nuclear Weapons & British Strategic Planning, 1955-1958. (Nuclear History Program Ser.). 280p. 1991. text 65.00 (*0-19-827754-7*, 12190) OUP.

Navias, Martin S. & Hooton, Edward. Tanker Wars: The Assault on Commercial Shipping during the Iran-Iraq Crisis 1980-1988. 256p. 1996. text 110.00 (*1-86064-032-X*) St Martin.

Navias, Martin S., jt. ed. see Willett, Susan.

Naviaux, Barbara. Miniature Horses: Their Care, Breeding & Coat Colors. Abramson, Joanne, ed. LC 98-87725. (Illus.). 272p. 1999. 42.00 (*0-9635964-1-1*) Raintree Pubns.

Navickas. Consciousness & Reality. 1976. pap. text 126.00 (*90-247-1775-2*) Kluwer Academic.

Navigation Commission of ICAO Staff, jt. auth. see Dangerous Goods Panel of Air Staff.

Navigator Staff. Acts. (LifeChange Ser.). 216p. (Orig.). 1987. pap. 7.00 (*0-89109-112-2*) NavPress.

— Exodus. (LifeChange Ser.). 165p. (Orig.). 1989. pap. 7.00 (*0-89109-283-8*) NavPress.

— First Peter. (LifeChange Ser.). 137p. (Orig.). 1986. pap. 7.00 (*0-89109-052-5*) NavPress.

— Galatians. (LifeChange Ser.). 137p. (Orig.). 1989. pap. 7.00 (*0-89109-562-4*) NavPress.

— Genesis. (LifeChange Ser.). 215p. 1987. pap. 7.00 (*0-89109-069-X*) NavPress.

— Hebrews. (LifeChange Ser.). 185p. (Orig.). 1989. pap. 7.00 (*0-89109-272-2*) NavPress.

— Isaiah. (LifeChange Ser.). 216p. (Orig.). 1987. pap. 7.00 (*0-89109-111-4*) NavPress.

— John. (LifeChange Ser.). 215p. (Orig.). 1989. pap. 7.00 (*0-89109-237-4*) NavPress.

— Leader's Guide. (Design for Discipleship Ser.). 80p. (Orig.). 1980. pap. 5.00 (*0-89109-043-6*) NavPress.

N

— Philippians. (LifeChange Ser.). 113p. (Orig.). 1986. pap. 7.00 (*0-89109-072-X*) NavPress.

— Romans. (LifeChange Ser.). 213p. (Orig.). 1987. pap. 7.00 (*0-89109-073-8*) NavPress.

Navigators Staff. Answering the Call. (Life & Ministry of Jesus Christ Ser.). 80p. (Orig.). 1996. pap. 6.00 (*0-89109-969-7*, 99697) NavPress.

***Navigators Staff.** Bearing Fruit in God's Family: A Course in Personal Discipleship to Strengthen Your Walk with God. 1999. pap. 12.00 (*1-57683-192-2*) NavPress.

Navigators Staff. The Beginning. (Life & Ministry of Jesus Christ Ser.). 80p. (Orig.). 1996. pap. 6.00 (*0-89109-965-4*) NavPress.

— Beginning a New Life. rev. ed. (Studies in Christian Living: Bk. 2). 32p. 1981. pap. 3.00 (*0-89109-078-9*) NavPress.

— Challenging Tradition. LC 96-205321. (Life & Ministry of Jesus Christ Ser.). 80p. (Orig.). 1996. pap. 6.00 (*0-89109-966-2*, 99662) NavPress.

— The Character of the Christian. rev. ed. (Design for Discipleship Ser.: Bk. 4). 48p. 1980. pap. 4.00 (*0-89109-039-8*) NavPress.

— The Cross & Resurrection. (Life & Ministry of Jesus Christ Ser.). 80p. (Orig.). 1996. pap. 6.00 (*0-89109-971-9*, 99719) NavPress.

***Navigators Staff.** Deepening Your Roots in God's Family: A Course in Personal Discipleship to Strengthen Your Walk. 1999. pap. 12.00 (*1-57683-190-6*) NavPress.

Navigators Staff. Developing Your Faith. rev. ed. (Studies in Christian Living: Bk. 5). 32p. 1981. pap. 3.00 (*0-89109-081-9*) NavPress.

— Final Teachings. (Life & Ministry of Jesus Christ Ser.). 80p. (Orig.). 1996. pap. 6.00 (*0-89109-970-0*, 99700) NavPress.

— First Timothy. (Life Change Ser.). 144p. 1996. pap. 7.00 (*0-89109-953-0*) NavPress.

— Following Jesus. LC 96-210813. (Life & Ministry of Jesus Christ Ser.). 80p. (Orig.). 1996. pap. 6.00 (*0-89109-968-9*, 99689) NavPress.

— Foundations for Faith. rev. ed. (Design for Discipleship Ser.: Bk. 5). 48p. 1980. pap. 4.00 (*0-89109-040-1*) NavPress.

— Growing As a Christian. rev. ed. (Studies in Christian Living: Bk. 4). 32p. 1981. pap. 3.00 (*0-89109-080-0*) NavPress.

— Growing in Christ. (Design for Discipleship Ser.). 1957. pap. 6.00 (*0-89109-157-2*) NavPress.

— Growing in Discipleship. rev. ed. (Design for Discipleship Ser.: Bk. 6). (Illus.). 48p. 1980. pap. 4.00 (*0-89109-041-X*) NavPress.

***Navigators Staff.** Growing Strong in God's Family: A Course in Personal Discipleship to Strengthen Your Walk with God. 1999. pap. 12.00 (*1-57683-191-4*) NavPress.

Navigators Staff. Knowing Jesus Christ. rev. ed. (Studies in Christian Living: Bk. 1). 32p. 1981. pap. 3.00 (*0-89109-077-0*) NavPress.

— Leader's Resource. (Life & Ministry of Jesus Christ Ser.). 200p. (Orig.). 1996. pap. 14.00 (*0-89109-972-7*) NavPress.

— Lessons on Assurance: Learn God's Promises for Salvation, Answered Prayer, Victory over Sin, Forgiveness & Guidance. rev. ed. (Growing in Christ Ser.). 32p. 1980. pap. 3.00 (*0-89109-160-2*) NavPress.

— Lessons on Christian Living: Learn & Apply God's Principles for Maturing in the Christian Life. rev. ed. (Growing in Christ Ser.). 48p. 1980. pap. 3.00 (*0-89109-162-9*) NavPress.

— The Messiah. (Life & Ministry of Jesus Christ Ser.). 80p. (Orig.). 1996. pap. 6.00 (*0-89109-967-0*, 99670) NavPress.

— The Navigator Bible Study Handbook. rev. ed. Lee-Thorp, Karen, ed. LC 79-87654. (Illus.). 120p. 1994. pap. 7.00 (*0-89109-075-4*) NavPress.

— Our Hope in Christ. rev. ed. (Design for Discipleship Ser.: Bk. 7). 48p. 1980. pap. 4.00 (*0-89109-042-8*) NavPress.

— Outreach: Sharing the Real Gospel with the World. (Foundations for Christian Living Ser.). 1997. pap. text 6.00 (*1-57683-012-8*) NavPress.

— Relationships: Resolving Conflict & Building Community. (Foundations for Christian Living Ser.). 1997. pap. text 6.00 (*1-57683-023-3*) NavPress.

— Second Corinthians. (Life Change Ser.). 176p. (Orig.). 1996. pap. 7.00 (*0-89109-951-4*) NavPress.

— Serving Others. rev. ed. (Studies in Christian Living: Bk. 6). 32p. 1981. pap. 3.00 (*0-89109-082-7*) NavPress.

— The Spirit-Filled Christian. rev. ed. (Design for Discipleship Ser.: Bk. 2). (Illus.). 48p. 1980. pap. 4.00 (*0-89109-037-1*) NavPress.

— Talking with Christ. rev. ed. (Studies in Christian Living: Bk. 3). 32p. 1981. pap. 3.00 (*0-89109-079-7*) NavPress.

— Walking with Christ. rev. ed. (Design for Discipleship Ser.: Bk. 3). (Illus.). 48p. 1980. pap. 4.00 (*0-89109-038-X*) NavPress.

— Warfare: Discovering the Reality of the Unseen World. (Foundations for Christian Living Ser.). 1997. pap. text 6.00 (*1-57683-026-8*) NavPress.

— Work: Serving God on the Job. (Foundations for Christian Living Ser.). 1997. pap. text 6.00 (*1-57683-024-1*) NavPress.

Navigators Staff, ed. LessonMaker - New Testament: Create Your Own Customized Bible Study on Any Passage in the New Testament in Minutes. LC 92-81117. 432p. (Orig.). 1992. pap. 26.00 (*0-89109-688-4*) NavPress.

— Your Life in Christ. rev. ed. (Design for Discipleship Ser.: Bk. 1). 31p. 1980. pap. 4.00 (*0-89109-036-3*) NavPress.

Naviglio, Antonio, ed. Heat & Mass Transfer in Chemical Process Industry Accidents. 465p. 1996. 99.50 (*1-56700-058-4*) Begell Hse.

Naviglio, Antonio, jt. auth. see Cumo, Maurizio.

Naviglio, Antonio, jt. ed. see Cumo, Maurizio.

Naville, Arnold. Bibliographie des Ecrits d'Andre Gide Depuis 1891 Jusqu'a Sa Mort. (FRE.). 15.95 (*0-8288-9780-8*, F102790) Fr & Eur.

Naville, E. The Text of the Old Testament. (British Academy, London, Schweich Lectures on Biblical Archaeology Series, 1930). 1974. reprint ed. pap. 25.00 (*0-8115-1257-6*) Periodicals Srv.

Naville, Pierre, et al, eds. Revolution Surrealiste. No. One - Twelve. LC 68-28660. (Contemporary Art Ser.). (FRE., Illus.). 1968. reprint ed. 74.95 (*0-405-00706-X*) Ayer.

Navin, Brian. Cruising Guide to Germany & Denmark. (Illus.). 200p. 1994. 125.00 (*0-85288-191-6*, Pub. by Laurie Norie & Wilson Ltd) St Mut.

— Cruising Guide to the Netherlands. 2nd rev. ed. (Illus.). 176p. (C). 1996. pap. 125.00 (*0-85288-375-7*, Pub. by Laurie Norie & Wilson Ltd) St Mut.

— Gatt 94 & the Paper Packaging Industry. 1997. 120.00 (*1-85802-081-6*, Pub. by Pira Pub) Bks Intl VA.

— North Sea Passage Pilot. 200p. 1987. 105.00 (*0-85288-102-9*, Pub. by Laurie Norie & Wilson Ltd) St Mut.

— North Sea Passage Pilot, Cromer to Dover & Calais to Den Helder. (Illus.). 1991. 51.95 (*0-85288-157-6*) Bluewater Bks.

Navin, Brian & Hawkins, Michael. World Pulp & Paper, 1997-2005: Trends & Forecasts. 120p. 1997. pap. 1040.00 (*1-85802-166-9*, Pub. by Pira Internatl) Bks Intl VA.

Navin, Brian & Helder, Den. North Sea Passage Pilot. 200p. 1998. pap. 125.00 (*0-85288-393-5*, Pub. by Laurie Norie & Wilson Ltd) St Mut.

Navin, Jacqueline. The Flower & the Sword. (Historical Ser.: Vol. 428). 1998. per. 4.99 (*0-373-29028-4*, 1-29028-7) Harlequin Bks.

— The Maiden & the Warrior. (Historical Ser.). 1998. per. 4.99 (*0-373-29003-9*, 1-29003-0) Harlequin Bks.

— A Rose at Midnight. 1999. mass mkt. 4.99 (*0-373-29047-0*, Harlequin) Harlequin Bks.

— Strathmere's Bride. (Historical Ser.: No. 479). 1999. per. 4.99 (*0-373-29079-9*, 1-29079-0) Harlequin Bks.

***Navin, Jacqueline.** The Viking's Heart. (Historical Ser.: Bk. 515). 2000. per. 4.99 (*0-373-29115-9*, 1-29115-2) Harlequin Bks.

Navin, Richard. Richard Navin: The Mycenae Circle. LC 80-1216. (Illus.). 20p. 1981. pap. 5.00 (*0-89207-028-5*) S R Guggenheim.

Navin, Sheryl & Cusack, Lynette. A Carer's Guide to Good Health. 61p. (Orig.). 1994. pap. 7.95 (*0-85572-207-X*, Pub. by Hill Content Pubng) Seven Hills Bk.

Navin, Thomas R. Copper Mining & Management. LC 78-2669. 450p. reprint ed. pap. 139.50 (*0-608-13845-2*, 202043800017) Bks Demand.

Navinchandra, D. Exploration & Innovation in Design: Towards a Computational Model. Loveland, D. W. et al, eds. (Symbolic Computation - Artificial Intelligence Ser.). (Illus.). xi, 194p. 1990. 65.95 (*0-387-97481-4*) Spr-Verlag.

Navius, Blake, ed. see Cooper, James Fenimore.

Navlakha, Suren. Elite & Social Change: A Study of Elite Formation in India. 180p. (C). 1989. text 24.00 (*0-8039-9627-6*) Sage.

***Navon, A. & Ascher, K. R. S., eds.** Bioassays of Entomopathogenic Microbes & Nematodes. (CABI Publishing Ser.). 352p. 2000. text 110.00 (*0-85199-422-9*) C A B Intl.

Navon, I. M., jt. auth. see Le Dimet, F. X.

Navon, Yitzhak. The Six Days & the Seven Gates. 1980. 6.00 (*0-930832-57-4*); pap. 4.00 (*0-686-70336-7*) Herzl Pr.

Navone, John. Communicating Christ. (C). 1988. 50.00 (*0-85439-127-4*, Pub. by St Paul Pubns) St Mut.

— Enjoying God's Beauty. LC 98-13343. (Illus.). 134p. 1999. pap. 12.95 (*0-8146-2486-3*) Liturgical Pr.

— The Land & Spirit of Italy: The Texture of Italian Religious Culture. rev. expanded ed. LC 96-3613. 1996. 16.00 (*1-881901-12-2*) LEGAS.

— Towards a Theology of Story. (C). 1988. 39.00 (*0-85439-136-3*, Pub. by St Paul Pubns) St Mut.

Navone, John & Cooper, Thomas. Tellers of the Word. 1981. 23.00 (*0-317-01341-6*); pap. 14.00 (*0-317-03298-4*) Haymkt-Doyma.

Navone, John & Stefanotti, Robert. Toward a Theology of Beauty. 96p. (Orig.). 1996. pap. 14.95 (*0-8146-2272-0*, Liturg Pr Bks) Liturgical Pr.

Navpress Publishing Staff. Christlikeness: Committing Ourselves to Be Changed by God. (Foundations for Christian Living Ser.). 1997. pap. text 6.00 (*1-57683-006-3*) NavPress.

— Intimacy: Pursuing Intimacy with God. (Foundations for Christian Living Ser.). 1997. pap. text 6.00 (*1-57683-010-1*) NavPress.

— Restoration: Discovering How All of God Meets Our Deepest Needs. (Foundations for Christian Living Ser.). 1997. pap. text 6.00 (*1-57683-009-8*) NavPress.

***Navpress Publishing Staff.** Seguridad en Cristo.Tr. of Lessons on Assurance. (SPA.). 32p. (YA). 2000. pap. 1.50 (*0-311-13666-4*, Edit Mundo) Casa Bautista.

Navpress Publishing Staff. Worship: Acknowledging God in All of Life. (Foundations for Christian Living Ser.). 1997. pap. 6.00 (*1-57683-007-1*) NavPress.

***NavPress Staff.** Beating Busyness: Busyness Discipleship Journal. 80p. 1999. pap. 5.00 (*1-57683-155-8*) NavPress.

— Becoming More Like Jesus: Character Discipleship Journal. 80p. 1999. pap. 5.00 (*1-57683-156-6*) NavPress.

Navpress Staff. First Thessalonians. (LifeChange Ser.). 1996. pap. 7.00 (*0-89109-932-8*) NavPress.

***NavPress Staff.** Following God in Tough Times: Suffering Discipleship Journal. 80p. 1999. pap. 5.00 (*1-57683-157-4*) NavPress.

— Growing Deeper with God: Loving God Discipleship Journal. 80p. 1999. pap. 5.00 (*1-57683-153-1*) NavPress.

Navpress Staff. Jesus' Farewell Teachings. (Radical Relationships Ser.). 1996. pap. 7.00 (*0-89109-929-8*) NavPress.

— Jesus on Relationships. (Radical Relationships Ser.). 1996. pap. 7.00 (*0-89109-933-6*) NavPress.

— Luke. (LifeChange Ser.). 1996. pap. 7.00 (*0-89109-930-1*) NavPress.

NavPress Staff. Matthew. (LifeChange Ser.). 1996. pap. text 7.00 (*0-89109-996-4*) NavPress.

— 2 Peter/Jude. (Lifechange Ser.). 1996. pap. text 7.00 (*0-89109-994-8*) NavPress.

Navpress Staff. The Uniqueness of Jesus. (Radical Relationships Ser.). 1996. pap. 7.00 (*0-89109-863-1*) NavPress.

Navratil, Christopher. In the House of Night: A Dream Reader. LC 97-29758. 1998. 18.95 (*0-8118-1762-8*) Chronicle Bks.

Navratil, Christopher, ed. Man of My Dreams: Provocative Writing on Men Loving Men. LC 96-26172. 192p. 1996. pap. 14.95 (*0-8118-1396-7*) Chronicle Bks.

Navratil, Helen L., ed. see Navratil, Sidney J., et al.

Navratil, James D. Science & Technology of Tributyl Phosphate, 2 vols., Set. Schultz, Wallace W., ed. LC 83-7774. 1987. 177.00 (*0-8493-6397-7*, QD305, CRC Reprint) Franklin.

Navratil, James D. & Schultz, Wallace W. Science & Technology of Tributyl Phosphate Vol. 2, Pt. A: Selected Technical & Industrial Uses. LC 83-7774. 1987. 84.00 (*0-8493-6398-5*, QD305, CRC Reprint) Franklin.

— Science & Technology of Tributyl Phosphate Vol. 2, Pt. B: Selected Technical & Industrial Uses. LC 83-7774. 1987. 94.00 (*0-8493-6399-3*, QD305, CRC Reprint) Franklin.

Navratil, James D. & Schulz, Wallace W. Actinide Recovery from Waste & Low Grade Sources. (Radioactive Waste Management Ser.: Vol. 6). xiv, 386p. 1982. text 306.00 (*3-7186-0105-2*) Gordon & Breach.

— Science & Technology of Tributyl Phosphate Vol. 1: Synthesis, Properties, Reactions, & Analysis. LC 83-774. 1984. 194.00 (*0-8493-6396-9*, QD305, CRC Reprint) Franklin.

Navratil, James D. & Schulz, Wallace W., eds. Transplutonium Elements: Production & Recovery. LC 81-7999. (ACS Symposium Ser.: Vol. 161). 314p. 1981. reprint ed. pap. 97.40 (*0-608-03049-X*, 206350200007) Bks Demand.

Navratil, James D., jt. auth. see Schultz, Wallace W.

Navratil, James D., jt. ed. see Li, Norman N.

Navratil, James D., jt. ed. see Schultz, Wallace W.

Navratil, James D., ed. see Tascher, Sylvia.

Navratil, James M. Medical Trivia. LC 86-82986. 200p. 1998. 12.50 (*0-937557-06-4*) Litarvan Lit.

***Navratil, Jaromir, ed.** The Prague Spring, 1968. LC 98-44001. 700p. (C). 1998. 59.95 (*963-9116-15-7*) Ctrl Europ Univ.

Navratil, Sidney J., et al. Alcan Trail Blazers. Lloyd, John K. & Navratil, Helen L., eds. (Illus.). 64p. (Orig.). 1992. pap. 14.00 (*0-9633018-0-2*) Six Hund Forty-Eight Mem.

Navratil, Thomas, ed. Trilateral Forum on North Pacific Security. LC 95-34882. (CSIS Panel Reports). 27p. (C). 1995. pap. text 10.95 (*0-89206-279-7*) CSIS.

Navratilova, Martina & Nickles, Liz. Killer Instinct. LC 97-97101. 322p. 1998. mass mkt. 6.99 (*0-345-38876-3*) Ballantine Pub Grp.

Navroth, Blaine. The Awataguchi Shinto School of Sword Making: A Monograph. (Illus.). 18p. 1980. reprint ed. pap. 4.95 (*0-910704-55-4*) Hawley.

— The Ito School of Tsuba Makers: A Monograph. (Illus.). 10p. 1986. reprint ed. pap. 4.95 (*0-910704-56-2*) Hawley.

Navrotsky, Alexandra. Physics & Chemistry of Earth Materials. LC 93-43135. (Cambridge Topics in Mineral Physics & Chemistry Ser.: No. 6). (Illus.). 431p. (C). 1994. text 90.00 (*0-521-35378-5*); pap. text 39.95 (*0-521-35894-9*) Cambridge U Pr.

Navrotsky, Alexandra & Weidner, D. J., eds. Perovskite: A Structure of Great Interest to Geophysics & Materials Sciences. (Geophysical Monograph Ser.: Vol. 45). 146p. 1989. 27.00 (*0-87590-071-2*) Am Geophysical.

Navrotsky, Alexandra, jt. ed. see Kieffer, S. W.

Navrozov, A., tr. see Pasternak, Boris.

Navrozov, Lev. Prose from the Book That Was Not Published in 1968. 112p. (Orig.). 1984. pap. 14.00 (*0-914265-00-8*) New Eng Pub MA.

Navy Department Staff. Manual for Overhaul, Repair & Handling of Hamilton 35-Size Chronometer Watch with Parts Catalog. (Illus.). 63p. 1988. pap. 9.95 (*0-930163-35-4*) Arlington Bk.

— Manual for Overhaul, Repair & Handling of U. S. Navy Mechanical, Boat & Deck Clocks: Chelsea Type with Parts Catalog. (Illus.). 101p. 1988. pap. 14.95 (*0-930163-20-6*) Arlington Bk.

Nawab, Ali. Some Moral & Religious Teachings of Al-Ghazzali. 1989. pap. 5.50 (*0-933511-60-4*) Kazi Pubns.

Nawab, Syed N. & Naqvi, Haider. Development Economics: A New Paradigm. LC 92-40700. 208p. (C). 1993. text 28.95 (*0-8039-9469-9*) Sage.

Nawalany, Marek, jt. auth. see Zijl, Wouter.

Nawalkha, Sanjay K. & Chambers, Donald R., eds. Interest Rate Risk Measurement & Management. (Illus.). 580p. 1999. pap. 95.00 (*0-9619446-9-2*, I I Bks) Institutional Investor.

Nawawi, Imam. Al-Maqasid. Keller, Noah H., tr. 1996. pap. 9.95 (*0-614-21202-2*, 1373) Kazi Pubns.

Nawawi, Imam An-. Riyad As-Salihin. Shad, Abdur R., tr. 1988. 29.00 (*0-933511-37-X*) Kazi Pubns.

Nawawi, Mahiudin A. Minhaj et Talibin: A Manual of Muhammadan Law According to the School of Shafii. 1992. reprint ed. 72.00 (*81-7013-097-2*, Pub. by Navarang) S Asia.

Nawaz, Ahmad. Adhunica, Pt. 3. LC 98-70776. (BEN.). xiv, 100p. 1998. pap. 10.00 (*1-58225-035-9*) Ananta Prakashani.

— Adhunica, Pt. 4. (BEN.). xiv, 100p. 1998. pap. 10.00 (*1-58225-036-7*) Ananta Prakashani.

— Adhunica, Pt. 5. (BEN.). xiv, 83p. 1998. pap. 10.00 (*1-58225-037-5*) Ananta Prakashani.

— Adhunica, Pt. 6. (BEN.). xiv, 100p. 1998. pap. 10.00 (*1-58225-038-3*) Ananta Prakashani.

— Adhunica, Pt. 9. LC 98-70776. (BEN.). xiv, 100p. 1998. pap. 10.00 (*1-58225-041-3*) Ananta Prakashani.

— Adhunica, Pt. 11. LC 98-70776. (BEN.). xiv, 100p. 1998. pap. 10.00 (*1-58225-043-X*) Ananta Prakashani.

— Adhunica, Pt. 12. (BEN.). xiv, 100p. 1998. pap. 10.00 (*1-58225-044-8*) Ananta Prakashani.

— Adhunica, Pts. 1 & 2. LC 98-70776. (BEN.). xiv, 132p. 1998. pap. 10.00 (*1-58225-034-0*) Ananta Prakashani.

— Adhunica Barnantar Pt. 7, Stet. 7. LC 98-70776. (BEN.). xiv, 100p. 1998. pap. 10.00 (*1-58225-039-1*) Ananta Prakashani.

— Adhunica Shabdantar, Stet. 8. (BEN.). xiv, 100p. 1998. pap. 10.00 (*1-58225-040-5*) Ananta Prakashani.

— Amitakhar Kabita. LC 98-70777. (BEN.). xiv, 108p. 1998. pap. 10.00 (*1-58225-045-6*) Ananta Prakashani.

— Anantica Adhunik Gan,1970, Pt. 30. LC 98-71112. (BEN.). xiv, 70p. 1998. pap. 10.00 (*1-58225-075-8*) Ananta Prakashani.

— Anantica Banibikash, Pt. 29. LC 98-71111. (BEN.). xiv, 98p. 1998. pap. 10.00 (*1-58225-074-X*) Ananta Prakashani.

— Anantica Banibina, Pt. 49. LC 98-71131. (BEN.). 100p. 1998. pap. 10.00 (*1-58225-094-4*) Ananta Prakashani.

— Anantica Banibithi, Pt. 34. LC 98-71116. (BEN.). xiv, 100p. 1998. pap. 10.00 (*1-58225-079-0*) Ananta Prakashani.

— Anantica Banibiua, Pt. 33. LC 98-71115. (BEN.). xiv, 100p. 1998. pap. 10.00 (*1-58225-078-2*) Ananta Prakashani.

— Anantica Banicandro, Pt. 45. LC 98-71127. (BEN.). xiv, 100p. 1998. pap. 10.00 (*1-58225-090-1*) Ananta Prakashani.

— Anantica Banichanda, Pt. 38. LC 98-71120. (BEN.). xiv, 100p. 1998. pap. 10.00 (*1-58225-083-9*) Ananta Prakashani.

— Anantica Banichia, Pt. 39. LC 98-71121. (BEN.). xiv, 101p. 1998. pap. 10.00 (*1-58225-084-7*) Ananta Prakashani.

— Anantica Banicona, Pt. 31. LC 98-71113. (BEN.). xiv, 100p. 1998. pap. 10.00 (*1-58225-076-6*) Ananta Prakashani.

— Anantica Banidhara, Pt. 27. LC 98-71109. (BEN.). xiv, 100p. 1998. pap. 10.00 (*1-58225-072-3*) Ananta Prakashani.

— Anantica Banighar, Pt. 43. LC 98-71125. (BEN.). xiv, 100p. 1998. pap. 10.00 (*1-58225-088-X*) Ananta Prakashani.

— Anantica Banikanti, Pt. 42. LC 98-71124. (BEN.). xiv, 100p. 1998. pap. 10.00 (*1-58225-087-1*) Ananta Prakashani.

— Anantica Banikhatro, Pt. 48. LC 98-71130. (BEN.). xiv, 100p. 1998. pap. 10.00 (*1-58225-093-6*) Ananta Prakashani.

— Anantica Banikunja, Pt. 35. LC 98-71117. (BEN.). xiv, 100p. 1998. pap. 10.00 (*1-58225-080-4*) Ananta Prakashani.

— Anantica Banilata, Pt. 40. LC 98-71122. (BEN.). xiv, 100p. 1998. pap. 10.00 (*1-58225-085-5*) Ananta Prakashani.

— Anantica Banilipi, Pt. 41. LC 98-71123. (BEN.). xiv, 100p. 1998. pap. 10.00 (*1-58225-086-3*) Ananta Prakashani.

— Anantica Banimala, Pt. 26. LC 98-71108. (BEN.). xiv, 100p. 1998. pap. 10.00 (*1-58225-071-5*) Ananta Prakashani.

— Anantica Banimancha, Pt. 47. LC 98-71129. (BEN.). xiv, 100p. 1998. pap. 10.00 (*1-58225-092-8*) Ananta Prakashani.

— Anantica Banimangal, Pt. 50. LC 98-71132. (BEN.). xiv, 100p. 1998. pap. 10.00 (*1-58225-095-2*) Ananta Prakashani.

— Anantica Banipatra, Pt. 44. LC 98-71126. (BEN.). xiv, 100p. 1998. pap. 10.00 (*1-58225-089-8*) Ananta Prakashani.

— Anantica Banirekha, Pt. 46. LC 98-71128. (BEN.). xiv, 100p. 1998. pap. 10.00 (*1-58225-091-X*) Ananta Prakashani.

— Anantica Banisagar, Pt. 36. LC 98-71118. (BEN.). xiv, 98p. 1998. pap. 10.00 (*1-58225-081-2*) Ananta Prakashani.

— Anantica Banisikha, Pt. 37. LC 98-71119. (BEN.). xiv, 100p. 1998. pap. 10.00 (*1-58225-082-0*) Ananta Prakashani.

— Anantica Banisutro, Pt. 32. LC 98-71114. (BEN.). xiv, 100p. 1998. pap. 10.00 (*1-58225-077-4*) Ananta Prakashani.

— Anantica Barnabicash, Pt. 5. LC 98-71087. (BEN.). xiv, 100p. 1998. pap. 10.00 (*1-58225-050-2*) Ananta Prakashani.

— Anantica Barnabina, Pt. 25. LC 98-71107. (BEN.). xiv, 100p. 1998. pap. 10.00 (*1-58225-070-7*) Ananta Prakashani.

— Anantica Barnabodh, Pt. 4. LC 98-71085. (BEN.). xiv, 100p. 1998. pap. 10.00 (*1-58225-049-9*) Ananta Prakashani.

— Anantica Barnachia, Pt. 15. LC 98-71097. (BEN.). xiv, 100p. 1998. pap. 10.00 (*1-58225-060-X*) Ananta Prakashani.

— Anantica Barnadhara, Pt. 3. LC 98-71084. (BEN.). xiv, 100p. 1998. pap. 10.00 (*1-58225-048-0*) Ananta Prakashani.

An Asterisk (*) at the beginning of an entry indicates that the title is appearing for the first time.

— Anantica Barnadhara, Pt. 20. LC 98-71102. (BEN.). xiv, 100p. 1998. pap. 10.00 (*1-58225-065-0*) Ananta Prakashani.
— Anantica Barnagar, Pt. 21. LC 98-71103. (BEN.). xiv, 100p. 1998. pap. 10.00 (*1-58225-066-9*) Ananta Prakashani.
— Anantica Barnakanti, Pt. 18. LC 98-71100. (BEN.). xiv, 100p. 1998. pap. 10.00 (*1-58225-063-4*) Ananta Prakashani.
— Anantica Barnalata, Pt. 16. LC 98-71098. (BEN.). xiv, 100p. 1998. pap. 10.00 (*1-58225-061-8*) Ananta Prakashani.
— Anantica Barnalay, Pt. 19. LC 98-71101. (BEN.). xiv, 100p. 1998. pap. 10.00 (*1-58225-064-2*) Ananta Prakashani.
— Anantica Barnalipi, Pt. 17. LC 98-71099. (BEN.). xiv, 100p. 1998. pap. 10.00 (*1-58225-062-6*) Ananta Prakashani.
— Anantica Barnamala, Pt. 2. LC 98-71086. (BEN.). xiv, 100p. 1998. pap. 10.00 (*1-58225-047-2*) Ananta Prakashani.
— Anantica Barnamancho, Pt. 23. LC 98-71105. (BEN.). xiv, 100p. 1998. pap. 10.00 (*1-58225-068-5*) Ananta Prakashani.
— Anantica Barnananda, Pt. 14. LC 98-71096. (BEN.). xiv, 100p. 1998. pap. 10.00 (*1-58225-059-6*) Ananta Prakashani.
— Anantica Barnarup, Pt. 6. LC 98-71088. (BEN.). xiv, 100p. 1998. pap. 10.00 (*1-58225-051-0*) Ananta Prakashani.
— Anantica Barnasar, Pt. 22. LC 98-71104. (BEN.). xiv, 100p. 1998. pap. 10.00 (*1-58225-067-7*) Ananta Prakashani.
— Anantica Barnasar, Pt. 24. LC 98-71106. (BEN.). xiv, 100p. 1998. pap. 10.00 (*1-58225-069-3*) Ananta Prakashani.
— Anantica Barnibodh, Pt. 28. LC 98-71110. (BEN.). xiv, 100p. 1998. pap. 10.00 (*1-58225-073-1*) Ananta Prakashani.
— Anantica Barnobithi, Pt. 10. LC 98-71092. (BEN.). xiv, 100p. 1998. pap. 10.00 (*1-58225-055-3*) Ananta Prakashani.
— Anantica Barnokona, Pt. 7. LC 98-71089. (BEN.). xiv, 100p. 1998. pap. 10.00 (*1-58225-052-9*) Ananta Prakashani.
— Anantica Barnokunjo, Pt. 11. LC 98-71093. (BEN.). xiv, 100p. 1998. pap. 10.00 (*1-58225-056-1*) Ananta Prakashani.
— Anantica Barnoloke, Pt. 13. LC 98-71095. (BEN.). xiv, 100p. 1998. pap. 10.00 (*1-58225-058-8*) Ananta Prakashani.
— Anantica Barnontor, Pt. 9. LC 98-71091. (BEN.). xiv, 100p. 1998. pap. 10.00 (*1-58225-054-5*) Ananta Prakashani.
— Anantica Barnosagor, Pt. 12. LC 98-71094. (BEN.). xiv, 100p. 1998. pap. 10.00 (*1-58225-057-X*) Ananta Prakashani.
— Anantica Barnosutro, Pt. 8. LC 98-71090. (BEN.). xiv, 100p. 1998. pap. 10.00 (*1-58225-053-7*) Ananta Prakashani.
— Anantica Gittarango, Pt. 1. LC 98-70835. (BEN.). xiv, 62p. 1998. pap. 10.00 (*1-58225-046-4*) Ananta Prakashani.
— Anantica Rangrekha, Pt. 51. LC 98-71133. (BEN.). xiv, 98p. 1998. pap. 10.00 (*1-58225-096-0*) Ananta Prakashani.
— Anchilica. LC 98-70781. (BEN.). xiv, 72p. 1998. pap. 10.00 (*1-58225-097-9*) Ananta Prakashani.
— Aponcika. LC 98-70782. (BEN.). xiv, 52p. 1998. pap. 10.00 (*1-58225-098-7*) Ananta Prakashani.
— Ashomica. LC 98-70783. (BEN.). xiv, 112p. 1998. pap. 10.00 (*1-58225-099-5*) Ananta Prakashani.
— Bani 1 Kanti. LC 98-70784. (BEN.). xiv, 100p. 1998. pap. 10.00 (*1-58225-100-2*) Ananta Prakashani.
— Bawul Gan. LC 98-70785. (BEN.). xiv, 100p. 1998. pap. 10.00 (*1-58225-101-0*) Ananta Prakashani.
— Bikashika. LC 98-70786. (BEN.). xiv, 91p. 1998. pap. 10.00 (*1-58225-102-9*) Ananta Prakashani.
— Chritrocona. LC 98-70787. (BEN.). xiv, 116p. 1998. pap. 10.00 (*1-58225-103-7*) Ananta Prakashani.
***Nawaz, Ahmad.** Collection, 1. LC 00-131426. 68p. 2000. pap. 10.00 (*1-58225-201-7*) Ananta Prakashani.
— Collection, 2. LC 00-131426. 116p. 2000. pap. 10.00 (*1-58225-377-3*) Ananta Prakashani.
— Collection, 3. LC 00-131426. 78p. 2000. pap. 10.00 (*1-58225-378-1*) Ananta Prakashani.
Nawaz, Ahmad. Collection, Vol. 1. LC 98-70747. xiv, 68p. 1998. pap. 10.00 (*1-58225-001-4*) Ananta Prakashani.
— Conversion. LC 98-70748. xiv, 72p. 1998. pap. 10.00 (*1-58225-002-2*) Ananta Prakashani.
***Nawaz, Ahmad.** Conversion. LC 00-131427. 72p. 2000. pap. 10.00 (*1-58225-202-5*) Ananta Prakashani.
Nawaz, Ahmad. Corporation. LC 98-70749. xiv, 82p. 1998. pap. 10.00 (*1-58225-003-0*) Ananta Prakashani.
***Nawaz, Ahmad.** Corporation. LC 00-131428. 82p. 2000. pap. 10.00 (*1-58225-203-3*) Ananta Prakashani.
Nawaz, Ahmad. Dispensation. LC 98-70750. xiv, 73p. 1998. pap. 10.00 (*1-58225-004-9*) Ananta Prakashani.
***Nawaz, Ahmad.** Dispensation. LC 00-131429. 73p. 2000. pap. 10.00 (*1-58225-204-1*) Ananta Prakashani.
Nawaz, Ahmad. Disquisition. LC 98-70752. xiv, 78p. 1998. pap. 10.00 (*1-58225-005-7*) Ananta Prakashani.
***Nawaz, Ahmad.** Disquisition. LC 00-131430. 78p. 2000. pap. 10.00 (*1-58225-205-X*) Ananta Prakashani.
Nawaz, Ahmad. Exposition of Words. LC 98-70753. xiv, 59p. 1998. pap. 10.00 (*1-58225-006-5*) Ananta Prakashani.
***Nawaz, Ahmad.** Exposition of Words. LC 00-131431. 59p. 2000. pap. 10.00 (*1-58225-206-8*) Ananta Prakashani.
Nawaz, Ahmad. Expression. xiv, 76p. 1998. pap. 10.00 (*1-58225-007-3*) Ananta Prakashani.
***Nawaz, Ahmad.** Expression. LC 00-131432. 76p. 2000. pap. 10.00 (*1-58225-207-6*) Ananta Prakashani.
Nawaz, Ahmad. Gan, 1964, Pt. 1. LC 98-70789. (BEN.). xiv, 117p. 1998. pap. 10.00 (*1-58225-105-3*) Ananta Prakashani.
— Gan, 1964, Pt. 2. LC 98-70789. (BEN.). xiv, 117p. 1998. pap. 10.00 (*1-58225-106-1*) Ananta Prakashani.
— Gan, 1963. LC 98-70788. (BEN.). xiv, 84p. 1998. pap. 10.00 (*1-58225-104-5*) Ananta Prakashani.
— Git Charan. LC 98-70792. (BEN.). xiv, 102p. 1998. pap. 10.00 (*1-58225-108-8*) Ananta Prakashani.
— Git Mahal. LC 98-70791. (BEN.). xiv, 80p. 1998. pap. 10.00 (*1-58225-107-X*) Ananta Prakashani.
— Gita Kar. LC 98-70790. (BEN.). xiv, 102p. 1998. pap. 10.00 (*1-58225-109-6*) Ananta Prakashani.
— Gita Khar. LC 98-70793. (BEN.). xiv, 108p. 1998. pap. 10.00 (*1-58225-110-X*) Ananta Prakashani.
— Gita Sor. LC 98-70794. (BEN.). xiv, 108p. 1998. pap. 10.00 (*1-58225-111-8*) Ananta Prakashani.
— Gitabash. LC 98-70795. (BEN.). xiv, 104p. 1998. pap. 10.00 (*1-58225-112-6*) Ananta Prakashani.
— Gitachar. LC 98-70796. (BEN.). xiv, 102p. 1998. pap. 10.00 (*1-58225-113-4*) Ananta Prakashani.
— Gitadhar. LC 98-70797. (BEN.). xiv, 104p. 1998. pap. 10.00 (*1-58225-114-2*) Ananta Prakashani.
— Gitagar. LC 98-70798. (BEN.). xiv, 102p. 1998. pap. 10.00 (*1-58225-115-0*) Ananta Prakashani.
— Gitalom. LC 98-70799. (BEN.). xiv, 100p. 1998. pap. 10.00 (*1-58225-116-9*) Ananta Prakashani.
— Gitandaz. LC 98-70800. (BEN.). xiv, 106p. 1998. pap. 10.00 (*1-58225-117-7*) Ananta Prakashani.
— Gitangon. LC 98-70801. (BEN.). xiv, 108p. 1998. pap. 10.00 (*1-58225-118-5*) Ananta Prakashani.
— Gitanjal. LC 98-70802. (BEN.). xiv, 111p. 1998. pap. 10.00 (*1-58225-119-3*) Ananta Prakashani.
— Gitanjan. LC 98-70803. (BEN.). xiv, 106p. 1998. pap. 10.00 (*1-58225-120-7*) Ananta Prakashani.
— Gitantar. LC 98-70804. (BEN.). xiv, 100p. 1998. pap. 10.00 (*1-58225-121-5*) Ananta Prakashani.
— Gitapan. LC 98-70805. (BEN.). xiv, 108p. 1998. pap. 10.00 (*1-58225-122-3*) Ananta Prakashani.
— Gitara. LC 98-70806. (BEN.). xiv, 100p. 1998. pap. 10.00 (*1-58225-123-1*) Ananta Prakashani.
— Gitarab. LC 98-70807. (BEN.). xiv, 102p. 1998. pap. 10.00 (*1-58225-124-X*) Ananta Prakashani.
— Gitargha. LC 98-70808. (BEN.). xiv, 104p. 1998. pap. 10.00 (*1-58225-125-8*) Ananta Prakashani.
— Gitasan. LC 98-70809. (BEN.). xiv, 107p. 1998. pap. 10.00 (*1-58225-126-6*) Ananta Prakashani.
— Giti Kona. LC 98-70810. (BEN.). xiv, 101p. 1998. pap. 10.00 (*1-58225-127-4*) Ananta Prakashani.
— Gitikumvo. LC 98-70811. (BEN.). xiv, 61p. 1998. pap. 10.00 (*1-58225-128-2*) Ananta Prakashani.
— Gitodoy. LC 98-70812. (BEN.). xiv, 801p. 1998. pap. 10.00 (*1-58225-129-0*) Ananta Prakashani.
— Gitoloke. LC 98-70813. (BEN.). xiv, 102p. 1998. pap. 10.00 (*1-58225-130-4*) Ananta Prakashani.
— Gitovoron. LC 98-70814. (BEN.). xiv, 102p. 1998. pap. 10.00 (*1-58225-131-2*) Ananta Prakashani.
— Hamd-o-Nath, Pt. 1. LC 98-70815. (BEN.). xiv, 100p. 1998. pap. 10.00 (*1-58225-132-0*) Ananta Prakashani.
— The Home of Number. LC 98-70770. xiv, 108p. 1998. pap. 10.00 (*1-58225-025-1*) Ananta Prakashani.
***Nawaz, Ahmad.** The Home of Numbers. LC 00-131823. 108p. 2000. pap. 10.00 (*1-58225-225-4*) Ananta Prakashani.
Nawaz, Ahmad. Immanation. LC 98-70756. xiv, 65p. 1998. pap. 10.00 (*1-58225-009-X*) Ananta Prakashani.
***Nawaz, Ahmad.** Immanation. LC 00-131434. 65p. 2000. pap. 10.00 (*1-58225-209-2*) Ananta Prakashani.
Nawaz, Ahmad. Impression. xiv, 93p. 1998. pap. 10.00 (*1-58225-010-3*) Ananta Prakashani.
***Nawaz, Ahmad.** Impression. LC 00-131435. 93p. 2000. pap. 10.00 (*1-58225-210-6*) Ananta Prakashani.
Nawaz, Ahmad. In Remembrance of the Prophet. LC 98-70758. xiv, 104p. 1998. pap. 10.00 (*1-58225-011-1*) Ananta Prakashani.
***Nawaz, Ahmad.** In Remembrance of the Prophet. LC 00-131436. 104p. 2000. pap. 10.00 (*1-58225-211-4*) Ananta Prakashani.
Nawaz, Ahmad. In the Land of Flowers & Birds. LC 98-70755. xiv, 59p. 1998. pap. 10.00 (*1-58225-008-1*) Ananta Prakashani.
***Nawaz, Ahmad.** In the Land of Flowers & Birds. LC 00-131433. 59p. 2000. pap. 10.00 (*1-58225-208-4*) Ananta Prakashani.
Nawaz, Ahmad. Interiorism. LC 98-70759. xiv, 59p. 1998. pap. 10.00 (*1-58225-012-X*) Ananta Prakashani.
***Nawaz, Ahmad.** Interiorism. LC 00-131437. 59p. 2000. pap. 10.00 (*1-58225-212-2*) Ananta Prakashani.
Nawaz, Ahmad. Jibon Bodh. LC 98-70816. (BEN.). xiv, 100p. 1998. pap. 10.00 (*1-58225-133-9*) Ananta Prakashani.
— Kabita. LC 98-70817. (BEN.). xiv, 100p. 1998. pap. 10.00 (*1-58225-134-7*) Ananta Prakashani.
— Kalpalata. LC 98-70818. (BEN.). xiv, 103p. 1998. pap. 10.00 (*1-58225-135-5*) Ananta Prakashani.
— Kathika. LC 98-70819. (BEN.). xiv, 98p. 1998. pap. 10.00 (*1-58225-136-3*) Ananta Prakashani.
— Krishna Sangit. LC 98-70820. (BEN.). xiv, 70p. 1998. pap. 10.00 (*1-58225-137-1*) Ananta Prakashani.
— The Light of the Prophet. LC 98-70771. xiv, 105p. 1998. pap. 10.00 (*1-58225-026-X*) Ananta Prakashani.
***Nawaz, Ahmad.** The Light of the Prophet. LC 00-131824. 105p. 2000. pap. 10.00 (*1-58225-226-2*) Ananta Prakashani.
Nawaz, Ahmad. Mahanabi Sharanika. LC 98-70821. (BEN.). xiv, 84p. 1998. pap. 10.00 (*1-58225-138-X*) Ananta Prakashani.
***Nawaz, Ahmad.** Miscellanea, 1. LC 00-133577. 180p. 2000. pap. 10.00 (*1-58225-379-X*) Ananta Prakashani.
— Miscellanea, 2. LC 00-133577. 71p. 2000. pap. 10.00 (*1-58225-380-3*) Ananta Prakashani.
— Modern Songs. LC 00-133576. 89p. 2000. pap. 10.00 (*1-58225-381-1*) Ananta Prakashani.
Nawaz, Ahmad. Mohanobi Mohammad. LC 98-70822. (BEN.). xiv, 98p. 1998. pap. 10.00 (*1-58225-139-8*) Ananta Prakashani.
— The Muse. LC 98-70772. xiv, 120p. 1998. pap. 10.00 (*1-58225-027-8*) Ananta Prakashani.
***Nawaz, Ahmad.** The Muse. LC 00-131825. 120p. 2000. pap. 10.00 (*1-58225-227-0*) Ananta Prakashani.
Nawaz, Ahmad. Nooron Nobi. LC 98-70823. (BEN.). xiv, 100p. 1998. pap. 10.00 (*1-58225-140-1*) Ananta Prakashani.
***Nawaz, Ahmad.** Nuzul-E-Quran. LC 00-133579. 80p. 2000. pap. 10.00 (*1-58225-382-X*) Ananta Prakashani.
Nawaz, Ahmad. On Spiritualism, Pt. 2. LC 98-71083. xiv, 66p. 1998. pap. 10.00 (*1-58225-024-3*) Ananta Prakashani.
***Nawaz, Ahmad.** On Spiritualism Part 1. LC 00-131827. 89p. 2000. pap. 10.00 (*1-58225-229-7*) Ananta Prakashani.
— On Spiritualism Part 2. LC 00-131822. 66p. 2000. pap. 10.00 (*1-58225-224-6*) Ananta Prakashani.
Nawaz, Ahmad. Palli Giti, Pt. 3. LC 98-71442. (BEN.). xiv, 100p. 1998. pap. 10.00 (*1-58225-141-X*) Ananta Prakashani.
— Panchadal. LC 98-70824. (BEN.). xiv, 61p. 1998. pap. 10.00 (*1-58225-142-8*) Ananta Prakashani.
— Paul Pakhider Desha. LC 98-70825. (BEN.). xiv, 63p. 1998. pap. 10.00 (*1-58225-143-6*) Ananta Prakashani.
***Nawaz, Ahmad.** Poetry of Dr. Ashraf Siddiqui. LC 00-133578. 56p. 2000. pap. 10.00 (*1-58225-383-8*) Ananta Prakashani.
Nawaz, Ahmad. Prakashika. LC 98-70826. (BEN.). xiv, 102p. 1998. pap. 10.00 (*1-58225-144-4*) Ananta Prakashani.
— Pravatica. LC 98-70827. (BEN.). xiv, 115p. 1998. pap. 10.00 (*1-58225-145-2*) Ananta Prakashani.
— Precursor. LC 98-70760. xiv, 64p. 1998. pap. 10.00 (*1-58225-013-8*) Ananta Prakashani.
***Nawaz, Ahmad.** Precursor. LC 00-131438. 64p. 2000. pap. 10.00 (*1-58225-213-0*) Ananta Prakashani.
Nawaz, Ahmad. Prominica. LC 98-70828. (BEN.). xiv, 79p. 1998. pap. 10.00 (*1-58225-146-0*) Ananta Prakashani.
— The Prophet of Light. LC 98-70773. xiv, 44p. 1998. pap. 10.00 (*1-58225-029-4*) Ananta Prakashani.
***Nawaz, Ahmad.** The Prophet of Light. LC 00-131826. 50p. 2000. pap. 10.00 (*1-58225-228-9*) Ananta Prakashani.
Nawaz, Ahmad. Purnima. LC 98-70829. (BEN.). xiv, 69p. 1998. pap. 10.00 (*1-58225-147-9*) Ananta Prakashani.
— Radiation. LC 98-70761. xiv, 97p. 1998. pap. 10.00 (*1-58225-014-6*) Ananta Prakashani.
***Nawaz, Ahmad.** Radiation. LC 00-131439. 100p. 2000. pap. 10.00 (*1-58225-214-9*) Ananta Prakashani.
— Rapture. LC 00-133581. 104p. 2000. pap. 10.00 (*1-58225-384-6*) Ananta Prakashani.
Nawaz, Ahmad. Rectitude. LC 98-70762. xiv, 79p. 1998. pap. 10.00 (*1-58225-015-4*) Ananta Prakashani.
***Nawaz, Ahmad.** Rectitude. LC 00-131440. 80p. 2000. pap. 10.00 (*1-58225-215-7*) Ananta Prakashani.
Nawaz, Ahmad. Rhymed Verses on the Holy Prophet. LC 98-70764. xiv, 100p. 1998. pap. 10.00 (*1-58225-017-0*) Ananta Prakashani.
***Nawaz, Ahmad.** Rhymed Verses on the Holy Prophet (SM) LC 00-131442. 100p. 2000. pap. 10.00 (*1-58225-217-3*) Ananta Prakashani.
Nawaz, Ahmad. Rumination. LC 98-70763. xiv, 84p. 1998. pap. 10.00 (*1-58225-016-2*) Ananta Prakashani.
***Nawaz, Ahmad.** Rumination. LC 00-131441. 84p. 2000. pap. 10.00 (*1-58225-216-5*) Ananta Prakashani.
Nawaz, Ahmad. Sagorica. LC 98-70830. (BEN.). 65p. 1998. pap. 10.00 (*1-58225-148-7*) Ananta Prakashani.
— Sata Namer Kabita, Pt. 1. LC 98-70831. (BEN.). xiv, 104p. 1998. pap. 10.00 (*1-58225-149-5*) Ananta Prakashani.
— Sata Namer Kabita, Pt. 2. LC 98-70831. (BEN.). xiv, 106p. 1998. pap. 10.00 (*1-58225-150-9*) Ananta Prakashani.
— Shonkolita, Pt. 1. LC 98-70778. (BEN.). xiv, 71p. 1998. pap. 10.00 (*1-58225-151-7*) Ananta Prakashani.
— Shonkolita, Pt. 2. LC 98-70778. (BEN.). xiv, 56p. 1998. pap. 10.00 (*1-58225-152-5*) Ananta Prakashani.
— Shonkolita, Pt. 3. LC 98-70778. (BEN.). xiv, 132p. 1998. pap. 10.00 (*1-58225-153-3*) Ananta Prakashani.
— Shonkolita, Pt. 4. LC 98-70778. (BEN.). xiv, 111p. 1998. pap. 10.00 (*1-58225-154-1*) Ananta Prakashani.
— Shonkolita, Pt. 5. LC 98-70778. (BEN.). xiv, 149p. 1998. pap. 10.00 (*1-58225-155-X*) Ananta Prakashani.
— Shonkolita, Pt. 6. LC 98-70778. (BEN.). xiv, 89p. 1998. pap. 10.00 (*1-58225-156-8*) Ananta Prakashani.
— Shonkolita, Pt. 7. LC 98-70778. (BEN.). xiv, 141p. 1998. pap. 10.00 (*1-58225-157-6*) Ananta Prakashani.
— Shonkolita, Pt. 9. LC 98-70778. (BEN.). xiv, 108p. 1998. pap. 10.00 (*1-58225-159-2*) Ananta Prakashani.
— Shonkolita, Pt. 10. LC 98-70778. (BEN.). xiv, 88p. 1998. pap. 10.00 (*1-58225-160-6*) Ananta Prakashani.
Shonkolita, Pt. 11. LC 98-70778. (BEN.). xiv, 88p. 1998. pap. 10.00 (*1-58225-161-4*) Ananta Prakashani.
— Shonkolita, Pt. 12. LC 98-70778. (BEN.). xiv, 98p. 1998. pap. 10.00 (*1-58225-162-2*) Ananta Prakashani.
— Shonkolita, Pt. 13. LC 98-70778. (BEN.). xiv, 119p. 1998. pap. 10.00 (*1-58225-163-0*) Ananta Prakashani.
— Shonkolita, Pt. 14. LC 98-70778. (BEN.). xiv, 80p. 1998. pap. 10.00 (*1-58225-164-9*) Ananta Prakashani.
— Shonkolita, Pt. 15. LC 98-70778. (BEN.). xiv, 105p. 1998. pap. 10.00 (*1-58225-165-7*) Ananta Prakashani.
— Shonkolita, Pt. 16. LC 98-70778. (BEN.). xiv, 95p. 1998. pap. 10.00 (*1-58225-166-5*) Ananta Prakashani.
— Shonkolita, Pt. 17. LC 98-70778. (BEN.). 114p. 1998. pap. 10.00 (*1-58225-167-3*) Ananta Prakashani.
— Shonkolita, Pt. 18. LC 98-70778. (BEN.). xiv, 98p. 1998. pap. 10.00 (*1-58225-168-1*) Ananta Prakashani.
— Shonkolita, Pt. 19. LC 98-70778. (BEN.). xiv, 118p. 1998. pap. 10.00 (*1-58225-169-X*) Ananta Prakashani.
— Shonkolita, Pt. 20. LC 98-70778. (BEN.). xiv, 75p. 1998. pap. 10.00 (*1-58225-170-3*) Ananta Prakashani.
— Shonkolita, Pt. 21. LC 98-70778. (BEN.). xiv, 73p. 1998. pap. 10.00 (*1-58225-171-1*) Ananta Prakashani.
— Shonkolita, Pt. 22. LC 98-70778. (BEN.). xiv, 127p. 1998. pap. 10.00 (*1-58225-172-X*) Ananta Prakashani.
— Shonkolita, Pt. 23. LC 98-70778. (BEN.). xiv, 101p. 1998. pap. 10.00 (*1-58225-173-8*) Ananta Prakashani.
— Shonkolita, Pt. 24. LC 98-70778. (BEN.). xiv, 143p. 1998. pap. 10.00 (*1-58225-174-6*) Ananta Prakashani.
— Shonkolita Palli Giti, Pts. 1, 2, & 8. LC 98-70778. (BEN.). xiv, 120p. 1998. pap. 10.00 (*1-58225-158-4*) Ananta Prakashani.
***Nawaz, Ahmad.** Some Festivals, 1. LC 00-133580. 236p. 2000. pap. 10.00 (*1-58225-385-4*) Ananta Prakashani.
— Some Festivals, 2. LC 00-133580. 124p. 2000. pap. 10.00 (*1-58225-386-2*) Ananta Prakashani.
— Some Sayings. LC 00-133583. 60p. 2000. pap. 10.00 (*1-58225-387-0*) Ananta Prakashani.
Nawaz, Ahmad. Song Poem, Vol. 1. LC 98-70765. xiv, 45p. 1998. pap. 10.00 (*1-58225-018-9*) Ananta Prakashani.
— Song Poem, Vol. 2. LC 98-70765. xiv, 97p. 1998. pap. 10.00 (*1-58225-019-7*) Ananta Prakashani.
***Nawaz, Ahmad.** Songpoem, 1. LC 00-131443. 50p. 2000. pap. 10.00 (*1-58225-218-1*) Ananta Prakashani.
— Songpoem, 2. LC 00-131443. 100p. 2000. pap. 10.00 (*1-58225-219-X*) Ananta Prakashani.
— Songpoem, 3. LC 00-131443. 120p. 2000. pap. 10.00 (*1-58225-388-9*) Ananta Prakashani.
Nawaz, Ahmad. Songs from Bangladesh. LC 98-70766. xiv, 100p. 1998. pap. 10.00 (*1-58225-020-0*) Ananta Prakashani.
***Nawaz, Ahmad.** Songs from Bangladesh. LC 00-131818. 100p. 2000. pap. 10.00 (*1-58225-220-3*) Ananta Prakashani.
Nawaz, Ahmad. Songs of Clouds. LC 98-70768. xiv, 100p. 1998. pap. 10.00 (*1-58225-022-7*) Ananta Prakashani.
***Nawaz, Ahmad.** Songs of Clouds. LC 00-131820. 100p. 2000. pap. 10.00 (*1-58225-222-X*) Ananta Prakashani.
Nawaz, Ahmad. Songs of Life. LC 98-70769. xiv, 100p. 1998. pap. 10.00 (*1-58225-023-5*) Ananta Prakashani.
***Nawaz, Ahmad.** Songs of Life. LC 00-131821. 100p. 2000. pap. 10.00 (*1-58225-223-8*) Ananta Prakashani.
Nawaz, Ahmad. Songs of 1980. LC 98-70767. xiv, 101p. 1998. pap. 10.00 (*1-58225-021-9*) Ananta Prakashani.
***Nawaz, Ahmad.** Songs of 1980. LC 00-131819. 101p. 2000. pap. 10.00 (*1-58225-221-1*) Ananta Prakashani.
— Songs on Jesus. LC 00-133582. 102p. 2000. pap. 10.00 (*1-58225-389-7*) Ananta Prakashani.
Nawaz, Ahmad. A Spiritual Autobiography. LC 98-70745. xiv, 155p. 1998. pap. 10.00 (*1-58225-000-6*) Ananta Prakashani.
***Nawaz, Ahmad.** A Spiritual Autobiography. LC 00-131425. 155p. 2000. pap. 10.00 (*1-58225-200-9*) Ananta Prakashani.
— Thoughtography. LC 00-133585. 156p. 2000. pap. 10.00 (*1-58225-390-0*) Ananta Prakashani.
Nawaz, Ahmad. Udbodhika. LC 98-70779. (BEN.). xiv, 78p. 1998. pap. 10.00 (*1-58225-175-4*) Ananta Prakashani.
— Unrhymed Verses, Bk. 1. LC 98-70774. xiv, 100p. 1998. pap. 10.00 (*1-58225-032-4*) Ananta Prakashani.
***Nawaz, Ahmad.** Unrhymed Verses, Bk. 1. LC 00-131828. 100p. 2000. pap. 10.00 (*1-58225-230-0*) Ananta Prakashani.
Nawaz, Ahmad. Unrhymed Verses, Bk. 2. LC 98-70774. xiv, 100p. 1998. pap. 10.00 (*1-58225-030-8*) Ananta Prakashani.
***Nawaz, Ahmad.** Unrhymed Verses, Bk. 2. LC 00-131828. 100p. 2000. pap. 10.00 (*1-58225-231-9*) Ananta Prakashani.
Nawaz, Ahmad. Unrhymed Verses, Bk. 3. LC 98-70774. xiv, 100p. 1998. pap. 10.00 (*1-58225-031-6*) Ananta Prakashani.
***Nawaz, Ahmad.** Unrhymed Verses, Bk. 3. LC 00-131828. 100p. 2000. pap. 10.00 (*1-58225-232-7*) Ananta Prakashani.
Nawaz, Ahmad. Utsobica. LC 98-70780. (BEN.). xiv, 52p. 1998. pap. 10.00 (*1-58225-176-2*) Ananta Prakashani.
Nawaz, Ahmad. Words of Wisdom. LC 98-70775. xiv, 100p. 1998. pap. 10.00 (*1-58225-033-2*) Ananta Prakashani.
***Nawaz, Ahmad.** Words of Wisdom. LC 00-131829. 100p. 2000. pap. 10.00 (*1-58225-233-5*) Ananta Prakashani.
Nawaz, Ahman. Adhunica, Pt. 10. LC 98-70776. (BEN.). xiv, 100p. 1998. pap. 10.00 (*1-58225-042-1*) Ananta Prakashani.
Nawaz, Shuja. Journeys. LC 98-136393. 52p. (C). 1998. text 16.95 (*0-19-577839-1*) OUP.
Nawaz, Tawfique, compiled by. The New International Economic Order: A Bibliography. LC 79-28077. 163p. 1980. lib. bdg. 52.95 (*0-313-22111-1*, NAI/, Greenwood Pr) Greenwood.
Nawid, Senzil K. Religious Response to Social Change in Afghanistan, 1919-1929: King Aman-Allah Khan & the Afghan Ulama. LC 98-22602. (Illus.). viii, 292p. 1998. lib. bdg. 45.00 (*1-56859-072-5*) Mazda Pubs.
Nawigmune, Anake, compiled by. A Century of Thai Graphic Design. (Illus.). 152p. 2000. 40.00 (*974-8225-42-9*, Pub. by River Books) Weatherhill.
Nawoczenski, Deborah A. & Epler, Marcia E. Orthotics in Functional Rehabilitation of the Lower Limb. LC 96-25618. (Illus.). 315p. 1997. text 47.00 (*0-7216-6134-3*, W B Saunders Co) Harcrt Hlth Sci Grp.
Naworski, Priscilla, jt. auth. see Ikeda, Joanne.

N

***Nawracaj, Carol Ann & Kosann, Monica Rich.** Thank Heaven for Little Girls. (Illus.). 128p. 2001. 27.50 (*1-58062-281-X*) Adams Media.

Nawrath, Alfred. The Aegean World. LC 77-87872. (Illus.). 1977. 30.00 (*0-88331-097-X*) J J Binns.

Nawratzki, I., ed. see Jersualem Conference on Impaired Vision In childho.

***Nawrocki, Dennis Alan.** Art in Detroit Public Places. rev. ed. LC 99-39813. 176p. 2000. pap. 19.95 (*0-8143-2702-8*) Wayne St U Pr.

Nawrocki, Helene K. The Nurse's Book of Courage. 61p. 1993. pap. 14.95 (*0-9636792-0-1*); audio 14.95 (*0-9636792-1-X*) Ctr Nursing Excell.

Nawrocki, Norman. Rebel Moon: Anarchist Rants & Poems. (Illus.). 112p. 1996. pap. 9.95 (*1-873176-08-2*, AK Pr San Fran) AK Pr Dist.

Nawrocki, Sarah. Camping with Strangers: And Other Stories. LC 99-17582. 160p. 1999. 20.00 (*0-9651879-9-3*, Pub. by Boaz Pubng) Publishers Group.

Nawrocki, Sarah, ed. see Wilkinson, D. Marion.

Nawrocki, Susan & Lair, Gerald. San Antonio: Portrait of the Fiesta City. LC 91-40861. (Illus.). 96p. 1992. pap. 16.95 (*0-89658-204-3*) Voyageur Pr.

Nawroth, Harry O. Lest We Forget. 97p. 1993. pap. 4.95 (*1-883537-51-7*) Nawroth Pub.

— Thoughts about Jesus & Mary. 109p. 1993. pap. 4.95 (*1-883537-50-9*) Nawroth Pub.

— We Do Have a Choice: Please Choose Jesus. 110p. 1993. pap. 4.95 (*1-883537-52-5*) Nawroth Pub.

Nawroth, P. P., jt. auth. see Hach-Wunderle, V.

Nawwab, Ismail I., et al, eds. Saudi Aramco & Its World: Arabia & the Middle East. rev. ed. LC 95-70752. (Illus.). 291p. 1995. 27.50 (*0-9601164-3-5*) Saudi Arab Oil Co.

Nawwab, Ismail I., ed. see Nance, Paul J.

Nawy, Edward G. Concrete Construction Engineering Handbook. LC 97-7652. 1232p. 1997. boxed set 124.95 (*0-8493-2666-4*) CRC Pr.

***Nawy, Edward G.** Fundamentals of High-Performance Concrete. 2nd ed. LC 00-33025. 2000. write for info. (*0-471-38555-7*) Wiley.

Nawy, Edward G. Prestressed Concrete: A Fundamental Approach. 2nd ed. LC 95-13788. (C). 1995. text 100.00 (*0-13-123480-3*) P-H.

***Nawy, Edward G.** Prestressed Concrete: A Fundamental Approach. 3rd ed. LC 99-38322. 939p. 1999. 105.00 (*0-13-020593-1*) P-H.

Nawy, Edward G. Simplified Reinforced Concrete. (Illus.). 320p. (C). 1986. text 29.95 (*0-317-29670-1*) P-H.

***Nawy, P.E. & Edwards, G.** Reinforced Concrete: A Fundamental Approach. 4th ed. LC 99-26348. (International Series in Civil Engineering). 777p. 1999. 105.00 (*0-13-020592-3*) P-H.

Nawyn, William E. American Protestantism's Response to Germany's Jews & Refugees, 1933-1941. LC 81-7552. (Studies in American History & Culture: No. 30). 342p. 1981. reprint ed. pap. 106.10 (*0-8357-1208-7*, 207010800064) Bks Demand.

Naxerova, A. Technisches Woerterbuch, Vol. 1. (CZE & GER.). 1970. 89.95 (*0-8288-6554-X*, M-7649, Pub. by O Brandstetter Verlag) Trafalgar.

— Technisches Woerterbuch, Vol. 2. (CZE & GER.). 1972. 89.95 (*0-8288-6422-5*, M-7650, Pub. by O Brandstetter Verlag) Trafalgar.

Naxon, Jan L. & Rosenthal, Beth E. Dallas Entrees: A Restaurant Guide & Celebrity Cookbook (with a Primer to California Wines) 144p. (Orig.). 1982. pap. 5.95 (*0-910163-00-6*) Artichoke Pub.

Nay, Catherine. The Black & the Red: Francois Mitterand & the Story of an Ambition. Sheridan, Alan, tr. LC 86-19382. 352p. 1987. 19.95 (*0-15-112885-5*) Harcourt.

Nay, Louise Le, see Le Nay, Louise.

Nay, Patricia, et al. Show What You Know on Ohio's Sixth Grade Proficiency Test. (Illus.). 1996. pap., teacher ed. write for info. (*1-884183-04-2*) Englfld & Arnold.

— Show What You Know on Ohio's Sixth Grade Proficiency Test. (Illus.). (J). (gr. 5-6). 1996. pap., student ed., wbk. ed. 9.95 (*1-884183-05-0*) Englfld & Arnold.

Nay, Robert L., ed. Firearms Regulations in Various Foreign Countries. 203p. (Orig.). (C). 1992. pap. text 40.00 (*1-56806-107-2*) DIANE Pub.

Nay, Tim. Legal-Financial Planning Guide for Families. 2nd ed. 100p. 1990. pap. text 15.00 (*1-877592-14-5*) GSH&MC.

Nay, Tim, jt. auth. see Byrlat, Katherine.

Naya, Seiji. Private Sector Development & Enterprise Reforms in Growing Asian Economies. 119p. 1990. pap. 14.95 (*1-55815-083-8*) ICS Pr.

— Relevance of Asian Development Experiences to African Problems. LC 93-50841. (Occasional Papers: No. 53). 1994. 9.95 (*1-55815-313-6*) ICS Pr.

Naya, Seiji, et al, eds. Lessons in Development: A Comparative Study of Asia & Latin America. LC 89-19996. 361p. 1989. 34.95 (*1-55815-051-X*); pap. 19.95 (*1-55815-052-8*) ICS Pr.

Naya, Seiji, et al. Asian Development: Economic Success & Policy Lessons. LC 88-40191. (C). 1989. pap. text 19.95 (*0-299-11784-7*) U of Wis Pr.

Nayacakalou, R. R. Leadership in Fiji. 1976. 22.00 (*0-19-550462-3*) OUP.

Nayak, A. K., jt. auth. see Kumar Singh, Uttam.

Nayak, Amiya, et al. 1997 Indian Medical Market Report Vol. 1: An Indepth Market Study on India's Pharmaceutical, Biotechnology & Medical Device Industries. 167p. (Orig.). 1997. pap. 299.95 (*0-9657889-1-1*) Golden Tri Org.

Nayak, B. U. New Trends in Indian Art & Archaeology: S. R. Rao's 70th Birthday Felicitation Volume, Vol. I. (C). 1992. write for info. (*81-85689-13-X*, Pub. by Aditya Prakashan) S Asia.

— New Trends in Indian Art & Archaeology: S. R. Rao's 70th Birthday Felicitation Volume, Vol. II. (C). 1992. write for info. (*81-85689-14-8*, Pub. by Aditya Prakashan) S Asia.

Nayak, B. U. & Ghosh, N. C. New Trends in Indian Art & Archaeology, 2 vols. 571p. 1991. pap. 183.50 (*81-85689-12-1*, Pub. by Aditya Prakashan) S Asia.

Nayak, Debi P., ed. The Molecular Biology of Animal Viruses, 2 vols., 2. LC 76-29295. (Illus.). 579p. reprint ed. pap. 179.50 (*0-8357-6220-3*, 203455600002) Bks Demand.

— The Molecular Biology of Animal Viruses, 2 vols., Vol. 1. LC 76-29295. (Illus.). 552p. reprint ed. pap. 171.20 (*0-8357-6219-X*, 203455600001) Bks Demand.

Nayak, G. C. Philosophical Reflections. (C). 1987. 11.50 (*81-208-0421-X*, Pub. by Motilal Bnarsidass) S Asia.

Nayak, Nitin & Ray, Asok. Intelligent Seam Tracking for Robotic Welding. LC 93-3303. 1993. 87.95 (*0-387-19826-1*) Spr-Verlag.

Nayak, P. K., jt. auth. see Samal, J. K.

Nayak, P. Pandurang. Automated Modelling of Physical Systems. LC 95-48030. (Lecture Notes in Artificial Intelligence: Vol. 1003). 232p. 1995. pap. 43.00 (*3-540-60641-6*) Spr-Verlag.

Nayak, P. Ranganath, jt. auth. see Deschamps, Jean-Philippe.

Nayak, Panda U. Pakistan Society & Politics. 1985. 22.50 (*0-8364-1348-2*, Pub. by S Asia Pubs) S Asia.

Nayak, Pandav. Pakistan: Political Economy of a Developing State. 1988. 48.50 (*81-7050-049-4*, Pub. by Patriot Pubs) S Asia.

Nayak, Pradeep. Politics of the Ayodhya Dispute. (C). 1993. 22.50 (*81-7169-252-4*, Commonwealth) S Asia.

Nayak, Purshottam. Disguised Unemployment & Under-Employment in Agriculture. 174p. 1990. text 27.50 (*0-685-33222-5*, Pub. by Radiant Pubs) S Asia.

Nayak, R. K. & Siddiqui, H. Y. Social Work & Social Development. 1989. 23.50 (*81-85060-32-0*, Pub. by Gitanjali Prakashan) S Asia.

Nayak, Radhakant. Administrative Justice in India. 248p. 1989. text 26.00 (*0-8039-9576-8*) Sage.

Nayak, Radhakant, ed. Fourth World. LC 97-905770. (C). 1997. 38.00 (*81-7304-182-2*, Pub. by Manohar) S Asia.

Nayak, Ragu, jt. auth. see Waters, Don.

***Nayak, Utpala.** Women's Development & Social Conflicts: Historical Perspectives on Indian Women (Study in Orissa) LC 98-915712. 1999. 34.00 (*81-7391-271-8*, Pub. by Kaniska Pubs Dist) S Asia.

Nayan, Deme, et al, eds. Aboriginal Pedagogy: Aboriginal Teachers Speak Out. 179p. (C). 1991. 80.00 (*0-7855-6749-6*, Pub. by Deakin Univ) St Mut.

Nayar, Alok. The Metal Databook. LC 97-218568. (Illus.). 768p. 1997. 89.95 (*0-07-046088-4*) McGraw.

Nayar, Baldar R. American Geopolitics & India. 246p. 1976. 15.95 (*0-318-37228-2*) Asia Bk Corp.

Nayar, Baldev R. India's Mixed Economy. (C). 1989. 57.00 (*0-86132-217-7*) S Asia.

— The Political Economy of India's Public Sector: Policy & Performance. 1990. 48.50 (*0-86132-264-9*, Pub. by Popular Prakashan) S Asia.

— State & International Aviation in India: Performance & Policy on the Eve of Aviation Globalization. LC 94-907490. (C). 1994. 34.00 (*81-7304-093-1*, Pub. by Manohar) S Asia.

Nayar, Indira, tr. see Bronshtein, Z. S.

Nayar, Kuldip. In Jail. 152p. 1978. 9.95 (*0-7069-0647-0*) Asia Bk Corp.

— The Judgement: Inside Story of the Emergency in India. 228p. 1977. 14.95 (*0-7069-0557-1*) Asia Bk Corp.

***Nayar, Kuldip.** Martyr: Bhagat Singh - Experiments in Revolution. 2000. 19.50 (*81-241-0700-9*, Pub. by Har-Anand Pubns) S Asia.

Nayar, Lali & Suxena, Rajul. Who's Afraid of Indian Cooking? Book of Menus. (C). 1994. 22.50 (*81-86112-64-2*, Pub. by UBS Pubs Dist) S Asia.

Nayar, M. P. Meaning of India Flowering Plants Name. (C). 1988. text 60.00 (*0-7855-3157-2*, Pub. by Scientific) St Mut.

Nayar, N. M. & More, T. A. Cucurbits. (Illus.). 352p. 1998. 75.00 (*1-57808-003-7*, V037) Science Pubs.

Nayar, Shree K. & Poggio, Tomaso, eds. Early Visual Learning. (Illus.). 384p. 1996. text 55.00 (*0-19-509522-7*) OUP.

Nayar, Sobhana. Bhatkhande's Contribution to Music: A Historical Perspective. (C). 1989. 32.00 (*0-86132-238-X*, Pub. by Popular Prakashan) S Asia.

Nayar, Sushila, tr. see Gandhi, Mohandas Karamchand.

Nayar, T. S. Pollen Flora of Maharashtra State. (International Bioscience Ser.: No. 14). (Illus.). 175p. 1990. 65.00 (*1-55528-221-0*) Scholarly Pubns.

Nayar, Usha. Women Teachers in South Asia, Nudity & Discontinuity With Change. (C). 1988. 22.50 (*81-7001-048-9*, Pub. by Chanakya) S Asia.

Nayatani, Yoshinobu, et al. The Seven New QC Tools: Practical Applications for Managers. Loftus, John H., tr. from JPN. (Illus.). 180p. 1994. pap. text 34.95 (*4-88319-004-8*, 190048, Pub. by Three A) Qual Resc.

Naydan, Theodore D. Secret Trout Flies: The Book of Unrevealed Patterns. (Illus.). 63p. 1989. pap. text. write for info. (*0-318-65818-6*) T D Naydan.

Nayder. Wilkie Collins. LC 97-21447. 1997. 32.00 (*0-8057-7059-3*, Twyne) Mac Lib Ref.

Naydler, Jeremy. Goethe on Science: An Anthology of Goethe's Scientific Writings. 1997. pap. text 16.95 (*0-86315-237-6*, Pub. by Floris Bks) Anthroposophic.

— The Temple of the Cosmos: The Ancient Egyptian Experience of the Sacred. LC 95-34644. 224p. 1995. pap. 19.95 (*0-89281-555-8*) Inner Tradit.

Nayer, Alor. Steel Handbook. 2000. 99.95 (*0-07-135573-1*) McGraw.

Nayer, H. S., et al, eds. Progress in Powder Metallurgy, Vol. 39. (Illus.). 696p. 1983. pap. 20.00 (*0-918404-61-4*) Metal Powder.

Nayer, Judy. Ants - Hormigas. Curry, Don, ed. Torres, Leyla, tr. from ENG. (Spanish Discovery Links Ser.). (SPA.). 8p. (J). (gr. k). 1997. pap. text 2.75 (*1-56784-919-9*) Newbridge Educ.

— Baby's Bath. (Baby's World Ser.). (Illus.). 10p. (J). 1996. bds. 2.99 (*1-56293-912-2*, McClanahan Book) Learn Horizon.

— Baby's Games. (Baby's World Ser.). (Illus.). 10p. (J). 1996. bds. 2.99 (*1-56293-911-4*, McClanahan Book) Learn Horizon.

— Baby's Rhymes. (Baby's World Ser.). (Illus.). 10p. (J). 1996. bds. 2.99 (*1-56293-910-6*, McClanahan Book) Learn Horizon.

— Baby's Toys. (Baby's World Ser.). (Illus.). 10p. (J). 1996. bds. 3.50 (*1-56293-913-0*, McClanahan Book) Learn Horizon.

— Birds. (At Your Fingertips Ser.). (Illus.). 10p. (J). (ps-3). 1995. bds. 6.95 (*1-56293-545-3*, McClanahan Book) Learn Horizon.

— Como Crecen las Ranas? Curry, Don, ed. Torres, Leyla, tr. from ENG. (Spanish Discovery Links Ser.). (SPA.). 8p. (J). (gr. k). 1997. pap. text 2.75 (*1-56784-993-8*) Newbridge Educ.

— Dinosaurs. (At Your Fingertips Ser.). (Illus.). 12p. (J). (ps-3). 1993. bds. 6.95 (*1-56293-336-1*, McClanahan Book) Learn Horizon.

— Dogs & Puppies. (At Your Fingertips Ser.). (Illus.). 10p. (J). (ps-3). 1996. bds. 6.95 (*1-56293-895-9*, McClanahan Book) Learn Horizon.

— The Eight Nights of Hanukkah. (Illus.). 32p. (J). (ps-3). 1998. pap. 3.50 (*0-8167-4550-1*) Troll Communs.

— En la Playa. Curry, Don, ed. Torres, Leyla, tr. from ENG. (Spanish Discovery Links Ser.). (SPA.). 8p. (J). (gr. k). 1997. pap. text 2.75 (*1-56784-971-7*) Newbridge Educ.

— En la Primavera. Curry, Don, ed. Torres, Leyla, tr. from ENG. (Spanish Discovery Links Ser.). (SPA.). 8p. (J). (gr. k). 1997. pap. text 2.75 (*1-56784-968-7*) Newbridge Educ.

— Fall. Mooney, Jennifer, ed. (Newbridge Links Ser.). 8p. (J). (gr. k up). 1997. pap. 2.75 (*1-56784-905-9*) Newbridge Educ.

— Frog Life Cycle. Curry, Don, ed. (Guided Reading Ser.). 8p. (J). (gr. k). 1997. pap. text 2.75 (*1-56784-925-3*) Newbridge Educ.

— Herramientas. Curry, Don, ed. Torres, Leyla, tr. (Spanish Discovery Links Ser.). (SPA.). 8p. (J). (gr. k). 1997. pap. text 2.75 (*1-56784-959-8*) Newbridge Educ.

— How Many? Ellis, Linette & Reed, Janet, eds. (Early Math Big Bks.). (Illus.). 16p. (J). (ps-2). 1996. pap. 16.95 (*1-56784-307-7*) Newbridge Educ.

— How Many? Mini-Book. Ellis, Linette & Reed, Janet, eds. (Early Learning Program Ser.). (Illus.). 16p. (J). (ps-1). 1996. pap. 3.95 (*1-56784-332-8*) Newbridge Educ.

— Human Body. rev. ed. LC QP37.N39 1998. (At Your Fingertips Ser.). (Illus.). 5p. (J). (ps-3). 1998. 6.95 (*0-7681-0065-8*, McClanahan Book) Learn Horizon.

— In the Sea. Evento, Susan, ed. (Guided Reading Ser.). 8p. (J). (gr. k). 1997. pap. text 2.75 (*1-56784-912-1*) Newbridge Educ.

— Insects. (At Your Fingertips Ser.). (Illus.). 12p. (J). (ps-3). 1993. bds. 6.95 (*1-56293-335-3*, McClanahan Book) Learn Horizon.

— Jungle Life. (At Your Fingertips Ser.). (Illus.). 10p. (J). (ps-3). 1992. bds. 6.95 (*1-56293-221-7*, McClanahan Book) Learn Horizon.

— Mammals. (At Your Fingertips Ser.). (Illus.). 12p. (J). (ps-3). 1993. bds. 6.95 (*1-56293-337-X*, McClanahan Book) Learn Horizon.

— Mis Cinco Sentidos: Cuento de un Leon. Palacios, Argentina, tr. (Spanish Whole Language Big Bks.).Tr. of My Five Senses. (SPA., Illus.). 16p. (Orig.). (J). (ps-2). 1994. pap. 16.95 (*1-56784-094-9*) Newbridge Educ.

— More or Less? Pliakas, Stephanie, ed. (Early Math Big Bks.). (Illus.). 16p. (J). (ps-2). 1997. pap. 16.95 (*1-56784-954-7*) Newbridge Educ.

— My First Numbers. (J). 1997. pap. text, wbk. ed. 2.25 (*1-56293-953-X*, McClanahan Book) Learn Horizon.

— My Five Senses. (Whole-Language Big Bks.). (Illus.). 16p. (Orig.). (J). (ps-2). 1994. pap. 16.95 (*1-56784-067-1*) Newbridge Educ.

— Night Animals. (At Your Fingertips Ser.). (Illus.). 10p. (J). (ps-3). 1992. bds. 6.95 (*1-56293-223-3*, McClanahan Book) Learn Horizon.

— North American Indians. (At Your Fingertips Ser.). (Illus.). 10p. (J). (ps-3). 1995. bds. 6.95 (*1-56293-548-8*, McClanahan Book) Learn Horizon.

— Otono. Curry, Don, ed. Torres, Leyla, tr. from ENG. (Spanish Discovery Links Ser.). (SPA.). 8p. (J). (gr. k). 1997. pap. text 2.75 (*1-56784-964-4*) Newbridge Educ.

— Projects for Preschoolers Arts & Crafts. (Projects for Preschoolers Ser.). 48p. (J). (ps-1). 1999. mass mkt. 4.99 (*0-7681-0080-1*, McClanahan Book) Learn Horizon.

— Projects for Preschoolers Make-Believe. (Projects for Preschoolers Ser.). 48p. (J). (ps-1). 1999. mass mkt. 4.99 (*0-7681-0081-X*, McClanahan Book) Learn Horizon.

— Projects for Preschoolers-Nature. (Projects for Preschoolers Ser.). 48p. (J). (ps-1). 1999. mass mkt. 4.99 (*0-7681-0079-8*, McClanahan Book) Learn Horizon.

— Projects for Preschoolers-Science. (Projects for Preschoolers Ser.). 48p. 1999. mass mkt. 4.99 (*0-7681-0078-X*, McClanahan Book) Learn Horizon.

— Reptiles. (At Your Fingertips Ser.). (Illus.). 10p. (J). (ps-3). 1992. bds. 6.95 (*1-56293-220-9*, McClanahan Book) Learn Horizon.

— Rocks & Minerals. (At Your Fingertips Ser.). (Illus.). 10p. (J). (ps-3). 1995. bds. 6.95 (*1-56293-547-X*, McClanahan Book) Learn Horizon.

— Sea Creatures. (At Your Fingertips Ser.). (Illus.). 10p. (J). (ps-3). 1992. bds. 6.95 (*1-56293-222-5*, McClanahan Book) Learn Horizon.

— Spring. Mooney, Jennifer, ed. (Newbridge Links Ser.). 8p. (J). (gr. k up). 1997. pap. 2.75 (*1-56784-909-1*) Newbridge Educ.

— Up, down, All Around: Big Book. Ellis, Linette, ed. (Early Math Ser.). (Illus.). 16p. (J). (ps-1). 1997. pap. 16.95 (*1-56784-952-0*) Newbridge Educ.

— Up, down, All Around: Mini Book. Ellis, Linette, ed. (Early Math Ser.). (Illus.). 16p. (J). (ps-1). 1997. pap. 3.16 (*1-56784-977-6*) Newbridge Educ.

— Weather. LC 98-66000. (At Your Fingertips Ser.). 5p. (J). (ps-3). 1999. mass mkt. 6.95 (*0-7681-0102-6*, McClanahan Book) Learn Horizon.

— What's the Shape? Big Book. Ellis, Linette, ed. (Newbridge Early Math Ser.). (Illus.). 16p. (J). (ps-1). 1997. pap. 16.95 (*1-56784-950-4*) Newbridge Educ.

— What's the Shape? Mini-Book. Ellis, Linette, ed. (Newbridge Early Math Ser.). (Illus.). 16p. (J). (ps-1). 1997. pap. 3.16 (*1-56784-975-X*) Newbridge Educ.

— Who Wears Shoes? Reed, Janet, ed. (Newbridge Early Learning Program Ser.). (Illus.). 16p. (J). (ps-1). 1996. pap. 16.95 (*1-56784-303-4*) Newbridge Educ.

— Who Wears Shoes? Mini Book. Reed, Janet, ed. (Early Learning Program Ser.). (Illus.). 16p. (J). (ps-1). 1996. pap. 3.16 (*1-56784-328-X*) Newbridge Educ.

— Zoo Animals. LC 97-76591. (At Your Fingertips Ser.). (Illus.). 5p. (J). (ps-3). 1998. 6.95 (*0-7681-0066-6*, McClanahan Book) Learn Horizon.

Nayer, Louise. The Houses Are Covered in Sound: Poems. LC 89-81826. 59p. (Orig.). 1990. pap. 10.00 (*0-9619744-2-7*) Blue Light Pr.

Nayer, Louise, jt. auth. see Lang, Virginia.

Nayfeh, Adnan H. Wave Propagation in Layered Anisotropic Media: With Application to Composites. LC 95-36456. (North-Holland Series in Applied Mathematics & Mechanics: Vol. 39). 346p. 1995. 155.00 (*0-444-89018-1*, North Holland) Elsevier.

Nayfeh, Ali H. Introduction to Perturbation Techniques. LC 80-15233. 536p. 1981. 169.00 (*0-471-08033-0*, Wiley-Interscience) Wiley.

— Introduction to Perturbation Techniques. (Classics Library). 536p. 1993. pap. 69.95 (*0-471-31013-1*) Wiley.

— Methods of Normal Form. LC 92-40113. 232p. 1993. 95.95 (*0-471-59354-0*) Wiley.

***Nayfeh, Ali H.** Nonlinear Interactions: Analytical, Computational, & Experimental Methods. LC 99-86738. 763p. 2000. text 110.00 (*0-471-17591-9*) Wiley.

Nayfeh, Ali H. Perturbation Methods. (Pure & Applied Mathematics: A Wiley-Interscience Series of Texts, Monographs & Tracts). 448p. 1973. 183.95 (*0-471-63059-4*) Wiley.

Nayfeh, Ali H. & Balachandran, Balakumar. Applied Nonlinear Dynamics: Analytical, Computational & Experimental Methods. (Nonlinear Science Ser.). 704p. 1995. 89.95 (*0-471-59348-6*) Wiley.

Nayfeh, Ali H. & Mook, Dean T. Nonlinear Oscillations. LC 78-27102. (Pure & Applied Mathematics: A Wiley-Interscience Series of Texts, Monographs & Tracts). 720p. 1979. 250.00 (*0-471-03555-6*) Wiley.

— Nonlinear Oscillations. LC 78-27102. (Classics Library). 720p. 1995. pap. 76.95 (*0-471-12142-8*) Wiley.

Nayfeh, Munir H. & Clark, C. W., eds. Atomic Excitation & Recombination in External Fields. LC 85-9780. viii, 526p. 1985. text 349.00 (*2-88124-043-7*) Gordon & Breach.

Nayler, G. H. Dictionary of Mechanical Engineering. 4th ed. 462p. 1995. 55.00 (*1-56091-754-7*, R-156) Soc Auto Engineers.

Nayler, G. H. F. Dictionary of Mechanical Engineering. 4th ed. 460p. 1997. pap. text 48.00 (*0-7506-3009-4*) Buttrwrth-Heinemann.

Nayler, W. G. Amlodipine. LC 93-23381. (Illus.). 325p. 1995. 137.00 (*0-387-56698-8*) Spr-Verlag.

— The Endothelins. (Illus.). 208p. 1990. 94.95 (*0-387-52856-3*) Spr-Verlag.

— Second Generation of Calcium Antagonists. (Illus.). xiii, 226p. 1991. 103.00 (*0-387-54215-9*) Spr-Verlag.

Naylor. Construction Project Management & Scheduling. 96p. 1995. teacher ed. 17.95 (*0-8273-5734-6*) Delmar.

— Picking up a Pin for the Lord. 1994. pap. 15.99 (*0-946462-25-9*, Pub. by Evangelical Pr) P & R Pubng.

— Water, Bread & Wine. 1994. pap. 3.99 (*0-946462-17-8*, Pub. by Evangelical Pr) P & R Pubng.

Naylor & Hagger. Paths to Proficiency. 1992. pap. text. write for info. (*0-582-06757-X*, Pub. by Addison-Wesley) Longman.

Naylor, A. R. Tarot Abecedarian: The Treasure House of Images. (Illus.). 160p. 1997. 27.50 (*1-872736-52-1*, Pub. by Mandrake Pr) Holmes Pub.

Naylor, A. R., ed. see Spare, Austin O. & Wallace, William.

***Naylor, A. W. & Sell, G. R.** Linear Operator Theory in Engineering & Science, (Applied Mathematical Sciences Ser.: 40). (Illus.). 664p. 2000. pap. 39.95 (*0-387-95001-X*) Spr-Verlag.

Naylor, A. W. & Sell, George R. Linear Operator Theory in Engineering & Science. (Applied Mathematical Sciences Ser.: Vol. 40). (Illus.). 624p. 1994. 69.95 (*0-387-90748-3*) Spr-Verlag.

Naylor, Anthony, ed. see Crowley, Aleister.

Naylor, B., jt. auth. see Kim, K.

Naylor, B. Phyllis, ed. see Hodges, William N.

***Naylor, Barbara & Clark, Pernell.** The Kid Citation Booklet. 1999. pap. 9.95 (*0-9669248-1-9*) Simply Frnds.

Naylor, Barbara & Clark, Pernell. The Relationship Citation. 1998. pap. 9.95 (*0-9669248-0-0*) Simply Frnds.

An Asterisk (*) at the beginning of an entry indicates that the title is appearing for the first time.

Naylor, C. David. Private Practice, Public Payment: Canadian Medicine & the Politics of Health Insurance, 1911-1966. 320p. (C). 1986. text 65.00 (*0-7735-0557-1*, Pub. by McG-Queens Univ Pr); pap. text 27.95 (*0-7735-0568-7*, Pub. by McG-Queens Univ Pr) CUP Services.

Naylor, C. David, ed. Canadian Health Care & the State: A Century of Evolution. 256p. 1992. pap. 27.95 (*0-7735-0949-6*, Pub. by McG-Queens Univ Pr) CUP Services.

— Canadian Health Care & the State: A Century of Evolution. 200p. 1992. 65.00 (*0-7735-0934-8*, Pub. by McG-Queens Univ Pr) CUP Services.

***Naylor, C. Scott.** Pocket OB/GYN. LC 99-44469. 1999. write for info. (*0-7817-1770-1*, Lippnctt) Lppncott W & W.

Naylor, C. W. God's Will & How to Know It. 1986. pap. 9.99 (*0-88019-200-3*) Schmul Pub Co.

— Heart Talks. 279p. 1982. reprint ed. pap. 5.00 (*0-686-36257-8*) Faith Pub Hse.

Naylor, C. W. The Redemption of Howard Gray. 72p. pap. 2.00 (*0-686-29162-X*) Faith Pub Hse.

Naylor, Charles, jt. auth. see Disch, Thomas M.

Naylor, Chris, jt. auth. see Forsyth, Richard S.

Naylor, Christopher. BBC Polish Phrase Book. (BBC Phrase Bks.). (ENG & POL., Illus.). 288p. 1996. pap. text 5.95 (*0-8442-9159-5*, 91595) NTC Contemp Pub Co.

— BBC Portuguese Phrase Book. (BBC Phrase Bks.). (Illus.). 288p. (Orig.). 1994. pap. 5.95 (*0-8442-9231-1*, 92311) NTC Contemp Pub Co.

— BBC Thai Phrase Book. (BBC Phrase Bks.). (ENG & THA., Illus.). 288p. (Orig.). 1996. pap. text 5.95 (*0-8442-9158-7*, 91587) NTC Contemp Pub Co.

— Greek Handy Dictionary. (BBC Phrase Bks.). (Illus.). 288p. 1994. 5.95 (*0-8442-9226-5*, 92265, Passprt Bks) NTC Contemp Pub Co.

— NTC's Compact Portuguese & English Dictionary. LC 95-35949. (POR., Illus.). 816p. 1995. pap. 19.95 (*0-8442-4691-3*, 46913) NTC Contemp Pub Co.

— Singapore. (Essential Guides Ser.). (Illus.). 128p. 1994. 7.95 (*0-8442-8933-7*, Passprt Bks) NTC Contemp Pub Co.

— Sixteen Short Plays for Young Actors. (Illus.). 226p. (YA). 1996. pap. 16.95 (*0-8442-5133-X*, 5133X, Natl Textbk Co) NTC Contemp Pub Co.

Naylor, Christopher. Speak French. (Speak Ser.). (FRE.). 1995. 59.95 incl. audio (*0-8442-1616-X*, 1616x, Natl Textbk Co) NTC Contemp Pub Co.

Naylor, Christopher. Vox Diccionario Actual de la Lengua Espanola. (SPA., Illus.). 1680p. 1996. 50.00 (*0-8442-7952-8*, 79528) NTC Contemp Pub Co.

— Vox Diccionario de Sinonimos y Antonimos. (SPA.). 672p. 1999. pap. 21.95 (*0-8442-0469-2*, 04692, Natl Textbk Co) NTC Contemp Pub Co.

— Vox Lengua Espanola Sinonimos y Antonimos. (SPA., Illus.). 672p. 1996. 27.95 (*0-8442-7950-1*, 79501) NTC Contemp Pub Co.

— Vox Spanish & English School Dictionary. LC 97-44969. 688p. 1997. 12.95 (*0-8442-7975-7*); pap. 8.95 (*0-8442-7976-5*) NTC Contemp Pub Co.

***Naylor, Clare.** Catching Alice. 2000. pap. 14.00 (*0-449-00557-7*, Ballantine) Ballantine Pub Grp.

Naylor, Clare. Love: A User's Guide. LC 98-49247. 1999. pap. 12.95 (*0-449-00556-9*) Fawcett.

***Naylor, Cliff & Hannan, Monica.** Dakota Day Trips: Discovering North Dakota's Hidden Treasures. (Illus.). 168p. 1999. pap. 10.95 (*0-9675758-0-X*) N D Dept of Tour.

Naylor, Colin, ed. Contemporary Artists. 3rd ed. 1989. 149.00 (*0-912289-96-1*) St James Pr.

— Contemporary Designers. 2nd ed. (Illus.). 641p. 1990. 155.00 (*0-912289-69-4*) St James Pr.

— Contemporary Masterworks. (Illus.). 933p. 1991. 160.00 (*1-55862-083-4*, 200104) St James Pr.

— Contemporary Photographers. 2nd ed. 1988. 145.00 (*0-912289-79-1*) St James Pr.

Naylor, D. Geology of Offshore Ireland & West Britain. Shannon, P. M., ed. 174p. 1982. pap. text 58.00 (*0-86010-430-3*); lib. bdg. 108.00 (*0-86010-340-4*) G & T Inc.

— Thinking about Buddhism LC 76-372774. (World Religions Ser.). 56p. 1976. write for info. (*0-7188-2158-0*) Lutterwrth.

Naylor, D. & Mounteney, S. N. Geology of the North-West European Continental Shelf. LC 75-329129. 1975. 6.50 (*0-86010-009-X*) G & T Inc.

Naylor, D., jt. auth. see Duff, George F.

Naylor, D., jt. auth. see Shannon, P. M.

Naylor, David, et al. Coronary Artery Bypass Graft Surgery & Percutaneous Transluminal Coronary Angioplasty: Ratings of Appropriateness & Necessity by a Canadian Panel. LC 93-33095. 1993. pap. text 15.00 (*0-8330-1452-8*, MR-128-CWF) Rand Corp.

Naylor, David, jt. auth. see Dillon, Jim.

Naylor, David, jt. auth. see Oosthuizen, P. H.

***Naylor, Doug.** Red Dwarf VIII: The Official Book. (Illus.). 192p. 2000. 19.95 (*1-85227-872-2*) Virgin Pubng.

Naylor, Edward W. An Elizabethan Virginal Book. LC 70-87638. (Music Ser.). 1970. reprint ed. lib. bdg. 35.00 (*0-306-71792-1*) Da Capo.

— The Poets & Music. LC 80-16489. (Music Reprint Ser.). 1980. reprint ed. 29.50 (*0-306-76038-X*) Da Capo.

— Shakespeare & Music. LC 06-1277. reprint ed. 20.00 (*0-404-04652-5*) AMS Pr.

— Shakespeare & Music. 2nd ed. LC 65-16244. (Illus.). 1972. reprint ed. 26.95 (*0-405-08814-0*) Ayer.

Naylor, Edward W., tr. see Bie, Oskar.

Naylor, Eric W., ed. The Text & Concordances of the Escorial Manuscript of the Arcipreste de Talavera of Alfonso Martinez de Toledo. (Spanish Ser.: No. 12). 6p. 1983. 10.00 incl. fiche (*0-942260-38-4*) Hispanic Seminary.

Naylor, Eric W., jt. auth. see Benson, Robert G.

Naylor, Eric W., ed. see De Avinon, Juan.

Naylor, Genevieve, jt. auth. see Levine, Robert M.

Naylor, Geoffrey, jt. auth. see McIver, Colin.

Naylor, Gloria. Bailey's Cafe. LC 91-42089. 229p. 1992. 19.95 (*0-15-110450-6*) Harcourt.

— Bailey's Cafe. LC 93-13117. (Vintage Contemporaries Ser.). 240p. 1993. pap. 12.00 (*0-679-74821-0*) Vin Bks.

— Bailey's Cafe. large type ed. LC 93-9846. 333p. 1993. pap. 17.95 (*0-8161-5720-0*, G K Hall Lrg Type) Mac Lib Ref.

— Linden Hills. (Contemporay American Fiction Ser.). 320p. 1986. pap. 12.95 (*0-14-008829-6*, Penguin Bks) Viking Penguin.

— Mama Day. 320p. 1988. 17.95 (*0-89919-716-7*, Pub. by Ticknor & Fields) HM.

— Mama Day. (Contemporaries Ser.). 320p. 1993. pap. 13.00 (*0-679-72181-9*) Vin Bks.

— Mama Day. 1993. pap. 10.00 (*0-394-25625-5*) Vin Bks.

— The Men of Brewster Place. 1998. 26.00 (*0-8050-5482-0*) H Holt & Co.

— The Men of Brewster Place. LC 97-45987. 173p. (J). 1998. 22.45 (*0-7868-6421-4*, Pub. by Hyperion) Time Warner.

***Naylor, Gloria.** The Men of Brewster Place. LC 99-18709. 1999. 25.95 (*1-56895-712-2*) Wheeler Pub.

Naylor, Gloria. The Men of Brewster Place: A Novel. 192p. 1999. pap. 11.95 (*0-7868-8405-3*, Pub. by Disney Pr) Time Warner.

— Selected from The Women of Brewster Place. abr. ed. (Writers' Voices Ser.). 64p. (Orig.). 1991. pap. text 3.95 (*0-929631-33-1*, Signal Hill) New Readers.

— Short Story, Vol. 2. 592p. 1997. pap. 14.95 (*0-316-59923-9*) Little.

— The Women of Brewster Place: A Novel in Seven Stories. (Contemporay American Fiction Ser.). 208p. 1983. pap. 11.95 (*0-14-006690-X*, Penguin Bks) Viking Penguin.

— The Women of Brewster Place: A Novel in Seven Stories. 1988. pap. 4.50 (*0-318-37688-1*, Penguin Bks) Viking Penguin.

Naylor, Gloria, ed. Children of the Night: The Best Short Stories by Black Writers, 1967 to the Present. LC 95-16356. 592p. (gr. 8). 1996. 24.95 (*0-316-59926-3*) Little.

Naylor, Grant. Red Dwarf: Better Than Life, Vol. 2. 304p. (Orig.). 1993. mass mkt. 5.99 (*0-451-45231-3*, ROC) NAL.

— Red Dwarf: Infinity Welcomes Careful Drivers. 304p. 1992. mass mkt. 5.99 (*0-451-45201-1*, ROC) NAL.

Naylor, Greg. A Supervisor's Guide to Preventing Sexual Harassment. LC 96-2807. 94p. 1996. spiral bd. 37.00 (*0-925773-26-3*) M Lee Smith.

Naylor, Harriet H. The Role of the Volunteer Director in the Care of the Terminal Patient & the Family. 1981. 19.95 (*0-405-13092-9*) Ayer.

— The Role of the Volunteer in the Care of the Terminal Patient & the Family. 1981. 17.95 (*0-405-13091-0*) Ayer.

Naylor, Helen & Murphy, Raymond. Essential Grammar in Use: Supplementary Exercises Edition Without Key. 100p. (J). 1997. pap. text, wbk. ed. 7.50 (*0-521-46998-8*) Cambridge U Pr.

Naylor, Henry F. Construction Project Management: Planning & Scheduling. 304p. (C). 1995. pap. 93.95 (*0-8273-5733-8*) Delmar.

Naylor, Honey. Insider's Guide to New Orleans. Rosenberg, Dan, ed. LC 93-41742. (Insider's Guide Ser.). (Illus.). 240p. (Orig.). 1994. pap. 9.95 (*1-55832-063-6*) Harvard Common Pr.

Naylor, J. Marketing. 1985. 60.00 (*0-85297-071-4*, Pub. by Chartered Bank) St Mut.

— Practical Theory of Tanning Leather, 1890-1987. (Illus.). 150p. 1991. pap. 20.00 (*0-87556-359-7*) Saifer.

Naylor, James. The New Democracy: Challenging the Social Order in Industrial Ontario, 1914-1925. 288p. 1992. text 55.00 (*0-8020-5953-8*); pap. text 18.95 (*0-8020-6886-3*) U of Toronto Pr.

Naylor, James B. Under Mad Anthony's Banner. 1993. reprint ed. lib. bdg. 89.00 (*0-7812-5393-4*) Rprt Serv.

Naylor, Jay H., jt. auth. see Jensen, Clayne R.

Naylor, John & Senior, Barbara. Incompressible Unemployment: Cause, Consequences & Alternatives. 214p. 1988. text 54.95 (*0-566-05530-9*, Pub. by Avebry) Ashgate Pub Co.

Naylor, John, jt. auth. see Senoir, Barbara.

Naylor, Joseph, ed. see Johnson, Vera H.

Naylor, Keith, jt. auth. see St. Clair, Barry.

Naylor, Kim. Discovery Guide to Rajasthan with Delhi & Agra. 224p. (C). 1995. pap. 39.00 (*0-902743-49-X*, Pub. by IMMEL Pubng) St Mut.

— Discovery Guide to Vietnam. 272p. (C). 1994. pap. 50.00 (*0-907151-71-X*, Pub. by IMMEL Pubng) St Mut.

— Discovery Guide to West Africa: The Niger & Gambia River Route. 224p. (C). 1995. pap. 50.00 (*0-902743-67-8*, Pub. by IMMEL Pubng) St Mut.

Naylor, Kim & Mendoza, David. Discovery Guide to Outer Mongolia. 240p. 1995. pap. 45.00 (*1-898162-95-6*, Pub. by IMMEL Pubng) St Mut.

Naylor, Larry L. American Culture: Myth & Reality of a Culture of Diversity. LC 97-31519. 184p. 1998. 55.00 (*0-89789-541-X*, Bergin & Garvey); pap. 19.95 (*0-89789-542-8*, Bergin & Garvey) Greenwood.

— Cultural Diversity in the United States. LC 96-26936. 392p. 1997. 69.50 (*0-89789-478-2*, Bergin & Garvey); pap. 25.95 (*0-89789-479-0*, Bergin & Garvey) Greenwood.

— Culture & Change: An Introduction. LC 95-36904. 256p. 1996. 69.50 (*0-89789-464-2*, Bergin & Garvey); pap. 24.95 (*0-89789-465-0*, Bergin & Garvey) Greenwood.

Naylor, Larry L., ed. Problems & Issues of Diversity in the United States. LC 98-41383. 232p. 1999. 65.00 (*0-89789-615-7*, Bergin & Garvey); pap. 22.95 (*0-89789-616-5*, Bergin & Garvey) Greenwood.

Naylor, Lynne. Television Writer's Guide. 4th ed. 1995. pap. text 50.00 (*0-943728-75-4*) Lone Eagle Pub.

Naylor, Lynne, ed. 1999 Television Writers Guide. 5th ed. 608p. 1999. pap. 55.00 (*0-943728-86-X*) Lone Eagle Pub.

— Television Directors Guide. 3rd ed. 350p. 1996. pap. 45.00 (*0-943728-76-2*) Lone Eagle Pub.

Naylor, Magdalena R., jt. auth. see Naylor, Phyllis Reynolds.

Naylor, Maria, ed. Authentic Indian Designs. LC 74-17711. (Illus.). 219p. 1975. reprint ed. pap. 11.95 (*0-486-23170-4*) Dover.

Naylor, Maria K., ed. The National Academy of Design Exhibition Record, 1861-1900. 1075p. 1973. 110.00 (*0-87920-055-3*) Kennedy Gall.

Naylor, Murray. Among Friends: The Scots Guards, 1956-1993. (Illus.). 284p. 1995. 32.95 (*0-85052-455-5*, Pub. by Leo Cooper) Trans-Atl Phila.

Naylor, N., ed. Marketing. (C). 1989. 40.00 (*0-85297-175-3*, Pub. by Chartered Bank) St Mut.

Naylor, N., jt. ed. see McIver, M.

Naylor, Natalie A., ed. The Roots & Heritage of Hempstead Town. LC 94-77120. (Illus.). 256p. 1994. 25.00 (*1-55787-124-8*, 71063); pap. 15.00 (*1-55787-109-4*, 71064) Hrt of the Lakes.

Naylor, Natalie A., et al, eds. Theodore Roosevelt: Many-Sided American. (Long Island Studies). (Illus.). 678p. 1992. lib. bdg. 55.00 (*1-55787-085-3*, NY71048) Hrt of the Lakes.

Naylor, Natalie A. & Murphy, Maureen O., eds. Long Island Women: Activists & Innovators. (Illus.). 340p. 1998. 38.00 (*1-55787-151-5*, NY71067); pap. 20.00 (*1-55787-150-7*, NY71067) Hrt of the Lakes.

Naylor, Natalie A., et al. Long Island's History & Cultural Heritage: An Integrative Curriculum Resource for Educators. LC 92-63132. (Illus.). 70p. 1992. pap. 7.00 (*0-943526-23-X*) Parrish Art.

Naylor, Natalie A., jt. ed. see Krieg, Joann P.

Naylor, Patrick. Introduction to Metal Ceramic Technology. (Illus.). 196p. 1992. text 72.00 (*0-86715-237-0*) Quint Pub Co.

Naylor, Paul. Poetic Investigations: Singing the Holes in History. LC 99-29032. (Avant-Garde & Modernism Studies). 222p. 1999. pap. 19.95 (*0-8101-1668-5*) Northwestern U Pr.

— Poetic Investigations: Singing the Holes in History. LC 99-29032. 208p. 1999. 59.95 (*0-8101-1667-7*) Northwestern U Pr.

Naylor, Peter. Discovering Dowsing & Divining. 1980. pap. 4.50 (*0-913714-54-2*) Shire Pubns.

— Discovering Dowsing & Divining. (Handbook Ser.: No. 251). (Illus.). 40p. 1989. pap. 30.00 (*0-85263-516-8*, Pub. by Shire Pubns) Parkwest Pubns.

— I Corinthians. 368p. (Orig.). 1996. pap. 19.99 (*0-85234-350-7*, Pub. by Evangelical Pr) P & R Pubng.

Naylor, Phillip C. & Heggoy, Alf A. The Historical Dictionary of Algeria. 2nd ed. LC 93-26302. (African Historical Dictionaries Ser.: No. 59). 488p. 1994. 64.00 (*0-8108-2748-4*) Scarecrow.

Naylor, Phyllis Reynolds. Achingly Alice. LC 97-12430. (Alice Ser.). 128p. (YA). (gr. 5-8). 1999. mass mkt. 4.50 (*0-689-80595-0*, 076714004504) Aladdin.

— The Agony of Alice. LC 85-7957. (Alice Ser.). 144p. (YA). (gr. 3-7). 1997. mass mkt. 3.99 (*0-689-81672-3*) Aladdin.

— The Agony of Alice. LC 85-7957. (Alice Ser.). 144p. (YA). (gr. 5-8). 1985. 16.00 (*0-689-31143-5*) Atheneum Yung Read.

Naylor, Phyllis Reynolds. The Agony of Alice. (Alice Ser.). (YA). (gr. 5-8). 1997. 9.09 (*0-606-12160-9*, Pub. by Turtleback) Demco.

Naylor, Phyllis Reynolds. Alice in April. LC 92-17016. (Alice Ser.). 176p. (YA). (gr. 5-8). 1993. 15.00 (*0-689-31805-7*) Atheneum Yung Read.

— Alice in April. (Alice Ser.). (YA). (gr. 5-8). 1994. pap. 4.50 (*0-440-91032-3*) BDD Bks Young Read.

— Alice in April. (Alice Ser.). 176p. (YA). (gr. 4-7). 1995. pap. 3.99 (*0-440-40944-6*) Dell.

Naylor, Phyllis Reynolds. Alice in April. (Alice Ser.). (YA). (gr. 5-8). 1995. 9.09 (*0-606-07181-4*, Pub. by Turtleback) Demco.

Naylor, Phyllis Reynolds. Alice In-Between. LC 93-8167. (Alice Ser.). 160p. (YA). (gr. 5-8). 1994. 15.00 (*0-689-31890-1*) Atheneum Yung Read.

— Alice In-Between. LC 00-5643. (Alice Ser.). 160p. (YA). (gr. 4-7). 1996. pap. 4.50 (*0-440-41064-9*) Dell.

Naylor, Phyllis Reynolds. Alice In-Between. (Alice Ser.). (YA). (gr. 5-8). 1996. 9.09 (*0-606-08976-4*, Pub. by Turtleback) Demco.

Naylor, Phyllis Reynolds. Alice In-Between. (Alice Ser.). (YA). (gr. 5-8). reprint ed. pap. 3.99 (*0-614-15577-0*, YB BDD) BDD Bks Young Read.

— Alice in Lace. LC 95-30903. (Alice Ser.). 144p. (YA). (gr. 4-8). 1997. per. 3.99 (*0-689-80597-7*) Aladdin.

— Alice in Lace. LC 95-30903. (Alice Ser.). 144p. (J). (gr. 5-8). 1996. 15.00 (*0-689-80358-3*) Atheneum Yung Read.

Naylor, Phyllis Reynolds. Alice in Lace. (Alice Ser.). (YA). (gr. 5-8). 1997. 9.09 (*0-606-13114-0*, Pub. by Turtleback) Demco.

Naylor, Phyllis Reynolds. Alice in Rapture, Sort Of. LC 88-8174. (Alice Ser.). 176p. (YA). (gr. 4-7). 1991. pap. 4.50 (*0-440-40462-2*) Aladdin.

— Alice in Rapture, Sort Of. LC 88-8174. (Alice Ser.). 176p. (YA). (gr. 5-8). 1989. lib. bdg. 16.00 (*0-689-31466-3*) Atheneum Yung Read.

— Alice in Rapture, Sort Of. (Alice Ser.). (YA). (gr. 5-8). 1989. 8.60 (*0-606-04858-8*, Pub. by Turtleback) Demco.

— Alice on the Outside. (Alice Ser.). (YA). (gr. 5-8). 2000. per. 3.95 (*0-689-80594-2*) Aladdin.

— Alice on the Outside. LC 98-7992. (Alice Ser.). 176p. (YA). (gr. 5-8). 1999. lib. bdg. 15.00 (*0-689-80359-1*) Atheneum Yung Read.

— Alice the Brave. LC 94-32340. (Alice Ser.). 144p. (YA). (gr. 5-8). 1997. 15.00 (*0-689-80095-9*) Atheneum Yung Read.

— Alice the Brave. LC 94-32340. (Alice Ser.). 144p. (YA). (ps-3). 1996. per. 3.99 (*0-689-80598-5*) S&S Childrens.

— Alice the Brave. (Alice Ser.). (YA). (gr. 5-8). 1995. 9.09 (*0-606-10737-1*, Pub. by Turtleback) Demco.

— All but Alice. LC 91-28722. (Alice Ser.). 128p. (YA). (gr. 5-8). 1992. 14.00 (*0-689-31773-5*) Atheneum Yung Read.

— All but Alice. LC 91-28722. (Alice Ser.). 160p. (YA). (gr. 4-7). 1994. pap. 3.99 (*0-440-40918-7*) Dell.

— All but Alice. (Alice Ser.). (YA). (gr. 5-8). 1992. 9.09 (*0-606-06172-X*, Pub. by Turtleback) Demco.

— An Amish Family. 20.95 (*0-8488-0109-1*) Amereon Ltd.

— Beetles, Lightly Toasted. LC 87-911. 144p. (J). (gr. 3-7). 1987. 16.00 (*0-689-31355-1*) Atheneum Yung Read.

— Beetles, Lightly Toasted. (J). 1987. 9.09 (*0-606-04127-3*, Pub. by Turtleback) Demco.

— Beetles, Lightly Toasted. 144p. (J). (gr. k-6). 1989. reprint ed. pap. 4.50 (*0-440-40143-7*, YB BDD) BDD Bks Young Read.

— Being Danny's Dog. LC 95-5280. 160p. (J). (gr. 3-7). 1995. 15.00 (*0-689-31756-5*) Atheneum Yung Read.

— Being Danny's Dog. LC 95-5280. (Illus.). 160p. (J). 1997. per. 3.99 (*0-689-81472-0*) Atheneum Yung Read.

— Being Danny's Dog. 1997. 9.09 (*0-606-11105-0*, Pub. by Turtleback) Demco.

— Bernie & the Bessledorf Ghost. LC 88-29389. (Bessledorf Mysteries Ser.). 144p. (J). (gr. 3-7). 1990. 15.00 (*0-689-31499-X*) Atheneum Yung Read.

— Bernie & the Bessledorf Ghost. 144p. (J). 1992. pap. 3.50 (*0-380-71351-9*, Avon Bks) Morrow Avon.

— The Bodies in the Bessledorf Hotel. LC 86-3602. 144p. (J). (gr. 3-7). 1986. lib. bdg. 15.00 (*0-689-31304-7*) Atheneum Yung Read.

— The Bodies in the Bessledorf Hotel. 112p. 1988. pap. 2.99 (*0-380-70485-4*, Avon Bks) Morrow Avon.

— The Bomb in the Bessledorf Bus Depot. LC 95-30295. 144p. (J). (gr. 3-7). 1997. per. 3.99 (*0-689-80599-3*) Aladdin.

— The Bomb in the Bessledorf Bus Depot. 1997. 9.09 (*0-606-11147-6*, Pub. by Turtleback) Demco.

— The Bomb in the Bessledorf Bus Depot: Is There a Bomber in the Magruder Family? Bernie Magruder Is Afraid There May Be. LC 95-30295. 144p. (J). (gr. 3-7). 1996. 15.00 (*0-689-80461-X*) Atheneum Yung Read.

— The Boy with the Helium Head. (Illus.). 64p. (J). (ps-4). 1998. pap. 4.50 (*0-440-41498-9*) BDD Bks Young Read.

— Boy with the Helium Head. 1998. 9.70 (*0-606-13224-4*, Pub. by Turtleback) Demco.

— Boys Against Girls. (J). 1995. pap. 4.99 (*0-440-91052-8*) BDD Bks Young Read.

— Boys Against Girls. 160p. (J). (gr. 3-7). 1995. pap. 4.99 (*0-440-41123-8*, YB BDD) BDD Bks Young Read.

— Boys Against Girls. LC 93-37683. (Illus.). 160p. (J). 1994. 14.95 (*0-385-32081-7*) Delacorte.

— Boys Against Girls. (J). 1995. 18.95 (*0-385-30982-1*) Doubleday.

***Naylor, Phyllis Reynolds.** Boys Against Girls. (Illus.). (J). (gr. 4-7). 2000. mass mkt. 2.99 (*0-375-80673-3*, Pub. by Random Bks Yng Read) Random.

Naylor, Phyllis Reynolds. Boys Against Girls. LC 93-37683. 1995. 9.60 (*0-606-09101-7*, Pub. by Turtleback) Demco.

— The Boys Start the War. (J). 1994. pap. 6.50 (*0-440-91026-9*) BDD Bks Young Read.

— The Boys Start the War: The Girls Get Even. LC 92-249. (J). 1993. 11.09 (*0-606-06248-3*, Pub. by Turtleback) Demco.

— The Boys Start the War - The Girls Get Even. LC 92-249. 272p. (J). (gr. 3-7). 1994. pap. 5.99 (*0-440-40971-3*) Dell.

— Danny's Desert Rats. 144p. (J). 1999. per. 4.50 (*0-689-83133-1*) Aladdin.

— Danny's Desert Rats. LC 97-28006. 144p. (J). (gr. 5 up). 1998. 16.00 (*0-689-81776-2*) S&S Childrens.

— Ducks Disappearing. LC 95-10281. (Illus.). 32p. (J). (gr. k-3). 1997. 13.00 (*0-689-31902-9*) S&S Bks Yung.

— Eddie, Incorporated. LC 79-22589. (Illus.). 112p. (J). (gr. 4-6). 1980. text 15.00 (*0-689-30754-3*) Atheneum Yung Read.

— The Face in the Bessledorf Funeral Parlor. LC 92-32613. 160p. (J). (gr. 3-7). 1993. 14.00 (*0-689-31802-2*) Atheneum Yung Read.

— The Face in the Bessledorf Funeral Parlor. LC 92-32613. 160p. (J). (gr. 3-7). 1995. mass mkt. 4.50 (*0-689-80603-5*) S&S Childrens.

— Face in the Bessledorf Funeral Parlor. 1995. 9.05 (*0-606-07494-5*, Pub. by Turtleback) Demco.

— The Fear Place. LC 93-38891. 128p. (J). (gr. 4-7). 1996. per. 3.95 (*0-689-80442-3*) Aladdin.

— The Fear Place. LC 93-38891. 128p. (J). (gr. 3-7). 1994. 16.00 (*0-689-31866-9*) Atheneum Yung Read.

— The Fear Plance. LC 93-38891. 1996. 9.05 (*0-606-09269-2*, Pub. by Turtleback) Demco.

— The Girls' Revenge. LC 97-44156. 160p. (J). (gr. 3-6). 1998. 15.95 (*0-385-32334-4*) BDD Bks Young Read.

***Naylor, Phyllis Reynolds.** The Girls' Revenge. 176p. 1999. pap. 4.99 (*0-440-41383-4*) Bantam.

N

Naylor, Phyllis Reynolds. The Grand Escape. LC 91-40816. (Illus.). 144p. (J). (gr. 3-7). 1993. 15.00 (*0-689-31722-0*) Atheneum Yung Read.

— The Grand Escape. 160p. (J). 1994. pap. 4.99 (*0-440-40968-3*) Dell.

Naylor, Phyllis Reynolds. The Grand Escape. (J). 1993. 10.09 (*0-606-06991-7*, Pub. by Turtleback) Demco.

— The Grooming of Alice. LC 99-32184. (Alice Ser.). (Illus.). 224p. (YA). (gr. 5-8). 2000. 16.00 (*0-689-82633-8*) Atheneum Yung Read.

Naylor, Phyllis Reynolds. The Healing of Texas Jake. LC 96-22025. (Illus.). 128p. (J). (gr. 4-6). 1998. per. 3.99 (*0-689-82243-X*) Aladdin.

— The Healing of Texas Jake. LC 96-22025. (Illus.). 128p. (J). (gr. 3-7). 1997. 15.00 (*0-689-81124-1*) Atheneum Yung Read.

— How I Came to Be a Writer. LC 86-32283. (Illus.). 144p. (J). (gr. 4 up). 1987. reprint ed. mass mkt. 4.95 (*0-689-71129-8*) Aladdin.

— I Can't Take You Anywhere. LC 96-7768. (Illus.). 32p. (J). (ps-4). 1997. 15.00 (*0-689-31966-5*) S&S Bks Yung.

— Ice. 224p. (J). (gr. 7 up). 1998. per. 4.50 (*0-689-81872-6*) Aladdin.

— Ice. LC 95-5279. 208p. (J). (gr. 4-9). 1995. 16.00 (*0-689-80005-3*) Atheneum Yung Read.

— Ice. (J). 1998. 9.60 (*0-606-12970-7*, Pub. by Turtleback) Demco.

— Jade Green. (J). 2001. per. 4.50 (*0-689-82002-X*) S&S Childrens.

— Jade Green: A Ghost Story. LC PZ7.N24Jad 2000. 176p. (J). (gr. 5-8). 2000. 16.00 (*0-689-82005-4*) S&S Childrens.

— Josie's Troubles. LC 90-47641. (Illus.). 112p. (J). (gr. 3-7). 1992. text, lib. bdg. 13.95 (*0-689-31659-3*) Atheneum Yung Read.

— The Keeper. LC 85-20029. 228p. (YA). (gr. 5 up). 1986. 16.00 (*0-689-31204-0*) Atheneum Yung Read.

— Keeping a Christmas Secret. LC 88-29277. (Illus.). 32p. (J). (ps-2). 1989. 15.00 (*0-689-31447-7*) Atheneum Yung Read.

— Keeping a Christmas Secret. (J). 1993. 10.15 (*0-606-05391-3*, Pub. by Turtleback) Demco.

— Keeping a Christmas Secret. LC 93-12248. (Illus.). 32p. (J). (gr. k-2). 1993. reprint ed. mass mkt. 4.95 (*0-689-71760-1*) Aladdin.

— King of the Playground. (Illus.). 32p. (J). (ps-3). 1991. 16.00 (*0-689-31558-9*) Atheneum Yung Read.

— King of the Playground. (J). 1994. 10.15 (*0-606-05901-6*, Pub. by Turtleback) Demco.

— King of the Playground. LC 93-25125. (Illus.). 32p. (J). (ps-3). 1994. reprint ed. mass mkt. 5.99 (*0-689-71802-0*) Aladdin.

— The Mad Gasser of Bessledorf Street. 112p. (J). 1992. pap. 3.50 (*0-380-71350-0*, Avon Bks) Morrow Avon.

— Night Cry. LC 83-15569. 168p. (J). (gr. 5-9). 1984. 16.00 (*0-689-31017-X*) Atheneum Yung Read.

— Night Cry. 160p. (J). (gr. 4-7). 1993. pap. 3.99 (*0-440-40017-1*, YB BDD) BDD Bks Young Read.

— Night Cry. 1988. 9.09 (*0-606-12450-0*, Pub. by Turtleback) Demco.

— Old Sadie & the Christmas Bear. LC 84-2995. (Illus.). 32p. (J). (ps-2). 1984. 15.00 (*0-689-31052-8*) Atheneum Yung Read.

— One of the Third Grade Thinkers. LC 88-3130. (Illus.). 144p. (J). (gr. 3-7). 1988. 15.00 (*0-689-31424-8*) Atheneum Yung Read.

— One of the Third Grade Thinkers. LC 88-3130. 144p. (J). (gr. 4-7). 1991. pap. 4.50 (*0-440-40407-X*) Dell.

— One of the Third Grade Thinkers. (J). 1988. 8.60 (*0-606-04763-8*, Pub. by Turtleback) Demco.

— Outrageously Alice. LC 96-7744. (Alice Ser.). 144p. (YA). (gr. 4-8). 1998. per. 3.99 (*0-689-80596-9*) Aladdin.

— Outrageously Alice. LC 96-7744. (Alice Ser.). 144p. (YA). (gr. 5-8). 1997. 15.00 (*0-689-80354-0*) Atheneum Yung Read.

***Naylor, Phyllis Reynolds.** Peril in the Bessledorf Parachute Factory. LC 98-36606. 160p. (J). (gr. 4-6). 2000. 16.00 (*0-689-82539-0*) Atheneum Yung Read.

— Reluctantly Alice. (Alice Ser.). (YA). (gr. 5-8). 2000. 3.99 (*0-689-81688-X*) Aladdin.

Naylor, Phyllis Reynolds. Reluctantly Alice. LC 90-37956. (Alice Ser.). 192p. (YA). (gr. 5-8). 1991. 15.00 (*0-689-31681-X*) Atheneum Yung Read.

— Sang Spell. (Illus.). 224p. (YA). (gr. 6-12). 2000. per. 4.50 (*0-689-82006-2*) Aladdin.

— Sang Spell. LC 97-34067. 192p. (J). (gr. 7 up). 1998. 16.00 (*0-689-82007-0*) Atheneum Yung Read.

Naylor, Phyllis Reynolds. Sang Spell. 224p. (YA). (gr. 5 up). pap. 4.99 (*0-8072-8294-4*) Listening Lib.

Naylor, Phyllis Reynolds. Saving Shiloh. LC 96-37373. 144p. (J). (gr. 3-7). 1997. 15.00 (*0-689-81460-7*) Atheneum Yung Read.

— Saving Shiloh. 144p. (J). (gr. 3-7). 1999. reprint ed. per. 4.50 (*0-689-81461-5*) S&S Childrens.

— Send No Blessings. LC 89-28024. 240p. (YA). (gr. 7 up). 1990. 16.00 (*0-689-31582-1*) Atheneum Yung Read.

— Send No Blessings. 1992. 10.09 (*0-606-00744-X*, Pub. by Turtleback) Demco.

— Shiloh. LC 90-603. 144p. (J). (gr. 3-7). 1991. 15.00 (*0-689-31614-3*) Atheneum Yung Read.

Naylor, Phyllis Reynolds. Shiloh. (J). 1992. pap. 3.50 (*0-440-80297-0*) BDD Bks Young Read.

Naylor, Phyllis Reynolds. Shiloh. 160p. (J). (gr. 3-7). 1992. pap. 5.50 (*0-440-40752-4*, YB BDD) BDD Bks Young Read.

Naylor, Phyllis Reynolds. Shiloh. 144p. (J). (gr. 3-5). pap. 4.99 (*0-8072-8330-4*) Listening Lib.

— Shiloh. (J). 1991. 10.09 (*0-606-01016-5*, Pub. by Turtleback) Demco.

Naylor, Phyllis Reynolds. Shiloh. large type ed. (J). 1993. 38.50 (*0-614-09869-6*, L-15921-00) Am Printing Hse.

***Naylor, Phyllis Reynolds.** Shiloh. large type ed. (LRS Large Print Cornerstone Ser.). 155p. (YA). (gr. 4-10). 2000. lib. bdg. 27.95 (*1-58118-058-6*, 23472) LRS.

Naylor, Phyllis Reynolds. Shiloh Season. 128p. (J). (gr. 3-7). 1998. per. 4.50 (*0-689-80646-9*) Aladdin.

***Naylor, Phyllis Reynolds.** Shiloh Season. (2000 Kids Picks Ser.). (J). (gr. 4-7). 2000. per. 2.99 (*0-689-83862-X*) Aladdin.

Naylor, Phyllis Reynolds. Shiloh Season. LC 95-32558. 128p. (J). (gr. 3-7). 1996. 15.00 (*0-689-80647-7*) Atheneum Yung Read.

— Shiloh Season. (J). 1998. 9.60 (*0-606-13085-3*, Pub. by Turtleback) Demco.

— Shiloh Season: Video Tie-In Edition. LC 95-32558. (Illus.). 128p. (J). (gr. 3-7). 1999. mass mkt. 4.50 (*0-689-82931-0*) Aladdin.

— Shiloh Trilogy. (J). (gr. 3-7). 1998. 35.00 (*0-689-82327-4*) Atheneum Yung Read.

***Naylor, Phyllis Reynolds.** A Spy among the Girls. LC 99-87931. (Illus.). 144p. (J). (gr. 4-7). 2000. 15.95 (*0-385-32336-0*) Delacorte.

Naylor, Phyllis Reynolds. Sweet Strawberries. LC 97-48411. (Illus.). 40p. (J). 1999. 16.00 (*0-689-81338-4*) S&S Childrens.

— To Walk the Sky Path. 1973. 9.09 (*0-606-00896-9*, Pub. by Turtleback) Demco.

— To Walk the Skypath. 144p. (J). (gr. 4-7). 1992. pap. 4.50 (*0-440-40636-6*, YB BDD) BDD Bks Young Read.

***Naylor, Phyllis Reynolds.** A Traitor Among the Boys. 144p. 2001. pap. 4.99 (*0-440-41386-9*) BDD Bks Young Read.

Naylor, Phyllis Reynolds. A Traitor Among the Boys. LC 98-54630. 144p. 1999. 15.95 (*0-385-32335-2*) Bantam.

— The Treasure of Bessledorf Hill. 144p. (J). 1999. per. 4.50 (*0-689-81856-4*) Aladdin.

— The Treasure of Bessledorf Hill. LC 96-30514. 136p. (J). (gr. 4-6). 1998. 15.00 (*0-689-81337-6*) Atheneum Yung Read.

***Naylor, Phyllis Reynolds.** Walker's Crossing. LC 98-50217. (Illus.). 240p. (YA). (gr. 7 up). 1999. 16.00 (*0-689-82939-6*) Atheneum Yung Read.

Naylor, Phyllis Reynolds. Witch Returns. (J). 1992. 8.60 (*0-606-05707-2*, Pub. by Turtleback) Demco.

— Witch Water. (J). 1977. 8.60 (*0-606-03957-0*, Pub. by Turtleback) Demco.

Naylor, Phyllis Reynolds & Naylor, Magdalena R. Achingly Alice. LC 97-12430. (Alice Ser.). 128p. (YA). (gr. 5-8). 1998. 15.00 (*0-689-80355-9*) Atheneum Yung Read.

Naylor, Phyllis Reynolds & Reynolds, Lura Schield. Maudie in the Middle. LC 87-3470. (Illus.). 176p. (J). (gr. 2-6). 1988. lib. bdg. 16.00 (*0-689-31395-0*) Atheneum Yung Read.

Naylor, R. H. Home Astrology: A Non-Technical Outline of Popular Astrology Tradition (1920) 222p. 1998. reprint ed. pap. 17.95 (*0-7661-0493-1*) Kessinger Pub.

Naylor, R. T. Bankers, Bagmen & Bandits: Business & Politics in the Age of Greed. LC 90-83630. 250p. (Orig.). (C). 1990. 47.99 (*0-921689-77-2*, Pub. by Black Rose); pap. 18.99 (*0-921689-76-4*, Pub. by Black Rose) Consort Bk Sales.

— Dominion of Debt: Centre, Periphery & the International Economic Order. 227p. 1985. 47.99 (*0-920057-51-9*, 1985, Pub. by Black Rose); pap. 18.99 (*0-920057-50-0*, Pub. by Black Rose) Consort Bk Sales.

— The History of Canadian Business 1867-1914. 2nd rev. ed. 660p. Date not set. 57.99 (*1-55164-065-1*, Pub. by Black Rose); pap. 28.99 (*1-55164-064-3*, Pub. by Black Rose) Consort Bk Sales.

— Hot Money: The Politics of Debt. 504p. (Orig.). 1990. pap. text 12.95 (*0-04-440188-4*) Routledge.

— Hot Money & the Politics of Debt. 2nd ed. LC 94-71245. 532p. 1994. 48.99 (*1-895431-95-6*, Pub. by Black Rose); pap. 19.99 (*1-895431-94-8*, Pub. by Black Rose) Consort Bk Sales.

***Naylor, Rachel.** Ghana. (Country Profiles Ser.: No. 20). (Illus.). 80p. 2000. pap. 9.95 (*0-85598-431-7*, Pub. by Oxfam Pub) Stylus Pub VA.

Naylor, Rachel, jt. auth. see Van Der Linde, Ada.

Naylor, Robert A. Influencia Britanica en el Comercio Centroamericano durante las Primeras Decadas de la Independencia: 1821-1851. LC 87-72666. (Monograph Ser.: No. 3). (SPA.). 400p. (Orig.). 1987. pap. 16.50 (*0-910443-04-1*) Plumsock Meso Studies.

— Penny Ante Imperialism: The Mosquito Shore & the Bay of Honduras, 1600-1914. LC 87-45735. (Illus.). 320p. 1989. 42.50 (*0-8386-3323-4*) Fairleigh Dickinson.

***Naylor, Robert E.** The Baptist Deacon. 1998. pap. text 11.99 (*0-8054-1986-1*) Broadman.

Naylor, Robert E. A Messenger's Memoirs: Sixty-One Southern Baptist Convention Meetings. LC 95-69284. (Illus.). 304p. (Orig.). 1995. pap. 16.95 (*1-881576-46-9*) Providence Hse.

Naylor, Ronald P., jt. ed. see Fiels, Keith M.

Naylor, Sean, jt. auth. see Donnelly, Tom.

***Naylor, Sharon.** How to Plan an Elegant Wedding in Six Months or Less. 2000. pap. 16.95 (*0-7615-2824-5*) Prima Pub.

Naylor, Sharon. Mother-of-the-Bride Book: Giving Your Daughter A Wonderful Wedding. LC 99-28530. 1999. 14.95 (*1-55972-531-1*, Birch Ln Pr) Carol Pub Group.

***Naylor, Sharon.** 100 Reasons to Keep Dumb. 2000. pap. 6.99 (*0-517-20965-9*) Random Hse Value.

— 1,001 Ways to Have a Dazzling Second Wedding. 288p. 2001. pap. 13.99 (*1-56414-520-4*, New Page Bks) Career Pr Inc.

Naylor, Sharon. One Thousand One Ways to Save Money...& Still Have a Dazzling Wedding. (Illus.). 320p. 1994. pap. 12.95 (*0-8092-3657-5*, 365750, Contemporary Bks) NTC Contemp Pub Co.

— Unofficial Guide to Divorce. LC 99-231514. 400p. 1998. pap. 16.00 (*0-02-862455-6*) Macmillan.

***Naylor, Simon & Ryan, James.** Cultural Turns/ Geographical Turns: Perspectives on Cultural Geography. LC 99-53634. 256p. 2000. write for info. (*0-582-36887-1*) P-H.

Naylor, Thomas. Search for Meaning. 1997. pap. 16.00 (*0-687-08176-9*) Abingdon.

Naylor, Thomas H. Corporate Planning Models. LC 77-93329. 1979. text. write for info. (*0-201-05226-1*) Addison-Wesley.

— Simulation Models in Corporate Planning. LC 78-31258. (Praeger Special Studies). 294p. 1979. 55.00 (*0-275-90398-2*, C0398, Praeger Pubs) Greenwood.

Naylor, Thomas H. & Polzer, Charles W., eds. Pedro de Rivera & the Military Regulations for Northern New Spain, 1724-1729: A Documentary History of His Frontier Inspection & the Reglamento de 1729. LC 88-26098. 367p. 1988. 51.00 (*0-8165-1070-9*) U of Ariz Pr.

— The Presidio & Militia on the Northern Frontier of New Spain: A Documentary History - 1570-1700, Vol. I. LC 86-13283. 756p. 1986. 72.00 (*0-8165-0903-4*) U of Ariz Pr.

Naylor, Thomas H. & Willimon, William H. Downsizing the U. S. A. LC 97-8919. 295p. (Orig.). 1997. pap. 25.00 (*0-8028-4330-1*) Eerdmans.

Naylor, Thomas H., et al. The Search for Meaning in the Workplace. LC 96-21841. 1996. pap. 12.95 (*0-687-01548-0*) Abingdon.

— The Search for Meaning Workbook. 88p. 1994. pap. 4.48 (*0-687-00440-3*) Abingdon.

— Simplan: A Computer Based Planning System for Government. LC 74-75956. 189p. reprint ed. pap. 58.60 (*0-608-11982-2*, 202342600033) Bks Demand.

Naylor, Thomas H., jt. auth. see Willimon, William H.

Naylor, Thomas H., ed. see Design of Computer Simulation Experiments Symposiu.

Naylor, Tom L. The Trumpet & Trombone in Graphic Arts, Fifteen Hundred to Eighteen Hundred. Glover, Stephen L., ed. LC 79-10044. (Brass Research Ser.: No. 9). (Illus.). 1979. lib. bdg. 30.00 (*0-914282-20-4*) Brass Pr.

Naylor, W. Patrick. 10 Steps to Financial Success: A Beginner's Guide to Saving & Investing. LC 96-49900. (Illus.). 272p. 1997. pap. 24.95 (*0-471-17533-1*) Wiley.

Nayor, Phyllis Reynolds. Alice in Rapture, Sort Of. (Alice Ser.). (YA). (gr. 4-7). 1999. pap. 4.50 (*0-689-81687-1*) Aladdin.

Naysmith, Kenneth J. Psychic Growth: Dangers & Ecstasies. 168p. 1977. pap. write for info. (*0-89540-037-5*, SB-037) Sun Pub.

Naythons, Matthew. American Reunion 1993. 1993. 39.95 (*0-446-51796-8*, Pub. by Warner Bks) Little.

Nayyar, Deepak. India's Exports & Export Policies in the 1960s. LC 75-46206. (Cambridge South Asian Studies: Vol. 19). 410p. reprint ed. pap. 116.90 (*0-608-16889-0*, 2027248) Bks Demand.

— Industrial Growth & Stagnation: The Debate in India. 364p. 1994. 21.00 (*0-19-563442-X*) OUP.

— Migration, Remittances & Capital Flow: The Indian Experience. 144p. (C). 1994. 14.95 (*0-19-563345-8*) OUP.

Nayyar, Deepak, ed. Economics As Ideology & Experience: Essays in Honour of Ashok Mitra. LC 97-17414. 291p. (C). 1998. text 59.50 (*0-7146-4723-3*, Pub. by F Cass Pubs); pap. text 25.00 (*0-7146-4273-8*, Pub. by F Cass Pubs) Intl Spec Bk.

— Trade & Industrialization. LC 97-903284. (Oxford in India Readings Ser.). 342p. 1998. text 32.00 (*0-19-563532-9*) OUP.

Nayyar, Harish & Ramaswamy, P., eds. Globalization & Agricultural Marketing. 1995. 40.00 (*0-614-25278-4*, Pub. by Rawat Pubns) S Asia.

Nayyar, Kuldip. Report on Afghanistan. 212p. 1980. 15.95 (*0-318-37264-9*) Asia Bk Corp.

***Nayyar, Mohinder L.** Piping Handbook. 7th ed. 1999. pap. text 125.00 (*0-07-047106-1*, McGrw-H College) McGrw-H Hghr Educ.

Nayyar, S. P. & Fanthome, Francis. Mental Mathematics, Vol. 1. 76p. 1997. pap. 25.00 (*81-209-0777-9*, Pub. by Pitambar Pub) St Mut.

— Mental Mathematics, Vol. 2. 72p. 1997. pap. 25.00 (*81-209-0778-7*, Pub. by Pitambar Pub) St Mut.

— Mental Mathematics, Vol. 3. 80p. 1997. pap. 25.00 (*81-209-0645-4*, Pub. by Pitambar Pub) St Mut.

— Mental Mathematics, Vol. 4. 80p. 1997. pap. 25.00 (*81-209-0651-9*, Pub. by Pitambar Pub) St Mut.

— Mental Mathematics, Vol. 5. 80p. 1997. pap. 25.00 (*81-209-0726-4*, Pub. by Pitambar Pub) St Mut.

Nayyar, Sushila. Kasturba, Wife of Gandhi. (C). 1948. pap. 7.00 (*0-87574-000-6*) Pendle Hill.

Naz, R. Dictionnaire de Droit Canonique, 7 vols., Set. (FRE.). 1965. 1195.00 (*0-8288-6739-9*, M-6423) Fr & Eur.

Naz, Rajesh K. Endocrine Disruptors Effects of Male & Female Reproductive Systems. LC 98-36723. 384p. 1999. boxed set 129.95 (*0-8493-3164-1*) CRC Pr.

— Prostate: Basic & Clinical Aspects. LC 96-49184. 400p. 1997. boxed set 104.95 (*0-8493-3159-5*) CRC Pr.

Naz, Rajesh K., ed. Immunology of Reproduction. 336p. 1992. lib. bdg. 198.95 (*0-8493-5191-X*, QP252) CRC Pr.

Nazaikinski, V. E., tr. see Davydov, I. A., et al.

Nazaikinskii, V. E., jt. auth. see Maslov, V. P.

Nazaikinskii, Vladimir E., et al. Contact Geometry & Linear Differential Equations. LC 92-24930. (Expositions in Mathematics Ser.: No. 6). vii, 216p. (C). 1992. lib. bdg. 85.95 (*3-11-013381-4*) De Gruyter.

— Methods of Noncommutative Analysis: Theory & Applications. LC 95-39641. (Studies in Mathematics: No. 22). x, 374p. (C). 1995. lib. bdg. 98.95 (*3-11-014632-0*) De Gruyter.

Nazar, David. There Is a Tomorrow. Tucker, Gary, ed. LC 96-83963. 265p. (Orig.). 1996. pap. 12.00 (*0-9651566-0-5*) Allastar.

Nazar, Krystyna, et al, eds. International Perspectives in Exercise Physiology. LC 89-37079. (Illus.). 243p. reprint ed. pap. 75.40 (*0-608-07041-6*, 206724800009) Bks Demand.

Nazarain, S., et al. Development & Testing of a Siesmic Pavement Analyzer. 165p. (C). 1993. pap. text 15.00 (*0-309-05753-1*, SHRP-H-375) SHRP.

Nazaraki, Muneshige & Frabetti, Guiliano. Ukiyo-E Masterpieces in European Collections Vol. 5: Victoria & Albert Museum II, Vol. 5. (Illus.). 272p. 1989. 300.00 (*0-87011-876-5*) Kodansha.

Nazare, Maria H., jt. ed. see Davies, Gordon.

Nazarea, et al. Yesterday's Ways, Tomorrow's Treasures: A Guide to Memory. 50p. (C). 1997. spiral bd. 12.95 (*0-7872-3895-3*, 41389501) Kendall-Hunt.

Nazarea-Sandoval, Virginia D. Local Knowledge & Rural Development in the Philippines. (Food Systems & Agrarian Change Ser.). (Illus.). 264p. 1995. 49.95 (*0-8014-2801-7*) Cornell U Pr.

Nazarea, Virginia D. Cultural Memory & Biodiversity. LC 97-45265. (Illus.). 200p. 1998. 40.00 (*0-8165-1681-2*) U of Ariz Pr.

Nazarea, Virginia D., ed. Ethnoecology: Situated Knowledge/Located Lives. LC 98-25481. (Illus.). 299 p. 1999. 40.00 (*0-8165-1882-3*) U of Ariz Pr.

Nazarenko, Alla L. & Rawson-Jones, Keith, eds. Passport to Russia. (SAP - Languages Ser.). 200p. 1999. pap. 19.95 (*1-85075-879-4*, Pub. by Sheffield Acad) CUP Services.

Nazarenko, O. K., jt. auth. see Paton, B. E.

Nazareno, Adrienne R., jt. auth. see Gahart, Betty L.

Nazareno, Rodolfo L., jt. auth. see Chua, Romulo L.

Nazareth, Brig J. Creative Thinking in Warfare. 1987. 34.00 (*81-7062-035-X*, Pub. by Lancer India) S Asia.

Nazareth, J. L. Computer Solution of Linear Programs. (Monographs on Numerical Analysis). (Illus.). 254p. 1988. text 60.00 (*0-19-504278-6*) OUP.

— The DLP Optimization Model & Decision Support System. LC 97-91623. 194p. (Orig.). (C). 1997. pap. 29.00 (*0-9657375-0-0*) Comput Decision.

Nazareth, John L. The Newton-Cauchy Framework: A Unified Approach to Unconstrained Nonlinear Minimization. LC 93-49417. (Lecture Notes in Computer Science Ser.: Vol. 769). xii, 101p. 1994. 29.95 (*0-387-57671-1*) Spr-Verlag.

Nazareth, Peter. The General Is up. 1995. pap. 10.95 (*0-920661-19-X*) LPC InBook.

Nazareth, Ralph, ed. see Gomes, Antonio.

Nazareth, Ralph, jt. ed. see Sorensen, Lynda.

Nazarieff, Serge. Jeux des Dames Cruelles. (FO Ser.). (Illus.). 1998. pap. 14.99 (*3-8228-9353-6*) Taschen Amer.

Nazario, Andy F. Watchman. 208p. 1998. pap. 18.95 (*1-58244-004-2*) Rutledge Bks.

Nazario, Edgar R. God Still Stops the Rain: Excerps of a Life Touched by God. Soto, Bobby, ed. 190p. (Orig.). 1996. pap. 11.88 (*1-57502-374-1*, P01195) Morris Pubng.

Nazario, Felix L. La Alucinacion y los Recursos Literarios en las Novelas de Reinaldo Arenas. LC 95-60175. (SPA.). 222p. (Orig.). 1995. pap. 19.00 (*0-89729-724-5*) Ediciones.

Nazario, Manuel A. El Habla Campesina del Pais. LC 89-5385. (SPA., Illus.). 616p. (Orig.). 1990. pap. 28.00 (*0-8477-3635-0*) U of PR Pr.

— Origenes y Desarrollo del Espanol en Puerto Rico: Siglos XVI y XVII. LC 80-21477. 470p. 1982. 15.00 (*0-8477-3197-9*); pap. 12.00 (*0-8477-3198-7*) U of PR Pr.

Nazarko, Linda. Nursing in Nursing Homes. LC 94-49058. 1995. pap. 21.95 (*0-632-03987-6*) Blackwell Sci.

Nazaroff. Environmental Engineering Science. text. write for info. (*0-471-14494-0*) Wiley.

Nazaroff, Alexandra I. Tolstoy, the Inconstant Genius: A Biography. 351p. 1977. 27.95 (*0-8369-6619-8*) Ayer.

Nazaroff, William W. & Nero, Anthony V., eds. Radon & Its Decay Products in Indoor Air. LC 87-8915. (Environmental Science & Technology Ser.). 518p. 1988. 185.00 (*0-471-62810-7*) Wiley.

Nazarov, Bakhtiyar & Sinor, Denis, eds. Essays on Uzbek History, Culture, & Language. LC 92-63232. (Uralic & Altaic Ser.: Vol. 156). 119p. 1993. 19.95 (*0-933070-29-2*) Ind U Res Inst.

Nazarov, S. A. & PLamenevsky, Boris A. Elliptic Problems in Domains with Piecewise Smooth Boundaries. LC 94-7660. (Expositions in Mathematics Ser.). vii, 525p. 1994. 159.95 (*3-11-013522-1*) De Gruyter.

Nazarov, V. M. & Frontasieva, M. V., eds. Activation Analysis in Environment Protection. 520p. (C). 1995. pap. 60.00 (*0-911767-90-8*) Hadronic Pr Inc.

***Nazarri, Marco.** The Arctic World: Landscapes, Wildlife & People. (Illus.). 228p. (J). 2000. 35.00 (*0-7892-0629-3*, Abbeville Kids) Abbeville Pr.

Nazel, Joe. B. B. King: King of the Blues. (Black-American Ser.). (Illus.). 192p. 1998. mass mkt. 4.95 (*0-87067-792-6*, Melrose Sq) Holloway.

Nazel, Joseph. Black Cop. 224p. 1993. mass mkt. 3.95 (*0-87067-761-6*) Holloway.

— Death for Hire. 224p. (Orig.). 1992. mass mkt. 3.50 (*0-87067-342-4*) Holloway.

— Delta Crossing. 256p. (Orig.). 1984. mass mkt. 2.75 (*0-87067-712-8*, BH712) Holloway.

Nazel, Joseph. Every Goodbye Ain't Gone. pap. text 3.95 (*0-87067-398-X*) Holloway.

Nazel, Joseph. Every Goodbye Ain't Gone. 224p. 1996. mass mkt. 5.99 (*0-87067-764-0*, BH764-0) Holloway.

— Finders Keepers, Losers Weepers. 272p. (Orig.). 1987. mass mkt. 3.25 (*0-87067-728-4*) Holloway.

An Asterisk (*) at the beginning of an entry indicates that the title is appearing for the first time.

— Iceman, No. Five: Spinning Target. 224p. (Orig.). 1983. mass mkt. 2.25 (*0-87067-090-5*, BH090) Holloway.
— Iceman, No. Four: Sunday Fix. (Orig.). 1983. mass mkt. 2.25 (*0-87067-089-1*, BH089) Holloway.
— Iceman, No. Six: Canadian Kill. (Orig.). 1983. mass mkt. 2.25 (*0-87067-091-3*, BH091) Holloway.
— Ida B. Wells: Activist. (Black American Ser.). (Illus.). 208p. (Orig.). (YA). (gr. 6-12). 1995. mass mkt. 4.95 (*0-87067-785-3*, BH-785-3, Melrose Sq) Holloway.
— Killer Cop. rev. ed. (Orig.). 1991. mass mkt. 3.50 (*0-87067-321-1*) Holloway.
— Langston Hughes: Poet. (Black American Ser.). (Illus.). 192p. (Orig.). (YA). 1994. mass mkt. 3.95 (*0-87067-591-5*, Melrose Sq) Holloway.
— Magic Johnson: The Rookie Year. 1990. pap. 3.95 (*0-87067-844-2*) Holloway.
— Martin Luther King, Jr. Civil Rights Leader. (Black American Ser.). (Illus.). 192p. (YA). 1992. mass mkt. 3.95 (*0-87067-573-7*, Melrose Sq) Holloway.
— Street Wars. 224p. (Orig.). 1987. mass mkt. 2.50 (*0-87067-284-3*) Holloway.
— Thurgood Marshall: Supreme Court Justice. (Black American Ser.). (Illus.). 192p. (YA). 1993. mass mkt. 3.95 (*0-87067-584-2*, Melrose Sq) Holloway.
— Uprising. 224p. (Orig.). 1987. mass mkt. 2.50 (*0-87067-295-9*, BH295) Holloway.

Nazem. Applied Time Series for Business & Economic Forecasting. (Statistics: Textbooks & Monographs: Vol. 93). (Illus.). 448p. 1988. text 157.50 (*0-8247-7913-4*) Dekker.

***Nazer, Hisham M.** Power of a Third Kind: The Western Attempt to Colonize the Global Village. LC 98-47761. 200p. 1999. 23.95 (*0-275-96489-2*, C6489, Praeger Pubs) Greenwood.

Nazik, Saba. Arab Travellers & Western Civilization. 252p. 69.95 (*0-86356-336-8*, Pub. by Saqi) Intl Spec Bk.

Nazim, M. Accountancy. 1987. 100.00 (*0-7855-1817-7*) St Mut.

Nazim, M. A Coprehensive Foundation in Accountancy. 1985. 90.00 (*0-946796-04-1*) St Mut.

Nazim, Sheikh. Islam the Freedom to Serve. 1997. pap. text 9.95 (*3-927606-15-4*, Pub. by Gorski & Spohr) Kazi Pubns.

Nazir A. Shah. Child Labour in India LC 92-906351. vii, 143 p. 1992. 175.00 (*81-7041-635-3*) S Asia.

***Nazir, Ahmed K.** Is God Man-Made? LC 99-97452. 2000. pap. 7.95 (*0-533-13430-7*) Vantage.

Nazir-Ali, Michael. Citizens & Exiles: Christian Faith in a Plural World. 184p. 1999. pap. 16.95 (*0-8298-1356-X*) Pilgrim OH.

Nazir, Osman El, see El Nazir, Osman.

Nazir, Pervaiz. Local Development in the Global Economy: The Case of Pakistan. 219p. 1991. text 82.95 (*1-85628-106-X*, Pub. by Avebry) Ashgate Pub Co.

Nazmi, Nader. Economic Policy & Stabilization in Latin America. LC 95-30476. (Illus.). 221p. (C). (gr. 13). 1996. text 76.95 (*1-56324-583-3*); pap. text 35.95 (*1-56324-584-1*) M E Sharpe.

Nazoa, Aquiles. Fabula de la Ratoncita Presumida (Fable of the Conceited Little Mouse) (SPA., Illus.). 36p. (J). (gr. 1-4). 5.95 (*980-257-074-5*, Pub. by Ediciones Ekare) Kane-Miller Bk.

Nazor, Anica, jt. comment see Panteli, Marija.

Nazraeli Press Staff. U. S. A. Photography Guide 2. 208p. 1996. pap. 29.00 (*3-923922-36-1*, 610402, Pub. by Nazraeli Pr) Dist Art Pubs.

Nazri, G., et al, eds. Solid-State Ionics V Vol. 548: Materials Research Society Symposium Proceedings. 726p. 1999. text 87.00 (*1-55899-454-8*) Materials Res.

Nazri, Gholam-Abbas, et al, eds. Solid State Ionics IV. (MRS Symposium Proceedings Ser.: Vol. 369). 715p. 1995. 82.00 (*1-55899-271-5*) Materials Res.

Nazri, Gholam-Abbas, ed. see Armand, M.

Nazri, Gholam-Abbas, jt. ed. see Julien, Christian.

Nazroo, James Y. The Health of Britain's Ethnic Minorities: Findings from a National Survey. LC 98-161210. (PSI Report Ser.). x, 219p. 1997. write for info. (*0-85374-709-1*) Pol Studies Inst.

Nazworth, Lenora H. Home Again. 320p. (Orig.). 1997. mass mkt. 4.99 (*0-505-52195-4*) Dorchester Pub Co.

Nazzal, Laila A., jt. auth. see Nazzal, Nafez.

Nazzal, Nafez & Nazzal, Laila A. Historical Dictionary of Palestine. LC 96-30594. (Asian Historical Dictionaries Ser.). 1997. 55.00 (*0-8108-3239-9*) Scarecrow.

Nazzari, Muriel. Disappearance of the Dowry: Women, Families, & Social Change in Sao Paulo, Brazil, 1600-1900. 272p. 1991. 39.50 (*0-8047-1928-4*) Stanford U Pr.

Nazzaro, Ann, et al. The PMS Solution: A Nutritional Approach to Premenstrual Syndrome. 156p. (Orig.). 1985. 7.95 (*0-86683-793-0*, AY8554) Harper SF.

Nazzaro, Joe & Wells, Sheelagh. Blake's 7: The Inside Story. (Illus.). 144p. (Orig.). 1997. pap. text 19.95 (*0-7535-0044-2*, Pub. by Virgin Bks) London Brdge.

Nazzaro, Robin & Lilly, Robert. Department of Energy: Fossil Energy Programs. (Illus.). 43p. (C). 1998. pap. text 15.00 (*0-7881-7485-1*) DIANE Pub.

NBA Staff, photos by. Basketball. (Illus.). 290p. 1997. pap. 29.95 (*0-7893-0107-5*, Pub. by Universe) St Martin.

NBC News Division Staff & Pearce, Alan. NBC News Division & the Economics of Prime Time Access, Washington D. C., September 1973: Proceedings, 2 vols. Sterling, Christopher H., ed. LC 78-21730. (Dissertations in Broadcasting Ser.). 1980. lib. bdg. 31.95 (*0-405-11768-X*) Ayer.

***NBC News Staff.** Dateline Survivors: Tales of Extraordinary Heroism by Everyday People. 1999. 19.95 (*0-07-134250-8*) McGraw.

NBC News Staff, jt. auth. see Ball, Rick.

NBCCA Staff. NBA Power Conditioning. LC 97-19426. (Illus.). 216p. (Orig.). 1997. pap. 17.95 (*0-88011-687-0*) Human Kinetics.

***Nbi Mhurchadha, Maighread.** Sober, Active & Bred to the Sea: The Customs & Excise Service in Fingal, 1684-1765. LC 99-29352. (Maynooth Studies in Local History). 64p. 1999. 10.95 (*0-7165-2672-7*, Pub. by Irish Acad Pr) Intl Spec Bk.

NBPA Staff & Armstead. Sergeant's Assessment Center: A Training Manual for Law Enforcement Officers, Vol. I. 224p. 1993. per. 19.95 (*0-8403-8713-X*) Kendall-Hunt.
— Sergeant's Assessment Center: A Training Manual for Law Enforcement Officers, Vol. II. 176p. 1993. per. 19.95 (*0-8403-8714-8*) Kendall-Hunt.

NC Museum of Art Staff, compiled by. The Store of Joys: Writers Celebrate the North Carolina Museum of Art. LC 97-7004. (Orig.). 1997. pap. 22.00 (*0-89587-174-2*) Blair.

N.C. Poetry Society Staff. Here's to the Land: A Celebration of Sixty Years. (Harperprints Chapbook Ser.). 216p. 1992. text 15.00 (*0-9633529-0-3*); pap. text 10.00 (*0-9633529-1-1*) NC Poetry Soc.

***NC Rural Aging Program Staff.** Rural Health & Aging Research: Theory, Methods & Practical Applications. Gesler, Wilbert M. et al, eds. LC 97-28444. (Society & Aging Ser.). 260p. 1998. text 46.00 (*0-89503-183-3*) Baywood Pub.

NC Wildlife Resources Commission, jt. auth. see Earley, Lawrence S.

NCA Staff. NCA Review for the Clinical Laboratory Sciences. 2nd ed. 1989. 32.95 (*0-316-59925-5*, Little Brwn Med Div) Lppncott W & W.

NCAA Staff. Official NCAA Football Records Book, 1998-1999. (Illus.). 568p. 1998. pap. 16.95 (*1-57243-269-1*) Triumph Bks.

NCARB Staff. Architect Overseas Practice Standards: A Guide to Selected Countries. 115p. (Orig.). 1987. pap. text 5.00 (*0-941575-02-0*) NCARB.
— Architect Overseas Practice Standards: A Guide to Selected Countries. 94p. (Orig.). 1996. pap. text 50.00 (*0-941575-26-8*) NCARB.
— Preparing for the Architect Registration Examination. (Illus.). 148p. 1997. pap. text 85.00 incl. vdisk (*0-941575-28-4*) NCARB.

NCCB, Bishops' Committee for Pastoral Research & P. Faithful to Each Other Forever. (Marriage Is a Sacrament Ser.). 164p. 1989. 22.95 (*1-55586-252-7*) US Catholic.

NCCB, Bishops' Committee on the Liturgy Staff, jt. auth. see NCCB, International Commission on English in the L.

NCCB Committee on Priestly Life & Ministry. A Shepherd's Care: Reflections on the Changing Role of Pastor. 84p. (Orig.). 1987. pap. 4.95 (*1-55586-166-0*) US Catholic.

NCCB Committee on the Liturgy Staff, jt. auth. see International Commission on English in the Liturgy.

NCCB, International Commission on English in the L & NCCB, Bishops' Committee on the Liturgy Staff. Rite of Christian Initiation of Adults: Study Edition. 396p. 1988. 7.95 (*1-55586-214-4*) US Catholic.

NCCB, Secretariat of the Bishops' Committee on the. Norms Governing Liturgical Calendars. (Liturgy Documentary Ser.: No. 6). 176p. 1984. 6.95 (*1-55586-928-9*) US Catholic.

NCCB Staff. Rito de la Iniciacion Cristiana de Adultos. (SPA.). 384p. 1991. student ed. 12.95 (*1-55586-509-7*) US Catholic.
— Rito de la Iniciacion Cristiana de Adultos. (SPA.). 384p. 1993. 34.95 (*1-55586-435-X*) US Catholic.

NCCB Staff, jt. auth. see Committee for Pro-Life Activities Staff.

***Nccer.** Advanced Electrical Topics, Binder, Instructor's Guide, 1. 1999. pap. text 80.00 (*0-13-909797-X*) P-H.
— Advanced Electrical Topics: Binder, Trainee Guide, 2. 1998. pap. text 80.00 (*0-13-909805-4*) P-H.
— Advanced Electrical Topics: 20509 Power Quality Perfect Bound, Trainee Guide. 1998. pap. text 20.00 (*0-13-909888-7*) P-H.
— Advanced Electrical Topics: 20510 Energy Management Perfect Bound, Instructor's Guide. 1998. pap. text 20.00 (*0-13-910019-9*) P-H.
— Advanced Electrical Topics: 20513 Process & Distributed Control Systems Perfect Bound, Instructor's Guide. 1999. pap. text 20.00 (*0-13-910076-8*) P-H.
— Advanced Electrical Topics: 20513 Process & Distributed Control Systems Perfect Bound, Trainee Guide. 1999. pap. text 20.00 (*0-13-910068-7*) P-H.
— Advanced Electronic Topics 20512 Sound & Instructor's Guide, Perfect Bound. 1999. pap. text 20.00 (*0-13-910050-4*) P-H.
— Carpentry Level 1: Trainee Guide '98 Revised With Core (ringbound) 1998. ring bd. 80.00 (*0-13-011737-4*) P-H.
— Curriculum Basico Instructor's Guide. 1999. teacher ed., per. 50.00 (*0-13-085348-8*) P-H.

Nccer. Electrical: Level 1. 1998. pap. text, wbk. ed. 8.00 (*0-13-012812-0*) P-H.
— Electrical: Level 2. 1998. pap. text, wbk. ed. 8.00 (*0-13-012813-9*) P-H.

***Nccer.** Electrical Level Two: Perfect Bound Trainee Guide, 98 Revision. 1998. pap. text 80.00 (*0-13-975301-X*) P-H.
— Heavy Equipment Operations Level Two. 1998. teacher ed., ring bd. 80.00 (*0-13-909581-0*) P-H.
— Heavy Equipment Operations Level Three: Perfect Bound, Instructor's Guide. 1998. pap. text 80.00 (*0-13-909615-9*) P-H.

Nccer. Ninteen Thousand Three Hundred Six Large Boilers. 1997. pap. text 12.00 (*0-13-910415-1*) P-H.

***Nccer.** Welding Level One: Perfect Bound With Aws Certificates, Trainee Gde. 1998. pap. text 100.00 (*0-13-982315-8*) P-H.
— Welding Level Three: Perfect Bound with Aws Certificates, Instructor's Guide. 1998. pap. text 80.00 (*0-13-982653-X*) P-H.
— Welding Level Three: Perfect Bound With Aws Certificates, Trainee Guide. 1998. pap. text 80.00 (*0-13-982505-3*) P-H.
— Welding Level Two: Perfect Bound With Aws Certificates, Instructor's Guide. 1998. pap. text 80.00 (*0-13-982554-1*) P-H.
— Welding Level Two: Perfect Bound With Aws Certificates, Trainee Guide. 1998. pap. text 80.00 (*0-13-982331-X*) P-H.

Nccer, ed. Electronic lg 98: Level 1. rev. ed. 1998. ring bd. 50.00 (*0-13-975335-4*) P-H.
— Sprinkler Fitter, Level 2. (C). 1996. pap. text, student ed. 80.00 (*0-13-490020-0*) P-H.

Nccer, ed. Sprinkler Fitter, Level 2. (C). 1996. pap. text, teacher ed. 80.00 (*0-13-490491-5*, Macmillan Coll) P-H.
— Sprinkler Fitter, Level 3. (C). 1996. pap. text, teacher ed. 80.00 (*0-13-490509-1*, Macmillan Coll) P-H.

***NCCER Staff.** Advanced Electrical Topics, 2. 1999. pap. text, teacher ed. 80.00 (*0-13-909813-5*, Prentice Hall) P-H.
— Advanced Electrical Topics: 20501 Advanced Electronic Theory. 1997. pap. text 20.00 (*0-13-909839-9*, Prentice Hall) P-H.
— Advanced Test Equipment 20514. 1999. pap. text 20.00 (*0-13-910084-9*, Prentice Hall); pap. text 20.00 (*0-13-910092-X*, Prentice Hall) P-H.
— Busses & Networks 20503. 1999. pap. text 20.00 (*0-13-909946-8*, Prentice Hall); pap. text, teacher ed. 20.00 (*0-13-909953-0*, Prentice Hall) P-H.
— CARPEN LV2 TG RB 99 REV, Level 2. rev. ed. 1999. pap. 80.00 (*0-13-772096-3*) P-H.
— Carpenter. rev. ed. 1998. teacher ed., ring bd. 50.00 (*0-13-772088-2*) P-H.

NCCER Staff. Carpenter Trainee. rev. ed. 1999. teacher ed., ring bd. 80.00 (*0-13-772104-8*) P-H.

***NCCER Staff.** Carpenter Trainee, Level 1. rev. ed. 1998. ring bd. 50.00 (*0-13-772070-X*) P-H.

NCCER Staff. Carpentry Level Four. rev. ed. 334p. (C). 1997. pap. text, teacher ed. 80.00 (*0-13-772146-3*, Prentice Hall) P-H.

***NCCER Staff.** Carpentry Level One. 1998. pap. text 80.00 (*0-13-789322-1*, Prentice Hall) P-H.
— Carpentry Level Two, 1999. 1999. pap. text, teacher ed. 80.00 (*0-13-014836-9*, Prentice Hall) P-H.
— Carpentry Level 3, 1999. 2000. ring bd. 80.00 (*0-13-018306-7*, Prentice Hall) P-H.
— Carpentry Level 3, 1999. 2000. teacher ed., ring bd. 80.00 (*0-13-018308-3*, Prentice Hall) P-H.
— Carpentry Level 3, 1999. rev. ed. 2000. pap. text, teacher ed. 80.00 (*0-13-018307-5*, Prentice Hall); pap. text, student ed. 80.00 (*0-13-018305-9*, Prentice Hall) P-H.
— Carpentry '98. rev. ed. 1998. pap. text 50.00 (*0-13-770421-6*) P-H.
— Concrete Finishing Level Two. 1999. pap. text 80.00 (*0-13-014860-1*, Prentice Hall); pap. text 80.00 (*0-13-014872-5*, Prentice Hall); ring bd. 80.00 (*0-13-014871-7*, Prentice Hall); ring bd. 80.00 (*0-13-014873-3*, Prentice Hall) P-H.
— Curriculum Basico. 1999. pap. text 50.00 (*0-13-085347-X*, Prentice Hall) P-H.

NCCER Staff. Electrical: Instructor's Guide, Level 3. (C). 1996. teacher ed., ring bd. 80.00 (*0-13-265174-2*, Prentice Hall) P-H.
— Electrical: Instructor's Guide, Level 4. (C). 1996. teacher ed., ring bd. 80.00 (*0-13-265182-3*, Prentice Hall) P-H.
— Electrical: Trainee Guide, Level 3. (Trainee Ser.). 1996. student ed., ring bd. 80.00 (*0-13-264987-X*, Prentice Hall) P-H.

***NCCER Staff.** Electrical Level 1. rev. ed. 2000. student ed., ring bd. 50.00 (*0-13-014843-1*) P-H.
— Electrical Level 3. 1999. pap. text, student ed. 80.00 (*0-13-014848-2*) P-H.
— Electrical Level Four, 1999. rev. ed. 1999. teacher ed., ring bd. 80.00 (*0-13-014854-7*, Prentice Hall) P-H.
— Electrical Level Four, 1999. rev. ed. 1999. teacher ed., ring bd. 80.00 (*0-13-014856-3*, Prentice Hall) P-H.
— Electrical Level Four ,1999. rev. ed. 1999. pap. text, teacher ed. 80.00 (*0-13-014855-5*, Prentice Hall) P-H.
— Electrical Level One: Binder With Core, Update. 1998. teacher ed., ring bd. 80.00 (*0-13-780628-0*, Prentice Hall) P-H.
— Electrical Level One, 1999. 1999. ring bd. 80.00 (*0-13-014844-X*, Prentice Hall) P-H.
— Electrical Level Three, 1999. 1999. student ed., ring bd. 80.00 (*0-13-014849-0*, Prentice Hall) P-H.
— Electrical Level Three, 1999. rev. ed. 1999. teacher ed., ring bd. 80.00 (*0-13-014851-2*, Prentice Hall) P-H.
— Electrical Level Two, 1999. 1999. pap. text 80.00 (*0-13-014845-8*, Prentice Hall); ring bd. 80.00 (*0-13-014847-4*, Prentice Hall) P-H.
— Electrical Level Two, '98. 1998. pap. text, teacher ed. 80.00 (*0-13-975319-2*, Prentice Hall) P-H.
— Electrical Trainee Guide, Level 4. 1996. ring bd. 80.00 (*0-13-264995-0*) P-H.
— Electrician, Level 1. 1998. pap. text, teacher ed. 50.00 (*0-13-770786-X*) P-H.
— Electrician Trainee, Level 1. rev. ed. 1998. ring bd. 50.00 (*0-13-772153-6*) P-H.
— Fiber Optics 20504. 1999. pap. text 20.00 (*0-13-909920-4*, Prentice Hall); pap. text, teacher ed. 20.00 (*0-13-909938-7*, Prentice Hall) P-H.
— Glazier Level Three. 1996. pap. text, teacher ed. 75.00 (*0-13-530718-X*, Prentice Hall) P-H.
— Heavy Equipment Operations Level One: Binder Without Core. 1997. student ed., ring bd. 50.00 (*0-13-909508-X*, Prentice Hall) P-H.
— Heavy Equipment Operations Level Three. 1998. teacher ed., ring bd. 80.00 (*0-13-909623-X*, Prentice Hall); student ed., ring bd. 80.00 (*0-13-909607-8*, Prentice Hall) P-H.

NCCER Staff. HVAC Level Two: Perfect Bound, Instructor's Guide, Level 2. (C). 1996. pap. text, teacher ed. 80.00 (*0-13-245242-1*) P-H.

***NCCER Staff.** Industrial Maintenance Level 3. 1999. pap. text 80.00 (*0-13-012583-0*); pap. text, teacher ed. 80.00 (*0-13-012587-3*) P-H.
— Industrial Maintenance Level 4. 1999. pap. text 80.00 (*0-13-012586-5*) P-H.
— Industrial Maintenance Level 5. 1999. pap. text 80.00 (*0-13-012588-1*) P-H.
— Instrumentation, Level 1. 1996. teacher ed., ring bd. 50.00 (*0-13-265273-0*) P-H.

NCCER Staff. Instrumentation: Trainee Guide, Vol. 1, Level 2. 1460p. (C). 1996. teacher ed., per. 80.00 (*0-13-245516-1*) P-H.

NCCER Staff. Instrumentation Level Two, 1 & 2. 1996. teacher ed., ring bd. 80.00 (*0-13-265075-4*, Prentice Hall) P-H.
— Instrumentation Level Two, 1 & 2. 1996. pap. text, teacher ed. 80.00 (*0-13-265695-7*, Prentice Hall) P-H.
— Instrumentation Level Two, 1 & 2. 1996. pap. text 80.00 (*0-13-261801-X*, Prentice Hall) P-H.
— Ironworking Lv. 2. 1999. student ed., ring bd. 80.00 (*0-13-018315-6*) P-H.
— Ironworking Level One, 1999. 1999. ring bd. 50.00 (*0-13-014868-7*, Prentice Hall) P-H.
— Ironworking Level One, 1999. 1999. teacher ed., ring bd. 80.00 (*0-13-014869-5*, Prentice Hall) P-H.
— Ironworking Level One, 1999. rev. ed. 1999. pap. text, teacher ed. 50.00 (*0-13-014864-4*, Prentice Hall); pap. text, teacher ed. 50.00 (*0-13-014867-9*, Prentice Hall) P-H.
— Ironworking Level One, 1999. rev. ed. 1999. teacher ed., ring bd. 50.00 (*0-13-014865-2*, Prentice Hall); teacher ed., ring bd. 80.00 (*0-13-014866-0*, Prentice Hall) P-H.
— Low Voltage Level One. 1999. pap. text 50.00 (*0-13-014874-1*, Prentice Hall); pap. text 50.00 (*0-13-014875-X*, Prentice Hall) P-H.
— Masonry Level 2. 1999. pap. text, teacher ed. 80.00 (*0-13-014830-X*); student ed., ring bd. 80.00 (*0-13-014839-3*) P-H.
— Masonry Level 2. rev. ed. 1999. teacher ed., ring bd. 80.00 (*0-13-014841-5*) P-H.
— Masonry Level Two, 1999. rev. ed. 1999. pap. text, teacher ed. 80.00 (*0-13-014837-7*, Prentice Hall) P-H.
— Masonry 1 '98. rev. ed. 1998. ring bd. 50.00 (*0-13-012260-2*) P-H.
— Masory Level 1, '98. 1998. teacher ed., ring bd. 50.00 (*0-13-012273-4*) P-H.
— Medical Systems 20506. 1997. pap. text 20.00 (*0-13-909904-2*, Prentice Hall); pap. text, teacher ed. 20.00 (*0-13-909912-3*, Prentice Hall) P-H.
— Medium Voltage 20508. 1997. pap. text 20.00 (*0-13-909862-3*, Prentice Hall) P-H.
— Medium Voltage 20508. 1997. pap. text, teacher ed. 20.00 (*0-13-909870-4*, Prentice Hall) P-H.

NCCER Staff. Millwright: Level Two, Level 2. rev. ed. 488p. (C). 1997. pap. text, teacher ed. 80.00 (*0-13-772245-1*, Prentice Hall) P-H.

***NCCER Staff.** Millwright Trainee, Level 2. rev. ed. 1998. pap. text 80.00 (*0-13-770900-5*) P-H.
— Mobile Crane Operations Level One. 1997. pap. text, teacher ed. 50.00 (*0-13-909664-7*, Prentice Hall); pap. text, student ed. 50.00 (*0-13-909631-0*, Prentice Hall); teacher ed., ring bd. 50.00 (*0-13-909672-8*, Prentice Hall); student ed., ring bd. 50.00 (*0-13-909649-3*, Prentice Hall) P-H.

NCCER Staff. Painting: Commercial & Residential, Level 1. rev. ed. 392p. (C). 1997. pap. text 50.00 (*0-13-771239-1*) P-H.
— Painting: Commercial & Residential, Level One, Level 1. 460p. (C). 1997. teacher ed., ring bd. 50.00 (*0-13-772922-7*) P-H.
— Painting: Commercial & Residential, Level One, Level 1. rev. ed. 404p. (C). 1997. ring bd. 50.00 (*0-13-772914-6*) P-H.
— Painting: Commercial & Residential Level One: Perfect Bound Without Core, Level 1. 442p. (C). 1997. pap. text, teacher ed. 50.00 (*0-13-771288-X*) P-H.
— Painting: Level Two, Level 2. rev. ed. 532p. (C). 1997. student ed., ring bd. 80.00 (*0-13-772930-8*, Prentice Hall) P-H.
— Painting Level Two, Level 2. rev. ed. 524p. (C). 1997. teacher ed., ring bd. 80.00 (*0-13-772948-0*, Prentice Hall) P-H.
— Painting Level Two, Level 2. rev. ed. 516p. (C). 1997. pap. text, student ed. 80.00 (*0-13-771296-0*, Prentice Hall) P-H.
— Painting Level Two, Level 2. rev. ed. 508p. (C). 1997. pap. text, teacher ed. 80.00 (*0-13-771304-5*, Prentice Hall) P-H.

***NCCER Staff.** Painting Level 3. rev. ed. 1998. pap. text, teacher ed. 80.00 (*0-13-949066-3*, Prentice Hall); pap. text, student ed. 80.00 (*0-13-949041-8*, Prentice Hall); teacher ed., ring bd. 80.00 (*0-13-949058-2*, Prentice Hall); teacher ed., ring bd. 80.00 (*0-13-949074-4*, Prentice Hall) P-H.

NCCER Staff. Pipefitter: Binder, Trainee Guide, Update, Level 4. rev. ed. 1997. pap. text, student ed. 80.00 (*0-13-773011-X*, Prentice Hall) P-H.
— Pipefitter: Trainee Guide, Level 3. 1996. student ed., ring bd. 80.00 (*0-13-265893-3*, Prentice Hall) P-H.
— Pipefitter Level Three, Level 3. rev. ed. 378p. (C). 1997. pap. text 80.00 (*0-13-771353-3*) P-H.

N

— Pipefitter Wheels, Level 1. 1996. pap. text, teacher ed. 50.00 (*0-13-265471-7*) P-H.

NCCER Staff. Pipefitter Wheels, Level 2. 1996. teacher ed., ring bd. 80.00 (*0-13-265489-X*) P-H.

— Pipefitter Wheels, Level 3. 1996. teacher ed., ring bd. 80.00 (*0-13-265497-0*) P-H.

— Programmable Logic Controllers 20505. 1998. pap. text 20.00 (*0-13-909979-4*, Prentice Hall) P-H.

— Scaffolding. 1999. pap. text 50.00 (*0-13-014876-8*, Prentice Hall); pap. text 50.00 (*0-13-014877-6*, Prentice Hall) P-H.

NCCER Staff. Sheet Metal: Level Four. rev. ed. 266p. (C). 1997. pap. text, student ed. 80.00 (*0-13-771452-1*, Prentice Hall) P-H.

NCCER Staff. Sheet Metal Level One: Binder with Core, Trainee Guide. 1996. ring bd. 80.00 (*0-13-264912-8*, Prentice Hall) P-H.

— Sound 20512. 1999. pap. text 20.00 (*0-13-910043-1*, Prentice Hall) P-H.

— Traffic Signals 20511. 1997. pap. text 20.00 (*0-13-909847-X*, Prentice Hall); pap. text, teacher ed. 20.00 (*0-13-909854-2*, Prentice Hall) P-H.

— Tv 20507. 1999. pap. text 20.00 (*0-13-909987-5*, Prentice Hall); pap. text, teacher ed. 20.00 (*0-13-909995-6*, Prentice Hall) P-H.

— Voice & Data Systems 20502. 1999. pap. text 20.00 (*0-13-910027-X*, Prentice Hall); pap. text 20.00 (*0-13-910035-0*, Prentice Hall) P-H.

NCCER Staff. Welding: Level Three, Level 3. rev. ed. 452p. (C). 1997. pap. text, student ed. 80.00 (*0-13-771536-6*, Prentice Hall) P-H.

***NCCER Staff.** Welding Level 1. 1999. pap. text, student ed. 50.00 (*0-13-014857-1*) P-H.

— Welding Lv. 2. 1999. pap., teacher ed. 80.00 (*0-13-018300-8*); pap., teacher ed. 80.00 (*0-13-018312-1*); teacher ed., ring bd. 80.00 (*0-13-018311-3*) P-H.

— Welding Level One: With Aws Certificates. 1998. pap. text 100.00 (*0-13-982513-4*, Prentice Hall) P-H.

— Welding Level One, 1999. 1999. teacher ed., ring bd. 50.00 (*0-13-014862-8*, Prentice Hall) P-H.

— Welding Level One, 1999. rev. ed. 1999. teacher ed., ring bd. 50.00 (*0-13-014858-X*, Prentice Hall); teacher ed., ring bd. 80.00 (*0-13-014863-6*, Prentice Hall) P-H.

— Welding with Aws Certification Level Three: Binder, Instructor's Guide. 1997. ring bd. 80.00 (*0-13-079837-1*, Prentice Hall) P-H.

— Welding with Aws Certification Level Three: Binder, Trainee Guide. 1997. ring bd. 80.00 (*0-13-079834-7*, Prentice Hall) P-H.

— Welding with Aws Certification Level Two: Binder, Instructor's Guide. 1997. ring bd. 80.00 (*0-13-079836-3*, Prentice Hall) P-H.

— Welding with Aws Certification Level Two: Binder, Trainee Guide. 1997. ring bd. 80.00 (*0-13-079833-9*, Prentice Hall) P-H.

NCCL Inquiry Staff. Stonehenge. (C). 1988. 21.00 (*0-946088-28-4*, Pub. by NCCL) St Mut.

NCCL Staff. The Attack on Higher Education. 1978. 25.00 (*0-7855-1327-2*, Pub. by NCCL) St Mut.

— Civil Disorder & Civil Liberties: Evidence to the Scarman Inquiry. 1981. 30.00 (*0-901108-96-0*, Pub. by NCCL) St Mut.

— Civil Liberties & the Miners' Dispute. 40p. (C). 1988. 30.00 (*0-946088-11-X*, Pub. by NCCL) St Mut.

— Civil Liberties, 1984. Wallington, Peter, ed. 1984. 40.00 (*0-7855-1341-8*, Pub. by NCCL) St Mut.

— Civil Liberty Briefings: Campaigning on the Public Order Bill, No. 2. 40p. 1984. 20.00 (*0-7855-1334-5*, Pub. by NCCL) St Mut.

— Civil Liberty Briefings: Police Accountability, No. 3. 40p. 1984. 25.00 (*0-7855-1338-8*, Pub. by NCCL) St Mut.

— Civil Liberty Briefings: Police & Criminal Evidence, No. 1. 40p. 1984. 50.00 (*0-7855-2995-0*, Pub. by NCCL) St Mut.

— Civil Rights for Civil Servants. 95p. 1988. 50.00 (*0-946088-09-8*, Pub. by NCCL) St Mut.

— The Death of Blair Peach. (C). 1988. 30.00 (*0-901108-91-X*, Pub. by NCCL) St Mut.

— Ethnic Minority Language Leaflets. (PAN.). (C). 1988. 30.00 (*0-7855-4416-X*, Pub. by NCCL) St Mut.

— Hereford, 1984. 1984. 20.00 (*0-7855-1460-0*, Pub. by NCCL) St Mut.

— Information Sheets on the Prevention of Terrorism Act. (C). 1988. 21.00 (*0-946088-14-4*, Pub. by NCCL) St Mut.

— Know Your Rights! (C). 1990. pap. text 39.00 (*0-946088-38-1*, Pub. by NCCL) St Mut.

— Making a Complaint Against the Police. (URD.). (C). 1988. 30.00 (*0-7855-6067-X*, Pub. by NCCL) St Mut.

— No Way in Wapping. 1988. 21.00 (*0-946088-27-6*, Pub. by NCCL) St Mut.

— A People's Charter: Liberty's Bill of Rights: A Consultation Document. 80p. (C). 1991. text 45.00 (*0-946088-39-X*, Pub. by NCCL) St Mut.

— Public Order Campaign Badges: Protest: While You Still Can in Red & Black. 1988. 30.00 (*0-7855-1466-X*, Pub. by NCCL) St Mut.

— The Purging of the Civil Service. 95p. 1988. 30.00 (*0-946088-17-9*, Pub. by NCCL) St Mut.

— Southall: April 23, 1979. (C). 1988. 30.00 (*0-901108-85-5*) St Mut.

— Strip Searching: Women Remand Prisoners at Armagh Prison, 1982-85. (C). 1988. 40.00 (*0-946088-20-9*, Pub. by NCCL) St Mut.

— Submissions to the Royal Commission on Criminal Procedure. 1979. 25.00 (*0-7855-1469-4*, Pub. by NCCL) St Mut.

NCCLS Staff. Physician's Office Laboratory Guidelines, Procedure Manual: Tentative Guideline. 3rd ed. 200p. 1995. pap. text 150.00 (*1-56238-159-8*, POL1/2-T3) NCCLS.

***NCCR Staff.** Welding. 1999. pap. 50.00 (*0-13-014850-4*) P-H.

***NCEER Staff.** Core Curriculum. 435p. 2000. pap. 50.00 (*0-13-018904-9*); ring bd. 50.00 (*0-13-018905-7*) P-H.

— Core Curriculum. annot. ed. 2000. teacher ed., ring bd. 50.00 (*0-13-018907-3*) P-H.

— Core Curriculum Guide 2001 Revision. annot. ed. 2000. pap., teacher ed. 50.00 (*0-13-018906-5*) P-H.

— Electrical Lv. 1. 2000. pap., student ed. 50.00 (*0-13-018899-9*) P-H.

— Electrical Lv. 1. 2000. student ed., ring bd. 50.00 (*0-13-018890-5*) P-H.

— Electrical Lv. 1. annot. ed. 2000. pap., teacher ed. 50.00 (*0-13-018901-4*) P-H.

— Electrical Level 1 Annotated Instructor's Guide 2001 Revision, Looseleaf. annot. ed. 2000. teacher ed., ring bd. 50.00 (*0-13-018902-2*) P-H.

— Ironworking. 1999. teacher ed., ring bd. 80.00 (*0-13-018318-0*) P-H.

— Ironworking Lv. 2. 1999. pap., teacher ed. 80.00 (*0-13-018316-4*); pap., student ed. 80.00 (*0-13-018314-8*) P-H.

— Welding Lv. 2. 1999. teacher ed., ring bd. 80.00 (*0-13-018313-X*) P-H.

NCEET Staff. Approaching Environmental Issues in the Classroom. 64p. (C). 1996. pap. text 10.95 (*0-7872-2195-3*, 41219501) Kendall-Hunt.

NCEET Staff. Designing Effective Workshops. 40p. (C). 1996. pap. text 10.95 (*0-7872-2197-X*) Kendall-Hunt.

NCEET Staff. EE Reference Collection. 304p. (C). 1996. pap. text, ring bd. 47.95 (*0-7872-2190-2*, 41219001) Kendall-Hunt.

— Evaluating Environmental Education Materials. 52p. (C). 1996. pap. text 10.95 (*0-7872-2192-9*, 41219201) Kendall-Hunt.

— Getting Started: A Guide to Bringing Environmental Education into Your Classroom. 144p. (C). 1996. pap. text, per. 18.95 (*0-7872-2191-0*, 41219101) Kendall-Hunt.

— Integrating Environmental Education into the School Curriculum. 60p. (C). 1996. pap. text 10.95 (*0-7872-2194-5*, 41219401) Kendall-Hunt.

— Resource Pak. 624p. (C). 1996. pap. text 65.95 (*0-7872-2235-6*, 41223501) Kendall-Hunt.

— Urban Environmental Education. 52p. (C). 1996. pap. text 10.95 (*0-7872-2199-6*, 41219901) Kendall-Hunt.

NCEET Staff. Using Community Resources. 48p. (C). 1996. pap. text 10.95 (*0-7872-2198-8*) Kendall-Hunt.

NCEET Staff. Using Computer in Environmental Education: Interactive Multimedia & On-Line Learning. 76p. (C). 1996. pap. text 10.95 (*0-7872-2193-7*, 41219301) Kendall-Hunt.

NCEO Staff. The Employee Ownership Communications Sourcebook. (Illus.). 154p. (Orig.). pap. 50.00 (*0-926902-28-8*) NCEO.

NcKeague. Algebra with Trigonometry for College Students. 3rd ed. (C). 1993. pap. text, teacher ed., suppl. ed. 24.50 (*0-03-097779-7*, Pub. by Harcourt Coll Pubs) Harcourt.

NCOA's National Eldercare Institute on Multipurpos, contrib. by. Senior Centers in America: A Blueprint for the Future. 54p. 1995. pap. 25.00 (*0-910883-83-1*, 864) Natl Coun Aging.

NCOHA Staff, ed. The Homestead Laws of Oklahoma Territory: Including the Celebrated Cherokee Outlet Indian Strip. rev. ed. LC 97-69502. (Illus.). 36p. 1998. reprint ed. pap. 9.95 (*0-9660090-3-7*) NCOHA.

— North Central Oklahoma: Rooted in the Past - Growing for the Future, Vol. 1. (Illus.). 1008p. 1995. 70.00 (*0-9660090-4-5*) NCOHA.

Ncozana, Silas S. Sangaya. 56p. 1996. pap. 24.95 (*99908-16-00-X*, U Pr W Africa) Intl Scholars.

NCPTA Staff. Addition & Subtraction. (Illus.). (J). (gr. 5-7). 1996. mass mkt. 6.95 (*0-340-62983-5*, Pub. by Hodder & Stought Ltd) Trafalgar.

— Better English. (J). (gr. 7-9). 1996. mass mkt. 6.95 (*0-340-64669-1*, Pub. by Hodder & Stought Ltd) Trafalgar.

— English Grammar. (Illus.). (YA). (gr. 9-11). 1996. mass mkt. 6.95 (*0-340-65109-1*, Pub. by Hodder & Stought Ltd) Trafalgar.

— General Knowledge. (Illus.). (YA). (gr. 9-11). 1996. mass mkt. 6.95 (*0-340-65112-1*, Pub. by Hodder & Stought Ltd) Trafalgar.

— Handwriting. (J). 1996. mass mkt. 6.95 (*0-340-65108-3*, Pub. by Hodder & Stought Ltd) Trafalgar.

— Home Learning 5-7 Parents' Guide. mass mkt. 6.95 (*0-340-69353-3*, Pub. by Hodder & Stought Ltd) Trafalgar.

— Home Learning 3-5 Maths. (Illus.). (J). mass mkt. 6.95 (*0-340-69382-7*, Pub. by Hodder & Stought Ltd) Trafalgar.

— Home Learning 3-5 Number Practice. (Illus.). (J). 1996. mass mkt. 5.95 (*0-340-65693-X*, Pub. by Hodder & Stought Ltd) Trafalgar.

— Home Learning 3-5 Reading. (Illus.). (J). mass mkt. 6.95 (*0-340-69381-9*, Pub. by Hodder & Stought Ltd) Trafalgar.

— Home Learning 3-5 Reading Practice. (Illus.). (J). 1996. mass mkt. 5.95 (*0-340-65691-3*, Pub. by Hodder & Stought Ltd) Trafalgar.

— Home Learning 3-5 Writing Practice. (Illus.). (J). 1996. mass mkt. 6.95 (*0-340-65692-1*, Pub. by Hodder & Stought Ltd) Trafalgar.

— Home Learning 3-5 Tables. (Illus.). (J). 1996. mass mkt. 6.95 (*0-340-62982-7*, Pub. by Hodder & Stought Ltd) Trafalgar.

— Home Learning 3-5 Weights & Measures. (Illus.). (J). 1996. mass mkt. 5.95 (*0-340-62985-1*, Pub. by Hodder & Stought Ltd) Trafalgar.

— Mental Arithmetic. (Illus.). (YA). (gr. 9-11). 1996. mass mkt. 6.95 (*0-340-65110-5*, Pub. by Hodder & Stought Ltd) Trafalgar.

— Multiplication & Division. (Illus.). (J). 1996. mass mkt. 6.95 (*0-340-62984-3*, Pub. by Hodder & Stought Ltd) Trafalgar.

— Numbers. (Home Learning Ser.). (J). 1996. mass mkt. 6.96 (*0-340-64658-6*, Pub. by Hodder & Stought Ltd) Trafalgar.

— Punctuation & Grammar. (Illus.). (J). 1996. mass mkt. 6.95 (*0-340-65106-7*, Pub. by Hodder & Stought Ltd) Trafalgar.

— Reading. (J). (gr. 3-5). 1996. mass mkt. 6.95 (*0-340-64656-X*, Pub. by Hodder & Stought Ltd) Trafalgar.

— Reading. (Illus.). (J). 1996. mass mkt. 6.95 (*0-340-65107-5*, Pub. by Hodder & Stought Ltd) Trafalgar.

— Reasoning. (YA). (gr. 9-11). 1996. mass mkt. 6.95 (*0-340-65113-X*, Pub. by Hodder & Stought Ltd) Trafalgar.

— Spelling. (Illus.). (J). (gr. 5-7). 1996. mass mkt. 6.95 (*0-340-65105-9*, Pub. by Hodder & Stought Ltd) Trafalgar.

— Writing. (J). 1996. mass mkt. 6.95 (*0-340-64657-8*, Pub. by Hodder & Stought Ltd) Trafalgar.

NCR Corporation Staff. NCR Stakeholder Essay Competition National Winners, 1988: Creating Value for Stakeholders. (Illus.). 73p. (Orig.). 1988. pap. text 11.95 (*0-925738-00-X*) NCR Law.

NCRA Staff. Cancer Registry Management: Principles & Practice. LC 97-156053. 720p. Date not set. 99.95 (*0-7872-2120-1*) Kendall-Hunt.

NCS Staff. NCS Carreer Assessment Keys. 1996. pap. text 7.40 (*0-13-244559-X*) P-H.

***NCSF Staff & SOWF Staff.** The CARE Book: College Aid Resources for Education. The Scholarship Financial Aid Guide for Tomorrow. 1998. pap. 29.95 (*0-9656724-0-9*) Nat Coll Scholarship.

NCSL Children & Families Program Staff, prod. 1997 State Legislative Summary: Children, Youth & Family Issues. 163p. 1998. 25.00 (*1-55516-755-1*, 6139) Natl Conf State Legis.

NCSL Children Families Program Staff. 1994 Summary of Children Youth & Family Legislation. 200p. 1994. 20.00 (*1-55516-649-0*, 6131) Natl Conf State Legis.

NCSL Fiscal Affairs Staff. NCSL State Budget Update: February, 1992. (State Legislative Reports: Vol. 17, No. 4). 22p. 1992. pap. text 15.00 (*1-55516-276-2*, 7302-1704) Natl Conf State Legis.

NCSL Fiscal Dept. & Oversight & Intergovrmtl. Affa. Public Pensions: A Legislator's Guide. 50p. 1995. 10.00 (*1-55516-085-9*, 5327) Natl Conf State Legis.

NCSL Foundation Fiscal Partners Staff. Critical Issues in State-Local Fiscal Policy: A Guide to Local Option Taxes. LC 99-195841. 33p. 1997. 20.00 (*1-55516-562-1*, 5337) Natl Conf State Legis.

NCSL Health Care Program Staff. Health Care Legislation, 1996: Executive Summary. 27p. 1997. 10.00 (*1-55516-756-X*) Natl Conf State Legis.

— Health Care Legislation,1997. 1998. 25.00 (*1-55516-826-4*) Natl Conf State Legis.

NCSL Health Program Staff. Maternal & Child Health Legislation, 1994. 75p. 1995. 15.00 (*1-55516-609-1*, 6650) Natl Conf State Legis.

— Medicaid Survival Kit. LC 99-162571. 322p. 1996. 75.00 (*1-55516-655-5*, 6654) Natl Conf State Legis.

NCSL Health Program Staff, compiled by. Health Care Legislation, 1995. 150p. 1996. 25.00 (*1-55516-606-7*, 6655) Natl Conf State Legis.

— 1997 Directory of Key Health Legislators & Legislative Staff. 79p. 1997. 20.00 (*1-55516-651-2*, 6661) Natl Conf State Legis.

NCSL Health Services Program Staff. 1995-96 Directory of Key Health Legislators & Legislative Staff. 1995. 20.00 (*1-55516-608-3*, 6653) Natl Conf State Legis.

NCSL Legislative Management Staff. Campaign Finance Legislation, 1993. 28p. (Orig.). 1994. 5.00 (*1-55516-745-4*, 9363) Natl Conf State Legis.

— Directory of Legislative Leaders, 1996. 137p. 1996. pap. 20.00 (*1-55516-778-0*, 7145) Natl Conf State Legis.

— State Legislators' Occupations, 1994: A Survey. LC 97-211249. 35p. 1994. 20.00 (*1-55516-746-2*, 7138) Natl Conf State Legis.

NCSL Legislative Management Staff & Root, Monica. Directory of Legislative Leaders, 1994. 137p. 1994. 15.00 (*1-55516-744-6*, 7136) Natl Conf State Legis.

NCSL Prevention Projects Program Staff. Adolescent Health Issues: State Actions, 1998. 1998. 20.00 (*1-55516-794-2*) Natl Conf State Legis.

NCSL Staff. Directory of Legislative Leaders: 1995. 137p. 1995. 15.00 (*1-55516-775-6*, 7141) Natl Conf State Legis.

— Directory of Legislative Leaders, 1993. 112p. 1993. pap. text 15.00 (*1-55516-742-X*, 7135) Natl Conf State Legis.

— The HIV-AIDS Fact Finder. 125p. 1993. pap. 25.00 (*1-55516-702-0*, 6640) Natl Conf State Legis.

— Issues Outlook, 1994. 45p. 1994. 30.00 (*1-55516-992-9*, 9355) Natl Conf State Legis.

— Metrology, Why Not?!! Proceedings of the 1998 Workshop & Symposium. unabridged ed. (Illus.). 1046p. 1998. 40.00 (*1-58464-022-7*) Natl Conf Stds Labs.

— 1995 State Legislative Priorities: An Opinion Survey of Leading Lawmakers. 45p. 1995. 30.00 (*1-55516-925-2*, 9368) Natl Conf State Legis.

NCSL Staff, comment. Election Results Directory, 1996. 282p. 1996. 35.00 (*1-55516-777-2*) Natl Conf State Legis.

NCSL State-Federal Relations Staff. Summary of One Hundred Second Congress, Second Session, (1992) (State-Federal Issue Brief Ser.: Vol. 5, No. 5). 13p. 1992. 6.50 (*1-55516-899-X*, 8500-0505) Natl Conf State Legis.

***NCSO Intrinsic & Derived Committee.** Catalogue of Intrinsic & Derived Standards. unabridged ed. 58p. 1999. 15.00 (*1-58464-024-3*) Natl Conf Stds Labs.

NCSS Staff. Alan F. Griffin on Teaching. 92p. 1995. per. 18.95 (*0-8403-8147-6*) Kendall-Hunt.

— Children's Literature & Social Studies: Selecting & Using Notable Books in the Classroom. 96p. 1996. per. 14.95 (*0-8403-8951-5*) Kendall-Hunt.

NCSU (Gilligan) Staff. College of Engineering: Student Handbook. 5th ed. 124p. (C). 1997. per. 10.95 (*0-7872-3939-9*) Kendall-Hunt.

— Introduction to College of Engineering E-100 Student Handbook, 1996-1997. 4th ed. 120p. (C). 1996. pap. text, per. 10.95 (*0-7872-2499-5*) Kendall-Hunt.

— The Widener Experience. 220p. (C). 1998. ring bd. 32.95 (*0-7872-5374-X*) Kendall-Hunt.

NCSU (Wilson) Staff. Introduction to the College of Management. 88p. (C). 1996. pap. text, ring bd. 14.17 (*0-7872-2678-5*) Kendall-Hunt.

NCTE Committee on Alternatives to Grading Student. Alternatives to Grading Student Writing. Tchudi, Stephen, ed. LC 97-10157. 308p. 1997. 22.95 (*0-8141-0130-5*) NCTE.

NCTE Committee on Classroom Practices[<]fv;0

NCTE Elementary Section Steering Committee & National Council of Teachers of English Staff. The Literate Life: Exploring Language Arts Standards Within a Cycle of Learning. LC 97-1785. 56p. pap. 8.95 (*0-8141-2976-5*) NCTE.

NCTM Commission on Teaching Standards for School M. Professional Standards for Teaching Mathematics. LC 90-26154. (Illus.). 196p. 1991. pap. 29.50 (*0-87353-307-0*) NCTM.

NCTM Staff. Connecting Mathematics Across the Curriculum: 1995 Yearbook. House, Peggy A. & Coxford, Arthur F., eds. LC 94-48261. (Yearbook Ser.: 1995). (Illus.). 248p. 1995. 25.95 (*0-87353-394-1*) NCTM.

— Cumulative Index: The Mathematics Teacher, 1908-1965. LC 42-24844. 207p. 1967. pap. 12.00 (*0-87353-028-4*) NCTM.

— A General Survey of Progress in the Last Twenty-Five Years: First Yearbook. 210p. 1995. reprint ed. pap. 15.95 (*0-87353-396-8*) NCTM.

— The Learning of Mathematics - Its Theory & Practice: Twenty-First Yearbook. Fehr, Howard F., ed. 353p. 1995. reprint ed. pap. 17.95 (*0-87353-404-2*) NCTM.

— Mathematics in Modern Life: Sixth Yearbook. Reeve, W. D., ed. 195p. 1995. reprint ed. pap. 15.95 (*0-87353-398-4*) NCTM.

— The Nature of Proof: Thirteenth Yearbook. Fawcett, Harold P., ed. 146p. 1995. reprint ed. pap. 15.95 (*0-87353-402-6*) NCTM.

— The Place of Mathematics in Education: 11th Yearbook. Reeve, W. D., ed. 258p. 1995. reprint ed. pap. 15.00 (*0-87353-400-X*) NCTM.

Ncube, Welchman. Law, Culture, Tradition, & Children's Rights in Eastern & Southern Africa. LC 98-19214. (Issues in Law & Society Ser.). 358p. (C). 1998. text 76.95 (*1-84014-047-X*, KQC145.M55N38, Pub. by Ashgate Pub); pap. text 31.95 (*1-84014-477-7*, KQC145.M44N38, Pub. by Ashgate Pub) Ashgate Pub Co.

NCYM Peace Committee, ed. Faith into Action. 40p. (Orig.). 1985. pap. 2.00 (*0-942727-13-4*) NC Yrly Pubns Bd.

N'Daba, Louis & Hodges-Aeberhard, Jane. HIV/AIDS & Employment. LC 98-176649. 71p. 1999. pap. 20.00 (*92-2-110334-X*, Pub. by Statnry Office) Balogh.

Ndachi, Teresa, ed. see True, Adiaha.

Ndagala, Daniel K. Territory, Pastoralists & Livestock: Resource Control among the Kisongo Maasai. (Uppsala Studies in Cultural Anthropology: No. 18). 192p. (Orig.). 1992. pap. 47.50 (*91-554-2877-0*) Coronet Bks.

***Ndambuki, Berida & Robertson, Claire C.** We Only Come Here to Struggle: Stories from Berida's Life. LC 99-48576. (Illus.). 240p. 2000. pap. 17.95 (*0-253-21366-5*); lib. bdg. 39.95 (*0-253-33701-1*) Ind U Pr.

Ndatshe, Vivienne, jt. auth. see Moodie, T. Dunbar.

Ndayizigiye, Thaddee. L' Anthropologie Biblique sous l'Eclairage de la Philosophie de l'Alterite Selon Emmanuel Levinas: Essai d'Analyse. (Publications Universitaires Europeennes Ser.: Series 23, Vol. 595). (FRE.). 454p. 1997. 60.95 (*3-906758-02-8*, Pub. by P Lang) P Lang Pubng.

— Reexamen Ethique des Droits de l'Homme Sous l'Eclairage de la Pensee d'Emmanuel Levinas. (Publications Universitaires Europeennes, Serie 28: Vol. 607). (FRE.). xxii, 559p. 1997. 60.95 (*3-906757-83-8*, Pub. by P Lang) P Lang Pubng.

Ndebe, Barnabas S., as told by. Tales from Bandiland. (Liberian Research Working Papers: No. 4). (Illus.). 311p. 1974. 12.00 (*0-916712-07-9*) Arden Assocs.

Ndebele, Njabulo S. Bonolo & the Peach Tree. large type ed. (Illus.). 1994. 21.50 (*0-614-09802-5*, L-34109-00) Am Printing Hse.

— Fools & Other Stories. (Readers International Ser.). 280p. (C). 1986. reprint ed. pap. 12.95 (*0-930523-20-2*) Readers Intl.

Ndego, Anne, ed. see Onuzo, Okey.

***Ndegwa, David & Olajide, D., eds.** Main Issues in Mental Health & Race. 278p. 2000. 74.95 (*1-84014-812-8*) Ashgate Pub Co.

An Asterisk (*) at the beginning of an entry indicates that the title is appearing for the first time.

Ndegwa, Stephen N. The Two Faces of Civil Society: NGOs & Politics in Africa. LC 95-38747. (Books on International Development). (Illus.). 160p. 1996. pap. 21.95 (*1-56549-055-X*); text 35.00 (*1-56549-056-8*) Kumarian Pr.

Ndegwa, Stephen N., jt. auth. see Bradshaw, York W.

Ndeti, Kivuto & Gray, Kenneth R., eds. The Second Scramble for Africa: A Response & a Critical Analysis of the Challenges Facing Contemporary Sub-Saharan Africa. 417p. 1992. pap. text 19.95 (*9966-835-73-3*) Prof World Peace.

***Ndiokwere, Nathaniel.** At the Crossroads: Dilemma of the Man of God. 228p. 1999. pap. write for info. (*0-7392-0472-6*, P03799) Morris Pubng.

Ndiokwere, Nathaniel. Prophecy & Revolution. 350p. 1996. pap. 32.50 (*0-7618-0602-4*) U Pr of Amer.

— Search for Greener Pastures: Igbo & African Experience. 336p. 1998. pap. 15.00 (*1-57502-945-6*, PO2601) Morris Pubng.

— The Third Millennium Church: The Church That Will Survive. 1998. pap. 18.00 (*1-57502-931-6*, PO2567) Morris Pubng.

Ndiokwere, Nathaniel I. Search for Greener Pastures: Igbo & African Experience. LC 98-21203. 348p. (C). 1998. 62.00 (*0-7618-1150-8*); pap. 42.50 (*0-7618-1151-6*) U Pr of Amer.

Ndione, Emmanuel, et al. The Future of Community Lands: Human Resources. LC 96-175904. 236p. 1995. pap. 29.50 (*1-85339-248-0*, Pub. by Intermed Tech) Stylus Pub VA.

Ndir. America, Teacher's Guide, 001. 1985. mass mkt. 8.24 (*0-395-39028-1*) HM.

Ndir. Orbits Voyagers. 1989. text 58.36 (*0-395-52131-9*) HM.

Ndlovu, Jacob M. African Pride: From the Other Side. (Illus.). 132p. 1994. pap. text 10.75 (*0-9644137-0-1*) NOA Intl.

Ndlovu, Lindani B. The System of Protection & Industrial Development in Zimbabwe. 246p. 1994. 77.95 (*1-85628-870-6*, Pub. by Avebry) Ashgate Pub Co.

Ndongko, Wilfred. Regional Economic Planning in Cameroon. (Research Report Ser.: No. 21). 21p. 1974. write for info. (*91-7106-073-1*, Pub. by Nordic Africa) Transaction Pubs.

Ndongko, Wilfred A. & Vivekananda, Franklin. Critical Essays on African & Third World Economic Development, Vol. 1: Africa, the Awakening Giant. 218p. (Orig.). 1989. pap. 84.50 (*91-86702-05-X*) Coronet Bks.

Ndreca, Mikel. Albanian-Serbocroatian Dictionary: Fjalor Shallor Shqip-Serbokrpatisht-Shqip. (ALB, CRO & SER.). 228p. 1987. pap. 19.95 (*0-8288-1091-5*, F78710) Fr & Eur.

Ndu, Pol. Songs for Seers. LC 73-91413. 35p. 1974. pap. 2.95 (*0-88357-036-X*) NOK Pubs.

Nduati, Ruth & Kiai, Wambui. Communicating with Adolescents with AIDS. 248p. 1997. pap. 19.95 (*0-88936-832-5*, Pub. by IDRC Bks) Stylus Pub VA.

Ndubisi, Forster O. Planning Implementation Tools & Techniques: A Resource Book for Local Governments. (Illus.). 224p. (Orig.). 1992. pap. text 20.00 (*0-911847-04-9*) U GA Inst Community.

— Public Policy & Land Use in Georgia: A Concise Reference Book. LC 96-11689. 1996. pap. write for info. (*0-911847-09-X*) U GA Inst Community.

Ndukwe, Ernest. Rushing to Deceive: Disagreements with Rush Limbaugh. LC 95-976890. 140p. 1995. pap. 9.95 (*1-885487-14-2*) Brownell & Carroll.

Ndukwe, P., jt. auth. see Kaschula, Russell.

Ndulo, Muna, jt. ed. see Osei-Hwedie, Kwaku.

***Ndulu, Benno J.** Economic Develop Sub-saharan. 2000. text 85.00 (*0-312-23206-3*) St Martin.

Ndulu, Benno J., jt. ed. see Lundahl, Mats.

Ndulu, Benno J., jt. ed. see Van De Walle, Nicolas.

Ndumbaro, Paul, jt. auth. see Broughton, Peter.

Nduwke, Pat I. Fulani. Bond, George & Wyck, Gary V., eds. (Heritage Library of African Peoples). (Illus.). 64p. (YA). (gr. 7-12). 1995. lib. bdg. 16.95 (*0-8239-1982-X*) Rosen Group.

Ndyajunwoha, Gaston Z., jt. auth. see Nagel, Walter H.

N.E. Thing Enterprises Staff. Garfield's Magic Eye. (Illus.). 32p. 1995. pap. 6.95 (*0-8362-7054-1*) Andrews & McMeel.

— Looney Tunes' Magic Eye. (Illus.). 32p. (J). 1995. 14.95 (*0-8362-7053-3*) Andrews & McMeel.

N.E. Thing Enterprises Staff, et al. Magic Eye: The 3D Guide. (Illus.). 64p. 1995. 10.95 (*0-8362-0467-0*) Andrews & McMeel.

***NEA Professional Library Association Staff & National Education Associaton of the United States Staff.** Works4Me: Practical Classroom Tips from Your Colleagues. LC 00-41578. 2000. write for info. (*0-8106-2161-4*) NEA.

***NEA Staff.** Advanced Reactors with Innovative Fuels: Workshop Proceedings, Villigen, Switzerland 21-23 October 1998. (OECD Proceedings Ser.). 464p. 1999. pap. 117.00 (*92-64-17117-7*, 66 1999 14 1 P, Pub. by Org for Econ) OECD.

NEA Staff. Agricultural Aspects of Nuclear and/or Radiological Emergency Situations. 192p. 1997. pap. 28.00 (*92-64-15614-3*, 66-97-08-1, Pub. by Org for Econ) OECD.

***NEA Staff.** Back-End of the Fuel Cycle in a 1000 Gwe Nuclear Scenario: Workshop Proceedings, Avignon, France, 6-7 October 1998. (OECD Proceedings Ser.). 124p. 1999. pap. 34.00 (*92-64-17116-9*, 66 1999 13 1 P, Pub. by Org for Econ) OECD.

— Core Monitoring the Commercial Reactors: Improvements in Systems & Methods, Workshop Proceedings, Stockholm 4-5 October 1999. (Proceedings Ser.). 296p. 2000. pap. 71.00 (*92-64-17659-4*, 66 2000 11 1 P, Pub. by Org for Econ) OECD.

— Environmental Activities in Uranium Mining & Milling. 176p. 1999. pap. 47.00 (*92-64-17064-2*, 66 1999 09 1 P, Pub. by Org for Econ) OECD.

NEA Staff. Field Tracer Experiments: Role in the Prediction of Radionuclide Migration. LC 98-144358. 250p. 1998. pap. 40.00 (*92-64-16013-2*, 66-97-13-1, Pub. by Org for Econ) OECD.

— Fluid Flow Through Faults & Fractures in Argillaceous Formations: Proceedings of a Joint NEA - EC Workshop Held in Berne, Switzerland, 10-12 June, 1996. LC 98-145994. 404p. 1998. pap. 67.00 (*92-64-16021-3*, 66-98-03-1-P, Pub. by Org for Econ) OECD.

— Future Nuclear Regulatory Challenges: A Report by the NEA Committee on Nuclear Regulatory Activities. LC 98-196457. 48p. 1998. pap. 20.00 (*92-64-16106-6*, 66 98 10 1 P, Pub. by European Conference Ministers Transp) OECD.

***NEA Staff.** Glossary of Nuclear Power Plant Ageing. 130p. 1999. pap. 52.00 (*92-64-05842-7*, Pub. by Org for Econ) OECD.

NEA Staff. In-Core Instrumentation & Reactor Core Assessment: Proceedings of a Specialist Meeting, Mito-shi, Japan, 16-17 October, 1996. 428p. 1997. pap. 58.00 (*92-64-15616-X*, 66-97-09-1, Pub. by Org for Econ) OECD.

— Informing the Public about Radioactive Waste Management: Proceedings of an NEA International Seminar, Rauma, Finland, 13-15 June 1995. (Nuclear Energy & Information Ser.). 332p. (Orig.). 1996. pap. 45.00 (*92-64-04860-X*, 66-96-09-3) OECD.

***NEA Staff.** Ion & Slow Positron Beam Utilisation. (OECD Proceedings Ser.). 240p. (Orig.). 1999. pap. 72.00 (*92-64-17025-1*, 66/1999/04/1/P, Pub. by Org for Econ) OECD.

NEA Staff. Long-Lived Radionuclide Chemistry in Nuclear Waste Treatment. LC 98-222844. (OECD Proceedings Ser.). 272p. 1998. pap. 65.00 (*92-64-16148-1*, 6698131P) OECD.

— Low-Level Radioactive Waste Repositories: An Analysis of Costs. 180p. 1999. pap. 50.00 (*92-64-16154-6*, 66 99 03 1 P) Org for Econ.

— The Management of Separated Plutonium: The Technical Options. 164p. 1997. pap. 47.00 (*92-64-15410-8*, 66-97-01-1, Pub. by Org for Econ) OECD.

***NEA Staff.** Methodologies for Assessing the Economic Consequences of Nuclear Reactor Accidents. (Radiation Protection Ser.). 116p. 2000. pap. 31.00 (*92-64-17658-6*, 66 2000 10 1 P, Pub. by Org for Econ) OECD.

NEA Staff. Modelling the Effects of Spatial Variability on Radionuclide Miigration. 320p. 1998. pap. 74.00 (*92-64-16099-X*, 66 98 09 1 P, Pub. by European Conference Ministers Transp) OECD.

— Nuclear Emergency Data Management. LC 98-145150. (Proceedings Ser.). 480p. 1998. pap. 79.00 (*92-64-16037-X*, 66-98-02-1-P, Pub. by Org for Econ) OECD.

— Nuclear Energy Data, 1998. 48p. 1998. pap. 20.00 (*92-64-05762-5*, 66 98 11 3 P, Pub. by European Conference Ministers Transp) OECD.

***NEA Staff.** Nuclear Energy Data 1999. 48p. 1999. pap. 21.00 (*92-64-05856-7*, 66 1999 08 3 P, Pub. by Org for Econ) OECD.

NEA Staff. Nuclear Energy Data 1997. 52p. 1997. pap. 20.00 (*92-64-05520-7*, 66-97-05-3, Pub. by Org for Econ) OECD.

— Nuclear Legislation Analytical Study: Regulatory & Institutional Framework for Nuclear Activities. (ENG & FRE.). 582p. 1995. 190.00 (*92-64-14586-9*, Pub. by Org for Econ) OECD.

— Nuclear Power: Sustainability, Climate Change & Competition. 88p. 1998. pap. 60.00 (*92-64-16954-7*, 6198291P) OECD.

— Nuclear Safety Research in OECD Countries: Areas of Agreement, Areas for Further Action, Increasing Need for Further Collaboration. LC 97-182172. 80p. (Orig.). 1996. pap. 20.00 (*92-64-15336-5*, 66-96-15-1, Pub. by Org for Econ) OECD.

— Overview of Nuclear Legislation in Central & Eastern Europe & in the NIS. LC 98-144342. 132p. 1998. pap. 25.00 (*92-64-16018-3*, 66 98 05 1 P, Pub. by Org for Econ) OECD.

— Projected Costs of Generating Electricity: Update 1998. LC 98-222889. 244p. 1998. pap. 66.00 (*92-64-16162-7*, 6698161P) OECD.

— Radiation in Perspective: Applications, Risks, & Protection. (Nuclear Energy & Information Ser.). 96p. 1997. pap. 27.00 (*92-64-15483-3*, 66-97-04-1, Pub. by Org for Econ) OECD.

***NEA Staff.** Radiation Waste Management: Water-Conducting Features in Radionuclide Migration. Workshop Proceedings, Barcelona, Spain, 10-12 June 1998. (OECD Proceedings Ser.). 380p. 1999. pap. 96.00 (*92-64-17124-X*, 66 1999 16 1 P, Pub. by Org for Econ) OECD.

— Regulatory Reviews of Assessments of Deep Geologic Repositories: Lessons Learnt. (Radioactive Waste Management Ser.). 136p. 2000. pap. 32.00 (*92-64-05886-9*, 2000 06 3 P, Pub. by Org for Econ) OECD.

NEA Staff. Safety Research Needs for Russian-Designed Reactors. LC 98-144331. 68p. 1998. pap. 16.00 (*92-64-15669-0*, 66 98 04 1 P, Pub. by Org for Econ) OECD.

— SATIF-2 - Shielding Aspects of Accelerators, Targets & Irradiation Facilities: Proceedings of the 2nd Specialists Meeting. LC 97-120824. 324p. (Orig.). 1996. pap. 69.00 (*92-64-15287-3*, 66-96-11-1) OECD.

***NEA Staff.** Shielding Aspects of Accelerators, Targets & Irradiation Facilities: SATIF 4 Workshop Proceedings. (OECD Proceedings Ser.). 308p. 1999. pap. 88.00 (*92-64-17044-8*, 66 1999 06 1 P, Pub. by Org for Econ) OECD.

NEA Staff. 3-D Deterministic Radiation Transport Computer Programmes: Features, Applications, & Perspectives. LC 98-121906. 432p. 1998. pap. 70.00 (*92-64-16020-5*, 66-97-16-1, Pub. by Org for Econ) OECD.

— Uranium Resources, Production & Demand, 1997 (1998 Edition) 400p. 1998. pap. 79.00 (*92-64-16050-7*, 66 98 06 1 P, Pub. by European Conference Ministers Transp) OECD.

— Use of Hydrogeochemical Information on Testing Groundwater Flow Models. 370p. 1999. pap. 91.00 (*92-64-16153-8*, 66 98 14 1 P) Org for Econ.

***NEA Staff.** Utilisation & Reliability of High Power Proton Accelerators: Workshop Proceedings, Mito, Japan, 13-15 October 1998. (OECD Proceedings Ser.). 444p. 1999. pap. 113.00 (*92-64-17068-5*, Pub. by Org for Econ) OECD.

NEA Staff, jt. auth. see OECD Staff.

Neach, David, jt. auth. see McGimpsey, Kevin.

Neacsu, L. Dictionary of Ecology: Dictionar de Ecologie. (RUM.). 1982. write for info. (*0-8288-1405-8*, M15838) Fr & Eur.

Nead. Law & the Image. LC 98-50313. 1999. pap. text 19.00 (*0-226-56954-3*) U Ch Pr.

— Law & the Image. LC 98-50313. (Illus.). 288p. 1999. lib. bdg. 47.00 (*0-226-56953-5*) U Ch Pr.

Nead, Benjamin M. Waynesboro: History of Settlements in the County Formerly Called Cumberland...in Its Beginnings Through Its Growth. (Illus.). 427p. 1997. reprint ed. lib. bdg. 45.00 (*0-8328-6460-9*) Higginson Bk Co.

Nead, Daniel W. Pennsylvania-German Settlement of Maryland. (Illus.). 304p. 1997. reprint ed. lib. bdg. 38.50 (*0-8328-5934-3*) Higginson Bk Co.

Nead, Kimberly, jt. ed. see Van De Walle, Dominique.

Nead, Lynda. Chila Kumari Burman: Beyond Two Cultures. 80p. 1995. 13.95 (*0-947753-07-9*, Pub. by Kala Pr) SPD-Small Pr Dist.

— The Female Nude: Art, Obscenity, & Sexuality. LC 92-10516. (Illus.). 240p. (C). (gr. 13). 1992. pap. 20.99 (*0-415-02678-4*, A9659) Routledge.

***Nead, Lynda.** Victorian Babylon: People, Streets & Images in Nineteenth-Century London. LC 00-31037. (Illus.). 256p. 2000. 35.00 (*0-300-08505-2*) Yale U Pr.

Nead, Lynda, jt. ed. see Marcus, Laura.

Nead, Stephanie K. Healing Food Allergies: It Can Be Delicious!: Detox & Food Testing; Alternative Ingredients & Recipes; Lifestyle Changes & Maintenance; Chemical Environmental Sensitivities. 192p. 1997. pap. 18.95 (*0-9661918-0-3*) S K Nead.

Neaderland, Louise. Alphagami: An Alphabet Book. (Illus.). 14p. 1998. 10.00 (*0-942561-32-5*) Bone Hollow.

— Black Holes. (Illus.). 1997. 25.00 (*0-942561-30-9*) Bone Hollow.

Neaderland, Louise O. Artist at Work. 1982. 5.00 (*0-942561 08 2*) Bone Hollow.

— The Book of Hours, Minutes & Seconds in 12 Volumes!, 12 vols., Set. (Illus.). 1500p. 1994. 300.00 (*0-942561-24-4*) Bone Hollow.

— A Book of Short Stories. (Illus.). 1986. 25.00 (*0-942561-11-2*) Bone Hollow.

— The Case for Gun Control. (Illus.). 10p. 1994. 15.00 (*0-942561-22-8*) Bone Hollow.

— Desert Storm - Desert Sand. (Illus.). 1992. 12.00 (*0-942561-17-1*) Bone Hollow.

— Dialogues. deluxe ed. (Illus.). 13p. (Orig.). 1990. boxed set 12.00 (*0-942561-15-5*) Bone Hollow.

— The Disposable History of the World. (Illus.). (C). 1987. boxed set 15.00 (*0-942561-01-5*) Bone Hollow.

— Distress Signals. 58p. 1985. 3.00 (*0-942561-07-4*) Bone Hollow.

— Farewells. (Illus.). 20p. 1990. boxed set. write for info. (*0-942561-16-3*) Bone Hollow.

— Journeys. (Illus.). (Orig.). (C). 1996. pap. 6.00 (*0-942561-27-9*) Bone Hollow.

— Leningrad, Aug. 9, 1991-Aug. 24, 1991: St. Petersburg, 1903. (Illus.). 65p. 1992. 35.00 (*0-942561-19-8*) Bone Hollow.

— A Mideast Kaleidoscope. (Illus.). 45p. 1983. 15.00 (*0-942561-05-8*) Bone Hollow.

— Missing Persons. 32p. 1988. spiral bd. 15.00 (*0-942561-10-4*) Bone Hollow.

— Nuclear Fan. (Illus.). 1984. 10.00 (*0-942561-02-3*) Bone Hollow.

— Open Roads - Empty Nests. (Illus.). 16p. 1988. 5.00 (*0-942561-12-0*) Bone Hollow.

— Our Glass. (Illus.). 1984. 25.00 (*0-942561-04-X*) Bone Hollow.

— Sadat's Journey. (Illus.). 1981. 10.00 (*0-942561-14-7*) Bone Hollow.

— Scenic Tunnels. (Illus.). 16p. (Orig.). 1983. pap. 12.00 (*0-942561-03-1*) Bone Hollow.

— La Strada. deluxe ed. (Illus.). 1986. boxed set 12.00 (*0-942561-06-6*) Bone Hollow.

— Straitjacket. (Illus.). 1987. 5.00 (*0-942561-00-7*) Bone Hollow.

— Where Could the Dark Matter Be. (Illus.). 1992. 5.00 (*0-942561-21-X*) Bone Hollow.

— Where Is Home? Basic Elements. deluxe ed. (Illus.). 1986. boxed set 10.00 (*0-942561-09-0*) Bone Hollow.

Neaderland, Louise O. & Christ, Steve. Empress Bullett. (Illus.). 1982. 12.00 (*0-942561-13-9*) Bone Hollow.

Neaderland, Louise Odes. The Sound of One Hand Clapping. (Illus.). 1995. pap. 25.00 (*0-942561-23-6*) Bone Hollow.

Neag, Michael, jt. ed. see Riga, Alan T.

Neagel, jt. auth. see Randell, Roscoe.

Neagles, James C. Confederate Research Sources: A Guide to Archive Collections. LC 85-52453. (Illus.). 286p. 1986. pap. 15.95 (*0-916489-16-7*) Ancestry.

— The Library of Congress: A Guide to Genealogical & Historical Research. 381p. 1990. 39.95 (*0-916489-48-5*) Ancestry.

— U. S. Military Records: A Guide to Federal & State Sources, Colonial America to the Present. LC 94-3848. (Illus.). 455p. 1994. 39.95 (*0-916489-55-8*) Ancestry.

Neagley, Linda E. Disciplined Exuberance: The Parish Church of Saint-Maclou & Late Gothic Architecture in Rouen. LC 96-38117. 1998. 55.00 (*0-271-01716-3*) Pa St U Pr.

Neagoe, Peter. Winning a Wife, & Other Stories. LC 78-152951. (Short Story Index Reprint Ser.). 1977. reprint ed. 20.95 (*0-8369-3866-6*) Ayer.

Neal. Beginners Guide T1-85: Custom Publishing. 2nd ed. 1996. 7.74 (*0-07-046290-9*) McGraw.

— MCSE Study Tips for Dummies. LC 99-474246. (For Dummies Ser.). 288p. 1998. pap. 16.99 (*0-7645-0484-3*) IDG Bks.

— Site Surveying Level 3. 1985. pap. text. write for info. (*0-582-41291-9*, Pub. by Addison-Wesley) Longman.

— Windows 98 Exam 70-98: Accelerated MCSE Study Guide. 1998. 24.99 (*0-07-134555-8*) McGraw.

Neal & Associates Staff, ed. see Swift, Catherine G.

Neal, A. W. Formation & Use of Industrial by-Products: A Guide. 1975. pap. 25.00 (*0-8464-0420-6*) Beekman Pubs.

Neal, Al. The Infinity Bible Code. (Illus.). 172p. 1999. pap. 15.00 (*1-58538-003-2*) Prophecy Club.

Neal, Alan C. European Communities' Health & Safety Legislation, Vol. 2. 1995. pap. 77.95 (*0-412-57760-7*) Chapman & Hall.

— European Communities' Health & Safety Legislation, Vol. 3. 1995. pap. 52.00 (*0-412-57770-4*) Chapman & Hall.

***Neal, Alan C.** Fundamental Social Rights at Work in the European Community. LC 99-224608. 242p. 1999. text 61.95 (*0-7546-2054-9*, Pub. by Ashgate Pub) Ashgate Pub Co.

Neal, Alan C. & Foyn, Sten. Developing the Social Dimension in an Enlarged European Union. (IUSEF Ser.: No. 16). 141p. (C). 1994. pap. 22.00 (*82-00-22648-4*, Pub. by Scand Univ Pr) IBD Ltd.

Neal, Alfred C. Business Power & Public Policy. LC 81-7348. 163p. 1981. 45.00 (*0-275-90686-8*, C0686, Praeger Pubs) Greenwood.

Neal, Anthony. Psychological Cinemas: A Poetical Autobiography. 1998. pap. 15.95 (*1-890301-06-X*) M Bey.

Neal, Anthony J. & Hoskin, Peter J. Clinical Oncology: Basic Principles & Practice. 2nd ed. LC 96-39632. (Illus.). 256p. 1997. pap. text 29.95 (*0-340-67748-1*, Pub. by E A) OUP.

— Clinical Oncology: A Textbook for Students. 328p. 1994. 24.95 (*0-340-59436-5*, Pub. by E A) OUP.

Neal, April K. & Taleff, Michael J. A Recovery Workbook: The Road Back from Substance Abuse. 36p. 1999. ring bd. 9.95 (*1-892132-01-X*, No. NRK105) Venture Pub PA.

Neal, Arminta. Exhibits for the Small Museum: A Handbook. LC 76-21812. 181p. 1976. reprint ed. pap. 56.20 (*0-608-07561-2*, 205266100009) Bks Demand.

— Help for the Small Museum: Handbook of Exhibit Ideas & Methods. 2nd ed. LC 86-30407. (Illus.). 176p. 1987. pap. 21.95 (*0-87108-720-0*) Pruett.

Neal, Arthur G. National Trauma & Collective Memory: Major Events in the American Century. LC 97-46625. 240p. (C). (gr. 13). 1998. text 65.95 (*0-7656-0286-5*) M E Sharpe.

***Neal, Arthur G.** National Trauma & Collective Memory: Major Events in the American Century. LC 97-46625. 240p. (C). (gr. 13). 1998. pap. text 27.95 (*0-7656-0287-3*) M E Sharpe.

***Neal, Arthur G. & Collas, Sara F.** Intimacy & Alienation: Forms of Estrangement in Female/Male Relationships. LC 00-27979. (Reference Library of Social Science). 2000. write for info. (*0-8153-3334-X*) Garland.

Neal-Barnett, Angela M. Family & Peers: Linking Two Social Worlds. Kerns, Kathryn A. & Contreras, Josefina M., eds. LC 99-16059. (Series in Applied Psychology). 280p. 2000. 69.50 (*0-275-96506-6*) Greenwood.

Neal-Barnett, Angela M., ed. see Kerns, Kathryn A.

Neal-Beckum, Sandra. A Typical Southern Family. 24p. 1999. pap. 7.00 (*0-8059-4752-3*) Dorrance.

Neal, Bill. Bill Neal's Southern Cooking. enl. rev. ed. LC 88-37258. xv, 204p. 1989. 29.95 (*0-8078-1859-3*); pap. 17.95 (*0-8078-4255-9*) U of NC Pr.

— Biscuits, Spoonbread & Sweet Potato Pie. 352p. 1996. pap. 18.00 (*0-679-76580-8*) Knopf.

— Gardener's Latin: A Lexicon. 144p. 1992. 14.95 (*0-945575-94-7*) Algonquin Bks.

Neal, Bill. The Last Frontier: History of Hardeman County, Texas. (Illus.). 296p. 1997. 29.95 (*1-57168-157-4*) Sunbelt Media.

Neal, Bill & Perry, David. Good Old Grits Cookbook: Have Grits Your Way. LC 90-50946. (Illus.). 160p. (Orig.). 1991. pap. 6.95 (*0-89480-865-6*, 1865) Workman Pub.

Neal, Bill, ed. see Lawrence, Elizabeth.

Neal, C. L. Manual para Obreros Cristianos.Tr. of Manual for Christian Workers. (SPA.). 184p. 1961. pap. 6.99 (*0-311-05017-4*) Casa Bautista.

Neal, C. W. Holding on to Heaven: While Your Husband Goes Through Hell. LC 97-44360. 1998. 12.99 (*0-8499-4065-6*) Word Pub.

Neal, C. W., jt. auth. see Dravecky, Dave.

Neal, Carl B. Leonard Shoun & His Wife Barbara Slemp of Johnson County, Tennessee & Their Descendants. 283p. 1985. reprint ed. 28.95 (*0-932807-10-0*); reprint ed. pap. 21.95 (*0-932807-09-7*) Overmountain Pr.

Neal, Cerla, et al. Brief Calculus: A Graphing Calculator Approach. abr. ed. LC 95-41658. 48p. 1996. text 61.95 (*0-471-05721-5*) Wiley.

N

— College Mathematics: A Graphing Calculator Approach. LC 95-41657. 861p. 1996. text 99.95 (*0-471-05720-7*) Wiley.

Neal, Charles. Armagnac: The Definitive Guide to France's Premier Brandy. 319p. 30.00 (*1-891267-20-5*) Wine Appreciation.

— Revelation: The Road to Overcoming. 2nd ed. LC 99-75698. 225p. 2000. reprint ed. pap. 9.95 (*0-87159-260-6*, 149) Unity Bks.

Neal, Charles, jt. ed. see Davies, Dominic.

Neal, Connie. 52 Maneras de Reducir el Estres en Tu Vida. (Fifty-Two Maneras de...Ser.). (SPA.). 150p. 1995. pap. 7.99 (*0-88113-226-8*) Caribe Betania.

— Dancing in the Arms of God: Finding Intimacy & Fulfillment in Your Only True Love. 176p. 1995. 14.99 (*0-310-20113-6*) Zondervan.

— Dancing in the Arms of God With Guide: Finding Intimacy & Fulfillment in Your Only True Love. 240p. 1997. pap. 12.99 (*0-310-21915-9*) Zondervan.

— Getting Your House (& Life) in Order. 1994. 8.98 (*0-88365-859-3*) Galahad Bks.

***Neal, Connie.** Holding on to Heaven: While Your Friend Goes Through Hell. LC 99-16792. 160p. 1999. pap. 10.99 (*0-8499-3764-7*) Tommy Nelson.

Neal, Connie, jt. auth. see Arterburn, Stephen.

Neal, Connie, jt. auth. see Dravecky, Jan.

Neal, Cynthia E., ed. & illus. see Kozlowski, Cheryl M.

Neal, D. E. Tumors in Urology. LC 94-14579. (Illus.). 298p. 1995. 136.00 (*3-540-19867-9*) Spr-Verlag.

Neal, Daniel. The History of New-England... to the Year of Our Lord, 1700, 2 vols., Set. LC 75-31125. reprint ed. 87.50 (*0-404-13760-1*) AMS Pr.

Neal, David. The Excavation of the Roman Villa in Gadebridge Park, Hemel Hempstead. (Illus.). 270p. 1975. 25.00 (*0-85431-231-5*, Pub. by Soc Antiquaries) David Brown.

— The Rule of Law in a Penal Colony: Law & Politics in Early New South Wales. (Studies in Australian History). 280p. (C). 1992. text 64.95 (*0-521-37264-X*) Cambridge U Pr.

Neal, David E., ed. Tumors in Urology: Biology & Clinical Management. LC 94-14579. 1994. 149.00 (*0-387-19867-9*) Spr-Verlag.

Neal, Diane. The Lion of the South: General Thomas C. Hindman. 1997. pap. text 17.95 (*0-86554-556-1*, P165) Mercer Univ Pr.

Neal, Donn C., ed. Consortia & Interinstitutional Cooperation. (ACE-Oryx Series on Higher Education). 224p. (C). 1988. 27.95 (*0-02-922510-8*) Free Pr.

***Neal, Dorothy.** Telephone Techniques. 2nd ed. 1998. teacher ed. 11.99 (*0-02-802012-X*) Glencoe.

Neal, Dorothy A. Telephone Techniques. 1990. pap. 19.20 (*0-07-046156-2*) McGraw.

— Telephone Techniques. 2nd ed. LC 97-26449. 1997. write for info. (*0-02-802011-1*) Glencoe.

Neal, Dorothy J. The Cloud-Climbing Railroad: Highest Point on the Southern Pacific. LC 98-85147. (Illus.). 134p. 1998. reprint ed. pap. 15.00 (*0-87404-280-1*, 280-1) Tex Western.

Neal, Dorothy J., jt. auth. see Neal, James E., Jr.

Neal, Ernest G. The Natural History of Badgers. LC 85-29248. (Illus.). 264p. reprint ed. pap. 81.90 (*0-7837-6690-4*, 204630700011) Bks Demand.

Neal, Ernest G. & Cheeseman, Chris. Badgers. (Poyser Natural History Ser.). (Illus.). 328p. 1996. text 36.00 (*0-85661-082-8*) Poyser.

Neal, Frank R. Concrete Industrial Ground Floors: ICE Design & Practice Guide. LC 97-135657. 56p. 1996. 24.00 (*0-7277-2521-1*) Am Soc Civil Eng.

Neal, Gregory, jt. auth. see Krasny, Marianne E.

Neal, H. Roger. Streetwise Investing in Rental Properties: A Detailed Strategy for Financial Independence. LC 93-32874. 1994. 15.95 (*1-882877-03-9*) Panoply Pr.

Neal, J. Matthew. Basic Endocrinology: An Interactive Approach. LC 99-30331. (Illus.). 1999. pap. 29.95 (*0-632-04429-2*) Blackwell Sci.

Neal, J. S., jt. auth. see Dawson, Tim P.

Neal, James E., Jr. Effective Phrases for Performance Appraisals: A Guide to Successful Evaluations. 8th rev. ed. LC 96-70322. 208p. 1997. mass mkt. 9.95 (*1-882423-08-9*) Neal Pubns Inc.

***Neal, James E., Jr.** Effective Phrases for Performance Appraisals: A Guide to Successful Evaluations. 9th ed. LC 99-74681. 208p. 2000. spiral bd. 10.95 (*1-882423-09-7*) Neal Pubns Inc.

Neal, James E., Jr. Effective Resume Writing: A Guide to Successful Employment. 2nd ed. LC 95-92744. 132p. (Orig.). 1996. pap. 7.95 (*1-882423-40-2*) Neal Pubns Inc.

— How to Make a Fortune in Self-Publishing. LC 93-92808. 106p. (Orig.). 1994. pap. text 7.95 (*1-882423-29-1*) Neal Pubns Inc.

— Your Slice of the Melon: A Guide to Greater Job Success. 2nd ed. LC 87-92044. 144p. (C). 1989. pap. 4.95 (*0-9609006-1-6*) Neal Pubns Inc.

***Neal, James E., Jr. & Neal, Dorothy J.** Effective Letters for Business, Professional & Personal Use: A Guide to Successful Correspondence. 3rd rev. ed. LC 98-91432. 179p. 1999. pap. 6.95 (*1-882423-14-3*, 1882423143) Neal Pubns Inc.

Neal, James G., jt. ed. see Bonta, Bruce D.

Neal, Jo. Coloring Book for Fourth Grade. (Word of the Week Ser.). 41p. (J). (gr. 4 up). 1997. pap. 4.00 (*1-57074-339-8*) Greyden Pr.

— My Character Growth Journal: Intermediate & Middle Grades. Warren, Sally E., ed. (Word of the Week Ser.). 152p. 1997. pap. 10.00 (*1-57074-350-9*) Greyden Pr.

— My Character Growth Journal: Primary Grades. Warren, Sally E., ed. (Word of the Week Ser.). 80p. (J). (gr. 1-3). 1997. pap. 8.00 (*1-57074-324-X*) Greyden Pr.

— Preschool Coloring Book. (Word of the Week Ser.). (Illus.). 40p. (J). (ps up). 1997. pap. 4.00 (*1-57074-359-2*) Greyden Pr.

— Student Activity Book for Intermediate & Middle Grades. Warren, Sally E., ed. (Word of the Week Ser.). (Illus.). 48p. (J). (gr. 4-8). 1997. pap. 4.00 (*1-57074-334-7*) Greyden Pr.

— Student Activity Book for Second Grade. Warren, Sally E., ed. (Word of the Week Ser.). (Illus.). 41p. (J). (gr. 2 up). 1997. pap. 5.00 (*1-57074-337-1*) Greyden Pr.

— Student Activity Book for Third Grade. Warren, Sally E., ed. (Word of the Week Ser.). (Illus.). 40p. pap. 5.00 (*1-57074-338-X*) Greyden Pr.

— Student Coloring Book for Second Grade. (Word of the Week Ser.). (Illus.). 41p. (J). (gr. 2 up). 1997. pap. 4.00 (*1-57074-331-2*) Greyden Pr.

— Student Coloring Book for Third Grade. (Word of the Week Ser.). (Illus.). 39p. (J). (gr. 3 up). 1997. pap. 4.00 (*1-57074-333-9*) Greyden Pr.

— Student Coloring/Activity Book for First Grade. Warren, Sally E., ed. (Word of the Week Ser.). (Illus.). 78p. (J). (gr. 1 up). 1997. pap. 5.00 (*1-57074-336-3*) Greyden Pr.

— Teacher's Guide for First Grade. Warren, Sally E., ed. (Word of the Week Ser.). 228p. 1997. pap. 20.00 (*1-57074-326-6*) Greyden Pr.

— Teacher's Guide for Intermediate Grades. Warren, Sally E., ed. (Word of the Week Ser.). 229p. 1997. pap. text 20.00 (*1-57074-329-0*) Greyden Pr.

— Teacher's Guide for Second Grade. Warren, Sally E., ed. (Word of the Week Ser.). 229p. 1997. pap. 20.00 (*1-57074-327-4*) Greyden Pr.

— Teacher's Guide for Third Grade. Warren, Sally E., ed. (Word of the Week Ser.). 229p. 1997. pap. 20.00 (*1-57074-328-2*) Greyden Pr.

— Uncoloring Book for Fifth & Sixth Grades. (Word of the Week Ser.). 41p. (J). (gr. 5-6). 1997. pap. 4.00 (*1-57074-340-1*) Greyden Pr.

Neal, John. The Down-Easters, 2 vols. LC 78-64083. reprint ed. 75.00 (*0-404-17310-1*) AMS Pr.

— Log of the Mahina. LC 76-150419. (Illus.). 284p. 1995. pap. 16.95 (*0-918074-02-9*) Pacific Intl.

— Logan, a Family History, 2 vols. LC 78-64085. reprint ed. 75.00 (*0-404-17330-6*) AMS Pr.

— Rachel Dyer. LC 96-1253. 284p. 1996. pap. text 6.95 (*1-57392-049-5*) Prometheus Bks.

— Rachel Dyer. LC 64-10667. 288p. 1979. reprint ed. 50.00 (*0-8201-1263-1*) Schol Facsimiles.

— Rachel Dyer, a North American Story. 1988. reprint ed. lib. bdg. 49.00 (*0-7812-0003-2*) Rprt Serv.

Neal, John, jt. auth. see Marrett, Barbara.

Neal, John D., et al. Worker's Compensation Handbook. 4th ed. LC 97-20729. 1997. ring bd. 90.00 (*1-57862-003-1*) State Bar WI.

Neal, John L., et al. Burning Douglas-Fir Slash: Physical, Chemical & Microbial Effects in the Soil. LC S 0602.87. (Oregon State University, Forest Research Laboratory, Research Papers: No. 1). 35p. reprint ed. pap. 30.00 (*0-8357-7482-1*, 202610900048) Bks Demand.

Neal, John R. Disunion & Restoration in Tennessee. LC 78-164390. (Black Heritage Library Collection). 1977. reprint ed. 15.95 (*0-8369-8849-3*) Ayer.

Neal, John W. Mother Was a Minister: Evangelizing the World - Beginning at Home. 64p. 1994. pap. 9.95 (*1-881576-32-9*) Providence Hse.

Neal, Joseph C., Jr. Getting Serious about Stewardship. LC 93-80741. 100p. (Orig.). 1993. pap. text 6.00 (*1-883667-05-4*) Christian Meth.

Neal, Joseph C., jt. auth. see James, Douglas A.

Neal, Julia. The Kentucky Shakers. 120p. 1996. pap. 16.00 (*0-8131-0897-7*) U Pr of Ky.

Neal, Kenneth. A Wise Extravagance: The Founding of the Carnegie International Exhibitions 1895-1901. LC 95-50881. (Illus.). 273p. 1996. pap. 14.95 (*0-8229-5584-9*) U of Pittsburgh Pr.

— A Wise Extravagance: The Founding of the Carnegie International Exhibitions 1895-1901. LC 95-50881. (Illus.). 273p. (C). 1996. text 29.95 (*0-8229-3925-8*) U of Pittsburgh Pr.

Neal, Kenneth G. Anatomy & Physiology. 4th ed. 424p. 1986. pap. text, student ed., lab manual ed. 36.80 (*0-02-386180-0*, Pub. by P-H) S&S Trade.

— Dissection Guide for Cats. (C). 1986. pap. text 20.80 (*0-02-386191-6*, Macmillan Coll) P-H.

Neal, Kris P., ed. see Schutte, Jim.

Neal, Larry. Archeological Survey of Clearcut Areas along Little River, McCurtain & Pushmataha Counties, Oklahoma. George, Preston, ed. (Archeological Resource Survey Report: No. 32). (Illus.). 201p. (C). 1988. pap. text 6.00 (*1-881346-21-8*) Univ OK Archeol.

— Hoodoo Hollerin Bebop Ghosts. LC 73-88972. (Illus.). 87p. 1974. 14.95 (*0-88258-011-6*) Howard U Pr.

— The Rise of Financial Capitalism: International Capital Markets in the Age of Reason. (Studies in Monetary & Financial History). (Illus.). 288p. (C). 1993. pap. text 18.95 (*0-521-45738-6*) Cambridge U Pr.

Neal, Larry, ed. War Finance, 2 vols. (International Library of Macroeconomic & Financial History: Vol. 12). 1880p. 1994. 610.00 (*1-85278-663-9*) E Elgar.

Neal, Larry D. & Barbezat, Daniel. The Economics of the European Union & the Economies of Europe. LC 97-4221. (Illus.). 416p. (C). 1998. pap. text 34.95 (*0-19-511068-4*) OUP.

Neal, Larry L., ed. The Next Fifty Years: Health, Physical Education, Recreation, Dance. 179p. 1971. pap. 10.00 (*0-943272-08-4*) Inst Recreation Res.

Neal, Larry L. & Edginton, Christopher R., eds. Exetra Perspectives: Concepts in Therapeutic Recreation. (Illus.). 232p. 1982. 10.00 (*0-943272-03-3*) Inst Recreation Res.

Neal, Larry L., jt. ed. see Fairchild, Effie L.

Neal, Linda, jt. auth. see Dennis, Cindy.

***Neal, Lisa.** France: An Illustrated History. (Illus.). 150p. 2000. 14.95 (*0-7818-0835-9*) Hippocrene Bks.

Neal, Lisa, ed. Treasury of Classic French Love Short Stories in French & English. LC 97-8212. (Hippocrene Bilingual Love Short Stories Ser.). (ENG & FRE.). 128p. 1997. 11.95 (*0-7818-0511-2*) Hippocrene Bks.

Neal, Lisa, jt. ed. see Szwillus, Gerd.

Neal, Lisa, ed. & tr. see De Crenne, Helisenne.

Neal, Lisa, tr. see Verger, Jacques.

Neal, Lois S. Abstracts of Vital Records from Raleigh, NC Newspapers 1799-1819, Vol. 1. 673p. 1979. reprint ed. 35.00 (*0-87152-297-7*) N C Genealogical.

— Abstracts of Vital Records from Raleigh, NC Newspapers 1830-1839, 2 vols., Vol. III, Pts. 1 & 2. 655p. 1995. 75.00 (*0-936370-05-X*) N C Genealogical.

Neal, Lula M. The Roast Pan . . . the Cat . . . & the Rat. (Illus.). (Orig.). (J). (gr. k-3). 1997. pap. 6.95 (*0-533-11742-9*) Vantage.

Neal, M. Custom Draperies in Interior Design. 208p. 1982. 40.25 (*0-444-00640-0*) P-H.

Neal, M. C. Hawaiian Helicinidae. (BMB Ser.). 1969. reprint ed. 25.00 (*0-527-02231-4*) Periodicals Srv.

— Hawaiian Marine Algae. (BMB Ser.). 1969. reprint ed. 25.00 (*0-527-02173-3*) Periodicals Srv.

Neal, M. J. Medical Pharmacology at a Glance. 3rd ed. LC 97-2123. (At a Glance Ser.). (Illus.). 1997. pap. 29.95 (*0-86542-719-4*) Blackwell Sci.

Neal, M. Pinson. Emergency Interventional Radiology. 1989. 115.00 (*0-316-59927-1*, Little Brwn Med Div) Lppncott W & W.

***Neal, Margaret, ed.** Hardwood Lumber: Buying & Selling. unabridged ed. 230p. 1999. pap. 39.95 (*0-9621022-2-9*) Highland Oregon.

Neal, Margaret B., et al. Balancing Work & Caregiving: For Children, Adults & Elders. (Applications of Family Caregiving Ser.: Vol. 3). (Illus.). 292p. (C). 1993. text 49.95 (*0-8039-4281-8*) Sage.

Neal, Margaret B., jt. ed. see Lechner, Viola M.

Neal, Margaret T. And Set Aglow a Sacred Flame. (Illus.). 1983. 8.50 (*0-317-00833-1*) Puddingstone.

Neal, Mark A. What the Music Said: Black Popular Music & Black Public Culture. LC 98-3639. (Illus.). 183p. (C). 1998. pap. 19.99 (*0-415-92072-8*) Routledge.

— What the Music Said: Black Popular Music & the Black Public Sphere. LC 98-3639. (Illus.). 336p. (C). 1998. 75.00 (*0-415-92071-X*) Routledge.

Neal, Marshall. Seven Churches. (Illus.). 108p. (Orig.). 1977. pap. 4.25 (*0-89084-062-8*, 003624) Bob Jones Univ.

Neal, Matthew J. Case Studies in Endocrinology, Diabetes, & Metabolism: A Problem-Oriented Approach. LC 95-32574. (Illus.). 248p. 1996. pap. 39.50 (*0-89640-297-5*) Igaku-Shoin.

Neal, Maynard, et al, intros. Hydraulic Institute Engineering Data Book. 2nd ed. (Hydraulic Institute Ser.). (Illus.). 205p. 1991. text 79.00 (*1-880952-01-7*, S200) Hydraulic Inst.

Neal, McClinton E., jt. ed. see Harper, Angela W.

Neal, Michael J., ed. The Tribology Handbook. 2nd ed. (Illus.). 640p. 2000. pap. text 170.00 (*0-7506-1198-7*) Buttrwrth-Heinemann.

Neal, Michael W., jt. auth. see Howard, Philip H.

Neal, Moira. The Weekend Crafter - Dough Craft: More Than 50 Stylish Designs to Make & Decorate in a Weekend. LC 97-28540. (Weekend Crafter Ser.). Orig. Title: Doughcraft in a Weekend. (Illus.). 80p. 1998. pap. 14.95 (*1-57990-028-3*, Pub. by Lark Books) Random.

Neal, Moira & Howarth, Lynda. Painting Ceramics: Easy Projects & Stylish Designs in a Weekend. LC 98-34767. (Weekend Crafter Ser.). (Illus.). 80p. 1999. pap. 14.95 (*1-57990-090-9*) Lark Books.

— The Weekend Crafter - Painting Glass: Stylish Designs & Practical Projects to Paint in a Weekend. LC 97-28543. (Weekend Crafter Ser.). Orig. Title: Painting Glass in a Weekend. (Illus.). 80p. 1998. pap. 14.95 (*1-57990-029-1*, Pub. by Lark Books) Random.

Neal, Patrick. Liberalism & Its Discontents. LC 97-8084. 1997. text 40.00 (*0-8147-5796-0*) NYU Pr.

— Liberalism & Its Discontents. 1999. pap. text 20.00 (*0-8147-5798-7*) NYU Pr.

***Neal, Patsy.** Basketballs, Goldfish & World Championships. LC 99-93150. (Illus.). 128p. 1999. pap. 9.95 (*0-9671493-0-4*) Playbacks.

Neal, Patsy. Psalms & Proverbs on the Playing Field. LC 99-71677. (Illus.). 127p. (Orig.). 1999. pap. 9.95 (*0-9657561-7-3*, Pub. by Reflection TX) Spring Arbor Dist.

— So Run Your Race: An Athlete's View of God. rev. ed. LC 99-71676. (Illus.). 63p. (Orig.). 1999. pap. 9.95 (*0-9657561-6-5*, Pub. by Reflection TX) Spring Arbor Dist.

— Wellness Made Simple. 175p. 1997. pap. 17.95 (*1-56072-477-3*, Nova Kroshka Bks) Nova Sci Pubs.

Neal, R. J. & Jinks, R. G. The History of Smith & Wesson 1857-1945. (Illus.). 436p. 1996. 50.00 (*1-884849-19-9*) R&R Bks.

Neal, R. M. Bayesian Learning for Neural Networks. LC 96-22079. (Lecture Notes in Statistics Ser.: Vol. 118). (Illus.). 200p. 1996. pap. 34.95 (*0-387-94724-8*) Spr-Verlag.

***Neal, Raymond E.** The American Railroad. 318p. 2000. mass mkt. write for info. (*0-7541-0954-2*, Pub. by Minerva Pr) Unity Dist.

Neal, Richard A., ed. International Development Projects: Proceedings of the World Fisheries Congress, Athens, Greece, Theme 4. (Illus.). 1996. lib. bdg. 58.00 (*1-886106-28-2*) Science Pubs.

Neal, Richard B., ed. The Stanford Two-Mile Accelerator. LC 68-24364. (Illus.). 1183p. reprint ed. pap. 200.00 (*0-8357-3820-5*, 205703000003) Bks Demand.

Neal, Richard G. School Based Management: A Detailed Guide for Successful Implementation. LC 98-160772. 211p. (Orig.). 1991. pap. 21.95 (*1-879639-15-7*) Natl Educ Serv.

Neal, Robert D., jt. ed. see Lorentzen, Karen M.

Neal, Robert H. Moodus: Poems by Robert H. Neal. (Illus.). 1988. pap. 9.00 (*0-917764-03-X*) Hog Hill Pr.

Neal, Robert J. Master Motor Builders: The Inception, Design, Production & Uses of the Non-Automotive Engines of Packard. unabridged ed. (Illus.). 384p. 1998. 65.00 (*0-9647483-1-2*) Aero-Marine Hist Pubng.

— Packards at Speed. unabridged ed. LC 95-78246. (Illus.). 352p. 1995. 65.00 (*0-9647483-0-4*) Aero-Marine Hist Pubng.

Neal, S. Lincoln, the Politician. 1999. text. write for info. (*0-670-80883-0*) Viking Penguin.

— Making of Equal Opportunities: Policies in Universities. LC 97-12934. 176p. 1997. pap. 37.95 (*0-335-19807-4*) OpUniv Pr.

— Racism & Anti-Racism in Higher: Policies in Universities. LC 97-12934. 176p. 1997. pap. 119.00 (*0-335-19808-2*) Taylor & Francis.

Neal, S., tr. see Anderson, L. J. & Young, N. S., eds.

Neal, Sandra S. Discipleship. 72p. 1998. pap. 10.00 (*0-9641845-5-9*) Wingspan Christian.

— Grow Rich Without Thinking: A Biblical Perspective. 200p. 1998. text 17.95 (*0-9641845-9-1*) Wingspan Christian.

— Holy Spirit. 40p. 1998. pap. 6.95 (*0-9641845-8-3*) Wingspan Christian.

— Putting God First. 1998. pap. 6.95 (*0-9641845-6-7*) Wingspan Christian.

— Sanctification. 40p. 1998. pap. 6.95 (*0-9641845-7-5*) Wingspan Christian.

— Sowing in the Kingdom of God. (Illus.). 68p. 1998. pap. 10.00 (*0-9641845-4-0*) Wingspan Christian.

— The Trinity. 40p. 1998. pap. 6.95 (*0-9641845-3-2*) Wingspan Christian.

— Understanding Salvation. 48p. 1998. pap. text 6.95 (*0-9641845-2-4*) Wingspan Christian.

Neal, Saundra K., jt. auth. see Culbreath, Alice N.

Neal, Steve. Dark Horse: A Biography of Wendell Wilkie. LC 89-22614. (Illus.). xii, 371p. 1989. reprint ed. 35.00 (*0-7006-0454-5*); reprint ed. pap. 14.95 (*0-7006-0453-7*) U Pr of KS.

— The Eisenhowers. LC 84-40412. (Illus.). xii, 508p. 1984. reprint ed. pap. 14.95 (*0-7006-0260-7*) U Pr of KS.

— McNary of Oregon: A Political Biography. LC 85-13692. 1985. 17.95 (*0-87595-173-2*) Oregon Hist.

***Neal, Steve.** Rolling on the River: The Best of Steve Neal. LC 99-21324. 200p. 1999. 24.95 (*0-8093-2282-X*) S Ill U Pr.

Neal, Steve, ed. see Neuberger, Richard L.

Neal, Terry. Barter & the Future of Money: Your Guide to New Forms of Money. 1996. 24.95 (*1-57101-061-0*) MasterMedia Pub.

Neal, Terry L. The Offshore Advantage. LC 98-40732. 272p. 1998. 29.95 (*1-57101-331-8*) MasterMedia Pub.

Neal, Thomas A. Farewell My Book. (Los Angeles Miscellany Ser.: No. 14). (Illus.). 44p. 1983. 30.00 (*0-87093-314-0*) Dawsons.

***Neal, Tim & McCormack, Joe.** Warriors of the Realms. (Illus.). iv, 139p. 1999. vinyl bd. 21.00 (*0-9672273-0-5*, WOTR#1) MnetWeb.

Neal, Timothy R. The Cherubim Unveiled: Wings of the Spirit. LC 97-94109. (Illus.). 68p. 1998. pap. 12.95 (*0-9660457-1-8*) Morn Star CA.

Neal, Tommy, jt. auth. see National Conference of State Legislatures Staff.

Neal, Tommy, jt. auth. see Walker, Robert J.

Neal, Valerie, et al. SpaceFlight. (Illus.). 256p. 1995. 24.95 (*0-02-860007-X*); 18.00 (*0-02-860040-1*) Macmillan.

Neal, Valerie, ed. see Tipler, Paul A.

Neal, Vernon Edwin, jt. auth. see Fraser, Peter.

Neal, Viola P. Fragments of Experience: A Spiritual Journey. LC 78-822. 1978. pap. 4.95 (*0-87516-280-0*) DeVorss.

Neal, Viola P. & Karagulla, Shafica. Through the Curtain. 2nd ed. LC 83-71171. 360p. 1993. reprint ed. pap. 15.95 (*0-87516-517-6*) DeVorss.

Neal, Virgil. Hypnotism & Hypnotic Suggestion. (Illus.). 93p. 1984. reprint ed. pap. text 15.00 (*0-87556-379-1*) Saifer.

Neal, W. G., jt. auth. see Hall, Richard N.

Neal, Wes. The Handbook on Athletic Perfection. 248p. (Orig.). (YA). (gr. 6 up). 1993. pap. 8.95 (*1-887002-07-3*) Cross Trng.

— The Handbook on Coaching Perfection. 248p. (YA). (gr. 6 up). 1993. pap. 8.95 (*1-887002-08-1*) Cross Trng.

Neal, William, jt. auth. see Bittenbinder, J. J.

Neal, William A., jt. auth. see Moller, James H.

Nealand-Staley, Harriet C. Mariner Cheney: My Dad. (Illus.). 136p. 1992. 19.95 (*1-882266-00-5*) Newburyport.

Neale. Exploring. 212p. 1995. pap. 31.95 (*0-471-13237-3*) Wiley.

***Neale.** Philosophy of Language. 2000. 49.95 (*0-8133-1858-0*, Pub. by Westview); pap. 17.95 (*0-8133-1859-9*, Pub. by Westview) HarpC.

Neale, Alan D., jt. auth. see Haslam, C.

Neale, Andrew. Narrow Gauge & Miniature Railways from Old Picture Postcards. 60p. (C). 1987. 35.00 (*0-9511108-0-2*, Pub. by Picton) St Mut.

Neale, Arthur. The Great Weird Stories. 409p. 1977. 23.95 (*0-8369-4156-X*) Ayer.

Neale, Bren, jt. auth. see Smart, Carol.

Neale, Caroline. Writing "Independent" History: African Historiography, 1960-1980, 85. LC 84-15756. (Contributions in Afro-American & African Studies: No. 85). 208p. 1985. 55.00 (*0-313-24652-1*, NID/, Greenwood Pr) Greenwood.

N

An Asterisk (*) at the beginning of an entry indicates that the title is appearing for the first time.

An Asterisk (*) at the beginning of an entry indicates that the title is appearing for the first time.

Nearing, Scott. The Making of a Radical: A Political Autobiography. LC 78-180725. 1972. pap. 11.95 (*0-911394-07-9*) Good Life Ctr.

— The Making of a Radical: A Political Autobiography. LC 78-180725. 308p. 1976. 16.95 (*0-911394-06-0*) Good Life Ctr.

— Man's Search for the Good Life. 143p. 1974. pap. 9.95 (*0-911394-12-5*) Good Life Ctr.

— New Education: A Review of Progressive Education Movements of the Day. LC 75-89210. (American Education: Its Men, Institutions, & Ideas. Series 1). 1974. reprint ed. 19.95 (*0-405-01449-X*) Ayer.

— A Scott Nearing Reader: The Good Life in Bad Times. Sherman, Steve, ed. LC 88-29528. (Illus.). 333p. 1989. 34.50 (*0-8108-2144-3*) Scarecrow.

— United World. 265p. 1945. pap. 9.95 (*0-911394-18-4*) Good Life Ctr.

Nearing, Scott & Freeman, Joseph. Dollar Diplomacy: A Study in American Imperialism. LC 74-111703. (American Imperialism: Viewpoints of United States Foreign Policy, 1898-1941 Ser.). 1979. reprint ed. 25.95 (*0-405-02040-6*) Ayer.

Nearing, Scott & Nearing, Helen. U. S. A. Today. 2nd ed. LC 55-12158. 1956. 15.00 (*0-911394-14-1*) Good Life Ctr.

Nearing, Scott & Russell, Bertrand. Bolshevism & the West: A Debate. 1973. 250.00 (*0-87968-070-9*) Gordon Pr.

Nearing, Scott, jt. auth. see Nearing, Helen.

***Nearman, Herbert, et al.** Buddhist Writings on Meditation & Daily Practice: The Serene Reflection Meditation Tradition : Including the Complete Scripture of Brahma's Net. 2nd ed. LC 98-60114. 1998. write for info. (*0-930066-18-9*) Shasta Abbey.

Nearman, Hubert, et al. No - Kyogen Masks & Performance. (Mime Journal Ser.). (Illus.). 236p. (Orig.). 1984. pap. 12.00 (*0-9611066-6-2*) Mime Jour.

Nearman, Hubert, tr. see Great Master Dogen.

Nearman, Hubert, tr. see Jiyu-Kennett, P. T., ed.

Nearman, Hubert, tr. see Jiyu-Kennett, P. T. & MacPhillamy, Daizui, eds.

Nearman, Hubert, tr. see Zenji, Keizan.

Nearman, Lesley. Pennsylvania Perspective, 1997. Shoop, Diane, ed. (Illus.). 20p. 1998. pap. 20.00 (*1-58036-057-2*) Penn State Data Ctr.

Neary, et al, eds. The Urban Experience: A People-Environment Perspective. (Illus.). 544p. (C). 1995. 110.00 (*0-419-20160-2*, E & FN Spon) Routledge.

Neary, D., jt. auth. see Crossman, A. R.

Neary, Dan, et al, eds. National Hydrology Workshop Proceedings. (Illus.). 210p. (Orig.). (C). 1997. pap. text 50.00 (*0-7881-3982-7*) DIANE Pub.

Neary, Daniel A. Rage in the Hills. Mueller, Kate, ed. LC 99-21170. 195p. 1999. pap. text 17.95 (*0-9630460-1-2*) Plateau.

— Vanishing Vermont: Photographs & Essay LC 93-193034. 64 p. 1991. 8.95 (*0-9630460-0-4*) Plateau.

Neary, Donal. The Calm Beneath the Storm: Reflections & Prayers for Young People. 77p. 1989. pap. 30.00 (*0-86217-096-6*, Pub. by Veritas Pubns) St Mut.

— Pilgrim in Lent: Prayer for Every Day. 96p. (Orig.). 1992. pap. 4.95 (*0-8146-2123-6*) Liturgical Pr.

Neary, Donna M. Designing a Career in Public History: Becoming a Professional Historian. Date not set. write for info. (*1-57524-098-X*) Krieger.

Neary, Ian, ed. Leaders & Leadership in Japan. (Japan Library). 224p. (C). 1996. text 45.00 (*1-873410-41-7*, Pub. by Curzon Pr Ltd) UH Pr.

— War, Revolution & Japan. 128p. (C). 1996. pap. text 15.00 (*1-873410-08-5*, Pub. by Curzon Pr Ltd) UH Pr.

Neary, Ian & Goodman, Roger, eds. Case Studies on Human Rights in Japan. (Japan Library). 192p. (C). 1996. text 45.00 (*1-873410-35-2*, Pub. by Curzon Pr Ltd) UH Pr.

Neary, J. Peter, ed. International Trade, 2, Set. LC 95-32856. (International Library of Critical Writings in Economics Ser.: Vol. 59). 1296p. (C). 1995. text 465.00 (*1-85278-361-3*) E Elgar.

Neary, J. Peter & Van Wijnbergen, Sweder, eds. Natural Resources & the Macroeconomy. 336p. 1986. 40.00 (*0-262-14041-1*) MIT Pr.

Neary, Jack. Jerry Finnegan's Sister. 1993. pap. 5.50 (*0-87129-300-5*, J23) Dramatic Pub.

— To Forgive, Divine. 1990. pap. 5.25 (*0-8222-1159-9*) Dramatists Play.

Neary, Jack, adapted by. The Little Match Girl. 44p. 1996. pap. 5.00 (*0-87440-025-2*) Bakers Plays.

***Neary, John.** Like & Unlike God. (AAR Reflection & Theory in the Study of Religion Ser.). 201p. 1999. pap. text 34.95 (*0-7885-0569-6*) OUP.

Neary, John. Something & Nothingness: The Fiction of John Updike & John Fowles. LC 90-25137. 288p. (C). 1991. 26.95 (*0-8093-1742-7*) S Ill U Pr.

Neary, Kevin & Smith, Dave. The Ultimate Disney Trivia Book, No. 3. LC 97-2506. (Illus.). 224p. (J). 1997. pap. 9.70 (*0-7868-8253-0*, Pub. by Hyperion) Time Warner.

Neary, Kevin, jt. auth. see Smith, Dave.

***Neary, M.** Teaching, Assessing & Evaluation for Clinical Competence. (Illus.). 224p. 2000. pap. 32.95 (*0-7487-4417-7*, Pub. by S Thornes Pubs) Intl Spec Bk.

Neary, Michael, ed. Global Humanization: Studies in the Manufacture of Labour. LC 99-10527. 224p. 1999. 80.00 (*0-7201-2340-2*) Continuum.

Neary, Peter. Newfoundland in the North Atlantic World, 1929-1949. (Illus.). 488p. (C). 1988. text 65.00 (*0-7735-0668-3*, Pub. by McG-Queens Univ Pr) CUP Services.

— Newfoundland in the North Atlantic World, 1929-1949. 400p. 1996. pap. text 24.95 (*0-7735-1518-6*, F1123, Pub. by McG-Queens Univ Pr) CUP Services.

— White Tie & Decorations: Sir John & Lady Hope Simpson in Newfoundland, 1934-1936. 408p. 1997. reprint ed. pap. 21.95 (*0-8020-8085-5*) U of Toronto Pr.

Neary, Peter, ed. White Tie & Decorations: Sir John & Lady Hope Simpson in Newfoundland, 1934-1936. (Illus.). 392p. 1996. reprint ed. text 39.95 (*0-8020-0719-8*) U of Toronto Pr.

Neary, Peter & Granatstein, Jack L., eds. The Veterans Charter & Post World War II Canada. (Illus.). 336p. 1997. text 55.00 (*0-7735-1678-6*, Pub. by McG-Queens Univ Pr) CUP Services.

— Veterans Charter & Post-WW II Canada. pap. 22.95 (*0-7735-1697-2*) McG-Queens Univ Pr.

Neary, Peter & O'Flaherty, Patrick, eds. By Great Waters: A Newfoundland & Labrador Anthology. LC 73-91561. (Social History of Canada Ser.). 1974. pap. 10.95 (*0-8020-6233-4*) U of Toronto Pr.

Neary, Peter, jt. ed. see Granatstein, Jack L.

Neary, Peter, jt. ed. see Hiller, James.

Neary, R. Patrick, ed. see Moran, John P.

Neary, Robert D., jt. auth. see Herdman, Robert K.

Neary, Sally, ed. see Pellham, Brian.

Neary, Sally, ed. see Pellham, Brian L. & Kent, Allison.

Neary, Timothy J. & Fritzsch, Bernd, eds. Development & Evolution: 9th Annual Karger workshop, New Orleans, La., October 1997, No.4-5, No.52. (Brain, Behavior & Evolution Ser.: Vol. 52, No. 4-5 (1998)). (Illus.). 84p. 1998. pap. 38.25 (*3-8055-6770-7*) S Karger.

Neas, Virginia L. Knife Rests. LC 86-90691. (Illus.). 87p. (Orig.). 1987. 16.95 (*0-9617836-0-5*); pap. 11.95 (*0-9617836-1-3*) Glassy Mount.

Neasi. Igual Que Yo. (J). 1989. 19.87 (*0-516-37299-8*) Childrens.

Neasi, Barbara J. Igual Que Yo (Just Like Me) LC 83-23154. (Rookie Readers - Spanish Ser.). (SPA., Illus.). 32p. (J). (ps-2). 1988. pap. 3.50 (*0-516-52047-4*) Childrens.

— Just Like Me. LC 83-23154. (Rookie Readers Ser.). (Illus.). 32p. (J). (ps-3). 1984. pap. 4.95 (*0-516-42047-X*); lib. bdg. 17.00 (*0-516-02047-1*) Childrens.

— Listen to Me. LC 86-10664. (Rookie Readers Ser.). (Illus.). 32p. (J). (ps-3). 1986. pap. 4.95 (*0-516-42072-0*); lib. bdg. 17.00 (*0-516-02072-2*) Childrens.

Neason, Rebecca. Highlander: Shadow of Obsession, No. 7. 240p. (Orig.). 1998. mass mkt. 5.99 (*0-446-60547-6*, Pub. by Warner Bks) Little.

Neason, Rebecca V. Guises of the Mind, No. 27. Ryan, Kevin, ed. (Star Trek: The Next Generation Ser.). 288p. (Orig.). 1993. mass mkt. 5.50 (*0-671-79831-6*) PB.

— Highlander: The Path. 224p. (Orig.). 1997. reprint ed. mass mkt. 5.99 (*0-446-60456-9*, Pub. by Warner Bks) Little.

Neat, James. Foxtrot, Oscar, X-Ray. 1992. 7.95 (*0-947533-30-3*, Pub. by Breese Bks) Firebird Dist.

Neat, Kenneth P., ed. see Alekhine, A.

Neat, Kenneth P., jt. ed. see Livshitz, August.

Neat, Kenneth P., tr. see Averbakh, Yuri.

Neat, Kenneth P., tr. see Averbakh, Yuri & Checkover, V.

Neat, Kenneth P., tr. see Botvinnik, Mikhael M.

Neat, Kenneth P., tr. see Bronstein, David & Smolyan, Georgy.

Neat, Kenneth P., tr. see Estrin, Yakov B. & Glaskov, I. B.

Neat, Kenneth P., tr. see Karpov, Anatoly.

Neat, Kenneth P., tr. see Kasparov, Garry.

Neat, Kenneth P., tr. see Livshitz, August.

Neat, Kenneth P., tr. see Neishtadt, J.

Neat, Kenneth P., tr. see Polugayevsky, Lyev.

Neat, Kenneth P., tr. see Shereshevsky, Mikhail I.

Neat, Kenneth P., tr. see Shereshevsky, Mikhail I. & Slutsky, Leonid M.

Neat, Kenneth P., tr. see Shereshevsky, Mikhail I. & Slutsky, L.M.

Neat, Kenneth P., tr. see Suetin, A. S.

Neat, Kenneth P., tr. see Tal, M., et al.

Neat, Kenneth P., tr. see Vainstein, B. S.

Neat, Timothy. Part Seen, Part Imagined: Meaning & Symbolism in the Works of Charles Rennie Mackintosh & Margaret Macdonald. (Illus.). 208p. 1995. 49.95 (*0-86241-366-4*, Pub. by Canongate Books) Interlink Pub.

— The Summer Walkers. (Classics Ser.). (Illus.). 224p. 1996. pap. 22.95 (*0-86241-576-4*, Pub. by Canongate Books) Interlink Pub.

— The Voice of the Bard: Living Poets & Ancient Tradition in the Highlands & Islands. 256p. 1999. pap. 22.95 (*0-86241-842-9*, Pub. by Canongate Books) Interlink Pub.

Neatby, Nicole. Carabins ou activistes? L'idealisme et la radicalisation de la pensee etudiante a l'Universite de Montreal au temps du Duplessisme. 55.00 (*0-7735-1834-7*) McG-Queens Univ Pr.

Neatby, H. Blair. William Lyon MacKenzie King: The Lonely Heights. LC 79-9143. (Scholarly Reprint Ser.: Vol. 2, 1924-1932). 464p. 1980. reprint ed. pap. 143.90 (*0-608-10397-7*, 202365600033) Bks Demand.

— William Lyon Mackenzie King Vol. 2: A Political Biography: 1924-1932: The Lonely Heights. LC 59-347. (Illus.). 474p. reprint ed. pap. 147.00 (*0-8357-8375-8*, 203405700088) Bks Demand.

— William Lyon Mackenzie King Vol. II: The Lonely Heights, 1924-1932. 366p. 1963. text 100.00 (*0-8020-1261-2*) U of Toronto Pr.

Neatby, H. Blair, et al. Imperial Relations in the Age of Laurier: Essays. LC 72-431730. (Canadian Historical Readings Ser.: No. 6). 92p. reprint ed. pap. 30.00 (*0-8357-3630-X*, 203635800003) Bks Demand.

Neatby, Hilda, et al. Queen's University, 1841-1914: And Not to Yield, Vol. I. Gibson, Frederick W. & Graham, Roger, eds. (Illus.). 1978. 65.00 (*0-7735-0336-6*, Pub. by McG-Queens Univ Pr) CUP Services.

Neatby, Leslie H. The Search for Franklin. LC 78-520758. (Illus.). 281p. 1970. write for info. (*0-213-17958-X*) Art Barker.

Neate, Francis W., ed. Using Set-Off As Security: A Comparative Survey for Practitioners. (C). 1990. lib. bdg. 181.00 (*1-85333-363-8*, Pub. by Graham & Trotman) Kluwer Academic.

Neate, Jill. Mountaineering Literature: A Bibliography of Material Published in English. 2nd enl. rev. ed. 296p. 1987. pap. 29.95 (*0-938567-04-7*) Mountaineers.

Neate, Jill, ed. Mountaineering in the Andes. (C). 1993. 60.00 (*0-907649-64-5*, Pub. by Expedit Advisory Ctr) St Mut.

Neate, Jill, tr. see Messner, Reinhold.

Neate, Tony. Channeling for Everyone: A Safe, Step-by-Step Guide to Developing Your Intuition & Psychic Awareness. LC 98-5024. (Illus.). 176p. 1998. pap. 12.95 (*0-89594-922-9*) Crossing Pr.

Neate, Wilson. Tolerating Ambiguity: Ethnicity & Community in Chicano/a Writing. LC 95-50140. (Many Voices Ser.). VI, 305p. 1998. 53.95 (*0-8204-3094-3*) P Lang Pubng.

Neath, Ian. Human Memory: Introduction to Research, Data & Theory. LC 97-24356. (Psychology Ser.). 424p. 1997. mass mkt. 65.95 (*0-534-34197-7*) Brooks-Cole.

Neather, E. J. Mastering French. (Mastering Languages Ser.). (Illus.). 262p. (Orig.). 1991. pap. 14.95 (*0-87052-055-5*); audio 12.95 (*0-87052-060-1*) Hippocrene Bks.

Neather, Ted, et al. Realisations: Students Book. 160p. 1998. pap., student ed. 35.00 (*0-7487-3702-2*) St Mut.

— Realisations: Teacher's Resource Book. 128p. 1998. pap., teacher ed. 113.00 (*0-7487-3703-0*) St Mut.

Neathery, Raymond F. Applied Mechanics: Statistics. (C). 2001. 67.00 (*0-13-378803-2*, Macmillan Coll) P-H.

— Applied Mechanics: Strength of Materials. (C). 2001. 67.00 (*0-13-378795-8*, Macmillan Coll) P-H.

Neathery, Raymond F. & Magill, Michael A. Applied Mechanics: Dynamics. (C). 2001. 67.00 (*0-13-378811-3*, Macmillan Coll) P-H.

Neathery, T. L., ed. Southeastern Section Field Guide. (DNAG Centennial Field Guides Ser.: No. 6). (Illus.). 477p. 1986. 20.25 (*0-8137-5406-2*) Geol Soc.

Neaum, Sally & Tallack, Jill. Good Practice in Implementing the Pre-School Curriculum. (Illus.). 200p. (Orig.). 1997. pap. 37.50 (*0-7487-2882-1*, Pub. by S Thornes Pubs) Trans-Atl Phila.

Neave, jt. auth. see Moffat.

Neave, Charles, jt. auth. see St. Laurent, Jonathan.

Neave, David & Waterson, Edward. Lost Houses of East Yorkshire. (C). 1989. text 35.00 (*0-9513966-0-9*) St Mut.

Neave, Edwin H. Financial Systems: Principles & Organization. LC 97-32079. 336p. (C). 1998. 100.00 (*0-415-11056-4*); pap. 49.99 (*0-415-11057-2*) Routledge.

Neave, Edwin H., jt. ed. see Courchene, Thomas J.

Neave, Guy. The Teaching Nation: Prospects for Teachers in the European Community. 180p. 1992. text 79.25 (*0-08-041381-1*, Pergamon Pr) Elsevier.

Neave, Guy & Jenkinson, Sally. Research & Higher Education in Sweden. 112p. 1983. pap. text 32.00 (*91-22-00624-9*) Coronet Bks.

Neave, Guy & Van Vught, Frans A., eds. The Winds of Change: Government & Higher Education Relationships over Three Continents: A Report to the World Bank. LC 93-23566. (Issues in Higher Education Ser.). 334p. 1994. text 86.50 (*0-08-042391-4*) Elsevier.

Neave, Guy, jt. auth. see Clark.

Neave, Guy, jt. ed. see Clark, Burton R.

Neave, Guy, ed. see van Vught, Frans.

***Neave, Guy R. & International Association of Universities Staff.** The Universities' Responsibilities to Society: International Perspectives. LC 99-27815. (Issues in Higher Education Ser.). 2000. 56.00 (*0-08-043569-6*, Pergamon Pr) Elsevier.

Neave, Henry R. The Deming Dimension. 464p. (C). 1990. pap. 20.00 (*0-945320-36-1*) Stat Process Contrl.

— Elementary Statistics Tables. LC 92-22598. 48p. (Orig.). (C). 1998. pap. 12.99 (*0-415-08458-X*) Routledge.

Neave, Judy. Pressed Flower Crafting. (Illus.). 32p. (Orig.). 1994. pap. 8.95 (*1-884555-03-9*) P Depke Bks.

Neave, M. A., jt. auth. see Bradbrook, A. J.

Neave, Richard, jt. auth. see Prag, John.

Neave, Susan & Ellis, Stephen, eds. An Historical Atlas of East Yorkshire. (Illus.). 172p. 1997. 35.00 (*0-85958-652-9*, Pub. by Univ of Hull Pr) Paul & Co Pubs.

Neaverson, Bob. The Beatles Movies. LC 96-52933. (Film Studies). (Illus.). 224p. 1997. pap. 21.95 (*0-304-33797-8*) Continuum.

Neaverson, Peter, jt. auth. see Palmer, Marilyn.

Neaves, Pat. From Granny with Love Recipes from My Heart. (Illus.). 184p. 1991. spiral bd. 10.95 (*1-879806-00-2*) From My Heart.

— Little Black CookBook. (Illus.). 140p. 1992. spiral bd. 9.95 (*1-879806-01-0*) From My Heart.

Neba, Aaron S. Modern Geography of the Republic of Cameroon. 2nd ed. LC 87-70017. (Illus.). xii, 204p. 1987. 32.50 (*0-941815-01-3*); pap. 22.50 (*0-941815-00-5*) Neba Pubs.

Nebabin, V. G. Methods & Techniques of Radar Recognition. LC 94-29478.Tr. of Metody i Tekhnika Radiolokatsionnogo Raspoznavaniia. 1994. 39.00 (*0-89006-719-8*) Artech Hse.

Nebauer, Alan. Against All Odds: Around Alone in the BOC Challenge. (Illus.). 166p. 1997. 19.95 (*0-07-470331-5*) McGraw.

Nebbe, Linda L. Nature As a Guide: Using Nature in Counseling, Therapy, & Education. LC 95-60563. (Illus.). 256p. (C). 1995. pap. text 14.95 (*0-932796-72-9*) Ed Media Corp.

Nebbia, G. & Namboodiri, M. N. Heavy-Ion Dynamics & Hot Nuclei: Proceedings of the 1995 ACS Nuclear Chemical Award Symposium. 200p. 1995. text 56.00 (*981-02-2355-2*) World Scientific Pub.

***Nebbia, Ruth.** Burnishings of the Heart. LC 99-96664. 2000. 17.95 (*0-533-13328-9*) Vantage.

Nebe, G., jt. auth. see Plesken, W.

Nebebe, Fassil. Statistics with Minitab. 1990. 9.25 (*0-685-51813-2*) Pearson Custom.

Nebehay, Christian M. Gustav Klimt: From Drawing to Painting. LC 94-1415. (Illus.). 288p. 1994. 75.00 (*0-8109-3510-4*, Pub. by Abrams) Time Warner.

Nebeker, Frederick. Sparks of Genius: Portraits of Electrical Engineering Excellence. LC 93-15916. (Illus.). 280p. 1993. text 39.95 (*0-7803-1033-0*, PC03822) Inst Electrical.

Nebeker, Frederik. Calculating the Weather: Meteorology in the 20th Century. (International Geophysics Ser.: Vol. 60). (Illus.). 255p. 1995. text 63.00 (*0-12-515175-6*) Acad Pr.

Nebeksy, Richard, jt. auth. see McNeely, Scott.

***Nebel & Wright.** Environmental Science: The Way the World Works. 7th ed. 1999. write for info. (*0-13-018835-2*) P-H.

Nebel, Anne, jt. auth. see Ackert, Patricia.

Nebel, Bernard J. Environmental Science. 3rd ed. 1989. pap. text, lab manual ed. 39.20 (*0-13-282245-8*) P-H.

— Environmental Science. 3rd ed. 560p. (C). 1990. text 57.00 (*0-13-282203-2*) P-H.

***Nebel, Bernard J. & Wright, Richard T.** Environmental Science: The Way the World Works. 7th ed. LC 99-25188. 664p. (C). 1999. pap. text 86.00 (*0-13-083134-4*) P-H.

Nebel, Bernhard. Reasoning & Revision in Hybrid Representation Systems. Siekmann, Joerg H., ed. (Lecture Notes in Artificial Intelligence Ser.: Vol. 422). xii, 270p. 1990. pap. 32.70 (*0-387-52443-6*) Spr-Verlag.

Nebel, Bernhard, et al, eds. Proceedings of the 3rd International Conference on Principles of Knowledge Representation & Reasoning. LC 92-34433. (Representation & Reasoning Ser.). 615p. (C). 1992. pap. text 49.95 (*1-55860-262-3*) Morgan Kaufmann.

Nebel, Bernhard & Dreschler-Fischer, Leonie, eds. KI-94: Advances in Artificial Intelligence: Proceedings of the 18th German Annual Conference on Artificial Intelligence, Saarbrucken, Germany, September 18-23, 1994. LC 94-35132. (Lecture Notes in Computer Science: Vol. 861). 1994. 58.00 (*0-387-58467-6*) Spr-Verlag.

— KI-94: Advances in Artificial Intelligence: Proceedings of the 18th German Annual Conference on Artificial Intelligence, Saarbrucken, Germany, September 18-23, 1994. LC 94-35132. (Artificial Intelligence: Vol. 861). 1994. 61.95 (*3-540-58467-6*) Spr-Verlag.

Nebel, Bernhard, jt. ed. see Lakemeyer, Gerhard.

Nebel, Cecile. The Dark Side of Creativity: Blocks, Unfinished Works & the Urge to Destroy. viii, 162p. 1988. 35.00 (*0-87875-346-X*) Whitston Pub.

Nebel, Constance, jt. auth. see Begin, Carmelle.

Nebel, Ed. Managing Hotels Effectively. (Illus.). 436p. 1991. text 55.95 (*0-442-23814-2*, VNR) Wiley.

— Managing Hotels Effectively. 1993. pap. 22.95 (*0-442-01501-1*, VNR) Wiley.

Nebel, Eddystone C. Managing Hotels Effectively: Lessons from Outstanding General Managers. 464p. 1991. 59.95 (*0-471-28909-4*, VNR) Wiley.

***Nebel, Laurel.** Iron Road Home. 186p. 1999. pap. 9.99 (*0-88092-466-7*) Royal Fireworks.

— Stop That Thief! 186p. (J). (gr. 4-7). 1999. pap. 9.99 (*0-88092-474-8*, 4748) Royal Fireworks.

Nebel, Martin. Vegetationskundliche Untersuchungen In Hohenlohe. (Dissertationes Botanicae Ser.: Band 97). (GER., Illus.). vi, 253p. 1986. pap. 77.00 (*3-443-64009-5*, Pub. by Gebruder Borntraeger) Balogh.

Nebel, Richard. Santa Maria Tonantzin, Virgen de Guadalupe (Santa Maria Tonantzin, Virgen of Guadalupe) (SPA.). 372p. 1995. pap. 12.99 (*968-16-4536-7*, Pub. by Fondo) Continental Bk.

Nebel, Thomas P., jt. auth. see Ogne, Steven L.

Nebel, Wolfgang & Mermet, Jean P., eds. Low Power Design in Deep Submicron Electronics. LC 97-16495. 1997. text 318.00 (*0-7923-4569-X*) Kluwer Academic.

— Low Power Design in Deep Submicron Electronics. LC 97-42789. 596p. 1998. pap. text 120.00 (*0-7923-8103-3*) Kluwer Academic.

Nebendahl, D., ed. Expert Systems Pt. 1: Introduction to the Technique & Applications. (Illus.). 260p. 1988. 30.00 (*3-8009-1513-8*, Wiley-VCH) Wiley.

— Expert Systems Pt. 2: Practical Applications. (Illus.). 328p. 1991. text 20.00 (*3-8009-4104-X*, Wiley-VCH) Wiley.

Nebenzahl, Avigdor. Tiku Bachodesh Shofer: Thoughts for Rosh Hashanah. 1997. 18.95 (*0-87306-836-X*) Feldheim.

Nebenzahl, Kenneth. Atlas of Columbus & the Great Discoveries. Fagan, Elizabeth G. & Leverenz, Jon, eds. (GER & SPA., Illus.). 176p. 1990. 75.00 (*0-528-83407-X*) Rand McNally.

— Bibliography of Printed Battle Plans of the American Revolution, 1775-1795. LC 74-16679. (C). 1993. lib. bdg. 12.00 (*0-226-56958-6*) U Ch Pr.

Neber-Aeschbacher, Hans, ed. Hydrogenated Amorphous Silicon. (Solid State Phenomena Ser.: Vols. 44-46). (Illus.). 1080p. (C). 1995. text 272.00 (*3-908450-10-1*, Pub. by Scitec Pubs) Enfield Pubs NH.

Neberizahl, Avigdor. Ani Ledodi: Thoughts for the Month of Elul. 1994. 16.95 (*0-87306-684-7*) Feldheim.

Nebert, D., jt. auth. see Burrell.

N

An Asterisk (*) at the beginning of an entry indicates that the title is appearing for the first time.

Nebes, Norbert. Funktionsanalyse Von Kana Yaf Alu. (Studien Zur Sprachwissenschaft Ser.: Vol. 1). xiv, 222p. 1982. write for info. (*3-487-07300-5*) G Olms Pubs.

Nebes, R. D. & Corkin, S., eds. Handbook of Neuropsychology, Vol. 4. 384p. 1990. 284.00 (*0-444-81234-2*) Elsevier.

— Handbook of Neuropsychology, Vol. 4. 384p. 1991. pap. 90.75 (*0-444-89169-2*) Elsevier.

Nebesky, Richard, et al. Lonely Planet Russia, Ukraine & Belarus: Travel Survival Kit. (Illus.). 1200p. 1996. pap. 27.95 (*0-86442-320-9*) Lonely Planet.

Nebesky, Richard, jt. auth. see King, John, III.

Nebesky-Wojkowitz, Rene De. Oracles & Demons of Tibet: The Cult & Iconography of the Tibetan Protective Deities. (C). 1993. 68.00 (*0-8364-2866-8*, Pub. by Book Faith) S Asia.

— Tibetan Religious Dances. Von Furer-Haimendorf, Christoph, ed. (Religion & Society Ser.: No. 2). 1976. text 69.25 (*90-279-7621-X*) Mouton.

Nebesky-Wojkowitz, Rene De, see De Nebesky-Wojkowitz, Rene.

Neblett, Elizabeth, jt. auth. see Foley, Barbara.

Neblett, Elizabeth R., jt. auth. see Foley, Barbara H.

Neblett, Genon H., jt. auth. see Wheeler, Mary B.

Neblett, Hester, jt. auth. see Hart, Martha A.

Neblett, Lester. Awakening Motion: A Journey. (Illus.). 72p. (Orig.). 1997. pap. 12.00 (*0-9656072-0-8*) Neblett Fnd.

Neblett, Pat. Circles of Sisterhood: A Book Discussion Group Guide for Women of Color. LC 96-41222. 224p. 1996. 14.00 (*0-86316-245-2*) Writers & Readers.

Neblett Perkins, Dorothy. Hopson: A Genealogy. LC 98-65311. (Illus.). 570p. 1998. 98.00 (*1-890240-03-6*) Neblett Pr.

Neblock, Nita, ed. Breaking Through Stone Walls: Where Do I Go From Here? (Illus.). 1989. pap. 5.00 (*0-913233-15-3*) AFRA.

— Genealogy Potpourri: Everything You Always Wanted to Know - But Didn't Know Who to Ask. (Illus.). 1988. pap. 5.00 (*0-913233-14-5*) AFRA.

— Migration of Church Groups to Midwest: Routes & Sources. (Illus.). 52p. 1987. pap. 5.00 (*0-913233-12-9*) AFRA.

— Roots in the Mid-West. (Illus.). 79p. 1991. pap. 5.00 (*0-913233-22-6*) AFRA.

— Threads in the Genealogical Tapestry. (Illus.). 38p. 1990. pap. 5.00 (*0-913233-18-8*) AFRA.

Neboiss, Arthur. Atlas of Trichoptera of the SW Pacific: Australian Region. (Entomologica Ser.). 1986. text 234.00 (*90-6193-575-X*) Kluwer Academic.

***Nebold, Allyson Hicks.** The Treasure of All Time. (Illus.). 40p. (J). (gr. 2-4). 2000. 6.95 (*1-880710-43-9*) Monterey Pacific.

Nebot, Didier. The Road to Exile. Moyal, Henri M., tr. from FRE. Orig. Title: Le Chemin de L'Exil. 312p. (Orig.). 1998. pap. 18.50 (*1-881283-16-X*) Alef Design.

Nebraska Curriculum Development Center Staff. A Curriculum for English, Units 82-84: Student Manual: The Hero. LC LB1631.N46. 197p. reprint ed. pap. 61.10 (*0-8357-3819-1*, 205233200003) Bks Demand.

***Nebraska Educational Media Association Staff.** Guide for Developing & Evaluating School Library Media Programs. 200p. 2000. pap. 39.00 (*1-56308-640-9*) Libs Unl.

Nebraska Flying Boxcars Staff. The Fightn' 451st Bombardment Group (So) LC 89-51930. 240p. 1990. 52.50 (*0-938021-77-X*) Turner Pub KY.

Nebraska Sociological Feminist Collective. A Feminist Ethic for Social Science Research. LC 87-27377. (Women's Studies: Vol. 1). 250p. 1988. lib. bdg. 89.95 (*0-88946-120-1*) E Mellen.

***Nebraska staff.** Related Laws to the Insurance Laws. LC 98-68506. 1998. write for info. (*0-89246-511-5*) NILS Pub.

Nebraska Symposium on Motivation Staff. Nebraska Symposium on Motivation, 1955. Jones, Marshall R., ed. LC 53-11655. (Current Theory & Research in Motivation Ser.: No. 3). 284p. reprint ed. pap. 88.10 (*0-7837-6597-5*, 204616300011) Bks Demand.

— Nebraska Symposium on Motivation, 1956. Jones, Marshall R., ed. LC 53-11655. (Current Theory & Research in Motivation Ser.: No. 4). 319p. reprint ed. pap. 98.90 (*0-7837-6598-3*, 204616400011) Bks Demand.

— Nebraska Symposium on Motivation, 1957. Jones, Marshall R., ed. LC 53-11655. (Current Theory & Research in Motivation Ser.: No. 5). 442p. reprint ed. pap. 137.10 (*0-7837-6599-1*, 204616500011) Bks Demand.

— Nebraska Symposium on Motivation, 1958. Jones, Marshall R., ed. LC 53-11655. (Current Theory & Research in Motivation Ser.: No. 6). 288p. reprint ed. pap. 89.30 (*0-7837-6600-9*, 204616600011) Bks Demand.

— Nebraska Symposium on Motivation, 1959. Jones, Marshall R., ed. LC 53-11655. (Current Theory & Research in Motivation Ser.: No. 7). 253p. reprint ed. pap. 78.50 (*0-7837-6601-7*, 204616700011) Bks Demand.

— Nebraska Symposium on Motivation, 1960. Jones, Marshall R., ed. LC 53-11655. (Current Theory & Research in Motivation Ser.: No. 8). 280p. reprint ed. pap. 86.80 (*0-7837-6602-5*, 204616800011) Bks Demand.

— Nebraska Symposium on Motivation, 1961. Jones, Marshall R., ed. LC 53-11655. (Current Theory & Research in Motivation Ser.: No. 9). 220p. reprint ed. pap. 68.20 (*0-7837-6603-3*, 204616900011) Bks Demand.

— Nebraska Symposium on Motivation, 1962. Jones, Marshall R., ed. LC 53-11655. (Current Theory & Research in Motivation Ser.: No. 10). 344p. reprint ed. pap. 106.70 (*0-7837-6604-1*, 204617000011) Bks Demand.

— Nebraska Symposium on Motivation, 1963. Jones, Marshall R., ed. LC 53-11655. (Current Theory & Research in Motivation Ser.: No. 11). 214p. reprint ed. pap. 66.40 (*0-7837-6605-X*, 204617100011) Bks Demand.

— Nebraska Symposium on Motivation, 1964. Levine, David, ed. LC 53-11655. (Current Theory & Research in Motivation Ser.: No. 12). 294p. reprint ed. pap. 91.20 (*0-7837-6606-8*, 204617200011) Bks Demand.

— Nebraska Symposium on Motivation, 1965. Levine, David, ed. LC 53-11655. (Current Theory & Research in Motivation Ser.: No. 13). 356p. reprint ed. pap. 110.40 (*0-7837-6607-6*, 204617300011) Bks Demand.

— Nebraska Symposium on Motivation, 1966. Levine, David, ed. LC 53-11655. (Current Theory & Research in Motivation Ser.: No. 14). 219p. reprint ed. pap. 67.90 (*0-7837-6608-4*, 204617400011) Bks Demand.

— Nebraska Symposium on Motivation, 1967. Levine, David, ed. LC 53-11655. (Current Theory & Research in Motivation Ser.: No. 15). 345p. reprint ed. pap. 107.00 (*0-7837-6609-2*, 204617500011) Bks Demand.

— Nebraska Symposium on Motivation, 1968. Arnold, William J., ed. LC 53-11655. (Current Theory & Research in Motivation Ser.: No. 16). 347p. reprint ed. pap. 107.60 (*0-7837-6610-6*, 204617800011) Bks Demand.

— Nebraska Symposium on Motivation, 1970. Arnold, William J. & Page, Monte M., eds. LC 53-11655. (Current Theory & Research in Motivation Ser.: No. 18). 302p. reprint ed. pap. 93.70 (*0-7837-6611-4*, 204617600011) Bks Demand.

— Nebraska Symposium on Motivation, 1971. Cole, James K., ed. LC 53-11655. (Current Theory & Research in Motivation Ser.: No. 19). 316p. reprint ed. pap. 98.00 (*0-7837-6612-2*, 204617700011) Bks Demand.

— Nebraska Symposium on Motivation, 1972. Cole, James K. & Jensen, Donald D., eds. LC 53-11655. (Current Theory & Research in Motivation Ser.: No. 20). 353p. reprint ed. pap. 109.50 (*0-7837-6613-0*, 204617900011) Bks Demand.

— Nebraska Symposium on Motivation, 1973. Cole, James K. & Dienstbier, Richard, eds. LC 53-11655. (Current Theory & Research in Motivation Ser.: No. 21). 339p. reprint ed. pap. 105.10 (*0-7837-6614-9*, 204618000011) Bks Demand.

— Nebraska Symposium on Motivation, 1974. Cole, James K. & Sonderegger, Theo B., eds. LC 53-11655. (Current Theory & Research in Motivation Ser.: No. 22). 328p. reprint ed. pap. 101.70 (*0-7837-6615-7*, 204618100011) Bks Demand.

— Nebraska Symposium on Motivation, 1979: Beliefs, Attitudes & Values. Page, Monte M., ed. LC 53-11655. (Current Theory & Research in Motivation Ser.: No. 27). 377p. reprint ed. pap. 116.90 (*0-7837-6620-3*, 204618600011) Bks Demand.

— Nebraska Symposium on Motivation, 1980: Cognitive Processes. Flowers, John H., ed. LC 53-11655. (Current Theory & Research in Motivation Ser.: No. 28). 265p. reprint ed. pap. 82.20 (*0-7837-6621-1*, 204618700011) Bks Demand.

— Nebraska Symposium on Motivation, 1975: Conceptual Foundations of Psychology. Arnold, William J., ed. LC 53-11655. (Current Theory & Research in Motivation Ser.: No. 23). 614p. reprint ed. pap. 190.40 (*0-7837-6616-5*, 204618200011) Bks Demand.

— Nebraska Symposium on Motivation, 1989: Cross-Cultural Perspectives. Berman, John J. & Dienstbier, Richard A., eds. LC 53-11655. (Current Theory & Research in Motivation Ser.: Vol. 37). 375p. reprint ed. pap. 116.30 (*0-608-08689-4*, 206921200003) Bks Demand.

— Nebraska Symposium on Motivation, 1978: Human Emotion. Dienstbier, Richard A., ed. LC 53-11655. (Current Theory & Research in Motivation Ser.: No. 26). 347p. reprint ed. pap. 107.60 (*0-7837-6619-X*, 204618500011) Bks Demand.

— Nebraska Symposium on Motivation, 1976: Personal Construct Psychology. Landfield, Alvin W., ed. LC 53-11655. (Current Theory & Research in Motivation Ser.: No. 24). 379p. reprint ed. pap. 117.50 (*0-7837-6617-3*, 204618300011) Bks Demand.

— Nebraska Symposium on Motivation, 1982: Personality - Current Theory & Research. Page, Monte M., ed. LC 53-11655. (Current Theory & Research in Motivation Ser.: No. 30). 292p. reprint ed. pap. 90.60 (*0-7837-6623-8*, 204618900011) Bks Demand.

— Nebraska Symposium on Motivation, 1981: Response Structure & Organization. Bernstein, Daniel J., ed. LC 53-11655. (Current Theory & Research in Motivation Ser.: No. 29). 279p. reprint ed. pap. 86.50 (*0-7837-6622-X*, 204618800011) Bks Demand.

— Nebraska Symposium on Motivation, 1977: Social Cognitive Development. Keasey, Charles B., ed. LC 53-11655. (Current Theory & Research in Motivation Ser.: No. 25). 373p. reprint ed. pap. 115.70 (*0-7837-6618-1*, 204618400011) Bks Demand.

— Nebraska Symposium on Motivation, 1983. Theories of Schizophrenia & Psychosis. Spaulding, William D. & Cole, James K., eds. LC 53-11655. (Current Theory & Research in Motivation Ser.: No. 31). 391p. reprint ed. pap. 121.30 (*0-7837-6624-6*, 204619000011) Bks Demand.

Nebreda, E. Bibliographia Augustiniana Seu Operum Collectio Quae, Divi Augustini Vitam et Doctrinam Quadantenus exponunt. (Classical Studies). (LAT.). reprint ed. lib. bdg. 39.50 (*0-697-00013-3*) Irvington.

Nebrera, Gregorio T., ed. see Quintero, Serafin Y.

Nebrija, A. Romance Vocabulary in Latin: Vocabulario de Romance en Latin. (LAT & SPA.). 200p. 1981. pap. 45.00 (*0-8288-1617-4*, S39785) Fr & Eur.

Nebrija, Elio A. De, see De Nebrija, Elio A.

Nebs Management. Managing Energy Efficiency. 72p. pap. text 34.95 (*0-7506-4092-8*) Buttrwrth-Heinemann.

Nebs Management Staff. Auditing Quality. 96p. Date not set. pap. text 34.95 (*0-7506-4091-X*) Buttrwrth-Heinemann.

Nebsm. Achieving Quality. 96p. pap. text. write for info. (*0-7506-3297-6*) Buttrwrth-Heinemann.

— Becoming More Effective. 88p. 1999. pap. text 29.95 (*0-7506-3322-0*) Buttrwrth-Heinemann.

— Caring for the Customer. 96p. 1999. pap. text 29.95 (*0-7506-3298-4*) Buttrwrth-Heinemann.

— Controlling Costs. 88p. pap. text. write for info. (*0-7506-3307-7*) Buttrwrth-Heinemann.

— How Organizations Work. 80p. pap. text. write for info. (*0-7506-3309-3*) Buttrwrth-Heinemann.

— Leading Change. 96p. pap. text. write for info. (*0-7506-3302-6*) Buttrwrth-Heinemann.

— Making a Financial Case. 96p. pap. text. write for info. (*0-7506-3308-5*) Buttrwrth-Heinemann.

— Marketing & Selling. 88p. pap. text. write for info. (*0-7506-3299-2*) Buttrwrth-Heinemann.

— Nebsm Planning & Controlling. 88p. pap. text. write for info. (*0-7506-3295-X*) Buttrwrth-Heinemann.

— Understanding Quality. 96p. pap. text. write for info. (*0-7506-3296-8*) Buttrwrth-Heinemann.

Nebsm. Using Graphs. (Open Learning for Supervisory Management). 1986. pap. text 19.50 (*0-08-033966-2*, Pergamon Pr) Elsevier.

Nebsm. Working with Budgets. 80p. pap. text. write for info. (*0-7506-3306-9*) Buttrwrth-Heinemann.

NEBSM Staff. Accounting Money. (Open Learning for Supervisory Management Ser.). 1986. pap. text 19.50 (*0-08-034056-3*, Pergamon Pr) Elsevier.

Nebsm Staff. Communicating. (Open Learning for Supervisory Management Ser.). 1985. pap. text 19.50 (*0-08-033394-X*, Pergamon Pr) Elsevier.

NEBSM Staff. Computers. (Open Learning for Supervisory Management Ser.). 1986. pap. text 19.50 (*0-08-034054-7*, Pergamon Pr) Elsevier.

Nebsm Staff. Enriching Work. (Open Learning for Supervisory Management). 1985. pap. text 19.50 (*0-08-033391-5*, Pergamon Pr) Elsevier.

— Health & Safety. (Open Learning for Supervisory Management Ser.). 1986. pap. text 19.50 (*0-08-033961-1*, Pergamon Pr) Elsevier.

NEBSM Staff. Hiring People. (Open Learning for Supervisory Management Ser.). 1986. pap. text 19.50 (*0-08-034033-4*, Pergamon Pr) Elsevier.

Nebsm Staff. Industrial Relations in Action. (Open Learning for Supervisory Management Ser.). 1986. pap. text 19.50 (*0-08-033962-X*, Pergamon Pr) Elsevier.

— Looking at Figures. (Open Learning for Supervisory Management). 1986. pap. text 19.50 (*0-08-033965-4*, Pergamon Pr) Elsevier.

NEBSM Staff. Managing Time. (Open Learning for Supervisory Management Ser.). 1986. pap. text 19.50 (*0-08-034055-5*, Pergamon Pr) Elsevier.

Nebsm Staff. Managing with Authority. 96p. pap. text. write for info. (*0-7506-3310-7*) Buttrwrth-Heinemann.

NEBSM Staff. NEBSM Leading Your Team. 96p. 1997. pap. text 36.95 (*0-7506-3311-5*) Buttrwrth-Heinemann.

— NEBSM Support Guide. 64p. 1997. pap. text 34.95 (*0-7506-3704-8*) Buttrwrth-Heinemann.

Nebsm Staff. Needs & Rewards. (Open Learning for Supervisory Management Ser.). 1985. pap. text 19.50 (*0-08-033368-0*, Pergamon Pr) Elsevier.

— Needs & Rewards. (Open Learning for Supervisory Management). 1986. pap. text 19.50 (*0-08-033960-3*, Pergamon Pr) Elsevier.

— Orders & Instructions. (Open Learning for Supervisory Management Ser.). 1986. pap. text 19.50 (*0-08-033964-6*, Pergamon Pr) Elsevier.

NEBSM Staff. Supervising the Law. (Open Learning for Supervisory Management Ser.). 1986. pap. text 19.50 (*0-08-034034-2*, Pergamon Pr) Elsevier.

Nebsm Staff. Training Plans. (Open Learning for Supervisory Management Ser.). 1985. pap. text 19.50 (*0-08-033392-3*, Pergamon Pr) Elsevier.

— Training Sessions. (Open Learning for Supervisory Management Ser.). 1985. pap. text 19.50 (*0-08-033393-1*, Pergamon Pr) Elsevier.

— Writing Skills. (Open Learning for Supervisory Management). 1985. pap. text 19.50 (*0-08-033963-8*, Pergamon Pr) Elsevier.

NEBSS Staff & NRMC Staff, eds. Writing Skills. (Open Learning for Supervisory Management Ser.: 302). (Illus.). 106p. 1986. 25.95 (*0-08-070072-1*, Pub. by PPL) Elsevier.

Nebylov, A., jt. auth. see Wilson, P. A.

NEC Corporation, Biological Simulators Inc. Staff, et al, eds. CritiControl. (ENG, FRE & GER.). 1998. 152.00 incl. cd-rom (*3-540-14682-2*) Spr-Verlag.

NEC-TAS Health Focus Group Staff & Fenichel, Emily. Promoting Health Through Part H: Promoting the Health of Infants & Toddlers with Disabilities Through Part H of the Individuals with Disabilities Evaluation Act. 49p. (Orig.). 1991. pap. 7.00 (*0-943657-17-2*) ZERO TO THREE.

Necas, Jindrich. Weak & Young Measure Valued Solutions to Evolution. 288p. 1996. lib. bdg. 69.95 (*0-412-57750-X*) Chapman & Hall.

***Necas, Petr.** Chameleons: Nature's Hidden Jewels. 348p. 1999. 47.50 (*1-57524-137-4*) Krieger.

Necatigil, Zaim M. The Cyprus Question & the Turkish Position in International Law. 2nd ed. LC 92-28431. (Illus.). 538p. 1993. text 95.00 (*0-19-825846-1*) OUP.

Necchi, Orlando, Jr. Revision of the Genus Batrachospermum Roth (Rhodophyta, Batrachospermales) in Brazil. (Bibliotheca Phycologica Ser.: Vol. 84). (Illus.). 201p. 1990. 65.00 (*3-443-60011-5*, Pub. by Gebruder Borntraeger) Balogh.

Necessary, Frank. Rustler's Hide-a-Way. 56p. 1999. pap. 8.00 (*0-8059-4640-3*) Dorrance.

Nechaer, Michelle W. Apron Annie's Pies, Vol. 4467. Kupperstein, Joel, ed. (Learn to Read Math Ser.). (Illus.). 16p. (J). 1998. pap. 2.75 (*1-57471-374-4*, 4467) Creat Teach Pr.

— The Hungry Farmer, Vol. 4417. Kupperstein, Joel, ed. (Learn to Read Social Studies). (Illus.). 16p. (J). (ps-2). 1998. pap. 2.75 (*1-57471-340-X*, 4417) Creat Teach Pr.

— Our Favorites, Vol. 4473. Kupperstein, Joel, ed. (Learn to Read Math Ser.). (Illus.). 16p. (J). 1998. pap. 2.75 (*1-57471-380-9*, 4473) Creat Teach Pr.

Nechaeva, Nina T., ed. Improvement in Desert Ranges in Soviet Central Asia, Vol.4. (Advances in Desert & Arid Land Technology & Development Ser.). xiv, 328p. 1985. text 477.00 (*3-7186-0222-9*) Gordon & Breach.

Nechas, Eileen. Unequal Treatment. 1994. 22.00 (*0-671-79186-9*) S&S Trade.

Necheles-Jansyn, Ruth F. The Mediator Revisited: Profile of a Profession, 1960s & 1985. LC 90-42215. (Institute of Management & Labor Relations Ser.: No. 3). 209p. 1990. 30.00 (*0-8108-2351-9*) Scarecrow.

Necheles, Ruth F. Abbe Gregoire, 1787-1831: The Odyssey of an Egalitarian, 9. LC 75-105987. 333p. (C). 1971. 59.95 (*0-8371-3312-2*, NAG/&, Greenwood Pr) Greenwood.

Neches, Neil, et al. Poetry in Motion: 100 Poems from the Subways & Buses. (Illus.). 128p. 1996. pap. 13.00 (*0-393-31458-8*, Norton Paperbks) Norton.

Nechiporenko, Oleg. Passport to Assassination: The Never Before Told Story of Lee Harvey Oswald by the KGB Colonel. 1993. 22.50 (*1-55972-210-X*, Birch Ln Pr) Carol Pub Group.

Nechis, Barbara. Watercolor from the Heart. (Illus.). 144p. (Orig.). 1993. 29.95 (*0-8230-1624-2*) Watsn-Guptill.

Nechita, Alexandra. Outside the Lines: Paintings by Alexandra Nechita. LC 95-82242. (Illus.). 100p. 1996. 29.95 (*1-56352-454-6*) Longstreet.

Nechodom, Kerry. The Rainbow Bridge: A Chumash Legend. 32p. (Orig.). (J). (gr. k-3). 1992. pap. 6.95 (*0-944627-36-6*) Sand River Pr.

Nechols, J. R., ed. Biological Control in the Western United States: Accomplishments & Benefits of Regional Research Project W-84, 1964-1989. LC 94-61791. 366p. 1995. 45.00 (*1-879906-25-2*, 3361-H); pap. 25.00 (*1-879906-21-X*, 3361) ANR Pubns CA.

Nechvatal, A., jt. auth. see Tedder, John M.

Necipo Lu, Gulru, ed. Muqarnas Vol. 14: An Annual on the Visual Culture of the Islamic World. (Illus.). iv, 188p. 1997. 54.50 (*90-04-10872-6*) Brill Academic Pubs.

Necipoglu, Gulru. Architecture, Ceremonial, & Power: The Topkapi Palace in the Fifteenth & Sixteenth Centurics. (Illus.). 356p. 1992. 60.00 (*0-262-14050-0*) MIT Pr.

— Topkapa Scroll-Geometry & Ornament in Islamic Architecture. 384p. 1996. 160.00 (*0-614-21592-7*, 1432) Kazi Pubns.

— The Topkapi Scroll: Geometry & Ornament in Islamic Architecture. LC 95-14621. (Sketchbooks & Albums Ser.). (Illus.). 412p. 1995. 160.00 (*0-89236-335-5*, Pub. by J P Getty Trust) OUP.

***Necipoglu, Gulru, ed.** Muqarnas. (Illus.). 200p. 1999. 54.50 (*90-04-11482-3*) Brill Academic Pubs.

Necipoglu, Gulru, ed. Muqarnas: An Annual on the Visual Culture of the Islamic World. (Muquarnas. An Annual on Islamic Art & Architecture Ser.: Vol. 13). viii, 211p. 1996. 54.50 (*90-04-10633-2*) Brill Academic Pubs.

Neck, Christopher. Medicine for the Mind: Healing Words to Help You Soar. 212p. 1995. pap. 10.00 (*0-07-046292-5*) McGraw.

Neck, Christopher P., jt. auth. see Manz, Charles C.

Neck, Philip A. & Nelson, Robert E., eds. Small Enterprise Development: Policies & Programmes. 2nd rev. ed. (Management Development Ser.: No. 14). xiii, 282p. (Orig.). 1987. pap. 31.50 (*92-2-105699-6*) Intl Labour Office.

Neck, Philip A., et al. The Practice of Entrepreneurship. ix, 196p. 1982. text 27.00 (*92-2-102839-9*); pap. text 20.25 (*92-2-102846-1*) Intl Labour Office.

Neckar, Lance, jt. ed. see Condon, Patrick M.

Neckebrouck, Valeer, jt. ed. see Cornille, Catherine.

Necker, Maksymilian B. The Auschwitz Chimneys Smoke. rev. ed. (Illus.). 140p. 1993. pap. 12.50 (*1-877582-19-0*) Ardor Pub.

— The Essence & Meaning of Life. (Illus.). 160p. (Orig.). 1991. write for info. (*1-877582-10-7*); pap. 18.50 (*1-877582-11-5*) Ardor Pub.

— Folks in Cockeyed Pictures: Collection of Parodies, Japes, Jokes, Anectodes & Pastiches. (Illus.). 116p. (Orig.). 1989. pap. 9.95 (*1-877582-09-3*) Ardor Pub.

— Gold, Silver & Uranium from Seas & Oceans: The Emerging Technology. rev. ed. (Illus.). 330p. (C). 1991. 77.00 (*1-877582-17-4*); pap. 68.00 (*1-877582-12-3*) Ardor Pub.

— Heart & Wit: Short Stories. (Illus.). 210p. (Orig.). 1991. pap. 16.50 (*1-877582-16-6*) Ardor Pub.

— The Holocaust Verses. rev. ed. (Illus.). 140p. (Orig.). 1990. pap. 12.50 (*1-877582-13-1*) Ardor Pub.

— The Human Menagerie: Collection of Satires & Parodies. rev. ed. (Illus.). 126p. (Orig.). 1990. pap. 14.50 (*1-877582-14-X*) Ardor Pub.

— Politicos, Dumbbells & Quacks. (Illus.). 170p. (Orig.). 1993. pap. 14.50 (*1-877582-15-8*) Ardor Pub.

— Sir Mistake & Mister Blunder: Collection of Satires & Parodies. 122p. (Orig.). 1989. pap. 13.50 (*1-877582-07-7*) Ardor Pub.

N

An Asterisk (*) at the beginning of an entry indicates that the title is appearing for the first time.

***Neckerman, Kathryn M.** Opposing Schools. 1998. 21.00 (*0-226-56960-8*) U Ch Pr.

Neckermann, Peter. The Unification of Germany: The Anatomy of a Peaceful Revolution. 160p. 1992. text 34.50 (*0-88033-230-1*, 333, Pub. by East Eur Monographs) Col U Pr.

Neckers, D. C. Photo-Initiation for Polymerization: UV & EB at the Millenium. LC 99-184625. (Chemistry & Technology of UV & EB Formations for Coatings, Inks & Paints Ser.). 410p. 1999. 185.00 (*0-471-98235-0*) Wiley.

Neckers, Douglas C., ed. Selected Papers on Photochemistry. LC 92-29753. (Milestone Ser.: Vol. MS 65). 1992. pap. 45.00 (*0-8194-1056-X*) SPIE.

— Selected Papers on Photochemistry. LC 92-29753. (Milestone Ser.: Vol. MS 65/HC). 1992. 55.00 (*0-8194-1057-8*) SPIE.

Neckers, Douglas C., et al, eds. Advances in Photochemistry, Vol. 20. LC 63-13592. 301p. 1995. 125.00 (*0-471-11469-3*) Wiley.

— Advances in Photochemistry, Vol. 21. LC 63-13592. 309p. 1996. 125.00 (*0-471-14332-4*) Wiley.

— Advances in Photochemistry, Vol. 22. LC 63-13592. 288p. 1997. 140.00 (*0-471-16999-4*) Wiley.

— Advances in Photochemistry, Vol. 23. (Advances in Photochemistry Ser.: Vol. 23). 361p. 1997. 150.00 (*0-471-19289-9*) Wiley.

***Neckers, Douglas C., et al, eds.** Advances in Photochemistry, Vol. 25. 256p. 1999. 120.00 (*0-471-32708-5*) Wiley.

Neckers, Douglas C., et al. Advances in Photochemistry, Vol. 19. LC 63-13592. 325p. 1994. 175.00 (*0-471-04912-3*) Wiley.

***Neckers, Douglas C., et al.** Advances in Photochemistry, Vol. 24. 368p. 1998. 150.00 (*0-471-28273-1*) Wiley.

Neckers, Douglas C., jt. auth. see Kumar, G. Sudesh.

Necoechea, Miguel. In Defense of Mexico. 1976. lib. bdg. 59.95 (*0-8490-2042-5*) Gordon Pr.

Necsulescu, Dan-Sorin & Baican, R. Applied Virtual Instrumentation. 276p. 2000. 138.00 (*1-85312-800-7*, 8007) Computational Mech MA.

Nectario, M. Juan Colon, Alias Cristobal Colon, Alias Christopher Columbus, Was a Spanish Jew. Josephson, E., ed. 1985. lib. bdg. 250.00 (*0-87700-867-1*) Revisionist Pr.

Nectoux, Jean M. New Grove Twentieth Century French. pap. write for info. (*0-393-31589-4*) Norton.

Nectoux, Jean-Michel. The New Grove Twentieth Century French Masters. 1986. 25.00 (*0-393-02284-6*) Norton.

— The New Grove Twentieth Century French Masters: Faure, Debussy, Satie, Ravel, Poulenc, Messaien. 1986. pap. 14.95 (*0-393-30350-0*) Norton.

Nedd, Kester J., ed. South Florida Rehab & Healthcare Directory, 1991. 490p. 1991. 39.00 (*1-879657-00-7*, Nedmar Graphics) HealthNet Pages.

Nedderman, R. M. Statics & Kinematics of Granular Materials. (Illus.). 368p. (C). 1992. text 115.00 (*0-521-40435-5*) Cambridge U Pr.

Nedderman, R. M., jt. auth. see Kay, John M.

Neddermeyer, Dorothy M. Protect Your Child from Sexual Abuse Perpetrators. 55p. 1995. pap. text 8.95 (*0-9647757-0-0*) Genesis Consult.

Neddermeyer, Dorothy M. & Parker, Bradley. Hit the Ground Running after Landing a Great Job: Start Your New Job the Right Way for Success. 60p. 1995. pap. text. write for info. (*0-9647757-1-9*) Genesis Consult.

Neddermeyer, Henning, ed. Scanning Tunneling Microscopy. LC 92-38479. (Perspectives in Condensed Matter Physics Ser.: Vol. 6). 272p. (C). 1993. text 174.50 (*0-7923-2065-4*) Kluwer Academic.

Nedeljkov, M., et al. The Linear Theory of Colombeau Generalized Functions. (Pitman Research Notes in Mathematics Ser.: No. 385). 168p. 1998. pap. 42.00 (*0-582-35683-0*, LM5683, Chap & Hall CRC) Addison-Wesley.

***Nedeljkovic.** Pain Management of HIV AIDS Patients. (Illus.). 304p. 2000. pap. text 65.00 (*0-7506-7167-X*) Buttrwrth-Heinemann.

Nedelkoff, D. Dan. One-Half of a Telephone Conversation. 1976. 4.00 (*0-685-67938-1*) Windless Orchard.

Nedell, Michael J. Saint Michael's Letters to the Aesthesians. 198p. 1999. pap. 14.95 (*0-9658903-5-X*) Writers Pubg Coop.

Nedellec, Claire & Rouveirol, Celine, eds. Machine Learning - ECML-98: Proceedings 10th European Conference on Machine Learning, Chemnitz, Germany, April 21-23, 1998. LC 98-18109. (Lecture Notes in Artificial Intelligence: Vol. 1398). xii, 420p. 1998. pap. 67.00 (*3-540-64417-2*) Spr-Verlag.

Nedelsky, Jennifer. Private Property & the Limits of American Constitutionalism: The Madisonian Framework & Its Legacy. xiv, 357p. 1994. pap. text 15.95 (*0-226-56971-3*) U Ch Pr.

— Private Property & the Limits of American Constitutionalism: The Madisonian Framework & Its Legacy. 360p. 1998. 35.95 (*0-226-56970-5*) U Ch Pr.

***Nederhood, Joel.** This Splendid Journey. 1998. pap. 11.99 (*0-87552-364-1*) P & R Pubng.

Nederhood, Joel H. This Splendid Journey. LC 98-28950. 207p. 1998. pap. 11.95 (*1-56212-359-9*, 1701-0620) CRC Pubns.

Nederkoorn, Paul & Timmerman, Henk. Signal Transduction by G Protein-Coupled Receptors: Bioenergetics & G Protein Activation; Proton Transfer & GTP Synthesis to Explain the Experimental Findings. LC 96-47443. (Molecular Biology Intelligence Unit Ser.). 1997. 99.00 (*1-57059-415-5*, 0-412-137119) Landes Bioscience.

Nederlander, Caren. Changing Views - The Impressionist Photographs of Caren Nederlander, Ph.D. (Illus.). 30p. (Orig.). 1988. pap. 10.00 (*0-9622466-0-3*) C Nederlander.

Nederlander, Munin. Kitezh: The Russian Grail Legends. 304p. 1991. 29.95 (*1-85538-037-4*, Pub. by Aqn Pr) Harper SF.

Nederlands Instituut Voor Hersenonderzoek Staff & Buijs, R. M. Hypothalamic Integration of Circadian Rhythms: Proceedings of the 19th International Summer School of Brain Research, Held at the Royal Netherlands Academy of Sciences, Amsterdam, the Netherlands, from 28-31 August 1995. LC 96-30122. (Progress in Brain Research Ser.: III). 408p. 1996. 218.50 (*0-444-82443-X*) Elsevier.

Nederlands Instituut Voor Internationale Betrekkin, jt. auth. see Nooy, G. C.

Nederlands Instituut Voor Internationale Betrekkingen "Clingendael" Staff. Early Warning & Conflict Prevention: Limitations & Possibilities. Van Walraven, Klaas, ed. LC 98-30405. (Law Specials Ser.). 224p. 1998. pap. 57.00 (*90-411-1064-X*, Pub. by M Nijhoff) Kluwer Academic.

***Nederlandse Vereniging voor Rechtsvergelijking Staff.** Introduction to Dutch Law. 3rd rev. ed. Chorus, J. M., ed. LC 98-46514. xiv, 574 p. 1998. 75.00 (*90-411-1121-2*) Kluwer Law Intl.

Nederman, Cary J. Community & Consent: The Secular Political Theory of Marsiglio of Padua's Defensor Pacis. LC 94-16779. 192p. 1994. reprint ed. pap. text 25.95 (*0-8476-7944-6*); reprint ed. lib. bdg. 65.00 (*0-8476-7943-8*) Rowman.

— Medieval Aristotelianism & Its Limits: Classical Traditions in Moral & Political Philosophy, 12-15th Centuries. LC 96-48557. (Collected Studies: No. 565). 352p. 1997. 106.95 (*0-86078-622-6*, Pub. by Variorum) Ashgate Pub Co.

***Nederman, Cary J.** Worlds of Difference: European Discourses of Toleration, C. 1100-1550. LC 99-42596. 2000. text. write for info. (*0-271-02017-2*) Pa St U Pr.

Nederman, Cary J. & Laursen, John C., eds. Difference & Dissent: Theories of Toleration in Medieval & Early Modern Europe. LC 96-32889. 250p. 1996. 66.00 (*0-8476-8375-3*); pap. 25.95 (*0-8476-8376-1*) Rowman.

Nederman, Cary J., ed. see John of Salisbury.

Nederman, Cary J., jt. ed. see Laursen, John C.

Nederman, Cary J., ed. see Marsiglio of Padua.

Nederpelt, R. P., et al. Selected Papers on Automath. LC 94-34022. (Studies in Logic & the Foundations of Mathematics: Vol. 133). 1044p. 1994. 238.00 (*0-444-89822-0*) Elsevier.

Nederveen, A., jt. auth. see Houtman, P.

Nederveen, Cornelis J. Accoustical Aspects of Woodwind Instruments. 2nd rev. ed. LC 98-3054. 1998. pap. 28.00 (*0-87580-577-9*) N Ill U Pr.

***Nederveen Pieterse, Jan.** Global Futures: Shaping Globalization. LC 99-54579. 2000. pap. write for info. (*1-85649-802-6*, Pub. by Zed Books) St Martin.

Nederveld, Patricia L. Adam & Eve: The Story of the First Man & Woman. LC 97-37044. (God Loves Me Ser.). (Illus.). 24p. (J). (ps-3). 1998. pap. 2.45 (*1-56212-272-X*, 1105-0103) CRC Pubns.

— An Amazing Star! The Story of the Wise Men. LC 97-53308. (God Loves Me Ser.). (Illus.). 24p. (J). (ps). 1998. pap. 2.45 (*1-56212-295-9*, 1105-0126) CRC Pubns.

— A Baby for Hannah: The Story of an Answered Prayer. LC 97-32474. (God Loves Me Ser.). (Illus.). 24p. (J). (ps). 1998. pap. 2.45 (*1-56212-285-1*, 1105-0116) CRC Pubns.

— The Best Day Ever! The Story of Easter. LC 98-15639. (God Loves Me Ser.). (Illus.). 24p. (J). (ps). 1998. pap. 2.45 (*1-56212-313-0*, 1105-0144) CRC Pubns.

— A Better Thing to Do: The Story of Jesus & Mary & Martha. LC 98-16965. (God Loves Me Ser.). (Illus.). 24p. (J). (ps). 1998. pap. 2.45 (*1-56212-307-6*, 1105-0138) CRC Pubns.

— A Big Fish Story: The Story of Jonah. LC 97-32477. (God Loves Me Ser.). (Illus.). 24p. (J). (ps). 1998. pap. 2.45 (*1-56212-291-6*, 1105-0122) CRC Pubns.

— Blue & Green & Purple Too! The Story of God's Colorful World. LC 97-37046. (God Loves Me Ser.). (Illus.). 24p. (J). 1998. pap. 2.45 (*1-56212-270-3*, 1105-0101) CRC Pubns.

— Come to Me! The Story of Jesus & the Children. LC 98-15643. (God Loves Me Ser.). (Illus.). 24p. (J). (ps). 1998. pap. 2.45 (*1-56212-309-2*, 1105-0140) CRC Pubns.

— Count the Stars! The Story of God's Promise to Abraham & Sarah. LC 97-37039. (God Loves Me Ser.). (Illus.). 24p. (J). (ps). 1998. pap. 2.45 (*1-56212-276-2*, 1105-0107) CRC Pubns.

— David & the Giant: The Story of David & Goliath. LC 97-32480. (God Loves Me Ser.). (Illus.). 24p. (J). (ps). 1998. pap. 2.45 (*1-56212-288-6*, 1105-0119) CRC Pubns.

— A Father's Wish: The Story of Jesus & a Little Boy. LC 97-53313. (God Loves Me Ser.). (Illus.). 24p. (J). (ps). 1998. pap. 2.45 (*1-56212-300-9*, 1105-0131) CRC Pubns.

— Follow Me! The Story of Jesus & His Twelve Helpers. LC 97-53317. (God Loves Me Ser.). (Illus.). 24p. (J). (ps). 1998. pap. 2.45 (*1-56212-298-3*, 1105-0129) CRC Pubns.

***Nederveld, Patricia L.** Get Up & Walk! The Story of Jesus & a Man Who Couldn't Walk. LC 97-53314. (God Loves Me Ser.). (Illus.). 24p. (J). (ps). 1998. pap. 2.45 (*1-56212-302-5*, 1105-0133) CRC Pubns.

Nederveld, Patricia L. A Girl Named Rebekah: The Story of God's Answer to Abraham. LC 97-37041. (God Loves Me Ser.). (Illus.). 24p. (J). (ps). 1998. pap. 2.45 (*1-56212-277-0*, 1105-0108) CRC Pubns.

— God Loves Me Complete Set, 52 vols. 1998. pap. 99.95 (*1-56212-367-X*) CRC Pubns.

— God Loves Me Take Home Cards. 1998. pap. text 6.75 (*1-56212-368-8*) CRC Pubns.

— Good News! The Story of the Shepherds. LC 97-53310. (God Loves Me Ser.). (Illus.). 24p. (J). (ps). 1998. pap. 2.45 (*1-56212-294-0*, 1105-0125) CRC Pubns.

— Goodbye for Now! The Story of Jesus' Return to Heaven. LC 98-15637. (God Loves Me Ser.). (Illus.). 24p. (J). (ps). 1998. pap. 2.45 (*1-56212-314-9*, 1105-0145) CRC Pubns.

— The Greatest Gift: The Story of Jesus & the Woman at the Well. LC 98-10843. (God Loves Me Ser.). (Illus.). 24p. (J). (ps). 1998. pap. 2.45 (*1-56212-299-1*, 1105-0130) CRC Pubns.

— Have a Great Day! The Story of Jesus & Zacchaeus. LC 98-15642. (God Loves Me Ser.). (Illus.). 24p. (J). (ps). 1998. pap. 2.45 (*1-56212-310-6*, 1105-0141) CRC Pubns.

— Hosannah! The Story of Palm Sunday. LC 98-15645. (God Loves Me Ser.). (Illus.). 24p. (J). (ps). 1998. pap. 2.45 (*1-56212-312-2*, 1105-0143) CRC Pubns.

— I Love You, Jesus! The Story of Mary's Gift to Jesus. LC 98-15644. (God Loves Me Ser.). (Illus.). 24p. (J). (ps). 1998. pap. 2.45 (*1-56212-311-4*, 1105-0142) CRC Pubns.

— I'll Do It! The Story of Moses & the Burning Bush. LC 97-37035. (God Loves Me Ser.). (Illus.). 24p. (J). (ps). 1998. pap. 2.45 (*1-56212-281-9*, 1105-0112) CRC Pubns.

— It's a Noisy Place! The Story of the First Creatures. LC 97-37045. (God Loves Me Ser.). (Illus.). 24p. (J). (ps). 1998. pap. 2.45 (*1-56212-271-1*, 1105-0102) CRC Pubns.

— Jesus Is Born! The Story of Christmas. LC 97-32485. (God Loves Me Ser.). (Illus.). 24p. (J). (ps). 1998. pap. 2.45 (*1-56212-293-2*, 1105-0124) CRC Pubns.

— Just Believe! The Story of Jesus & a Little Girl. LC 97-53312. (God Loves Me Ser.). (Illus.). 24p. (J). (ps). 1998. pap. 2.45 (*1-56212-301-7*, 1105-0132) CRC Pubns.

— Lions & Bears! The Story of David the Shepherd Boy. LC 97-32476. (God Loves Me Ser.). (Illus.). 24p. (J). (ps). 1998. pap. 2.45 (*1-56212-287-8*, 1105-0118) CRC Pubns.

— Lions, Lions! The Story of Daniel. LC 97-32484. (God Loves Me Ser.). (Illus.). 24p. (J). (ps). 1998. pap. 2.45 (*1-56212-292-4*, 1105-0123) CRC Pubns.

— A Little Jar of Oil: The Story of Elisha & the Widow. LC 97-32478. (God Loves Me Ser.). (Illus.). 24p. (J). (ps). 1998. pap. 2.45 (*1-56212-289-4*, 1105-0120) CRC Pubns.

— A Little Lunch: The Story of Jesus & the Hungry Crowd. LC 97-53315. (God Loves Me Ser.). (Illus.). 24p. (J). (ps). 1998. pap. 2.45 (*1-56212-303-3*, 1105-0134) CRC Pubns.

— A Lost Lamb: The Story of the Good Shepherd. LC 98-15641. (God Loves Me Ser.). (Illus.). 24p. (J). (ps). 1998. pap. 2.45 (*1-56212-308-4*, 1105-0139) CRC Pubns.

— A New Friend: The Story of Paul's Conversion. LC 98-16962. (God Loves Me Ser.). (Illus.). 24p. (J). (ps). 1998. pap. 2.45 (*1-56212-317-3*, 1105-0148) CRC Pubns.

— One, Two, Three, Four, Five, Six, Seven! The Story of Elisha & Naaman. LC 97-32472. (God Loves Me Ser.). (Illus.). 24p. (J). (ps). 1998. pap. 2.45 (*1-56212-290-8*, 1105-0121) CRC Pubns.

— Over the Wall: The Story of Paul's Escape in a Basket. LC 98-15638. (God Loves Me Ser.). (Illus.). 24p. (J). (ps). 1998. pap. 2.45 (*1-56212-318-1*, 1105-0149) CRC Pubns.

— Plenty to Eat: The Story of Joseph & His Brothers. LC 97-37036. (God Loves Me Ser.). (Illus.). 24p. (J). (ps). 1998. pap. 2.45 (*1-56212-279-7*, 1105-0110) CRC Pubns.

— A Prayer for Peter: The Story of Peter in Prison. LC 98-16961. (God Loves Me Ser.). (Illus.). 24p. (J). (ps). 1998. pap. 2.45 (*1-56212-315-7*, 1105-0146) CRC Pubns.

— A Rainy, Rainy Day: The Story of Noah. LC 97-37040. (God Loves Me Ser.). (Illus.). 24p. (J). (ps-3). 1998. pap. 2.45 (*1-56212-275-4*, 1105-0106) CRC Pubns.

— A Ride in the Night: The Story of Paul's Escape on Horseback. LC 98-15636. (God Loves Me Ser.). (Illus.). 24p. (J). (ps). 1998. pap. 2.45 (*1-56212-320-3*, 1105-0151) CRC Pubns.

— Sad Day, Happy Day! The Story of Peter & Dorcas. LC 98-18517. (God Loves Me Ser.). (Illus.). 24p. (J). (ps). 1998. pap. 2.45 (*1-56212-316-5*, 1105-0147) CRC Pubns.

— Safe at Last! The Story of Moses & the Red Sea. LC 97-37031. (God Loves Me Ser.). (Illus.). 24p. (J). (ps). 1998. pap. 2.45 (*1-56212-282-7*, 1105-0113) CRC Pubns.

— Safe in a Basket: The Story of Baby Moses. LC 97-37037. (God Loves Me Ser.). (Illus.). 24p. (J). (ps). 1998. pap. 2.45 (*1-56212-280-0*, 1105-0111) CRC Pubns.

— Samuel! Samuel! The Story of God's Call to Samuel. LC 97-32475. (God Loves Me Ser.). (Illus.). 24p. (J). (ps). 1998. pap. 2.45 (*1-56212-286-X*, 1105-0117) CRC Pubns.

— A Scary Storm: The Story of Jesus & a Stormy Sea. LC 97-52272. (God Loves Me Ser.). (Illus.). 24p. (J). (ps). 1998. pap. 2.45 (*1-56212-304-1*, 1105-0135) CRC Pubns.

— The Shipwreck: The Story of Paul's Rescue at Sea. LC 98-15634. (God Loves Me Ser.). (Illus.). 24p. (J). (ps). 1998. pap. 2.45 (*1-56212-321-1*, 1105-0152) CRC Pubns.

— A Song in the Night: The Story of Paul & Silas in Prison. LC 98-15640. (God Loves Me Ser.). (Illus.). 24p. (J). (ps). 1998. pap. 2.45 (*1-56212-319-X*, 1105-0150) CRC Pubns.

— Take Good Care of My World! The Story of Adam & Eve in the Garden. LC 97-37043. (God Loves Me Ser.). (Illus.). 24p. (J). (ps). 1998. pap. 2.45 (*1-56212-273-8*, 1105-0104) CRC Pubns.

— A Tall Wall: The Story of Jericho. LC 97-32482. (God Loves Me Ser.). (Illus.). 24p. (J). (ps). 1998. pap. 2.45 (*1-56212-284-3*, 1105-0115) CRC Pubns.

— Thank You, Jesus! The Story of Jesus & One Thankful Man. LC 97-52790. (God Loves Me Ser.). (Illus.). 24p. (J). (ps). 1998. pap. 2.45 (*1-56212-305-X*, 1105-0136) CRC Pubns.

— Two Coats for Joseph: The Story of Young Joseph. LC 97-37038. (God Loves Me Ser.). (Illus.). 24p. (J). (ps). 1998. pap. 2.45 (*1-56212-278-9*, 1105-0109) CRC Pubns.

— A Very Sad Day: The Story of Adam & Eve's Disobedience. LC 97-37042. (God Loves Me Ser.). (Illus.). 24p. (J). (ps). 1998. pap. 2.45 (*1-56212-274-6*, 1105-0105) CRC Pubns.

— Waiting, Waiting, Waiting! The Story of Simeon & Anna. LC 97-53309. (God Loves Me Ser.). (Illus.). 24p. (J). (ps). 1998. pap. 2.45 (*1-56212-296-7*, 1105-0127) CRC Pubns.

— What Is It? The Story of Manna in the Desert. LC 97-32479. (God Loves Me Ser.). (Illus.). 24p. (J). (ps). 1998. pap. 2.45 (*1-56212-283-5*, 1105-0114) CRC Pubns.

***Nederveld, Patricia L.** Who Is This Child? The Story of Jesus in the Temple. LC 97-53311. (God Loves Me). (Illus.). 24p. (J). (ps). 1998. pap. 2.45 (*1-56212-297-5*, 1105-0128) CRC Pubns.

Nederveld, Patricia L. A Wonderful Sight! The Story of Jesus & a Man Who Couldn't See. LC 98-16963. (God Loves Me Ser.). (Illus.). 24p. (J). (ps). 1998. pap. 2.45 (*1-56212-306-8*, 1105-0137) CRC Pubns.

Nedham, Marchamont, tr. see Selden, John.

Nedjalkov, Igor. Evenki. LC 96-11437. (Descriptive Grammars Ser.). 368p. (C). 1997. 190.00 (*0-415-02640-7*) Routledge.

Nedjalkov, Vladimir P. & Comrie, Bernard, eds. Typology of Resultative Constructions. LC 88-2598. (Typological Studies in Language: Vol. 12). xx, 573p. (C). 1988. reprint ed. 144.00 (*0-915027-78-X*); reprint ed. pap. 48.95 (*0-915027-79-8*) J Benjamins Pubng Co.

***Nedkilalkov, V. P.** Tense-Aspect, Transitivity & Causativity: Essays in Honor of Vladimir Nedjalkov. Abraham, Werner & Kulikov, Leonid, eds. LC 99-40613. (Studies in Language Companion : Vol. 50). xxxiv, 359p. 1999. 95.00 (*1-55619-936-8*) J Benjamins Pubng Co.

Nedley, Neil. Proof Positive: How to Reliably Combat Diseases & Achieve Optimal Health. De Rose, David, ed. (Illus.). 560p. 1998. text 49.00 (*0-9661979-3-3*) Nedley Publishing.

Nedo, M. Ludwig Wittgenstein-Wiener Ausgabe: Einfuhrung-Introduction. (Illus.). 148p. 1994. 26.95 (*0-387-82498-7*) Spr-Verlag.

— Philosophische Bemerkungen, 1. (Ludwig Wittgenstein, Wiener Ausgabe Ser.). 196p. 1994. 98.00 (*0-387-82499-5*) Spr-Verlag.

— Philosophische Betrachtungen, 2. (Ludwig Wittengenstien, Wiener Ausgabe Ser.). 333p. 1994. 125.00 (*0-387-82502-9*) Spr-Verlag.

Nedo, M., ed. Ludwig Wittgenstein - Vienna Edition Vol. 3: Bemerkungen Philosophische Bemerkungen. xv, 334p. 1995. 159.95 (*3-211-82534-7*) Spr-Verlag.

***Nedo, M., ed.** Ludwig Wittgenstein, Weiner Ausgabe Studien Texte, Bande 1-5. (ENG & GER.). 1999. pap. 143.00 (*3-211-83271-8*) Spr-Verlag.

— Ludwig Wittgenstein, Weiner Ausgabe Studien Texte Band 1: Philosophische Bemerkungen. (ENG & GER.). xix, 196p. 1999. pap. 36.00 (*3-211-83266-1*) Spr-Verlag.

— Ludwig Wittgenstein, Weiner Ausgabe Studien Texte Band 2: Philosophische Betrachtungen. Philosophische Bemerkungen. (ENG & GER.). xiii, 333p. 1999. pap. 36.00 (*3-211-83267-X*) Spr-Verlag.

— Ludwig Wittgenstein, Weiner Ausgabe Studien Texte Band 3: Bemerkungen. Philosophische Bemerkungen. (ENG & GER.). xv, 334p. 1999. pap. 36.00 (*3-211-83268-8*) Spr-Verlag.

— Ludwig Wittgenstein, Weiner Ausgabe Studien Texte Band 4: Bemerkungen zur Philosophie. Bemerkungen zur Philosophischen Grammatik. (ENG & GER.). xiii, 240p. 1999. pap. 36.00 (*3-211-83269-6*) Spr-Verlag.

— Ludwig Wittgenstein, Weiner Ausgabe Studien Texte Band 5: Philosophische Grammatik. (ENG & GER.). xxvii, 195p. 1999. pap. 36.00 (*3-211-83270-X*) Spr-Verlag.

Nedo, M., ed. Register zu den Banden 1 - 5: Ludwig Wittgenstein, Wiener Ausgabe. xxv, 293p. 1998. 129.00 (*3-211-82858-3*) Spr-Verlag.

***Nedo, M., ed.** Synopse der Manuskriptbande V-X. (Ludwig Wittgenstein, Wiener Ausgabe Ser.: Vol. 8, 1). 250p. 2000. 89.95 (*3-211-82562-2*) Spr-Verlag.

Nedobeck, Don. Nedobeck's Alphabet Book. (Illus.). 16p. (J). (gr. 1-8). 1993. reprint ed. 15.00 (*0-944314-00-7*) New Wrinkle.

— Nedobeck's Numbers Book. 26p. (J). (gr. 1-8). 1988. 15.00 (*0-944314-01-5*) New Wrinkle.

Nedobeck, Don. Nedobeck's Twelve Days of Christmas. (J). (gr. 1-8). 1988. reprint ed. lib. bdg. 15.00 (*0-944314-02-3*) New Wrinkle.

Nedoluha, Gerald E., jt. ed. see Clegg, Andrew W.

Nedoma, Josef. Numerical Modelling in Geodynamics: With Applications. LC 97-20322. 990p. 1998. 160.00 (*0-471-97461-7*) Wiley.

Nedoncelle, Maurice. The Personalist Challenge: Intersubjectivity & Ontology. Gerard, Francois C. et al, trs. LC 83-26293. (Pittsburgh Theological Monographs: No. 27). 1994. pap. 10.00 (*0-915138-29-8*) Pickwick.

Nedoroscik, Jeffrey A. The City of the Dead: A History of Cairo's Cemetery Communities. LC 97-10409. 152p. 1997. 57.95 (*0-89789-533-9*, Bergin & Garvey) Greenwood.

An Asterisk (*) at the beginning of an entry indicates that the title is appearing for the first time.

Nedoseka, A. Y. Fundamentals of Calculations & Diagnostics of Welded Structures. 260p. 1997. pap. 96.00 (*1-898326-46-0*, Pub. by CISP) Balogh.

Nedreaas, Torborg. Music from a Blue Well. Lee, Bibbi, tr. LC 87-19026. (European Women Writers Ser.). 244p. 1988. reprint ed. pap. 75.70 (*0-608-02669-7*, 206332200004) Bks Demand.

— Nothing Grows by Moonlight. Lee, Bibbi, tr. from NOR. LC 87-5000. (European Women Writers Ser.).Tr. of Av Maneskinn Gror det Ingenting. vi, 198p. 1987. text 30.00 (*0-8032-3313-2*) U of Nebr Pr.

Nedreberg, Sherry. More Conference Activities. (Gospel Games Ser.). (Illus.). 60p. 1997. pap. 5.95 (*1-57665-039-1*) Muggli Graphics.

Nedreberg, Sherry & Muggli, Glorianne. Classroom Activity Book: Book of Mormon. (Illus.). 96p. (Orig.). 1995. pap. 7.95 (*1-57665-010-3*) Muggli Graphics.

— Classroom Activity Book: Choose the Right A. (Illus.). 100p. (Orig.). 1996. pap. 7.95 (*1-57665-020-0*) Muggli Graphics.

— Classroom Activity Book: Choose the Right B. (Illus.). 100p. (Orig.). 1996. pap. 7.95 (*1-57665-026-X*) Muggli Graphics.

— Classroom Activity Book: Nursery Book. (Illus.). 76p. (Orig.). 1995. pap. 6.95 (*1-57665-012-X*) Muggli Graphics.

— Classroom Activity Book: Sunbeam Book. (Illus.). 84p. (Orig.). 1995. pap. 6.95 (*1-57665-011-1*) Muggli Graphics.

— Old Testament. (Classroom Activity Book Ser.). (Illus.). 100p. 1997. pap. 7.95 (*1-57665-036-7*) Muggli Graphics.

Nedved, Gregory J. South Dakota Presidential Trivia. 57p. 1995. pap. write for info. (*0-9651949-0-6*) G J Nedved.

— South Dakota Presidential Trivia. 57p. 1995. pap. 6.00 (*0-614-24798-5*) Tesseract SD.

Nedwek, Brian P., ed. Doing Academic Planning: Effective Tools for Decision Making. LC 97-6286. (Illus.). 160p. (Orig.). 1996. pap. text 60.00 (*0-9601608-3-3*) Soc Coll & Univ Planning.

Nedwell, D. B., jt. ed. see Swamy.

***Nedwell, D.B., ed.** Advances in Ecological Research Vol. 29: Estuaries. 330p. 1999. 99.95 (*0-12-013929-4*) Acad Pr.

Nee, A. Y., et al, eds. Advanced Fixture Design for FMS. (Advanced Manufacturing Ser.). 1994. 114.95 (*0-387-19908-X*) Spr-Verlag.

***Nee, A. Y. C., et al, eds.** Computer Applications in Near Net-Shape Operations. LC 99-35688. (Advanced Manufacturing Ser.). (Illus.). xviii, 322p. 1999. 116.00 (*1-85233-186-0*, Pub. by Spr-Verlag) Spr-Verlag.

Nee-Benham, Maenette K. & Cooper, Joanne E. Let My Spirit Soar! Narratives of Diverse Women in School Leadership. LC 97-33952. (1-Off Ser.). 176p. 1998. 51.95 (*0-8039-6671-7*); pap. 22.95 (*0-8039-6672-5*) Corwin Pr.

Nee-Benham, Maenette K. Ah, see Ah Nee-Benham, Maenette K.

Nee, Brett De Bary, see Nee, Victor G. & De Bary Nee, Brett.

Nee, D. Y. The Destiny of Humanity. (C). 1998. pap. 48.00 (*0-9639876-2-3*) Inst For Systs.

— Radicalizinag the World Through Social Engineering: The New World Order. 272p. (Orig.). (C). 1993. pap. 38.00 (*0-9639876-0-7*) Inst For Systs.

Nee, Eric. The UniForum Guide to Graphical User Interfaces. Gold, Jordan, ed. (Illus.). 25p. (Orig.). pap. text 9.95 (*0-936593-16-4*) UniForum.

Nee, John. Fundamentals of Tool Design. 4th ed. SME Staff, ed. LC 97-61865. (Illus.). 769 p. 1998. 75.00 (*0-87263-490-6*, PI2642) SME.

Nee, John G. Jig & Fixture Design & Detailing. LC 78-71562. (Illus.). (C). 1979. pap. 17.95 (*0-911168-41-9*) Prakken.

— Mechanical Engineering Technology: Product Design & Drafting Problems. LC 83-60332. (Illus.). 163p. (C). 1983. pap. 11.95 (*0-911168-52-4*) Prakken.

Nee, Kathie, ed. see Belk, Clothilde.

Nee, Patrick W. The Internationalist Business Guides Series: Guide for International Business & Investment, 6 bks., Set. (Orig.). 1998. pap. 99.95 (*0-9633905-7-0*) Intrntnlst.

— Top 10 Guide to New York City. (Top Ten Travel Guides Ser.). (Illus.). 200p. 1999. pap. 14.95 (*1-891382-21-7*) Intrntnlst.

Nee, Patrick W., ed. Business Guide to Middle East & Southern Asia: Guide for International Business & Investment. (Business Guides to the World Ser.). (Illus.). 200p. (Orig.). 1999. pap. 24.95 (*0-9633905-5-4*) Intrntnlst.

— The Euro. (Making Money Internationally Ser.). (Illus.). 200p. 1998. pap. 34.95 (*1-891382-27-6*) Intrntnlst.

— Making Money in China: All You Need to Know about Doing Business Internationally. (Making Money Internationally Ser.). (Illus.). 200p. 1998. pap. 24.95 (*1-891382-01-2*) Intrntnlst.

— Making Money in Mexico: All You Need to Know about Doing Business Internationally. (Making Money Internationally Ser.). (Illus.). 200p. 1998. pap. 24.95 (*1-891382-00-4*); pap. 24.95 (*1-891382-02-0*) Intrntnlst.

— Making Money in South America: All You Need to Know about Doing Business Internationally. (Making Money Internationally Ser.). (Illus.). 200p. 1998. pap. 24.95 (*1-891382-03-9*) Intrntnlst.

— Road Map of Florence. (Road Maps of the World Ser.). (Illus.). 1998. pap. 14.95 (*1-891382-16-0*, Pub. by Intrntnlst) BookWorld.

— Road Map of France. (Road Maps of the World Ser.). (Illus.). 1998. pap. 14.95 (*1-891382-12-8*, Pub. by Intrntnlst) BookWorld.

— Road Map of Italy. (Road Maps of the World Ser.). (Illus.). 1998. pap. 14.95 (*1-891382-13-6*, Pub. by Intrntnlst) BookWorld.

— Road Map of Mexico & Central America. (Road Maps of the World Ser.). (Illus.). 1999. pap. 14.95 (*1-891382-19-5*, 665-022, Pub. by Intrntnlst) BookWorld.

— Road Map of Russia. (Road Maps of the World Ser.). (Illus.). 1998. pap. 14.95 (*1-891382-11-X*) Intrntnlst.

— Road Map of South America. (Road Maps of the World Ser.). (Illus.). 1998. pap. 14.95 (*1-891382-18-7*) Intrntnlst.

— Road Map of Umbria Provincial Area: Easy to Read Road Maps for Safe & Enjoyable Travel. (Road Maps of the World Ser.). (Illus.). 1998. pap. 14.95 (*1-891382-10-1*) Intrntnlst.

— Road Map to Australia: Easy to Read Road Maps for Safe & Enjoyable Travel. (Road Maps of the World Ser.). (Illus.). 1998. pap. 11.95 (*1-891382-17-9*, Pub. by Intrntnlst) BookWorld.

— Road Map to Great Britain & Ireland: Easy to Read Road Maps for Safe & Enjoyable Travel. (Road Maps of the World Ser.). (Illus.). 1998. 11.95 (*1-891382-15-2*, Pub. by Intrntnlst) BookWorld.

— Road Map to Roma Provincial Area: Easy to Read Road Maps for Safe & Enjoyable Travel. (Road Maps of the World Ser.). (Illus.). 1998. pap. 11.95 (*1-891382-14-4*) Intrntnlst.

— Top Ten Guide to Florence: The Best of Travel. (Top Ten Travel Guides Ser.). (Illus.). 200p. 1998. pap. 14.95 (*1-891382-05-5*) Intrntnlst.

— Top Ten Guide to Hong Kong. (Top Ten Travel Guides Ser.). (Illus.). 200p. 1998. pap. 14.95 (*1-891382-07-1*) Intrntnlst.

— Top Ten Guide to Milan. (Top Ten Travel Guides Ser.). (Illus.). 200p. 1998. pap. 14.95 (*1-891382-26-8*) Intrntnlst.

— Top Ten Guide to Orlando & Disney World. (Top Ten Travel Guides Ser.). (Illus.). 200p. 1998. pap. 14.95 (*1-891382-22-5*) Intrntnlst.

— Top Ten Guide to Rome: The Best of Travel. (Top Ten Travel Guides Ser.). (Illus.). 200p. 1998. pap. 14.95 (*1-891382-20-9*) Intrntnlst.

— Top Ten Guide to Singapore: The Best of Travel. (Top Ten Travel Guides Ser.). (Illus.). 200p. 1998. pap. 14.95 (*1-891382-09-8*) Intrntnlst.

— Top 10 Guide to Tokyo: The Best of Travel. (Top 10 Travel Guides Ser.). 1998. pap. text 14.95 (*1-891382-08-X*) Intrntnlst.

Nee, Patrick W., ed. see Osborn, Meredith B.

Nee, Paul A. ISO 9000 in Construction. LC 95-26005. 224p. 1996. 80.00 (*0-471-12121-5*) Wiley.

Nee, Paul V. Chains & Other Things. 1998. pap. write for info. (*1-57553-647-1*) Watermrk Pr.

— How Things Change. 1998. pap. write for info. (*1-57553-869-5*) Watermrk Pr.

— In Tribute. 1997. pap. 56.95 (*1-57553-694-3*) Watermrk Pr.

Nee, Richard D. Van, see Van Nee, Richard D.

Nee, Robert H., jt. ed. see Roberts, Robert W.

Nee, T. S. Aguas Refrescantes. Orig. Title: Through the Year. (SPA.). 216p. 1992. pap. 8.99 (*0-8254-1500-4*, Edit Portavoz) Kregel.

— Autoridad Espiritual.Tr. of Spiritual Authority. (SPA.). 204p. 1978. pap. 6.99 (*0-8297-0805-7*) Vida Pubs.

— Conhecimento Espiritual. Orig. Title: Spiritual Knowledge. (POR.). 144p. 1986. pap. 3.95 (*0-8297-0781-6*) Vida Pubs.

— La Cruz en la Vida Cristiana Normal. Orig. Title: The Cross in the Normal Christian Life. (SPA.). 144p. 1992. mass mkt. 4.99 (*0-8254-1501-2*, Edit Portavoz) Kregel.

— L' Homme Spirituel.Tr. of Spiritual Man. (FRE.). 434p. 1991. pap. 27.95 (*0-8297-1527-4*) Vida Pubs.

— Mejor Pacto.Tr. of Better Covenant. (SPA.). 208p. 1984. pap. 5.99 (*0-8297-0958-4*) Vida Pubs.

— No Ameis al Mundo. Orig. Title: Love Not the World. (SPA.). 96p. 1992. mass mkt. 3.99 (*0-8254-1502-0*, Edit Portavoz) Kregel.

— El Obrero Cristiano Normal. Orig. Title: The Normal Christian Worker. (SPA.). 112p. 1992. mass mkt. 3.99 (*0-8254-1503-9*, Edit Portavoz) Kregel.

— Oremos.Tr. of Let Us Pray. (SPA.). 120p. 1980. pap. 4.99 (*0-8297-1046-9*) Vida Pubs.

— Que Hare, Senor? Orig. Title: What Shall This Man Do?. (SPA.). 272p. 1992. mass mkt. 6.99 (*0-8254-1504-7*, Edit Portavoz) Kregel.

— Sentaos, Andad, Estad Firmes. Orig. Title: Sit, Walk, Stand. (SPA.). 80p. 1992. mass mkt. 3.99 (*0-8254-1505-5*, Edit Portavoz) Kregel.

— Transformados en Su Semejanza. Orig. Title: Transformed into His Image. (SPA.). 144p. 1992. mass mkt. 4.99 (*0-8254-1506-3*, Edit Portavoz) Kregel.

— La Vida Cristiana Normal. Orig. Title: Normal Christian Worker. (SPA.). 128p. 1992. mass mkt. 4.99 (*0-8254-1509-8*, Edit Portavoz) Kregel.

— Vida Cristiana Victoriosa.Tr. of Life That Wins. (SPA.). 160p. 1995. pap. 8.99 (*0-8297-0399-3*) Vida Pubs.

Nee, Victor, jt. ed. see Brinton, Mary C.

Nee, Victor G. The Cultural Revolution at Peking University. LC 77-81790. 91p. reprint ed. pap. 30.00 (*0-608-15884-4*, 203076500070) Bks Demand.

Nee, Victor G. & De Bary Nee, Brett. Longtime Californ' A Documentary Study of an American Chinatown. 438p. 1986. reprint ed. pap. 16.95 (*0-8047-1336-7*) Stanford U Pr.

Nee, Victor G. & Lyons, Thomas P., eds. The Economic Transformation of South China: Reform & Development in the Post-Mao Era. 298p. (C). 1994. 23.80 (*0-939657-82-1*) Cornell East Asia Pgm.

— The Economic Transformation of South China: Reform & Development in the Post-Mao Era, No. 70. 304p. (C). 1994. pap. 14.45 (*0-939657-70-8*) Cornell East Asia Pgm.

Nee, Victor G., jt. ed. see Mozingo, David.

Nee, Victor G., jt. ed. see Stark, David.

Nee, Watchman. Aids to "Revelation" Kaung, Stephen, tr. 122p. 1983. pap. 4.00 (*0-935008-60-8*) Christian Fellow Pubs.

— Assembling Together. Kaung, Stephen, tr. (Basic Lesson Ser.: Vol. 3). 147p. 1973. 6.50 (*0-935008-01-2*); pap. 4.50 (*0-935008-02-0*) Christian Fellow Pubs.

— The Assembly Life. 131p. 1995. per. 7.00 (*0-87083-855-5*, 08-043-001) Living Stream Ministry.

— Los Asuntos De La Iglesia.Tr. of Church Affairs. (SPA.). 259p. 1995. per. 9.25 (*0-87083-555-6*, 08-003-002) Living Stream Ministry.

— Authority & Submission. 101p. 1993. per. 3.75 (*0-87083-404-5*, 07001001) Living Stream Ministry.

— Back to the Cross. Fader, Herbert L., ed. Kaung, Stephen, tr. from CHI. 171p. (Orig.). 1988. pap. 4.50 (*0-935008-70-5*) Christian Fellow Pubs.

— A Balanced Christian Life. Kaung, Stephen, tr. 174p. 1981. pap. 4.50 (*0-935008-53-5*) Christian Fellow Pubs.

— Baptism Nbs-1: Spanish. 1998. pap. text 2.00 (*1-57593-939-8*) Living Stream Ministry.

— The Better Covenant. Kaung, Stephen, tr. 167p. 1982. pap. 5.00 (*0-935008-55-1*) Christian Fellow Pubs.

***Nee, Watchman.** Body Christ. 6p. 1998. per. 1.00 (*0-7363-0307-3*, 18-071-002) Living Stream Ministry.

— Body of Christ. 1998. pap. 2.00 (*0-7363-0126-7*) Living Stream Ministry.

Nee, Watchman. The Body of Christ: A Reality. Kaung, Stephen, tr. 90p. 1978. pap. 3.50 (*0-935008-13-6*) Christian Fellow Pubs.

— Breaking of the Outer Man & the Release of the Spirit. 116p. 1998. per. 7.75 (*1-57593-380-2*, 07-068-002) Living Stream Ministry.

— The Breaking of the Outer Man for the Release of the Spirit. 116p. 1997. per. 7.75 (*1-57593-955-X*, 07-068-001) Living Stream Ministry.

***Nee, Watchman.** Called to Commitment. LC 99-30462. (Life Messages of Great Christians Ser.). 185p. 1999. pap. 10.99 (*1-56955-094-8*, Vine Bks) Servant.

Nee, Watchman. Catching Men. (Vital Ser.). 1997. pap. 0.75 (*0-87508-501-6*) Chr Lit.

— Changed into His Likeness. 1992. mass mkt. 4.95 (*0-87508-410-9*) Chr Lit.

— Changed into His Likeness. 176p. 1978. pap. 4.99 (*0-8423-0228-X*) Tyndale Hse.

— The Character of God's Workman. Fader, Herbert L., ed. Kaung, Stephen, tr. from CHI. 229p. (Orig.). 1988. pap. 5.50 (*0-935008-69-1*) Christian Fellow Pubs.

— Character of the Lord's Worker. 163p. 1998. per. 9.00 (*1-57593-322-5*, 13-063-401) Living Stream Ministry.

— Christ Becoming our Wisdom. 38p. 1998. pap. 1.00 (*0-7363-0085-6*, 18-070-002) Living Stream Ministry.

— Christ Our Righteousness, 10 Vols. 10p. 1998. pap. 1.00 (*1-57593-397-7*, 18-069-002) Living Stream Ministry.

— Christ the Sum of All Spiritual Things. Kaung, Stephen, tr. 96p. 1973. pap. 3.50 (*0-935008-14-4*) Christian Fellow Pubs.

— The Church: The Building of God. (Vital Ser.). 1997. pap. 0.75 (*0-87508-504-0*) Chr Lit.

— Church Affairs. 244p. pap. 9.25 (*0-87083-378-2*, 08003001) Living Stream Ministry.

— Church Affairs. 244p. 1996. per. 11.75 (*1-57593-804-9*, 08-003-001) Living Stream Ministry.

— The Church & the Work, 3 vols. Kaung, Stephen, tr. (CHI.). 550p. 1982. reprint ed. 30.00 (*0-935008-57-8*); reprint ed. pap. text 17.00 (*0-935008-58-6*) Christian Fellow Pubs.

— The Collected Works of Watchman Nee. 4386p. 1994. boxed set 240.00 (*0-87083-591-2*, 03-003-001) Living Stream Ministry.

— The Collected Works of Watchman Nee, Set #1. Vol. 1. 4917p. 1992. boxed set 300.00 (*0-87083-589-0*, 03-001-001) Living Stream Ministry.

— The Collected Works of Watchman Nee, Set #2. 5876p. 1993. boxed set 390.00 (*0-87083-590-4*, 03-002-001) Living Stream Ministry.

— Come, Lord Jesus. Kaung, Stephen, tr. 258p. 1976. 8.00 (*0-935008-15-2*); pap. 6.00 (*0-935008-16-0*) Christian Fellow Pubs.

***Nee, Watchman.** Comision Especifica en la Oracion. 1998. pap. text 10.00 (*0-7363-0037-6*) Living Stream Ministry.

Nee, Watchman. The Communion of the Holy Spirit. Fader, Herbert L., ed. Kaung, Stephen, tr. 1994. pap. 4.50 (*0-935008-79-9*) Christian Fellow Pubs.

***Nee, Watchman.** Como Estudiar la Biblia. 1999. pap. text 8.25 (*0-7363-0539-4*) Living Stream Ministry.

Nee, Watchman. Concerning the Lord's Day Message Meeting. 56p. 1988. pap. 3.75 (*0-87083-381-2*, 08-005-001) Living Stream Ministry.

***Nee, Watchman.** Confession & Recompense Nbs 13 Spanish: New Believers 13. (SPA.). 1998. pap. 2.00 (*1-57593-443-4*) Living Stream Ministry.

Nee, Watchman. Conocimiento Espiritual. Orig. Title: Spiritual Knowledge. (SPA.). 1986. mass mkt. 3.95 (*0-8297-0782-4*) Vida Pubs.

***Nee, Watchman.** Cristo Es Todas las Cosas y los Asuntos Espirituales. (SPA.). 1999. pap. 5.25 (*0-7363-0698-6*) Living Stream Ministry.

Nee, Watchman. La Disciplina de Dios, 19. (Mensajes Para Creyentes Nuevos Ser). 1998. pap. text 2.00 (*0-7363-0096-1*) Living Stream Ministry.

***Nee, Watchman.** Discipline of the Holy Spirit. 1998. pap. 2.00 (*0-7363-0097-X*) Living Stream Ministry.

Nee, Watchman. Do All to the Glory of God. Kaung, Stephen, tr. (Basic Lesson Ser.: Vol. 5). 214p. 1974. 7.00 (*0-935008-03-9*); pap. 5.50 (*0-935008-04-7*) Christian Fellow Pubs.

— Las Dos Naturalezas.Tr. of Two Natures. (SPA.). 19p. 1994. pap. 2.00 (*0-87083-794-X*, 07-035-002) Living Stream Ministry.

— El Evangelio De Dios, 3.Tr. of GOSPEL OF GOD. (SPA.). 519p. per. 18.50 (*0-87083-753-2*, 11009002) Living Stream Ministry.

— La Fe Cristiana Normal.Tr. of NORMAL CHRISTIAN FAITH. (SPA.). 225p. 1994. per. 9.00 (*0-87083-779-6*, 11-010-002) Living Stream Ministry.

— The Finest of the Wheat, Vol. 1. Kaung, Stephen & Fader, Herbert L., eds. 456p. 1992. pap. 10.00 (*0-935008-76-4*) Christian Fellow Pubs.

— The Finest of the Wheat, Vol. I. Kaung, Stephen & Fader, Herbert L., eds. 456p. 1992. 15.00 (*0-935008-75-6*) Christian Fellow Pubs.

— The Finest of the Wheat, Vol. 2. Kaung, Stephen & Fader, Herbert L., eds. 527p. 1993. pap. 10.00 (*0-935008-78-0*) Christian Fellow Pubs.

— The Finest of the Wheat, Vol. II. Kaung, Stephen & Fader, Herbert L., eds. 527p. 1993. 15.00 (*0-935008-77-2*) Christian Fellow Pubs.

***Nee, Watchman.** Flow of the Spirit. 9p. 1998. pap. 1.00 (*0-7363-0352-9*, 18-068-002) Living Stream Ministry.

Nee, Watchman. From Faith to Faith. Fader, Herbert L., ed. 120p. 1984. pap. 4.50 (*0-935008-62-4*) Christian Fellow Pubs.

— From Glory to Glory. Fader, Herbert L., ed. Kaung, Stephen, tr. from CHI. & intro. by. 142p. (Orig.). 1985. pap. 4.50 (*0-935008-64-0*) Christian Fellow Pubs.

— Full of Grace & Truth, Vol. I. Kaung, Stephen, tr. 205p. 1980. pap. 4.50 (*0-935008-49-7*) Christian Fellow Pubs.

— Full of Grace & Truth, Vol. II. Kaung, Stephen, tr. 147p. 1981. pap. 4.50 (*0-935008-51-9*) Christian Fellow Pubs.

— Further Talks on The Church Life. 170p. 1997. per. 8.50 (*0-87083-003-1*, 08-010-001) Living Stream Ministry.

— Gleanings in the Fields of Boaz. Fader, Herbert L., ed. Kaung, Stephen, tr. from CHI. 136p. (Orig.). 1987. pap. 4.50 (*0-935008-68-3*) Christian Fellow Pubs.

— The Glorious Church. 157p. 1968. per. 8.75 (*0-87083-745-1*, 08-012-001) Living Stream Ministry.

— The Glory of His Life. Kaung, Stephen, tr. 117p. 1976. pap. 4.50 (*0-935008-18-7*) Christian Fellow Pubs.

— The God of Abraham, Isaac & Jacob. 178p. 1995. per. 9.00 (*0-87083-932-2*, 05-004-001) Living Stream Ministry.

— God of Abraham, Isaac & Jacob. (SPA.). 176p. 1998. per. 9.00 (*1-57593-377-2*, 05-004-002) Living Stream Ministry.

***Nee, Watchman.** God's Keeping. 11p. 1998. pap. 1.00 (*0-7363-0347-2*, 18-058-002) Living Stream Ministry.

Nee, Watchman. God's Plan & the Overcomers. Kaung, Stephen, tr. from CHI. 83p. 1977. pap. 3.50 (*0-935008-19-5*) Christian Fellow Pubs.

— God's Work. Kaung, Stephen, tr. 64p. 1974. pap. 3.50 (*0-935008-20-9*) Christian Fellow Pubs.

— The Good Confession. Kaung, Stephen, tr. (Basic Lesson Ser.: Vol. 2). 114p. 1973. 6.00 (*0-935008-05-5*); pap. 4.00 (*0-935008-06-3*) Christian Fellow Pubs.

— Gospel Dialogue. Kaung, Stephen, tr. 197p. 1975. 8.00 (*0-935008-21-7*); pap. 5.00 (*0-935008-22-5*) Christian Fellow Pubs.

— The Gospel Of God, 3. 492p. per. 18.50 (*0-87083-533-5*, 11009001) Living Stream Ministry.

— Grace for Grace. Kaung, Stephen, tr. from CHI. 114p. 1983. pap. text 4.00 (*0-935008-59-4*) Christian Fellow Pubs.

***Nee, Watchman.** How to Know God's Will. 15p. 1998. pap. 1.00 (*0-7363-0349-9*, 18-066-002) Living Stream Ministry.

— How to Study the Bible. 1999. pap. text 8.25 (*0-7363-0407-X*) Living Stream Ministry.

Nee, Watchman. La Iglesia Gloriosa (The Glorious Church) (SPA.). 161p. 1996. per. 8.75 (*0-87083-971-3*, 08-012-002) Living Stream Ministry.

— Interpreting Matthew. Fader, Herbert L., ed. Kaung, Stephen, tr. from CHI. 288p. (Orig.). 1989. 12.00 (*0-935008-71-3*); pap. 6.50 (*0-935008-72-1*) Christian Fellow Pubs.

— The Joyful Heart. 1979. pap. 5.95 (*0-87508-417-6*) Chr Lit.

— The Joyful Heart. Chen, Ruth T., tr. (CHI.). 1985. write for info. (*0-941598-91-8*); pap. write for info. (*0-941598-24-1*) Living Spring Pubns.

— The King & the Kingdom of Heaven. Kaung, Stephen, tr. from CHI. 386p. 1978. pap. 7.00 (*0-935008-24-1*) Christian Fellow Pubs.

— The Latent Power of the Soul. Kaung, Stephen, tr. 86p. 1972. pap. 3.50 (*0-935008-25-X*) Christian Fellow Pubs.

— Let Us Pray. Kaung, Stephen, tr. from CHI. 87p. 1977. pap. 3.50 (*0-935008-26-8*) Christian Fellow Pubs.

— La Liberacion Del Espiritu.Tr. of Release of the Spirit. 112p. 1992. 6.99 (*0-88113-255-1*) Caribe Betania.

— The Life that Wins. Fader, Herbert L., ed. Kaung, Stephen, tr. from CHI. & intro. by. 157p. (Orig.). 1986. 11.00 (*0-935008-65-9*); pap. 5.00 (*0-935008-66-7*) Christian Fellow Pubs.

— A Living Sacrifice. Kaung, Stephen, tr. (Basic Lesson Ser.: Vol. 1). 115p. 1972. 6.00 (*0-935008-07-1*); pap. 4.00 (*0-935008-08-X*) Christian Fellow Pubs.

— The Lord My Portion. Fader, Herbert L. & O'Dell, James P., eds. (Illus.). 246p. (Orig.). 1984. pap. 4.50 (*0-935008-61-6*) Christian Fellow Pubs.

— Love Not the World. 124p. 1993. pap. text 5.70 (*1-883137-05-5*) Christ Stewards.

— Love Not the World. rev. ed. 13p. 1998. mass mkt. 5.99 (*0-87508-489-3*, 489) Chr Lit.

N

An Asterisk (*) at the beginning of an entry indicates that the title is appearing for the first time.

— Love One Another. Kaung, Stephen, tr. (Basic Lesson Ser.: Vol. 6). 235p. 1975. 7.00 (0-935008-09-8); pap. 5.50 (0-935008-10-1) Christian Fellow Pubs.

— Mensajes para Creyentes Nuevos, 24. 1998. pap. text 36.00 (0-7363-0321-9) Living Stream Ministry.

— The Messenger of the Cross. Kaung, Stephen, tr. 154p. 1980. pap. text 4.50 (0-935008-50-0) Christian Fellow Pubs.

— The Messenger of the Cross. 44p. (J). 1991. pap. 2.50 (0-87083-605-6, 07-033-001) Living Stream Ministry.

***Nee, Watchman.** Messenger of the Cross. 17p. 1998. pap. 1.00 (0-7363-0308-1, 18-074-002) Living Stream Ministry.

— Ministramos al Templo Ministramos a Dios, Vol. 10. 1999. pap. 10.00 (0-7363-0305-7) Living Stream Ministry.

Nee, Watchman. The Ministry of God's Word. Kaung, Stephen, tr. 282p. 1971. 8.00 (0-935008-27-6); pap. 6.00 (0-935008-28-4) Christian Fellow Pubs.

— The Mystery of Christ: Knowing Christ in the Church & As the Church. 70p. 1997. per. 6.50 (1-57593-954-1, 08-045-001) Living Stream Ministry.

— The Mystery of Creation. Kaung, Stephen, tr. 149p. 1981. pap. 4.50 (0-935008-52-7) Christian Fellow Pubs.

— New Covenant Spanish. 100p. 1999. per. 6.50 (0-7363-0064-3, 07-050-402) Living Stream Ministry.

— The Normal Christian Church Life. 188p. 1980. per. 8.75 (0-87083-027-9, 08-013-001) Living Stream Ministry.

— The Normal Christian Faith. 213p. per. 8.00 (0-87083-006-6, 11010001) Living Stream Ministry.

***Nee, Watchman.** The Normal Christian Life. (Deluxe Christian Classics). 204p. 2000. 9.97 (1-57748-915-2) Barbour Pub.

Nee, Watchman. The Normal Christian Life. 1979. mass mkt. 5.95 (0-87508-414-1) Chr Lit.

— The Normal Christian Life. 285p. 1977. mass mkt. 5.99 (0-8423-4710-0) Tyndale Hse.

— The Normal Christian Life: Also Including the Overcoming Life. (Essential Christian Library Ser.). 412p. 1999. 9.97 (1-57748-519-X) Barbour Pub.

— Not I, but Christ. Kaung, Stephen, tr. (Basic Lesson Ser.: Vol. 4). 143p. 1974. 6.50 (0-935008-11-X); pap. 4.50 (0-935008-12-8) Christian Fellow Pubs.

— The Orthodoxy of the Church. 102p. 1973. per. 7.25 (0-87083-007-4, 08-017-001) Living Stream Ministry.

— The Overcoming Life: The Basis for the Normal Christian Life. 180p. 1997. 18.00 (1-57593-817-0, 07-061-901) Living Stream Ministry.

— Platicas Adicionales Sobre la Vida de la Iglesia.Tr. of FURTHER TALKS ON THE CHURCH LIFE. (SPA.). 189p. per. 6.50 (0-87083-090-2, 08010002) Living Stream Ministry.

— Platicas Adicionales Sobre la Vida de la Iglesia (Further Talks on the Church Life) (SPA.). 189p. 1982. per. 8.50 (0-87083-236-0, 08-010-002) Living Stream Ministry.

— Practical Issues of This Life. Kaung, Stephen, tr. 163p. 1975. pap. 5.00 (0-935008-29-2) Christian Fellow Pubs.

— The Prayer Ministry of the Church. Kaung, Stephen, tr. 128p. 1973. pap. 4.50 (0-935008-30-6) Christian Fellow Pubs.

— The Prayer Ministry of the Church. 84p. 1995. per. 6.00 (0-87083-860-1, 04-038-001) Living Stream Ministry.

***Nee, Watchman.** Release of the Spirit. 1999. pap. 7.00 (0-935008-83-7) Christian Fellow Pubs.

Nee, Watchman. Revive Thy Work. Fader, Herbert L., ed. Kaung, Stephen, tr. from CHI. LC 96-229614. (Orig.). 1996. pap. 5.50 (0-935008-81-0) Christian Fellow Pubs.

— The Riches of Watchman Nee. (Essential Christian Library Ser.). 320p. 1999. 9.97 (1-57748-585-8) Barbour Pub.

— El Sacerdocio, 23. (Mensajes Para Creyentes Nuevos Ser). 1998. pap. text 2.00 (0-7363-0125-9) Living Stream Ministry.

— The Salvation of the Soul. Kaung, Stephen, tr. 115p. 1978. pap. 4.50 (0-935008-31-4) Christian Fellow Pubs.

— Secrets to Spiritual Power: From the Writings of Watchman Nee. LC 98-47850. 303p. 1999. pap. 12.99 (0-88368-498-5) Whitaker Hse.

— Selections from the Normal Christian Life. (Vital Ser.). 1997. pap. 0.75 (0-87508-514-8) Chr Lit.

— Sit, Walk, Stand. 1991. pap. 4.95 (0-87508-419-2) Chr Lit.

— Sit, Walk, Stand. 77p. 1977. mass mkt. 4.99 (0-8423-5893-5) Tyndale Hse.

— Song of Songs. 1992. pap. 9.99 (0-87508-442-7) Chr Lit.

— Song of Songs. 126p. 1998. per. 8.00 (1-57593-956-8, 07-048-002) Living Stream Ministry.

— The Song of Songs. 126p. 1995. per. 8.00 (0-87083-872-5, 07-048-001) Living Stream Ministry.

— Special Grace & Reserve Grace. 1998. pap. text 10.00 (0-7363-0145-3) Living Stream Ministry.

— The Spirit of Judgment. Fader, Herbert L. et al, eds. Kaung, Stephen, tr. from CHI. 158p. (Orig.). 1984. pap. 4.50 (0-935008-63-2) Christian Fellow Pubs.

— The Spirit of the Gospel. Fader, Herbert L., ed. 100p. (Orig.). 1986. pap. 4.50 (0-935008-67-5) Christian Fellow Pubs.

— The Spirit of Wisdom & Revelation. Kaung, Stephen, tr. 160p. 1980. pap. 4.50 (0-935008-48-9) Christian Fellow Pubs.

— Spiritual Authority. Kaung, Stephen, tr. 191p. 1972. pap. 5.00 (0-935008-35-7) Christian Fellow Pubs.

— Spiritual Knowledge. Kaung, Stephen, tr. 124p. 1973. 5.50 (0-935008-36-5); pap. 4.50 (0-935008-37-3) Christian Fellow Pubs.

— Spiritual Man. Kaung, Stephen, tr. 694p. 1968. pap. 10.00 (0-935008-39-X) Christian Fellow Pubs.

***Nee, Watchman.** Spiritual Progress. 9p. 1998. pap. 1.00 (0-7363-0354-5, 18-072-002) Living Stream Ministry.

Nee, Watchman. Spiritual Reality or Obsession. Kaung, Stephen, tr. 64p. 1970. pap. 3.50 (0-935008-41-1) Christian Fellow Pubs.

— Table in the Wilderness. 1979. pap. 5.95 (0-87508-422-2) Chr Lit.

— Take Heed. Kaung, Stephen & Fader, Herbert L., eds. 204p. (Orig.). 1991. pap. 5.00 (0-935008-74-8) Christian Fellow Pubs.

— Testimony of God. Kaung, Stephen, tr. 123p. 1979. pap. 4.00 (0-935008-44-6) Christian Fellow Pubs.

— The Time of the Cross. 21p. 1991. pap. 2.00 (0-87083-607-2, 07-034-001) Living Stream Ministry.

— Treasure in Earthen Vessels, 10 vols. 21p. 1998. pap. 1.00 (1-57593-989-4, 18-006-001) Living Stream Ministry.

— Twelve Baskets Full, Vol. 1. 168p. 1982. per. 6.50 (0-87083-086-4, 07-019-001) Living Stream Ministry.

— Twelve Baskets Full, Vol. 2. 155p. 1981. per. 6.00 (0-87083-049-X, 07-020-001) Living Stream Ministry.

— Twelve Baskets Full, Vol. 3. 91p. 1981. per. 4.50 (0-87083-050-3, 07-021-001) Living Stream Ministry.

— Twelve Baskets Full, Vol. 4. 154p. 1982. per. 5.75 (0-87083-087-2, 07-022-001) Living Stream Ministry.

— The Two Natures. 19p. 1991. pap. 1.00 (0-87083-608-0, 07-035-001) Living Stream Ministry.

— Two Principles of Living, 10 Vols. 29p. 1999. pap. 1.00 (1-57593-990-8, 18-020-002) Living Stream Ministry.

— La Vida Cristiana Normal de la Iglesia.Tr. of NORMAL CHRISTIAN CHURCH LIFE. (SPA.). 229p. 1989. per. 8.75 (0-87083-495-9, 08-013-002) Living Stream Ministry.

***Nee, Watchman.** Watchman Nee: Man of Suffering. LC 99-163002. (Heroes of the Faith Ser.). 208p. 1998. pap. 3.97 (1-57748-223-9) Barbour Pub.

Nee, Watchman. Watchman Nee's Testimony. 57p. 1991. per. 5.50 (0-87083-051-1, 20-006-001) Living Stream Ministry.

— The Way to Self-Knowledge. (Vital Ser.). 1997. pap. 0.75 (0-87508-519-9) Chr Lit.

— Wayfarer in the Land. 176p. 1975. reprint ed. mass mkt. 4.99 (0-8423-7823-5) Tyndale Hse.

— What Are We? 26p. 1991. pap. 2.00 (0-87083-600-5, 08-034-001) Living Stream Ministry.

— What Shall This Man Do. rev. ed. 208p. 1998. mass mkt. 9.99 (0-87508-488-5, 188) Chr Lit.

— Whom Shall I Send? Kaung, Stephen, tr. 89p. 1979. pap. 3.50 (0-935008-45-4) Christian Fellow Pubs.

— Why This Waste? (Vital Ser.). 1997. pap. 0.75 (0-87508-522-9) Chr Lit.

***Nee, Watchman.** Withstanding the Devil. 1998. pap. 2.00 (0-7363-0098-8) Living Stream Ministry.

Nee, Watchman. The Word of the Cross. Fader, Herbert L., ed. Kaung, Stephen, tr. from CHI. LC 96-129351. 165p. (Orig.). 1995. pap. 5.00 (0-935008-80-2) Christian Fellow Pubs.

— The Word of the Cross. 34p. (Orig.). 1991. pap. 2.50 (0-87083-606-4, 07-032-001) Living Stream Ministry.

— Worship God. Kaung, Stephen & Fader, Herbert L., eds. 107p. (Orig.). 1990. pap. 4.50 (0-935008-73-X) Christian Fellow Pubs.

***Nee, Watchman.** Worshipping the Ways of God, 10 vols. 1998. pap. text 10.00 (0-7363-0184-4) Living Stream Ministry.

Nee, Watchman. Ye Search the Scriptures. Kaung, Stephen, tr. 173p. 1974. 8.00 (0-935008-46-2); pap. 5.00 (0-935008-47-0) Christian Fellow Pubs.

Nee, Watchman & Lee, Witness. Messages Given During the Resumption of Watchman Nee's Ministry, 2 vols. 604p. 1991. per. 21.50 (0-87083-028-7, 14-006-001) Living Stream Ministry.

— The New Covenant. 174p. 1981. per. 7.50 (0-87083-048-1, 07-007-001) Living Stream Ministry.

Neeb, Karl-Heinz. Radiochemistry of Light Water Reactor Nuclear Power Plants. LC 97-31125. 720p. (C). 1997. lib. bdg. 368.90 (3-11-013242-7) De Gruyter.

***Neeb, Karl-Hermann.** Holomorphy & Convexity in Lie Theory. LC 99-47514. (Expositions in Mathematics Ser.). 778p. 1999. write for info. (3-11-015669-5) De Gruyter.

Neeb, Karl-Hermann. Invariant Subsemigroups of Lie Groups. LC 93-17164. (Memoirs of the American Mathematical Society Ser.: No. 499). 193p. 1993. pap. 36.00 (0-8218-2562-3, MEMO/104/499) Am Math.

Neeb, Karl-Hermann, jt. auth. see Hilgert, J.

Neeb, Karl-Hermann, jt. auth. see Hilgert, Joachim.

Neeb, Kathryn C. Fundamentals of Mental Health Nursing. LC 96-37436. (Illus.). 411p. (C). 1997. pap. text 27.95 (0-8036-0205-7) Davis Co.

Neebascher, B. Official Beanie Basher Handbook. LC 98-86600. 1998. pap. text 7.95 (0-8362-8186-1) Andrews & McMeel.

Neebe. Primer on Linear Programming. 56p. (C). 1991. pap. text 10.00 (0-536-58006-5) Pearson Custom.

Neebe, Gudrun. Apostolische Kirche: Grundunterscheidungen an Luthers Kirchenbegriff unter Besonderer Beruecksichtigung Seiner Lehre von den Notae Ecclesiae. (Theologische Bibliothek Toepelmann Ser.: Vol. 82). (GER.). 300p. (C). 1997. lib. bdg. 110.00 (3-11-015628-8) De Gruyter.

Need, Ovid. The Death of Victory: Tracing the Roots & Implications of Otherworldliness. 500p. 1997. text. write for info. (1-879998-11-4) Ross Hse Bks.

Need, Stephen W. Human Language & Knowledge in the Light of Chalcedon. (American University Studies VII: Vol. 187). XIII, 248p. (C). 1996. text 44.95 (0-8204-2728-4) P Lang Pubng.

***Needell, Allan.** Science, Cold War & the American State: Lloyd V. Berkner & the Balance of Professional Ideals. (Studies in the History of Science, Technology & Medicine). 428p. 2000. 60.00 (90-5702-621-X, Harwood Acad Pubs); pap. 28.00 (90-5702-622-8, Harwood Acad Pubs) Gordon & Breach.

Needell, Allan, ed. The First Twenty-Five Years in Space. LC 83-600210. 166p. (C). 1989. pap. 17.50 (0-87474-713-9) Smithsonian.

Needell, Claire. Migrations. 32p. 1998. pap. 4.00 (1-893032-03-5) Jensen Daniels.

— Not a Balancing Act: Poems. (Burning Deck Poetry Ser.). 64p. 1993. pap. 8.00 (0-930901-89-4) Burning Deck.

— Not a Balancing Act: Poems. limited ed. (Burning Deck Poetry Ser.). 64p. 1993. pap. 15.00 (0-930901-90-8) Burning Deck.

Needell, Jeffrey D. A Tropical Belle Epoque: Elite Culture & Society in Turn-of-the-Century Rio de Janeiro. (Cambridge Latin American Studies: No. 62). (Illus.). 384p. 1988. text 85.00 (0-521-33374-1) Cambridge U Pr.

Needes, Robin. You Don't Have to Feel Unwell: Nutrition, Lifestyle, Herbs & Homeopathy - A Home Guide. 2nd ed. 336p. 1994. pap. write for info. (1-85860-009-X) ACCESS Pubs Network.

Needham. Organizing Knowledge. (C). 1977. text 23.00 (0-233-95836-3) Westview.

— Urban Land Property Mark Netherlands. 240p. 1993. 75.00 (1-85728-051-2, Pub. by UCL Pr Ltd) Taylor & Francis.

Needham, jt. auth. see Dransfield.

Needham, A. & Kerkut, G. A. Uniqueness of Biological Materials. LC 64-21694. (International Series of Monographs on Pure & Applied Mathematics: Vol. 25). 1965. 268.00 (0-08-010748-6, Pub. by Pergamon Repr) Franklin.

Needham, Alix. The Stress Management Kit. LC 96-229557. 112p. 1997. 24.95 (1-885203-39-X) Jrny Editions.

***Needham, Anuradha Dingwan.** Resistance & the Literature of the African & South Asian Dias. LC 99-54551. 208p. 1999. text 45.00 (0-312-22542-3) St Martin.

Needham, Barrie. Physical Planning & Environmental Policy in the Netherlands: A Guide to English-Language Publications. LC 92-5721. (CPL Bibliographies Ser.: No. 280). (Illus.). 1992. 10.00 (0-86602-280-5, Sage Prdcls Pr) Sage.

Needham, Bobbe. Beastly Abodes: Homes for Birds, Bats, Butterflies & Other Backyard Wildlife. (Illus.). 144p. 1996. pap. 14.95 (0-8069-3169-8) Sterling.

— Beastly Abodes Book & Kit. (Illus.). 1995. 29.95 (0-8069-4350-5) Lark Books.

— Dog Crafts. LC 96-36803. (Illus.). 128p. 1997. 14.95 (0-8069-9565-3) Sterling.

— Ecology Crafts for Kids: 50 Great Ways to Make Friends with Planet Earth. LC 98-3565. (Illus.). 144p. (J). (gr. 4-7). 1998. 24.95 (0-8069-0685-5) Sterling.

— Ecology Crafts for Kids: 50 Great Ways to Make Friends with Planet Earth. (J). 1999. pap. text 14.95 (0-8069-2024-6) Sterling.

— Fantastic Flowerpots: 50 Creative Ways to Decorate a Plain Pot. LC 98-3960. 128p. 1998. 24.95 (1-57990-065-8, Pub. by Lark Books) Random.

— Fantastic Flowerpots: 50 Creative Ways to Decorate a Plain Pot. LC 98-3960. 1999. pap. 14.95 (1-57990-143-3, Pub. by Lark Books) Random.

Needham, Bobbe, ed. see Crandall-Frazier, Cindy.

Needham, Bobbe, ed. see Langsner, Drew.

Needham, Brian, ed. Case Studies of Coastal Management: Experience from the U. S. (Illus.). 117p. (Orig.). (C). 1993. pap. text 25.00 (1-56806-579-5) DIANE Pub.

Needham, Christina W. & Morales, Carmen A. Manual Para la Practica Docente: Programa a Base de Competencias. Objectivos Operacionales-Instrumentos de Evaluacion. (SPA.). 82p. 1980. pap. 5.00 (0-8477-2744-0) U of PR Pr.

Needham, Christopher D., ed. Reader in Social Science Documentation. LC 75-8049. 538p. 1983. lib. bdg. 69.50 (0-313-24047-7, ZRO/, Greenwood Pr) Greenwood.

Needham, Christopher D. & Herman, Esther, eds. Study of Subject Bibliography with Special Reference to the Social Sciences. LC 75-630095. (Student Contribution Ser.: No. 3). 1970. pap. 5.00 (0-911808-05-1) U of Md Lib Serv.

Needham, Claude. The Original Handbook for the Recently Deceased. (Illus.). 144p. 1992. 100.00 (0-89556-093-3) Gateways Bks & Tapes.

— The Original Handbook for the Recently Deceased. (Illus.). 144p. 1993. pap. 12.50 (0-89556-068-2) Gateways Bks & Tapes.

***Needham, Cynthia, et al.** Intimate Strangers: Unseen Life on Earth. LC 99-59802. (Illus.). 240p. 2000. 39.95 (1-55581-163-9) ASM Pr.

Needham, D. Descubriendo la Oracion. (Serie Discipulado - Discipleship Ser.).Tr. of Discovering Prayer. (SPA.). 1.99 (1-56063-359-X, 498252) Editorial Unilit.

Needham, David. Close to His Majesty: A Road Map to God. LC 96-143440. 1996. pap. 10.99 (0-88070-860-3, Multnomah Bks) Multnomah Pubs.

Needham, David & Dransfield, Rob. Business Studies. 3rd ed. 768p. (Orig.). 1997. pap. 52.50 (0-7487-3061-3, Pub. by S Thornes Pubs) Trans-Atl Phila.

— Business Studies: A-Level Workbook. 3rd ed. 230p. 1998. pap., wbk. ed. 39.00 (0-7487-1891-5) St Mut.

— Business Studies for You. 320p. 1998. pap. 41.00 (0-7487-2490-7) St Mut.

— Business Studies for You: Teacher Support Pack. 186p. 1998. pap., teacher ed. 195.00 (0-7487-2491-5) St Mut.

— European Business Studies. 288p. 1994. pap. 39.50 (0-7487-1895-8, Pub. by S Thornes Pubs) Trans-Atl Phila.

— Understanding Business Studies. (Illus.). 658p. 1998. pap. 52.50 (0-7487-3346-9, Pub. by S Thornes Pubs) Trans-Atl Phila.

Needham, David & Dransfield, Robert. Business Studies "A" Level Workbook. LC 92-43624. 1993. 10.99 (0-07-707607-9) McGraw.

Needham, David & Dransfield, Robert, eds. Understanding Business Studies: Teacher's Guide. 200p. (Orig.). 1998. pap., teacher ed. 195.00 (0-7487-3846-0) St Mut.

Needham, David, et al. Teaching Business Studies. LC 92-20520. 1992. 15.99 (0-07-707602-8) McGraw.

Needham, David, jt. auth. see Dransfield, Robert.

Needham, Dennis. Derry, Donegal, Tyrone Walks. 160p. 1998. pap. 10.95 (0-86278-549-9, Pub. by OBrien Pr) Irish Amer Bk.

***Needham, Dennis.** Welsh Canals: Then & Now LC 99-171078. 143p. 1998. write for info. (0-86243-421-1) Y Lolfa.

Needham, Dorothy M., jt. auth. see Teich, Mikulas.

Needham, Francine L. Get Rid of Your Hang-ups with the Key to Your Unconscious. LC 91-76665. (Illus.). 224p. (Orig.). 1993. pap. 9.95 (0-9630889-4-7) Gallandat.

Needham, G. I., ed. see Aelfric.

***Needham, Glen R., et al, eds.** Acarology IV Symposia: IX International Congress, July 17-22, 1994, 2 vols., Vol. 2. LC 99-70956. 507p. 1999. pap. text 70.00 (0-86727-134-5) Ohio Bio Survey.

Needham, Glen R., et al. Africanized Honey Bees & Bee Mites. (Entomology & Acarlogy Ser.). 1988. text 99.95 (0-470-21113-X) P-H.

Needham, H. A. Taste & Criticism in the Eighteenth Century. (Illus.). 231p. 1977. 19.95 (0-8369-5035-6) Ayer.

Needham, Henry B. Double Squeeze. LC 75-150557. (Short Story Index Reprint Ser.). (Illus.). 1977. reprint ed. 20.95 (0-8369-3854-2) Ayer.

Needham, Henry E., Jr., jt. auth. see Henley, Victoria B.

Needham Historical Society Staff. Needham. (Images of America Ser.). 1997. pap. 16.99 (0-7524-0578-0) Arcadia Publng.

Needham, J. Trans-Pacific Echoes & Resonance: Listening Once Again. 132p. 1991. pap. text 7.00 (0-9625118-8-9) World Scientific Pub.

Needham, Jack E., Jr. The Zebra Hunter: A Journey of Truth, Love & Compassion. Jordan, Janet, ed. & illus. by. 1998. mass mkt. 12.95 (0-9663960-0-6) Mind Solutions.

Needham, James, jt. auth. see Wadsworth, Ginger.

Needham, James G. Guide to the Study of Freshwater Biology. 5th ed. 1989. pap. 10.95 (0-8162-6310-8) Holden-Day.

Needham, James G. & Needham, Paul R. A Guide to the Study of Fresh-Water Biology: With Special Reference to Aquatic Insects & Other Invertebrate Animals. (Illus.). 88p. 1930. pap. 33.95 (0-398-04377-9) C C Thomas.

— A Guide to the Study of Freshwater Biology. 5th ed. (C). 1988. 30.00 (0-07-046137-6) McGraw.

***Needham, James G., et al.** Dragonflies of North America. LC 99-55363. (Illus.). 650p. 2000. text 85.00 (0-945417-94-2) Sci Pubs.

Needham, Joan F. Gerontological Nursing. LC 94-25559. (Plans of Care for Specialty Practice Ser.). 384p. (C). 1994. pap. 51.95 (0-8273-6226-9) Delmar.

— Nursing Assistant. (Home Care Aide Ser.). 1999. teacher ed. 18.00 (0-8273-6488-1); wbk. ed. 12.95 (0-8273-6487-3); pap. 27.95 (0-8273-6486-5) Delmar.

Needham, Joan F., jt. auth. see Hegner, Barbara R.

***Needham, John.** The Departure Lounge. 220p. 2000. pap. 24.95 (1-85754-443-9, Pub. by Carcanet Pr) Paul & Co Pubs.

Needham, John K. Privatization: Lessons Learned by State & Local Governments. (Illus.). 48p. (C). 1999. pap. text 20.00 (0-7881-7643-9) DIANE Pub.

Needham, Joseph. The Grand Titration: Science & Society in East & West. LC 76-483302. (Canadian University Paperbooks Ser.: No. 226). 350p. reprint ed. pap. 108.50 (0-8357-4161-3, 203693500007) Bks Demand.

— Gunpowder As the Fourth Power, East & West: First East Asian History of Science Foundation Lecture, Presented at the University of Hong Kong, 20 October 1983. LC 86-101420. (Occasional Papers: No. 3). 76p. 1985. reprint ed. pap. 30.00 (0-608-01387-0, 206214800002) Bks Demand.

— A History of Embryology. 2nd ed. LC 74-26280. (History, Philosophy & Sociology of Science Ser.). 1979. reprint ed. 33.95 (0-405-06607-4) Ayer.

— Moulds of Understanding: A Pattern of Natural Philosophy. (Modern Revivals in Philosophy Ser.). 320p. 1993. 72.95 (0-7512-0209-6, Pub. by Gregg Revivals) Ashgate Pub Co.

— Order & Life. 1968. pap. text 11.50 (0-262-64001-5) MIT Pr.

— Science & Civilisation in China, 6 vols. Incl. Vol. 1. Introductory Orientations. (Illus.). 352p. 1956. text 120.00 (0-521-05799-X); Vol. 2. History of Scientific Thought. (Illus.). 722p. 1991. text 160.00 (0-521-05800-7); Vol. 3. Mathematics & the Sciences of the Heavens & the Earth. (Illus.). 926p. 1959. text 200.00 (0-521-05801-5); Vol. 4. Chemistry & Chemical Technology Pt. 4: Spagyrical Discovery & Invention: Apparatus & Theory. (Illus.). 804p. 1980. text 175.00 (0-521-08573-X); Vol. 4. Physics & Physical Technology Pt. 1: Physics. (Illus.). 468p. 1962. text 130.00 (0-521-05802-3); Vol. 4. Physics & Physical Technology Pt. 2: Mechanical Engineering. (Illus.). 816p. 1991. text 180.00 (0-521-05803-1); Vol. 4. Physics & Physical Technology Pt. 3: Civil Engineering & Nautics. (Illus.). 990p. 1971. text 200.00 (0-521-07060-0); Vol. 5. Chemistry & Chemical Technology Pt. 1: Paper & Printing. (Illus.). 504p. 1985. text 140.00 (0-521-08690-6); Vol. 5. Chemistry & Chemical Technology Pt. 2: Spagyrical Discovery & Invention: Magisteries of Gold & Immortality. (Illus.). 600p. 1974. text 145.00 (0-521-08571-3); Vol. 5. Chemistry & Chemical Technology Pt. 3: Spagyrical Discovery & Invention: Historical Survey from Cinnabar Elixirs to Synthetic Insulin. (Illus.). 516p. 1976. text 145.00 (0-521-21028-3); Vol. 5. Chemistry & Chemical Technology Pt. 5: Spagyrical Discovery & Invention: Physiological Alchemy. (Illus.). 550p. 1983. text 150.00 (0-521-08574-8); Vol. 5. Military Technology Pt. 7: The

An Asterisk (*) at the beginning of an entry indicates that the title is appearing for the first time.

Gunpowder Epic. (Illus.). 742p. 1987. text 155.00 (*0-521-30358-3*); Vol. 6. Biology & Biological Technology Pt. 1: Botany. (Illus.). 756p. 1986. text 155.00 (*0-521-08731-7*); Vol. 6. Biology & Biological Technology Pt. 2: Agriculture. (Illus.). 768p. 1984. text 155.00 (*0-521-25076-5*); write for info. (*0-318-51294-7*) Cambridge U Pr.

***Needham, Joseph.** Science & Civilisation in China Vol. 6, Pt. 6: Biology & Biological Technology: Medicine. Sivin, Nathan, ed. (Science & Civilisation in China Ser.). (Illus.). 350p. (C). 2000. 75.00 (*0-521-63262-5*) Cambridge U Pr.

Needham, Joseph. Science in Traditional China. (Illus.). 144p. (C). 1981. pap. text 14.00 (*0-674-79439-7*) HUP.

— Time & Eastern Man. LC 65-29667. (Royal Anthropological Institute, Occasional Paper Ser.: No. 21). 62p. reprint ed. pap. 30.00 (*0-608-13749-9*, 205549200023) Bks Demand.

— Time, the Refreshing River. 280p. 1986. reprint ed. 57.50 (*0-85124-429-7*, Pub. by Spkesman); reprint ed. pap. 26.50 (*0-85124-439-4*, Pub. by Spkesman) Coronet Bks.

— Within the Four Seas: The Dialogue of East & West. 1979. pap. 8.95 (*0-8020-6360-8*) U of Toronto Pr.

Needham, Joseph & Gwei-Djen. Trans-Pacific Echoes & Resonances: Listening Once Again. 106p. 1985. text 30.00 (*9971-950-86-3*) World Scientific Pub.

Needham, Joseph & Pagel, Walter, eds. Background to Modern Science. LC 74-26281. (History, Philosophy & Sociology of Science Ser.). 1975. reprint ed. 21.95 (*0-405-06608-2*) Ayer.

Needham, Joseph & Yates, Robin D. Science & Civilisation in China - Military Technology Pt. 6: Military Technology, Pt. 6, Missiles & Sieges; Vol. 5 Chemistry & Chemical Technology. (Science & Civilisation in China Ser.). (Illus.). 630p. (C). 1995. text 145.00 (*0-521-32727-X*) Cambridge U Pr.

Needham, Joseph, et al. The Hall of Heavenly Records: Korean Astronomical Instruments & Clocks 1380-1780. (Illus.). 223p. 1986. text 80.00 (*0-521-30368-0*) Cambridge U Pr.

Needham, K. Essential German Dictionary. (Essential Dictionaries Ser.). (Illus.). 64p. (YA). (gr. 7-12). 1995. pap. 6.95 (*0-7460-1006-0*, Usborne) EDC.

— You & Your Body. (Starting Point Science Ser.). (Illus.). 120p. (J). (gr. 1-4). 1994. 17.95 (*0-7460-1858-4*, Usborne) EDC.

Needham, Kate. Dinosaurs. (Time Trekkers Visit The--). 1995. 11.15 (*0-606-09975-1*, Pub. by Turtleback) Demco.

— Essential French Dictionary. (Essential Guides Ser.). (Illus.). 64p. (J). (gr. 7-12). 1994. pap. 6.95 (*0-7460-1004-4*, Usborne) EDC.

— Essential French Dictionary. (Essential Guides Ser.). (Illus.). 64p. (J). (gr. 6 up). 1999. lib. bdg. 14.95 (*0-88110-709-3*, Usborne) EDC.

— Essential German Dictionary. (Essential Dictionaries Ser.). (Illus.). 64p. (YA). (gr. 6 up). 1999. lib. bdg. 14.95 (*0-88110-739-5*, Usborne) EDC.

— First Pony. (Riding School Ser.). (Illus.). 32p. (J). (gr. 3 up). 1996. pap. 5.95 (*0-7460-2436-3*, Usborne); lib. bdg. 13.95 (*0-88110-841-3*, Usborne) EDC.

— Great Undersea Search. (Great Searches Ser.). (Illus.). 47p. (J). (ps-3). 1996. pap. 8.95 (*0-7460-2341-3*, Usborne); lib. bdg. 16.95 (*0-88110-820-0*, Usborne) EDC.

— Grooming & Stable Management. (Riding School Ser.). 32p. (J). (gr. 3 up). 1996. pap. 5.95 (*0-7460-2438-X*, Usborne); lib. bdg. 13.95 (*0-88110-840-5*, Usborne) EDC.

— Jumping. (Riding School Ser.). (Illus.). 32p. (J). (gr. 3 up). 1997. pap. 5.95 (*0-7460-2442-8*, Usborne); lib. bdg. 13.95 (*0-88110-905-3*, Usborne) EDC.

Needham, Kate. The Middle Ages. LC 95-39832. (Time Trekkers Visit The--). 1996. 11.15 (*0-606-09976-X*, Pub. by Turtleback) Demco.

Needham, Kate. Starting Point Science #4: Science, Vol. 4. (gr. 1 up). 1996. 12.95 (*0-7460-1307-8*) EDC.

— Time Trekkers Visit the Dinosaurs. LC 95-14023. (Time Trekkers Ser.). (Illus.). 32p. (J). (gr. 2-4). 1995. lib. bdg. 20.90 (*1-56294-942-X*, Copper Beech Bks) Millbrook Pr.

— Time Trekkers Visit the Middle Ages. (Time Trekkers Ser.). (Illus.). 32p. (J). (gr. 2-4). 1996. lib. bdg. 20.90 (*0-7613-0481-9*, Copper Beech Bks) Millbrook Pr.

— Why Do People Eat? (Starting Point Science Ser.). (Illus.). 24p. (J). (gr. 1 up). 1993. pap. 3.95 (*0-7460-1302-7*, Usborne); lib. bdg. 12.95 (*0-88110-638-0*, Usborne) EDC.

Needham, Kate, ed. Cross Country. (Riding School Ser.). (Illus.). 32p. (YA). (gr. 3 up). 1999. pap. 5.95 (*0-7460-2927-6*, Usborne); lib. bdg. 13.95 (*1-58086-157-1*, Usborne) EDC.

— En el Fondo del Mar/Great Animals Search. (Great Searches Ser.). (Illus.). 32p. (J). (ps up). 1999. pap. 8.95 (*0-7460-3438-5*, Usborne) EDC.

— ESP: The Evidence & the Arguments. (Paranormal Guides Ser.). (Illus.). 48p. (YA). (gr. 5 up). 1999. 5.95 (*0-7460-3060-6*, Usborne) EDC.

Needham, Kate & Gibson, Gay. Collecting Things. (How to Make Ser.). (Illus.). 32p. (J). (gr. 3-7). 1995. pap. 6.95 (*0-7460-2081-3*, Usborne); lib. bdg. 14.95 (*0-88110-774-3*, Usborne) EDC.

Needham, Kate & Smith, Lucy. Riding School: Bind-Up. (Riding School Ser.). (Illus.). 128p. (Orig.). (YA). (gr. 3 up). 1997. pap. 14.95 (*0-7460-2929-2*, Usborne); lib. bdg. 22.95 (*0-88110-941-X*, Usborne) EDC.

Needham, Kate, jt. auth. see O'Brien, Eileen.

Needham, Lana. A Bride's Dream Vol. 1: The Perfect Wedding on Any Budget. 100p. 1995. write for info. (*0-9654320-0-9*) Brides Dream.

Needham, Lawrence D., jt. ed. see Bialostosky, Don H.

Needham, Lesley, tr. see McCallum, H. J.

Needham, Linda. Ever His Bride. 384p. 1997. mass mkt. 5.99 (*0-380-78756-3*, Avon Bks) Morrow Avon.

— For My Lady's Kiss. 1997. mass mkt. 5.99 (*0-380-78755-5*, Avon Bks) Morrow Avon.

***Needham, Linda.** The Maiden Bride. LC 99-96443. 384p. 2000. mass mkt. 5.99 (*0-380-79636-8*, Avon Bks) Morrow Avon.

Needham, Linda. Secret Guardian. 384p. 1998. mass mkt. 5.99 (*0-380-79634-1*, Avon Bks) Morrow Avon.

— The Wedding Night. 384p. 1999. mass mkt. 5.99 (*0-380-79635-X*, Avon Bks) Morrow Avon.

***Needham, Nancy.** They Called Me Kite. 2000. pap. 18.00 (*0-7388-2199-3*) Xlibris Corp.

Needham, Nicholas R. Thomas Erskine of Linlathen: His Life & Theology, 1788-1837. LC 92-7135. (Rutherford Studies in Historical Theology). 452p. 1992. reprint ed. lib. bdg. 109.95 (*0-7734-1645-5*) E Mellen.

— 2,000 Years of Christ Power. 1998. pap. 17.99 (*0-946462-49-6*, Pub. by Evangelical Pr) P & R Pubng.

Needham, Paul. The Printer & the Pardoner: An Unrecorded Indulgence, Printed by William Caxton for the Hospital of St. Mary Rounceval, Charing Cross. LC 85-18120. 101p. 1986. 35.00 (*0-8444-0508-6*) Lib Congress.

Needham, Paul & Joseph, Michael. Adventure & Art: The First Hundred Years of Printing. (Illus.). 96p. 1999. pap. text 35.00 (*0-8135-2727-9*) Rutgers U Pr.

Needham, Paul R., jt. auth. see Needham, James G.

Needham, Phil. Community in Mission: A Salvationist Ecclesiology. (Orig.). 1987. pap. 6.95 (*0-86544-043-3*) Salv Army Suppl South.

***Needham, Phil.** He Who Laughed First: Delighting in a Holy God. LC 99-58946. 2000. pap. 12.99 (*0-8341-1872-6*) Beacon Hill.

Needham, Randall W. When the Tempter Comes: Victory over Habits. 60p. (Orig.). 1994. pap. 4.95 (*0-9636067-0-0*) Grace TX.

Needham, Richard L. Battling for Peace. LC 99-174341. 1999. 35.00 (*0-85640-637-6*) Blackstaff Pr.

***Needham, Richard L.** Battling for Peace. 344p. 1999. pap. 28.95 (*0-85640-654-6*, Pub. by Blackstaff Pr) Dufour.

Needham, Richard L., ed. see Tehabi Books Staff.

Needham, Rodney. Circumstantial Deliveries. LC 81-1247. (Quantum Bks.: No. 21). (Illus.). 100p. 1981. 40.00 (*0-520-04389-8*, Pub. by U CA Pr) Cal Prin Full Svc.

— Mamboru: History & Structure in a Domain of Northwestern Sumba. LC 86-18061. (Illus.). 320p. 1987. text 55.00 (*0-19-823400-7*) OUP.

— Primordial Characters. LC 78-17230. 104p. reprint ed. pap. 32.30 (*0-7837-5314-4*, 204471200004) Bks Demand.

— Reconnaissances. LC 81-160186. 132p. reprint ed. pap. 41.00 (*0-8357-8298-0*, 203401300088) Bks Demand.

Needham, Rodney, ed. Right & Left: Essays on Dual Symbolic Classification. LC 73-82982. 488p. reprint ed. pap. 151.30 (*0-608-18210-9*, 205661400078) Bks Demand.

— Structure & Sentiment: A Test Case in Social Anthropology. LC 62-9738. xii, 148p. 1984. pap. text 14.50 (*0-226-56989-6*, Midway Reprint) U Ch Pr.

Needham, Rodney, ed. see Hocart, A. M.

Needham, Rodney, ed. see Starcke, Carl N.

Needham, Rodney, ed. see Wake, Charles S.

Needham, Rodney, tr. see Durkheim, Emile & Mauss, Marcel.

Needham, Rodney, tr. see Levi-Strauss, Claude.

Needham, Sara L. Heart of the Gods. Wells, Helen S., ed. (Illus.). 101p. (Orig.). (C). 1993. pap. 10.00 (*0-9639901-0-1*) Fascinatn.

Needham, Stuart & Macklin, Mark G., eds. Alluvial Archaeology in Britain. (Oxbow Monographs in Archaeology: No. 27). (Illus.). 276p. 1992. pap. 60.00 (*0-946897-52-2*, Pub. by Oxbow Bks) David Brown.

Needham, Terence. Vascular Laboratory Quality Assurance Manual. Date not set. write for info. (*0-941022-26-9*) Davies Pubng.

Needham, Tristan. Visual Complex Analysis. (Illus.). 616p. 1997. text 55.00 (*0-19-853447-7*) OUP.

— Visual Complex Analysis. (Illus.). 592p. 1999. pap. 45.00 (*0-19-853446-9*) OUP.

Needham, W. Designer's Guide to Testable ASIC Device. (Electrical Engineering Ser.). 1991. 59.95 (*0-442-00221-1*, VNR) Wiley.

Needham, Woody. The Engagement. 290p. mass mkt. 4.99 (*1-896329-79-9*) Picasso Publ.

— The Federal Budget, a Primer for the American People. (Illus.). 120p. 2000. pap. 9.95 (*0-9662893-0-7*) Prime Pump.

Needham, Woody. Joseph: A Screenplay. 118p. 1998. pap. 9.00 (*0-9662893-1-5*) Prime Pump.

***Needham, Woody.** A Toe on the Steps of Time. 2nd rev. ed. 36p. 1999. pap. 8.00 (*0-9662893-2-3*) Prime Pump.

Needle. Business in Context. 2nd ed. 1994. pap. write for info. (*1-86152-353-X*) ITBP.

— Business in Context. 3rd ed. 2000. 24.99 (*1-86152-358-0*) Thomson Learn.

***Needle, Barry.** South Wales in Focus: One Hundred Images of South Wales. (Illus.). 120p. 1999. 39.95 (*1-85411-257-0*, Pub. by Seren Bks) Dufour.

***Needle, Barry & Barrington, T. J.** Discovering Kerry: The History, Heritage & Topography. LC 99-490283. (Illus.). 340p. 1999. reprint ed. 55.00 (*1-898256-71-3*) Irish Bks Media.

Needle Craft Shop Staff. Threads of Time Cross Stitch. 1998. 19.96 (*1-57367-026-X*) Needlecrft Shop.

Needle, D. Business in Context. 384p. 1990. pap. 34.50 (*0-412-02661-9*, A4463, Chap & Hall NY) Chapman & Hall.

— Business in Context: An Introduction to Business & Its Environment. 2nd ed. (Business Context Ser.). 416p. 1994. pap. 29.95 (*0-412-48410-2*) Thomson Learn.

***Needle, Jan.** A Fine Boy for Killing. (Sea Officer William Bentley Novels Ser.: Vol. 1). 384p. 2000. pap. 15.95 (*0-935526-86-2*) McBooks Pr.

Needle, Jan. El Ladron (The Thief) Ultrilla, Juan J., tr. (SPA., Illus.). 116p. (YA). 1991. pap. 6.99 (*968-16-3680-5*, Pub. by Fondo) Continental Bk.

Needle, Jan & Thompson, Peter. Brecht. LC 80-29387. (Illus.). 252p. reprint ed. pap. 78.20 (*0-608-09487-0*, 205428800005) Bks Demand.

Needle, Jan & Thomson, Peter. Brecht. LC 80-29387. 1981. 20.00 (*0-226-57022-3*) U Ch Pr.

***Needle, Richard H., ed.** HIV Prevention with Drug-Using Populations: Current Status & Future Prospects. (Illus.). 204p. (C). 2000. reprint ed. pap. text 35.00 (*0-7881-8532-2*) DIANE Pub.

Needle, Sheldon. Guide to Accounting Software for Microcomputers: And The Requirements Analyst. rev. ed. (Illus.). 396p. 1997. ring bd. 795.00 incl. disk (*0-917429-04-4*) CTS.

— Guide to PC-Based Software for Property Management: And The Requirements Analyst, 9 disks. 144p. 1994. ring bd. 595.00 incl. disk (*0-917429-10-9*) CTS.

— Guide to PC-Based Software for the Manufacturing Industry: And The Requirements Analyst. rev. ed. (Illus.). 302p. 1997. ring bd. 895.00 incl. disk (*0-917429-18-4*) CTS.

— Guide to Small Business Accounting Software Priced under $500: And The Requirements Analyst. rev. ed. (Illus.). 138p. 1996. pap. 145.00 incl. disk (*0-917429-13-3*) CTS.

— How I Recovered from Chronic Back & Neck Pain: An Odyssey of Pain & Learning. (Illus.). 99p. 1997. pap. 19.95 (*0-917429-15-X*) CTS.

Needle, Sheldon & Hollander, Nathan. Handbook of Computer & Management Consulting: Strategies for Increasing Profits. rev. ed. Majumder, Kiganta, ed. (Illus.). 501p. 1997. pap. 125.00 (*0-917429-16-8*) CTS.

Needle, Sheldon & Jewell, June R. Selecting Software for Non-Profit Organizations & Trade Associations. 321p. (Orig.). 1995. pap. 99.00 (*0-917429-17-6*) CTS.

Needle, Sheldon & Maltzman, Steve. Guide to Accounting Software for the Construction Industry: And The Requirements Analyst. rev. ed. (Illus.). 232p. 1997. ring bd. 795.00 incl. disk (*0-917429-11-7*) CTS.

Needle, Sheldon, jt. auth. see Sterling, Ronald B.

***Needlecraft Shop Staff.** Ultimate Christmas Companion. (Illus.). 1999. 19.96 (*1-57367-107-X*) Needlecrft Shop.

***Needlecraft Shop Staff, ed.** Afghan Romance. (Illus.). 2000. 19.96 (*1-57367-108-8*) Needlecrft Shop.

Needleman, A., et al, eds. Fundamentals of Metal-Matrix Composites. 700p. 1994. text 120.00 (*0-7506-9321-5*, 6513U) Buttrwrth-Heinemann.

Needleman, A., jt. ed. see Noor, A. K.

Needleman, Carla. The Work of Craft: An Inquiry into the Nature of Crafts & Craftsmanship. LC 92-16920. 160p. 1993. reprint ed. pap. 10.00 (*4-7700-1701-4*) Kodansha.

Needleman, Carolyn E., jt. auth. see Needleman, Martin L.

Needleman, Herbert L. Human Lead Exposure. 290p. 1991. lib. bdg. 199.00 (*0-8493-6034-X*, RC347) CRC Pr.

Needleman, Herbert L. & Bellinger, David, eds. Prenatal Exposure to Toxicants: Developmental Consequences. LC 93-34394. (Series in Environmental Toxicology). 352p. 1994. 90.00 (*0-8018-4704-4*) Johns Hopkins.

Needleman, Herbert L. & Landrigan, Philip J. Raising Children Toxic Free: How to Keep Your Child Safe from Lead, Asbestos, Pesticides... 272p. 1995. pap. 12.00 (*0-380-72577-0*, Avon Bks) Morrow Avon.

— Raising Toxic Free Children: Protecting Your Child from Common Environmental Health Threats. LC 93-38108. 1994. 20.00 (*0-374-24643-2*) FS&G.

Needleman, Jacob. A Little Book on Love. LC 96-1. 1996. 90.00 (*0-385-48289-2*) Doubleday.

***Needleman, Jacob.** A Little Book on Love: A Wise & Inspiring Guide to Discovering the Gift of Love. 192p. 2000. pap. 9.95 (*0-385-33432-X*, Delta Trade) Dell.

Needleman, Jacob. Lost Christianity: A Journey of Rediscovery to the Center of Christian Experience. 2nd ed. (Classic Edition Ser.). 238p. 1993. pap. 15.95 (*1-85230-132-5*, Pub. by Element MA) Penguin Putnam.

— Money & the Meaning of Life. 352p. 1994. pap. 16.95 (*0-385-26242-6*) Doubleday.

Needleman, Jacob. Money & the Meaning of Life, Set. abr. ed. 1997. text 17.95 incl. audio (*1-57453-213-8*) Audio Lit.

Needleman, Jacob. Sin & Scientism. (Broadside Editions Ser.). 26p. (Orig.). (C). 1986. pap. 4.95 (*0-9609850-7-7*) Rob Briggs.

— The Sword of Gnosis. 1996. pap. 21.95 (*0-614-21366-5*, 1205) Kazi Pubns.

— Time & the Soul: Where Has All the Meaningful Time Gone? & How to Get It Back. LC 97-29929. 176p. 1997. 16.00 (*0-385-48177-2*) Doubleday.

Needleman, Jacob, ed. Speaking of My Life. 149p. 1979. pap. 7.00 (*0-06-250643-9*) Far West Edns.

Needleman, Jacob & Appelbaum, David, eds. Real Philosophy: An Anthology of the Universal Search for Meaning. 352p. 1991. pap. 13.95 (*0-14-019256-5*, Arkana) Viking Penguin.

Needleman, Jacob & Baker, George, eds. Gurdjieff: Essays & Reflections on the Man & His Teachings. 462p. 1997. pap. 27.50 (*0-8264-1049-9*) Continuum.

Needleman, Jacob, et al. Religion for a New Generation. 2nd ed. Scott, Kenneth J., ed. 592p. (C). 1977. pap. text 34.60 (*0-02-385990-3*, Macmillan Coll) P-H.

Needleman, Jacob, jt. auth. see Tsu, Lao.

Needleman, Lawrence D. Cognitive Case Conceptualization: A Guidebook for Practitioners. LC 98-31852. (Personality & Clinical Psychology Ser.). 352p. 1999. 39.95 (*0-8058-1908-8*) L Erlbaum Assocs.

Needleman, Marilyn J. Werbel Multiple Choice Practice Questions for New York Law Addendum Property & Casualty Insurance. rev. ed. 112p. (C). 1999. pap. text 12.95 (*1-884803-00-8*) Werbel Pub.

Needleman, Martin L. & Needleman, Carolyn E. Guerrillas in Bureaucracy: The Community Planning Experiment in the United States. LC 73-19806. (Wiley Series in Urban Research). 384p. reprint ed. pap. 119.10 (*0-608-30187-6*, 201517600092) Bks Demand.

Needler-Arai, M. Functional Biology of Scyphozoa. (Illus.). 336p. 1996. pap. write for info. (*0-412-45110-7*) Kluwer Academic.

Needler, Martin C. The Concepts of Comparative Politics. LC 90-43159. 176p. 1991. 49.95 (*0-275-93652-X*, C3652, Praeger Pubs); pap. 19.95 (*0-275-93653-8*, B3653, Praeger Pubs) Greenwood.

— Identity, Interest & Ideology: An Introduction to Politics. LC 95-50731. 272p. 1996. 69.50 (*0-275-95440-4*, Praeger Pubs) Greenwood.

— Identity, Interest, & Ideology: An Introduction to Politics. LC 95-50731. 272p. 1996. pap. 24.95 (*0-275-95441-2*, Praeger Pubs) Greenwood.

— Latin American Politics in Perspective. 1990. 16.50 (*0-8446-2639-2*) Peter Smith.

— Mexican Politics: The Containment of Conflict. 3rd ed. LC 95-34439. 168p. 1995. 59.95 (*0-275-95251-7*, Praeger Pubs); pap. 18.95 (*0-275-95252-5*, Praeger Pubs) Greenwood.

Needler, Marvin A. & Baker, Don E. Digital & Analog Controls. (Illus.). 432p. (C). 1992. reprint ed. text 101.00 (*1-878907-64-6*) TechBooks.

Needler, Toby & Goodman, Bonnie. Exploring Global Art. 198p. 1991. ring bd. 25.00 (*0-944675-46-8*) Amer Forum.

***Needles.** General Mills. 3rd ed. 1999. pap. text, teacher ed. 14.97 (*0-395-93559-8*) HM.

Needles. Needles Finman , Vol. 2. 5th ed. 1999. pap. text 8.97 (*0-395-93570-9*) HM.

— Partnership, 6 vols. (C). 1996. pap., suppl. ed. write for info. (*0-395-81875-3*) HM.

Needles, Belvard E., Jr., et al. Financial & Managerial Accounting: A Sole Proprietorship Approach, 4 vols. 4th ed. 1400p. (C). 1995. text 86.36 (*0-395-74565-9*) HM.

Needles, Belverd E. Accounting Education for the 21st Century: The Global Challenges. Burns, Jane O., ed. LC 94-9175. 1994. 228.00 (*0-08-042405-8*, Pub. by Pergamon Repr) Franklin.

N

Needles, Belverd E., Jr. Collegiate T's: Three-in-One Financial Practice Set, 5 vols. (C). 1993. text, teacher ed. 3.96 (*0-395-65515-3*) HM.

Needles, Belverd E. Edwards Cook's Solar Energy, 3 vols. (C). 1986. pap. text 20.76 (*0-395-43757-1*) HM.

Needles, Belverd E., Jr. Financial Accounting. 1982. 11.95 (*0-685-42657-2*); 3.50 (*0-685-42658-0*) HM.

Needles, Belverd E. Financial Accounting, 5 vols. (C). 1994. pap., student ed. 19.96 (*0-395-71973-9*) HM.

— Financial Accounting, 5 vols. (C). 1994. pap., teacher ed. 11.96 (*0-395-71974-7*); pap., teacher ed., suppl. ed. 11.96 (*0-395-71975-5*) HM.

Needles, Belverd E., Jr. Financial Accounting. 3rd ed. 1988. write for info. (*0-318-63324-8*); student ed. 17.56 (*0-318-36901-X*); trans. write for info. (*0-318-63325-6*) HM.

Needles, Belverd E. Financial Accounting, 5 vols. 5th ed. LC 94-76533. (C). 1994. text 82.36 (*0-395-69802-2*); pap. text, suppl. ed. 14.76 (*0-395-71976-3*) HM.

— Financial Management, 3 vols. (C). 1993. pap., teacher ed. 9.96 (*0-395-68549-4*); pap., teacher ed., suppl. ed. 9.96 (*0-395-68550-8*) HM.

— Financial Management, 3 vols. (C). 1994. pap., teacher ed., suppl. ed. 9.96 (*0-395-69197-4*) HM.

— Financial Management Accounting, 3 vols. 3rd ed. LC 93-78706. (C). 1993. text 86.36 (*0-395-67693-2*) HM.

— Financial Management Accounting. 5th ed. LC 98-72067. 1998. text 69.87 (*0-395-92098-1*) HM.

— Financial Management Accounting: Sole Proprietorship Exam, 4 vols. LC 95-76963. (C). 1996. text 86.36 (*0-395-76597-8*) HM.

— Financial Management & Accounting, 3 vols. (C). 1993. pap., student ed. 23.96 (*0-395-68552-4*) HM.

— Financial Management & Accounting, 3 vols. 3rd ed. (C). 1993. pap. text, teacher ed. 7.96 (*0-395-68144-8*) HM.

— Financial Management & Accounting: Student Video Guide, 4 vols. 4th ed. (C). 1993. pap. text 6.76 (*0-395-68555-9*) HM.

— Introduction to Algebra, 4 vols. (C). 1994. pap., teacher ed., suppl. ed. 11.96 (*0-395-71928-3*) HM.

— Managerial Accounting, 4 vols. 4th ed. LC 95-76964. (C). 1995. pap. text 60.36 (*0-395-74567-5*) HM.

Needles, Belverd E., Jr. Micro-Tec: A Merchandising Sole Proprietorship Practice Set, 6 vols. 4th ed. (C). 1995. text, teacher ed. 11.96 (*0-395-75952-8*) HM.

Needles, Belverd E. Principles of Accounting 7th ed. LC 98-72069. 1229 p. 1999. text 69.57 (*0-395-92758-7*) HM.

— Principles of Financial Accounting, 6 vols. 6th ed. (C). 1995. pap. text 60.36 (*0-395-74566-7*) HM.

— Principles of Financial Accounting. 7th ed. LC 98-72070. 884 p. 1999. text 49.47 (*0-395-92629-7*) HM.

— Words & Sounds, 5 vols. (C). 1994. pap., teacher ed. 3.96 (*0-395-65625-7*) HM.

Needles, Belverd E., Jr. & McWhorter. Soft-Tec, Inc: Practice Case, 5 vols. 5th ed. (C). 1994. pap. text, teacher ed. 20.36 (*0-395-71979-8*) HM.

Needles, Belverd F., Jr., et al. Accounting: Instructor's Solutions Manual, 4 vols., Vol. I. 4th ed. (C). 1995. text, teacher ed. 11.96 (*0-395-75983-8*) HM.

— Accounting: Instructor's Solutions Manual, 4 vols., Vol. II. 4th ed. (C). 1995. text, teacher ed. 11.96 (*0-395-75984-6*) HM.

— Financial & Managerial Accounting: A Corporate Approach, 4 vols. 4th ed. 1400p. (C). 1995. text 86.36 (*0-395-72221-7*) HM.
— Principles of Accounting, 001. LC 80-80503. (Illus.). 1008p. (C). 1980. text 27.95 (*0-395-29527-0*) HM.
— Principles of Accounting, 3 vols. 3rd ed. 1058p. (C). 1987. pap. 15.16 (*0-395-43144-1*); text 47.16 (*0-685-18701-2*); 17.56 (*0-685-18702-0*) HM.
— Principles of Accounting, 4 vols. 4th ed. (C). 1990. pap. 5.96 (*0-395-53274-4*); text 32.06 (*0-395-43350-9*) HM.
— Principles of Accounting, 4 vols. 4th ed. (C). 1990. pap. text 3.96 (*0-395-52758-9*) HM.
— Principles of Accounting, 4 vols. 4th ed. (C). 1990. pap. 21.96 (*0-395-52961-1*) HM.
— Principles of Accounting, 4 vols. 4th ed. (C). 1990. pap. 21.96 (*0-395-52963-8*) HM.
— Principles of Accounting, 4 vols. 4th ed. (C). 1990. pap. 21.96 (*0-395-52962-X*); pap., student ed. 19.16 (*0-395-52960-3*); text 58.36 (*0-395-53506-9*) HM.
— Principles of Accounting, 4 vols. 4th ed. (C). 1990. text 58.36 (*0-395-53507-7*) HM.
— Principles of Accounting, 6 vols. 6th ed. 1344p. (C). 1995. text 80.76 (*0-395-72219-5*) HM.
— Principles of Accounting, 6 vols., Vol. I. 6th ed. (C). 1995. text, teacher ed. 11.96 (*0-395-75278-7*) HM.
— Principles of Accounting, 6 vols., Vol. II. 6th ed. (C). 1995. text, teacher ed. 11.96 (*0-395-75279-5*) HM.
— Principles of Financial & Managerial Accounting. LC 87-80110. 950p. (C). 1988. 15.96 (*0-685-73859-0*); trans. 159.96 (*0-685-73860-4*) HM.

Needles, Belverd E., jt. auth. see Powers, Marian.

***Needles, Colleen & Carlson, Kit.** Working Dogs: Tales from the K-9 to 5 World. LC 99-44118. 2000. 15.95 (*1-56331-843-1*, Pub. by Discovery) Random.

Needles, Dan. Letters from Wingfield Farm. 160p. 1990. pap. 7.99 (*0-7704-2386-8*) Bantam.

Needles, Edward, compiled by. Historical Memoir of the Pennsylvania Society for Promoting the Abolition of Slavery for the Relief of Free Negroes Unlawfully Held in Bondage & for Improving the Condition of the African Race. LC 77-82207. (Anti-Slavery Crusade in America Ser.). 1980. reprint ed. 23.95 (*0-405-00645-4*) Ayer.

Needles, Howard L. & Zeronian, S. Haig, eds. Historic Textile & Paper Materials: Conservation & Characterization. LC 85-20094. (Advances in Chemistry Ser.: No. 212). (Illus.). xii, 464p. 1986. 76.95 (*0-8412-0900-6*) Am Chemical.
— Historic Textile & Paper Materials: Conservation & Characterization: Developed from a Symposium. LC 85-20094. (Advances in Chemistry Ser.: No. 212). (Illus.). 476p. 1986. reprint ed. pap. 147.60 (*0-608-04361-3*, 206514200001) Bks Demand.
— Historic Textile & Paper Materials, No. 2: Conservation & Characterization. LC 89-38410. (Symposium Ser.: No. 410). (Illus.). 249p. 1989. text 62.00 (*0-8412-1683-5*, Pub. by Am Chemical) OUP.

Needles, Mark. Electronic Calculators in Business. LC 81-6599. 349p. reprint ed. pap. 108.20 (*0-7837-4051-4*, 204388100011) Bks Demand.

Needle's Prayse Staff & O'Steen, Darlene. The Proper Stitch: A Guide for Counted Thread. Cockerham, Barbara, ed. (Illus.). 144p. 1994. 39.95 (*0-932437-03-6*) Symbol Exc Pubs.

Needman, J. R. Handbook of Microbiological Investigations for Laboratory Animal Health. 1979. text 104.00 (*0-12-515950-1*) Acad Pr.

***Neef, Andreas.** Auswirkungen Von Bodenrechtswandel Auf Ressourcennutzung und Wirtschaftliches Verhalten Von Kleinbauern In Niger und Benin. (GER., Illus.). xxxiv, 290p. 1999. 57.00 (*3-631-34782-0*) P Lang Pubng.

Neef, Dale. Economic Impact of Knowledge. LC 98-14676. 384p. 1998. pap. text 21.95 (*0-7506-7009-6*) Buttrwrth-Heinemann.
— The Knowledge Economy. LC 97-34241. 278p. 1997. pap. 21.95 (*0-7506-9936-1*) Buttrwrth-Heinemann.
— A Little Knowledge Is a Dangerous Thing: Understanding Our Global Knowledge of Economy. LC 98-36796. 1998. 19.95 (*0-7506-7061-4*) Buttrwrth-Heinemann.

Neef, Heinz-Dieter. Ephraim: Studien Zur Geschichte des Stammes Ephraim Von der Landnahme Bis Zur Fruehen Koenigszeit. (Beiheft zur Zeitschrift fuer die Alttestamentliche Wissenschaft Ser.: Vol. 238). (GER.). xvi, 389p. (C). 1995. lib. bdg. 152.30 (*3-11-014756-4*) De Gruyter.

Neef, Joseph. Sketch of a Plan: Method of Education. LC 79-89211. (American Education: Its Men, Institutions, & Ideas. Series 1). 1977. reprint ed. 18.95 (*0-405-01450-3*) Ayer.
— Sketch of a Plan & Method of Education: 1808 Edition. Stern, Jeffrey, ed. & intro. by. (Classics in Education Ser.). 176p. 1996. reprint ed. 75.00 (*1-85506-299-2*) Bks Intl VA.

Neef, Marian, jt. auth. see Nagel, Stuart S.

Neef, Marian, jt. ed. see Nagel, Stuart S.

Neegele, N., ed. Air Pollution Damage to Vegetation. (C). 1991. text 375.00 (*0-89771-612-4*, Pub. by Intl Bk Distr) St Mut.

Neel, Boyd. The Story of an Orchestra. 1988. reprint ed. lib. bdg. 49.00 (*0-7812-0773-8*) Rprt Serv.
— The Story of an Orchestra. LC 71-181218. 133p. 1950. reprint ed. 19.00 (*0-403-01629-0*) Scholarly.

Neel, Carol & Wallerstein, Mark. A Pocket Guide for Medical-Surgical Nursing. (Illus.). 448p. (C). 1985. pap. text 27.95 (*0-89303-772-9*, D7729-9) Appleton & Lange.

Neel, Carol, tr. see Dhuoda.

Neel, Carol, tr. & intro. see Dhuoda.

Neel, Charles D. & Sampson, Kenneth. Prehistoric Rock Art of the Cross Timbers Management Unit, East Central Oklahoma: An Introductory Study. (Archeological Resource Survey Report: No. 27). (Illus.). 130p. (C). 1986. pap. text 8.50 (*1-881346-18-8*) Univ OK Archeol.

Neel, David. The Great Canoes. LC 95-10804. (Illus.). 136p. (C). 1995. pap. 27.95 (*0-295-97482-6*) U of Wash Pr.
— Our Chiefs & Elders: Words & Photographs of Native Leaders. LC 92-24652. (Illus.). 160p. 1992. pap. 25.95 (*0-7748-0502-1*) U of Wash Pr.
— Our Chiefs & Elders: Words & Photographs of Native Leaders. LC 92-24652. (Illus.). 192p. 1992. 39.95 (*0-295-97217-3*) U of Wash Pr.

Neel, Eudie P. Wilford - Williford Family Treks into America. (Illus.). 531p. 1998. reprint ed. pap. 84.00 (*0-8328-9549-0*); reprint ed. lib. bdg. 94.00 (*0-8328-9548-2*) Higginson Bk Co.

Neel, James V. & Schull, William J. Human Heredity. LC 54-12698. (College Library of Biolobical Sciences Ser.). 369p. reprint ed. pap. 114.40 (*0-608-12086-3*, 202412200035) Bks Demand.

Neel, James V. & Schull, William J., eds. The Children of Atomic Bomb Survivors: A Genetic Study. fac. ed. LC 91-10042. (Illus.). 523p. 1994. pap. 162.20 (*0-7837-7566-0*, 204731900007) Bks Demand.

Neel, Janet. Death among the Dons. (Illus.). (J). 1995. mass mkt. 5.50 (*0-671-89952-X*) PB.
— Death among the Dons. large type ed. LC 94-14548. 369p. 1994. lib. bdg. 21.95 (*0-8161-7439-3*, G K Hall Lrg Type) Mac Lib Ref.
— Death of a Partner. large type ed. LC 96-7759. 384p. 1996. pap. 20.95 (*0-7838-1641-3*, G K Hall Lrg Type) Mac Lib Ref.
— Death of a Partner. Chelius, Jane, ed. 256p. 1994. reprint ed. mass mkt. 4.99 (*0-671-74839-4*) PB.
— Death on Site. Chelius, Jane, ed. 288p. 1993. reprint ed. mass mkt. 4.99 (*0-671-73581-0*) PB.
— Death's Bright Angel. large type ed. LC 97-91165. (General Ser.). 365p. 1998. pap. 21.95 (*0-7862-1289-6*) Mac Lib Ref.
— Death's Bright Angel. Chelius, Jane, ed. 288p. 1991. reprint ed. mass mkt. 4.99 (*0-671-73579-9*) PB.
— A Timely Death. large type ed. LC 97-9881. 382p. 1997. pap. 21.95 (*0-7838-8140-1*, G K Hall Lrg Type) Mac Lib Ref.

***Neel, Janet.** To Die For: A Mystery. LC 99-18077. 240p. 1999. text 21.95 (*0-312-20598-8*) St Martin.

Neel, Jasper P. Aristotle's Voice: Rhetoric, Theory, & Writing in America. LC 94-9931. 264p. (C). 1995. 36.95 (*0-8093-1933-0*) S Ill U Pr.
— Plato, Derrida, & Writing. LC 87-28439. 268p. (C). 1988. text 31.95 (*0-8093-1440-1*) S Ill U Pr.

Neel, Jasper P., ed. Freshman Composition. LC 78-62655. (Options for the Teaching of English Ser.: No. 2). 128p. 1978. pap. 39.70 (*0-608-05588-3*, 206604800006) Bks Demand.

Neel, Jasper P., ed. see Modern Language Association of America Staff.

Neel, Jim & Springer, Melissa, photos by. Salvation on Sand Mountain. LC 95-48176. (Illus.). 1996. write for info. (*0-944564-05-4*) Alex Mus.

Neel, John, ed. see Gentry, Roosevelt & Henderson, William T.

Neel, Paul R., jt. auth. see Harrigan, John E.

Neel, Peg. How to Pray According to God's Word. 72p. 1982. pap. 2.25 (*0-88144-004-3*, CPS-004) Christian Pub.

Neel, Steven M. Saying "I Do" - the Wedding Ceremony: The Complete Guide to a Perfect Wedding. Wray, Rhonda, ed. LC 95-31890. (Illus.). 256p. 1995. pap. 12.95 (*1-56608-012-6*, B122) Meriwether Pub.

Neelakanta, P. S. A Textbook on ATM Telecommunications. 1999. 85.00 (*0-8493-1805-X*) CRC Pr.

Neelakanta, Perambur S., ed. Handbook of Electromagnetic Monolithic & Composite Materials. LC 95-2747. 608p. 1995. boxed set 159.95 (*0-8493-2500-5*, 2500) CRC Pr.

Neelakanta, Perambur S. & DeGroff, Dolores F. Neural Network Modeling: Statistical Mechanics & Cybernetic Perspectives. 256p. 1994. boxed set 99.95 (*0-8493-2488-2*, 2488) CRC Pr.

Neelamkavil. Computer Simulation & Modelling. 1987. pap. text 75.00 (*0-471-91130-5*) Wiley.

Neelamkavil, Francis. Computer Simulation & Modelling. LC 86-9263. 324p. 1987. 135.00 (*0-471-91129-1*) Wiley.

Neelands, Jonathan. Beginning Drama 11-14. LC 98-185992. (Illus.). 112p. 1998. pap. text 22.50 (*1-85346-528-3*, 465283, Pub. by David Fulton) Calendar Islands.
— Making Sense of Drama: A Guide to Classroom Practice. 122p. (Orig.). (C). 1985. pap. text 19.50 (*0-435-18658-2*, 18658) Heinemann.
— Structuring Drama Work: A Handbook of Available Forms in Theatre & Drama. Goode, Tony, ed. (Illus.). 88p. (C). 1990. pap. text 22.95 (*0-521-37635-1*) Cambridge U Pr.

Neelankanta, P. S. Information Theoretic Aspects of Neural Networks. LC 99-203978. 1999. lib. bdg. 74.95 (*0-8493-3198-6*, 3198) CRC Pr.

Neeld, Elizabeth H. A Sacred Primer: The Essential Guide to Quiet Time & Prayer. LC 98-50355. 240p. 1999. 17.95 (*1-58063-059-6*, Pub. by Renaissance) St Martin.

— Seven Choices: Taking the Steps to New Life after Losing Someone You Love: A Pocket Reference Guide. 58p. 1998. pap. 4.95 (*0-937897-60-4*) Centerpoint Pr.

Neeld, Elizabeth H., jt. auth. see Muller, Mary B.

Neeld, Elizabeth H., ed. & pref. see Harper, Tommie F.

Neeld, Judith. Naming the Island. 64p. (Orig.). 1988. pap. 5.95 (*0-939395-08-8*) Thorntree Pr.
— To Fit Your Heart into the Body: Poems LC 98-50517. 1999. write for info. (*1-892471-00-0*) Bright Hill.

***Neeleman, Ad & Weerman, Fred.** Flexible Syntax: A Theory of Case & Arguments. LC 99-51814. (Studies in Natural Language & Linguistic Theory). 264p. 1999. 104.00 (*0-7923-6058-3*) Kluwer Academic.

Neeley, Bill. The Last Comanche Chief: The Life & Times of Quanah Parker. LC 94-38101. (Illus.). 276p. 1996. pap. 16.95 (*0-471-16076-8*) Wiley.
— The Last Comanche Chief: The Life & Times of Quanah Parks. LC 94-38101. (Illus.). 276p. 1995. 24.95 (*0-471-11722-6*) Wiley.

Neeley, Dennis. Softdesk Solutions: The Essential Guide to Auto-Architect LC 96-7187. 456p. 1996. pap. 32.95 incl. cd-rom (*0-471-15418-0*) Wiley.

Neeley, Deta P. A Child's Story of the Book of Mormon. LC 87-19903. 382p. (J). (gr. 1-6). 1987. 13.95 (*0-87579-101-8*) Deseret Bk.

Neeley, G. Steven. The Constitutional Right to Suicide: A Legal & Philosophical Examination. 2nd ed. LC 96-14979. (Studies in Law & Politics: Vol. 1). X, 230p. (C). 1996. 41.95 (*0-8204-3453-1*) P Lang Pubng.

Neeley, Gwen C. Miss Ima & the Hogg Family. (Illus.). 96p. (J). (gr. 7 up). 1992. pap. 8.95 (*0-937460-79-6*) Hendrick-Long.

Neeley, Imke. Accounting: Principles & Practices. 4th ed. (SWC-Accounting Ser.). (C). 1990. pap. 3.75 (*0-538-80821-7*) Sth-Wstrn College.

Neeley, L. P. Accounting Principles & Practices: Key for Practice. 4th ed. 1990. 11.50 (*0-538-80826-8*) Sth-Wstrn College.

Neeley, L. Paden. Mls Accounting Module 2. (SWC-Accounting). (C). 1999. mass mkt. 47.95 (*0-538-26645-7*) S-W Pub.

Neeley, L. Paden & Imke, Frank. Accounting Principles & Practices. 4th ed. 1072p. (C). 1990. text. write for info. (*0-318-68084-X*, AV63DA) S-W Pub.

Neeley, Mary A., jt. auth. see Muskat, Beth T.

Neeley, Mary Ann. Montgomery: Capital City Corners. (Images of America Ser.). 1997. pap. 16.99 (*0-7524-0553-5*) Arcadia Publng.

Neeley, Patty A. Miracle Muffins: Amazingly Delicious Treats Without All That Fat! (Illus.). 160p. 1996. pap., per. 12.00 (*0-7615-0423-0*) Prima Pub.

Neeley, Patty A. Sweet Deceptions: Create Decadent Desserts Without All That Fat (or Guilt)! LC 95-42385. (Illus.). 240p. 1996. spiral bd. 14.95 (*0-7615-0287-4*) Prima Pub.

***Neeley, Paul L.** People of the Drum of God - Come? (Publications in Ethnography). 1999. pap. 29.00 (*1-55671-013-5*) S I L Intl.

Neelon, Ann. Easter Vigil. (Anhinga Prize for Poetry Ser.). 80p. (Orig.). 1996. pap. 10.00 (*0-938078-44-5*) Anhinga Pr.

Neels. The Mistletoe Kiss. 1997. per. 3.25 (*0-373-15729-0*) Harlequin Bks.

***Neels, Betty.** A Good Wife. large type ed. 2000. 22.95 (*0-263-16447-0*) Mac Lib Ref.

***Neels, Betty, et al.** Mistletoe Magic. 2000. mass mkt. 6.50 (*0-373-83440-3*) Harlequin Bks.

Neels, Betty A. Apple from Eve. large type ed. 1990. pap. 5.00 (*0-7451-1283-8*, Pub. by Chivers N Amer) Chivers N Amer.
— At Odds with Love. (Romance Ser.). 1994. per. 2.99 (*0-373-03323-0*, 1-03323-2) Harlequin Bks.
— At Odds with Love. large type ed. 1994. per. 2.99 (*0-373-15569-7*) Harlequin Bks.
— The Awakened Heart. LC 97-10517. (Romance Ser.). 189p. 1994. per. 2.99 (*0-373-03339-7*, 1-03339-8) Harlequin Bks.
— The Awakened Heart. large type ed. (Harlequin Romance Ser.). 1994. lib. bdg. 18.95 (*0-263-13824-0*) Thorndike Pr.
— The Bachelor's Wedding. (Harlequin Romance Ser.: No. 3415). 1996. per. 3.25 (*0-373-03415-6*, 1-03415-6) Harlequin Bks.
— Cassandra by Chance. (Promo Ser.). 1999. per. 3.99 (*0-373-83390-3*, 1-83390-4) Harlequin Bks.
— A Christmas Wish. LC 96-291. 187p. 1995. per. 2.99 (*0-373-03389-3*, 1-03389-3) Harlequin Bks.
— A Christmas Wish. large type ed. (Harlequin Romance Ser.). 1995. 19.95 (*0-263-14286-8*) Mac Lib Ref.
— Cobweb Morning. (Promo Ser.). 1999. per. 3.99 (*0-373-83388-1*, 1-83388-8) Harlequin Bks.
— The Convenient Wife. (And the Winner Is...Ser.). 1997. mass mkt. 3.99 (*0-373-48344-9*, 1-48344-5) Harlequin Bks.
— The Convenient Wife. 1999. per. 4.50 (*0-373-65104-X*) Harlequin Bks.
— The Daughter of the Manor. (Romance Ser.: Bk. 3583). 1999. per. 3.50 (*0-373-03583-7*, 1-03583-1) Harlequin Bks.
— Daughter of the Manor. large type ed. (Harlequin Romance Ser.). 1997. 20.95 (*0-263-15169-7*) Mac Lib Ref.
— Dearest Love. (Promo Ser.). 1999. per. 4.50 (*0-373-21956-3*, 1-21956-7) Harlequin Bks.
— Dearest Love: (Sealed with a Kiss) LC 95-6952. (Romance Ser.). 187p. 1995. per. 2.99 (*0-373-03355-9*, 1-03355-4) Harlequin Bks.
— Dearest Mary Jane. 1996. per. 3.25 (*0-373-03435-0*, 1-03435-4) Harlequin Bks.
— Dearest Mary Jane. large type ed. (Christmas Ser.). 1996. per. 3.25 (*0-373-15681-2*) Harlequin Bks.

***Neels, Betty A.** Discovering Daisy. large type ed. (Thorndike Harlequin Romance Ser.). 2000. 22.95 (*0-263-16287-7*) Mills & Boon.

Neels, Betty A. The Doubtful Marriage, - 1997. per. 3.99 (*0-373-83337-7*, 1-83337-5) Harlequin Bks.
— End of the Rainbow. 1997. per. 3.99 (*0-373-83338-5*) Harlequin Bks.
— Fate Is Remarkable. 1998. pap. 3.99 (*0-373-83395-4*, 1-83395-3) Harlequin Bks.
— Fate Takes a Hand. 1997. per. 3.25 (*0-373-03454-7*, 1-03454-5) Harlequin Bks.
— Fate Takes a Hand. (Harlequin Romance Ser.). 1996. 19.95 (*0-263-14482-8*) Mac Lib Ref.
— Fate Takes a Hand. large type ed. 1997. per. 3.25 (*0-373-15700-2*, 1-15700-7) Harlequin Bks.
— The Final Touch. (Romance Ser.: No. 197). 1992. pap. 2.89 (*0-373-03197-1*, 1-03197-0) Harlequin Bks.
— The Final Touch. large type ed. 1992. reprint ed. 18.95 (*0-263-12902-0*) Thorndike Pr.
— Fortunes of Francesca. large type ed. 1998. 21.95 (*0-263-15563-3*, G K Hall & Co) Mac Lib Ref.
— A Gem of a Girl. (Promo Ser.). 1999. per. 3.99 (*0-373-83386-5*, 1-83386-2) Harlequin Bks.
— A Girl in a Million. 1994. per. 2.99 (*0-373-03315-X*, 1-03315-8) Harlequin Bks.
— A Girl in a Million. (Promo Ser.). 1999. per. 4.50 (*0-373-21976-8*, 1-21976-5) Harlequin Bks.
— A Girl in a Million. large type ed. 1994. per. 2.99 (*0-373-15561-1*) Harlequin Bks.
— A Happy Meeting. (Romance Ser.). 1993. per. 2.99 (*0-373-03267-6*, 1-03267-1) Harlequin Bks.
— A Happy Meeting. large type ed. (Harlequin Ser.). 1993. reprint ed. lib. bdg. 18.95 (*0-263-13278-1*) Mac Lib Ref.
— Heaven Is Gentle. 1998. pap. 3.99 (*0-373-83397-0*, 1-83397-9) Harlequin Bks.
— Henrietta's Own Castle. (Promo Ser.). 1999. per. 3.99 (*0-373-83389-X*, 1-83389-6) Harlequin Bks.
— Henrietta's Own Castle. large type ed. 257p. 1995. 27.99 (*0-7505-0688-1*, Pub. by Mgna Lrg Print) Ulverscroft.
— Ideal Wife. 1998. 21.95 (*0-263-15654-0*, Harlequin) Harlequin Bks.

***Neels, Betty A.** An Innocent Bride: White Weddings. (Romance Ser.: No. 3577). 1999. per. 3.50 (*0-373-03577-2*, 1-03577-3) Harlequin Bks.
— An Innocent Bride: White Weddings. large type ed. (Larger Print Ser.: No. 423). 1999. per. 3.50 (*0-373-15823-8*, 1-15823-7) Harlequin Bks.
— An Innocent Bride: White Weddings. large type ed. 1999. write for info. (*0-263-16176-5*, Pub. by Mills & Boon) Ulverscroft.

Neels, Betty A. A Kiss for Julie. (Romance Ser.: Vol. 3512). 1998. per. 3.50 (*0-373-03512-8*, 1-03512-0) Harlequin Bks.
— A Kiss for Julie. large type ed. (Larger Print Ser.: Vol. 358). 1998. per. 3.50 (*0-373-15758-4*, 1-15758-5) Harlequin Bks.
— Magic in Vienna. large type ed. LC 94-3361. 253p. 1994. lib. bdg. 16.95 (*0-8161-7455-5*, G K Hall Lrg Type) Mac Lib Ref.
— The Magic of Living. 1998. pap. 3.99 (*0-373-83393-8*, 1-83393-8) Harlequin Bks.
— Marrying Mary. (Romance Ser.: No. 3492). 1998. per. 3.50 (*0-373-03492-X*, 1-03492-5) Harlequin Bks.
— Marrying Mary. large type ed. 1998. per. 3.50 (*0-373-15738-X*, Harlequin) Harlequin Bks.
— Marrying Mary. large type ed. (Harlequin Romance Ser.). 1996. lib. bdg. 19.95 (*0-263-14594-8*) Mac Lib Ref.
— The Mistletoe Kiss. (Romance Ser.: No. 3483). 1997. per. 3.25 (*0-373-03483-0*, 1-03483-4) Harlequin Bks.
— The Moon for Lavinia. (Promo Ser.). 1999. per. 3.99 (*0-373-63104-9*, 1-63104-3) Harlequin Bks.
— The Most Marvellous Summer. (Romance Ser.: No. 185). 1992. pap. 2.89 (*0-373-03185-8*, 1-03185-5) Harlequin Bks.
— The Nasty Marriage. deluxe ed. 1998. per. 3.99 (*0-373-83341-5*) Harlequin Bks.

An Asterisk (*) at the beginning of an entry indicates that the title is appearing for the first time.

— Off with the Old Love. (Promo Ser.). 1999. per. 3.99 (*0-373-63103-0*, 1-63103-5) Harlequin Bks.
— An Old-Fashioned Girl. 1993. per. 2.99 (*0-373-15533-6*) Harlequin Bks.
— Only by Chance. 1998. per. 3.50 (*0-373-03537-3*, 1-03537-7, Mira Bks) Harlequin Bks.
— Only by Chance. large type ed. (Larger Print Ser.). 1999. per. 3.50 (*0-373-15783-5*, 1-15783-3) Harlequin Bks.
— Only by Chance. large type ed. Vol. 431. 251p. 1999. per. 3.50 (*0-373-15831-9*, 1-15831-0) Harlequin Bks.
— Only by Chance. large type ed. (Harlequin Ser.). 1996. 19.95 (*0-263-14751-7*) Thorndike Pr.
— The Quiet Professor. (Romance Ser.). 1993. mass mkt. 2.99 (*0-373-03279-X*, 1-03279-6) Harlequin Bks.
— The Right Kind of Girl. 1997. per. 3.25 (*0-373-15713-4*, 1-15713-0); per. 3.25 (*0-373-03467-9*, 1-03467-7) Harlequin Bks.
— The Right Kind of Girl. large type ed. 1996. 19.95 (*0-263-14579-4*) Mac Lib Ref.
— Ring in a Teacup. (Promo Ser.). 1999. per. 3.99 (*0-373-63102-2*, 1-63102-7) Harlequin Bks.
— Romantic Encounter. (Romance Ser.). 1993. per. 2.89 (*0-373-03249-8*, 1-03249-9) Harlequin Bks.
— Romantic Encounter. large type ed. 1993. reprint ed. lib. bdg. 18.95 (*0-263-13184-X*) Mac Lib Ref.
— Roses for Christmas: Collector's Edition. 1997. per. 3.99 (*0-373-83340-7*) Harlequin Bks.
— Saturday's Child. 1998. pap. 3.99 (*0-373-83394-6*, 1-83394-6) Harlequin Bks.
— A Secret Infatuation. LC 95-6868. (Romance Ser.). 189p. 1995. mass mkt. 2.99 (*0-373-03363-X*, 1-03363-8) Harlequin Bks.
— Sister Peters in Amsterdam. 1998. pap. 3.99 (*0-373-83392-X*, 1-83392-0) Harlequin Bks.
— A Star Looks Down. 1998. pap. 3.99 (*0-373-83396-2*, 1-83396-1) Harlequin Bks.
— Stars Through the Mist. 1997. per. 3.99 (*0-373-83336-9*) Harlequin Bks.
— Three for a Wedding. 1997. per. 3.99 (*0-373-83339-3*) Harlequin Bks.
— Two for the Heart. 1994. per. 2.99 (*0-373-15545-X*) Harlequin Bks.
— An Unlikely Romance. large type ed. 1992. reprint ed. lib. bdg. 18.95 (*0-263-13091-6*) Mac Lib Ref.
— A Valentine for Daisy. large type ed. (Harlequin Ser.). 1994. lib. bdg. 18.95 (*0-263-13723-6*) Mac Lib Ref.
— A Valentine for Daisy: (Kids & Kisses) LC 95-4584. (Romance Ser.). 189p. 1995. per. 2.99 (*0-373-03347-8*, 1-03347-1) Harlequin Bks.
— The Vicar's Daughter. 1998. pap. 3.50 (*0-373-03527-6*, 1-03527-8) Harlequin Bks.
— The Vicar's Daughter. large type ed. 1998. pap. 3.50 (*0-373-15773-8*, 1-15773-4) Harlequin Bks.
— The Vicar's Daughter. large type ed. (Harlequin Romance Ser.). 1997. 20.95 (*0-263-15008-9*) Mac Lib Ref.
— Victory for Victoria. (Promo Ser.). 1999. per. 3.99 (*0-373-83391-1*, 1-83391-2) Harlequin Bks.
— Waiting for Deborah. LC 96-729. (Romance Ser.). 186p. 1996. per. 3.25 (*0-373-03400-8*, 1-03400-8) Harlequin Bks.
— Wedding Bells for Beatrice. LC 95-13698. (Romance Ser.). 186p. 1995. per. 2.99 (*0-373-03371-0*, 1-03371-1) Harlequin Bks.
— Wedding Bells for Beatrice. large type ed. 1995. lib. bdg. 18.95 (*0-263-13939-5*) Thorndike Pr.
*__Neels, Betty A.__ A Winter Love Story. (Romance Ser.: Bk. 3626). 2000. mass mkt. 3.50 (*0-373-03626-4*, 1-03626-4) Harlequin Bks.
__Neels, Betty A.__ Wish with the Candles. (Promo Ser.). 1999. per. 3.99 (*0-373-83387-3*, 1-83387-0) Harlequin Bks.
__Neels, Betty A. & Goldrick, Emma.__ Love & Marriage: Making Sure of Sarah; Something Blue - 50th Anniversary. anniversary ed. (Romance Ser.: No. 3554). 1999. per. 3.50 (*0-373-03554-3*, 1-03554-2) Harlequin Bks.
— Love & Marriage: Making Sure of Sarah; Something Blue - 50th Anniversary. anniversary large type ed. (Romance Ser.: No. 3554). 1999. per. 3.50 (*0-373-15800-9*, 1-15800-5) Harlequin Bks.
__Neels, Betty A. & James, Ellen.__ Two for the Heart. (Romance Ser.). 1994. mass mkt. 2.99 (*0-373-03299-4*, 1-03299-4) Harlequin Bks.
— Two for the Heart. large type ed. LC 94-43668. 240p. 1995. pap. 17.95 (*0-7838-1213-2*, G K Hall Lrg Type) Mac Lib Ref.
__Neels, Betty A. & Mortimer, Carole.__ Christmas Miracles. 1997. per. 4.99 (*0-373-15265-5*) Harlequin Bks.
__Neels, Betty A., et al.__ Harlequin Romance Fortieth Anniversary Collection: Paradise for Two; Fallen Idol; Both of Them. anniversary ed. 1997. pap. write for info. (*0-373-15319-8*, 1-15319-6) Harlequin Bks.
__Neelsen, John P., ed.__ Gender, Caste & Power in South Asia: Social Status & Mobility in a Transitional Society. (C). 1991. 30.00 (*81-85425-44-2*, Pub. by Manohar) S Asia.
— Social Inequality & Political Structures: Studies in Class Formation & Interest Articulation in an Indian Coalfield & Its Rural Hinterland. 1983. 27.50 (*0-8364-1071-8*, Pub. by Manohar) S Asia.
__Neely.__ Ecology & Field Biology. 5th ed. 272p. (C). 1997. pap. text, teacher ed., suppl. ed. write for info. (*0-06-501897-4*) Addson-Wesley Educ.
— Machine Tool. 6th ed. (C). 1998. pap. text, student ed., wbk. ed. write for info. (*0-13-099671-8*) P-H.
__Neely, Alan.__ Christian Mission: A Case Study Approach. LC 95-18044. (American Society of Missiology Ser.: No. 21). 250p. (Orig.). 1995. pap. 20.00 (*1-57075-008-4*) Orbis Bks.
*__Neely, Alan.__ A New Call to Mission: Help for Perplexed Churches. LC 99-38748. 1999. 15.00 (*1-57312-296-3*) Smyth & Helwys.
__Neely, Alan, ed. see Bosch, David J.__
__Neely, Alan, ed. see Shenk, Wilbert R.__
__Neely, Alan, tr. & rev. see Dussel, Enrique D.__
__Neely, Barbara.__ Blanche among the Talented Tenth. 240p. 1995. mass mkt. 5.99 (*0-14-025036-0*, Penguin Bks) Viking Penguin.
— Blanche Cleans Up. 272p. 1999. mass mkt. 5.99 (*0-14-027747-1*) Viking Penguin.
— Blanche on the Lam. 192p. 1993. pap. 5.99 (*0-14-017439-7*, Penguin Bks) Viking Penguin.
*__Neely, Barbara.__ Blanche Passes Go. LC 99-462184. 272p. 2000. 22.95 (*0-670-89165-7*, Viking) Viking Penguin.
— Phonics Magic. (Illus.). 354p. 1999. ring bd. 79.95 (*1-929343-04-3*) Peer Tutor Pr.
*__Neely, Blake.__ Bass Method. (Fast Track Ser.). (Illus.). 96p. 2000. per. 7.95 (*0-634-01143-X*) H Leonard.
— Drum Method. (Fast Track Ser.). (Illus.). 96p. 2000. per. 7.95 (*0-634-00941-9*) H Leonard.
— E-Flat Sax Method. (Fast Track Ser.). (Illus.). 2000. pap. 7.95 (*0-634-00939-7*) H Leonard.
— Guitar Method: For Electric or Acoustic Guitar. (Fast Track Ser.). (Illus.). 96p. 2000. per. 7.95 (*0-634-01142-1*) H Leonard.
— Harmonica Method. (Fast Track Ser.). (Illus.). 96p. 2000. pap. 7.95 (*0-634-01427-7*) H Leonard.
__Neely, Blake.__ How to Play a Fake Book Faking Your Own Arrangements from Melodies & Chords. 88p. 1999. otabind 10.95 (*0-634-00206-6*) H Leonard.
*__Neely, Blake.__ Keyboard Method: For Electronic Keyboard, Synthesizer or Piano. (Fast Track Ser.). (Illus.). 96p. 2000. per. 7.95 (*0-634-00940-0*) H Leonard.
— Lead Singer's Method. (Fast Track Ser.). (Illus.). 2000. pap. 7.95 (*0-634-01426-9*) H Leonard.
__Neely, Cam & Tarcy, Brain.__ Hockey for Everybody: Cam Neely's Guide to the Red-Hot Game on Ice. LC 98-72599. 300p. 1998. pap. 19.95 (*1-886284-17-2*, Pub. by Chandler Hse) Natl Bk Netwk.
__Neely, Carol T.__ Broken Nuptials in Shakespeare's Plays. LC 84-29947. 272p. reprint ed. pap. 84.40 (*0-7837-3325-9*, 205773100007) Bks Demand.
— Broken Nuptials in Shakespeare's Plays. LC 93-24730. 264p. 1993. reprint ed. pap. text 14.95 (*0-252-06362-7*) U of Ill Pr.
__Neely, Charles.__ Tales & Songs of Southern Illinois: Timeless Folklore in Story & Verse. 296p. 1989. reprint ed. 18.95 (*0-9623990-3-5*); reprint ed. pap. 12.95 (*0-9623990-2-7*) Crossfire Pr.
__Neely, Charles & Spargo, John W.__ Tales & Songs of Southern Illinois. LC 97-34077. 270p. 1998. pap. 12.95 (*0-8093-2183-1*) S Ill U Pr.
__Neely, Cynthia, et al.__ Guide to Georgetown - Silver Plume. 3rd ed. LC 95-7719. (Historic Mining District Ser.). 48p. 1995. pap. 6.95 (*1-55566-151-3*) Johnson Bks.
__Neely, Dan & Watson, Gary, eds.__ The Landscape below Ground. 222p. (C). 1994. pap. text 60.00 (*0-685-75083-3*) Int Soc Arboricult.
— The Landscape below Ground II. 266p. (C). 1998. pap 40.00 (*1-881956-06-7*) Int Soc Arboricult.
__Neely, Glenn.__ Mastering Elliott Wave: Presenting the Neely Method. 223p. 1990. 95.00 (*0-930233-44-1*) Windsor.
__Neely, Jack.__ The Marble City: A Photographic Tour of Knoxville's Graveyards. LC 98-40116. (Illus.). 88p. 1999. 34.00 (*1-57233-043-0*); pap. 16.00 (*1-57233-036-8*, 9840116) U of Tenn Pr.
__Neely, James A. & Wright, Henry T.__ Early Settlement & Irrigation on the Deh Luran Plain: Village & Early State Societies in Southwestern Iran. (Technical Reports Ser.: No. 26). (Illus.). viii, 234p. (Orig.). 1994. pap. 20.00 (*0-915703-36-X*) U Mich Mus Anthro.
__Neely, James W. & Isacoff, Eric G.__ Carbonaceous Adsorbents for the Treatment of Ground & Surface Waters. LC 82-8930. (Pollution Engineering & Technology Ser.: No. 21). (Illus.). 240p. reprint ed. pap. 74.40 (*0-7837-5373-X*, 204513700005) Bks Demand.
*__Neely, John.__ Practical Metallurgy & Materials of Industry. 5th ed. 461p. 1999. 90.00 (*0-13-624552-8*) P-H.
__Neely, John E.__ Basic Machine Tool Operations. LC 99-19572. (Illus.). 441p. (C). 1999. pap. 67.00 (*0-13-099677-7*) P-H.
— Practical Metallurgy & Materials of Industry. 2nd ed. 406p. 1984. pap. text 6.00 (*0-471-80125-9*) P-H.
— Practical Metallurgy & Materials of Industry. 3rd ed. 1989. text 40.95 (*0-471-60923-4*) P-H.
__Neely, Joseph L.__ Chosen Words, Favorite Sayings of Famous People. 1994. 6.50 (*1-56245-163-4*) Great Quotations.
— The Journey to Success. Caton, Patrick, ed. LC 96-78970. 68p. 1997. 6.50 (*1-56245-285-1*) Great Quotations.
*__Neely, Keith.__ Memories of the Dance. Clutter, Patricia, ed. LC 98-61857. 368p. 1999. pap. 18.95 (*1-880254-59-X*) Vista.
__Neely, Keith R.__ Street Dancer. Forman, David B., ed. LC 90-91640. 265p. (Orig.). 1990. pap. 8.95 (*0-936174-06-4*) Jems Comm.
__Neely, Kim.__ Five Against One: The Story of Pearl Jam. LC 98-12196. 1998. pap. 14.95 (*0-14-027642-4*) Viking Penguin.
__Neely, Kris.__ AS/400 Networking & Data Communications Sourcebook. (Illus.). 585p. (Orig.). 1995. pap. 99.00 (*1-883884-21-7*, 522) Midrange Comput.
— How to Design a Universal Cabling System. (Illus.). 111p. (Orig.). 1994. pap. 49.00 (*1-883884-20-9*, 519) Midrange Comput.
__Neely, Kris & Hoopes, Jim.__ AS/400 Network Computing Professional Reference: A Guide to System Administration & Software Development. (IBM/Network Computing Ser.). (Illus.). 960p. 1997. 79.95 (*0-07-046624-6*) McGraw.
__Neely, Kris, et al.__ Building AS/400 Client/Server Solutions Using Shrink-Wrapped Software & Off-the-Shelf Hardware. LC 98-10137. (Illus.). 384p. 1997. pap. 69.00 (*1-883884-44-6*, 572) Midrange Comput.
__Neely, L.__ What Doctor's, Hospitals & HMO's Don't Want You to Know: Blind Faith in the Medical System Can Kill You, You Can Take Control. 285p. pap. 34.95 (*0-9675896-6-5*) Gale Pubng.
__Neely, Letta.__ Juba. LC 98-90181. (Illus.). 1998. pap. 12.00 (*0-9663097-2-3*) Wildheart Pr.
__Neely, Margery A.__ Quality Interviews with Adult Students & Trainees: A Communication Course in Student Personnel & In-Service Training. (Illus.). 384p. 1992. pap. 49.95 (*0-398-06302-8*) C C Thomas.
— Quality Interviews with Adult Students & Trainees: A Communication Course in Student Personnel & In-Service Training. (Illus.). 384p. (C). 1992. text 75.95 (*0-398-05813-X*) C C Thomas.
*__Neely, Margery A. & Maass, Vera S.__ Counseling Single Parents. LC 99-55582. 2000. write for info. (*0-8261-1313-3*) Springer Pub.
__Neely, Margery A., jt. auth. see Haines, James.__
__Neely, Mark E., Jr.__ The Abraham Lincoln Encyclopedia. (Quality Paperbacks Ser.). (Illus.). 368p. 1984. pap. 19.95 (*0-306-80209-0*) Da Capo.
— Confederate Bastille: Jefferson Davis & Civil Liberties. (Klement Lecture Ser.: No. 1). 25p. 1993. pap. 5.00 (*0-87462-325-1*) Marquette.
— The Fate of Liberty: Abraham Lincoln & Civil Liberties. 304p. 1992. reprint ed. pap. text 17.95 (*0-19-508032-7*) OUP.
— The Last Best Hope of Earth: Abraham Lincoln & the Promise of America. LC 93-22863. (Illus.). 304p. 1993. text 24.95 (*0-674-51125-5*) HUP.
— The Last Best Hope of Earth: Abraham Lincoln & the Promise of America. 320p. 1995. pap. 14.95 (*0-674-51126-3*, NEELAX) HUP.
— Southern Rights: Political Prisoners & the Myth of Confederate Constitutionalism. LC 99-25230. (Nation Divided Ser.). 1999. 35.00 (*0-8139-1894-4*) U Pr of Va.
__Neely, Mark E. & Holzer, Harold.__ The Union Image: Popular Prints of the Civil War North. LC 99-18486. (Illus.). 296p. 1999. 45.00 (*0-8078-2510-7*) U of NC Pr.
__Neely, Mark E., Jr. & McMurtry, R. Gerald.__ The Insanity File: The Case of Mary Todd Lincoln. LC 92-33847. 420p. (C). 1993. reprint ed. pap. 14.95 (*0-8093-1895-4*) S Ill U Pr.
*__Neely, Mark E., Jr., et al.__ The Confederate Image: Prints of the Lost Cause. LC 86-30797. (Illus.). 288p. 2000. reprint ed. pap. 34.95 (*0-8078-4905-7*) U of NC Pr.
__Neely, Mark E., et al.__ The Confederate Image: Prints of the Lost Cause. LC 86-30797. 287p. reprint ed. pap. 89.00 (*0-608-08609-6*, 206913200003) Bks Demand.
__Neely, Martina.__ West Virginia Italian Heritage Festival Cookbook. (Illus.). 112p. (Orig.). 1980. pap. 5.00 (*0-686-37047-3*) Back Fork Bks.
__Neely, Patricia A., jt. auth. see Chancey, Tina.__
__Neely, Paula K. & Croxton, Ryan.__ The Insiders' Guide to Richmond. 7th rev. ed. (Insiders' Guide Ser.). (Illus.). 360p. 1999. pap. 15.95 (*1-57380-097-X*, The Insiders Guide) Falcon Pub Inc.
__Neely, R. Dan & Watson, Gary.__ Proceedings of the Trees & Buildings Conference. 191p. (C). 1995. pap. text 45.00 (*1-881956-15-6*) Int Soc Arboricult.
__Neely, Richard.__ Tragedies of Our Own Making: How Private Choices Have Created Public Bankruptcy. 184p. 1993. 21.95 (*0-252-02038-3*) U of Ill Pr.
__Neely, Richard D., jt. auth. see Hale, Lee.__
*__Neely, Robert D.__ The Lawyers of Dickens & Their Clerks. LC 00-21520. 2000. write for info. (*1-58477-091-0*) Lawbk Exchange.
__Neely, Robert M., et al.__ The Business of Boating Recreation in Oregon. (Illus.). 28p. 1998. pap. 5.00 (*1-881826-14-7*) OR Sea Grant.
__Neely, Sharlotte.__ Snowbird Cherokees: People of Persistence. LC 90-11308. (Brown Thrasher Bks.). (Illus.). 192p. 1993. pap. 15.95 (*0-8203-1575-3*) U of Ga Pr.
__Neely, Sharlotte, jt. auth. see Oswalt, Wendell H.__
__Neely, Sylvia.__ Lafayette & the Liberal Ideal, 1814-1824: Politics & Conspiracy in an Age of Reaction. LC 90-25649. (Illus.). 368p. (C). 1991. 41.95 (*0-8093-1733-8*) S Ill U Pr.
__Neely, Sylvia, tr. see Fraysse, Olivier.__
__Neely, Teresa Y., jt. ed. see Abif, Khafre K.__
__Neely, Tim.__ Goldmine Christmas Record Price Guide. LC 97-73028. (Illus.). 400p. (Orig.). 1997. pap. 19.95 (*0-87341-524-8*, XREC) Krause Pubns.
*__Neely, Tim.__ Goldmine Jazz Album Price Guide. LC 99-68155. (Illus.). 544p. 2000. pap. 24.95 (*0-87341-384-9*, RJ04) Krause Pubns.
__Neely, Tim.__ Goldmine Price Guide to Alternative Records. LC 96-76694. 528p. 1996. pap. 23.95 (*0-87341-463-2*, NWR) Krause Pubns.
— Goldmine Price Guide to 45 RPM Records. 2nd ed. LC 96-76685. (Illus.). 544p. 1999. pap. 22.95 (*0-87341-748-8*, R452) Krause Pubns.
*__Neely, Tim.__ Goldmine Record Album Price Guide. LC 99-63746. (Illus.). 552p. 1999. pap. 24.95 (*0-87341-780-1*) Krause Pubns.
— Goldmine's Country Western Record Price Guide. 2nd rev. ed. LC 96-76683. (Illus.). 544p. 2000. pap. 24.95 (*0-87341-949-9*, RCW02) Krause Pubns.
__Neely, Tim.__ Standard Catalog of American Records. LC 98-84618. (Goldmine Price Guide to Collectible Record Albums Ser.). (Illus.). 1200p. 1998. pap. 29.95 (*0-87341-633-3*, REC1) Krause Pubns.
*__Neely, Tim.__ Standard Catalog of American Records, 1950-1975. 2nd rev. ed. LC 98-84618. (Goldmine Price Guide to Collectible Record Albums Ser.). (Illus.). 1,296p. 2000. pap. 34.95 (*0-87341-934-0*, REC2) Krause Pubns.
__Neely, Tim & Thompson, Dave.__ Goldmine British Invasion Record Price Guide. LC 97-73031. (Illus.). 400p. 1997. pap. 22.95 (*0-87341-535-3*, BRIT) Krause Pubns.
__Neely, Tim, ed. see Heggeness, Fred.__
__Neely, Virginia L.__ Alaska Calls. (Illus.). 208p. (Orig.). 1983. pap. 9.95 (*0-88839-970-7*) Hancock House.
__Neely, W. Brock.__ Introduction to Chemical Exposure & Risk Assessment. LC 94-22452. 208p. 1994. lib. bdg. 65.00 (*1-56670-094-9*, L1094) Lewis Pubs.
__Neely, W. Brock & Blau, Gary E.__ Environmental Exposure from Chemicals, Vol. 2. LC 84-7765. 192p. 1989. 96.00 (*0-8493-6166-4*, TD196) Franklin.
__Neely, W. Brock & Blau, Gary E., eds.__ Environmental Exposure from Chemicals. 256p. 1985. 146.00 (*0-8493-6165-6*, TD196, CRC Reprint) Franklin.
__Neely, W. Brook.__ Emergency Response to Chemical Spills. 96p. 1992. lib. bdg. 450.00 (*0-87371-733-3*, L733) Lewis Pubs.
__Neely, Wayne C.__ Agricultural Fair. LC 73-181962. reprint ed. 27.50 (*0-404-04669-X*) AMS Pr.
__Neely, Wesley B.__ Chemicals in the Environment: Distribution, Transport, Fate, Analysis. LC 80-23443. (Pollution Engineering & Technology Ser.: Vol. 13). (Illus.). 255p. reprint ed. pap. 79.10 (*0-608-18334-2*, 203301000082) Bks Demand.
__Neely, William.__ Alone in the Crowd: The Jim Gilmore Story. LC 88-70765. (Illus.). 192p. 1988. 22.95 (*0-89404-083-9*) Aztex.
— Stand on It: A Novel by Stroker Ace. LC 73-10414. 294p. 1990. reprint ed. pap. 12.95 (*0-89404-081-2*) Aztex.
— Tire Wars: Racing with Goodyear. LC 93-72137. (Illus.). 192p. 1993. 34.95 (*0-89404-091-X*) Aztex.
__Neely, William C.__ I Can't Be Addicted Because. 7p. (Orig.). 1986. pap. 1.50 (*0-89486-391-6*, 5308B) Hazelden.
__Neely, William T., jt. auth. see Esterly, Richard W.__
__Neelyand & William.__ Artsquest Preliminary Education. 222p. 1995. pap. text 38.80 (*0-536-58992-5*) Pearson Custom.
__Neeman, A.__ Ueda Theory: Theorems & Problems. LC 89-15176. (Memoirs Ser.: Vol. 81/415). 123p. 1989. pap. 21.00 (*0-8218-2478-3*, MEMO/81/415) Am Math.
*__Ne'eman, Gidi & Trabaud, Louis.__ Ecology, Biogeography & Management of Pinus Halepensis & P. Brutia Forest Ecosystems in the Mediterranean Basin. (Illus.). xii, 412p. 2000. 130.00 (*90-5782-055-2*, Pub. by Backhuys Pubs) Balogh.
__Neeman, Michael.__ Rational Emotive Behavior Therapy: Advances in Theory & Practice. 1998. pap. text 32.95 (*1-86156-104-0*) Whurr Pub.
__Ne'eman, Nira & Barthal, Lea.__ The Metaphoric Body: Guide to Expressive Therapy Through Images & Archetypes. 200p. 1993. pap. 25.95 (*1-85302-152-0*) Taylor & Francis.
__Neeman, Yaakov, ed.__ Conference on the Tax Consequences of American Investments in Israel: Proceedings, November 12-14, 1972. x, 337p. 1974. 20.00 (*0-8377-0902-4*, Rothman) W S Hein.
__Ne'Eman, Yuval & Eizenberg, E.__ Membranes & Other Extendons. 250p. (C). 1995. text 68.00 (*981-02-0630-5*); pap. text 36.00 (*981-02-0631-3*) World Scientific Pub.
__Ne'eman, Yuval & Kirsh, Yoram.__ The Particle Hunters. 2nd ed. (Illus.). 316p. (C). 1996. pap. 27.95 (*0-521-47686-0*); text 69.95 (*0-521-47107-9*) Cambridge U Pr.
__Neemann, Ursula.__ Gegensatze und Syntheseversuche im Methodenstreit der Neuzeit, 2 vols. Incl. Band 1. Gegensatze. (GER.). xii, 298p. 1993. (*3-487-09778-8*); Band 2. Syntheseversuche. (GER.). x, 695p. 1994. (*3-487-09779-6*); write for info. (*3-487-09777-X*) G Olms Pubs.
*__Neenan, Benedict.__ Thomas Verner Moore: Psychiatrist, Educator & Monk. 320p. 2000. pap. 22.95 (*0-8091-3987-1*) Paulist Pr.
__Neenan, Colin.__ In Your Dreams. LC 94-31058. 256p. (YA). (gr. 7 up). 1995. 11.00 (*0-15-200885-3*); pap. 5.00 (*0-15-200884-5*) Harcourt.
— Live a Little. LC 95-53259. 264p. 1996. pap. 6.00 (*0-15-201243-5*) Harcourt.
— Live a Little. LC 95-53259. 264p. (J). 1996. 12.00 (*0-15-201212-7*) Harcourt.
__Neenan, Michael & Dryden, Windy.__ Dealing with Difficulties in Rational Emotive Behavior Therapy. (Illus.). 120p. (Orig.). 1996. pap. 29.95 (*1-56593-815-1*, 1602) Singular Publishing.
__Neenan, Michael, jt. auth. see Dryden, Windy.__
__Neenan, Thomas, et al, eds.__ Biomedical Materials Vol. 550: Drug Delivery, Implants & Tissue Engineering. LC 99-25874. (Symposium Proceedings Ser.). 376p. 1999. 89.00 (*1-55899-456-4*) Materials Res.
__Neenan, Thomas & Hancock, Greg.__ Let's Blow Thru Europe. rev. ed. LC 91-50886. (Illus.). 256p. 1992. pap. 12.95 (*0-914457-46-2*) Mustang Pub.
__Neenan, William B., jt. ed. see Mathewson, Kent.__
__Neenan, William B., ed. see Social Security Conference Staff.__
__Neer.__ Shoulder Reconstruction. 624p. 1990. text 189.00 (*0-7216-2832-X*, W B Saunders Co) Harcrt Hlth Sci Grp.
__Neer, Frances L., ed.__ Perceiving the Elephant: Essays on Eyesight. LC 97-65992. 218p. 1998. pap. 14.95 (*0-88739-122-2*) Creat Arts Bk.
*__Neer, Frances Lief, ed.__ Breaking Barriers: The Extraordinary Stories of Uncommon People. LC 99-64932. 208p. 2000. pap. 13.95 (*0-88739-299-7*) Creat Arts Bk
__Neer, Richard T.__ Corpus Vasorum Antiquorum, United States of America, Fascicule 31 Fascicule 7: The J. Paul Getty Museum, Fascicule 7. LC 88-12781. (Getty Trust Publications: J. Paul Getty Museum). (Illus.). 116p. 1997. 90.00 (*0-89236-294-4*, Pub. by J P Getty Trust) OUP.
__Neera.__ Teresa. King, Martha, tr. from ITA. LC 98-31619. (European Classics). 160p. 1999. pap. 15.95 (*0-8101-1662-6*) Northwestern U Pr.

N

An Asterisk (*) at the beginning of an entry indicates that the title is appearing for the first time.

Neerakuckrejasohoni. Status of Girls in Development Strategies. (C). 1994. text 28.00 (*81-241-0019-5*, Pub. by Har-Anand Pubns) S Asia.

Neergaard, Ejler B., jt. auth. see Richardson, I. W.

Neergaard, Helene Gaillard De, see Gaillard de Neergaard, Helene.

Neergard, Jacobsen B., jt. ed. see Nyholm, N.

Neering, Rosemary. Backroading Vancouver Island. rev. ed. (Illus.). 192p. 1996. pap. text 14.95 (*1-55110-401-6*) Whitecap Bks.

***Neering, Rosemary.** Emily Carr. 64p. 1999. pap. 6.95 (*1-55041-483-6*) Fitzhenry & W Ltd.

Neerskov, Hans K. & Hunt, Dave. A Invasao Secreta.Tr. of Secret Invasion. (POR.). 212p. 1991. pap. 8.95 (*0-8297-1640-8*) Vida Pubs.

Neerven, Jan Van, see Van Neerven, Jan.

***Nees, Greg.** Germany: Unraveling an Enigma. LC 99-46629. 2000. write for info. (*1-877864-75-7*) Intercult Pr.

Nees-Hatlen, Virginia, jt. ed. see Burnes, A. Patricia.

Nees, Lawrence. Approaches to Early-Medieval Art. LC 97-76173. (Speculum Bks.). (Illus.). xi, 185p. 1998. pap. 20.00 (*0-915651-09-2*) Medieval Acad.

— The Gundohinus Gospels. LC 80-82036. (Medieval Academy Bks.: No. 95). 1987. 40.00 (*0-910956-93-6*) Medieval Acad.

Nees, Richard. Electronic Image Communications: A Guide to Networking Image Files. LC 93-182918. (Illus.). 95p. 1994. 39.50 (*0-938734-87-3*) Info Today Inc.

Nees, Thomas. Compassion Evangelism: Meeting Human Needs. 120p. (Orig.). 1996. pap. 8.99 (*0-8341-1623-5*) Beacon Hill.

Nees, Tom. The Changing Face of the Church: From American to Global. LC 97-11266. 120p. (Orig.). 1997. pap. 10.99 (*0-8341-1672-3*) Beacon Hill.

Neese, A. A., jt. auth. see Neese, Lon.

***Neese, Amberly.** Miracles of Jesus, Vol. 8. (Pulse Ser.). 2000. pap. 14.99 (*0-8307-2509-1*) Gospel Lght.

***Neese, Harvey & O'Donnell, John, eds.** Prelude to Tragedy: Vietnam, 1960-1965. (Illus.). 344p. 2000. 32.95 (*1-55750-491-1*) Naval Inst Pr.

Neese, Harvey C. The Almanac of Rural Living. (Illus.). 1976. per. 6.95 (*0-686-16740-6*) N & N Resources.

— Home Gardening: Practical & Simple. 1978. write for info. (*0-686-23016-7*) N & N Resources.

***Neese, Lon & Neese, A. A.** Cutting the Gordian Knot: Understanding Investing. LC 99-60694. 191p. 1999. 21.95 (*1-56167-496-6*) Am Literary Pr.

Neese, Randolph M. & Williams, George C. Why We Get Sick: How Darwinian Medicine is Revolutionizing the Science of Healing. 304p. 1996. pap. 13.00 (*0-679-74674-9*) Vin Bks.

Neese, William A. Aircraft Hydraulic Systems. 3rd ed. 526p. (C). 1991. 52.50 (*0-89464-562-5*) Krieger.

Neeser, Robert W. Statistical & Chronological History of the United States Navy, 1775-1907, 2 vols., Set. (BCL1 - U. S. History Ser.). 1991. reprint ed. lib. bdg. 150.00 (*0-7812-6044-2*) Rprt Serv.

Neeson, Eoin. Celtic Myths & Legends. 160p. 1998. pap. 9.95 (*1-85635-222-6*, Pub. by Mercier Pr) Irish Amer Bk.

— Civil War, 1922-23. 350p. 1988. pap. 19.95 (*1-85371-013-X*, Pub. by Poolbeg Pr) Dufour.

Neeson, Francis J., jt. auth. see McCalley, Stuart W.

Neeson, J. M. Commoners: Common Right, Enclosure & Social Change in England, 1700-1820. (Past & Present Publications). 398p. 1996. pap. text 24.95 (*0-521-56774-2*) Cambridge U Pr.

Neeson, Jack H. Footprints of St. Peter's: The First Fifty Years, 1852-1902. LC 97-74914. (Illus.). 198p. 1997. pap. 12.95 (*0-9661371-0-8*) Long Pt Pr.

***Neeson, Margaret G.** White Rock Ways. LC 98-92145. (Illus.). 196p. 1999. per. 15.95 (*0-9661371-1-6*) Long Pt Pr.

Neesse, Gottfried. Heraklit Heute. viii, 148p. 1982. write for info. (*3-487-07157-6*) G Olms Pubs.

Neetens, A., ed. Intraocular Lenses & Corneal Endothelium. (Journal: Ophthalmologica: Vol. 187, No. 2). (Illus.). x, 68p. 1983. pap. 45.25 (*3-8055-3758-1*) S Karger.

Neetens, A., et al, eds. The Visual System in Meyelin Disorders. (Monographs in Ophthalmology). 1984. text 289.00 (*90-6193-807-4*) Kluwer Academic.

Neetens, A., jt. ed. see Daroff, R.

Neethling, J. Persoonlikheidsreg. (AFR.). 332p. 1991. pap. write for info. (*0-409-04560-8*, MICHIE) LEXIS Pub.

Neethling, J., et al. Case Book on the Law of Delict: Vonnisbundel oor die Deliktereg. 759p. 1991. pap. write for info. (*0-7021-2593-8*, Pub. by Juta & Co) Gaunt.

— Case Book on the Law of Delict: Vonnisbundel oor die Deliktereg. 2nd ed. LC 97-198507. (ENG & SPA.). 830p. 1995. pap. 42.50 (*0-7021-3384-1*, Pub. by Juta & Co) Gaunt.

***Neethling, J., et al.** Case Book on the Law of Delict: Vonnisbundel oor die Deliktereg. 3rd ed. 985p. 1999. pap. 61.50 (*0-7021-5123-8*, Pub. by Juta & Co) Gaunt.

Neethling, J., et al. Delict, Law Of. 2nd ed. LC 94-164116. 367p. 1994. pap. write for info. (*0-409-04566-7*, MICHIE) LEXIS Pub.

— Deliktereg. 3rd ed. (AFR.). 430p. 1996. pap. write for info. (*0-409-04564-0*, MICHIE) LEXIS Pub.

— Neethling's Law of Personality. expanded rev. ed. LC 97-162562. 450p. 1996. pap. write for info. (*0-409-06124-7*, MICHIE) LEXIS Pub.

— Tydskrif Vir Hedendaagse Romeins-Hollandse Reg/The Journal of Contemporary Roman-Dutch Law. (AFR & ENG.). Date not set. write for info. (*0-409-07917-0*, MICHIE) LEXIS Pub.

Neethling, J., jt. auth. see Van Heerden, H. J.

Neev, David, jt. auth. see Emery, K. O.

Neev, Elan Z. Cosmic Doodlings for Self-Realization & Self-Coloring. (Illus.). (Orig.). 1980. pap. 9.95 (*0-918482-03-8*) Ageless Bks.

— God the Generous Capitalist or How to Borrow All You Need from the Universal Bank of Infinite Abundance. (Illus.). (Orig.). pap. text 7.95 (*0-918482-05-4*) Ageless Bks.

— How to Be Selfishly Good. (Illus.). (Orig.). 6.95 (*0-918482-06-2*) Ageless Bks.

— Wholistic Healing: How to Harmonize Your Body, Mind & Spirit with Life, for Freedom, Joy, Health, Beauty, Love, Money & Psychic Powers. rev. ed. LC 77-71152. (Illus.). 1977. pap. 10.95 (*0-918482-00-3*) Ageless Bks.

Neev, Joseph, ed. Applications of Ultrashort-Pulse Lasers in Medicine & Biology, Vol. 3255. 130p. 1998. 59.00 (*0-8194-2694-6*) SPIE.

Neev, Joseph, jt. ed. see Reed, Murray K.

Neeves, Robert, jt. auth. see Sweetgall, R.

Neeves, Robert, jt. auth. see Sweetgall, Robert.

Neeves, Robert, ed. see Sweetgall, Robert.

Nef. Princess Navina Visits Malvolia. (Illus.). 64p. (Orig.). 1990. pap. 9.95 (*0-915728-09-5*) Lytton Pub.

Nef, Count. Princess Navina Visits Nueva Malvolia. (Illus.). 52p. (Orig.). 1999. pap. 9.95 (*0-915728-14-1*) Lytton Pub.

Nef, John U. Conquest of the Material World. LC 64-15804. 420p. 1998. lib. bdg. 30.00 (*0-226-57121-1*) U Ch Pr.

— The Rise of the British Coal Industry, 2 Vols. LC 71-37902. (Select Bibliographies Reprint Ser.). 1977. reprint ed. 89.95 (*0-8369-6740-2*) Ayer.

— The Rise of the British Coal Industry, 2 vols. (Illus.). 1966. reprint ed. 95.00 (*0-7146-1346-0*, BHA-01346, Pub. by F Cass Pubs) Intl Spec Bk.

— The United States & Civilization. 2nd ed. LC 67-20465. (Walgreen Foundation Lectures). 1994. lib. bdg. 30.00 (*0-226-57123-8*) U Ch Pr.

***Nef, Jorge.** Human Security & Mutual Vulnerability. 2nd ed. 130p. 1999. pap. 16.95 (*0-88936-879-1*, Pub. by IDRC Bks) Stylus Pub VA.

Nef, Karl. Outline of the History of Music. (Music Book Index Ser.). 400p. 1992. reprint ed. lib. bdg. 89.00 (*0-7812-9483-5*) Rprt Serv.

Nef, Walter. Linear Algebra. 320p. 1988. pap. 9.95 (*0-486-65772-8*) Dover.

Nefedov, O. M., et al. Synthesis Structure & Properties of the First Examples of Germacyclopropenes (Germirenes) & 1,2-Digermacyclobutenes. (SSR Chemistry Reviews Ser.). 64p. 1988. 39.00 (*0-318-39941-5*) Gordon & Breach.

Nefedov, O. M., jt. auth. see Kolesnikov, S. P.

Nefedov, V. I. X-Ray Photoelectron Spectroscopy of Solid Surfaces. viii, 200p. 1987. lib. bdg. 133.00 (*90-6764-080-8*, Pub. by VSP) Coronet Bks.

Nefedova, T. G., jt. auth. see Ioffe, G. V.

Nefedova, Tatyana, jt. auth. see Ioffe, Grigory.

Neff. Los Milagros de Jesus (Miracles of Jesus. (SPA.). (J). 1995. write for info. (*0-7899-0034-3*) Editorial Unilit.

Neff, jt. auth. see Nathan.

Neff, Bettye C., jt. auth. see Fox, Janet.

Neff, Blake J. & Ratcliff, Donald, eds. Handbook of Family Religious Education. 290p. 1995. pap. 24.95 (*0-89135-095-0*) Religious Educ.

Neff, Blake J., jt. auth. see Ratcliff, Donald.

Neff, Carole C., jt. auth. see Nathan, Max, Jr.

Neff, Donald. Fallen Pillars: U. S. Policy Towards Palestine & Israel since 1945. 200p. 1995. 25.00 (*0-88728-262-8*) Inst Palestine.

— 50 Years of Israel. LC 98-25834. 1998. pap. write for info. (*0-937165-08-5*) Am Educ Trust.

— Warriors Against Israel. 600p. (Orig.). 1988. 19.95 (*0-915597-59-4*) Amana Bks.

— Warriors at Suez. 479p. 1987. pap. 9.95 (*0-915597-58-6*) Amana Bks.

— Warriors for Jerusalem. 430p. pap. 9.95 (*0-915597-57-8*) Amana Bks.

Neff, E. C. A Chronicle, Together with a Little Romance, Regarding Rudolf & Jacob Naf, of Frankford Pennsylvania, & Their Descendants, Including an Account of the Neffs in Switzerland & America. (Illus.). 352p. 1989. reprint ed. pap. 55.50 (*0-8328-0899-7*); reprint ed. lib. bdg. 65.50 (*0-8328-0898-9*) Higginson Bk Co.

Neff, E. Richard. Oil History: A Selected & Annotated Bibliography. Williford, George A., ed. 373p. 1995. 35.00 (*0-9648314-0-6*) Intl Assn Drill.

Neff, Eileen, ed. Arcades of Philadelphia the Present: Manuscripts of the 1992-93 Pew Fellowships in the Arts Disciplinary Winners in Poetry. (Illus.). 36p. (Orig.). 1995. 10.00 (*0-939084-26-0*) R Mus & Lib.

Neff, Eileen, et al. William Anastasi: A Retrospective (1960-1995) LC 95-79668. (Illus.). 32p. 1994. pap. 30.00 (*1-58442-002-2*) Galleries at Moore.

Neff, Emery E. Carlyle & Mill: An Introduction to Victorian Thought. (BCL1-PR English Literature Ser.). 435p. 1992. reprint ed. lib. bdg. 99.00 (*0-7812-7492-3*) Rprt Serv.

— The Poetry of History: The Contribution of Literature & Literary Scholarship to the Writing of History Since Voltaire. LC 47-30933. 258p. (C). 1961. pap. text 23.00 (*0-231-08525-7*) Col U Pr.

Neff, Emily B. John Singleton Copley in England. LC 95-24702. 1995. write for info. (*0-89090-070-1*) Mus Fine TX.

***Neff, Emily B. & Remington, Frederic.** Frederic Remington: The Hogg Brothers Collection of the Museum of Fine Arts, Houston. LC 99-39063. (Illus.). 2000. pap. write for info. (*0-89090-092-2*) Mus Fine TX.

Neff, Emily B. & Shackelford, George T. American Painters in the Age of Impressionism: Distributed for the Museum of Fine Arts, Houston. LC 94-40856. (Illus.). 144p. 1994. pap. 35.00 (*0-89090-064-7*) Mus Fine TX.

***Neff, Emily Ballew & Phelan, Wynne H.** Frederic Remington: The Hogg Brothers Collection of the Museum of Fine Arts, Houston. LC 99-39063. (Illus.). 146p. 2000. 49.95 (*0-691-04928-9*) Princeton U Pr.

Neff, Fred. Great Puzzles of History. LC 96-50925. (J). (gr. 6-9). 1996. lib. bdg. 19.93 (*0-8225-3931-4*, Runestone Pr) Lerner Pub.

— Mysterious Persons in History. LC 96-51182. 1996. lib. bdg. 19.93 (*0-8225-3932-2*, Lerner Publctns) Lerner Pub.

Neff, Genevieve C. Happy Thoughts for a Secret Pal. (Charming Petites Ser.). (Illus.). 80p. 1998. 4.95 (*0-88088-381-2*) Peter Pauper.

Neff, George E., jt. auth. see Amara, Mark S.

***Neff, Heather.** Blackgammon. 368p. 2000. 24.00 (*0-345-43611-3*) Ballantine Pub Grp.

Neff, Heln, jt. auth. see Westminster Presbyterian Church, Interpre Staff.

Neff, Herbert P., Jr. Continuous & Discrete Linear Systems. LC 90-48559. 530p. (C). 1991. reprint ed. lib. bdg. 62.50 (*0-89464-541-2*) Krieger.

Neff, Jack. Make Your Woodworking Pay for Itself. rev. ed. (Illus.). 128p. 1996. pap. 18.99 (*1-55870-418-3*, Betrwy Bks) F & W Pubns Inc.

***Neff, Jack, et al.** Formatting & Submitting Your Manuscript. LC 99-43650. (Writers' Market Library). (Illus.). 208p. 1999. pap. 18.99 (*0-89879-921-X*, 10618, Wrtrs Digest Bks) F & W Pubns Inc.

Neff, Jack, jt. auth. see Luken, Charlie.

Neff, James. City Beat: Stories from the Heart of Cleveland. ix, 231p. 1983. 13.95 (*0-939738-55-4*) Zubal Inc.

— Unfinished Murder: The Capture of a Serial Rapist. 368p. 1996. per. 5.99 (*0-671-73186-6*) PB.

Neff, Janet A. & Kidd, Pamela S. Trauma Nursing: The Art & Science. LC 92-16291. (Illus.). 808p. (C). (gr. 13). 1992. text 57.95 (*0-8016-6655-4*, 06655) Mosby Inc.

Neff, Joanna, ed. see Altman, Sandra.

Neff, John A. & Javidi, Bahram, eds. Materials, Devices, & Systems for Optoelectronic Processing. 206p. 1996. 56.00 (*0-8194-2236-3*) SPIE.

Neff, John B. & Mintz, S. L. John Neff on Investing. LC 99-16345. 288p. 1999. 27.95 (*0-471-19717-3*) Wiley.

Neff, John H. & Fineberg, Jonathan. Roxy Paine. (FRE & ENG.). 40p. 1998. pap. 30.00 (*0-932171-08-7*, Museed Art) Terra Found Arts.

Neff, Kelly J. Dear Companion: The Inner Life of Martha Jefferson. LC 98-112847. 632p. 1997. pap. 14.95 (*1-57174-075-9*) Hampton Roads Pub Co.

— Everyday Life in Two Worlds: A Psychic's Experience. LC 95-131053. 200p. 1994. pap. 9.95 (*1-878901-95-8*) Hampton Roads Pub Co.

Neff, Ken, jt. auth. see Day, Michael.

Neff, Kirk, jt. auth. see Schultz, Alfred W.

Neff, Larry M. Ha Nacido Jesus (Vida de Cristo)Tr. of Jesus Is Born. (SPA.). 12p. (J). 5.99 (*0-7899-0033-5*, 497759) Editorial Unilit.

Neff, Larry M., ed. Selections from Arthur D. Graeff's Scholla. LC 79-166008. (Pennsylvania German Folklore Ser.: Vol. 5). 1971. 15.00 (*0-911122-27-3*) Penn German Soc.

Neff, Larry M. & Weiser, Frederick S., eds. The Account Book of Conrad Weiser: Berks County, Pennsylvania, 1746-1760. LC 81-84666. (Sources & Documents Ser.: No. 6). (Illus.). 1981. 15.00 (*0-911122-43-5*) Penn German Soc.

***Neff, LaVonne.** The Jesus Book: 40 Bible Stories. LC 99-208229. (Life of Christ for Children Ser.). (Illus.). 83p. (J). (ps-k). 1999. 9.95 (*0-8294-1373-1*) Loyola Pr.

Neff, LaVonne. One of a Kind: Making the Most of Your Child's Uniqueness. rev. ed. Heaney, Liz, ed. LC 93-40255. 147p. (Orig.). 1995. pap. 14.00 (*0-935652-20-5*) Ctr Applications Psych.

Neff, LaVonne, ed. see Hope, Mary.

Neff, LaVonne, ed. see Hybels, Bill.

Neff, Liz, tr. see McIntyre, Sally.

Neff, M. Devocional para Mujeres Que Trabajan.Tr. of Devotions for Women in the Workplace. 6.99 (*1-56063-578-9*, 495011) Editorial Unilit.

Neff, M. Christine. Las Mujeres y Sus Emociones.Tr. of Women & Their Emotions. (SPA.). pap. 8.99 (*1-56063-579-7*, 495012) Editorial Unilit.

Neff, M. Christine & Spray, Martha. Introduction to Maternal & Child Health Nursing. LC 95-45452. 800p. 1996. text 41.95 (*0-397-55025-1*) Lppncott W & W.

Neff, Marsha J., jt. auth. see Dietl, L. Kay.

Neff, Michael W., ed. The Brooks & Olmo Register of Fruit & Nut Varieties. 3rd ed. 744p. 1997. lib. bdg. 150.00 (*0-9615027-4-6*) Am Soc Horticult.

Neff, Michael W., jt. ed. see McGiffen, Milt, Jr.

Neff, Michael W., ed. see Tyler, Rodney W.

Neff, Mindy. Adam's Kiss. 1997. per. 3.75 (*0-373-16663-X*, 1-16663-6) Silhouette.

— A Bachelor for the Bride: The Bride of Grazer's Corners. (American Romance Ser.: Vol. 739). 1998. per. 3.99 (*0-373-16739-3*, 1-16739-4) Harlequin Bks.

— The Bad Boy Next Door. (How to Marry...Ser.). 1997. per. 3.75 (*0-373-16679-6*, 1-16679-2) Harlequin Bks.

— The Cowboy Is a Daddy. 1998. per. 3.99 (*0-373-16759-8*, 1-16759-2, Mira Bks) Harlequin Bks.

— A Family Man. (American Romance Ser.). 1996. per. 3.75 (*0-373-16644-3*, 1-16644-6) Harlequin Bks.

***Neff, Mindy.** The Horseman's Convenient Wife. (American Romance Ser.). 2000. mass mkt. 4.25 (*0-373-16838-1*, 1-16838-4) Harlequin Bks.

Neff, Mindy. The Playboy & the Mommy: Tall, Dark & Irresistible. (American Romance Ser.: No. 800). 1999. per. 3.99 (*0-373-16800-4*, 1-16800-4) Harlequin Bks.

***Neff, Mindy.** A Pregnancy & a Proposal: (The Daddy Club) (American Romance Ser.: No. 809). 2000. per. 4.25 (*0-373-16809-8*, 1-16809-5, Harlequin) Harlequin Bks.

— Suddenly a Daddy. 1999. per. 3.99 (*0-373-16769-5*, 1-16769-1, Harlequin) Harlequin Bks.

Neff, Mindy. They're the Ones! The Ultimate . . . (American Romance Ser.: No. 711). 1998. per. 3.75 (*0-373-16711-3*, 1-16711-3) Harlequin Bks.

— The Virgin & Her Bodyguard: Tall, Dark & Irresistible. (American Romance Ser.: No. 795). 1999. per. 3.99 (*0-373-16795-4*, 1-16795-6) Harlequin Bks.

Neff, Miriam. Women & Their Emotions. expanded rev. ed. (Orig.). pap. 10.99 (*0-8024-9531-1*, 329) Moody.

Neff, Miriam & Klingsporn, Debra. Shattering Our Assumptions: Breaking Free of Expectations - Others & Our Own. LC 96-45769. 224p. 1996. pap. 10.99 (*1-55661-686-4*) Bethany Hse.

Neff, Norman D. & Naus, Joseph I. The Distribution of the Size of the Maximum Cluster of Points on a Line. LC 74-6283. (Selected Tables in Mathematical Statistics Ser.: No. 6). 207p. 1980. text 27.00 (*0-8218-1906-2*, TABLES/6) Am Math.

Neff, Pauline. Tough Love: How Parents Can Deal with Drug Abuse. 160p. 1984. reprint ed. pap. 10.95 (*0-687-42407-0*) Abingdon.

— Tough Love: How Parents Can Deal With Drug Abuse. rev. ed. 160p. 1996. pap. text 10.95 (*0-687-01825-0*) Abingdon.

Neff Perkins, Hilda. Tri-Tuning: Harmonizing Your Mind, Body & Spirit to Live Beyond Fear a Quest for the Key to Ki; The Essence of Life. LC 97-91369. (Illus.). 304p. 1999. pap. 18.95 (*0-9662618-0-1*) Universal Quest.

***Neff, Philip.** Grail Quest. 2000. pap. 18.00 (*0-7388-2145-4*) Xlibris Corp.

Neff, Rena. Napkin Magic. Pemno, Karen, ed. 64p. (Orig.). 1990. pap., per. 3.95 (*0-942320-36-0*) Am Cooking.

Neff, Rena & Perrino, Karen. The Junior Chef, Vol. 33. 64p. 1992. pap., per. 3.95 (*0-942320-41-7*) Am Cooking.

Neff, Richard B. & Smallson, Fran. NAFTA: Protecting & Enforcing Intellectual Property Rights in North America. LC 94-26390. 1994. write for info. (*0-07-172611-X*) Shepards.

***Neff, Robert & Connor, Anthony.** The Blues: In Images & Interviews. (Illus.). 152p. 1999. pap. 17.95 (*0-8154-1003-4*) Cooper Sq.

Neff, Robert C. Japan's Hidden Hot Springs. (Illus.). 196p. (Orig.). 1995. pap. 12.95 (*0-8048-1949-1*) Tuttle Pubng.

Neff, Ronald L., jt. auth. see Mey, Vander Brenda J.

Neff, Rose A. & Weimer, Maryellen, eds. Classroom Communication: Collected Readings for Effective Discussion & Questioning. 93p. (Orig.). (C). 1989. pap. text 22.50 (*0-912150-08-4*) Atwood Pub LLC.

Neff, Rose A. & Weimer, Maryellen G. Teaching College: Collected Readings for the New Instructor. 146p. 1990. pap. 21.95 (*0-912150-12-2*) Atwood Pub LLC.

Neff, Rose Ann & Weimer, Maryellen, eds. Classroom Communication: Collected Readings for Effective Discussion & Questioning. 93p. 1989. reprint ed. pap. text 22.50 (*1-891859-00-5*) Atwood Pub LLC.

Neff, Rose Ann, jt. ed. see Weimer, Maryellen.

Neff, Severine, ed. & tr. see Schoenberg, Arnold.

Neff, Stephen. Friends but No Allies: The Triumph of Capitalism & the Law of Nations. 1990. text 57.50 (*0-231-07142-6*) Col U Pr.

Neff, Susan A., jt. auth. see Lunn, Terry.

Neff, Terry A., ed. Open Spain - Espana Abierta: Contemporary Documentary Photography in Spain. Fontanella, Lee, tr. (ENG & SPA., Illus.). 264p. 1992. write for info. (*0-932026-27-3*) Columbia College Chi.

— Within This Garden. (Illus.). (Orig.). (C). 1993. pap. 29.95 (*0-932026-30-3*) Columbia College Chi.

— Within This Garden: Photographs by Ruth Thorne-Thomsen. (Illus.). (Orig.). 1993. 68.00 (*0-89381-549-7*) Aperture.

Neff, Terry A., ed. see Bantel, Linda, et al.

Neff, Terry A., ed. see Csikszentmihalyi, Mihaly, et al.

Neff, Terry A., ed. see Cuenther, Bruce.

Neff, Terry A., ed. see Hazzard, Shirley & Richardson, Nan.

Neff, Terry A., ed. see Hooks, Bell.

Neff, Terry A., ed. see Paschke, Ed, et al.

Neff, Terry A., ed. see Plagens, Peter & Guenther, Bruce.

Neff, Terry A., ed. see Warren, Lynne.

Neff, Terry A., ed. see Warren, Lynne & Dunlop, Ian.

Neff, Terry A., ed. see Winters, Laurie, et al.

Neff, Terry A., ed. see Wright, Beryl J., et al.

Neff, Thomas J., et al. Lessons from the Top: The Search of America's Best Business Leaders. LC 99-21724. 448p. 1999. 24.95 (*0-385-49343-6*) Doubleday.

Neff, Wallace, jt. auth. see Clark, Alson.

Neff, Walter S., ed. see National Conference on the Psychological Aspects o.

Neff, Wanda F. Victorian Working Women. LC 77-181963. reprint ed. 29.50 (*0-404-04676-2*) AMS Pr.

Neff, William A. The Neff-Naf Family History. LC 91-66144. (Illus.). 480p. 1991. 42.50 (*0-9630457-0-9*) Neff & Assocs.

***Neff, Windy.** The Playboy's Own Miss Prim: Bachelors of Shotgun Ridge, Vol. 834. (American Romance Ser.). 2000. mass mkt. 4.25 (*0-373-16834-9*, 1-16834-3) Harlequin Bks.

— The Rancher's Mail-Order Bride: Men of Malone County. (American Romance Ser.: Bk. 830). 2000. per. 4.25 (*0-373-16830-6*, 1-16830-1) Harlequin Bks.

***Neffen, Hugo E., et al, eds.** Asthma: A Link Between Environment, Immunology & the Airways. LC 99-65053. (Illus.). 300p. 1999. 69.00 (*0-88937-220-9*) Hogrefe & Huber Pubs.

Neffgen, H. Grammar & Vocabulary of the Samoan Language. Stock, Arnold B., tr. from GER. LC 75-35206. reprint ed. 21.50 (*0-404-14229-X*) AMS Pr.

N

Nefsky, Marilyn F. Stone Houses & Iron Bridges: Tradition & the Place of Women in Contemporary Japan. LC 91-18444. (Toronto Studies in Religion: Vol. 12). 260p. (C). 1992. text 47.95 (*0-8204-1568-5*) P Lang Pubng.

Nefsky, Marilyn F., jt. auth. see Davies, Alan.

Neft. Sports Encyclopedia Baseball, Vol. 9. 752p. 1999. pap. 19.99 (*0-312-20018-8*) St Martin.

Neft, David S. Cincinnati Reds Trivia Book. 1993. pap. 9.99 (*0-312-08736-5*) St Martin.

— The Sports Encyclopedia: Baseball. 1989. 29.95 (*0-312-02033-3*) St Martin.

— Sports Encyclopedia: Baseball 1998 Edition. 98th ed. 736p. 1998. pap. 19.99 (*0-312-18183-3*, St Martin Griffin) St Martin.

— Sports Encyclopedia: Pro Football: The Modern Era, 1973-1997. 16th ed. 672p. 1998. pap. 19.99 (*0-312-18761-0*) St Martin.

Neft, David S. & Cohen. The Sports Encyclopedia: Pro Football. 17th ed. 1999. pap. 19.99 (*0-312-20438-8*) St Martin.

Neft, David S. & Cohen, Richard M. The Sports Encyclopedia: Baseball. 8th ed. LC 85-1833. 610p. 1988. 29.95 (*0-685-20014-0*) St Martin.

***Neft, David S. & Cohen, Richard M.** Sports Encyclopedia: Baseball 2000. 752p. 2000. pap. 19.99 (*0-312-20437-X*) Griffin Assocs.

Neft, David S. & Cohen, Richard M. The Sports Encyclopedia: Pro Football. 1989. pap. 18.95 (*0-318-42737-0*) St Martin.

Neft, David S., et al. The Boston Red Sox Trivia Book. LC 92-44102. 1993. pap. 10.95 (*0-312-08712-8*) St Martin.

— The Cincinnati Reds Trivia Book. LC 92-44101. 1993. write for info. (*0-312-98736-6*) St Martin.

Neft, David S., jt. auth. see Carroll.

Neft, David S., jt. auth. see Cohen, Richard M.

Neft, N. & Levine, A. Where Women Stand: An International Report on the Status of Women in Over 140 Countries 1997 - 1998. LC 97-1728. 1997. pap. 20.00 (*0-679-78015-7*) Random Ref & Info.

Neftci, Salih N. An Introduction to the Mathematics of Financial Derivatives. LC 96-13492. (Illus.). 352p. 1996. text 49.95 (*0-12-515390-2*) Acad Pr.

***Neftci, Salih N.** Introduction to the Mathematics of Financial Derivatives. 2nd ed. 540p. 2000. 59.95 (*0-12-515392-9*) Acad Pr.

Neftci, Salih N., jt. auth. see Dunn, Robert M., Jr.

Nefzger, Carl. Traits of a Winner: The Formula for Developing Thoroughbred Racehorses. (Illus.). 320p. 1994. 30.00 (*0-929346-33-5*) R Meerdink Co Ltd.

Nega, Susan L., jt. photos by see Levinson, Joel B.

Negahban, Ezat O. Excavations at Haft Tepe, Iran. (University Museum Monographs: No. 70). (Illus.). xx, 156p. 1990. 75.00 (*0-934718-89-X*) U Museum Pubns.

— Marlik: The Complete Excavation Report. LC 94-32410. (University Museum Monographs: Vol. 87). (Illus.). 408p. 1996. 195.00 (*0-924171-32-4*) U Museum Pubns.

Negahban, Mehrdad, ed. Current Research in the Thermo-Mechanics of Polymers in the Rubbery-Glassy Range - 1995 Vol. 203: Current Research in the Thermo-Mechanics of Polymers in the Rubbery-Glassy Range - 1995. LC 95-77199. (1995 Joint ASME Applied Mechanics & Materials Summer Meeting Ser.: Vol. 203). 184p. 1995. 100.00 (*0-7918-1318-5*, H00950) ASME.

Negandhi, Anant R., ed. Interorganization Theory. LC 74-21887. 293p. reprint ed. pap. 90.90 (*0-7837-0503-4*, 204082700018) Bks Demand.

Negandhi, Arnant R. Advances in International Comparative Management: Beyond Theory Z, Suppl. 1. Farmer, Richard N. et al, eds. 206p. 1984. suppl. ed. 73.25 (*0-89232-445-7*) Jai Pr.

Negas, T., ed. see Symposium on Materials & Processes for Wireless Co, et al.

Negash, Tekeste. The Crisis of Ethiopian Education: Some Implications for Nation-Building. 112p. 1990. write for info. (*91-86744-40-2*, Pub. by Nordic Africa) Transaction Pubs.

— Eritrea & Ethiopia: The Federal Experience. LC 97-3089. 225p. 1997. pap. text 26.95 (*1-56000-992-6*) Transaction Pubs.

— Eritrea & Ethiopoa: The Federal Experience. 234p. 1997. 26.95 (*91-7106-406-0*, Pub. by Nordic Africa) Transaction Pubs.

— Italian Colonialism in Eritrea, 1882-1941: Policies, Praxis, & Impact. (Studia Historica Upsaliensia: No. 148). 217p. (Orig.). 1987. pap. 43.50 (*91-554-2111-3*, Pub. by Uppsala Univ Acta Univ Uppsaliensis) Coronet Bks.

— Rethinking Education in Ethiopia. LC 97-145766. 118p. (Orig.). 1996. pap. 37.50 (*91-7106-383-8*, Pub. by Nordisk Afrikainstitutet) Coronet Bks.

Negash, Tekeste & Rudebeck, Lars, eds. Dimensions of Development with Emphasis on Africa. 279p. 1995. write for info. (*91-7106-378-1*, Pub. by Nordic Africa) Transaction Pubs.

Negativland. Fair Use: The Story of the Letter U & the Numeral 2. LC 94-69077. (Illus.). 288p. (Orig.). 1995. pap. 19.95 (*0-9643496-0-4*) Seeland.

***Negbi, Moshe, ed.** Saffron: Crocus Sativus L. 172p. 1999. text 80.00 (*90-5702-394-6*, Harwood Acad Pubs) Gordon & Breach.

Negedly, R. Elsevier's Dictionary of Fishery, Processing, Fish & Shellfish Names of the World. (ENG, FRE, GER, LAT & SPA.). 632p. 1990. 250.00 (*0-444-88039-9*) Elsevier.

— Elsevier's Dictionary of Fishery, Processing, Fish & Shellfish Names of the World. (ENG, FRE, GER, LAT & SPA.). 624p. 1990. 295.00 (*0-8288-9214-8*) Fr & Eur.

Negele, J. W. & Vogt, E. Advances in Nuclear Physics, Vol. 18. LC 67-29001. (Illus.). 474p. (C). 1988. text 110.00 (*0-306-42700-1*, Kluwer Plenum) Kluwer Academic.

— Advances in Nuclear Physics, Vol. 19. (Illus.). 396p. (C). 1989. text 110.00 (*0-306-43046-0*, Kluwer Plenum) Kluwer Academic.

Negele, J. W. & Vogt, E. Advances in Nuclear Physics, Vol. 20. (Illus.). 500p. (C). 1991. text 110.00 (*0-306-43861-5*, Kluwer Plenum) Kluwer Academic.

Negele, J. W. & Vogt, E. Advances in Nuclear Physics, Vol. 21. (Illus.). 464p. (C). 1994. text 110.00 (*0-306-44548-4*, Kluwer Plenum) Kluwer Academic.

— Advances in Nuclear Physics, Vol. 22. (Illus.). 282p. (C). 1996. text 107.00 (*0-306-45157-3*, Kluwer Plenum) Kluwer Academic.

— Advances in Nuclear Physics, Vol. 23. (Illus.). 318p. (C). 1996. text 114.00 (*0-306-45220-0*, Kluwer Plenum) Kluwer Academic.

— Advances in Nuclear Physics, Vol. 24. (Illus.). 228p. (C). 1998. text 89.50 (*0-306-45757-1*, Kluwer Plenum) Kluwer Academic.

Negele, John W. & Orland, Henri. Quantum Many-Particle Systems. (Frontiers in Physics Ser.). (Illus.). 500p. (C). 1988. 54.95 (*0-201-12593-5*) Addison-Wesley.

Negele, John W. & Orlando, Henri. Quantum Many-Particle Systems. LC 98-88186. (Advanced Book Classics Ser.). 480p. 1998. pap. text 39.00 (*0-7382-0052-2*) Perseus Pubng.

Negele, John W. & Vogt, Erich, eds. Advances in Nuclear Physics, Vol. 16. LC 67-29001. 342p. 1985. 89.50 (*0-306-41997-1*, Plenum Trade) Perseus Pubng.

Negendank, Jorg F. & Zolitschka, Bernd, eds. Paleolimnology of European Maar Lakes. LC 93-4663. (Lecture Notes in Earth Sciences Ser.: Vol. 49). 1993. 126.95 (*0-387-56570-1*) Spr-Verlag.

— Paleolimnology of European Maar Lakes. (Lecture Notes in Earth Sciences Ser.: Vol. 49). (Illus.). x, 514p. 1993. pap. write for info. (*3-540-56570-1*) Spr-Verlag.

Negev, Abraham, ed. Dictionnaire Archeologique de la Bible.Tr. of Archeological Dictionary of the Bible. (FRE.). 350p. 1970. 75.00 (*0-8288-6510-8*, M-6117) Fr & Eur.

Negev, Avraham, ed. The Archaeological Encyclopedia of the Holy Land. 3rd ed. (Illus.). 420p. 1990. 29.95 (*0-13-044090-6*) Prntice Hall Bks.

Neggers, Carla. Bewitching. (Temptation Ser.). 1993. per. 2.99 (*0-373-25552-7*, 1-25552-0) Harlequin Bks.

***Neggers, Carla.** The Carriage House. 2001. mass mkt. 6.50 (*1-55166-790-8*, Mira Bks) Harlequin Bks.

Neggers, Carla. Claim the Crown. 1997. per. 5.50 (*1-55166-266-3*, 1-66266-7, Mira Bks) Harlequin Bks.

— Finders Keepers. (Men Made in America Ser.). 1994. pap. 3.99 (*0-373-45195-4*, 1-45195-4) Harlequin Bks.

— Finding You. 1996. mass mkt. 5.99 (*0-671-88320-8*) PB.

— The Groom Who (Almost) Got Away. (Yours Truly Ser.). 1996. per. 3.50 (*0-373-52022-0*, 1-52022-0) Silhouette.

— Just Before Sunrise. 1997. per. 5.99 (*0-671-88322-4*, Pocket Books) PB.

— Kiss the Moon. 384p. (Orig.). 1999. per. 5.99 (*1-55166-485-2*, 1-66485-3, Mira Bks) Harlequin Bks.

— Night Scents. 1997. per. 5.99 (*0-671-56769-1*) PB.

— Night Watch: Lovers & Legends. (Temptation Ser.). 1993. per. 2.99 (*0-373-25561-6*, 1-25561-1) Harlequin Bks.

— On Fire. 384p. 1999. per. 5.99 (*1-55166-541-7*, 1-66541-3, Mira Bks) Harlequin Bks.

— A Rare Chance. 1996. mass mkt. 5.99 (*0-671-88321-6*) PB.

***Neggers, Carla.** The Waterfall. 378p. 2000. per. 6.50 (*1-55166-582-4*, Mira Bks) Harlequin Bks.

— White Hot. 320p. 1998. mass mkt. 6.50 (*0-671-56770-5*, Pocket Books) PB.

Neggers, Carla. Wisconsin Wedding. (Tyler Ser.: No. 3). 1999. mass mkt. 3.99 (*0-373-82503-X*, 0-82503-4) Harlequin Bks.

Neggers, Carla, et al. Once upon a Time: Night Watch, A Wish... & a Kiss, the Missing Heir, 3 bks. in 1. rev. ed. (By Request Ser.). 1999. per. 6.99 (*0 373 20159-1*, 1-20159-9) Harlequin Bks.

Neggers, Gladys. Vocabulario Culto. 2nd ed. (SPA.). 168p. 1977. pap. 17.95 (*0-8288-5535-8*, S50023) Fr & Eur.

Neggers, Joseph. Basic Posets. 1998. 28.00 (*981-02-3589-5*) World Scientific Pub.

Neggi, Dwijendra N. Sacred Tales of India. (C). 1991. reprint ed. 8.50 (*0-685-48886-1*, Pub. by Asian Educ Servs) S Asia.

Negi, Jagmohan. Travel Agency & Tour Operation: Concepts & Principles. (C). 1997. 58.00 (*81-7391-177-0*, Pub. by Abhinav) S Asia.

Negi, S. S. Biodiversity & Its Conservation in India. (C). 1993. 31.00 (*81-85182-88-4*, Pub. by Indus Pub) S Asia.

— A Dictionary of Forestry. (C). 1988. 80.00 (*81-7136-010-6*, Pub. by Periodical Expert) St Mut.

— Elements of General Silviculture. 316p. 1988. 115.00 (*81-7089-092-6*, Pub. by Intl Bk Distr) St Mut.

— Forest Policy & Law. 261p. 1997. pap. 113.00 (*81-7089-244-9*, Pub. by Intl Bk Distr) St Mut.

— Forest Types of India, Nepal & Bhutan. (C). 1989. 200.00 (*81-7136-012-2*, Pub. by Periodical Expert) St Mut.

— Forestry in India, 2 vols. Incl. Forestry in India Vol. 1: Research, Extension, Training & Education. 237p. 1997. pap. 213.00 (*81-7533-035-X*, Pub. by Print Hse); Forestry in India Vol. 2: Administration, Organization, Policy & Legislation. 213p. 1997. pap. 175.00 (*81-7533-046-5*, Pub. by Print Hse); 450p. 1997. Set pap. 390.00 (*81-7533-047-3*, Pub. by Print Hse) St Mut.

— Forestry in SAARC Countries. (C). 1992. 225.00 (*81-7136-035-1*, Pub. by Periodical Expert) St Mut.

— Forestry Research in Tropical Asia-Pacific. 228p. 1995. pap. 150.00 (*81-85880-80-8*, Pub. by Print Hse) St Mut.

— Forests & Forestry in Nepal. (Illus.). 205p. (C). 1994. 20.00 (*81-7024-581-8*, Pub. by Ashish Pub Hse) Nataraj Bks.

— Forests for Socio-Economic & Rural Development in India. LC 95-911606. 222p. 1996. pap. 162.50 (*81-85880-99-9*, Pub. by Print Hse) St Mut.

— Fundamentals of Forestry Vol. 3: Introductory Soil Science. 101p. (C). 1983. 60.00 (*0-7855-3248-X*, Pub. by Scientific) St Mut.

— Fundamentals of Silviculture. (C). 1987. 95.00 (*0-7855-3107-6*, Pub. by Intl Bk Distr) St Mut.

— Garhwal: The Land & People. (C). 1994. 20.00 (*81-85182-91-4*, Pub. by Indus Pub) S Asia.

— Geo-Botany of India. (C). 1986. 75.00 (*81-7136-005-X*, Pub. by Periodical Expert) St Mut.

Negi, S. S. Handbook of Forest. 690p. (C). 1986. 175.00 (*0-7855-3108-4*, Pub. by Intl Bk Distr) St Mut.

Negi, S. S. Handbook of Forest Ecology & Biology. 1994. pap. 200.00 (*81-7089-146-9*, Pub. by Intl Bk Distr) St Mut.

— A Handbook of Forest Protection. 1995. pap. 70.00 (*81-7089-234-1*, Pub. by Intl Bk Distr) St Mut.

— Handbook of Forestry. 690p. 1986. 90.00 (*0-7855-6543-4*, Pub. by Intl Bk Distr) St Mut.

— Handbook of Forestry. 690p. (C). 1986. 275.00 (*0-7855-6879-4*, Pub. by Intl Bk Distr); text 175.00 (*0-7855-6590-6*, Pub. by Intl Bk Distr) St Mut.

— Handbook of National Parks, Sanctuaries & Bisphere Reserves in India. (C). 1991. 25.00 (*81-85182-59-0*, Pub. by Indus Pub) S Asia.

— Handbook of Social Forestry. 178p. 1986. 75.00 (*0-7855-6542-6*, Pub. by Intl Bk Distr) St Mut.

— Handbook of Social Forestry. 178p. (C). 1986. 150.00 (*0-7855-6878-6*, Pub. by Intl Bk Distr); text 110.00 (*0-7855-6591-4*, Pub. by Intl Bk Distr) St Mut.

Negi, S. S. Handbook of Social Forestry. 178p. (C). 1986. 100.00 (*81-7089-037-3*, Pub. by Intl Bk Distr) St Mut.

Negi, S. S. A Handbook of the Himalaya. (C). 1990. 58.50 (*81-85182-35-3*, Pub. by Indus Pub) S Asia.

— Himachal Pradesh: The Land & People. (C). 1993. 24.00 (*81-85182-90-6*, Pub. by Indus Pub) S Asia.

— Himalayan Fishes & Fisheries. LC 94-905651. (Illus.). v, 291p. 1994. 32.00 (*81-7024-638-5*, Pub. by Ashish Pub Hse) Nataraj Bks.

— Himalayan Forests & Forestry. (C). 1990. 48.00 (*81-85182-44-2*, Pub. by Indus Pub) S Asia.

— Himalayan Rivers, Lakes & Glaciers. (C). 1991. 20.00 (*81-85182-61-2*, Pub. by Indus Pub) S Asia.

— Himalayan Wildlife: Habitat & Conservation. (C). 1992. 24.00 (*81-85182-68-X*, Pub. by Indus Pub) S Asia.

***Negi, S. S.** Indian Forestry 1947-1997. 1998. pap. 120.00 (*81-7089-253-8*, Pub. by Intl Bk Distr) St Mut.

Negi, S. S. Indian Forestry Through the Ages. (C). 1995. 28.00 (*81-7387-020-9*, Pub. by Indus Pub) S Asia.

— India's Forests, Forestry & Wildlife. (C). 1994. text 48.00 (*81-7387-010-1*, Pub. by Indus Pub) S Asia.

— An Introduction to Forest Pathology. 285p. 1996. pap. 99.00 (*81-7089-240-6*, Pub. by Intl Bk Distr) St Mut.

— Managing the Himalayan Environment. (C). 1986. 75.00 (*81-7136-006-8*, Pub. by Periodical Expert) St Mut.

— Manual of Wildlife in India. 1993. pap. 175.00 (*81-7089-166-3*, Pub. by Intl Bk Distr) St Mut.

— Minor Forest Products. (C). 1992. 125.00 (*81-7136-038-6*, Pub. by Periodical Expert) St Mut.

— Operation Pushpak. (C). 1987. 45.00 (*81-7136-008-4*, Pub. by Periodical Expert) St Mut.

— Principal of Land Management & Soil Conservation. (C). 1991. 170.00 (*81-7136-016-5*, Pub. by Periodical Expert) St Mut.

— Tribal Development & Administration, 1986. 167p. (C). 1986. 125.00 (*81-7089-038-1*, Pub. by Intl Bk Distr) St Mut.

— Tribal Welfare Development & Administration. 167p. (C). 1986. text 125.00 (*0-7855-6592-2*, Pub. by Intl Bk Distr) St Mut.

— Uttarakhand: Land & People. LC 95-901624. 149p. 1995. pap. 100.00 (*81-85880-73-5*, Pub. by Print Hse) St Mut.

Negi, S. S., ed. Forests & Forestry in Nepal. 1994. pap. 60.00 (*0-7855-0442-7*, Pub. by Ratna Pustak Bhandar) St Mut.

Negi, S. S. & Naithani, H. B. Oaks of India, Nepal & Bhutan. LC 95-911159. 1995. pap. 90.00 (*81-7089-233-3*, Pub. by Intl Bk Distr) St Mut.

Negishi, Kazuki, et al. Tadao Ando: Dormant Lines. (Illus.). 48p. 1991. 30.00 (*0-614-14666-6*) Harvard Univ Graduate Schl of.

Negishi, Takashi. Economic Theories in a Non-Walrasian Tradition. (Historical Perspectives on Modern Economics Ser.). (Illus.). 208p. 1985. text 80.00 (*0-521-25967-3*) Cambridge U Pr.

— Economic Theories in a Non-Walrasian Tradition. (Historical Perspectives on Modern Economics Ser.). (Illus.). 224p. (C). 1989. pap. text 25.95 (*0-521-37860-5*) Cambridge U Pr.

***Negishi, Takashi.** Economic Thought from Smith to Keyes. LC 00-34120. (Collected Essays of Takashi Negishi Ser.). 2000. write for info. (*1-85898-764-4*) E Elgar.

Negishi, Takashi. General Equilibrium Theory: The Collected Essays of Takashi Negishi, Vol. I. (Economists of the Twentieth Century Ser.). 448p. 1994. 110.00 (*1-85278-937-9*) E Elgar.

— History of Economic Theory. (Advanced Textbooks in Economics Ser.: No. 26). 398p. 1989. 75.00 (*0-444-70437-X*, North Holland) Elsevier.

— The History of Economics: The Collected Essays of Takashi Negishi, Vol. II. (Economists of the Twentieth Century Ser.). 272p. 1994. 95.00 (*1-85278-938-7*) E Elgar.

Negishi, Takashi, jt. auth. see Itoh, Motoshige.

Negley, Betty J. Divine Legacy. LC 96-176695. 256p. (Orig.). 1996. pap. 10.99 (*1-56043-273-X*, Treasure Hse) Destiny Image.

Negley, Brooke. The World by the Tail. LC 99-71051. x, 244p. 1999. pap. 15.95 (*0-934955-38-7*) Watercress Pr.

Negley, Glenn R. Political Authority & Moral Judgement. LC 65-13654. 173p. reprint ed. pap. 53.70 (*0-608-11981-4*, 202342700033) Bks Demand.

Negley, Oka, ed. see Bane, William F.

Negley-Parker, Esther, jt. auth. see Araoz, Daniel L.

Negley, Sandra. Crossing the Bridge: A Journey in Self-Esteem, Relationships & Life Balance. LC 97-61641. (Illus.). 128p. 1997. pap., spiral bd. 29.95 (*0-9622022-9-0*) Wellness Reprodns.

Neglia, Herminio G. & Ordaz, Luis. Repertorio Selecto del Teatro Hispanoamericano Contemporaneo. LC 79-15199. 110p. 1982. 22.50 (*0-87918-042-0*) ASU Lat Am St.

Neglia, J. P., jt. auth. see Cheremisinoff, Nicholas P.

Negm, Maged. The Tomb of Simut (Kyky) Theban Tomb 409 at Qurnah. (Illus.). 120p. 1997. pap. 80.00 (*0-85668-698-0*) David Brown.

***Negnevitsky, Michael.** Intelligent Systems. (Illus.). 352p. 2001. pap. 47.95 (*0-7506-4905-4*) Buttrwrth-Heinemann.

Negoesco, Stephen. Soccer. 144p. (C). 1992. text. write for info. (*0-697-10059-6*) Brown & Benchmark.

Negoita, Constantin V. The Cybernetic Conspiracy: Mind over Matter. LC 88-80257. 144p. 1988. pap. 8.95 (*0-941404-69-2*) New Falcon Pubns.

***Negoita, Constantin V.** Fuzzy Sets. LC 99-69396. 160p. 2000. pap. 12.95 (*1-56184-146-3*) New Falcon Pubns.

Negoita, Constantin V. Fuzzy Systems, Vol. 2. (Cybernetics & Systems Ser., Abacus Bks.). (Illus.). viii, 112p. 1981. text 85.00 (*0-85626-164-5*) Gordon & Breach.

Negoita, Constantin V., ed. Cybernetics & Applied Systems. (Illus.). 376p. 1992. text 185.00 (*0-8247-8677-7*) Dekker.

Negovskii, Vladimir A. Acute Problems in Resuscitation & Hypothermia: Proceedings of a Symposium on the Application of Deep Hypothermia in Terminal States, Sept. 15-19, 1964. Haigh, Basil, tr. from RUS. LC 65-20214. 98p. reprint ed. pap. 30.40 (*0-8357-5090-6*, 202066700018) Bks Demand.

— Resuscitation & Artificial Hypothermia. Haigh, Basil, tr. LC 62-21589. 328p. reprint ed. pap. 101.70 (*0-608-30223-6*, 202065800018) Bks Demand.

Negre, Herve. Petit Larousse de la Medecine, Vol. 1. (FRE.). 975p. 1988. pap. 19.95 (*0-7859-4845-7*) Fr & Eur.

Negreiros, Almada, jt. illus. see Levine, David.

Negrepontis, S., jt. auth. see Comfort, W. W.

Negrete, Omar Ibanez, tr. see Brooks, Thomas.

Negrete, Omar Ibanez, tr. see Burroughs, Jeremiah.

Negrete, Omar Ibanez, tr. see Flavel, John.

Negrete, Omar Ibanez, tr. see Montgomery, Thomas.

Negrete, Omar Ibanez, tr. see Montgomery, Thomas, ed.

Negrete, Omar Ibanez, tr. see Owen, John.

Negrete, Omar Ibanez, tr. see Pink, A. W.

Negrete, Omar Ibanez, tr. see Ryle, J. C.

Negrey, Cynthia. Gender, Time, & Reduced Work. LC 92-11955. (SUNY Series in the Sociology of Work). (Illus.). 148p. (C). 1993. text 64.50 (*0-7914-1407-8*); pap. text 21.95 (*0-7914-1408-6*) State U NY Pr.

Negri. Marx Beyond Marx. (C). 1996. 80.95 (*0-7453-0575-X*); pap. 23.00 (*0-7453-0576-8*) Westview.

Negri, Antonio. Insurgencies: Constituent Power & the Modern State. LC 99-30982. (Theory Out of Bounds Ser.: Vol. 15). 344p. 1999. pap. 25.95 (*0-8166-2275-2*, Pub. by U of Minn Pr); lib. bdg. 64.95 (*0-8166-2274-4*, Pub. by U of Minn Pr) Chicago Distribution Ctr.

— Marx Beyond Marx: Lessons on the Grundrisse. Orig. Title: Marx Oltre Marx. 248p. 1991. pap. 10.00 (*0-936756-25-X*) Autonomedia.

— The Politics of Subversion: A Manifesto for the Twenty-First Century. Newell, James, tr. 200p. 1989. text 61.95 (*0-7456-0601-6*) Blackwell Pubs.

***Negri, Antonio.** The Politics of Subversion: A Manifesto for the Twenty-First Century. Newell, James, tr. 232p. 2000. reprint ed. text 25.00 (*0-7881-6969-6*) DIANE Pub.

Negri, Antonio. The Savage Anomaly: The Power of Spinoza's Metaphysics & Politics. Hardt, Michael, tr. & frwd. by. 284p. 1990. pap. 19.95 (*0-8166-1877-1*) U of Minn Pr.

***Negri, Antonio.** Savage Anomaly: The Power of Spinoza's Metaphysics & Politics. 2000. pap. 19.95 (*0-8166-3670-2*) U of Minn Pr.

Negri, Antonio, jt. auth. see Hardt, Michael.

Negri, Cesare. Le Gratie d'Amore. fac. ed. (Monuments of Music & Music Literature in Facsimile, II Ser.: Vol. 141). (Illus.). 1969. lib. bdg. 75.00 (*0-8450-2341-1*) Broude.

Negri, Paul, ed. Civil War Poetry: An Anthology. LC 97-20645. (Dover Thrift Editions Ser.). (Illus.). 128p. 1998. pap. 1.50 (*0-486-29883-3*) Dover.

— English Victorian Poetry: An Anthology. LC 99-10649. (Thrift Editions Ser.). 256p. 1999. pap. 2.00 (*0-486-40425-0*) Dover.

— Great Sonnets. LC 94-6460. 112p. (Orig.). 1994. pap. 1.00 (*0-486-28052-7*) Dover.

Negri, Paul & Dover Staff, eds. Civil War Stories & Poems, 5 bks. 544p. 1998. pap., boxed set 5.50 (*0-486-29994-5*) Dover.

Negri, Richard F., ed. Tales of Canyonlands Cowboys. LC 97-4900. 240p. (Orig.). 1997. pap. 17.95 (*0-87421-229-4*) Utah St U Pr.

Tales of Canyonlands Cowboys. LC 97-4900. 240p. (Orig.). 1997. 34.95 (*0-87421-231-6*) Utah St U Pr.

Negri, Romana. The Newborn in the Intensive Care Unit: A Neuropsychoanalytic Prevention Model. 288p. 1994. pap. text 32.00 (*1-85575-073-2*, Pub. by H Karnac Bks Ltd) Other Pr LLC.

— The Newborn in the Intensive Care Unit: A Neuropsychoanalytic Prevention Model. 285p. 1994. pap. text 34.95 (*0-614-07215-8*, Pub. by H Karnac Bks Ltd) Brunner-Mazel.

N

Negri, Sam. Arizona: The Beauty of It All. 3rd ed. LC 96-84047. (Illus.). 96p. 2000. 24.95 (*0-916179-58-3*) Ariz Hwy.

Negri, Sharon. The Other Side of Now. LC 88-26870. 72p. (Orig.). 1989. pap. 7.00 (*0-931846-35-8*) Wash Writers Pub.

— Ruby & Other Lives: Poems by Sharon Negri. Baker, R. D., ed. (Poetry Chapbook Ser.). (Illus.). 28p. (Orig.). 1996. pap. 4.00 (*1-887641-11-4*) Argonne Hotel Pr.

Negri, Toni. Revolution Retrieved: Writings on Marx, Keynes, Capitalist Crisis & New Social Subjects (1967-83) (Red Notes Italy Archive Ser.: Vol. 1). 274p. (Orig.). 1988. pap. 22.00 (*0-906305-10-1*, Pub. by Red Notes) AK Pr Dist.

Negri, Toni, jt. auth. see Guattari, Felix.

Negri Zamagni, Vera, jt. auth. see Engwall, Lars.

Negrin, Howard, jt. ed. see Lightman, Marjorie.

***Negrin, Maria Luisa.** El Circulo del Exilio y la Enajenacion en la Obra de Reinaldo Arenas. LC 99-48754. (Hispanic Literature Ser.: Vol. 50). 188p. 2000. text 79.95 (*0-7734-7909-0*) E Mellen.

Negrin, Salvador. El Divorcio No Es la Solucion.Tr. of Divorce Is Not the Solution. (SPA.). 96p. 1994. 7.99 (*0-88113-267-5*, B065-2675) Caribe Betania.

Negrin Sosa, Lourdes, et al. Revision Taxonomica de Sideritis L. Subgenera Marrubiastrum (Moench) Mend.-Heuer (Endemismo Macaronesico) (Phanerogamarum Monographiae Ser.: Tomus XX). (GER., Illus.). 328p. 1992. 95.00 (*3-443-78002-4*, Pub. by Gebruder Borntraeger) Balogh.

Negrin, Su. Begin at Start: Some Thoughts on Personal Liberation & World Change. LC 72-87031. (Illus.). 176p. (Orig.). 1972. 15.95 (*0-87810-520-4*); pap. 7.95 (*0-87810-020-2*) Times Change.

Negrin, Su, ed. The Great Harmony: Teachings & Observations of the Way of the Universe. LC 77-77387. (Illus.). 128p. (Orig.). 1977. pap. 5.95 (*0-87810-033-4*) Times Change.

Negrine. Television & Press since 1945. 208p. 2000. text 79.95 (*0-7190-4920-2*, Pub. by Manchester Univ Pr); pap. text 29.95 (*0-7190-4921-0*, Pub. by Manchester Univ Pr) St Martin.

Negrine, Ralph M. The Communication of Politics. 240p. 1996. 69.95 (*0-8039-7738-7*); pap. 22.95 (*0-8039-7739-5*) Sage.

— The Internationalisation of Television. 1991. text 54.00 (*0-86187-761-6*) St Martin.

— Parliament & the Media: A Study of Britain, Germany & France. LC 97-52202. (Chatham House Papers Ser.). 140p. 1998. 44.95 (*1-85567-555-2*, Pub. by P P Pubs); pap. 15.95 (*1-85567-556-0*, Pub. by P P Pubs) Cassell & Continuum.

— Politics & the Mass Media in Britain. (Illus.). 284p. 1989. 45.00 (*0-415-01529-4*, A3282); pap. 17.95 (*0-415-01530-8*, A3286) Routledge.

Negrine, Ralph M., ed. Satellite Broadcasting: The Politics & Implications of the New Media. 320p. 1988. lib. bdg. 65.00 (*0-415-00109-9*) Routledge.

Negrini, R., et al. Fault Tolerance Through Reconfiguration in VLSI & WSI Arrays. (Computer Systems Ser.). 320p. 1989. 47.50 (*0-262-14044-6*) MIT Pr.

Negrino, Tom. Microsoft Office 98 for Macs for Dummies. LC HF5548.4.M525N43. 384p. 1998. pap. 19.99 (*0-7645-0229-8*) IDG Bks.

***Negrino, Tom.** Microsoft Office "X" for Macs for Dummies. (For Dummies Ser.). (Illus.). 384p. 2000. pap. 19.99 (*0-7645-0702-8*) IDG Bks.

Negrino, Tom. Quicken 98 for Macintosh: Visual QuickStart Guide. LC 99-162315. (Visual QuickStart Guide Ser.). 168p. (C). 1998. pap. text 16.99 (*0-201-35401-2*, Pub. by Peachpit Pr) Addison-Wesley.

— Quicken 99 for Windows: Visual QuickStart Guide. LC 99-219513. (Visual QuickStart Guide Ser.). (Illus.). 256p. 1999. pap. 16.99 (*0-201-35426-8*, Pub. by Peachpit Pr) Addison-Wesley.

***Negrino, Tom.** Quicken 2000 for Macintosh: Visual QuickStart Guide. 2nd ed. (Visual QuickStart Guide Ser.). 256p. (C). 1999. pap. text, student ed. 16.99 (*0-201-69964-8*) Peachpit Pr.

— Quicken 2000 for Windows: Visual QuickStart Guide. 2nd ed. (Visual QuickStart Guide Ser.). 256p. (C). 1999. pap. text, teacher ed. 16.99 (*0-201-69965-6*) Peachpit Pr.

Negrino, Tom & Smith, Dori. JavaScript for the World Wide Web: Visual QuickStart Guide. 2nd ed. LC 98-137901. 208p. (C). 1997. pap. text 17.95 (*0-201-69648-7*) Peachpit Pr.

***Negrino, Tom & Smith, Dori.** JavaScript for the World Wide Web: Visual QuickStart Guide. 3rd ed. LC 99-461837. (Visual QuickStart Guides Ser.). (Illus.). 304p. (C). 1999. pap. 17.99 (*0-201-35463-2*) Peachpit Pr.

Negro, A., Jr. & Ferreira, A. A., eds. Tunnels & Metropolises: Proceedings of the World Tunnel Congress '98, 2 vols. (Illus.). 1264p. (C). 1998. text 201.00 (*90-5410-936-X*, Pub. by A A Balkema) Ashgate Pub Co.

***Negro, Brujo.** Voodoo Sorcery Grimoire: Voodoo Course. (Illus.). 140p. 2000. 50.00 (*1-57179-076-4*) Intern Guild ASRS.

Negro, J. M. Del, see Stevenson, D. & Del Negro, J. M.

Negro, Pavon D., ed. see Mill, John Stuart.

Negro, Sergio P. Times & Seasons: Homilies for the Church Year. LC 94-76370. (Illus.). 200p. 1994. pap. 15.00 (*0-9641404-9-7*, WordWrks) Sixth St Pr.

***Negro, Sergio P.** Times & Seasons Vol. II: Homilies for Church Year B. Young, Sharon M., ed. (Illus.). 256p. 1999. pap. 20.00 (*0-9641404-6-2*, WordWrks) Sixth St Pr.

Negro-Vilar, Andrea & Conn, P. Michael. Peptide Hormones: Effects & Mechanisms of Action, Vol. 3. 224p. 1988. 125.00 (*0-8493-6721-2*, CRC Reprint) Franklin.

Negro-Vilar, Andrea & Conn, P. Michael, eds. Peptide Hormones: Effects & Mechanisms of Action, Vol. 1. LC 87-35530. 272p. 1988. 167.00 (*0-8493-6719-0*, QP572, CRC Reprint) Franklin.

— Peptide Hormones: Effects & Mechanisms of Action, Vol. II. 224p. 1988. 148.00 (*0-8493-6720-4*, CRC Reprint) Franklin.

Negro-Vilar, Andres, ed. Male Reproduction & Fertility. LC 81-40374. 406p. 1983. reprint ed. pap. 125.90 (*0-608-00446-4*, 206116100007) Bks Demand.

Negro-Vilar, Andres & Horowitz, Kathryn B., eds. Endocrine Aspects of Cancer. (Illus.). 256p. 1993. pap. 15.00 (*1-879225-10-7*) Endocrine Soc.

Negro-Vilar, Andres, jt. ed. see Bikle, Daniel E.

Negron, Chuck. Three Dog Nightmare. (Illus.). 256p. 1999. 22.95 (*1-58063-040-5*) Renaissance.

***Negron, Chuck.** Three Dog Nightmare. 368p. 2000. pap. text 15.95 (*1-58063-155-X*) Renaissance.

Negron De Montilla, Aida. Americanization in Puerto Rico & the Public School System, 1900-1930. 282p. 1975. 5.00 (*0-8477-2727-0*) U of PR Pr.

Negron-Muntaner, Frances & Grosfoguel, Ramon, eds. Puerto Rican Jam: Rethinking Colonialism & Nationalism. LC 97-9569. 256p. (C). 1997. pap. 19.95 (*0-8166-2849-1*); text 49.95 (*0-8166-2848-3*) U of Minn Pr.

Negron-Portillo, Mariano & Mayo-Santana, Raul. La Esclavitud Urbana en San Juan de Puerto Rico. LC 92-72980. (SPA., Illus.). 137p. (Orig.). (C). 1992. pap. 7.50 (*0-929157-19-2*) Ediciones Huracan.

Negron, Victor E. Copani. LC 95-83837. 1996. pap. 19.95 (*1-884092-03-9*) R Altschuler.

Negroni & Winston PLLC Staff, jt. auth. see RSM McGladrey Inc. Staff.

Negroni, Andrea L. & Platt, Larry. Residential Mortgage Lending: State Regulation Manual, 6 vols. 1990. 275.00 (*0-685-74210-5*) West Group.

Negroni, Christine. Deadly Departure. pap. 13.00 (*0-06-093265-1*) HarpC.

— Deadly Departure: Why the Experts Failed to Prevent the TWA 800 Disaster & How It Could Happen Again. 272p. 2000. 25.00 (*0-06-019477-4*, Cliff Street) HarperTrade.

Negroni, Francois de & Moncel, Corinne. Suicidologe - Dictionnaire Suicides Celebres. (FRE.). 576p. 1997. 69.95 (*0-320-00484-8*) Fr & Eur.

Negroni, Iraida. El Gran Dilema Humano: La Vida, Complicada e Incomprendida. (SPA., Illus.). 372p. (Orig.). (C). 1988. pap. 12.00 (*0-9620054-0-1*) I Negroni.

Negroni, Maria, tr. see Ransome, Arthur.

Negroni, Maria, tr. see Scieszka, Jon.

Negroni, Maria, tr. see Shulevitz, Uri.

Negroni, Maria, tr. see Steig, William.

Negroponte, Nicholas. Being Digital. Asher, Marty, ed. LC 94-45971. 256p. 1995. 28.00 (*0-679-43919-6*) Vin Bks.

— Being Digital. Asher, Marty, ed. LC 94-45971. 256p. 1996. pap. 12.00 (*0-679-76290-6*) Vin Bks.

Negrotti, M., ed. Understanding the Artificial: On the Future Shape of Artificial Intelligence. (Artificial Intelligence & Society Ser.). (Illus.). xi, 164p. 1991. pap. 69.00 (*0-387-19612-9*) Spr-Verlag.

***Negrotti, Massimo.** Theory of the Artificial: Virtual Replications & the Revenge of Reality. LC 99-487829. 160p. 1999. 24.95 (*1-871516-55-2*, Pub. by Intellect) Intl Spec Bk.

Negrutiu, I. & Gharti-Chhetri, G., eds. A Laboratory Guide to Cellular & Molecular Techniques for Higher Plants. (Biomethods Ser.: Vol. 4). 392p. 1991. 174.50 (*0-8176-2542-9*) Birkhauser.

Negrutiu, Radu. Elastic Analysis of Slab Structures. 1987. text 261.50 (*90-247-3367-7*) Kluwer Academic.

Negt, Oskar & Kluge, Alexander. Public Sphere & Experience: Analysis of the Bourgeois & Proletarian Public Sphere. Labanyi, Peter et al, trs. LC 93-610. (Theory & History of Literature Ser.: Vol. 85). 327p. (C). 1993. 44.95 (*0-8166-2031-8*) U of Minn Pr.

Negulescu, Ioan A., jt. auth. see Uglea, Constantin V.

***Negus, Christopher.** Caldera OpenLinux Bible. (Illus.). 900p. 2000. pap. text 39.99 (*0-7645-4706-2*) IDG Bks.

— Red Hat Linux Bible. LC 99-48375. 700p. 1999. pap. 39.99 (*0-7645-4574-4*) IDG Bks.

Negus, David, et al, eds. Phlebology, '95: Proceedings of the XII World Congress Union Internationale de Phlebologie, 2 vols. 1264p. 1996. 190.00 (*3-540-19999-3*) Spr-Verlag.

Negus, Joan. Astro-Alchemy: Making the Most of Your Transits. 156p. 1985. pap. 9.95 (*0-917086-82-1*) ACS Pubns.

— Basic Astrology: A Workbook for Students. 64p. 1978. pap. 6.95 (*0-917086-15-5*) ACS Pubns.

— Interpreting Composite & Relationship Charts. 16p. 1985. pap. 3.95 (*0-917086-71-6*) ACS Pubns.

***Negus, Keith.** Music Genres & Corporate Cultures. LC 98-51909. 1999. pap. 22.99 (*0-415-17400-7*); text. write for info. (*0-415-17399-X*) Routledge.

— Popular Music in Theory: An Introduction. LC 96-61301. (Music - Culture Ser.). 249p. 1996. pap. text 19.95 (*0-8195-6310-2*, Wesleyan Univ Pr) U Pr of New Eng.

Negus, Keith. Producing Pop: Culture & Conflict in the Popular Music Industry. 192p. 1995. pap. text 16.95 (*0-340-57512-3*, B0097, Pub. by E A) OUP.

Negus, Kenneth. Grimmelshausen. LC 73-17215. (Twayne's World Authors Ser.). (GER.). 178p. (C). 1974. lib. bdg. 17.95 (*0-8057-2405-2*) Irvington.

Negwer, Martin. Organic-Chemical Drugs & Their Synonyms: An International Survey, 4 vols., Set. 7th ed. LC 94-27326. 3952p. 1994. text 925.00 (*3-527-40040-0*, Pub. by Akademie Verlag) Wiley.

NEHA Staff, jt. auth. see EPA Staff.

Nehamas, Alexander. The Art of Living: Socratic Reflections from Plato to Foucault. LC 97-25834. (Sather Classical Lectures Ser.). 356p. 1998. 45.00 (*0-520-21173-1*, Pub. by U CA Pr) Cal Prin Full Svc.

***Nehamas, Alexander.** The Art of Living: Socratic Reflections from Plato to Foucault. 294p. 2000. pap. 17.95 (*0-520-22490-6*, Pub. by U CA Pr) Cal Prin Full Svc.

Nehamas, Alexander. Nietzsche: Life As Literature. LC 85-5589. 240p. 1985. 29.95 (*0-674-62435-1*) HUP.

— Nietzsche: Life as Literature. LC 85-5589. 240p. 1985. pap. 17.95 (*0-674-62426-2*) HUP.

— Virtues of Authenticity: Essays on Plato & Socrates. LC 98-7109. 376p. 1998. text 65.00 (*0-691-00177-4*, Pub. by Princeton U Pr) Cal Prin Full Svc.

***Nehamas, Alexander.** Virtues of Authenticity: Essays on Plato & Socrates. LC 98-7109. 358p. 1998. pap. text 21.95 (*0-691-00178-2*, Pub. by Princeton U Pr) Cal Prin Full Svc.

Nehamas, Alexander, jt. ed. see Furley, David J.

Nehamas, Alexander, tr. see Plato.

Nehaniv, Chrystopher L., jt. auth. see International Workshop on Mathematical & Computational Staff.

Nehaniv, C., et al, eds. Computer for Metaphors, Analogy & Agents. LC 99-15708. (Lecture Notes in Artificial Intelligence Ser.: Vol. 1562). x, 389p. 1999. pap. 62.00 (*3-540-65959-5*) Spr-Verlag.

Nehaniv, C. L. & Ito, M., eds. Algebraic Engineering: Proceedings of the 1st International Conference on Semigroups & Algebraic Engineering University of Kyoto, Japan 18-21 March 1997; Proceedings of the Workshop on Formal Languages & Computer Systems University of Aizu, Japan 24-28 March 1997. LC 99-25180. 650p. 1998. 128.00 (*981-02-3667-0*) World Scientific Pub.

Nehari, Zeev. Conformal Mapping. LC 74-27513. (Illus.). 396p. 1975. reprint ed. pap. text 10.95 (*0-486-61137-X*) Dover.

***Nehemiah Progressive Housing Development Corporation, Inc. Staff.** The New Homeowner's Handbook: What to Do after You Move In. 2000. pap. 13.95 (*0-7931-3818-3*) Dearborn.

Nehemkis, Peter, jt. auth. see Eells, Richard.

Neher, et al. Public Communication: Rhetoric & Leadership. 352p. (C). 1998. per. 54.95 (*0-7872-5267-0*) Kendall-Hunt.

Neher, Andre. They Made Their Souls Anew: Ils Ont Refait Leur Ame. Maisel, David, tr. LC 89-38685. (SUNY Series in Modern Jewish Literature & Culture). 179p. (C). 1990. text 21.50 (*0-7914-0315-7*) State U NY Pr.

Neher, Andrew. The Psychology of Transcendence. 384p. 1990. pap. 12.95 (*0-486-26167-0*) Dover.

Neher, Barbara L. From the Kitchen of the Royal Chef. (Illus.). 200p. (Orig.). 1985. ring bd. 14.95 (*0-685-10568-7*) Directed Media.

***Neher, Clark.** Southeast Asia: Crossroads of the World, Edition 2000. (Illus.). 2000. pap. text 14.95 (*1-891134-06-X*) SE Asia.

— Southeast Asia: Crossroads of the World, Pilot Edition. (Illus.). 125p. (C). 2000. pap. text 14.95 (*1-891134-03-5*) SE Asia.

Neher, Clark D. Politics in Southeast Asia. rev. ed. 322p. 1987. 24.95 (*0-87047-010-8*); pap. 18.95 (*0-87047-011-6*) Schenkman Bks Inc.

— Southeast Asia in the New International Era. 3rd ed. LC 98-15907. (Politics in Asia & the Pacific). 288p. 1998. pap. 28.00 (*0-8133-3390-3*, Pub. by Westview) HarpC.

Neher, Clark D., ed. Modern Thai Politics: From Village to Nation. LC 78-25917. 491p. 1979. reprint ed. pap., student ed. 152.30 (*0-608-05334-1*, 206503900012) Bks Demand.

Neher, Clark D. & Marlay, Ross. Democracy & Development in Southeast Asia: The Winds of Change. LC 95-23653. (C). 1995. pap. 25.00 (*0-8133-1985-4*, Pub. by Westview) HarpC.

Neher, Clark D., jt. auth. see Marlay, Ross.

Neher, Clark D., jt. ed. see Mungkandi, Wiwat.

Neher, Deborah A., jt. ed. see Francl, Leonard J.

Neher, E. Jordan Triple Systems by the Grid Approach. (Lecture Notes in Mathematics Ser.: Vol. 1280). xii, 193p. 1987. 38.95 (*0-387-18362-0*) Spr-Verlag.

Neher, E. C., tr. The Creative Power of Chance. LC 97-45250. 272p. 1998. 18.95 (*0-252-06686-3*); text 49.95 (*0-252-02386-2*) U of Ill Pr.

Neher, E. C., tr. see Lestienne, Remy.

Neher, Erwin, jt. ed. see Sakmann, Bert.

Neher, Evelyn. Four-Harness Huck. (Illus.). 40p. 1967. reprint ed. pap. text 10.00 (*0-9600854-1-6*) E Neher.

— Inkle. (Illus.). 313p. 1974. 25.00 (*0-9600854-2-4*) E Neher.

***Neher, Gabriele & Shepherd, Rupert.** Revaluing Renaissance Art. LC 00-25211. (Illus.). 2000. write for info. (*0-7546-0169-2*) Ashgate Pub Co.

Neher, James A. A Christian's Guide to Today's Catholic Charismatic Movement. vi, 134p. 1987. pap. 9.95 (*0-944788-99-8*) IBRI.

Neher, Philip A., et al, eds. Rights Based Fishing. (C). 1989. lib. bdg. 260.00 (*0-7923-0246-X*) Kluwer Academic.

***Neher, Ross.** Blindfolding the Muse: The Plight of Painting in the Age of Conceptual Art. Takiff, Michael, ed. (Illus.). 110p. 1999. pap. text 15.00 (*0-9671808-0-5*, Pub. by Prenom Pr) Ursus Bks.

Neher, William & Waite, David. The Business & Professional Communicator. (C). 1993. pap. text, teacher ed. write for info. (*0-205-14437-3*, H4437-3) Allyn.

Neher, William W. Organizational Communication: Challenges of Change, Diversity, & Continuity. 382p. 1996. 59.00 (*0-205-15006-3*) Allyn.

NEHGS Staff. The New England Historical & Genealogical Register, 1896, Vol. L. 612p. 1998. reprint ed. pap. 29.50 (*0-7884-0865-8*, NR50) Heritage Bk.

N.E.H.G.S. Staff. The New England Historical & Genealogical Register, Vol. 39. (Illus.). 425p. 1996. pap. 29.50 (*0-7884-0498-9*, NR39) Heritage Bk.

NEHGS Staff. The New England Historical & Genealogical Register, 1851, Vol. 5. 486p. 1857. reprint ed. pap. 25.00 (*1-55613-708-7*) Heritage Bk.

— The New England Historical & Genealogical Register, 1865 Vol. XIX, Vol. X. 394p. (Orig.). 1994. pap. 25.00 (*1-55613-976-4*) Heritage Bk.

— The New England Historical & Genealogical Register, 1866, XX. 398p. (Orig.). 1994. pap. 25.00 (*1-55613-977-2*) Heritage Bk.

— The New England Historical & Genealogical Register, 1874, Vol. 28. (Illus.). 500p. 1995. reprint ed. pap. text 25.00 (*0-7884-0194-7*) Heritage Bk.

— The New England Historical & Genealogical Register, 1875, Vol. 29. (Illus.). 513p. (Orig.). 1995. pap. text 25.00 (*0-7884-0195-5*) Heritage Bk.

N.E.H.G.S. Staff. The New England Historical & Genealogical Register, 1884, Vol. 38. (Illus.). 476p. 1996. pap. 29.50 (*0-7884-0497-0*, NR38) Heritage Bk.

NEHGS Staff. The New England Historical & Genealogical Register, 1897, Ll. 575p. 1998. pap. 29.50 (*0-7884-0866-6*, NR51) Heritage Bk.

— New England History & Genealogy Reg., 1872, Vol. 26. 464p. 1995. reprint ed. pap. text 25.00 (*0-7884-0126-2*) Heritage Bk.

NEHGS Staff, ed. The New England Historical & Genealogical Register, 1852, Vol. VI. 402p. 1852. reprint ed. pap. 25.00 (*1-55613-709-5*) Heritage Bk.

Nehil. Cultural Guide to the Global Village. 320p. (C). 1996. pap. text 45.00 (*0-536-59816-9*) Pearson Custom.

Nehl, Jans Peter. Principles of Administrative Procedure in EC Law. LC 98-198357. 220p. 1998. 45.00 (*1-84113-008-7*, Pub. by Hart Pub) Intl Spec Bk.

Nehlig. Childhood Epilepsies & Brain Development. 320p. 96.00 (*0-86196-578-7*, Pub. by J Libbey Med) Bks Intl VA.

Nehls, Edward, compiled by. D. H. Lawrence Vol. 2, 1919-1925: A Composite Biography. LC 57-9817. (Illus.). 559p. reprint ed. pap. 173.30 (*0-608-20459-5*, 207171100002) Bks Demand.

— D. H. Lawrence Vol. VI, 1885-1919: A Composite Biography. LC 57-9817. (Illus.). 640p. reprint ed. pap. 198.40 (*0-608-20458-7*, 207171100001) Bks Demand.

Nehls, H. Michael. The Colors of Christmas. Sherer, Michael L., ed. (Orig.). 1986. pap. 4.95 (*0-89536-838-2*, 6862) CSS OH.

Nehls, Harry B. Familiar Birds of the Northwest. 3rd ed. (Illus.). 184p. 1990. pap. 11.95 (*0-931686-08-3*) Audubon Soc Portland.

Nehls, Nadine, jt. auth. see Morgenbesser, Mel.

Nehlsen, Sonke-Peter. Nutzungsausfallersatz ein Notwendiges Ubel? Versuch einer Dogmatischen Begrundung und Alternativlosungen. (Aivilrechtliche Schriften Ser.: Bd. 11). (GER.). 237p. 1996. pap. 44.95 (*3-631-30773-X*) P Lang Pubng.

Nehmer, J., ed. Experiences with Distributed Systems. (Lecture Notes in Computer Science Ser.: Vol. 309). 292p. 1988. 36.00 (*0-387-19333-2*) Spr-Verlag.

Nehmsmann, Camille. Discover Hidden Treasure. 80p. 1998. pap. text 5.95 (*0-9657682-4-4*) Moriah Pr.

— Meet the God Who Loves You. 100p. 1998. pap. 6.95 (*0-9657682-2-8*) Moriah Pr.

— Power of Intercessory Prayer. 104p. 1998. pap. text 6.95 (*0-9657682-3-6*) Moriah Pr.

***Nehmzow, Ulrich.** Mobile Robotics: A Practical Introduction. LC 99-43763. (Applied Computing Ser.). xii, 244p. 1999. pap. 49.95 (*1-85233-173-9*, Pub. by Spr-Verlag) Spr-Verlag.

Nehr, Ellen. Doubleday Crime Club Compendium, 1928-1991. 1992. lib. bdg. 75.00 (*0-9634420-0-7*) Offspring Pr.

Nehring, James. The School Within Us: The Creation of an Innovative Public School. LC 97-37704. (SUNY Series, Restructuring & School Change). 234p. (C). 1998. text 34.50 (*0-7914-3589-X*); pap. text 10.95 (*0-7914-3590-3*) State U NY Pr.

— Why Do We Gotta Do This Stuff, Mr. Nehring? Notes from a Teacher's Day in School. LC 89-1352. 204p. 1989. 15.95 (*0-87131-574-2*) M Evans.

Nehring, Nancy. 50 Heirloom Buttons to Make. LC 95-51690. (Illus.). 128p. 1996. pap. 19.95 (*1-56158-146-1*, 070247) Taunton.

— The Lacy Knitting of Mary Schiffmann. LC 97-53191. 95p. 1998. pap. 17.95 (*1-883010-42-X*) Interweave.

— Ribbon Trims. LC 99-18060. 144p. 1999. 19.95 (*1-56158-308-1*) Taunton.

Nehring, Neil. Flowers in the Dustbin: Culture, Anarchy, & Postwar England. LC 92-42085. 416p. 1993. text 49.50 (*0-472-09526-9*, 09526) U of Mich Pr.

— Popular Music, Gender & Postmodernism: Anger Is an Energy. LC 97-4590. 240p. 1997. 48.00 (*0-7619-0835-8*); pap. 21.95 (*0-7619-0836-6*) Sage.

Nehring, Radine T. Dear Earth . . . A Love Letter from Spring Hollow. LC 94-28966. 176p. 1995. 17.95 (*0-9636620-2-3*) Brett Bks.

***Nehring, Ron.** Persecution of Microsoft Hurts Consumers. 1999. pap. write for info. (*1-57655-180-6*) Independ Inst.

***Nehring, Wendy M..** A History of Nursing in the Field of Mental Retardation & Development Disabilities. LC 99-41728. 205p. 1999. 39.95 (*0-940898-68-3*) Am Assn Mental.

Nehrling, Arno & Nehrling, Irene. Gardening for Flower Arrangement. LC 75-20966. Orig. Title: Flower Growing for Flower Arrangement. 256p. 1976. reprint ed. pap. 5.95 (*0-486-23263-8*) Dover.

Nehrling, Irene, jt. auth. see Nehrling, Arno.

An Asterisk (*) at the beginning of an entry indicates that the title is appearing for the first time.

Nehrt, Lee C. International Marketing of Nuclear Power Plants. LC 65-24596. (Indiana University Social Science Ser.: No. 22). 419p. reprint ed. 129.90 (*0-8357-9220-X*, 201546200094) Bks Demand.

Nehru, Jawaharlal. An Autobiography: Centenary Edition. 640p. 1989. 21.00 (*0-19-562395-9*); pap. text 15.95 (*0-19-562361-4*) OUP.

— Discovery of India. 582p. 1990. pap. 14.95 (*0-19-562359-2*) OUP.

— Independence & After. LC 75-134120. (Essay Index Reprint Ser.). 1977. 29.95 (*0-8369-2003-1*) Ayer.

— India's Foreign Policy. 612p. 1985. reprint ed. 34.95 (*0-940500-94-9*, Pub. by Pubns Div) Asia Bk Corp.

— Letters to Chief Ministers, 1947-1964 Vol. 1: 1947-1949. Parthasarathi, G., ed. (Illus.). 584p. 1988. 36.00 (*0-19-561881-5*) OUP.

— Letters to Chief Ministers, 1947-1964 Vol. 2: 1950-1952. (Illus.). 600p. 1987. 36.00 (*0-19-562012-7*) OUP.

— Letters to Chief Ministers, 1947-1964 Vol. 3: 1952-1954. (Illus.). 706p. 1988. 36.00 (*0-19-562180-8*) OUP.

— Letters to Chief Ministers, 1947-1964 Vol. 4: 1954-1957, Vol. 4. (Illus.). 684p. 1990. text 36.00 (*0-19-562338-X*) OUP.

— Letters to Chief Ministers, 1947-1964 Vol. 5: 1958-1964, Vol. 5. (Illus.). 664p. 1990. text 36.00 (*0-19-562512-9*) OUP.

— Selected Works of Jamaharlal Nehru: 1 July 1951 - 31 October 1951, Vol. 16, Pt. II. Gopal, S., ed. (Second Ser.). (Illus.). 834p. 1995. 16.95 (*0-19-563681-3*) OUP.

— Selected Works of Jawaharlal Nehru, Vol. 3. Gopal, Sarvepalli, ed. (Illus.). 556p. 1987. 36.00 (*0-19-561849-1*) OUP.

— Selected Works of Jawaharlal Nehru, Vol. 4. Gopal, Sarvepalli, ed. (Illus.). 727p. 1987. 34.50 (*0-19-561948-X*) OUP.

— Selected Works of Jawaharlal Nehru, Vol. 13. Gopal, Sarvepalli, ed. (Illus.). 538p. 1993. 24.00 (*0-19-563086-6*) OUP.

— Selected Works of Jawaharlal Nehru, Vol. 14. Gopal, Sarvepalli, ed. (Second Ser.). (Illus.). 660p. 1993. 24.00 (*0-19-563096-3*) OUP.

— Selected Works of Jawaharlal Nehru, Vol. 15, Pt. I. 2nd ed. Gopal, S., ed. 593p. write for info. (*0-318-72311-5*) OUP.

— Selected Works of Jawaharlal Nehru: Second Series, Second Series. Gopal, Sarvepalli, ed. (Second Ser.). (Illus.). 692p. 1984. text 34.95 (*0-19-561636-7*) OUP.

— Selected Works of Jawaharlal Nehru: Second Series, Second Series. Gopal, Sarvepalli, ed. (Second Ser.). (Illus.). 690p. 1985. text 29.95 (*0-19-561689-8*) OUP.

— Selected Works of Jawaharlal Nehru: Second Series, Second Series. Gopal, Sarvepalli, ed. (Illus.). 646p. 1988. 34.50 (*0-19-562011-9*) OUP.

— Selected Works of Jawaharlal Nehru: Second Series, Second Series. Gopal, Sarvepalli, ed. (Illus.). 582p. 1989. 36.00 (*0-19-562141-7*) OUP.

— Selected Works of Jawaharlal Nehru: Second Series, Second Series. Gopal, Sarvepalli, ed. (Illus.). 814p. 1989. 36.00 (*0-19-562337-1*) OUP.

— Selected Works of Jawaharlal Nehru: Second Series, Second Series. Gopal, Sarvepalli, ed. 514p. 1990. 32.00 (*0-19-562513-7*) OUP.

— Selected Works of Jawaharlal Nehru: Second Series, Second Series. Gopal, Sarvepalli, ed. (Illus.). 588p. 1991. 26.00 (*0-19-562838-1*) OUP.

— Selected Works of Jawaharlal Nehru: Second Series, Second Series. Gopal, Sarvepalli, ed. (Illus.). 598p. 1992. 32.00 (*0-19-562654-0*) OUP.

— Selected Works of Jawaharlal Nehru: Second Series, Second Series. Gopal, Sarvepalli, ed. (Illus.). 550p. 1992. 26.00 (*0-19-562964-7*) OUP.

***Nehru, Jawaharlal.** Selected Works of Jawaharlal Nehru: 1 April 1953-30 June 1953, Vol. 22. Gopal, S. et al, eds. (Second Ser.). (Illus.). 662p. 1999. text 29.95 (*0 19 564785-8*) OUP.

— Selected Works of Jawaharlal Nehru: 1 August- 25 October 1950, Vol. 15, Pt. I. Gopal, S., ed. (Second Ser.). 636p. 1994. 19.95 (*0-19-563310-5*) OUP.

Nehru, Jawaharlal. Selected Works of Jawaharlal Nehru: 1 January 1953-31 March 1953, Vol. 21. Gopal, S., ed. (Second Ser.). (Illus.). 676p. 1998. 32.00 incl. disk (*0-19-564539-1*) OUP.

— Selected Works of Jawaharlal Nehru: 1 July 19535-30 September 1953, Vol. 23. Gopal, S. et al, eds. (Second Ser.). (Illus.). 666p. 1999. text 29.95 (*0-19-564944-3*) OUP.

— Selected Works of Jawaharlal Nehru: 1 March 1951 - 30 June 1951, Vol. 16, Pt. 1. Gopal, S., ed. (Second Ser.). (Illus.). 700p. 1996. text 10.95 (*0-19-563478-0*) OUP.

— Selected Works of Jawaharlal Nehru: 16 July 1952 - 18 October 1952, Vol. 19. Gopal, S., ed. (Second Ser.). (Illus.). 828p. 1998. 32.00 incl. cd-rom (*0-19-564193-0*) OUP.

— Selected Works of Jawaharlal Nehru: 19 October 1952-31 December 1952, Vol. 20. Gopal, S., ed. (Second Ser.). (Illus.). 648p. 1998. text 29.95 (*0-19-564364-X*) OUP.

— Selected Works of Jawaharlal Nehru: 26 October 1950 - 28 February 1951, Vol. 15, Pt. 2. Gopal, S., ed. 742p. 1994. 16.95 (*0-19-563477-2*) OUP.

— Selected Works of Jawaharlal Nehru: 8 April- 31 July 1950, Vol. 14, Pt. II. Gopal, S., ed. (Second Ser.). 574p. 1995. 14.95 (*0-19-563309-1*) OUP.

— Selected Works of Jawaharlal Nehru Vol. 17, Second Series. (Illus.). 700p. (C). 1996. text 36.00 (*0-19-563745-3*) OUP.

***Nehru, Jawaharlal.** Selected Works of Jawaharlal Nehru Vol. 25 (1 February-31 May 1954) Gopal, S. et al, eds. (Illus.). 640p. 2000. text 27.00 (*0-19-565275-4*) OUP.

Nehru, Lolita. Origins of the Gandharan Style: A Study of Contributory Influences. (Illus.). 252p. 1990. 55.00 (*0-19-562472-6*) OUP.

Nehusi, Kimani S. K., jt. ed. see Smart, Ian Isidore.

Nei, Masatoshi. Molecular Evolutionary Genetics. 448p. 1987. text 105.50 (*0-231-06320-2*) Col U Pr.

— Molecular Evolutionary Genetics. 448p. 1989. pap. text 38.50 (*0-231-06321-0*) Col U Pr.

***Nei, Masatoshi & Kumar, Sudhir.** Molecular Evolution & Phylogenetics. LC 99-39160. 336p. 2000. write for info. (*0-19-513584-9*); write for info. (*0-19-513585-7*) OUP.

Neib, Alan. Running Microsoft Outlook 2000. LC 98-31910. 1998. 39.99 (*1-57231-939-9*) Microsoft.

Neibacher, Susan. Homeless People & Health Care: An Unrelenting Challenge. (Papers: No. 14). 32p. 1990. 5.00 (*0-934459-62-2*) United Hosp Fund.

Neibauer, Alan. The ABCs of Word Perfect 8. 2nd ed. LC 97-67591. 368p. 1997. pap. text 19.99 (*0-7821-2087-3*) Sybex.

— Access for Windows 95 for Busy People. (Busy People Ser.). 304p. 1996. pap. text 22.95 (*0-07-882112-6*) McGraw.

— Access 97 for Busy People. LC 97-138564. 1997. pap. text 24.99 (*0-07-882281-5*) Osborne-McGraw.

***Neibauer, Alan.** Access 2000 for Busy People. LC 99-461846. 336p. 1999. pap. 19.99 (*0-07-211983-7*) McGraw.

Neibauer, Alan. Corel WordPerfect Suite 8: The Official Guide. 2nd ed. LC 97-202554. 1997. pap. text 34.99 (*0-07-882327-7*) Osborne-McGraw.

— Corel WordPerfect Suite 8 Professional: The Official Guide. LC 98-108281. 1104p. 1997. pap., pap. text 49.99 incl. cd-rom (*0-07-882439-7*) McGraw.

— Excel 97 One Step at a Time. LC 97-76685. (New Tutorial Ser.). (Illus.). 464p. 1997. pap. 29.99 (*0-7645-3139-5*) IDG Bks.

***Neibauer, Alan.** How to Do Everything with Yahoo! 2000. 24.99 (*0-07-212561-6*) Osborne-McGraw.

— Internet! I Didn't Know You Could Do That... 4th ed. 320p. 1999. pap. text 19.99 incl. audio compact disk (*0-7821-2587-5*) Sybex.

— Microsoft Excel 2000. LC 99-15718. (One Step at a Time Ser.). 400p. 1999. pap. 29.99 (*0-7645-3291-X*) IDG Bks.

Neibauer, Alan. Microsoft Word for Windows 95 Made Easy: The Basics & Beyond! (Made Easy Ser.). 480p. 1995. pap. text 24.95 (*0-07-882152-5*) McGraw.

— Office 2000 Made Easy: The Basics & Beyond. (Made Easy Ser.). 608p. 1999. pap. text 24.99 (*0-07-882585-7*) Osborne-McGraw.

— The Official Guide to Corel Wordperfect Suite 7 for Windows 95. LC 96-219758. 656p. 1996. pap. text 34.99 (*0-07-882237-8*) Osborne-McGraw.

***Neibauer, Alan.** Running Microsoft Outlook 98. LC 98-4617. (Running Ser.). (Illus.). 627p. 1998. pap. 34.99 incl. cd-rom (*1-57231-840-6*) Microsoft.

Neibauer, Alan. Smart Business Solutions for Networking. LC 99-57856. 2000. pap. text 29.99 (*0-7356-0685-4*) Microsoft.

***Neibauer, Alan.** This Wired Home: The Microsoft Guide to Home Networking. LC 99-42530. 1999. pap. text 29.99 (*0-7356-0847-4*) Microsoft.

— This Wired Home: The Microsoft Guide To Home Networking. 432p. 2000. pap. 29.99 (*0-7356-1158-0*) Microsoft Pr.

Neibauer, Alan. WordPerfect Office 2000: The Official Guide. LC 99-234992. 1998. pap. text 39.99 (*0-07-882569-5*) Osborne-McGraw.

Neibauer Press Staff. Childrens Church Promotion. (Illus.). 48p. 1990. pap. 7.95 (*1-878259-06-7*) Neibauer Pr.

— Church Year I. (Illus.). 48p. 1987. pap. 5.95 (*0-685-28913-3*, 1451) Neibauer Pr.

— Clip Art for Afro American Churches. (Illus.). 48p. 1990. pap. 7.95 (*1-878259-00-8*) Neibauer Pr.

— How to Organize a Mission Program. 166p. 1990. ring bd. 27.95 (*1-878259-02-4*) Neibauer Pr.

Neibaur, Alexander, jt. auth. see Lebeda, Guy.

Neibaur, James L. The RKO Features: A Complete Filmography of the Feature Films Released or Produced by RKO Radio Pictures, 1929-1960. LC 92-56669. (Illus.). 344p. 1994. lib. bdg. 52.50 (*0-89950-787-5*) McFarland & Co.

Neibaur, James L. & Okuda, Ted. The Jerry Lewis Films: An Analytical Filmography of the Innovative Comic. LC 94-30905. (Illus.). 295p. 1994. lib. bdg. 39.95 (*0-89950-961-4*) McFarland & Co.

Neibel, Benjamin W. & Gjesdahl, Maurice S. Production Engineering. (Illus.). 148p. 1971. text 14.75 (*92-833-1003-9*, 310039); pap. text 11.00 (*92-833-1004-7*, 310047) Productivity Inc.

***Neiberg, Michael S.** Making Citizen Soldiers: ROTC & the Ideology of American Military Service. LC 99-44354. 288p. 2000. 39.95 (*0-674-54312-2*) HUP.

Neible, Stephen, jt. ed. see Waring, Michael J.

Neiburger, Ellis J. Computers for Professional Practice. LC 83-72626. (Illus.). 281p. 1984. pap. 14.95 (*0-914555-00-6*) Andent Inc.

Neiburger, Ellis J. & Neiburger, S. The Dentists' Handbook. LC 92-73278. (Illus.). 350p. (Orig.). 1993. pap. text 37.50 (*0-914555-01-4*) Andent Inc.

Neiburger, S., jt. auth. see Neiburger, Ellis J.

***Neicas, Jindirich, et al.** Partial Differential Equations: Theory & Numerical Solutions LC 99-27317. (Research Notes in Mathematics Ser.). 360p. 1999. per. 79.95 (*1-58488-022-8*, Chap & Hall CRC) CRC Pr.

Neice, K. C. & Bartell, D. P. A Faunistic Survey of the Organisms Associated with Ants of Western Texas. (Graduate Studies: No. 25). (Illus.). 36p. (Orig.). 1982. pap. 6.00 (*0-89672-096-9*) Tex Tech Univ Pr.

Neice, Susan L. & Craddock, Paul, eds. Metal Plating & Patination: Cultural, Technical, & Historical Developments. LC 93-18065. 327p. Date not set. reprint ed. pap. 101.40 (*0-608-20657-1*, 207209400003) Bks Demand.

Neich, Roger & Pendergrast, Mick. Traditional Tapa Textiles of the Pacific. LC 97-61529. (Illus.). 160p. 1998. pap. 24.95 (*0-500-27989-6*, Pub. by Thames Hudson) Norton.

Neidaspreum, Mike, et al. 6 Steps to Winning Time Trials: For Beginning & Sport Levels. (Illus.). 36p. 1997. pap. 5.95 (*1-891200-02-X*) Performance Conditioning.

Neidecker, Betty. The Marblehead Lighthouse: Lake Erie's Eternal Flame. Kernan, Rose, ed. (Illus.). 112p. (Orig.). 1996. pap. 16.95 (*0-9649679-0-1*) Hawks Cry.

Neidecker, Elizabeth A. & Blosser, Jean L. School Programs in Speech-Language: Organization & Management. 3rd ed. 400p. 1992. 84.00 (*0-13-792268-X*) P-H.

Neidel-Greenlee, Rosemary, jt. auth. see Monahan, Evelyn M.

Neidell, Norman S. Geophysical Determination of Lithology: Using Shear Waves & Amplitudes with Offsets - a Progress Update. LC QE0431.6.G4N. (Continuing Education Course Notes Ser.: Vol. 29). 55p. 1987. reprint ed. pap. 30.00 (*0-608-03026-0*, 206347600006) Bks Demand.

— Stratigraphic Modeling & Interpretation: Geophysical Principles & Techniques. LC QE0651.N45. (Education Course Note Ser.: No. 13). (Illus.). 145p. 1979. reprint ed. pap. 45.00 (*0-608-04226-9*, 206498300012) Bks Demand.

***Neider, Charles.** Antarctica: Firsthand Accounts of Exploration & Endurance. (Illus.). 2000. pap. 18.95 (*0-8154-1023-9*, Pub. by Cooper Sq) Natl Bk Netwk.

Neider, Charles. The Authentic Death of Hendry Jones. LC 92-30094. (Western Literature Ser.). 227p. reprint ed. pap. 70.40 (*0-608-10640-2*, 207126200009) Bks Demand.

***Neider, Charles.** The Autobiography of Mark Twain. LC 99-55390. (Perennial Classics Ser.). 560p. 2000. pap. 15.00 (*0-06-095542-2*, Perennial) HarperTrade.

— Essays of the Masters. 2000. reprint ed. pap. 8.95 (*0-8154-1097-2*, Pub. by Cooper Sq) Natl Bk Netwk.

— Great Shipwrecks & Castaways: Firsthand Accounts of Disasters at Sea. LC 00-34544. 2000. reprint ed. pap. write for info. (*0-8154-1094-8*, Pub. by Cooper Sq) Natl Bk Netwk.

— Life as I Find It: A Treasury of Mark Twain Rarities. LC 99-50204. 2000. pap. write for info. (*0-8154-1027-1*) Cooper Sq.

— Man Against Nature: Firsthand Accounts of Adventure & Exploration. (Illus.). 2000. pap. write for info. (*0-8154-1040-9*) Cooper Sq.

Neider, Charles. Overflight. 235p. 1986. 15.95 (*0-88282-026-5*) New Horizon NJ.

***Neider, Charles.** Travels of Mark Twain. 2000. pap. 19.95 (*0-8154-1039-5*, Pub. by Cooper Sq) Natl Bk Netwk.

Neider, Charles, ed. The Autobiography of Mark Twain. LC 90-55053. (Illus.). 432p. 1990. reprint ed. pap. 14.00 (*0-06-092025-4*, Perennial) HarperTrade.

***Neider, Charles, ed.** The Complete Essays of Mark Twain. 2000. pap. 23.00 (*0-306-80957-3*, Pub. by Da Capo) HarpC.

Neider, Charles, ed. Fabulous Insects. LC 68-16960. (Essay Index Reprint Ser.). 1977. 20.95 (*0-8369-0736-1*) Ayer.

***Neider, Charles, ed.** The Fabulous Insects: Essays by the Foremost Nature Writers. 2000. reprint ed. pap. 17.95 (*0-8154-1100-6*, Pub. by Cooper Sq) Natl Bk Netwk.

Neider, Charles, ed. Great Short Stories: Fiction from the Masters of World Literature. 560p. 1995. pap. 16.95 (*0-7867-0268-0*) Carroll & Graf.

— The Great West: A Treasury of Firsthand Accounts. LC 96-45126. (Illus.). 460p. 1997. reprint ed. pap. 22.95 (*0-306-80761-0*) Da Capo.

— Stature of Thomas Mann. LC 68-16961. (Essay Index Reprint Ser.). 1977. 29.95 (*0-8369-0737-X*) Ayer.

Neider, Charles, ed. Short Novels of the Masters. 656p. 1996. pap. 15.95 (*0-7867-0324-5*) Carroll & Graf.

Neider, Charles, ed. see Irving, Washington.

Neider, Charles, ed. see Tolstoy, Leo.

Neider, Charles, ed. see Twain, Mark, pseud.

Neider, Charles, ed. & intro. see Stevenson, Robert Louis.

Neider, Charles, ed. & intro. see Tolstoy, Leo.

Neider, John. Perdona y Ama Otra Vez.Tr. of Forgive & Love Again. (SPA.). 210p. 1995. 8.99 (*1-56063-521-5*, 498578) Editorial Unilit.

Neiderbach, Shelley. Invisible Wounds: Crime Victims Speak. LC 86-14831. 281p. 1986. 3.95 (*0-86656-525-6*) Haworth Pr.

— Invisible Wounds: Crime Victims Speak. LC 86-14831. 281p. 1986. text 49.95 (*0-86656-460-8*) Haworth Pr.

— Invisible Wounds: Crime Victims Speak. LC 86-22742. 281p. 1986. pap. 19.95 (*0-918393-30-2*, Harrington Park) Haworth Pr.

Neiderhiser, Richard. You Can Be Sanctified Wholly. (Christian Living Ser.). 40p. 1988. pap. 3.50 (*0-8341-1217-5*) Beacon Hill.

***Neiderman, Andrew.** Curse. 384p. 2000. 6.99 (*0-671-04172-X*) PB.

Neiderman, Andrew. The Dark. 1997. per. 6.99 (*0-671-00796-3*) PB.

— The Devil's Advocate Movie Tie In. 1997. per. 5.99 (*0-671-01410-2*) PB.

— In Double Jeopardy. 376p. 1998. mass mkt. 6.99 (*0-671-01561-3*) S&S Trade.

— Perfect Little Angels. (Orig.). 1991. 19.00 (*0-7278-4150-5*) Severn Hse.

— Reflection. 384p. (Orig.). 1986. mass mkt. 3.50 (*0-373-97027-7*, Wrldwide Lib) Harlequin Bks.

Neiderman, Beth R. Star Light, Star Bright: Whole Language Activities Through Nursery Rhymes. 1992. pap. 18.95 (*0-201-81537-0*) Addison-Wesley.

Neidermeyer, Dan. Cage Boy: The Story of Clyde Beatty. 1997. pap. 3.00 (*1-57514-309-7*, 1176) Encore Perform Pub.

Neidert, David. The Season of Leadership. 1999. 18.95 (*1-890009-57-1*) Exec Excell.

Neides, Daniel M., jt. auth. see Weinstock, Michael B.

Neidhardt, Elizabeth R. & Allen, Jo A. Family Therapy with the Elderly. (Sourcebooks for the Human Services Ser.: Vol. 22). (Illus.). 225p. (C). 1992. 56.00 (*0-8039-4498-5*); pap. 26.00 (*0-8039-4499-3*) Sage.

Neidhardt, Elizabeth R. & Allen, Jo Ann. Family Therapy with the Elderly. LC 92-49538. (Sage Sourcebooks for the Human Services Ser.: Vol. 22). (Illus.). 222p. reprint ed. pap. 68.90 (*0-608-09782-9*, 206995600007) Bks Demand.

Neidhardt, Frances. Things Seen & Seen Again. LC 97-67189. 57p. 1997. 10.00 (*0-9657687-1-6*) Sulphur River.

Neidhardt, H., jt. auth. see Exner, P.

Neidhardt, Jane E., ed. see Drucker, Johanna, et al.

Neidhardt, Jane E., ed. see Ketner, Joseph D., et al.

Neidhardt, Ralph, jt. auth. see Pellerin, Bill.

Neidhardt, W. Jim, jt. auth. see Loder, James E.

***Neidhart, Bernd.** Quality in Chemical Measurement: Current Concepts in Training & Teaching. 150p. 2000. 79.95 (*3-540-65994-3*) Spr-Verlag.

Neidig, D. F. & Hudson, H. S., eds. Solar Physics in the 1990s: Proceedings of Workshop XV & of the COSPAR Interdisciplinary Scientific Commission E (Meeting E1) of the COSPAR 27th Plenary Meeting Held in Espoo, Finland 18-29 July, 1988. (Advances in Space Research Ser.: Vol. 8). 286p. 1989. pap. 78.00 (*0-08-037371-2*, Pergamon Pr) Elsevier.

Neidig, H. A., jt. auth. see Gillette, M. L.

Neidig, H. Anthony. Enthalpy of Hydration. (Modular Laboratory Program in Chemistry Ser.). 12p. (C). 1989. pap. text 1.50 (*0-87540-370-0*, THER 370-0) Chem Educ Res.

— Enthalpy of Neutralization. (Modular Laboratory Program in Chemistry Ser.). 16p. (C). 1988. pap. text 1.50 (*0-87540-346-8*, THER 346-8) Chem Educ Res.

Neidig, H. Anthony & Gillette, M. L. Separating & Determining the Mass of Calcium Ion in a Calcium-Enriched Tablet. (Modular Laboratory Program in Chemistry Ser.). 12p. (C). 1995. pap. text 1.50 (*0-87540-455-3*, ANAL 455-3) Chem Educ Res.

Neidig, H. Anthony & Gillette, Marcia L. Detecting Signs of Chemical Change. (Modular Laboratory Program in Chemistry Ser.). 12p. (C). 1992. pap. text 1.50 (*0-87540-399-9*, REAC 399-9) Chem Educ Res.

— Determining the Comparative Reactivities of Several Metals. (Modular Laboratory Program in Chemistry Ser.). 7p. (C). 1992. pap. text 1.50 (*0-87540-414-6*, REAC 414-6) Chem Educ Res.

Neidig, H. Anthony & Spencer, James N. Charles's Law. (Modular Laboratory Program in Chemistry Ser.). 8p. (C). 1990. pap. text 1.50 (*0-87540-384-0*, PROP 384-0) Chem Educ Res.

— Chemical Models: Ball-&-Stick Models of Organic Compounds. (Modular Laboratory Program in Chemistry Ser.). 10p. (C). 1994. pap. text 1.50 (*0-87540-435-9*, STRC 435-9) Chem Educ Res.

— Density of Liquids & Solids. (Modular Laboratory Program in Chemistry Ser.). 12p. (C). 1990. pap. text 1.50 (*0-87540-383-2*, PROP 383-2) Chem Educ Res.

— Determining the Molar Concentration of a Sodium Hydroxide Solution. (Modular Laboratory Program in Chemistry Ser.). 12p. (C). 1992. pap. text 1.50 (*0-87540-394-8*, ANAL 394-8) Chem Educ Res.

— Diffusion of Gases. (Modular Laboratory Program in Chemistry Ser.). 7p. (C). 1990. pap. text 1.50 (*0-87540-385-9*, PROP 385-9) Chem Educ Res.

— Double Replacement Reactions. (Modular Laboratory Program in Chemistry Ser.). 12p. (C). 1991. pap. text 1.50 (*0-87540-390-5*, REAC 390-5) Chem Educ Res.

— The Empirical Formula of an Oxide. (Modular Laboratory Program in Chemistry Ser.). 12p. (C). 1990. pap. text 1.50 (*0-87540-388-3*, STOI 388-3) Chem Educ Res.

— Evaluation of the Gas Law Constant. (Modular Laboratory Program in Chemistry Ser.). 8p. (C). 1986. pap. text 1.50 (*0-87540-332-8*, PROP 332-8) Chem Educ Res.

— The Gas Burner & Glass Working. (Modular Laboratory Program in Chemistry Ser.). 12p. (C). 1990. pap. text 1.50 (*0-87540-381-6*, TECH 381-6) Chem Educ Res.

— Gravimetric Determination of Sulfate. (Modular Laboratory Program in Chemistry Ser.). 12p. (C). 1988. pap. text 1.50 (*0-87540-356-5*, ANAL 356-5) Chem Educ Res.

— Heat of Neutralization. (Modular Laboratory Program in Chemistry Ser.). 12p. (C). 1989. pap. text 1.50 (*0-87540-368-9*, THER 368-9) Chem Educ Res.

— Introducing Equilibrium. (Modular Laboratory Program in Chemistry Ser.). 12p. (C). 1991. pap. text 1.50 (*0-87540-392-1*, EQUL 392-1) Chem Educ Res.

— Introducing the Qualitative Analysis of a Group of Cations. (Modular Laboratory Program in Chemistry Ser.). 12p. (C). 1992. pap. text 1.50 (*0-87540-396-4*, ANAL 396-4) Chem Educ Res.

— Percent Water in a Hydrate. (Modular Laboratory Program in Chemistry Ser.). 7p. (C). 1990. pap. text 1.50 (*0-87540-387-5*, ANAL 387-5) Chem Educ Res.

— PH, Acids, & Bases. (Modular Laboratory Program in Chemistry Ser.). 11p. 1992. pap. text 1.50 (*0-87540-397-2*, EQUL 397-2) Chem Educ Res.

— Precipitating Lead Chromate on a Small Scale. (Modular Laboratory Program in Chemistry Ser.). 12p. (C). 1992. pap. text 1.50 (*0-87540-420-0*, STOI 420-0) Chem Educ Res.

— Safety Practices in the Chemistry Laboratory. (Modular Laboratory Program in Chemistry Ser.). 8p. (C). 1994. pap. text 1.50 (*0-87540-380-8*, TECH 380-8) Chem Educ Res.

N

— Single Replacement Reactions & Relative Reactivity. (Modular Laboratory Program in Chemistry Ser.). 12p. (C). 1990. pap. text 1.50 (0-87540-389-1, REAC 389-1) Chem Educ Res.
— Solutions. (Modular Laboratory Program in Chemistry Ser.). 12p. (C). 1991. pap. text 1.50 (0-87540-391-3, PROP 391-3) Chem Educ Res.
— Stoichiometry of the Reaction of Magnesium with Hydrochloric Acid. (Modular Laboratory Program in Chemistry Ser.). 12p. (C). 1989. pap. text 1.50 (0-87540-369-7, STOI 369-7) Chem Educ Res.
— Titrating Vinegar. (Modular Laboratory Program in Chemistry Ser.). 11p. (C). 1992. pap. text 1.50 (0-87540-395-6, ANAL 395-6) Chem Educ Res.
— Transfer & Measurement of Chemicals. (Modular Laboratory Program in Chemistry Ser.). 12p. (C). 1990. pap. text 1.50 (0-87540-382-4, TECH 382-4) Chem Educ Res.
— Writing Lewis Symbols & Lewis Structures. (Modular Laboratory Program in Chemistry Ser.). 8p. (C). 1994. pap. text 1.50 (0-87540-434-0, STRC 434-0) Chem Educ Res.
Neidig, H. Anthony, et al. Evaluating the Equilibrium Constant for the Reaction of Iron (III) Ion with Thiocyanate Ion. (Modular Laboratory Program in Chemistry Ser.). 16p. (C). 1994. pap. text 1.50 (0-87540-441-3, EQUL 441-3) Chem Educ Res.
— Identifying Six Solutions by Their Interactions. (Modular Laboratory Program in Chemistry Ser.). 16p. (C). 1993. pap. text 1.50 (0-87540-405-7, REAC 405-7) Chem Educ Res.
— Separating the Components of a Binary Mixture. (Modular Laboratory Program in Chemistry Ser.). 11p. (C). 1989. pap. text 1.50 (0-87540-374-3, PROP 374-3) Chem Educ Res.
— Separating the Components of a Ternary Mixture. (Modular Laboratory Program in Chemistry Ser.). 12p. (C). 1989. pap. text 1.50 (0-87540-375-1, PROP 375-1) Chem Educ Res.
Neidig, H. Anthony, jt. auth. see Gillette, M. L.
Neidig, H. Anthony, jt. auth. see Gillette, Marcia L.
Neidig, H. Anthony, jt. auth. see Stanitski, Conrad L.
Neidig, H. Anthony, ed. see Bailey, David N.
Neidig, H. Anthony, ed. see Bedenbaugh, Angela O., et al.
Neidig, H. Anthony, ed. see Billingham, E. J.
Neidig, H. Anthony, ed. see Brown, William H.
Neidig, H. Anthony, ed. see Carter, K. N.
Neidig, H. Anthony, ed. see Clemens, Donald F. & McAllister, Warren A.
Neidig, H. Anthony, ed. see Deckey, George.
Neidig, H. Anthony, ed. see Dingledy, David P.
Neidig, H. Anthony, ed. see Everett, Grover W., Jr.
Neidig, H. Anthony, ed. see Farrer, Leslie.
Neidig, H. Anthony, ed. see Foster, Judith C.
Neidig, H. Anthony, ed. see Foster, Judith C., et al.
Neidig, H. Anthony, ed. see Gillette, M. L. & Raney, Donald C.
Neidig, H. Anthony, ed. see Glogovsky, Robert L.
Neidig, H. Anthony, ed. see Griswold, Norman E.
Neidig, H. Anthony, ed. see Gunter, S. Kay & Birk, James P.
Neidig, H. Anthony, ed. see Hudak, Norman J.
Neidig, H. Anthony, ed. see Johnson, S. R. & Gillette, Marcia L.
Neidig, H. Anthony, ed. see Kieffer, William F.
Neidig, H. Anthony, ed. see Kotz, John C. & Reed, Roberta G.
Neidig, H. Anthony, ed. see Markow, Peter G.
Neidig, H. Anthony, ed. see Marks, R. L.
Neidig, H. Anthony, ed. see McKone, Harold T.
Neidig, H. Anthony, ed. see Melford, S. J. & Anysas, J. A.
Neidig, H. Anthony, ed. see Metz, Clyde R.
Neidig, H. Anthony, ed. see Milio, Frank R. & Loffredo, William M.
Neidig, H. Anthony, ed. see Mitchell, Richard S.
Neidig, H. Anthony, ed. see Patterson, George S.
Neidig, H. Anthony, ed. see Patterson, George S. & Good, William E., Jr.
Neidig, H. Anthony, ed. see Pinnell, Robert P.
Neidig, H. Anthony, ed. see Ramsay, O. Bertrand & Nicholson, Elva M.
Neidig, H. Anthony, ed. see Reichenbach, Wendy A.
Neidig, H. Anthony, ed. see Royer, M., et al.
Neidig, H. Anthony, ed. see Schreck, James O. & Loffredo, William M.
Neidig, H. Anthony, ed. see Squattrito, Philip J.
Neidig, H. Anthony, ed. see Stafford, Don.
Neidig, H. Anthony, ed. see Suffredini, Constance.
Neidig, H. Anthony, ed. see Suttles, Nancy L.
Neidig, H. Anthony, ed. see Wolthuis, Enno.
Neidig, H. Anthony, ed. see Zanella, Andrew W.
***Neidig, Isabel.** Winding Paths. 1999. pap. write for info. (1-58235-166-X) Watermrk Pr.
Neidig, Peter H. & Friedman, Dale H. Spouse Abuse: A Treatment Program for Couples. LC 84-61187. 256p. (Orig.). 1984. pap. text 17.95 (0-87822-234-0, 2340) Res Press.
Neidigh, Sherry. 1, 2 Buckle My Shoe. LC 98-100416. (Illus.). 1997. write for info. (0-7853-2364-3) Pubns Intl Ltd.
Neidigh, Sherry. The Story of the Sermon on the Mount. LC 97-218425. (Story of...Ser.). 24p. (Orig.). (J). (ps-2). 1997. pap. 3.95 (1-57102-109-4, Ideals Child) Hambleton-Hill.
Neidigk, Donald H. The Gifts of Lent: Sermons & Children's Sermons. LC 98-48039. 76p. 1999. pap. 7.75 (0-7880-1307-6) CSS OH.

***Neiditz, Minerva H.** Angels Tongues & Lobster Tails. LC 99-34519. 80p. 1999. pap. 12.95 (1-928755-01-1) Dryad Pr.
Neiditz, Minerva H. Business Writing at Its Best. 288p. 1993. 22.50 (0-7863-0137-6, Irwn Prfssnl) McGraw-Hill Prof.
Neidjie, Bill. Story about Feeling. 180p. (C). 1990. 45.00 (0-9588101-0-9, Pub. by Pascoe Pub) St Mut.
Neidl, Raymond E., jt. auth. see Ott, James.
Neidle, Alan F. Nuclear Negotiations: Reassessing Arms Control Goals in U. S.-Soviet Relations. LC 82-83390. (Tom Slick World Peace Ser.). 204p. 1982. pap. 5.00 (0-89940-004-3) LBJ Sch Pub Aff.
Neidle, Amos, jt. ed. see Ehrenpreis, Seymour.
Neidle, Carol. The Role of Case in Russian Syntax. (C). 1988. text 173.50 (1-55608-042-5) Kluwer Academic.
— Syntax of American Sign Language: Functional Categories & Hierarchical Structure. LC 99-15444. (Language, Speech & Communication Ser.). (Illus.). 224p. 1999. 32.50 (0-262-14067-5) MIT Pr.
Neidle, Enid A., jt. auth. see Hargreaves, Yagiela.
Neidle, Stephen. DNA Structure & Recognition: In Focus. (In Focus Ser.). (Illus.). 118p. (C). 1994. pap. text 19.95 (0-19-963419-X) OUP.
Neidle, Stephen, ed. Nucleic Acid Structure, Pt. 3. LC 87-6137. (Topics in Molecular & Structural Biology Ser.). 230p. 1987. 130.00 (0-89573-606-3, Wiley-VCH) Wiley.
— Oxford Handbook of Nucleic Acid Structure. LC 98-34431. (Illus.). 680p. 1999. text 140.00 (0-19-850038-6) OUP.
Neidle, Stephen & Waring, Michael J., eds. Molecular Aspects of Anticancer Drug-DNA Interactions, Vol. 1. LC 93-8201. (Topics in Molecular & Structural Biology Ser.). 1993. 110.00 (0-8493-7770-6) CRC Pr.
***Neidleman, Jason Andrew.** The General Will Is Citizenship: Inquiries into French Political Thought. LC 00-31103. 2000. pap. write for info. (0-7425-0789-0) Rowman.
Neidleman, Saul & Laskin, Allen I., eds. Advances in Applied Microbiology, Vol. 43. (Illus.). 254p. 1997. text 85.00 (0-12-002643-0) Morgan Kaufmann.
Neidleman, Saul L. & Laskin, Allen I., eds. Advances in Applied Microbiology, Vol. 41. (Illus.). 290p. 1995. text 83.00 (0-12-002641-4) Acad Pr.
— Advances in Applied Microbiology, Vol. 44. (Illus.). 358p. 1997. text 89.95 (0-12-002644-9) Morgan Kaufmann.
— Advances in Applied Microbiology Vol. 46: Cumulative Subject Index, Vols. 22-44, Vol. 46. (Illus.). 170p. 1997. text 89.95 (0-12-002646-5) Morgan Kaufmann.
Neidleman, Saul L. & Laskin, Allen I., eds. Advances in Applied Microbiology, Vol. 40. (Illus.). 334p. 1995. text 83.00 (0-12-002640-6) Acad Pr.
Neidlleman, Saul L. & Laskin, Allen I., eds. Advances in Applied Microbiology, Vol. 45. (Illus.). 326p. 1997. text 89.95 (0-12-002645-7) Acad Pr.
Neidner, James Q. Angel from Heaven. (Illus.). 120p. (Orig.). 1995. pap. 9.95 (0-9642737-0-5) J Q Neidner.
Neidorf, Mary. Operantics with Wolfgang Amadeus Mozart: A Workbook. LC 86-14435. 32p. (Orig.). (J). (gr. 3-6). 1987. pap. 4.95 (0-86534-092-7) Sunstone Pr.
Neidthardt, Hans Joachim. Ein Dresdner Malt Venedig: Bilder Von Ernst Hassebrauk. (GER., Illus.). 96p. 1995. text 23.00 (3-364-00363-7, Verlag Kunst) Gordon & Breach.
Neie, Herbert. The Doctrine of the Atonement in the Theology of Wolfhart Pannenberg. (Theologische Bibliothek Toepelmann Ser.: Vol. 36). (C). 1978. 80.80 (3-11-007506-7) De Gruyter.
Neier, Areyeh, ed. see Helsinki Watch Staff.
Neier, Areyeh, ed. see Kushen, Robert.
Neier, Aryeh, ed. see Goldstein, Eric.
Neier, Aryen. War Crimes: Brutality, Genocide, Terror & the Struggle for Justice. LC 98-5783. 288p. 1998. 25.00 (0-8129-2381-2, Times Bks) Crown Pub Group.
Neifeld, J. P., et al. Manual of Soft-Tissue Tumor Surgery. (Comprehensive Manuals of Surgical Specialties Ser.). (Illus.). 214p. 1983. 189.00 (0-387-90843-9) Spr-Verlag.
Neifeld, Morris R. Cooperative Consumer Credit. Bruchey, Stuart & Carosso, Vincent P., eds. LC 78-18972. (Small Business Enterprise in America Ser.). (Illus.). 1979. reprint ed. lib. bdg. 19.95 (0-405-11475-3) Ayer.
Neifert, Marianne E., et al. Dr. Mom. 544p. 1987. mass mkt. 6.99 (0-451-16311-7, Sig) NAL.
Neifert, Marianne R. Dr. Mom's Guide to Breastfeeding. LC 98-19125. (Illus.). 464p. 1998. pap. 14.95 (0-452-27990-9, Plume) Dutton Plume.
Neifert, Marianne R., jt. ed. see Neville, Margaret C.
Neiger, Alexander. Atlas of Practical Proctology. 2nd enl. rev. ed. LC 89-71714. 170p. 1990. text 98.00 (0-920887-76-7) Hogrefe & Huber Pubs.
Neiger, E. Dictionary Gastronomy: English/French/German/Italian/Spanish. 10th ed. (ENG, FRE, GER, ITA & SPA.). 164p. 1997. 59.95 (0-320-00439-2) Fr & Eur.
Neiger, Elisabeth. Food in Five Languages: An International Menu Guide. LC 96-9927. (ENG, FRE, GER, ITA & SPA.). 144p. 1997. pap. 9.95 (1-56656-215-5) Interlink Pub.
— Gastronomic Dictionary in Five Languages. 5th ed. (ENG, FRE, GER, ITA & SPA.). 144p. 1986. pap. 49.95 (0-8288-0159-2, M8448) Fr & Eur.
— Gastronomisches Woerterbuch: German, French, English, Italian, Spanish. 8th ed. (ENG, FRE & GER.). 144p. 1991. pap. 49.95 (0-7859-7080-0) Fr & Eur.
Neiger, L., jt. auth. see Beekman-Love, Gilian.
Neighbarger, Randy L. An Outward Show: Music for Shakespeare on the London Stage, 1660-1830, 27. LC 92-5423. (Contributions to the Study of Music & Dance Ser.: No. 27). 340p. 1992. 59.95 (0-313-27805-9, NML, Greenwood Pr) Greenwood.

Neighbor, R. Where Do We Go from Here? 1996. pap. 14.95 (1-880828-54-5) Touch Pubns.
Neighbor, Ralph W., Jr. & Latham, Bill. Survival Kit: Five Keys to Effective Spiritual Growth. 128p. 1979. pap. text 4.95 (0-8054-9770-6, LifeWy Press) LifeWay Christian.
Neighbor, Travis & Larner, Monica. Living, Studying & Working in Italy: Everything You Need to Know to Fulfill YOur Dreams of Living Abroad. LC 97-30702. 288p. 1998. pap. 14.95 (0-8050-5102-3) H Holt & Co.
Neighbors, Charles, ed. see Carlson, Richard R.
Neighbors, Harold W. & Jackson, James S., eds. Mental Health in Black America. LC 95-50210. 248p. (C). 1996. 44.00 (0-8039-3539-0); pap. 19.95 (0-8039-3540-4) Sage.
Neighbors, Marianne. Practical Guide to Medical-Surgical Nursing in the Home. 670p. 1997. pap. write for info. (0-7216-7331-7, W B Saunders Co) Harcrt Hlth Sci Grp.
Neighbors, Marianne, jt. auth. see Jackson, Janet E.
Neighbors, Marianne, jt. auth. see Monahan, Frances D.
Neighbors, Marianne, jt. ed. see Monahan, Frances D.
Neighbour, Oliver. Second Viennese School: Schoenberg, Webern & Berg. (New Grove Composer Biography Ser.). 1997. pap. 16.95 (0-393-31587-8) Norton.
***Neighbour, Ralph.** Living Your Christian Values. 128p. 1999. pap. text 4.95 (0-7673-9337-6, LifeWy Press) LifeWay Christian.
Neighbour, Ralph W., Jr. The Arrival Kit. 1993. pap. text 5.95 (1-880828-70-7) Touch Pubns.
— Bienvido a Tu Nueva Vida. (SPA.). 1997. pap. text 1.95 (1-880828-99-5) Touch Pubns.
— Cell Leader Intern Trainer's Guide. 1996. ring bd. 24.95 (1-880828-93-6) Touch Pubns.
— La Guia de Viaje. 1997. pap. text 1.45 (1-880828-98-7) Touch Pubns.
— La Guia del Mentor. 1997. pap. text 5.95 (1-880828-04-9) Touch Pubns.
— Handbook for Successful Living. 1992. pap. text 1.99 (1-880828-95-2) Touch Pubns.
— Life Basic Training Workbook. 1992. pap. text 7.95 (1-880828-57-X) Touch Pubns.
— The Shepherd's Guidebook. 1996. pap. 10.95 (1-880828-55-3) Touch Pubns.
— Sigueme: Survival Kit for New Christians. 128p. 1981. reprint ed. teacher ed. 5.50 (0-311-13837-3) Casa Bautista.
— Sigueme: Una Guia Practica Para Crecer Espiritualmente.Tr. of Survival Kit for New Christians. 128p. 1981. reprint ed. student ed. 7.50 (0-311-13836-5) Casa Bautista.
— Sigueme, Edicion Para Ninos: Survival Kit for New Christians, Childrens Edition. Geiger, Mary J. & Ditmore, Shirley, trs. from ENG. (SPA., Illus.). 64p. (Orig.). (J). 1989. pap. 5.99 (0-311-13848-9) Casa Bautista.
— Sigueme 2: Survival Kit II. Martinez, Mario, tr. from ENG. (SPA., Illus.). 128p. (Orig.). (J). 1989. pap. 7.50 (0-311-13843-8) Casa Bautista.
— The Sponsor's Guidebook. 1996. pap. text 5.95 (1-880828-89-8) Touch Pubns.
— Touching Hearts Guidebook. 1997. pap. text 5.95 (1-880828-92-8) Touch Pubns.
— La Vida en el Reino. 1996. pap. text 5.95 (1-880828-00-6) Touch Pubns.
— Welcome to Your Changed Life. 1997. 1.95 (1-880828-73-1) Touch Pubns.
***Neighbour, Ralph W.** Where Do We Go from Here? A Guidebook for the Cell Group Church. 10th ed. 2000. pap. 14.95 (1-880828-17-0) Touch Pubns.
Neighbour, Ralph W., Jr. & Egli, Jim. La Estacion del Nuevo Creyente. (SPA.). 1995. pap. text 4.95 (1-880828-05-7) Touch Pubns.
Neighbours, John T., et al, eds. The Developing Labor Law: 1999 Cumulative Supplement. 887p. 1999. pap., suppl. ed. 205.00 (1-57018-136-5, 1136) BNA Books.
***Neihardt, Hilda.** Black Elk & Flaming Rainbow: Personal Memories of the Lakota Holy Man & John Neihardt. LC 94-26350. (Illus.). 160p. 1999. pap. 12.00 (0-8032-8376-8) U of Nebr Pr.
Neihardt, Hilda, ed. The Ancient Memory & Other Stories. LC 91-2603. (Illus.). xiii, 230p. 1998. reprint ed. pap. 10.00 (0-8032-8374-1, NEIANX, Bison Books) U of Nebr Pr.
Neihardt, Hilda, ed. see DeSersa, Esther Black Elk, et al.
Neihardt, John G. All Is but a Beginning: Youth Remembered, 1881-1901. LC 85-28955. x, 173p. 1986. reprint ed. pap. 9.95 (0-8032-8355-5, Bison Books); reprint ed. text 30.00 (0-8032-3311-6) U of Nebr Pr.
— The Ancient Memory & Other Stories. Petri, Hilda N., ed. LC 91-2603. (Illus.). xiii, 230p. 1991. text 30.00 (0-8032-3327-2) U of Nebr Pr.
— Black Elk Speaks. (Illus.). 320p. 1996. reprint ed. 8.98 (1-56731-111-3, MJF Bks) Fine Comms.
— Black Elk Speaks. rev. ed. 100p. 1996. pap. 5.95 (0-87129-615-2, B80) Dramatic Pub.
— Black Elk Speaks: Being the Life Story of a Holy Man of the Oglala Sioux. LC 88-14317. (Illus.). xx, 298p. 1979. text 40.00 (0-8032-3301-9) U of Nebr Pr.
— Black Elk Speaks: Being the Life Story of a Holy Man of the Oglala Sioux. LC 88-14317. (Illus.). 298p. 1988. pap. 11.95 (0-8032-8359-8, Bison Books) U of Nebr Pr.
— A Bundle of Myrrh. (Collected Works of John G. Neihardt). 60p. 1999. reprint ed. lib. bdg. 88.00 (1-58201-780-8) Classic Bks.
— A Cycle of the West: Golden Anniversary Edition. LC 91-38033. (Illus.). xiv, 524p. 1992. text 115.00 (0-8032-3323-X) U of Nebr Pr.
— The Dawn Builder. LC 90-21279. (Landmark Edition Ser.). 335p. 1991. reprint ed. text 45.00 (0-8032-3330-2) U of Nebr Pr.

— The Dawn-Builder. (Collected Works of John G. Neihardt). 335p. 1999. reprint ed. lib. bdg. 88.00 (1-58201-781-6) Classic Bks.
— The Divine Enchantment: A Mystical Poem. 1974. 250.00 (0-87968-168-3) Gordon Pr.
— The Divine Enchantment: A Mystical Poem. (Collected Works of John G. Neihardt). 335p. 1999. reprint ed. lib. bdg. 108.00 (1-58201-782-4) Classic Bks.
— The Divine Enchantment: A Mystical Poem & Poetic Values: Their Reality & Our Need of Them. LC 88-38263. (Landmark Edition Ser.). iv, 144p. 1989. reprint ed. text 45.00 (0-8032-3319-1) U of Nebr Pr.
— The End of the Dream & Other Stories. LC 90-43667. xxviii, 115p. 1991. text 25.00 (0-8032-3326-4) U of Nebr Pr.
— Giving Earth: A John G. Neihardt Reader. Petri, Hilda N., ed. LC 90-28609. (Illus.). xviii, 301p. 1991. pap. 12.95 (0-8032-8373-3) U of Nebr Pr.
— Life's Lure. LC 91-21490. (Landmark Edition Ser.). 277p. 1991. text 50.00 (0-8032-3333-7) U of Nebr Pr.
— Life's Lure. (Collected Works of John G. Neihardt). 277p. 1999. reprint ed. lib. bdg. 98.00 (1-58201-783-2) Classic Bks.
— The Lonesome Trail. (Collected Works of John G. Neihardt). 303p. 1999. reprint ed. lib. bdg. 98.00 (1-58201-784-0) Classic Bks.
— Man-Song. LC 91-19103. (Landmark Edition Ser.). viii, 117p. 1991. text 45.00 (0-8032-3332-9) U of Nebr Pr.
— Man-Song. (Collected Works of John G. Neihardt). 124p. 1999. reprint ed. lib. bdg. 88.00 (1-58201-785-9) Classic Bks.
— The Mountain Men. LC 70-134770. (Cycle of the West Ser.: Vol. 1). (Illus.). xvi, 369p. 1971. reprint ed. pap. text 20.00 (0-8032-5733-3, Bison Books) U of Nebr Pr.
— Patterns & Coincidences: A Sequel to "All Is But a Beginning" LC 77-24199. x, 123p. 1978. text 20.00 (0-8032-3312-4) U of Nebr Pr.
— The River & I. (Collected Works of John G. Neihardt). 325p. 1999. reprint ed. lib. bdg. 98.00 (1-58201-786-7) Classic Bks.
— The River & I. LC 92-15792. (Landmark Edition Ser.). (Illus.). xix, 325p. 1992. reprint ed. text 50.00 (0-8032-3335-3) U of Nebr Pr.
— The Song of Hugh Glass. (Collected Works of John G. Neihardt). 181p. 1999. reprint ed. lib. bdg. 88.00 (1-58201-787-5) Classic Bks.
— The Song of Three Friends. (Collected Works of John G. Neihardt). 126p. 1999. reprint ed. lib. bdg. 88.00 (1-58201-788-3) Classic Bks.
— The Splendid Wayfaring: Jedediah Smith & the Ashley-Henry Men, 1822-1831. LC 71-116054. (Illus.). xii, 290p. 1970. reprint ed. pap. 9.95 (0-8032-5723-6, Bison Books) U of Nebr Pr.
— Splendid Wayfaring: The Story of the Exploits & Adventures of Jedediah Smith & His Comrades, the Ashley-Henry Men, Discoverers & Explorers of the Great Central Route from the Missouri River to the Pacific Ocean, 1822-1831. (Collected Works of John G. Neihardt). 290p. 1999. reprint ed. lib. bdg. 98.00 (1-58201-789-1) Classic Bks.
— The Stranger at the Gate. (Collected Works of John G. Neihardt). 70p. 1999. reprint ed. lib. bdg. 88.00 (1-58201-790-5) Classic Bks.
— Two Mothers. (Collected Works of John G. Neihardt). 82p. 1999. reprint ed. lib. bdg. 88.00 (1-58201-791-3) Classic Bks.
— When the Tree Flowered: The Story of Eagle Voice, a Sioux Indian (New Edition) LC 90-19669. xx, 250p. 1991. reprint ed. pap. 11.95 (0-8032-8363-6, Bison Books) U of Nebr Pr.
Neihardt, John G. & Sodaro, Craig. Another Side of Eden. LC 88-14317. 71p. 1993. pap. 5.50 (0-87129-304-8, A52) Dramatic Pub.
Neihardt, John G., jt. auth. see Sergel, Christopher.
Neihardt, John Gneisenau, jt. auth. see Black Elk, Wallace.
***Neihart, Ben.** Burning Girl. 256p. 2000. pap. 13.00 (0-688-17689-5, Wm Morrow) Morrow Avon.
Neihart, Ben. Burning Girl: A Novel. LC 98-42117. 256p. 1999. 24.00 (0-688-15691-6, Wm Morrow) Morrow Avon.
— Hey, Joe. 224p. 1997. mass mkt. 6.99 (0-425-15972-8) Berkley Pub.
Neiheisel. Politics in Texasville: Locating the Texasville Regional Medical. 1998. pap. text 15.73 (0-205-29758-7) Allyn.
Neiheisel, Steven R. Corporate Strategy & the Politics of Goodwill Vol. 40: A Political Analysis of Corporate Philanthropy in America. LC 93-6959. (American University Studies: No. X). XV, 202p. (C). 1995. text 38.95 (0-8204-2128-6) P Lang Pubng.
Neihsial, Tualchin. Burma Frontier Areas Committee of Enquiry Report. 1998. pap. 15.00 (81-210-0380-6) Inter-India Pubns.
Neiiendam, Maureen, tr. see Sorensen, Villy.
Neil & McIntyre. Lipids & Lipoproteins in Clinical Practice. 160p. (C). (gr. 13). 1990. text 59.00 (0-7234-0946-3) Mosby Inc.
Neil, Abbot. Hulkamania! Hulk Hogan America's Hero. 1985. pap. 3.50 (0-317-19507-7) PB.
Neil, Andrew, et al, eds. Prevention of Cardiovascular Disease in Primary Care: An Evidence-Based Approach. (General Practice Ser.). (Illus.). 352p. 1996. pap. text 59.50 (0-19-262397-4) OUP.
Neil, Barbara. Bella. (Regency Romance Ser.: No. 172). 1992. mass mkt. 2.99 (0-373-31172-9, 1-31172-9) Harlequin Bks.
— Gentleman Rogue. 1999. per. 3.75 (0-373-31227-X) Harlequin Bks.
— A History of Silence: A Novel. LC 98-14335. 352p. 1998. 23.00 (0-385-49178-6) Doubleday.

N

An Asterisk (*) at the beginning of an entry indicates that the title is appearing for the first time.

— The Possession of Delia Sutherland. large type ed. LC 94-25968. 453p. 1995. pap. 19.95 (*0-7862-0293-9*) Thorndike Pr.

Neil, Cecily & Tykkylainen, Markku, eds. Local Economic Development: A Geographical Comparison of Rural Community Restructuring. LC 98-40088. 368p. 1998. pap. 24.95 (*92-808-0998-9*, Pub. by UN Univ Pr) Brookings.

Neil, Clive. Dancing with Danger: Turning Obstacles into Opportunities. 127p. (Orig.). 1997. pap. 9.99 (*1-889389-11-0*) End-Time Wave.

Neil, Clive E. Breaking Through: Developing Healthy Relationships. 156p. (Orig.). 1996. pap. 9.99 (*1-889389-06-4*) End-Time Wave.

— Unleashing the Truth: How to Be Intimate with God. 128p. (Orig.). 1996. pap. 8.99 (*0-9634306-8-8*) End-Time Wave.

Neil, David H., jt. auth. see Rutherford, Clarice.

Neil, Deborah M. Collaboration in Intercultural Discourse: Examples from a Multicultural Australian Workplace. Hess-Luttich, Ernest W. & Watts, Richard, eds. (Cross Cultural Communication Ser.: Vol. 3). 218p. 1996. pap. 42.95 (*3-631-49930-2*) P Lang Pubng.

— Collaboration in Intercultural Discourse: Examples from a Multicultural Australian Workplace. Hess-Luttich, Ernest W. & Watts, Richard, eds. (Cross Cultural Communication Ser.: Vol. 3). 218p. 1996. pap. 42.95 (*0-8204-3162-1*) P Lang Pubng.

Neil, Dorothy. Age Is In. 80p. 1998. pap. 12.00 (*0-8059-4314-5*) Dorrance.

— Face the Nation. 72p. 1998. pap. 8.00 (*0-8059-4303-X*) Dorrance.

Neil, Dorothy M. Age Is In. (Orig.). 1996. pap. write for info. (*1-57553-362-6*) Watermrk Pr.

— By Canoe & Sailing Ship They Came. Brainard, Lee, ed. LC 89-63170. (Illus.). 296p. (Orig.). 1989. pap. 21.95 (*0-9624462-0-3*) Spindrift Pub.

— I Wonder Why. 80p. 1998. pap. 8.00 (*0-8059-4266-1*) Dorrance.

***Neil F. Jones & Co Staff.** Set-Off in the Construction Industry. 2nd ed. LC 99-34681. 1999. write for info. (*0-632-04824-7*) Blackwell Sci.

Neil, Fred, jt. auth. see Eckman, Charlie.

***Neil, G. R. & Benson, S. V., eds.** Free Electron Lasers 1998. 662p. 1999. 175.00 (*0-444-50248-3*, North Holland) Elsevier.

Neil, Garry A., jt. ed. see Zimmermann, Ulrich.

***Neil, J. Murray.** The Scots Fiddle: Tunes, Tales & Traditions of the North-East & Central Highlands. (Illus.). 2000. pap. 29.95 (*1-897784-86-4*, Pub. by N Wilson Pubng) Interlink Pub.

Neil, Joanna. La Comedie de l'Innocence. (Horizon Ser.). (FRE.). 1994. pap. 3.50 (*0-373-39292-3*, 1-39292-7) Harlequin Bks.

— Loving Remedy. large type ed. 288p. 1995. 23.99 (*0-263-14338-4*, Pub. by Mills & Boon) Ulverscroft.

***Neil, Kate & Holford, Patrick.** Balance Hormones Naturally. LC 99-33919. 168p. 1999. pap. 12.95 (*1-58091-041-6*) Crossing Pr.

Neil, Marilyn. Stars, Wings, & Fun Things: Three Hundred Sixty-Five Activities for Children. (Illus.). 68p. (Orig.). (J). (gr. k-3). 1991. pap. text 8.95 (*0-945301-05-7*) Druid Pr.

Neil, Marilyn S. Mathematics the Write Way: Activities for Every Elementary Classroom. LC 96-3313. 200p. 1996. pap. 29.95 (*1-883001-19-6*) Eye On Educ.

Neil, Pagan. Book of Love: An Encyclopedic Lexicon & Consulting Dictionary of the Word Love. 121p. 1985. pap. 7.95 (*0-935865-00-4*) SFX Pr.

Neil, R. & Watts, R., eds. Caring & Nursing: Explorations in Feminist Perspectives. 275p. 1990. pap. 29.95 (*0-88737-501-4*) Natl League Nurse.

Neil, Richard. Stress: Taming the Tyrant. LC 94-60991. 118p. 1994. per. 8.95 (*1-57258-001-1*) Teach Servs.

Neil Sharr & Associates Staff. Saninista Nicaragua Pt. 2: Economy, Politics, & Foreign Policy: an Annotated Bibliography with Analytical Introductions, Pt. 2. (Resources on Contemporary Issues Ser.: No. 5). 194p. 1990. pap. 40.00 (*0-87650-256-7*) Pierian.

Neil, Thomas. Chinese Meals in Minutes: Quick & Easy. (Illus.). 160p. 1997. pap. text 11.95 (*0-572-02186-0*, Pub. by W Foulsham) Trans-Atl Phila.

— Indian Meals in Minutes: Quick & Easy. (Illus.). 160p. 1997. pap. text 11.95 (*0-572-02187-9*, Pub. by W Foulsham) Trans-Atl Phila.

Neil, William. Acts. (New Century Bible Ser.). 272p. 1973. 8.95 (*0-551-00336-7*) Attic Pr.

— The Pocket Bible Commentary. 1997. 10.98 (*0-7858-0813-2*) Bk Sales Inc.

Neil, Winter C., ed. Short Stories, Vol. 1. 1999. pap. 13.95 (*0-9653145-3-7*, Winter Bks LA) Pontalba Pr.

Neil, Winter C., ed. see D'Acre, Jacqueline.

Neil, Winter C., ed. see Hebert, Charles J.

Neil, Winter C., ed. see Jacobs, Beth.

Neil, Winter C., III, ed. see Lemann, Arthur A., III.

Neil, Winter C., ed. see Losee, Rita H.

Neil, Winter C., ed. see Van Campe, Honey.

Neil, Winter C., ed. see Zimmermann, L. F.

Neilan, Ruth E. American Military Movement Relating Sacred Dance. Adams, Doug, ed. & intro. by. (Orig.). 1985. pap. 3.00 (*0-941500-37-3*) Sharing Co.

Neilan, Sarah. The Braganza Pursuit. large type ed. 400p. 1984. 27.99 (*0-7089-1076-9*) Ulverscroft.

Neilands, L. & MacKinnon, K. A Friend for Life. 5.99 (*1-871676-78-9*, Pub. by Christian Focus) Spring Arbor Dist.

Neild, Eric. With Pegasus in India: The Story of 153rd Gurkha Parachute Battalion. (Airborne Ser.: No. 21). (Illus.). 110p. 1990. reprint ed. 29.95 (*0-89839-150-4*) Battery Pr.

Neild, Rachel, ed. see Washington Office on Latin America Staff.

Neild, Terry. Beyond Endurance. 284p. 1996. 15.95 (*1-57087-249-X*) Prof Pr NC.

Neill. Politics of Jane Austen. LC 98-31055. 192p. 1999. text 59.95 (*0-312-21872-9*) St Martin.

Neill, Alex & Ridley, Aaron. The Philosophy of Art: Readings Ancient & Modern. LC 94-37453. 592p. (C). 1994. pap. 38.75 (*0-07-046192-9*) McGraw.

Neill, Alexander S. Summerhill School: A New View of Childhood. Lamb, Albert, ed. LC 95-33481. 269p. 1995. pap. 12.95 (*0-312-14137-8*, St Martin Griffin) St Martin.

Neill, Alistair. Life Contingencies. LC 78-303002. (Illus.). 464p. reprint ed. pap. 143.90 (*0-608-09702-0*, 206986800007) Bks Demand.

Neill, Brian, ed. see Rampton, Richard & Sharp, Victoria.

Neill, C. R., ed. see Roads & Transportation Association of Canada, Proj.

Neill, Catherine A. & Clark, Edward B., eds. The Developing Heart: A History of Pediatric Cardiology. LC 95-3082. (Developments in Cardiovascular Medicine Ser.: Vol. 162). 176p. (C). 1995. text 70.50 (*0-7923-3375-6*) Kluwer Academic.

Neill, Catherine A., et al. The Heart of a Child: What Families Need to Know about Heart Disorders in Children. 326p. 1993. 24.95 (*0-8018-4234-4*) Johns Hopkins.

***Neill, Chris.** F/A-18 Hornet Walk Around. (Walk Around Ser.). (Illus.). 80p. 1999. pap. 14.95 (*0-89747-401-5*) Squad Sig Pubns.

Neill, Derrick. Duck Egg Blue: A Novel. LC 99-10415. 280p. 1999. 24.95 (*1-57392-685-X*) Prometheus Bks.

***Neill, Edw. D.** John Neill of Lewes, Delaware, 1739 & His Descendants. fac. ed. 127p. 1999. reprint ed. 31.00 (*0-8328-9921-6*); reprint ed. pap. 21.00 (*0-8328-9922-4*) Higginson Bk Co.

Neill, Edward. Trial by Ordeal: Thomas Hardy & the Critics. LC 98-37818. 159p. 1999. 55.00 (*1-57113-140-X*) Camden Hse.

Neill, Edward D. Abraham Lincoln & His Mailbag: Two Documents. Blegen, Theodore C., ed. LC 64-23313. (Publications of the Minnesota Historical Society). 60p. reprint ed. pap. 30.00 (*0-8357-3316-5*, 203954000013) Bks Demand.

— Founders of Maryland, As Portrayed in Manuscripts, Provincial Records & Early Documents. (Illus.). 193p. 1997. reprint ed. pap. 22.50 (*0-8328-5942-7*) Higginson Bk Co.

— The History of Minnesota: From the Earliest French Explorations to the Present Time. LC 75-112. (Mid-American Frontier Ser.). 1975. reprint ed. 51.95 (*0-405-06879-4*) Ayer.

— History of Minnesota: From the Earliest French Explorations to the Present Time (1883) 5th enl. rev. ed. (Illus.). 947p. 1997. reprint ed. lib. bdg. 94.50 (*0-8328-6794-2*) Higginson Bk Co.

— History of Ramsey County & City of St. Paul, Minnesota. 650p. 1994. reprint ed. lib. bdg. 65.00 (*0-8328-3851-9*) Higginson Bk Co.

— History of Ramsey County & the City of St. Paul, MN. 650p. 1993. reprint ed. lib. bdg. 67.50 (*0-8328-3487-4*) Higginson Bk Co.

— History of the Upper Mississippi Valley. 717p. 1994. reprint ed. lib. bdg. 72.50 (*0-8328-3850-0*) Higginson Bk Co.

— Terra Maria: or Threads of Maryland Colonial History. (Illus.). 260p. 1997. reprint ed. lib. bdg. 32.50 (*0-8328-5940-0*) Higginson Bk Co.

— Virginia Carolorum: The Colony under the Rule of Charles the First & Second, 1625-1865. 417p. 1996. pap. 31.00 (*0-7884-0478-4*, N134) Heritage Bk.

Neill, Edward D. & Bryant, Charles S. History of Rice County, Minnesota. 603p. 1994. reprint ed. lib. bdg. 62.50 (*0-8328-3856-X*) Higginson Bk Co.

— History of the Minnesota Valley. 1016p. 1994. reprint ed. lib. bdg. 105.00 (*0-8328-3838-1*) Higginson Bk Co.

Neill, Gene. I'm Gonna Bury You! LC 79-23314. 205p. 1975. write for info. (*0-932294-05-7*) Acclaimed Bks.

— I'm Gonna Bury You! 11th rev. ed. (Illus.). 210p. 1991. reprint ed. pap. 5.00 (*0-9608028-0-0*) Voice of Triumph.

***Neill, George W.** Infantry Soldier: Holding the Line at the Battle of the Bulge. LC 99-48506. (Illus.). 384p. 2000. 24.95 (*0-8061-3222-1*) U of Okla Pr.

Neill, George W., jt. auth. see Neill, Shirley B.

Neill, Hugh, jt. auth. see Abbott, P.

Neill, Hugh, jt. auth. see Barnard, Tony.

Neill, Hugh, jt. auth. see Ralston, Anthony.

Neill, Humphrey B. Art of Contrary Thinking. 5th ed. LC 54-7837. 201p. 1963. pap. 9.95 (*0-87004-110-X*) Caxton.

— The Ruminator: A Collection of Thoughts & Suggestions on Contrary Thinking. LC 92-82739. 128p. (C). 1992. reprint ed. pap. 12.00 (*0-87034-105-7*) Fraser Pub Co.

— Tape Reading & Market Tactics: The Three Steps to Successful Stock Trading. LC 73-115001. 224p. 1970. reprint ed. pap. 17.00 (*0-87034-074-3*) Fraser Pub Co.

Neill, Isobel. An End of Darkness. large type ed. 272p. 1994. pap. 16.99 (*0-7089-7546-1*) Ulverscroft.

— The Law of Love. large type ed. (Romance Ser.). 1994. pap. 16.99 (*0-7089-7621-2*, Linford) Ulverscroft.

— Nothing to Lose. large type ed. (Romance Ser.). 1994. pap. 16.99 (*0-7089-7610-7*, Linford) Ulverscroft.

Neill, J., jt. auth. see Woodhouse, Roger G.

Neill, Jimmy D., jt. ed. see Knobil, Ernst.

Neill, John. Records & Reminiscences of Bonhill Parish. 280p. (C). 1986. 49.00 (*0-9506620-0-3*) St Mut.

Neill, John & Neill, Lois. Fun Times & Rhymes. 176p. (J). 1998. pap. 14.00 (*0-8059-4284-X*) Dorrance.

Neill, John R. Lucky Bucky in Oz. (Illus.). 289p. (J). (gr. 3 up). 1992. 24.95 (*0-929605-17-9*) Books of Wonder.

— The Scalawagons in Oz. (Illus.). 309p. (J). (gr. 3 up). 1991. 24.95 (*0-929605-12-8*) Books of Wonder.

— Wonder City of Oz. (Illus.). 318p. (J). (gr. 2 up). 1990. 24.95 (*0-929605-07-1*) Books of Wonder.

Neill, John R. Wonder City of Oz. (Illus.). 318p. (J). (gr. 3 up). 1996. reprint ed. pap. 12.95 (*0-929605-61-6*) Books of Wonder.

Neill, John R. & Baum, L. Frank. The Runaway in Oz. (Illus.). 254p. (J). (gr. 3 up). 1995. 24.95 (*0-929605-39-X*) Books of Wonder.

Neill, Jon. Poverty & Inequality: The Political Economy of Redistribution. LC 97-32412. (C). 1997. pap. 14.00 (*0-88099-181-X*); text 33.00 (*0-88099-182-8*) W E Upjohn.

Neill, June. Assessing Elderly People for Residential Care: A Practical Guide. (C). 1989. 59.00 (*0-7855-3728-7*, Pub. by Natl Inst Soc Work); 40.00 (*0-7855-0087-1*, Pub. by Natl Inst Soc Work) St Mut.

Neill, June, ed. Assessing Elderly People for Residential Care: A Practical Guide. (C). 1989. pap. 30.00 (*0-902789-59-7*, Pub. by Natl Inst Soc Work) St Mut.

Neill, Kenneth, jt. auth. see Branston, John.

Neill, Lois, jt. auth. see Neill, John.

Neill, Mary, et al. How Shall We Find the Father? Meditations for Mixed Voices. 160p. (Orig.). 1984. 8.95 (*0-8164-2623-6*) Harper SF.

Neill, Mary, jt. auth. see Chervin, Rhonda D.

Neill, Merrily & Tangedahl, Joanne. A New Blueprint for Marriage. 256p. 1981. pap. 6.50 (*0-942494-65-2*) Coleman Pub.

Neill, Michael. Issues of Death: Mortality & Identity in English Renaissance Tragedy. (Illus.). 418p. 1999. pap. text 24.95 (*0-19-818493-X*) OUP.

***Neill, Michael.** Putting History to the Question: Power, Politics & Society in English Renaissance Drama. LC 99-29886. 464p. 1999. 37.50 (*0-231-11332-3*) Col U Pr.

Neill, Michael, ed. Issues of Death: Mortality & Identity in English Renaissance Tragedy. (Illus.). 418p. 1997. text 85.00 (*0-19-818386-0*) OUP.

Neill, Michael, ed. see Shakespeare, William.

Neill, Nancy, jt. auth. see Atlanta Athletic Club Staff.

Neill, Peter. Acoma. LC 77-92932. 1978. pap. 3.95 (*0-918172-03-9*) Leetes Isl.

— Maritime America: Art & Artifacts from America's Great Nautical Collections. (Illus.). 256p. 1988. 45.00 (*0-917439-11-2*) Balsam Pr.

***Neill, Peter, ed.** American Sea Writing: A Literary Anthology. 2000. 35.00 (*1-883011-83-3*, Pub. by Library of America) Penguin Putnam.

Neill, Peter, ed. Maritime America: Art & Artifacts from America's Great Nautical Collections. (Illus.). 250p. 1988. 45.00 (*0-8109-1527-8*, PEMP141) Peabody Essex Mus.

Neill, Peter & Ehrenwald, Barbara, eds. Great Maritime Museums of the World. (Illus.). 304p. 1991. 30.00 (*0-917439-12-0*) Mariners Mus.

Neill, Peter, et al. On a Painted Ocean: Art of the Seven Seas. Steen, Gareth L., ed. LC 95-32496. 188p. (C). 1995. text 45.00 (*0-8147-5787-1*) NYU Pr.

Neill, Peter, ed. see Cunningham, Louisa.

Neill, Richard, jt. auth. see Sturges, R. P.

Neill, Robert H. Don't Fish under the Dingleberry Tree. 1991. 19.95 (*0-9617591-9-4*) MS River Pub.

— The Flaming Turkey. LC 86-62509. (Illus.). 208p. 1986. 17.95 (*0-9617591-0-0*) MS River Pub.

— Going Home. (Illus.). 200p. 1987. 17.95 (*0-9617591-2-7*) MS River Pub.

— The Jakes. 1989. 17.95 (*0-9617591-4-3*) MS River Pub.

— Magnolia Club. 1990. 25.00 (*0-9617591-7-8*) MS River Pub.

— Voice of Jupiter Pluvius. 1990. 17.95 (*0-9617591-8-6*) MS River Pub.

Neill, Robert H. & Baugh, Jim R. How to Lose Your Farm in Ten Easy Lessons & Cope with It. 150p. 1987. 6.95 (*0-9617591-1-9*) MS River Pub.

Neill, Robert H., ed. see Southeast Out Press Writers Assoc. Staff.

Neill, Robin. A New Theory of Value: The Canadian Economics of H. A. Innis. LC 77-185867. (Canadian University Paperbooks Ser.: No. 120). 167p. reprint ed. pap. 51.80 (*0-8357-4162-1*, 203693600007) Bks Demand.

Neill, Rocky. Complete Double Bass Drum Cookbook. 160p. 1995. pap. 15.00 (*0-7866-0236-8*, 95340) Mel Bay.

Neill, S. D. Clarifying McLuhan: An Assessment of Process & Product, 37. LC 92-36609. (Contributions to the Study of Mass Media & Communications Ser.: No. 37). 168p. 1993. 49.95 (*0-313-28444-X*, NCM, Greenwood Pr) Greenwood.

— Dilemmas in the Study of Information: Exploring the Boundaries of Information Science, 70. LC 91-24835. (Contributions in Librarianship & Information Science Ser.: No. 70). 200p. 1992. 52.95 (*0-313-27734-6*, NDN, Greenwood Pr) Greenwood.

Neill, S. E. Lexikon Zur Weltmission. (GER.). 95.00 (*3-7974-0054-3*, M-7190); 95.00 (*0-8288-7912-5*, M7190) Fr & Eur.

Neill, Sarah M., jt. auth. see Ridley, C. Marjorie.

Neill, Shirley B. & Neill, George W. Only the Best: Annual Guide to Highest-Rated Education Software-Multimedia for Preschool-Grade 12. 144p. 1991. 27.95 (*0-936423-04-8*) Ed News Serv.

Neill, Stephen. Penguin History of the Church Vol. 6: A History of Christian Missions. 2nd ed. 1991. pap. 15.95 (*0-14-013763-7*) Viking Penguin.

Neill, Stephen & Wright, N. T. The Interpretation of the New Testament, 1861-1986. 2nd ed. 474p. 1988. pap. text 17.95 (*0-19-283057-0*) OUP.

Neill, Stephen, et al. When Will Ye Be Wise? Kilmister, C. A., ed. 208p. (Orig.). 1984. reprint ed. pap. 6.95 (*0-685-09580-0*) St Thomas.

Neill, Stephen, jt. auth. see Clark, Peter J.

Neill, Thomas. Incidents in the Early History of Pullman & the State College of Washington. 1977. pap. 6.95 (*0-87770-175-X*) Ye Galleon.

Neill, Wilfred T. Twentieth-Century Indonesia. LC 72-11718. (Illus.). 413p. 1973. pap. text 26.00 (*0-231-08316-5*) Col U Pr.

Neill, Wilfred T. & Allen, E. Ross. Florida's Seminole Indians. rev. ed. LC 65-3660. (Illus.). 128p. 1965. reprint ed. pap. 4.95 (*0-8200-1018-9*) Great Outdoors.

***Neill, William.** Caledonian Cramboclink: The Poetry of William Neill. 2000. pap. 16.95 (*0-946487-53-7*) Luath Pr Ltd.

Neill, William. Making Tracks: Poems in Scots, English & Gaelic with Translation. 96p. (C). 1989. 45.00 (*0-903065-65-7*, Pub. by G Wright Pub) St Mut.

— Straight Lines. 98p. (Orig.). 1992. pap. 12.95 (*0-85640-475-6*, Pub. by Blackstaff Pr) Dufour.

— Tales Frae the Odyssey & Homer. (C). 1993. pap. 32.00 (*0-85411-049-6*, Pub. by Saltire Soc) St Mut.

— Wild Places. 200p. 1989. pap. write for info. (*0-946487-11-1*) Luath Pr Ltd.

Neill, William, photos by. Landscapes of the Spirit. LC 96-48370. (Illus.). 120p. (gr. 8). 1998. 40.00 (*0-8212-2338-0*) Little.

Neill, William J., et al. Reimaging the Pariah City: Urban Development in Belfast & Detroit. LC 95-75556. 251p. 1995. 74.95 (*1-85628-480-8*, Pub. by Avebry) Ashgate Pub Co.

Neillands, Robin. The Conquest of the Reich: D-Day to VE Day - A Soldier's History. LC 94-23982. (Illus.). 301p. (C). 1995. text 37.50 (*0-8147-5781-2*) NYU Pr.

— The Conquest of the Reich: D-Day to VE Day - A Soldier's History. (Illus.). 301p. (C). 1997. pap. text 19.50 (*0-8147-5789-8*) NYU Pr.

— The Hundred Years War. (Illus.). 370p. (C). 1991. pap. 25.99 (*0-415-07149-6*, A6681) Routledge.

— In the Combat Zone: Special Forces since 1945. LC 97-35389. 388p. 1998. text 26.00 (*0-8147-5795-2*) NYU Pr.

— Walking Through France. 1995. pap. text 10.95 (*1-85253-312-9*, Pub. by Quiller Pr) St Mut.

— Wining & Dining in France. 1995. pap. text 40.00 (*1-85253-313-7*, Pub. by Quiller Pr) St Mut.

Neillands, Robin, jt. auth. see Bartelski, Konrad.

***Neilly, Julia M.** Counting My Blessings. 16p. (J). 2001. 9.95 (*0-8192-1842-1*, 6286) Morehouse Pub.

Neils, Elaine M. Reservation to City: Indian Migration & Federal Relocation. LC 78-144044. (University of Chicago, Department of Geography, Research Paper Ser.: No. 131). 214p. 1971. reprint ed. pap. 66.40 (*0-608-02282-9*, 206292300004) Bks Demand.

Neils, Jenifer, ed. Worshipping Athena: Panathenaia & Parthenon. LC 96-8274. (Wisconsin Studies in Classics). (Illus.). 262p. (Orig.). 1996. 55.00 (*0-299-15110-7*); pap. 22.95 (*0-299-15114-X*) U of Wis Pr.

Neils, Jenifer, ed. see Cleveland Museum of Art Staff.

Neils, Patricia. China Images in the Life & Times of Henry Luce. 384p. 1990. lib. bdg. 55.00 (*0-8476-7634-X*) Rowman.

Neils, Patricia, ed. United States Attitudes Toward China: The Impact of American Missionaries. LC 89-78510. (Studies on Modern China). 304p. (C). (gr. 13). 1990. text 68.95 (*0-87332-632-6*, East Gate Bk) M E Sharpe.

Neils, Rob. Death with Dignity: Frequently Asked Questions. 3rd ed. LC 97-71062. 160p. 1997. per. 14.95 (*0-7872-3611-X*) Kendall-Hunt.

Neils, Selma M. The Klickitat Indians. LC 85-72818. (Illus.). 240p. (Orig.). 1985. pap. 12.95 (*0-8323-0446-8*) Binford Mort.

Neilsen. OSHA Compendium for Health Care Professional. LC 99-11382. (Allied Health Ser.). (C). 1999. pap. 40.95 (*0-7668-0478-X*) Delmar.

Neilsen, Allan R. Critical Thinking & Reading: Empowering Learners to Think & Act. (Monographs on Teaching Critical Thinking). (Illus.). 54p. (C). 1989. pap. 8.95 (*0-927516-02-0*) ERIC-REC.

Neilsen, Allan R., ed. Daily Meaning: Counternarratives on Teachers' Work. 1999. pap. 16.00 (*0-9696985-5-0*) Bendall Bks.

Neilsen, Irene E., jt. ed. see Paton, Ray.

Neilsen, Jakob, ed. see Bergman, Eric.

Neilsen, Jakob, ed. see Druin, Allison & Hendler, Jim.

Neilsen, Jakob, ed. see Johnson, Jeff.

Neilsen, Jakob, ed. see Mayhew, Deborah J.

Neilsen, Jakob, ed. see Ware, Colin.

Neilsen, Lorri. Knowing Her Place: Research Literacies & Feminist Occasions. LC 98-16745. 1998. 24.95 (*1-880192-27-6*) Caddo Gap Pr.

— Literacy & Living: The Literate Lives of Three Adults. LC 88-35973. 150p. (Orig.). (C). 1989. pap. 14.95 (*0-435-08493-3*, 08493) Heinemann.

— A Stone in My Shoe: Teaching Literacy in Times of Change. LC 96-133075. (Illus.). 141p. 1994. pap. 12.00 (*1-895411-73-4*) Peguis Pubs Ltd.

Neilsen, Mark. Reaffirming Life in a Culture of Death: A Catholic Response to Critical Issues. LC 95-80149. 112p. (Orig.). 1995. pap. 6.95 (*0-89243-871-1*) Liguori Pubns.

Neilsen, Mark, ed. I Am with You Always: A Living Faith Prayer Companion. (Illus.). 169p. (Orig.). 1991. pap. 7.95 (*0-9629585-0-6*) Crtve Commns MO.

Neilsen, Nicki J. The Red Dragon & St. George's. (Illus.). 66p. 1983. pap. 7.50 (*0-9607358-2-8*) Fathom Pub.

Neilsen, Philip, ed. The Sting in the Wattle. 270p. 1994. pap. 16.95 (*0-7022-2565-7*, Pub. by Univ Queensland Pr) Intl Spec Bk.

Neilsen, Philip, jt. ed. see Horton, Helen.

N

Neilsen, Richard P. The Politics of Ethics: Methods for Acting, Learning & Sometimes Fighting with Others in Addressing Problems in Organizational Life. (Ruffin Series in Business Ethics). (Illus.). 272p. 1996. pap. 35.00 (*0-19-509666-5*) OUP.

Neilsen, Shelley, et al. On Track: A Comprehensive System for Early Childhood Intervention. 426p. 1994. pap. text, teacher ed. 47.50 (*1-57035-034-5*, C66MAN) Sopris.

Neilsen, Therese & Martin, David. Mage Chronicles, Vol. 2. (Werewolf Ser.). (Illus.). (Orig.). 1997. pap. 20.00 (*1-56504-443-6*, 4015) White Wolf.

Neilson. Intermediate Microeconomics. LC 97-15185. (HB - Economics Ser.). (C). 1997. mass mkt. 92.95 (*0-538-84582-1*) S-W Pub.

Neilson & Winter. Intermediate Macroeconomics. 2nd ed. (SWC-Economics Ser.). 2001. pap. text 56.25 (*0-324-02395-2*) Sth-Wstrn College.

Neilson, A. H. & Hutzinger, O., eds. PAHs & Related Compounds: Biology. (Handbook of Environmental Chemistry Ser.: Vol. 3, Pt. J). (Illus.). 400p. 1997. 198.00 (*3-540-63422-3*) Spr-Verlag.

Neilson, A. N. & Hutzinger, O., eds. PAHs & Related Compounds: Chemistry. (Handbook of Environmental Chemistry Ser.: Vol. 3, Pt. I). (Illus.). 326p. 1997. 198.00 (*3-540-62394-9*) Spr-Verlag.

Neilson, Alasdair. Fate of Organic Chemicals in the Aquatic Environment. 448p. 1994. lib. bdg. 95.00 (*0-87371-597-7*, L597) Lewis Pubs.

***Neilson, Alasdair H.** Organic Chemicals: An Environmental Perspective. LC 99-52061. 912p. 1999. boxed set 99.95 (*1-56670-376-X*) Lewis Pubs.

***Neilson, Anthony.** Anthony Neilson Plays. LC 00-303029. (Drama Ser.). 1998. pap. 14.95 (*0-413-72460-3*) Methn.

— The Censor. LC 98-195311. (Royal Court Writers Ser.). 1997. pap. 10.95 (*0-413-72130-2*) Methn.

Neilson, Bruce J., et al, eds. Estuarine Circulation. LC 89-1725. (Contemporary Issues in Science & Society Ser.). (Illus.). 394p. 1989. 125.00 (*0-89603-155-1*) Humana.

Neilson, Bruce J. & Cronin, L. Eugene, eds. Estuaries & Nutrients. LC 81-83901. (Contemporary Issues in Science & Society Ser.). (Illus.). 658p. 1981. 120.00 (*0-89603-035-0*) Humana.

Neilson, Colin. Bliss Bibliographic Classification: Class R: Politics & Public Administration. (Bliss Bibliographic Classification Ser.). 155p. 1996. 50.00 (*1-85739-077-6*) Bowker-Saur.

— Bliss Bibliographic Classification: Class S: Law. (Bliss Bibliographic Classification Ser.). 255p. 1996. 60.00 (*1-85739-067-9*) Bowker-Saur.

Neilson, D. & Das, M. P. Computational Approaches to Novel Condensed Matter Systems: Applications to Classical & Quantum Systems. LC 95-13989. (Illus.). 288p. (C). 1995. text 95.00 (*0-306-44986-2*, Kluwer Plenum) Kluwer Academic.

Neilson, D., jt. ed. see Das, M. P.

Neilson, DeAnne. Perfect Neighbors. LC 94-77979. 207p. 1994. pap. 7.95 (*0-9624049-6-9*) Hatrack River.

Neilson, Eric. Immunologic Renal Diseases. 1,056p. 1996. text 213.00 (*0-397-51671-1*) Lppncott W & W.

Neilson, Francis. Churchill & Yalta. (Revisionist Historiography Ser.). 1979. lib. bdg. 250.00 (*0-685-96613-5*) Revisionist Pr.

— The Churchill Legend: Winston Churchill As Fraud, Fakir & War-Monger. 1983. lib. bdg. 250.00 (*0-87700-001-8*) Revisionist Pr.

— Churchill's War Memoirs. (Revisionist Historiography Ser.). 1979. lib. bdg. 250.00 (*0-87700-275-4*) Revisionist Pr.

— Cultural Tradition & Other Essays. LC 69-18935. (Essay Index Reprint Ser.). 1977. 20.95 (*0-8369-1046-X*) Ayer.

— The Devil & All: A Churchill Satire. 1971. 250.00 (*0-87700-019-0*) Revisionist Pr.

— The Freudians & the Oedipus Complex. 1971. 250.00 (*0-87700-013-1*) Revisionist Pr.

— From Ur to Nazareth: An Economic Inquiry into the Religious & Political History of Israel. 1971. 300.00 (*0-87700-010-7*) Revisionist Pr.

— The Garden of Doctor Persuasion. 1971. 250.00 (*0-87700-018-2*) Revisionist Pr.

— Hate, the Enemy of Peace. (Studies in Pacifism). 1991. lib. bdg. 75.00 (*0-8490-4405-7*) Gordon Pr.

— History Versus Patriotism: Diplomacy Up a Blind Alley. (Revisionist Historiography Ser.). 1979. lib. bdg. 44.50 (*0-685-96625-9*) Revisionist Pr.

— How Diplomats Make War. 1986. lib. bdg. 250.00 (*0-8490-3847-2*) Gordon Pr.

— In Quest of Justice. 135p. 1944. 4.00 (*0-911312-31-5*) Schalkenbach.

— The Last Mile. 1971. 250.00 (*0-685-26316-9*) Revisionist Pr.

— The Makers of War. 1971. 250.00 (*0-87700-002-6*) Revisionist Pr.

— My Life in Two Worlds, 2 vols., Set. 1971. 300.00 (*0-87700-004-2*) Revisionist Pr.

— The Nietzsche-Wagner Rift. 1979. lib. bdg. 150.00 (*0-685-96632-1*) Revisionist Pr.

— Our Garden: Reflections on Nature. 1971. 250.00 (*0-87700-015-8*) Revisionist Pr.

— Philanthropy & Peace. 1979. lib. bdg. 79.95 (*0-685-96634-8*) Revisionist Pr.

— A Poem. 1971. 59.95 (*0-87700-066-2*) Revisionist Pr.

— Poems. 1971. 250.00 (*0-87700-006-9*) Revisionist Pr.

— Portents: Scares Old & New. 1979. lib. bdg. 39.00 (*0-685-96635-6*) Revisionist Pr.

— Recent Books on World War II. (Revisionist Historiography Ser.). 1979. lib. bdg. 39.95 (*0-685-96636-4*) Revisionist Pr.

— Shakespeare & the Tempest. LC 74-30004. 181p. 1970. reprint ed. lib. bdg. 65.00 (*0-8371-7385-X*, NEST, Greenwood Pr) Greenwood.

— The Story of the Freeman. 1971. 250.00 (*0-87700-011-5*) Revisionist Pr.

— A Task for Diogenes: A Satire. 1971. 250.00 (*0-87700-017-4*) Revisionist Pr.

— Taxes Are Devilish Things. 1979. lib. bdg. 79.95 (*0-685-96638-0*) Revisionist Pr.

— Teilhard de Chardin's Vision of the Future. 1979. lib. bdg. 250.00 (*0-685-96640-2*) Revisionist Pr.

— The Threat of International Chaos. 1979. lib. bdg. 39.95 (*0-685-96641-0*) Revisionist Pr.

— Tolstoy's Message for Our Times. 1979. lib. bdg. 39.00 (*0-685-96643-7*) Revisionist Pr.

— Toynbee's Study of History. 1979. lib. bdg. 250.00 (*0-685-96644-5*) Revisionist Pr.

— The Tragedy of Europe. 1971. 300.00 (*0-87700-003-4*) Revisionist Pr.

Neilson, G. W. & Enderby, J. E., eds. Water & Aqueous Solutions. (Illus.). 362p. 1986. 105.00 (*0-85274-576-1*) IOP Pub.

Neilson, G. W., jt. auth. see Bellisent-Funel, M. C.

Neilson, Gena. Favorite Rhymes. (Illus.). (J). (ps-1). 1986. pap. 9.95 (*0-937763-02-0*) Lauri Inc.

Neilson, Gena. Dinosaurs. (J). (ps-1). 1986. spiral bd. 9.95 (*0-937763-00-4*) Lauri Inc.

— It's Your Birthday. (J). (ps-1). 1986. spiral bd. 9.95 (*0-937763-03-9*) Lauri Inc.

— Noah's Ark. (J). (ps-1). 1986. spiral bd. 9.95 (*0-937763-01-2*) Lauri Inc.

Neilson, George. John Barbour: Poet & Translator. (BCL1-PR English Literature Ser.). 57p. 1992. reprint ed. lib. bdg. 59.00 (*0-7812-7167-3*) Rprt Serv.

***Neilson, George.** Trial by Combat, 1890. fac. ed. LC 99-59101. 2000. 75.00 (*1-58477-075-9*) Lawbk Exchange.

Neilson, Gregory G. Karl the Kodiak & the Scratching Bear Contest. (Illus.). 18p. (J). 1994. text 12.50 (*0-930329-84-8*) Kabel Pubs.

***Neilson, Gregory G.** Lotus Domino Administration in a Nutshell. Denn, Robert, ed. (In a Nutshell Ser.). (Illus.). 400p. 2000. pap. 24.95 (*1-56592-717-6*) OReilly & Assocs.

Neilson, Helen P. What the Cow Said to the Calf: Native American Historical Biography. LC 93-84752. 200p. (Orig.). (C). 1993. pap. text 17.95 (*1-880222-15-9*) Red Apple Pub.

Neilson, James P. & Chambers, S. E., eds. Obstetric Ultrasound, Vol. 1. (Illus.). 320p. 1993. 79.00 (*0-19-262224-2*) OUP.

— Obstetric Ultrasound, Vol. 2. (Illus.). 258p. 1995. text 79.00 (*0-19-262373-7*) OUP.

Neilson, Jim. Warring Fictions: Cultural Politics & the Vietnam War Narrative. LC 98-33587. 248p. 1998. 45.00 (*1-57806-087-7*); pap. 18.00 (*1-57806-088-5*) U Pr of Miss.

Neilson, Joe, jt. auth. see Ray, Blaine.

***Neilson, Jonathan M.** Paths Not Taken: Speculations on American Foreign Policy & Diplomatic History, Interests, Ideals & Power LC 99-37524. (Studies in Diplomacy & Strategic Thought). 240p. 2000. 65.00 (*0-275-96769-7*, Praeger Pubs) Greenwood.

Neilson, Joseph. Memories of Rufus Choate: With Some Consideration of His Studies, Methods & Opinions & of His Style As a Speaker & Writer. xx, 460p. 1985. reprint ed. 55.00 (*0-8377-0909-1*, Rothman) W S Hein.

***Neilson, Joseph T.** Personally, I Wouldn't Buy It Either. 137p. 1999. pap. 11.95 (*0-7414-0317-X*) Buy Books.

Neilson, Keith. Strategy & Supply: The Anglo-Russian Alliance, 1914-17. 240p. 1984. text 55.00 (*0-04-940072-X*) Routledge.

Neilson, Keith & Errington, Elizabeth J., eds. Navies & Global Defense: Theories & Strategy. LC 95-2239. 256p. 1995. 62.95 (*0-275-94898-6*, Praeger Pubs) Greenwood.

Neilson, Keith & Haycock, Ronald G., eds. The Cold War & Defense. LC 90-30926. 216p. 1990. 55.00 (*0-275-93556-6*, C3556, Praeger Pubs) Greenwood.

Neilson, Keith & McKercher, B. J., eds. Go Spy the Land: Military Intelligence in History. LC 92-234. 222p. 1992. 47.95 (*0-275-93708-9*, C3708, Praeger Pubs) Greenwood.

Neilson, Keith, jt. ed. see Ion, A. Hamish.

Neilson, Keith, jt. ed. see Kennedy, Greg.

Neilson, M. Marguerite Neilson's Cats. McHattie, Grace, ed. (Illus.). 1999. pap. 23.00 (*0-900767-69-3*, Pub. by Univs Fed Animal Welfare) St Mut.

Neilson, Melanie. Civil Noir. LC 91-67073. (Roof Bks.). 96p. (Orig.). 1992. pap. 8.95 (*0-937804-45-2*) Segue NYC.

— Natural Facts. 68p. 1996. pap. 11.00 (*0-937013-57-9*) Potes Poets.

Neilson, Melanie, jt. auth. see Anderson, Michael, Jr.

Neilson, N., ed. The Cartulary & Terrier of the Priory of Bilsongton, Kent. (British Academy, London, Records of the Social & Economic History of England & Wales Ser.: Vol. 7). 1972. reprint ed. pap. 50.00 (*0-8115-1247-9*) Periodicals Srv.

— A Terrier of Fleete, Lincolnshire. (British Academy, London, Records of the Social & Economic History of Wngland & Wales. Series: Vol. 4). 1974. reprint ed. pap. 50.00 (*0-8115-1244-4*) Periodicals Srv.

Neilson, Nellie. Types of Manorial Structure in the Northern Danelaw. Customary Rents. LC 73-22286. iv, 219 p. 1974. write for info. (*0-374-96160-3*) FS&G.

Neilson, Peter, ed. Life-Adventures of Zamba, an African Negro King. LC 70-133162. (Black Heritage Library Collection). 1977. 27.95 (*0-8369-8717-9*) Ayer.

Neilson, Philip. Imagined Lives: A Study of David Malouf. 1990. pap. 14.95 (*0-7022-2274-7*, Pub. by Univ Queensland Pr) Intl Spec Bk.

— Imago. (Orig.). 1993. pap. 10.95 (*0-7022-2566-5*, Pub. by Univ Queensland Pr) Intl Spec Bk.

Neilson, Robert E. Collaborative Technologies & Organizational Learning. LC 96-40293. (Series in Information Technology Management). 160p. (C). 1997. pap. text 35.95 (*1-878289-39-X*) Idea Group Pub.

Neilson, Rosalie. The Thirty-Seven Interlacements of Hira Kara Gumi. LC 98-85354. (Illus.). 60p. 1998. 30.00 (*0-9664863-0-7*) Orions Plumage.

Neilson, Sandy, ed. see Bell, Keith F.

***Neilson, Stefan.** Financial & Personal Success: Keys to Wealth Through Leadership, Team Building & Empowerment Statements. (Illus.). 2000. pap. 29.95 (*1-880830-46-9*) AEON-Hierophant.

Neilson, Stefan & Theolke, Shay. Winning Colors for Elementary Students. (Personality Language & Winning Colors Ser.). (Illus.). 89p. 1990. teacher ed., spiral bd. 30.00 (*1-880830-12-4*); teacher ed., spiral bd. 30.00 (*1-880830-22-1*); student ed., spiral bd. 20.00 (*1-880830-13-2*) AEON-Hierophant.

***Neilson, Stefan & Thoelke, Shay.** Careers Unlimited, To Be or Not to Be Vol. II: Your 21st Century Blueprint for Selecting a Career Through the Winning Colors Process. Thoelke, Rich, ed. LC 99-9467. (Winning Colors Ser.). (Illus.). 240p. 1999. pap. text 29.95 (*1-880830-44-2*) AEON-Hierophant.

— Conflict Resolution Through Winning Colors Vol. I: A Workable Process for Resolving Personal Differences (Hostility, Anger, Miscommunication, Agendas) Thoelke, Rich, ed. LC 99-94766. (Winning Colors Ser.). (Illus.). 231p. 1999. pap. text 29.95 (*1-880830-43-4*) AEON-Hierophant.

Neilson, Stefan & Thoelke, Shay. Here's Looking at You Kid! Color Me Winning. LC 90-84509. (Personality Language Ser.). (Illus.). 118p. 1992. teacher ed., spiral bd. 35.00 (*1-880830-06-X*) AEON-Hierophant.

— Winning Colors Power Pack: Adult. rev. ed. (Illus.). 101p. (C). 1988. teacher ed., spiral bd. 30.00 (*1-880830-15-9*); spiral bd. 20.00 (*1-880830-14-0*) AEON-Hierophant.

— Winning Colors Power Pack: Student. rev. ed. (Personality Language Ser.). (Illus.). 102p. 1988. teacher ed., spiral bd. 30.00 (*1-880830-17-5*); student ed., spiral bd. 20.00 (*1-880830-16-7*) AEON-Hierophant.

Neilson, Suzanne, ed. see Wilson, James F., et al.

Neilson, William A. & Thorndike, Ashley H. The Facts About Shakespeare. reprint ed. 69.00 (*0-403-03058-7*) Somerset Pub.

Neily, Robert B. Archaeological Investigations in the Snowflake-Mesa Redonda Area, East-Central Arizona: The Apache-Navajo South Project. (Archaeological Ser.: Vol. 173). 388p. 1988. 16.95 (*1-889747-59-9*) Ariz St Mus.

***Neiman.** Defending the Idea of Governing. 260p. 1999. pap. text 26.67 (*0-13-373044-1*, Prentice Hall) P-H.

Neiman, Barbara L. Come Behind the Veil. Dean, Athena, ed. (Illus.). 112p. (Orig.). 1993. pap. 8.95 (*0-9622413-4-2*) WinePress Pub.

***Neiman, Charles.** Master Asker: Expect God to Answer Your Prayer! 2000. pap. 12.99 (*0-88419-694-1*) Creation House.

***Neiman, Cleo.** Can You Enjoy Being a Woman? A Guide to Getting What You Want in a Man's World. LC 00-190968. 145p. 2000. 25.00 (*0-7388-2144-6*); pap. 18.00 (*0-7388-2143-8*) Xlibris Corp.

Neiman, Harvey L. & Yao, James S., eds. Angiography of Vascular Disease. LC 84-17564. (Illus.). 624p. reprint ed. pap. 193.50 (*0-7837-6239-9*, 204595300010) Bks Demand.

Neiman, Irving G. Murder Once Removed. 1972. pap. 5.25 (*0-8222-0793-1*) Dramatists Play.

Neiman, LeRoy. An American in Paris. LC 94-263. (Illus.). 160p. 1994. 49.50 (*0-8109-1950-8*, Pub. by Abrams) Time Warner.

— Big-Time Golf. (Illus.). 176p. 1992. 45.00 (*0-8109-3666-6*, Pub. by Abrams) Time Warner.

— Carnaval. (Illus.). 1981. 100.00 (*0-937608-01-7*) Knoedler.

— LeRoy Neiman on Safari. LC 96-25980. (Illus.). 168p. 1997. 60.00 (*0-8109-6332-9*, Pub. by Abrams) Time Warner.

Neiman, M. B. & Gal, D. The Kinetic Isotope Method & Its Application. 310p. (C). 1971. 48.00 (*963-05-9999-6*, Pub. by Akade Kiado) St Mut.

Neiman Marcus InCirlce Staff. No Jacket Required: Another Great Collection of Recipes from Incircle. (Illus.). 292p. 1995. 25.00 (*0-15-100189-8*) Harcourt.

— Pure & Simple: An Incircle Cookbook. (Illus.). 320p. 1993. 19.95 (*0-15-175122-6*) Harcourt.

Neiman Marcus Staff. Pure & Simple: An Incircle Cookbook. 1991. 19.95 (*0-9629473-0-X*) Neiman-InCircle.

Neiman, Max, jt. ed. see Kempton, Willett.

Neiman, Morris. A Century of Modern Hebrew Literary Criticism, 1784-1884. 1983. 25.00 (*0-88125-011-2*) Ktav.

Neiman, Richard S., et al, eds. Hodgkin's Disease II: Pathological Considerations. LC 73-23030. (Hodgkin's Disease Ser.: Vol. 2). 141p. 1974. text 24.00 (*0-8422-7194-5*) Irvington.

Neiman, Richard S. & Orazi, Attilio. Disorders of the Spleen. 2nd ed. Strauss, Marc, ed. LC 99-31814. (Illus.). 230p. 1999. text. write for info. (*0-7216-7551-4*, W B Saunders Co) Harcrt Hlth Sci Grp.

Neiman, Richard S., jt. auth. see Wolf, Barbara C.

Neiman, Susan. The Unity of Reason: Rereading Kant. 224p. 1997. reprint ed. pap. 16.95 (*0-19-511388-8*) OUP.

Neiman, Tummy & Reynolds, Sue. Sirens for the Cross. Reynolds, Gaius & Sokoloski, Cherry, eds. (Illus.). 153p. 1998. pap. 12.95 (*0-9668878-0-8*, Pub. by Embrace Commns) Spring Arbor Dist.

Neiman, Valarie & Glick, Elleen J. No Apologies Pricing: How to Price Your Services & Products for Profit. 52p. 1995. pap. 9.95 (*1-887780-00-9*) HomeBased Busn Assn.

Neimanis, George J. The Collapse of the Soviet Empire: A View from Riga. LC 96-24332. 160p. 1997. 42.95 (*0-275-95713-6*, Praeger Pubs) Greenwood.

Neimark, A. V. Percolation & Fractals in Colloid & Interface Science. 400p. (C). 1997. text 48.00 (*981-02-0734-4*) World Scientific Pub.

Neimark, Anne E. Che! Latin America's Legendary Guerilla Leader. LC 88-23137. 128p. (J). (gr. 6 up). 1989. 13.95 (*0-397-32308-5*); lib. bdg. 13.89 (*0-397-32309-3*) HarpC Child Bks.

— Myth Maker: J. R. R. Tolkien. LC 96-4196. (Illus.). 128p. (J). 1996. 17.00 (*0-15-298847-5*) Harcourt.

— Myth Maker: J. R. R. Tolkien. LC 97-50380. (Illus.). 128p. (YA). (gr. 5-9). 1998. mass mkt. 4.95 (*0-688-15741-6*, Wm Morrow) Morrow Avon.

— Myth Maker: J. R. R. Tolkien. (J). 1998. 10.05 (*0-606-13639-8*, Pub. by Turtleback) Demco.

— Wild Heart: The Story of Joy Adamson, Author of Born Free. LC 98-26097. (Illus.). 128p. (YA). (gr. 7 up). 1999. 17.00 (*0-15-201368-7*) Harcourt.

Neimark, Edith D., et al, eds. Moderators of Competence. (Jean Piaget Symposia Ser.). 240p. (C). 1985. text 49.95 (*0-89859-531-2*) L Erlbaum Assocs.

Neimark, Jill, jt. auth. see Weiner, Marcella B.

Neimark, Lenny. The Pasta - Popcorn - Chocolate Diet. 32p. 1999. pap. 6.75 (*1-893557-03-0*, Pub. by R E P Tech) Soul Proprietor.

Neimark, Marilyn K. The Hidden Dimensions of Annual Reports: Sixty Years of Social Conflict at General Motors. (Critical Accounting Research Ser.). 207p. (C). 1995. text 39.95 (*1-55876-054-7*); pap. text 24.95 (*1-55876-100-4*) Wiener Pubs Inc.

Neimark, Neil F. The Handbook of Journaling: Tools for the Healing of Mind, Body & Spirit. 50p. 1999. pap. 7.95 (*1-893557-02-2*, Tools1) R E P Tech.

***Neimark, Neil F.** The Handbook of Journaling: Tools for the Healing of Mind, Body & Spirit. 2nd ed. 107p. 2000. pap. 10.00 (*1-893557-05-7*) R E P Tech.

— The Healing Power of Attitudes & Beliefs: A Journey Towards Self-Discovery. 77p. 1999. pap. 12.00 (*1-893557-45-6*) R E P Tech.

Neimark, Paul & Berkowitz, Gerald. A Doctor Discusses Care of the Back. 1990. pap. 6.00 (*0-910304-04-1*) Budlong.

Neimark, Paul & Matlin, Samuel. Doctor Discusses Female Surgery. (Illus.). 1992. pap. 6.00 (*0-686-65550-8*) Budlong.

Neimark, Paul, et al. A Doctor Discusses Your Life After the Baby Is Born. (Illus.). 1993. pap. 6.00 (*0-685-46338-9*) Budlong.

Neimark, Paul, jt. auth. see Scheimann, Eugene.

Neimark, Paul, ed. see Bockwinkel, Susan R.

Neimark, Peninah Rhodes & Mott, Peter, eds. The Environmental Debate: A Documentary History. LC 99-17844. (Primary Documents in American History & Contemporary Issues Ser.). 352p. 1999. 49.95 (*0-313-30020-8*) Greenwood.

Neimark, Philip J. The Way of Orisa: Empowering Your Life Through the Ancient African Religion of Ifa. LC 92-53903. 208p. 1993. pap. 14.00 (*0-06-250557-2*, Pub. by Harper SF) HarpC.

Neimark, Yu. I. & Landa, P. S. Stochastic & Chaotic Oscillations. (C). 1992. text 302.00 (*0-7923-1530-8*) Kluwer Academic.

Neimat, Marie-Anne K. Search Mechanisms for Large Files. Stone, Harold S., ed. LC 81-13036. (Computer Science: Distributed Database Systems Ser.: No. 11). 130p. 1981. reprint ed. pap. 40.30 (*0-8357-1231-1*, 207006400063) Bks Demand.

Neimeijer, Reint J. Doppler-Polarimetric Radar Signal Processing. (Illus.). 221p. (Orig.). 1996. pap. 57.50 (*90-407-1332-4*, Pub. by Delft U Pr) Coronet Bks.

Neimeijer, Rudo, jt. auth. see Hoorweg, Jan.

Neimeyer, Charles P. America Goes to War: A Social History of the Continental Army. (American Social Experience Ser.). (Illus.). 240p. (C). 1995. text 45.00 (*0-8147-5780-4*) NYU Pr.

— America Goes to War: A Social History of the Continental Army. (American Social Experience Ser.). 1997. pap. text 20.00 (*0-8147-5782-0*) NYU Pr.

Neimeyer, Greg J. Constructivist Assessment: A Casebook. (Counseling Psychologist Casebook Ser.: Vol. 2). (Illus.). 248p. (C). 1992. 42.00 (*0-8039-4830-1*); pap. 19.95 (*0-8039-4831-X*) Sage.

Neimeyer, Greg J. & Neimeyer, Robert A., eds. Advances in Personal Construct Psychology, Vol. 1. 287p. 1990. 78.50 (*1-55938-081-0*) Jai Pr.

— Advances in Personal Construct Psychology, Vol. 2. 272p. 1992. 78.50 (*1-55938-194-9*) Jai Pr.

— Advances in Personal Construct Psychology, Vol. 3. 336p. 1995. 78.50 (*1-55938-593-6*) Jai Pr.

— Advances in Personal Construct Psychology, Vol. 4. 296p. 1997. 78.50 (*0-7623-0083-3*) Jai Pr.

— Advances in Personal Construct Psychology, Vol. 5. Date not set. 78.50 (*0-7623-0431-6*) Jai Pr.

Neimeyer, Robert A. The Development of Personal Construct Psychology. LC 84-17367. 186p. reprint ed. pap. 57.70 (*0-7837-6806-0*, 204663800003) Bks Demand.

Neimeyer, Robert A., ed. Death Anxiety Handbook. (Series in Death Education, Aging, & Health Care). 312p. 1994. 54.50 (*1-56032-282-9*, Pub. by P Chapman) Taylor & Francis.

Neimeyer, Robert A., et al, eds. Treatment of Suicidal People. LC 94-12025. 240p. 1994. 54.95 (*1-56032-287-X*) Hemisp Pub.

***Neimeyer, Robert A. & Mahoney, Michael J., eds.** Constructivism in Psychotherapy. LC 94-23952. 436p. 1999. pap. 29.95 (*1-55798-645-2*) Am Psychol.

Neimeyer, Robert A., jt. auth. see Liles, Larry E.

Neimeyer, Robert A., jt. ed. see Epting, Franz R.

An Asterisk (*) at the beginning of an entry indicates that the title is appearing for the first time.

Neimeyer, Robert A., jt. ed. see Neimeyer, Greg J.

Neimeyer, Robert A., jt. ed. see Wass, Hannelore.

Neimi, Helena R. Porcelain Dollmaking in Detail. (Illus.). 60p. (Orig.). 1995. pap. text, student ed. 15.00 (*0-9607800-0-9*) H R Niemi.

Neinast, Helen & Ettinger, Thomas C. The Long & Winding Road: A Spiritual Guide for Baby Boomers. LC 98-42482. 96p. 1998. pap. 8.00 (*0-687-01593-6*) Dimen for Liv.

Neinast, Helen R. Albert Schweitzer. 1989. pap. 2.95 (*0-687-60015-4*) Abingdon.

— With Heart & Mind. 1994. pap. 14.95 (*0-687-61393-0*) Abingdon.

Neinast, Helen R., compiled by. Contemporary Spiritual Classics: Albert Schweitzer. LC 89-50644. 60p. 1989. pap. 3.00 (*0-8358-0605-7*) Upper Room Bks.

Neinast, Helen R. & Ettinger, Thomas C. What about God Now That You're off to College? A Prayers Guide for First-Year Students. LC 91-67171. 240p. 1992. text 20.00 (*0-8358-0655-3*) Upper Room Bks.

Neinast, Helen R. & Ettinger, Tom. With Heart & Mind & Soul. 250p. 1994. pap. 15.00 (*0-8358-0695-2*) Upper Room Bks.

Neinhuys, J. W., tr. see Temam, Roger.

Neininger, Falko, ed. London 1075-1187. (English Episcopal Acta Ser.: No. 15). (Illus.). 296p. 2000. text 49.95 (*0-19-726179-5*) OUP.

Neinken, Mortimer L. The U. S. Ten Cent Stamps of 1855-59. (Illus.). 252p. 1960. 30.00 (*0-912574-07-0*) Collectors.

Neinstein, Lawrence S. Adolescent Health Care: A Practical Guide. rev. ed. (Illus.). 1112p. 1990. pap. 59.00 (*0-683-06373-1*) Lppncott W & W.

— Adolescent Health Care: A Practical Guide. 2nd rev. ed. (Illus.). 1112p. 1990. 82.00 (*0-683-06374-X*) Lppncott W & W.

— Adolescent Health Care: A Practical Guide. 3rd ed. LC 95-47009. (Illus.). 1128p. 1996. pap. 69.00 (*0-683-06375-8*) Lppncott W & W.

— Issues in Reproductive Management. LC 93-33909. 1993. 55.00 (*0-86577-505-2*) Thieme Med Pubs.

Neipert, David M. A Tour of International Trade. LC 99-39220. (Illus.). 202p. 1999. pap. text 41.00 (*0-13-671744-6*) P-H.

Neira, Francisco J., et al. Larvae of Temperate Australian Fishes: Laboratory Guide for Larval Fish Identification. (Illus.). 436p. 1998. 125.00 (*1-875560-72-6*, Pub. by Univ of West Aust Pr); pap. 95.00 (*1-876268-17-4*, Pub. by Univ of West Aust Pr) Intl Spec Bk.

Neirynck, F. The Minor Agreements in a Horizontal-Line Synopsis. (Studiorum Novi Testamenti Auxilia: No. 15). 103p. (Orig.). 1991. pap. 24.00 (*90-6186-457-7*, Pub. by Leuven Univ) Coronet Bks.

Neis, Klaus J. & Hepp, Hermann. Hysteroscopy. (Illus.). 128p. 1994. text 89.00 (*0-86577-489-7*) Thieme Med Pubs.

Neisbitt, John. Megatrends Asia: Eight Asian Megatrends That Are Reshaping Our World. 320p. 1996. 24.00 (*0-684-81542-7*) S&S Trade.

Neisendorfer, Joseph. Primary Homotopy Theory. LC 80-12109. (Memoirs of the American Mathematical Society Ser.: No. 25/232). 67p. 1983. reprint ed. pap. 16.00 (*0-8218-2232-2*, MEMO/25/232) Am Math.

Neises, Amy, ed. see Pellham, Brian L.

Neises, Charles P. The Beatles Reader: A Selection of Contemporary Views, News & Reviews of the Beatles in Their Heyday. LC 84-60267. (Rock & Roll Remembrances Ser.: No. 6). 232p. 1991. reprint ed. 28.50 (*1-56075-024-3*) Popular Culture.

Neises, M., et al, eds. Der Geriatrische Tumorpatient. (Beitraege Zur Onkologie, Contributions to Oncology Ser.: Vol. 45). (Illus.). viii, 234p. 1994. 100.00 (*3-8055-5808-2*) S Karger.

Neish, W. J. Xanthines & Cancer: An Experimental Study of Tumour Inhibition. 192p. (C). 1988. pap. 35.00 (*0-08-036399-7*, Pub. by Aberdeen U Pr) Macmillan.

Neishtadt, Iakov. Paul Keres Chess Master Class. 182p. 1983. 29.90 (*0-08-023122-5*, Pergamon Pr); 17.90 (*0-08-029719-6*, Pergamon Pr) Elsevier.

— Queen Sacrifice. LC 90-40805. (Russian Chess Ser.). 266p. 1990. pap. 14.95 (*0-685-47231-0*, Pub. by CHES) Macmillan.

— Queen's Gambit Accepted. 1997. pap. 24.95 (*1-85744-114-1*, Pub. by Cadgn Bks) Macmillan.

— Winning Quickly with Black. 144p. 1996. pap. 19.95 (*1-85744-039-0*, Pub. by Cadgn Bks) Macmillan.

— Winning Quickly with White. 144p. 1996. pap. 19.95 (*1-85744-038-2*, Pub. by Cadgn Bks) Macmillan.

Neishtadt, J. Play the Catalan: Closed Variation & Catalan Opening after 1 d4 d5 2 c4. LC 87-2262. (Illus.). 190p. 1988. pap. 19.90 (*0-08-032062-7*, Pergamon Pr) Elsevier.

— Play the Catalan: Open Variation, Vol. 1. Neat, Kenneth P., tr. LC 87-2262. (Chess Ser.). (Illus.). 258p. 1987. pap. 23.90 (*0-08-029740-4*, Pergamon Pr) Elsevier.

Neiss, Peggy R. Opening the Door. (Illus.). 128p. (Orig.). 1997. pap. 15.95 (*0-9657305-0-6*) P R Neiss.

Neissa, Peter A. The Drug Lord. 210p. 1990. 23.00 (*0-685-38358-X*) Floricanto Pr.

Neisser. Memory Observed. 2nd ed. LC 99-49080. 1999. pap. text 27.95 (*0-7167-3319-6*) W H Freeman.

Neisser, Arden. The Other Side of Silence. LC 89-71507. 316p. 1990. pap. 15.95 (*0-930323-64-5*) Gallaudet Univ Pr.

Neisser, Eric. Recapturing the Spirit: Essays on the Bill of Rights at 200. 291p. 1991. pap. 12.95 (*0-945612-23-0*); text 19.95 (*0-945612-22-2*) Madison Hse.

Neisser, Philip T., jt. ed. see Schram, Sanford F.

Neisser, Ulric, ed. The Perceived Self: Ecological & Interpersonal Sources of Self Knowledge. (Emory Symposia in Cognition Ser.: No. 5). (Illus.). 333p. (C). 1994. text 54.95 (*0-521-41509-8*) Cambridge U Pr.

— The Rising Curve: Long-Term Gains in IQ & Related Measures. LC 97-52183. 415p. 1998. 39.95 (*1-55798-503-0*) Am Psychol.

— The School Achievement of Minority Children: New Perspectives. 208p. (C). 1986. text 39.95 (*0-89859-685-8*) L Erlbaum Assocs.

Neisser, Ulric & Fivush, Robyn, eds. The Remembering Self: Construction & Accuracy in the Self-Narrative. LC 93-40556. (Emory Symposia in Cognition Ser.: Vol. 6). 315p. (C). 1994. text 52.95 (*0-521-43194-8*) Cambridge U Pr.

Neisser, Ulric & Winograd, Eugene. Remembering Reconsidered: Ecological & Traditional Approaches to the Study of Memory. (Emory Symposia in Cognition Ser.: No. 2). (Illus.). 400p. 1988. text 64.95 (*0-521-33031-9*) Cambridge U Pr.

Neisser, Ulric & Winograd, Eugene, eds. Remembering Reconsidered: Ecological & Traditional Approaches to the Study of Memory. (Emory Symposia in Cognition Ser.: No. 2). (Illus.). 400p. (C). 1995. pap. text 25.95 (*0-521-48500-2*) Cambridge U Pr.

Neisser, Ulric, jt. ed. see Winograd, Eugene.

Neisser, Ulriv & Jopling, David, eds. The Conceptual Self in Context: Culture, Experience, Self Understanding. (Emory Symposia in Cognition Ser.: Vol. 7). (Illus.). 294p. (C). 1997. text 54.95 (*0-521-48203-8*) Cambridge U Pr.

Neist, Melinda. Melinda's Folk Art, Vol. 1. (Illus.). 1993. pap. 9.95 (*1-883675-00-6*, 100) J Shaw Studio.

— Melinda's Folk Art, Vol. 2. (Illus.). 1994. pap. 9.95 (*1-883675-02-2*, 102) J Shaw Studio.

— Melinda's Folk Art, Vol. 3. (Illus.). 1997. pap. 10.95 (*1-883675-19-7*, 119) J Shaw Studio.

Neistadt, Maureen E. Occupational Therapy Evaluation for Adults: A Pocket Guide. 256p. spiral bd. 34.95 (*0-7817-2495-3*) Lppncott W & W.

Neistadt, Maureen E. & Crepeau, Elizabeth Blesedell. Willard & Spackman's Occupational Therapy. 9th ed. LC 97-15395. 976p. 1997. text 57.95 (*0-397-55192-4*) Lppncott W & W.

Neistadt, Maureen E. & Freda, Maureen. Choices: A Guide to Sex Counseling with Physically Disabled Adults. LC 86-2888. 132p. 1987. pap. 9.95 (*0-89464-201-4*); text 15.50 (*0-89874-903-4*) Krieger.

Neisworth, John T., et al. Temperament & Typical Behavior Scale: Early Childhood Indicators of Developmental Dysfunction. LC 99-11263. 128p. 1999. pap. text 40.00 (*1-55766-422-6*) P H Brookes.

Neisworth, John T., jt. auth. see Bagnato, Stephen J.

Neisworth, John T., jt. auth. see Smith, Robert M.

Neitch, Shirley M. & Mufson, Maurice. Becoming a Clinician: A Primer for Students. LC 98-15024. (Illus.). 384p. 1998. pap. text 29.95 (*0-07-046515-0*) McGraw-Hill HPD.

Neito, Eva M., et al, eds. Notable Hispanic American Women. 485p. 1993. 75.00 (*0-8103-7578-8*, 003318) Gale.

Neito, M. M., jt. ed. see Goldman, T.

Neittaanmaki, P., ed. Numerical Methods for Free Boundary Problems. (International Series of Numerical Mathematics: Vol. 99). 439p. 1991. 59.00 (*3-7643-2641-7*) Birkhauser.

Neittaanmaki, Pekka, ed. Numerical Methods for Free Boundary Problems. (International Series of Numerical Mathematics: Vol. 99). xv, 439p. 1991. 137.00 (*0-8176-2641-7*) Birkhauser.

Neittaanmaki, Pekka & Krizek, Michael. Mathematical & Numerical Modelling in Electrical Engineering: Theory & Applications. LC 96-35769. (Mathematical Modelling Ser.). 316p. (C). 1996. text 169.00 (*0-7923-4249-6*) Kluwer Academic.

Neittaanmaki, Pekka & Makela, M. M. Nonsmooth Optimization: Analysis & Algorithms with Applications to Optimal Control. 300p. (C). 1992. text 48.00 (*981-02-0773-5*) World Scientific Pub.

Neittaanmaki, Pekka & Marinov, C. A. Mathematical Models in Electrical Circuits: Theory & Applications. (C). 1991. text 118.00 (*0-7923-1155-8*) Kluwer Academic.

Neittaanmaki, Pekka & Tiba, D. Optimal Control of Nonlinear Parabolic Systems: Theory, Algorithms & Applications. LC 93-45312. (Pure & Applied Mathematics Ser.: Vol. 179). (Illus.). 424p. 1994. text 165.00 (*0-8247-9081-2*) Dekker.

Neittaanmaki, Pekka, et al. Inverse Problems & Optimal Design in Electricity & Magnetism. (Monographs in Electrical & Electronic Engineering: No. 35). (Illus.). 380p. 1996. text 115.00 (*0-19-859383-X*) OUP.

Neittaanmaki, Pekka, jt. auth. see Haslinger, Jaroslav.

Neitz, Mary J. Charisma & Community: A Study of Religion in American Culture. 275p. 1987. 44.95 (*0-88738-130-8*) Transaction Pubs.

Neitzel, Charlotte L. RCRA Compliance Handbook. 2nd ed. (Environmental Compliance Handbook Ser.: Vol. 3). 1992. pap. 49.95 (*0-7816-0071-5*) Exec Ent Pubns.

— RCRA Compliance Handbook. 2nd rev. ed. (Environmental Compliance Handbook Ser.: Vol. 3). 152p. 1994. pap. 80.00 (*0-471-11266-6*) Wiley.

Neitzel, Duane A., jt. ed. see Becker, C. Dale.

Neitzel, J. E., jt. auth. see Carr, C.

Neitzel, Jill E. The Regional Organization of the Hohokam in the American Southwest: A Stylistic Analysis of Red-on-Buff Pottery. LC 90-28291. (Evolution of North American Indians Ser.). 215p. 1991. reprint ed. text 10.00 (*0-8240-2509-1*) Garland.

Neitzel, M., ed. Recycling Concepts & Procedures. 88p. 1993. 98.00 (*1-85573-145-2*, Pub. by Woodhead Pubng) Am Educ Systs.

Neitzel, Michael C. The Valencia Tragedy. (Illus.). 112p. 1995. pap. 11.95 (*1-895811-36-8*) Heritage Hse.

Neitzel, Robert S. The Grand Village of the Natchez Indians Revisited. Galloway, Patricia K., ed. LC 83-620022. (Mississippi Department of Archives & History Archaeological Reports). 215p. 1983. pap. 15.00 (*0-938896-35-0*) Mississippi Archives.

Neitzel, Shirley. The Bag I'm Taking to Grandma's. LC 94-4115. (IFAC Symposia Series). (Illus.). 32p. (J). (ps up). 1995. 15.00 (*0-688-12960-9*, Grenwillow Bks); lib. bdg. 14.93 (*0-688-12961-7*, Grenwillow Bks) HarpC Child Bks.

— The Bag I'm Taking to Grandma's. (J). 1998. 10.15 (*0-606-13176-0*, Pub. by Turtleback) Demco.

— Bag I'm Taking to Grandma's. (Illus.). 32p. (J). (gr. k-3). 1998. mass mkt. 4.95 (*0-688-15840-4*, Wm Morrow) Morrow Avon.

Neitzel, Shirley. The Dress I'll Wear to the Party. LC 91-30906. (Illus.). 32p. (J). (ps-3). 1992. 13.89 (*0-688-09960-2*, Grenwillow Bks) HarpC Child Bks.

— The Dress I'll Wear to the Party. LC 91-30906. (Illus.). 32p. (J). (ps-4). 1995. mass mkt. 6.95 (*0-688-14261-3*, Wm Morrow) Morrow Avon.

Neitzel, Shirley. The Dress I'll Wear to the Party. (J). (ps-4). 1995. 10.15 (*0-606-07453-8*, Pub. by Turtleback) Demco.

***Neitzel, Shirley.** From the Land of the White Birch: Three Ojibwa Legends. (Illus.). 32p. (J). (gr. 2-5). 2000. pap. 8.95 (*0-938682-56-3*) River Rd Pubns.

Neitzel, Shirley. From the Land of the White Birch Teacher's Guide. (Illus.). 32p. (J). (gr. 2-5). 1998. pap., wbk. ed. 8.95 (*0-938682-51-2*, 682-51-2) River Rd Pubns.

— The House I'll Build for the Wrens. LC 96-43679. (Illus.). 32p. (J). (gr. k-3). 1997. 15.00 (*0-688-14973-1*, Grenwillow Bks) HarpC Child Bks.

— The House I'll Build for the Wrens. LC 96-43679. (Illus.). 32p. (J). (gr. k up). 1997. lib. bdg. 14.93 (*0-688-14974-X*, Grenwillow Bks) HarpC Child Bks.

***Neitzel, Shirley.** I'm Not Feeling Well Today. (J). 2001. 15.95 (*0-688-17380-2*, Grenwillow Bks) HarpC Child Bks.

— I'm Not Feeling Well Today. (J). 2001. lib. bdg. 15.89 (*0-688-17381-0*, Grenwillow Bks) HarpC Child Bks.

Neitzel, Shirley. I'm Taking a Trip on My Train. LC 98-2979. (Illus.). 40p. (J). (ps-3). 1999. 15.00 (*0-688-15833-1*, Grenwillow Bks) HarpC Child Bks.

***Neitzel, Shirley.** I'm Taking a Trip on My Train. LC 98-2979. (Illus.). 40p. (J). (ps-3). 1999. 14.93 (*0-688-15834-X*, Grenwillow Bks) HarpC Child Bks.

Neitzel, Shirley. The Jacket I Wear in the Snow. LC 88-18767. (Illus.). 32p. (J). (ps up). 1989. 16.00 (*0-688-08028-6*, Grenwillow Bks) HarpC Child Bks.

Neitzel, Shirley. The Jacket I Wear in the Snow. LC 88-18767. (Illus.). 32p. 1997. pap. 18.95 (*0-688-12771-1*, Wm Morrow) Morrow Avon.

— The Jacket I Wear in the Snow. LC 92-43789. 1994. 10.15 (*0-606-06503-2*, Pub. by Turtleback) Demco.

— The Jacket I Wear in the Snow. Cohr, Amy, ed. LC 92-43789. (Illus.). 32p. (J). (ps up). 1994. reprint ed. mass mkt. 5.95 (*0-688-04587-1*, Wm Morrow) Morrow Avon.

Neitzel, Shirley. We're Making Breakfast for Mother. LC 96-10417. (Illus.). 32p. (J). (ps up). 1997. 15.00 (*0-688-14575-2*, Grenwillow Bks); lib. bdg. 14.93 (*0-688-14576-0*, Grenwillow Bks) HarpC Child Bks.

Neitzell, Jill E. Great Towns & Regional Polities in the Prehistoric American Southeast & Southwest. LC 98-40959. Vol. 3. (Illus.). xxii, 325 p. 1999. 45.00 (*0-8263-2001-5*) U of NM Pr.

Neitzert, Monica, jt. auth. see Handa, Sudhanshu.

***Neiva, Eduardo.** Mythologies of Vision: Image, Culture & Visuality. LC 98-25975. (Semiotics & the Human Sciences Ser.: Vol. 15). 254p. (C). 1999. text 50.95 (*0-8204-4184-8*, 41848) P Lang Pubng.

Neiwert, David A. In God's Country: The Patriot Movement & the Pacific Northwest. LC 98-50203. (Illus.). 384p. 1999. pap. 19.95 (*0-87422-175-7*) Wash St U Pr.

Nejar, Carlos. Carlos Nejar. Picciotto, tr. (QRL Poetry Bks.: Vol. XXII). 1981. 20.00 (*0-614-06392-2*) Quarterly Rev.

Nekam, Alexander. The Personality Conception of the Legal Entity. LC 38-37803. (Harvard Studies in the Conflict of Laws: Vol. 3). 131p. 1978. reprint ed. lib. bdg. 40.00 (*0-89941-128-2*, 301060) W S Hein.

***Nekimken, Albert.** Kocsis Scourged: Surviving the Art World. LC 92-81994. (Illus.). 260p. 1999. 95.00 (*0-9674199-0-5*) Paragon Pr PA.

Nekliudova, M. Ivanov, Alexander. (C). 1985. 50.00 (*0-7855-4526-3*, Pub. by Collets) St Mut.

Nekola, Charlotte. Dream House. 175p. 1993. pap. 12.00 (*1-55597-225-X*) Graywolf.

Nekola, Charlotte & Rabinowitz, Paula, eds. Writing Red: An Anthology of American Women Writers, 1930-1940. LC 89-25023. 368p. 1990. pap. 18.95 (*0-935312-76-5*) Feminist Pr.

Nekoogar, Farzad. Timing of Verification of Digital Systems. LC 99-33309. 208p. (C). 1999. 78.00 (*0-13-794348-2*, Macmillan Coll) P-H.

Nekoogar, Farzad & Moriarty, Gene. Digital Control Using Digital Signal Processing. LC 98-18811. (Illus.). 448p. 1998. 76.00 (*0-13-089103-7*) P-H.

Nekrasov, George M. North of Gallipoli No. 343: The Black Sea Fleet at War, 1914-1917. 200p. 1992. text 37.50 (*0-88033-240-9*, 343, Pub. by East Eur Monographs) Col U Pr.

Nekrasov, I. Ya. Geochemistry, Mineralogy & Genesis of Gold Deposits. (Illus.). 344p. (C). 1996. text 110.00 (*90-5410-723-5*, Pub. by A A Balkema) Ashgate Pub Co.

Nekrasov, Nikolai. Who Can Be Happy & Free in Russia? LC 72-120571. reprint ed. 39.50 (*0-404-04677-0*) AMS Pr.

Nekrasov, Victor. Po Obe Storony Steny. LC 84-81387. (Povesti i Rasskazy Ser.). (RUS.). 216p. 1985. 12.50 (*0-911971-12-2*) Effect Pub.

Nekrasova, Maria. Lacquer Miniatures from Palekh. (Illus.). 1984. 50.00 (*0-7855-1551-8*) St Mut.

Nekrich, Aleksandr M. Pariahs, Partners, Predators: German-Soviet Relations, 1922-1941. Freeze, Gregory L., tr. from RUS. LC 96-29605. 308p. 1997. 37.00 (*0-231-10676-9*) Col U Pr.

Nektaria, Veloff, tr. see Braga, Roman.

Nekuee, Shervin, jt. ed. see Hagendoorn, Louk.

Nel, Christo, jt. auth. see McLagan, Patricia.

Nel, Etienne L. Regional & Local Economic Development in South Africa: The Experience of the Eastern Cape. (Making of Modern Africa Ser.). 372p. 1999. text 78.95 (*1-84014-941-8*, Pub. by Ashgate Pub) Ashgate Pub Co.

Nel, Francisca & Bezuidenhout, Jan. Human Rights for the Police. 1995. pap. 41.50 (*0-7021-3323-X*, Pub. by Juta & Co) Intl Spec Bk.

Nel, Francisca & Bezuidenhout, Jan, eds. Policing & Human Rights. 2nd ed. LC 97-198501. 472p. 1997. pap. 52.50 (*0-7021-3905-X*, Pub. by Juta & Co) Gaunt.

Nel, H., jt. auth. see Jones, R. J.

Nel, Martini. Complete Quilt Book. 1997. pap. text 24.95 (*0-7981-3647-2*) Human & Rousseau.

Nel, Philip J. The Structure & Ethos of the Wisdom Admonitions in Proverbs. (Beiheft zur Zeitschrift fuer die Alttestamentliche Wissenschaft Ser.: Vol. 158). xii, 142p. 1982. 66.95 (*3-11-008750-2*) De Gruyter.

Nelder, J. A. & Kime, R. D. Computers in Biology. (Wykeham Science Ser.: No. 32). 168p. (C). 1974. 14.00 (*0-8448-1159-9*, Crane Russak) Taylor & Francis.

Nelder, J. A., jt. auth. see Baker, R. J.

Nelder, J. A., jt. auth. see McCullagh, Peter.

***Nele, Bill.** Business Finance. (C). 2000. pap. text. write for info. (*0-201-61904-0*) Addison-Wesley.

Neleheel, Sennovy. Sennovy Neleheels Poems: Poems of Reality. (Illus.). 50p. 1999. 24.95 (*1-893025-00-4*) P & F Pubg.

***Neleman, Hans, photos by.** Silence: Hans Neleman/Stills. (Illus.). 2000. 75.00 (*3-908163-30-7*, Pub. by Edit Stemmle) Abbeville Pr.

Nelesen, James H. Mr. Washington's Travelling Music. 32p. (J). (ps-4). 1987. 8.99 (*0-570-04151-1*, 56-1611) Concordia.

— The Most Important Christmas. 32p. (J). (gr. 5-9). 1985. 8.99 (*0-570-04110-4*, 56-1521) Concordia.

Nelessen, Anton C. Visions for a New American Dream. 2nd ed. LC 94-71145. (Illus.). 374p. 1994. reprint ed. pap. 55.95 (*1-884829-00-7*, Planners Press) Am Plan Assn.

— Visions for a New American Dream: Process, Principles, & an Ordinance to Plan & Design Small Communities. 2nd ed. LC 94-71145. (Illus.). 374p. 1994. reprint ed. lib. bdg. 70.00 (*1-884829-01-5*, Planners Press) Am Plan Assn.

Nelhybel, V. Eck Danza: Full Score String Orchestra. 12p. 1989. pap. 5.00 (*0-7935-5009-2*, 50480909) H Leonard.

— Eck Duets: For Horn/Trombone. 8p. 1989. pap. 4.50 (*0-7935-5181-1*, 50480916) H Leonard.

— Suite from Bohemia. 1989. pap. text 50.00 (*0-7935-2316-8*, 50481024) H Leonard.

***Neligan, David.** A Spy in the Castle. 189p. 1999. pap. 15.95 (*0-9535697-0-5*) Irish Bks Media.

Neligh, Robert D., ed. The Brownsea Trail: A Brave, Clean, & Reverent Path. LC 92-81312. (Illus.). 300p. 1993. 21.95 (*0-9631648-5-6*); pap. 12.95 (*0-9631648-6-4*) Ambush Pub.

***Nelik, Lev.** Centrifugal & Rotary Pumps: Fundamentals with Applications. LC 98-49382. 15p. 1999. boxed set 89.95 (*0-8493-0701-5*) CRC Pr.

Nelipa, N. F., jt. auth. see Chaichian, M.

Nelis, G. F., et al. Peptic Ulcer Diseases: Basic & Clinical Aspects. (Developments in Gastroenterology Ser.). 1985. text 237.50 (*0-89838-759-0*) Kluwer Academic.

Nellscher, Maurice, ed. Handbook of Landscape Architectural Construction, Vol. 1. 2nd ed. 385p. 1985. 45.00 (*0-941236-09-9*, 609B, Landscape Architecture) Am Landscape Arch.

— Handbook of Landscape Architectural Construction: Site Works, Vol. 2. LC 85-80042. 1988. 40.00 (*0-941236-31-5*) Am Landscape Arch.

Nelissen, A. M., et al. Future Scenarios on Dental Health Care: A Reconnaissance of the Period 1990-2020. LC 94-636. (Scenario Report Ser.). 1994. pap. text 136.00 (*0-7923-2694-6*) Kluwer Academic.

Nelissen, Nico, et al, eds. Classics in Environmental Studies: An Overview of Classic Texts. 400p. 1997. 69.90 (*90-6224-963-9*, Pub. by Uitgeverij Arkel) LPC InBook.

— Classics in Environmental Studies: An Overview of Classic Texts in Environmental Studies. 424p. (Orig.). 1997. pap. text 24.95 (*90-6224-973-6*, Pub. by Uitgeverij Arkel) LPC InBook.

— Renewing Government: Innovative & Inspiring Visions. 320p. 1998. pap. 24.95 (*90-5727-017-X*, Pub. by Intl Bks) Paul & Co Pubs.

Nelissen, Nico, jt. auth. see Leroy, Peter.

Nelken & Vogler. Comparative Criminal Justice. 148.95 (*1-85521-880-1*) Ashgate Pub Co.

Nelken, Andrea, ed. see Van Hook, Beverly.

Nelken, David. Contrasts in Criminal Justice. 78.95 (*1-84014-469-6*) Ashgate Pub Co.

Nelken, David. The Futures of Criminology. 256p. 1994. 69.95 (*0-8039-8714-5*); pap. 26.95 (*0-8039-8715-3*) Sage.

Nelken, David, ed. Comparing Legal Cultures. LC 96-43132. (Socio-Legal Ser.). 288p. 1997. text 82.95 (*1-85521-718-X*, Pub. by Dartmth Pub); pap. text 34.95 (*1-85521-898-4*, Pub. by Dartmth Pub) Ashgate Pub Co.

— Law As Communication. LC 95-46956. (Issues in Law &

N

Society Ser.). (Illus.). 288p. 1996. pap. 32.95 (1-85521-722-8, Pub. by Dartmth Pub); text 96.95 (1-85521-719-8, Pub. by Dartmth Pub) Ashgate Pub Co.
— White Collar Crime. (International Library of Criminology & Criminal Justice). 656p. 1994. 249.95 (1-85521-376-1, Pub. by Dartmth Pub) Ashgate Pub Co.
Nelken, David & Levi, Mike, eds. The Corruption of Politics & the Politics of Corruption. (Journal of Law & Society Ser.). 128p. (Orig.). (C). 1996. pap. text 26.95 (0-631-20014-2) Blackwell Pubs.
Nelken, David, jt. ed. see Beirne, Piers.
Nelken, Davis. Italian Politics: The Center-Left in Power. D'Alimonte, Roberto, ed. LC 97-30513. (Italian Politics Ser.). (C). 1997. pap. 28.00 (0-8133-3443-8, Pub. by Westview) HarpC.
Nelken, Halina. And Yet, I Am Here! LC 98-30275. (Illus.). 304p. 1999. 27.95 (1-55849-156-2) U of Mass Pr.
Nelken, Israel. Computerized Trading: How to Design, Build & Test Market a PC-Based Trading System. 300p. 1997. 50.00 incl. disk (0-7863-1069-3, Irwn Prfssnl) McGraw-Hill Prof.
— The Handbook of Exotic Options: Instruments, Analysis & Applications. 384p. 1995. text 70.00 (1-55738-904-7, Irwn Prfssnl) McGraw-Hill Prof.
*__Nelken, Israel.__ Handbook of Hybrid Instruments. LC 99-88565. (Illus.). 258p. 2000. 95.00 (0-471-89114-2) Wiley.
Nelken, Israel. Implementing Credit Derivatives: Strategies & Techniques for Using Credit Derivatives in Risk Management. LC 99-13976. (Illus.). 256p. 1999. 60.00 (0-07-047237-8, Irwn Prfssnl) McGraw-Hill Prof.
— Option Embedded Bonds: Price Analysis, Credit Risk, & Investment Strategies. 312p. 1996. 75.00 (0-7863-0818-4, Irwn Prfssnl) McGraw-Hill Prof.
— Pricing, Hedging, & Trading Exotic Options: Understand the Intricacies of Exotic Options & How to Use Them to Maximum Advantage. LC 99-34153. (Illus.). 256p. 1999. 60.00 (0-07-047236-X, Irwn Prfssnl) McGraw-Hill Prof.
— Volatility in the Capital Markets: State-of-the-Art Techniques for Modeling, Managing, & Trading Volatility. (Glenlake Business Monographs). 300p. 1998. 55.00 (1-884964-73-7) Fitzroy Dearborn.
Nelken, Israel, ed. Volatility in the Capital Markets: State-of-the-Art Techniques for Modeling, Managing, & Trading Volatility. (Finance Editions Ser.). 300p. 1997. 55.00 (1-888998-05-9) Glenlake Pub.
Nelken, Michael. Hitler Unmasked: The Romance of Racism & Suicide. LC 95-83613. (Illus.). 276p. 1996. 24.50 (0-9649979-0-8) Darkside Pr.
Nelken-Turner, Antoinette, et al. Second Annual Report of the Ayacucho Project. (Reports of the Ayacucho Archaeological-Botanical Project Ser.). 1970. pap. text 7.00 (0-939312-16-6) Peabody Found.
Nelkin, Barry D. Genetic Mechanisms in Multiple Endocrine Neoplasia Type 2A. LC 96-30948. (Medical Intelligence Unit Ser.). 202p. 1996. 99.00 (1-57059-402-3) Landes Bioscience.
Nelkin, Dorothy. Jetport: The Boston Airport Controversy. LC 74-78793. (Social Policy Ser.). 200p. 1974. 34.95 (0-87855-111-5); pap. 21.95 (0-87855-591-9) Transaction Pubs.
— Science As Intellectual Property: Who Controls Research? LC 83-3805. (AAAS Series on Issues in Science & Technology). 142p. reprint ed. pap. 44.10 (0-7837-6741-2, 204636900011) Bks Demand.
— Science As Intellectual Property: Who Controls Scientific Research. (AAAS Issues in Science & Technology Ser.). 130p. 1983. pap. text 15.95 (0-02-949090-1) Free Pr.
— Science As Intellectual Property: Who Controls Scientific Research. 130p. 1983. text. write for info. (0-318-57876-X) Macmillan.
— Selling Science: How the Press Covers Science & Technology. 2nd rev. ed. 217p. 1994. pap. text 15.95 (0-7167-2595-9) W H Freeman.
Nelkin, Dorothy, ed. Controversy: Politics of Technical Decisions. 3rd ed. (Focus Editions Ser.: Vol. 8). (Illus.). 320p. 1992. 59.95 (0-8039-4466-7); pap. 26.00 (0-8039-4467-5) Sage.
— The Language of Risk: Conflicting Perspectives on Occupational Health. LC 85-2211. (Sage Focus Edition Ser.: No. 71). 200p. reprint ed. pap. 62.00 (0-7837-4565-6, 204409400003) Bks Demand.
Nelkin, Dorothy, et al, eds. A Disease of Society: Cultural & Institutional Responses to AIDS. 295p. (C). 1991. text 59.95 (0-521-40411-8); pap. text 18.95 (0-521-40743-5) Cambridge U Pr.
Nelkin, Dorothy & Brown, Michael S. Workers at Risk: Voices from the Workplace. LC 83-9319. (Illus.). xviii, 238p. 1984. lib. bdg. 22.50 (0-226-57127-0) U Ch Pr.
— Workers at Risk: Voices from the Workplace. LC 83-9319. (Illus.). xviii, 338p. 1998. pap. text 12.00 (0-226-57128-9) U Ch Pr.
Nelkin, Dorothy & Lindee, M. Susan. The DNA Mystique: The Gene as a Cultural Icon. LC 94-48711. (Illus.). 276p. 1995. text 22.95 (0-7167-2709-9) W H Freeman.
— The DNA Mystique: The Gene as a Cultural Icon. 288p. 1996. pap. text 12.95 (0-7167-3049-9) W H Freeman.
Nelkin, Dorothy & Pollak, Michael. The Atom Besieged: Extraparliamentary Dissent in France & Germany. (Illus.). 256p. 1980. 30.00 (0-262-14034-9) MIT Pr.
— The Atom Besieged: Extraparliamentary Dissent in France & Germany. (Illus.). 248p. 1982. pap. text 10.95 (0-262-64021-X) MIT Pr.
Nelkin, Dorothy & Tancredi, Laurence. Dangerous Diagnostics: The Social Power of Biological Information. LC 93-32571. 232p. 1994. pap. text 12.95 (0-226-57129-7) U Ch Pr.
Nelkin, Dorothy, jt. auth. see Andrews, Lori B.
Nelkin, Dorothy, jt. auth. see Jasper, James M.
Nelkin, Norton. Consciousness & the Origins of Thought. (Cambridge Studies in Philosophy). 356p. (C). 1996. text 59.95 (0-521-56409-3) Cambridge U Pr.
Nelkowski, H., ed. Einstein Symposium Berlin, on Occasion of the One Hundredth Anniversary of His Birthday. (Lecture Notes in Physics Ser.: Vol. 100). 550p. 1980. pap. 34.00 (0-387-09718-X) Spr-Verlag.
Nell, Donald F. & Taylor, John E. Lewis & Clark in the Three Rivers Valleys. (Illus.). 299p. (Orig.). 1996. pap. text 23.40 (0-9651346-0-1) Headwaters Chapter.
Nell, Donald F., ed. see Lewis, Meriwether & Clark, William.
Nell, Edward J. The General Theory of Transformational Growth: Keynes after Sraffa. LC 98-24700. (Illus.). 658p. (C). 1998. text 135.00 (0-521-59006-X) Cambridge U Pr.
— Making Sense of a Changing Economy: Technology, Markets, & Morals. 240p. (C). 1996. pap. 22.99 (0-415-13640-7) Routledge.
— Prosperity & Public Spending: Transformation Growth & the Role of Government. (Studies in International Political Economy). 224p. 1988. text 37.95 (0-04-339044-7); pap. text 17.95 (0-04-339045-5) Routledge.
— Transformational Growth & Effective Demand: Economics after the Capital Critique. 675p. (C). 1991. text 100.00 (0-8147-5769-3) NYU Pr.
— Transformational Growth & the Business Cycle. LC 96-50075. 368p. (C). 1998. write for info. (0-415-14855-3) Routledge.
Nell, Lynda, et al. Hog Heaven: Recipes from the Durning House. 19.95 (0-9639218-0-0) Hog Heaven.
Nell, Onora. Acting on Principle: An Essay on Kantian Ethics. LC 74-20647. 167p. reprint ed. pap. 51.80 (0-8357-5083-3, 202272500029) Bks Demand.
Nell, Sharon, et al, eds. The French Novel from Lafayette to Desvignes: Collected Essays to Mark the 60th Birthday of Patrick Brady. 334p. 1995. pap. text 29.95 (1-886935-10-6) New Prdigm Pr.
Nell, Terril A. Flowering Potted Plants: Prolonging Shelf Performance: Postproduction Care & Handling. LC 92-45173. (Postproduction Ser.). (Illus.). 96p. (C). 1993. pap. text 19.95 (0-9626796-8-2, B014) Ball Pub.
Nell, Varney R., ed. Entitled! Free Papers in Appalachia Concerning Antebellum Freeborn Negroes & Emancipated Blacks of Montgomery County, Virginia. LC 81-80481. 102p. 1981. lib. bdg. 18.50 (0-915156-47-4) Natl Genealogical.
Nell, Victor. Cross-Cultural Neuropsychological Assessment: Theory & Practice. LC 99-32682. 250p. 1999. write for info. (0-8058-3355-2); pap. write for info. (0-8058-3356-0) L Erlbaum Assocs.
Nell, William C. The Colored Patriots of the American Revolution. LC 68-29013. (American Negro: His History & Literature, Ser. No. 1). 1978. reprint ed. 31.95 (0-405-01832-0) Ayer.
— Services of Colored Americans in the Wars of 1776 & 1812. LC 78-144663. reprint ed. 27.50 (0-404-00202-1) AMS Pr.
Nellas & Panayiotis. Deification in Christ: The Nature of the Human Person. LC 86-31479. (Contemporary Greek Theologians Ser.: No. 5). 254p. (Orig.). 1984. pap. 14.95 (0-88141-030-6) St Vladimirs.
Nelle, Susan. Using Workperfect Advanced Vol. 4: IBM 5.1. (C). 1991. text 24.75 (0-07-909587-9) McGraw.
— Using Workperfect IBM 5.1 with Disk: Beginner's Edition. (C). 1991. pap., text 27.75 incl. disk (0-07-909583-6) McGraw.
Nelleman, Beate, ed. see Jensen, Lynette.
Nelleman, Beate, ed. see Laporte, Gul.
Nelleman, Beate, ed. see Sundermann, Terrell.
*__Nellen, Annette.__ Tax Aspects of Business Transactions: A First Course. 706p. 1998. 97.00 (0-13-261751-X) P-H.
Nellen, Henk J. Hugo Grotius, Theologian: Essays in Honor of G.H.M Posthumus Meyjes. Rabbie, Edwin, ed. LC 93-46252. (Studies in the History of Christian Thought: Vol. 55). 1994. text 94.00 (90-04-10000-8) Brill Academic Pubs.
Nellen, Wolfgang, jt. ed. see Lichtenstein, Conrad.
Nelles, H. V. The Art of Nation Building: Pageanty & Spectacle at Quebec's Tercentenary. (Illus.). 408p. 1999. text 45.00 (0-8020-4271-6) U of Toronto Pr.
Nelles, H. V., jt. auth. see Armstrong, Christopher.
Nelles, Joachim & Fuhrer, Andreas, eds. Harm Reduction in Prison Risikominderung im Gefangnis: Strategies Against Drugs, AIDS & Risk Behaviour (Strategien Gegen Drogen, AIDS und Risikoverhalten) (Illus.). 264p. 1997. pap. 42.95 (3-906756-97-1, Pub. by P Lang) P Lang Pubng.
— Harm Reduction in Prison/Risikominderung im Gefangnis: Strategies Against Drugs, AIDS & Risk Behaviour/Strategien Gegen Drogen, AIDS und Risikoverhalten. LC 96-52165. 264p. (C). 1997. pap. text 42.95 (0-8204-3402-7, Pub. by P Lang) P Lang Pubng.
*__Nelles, Rick.__ Proof of Performance: How to Build a Career Portfolio to Land a Great New Job. 2000. pap. 17.95 (1-57023-148-6) Impact VA.
Nelles Staff. Australia Nelles Guide. 2nd ed. (Nelles Guides Ser.). (Illus.). 256p. 1997. pap. 14.95 (3-88618-118-9, Pub. by Nelles Verlag) Seven Hills Bk.
— Cambodia Laos Nelles Guide. 2nd ed. (Nelles Guides Ser.). (Illus.). 256p. 1997. pap. 14.95 (3-88618-102-2, Pub. by Nelles Verlag) Seven Hills Bk.
— Hawaii Nelles Guide. 2nd ed. (Nelles Guides Ser.). (Illus.). 256p. 1997. pap. 14.95 (3-88618-109-X, Pub. by Nelles Verlag) Seven Hills Bk.
— Vietnam Nelles Guide. 2nd ed. (Nelles Guides Ser.). (Illus.). 256p. 1997. pap. 14.95 (3-88618-116-2, Pub. by Nelles Verlag) Seven Hills Bk.
*__Nelles, Verlag.__ Maldives. (Nelles Guides Ser.). (Illus.). 256p. 1999. pap. 15.95 (3-88618-139-1) Hunter NJ.
— Recommended Country Hotels of Britain, 2000. 160p. 1999. pap. 9.95 (1-55650-874-3) Hunter NJ.
— Recommended Wayside & Country Inns of Britain, 2000. 160p. 1999. pap. 9.95 (1-55650-875-1) Hunter NJ.
Nelles Verlag Staff. Berlin & Potsdam. 3rd rev. ed. (Nelles Guides Ser.). (Illus.). 256p. 1999. pap. 15.95 (3-88618-029-8) Hunter NJ.
— Brittany. 2nd rev. ed. (Nelles Guides Ser.). (Illus.). 256p. 1999. pap. 15.95 (3-88618-072-7) Hunter NJ.
— Canada: Ontario, Quebec, Atlantic Provinces. 2nd rev. ed. (Nelles Guides Ser.). (Illus.). 256p. 1999. pap. 15.95 (3-88618-089-1) Hunter NJ.
— Canada: Rockies, Pacific, Prairie, Territories. (Nelles Guides Ser.). (Illus.). 256p. 1999. pap. 15.95 (3-88618-368-8) Hunter NJ.
— The Caribbean: The Lesser Antilles. (Nelles Guides Ser.). (Illus.). 256p. 1999. pap. 15.95 (3-88618-112-X) Hunter NJ.
— Costa Rica. (Nelles Guides Ser.). (Illus.). 256p. 1999. pap. 15.95 (3-88618-127-8) Hunter NJ.
— Croatia: Explore the World. (Guides Ser.). (Illus.). 1998. pap. text 14.95 (3-88618-395-5, Pub. by Nelles Verlag) Seven Hills Bk.
— Greek Islands. (Nelles Guides Ser.). (Illus.). 256p. 1999. pap. 15.95 (3-88618-024-7) Hunter NJ.
*__Nelles Verlag Staff.__ India: North & Central. 3rd rev. ed. (Nelles Guides Ser.). (Illus.). 256p. 1999. pap. 15.95 (3-88618-075-1) Hunter NJ.
— Indonesia: Sumatra, Java, Bali, Lombok, Sulawesi. 3rd rev. ed. (Nelles Guides Ser.). (Illus.). 256p. 1999. pap. 15.95 (3-88618-085-9) Hunter NJ.
Nelles Verlag Staff. Malaysia - Singapore - Brunei. 2nd rev. ed. (Nelles Guides Ser.). (Illus.). 256p. 1999. pap. 15.95 (3-88618-902-3) Hunter NJ.
— Mexico. 2nd rev. ed. (Nelles Guides Ser.). (Illus.). 256p. 1999. pap. 15.95 (3-88618-119-7) Hunter NJ.
— Morocco. 2nd rev. ed. (Nelles Guides Ser.). (Illus.). 256p. 1999. pap. 15.95 (3-88618-113-8) Hunter NJ.
— Moscow - St. Petersburg. 2nd rev. ed. (Nelles Guides Ser.). (Illus.). 256p. 1999. pap. 15.95 (3-88618-904-X) Hunter NJ.
— Munich: Including Excursions to Castles, Lakes & Mountains. 3rd rev. ed. (Nelles Guides Ser.). (Illus.). 256p. 1999. pap. 15.95 (3-88618-120-0) Hunter NJ.
— Munich & Surroundings. (Nelles Guides Ser.). (Illus.). 256p. (Orig.). 1995. pap. 14.95 (3-88618-039-5, Pub. by Nelles Verlag) Seven Hills Bk.
— Myanmar (Burma) (Nelles Guides Ser.). (Illus.). 256p. 1999. pap. 15.95 (3-88618-415-3) Hunter NJ.
— Nelles Guide: Portugal. 1996. pap. text 14.95 (3-88618-417-X, Pub. by Nelles Verlag) Seven Hills Bk.
— Nelles Guide to Egypt. (Nelles Guides Ser.). 1996. pap. text 14.95 (3-88618-107-3, Pub. by Nelles Verlag) Seven Hills Bk.
— Nelles Guide to Northern Spain: Pyrenees, Atlantic Coast, Central Spain. (Nelles Guides Ser.). 1997. pap. text 14.95 (3-88618-400-5, Pub. by Nelles Verlag) Seven Hills Bk.
— Nelles Guide to Paris. (Nelles Guides Ser.). 1997. pap. text 14.95 (3-88618-108-1, Pub. by Nelles Verlag) Seven Hills Bk.
— Nelles Guide to Sri Lanka. (Nelles Guides Ser.). 1997. pap. text 14.95 (3-88618-418-8, Pub. by Nelles Verlag) Seven Hills Bk.
— Nelles Guide to the Caribbean: The Greater Antilles, Bermuda, Bahamas. (Nelles Guides Ser.). 1997. pap. text 14.95 (3-88618-403-X, Pub. by Nelles Verlag) Seven Hills Bk.
— Nepal: Nelles Guide. rev. ed. (Nelles Guides Ser.). (Illus.). 256p. (Orig.). 1996. pap. 14.95 (3-88618-046-8, Pub. by Nelles Verlag) Seven Hills Bk.
— New Zealand. 3rd rev. ed. (Nelles Guides Ser.). (Illus.). 256p. 1999. pap. 15.95 (3-88618-905-8) Hunter NJ.
— Philippines. 2nd rev. ed. (Nelles Guides Ser.). (Illus.). 256p. 1999. pap. 15.95 (3-88618-106-5) Hunter NJ.
— Poland. (Nelles Guides Ser.). (Illus.). 256p. 1999. pap. 15.95 (3-88618-088-3) Hunter NJ.
— Prague - Czech Republic. 2nd rev. ed. (Nelles Guides Ser.). (Illus.). 256p. 1999. pap. 15.95 (3-88618-907-4) Hunter NJ.
— Provence - Cote D'Azur. 2nd rev. ed. (Nelles Guides Ser.). (Illus.). 256p. 1999. pap. 15.95 (3-88618-034-4) Hunter NJ.
— South Pacific Islands. (Nelles Guides Ser.). (Illus.). 256p. 1999. pap. 15.95 (3-88618-104-9) Hunter NJ.
— Sweden. (Nelles Guides Ser.). (Illus.). 256p. 1999. pap. 15.95 (3-88618-103-0) Hunter NJ.
— Syria - Lebanon. (Nelles Guides Ser.). (Illus.). 256p. 1999. pap. 15.95 (3-88618-105-7) Hunter NJ.
— Tanzania. (Nelles Guides Ser.). (Illus.). 256p. 1999. pap. 15.95 (3-88618-050-6) Hunter NJ.
— Thailand. 3rd rev. ed. (Nelles Guides Ser.). (Illus.). 256p. 1999. pap. 15.95 (3-88618-032-8) Hunter NJ.
— Thailand: Nelles Guide. rev. ed. (Nelles Guides Ser.). (Illus.). 256p. (Orig.). 1996. pap. 14.95 (3-88618-047-6, Pub. by Nelles Verlag) Seven Hills Bk.
— Turkey. 3rd rev. ed. (Nelles Guides Ser.). (Illus.). 256p. 1999. pap. 15.95 (3-88618-911-2, Pub. by Nelles Verlag) Hunter NJ.
Nelles Verlag Staff, compiled by. China. (Nelles Guides Ser.). (Illus.). 256p. 1993. pap. 14.95 (3-88618-393-9, Pub. by Nelles Verlag) Seven Hills Bk.
Nelles, William. Frameworks: Narrative Levels & Embedded Narrative. LC 96-34383. (American University Studies XIX: Vol. 33). 208p. (C). 1997. text 42.95 (0-8204-3039-0) P Lang Pubng.
Nelles/Verlag Staff. Corsica. (Nelles Guides Ser.). 1996. pap. text 14.95 (3-88618-036-0, Pub. by Nelles Verlag) Seven Hills Bk.
— Israel. (Nelles Guides Ser.). 1996. pap. text 14.95 (3-88618-412-9, Pub. by Nelles Verlag) Seven Hills Bk.
— Kenya. (Nelles Guides Ser.). 1996. pap. text 14.95 (3-88618-052-2, Pub. by Nelles Verlag) Seven Hills Bk.
— South Africa. (Nelles Guides Ser.). 1996. pap. text 14.95 (3-88618-411-0, Pub. by Nelles Verlag) Seven Hills Bk.
— Spain, South. (Nelles Guides Ser.). 1996. pap. text 14.95 (3-88618-399-8, Pub. by Nelles Verlag) Seven Hills Bk.
Nellhaus, Arlynn. Into the Heart of Jerusalem: A Traveler's Guide to Visits, Celebrations, & Sojourns. 2nd rev. ed. LC 98-43086. Orig. Title: Heart of Jerusalem. (Illus.). 360p. 1999. pap. 16.95 (1-56261-425-8) Avalon Travel.
Nellhaus, Gerald, tr. see Brecht, Bertolt.
Nelli, Humbert S. The Business of Crime: Italians & Syndicate Crime in the United States. LC 80-27196. xiv, 328p. (C). 1981. reprint ed. pap. text 19.95 (0-226-57132-7) U Ch Pr.
Nelli, Humbert S. & Nelli, Steve. The Winning Tradition: A History of Kentucky Wildcat Basketball. 2nd ed. LC 98-3788. 1998. 24.95 (0-8131-2087-X) U Pr of Ky.
Nelli, Rene. Dictionnaire des Heresies Meridionales. (FRE.). 384p. 18.50 (0-8288-9194-X) Fr & Eur.
— Spiritualite de L'Heresie: Le Catharisme. LC 78-63189. (Heresies of the Early Christian & Medieval Era Ser.: Second Ser.). reprint ed. 39.50 (0-404-16226-6) AMS Pr.
Nelli, Steve, jt. auth. see Nelli, Humbert S.
Nelligan, Emile. Selected Poems. Widdows, P. F., tr. from FRE. (Essential Poets Ser.: No. 73). 96p. pap. 8.00 (1-55071-034-6) Guernica Editions.
Nelligan, Emily. Heart of the Flower: Poems for the Sensuous Gardener. LC 90-24639. 128p. (Orig.). 1991. pap. 13.95 (0-9619111-2-3) Chicory Blue.
Nelligan, Frank A., jt. auth. see Siegel, Freyda.
Nelligan, Murray H. Old Arlington: The Story of the Lee Mansion National Memorial. LC F234.A7N45. (Illus.). 480p. 1996. pap. 29.95 (1-57420-051-8) Chatelaine.
Nelligan, Tom. Commuter Trains to Central Terminal. 1986. pap. 7.95 (0-915276-45-3) Quadrant Pr.
Nellis, jt. auth. see Fleming.
Nellis, David W. Poisonous Plants & Animals of Florida & the Caribbean. LC 96-21971. (Illus.). 416p. 1997. 29.95 (1-56164-111-1); pap. 21.95 (1-56164-113-8) Pineapple Pr.
*__Nellis, David W.__ Puerto Rico & Virgin Islands Wildlife Viewing Guide. LC 99-26752. (Watchable Wildlife Ser.). (Illus.). 93p. 1999. pap. text 8.95 (1-56044-836-9) Falcon Pub Inc.
Nellis, David W. Seashore Plants of South Florida & the Caribbean. LC 93-40713. (Illus.). 160p. 1994. 27.95 (1-56164-026-3); pap. 19.95 (1-56164-056-5) Pineapple Pr.
Nellis, David W., jt. auth. see Dammann, Arthur E.
Nellis, Elwyn A. A SCORE That Counts: The Story of the Service Corps of Retired Executives. (Illus.). 188p. 1989. 7.50 (0-9623466-0-8) SCOREA.
Nellis, Eric G., ed. The Records of the Boston Overseers of the Poor, 1735-1795. 550p. 1997. 49.50 (0-9620737-4-1) Colonial MA.
*__Nellis, John.__ Time to Rethink Privatization in Transition Economies? LC 99-23306. (IFC Discussion Paper Ser.: No. 38). 40p. 1999. pap. 22.00 (0-8213-4503-6, 14503) World Bank.
Nellis, John, et al. Privatization: The Lessons of Experience. LC 92-27381. 90p. 1992. pap. 22.00 (0-8213-2181-1, 12181) World Bank.
Nellis, John R. The Ethnic Composition of Leading Kenyan Government Positions. (Research Report Ser.: No. 24). 26p. 1974. write for info. (91-7106-079-0, Pub. by Nordic Africa) Transaction Pubs.
Nellis, John R. & Lee, Barbara. Enterprise Reform & Privitization in Socialist Economies. (Discussion Papers: No. 104). 34p. 1990. 22.00 (0-8213-1666-4, 11666) World Bank.
Nellis, John R. & Nunberg, Barbara. Civil Service Reform & the World Bank. LC 92-12847. (Discussion Paper Ser.: No. 161). 50p. 1995. pap. 22.00 (0-8213-2117-X, 12117) World Bank.
Nellis, Joseph. The Essence of Business Economics. 2nd ed. LC 97-12766. 248p. (C). 1997. pap. text 19.95 (0-13-573130-5) P-H.
Nellis, Joseph G. The Essence of the Economy. 2nd ed. LC 97-10601. (Essence of Management Ser.). 223p. (C). 1996. pap. text 19.95 (0-13-356502-5) P-H.
Nellis, Joseph G., jt. auth. see Fleming, M. C.
Nellis, Joseph G., jt. auth. see Fleming, Michael C.
Nellis, Lee. Protecting Stream Corridors. 27p. 1993. pap. 10.00 (0-86602-301-1, Sage Prdcls Pr) Sage.
Nellis, Micki. Logan & the Duck Patrol. LC 95-79218. (Illus.). 32p. (J). (gr. k-2). 1996. 14.95 (1-885534-04-3) Buffalo Creek.
Nellis, Micki, ed. see Schroder, Eugene & Schechter, David.
Nellis, Ryan G. The Wadiba Tree: A Photographic Story Book. LC 96-71185. (Illus.). 72p. 1997. 24.95 (0-9654895-0-7) Creat Media Wrks.
Nellis, W. J., et al, eds. Shock Waves in Condensed Matter, 1981: (Menlo Park) LC 82-70014. (AIP Conference Proceedings Ser.: No. 78). 715p. 1982. lib. bdg. 43.00 (0-88318-177-0) Am Inst Physics.
Nellist, Brian, ed. see Lodge, Thomas.
Nellist, Cassandra L. Child's First Book about Hawaii. (Illus.). 24p. (J). (ps). 1987. 9.95 (0-916630-58-7) Pr Pacifica.
Nellist, John G. Understanding Telecommunications & Lightwave Systems: An Entry-Level Guide. 2nd ed. LC 95-11535. 272p. 1995. pap. 39.95 (0-7803-1113-2, PP 4665) Inst Electrical.
Nellist, John G. & Gilbert, Elliot M. Understanding Modern Telecommunications & the Information Superhighway. LC 99-10793. (Illus.). 300p. 1999. 55.00 (0-89006-322-2) Artech Hse.
Nellist, John G., jt. auth. see Gilbert, Elliot M.

An Asterisk (*) at the beginning of an entry indicates that the title is appearing for the first time.

Nello, Arthur. Heriot. LC 91-9633. 1991. pap. 13.95 (*0-87949-335-6*) Ashley Bks.

Nello, Susan S. & Smith, Karen E. The European Union & Central & Eastern Europe: The Implications of Enlargement in Stages. LC 98-72627. 130p. 1998. text 55.95 (*1-84014-514-5*, Pub. by Ashgate Pub) Ashgate Pub Co.

Nellore, Usha, jt. ed. see Husta, Adriana.

Nells, Robert. Walk a Straight Line to Freedom. 1991. 7.95 (*0-533-08956-5*) Vantage.

Nells, Tara L., jt. auth. see Fox, Sharon E.

Nells, Tara L., jt. auth. see Telles, Carol A.

Nelmes, Jill. An Introduction to Film Studies. 2nd ed. LC 98-11724. 1999. 85.00 (*0-415-17309-4*); pap. 29.99 (*0-415-17310-8*) Routledge.

Nelms, Brenda. The Third Republic & the Centennial of 1789. (Modern European History Ser.). 312p. 1987. text 15.00 (*0-8240-8039-4*) Garland.

Nelms, C. Robert. The Dynamics of Inculcating the Root Cause Mentality. (Illus.). 145p. (Orig.). 1997. pap. text 30.00 (*1-886118-30-2*) Failsafe Netwrk.

— The Go-Book. (Illus.). 165p. (Orig.). 1996. pap. text 35.00 (*1-886118-20-5*) Failsafe Netwrk.

— The Go-Book. 3rd rev. ed. (Illus.). 165p. (Orig.). 1998. pap. 35.00 (*1-886118-21-3*) Failsafe Netwrk.

— What You Can Learn from Things That Go Wrong: A Guidebook to the Root Causes of Failure. (Illus.). 192p. (Orig.). 1996. pap. text 35.00 (*1-886118-10-8*) Failsafe Netwrk.

Nelms, David K. The H. A. M. R. Manual: How to Rewire Your Own Brain. LC 96-86026. (Illus.). x, 128p. (Orig.). 1997. pap. 19.95 (*0-9654169-6-8*) Billings Wrldwide.

***Nelms, Henning.** Magic & Showmanship: A Handbook for Conjurers. LC 99-52791. 2000. pap. 8.95 (*0-486-41087-0*) Dover.

Nelms, Henning. Only an Orphan Girl. 1944. pap. 5.25 (*0-8222-0855-5*) Dramatists Play.

— A Primer of Stagecraft. 1941. pap. 5.95 (*0-8222-0914-4*) Dramatists Play.

— Scene Design: A Guide to the Stage. LC 74-25249. (Illus.). 96p. 1975. reprint ed. pap. 7.95 (*0-486-23153-4*) Dover.

Nelms, Link. Remembering Vietnam: After the War in the Gulf. 188p. 1995. pap. 13.50 (*0-87012-531-1*) McClain.

Normally after military action or war, an official history is soon written but we are still waiting for one on the Vietnam War. The trouble is, a flood of "histories" hit the market first & became the politically correct version. Since the official historians are not yet writing fiction & truthful reports from them cause a storm of protests from Big Media, there has been no release of an official version of the war. Now, at last, you can read the non-politically correct side of the story by a retired USAF Intelligence Officer. *Publisher Paid Annotation.*

Nelms, R. M., ed. see De Doncker, R. W., et al.

Nelms, Sheryl L. Friday Night Desperate. (Illus.). 64p. (Orig.). 1997. pap. 7.00 (*0-9654651-4-4*) IM Press.

Nelms, Willie. Cora Wilson Stewart: Crusader Against Illiteracy. LC 97-25077. (Illus.). 239p. 1997. pap. 38.50 (*0-7864-0334-9*) McFarland & Co.

Nels, Rebecca, jt. auth. see Clancy, Pat.

Nelsbach, Hannah. Fairytale about the Phenomenon of Indian Summer. (Illus.). 30p. (J). (gr. k-6). 1997. pap. text 12.95 (*0-9660716-0-3*) H Nelsbach.

Nelscott, Kris. A Dangerous Road. mass mkt. write for info. (*0-312-97643-7*) St Martin.

— A Dangerous Road. LC 00-25137. 336p. 2000. 24.95 (*0-312-26264-7*, Minotaur) St Martin.

Nelsen, Brent F. The State Offshore: Petroleum, Politics, & State Intervention on the British & Norwegian Continental Shelves. LC 90-21037. 272p. 1991. 65.00 (*0-275-93835-2*, C3835, Praeger Pubs) Greenwood.

Nelsen, Brent F., ed. Norway & the European Community: The Political Economy of Integration. LC 92-45109. 264p. 1993. 57.95 (*0-275-94211-2*, C4211, Praeger Pubs) Greenwood.

Nelsen, Brent F. & Stubb, Alexander C., eds. The European Union. 2nd ed. LC 98-7423. 340p. 1998. pap. 22.50 (*1-55587-804-0*) L Rienner.

Nelsen, Brent F., ed. see Huff, A. V., et al.

***Nelsen, Frank C.** Public Education, Law & Religion in America: A Comprehensive History. 397p. 2000. pap. text 40.00 (*1-55605-302-9*) Wyndham Hall.

Nelsen, Jan L., jt. auth. see Nelsen, Marjorie R.

***Nelsen, Jane.** From Here to Serenity: Four Principles for Understanding Who You Really Are. 2000. pap. text 14.00 (*0-7615-2419-3*) Prima Pub.

Nelsen, Jane. Positive Discipline. rev. ed. 272p. 1996. pap. 11.00 (*0-345-40251-0*) Ballantine Pub Grp.

— Positive Discipline. 2nd ed. 242p. 1987. pap. 7.95 (*0-9606896-1-3*) Ballantine Pub Grp.

— Positive Discipline for Blended Families: Nurturing Harmony, Respect, & Unity in Your New Stepfamily. LC 97-25126. 208p. 1997. per. 15.00 (*0-7615-1035-4*) Prima Pub.

— Positive Discipline in the Classroom. 2nd expanded rev. ed. LC 97-9016. 240p. 1997. per. 15.00 (*0-7615-1059-1*) Prima Pub.

— Understanding. 2nd rev. ed. 224p. 1996. pap. 12.00 (*0-7615-0559-8*) Prima Pub.

Nelsen, Jane & Glenn, H. Stephen. Time Out: A Guide for Parents & Teachers Using Popular Discipline Methods to Empower & Encourage Children. 2nd ed. Erwin, Cheryl, ed. 111p. 1992. pap. 6.95 (*0-9606896-8-0*, B105) Empowering People.

Nelsen, Jane & Lott, Lynn. I'm on Your Side: Resolving Conflict with Your Teenage Son or Daughter. 304p. 1991. pap. 9.95 (*1-55958-059-3*) Prima Pub.

— Positive Discipline for Teenagers: Resolving Conflict with Your Teenager. LC 93-36383. 448p. 1994. pap. 14.95 (*1-55958-441-6*) Prima Pub.

Nelsen, Jane, et al. Clean & Sober Parenting: A Guide to Help Recovering Parents Rebuild Trust, Create Structure & Routine from Chaos, Improve Communication & Share Feelings, Learn Parenting Skills, & Give up Guilt & Shame. 288p. (Orig.). 1992. pap. 10.95 (*1-55958-165-4*) Prima Pub.

— Positive Discipline: A Teacher's A-Z Guide: Turn Common Behavioral Problems into Learning Opportunities. LC 95-47032. 384p. 1996. per. 14.95 (*0-7615-0499-0*) Prima Pub.

— Positive Discipline: The First Three Years: From Infant to Toddler - Laying the Foundation for Raising a Capable, Confident Child. LC 98-7750. 304p. 1998. pap. 16.00 (*0-7615-1505-4*) Prima Pub.

— Positive Discipline A-Z. 368p. 1993. pap. 14.95 (*1-55958-312-6*) Prima Pub.

— Positive Discipline for Parenting in Recovery: A Guide to Help Recovering Parents. LC 95-24341. 288p. 1995. pap. 12.95 (*0-7615-0130-4*) Prima Pub.

— Positive Discipline for Preschoolers, Age Three to Six: For Their Early Years - Raising Children Who Are Responsible, Respectful & Resourceful. 2nd rev. ed. LC 98-36006. 304p. 1998. pap. 16.00 (*0-7615-1515-1*) Prima Pub.

***Nelsen, Jane, et al.** Positive Discipline for Single Parents: A Practical Guide to Raising Children Who Are Responsibl. 2nd rev. ed. LC 99-27561. (Illus.). 288p. 1999. pap. 16.00 (*0-7615-2011-2*) Prima Pub.

Nelsen, Jane, et al. Positive Discipline for Single Parents: A Practical Guide to Raising Children Who Are Responsible, Respectful, & Resourceful. LC 93-17738. 208p. 1993. pap. 12.00 (*1-55958-355-X*) Prima Pub.

***Nelsen, Jane, et al.** Positive Discipline for Your Stepfamily. 4th ed. 2000. pap. 16.95 (*0-7615-2012-0*) Prima Pub.

— Positive Discipline in the Classroom. 3rd ed. LC 99-86308. (Positive Discipline Ser.). 272p. 2000. pap. text 16.95 (*0-7615-2421-5*) Prima Pub.

Nelsen, Jane, et al. Positive Discipline in the Classroom: How to Effectively Use Class Meetings & Other Positive Discipline Strategies. 192p. (Orig.). 1993. pap. 14.95 (*1-55958-311-8*) Prima Pub.

Nelsen, Jane, jt. auth. see Glenn, H. Stephen.

Nelsen, Jane T., ed. A Prairie Populist: The Memoirs of Luna Kellie. LC 91-41361. (Singular Lives: The Iowa Series in North American Autobiography). (Illus.). 209p. 1992. pap. text 13.95 (*0-87745-369-1*) U of Iowa Pr.

Nelsen, Jeffrey. Space Jokes & Riddles. 1988. pap. 1.95 (*0-02-689071-2*) Macmillan.

Nelsen, Judith C. Communication Theory & Social Work Practice. LC 79-20361. 224p. 1998. lib. bdg. 15.00 (*0-226-57151-3*) U Ch Pr.

— An Integrative Guide to Couple Treatment. LC 98-12033. 1998. 60.00 (*0-7657-0166-9*) Aronson.

Nelsen, Karen. Books by Kids! Helping Young Children Create Their Own Books. 1993. pap. 10.99 (*0-86653-930-1*) Fearon Teacher Aids.

Nelsen, Kirsten. Secrets of Making Bows. 1996. pap. text 11.95 (*1-56824-118-6*) Mark Inc CA.

— Wedding Bows Great Decorating. 1996. 13.95 (*1-56824-116-X*) Mark Inc CA.

Nelsen, Marjorie R. A Child's Book of Responsibilities: Developing Self-Reliance Through Guided Tasks; Ages 3-8 Years. LC 96-72559. (Illus.). 15p. (Orig.). 1997. pap. 14.95 (*0-9630495-3-4*) Partners in Learn.

— The Terrific, No Tears Bedtime Book: A Child's Delightful Bedtime Routine with a Definite Beginning & a Definite, No Tears Ending - Ages 2-6 Years. (Illus.). 8p. (Orig.). 1996. pap. 8.95 (*0-9630495-2-6*) Partners in Learn.

Nelsen, Marjorie R. & Nelsen, Jan L. Peak with Books: An Early Childhood Resource Guide. 2nd rev. ed. (Illus.). 228p. 1991. 21.95 (*0-9630495-1-8*) Partners in Learn.

Nelsen, Marjorie R. & Nelsen-Parish, Jan. Peak with Books: An Early Childhood Resource for Balanced Literacy. 3rd ed. LC 99-6080. (1-Off Ser.). (Illus.). 288p. 1999. pap. 34.95 (*0-8039-6796-9*) Corwin Pr.

Nelsen, Norman R. A Year Here in Basking Ridge. 1998. pap. write for info. (*1-57553-696-X*) Watermrk Pr.

Nelsen-Parish, Jan, jt. auth. see Nelsen, Marjorie R.

Nelsen, Philip T., jt. ed. see Hampton, Robert G.

Nelsen, R. B. An Introduction to Copulas. LC 98-41245. (Lecture Notes in Statistics Ser.: Vol. 139). 232p. 1999. pap. 39.95 (*0-387-98623-5*) Spr-Verlag.

Nelsen, Rodney, ed. see Westheimer, Mary.

Nelsen, Roger B. Proofs Without Words: Exercises in Visual Thinking. LC 93-86338. (Classroom Resource Materials Ser.). 160p. (Orig.). 1993. pap. text 34.95 (*0-88385-700-6*, PWW) Math Assn.

Nelsen, William C. Renewal of the Teacher-Scholar: Faculty Development in the Liberal Arts College. LC 82-135931. 116p. (Orig.). reprint ed. pap. 36.00 (*0-7837-1649-4*, 204194600024) Bks Demand.

Nelsen, William C. & Siegel, Michael E., eds. Effective Approaches to Faculty Development. LC 79-93173. 159p. (Orig.). reprint ed. pap. 49.30 (*0-7837-1647-8*, 204194100024) Bks Demand.

Nelson. Advanced Run Book. (Runner's World Ser.). 1983. 10.95 (*0-02-499480-4*, Macmillan Coll) P-H.

— African American Reader Custom. 1999. (*0-07-235684-7*) McGraw.

— Application Group Theory Bonding & Spectroscopy. (C). 1990. 56.00 (*0-205-12180-2*, Macmillan Coll) P-H.

— Applications of Group Theory to Bonding & Spectroscopy. (C). 1998. 51.00 (*0-13-041799-8*, Macmillan Coll) P-H.

***Nelson.** Applied Manufacturing Process Plan. 736p. 2000. 66.67 (*0-13-532458-0*) P-H.

Nelson. Ceramics: A Potter's Handbook. 6th ed. (C). 1998. pap. text 42.50 (*0-03-028937-8*) Harcourt Coll Pubs.

— Children & Social Studies. 3rd ed. LC 97-73574. (C). 1997. pap. text 65.50 (*0-15-505465-1*, Pub. by Harcourt Coll Pubs) Harcourt.

— Classics of Eastern Thought. 2nd ed. (C). Date not set. pap. text. write for info. (*0-15-507868-2*) Harcourt Coll Pubs.

— Confidence in Public Speaking. 7th ed. 2001. 28.50 (*0-697-35499-7*) McGraw.

Nelson. Elements of Biochemistry. pap. text. write for info. (*1-57259-158-7*) W H Freeman.

Nelson. Environmental Emergencies. 1985. pap. text 37.00 (*0-7216-1163-X*, W B Saunders Co) Harcrt Hlth Sci Grp.

— The Examined Life. 1997. 15.25 (*0-07-220149-5*) McGraw.

— The Global Perspective, Vol. 1. 2nd ed. (C). 2000. pap. text 31.00 (*0-15-505538-0*) Harcourt Coll Pubs.

— The Global Perspective, Vol. 2. 2nd ed. (C). 2000. pap. text 31.00 (*0-15-505539-9*) Harcourt Coll Pubs.

— Group Leadership, University of Indianapolis. (Counseling Ser.). 1998. 35.00 (*0-534-50138-9*) Brooks-Cole.

— Guillermo Cabrera Infante. 1998. 28.95 (*0-8057-1644-0*, Twyne) Mac Lib Ref.

— Gun, Butter, & Politics in Wars. 1999. text. write for info. (*0-312-04775-4*) St Martin.

— Human Geography. (C). 1995. pap. text, student ed. 24.00 (*0-03-043782-2*, Pub. by Harcourt Coll Pubs) Harcourt.

— Human Geography. (C). 1995. pap. text 19.50 (*0-03-016552-0*, Pub. by Harcourt Coll Pubs) Harcourt.

— Human Geography. (C). 2001. pap. text 60.00 (*0-03-005903-8*) Harcourt Coll Pubs.

— The Human Geography of NAFTA. (C). Date not set. pap. text 14.00 (*0-03-015937-7*) Harcourt Coll Pubs.

— The Human Perspective, No. VI. 2nd ed. LC 96-77709. (C). 1996. pap. text 35.50 (*0-15-501345-9*, Pub. by Harcourt Coll Pubs) Harcourt.

— Human Research & Labor Relations. 882p. (C). 1995. pap. text 83.00 (*0-536-59093-1*) Pearson Custom.

— A Manager's Guide to Exporting. (Management Ser.). 256p. 1999. pap. 19.99 (*1-86152-316-5*) Thomson Learn.

— A Manager's Guide to International Business. 256p. 1998. 20.00 (*1-86152-315-7*) Thomson Learn.

— Math in Context 7. (UM - International Math Ser.). 1992. teacher ed. 106.95 (*0-538-62698-4*) S-W Pub.

— NurseNotes: Medical-Surgical Nursing. LC 96-23717. 464p. 1997. pap. text 31.95 (*0-7817-1130-4*) Lppncott W & W.

— Oht T/A Human Geography. 1995. 288.00 (*0-03-044154-4*, Pub. by Harcourt Coll Pubs) Harcourt.

— Organizational Behaviour. 1994. pap., teacher ed. write for info. (*0-314-03553-2*); text. write for info. (*0-314-03498-6*) West Pub.

— Original Behavior. Date not set. pap. text, teacher ed. write for info. (*0-314-03367-X*) West Pub.

— Problems Book for Group Theory. (C). 1990. 33.33 (*0-205-12095-4*, Macmillan Coll) P-H.

— Protocol for Profit: A Manager's Guide to Competing Worldwide, Vol. 1. LC 98-218553. 256p. 1998. pap. 20.00 (*1-86152-314-9*) Thomson Learn.

***Nelson.** QuickBooks 99 for Dummies. LC HF5679.N4497 1998. 384p. 1999. pap. 19.99 (*0-7645-0521-1*) IDG Bks.

Nelson. Real Estate Law. Date not set. pap. text, teacher ed. write for info. (*0-314-03376-9*) West Pub.

***Nelson.** Small Animal Cardiology. 256p. 2001. pap. 25.00 (*0-7506-7298-6*) Buttrwrth-Heinemann.

Nelson. Sociology in the 21st Century. 200p. (C). 1996. pap. text, student ed. 15.20 (*0-13-476730-6*) P-H.

— To the Common Defense. 1999. per. write for info. (*0-671-51926-3*) S&S Trade.

— Ultimate Mens & Womens. 1995. pap. 6.95 (*0-7601-0151-5*) Brentwood Music.

— Year in Life of a Shinto Shrine. LC 95-23257. (Illus.). 288p. 1996. pap. 17.50 (*0-295-97500-8*) U of Wash Pr.

Nelson, et al, eds. Delaware, 1782 Tax Assessment & Census List. 270p. 1994. text 35.00 (*1-887061-04-5*) DE Geneal Soc.

Nelson & Catalano, Robert A. Atlas of Ocular Motility. 256p. 1989. text 145.00 (*0-7216-2628-9*, W B Saunders Co) Harcrt Hlth Sci Grp.

Nelson & Fene. Using Maps & Globes. (Illus.). 32p. (J). (gr. 4-6). 1996. pap., teacher ed. 2.95 (*1-55799-540-0*, 4142) Evan-Moor Edu Pubs.

Nelson & Pearson. Confidence in Public Speaking. 6th annot. ed. 1995. teacher ed. 40.31 (*0-697-25986-2*, WCB McGr Hill) McGrw-H Hghr Educ.

— Confidence Public Speaking. 6th ed. 1996. teacher ed. 20.62 (*0-697-24636-1*, WCB McGr Hill) McGrw-H Hghr Educ.

***Nelson & Quick.** Organizational Behavior. 3rd ed. 2000. pap., student ed. 13.00 (*0-324-07176-0*) Sth-Wstrn College.

Nelson & Quick. Organizational Behaviour: Foundation, Realities & Challenges. 2nd ed. 1997. 26.50 (*0-314-20566-7*) West Pub.

Nelson & Turk. Human Geography. (C). 1995. pap. text, teacher ed., suppl. ed. 47.75 (*0-03-025417-5*) Harcourt Coll Pubs.

***Nelson, et al.** Infectious Disease Epidemiology. 2000. 69.00 (*0-8342-1766-X*) Aspen Pub.

Nelson, et al. Proceedings of the Winter Simulation Conference, 1991. 1262p. 1991. 150.00 (*0-685-66846-0*, WSC-91) Soc Computer Sim.

Nelson, jt. auth. see Austin.

Nelson, jt. auth. see Ewen, Dale R.

Nelson, jt. auth. see Hart.

Nelson, jt. auth. see Holmes, Larry.

Nelson, jt. auth. see Jurmain, Robert.

Nelson, jt. auth. see Lorbeer.

***Nelson, Carol Ann.** Red & Red. 32p. (J). 1998. 16.95 (*1-893886-00-X*) Harmonic Computing.

— Sammy Knows What to Do. (J). (gr. 1-3). 2000. 11.95 (*1-893886-02-6*) Harmonic Computing.

Nelson, Keith S. It's Time to Start a Third Party. LC 98-72547. 1998. pap. text 12.99 (*0-933451-40-7*) Prescott Pr.

Nelson, Lynne R., jt. ed. see Drake, Frederick D.

Nelson, A. Stepping Stones Activity Book 1. 1997. pap. write for info. (*0-17-556498-1*, Pub. by ITP Nelson) Thomson Learn.

Nelson, A. Thomas & Miller, Paul B. Modern Management Accounting. 2nd ed. LC 80-23023. 589p. reprint ed. pap. 182.60 (*0-7837-6549-5*, 204568600007) Bks Demand.

Nelson, Adie & Robinson, Barrie W. Gigolos & Madames Bountiful: Illusions of Gender, Power & Intimacy. 344p. 1994. text 24.95 (*0-8020-0613-2*) U of Toronto Pr.

— Gigolos & Madames Bountiful: Illusions of Gender, Power & Intimacy. 344p. 1996. pap. 14.95 (*0-8020-7859-1*) U of Toronto Pr.

***Nelson, Al P. & Jones, Mel R.** A Silent Siren Song: The Aitken Brothers' Hollywood Odyssey, 1905-1926. LC 00-31781. 2000. 24.95 (*0-8154-1069-7*, Pub. by Cooper Sq) Natl Bk Netwk.

Nelson, Al P., jt. auth. see Keating, Lawrence A.

Nelson, Alan, ed. Cambridge, 2 vols. (Records of Early English Drama Ser.). 1100p. 1989. text 175.00 (*0-8020-5751-9*) U of Toronto Pr.

Nelson, Alan, jt. auth. see Toler, Stan.

Nelson, Alan E. Leading Your Ministry. Miller, Herb, ed. LC 96-12804. (Leadership Insights Ser.). 176p. 1996. pap. 14.95 (*0-687-01964-8*) Abingdon.

Nelson, Alan E., jt. auth. see Nelson, Linda S.

Nelson, Alan H. Early Cambridge Theatres: College, University, & Town Stages, 1464-1720. LC 93-31690. (Illus.). 208p. (C). 1994. text 59.95 (*0-521-43177-8*) Cambridge U Pr.

— The Medieval English Stage: Corpus Christi Pageants & Plays. LC 73-85247. (Patterns of Literary Criticism Ser.). 288p. 1992. lib. bdg. 21.00 (*0-226-57173-4*) U Ch Pr.

Nelson, Alan H., ed. see Medwall, Henry.

Nelson, Alan H., jt. ed. see Taylor, Jerome.

Nelson, Alan R., jt. ed. see McCalpin, James P.

Nelson, Albert J. Democrats under Siege in the Sunbelt Megastates: California, Florida, & Texas. LC 95-51425. 136p. 1996. 52.95 (*0-275-95568-0*, Praeger Pubs) Greenwood.

— Emerging Influentials in State Legislatures: Women, Blacks, & Hispanics. LC 91-8604. 168p. 1991. 47.95 (*0-275-93829-8*, C3829, Praeger Pubs) Greenwood.

Nelson, Alfred L., et al, eds. The Adelphi Calendar Project, 1806-1850: Sans Pareil Theatre 1806-1819 - Adelphi Theatre 1819-1850, 1. LC 89-11968. (London Stage, 1800-1900 Ser.: No. 1). 248p. 1990. text 195.00 (*0-313-25882-1*, DUG/, Greenwood Pr) Greenwood.

— The Adelphi Theatre Calendar: The Adelphi Calendar Project 1806-1900 - the Adelphi Theatre 1850-1900, Pt. II. LC 89-11968. (London Stage, 1800-1900 Ser.). 296p. 1993. text 225.00 (*0-313-28882-8*, GR8882) Greenwood.

Nelson, Alice J. Virginia Lineages, Letters & Memories. (Illus.). x, 302p. 21.50 (*0-9614497-0-5*) A J Nelson.

Nelson, Alice R. The Goodness of St. Rocque & Other Stories. LC 73-18594. reprint ed. 32.50 (*0-404-11405-9*) AMS Pr.

Nelson, Alicia, ed. see Lewis, Joe.

Nelson, Alvar. Responses to Crime: An Introduction to Swedish Criminal Law & Administration. (New York University Criminal Law Education & Research Center, Monograph Ser.: Vol. 6). vi, 90p. 1972. reprint ed. pap. 18.50 (*0-8377-0900-8*, Rothman) W S Hein.

Nelson, Alvin F. Inquiry & Reality: A Discourse in Pragmatic Synthesis. LC 75-46077. 192p. reprint ed. pap. 59.60 (*0-608-10312-8*, 202157300022) Bks Demand.

***Nelson, Amy.** Sweetners: Alternative. (Ingredient Handbook Ser.). (Illus.). 100p. 2000. pap. 59.00 (*1-891127-11-X*) Eagan Pr.

Nelson-Anderson, Danette L. Genetic Connections: A Guide to Documenting Your Individual & Family Health History (Special Condensed Edition) (Illus.). 88p. 1997. 19.95 (*0-9639154-4-4*) Sonters Pubng.

Nelson-Anderson, Danette L. & Waters, Cynthia V. Genetic Connections: A Guide to Documenting Your Individual & Family Health History. LC 94-67892. (Illus.). 335p. 1995. pap. 34.95 (*0-9639154-3-6*); text 39.95 (*0-9639154-2-8*) Sonters Pubng.

Nelson, Andrea, jt. auth. see Muehrcke, Jill.

Nelson, Andrea, jt. auth. see Nelson, John E.

Nelson, Andrew. Catch the Vision, Find Your Mission. 1997. pap. 12.95 (*0-9650275-1-1*) Holistic Health.

— Modern Reader's Japanese-English Character Dictionary. 2nd rev. ed. LC 61-11973. (ENG & JPN.). 1110p. 1962. 69.95 (*0-8048-0408-7*) Tuttle Pubng.

Nelson, Andy. Poker: A Winner's Guide. 288p. 1996. pap. 11.00 (*0-399-52212-3*, Perigee Bks) Berkley Pub.

Nelson, Angela, jt. auth. see Patterson, Karen F.

Nelson, Angela M. This Is How We Flow: Rhythm & Sensibility in Black Cultures. LC 98-40207. 166p. 1999. 24.95 (*1-57003-190-8*) U of SC Pr.

Nelson, Anita, jt. auth. see Hatcher, Robert A.

Nelson, Anita, jt. illus. see Schoonover, Pat.

Nelson, Anita, jt. illus. see Thiewes, Sam.

N

An Asterisk (*) at the beginning of an entry indicates that the title is appearing for the first time.

Nelson, Anitra. Marx's Concept of Money: The God of Commodities. LC 98-8109. 1998. 99.99 (*0-415-18200-X*) Routledge.

Nelson, Ann M. & Horsburgh, C. Robert, eds. Pathology of Emerging Infections 2. LC 98-8770. (Illus.). 460p. 1998. 89.95 (*1-55581-140-X*) ASM Pr.

Nelson, Ann M., jt. auth. see Horsburgh, C. Robert.

Nelson, Anna K., ed. see Kennan, George F.

***Nelson, Annabelle.** How to Use the Learning Wheel for Multicultural Learning & Training: Facilitators Guide. unabridged ed. (Illus.). 48p. 1999. pap. text 59.95 (*0-9656732-3-5*) WHEEL Council.

Nelson, Annabelle. The Learning Wheel: Ideas & Activities for Multicultural & Holistic Lesson Planning. rev. ed. LC 98-27890. (Illus.). 1998. pap. 30.00 (*0-9656732-1-9*) WHEEL Council.

— Living the Wheel: Working with Emotion, Terror & Bliss Through Imagery. LC 93-16810. (Illus.). 202p. (Orig.). 1993. pap. 10.95 (*0-87728-782-1*) Weiser.

— Storytelling Powerbook: Substance Abuse Prevention. (Illus.). 1p. (YA). 1997. pap., wbk. ed. 29.95 (*0-9656732-0-0*) WHEEL Council.

***Nelson, Annabelle.** The Storytelling Project: How to Tell Your Story to Impress Others & Find Your Voice. (Illus.). 38p. 1999. pap. text 19.95 (*0-9656732-2-7*) WHEEL Council.

Nelson, Anne-Marie, et al. Patient Satisfaction Pays: Quality Service for Practice Success. 2nd ed. LC 97-7706. 336p. 1997. 55.00 (*0-8342-0922-5*, 20922) Aspen Pub.

Nelson, Annie, ed. see Armstrong, Carol.

Nelson, Annie, ed. see Hargrave, Harriet & Craig, Sharyn S.

Nelson, Annie, ed. see Lawler, Mickey.

Nelson, Annie, ed. see Lose, Patrick.

Nelson, Annie, ed. see Sassaman, Jane A.

Nelson, Annie, ed. see Scherer, Deidre.

Nelson, Annie, ed. see Sienkiewicz, Elly.

Nelson, Annie, ed. see Wells, Valori & Wells, Jean.

Nelson, Annie G. After the Storm. LC 76-14493. 131p. 1976. reprint ed. 15.00 (*0-87152-243-8*) Reprint.

— The Dawn Appears. LC 76-18799. 135p. 1976. reprint ed. 15.00 (*0-87152-244-6*) Reprint.

— Don't Walk on My Dreams. LC 76-18308. (Illus.). 121p. 1976. reprint ed. 15.00 (*0-87152-245-4*) Reprint.

Nelson, Annika M. Folk Wisdom of Mexico - Proverbios y Dichos Mexicanos. LC 93-30338. (ENG & SPA.). 80p. 1994. 9.95 (*0-8118-0513-1*) Chronicle Bks.

Nelson, Anson & Nelson, Fanny. Memorials of Sarah Childress Polk: Wife of the Eleventh President of the United States. LC 73-22435. (Illus.). 298p. 1974. reprint ed. 25.00 (*0-87152-163-6*) Reprint.

— Sarah Childress Polk: Wife of the 11th President of the United States. Speirs, Katherine E., ed. LC 93-74429. (Signature Ser.). (Illus.). 284p. 1994. reprint ed. 30.00 (*0-945707-07-X*) Amer Political.

Nelson, Antonya. The Expendables. LC 89-31444. (Flannery O'Connor Award for Short Fiction Ser.). 208p. 1989. 19.95 (*0-8203-1156-1*) U of Ga Pr.

— The Expendables: Stories by Antonya Nelson. LC 98-51976. 208p. 1999. pap. 11.00 (*0-684-84685-3*) S&S Trade.

— Family Terrorists. LC 95-35507. 288p. 1996. per. 11.00 (*0-684-80224-4*, Scribner Pap Fic) S&S Trade Pap.

— In the Land of Men. 240p. 1993. reprint ed. pap. 8.00 (*0-380-71488-4*, Avon Bks) Morrow Avon.

— In The Land Of Men: Stories by Antonya Nelson. LC 98-32067. 240p. 1999. pap. 11.00 (*0-684-84686-1*) S&S Trade.

***Nelson, Antonya.** Living To Tell. LC 99-88529. 320p. 2000. 23.50 (*0-684-83933-4*) Scribner.

Nelson, Antonya. Nobody's Girl: A Novel. LC 97-34839. 285p. 1998. 21.50 (*0-684-83932-6*) S&S Trade.

— Nobody's Girl: A Novel. 288p. 1999. pap. 12.00 (*0-684-85207-1*) S&S Trade.

— Talking in Bed. LC 97-39945. 1998. per. 11.00 (*0-684-83800-1*) S&S Trade.

Nelson, Ardel E., jt. auth. see Gilbert, G. Ronald.

Nelson, Ardis L. Cabrera Infante in the Menippean Tradition. 124p. 1983. 15.75 (*0-936388-15-3*); pap. 10.75 (*0-936388-20-X*) Juan de la Cuesta.

Nelson, Ardys H. Growing up in Olcott Park. (Illus.). 128p. 1998. pap. 10.00 (*0-9664131-0-5*) Cal Creek Pub.

Nelson, Arlene J. Accounts, Designs & Roses. (Teachings of the Master, Sinat Schirah "Suggestions for Learning" Ser.). 240p. (Orig.). 1988. pap. 12.95 (*0-685-26083-6*, TXU 307-298) Loveline Prodns.

— Placements. (Teachings of the Master, Sinat Schirah, "Suggestions for Learning" Ser.). 200p. (Orig.). 1988. pap. 9.95 (*0-685-26084-4*, TXU 309-553) Loveline Prodns.

Nelson, Arthur C. System Development Charges for Water, Wastewater, & Stormwater Facilities. LC 94-23520. 192p. 1995. lib. bdg. 75.00 (*1-56670-037-X*, L1037) Lewis Pubs.

Nelson, Arthur C., ed. Development Impact Fees. LC 88-70565. (Illus.). 389p. 1988. pap. 36.95 (*0-918286-55-7*, Planners Press) Am Plan Assn.

Nelson, Arthur C., et al. Growth Management Principles & Practices. LC 94-70284. (Illus.). 184p. (Orig.). 1995. pap. 39.95 (*0-918286-92-1*, Planners Press); lib. bdg. 49.00 (*0-918286-93-X*, Planners Press) Am Plan Assn.

Nelson, Arthur C., jt. auth. see Knaap, Gerrit.

Nelson-Atkins Museum of Art Staff & Ward, Roger B. Durer to Matisse: Master Drawings from the Nelson-Atkins Museum of Art. LC 96-8563. 1996. 9.95 (*0-942614-27-5*) Nelson-Atkins.

Nelson, Barbara. Igniting the Flame: Clinical Pastoral Education for Nurses. LC 95-60616. xvii, 164p. (C). 1995. pap. 16.00 (*1-55605-258-8*) Wyndham Hall.

Nelson, Barbara & Timpson, William M. Advances in Instruction. pap. write for info. (*0-8290-1791-7*) Irvington.

Nelson, Barbara J. Making an Issue of Child Abuse: Political Agenda Setting for Social Problems. LC 83-18044. xiv, 184p. 1986. pap. text 13.00 (*0-226-57201-3*) U Ch Pr.

Nelson, Barbara J. & Chowdhury, Najma, eds. Women & Politics Worldwide. LC 93-28668. 818p. (C). 1994. pap. 30.00 (*0-300-05408-4*) Yale U Pr.

Nelson, Barbara J., jt. auth. see Evans, Sara M.

Nelson, Barbara N., jt. auth. see Evans, Sara M.

Nelson, Barbara S., jt. auth. see Fennema, Elizabeth.

Nelson, Barbara S., jt. ed. see Fennema, Elizabeth.

Nelson, Barbara W. The Share Rental Survival Guide: Open Your Door to Fun & Profit. (Orig.). 1989. write for info. (*0-318-63724-3*) Mediawrite.

***Nelson, Barney.** The Last Campfire: The Life Story of Ted Gray, A West Texas Rancher. 2nd ed. (Illus.). 196p. 2000. reprint ed. 29.95 (*0-9657985-1-8*); reprint ed. pap. 14.95 (*0-9657985-2-6*) Iron Mountain.

— The Wild & the Domestic: Animal Representation, Ecocriticism & Western American Literature. LC 99-45814. (Environmental Arts & Humanities Ser.). 232p. 2000. pap. 21.95 (*0-87417-347-7*) U of Nev Pr.

Nelson, Barry L. Stochastic Modeling: Analysis & Simulation. (Industrial Engineering & Management Science Ser.). 416p. (C). 1994. 82.81 (*0-07-046213-5*) McGraw.

Nelson, Becky, jt. auth. see Ingram, Laurie.

Nelson, Becky, ed. see Allen, Loyd.

Nelson, Becky, ed. see Bates, Beverly.

Nelson, Becky, ed. see Brown, Pam.

Nelson, Becky, ed. see Browning, James.

Nelson, Becky, ed. see Butler, Cathy.

Nelson, Becky, ed. see Clendinning, Monte M.

Nelson, Becky, ed. see Climer, Ron.

Nelson, Becky, ed. see Crim, Lottie & McAlister, Katsy.

Nelson, Becky, ed. see Dean, Jennifer K.

Nelson, Becky, ed. see Dickson, Charles.

Nelson, Becky, ed. see Dixon, Michael C.

Nelson, Becky, ed. see Dockrey, Karen.

Nelson, Becky, ed. see Edwards, Judy.

Nelson, Becky, ed. see Harris, Doris.

Nelson, Becky, ed. see Howard, David.

Nelson, Becky, ed. see Marler, Malcolm.

Nelson, Becky, ed. see Martin, Joyce.

Nelson, Becky, ed. see Parham, Robert.

Nelson, Becky, ed. see Perryman, Eunice & Waddell, Pam.

Nelson, Becky, ed. see Serratt, Mary L.

Nelson, Becky, ed. see Simons, Karen.

Nelson, Becky, ed. see Smith, Melanie.

Nelson, Becky, ed. see Taylor, Laurie.

Nelson, Benjamin. Monarch Notes on Tennessee Williams' Major Plays. (Orig.). (C). 3.95 (*0-671-00650-9*, Arco) Macmillan Gen Ref.

— On the Roads to Modernity - Conscience, Science, & Civilizations: Selected Writings. Huff, Toby E., ed. LC 79-21321. 340p. 1981. 41.00 (*0-8476-6209-8*) Rowman.

— Tennessee Williams. 1961. 20.00 (*0-8392-1111-2*) Astor-Honor.

Nelson, Benjamin, ed. Freud & the Twentieth Century. 1990. 16.50 (*0-8446-2097-1*) Peter Smith.

***Nelson, Benjamin F.** Bosnia Peace Operation: Mission, Structure & Transition Strategy of NATO's Stabilization Force. (Illus.). 60p. (C). 1999. pap. text 20.00 (*0-7881-8280-3*) DIANE Pub.

Nelson, Benjamin F. Infectious Diseases: Soundness of World Health Organization Estimates for Eradication or Elimination. (Illus.). 58p. 1999. pap. text 20.00 (*0-7881-7974-8*) DIANE Pub.

— International Affairs Budget: Framework for Assessing Relevance, Priority, & Efficiency. (Illus.). 56p. (C). 1998. pap. text 20.00 (*0-7881-7550-5*) DIANE Pub.

***Nelson, Benjamin F., ed.** Managing for Results: Agencies' Annual Performance Plans Can Help Address Strategic Planning Challenges. 143p. (C). 1999. pap. text 30.00 (*0-7881-8350-8*) DIANE Pub.

Nelson, Benjamin F., ed. United Nations: Financial Issues & U. S. Arrears. (Illus.). 61p. (C). 1998. pap. text 20.00 (*0-7881-7340-5*) DIANE Pub.

Nelson, Bernie. Mind Control Wars: They Promise Immortality Using New Human-Alien Technologies That Could Trigger the Apocalypse. LC 94-77607. 240p. (Orig.). 1995. pap. 12.95 (*0-9641923-0-6*) Lightwood Pubng.

***Nelson, Beryl.** State of Charter Schools, 2000, Fourth Year Report. 61p. 2000. pap. 6.25 (*0-16-050267-5*) USGPO.

***Nelson, Beth.** Caminante. 2000. 14.95 (*1-58479-001-6*) , Stewart Tabori & Chang.

Nelson, Beth. George Crabbe & the Progress of Eighteenth-Century Narrative Verse. LC 75-5147. 189p. 1976. 18.00 (*0-8387-1736-5*) Bucknell U Pr.

***Nelson, Beth.** Postcards from the Basque Country: A Journey of Enchantment & Imagination. LC 98-55675. (Illus.). 104p. 1999. text 19.95 (*1-55670-893-9*) Stewart Tabori & Chang.

— Suenos Journal. 2000. 14.95 (*1-58479-002-4*) Stewart Tabori & Chang.

— El Viajero. (SPA.). 2000. 15.95 (*1-58479-003-2*) Stewart Tabori & Chang.

Nelson, Betty P. Uncertain April. 336p. 1994. 20.95 (*0-312-11084-7*) St Martin.

Nelson, Bill. Implementing Standards of Good Behavior. LC 79-11414. 53p. 1979. pap. 3.75 (*0-934332-15-0*) LEpervier Pr.

— Manson Behind the Scenes. LC 97-65212. 400p. (Orig.). 1997. pap. 19.95 (*0-9629084-1-X*) Pen Power.

— Work Smarter, Not Harder! The Service That Sells Workbook for Alcohol Beverage Service. rev. ed. (Illus.). 1998. pap., wbk. ed. 6.95 (*1-879239-18-3*) Pencom.

— Work Smarter, Not Harder! The Service That Sells Workbook for Foodservice. rev. ed. (Illus.). 44p. 1998. pap., wbk. ed. 6.95 (*1-879239-17-5*) Pencom.

Nelson, Bill, ed. see Franz, Bill.

Nelson, Blake. Exile. LC 96-53106. 1997. per. 11.00 (*0-684-83838-9*, Scribner Pap Fic) S&S Trade Pap.

— Girl: A Novel. 256p. 1994. pap. 11.00 (*0-671-89707-1*, Touchstone) S&S Trade Pap.

— User. 1999. 19.00 (*1-888277-20-3*, Pub. by Incommcdo San Diego) Consort Bk Sales.

Nelson, Bob. 1001 Ways Employees Can Take Initiative. LC 99-21940. 304p. 1999. pap. 10.95 (*0-7611-1405-X*) Workman Pub.

— One Thousand One Ways to Energize Employees. 1997. pap. 87.60 (*0-7611-0861-0*) Workman Pub.

— One Thousand One Ways to Energize Employees. LC 97-10766. (Illus.). 224p. 1997. pap. 10.95 (*0-7611-0160-8*, 10160) Workman Pub.

— One Thousand One Ways to Reward Employees. LC 93-14449. (Illus.). 302p. (Orig.). 1994. pap. 9.95 (*1-56305-339-X*, 3339) Workman Pub.

— 365 Ways to Manage Better. 1997. pap. 10.95 (*0-7611-0835-1*) Workman Pub.

Nelson, Bob, ed. Sagas of the Central Coast: History from the Pages of Central Coast Magazine. (Illus.). 128p. (Orig.). 1995. pap. 14.95 (*0-9646930-0-3*) R J Nelson.

Nelson, Bob & Economy, Peter. Consulting for Dummies. LC 97-71815. (For Dummies Ser.). 384p. 1997. pap. 19.99 (*0-7645-5034-9*) IDG Bks.

— Managing for Dummies. (For Dummies Ser.). (Illus.). 384p. 1996. pap. 19.99 (*1-56884-858-7*) IDG Bks.

Nelson, Bobbe. Recipes from New Perry Hotel. Couey, Robin, ed. (Illus.). 264p. 1994. reprint ed. 16.95 (*0-9652529-0-6*) New Perry Hotel.

Nelson, Bobby J. Keepers: A Memoir. LC 97-26817. 288p. 1998. 23.95 (*0-393-04597-8*) Norton.

Nelson, Bonnie. The Big Show: Inside America's SportsCenter. LC 97-157284. 1975. 1.50 (*0-671-00918-4*) PB.

***Nelson, Bonnie.** It's Not Luck, It's God. (Illus.). 228p. 1999. pap. 19.95 (*0-7392-0265-0*, PO3342) Morris Pubng.

***Nelson, Bonnie Fay.** Crime Waves. LC 99-95039. 2000. pap. 10.95 (*0-533-13272-X*) Vantage.

Nelson, Bonnie R. Criminal Justice Research in Libraries & on the Internet. rev. ed. LC 97-16124. 304p. 1997. lib. bdg. 75.00 (*0-313-30048-8*, Greenwood Pr) Greenwood.

— A Guide to Published Library Catalogs. LC 81-16558. 358p. 1982. 29.00 (*0-8108-1477-3*) Scarecrow.

Nelson, Bonnie R., ed. The OPAC Directory: An Annual Guide to Internet-Accessible Online Public Access Catalogs. rev. ed. 500p. 1997. pap. 70.00 (*1-57387-031-5*) Info Today Inc.

***Nelson, Bradley J. & Breguet, Jean M., eds.** Microrobotics & Microassembly. 230p. 1999. pap. text 62.00 (*0-8194-3427-2*) SPIE.

***Nelson, Bradley J. & Miller, Dan.** Ham 'n' Egg on Golf: Why Won't This Game Just Leave Us Alone? LC 00-190590. 214p. 2000. pap. 14.00 (*0-9678453-2-7*) Whole in One.

Nelson, Bradley J., jt. ed. see Sulzmann, Armin.

Nelson, Brent A. America Balkanized: Immigration's Challenge to Government. LC 94-4306. 1994. 9.00 (*0-936247-14-2*) Amer Immigration.

Nelson, Brian, ed. Asian American Drama: 9 Plays from the Multiethnic Landscape. LC 97-27054. 420p. 1997. pap. 16.95 (*1-55783-314-1*) Applause Theatre Bk Pubs.

— Giono: Colline. (Bristol French Texts Ser.). (FRE.). 136p. 1992. 16.95 (*0-631-14296-7*) Blackwell Pubs.

— Naturalism in the European Novel: Critical Essays. LC 91-19724. (European Studies Ser.). 288p. 1992. 19.50 (*0-85496-627-7*) Berg Pubs.

Nelson, Brian, et al, eds. The European Community in the Nineteen Nineties: Economics, Politics, Defence. (International Issues - Questions Internationales Ser.). 246p. 1992. 49.95 (*0-85496-758-3*) Berg Pubs.

Nelson, Brian, ed. see Llobera, Josep R.

Nelson, Brian, ed. & intro. see Zola, Emile.

Nelson, Brian, tr. see Zola, Emile.

Nelson, Brian, tr. & intro. see Zola, Emile.

Nelson, Brian, tr. & tr. see Zola, Emile.

Nelson, Brian R. Western Political Thought: From Socrates to the Age of Ideology. 2nd ed. LC 94-48427. 392p. (C). 1995. 66.00 (*0-13-191172-4*) P-H.

Nelson, Brian W., jt. auth. see Zucker, William V.

***Nelson, Bruce.** Divided We Stand: American Workers & the Struggle for Black Equality. (Politics & Society in Twentieth-Century America Ser.). (Illus.). 424p. 2000. 39.50 (*0-691-01732-8*) Princeton U Pr.

— Workers on the Waterfront: Seamen, Longshoremen, & Unionism in the 1930s. LC 87-28749. 384p. 1990. pap. text 21.95 (*0-252-06144-6*) U of Ill Pr.

Nelson, Bruce, ed. Portland: A Collection of 19th Century Engravings. (Illus.). 1976. pap. 6.95 (*0-9600612-6-6*) Greater Portland.

Nelson, Bruce & Nelson, Dwight. And What Do You Do? Biblical Perspectives on Vocation & Work. 1984. pap. 1.95 (*0-910452-54-7*) Covenant.

Nelson, Bruce, jt. auth. see Zimmerman, David.

Nelson, Bruce C. Beyond the Martyrs: A Social History of Chicago's Anarchists, 1870-1900. (Class & Culture Ser.). 352p. (C). 1988. text 40.00 (*0-8135-1344-8*) Rutgers U Pr.

Nelson, Bruce L. Hunting Big Whitetails: Tactics Guaranteed to Make You a More Successful Whitetail Hunter. (Illus.). 272p. (Orig.). 1995. pap. 17.95 (*0-9645972-8-4*) Buck Pubng.

Nelson, Bruce W., ed. Environmental Framework of Coastal Plain Estuaries. LC 71-187849. (Geological Society of America, Memoir Ser.: No. 133). 640p. reprint ed. pap. 198.40 (*0-608-13954-8*, 202502700041) Bks Demand.

Nelson, Bryan. The Gannet. LC 78-57690. (Illus.). 1978. 30.00 (*0-931130-01-8*) Harrell Bks.

— The Gannet. (Illus.). 24p. 1989. pap. 5.25 (*0-7478-0018-9*, Pub. by Shire Pubns) Parkwest Pubns.

— Living with Seabirds. (Island Biology Ser.: Vol. 2). (Illus.). 240p. 1987. 35.00 (*0-85224-523-8*, Pub. by Edinburgh U Pr) Col U Pr.

Nelson, Bryce E. Good Schools: The Seattle Public School System, 1901-1930. LC 88-6916. (Illus.). 192p. 1988. 20.00 (*0-295-96668-8*) U of Wash Pr.

Nelson, Byron. Byron Nelson: The Little Black Book: Anecdotes, Memories & Lessons on the 50th Anniversary of One Man's Greatest Year in Golf. LC 95-15760. 192p. 1995. 20.00 (*1-56530-180-3*) Summit TX.

— How I Played the Game. LC 92-37339. 304p. 1993. 19.95 (*0-87833-819-5*) Taylor Pub.

Nelson, Byron & Dennis, Larry. Shape Your Swing the Modern Way. rev. ed. (Classics of Golf Ser.). (Illus.). 126p. 1985. 28.00 (*0-940889-06-4*) Classics Golf.

Nelson, C. TQM & ISO 9000 for Architects & Designers. LC 95-45348. (Illus.). 317p. 1995. 45.00 (*0-07-046277-1*) McGraw.

Nelson, C., jt. ed. see Gunnar, Megan R.

Nelson, C. A., jt. ed. see Ernst, W. G.

Nelson, C. B., jt. ed. see Wittchen, H. U.

Nelson, C. Donald. Practical Procedures for Children with Language . . . 94p. 1991. pap. text 27.00 (*0-7506-9734-2*) Buttrwrth-Heinemann.

Nelson, C. Ellis. Congregations: Their Power to Form & Transform. LC 87-35252. 264p. 1988. pap. 17.95 (*0-8042-1601-0*) Westminster John Knox.

***Nelson, C. F.** Aging & Loss of Coolant Accident Testing of Electrical Connections. 109p. 1998. per. 9.00 (*0-16-062881-4*) USGPO.

— Long-Term Aging & Loss-of-Coolant Accident Testing of Electrical Cables: United States/French Cooperative Research Program. 151p. 1996. per. 15.00 (*0-16-062784-2*) USGPO.

Nelson, C. Jerry, et al, eds. Forages Vol. 1: An Introduction to Grassland Agriculture. 5th ed. LC 94-37719. (Illus.). 532p. 1995. text 62.95 (*0-8138-0681-X*) Iowa St U Pr.

— Forages Vol. II: The Science of Grassland Agriculture. 5th ed. LC 94-37719. (Illus.). 416p. 1995. text 62.95 (*0-8138-0683-6*) Iowa St U Pr.

***Nelson, C. Michael, et al.** Perspective on Emotional/Behavioral Disorders: Assumptions & Their Implications for Education & Treatment. (What Works for Children & Youth with Emotional/Behavior Disorders Ser.). 42p. 1999. pap. 11.40 (*0-86586-350-4*) Coun Exc Child.

Nelson, C. Michael, jt. ed. see Illback, Robert J.

Nelson, C. Richard, ed. see Atlantic Council of the United States Staff.

***Nelson, C. Robert.** Building the Optimum Organization for Federal Agencies: The Hand Book for Developing the A-76 MEO. (Illus.). 193p. 1998. pap. 34.95 (*0-936295-91-0*) FPMI Comns.

Nelson, C. Robert, jt. auth. see Ewen, Dale R.

Nelson Canada Staff. Blackline Masters, Communication Handbook. (EC - HS Communication/English Ser.). 1996. 76.95 (*0-538-66151-8*) S-W Pub.

— Communication Handbook. (EC - HS Communication/ English Ser.). 1996. 18.95 (*0-538-66150-X*) S-W Pub.

— Math in Context 7. (UM - International Math Ser.). 1992. pap., suppl. ed. 106.95 (*0-538-62699-2*); pap., suppl. ed. 106.95 (*0-538-62700-X*); mass mkt., student ed. 53.95 (*0-538-62697-6*) S-W Pub.

— Math in Context 8. (UM - International Math Ser.). 1992. teacher ed. 106.95 (*0-538-62704-2*); pap., suppl. ed. 106.95 (*0-538-62705-0*); mass mkt., student ed. 53.95 (*0-538-62703-4*) S-W Pub.

Nelson, Candace, ed. An Institutional Guide for Enterprise Development Organizations: Facilitator's Manual. 247p. 1996. spiral bd. 40.00 (*1-888753-03-X*) PACT Pubns.

Nelson, Candace, ed. see Johnson, Bea.

Nelson, Candice J., jt. auth. see Magleby, David B.

Nelson, Candice J., jt. ed. see Thurber, James A.

***Nelson, Carl.** Advisor. 1999. 24.95 (*1-56311-513-1*) Turner Pub KY.

***Nelson, Carl A.** Import Export: How to Get Started in International Trade. 3rd ed. LC 00-29204. (Illus.). 272p. 2000. 16.95 (*0-07-135871-4*) McGraw.

Nelson, Carl A. Import/Export: How to Get Started in International Trade. 2nd ed. LC 95-16132. (Illus.). 224p. 1995. pap. 14.95 (*0-07-046276-3*) McGraw.

— Managing Globally: A Complete Guide to Competing Worldwide. 320p. 1993. text 65.00 (*0-7863-0121-X*, Irwn Prfssnl) McGraw-Hill Prof.

— Mechanical Trades Pocket Manual. 3rd ed. 364p. 1990. pap. 14.95 (*0-02-588665-7*, Aude IN) IDG Bks.

— Millwrights & Mechanics Guide. 4th ed. 1040p. 1989. 34.95 (*0-02-588591-X*, Aude IN) IDG Bks.

Nelson, Carl L., et al. Protecting the Past from Natural Disasters. (Illus.). 192p. (Orig.). 1995. pap. 14.95 (*0-471-14416-9*) Wiley.

Nelson, Carla A. The Path of Joy. 96p. (Orig.). 1996. pap. 8.95 (*0-9655078-0-7*) Windsong Pub ME.

Nelson, Carla J. Beyond Betwixt Between. LC 98-92970. (Illus.). v, 128p. 1998. 14.95 (*0-9664662-0-9*) Herb Gatherings.

***Nelson, Carla J.** Fairy Crafts, Gardens & Teas. (Illus.). 95p. 1999. pap. 9.95 (*0-9664662-1-7*) Herb Gatherings.

Nelson, Carletta L. Marriages of Alleghany County, Virginia, 1822-1872. 508p. (Orig.). 1994. pap. text 35.00 (*0-7884-0038-X*) Heritage Bk.

Nelson, Carlos I., jt. auth. see Mulvaney, Rebekah M.

N

An Asterisk (*) at the beginning of an entry indicates that the title is appearing for the first time.

Nelson, Carlton H. & Nilson, Tor H. Modern & Ancient Deep-Sea Fan Sedimentation. LC GC0087.6.S92. (SEPM Short Course Ser.: Vol. 14). (Illus.). 411p. 1984. reprint ed. pap. 127.50 (*0-608-05677-4*, 206619300006) Bks Demand.

Nelson, Carol. Integrated Advertising. 213p. 1992. 29.95 (*0-85013-218-5*) Dartnell Corp.

Nelson, Carol, ed. Women's Market Handbook. 400p. 1993. 75.00 (*0-8103-9139-2*, 101791) Gale.

Nelson, Carol, jt. auth. see Lewis, Herschell Gordon.

Nelson, Carol, jt. auth. see Musser, Charles.

Nelson, Carol C. Where to Have Affairs: Unique Locations for Business & Private Special Events in California's Historic Gold Country. (Illus.). 152p. (Orig.). 1996. pap. 14.95 (*0-9648292-6-6*) Riba Commun.

Nelson, Carol F., jt. auth. see Nelson, Horace G.

Nelson, Carolyn & Seccombe, Matthew, eds. British Newspapers & Periodicals, 1641-1700: A Short-Title Catalogue of Serials Printed in England, Scotland, Ireland & British America. LC 86-33171. xx, 724p. 1988. lib. bdg. 300.00 (*0-87352-174-9*, Z008C) Modern Lang.

Nelson, Carolyn C. British Women Fiction Writers of the 1890's. LC 96-33244. (Twayne's English Authors Ser.: No. 533). 115p. 1996. 32.00 (*0-8057-4570-X*, Twyne) Mac Lib Ref.

Nelson, Cary. Aura of the Cause. 206p. (C). 1997. 24.95 (*0-252-06680-4*) U of Ill Pr.

— Manifesto of a Tenured Radical. LC 96-51305. 1997. text 50.00 (*0-8147-5794-4*); pap. text 18.00 (*0-8147-5797-9*) NYU Pr.

— Our Last First Poets: Vision & History in Contemporary American Poetry. LC 81-5082. 239p. reprint ed. pap. 74.10 (*0-608-13447-3*, 202278300029) Bks Demand.

— Our Last First Poets: Vision & History in Contemporary American Poetry. LC 81-5082. 240p. 1984. reprint ed. pap. text 11.95 (*0-252-01140-6*) U of Ill Pr.

— Repression & Recovery: Modern American Poetry & the Politics of Cultural Memory, 1910-1945. LC 89-40264. (Wisconsin Project on American Writers Ser.). (Illus.). 352p. (C). 1992. reprint ed. pap. 12.95 (*0-299-12344-8*) U of Wis Pr.

— Shouts from the Wall: Posters & Photographs Brought Home from the Spanish Civil War by American Volunteers. LC 96-201807. 72p. 19.95 (*0-252-06606-5*) U of Ill Pr.

Nelson, Cary, ed. Disciplinarity & Dissent in Cultural Studies. (Illus.). 488p. (C). 1996. 80.00 (*0-415-91371-3*); pap. 25.99 (*0-415-91372-1*) Routledge.

— Remembering Spain: Hemingway's Civil War Eulogy & the Veterans of the Abraham Lincoln Brigade. 40p. 1994. text 14.95 (*0-252-02124-X*) U of Ill Pr.

— Theory in the Classroom. LC 85-16531. 288p. 1986. text 29.95 (*0-252-01265-8*); pap. text 13.95 (*0-252-01471-5*) U of Ill Pr.

— Will Teach for Food: Academic Labor in Crisis. LC 96-51992. (Cultural Politics Ser.: Vol. 12). (Illus.). 248p. (C). 1997. pap. 19.95 (*0-8166-3034-8*); text 49.95 (*0-8166-3033-X*) U of Minn Pr.

— A Yale Strike Dossier, Vol. 14, No. 4. 270p. 1997. pap. 12.00 (*0-8223-6443-3*) Duke.

Nelson, Cary, et al, eds. An Anthology of Modern American Poetry. LC 99-16339. (Illus.). 1296p. (C). 2000. pap. 45.00 (*0-19-512271-2*) OUP.

— Anthology of Modern American Poetry. (Illus.). 1296p. (C). 1999. 65.00 (*0-19-512270-4*) OUP.

— Cultural Studies. (Illus.). 800p. (C). (gr. 13). 1991. pap. 29.99 (*0-415-90345-9*, A4873) Routledge.

Nelson, Cary & Folsom, Ed, eds. W. S. Merwin: Essays on the Poetry. LC 85-24531. (Illus.). 424p. 1987. text 27.50 (*0-252-01277-1*) U of Ill Pr.

Nelson, Cary & Grossberg, Lawrence, eds. Marxism & the Interpretation of Culture. LC 87-5981. 752p. 1988. pap. text 21.95 (*0-252-01401-4*) U of Ill Pr.

Nelson, Cary & Hendricks, Jefferson. Edwin Rolfe: A Biographical Essay & Guide to the Rolfe Archive at the University of Illinois at Urbana-Champaign. (Illus.). 124p. 1990. text 24.95 (*0-252-01794-3*); pap. text 11.95 (*0-252-06179-9*) U of Ill Pr.

Nelson, Cary & Hendricks, Jefferson, eds. Madrid, 1937: Letters of the Abraham Lincoln Brigade from the Spanish Civil War. LC 98-138978. (Illus.). 624p. (C). 1996. 45.00 (*0-415-91408-6*) Routledge.

Nelson, Cary & Watt, Stephen. Academic Keywords: A Devil's Dictionary for Higher Education. LC 98-29067. 1999. 70.00 (*0-415-92202-X*) Routledge.

***Nelson, Cary & Watt, Stephen.** Academic Keywords: A Devil's Dictionary for Higher Education. LC 98-29067. 338p. 1999. pap. 20.00 (*0-415-92203-8*) Routledge.

Nelson, Cary, jt. ed. see Berube, Michael.

Nelson, Cary, ed. see Rolfe, Edwin.

***Nelson, Casey.** Nothing Gold Can Stay. LC 00-26233. 256p. 2000. pap. 12.95 (*1-55583-492-2*, Pub. by Alyson Pubns) Consort Bk Sales.

Nelson, Cathy. Being Grown up Is Not What I Thought! (Coralville Capers Ser.). (Illus.). 28p. (Orig.). (J). (gr. 1-3). 1994. pap. 6.00 (*0-9637845-0-1*) Thumbprnt Pub.

Nelson-Cave, Wendy. Who's Who in Shakespeare. 192p. 1995. 7.98 (*0-7858-0222-3*) Bk Sales Inc.

***Nelson-Cave, Wendy.** Who's Who in Shakespeare. (Illus.). 160p. 2000. reprint ed. text 20.00 (*0-7881-6938-6*) DIANE Pub.

Nelson, Charles. The Boy Who Picked the Bullets Up. (Meadowland Ser.). 1988. pap. 9.95 (*0-8216-2002-9*, Univ Books) Carol Pub Group.

— Panthers in the Skins of Men. 1989. pap. 9.95 (*0-8216-2006-1*, Univ Books) Carol Pub Group.

— The Trees of Ireland. (Illus.). 240p. 1993. 75.00 (*1-874675-24-4*, Pub. by Lilliput Pr) Irish Bks Media.

***Nelson, Charles.** Wild Plants of the Burren & the Aran Islands: A Field Guide. LC 99-229892. (Illus.). 144p. 1999. pap. 19.95 (*1-898256-70-5*, Pub. by Collins Press) Irish Bks Media.

Nelson, Charles & Rice, David. Archaeological Survey & Test Asotin Dam Reservoir Area, S. E. Washington. (Washington State University, Laboratory of Archaeology & History Ser.). (Illus.). 148p. (C). 1969. reprint ed. pap. text 16.25 (*1-55567-597-2*) Coyote Press.

Nelson, Charles, jt. illus. see Walsh, Wendy.

***Nelson, Charles A.** The Effects of Early Adversity on Neurobehavioral Development. LC 00-41100. (Minnesota Symposia on Child Psychology Ser.). 2000. write for info. (*0-8058-3406-0*) L Erlbaum Assocs.

Nelson, Charles A., ed. Basic & Applied Perspectives on Learning, Cognition, & Development: The Minnesota Symposia on Child Psychology, Vol. 28. (Minnesota Symposium on Child Psychology Ser.). 256p. 1995. text 49.95 (*0-8058-1833-2*) L Erlbaum Assocs.

— Memory & Affect in Development: The Minnesota Symposia on Child Psychology. (Minnesota Symposium on Child Psychology Ser.: Vol. 26). 288p. 1993. text 59.95 (*0-8058-1261-X*) L Erlbaum Assocs.

— Scott Buchanan: Recollections & Essays. 160p. 1996. 14.95 (*0-9603690-5-8*) SJC Annapolis.

— Stringfellow Barr: A Centennial Appreciation of His Life & Work, 1897-1982. LC 99-163004. (Illus.). 238p. 1997. 19.95 (*0-9603690-4-X*) SJC Annapolis.

— Threats to Optimal Development: Integrating Biological, Psychological, & Social Risk Factors: The Minnesota Symposia on Child Psychology, Vol. 29. 360p. 1994. text 69.95 (*0-8058-1510-4*) L Erlbaum Assocs.

Nelson, Charles A. & Cavey, Robert D. Ethics, Leadership & the Bottom Line: An Executive Reader. LC 90-14161. 1991. pap. 22.50 (*0-88427-081-5*) North River.

Nelson, Charles B. History of Stratham, 1631-1900. (Illus.). 308p. 1998. reprint ed. lib. bdg. 37.50 (*0-8328-9728-0*) Higginson Bk Co.

Nelson, Charles I. & Wendel, Peter T. A Possessory Estates & Future Interests Primer. LC 96-185579. (Paralegal). 200p. (C). 1996. pap. text 16.00 (*0-314-09730-9*) West Pub.

Nelson, Charles L. The Book of the Knight Zifar: A Translation of El Libro del Cavallero Zifar. LC 82-21940. (Studies in Romance Languages: No. 27). 328p. 1983. reprint ed. pap. 101.70 (*0-7837-9585-8*, 206033400005) Bks Demand.

Nelson, Charles R. Applied Time Series Analysis for Managerial Forecasting. LC 72-88942. 350p. 1973. text 42.95 (*0-8162-6366-3*) Holden-Day.

— The Investor's Guide to Economic Indicators. 208p. 1989. pap. 17.95 (*0-471-51329-6*) Wiley.

Nelson, Charles R., jt. auth. see Kim, Chang-Jin.

Nelson, Charles W., jt. auth. see Keedy, Mervin L.

Nelson, Charleszine T., jt. auth. see McCune, Bonnie F.

***Nelson, Cheryl.** National Ambulatory Medical Care Survey: 1993. 105p. 1998. per. 8.50 (*0-16-061487-2*) USGPO.

Nelson, Chris. Selecting the Best Dog for You. (Illus.). 64p. 1997. 12.95 (*0-7938-0144-3*, WW-033) TFH Pubns.

Nelson, Chris & American Society for the Prevention of Cruelty to. Dogs, Selecting the Best Dog for You: A Complete & Up-to-Date Guide. LC 97-4195. (Basic Domestic Pet Library). 76p. (J). (gr. 3 up). 1997. 19.95 (*0-7910-4606-0*) Chelsea Hse.

Nelson, Chris, jt. auth. see Webster, David.

Nelson, Chris, ed. see Thayer, Tom N.

Nelson, Chris, tr. see Zola, Emile.

***Nelson, Chrissy L.** Eagle Doctor: Stories of Stephen, My Child with Special Needs. LC 99-48932. xiv, 178p. 1999. pap. 12.95 (*1-929165-05-6*) Pangaea Pub.

— Eagle Doctor: Stories of Stephen, My Child with Special Needs. Hayskar, Bonnie J., ed. LC 99-48932. xii, 178p. 1999. 19.95 (*1-929165-02-1*) Pangaea Pub.

Nelson, Christena C. Sharing the Articles of Faith: Child-Centered Learning Activities. (Illus.). (Orig.). 1994. pap. 6.95 (*0-87579-943-4*) Deseret Bk.

— Sharing Time for Special Occassions. (Illus.). 51p. 1993. pap. 6.95 (*0-87579-815-2*) Deseret Bk.

Nelson, Christine A., jt. auth. see Pescar, Susan C.

Nelson, Christopher. Mapping the Civil War: Featuring Rare Maps from the Library of Congress. LC 92-17799. (Illus.). 176p. 1992. 39.95 (*1-56373-001-4*) Fulcrum Pub.

— TCL/TK Programmer's Reference. (Programmer's Reference Ser.). 539p. 1999. pap. text 19.99 (*0-07-212004-5*) Osborne.

Nelson, Christopher, et al. Photographs of American Civil War Cavalry. (Illus.). 100p. (Orig.). 1988. pap. 9.95 (*0-317-91045-0*) Guidon Pr.

Nelson, Clarence, ed. see Folsom, W. H.

Nelson, Claudia. Boys Will Be Girls: The Feminine Ethic & British Children's Fiction, 1857-1917. LC 90-20004. (Illus.). 216p. (C). 1991. text 35.00 (*0-8135-1681-1*) Rutgers U Pr.

— Invisible Men: Fatherhood in Victorian Periodicals, 1850-1910. LC 94-18033. 344p. 1995. 45.00 (*0-8203-1699-7*) U of Ga Pr.

— Maternal Instincts, 1875-1925. Holmes, Ann S., ed. LC 96-30027. 240p. 1997. text 59.95 (*0-312-17412-8*) St Martin.

***Nelson, Claudia & Vallone, Lynne, eds.** The Girl's Own: Cultural Histories of the Anglo-American Girl, 1830-1915. (Illus.). 296p. 1999. reprint ed. text 25.00 (*0-7881-6141-3*) DIANE Pub.

Nelson, Clifford A., ed. Pioneer Churchman: The Narrative & Journal of J. W. C. Dietrichson, 1844-1850. Rosholt, Malcom & Kaasa, Harris, trs. 265p. 1974. 20.00 (*0-87732-053-5*) Norwegian-Am Hist Assn.

Nelson, Clifford A., tr. see Giertz, Bo.

Nelson, Cordner. Careers in Pro Sports. rev. ed. Rosen, Ruth C., ed. LC 89-37641. (Careers Ser.). (Illus.). 143p. (YA). (gr. 7-12). 1996. 15.95 (*0-8239-2190-5*) Rosen Group.

— Runners' World Advanced Running Book. 200p. (Orig.). 1983. pap. 10.95 (*0-89037-273-X*) Anderson World.

Nelson, Corinna. Working in the Environment. LC 97-7394. (Exploring Careers Ser.). 112p. (YA). (gr. 6-8). 1997. lib. bdg. 23.93 (*0-8225-1763-9*, Lerner Publctns) Lerner Pub.

Nelson, Craig. Finding True Love in a Man-Eat-Man World: The Intelligent Guide to Gay Dating,Romance & Eternal Love. LC 95-24742. 320p. 1996. pap. 13.95 (*0-440-50689-1*, Dell Trade Pbks) Dell.

Nelson, Craig. Let's Get Lost: Adventures in the Great Wide Open. LC 98-49256. 320p. 1999. 24.00 (*0-446-52366-6*, Pub. by Warner Bks) Little.

***Nelson, Craig.** Let's Get Lost: Adventures in the Great Wide Open. 384p. 2000. pap. 14.95 (*0-446-67603-9*) Warner Bks.

Nelson, Craig, ed. see National Security Archive Staff & Chadwyck-Healey Staff.

***Nelson, Craig A.** Living Forgiven: An In-Depth Study of Forgiveness. 2000. pap. 11.99 (*0-939513-23-4*) Joy Pub SJC.

Nelson-Cullen, Barbara, ed. see Sinclair, Constance.

Nelson-Cullen, Barbara, ed. see VanRipper, Sharon & VanRipper, John.

***Nelson, Curt.** Darkstar. LC 00-190558. 2000. 25.00 (*0-7388-1824-0*); pap. 18.00 (*0-7388-1825-9*) Xlibris Corp.

Nelson, Curtis L. Hunters in the Shallows: A History of the PT Boat. LC 98-15797. (Illus.). 288p. 1998. 28.95 (*1-57488-167-1*) Brasseys.

Nelson, Cyndi, jt. auth. see Miller, Millie.

Nelson, Cynthia. Doria Shafik, Egyptian Feminist: A Woman Apart. LC 96-15389. (Illus.). 368p. 1996. 49.95 (*0-8130-1455-7*) U Press Fla.

— Kentucky Rules. 110p. 1998. pap. 10.00 (*1-887128-26-3*) Soft Skull Pr.

— Raven Days. 108p. 1994. pap. 8.00 (*1-887128-08-5*) Soft Skull Pr.

***Nelson, Cynthia & Altorki, Soraya.** Arab Regional Women's Studies Workshop. (Cairo Papers in Social Science: Vol. 20, No. 3). 1p. 1999. pap. 10.00 (*977-424-478-8*, Pub. by Am Univ Cairo Pr) Col U Pr.

Nelson, Cynthia, jt. auth. see Nelson, Maggie.

Nelson, Cyril I. & Houck, Carter. Treasury of American Quilts: Including Complete Patterns & Instructions for Making Your Own Quilts. (Illus.). 272p. 1998. text 25.00 (*0-7881-5779-5*) DIANE Pub.

Nelson, D. F., jt. ed. see Martienssen, W.

Nelson, D. W., et al, eds. Chemical Mobility & Reactivity in Soil Systems. (Special Publications: No. 11). 262p. 1983. pap. 12.00 (*0-89118-771-5*) Soil Sci Soc Am.

Nelson, Dalmas H. Administrative Agencies of the U. S. A. Their Decisions & Authority. LC 63-13433. (Wayne State University Studies: No. 15: Political Science). 352p. reprint ed. pap. 109.20 (*0-8357-5108-2*, 202765200055) Bks Demand.

***Nelson, Dan A.** The Best of the Pacific Crest Trail - Washington: 55 Hikes. LC 99-50669. (Illus.). 224p. 2000. pap. 14.95 (*0-89886-703-7*) Mountaineers.

— Predators at Risk in the Pacific Northwest. (Illus.). 144p. 2000. pap. 14.95 (*0-89886-733-9*) Mountaineers.

Nelson, Dan A. Snowshoe Routes - Washington. LC 98-22546. (Illus.). 256p. 1998. pap. 16.95 (*0-89886-585-9*) Mountaineers.

Nelson, Dan A., jt. auth. see Judd, Ron C.

Nelson, Dan A., ed. see Washington Trails Association Staff.

Nelson, Dana. Gonzalo de Berceo y el "Alixandre" Vindicacion de un Estilo. (Spanish Ser.: No. 63). (SPA.). xi, 505p. 1991. 30.00 (*0-940639-57-2*) Hispanic Seminary.

Nelson, Dana, ed. see Rush, Rebecca.

Nelson, Dana D. Naked Nature: Race & the Subject of National Manhood. LC 98-14396. (New Americanists Ser.). 1998. write for info. (*0-8223-2130-0*) Duke.

— National Manhood: Capitalist Citizenship & the Imagined Fraternity of White Men. LC 98-14396. (New Americanists Ser.). 1998. pap. 17.95 (*0-8223-2149-1*) Duke.

Nelson, Dana D., ed. & intro. see Child, Lydia Maria.

Nelson, Daniel. American Rubber Workers & Organized Labor, 1900-1941. LC 87-35404. 352p. 1988. reprint ed. pap. 109.20 (*0-608-04653-1*, 206533900003) Bks Demand.

— A Checklist of Writings on the Economic History of the Greater Philadelphia-Wilmington Region. 112p. 1974. pap. 3.50 (*0-914650-00-9*) Hagley Museum.

— Farm & Factory in the Heartland: Work & Workers in the American Midwest, 1880 to 1990. LC 94-45185. (Midwestern History & Culture Ser.). 320p. 1995. 29.95 (*0-253-32883-7*) Ind U Pr.

— Managers & Workers: Origins of the Twentieth-Century Factory System in the United States, 1880-1920. rev. ed. LC 95-6356. 262p. 1995. 40.00 (*0-299-14880-7*); pap. 17.95 (*0-299-14884-X*) U of Wis Pr.

— Shifting Fortunes: The Rise & Decline of American Labor, from the 1820s to the Present. LC 97-22108. (American Ways Ser.). 186p. 1997. 22.50 (*1-56663-179-3*, Pub. by I R Dee) Natl Bk Netwk.

— Shifting Fortunes: The Rise & Decline of American Labor, from the 1820s to the Present. LC 97-22108. (American Ways Ser.). 192p. 1998. pap. text 12.95 (*1-56663-180-7*) I R Dee.

— Unemployment Insurance: The American Experience, 1915-1935. LC 69-16114. (Illus.). 323p. reprint ed. pap. 100.20 (*0-7837-1660-5*, 204195700024) Bks Demand.

Nelson, Daniel, ed. A Mental Revolution: Scientific Management since Taylor. LC 91-33381. (Historical Perspectives on Business Enterprise Ser.). 259p. reprint ed. pap. 80.30 (*0-608-09860-4*, 206982500006) Bks Demand.

Nelson, Daniel, ed. see Jones, Alfred W.

Nelson, Daniel D. The Computer Numerical Control ToolBox: A New School in Machine Tool Service. LC 96-86188. (Illus.). 320p. (Orig.). 1997. pap. 54.95 (*0-9654314-4-4*, 3297) Aero Pubng.

***Nelson, Daniel D.** The Computer Numerical Control ToolBox: Top Service for Machine Tools. 2nd rev. ed. LC 99-72277. (Illus.). 320p. 1999. 54.95 (*0-9654314-7-9*, 3298) Aero Pubng.

Nelson, Daniel M. The Priority of Prudence: Virtue & Natural Law in Thomas Aquinas & the Implications for Modern Ethics. 224p. 1992. text 32.50 (*0-271-00778-8*) Pa St U Pr.

Nelson, Daniel N. Democratic Centralism in Romania: A Study of Local Communist Politics. (East European Monographs: No. 69). 186p. 1980. text 67.00 (*0-914710-63-X*, Pub. by East Eur Monographs) Col U Pr.

— Romanian Politics in the Ceausescu Era. xviii, 244p. 1988. text 141.00 (*2-88124-261-8*) Gordon & Breach.

Nelson, Daniel N., ed. After Authoritarianism: Democracy or Disorder? LC 95-5267. 200p. 1995. pap. 20.95 (*0-275-95330-0*, Greenwood Pr) Greenwood.

— After Authoritarianism: Democracy or Disorder?, 360. LC 95-5267. (Contributions in Political Science Ser.: Vol. 360). 200p. 1995. 65.00 (*0-313-29393-7*, Greenwood Pr) Greenwood.

— Local Politics in Communist Countries. LC 78-58121. 240p. 1980. 24.00 (*0-8131-1398-9*) U Pr of Ky.

Nelson, Daniel N. & Anderson, Roger B., eds. Soviet-American Relations: Understanding Differences, Avoiding Conflicts. LC 88-19726. 211p. (C). 1988. 45.00 (*0-8420-2300-3*); pap. text 17.95 (*0-8420-2326-7*) Scholarly Res Inc.

Nelson, Daniel N., jt. auth. see Markus, Ustina.

Nelson, Daniel N., jt. ed. see Lampe, John R.

Nelson, Daniel N., jt. ed. see Menon, Rajan.

***Nelson, Darlene Rose.** Stock Split Secrets: Profiting from a Powerful, Predictable, Price-Moving Event. 2000. 29.95 (*1-892008-51-3*, Pub. by Lghthse Pub Gp) Origin Bk Sales.

Nelson, Dave. I Never Pay Taxes - I Always Get a Refund: or Myths, Mysteries, Fallacies, Fables & Facts about the IRS & Taxes. 32p. 1992. pap. 7.95 (*0-9635607-0-0*) D S Nelson.

Nelson, Dave, et al. Powered by Honda: Developing Excellence in the Global Enterprise. LC 97-45106. 272p. 1998. 29.95 (*0-471-18182-X*) Wiley.

Nelson, David. Menu: San Diego County - The Best 200 Restaurants. (Illus.). 448p. 1994. pap. 12.95 (*0-9628274-7-9*) D Thomas Pub.

— Natural Immunity. 844p. 1990. text 132.00 (*0-12-514555-1*) Acad Pr.

— The Penguin Dictionary of Mathematics. 2nd ed. 461p. 1999. pap. 14.95 (*0-14-051342-6*, Pub. by Pnguin Bks Ltd) Trafalgar.

Nelson, David, et al, eds. Statistical Mechanics of Membranes & Surfaces: 5th Jerusalem Winter School for Theoretical Physics. 272p. (C). 1989. text 53.00 (*9971-5-0722-6*); pap. text 36.00 (*9971-5-0734-X*) World Scientific Pub.

Nelson, David & Wilson, Ruth A. Improving Study & Test-Taking Skills. (Illus.). 96p. (YA). (gr. 5). 1997. pap. text 10.95 (*1-58037-015-2*, Pub. by M Twain Media) Carson-Dellos.

Nelson, David, et al. Multicultural Mathematics. LC 92-17031. (Illus.). 238p. 1993. pap. text 14.95 (*0-19-282241-1*) OUP.

Nelson, David A., ed. see Lewis, Joe.

Nelson, David A., jt. ed. see Utterback, Paul J.

Nelson, David C., jt. auth. see Brown, Ronald C.

Nelson, David D. International Environmental Auditing. LC 98-16513. 787p. 1998. text 149.00 (*0-86587-588-X*, 588) Gov Insts.

Nelson, David J., Jr. Cracking the Pavement. (Minority Poet Ser.). (Illus.). 57p. 1989. pap. 4.00 (*1-880046-01-6*) Baculite Pub.

Nelson, David K., ed. see Nelson, Gail & Foard, Pamela.

Nelson, David L., et al, eds. Chemistry of High-Temperature Superconductors. LC 87-19314. (ACS Symposium Ser.: No. 351). (Illus.). xi, 349p. 1987. 69.95 (*0-8412-1431-X*) Am Chemical.

— Chemistry of High-Temperature Superconductors, Vol. 1. LC 87-19314. (ACS Symposium Ser.: Vol. 351). 368p. 1987. reprint ed. pap. 114.10 (*0-608-03874-1*, 206432100001) Bks Demand.

Nelson, David L. & Brownstein, Bernard H., eds. YAC Libraries: A User's Guide. LC 93-13780. (University of Wisconsin Biotechnology Center Biotechnical Resource Ser.). (Illus.). 240p. 1993. pap. text 48.00 (*0-7167-7014-8*) OUP.

Nelson, David L. & George, Thomas F., eds. Chemistry of High-Temperature Superconductors, No. 2. LC 88-19314. (ACS Symposium Ser.: No. 377). (Illus.). ix, 340p. 1988. 64.95 (*0-8412-1541-3*, Pub. by Am Chemical) OUP.

— Chemistry of High-Temperature Superconductors II. LC 87-19314. (ACS Symposium Ser.: Vol. 377). 352p. 1988. reprint ed. pap. 109.20 (*0-608-03291-3*, 206380900002) Bks Demand.

Nelson, David M. The Anatomy of a Game: Football, the Rules, & the Men Who Made the Game. LC 91 51009. 1994. 29.50 (*0-87413-455-2*) U Delaware Pr.

Nelson, David N. Bibliography of South Asia. LC 94-613. (Area Bibliographies Ser.: No. 4). 484p. 1994. text 60.00 (*0-8108-2854-5*) Scarecrow.

N

An Asterisk (*) at the beginning of an entry indicates that the title is appearing for the first time.

— Bridles & Bits of Cowboy Poetry. (Illus.). 60p. (Orig.). 1994. pap. text 8.00 (*1-886615-00-4*) D N Nelson.

— Reflections. (Illus.). 45p. (Orig.). 1994. pap. text 10.00 (*1-886615-03-9*) D N Nelson.

Nelson, David T., tr. see Koren, Elizabeth.

Nelson, Davis N. Stress Management: Does Anyone in Chicago Know about It? LC 92-93554. 90p. (Orig.). 1992. pap. 12.95 (*0-88100-078-7*) Natl Writ Pr.

Nelson, Dawn. Compassionate Touch: Hands-On Caregiving for the Elderly, the Ill & the Dying. 1993. pap. 17.95 (*0-88268-149-4*) Station Hill Pr.

Nelson, Dean, jt. auth. see Morsch, Gary.

Nelson, Deborah L. & Howicz, Jennifer L. Uniform Commercial Code Legal Forms, 2 vols. 3rd ed. LC 94-37285. 1994. 200.00 (*0-614-32152-2*) West Group.

— Williston on Sales, 3 vols. 5th ed. LC 94-46505. 1994. 265.00 (*0-614-32428-9*) West Group.

***Nelson, Debra L. & Quick, James C.** Organizational Behavior: Foundations, Realitie & Challenges. 3rd ed. LC 99-23693. 641p. 1999. pap. 86.95 (*0-324-00637-3*) Thomson Learn.

Nelson, Debra L. & Quick, James C. Organizational Behavior: Foundations, Realities & Challenges. Leyh, ed. LC 93-27987. 650p. (C). 1993. pap. 68.50 (*0-314-02640-1*) West Pub.

— Organizational Behavior: Foundations, Realities & Challenges. 2nd ed. 1997. teacher ed. write for info. (*0-314-20558-6*) West Pub.

— Organizational Behavior: Foundations, Realities & Challenges. 2nd ed. LC 96-35205. 1997. mass mkt. 61.25 (*0-314-20567-5*) West Pub.

— Organizational Behavior: Foundations, Realities & Challenges. 2nd ed. LC 96-35205. 650p. 1997. mass mkt. 70.25 (*0-314-09626-4*) West Pub.

— Organizational Behavior: The Essentials. LC 95-23788. 375p. (C). 1995. mass mkt. 46.95 (*0-314-06436-2*) West Pub.

Nelson, Debralee McKelvey. Saunders Review of Dental Hygiene. LC 99-27192. (Illus.). 510p. 2000. text 42.95 (*0-7216-7576-X*, W B Saunders Co) Harcrt Hlth Sci Grp.

Nelson, Dee W., ed. The Crisp Pine: A Collection of Winning Poems, 1980-1989. (Illus.). 120p. (Orig.). (C). 1990. pap. 10.00 (*0-9626793-0-5*) AAUW Pr.

Nelson, Dennis. Advanced Random Vibration & Shock. (Illus.). 250p. (C). 1990. student ed. 100.00 (*0-918247-10-1*) Tustin Tech.

— Food Combining Simplified: Twenty-Eight Recipes Included. rev. ed. (Illus.). 64p. 1988. pap. 3.00 (*0-9612188-2-7*) Nelsons Bks.

— Maximizing Your Nutrition. (Illus.). 128p. (Orig.). 1988. pap. 3.50 (*0-9612188-3-5*) Nelsons Bks.

***Nelson, Dennis.** Safety & Health in the Salon: Facilitator's Guide. LC 00-32462. (Illus.). 2000. write for info. (*1-56253-594-3*) Milady Pub.

Nelson, Dennis R., jt. ed. see Stanley-Samuelson, David W.

Nelson, Derek. The American State Fair. LC 99-14541. (Illus.). 160p. 1999. 29.95 (*0-7603-0656-7*, Pub. by MBI Pubg) Motorbooks Intl.

— Off the Map: The Curious Histories of Place Names. LC 97-25499. 192p. 1997. 19.00 (*1-56836-174-2*) Kodansha.

***Nelson, Derek.** Off the Map: The Curious Histories of Place Names. 208p. 1999. pap. 10.00 (*1-56836-298-6*) Kodansha.

Nelson, Diane C. Grammatical Case Assignment in Finnish. rev. ed. LC 98-25645. (Outstanding Dissertations in Linguistics Ser.). 270p. 1998. 65.00 (*0-8153-3180-0*) Garland.

***Nelson, Diane M.** A Finger in the Wound: Body Politics in Quincentennial Guatemala. LC 98-35061. 450p. 1999. 55.00 (*0-520-21284-3*, Pub. by U CA Pr); pap. 22.00 (*0-520-21285-1*, Pub. by U CA Pr) Cal Prin Full Svc.

***Nelson, Dianne.** A Brief History of Male Nudes in America: Stories by Dianne Nelson. 144p. 1999. pap. 12.00 (*1-893448-01-0*) Boaz Pubng.

Nelson, Dianne. A Brief History of Male Nudes in America: Stories by Dianne Nelson. LC 93-809. (Flannery O'Connor Award for Short Fiction Ser.). 136p. (C). 1993. 19.95 (*0-8203-1571-0*) U of Ga Pr.

Nelson, Dianne, ed. see Richmond, Mardi & Barash, Melanee L.

Nelson, Dick & Nelson, Sharon. Birds of the Desert. rev. ed. (Easy Field Guide Ser.). (Illus.). 32p. (J). 1995. pap. 1.50 (*0-935810-13-7*) R H Pub.

— Cactus of the Desert. rev. ed. (Easy Field Guide Ser.). (Illus.). 32p. (J). 1995. pap. 1.50 (*0-935810-15-3*) R H Pub.

— The Desert Survival Manual. 104p. 1997. pap. 5.95 (*0-915030-01-2*) Tecolote Pr.

— Insects of the Desert. rev. ed. (Easy Field Guide Ser.). (Illus.). 32p. (J). 1995. pap. 1.50 (*0-935810-14-5*) R H Pub.

— Mammals of Arizona. rev. ed. (Easy Field Guide Ser.). (Illus.). 32p. (J). 1994. pap. 1.50 (*0-935810-16-1*) R H Pub.

— Mammals of New Mexico. rev. ed. (Easy Field Guide Ser.). (Illus.). 32p. (J). 1985. pap. 1.50 (*0-935810-22-6*) R H Pub.

— Snakes of the Southwest. (Easy Field Guide Ser.). (Illus.). 32p. (J). 1994. pap. 1.50 (*0-935810-17-X*) R H Pub.

— Trees of Arizona. rev. ed. (Easy Field Guide Ser.). (Illus.). 32p. (J). 1994. pap. 1.50 (*0-935810-18-8*) R H Pub.

— Trees of New Mexico. rev. ed. (Easy Field Guide Ser.). (Illus.). 32p. (J). 1985. pap. 1.50 (*0-935810-23-4*) R H Pub.

Nelson, Don. Paddling Yellowstone & Grand Teton National Parks. (Illus.). 128p. 1999. pap. 10.95 (*1-56044-627-7*) Falcon Pub Inc.

Nelson, Donald, jt. auth. see Carolus, Roger.

Nelson, Donald E., jt. auth. see Humphrey, Sherry H.

Nelson, Donald F., ed. see COSASYL COBOL Committee.

Nelson, Donald M. Arsenal of Democracy: The Story of American War Production. LC 72-2378. (FDR & the Era of the New Deal Ser.). 439p. 1973. reprint ed. lib. bdg. 45.00 (*0-685-01352-9*) Da Capo.

Nelson, Donald T. & Schneiter, Paul H. Gifts-in-Kind: The Fund Raiser's Guide to Acquiring, Managing, & Selling Charitable Contributions Other than Cash & Securities. 178p. 1991. 29.95 (*0-930807-23-5*, 600318) Fund Raising.

Nelson, Donna. Reaction Guide for Organic Chemistry. (Chemistry Ser.). 1997. pap. 5.00 (*0-7637-0287-0*) Jones & Bartlett.

Nelson, Doris. Through a Looking Glass. Erickson, Richard D. & Bild, Sharon, eds. 142p. 1997. pap. 13.95 (*0-9649922-4-8*) Deforest Pr.

Nelson, Dorothy. At Final Anchor, Glengary. 146p. 1984. 14.95 (*0-87770-320-5*) Ye Galleon.

***Nelson, Dorothy N.** God Spoke to a Girl. (Illus.). 32p. (J). (ps-2). 1998. pap. 1.97 (*0-8163-1655-4*) Pacific Pr Pub Assn.

Nelson, Doug. Caleb & Me. (Illus.). 120p. (Orig.). 1995. pap. write for info. (*1-55059-126-6*) Detselig Ents.

— Hotcakes to High Stakes: The Chuckwagon Story. (Illus.). 192p. 1993. 39.95 (*1-55059-056-1*) Temeron Bks.

Nelson, Douglas, photos by. Day by Day: The Sixties, Vol. 1. (Illus.). 1983. pap. text 97.50 (*0-87196-384-1*) Facts on File.

Nelson, Douglas, jt. auth. see Nelson, Ray.

Nelson, Douglas, jt. auth. see Parker, Thomas.

Nelson, Doyal & Worth, Joan. How to Choose & Create Good Problems for Primary Children. LC 83-6218. (Illus.). 40p. 1983. pap. 9.95 (*0-87353-205-8*) NCTM.

Nelson, Dwight, jt. auth. see Nelson, Bruce.

Nelson, Dwight K. Built to Last: Creation & Evolution: A Thoughtful Look at the Evidence That a Master Designer Created Our Planet. LC 98-25932. 1998. 1.99 (*0-8163-1680-5*) Pacific Pr Pub Assn.

— The Claim: Nine Radical Claims of Jesus That Can Revolutionize Your Life. LC 94-26480. 1994. pap. 1.99 (*0-8163-1236-2*) Pacific Pr Pub Assn.

— Outrageous Grace: Finding a Forever Friendship with God. LC 98-25929. 1998. 1.99 (*0-8163-1679-1*) Pacific Pr Pub Assn.

Nelson, E. A., tr. see Speyr, Adrienne von.

Nelson, E. A., tr. see Von Balthasar, Hans U.

Nelson, E. B., ed. Well Cementing. (Developments in Petroleum Science Ser.: No. 28). 496p. 1990. 226.75 (*0-444-88751-2*) Elsevier.

Nelson, E. Clifford. The Rise of World Lutheranism: An American Perspective. LC 80-2376. 445p. reprint ed. pap. 138.00 (*0-608-15332-X*, 202961800061) Bks Demand.

Nelson, E. Clifford, ed. Lutherans in North America. rev. ed. LC 74-26337. (Illus.). 576p. 1980. 45.00 (*0-8006-1409-7*, 1-1409) Augsburg Fortress.

Nelson, E. E., et al. Are Seed & Cone Pathogens Causing Significant Losses in Pacific Northwest Seed Orchards? 10p. 1997. reprint ed. pap. 1.50 (*0-89904-765-3*, Ecosytems Resrch) Crumb Elbow Pub.

Nelson, E. W., et al. Schaum's Outline of Engineering Mechanics. 5th ed. LC 97-24244. (Illus.). 480p. (C). 1997. pap. 15.95 (*0-07-046193-7*) McGraw.

Nelson, E. W., jt. auth. see McLean, William G.

Nelson, Eastin, jt. auth. see Conference on Economic Development Staff.

Nelson, Edna C. Magnificent Percheron. (Illus.). 1963. pap. 8.95 (*0-87505-115-4*) Borden.

Nelson, Edward. Dynamical Theories of Brownian Motion. LC 72-38239. (Mathematical Notes Ser.). 146p. reprint ed. pap. 45.30 (*0-608-16410-0*, 205217800051) Bks Demand.

— Quantum Fluctuations. LC 84-26449. (Physics Ser.). 155p. 1985. pap. text 29.95 (*0-691-08379-7*, Pub. by Princeton U Pr) Cal Prin Full Svc.

— Radically Elementary Probability Theory. (Annals of Mathematics Studies: No. 117). (Illus.). 86p. 1987. pap. text 21.95 (*0-691-08474-2*, Pub. by Princeton U Pr) Cal Prin Full Svc.

Nelson, Edward W. The Eskimo about Bering Strait. LC 83-600094. (Classics of Smithsonian Anthropology Ser.: No. 4). (Illus.). 520p. 1983. pap. text 29.95 (*0-87474-671-X*, NEEBP) Smithsonian.

— Music & Worship. 176p. 1985. spiral bd. 11.99 (*0-311-72642-9*) Casa Bautista.

— Que Mi Pueblo Adore: Music & Worship. Mussiett, Salom, tr. from ENG. (SPA.). 184p. 1986. pap. 10.99 (*0-311-17029-3*) Casa Bautista.

Nelson, Edwin L., jt. auth. see Fuda, George E.

Nelson, Elden. I Hate WordPerfect: A Friendly Guide to WordPerfect. 338p. 1993. 16.95 (*1-56529-212-X*) Que.

— WordPerfect 8 for Busy People. LC 97-200297. 320p. 1997. pap. 24.99 (*0-07-882313-7*) Osborne-McGraw.

Nelson, Elizabeth. Professional Teaching Techniques: A Handbook for Teaching Adults Any Subject. rev. ed. LC 98-91328. 106p. (Orig.). 1998. pap. 15.00 (*0-918328-21-7*) We Unlimited.

Nelson, Elizabeth, ed. see Riviera Publications Staff.

Nelson, Elizabeth A. Coping with Drugs & Sports. rev. ed. (Coping Ser.). (YA). (gr. 7-12). 1995. lib. bdg. 17.95 (*0-8239-2213-8*) Rosen Group.

— Orange County Children's Directory, 1992. 1991. pap. 4.95 (*1-877609-05-6*) Riviera Pubns.

— San Diego Children's Directory, 1992. 1991. pap. 3.95 (*1-877609-04-8*) Riviera Pubns.

Nelson, Elizabeth A., ed. Orange County Children's Directory. 110p. 1989. pap. 4.95 (*1-877609-00-5*) Riviera Pubns.

Nelson, Elizabeth A. & Nelson Engineering & Research, Inc. Staff. San Diego Children's Directory, 1993. 1992. pap. 4.95 (*1-877609-06-4*) Riviera Pubns.

Nelson, Elizabeth A., ed. see Riviera Publications Staff.

Nelson, Elizabeth R. Monarch Notes: Hardy's Far from the Madding Crowd. (C). 1994. 3.95 (*0-671-00890-0*, Arc) IDG Bks.

Nelson, Elton W. District of Columbia Tax Handbook, 1998. rev. ed. 142p. 1997. pap. text 45.00 (*0-7811-0180-8*) Res Inst Am.

Nelson, Elva L., ed. see Ranganathananda, Swami.

Nelson, Emmanuel S. AIDS: The Literary Response. 360p. 1992. pap. 14.95 (*0-8057-9032-2*, Twyne); text 23.95 (*0-8057-9029-2*, Twyne) Mac Lib Ref.

***Nelson, Emmanuel S., ed.** African American Authors 1745-1945: A Bio-Bibliographical Critical Sourcebook. LC 99-32527. 544p. 2000. lib. bdg. 99.50 (*0-313-30910-8*) Greenwood.

— Asian American Novelists: A Bio-bibliographical Critical Sourcebook. LC 99-16099. 440p. 2000. lib. bdg. 89.50 (*0-313-30911-6*) Greenwood.

Nelson, Emmanuel S., ed. Bharati Mukherjee: Critical Perspectives. LC 93-18145. Vol. 1663. 256p. 1993. text 15.00 (*0-8153-1173-7*, H1663) Garland.

— Contemporary African American Novelists: A Bio-Bibliographical Critical Sourcebook. LC 98-26438. 552p. 1999. lib. bdg. 95.00 (*0-313-30501-3*, Greenwood Pr) Greenwood.

— Contemporary Gay American Novelists: A Bio-Bibliographical Critical Sourcebook. LC 92-25762. 456p. 1993. lib. bdg. 79.50 (*0-313-28019-3*, NCY, Greenwood Pr) Greenwood.

— Reworlding: The Literature of the Indian Diaspora, 42. LC 91-40939. (Contributions to the Study of World Literature Ser.: No. 42). 208p. 1992. 55.00 (*0-313-27794-X*, NLI, Greenwood Pr) Greenwood.

— Writers of the Indian Diaspora: A Bio-Bibliographical Critical Sourcebook. LC 92-27898. 504p. 1993. lib. bdg. 99.50 (*0-313-27904-7*, NWI/, Greenwood Pr) Greenwood.

Nelson, Emmanuel S., intro. Critical Essays: Gay & Lesbian Writers of Color. LC 93-30614. (Journal of Homosexuality: Vol. 26, Nos. 2-3). 250p. 1993. lib. bdg. 49.95 (*1-56024-482-8*) Haworth Pr.

— Critical Essays: Gay & Lesbian Writers of Color. LC 93-30614. (Journal of Homosexuality Ser.: Vol. 26, Nos. 2-3). 250p. 1994. pap. 19.95 (*1-56023-048-7*, Harrington Park) Haworth Pr.

Nelson Engineering & Research, Inc. Staff, jt. auth. see Nelson, Elizabeth A.

Nelson, Eric. The Interpretation of Waking Life. 80p. 1991. 20.00 (*1-55728-197-1*); pap. 12.00 (*1-55728-198-X*) U of Ark Pr.

— The Light Bringers. LC 83-50966. (Series Eight). 52p. 1983. pap. 7.00 (*0-931846-23-4*) Wash Writers Pub.

— Mall of America: Reflections of a Virtual Community. LC 97-45765. 272p. 1998. pap. 14.95 (*1-880090-58-9*) Galde Pr.

— On Call. (Moonsquilt Chadbook Ser.). 28p. (Orig.). 1983. pap. 3.50 (*0-943216-04-4*) MoonsQuilt Pr.

Nelson-Erichsen, Jean & Erichsen, Heino R. Butterflies in the Wind: Spanish - Indian Children with White Parents. Gantley, Juleen & Cramer, Lorraine, eds. (Illus.). 355p. (Orig.). (C). 1992. pap. 18.00 (*0-935366-19-9*) Los Ninos.

***Nelson-Erichsen, Jean & Erichsen, Heino R.** How to Adopt Internationally, 2000-2002 Edition: A Guide for Agency-Directed & Independent Adoptions. LC 00-100577. 296p. 2000. pap. 22.00 (*0-940352-13-3*) Mesa Hse.

Nelson, Erland, jt. ed. see Price, Thomas R.

Nelson, Esther. Blocks Are to Build. large type ed. Hirsch, Davida, ed. (Illus.). 28p. (Orig.). (J). (gr. k-1). 1999. pap. 7.95 (*0-945110-15-4*) Granny Pr.

— Chairs Are to Sit. large type ed. Hirsch, Davida, ed. (Illus.). 28p. (Orig.). (J). (gr. k-1). 1999. pap. 7.95 (*0-945110-14-6*) Granny Pr.

— Everybody Sing & Dance. Scholastic, Inc. Staff, ed. (J). 1993. pap. 12.95 (*0-590-49041-9*) Scholastic Inc.

Nelson, Esther M. An Analysis of Content of Student-Teaching Courses. LC 70-177100. (Columbia University. Teachers College. Contributions to Education Ser.: No. 723). reprint ed. 37.50 (*0-404-55723-6*) AMS Pr.

Nelson, Ethel, jt. auth. see Kang, C. H.

***Nelson, Ethel R.** Burkitt: Cancer, Fiber. LC 97-61573. xii, 264 p. 1998. 14.95 (*1-57258-093-3*) Teach Servs.

Nelson, Ethel R., ed. Three Hundred Seventy-Five Meatless Recipes: Century 21 Cookbook. LC 94-61582. 164p. (Orig.). 1993. spiral bd. 7.95 (*0-945383-41-X*) Teach Servs.

Nelson, Ethel R. & Broadberry, Richard E. Genesis & the Mystery Confucius Couldn't Solve. LC 93-50090. (Illus.). 184p. (Orig.). 1994. pap. 10.99 (*0-570-04635-1*, 12-3216) Concordia.

Nelson, Ethel R., et al. God's Promise to the Chinese. abr. rev. ed. Orig. Title: Mysteries Confucius Couldn't Solve/Genesis & Mystery Confucius Couldn't Solve. (CHI & ENG., Illus.). 140p. 1997. pap. 12.00 (*0-937869-01-5*) Read Bks Pubs.

Nelson, Ethel R., jt. auth. see Wang, Samuel.

Nelson, Eugene. Break Their Haughty Power: Joe Murphy in the Heyday of the Wobblies. LC 93-16106. (Illus.). 367p. (Orig.). 1993. pap. 12.00 (*0-910383-31-6*) Ism Pr.

***Nelson, Eugene C., et al.** Clinical Improvement Action Guide. LC 97-76552. 210p. 1998. 45.00 (*0-86688-553-6*, AG-100) Joint Comm Hlthcare.

Nelson, Eve, jt. ed. see DeMirjian, Arto, Jr.

Nelson, Evelyn G. & Nelson, Frederick J. The Island of Guam: Description & History from a 1934 Perspective. LC 92-85517. (Illus.). 250p. 1992. 15.00 (*0-9618941-2-1*) Ana Pubns.

Nelson, Fanny, jt. auth. see Nelson, Anson.

***Nelson, Felicitas H.** Talismans & Amulets of the World. LC 99-462008. 2000. 13.95 (*0-8069-2873-5*) Sterling.

Nelson-Ferguson, Rebecca. Handy History Answer Book. 600p. 1999. pap. text 19.95 (*1-57859-080-9*) Visible Ink Pr.

Nelson, Fern K. This Was Jackson's Hole: Incidents & Profiles from the Settlement of Jackson Hole. LC 94-25082. (Illus.). 384p. 1994. pap. 15.95 (*0-931271-25-8*) Hi Plains Pr.

Nelson, Fiona. Lesbian Motherhood: An Exploration of Canadian Lesbian Families. 176p. 1996. text 50.00 (*0-8020-0765-1*) U of Toronto Pr.

— Lesbian Motherhood: An Exploration of Canadian Lesbian Families. 176p. 1996. pap. text 18.95 (*0-8020-7135-X*) U of Toronto Pr.

Nelson, Florence E. & Dlugosch, Sharon. Games for Wedding Shower Fun. LC 83-73600. (Illus.). 112p. 1985. pap. 6.95 (*0-918420-12-1*) Brighton Pubns.

Nelson, Florence E., jt. auth. see Dlugosch, Sharon E.

Nelson, Florencia B. The School of the South (La Escuela del Sur) El Taller Torres-Garcia & Its Legacy. LC 91-73445. (Illus.). 22p. 1991. pap. 5.00 (*0-614-02733-0*) J S Blanton Mus.

Nelson, Florencia B., ed. see Barnitz, Jacqueline.

Nelson-Folkerson, Jeff. Windows 95 Essentials. 1996. teacher ed., ring bd. 49.99 (*1-57576-250-1*) Que Educ & Trng.

Nelson, Forrest D., jt. auth. see Aldrich, John H.

Nelson, Franklin W. Bridges of Promise: Taking Steps to Follow Jesus. 1990. pap., teacher ed. 6.00 (*0-8170-1168-4*) Judson.

— Bridges of Promises: Taking Steps to Follow Jesus. 1990. pap., student ed. 7.00 (*0-8170-1159-5*) Judson.

Nelson, Fred, jt. auth. see Blauvelt, Carolyn T.

Nelson, Frederick C., tr. & adapted by see Lalanne, Michel, et al.

Nelson, Frederick J., jt. auth. see Nelson, Evelyn G.

Nelson, Frieda, ed. see Tish, John.

Nelson-Fulkersen, Jeff. Windows 95 Essentials, IM, Level 2. 1996. pap. text, teacher ed. 49.99 (*1-57576-273-0*) Que Educ & Trng.

Nelson, G., et al. Training in the Community for People with Disabilities. (ARA, CHI, ENG, FRE & SPA., Illus.). 684p. 1989. pap. text 72.00 (*92-4-154401-5*, 1150330) World Health.

Nelson, G. Dudley. As the Cock Crows: Reflections of a Medical Missionary to Haiti. (Illus.). 160p. (Orig.). 1997. pap. 17.95 (*1-57736-047-8*) Providence Hse.

Nelson, G. E. Who's the Boss? Love. 1985. pap. 6.95 (*0-394-74223-0*) Random.

Nelson, G. Kenneth & Cramer, Joe J., Jr. Budgeting Problems. LC 68-28845. (Illus.). 182p. reprint ed. 56.50 (*0-8357-9849-6*, 201252400081) Bks Demand.

Nelson, G. Lynn. Writing & Being: Taking Back Our Lives Through the Power of Language. LC 94-3776. 160p. (Orig.). 1994. pap. 14.95 (*1-880913-11-9*) Innisfree Pr.

Nelson, G. R. The Basics of Morality & Its Relation to Dramatic Form in a Study of David Copperfield. LC 98-4387. (Studies in Comparative Literature: Vol. 3). 140p. 1998. text 69.95 (*0-7734-8390-X*) E Mellen.

Nelson, Gail & Foard, Pamela. In Concert: The Freelance Musician's Keys to Financial Success. Nelson, David K., ed. LC 94-92250. (Illus.). 96p. (Orig.). 1994. pap. 16.95 (*0-9633888-2-7*, KFS1) Preludes Nouveaux.

— Wedding Music Essentials. rev. ed. LC 93-85452. 90p. 1993. pap. 19.95 incl. audio (*0-9633888-1-9*, PNWM02) Preludes Nouveaux.

Nelson, Gail, jt. auth. see Foard, Pamela.

Nelson, Gail, jt. auth. see Nelson, Lynn.

Nelson, Gail A., jt. auth. see Hauser, Paula.

Nelson, Gail L., jt. auth. see Nelson, Lynn T.

***Nelson, Gale.** Ceteris Paribus: Poems. (Poetry Ser.: Vol. 41). 127p. 2000. pap. 12.50 (*1-886224-37-4*, Pub. by Burning Deck) SPD-Small Pr Dist.

— Ceteris Paribus: Poems. aut. ed. (Poetry Ser.: Vol. 41). 128p. 2000. pap. 20.00 (*1-886224-38-2*, Pub. by Burning Deck) SPD-Small Pr Dist.

Nelson, Gale. Stare Decisis: Poems. (Burning Deck Poetry Ser.). 144p. 1991. pap. 9.00 (*0-930901-72-X*) Burning Deck.

— Stare Decisis: Poems. limited ed. (Burning Deck Poetry Ser.). 144p. 1991. pap. 15.00 (*0-930901-73-8*) Burning Deck.

Nelson, Gary J., ed. Health Effects of Dietary Fatty Acids. 284p. (C). 1991. 95.00 (*0-935315-31-4*) Am Oil Chemists.

— Health Effects of Dietary Fatty Acids. 284p. 1992. pap. 40.00 (*0-935315-44-6*) Am Oil Chemists.

***Nelson, Gary M.** Self-Governance in Communities & Families. LC 99-86444. 230p. 2000. pap. 24.95 (*1-57675-086-8*, Pub. by Berrett-Koehler) Publishers Group.

Nelson, Gary M., et al. The Field of Adult Services: Social Work Practice & Administration. 400p. (C). 1995. lib. bdg. 34.95 (*0-87101-250-2*, 2502) Natl Assn Soc Wkrs.

Nelson, Gary O. Gas Mixtures: Preparation & Control. 304p. 1992. lib. bdg. 99.95 (*0-87371-298-6*, L298) Lewis Pubs.

Nelson, Gayle & Winter, Thomas. Operations in English: 55 Natural & Logical Sequences for Language Acquisition. Clark, Raymond C., ed. (Supplementary Materials Handbook Ser.: No. 2). (Illus.). 112p. 1993. pap. text 13.00 (*0-86647-074-3*) Pro Lingua.

***Nelson, Geneva E.** The Healing. 384p. 1999. pap. 19.00 (*1-57921-249-2*) WinePress Pub.

Nelson, George. The Alamo: An Illustrated History. LC 97-41181. (Illus.). 112p. 1998. per. 19.95 (*0-9659159-0-5*, 1) Aldine Pr.

***Nelson, George.** One Woman Short: A Novel. LC 00-20400. 256p. 2000. pap. 12.00 (*0-684-86461-4*, Fireside) S&S Trade Pap.

Nelson, George. Outside In. 63p. (Orig.). (YA). (gr. 5-12). 1994. pap. 4.00 (*1-57514-119-1*, 1075) Encore Perform Pub.

Nelson, George, ed. see Herman Miller Staff.

Nelson, George E. The Introductory Biological Sciences in the Traditional Liberal Arts College. LC 74-177101. (Columbia University. Teachers College. Contributions to Education Ser.: No. 501). (C). reprint ed. 37.50 (*0-404-55501-2*) AMS Pr.

Nelson, George R., ed. Freedom & Welfare: Social Patterns in the Northern Countries of Europe. LC 72-98784. 539p. 1970. reprint ed. lib. bdg. 79.50 (*0-8371-2903-6*, NEFR, Greenwood Pr) Greenwood.

Nelson, Gerald D. & Krause, John L. Clinical Photography in Plastic Surgery. (Illus.). 176p. 1987. 79.95 (*0-316-60315-5*, Little Brwn Med Div) Lppncott W & W.

***Nelson, Gerald E.** Good Discipline, Good Kids. 256p. 2000. pap. 10.95 (*1-58062-284-4*) Adams Media.

Nelson, Gerald E., jt. auth. see Do-Nguyen, Mariette.

Nelson, Gerry. Armageddon: The Diary of Vladimir Brezynski. 198p. 1983. 12.95 (*0-914701-00-2*) New Comet.

— 1999 - King of Terror. 200p. (Orig.). 1996. pap. 4.95 (*0-614-14396-9*) New Comet.

Nelson, Gertrud M. Child of God: A Book of Birthdays & Days in Between. (Illus.). 64p. 1997. 15.00 (*1-56854-178-3*, BDBOOK) Liturgy Tr Pubns.

— Here All Dwell Free: Stories to Heal the Wounded Feminine. LC 98-43808. (Illus.). 384p. 1999. pap. 23.95 (*0-8091-3872-7*) Paulist Pr.

— Pocket Prayers. 176p. 1995. pap. 6.00 (*0-385-47847-X*) Doubleday.

— To Dance with God: Family Ritual & Community Celebration. 256p. 1986. pap. 14.95 (*0-8091-2812-8*) Paulist Pr.

Nelson, Gertrud M. & Witt, Christopher. Sacred Threshold: Rituals & Readings for a Wedding with Spirit. LC 97-37656. 320p. 1998. pap. 11.00 (*0-385-48539-5*) Doubleday.

Nelson, Gertrud Mueller. A Walk Through Our Church. LC 97-41091. 64p. (J). (gr. 1 up). 1998. 14.95 (*0-8091-6648-8*) Paulist Pr.

Nelson-Giavanni, Marcus. A System in Denial: Nelson vs. the United States. Pritchard, John, ed. (Illus.). 416p. 1997. 23.95 (*0-914207-11-3*) Cornucopia Pubns.

Nelson, Gil. Exploring Wild North Florida. LC 95-22761. (Illus.). 256p. 1995. pap. 14.95 (*1-56164-091-3*) Pineapple Pr.

— Exploring Wild Northwest Florida. LC 95-22760. (Illus.). 288p. 1995. pap. 14.95 (*1-56164-086-7*) Pineapple Pr.

***Nelson, Gil.** The Ferns of Florida. LC 99-42528. (Illus.). 280p. 2000. 27.95 (*1-56164-193-6*); pap. 19.95 (*1-56164-197-9*) Pineapple Pr.

Nelson, Gil. Shrubs & Woody Vines of Florida. (Illus.). 464p. 1996. 30.95 (*1-56164-106-5*); pap. 21.95 (*1-56164-110-3*) Pineapple Pr.

— The Trees of Florida: A Reference & Field Guide. LC 93-41607. (Illus.). 338p. 1994. 29.95 (*1-56164-053-0*); pap. 19.95 (*1-56164-055-7*) Pineapple Pr.

Nelson, Gillian. Highland Bridges. (Illus.). 1990. pap. 17.75 (*0-08-037744-0*, Pub. by Aberdeen U Pr) Macmillan.

— Walking in the Garden. 1994. lib. bdg. 19.00 (*0-7278-4619-1*) Severn Hse.

Nelson, Glenn C. Ceramics: A Potter's Handbook. 5th ed. LC 83-12633. (Illus.). (C). 1984. pap. text 56.00 (*0-03-063227-7*, Pub. by Harcourt Coll Pubs) Harcourt.

— Ceramics: A Potter's Handbook. 5th ed. LC 83-12633. (Illus.). (C). 1984. 34.50 (*0-03-064163-2*) Harcourt Coll Pubs.

Nelson, Gloria B. Documentation Manual for Speech Language Pathology. 240p. 1998. ring bd. 115.00 (*0-8342-0991-8*, 20991) Aspen Pub.

Nelson, Gordon L., ed. Fire & Polymers: Hazards Identification & Prevention. LC 90-34195. (ACS Symposium Ser.: No. 425). (Illus.). 610p. 1990. text 105.00 (*0-8412-1779-3*, Pub. by Am Chemical) OUP.

— Fire & Polymers II: Materials & Tests for Hazard Prevention. LC 95-17788. (ACS Symposium Ser.: No. 599). (Illus.). 642p. 1995. text 140.00 (*0-8412-3231-8*, Pub. by Am Chemical) OUP.

Nelson, Gordon L., jt. auth. see Alper, Joseph.

Nelson, Grant S. & Whitman, Dale A. Cases & Materials on Real Estate Transfer, Finance & Development. 4th ed. (American Casebook Ser.). 1346p. (C). 1992. reprint ed. text 52.00 (*0-314-00568-4*) West Pub.

— Cases & Materials on Real Estate Transfer, Finance & Development. 5th ed. LC 98-4457. (Paralegal). 1400p. 1999. text 47.25 (*0-314-22664-8*) West Pub.

— Land Transactions & Finance. 2nd ed. (Black Letter Ser.). 466p. (C). 1988. reprint ed. pap., pap. text 24.50 incl. disk (*0-314-68969-9*) West Pub.

— Land Transactions & Finance. 3rd ed. LC 97-35491. (Block Letter Ser.). 497p. (C). 1997. pap., suppl. ed. 24.50 incl. disk (*0-314-21104-7*) West Pub.

— Real Estate Finance Law. LC 93-43024. (Paralegal). 1091p. 1997. text 39.00 (*0-314-03453-6*) West Pub.

— Real Estate Finance Law. LC 85-13660. (Hornbook Ser.). 1052p. 1991. reprint ed. text, student ed. 36.50 (*0-314-91412-9*) West Pub.

— Real Estate Finance Law, 2 vols., Vol. 1. 3rd ed. (Practitioner's Treatise Ser.). 842p. 1993. text 62.50 (*0-314-02296-1*) West Pub.

— Real Estate Finance Law, 2 vols., Vol. 2. (Practitioner Treatise Ser.). 825p. 1993. text 62.50 (*0-314-02434-4*) West Pub.

Nelson, Grant S., et al. Contemporary Property. (American Casebook Ser.). 382p. 1996. pap. text, teacher ed. write for info. (*0-314-21772-X*) West Pub.

— Contemporary Property: American Casebook Series. (Paralegal). 1201p. (C). 1996. text 47.50 (*0-314-07215-2*) West Pub.

***Nelson, Greg.** High Frequency & Microwave Circuit Design. LC 99-40461. 165p. 1999. boxed set 79.95 (*0-8493-0249-8*) CRC Pr.

Nelson, Greg. Speak: A Comedy. 96p. 1998. pap. 13.95 (*0-88754-566-1*, Pub. by Theatre Comm) Consort Bk Sales.

— Spirit Wrestler. (Illus.). 96p. 1998. pap. 10.95 (*1-55050-126-7*, Pub. by Coteau) Genl Dist Srvs.

***Nelson, Gregory P.** A Touch of Heaven: Finding New Meaning in Sabbath Rest. LC 99-17393. 1999. 11.99 (*0-8163-1721-6*) Pacific Pr Pub Assn.

***Nelson, Gustav.** Service Is the Point: Members as Ministers to the World. LC 99-86408. 144p. 2000. pap. 14.00 (*0-687-08789-9*) Abingdon.

Nelson, H. F., ed. Thermal Design of Aeroassisted Orbital Transfer Vehicles. LC 85-3853. (PAAS Ser.: Vol. 96). (Illus.). 566p. 1985. 81.95 (*0-915928-94-9*, V-96) AIAA.

Nelson, H. H. The Registry of the Photographic Archives of the Epigraphic Survey: With Plates from Key Plans Showing Locations of Theban Temple Decorations. LC 94-69120. (Epigraphic Survey - Communications Ser.: No. 27). (Illus.). xviii, 270p. 1995. pap. text 25.00 (*0-918986-98-2*) Orient Inst.

Nelson, H. Roice. New Technologies in Exploration Geophysics. LC 82-21120. 293p. 1983. reprint ed. pap. 90.90 (*0-608-01577-6*, 206199700001) Bks Demand.

Nelson-Haber, Molly. Internationally Yours: Two Hundred Topics & Activities for English Conversation Practice. 273p. 1995. pap. text 14.00 (*0-9652597-0-6*) Intl Ctr NY.

Nelson, Hank & McCormack, Gavan. The Burma-Thailand Railway. 192p. 1994. pap. 17.95 (*1-86373-577-1*, Pub. by Allen & Unwin Pty) Paul & Co Pubs.

Nelson, Hanna. The Z-Mail Handbook: Three Interfaces for E-Mail. (Nutshell Handbook Ser.). 462p. (Orig.). 1993. pap. 29.95 (*0-937175-76-5*) Thomson Learn.

Nelson, Harland S. Charles Dickens. (English Authors Ser.: No. 314). 264p. (C). 1981. 32.00 (*0-8057-6805-X*, Twyne) Mac Lib Ref.

Nelson, Harold. Asthma: A Guide for Patients. Wilson, Archie, ed. (Allergy Ser.). (Illus.). 32p. (Orig.). 1996. pap. 2.95 (*1-885274-34-3*) Health InfoNet Inc.

Nelson, Harold D., ed. Liberia: A Country Study. LC 85-7393. (Army Department Pamphlet Area Handbook Ser.: No. 550-38). (Illus.). 371p. 1985. 16.00 (*0-318-18782-5*, S/N 008-020-01041-3) USGPO.

— Morocco: A Country Study. LC 85-600265. (DA Pam Area Handbook Ser.: No. 550-49). (Illus.). 476p. (YA). (gr. 9-12). 1986. 20.00 (*0-16-001640-1*, S/N 008-020-01072-3) USGPO.

— Mozambique: A Country Study. LC 85-6027. (DA Pam Area Handbook Ser.: No. 550-61). (Illus.). 375p. 1985. text 16.00 (*0-16-001622-3*, S/N 008-020-01033-2) USGPO.

— Tunisia: A Country Study. 3rd ed. LC 86-3351. (DA Pam Area Handbook Ser.: No. 550-89). Orig. Title: Area Handbook for the Republic of Tunisia. (Illus.). 407p. 1988. 17.00 (*0-16-001651-7*, S/N 008-020-01092-8) USGPO.

Nelson, Harold E., et al. Quantitative Methods for Life Safety Analysis: Proceedings of the 1986 Symposium. 1988. 35.30 (*0-318-24020-3*) Society Fire Protect.

Nelson, Harold H. The Great Hypostyle Hall at Karnak Vol. 1: The Wall Reliefs. Murnane, William J., ed. LC 81-80596. (Oriental Institute Publications: No. 106). (Illus.). 1981. lib. bdg. 90.00 (*0-918986-30-3*) Orient Inst.

— Key Plans Showing Locations of Theban Temple Decorations. LC 42-21551. (Oriental Institute Publications: No. 56). (Illus.). 1995. lib. bdg. 36.00 (*0-226-62154-5*, OIP56) U Ch Pr.

— Medinet Habu - Epigraphic Survey: The Calendar, the Slaughterhouse, & Minor Records of Ramses III, Vol. 3. LC 30-6904. (Oriental Institute Publications: No. 23). 1934. lib. bdg. 70.00 (*0-226-62119-7*, OIP23) U Ch Pr.

Nelson, Harold H. & Holscher, Uvo. Medinet Habu, 1924-28. LC 29-13423. (Illus.). 50p. 1998. pap. text 6.00 (*0-226-62320-3*, OIC5) U Ch Pr.

Nelson, Harold N., ed. Freedom of the Press from Hamilton to the Warren Court. LC 66-22578. (Orig.). (C). 1967. write for info. (*0-672-51005-7*, Bobbs); pap. 8.40 (*0-672-60120-6*, AHS74, Bobbs) Macmillan.

Nelson, Harold W. Leon Trotsky & the Art of Insurrection, 1905-1917. 250p. 1986. 49.50 (*0-7146-3272-4*, Pub. by F Cass Pubs); pap. text 22.50 (*0-7146-4065-4*, Pub. by F Cass Pubs) Intl Spec Bk.

Nelson, Harold W., jt. auth. see Luvaas, Jay.

Nelson, Harold W., jt. ed. see Luvaas, Jay.

Nelson, Harry. Federalism in Health Reform: Views from the States That Could Not Wait. (Illus.). 36p. 1994. pap. text. write for info. (*0-9629870-6-9*) Milbank Memorial.

— Knowing What the Problem Is & Getting It Solved: State Reform in Long-Term Care. 28p. (Orig.). 1994. pap. text. write for info. (*0-9629870-3-4*) Milbank Memorial.

— Nonprofit & For-Profit HMOs: Converging Practices but Different Goals? 36p. (Orig.). 1997. pap. write for info. (*1-887748-13-X*) Milbank Memorial.

— The Question of Primary Care: Legislators Get the Answers. 40p. (Orig.). 1995. pap. write for info. (*0-9629870-9-3*) Milbank Memorial.

— The Resistance of the Air to Stone-Dropping Meteors. LC 53-12359. (Augustana College Library Publications: No. 24). 37p. 1953. pap. 6.00 (*0-910182-19-1*) Augustana Coll.

— Treating Drug Abusers Effectively: Researchers Talk with Policy Makers. (Illus.). 28p. (Orig.). 1996. pap. write for info. (*1-887748-01-6*) Milbank Memorial.

— What Is Appropriate Care for Children of Troubled Families? 40p. (Orig.). 1996. pap. write for info. (*1-887748-06-7*) Milbank Memorial.

Nelson, Harry & Monroe, Ann F. Converting & Merging Hospitals: Trustees Talk to Each Other. 28p. 1999. pap. write for info. (*1-887748-24-5*) Milbank Memorial.

Nelson, Harry, et al. Essentials of Physical Anthropology. Perlee, Clyde & Simon, eds. 352p. (C). 1992. pap. text 38.25 (*0-314-93440-5*) West Pub.

Nelson, Harry, jt. auth. see Jurmain, Robert.

Nelson, Harry E. In the Astronomy Tradition at Augustana. 59p. 1992. pap. 8.00 (*1-878326-04-X*) Augustana.

Nelson, Harvey K. Proceedings & Papers of the Fourteenth Trumpeter Swan Society Conference: Trumpeter Swans - An Asset or a Liability? Compton, Donna C. et al, eds. (Illus.). 170p. (Orig.). 1994. pap. text 15.00 (*0-9619936-9-3*) Trumpeter Swan Soc.

Nelson, Hazel. Cognitive Behavioral Therapy with Schizophrenia: A Practice Manual. 224p. 1997. 39.95 (*1-56593-934-4*, 1854) Singular Publishing.

Nelson, Hazel E. Cognitive Behavioural Therapy with Schizophrenia: A Practice Manual. (Illus.). 262p. (Orig.). 1997. pap. 39.50 (*0-7487-3305-1*, Pub. by S Thornes Pubs) Trans-Atl Phila.

Nelson, Hazel J. Jackrabbit Road & Me: A History of Humble Texas & Personal Autobiography. Richards, Jerri S., ed. (Illus.). 48p. (Orig.). 1996. pap. 8.00 (*1-887303-12-X*) Blu Lantern Pub.

Nelson, Helen, et al. Growing up in Paradise: The History of Nelson's Spring Creek Ranch. LC 98-86653. (Illus.). 80p. 1998. pap. 11.95 (*0-9665751-0-5*) Clairmont Pubg.

Nelson, Helge. The Swedes & the Swedish Settlements in North America, 2 vols. Scott, Franklyn D., ed. LC 78-15197. (Scandinavians in America Ser.). (Illus.). 1979. reprint ed. lib. bdg. 50.95 (*0-405-11654-3*) Ayer.

Nelson, Henry S. Doctor with Big Shoes: Missionary Experiences in China & Africa. LC 95-70539. (Illus.). 288p. (Orig.). 1995. pap. 17.95 (*1-881576-45-0*) Providence Hse.

Nelson, Herbert B., ed. see Hilleary, William M.

Nelson-Hernandez, Natalie. Mapmakers of the Western Trails: The Story of John Charles Fremont. LC 97-181478. (Illus.). 128p. (J). (gr. 3-8). 1997. pap. 9.95 (*0-9644386-2-3*) Santa Ines Pub.

— Stowaway to California: Adventures with Father Serra. LC 95-125156. (Illus.). 136p. (Orig.). (J). (gr. 3-8). 1994. pap. 9.95 (*0-9644386-0-7*) Santa Ines Pub.

Nelson, Hilda. Francois Baucher: The Man & His Method. 192p. 1990. 110.00 (*0-85131-534-8*, Pub. by J A Allen) Trafalgar.

— L 'Hotte & the Quest for Lightness. 1997. 110.00 (*0-85131-705-7*, Pub. by J A Allen) Trafalgar.

Nelson, Hilda, tr. see De Pluvinel, Antoine.

Nelson, Hilde L. Feminism & Families. 272p. (C). 1996. pap. 18.99 (*0-415-91254-7*) Routledge.

Nelson, Hilde L., ed. Stories & Their Limits: Narrative Approaches to Bioethics. LC 97-36487. (Reflective Bioethics Ser.). 288p. (C). 1997. 80.00 (*0-415-91909-6*); pap. 19.99 (*0-415-91910-X*) Routledge.

Nelson, Hilde L. & Nelson, James L. The Patient in the Family: An Ethics of Medicine & Families. LC 94-33652. 224p. (C). (gr. 13). 1995. pap. 18.99 (*0-415-91129-X*, B4914) Routledge.

Nelson, Hilde L., jt. auth. see Lindemann, James.

Nelson, Hilde L., jt. auth. see Nelson, James L.

Nelson, Hilde Lindemann, ed. Feminism & Families. 272p. (C). 1996. 70.00 (*0-415-91253-9*) Routledge.

Nelson, Horace G. & Nelson, Carol F. The College Journal. 320p. 1994. 28.95 (*0-9638311-0-0*) Primary Publns.

Nelson, Horatio. Dispatches & Letters of Vice Admiral Lord Viscount Nelson. LC 98-151521. (Dispatches & Letters of Lord Nelson Ser.). 1999. pap. text 32.95 (*1-86176-050-7*) Chatham Pr.

— Dispatches & Letters of Vice Admiral Lord Viscount Nelson. LC 98 151521. (Dispatches & Letters of Lord Nelson Ser.). 1999. pap. text 32.95 (*1-86176-049-3*) Chatman Pub.

— Nelson's Last Diary: A Facsimile. Warner, Oliver, ed. LC 70-165752. 80p. reprint ed. pap. 30.00 (*0-608-14574-2*, 202492400039) Bks Demand.

Nelson, Howard. Bone Music. (Poetry Chapbook Ser.). 36p. 1997. pap. 7.95 (*1-879205-72-6*) Nightshade Pr.

— Creatures. (CSU Poetry Ser.: Vol. XIII). 47p. (Orig.). 1983. pap. 4.50 (*0-914946-40-4*) Cleveland St Univ Poetry Ctr.

— Robert Bly: An Introduction to the Poetry. Unterecker, John, ed. LC 83-14481. (Columbia Introductions to Twentieth-Century American Poetry Ser.). 1984. text 39.00 (*0-231-05310-X*) Col U Pr.

— Shelling Peanuts: And Other Odd Odes. 118p. (Orig.). 1996. pap. 5.00 (*1-57502-240-0*, P0913) Morris Pubng.

Nelson, Howard, ed. On the Poetry of Galway Kinnell: The Wages of Dying. 304p. 1988. text 42.50 (*0-472-09376-2*, 09376); pap. text 18.95 (*0-472-06376-6*, 06376) U of Mich Pr.

Nelson, Humphrey. The Little Man & the Little Oyster. LC 89-21489. 1990. 9.95 (*0-87770-479-1*) Ye Galleon.

Nelson, J. Black Beauty: Poems about Our People. 175p. 1995. 7.95 (*0-614-05145-2*) House Nia.

Nelson, J. C. Operational Amplifier Circuits: Analysis & Design. LC 94-32724. (EDN Ser.). 152p. 1994. pap. text 28.95 (*0-7506-9468-8*) Buttrwrth-Heinemann.

Nelson, J. C., tr. see Jagoda, A. & De Villepin, M.

Nelson, J. Craig. Geriatric Psychopharmacology. LC 97-42394. (Medical Psychiatry Ser.). (Illus.). 488p. 1997. text 175.00 (*0-8247-9851-1*) Dekker.

Nelson, J. H., compiled by. The Madura Country: A Manual. (Illus.). (C). 1989. reprint ed. 62.50 (*81-206-0424-5*, Pub. by Asian Educ Servs) S Asia.

Nelson, J. R. Bonnie: The Development of the Triumph Bonneville. 2nd ed. (Illus.). 184p. 1995. pap. 24.95 (*0-85429-957-2*) MBI Pubg.

Nelson, J. Robert. Science & Our Troubled Conscience. LC 80-8045. 187p. (Orig.). reprint ed. pap. 58.00 (*0-608-15333-8*, 202961900061) Bks Demand.

Nelson, J. Robert, ed. Life As Liberty, Life As Trust. fac. ed. LC 92-6287. 104p. 1992. reprint ed. pap. 32.30 (*0-7837-7968-2*, 204772400008) Bks Demand.

***Nelson, J. Ron & Carr, Beth Ann.** The Thinktime Strategy for Schools, Set. 2nd rev. ed. (Illus.). 26p. 2000. 49.00 incl. VHS (*1-57035-223-2*, 130THINK) Sopris.

***Nelson, J. Ron, et al.** Conducting Functional Behavioral Assessments: A Practical Guide. 50p. 1998. pap. 19.50 (*1-57035-198-8*) Sopris.

Nelson, J. Russell, ed. see Conference on Understanding Profits (1964: Macales.

Nelson, J. S. & Dunham, S. T., eds. Semiconductor Process & Device Performance Modeling Vol. 490: Materials Research Society Symposium Proceedings. LC 98-33841. 273p. 1998. text 66.00 (*1-55899-395-9*) Materials Res.

Nelson, Jack. Feminism, Science & the Philosophy of Science. Nelson, Lynn H., ed. LC 96-25075. (Synthese Library SYLI: Vol. 256). 336p. (C). 1996. text 117.50 (*0-7923-4162-7*) Kluwer Academic.

— Terror in the Night: The Klan's Campaign Against the Jews. LC 92-29539. (Illus.). 304p. 1993. 22.00 (*0-671-69223-2*) S&S Trade.

— Terror in the Night: The Klan's Campaign Against the Jews. LC 96-2905. (Illus.). 288p. 1996. reprint ed. pap. 16.00 (*0-87805-907-5*) U Pr of Miss.

Nelson, Jack & Roberts, Gene, Jr. The Censors & the Schools. LC 77-23390. 208p. 1977. reprint ed. lib. bdg. 59.50 (*0-8371-9687-6*, NECE, Greenwood Pr) Greenwood.

Nelson, Jack, jt. auth. see Bass, Jack.

Nelson, Jack, jt. auth. see Hankinson-Nelson, Lynn.

Nelson, Jack A., ed. The Disabled, the Media, & the Information Age, 42. LC 93-7700. (Contributions to the Study of Mass Media & Communications Ser.: No. 42). 264p. 1994. 59.95 (*0-313-28472-5*, NDM/, Greenwood Pr) Greenwood.

Nelson, Jack E. Christian Missionizing & Social Transformation: A History of Conflict & Change in Eastern Zaire. LC 91-46755. 224p. 1992. 55.00 (*0-275-94246-5*, C4246, Praeger Pubs) Greenwood.

Nelson, Jack K., jt. auth. see Thomas, Jerry R.

Nelson, Jack L. Introduction to Value Inquiry: A Student Process Book. LC 73-18118. (Hayden American Values Ser.). 47p. 1974. write for info. (*0-8104-5900-0*) Sams.

Nelson, Jack L., et al. Critical Issues in Education: A Dialectic Approach. 3rd ed. LC 95-39695. (C). 1995. pap. text 26.74 (*0-07-046212-7*) McGraw.

***Nelson, Jack L., et al.** Critical Issues in Education: Dialogues & Dialectics 4th ed. LC 99-32995. 528p. 1999. pap. 34.68 (*0-07-228661-X*) McGraw.

Nelson, Jackie & Halpern-Segal, Janice. My Trip. (Illus.). 24p. (Orig.). (J). (ps-3). 1989. pap. 6.95 (*0-685-29177-4*) Take Along Pubns.

Nelson, Jacquelyn S. Indiana Quakers Confront the Civil War. LC 91-8983. xvii, 303p. 1991. 19.95 (*0-87195-064-2*) Ind Hist Soc.

Nelson, James. Health & Welfare Benefit Plans: A Legal Guide to Planning & Management. 1991. ring bd. 95.00 (*0-327-03921-3*, 80984-10, MICHIE) LEXIS Pub.

Nelson, James, ed. Alaska Review. (Illus.). 84p. (Orig.). 1989. pap. 11.95 (*0-9623681-0-5*, Moosehorn Pubns) AK ReView Inc.

Nelson, James B. Between Two Gardens: Reflections on Sexuality & Religious Experience. LC 83-11119. 208p. (Orig.). 1983. pap. 12.95 (*0-8298-0681-4*) Pilgrim OH.

— Body Theology. 176p. (Orig.). 1992. pap. 19.95 (*0-664-25379-2*) Westminster John Knox.

— Embodiment: An Approach to Sexuality & Christian Theology. LC 78-55589. 304p. 1979. pap. 19.99 (*0-8066-1701-2*, 10-2071, Augsburg) Augsburg Fortress.

— The Intimate Connection: Male Sexuality, Masculine Spirituality. LC 87-29487. 144p. (Orig.). 1988. pap. 17.95 (*0-664-24065-8*) Westminster John Knox.

— Moral Nexus: Ethics of Christian Identity & Community. 25th anniversary ed. LC 96-22894. 264p. 1996. pap. 24.95 (*0-664-25678-3*) Westminster John Knox.

Nelson, James B. & Longfellow, Sandra P., eds. Sexuality & the Sacred: Sources for Theological Reflection. LC 93-39390. 432p. (Orig.). 1994. pap. 29.95 (*0-664-25529-9*) Westminster John Knox.

Nelson, James B. & Rohricht, Jo A. Human Medicine: Ethical Perspective on Today's Medical Issues. expanded rev. ed. LC 84-12411. 224p. (Orig.). 1984. pap. 19.99 (*0-8066-2086-2*, 10-3187, Augsburg) Augsburg Fortress.

Nelson, James D. Awakening. 1989. pap. 9.95 (*0-8306-9000-X*) McGraw-Hill Prof.

Nelson, James D., ed. see Pregnancy & Infant Loss Center Staff.

Nelson, James G. The Early Nineties: A View from the Bodley Head. LC 70-139718. 403p. 1971. reprint ed. pap. 125.00 (*0-7837-2303-2*, 205739100004) Bks Demand.

— Elkin Mathews: Publisher to Yeats, Joyce, Pound. LC 89-40265. xiii, 299 p. (Orig.). (C). 1989. pap. text 17.95 (*0-299-12244-1*) U of Wis Pr.

— The Last Refuge. LC 72-87214. 230p. reprint ed. pap. 71.30 (*0-608-13592-5*, 202231400026) Bks Demand.

***Nelson, James G.** Publisher to the Decadents: Leonard Smithers in the Careers of Beardsley, Wilde & Dowson. 2000. 35.00 (*0-271-01974-3*) Pa St U Pr.

Nelson, James G. Sir William Watson. LC 66-28912. (Twayne's English Authors Ser.). 1966. pap. text 6.95 (*0-8290-2025-X*); lib. bdg. 20.95 (*0-89197-938-7*) Irvington.

N

— The Sublime Puritan: Milton & the Victorians. LC 74-8794. (Illus.). 209p. 1974. reprint ed. lib. bdg. 38.50 (0-8371-7586-0, NESP, Greenwood Pr) Greenwood.

Nelson, James G. & Serafin, Rafal, eds. National Parks & Protected Areas: Keystones to Conservation & Sustainable Development. LC 97-37830. (NATO ASI Series G: Vol. 40). (Illus.). ix, 292p. 1997. text 109.00 (3-540-63527-0) Spr-Verlag.

Nelson, James H. Threshold of Empire: Battle for Manila, 1898-1899. 288p. (Orig.). 1997. pap. 19.95 (1-884570-71-2) Research Triangle.

Nelson, James K., Jr., ed. Computer Utilization in Structural Engineering. LC 89-6774. 574p. 1989. pap. text 8.00 (0-87262-698-9, 698) Am Soc Civil Eng.

— Electronic Computation. LC 59-65010. (Conference Proceedings Ser.). 794p. 1983. pap. 8.00 (0-87262-351-3) Am Soc Civil Eng.

Nelson, James K., jt. auth. see McCormac, Jack C.

***Nelson, James L.** All the Brave Fellows. LC 99-88031. Vol. 5. 416p. 2000. 25.95 (0-671-03846-X, Pocket Books) PB.

Nelson, James L. By Force of Arms. Wolverton, Peter, ed. 336p. 1996. per. 14.00 (0-671-51924-7, PB Trade Paper) PB.

— By Force of Arms. large type ed. LC 98-52521. (G. K. Hall Core Ser.). 1999. 27.95 (0-7838-8526-1, G K Hall Lrg Type) Mac Lib Ref.

— The Continental Risque. 384p. 1998. per. 14.00 (0-671-01381-5, Pocket Books) PB.

***Nelson, James L.** The Guardship: Book One of the Brethren of the Coast. LC 99-39239. (Brethren of the Coast Ser.). 384p. 2000. pap. 14.00 (0-380-80452-2, Avon Bks) Morrow Avon.

Nelson, James L. Lords of the Ocean. LC 99-26943. 352p. 1999. 23.00 (0-671-03490-1, PB Hardcover) PB.

— Lords of the Ocean. 368p. 2000. reprint ed. per. 13.95 (0-671-01383-1) PB.

— The Maddest Idea. LC 96-42484. 432p. 1997. per. 14.00 (0-671-51925-5) PB.

Nelson, James L. & Nelson, Hilde L. Alzheimer's: Answers to Hard Questions for Families. 224p. 1997. pap. 12.95 (0-385-48534-4, Main St Bks) Doubleday.

Nelson, James L., jt. auth. see Nelson, Hilde L.

Nelson, James M. Health & Welfare Benefit Plans: A Legal Guide to Planning & Management. 1994. ring bd., suppl. ed. 37.50 (0-685-74395-0, MICHIE) LEXIS Pub.

— Health & Welfare Benefit Plans: A Legal Guide to Planning & Management. 440p. 1994. spiral bd. 95.00 (0-88063-371-9, MICHIE) LEXIS Pub.

***Nelson, James M.** Health & Welfare Benefits Plan, 1999 Edition. 600p. 1999. ring bd. write for info. (0-327-01377-X, 8098411) LEXIS Pub.

Nelson, James S. & McKeever, Paul E. Clinical Neuropathology. (C). 1994. text 600.00 incl. disk (1-56815-020-2) Mosby Inc.

Nelson, Jan A., ed. Le Chevalier au Cygne & La Fin d'Elias. LC 85-8443. (Old French Crusade Cycle Ser.: Vol. II). (FRE., Illus.). 608p. 1985. text 60.00 (0-8173-0272-7) U of Ala Pr.

Nelson, Jan A. & Mickel, Emanuel J., eds. La Naissance du Chevalier au Cygne. LC 76-30489. (Old French Crusade Cycle Ser.: Vol. 1). 496p. 1977. text 34.50 (0-8173-8501-0) U of Ala Pr.

Nelson, Jan A., ed. see De Troyes, Chretien.

Nelson, Jan C. & Aaker, David A. The Bereavement Ministry Program: A Comprehensive Guide for Churches. LC 97-35308. 336p. 1998. spiral bd. 35.95 (0-87793-645-5) Ave Maria.

***Nelson, Jane & Evertz, Kathy.** The Politics of Writing Centers. 2000. pap. write for info. (0-86709-569-5, Pub. by Boynton Cook Pubs) Heinemann.

***Nelson, Jane & Lott, Lynn.** Positive Discipline for Teenagers. 2nd ed. LC 99-59674. (Positive Discipline Library). 2000. pap. 16.95 (0-7615-2181-X) Prima Pub.

Nelson, Jane, jt. auth. see Fogarty, James.

Nelson, Jane A. Form & Image in the Fiction of Henry Miller. LC 69-10515. 230p. reprint ed. pap. 71.30 (0-608-16593-X, 202767300055) Bks Demand.

Nelson, Jane S. Christ-Centered Crafts for Children's Classes. LC 81-8711. (Illus.). 102p. (Orig.). 1981. pap. 4.99 (0-87227-078-5, RBP5093) Reg Baptist.

Nelson, Jane V. Mabel Dodge Luhan. (Western Writers Ser.: No. 55). (Illus.). 50p. (Orig.). 1982. pap. 4.95 (0-88430-029-3) Boise St U W Writ Ser.

Nelson, Jane V., jt. ed. see Wangberg, James K.

Nelson, Janet L. Charles the Bald. LC 91-17355. (Medieval World Ser.). 1992. write for info. (0-582-05585-7, Drumbeat) Longman.

— The Frankish World, 750-900. LC 95-47680. xxxi, 256 p. 1996. 60.00 (1-85285-105-8) Hambledon Press.

— Rulers & Ruling Families in Early Medieval Europe: Alfred, Charles the Bald & Others LC 99-29851. (Variorum Collected Studies Ser.). 1999. 106.95 (0-86078-802-4, Pub. by Ashgate Pub) Ashgate Pub Co.

Nelson, Janet L., ed. The Annals of St-Bertin: Ninth-Century Histories, Vol. 1. LC 91-4030. 256p. 1992. text 29.95 (0-7190-3426-4, Pub. by Manchester Univ Pr) St Martin.

Nelson, Janet L., jt. auth. see Theuws, Frans.

Nelson, Janet L., jt. ed. see Gibson, Margaret T.

Nelson, Jason M. When You Become an Adult. (Stepping Stones Ser.). 32p. (Orig.). 1992. pap. 1.95 (0-8100-0460-7, 12N2007) Northwest Pub.

Nelson, Jay & Robinson, G. D. Adventures in Human Physiology. 60p. (C). 1996. pap. text, spiral bd. 11.95 (0-7872-2859-1) Kendall-Hunt.

Nelson, Jeannie, jt. auth. see Beechick, Ruth.

Nelson, Jeff. Programming Mobile Objects with Java. LC 98-50956. 601p. 1999. pap. 49.99 incl. cd-rom (0-471-25406-1) Wiley.

Nelson, Jefferson E., jt. auth. see Good, William V.

***Nelson, Jeffery.** Pokemon Stadium Official Strategy Guide. (Strategy Guides Ser.). (Illus.). 128p. (J). 2000. pap. 12.99 (1-56686-974-9, BradyGAMES) Brady Pub.

Nelson, Jeffrey. Monster Hunt Activity Book. (Orig.). (YA). 1994. pap. 2.99 (0-8125-9434-7, Pub. by Tor Bks) St Martin.

— Scary, Spooky Hunt Activity Book. 48p. (Orig.). (YA). 1994. pap. 2.99 (0-8125-9436-3, Pub. by Tor Bks) St Martin.

Nelson, Jeffrey, ed. see Regnery, Henry.

Nelson, Jeffrey A., jt. auth. see Fox, Gerard P.

Nelson, Jeffrey A., jt. auth. see McNichol, Andrea.

Nelson, Jeffrey N., ed. The Poetry of Robert Tofte, 1597-1620: A Critical Old-Spelling Edition. LC 94-9802. (Renaissance Imagination Ser.). 360p. 1994. text 35.00 (0-8153-1091-9) Garland.

Nelson, Jeffrey R. Around Union City. LC 96-231018. (Images of America Ser.). 1996. pap. 16.99 (0-7524-0460-1) Arcadia Publng.

— Erie. (Images of America Ser.). (Illus.). 128p. 1998. pap. 16.99 (0-7524-0903-4) Arcadia Publng.

Nelson, Jeffrey S. Animal Jokes & Riddles. LC 90-27676. (Illus.). 24p. (J). (gr. 3 up). 1991. pap. 1.95 (1-56288-016-0) Checkerboard.

— The Dinosaur Hunt Activity Book. (Orig.). (J). 1994. pap. 2.99 (0-8125-9439-8, Pub. by Tor Bks) St Martin.

— Dinosaur Jokes & Riddles Book. (Illus.). 24p. (J). (gr. 3 up). 1988. pap. 1.95 (1-56288-341-0) Checkerboard.

— Family Jokes & Riddles. (Illus.). 24p. (J). (gr. 3 up). 1991. pap. 1.95 (1-56288-015-2) Checkerboard.

— Jungle Jokes & Riddles. (Illus.). 24p. (J). (gr. 3 up). 1991. pap. 1.95 (1-56288-017-9) Checkerboard.

— Monster Jokes & Riddles. (Illus.). 24p. (J). (gr. 3 up). 1988. pap. 1.95 (1-56288-342-9) Checkerboard.

— Outerspace Jokes & Riddles Book. (Jokes & Riddles Bks.). (Illus.). 24p. (J). (gr. 3 up). 1988. pap. 1.95 (1-56288-343-7) Checkerboard.

— Spooky Jokes & Riddles. LC 89-123851. (J). 1988. pap. 1.95 (0-02-689070-4, Mac Bks Young Read) S&S Childrens.

— Spooky Jokes & Riddles Book. (Illus.). 24p. (J). (gr. 3 up). 1988. pap. 1.95 (1-56288-344-5) Checkerboard.

— Yucky Jokes & Riddles. (Illus.). 24p. (J). (gr. 3 up). 1991. pap. 1.95 (1-56288-014-4) Checkerboard.

Nelson, Jeffrey S., ed. The Theology of Inexpedience: Two Case Studies in "Moderate" Congregational Dissent in the Lutheran Church - Missouri Synod. LC 97-26650. 184p. (C). 1997. 39.00 (0-7618-0868-X) U Pr of Amer.

Nelson, Jennie, et al. Education in the U. S. A. Readings on the Problems & Promis of Education. 352p. (C). 1996. pap. text, per. 41.95 (0-7872-2472-3, 41247201) Kendall-Hunt.

Nelson, Jennifer, jt. auth. see Austin, Rebecca.

Nelson, Jennifer K., et al. Mayo Clinic Diet Manual: A Handbook of Nutrition Practices. 7th ed. LC 93-43747. (Illus.). 912p. (C). (gr. 13). 1994. pap. text 75.00 (0-8151-6348-7, 23782) Mosby Inc.

Nelson, Jerome, jt. auth. see Edies, Gary J.

Nelson, Jerome L. Libel: A Basic Program for Beginning Journalists. LC 73-13006. 121p. reprint ed. pap. 37.60 (0-608-16266-3, 202665900051) Bks Demand.

Nelson, Jerry R. Alaska Burning. (Illus.). 160p. 1998. pap. 16.95 (1-896754-04-X, Pub. by Sh1oreline) Partners Pubs Grp.

Nelson, Jill. Straight No Chaser: How I Became a Grown-Up Black Woman. 240p. 1999. pap. 12.95 (0-14-027724-2) Penguin Putnam.

— Volunteer Slavery: My Authentic Negro Experience. LC 92-51078. 243p. 1993. 21.95 (1-879360-24-1) Noble Pr.

— Volunteer Slavery: My Authentic Negro Experience. 256p. 1994. pap. 12.95 (0-14-023716-X, Penguin Bks) Viking Penguin.

— Volunteer Slavery: My Authentic Negro Experience. 1994. audio 15.00 (1-57042-207-9, Pub. by Warner Bks) Little.

***Nelson, Jill, ed.** Police Brutality: An Anthology. 320p. 2000. 24.95 (0-393-04883-7) Norton.

Nelson, Jim. Careers in Law Enforcement: Interviewing for Results. 1996. pap. 30.00 (0-938609-01-7) Graduate Group.

***Nelson, Jim.** Compulsive. 265p. 1998. pap. 14.95 (1-928971-01-6) Blue Chicken.

— Glenwood Caverns & the Historic Fairy Caves. (Illus.). 36p. 2000. pap. 7.95 (1-928971-03-2) Blue Chicken.

— Glenwood Springs: The History of a Rocky Mountain River. LC 99-64980. (Illus.). 260p. 1999. pap. 14.95 (1-890437-39-5) Western Reflections.

— A Quick History of Glenwood Springs. 125p. 1999. pap. 7.95 (1-928971-00-8) Blue Chicken.

— A Quick History of Marble & Redstone. 135p. 1999. pap. 7.95 (1-928971-02-4) Blue Chicken.

***Nelson, Jim & Potterfield, Peter.** Selected Climbs in the Cascades Vol. 2: Alpine Routes, Sport Climbs & Crag Climbs. (Illus.). 336p. 2000. pap. 22.95 (0-89886-561-1) Mountaineers.

Nelson, Jim, jt. auth. see Ellrod, Gary.

Nelson, Jim, jt. auth. see Potterfield, Peter.

Nelson, Jo, jt. auth. see Munson, Shirley.

Nelson, Joan, ed. Precarious Balance Vol. I: Democratic Consolidation & Economic Reform in Eastern Europe & Latin America. LC 94-20970. 1994. pap. 19.95 (1-55815-322-5) ICS Pr.

— Precarious Balance Vol. II: Democratic Consolidation & Economic Reform in Eastern Europe & Latin America. 1994. pap. 19.95 (1-55815-323-3) ICS Pr.

Nelson, Joan E. Kids Who Kill Kids. LC 93-85136. 284p. (Orig.). (YA). (gr. 8-12). 1994. pap. 12.95 (0-9637293-1-4) Storm Pub.

— Mommy, Where Are You? (Orig.). 1994. reprint ed. pap. 10.95 (0-9637293-7-3) Storm Pub.

Nelson, Joan M. Migrants, Urban Poverty, & Instability in Developing Nations. LC 74-9752. (Harvard University. Center for International Affairs. Occasional Papers in International Affairs: No. 22). reprint ed. 27.50 (0-404-54622-6) AMS Pr.

— Self-Defense: Steps to Success. LC 90-25460. (Steps to Success Activity Ser.). (Illus.). 160p. (Orig.). 1991. pap. 15.95 (0-88011-430-4, PNEL0430) Human Kinetics.

— Teaching Self-Defense: Steps to Success. LC 93-31620. (Steps to Success Activity Ser.). (Illus.). 160p. 1994. pap. text 15.95 (0-87322-620-8, PNEL0620) Human Kinetics.

— Transforming Post-Communist Political Economies. Walker, Lee & Tilly, Charles, eds. LC 97-45305. 1998. 54.00 (0-309-05929-1) Natl Acad Pr.

Nelson, Joan M., ed. Intricate Links: Democratization & Market Reforms in Latin America & Eastern Europe. LC 94-39868. (U. S. Third World Policy Perspectives Ser.: No. 20). 256p. (C). 1994. 32.95 (1-56000-177-1); pap. 17.95 (1-56000-759-1) Transaction Pubs.

Nelson, Joan M., et al, eds. Fragile Coalitions: The Politics of Economic Adjustment. 224p. 1990. 32.95 (0-88738-283-5) Transaction Pubs.

— The Politics of Economic Adjustment: Fragile Coalitions. 224p. 1990. pap. 17.95 (0-88738-787-X) Transaction Pubs.

Nelson, Joan M. & Eglinton, Stephanie J. Encouraging Democracy: What Role for Conditioned Aid? LC 92-14033. (Policy Essay Ser.: No. 4). 80p. (Orig.). 1992. pap. text 13.95 (1-56517-004-0) Overseas Dev Council.

— Global Goals, Contentious Means: Issues of Multiple Aid Conditionality. LC 93-23293. (Policy Essay Ser.: No. 10). 136p. (C). 1993. pap. text 13.95 (1-56517-012-1) Overseas Dev Council.

Nelson, Joan M., jt. auth. see Huntington, Samuel P.

***Nelson, Joan Marie.** Reforming Health & Education: The Multilateral Development Banks & Complex Institutional Change. LC 99-58625. 112p. 1999. pap. text 13.95 (1-56517-030-X) Overseas Dev Council.

Nelson, JoAnne. Feeling Fit, That's It! LC 92-37719. (Primarily Health Ser.). (Illus.). (J). (ps-2). 1995. pap. 6.00 (0-7802-3249-6) Wright Group.

— Friends All Around. LC 92-4657. (Primarily Health Ser.). (Illus.). 24p. (Orig.). (J). (ps-2). 1995. pap. 6.00 (0-7802-3243-7) Wright Group.

— Good Grief! Good Grief! LC 92-6685. (Primarily Health Ser.). (Illus.). 24p. (Orig.). (J). (ps-2). 1995. pap. 6.00 (0-7802-3237-2) Wright Group.

— How Do You Feel? LC 91-36336. (Primarily Health Ser.). (Illus.). 24p. (Orig.). (J). (ps-2). 1995. pap. 6.00 (0-7802-3241-0) Wright Group.

— It's up to Me! LC 93-9349. (Primarily Health Ser.). (Illus.). (J). (ps-2). 1995. 6.00 (0-7802-3251-8) Wright Group.

— Nose to Toes. LC 91-34706. (Primarily Health Ser.). (Illus.). (J). (ps-2). 1995. pap. 6.00 (0-7802-3245-3) Wright Group.

— Our Friend, the Earth. LC 92-37716. (Primarily Health Ser.). (Illus.). (J). (gr. k-2). 1995. pap. 6.00 (0-935529-59-4) Wright Group.

— Play It Safe. LC 93-12173. (Primarily Health Ser.). (Illus.). (J). (ps-2). 1995. 6.00 (0-7802-3255-0) Wright Group.

— We Are Family. LC 93-12176. (Primarily Health Ser.). (Illus.). (J). (ps-2). 1995. 6.00 (0-7802-3257-7) Wright Group.

— What Next? LC 91-35731. (Primarily Health Ser.). (Illus.). 24p. (Orig.). (J). (ps-2). 1995. pap. 6.00 (0-7802-3247-X) Wright Group.

— When I'm Sick. LC 93-9348. (Primarily Health Ser.). (Illus.). (J). (ps-2). 1995. 6.00 (0-7802-3259-3) Wright Group.

— Where's Mittens? LC 91-9373. (Primarily Health Ser.). (Illus.). 24p. (Orig.). (J). (ps-2). 1995. pap. 6.00 (0-7802-3239-9) Wright Group.

Nelson, Joel A. When Your Child Begins School. (Stepping Stones Ser.). 32p. (Orig.). 1992. pap. 1.95 (0-8100-0456-9, 12N2003) Northwest Pub.

Nelson, Joel I. Post-Industrial Capitalism. 206p. (C). 1995. 52.00 (0-8039-7332-2); pap. 23.50 (0-8039-7333-0) Sage.

Nelson, John. Advanced Scroll Saw Clocks: Measured Drawings for Five Antique Examples. (Scroll Saw Favorites Ser.: Bk. 3). 58p. 1998. pap. 9.95 (1-56523-110-4) Fox Chapel Pub.

— 50 Easy Weekend Scroll Saw Projects. (Scroll Saw Favorites Ser.: Bk. 1). 58p. 1998. pap. 9.95 (1-56523-108-2) Fox Chapel Pub.

— Horse Lover's Scroll Saw Patterns. (Scroll Saw Favorites Ser.: Bk. 2). 58p. 1998. pap. 9.95 (1-56523-109-0) Fox Chapel Pub.

— Living the Little Way: Therese of Lisieux. LC 99-50280. (Christian Living Ser.). 160p. 1999. pap. 10.95 (1-56548-133-X) New City.

— Matrix of the Gods. LC 95-128580. 288p. 1994. pap. 10.95 (1-878901-97-4) Hampton Roads Pub Co.

***Nelson, John.** Scroll Saw Workbook. (Illus.). 96p. (Orig.). 2000. pap., wbk. ed. 14.95 (1-56523-117-1, Pub. by Fox Chapel Pub) IPG Chicago.

Nelson, John. Starborn: A Mystical Tale. (Mystical Tale Ser.). 136p. 1993. pap. 8.95 (1-878901-59-1) Hampton Roads Pub Co.

— Super Simple Scroll Saw Clocks. (Scroll Saw Favorites Ser.: Bk. 4). 58p. 1998. pap. 9.95 (1-56523-111-2) Fox Chapel Pub.

— Transformations. 272p. 1997. pap. 12.95 (1-57174-077-5) Hampton Roads Pub Co.

— Triumph: The Tiger 100/Daytona. 1998. pap. text 22.95 (0-85429-489-9, Pub. by GT Foulis) Haynes Manuals.

— Wintering on the Cortez. 235p. 1999. pap. 12.95 (1-891929-18-6) Four Seasons.

Nelson, John, compiled by. The Little Way of Saint Theresa of Lisieux: Readings for Prayer & Meditation. LC 97-32384. 160p. 1998. pap. 9.00 (0-7648-0199-6) Liguori Pubns.

Nelson, John, ed. Solstice Shift: Magical Blend's Synergistic Guide to the Coming Age. LC 98-101484. (Illus.). 240p. 1997. pap. 16.95 (1-57174-063-5) Hampton Roads Pub Co.

Nelson, John, et al, prefs. Management of Uranium Mill Tailings, Low-Level Waste & Hazardous Waste: Proceedings of the 7th Symposium, 2 vols. (Orig.). 1985. pap. text 38.00 (0-910069-08-5) Geotech Engineer Prog.

Nelson, John & Guimand, Bill. Scroll Saw Basketweave Projects. 62p. 1999. pap. 9.95 (1-56523-103-1) Fox Chapel Pub.

Nelson, John & Guimond, William. Making Wooden Baskets on Your Scroll Saw. (Illus.). 60p. 1998. pap. 9.95 (1-56523-099-X) Fox Chapel Pub.

Nelson, John, et al. The Rhetoric of the Human Sciences: Language & Argument in Scholarship & Public Affairs. LC 86-34030. (Illus.). 408p. 1990. pap. 19.95 (0-299-11024-9) U of Wis Pr.

Nelson, John A. Basic Blueprint Reading. (Illus.). 256p. 1989. 28.95 (0-8306-4273-0); pap. 19.95 (0-8306-3273-5) McGraw-Hill Prof.

— Build Your Own Grandfather Clock & Save. (Illus.). 144p. 1988. 19.95 (0-8306-9053-0, 3053); pap. 12.95 (0-8306-9353-X, 3053) McGraw-Hill Prof.

— Clockmaking: Eighteen Antique Designs for the Woodworker. (Illus.). 176p. (Orig.). 1989. 25.95 (0-8306-9164-2); pap. 18.95 (0-8306-3164-X) McGraw-Hill Prof.

— Clockmaking: Eighteen Antique Designs for the Woodworker. (Illus.). 240p. (Orig.). 1994. pap. 16.95 (0-8117-2526-X) Stackpole.

— Clocks: Full-Size Designs, Ready to Cut. (Scroll Saw Pattern Bks.). (Illus.). 96p. 1995. pap. 14.95 (0-8117-3073-5) Stackpole.

— Colonial Classics You Can Build Today: Plans & Drawings for 80 Authentic Projects, All Exact Replicas of Early American Antiques. LC 85-26171. (Illus.). 256p. (Orig.). 1986. pap. 19.95 (0-8117-2025-X) Stackpole.

***Nelson, John A.** Complete Guide to Making Wooden Clocks: 37 Beautiful Projects for the Home Workshop. (Illus.). 180p. 2000. pap. 24.95 (1-56523-119-8, Pub. by Fox Chapel Pub) IPG Chicago.

Nelson, John A. Country Classics: Authentic Projects You Can Build in One Weekend. Atwater, Sally, ed. LC 88-20027. (Illus.). 224p. (Orig.). 1989. pap. 16.95 (0-8117-2277-5) Stackpole.

— Drafting for Trades & Industry. LC 77-91450. (Drafting Ser.). 1979. pap., teacher ed. 14.00 (0-8273-1641-0) Delmar.

— Drafting for Trades & Industry - Architectural. LC 77-91450. (Drafting Ser.). 138p. (C). 1979. pap. 26.95 (0-8273-1839-1) Delmar.

— Drafting for Trades & Industry - Basic Skills. LC 77-91450. (Drafting Ser.). 464p. (C). 1979. pap. 36.95 (0-8273-1841-3) Delmar.

— Drafting for Trades & Industry - Civil. LC 77-91450. (Drafting Ser.). 942p. (C). 1979. pap. 34.25 (0-8273-1844-8) Delmar.

— Drafting for Trades & Industry - Mechanical & Electronic. LC 77-91450. (Drafting Ser.). 328p. (C). 1979. pap. 27.50 (0-8273-1846-4) Delmar.

— Early American Classics. 1993. 26.00 (0-8446-6720-X) Peter Smith.

— Easy Clocks: Full-Size Designs, Ready to Cut. (Scroll Saw Pattern Bks.). (Illus.). 96p. 1996. pap. 14.95 (0-8117-3074-3) Stackpole.

— Easy-to-Make Antique Furniture Reproductions: 15 Small Projects. (Illus.). 128p. 1988. reprint ed. pap. 8.95 (0-486-25671-5) Dover.

— Fancy Fretwork: 39 Full-Size Designs, Ready to Cut. LC 94-33616. (Scroll Saw Pattern Bks.). (Illus.). 96p. 1995. pap. 14.95 (0-8117-3024-7) Stackpole.

— Fifty-Two Holiday Wood Projects. LC 94-42100. (Illus.). 164p. 1995. pap. 14.95 (0-8069-0652-9) Sterling.

— Folk Art Weather Vanes: Authentic American Patterns for Wood & Metal. LC 89-26368. (Illus.). 160p. (Orig.). 1990. pap. 16.95 (0-8117-2406-9) Stackpole.

— Handbook of Architectural & Civil Drafting. 296p. 1983. pap. 33.95 (0-442-26864-5) Chapman & Hall.

— Inspirational Scroll Saw Projects. (Scroll Saw Favorites Ser.: Bk. 5). 58p. 1998. pap. 9.95 (1-56523-112-0) Fox Chapel Pub.

— Letters & Numbers: Full Size Designs, Ready to Cut. (Scroll Saw Pattern Bks.). (Illus.). 96p. 1996. pap. 14.95 (0-8117-3075-1) Stackpole.

— Plain & Simple Fun: 59 Full-Size Designs, Ready to Cut. (Scroll Saw Pattern Bks.). (Illus.). 96p. 1995. pap. 14.95 (0-8117-3025-5) Stackpole.

— Trains, Planes, & Automobiles: Full-Size Designs, Ready to Cut. (Scroll Saw Pattern Bks.). (Illus.). 96p. 1995. pap. 14.95 (0-8117-3072-7) Stackpole.

— Woodworker's Jackpot. 1991. 24.95 (0-8306-5316-3) McGraw-Hill Prof.

— Woodworker's Jackpot: Forty-Nine Step-by-Step Projects. (Illus.). 240p. (Orig.). 1989. 22.95 (0-8306-9154-5); pap. 16.95 (0-8306-3154-2) McGraw-Hill Prof.

Nelson, John A. & Nelson, Joyce C. Holiday Woodworking Projects: 90 Patterns for Festive Decorations. LC 93-17075. (Illus.). 160p. 1993. pap. 12.95 (0-8117-2547-2) Stackpole.

— Patterns & Projects for the Scroll Saw. LC 90-44284. 224p. (Orig.). 1991. pap. 14.95 (0-8117-3040-9) Stackpole.

Nelson, John A., jt. auth. see Goetsch, David L.

Nelson, John C., tr. see Halley, Pierre.

Nelson, John C., tr. see Pelloso, Pierre.

Nelson, John D. 1998-1999 Pocket Book of Pediatric Antimicrobial Therapy. 13th ed. 116p. 1997. pap. 14.95 (*0-683-30484-4*) Lppncott W & W.

— Pocket Book of Pediatric Antimicrobial Therapy, 1995. 11th ed. LC 88-26186. (Illus.). 106p. 1995. pap. 13.95 (*0-683-06406-1*) Lppncott W & W.

— Pocket Book of Pediatric Antimicrobial Therapy, 1996-1997. 12th ed. 108p. 1997. pap. 14.95 (*0-683-18053-3*) Lppncott W & W.

Nelson, John D. & Bradley, John S. Nelson's 2000-2001 Pocket Book of Pediatric Antimicrobial Therapy. 14th ed. 120p. pap. text 14.95 (*0-7817-2570-4*) Lppncott W & W.

Nelson, John D. & Miller, Debora J. Expansive Soils: Problems & Practice in Foundation & Pavement Engineering. LC 91-42720. 288p. 1997. pap. 75.00 (*0-471-18114-5*) Wiley.

Nelson, John E. Healing the Split: Integrating Spirit into Our Understanding of the Mentally Ill. rev. ed. LC 93-32115. (SUNY Series in the Philosophy of Psychology). 442p. (C). 1994. pap. text 21.95 (*0-7914-1986-X*) State U NY Pr.

— Healing the Split: Integrating Spirit into Our Understanding of the Mentally Ill. rev. ed. LC 93-32115. (SUNY Series in the Philosophy of Psychology). 442p. (C). 1994. text 59.50 (*0-7914-1985-1*) State U NY Pr.

Nelson, John E. & Nelson, Andrea. Sacred Sorrows: Embracing & Transforming Depression. LC 95-24790. (New Consciousness Reader Ser.). 288p. (Orig.). 1996. pap. 14.95 (*0-87477-822-0*, Tarcher Putnam) Putnam Pub Group.

Nelson, John G. Wheelchair Vagabond. 14.95 (*0-933261-10-1*) Twin Peaks Pr.

— Wheelchair Vagabond. 1975. pap. 9.95 (*0-933261-07-1*) Twin Peaks Pr.

Nelson, John H. Laboratory Experiments for Chemistry. 7th ed. 1996. pap. text 49.00 (*0-13-578360-7*) P-H.

— The Negro Character in American Literature. LC 73-128982. reprint ed. 29.50 (*0-404-00203-X*) AMS Pr.

— The Negro Character in American Literature. (BCL1-PS American Literature Ser.). 146p. 1992. reprint ed. lib. bdg. 69.00 (*0-7812-6616-5*) Rprt Serv.

Nelson, John H. & Kemp, Kenneth C. Chemistry. 6th ed. 544p. (C). 1994. pap. text, lab manual ed. 53.00 (*0-13-338708-9*) P-H.

***Nelson, John K.** Enduring Identities: The Guise of Shinto in Contemporary Japan. LC 99-44520. 336p. 2000. text 60.00 (*0-8248-2120-3*); pap. text 29.95 (*0-8248-2259-5*) UH Pr.

Nelson, John L. The Beginner's Guide to Flight Instruction. 2nd ed. (Practical Flying Ser.). (Illus.). 208p. (Orig.). 1989. pap. 15.95 (*0-8306-2443-0*) McGraw-Hill Prof.

Nelson, John O. Opportunities in Religious Service Careers. LC 97-41453. (Opportunities in...Ser.). (Illus.). 160p. 1998. 14.95 (*0-8442-2340-9*, 23409, VGM Career); pap. 11.95 (*0-8442-2341-7*, 23417, VGM Career) NTC Contemp Pub Co.

Nelson, John O., jt. auth. see Machan, Tibor R.

Nelson, John Oliver. Opportunities in Religious Service Careers. (Opportunities In . . . Ser.). (Illus.). 160p. pap. 12.95 (*0-8442-6485-7*, 297OIRS, VGM Career) NTC Contemp Pub Co.

— Opportunities in Religious Service Careers. (Illus.). 160p. 1992. 14.95 (*0-8442-6484-9*, VGM Career) NTC Contemp Pub Co.

Nelson, John P., jt. auth. see Werner, Patricia K.

Nelson, John R., Jr. American Folk Toys. LC 97-46760. (Illus.). 176p. 1998. 24.95 (*1-56158-221-2*, 070350) Taunton.

Nelson, John R. Liberty & Property: Political Economy & Policymaking in the New Nation, 1789-1812. LC 86-21373. (Johns Hopkins University Studies in Historical & Political Science: 105th Series, No. 2). 240p. 1987. reprint ed. pap. 74.40 (*0-608-03739-7*, 206456400009) Bks Demand.

— Triumph Tiger 100 & Daytona: The Development & History of the Pre-Unit & Unit Construction 500cc. (Illus.). 232p. 1998. pap. 22.95 (*1-85960-428-5*, Pub. by J H Haynes & Co) Motorbooks Intl.

Nelson, John S. Tropes of Politics: Science, Theory, Rhetoric, Action. LC 97-36581. (Rhetoric of the Human Sciences Ser.). (Illus.). 312p. (Orig.). 1998. pap. text 21.95 (*0-299-15834-9*) U of Wis Pr.

— Tropes of Politics: Science, Theory, Rhetoric, Action. LC 97-36581. (Rhetoric of the Human Sciences Ser.). (Illus.). xvii, 291p. (Orig.). 1998. text 59.95 (*0-299-15830-6*) U of Wis Pr.

Nelson, John S., ed. Tradition, Interpretation, & Science: Political Theory in the American Academy. LC 86-7098. (SUNY Series in Political Theory: Contemporary Issues). 372p. (C). 1986. pap. text 21.95 (*0-88706-373-X*) State U NY Pr.

— What Should Political Theory Be Now? LC 82-19167. (SUNY Series in Political Theory: Contemporary Issues). 607p. (C). 1984. text 19.50 (*0-87395-694-X*) State U NY Pr.

Nelson, John S. & Boynton, G. R. Video Rhetorics: Televised Advertising in American Politics. LC 97-4580. 1997. write for info. (*0-252-02345-5*) U of Ill Pr.

Nelson, John S. & Boynton, G. R. Video Rhetorics: Televised Advertising in American Politics. LC 97-4580. 208p. 1997. pap. text 29.95 incl. VHS (*0-252-06648-0*) U of Ill Pr.

Nelson, Johnnierenee. Kwanzaa Love. (Illus.). 40p. (Orig.). 1994. pap. 6.00 (*0-9623205-3-6*) House Nia.

— Pissed-Off Poems. 48p. (Orig.). 1996. pap. 10.95 (*0-9623205-4-4*) House Nia.

— Positive Passage: Everyday Kwanzaa Poems. (Illus.). 48p. (Orig.). (J). (gr. 1 up). 1991. pap. 7.00 (*0-9623205-1-X*) House Nia.

— A Quest for Kwanzaa: Poems by Johnnierenee Nelson. (Illus.). 40p. (Orig.). 1988. pap. 6.00 (*0-9623205-0-1*) House Nia.

— Values of the African American Family: The Kwanzaa Canons. (Illus.). 48p. (Orig.). 1993. pap. 9.00 (*0-9623205-2-8*) House Nia.

Nelson, Jon, jt. auth. see Crump, Robert.

Nelson, Jon, jt. auth. see Wooley, Dave.

Nelson-Jones, John & Nuttall, Graeme. Employee Ownership: Legal & Tax Aspects. 170p. 1987. 120.00 (*1-85190-033-0*, Pub. by Fourmat Pub) St Mut.

Nelson-Jones, John & Stewart, Peter. A Practical Guide to Package Holiday Law & Contracts. 1987. 120.00 (*1-85190-041-1*, Pub. by Fourmat Pub) St Mut.

— A Practical Guide to Package Holiday Law & Contracts. 300p. 1993. 105.00 (*0-85459-810-3*, Pub. by Tolley Pubng) St Mut.

Nelson-Jones, Richard. Creating Happy Relationships: A Guide to Partner Skills. LC 83-26158. 224p. 1999. pap. 19.95 (*0-304-70506-3*) Continuum.

— Group Leadership: A Training Approach. LC 91-25842. 336p. (C). 1992. pap. 40.95 (*0-534-17010-2*) Brooks-Cole.

— Lifeskills Helping. (Counseling Ser.). 1993. pap., student ed. 20.95 (*0-534-19675-6*) Brooks-Cole.

— Lifeskills Helping: Helping Others Through a Systematic People Approach. 436p. (C). 1993. pap. 31.95 (*0-534-19674-8*) Brooks-Cole.

— Personal Responsibility & Therapy: An Integrative Approach. 214p. 1987. 49.95 (*0-89116-777-3*) Hemisp Pub.

***Nelson-Jones, Richard.** Six Key Approaches to Counselling & Therapy. 256p. 2000. pap. text 21.95 (*0-8264-4969-7*) Continuum.

Nelson-Jones, Richard. Using Your Mind: Creative Thinking Skills for Work & Business Success. 1997. pap. text 25.95 (*0-304-70185-8*) Continuum.

— You Can Help! Introducing Lifeskills Helping. 176p. 1993. pap. 24.95 (*1-86373-617-4*, Pub. by Allen & Unwin Pty) Paul & Co Pubs.

Nelson-Jones, Rodney & Burton, Frank. Medical Negligence Case Law. 432p. (C). 1990. text 150.00 (*1-85190-087-X*, Pub. by Tolley Pubng) St Mut.

— Nelson-Jones & Burton: Medical Negligence Case Law. 2nd ed. 1995. write for info. (*0-406-03601-2*, NJBM2, MICHIE) LEXIS Pub.

— Personal Injury Limitation Law. 362p. 1994. pap. text 75.00 (*0-406-02447-2*, UK, MICHIE) LEXIS Pub.

Nelson-Jones, Rodney & Nuttall, Graeme. Tax & Interest Tables, 1988-89. (Illus.). 80p. (C). 1988. 100.00 (*1-85190-047-0*, Pub. by Fourmat Pub) St Mut.

Nelson-Jones, Rodney & Stewart, P. Product Liability: The New Law under the Consumer Protection Act, 1987. 208p. (C). 1988. 90.00 (*1-85190-049-7*, Pub. by Fourmat Pub) St Mut.

Nelson-Jones, Rodney & Stewart, Peter. Product Liability. The New Law under the Consumer Protection Act 1987. 208p. 1987. 128.00 (*1-85190-034-9*, Pub. by Fourmat Pub) St Mut.

Nelson, Joseph C. Spanning Time: Vermont's Covered Bridges. LC 97-23083. (Illus.). 288p. 1997. 60.00 (*1-881535-25-8*) New Eng Pr VT.

Nelson, Joseph F. So You Want to Build a Live Steam Locomotive. LC 74-75879. (Illus.). 164p. 1978. reprint ed. 20.95 (*0-914104-01-2*) Wildwood Pubns MI.

Nelson, Joseph L., jt. auth. see Darwin, Charles.

Nelson, Joseph S. Fishes of the World. 3rd ed. 624p. 1994. 125.00 (*0-471-54713-1*) Wiley.

Nelson, Josephus & Farley, Judith. Full Circle: Ninety Years of Service in the Main Reading Room. LC 91-14571. 64p. 1991. 6.00 (*0-8444-0726-7*) Lib Congress.

Nelson, Joyce. Sultans of Sleaze: Public Relations & the Media. 160p. (Orig.). 1998. pap. text 13.00 (*0-7881-5544-X*) DIANE Pub.

Nelson, Joyce C., jt. auth. see Nelson, John A.

***Nelson, Joyce E.** The Alpha Omega Story. 116p. 2000. pap. 12.95 (*0-7880-1618-0*, Fairway Pr) CSS OH.

Nelson, Joyce I. A Matter of Life & Death: Recent Death Rates among the South Dakotan Elderly. (Studies in Historical Demography). 225p. 1990. reprint ed. text 50.00 (*0-8240-3361-2*) Garland.

Nelson, Judd O., et al, eds. Immunmoanalysis of Agrochemicals: Emerging Technologies. LC 95-5968. (ACS Symposium Ser.: No. 586). 376p. 1995. text 110.00 (*0-8412-3149-4*, Pub. by Am Chemical) OUP.

Nelson, Judith. The Accidental Match. 240p. (Orig.). 1995. mass mkt. 4.99 (*0-515-11749-8*, Jove) Berkley Pub.

— Julianna. 208p. (Orig.). 1989. mass mkt. 3.50 (*0-446-35058-3*, Pub. by Warner Bks) Little.

Nelson, Judith G. Seis Chaves para Recrutar, Orientar e Envolver Membros Do Conselho Diretor de Organizacoes Sem Fins Lucrativos.Tr. of Six Keys to Recruiting, Orienting, & Involving Nonprofit Board Members. (POR.). 61p. (Orig.). 1996. pap. write for info. (*0-925299-64-2*) Natl Ctr Nonprofit.

— Six Keys to Recruiting, Orienting & Involving Nonprofit Board Members: A Guide to Building Your Board, No. 42. 64p. 1992. reprint ed. pap. text 26.00 (*0-925299-11-1*) Natl Ctr Nonprofit.

Nelson, Judith Grummon, et al. Tools for Recruiting, Orienting, & Involving YMCA Board Members: A Guide. LC 98-176299. (Making Great Boards Better Ser.). 60p. 1997. 10.00 (*0-88011-894-6*) Human Kinetics.

Nelson, Judith N. Fish & Visitors: A Getaway Journal. (Illus.). 128p. 1997. pap. 11.95 (*0-9657498-0-0*) Openbook Pr.

Nelson, Judy, jt. auth. see Akers, Michelle.

Nelson, Judy A. & Faulker, Sandra. Love Match. (Illus.). 256p. 1993. 19.95 (*1-55972-157-X*, Birch Ln Pr) Carol Pub Group.

Nelson, Judy H. Choices: My Journey after Leaving My Husband for Martina & a Lesbian Life. (Illus.). 256p. 1996. 21.95 (*1-55972-328-9*, Birch Ln Pr) Carol Pub Group.

Nelson, Julia. My Book of Birthdays. Date not set. write for info. (*0-9673230-1-0*) Allyn Group Pubns.

— New-Fashioned Grandparenting: Changing America One Grandchild at a Time. Allen-Goad, Pamela, ed. 256p. 1999. pap. 14.95 (*0-9673230-0-2*) Allyn Group Pubns.

Nelson, Julianne, jt. ed. see Sato, Ryuzo.

***Nelson, Julie.** Indianapolis Colts. 3rd rev. ed. (Pro Football Today Ser.). (Illus.). 32p. (YA). (gr. 3-12). 2000. lib. bdg. 22.60 (*1-58341-045-7*, Creat Educ) Creative Co.

— Jacksonville Jaguars. 3rd rev. ed. (Pro Football Today Ser.). (Illus.). 32p. (YA). (gr. 3-12). 2000. lib. bdg. 22.60 (*1-58341-046-5*, Creat Educ) Creative Co.

— Kansas City Chiefs. 3rd rev. ed. (Pro Football Today Ser.). (Illus.). 32p. (YA). (gr. 3-12). 2000. lib. bdg. 22.60 (*1-58341-047-3*, Creat Educ) Creative Co.

— Miami Dolphins. 3rd rev. ed. (Pro Football Today Ser.). (Illus.). 32p. (YA). (gr. 3-12). 2000. lib. bdg. 22.60 (*1-58341-048-1*, Creat Educ) Creative Co.

— Minnesota Vikings. 3rd rev. ed. (Pro Football Today Ser.). (Illus.). 32p. (YA). (gr. 3-12). 2000. lib. bdg. 22.60 (*1-58341-049-X*, Creat Educ) Creative Co.

— New England Patriots. 3rd rev. ed. (Pro Football Today Ser.). (Illus.). 32p. (YA). (gr. 3-12). 2000. lib. bdg. 22.60 (*1-58341-050-3*, Creat Educ) Creative Co.

— New Orleans Saints. 3rd rev. ed. (Pro Football Today Ser.). (Illus.). 32p. 2000. lib. bdg. 22.60 (*1-58341-051-1*, Creat Educ) Creative Co.

— New York Giants. 3rd rev. ed. (Pro Football Today Ser.). (Illus.). 32p. (YA). (gr. 3-12). 2000. lib. bdg. 22.60 (*1-58341-052-X*, Creat Educ) Creative Co.

— New York Jets. 3rd rev. ed. LC 99-15747. (Pro Football Today Ser.). (Illus.). 32p. (YA). 2000. lib. bdg. 22.60 (*1-58341-053-8*, Creat Educ) Creative Co.

— Oakland Raiders. 3rd rev. ed. LC 99-23742. (Pro Football Today Ser.). (Illus.). 32p. (YA). (gr. 3-12). 2000. lib. bdg. 22.60 (*1-58341-054-6*, Creat Educ) Creative Co.

— Philadelphia Eagles. 3rd rev. ed. (Pro Football Today Ser.). (Illus.). 32p. (YA). (gr. 3-12). 2000. lib. bdg. 22.60 (*1-58341-055-4*, Creat Educ) Creative Co.

— Pittsburgh Steelers. 3rd rev. ed. (Pro Football Today Ser.). (Illus.). 32p. (YA). (gr. 3-12). 2000. lib. bdg. 22.60 (*1-58341-056-2*, Creat Educ) Creative Co.

— St. Louis Rams. 3rd rev. ed. (Pro Football Today Ser.). (Illus.). 32p. (YA). (gr. 3-12). 2000. lib. bdg. 22.60 (*1-58341-057-0*, Creat Educ) Creative Co.

— San Diego Chargers. 3rd rev. ed. (Pro Football Today Ser.). (Illus.). 32p. (YA). (gr. 3-12). 2000. lib. bdg. 22.60 (*1-58341-058-9*, Creat Educ) Creative Co.

— San Francisco 49ers. 3rd rev. ed. (Pro Football Today Ser.). (Illus.). 32p. (YA). (gr. 3-12). 2000. lib. bdg. 22.60 (*1-58341-059-7*, Creat Educ) Creative Co.

— Seattle Seahawks. 3rd rev. ed. (Pro Football Today Ser.). (Illus.). 32p. (YA). (gr. 3-12). 2000. lib. bdg. 22.60 (*1-58341-060-0*, Creat Educ) Creative Co.

— Tampa Bay Buccaneers. 3rd rev. ed. (Pro Football Today Ser.). (Illus.). 32p. (YA). (gr. 3-12). 2000. lib. bdg. 22.60 (*1-58341-061-9*, Creat Educ) Creative Co.

— Tennessee Titans. 3rd rev. ed. (Pro Football Today Ser.). (Illus.). 32p. (YA). (gr. 3-12). 2000. lib. bdg. 22.60 (*1-58341-062-7*, Creat Educ) Creative Co.

— Washington Redskins. 3rd rev. ed. (Pro Football Today Ser.). (Illus.). 32p. (YA). (gr. 3-12). 2000. lib. bdg. 22.60 (*1-58341-063-5*, Creat Educ) Creative Co.

Nelson, Julie, jt. auth. see Nichols, John.

Nelson, Julie A. Economics: Discipline Analysis, Vol. 7F. (Women in the Curriculum Ser.). 22p. (Orig.). 1997. pap. 7.00 (*1-885303-28-9*) Towson St Univ.

— Feminism, Objectivity & Economics. LC 95-21629. (Economics as Social Theory Ser.). 192p. (C). 1995. pap. 22.99 (*0-415-13337-8*) Routledge.

— Feminism, Objectivity & Economics. LC 95-21629. (Economics as Social Theory Ser.). 192p. (C). (gr. 13). 1995. 75.00 (*0-415-13336-X*) Routledge.

***Nelson, Julie A.** The History of the Los Angeles Sparks. LC 99-18890. (Women's Pro Basketball Today Ser.). 1999. lib. bdg. 21.30 (*1-58341-014-7*, Creat Educ) Creative Co.

Nelson, Julie A., jt. ed. see Ferber, Marianne A.

Nelson, June K. Harry Bertoia, Printmaker: Monotypes & Other Monographics. LC 87-32780. (Great Lakes Bks.). (Illus.). 236p. 1987. pap. 19.95 (*0-8143-2063-5*) Wayne St U Pr.

— Harry Bertoia, Printmaker: Monotypes & Other Monographics. LC 87-32780. (Great Lakes Bks.). (Illus.). 235p. reprint ed. pap. 72.90 (*0-608-10559-7*, 207117900009) Bks Demand.

Nelson, K., ed. Internationales Zuchtbuch, 1988. (GER., Illus.). 1988. write for info. (*0-913934-13-5*) Chicago Zoo.

Nelson, K., jt. auth. see French, L. A.

Nelson, K. D. Design & Construction of Small Earth Dams. (C). 1991. text 125.00 (*81-7233-003-0*, Pub. by Scientific Pubs) St Mut.

— Design & Construction of Small Earth Dams. 128p. (C). 1988. reprint ed. 160.00 (*0-7855-6711-9*, Pub. by Scientific) St Mut.

Nelson, K. E., jt. ed. see Speidel, G.

Nelson, K. M., tr. see Howorka, K.

Nelson, K. Ray, jt. auth. see Smith, J. David.

Nelson, Kai. Moral Concerns. 240p. Date not set. 16.95 (*1-55111-013-X*) Broadview Pr.

Nelson, Karin B. & Ellenberg, Jonas H., eds. Febrile Seizures. fac. ed. LC 80-5898. (Illus.). 378p. pap. 117.20 (*0-7837-7526-1*, 204697900005) Bks Demand.

Nelson, Katherine. Language in Cognitive Development: The Emergence of the Mediated Mind. (Illus.). 448p. (C). 1996. text 54.95 (*0-521-55123-4*) Cambridge U Pr.

— Language in Cognitive Development: The Emergence of the Mediated Mind. (Illus.). 448p. (C). 1998. reprint ed. pap. text 21.95 (*0-521-62987-X*) Cambridge U Pr.

***Nelson, Katherine.** Websights: The Future of Business & Design on the Internet. (Illus.). 192p. 2000. 35.00 (*1-883915-07-4*) RC Pubns.

Nelson, Katherine, ed. Event Knowledge: Structure & Function in Development. 288p. (C). 1986. text 59.95 (*0-89859-657-2*) L Erlbaum Assocs.

— Narratives from the Crib. LC 88-28455. (Illus.). 400p. 1989. 41.50 (*0-674-60118-1*) HUP.

Nelson, Katherine, jt. auth. see Mutz, John.

Nelson, Katherine, ed. see Scholnich, Ellin K.

Nelson, Katherine A., jt. auth. see Trevino, Linda K.

Nelson, Katherine M. Night Fishing: A Woman's Dream Journal. LC 96-40966. (Illus.). 160p. 1997. pap. 19.95 (*0-87905-790-4*) Gibbs Smith Pub.

Nelson, Kathleen E. Medieval Liturgical Music of Zamora. LC 96-148301. (Wissenschaftliche Abhandlungen-Musicological Studies: No. 67). (ENG & LAT., Illus.). 330p. 1996. lib. bdg. 86.00 (*0-931902-40-1*) Inst Mediaeval Mus.

Nelson, Kathleen H. Daughter of Dragons. 2nd ed. LC 98-10348. 478p. 1998. 19.95 (*1-896944-00-0*) Dragon Moon Pr.

***Nelson, Kathleen H.** Human Thing. 1999. 19.95 (*1-896944-03-5*) Dragon Moon Pr.

Nelson, Kathryn, jt. auth. see Duerksen, Lu.

Nelson, Kathryn E., et al. Voices from the Field: Lessons from the Family Academy. LC 94-18656. 1994. 16.95 (*0-934842-30-2*) CSPA.

Nelson, Kathryn P. Gentrification & Distressed Cities: An Assessment of Trends in Intrametropolitan Migration. LC 87-40370. (Social Demography Ser.). 224p. (C). 1988. pap. text 16.25 (*0-299-11164-4*) U of Wis Pr.

— Gentrification & Distressed Cities: An Assessment of Trends in Intrametropolitan Migration. LC 87-40370. (Social Demography Ser.). 203p. reprint ed. pap. 63.00 (*0-608-20460-9*, 207171200002) Bks Demand.

***Nelson, Kathryn P.** Rental Housing Assistance - the Worsening Crisis: A Report to Congress on Worst Case Housing Needs. (Illus.). 83p. (C). 2000. pap. text 20.00 (*0-7567-0031-0*) DIANE Pub.

Nelson, Kay H. & Huse, Nancy, eds. The Critical Response to Tillie Olsen, 10. LC 93-41228. (Critical Responses in Arts & Letters Ser.: No. 10). 304p. 1994. lib. bdg. 69.50 (*0-313-28714-7*, Greenwood Pr) Greenwood.

Nelson, Kay S. A Bonnie Scottish Cookbook. LC 89-7778. 144p. 1989. spiral bd. 10.95 (*0-939009-25-0*) EPM Pubns.

— One-Dish Meals from Around the World. 1993. pap. 14.95 (*0-8128-8551-1*, Scrbrough Hse) Madison Bks UPA.

— The Scottish-Irish Pub & Hearth Cookbook: Recipes & More from Celtic Kitchens. (Illus.). 272p. 1999. 24.95 (*0-7818-0741-7*) Hippocrene Bks.

— Soups from Around the World. 1993. pap. 14.95 (*0-8128-8552-X*, Scrbrough Hse) Madison Bks UPA.

— Stews & Ragouts: Simple & Hearty One-Dish Meals. 1978. reprint ed. pap. 7.95 (*0-486-23662-5*) Dover.

***Nelson, Kay Shaw.** All along the Rhine: Recipes, Wine & Lore from Germany, France, Switzerland, Austria, Lichtenstein & Holland. 220p. 2000. 24.95 (*0-7818-0830-8*) Hippocrene Bks.

Nelson, Kay Y. 1-2-3 for Windows Answers: Certified Technical Support. (Certified Tech Support Ser.). 352p. 1994. pap. text 16.95 (*0-07-882068-5*) Osborne-McGraw.

Nelson, Kay Yarborough. The Little System 7.1-7.5 Book. 3rd ed. 208p. (C). 1995. pap. text 13.95 (*1-56609-151-9*) Peachpit Pr.

Nelson, Kay Yarborough. The Little Windows Book, 3.1 Edition. (Illus.). 144p. 1995. pap. text 12.95 (*0-938151-81-9*) Peachpit Pr.

— The Little Windows 95 Book. 3rd ed. 144p. (C). 1995. pap. text 12.95 (*1-56609-181-0*, Pub. by Peachpit Pr) Addison-Wesley.

Nelson, Kay Yarborough. Windows 95 Is Driving Me Crazy! A Practical Guide to Windows 95 Headaches, Hassles, Bugs, Potholes & Installation Problems for Luddites, Power Users & the Rest of Us. (Illus.). 400p. (C). 1996. pap. 24.95 (*0-201-88626-X*) Peachpit Pr.

Nelson, Keith, jt. ed. see Geiger, Dan.

Nelson, Keith E., ed. Children's Language, Vol. 3. 522p. (C). 1982. text 99.95 (*0-89859-264-X*) L Erlbaum Assocs.

— Children's Language, Vol. 4. 496p. 1983. text 89.95 (*0-89859-272-0*) L Erlbaum Assocs.

— Children's Language, Vol. 5. 472p. (C). 1985. text 89.95 (*0-89859-346-8*) L Erlbaum Assocs.

Nelson, Keith E. & Reger, Zita, eds. Children's Language, Vol. 8. 304p. 1994. text 59.95 (*0-8058-1367-5*) L Erlbaum Assocs.

Nelson, Keith E. & Van Kleeck, Anne E., eds. Children's Language, Vol. 6. 366p. 1987. text 89.95 (*0-89859-760-9*) L Erlbaum Assocs.

Nelson, Keith L. The Making of Detente: Soviet-American Relations in the Shadow of Vietnam. LC 94-34423. 248p. 1995. text 35.00 (*0-8018-4883-0*) Johns Hopkins.

— Victors Divided: America & the Allies in Germany, 1918-1923. LC 72-87203. 463p. reprint ed. pap. 143.60 (*0-608-15827-5*, 203130800074) Bks Demand.

Nelson, Keith L. & Olin, Spencer C. Why War? Ideology, Theory, & History. LC 78-51746. 1980. pap. 15.95 (*0-520-04279-4*, Pub. by U CA Pr) Cal Prin Full Svc.

Nelson, Keith L., ed. see Grattan, C. H.

Nelson, Keith L., jt. ed. see Morgan, Patrick M.

Nelson, Kelly, jt. ed. see Atkinson, Robert.

N

An Asterisk (*) at the beginning of an entry indicates that the title is appearing for the first time.

***Nelson, Ken.** Inventory of Academic Standards-Related Activities: National Education Goals Panel. 62p. (C). 2000. reprint ed. pap. text 20.00 (*0-7881-8952-2*) DIANE Pub.

***Nelson, Ken, ed.** The National Education Goals Report: Building a Nation of Learners 1999. 88p. 2000. pap. text 20.00 (*0-7881-8834-8*) DIANE Pub.

Nelson, Ken, ed. National Education Goals Report Summary, 1997: Mathematics & Science Achievement for the 21st Century. (Illus.). 48p. 1998. pap. text 20.00 (*0-7881-7175-5*) DIANE Pub.

— Principles & Recommendations for Early Childhood Assessments. (Illus.). 40p. 1998. pap. text 15.00 (*0-7881-7361-8*) DIANE Pub.

Nelson, Ken & Dyville, Jack. A Country Christmas Carol: 2-Act Musical Comedy. (Illus.). 36p. 1985. pap. 4.50 (*0-88680-235-0*) I E Clark.

Nelson, Kenneth A. Quick Reference for the Electrical Engineering PE Exam. LC 96-35106. 1996. pap. 33.95 (*1-888577-02-9*) Prof Pubns CA.

Nelson, Kenneth C. Understanding Station Carrier. LC 73-85629. (Basic Ser.). (Illus.). 55p. (Orig.). (C). 1983. spiral bd. 17.95 (*1-56016-058-6*) ABC TeleTraining.

Nelson, Kenneth E. Thoughts of a Boy Growing Up, Vol. 1. LC 96-86565. 176p. 1999. 11.95 (*0-8158-0525-X*) Chris Mass.

Nelson, Kent. Discoveries: Short Stories of the San Juan Mountains. LC 98-60196. 152p. 1998. 24.95 (*1-890437-16-6*); pap. 15.95 (*1-890437-15-8*) Western Reflections.

— Toward the Sun: The Collected Sports Stories of Kent Nelson. LC 98-71736. 240p. 1998. 20.00 (*1-891369-05-9*, Pub. by Breakaway Bks) Consort Bk Sales.

Nelson, Kerri. A Road Guide to the Geology of Big Bend National Park. (Illus.). 76p. (Orig.). 1995. spiral bd. 6.95 (*0-912001-15-1*) Big Bend.

Nelson, Kerry, ed. see Douglas County Historical Society Staff.

Nelson, Kevin. The Angler's Book of Daily Inspiration. LC 96-40271. 384p. 1997. 14.95 (*0-8092-3069-0*, 306900, Contemporary Bks) NTC Contemp Pub Co.

— The Daddy Guide. LC 97-47047. 336p. 1998. pap. 16.95 (*0-8092-2963-3*, 296330, Contemporary Bks) NTC Contemp Pub Co.

— The Golfer's Book of Daily Inspiration. 384p. 1996. 14.95 (*0-8092-3213-8*, 321380, Contemporary Bks) NTC Contemp Pub Co.

— The Greatest Golf Shot Ever Made: And Other Lively & Entertaining Tales from the Lore & History of Golf. (Illus.). 256p. (Orig.). 1992. 21.00 (*0-671-75002-X*, Fireside) S&S Trade Pap.

— Pickle, Pepper, & Tip-in-Too: 275 Sports-Derived Games & Activities for Kids. (Illus.). 208p. 1994. pap. 15.00 (*0-671-87956-1*, Fireside) S&S Trade Pap.

— The Runner's Book of Daily Inspiration. LC 98-33517. 384p. 1999. 14.95 (*0-8092-2962-5*, 296250, Contemporary Bks) NTC Contemp Pub Co.

— Slap Shots. LC 95-18215. (Illus.). 208p. 1995. per. 10.00 (*0-684-81075-1*) S&S Trade.

***Nelson, Kim.** A Desert Gardener's Companion. (Illus.). 304p. 2000. pap. 19.95 (*1-887896-20-1*, Rio Nuevo) Treas Chest Bks.

Nelson, Kim L. Bioprocess Engineering: Systems, Equipment & Facilities. Lyderson, Bjorn K. et al, eds. 832p. 1994. 125.00 (*0-471-03544-0*) Wiley.

Nelson, Kimberly, jt. auth. see Justice, Rita.

Nelson, Kimberly K. I Will Remember. Nijholm, Earl, tr.Tr. of Inga-Minjimendam. (ENG & OJI., Illus.). 28p. (Orig.). (J). (gr. k-3). 1995. pap. 10.95 (*0-926147-06-4*) Loonfeather.

***Nelson, Kirk.** Edgar Cayce's Hidden History of Jesus. LC 99-40896. Orig. Title: The Greatest Story Never Told. 172p. 1999. pap. 12.95 (*0-87604-461-5*, 537) ARE Pr.

Nelson, Kirk. Edgar Cayce's Secrets of Astrology: Planets, Signs, Aspects, & Sojourns. LC 98-45857. (Illus.). 2000. pap. 12.95 (*0-87604-420-8*, 541) ARE Pr.

— The Greatest Story Never Told. 115p. (Orig.). 1995. pap. 12.95 (*0-9617119-1-4*) Wright Pub VA.

— The Second Coming. (Orig.). 1986. pap. 8.95 (*0-9617119-0-6*) Wright Pub VA.

— The Second Coming: Edgar Cayce's Earth Changes Prophecies. rev. ed. LC 97-49140. (Illus.). 149p. 1998. pap. 12.95 (*0-87604-406-2*, 518) ARE Pr.

Nelson-Kjenstad, J. Introduction to Tole & Decorative Painting. (Illus.). 112p. 1999. 29.95 (*4-7661-1103-6*, Pub. by Graphic-Sha) Bks Nippan.

Nelson, Klayton E. Harvesting & Handling California Table Grapes for Market. LC 79-51948. (Illus.). 76p. 1979. pap. 10.00 (*0-931876-33-8*, 1913) ANR Pubns CA.

Nelson, Kou K., jt. auth. see Frost, Dan R.

Nelson, Kristen. Developing Students Multiple I: Hundreds of Practical Ideas Easily Integrated. 128p. 1998. 15.95 (*0-590-93101-6*) Scholastic Inc.

***Nelson, Kristi.** The Chamique Holdsclaw Story. 80p. (gr. 2-5). 2000. pap. 4.99 (*0-439-16948-8*) Scholastic Inc.

Nelson, Kristi. Dutch Drawings & Watercolors from the Kharkiv Art Museum. LC 97-62116. (Illus.). 60p. 1997. pap. 12.95 (*0-915577-28-3*) Taft Museum.

***Nelson, Kristin.** Clever Raccoons. LC 99-50405. (Pull Ahead Bks.). (Illus.). 32p. (J). 2000. pap. 6.95 (*0-8225-3644-7*, Lerner Publctns) Lerner Pub.

— Clever Raccoons. LC 99-50405. (Pull Ahead Ser.). (Illus.). 32p. (J). (gr. k-2). 2000. 21.27 (*0-8225-3763-X*, Lerner Publctns) Lerner Pub.

***Nelson, Kristina R.** Love Note's: Poetic Justice for the Soul. 72p. 1999. pap. text 10.00 (*0-9678537-0-2*, 1337) New Hope Local.

Nelson, Kristine E., jt. ed. see Adams, Paul.

Nelson, Kurt R. Policing Mass Transit: A Comprehensive Approach to Designing a Safe, Secure, & Desirable Transit Policing & Management System. LC 98-44029. 224p. 1999. text 46.95 (*0-398-06919-0*); pap. text 33.95 (*0-398-06920-4*) C C Thomas.

Nelson, Kyerstie. Marriage & Divorce Practices in Native California. (Archaeological Research Facility, Dept. of Anthropology, Miscellaneous Papers, Berkeley CA). 51p. (C). 1975. pap. 6.25 (*1-55567-647-2*) Coyote Press.

Nelson, L. Ted, jt. auth. see Maier, Eugene.

Nelson-L'Aloge, Virginia, ed. see L'Aloge, Bob.

Nelson, Larry E. Bullets, Ballots & Rhetoric: Confederate Policy for the U. S. Presidential Contest of 1864. LC 79-27869. 249p. pap. 77.20 (*0-7837-8396-5*, 205920700009) Bks Demand.

Nelson, Larry L. A Man of Distinction among Them: Alexander Mckee & British-Indian Affairs along the Ohio Country Frontier, 1754-1799. LC 98-43050. (Illus.). 280p. 1999. text 35.00 (*0-87338-620-5*) Kent St U Pr.

— Men of Patriotism, Courage & Enterprise: Fort Meigs in the War of 1812. (Illus.). 174p. 1998. reprint ed. pap. 16.00 (*0-7884-0728-7*, N151) Heritage Bk.

Nelson, Larry R., jt. auth. see Clancy, Gary.

Nelson, Laura A., et al, eds. A Book of Meditations: Readings from Phillips Exeter Academy, 1983-1994. (Orig.). 1995. pap. 14.95 (*0-939618-09-5*) Phillips Exeter.

***Nelson, Laura C.** Measured Excess: Status, Gender & Consumer Nationalism in South Korea. LC 00-21051. 2000. pap. 18.50 (*0-231-11617-9*) Col U Pr.

— Measured Excess: Status, Gender, & Consumer Nationalism in South Korea. 224p. 2000. text 45.00 (*0-231-11616-0*) Col U Pr.

Nelson, Laura H. & Starkey, Deb. Packaging & Solid Waste Management. 5th ed. Thorman, Judith, ed. 1996. pap. 5.00 (*1-55516-510-9*, 4656) Natl Conf State Legis.

Nelson, Laura H., et al. Public Policy & Markets for Recycled Materials. 4th ed. 1996. pap. 5.00 (*1-55516-509-5*, 4655) Natl Conf State Legis.

Nelson, Laura H., jt. auth. see Starkey, Deb.

Nelson, Laura Hagg. Emergency Management: A Legislator's Guide. LC 97-215288. 47p. 1997. 20.00 (*1-55516-588-5*, 4347) Natl Conf State Legis.

Nelson, Laura L., et al, eds. A Terrible Thing. (Drugless Douglass Tales Ser.). (Illus.). 20p. (J). (ps-k). 1994. 6.95 (*1-884307-14-0*) Dev Res Educ.

Nelson, Laura L., ed. see Milam, June M.

Nelson, Lawrence J. King Cotton's Advocate: Oscar G. Johnston & the New Deal. LC 98-19739. (Illus.). 352p. 1999. text 38.00 (*1-57233-025-2*) U of Tenn Pr.

Nelson, Lee. Beyond the Veil, 4 vols. pap. 45.95 (*1-55517-363-2*) CFI Dist.

Nelson, Lee. Beyond the Veil, Vol. I. 142p. 1994. pap. 12.95 (*1-55517-166-4*) CFI Dist.

— Beyond the Veil, Vol. II. 163p. 1995. pap. 12.95 (*1-55517-172-9*) CFI Dist.

— Beyond the Veil, Vol. III. 151p. 1994. pap. 12.95 (*1-55517-165-6*) CFI Dist.

Nelson, Lee. Beyond the Veil, Vols. 1, 2 & 3. pap. 29.95 (*1-55517-117-6*) CFI Dist.

— The Blackhawk Journey. 1999. 17.95 (*1-55517-451-5*) CFI Dist.

— Dance of Courage. pap. 8.95 (*1-55517-375-6*) CFI Dist.

Nelson, Lee. NDE Near Death Experiences. 1994. pap. 12.95 (*1-55517-366-7*) CFI Dist.

— NDE Near Death Experiences. 177p. 1995. 14.95 (*1-55517-160-5*) CFI Dist.

Nelson, Lee. The Storm Testament V. pap. 14.95 (*1-55517-356-X*) CFI Dist.

— The Storm Testament IV. pap. 14.95 (*1-55517-413-2*) CFI Dist.

— The Storm Testament III. pap. 14.95 (*1-55517-374-8*) CFI Dist.

— Taming the Sasquatch. pap. 9.95 (*1-55517-372-1*) CFI Dist.

Nelson, Lee, compiled by. Brigham Young's Journal. pap. 13.95 (*1-55517-364-0*) CFI Dist.

— Joseph Smith's Journal. pap. 13.95 (*1-55517-365-9*) CFI Dist.

Nelson, Lee, ed. The Storm Testament: Porter Rockwell, Walkara, Butch Cassidy, Storm Testament, 4 bks., Set. 1992. boxed set 39.95 (*1-55684-009-0*) Evans Bk Dist.

Nelson, Lee, jt. auth. see Coonradt, Charles A.

Nelson, Lee, ed. see Harris, Blaine & Coonradt, Charles.

Nelson, Lee H. The Colossus of 1812: An American Engineering Superlative. 64p. 1989. pap. text 27.00 (*0-87262-737-3*) Am Soc Civil Eng.

Nelson, Leon. The Bonding Book. 1985. 25.00 (*0-87814-267-3*) PennWell Bks.

Nelson, Leonard B. Harley's Pediatric Opthalmology. 4th ed. Lampert, Richard, ed. LC 97-13498. (Illus.). 576p. 1998. text 185.00 (*0-7216-6842-9*, W B Saunders Co) Harcrt Hlth Sci Grp.

— Pediatric Ophthalmology. (Major Problems in Clinical Pediatrics Ser.: Vol. 25). (Illus.). 288p. 1984. text 84.00 (*0-7216-1191-5*, W B Saunders Co) Harcrt Hlth Sci Grp.

Nelson, Leonard B., jt. auth. see Catalano, Robert A.

Nelson, Leonard T., jt. auth. see Bennett, Albert B.

Nelson, Leonard T., jt. auth. see Bennett, Albert B., Jr.

Nelson, Leslie W., jt. auth. see Lorbeer, George C.

Nelson, Lewis B. History of the U. S. Fertilizer Industry. Parker, J. Harold, ed. LC 91-205883. (Illus.). 522p. 1990. text 45.00 (*0-87077-004-7*) TVA.

Nelson, Lewis H., III. Ultrasonography of the Placenta: A Review. (Illus.). 49p. 1994. pap. 57.00 (*1-930047-17-7*, UP) Am Inst Ultrasound.

Nelson, Libby. Projects & Layouts. (J). (gr. 4-7). pap. 5.95 (*0-8225-9831-0*) Lerner Pub.

Nelson, Libby & Cornell, Kari A. Projects & Layouts. LC 97-8482. (California Missions Ser.). (J). 1997. lib. bdg. 23.93 (*0-8225-1931-3*) Lerner Pub.

Nelson, Lin, et al. Turning Things Around: A Women's Occupational & Environmental Health Resource Guide. (Illus.). 162p. (Orig.). 1990. pap. 12.95 (*0-939522-01-2*) Nat Womens Hlth Netwk.

Nelson, Lincoln D. With Scapel & the Sword: An American Doctor's Odyssey in the Philippines. (Illus.). 198p. 1997. pap. text 8.95 (*1-888796-12-X*) ABWE Pubng.

Nelson, Linda, jt. ed. see Little, Judith W.

Nelson, Linda, ed. see McKinley, Robert K.

Nelson, Linda L., jt. ed. see Spence, Richard B.

***Nelson, Linda S. & Nelson, Alan E.** Child Care Administration: Planning Quality Programs for Young Children. LC 99-57511. (Illus.). 400p. 2000. pap. text 37.28 (*1-56637-720-X*) Goodheart.

Nelson, Lisa, jt. ed. see Smith, Nancy S.

Nelson, Lisa M. Freddy Bear's Wakeful Winter. LC 95-206035. (Illus.). 32p. (Orig.). (J). (ps-4). 1994. pap. text 6.95 (*1-883212-02-2*, BIP401) Brght Ideas CA.

— Positive Music for Today's Kids! Bright Smiles & Blue Skies. unabridged ed. (Illus.). 16p. (J). (gr. k-6). 1990. pap. 9.95 incl. audio (*0-9627863-0-6*) Brght Ideas CA.

Nelson, Lisa M., jt. auth. see Taylor, Louise.

Nelson, Lisa M., ed. see Charlip, Remy.

***Nelson, Lisa Marie.** Getting There: 9 Ways to Help Your Kids Learn What Matters Most in Life. 192p. 2000. 22.95 (*1-885203-82-9*, Pub. by Jrny Editions) Tuttle Pubng.

***Nelson, Liza.** Newburyport: Stories from the Waterside. (Town Memoirs Ser.). (Illus.). 144p. 2000. pap. 14.95 (*1-889833-12-6*, Commonwealth Eds) Memoirs Unltd.

— Playing Botticelli. LC 99-47292. 288p. 2000. 23.95 (*0-399-14601-6*, Marion Wood) Putnam Pub Group.

Nelson, Liza, jt. auth. see Goldstein, Kay.

Nelson, Louella. Days of Fire. (American Romance Ser.). 1993. per. 3.39 (*0-373-16479-3*, 1-16479-7) Harlequin Bks.

— Emerald Fortune. (American Romance Ser.: No. 379). 1991. per. 2.95 (*0-373-16379-7*) Harlequin Bks.

Nelson, Louis J., jt. auth. see Donnelly, Dennis M.

Nelson, Louis J., jt. auth. see Sorg, Cindy F.

Nelson, Louise E. Project-Readiness: A Guide to Family Emergency Preparedness. rev. ed. 272p. 1999. pap. 18.95 (*0-88290-657-7*) Horizon Utah.

Nelson, Louise K. The Aroma & Memories of Grandma's & Mama's Kitchen: Plus Great Smoky Mountain Memories. LC 98-877463. (Illus.). 104p. 1999. pap. 9.95 (*1-56664-143-8*) WorldComm.

— Country Folklore: 1920s & 1930s & That's the Way It Was. LC 96-61902. (Illus.). 160p. (Orig.). 1997. pap. 9.95 (*1-56664-113-6*) WorldComm.

Nelson, Lowry. Cuba: The Measure of a Revolution. LC 77-187163. 258p. reprint ed. pap. 80.00 (*0-8357-8855-5*, 203327500085) Bks Demand.

— The Minnesota Community: Country & Town in Transition. LC 60-10191. 185p. reprint ed. pap. 57.40 (*0-608-18647-3*, 205589300039) Bks Demand.

— The Mormon Village: A Study in Social Origins. 1972. 250.00 (*0-8490-0673-2*) Gordon Pr.

Nelson, Lowry, Jr. Poetic Configurations: Essays in Literary History & Criticism. 352p. 1992. text 45.00 (*0-271-00800-8*) Pa St U Pr.

Nelson, Lowry, Jr., jt. ed. see Jackson, Robert L.

Nelson, Lucille, tr. see Alonzo, Anne-Marie.

Nelson, Lycette. Breaking the Rules of Graphic Design. 1997. 49.99 (*1-56830-435-8*) Hayden.

— Shattering Rules of Graphic Design. 1997. 55.00 (*1-56830-417-X*) Hayden.

Nelson, Lycette, jt. auth. see Joss, Molly.

Nelson, Lycette, tr. see Blanchot, Maurice.

Nelson, Lycette, tr. & intro. see Blanchot, Maurice.

Nelson, Lyle, et al. Spirit of Champions: Great Achievers Reveal How to Integrate Mind, Body & Spirit. 288p. 1997. pap. 14.95 (*1-885221-49-5*) BookPartners.

***Nelson, Lyle H.** SnoWhite & BenAdam. LC 99-93573. (J). (gr. k-3). 1999. pap. 12.95 (*0-533-13065-4*) Vantage.

Nelson, Lyle M., jt. ed. see Lerner, Daniel.

Nelson, Lynda. Mi Historia: Compendio Historico de Vida Tradicional - Non-Denominational. 2nd ed.Tr. of My Story: Life History Outline Non-Denominational. (SPA.). 97p. 1992. reprint ed. ring bd. 12.95 (*0-9652557-3-5*) Hist Happenings.

— Mi Historia Compendio Historico de Vida: Para Miembros de la Iglesia de los Santos de los Ultimos Dias. 2nd ed.Tr. of My Story Life History Outline for Latter-Day Saints. (SPA.). 127p. 1992. reprint ed. ring bd. 14.95 (*0-9652557-2-7*, LDSS) Hist Happenings.

— My Master's Touch: A Heartwarming Tale of Love, Loyalty, & Devotion. LC 97-51820. (Illus.). 120p. (J). 1998. 13.00 (*0-399-52443-6*, Perigee Bks) Berkley Pub.

— My Story: Life History Outline - Non-Denominational. 4th ed. 97p. 1992. reprint ed. ring bd. 13.95 (*0-9652557-1-9*, NDE) Hist Happenings.

— My Story: Life History Outline for Latterday Saints. 4th ed. 127p. 1992. reprint ed. ring bd. 16.95 (*0-9652557-0-0*, LDSE) Hist Happenings.

Nelson, Lynda B., jt. auth. see Madsen, Donna L.

Nelson, Lynda M. The Little Red Buckets: A Story of Family & Giving. LC 97-6696. 128p. (J). 1997. pap. 13.00 (*0-399-52357-X*, Perigee Bks) Berkley Pub.

***Nelson, Lynn.** Book of the Abacus. (Illus.). 16p. (J). (gr. 2-12). 1998. pap. 4.95 (*1-884727-11-5*) Digits Intl.

— Creating CL Commands by Example. LC 99-6967. 1999. pap. 49.00 (*1-58304-058-7*) News Four-Hund.

Nelson, Lynn. Desktop Guide to Creating CL Commands. LC 96-10149. (News/400 Technical Reference Ser.). 266p. 1996. pap. 34.95 (*1-882419-56-1*) News Four-Hund.

— A Genealogist's Guide to Discovering Your Italian Ancestors. LC 97-8280. (Genealogist's Guide to Discovering Your Ancestors Ser.). (Illus.). 128p. 1997. pap. 16.99 (*1-55870-426-4*, Betrwy Bks) F & W Pubns Inc.

Nelson, Lynn & Nelson, Gail. Enciclopedia de Reflejologia Vol. 1: El Texto de un Profesional del Funcionamiento. (SPA., Illus.). 608p. 1996. ring bd. 125.00 (*1-884727-25-5*) Digits Intl.

Nelson, Lynn & Nelson, Gail. Encyclopedia of Reflexology: A Working Professionals Text. 7th ed. (Illus.). 610p. (C). 1996. ring bd. 125.00 (*1-884727-14-X*) Digits Intl.

Nelson, Lynn & Nelson, Gail. Reflejologia a Introduccion. (SPA., Illus.). 78p. 1996. pap. 19.95 (*1-884727-45-X*) Digits Intl.

***Nelson, Lynn D.** Sociology in Global Perspective. (Illus.). 430p. (C). 1998. pap. text 5.00 (*0-9663792-0-9*) Digital Text.

Nelson, Lynn D. & Kuzes, Irina Y. Property to the People: The Struggle for Radical Economic Reform in Russia. LC 93-5692. 280p. (C). (gr. 13). 1994. text 85.95 (*1-56324-273-7*) M E Sharpe.

— Radical Reform in Yeltsin's Russia: Political, Economic & Social Dimensions. LC 94-41114. (Illus.). 272p. (C). (gr. 13). 1995. text 81.95 (*1-56324-479-9*); pap. text 36.95 (*1-56324-480-2*) M E Sharpe.

Nelson, Lynn D., et al. Property to the People: The Struggle for Radical Economic Reform in Russia. LC 93-5692. 280p. (gr. 13). 1994. pap. text 36.95 (*1-56324-274-5*) M E Sharpe.

Nelson, Lynn H. The Chronicle of San Juan de la Pena: A Fourteenth-Century Official History of the Crown of Aragon. LC 91-8495. (Middle Ages Ser.). 160p. (C). 1991. text 32.50 (*0-8122-3068-X*); pap. text 14.95 (*0-8122-1352-1*) U of Pa Pr.

— Global Perspectives, Vol. II, Since 1600: Source Readings from World Civilizations. 492p. (C). 1989. pap. text 35.50 (*0-15-529617-5*, Pub. by Harcourt Coll Pubs) Harcourt.

— Who Knows: From Quine to a Feminist Empiricism. 336p. (C). 1990. 37.95 (*0-87722-647-4*) Temple U Pr.

— Who Knows: From Quine to a Feminist Empiricism. 336p. 1992. pap. 22.95 (*1-56639-007-9*) Temple U Pr.

Nelson, Lynn H., ed. Global Perspectives, Vol. I, 3000 B.C. to 1600 A.D. Source Readings from World Civilizations. 430p. (C). 1988. pap. text 35.50 (*0-15-529616-7*, Pub. by Harcourt Coll Pubs) Harcourt.

Nelson, Lynn H., tr. The Restoration of the Monastery of Saint Martin of Tournai. LC 95-40170. 248p. 1996. pap. 19.95 (*0-8132-0851-3*) Cath U Pr.

Nelson, Lynn H. & Drummond, Steven K. The Human Perspective Vol. II: The Modern World Through the Twentieth Century, Vol. II. 2nd ed. LC 96-77709. 448p. (C). 1996. pap. text 35.50 (*0-15-501346-7*, Pub. by Harcourt Coll Pubs) Harcourt.

Nelson, Lynn H. & Shirk, Melanie. Liutprand of Cremona, Mission to Constantinople, 968 A. D. 62p. 1972. pap. 5.00 (*0-87291-039-3*) Coronado Pr.

Nelson, Lynn H., jt. auth. see Drummond, Steven K.

Nelson, Lynn H., ed. see Nelson, Jack.

Nelson, Lynn H., tr. & notes see Herman of Tournai.

***Nelson, Lynn Ingrid.** Helping Youth Thrive: How Youth Organizations Can - And Do - Build Developmental Assets. 28p. 1998. pap. 5.95 (*1-57482-379-5*) Search Inst.

Nelson, Lynn T. & Nelson, Gail L. Encyclopedia of Reflexology: A Working Professional's Text. 6th ed. (Illus.). 610p. 1995. ring bd. 125.00 (*1-884727-13-1*) Digits Intl.

— Introduction to Reflexology. 3rd ed. (Illus.). 70p. (Orig.). (C). 1995. pap. 19.95 (*1-884727-01-8*) Digits Intl.

Nelson, M. E., ed. Pets-R-Permitted Hotel, Motel, Kennel & Petsitter Directory: Over 10,000 Petcare Options When You Travel. 5th rev. ed. (Illus.). 320p. (Orig.). 1995. pap. 10.95 (*1-56471-795-X*) Annenberg.

— Pets-R-Permitted Hotel, Motel, Kennel & Petsitter Directory: Petcare Options When You Travel. 288p. (Orig.). 1993. pap. 9.95 (*1-56471-779-8*) Annenberg.

Nelson, M. E., ed. see ACI Staff.

Nelson, M. E., ed. see Annenberg Communications Staff.

Nelson, M. E., ed. see Loeffler, L. L.

Nelson, M. J., et al. Denny Reading Test. 1973. text 22.72 (*0-395-17986-6*) HM.

Nelson, Maggie. Pacific. 55p. 1997. pap. 8.00 (*1-887128-98-0*) Soft Skull Pr.

Nelson, Maggie & Nelson, Cynthia. Not Sisters. 56p. 1996. pap. 8.00 (*1-887128-17-4*) Soft Skull Pr.

Nelson, Malcolm A., jt. auth. see George, Diana Hume.

Nelson, Margaret, et al. Ladder Ranch Research Project: A Report of the First Season. (Maxwell Museum Papers: No. 1). (Illus.). 105p. 1984. pap. 10.00 (*0-912535-02-4*) Max Mus.

Nelson, Margaret C. Mimbres During the Twelfth Century Abandonment, Continuity, & Reorganization. LC 98-40197. 1999. 35.00 (*0-8165-1868-8*) U of Ariz Pr.

Nelson, Margaret K. Negotiated Care: The Experience of Family Day Care Providers. 400p. 1991. 37.95 (*0-87722-728-4*) Temple U Pr.

Nelson, Margaret K. & Smith, Joan. When Good Work Disappears: Survival Strategies in Rural America. LC 98-20758. 289p. 1999. 45.00 (*0-520-21574-5*, Pub. by U CA Pr); pap. 16.95 (*0-520-21575-3*, Pub. by U CA Pr) Cal Prin Full Svc.

Nelson, Margaret K., jt. ed. see Abel, Emily K.

Nelson, Margaret V. Study of Judicial Review in Virginia, 1789-1928. LC 47-31482. (Columbia University. Studies in the Social Sciences: No. 532). reprint ed. 27.50 (*0-404-51532-0*) AMS Pr.

Nelson, Margie, jt. auth. see Johnson, Marael.

Nelson, Marguerite. Desert Nurse. large type ed. (Linford Romance Library). 240p. 1992. pap. 16.99 (*0-7089-7211-X*) Ulverscroft.

N

An Asterisk (*) at the beginning of an entry indicates that the title is appearing for the first time.

Nelson, Marguerite H. Teacher Stories: Teaching Archetypes Revealed by Analysis. 122p. (Orig.). 1993. pap. text 10.40 (*0-911168-86-9*) Prakken.

Nelson, Mariah. Essential Monastic Wisdom: Writings on the Contemplative Life. Feiss, Hugh, ed. LC 98-49369. 240p. 2000. pap. 16.00 (*0-06-062482-5*, Pub. by Harper SF) HarpC.

— The Unburdened Heart. LC 99-59763. 2000. 13.00 (*0-06-251600-0*) HarpC.

Nelson, Mariah B. Embracing Victory: How Women Can Compete Joyously, Compassionately, & Successfully in the Workplace & on the Playing Field. LC 97-30454. 352p. 1999. pap. 12.50 (*0-380-72720-X*, Avon Bks) Morrow Avon.

— Embracing Victory: Life Lessons in Cmpetition & Compassion. LC 97-30454. 288p. 1998. 23.00 (*0-688-14649-X*, Wm Morrow) Morrow Avon.

— Stronger Women Get More. 320p. 1995. reprint ed. pap. 12.00 (*0-380-72527-4*, Avon Bks) Morrow Avon.

— The Stronger Women Get, the More Men Love Football: Sex & Sports in America. LC 93-44358. 1994. 22.95 (*0-15-181393-0*) Harcourt.

— The Unburdened Heart: 5 Keys to Forgiveness & Freedom. LC 99-59763. 224p. 2000. 22.00 (*0-06-251599-3*, Pub. by Harper SF) HarpC.

***Nelson, Mariah Burton.** Embracing Victory: Life Lessons in Competition & Compassion. 337p. 2000. reprint ed. text 23.00 (*0-7881-9266-3*) DIANE Pub.

Nelson, Marian, jt. ed. see Goodloe, Alfred M.

Nelson, Marian F. Priscilla's Patch. LC 97-69071. (Illus.). 32p. (J). (ps-2). 1997. 14.95 (*1-882792-52-1*) Proctor Pubns.

Nelson, Marie. Judith, Juliana, & Elene: Three Fighting Saints. LC 91-17515. (American University Studies: English Language & Literature: Ser. IV, Vol. 135). (Illus.). IX, 210p. 1991. 37.95 (*0-8204-1576-6*) P Lang Pubng.

Nelson, Marie C. Bitter Bread: The Famine in Norrbotten, 1867-1868. (Studia Historica Upsaliensia: No. 153). 192p. (Orig.). 1988. pap. 43.50 (*91-554-2264-0*, Pub. by Uppsala Univ Acta Univ Uppsaliensis) Coronet Bks.

Nelson, Marie C., ed. The Narcissistic Condition: A Fact of Our Lives & Times. LC 76-20724. (Self-in-Process Ser.: Vol. 1). 300p. 1977. 43.95 (*0-87705-250-6*, Kluwer Acad Hman Sci) Kluwer Academic.

Nelson, Marie C. & Eigen, Michael, eds. Evil: Self & Culture. (Self-in-Process Ser.: Vol. 4). 352p. 1984. 42.95 (*0-89885-143-2*, Kluwer Acad Hman Sci) Kluwer Academic.

Nelson, Marie C. & Ikenberry, Jean, eds. Psychosexual Imperatives: Their Role in Identity Formation. LC 78-17739. (Self-in-Process Ser.: Vol. 2). 397p. 1979. 45.95 (*0-87705-302-2*, Kluwer Acad Hman Sci) Kluwer Academic.

Nelson, Marie W. At the Point of Need: Teaching Basic & ESL Writers. LC 90-44002. 269p. (C). 1990. pap. text 27.50 (*0-86709-265-3*, 0265, Pub. by Boynton Cook Pubs) Heinemann.

Nelson, Marilyn. The Fields of Praise: New & Selected Poems. LC 97-8107. 216p. 1997. pap. 16.95 (*0-8071-2175-4*); text 24.95 (*0-8071-2174-6*) La State U Pr.

Nelson, Marilyn M. Practcl Gd Neural Netwrk. 368p. 1991. pap. text 39.95 (*0-201-52376-0*) Addison-Wesley.

Nelson, Marilyn M. Practical Guide to Neural Networks. 352p. (C). 1994. pap. 40.00 (*0-201-63378-7*) Addison-Wesley.

Nelson, Marion, ed. Norwegian Folk Art: The Migration of a Tradition. LC 97-175773. (Illus.). 280p. 1996. pap. 55.00 (*0-7892-0196-8*) Abbeville Pr.

Nelson, Marion, et al. Material Culture & People's Art among the Norwegians in America. (Special Publications). 228p. 1994. 30.00 (*0-87732-082-9*) Norwegian-Am Hist Assn.

Nelson, Marion J. Art Pottery of the Midwest. Brown, Susan Taylor, ed. LC 88-51176. (Illus.). 120p. (Orig.). 1988. pap. text 25.00 (*0-938713-03-5*) Univ MN Art Mus.

Nelson, Mark. Complete Book of Celtic Music for Appalachian Dulcimer. 168p. 1995. pap. 19.95 (*0-7866-0850-1*, MB95530) Mel Bay.

Nelson, Mark. Complete Book of Celtic Music for Appalachian Dulcimer. 168p. 1996. pap. 34.95 incl. audio compact disk (*0-7866-0852-8*, 95530CDP) Mel Bay.

Nelson, Mark. The Data Compression Book. 527p. (Orig.). 1995. pap. 39.95 incl. disk (*1-55851-216-0*, M&T Bks) IDG Bks.

Nelson, Mark. Scottish Airs & Ballads for Appalachian Dulcimer: Intermediate Level. 104p. 1997. spiral bd. 22.95 incl. audio compact disk (*0-7866-2321-7*, 96022BCD) Mel Bay.

Nelson, Mark. Serial Communications. 2nd ed. 1998. 49.95 (*1-55851-571-2*, MIS Pr) IDG Bks.

— Serial Communications Developer's Guide. 888p. 1999. pap. 49.99 (*0-7645-4570-1*) IDG Bks.

Nelson, Mark. You Can Teach Yourself to Make Music with Homemade Instruments. (You Can Teach Yourself Ser.). 112p. 1995. pap. 9.95 (*0-7866-0230-9*, 95329) Mel Bay.

***Nelson, Mark & Beamer, Keola.** Learn to Play Hawaiian Slack Key Guitar. 160p. 1999. pap. 24.95 incl. audio compact disk (*0-7866-4109-6*, 96695BCD) Mel Bay.

Nelson, Mark & Gailly, Jean-Loup. The Data Compression Book. 2nd ed. 557p. (Orig.). 1995. pap. 39.95 incl. disk (*1-55851-434-1*, M&T Bks) IDG Bks.

Nelson, Mark, jt. auth. see Allen, John.

Nelson, Mark, jt. auth. see Alling, Abigail.

Nelson, Mark A., jt. auth. see Verheiden, Mark.

Nelson, Mark E. An Econometric Study of Residential Electricity Demand: A Conditional Demand Analysis of End-Use Equipment Consumption. Sweeney, T. J. & Loeffler, L. L., eds. (Illus.). 155p. 1994. 795.00 (*1-56471-005-X*) Annenberg.

Nelson, Mark L. Bibliography of Old Time Saddlemakers. 98p. (Orig.). 1992. pap. 20.00 (*0-9632094-1-8*) Nelson Pub.

Nelson, Marte. To the Final Journey: The Final Journey of America. (Illus.). 400p. 1998. 15.00 (*0-9665243-0-6*) Lbrty Ent.

Nelson, Martia. Coming Home: The Return to True Self. rev. ed. 232p. 1995. pap. 12.95 (*1-882591-23-2*) New Wrld Lib.

Nelson, Mary & Clark, Kay, eds. The Educator's Guide to Preventing Child Sexual Abuse. 250p. 1986. pap. text 19.95 (*0-941816-17-6*) ETR Assocs.

Nelson, Mary, ed. see Bignell, Steven.

Nelson, Mary, ed. see Nichols, Lyn.

Nelson, Mary, ed. see Strong, Bryan & DeVault, Christine.

Nelson, Mary A. & Reams, Bernard D., Jr., eds. Export Trading Company Act of 1982: Including the Foreign Trade Antitrust Improvement Act, 9 vols., Set. LC 88-83622. (Federal Legislative Histories of Laws & Legislation on Trade Law & Economic Policy Ser.: Part 1). 8900p. 1988. lib. bdg. 725.00 (*0-89941-666-7*, 305760) W S Hein.

Nelson, Mary A., jt. auth. see Reams, Bernard D., Jr.

Nelson, Mary A., jt. ed. see Reams, Bernard D., Jr.

Nelson, Mary Ann, jt. auth. see Means, J. Jeffrey.

Nelson, Mary C. Artists of the Spirit: New Prophets in Art & Mysticism. Mackenzie, Anne, ed. LC 94-10117. (Illus.). 264p. (Orig.). 1994. pap. 12.95 (*0-916955-14-1*) Bro Life Inc.

— Maria Martinez. LC 78-172871. (Story of an American Indian Ser.). 77 p. 1972. write for info. (*0-87518-038-8*, Dillon Silver Burdett) Silver Burdett Pr.

— Maria Martinez. LC 74-12323. (Story of an American Indian Ser.). 74 p. 1974. write for info. (*0-87518-098-1*, Dillon Silver Burdett) Silver Burdett Pr.

Nelson, Mary C. & Ruiz, Nagual Miguel. Beyond Fear: A Toltec's Guide to Freedom & Joy - Teachings of Miguel Angel Ruiz, M. D. LC 97-29355. (Illus.). 224p. (Orig.). 1997. pap. 16.95 (*1-57178-038-6*) Coun Oak Bks.

***Nelson, Mary D.** Madame Nelson's French Verb Book with All the Answers. (FRE & ENG.). 332p. 1999. 25.00 (*0-8425-2463-0*) Brigham.

Nelson, Mary D. Motivating with Love: A Memoir. LC 89-10021. (Illus.). xxii, 327p. 1989. pap. 17.50 (*0-8425-2372-3*, BYU DMK Ctr Intl) Brigham.

Nelson, Matthew. Java Foundation Classes. LC 98-6455. (Java Masters Ser.). 1040p. 1998. pap. 49.95 incl. cd-rom (*0-07-913758-X*) McGraw.

Nelson, Max & Shipbaugh, Calvin. The Potential of Nanotechnology for Molecular Manufacturing. 62p. (Orig.). 1995. pap. text 7.50 (*0-8330-2287-3*, MR-615-RC) Rand Corp.

Nelson, Melinda. Imagine You Are a Hang Glider. LC 98-26365. (Action Sports Library). (J). 2002. lib. bdg 21.35 (*1-57765-202-9*) ABDO Pub Co.

— Imagine You Are a Snowboarder. LC 98-26363. (Action Sports Library). (J). 2002. lib. bdg. 21.35 (*1-57765-199-5*) ABDO Pub Co.

Nelson, Melinda & Wallner, Rosemary. Imagine You Are a Whitewater Rafter. LC 98-26315. (Action Sports Library). (J). 2002. lib. bdg. 21.35 (*1-57765-203-7*) ABDO Pub Co.

Nelson, Meryl. Meryl Nelson's When You're Out Of . . . Cookbook. rev. ed. Sing, Shirley, ed. LC 83-51044. (Illus.). 104p. 1983. pap. 4.95 (*0-941900-06-1*) This N That.

— The New Low Fat This for That: A Cooks Handbook of Savvy Substitutions. (Illus.). 138p. 1998. pap. 7.95 (*0-941900-07-X*) This N That.

Nelson, Meryl & Thoman, Frances. Meryl Nelson's Cooking Coast to Coast. Sing, Shirley, ed. LC 83-51697. (Illus.). 120p. (Orig.). 1984. pap. 3.95 (*0-941900-08-8*) This N That.

Nelson-Metlay, Valerie, tr. see Graham, Bill.

Nelson, Mexico Mike. Mexico's Colonial Heart. LC 94-90360. (Sanborn's Travelog - Mexico by Land Ser.). (Illus.). 336p. (Orig.). 1995. pap. 5.00 (*1-878166-17-4*) Wanderlust Pubns.

— Spas & Hot Springs of Mexico: Over 60 Restful Places from World-Class Spas to Simple Hot Springs. 2nd rev. ed. 232p. 1998. pap. 16.95 (*1-889489-04-2*) Rds Scholar.

Nelson, Michael. The Development of Tropical Lands: Policy Issues in Latin America. LC 72-12363. (Resources for the Future Ser.). 323p. 1973. 27.00 (*0-8018-1488-X*) Johns Hopkins.

— The Development of Tropical Lands: Policy Issues in Latin America. LC 72-12363. (Illus.). 326p. reprint ed. pap. 101.10 (*0-608-17388-6*, 203021200067) Bks Demand.

— The Elections of 1996. LC 97-2059. 182p. (YA). (gr. 11). 1997. text 23.97 (*1-56802-247-6*); pap. text 13.17 (*1-56802-219-0*) Congr Quarterly.

— The Presidency & the Political System. 5th ed. LC 97-40586. 607p. (YA). 1997. text 41.95 (*1-56802-305-7*) Congr Quarterly.

— The Presidency & the Political System. 5th ed. LC 97-40586. 607p. (YA). 1997. pap. text 30.95 (*1-56802-304-9*) Congr Quarterly.

***Nelson, Michael.** The Presidency & the Political System. 6th ed. LC 99-54451. 600p. 2000. pap. 35.95 (*1-56802-496-7*) CQ Pr.

— Presidency & the Political System. 6th ed. 2000. 45.95 (*1-56802-497-5*) CQ Pr.

Nelson, Michael. War of the Black Heavens: The Battles of Western Broadcasting in the Cold War. LC 97-13789. (Illus.). 277p. 1997. 34.95 (*0-8156-0479-3*) Syracuse U Pr.

Nelson, Michael, ed. The Evolving Presidency. LC 98-27073. 50p. 1981. pap. text 15.95 (*1-56802-369-3*) Congr Quarterly.

***Nelson, Michael, ed.** The Evolving Presidency. LC 98-27073. 33p. 1998. text 29.95 (*1-56802-370-7*) Congr Quarterly.

— Guide to the Presidency, 2 vols. 2nd ed. LC 96-18543. 1800p. 1996. text 315.00 (*1-56802-018-X*) Congr Quarterly.

Nelson, Michael, ed. A Heartbeat Away: Report of the Task Force on the Vice-Presidency. 120p. 1988. text 18.95 (*0-318-35969-3*); pap. text 9.95 (*0-318-35970-7*) Routledge.

— Historical Documents on Presidential Elections, 1787-1988. LC 91-18729. 902p. 1991. 95.00 (*0-87187-607-8*) Congr Quarterly.

— The Presidency A to Z: A Ready Reference Encyclopedia. rev. ed. LC 94-17668. (Encyclopedia of American Government Ser.: Vol. 2). 574p. (YA). (gr. 11). 1994. text 145.00 (*1-56802-056-2*) Congr Quarterly.

Nelson, Michael, jt. auth. see Congressional Quarterly, Inc, Staff.

Nelson, Michael, jt. auth. see CQ Inc. Staff.

Nelson, Michael, jt. auth. see Hargrove, Erwin C.

Nelson, Michael, jt. auth. see Milkis, Sidney M.

Nelson, Michael, jt. ed. see Heard, Alexander.

Nelson, Michael, jt. ed. see Margetts, Barrie.

Nelson, Michael C., jt. auth. see Kerr, Mary M.

***Nelson, Michael E.** Welcome to Our Neighborhood. 2000. pap. 15.00 (*0-938708-96-1*) L F Garlinghouse Co.

Nelson, Michael E., jt. auth. see Watts, Mark T.

Nelson, Michael G., jt. ed. see Bandopadhyay, Sukumar.

Nelson, Michael J. Managing Health Professionals. 216p. 1990. pap. 25.50 (*0-412-33350-3*, A4446) Chapman & Hall.

***Nelson, Michael J.** Mike Nelson's Movie Megacheese. 288p. 2000. pap. 15.00 (*0-380-81467-6*) Morrow Avon.

Nelson, Michael P., jt. auth. see Callicott, J. Baird.

Nelson, Michael P., jt. ed. see Callicott, J. Baird.

Nelson, Mico. Cutting Edge of Audio Production & Audio Post-Production: Theory, Equipment & Techniques. 285p. 1995. pap. text 48.95 (*0-86729-305-5*, Focal) Buttrwrth-Heinemann.

Nelson, Mike. Baja Driver's Travelog. (Mexico by Land Ser.). 52p. (Orig.). 1993. pap. 15.95 (*1-878166-07-7*) Wanderlust Pubns.

— Central America by Car. LC 91-62784. (Sanborn's Travelog Ser.). 108p. 1997. pap. 19.95 (*1-878166-23-9*) Wanderlust Pubns.

***Nelson, Mike.** Live Better South of the Border in Mexico: Practical Advice for Living & Working. 168p. 2000. pap. 16.95 (*1-55591-394-6*) Fulcrum Pub.

Nelson, Mike. Mexico's Gulf Coast: And Costa Esmeralda. (Sanborn's Travelog Ser.). 90p. 1997. pap. 15.95 (*1-878166-27-1*) Wanderlust Pubns.

— Mexico's Pacific Coast: And Copper Canyon. (Sanborn's Travelog Ser.). 150p. 1996. pap. 15.95 (*1-878166-26-3*). Wanderlust Pubns.

— Mexico's Ruta Maya: Yucatan Penisula Cancune & Belize. LC 97-60402. (Sanborn's Travelog Ser.). 142p. (Orig.). 1997. pap. 15.95 (*1-878166-08-5*) Wanderlust Pubns.

***Nelson, Mike.** Stop Clutter from Stealing Your Life: Discover Why You Clutter & How You Can Stop. 224p. 2001. pap. 14.99 (*1-56414-502-6*, New Page Bks) Career Pr Inc.

Nelson, Mike & Romer, George, eds. Northeastern Mexico: Coahuila, Nuevo Leon & Tamaulipas. 2nd rev. ed. (Sanborn's Travelog - Mexico by Land Ser.). 110p. 1995. pap. 9.95 (*1-878166-24-7*) Wanderlust Pubns.

Nelson, Mike & 9News Weather Team. The Colorado Weather Book. LC 99-17298. (Illus.). 136p. 1999. pap. 24.95 (*1-56579-342-0*) Westcliffe Pubs.

Nelson, Mike, ed. see Shroeder, Rick & Riser, Mel.

***Nelson, Miriam & Wernick, Sarah.** Strong Women Stay Young. rev ed. 304p. 2000. pap. 13.95 (*0-553-38077-X*) Bantam.

Nelson, Miriam E. & Wernick, Sarah. Strong Women Stay Slim. LC 97-44179. 336p. 1998. 24.95 (*0-553-10931-6*) Bantam.

— Strong Women Stay Slim. 336p. 1999. pap. 11.95 (*0-553-37945-3*) Broadway BDD.

— Strong Women Stay Young. LC 96-41541. 288p. 1997. 24.95 (*0-553-10347-4*) Bantam.

***Nelson, Miriam E. & Wernick, Sarah.** Strong Women, Strong Bones: Everything You Need to Know to Prevent, Treat & Beat Osteoporosis. LC 99-57570. (Illus.). 304p. 2000. 23.95 (*0-399-14597-4*) Putnam Pub Group.

Nelson-Morrill, Creston, ed. see Polangin, Richard F. & Feigenbaum, Ernest.

Nelson, Morton, jt. auth. see Larson, Kermit.

Nelson, Murray R. Multiculturalism & the School Curriculum: Historical Case Studies. Kincheloe, Joe & Steinberg, Shirley R., eds. (Critical Education Practice Ser.). 350p. Date not set. text 52.00 (*0-8153-2106-6*); pap. text 18.95 (*0-8153-2326-3*) Garland.

***Nelson, Murry.** The Originals: The New York Celtics Invent Modern Basketball. LC 99-22733. 225p. 1999. 51.95 (*0-87972-793-4*); pap. 25.95 (*0-87972-794-2*) Bowling Green Univ Popular Press.

Nelson, Murry R., ed. The Future of the Social Studies. 90p. (Orig.). 1994. pap. 14.95 (*0-89994-378-0*) Soc Sci Ed.

Nelson, N. C. The Ellis Landing Shellmound. fac. ed. (University of California Publications in American Archaeology & Ethnology: Vol. 7: 5). 76p. (C). 1910. reprint ed. pap. text 8.75 (*1-55567-179-9*) Coyote Press.

— Shellmounds of the San Francisco Bay Region. fac. ed. (University of California Publications in American Archaeology & Ethnology: Vol. 7: 4). 51p. (C). 1909. reprint ed. pap. text 6.25 (*1-55567-178-0*) Coyote Press.

— Winner Takes All: Exceptional People Teach Us How to Find Career & Personal Success in the 21st. LC BF637.S8N425 1999. (Illus.). 216p. (C). 1999. 24.95 (*0-306-46005-X*, Pub. by Perseus Pubng) HarpC.

Nelson, N. S. The Compleat Slug. LC 85-61964. (Illus.). 76p. (Orig.). 1986. pap. 6.50 (*0-935195-12-2*) Plaid Pony Pubns.

Nelson, Nan F. My Day with Anka. LC 95-25425. (Illus.). 24p. (J). (ps up). 1996. 16.00 (*0-688-11058-4*); lib. bdg. 15.93 (*0-688-11059-2*) Lothrop.

Nelson, Nancy. Any Time, Any Place, Any River: The Nevills of Mexican Hat. LC 91-67399. (Illus.). 85p. (Orig.). 1991. pap. 9.95 (*0-9611678-8-2*) Red Lake Bks.

— Evenings with Cary Grant. large type ed. 748p. 1992. lib. bdg. 14.95 (*1-56054-937-8*) Thorndike Pr.

— Evenings with Cary Grant. large type ed. 748p. 1992. reprint ed. 22.95 (*1-56054-342-6*) Thorndike Pr.

Nelson, Nancy D., tr. see Gilles, Jean-Elie.

Nelson, Nancy J., jt. auth. see Labat, Karen L.

Nelson, Nancy O. The Lizard Speaks: Essays on the Writings of Frederick Manfred. LC 98-23330. (Prairie Plains Ser.: Vol. 6). 250p. 1998. pap. 15.95 (*0-931170-67-2*) Ctr Western Studies.

Nelson, Nancy O., ed. Private Voices, Public Lives: Women Speak on the Literary Life. LC 94-48327. 345p. (Orig.). 1995. pap. 18.95 (*0-929398-88-2*) UNTX Pr.

Nelson, Nancy O., ed. see Manfred, Frederick, pseud.

Nelson, Nathan H. Spiritual Devotion: Intimacy with God. LC 95-77705. 112p. 1996. pap. 4.95 (*0-88243-107-2*); pap., teacher ed. 9.95 (*0-88243-207-9*) Gospel Pub.

Nelson, Ned. Pequeno Gigante de la Cancion. (SPA.). 1998. pap. 6.99 (*0-8297-0372-1*) Zondervan.

Nelson-Nesvig, Carleen. Outsourcing Solutions: Workforce Strategies That Improve Profitability. LC 97-67219. 160p. (Orig.). 1997. pap. 12.95 (*1-890394-01-7*) Rhodes & Easton.

Nelson, Nici, ed. African Women in the Development Process. 144p. 1981. 35.00 (*0-7146-3175-2*, Pub. by F Cass Pubs) Intl Spec Bk.

Nelson, Nici, jt. ed. see Wright, Susan.

Nelson, Nickola W. Childhood Language Disorders. 2nd ed. LC 97-32508. 594p. 1998. 62.00 (*0-205-19787-6*) Allyn.

— Childhood Language Disorders in Context: Infancy Through Adolescence. 2nd ed. 224p. (C). 1998. text, teacher ed. write for info. (*0-205-27814-0*, T7814-1) Allyn.

Nelson, Nickola W. & Hoskins, Barbara, eds. Strategies for Supporting Classroom Success: Focus on Communication - an Audio Workshop, 6 cass. (School-Age Children Ser.). (Illus.). 132p. (Orig.). 1997. pap. 125.00 incl. audio (*1-56593-810-0*, 1586) Singular Publishing.

Nelson, Nina. Essential Egypt. (Essential Travel Guides Ser.). 128p. 1994. pap. 7.95 (*0-8442-8908-6*, Passprt Bks) NTC Contemp Pub Co.

Nelson, Noelle. Dangerous Relationships: How to Stop Domestic Violence Before It Stops You. LC 97-26645. (Illus.). 332p. (C). 1997. 27.95 (*0-306-45625-7*; Plen Insight) Perseus Pubng.

***Nelson, Noelle.** Everyday Miracles: Transform Your Life Using What You Already Have. LC 99-88621. 224p. 2000. pap. 12.00 (*0-7352-0159-5*) PH Pr.

Nelson, Noelle. Get Your Way! Put a Lawyer's Power of Persuasion to Use in Your Everyday Life. LC 98-13852. (Illus.). 400p. 1998. reprint ed. pap. 14.00 (*0-7352-0026-2*) PH Pr.

Nelson, Norm, ed. see Strain, Dave & Nauman, Chuck.

Nelson, O., ed. Plant Transposable Elements: Alaskan Aviation History. LC 88-21917. (Basic Life Sciences Ser.: Vol. 47). (Illus.). 416p. 1990. 105.00 (*0-306-43001-0*, Plenum Trade) Perseus Pubng.

Nelson, O. N. History of the Scandinavians & Successful Scandinavians in the U. S., 2 vols., Set. LC 68-31266. (American History & Americana Ser.: No. 47). 1969. reprint ed. lib. bdg. 150.00 (*0-8383-0198-3*) M S G Haskell Hse.

Nelson, O. T. The Girl Who Owned a City. 192p. (YA). (gr. 6 up). 1977. mass mkt. 4.99 (*0-440-92893-1*, LLL BDD) BDD Bks Young Read.

— The Girl Who Owned a City. 204p. (YA). (gr. 5 up). 1995. pap. 3.95 (*0-8225-9670-9*, Runestone Pr); lib. bdg. 19.95 (*0-8225-3152-6*, Runestone Pr) Lerner Pub.

— The Girl Who Owned a City. (Laurel-Leaf Science Fiction Ser.). (J). 1975. 9.60 (*0-606-01096-3*, Pub. by Turtleback) Demco.

***Nelson, O. T.** The Girl Who Owned a City. unabridged ed. (J). (gr. 7). 1998. 50.75 incl. audio (*0-7887-2664-1*, 40824) Recorded Bks.

Nelson Oberhansly, Dianne, jt. auth. see Oberttansky, Curtis.

Nelson, Olga G., et al. Practical Classroom Applications of Language Experience: Looking Back, Looking Forward. LC 98-21656. 280p. 1998. pap. text 34.00 (*0-205-26156-6*) Allyn.

Nelson, Otto, jt. ed. see Goebel, Ulrich.

Nelson, P. Doctrinas Biblicas.Tr. of Bible Doctrines. (SPA.). 192p. 1964. pap. 5.99 (*0-8297-0539-2*) Vida Pubs.

Nelson, P. A. & Elliott, S. J. Active Control of Sound. 436p. 1993. pap. text 59.00 (*0-12-515426-7*) Acad Pr.

Nelson, P. C. Bible Doctrines. LC 81-82738. 126p. (YA). (gr. 9). 1981. pap. 3.95 (*0-88243-479-9*, 02-0479) Gospel Pub.

Nelson, P. C. & Wawire, Plus. Bible Doctrines. (Discovery Ser.). 121p. 1999. pap. text. write for info. (*1-891110-00-4*) Africa Theolog Trng.

Nelson-Pallmeyer, Jack. Brave New World Order: Must We Pledge Allegiance? LC 91-37238. 192p. reprint ed. pap. 59.60 (*0-608-20198-7*, 207145700012) Bks Demand.

— Families Valued: Parenting & Politics for the Good of All Children. LC 96-24592. 1996. 9.95 (*0-377-00309-3*) Friendship Pr.

N

An Asterisk (*) at the beginning of an entry indicates that the title is appearing for the first time.

— School of Assassins: The Case for Closing the School of the Americas & for Fundamentally Changing U. S. Foreign Policy. LC 97-3390. 128p. (Orig.). 1997. pap. 12.00 (*1-57075-134-X*) Orbis Bks.

Nelson-Pallmeyer, Jack, jt. auth. see Leonard, Joe.

Nelson, Pam, tr. see Jeunesse, Gallimard, et al.

Nelson, Pamela & Museum of Science & Industry Staff. Every Teacher's Science. Scholastic, Inc. Staff, ed. 1994. pap. 12.95 (*0-590-49381-7*) Scholastic Inc.

Nelson, Pamela, ed. see Chipman, Dawn, et al.

Nelson, Pamela, tr. see Delafosse, Claude.

Nelson, Pamela B. Ethnic Images in Toys & Games. LC 90-81444. (Illus.). 51p. 1990. 5.00 (*0-937437-07-7*) Balch IES Pr.

Nelson, Pamela B., ed. Armenian Rugs: Fabric of a Culture. LC 87-71500. (Illus.). 40p. 1988. 10.00 (*0-937437-04-2*) Balch Inst Ethnic Studies.

Nelson, Pamela B., et al. Something Old, Something New: Ethnic Weddings in America. LC 87-71305. (Illus.). 35p. (Orig.). 1987. pap. 5.25 (*0-937437-02-6*) Balch Inst Ethnic Studies.

Nelson, Pat. Magic Minutes: Quick Read-Alouds for Every Day. LC 92-35887. (Illus.). 151p. 1993. pap. text 18.50 (*0-87287-996-8*) Libs Unl.

***Nelson, Pat.** Stylish Sewing. (Illus.). 112p. 2000. pap. write for info. (*1-56477-299-3*, B427, Pub. by Martingale & Co) F & W Pubns Inc.

Nelson, Patty. Teacher's Bag of Tricks. (Illus.). 80p. (J). (gr. k-6). 1986. pap. text 9.95 (*0-86530-132-8*, 76-7) Incentive Pubns.

Nelson, Paul. Average Nights. LC 77-75758. 62p. 1977. per. 3.75 (*0-934332-04-5*) LEpervier Pr.

***Nelson, Paul.** Internet Business Concepts. (Illus.). (YA). 2000. pap. write for info. (*0-7423-0440-X*) ComputerPREP.

Nelson, Paul. Narrative & Morality: A Theological Inquiry. LC 86-43034. 192p. 1987. 35.00 (*0-271-00485-1*) Pa St U Pr.

— Out of Sight, Out of Mind: Invisible Maniac. (Illus.). 44p. (Orig.). 1997. pap. 5.00 (*1-890051-03-9*) It Plays in Peoria.

Nelson, Paul, ed. The Creationist Writings of Byron C. Nelson. LC 95-1065. (Creationism in Twentieth-Century America Ser.: Vol. 5). 536p. 1995. text 116.00 (*0-8153-1806-5*) Garland.

***Nelson, Paul & Lanier-Graham, Susan D.** Internet Basics & Infrastructure. Dietz, Kevin C. & Tillman, Jamie, eds. (Illus.). (YA). 2000. pap. write for info. (*0-7423-0444-2*) ComputerPREP.

— Internet Client & Server Information. Dietz, Kevin C. & Tillman, Jamie, eds. (Illus.). (YA). 2000. pap. write for info. (*0-7423-0443-4*) ComputerPREP.

— Internet Development. Dietz, Kevin C., ed. (Illus.). (YA). 2000. pap. write for info. (*0-7423-0442-6*) ComputerPREP.

— Intranets, Extranets & Security. Dietz, Kevin C., ed. (Illus.). (YA). 2000. pap. write for info. (*0-7423-0441-8*) ComputerPREP.

— Preparing for iNet+ Certification. Tillman, Jamie & Dietz, Kevin C., eds. (Illus.). (YA). 2000. pap. write for info. (*0-7423-0471-X*) ComputerPREP.

Nelson, Paul, et al. Transport Theory, Invariant Imbedding, & Integral Equations: Proceedings in Honor of G. M. Wing's 65th Birthday. (Lecture Notes in Pure & Applied Mathematics Ser.: Vol. 115). (Illus.). 480p. 1989. pap. text 195.00 (*0-8247-8158-9*) Dekker.

Nelson, Paul, jt. auth. see MacAdams, William.

Nelson, Paul A., ed. see Poulsen, Peter.

Nelson, Paul C. Gilbert's Famous American Flyer Trains. LC 97-78056. 200p. 1999. write for info. (*0-911581-48-0*) Heimburger Hse Pub.

Nelson, Paul D. Anthony Wayne, Soldier of the Early Republic. LC 84-48543. (Illus.). 380p. 1985. reprint ed. pap. 117.80 (*0-608-01067-7*, 205937500001) Bks Demand.

— General James Grant: Scottish Soldier & Royal Governor of East Florida. LC 92-28134. 216p. 1993. 22.95 (*0-8130-1175-2*) U Press Fla.

— Sir Charles Grey, First Earl Grey: Royal Soldier, Family Patriarch. LC 95-26341. (Illus.). 256p. 1996. 37.50 (*0-8386-3673-X*) Fairleigh Dickinson.

— William Alexander, Lord Stirling. LC 85-16473. (Illus.). 258p. pap. 80.00 (*0-608-05143-8*, 206570400005) Bks Demand.

— William Tryon & the Course of Empire: A Life in British Imperial Service. LC 90-11998. (Illus.). xiii, 250p. (C). 1990. 34.95 (*0-8078-1917-4*) U of NC Pr.

***Nelson, Paul David.** General Sir Guy Carleton, Lord Dorchester: Soldier-Statesman of Early British Canada. LC 99-35399. (Illus.). 296p. 2000. 45.00 (*0-8386-3838-4*) Fairleigh Dickinson.

Nelson, Paul E. Understanding & Sharing. 6th ed. (C). 1994. audio. write for info. (*0-697-26038-0*) Brown & Benchmark.

Nelson, Paul E. & Pearson, Judy c. Confidence in Public. 6th ed. 100p. (C). 1996. text, student ed. 17.50 (*0-697-32701-9*, WCB McGr Hill) McGrw-H Hghr Educ.

Nelson, Paul E. & Pearson, Judy C. Core Volume Confidence in Public Speaking. 6th ed. LC 95-77677. 368p. (C). 1995. text. write for info. (*0-697-33341-8*) Brown & Benchmark.

— An Introduction to Human Communication. 7th ed. LC 96-83903. 512p. (C). 1996. text. write for info. (*0-697-28898-6*, WCB McGr Hill) McGrw-H Hghr Educ.

Nelson, Paul E., jt. auth. see Pearson, Judy.

Nelson, Paul E., jt. auth. see Pearson, Judy C.

Nelson, Paul E., jt. ed. see Horst, R. Kenneth.

Nelson, Paul Y. Greenhouse Operation & Management. 5th ed. LC 97-24640. 637p. (C). 1997. 100.00 (*0-13-374687-9*) P-H.

Nelson, Paula, jt. auth. see Clifton, Donald O.

Nelson, Paula M. After the West Was Won: Homesteaders & Town-Builders in Western South Dakota, 1900-1917. LC 86-11405. (Illus.). 238p. (C). 1986. reprint ed. pap. text 14.95 (*0-87745-250-4*) U of Iowa Pr.

— The Prairie Winnows Out Its Own: The West River Country of South Dakota in the Years of Depression & Dust. LC 95-24904. (Illus.). 276p. 1996. text 27.95 (*0-87745-525-2*) U of Iowa Pr.

Nelson, Pauline & Daubert, Todd. Starting with Shakespeare: Successfully Introducing Shakespeare to Children. LC 99-38709. 175p. 1999. pap. 23.50 (*1-56308-753-7*) Libs Unl.

Nelson, Pauline, jt. auth. see Daubert, Todd.

Nelson, Pearl A. The First Year: Retirement Journal. Kirchhofer, M. V., ed. (Illus.). 163p. (Orig.). 1982. pap. 6.95 (*0-932910-41-6*) Potentials Development.

Nelson, Peggy. How to Create Powerful Newsletters: Easy Ways to Avoid the Pitfalls that 80 Percent of All Newsletters Face. 212p. 1992. 30.00 (*0-929387-86-4*) Bonus Books.

Nelson, Perry. Resoundings. 1998. 6.00 (*0-937690-54-6*, 3420) Wrld Lib Pubns.

***Nelson, Pete & Brehm, Jack W.** That Others May Live: The True Story of a P. J., a Member of America's Most Daring Rescue Force. LC 99-46251. 288p. 2000. 24.00 (*0-609-60504-6*, Crown) Crown Pub Group.

Nelson, Pete, jt. auth. see Brehm, Jack.

Nelson, Peter. Dangerous Waters. Ashby, Ruth, ed. (Sylvia Smith-Smith Novel Ser.). 224p. (Orig.). (J). 1992. per. 3.50 (*0-671-74891-2*, Archway) PB.

— Ten Practical Tips for Environmental Reporting. 57p. 1995. pap. text 7.50 (*0-9626584-6-4*) Intl Ctr Journal.

— Treehouses. LC 93-32568. (Illus.). 128p. 1994. pap. 19.95 (*0-395-62949-7*) HM.

Nelson, Peter & Hadden, Gerry. Home Tree Home: Principles of Tree House Construction & Other Tall Tales. LC 96-54737. (Illus.). 179p. 1997. pap. 17.95 (*0-14-025998-8*) Viking Penguin.

***Nelson, Peter, et al.** Treehouse Book. (Illus.). 224p. 2000. pap. 25.00 (*0-7893-0411-2*) Universe.

Nelson, Peter, tr. see Antoine, Charles.

Nelson, Peter E., ed. see American Society for Testing & Materials Staff, et al.

Nelson, Peter R., et al, eds. The Frontiers of Statistical Computation, Simulation, & Modeling Vol. 1: Proceedings of the ICOSCO-I Conference (First International Conference on Statistical Computing, Cesme, Izmir, Turkey, March-April 1987) LC 90-85328. (Series in Mathematical & Management Sciences: Vol. 25). 450p. 1991. 195.00 (*0-935950-27-3*) Am Sciences Pr.

Nelson, Philip. Coinage of William Wood. (Illus.). 1978. reprint ed. pap. 8.00 (*0-915262-21-5*) S J Durst.

Nelson, Philip B. Corporations in Crisis: Behavioral Observations for Bankruptcy Policy. LC 81-1415. 206p. 1981. 49.95 (*0-275-90687-6*, C0687, Praeger Pubs) Greenwood.

Nelson, Philip B., jt. auth. see Hegarty, Christopher J.

Nelson, Philip B., jt. auth. see Hilke, John C.

Nelson, Phillip G. & Lieberman, Melvyn, eds. Excitable Cells in Tissue Culture. LC 80-8106. 440p. 1981. 95.00 (*0-306-40516-4*, Plenum Trade) Perseus Pubng.

Nelson, Portia. There's a Hole in My Sidewalk. 128p. 1989. reprint ed. pap. 6.95 (*0-9621159-0-8*) Stonebarn.

— There's a Hole in My Sidewalk: The Romance of Self-Discovery. 2nd ed. LC 93-18380. 144p. 1993. pap. 7.95 (*0-941831-87-6*) Beyond Words Pub.

Nelson, Priscilla P., et al, eds. Design & Performance for Deep Foundations, Piles & Piers in Soil & Soft Rock: Proceedings of a Session Sponsored by the Committees on Deep Foundations & Rock Mechanics of the Geotechnical Engineering Division of the American Society of Civil Engineers in Conjunction with the ASCE Convention in Dallas, Texas, October 24-28, 1993. LC 93-31658. (Geotechnical Special Publications: No. 38). 288p. 1993. 28.00 (*0-87262-987-2*) Am Soc Civil Eng.

***Nelson Publishing Staff.** Natures Wonders, 3. 2000. 35.97 (*0-7852-3712-7*) Nelson.

— Nelson Reference Bible. 2000. 12.97 (*0-7852-5512-5*) Nelson.

Nelson, R. An American Comedy. 1991. pap. 6.95 (*0-88145-097-9*) Broadway Play.

— Between East & West. 1989. pap. 6.95 (*0-88145-077-4*) Broadway Play.

— Graph Colourings. 1990. pap. 58.00 (*0-582-05120-7*, Pub. by Addison-Wesley) Longman.

Nelson, R., jt. auth. see Goldoni, Carlo.

Nelson, R., jt. auth. see Moliere.

Nelson, R., ed. see Chekhov, Anton.

Nelson, R. D., Jr. Dispersing Powders in Liquids. (Handbook of Powder Technology Ser.: No. 7). 246p. 1988. 173.50 (*0-444-43004-0*) Elsevier.

Nelson, R. J. The Logic of Mind. 1982. lib. bdg. 171.00 (*90-277-1399-5*) Kluwer Academic.

— The Logic of Mind. enl. ed. 410p. (C). 1989. pap. text 59.50 (*90-277-2822-4*, Pub. by Kluwer Academic) Kluwer Academic.

— The Logic of Mind. 2nd enl. rev. ed. 410p. (C). 1989. lib. bdg. 171.50 (*90-277-2819-4*, Pub. by Kluwer Academic) Kluwer Academic.

— Naming & Reference. LC 91-45969. (Problems of Philosophy Series: Their Past & Present). (Illus.). 304p. (C). (gr. 13). 1992. 80.00 (*0-415-00939-1*, A1619) Routledge.

— Play Within a Play. LC 72-87356. (Theatre, Film & the Performing Arts Ser.). 182p. 1971. reprint ed. lib. bdg. 29.50 (*0-306-71580-5*) Da Capo.

Nelson, Rachel W., jt. auth. see Webb, Sheyann.

Nelson, Rachelle. A Cherished Reward. 304p. 1996. mass mkt. 5.99 (*0-515-11897-4*, Jove) Berkley Pub.

— Flirt: Sons & Daughters. 1995. mass mkt. 4.99 (*0-515-11768-4*, Jove) Berkley Pub.

— Heartbound. 288p. 1997. mass mkt. 5.99 (*0-515-12034-0*, Jove) Berkley Pub.

Nelson, Ralph, ed. & tr. see Simon, Yves R.

Nelson, Ralph A., et al, eds. Heat Transfer Division, 1998; Proceedings: ASME International Mechanical Engineering Congress & Exposition (1998: Anaheim, California) LC 99-191721. 1951p. 1998. pap. 690.00 (*0-7918-1597-8*) ASME Pr.

Nelson, Ralph L. Economic Factors in the Growth of Corporation Giving. LC 70-104182. 116p. 1970. 19.95 (*0-87154-615-9*) Russell Sage.

— The Investment Policies of Foundations. LC 66-30032. 204p. 1967. 24.95 (*0-87154-614-0*) Russell Sage.

— Merger Movements in American Industry, 1895-1956. (General Ser.: No. 66). 198p. 1975. reprint ed. 49.50 (*0-87014-065-5*) Ayer.

— Merger Movements in American Industry, 1895-1956. LC 59-11082. (National Bureau of Economic Research. General Ser.: No. 66). 198p. reprint ed. pap. 61.40 (*0-608-30171-X*, 205175600007) Bks Demand.

Nelson, Ramon W. & Woodward, John B. Island Life, Island Toil: The House of David on High Island. (Illus.). 192p. 1991. 29.00 (*0-931781-07-8*) Jennings Pr.

Nelson, Rand H. & Trafford, Charles H. ABC's & 123's: Physical Language Readiness. (Illus.). iii, 62p. (J). (ps-2). 1997. student ed., spiral bd. 7.95 (*1-890666-00-9*, 102097) Peterson Direct.

— ABC's & 123's Big Book. (Illus.). 28p. 1997. teacher ed., ring bd. 35.00 (*1-890666-06-8*, K197) Peterson Direct.

— We Write to Read: Teacher Handbook for Early Childhood & Kindergarten. 5th rev. ed. (Illus.). 28p. 1997. pap. text, teacher ed. 4.40 (*1-890666-07-6*, 112007) Peterson Direct.

— We Write to Read Home School Handwriting: A Practical Transition to Cursive, Grade Three, 2 bks. (We Write to Read Ser.). (Illus.). 1997. pap. text, teacher ed., student ed. 9.95 (*1-890666-21-1*, 038897) Peterson Direct.

— We Write to Read Home School Handwriting: Advanced Cursive, Grades 5-8, 2 bks. (We Write to Read Ser.). (Illus.). 1997. pap. text, teacher ed., student ed. 6.95 (*1-890666-23-8*, 588897) Peterson Direct.

— We Write to Read Home School Handwriting: Integrating Fluent Patterns, Vertical Print Grade One, 2 bks. (We Write to Read Ser.). (Illus.). 1997. pap. text, teacher ed., student ed. 9.95 (*1-890666-19-X*, 018897) Peterson Direct.

— We Write to Read Home School Handwriting: Introducing Adult Tools & Proportion, Grade Four, 2 bks. (We Write to Read Ser.). (Illus.). 1997. pap. text, teacher ed., student ed. 6.95 (*1-890666-22-X*, 048897) Peterson Direct.

— We Write to Read Home School Handwriting: Introducing Cursive Readiness, Grade 2, 2 bks. (We Write to Read Ser.). (Illus.). 1997. pap. text, teacher ed., student ed. 9.95 (*1-890666-20-3*, 028897) Peterson Direct.

— We Write to Read Home School Handwriting: Print Readiness, Preschool & Kindergarten, 2 bks. (We Write to Read Ser.). (Illus.). 1997. pap. text, teacher ed., student ed. 14.95 (*1-890666-18-1*, 118897) Peterson Direct.

Nelson, Rand H., jt. auth. see Trafford, Charles H.

Nelson, Randolph. Probability, Stochastic Processes & Queueing Theory: The Mathematics of Computer Performance Modelling. LC 95-4041. (Illus.). 583p. 1995. 54.95 (*0-387-94452-4*) Spr-Verlag.

Nelson, Randy F. The Martial Arts Index: An Annotated Bibliography. LC 88-11243. 456p. 1988. text 25.00 (*0-8240-4435-5*, SS451) Garland.

Nelson, Randy F., ed. The Overlook Martial Arts Reader. 356p. 1989. 19.95 (*0-87951-347-0*, Pub. by Overlook Pr) Penguin Putnam.

— The Overlook Martial Arts Reader: Classic Writings on Philosophy & Technique. 356p. 1992. reprint ed. pap. 15.95 (*0-87951-459-0*, Pub. by Overlook Pr) Penguin Putnam.

Nelson, Randy J. An Introduction to Behavioral Endocrinology. 2nd rev. ed. (C). 1999. text 64.95 (*0-87893-616-5*) Sinauer Assocs.

Nelson, Ray. Shrews Can't Hoop!? LC 94-78337. (Illus.). 48p. (J). (gr. 3-6). 1994. 9.95 (*1-883772-04-4*) Flying Rhino.

— Sleeper. (Illus.). 105p. (YA). 1995. pap. 9.95 (*0-9623068-1-9*) Raynel.

— Virtual Zen. 224p. (Orig.). 1996. mass mkt. 5.50 (*0-380-78185-9*, Avon Bks) Morrow Avon.

Nelson, Ray & Kelly, Doug. Connie & Bonnie's Birthday Blastoff. rev. ed. Siegal, Joseph, ed. (Illus.). 48p. (J). (gr. 3-6). 1997. 16.95 (*1-883772-10-9*) Flying Rhino.

— Greetings from America. rev. ed. McLane, Mike & Siegal, Joseph, eds. (Illus.). 48p. (J). (gr. 3-6). 1997. 16.95 (*1-883772-13-3*) Flying Rhino.

— The Seven Seas of Billy's Bathtub. rev. ed. McLane, Mike & Siegal, Joseph, eds. (Illus.). 48p. (J). (gr. 3-6). 1997. 16.95 (*1-883772-12-5*) Flying Rhino.

Nelson, Ray & Kelly, Douglas. Connie & Bonnie's Birthday Blastoff. (Illus.). 48p. (J). (gr. 3-6). 1994. 14.95 (*1-56977-403-X*) Flying Rhino.

— The Seven Seas of Billy's Bathtub. (Illus.). 48p. (J). (gr. 3-6). 1994. 14.95 (*1-56977-406-4*) Flying Rhino.

Nelson, Ray & Mohr, Julie. I Am Hercules. McLane, Mike, ed. (Farmer Bob Ser.). (Illus.). 32p. (J). (gr. 1-3). 2000. pap. text 9.95 (*1-883772-16-8*) Flying Rhino.

— I Am Jenny. (Farmer Bob Ser.). (Illus.). 32p. (J). (gr. 1-3). 2000. pap. text 9.95 (*1-883772-18-4*) Flying Rhino.

— I Am Porkchop. (Farmer Bob Ser.). (Illus.). 32p. (J). (gr. 1-2). 2000. pap. text 9.95 (*1-883772-17-6*) Flying Rhino.

— I Am Sam. McLane, Mike et al, eds. (Farmer Bob Ser.). (Illus.). 32p. (J). (gr. 1-3). 2000. pap. text 9.95 (*1-883772-15-X*) Flying Rhino.

— Today I Will Moo. (Farmer Bob Ser.). (Illus.). 32p. (J). (gr. 1-3). 2000. pap. text 9.95 (*1-883772-19-2*) Flying Rhino.

Nelson, Ray & Nelson, Douglas. Greetings from America: Postcards from Donovan Willoughby. 2nd ed. Tronslin, Andrea, ed. LC 92-14819. (Illus.). 48p. (J). (gr. k-5). 14.95 (*1-56977-409-9*) Flying Rhino.

Nelson, Ray, et al. The Battle Against Boredom. (Illus.). 48p. (J). (gr. 3-6). 2000. 16.95 (*1-883772-20-6*) Flying Rhino.

— A Dinosaur Ate My Homework. (Illus.). 48p. (J). (gr. 3-6). 1994. 14.95 (*1-56977-400-5*) Flying Rhino.

— A Dinosaur Ate My Homework. rev. ed. Siegel, Joseph, ed. (Illus.). 48p. (J). (gr. 3-6). 1997. 16.95 (*1-883772-09-5*) Flying Rhino.

***Nelson, Ray, et al.** Hercules' Spring Book. Siegel, Joseph & Habecker, Mary Beth, eds. (Illus.). 32p. (J). (gr. 1-3). 2000. pap. 9.95 (*1-883772-23-0*) Flying Rhino.

Nelson, Ray, et al. The Internal Adventures of Marcus Snarkis. McLane, Mike, ed. (Farmer Bob Ser.). 48p. (J). (gr. 3-6). 2000. 16.95 (*1-883772-14-1*) Flying Rhino.

***Nelson, Ray, et al.** Jenny's Autumn Book. Siegel, Joseph & Habecker, Mary Beth, eds. (Illus.). 32p. (J). (gr. 1-3). 2000. pap. 9.95 (*1-883772-50-8*) Flying Rhino.

Nelson, Ray, Jr., et al. The Munchy Crunchy Bug Book. Siegel, Joseph, ed. (Illus.). 48p. (J). (gr. 3-6). 1997. 16.95 (*1-883772-08-7*) Flying Rhino.

***Nelson, Ray, et al.** Porkchop's Summer Book. Siegel, Joseph & Habecker, Mary Beth, eds. (Illus.). 32p. (J). (gr. k-3). 1999. pap. 9.95 (*1-883772-24-9*) Flying Rhino.

— Sam's Winter Book. Siegel, Joseph & Habecker, Mary Beth, eds. (Illus.). 32p. (J). (gr. 1-3). 2000. pap. 9.95 (*1-883772-22-2*) Flying Rhino.

— A Snack for Phillip. Siegel, Joseph & Habecker, Mary Beth, eds. (Illus.). 32p. (J). (gr. 1-3). 2000. pap. 9.95 (*1-883772-51-6*) Flying Rhino.

— A Snack for Phillip: Big Book. Siegel, Joseph & Habecker, Mary Beth, eds. (Illus.). 32p. (J). (gr. 1-3). 1999. spiral bd. 39.95 (*1-883772-52-4*) Flying Rhino.

Nelson, Ray, et al. Wooden Teeth & Jelly Beans: The Tupperman Files. rev. ed. Siegal, Joseph, ed. (Illus.). 48p. (J). (gr. 3-6). 1997. 16.95 (*1-883772-11-7*) Flying Rhino.

Nelson, Ray F. Dogheaded Death. (Centurion Bks.). 184p. (Orig.). 1989. pap. 9.95 (*0-89407-079-7*) Strawberry Hill.

Nelson, Ray R. I Never Met One Stranger: A Personal Journey. 435p. (Orig.). (YA). (gr. 12). 1989. pap. 10.45 (*0-9623068-0-0*) Raynel.

Nelson, Raymond. Kenneth Patchen & American Mysticism. LC 83-27384. 211p. reprint ed. pap. 65.50 (*0-608-20085-9*, 207135700011) Bks Demand.

Nelson, Raymond, jt. auth. see Sharkey, Robert.

Nelson, Raymond, ed. see Tolson, Melvin B.

Nelson, Raymond D. Flying Rhino Cartooning Kit. (Walter Foster Art Products Ser.). (Illus.). 32p. 1997. pap. 14.95 (*1-56010-202-0*, FR01) W Foster Pub.

Nelson, Raymond S. And the Kansas Wind Blows: Poems about the People, the Land. LC 91-70831. (Illus.). 96p. (Orig.). 1991. pap. 7.95 (*0-9627947-1-6*) Hearth KS.

— At Home in Kansas LC 98-75559. 88 p. 1998. write for info. (*1-882420-32-2*, Prairie Bks) Hearth KS.

— Hemingway: Expressionist Artist. LC 79-4640. 113p. reprint ed. pap. 35.10 (*0-608-14588-2*, 202482200038) Bks Demand.

— Prairie Sketches. LC 92-73894. (Illus.). 96p. (Orig.). 1992. pap. 8.95 (*0-9627947-8-3*) Hearth KS.

— Thy Love Is Better Than Wine. LC 93-81210. (Illus.). 96p. (Orig.). 1994. pap. 9.95 (*1-882420-11-X*, 1-882420-11-X) Hearth KS.

Nelson, Raymond S., ed. see Shaw, George Bernard.

Nelson Readers Staff. Four Short Stories. 1997. pap. write for info. (*0-17-556690-9*, Pub. by ITP Nelson) Thomson Learn.

Nelson, Rebecca, ed. see Gray, Charlene.

Nelson, Rebecca, ed. see Johnston, Sammie.

Nelson, Rebecca, ed. see Serratt, Mary L.

Nelson, Rebecca S. Games & Activities with Base, Bk. 1. (J). 1995. pap. 9.50 (*0-201-48009-3*) Addison-Wesley.

— Games & Activities with Base, Bk. 2. (J). 1995. pap. 9.50 (*0-201-48010-7*) Addison-Wesley.

— Games & Activities with Base Ten Blocks, Bk. 1. (Illus.). 64p. (J). (gr. 1-4). 1987. pap. text 9.50 (*0-914040-57-X*) Cuisenaire.

— Games & Activities with Base Ten Blocks, Bk. 2. 64p. (J). (gr. 1-4). 1987. pap. text 9.50 (*0-914040-58-8*) Cuisenaire.

Nelson, Reed E. Organizational Troubleshooting: Asking the Right Questions, Finding the Right Answers. LC 95-51414. 184p. 1997. 55.00 (*1-56720-046-X*, Quorum Bks) Greenwood.

***Nelson Reference Books Staff.** Nelson's Amazing Bible Trivia, Vol. 2. 2000. pap. 9.99 (*0-7852-4528-6*) Nelson.

— Supervalue Reference Superset: The New Strong's Exhaustive Concordance of the Bible/Matthew Henry's Concise Commentary on the Whole Bible/Illustrated, 4 vols. (Illus.). 2000. 59.97 (*0-7852-4519-7*) Nelson.

Nelson, Rex. The Hillary Factor: The Story of America's First Lady. 256p. 1993. 21.95 (*0-9636477-0-9*) Gallen Pub Fnd.

— The Hillary Factor: The Story of America's First Lady. (Illus.). 258p. 1993. pap. 5.99 (*0-9636477-1-7*) Gallen Pub Fnd.

An Asterisk (*) at the beginning of an entry indicates that the title is appearing for the first time.

Nelson, Richard. Aesthetic Frontiers: The Machiavellian Tradition & the Southern Imagination. LC 90-32055. 296p. reprint ed. pap. 91.80 (*0-608-08719-X*, 206928700003) Bks Demand.
— An American Comedy & Other Plays. 1984. pap. 12.95 (*0-933826-70-2*) PAJ Pubns.
— A Culture of Confidence: Politics, Performance & the Idea of America. LC 95-44457. (C). 1996. 47.50 (*0-87805-868-0*); pap. 19.50 (*0-87805-869-9*) U Pr of Miss.
— The General from America. 96p. (Orig.). 1996. pap. 11.95 (*0-571-19018-9*) Faber & Faber.
— Goodnight Children Everywhere. 1998. pap. 11.95 (*0-571-19430-3*) Faber & Faber.
— Heart & Blood. 1998. pap. 14.00 (*0-679-73686-7*) Vin Bks.
— The Island Within. LC 90-55685. 304p. 1991. pap. 13.00 (*0-679-73239-X*) Vin Bks.
— Life Sentences. 96p. (Orig.). 1993. pap. 8.95 (*0-571-19831-7*) Faber & Faber.
— Richard Nelson Plays 1: Some Americans Abroad, Two Shakespearean Actors, New England, Principia Scriptoriae & Left. 320p. 1999. pap. 20.00 (*0-571-19708-6*) Faber & Faber.
— Roots in Water. 1991. pap. 6.95 (*0-88145-093-6*) Broadway Play.
— Two Shakespearean Actors. 103p. (Orig.). 1991. pap. 8.95 (*0-571-16103-0*) Faber & Faber.
Nelson, Richard, ed. Strictly Dishonorable & Other Lost American Plays. LC 86-5782. (Illus.). 260p. (Orig.). (C). 1986. pap. 10.95 (*0-930452-55-0*) Theatre Comm.
Nelson, Richard & Jones, David. Making Plays: The Writer-Director Relationship in the Theater Today. Chambers, Colin, ed. 165p. 1995. pap. 13.95 (*0-571-16354-8*) Faber & Faber.
Nelson, Richard, tr. see Strindberg, August.
Nelson, Richard A. A Chronology & Glossary of Propaganda in the United States. LC 94-47427. 360p. 1996. lib. bdg. 82.95 (*0-313-29261-2*, Greenwood Pr) Greenwood.
Nelson, Richard A., jt. auth. see Heath, Robert L.
Nelson, Richard B., jt. auth. see Felton, Lewis P.
Nelson, Richard B., jt. ed. see Hart, Gary C.
Nelson, Richard C. Choice Awareness: Systematic, Eclectic Counseling Theory. LC 90-81967. 352p. (Orig.). (C). 1990. pap. text 17.95 (*0-932796-30-3*) Ed Media Corp.
— Choosing: A Better Way to Live. LC 78-67188. (Illus.). 1978. pap. 5.95 (*0-932570-00-3*) Guidelines Pr.
— On the Crest: Growing Through Effective Choices. LC 92-70821. (Illus.). 192p. (Orig.). (C). 1992. pap. text 9.95 (*0-932796-39-7*) Ed Media Corp.
— Success Is a Choice. (Orig.). 1979. pap. write for info. (*0-932570-01-1*) Guidelines Pr.
Nelson, Richard C., et al. Working with Adolescents: Building Effective Communication & Choice-Making Skills. LC 94-70340. 144p. (Orig.). (C). 1994. pap. text 16.95 (*0-932796-61-3*) Ed Media Corp.
Nelson, Richard C., jt. auth. see Miller, Doris I.
Nelson, Richard C., jt. ed. see Mowery, David C.
Nelson, Richard D. First & Second Kings. LC 87-9883. (Interpretation: A Bible Commentary for Teaching & Preaching Ser.). 252p. 1987. 25.00 (*0-8042-3109-5*) Westminster John Knox.
— The Historical Books. Matthews, Rex, ed. LC 98-28160. (Interpreting Biblical Texts Ser.). 192p. 1998. pap. 18.95 (*0-687-00843-3*) Abingdon.
— Joshua: A Commentary. LC 97-8356. (Old Testament Library). 328p. 1999. 40.00 (*0-664-21941-1*) Westminster John Knox.
— Raising up a Faithful Priest: Community & Priesthood in Biblical Theology. LC 93-10361. 1993. pap. 22.95 (*0-664-25437-3*) Westminster John Knox.
Nelson, Richard E. Power to Prevent Suicide: A Guide for Teens Helping Teens. LC 94-5594. 1994. 17.05 (*0-606 06678-0*, Pub. by Turtleback) Demco.
Nelson, Richard E. & Galas, Judith C. The Power to Prevent Suicide: A Guide for Teens Helping Teens. Espeland, Pamela, ed. LC 94-5594. (Illus.). 136p. (YA). (gr. 5 up). 1994. pap. 12.95 (*0-915793-70-9*) Free Spirit Pub.
Nelson, Richard G., et al, eds. Biodiesel 1994: Proceedings of the Conference on Technologies, Trends & Case Studies about the Benefits & Use of Biodiesel. (Illus.). 218p. (Orig.). (C). 1995. pap. text 50.00 (*0-7881-2118-9*) DIANE Pub.
Nelson, Richard K. Hunters of the Northern Forest: Designs for Survival among the Alaskan Kutchin. 2nd ed. LC 86-7085. (Illus.). 320p. (C). 1986. pap. text 16.00 (*0-226-57181-5*) U Ch Pr.
— Hunters of the Northern Ice. LC 78-75136. (Illus.). 454p. 1997. pap. text 15.95 (*0-226-57176-9*) U Ch Pr.
— Make Prayers to the Raven: A Koyukon View of the Northern Forest. LC 82-8441. xvi, 320p. 1986. pap. 15.00 (*0-226-57163-7*) U Ch Pr.
— Shadow of the Hunter: Stories of Eskimo Life. LC 80-11091. (Illus.). xiv, 296p. 1983. pap. 12.95 (*0-226-57180-7*) U Ch Pr.
— Shadow of the Hunter: Stories of Eskimo Life. LC 80-11091. 296p. reprint ed. pap. 91.80 (*0-608-18045-9*, 202649400049) Bks Demand.
Nelson, Richard R. The Sources of Economic Growth. LC 96-16498. (Illus.). 288p. 1996. 43.00 (*0-674-82145-9*) HUP.
***Nelson, Richard R.** Sources of Economic Growth. 2000. pap. text 19.95 (*0-674-00172-9*) HUP.
Nelson, Richard R., ed. National Innovation Systems. (Illus.). 560p. 1993. pap. text 39.95 (*0-19-507617-6*) OUP.
Nelson, Richard R. & Winter, Sidney G. An Evolutionary Theory of Economic Change. (Illus.). 400p. 1982. pap. 23.95 (*0-674-27228-5*) HUP.
Nelson, Richard R., et al. Structural Change in a Developing Economy: Colombia's Problems & Prospects. LC 72-146645. (Rand Corporation Research Study). (Illus.). 336p. reprint ed. pap. 104.20 (*0-608-18441-1*, 203264200080) Bks Demand.
Nelson, Richard R., jt. auth. see Ostry, Sylvia.
Nelson, Richard R., ed. see Conference on Families & the Economy Staff.
Nelson, Richard R., jt. ed. see Kim, Linsu.
Nelson, Richard S. Hohokam Marine Shell Exchange & Artifacts. (Archaeological Ser.: No. 179). (Illus.). 108p. 1991. pap. 12.95 (*1-889747-44-0*) Ariz St Mus.
Nelson, Richard W. Credit Card Risk Management. LC 96-90478. (Illus.). 280p. 1996. 67.95 (*0-9653865-0-3*) Warren-Taylor.
***Nelson, Richard W. & Couto, C. Guillermo.** Manual of Small Animal Internal Medicine. (Illus.). 944p. (C). (gr. 13). 1998. pap. text 39.95 (*0-8151-7297-4*, 27769) Mosby Inc.
Nelson, Richard W. & Couto, C. Guillermo. Small Animal Internal Medicine. 2nd ed. LC 98-221791. (Illus.). 1376p. (C). (gr. 13). 1998. text 125.00 (*0-8151-6351-7*, 26032) Mosby Inc.
Nelson, Richard W., jt. auth. see Feldman, Edward C.
Nelson, Richard W., jt. auth. see Rubin, Seymour J.
Nelson-Richards, Melsome. Beyond the Sociology of Agrarian Transformation: Economy & Society in Zambia, Nepal & Zanzibar. Ishwaran, K., ed. LC 87-20931. (Monographs & Theoretical Studies in Sociology & Anthropology in Honour of Nels Anderson: Vol. 20). (Illus.). v, 141p. (Orig.). 1988. pap. 45.50 (*90-04-08282-4*) Brill Academic Pubs.
Nelson, Rick. City Smart: Minneapolis/St. Paul. 2nd rev. ed. (City Smart Ser.). (Illus.). 224p. 1999. pap. 14.95 (*1-56261-471-1*, City Smart) Avalon Travel.
Nelson, Rick & Nelson, Sheila. A Cruising Guide to the Black Sea. (Illus.). 130p. 1995. pap. 125.00 (*0-85288-173-8*, Pub. by Laurie Norie & Wilson Ltd) St Mut.
Nelson, Riki K. Borders - Grenzen. (ENG & GER., Illus.). 128p. 1991. pap. 10.00 (*0-9614462-4-2*) Black Hat Pr.
Nelson, Riki K. The Fall Heart, Vol. 7. (Northfield Women Poets Chapbook Ser.). (Illus.). 24p. 1992. 4.00 (*0-9614314-5-8*) Heywood Pr.
***Nelson, Rob.** Last Call: 10 Common Sense Solutions to America's Biggest Problems. 304p. 2000. pap. 12.95 (*0-440-50903-3*) Delacorte.
— Last Call: 10 Commonsense Solutions to America's Biggest Problems. LC 99-55447. 2000. 12.95 (*0-385-33408-7*, Delta Trade) Dell.
***Nelson, Robert.** A Burning Issue: A Case for Abolishing the U. S. Forest Service. LC 99-57704. (The Political Economy Forum Ser.). 288p. 2000. pap. 24.95 (*0-8476-9735-5*); text 60.00 (*0-8476-9734-7*) Rowman.
Nelson, Robert, Jr. Finnish Magic. LC 98-31527. (World of Magic & Religion Ser.). (Illus.). 192p. 1999. pap. 7.95 (*1-56718-489-8*) Llewellyn Pubns.
***Nelson, Robert.** The Greatest Sales Training in the World. 224p. 2000. 20.00 (*0-88391-002-0*) F Fell Pubs Inc.
Nelson, Robert. The Job Hunt. LC 85-27921. 83p. (Orig.). 1986. pap. 2.95 (*0-89815-160-0*) Ten Speed Pr.
Nelson, Robert & Christensen, Carl J. Foundations of Music: A Computer-Assisted Introduction. 221p. (C). 1986. pap. write for info. (*0-534-06894-4*) Wadsworth Pub.
***Nelson, Robert & Christensen, Carl J.** Foundations of Music: A Computer-Assisted Introduction 4th ed. LC 99-27833. 1999. 40.50 (*0-534-56764-9*) Wadsworth Pub.
Nelson, Robert & Christensen, Carl J. Foundations of Music: A Computer-Assisted Introduction (Apple II) 2nd ed. LC 92-12695. 236p. (C). 1992. 42.75 (*0-534-18829-X*) Wadsworth Pub.
— Foundations of Music: A Computer-Assisted Introduction (IBM) 3rd ed. LC 96-22949. (C). 1996. pap. 42.75 (*0-534-50740-9*) Wadsworth Pub.
— Foundations of Music: A Computer-Assisted Introduction (Macintosh) 2nd ed. 236p. (C). 1992. mass mkt. 37.50 (*0-534-18828-1*) Wadsworth Pub.
— Foundations of Music: A Computer-Assisted Introduction (Macintosh) 3rd ed. LC 96-186488. (C). 1996. pap. 67.95 (*0-534-50741-7*) Wadsworth Pub.
Nelson, Robert, et al. Exploring the World of Business. 807p. 1995. text 49.20 (*1-57259-070-X*) Worth.
— Exploring the World of Business. 416p. 1996. pap. text, student ed. 13.20 (*1-57259-071-8*) Worth.
Nelson, Robert, tr. see Sanchez, Victor.
Nelson, Robert A. International System of Units. 2nd ed. (Illus.). 132p. 1983. per. 11.00 (*0-917853-84-9*, OP-45) Am Assn Physics.
Nelson, Robert B. Empowering Employees Through Delegation. LC 93-5929. 175p. 1993. 19.95 (*1-55623-847-9*, Irwn Prfssnl) McGraw-Hill Prof.
Nelson, Robert B. & Economy, Peter J. Better Business Meetings. LC 94-9330. (Briefcase Bks.). 175p. 1994. text 19.95 (*0-7863-0188-0*, Irwn Prfssnl) McGraw-Hill Prof.
— Better Business Meetings International Editon. LC 94-9330. (Briefcase Bks.). 192p. 1994. per. 13.95 (*0-7863-0205-4*, Irwn Prfssnl) McGraw-Hill Prof.
Nelson, Robert B. & Wallick, Jennifer. The Presentation Primer: Getting Your Point Across. LC 93-29855. 168p. 1993. 19.95 (*1-55623-846-0*, Irwn Prfssnl) McGraw-Hill Prof.
Nelson, Robert B., jt. auth. see Mosvick, Roger K.
Nelson, Robert C. Elementary Technical Mathematics. 6th ed. LC 94-26683. (Math). 640p. 1994. mass mkt. 51.75 (*0-534-94554-6*) PWS Pubs.
— Flight Stability & Automatic Control. 2nd ed. LC 97-26109. 456p. 1997. 86.88 (*0-07-046273-9*) McGraw.
***Nelson, Robert E., ed.** Directory of American Toolmakers: A Listing of Identified Makers of Tools Who Worked in Canada & the United States Before 1900. 1176p. 1999. pap. 65.00 (*0-9619425-3-5*) Early Am Indus.
Nelson, Robert E., jt. ed. see Neck, Philip A.
Nelson, Robert H. The Making of Federal Coal Policy. LC 83-7155. (Duke Press Policy Studies). (Illus.). xi, 261p. (C). 1983. text 46.95 (*0-8223-0497-X*) Duke.
— Public Lands & Private Rights: The Failure of Scientific Management. 400p. (C). 1995. lib. bdg. 73.00 (*0-8476-8008-8*) Rowman.
— Reaching for Heaven on Earth: The Theological Meaning of Economics. 320p. 1993. pap. 16.95 (*0-8226-3024-9*) Littlefield.
Nelson, Robert J. Pascal: Adversary & Advocate. LC 81-6330. (Illus.). 296p. 1982. 43.00 (*0-674-65615-6*) HUP.
— Willa Cather & France: In Search of the Lost Language. LC 87-24484. 192p. (C). 1988. text 24.95 (*0-252-01502-9*) U of Ill Pr.
Nelson, Robert J. & Oxenhandler, Neal, eds. Aspects of French Literature. LC 61-5992. (FRE.). 1961. 49.50 (*0-89197-037-1*); pap. text 29.95 (*0-89197-038-X*) Irvington.
Nelson, Robert J. & Weales, Gerald, eds. Enclosure: A Collection of Plays. LC 74-23084. 282p. 1975. 16.95 (*0-679-50531-8*) Boulevard.
Nelson, Robert J., jt. ed. see Weales, Gerald.
Nelson, Robert L. Our Ocean Home. LC 96-46822. (Illus.). 48p. (Orig.). (J). (ps-1). 1997. 11.95 (*1-55971-596-0*, NorthWord Pr) Creat Pub Intl.
— Underwater Fantasies. 1995. pap. 10.99 (*1-57081-770-7*) At-A-Glance Consumer.
Nelson, Robert L. & Bridges, William P. Legalizing Gender Inequality: Courts, Markets & Unequal Pay for Women in America. LC 98-38432. (Structural Analysis in the Social Sciences Ser.: No. 16). (Illus.). 368p. (C). 1999. text 59.95 (*0-521-62169-0*); pap. text 19.95 (*0-521-62750-8*) Cambridge U Pr.
Nelson, Robert L. & Trubek, David M., eds. Lawyers' Ideals - Lawyers' Practices: Transformations in the American Legal System. LC 91-55533. 320p. 1992. text 47.50 (*0-8014-2461-5*); pap. text 18.95 (*0-8014-9710-8*) Cornell U Pr.
Nelson, Robert S. The Iconography of Preface & Miniature in the Byzantine Gospel Book. LC 80-15335. (College Art Association Monographs: Vol. 36). (Illus.). 180p. 1985. reprint ed. 40.00 (*0-271-00404-5*) Pa St U Pr.
***Nelson, Robert S., ed.** Visuality Before & Beyond the Renaissance. (Cambridge Studies in New Art History & Criticism). (Illus.). 288p. (C). 2000. 80.00 (*0-521-65222-7*) Cambridge U Pr.
Nelson, Robert S. & Shiff, Richard, eds. Critical Terms for Art History. (Illus.). 360p. 1999. lib. bdg. 48.00 (*0-226-57164-5*) U Ch Pr.
Nelson, Robert S., ed. see Shiff, Richard.
Nelson, Robert V. Understanding Basic Energy Terms. LC 81-2888. 1981. pap. text 8.00 (*0-86663-807-5*); lib. bdg. 10.00 (*0-86663-806-7*) Ide Hse.
Nelson, Robert V., et al. E Equals MC Squared: Energy - Management, Conservation & Communication, 17 vols. Ide, Arthur F., ed. (Illus.). (Orig.). 1981. write for info. (*0-86663-800-8*); pap. write for info. (*0-86663-801-6*) Ide Hse.
Nelson, Robyn M., et al. Little, Brown's Medical-Surgical Nursing Review. LC 96-23717. 1997. pap. text 22.95 (*0-316-81169-6*) Lppncott W & W.
Nelson, Rodney. The Boots Brevik Saga. LC 78-11771. 1978. pap. 10.95 (*0-914974-19-X*) Holmgangers.
— Home River. LC 83-63482. 76p. 1984. pap. 4.85 (*0-911042-28-8*) NDSU Inst Reg.
— Oregon Scroll. 1976. pap. 3.00 (*0-914974-11-4*) Holmgangers.
— Thor's Home. (Kestrel Ser.: No. 8). 28p. 1983. pap. 5.00 (*0-914974-40-8*) Holmgangers.
— Villy Sadness: A Novella. 114p. 1987. pap. 7.95 (*0-89823-093-1*) New Rivers Pr.
Nelson, Rodney, ed. see Blanc, Tara.
Nelson, Rodney, ed. see Eskes, David.
Nelson, Rodney, ed. see Finnerty, Margaret.
Nelson, Rodney, ed. see Phillips, Amy.
Nelson, Rodney, ed. see Sanford, Charles W., Jr.
Nelson, Rodney B., III. Beaumont: America's First Physiologist. LC 89-82643. (Illus.). 400p. 1990. 42.00 (*0-9625624-0-8*) Grant Hse Pr.
— The Franklin Institute Illinois' First Medical School. (Illus.). v, 94p. (Orig.). 1991. pap. 9.95 (*0-9625624-2-4*) Grant Hse Pr.
Nelson, Roger. Does God Watch the Superbowl? Leader's Guide. (Life Wise Ser.). 34p. 1998. pap., teacher ed. 7.95 (*1-56212-357-2*, 1210-4020) CRC Pubns.
— The Vision Thing: Making Sense of Life. (Life Wise Ser.). 36p. (Orig.). (YA). 1996. pap., teacher ed. 7.95 (*1-56212-188-X*, 1210-4016) CRC Pubns.
Nelson, Roger M. & Currier, Dean P. Clinical Electrotherapy. 2nd ed. (Illus.). 422p. (C). 1990. pap. text 49.95 (*0-8385-1334-4*, A1334-0) Appleton & Lange.
Nelson, Roger M., et al. Clinical Electrotherapy. 3rd rev. ed. LC 98-50864. (Illus.). 420p. (C). 1999. text 49.95 (*0-8385-1491-X*) Appleton & Lange.
Nelson, Roger M., jt. auth. see Currier, Dean P.
Nelson, Ronald, jt. ed. see Lees, Alfred.
Nelson, Ronald A. Stepping Stones: Early Childhood, Year 1, 7 vols. Hawn, C. Michael, ed. (Stepping Stones Ser.). 64p. 1995. reprint ed. pap. text 22.95 (*1-929187-04-1*, CGBK55, Pub. by Choristers) Lorenz Corp.
Nelson, Ronald B. The Control of Man & the Enslavement of Women. LC 97-91191. 243p. 1998. 19.95 (*0-533-12580-4*) Vantage.
— A Gateway to the Past. LC 98-90861. 1999. 17.95 (*0-533-12952-4*) Vantage.
Nelson, Ronald E. Human Geography: People, Cultures & Landscapes. LC 94-67522. (C). 1994. pap. text 72.50 (*0-03-025414-0*, Pub. by Harcourt Coll Pubs) Harcourt.
Nelson, Ronald E. & IGS (Sublett) Staff. Illinois: Geographical Society. rev. ed. 352p. 1995. pap. text, per. 39.95 (*0-7872-1714-X*) Kendall-Hunt.
Nelson, Ronald R. & Schweizer, Peter. The Soviet Concepts of Peace, Peaceful Coexistence & Detente. LC 87-34520. 198p. (Orig.). (C). 1988. pap. text 22.50 (*0-8191-6833-5*); lib. bdg. 47.00 (*0-8191-6832-7*) U Pr of Amer.
Nelson, Rosemary. Galena's Gift. 144p. (J). (gr. 4-7). 1997. pap. 6.95 (*0-929141-56-3*) Napoleon Publ.
— The Golden Grasshopper. 128p. (J). (gr. 4-7). 1996. pap. 5.95 (*0-929141-50-4*) Napoleon Publ.
Nelson, Rosemary O. & Hayes, Steven C., eds. Conceptual Foundations of Behavioral Assessment. LC 85-27363. (Behavioral Assessment Ser.). 544p. 1986. lib. bdg. 75.00 (*0-89862-142-9*) Guilford Pubns.
Nelson, Roy, ed. Vingtieme Siecle: La Problematique du Discours. LC 81-50963. (Michigan Romance Studies: vol. 6). 127p. 1986. pap. 15.00 (*0-939730-05-7*) Mich Romance.
Nelson, Roy & Wilson, Robin J., eds. Graph Colourings. LC 89-34242. (Pitman Research Notes in Mathematics Ser.: No. 218). 157p. 1991. pap. 48.70 (*0-608-05240-X*, 206577700001) Bks Demand.
Nelson, Roy C. Industrialization & Political Affinity: Industrial Policy in Brazil. LC 95-3434. (Thunderbird/Routledge Series in International Management). 144p. (C). (gr. 13). 1995. pap. 49.00 (*0-415-12528-6*) Thomson Learn.
Nelson, Roy J. Casuality & Narrative in French Fiction from Zola to Robbe-Grillet. LC 89-34065. 277p. reprint ed. pap. 85.90 (*0-608-09861-2*, 206982600006) Bks Demand.
Nelson, Roy P. The Design of Advertising. 7th ed. 432p. (C). 1996. text. write for info. (*0-697-38766-6*) Brown & Benchmark.
— Publication Design. 5th ed. 336p. (C). 1990. text. write for info. (*0-697-08620-8*) Brown & Benchmark.
Nelson, Roy P., jt. auth. see Copperud, Roy H.
Nelson, Roy Paul. Publication Design. LC 78-176306. 232 p. 1972. write for info. (*0-697-04323-1*) Brown & Benchmark.
Nelson, Ruby. Door of Everything. 1963. pap. 8.95 (*0-87516-069-7*) DeVorss.
Nelson, Rudolph. The Making & Unmaking of an Evangelical Mind: The Case of Edward Carnell. 272p. 1988. text 69.95 (*0-521-34263-5*) Cambridge U Pr.
Nelson, Russell, jt. auth. see Levine, John R.
Nelson, Russell M. The Gateway We Call Death. LC 95-3147. 128p. 1995. 10.95 (*0-87579-953-1*) Deseret Bk.
— Perfection Pending & Other Favorite Discourses. LC 98-24542. 1998. 17.95 (*1-57345-405-2*) Deseret Bk.
— The Power Within Us. LC 88-20299. ix, 160p. 1988. 15.95 (*0-87579-154-9*) Deseret Bk.
Nelson, Russell M. The Magnificence of Man & Truth--and More. LC 97-78187. 58 p. 1998. write for info. (*0-87579-985-X*) Deseret Bk.
Nelson, Russell S., jt. ed. see Wrone, David R.
Nelson, Ruth A. & Williams, Roger. Handbook of Rocky Mountain Plants. 4th ed. (Illus.). 444p. 1992. pap. 19.95 (*0-911797-96-3*) Roberts Rinehart.
Nelson, S. A. The ABC of Stock Speculation. LC 63-22761. 1964. reprint ed. pap. 16.00 (*0-87034-054-9*) Fraser Pub Co.
Nelson, S. D. Gift Horse. LC 98-51666. (Illus.). 32p. (J). (gr. 2-6). 1999. 14.95 (*0-8109-4127-9*, Pub. by Abrams) Time Warner.
Nelson, S. H., jt. auth. see Grogono, Peter.
***Nelson-Saginor, Page.** Gallery Effects. vi, 22p. 1999. pap. write for info. (*0-9674900-1-4*) Wordrunner.
Nelson, Sally, et al. Microcomputer Accounting: Tutorial & Applications with Peachtree. LC 93-44207. 1994. 35.95 (*0-02-801065-5*) Glencoe.
Nelson, Sally, jt. auth. see Spiegelberg, Emma J.
Nelson, Samuel A. The A B C of Stock Speculation. LC 89-60256. 232p. 1989. reprint ed. 45.00 (*1-55888-805-5*) Omnigraphics Inc.
Nelson, Samuel H. Colonialism in the Congo Basin, 1880-1940. LC 94-18278. (Monographs in International Studies, Africa: No. 64). 290p. (Orig.). (C). 1994. pap. text 23.00 (*0-89680-180-2*) Ohio U Pr.
Nelson, Samuel J. Mississippian Faunas of Western Canada. LC QE0729.N36. (Geological Association of Canada. Special Paper: No. 2). 100p. reprint ed. pap. 31.00 (*0-608-18711-9*, 202783700056) Bks Demand.
Nelson, Sandra S., et al. Managing for Results: Effective Resource Allocation for Libraries. LC 99-33130. (Illus.). 320p. 1999. pap. 45.00 (*0-8389-3498-6*) ALA.
Nelson, Sara, tr. see Vierci, Pablo.
Nelson, Sarah. The Archaeology of Korea. (World Archaeology Ser.). (Illus.). 323p. (C). 1993. text 80.00 (*0-521-40443-6*); pap. text 29.95 (*0-521-40783-4*) Cambridge U Pr.
— Ulster's Uncertain Defenders: Protestant Political, Paramilitary, & Community Groups, & the Northern Ireland Conflict. LC 84-132570. (Irish Studies). 219p. 1984. reprint ed. pap. 67.90 (*0 608 06978-7*, 206718600009) Bks Demand.
Nelson, Sarah M. Gender in Archaeology: Analyzing Power & Prestige. LC 97-4860. 240p. 1997. 62.00 (*0-7619-9115-8*); pap. 22.95 (*0-7619-9116-6*) AltaMira Pr.
Nelson, Sarah M., ed. The Archaeology of Northeast China: Beyond the Great Wall. LC 94-9966. (Illus.). 288p. (C). (gr. 13). 1995. 85.00 (*0-415-11755-0*, B4521) Routledge.

Nelson, Sarah M. & Kehoe, Alice B., eds. Powers of Observation: Alternative Views in Archeology. 1990. write for info. (0-913167-42-8) Am Anthro Assn.

Nelson, Scott. No Experience Necessary. LC 90-60085. 1990. pap. 12.95 (0-916990-25-7) META Pubns.

Nelson, Scott A. The Discourses of Algernon Sidney, Vol. 24, No. 45. LC 91-58939. 176p. 1993. 33.50 (0-8386-3438-9) Fairleigh Dickinson.

Nelson, Scott R. Iron Confederacies: Southern Railways, Klan Violence & Reconstruction. LC 98-41228. (Illus.). 272p. 1999. pap. 18.95 (0-8078-4803-4); lib. bdg. 39.95 (0-8078-2476-3) U of NC Pr.

Nelson, Sean, jt. auth. see Grubbs, John.

Nelson, Sean M., jt. auth. see Grubbs, John R.

Nelson, Sharlene. Mount St. Helens National Volcanic Monument. (True Bks.). (J). 1998. pap. text 6.95 (0-516-26269-6) Childrens.

— Olympic National Park. (True Bks.). (J). 1998. pap. text 6.95 (0-516-26271-8) Childrens.

***Nelson, Sharlene.** Umbrella Guide to California Lighthouses. (Illus.). 2000. pap. 12.95 (0-945397-86-0) Epicenter Pr.

***Nelson, Sharlene & Nelson, Ted.** Brett Favre. (Sports Heroes Ser.). 48p. (YA). (gr. 5 up). 2000. lib. bdg. 21.26 (0-7368-0576-1, Capstone Bks) Capstone Pr.

Nelson, Sharlene & Nelson, Ted. Hawaii Volcanoes National Park. (True Bks.). (Illus.). 48p. (J). (gr. 3-5). 1998. pap. 6.95 (0-516-26378-1) Childrens.

— Mount Rainier National Park. DeCapua, Sarah, ed. (True Bks.). (Illus.). 48p. (J). 1998. pap. 6.95 (0-516-26381-1) Childrens.

— Unbrella Guide to Washington Lighthouses. 2nd rev. ed. Mattson, Sue, ed. (Umbrella Bks.: Vol. 11). 1998. pap. 12.95 (0-945397-70-4) Epicenter Pr.

Nelson, Sharlene P. William Boeing: Builder of Planes. LC 98-27760. (Community Builders Ser.). 48p. (J). (gr. 3-5). 1999. lib. bdg. 23.00 (0-516-20973-6) Childrens.

***Nelson, Sharlene P.** William Boeing: Builder of Planes. (Community Builders Ser.). (J). 2000. pap. text 6.95 (0-516-27012-5) Childrens.

Nelson, Sharlene P. & Nelson, Ted. Bull Whackers to Whistle Punks: Logging in the Old West. (First Bks.). (Illus.). 64p. (J). (gr. 4-6). 1996. lib. bdg. 22.00 (0-531-20228-3) Watts.

— Umbrella Guide to California Lighthouses. Olson, B. G., ed. (Umbrella Guides Ser.). (Illus.). 192p. (Orig.). 1993. pap. 12.95 (0-945397-21-6, Umbrella Bks) Epicenter Pr.

— Umbrella Guide to Exploring the Columbia-Snake River Inland Waterway: By River & by Road. (Umbrella Guides Ser.). (Illus.). 160p. (Orig.). (C). 1997. pap. 12.95 (0-945397-58-5, Umbrella Bks) Epicenter Pr.

— Umbrella Guide to Oregon Lighthouses. (Illus.). 128p. 1994. pap. 10.95 (0-945397-27-5, Umbrella Bks) Epicenter Pr.

Nelson, Sharlene P. & Nelson, Ted W. Hawaii Volcanoes National Park. LC 97-8232. (True Bks.). (Illus.). 48p. (J). (gr. 2-4). 1998. 21.00 (0-516-20623-0) Childrens.

— Mount Rainier National Park. LC 97-8233. (True Bks.). (Illus.). 48p. (J). (gr. 2-4). 1998. 21.00 (0-516-20624-9) Childrens.

— Mount St. Helens National Volcanic Monument. LC 96-46738. (True Bk.). (J). 1997. lib. bdg. 21.00 (0-516-20444-0) Childrens.

— Olympic National Park. LC 96-39888. (True Bk.). (J). 1997. lib. bdg. 21.00 (0-516-20446-7) Childrens.

Nelson, Sharon, jt. auth. see Nelson, Dick.

Nelson, Sharon R., jt. auth. see Reed, Kathlyn L.

Nelson, Shawn. The Easiest Guide to Exercise & Diet...Ever. 90p. (Orig.). 1997. mass mkt. 10.95 (0-9658265-0-3) Schooner Publ.

Nelson, Sheila, jt. auth. see Nelson, Rick.

Nelson, Sherry & Shaw, Jackie. You Can Paint Anything in Oils or Acrylics. (Illus.). 32p. (Orig.). 1987. pap. 7.95 (0-941284-38-7) J Shaw Studio.

***Nelson, Sherry C.** Painting Flowers from A to Z. LC 99-55967. (Illus.). 144p. 2000. pap. 24.99 (0-89134-938-3, North Lght Bks) F & W Pubns Inc.

Nelson, Sherry C. Painting Garden Birds with Sherry C. Nelson. LC 97-36341. (Illus.). 128p. 1998. pap. 24.99 (0-89134-771-2, North Lght Bks) F & W Pubns Inc.

Nelson, Sigurd, et al, eds. Veterans' Employment & Training: Services Provided by Labor Department Programs. (Illus.). 80p. (C). 1999. pap. text 20.00 (0-7881-7692-7) DIANE Pub.

***Nelson, Sonja.** Rhododendrons in the Landscape. LC 99-31316. (Illus.). 255p. 2000. 29.95 (0-88192-440-7) Timber.

Nelson, Sonya & Jackson, Melody, eds. 18 Kids & a Mule Named Tom: The Nelson Family Stories. 100p. 1997. pap. 10.00 (1-886583-21-8) SeaStar Pub.

Nelson, Stacey. The Destiny of America & the Universal Law of Cause & Effect. 80p. 1998. pap. 7.40 (0-9663941-0-0) Flame of Freedom.

Nelson-Stafford, Barbara. From Kitchen to Consumer: An Entrepreneur's Guide to Commercial Food Production. (Illus.). 343p. (C). 1991. pap. text 37.00 (0-12-662770-3) Acad Pr.

Nelson, Stanley. The Brooklyn Book of the Dead. 108p. 1971. pap. 10.00 (0-912292-22-9) Smith.

— The Brooklyn Book of the Dead. deluxe limited ed. 108p. 1971. 50.00 (1-882986-01-6) Smith.

— Driftin on a Nightriff. (Illus.). 24p. (Orig.). 1988. pap. 3.50 (0-945085-04-4) Sub Rosa.

— Immigrant, Bk. I. 84p. 1990. pap. 9.95 (0-913559-14-8) Birch Brook Pr.

— Immigrant, Bk. II. 112p. 1993. pap. 11.95 (0-913559-21-0) Birch Brook Pr.

— Immigrant, Bk. III. 1996. pap. 12.50 (0-913559-31-8) Birch Brook Pr.

— Immigrant, Bk. IV. 1998. pap. 13.00 (0-913559-42-3) Birch Brook Pr.

— Nightriffer. (Illus.). 108p. 1988. pap. 5.95 (0-913559-02-4) Birch Brook Pr.

— Nightriffer. deluxe ed. (Illus.). 108p. 1988. pap. 30.00 (0-913559-01-6) Birch Brook Pr.

— One Hundred One Fragments of a Prayer. Gauthier, Guy, ed. (Midnight Sun Ser.). (Illus.). 1979. 2.00 (0-935292-00-4) Midnight Sun.

— The Travels of Ben Sira. LC 77-82687. 70p. 1978. pap. 10.00 (0-912292-44-X) Smith.

— The Unknowable Light of the Alien. LC 80-53431. 180p. 1981. pap. 10.00 (0-912292-65-2) Smith.

Nelson, Stanley, ed. The Scene 4. LC 77-70415. (Scene Award Ser.). (Illus.). 272p. 1977. pap. 8.00 (0-912292-42-3) Smith.

— The Scene 1. LC 72-89382. (Scene Award Ser.). 212p. 1972. pap. 8.00 (0-912292-27-X) Smith.

— The Scene 3. LC 72-89382. (Scene Award Ser.). 196p. 1975. pap. 8.00 (0-912292-38-5) Smith.

— The Scene 2. LC 70-94633. (Scene Award Ser.). 192p. 1974. pap. 8.00 (0-912292-34-2) Smith.

Nelson, Stephanie. God & the Land: The Metaphysics of Farming in Hesiod & Vergil. Grene, David, tr. 272p. 1998. text 55.00 (0-19-511740-9) OUP.

Nelson, Stephen. Microsoft Frontpage 98 at a Glance. LC 97-33676. 288p. 1997. pap. text 16.99 (1-57231-637-3) Microsoft.

— Microsoft Frontpage 98 Step by Step. LC 97-37380. 352p. 1997. pap. text 29.99 incl. cd-rom (1-57231-636-5) Microsoft.

— Microsoft Money 98 at a Glance. LC 97-29787. 352p. 1997. pap. 16.99 (1-57231-639-X) Microsoft.

— Office 97 for Busy People. LC 97-128635. 304p. 1997. pap. text 24.99 (0-07-882280-7) Osborne-McGraw.

— Only a Paper Moon: The Theatre of Billy Rose. Brockett, Oscar G., ed. LC 87-5001. (Theater & Dramatic Studies: No. 42). 183p. reprint ed. 56.80 (0-8357-1796-8, 207074600004) Bks Demand.

— Quickbooks 5 for Dummies. 3rd ed. LC 96-77701. (Illus.). 384p. 1997. pap. 19.99 (0-7645-0043-0) IDG Bks.

— Quickbooks 4 for Dummies. 2nd ed. 384p. 1993. pap. 19.99 (1-56884-947-8) IDG Bks.

— Windows NT for Busy People. LC 97-138983. 304p. 1996. pap. text 22.95 (0-07-882254-8) Osborne-McGraw.

— The World Wide Web for Busy People: Surf the Web without Drowning in Information Overload. LC 96-223114. (Busy People Bks.). 304p. 1996. pap. text 22.95 (0-07-882244-0) Osborne-McGraw.

Nelson, Stephen & Weverka, Peter. Office 2000 for Busy People. 305p. 1999. pap. 19.99 (0-07-211857-1) McGraw.

Nelson, Stephen, jt. auth. see Heady, Christy.

Nelson, Stephen D., et al, eds. AAAS Science & Technology Policy Yearbook, 1992. 400p. 1993. pap. 19.95 (0-87168-503-5, 92-24S) AAAS.

***Nelson, Stephen James.** Leaders in the Crucible: The Moral Voice of College Presidents. LC 00-20485. 250p. 2000. 61.00 (0-89789-742-0, H742, Bergin & Garvey) Greenwood.

Nelson, Stephen L. Excel 4 pour Windows Memopoche. 250p. 1993. pap. 32.95 (0-7859-5642-5, 2736110080) Fr & Eur.

***Nelson, Stephen L.** Field Guide to Microsoft Access for Windows 95. (Field Guide Ser.). 2000. pap. 7.99 (0-7356-1057-6) Microsoft.

— Field Guide to Microsoft Excel for Windows 95. (Field Guide Ser.). (Illus.). 2000. pap. 7.99 (0-7356-1055-X) Microsoft.

— Field Guide to Microsoft Exchange. (Field Guide Ser.). 2000. pap. 7.99 (0-7356-1058-4) Microsoft.

— Field Guide to Microsoft PowerPoint for Windows 95. (Field Guide Ser.). (Illus.). 2000. pap. 7.99 (0-7356-1056-8) Microsoft.

— Field Guide to Microsoft Word for Windows 95. (Field Guide Ser.). (Illus.). 2000. pap. text 7.99 (0-7356-1054-1) Microsoft.

— Field Guide to Windows 95. 2nd ed. (Field Guide Ser.). (Illus.). 2000. pap. text 7.99 (0-7356-1053-3) Microsoft.

Nelson, Stephen L. Forever Friends. (Pop-Up Victorian Bks.). 1994. 4.99 (0-8407-6959-8) Nelson.

— Friendship Garden: Victoria Pop-Up. 1994. 4.99 (0-8407-6960-1) Nelson.

— Furry Friends: Victorian Pop-Up. 1994. 4.99 (0-8407-6956-3) Nelson.

— The Heritage of Great Evangelical Teaching. 1200p. 1996. 29.99 (0-7852-1161-6) Nelson.

***Nelson, Stephen L.** Mastering Quicken 2000. 3rd ed. 672p. 1999. pap. 29.99 (0-7821-2596-4) Sybex.

Nelson, Stephen L. MBA's Guide to Microsoft Excel 2000: The Essential Reference for Business Professionals. (Illus.). 512p. 1999. pap. 39.99 (0-9672981-0-5) Redmond Technology Pr.

***Nelson, Stephen L.** Microsoft Access 97 Field Guide. (Field Guide Ser.). (Illus.). 2000. pap. 7.99 (0-7356-1062-2) Microsoft.

— Microsoft Excel 97 Field Guide. (Field Guide Ser.). (Illus.). 2000. pap. 7.99 (0-7356-1060-6) Microsoft.

Nelson, Stephen L. Microsoft Exchange 5.0 Field Guide. LC 97-26072. 192p. 1997. 9.99 (1-57231-705-1) Microsoft.

— Microsoft Frontpage 97 at a Glance. LC 96-29987. (Field Guide Ser.). 288p. 1997. pap. 16.99 (1-57231-573-3) Microsoft.

— Microsoft FrontPage 2000 at a Glance. LC 98-43586. (At A Glance Ser.). (Illus.). 211p. 1999. pap. 19.99 (1-57231-951-8) Microsoft.

***Nelson, Stephen L.** Microsoft Help Desk for Microsoft Office 2000: Support Solutions Direct from Microsoft. LC 99-56530. (EU-Help Desk Ser.). (Illus.). 2000. pap. 39.99 (0-7356-0850-4) Microsoft.

— Microsoft Help Desk for Microsoft Windows 98. (Help Desk Ser.). (Illus.). 2000. pap. 39.99 (0-7356-1096-7) Microsoft.

Nelson, Stephen L. Microsoft Internet Explorer 4 Field Guide. LC 97-42102. 192p. pap. write for info. (1-57231-741-8) Microsoft.

— Microsoft Money 99 at a Glance. LC 98-29960. 224p. 1998. pap. 16.99 (1-57231-993-3) Microsoft.

***Nelson, Stephen L.** Microsoft Money 99 at a Glance. (Illus.). 205p. 1999. pap. write for info. (0-7356-0696-X) Microsoft.

— Microsoft Money 2000 at a Glance. LC 99-33880. (At a Glance Ser.). 1999. pap. text 19.99 (0-7356-0811-3) Microsoft.

Nelson, Stephen L. Microsoft Outlook 98 at a Glance: The Easy Way to Find the Right Answers, Right Now. LC 97-52075. (At A Glance Ser.). 224p. 16.99 (1-57231-719-1) Microsoft.

***Nelson, Stephen L.** Microsoft Outlook 98 Field Guide. (Field Guide Ser.). (Illus.). 2000. pap. 7.99 (0-7356-1065-7) Microsoft.

Nelson, Stephen L. Microsoft Outlook 97 at a Glance. LC 97-7750. (Field Guide Ser.). 208p. 16.99 (1-57231-390-0) Microsoft.

***Nelson, Stephen L.** Microsoft Outlook 97 Field Guide. (Field Guide Ser.). (Illus.). 2000. pap. text 7.99 (0-7356-1063-0) Microsoft.

Nelson, Stephen L. Microsoft Outlook 2000 at a Glance. LC 98-43579. 208p. 1999. pap. 19.99 (1-57231-948-8) Microsoft.

***Nelson, Stephen L.** Microsoft Pocket Guide to Microsoft Access 2000. (Microsoft Pocket Guides Ser.). 2000. pap. 7.99 (0-7356-1066-5) Microsoft.

— Microsoft Pocket Guide to Microsoft Excel 2000. (Pocket Guides Ser.). (Illus.). 2000. pap. 7.99 (0-7356-1067-3) Microsoft.

— Microsoft Pocket Guide to Microsoft Internet Explorer 5. (Pocket Guides Ser.). (Illus.). 2000. pap. 7.99 (0-7356-1071-1) Microsoft.

— Microsoft Pocket Guide to Microsoft Outlook 2000. (Pocket Guides Ser.). (Illus.). 2000. pap. 7.99 (0-7356-1070-3) Microsoft.

— Microsoft Pocket Guide to Microsoft PowerPoint 2000. (Pocket Guides Ser.). (Illus.). 2000. pap. 7.99 (0-7356-1068-1) Microsoft.

Nelson, Stephen L. Microsoft Pocket Guide To Microsoft Windows **Canceled 2000 Professional. (C). (gr. 8). 1999. pap. 12.99 (1-57231-844-9) Little.

***Nelson, Stephen L.** Microsoft Pocket Guide to Microsoft Word 2000. (Pocket Guides Ser.). (Illus.). 2000. pap. 7.99 (0-7356-1069-X) Microsoft.

Nelson, Stephen L. Microsoft PowerPoint 97 Field Guide. LC 96-36634. 192p. pap. 9.95 (1-57231-327-7) Microsoft.

***Nelson, Stephen L.** Microsoft PowerPoint 97 Field Guide. (Field Guide Ser.). 2000. pap. 7.99 (0-7356-1061-4) Microsoft.

— Microsoft Windows 98 Field Guide. (Field Guide Ser.). (Illus.). 2000. pap. text 7.99 (0-7356-1064-9) Microsoft.

— Microsoft Word 97 Field Guide. (Field Guide Ser.). (Illus.). 2000. pap. 7.99 (0-7356-1059-2) Microsoft.

Nelson, Stephen L. The Millionaire Kit: Surprisingly Simple Strategies for Building Real Wealth. LC 98-16182. 224p. 1998. pap. 29.95 (0-8129-3004-5, Times Bks) Crown Pub Group.

— Playtime Friends: Victorian Pop-Up. 1994. 4.99 (0-8407-6957-1) Nelson.

— QuickBooks 6 for Dummies. (For Dummies Ser.). 384p. 1998. pap. 19.99 (0-7645-0330-8) IDG Bks.

***Nelson, Stephen L.** QuickBooks X for Dummies. (For Dummies Ser.). (Illus.). 384p. 2000. pap. 19.99 (0-7645-0665-X) IDG Bks.

Nelson, Stephen L. Quicken 98 for Windows for Dummies. 5th ed. LC 97-80308. 400p. 1997. pap. 19.99 (0-7645-0243-3) IDG Bks.

— Quicken 99 for Dummies. LC HG179.N42658 1998. (For Dummies Ser.). 408p. 1998. pap. 19.99 (0-7645-0432-0) IDG Bks.

***Nelson, Stephen L.** Quicken X for Dummies. 408p. 1999. pap. 19.99 (0-7645-0607-2) IDG Bks.

Nelson, Stephen L. Small Business Windows 98 for Dummies. LC HF5548.4.M527N453. (For Dummies Ser.). 368p. 1998. 24.99 incl. cd-rom (0-7645-0425-8) IDG Bks.

— Thing of Beauty. (Flower Pop-up Gift Bks.). 1994. 5.99 (0-8407-6964-4) Nelson.

***Nelson, Stephen L., compiled by.** Microsoft Help Desk for Microsoft Windows NT Workstation 4.0. LC 99-21355. (Illus.). 1116p. 2000. pap. 39.99 (0-7356-1097-5) Microsoft.

***Nelson, Stephen L. & Buschmohle, Michael.** Effective Executive's Guide to PowerPoint 2000: The Seven Steps for Creating High-Value, High-Impact PowerPoint Presentations. 288p. 2000. pap. 24.95 (0-9672981-4-8) Redmond Technology Pr.

***Nelson, Stephen L. & Coleman, Pat.** Effective Executive's Guide to the Internet: The Seven Core Skills Required to Turn the Internet into a Business. 288p. 2001. pap. 24.95 (0-9672981-7-2) Redmond Technology Pr.

— Effective Executive's Guide to Windows 2000: The Seven Core Skills Required to Turn Windows 2000 Professional. 288p. 2000. pap. 24.95 (0-9672981-8-0) Redmond Technology Pr.

***Nelson, Stephen L. & Gerend, Jason.** Effective Executive's Guide to Dreamweaver Web Sites: The Seven Steps for Designing, Building & Managing Dreamweaver Web Sites. 320p. 2000. pap. 24.95 (0-9672981-9-9) Redmond Technology Pr.

— Effective Executive's Guide to FrontPage Web Sites: The Eight Steps for Designing, Building & Managing FrontPage Web Sites. 288p. 2000. pap. 24.95 (0-9672981-3-X) Redmond Technology Pr.

***Nelson, Stephen L. & Maguiness, David.** Ask the Expert Guide to Microsoft Money 2001: Expert Help for Using Microsoft Money at Home, for Investments, or in a Small Business. 304p. 2000. pap. 19.95 (0-9672981-2-1, Pub. by Redmond Technology Pr) IPG Chicago.

Nelson, Stephen L. & Weverka, Peter. Microsoft Office 97: The Complete Reference. LC 97-208953. 967p. 1997. pap., pap. text 39.99 incl. cd-rom (0-07-882338-2) Osborne-McGraw.

— Office 2000: The Complete Reference. LC 99-228522. (The Complete Reference Ser.). (Illus.). 1040p. 1999. pap. 39.99 incl. audio compact disk (0-07-211859-8) Osborne-McGraw.

Nelson, Stephen L., et al. Effective Executive's Guide to Project 2000: The Eight Steps for Using Microsoft Project 2000 to Organize, Manage & Finish Critically Important Projects. (Illus.). 304p. 2000. pap. 24.95 (0-9672981-1-3) Redmond Technology Pr.

***Nelson, Stephen L., et al.** MBA's Guide to the Internet: The Essential Internet Reference for Business Professionals. 624p. 2000. pap. 39.95 (0-9672981-6-4) Redmond Technology Pr.

— MBA's Guide to Windows 2000: The Essential Windows 2000 Reference for Business Professionals. 624p. 2000. pap. 39.95 (0-9672981-5-6) Redmond Technology Pr.

Nelson, Stephen T., et al. New 40Ar/39Ar Ages of Intrusive Rocks from the Henry & La Sal Mountains, Utah. (Miscellaneous Publications: 92-2). (Illus.). 24p. 1992. pap. 4.50 (1-55791-318-8, MP-92-2) Utah Geological Survey.

Nelson, Steve. Excel Power Presentations: High-Impact Graphics That Make You Look Good. LC 92-36799. 320p. 1992. pap. 34.95 incl. disk (0-201-63294-2) Addison-Wesley.

— Mastering Quicken 99. LC 98-87089. (Mastering Ser.). (Illus.). 736p. 1998. pap. 34.99 (0-7821-2359-7) Sybex.

***Nelson, Steve & Martin, Thomas R., eds.** Cytokines in Pulmonary Disease: Infection & Inflammation. (Lung Biology in Health & Disease Ser.: Vol. 141). 598p. 2000. 195.00 (0-8247-1931-X) Dekker.

Nelson, Steve & Rollins, Jack. Frosty the Snowman: Book & Cookie Cutter Set. (Illus.). 16p. (J). (ps-2). 1993. pap. 3.95 (0-590-69016-7, Cartwheel) Scholastic Inc.

Nelson, Steve, et al. Steve Nelson, American Radical. LC 80-26528. (Series in Social & Labor History). (Illus.). 475p. 1992. pap. 19.95 (0-8229-5471-0) U of Pittsburgh Pr.

Nelson, Steven. Guinea Pigs As a New Pet. (Illus.). 64p. (Orig.). 1990. pap. 6.95 (0-86622-613-3, TU-006) TFH Pubns.

Nelson, Steven L. QR-Quicken 4 for Windows for Dummies. 224p. 1994. spiral bd. 9.95 (1-56884-950-8) IDG Bks.

— Quickbooks 3 for Dummies. LC 94-79876. 384p. 1993. pap. 19.99 (1-56884-227-9) IDG Bks.

— Quicken 8 for DOS for Dummies. 2nd ed. LC 94-78901. 352p. 1994. pap. 19.95 (1-56884-210-4) IDG Bks.

— Quicken 5 for MACs for Dummies. LC 94-78902. 360p. 1995. pap. 19.95 (1-56884-211-2) IDG Bks.

— Quicken 5 for Windows for Dummies Quick Reference. 2nd ed. 196p. 1995. spiral bd. 9.99 (1-56884-963-X) IDG Bks.

— Quicken 5 for Windows for Dummies. 3rd ed. 408p. 1995. pap. 19.99 (1-56884-923-0) IDG Bks.

— Quicken for DOS for Dummies. (Illus.). 300p. 1994. pap. 16.95 (1-56884-006-3) IDG Bks.

— Quicken 4 for Windows for Dummies. 2nd ed. LC 95-128430. 352p. 1994. pap. 19.95 (1-56884-209-0) IDG Bks.

— Quicken 6 for Macs for Dummies. 2nd ed. 384p. 1995. pap. 19.99 (1-56884-924-9) IDG Bks.

— Quicken 3 for Windows Made Easy. (Illus.). 300p. 1993. pap. 16.95 (1-56884-005-5) IDG Bks.

Nelson, Susan & Strobel, Gary. Guide to Owning a Ragdoll Cat. (Illus.). 64p. 1997. pap. 6.95 (0-7938-2164-9, RE410) TFH Pubns.

Nelson, Susan C., jt. auth. see Breneman, David.

Nelson, Susan L. Healing the Broken Heart: Sin, Alienation, & the Gift of Grace. LC 96-36859. 136p. (Orig.). 1997. pap. 14.99 (0-8272-1427-8) Chalice Pr.

Nelson, Susan R., ed. Groundworks: North American Underground Projects, 1980-1989. (Illus.). (Orig.). 1989. pap. 45.00 (0-9622383-0-9) AUSA.

Nelson, Suzann, ed. see Martin, Janet L.

Nelson, Suzann J. & Martin, Janet L. Is It Too Windy Back There, Then? 1996. pap. 7.95 (1-886627-01-0, Caragana Pr) Redbird Prods.

Nelson, Suzann J., jt. auth. see Martin, Janet L.

Nelson, Suzann Johnson, jt. auth. see Martin, Janet Letnes.

Nelson, Suzanne, ed. Fast, Fun & Fabulous Quilts: 30 Terrific Projects from the Country's Most Creative Designers. LC 95-38002. (Illus.). 256p. 1996. text 27.95 (0-87596-709-4) Rodale Pr Inc.

***Nelson, Suzanne, ed.** Fast, Fun & Fabulous Quilts: 30 Terrific Projects from the Country's Most Creative Designers. (Illus.). 256p. 2000. pap. 18.95 (1-57954-297-2) Rodale Pr Inc.

***Nelson, Sylvia.** Island Fisherman & Their Boats. (Illus.). 27p. 1999. pap. 2.00 (1-890352-07-1) Jackson Harbor.

Nelson, Sylvia & Berquist, Goodwin F., eds. Island Schools Then & Now. LC 98-65762. (Illus.). 78p. 1998. pap. 6.95 (1-890352-04-7) Jackson Harbor.

Nelson, T. G. Children, Parents, & the Rise of the Novel. LC 94-47663. 256p. 1995. 37.50 (0-87413-558-3) U Delaware Pr.

Nelson, T. J. & Wullert, J. R., II. Electronic Information Display Technologies. LC 96-25998. 250p. 1997. text 53.00 (981-02-1301-8) World Scientific Pub.

Nelson, T. P. & Wevill, S. L. Alternative Formulations & Packaging to Reduce Use of Chlorofluorocarbons. 361p. 1998. 109.00 (0-8155-1257-0) Noyes.

An Asterisk (*) at the beginning of an entry indicates that the title is appearing for the first time.

Nelson, Ted. The Nature of Kensington: A Photographic Portrayal. LC 98-89962. (Illus.). 112p. 1999. 32.00 (*0-9669880-0-0*) Austin-Carol.

Nelson, Ted, et al, eds. Legal & Regulatory Affairs Manual. 1982. pap. 15.00 (*0-686-37426-6*) Coun NY Law.

Nelson, Ted, jt. auth. see Nelson, Sharlene.

Nelson, Ted, jt. auth. see Nelson, Sharlene P.

Nelson, Ted W., jt. auth. see Nelson, Sharlene P.

Nelson, Teresa. Cherished Weddings: 17 Floral Projects for Two Romantic Weddings LC 92-149723. 28p. 1992. write for info. (*1-56231-067-4*) Hot off Pr.

— Special Occasions. (Illus.). 28p. 1985. pap. 5.95 (*0-933491-02-6*) Hot off Pr.

Nelson, Teresa, ed. Creative Wedding Decorations You Can Make. LC 97-49012. (Illus.). 128p. 1998. pap. 19.99 (*1-55870-484-1*, Betrwy Bks) F & W Pubns Inc.

Nelson, Terri. On the Way to Finding Your Soulmate, Vol. 1. Stone, Victorya, ed. LC 97-73855. 226p. 1997. pap. 19.95 (*0-9659600-3-X*) Above The Din.

Nelson, Thelma R. Hughes of North Carolina Ancestral Journal of the Hughes Families & Their Interlinks. (Illus.). 380p. 1994. reprint ed. pap. 57.00 (*0-8328-4081-5*); reprint ed. lib. bdg. 67.00 (*0-8328-4080-7*) Higginson Bk Co.

Nelson, Theodor H. Literary Machines 93.1. rev. ed. (Illus.). 286p. 1992. pap. 25.00 (*0-89347-062-7*) Mindful Pr.

Nelson, Theresa. And One for All. 192p. (J). (gr. 4-7). 1991. pap. 4.50 (*0-440-40456-8*) Dell.

— And One for All. LC 88-22490. 192p. (J). (gr. 6-8). 1989. 16.95 (*0-531-05804-2*) Orchard Bks Watts.

— And One for All. 1991. 9.09 (*0-606-04866-9*, Pub. by Turtleback) Demco.

— The Beggars' Ride. LC 90-52515. 256p. (YA). (gr. 6 up). 1992. 16.95 (*0-531-05896-4*) Orchard Bks Watts.

— The Beggars' Ride. LC 90-52515. 256p. (YA). (gr. 7 up). 1992. lib. bdg. 17.99 (*0-531-08496-5*) Orchard Bks Watts.

— Earthshine. (YA). (gr. 6 up). 1995. mass mkt. 5.99 (*0-440-91082-X*) BDD Bks Young Read.

— Earthshine. 192p. (YA). (gr. 6 up). 1996. mass mkt. 4.99 (*0-440-21989-2*) Dell.

— Earthshine. LC 94-8793. 192p. (YA). (gr. 6 up). 1994. 16.95 (*0-531-06867-6*); lib. bdg. 17.99 (*0-531-08717-4*) Orchard Bks Watts.

Nelson, Theresa. Earthshine: A Novel. LC 94-8793. (J). 1996. 9.60 (*0-606-09222-6*, Pub. by Turtleback) Demco.

Nelson, Theresa. The Empress of Elsewhere. LC 98-13209. 288p. (J). (gr. 4-8). 1998. 17.95 (*0-7894-2498-3*) DK Pub Inc.

***Nelson, Theresa.** Empress of Elsewhere. (Illus.). 288p. (J). (gr. 5-9). 2000. pap. 5.99 (*0-14-130813-3*, PuffinBks) Peng Put Young Read.

— Empress of Elsewhere. (Illus.). (J). 2000. 11.34 (*0-606-18836-3*) Turtleback.

Nelson, Theresa, ed. Grand Traverse Commerce Information Guidebook: Resources for Business Start-ups, Relocations, Expansions. 240p. (Orig.). 1997. pap. 10.00 (*1-890587-01-X*) Jenkins Group Inc.

Nelson, Theron R. & Potter, Thomas A. Real Estate Law Hc. Burvikovs, ed. LC 93-36562. (Paralegal). 600p. (C). 1994. mass mkt. 50.25 (*0-314-02824-2*) West Pub.

Nelson, Thomas. Daily Guideposts: 1990. large type ed. 1989. 9.95 (*0-317-02410-8*) Guideposts.

***Nelson, Thomas.** Three-Dimensional Ultrasound. LC 98-32024. 252p. 1999. write for info. (*0-7817-1997-6*) Lppncott W & W.

Nelson, Thomas A., jt. auth. see Cirrincione, Joseph A.

Nelson, Thomas A., jt. auth. see Schouppe, F. X.

Nelson, Thomas Allen. Kubrick: Inside a Film Artist's Maze. LC 80-8845. (Illus.). 288p. 1982. pap. 13.95 (*0-253-20283-3*, MB-283) Ind U Pr.

***Nelson, Thomas Allen.** Kubrick: Inside a Film Artist's Maze. expanded ed. LC 99-87689. (Illus.). 340p. 2000. pap. 14.95 (*0-253-21390-8*); lib. bdg. 39.95 (*0-253-33742-9*) Ind U Pr.

Nelson, Thomas Allen. Shakespeare's Comic Theory: A Study of Art & Artifice in the Last Plays. (De Proprietatibus Litterarum, Ser. Practica: No. 57). 95p. (Orig.). 1972. text 13.85 (*3-10-800281-3*) Mouton.

Nelson, Thomas Allen, jt. auth. see Cirrincione, J. A.

Nelson, Thomas C. It's Your Choice: The Practical Guide to Planning a Funeral. LC 81-21362. 1982. pap. 4.95 (*0-673-24802-X*) Addison-Wesley.

***Nelson, Thomas Laurence.** Dance Book 2001, 1 vol. 2nd rev. ed. Orig. Title: Dance Handbook. (Illus.). 1000p. 2000. 180.00 (*1-930475-01-2*) CoupleDanceWorld.

— Dance Handbook: A Glossary for Coupledancers. xxii, 561p. 2000. 180.00 (*1-930475-00-4*) CoupleDanceWorld.

Nelson, Thomas O., jt. ed. see Mazzoni, Giuliana.

Nelson, Thorana S. & Trepper, Terry S., eds. 101 Interventions in Family Therapy. 428p. 1993. pap. 24.95 (*1-56024-193-4*); lib. bdg. 54.95 (*0-86656-902-2*) Haworth Pr.

— 101 More Interventions in Family Therapy. LC 97-51448. (Illus.). 511p. (C). 1998. 69.96 (*0-7890-0058-X*); pap. 39.95 (*0-7890-0570-0*) Haworth Pr.

Nelson, Tim B. Eye of God. LC 99-205948. 1997. pap. 5.25 (*0-8222-1575-6*) Dramatists Play.

— The Grey Zone. LC 98-146947. 1998. pap. 5.25 (*0-8222-1574-8*) Dramatists Play.

Nelson, Tina & Lanza, Janet. An Illustrated Guide to Northeastern Forest Trees. (Marginal Media Bioguide Ser.: No. 4). (Illus.). 50p. (J). 1983. pap. 3.00 (*0-942788-11-7*) Iris Visual.

Nelson, Tom. Don't Just Say No: Daniel 1. (Inter Acta Ser.). (Illus.). 6p. (C). 1994. teacher ed., ring bd. 1.25 (*1-885702-77-9*, 741-052t, Inter Acta); student ed., ring bd. 3.25 (*1-885702-76-0*, 741-052s, Inter Acta) WSN Pr.

— Math in Geography. (Math Is Everywhere Ser.). (Illus.). 48p. (J). (gr. 4-6). 1994. pap. text, teacher ed. 6.45 (*1-55799-331-9*, EMC 115) Evan-Moor Edu Pubs.

— Mega-Choices. rev. ed. (Inter Acta Ser.). (Illus.). 6p. (C). 1996. teacher ed., ring bd. 1.25 (*1-57334-024-3*, 741-053t, Inter Acta); student ed., ring bd. 3.25 (*1-885702-86-8*, 741-053s, Inter Acta) WSN Pr.

Nelson, Tommy. The Big Picture: Understanding the Story of the Bible. 2nd rev. ed. 264p. 1999. pap. 13.99 (*1-928828-03-5*) Hudson Prods.

— The Book of Romance: What Solomon Says about Love, Sex & Intimacy. LC 98-8503. 224p. 1999. 14.99 (*0-7852-7471-5*) Nelson.

— The Song of Solomon Study Guide: A Study of Love, Sex, Marriage & Romance. 96p. 1999. pap., student ed. 5.95 (*1-928828-00-0*) Hudson Prods.

Nelson, Tracy, ed. see Stafford, Deborah K. & Victory Press Pubns. Staff.

***Nelson, Trish.** My Name Is A: Meeting the Letters of the Alphabet. LC 99-93419. (Illus.). 32p. (J). (ps-1). 1999. pap. 6.95 (*0-9673943-0-9*) Nelson Bldg Blk.

Nelson, Turnel. Church: A Mystery Revealed. 1995. pap. 7.95 (*1-56229-431-8*) Pneuma Life Pub.

Nelson U. K. Staff. Basic English for Arabs. 1991. pap. text, student ed. write for info. (*0-17-556030-7*) Addison-Wesley.

— Two Roman Stories. 1991. pap. text. write for info. (*0-17-556646-1*) Addison-Wesley.

Nelson, Vaunda M. Beyond Mayfield. LC 98-35692. (J). (gr. 5 up). 1999. 15.99 (*0-399-23355-5*, G P Putnam) Peng Put Young Read.

— Mayfield Crossing. LC 92-10564. 96p. (YA). (gr. 4-7). 1994. mass mkt. 4.50 (*0-380-72179-1*, Avon Bks) Morrow Avon.

— Mayfield Crossing. LC 92-10564. (Illus.). 96p. (J). (gr. 4-7). 1993. 14.95 (*0-399-22331-2*, G P Putnam) Peng Put Young Read.

— Mayfield Crossing. (J). 1993. 9.70 (*0-606-05922-9*, Pub. by Turtleback) Demco.

Nelson, Vaunda M. & Burgender, Anne S. Zoolutions: A Mathematical Expedition with Topics for Grades 4 Through 8. (School Library Media Ser.: Vol. 6). 120p. 1996. pap. 24.50 (*0-8108-3075-2*) Scarecrow.

Nelson, Vaunda Micheaux. Possibles. LC 94-44386. (Illus.). 192p. (J). (gr. 5-8). 1997. pap. 5.99 (*0-698-11551-1*, PapStar) Peng Put Young Read.

Nelson, Vaunda Micheaux. Possibles. (J). 1997. 11.05 (*0-606-10989-7*, Pub. by Turtleback) Demco.

Nelson, Velda, ed. see Beerman, Merlin.

Nelson, Victor P., et al. Digital Logic Circuit Analysis & Design. LC 94-35122. 896p. (C). 1995. 100.00 (*0-13-463894-8*) P-H.

Nelson, Victoria. On Writer's Block: Removing the Barriers to Creativity. LC 92-38147. 192p. 1993. pap. 14.00 (*0-395-64727-4*) HM.

Nelson, Vincent. Entertainment Law, Vol. 1. 1994. 112.00 (*0-421-50150-2*, Pub. by Sweet & Maxwll) Gaunt.

Nelson, Vincent E. The Structural Geology of the Cache Creek Area, Gros Ventre Mountains, Wyoming. LC 43-15519. (Augustana College Library Publications: No. 18). 46p. 1942. pap. 6.00 (*0-910182-13-2*) Augustana Coll.

Nelson, Virginia. Learning to Listen in English. 144p. 1991. pap. 39.95 incl. audio (*0-8442-0689-X*, 0689X, Natl Textbk Co) NTC Contemp Pub Co.

— Learning to Listen in English: Content-Area Information & Skill-Building Activities on a Variety of Subjects. 1997. pap., teacher ed. 19.95 (*0-8442-0526-5*); pap., student ed., wbk. ed. 14.60 (*0-8442-0525-7*) NTC Contemp Pub Co.

— Listening to Communicate in English. 1997. pap. text. write for info. (*0-8442-0693-8*) NTC Contemp Pub Co.

— Listening to Communicate in English, Set. 176p. 1995. student ed. 39.95 incl. audio (*0-8442-0692-X*, Natl Textbk Co) NTC Contemp Pub Co.

— Listening to Communicate in English: 30 Engaging Conversations & Skill-Building Activities with Functional Goals. 1997. pap., teacher ed., wbk. ed. 19.95 (*0-8442-0530-3*); pap., student ed., wbk. ed. 14.60 (*0-8442-0528-1*) NTC Contemp Pub Co.

Nelson, Virginia, ed. Learning to Listen in English: Content-Area Information & Skill-Building Activities on a Variety of Subjects. 1997. pap., student ed. 5.25 (*0-8442-0527-3*) NTC Contemp Pub Co.

Nelson, Virginia D. There's a Cow in the Kitchen: A Guide to Cooking with Powdered Milk. rev. ed. (Illus.). 87p. 1999. spiral bd. 6.95 (*0-9660284-8-1*) Nelson Bk.

Nelson, Vivian, jt. auth. see Roller, Bill.

Nelson, W. Checklist of the Issues of the Press of New Jersey, 1723-1800. 1969. 5.00 (*0-87556-223-X*) Saifer.

— Life of Sir George by Alexander Barclay. (EETS Original Ser.: Vol. 230). 1963. reprint ed. 30.00 (*0-19-722230-7*, Pub. by EETS) Boydell & Brewer.

Nelson, W. Modern Techniques for Rapid Microbiological Analysis. 263p. 1991. 99.95 (*0-471-18777-1*, Wiley-VCH) Wiley.

Nelson, W. Dale. The President Is at Camp David. LC 94-37083. (Illus.). 260p. 1995. 29.95 (*0-8156-0318-5*) Syracuse U Pr.

***Nelson, W. Dale.** The President Is at Camp David. (Illus.). 344p. 2000. pap. 18.95 (*0-8156-0628-1*) Syracuse U Pr.

— Who Speaks for the President? The White House Press Secretary from Cleveland to Clinton. LC 97-40236. 325p. (YA). (gr. 8 up). 1998. 29.95 (*0-8156-0514-5*) Syracuse U Pr.

***Nelson, W. Dale.** Who Speaks for the President? The White House Press Secretary from Cleveland to Clinton. (Illus.). 216p. 2000. pap. 16.95 (*0-8156-0632-X*) Syracuse U Pr.

Nelson, W. James, ed. Current Topics in Membranes, Vol. 4. 1996. text 85.00 (*0-12-153343-3*) Acad Pr.

Nelson, W. M., jt. auth. see Lee, Edward G.

Nelson, W. Michael, III & Finch, A. J., Jr. Cognitive-Behavioral Therapy for Aggressive Children: Therapist Manual. 72p. 1996. 13.00 (*1-888805-08-0*) Wrkbk Pubng.

— Keeping Your Cool: The Anger Management Workbook. 168p. 1996. wbk. ed. 22.95 (*1-888805-09-9*) Wrkbk Pubng.

— Keeping Your Cool Pt. 2: Additional Sessions for the Anger Management Workbook. 71p. 1996. wbk. ed. 16.95 (*1-888805-10-2*) Wrkbk Pubng.

Nelson, W. N. Illustrated Dictionary of the Bible: Diccionario Ilustrado de la Biblia. 10th ed. (SPA., Illus.). 735p. 1982. 59.95 (*0-8288-1204-7*, S34921) Fr & Eur.

Nelson, Waldo E., ed. see Behrman, Richard E., et al.

Nelson, Walter C. Home on the Range. LC 96-92788. (Illus.). 192p. (Orig.). 1998. pap. 12.95 (*0-9654298-0-6*) Pyramid FL.

***Nelson, Walter H.** Bikram's Beginning Yoga Class. rev. ed. LC 99-41849. 2000. pap. 16.95 (*1-58542-020-4*, Tarcher Putnam) Putnam Pub Group.

— Buddha: His Life & His Teaching. 160p. 2000. pap. 12.95 (*1-58542-001-8*, Tarcher Putnam) Putnam Pub Group.

Nelson, Walter H. Small Wonder: The Amazing Story of the Volkswagen Beetle. 2nd ed. LC 98-22447. (Illus.). 380p. 1998. pap. text 17.95 (*0-8376-0147-9*) Bentley Pubs.

Nelson, Walter R. History of Goshen. (Illus.). 471p. 1992. reprint ed. lib. bdg. 47.00 (*0-8328-0133-X*) Higginson Bk Co.

***Nelson, Warren.** A Ditch of Witches. LC 99-61576. (Illus.). 32p. (J). (gr. k-4). 1999. 16.95 (*0-9670683-0-4*) Bayfield St Pubg.

Nelson, Warren. T. C. Hammond. 178p. 1994. pap. 9.99 (*0-85151-672-6*) Banner of Truth.

Nelson, Warren L., et al. Always Bet on the Butcher: Warren Nelson & Casino Gaming, 1930s-1980s. LC 94-21183. (Illus.). 242p. 1994. 21.95 (*1-56475-368-9*) U NV Oral Hist.

Nelson, Wayne. Accelerated Testing: Statistical Models, Test Plans & Data Analysis. LC 89-24853. (Series in Probability & Mathematics). 616p. 1990. 175.00 (*0-471-52277-5*) Wiley.

— Applied Life Data Analysis. LC 81-14779. (Probability & Mathematical Statistics: Applied Probability & Statistics Section Ser.). 656p. 1982. 145.00 (*0-471-09458-7*, Wiley-Interscience) Wiley.

— How to Analyze Data with Simple Plots, Vol. 1. 38p. 1979. pap. 20.00 (*0-87389-011-6*, T3501) ASQ Qual Pr.

— How to Analyze Reliability Data, Vol. 6. 54p. 1983. pap. 21.00 (*0-87389-018-3*, T3506) ASQ Qual Pr.

Nelson, Wayne E. & Glass, Henry. International Playtime. 1992. pap. 22.99 (*0-86653-990-5*) Fearon Teacher Aids.

Nelson, Wendell. Of Stones, Steam & the Earth: The Pleasures & Meanings of a Sauna. (Illus.). 88p. (Orig.). 1993. pap. 9.95 (*0-9632975-3-8*) Sampo Pub.

Of Stones, Steam & the Earth: The Pleasures & Meanings of a Sauna. (Illus.). 88p. (Orig.). 1994. pap. 9.95 (*0-9632975-7-0*) Sampo Pub.

Nelson, Wendy, jt. auth. see Syracuse Language Systems Staff.

Nelson, Wesley W. The Art of Bridge Building. 1989. pap. 2.95 (*0-910452-69-5*) Covenant.

— God's Friends: Called to Believe & Belong. 1985. 15.95 (*0-910452-59-8*) Covenant.

Nelson-Weyh, Christie. Woodacre: A Novel. LC 99-192602. 258p. 1998. write for info. (*0-9654951-2-4*) Thumbprint CA.

Nelson, Wilfred H. Instrumental Methods for Rapid Microbiological Analysis. LC 85-15726. 219p. 1985. 60.00 (*0-89573-137-1*, Wiley-VCH) Wiley.

— Physical Methods for Microorganisms Detection. 176p. 1991. lib. bdg. 149.00 (*0-8493-4140-X*, QR69) CRC Pr.

Nelson, Wilfred H., ed. Modern Techniques for Rapid Microbial Analysis. (Illus.). xiv, 263p. 1991. 69.50 (*1-56081-001-7*, Wiley-VCH) Wiley.

Nelson, William. Documents Relating to the Colonial History of the State of New Jersey, Vol. XXIII Vol. XXIII: Calendar of New Jersey Wills, 1670-1730, Vol. 1. (Illus.). 662p. 1994. reprint ed. pap. text 42.00 (*1-55613-988-8*) Heritage Bk.

— Doremus: Genealogy of the Doremus Family in America, Descendants of Cornelis Doremus from Breskens & Middleburg, in Holland, Who Emigrated to America about 1685-6 & Settled at Paterson, N. J. (Illus.). 232p. 1997. reprint ed. pap. 38.00 (*0-8328-8330-1*); reprint ed. lib. bdg. 28.00 (*0-8328-8329-8*) Higginson Bk Co.

— Fact or Fiction: The Dilemma of the Renaissance Storyteller. LC 73-77990. 131p. 1973. reprint ed. pap. 40.70 (*0-7837-4096-4*, 205791900011) Bks Demand.

— Interference Handbook. Orr, William I., ed. (Illus.). 252p. 1991. pap. 13.95 (*0-8230-8709-3*, RAC Bks) Watsn-Guptill.

— New Jersey Biographical & Genealogical Notes. 222p. 1997. reprint ed. pap. 22.00 (*0-8063-0562-2*, 4005) Clearfield Co.

— New Jersey Marriage Records, 1665-1800. LC 67-18088. (Illus.). 804p. 1997. reprint ed. 40.00 (*0-8063-0254-2*) Genealog Pub.

— Patents & Deeds & Other Early Records of New Jersey, 1664-1703. LC 76-252. 770p. 2000. reprint ed. 57.50 (*0-8063-0711-0*, Pub. by Clearfield Co) ACCESS Pubs Network.

Nelson, William & Van Doren Honeyman, A. Documents Relating to the Colonial History of the State of New Jersey: Calendar of N. J. Wills, Administrations, Etc., 1730 - 1750, 2 vols., No. 2. 708p. (Orig.). 1994. pap. text 42.00 (*0-7884-0041-X*) Heritage Bk.

Nelson, William, jt. ed. see Clayton, W. Woodford.

Nelson, William, jt. ed. see Ferguson, John.

Nelson, William A. Vermont Criminal Practice & Procedure. 1993. ring bd. 170.00 (*0-88063-788-9*, MICHIE) LEXIS Pub.

Nelson, William E. The Americanization of the Common Law: The Impact of Legal Change of Massachusetts Society, 1760-1830. LC 74-21231. (Studies in Legal History). 288p. (C). 1975. pap. 13.95 (*0-674-02972-0*) HUP.

— Americanization of the Common Law: The Impact of Legal Change on Massachusetts Society, 1760-1830. LC 74-21231. 288p. 1994. reprint ed. pap. 20.00 (*0-8203-1587-7*) U of Ga Pr.

***Nelson, William E., Jr.** Black Atlantic Politics: Dilemmas of Political Empowerment in Boston & Liverpool. (C). 2000. pap. text 24.95 (*0-7914-4672-7*) State U NY Pr.

— Black Atlantic Politics: Dilemmas of Political Empowerment in Boston & Liverpool. (C). 2000. text 73.50 (*0-7914-4671-9*) State U NY Pr.

Nelson, William E. Dispute & Conflict Resolution in Plymouth County, Massachusetts, 1725-1825. LC 80-17403. (Studies in Legal History). 224p. reprint ed. pap. 69.50 (*0-8357-3900-7*, 203663200004) Bks Demand.

— The Fourteenth Amendment: From Political Principle to Judicial Doctrine. LC 87-35226. 288p. (Orig.). 1990. text 37.95 (*0-674-31625-8*) HUP.

— The Fourteenth Amendment: From Political Principle to Judicial Doctrine. 272p. (Orig.). (C). 1995. pap. text 16.50 (*0-674-31626-6*) HUP.

***Nelson, William E.** Marbury vs. Madison: The Origins & Legacy of Judicial Review. (Landmark Law Cases & American Society Ser.). 2000. 29.95 (*0-7006-1061-8*) U Pr of KS.

— Marbury vs. Madison: The Origins & Legacy of Judicial Review. 2000. pap. 12.95 (*0-7006-1062-6*) U Pr of KS.

Nelson, William F., jt. auth. see Davis, Harold T.

Nelson, William J. Almost a Territory: America's Attempt to Annex the Dominican Republic. LC 89-40204. (Illus.). 152p. 1990. 32.50 (*0-87413-380-7*) U Delaware Pr.

Nelson, William R. Interference Handbook. 2nd ed. LC 81-51709. (Illus.). 247p. 1981. 11.95 (*0-933616-01-5*) Radio Pubns.

— Planting Design: A Manual of Theory & Practice. (Illus.). 1985. text 25.80 (*0-87563-268-8*) Stipes.

Nelson, William S. Mid-Continent Area Power Planners: A New Approach to Planning in the Electric Power Industry. LC 68-63563. (MSU Public Utilities Studies: Vol. 1968). 141p. reprint ed. pap. 43.80 (*0-608-20507-9*, 207175900002) Bks Demand.

Nelson, William S., ed. Christian Way in Race Relations. LC 79-134121. (Essay Index Reprint Ser.). 1977. 21.95 (*0-8369-2004-X*) Ayer.

***Nelson, William T.** A Treatise of the Law of Divorce & Annulment of Marriage: Including the Adjustment of Property Rights upon Divorce, the Procedure in Suites for Divorce & the Validity & Extraterritorial Effect of Decrees of Divorce, 2 vols. cxxxi, 1197p. 2000. reprint ed. 336.00 (*1-56169-577-7*) Gaunt.

***Nelson, Willie & Shrake, Bud.** Willie: An Autobiography. 2000. reprint ed. pap. 18.95 (*0-8154-1080-8*, Pub. by Cooper Sq) Natl Bk Netwk.

Nelson, Wilson E. The Roots of American Bureaucracy, 1830-1900. 224p. 1982. 34.50 (*0-674-77945-2*) HUP.

Nelson, Wilton M. Nuevo Diccionario Ilustrado de la Biblia.Tr. of New Illustrated Bible Dictionary. (SPA., Illus.). 1392p. 1998. 39.99 (*0-89922-285-4*, C010-2854) Caribe Betania.

— Protestantism in Central America. LC 84-13727. 96p. reprint ed. pap. 30.00 (*0-608-17708-3*, 203006900067) Bks Demand.

Nelson, Word Publishing Group. Living Abundantly. 1999. pap. 2.99 (*0-7852-0057-6*) Nelson.

***Nelson Word Publishing Group Staff.** Blessed Beginnings. (Precious Moments Seasons of Faith Ser.). (Illus.). 32p. 2000. 7.99 (*0-7852-5535-4*) Nelson.

Nelson Word Publishing Group Staff. Forgiving Hearts. 1999. pap. 2.99 (*0-7852-0059-2*) Nelson.

***Nelson Word Publishing Group Staff.** Gifts from the Heart: Selected Scriptures from the New King James Version. (Precious Moments Seasons of Faith Ser.). (Illus.). 32p. 2000. pap. 7.99 (*0-7852-0499-7*) W1CL.

— God's Promises & Answers. 1999. pap. 7.97 (*0-8499-5615-3*) J Countryman.

— Hand in Hand with Jesus: A Bible Verse for Every Day, to Help Me Live a Better Way. (Illus.). 64p. (J). (ps-3). 2000. pap. 2.99 (*0-7852-0026-6*) W1CL.

— He is Risen: Selected Scriptures from the New King James Version. (Precious Moments Seasons of Faith Ser.). (Illus.). 32p. (ps-3). 2000. pap. 7.99 (*0-7852-0509-8*) W1CL.

Nelson Word Publishing Group Staff. Jesus Is My Special Friend. 1999. pap. 2.99 (*0-7852-0063-0*) Nelson.

— Jesus, Jesus Everywhere. 1999. pap. 2.99 (*0-7852-0060-6*) Nelson.

— Jesus Loves You & Me. 1999. pap. 2.99 (*0-7852-0062-2*) Nelson.

— Jesus Made a Marvelous Me. 1999. pap. 2.99 (*0-7852-0061-4*) Nelson.

***Nelson Word Publishing Group Staff.** Little Flowers New Testament with Psalms, 1. 640p. 2000. pap. 4.99 (*0-7852-0486-5*); pap. 4.99 (*0-7852-0493-8*); pap. 4.99 (*0-7852-0496-2*); pap. 4.99 (*0-7852-0498-9*) W1CL.

Nelson Word Publishing Group Staff. Living Each Day with Jesus. 1999. pap. 0.99 (*0-7852-0056-8*) Nelson.

***Nelson Word Publishing Group Staff.** Love Forever True. (Precious Moments Seasons of Faith Ser.). (Illus.). 32p. 2000. 7.99 (*0-7852-5534-6*) Nelson.

— Precious Moments Bible. (Illus.). 1104p. (ps-3). 2000. 24.99 (*0-7852-0453-9*); 24.99 (*0-7852-0485-7*) W1CL.

Nelson Word Publishing Group Staff. Walking in Love with Jesus. 1999. pap. 2.99 (*0-7852-0058-4*) Nelson.

N

*Nelson Word Publishing Group Staff. Women of Destiny: A Spirit-Filled Life Bible. (Illus.). 1696p. 2000. 44.99 (0-7852-0006-1); 52.99 (0-7852-0008-8); pap. 19.99 (0-7852-0099-1) W1CL.

*Nelson Word Publishing Group Staff, contrib. by. Women of Destiny Bible. 1696p. 2000. 29.99 (0-7852-0000-2); 44.99 (0-7852-0002-9); 54.99 (0-7852-0003-7); 54.99 (0-7852-0005-3) W1CL.

*Nelson Word Publishing Staff. Discovering Who You Are in Jesus: Daily Encouragement as Close as Your Heart, New King James Version. (Jesus in My Pocket Ser.). 64p. 2000. pap. 2.99 (0-7852-0020-7) W1CL.

— Jesus is My Superhero: A Bible Verse for Every Day, to Help Me Live a Better Way, 1. (Jesus in My Pocket Ser.). 2000. pap. 2.99 (0-7852-0022-3) W1CL.

— Living Your Dreams: Daily Encouragement as Close as Your Heart, New King James Version. (Jesus in My Pocket Ser.). 2000. pap. 2.99 (0-7852-0018-5) W1CL.

— My Bible Talks to Me: A Bible Verse for Every Day, to Help Me Live a Better Way, 1. (Jesus in My Pocket Ser.). (Illus.). 64p. (J). (ps-3). 2000. pap. 2.99 (0-7852-0023-1) W1CL.

— Precious Moments Small Hands Bible: Supersaver Edition. 1999. 16.97 (0-7852-0045-2) Nelson.

— Proverbs to Grow By: A Bible Verse for Every Day, to Help Me Live a Better Way. (Jesus in My Pocket Ser.). (Illus.). 64p. (J). (ps-3). 2000. pap. 2.99 (0-7852-0025-8) W1CL.

— Psalms to Live & Love By: Daily Encouragement as Close as Your Heart, New King James Version, 1. (Jesus in My Pocket Ser.). (Illus.). 64p. 2000. pap. 2.99 (0-7852-0019-3) W1CL.

— Seeking Jesus in Times of Trouble: Daily Encouragement as Close as Your Heart, New King James Version. (Jesus in My Pocket Ser.). 64p. 2000. pap. 2.99 (0-7852-0021-5) W1CL.

Nelson, Yvette. Celebrating the Eucharist. Zanzig, Thomas, ed. (Discovering Program Ser.). (Illus.). 49p. (YA). (gr. 6-8). 1992. teacher ed. 6.00 (0-88489-270-0); pap. text 3.00 (0-88489-269-7) St Marys.

— Exploring the Story of Israel: Discovering Program. (Illus.). 52p. (Orig.). 1992. teacher ed. 6.00 (0-88489-268-9); student ed. 3.00 (0-88489-267-0) St Marys.

— Gathering to Celebrate. Zanzig, Thomas, ed. (Discovering Program Ser.). (Illus.). 52p. (J). (gr. 6-8). 1994. teacher ed. 6.00 (0-88489-301-4); pap. text 3.00 (0-88489-300-6) St Marys.

NelsonWord Staff. Gods Gift for Mothers, 1. 1999. pap. text 2.97 (90-71676-27-7) Word Pub.

— Gods Power for Fathers, 1. 1999. pap. text 2.97 (90-71676-29-3) Word Pub.

*NelsonWord Staff. Precious Moments Baby Bible for Catholics. (Illus.). (J). 1999. 19.99 (0-7852-0083-5) Nelson.

NelsonWord Staff. Road to Armageddon & Beyond: Participant's Study Guide Edition. 1999. pap. text 9.99 (0-8499-8774-1) Word Pub.

— Seven Promises Practiced, Participant's Workbook Edition. 1999. pap. text 9.99 (0-8499-8765-2) Word Pub.

Nelsson, James & Riedel, Susan A. VL2 S/M W/TRAN MSTR ELEC. 5th ed. Cote, Lynne D., ed. (C). 1995. pap. text 25.67 (0-201-84712-4) Addison-Wesley.

Nelt, M. Madres Que Trabajan - Working Moms. (SPA.). 150p. 1995. write for info. (1-56063-524-X) Editorial Unilit.

Nelting, David, jt. ed. see Felten, Hans.

Neltz, Mary A. Dysfunctional Family Cooking. 32p. 1993. pap. 4.95 (1-883849-02-0) Nine Hund Forty Six Pr.

Nelvana (Firm) Staff, jt. auth. see Moore, Eva.

Nelville, David, et al. Promoting Positive Parenting. 160p. 1995. pap. 26.95 (1-85742-266-X, Pub. by Arena) Ashgate Pub Co.

Nema. Maat Magick: A Guide to Self-Initiation. LC 95-18084. 256p. 1995. reprint ed. pap. 14.95 (0-87728-827-5) Weiser.

Nema, N. Phytomedicine, a Treatise on Plant Diseases. (C). 1988. 197.50 (81-7136-009-2, Pub. by Periodical Expert) St Mut.

Neman, Beth S. Teaching Students to Write. 2nd ed. (Illus.). 624p. (C). 1995. pap. text 31.95 (0-19-506428-3) OUP.

Neman, Beth S. & Smythe, Sandra H. Writing Effectively in Business. 576p. (C). 1997. pap. text 72.00 (0-06-044809-1) Addson-Wesley Educ.

Nemanich, R. J., et al, eds. Chemical Surface Preparation, Passivation & Cleaning for Semiconductor Growth & Processing. (Materials Research Society Symposium Proceedings Ser.: Vol. 259). 527p. 1992. text 30.00 (1-55899-154-9) Materials Res.

Nemanich, R. J., et al, eds. Thin Films - Interfaces & Phenomena, Vol. 54. (Materials Research Society Symposium Proceedings Ser.). 1986. text 17.50 (0-931837-19-7) Materials Res.

Nemaniec, Allison. Diabetes Care Made Easy, in Spanish: A Simple Step by Step Guide for Controlling Your Diabetes. (SPA.). 1993. pap. 9.95 (1-56561-014-8) Wiley.

Nemapare, Prisca & Neumann, Richard. Fundamentals of Meal Management. LC 95-3064. (Illus.). 242p. (C). 1995. text 55.95 (0-398-05991-8); pap. text 38.95 (0-398-05992-6) C C Thomas.

Nemat-Nasser, S. Micromechanics: Overall Properties of Heterogeneous Materials. 2nd rev. ed. LC 98-48057. 810p. 1999. pap. 94.00 (0-444-50084-7, North Holland) Elsevier.

Nemat-Nasser, S., ed. Hydraulic Fracturing & Geothermal Energy. 1983. text 255.50 (90-247-2855-X) Kluwer Academic.

— Mechanics Today, Set. Incl. Vol. 6. 1981. pap. text 40.00 (0-08-027318-1); 1978. 121.00 (0-08-022682-5, Pub. by Pergamon Repr) Franklin.

Nemat-Nasser, S. & Hori, Motoo. Micromechanics: Overall Properties of Heterogeneous Materials. LC 93-11093. (Applied Mathematics & Mechanics Ser.). 708p. 1993. 173.00 (0-444-89881-6, North Holland) Elsevier.

Nemat-Nasser, S., ed. see American Society of Mechanical Engineers Staff.

Nemati, Parviz. Splendors of Rugs & Tapestries: Past & Present. 400p. Date not set. write for info. (0-937266-02-7) Agate Pr.

Nembach, Eckhard. Particle Strengthening of Metals & Alloys. LC 96-14932. 285p. 1996. 98.50 (0-471-12072-3) Wiley.

Nembach, Paul A., jt. auth. see Douglas, James A.

Nembach, Ulrich. Informationes Theologiae Europae. (GER.). 399p. 1995. 61.95 (3-631-49452-1) P Lang Pubng.

*Nembach, Ulrich. Informationes Theologiae Europae: Internationales Okumenisches Jahrbuch fur Theologie. 354p. 1999. 51.95 (3-631-35751-6) P Lang Pubng.

Nembach, Ulrich. Informationes Theologiae Europae: Internationales Okumenisches Jahrbuch Fur Theologie 7.jg. 1998. (Illus.). 366p. 1998. 48.00 (3-631-34098-2) P Lang Pubng.

Nembach, Ulrich, ed. Informationes Theologiae Europae: Internationales Okumenisches Jahrbuch fur Theologie. (GER.). 1996. 61.95 (3-631-30957-0) P Lang Pubng.

— Jugend - 2000 Jahre Nach Jesus: Jugend und Religion in Europa II Bericht vom 2. Internationalen Gottinger Religionssoziologischen Symposion. (Forschungen zur Praktischen Theologie Ser.: Bd. 16). (GER., Illus.). 275p. 1996. 19.95 (3-631-30880-9) P Lang Pubng.

— Jugend und Religion in Europa: Bericht Eines Symposions. 2nd ed. (Forschungen zur Praktischen Theologie Ser.: Bd. 2). (GER., Illus.). 384p. 1990. 60.80 (3-631-42564-3) P Lang Pubng.

Nembach, Ulrich, ed. see Ahonen, Risto.

Nembhard, Jessica G. Capital Control, Financial Regulation, & Industrial Policy in South Korea & Brazil. LC 95-30554. 296p. 1996. 69.50 (0-275-95126-X, Praeger Pubs) Greenwood.

Nembhard, Ralston. You & Your Neighbour in a Broken World. 68p. (Orig.). 1997. pap. 8.75 (1-57502-516-7, P01532) Morris Pubng.

Nemcek, Kathleen, ed. & illus. see Nemcek, Mark.

Nemcek, Mark. Iggs' Florida Adventure. Nemcek, Kathleen, ed. & illus. by. 18p. (Orig.). (J). (ps-6). 1999. pap. write for info. (0-9669289-0-3) Iguana Adventures.

*Nemcosky, K. B. Drift. 88p. 2000. pap. 12.00 (1-930330-03-0) Ten Pell Bks.

Nemcova, Bozena. Fairy Tales from Czechoslovakia Vol. I, Vol. I. Velinsky, L., tr. (CZE., Illus.). 305p. (Orig.). (J). (gr. 4 up). 1987. pap. 39.50 (0-930329-35-X) Kabel Pubs.

Nemcova, Irena, et al, eds. Spectrophotometric Reactions. (Practical Spectroscopy Ser.: Vol. 22). (Illus.). 264p. 1996. text 145.00 (0-8247-9451-6) Dekker.

Nemcova, Jeanne, tr. see Skvorecky, Josef.

Nemec, Brian. Helmzier Vol. 1: German Military Helmet Plates 1842-1918. (Illus.). 68p. (Orig.). 1996. pap. 24.95 (0-9653637-0-8) Nemeco.

Nemec, David. The Baseball Challenger Quiz Book. 192p. (Orig.). 1991. mass mkt. 3.99 (0-451-16943-3, Sig) NAL.

— The Beer & Whiskey League. LC 94-27805. 272p. 1994. 27.95 (1-55821-285-X) Lyons Pr.

— Early Dreams. 150p. 1998. 17.95 (1-893392-02-3) Baseball Pr Bks.

— The Great American Baseball Team Book: 1995 Updated Edition. 432p. (Orig.). 1999. mass mkt. 4.99 (0-451-18336-3, Sig) NAL.

— Great Baseball Feats Facts & Firsts, 1 vol. rev. ed. 1999. mass mkt. 6.99 (0-451-19844-1) NAL.

*Nemec, David. Great Baseball Feats, Facts & Firsts 2000. 2000. mass mkt. 6.99 (0-451-20084-5, Sig) NAL.

— The Great Book of Baseball Knowledge. LC 98-45461. (Illus.). 488p. 1999. pap. 19.95 (0-8092-2659-6, 265960, Mstrs Pr) NTC Contemp Pub Co.

Nemec, David. The Rules of Baseball. LC 93-48361. (Illus.). 272p. 1994. pap. 16.95 (1-55821-280-9) Lyons Pr.

— Stonesifer. 277p. 1999. 25.00 (1-885003-19-6) R D Reed Pubs.

Nemec, Dulci. White Fury. (Illus.). 150p. (Orig.). 1989. pap. 3.49 (0-9618998-4-0) Nemec Pub.

Nemec, E. P. Manager's Handbook. LC 87-71781. (Illus.). 158p. (Orig.). 1987. pap. 4.45 (0-9618998-0-8) Nemec Pub.

Nemec, Gale B. Living with Cats. (Illus.). 224p. 1997. reprint ed. pap. text 8.00 (0-7881-5118-5) DIANE Pub.

Nemec, Jack. Universe of Cartoons. LC 87-91984. (Illus.). 120p. (Orig.). 1987. pap. 3.95 (0-9618998-3-2) Nemec Pub.

Nemec, James M. & Matthews, Jaymie M., eds. New Perspectives on Stellar Pulsation & Pulsating Variable Stars. (Illus.). 463p. (C). 1993. text 74.95 (0-521-44382-2) Cambridge U Pr.

Nemec, Jaromir. Design & Operation of Hydrological Forecasting Systems. 1986. text 151.50 (90-277-2259-5) Kluwer Academic.

Nemec, Jaromir, et al, eds. Prediction & Perception of Natural Hazards: Proceedings Symposium, 22-26 October 1990, Perugia, Italy. LC 93-4585. (Advances in Natural & Technological Hazards Research Ser.: Vol. 2). 216p. (C). 1993. lib. bdg. 100.00 (0-7923-2355-6) Kluwer Academic.

Nemec, John. Article Writing Guidelines. 14p. 1987. pap. 1.75 (0-9618998-2-4) Nemec Pub.

— Naked in the Night. 160p. (Orig.). 1991. pap. 3.49 (0-9618998-8-3) Nemec Pub.

— Present Your Sale. LC 87-90713. 50p. (Orig.). 1987. pap. 2.95 (0-9618998-1-6) Nemec Pub.

— Raging Passion. 160p. (Orig.). 1991. pap. 3.49 (0-9618998-7-5) Nemec Pub.

— Vacationer's Choice. (Illus.). 163p. (Orig.). 1989. pap. 4.45 (0-9618998-5-9) Nemec Pub.

— Wild for Kicks. 160p. (Orig.). 1991. pap. 3.49 (0-9618998-6-7) Nemec Pub.

Nemec, Ludvik. Infant Jesus of Prague. 1978. pap. 2.95 (0-89942-129-6, 129/04) Catholic Bk Pub.

— El Nino Jesus de Praga. (SPA.). 1987. pap. 2.95 (0-89942-439-2, 439/S) Catholic Bk Pub.

Nemecek, Larry. Star Trek: The Next Generation Companion. rev. ed. 1995. pap. 18.00 (0-671-88340-2) PB.

Nemechek, Nadine & Gerardi, Sharon N. The 7 Day Cookbook: The Easy Answer to "What's for Dinner?" unabridged ed. (Illus.). 256p. 1997. 13.95 (0-9657500-0-0) Redbank Ranch.

Nemechek, Nadine, et al. The Golf Cookbook: Easy Recipes for People Who Would Rather Golf Than Cook. LC 98-91266. (Illus.). 144p. 1998. 10.95 (0-9657500-1-9) Redbank Ranch.

Nemeck, Francis K. & Coombs, Marie T. Contemplation. (Ways of Prayer Ser.). 151p. 1982. pap. 11.95 (0-8146-5283-2, M Glazier) Liturgical Pr.

— Spiritual Journey: Critical Thresholds & Stages of Adult Spiritual Genesis. LC 85-45664. 230p. (Orig.). 1986. pap. 14.95 (0-8146-5546-7) Liturgical Pr.

— The Way of Spiritual Direction. LC 84-81254. 220p. 1985. pap. 14.95 (0-8146-5447-9) Liturgical Pr.

Nemeck, Francis K., jt. auth. see Coombs, Marie T.

Nemecz, E. Clay Minerals. 548p. 1981. 227.00 (0-569-08686-8) St Mut.

*Nemeczek, Alfred. Van Gogh in Arles. (Pegasus Library Ser.). (Illus.). 128p. 1999. 9.95 (3-7913-2230-3, Pub. by Prestel) te Neues.

Nemeczek, Alfred, et al. Van Gogh in Arles. (Pegasus Library). (Illus.). 128p. 1995. 25.00 (3-7913-1484-X, Pub. by Prestel) te Neues.

Nemeroff, Charles B. Neuroendocrinology. 640p. 1992. lib. bdg. 110.00 (0-8493-8844-9, QP356) CRC Pr.

— Neuropeptides in Psychiatric & Neurological Disorders. LC 87-45487. (Johns Hopkins Series in Contemporary Medicine & Public Health). (Illus.). 326p. reprint ed. pap. 101.10 (0-608-08792-0, 206943100004) Bks Demand.

Nemeroff, Charles B. & Dunn, A. J., eds. Peptides, Hormones & Behavior. (Illus.). 944p. 1984. text 150.00 (0-88331-174-7) R B Luce.

Nemeroff, Charles B. & Loosen, Peter T., eds. Handbook of Clinical Psychoneuroendocrinology. LC 86-31837. 502p. 1987. lib. bdg. 80.95 (0-89862-698-6) Guilford Pubns.

Nemeroff, Charles B. & Schatzberg, Alan F. Recognition & Treatment of Psychiatric Disorders: A Psychopharmacology Handbook for Primary Care. LC 99-15420. 269p. 1999. 35.00 (0-88048-990-1) Am Psychiatric.

Nemeroff, Charles B., jt. auth. see Craighead, W. Edward.

Nemeroff, Charles B., jt. auth. see Schatzberg, Alan F.

Nemeroff, Charles B., jt. ed. see De Souza, Errol B.

Nemeroff, Charles B., jt. ed. see Schatzberg, Alan F.

*Nemerov, Alexander. The Body of Raphaelle Peale. LC 00-37407. (Illus.). 2001. write for info. (0-520-22498-1) U CA Pr.

Nemerov, Alexander. Frederic Remington & Turn-of-the-Century America. LC 95-1223. (Publications in the History of Art). 1995. 47.00 (0-300-05566-8) Yale U Pr.

Nemerov, Howard. The Collected Poems of Howard Nemerov. LC 77-544. (Illus.). 1977. 20.00 (0-226-57258-7) U Ch Pr.

— The Collected Poems of Howard Nemerov. LC 77-544. 536p. 1981. pap. 19.95 (0-226-57259-5) U Ch Pr.

— Gnomes & Occasions. 1992. pap. 1.95 (0-226-57255-2) U Ch Pr.

— The Homecoming Game: A Novel. LC 92-15687. 264p. (Orig.). 1992. reprint ed. pap. 18.95 (0-8262-0870-3) U of Mo Pr.

— A Howard Nemerov Reader. 552p. 1991. 34.95 (0-8262-0776-6) U of Mo Pr.

— A Howard Nemerov Reader. 552p. 1993. pap. 22.50 (0-8262-0936-X) U of Mo Pr.

— Inside the Onion. LC 83-9312. 72p. (C). 1995. 11.95 (0-226-57244-7) U Ch Pr.

— Inside the Onion. LC 83-9312. 72p. (C). 1996. pap. 9.95 (0-226-57245-5) U Ch Pr.

— Journal of the Fictive Life. LC 81-10449. 196p. (C). 1981. pap. 7.95 (0-226-57261-7) U Ch Pr.

— The Melodramatists. LC 91-40801. 352p. (C). 1992. reprint ed. pap. 18.95 (0-8262-0846-0) U of Mo Pr.

— New & Selected Poems. LC 60-14236. 122p. 1998. pap. 11.95 (0-226-57247-1, PP6) U Ch Pr.

— Oak in the Acorn: On Remembrance of Things Past & on Teaching Proust, Who Will Never Learn. LC 86-21087. 168p. 1987. text 27.50 (0-8071-1385-9) La State U Pr.

— Sentences. LC 80-17702. 86p. 1980. 8.95 (0-226-57260-9) U Ch Pr.

— Sentences. LC 80-17702. 96p. 1983. pap. 10.95 (0-226-57262-5) U Ch Pr.

— Tall Story. adapted ed. Lindsey, Howard, ed. 1959. pap. 5.25 (0-8222-1109-2) Dramatists Play.

— Trying Conclusions: New & Selected Poems, 1961-1991. 174p. 1991. 18.95 (0-226-57263-3) U Ch Pr.

— War Stories: Poems about Long Ago & Now. LC 87-5097. (Illus.). x, 70p. 1989. pap. 9.95 (0-226-57243-9) U Ch Pr.

— War Stories: Poems about Long Ago & Now. LC 87-5097. 72p. (C). 1996. 13.50 (0-226-57242-0) U Ch Pr.

Nemerow, Nelson L. Industrial Solid Waste. LC 82-13866. 384p. 1983. text 45.00 (0-88410-876-7, HarpBusn) HarpInfo.

— Zero Pollution for Industry: Waste Minimization Through Industrial Complexes. LC 95-10072. 240p. 1995. 90.00 (0-471-12164-9) Wiley.

Nemerow, Nelson L. & Agardy, Frank P. Strategies of Industrial & Hazardous Waste Management. 2nd ed. LC 97-41195. (Illus.). 750p. 1997. 99.95 (0-442-02445-2, VNR) Wiley.

Nemerow, Nelson L. & Agardy, Franklin J. Strategies of Industrial & Hazardous Waste Management. 2nd ed. LC 97-41195. (Environmental Engineering Ser.). 748p. 1998. 150.00 (0-471-29216-8) Wiley.

Nemerow, Nelson L. & Dasgupta, Avijit. Industrial & Hazardous Waste Treatment. LC 90-49704. (Illus.). 752p. 1991. text 108.95 (0-442-31934-7, VNR) Wiley.

Nemerowicz, Gloria & Rosi, Eugene. Education for Leadership & Social Responsibility. 160p. 1997. pap. 27.95 (0-7507-0608-2, Falmer Pr) Taylor & Francis.

Nemerowicz, Gloria M. Children's Perceptions of Gender & Work Roles. LC 79-11783. 201p. 1979. 49.95 (0-275-90399-0, C0399, Praeger Pubs) Greenwood.

Nemerowicz, Gloria M. & Gora, Joann. Emergency Squad Volunteers: Professionalism in Unpaid Work. LC 85-12310. 176p. 1985. 49.95 (0-275-90206-4, C0206, Praeger Pubs) Greenwood.

Nemerson, Roy, jt. auth. see Buono, Anthony.

Nemes, Claire. A Picture Book of Dinosaurs. LC 89-37331. (Picture Book of...Ser.). (Illus.). 24p. (J). (gr. 1-4). 1990. lib. bdg. 14.50 (0-8167-1900-4) Troll Communs.

— A Picture Book of Dinosaurs. LC 89-37331. (Picture Book of...Ser.). 24p. (J). (gr. 1-4). 1996. pap. 2.95 (0-8167-1901-2) Troll Communs.

— Picture Book of Dinosaurs. (Illus.). (J). 1990. 8.15 (0-606-04514-7, Pub. by Turtleback) Demco.

Nemes, Claire, ed. Young Thomas Edison: Great Inventor. LC 95-8107. (First-Start Biography Ser.). (Illus.). 32p. (J). (gr. k-2). 1995. pap. text 3.50 (0-8167-3777-0) Troll Communs.

— Young Thomas Edison: Great Inventor. LC 95-8107. (First-Start Biography Ser.). (Illus.). 32p. (J). (gr. k-2). 1997. lib. bdg. 17.25 (0-8167-3776-2) Troll Communs.

Nemes, Gabrielle. 10 Minute Guide to Microsoft Exchange. (Illus.). 208p. 1996. 14.99 (0-7897-0677-6) Que.

*Nemes, Gabrielle. Write Your Own Will in a Weekend. (In a Weekend Ser.). 2000. pap. 24.99 (0-7615-2378-2, Prima Tech) Prima Pub.

Nemes, L. Information Control Problems in Manufacturing Automation, Vol. 5. 500p. 1993. text 69.00 (9971-5-0100-7) World Scientific Pub.

Nemes, L., jt. ed. see Puente, E. A.

Nemes, Laszlo, tr. see Mika, Jozsef & Torok, Tibor.

*Nemes, Livia & Berenyi, Gabor. Die Budapester Schule der Psychoanalyse. 408p. 1999. 80.00 (963-05-7625-2) Intl Spec Bk.

Nemes, Sylvester. Learn How to Fly Fish in One Day: Quickest Way to Start Tying Flies, Casting Flies, & Catching Fish. LC 85-20802. (Illus.). 128p. (Orig.). 1986. pap. 11.95 (0-8117-2185-X) Stackpole.

— The Soft-Hackled Fly: A Trout Fisherman's Guide. LC 93-12705. (Illus.). 130p. 1993. reprint ed. 22.95 (0-8117-1670-8) Stackpole.

— The Soft-Hackled Fly Addict. LC 93-12707. (Illus.). 144p. 1993. reprint ed. 19.95 (0-8117-1671-6) Stackpole.

Nemeshegyi, Peter. The Meaning of Christianity. 128p. 1982. pap. 3.95 (0-8091-2464-5) Paulist Pr.

Nemessuri, Mihaly & Szende, O. The Physiology of Violin Playing. 202p. (C). 1988. 75.00 (0-569-06196-2, Pub. by Collets) St Mut.

Nemesvari, Richard, ed. see Braddon, Mary Elizabeth.

Nemesvari, Richard, ed. see Bronte, Charlotte.

Nemesvari, Richard, ed. & intro. see Hardy, Thomas.

Nemet-Nejat, Karen R. Cuneiform Mathematical Texts As a Reflection of Everyday Life in Mesopotamia. (American Oriental Ser.: Vol. 75). xii, 335p. 1993. 42.00 (0-940490-75-7) Am Orient Soc.

— Daily Life in Ancient Mesopotamia. LC 97-53110. (Greenwood Press "Daily Life Through History" Ser.). 368p. 1998. 45.00 (0-313-29497-6, Greenwood Pr) Greenwood.

*Nemet-Nejat, Murat. Peripheral Space of Photography. (Illus.). 76p. 2000. pap. 9.95 (1-892295-90-3) Green Integer.

Nemet-Nejat, Murat, tr. see Ayham, Ece.

Nemet-Nejat, Murat, tr. see Veli, Orhan.

Nemeth, Bonnie. Take-Off Tappers. Nemeth, Wolf & Bouldin, Debby, eds. (Timeless Tap Ser.: Level 3, Bk. 3, Vol. 3). (Illus.). 72p. (Orig.). (J). (gr. 1-3). 1996. pap. 12.00 (1-888199-53-9) Dance Innovators.

— Terrific Tappers. Nemeth, Wolf & Bouldin, Debby, eds. (Timeless Tap Ser.: Level 4, Bk. 4, Vol. 4). (Illus.). 72p. (Orig.). (J). (gr. 4-7). 1996. pap. 12.00 (1-888199-54-7) Dance Innovators.

— Tiny Tappers Level 1: Book One. (Timeless Tap Ser.). 72p. (J). (ps-k). 1995. pap. 12.00 (1-888199-50-4) Dance Innovators.

— Tip-Toe Tappers. Nemeth, Wolf & Bouldin, Debby, eds. (Timeless Tap Ser.: Level 2, Bk. 2, Vol. 2). (Illus.). 72p. (Orig.). (J). (ps-1). 1996. pap. 12.00 (1-888199-52-0) Dance Innovators.

— Tip-Top Tappers. Nemeth, Wolf & Bouldin, Debby, eds. (Timeless Tap Ser.: Level 5, Bk.5, Vol. 5). (Illus.). 72p. (Orig.). (YA). (gr. 8 up). 1996. pap. 12.00 (1-888199-55-5) Dance Innovators.

Nemeth, Charles P. Bankruptcy. (Paralegal Workbook Ser.). 67p. (C). 1995. pap. text 9.95 (0-87084-572-1) Anderson Pub Co.

— Careers in the Law. (Paralegal Workbook Ser.). 86p. (C). 1995. pap. text 10.95 (0-87084-607-8) Anderson Pub Co.

— The Case of Archbishop Lefebvre: Trial by Canon Law. LC 98-118520. 173p. 1994. pap. text 9.95 (0-935952-50-0) Angelus Pr.

An Asterisk (*) at the beginning of an entry indicates that the title is appearing for the first time.

— Consumer, Contract & Commercial Applications. (Paralegal Workbook Ser.). 67p. (C). 1995. pap. text 9.95 (*0-87084-571-3*) Anderson Pub Co.
— Criminal Law & Procedure. (Paralegal Workbook Ser.). (Illus.). 97p. (C). 1995. pap. text 11.95 (*0-87084-585-3*) Anderson Pub Co.
— Delaware Corporate Practice for the Paralegal: With Forms. LC 94-70885. 400p. 1995. ring bd. 89.50 (*1-887024-29-8*) Bisel Co.
— Estate Planning & Administration for Paralegals. 688p. (C). 1993. text 42.95 (*0-929563-35-2*) Pearson Pubns.
— Estates & Trusts. (Paralegal Workbook Ser.). 152p. (C). 1995. pap. text 12.95 (*0-87084-569-1*) Anderson Pub Co.
— Evidence Handbook for Paralegals. 304p. (C). 1993. text 39.95 (*0-929563-36-0*) Pearson Pubns.
— Family Law. (Paralegal Workbook Ser.). 72p. (C). 1995. pap. text 10.95 (*0-87084-586-1*) Anderson Pub Co.
— Florida Corporate Practice for the Paralegal: With Forms. 403p. 1995. ring bd. 89.50 (*1-887024-30-1*) Bisel Co.
— Incorporation of a Business. (Paralegal Workbook Ser.). 79p. (C). 1995. pap. text 10.95 (*0-87084-608-6*) Anderson Pub Co.
***Nemeth, Charles P.** Law & Evidence: Criminal Justice, Criminology, Law & Legal Studies. 450p. 2000. 66.67 (*0-13-030811-0*, Prentice Hall) P-H.
Nemeth, Charles P. Legal Research & Writing Exercises for Paralegals. (Illus.). 171p. (Orig.). (C). 1992. pap., student ed. 8.95 (*0-916951-00-6*) Adams & Ambrose.
— Legal Research & Writing Exercises for Paralegals: Teacher's Answer Key. 41p. (Orig.). (C). 1992. pap., student ed. 7.50 (*0-916951-01-4*) Adams & Ambrose.
— Litigation & Pleadings. (Paralegal Workbook Ser.). 60p. (C). 1996. pap. text 9.95 (*0-87084-614-0*) Anderson Pub Co.
— Litigation, Pleadings & Arbitration. 2nd ed. LC 97-70034. 668p. (C). 1997. pap. 52.95 (*0-87084-543-8*) Anderson Pub Co.
— New Jersey Corporate Practice for the Paralegal: With Forms. LC 94-72418. 399p. 1995. ring bd. 89.50 (*1-887024-37-9*) Bisel Co.
— Paralegal Internships Manual. 2nd ed. 205p. (C). 1996. per. 34.95 (*0-929563-32-8*) Pearson Pubns.
— The Paralegal Resource Manual, 2 vols., Vols. I-II. 2nd ed. LC 94-71863. (Illus.). (C). 1994. pap. text 99.95 (*0-87084-612-4*) Anderson Pub Co.
— Pennsylvania Corporate Practice for the Paralegal: With Forms. LC 94-70887. 494p. 1994. ring bd. 89.50 (*1-887024-43-3*) Bisel Co.
— Pennsylvania Real Estate Agreements. LC 95-76463. 1996. ring bd. 79.50 (*1-887024-63-8*) Bisel Co.
— Pennsylvania Real Estate Practice. LC 95-76462. 1996. ring bd. 79.50 (*1-887024-64-6*) Bisel Co.
— Private Security & the Investigative Process. 2nd ed. LC 97-49930. 360p. 1998. pap. 34.95 (*0-7506-9087-9*) Buttrwrth-Heinemann.
— Private Security & the Law. 2nd ed. LC 94 73212. 426p. (C). 1995. pap. 37.95 (*0-87084-599-3*) Anderson Pub Co.
— Real Estate. (Paralegal Workbook Ser.). 104p. (C). 1995. pap. 11.95 (*0-87084-584-5*) Anderson Pub Co.
***Nemeth, Charles P.** The Reality of Real Estate. (Illus.). 300p. (C). 2000. ring bd. 45.50 (*0-929563-23-9*) Pearson Pubns.
Nemeth, Charles P. A Status Report on Contemporary Criminal Justice Education: A Definition of the Discipline & an Assessment of Its Curricula, Faculty & Program Characteristics. LC 88-7998. (Mellen Studies in Education: Vol. 3). 250p. 1989. lib. bdg. 89.95 (*0-88946-938-5*) E Mellen.
— Torts & Personal Injury. (Paralegal Workbook Ser.). (Illus.). 124p. (C). 1995. pap. text 12.95 (*0-87084-613-2*) Anderson Pub Co.
Nemeth, Charles P., ed. Biographical Directory of Legal Administration Professionals. 1996. pap. 79.00 (*1-888286-10-5*) Altman Weil.
Nemeth, David J. The Architecture of Ideology: Neo-Confucian Imprinting on Cheju Island, Korea. (UC Publications in Geography: Vol. 26). (Orig.). 1988. pap. 60.00 (*0-520-09713-0*, Pub. by U CA Pr) Cal Prin Full Svc.
Nemeth, Doris I., et al, eds. The Poet, 1981. (Autumn Ser.). (Illus.). 400p. 1981. pap. 11.00 (*0-932192-03-3*) Fine Arts Soc.
— The Poet, 1983. (Autumn Ser.: 1983). (Illus.). 400p. 1983. pap. 11.50 (*0-932192-05-X*) Fine Arts Soc.
Nemeth, Elisabeth, ed. Encyclopedia & Utopia: The Life & Work of Otto Neurath (1882-1945) (Vienna Circle Institute Yearbook VCIY Ser.: No. 4). 416p. (C). 1996. text 144.00 (*0-7923-4161-9*) Kluwer Academic.
Nemeth, Eva, ed. Caraway. 195p. 1998. text 70.00 (*90-5702-395-4*, Harwood Acad Pubs) Gordon & Breach.
Nemeth, Evi. TEC UNIX System Administration. 1991. pap. write for info. (*0-201-41895-9*) Addison-Wesley.
— UNIX System Administration Handbook. 2nd ed. 780p. 1995. pap. 74.00 incl. cd-rom (*0-13-151051-7*) P-H.
Nemeth, Evi, et al. UNIX Systems Administration Handbook. 3rd ed. 1200p. (C). 2000. pap. 68.00 (*0-13-020601-6*) P-H.
Nemeth, G. & Kuttig, H. Isodose Atlas for Use in Radiotherapy. 272p. 1981. text 176.50 (*90-247-2476-7*) Kluwer Academic.
Nemeth, Gerry, jt. auth. see Mogan, Peter J.
Nemeth, Geza. Mathematical Approximations of Special Functions: Ten Papers on Chebyshev Expansions. 185p. (C). 1992. pap. text 165.00 (*1-56072-052-2*) Nova Sci Pubs.
Nemeth, Gyula. Hungary: A Complete Guide. 288p. 1989. pap. 60.00 (*963-13-3740-5*, Pub. by Corvina Bks) St Mut.
— Hungary: A Pocket Guide. 172p. 1999. pap. 40.00 (*963-13-3812-6*, Pub. by Corvina Bks) St Mut.
Nemeth, K. Application of Electro-Ultrafiltration (EUF) in Agricultural Production. 1982. pap. text 73.50 (*90-247-2641-7*) Kluwer Academic.
***Nemeth, Lane.** Discovering Another Way: Raising Brighter Children while Having a Meaningful Career. LC 98-32776. 256p. 1999. pap. 16.95 (*1-58270-010-9*, Pub. by Beyond Words Pub) Publishers Group.
Nemeth, Laszlo. Guilt. Gulyas, Gyula, tr. from HUN. LC 66-76589. 1966. 22.50 (*0-7206-3845-3*) Dufour.
Nemeth, M. Virus, Mycoplasm & Rickettsia Diseases of Fruit Trees. (Forestry Sciences Ser.). 1987. text 389.50 (*90-247-2868-1*) Kluwer Academic.
***Nemeth, Maria.** The Energy of Money: A Spiritual Guide to Financial & Personal Fulfillment. 336p. 2000. pap. 14.95 (*0-345-43497-8*) Ball Well.
Nemeth, Maria. The Energy of Money: A Spiritual Guide to Financial & Personal Fulfilment. LC 98-48294. (Illus.). 317p. 1999. 24.95 (*0-345-43099-9*) Ballantine Pub Grp.
— You & Money: Would It Be All Right with You If Life Got Easier? (Illus.). viii, 348p. (Orig.). 1997. pap. 18.95 (*1-890507-50-4*) Vildehiya.
Nemeth, Sally. Holy Days. 1991. pap. 6.95 (*0-88145-095-2*) Broadway Play.
— Sally's Shorts. 1995. pap. 5.25 (*0-8222-1454-7*) Dramatists Play.
Nemeth, Wolf, ed. see Nemeth, Bonnie.
Nemethy, Andrew L. Travel Vermont: The Best of the Green Mountain State. 3rd ed. LC 95-38316. (Illus.). 1995. pap. text 24.95 (*0-936896-39-6*) VT Life Mag.
Nemets, Alexander. The Growth of China & Prospects for the Eastern Regions of the Former U. S. S. R. LC 95-49264. 116p. 1996. text 59.95 (*0-7734-8798-0*) E Mellen.
Nemett, Barry. Crooked Tracks. LC 99-46880. write for info. (*1-57400-043-8*) Data Trace Pubng.
Nemett, Barry. Images, Objects & Ideas. 324p. (C). 1994. text. write for info. (*0-697-27459-4*) Brown & Benchmark.
Nemetz, Rowena. Bo's Search for Love & Understanding. LC 86-10379. (Illus.). 48p. (Orig.). (J). (gr. 1-6). 1986. pap. 5.95 (*0-941992-09-8*) Los Arboles Pub.
Nemhauser, Ellen. The Book of the Jewish Life. (Illus.). 96p. (Orig.). 1997. pap. text, teacher ed. 15.00 (*0-8074-0558-2*, 208045) UAHC.
Nemhauser, George L. Introduction to Dynamic Programming. LC 66-21046. (Series in Decision & Control). 270p. reprint ed. pap. 83.70 (*0-608-30977-X*, 201305300085) Bks Demand.
Nemhauser, George L., et al, eds. Optizmation: Handbooks in Operations Research & Management Science, Vol. 1. 710p. 1989. 165.00 (*0-444-87284-1*, North Holland) Elsevier.
Nemhauser, George L. & Wolsey, Laurence A. Integer & Combinatorial Optimization. LC 87-34067. (Discrete Mathematics Ser.). 784p. 1988. 165.00 (*0-471-82819-X*) Wiley.
— Integer & Combinatorial Optimization. (Wiley-Interscience Series in Discrete Mathematics). 766p. 1999. pap. 84.95 (*0-471-35943-2*) Wiley.
Nemhauser, George L., et al. Handbooks in Operations Research & Management Science, Vol. 7. LC 95-175001. 798p. 1995. 165.00 (*0-444-89292-3*, North Holland) Elsevier.
Nemiah, J. C. & Gallardo, F. P. Spanish-English - English-Spanish Glossary of Psychiatric Terminology. (ENG & SPA.). 504p. 1996. pap. 32.00 (*84-7978-234-X*, Pub. by Ediciones Diaz) IBD Ltd.
Nemiah, John C. Foundations of Psychopathology. 352p. 1966. pap. text 24.50 (*0-19-501137-6*) OUP.
Nemiah, John C., jt. ed. see Gold, Judith H.
Nemiah, John C., jt. ed. see Menninger, Roy W.
Nemilov, Sergei V. Vitreous State: Thermodynamic & Kinetic Aspects. 224p. 1994. boxed set 152.95 (*0-8493-3782-8*) CRC Pr.
Nemilova, I. S. French Painting of the Eighteenth Century in the State Hermitage. 268p. 1985. 175.00 (*0-7855-1778-2*) St Mut.
Nemiro, Beverly A. & Hamilton, Donna M. High Altitude Cookbook. LC 67-12738. 1980. 29.95 (*0-394-51308-8*) Random.
Nemiroff, Diana. Canadian Biennial of Contemporary Art. (FRE & ENG., Illus.). 188p. 1996. pap. 24.95 (*0-88884-595-2*) U Ch Pr.
— Jana Sterbak: States of Being. (FRE & ENG., Illus.). 96p. 1991. pap. 24.95 (*0-88884-616-9*) U Ch Pr.
Nemiroff, Diana, ed. Land, Spirit, Power: First Nations at the National Gallery of Canada. (Illus.). 96p. 1996. pap. 43.95 (*0-88884-650-9*) U Ch Pr.
Nemiroff, Diana & Kuspit, Donald. Roland Poulin: Sculpture. 160p. 1996. pap. text 29.95 (*0-88884-634-7*) U Ch Pr.
Nemiroff, Greta H. Reconstructing Education: Towards a Pedagogy of Critical Humanism. LC 91-33944. 224p. 1992. 55.00 (*0-89789-266-6*, H266, Bergin & Garvey); pap. 22.95 (*0-89789-267-4*, G267, Bergin & Garvey) Greenwood.
Nemiroff, Marc, jt. auth. see Rasmussen, Anne.
Nemiroff, Marc A. & Annunziata, Jane. A Child's First Book about Play Therapy. LC 90-49954. (Illus.). 60p. (J). 1990. pap. text 39.95 (*1-55798-089-6*) Am Psychol.
— A Child's First Book about Play Therapy. LC 90-49954. (Illus.). 60p. (J). (gr. 1-4). 1990. 19.95 (*1-55798-112-4*) Am Psychol.
— Help Is on the Way: A Child's Book about ADD. LC 98-3114. (Illus.). 64p. (J). (gr. k-4). 1998. 19.95 (*1-55798-505-7*, 441-5057) Am Psychol.
Nemiroff, Marc A., jt. auth. see Annunziata, Jane.
Nemiroff, R. A. & Colarusso, C. A. The Race Against Time: Psychotherapy & Psychoanalysis in the Second Half of Life. LC 84-17683. (Critical Issues in Psychiatry Ser.). (Illus.). 350p. (C). 1985. 55.00 (*0-306-41753-7*, Plenum Trade) Perseus Pubng.
Nemiroff, Robert. To Be Young, Gifted & Black: Lorraine Hansberry in Her Own Words. 1970. 11.09 (*0-606-01479-9*, Pub. by Turtleback) Demco.
Nemiroff, Robert, ed. & frwd. see Hansberry, Lorraine.
Nemiroff, Robert A., et al, eds. On Loving, Hating, & Living Well: The Public Psychoanalytic Lectures of Ralph R. Greenson, M.D. LC 92-1438. (Monograph Series of the Ralph R. Greenson Memorial Library of the San Diego Psychoanalytic Institute & Society). 382p. 1992. 55.00 (*0-8236-3790-5*) Intl Univs Pr.
Nemiroff, Robert A., jt. auth. see Colarusso, Calvin A.
Nemirovitch-Dantchenko, Vladimir. My Life in the Russian Theatre. LC 67-18053. (Illus.). 365p. 1987. pap. 69.90 (*0-87830-520-3*, Thtre Arts Bks) Routledge.
Nemirovskaias, M. A. Watercolours & Drawings of the Eighteenth & First Half of the Nineteenth Century in the Tretyakov Gallery. (ENG & RUS., Illus.). 162p. 1982. 173.00 (*0-7855-1682-4*) St Mut.
Nemirovskaya. Inside the Russian Soul. 1997. pap., student ed. 46.88 (*0-07-012225-3*) McGraw.
Nemirovski, Arkadii, jt. auth. see Nesterov, Yurii.
Nemirovsky, Irene. Life of Chekhov. LC 74-7101. (Studies in Russian Literature & Life: No. 100). 1974. lib. bdg. 75.00 (*0-8383-1865-7*) M S G Haskell Hse.
Nemitz, Barbara. Trans Plant: Living Vegetation in Contemporary Art. 1999. pap. text 45.00 (*3-89322-971-X*) Dr Cantz sche Druckerei GmbH.
Nemko, Martin. The College Matchmaker: Dr. Nemko Helps to find the Right College for You. 1996. pap. write for info. (*0-316-60369-4*) Little.
— How to Get an Ivy League Education at a State University. 784p. 1988. pap. 10.95 (*0-380-75375-8*, Avon Bks) Morrow Avon.
***Nemko, Martin.** You're Gonna Love This College Guide. LC 98-54148. 200p. (YA). 1999. pap. 9.95 (*0-7641-0816-6*) Barron.
Nemko, Martin & Hatfield, Susan R., eds. The Seven Principles in Action: Improving Undergraduate Education. 168p. (C). 1995. pap. text 24.95 (*1-882982-05-3*) Anker Pub.
Nemko, Marty. Cool Careers for Dummies. LC HF5382.5.U5N37 1998. (For Dummies Ser.). 432p. 1998. pap. 16.99 (*0-7645-5095-0*) IDG Bks.
Nemmers, Erwin E. Hobson & Underconsumption. LC 73-186784. (Reprints of Economic Classics Ser.). xi, 152p. 1972. reprint ed. 35.00 (*0-678-00672-5*) Kelley.
— Twenty Centuries of Catholic Church Music. LC 78-17248. 213p. 1978. reprint ed. lib. bdg. 35.00 (*0-313-20542-6*, NETW, Greenwood Pr) Greenwood.
Nemnich, Mary B., jt. auth. see Jandt, Fred E.
Nemnick, Mary B., jt. auth. see Jandt, Fred E.
***Nemo, Francois.** Semantique des Pertinences Enociatives. (Sciences pour la Communication Ser.: Vol. 58). 300p. 1999. 47.95 (*3-906761-98-3*, Pub. by P Lang) P Lang Pubng.
Nemo, John, ed. see Kavanagh, Patrick & O'Connor, P. J.
Nemo, Phillipe. Job & the Excess of Evil. Kigel, Michael, tr. from FRE. LC 98-9000. 255p. 1998. text 45.00 (*0-8207-0285-4*); pap. text 18.95 (*0-8207-0286-2*) Duquesne.
Nemoianu, Anca M. The Boat's Gonna Leave: A Study of Children Learning a Second Language from Conversations with Other Children. (Pragmatics & Beyond Ser.: Vol. 1:1). vi, 116p. 1980. pap. 29.00 (*90-272-2507-9*) J Benjamins Pubng Co.
Nemoianu, Virgil. The Taming of Romanticism: European Literature & the Age of the Biedermeier. (Studies in Comparative Literature: No. 37). 320p. 1984. 43.00 (*0-674-86802-1*) HUP.
— A Theory of the Secondary: Literature, Progress, & Reaction. LC 88-8362. (Parallax Ser.). 262p. reprint ed. pap. 81.30 (*0-608-06173-5*, 206650600008) Bks Demand.
Nemoianu, Virgil, ed. Romanticism in Its Modern Aspects & Early Discussions on Expanding Comparative Literary Studies. (Review of National Literatures & World Report Ser.: Vol. 1). 1998. 40.00 (*0-918680-73-5*) Griffon House.
Nemoianu, Virgil & Royal, Robert, eds. The Hospitable Canon: Essays on Literary Play, Scholarly Choice & Popular Pressures. LC 91-8337. (Cultura Ludens Ser.: Vol. 4). x, 252p. 1991. 74.00 (*1-55619-152-9*) J Benjamins Pubng Co.
— Play, Literature, Religion: Essays in Cultural Intertextuality. LC 91-4056. 221p. (C). 1992. pap. text 18.95 (*0-7914-0936-8*) State U NY Pr.
Nemore, Arnold L. & Mangum, Garth L. Reorienting the Federal - State Employment Service. (Policy Papers in Human Resources & Industrial Relations Ser.: No. 8). (Orig.). 1968. pap. 5.00 (*0-87736-108-8*) U of Mich Inst Labor.
Nemoshkalenko, V. V. & Antonov, V. N. Computational Methods in Solid State Physics. 312p. 1999. text 69.00 (*90-5699-094-2*, ECU88) Gordon & Breach.
Nemoto, Edwin M. & LaManna, Joseph C., eds. Oxygen Transport to Tissue, Vol. 18. LC 97-4326. (Advances in Experimental Medicine & Biology Ser.: Vol. 411). (Illus.). 624p. (C). 1997. text 159.50 (*0-306-45516-1*, Kluwer Plenum) Kluwer Academic.
Nemoy, Elizabeth M. Speech Correction Through Story-Telling Units. 1973. text 6.00 (*0-686-09399-2*) Expression.
Nemoy, Leon. Arabic Manuscripts in the Yale University Library. (Connecticut Academy of Arts & Sciences Ser., Trans.: Vol. 40). 1956. pap. 100.00 (*0-685-22894-0*) Elliots Bks.
— Karaite Anthology: Excerpts from the Early Literature. 1987. pap. 22.00 (*0-300-03929-8*) Yale U Pr.
Nemoy, Leon, jt. ed. see Katsh, Abraham I.
Nemschak, F., ed. World Economy & East-West Trade, Vol. 1. 1977. 39.95 (*0-387-81390-X*) Spr-Verlag.
Nemser, Cindy. Art Talk. enl. rev. ed. LC 95-45404. (Illus.). 368p. 1995. pap. 30.00 (*0-06-430983-5*) HarpC.
Nemser, Cindy. Ben Cunningham: A Life with Color. 92p. 1989. text 25.00 (*0-9622235-0-6*) Gordon & Breach.
— Ben Cunningham - A Life with Color. (Illus.). 92p. 1989. write for info. (*0-318-64797-4*) JPL Art Pubs.
Nemser, W., jt. ed. see Dezso, L.
Nemser, William. Experimental Study of Phonological Interference in the English of Hungarians. LC 68-66741. (Uralic & Altaic Ser.: Vol. 105). 191p. (Orig.). 1971. pap. text 12.00 (*0-87750-043-6*) Res Inst Inner Asian Studies.
***Nemtin, Frances.** Frank Lloyd Wright & Taliesin. LC 99-57563. 2000. 19.95 (*0-7649-1261-5*) Pomegranate Calif.
Nemvalts, Peep. Case Markings of Subject Phrases in Modern Standard Estonian. LC 96-209139. (Studia Uralica Upsaliensia: No. 25). 151p. (Orig.). 1996. pap. 39.50 (*91-554-3776-1*) Coronet Bks.
Nemy, Enid. Judith Leiber: The Art of the Handbag. LC 94-17787. (Illus.). 1995. pap. 17.50 (*0-8109-2609-1*, Pub. by Abrams) Time Warner.
— Judith Leiber: The Art of the Handbag. LC 94-17787. (Illus.). 192p. 1995. 39.95 (*0-8109-3571-6*, Pub. by Abrams) Time Warner.
Nemytskii, V. V. & Stepanov, V. V. Qualitative Theory of Differential Equations. 523p. 1989. pap. 14.95 (*0-486-65954-2*) Dover.
Nemzow, Martin A. Building Cyberstores: Installation, Transaction Processing, & Management. LC 97-2163. (Illus.). 522p. 1997. pap. 39.95 incl. cd-rom (*0-07-913090-9*) McGraw.
— Fast EtherNet: Implementations & Migration Solutions. LC 96-33935. (Illus.). 320p. 1997. pap. 40.00 (*0-07-046385-9*) McGraw.
— Implementing Wireless Networks. LC 94-43753. 241p. 1995. 45.00 (*0-07-046377-8*) McGraw.
— LAN Performance Optimization. 1993. pap. text 29.95 (*0-07-852659-0*) McGraw.
— The McGraw-Hill Essential ISDN Sourcebook. (Illus.). 366p. 1997. pap. 39.95 (*0-07-046384-0*) McGraw.
— Visual Basic Developer's Toolkit: Performance Optimization, Rapid Application Development, Debugging & Distribution. (Illus.). 464p. 1996. pap., pap. text 44.95 incl. cd-rom (*0-07-912309-0*) McGraw.
— Web Video Complete. LC 97-227213. (Illus.). 607p. 1997. pap. 54.95 incl. cd-rom (*0-07-046404-9*) McGraw.
Nenarkomova, I. Sizov. Art Treasures from the Museums of the Moscow Kremlin. 111p. 1980. 75.00 (*0-569-08692-2*) St Mut.
Nenaskev, Mikhail. An Ideal Betrayed: Testimonies of a Prominent & Loyal Member of the Soviet Establishment. 176p. 1995. pap. 14.95 (*1-871871-25-5*) Paul & Co Pubs.
***Nencel, Lorraine.** Ethnography & Prostitution in Peru. LC 00-9132. (Anthropolgy, Culture & Society Ser.). 2001. write for info. (*0-7453-1662-X*) Pluto GBR.
Nencel, Lorraine & Pels, Peter, eds. Constructing Knowledge: Authority & Critique in Social Science. (Inquiries in Social Construction Ser.). 256p. (C). 1991. text 55.00 (*0-8039-8401-4*); pap. text 22.50 (*0-8039-8402-2*) Sage.
Nenci, Italo & Castagnetta, L. Biology & Biochemistry of Normal & Cancer Cell Growth. xiv, 274p. 1988. text 258.00 (*3-7186-4816-4*) Gordon & Breach.
Nencka, Hanna. Low Dimensional Topology. LC 99-14986. (Contemporary Mathematics Ser.). 1999. write for info. (*0-8218-0884-2*) Am Math.
Nene, Y. L. & Thapliyal, P. N. Fungicides in Plant Disease Control. 3rd ed. 670p. (C). 1993. text 75.00 (*1-881570-22-3*) Science Pubs.
Nengel, John Gareh. Precolonial African Intergroup Relations in Kaura & Pengana Polities of Central Nigerian Highlands 1800-1900. LC 98-33249. (European University Studies: Vol. 814). (Illus.). 260p. 1999. pap. 45.95 (*0-8204-3231-8*) P Lang Pubng.
Nenneman, Richard A. Persistent Pilgrim: The Life of Mary Baker Eddy. LC 97-38216. 1997. 30.00 (*1-891331-02-7*, 1003) Nebbadoon Pr.
Nenner & Nyif. Over the Counter Trading. 1998. text. write for info. (*0-7352-0047-5*) P-H.
Nenner, Howard. The Right to Be King: The Succession to the Crown of England, 1603-1714. LC 95-14389. (Studies in Legal History). 450p. (C). 1995. reprint ed. text 49.95 (*0-8078-2247-7*) U of NC Pr.
Nenner, Howard, ed. Politics & the Political Imagination in Later Stuart Britain: Essays Presented to Lois Green Schwoerer. LC 97-40133. 240p. 1998. 75.00 (*1-878822-95-0*) Univ Rochester Pr.
Nenner, Irene, et al, eds. Molecules & Grains in Space. (AIP Conference Proceedings Ser.: No. 312). 832p. 1994. text 145.00 (*1-56396-355-8*) Am Inst Physics.
Nennessy, John. Second Manassas Battlefield Map Study. (Virginia Civil War Battles & Leaders Ser.). (Illus.). 504p. 1991. 39.95 (*1-56190-009-5*) H E Howard.
Nenninger, Timothy K. The Leavenworth Schools & the Old Army: Education, Professionalism, & the Officer Corps of the United States Army, 1881-1918., 15. LC 77-91105. (Contributions in Military History Ser.: No. 15). 173p. 1978. 49.95 (*0-313-20047-5*, NFL/) Greenwood.
Nenninger, Timothy K., jt. ed. see Ryan, Garry D.
Nennius. History of the Britons. Giles, J. A., tr. 1987. pap. 3.95 (*0-89979-019-4*) British Am Bks.

N

Nennius Abbot of Bangor. The Irish Nennius from Leabhar Na H-Uidre & Homilies & Legends from Leabhar Breac. Hogan, Edmund, ed. LC 78-72685. (Royal Irish Academy. Todd Lecture Ser.: Vol. 6). reprint ed. 16.50 (*0-404-60566-4*) AMS Pr.

Nenno, Mary K. Ending the Stalemate: Moving Housing & the Urban Development into the Mainstream of America's Future. 354p. (C). 1996. pap. text 32.50 (*0-7618-0217-7*); lib. bdg. 67.50 (*0-7618-0216-9*) U Pr of Amer.

Nenno, Robert B., jt. auth. see Gilligan, Lawrence G.

Nenon, T., ed. see Husserl, Edmund.

Nenon, Thomas, ed. see Embree, Lester E.

Nenon, Thomas J., Jr., tr. see Marx, Werner.

Nenov, Toshka G. & Yordanov, Stefcho P. Ceramic Sensors: Technology & Applications. LC 95-78690. 390p. 1995. pap. text 164.95 (*1-56676-309-6*) Technomic.

Nenshel, Robert P. The Servant Leader: Unleashing the Power of Your People. large type ed. Landau, Ken, ed. LC 98-165917. 198p. 1998. 25.00 (*0-9658933-2-4*) Visions Sports.

Nentvig, Juan. Rudo Ensayo: A Description of Sonora & Arizona in 1764. Pradeau, Alberto F. & Rasmussen, Robert R., trs. LC 79-20420. 188p. 1980. reprint ed. pap. 58.30 (*0-608-02353-1*, 206299400004) Bks Demand.

Nentwich, Michael & Weale, Albert, eds. Political Theory & the European Union: Legitimacy, Constitutional Choice & Citizenship. LC 98-4174. (European Political Science Ser.). (Illus.). 232p. (C). (gr. 13). 1998. 75.00 (*0-415-17313-2*, D5999) Routledge.

Nentwich, Phyllis F. Handbook of IV Medications, 1991. 544p. 1991. pap. 30.00 (*0-86720-441-9*) Jones & Bartlett.

— Intravenous Therapy. 512p. 1990. 50.00 (*0-86720-419-2*) Jones & Bartlett.

Nentwig, J. & Kreuder, M. General & Inorganic Chemistry Made Easy. 727p. 1992. pap. 54.95 (*0-471-18812-3*, Wiley-VCH) Wiley.

Nentwig, J. & Kreuder, M. Organic Chemistry Made Easy. 576p. 1992. pap. 89.95 (*0-471-18827-1*, Wiley-VCH) Wiley.

N

Nentwig, Joachim. Parat Lexikon Folientechnik. (GER.). 550p. 1991. 165.00 (*0-7859-8417-8*, 3527281819) Fr & Eur.

Nentwig, Joachim, et al. Chemistry Made Easy, 2 vols., Set, Pts. I & II. 750p. (C). 1992. pap. text 59.95 (*1-56081-549-3*, Wiley-VCH) Wiley.

— General & Inorganic Chemistry Made Easy. 744p. (C). 1992. pap. text 34.95 (*1-56081-502-7*, Wiley-VCH) Wiley.

— Organic Chemistry Made Easy. 558p. (C). 1992. pap. text 59.95 (*1-56081-548-5*, Wiley-VCH) Wiley.

Nentwig, K. Elsevier's Dictionary of Opto-Electronics & Electro-Optics: In English, German, French & Spanish. viii, 296p. 1986. 232.75 (*0-444-42617-5*) Elsevier.

— Elsevier's Dictionary of Opto-Electronics & Electro-Optics in English, German, French & Spanish. (ENG, FRE, GER & SPA.). 296p. 1986. 295.00 (*0-8288-9242-3*, F92345) Fr & Eur.

— Elsevier's Dictionary of Solar Technology. (ENG, FRE, GER, ITA & SPA.). 214p. 1985. 250.00 (*0-8288-9255-5*, M15475) Fr & Eur.

— Elsevier's Dictionary of Solar Technology: In English, German, French, Spanish & Italian. 222p. 1985. 199.00 (*0-444-42459-8*) Elsevier.

Nentwig, W. Spiders of Panama. (Flora & Fauna Handbook Ser.: No. 12). (Illus.). 288p. (Orig.). 1993. lib. bdg. 65.00 (*1-877743-18-6*) Sandhill Crane.

Nentwig, W., ed. Ecophysiology of Spiders. (Illus.). 465p. 1987. 341.95 (*0-387-17034-0*) Spr-Verlag.

Nentwig, Wendy L. Moonstruck in Manhattan. (Unmistakably Cooper Ellis Ser.). 16p. 1998. pap. 5.99 (*0-7642-2066-7*) Bethany Hse.

— Subway Tokens in the Sand, Vol. 3. (Unmistakably Cooper Ellis Ser.). 160p. 1999. pap. text 5.99 (*0-7642-2067-5*) Bethany Hse.

— Tripping over Skyscrapers. LC 98-220295. (Unmistakably Cooper Ellis Ser.). 16p. 1998. pap. 5.99 (*0-7642-2065-9*) Bethany Hse.

***Nentwig, Wendy Lee.** Cabs, Cameras & Catastrophes, 4. (Unmistakably Cooper Ellis Ser.). 160p. 1999. pap. text 5.99 (*0-7642-2068-3*) Bethany Hse.

Nentwig, Wolfgang, jt. auth. see Heimer, Stefan.

Neocleous. Administering Civil Society. LC 96-8631. 240p. 1996. text 65.00 (*0-312-16155-7*) St Martin.

— Fascism. LC 96-45152. (Concepts in the Social Sciences Ser.). 1997. 2.00 (*0-335-19487-7*); 9.00 (*0-335-19488-5*) OpUniv Pr.

***Neocleous, Mark.** The Fabrication of Order: A Critical Theory of Police Power. LC 00-22301. 160p. 2000. 69.95 (*0-7453-1489-9*, Pub. by Pluto GBR); pap. 22.50 (*0-7453-1484-8*, Pub. by Pluto GBR) Stylus Pub VA.

Neocleous, Mark. Fascism. LC 96-48811. (Concepts in Social Thought Ser.). 1997. pap. 14.95 (*0-8166-3040-2*) U of Minn Pr.

Neocleous, Martha W. Personal Injury Practice & Procedure in Europe. LC 98-158744. xi, 182p. 1997. pap. 68.50 (*1-85941-179-7*, Pub. by Cavendish Pubng) Gaunt.

Neocosmos, Michael. Agrarian Question in Southern Africa & Accumulation from Below: Economics & Politics in the Struggle for Democracy. (Research Reports: Vol. 93). 109p. 1993. pap. text 16.95 (*91-7106-342-0*, Pub. by Nordic Africa) Transaction Pubs.

Neog, Maheswar. Srihastamuktavali: A Text of Ancient Indian Aescetics. (C). 1991. 30.00 (*81-208-0829-0*, Pub. by Motilal Bnarsidass) S Asia.

Neogi, P., ed. Diffusion in Polymers. (Plastics Engineering Ser.: Vol. 32). (Illus.). 328p. 1996. text 165.00 (*0-8247-9530-X*) Dekker.

Neogi, P., jt. auth. see Miller, C.

Neogy, Rathin. Two Canadians?? LC 98-96905. ix, 124p. 1998. pap. 14.00 (*0-9669227-0-0*) CTS Intl.

Neophyton, Andrea. Fresh Flower Arranger's Companion. 1994. 10.98 (*0-7858-0099-9*) Bk Sales Inc.

Neoptolemos, John, et al, eds. Pancreatic Cancer: Molecular & Clinical Advances. LC 95-35297. 360p. 1995. 150.00 (*0-86542-973-1*) Blackwell Sci.

Neoptolemos, John P., et al, eds. Surgical Treatment of Chronic Pancreatitis: New Standards. (Journal: Digestive Surgery: Vol. 13, No. 2, 1996). (Illus.). 96p. 1996. pap. 54.00 (*3-8055-6323-X*) S Karger.

Neou, Vivian. Internet: Domain Administration. 250p. (C). 2000. pap. 32.00 (*0-13-511180-3*) P-H.

Nepal, M. P. Socio-Economic History of Ancient & Medieval Nepal. 1997. pap. 22.00 (*0-7855-7494-8*, Pub. by Ratna Pustak Bhandar) St Mut.

Nepaulsingh, Colbert I. Apples of Gold in Filigrees of Silver: Jewish Writing in the Eye of the Inquisition. (New Perspectives: Jewish Life & Thought Ser.). 200p. (C). 1995. 40.00 (*0-8419-1358-7*); pap. 18.00 (*0-8419-1361-7*) Holmes & Meier.

— Towards a History of Literary Composition in Medieval Spain. (Romance Ser.). 302p. 1986. text 45.00 (*0-8020-2570-6*) U of Toronto Pr.

Nepaulsingh, Colbert I., tr. Pero Tafur & Cyprus. (Sources for the History of Cyprus Ser.: Vol. IV). 85p. (Orig.). 1997. pap. 25.00 (*0-9651704-4-6*) Greece & Cyprus Res.

Nepershin, R., jt. auth. see Druyanov, B.

Neperud, Ron, ed. Context, Content, & Community in Art Education: Beyond Postmodernism. 272p. (C). 1995. text 48.00 (*0-8077-3445-4*); pap. text 22.95 (*0-8077-3444-6*) Tchrs Coll.

Neperud, Ronald W., jt. ed. see Farley, Frank H.

***Neph, Joan.** Inner Thoughts. 1999. pap. write for info. (*1-58235-283-6*) Watermrk Pr.

Nephew, John. Arcana. (On the Edge Ser.). 1995. 1.95 (*1-887801-27-8*, Atlas Games) Trident MN.

— Monstrous Compendium: Mystara, Vol. 19. LC 94-215338. (Advanced Dungeons & Dragons, 2nd Edition Ser.: MC19). 1994. 18.00 (*1-56076-875-4*) TSR Inc.

Nephew, John, ed. Forgotten Lives: An Over the Edge Adventure Anthology. (Over the Edge Ser.). (Illus.). 112p. 1997. pap. 19.95 (*1-887801-51-0*) Trident MN.

Nephew, John, jt. auth. see Tweet, Jonathan.

Nephew, John, ed. see Laws, Robin D.

Nephew, John, ed. see Tweet, Jonathan & Laws, Robin D.

Nephew, Sara. Happy Halloween. (Illus.). 36p. 1997. pap. 9.95 (*0-9621172-6-9*) Clearview Triangle.

— Merry Christmas. (Illus.). 36p. (Orig.). 1997. pap. 4.00 (*0-9621172-5-0*) Clearview Triangle.

— New Labels. (Illus.). 16p. 1998. pap. 6.95 (*0-9621172-8-5*) Clearview Triangle.

— Patchwork Zoo. (Illus.). 144p. 1998. pap. 24.95 (*0-9621172-7-7*) Clearview Triangle.

***Nephew, Sara.** Special Times. 36p. 2000. pap. 9.95 (*1-930294-00-X*) Clearview Triangle.

— Town & Country. 36p. 2000. pap. 9.95 (*1-930294-01-8*) Clearview Triangle.

Nephew, Sara A. Building Block Quilts. LC 89-82476. (Illus.). 64p. (Orig.). 1990. pap. 14.95 (*0-9621172-1-8*) Clearview Triangle.

— Easy & Elegant Quilts. LC 93-72737. (Illus.). 64p. (Orig.). 1994. pap. 5.00 (*0-9621172-3-4*) Clearview Triangle.

— Equilateral Triangle Patchwork: Complete Instructions for 11 Quilts. (Illus.). 56p. 1992. reprint ed. pap. 4.95 (*0-486-27048-3*) Dover.

— Mock Applique. LC 95-67105. (Illus.). 72p. (Orig.). 1995. pap. 5.00 (*0-9621172-4-2*) Clearview Triangle.

— Quilt Designs from the Thirties. LC 93-41394. (Illus.). 64p. 1994. reprint ed. pap. 7.95 (*0-486-28156-6*) Dover.

— Sensational 6-Pointed Star Quilts. LC 99-94905. (Illus.). 56p. 1999. pap. 14.95 (*0-9621172-9-3*, B-21) Clearview Triangle.

— Stars & Flowers: Three-Sided Patchwork. LC 88-72380. (Illus.), 56p. (Orig.). 1989. pap. 5.00 (*0-9621172-0-X*) Clearview Triangle.

Nephrology Symposium Staff. Glomerulonephritis: Proceedings of the Nephrology Symposium, 3rd, Hannover, June 1975. Sterzel, R. B., ed. (Contributions to Nephrology Ser.: Vol. 2). (Illus.). 200p. 1976. 29.75 (*3-8055-2318-1*) S Karger.

— Interstitial Nephropathies: Proceedings of the Nephrology Symposium, 6th, Hannover, May 1978. Kuhn, K., ed. (Contributions to Nephrology Ser.: Vol. 16). (Illus.). 1979. pap. 29.75 (*3-8055-2979-1*) S Karger.

Nepo, Mark. Acre of Light: Living with Cancer. 1994. pap. 9.95 (*0-87886-138-6*) Greenfld Rev Lit.

***Nepo, Mark.** The Book of Awakening: Having the Life You Want By Being Present to the Life You Have. 378p. 2000. pap. 16.95 (*1-57324-117-2*) Conari Press.

Nepomnyashchy, A. A., jt. auth. see Simanovskii, I. B.

Nepomnyashchy, Catharine T. Abram Tertz & the Poetics of Crime. LC 94-40946. (Studies of the Harriman Institute; Russian Literature & Thought Ser.). 368p. 1995. 35.00 (*0-300-06210-9*) Yale U Pr.

***Neporent, Liz.** Fitness Walking for Dummies. 350p. 1999. pap. 19.99 (*0-7645-5192-2*) IDG Bks.

Neporent, Liz, jt. auth. see Schlosberg, Suzanne.

Neporent, Liz W. Crunch: A Complete Guide to Health & Fitness. LC 96-30821. 240p. 1997. pap. 14.95 (*0-385-48809-2*, Main St Bks) Doubleday.

Neporent, Liz W. & Hart, Leisa. Buns of Steel Total Body Workout. (Illus.). 272p. (Orig.). 1995. mass mkt. 13.99 (*0-446-67089-8*, Pub. by Warner Bks) Little.

Neporent, Liz W., et al. Crunch! A Complete Guide to Health & Fitness for Men & Women from the Hottest Gym in America. 1996. 16.00 (*0-614-99276-1*) Vin Bks.

Nepote, Jacques. Vietnam. 2nd rev. ed. LC 98-32320. (Odyssey Passport Ser.). (Illus.). 240p. 1999. pap. 19.95 (*962-217-355-1*) China Guides.

Neppe, Vernon M. Cry the Beloved Mind: A Voyage of Hope. LC 98-67899. (Illus.). 383p. 1999. write for info. (*1-58412-000-2*); cd-rom. write for info. (*1-58412-001-0*) Brainvoyage.

— Cry the Beloved Mind: A Voyage of Hope. LC 98-67899. (Illus.). 366p. 1999. pap. 22.95 (*0-89716-823-2*, Peanut Btr Pubng) Elton-Wolf Pub.

— Innovative Psychopharmacotherapy. LC 88-30741. 237p. 1989. reprint ed. pap. 73.50 (*0-608-03435-5*, 206413600008) Bks Demand.

Neppi, Enzo. Le Babil et la Caresse: Pensee du Maternel Chez Sartre, Vol. 210. (American University Studies: Romance Languages & Literature: No. II). (FRE.). XI, 180p. (C). 1995. 32.95 (*0-8204-2393-9*) P Lang Pubng.

Neprash, Ivan V., et al. Glory Filled the Land. 205p. 1989. lib. bdg. 17.95 (*0-926474-00-6*) Intl Awakening Pr.

— Glory Filled the Land: A Trilogy on the Welsh Revival of 1904-1905. Roberts, Richard O., ed. xvi, 204p. 1989. 17.95 (*0-940033-38-0*) R O Roberts.

Neprash, Jerry A. Brookhart Campaigns in Iowa, 1920-1926. LC 68-58612. (Columbia University. Studies in the Social Sciences: No. 366). reprint ed. 20.00 (*0-404-51366-2*) AMS Pr.

Nepstad, Daniel & Schwartzman, Stephen, eds. Non-Timber Products from Tropical Forests: Evaluation of a Conservation & Development Strategy. LC 92-14911. (Advances in Economic Botany Ser.: Vol. 9). 176p. 1992. pap. text 18.95 (*0-89327-376-7*) NY Botanical.

Neptume, Arnold, jt. ed. see Mead, Alice.

Neptune, Vincent J. A Jackass in Moonlight. LC 98-96792. 72p. 1998. boxed set 24.95 (*1-893334-00-7*) Trident Pr.

Nequam, Alexander, jt. auth. see Thomson, Rodney M.

***Ner-David, Haviva.** Life on the Fringes: A Feminist Journey Toward. 2000. 21.95 (*0-9664306-7-0*) JFL Bks.

Ner, Sonia, ed. see O'Boyle, Lily G. & Alejandro, Reynaldo.

Nera, Franca. All That Glitters. (Sapphire Ser.). 1999. pap. text 9.95 (*0-352-33426-6*) London Brdge.

Neracher, Mark, see Training Mark, pseud.

Neracher, Mark R. Car Buying - "Why Won't Anyone Tell Me the Price?" A Gold Level General Sales Manager Reveals Trade Secrets, Tips to Successful Car Buying. 2nd ed. 112p. (Orig.). 1996. per. 7.95 (*0-9631803-1-2*) Bookmark AZ.

Nerad, Hasan. Essentials of Infectious Diseases. 2000. pap. text Price not set. (*0-7216-8114-X*, W B Saunders Co) Harcrt Hlth Sci Grp.

Nerad, Jack R. Fatal Photographs: The True Story of a Model's Brutal Murder & the Search for Justice. LC 98-93297. (Illus.). 352p. 1998. mass mkt. 6.99 (*0-380-79770-4*, Avon Bks) Morrow Avon.

— 50 Greatest Cars of All Time: From the Ford Model T to the Ferrari Testarossa. LC 97-40465. (Illus.). 224p. 1997. pap. text 16.95 (*0-8065-1935-5*, Citadel Pr) Carol Pub Group.

***Nerad, Jeffrey A.** The Requisites in Ophthalmology: Oculoplastic Surgery. (Illus.). 450p. (C). 1999. text. write for info. (*0-323-00174-2*) Mosby Inc.

Nerad, Maresi. The Academic Kitchen: A Social History of Gender Stratification at the University of California, Berkeley. LC 98-11597. (SUNY Series in Frontiers in Education). (Illus.). 224p. (C). 1999. text 59.50 (*0-7914-3969-0*); pap. text 19.95 (*0-7914-3970-4*) State U NY Pr.

Nerad, Thomas A., ed. American Type Culture Collection Catalogue of Protists. 18th ed. 100p. 1993. pap. text. write for info. (*0-930009-50-9*) ATCC.

Neraudau, Jean-Pierre. Dictionnaire d'Histoire de l'Art. (FRE.). 544p. 1985. 125.00 (*0-8288-1417-1*, F26160) Fr & Eur.

Neray, Ruth B. To Auschwitz & Back: My Personal Journey. unabridged ed. 152p. 1998. 19.95 (*0-9660026-0-1*) Sudbury Pr.

Nerbonne, John, ed. Linguistic Databases. LC 97-15734. (Lecture Notes Ser.: Vol. 77). 243p. (C). 1998. text 64.95 (*1-57586-093-7*); pap. text 24.95 (*1-57586-092-9*) CSLI.

Nerbonne, John, et al. German in Head-Driven Phrase Structure Grammar. LC 93-40350. (CSLI Lecture Notes Ser.: No. 46). 420p. 1995. 49.95 (*1-881526-30-5*); pap. 21.95 (*1-881526-29-1*) CSLI.

Nerbonne, Michael A., jt. ed. see Schow, Ronald L.

***Nerburn, Kent.** Calm Surrender: Walking the Hard Road of Forgiveness. LC 99-42245. 128p. 2000. 16.00 (*1-57731-119-1*) New Wrld Lib.

Nerburn, Kent. A Haunting Reverence: Meditations on a Northern Land. LC 98-33191. 1999. reprint ed. pap. 14.95 (*0-8166-3384-3*) U of Minn Pr.

— Letters to My Son: A Father's Wisdom on Manhood, Life & Love. 2nd rev. ed. LC 98-51499. 240p. 1999. pap. 12.95 (*1-57731-031-4*, Pub. by New Wrld Lib) Publishers Group.

***Nerburn, Kent.** Make Me an Instrument of Your Peace: Living in the Spirit of the Prayer of Saint Francis. LC 98-43675. 1999. pap. write for info. (*0-06-251582-9*) Harper SF.

Nerburn, Kent. Make Me an Instrument of Your Peace: Living in the Spirit of the Prayer of Saint Francis. LC 98-43675. 144p. 1999. 16.00 (*0-06-251581-0*, Pub. by Harper SF) HarpC.

— Neither Wolf nor Dog: On Forgotten Roads with an Indian Elder. LC 94-21558. 308p. 1994. pap. 14.00 (*1-880032-37-6*) New Wrld Lib.

— Simple Truths: Clear & Gentle Guidance on the Big Issues in Life. LC 96-5130. 112p. 1996. 15.00 (*1-880032-92-9*) New Wrld Lib.

— Small Graces: The Quiet Gifts of Everyday Life. LC 98-5115. 128p. 1998. 15.00 (*1-57731-072-1*) New Wrld Lib.

Nerburn, Kent, ed. The Soul of an Indian: And Other Writings from Ohiyesa (Charles Alexander Eastman) LC 93-24678. (Classic Wisdom Collection). 96p. 1993. 15.00 (*1-880032-23-6*) New Wrld Lib.

— The Wisdom of the Native Americans: Includes the Soul of an Indian & Other Writings by Ohiyesa, & the Great Speeches of Red Jacket, Chief Joseph & Chief Seattle. LC 98-42936. 272p. 1999. text 16.95 (*1-57731-079-9*) New Wrld Lib.

Nerburn, Kent & Mengelkoch, Louise, compiled by. Native American Wisdom. LC 91-21315. (Classic Wisdom Collection). 128p. 1991. 15.00 (*0-931432-78-2*) New Wrld Lib.

Nercessian, Y. T. Armenian Coins & Their Values. LC 94-94430. (Illus.). 297p. 1995. lib. bdg. 48.00 (*0-9606842-8-X*) ANS.

— Armenian Numismatic Bibliography & Literature. LC 83-73256. 729p. 1984. boxed set 50.00 (*0-9606842-2-0*) ANS.

***Nercessian, Y. T.** Armenian Numismatic Studies. LC 99-72221. (Illus.). viii, 774p. 2000. boxed set 75.00 (*0-9606842-9-8*) ANS.

Nercessian, Y. T. Attribution & Dating of Armenian Bilingual Trams. (Illus.). 48p. (Orig.). 1983. 6.75 (*0-9606842-1-2*) ANS.

— Bank Notes of Armenia. LC 86-70860. 416p. 1988. boxed set 30.00 (*0-9606842-5-5*) ANS.

Nercessian, Y. T., ed. Studies in Honor of Dr. Paul Z. Bedoukian, Armenian Numismatic Journal, 1989, Vol. 15: Essays Dedicated in Honor of Dr. Paul Z. Bedoukian on the Fortieth Year of His Contributions. (ARM & ENG., Illus.). 192p. 1989. 30.00 (*0-9606842-6-3*) ANS.

***Nerdel, Carol.** Divorce, Remarriage & the Falling Away. 152p. 1999. pap. 10.00 (*0-9667651-1-7*) Complete in Christ.

Nerdeman, Cary J. Defensor Minor & de Translatione Imperli. LC 92-33311. (Cambridge Texts in the History of Political Thought Ser.). 120p. (C). 1993. pap. text 16.95 (*0-521-40846-6*) Cambridge U Pr.

Nerdinger, Winfried. Architectural Guide Germany, 20th Century. LC 96-218056. (Illus.). 540p. 1996. 40.00 (*3-7643-5315-5*, Pub. by Birkhauser) Princeton Arch.

— Gropius Archive, 1930-1936, Vol. II. LC 90-3058. 500p. 1990. reprint ed. text 175.00 (*0-8240-3341-8*) Garland.

— The Walter Gropius Archive, 1936-1957, Vol. III. LC 90-3058. (Illus.). 500p. 1990. reprint ed. text 200.00 (*0-8240-3342-6*) Garland.

Nerdinger, Winfried, ed. Alvar Aalto: Toward A Human Modernism. LC 99-18300. (Illus.). 168p. 1999. 29.95 (*3-7913-2049-1*) te Neues.

Nerdinger, Winifred, ed. Walter Gropius, 1911-1930: Collection of the Busch-Reisinger Museum. LC 90-3058. (Walter Gropius Archive Ser.: Vol. I of 4). (Illus.). 500p. 1990. reprint ed. text 175.00 (*0-8240-3340-X*) Garland.

***Nerdrum, Lars.** The Economics of Human Capital. 274p. (C). 1999. pap. 37.00 (*82-00-45161-5*, Pub. by Scand Univ Pr) IBD Ltd.

Nerenberg, Arnie. Love & Estrangement in the Baha'i Community. 137p. (Orig.). 1986. 14.95 (*0-933770-47-2*) Kalimat.

Nerenberg, Arnold. Hi Mom & Dad, I'm Here. (Orig.). 1994. pap. text 9.95 (*1-878113-06-2*) Bell Pubns.

— Path of the Wrong Way. (C). 1987. pap. write for info. (*1-878113-00-3*) Bell Pubns.

Nerenberg, Ellen V., jt. auth. see Galluci, Carole C.

Nerenberg, Jack. Living off the Earnings of a Hooker: The Seafood Recipes of Jack Nerenberg, PhD. unabridged ed. (Illus.). 95p. 1997. mass mkt. 15.95 (*0-9661559-0-4*) Aunt Chelada.

Nerenberg, Lisa. Innovative Training Package for Detecting & Aiding Victims of Domestic Elder Abuse. LC 94-65125. 474p. 1993. ring bd. 55.00 (*1-878734-32-6*) Police Exec Res.

Nerenz, Anne & Ariew. C'Est a Dire: Premiers Echanges. (C). 1989. text, mass mkt. 42.95 incl. audio (*0-8384-1696-9*) Heinle & Heinle.

— C'Est a Dire: Premiers Echanges. (FRE.). (C). 1989. suppl. ed. 23.95 incl. audio (*0-8384-1703-5*) Heinle & Heinle.

— A Proposito! 1992. mass mkt. 16.95 (*0-8384-2369-8*) Heinle & Heinle.

— Sans Doute. 1992. mass mkt. 15.95 (*0-8384-2379-5*) Heinle & Heinle.

Nerenz, Anne, jt. auth. see Ariew, Robert.

Nereson, Sally. Outside the Lines but on the Page: Perspectives on Writing in an Individualized, Writing-Intensive Baccalaureate Degree Program. Bridwell-Bowles, Lillian & Olson, Mark, eds. (Technical Reports: No. 8). 38p. (Orig.). (C). 1994. pap. 3.50 (*1-881221-14-8*) U Minn Ctr Interdis.

Neressian, Nancy J. Faraday to Einstein: Constructing Meaning in Scientific Theories. 210p. 1984. lib. bdg. 107.50 (*90-247-2997-1*, Pub. by M Nijhoff) Kluwer Academic.

Neret, G., jt. auth. see Muthesius, A.

Neret, Giles. Dali, Vol. II. LC 97-6596. (Thunder Bay Artists Ser.). 1997. 4.99 (*1-57145-096-3*, Thunder Bay) Advantage Pubs.

Neret, Gilles. Aubrey Beardsley. 1998. pap. 9.99 (*3-8228-7173-7*) Taschen Amer.

— Aubrey Beardsley. (Albums Ser.). 1998. pap. 9.99 (*3-8228-7200-8*) Taschen Amer.

— Auguste Rodin. (Albums Ser.). (Illus.). 95p. 1997. pap. 9.99 (*3-8228-8662-9*) Taschen Amer.

— Dali. 96p. 1994. pap. 9.99 (*3-8228-9326-9*) Taschen Amer.

— Dali. (SPA.). 1996. pap. 9.99 (*3-8228-9549-0*) Taschen Amer.

An Asterisk (*) at the beginning of an entry indicates that the title is appearing for the first time.

— De Lempicka. (Basic Ser.). 1994. pap. 9.99 (*3-8228-0558-0*) Taschen Amer.
— Delacroix. (Basic Art Ser.). 96p. 1999. pap. 9.99 (*3-8228-7640-2*) Taschen Amer.
— Description of Egypt. 1995. pap. 29.99 (*3-8228-8964-4*) Taschen Amer.
— Erotic Art. 200p. 1994. pap. 19.99 (*3-8228-9652-7*) Taschen Amer.
— Erotica Universalis. 1995. pap. 29.99 (*3-8228-8963-6*) Taschen Amer.
***Neret, Gilles.** Erotica Universalis. 2000. pap. text 29.99 (*3-8228-6418-8*) Taschen Amer.
Neret, Gilles. Furniture Design. 1994. pap. 24.99 (*3-8228-0276-X*) Taschen Amer.
— Klimt. (Basic Ser.). 1994. pap. 9.99 (*3-8228-9647-0*) Taschen Amer.
— Klimt. (SPA.). 1996. pap. 9.99 (*3-8228-0683-8*) Taschen Amer.
Neret, Gilles. KR - Lempicka - Spanish. 1996. 12.99 (*3-8228-0662-5*) Benedikt Taschen.
Neret, Gilles. Matisse. (Big Ser.). 1997. pap. 19.99 (*3-8228-8276-3*) Taschen Amer.
***Neret, Gilles.** Matisse. 1999. 19.99 (*3-8228-6543-5*) Taschen Amer.
Neret, Gilles. Matisse Cut-Outs. (Illus.). 95p. 1997. pap. 9.99 (*3-8228-8658-0*) Taschen Amer.
— Michelangelo. 1998. 9.99 (*3-8228-8272-0*, Pub. by Taschen Amer) Bks Nippan.
— Michelangelo Postcard Book. 1998. pap. 5.99 (*3-8228-7985-1*) Taschen Amer.
— 1000 Dessous: A History of Lingerie. 1998. pap. 29.99 (*3-8228-7629-1*) Taschen Amer.
— Serge Jacques. 1998. pap. 29.99 (*3-8228-7880-4*) Taschen Amer.
Neret, Gilles. Toulouse-Lautrec. LC 00-9282. 200p. 1995. pap. 19.99 (*3-8228-9036-7*) Taschen Amer.
***Neret, Gilles.** Toulouse-Lautrec. 1999. 19.99 (*3-8228-7018-8*) Taschen Amer.
Neret, Gilles, ed. see Wildenstein, Daniel.
Neretin, Yu A. Categories of Symmetries & Infinite-Dimensional Groups. Gould, G. G., tr. (London Mathematical Society Monographs: No. 16). (Illus.). 432p. 1996. text 115.00 (*0-19-851186-8*) OUP.
***Nergaard, Bea.** Boffin's Journey. LC 98-68154. (Illus.). 95p. 1999. pap. 11.95 (*1-882792-72-6*) Proctor Pubns.
Nergaard, Bea, ed. see Nightingale, Florence.
Nergaard, R. Arnfinn. The Smedvig Production Unit. 1989. 150.00 (*90-6314-520-9*, Pub. by Lorne & MacLean Marine) St Mut.
Nerhood, Harry W., jt. ed. see Tupper, Harmon.
Nerhot, Patrick. Law, Writing, Meaning: An Essay in Legal Hermeneutics. (Law & Society Ser.). 224p. (C). 1993. text 65.00 (*0-7486-0391-3*, Pub. by Edinburgh U Pr) Col U Pr.
Nerhot, Patrick, ed. Law, Interpretation & Reality: Essays in Epistemology, Hermeneutics & Jurisprudence. (Law & Philosophy Library). 470p. (C). 1990. lib. bdg. 207.50 (*0-7923-0593-0*, Pub. by Kluwer Academic) Kluwer Academic.
— Legal Knowledge & Analogy: Fragments of Legal Epistemology, Hermeneutics & Linguistics. 250p. (C). 1991. lib. bdg. 135.00 (*0-7923-1065-9*, Pub. by Kluwer Academic) Kluwer Academic.
Neri, Ana, tr. see Jaramillo, Carmen M.
Neri, Claudio. Group. Trollope, Christine, tr. from ITA. LC 98-147966. 260p. 1996. pap. 29.95 (*1-85302-416-3*, Pub. by Jessica Kingsley) Taylor & Francis.
Neri, Helene M., tr. see Schaefer, Udo.
Neri, Joseph. So I Said to the Little Old Man. Edwards, Kristen, ed. (Illus.). 96p. (Orig.). (J). (gr. k-6). 1994. pap. 12.95 (*0-9639428-3-2*); lib. bdg. 14.99 (*0-9639428-1-6*) Tympanon Prods.
Neri, Kirs. Revenge of the Gypsy Queen: A Tracy Eaton Mystery. LC 99-22401. 272p. 1999. 20.00 (*1-56825-043-6*, 043-6) Rainbow Books.
Neri, Louise, ed. Rachel Whiteread's Water Tower. (Illus.). 176p. 1999. 39.95 (*3-908247-16-0*, Pub. by Scalo Pubs) Dist Art Pubs.
Neri, Louise & Crugier, Bice, eds. Collaboration Sigmar Polke. (Parkett Art Magazine Ser.: No. 30). (Illus.). 220p. 1991. pap. 19.50 (*3-907509-80-3*, Pub. by Parkett Verlag AG) Dist Art Pubs.
Neri, Louise, jt. auth. see Phillips, Lisa.
Neri, Max, jt. auth. see Hamilton, Jeffrey.
Neri, Michael C. Hispanic Catholicism in Transitional California: The Life of Jose Gonzalez Rubio, O.F.M. (1804-1875) LC 95-33585. 164p. (C). 1997. 30.00 (*0-88382-065-X*) AAFH.
Neri, P. J. The Curse of Pele. LC 98-147356. (Hawaii Chillers Ser.: No. 2). 112p. (Orig.). (J). (gr. 3-6). 1997. pap. 4.95 (*1-57306-028-3*) Bess Pr.
— The Ghost-Dog of Makaena Point. (Hawaii Chillers Ser.: Vol. 5). 128p. (J). (gr. 3-6). 1998. pap. 4.95 (*1-57306-044-5*) Bess Pr.
— In Perfect Harmony. (Diamond Head High Ser.). 144p. (YA). (gr. 5-8). 1999. pap. 4.95 (*1-57306-105-0*) Bess Pr.
— Killer Cockroaches. (Hawaii Chillers Ser.: Vol. 6). 128p. (J). (gr. 3-6). 1998. pap. 4.95 (*1-57306-045-3*) Bess Pr.
— The Missionary's Ghost. LC 98-149722. (Hawaii Chillers Ser.: No. 3). 104p. (Orig.). (J). (gr. 3-6). 1997. pap. 4.95 (*1-57306-029-1*) Bess Pr.
— The Night of the Living Tiki. (Hawaii Chillers Ser.: Vol. 4). 128p. (J). (gr. 3-6). 1998. pap. 4.95 (*1-57306-043-7*) Bess Pr.
— The Shark-Man of Kapu Bay. LC 98-234411. (Hawaii Chillers Ser.: No. 1). 104p. (Orig.). (J). (gr. 3-6). 1997. pap. 4.95 (*1-57306-030-5*) Bess Pr.
Neri, Penelope. Beloved Scoundrel. 1983. mass mkt. 3.75 (*0-8217-1259-4*, Zebra Kensgtn) Kensgtn Pub Corp.
— Cherish the Night. 1992. mass mkt. 5.99 (*0-8217-3654-X*, Zebra Kensgtn) Kensgtn Pub Corp.
— Crimson Angel. 1986. mass mkt. 3.95 (*0-317-39257-3*, Zebra Kensgtn) Kensgtn Pub Corp.
***Neri, Penelope.** Highland Lovesong. 368p. 2000. mass mkt. 5.99 (*0-8439-4724-1*, Leisure Bks) Dorchester Pub Co.
Neri, Penelope. Jasmine Paradise. 1983. mass mkt. 3.75 (*0-8217-1170-9*, Zebra Kensgtn) Kensgtn Pub Corp.
***Neri, Penelope.** Keeper of My Heart. 400p. (Orig.). 1999. mass mkt. 5.99 (*0-8439-4647-4*, Leisure Bks) Dorchester Pub Co.
Neri, Penelope. The Love Within. 320p. 1997. mass mkt. 5.99 (*0-8217-5398-3*, Zebra Kensgtn) Kensgtn Pub Corp.
— Master of Midnight. 1995. pap. 4.99 (*0-8217-5035-6*) NAL.
— Passion's Betrayal. 1985. mass mkt. 3.95 (*0-8217-1568-2*, Zebra Kensgtn) Kensgtn Pub Corp.
— Passion's Rapture. 1982. mass mkt. 3.50 (*0-89083-912-3*, Zebra Kensgtn) Kensgtn Pub Corp.
***Neri, Penelope.** Scandals. 400p. 1999. mass mkt. 5.99 (*0-8439-4470-6*, Leisure Bks) Dorchester Pub Co.
Neri, Penelope. Sea Jewel. 496p. 1986. mass mkt. 3.95 (*0-8217-1888-6*, Zebra Kensgtn) Kensgtn Pub Corp.
Neri, Rita, ed. U. S. & Japan Foreign Trade: An Annotated Bibliography of Socioeconomic Perspectives. LC 87-34805. 332p. 1988. text 20.00 (*0-8240-8471-3*) Garland.
Nerin, William F. Family Reconstruction: Long Day's Journey into Light. (Professional Bks.). (Illus.). 1986. 22.95 (*0-393-70017-8*) Norton.
— You Can't Grow up Till You Go Back Home: A Safe Journey to See Your Parents As Human. LC 92-42915. (Illus.). 194p. 1995. reprint ed. 22.95 (*0-9646789-0-X*) Magic Mtn.
Nering, Evar D. Linear Algebra & Matrix Theory. 2nd ed. 368p. (C). 1976. text 106.95 (*0-471-63178-7*) Wiley.
Nering, Evar D. & Tucker, Albert W. Linear Programs & Related Problems. (Computer Science & Scientific Computing Ser.). 584p. 1992. text 59.00 (*0-12-515440-2*) Acad Pr.
***Nerius, Maria.** Holiday Decorations for Fun & Profit. LC 99-39227. 1999. pap. 19.99 (*0-7615-2041-4*) Prima Pub.
— Rubberstamp for Fun & Profit. LC 00-38549. (Illus.). 320p. 2000. pap. 19.99 (*0-7615-2039-2*) Prima Pub.
— Soapmaking for Fun & Profit. LC 99-39228. 1999. pap. 16.99 (*0-7615-2042-2*) Prima Pub.
***Nerius, Maria Given & Gardner, Bill.** Creating Your Family Heritage Scrapbook. 2000. pap. 24.95 (*0-7615-3014-2*) Prima Pub.
Nerlich, Brigitte. Semantic Theories in Europe, 1830-1930: From Etymology to Contextuality. LC 91-42523. (Studies in the History of the Language Sciences: No. 59). xi, 359p. 1992. 74.00 (*1-55619-354-8*) J Benjamins Pubng Co.
Nerlich, Brigitte & Clarke, David D. Language, Action & Context: The Early History of Pragmatics in Europe & America 1780-1930. LC 96-13678. (Studies in the History of the Language Sciences: Vol. 80). xiv, 497p. 1996. lib. bdg. 115.00 (*1-55619-616-4*) J Benjamins Pubng Co.
Nerlich, Brigitte, tr. see Keller, Rudi.
***Nerlich, Daniel.** Diplomatische Gesandtschaften Zwischen Ost und Westkaisern, 756-1002. (Geist und Werk der Zeiten Ser.). 337p. 1999. 46.95 (*3-906763-35-8*, Pub. by P Lang) P Lang Pubng.
Nerlich, Graham. The Shape of Space. 2nd ed. LC 93-28935. 306p. (C). 1994. text 69.95 (*0-521-45014-4*) Cambridge U Pr.
— Values & Valuing: Speculations on the Ethical Life of Persons. 226p. 1990. text 65.00 (*0-19-824847-4*) OUP.
— What Spacetime Explains: Metaphysical Essays on Space & Time. LC 93-27336. 297p. (C). 1994. text 57.95 (*0-521-45261-9*) Cambridge U Pr.
Nerlich, Michael. Ideology of Adventure: Studies in Modern Consciousness, 1100-1750. 2 vols., 1. LC 86-19354. (Theory & History of Literature Ser.: Vols. 42 & 43). 1988. pap. 17.95 (*0-8166-1538-1*) U of Minn Pr.
Nerlich, Michael & Spadaccini, Nicholas, eds. Cervantes's Exemplary Novels & the Adventure of Writing. (Hispanic Issues Ser.). 365p. (Orig.). (C). 1990. pap. 14.95 (*0-910235-35-X*) Prisma Bks.
Nerlich, Michael, jt. auth. see Talens, Jenaro.
Nerlich, Uwe, ed. Soviet Power & Western Negotiating Policies Vol. II: The Western Panacea; Constraining Soviet Power Through Negotiation. LC 82-22694. 456p. 1983. text 39.95 (*0-88410-921-6*, HarpBusn) HarpInfo.
Nerlove, Marc. Issues in Contemporary Economics Vol. 2: Aspects of Macroeconomics & Econometrics. (International Economic Association Book Ser.). 300p. (C). 1991. text 100.00 (*0-8147-5767-7*) NYU Pr.
— Modernizing Traditional Agriculture. 20p. 1988. pap. 9.95 (*1-55815-033-1*) ICS Pr.
Nerlove, Marc, et al. Analysis of Economic Time Series: A Synthesis. 2nd rev. ed. (Economic Theory, Econometrics & Mathematical Economics Ser.). (Illus.). 468p. 1995. text 39.95 (*0-12-515751-7*) Acad Pr.
— Role of Farm-Level Diversification in the Adoption of Modern Technology in Brazil. Vol. 104. LC 96-49242. (Research Reports). 1996. write for info. (*0-89629-107-3*) Intl Food Policy.
Nerlove, Miriam. Christmas. (Illus.). 32p. (J). (ps-1). 1993. pap. 4.95 (*0-8075-1147-1*) A Whitman.
— Easter. Mathews, Judith, ed. LC 89-35394. (Illus.). 24p. (J). (ps-1). 1989. pap. 4.95 (*0-8075-1872-7*) A Whitman.
Nerlove, Miriam. Flowers on the Wall. LC 94-31289. (Illus.). 32p. (J). (ps-3). 1996. pap. 16.00 (*0-689-50614-7*) McElderry Bks.
Nerlove, Miriam. Halloween. Levine, Abby, ed. LC 88-36858. (Illus.). 24p. (J). (ps-1). 1989. pap. 4.95 (*0-8075-3130-8*) A Whitman.
— Hanukkah. Levine, Abby, ed. LC 88-36648. (Illus.). 24p. (J). (ps-1). 1989. pap. 5.95 (*0-8075-3142-1*) A Whitman.
— Passover. Levine, Abby, ed. LC 89-35393. (Illus.). 24p. (J). (ps-1). 1989. pap. 4.95 (*0-8075-6361-7*); lib. bdg. 13.95 (*0-8075-6360-9*) A Whitman.
— Purim. Levine, Abby, ed. LC 91-19516. (Illus.). 24p. (J). (ps-1). 1992. lib. bdg. 13.95 (*0-8075-6682-9*) A Whitman.
— Purim. LC 91-19516. (Albert Whitman Prairie Bks.). (Illus.). 24p. (J). (ps-1). 1994. pap. 4.95 (*0-8075-6683-7*) A Whitman.
— Shabbat. LC 98-14412. (Illus.). 24p. (J). (ps-1). 1998. lib. bdg. 13.95 (*0-8075-7324-8*) A Whitman.
***Nerlove, Miriam.** Shabbat. (Illus.). 24p. (J). (ps-1). 2000. pap. 5.95 (*0-8075-7323-X*) A Whitman.
Nerlove, Miriam. The Ten Commandments for Jewish Children. LC 99-10667. (Illus.). 32p. (J). (ps-2). 1999. lib. bdg. 14.95 (*0-8075-7770-7*) A Whitman.
— Thanksgiving. Mathews, Judith, ed. LC 89-49363. (Illus.). 24p. (J). (ps-1). 1990. lib. bdg. 13.95 (*0-8075-7818-5*) A Whitman.
— Thanksgiving. (Illus.). 32p. (J). (ps-3). 1993. pap. 5.95 (*0-8075-7817-7*) A Whitman.
— Valentine's Day. Mathews, Judith, ed. LC 91-19289. (Illus.). 24p. (J). (ps-1). 1992. lib. bdg. 13.95 (*0-8075-8454-1*) A Whitman.
— Valentine's Day. LC 91-19289. (Albert Whitman Prairie Bks.). (Illus.). 24p. (J). (ps-1). 1994. pap. 5.95 (*0-8075-8455-X*) A Whitman.
Nerman, Birger. Poetic Edda in the Light of Archaeology. LC 76-43954. (Viking Society for Northern Research: Extra Ser.: Vol. 4). (Illus.). reprint ed. 39.50 (*0-404-60024-7*) AMS Pr.
Nerney, Catherine. Mark's Gospel Enrollment in the School of Discipleship. 1987. pap. 2.50 (*0-8091-9331-0*) Paulist Pr.
— Promise of Glory. 1985. pap. 1.25 (*0-8091-9334-5*) Paulist Pr.
Nerney, Catherine T. Lenten Longings: Let Yourself Be. pap. 2.25 (*0-7648-0444-8*) Liguori Pubns.
Nero, Ann B. Essential Skills in Geography. Radner, Barbara, ed. (Illus.). 94p. (Orig.). (J). (gr. 4-9). 1987. teacher ed. 7.92 (*0-528-17919-5*); pap. text 3.96 (*0-528-17918-7*) Rand McNally.
Nero, Anthony V., Jr. A Guidebook to Nuclear Reactors. (Illus.). 303p. (C). 1993. pap. text 80.00 (*1-878907-76-X*) TechBooks.
Nero, Anthony V. A Guidebook to Nuclear Reactors. LC 77-76183. (Illus.). 304p. reprint ed. pap. 94.30 (*0-7837-4676-8*, 204442200003) Bks Demand.
Nero, Anthony V., jt. ed. see Nazaroff, William W.
Nero, Clarence. Cheekie: Child out of the Desire. LC 98-12143. 288p. 1998. 18.95 (*1-57178-063-7*) Coun Oak Bks.
Nero, Cotton. Pearl, Cleanness, Patience & Sir Gawain. (OS 162 Ser.). 1972. reprint ed. 76.00 (*0-19-722162-9*) OUP.
Nero, Greg. Musclesex: A Collection of Erotic Short Stories. 160p. (Orig.). 1995. pap. 14.95 (*0-943595-59-2*) Leyland Pubns.
Nero International Holding Company, Inc. Staff. NERO Rule Book. (Illus.). (YA). pap. 10.00 (*0-9700563-0-3*) N E R O Inter.
Nero, Karen, ed. The Arts & Politics in Oceania. (Pacific Studies: Vol. 15, No. 4). (Illus.). 358p. (C). 1992. pap. text 15.00 (*0-939154-60-9*) Inst Polynesian.
Nerode, Anil, et al, eds. Logical Foundations of Computer Science - Tver '92: Second International Symposium, Tver, Russia, July 20-24, 1992, Proceedings. LC 92-18642. (Lecture Notes in Computer Science Ser.: Vol. 620). ix, 514p. 1992. 76.95 (*0-387-55707-5*) Spr-Verlag.
Nerode, Anil & Matiyasevich, Y. V., eds. Logical Foundations of Computer Science: Proceedings of the Third International Symposium, LFCS '94, St. Petersburg, Russia, July 11-14, 1994. LC 94-19257. 1994. 61.95 (*0 387 58140-5*) Spr-Verlag.
Nerode, Anil & Metakides, G. Principles of Logic & Logic Programming. LC 96-12490. (Studies in Computer Science & Artificial Intelligence: No. 13). 344p. 1996. 149.50 (*0-444-81644-5*, North Holland) Elsevier.
Nerode, Anil & Shore, R., eds. Recursion Theory. LC 84-18525. (Proceedings of Symposia in Pure Mathematics Ser.: Vol. 42). 528p. 1985. text 82.00 (*0-8218-1447-8*, PSPUM/42) Am Math.
Nerode, Anil & Shore, Richard. Logic for Applications. LC 93-27846. (Texts & Monographs in Computer Science). (Illus.). 365p. 1993. 48.95 (*0-387-94129-0*) Spr-Verlag.
— Logic for Applications. 2nd ed. LC 96-43297. (Graduate Texts in Computer Science Ser.). (Illus.). 456p. 1997. 49.95 (*0-387-94893-7*) Spr-Verlag.
Nerode, Anil, jt. auth. see Crossley, J. N.
Nerode, Anil, jt. ed. see Pereira, Luis M.
Nerone, Barbara J., jt. auth. see Fondiller, Shirley H.
Nerone, John. The Culture of the Press in the Early Republic: Cincinnati, 1793-1848. (Nineteenth Century American Political & Social History Ser.). 310p. 1989. reprint ed. 20.00 (*0-8240-4070-8*) Garland.
— Violence Against the Press: Policing the Public Sphere in U. S. Histgory. (Communication & Society Ser.). 320p. (C). 1994. pap. text 23.95 (*0-19-508698-8*) OUP.
Nerone, John C., ed. see Berry, William E.
Neroni, Rosalind. The Porcupine's Princess. (Cleveland Poets Ser.: No. 18). 29p. 1978. pap. 2.50 (*0-914946-12-9*) Cleveland St Univ Poetry Ctr.
Nerou, Jean-Pierre, jt. auth. see Bergeron, Marcel.
Nerovich, Peter. Reupholstering at Home. LC 91-67017. (Illus.). 176p. 1992. pap. 14.95 (*0-88740-376-X*) Schiffer.
Neroznak, V. P., jt. auth. see Diakonov, I. M.
Nerozzi, Dina, et al, eds. Hypothalamic Dysfunction in Neuropsychiatric Disorders. LC 86-42680. (Advances in Biochemical Psychopharmacology Ser.: Vol. 43). 382p. 1987. reprint ed. pap. 118.50 (*0-608-04723-6*, 206544400004) Bks Demand.
Nerpin, S. V. & Chudnovskii, A. F. Heat & Mass Transfer in the Plant-Soil-Air System. Sivaramakrishnan, M. M., tr. from RUS. 367p. (C). 1985. text 123.00 (*90-6191-446-9*, Pub. by A A Balkema) Ashgate Pub Co.
Ners, Krzysztof J., et al. Assistance to Transition: 1995 Survey. (POL.). 1995. 20.00 (*0-913449-38-5*); write for info. (*0-913449-39-3*) Inst EW Stud.
— Beyond Assistance: Report of the IEWS Task Force on Western Assistance to Transition in the Czech & Slovak Federal Republic, Hungary, & Poland. LC 92-18010. 1992. 12.85 (*0-913449-32-6*) Inst EW Stud.
***Nersesian, Arthur.** Dogrun. 256p. 2000. 12.95 (*0-671-77542-1*) PB.
Nersesian, Arthur. The Fuck-Up. LC 96-80302. 274p. 1997. pap. 13.00 (*1-888451-03-3*) Akashic Bks.
— The Fuck-Up. 296p. 1999. per. 12.00 (*0-671-02763-8*, MTV Bks) PB.
***Nersesian, Arthur.** Manhattan Loverboy. LC 99-96428. 203p. 2000. pap. 13.95 (*1-888451-09-2*, AKB06, Pub. by Akashic Bks) SPD-Small Pr Dist.
Nersesian, Roy L. Computer Simulation in Business Decision Making: A Guide for Managers, Planners, & MIS Professionals. LC 88-32390. 268p. 1989. 72.95 (*0-89930-408-7*, NCR/, Quorum Bks) Greenwood.
— Computer Simulation in Financial Risk Management: A Guide for Business Planners & Strategists. LC 90-45146. 240p. 1991. 72.95 (*0-89930-578-4*, NCD, Quorum Bks) Greenwood.
— Corporate Planning, Human Behavior, & Computer Simulation: Forecasting Business Cycles. LC 89-37650. 249p. 1990. 72.95 (*0-89930-458-3*, NCB/, Greenwood Pr) Greenwood.
***Nersesian, Roy L.** Trends & Tools for Operations Management: An Updated Guide for Executives & Managers. LC 99-40349. 288p. 2000. write for info. (*1-56720-225-X*, Quorum Bks) Greenwood.
Nersesian, Roy L. & Swartz, G. B. Computer Simulation in Logistics: With Visual Basic Application. LC 95-50741. 264p. 1996. 69.50 (*0-89930-985-2*, Quorum Bks) Greenwood.
Nersesian, Roy L., jt. auth. see Heely, James A.
Nersessian, Edward & Kopff, Richard G., Jr., eds. Textbook of Psychoanalysis. 768p. 1995. text 115.00 (*0-88048-507-8*, 8507) Am Psychiatric.
Nersessian, N. V. A Bibliography of Articles on Armenian Studies in Western Journals: 1869-1995. 260p. 1997. 55.00 (*0-7007-0635-6*, Pub. by Curzon Pr Ltd) Paul & Co Pubs.
Nersessian, N. V., tr. see At'ayan, R. A.
Nersessian, N. V., tr. see Khusnaryan, Kh. S.
Nersessian, Nancy J. Faraday to Einstein: Constructing Meaning in Scientific Theories. (Science & Philosophy Ser.). 216p. 1990. pap. text 49.00 (*0-7923-0950-2*, Pub. by M Nijhoff) Kluwer Academic.
Nersessian, Nancy J., ed. The Process of Science: Contemporary Philosophical Approaches to Understanding Scientific Practice. (Science & Philosophy Ser.: No. 3). 234p. 1987. lib. bdg. 151.50 (*90-247-3425-8*, Pub. by M Nijhoff) Kluwer Academic.
Nersessian, Sirarpie Der, see Der Nersessian, Sirarpie.
Nersessian, Vrej. The Tondrakian Movement: Religious Movements in the Armenian Church from the Fourth to the Tenth Centuries. LC 88-4066. (Princeton Theological Monographs: No. 15). 156p. 1988. reprint ed. pap. 10.00 (*0-915138-99-9*) Pickwick.
— The Tondrakian Movement: Religious Movements in the Armenian Church from the 4th to the 10th Centuries. 145p. 1998. 45.00 (*0-900707-92-5*, Pub. by Curzon Pr Ltd) Paul & Co Pubs.
Nersessian, Vrej Nerses. Armenia. LC 94-231103. (World Bibliographical Ser.). 330p. 1993. lib. bdg. 92.00 (*1-85109-144-0*) ABC-CLIO.
Nersoyan, Abp T. Armenian Church Historical Studies: Matters of Doctrine & Administration. LC 98-192524. 460p. 1998. 85.00 (*0-934728-29-1*) Curzon Pubns.
Nersoyan, Hagop J. Andre Gide: The Theism of an Atheist. LC 69-17717. 222p. 1969. reprint ed. pap. 68.90 (*0-608-07621-X*, 205993600010) Bks Demand.
Nersoyan, Tiran, jt. ed. see Fries, Paul R.
Neruda, Jan. Prague Tales. (Central European Classics). 1993. pap. text 16.95 (*963-9116-23-8*) Ctrl Europ Univ.
Neruda, Jan. Prague Tales. Heim, Michael H., tr. (Central European Classics Ser.). 368p. (C). 1996. pap. 16.95 (*1-85866-058-0*) Ctrl Europ Univ.
— Tales of the Little Quarter. Pargeter, Edith, tr. from CZE. LC 76-49935. 296p. 1977. reprint ed. lib. bdg. 59.50 (*0-8371-9344-3*, NELQ, Greenwood Pr) Greenwood.
Neruda, Matilde, ed. see Neruda, Pablo.
Neruda, Pablo. Antologia Essencial. (SPA.). 1971. 14.95 (*0-8288-2542-4*, S20078) Fr & Eur.
— Antologia Poetica. (SPA.). 509p. 1982. 9.95 (*0-685-60725-9*, S39023) Fr & Eur.
— Antologia Poetica 1. 43rd ed. (SPA.). 304p. 1990. pap. 12.95 (*0-7859-5197-0*) Fr & Eur.
— Antologia Poetica 2. 3rd ed. (SPA.). 256p. 1988. pap. write for info. (*0-7859-5198-9*) Fr & Eur.
— The Book of Questions. O'Daly, William, tr. from SPA. LC 91-72064. 96p. (Orig.). 1991. 19.00 (*1-55659-040-7*) Copper Canyon.
— The Book of Questions. O'Daly, William, tr. from SPA. LC 91-72064. 96p. (Orig.). 1998. pap. 11.00 (*1-55659-041-5*, Pub. by Copper Canyon) Consort Bk Sales.
— Canto General. (SPA.). 1968. 12.50 (*0-8288-2532-7*) Fr & Eur.

N

An Asterisk (*) at the beginning of an entry indicates that the title is appearing for the first time.

— Canto General. 1993. pap. 17.95 (*0-520-08279-6*, Pub. by U CA Pr) Cal Prin Full Svc.

— Canto General. 2nd ed. 496p. 1988. pap. 13.95 (*0-7859-5186-5*) Fr & Eur.

***Neruda, Pablo.** Canto General. 50th anniversary ed. Schmitt, Jack, tr. (Latin American Literature & Culture Ser.). (Illus.). 418p. 2000. pap. 17.95 (*0-520-22709-3*) U CA Pr.

Neruda, Pablo. Captain's Verses. Walsh, Donald D., tr. from SPA. & intro. by. LC 72-80977. 151p. 1988. pap. 9.95 (*0-8112-0457-X*, NDP345, Pub. by New Directions) Norton.

— Ceremonial Songs. Jacketti, Maria, tr. from SPA. LC 96-15032. (Discoveries Ser.). (ENG & SPA.). 130p. (C). 1996. pap. 13.95 (*0-935480-80-3*) Lat Am Lit Rev Pr.

***Neruda, Pablo.** Cien Sonetos de Amor. (Biblioteca Breve Ser.: Vol. 407). (SPA.). 2000. pap. 14.95 (*84-322-0311-4*) E Seix Barral.

Neruda, Pablo. Cien Sonetos de Amor/100 Love Sonnets. 1997. pap. 11.95 (*84-322-0411-0*, Pub. by E Seix Barral) Continental Bk.

— Confieso Que He Vivido. (SPA.). 464p. 1984. pap. 10.95 (*0-7859-5004-4*) Fr & Eur.

— Confieso Que He Vivido. 1998. pap. 8.50 (*84-01-42521-2*) Lectorum Pubns.

— Crepusculario. 3rd ed. (SPA.). 104p. 1987. pap. 12.95 (*0-7859-5199-7*) Fr & Eur.

— Cuadernos de Temuco.Tr. of Notes from Temuco. (SPA.). Date not set. pap. 20.95 (*84-322-0733-0*, Pub. by E Seix Barral) Continental Bk.

— Epic Song. 144p. 1998. pap. 12.95 (*1-885214-15-4*) Azul Edits.

— Extravagaria. Reid, Alastair, tr. from SPA. LC 92-37189. (Texas Pan American Ser.). 303p. (C). 1993. reprint ed. pap. 16.95 (*0-292-72083-1*) U of Tex Pr.

— Extravagaria: A Bilingual Edition. Reid, Alastair, tr. from SPA. LC 72-84773. 304p. 2001. pap. 16.00 (*0-374-51238-8*) FS&G.

— Five Decades: Poems, 1925-1970. Belitt, Ben, ed. & tr. by. from SPA. LC 73-21033. 464p. 1988. pap. 15.00 (*0-8021-3035-6*, Grove) Grove-Atltic.

— Geografia Infructuosa. (SPA.). 1973. write for info. (*0-8288-2537-8*) Fr & Eur.

— Heaven Stones. Barkan, Stanley H., ed. Jacketti, Maria, tr. (Review International Writers Ser.: No. 2).Tr. of Las Piedras del Cielo. (ENG & SPA.). 80p. 1992. 30.00 (*0-89304-746-5*); pap. 15.00 (*0-89304-747-3*) Cross-Cultrl NY.

— The Heights of Macchu Picchu: Bilingual Edition. Tarn, Nathaniel, tr. from SPA. 80p. 1967. pap. 12.00 (*0-374-50648-5*) FS&G.

— Incitement to Nixonicide. Kowit, Steve, tr. 1076p. 27.50 (*0-9600306-3-8*) Fr & Eur.

— Incitement to Nixonicide. Kowit, Steve, tr. 1979. pap. 5.00 (*0-685-04198-0*) Quixote.

— Incitement to Nixonicide & Praise for the Chilean Revolution. 2nd ed. Kowit, Steve, tr. from SPA. (Illus.). 82p. 1980. pap. 6.00 (*0-686-68219-X*) Quixote.

***Neruda, Pablo.** Isla Negra. Maloney, Dennis, ed. (Illus.). 96p. 2000. pap. 12.00 (*1-893996-07-7*, Pub. by White Pine) Consort Bk Sales.

Neruda, Pablo. Isla Negra: A Notebook. Reid, Alastair, tr. from SPA. 432p. 1982. pap. 16.00 (*0-374-51734-7*) FS&G.

— Jardin de Invierno. 3rd ed. (SPA.). 104p. 1983. pap. 12.95 (*0-685-74087-0*) Fr & Eur.

Neruda, Pablo. El Libro de las Preguntas: Seleccion. (Coleccion Estrella de los Andes). (SPA.). 1991. 12.70 (*0-606-05257-7*, Pub. by Turtleback) Demco.

Neruda, Pablo. Love: Ten Poems by Pablo Neruda. LC 97-193693. 48p. (J). 1995. pap. 6.70 (*0-7868-8148-8*, Pub. by Hyperion) Time Warner.

— El Mary y las Campanas. (SPA.). 80p. 1976. pap. 19.95 (*0-7859-5003-6*) Fr & Eur.

***Neruda, Pablo.** Memoirs. St. Martin, Hardie, tr. from SPA. 384p. 2001. pap. 15.00 (*0-374-52753-9*) FS&G.

Neruda, Pablo. Memoirs. 1992. pap. 13.95 (*0-14-018628-X*, Penguin Bks) Viking Penguin.

— Memorial de Isla Negra. 2nd ed. (SPA.). 312p. 1982. pap. 12.95 (*0-7859-5000-1*) Fr & Eur.

— Neruda at Isla Negra. Jacketti, Maria et al, trs. LC 98-14080. (Illus.). 128p. 1998. pap. text 15.00 (*1-877727-83-0*) White Pine.

— Neruda's Garden: An Anthology of Odes. Miller, Yvette E., ed. Jacketti, Maria, tr. from SPA. LC 94-25088. (Discoveries Ser.). (ENG & SPA.). 256p. 1995. pap. 17.95 (*0-935480-68-4*) Lat Am Lit Rev Pr.

— Nuevas Odas Elementales. (SPA.). 1964. 9.95 (*0-8288-2535-1*, S20092) Fr & Eur.

— Odas Elementales. (SPA.). pap. 12.95 (*84-376-0366-8*, Pub. by Ediciones Catedra) Continental Bk.

— Odas Elementales. 3rd ed. (SPA.). 276p. 1988. pap. 12.95 (*0-7859-4999-2*) Fr & Eur.

Neruda, Pablo. Odes to Common Things. Krabbenhoft, Kenneth, tr. LC 93-39665. (ENG & SPA., Illus.). 152p. 1994. 23.95 (*0-8212-2080-2*, Pub. by Bulfinch Pr) Little.

— Odes to Opposites. Krabbenhoft, Kenneth, tr. LC 95-22412. (SPA., Illus.). 152p. 1995. 22.95 (*0-8212-2227-9*, Pub. by Bulfinch Pr) Little.

Neruda, Pablo. One Hundred Love Sonnets: Cien Sonetos de Amor. Tapscott, Stephen, tr. from SPA. (Texas Pan American Ser.). 232p. 1986. pap. 12.95 (*0-292-76028-0*) U of Tex Pr.

— Pablo Neruda: Fifty Odes. Schade, George D., ed. & tr. by. iv, 349p. (C). 1996. 35.00 (*0-924047-13-5*); pap. 17.00 (*0-924047-14-3*) Host Pubns.

— Pablo Neruda: Selected Poems. Tarn, Nathaniel, ed. Kerrigan, Anthony, tr. 508p. 1990. pap. 15.95 (*0-395-54418-1*) HM.

Neruda, Pablo. Pablo Neruda Reading His Poetry: Neruda,&Pablo. abr. ed. (SPA.). 1995. audio 12.00 (*0-694-51710-0*, CPN 1215) HarperAudio.

Neruda, Pablo. Passions & Impressions. Neruda, Matilde & Silva, Miguel Otero, eds. Peden, Margaret Sayers, tr. from SPA. 400p. 2001. reprint ed. pap. 16.00 (*0-374-51811-4*) FS&G.

— Residence on Earth & Other Poems. Walsh, Donald D., tr. from SPA. & intro. by. LC 72-93972. Orig. Title: Residencia en la Tierra. 1973. pap. 12.95 (*0-8112-0467-7*, NDP340, Pub. by New Directions) Norton.

— Residence on Earth & Other Poems: Bilingual Edition. Flores, Angel, tr. LC 76-75462. 205p. 1976. 50.00 (*0-87752-205-7*) Gordian.

— Residencia en la Tierra. 5th ed. (SPA.). 160p. 1989. pap. 16.95 (*0-7859-4996-8*) Fr & Eur.

— La Rosa Separada. 4th ed. (SPA.). 112p. 1990. pap. 16.95 (*0-7859-5001-X*) Fr & Eur.

— The Sea & the Bells. O'Daly, William, tr. from SPA. LC 88-70585. 136p. (Orig.). 1988. pap. 10.00 (*1-55659-019-9*) Copper Canyon.

— Selected Odes of Pablo Neruda. Peden, Margaret Sayers, tr. LC 90-10707. 388p. 1990. pap. 16.95 (*0-520-07172-7*, Pub. by U CA Pr) Cal Prin Full Svc.

***Neruda, Pablo.** Selected Odes of Pablo Neruda. (Latin American Literature & Culture Ser.). 388p. 2000. pap. 16.95 (*0-520-22708-5*) U CA Pr.

Neruda, Pablo. Selected Poems. Belitt, Ben, ed. & tr. by. LC 61-11772. (SPA.). 320p. 1989. pap. 14.00 (*0-8021-5102-7*, Grove) Grove-Atltic.

— The Separate Rose. O'Daly, William, tr. from SPA. LC 84-73338. 64p. (Orig.). 1985. pap. 9.00 (*0-914742-88-4*) Copper Canyon.

— Spain in the Heart. 1997. pap. text 12.95 (*1-885214-14-6*) Azul Edits.

— Spain in the Heart: Hymn to the Glories of the People at War. Schaaf, Richard, tr. from SPA. LC 92-71332. 150p. (Orig.). 1993. pap. 12.95 (*0-9632363-1-8*) Azul Edits.

— Still Another Day. O'Daly, William, tr. LC 84-70299. (ENG & SPA.). 80p. 1984. pap. 9.00 (*0-914742-77-9*) Copper Canyon.

— Stones of the Sky. Nolan, James, tr. from SPA. LC 87-71140. 80p. (Orig.). 1987. 15.00 (*1-55659-006-7*); pap. 10.00 (*1-55659-007-5*) Copper Canyon.

— Tercera Residencia. 4th ed. (SPA.). 112p. 1990. pap. 14.95 (*0-7859-4997-6*) Fr & Eur.

— Twenty Love Poems & a Song of Despair. Merwin, W. S., tr. (Illus.). 80p. 1993. 12.95 (*0-8118-0320-1*) Chronicle Bks.

— Twenty Love Poems & a Song of Despair. Merwin, W. S., tr. 88p. 1993. pap. 9.95 (*0-14-018648-4*, Penguin Classics) Viking Penguin.

— Twenty Love Poems & a Song of Despair. abr. ed. Merwin, W. S., tr. 1999. audio 8.95 (*0-14-086293-5*, Png AudioBks) Viking Penguin.

— 2000. Schaaf, Richard, tr. from SPA. LC 92-70941. 88p. 1992. pap. 10.95 (*0-9632363-0-X*) Azul Edits.

— Veinte Poemas de Amor.Tr. of Twenty Love Sonnets. 1997. pap. 7.95 (*84-322-0327-0*, Pub. by E Seix Barral) Continental Bk.

— Veinte Poemas de Amor y una Cancion Desesperada. 1998. pap. 6.50 (*84-01-42522-0*) Lectorum Pubns.

— Veinte Poemas de Amor y una Cancion Desesperada. 3rd ed. (SPA.). 129p. 1991. pap. 10.95 (*0-7859-4995-X*) Fr & Eur.

— Venture of the Infinite Man. King, Scott & Parish, Roger, trs. from SPA. Orig. Title: Tentative del Hombre Infinito. 36p. 1998. 9.00 (*1-890193-06-2*) Red Dragonfly.

— Los Versos del Capitan. 2nd ed. (SPA.). 126p. 1977. pap. 19.95 (*0-7859-4998-4*) Fr & Eur.

***Neruda, Pablo.** Viente Peomas de Amor: Y una Canion Desperada. 1999. pap. 8.95 (*84-322-0773-X*) E Seix Barral.

Neruda, Pablo. Windows That Open Inward: Images of Chile. rev. ed. Maloney, Dennis, ed. & tr. by. from SPA. Bly, Robert, tr. from SPA. (Illus.). 96p. 1999. pap. 20.00 (*1-877727-89-X*, Pub. by White Pine) Consort Bk Sales.

— Winter Garden. O'Daly, William, tr. from SPA. LC 86-71837.Tr. of Jardin de Invierno. 80p. (Orig.). 1986. 15.00 (*0-914742-99-X*); pap. 9.00 (*0-914742-93-0*) Copper Canyon.

— The Yellow Heart. O'Daly, William, tr. from SPA. LC 89-81834. (Illus.). 96p. 1990. pap. 10.00 (*1-55659-029-6*) Copper Canyon.

Neruda, Pablo & Parra, Nicanor. Pablo Neruda & Nicanor Parra Face to Face: A Bilingual & Critical Edition of Their Speeches on the Occasion of Neruda's Appointment to the Faculty of the University of Chile. Gottlieb, Marlene, tr. LC 97-2196. (Hispanic Literature Ser.: Vol. 36). 120p. 1997. text 59.95 (*0-7734-8673-9*) E Mellen.

Neruda, Pablo & Reid, Alastair. Fully Empowered. LC 94-7998. 135p. 1995. reprint ed. pap. 10.95 (*0-8112-1281-5*, NDP 792, Pub. by New Directions) Norton.

Neruda, Pablo & Vallejo, Cesar. Neruda & Vallejo: Selected Poems. Bly, Robert, ed. & tr. by. Knoepfle, John et al, trs. LC 93-10400. (SPA., Illus.). 288p. 1993. pap. 16.00 (*0-8070-6489-0*) Beacon Pr.

Neruda, Pablo, jt. auth. see Rodriguez, Osvaldo.

Nerurkar, Mahesh G., jt. auth. see Johnson, Russell.

Neruzow, Martin. Enterprise Network Performance Optimization. LC 94-3427. 1995. 50.00 (*0-07-911889-5*) McGraw.

Nerval, Gerard De. Aurelia. (Livre de Poche Classique Ser.). (FRE.). pap. 10.95 (*0-8288-9653-4*, F69730) Fr & Eur.

— Aurelia. Aldington, Richard, tr. LC 77-10265. (Illus.). 200p. reprint ed. 23.50 (*0-404-16317-3*) AMS Pr.

***Nerval, Gerard De.** Aurelia, Vol. 57. 2000. pap. 11.95 (*1-892295-46-6*) Green Integer.

Nerval, Gerard De. Aurelia & Other Writings. Wagner, Geoffrey, tr. from FRE. 224p. 1996. pap. 13.95 (*1-878972-09-X*) Exact Change.

— Aurelia Followed by Sylvie. 2nd rev. ed. Lappin, Kendall, tr. from FRE. 160p. 1993. pap. 14.00 (*1-878580-07-8*) Asylum Arts.

— Aurelia, Les Chimeres, La Pandora. (FRE., Illus.). 1984. pap. 8.95 (*0-7859-3079-5*) Fr & Eur.

— Les Chimeres. (FRE.). 94p. 1966. pap. 11.95 (*0-7859-5388-4*) Fr & Eur.

***Nerval, Gerard De.** Les Chimeres. Stone, William, tr. 64p. 1999. pap. 12.95 (*1-874320-22-5*, Pub. by Menard Pr.) SPD-Small Pr Dist.

Nerval, Gerard De. Les Confidences de Nicolas. 236p. 1945. 50.00 (*0-686-54813-2*) Fr & Eur.

— Les Filles de Feu. unabridged ed. (FRE.). Date not set. reprint ed. pap. 7.95 (*2-87714-348-1*, Pub. by Bookking Intl) Distribks Inc.

— Les Filles du Feu. (Coll. GF). (FRE.). 448p. 1989. reprint ed. pap. 11.95 (*0-7859-4702-7*) Fr & Eur.

— Les Filles du Feu: Les Chimeres. (FRE.). 1992. pap. 12.95 (*0-7859-2957-6*) Fr & Eur.

— Les Filles du Feu: Petits Chateaux de Boheme. (FRE.). 1973. pap. 11.95 (*0-7859-3411-1*) Fr & Eur.

— Les Filles du Feu, La Pandora, Aurelia. (FRE.). 120p. 1963. pap. 11.95 (*0-7859-4588-1*) Fr & Eur.

— Les Filles du Feu, La Pandora, Aurelia. (Folio Ser.: No. 179). (FRE.). pap. 9.95 (*2-07-036179-9*) Schoenhof.

— Les Illumines. (FRE.). 1976. pap. 11.95 (*0-685-68094-0*, 2070368483) Fr & Eur.

— Le Nouveau Genre ou le Cafe d'un Theatre: Scenes I a X. 112p. 1969. 6.95 (*0-686-54816-7*) Fr & Eur.

— Oeuvres, 2 vols., Vol. 1. deluxe ed. Beguin & Richer, eds. (Pleiade Ser.). (FRE.). 99.95 (*2-07-011067-2*) Schoenhof.

— Oeuvres, 2 vols., Vol. 2. Beguin & Richer, eds. (Pleiade Ser.). (FRE.). 88.95 (*2-07-011029-X*) Schoenhof.

— Oeuvres Completes, Vol. 2. Guillaume, Jean, ed. (FRE.). 1984. lib. bdg. 135.00 (*0-7859-3928-8*) Fr & Eur.

— Petits Chateaux de Boheme. (Class. Garnier Ser.). write for info. Schoenhof.

— Petits Chateaux de Boheme: Prose et Poesie. 96p. 1973. reprint ed. 32.00 (*0-686-54808-6*) Fr & Eur.

— Poesies et Souvenirs. Richer, Maurice, ed. (FRE.). 1974. pap. 18.95 (*0-7859-2775-1*) Fr & Eur.

— Poesies et Souvenirs. (Poesie Ser.). (FRE.). 1974. pap. 14.95 (*2-07-032127-4*) Schoenhof.

— Selected Prose. 400p. 1999. pap. 13.95 (*0-14-044601-X*, PuffinBks) Peng Put Young Read.

— Sylvie: Recollections of Valois. LC 77-10266. (Illus.). 168p. reprint ed. 55.00 (*0-404-16318-1*) AMS Pr.

— Le Voyage en Orient, 2 vols. (FRE.). 1980. pap. 12.95 (*0-7859-2976-2*) Fr & Eur.

— Le Voyage en Orient, 2 vols., 1. (FRE.). 1980. pap. 12.95 (*0-7859-2975-4*) Fr & Eur.

— The Women of Cairo: Scenes of Life on the Orient, 2 vols. LC 77-87652. 720p. reprint ed. 115.00 (*0-404-16420-X*) AMS Pr.

Nerval, Gerard De & Guillaume, Leon. Oeuvres Completes, Vol. 1. (FRE.). 1989. lib. bdg. 175.00 (*0-7859-3865-6*) Fr & Eur.

Nerval, Gerard De, et al. The Chimeras. 76p. 1984. 24.95 (*0-85646-125-3*, Pub. by Anvil Press) Dufour.

Nervi, Pier L. Aesthetics & Technology in Building. Einaudi, R., tr. LC 65-16686. (Charles Eliot Norton Lectures: 1961-1962). (Illus.). 210p. 1965. 22.00 (*0-674-00701-8*) HUP.

Nervo, A. Amada Inmovil. (SPA.). 143p. 1972. 9.95 (*0-8288-7128-0*, S8371) Fr & Eur.

— Perlas Misticas. (SPA.). 147p. 1973. 9.95 (*0-8288-7122-1*) Fr & Eur.

Nervo, Amado. Amado Nervo, Antologia Poetica 5th ed.Tr. of Poetic Anthlogy. (SPA., Illus.). 158p. (Orig.). 1997. pap. text 4.98 (*968-15-0308-2*) Ed Mex.

— Federico Garcia Lorca. (SPA., Illus.). 102p. 1997. pap. text 4.98 (*968-15-0315-5*) Ed Mex.

Nervo, Amado. The Soul-Giver/El Donador De Almas: Hispanic Literature, No.46. Capobianco, Michael F. & Mele'ndez, Gloria S., trs. LC 98-46804. 240p. 1999. 89.95 (*0-7734-8206-7*) E Mellen.

***Nervo, Amado, et al.** The Soul-Giver El Donador de Almas LC 98-46804. (Hispanic Literature Ser.). (ENG & SPA.). x, 169 p. 1999. write for info. (*0-88946-386-7*) E Mellen.

Nervoa, Pablo. Epic Song. Schaaf, Richard, tr. from SPA. 126p. 1998. pap. 12.95 (*1-885214-11-1*) Azul Edits.

***Nervy, Paul.** Notes, 1998. 102p. 1999. pap. 6.00 (*0-9670613-6-9*) Protean Pub.

— Notes, 1999. 80p. 2000. pap. 6.00 (*0-9670613-8-5*) Protean Pub.

— Notes 1988-1997. 545p. 1999. spiral bd. 10.00 (*0-9670613-3-4*) Protean Pub.

Nerwitz, David R. & Barrett, Matthew J. Materials on Accounting for Lawyers. 2nd ed. LC 97-25345. (University Casebook Ser.). 749p. 1997. text. write for info. (*1-56662-451-7*) Foundation Pr.

Nerys, Dee. Fortune-Telling by Playing Cards: A New Guide to the Ancient Art of Cartomancy. (Illus.). 160p. 1981. pap. 9.95 (*0-85030-266-8*) Sterling.

***Nerz, A. Ryan.** Digimon: Invasion of the Black Gears!, No. 2. (Digimon Ser.: No. 2). (Illus.). 96p. (gr. 4-7). 2000. pap. 4.50 (*0-06-107187-0*, HarpEntertain) Morrow Avon.

— Digimon: The Official Character Guide. (Illus.). 144p. (J). (gr. 1-4). 2000. pap. 9.99 (*0-06-107184-6*, HarpEntertain) Morrow Avon.

Nerz, A. Ryan. Jennifer Love Hewitt, Scene 2. (Illus.). 32p. (YA). (gr. 4-9). 1998. pap. 6.99 (*0-689-82403-3*) Aladdin.

Nes, jt. auth. see Green, Nessen.

Nes, Patricia Van, see Van Nes, Patricia.

Nes, W. David. Isopentenoids & Other Natural Products: Evolution & Function. LC 94-25742. (ACS Symposium Ser.: No. 562). (Illus.). 240p. 1994. text 76.00 (*0-8412-2934-1*, Pub. by Am Chemical) OUP.

Nes, W. David, et al, eds. Isopentenoids in Plants: Biochemistry & Function. LC 83-23167. (Illus.). 614p. reprint ed. pap. 190.40 (*0-7837-4307-6*, 204399800012) Bks Demand.

— Regulation of Isopentenoid Metabolism. LC 92-17807. (ACS Symposium Ser.: Vol. 497). (Illus.). 270p. 1992. text 75.00 (*0-8412-2457-9*, Pub. by Am Chemical) OUP.

Nes, W. David, jt. auth. see Parish, Edward J.

Nes, W. David, jt. ed. see Fuller, Glenn.

Nes, W. David, jt. ed. see Patterson, Glenn W.

***Nesathurai, Shanker.** The Rehabilitation of People with Traumatic Brain Injury. (Illus.). 128p. 2000. pap. 14.95 (*0-632-04517-5*) Blackwell Sci.

Nesaule, Agate. A Woman in Amber: Healing the Trauma of War & Exile. LC 95-18907. 284p. 1995. 24.00 (*1-56947-046-4*) Soho Press.

— A Woman in Amber: Healing the Trauma of War & Exile. 288p. 1997. pap. 11.95 (*0-14-026190-7*) Viking Penguin.

Nesbary. An Index to the Signatures of Deposit for the Freedman's Savings & Loan Bank, 1865-1869: For the State of Mississippi, Columbia, Natchez & Vicksburg. 148p. 1997. pap. 15.50 (*0-7884-0791-0*, N170) Heritage Bk.

***Nesbett, Peter T. & DuBois, Michelle.** The Complete Jacob Lawrence, 2 vols. (Illus.). 2000. 125.00 (*0-295-97963-1*) U of Wash Pr.

Nesbit. Treat Plan Dent. 2000. text 59.00 (*0-323-00395-8*) Harcourt Coll Pubs.

Nesbit, Charles B. The Meter's Running. 1998. pap. write for info. (*1-57553-907-1*) Watermrk Pr.

Nesbit, Dorothy D. Videostyle in Senate Campaigns. LC 88-2166. 192p. 1988. text 26.00 (*0-87049-582-8*) U of Tenn Pr.

***Nesbit, E.** The Children's Shakespeare. (Illus.). 117p. (J). (gr. 2-9). 2000. reprint ed. pap. 12.95 (*0-89733-485-X*) Academy Chi Pubs.

Nesbit, E. Enchanted Castle. (Children's Library). 1998. pap. 3.95 (*1-85326-129-7*, 1297WW, Pub. by Wrdsworth Edits) NTC Contemp Pub Co.

— English Fairy Tales. (Children's Library). 1998. pap. 3.95 (*1-85326-133-5*, 1335WW) NTC Contemp Pub Co.

— Harding's Luck. (Illus.). 272p. (J). (gr. 5 up). 1998. pap. 12.95 (*0-929605-90-X*) Books of Wonder.

***Nesbit, E.** Harding's Luck. (Illus.). 272p. (YA). (gr. 5 up). 1998. 19.95 (*0-929605-91-8*) Books of Wonder.

Nesbit, E. The House of Arden. 1997. 19.95 (*0-929605-70-5*) Books of Wonder.

— The House of Arden. (Illus.). 272p. 1997. pap. 12.95 (*0-929605-69-1*) Books of Wonder.

***Nesbit, E.** The House of Arden, Set. unabridged ed. (J). (gr. 1-3). 1998. 35.95 incl. audio (*1-55685-593-1*) Audio Bk Con.

— In the Dark. (Classic Frights Ser.). (Illus.). 64p. (YA). (gr. 5 up). 1998. pap. 5.95 (*0-929605-87-X*, Classic Frights) Books of Wonder.

Nesbit, E. Irish Fairy Tales. (Children's Library). 1998. pap. 3.95 (*1-85326-157-2*, 1572WW, Pub. by Wrdsworth Edits) NTC Contemp Pub Co.

***Nesbit, E.** Magic City. (Illus.). (J). 2000. 14.95 (*1-58717-024-8*) SeaStar.

Nesbit, E. Man Size in Marble. LC 99-214309. 64p. 1997. pap. 5.95 (*0-929605-72-1*) Books of Wonder.

— Man-Size in Marble. (Classic Frights Ser.). 1997. 11.05 (*0-606-13595-2*, Pub. by Turtleback) Demco.

— Melisande. LC 98-33875. (Illus.). 48p. (J). (gr. k-3). 1999. pap. 7.99 (*0-7636-0717-7*, Pub. by Candlewick Pr) Penguin Putnam.

— The Railway Children. (Andre Deutsch Classics). 223p. (J). (gr. 5-8). 1996. 9.95 (*0-233-99037-2*, Pub. by Andre Deutsch) Trafalgar.

— The Railway Children. (J). 1993. 12.95 (*0-679-42534-9*) Everymns Lib.

***Nesbit, E.** The Railway Children. LC 98-46150. (Chapter Book Charmers Ser.). (Illus.). 80p. (J). (gr. 2-5). 1999. 2.99 (*0-694-01285-8*) HarpC Child Bks.

Nesbit, E. The Railway Children. (J). 1997. pap. 2.95 (*0-8167-0469-4*) Troll Communs.

***Nesbit, E.** Railway Children. LC 99-89349. (Juvenile Classics). (Illus.). 208p. (J). 2000. pap. 2.50 (*0-486-41022-6*) Dover.

Nesbit, E. The Railway Children. abr. ed. (Children's Classics Ser.). (J). 1994. mass mkt. 14.95 incl. audio (*1-85998-081-3*) Trafalgar.

— Story of the Treasure: Penguin Readers Level 2. 48p. 1998. pap. 7.00 (*0-14-081628-3*) Viking Penguin.

***Nesbit, E.** Story of the Treasure Seekers. rev. ed. (Penguin Readers : Level 2). (J). 1999. pap. text 7.00 (*0-582-40153-4*) Longman.

Nesbit, E., adapted by. The Best of Shakespeare. LC 97-15223. (The Iona & Peter Opie Library of Children's Literature). (Illus.). 112p. (J). (gr. 6 up). 1997. 18.95 (*0-19-511689-5*) OUP.

— The Best of Shakespeare: Retellings of 10 Classic Plays. (Opie Library). (YA). (gr. 4 up). 1997. 16.95 (*0-614-28877-0*) OUP.

— The Best of Shakespeare: Retellings of 10 Classic Plays. (Illus.). 112p. (YA). 1999. pap. 9.95 (*0-19-513213-0*) OUP.

***Nesbit, E. & Millar, H. R.** The Magic City. LC 00-25204. (Illus.). (J). 2000. pap. write for info. (*1-58717-025-6*) SeaStar.

Nesbit, Edith. Book of Dragons. (J). 1997. pap. 2.95 (*0-8167-0852-5*) Troll Communs.

— Caesars Dialogue. LC 73-38215. (English Experience Ser.: No. 480). 154p. 1972. reprint ed. 20.00 (*90-221-0480-X*) Walter J Johnson.

— The Deliverers of Their Country. LC 96-21676. (Illus.).

N

An Asterisk (*) at the beginning of an entry indicates that the title is appearing for the first time.

32p. (J). (gr. 2-4). 1996. 16.95 (*1-55858-623-7*, Pub. by North-South Bks NYC); pap. 6.95 (*1-55858-612-1*, Pub. by North-South Bks NYC) Chronicle Bks.
— The Deliverers of Their Country. LC 85-9389. (Illus.). 32p. (J). (gr. 3-5). 1991. pap. 15.95 (*0-88708-005-7*, Picture Book Studio) S&S Childrens.
— Enchanted Castle. (Illus.). (YA). (gr. 5 up). 1995. pap. 4.99 (*0-14-036743-8*) Viking Penguin.
— The Enchanted Castle. LC 91-46267. (Books of Wonder: Vol. 1). (Illus.). 304p. (YA). (gr. 7 up). 1992. 20.00 (*0-688-05435-8*, Wm Morrow) Morrow Avon.
— Enchanted Castle. 231p. (J). 1981. reprint ed. lib. bdg. 25.95 (*0-89966-361-3*); reprint ed. lib. bdg. 16.95 (*0-89967-035-0*, Harmony Rain) Buccaneer Bks.
— Five Children & It. 207p. 20.95 (*0-8488-2523-3*) Amereon Ltd.
— Five Children & It. (J). 1997. pap. 1.95 (*0-8167-0797-9*) Troll Communs.
— Five Children & It. (Illus.). 256p. (YA). (gr. 5 up). 1996. pap. 4.99 (*0-14-036735-7*) Viking Penguin.
— Five Children & It. 188p. (J). 1981. reprint ed. lib. bdg. 25.95 (*0-89966-362-1*); reprint ed. lib. bdg. 21.95 (*0-89967-036-9*, Harmony Rain) Buccaneer Bks.
— The Magic City. (Illus.). 224p. (J). (gr. 3 up). 1996. reprint ed. 24.95 (*0-929605-62-4*); reprint ed. pap. 12.95 (*0-929605-53-5*) Books of Wonder.
— The Magic World. (Illus.). (YA). (gr. 5 up). 1996. pap. 4.99 (*0-14-036765-9*) Viking Penguin.
— Melisande. 41p. (J). (gr. k-3). 1989. 13.95 (*0-15-253164-5*) Harcourt.
— The Phoenix & the Carpet. (Illus.). (YA). (gr. 5 up). 1996. pap. 4.99 (*0-14-036739-X*) Viking Penguin.
— The Phoenix & the Carpet. 1999. lib. bdg. 23.95 (*1-56723-170-5*) Yestermorrow.
— The Rail: Penguin Readers Level 2. 1998. pap. 7.00 (*0-14-081463-9*) Viking Penguin.
— The Railway Children. (J). 1995. write for info. (*0-8050-3129-4*) H Holt & Co.
— The Railway Children. (Classics for Young Readers Ser.). (Illus.). 240p. (J). (gr. 4-7). 1994. pap. 3.99 (*0-14-036671-7*, PuffinBks) Peng Put Young Read.
— The Railway Children. (Children's Library). 368p. 1998. pap. 3.95 (*1-85326-107-6*, 1076WW, Pub. by Wrdsworth Edits) NTC Contemp Pub Co.
— Story of the Amulet. (Illus.). (YA). (gr. 5 up). 1996. pap. 3.99 (*0-14-036752-7*) Viking Penguin.
— The Story of the Amulet. (J). 1992. pap. 2.95 (*0-8167-2901-8*) Troll Communs.
— Story of the Treasure Seekers. (Classics for Young Readers Ser.). (J). (gr. 4-6). 1987. pap. 2.25 (*0-685-03990-0*, PuffinBks) Peng Put Young Read.
— Wet Magic. (Illus.). 192p. (J). (gr. 3 up). 1996. reprint ed. 24.95 (*0-929605-63-2*); reprint ed. pap. 12.95 (*0-929605-54-3*) Books of Wonder.
— The Wouldbegoods. (J). (gr. 5-8). 1988. 18.25 (*0-8446-6347-6*) Peter Smith.
Nesbit, Edith, ed. Beautiful Stories from Shakespeare for Children. (Illus.). 320p. (J). (gr. 4-7). 1997. reprint ed. 12.98 (*0-7651-9490-2*) Smithmark.
Nesbit, Evelyn. Book of Dragons Digest. (J). 1997. pap. 4.95 (*0-8167-2879-8*) Troll Communs.
Nesbit, Frederick. Psychology Guide to Understanding & Enjoyment Human Behavior. 6th ed. 170p. (C). 1994. text 25.00 (*0-536-58736-1*) Pearson Custom.
Nesbit, Frederick. Sweet Auburn: Recollections of a Prison Psychiatrist. LC 99-93298. 100p. 1999. pap. 14.95 (*0-9659506-1-1*) Eastern Offset.
Nesbit, James M. A Lifestyle of Light. LC 96-95031. 333p. 1996. write for info. (*0-9654294-0-7*) J Nesbit.
Nesbit, Jan, jt. auth. see Cameron, Sandra J.
Nesbit, Jeff. Setting the Trap. LC 93-41025. (High Sierra Adventure Ser.: Vol. 3). 162p. (J). (gr. 5-9). 1994. pap. 5.99 (*0-8407-9256-5*) Nelson.
Nesbit, Jeffrey A. The Puzzled Prodigy. (Capital Crew Ser.). (Orig.). (J). (gr. 3-6). 1992. pap. 1.00 (*0-89693-075-0*, Victor Bks) Chariot Victor.
Nesbit, Lois. Richard Meier Sculpture. (Illus.). 56p. 1994. pap. 25.00 (*0-8478-1848-9*, Pub. by Rizzoli Intl) St Martin.
Nesbit, Martha G. Savannah Collection: Favorite Recipes from Savannah Cooks. (Illus.). 250p. 1986. bds. 10.95 (*0-9617126-0-0*) M Nesbit.
— Savannah Entertains. (Illus.). 144p. 1996. 29.95 (*0-941711-35-8*) Wyrick & Co.
Nesbit, Micki. Out to Win. (Illus.). 78p. (Orig.). Date not set. pap. 7.99 (*0-9659759-0-8*) Nat Tech Inst.
Nesbit, Molly. Atget's Seven Albums. (Illus.). 440p. (C). 1994. pap. 35.00 (*0-300-05916-7*) Yale U Pr.
Nesbit, Paul W. Garden of God's. 5th rev. ed. LC 88-90928. (Illus.). 1996. pap. 6.00 (*0-911746-09-9*) Nesbit.
— New Techniques for Efficient Teaching. (Illus.). 1947. 1.75 (*0-911746-03-X*); pap. 1.00 (*0-911746-05-6*) Nesbit.
— Nez-Bits. (Illus.). 1946. pap. 0.75 (*0-911746-04-8*) Nesbit.
Nesbit, Robert & Miller, Arthur. Making Sales Manager: All You Need to Know to Lead & Succeed. 225p. 1992. 24.95 (*1-55738-400-2*, Irwn Prfssnl) McGraw-Hill Prof.
Nesbit, Robert C. Wisconsin: A History. 2nd rev. ed. (Illus.). 600p. (C). 1990. 34.95 (*0-299-10800-7*) U of Wis Pr.
Nesbit, Roy C. Eyes of the RAF: A History of Photo-Reconnaissance. LC 96-22049. (Illus.). 352p. 1996. 44.95 (*0-7509-1130-1*, Pub. by Sutton Pub Ltd) Intl Pubs Mktg.
— Eyes of the RAF: A History of Photo-Reconnaissance. (Aviation History Ser.). (Illus.). 352p. 1998. pap. 24.95 (*0-7509-1729-6*, Pub. by Sutton Pub Ltd) Intl Pubs Mktg.
— RAF: An Illustrated History from 1918. LC 99-193257. (Illus.). 288p. 1998. 49.95 (*0-7509-1949-3*, Pub. by Sutton Pub Ltd) Intl Pubs Mktg.
— RAF Coastal Command in Action, 1939-1945: Archive Photographs from the Public Record Office. LC 98-113376. (Illus.). 192p. 1998. 35.95 (*0-7509-1565-X*, Pub. by Sutton Pub Ltd) Intl Pubs Mktg.
***Nesbit, Roy C.** RAF in Action: Images from Gun Cameras & War Artists. (Illus.). 288p. 2000. 39.95 (*1-873162-82-0*, Pub. by PRO Pubns) Midpt Trade.
Nesbit, Roy C. The RAF in Camera, 1946-1995. (Illus.). 192p. 1996. 33.95 (*0-7509-1056-9*, Pub. by Sutton Pub Ltd) Intl Pubs Mktg.
— The RAF in Camera, 1946-1995 Vol. 3: Archive Photographs from the Public Record Office & the Ministry of Defence. (Illus.). 192p. (Orig.). 1997. pap. 17.95 (*0-7509-1522-6*, Pub. by Sutton Pub Ltd) Intl Pubs Mktg.
— The RAF in Camera, 1903-1939: Archive Photographs from the Public Record Office & the Ministry of Defence. (Illus.). 192p. (Orig.). 1997. pap. 17.95 (*0-7509-1514-5*, Pub. by Sutton Pub Ltd) Intl Pubs Mktg.
— The RAF in Camera, 1939-1945 Vol. 2: Archive Photographs from the Public Record Office & the Ministry of Defence. (Illus.). 192p. (Orig.). 1997. pap. 17.95 (*0-7509-1521-8*, Pub. by Sutton Pub Ltd) Intl Pubs Mktg.
Nesbit, Roy Conyers. Britain's Rebel Air Force: The War from the Air in Rhodesia, 1965-1980. 288p. 1998. 34.95 (*1-902304-05-5*, Pub. by Grub St) Seven Hills Bk.
***Nesbit, Roy Conyers.** Raf Records in the Pro. 1999. pap. 8.95 (*1-873162-14-6*) PRO Pubns.
***Nesbit, Roy Conyers & van Acker, Georges.** The Flight of Rudolf Hess: Myths & Reality. (Illus.). 192p. 2000. 34.95 (*0-7509-2386-5*) Sutton Publng.
Nesbit, William & Williams, Samuel W. Two Black Views of Liberia: Four Months in Liberia, or African Colonization Exposed Four Years in Liberia, a Sketch of the Life of Rev. Samuel Williams. LC 70-92234. (American Negro: His History & Literature. Series 3). 1970. reprint ed. 16.95 (*0-405-01936-X*) Ayer.
Nesbit, William M. Sumerian Records from Drehem. LC 15-2779. (Columbia University. Oriental Studies: No. 8). (Illus.). reprint ed. 32.50 (*0-404-50498-1*) AMS Pr.
Nesbitt. Wild Rose of Ruby Canyon. large type ed. LC 98-31494. 1999. 30.00 (*0-7838-0434-2*, G K Hall Lrg Type) Mac Lib Ref.
Nesbitt, Alexander. Decorative Alphabets & Initials. (Illus.). 1990. 24.25 (*0-8446-0820-3*) Peter Smith.
— Decorative Initials & Alphabets. (Illus.). 192p. 1959. pap. 9.95 (*0-486-20544-4*) Dover.
— The History & Technique of Lettering. unabridged ed. LC 98-35000. Orig. Title: Lettering: The History & Technique of Lettering As Design. (Illus.). 320p. 1998. pap. 9.95 (*0-486-40281-9*) Dover.
— Two Hundred Decorative Title-Pages. (Illus.). 213p. (Orig.). 1964. pap. 9.95 (*0-486-21264-5*) Dover.
Nesbitt, C. C., jt. ed. see Ramachandran, V.
Nesbitt, Caroline. The Pony Breeder's Companion: A Practical Guide for Owners & Breeders. LC 95-15647. (Illus.). 288p. 1995. pap. 29.95 (*0-87605-996-5*) Howell Bks.
Nesbitt, Cecil J., jt. auth. see Butcher, Marjorie V.
Nesbitt, Charlie. Stiffed on Christmas Eve: A Simple & Practical Guide to Tipping. LC 95-42644. 1996. pap. 12.95 (*1-56072-276-2*, Nova Kroshka Bks) Nova Sci Pubs.
Nesbitt, Ellen M., ed. see Nesbitt, Robert E. L., Jr.
Nesbitt, Ellen Morrissey, ed. see Nesbitt, Robert E. L., Jr.
Nesbitt, Gemma. Garden Graphics: How to Map & Plan Your Garden. (Illus.). 192p. 1993. 25.00 (*0-913643-11-4*) Capabilitys.
***Nesbitt, Gene & Ackerman, Lowell.** Canine & Feline Dermatology: Diagnosis & Treatment. LC 98-175581. 300p. 1998. pap. text 99.00 (*1-884254-39-X*) Vet Lrn Syst.
Nesbitt, Hadley. Southern Oregon Restaurants: A Guide to Pleasant Dining in & Around Ashland & Medford. LC 96-84998. 144p. (Orig.). 1996. pap. 10.95 (*0-9652271-5-4*) Bell Rose.
Nesbitt, Henrietta. White House Diary. (American Autobiography Ser.). 314p. 1995. reprint ed. lib. bdg. 89.00 (*0-7812-8600-X*) Rprt Serv.
Nesbitt, James H., ed. see Dowdy, Homer E.
Nesbitt, John, ed. Wyoming Journeys. (Illus.). 32p. (Orig.). 1995. pap. 5.00 (*0-917557-04-2*) Wyo Writers.
Nesbitt, John & Oikonomides, Nicolas. Catalogue of Byzantine Seals at Dumbarton Oaks & in the Fogg Museum of Art: West, Northwest, & Central Asia Minor & the Orient. (Catalogue of Byzantine Seals Ser.: Vol. 3). 1996. 45.00 (*0-88402-250-1*, BYS3) Dumbarton Oaks.
Nesbitt, John & Oikonomides, Nicolas, eds. Catalogue of Byzantine Seals at Dumbarton Oaks & in the Fogg Museum of Art Vol. 2: South of the Balkans, the Islands, South of Asia Minor. LC 91-12861. (Illus.). 248p. 1994. 35.00 (*0-88402-226-9*, BYS2, Dumbarton Rsch Lib) Dumbarton Oaks.
— Catalogue of Byzantine Seals at Dumbarton Oaks & in the Fogg Museum of Art, Vol. 1: Italy, North of the Balkans, North of the Black Sea. LC 91-12861. (Illus.). 276p. 1991. 30.00 (*0-88402-194-7*, BYS1) Dumbarton Oaks.
Nesbitt, John, jt. ed. see Miller, Timothy S.
Nesbitt, John A., et al, eds. Recreation & Leisure Service for the Disadvantaged. LC 76-115026. (Illus.). 612p. reprint ed. 189.80 (*0-8357-9419-9*, 201456800092) Bks Demand.
***Nesbitt, John D.** The Adventures of the Ramrod Rider. (Illus.). 214p. 1999. pap. 9.95 (*1-892944-07-3*) Endeavor Bks.
Nesbitt, John D. Antelope Sky: Stories of the Modern West. 166p. (Orig.). 1997. pap. 8.95 (*0-9651856-4-8*) R R Prodns.
— Black Diamond Rendezvous. 256p. 1998. mass mkt. 4.50 (*0-8439-4388-2*, Leisure Bks) Dorchester Pub Co.
***Nesbitt, John D.** Black Diamond Rendezvous. large type ed. (G. K. Hall Western Ser.). 2000. 23.95 (*0-7838-8955-0*, G K Hall Lrg Type) Mac Lib Ref.
Nesbitt, John D. Blue Book of Basic Writing. 4th ed. (Illus.). 388p. (C). 1996. pap. text 21.00 (*0-9653706-1-5*, EB-102) Endeavor Bks.
***Nesbitt, John D.** Blue Book of Basic Writing. 5th rev. ed. 394p. 1999. pap. text 21.00 (*1-892944-05-7*, EB-112) Endeavor Bks.
— Coyote Trail. 272p. (Orig.). 2000. pap. 4.50 (*0-8439-4671-7*, Leisure Bks) Dorchester Pub Co.
Nesbitt, John D. A Good Man to Have in Camp. 172p. 1999. pap. 10.95 (*1-892944-01-4*) Endeavor Bks.
— I'll Tell You What: Fiction with Voice. 105p. 1996. pap. 6.95 (*0-9651856-1-3*) R R Prodns.
— Keep the Wind in Your Face. 253p. 1998. pap., per. 14.95 (*0-9653706-9-0*, EB-108) Endeavor Bks.
— One-Eyed Cowboy Wild. LC 93-32741. 180p. 1994. 19.95 (*0-8027-4135-5*) Walker & Co.
— One-Eyed Cowboy Wild. large type ed. LC 94-26349. 221p. 1994. pap. 18.95 (*0-8161-7477-6*, G K Hall Lrg Type) Mac Lib Ref.
— One Foot in the Stirrup: Western Stories. 126p. 1998. reprint ed. pap. 7.95 (*0-9651856-3-X*) R R Prodns.
— Seasons in the Fields: Stories of a Golden West. 173p. 1998. pap. 8.95 (*0-9651856-5-6*) R R Prodns.
— Twin Rivers. 192p. 1995. 19.95 (*0-8027-4152-5*) Walker & Co.
— Wild Rose of Ruby Canyon. LC 96-51010. 179p. 1997. 20.95 (*0-8027-4159-2*) Walker & Co.
Nesbitt, Jonathan C. & Wind, Gary G. General Thoracic Surgical Anatomy & Procedures. 500p. 1998. write for info. (*0-683-06429-0*) Lppncott W & W.
Nesbitt, Kate, ed. Theorizing a New Agenda for Architecture: An Anthology of Architectural Theory 1965-1995. (Illus.). 608p. 1996. 50.00 (*1-56898-053-1*); pap. 34.95 (*1-56898-054-X*) Princeton Arch.
Nesbitt, Kate D. Gwinnett County, Georgia: 1850 Census with Mortality Schedule. 242p. 1986. 20.00 (*0-914923-13-7*) Gwinnett Hist.
***Nesbitt, Kris.** My Amazon River Day. (Illus.). 48p. (J). (gr. 3-8). 2000. 23.95 (*0-9701035-0-6*) Shedd Aquarium.
Nesbitt, Lee T., Jr., jt. ed. see Sanders, Charles V.
Nesbitt, Lewis M. Gold Fever, Vol. 11. LC 74-355. 214p. 1974. reprint ed. 20.95 (*0-405-05916-7*) Ayer.
— Hell Hole of Creation: The Exploration of Abyssinian Danakil. LC 74-15072. (Illus.). reprint ed. 34.50 (*0-404-12116-0*) AMS Pr.
Nesbitt, Lois, ed. see Willis, Beverly.
Nesbitt, Lois, jt. ed. see Wong, Tony.
Nesbitt, Marilyn, ed. see Mansfield, Marilynn.
Nesbitt, Mark. Ghosts of Gettysburg IV. LC 98-85175. (Illus.). 96p. 1998. pap. 5.95 (*1-57747-038-9*) Thomas Publications.
Nesbitt, Mark V. Ghosts of Gettysburg, Vol. V. (Illus.). Date not set. pap. write for info. (*1-57747-054-0*) Thomas Publications.
Nesbitt, Mark V. Ghosts of Gettysburg: Spirits, Apparitions & Haunted Places of the Battlefield. (Illus.). 84p. (C). 1991. pap. text 5.95 (*0-939631-41-5*) Thomas Publications.
— Ghosts of Gettysburg III. LC 97-164270. (Illus.). 76p. 1995. pap. 5.95 (*0-939631-90-3*) Thomas Publications.
— If the South Won Gettysburg. LC 80-52561. (Illus.). 107p. (Orig.). 1980. pap. 6.95 (*0-937740-01-2*) Reliance Pub.
— If the South Won Gettysburg. LC 80-52561. (Illus.). 124p. (Orig.). (C). 1993. reprint ed. pap. text 6.95 (*0-939631-69-5*) Thomas Publications.
— More Ghosts of Gettysburg: Spirits, Apparitions & Haunted Places of the Battlefield. (Illus.). 100p. (C). 1992. pap. text 5.95 (*0-939631-51-2*) Thomas Publications.
— Rebel Rivers: A Guide to the Civil War Sites on the Potomac, Rappahannock, York, & James. LC 93-20180. (Illus.). 166p. 1993. pap. 12.95 (*0-8117-2538-3*) Stackpole.
— Saber & Scapegoat: J. E. B. Stuart & the Gettysburg Controversy. (Illus.). 272p. 1994. 19.95 (*0-8117-0915-9*) Stackpole.
— 35 Days to Gettysburg: The Campaign Diaries of Two American Enemies. LC 92-13397. (Illus.). 208p. 1992. 19.95 (*0-8117-1757-7*) Stackpole.
Nesbitt, Murray B. Labor Relations in the Federal Government Service. LC 75-44255. 559p. reprint ed. pap. 173.30 (*0-608-14107-0*, 202430600036) Bks Demand.
Nesbitt, Paula D. Feminization of the Clergy in America: Occupational & Organizational Perspectives. LC 96-22281. (Illus.). 304p. 1997. text 45.00 (*0-19-510686-5*) OUP.
Nesbitt, Perry L., ed. & intro. see Phillips, Patricia C.
Nesbitt, Prexy. Apartheid in Our Living Rooms: U. S. Foreign Policy & South Africa. (Midwest Research Monographs: No. 3). 58p. 1986. pap. 5.50 (*0-915987-02-3*) Political Rsch Assocs.
***Nesbitt, Robert E., Jr.** Chorales for Arid Souls. 1999. pap. write for info. (*1-58235-362-X*) Watermrk Pr.
— The Fullness Search. 2000. write for info. (*1-58235-456-1*) Watermrk Pr.
— Visions Shared. 2000. write for info. (*1-58235-500-2*) Watermrk Pr.
***Nesbitt, Robert E. L., Jr.** Hearts of Flesh. Nesbitt, Ellen Morrissey, ed. LC 99-75242. 240p. 2001. 18.95 (*0-8158-0541-1*) Chris Mass.
Nesbitt, Robert E. L., Jr. In the Fullness of Time. Nesbitt, Ellen M., ed. LC 97-66582. 256p. 1999. 18.95 (*0-8158-0531-4*) Chris Mass.
— The Last Twig on the Bush. Nesbitt, Ellen M., ed. LC 97-66583. 224p. 1999. 16.95 (*0-8158-0530-6*) Chris Mass.
Nesbitt, Steven M. British Pensions Policy Making in the 1980's: The Rise & Fall of a Policy Community. 176p. 1995. 72.95 (*1-85628-498-0*, Pub. by Avebry) Ashgate Pub Co.
Nesbitt, Susan & Krasner, Melvin I. The Financial Condition of New York City Voluntary Hospitals: The First Year of NYPHRM. (Papers: No. 2). 24p. 1985. 5.00 (*0-934459-10-X*) United Hosp Fund.
Nesbitt, Thomas, ed. see Files, L. Burke.
Nesbitt, Verne. The Servant King. 176p. (Orig.). 1996. mass mkt. 5.99 (*0-88368-436-5*) Whitaker Hse.
Nesbitt, W. H. & Reneau, Jack, eds. Records of North American Big Game, 1988. 9th ed. LC 88-72182. (Illus.). 512p. 1988. 49.95 (*0-940864-13-4*) Boone & Crockett.
— Records of North American Elk & Mule Deer, 1991. LC 91-73121. (Illus.). viii, 264p. (Orig.). 1991. pap. 16.95 (*0-940864-18-5*) Boone & Crockett.
— Records of North American Whitetail Deer, 1987. LC 87-72474. (Illus.). 246p. 1987. pap. 14.95 (*0-940864-12-6*) Boone & Crockett.
Nesbitt, W. H. & Wright, Philip L., eds. Records of North American Big Game, 1981. 8th limited ed. LC 81-68426. (Records of North American Big Game Ser.). (Illus.). xii, 412p. 1981. 199.00 (*0-940864-01-0*) Boone & Crockett.
Nesbitt, William A. & Abramowitz, Norman. Teaching Youth about Conflict & War. Bloomstein, Charles, ed. LC 73-75291. (Teaching Social Studies in Age of Crisis: No. 5). 112p. reprint ed. pap. 34.80 (*0-608-30743-2*, 200509900049) Bks Demand.
Nesbitt, William H. Boone & Crockett Clubs Twenty-First Big Game Award, 1989-1991. 1992. 39.95 (*1-879356-19-8*) Wolfe Pub Co.
Nesbitt, William H., ed. Boone & Crockett Club's 18th Big Game Awards. LC 84-71676. (Illus.). 306p. 1984. 24.95 (*0-940864-05-3*) Boone & Crockett.
Nesbitt, William H. & Reneau, Jack, eds. Boone & Crockett Club's Twentieth Big Game Awards. LC 90-82934. (Illus.). 480p. 1990. 34.95 (*0-940864-16-9*) Boone & Crockett.
Nesbitt, William H. & Wright, Philip L. Measuring & Scoring North American Big Game. Byers, C. Randall & Reneau, Jack, eds. (Illus.). 160p. 1997. ring bd. 34.95 (*0-940864-32-0*) Boone & Crockett.
Nesbitt, William R. Manual of First-Aid Practices for School Bus Drivers. (Illus.). 80p. 1998. pap. text 20.00 (*0-7881-7122-4*) DIANE Pub.
Nesci, Catherine. La Femme mode d'emploi: Balzac, de la Physiologie du mariage a La Comedie humaine. LC 92-71331. (French Forum Monographs: No. 81). (FRE.). 247p. (Orig.). 1992. pap. 17.95 (*0-917058-86-0*) French Forum.
Nescio. Devious Minds: A Novel. 300p. 1998. 19.95 (*0-9662411-0-X*) Flying Goose.
Nese & Grenci. A World of Weather: Fundamentals of Meteorology. 2nd ed. 496p. (C). 1997. pap. text 52.95 (*0-7872-3578-4*, 41357801) Kendall-Hunt.
Nese, Jon, et al. World of Weather. LC 96-152422. 400p. (C). 1996. spiral bd. 52.95 (*0-7872-0593-1*) Kendall-Hunt.
Nese, Marco. Soziologie und Positivismus im prafaschistischen Italien 1870, 1922. 1993. 22.95 (*3-906764-12-5*, Pub. by P Lang) P Lang Pubng.
Neseman, Dale & Thebo, Jack. So That's How They're Spending Our Money! Your Federal Taxes at Work. (Illus.). 144p. (Orig.). 1991. pap. 6.95 (*0-9629343-0-5*) Neseman Enter.
***Nesenoff, Mitchell B.** Computer Repair Program: Instructor Manual. (Illus.). 192p. 1999. pap. write for info. (*0-86711-290-5*) CES Industries.
— Computer Repair Program: Safety Lesson & Introduction to Computer Repair. (Illus.). 130p. 1999. pap. 33.34 (*0-86711-258-1*) CES Industries.
— Computer Repair Program Vol. II: Identifying Hardware Components. (Illus.). 244p. 1999. pap. 33.34 (*0-86711-272-7*) CES Industries.
— Computer Repair Program Vol. 3: System Construction. (Illus.). 163p. 1999. pap. 33.34 (*0-86711-273-5*) CES Industries.
— Computer Repair Program Vol. IV: Operating Systems for Dos & Windows for Work Groups. (Illus.). 263p. 1999. pap. 33.34 (*0-86711-284-0*) CES Industries.
— Computer Repair Program Vol. 5: Operating System for Windows 95, 7 vol.s. 237p. 1999. pap. 33.34 (*0-86711-287-5*) CES Industries.
— Computer Repair Program Vol. VI: Troubleshooting the System & Peripheral Repair. (Illus.). 282p. 1999. pap. 33.34 (*0-86711-288-3*) CES Industries.
— Computer Repair Program Vol. VII: Networking. 245p. 1999. pap. 33.34 (*0-86711-289-1*) CES Industries.
— Ed-Lab 500 - Modern Electronics. 3rd ed. (Illus.). 323p. 1997. pap. 33.00 (*0-86711-222-0*) CES Industries.
Nesenoff, Norman. CES 381 - Micrprocessor Techniques: Unit M2. (Illus.). 172p. 1995. pap. 10.00 (*0-86711-159-3*) CES Industries.
— CES 381 - Microprocessor Concepts: Unit M1, 3 vols. (Illus.). 158p. 1995. pap. 10.00 (*0-86711-077-5*) CES Industries.
— CES 381 - Microprocessor Appendices: Unit M3, 3 vols. (Illus.). 76p. 1995. pap. 10.00 (*0-86711-160-7*) CES Industries.
— ED-Lab 400: Jobs for Electrical Circuits Parts 1-3. (Illus.). 184p. 1990. pap. 35.00 (*0-86711-198-4*) CES Industries.
— Ed-Lab 400 Instructor Guide: Jobs for Electrical Circuits Parts 1-3. (Illus.). 215p. 1996. pap. write for info. (*0-86711-241-7*) CES Industries.
— ED-Lab 702: D1 - Basic Digital Concepts. (Illus.). 158p. 1995. pap. 11.00 (*0-86711-086-4*) CES Industries.
— ED-Lab 702: D2 - Logic Arithmetic Techniques. (Illus.). 176p. 1995. pap. 12.00 (*0-86711-093-7*) CES Industries.

N

— ED-Lab 702: D3 - Counter Logic Systems. (Illus.). 111p. 1995. pap. 10.00 (*0-86711-094-5*) CES Industries.

— ED-Lab 702 Vol. D4: D4 - Registers & Timing Logic. (Illus.). 167p. 1995. pap. 10.00 (*0-86711-095-3*) CES Industries.

— ED-Lab 702 Instructor's Manual: D1-D4 Digital Systems. (Illus.). 141p. 1986. pap., teacher ed. 11.00 (*0-86711-111-9*) CES Industries.

— ED-Lab 651: G2 - AC Components. (Illus.). 265p. 1995. 20.00 (*0-86711-122-4*) CES Industries.

— ED-Lab 651 Instructor's Manual for Unit J1: Transistors & Circuits. (Illus.). 68p. 1995. pap., teacher ed. 10.00 (*0-86711-143-7*) CES Industries.

— Ed-Lab 651: Unit E1 - DC Electricity Concepts. (Illus.). 135p. 1985. pap. 22.00 (*0-86711-099-6*) CES Industries.

— Ed-Lab 651: Unit E2 - DC Electrical Circuits. (Illus.). 118p. (YA). (gr. 9-12). 1986. pap. 19.00 (*0-86711-102-X*) CES Industries.

— ED-Lab 651: Unit E3 - DC OHM's Law. (Illus.). 166p. (YA). (gr. 9-12). 1995. pap. 27.00 (*0-86711-104-6*) CES Industries.

— ED-Lab 651: Unit E4 - DC Circuits & Laws. (Illus.). 159p. (YA). (gr. 9-12). 1995. pap. 26.00 (*0-86711-103-8*) CES Industries.

— ED-Lab 651: Unit E5. (Illus.). 82p. (YA). (gr. 9-12). 1995. pap. 14.00 (*0-86711-106-2*) CES Industries.

— ED-Lab 651: Unit F1 - Magnetism & Motors. (Illus.). 220p. 1995. pap. 35.00 (*0-86711-109-7*) CES Industries.

— ED-Lab 651: Unit G1 - AC Voltages & Components. (Illus.). 149p. 1995. pap. 24.00 (*0-86711-114-3*) CES Industries.

— ED-Lab 651: Unit G3 - Oscilloscope Operation & Applications. (Illus.). 153p. 1995. pap. 24.00 (*0-86711-115-1*) CES Industries.

— ED-Lab 651: Unit G4 - AC RLC Circuits. (Illus.). 201p. 1995. pap. 30.00 (*0-86711-116-X*) CES Industries.

— ED-Lab 651: Unit G5 - AC Circuits. (Illus.). 201p. 1995. pap. 30.00 (*0-86711-123-2*) CES Industries.

— ED-Lab 651: Unit H1 - Diodes & Power Supplies. (Illus.). 193p. 1995. pap. 30.00 (*0-86711-182-8*) CES Industries.

— ED-Lab 651: Unit J1 - Transistors & Circuits. (Illus.). 335p. 1995. pap. 50.00 (*0-86711-139-9*) CES Industries.

— ED-Lab 651 Instructor's Guide Units G1-G5: AC Concepts & Circuits. (Illus.). 193p. 1995. pap. 16.00 (*0-86711-132-1*) CES Industries.

— Ed-Lab 651 Instructor's Manual E1-E5: DC Electronics. (Illus.). 241p. 1995. pap. 16.00 (*0-86711-110-0*) CES Industries.

— ED-Lab 651 Instructor's Manual for Unit H1: Diodes & Power Supplies. (Illus.). 42p. 1995. pap., teacher ed. 10.00 (*0-86711-186-0*) CES Industries.

— ED-Lab 651 Instructor's Manual for Unit F1: Magnetism & Motors. (Illus.). 45p. 1995. pap. 10.00 (*0-86711-133-X*) CES Industries.

Nesenoff, Norman, jt. auth. see CES Industries, Inc. Staff.

Nesenoff, Norman, ed. see CES Industries, Inc. Staff.

***Nesetril, J., ed.** Algorithms - ESA '99: 7th Annual European Symposium, Prague, Czech Republic, July 16-18, 1999, Proceedings. LC 99-37541. (Lecture Notes in Computer Science Ser.: Vol. 1643). xii, 552p. 1999. pap. 85.00 (*3-540-66251-0*) Spr-Verlag.

Nesetril, J., et al, eds. Mathematics of Ramsey Theory. (Algorithms & Combinatorics Ser.: Vol. 5). (Illus.). 281p. 1990. 135.95 (*0-387-18191-1*) Spr-Verlag.

Nesetril, J., jt. auth. see Graham, R. L.

Nesetril, Jaroslav, jt. auth. see Matousek, Jiri.

***Nesfield-Cookson, Bernard.** Michael & the Two Horned Beast: Challenge of Evil Today in the Light of Rudolf Steiner's Science of the Spirit. 384p. 1998. pap. 29.95 (*0-904693-98-8*, Pub. by Temple Lodge) Anthroposophic.

Nesfield-Cookson, Bernard. Rodolf Steiners Visions of Love. 1989. pap. 12.95 (*1-85274-063-9*, Pub. by Crucible Pr) Cavendish Bks.

***Nesfield-Cookson, Bernard.** Rudolf Steiner's Vision of Love: Spiritual Science & the Logic of the Heart. 352p. 1999. reprint ed. pap. 24.95 (*1-85584-048-0*, Pub. by R Steiner Pr) Anthroposophic.

Nesfield-Cookson, Bernard. William Blake: Prophet of Universal Brotherhood. 480p. (Orig.). 1989. pap. 14.95 (*0-85030-562-4*, Pub. by Aqm Pr) HarpC.

***Neshama, Rivvy.** Nat Turner & the Virginia Slave Revolt. LC 00-21399. (Illus.). (J). 2000. lib. bdg. write for info. (*1-56766-744-9*) Childs World.

***Neshanic Station Historical Society Staff.** Neshanic Station. (Images of America Ser.). 128p. 1999. pap. 18.99 (*0-7385-0140-9*) Arcadia Publng.

Neshat, Shirin. Women of Allah. LC 98-142908. 1998. pap. text 35.00 (*88-900202-0-2*, Pub. by Noire) Dist Art Pubs.

Neshati, Amin, tr. see Al-Saltana, Taj.

Neshati, Amin, tr. see Danishvar, Simin.

Nesheim, Eric. Saucer Attack. 1997. pap. text 16.95 (*0-87816-603-3*) Kitchen Sink.

Nesheim, Eric, ed. see Rude, Steve.

Nesheim, Gisela. High Tech Murder: A Silicon Valley Murder Mystery. McGuire, Beverly, ed. 316p. 1998. 17.95 (*0-9663167-0-3*) Strategic Ent.

***Nesheim, John L.** High Tech Start Up: The Complete Handbook for Creating Successful New High Tech Companies. rev. ed. LC 99-45249. (Illus.). 352p. 2000. 50.00 (*0-684-87170-X*) Free Pr.

Nesheim, John L. High Tech Start Up: The Complete How-to-Handbook for Creating Successful New High Tech Companies. Brett, Elaine, ed. LC 91-29695. 303p. 1992. reprint ed. 49.95 (*0-914405-71-3*) Strategic Ent.

Nesheim, Malden C., et al. Nutrition of the Chicken. 3rd ed. 555p. 1982. 32.00 (*0-9602726-2-3*, 76-49249) Scott & Assocs.

Nesheim, Malden C., jt. auth. see Austic, Richard E.

Nesheim, Paul & Noble, Weston. Building Beautiful Voices. Foss, Scott, ed. 180p. (Orig.). (C). 1995. pap. text 25.00 (*0-89328-138-7*, 30-1054R) Lorenz Corp.

Neshyba, Steve, et al, eds. Poleward Flows along Eastern Ocean Boundaries. (Coastal & Estuarine Studies: Vol. 34). ix, 374p. 1989. 65.00 (*0-387-97175-0*) Spr-Verlag.

Nesi & Smith, Byron. Ophthalmic Plastic & Reconstructive Surgery. 2nd ed. LC 97-26132. (Illus.). 1248p. (C). (gr. 13). 1997. text 295.00 (*0-8151-6356-8*, 24723) Mosby Inc.

Nesi, Frank A., jt. ed. see Spoor, Thomas C.

Nesi, Paolo, ed. Software Quality: Objective Quality: Second Symposium on Software Quality Techniques & Acquisition Criteria, Florence, Italy, May 28-30, 1995: Proceedings. (Lecture Notes in Computer Science Ser.: Vol. 926). 1995. write for info. (*0-387-59449-3*) Spr-Verlag.

Nesi, Paolo, et al, eds. Software Quality: Objective Quality: Second Symposium on Software Quality Techniques & Acquisition Criteria, Florence, Italy, May 28-30, 1995: Proceedings. (Lecture Notes in Computer Science Ser.: Vol. 926). 249p. 1995. 49.00 (*3-540-59449-3*) Spr-Verlag.

Nesi, Thomas J. & Wolfe, M. Michael. Heartburn: Extinguishing the Fire Inside. LC 96-35815. 192p. 1997. pap. 12.95 (*0-393-31634-3*) Norton.

Nesi, Thomas J., jt. auth. see Wolfe, M. Michael.

Nesiah, Devanesan. Discrimination with Reason? The Policy of Reservations in the United States, India & Malaysia. LC 97-903273. (Illus.). 356p. (C). 1997. text 32.00 (*0-19-563983-9*) OUP.

Nesin, Ali, jt. auth. see Borovik, Alexandre.

Nesin, Aziz. Turkish Stories from Four Decades. Mitler, Louis, tr. from TUR. 200p. (Orig.). 1991. pap. 13.95 (*0-89410-688-0*, Three Contnts); text 28.00 (*0-89410-687-2*, Three Contnts) L Rienner.

***Nesin, Aziz & Jacobson, Joseph S.** Dog Tails. 134p. 2000. pap. 9.95 (*0-9673703-4-5*) Southmoor Stud.

Nesin, Diane, ed. see Hoyle, Fred.

Nesin, Gert, jt. auth. see Lounsbury, John.

***Nesis, Gennady.** Khalifman: Life & Games. (Illus.). 2000. pap. 22.95 (*1-85744-212-1*, Pub. by Everyman Chess) Globe Pequot.

Nesis, Gennady. Tactics in the Grunfeld. (Batsford Chess Library). 176p. 1993. pap. 19.95 (*0-8050-2638-X*, Owl) H Holt & Co.

Nesius, Kneeland K. Life Science II. 2nd ed. 246p. (C). per. 24.95 (*0-7872-6610-8*) Kendall-Hunt.

***Nesje, Atle & Dahl, Svein Olaf.** Glaciers & Environmental Change. (Key Issues in Environmental Change). 224p. 2000. pap. 29.95 (*0-340-70634-1*); text 72.00 (*0-340-70637-6*) E A.

Nesle, Solange De Mailly, see De Mailly Nesle, Solange.

Nesler, T. P. & Bergersen, E. P. Mysids in Fisheries. LC 91-71560. (Symposium Ser.: No. 9). 199p. 1991. pap. 42.00 (*0-913235-71-7*, 540.09) Am Fisheries Soc.

Neslon, Lance E., ed. Purifying the Earthly Body of God: Religion & Ecology in Hindu India. LC 97-50608. (Series in Religious Studies). 352p. (C). 1998. text 73.50 (*0-7914-3923-2*); pap. text 24.95 (*0-7914-3924-0*) State U NY Pr.

Nesman, Edgar G. Peasant Mobilization & Rural Development. 148p. 1981. pap. text 13.95 (*0-87073-718-X*) Schenkman Bks Inc.

Nesme-Ribes, Elizabeth. The Solar Engine & Its Influence of Terrestrial Atmosphere & Climate. LC 94-34430. 1994. 262.95 (*3-540-58417-X*) Spr-Verlag.

Nesmelov, Arsenij. Bez Rossii. (Illus.). 480p. (Orig.). 1990. 35.00 (*1-878445-57-X*) Antiquary CT.

Nesmith, Alisa A., ed. see Peppers, Jerome G.

Nesmith, Anna M., ed. see Kissinger, Charles C.

Nesmith, Bruce. The New Republican Coalition: The Reagan Campaigns & White Evangelicals. LC 92-40964. (American University Studies, X, Political Science: Vol. 41). (Illus.). VIII, 182p. (C). 1994. text 39.95 (*0-8204-2138-3*) P Lang Pubng.

Nesmith, Eleanor L. Showcase of Interior Design: Southern. 3rd ed. (Illus.). 192p. 1998. write for info. (*1-56496-500-7*) Rockport Pubs.

Nesmith, James W. Two Addresses. 56p. 1978. pap. 9.95 (*0-87770-202-0*) Ye Galleon.

***Nesmith, Jeff.** No Higher Honor: The U. S. S. Yorktown at the Battle of Midway. LC 99-61750. (Illus.). 304p. 1999. 24.00 (*1-56352-552-6*) Longstreet.

NeSmith, Keao, ed. see Kai, Mahele Kumuwaiwai.

Nesmith, Lynn. Health Care Architecture Designs for the Future. 1994. 39.99 (*1-56496-136-2*) Rockport Pubs.

Nesmith, Mary E. An Objective Determination of Stories & Poems for the Primary Grades. LC 78-117102. (Columbia University. Teachers College. Contributions to Education Ser.: No. 255). reprint ed. 37.50 (*0-404-55255-2*) AMS Pr.

Nesmith, Michael. The Long Sandy Hair of Neftoon Zamora. LC 98-19510. 256p. 1998. 24.95 (*0-312-19296-7*, Thomas Dunne) St Martin.

Nesmith, Samuel P. Belgian Texans. 2nd rev. ed. (Texians & the Texans Ser.). 22p. 1982. pap. 4.95 (*0-933164-97-1*) U of Tex Inst Tex Culture.

Nesmith, Samuel P., jt. auth. see Martinello, Marian L.

Nesmith, Timothy E., jt. auth. see Batchelor, Andrew J., Jr.

Nesmith, Tom, ed. Canadian Archival Studies & the Rediscovery of Provenance. (Society of American Archivists & Association of Canadian Archivists Ser.). (Illus.). 526p. 1993. 68.50 (*0-8108-2660-7*) Scarecrow.

***Nesom, Joe.** Be Sure What You Believe: The Christian Faith Simply Explained. 1999. pap. text 11.99 (*0-85234-427-9*) Evangelical Pr.

Nespeca, Sue M. Library Programming for Families with Young Children: A How-to-Do-It Manual. LC 94-37894. (A How-to-do-it Manual Ser.: 45). 180p. 1994. 38.50 (*1-55570-181-7*) Neal-Schuman.

Nesper, Kathy, jt. auth. see Wessel, Helen.

Nespitz, Charles K. Childhood Rhinitis & Sinusitis: Pathophysiology & Treatment. Tinkelman, David G., ed. (Allergic Disease & Therapy Ser.: Vol. 3). (Illus.). 304p. 1990. text 125.00 (*0-8247-8228-3*) Dekker.

Nespor, Jan. Knowledge in Motion: Space, Time & Curriculum in Undergraduate Physics & Management. LC 94-31140. 172p. 1994. 85.00 (*0-7507-0270-2*) Taylor & Francis.

— Knowledge in Motion: Space, Time & Curriculum in Undergraduate Physics & Management. LC 94-31140. (Knowledge, Identity & School Life Ser.: Vol. 2). 166p. 1994. pap. 29.95 (*0-7507-0271-0*, Falmer Pr) Taylor & Francis.

— Tangled up in School: Politics, Space, Bodies, & Signs in the Educational Process. LC 97-1959. (Sociocultural, Political, & Historical Studies in Education). 304p. 1997. pap. 24.50 (*0-8058-2653-X*) L Erlbaum Assocs.

— Tangled up in School: Politics, Space, Bodies, & Signs in the Educational Process. LC 97-1959. (Sociocultural, Political, & Historical Studies in Education). 304p. 1997. text 59.95 (*0-8058-2652-1*) L Erlbaum Assocs.

Nespor, Marina & Vogel, G. Prosodic Phonology. (Studies in Generative Grammar). xiv, 328p. 1986. pap. 80.80 (*90-6765-242-3*) Mouton.

Nespor, Marina, jt. ed. see Mascaro, Joan.

Nespote, Jacques. Vietnam. (Illus.). 304p. 1995. pap. 15.95 (*0-8442-9691-0*, Natl Textbk Co) NTC Contemp Pub Co.

Nespoulous, J. L. & Villiard, P., eds. Morphology, Phonology & Aphasia. (Neuropsychology Ser.). (Illus.). 304p. 1990. 89.95 (*0-387-97183-1*) Spr-Verlag.

Nespoulous, J. L., et al. The Biological Foundations of Gesture: Motor & Semiotic Aspects. 336p. (C). 1986. text 69.95 (*0-89859-645-9*) L Erlbaum Assocs.

Ness, Arlin E., jt. auth. see Brendtro, Larry K.

Ness, Arthur J., ed. The Lute Music of Francesco Canova da Milano. LC 79-103671. (Harvard Publications in Music: Vols. 3 & 4). 507p. 1970. reprint ed. pap. 157.20 (*0-608-02224-1*, 205794600011) Bks Demand.

Ness, Arthur J. & Ward, John M. The Konigsberg Manuscript. LC 89-80415. (Illus.). 196p. 1989. 89.00 (*0-936186-31-3*) Edit Orphee.

Ness, Beatrice. Mystification et Creativite dans l'Oeuvre Romanesque de Marguerite Yourcenar: Cinq Lectures Genetiques. LC 93-85869. (North Carolina Studies in the Romance Languages & Literatures). 210p. (C). 1994. pap. text 32.50 (*0-8078-9251-3*) U of NC Pr.

Ness, Caro, ed. In a Nutshell: Aromatherapy: A Step-by-Step Guide. LC 98-193500. 64p. 1997. pap. 7.95 (*1-86204-012-5*, Pub. by Element MA) Penguin Putnam.

— In a Nutshell: Homeopathy: A Step-by-Step Guide. 64p. 1997. pap. 7.95 (*1-86204-007-9*, Pub. by Element MA) Penguin Putnam.

— In a Nutshell: Reflexology: A Step-by-Step Guide. 64p. 1997. pap. 7.95 (*1-86204-010-9*, Pub. by Element MA) Penguin Putnam.

— In a Nutshell: Vitamins & Minerals: A Step-by-Step Guide. 64p. 1997. pap. 7.95 (*1-86204-011-7*, Pub. by Element MA) Penguin Putnam.

Ness, Caroline. The Ocean of Story: Fairy Tales from India. Philip, Neil, ed. LC 95-76366. (Illus.). 128p. (J). (gr. 2 up). 1996. 17.00 (*0-688-13584-6*) Lothrop.

Ness, Christine M. Van, see Van Ness, John R. & Van Ness, Christine M., eds.

Ness, Daniel V. & Strong, Karen H. Restoring Justice. LC 97-71386. 228p. (C). 1997. pap. 27.95 (*0-87084-890-9*) Anderson Pub Co.

Ness, Daniel W. Van, see Van Ness, Daniel W.

Ness, Eliot & Fraley, Oscar. The Untouchables. 224p. 1987. mass mkt. 4.99 (*0-671-64449-1*) PB.

Ness, Eliot, jt. auth. see Fraley, Oscar.

Ness, Elliott & Fraley, Oscar. The Untouchables. 1993. reprint ed. lib. bdg. 27.95 (*1-56849-198-0*) Buccaneer Bks.

Ness, Evaline. Sam, Bangs, & Moonshine. LC 66-10113. (Illus.). 48p. (J). (ps-2). 1995. 14.95 (*0-8050-0314-2*, Bks Young Read); pap. 5.95 (*0-8050-0315-0*, Bks Young Read) H Holt & Co.

— Sam, Bangs, & Moonshine. (J). 1966. 11.15 (*0-606-01326-1*, Pub. by Turtleback) Demco.

— Sam, Bangs y Hechizo de Luna (Sam, Bangs & Moonshine) Alonso, Liwayway, tr. from ENG. (SPA., Illus.). 48p. (J). 1994. 14.95 (*1-880507-12-9*) Lectorum Pubns.

Ness, Evaline. Tom Tit Tat. (Illus.). (J). 1997. pap. 13.40 (*0-613-06055-5*) Econo-Clad Bks.

Ness, Evaline. Tom Tit Tot. LC 97-202926. (Illus.). 32p. (J). (gr. k-3). 1997. mass mkt. 5.99 (*0-689-81398-8*) Aladdin.

— Tom Tit Tot. (J). 1997. 11.19 (*0-606-13854-4*, Pub. by Turtleback) Demco.

Ness, Frederic W. An Uncertain Glory: Letters of Cautious but Sound Advice. LC 74-152812. (Jossey-Bass Higher Education Ser.). 168p. reprint ed. 52.10 (*0-8357-9353-2*, 201382000087) Bks Demand.

Ness, Frederic W., jt. ed. see Jellema, William W.

***Ness, Gayl D.** Five Cities: Studies in Asian Urban Population Environment Dynamics. 2000. pap. 24.95 (*0-19-588693-3*) OUP.

Ness, Gayl D. & Ando, Hirofumi. The Land Is Shrinking: Population Planning in Asia. LC 83-48048. (Johns Hopkins Studies in Development). (Illus.). 253p. reprint ed. pap. 78.50 (*0-608-06174-3*, 206650700008) Bks Demand.

Ness, George T., Jr. The Regular Army on the Eve of the Civil War. LC 89-52137. (Illus.). 326p. 1990. 20.00 (*0-9612670-1-1*) Toomey Pr.

Ness, George T., Jr. Under the Eagle's Wings: The Army on the Eve of Civil War, 2 vols. 650p. 1983. 87.95 (*0-89126-112-5*) MA-AH Pub.

Ness, Gordon Van, see Van Ness, Gordon.

Ness, H. C. van, see Smith, J. M. & Van Ness, H. C.

Ness, H. C. van, see Van Ness, H. C.

Ness, Immanuel. Enclopedia of World Cities. 650p. 1999. lib. bdg. 145.00 (*1-57958-131-5*) Fitzroy Dearborn.

— Encyclopedia of Interest Groups & Lobbyists in the United States, 2 vols. LC 99-48849. 800p. 2000. text 185.00 (*0-7656-8022-X*, Sharpe Ref) M E Sharpe.

— Encyclopedia of World Cities, 2 vols. LC 98-29844. (Illus.). 768p. 1998. text 179.00 (*0-7656-8017-3*) M E Sharpe.

— Trade Unions & the Betrayal of the Unemployed Labor Conflicts During the 1990's. LC 98-18640. (Studies in the History of American Labor). 268p. 1998. 60.00 (*0-8153-3179-7*) Garland.

Ness, Immanuel & Ciment, James. The Encyclopedia of Global Population & Demographics, 2 vols. Set. LC 98-46436. (Illus.). 984p. 1998. text 185.00 (*1-56324-710-0*, Sharpe Ref) M E Sharpe.

— The Encyclopedia of Third Parties in America, 3 Vols. LC 98-29844. (Illus.). 880p. 2000. text 275.00 (*0-7656-8020-3*, Sharpe Ref) M E Sharpe.

***Ness, Immanuel & Eimer, Stuart, eds.** Organizing for Justice: Central Labor Councils & the Revival of American Unionism. (Illus.). 256p. 2000. 64.95 (*0-7656-0599-6*) M E Sharpe.

Ness, Immanuel, jt. auth. see Ciment, James.

Ness, Indoe. Tax Planning for Disposition of Business Interest. 2nd ed. 704p. suppl. ed. 48.00 (*0-7913-0932-0*); suppl. ed. 50.75 (*0-685-51110-3*) Warren Gorham & Lamont.

— Tax Planning for Disposition of Business Interest. 2nd ed. 704p. 1990. suppl. ed. 175.00 (*0-7913-0627-5*, TPB) Warren Gorham & Lamont.

Ness, Jean, jt. auth. see Aune, Elizabeth.

Ness, Joanne. Calcium-Requirement Cookbook. 192p. 1998. pap. text 12.95 (*0-87131-850-4*) M Evans.

Ness, John R. Van, see Van Ness, John R.

Ness, John R. Van, see Briggs, Charles L. & Van Ness, John R., eds.

Ness, John R. Van, see Van Ness, John R., ed.

Ness, John W. Van, see Cheng, Chi-Lun & Van Ness, John W.

Ness, Judy & Hoffman, Connie. Putting Sense into Consensus: Solving the Puzzle of Making Team Decisions. (Illus.). 127p. 1998. pap. text 26.50 (*0-9665529-0-3*) Vista Assocs.

Ness, Pamela M. Assisi Embroidery. (Illus.). 48p. 1979. pap. 3.50 (*0-486-23743-5*) Dover.

Ness, Paul D. Van, see Van Ness, Paul D.

Ness, Paul D. Van, see Hartman, Walter & Van Ness, Paul D.

Ness, Paul D. Van, see Van Ness, Paul D.

Ness, Paul M., jt. auth. see Anderson, Kenneth C.

Ness, Paul N. Van, see Van Ness, Paul N.

Ness, Peter H. Van, see Van Ness, Peter H.

Ness, Richard. Alan Rudolph: Richard Ness. LC 96-27579. (Twayne's Filmmakers Ser.). 1996. 33.00 (*0-8057-7847-0*, Twyne); pap. 20.00 (*0-8057-9247-3*, Twyne) Mac Lib Ref.

— From Headline Hunter to Superman: A Journalism Filmography. LC 97-5526. 1997. 89.50 (*0-8108-3291-7*) Scarecrow.

Ness, Richard H. Van, see Van Ness, Richard H.

Ness, Richard J. Van, see Van Ness, Richard J.

Ness, Roberta B. & Kuller, Lewis H., eds. Health & Disease among Women: Biological & Environmental Influences. (Illus.). 488p. 1998. text 65.00 (*0-19-511396-9*) OUP.

Ness, Sally A. Body, Movement, & Culture: Kinesthetic & Visual Symbolism in a Philippine Community. LC 92-15310. (Contemporary Ethnography Ser.). (Illus.). 312p. (Orig.). (C). 1992. text 45.00 (*0-8122-3110-4*) U of Pa Pr.

Ness Seymour, Tryntje Van, see Van Ness Seymour, Tryntje.

Ness, Shirley A. Air Monitoring for Toxic Exposures. LC 90-38159. (Illus.). 534p. 1991. text 103.95 (*0-442-20639-9*, VNR) Wiley.

— Air Monitoring For Toxic Exposures. 2nd ed. (Industrial Health & Safety Ser.). 1997. text 109.95 (*0-442-02284-0*, VNR) Wiley.

— Air Monitoring for Toxic Exposures: An Integrated Approach. (Industrial Health & Safety Ser.). 544p. 1991. 115.00 (*0-471-28860-8*, VNR) Wiley.

Ness, Shirley A. Surface & Dermal Monitoring for Toxic Exposures. (Industrial Health & Safety Ser.). 576p. 1994. 115.00 (*0-471-28564-1*, VNR) Wiley.

Ness, Shirley A. Surface & Dermal Sampling for Toxic Exposures. 562p. 1994. text 79.95 (*0-442-01465-1*, VNR) Wiley.

Ness, Shirley A., ed. NIOSH Case Studies in Bioaerosols. LC 96-182386. 316p. 1996. pap. text 39.00 (*0-86587-485-9*) Gov Insts.

— NIOSH Case Studies in Ergonomics. LC 96-183186. 321p. 1996. pap. text 39.00 (*0-86587-483-2*) Gov Insts.

— NIOSH Case Studies in Indoor Air Quality. LC 96-182385. 430p. 1996. pap. text 39.00 (*0-86587-482-4*) Gov Insts.

— NIOSH Case Studies in Lead. LC 96-183160. 308p. 1996. pap. text 39.00 (*0-86587-484-0*) Gov Insts.

— NIOSH Case Studies in Personal Protective Equipment. 309p. 1996. pap. text 39.00 (*0-86587-529-4*) Gov Insts.

An Asterisk (*) at the beginning of an entry indicates that the title is appearing for the first time.

Ness, Stanley & Sherlock, Charles N., eds. ASNT Nondestructive Testing Handbook: Nondestructive Testing Overview. 2nd ed. LC 96-25138. (Nondestructive Testing Handbook Ser.: Vol. 10). 581p. 1996. 97.25 (*1-57117-018-9*) Am Soc Nondestructive.

Ness, Theodore & Vogel, Eugene L. Taxation of the Closely Held Corporation. 4th ed. 1991. suppl. ed. 160.00 (*0-685-45578-5*, TCHC) Warren Gorham & Lamont.

Ness, Tor, jt. auth. see Andenaes, Olav.

Ness, William P. Van, see Van Ness, William P.

Nessan, Craig L. Beyond Maintenance to Mission: A Theology of the Congregation. LC 98-48889. 128p. 1999. pap. 14.00 (*0-8006-3152-8*, 1-3152, Fortress Pr) Augsburg Fortress.

***Nesse, William D.** Introduction to Mineralogy. LC 98-45279. (Illus.). 464p. (C). 1999. text 70.00 (*0-19-510691-1*) OUP.

Nesse, William D. Introduction to Optical Mineralogy. 2nd ed. (Illus.). 352p. (C). 1991. text 64.95 (*0-19-506024-5*) OUP.

Nessel, Brian. What a Life: One Man, One Mind, One Mistake after Another. (Illus.). 163p. (Orig.). 1996. pap. 10.00 (*1-889934-00-3*) Bs Hive Pub.

Nessel, Denise D., ed. Awakening Young Minds: Perspectives on Education. LC 96-28684. 224p. (Orig.). 1997. pap. 14.00 (*1-883536-05-7*, Malor Bks) ISHK.

Nessel, Denise D. & Jones, Margaret B. Language-Experience Approach to Reading: A Handbook for Teachers of Reading. LC 80-27822. 280p. (Orig.). 1981. pap. 15.95 (*0-8077-2596-X*) Tchrs Coll.

Nesselrath, Arnold, et al, contrib. by. Angels from the Vatican: The Invisible Made Visible. (Illus.). 320p. 1998. 60.00 (*0-8109-6355-8*) Abrams.

Nesselrath, Heinz-Gunther. Die Atticshe Mittlere Komodie: Ihre Stellung in der Antiken Literatur & Literaturgeschichte. (Untersuchungen zur Antiken Literatur und Geschichte Ser.: No. 36). (GER.). x, 395p. (C). 1990. lib. bdg. 166.15 (*3-11-012196-4*) De Gruyter.

— Lukians Parasitendialog: Untersuchungen und Kommentar. (Untersuchungen zur Antiken Literatur und Geschichte Ser.: Vol. 22). (GER.). xi, 559p. 1985. 234.65 (*3-11-010277-3*) De Gruyter.

Nesselrath, Heinz-Gunther, et al, eds. Supplementum Hellenisticum. (GRE.). 863p. 1983. 476.95 (*3-11-008171-7*) De Gruyter.

Nesselrath, Heinz-Gunther, ed. see Kassel, Rudolf.

Nesselroade, J. R. & Cattell, R. B. Handbook of Multivariate Experimental Psychology. 2nd ed. LC 88-9806. (Perspectives on Individual Differences Ser.). (Illus.). 996p. (C). 1988. 150.00 (*0-306-42526-2*, Plenum Trade) Perseus Pubng.

Nesselrod, Piri K. Rubezahl: The Adventurous Mountain Spirit. LC 97-90839. (J). 1998. 10.95 (*0-533-12490-5*) Vantage.

Nesselroth. Lautreamont's Imagery: A Stylistic Approach. 14.95 (*0-685-34929-2*) Fr & Eur.

Nesselson, Lisa, jt. auth. see Fitch, Brian T.

***Nesselson, Mark.** The Whole Child Pediatrician. 2000. 26.00 (*0-8129-3223-4*, Times Bks) Random.

Nessen, Julie, jt. auth. see Nessen, Robert L.

Nessen, Robert L. Real Estate Finance & Taxation: Structuring Complex Transactions. unabridged ed. (Illus.). 350p. 1998. pap. text 35.00 (*0-9667170-1-5*) Millenim III Pr.

Nessen, Robert L. & Nessen, Julie. A Need to Die. unabridged ed. 170p. 1998. mass mkt. 9.50 (*0-9667170-0-7*) Millenim III Pr.

Nessen, Ron. Knight & Day. 1996. mass mkt. 5.99 (*0-8125-5053-6*, Pub. by Forge NYC) St Martin.

— Press Corpse. (Knight & Day Ser.). 224p. 1997. mass mkt. 5.99 (*0-8125-6793-5*, Pub. by Forge NYC) St Martin.

Nessen, Ron & Neuman, Johanna. Death with Honors, No. 3. LC 97-37099. 288p. 1998. text 22.95 (*0-312-85594-X*) St Martin.

— Knight & Day. 256p. 1995. 21.95 (*0-312-85588-5*) Tor Bks.

Nesser, H. J., et al, eds. Atlas of Tissue Doppler Echocardiography TDE. (Illus.). 150p. 1995. 145.00 (*3-7985-1020-2*) Spr-Verlag.

Nesser, Joann. Journey into Reality: Through Prayer & God-Centeredness. LC 24-832. 96p. 1998. pap. 9.95 (*0-9659320-4-4*) Lvg Waters.

Nesset, Kirk. The Stories of Raymond Carver: A Critical Study. LC 94-30322. 140p. (C). 1995. pap. text 14.95 (*0-8214-1100-4*) Ohio U Pr.

Nessheim, Ragnhild. Press, Politics & Votes for women, 1910, 1918. 384p. 1997. pap. 45.00 (*82-00-12695-1*) Scandnvan Univ Pr.

Nessmith. Thinking Sociologically. (C). 1994. pap. text, teacher ed. 33.75 (*0-15-501870-1*) Harcourt Coll Pubs.

Nessmuk, pseud. Woodcraft & Camping. (Illus.). 105p. 1963. pap. 4.95 (*0-486-21145-2*) Dover.

Nesson, Charles, jt. ed. see Kahin, Brian.

Nesson, Charles R. Evidence, 1988. 1988. 25.00 (*1-55917-164-2*, 7306); audio 135.00 (*1-55917-162-6*); VHS 495.00 (*1-55917-163-4*) Natl Prac Inst.

Nesson, Charles R., jt. auth. see Green, Eric D.

Nesson, Fern L. Great Waters: A History of Boston's Water Supply. LC 82-40342. (Illus.). 134p. reprint ed. pap. 41.60 (*0-8357-6521-0*, 203589200097) Bks Demand.

Nesss. Problem Solving for Air Monitoring. (Biology Ser.). 1998. pap. 34.95 (*0-442-02484-3*, VNR) Wiley.

Nest, Dean G. Van, see Van Nest, Dean G.

Neste, Dominique Van, see Dawber, Rodney & Van Neste, Dominique.

Nestel, Barry, jt. auth. see Daniels, Doug.

Nestel, Glenn, et al. QualServe Guidance for Peer Review. LC 97-184383. (Illus.). 184p. 1997. pap. 195.00 (*0-89867-908-7*, 90730) Am Water Wks Assn.

Nestel, P. J., jt. ed. see Simopoulos, A. P.

Nestell, Merlynd, tr. see Akhiezer, N. I. & Glazman, I. M.

Nester. International Relations. (Political Science Ser.). 2000. text 36.50 (*0-8304-1552-1*) Wadsworth Pub.

— Microbiology. 1994. teacher ed. 50.00 (*0-697-12761-3*) McGraw.

— Microbiology. 3rd ed. 2000. student ed. 20.00 (*0-07-231884-8*) McGraw.

— Microbiology: A Human Perspective. 3rd ed. 2000. 63.00 (*0-07-231878-3*) McGraw.

— Microbiology: Human Perspective. 2nd ed. 1998. 31.25 (*0-697-28598-7*, WCB McGr Hill) McGraw-H Hghr Educ.

— Microbiology: Human Perspective & Student Study Art Notebook. 2nd ed. 1994. student ed. 66.00 (*0-697-26398-3*, WCB McGr Hill) McGraw-H Hghr Educ.

— Microbiology & Study Cards & Student Study Art Notebook: Study Cards, Student Study Art Notebook. 1996. incl. cd-rom (*0-697-36802-5*, WCB McGr Hill) McGraw-H Hghr Educ.

Nester, Dean. A Second Chance: A True Story of Tragedy Turned to Triumph. 283p. (Orig.). 1995. pap. 9.95 (*0-9647710-0-4*) Sable Pubng.

Nester, Eugene W. Microbiology: A Human Perspective. 2nd ed. 206p. 1998. pap., student ed. 22.19 (*0-697-28605-3*) McGraw.

Nester, Eugene W. & Nester, Martha T. Microbiology: A Human Perspective. 2nd ed. LC 97-15264. 864p. (C). 1997. text. write for info. (*0-697-28602-9*, WCB McGr Hill) McGraw-H Hghr Educ.

Nester, Eugene W. & Verma, Desh P., eds. Advances in Molecular Genetics of Plant-Microbe Interactions, Vol. 2. LC 92-35081. 640p. (C). 1992. text 208.00 (*0-7923-2045-X*) Kluwer Academic.

Nester, Eugene W., et al. Microbiology: A Human Perspective. 832p. (C). 1994. text, student ed. 23.12 (*0-697-14788-6*, WCB McGr Hill) McGraw-H Hghr Educ.

Nester, Martha T., jt. auth. see Nester, Eugene W.

Nester, Mary A. Pre-Employment Testing & the ADA. (ADA Practice Ser.). 16p. 1994. pap. 9.00 (*0-685-72821-8*) LRP Pubns.

***Nester, William.** From Mountain Man to Millionaire: The "Bold & Dashing Life" of Robert Campbell. LC 98-54962. (Illus.). 288p. 1999. 29.95 (*0-8262-1218-2*) U of Mo Pr.

Nester, William R. American Industrial Policy: Free or Managed Markets. LC 96-35137. 256p. 1997. text 39.95 (*0-312-16592-7*) St Martin.

— American Power, the New World Order, & the Japanese Challenge. LC 92-28897. 400p. 1993. text 39.95 (*0-312-08991-0*) St Martin.

— European Power & the Japanese Challenge. LC 93-17512. 304p. (C). 1993. text 55.00 (*0-8147-5777-4*) NYU Pr.

***Nester, William R.** The First Global War 1756-1775: Britain, France & The Fate of North America. LC 99-32051. 320p. 2000. 69.95 (*0-275-96771-9*) Greenwood.

Nester, William R. The Foundation of Japanese Power. LC 90-34055. 418p. (gr. 13). 1990. text 83.95 (*0-87332-755-1*) M E Sharpe.

***Nester, William R.** The Great Frontier War 1607-1755: Britain, France & The Imperial Struggle for North America. LC 99-32050. 344p. 2000. 69.50 (*0-275-96772-7*) Greenwood.

— Haughty Conquerors: Amherst & the Great Indian Uprising of 1763. LC 99-55020. 328p. 2000. 68.00 (*0-275-96770-0*, C6770, Praeger Pubs) Greenwood.

Nester, William R. Japanese Industrial Targeting: The Neomercantilist Path to Economic Superpower. LC 90-20560. 312p. 1991. text 55.00 (*0-312-05782-2*) St Martin.

— Power Across the Pacific: A History of America's Relations with Japan. 480p. (C). 1996. text 55.00 (*0-8147-5788-X*) NYU Pr.

— The War for America's Natural Resources. LC 96-35139. 256p. 1997. pap. 18.95 (*0-312-16591-9*); text 59.95 (*0-312-16589-7*) St Martin.

Nesterenko, V. V., jt. auth. see Barbashov, B. M.

Nesterenko, Yu V., tr. & contrib. by see Parshin, A. N., et al, eds.

Nesterov, A. Physicochemical Aspects of Medicine Reviews Vol. 3, Pt. 2: Hydromechanics of the Eye, Vol. 3. (Soviet Medical Reviews Ser.: Section B). 68p. 1992. pap. text 71.00 (*3-7186-5256-0*, Harwood Acad Pubs) Gordon & Breach.

Nesterov, Anatoly E., jt. auth. see Lipatov, Yuri S.

Nesterov, Yurii & Nemirovski, Arkadii. Interior Point Polynomial Methods in Convex Programming. LC 93-38912. (Studies in Applied Mathematics: No. 13). ix, 405p. 1994. 77.50 (*0-89871-319-6*) Soc Indus-Appl Math.

Nesterova, Elena. Itinerants: The Masters of Russian Realism. (Schools & Movements Ser.). (Illus.). 240p. 1996. 55.00 (*1-85995-254-2*) Parkstone Pr.

Nesterowicz, C., ed. Extramural Grant Program, 1998: Chicago, Ill., May 1998: Abstract. (Blood Purification Ser.: Vol. 17, Suppl. 1 (1999)). (Illus.). vi, 68p. 1999. pap. 25.25 (*3-8055-6894-0*) S Karger.

***Nesterowicz, C., ed.** Extramural Grant Program 1999: Chicago (Ill.), May 1999 - Abstracts. (Blood Purification Ser.: Vol. 18). (Illus.). vi, 62p. 2000. pap. 25.25 (*3-8055-7117-8*) S Karger.

Nestingen, Jan, ed. see Brandt, Betty.

Nestingen, Signe L. & Lewis, Laurel. Growing Beyond Abuse: A Workbook for Survivors of Sexual Exploitation or Childhood Sexual Abuse. 192p. 1991. wbk. ed. 18.95 (*0-9628703-0-7*) Omni Recovery.

***Nestle, Aland.** Novum Testamentum Greece. 27th ed. 1999. 33.99 (*5-550-00786-X*) Nairi.

***Nestle Company Staff.** Nestle Toll House Best-Ever Cookies. LC 98-66559. (Illus.). 240p. 1999. 24.95 (*0-696-20904-7*) Meredith Bks.

Nestle Company Staff. Polyunsaturated Fatty Acids in Human Nutrition. Bracco, Umberto & Deckelbaum, Richard J., eds. LC 92-11920. (Nestle Nutrition Workshop Ser.: Vol. 28). (Illus.). 255p. 1992. reprint ed. pap. 79.10 (*0-608-07259-1*, 206748700009) Bks Demand.

— Rickets. Glorieux, Francis H., ed. LC 91-11849. (Nestle Nutrition Workshop Ser.: No. 21). (Illus.). 300p. 1991. reprint ed. pap. 93.00 (*0-608-05852-1*, 205981900007) Bks Demand.

Nestle Company Staff, et al. Diarrheal Disease. LC 96-43035. (Nestle Nutrition Workshop Ser.). 368p. 1997. text 74.00 (*0-397-58771-6*) Lppncott W & W.

Nestle, Joan. A Fragile Union: New & Selected Writings. LC 98-31261. 230p. 1998. pap. 14.95 (*1-57344-040-X*) Cleis Pr.

— A Restricted Country. LC 87-26671. 192p. (Orig.). 1987. pap. 10.95 (*0-932379-37-0*); lib. bdg. 22.95 (*0-932379-38-9*) Firebrand Bks.

Nestle, Joan, ed. The Persistent Desire: A Femme-Butch Reader. LC 92-6166. 502p. (Orig.). 1992. pap. 14.95 (*1-55583-190-7*) Alyson Pubns.

Nestle, Joan & Holoch, Naomi, eds. The Vintage Book of International Lesbian Fiction: An Anthology. LC 98-32138. 384p. 1999. pap. 15.00 (*0-679-75952-2*) Vin Bks.

— Women on Women: An Anthology of American Lesbian Short Fiction. 1990. pap. 13.95 (*0-452-26388-3*, Plume) Dutton Plume.

Nestle, Joan, jt. ed. see Holoch, Naomi.

Nestle, Marion. Nutrition in Clinical Practice. LC 85-60806. 330p. (Orig.). 1986. pap. 19.95 (*0-930010-11-6*) Jones Med.

Nestle, Wilhelm. Vom Mythos Zum Logos: Die Selbstentfaltung Des Griechischen Denkens Von Homer Bis Auf Die Sophistik und Sokrates. Bolle, Kees W., ed. LC 77-79147. (Mythology Ser.). (GER.). 1978. reprint ed. lib. bdg. 50.95 (*0-405-10556-8*) Ayer.

Nestlebaum, Chana. The Mookster's Mitzvah Mishaps. LC 91-75362. (Illus.). 32p. (J). (gr. k-4). 1991. 12.95 (*0-910818-26-6*); pap. 9.95 (*0-910818-27-4*) Judaica Pr.

***Nestler, Brigitte.** Bibliographie Willi Bredel. 709p. 1999. 85.95 (*3-631-32809-5*) P Lang Pubng.

Nestler, Eric J., jt. auth. see Hyman, Steven E.

Nestler, Erich, jt. auth. see Henning, Christian.

Nestler, Harold. A Bibliography of New York State Communities. 3rd ed. 312p. 1990. pap. 20.00 (*1-55613-330-8*) Heritage Bk.

Nestmann, Frank & Hurrelman, Klaus, eds. Social Networks & Social Support in Childhood & Adolescence. LC 94-544. (Prevention & Intervention in Childhood & Adolescence Ser.: Vol. 16). xii, 441p. (C). 1994. lib. bdg. 79.95 (*3-11-014360-7*) De Gruyter.

Nestmann, Mark. Asset Protection 2000. 2nd rev. ed. 245p. 1998. per. 75.00 (*1-891266-06-3*, Pub. by Asset Protection Intl) Pathway Bk Serv.

— Big Brother Goes Global: Financial Intelligence Units Proliferate, Worldwide. 32p. 1998. 25.00 (*1-891266-08-X*, Pub. by Asset Protection Intl) Pathway Bk Serv.

— Counter-Surveillance. 33p. 1997. pap. 25.00 (*0-9657151-6-7*, Pub. by Asset Protection Intl) Pathway Bk Serv.

— A Critical Analysis of the Cook Islands As an Asset Protection Haven. 2nd rev. ed. 17p. 1998. spiral bd. 25.00 (*1-891266-11-X*, Pub. by Asset Protection Intl) Pathway Bk Serv.

— Mutual Legal Assistance Treaties. 2nd rev. ed. 15p. 1998. spiral bd. 25.00 (*1-891266-10-1*, Pub. by Asset Protection Intl) Pathway Bk Serv.

***Nestmann, Mark.** Practical Privacy Strategies for Windows 95/98. 2nd ed. Orig. Title: Practical Privacy Strategies for Windows 95. 45p. 2000. spiral bd. 25.00 (*1-891266-17-9*, Pub. by Asset Protection Intl) Pathway Bk Serv.

Nestmann, Mark. Privacy 1995. 208p. 1995. 100.00 (*3-9520851-0-3*, Pub. by W Beck Verlag) Tattered Cover.

— Privacy 2000. 264p. 1997. pap. 75.00 (*0-9657151-3-2*, Pub. by Asset Protection Intl) Pathway Bk Serv.

Nestmann, Mark, ed. 97 Ways to Protect What's Left of Your Privacy & Property Rights. 2nd ed. 35p. 1998. 25.00 (*1-891266-07-1*, Pub. by Asset Protection Intl) Pathway Bk Serv.

***Nesto, Richard W.** Cholesterol-Lowering Drugs: Everything You & Your Family Need to Know. 288p. 2000. mass mkt. 5.99 (*0-380-80779-3*, Avon Bks) Morrow Avon.

Nestor, Basil. Judy: A Life in Pictures. LC 96-30067. 1997. 12.98 (*1-56799-436-9*, MetroBooks) M Friedman Pub Grp Inc.

Nestor, Darryl, jt. auth. see Moore, David S.

Nestor, Helen. Family Portraits in Changing Times. (Illus.). 144p. 1992. 39.95 (*0-939165-16-3*); pap. 22.95 (*0-939165-15-5*) NewSage Press.

Nestor-Iskander. The Tale of Constantinople: Of Its Origin & Capture in the Year 1453. Hanak, Walter & Philippides, Marios, eds. & trs. by. from CHU. (Late Byzantine & Ottoman Studies: No. 5). (ENG & SLA.). 192p. 1996. text 60.00 (*0-89241-503-7*) Caratzas.

Nestor, J., jt. auth. see Mendez, V.

Nestor, J. J., Jr., jt. ed. see Vickery, B. H.

Nestor, Joanne P. & Glotzer, Judith A. Teaching Nutrition. 302p. 1981. pap. text 20.00 (*0-89011-559-1*) Abt Bks.

Nestor, Joanne P. & Glotzer, Judith A., eds. Teaching Nutrition: A Review of Programs & Research. 302p. 1984. reprint ed. pap. text 27.00 (*0-8191-4115-1*) U Pr of Amer.

Nestor, Larry, jt. auth. see Peterson, Gary.

Nestor, Pauline. Charlotte Bronte's "Jane Eyre" LC 92-17623. (Critical Studies of Key Texts). 114 p. 1992. pap. 12.95 (*0-312-08601-6*) St Martin.

Nestor, Pauline, ed. see Bronte, Emily Jane.

Nestor, Sarah & Robertson, Edna E. Artists of the Canyons & Caminos: Sante Fe, the Early Years. 2nd unabridged ed. Noble, David, ed. LC 96-85134. (Illus.). 176p. 1996. reprint ed. pap. 16.95 (*0-941270-92-0*) Ancient City Pr.

Nestor, Sarah A., et al. Harmony by Hand: Art of the Southwest Indians. LC 87-6321. (Illus.). 108p. 1987. 30.00 (*0-87701-455-8*); pap. 18.95 (*0-87701-426-4*) Chronicle Bks.

Nestor, Thomay. Macedonia to America & Back: A Biographical History of Dmitri Nasos. LC 96-69028. 335p. (Orig.). 1996. pap. 18.95 (*1-880222-25-6*) Red Apple Pub.

***Nestor, Tom.** The Keeper of Absalom's Island: A Lyrical Tribute to a Rural Childhood. LC 99-492140. 238p. 2000. pap. 17.95 (*1-898256-82-9*, Pub. by Collins Press) Irish Bks Media.

Nestorian Church Staff. Liturgy & Ritual: The Liturgy of the Holy Apostles Adai & Mari. LC 79-131032. reprint ed. 29.50 (*0-404-03997-9*) AMS Pr.

Nestorius Patriarch Of Constantinople. The Bazaar of Heracleides. Driver, G. R., tr. LC 77-84705. reprint ed. 42.00 (*0-404-16112-X*) AMS Pr.

Nestorova, Tatyana. Rise & Fall Soviet Union. 176p. 1993. per. 31.95 (*0-8403-8467-X*) Kendall-Hunt.

Nestorva, Tatyana. American Missionaries among the Bulgarians: 1858-1912. 151p. 1987. text 47.50 (*0-88033-114-3*, 218, Pub. by East Eur Monographs) Col U Pr.

Nestrick, William V. Constructional Activities of Adult Males. LC 76-177115. (Columbia University. Teachers College. Contributions to Education Ser.: No. 780). reprint ed. 37.50 (*0-404-55780-5*) AMS Pr.

Nestroy, Johann. Three Viennese Comedies. Harrison, Robert & Wilson, Katharina M., trs. from GER. LC 85-71916. (GERM Ser.: Vol. 21). (Illus.). viii, 264p. 1986. 29.95 (*0-938100-37-8*) Camden Hse.

Nestroy, Johann N. Johann Nestroy's Saemtliche Werke, 15 vols. Von Brukner, Fritz & Rommell, Otto, eds. LC 77-173072. reprint ed. 1147.50 (*0-404-04690-8*) AMS Pr.

— Der Talisman: Posse mit Gesanf in Drei Akten. Herles, Helmut, ed. 135p. (C). 1971. 15.25 (*3-11-001869-1*) De Gruyter.

Nestroy, Johann N., et al. Nineteenth-Century German Plays: King Ottocar's Rise & Fall; The Talisman, & Agnes Bernauer. Schwarz, Egon, ed. LC 78-4300. (German Library: Vol. 31). 320p. 1990. 39.50 (*0-8264-0331-X*); pap. 19.95 (*0-8264-0332-8*) Continuum.

Nestyev, Israel V. Prokofiev. Jonas, Florence, tr. from RUS. LC 60-11631. 556p. 1960. reprint ed. pap. 30.00 (*0-7837-1224-3*, 204175500023) Bks Demand.

Nesvada, Josef. In the Footsteps of the Abominable Snowman: Stories of Science & Fantasy. LC 75-510081. 215p. 1970. write for info. (*0-575-00427-4*) Trafalgar.

Net Guru Technologies, Inc. Staff. Webmaster Administrator: Certification Exam Guide. LC 97-41803. (Illus.). 960p. 1997. 74.95 incl. cd-rom (*0-07-913287-1*) McGraw.

Neta, B. In Memory of Leeor Merkine. 318p. 1991. pap. text 1265.00 (*2-88124-827-6*) Gordon & Breach.

Netanyahu, B. Don Isaac Abravanel: Statesman & Philosopher. 5th ed. LC 97-50254. 368p. 1998. text 49.95 (*0-8014-3487-4*); pap. text 16.95 (*0-8014-8485-5*) Cornell U Pr.

— The Marranos of Spain: From the Late 14th to the Early 16th Century (According to Contemporary Hebrew Sources) 3rd expanded rev. ed. LC 98-55165. 304p. 1999. 42.50 (*0-8014-3586-2*) Cornell U Pr.

— The Marranos of Spain: From the Late 14th to the Early 16th Century According to Contemporary Hebrew Sources. 3rd expanded rev. ed. LC 98-55165. 302p. 1999. pap. 16.95 (*0-8014-8568-1*) Cornell U Pr.

***Netanyahu, B.** Origins of the Inquisition in Fifteenth Century Spain. 2000. pap. 29.95 (*0-940322-39-0*) NY Rev Bks.

Netanyahu, B. Toward the Inquisition: Essays on Jewish & Converso History in Late Medieval Spain. LC 97-19283. 272p. 1997. text 32.50 (*0-8014-3410-6*) Cornell U Pr.

Netanyahu, Benjamin. A Durable Peace: Israel & Its Place among the Nations. LC 98-37522. 496p. 2000. 30.00 (*0-446-52306-2*, Pub. by Warner Bks) Little.

— Fighting Terrorism: How Democracies Can Defeat Domestic & International Terrorism. 152p. 1998. text 17.00 (*0-7881-5514-8*) DIANE Pub.

— Fighting Terrorism: How Democracies Can Defeat Domestic & International Terrorists. 153p. 1995. text 17.00 (*0-374-15492-9*) FS&G.

— Fighting Terrorism: How Democracies Can Defeat Domestic & International Terrorists. LC 95-4849. 160p. 1997. pap. 12.00 (*0-374-52497-1*, Noonday) FS&G.

Netanyahu, Benjamin, ed. International Terrorism: Challenge & Response. 383p. 1982. pap. 24.95 (*0-87855-894-2*) Transaction Pubs.

— Terrorism: How the West Can Win. 272p. 1987. mass mkt. 4.50 (*0-380-70321-1*, Avon Bks) Morrow Avon.

Netanyahu, Johnathan. Self-Portrait of a Hero: From the Letters of Jonathan Netanyahu, 1963-1976. LC 98-10170. (Illus.). 336p. 1998. mass mkt. 14.00 (*0-446-67461-3*, Pub. by Warner Bks) Little.

Netanyahu, Sinaia, jt. ed. see Just, Richard.

Netcott, Rachel, ed. see Rilyeu, Gary.

Netek, Don F. The Sportsman's Cookbook & Then Some. 2nd rev. ed. 100p. 1998. spiral bd. 14.95 (*0-9671457-0-8*) Netek Enterp.

N

An Asterisk (*) at the beginning of an entry indicates that the title is appearing for the first time.

Netemeyer, Richard G. Handbook of Marketing Scales: Multi-Item Measures for Marketing & Consumer Behavior Research. 2nd ed. Bearden, William O., ed. LC 98-25452. (Association for Consumer Research Ser.). 537p. 1998. 75.00 (*0-7619-1000-X*) Sage.

Neter. Applied Linear Stat. Models. 4th ed. 1996. pap., student ed. 22.81 (*0-256-11987-2*) McGraw.

Neter, E., ed. see International Convocation on Immunology Staff.

Neter, John, et al. Applied Linear Regression Models. 3rd ed. LC 95-37444. 720p. (C). 1996. text 68.95 (*0-256-08601-X*, Irwn McGrw-H) McGrw-H Hghr Educ.

— Applied Linear Statistical Models. 4th ed. LC 95-37447. 1408p. (C). 1996. text 77.50 (*0-256-11736-5*, Irwn McGrw-H) McGrw-H Hghr Educ.

— Applied Statistics. 3rd ed. 1006p. (C). 1988. teacher ed. write for info. (*0-205-10331-6*, H03296); boxed set 56.00 (*0-205-10328-6*, H03288) Allyn.

— Applied Statistics. 3rd ed. 1006p. (C). 1988. student ed. 19.00 (*0-685-18748-9*, H03312); student ed. write for info. (*0-318-62190-8*, H03304) P-H.

Neterer, Chris. Unknown Soldiers. 295p. 1998. mass mkt. 4.99 (*1-55197-041-4*) Picasso Publ.

Neterowicz, Eva M., jt. auth. see Bowers, Stephen R.

Neth, Mary C. Preserving the Family Farm: Women, Community & the Foundations of Agribusiness in the Midwest, 1900-1940. (Revisiting Rural America Ser.). 272p. 1995. text 39.95 (*0-8018-4898-9*) Johns Hopkins.

Neth, Rolf, et al, eds. Modern Trends in Human Leukemia, No. VIII. (Haematology & Blood Transfusion Ser.: Vol. 32). (Illus.). 592p. 1990. 224.00 (*0-387-50967-4*) Spr-Verlag.

— Modern Trends in Human Leukemia IX: New Results in Clinical & Biological Research Including Pediatric Oncology; Organized on Behalf of the Deutsche Gesellschaft fur Hamatologie und Onkologie, Wilsede, June 17-21, 1990. LC 92-2334. (Haematology & Blood Transfusion - Haematologie und Bluttransfusion Ser.: Vol. 35). (Illus.). 480p. 1992. 239.00 (*0-387-54360-0*); pap. 198.00 (*3-540-54360-0*) Spr-Verlag.

— Modern Trends in Human Leukemia Three. (Illus.). 1979. 100.00 (*0-387-08999-3*) Spr-Verlag.

Nethercot, Arthur H. First Five Lives of Annie Besant. LC 59-11624. (Illus.). 431p. reprint ed. pap. 133.70 (*0-8357-9645-0*, 201362100087) Bks Demand.

— The Last Four Lives of Annie Beasant. LC 63-25862. 499p. reprint ed. pap. 154.70 (*0-608-13404-X*, 202410200035) Bks Demand.

— Men & Supermen: The Shavian Portrait Gallery. 2nd ed. LC 65-16245. 1972. 23.95 (*0-405-08815-9*) Ayer.

Nethercot, D. A. Limit States Design of Structural Steelwork. 2nd ed. (Illus.). 274p. (C). (gr. 13). 1991. pap. 45.00 (*0-412-39700-5*) Chapman & Hall.

***Nethercot, D. A.** Limit States Design of Structural Steelwork. 3rd ed. LC 00-55646. (Illus.). 2001. write for info. (*0-419-26090-0*, E & FN Spon) Routledge.

Nethercote, J. R., jt. ed. see Disney, Julian.

Nethercott, Arthur H. Reputation of Abraham Cowley, 1660-1800. (English Literature Ser.: No. 33). 1970. reprint ed. pap. 22.95 (*0-8383-0057-X*) M S G Haskell Hse.

— Reputation of the Metaphysical Poets During the Age of Johnson & the Romantic Revival. LC 72-98993. (English Literature Ser.: No. 33). 1970. reprint ed. pap. 22.95 (*0-8383-0058-8*) M S G Haskell Hse.

Netherland, E. Lane, et al. Perspectives in Introductory Biology. 7th rev. ed. 168p. 1996. pap. text 21.95 (*0-88725-234-6*) Hunter Textbks.

Netherlands Agency of Energy & the Environment Sta. Building with Photovoltaics. 88p. 1995. 60.00 (*90-71694-37-2*) Bks Intl VA.

Netherlands Centre for Civil Engineering Research. Manual on the Use of Rock in Hydraulic Engineering. 800p. 1995. 368.00 (*90-5410-605-0*, Pub. by A A Balkema) Ashgate Pub Co.

Netherlands Committee on Bone Tumours. Radiological Atlas of Bone Tumours, 2 vols. Incl. Vol. II. 1972. 261.55 (*3-10-800119-1*); (Illus.). write for info. (*0-318-54405-9*) Mouton.

Netherlands for the Law of the Sea (NILOS) Sta, ed. International Organizations & the Law of the Sea, Vol. IOLS 1. 1024p. 1998. 375.00 (*90-411-0435-6*) Kluwer Law Intl.

Netherlands Institute for the Law of the Sea Staff. International Organizations & the Law of the Sea: Documentary Yearbook, 1992. 944p. (C). 1994. lib. bdg. 358.50 (*0-7923-2614-8*) Kluwer Academic.

Netherlands Institute for the Law of the Sea Staff, ed. International Organizations & the Law of the Sea: Documentary Yearbook, 1985. 650p. 1987. lib. bdg. 217.50 (*90-247-3488-6*) Kluwer Academic.

— International Organizations & the Law of the Sea: Documentary Yearbook, 1986. (C). 1988. lib. bdg. 231.50 (*1-85333-104-X*) Kluwer Academic.

— International Organizations & the Law of the Sea: Documentary Yearbook, 1987. (C). 1990. lib. bdg. 220.50 (*1-85333-162-7*) Kluwer Academic.

— International Organizations & the Law of the Sea: Documentary Yearbook, 1988. 680p. 1990. lib. bdg. 231.50 (*1-85333-455-3*, Pub. by Graham & Trotman) Kluwer Academic.

— International Organizations & the Law of the Sea: Documentary Yearbook, 1989. 800p. (C). 1991. lib. bdg. 273.50 (*0-7923-1201-5*) Kluwer Academic.

— International Organizations & the Law of the Sea: Documentary Yearbook, 1990. 752p. (C). 1992. lib. bdg. 266.00 (*0-7923-1600-2*) Kluwer Academic.

Netherlands State Archive Service Staff, ed. Guide to the Sources on the History of Africa South of the Sahara in the Netherlands, Vol. 9. (Africa South of Sahara; Second Ser.). 451p. 1991. lib. bdg. 82.00 (*0-614-03097-8*) K G Saur Verlag.

Netherly, Patricia J., jt. ed. see Henderson, John S.

Nethersole, Reingard, ed. Emerging Literatures. (Johannesburg Forum. Contributions to Literary Studies: Vol. 1). (Illus.). XXXVI, 197p. 1991. 59.00 (*3-261-04308-3*) P Lang Pubng.

Nethersole-Thompson, Desmond. The Oystercatcher. (Natural History Ser.: No. 28). (Illus.). 24p. 1989. pap. 5.25 (*0-85263-949-X*, Pub. by Shire Pubns) Parkwest Pubns.

Nethersole-Thompson, Desmond & Nethersole-Thompson, Maimie. Greenshanks. LC 78-67031. (Illus.). 1979. 27.50 (*0-931130-02-6*) Harrell Bks.

— Waders: Their Breeding Haunts & Watchers. (Illus.). 424p. 1991. text 35.00 (*0-85661-042-9*, 784642) Poyser.

Nethersole-Thompson, Desmond & Watson, Adam. The Cairngorms. 324p. (C). 1986. 45.00 (*0-906664-12-8*, Pub. by Mercat Pr Bks) St Mut.

Nethersole-Thompson, Maimie, jt. auth. see Nethersole-Thompson, Desmond.

Netherton, Cliff. History of the Sport of Casting: Golden Years. LC 83-72846. (Illus.). 388p. 1983. pap. 14.95 (*0-9605960-3-8*); lib. bdg. 24.95 (*0-9605960-2-X*) Am Casting.

— History of the Sport of Casting: People, Events, Records, Tackle & Literature - Early Times. LC 81-65632. (Illus.). 404p. 1981. pap. 14.95 (*0-9605960-1-1*); lib. bdg. 24.95 (*0-9605960-0-3*) Am Casting.

Netherton, John. Florida - A Guide to Nature & Photography. Badger, David, ed. LC 90-81715. (Illus.). 96p. 1990. 29.95 (*0-9620582-2-X*); pap. 19.95 (*0-9620582-1-1*) Cumberland Val Pr.

— Great Smoky Mountains National Park. LC 96-38592. (Tiny Folio Ser.). (Illus.). 288p. 1998. pap. 11.95 (*0-7892-0149-6*) Abbeville Pr.

— North American Wading Birds. LC 98-13105. (Illus.). 128p. 1998. pap. 16.95 (*0-89658-402-X*) Voyageur Pr.

— Of Breath & Earth: A Book of Days with Wisdom from Native America. (Illus.). 120p. 1999. 14.95 (*0-87358-589-5*) Northland AZ.

***Netherton, John.** Red-Eyed Tree Frogs. LC 99-38915. (Early Bird Nature Bks.). (Illus.). 48p. (J). (ps-3). 2000. 22.60 (*0-8225-3037-6*, Lerner Publctns) Lerner Pub.

Netherton, John. Tennessee: A Bicentennial Celebration. (Illus.). 128p. 1995. 39.95 (*1-56579-126-6*) Westcliffe Pubs.

Netherton, John, photos by. Big South Fork Country. LC 93-28260. (Illus.). 120p. (YA). (gr. 9 up). 1993. 29.95 (*1-55853-258-7*) Rutledge Hill Pr.

— Frogs. LC 95-9828. (Illus.). 144p. 1995. 35.00 (*0-89658-314-7*) Voyageur Pr.

— Frogs. LC 95-9828. (Illus.). 144p. 1999. pap. 19.95 (*0-89658-427-5*) Voyageur Pr.

— Radnor Lake: Nashville's Walden Pond. LC 84-51576. (Illus.). 72p. 1994. reprint ed. 18.95 (*0-934395-17-9*) Rutledge Hill Pr.

Netherton, John & Duhl, David. A Guide to Photography & the Smoky Mountains. Badger, David, ed. LC 88-70895. (Illus.). 96p. (Orig.). 1988. pap. 17.95 (*0-9620582-0-3*) Cumberland Val Pr.

Netherton, Nan. Books & Beyond: Fairfax County Public Library's First Fifty Years. (Illus.). (Orig.). 1990. pap. 9.95 (*0-9623689-0-3*) Fairfax Cnty Pub Lib.

Netherton, Nan & City of Fairfax Round Table (Fairfax, Va.). Fairfax, Virginia: A City Traveling Through Time. LC 97-77248. (Illus.). 1997. write for info. (*0-914927-26-4*) Higher Ed Pubns.

Netherton, Nan & Rose, Ruth P. Memories of Beautiful Burke, Virginia. LC 88-71085. (Illus.). 1988. 19.95 (*0-9620619-0-5*) Burke Hist Soc.

Netherton, Nan, et al. Fairfax County, Virginia: A History. LC 77-95356. (Illus.). 1978. 15.00 (*0-686-24339-0*) Fairfax County.

Netherton, Sandra D., et al, eds. Child & Adolescent Psychological Disorders: A Comprehensive Textbook. LC 98-7279. (Oxford Textbooks in Clinical Psychology Ser.). (Illus.). 624p. (C). 1999. text 69.95 (*0-19-509961-3*) OUP.

Nethery, Mary. Hannah & Jack. LC 93-4651. (Illus.). (J). 1995. text 16.00 (*0-02-768125-4*, Mac Bks Young Read) S&S Childrens.

— Hannah & Jack: A Very Special Friendship. (Illus.). 32p. (J). (ps-2). 1996. 15.00 (*0-689-80533-0*) Atheneum Yung Read.

— Mary Veronica's Egg. LC 98-35723. (Illus.). 32p. (J). (ps-2). 1999. 15.95 (*0-531-30134-6*); lib. bdg. 16.99 (*0-531-33134-2*) Orchard Bks Watts.

Nethery, Susan, jt. auth. see McIlhaney, Joe S., Jr.

Nethus, Marie, ed. Video Forum - A Videography for Libraries: Latino Issue. 60p. write for info. (*1-884188-02-8*) Nat Video.

Netland, Campbell. Stereo Atlas of Glaucoma. LC 97-22257. (Illus.). 272p. 1997. text 149.00 (*0-8151-1399-4*, 26953) Mosby Inc.

Netland, Harold, jt. ed. see Rommen, Edward.

Netley, Jayne. Animals in Cross Stitch. 1998. pap. 16.95 (*0-7153-0823-8*, Pub. by D & C Pub) Sterling.

Neto, A. Lins, jt. auth. see Camacho, Cesar.

Neto, A. M., jt. ed. see Toledano, Pierre.

Neto-Advogados, Pinhiero, ed. Doing Business in Brazil. 1200p. 1982. ring bd., suppl. ed. 525.00 (*1-56425-008-3*) Juris Pubng.

Neto, J. V. Dictionary of Telecommunications: Dicionario de Telecommunicacoes. (ENG & POR.). 689p. 1981. 75.00 (*0-8288-0184-3*, F45000) Fr & Eur.

Neto, Joao Cabral De Melo, see Cabral De Melo Neto, Joao.

Neto, Jose R. The Christianization of Pyrrhonism: Scepticism & Faith in Pascal, Kierkegaard & Shestov. LC 95-1251. (International Archives of the History of Ideas Ser.: Vol. 144). 1995. lib. bdg. 125.00 (*0-7923-3381-0*, Pub. by Kluwer Academic) Kluwer Academic.

Neto, Teixeira A. Pomba-Gira: Enchantments to Invoke the Formidable Powers of the Female Messenger of the Gods. Dow, Carol L., tr. from POR. & intro. by. (Illus.). 84p. 1992. pap. 11.95 (*1-878738-04-6*) Tech Sacred.

Netravali, Arun N. Computational Aspect. (C). 1991. text. write for info. (*0-7167-8214-6*) W H Freeman.

Netravali, Arun N. & Haskell, Barry G. Digital Pictures: Representation, Compression & Standards. 2nd ed. LC 94-42988. (Applications of Communications Theory Ser.). (Illus.). 706p. (C). 1995. 110.00 (*0-306-44917-X*, Plenum Trade) Perseus Pubng.

Netravali, Arun N. & Prasada, Birendra, eds. Visual Communications Systems. LC 88-34726. (Illus.). 552p. 1989. text 79.95 (*0-87942-250-5*, PC02410) Inst Electrical.

***NETS Project Staff.** National Educational Technology Standards for Students: Connecting Curriculum & Technology. (Illus.). 378p. (YA). (gr. 5-12). 1999. spiral bd. 29.95 (*1-56484-150-2*) Intl Society Tech Educ.

***NETS Standards Development Team Staff.** National Educational Technology Standards for Students. (Illus.). 19p. 1998. pap. 5.00 (*1-56484-164-2*) Intl Society Tech Educ.

Netsch, Dawn Clark, jt. auth. see Mandelker, Daniel R.

Netsch, Walter. Living with Art Three: The Collection of Walter & Dawn Clark Netsch. LC 91-60799. 40p. (Orig.). 1991. 12.00 (*0-940784-14-9*) Miami Univ Art.

Netschert, Bruce C. The Mineral Foreign Trade of the United States in the 20th Century: A Study in Mineral Economics. Bruchey, Stuart, ed. LC 76-39836. (Nineteen Seventy-Seven Dissertations Ser.). (Illus.). 1977. lib. bdg. 47.95 (*0-405-09916-9*) Ayer.

Netschert, Bruce C. & Landsberg, Hans H. The Future Supply of the Major Metals: A Reconnaissance Survey. LC 61-18125. 71p. reprint ed. pap. 30.00 (*0-7837-3047-0*, 204287100006) Bks Demand.

— The Future Supply of the Major Metals: A Reconnaissance Survey. LC 76-58923. (Resources for the Future Ser.). (Illus.). 65p. 1978. reprint ed. lib. bdg. 49.75 (*0-8371-9472-5*, NEMM, Greenwood Pr) Greenwood.

Netschert, Bruce C. & Schurr, S. H. Atomic Energy Applications with Reference to Underdeveloped Countries: A Preliminary Survey. LC 57-1745. 143p. reprint ed. pap. 44.40 (*0-7837-3046-2*, 204287200006) Bks Demand.

Netsell, Ronald. A Neurobiologic View of Speech Production & the Dysarthrias. (Illus.). 164p. (C). 1991. reprint ed. pap. text 37.95 (*1-879105-25-X*, 0080) Thomson Learn.

Netsky, Ron. The Graphic Art of Harold Faye. LC 87-3223. (Illus.). 32p. (Orig.). 1987. pap. 3.50 (*0-943651-00-X*) Hudson Riv.

Nett, Bernhard, et al, eds. Agricultural Transformation & Social Change in Africa. LC 92-46128. (Aachener Studies on Comparative Sociology & China Research; Aachener Beitr Age Zur Vergleichenden Soziologie und Zur China-Forschung: No. 10). (Illus.). XIV, 252p. 1993. 47.00 (*3-631-45360-4*) P Lang Pubng.

Nett, Del, ed. see Marino, Martha.

Nett, Lewis. Magazine Beach. 1996. 23.00 (*0-614-96943-3*, HarperPrism) HarpC.

Nett, Louise M., jt. auth. see Petty, Thomas L.

Nett, Roger, jt. auth. see Sjoberg, Gideon.

Netta, Irene. Das Phanomen Zeit Bei Jan Vermeer van Delft. (Studien Zur Kunstgeschichte Ser.: Bd. 105). (GER., Illus.). 270p. 1996. write for info. (*3-487-10160-2*) G Olms Pubs.

Nettancourt, D. Incompatibility in Angiosperms. (Monographs on Theoretical & Applied Genetics: Vol. 3). 1977. 55.95 (*0-387-08112-7*) Spr-Verlag.

Nette, Heinz. Untersuchungen Ueber Veraenderungen in Den Buchenschuerzen der Kalk-Buchenwaelder des Teutoburger Waldes. (Dissertationes Botanicae Ser.: Band 108). (Illus.). x, 104p. 1987. pap. 36.00 (*3-443-64020-6*, Pub. by Gebruder Borntraeger) Balogh.

Nettel, Reginald. The Orchestra in England: A Social History. 1988. reprint ed. lib. bdg. 49.00 (*0-7812-0774-6*) Rprt Serv.

Nettel, Stephen. Wave Physics: Oscillations, Solitons & Chaos. 1992. 39.00 (*0-387-55715-6*) Spr-Verlag.

— Wave Physics: Oscillations, Solitons & Chaos. 2nd ed. (Illus.). 272p. 1997. 39.00 (*3-540-58504-4*) Spr-Verlag.

— Wave Physics: Oscillations, Solitons & Chaos. 2nd enl. ed. 1994. write for info. (*0-387-58504-4*) Spr-Verlag.

— Wave Physics: Up to Solitons & Chaos. (Illus.). 260p. (C). 1992. text 33.00 (*0-387-53295-1*) Spr-Verlag.

Nettelbeck, Amanda, jt. ed. see Kerr, Heather.

Nettelbeck, Colin W. Forever French: Exile in the United States, 1939-1945. 211p. 1992. 19.50 (*0-85496-632-3*) Berg Pubs.

Nettelbeck, Colin W., ed. War & Identity in France. 176p. (C). 1994. pap. text 22.95 (*0-423-51700-7*) Routledge.

Nettelbladt, Daniel. Sammlung Kleiner Juristischer Abhandlungen Band 38: Nebst Desselben Leben und Vollstandigem Verzeichni Seiner Schriften. (GER.). 5856p. 1997. reprint ed. 160.00 (*3-487-10283-8*) G Olms Pubs.

— Systema Elementare Universae Jurisprudentiae Naturalis in Usum Praelectionum Academicarum Adornatum, Band 39. (GER.). 806p. 1996. reprint ed. 145.00 (*3-487-10284-6*) G Olms Pubs.

Nettelbladt, Daniel, jt. auth. see Wolff, Christian.

Nettels, Curtis P. The Emergence of a National Economy, 1775-1815. LC 89-10649. (The Economic History of the United States Ser.). 451p. (gr. 13). 1977. reprint ed. pap. text 35.95 (*0-87332-096-4*) M E Sharpe.

— The Money Supply of the American Colonies. 1972. 250.00 (*0-8490-0663-5*) Gordon Pr.

— The Money Supply of the American Colonies Before 1720. LC 64-22242. (Library of Money & Banking History). 300p. 1964. reprint ed. 45.00 (*0-678-00061-1*) Kelley.

— Roots of American Civilization: A History of American Colonial Life. 2nd ed. LC 63-8707. (Illus.). reprint ed. write for info. (*0-89197-386-9*); reprint ed. pap. text. write for info. (*0-89197-925-5*) Irvington.

Nettels, Elsa. Language & Gender in American Fiction: Howells, James, Wharton, & Cather. LC 96-3429. 200p. (C). 1997. text 29.50 (*0-8139-1724-7*) U Pr of Va.

— Language, Race & Social Class in Howells's America. LC 87-18895. 328p. 1988. text 29.95 (*0-8131-1629-5*) U Pr of Ky.

Netten, Ann. A Positive Environment: Physical & Social Influences on People with Senile Dementia in Residential Care. LC 92-44396. 110p. 1993. pap. 28.95 (*1-85742-112-4*, Pub. by Arena) Ashgate Pub Co.

— A Positive Environment: Physical & Social Influences on People with Senile Dementia in Residential Care. LC 92-44396. 110p. 1993. 54.95 (*1-85742-107-8*, Pub. by Arena) Ashgate Pub Co.

Netten, Ann & Beecham, Jennifer. Costing Community Care: Theory & Practice. LC 93-16351. 214p. 1993. 64.95 (*1-85742-098-5*, Pub. by Arena); pap. 31.95 (*1-85742-102-7*, Pub. by Arena) Ashgate Pub Co.

Netten, Hans. Automated Image Analysis of Fish-Stained Cell Nuclei. 131p. (Orig.). 1997. pap. 44.50 (*90-407-1431-2*, Pub. by Delft U Pr) Coronet Bks.

Netten, J. H., jt. auth. see Van Remmerden, H.

Netten, S. Van, see Duifhuis, H & Van Netten, S.

Netter, Klaus, jt. ed. see Hiader, Hubert.

Netter, Matt. Backstreet Boys & Aaron Carter, Vol. 1. 1998. per. 4.99 (*0-671-03539-8*) PB.

— Hanson. (J). 1998. per. 3.99 (*0-671-02488-4*, Archway) PB.

***Netter, Matt.** Meet the Stars of 7th Heaven: The Unofficial Scrapbook. LC 99-230478. (Illus.). 48p. (J). (gr. 3-10). 1999. pap. text 5.99 (*0-439-04299-2*) Scholastic Inc.

Netter, Matt. 'N Sync: Tearin' up the Charts. 1998. per. 4.99 (*0-671-03470-7*, Archway) PB.

— 'N Sync with Justin. (Illus.). 123p. (J). (gr. 3-7). 1999. per. 4.99 (*0-671-03276-3*, Archway) PB.

— Zac Hanson: Totally Zac! (J). 1998. mass mkt. 3.99 (*0-671-02445-0*, Archway) PB.

Netter, P., ed. Psychobiology: Psychophysiological & Psychohumoral Processes Combined. (Journal: Neuropsychobiology: Vol. 28, No. 1-2, 1993). (Illus.). 112p. 1993. pap. 117.50 (*3-8055-5853-8*) S Karger.

***Netter, Petra & Brocke, Burkhard, eds.** Traits as Dispositions for Psychopathology: Congress, Dresden, September 1998. (Neuropsychobiology Ser.: Vol. 41, No. 1). (Illus.). 54p. 2000. pap. 25.25 (*3-8055-6911-4*) S Karger.

Netter, Thomas. Fasciculi Zizaniorium Magistri Johannis Wyclif Cum Tritico. Shirley, Walter W., ed. (Rolls Ser.: No. 5). 1972. reprint ed. 70.00 (*0-8115-1006-9*) Periodicals Srv.

Nettesheim, Paul, et al, eds. Inhalation Carcinogenesis: Proceedings. LC 76-605835. (AEC Symposium Ser.). 524p. 1970. pap. 21.00 (*0-87079-246-6*, CONF-691001); fiche 9.00 (*0-87079-247-4*, CONF-691001) DOE.

— Morphology of Experimental Respiratory Carcinogenesis: Proceedings. LC 73-609398. (AEC Symposium Ser.). 500p. 1970. pap. 20.50 (*0-87079-277-6*, CONF-700501); fiche 9.00 (*0-87079-278-4*, CONF-700501) DOE.

Nettesheim, Paul & Witschi, Hanspeter R. Mechanisms in Respiratory Toxicology, 2 vols., Vol. I. 288p. 1982. 168.00 (*0-8493-5689-X*, RC732, CRC Reprint) Franklin.

— Mechanisms in Respiratory Toxicology, 2 vols., Vol. II. 240p. 1982. 138.00 (*0-8493-5690-3*, CRC Reprint) Franklin.

Nettesheim, Paul, jt. auth. see Thomassen, David G.

Nettheim, Garth & Chisholm, R. Understanding Law: An Introduction to Australia's Legal System. 4th ed. 160p. 1992. pap. 22.00 (*0-409-30486-7*, MICHIE) LEXIS Pub.

Nettheim, Garth, et al. Aboriginal Legal Issues: Commentary & Materials. 350p. 1991. pap. 69.00 (*0-455-21017-9*, Pub. by LawBk Co) Gaunt.

Nettick, Geri & Elliot, Beth. Mirrors: Portrait of a Lesbian Transsexual. (Orig.). 1996. mass mkt. 6.95 (*1-56333-435-6*, Rhinoceros) Masquerade.

Nettime Staff, ed. see Bosma, Josephine.

Nettina, Sandra. Lippincott's Pocket Manual of Nursing Practice. LC 96-15107. 976p. 1996. pap. text 25.95 (*0-397-55355-2*) Lppncott W & W.

Nettina, Sandra M. The Lippincott Manual of Nursing Practice. 7th ed. 1728p. text 58.95 (*0-7817-2296-9*) Lppncott W & W.

Netting, Ellen. Social Work Macro Practice. 2nd ed. LC 97-13944. 320p. (C). 1997. text 65.00 (*0-8013-1611-1*) Allyn.

Netting, F. Ellen & Williams, Frank G. Enhancing Primary Care of Elderly People. LC 98-21725. 272p. 1998. 57.00 (*0-8153-2531-2*); pap. text 24.95 (*0-8153-2532-0*) Garland.

Netting, F. Ellen, et al. Social Work Macro Practice. 320p. 1998. write for info. (*0-8013-3050-5*) Longman.

Netting, Robert M. Cultural Ecology. (Modular Program in Anthropology Ser.). pap. 9.00 (*0-8465-4840-2*) Benjamin-Cummings.

— Cultural Ecology. 2nd ed. (Illus.). 131p. 1986. pap. text 10.50 (*0-88133-204-6*) Waveland Pr.

— Hill Farmers of Nigeria. LC 84-45539. (American Ethnological Society Monographs: No. 46). 1988. reprint ed. 37.50 (*0-404-62944-X*) AMS Pr.

— Smallholders, Householders: Farm Families & the

An Asterisk (*) at the beginning of an entry indicates that the title is appearing for the first time.

Ecology of Intensive, Sustainable Agriculture. (Illus.). 416p. (C). 1993. 49.50 (*0-8047-2061-4*); pap. 16.95 (*0-8047-2102-5*) Stanford U Pr.

Nettl. In Course of Performance. LC 98-3640. 1998. pap. text 25.00 (*0-226-57411-3*) U Ch Pr.

— In Course Performance. LC 98-3640. 1998. lib. bdg. 65.00 (*0-226-57410-5*) U Ch Pr.

Nettl, Bruno. Blackfoot Musical Thought: Comparative Perspectives. LC 88-28450. 210p. 1989. reprint ed. pap. 65.10 (*0-608-07358-X*, 206758600009) Bks Demand.

— Cheremis Musical Styles. LC 60-64259. (Indiana University Folklore Institute Monograph Ser.: Vol. 14). 126p. reprint ed. pap. 39.10 (*0-608-30068-3*, 205004500059) Bks Demand.

— Heartland Excursions: Ethnomusicological Reflections on Schools of Music. 192p. 1995. 13.95 (*0-252-06468-2*) U of Ill Pr.

— Heartland Excursions: Ethnomusicological Reflections on Schools of Music. (Music in American Life Ser.). 192p. 1995. text 35.00 (*0-252-02135-5*) U of Ill Pr.

— Music in Primitive Culture. LC 56-8551. 220p. reprint ed. 68.20 (*0-8357-9167-X*, 201673000005) Bks Demand.

— The Study of Ethnomusicology: Twenty-Nine Issues & Concepts. LC 82-7065. 424p. 1983. pap. text 19.95 (*0-252-01039-6*) U of Ill Pr.

— The Study of Ethnomusicology: Twenty-Nine Issues & Concepts. LC 82-7065. 422p. reprint ed. pap. 130.90 (*0-8357-3554-0*, 203445400090) Bks Demand.

— The Western Impact on World Music Change, Adaption, & Survival. 232p. 1985. write for info. (*0-317-46649-6*) Macmillan.

Nettl, Bruno, ed. Eight Urban Musical Cultures: Tradition & Change. LC 77-25041. (Illus.). 336p. 1978. text 29.95 (*0-252-00208-3*) U of Ill Pr.

Nettl, Bruno & Bohlman, Philip V. Comparative Musicology & Anthropology of Music: Essays in the History of Ethnomusicology. (Chicago Studies in Ethnomusicology). (Illus.). 400p. 1991. pap. text 23.00 (*0-226-57409-1*) U Ch Pr.

— Comparative Musicology & Anthropology of Music: Essays in the History of Ethnomusicology. (Chicago Studies in Ethnomusicology). (Illus.). 400p. 1993. lib. bdg. 49.95 (*0-226-57408-3*) U Ch Pr.

Nettl, Bruno & Myers, Helen. Folk Music in the United States: An Introduction. exp. rev. ed. LC 76-84. 190p. 1976. pap. 15.95 (*0-8143-1557-7*) Wayne St U Pr.

Nettl, Bruno, et al. Excursions in World Music. 2nd ed. LC 96-14971. 340p. (C). 1996. pap. 52.00 (*0-13-230632-8*, Pub. by P-H) S&S Trade.

Nettl, Bruno, jt. auth. see Blacking, John.

Nettl, Paul. The Beethoven Encyclopedia: His Life & Art from A to Z. LC 94-17636. 336p. 1994. 12.95 (*0-8065-1539-2*, Citadel Pr) Carol Pub Group.

— The Beethoven Encyclopedia: His Life & Art from A to Z. 336p. 1999. reprint ed. 32.95 (*0-7351-0113-2*) Replica Bks.

— Beethoven Handbook. LC 75-33885. 335p. 1975. reprint ed. lib. bdg. 38.50 (*0-8371-8540-8*, NEBH, Greenwood Pr) Greenwood.

— Book of Musical Documents. LC 73-88991. 381p. 1969. lib. bdg. 69.50 (*0-8371-2116-7*, NEMD, Greenwood Pr) Greenwood.

— Mozart & Masonry. LC 78-114564. (Music Ser.). 1970. reprint ed. lib. bdg. 25.00 (*0-306-71922-3*) Da Capo.

— The Other Casanova: A Contribution to 18th-Century Music & Manners. LC 73-107872. (Music Ser.). (Illus.). 1970. reprint ed. lib. bdg. 39.50 (*0-306-71896-0*) Da Capo.

— Story of Dance Music. (Ballroom Dance Ser.). 1986. lib. bdg. 79.95 (*0-8490-3253-9*) Gordon Pr.

Nettlau, M. La Premiere Internationale en Espagne. (FRE., Illus.). 683p. 1969. lib. bdg. 296.00 (*90-277-0103-2*) Kluwer Academic.

Nettlau, Max. Anarchism in England One Hundred Years Ago. 1971. 59.95 (*0-8490-1422-0*) Gordon Pr.

— Anarchy Through the Times. Johnson, Scott, tr. 1978. lib. bdg. 300.00 (*0-8490-1397-6*) Gordon Pr.

— History of Anarchism, 3 vols., Set. (Men & Movements in the History & Philosophy of Anarchism Ser.). 1978. lib. bdg. 900.00 (*0-685-57774-0*) Revisionist Pr.

— The Unfolding of Anarchism: Its Origins & Historical Development to the Year 1864. (Men & Movements in the History & Philosophy of Anarchism Ser.). 1978. lib. bdg. 49.95 (*0-685-06650-9*) Revisionist Pr.

***Nettle, Daniel & Romaine, Suzanne.** Vanishing Voices: The Extinction of the World's Languages. 256p. 2000. 27.50 (*0-19-513624-1*) OUP.

Nettle, Daniel, jt. ed. see Renfrew, A. Colin.

Nettlebeck, Amanda, ed. Provisional Maps: Critical Essays on David Malouf. LC 94-213430. pap. 18.00 (*0-86422-300-5*, Pub. by Univ of West Aust Pr) Intl Spec Bk.

Nettleford, Rex. Inward Stretch - Outward Reach: A Voice from the Caribbean. 212p. (Orig.). 1995. pap. 15.00 (*1-878433-19-9*) Caribbean Diaspora Pr.

Nettleford, Rex, ed. Jamaica in Independence: Essays on the Early Years. 364p. (C). 1991. pap. text 19.95 (*976-605-094-5*, 00685) Heinemann.

Nettler, Gwynn. The Relationship Between Attitude & Information Concerning the Japanese in America. Merton, Robert K. & Zuckerman, Harriet, eds. LC 79-9016. (Dissertations on Sociology Ser.). 1980. lib. bdg. 21.95 (*0-405-12984-X*) Ayer.

Nettler, Ronald L., ed. Medieval & Modern Perspectives on Muslim-Jewish Relations. (Studies in Muslim-Jewish Relations). 205p. 1995. text 64.00 (*3-7186-5727-9*, Harwood Acad Pubs) Gordon & Breach.

— Studies in Muslim-Jewish Relations, Vol. 1. 204p. 1993. text 62.00 (*3-7186-5283-8*, Harwood Acad Pubs) Gordon & Breach.

Nettler, Ronald L. & Taji-Farouki, Suha, eds. Muslim-Jewish Encounters: Intellectual Expressions & Modern Politics, Vol. 4. (Studies in Mulsim-Jewish Relations). 219p. 1998. text 30.00 (*90-5702-195-1*, Harwood Acad Pubs); pap. text 14.00 (*90-5702-196-X*, Harwood Acad Pubs) Gordon & Breach.

***Nettles, Arie L. & Nettles, Michael T.** Measuring Up: Challenges Minorities Face in Educational Assessment LC 99-12925. (Evaluation in Education & Human Services Ser.). xvi, 266p. 1999. write for info. (*0-7923-8401-6*) Kluwer Academic.

Nettles, Bea. Breaking the Rules: A Photo Media Cookbook. 3rd ed. LC 77-12930. (Illus.). 64p. (C). 1992. pap. text 15.00 (*0-930810-08-2*) Inky Pr.

— Flamingo in the Dark: Images. (Orig.). 1979. 35.00 (*0-930810-01-5*) Inky Pr.

— Knights of Assisi: A Journey Through the Tarot. (Illus.). 24p. (Orig.). 1990. pap. 10.00 (*0-930810-06-6*) Inky Pr.

— Life's Lessons: A Mother's Journal. (Illus.). 72p. (Orig.). 1990. pap. 15.00 (*0-930810-05-8*) Inky Pr.

— Skirted Garden, 1970-1990: Nineteen Seventy to Nineteen Ninety. (Illus.). 80p. (Orig.). 1990. pap. 5.00 (*0-930810-04-X*) Inky Pr.

Nettles, Bea, photos by. Complexities. (Illus.). 48p. (Orig.). 1992. pap. 15.00 (*0-930810-07-4*) Inky Pr.

— Grace's Daughter. (Illus.). 48p. (Orig.). 1994. pap. 8.00 (*0-930810-09-0*) Inky Pr.

— Turning Fifty. (Illus.). 64p. (Orig.). 1995. pap. 10.00 (*0-930810-11-2*) Inky Pr.

Nettles, Bea, jt. auth. see Nettles, Grace.

Nettles, Gala. Basic Horsemanship with Nancy Cahill. Date not set. write for info. (*0-9649288-3-3*) LMH Pubng.

— Doc Bar. 144p. 1995. reprint ed. pap. 21.95 (*0-9649288-0-9*) LMH Pubng.

— Don Dodge: The Way It Was: The Life of Legendary Horseman, Don Dodge. Kurtz, Glory A., ed. 1998. 34.95 (*0-9649288-4-1*) LMH Pubng.

— Helpful Hints for Horsemen. Kurtz, Glory A., ed. 1998. pap. 15.95 (*0-9649288-2-5*) LMH Pubng.

— King Ranch & Little Peppy: The Legacy & the Legend. Kurtz, Gory A., ed. LC 96-78900. (Illus.). 221p. 1996. 29.95 (*0-9649288-1-7*) LMH Pubng.

Nettles, Gala, jt. auth. see Freeman, Bill.

Nettles, Grace & Nettles, Bea. Corners. (Illus.). 104p. 1989. pap. 14.95 (*0-930810-03-1*) Inky Pr.

Nettles, Hafeesa. Prayers & Meditations for Our Little Angels. LC 96-5895. (Illus.). (J). 1996. 14.95 (*1-881316-49-1*); pap. 7.95 (*1-881316-33-5*) A&B Bks.

Nettles, Jack, jt. auth. see McNellis, Jerry.

Nettles, Joseph E. So Beloved Cousins: The Life & Times of Solon B. Cousins, Jr. LC 82-23986. x, 178p. 1983. 12.95 (*0-86554-070-5*, MUP/H053) Mercer Univ Pr.

Nettles, Margaret F. A Study of Wives. 35p. 1997. pap. 7.95 (*0-9653688-6-6*) P & P Ent.

Nettles, Michael T. Equity & Excellence in Educational Testing & Assessment. (Evaluation in Education & Human Services Ser.). 400p. (C). 1994. lib. bdg. 98.50 (*0-7923-9531-X*) Kluwer Academic.

***Nettles, Michael T.** Salary, Promotion & Tenure Status of Minority & Women Faculty in United States Colleges & Universities. 127p. 2000. per. 12.00 (*0-16-050303-5*) USGPO.

Nettles, Michael T., ed. The Effect of Assessment on Minority Student Participation. LC 85-645339. (New Directions for Institutional Research Ser.: No. IR 65). 1990. pap. 22.00 (*1-55542-828-2*) Jossey-Bass.

— Toward Black Undergraduate Student Equality in American Higher Education, 25. LC 87-24956. (Contributions to the Study of Education Ser.: No. 25). 234p. 1988. 55.00 (*0-313-25616-0*, NBK/, Greenwood Pr) Greenwood.

Nettles, Michael T., et al. The African American Education Data Book Vol. I: Higher & Adult Education. 504p. 1997. 25.00 (*0-9657873-0-3*) Frederick Patterson.

— The African American Education Data Book Vol. II: Pre-School Through High School Education. (Illus.). 1997. 25.00 (*0-9657873-1-1*) Frederick Patterson.

— The African American Education Data Book Vol. III: The Transition from School to College & School to Work. (Illus.). 1997. 25.00 (*0-9657873-2-X*) Frederick Patterson.

Nettles, Michael T., jt. auth. see Nettles, Arie L.

Nettles, Sarah A. Growing up with E. Z. Mezure: E. Z. Makes Measuring Easy! (Illus.). 64p. (Orig.). (J). (gr. 3-5). 1995. pap. text 8.95 (*1-882293-06-1*, A-1705) Activity Resources.

Nettles, Scott & Connor, Richard, eds. Advances in Persitent Object Systems: Proceedings of the 7th Workshop. 1998. pap. text 53.00 (*1-55860-447-2*) Morgan Kaufmann.

Nettles, Thomas J. A Foundation for the Future: The Southern Baptist Message & Mission. LC 98-117254. (Illus.). 60p. 1997. pap. 4.95 (*0-9654955-1-5*) Founders Pr.

Nettles, Tom J. Teaching Truth, Training Hearts: The Study of Catechisms in Baptist Life. 256p. 1998. pap. 13.95 (*1-879737-38-8*) Calvary Press.

Nettles, Tom J., jt. auth. see Bush, L. Russ.

Nettleship, David N., et al, eds. Seabirds on Islands: Threats, Case Studies & Action Plans. (Birdlife Conservation Ser.). (Illus.). 350p. 1994. pap. text 47.95 (*1-56098-526-7*) Smithsonian.

Nettleship, David N. & Birkhead, Tim R., eds. The Atlantic Alcidae: The Evolution, Distribution & Biology of the Auks Inhabiting the Atlantic Ocean & Adjacent Water Areas. 1986. text 125.00 (*0-12-515670-7*); pap. text 48.00 (*0-12-515671-5*) Acad Pr.

Nettleship, David N. & Duffy, David C. The Double-Crested Cormorant: Biology, Conservation & Management. (Colonial Waterbirds Ser.: Vol. 18, No. 1). (Illus.). 256p. (Orig.). (C). 1995. pap. text 25.00 (*0-9651399-0-5*) Colonial Wtrbird.

Nettleship, H., ed. see Persius.

Nettleship, Henry. Lectures & Essays, Second Series. Haverfield, F., ed. LC 72-336. (Essay Index Reprint Ser.). 1977. reprint ed. 23.95 (*0-8369-2812-1*) Ayer.

Nettleship, Henry, ed. see Virgil.

Nettleship, Martin, jt. ed. see Givens, R. Dale.

Nettleship, Martin A., et al, eds. War, Its Causes & Correlates. (World Anthropology Ser.). (Illus.). xviii, 814p. 1975. 82.35 (*90-279-7659-7*) Mouton.

Nettleship, R. L. Memoirs of Thomas Hill Green: 1906 Edition. 272p. 1996. reprint ed. 70.00 (*1-85506-197-X*) Bks Intl VA.

Nettleship, R. L., ed. see Green, Thomas Hill.

Nettleship, Richard L. Theory of Education in the Republic of Plato. LC 68-54676. (Classics in Education Ser.). 1968. pap. text 6.00 (*0-8077-1849-1*) Tchrs Coll.

Nettleton, Asabel. Village Hymns for Social Worship. Nichols, William C., ed. 576p. 1998. 39.95 (*0-9641803-8-3*) Internat Outreach.

Nettleton, Asahel. Asahel Nettleton: Sermons from the Second Great Awakening. 500p. 1995. 35.95 (*0-9641803-3-2*) Internat Outreach.

— Door is Open. 1998. pap. text 2.99 (*0-85234-409-0*) P & R Pubng.

Nettleton, D. H. Linguistic Diversity. LC 98-53373. (Illus.). 180p. 1999. text 65.00 (*0-19-823858-4*); pap. text 19.95 (*0-19-823857-6*) OUP.

Nettleton, D. H., jt. ed. see Fox, N. P.

Nettleton, David. Conozca a los Profetas Menores. Meyer, Richard, ed. (Adult Sunday School Ser.). (SPA.). 88p. 1993. 4.40 (*1-879892-36-7*) Editorial Bautista.

Nettleton, George H. Yale in the World War, 2 vols. 1925. 300.00 (*0-685-40002-6*) Elliots Bks.

Nettleton, George H., ed. Specimens of the Short Story. LC 75-94740. (Short Story Index Reprint Ser.). 1977. 19.95 (*0-8369-3120-3*) Ayer.

Nettleton, George H. & Case, Arthur E., eds. British Dramatists from Dryden to Sheridan. 2nd ed. LC 75-2443. 975p. (C). 1975. pap. 31.95 (*0-8093-0743-X*) S Ill U Pr.

Nettleton, John A. Cumbria. (Country Guide Ser.: No. 25). (Illus.). 128p. 1996. pap. 12.50 (*0-7478-0315-3*, Pub. by Shire Pubns) Parkwest Pubns.

Nettleton, L. L. Gravity & Magnetics for Geologists & Seismologists. (Geophysical Monographs: No. 1). 121p. 1971. pap. 14.00 (*0-931830-10-9*, 141A) Soc Expl Geophys.

Nettleton, Sarah. The Body in Everyday Life. LC 97-44695. 280p. (C). 1998. pap. 25.99 (*0-415-16201-7*) Routledge.

— Power, Pain & Dentistry. 192p. 1992. 113.00 (*0-335-09723-5*); pap. 36.95 (*0-335-09722-7*) OpUniv Pr.

— The Sociology of Health & Illness. 280p. (C). 1995. pap. 29.95 (*0-7456-0894-9*) Blackwell Pubs.

— The Sociology of Health & Illness. 280p. (C). 1995. 64.95 (*0-7456-0893-0*) Blackwell Pubs.

Nettleton, Sarah & Watson, Jonathan, eds. Body in Everyday Life. LC 97-44695. 320p. (C). 1998. 85.00 (*0-415-16200-9*) Routledge.

Nettleton, T., jt. auth. see Harrison, H. R.

Nettleton, W. D., et al. Data Reliability & Risk Assessment. (SSSA Special Publications: No. 47). 164p. 1996. 34.00 (*0-89118-823-1*) Soil Sci Soc Am.

***Netton, Ian R.** Al-Farabi & His School. 288p. 1999. pap. (*0-7007-1064-7*, Pub. by Curzon Pr Ltd) Paul & Co Pubs.

Netton, Ian R. Al-Farabi & His School. 130p. 1996. pap. 15.95 (*0-614-21218-9*, 290) Kazi Pubns.

— Allah Transcendant: Studies in the Structure & Semiotics of Islamic Philosophy, Theology & Cosmology. 448p. (C). 1994. pap. 29.95 (*0-7007-0287-3*) Paul & Co Pubs.

— Middle East Sources: A MELCOM Guide to Middle Eastern & Islamic Books & Materials in the United Kingdom & Irish Libraries. LC 98-179259. 260p. 1998. 75.00 (*0-7007-1029-9*, Pub. by Curzon Pr Ltd) Paul & Co Pubs.

— Muslim Neoplatonism. 1991. pap. text 27.00 (*0-7486-0251-8*, Pub. by Edinburgh U Pr) Col U Pr.

— A Popular Dictionary of Islam. LC 92-13600. 288p. (C). 1992. pap. 19.95 (*0-7007-0233-4*, Pub. by Curzon Pr Ltd) Paul & Co Pubs.

— A Popular Dictionary of Islam. LC 92-13600. 244p. 1992. pap. 18.50 (*0-391-03756-0*) Humanities.

— A Popular Dictionary of Islam. LC 97-23830. (Illus.). 288p. 1997. pap. 14.95 (*0-8442-0422-6*, 04226) NTC Contemp Pub Co.

— Seek Knowledge: Thought & Travel in the House of Islam. 176p. (C). 1996. 75.00 (*0-7007-0339-X*, Pub. by Curzon Pr Ltd); pap. 25.00 (*0-7007-0340-3*, Pub. by Curzon Pr Ltd) Paul & Co Pubs.

— Text & Trauma: An East-West Primer. LC 96-119348. 176p. (C). 1995. 65.00 (*0-7007-0325-X*, Pub. by Curzon Pr Ltd); pap. 25.00 (*0-7007-0326-8*, Pub. by Curzon Pr Ltd) Paul & Co Pubs.

Netton, Ian R., ed. Golden Roads: Migration, Pilgrimage & Travel in Medieval & Modern Islam. 288p. (C). 1993. pap. 37.50 (*0-7007-0243-1*, Pub. by Curzon Pr Ltd) Paul & Co Pubs.

— Middle East Materials in United Kingdom & Irish Libraries: A Directory: a MELCOM Guide to Libraries & Other Institutions in Britain & Ireland with Islamic & Middle Eastern Books & Materials. LC 82-23574. 136p. reprint ed. pap. 42.20 (*0-7837-5318-7*, 204505700005) Bks Demand.

Netton, Ian R. & Bosworth, Clifford E. Hunter of the East: Studies in Honour of Clifford Edmund Bosworth. LC 98-28814. 464p. 1999. 147.50 (*90-04-11076-3*) Brill Academic Pubs.

***Netton, Ian Richard.** Sufi Ritual: The Parallel Universe. 248p. 2000. 85.00 (*0-7007-1242-9*, Pub. by Curzon Pr Ltd); pap. 29.95 (*0-7007-1254-2*, Pub. by Curzon Pr Ltd) Paul & Co Pubs.

***Network Action Company Staff.** Benefits & Deductions of the Home Based Business with 12 Receipt Envelopes Kit: A Professional & Easy to Use Tax Diary System. (Illus.). 48p. 2000. pap. 39.95 (*0-9664224-1-4*) Netwrk Action.

— Network Marketing Business Builder Action Pack. (Illus.). 580p. 1997. ring bd. 124.95 incl. audio, VHS (*0-9664224-0-6*, 02BBAP) Netwrk Action.

Network Development & MARC Standards Office. USMARC Format for Authority Data: Including Guidelines for Content Designation. LC 93-26502. 1993. write for info. (*0-8444-0802-6*) Lib Congress.

— USMARC Format for Community Information: Including Guidelines for Content Designation. LC 92-45199. 1993. write for info. (*0-8444-0779-8*) Lib Congress.

Network Development & MARC Standards Office Staff, ed. USMARC Code List for Geographic Areas. LC 94-9550. 1994. write for info. (*0-8444-0812-3*) Lib Congress.

Network Development Staff & MARC Standards Office Staff. USMARC Code List for Relators, Sources, Description Conventions. LC 93-30404. 1993. write for info. (*0-8444-0806-9*) Lib Congress.

Network Development Staff & MARC Standards Office Staff, eds. Format Integration & Its Effect on the USMARC Bibliographic Format. LC 94-49541. 1995. pap. write for info. (*0-8444-0873-5*) Lib Congress.

***Network Magazine Editors.** Network Tutorial: A Complete Introduction to Networks. 480p. 1999. pap. 29.95 (*1-57820-044-X*, Pub. by Telecom Bks) Publishers Group.

Network of Black Organizers Staff. Black Prison Movements/U. S. A. 200p. 1996. 45.95 (*0-86543-494-8*) Africa World.

Network of Egyptian Professional Women Staff. Egyptian Women in Social Development: A Resource Guide. 550p. 1988. pap. 35.00 (*977-424-184-3*, Pub. by Am Univ Cairo Pr) Col U Pr.

***Netz, Amir & Gill, Samuel.** Inside Microsoft SQL Server 2000 Analysis Services. 500p. 2000. pap. 49.99 (*0-7356-0697-8*) Microsoft Pr.

Netz, Reviel. The Shaping of Deduction in Greek Mathematics: A Study in Cognitive History. LC 98-20463. (Ideas in Context Ser.: No. 51). (Illus.). 432p. (C). 1999. text 64.95 (*0-521-62279-4*) Cambridge U Pr.

Netzel, J. P. & Gordon, B. Mechanical Seal Design & Technology. Date not set. write for info. (*0-8247-8950-4*) Dekker.

Netzel, Sally. Alice in Wonderland - the Musical: In 2 Acts. (Stage Magic Play Ser.). (Illus.). 56p. 1991. pap. 4.50 (*0-88680-342-X*) I E Clark.

— Cinderella: In 2 Acts. (Illus.). 32p. (J). (ps up). 1981. pap. 3.50 (*0-88680-028-5*) I E Clark.

— The Dark Castle: 2 Act Play with Audience Participation. (Illus.). 27p. 1993. pap. 4.00 (*0-88680-379-9*) I E Clark.

— The Jest. (YA). (gr. 5-12). 1996. pap. 6.00 (*0-87602-341-3*) Anchorage.

Netzel, Sally. Mr. Clemens & Mr. Brown. 83p. Date not set. pap. write for info. (*0-87129-820-1*, MC1) Dramatic Pub.

Netzel, Sally. Puss in Boots: A One-Act Play. (Illus.). 32p. (J). (gr. k up). 1979. pap. 3.50 (*0-88680-157-5*) I E Clark.

Netzer, A. Ambrose. The Healing Power of Forgiveness: A Guide to Healing Life's Hurts. rev. ed. 273p. 1998. pap. 15.00 (*0-9614588-1-X*) Center Creative Life.

— How to Parent Carefully: A Handbook on Parenting & Self Care. LC 85-70262. (Illus.). 146p. (Orig.). 1985. pap. 9.95 (*0-9614588-0-1*) Center Creative Life.

Netzer, Amnon, ed. Padyavand, Vol. I. LC 95-37762. (Judeo-Iranian & Jewish Studies Ser.). (Illus.). 470p. 1995. lib. bdg. 35.00 (*1-56859-036-9*) Mazda Pubs.

— Padyavand, Vol. II. (Judeo-Iranian & Jewish Studies Ser.: Vol. 1). (Illus.). 682p. 1998. lib. bdg. 40.00 (*1-56859-063-6*) Mazda Pubs.

***Netzer, Amnon, ed.** Padyavand, Vol. III. (Judeo-Iranian & Jewish Studies Ser.). 420p. 2000. 40.00 (*1-56859-127-6*) Mazda Pubs.

Netzer, Carol. Cutoffs: How Family Members Who Sever Relationships Can Reconnect. 256p. 1995. pap. 13.95 (*0-88282-138-5*) New Horizon NJ.

***Netzer, Corinne T.** The Century 2001 Calorie Counter. 2000. mass mkt. 6.99 (*0-440-23642-8*) Dell.

— The Complete Book of Food Counts. 5th ed. (Illus.). 848p. 2000. mass mkt. 7.50 (*0-440-22563-9*) Dell.

Netzer, Corinne T. The Complete Book of Vitamin & Mineral Counts. rev. ed. LC 97-128622. 448p. 1997. mass mkt. 5.99 (*0-440-22335-0*) Dell.

— The Corinne T. Netzer Carbohydrate Counter. LC 98-155045. 496p. 1998. mass mkt. 6.50 (*0-440-22550-7*, Dell Trade Pbks) Dell.

— The Corinne T. Netzer Carbohydrate Dieter's Diary. 176p. 1999. pap. 8.95 (*0-440-50852-5*) Dell.

— The Corinne T. Netzer Dieter's Diary. 176p. 1992. pap. 8.95 (*0-440-50410-4*) Dell.

— Corinne T. Netzer Encyclopedia of Food Values. 928p. 1992. 28.95 (*0-440-50367-1*) Dell.

— The Corinne T. Netzer Fat Counter. 512p. 1996. mass mkt. 5.99 (*0-440-22055-6*) Dell.

— The Corinne T. Netzer Low-Fat Diary. 192p. 1995. pap. 7.95 (*0-440-50695-6*) Dell.

— The Corinne T. Netzer 1998 Calorie Counter. rev. ed. 240p. 1998. mass mkt. 5.50 (*0-440-22415-2*) Dell.

N

— Corinne T. Netzer's, 3 vols. 1990. boxed set 12.85 (*0-440-36012-9*) Dell.

— Corinne T. Netzer's Big Book of Miracle Cures. LC 99-212487. 400p. 1999. mass mkt. 6.99 (*0-440-22609-0*) Dell.

***Netzer, Corinne T.** Corinne T. Netzer Calorie Counter for the Year 2000. 272p. 1999. mass mkt. 6.99 (*0-440-23498-0*) Dell.

Netzer, Corinne T. Counting on Corinne. Date not set. mass mkt. write for info. (*0-614-25230-X*) Dell.

— The CTN Brand-Name Calorie Counter. 7th ed. 480p. 1998. mass mkt. 5.99 (*0-440-22289-3*) Dell.

— The Dieter's Calorie Counter. 4th ed. LC 97-29839. 432p. 1998. pap. 10.95 (*0-440-50821-5*, Dell Trade Pbks) Dell.

— Fiber Counter. 224p. 1994. mass mkt. 5.50 (*0-440-21483-1*) Dell.

— 100 Low Fat Small Meals & Salads, 100 Low Fat Pasta & Grain Recipes, 100 Low Fat Vegetable & Legume Recipes, 100 Low Fat Soup & Stew Recipes, 100 Low Fat Fish & Shellfish Recipes & 100 Low Fat Chicken & Turkey Recipes. 1997. mass mkt. 5.99 (*0-614-27732-9*) Dell.

— Salads & Small Meals. LC 97-153288. (Corinne T. Netzer Good Eating Gourmet Ser.). 224p. 1997. mass mkt. 5.99 (*0-440-22349-0*) Dell.

Netzer, Corrine T. The Complete Book of Food Counts. LC 97-70829. 784p. 1997. 14.98 (*1-56731-213-6*, MJF Bks) Fine Comms.

Netzer, David W., jt. ed. see Jensen, Gordon E.

Netzer, Dick. Economics of the Property Tax. LC 65-28602. (Studies of Government Finance). 344p. reprint ed. pap. 106.70 (*0-608-18701-1*, 205625300056) Bks Demand.

***Netzer, Dick.** Land Value Taxation: Can It & Will It Work Today? LC 98-49916. 284p. 1998. pap. 25.00 (*1-55844-133-6*) Lincoln Ingalls Bks.

Netzer, Dick, jt. ed. see Bellush, Jewel.

Netzer, Dick, ed. see Drennan, Matthew P.

Netzer, Nancy. Cultural Interplay in the Eighth Century: The Trier Gospels & the Makings of a Scriptorium at Echternach. LC 93-17800. (Studies in Palaeography & Codicology: No. 3). (Illus.). 274p. (C). 1994. text 74.95 (*0-521-41255-2*) Cambridge U Pr.

— Medieval Objects in the Museum of Fine Arts, Boston: Metalwork. LC 90-63004. (Illus.). 200p. 1991. pap. 11.95 (*0-87846-327-5*) Mus Fine Arts Boston.

***Netzer, Nancy & Reinburg, Virginia, eds.** Fragmented Devotion: Medieval Objects from the Schnutgen Museum, Cologne. (Illus.). 180p. 2000. pap. 40.00 (*1-892850-01-X*) McMullen Mus Art.

Netzer, Nancy, ed. see Boston College Museum of Art Staff.

***Netzer, Roland Lee.** Echoes from the Hills Vol. 1: A Defined Guide to Country Sayings. LC 90-80819. 270p. 1999. pap. 14.95 (*0-9625768-1-6*) Echo Pub MO.

Netzer, Roland Lee. Echoes from the Hills Vol. 1: A Defined Guide to Country Sayings. LC 90-80819. 272p. 2000. 19.95 (*0-9625768-0-8*) Echo Pub MO.

Netzhammer, Beverly S., jt. auth. see Lerner, B. Rosie.

Netzler, Lee. Love Poems from a Poor Man. LC 84-91012. 54p. (Orig.). 1984. pap. 6.95 (*0-9647696-1-1*) Netzler Pubng.

— Oh How My Piper Played. LC 95-94703. (Illus.). 72p. (Orig.). 1995. pap. 11.95 (*0-9647696-2-X*) Netzler Pubng.

— Once in Love with a Puppy. 38p. 1984. reprint ed. pap. 6.95 (*0-9647696-0-3*) Netzler Pubng.

***Netzley, Patricia.** Encyclopedia of Movie Special Effects. LC 99-47733. (Illus.). 291p. 1999. 59.50 (*1-57356-167-3*) Oryx Pr.

Netzley, Patricia. Encyclopedia of Women's Travel & Exploration. (Illus.). 224p. 2000. text, boxed set 65.00 (*1-57356-238-6*) Oryx Pr.

***Netzley, Patricia D.** Alien Abductions. LC 00-9165. (Mystery Library). 2000. write for info. (*1-56006-767-5*) Lucent Bks.

— Alien Abductions: Opposing Viewpoints. LC 95-25106. (Great Mysteries Ser.). (Illus.). 112p. (J). (gr. 4-7). 1996. lib. bdg. 22.45 (*1-56510-352-1*) Greenhaven.

— Angels. LC 00-9442. (Mystery Library). (YA). 2001. write for info. (*1-56006-768-3*) Lucent Bks.

Netzley, Patricia D. The Assassination of President John F. Kennedy. LC 93-20818. (American Events Ser.). (Illus.). 96p. (YA). (gr. 6 up). 1994. lib. bdg. 18.95 (*0-02-768127-0*, New Dscvry Bks) Silver Burdett Pr.

***Netzley, Patricia D.** The Curse of King Tut. (Mystery Library). 144p. (YA). (gr. 4-12). 2000. 18.96 (*1-56006-684-9*) Lucent Bks.

Netzley, Patricia D. Environmental Groups. LC 98-12735. (Overview Ser.). (Illus.). 96p. (YA). (gr. 4-12). 1997. lib. bdg. 22.45 (*1-56006-195-2*) Lucent Bks.

— Environmental Literature: An Encyclopedia of Works, Characters, Authors & Themes. LC 99-35271. 337p. 1999. 75.00 (*1-57607-000-X*) ABC-CLIO.

***Netzley, Patricia D.** Haunted Houses. LC 00-8129. (Mystery Library). (Illus.). 144p. (YA). (gr. 4-8). 2000. 18.96 (*1-56006-685-7*) Lucent Bks.

— Issues in Censorship. LC 99-30281. (Contemporary Issues Ser.). (Illus.). 128p. (YA). (gr. 6-9). 2000. lib. bdg. 23.70 (*1-56006-609-1*) Lucent Bks.

— Issues in Crime. LC 99-44980. (Contemporary Issues Ser.). (Illus.). 128p. (YA). (gr. 6-9). 2000. lib. bdg. 23.70 (*1-56006-480-3*) Lucent Bks.

Netzley, Patricia D. Issues in the Environment. LC 97-25894. (Contemporary Issues Ser.). (Illus.). 95p. (YA). (gr. 4-12). 1997. lib. bdg. 22.45 (*1-56006-475-7*) Lucent Bks.

***Netzley, Patricia D.** Japan. LC 99-37253. (Overview Ser.). (Illus.). 144p. (YA). (gr. 6-9). 2000. lib. bdg. 23.70 (*1-56006-599-0*) Lucent Bks.

Netzley, Patricia D. Life During the Renaissance. LC 97-39781. (Way People Live Ser.). (Illus.). (YA). (gr. 4-12). 1997. lib. bdg. 22.45 (*1-56006-375-0*) Lucent Bks.

***Netzley, Patricia D.** Paranormal Phenomena. LC 99-40473. (Overview Ser.). (Illus.). 128p. (YA). (gr. 6-9). 2000. lib. bdg. 23.70 (*1-56006-622-9*) Lucent Bks.

— Presidential Assasins. (History Makers Ser.). (Illus.). 144p. (YA). (gr. 6-9). 2000. lib. bdg. 23.70 (*1-56006-623-7*) Lucent Bks.

— Social Protest Literature: An Encyclopedia of Works, Characters, Authors & Themes. LC 98-43005. 295p. (YA). 1999. lib. bdg. 75.00 (*0-87436-980-0*) ABC-CLIO.

Netzley, Patricia D. The Stone Age. LC 97-33613. (World History Ser.). (Illus.). 96p. (YA). (gr. 6-10). 1997. lib. bdg. 22.45 (*1-56006-316-5*) Lucent Bks.

***Netzley, Patricia D.** UFO's. LC 00-8154. (Mystery Library). 144p. (YA). (gr. 4-12). 2000. lib. bdg. 18.96 (*1-56006-686-5*) Lucent Bks.

— Unicorns. LC 00-8640. 2000. write for info. (*1-56006-687-3*) Lucent Bks.

Neu. Focus on HIV. 1994. pap. text 82.00 (*0-443-04919-X*, W B Saunders Co) Harcrt Hlth Sci Grp.

Neu, Axel D. Geburtentaler, Rentenberge & Wanderungen: Bevolkerungsentwicklung, Arbeitsmarkt & Altersversorgung in Deutschland & Westeuropa. (GER., Illus.). 309p. 1996. 50.95 (*3-631-30763-2*) P Lang Pubng.

Neu, C. R. A New Bretton Woods: Rethinking International Economic Institutions & Arrangements. 102p. 1993. pap. 15.00 (*0-8330-1304-1*, MR-116) Rand Corp.

Neu, C. R., jt. auth. see Steiner, Andrea.

Neu, C. Richard, et al. Sending Your Government a Message: E-Mail Communications Between Citizens & Government. LC 99-37564. (Illus.). 226p. 1999. pap. 20.00 (*0-8330-2754-9*, MR-1095-MF) Rand Corp.

***Neu, Charles, ed.** After Vietnam: Legacies of a Lost War. LC 99-53818. 192p. 2000. 34.95 (*0-8018-6327-9*); pap. 14.95 (*0-8018-6332-5*) Johns Hopkins.

Neu, Charles E. The Troubled Encounter: The United States & Japan. LC 79-4541. 272p. 1979. reprint ed. pap. 21.50 (*0-88275-951-5*) Krieger.

— An Uncertain Friendship: Theodore Roosevelt & Japan, 1906-1909. LC 67-27091. 359p. 1967. reprint ed. pap. 111.30 (*0-7837-4172-3*, 205902100012) Bks Demand.

Neu, Charles E., jt. ed. see Cooper, John M., Jr.

Neu, Clyde W., jt. auth. see Redinbaugh, Larry D.

Neu, Elisabeth, tr. see Van Dulmen, Richard.

Neu, H. & Bain, D., eds. National Energy Planning & Management in Developing Countries. 1983. text 199.50 (*90-277-1589-0*) Kluwer Academic.

Neu, H. C., ed. Fosfomycin Trometamol Single Dose: Significance & Management of Lower UTI's - Journal: Chemotherapy, Vol. 36, Suppl. 1, 1990. (Illus.). iv, 56p. 1990. pap. 18.50 (*3-8055-5325-0*) S Karger.

Neu, H. C. & Sabath, L. D., eds. Ein Praktischer Leitfaden fuer die Therapeutische Anwendung von Cefotiam. (Pharmanual Ser.: Vol. 3). (Illus.). vi, 182p. 1983. pap. 48.75 (*3-8055-3694-1*) S Karger.

Neu, H. C. & Williams, J. D., eds. New Trends in Urinary Tract Infections. (Illus.). x, 358p. 1988. 214.00 (*3-8055-4637-8*) S Karger.

Neu, Harold C., ed. New Antibacterial Strategies. (Illus.). 340p. (Orig.). 1991. pap. text 87.00 (*0-443-04448-1*) Church.

Neu, Harold C., ed. see Acar, et al.

Neu, Harold C., jt. ed. see Welton, Andrew.

Neu, Harold C., ed. see Young, Lowell S., et al.

Neu, Irene D. Erastus Corning, Merchant & Financier: 1794-1872. LC 77-22015. (Illus.). 212p. 1977. reprint ed. lib. bdg. 38.50 (*0-8371-9791-0*, NEEC, Greenwood Pr) Greenwood.

Neu, Irene D., jt. auth. see Taylor, George.

Neu, Jerome. A Tear Is an Intellectual Thing: The Meanings of Emotion. LC 99-10364. 352p. 2000. text 45.00 (*0-19-512337-9*) OUP.

Neu, Jerome, ed. The Cambridge Companion to Freud. (Companions to Philosophy Ser.). 368p. (C). 1991. text 80.00 (*0-521-37424-3*); pap. text 22.95 (*0-521-37779-X*) Cambridge U Pr.

— Guia de Freud. Santana, Mario, tr.Tr. of Cambridge Companion to Freud. (SPA.). 439p. (C). 1996. pap. 18.95 (*0-521-47838-3*) Cambridge U Pr.

Neu, John. Isis Cumulative Bibliography, 1986-1995. LC 97-18452. 1997. write for info. (*0-88135-131-8*); write for info. (*0-88135-132-6*); write for info. (*0-88135-133-4*); write for info. (*0-88135-134-2*) Watson Pub Intl.

Neu, John, ed. Isis Cumulative Bibliography, 1966-1975 Vol. 2: Subjects, Periods & Civilizations. 720p. 1985. text 200.00 (*0-7201-1516-7*) Continuum.

Neu, John, jt. auth. see Lindsay, Robert O.

Neu, Joyce, jt. ed. see Gass, Susan M.

Neu, Lynn. Seeking Justice. Zanzig, Thomas, ed. (Discovering Program Ser.). (Illus.). 24p. 1990. 3.00 (*0-88489-208-5*); teacher ed. 6.00 (*0-88489-209-3*) St Marys.

Neu, Ray. Actual Reality. (Illus.). 125p. (YA). (gr. 9-12). 1996. pap. 9.95 (*1-886461-33-3*) Lydia Press.

Neu Watkins, Renee, tr. see Alberti, Leon Battista.

Neubacher-Fesser, Monika & Kohner, Dieter. Paint Your Own T-Shirts: Including 20 Iron-On Transfers. (Illus.). 96p. 1996. pap. 19.95 (*0-85532-811-8*, 8118, Pub. by Srch Pr) A Schwartz & Co.

Neubacher, Helen Copan, jt. compiled by see Copan, Lil.

Neubart, Jack. Electronic Flash. LC 96-67853. (Kodak Workshop Ser.). (Illus.). 110p. (C). 1998. pap. 22.95 (*0-87985-772-2*, KW-12e, Kodak) Saunders Photo.

— The Photographer's Guide to Exposure. (Illus.). 144p. 1988. pap. 18.95 (*0-8174-5424-1*, Amphoto) Watsn-Guptill.

Neubauer. The American Courts & Criminal Justice System. (Criminal Justice Ser.). 1979. pap. write for info. (*0-534-02437-8*) Wadsworth Pub.

— Americas Courts. 4th ed. (Criminal Justice Ser.). 1992. text. write for info. (*0-534-15433-6*) Wadsworth Pub.

— America's Courts & Criminal Justice System. 6th ed. LC 98-16505. (Criminal Justice Ser.). 1998. pap. 70.95 (*0-534-54702-8*) Wadsworth Pub.

— America's Courts & Criminal Justice System. 6th ed. (Criminal Justice). 1998. pap., student ed. 18.75 (*0-534-54703-6*) Wadsworth Pub.

Neubauer, Adolf, jt. auth. see Driver, Samuel R.

Neubauer, Adolphe & Stern, Moritz, eds. Hebraische Berichte Uber die Judenverfolgung Wahrend der Kreuzzuge. (Quellen zur Geschichte der Juden in Deutschland Ser.: Vol. II). (GER.). xxxiv, 226p. 1997. reprint ed. 65.00 (*3-487-10460-1*) G Olms Pubs.

Neubauer, Adolphe D. Catalogue of the Hebrew Manuscripts in the Bodleian Library & in the College Libraries of Oxford, Vol. I. 1,120p. 1995. text 145.00 (*0-19-951357-0*) OUP.

— La Geographie Du Talmud. xl, 468p. 1967. reprint ed. write for info. (*0-318-71381-0*) G Olms Pubs.

Neubauer, Alexander, jt. auth. see Neubauer, Peter S.

Neubauer, David W. America's Court & the Criminal Justice System. 2nd ed. LC 83-15167. 500p. (C). 1984. pap. 23.25 (*0-534-02955-8*) Brooks-Cole.

— America's Courts & Criminal Justice System. 5th ed. (Criminal Justice Ser.). 1995. pap., student ed. 18.75 (*0-534-25266-4*) Wadsworth Pub.

— America's Courts & the Criminal Justice System. 3rd ed. LC 87-27860. 420p. (C). 1988. pap. 38.95 (*0-534-09090-7*) Brooks-Cole.

— America's Courts & the Criminal Justice System. 4th ed. LC 91-32391. 489p. (C). 1992. mass mkt. 44.95 (*0-534-15432-8*) Wadsworth Pub.

— America's Courts & the Criminal Justice System. 5th ed. LC 95-2518. 1995. pap. 45.00 (*0-534-23952-8*) Wadsworth Pub.

— Judicial Process: Law, Courts, & Politics in the U. S. 2nd ed. 560p. (C). 1996. text 50.00 (*0-03-019384-2*, Pub. by Harcourt Coll Pubs) Harcourt.

— Judicial Process: Law, Courts, & Politics in the U. S. 2nd ed. (Political Science Ser.). 1998. text 33.95 (*0-534-23946-3*) Wadsworth Pub.

Neubauer, F., jt. ed. see Von Raumer, J. F.

Neubauer, F. F. Portfolio Management: The Concept of Profit Potentials; Its Application. 3rd ed. 110p. 1990. 52.00 (*90-6544-500-5*) Kluwer Law Intl.

Neubauer, Franz C. Franz Christoph Neubauer: Chamber Music. Sjoerdsma, Richar, ed. (Recent Researches in Music of the Classic Era Ser.: Vol. RRC21). (Illus.). xiii, 96p. 1985. pap. 40.00 (*0-89579-175-7*) A-R Eds.

Neubauer, Franz-Friedrich, jt. auth. see Demb, Ada.

Neubauer, Fred & Lank, Alden. Family Business: Its Governance & Sustainability. 272p. (C). (gr. 13). 1998. 40.00 (*0-415-92094-9*) Routledge.

Neubauer, Fred, jt. auth. see Lessem, Ronnie.

Neubauer, Georg & Hurrelmann, Klaus, eds. Individualization in Childhood & Adolescence Ser. (Prevention & Intervention in Childhood & Adolescence: No. 15). vi, 348p. (C). 1995. lib. bdg. 54.95 (*3-11-014681-9*) De Gruyter.

***Neubauer, Hans-Joachim.** The Rumour: A Cultural History. (Illus.). 260p. 1999. 30.00 (*1-85343-472-8*, Pub. by Free Assoc Bks) Intl Spec Bk.

Neubauer, Hendrik. Black Star: 60 Years of Photojournalism. (ENG, FRE & GER., Illus.). 400p. 1998. 39.95 (*3-89508-250-3*, 810089) Konemann.

***Neubauer, Hendrik.** Curious Moments in Photographs. (Illus.). 800p. 1999. pap. 19.95 (*3-8290-2988-8*) Konemann.

***Neubauer, Joan.** The Complete Idiot's Guide to Journaling. 2001. pap. 16.95 (*0-02-863980-4*, Alpha Ref) Macmillan Gen Ref.

Neubauer, Joan R. Dear Diary: The Art & Craft of Writing a Creative Journal. LC 95-49501. 64p. 1985. pap. 5.95 (*0-916489-61-2*) Ancestry.

— From Memories to Manuscript: The Five-Step Method of Writing Your Life Story. LC 93-43942. 40p. 1994. pap. 5.95 (*0-916489-56-6*) Ancestry.

***Neubauer, John, ed.** Cultural History after Foucault. LC 99-22892. 259p. 1999. reprint ed. pap. text 23.95 (*0-202-30585-6*) Aldine de Gruyter.

Neubauer, Karl W., ed. European Library Networks. LC 89-37179. 448p. (C). 1990. text 82.50 (*0-89391-157-7*) Ablx Pub.

Neubauer, Larry. She Married an American Idiot: Love & Romance Are Still Alive in the 1990's. 96p. 1998. pap. 9.00 (*0-8059-4246-7*) Dorrance.

Neubauer, Patricia. Beneath Bare Cherry Trees: Haiku for Winter. LC 87-90531. (Illus.). 56p. (Orig.). 1987. 45.00 (*0-9617265-2-0*); pap. 15.00 (*0-9617265-3-9*) Neubauer Pr.

— Beneath Bare Cherry Trees: Haiku for Winter. limited ed. LC 87-90531. (Illus.). 56p. (Orig.). 1987. write for info. (*0-9617265-4-7*) Neubauer Pr.

— Leaves & Wind Chimes: Haiku for Autumn. LC 86-90529. (Illus.). 50p. (Orig.). 1986. write for info. (*0-9617265-0-4*); pap. 15.00 (*0-9617265-1-2*) Neubauer Pr.

Neubauer, Peter B. Nature's Thumbprint: The Role of Genetics in Human Development. 1990. 17.26 (*0-201-09254-9*) Addison-Wesley.

Neubauer, Peter B. & Solnit, Albert J., eds. The Psychoanalytic Study of the Child, Vol. 42. LC 45-11304. Vol. 42. 609p. 1987. 60.00 (*0-300-04057-1*) Yale U Pr.

Neubauer, Peter B., jt. auth. see Eissler, Ruth S.

Neubauer, Peter B., jt. auth. see Flapan, Dorothy.

Neubauer, Peter S. & Neubauer, Alexander. Nature's Thumbprint: The New Genetics of Personality. LC 95-37858. 224p. (C). 1996. pap. 18.50 (*0-231-10441-3*) Col U Pr.

Neubauer, Raymond L. The Banquet of Eternity: 20th Century Psalms. LC 96-35633. 1996. 14.95 (*1-879007-20-7*) St Bedes Pubns.

— The Visionary Universe: A Prophecy. (Illus.). 273p. (Orig.). 1995. pap. 8.95 (*0-914220-00-4*, A441941) Bay Rainbows Pr.

Neubauer, Richard A. & Walker, Morton. Hyperbaric Oxygen Therapy: Using HBO Therapy to Increase Circulation, Repair Damaged Tissue, Fight Infection, Save Limbs, & Relieve Pain. LC 97-30980. 216p. pap. 13.95 (*0-89529-759-0*, Avery) Penguin Putnam.

Neubauer, Richard E. The Intelligent Building Sourcebook. LC 85-45877. 350p. 1987. text 68.00 (*0-88173-019-X*) Fairmont Pr.

Neubauer, Russell H. Naturally Occurring Biological Immunosuppressive Factors & Their Relationship to Disease. 304p. 1979. 170.00 (*0-8493-5243-6*, RC268, CRC Reprint) Franklin.

Neubauer, William. The Trouble in Ward J. large type ed. (Linford Romance Library). 240p. 1996. pap. 16.99 (*0-7089-7972-6*) Ulverscroft.

Neubaur, William. Angel Mountain. large type ed. (Linford Romance Library). 288p. 1996. pap. 16.99 (*0-7089-7844-4*, Linford) Ulverscroft.

Neubauser, Duncan, et al, eds. Clinical CQI: A Book of Readings. (Illus.). 254p. 1995. pap. 38.00 (*0-86688-418-1*, CQI-105) Joint Comm Hlthcare.

Neubeck, Deborah K. Guide to the Microfilm Edition of The Frank B. Kellogg Papers. LC 78-63612. 56p. 1978. pap. 2.00 (*0-87351-126-3*) Minn Hist.

Neubeck, Ken. A-10 "Mini" in Action. (Mini in Action Ser.). (Illus.). 50p. 1995. pap. 5.95 (*0-89747-335-3*) Squad Sig Pubns.

***Neubeck, Ken.** A-10 Warthog Walk Around. (Walk Around Ser.: Vol. 17). (Illus.). 80p. 1999. pap. 14.95 (*0-89747-400-7*) Squad Sig Pubns.

— F-105 Thunderchief Walk Around. (Walk Around Ser.: Vol. 23). (Illus.). 80p. 2000. pap. 414.95 (*0-89747-418-X*, 5523) Squad Sig Pubns.

Neubeck, Kenneth J. Sociology: A Critical Approach. 1995. pap., student ed. 44.06 (*0-07-046394-8*) McGraw.

Neubeck, Mary A., jt. auth. see Nuebeck, Kenneth J.

Neubecker, Ottfried. German & French for Heraldry: Deutsch und Franzoesisch Fuer Heraldiker. (FRE & GER.). 108p. 1983. 59.95 (*0-8288-1480-5*, M15253) Fr & Eur.

— Grosses Wappen-Bilder-Lexikon. 2nd ed. (GER.). 1147p. 1992. 150.00 (*0-7859-8544-1*, 3894410302) Fr & Eur.

— Wappen-Bilder-Lexikon: German, French & English. (ENG, FRE & GER.). 418p. 1974. 49.95 (*0-7859-8519-0*, 3870450223) Fr & Eur.

***Neubecker, Ottfried & Brooke-Little, J. P.** Heraldry: Sources, Symbols & Meaning. (Illus.). 288p. 1999. reprint ed. text 40.00 (*0-7881-6583-6*) DIANE Pub.

Neubecker, William, ed. Antique Auto Body Metal Work for the Restorer. LC 82-62579. (Vintage Craft Ser.: No. 1). (Illus.). 1969. pap. 6.95 (*0-911160-01-9*) Post Group.

Neuber, Baldur. Sprechwissenschaft und Sprecherziehung In der Lehrerbildung der Ehemaligen Ddr: Versuch Einer Kritischen Betrachtung Mit Dem Ziel Neuer Konzeptioneller Losungsansatze Unter Besonderer Berucksichtigung der Arbeit In Den Neuen Bundeslandern. (Illus.). 181p. 1998. 37.95 (*3-631-33982-8*) P Lang Pubng.

Neuber, Keith A., et al. Needs Assessment: A Model for Community Planning. (Human Services Guides Ser.: Vol. 14). 107p. 1980. pap. 18.95 (*0-8039-1396-6*) Sage.

Neuberg, jt. auth. see Kenrick.

Neùberg, Albert S. Indexing for Maximum Investment Results. (Glenlake Business Monographs). 275p. 1998. 65.00 (*1-884964-50-8*) Fitzroy Dearborn.

Neuberg, Leland G. Conceptual Anomalies in Economics & Statistics: Lessons from the Social Experiment. (Illus.). 384p. 1989. text 95.00 (*0-521-30444-X*) Cambridge U Pr.

Neuberg, Roger. Obstetrics: A Practical Manual. (Illus.). 302p. 1995. pap. text 49.95 (*0-19-263007-5*) OUP.

Neuberg, Victor. The Popular Press Companion to Popular Literature. LC 82-74162. 207p. 1983. 20.95 (*0-87972-233-9*) Bowling Green Univ Popular Press.

Neuberger, A. & Van Deenen, L. L. Comprehensive Biochemistry, Section 6: History of Biochemistry, Vols. 30-32. Incl. Vol. 32. Early Studies on Biosynthesis. 362p. 1977. 167.00 (*0-444-41544-0*); 1977. write for info. (*0-318-51831-7*, North Holland) Elsevier.

Neuberger, A. & Van Deenen, L. L., eds. Modern Physical Methods in Biochemistry, Pt. A. (New Comprehensive Biochemistry Ser.: Vol. 11). 428p. 1985. 170.75 (*0-444-80649-0*) Elsevier.

Neuberger, Anne E. Advent Stories & Activities: Meeting Jesus Through the Jesse Tree. LC 96-61817. 96p. 1997. pap. 12.95 (*0-89622-734-0*) Twenty-Third.

— Girl-Son. LC 94-6725. (Adventures in Time Ser.). 132p. (J). (gr. 4 up). 1994. lib. bdg. 21.27 (*0-87614-846-1*, Carolrhoda) Lerner Pub.

— Girl-Son. (Illus.). 131p. (J). 1995. pap. text 6.95 (*1-57505-077-3*, Carolrhoda) Lerner Pub.

***Neuberger, Anne E.** St Nicholas, the Wonder Worker. LC 00-130462. 120p. 2000. pap. 8.95 (*0-87973-481-7*) Our Sunday Visitor.

Neuberger, Anne E. Stories of Saints Through the Centuries: Mystics & Martyrs, Healers & Hermits, Soldiers & Seekers... (Illus.). 121p. (J). 1999. pap. 12.95 (*0-89622-984-X*) Twenty-Third.

Neuberger, Benjamin. Involvement, Invasion & Withdrawal: Qadhdhafi's Libya & Chad, 1969-1981. 80p. (Orig.). 1982. pap. text 9.95 (*0-8156-7049-4*) Syracuse U Pr.

Neuberger, Egon & Lara, Juan. The Foreign Trade Practices of Centrally Planned Economies & Their Effects on U. S. International Competitiveness. LC 77-90040. 56p. 1977. 3.00 (*0-89068-043-4*) Natl Planning.

Neuberger, Egon, ed. see Conference on International Trade & Central Planni.

Neuberger, I., ed. Arne Beurling: Collected Works, 2 vols., Set. (Contemporary Mathematicians Ser.). 900p. 1990. 115.00 (*0-8176-3412-6*) Birkhauser.

— Arne Beurling: Collected Works, 2 vols., Vol. I. (Contemporary Mathematicians Ser.). 512p. 1989. 63.00 (*0-8176-3415-0*) Birkhauser.

— Arne Beurling: Collected Works, 2 vols., Vol. II. (Contemporary Mathematicians Ser.). 384p. 1989. 63.00 (*0-8176-3416-9*) Birkhauser.

Neuberger, James & Adams, David, eds. Immunology of Liver Transplantation. 320p. 1993. text 129.50 (*0-340-55310-3*, Pub. by E A) OUP.

Neuberger, James & Lucey, Michael, eds. Liver Transplantation: Practice & Management. 420p. 1994. pap. text 59.00 (*0-7279-0787-5*, Pub. by BMJ Pub) Login Brothers Bk Co.

Neuberger, Joan. Hooliganism: Crime, Culture, & Power in St. Petersburg, 1900-1914. LC 92-34003. (Studies on the History of Society & Culture: Vol. 19). 324p. 1993. 50.00 (*0-520-08011-4*, Pub. by U CA Pr) Cal Prin Full Svc.

Neuberger, John W. Sobolev Gradients & Differential Equations. Vol. 167. Dold, A. & Takens, F., eds. LC 97-37832. (Lecture Notes in Mathematics Ser.: Vol. 1670). viii, 150p. 1997. pap. text 33.00 (*3-540-63537-8*) Spr-Verlag.

Neuberger, Julia. Dying Well. 175p. 1999. pap. text 25.00 (*1-898507-26-0*) Buttrwrth-Heinemann.

Neuberger, Marc J. & Dorfman, Len. Microsoft Macro Assembler 6.0 Programming. 1993. pap. 34.95 (*0-07-017809-7*) McGraw.

Neuberger, Marc J., jt. auth. see Dorfman, Len.

Neuberger, Max. The Historical Development of Experimental Brain & Spinal Cord Physiology Before Flourens. Clarke, Edwin, ed. & tr. by. from GER. LC 81-47604. 424p. 1982. text 70.00 (*0-8018-2380-3*) Johns Hopkins.

Neuberger, Phyllis J. Suppose You Were a Kitten. LC 82-91105. (Illus.). (J). (gr. 1-3). 1982. pap. 2.95 (*0-9610050-0-9*) P J Neuberger.

Neuberger, Richard L. They Never Go Back to Pocatello: The Selected Essays of Richard Neuberger. Neal, Steve, ed. LC 88-17935. (Illus.). 416p. 1988. 22.50 (*0-87595-201-1*) Oregon Hist.

Neuberger, Richard L. & Loe, Kelley. An Army of the Aged. LC 72-2379. (FDR & the Era of the New Deal Ser.). 332p. 1973. reprint ed. lib. bdg. 39.50 (*0-306-70518-4*) Da Capo.

Neuberger, Roy R. So Far, So Good: The First 94 Years. LC 97-14193. (Illus.). 240p. 1997. 29.95 (*0-471-17186-7*) Wiley.

***Neuberger, Roy S.** From Central Park to Sinai: How I Found My Jewish Soul. LC 00-31452. 2000. write for info. (*0-8246-0431-8*) Jonathan David.

Neuberger, Ruth, ed. see Longinus.

Neuberger, Thomas. Foundation: Building Sentence Skills. 3rd ed. 432p. 1988. teacher ed. write for info. (*0-318-63326-4*) HM.

Neuberger, Thomas. Foundation: Building Sentence Skills, 3 vols. 3rd ed. LC 88-81352. 432p. (C). 1988. pap. 44.76 (*0-395-35028-X*) HM.

Neubert, Albert S. Indexing for Maximum Investment Results. 260p. 1997. 65.00 (*1-888998-11-3*) Glenlake Pub.

Neubert, Albert S., ed. Indexing for Maximum Investment Results. 250p. 1998. 45.00 (*0-8144-0443-X*) AMACOM.

Neubert, Albrecht & Shreve, Gregory M. Translation As Text. LC 92-7731. (Translation Studies: No. 1). 184p. (C). 1992. 27.00 (*0-87338-469-5*) Kent St U Pr.

Neubert, Christopher & Withiam, Jack, Jr. How to Handle Your Own Contracts. exp. rev. ed. LC 90-23740. (Illus.). 256p. 1991. pap. 14.95 (*0-8069-8256-X*) Sterling.

Neubert, Diether, et al. Risk Assessment of Prenatally-Induced Adverse Health Effects. LC 92-26482. 1992. 125.00 (*0-387-55890-X*) Spr-Verlag.

Neubert, Emil. My Ideal-Jesus, Son of Mary. LC 88-50578. 111p. 1988. reprint ed. pap. 4.00 (*0-89555-338-4*) TAN Bks Pubs.

Neubert, George W., text. Paul Wonner: Abstract Realist. LC 81-67616. (Illus.). 72p. 1981. pap. 15.00 (*0-911291-07-5*, Pub. by Fellows Cont Art) RAM Publications.

Neubert, Gloria A. & Binko, James B. Inductive Reasoning in the Secondary Classroom. 128p. 1992. pap. 11.95 (*0-8106-3010-9*) NEA.

Neubert, Gloria A., jt. auth. see Binko, James B.

Neubert, Gloria A., jt. auth. see McAllister, Elizabeth A.

Neubert, Gunter. Dictionary of Hydraulics & Pneumatics. 226p. 1980. 60.00 (*0-569-08523-3*) St Mut.

— Dictionary of Hydraulics & Pneumatics: English-German-Russian-Spanish & French. (ENG, FRE, GER, RUS & SPA.). 226p. 1973. 95.00 (*0-7859-0814-5*, M-8178) Fr & Eur.

— Parat Dictionary of Fluidics: English-German, German-English. (ENG & GER.). 259p. 1993. 150.00 (*0-7859-6959-4*) Fr & Eur.

Neubert, Kevin, jt. auth. see Buehrens, Carol.

Neubert-Mader, Laila, jt. auth. see Mader, Gunter.

***Neubert, Susanne.** Social Impact Analysis of Poverty Alleviation Programmes & Projects: A Contribution to the Debate on the Methodology of Evaluation in Development Cooperation. LC 00-22704. (GDI Book Ser.). (Illus.). 2000. write for info. (*0-7146-5049-8*) F Cass Pubs.

Neuborne, Burt, jt. auth. see Friedman, Leon.

Neubort, Shimon, tr. Branches of the Chassidic Menorah No. 1: Biographical Sketches Based on the Essay "Fathers of Chassidus" LC 98-224667. 224p. 1998. 18.00 (*1-881400-31-X*) S I E.

— Links in the Chassidic Legacy No. 1: Biographical Sketches That First Appeared in the Classical Columns of HaTamim. LC 97-141956. 224p. 1997. 18.00 (*1-881400-23-9*) S I E.

— The Making of Chassidim: A Letter Written by the Previous Lubavitcher Rebbe Rabbi Yosef Yitzchak Schneersohn. LC 97-124335. 224p. 1996. 18.00 (*1-881400-19-0*) S I E.

Neuburg, Matt. Frontier: The Definitive Guide. (Illus.). 560p. 1998. pap. 34.95 (*1-56592-383-9*) OReilly & Assocs.

Neuburg, Matt, ed. & tr. see Aristophanes.

Neuburger, jt. auth. see Koneman, Elmer W.

Neuburger, Henry & Fraser, Neil. Economic Policy Analysis: A Rights-Based Approach. 224p. 1993. 72.95 (*1-85628-505-7*, Pub. by Avebry) Ashgate Pub Co.

Neuburger, Hugh M. German Banks & German Economic Growth from Unification to World War I. Bruchey, Stuart, ed. LC 77-77182. (Dissertations in European Economic History Ser.). 1978. lib. bdg. 23.95 (*0-405-10795-1*) Ayer.

Neuburger, Hugh M., jt. auth. see Stokes, Houston H.

Neuby, Barbara, ed. Relevancy of the Social Sciences in the Next Millennium. (Studies in Social Sciences). 124p. 1998. pap. text. write for info. (*1-883199-08-5*) St U W Georgia.

Neudeck-Dicken, Marilyn. Cumulative Stress Management for Search & Rescue: A Workbook for Emergency Personnel. (Illus.). (Orig.). 1997. pap., wbk. ed. 15.95 (*0-86541-039-9*) Filter.

Neudeck, Gerald W. El Diodo Pn. de Union. (SPA.). 208p. (C). 1993. pap. text 12.66 (*0-201-60142-7*) Addison-Wesley.

— El Transistor Bipolar de Union. (SPA.). 128p. (C). 1994. pap. text 11.66 (*0-201-60143-5*) Addison-Wesley.

Neudeck, Gerold W. The Bipolar Junction Transistor. LC 81-14977. (Modular Series on Solid State Devices: No. 3). (Illus.). 85p. 1983. pap. write for info. (*0-201-05322-5*) Addison-Wesley.

— The PN Junction Diode. LC 81-14979. (Modular Series on Solid State Devices: No. 2). (Illus.). 120p. 1983. pap. 7.00 (*0-201-05321-7*) Addison-Wesley.

— The PN Junction Diode. 2nd ed. (Modular Series on Solid State Devices). (Illus.). 176p. (C). 1988. pap. text 23.40 (*0-201-12296-0*) Addison-Wesley.

Neudeck, Gerold W., jt. auth. see Hayt, William H.

Neudeck, Gerold W., jt. auth. see Pierret, Robert F.

Neudecker, H., jt. auth. see Magnus, J. R.

Neuder, Gustav F. & Ullrich, Heinz M. Dictionary of Radiological Engineering. (ENG, FRE & GER.). (C). 1979. pap. text 53.10 (*3 11 007807-4*) De Gruyter.

Neudorf, Eugene. A Light to All Japan: The Story of Susan Dyck. 30p. 1998. pap. 3.99 (*0-87509-775-8*) Chr Pubns.

— A Light to All Japan: The Story of Susan Dyck. LC 97-77647. Vol. 19. (Illus.). 206p. (gr. 4-7). 1998. pap. 9.99 (*0-87509-724-3*) Chr Pubns.

Neudorfer, Paul O. & Hassul, Michael. Introduction to Circuit Analysis. 600p. 1990. teacher ed. write for info. (*0-318-63886-X*, H13741) P-H.

Neue, Friedrich. Formenlehre der Lateinischen Sprache, 4 vols. in 3, Set. 3151p. 1985. reprint ed. write for info. (*3-487-07703-5*) G Olms Pubs.

— Formenlehre der Lateinischen Sprache, 4 vols. in 3, Vol. I: Das Substantivum. 3151p. 1985. reprint ed. write for info. (*0-318-71183-4*) G Olms Pubs.

— Formenlehre der Lateinischen Sprache, 4 vols. in 3, Vol. II: Adjektiva, Numeralia etc. 3151p. 1985. reprint ed. write for info. (*0-318-71184-2*) G Olms Pubs.

— Formenlehre der Lateinischen Sprache, 4 vols. in 3, Vol. III: Das Verbum. 3151p. 1985. reprint ed. write for info. (*0-318-71185-0*) G Olms Pubs.

— Formenlehre der Lateinischen Sprache, 4 vols. in 3, Vol. IV: Register Mit Zusatzen und Verbesserungen. 3151p. 1985. reprint ed. write for info. (*0-318-71186-9*) G Olms Pubs.

Neue Gesellschaft Bildende Kunst Berlin Staff. Der Wettbewerb Fur Das "denkmal Fur Die Ermordeten Juden Europas" - Eine Streitschrift. (GER.). 196p. 1995. pap. text 9.00 (*3-364-00362-9*, Verlag Kunst) Gordon & Breach.

Neue, Michael, ed. see Darwin, Charles.

Neue, Uwe D. HPLC Columns: Theory, Technology & Practice. LC 97-3994. (Illus.). 416p. 1997. 94.95 (*0-471-19037-3*) Wiley.

Neueder, R., et al. Electrolyte Data Collection: Conductivities Transference Numbers & Limiting Ionic Conductivities of Solutions of Propanol. Kreysa, Gerhard, ed. (Dechema Chemistry Data Ser.: Vol. 12, Pt. 1B). (Illus.). 635p. 1994. text, lib. bdg. 360.00 (*3-926959-41-X*, Pub. by Dechema) Scholium Intl.

Neueder, R., jt. auth. see Barthel, J.

Neueder, R., jt. auth. see Barthel, Josef.

Neuefeind, Wilhelm & Riezman, Raymond G., eds. Economic Theory & International Trade: Essays in Memoriam J. Trout Radar. LC 92-26243. (Illus.). x, 306p. 1992. 133.95 (*0-387-55737-7*) Spr-Verlag.

Neuen. Choral Techniques & Conducting. 1999. 39.00 (*0-02-864749-1*) Intrepid Travel.

Neuendorf, Wayne. An Engineer's Notebook: A Collection of Original Articles, Practical Ideas & Other Stuff about Recording. LC 89-92332. (Illus.). 155p. (Orig.). 1990. pap. 12.95 (*0-9624890-6-9*) Spiral Pr.

Neuenfeldt, Karl, ed. The Didjeridu: From Arnhem Land to Internet. LC 97-149528. (Illus.). 192p. 1998. 35.00 (*1-86462-003-X*); pap. 19.95 (*1-86462-004-8*) Ind U Pr.

Neuenschwander, B. Mystik im Johannesevangelium: Eine Hermeneutische Untersuchung Aufgrund der Auseinandersetzung mit Zen-Meister Hisamatsu Shin'Ichi. (Biblical Interpretation Ser.: No. 31). (GER.). xiv, 370p. 1998. 134.00 (*90-04-11035-6*) Brill Academic Pubs.

Neuenschwander, Brody. Letterwork: Creative Letterforms in Graphic Design. (Illus.). 160p. (C). 1993. pap. 29.95 (*0-7148-2909-9*, Pub. by Phaidon Press) Phaidon Pr.

Neuenschwander, D. Probabilities on the Heisenberg Group: Limit Theorems & Brownian Motion, Vol. 163. LC 96-26210. (Lecture Notes in Mathematics Ser.). 139p. 1996. pap. 29.00 (*3-540-61453-2*) Spr-Verlag.

Neuenschwander, Evonne, et al, eds. Tapestry of Praise. 44p. 1986. 9.99 (*0-8341-9340-X*, MB-566) Lillenas.

Neuenschwander, Jan, jt. auth. see Ottensmann, John R.

Neuenschwander, John A. Oral History & the Law. LC 85-13686. (Oral History Association Pamphlet Ser.: No. 1). 1993. pap. 8.00 (*0-317-01097-2*) Oral Hist.

Neuenschwander, Mark. Crisis Evangelism: How You Can Be Prepared to Give an Account of the Hope That Is in You. LC 99-20546. 290p. 1999. pap. 11.99 (*0-8307-2490-7*) Gospel Lght.

Neuenschwander, Robert. Carving Comical Bears. LC 95-45768. 1996. pap. 12.95 (*0-88740-896-6*) Schiffer.

Neuenswander, Helen L. & Arnold, Dean E. Cognitive Studies of Southern Mesoamerica. LC 77-80015. (Museum of Anthropology Publications: No. 3). 283p. 1977. pap. 11.00 (*0-88312-152-2*) S I L Intl.

Neuerburg-Heusler, Doris, et al, eds. Diagnostic Vascular Ultrasound. 384p. 1992. text 195.00 (*0-340-55399-5*, Pub. by E A) OUP.

Neuerburg-Heusler, Doris, jt. auth. see Hennerici, M.

Neuerburg-Heusler, Doris, jt. auth. see Hennerici, Michael.

Neuerburg, Norman. California Missions to Cut Out, Vol. I. (J). (gr. 4-9). 1993. pap. 5.95 (*0-88388-177-2*) Bellerophon Bks.

— California Missions to Cut Out, Vol. II. (J). (gr. 4-9). 1993. pap. 6.95 (*0-88388-185-3*) Bellerophon Bks.

— The Decoration of the California Missions. (Illus.). 80p. (Orig.). 1987. pap. 9.95 (*0-88388-131-4*) Bellerophon Bks.

— Saints of the California Missions. (Illus.). 48p. (Orig.). 1989. pap. 9.95 (*0-88388-139-X*) Bellerophon Bks.

Neufang, Otger. Electronics Lexicon: Lexikon der Elektronik. (ENG & GER.). 815p. 1983. 185.00 (*0-8288-0292-0*, M8754) Fr & Eur.

Neufang, Otger & Ruhl, Horst. German & English Electronics Dictionary: Elektronik-Worterbuch. (ENG & GER.). 421p. 1986. pap. 185.00 (*0-8288-1376-0*, M426) Fr & Eur.

Neufeld. Bombing of Auschwitz. LC 99-15907. 2000. text 27.50 (*0-312-19838-8*) St Martin.

Neufeld, Bernie. Music in Worship: A Mennonite Perspective. LC 99-188757. 260p. 1999. pap. text 14.99 (*0-8361-9459-4*) Herald Pr.

Neufeld, Beverly, jt. auth. see Eata, Michi.

Neufeld, Christine. Peace Heroes. (Fast Lane Bible Studies Ser.). 48p. (J). (gr. 7-9). 1996. pap. 9.95 (*0-87303-306-X*) Faith & Life.

— Peace-Just Live It! A Challenge to Youth for the 21st Century. LC 94-61723. 104p. (YA). (gr. 9-12). 1995. pap., spiral bd. 18.95 (*0-87303-239-X*) Faith & Life.

Neufeld, David & Habiluk, Patrick. Make It Pay Gold Dredge No. 4: Klondike, Yukon, Canada. abr. ed. LC 94-66660. (Illus.). 64p. 1994. pap. 7.95 (*0-929521-88-9*) Pictorial Hist.

Neufeld, David & Norris, Frank. Chilkoot Trail: Heritage Route to the Klondike. LC 96-205482. (Illus.). 192p. 1996. pap. text 19.95 (*0-9694612-9-1*, Pub. by Lost Moose) Genl Dist Srvs.

Neufeld, Dietmar. Reconceiving Texts As Speech Acts: An Analysis of 1 John. LC 94-1367. (Biblical Interpretation Ser.: Vol. 7). xi, 152p. 1994. 71.00 (*90-04-09853-4*) Brill Academic Pubs.

Neufeld, Edward P. A Global Corporation: A History of the International Development of Massey-Ferguson Limited. LC 76-403976. (Illus.). 474p. reprint ed. pap. 147.00 (*0-8357-4740-9*, 203766000009) Bks Demand.

Neufeld, Elsie K. Dancing in the Dark: A Sister Grieves. LC 90-83830. 200p. (Orig.). 1990. pap. 8.99 (*0-8361-3537-7*) Herald Pr.

Neufeld, Evelyn. Homework! 64p. (J). (gr. k-2). 1987. pap. text 9.50 (*0-914040-56-1*) Cuisenaire.

Neufeld, Gerald G. & Immers, Richard C. Inside Commodore DOS. (Illus.). 250p. 19.95 (*0-317-13067-6*) P-H.

Neufeld, Henry N. & Schneeweiss, Adam. Coronary Artery Disease in Infants & Children. LC 83-766. (Illus.). 189p. reprint ed. pap. 58.60 (*0-7837-1491-2*, 205718700023) Bks Demand.

***Neufeld, Herb.** Jacob's Journey. LC 99-96810. 2000. 18.95 (*0-533-13352-1*) Vantage.

Neufeld, Herman A. Mary Neufeld & the Repphun Story: From the Molotschna to Manitoba. LC 88-70276. (Illus.). 240p. 1988. 16.75 (*0-945608-07-1*) C Joyce Gall.

— The Repphun Family: Circas: 1840-50s to 1988. LC 88-192584. 57p. 1988. 15.00 (*0-945608-10-1*) C Joyce Gall.

Neufeld, Herman A., compiled by. Flashback: Neufeld Family Newsletters, March 1977 to Dec. 1989, Vol. II. (Illus.). 360p. 1990. 49.50 (*0-945608-08-X*) C Joyce Gall.

— Flashback: Neufeld Family Newsletters, Oct. 1959 - Dec. 1976, Vol. I. (Illus.). 342p. 1988. pap. write for info. (*0-945608-06-3*) C Joyce Gall.

Neufeld, Jacob, jt. auth. see Hall, R. Cargill.

Neufeld, James. Power to Rise: The Story of the National Ballet of Canada. (Illus.). 320p. 1996. text 45.00 (*0-8020-4109-4*) U of Toronto Pr.

Neufeld, Jamie, jt. ed. see Reid, Louann.

Neufeld, John. Almost a Hero. LC 94-12785. 160p. (J). (gr. 3-7). 1995. 15.00 (*0-689-31971-1*) Atheneum Yung Read.

Neufeld, John. Almost a Hero. (J). (gr. 3-7). 1996. mass mkt. 3.99 (*0-689-80740-6*) S&S Childrens.

Neufeld, John. Almost a Hero. 1996. 9.09 (*0-606-10738-X*, Pub. by Turtleback) Demco.

— Boys Lie. LC 98-34546. 176p. (YA). (gr. 7-12). 1999. text 16.95 (*0-7894-2624-2*, D K Ink) DK Pub Inc.

— Edgar Allan. LC 99-25968. 128p. (YA). (gr. 5-9). 1999. pap. 4.99 (*0-14-130432-4*, PuffinBks) Peng Put Young Read.

— Edgar Allan. LC 68-31175. (Illus.). (J). (gr. 5-8). 1968. 26.95 (*0-87599-149-1*) S G Phillips.

— Edgar Allan. (J). 1968. 10.09 (*0-606-03122-7*, Pub. by Turtleback) Demco.

— Lisa, Bright & Dark. LC 75-85002. (YA). (gr. 7-12). 1970. mass mkt. 4.99 (*0-451-16684-1*) NAL.

— Lisa, Bright & Dark. (YA). (gr. 7 up). 1969. 26.95 (*0-87599-153-X*) S G Phillips.

— Lisa Bright & Dark. 1987. 10.09 (*0-606-12396-2*, Pub. by Turtleback) Demco.

— Lisa, Bright & Dark: A Novel. LC 99-25551. (Illus.). 143p. (YA). (gr. 5-9). 1999. pap. 4.99 (*0-14-130434-0*, PuffinBks) Peng Put Young Read.

— A Small Civil War. 1996. pap. 3.99 (*0-689-80771-6*) S&S Bks Yung.

— A Small Civil War. 192p. (J). (gr. 5 up). 1996. 16.00 (*0-689-80770-8*) S&S Bks Yung.

Neufeld, John J., tr. Daut Niehe Tastament en Psalme. (GER.). 483p. 1996. reprint ed. pap. 18.95 (*0-919797-76-8*) Kindred Prods.

Neufeld, John L. Learning Business Statistics with Microsoft Excel 97. 2nd ed. LC 98-11985. 436p. (C). 1998. pap. text 36.00 (*0-13-923442-X*) P-H.

Neufeld, Jonathan, jt. auth. see Grimmett, Peter P.

Neufeld, Jonathan, tr. see Huberman, Michael, et al.

Neufeld, Judith B., ed. LILRC Handbook of Programs & Services. 1994. ring bd. 25.00 (*0-938435-34-5*) LI Lib Resources.

— Long Island Union List of Periodicals, 5 vols., Set. (Orig.). 1996. pap. write for info. (*0-938435-41-8*) LI Lib Resources.

— Long Island Union List of Periodicals, Vol. 1. (Orig.). 1996. pap. write for info. (*0-938435-42-6*) LI Lib Resources.

— Long Island Union List of Periodicals, Vol. 2. (Orig.). 1996. pap. write for info. (*0-938435-43-4*) LI Lib Resources.

— Long Island Union List of Periodicals, Vol. 3. (Orig.). 1996. pap. write for info. (*0-938435-44-2*) LI Lib Resources.

— Long Island Union List of Periodicals, Vol. 4. (Orig.). 1996. pap. write for info. (*0-938435-45-0*) LI Lib Resources.

— Long Island Union List of Periodicals, Vol. 5. (Orig.). 1996. pap. write for info. (*0-938435-46-9*) LI Lib Resources.

— Long Island Union List of Periodicals 1998. 1998. lib. bdg. 400.00 (*0-938435-47-7*) LI Lib Resources.

Neufeld, Karl H., ed. see Nyiri, Tamas.

Neufeld, Mark. The Restructuring of International Relations Theory. (Studies in International Relations: No. 43). 188p. (C). 1995. text 59.95 (*0-521-47394-2*); pap. text 18.95 (*0-521-47936-3*) Cambridge U Pr.

Neufeld, Michael, jt. ed. see Dobell, Rod.

Neufeld, Michael J. The Rocket & the Reich: Peenemunde & the Coming of the Ballistic Missile Era. 400p. 1996. pap. 15.95 (*0-674-77650-X*) HUP.

— The Skilled Metalworkers of Nuremberg: Craft & Class in the Industrial Revolution. LC 88-23875. (Class & Culture Ser.). 240p. (C). 1989. text 45.00 (*0-8135-1394-4*) Rutgers U Pr.

Neufeld, P. Elementary Aspects of Corrosion. (C). 1988. 180.00 (*0-901994-56-1*, Pub. by Fuel Metallurgical Jrnl) St Mut.

Neufeld, Ronald D., ed. Energy - Environmental Opportunities for Civil Engineers. 154p. 1988. 18.00 (*0-87262-655-5*) Am Soc Civil Eng.

Neufeld, Ronald D. & Goodwin, Richard W., eds. Emerging Energy - Environmental Trends & the Engineer. 59p. 1983. pap. 5.00 (*0-87262-380-7*) Am Soc Civil Eng.

Neufeld, W. P. The Liver Causes Heart Attacks. 159p. (Orig.). 1991. pap. 14.95 (*0-88925-816-3*) Gordon Soules Bk.

Neufeld, William. From Faith to Faith: The History of the Manitoba Mennonite Brethren Church. (Illus.). 260p. (Orig.). 1989. pap. 15.95 (*0-919797-92-X*) Kindred Prods.

Neufelder, Ann M. Ensuring Software Reliability. LC 92-25561. (Quality & Reliability Ser.: Vol. 38). (Illus.). 264p. 1992. text 85.00 (*0-8247-8762-5*) Dekker.

Neufeldt. Dictionary. 1992. mass mkt. 4.50 (*0-446-36489-4*, Pub. by Warner Bks) Little.

— New Webster's Dictionary. 1992. 4.50 (*0-446-77618-1*) Warner Bks.

***Neufeldt, Alfred & Albright, Alison.** Disability & Self-Directed Employment: Entrepreneurship & Cooperatives. LC 98-175324. 325p. 1998. pap. 19.95 (*0-88936-760-4*, Pub. by IDRC Bks) Stylus Pub VA.

Neufeldt-Fast, Arnold, tr. see Jungel, Eberhard.

Neufeldt, Harvey G. & McGee, Leo, eds. Education of the African American Adult: An Historical Overview, 134. LC 89-25925. (Contributions in Afro-American & African Studies: No. 134). 285p. 1990. 59.95 (*0-313-25972-0*, MGK/, Greenwood Pr) Greenwood.

Neufeldt, Harvey G., jt. compiled by see McGee, Leo.

N

An Asterisk (*) at the beginning of an entry indicates that the title is appearing for the first time.

Neufeldt, Leonard. The House of Emerson. LC 81-16208. 272p. reprint ed. pap. 84.40 (*0-7837-6174-0*, 20458960009) Bks Demand.

Neufeldt, Leonard N. & Simmons, Nancy C., eds. The Writings of Henry D. Thoreau Journal, 1851-1852, Vol. 4. (Illus.). 450p. 1992. text 65.00 (*0-691-06535-7*, Pub. by Princeton U Pr) Cal Prin Full Svc.

Neufeldt, Ronald. F. Max Muller & the Rg-Veda. 1980. 16.00 (*0-8364-0040-2*) S Asia.

Neufeldt, Ronald W. Religious Studies in Alberta: A State-of-the-Art Review. (Study of Religion in Canada Ser.: Vol. 1). 160p. (C). 1983. pap. 8.50 (*0-919812-18-X*) W Laurier U Pr.

Neufeldt, Ronald W., et al, eds. Readings in Eastern Religions. (C). 1988. pap. 24.95 (*0-88920-955-3*) W Laurier U Pr.

Neufeldt, Susan A. Supervision Strategies for the First Practicum. 2nd ed. LC 98-49915. 226p. 1999. 33.95 (*1-55620-218-0*) Am Coun Assn.

Neufeldt, Victor, ed. The Works of Patrick Branwell Bronte, 1834-1836, Vol. 2. 720p. 1998. 115.00 (*0-8153-0225-8*, SS1238) Garland.

Neufeldt, Victor A. The Poems of Patrick Branwell Bronte: A New Text & Commentary. LC 90-38464. 590p. 1990. text 25.00 (*0-8240-4590-4*, H1050) Garland.

Neufeldt, Victor A., ed. A Bibliography of the Manuscripts of Patrick Branwell Bronte. LC 93-8646. 184p. 1993. text 20.00 (*0-8153-1563-5*) Garland.

— The Works of Patrick Branwell Bronte: An Edition, Vol. 1. LC 97-11630. (Literature Reference Ser.). 496p. 1997. text 100.00 (*0-8153-0224-X*, SS1238) Garland.

***Neufeldt, Victor A., ed.** The Works of Patrick Branwell Bronte, 1834-1836, Vol. 3. LC 97-11630. (Reference Library of the Humanities). 531p. 1999. 95.00 (*0-8153-0226-6*, SS1238) Garland.

Neufeldt, Victoria & Guralnik, David B. Webster's New World College Dictionary, Thumb-Index. 3rd deluxe ed. LC 96-44362. (Illus.). 1616p. 1997. 27.95 (*0-02-861674-X*) Macmillan.

Neufeldt, Victoria, ed. see Webster's New World Dictionaries Editors.

Neufeldt, Victoria E. Webster's New World Dictionary. 1995. 10.09 (*0-606-08954-3*, Pub. by Turtleback) Demco.

Neufeldt, Victoria E. & Sparks, Andrew N., eds. Webster's New World Dictionary. 704p. 1995. per. 4.99 (*0-671-51982-4*) PB.

***Neufert, Ernst, et al.** Architects' Data. 3rd ed. LC 00-42905. (ENG.). 2000. write for info. (*0-632-05771-8*) Blackwell Sci.

Neuffer, Claude H. The Name Game: From Oyster Point to Keowee. LC 72-76383. (Illus.). 1979. 6.00 (*0-87844-009-7*) C H Neuffer.

— Names in South Carolina, 1954-65, Vols. I-XII. LC 76-29026. 1976. reprint ed. 25.00 (*0-87152-248-9*) C H Neuffer.

— Names in South Carolina, 1966-83, Vols. XIII-XXX. 1983. 5.00 (*0-686-18734-2*) C H Neuffer.

Neuffer, M. G., et al. Mutants of Maize. LC 96-44280. (Illus.). 468p. (C). 1997. 150.00 (*0-87969-443-2*); pap. 60.00 (*0-87969-444-0*) Cold Spring Harbor.

Neuffer, Mark, jt. auth. see Amigo, Eleanor.

Neuffler, Janice, jt. ed. see Worthy, Luke.

Neufield, Michael J. The Rocket & the Reich: Peenemunde & the Coming of the Ballistic Missile Era. (Illus.). 350p. 1994. 25.00 (*0-02-922895-6*) Free Pr.

Neufville, Judith I. De, see De Neufville, Judith I., ed.

Neugaard, Edward, ed. Motif-Index of Medieval Catalan Folktales. LC 92-16905. (Medieval & Renaissance Texts & Studies: Vol. 96). 160p. 1993. 22.00 (*0-86698-110-1*, MR96) MRTS.

Neugaard, Edward, tr. from SPA. Anthology of Catalan Folktales. LC 94-16323. (Catalan Studies: Vol. 16). 168p. (C). 1995. text 44.95 (*0-8204-2530-3*) P Lang Pubng.

***Neugart, Michael.** Nonlinear Labor Market Dynamics. LC 00-26593. (Lecture Notes in Economics & Mathematical Systems Ser.: Vol. 486). (Illus.). x, 175p. 2000. pap. 53.00 (*3-540-67279-6*) Spr-Verlag.

Neugart, R. & Wohr, A. Nuclei Far from Stability & Atomic Masses & Fundamental Constants, 1992: The Proceedings of the 6th International Conference on Nuclei Far from Stability & the 9th International Conference on Atomic Masses & Fundamental Constants Held in Mainz, Germany, 19-24 July 1992. (Institute of Physics Conference Ser.: No. 132). 1040p. 1993. 373.00 (*0-7503-0262-3*) IOP Pub.

Neugarten, Bernice L. The Meanings of Age: Selected Papers. Neugarten, Dail A., ed. & frwd. by. LC 96-14865. (Illus.). 440p. 1996. pap. text 24.95 (*0-226-57384-2*); lib. bdg. 68.00 (*0-226-57383-4*) U Ch Pr.

Neugarten, Bernice L., ed. Age or Need? Public Policies for Older People. LC 82-16726. (Sage Focus Editions Ser.: No. 59). 288p. 1982. reprint ed. pap. 89.30 (*0-608-01085-5*, 205939400001) Bks Demand.

— Middle Age & Aging: A Reader in Social Psychology. LC 68-55150. 610p. 1968. pap. text 24.00 (*0-226-57382-6*) U Ch Pr.

Neugarten, Bernice L., et al. Personality in Middle Life & Late Life: Empirical Studies. Stein, Leon, ed. LC 79-8677. (Growing Old Ser.). (Illus.). 1980. reprint ed. lib. bdg. 25.95 (*0-405-12794-4*) Ayer.

Neugarten, Bernice L., jt. auth. see Coleman, Richard P.

Neugarten, Dail A., ed. & frwd. see Neugarten, Bernice L.

Neugebauer, A., ed. Macromolecular Interplay in Brain Associative Mechanisms. LC 98-214620. 350p. 1997. text 78.00 (*981-02-3212-8*) World Scientific Pub.

Neugebauer, Bonnie, ed. Alike & Different: Exploring Our Humanity with Young Children. rev. ed. LC 92-61315. (Illus.). 186p. 1992. reprint ed. pap. 8.00 (*0-935989-52-8*, 240) Natl Assn Child Ed.

— The Anti-Ordinary Thinkbook: A Stimulating Tool for Staff Training & Team-Building in Early Childhood Programs. (Illus.). 24p. (Orig.). (C). 1991. pap. 10.00 (*0-942702-08-5*) Child Care.

— The Wonder of It: Exploring How the World Works. rev. ed. (Illus.). 88p. (Orig.). (C). 1996. pap. 16.00 (*0-942702-05-0*) Child Care.

Neugebauer, Bonnie, jt. ed. see Neugebauer, Roger.

Neugebauer, Bonnie, jt. ed. see Wolf, Dennie P.

Neugebauer, C. A., et al. The Packaging of Power Semiconductor Devices. (Electrocomponent Science Monographs: Vol. 7). viii, 86p. 1986. text 75.00 (*2-88124-135-2*) Gordon & Breach.

Neugebauer, C. A., ed. see International Conference on Structure & Properties.

***Neugebauer, Charise.** The Real Winner. LC 99-57863. (Illus.). 32p. (J). (gr. k-3). 2000. 15.95 (*0-7358-1252-7*, Pub. by North-South Bks NYC) Chronicle Bks.

— Santa's Gift. LC 99-17372. (Illus.). 32p. (J). (ps-3). 1999. lib. bdg. 15.88 (*0-7358-1146-6*, Pub. by North-South Bks NYC) Chronicle Bks.

***Neugebauer, Charise.** Santa's Gift. LC 99-17372. (Illus.). 32p. (J). (ps-3). 1999. 15.95 (*0-7358-1145-8*, Pub. by North-South Bks NYC) Chronicle Bks.

Neugebauer, Dunn. Alumni Hall, Room 34. vi, 263p. (Orig.). 1997. pap. 11.95 (*0-9658729-0-4*) Patek Pr.

Neugebauer, Edmund A. Handbook of Mediators in Septic Shock. 608p. 1993. lib. bdg. 220.00 (*0-8493-3548-5*, RC182) CRC Pr.

Neugebauer, Gerry, jt. auth. see Goodstein, David.

Neugebauer, H. J., ed. see Muller, D.

Neugebauer, Horst, jt. auth. see Hergarten, Stefan.

Neugebauer, Janet M., ed. All That Matters: The Texas Plains in Photographs & Poems. LC 92-16575. 144p. 1992. 22.50 (*0-89672-291-0*) Tex Tech Univ Pr.

— Lambshead Legacy: The Ranch Diary of Watt R. Matthews. LC 96-41415. (Centennial Series of the Association of Former Students: Vol. 66). (Illus.). 304p. (C). 1997. text 24.95 (*0-89096-738-5*) Tex A&M Univ Pr.

Neugebauer, O. Astronomy & History: Selected Essays. (Illus.). 538p. 1983. 70.95 (*0-387-90844-7*) Spr-Verlag.

Neugebauer, O. & Parker, R. A. Egyptian Astronomical Texts: Decans, Planets, Constellations & Zodiacs, Vol. 3. LC 60-15723. (Brown Egyptological Studies: No. 6). (Illus.). 148p. 1969. reprint ed. pap. text 45.90 (*0-8357-9045-2*, 201229200081) Bks Demand.

Neugebauer, O. & Parker, R. A. Egyptian Astronomical Texts: Decans, Planets, Constellations & Zodiacs Including Plates, Vol. 3. LC 60-15723. (Brown Egyptological Studies: No. 6). (Illus.). 283p. reprint ed. pap. 87.80 (*0-608-16104-7*, 201229200082) Bks Demand.

Neugebauer, O. & Sachs, A. Mathematical Cuneiform Texts. (American Oriental Ser.: Vol. 29). x, 177p. 1945. 32.00 (*0-940490-29-3*) Am Orient Soc.

Neugebauer, O., jt. auth. see Swerdlow, N. M.

Neugebauer, Otto. The Exact Sciences in Antiquity. 2nd ed. LC 69-20421. (Illus.). 240p. 1969. reprint ed. pap. 7.95 (*0-486-22332-9*) Dover.

Neugebauer, Otto & Van Hoesen, H. B. Greek Horoscopes. LC 59-11559. (Memoirs Ser.: 48). 1959. 20.00 (*0-87169-048-9*, M048-neo) Am Philos.

Neugebauer, Peter. Sherlock Holmes: The Truth about Ludwig II. Rutter, Richard R., tr. from GER. (GER.). 232p. 1995. text 24.00 (*1-896032-42-7*) Battered Silicon.

Neugebauer, Philip. The Cabin. (Illus.). 190p. (Orig.). (C). 1996. pap. 15.00 (*1-57502-297-4*, P1013) Morris Pubng.

Neugebauer, Phillip D. That & This. (Illus.). 228p. (Orig.). 1997. pap. 15.00 (*1-57502-494-2*, P01466) Morris Pubng.

Neugebauer, Richard. Certuv Kamen. (CZE., Illus.). 110p. 1983. reprint ed. pap. 10.00 (*0-86516-024-4*) Bolchazy-Carducci.

Neugebauer, Richard & Sebesta, Judith L. Certuv Kamen. (Illus.). 110p. 1983. 17.00 (*0-86516-049-X*) Bolchazy-Carducci.

Neugebauer, Roger, ed. Developing Staff Skills. (Best of Exchange Ser.). (Illus.). 48p. (Orig.). (C). 1990. pap. 10.00 (*0-942702-07-7*) Child Care.

— Fostering Improved Staff Performance. (Best of Exchange Ser.). 48p. (Orig.). (C). 1991. pap. 10.00 (*0-942702-10-7*) Child Care.

— Inside Child Care: Trend Report. 96p. 1997. pap. 75.00 (*0-942702-22-0*) Child Care.

— On Being a Leader. (Best of Exchange Ser.). (Illus.). 48p. (Orig.). (C). 1990. pap. 10.00 (*0-942702-06-9*) Child Care.

— On-Target Marketing: Promotion Strategies for Child Care Centers. (Best of Exchange Ser.). 48p. (Orig.). 1996. pap. 10.00 (*0-942702-18-2*) Child Care.

— Parent Relations: Building an Active Partnership. (Best of Exchange Ser.). 48p. (Orig.). (C). 1994. pap. 10.00 (*0-942702-13-1*) Child Care.

— Survival Skills for Center Directors. (Best of Exchange Ser.). 48p. (Orig.). (C). 1994. pap. 10.00 (*0-942702-11-5*) Child Care.

— Taking Stock: Tools for Teacher, Director, & Center Evaluation. (Best of Exchange Ser.). 48p. (Orig.). (C). 1994. pap. 10.00 (*0-942702-12-3*) Child Care.

— 250 Management Success Stories: From Child Care Center Directors. 48p. (Orig.). 1995. pap. 10.00 (*0-942702-16-6*) Child Care.

Neugebauer, Roger & Neugebauer, Bonnie, eds. The Art of Leadership: Managing Early Childhood Organizations. 350p. 1998. pap. 63.00 (*0-942702-24-7*) Child Care.

— Does Your Team Work? Ideas for Bringing Your Staff Together. (Illus.). 48p. 1997. pap. 10.00 (*0-942702-20-4*) Child Care.

— Managing Money: A Center Director's Guidebook. (Illus.). 160p. 1997. pap. 20.00 (*0-942702-21-2*) Child Care.

— Top 20 Classics: The Best of Exchange from the First 20 Years. 80p. 1998. pap. 16.00 (*0-942702-23-9*) Child Care.

Neugebauer, Wolfgang, ed. Schule & Absolutismus in Preussen: Akten zum Preussischen Elementarschulwesen Bis 1806. (Veroeffentlichungen der Historischen Kommission zu Berlin, Band 67, Beitraege zu Inflation und Wiederaufbau in Deutschland und Europa 1914-1924: Vol. 33). vii, 814p. (C). 1992. lib. bdg. 195.40 (*3-11-012304-5*) De Gruyter.

Neugeboren, Bernard. Environmental Practice in the Human Services: Integration of Micro & Macro Roles, Skills, & Contexts. LC 95-25071. 384p. 1996. 49.95 (*1-56024-944-7*); pap. 22.95 (*0-7890-6025-6*) Haworth Pr.

— Organization, Policy & Practice in the Human Services. 319p. 1991. pap. 19.95 (*1-56024-159-4*) Haworth Pr.

***Neugeboren, Jay.** Big Man: A Novel. 224p. 2001. pap. 13.00 (*0-618-07922-X*, Mariner Bks) HM.

Neugeboren, Jay. Don't Worry about the Kids: Stories. LC 97-14706. 208p. 1997. 24.95 (*1-55849-113-9*) U of Mass Pr.

— Imagining Robert: My Brother, Madness & Survival: A Memoir. LC 97-46786. 304p. 1998. pap. 14.95 (*0-8050-5730-7*, Owl) H Holt & Co.

— Poli - A Mexican Boy in Early Texas. LC 88-64094. (Multicultural Texas Ser.). (Illus.). 120p. (YA). (gr. 7 up). 1992. pap. 7.95 (*0-931722-74-8*) Corona Pub.

— The Stolen Jew. LC 98-19554. (Library of Modern Jewish Literature). 1998. pap. 21.95 (*0-8156-0536-6*) Syracuse U Pr.

— Transforming Madness: New Lives for People Living with Mental Illness. LC 98-50056. 400p. 1999. 25.00 (*0-688-15655-X*, Wm Morrow) Morrow Avon.

Neuger, Christie C., ed. The Arts of Ministry: Feminist-Womanist Approaches. LC 95-46683. 204p. (Orig.). 1996. pap. 24.95 (*0-664-25593-0*) Westminster John Knox.

Neuger, Christie C. & Poling, James N., eds. The Care of Men. LC 96-43401. 256p. 1997. pap. 18.95 (*0-687-01451-4*) Abingdon.

***Neugroschel, Joachim.** Anskys World War 1 Diaries & Reports. 1999. text 35.00 (*0-8050-5944-X*) St Martin.

— Anskys Worldwar 1Reports & Diaries. 1999. pap. write for info. (*0-8050-5945-8*) St Martin.

Neugroschel, Joachim. Great Works of Jewish Fantasy: Yenne Velt. LC 77-373797. 713 p. 1976. 7.50 (*0-304-29767-4*) Continuum.

Neugroschel, Joachim, ed. The Shtetl: A Creative Anthology of Jewish Life in Eastern Europe. 584p. 1989. 25.00 (*0-87951-356-X*, Pub. by Overlook Pr) Penguin Putnam.

— The Shtetl: A Creative Anthology of Jewish Life in Eastern Europe. 584p. 1990. pap. 15.95 (*0-87951-380-2*, Pub. by Overlook Pr) Penguin Putnam.

Neugroschel, Joachim, tr. Great Tales of Jewish Fantasy. LC 85-900. (Illus.). 710p. 1987. 27.95 (*0-87951-229-6*, Pub. by Overlook Pr) Penguin Putnam.

— Great Works of Jewish Fantasy. LC 85-900. (Illus.). 710p. 1987. pap. 15.95 (*0-87951-242-3*, Pub. by Overlook Pr) Penguin Putnam.

Neugroschel, Joachim & Zucker, Barbara. Barbara Zucker: For Beauty's Sake. Longhauser, Elsa, ed. (Illus.). 8p. 1996. pap. 10.00 (*1-58442-046-4*) Galleries at Moore.

Neugroschel, Joachim, jt. tr. see Ansky, S.

Neugroschel, Joachim, tr. see Arp, J. Hans.

Neugroschel, Joachim, tr. see Barbieri, Renzo.

Neugroschel, Joachim, tr. see Bataille, Georges.

Neugroschel, Joachim, tr. see Cirillo, Stefano & DiBlasio, Paola.

Neugroschel, Joachim, tr. see Ellul, Jacques.

Neugroschel, Joachim, tr. see Hartling, Peter.

Neugroschel, Joachim, tr. see Hervier, Julien.

Neugroschel, Joachim, tr. see Hesse, Hermann.

Neugroschel, Joachim, tr. see Junger, Ernst.

Neugroschel, Joachim, tr. see Kafka, Franz.

Neugroschel, Joachim, tr. see Kolbowski, Silvia, et al.

Neugroschel, Joachim, tr. see Landolfi, Tommaso.

Neugroschel, Joachim, tr. see Lernet-Holenia, Alexander.

Neugroschel, Joachim, tr. see Levi-Strauss, Claude.

Neugroschel, Joachim, tr. see Nossack, Hans E.

Neugroschel, Joachim, tr. see Roth, Joseph.

Neugroschel, Joachim, tr. see Seel, Pierre.

Neugroschel, Joachim, tr. see Sergeant, Philippe.

Neugroschel, Joachim, tr. see Vogt, Paul, et al.

Neugroschel, Joachim, tr. see Von Sacher-Masoch, Leopold.

Neugroschel, Joachim, tr. see Weiss, Peter.

Neugrostel, Joachim, ed. Great Tales of Jewish Fantasy & the Occult: The Dybbuk & 30 Other Classic Stories. LC 85-9000. 720p. 1997. reprint ed. pap. 22.95 (*0-87951-782-4*, Pub. by Overlook Pr) Penguin Putnam.

Neugut, Alfred I., et al. Multiple Primary Cancers in Connecticut & Denmark. LC 98-52750. 484p. 1999. write for info. (*0-683-30124-1*) Lppncott W & W.

Neuhart, John, et al. Eames Design: The Work of the Office of Charles & Ray Eames 1941-1978. (Illus.). 464p. 1989. 95.00 (*0-8109-0879-4*, Pub. by Abrams) Time Warner.

Neuhart, John, jt. auth. see Neuhart, Marilyn.

Neuhart, Marilyn & Neuhart, John. Eames House. (Illus.). 64p. 1994. 19.95 (*1-85490-905-3*) Academy Ed UK.

Neuharth, Allen H. Buscapade: Plain Talk Across the U. S. A. 1987. 16.95 (*0-944347-00-2*) USA Today Bks.

— Window on the World: Faces, Places & Plain Talk from 32 Countries. LC 88-30708. (Illus.). 256p. 1988. write for info. (*0-944347-16-9*) USA Today Bks.

Neuharth, Allen H., et al. Profiles of Power: How the Governors Run Our 50 States. (Illus.). 1988. 9.95 (*0-944347-14-2*) USA Today Bks.

***Neuharth, Dan.** If You Had Controlling Parents: How to Make Peace with Your Past & Take Your Place in the World. 245p. 2000. 25.00 (*0-7881-9383-X*) DIANE Pub.

— If You Had Controlling Parents: How to Make Peace with Your Past & Take Your Place in the World. LC 98-8650. 272p. 1999. pap. 14.00 (*0-06-092932-4*) HarpC.

Neuharth, Dan. If You Had Controlling Parents: How to Make Peace with Your Past & Take Your Place in the World. LC 98-8650. 272p. 1998. 25.00 (*0-06-019191-0*, Cliff Street) HarperTrade.

***Neuharth, Dan.** If You Had Controlling Parents: Neuharth,&Dan, Set. 1998. audio 18.00 (*0-694-52022-5*, CPN2779) HarperAudio.

Neuhaus, D. & Williamson, M. P. The Nuclear Overhauser Effect in Structural & Conformational Analysis. (Methods in Stereochemical Analysis Ser.). 522p. 1992. pap. 89.95 (*0-471-18851-4*, Wiley-VCH) Wiley.

Neuhaus, David & Williamson, Michael. The Nuclear Overhauser Effect in Stereochemical & Conformational Analysis. LC 88-33963. 522p. 1989. lib. bdg. 110.00 (*1-56081-616-3*, Wiley-VCH) Wiley.

— The Nuclear Overhauser Effect in Stereochemical & Conformational Analysis. LC 88-33963. 522p. 1989. 170.00 (*0-471-18684-8*, Wiley-VCH) Wiley.

***Neuhaus, David & Williamson, Michael P.** The Nuclear Overhauser Effect in Structural & Conformational Analysis. 2nd ed. LC 99-49630. 640p. 2000. 125.00 (*0-471-24675-1*) Wiley.

Neuhaus, Edmund C. & Astwood, William. Practicing Psychotherapy: Basic Techniques & Practical Issues. LC 79-25464. 208p. 1980. 35.95 (*0-87705-467-3*, Kluwer Acad Hman Sci); pap. 22.95 (*0-89885-230-7*, Kluwer Acad Hman Sci) Kluwer Academic.

Neuhaus, Eugen. Drawn from Memory: A Self-Portrait. LC 64-23486. (Illus.). 208p. 1964. 21.95 (*0-87015-129-0*) Pacific Bks.

— The History & Ideals of American Art. LC 31-15082. 462p. reprint ed. pap. 143.30 (*0-608-11067-1*, 205085900061) Bks Demand.

Neuhaus, Eugen, tr. see Doerner, Max.

Neuhaus, H. Joachim. A Phonetic Concordance to Daniel Jones: Phonetic Readings in English. (Alpha-Omega, Series C: Vol. 6). 174p. 1973. pap. write for info. (*3-487-10052-5*) G Olms Pubs.

— Shakespeare's Word-Formations. (GER.). 600p. 1999. write for info. (*3-487-09994-2*); write for info. (*3-487-09995-0*) G Olms Pubs.

Neuhaus, Heike. Plastidaere Mosaikgene: Struktur und Funktion Des Chloroplasten-Gens Fuer die tRNALys Aus Sinapis Alba L. 1988. (Dissertationes Botanicae Ser.: Band 115). (GER., Illus.). v, 100p. 1988. pap. 36.00 (*3-443-64027-3*, Pub. by Gebruder Borntraeger) Balogh.

Neuhaus, Heinrich. The Art of Piano Playing. Leibovitch, K. A., tr. from RUS. LC 89-2585. 240p. 1995. pap. 22.50 (*0-89341-756-4*, Longwood Academic) Hollowbrook.

Neuhaus, John W. Toward a Biocritical Sociology. LC 95-44341. X, 210p. (C). 1996. pap. text 29.95 (*0-8204-3081-1*) P Lang Pubng.

Neuhaus, Joseph E., jt. auth. see Holtzmann, Howard M.

Neuhaus, Richard J. America Against Itself: Moral Vision & the Public Order. LC 91-51112. (C). 1992. text 23.00 (*0-268-00633-4*) U of Notre Dame Pr.

— The Best of the Public Square: Selections from Richard John Neuhaus' Celebrated Column in "First Things" LC 97-74385. 160p. 1997. pap. write for info. (*0-9659507-0-0*) Inst on Religion.

Neuhaus, Richard J. Death on a Friday Afternoon: Meditations on the Seven Last Words of Christ. pap. 14.00 (*0-465-04933-8*, Pub. by Basic) HarpC.

— Death on a Friday Afternoon: Meditations on the Seven Last Words of Christ. LC 99-50283. 288p. 2000. 24.00 (*0-465-04932-X*, Pub. by Basic) HarpC.

Neuhaus, Richard J. Dispensations: The Future of South Africa as South Africans See It. LC 86-2150. 333p. reprint ed. pap. 103.30 (*0-8357-8562-9*, 203492200091) Bks Demand.

— The End of Democracy? The Celebrated First Things Debate with Arguments Pro & Con. LC 97-22959. 1997. 22.95 (*1-890626-03-1*); pap. 11.95 (*1-890626-04-X*) Spence Pub.

— The Naked Public Square: Religion & Democracy in America. 292p. 1988. reprint ed. pap. 20.00 (*0-8028-0080-7*) Eerdmans.

Neuhaus, Richard J., ed. The Eternal Pity: Reflections on Dying. (Ethics of Everyday Life Ser.). 124p. 2000. 15.00 (*0-268-02756-0*, Pub. by U of Notre Dame Pr); pap. 15.00 (*0-268-02757-9*, Pub. by U of Notre Dame Pr) Chicago Distribution Ctr.

Neuhaus, Richard J. & Colson, Charles. Evangelicals & Catholics Together: Working Toward a Common Mission. 224p. pap. 15.99 (*0-8499-3860-0*) Word Pub.

Neuhaus, Richard J. & Cromartie, Michael, eds. Piety & Politics: Evangelicals & Fundamentalists Confront the World. LC 87-19942. 434p. (Orig.). (C). 1988. pap. text 12.95 (*0-89633-108-3*) Ethics & Public Policy.

Neuhaus, Richard J. & Weigel, George, eds. Being Christian Today: An American Conversation. 310p. (C). 1992. 24.95 (*0-89633-164-4*) Ethics & Public Policy.

Neuhaus, Richard J., jt. auth. see Berger, Peter L.

Neuhaus, Richard J., jt. auth. see Klenicki, Leon.

Neuhaus, Ruby H. Long Term Care Administration: Teamwork & Effective Management. 200p. (Orig.). (C). 1990. pap. text 23.50 (*0-8191-7861-6*); lib. bdg. 45.00 (*0-8191-7860-8*) U Pr of Amer.

Neuhaus, Ruby H. & Aaronson, William N. Core Technology for Long-Term Care: Team Delivery. (Learning the Continuum). (Illus.). 84p. (Orig.). (C). 1989. pap. text 20.00 (*0-910591-19-9*) AUPHA Pr.

N

An Asterisk (*) at the beginning of an entry indicates that the title is appearing for the first time.

Neuhaus, Thomas & O'Connor, Therese. Culinary Theory & Practice. 318p. (C). 1995. text 43.00 (*0-536-58693-4*) Pearson Custom.

Neuhaus, Tom. The Informed Chef. 1998. reprint ed. pap. text 54.95 (*0-9665117-1-9*) Neuhaus Features.

Neuhaus, Volker, ed. see Jacobs, Dietmar.

Neuhaus, W., tr. see Gerber, H. U.

Neuhausel, Patricia A., jt. auth. see Mansmann, Patricia A.

Neuhauser, Charles. Third World Politics: China & the Afro-Asian People's Solidarity Organization, 1957-1967. LC 76-2492. (East Asian Monographs: No. 27). 107p. 1968. pap. 20.00 (*0-674-88455-8*) HUP.

***Neuhauser, Claudia.** Calculus for Biological & Medical Sciences. LC 99-52144. 766p. 1999. 96.00 (*0-13-085137-X*) P-H.

Neuhauser, Duncan. Coming of Age. 2nd ed. LC 93-81268. 361p. 1995. 25.00 (*1-56793-009-3*, 0519) Health Admin Pr.

Neuhauser, Duncan, jt. auth. see Kovner, Anthony R.

Neuhauser, Duncan, jt. ed. see Crichton, Anne.

Neuhauser, E. F., jt. ed. see Edwards, C. A.

Neuhauser, Peg C. Tribal Warfare in Organizations. 240p. 1989. 24.95 (*0-88730-355-2*, HarpBusn) HarpInfo.

***Neuhauser, Peg C., et al.** Culture.Com: Building Corporate Culture in the Connected Workplace. 288p. 2000. 27.95 (*0-471-64539-7*) Wiley.

Neuhausl, R., et al, eds. Chorological Phenomena in Plant Communities. (Advances in Vegetation Science Ser.). 1985. text 274.00 (*90-6193-515-6*) Kluwer Academic.

Neuhausl, R., jt. ed. see Bohn, U.

Neuhausler, Johann. Dachau. (Holocaust Ser.). 1991. lib. bdg. 62.95 (*0-8490-4465-0*) Gordon Pr.

***Neuhofer, M. Dorothy.** In the Benedictine Tradition: The Origins & Early Development of Two College Libraries. 264p. 1999. 48.00 (*0-7618-1463-9*) U Pr of Amer.

Neuhoff, V. & Friend, J., eds. Cell to Cell Signals in Plants & Animals Progress Report. (NATO ASI Series H: Cell Biology: Vol. 51). (Illus.). 386p. 1991. 152.95 (*0-387-53739-2*) Spr-Verlag.

***Neuhold, Andreas & Patscheider, Herwig.** Universitare Weiterbildung In Osterreich. (GER.). 206p. 1999. 38.00 (*3-631-34355-8*) P Lang Pubng.

Neuhold, Erich J. & Paul, M., eds. Formal Description of Programming Concepts. (IFIP State-of-the-Art Reports). (Illus.). ix, 507p. 1991. 78.95 (*0-387-53961-1*) Spr-Verlag.

Neuhold, Erich J., jt. auth. see Furtado, A. L.

Neuhold, R. Trilingual Dictionary of Telecommunications Technology, English-German-French. 3rd ed. (ENG, FRE & GER.). 610p. 1997. 250.00 (*0-7859-9517-X*) Fr & Eur.

Neuhold, Roberty J., jt. auth. see Ott, Karl Otto.

Neuhouser, David L., ed. see MacDonald, George.

***Neuhouser, Frederick.** Foundations of Hegel's Social Theory: Actualizing Freedom. 2000. text 49.95 (*0-674-00152-4*) HUP.

Neuhouser, Frederick, ed. see Fichte, Johann Gottlieb.

Neuhuber, W. L., jt. ed. see Zenker, W.

Neuhuis, Jacob E., jt. auth. see Goldman, Norman.

***Neuilly, Michele.** Modelling & Estimation of Measurement Errors. Pike, Derek J., tr. from FRE. (Illus.). 704p. 1999. 198.00 (*1-898298-59-9*, Pub. by Intercept UK) Spr-Verlag.

Neuitt, Jennifer, et al. How to Excel in Leasing Apartments. (Illus.). 325p. (Orig.). 1995. pap. 29.95 (*0-9645538-0-5*) NCMHI.

Neujahr, Philip J. Kant's Idealism. LC 95-23145. 1995. 16.00 (*0-86554-476-X*, MUP-P122) Mercer Univ Pr.

Neukirch, J. Algebraic Number Theory. Chern, S. S. et al, eds. Schappacher, N., tr. from GER. LC 99-21030. (Illus.). xv, 565p. 1999. 99.00 (*3-540-65399-6*) Spr-Verlag.

— Class Field Theory. LC 85-14846. (Grundlehren der Mathematischen Wissenschaften Ser.: Vol. 280). 155p. 1986. 94.95 (*0-387-15251-2*) Spr-Verlag.

***Neukirch, J., et al.** Cohomology of Number Fields. LC 99-56700. (Grundlehren der Mathematischen Wissenschaften Ser.: Bd. 323). 600p. 2000. 109.00 (*3-540-66671-0*) Spr-Verlag.

Neukom, Marius. Franz Kafkas Tagebucheintrag 'Verlockung Im Dorf' Eine Erzahlanalytische Untersuchung Mit Dem Verfahren Jakob. Boothe, Brigitte & Volkart, Reto, eds. (Psychoanalyse in Dialog Ser.: Bd. 5). 238p. 1997. 39.95 (*3-906757-07-2*, Pub. by P Lang) P Lang Pubng.

Neukomm, P. A., ed. see Biotelemetry International Symposium Staff.

Neukrantz, Klaus. Barricades in Berlin. LC 78-68131. 1978. pap. 2.95 (*0-916650-07-3*) Banner Pr Intl.

Neukrug. Theory, Practice & Trends in Human Services. 2nd ed. LC 99-31828. (Counseling Ser.). 1999. pap. text 58.95 (*0-534-35726-1*) Brooks-Cole.

— World of the Counselor. (Counseling Ser.). 1998. pap., wbk. ed. 27.95 (*0-534-35586-2*) Brooks-Cole.

Neukrug, Ed. Theory, Practice, & Trends in Human Services: An Overview of an Emerging Profession. LC 93-20941. 350p. 1993. mass mkt. 46.25 (*0-534-22278-1*) Brooks-Cole.

— The World of the Counselor: An Introduction to the Counseling Profession. LC 98-15140. 1998. pap. 71.95 (*0-534-35828-4*) Brooks-Cole.

Neukrug, Edward S. Theory, Practice, & Trends in Human Services: An Overview of an Emerging Profession. 1994. pap., teacher ed. write for info. (*0-534-22279-X*) Brooks-Cole.

Neuleib & Scharton. Things Your Grammar Never Told You. 184p. 1998. spiral bd. 17.00 (*0-205-16269-X*) Allyn.

***Neulen, Hans Werner.** In the Skies of Europe. (Illus.). 392p. 2000. 44.95 (*1-86126-326-0*, 130655AE, Pub. by Crolwood) Motorbooks Intl.

Neulen, Leon N. Problem Solving in Arithmetic. LC 70-177116. (Columbia University. Teachers College. Contributions to Education Ser.: No. 483). (C). reprint ed. 37.50 (*0-404-55483-0*) AMS Pr.

Neulen, Lester N. State Aid for Educational Projects in the Public Schools. LC 73-177117. (Columbia University. Teachers College. Contributions to Education Ser.: No. 308). reprint ed. 37.50 (*0-404-55308-7*) AMS Pr.

Neuliep, James W. Human Communication Theory: Applications & Case Studies. (C). 1996. pap. text, teacher ed. write for info. (*0-205-26357-7*, T6357-2) Allyn.

Neuliep, James W., ed. Replication Research in the Social Sciences. 530p. 1991. 55.00 (*0-8039-4091-2*); pap. 25.95 (*0-8039-4092-0*) Sage.

Neuling, Donna. Down Separate Paths Together. (Illus.). 224p. 1998. mass mkt. 8.99 (*1-891635-09-3*) Moore Bks.

Neuls-Bates, Carol, ed. Women in Music: An Anthology of Source Readings from the Middle Ages to the Present. 2nd ed. LC 95-17460. 400p. 1995. pap. text 17.95 (*1-55553-240-3*) NE U Pr.

Neuls-Bates, Carol, jt. ed. see Block, Adrienne F.

Neumaier, A. Introduction to Numerical Analysis. (Illus.). 300p. (C). 1999. text 44.95 (*0-521-33323-7*) Cambridge U Pr.

Neumaier-Dargyay, E. K. The Sovereign All-Creating Mind-The Motherly Buddha: A Translation of the Kun Byed Rgyal Po'i Mdo. LC 91-2500. (SUNY Series in Buddhist Studies). 246p. (C). 1992. text 19.50 (*0-7914-0895-7*) State U NY Pr.

Neumaier-Dargyay, Eva K., jt. ed. see Joy, Morny.

Neumaier, Diane, ed. Reframings: New American Feminist Photographies. LC 94-46914. (Illus.). 304p. 1996. 49.95 (*1-56639-331-0*) Temple U Pr.

— Reframings: New American Feminist Photographies. LC 94-46914. (Illus.). 336p. (C). 1998. pap. 24.95 (*1-56639-332-9*) Temple U Pr.

Neumaier, Diane & Tannenbaum, Judith. Boris Mihailov. (Illus.). 36p. 1995. pap. 12.00 (*0-88454-082-0*) U of Pa Contemp Art.

Neumaier, Diane, jt. ed. see Kahn, Douglas.

Neumaier, J. J., ed. see Durrenmatt, Friedrich.

Neumaier, Joe, ed. see Stern, Bret.

Neumaier, Robert, ed. Hermetic Pumps: The Ecological Solution, Centrifugal Pumps & Rotary Displacement Pumps. LC 97-11477. 620p. 1997. 125.00 (*0-88415-801-2*, 5801) Gulf Pub.

Neuman, Alma. Always Straight Ahead: A Memoir. LC 92-20844. viii, 176p. (C). 1993. 24.95 (*0-8071-1792-7*) La State U Pr.

Neuman, Andrew, jt. auth. see Kaufman, Elizabeth.

Neuman, Betty M., ed. The Neuman Systems Model. 3rd ed. LC 94-30479. (C). 1994. pap. text 45.00 (*0-8385-6701-0*, A6701-5) Appleton & Lange.

Neuman, Betty M., jt. auth. see Walker, Patricia H.

Neuman, Brunon. Polish-French Medical Dictionary: Dictionnaire Medical Polonais-Francais. 2nd ed. 1984. 50.00 (*0-8288-1854-1*, M15407) Fr & Eur.

Neuman, Colleen. The Princess Plays. 96p. (YA). 1996. pap. 5.00 (*0-87440-030-9*) Bakers Plays.

— Riverview, Tape 23. 1993. pap. 3.50 (*0-87129-286-6*, R53) Dramatic Pub.

Neuman, Dagmar. The Origin of Arithmetic Skills: A Phenomenographic Approach. (Goteborg Studies in Educational Sciences: No. 62). 352p. 1987. pap. 59.50 (*91-7346-194-6*, Pub. by Acta U Gothenburg) Coronet Bks.

Neuman, Daniel M. The Life of Music in North India: The Organization of an Artistic Tradition. LC 89-20604. (Illus.). 302p. 1990. reprint ed. pap. text 25.00 (*0-226-57516-0*) U Ch Pr.

Neuman de Veguar, C., jt. auth. see Farrell, R. T.

Neuman, Donald B. Experiences in Science for Young Children. LC 76-53185. (C). 1978. teacher ed. 10.00 (*0-8273-1643-7*) Delmar.

— Experiences in Science for Young Children. (Illus.). 176p. (C). 1992. reprint ed. pap. text 16.50 (*0-88133-682-3*) Waveland Pr.

— Experiencing Elementary Science. 434p. (C). 1993. 48.50 (*0-534-18822-2*) Wadsworth Pub.

Neuman, Ewald & Neumann, Ewald. TOEFL Vocabulary Builder. unabridged rev. ed. (Vocabulary Builder Ser.). 80p. (C). (gr. 11 up). 1994. pap., pap. text 24.95 incl. audio (*0-9625001-4-3*) Spargo Comns.

Neuman, Frantisek. Global Properties of Linear Ordinary Differential Equations. (C). 1992. text 199.50 (*0-7923-1269-4*) Kluwer Academic.

***Neuman, Fred G.** The Story of Paducah. 3rd rev. ed. (Illus.). 280p. 2000. 21.95 (*0-615-11775-9*) M D Jones.

Neuman, Gerald L. Strangers to the Constitution: Immigrants, Borders, & Fundamental Law. LC 95-39587. 296p. (C). 1996. text 39.50 (*0-691-04360-4*, Pub. by Princeton U Pr) Cal Prin Full Svc.

Neuman, Gerard G. Origins of Human Aggression: Dynamics & Etiology. LC 86-15370. 200p. 1987. 35.95 (*0-89885-324-9*, Kluwer Acad Hman Sci) Kluwer Academic.

***Neuman, Isaac & Palencia-Roth, Michael.** The Narrow Bridge: Beyond the Holocaust. 224p. 2000. 22.50 (*0-252-02561-X*) U of Ill Pr.

Neuman, Johanna, jt. auth. see Nessen, Ron.

Neuman, John E. Guide to Policy, Certification, & Qualification: WTCA Member Guide. Neuman, Sally E., ed. (Illus.). 202p. 1997. text 60.00 (*1-888282-05-3*) Little Otter.

Neuman, M. Useful & Harmful Interactions of Antibiotics. LC 84-1607. 288p. 1985. 164.00 (*0-8493-6061-7*, CRC Reprint) Franklin.

Neuman, M. Gary. Helping Your Kids Cope with Divorce the Sandcastles (TM) Way. LC 97-26653. 464p. 1998. 25.00 (*0-8129-2902-0*, Times Bks) Crown Pub Group.

Neuman, M. Gary & Romanowski, Patricia. Helping Kids Cope with Divorce. 460p. 1999. pap. 16.95 (*0-679-77801-2*) Villard Books.

Neuman, Margaret W., jt. auth. see Neuman, William F.

Neuman, Mark & Payne, Michael, eds. Perspective: Art, Literature, Participation. LC 85-24330. (Review Ser.: Vol. 30, No. 1). (Illus.). 160p. 1986. 22.00 (*0-8387-5104-0*) Bucknell U Pr.

Neuman, Maurice. Dictionnaire des Medicaments.Tr. of Dictionary of Medications. (FRE.). 432p. 1971. pap. 35.00 (*0-8288-6446-2*, M-6424) Fr & Eur.

***Neuman, Michael & Whittington, Janice.** Building California's Future: Current Conditions in California's Infrastructure Planning, Budgeting & Financing. Public Policy Institute of California Staff, ed. LC 00-27817. (Illus.). 2000. write for info. (*1-58213-024-8*) Pub Policy Inst.

Neuman, Michael, jt. auth. see Laursen, Kjeld.

Neuman, Michael R., et al, eds. Physical Sensors for Biomedical Applications. 168p. 1980. 101.00 (*0-8493-5975-9*, R857, CRC Reprint) Franklin.

Neuman, Nancy, jt. auth. see Greenberg, Michael R.

Neuman, Nancy M., ed. True to Ourselves: A Celebration of Women Making a Difference. LC 98-25436. (Health & Psychology Ser.). (Illus.). 256p. 1998. 22.00 (*0-7879-4175-1*) Jossey-Bass.

— A Voice of Our Own Leading American Women Celebrate the Right to Vote. (Public Administration Ser.). (Illus.). 304p. 1996. 25.00 (*0-7879-0231-4*, 1045) LWVUS.

Neuman-Nowicki, Adam. Struggle for Life During the Nazi Occupation of Poland. Strosberg, Sharon S., ed. & tr. by. from POL. LC 98-3654. (Symposium Ser.: Vol. 47). (Illus.). 180p. 1998. text 79.95 (*0-7734-8378-0*) E Mellen.

Neuman, Patricia O. Moving: The What, When, Where, & How of It. (Illus.). 132p. 1981. pap. 5.95 (*0-89651-450-1*) M & O Pub.

Neuman, Pearl. The Egypt Game: A Study Guide. Friedland, J. & Kessler, R., eds. (Novel-Ties Ser.). (J). (gr. 5-7). 1994. pap. text, student ed. 15.95 (*1-56982-067-8*) Lrn Links.

— The Stories Julian Tells: A Study Guide. Friedland, J. & Kessler, R., eds. (Novel-Ties Ser.). (J). (gr. 1-3). 1994. pap. text 15.95 (*1-56982-054-6*) Lrn Links.

— When Winter Comes. (Real Readers Ser.: Level Blue). (Illus.). 32p. (J). (ps-3). 1989. lib. bdg. 21.40 (*0-8172-3519-1*) Raintree Steck-V.

— When Winter Comes. (Real Readers Ser.: Level Blue). (Illus.). 32p. (J). (gr. 1-4). 1989. pap. 4.95 (*0-8114-6723-6*) Raintree Steck-V.

Neuman, Phyllis. Conveyancing of Freehold Property. 1980. 45.00 (*0-7855-7330-5*, Pub. by Fourmat Pub) St Mut.

Neuman, R. Emil. The Complete Handbook of Health Tips. rev. ed. 256p. 1995. pap. 12.95 (*0-9614924-1-4*) United Res CA.

— The Complete Handbook of U. S. Government Benefits: How to Collect BIG from Uncle Sam. rev. ed. LC 97-183390. (Illus.). 325p. 1997. pap. 14.95 (*0-9614924-2-2*) United Res CA.

— How You Can Achieve Financial Independence in Mail Order Working Out of Your Home. (Illus.). 176p. (Orig.). 1986. pap. 12.95 (*0-9614924-3-0*) United Res CA.

— Paradise Found: How to Live in North America's Best Climate for under 500 Dollars a Month. rev. ed. (Illus.). 176p. 1989. pap. 12.95 (*0-9614924-0-6*) United Res CA.

— Write Perfect Letters for Any Occasion. (Illus.). 240p. (Orig.). 1995. pap. 14.95 (*0-9614924-5-7*) United Res CA.

***Neuman, R. Emil, ed.** Art History Goes to the Magic Kingdom. 120p. 1999. pap. text 35.00 (*90-5700-556-5*) Gordon & Breach.

Neuman, Regina, jt. auth. see Brinton, Donna.

Neuman, Richard C. Experimental Strategies for Polymer Scientists & Plastics Engineers. LC 97-16635. 1997. 62.50 (*1-56990-224-0*) Hanser-Gardner.

Neuman, Robert. Robert de Cotte & the Perfection of Architecture in Eighteenth-Century France. LC 93-30046. 266p. 1994. 55.00 (*0-226-57437-7*) U Ch Pr.

Neuman, Robert W. The Good Soldier Site (39LM238), Big Bend Reservoir, Lyman County, South Dakota, Vol. 37. fac. ed. (Smithsonian Institution, Bureau of American Ethnology Ser.: Bulletin 189). (Illus.). 33p. (C). 1964. reprint ed. pap. text 4.05 (*1-55567-706-1*) Coyote Press.

— An Introduction to Louisiana Archaeology. LC 83-19973. (Illus.). xvi, 368p. 1990. pap. 19.95 (*0-8071-1651-3*) La State U Pr.

— The Sonota Complex & Associated Sites on the Northern Great Plains. (Publications in Anthropology: No. 6). 216p. 1975. pap. 2.00 (*0-933307-11-X*) Nebraska Hist.

Neuman, Robert W., ed. Historical Archaeology of the Eastern United States: Papers from the R. J. Russell Symposium. LC 82-84033. (Geoscience & Man Ser.: Vol. 23). (Illus.). 76p. 1983. pap. 10.00 (*0-938909-31-2*) Geosci Pubns LSU.

Neuman, Robert W., jt. ed. see West, Frederick H.

Neuman, Ronald H. GMDSS: Sailor/Sperry Operational Guidelines. 32p. 1999. pap. 25.75 (*1-879778-78-5*, BK-0831) Marine Educ.

***Neuman, S. P., et al.** Theory, Modeling & Field Investigation in Hydrogeology: A Special Volume in Honor of Shlomo P. Neuman's 60th Birthday. LC 00-35327. 2000. write for info. (*0-8137-2348-5*) Geol Soc.

Neuman, Sally. MS-DOS Quick Reference. 1993. pap. 9.95 (*1-56539-137-3*) Color Cnty.

— MS DOS 6.2 Quick Reference. 200p. 1993. 9.99 (*1-56529-645-1*) Que.

— PC Magazine's 1997 Computer Buyer's Guide. 544p. 1996. 24.99 (*1-56276-434-9*, Ziff-Davis Pr) Que.

Neuman, Sally E., ed. see Neuman, John E.

Neuman, Shirley. Some One Myth: Yeat's Autobiographical Prose. (Illus.). 160p. 1982. pap. 19.95 (*0-318-40003-0*, Pub. by Smyth) Dufour.

Neuman, Shirley, ed. Autobiography & Questions of Gender. 1992. text 29.50 (*0-7146-3422-0*, Pub. by F Cass Pubs) Intl Spec Bk.

Neuman, Shirley & Nadel, Ira B., eds. Gertrude Stein & the Making of Literature. 236p. 1988. text 45.00 (*1-55553-025-7*) NE U Pr.

Neuman, Shirley & Stephenson, Glennis, eds. Reimagining Women: Representations of Women in Culture. 352p. 1993. text 60.00 (*0-8020-2777-6*); pap. text 24.95 (*0-8020-6825-1*) U of Toronto Pr.

Neuman, Shlomo P., jt. ed. see Dagan, Gedeon.

Neuman, Stephanie G. Military Assistance in Recent Wars: The Dominance of the Superpowers, 122. LC 86-16911. (Washington Papers: No. 122). 199p. 1987. 45.00 (*0-275-92219-7*, C2219, Praeger Pubs) Greenwood.

Neuman, Stephanie G., ed. International Relations Theory & the Third World. LC 97-13407. 224p. 1998. pap. 19.95 (*0-312-17706-2*); text 59.95 (*0-312-17299-0*) St Martin.

Neuman, Stephanie G., jt. ed. see Harkavy, Robert E.

Neuman, Susan B. Exploring Feelings. LC 82-81894. (Illus.). 230p. (Orig.). 1983. lib. bdg. 28.95 (*0-89334-205-X*, 205-X) Humanics Ltd.

Neuman, Susan B. & McCormick, Sandra, eds. Single-Subject Experimental Research: Applications for Literacy. 256p. 1995. pap. 20.95 (*0-87207-128-6*) Intl Reading.

Neuman, Susan B. & Roskos, Kathleen A. Language & Literacy Learning in the Early Years: An Integrated Approach. (Illus.). 320p. (C). 1993. pap. text 46.50 (*0-03-076846-2*, Pub. by Harcourt Coll Pubs) Harcourt.

Neuman, Susan B., et al. Children Achieving: Best Practices in Early Literacy. LC 98-29709. 1998. 28.95 (*0-87207-193-6*) Intl Reading.

***Neuman, Susan B., et al.** Learning to Read & Write: Developmentally Appropriate Practices for Young Children. LC 99-67613. (Illus.). 144p. 1999. pap. text 10.00 (*0-935989-87-0*, NAEYC161) Natl Assn Child Ed.

Neuman, W. Lawrence & Weigand, Bruce. Criminal Justice Research Methods: Qualitative & Quantitative Approaches. LC 98-43813. 515p. (C). 1999. 70.00 (*0-205-28710-7*, Macmillan Coll) P-H.

Neuman, W. Russell. The Future of the Mass Audience. (Illus.). 218p. (C). 1991. pap. text 17.95 (*0-521-42404-6*) Cambridge U Pr.

— The Future of the Mass Audience. (Illus.). 218p. (C). 1992. text 59.95 (*0-521-41347-8*) Cambridge U Pr.

— The Paradox of Mass Politics: Knowledge & Opinion in the American Electorate. LC 86-288. (Illus.). 264p. 1986. pap. 18.50 (*0-674-65460-9*) HUP.

Neuman, W. Russell, et al. Common Knowledge: News & the Construction of Political Meaning. LC 92-5992. (American Politics & Political Economy Ser.). (Illus.). 190p. (C). 1992. pap. text 11.95 (*0-226-57440-7*) U Ch Pr.

— Common Knowledge: News & the Construction of Political Meaning. LC 92-5992. (American Politics & Political Economy Ser.). (Illus.). 168p. (C). 1993. lib. bdg. 29.95 (*0-226-57439-3*) U Ch Pr.

— The Gordian Knot: Political Gridlock on the Information Highway. LC 97-1580. (Illus.). 342p. 1997. 22.50 (*0-262-14061-6*) MIT Pr.

— The Gordian Knot: Political Gridlock on the Information Highway. (Illus.). 344p. 1999. reprint ed. pap. 16.00 (*0-262-64039-2*) MIT Pr.

Neuman, William F. & Neuman, Margaret W. The Chemical Dynamics of Bone Mineral. LC 58-5491. 221p. 1958. reprint ed. pap. 68.60 (*0-608-04761-9*, 202020200016) Bks Demand.

Neuman, William I., tr. see Ignacio Talbo, Paco, II.

Neuman, William I., tr. see Taibo, Paco I., II.

Neuman, William Lawrence. Social Research Methods: Qualitative & Quantitative Approaches. 4th ed. LC 99-26312. 558p. 1999. 70.00 (*0-205-29771-4*) Allyn.

Neumann. Human Kinesiology: Applications to Physical Rehabilitation. (Illus.). 496p. (gr. 13). 2000. text 42.95 (*0-8151-6349-5*, 23746) Mosby Inc.

— Legal Reasoning & Legal Writing. 1990. 22.00 (*0-316-60379-1*, Aspen Law & Bus) Aspen Pub.

Neumann, A. L. & Lusby, Keith S. Beef Cattle. 8th ed. LC 86-16. 336p. 1986. text 95.95 (*0-471-82535-2*) Wiley.

Neumann, A. W. & Spelt, Jan K., eds. Applied Surface Thermodynamics. (Surfactant Science Ser.: Vol. 63). (Illus.). 664p. 1996. text 215.00 (*0-8247-9096-0*) Dekker.

Neumann, Adolf. Sicilian Defence Closed Variation Vol. 1: (B23) Edritrice, S. L., ed. (Illus.). 176p. 1996. pap. 17.95 (*88-86127-48-0*) Thinkers Pr.

— Sicilian Defence Closed Variation Vol. 2: (B24-B25) Edritrice, S. L., ed. (Illus.). 234p. 1996. pap. 19.95 (*88-86127-49-9*) Thinkers Pr.

— Sicilian Defence Closed Variation Vol. 3: (B26) Edritrice, S. L., ed. (Illus.). 160p. 1996. pap. 17.50 (*88-86127-50-2*) Thinkers Pr.

— Sicilian Defence 5.f3. Edritrice, S. L., ed. (Illus.). 60p. 1996. pap. 15.50 (*88-86127-55-3*) Thinkers Pr.

Neumann, Alfred. King Haber, & Other Stories. LC 71-128743. (Short Story Index Reprint Ser.). 1977. 19.95 (*0-8369-3634-5*) Ayer.

Neumann, Angelo. Personal Recollections of Wagner. LC 76-16506. (Music Reprint Ser.). 329p. 1976. reprint ed. 45.00 (*0-306-70843-4*) Da Capo.

N

An Asterisk (*) at the beginning of an entry indicates that the title is appearing for the first time.

Neumann, Anna & Peterson, Penelope L., eds. Learning from Our Lives: Women, Research, & Biography in Education. 288p. (C). 1997. text 46.00 (0-8077-3594-9); pap. text 21.95 (0-8077-3593-0) Tchrs Coll.

Neumann, Anna, jt. auth. see Bensimon, Estela M.

Neumann, Anne W. Should You Read Shakespeare? Literature, Popular Culture & Morality. 192p. 1998. pap. 24.95 (0-86840-489-6) Intl Spec Bk.

Neumann, B. H., jt. auth. see Kim, A. C.

Neumann, B. H., jt. ed. see Kim, A. C.

Neumann, Balthasar, ed. Neresheim Abbey Church: Balthasar Neumann. (Opus Ser.). (Illus.). 60p. 1993. 39.95 (3-8030-2706-3, Pub. by E J Wasmuth) Dist Art Pubs.

Neumann, Bernard De, see De Neumann, Bernard.

Neumann, Bernd & Horn, Werner, eds. ECAI 92: 10th European Conference on Artificial Intelligence. 898p. 1992. pap. 300.00 (0-471-93608-1) Wiley.

Neumann, Berndt. Texturbildende Prozesse in Re-Kristallisierten Quarzpolykristallen. (Geotektonische Forschungen Ser.: Vol. 87). (GER.). 154p. 1996. 77.00 (3-510-50053-9, Pub. by E Schweizerbartsche) Balogh.

Neumann, Bonnie H. & McDonnell, Helen M., eds. Teaching the Short Story: A Guide to Using Stories from Around the World. 302p. 1996. pap. 21.95 (0-8141-1947-6) NCTE.

Neumann, Bruce R. & Boles, Keith E. Management Accounting for Healthcare Organizations. 5th rev. ed. LC 97-75989. 745p. 1998. 65.00 (0-944496-60-1) Teach-em.

Neumann, Carrie & Ballor, Ginny, eds. Cranberry Island. 40p. (Orig.). (C). 1996. pap. 3.00 (1-882294-22-X) Green Gate.

— Porches. 40p. (C). 1997. pap. text 3.00 (1-882294-27-0) Green Gate.

— This Ordinary World. 40p. (C). 1997. pap. text 3.00 (1-882294-24-6) Green Gate.

Neumann, Carrie & Ballor, Ginny L., eds. There's a Star Spangled Banner Waving Somewhere. (Illus.). 40p. (Orig.). 1996. pap. 3.00 (1-882294-12-2) Green Gate.

Neumann, Carrie, jt. auth. see Ballor, Ginny L.

Neumann, Carrie, jt. ed. see Ballor, Ginny L.

Neumann, Carrie, ed. see Gilliland, Brian.

Neumann, Carrie, ed. see Haskin, Connie.

Neumann, Carrie, ed. see Hay, C. David.

Neumann, Carrie, ed. see Henson, Grant E.

Neumann, Carrie, ed. see Wise, Norma.

Neumann, Carry, ed. see Schmidt, Rosemary.

Neumann, Claudia. Design Directory: Italian. LC 99-24734. (Illus.). 84p. 1999. pap. 24.95 (0-7893-0335-3, Pub. by Universe) St Martin.

Neumann, D. A., et al, eds. Neutron Scattering in Materials Science II, Vol. 376. (MRS Symposium Proceedings Ser.). 795p. 1995. 77.00 (1-55899-278-2) Materials Res.

Neumann, Daniele, jt. auth. see Limousin, Odile.

Neumann, David A., et al. Human Variability in Response to Chemical Exposures: Measures, Modeling & Risk Assessment. LC 98-3610. 257p. 1998. write for info. (1-57881-000-0) CRC Pr.

— Human Variability in Response to Chemical Exposures: Measures, Modeling & Risk Assessment. LC 98-3610. 272p. 1998. boxed set 104.95 (0-8493-2805-5, 2805) CRC Pr.

Neumann, Diane. Choosing a Divorce Mediator: A Guide to Help Divorcing Couples Find a Competent Mediator. LC 96-24891. 192p. 1995. pap. 16.95 (0-8050-4762-X, Owl) H Holt & Co.

— Choosing a Divorce Mediator: A Guide to Help Divorcing Couples Find a Competent Mediator. 204p. 1999. reprint ed. pap. text 17.00 (0-7881-6278-0) DIANE Pub.

*__Neumann, Dietrich.__ Joe & the Skyscraper. (Adventures in Architecture Ser.). (Illus.). 30p. (YA). (gr. 3-10). 1999. 14.95 (3-7913-2103-X, Pub. by Prestel) te Neues.

Neumann, Dietrich, ed. Film Architecture: Set Designs from Metropolis to Blade Runner. (Illus.). 220p. 1999. pap. 29.95 (3-7913-2163-3, Pub. by Prestel) te Neues.

Neumann, Dietrich, et al, eds. Film Architecture: Set Designs from "Metropolis" to "Blade Runner" LC 97-16619. (Illus.). 220p. (Orig.). 1996. 65.00 (3-7913-1605-2, Pub. by Prestel) te Neues.

Neumann, Dietrich & Jenner, Henk A., eds. The Zebra Mussel Dreissena Polymorpha. (Limnologie Aktuell Ser.: Band 4). (Illus.). 280p. 1992. 80.00 (3-437-30689-8, Pub. by Gustav Fischer) Balogh.

Neumann-Duscha. Beverages: Three-Language Technical Dictionary. (ENG, FRE & GER.). 424p. 1986. 225.00 (0-8288-7915-X) Fr & Eur.

Neumann, E., et al. Electroporation & Electrofusion in Cell Biology. (Illus.). 454p. (C). 1989. text 120.00 (0-306-43043-6, Kluwer Plenum) Kluwer Academic.

Neumann, E. G. Single-Mode Fibers. (Optical Sciences Ser.: Vol. 57). (Illus.). 560p. 1988. 123.95 (0-387-18745-6) Spr-Verlag.

Neumann, Eberhard G. Gedanken Zur Industriearchaologie. (GER.). 1997. 44.80 (3-487-07735-3) G Olms Pubs.

Neumann, Eckhard. Bauhaus & Bauhaus People: Personal Opinions & Recollections of Former Bauhaus Members & Their Contemporaries. rev. ed. Richter, Eva & Lorman, Alba, trs. LC 92-19324. 1993. text 42.95 (0-442-01279-9, VNR) Wiley.

Neumann, Eduardo G. Benefactors & Notable Men of Puerto Rico, 2 vols., Set. (Puerto Rico Ser.). 1979. lib. bdg. 250.00 (0-8490-2871-X) Gordon Pr.

Neumann, Edward S. & Bondada, Murthy V., eds. Automated People Movers: Engineering & Management in Major Activity Centers. 846p. 1985. 66.00 (0-87262-488-9) Am Soc Civil Eng.

Neumann, Else-Ragnhild & Ramberg, Ivar B., eds. Petrology & Geochemistry of Continental Rifts. (NATO Advanced Study Institutes Series C: No. 36). 1978. text 177.50 (90-277-0866-5) Kluwer Academic.

Neumann, Else-Ragnhild, jt. ed. see Ramberg, Ivar B.

Neumann, Emanuel. In the Arena. 1976. 10.00 (0-685-82596-5) Herzl Pr.

Neumann, Erich. Amor & Psyche: The Psychic Development of the Feminine: A Commentary on the Tale by Apuleius. Manheim, Ralph, tr. from GER. (Works by Erich Neumann). 192p. (C). 1956. pap. 10.95 (0-691-01772-7, Pub. by Princeton U Pr) Cal Prin Full Svc.

— Fear of the Feminine & Other Essays on Feminine Psychology: Five Essays. Matthews, Boris et al, trs. from GER. LC 93-32444. (Essays of Erich Neumann Ser.: Vol. 4). 524p. 1994. text 55.00 (0-691-03474-5, Pub. by Princeton U Pr); pap. text 16.95 (0-691-03473-7, Pub. by Princeton U Pr) Cal Prin Full Svc.

— The Great Mother: An Analysis of the Archetype. Manheim, Ralph, tr. (Works by Erich Neumann: Vol. 47). 432p. 1991. pap. 18.95 (0-691-01780-8, Pub. by Princeton U Pr) Cal Prin Full Svc.

— The Place of Creation: Six Essays. LC 88-25297. (Essays of Erich Neumann: Vol. 3). 410p. 1989. reprint ed. pap. 127.10 (0-608-07136-6, 206736200009) Bks Demand.

Neumann, Erich & Hull, R. F. C. The Origins & History of Consciousness. (Works by Erich Neumann: Vol. 42). (Illus.). 520p. 1954. pap. 17.95 (0-691-01761-1, Pub. by Princeton U Pr) Cal Prin Full Svc.

Neumann, Erich P., jt. ed. see Noelle-Neumann, Elisabeth.

Neumann, Ewald. GRE Vocabulary Builder. 2nd unabridged rev. ed. (Vocabulary Builder Ser.). 64p. (C). 1994. pap., pap. text 24.95 incl. audio (0-9625001-1-9) Spargo Comns.

— SAT Vocabulary Builder. unabridged ed. (Vocabulary Builder Ser.). 64p. (C). (gr. 11-12). 1992. pap., pap. text 24.95 incl. audio (0-9625001-2-7) Spargo Comns.

Neumann, Ewald, jt. auth. see Neuman, Ewald.

Neumann, F. Questions & Problems in Auditing. 484p. 1998. spiral bd. 33.80 (0-87563-774-4) Stipes.

— Uber das Lachen und Studien: Uber den Platonischen Sokrates. 177p. 1971. pap. text 57.00 (90-247-5118-7) Kluwer Academic.

Neumann, F., jt. auth. see Habenicht, U. F.

Neumann, Franz. Gesammelte Werke, 3 vols., Set. 1990. reprint ed. 300.00 (3-262-01422-2) Periodicals Srv.

Neumann, Franz L., et al. The Cultural Migration: The European Scholar in America. Metzger, Walter P., ed. LC 76-55140. (Academic Profession Ser.). 1977. reprint ed. lib. bdg. 17.96 (0-405-10041-8) Ayer.

Neumann, Frederick. New Essays on Performance Practice. LC 89-34600. 267p. (C). 1992. reprint ed. pap. 29.95 (1-878822-13-6) Univ Rochester Pr.

— Ornamentation & Improvisation in Mozart. LC 90-31538. 316p. 1986. reprint ed. pap. 98.00 (0-608-07638-4, 205995400010) Bks Demand.

— Ornamentation in Baroque & Post-Baroque Music. LC 77-72130. (Illus.). 630p. 1978. pap. text 45.00 (0-691-02707-2, Pub. by Princeton U Pr) Cal Prin Full Svc.

— Performance Practices of the Seventeenth & Eighteenth Centuries. 605p. 1993. 50.00 (0-02-873300-2, Schirmer Books) Mac Lib Ref.

Neumann, G. Dictionary of Homeopathy: German/English/German. (ENG & GER.). 630p. 1996. 95.00 (0-320-00507-0) Fr & Eur.

— Surface Self-Diffusion of Metals. 1972. 36.00 (0-87849-501-0, Pub. by Trans T Pub) Enfield Pubs NH.

Neumann, G., jt. ed. see Conen, W.

Neumann, George B. A Study of International Attitudes of High School Students with Special Reference to Those Nearing Completion of Their High School Courses. LC 77-177118. (Columbia University. Teachers College. Contributions to Education Ser.: No. 239). reprint ed. 37.50 (0-404-55239-0) AMS Pr.

Neumann, George C. Battle Weapons of the American Revolution: The Historian's Complete Reference. (Illus.). 393 p. 1998. 65.00 (1-880655-07-1) Scurlock Pub.

Neumann, George C. & Kravic, Frank J. Collector's Illustrated Encyclopedia of the American Revolution. LC 89-64003. (Illus.). 286p. 1990. reprint ed. 36.95 (0-9605666-7-8); reprint ed. pap. 24.95 (0-9605666-8-6) Scurlock Pub.

— Swords & Blades of the American Revolution. LC 91-66957. (Illus.). 288p. 1991. reprint ed. 36.95 (0-9605666-9-4) Scurlock Pub.

Neumann, George C. & Kravic, Frank J. Swords & Blades of the American Revolution. (Illus.). 288p. 1991. reprint ed. pap. 24.95 (1-880655-00-4) Scurlock Pub.

Neumann, George R., jt. auth. see Kiefer, Nicholas M.

Neumann, H. Varieties of Groups. (Ergebnisse der Mathematik und Ihrer Grenzgebiete Ser.: Vol. 37). 1967. 71.95 (0-387-03779-9) Spr-Verlag.

Neumann, H. D. Introduction to Manual Medicine. (Illus.). 130p. 1989. 38.95 (0-387-50612-8) Spr-Verlag.

Neumann, H. G., jt. ed. see Dekant, Wolfgang.

Neumann, Harry. Liberalism. LC 91-70429. 359p. 1991. 29.95 (0-89089-455-8) Carolina Acad Pr.

Neumann, I. Biotaxonomische Untersuchungen an Einigen Hefen der Gattung Saccharomyces. 1972. 24.00 (3-7682-5440-2) Lubrecht & Cramer.

Neumann, Inge S. European War Crimes Trials: A Bibliography. Rosebaum, Robert A., ed. LC 77-18934. 113p. 1978. reprint ed. lib. bdg. 38.50 (0-313-20210-9, NEEW) Greenwood.

Neumann, Iver B. Russia & the Idea of Europe: A Study in Identity & International Relations. LC 95-22617. (New International Relations Ser.). 272p. (C). (gr. 13). 1995. 90.00 (0-415-11370-9) Routledge.

— Russia & the Idea of Europe: A Study in Identity & International Relations. 906th ed. LC 95-22617. (New International Relations Ser.). 272p. (C). 1995. pap. 27.99 (0-415-11371-7) Routledge.

— Uses of the Other: "The East" in European Identity Formation. LC 98-11627. (Borderlines Ser.: Vol. 9). 248p. 1998. 49.95 (0-8166-3082-8); pap. 19.95 (0-8166-3083-6) U of Minn Pr.

Neumann, Iver B. & Waever, Ole, eds. The Future of International Relations: Masters in the Making? (New International Relations Ser.). 400p. (C). 1997. 90.00 (0-415-14407-8); pap. 27.99 (0-415-14408-6) Routledge.

Neumann, J. Multilingual Dictionary of Technical Terms in Cartography. (ENG, FRE & SPA.). 500p. 1992. 450.00 (0-8288-7914-1, 3598107641) Fr & Eur.

Neumann, J. J. The Polyporaceae of Wisconsin. 1971. reprint ed. 36.00 (3-7682-0704-8) Lubrecht & Cramer.

Neumann, James E., jt. ed. see Mendelsohn, Robert.

Neumann, Jean E., et al. Developing Organizational Consultancy. LC 96-50308. (Illus.). 312p. (C). 1997. 85.00 (0-415-15702-1); pap. 29.99 (0-415-15703-X) Routledge.

Neumann, Jeff & Ruth, Romy. The Naturalist Collector: The Best Book on Card Collecting. Robinson, Rita & Frank, Alan, eds. LC 94-69480. (Illus.). 128p. (YA). (gr. 9 up). 1994. pap. 14.95 (0-9643339-0-2) Romy Pubns.

*__Neumann, Jeffrey.__ Thirty Years As Jehovah's Slave. LC 99-93339. (Illus.). 218p. 1999. pap. 19.99 (0-9674014-0-2) New Millen Bk.

Neumann, Jens, jt. auth. see Hufner, Klaus.

Neumann, K. Stochastic Project Networks: Temporal Analysis, Scheduling & Cost Minimization. (Lecture Notes in Economics & Mathematical Systems Ser.: Vol. 344). (Illus.). xii, 237p. 1990. 34.00 (0-387-52664-1) Spr-Verlag.

Neumann, K. & Pallaschke, D., eds. Contributions to Operations Research. (Lecture Notes in Economics & Mathematical Systems Ser.: Vol. 240). v, 190p. 1985. 36.00 (0-387-15205-9) Spr-Verlag.

Neumann, K. & Steinhardt, U. GERT Networks & the Time-Oriented Evaluation of Projects. (Lecture Notes in Economics & Mathematical Systems Ser.: Vol. 172). (Illus.). 1979. 31.00 (0-387-09705-8) Spr-Verlag.

Neumann, K. H., et al, eds. Primary & Secondary Metabolism of Plant Cell Cultures. LC 85-17257. (Proceedings in Life Sciences Ser.). (Illus.). 400p. 1985. 167.95 (0-387-15797-2) Spr-Verlag.

Neumann, K. H., jt. ed. see Elixmann, D.

Neumann, Karl & Rosenbaum, Maury, eds. The Business Traveler's Guide to Good Health on the Road: The Nation's Leading Health, Travel, & Business Experts Tell How to Maximize Your Health While Traveling. LC 93-31497. 224p. 1993. pap. 12.95 (1-56561-036-9, 004233) Wiley.

Neumann, Karl, ed. see Rosenbaum, Maury.

Neumann, Klaus. Not the Way It Really Was: Constructing the Tolai Past. LC 91-28884. (Pacific Islands Monographs: No. 10). (Illus.). 328p. (C). 1992. text 32.00 (0-8248-1333-2) UH Pr.

*__Neumann, Klaus.__ Shifting Memories: The Nazi Past in the New Germany. (Social History, Popular Culture & Politics in Germany Ser.). (Illus.). 360p. (C). 2000. text 54.50 (0-472-11147-7, 11147); pap. text 22.95 (0-472-08710-X, 08710) U of Mich Pr.

*__Neumann, Liisa.__ A Visual Teaching Method for Children with Autism. 68p. 2000. pap. 5.95 (0-615-11310-9) Willerik Pub.

Neumann, Linda C. Partners in Play: Parent-Made Toys for Toddlers. LC 94-37777. 1995. pap. 12.95 (0-8050-3673-3, Owl) H Holt & Co.

Neumann, Linda C., jt. auth. see Anderson, Rita.

Neumann, Manfred. The Rise & Fall of the Wealth of Nations: Long Waves in Economics & International Politics. LC 96-48052. 192p. 1997. 85.00 (1-85898-548-X) E Elgar.

Neumann, Manfred, et al. Competition, Efficiency, & Welfare: Essays in Honor of Manfred Neumann. LC 98-41136. 1998. 140.00 (0-7923-8293-5) Kluwer Academic.

Neumann, Manfred, ed. see International Institute of Public Finance Congress.

Neumann, Manfred J., ed. Monetary Policy & Uncertainty: Collected Papers from the 1982-1984 Konstanz Seminars. 262p. 1986. pap. 54.00 (3-7890-1257-2, Pub. by Nomos Verlags) Intl Bk Import.

Neumann, Manfred J. & Roskamp, Karl W., eds. Public Finance & Performance of Enterprises: Proceedings of the 43rd Congress of the International Institute of Public Finance, Paris, 1987. LC 89-5521. 512p. (C). 1989. 49.95 (0-8143-2269-7) Wayne St U Pr.

Neumann, Marguerite, ed. The Tricentennial People: Human Applications of the New Genetics. LC 78-8420. 114p. 1978. reprint ed. pap. 35.40 (0-608-00108-2, 206087300006) Bks Demand.

*__Neumann, Mark.__ On the Rim: Looking for the Grand Canyon. LC 99-35133. 320p. 1999. 29.95 (0-8166-2784-3, Pub. by U of Minn Pr) Chicago Distribution Ctr.

— On the Rim: Looking for the Grand Canyon LC 99-35133. 1999. pap. write for info. (0-8166-2785-1) U of Minn Pr.

Neumann, Michael. What's Left? Radical Politics & the Radical Psyche. 240p. 1988. pap. 7.95 (0-921149-22-0) Broadview Pr.

*__Neumann, Mikel.__ Home Groups for Urban Cultures: Biblical Small Group Ministry on Five Continents. 198p. 1999. pap. 14.95 (1-879089-29-7) B Graham Ctr.

Neumann, Odmar & Sanders, Andries F., eds. Handbook of Perception & Action Vol. 3: Attention, Vol. 3. (Illus.). 448p. 1996. text 99.95 (0-12-516163-8) Acad Pr.

Neumann, P. M., jt. auth. see Adeleke, S. A.

Neumann, Peter, jt. auth. see Wright, Rebecca N.

Neumann, Peter G. Computer-Related Risks. 384p. (C). 1994. pap. text 29.95 (0-201-55805-X) Addison-Wesley.

*__Neumann, Peter J.__ Playing a Virginia Moon. 248p. (YA). (gr. 11-12). 1999. reprint ed. text 15.00 (0-7881-6636-0) DIANE Pub.

Neumann, Peter M., ed. Plant Growth & Leaf-Applied Chemicals. 192p. 1988. lib. bdg. 183.00 (0-8493-5414-5, SB128) CRC Pr.

*__Neumann, Peter M., et al.__ The Collected Papers of William Burnside. (Illus.). 1408p. 2000. text 180.00 (0-19-850585-X) OUP.

Neumann, Peter M., et al. Groups & Geometry. LC 93-270. (Illus.). 264p. (C). 1994. pap. text 35.00 (0-19-853451-5) OUP.

*__Neumann, Petra.__ Untersuchungen Zu Werk und Rezeption des Katalanischen Dramatikers Angel Guimera. (GER.). 210p. 1999. 38.00 (3-631-34583-6) P Lang Pubng.

Neumann, Phyllis L. Marin County Bike Trails: Easy to Challenging Bicycle Rides for Touring & Mountain Bikes. (Bay Area Bike Trails Ser.). (Illus.). 128p. (Orig.). 1996. pap. 12.95 (0-9621694-0-4) Penngrove Pubns.

— Sonoma County Bike Trails. 2nd ed. (Illus.). 128p. 1996. pap. 11.95 (0-9621694-1-2) Penngrove Pubns.

— Sonoma County Bike Trails. 3rd rev. ed. (Bay Area Bike Trails Ser.). (Illus.). 128p. 1999. pap. 13.95 (0-9621694-7-1) Penngrove Pubns.

Neumann, Randall D., jt. auth. see Brown, David E.

Neumann, Randall D., jt. ed. see Brown, David E.

Neumann, Richard, jt. auth. see Nemapare, Prisca.

Neumann, Richard K., Jr. Legal Reasoning & Legal Writing: Structure, Strategy, & Style. 2nd ed. 512p. 1994. teacher ed. write for info. (0-316-57151-2, 71512) Aspen Law.

Neumann, Richard K. Legal Reasoning & Legal Writing: Structure, Strategy, & Style. 3rd ed. LC 97-50018. 1998. pap. text 34.95 (1-56706-694-1) Aspen Law.

Neumann, Richard K., Jr. Legal Reasoning & Legal Writing: Structure, Strategy, & Style, Vol. 2. 2nd ed. LC 93-80973. 512p. 1994. pap. 26.50 (0-316-60390-2, 03902) Aspen Law.

Neumann, Richard K. The Stephan Problem. Wells et al, eds. Niezgodka, Marek & Crowley, Anna, trs. from RUS. (Expositions in Mathematics Ser.: No. 3). ix, 245p. (C). 1992. lib. bdg. write for info. (3-11-011479-8) De Gruyter.

*__Neumann, Robert L.__ Twilight Shades, Day Echoes. LC 00-90301. 2000. 12.50 (0-533-13515-X) Vantage.

Neumann, Roderick P. Imposing Wilderness: Struggles over Livelihood & Nature Preservation in Africa. LC 98-12746. 271p. 1998. 35.00 (0-520-21178-2, Pub. by U CA Pr) Cal Prin Full Svc.

Neumann, Ruth, jt. auth. see Lindsay, Alan.

*__Neumann, Sabine.__ The Locative Class in Shengologa (Kgalagadi) (Research in African Studies). 240p. 1999. 45.95 (3-631-34938-6) P Lang Pubng.

— The Locative Class in Shengologa (Kgalagadi) LC 99-37953. (Schriften zur Afrikanistik - Research in African Studies: Vol. 2). (Illus.). 240p. (C). 1999. pap. text 45.95 (0-8204-4347-6) P Lang Pubng.

Neumann, Sarah, ed. see Ouellette, Deborah.

Neumann, Shosh, jt. auth. see Bismuth, Gil.

Neumann, Siegfried P. Hunger und Liebe: Der Mensch: das Poetische Wesen. (GER., Illus.). 437p. 1995. 68.95 (3-631-47915-8) P Lang Pubng.

*__Neumann, Sven.__ The GIMP Pocket Reference. Toporek, Chuck, ed. (Illus.). 112p. 2000. pap. 9.95 (1-56592-731-1) OReilly & Assocs.

Neumann, Thomas, jt. ed. see Hardmeier, Christof.

Neumann, Udo, jt. auth. see Goddard, Dale.

Neumann, Uwe. Uwe Johnson und der Nouveau Roman: Komparatistische Untersuchungen Zur Stellung Von Uwe Johnsons Erzahlwerk Zur Theorie und Praxis des Nouveau Roman. (GER.). IV, 567p. 1992. 87.80 (3-631-45036-2) P Lang Pubng.

Neumann, Victor. The Temptation of Homo Europaeus. LC 93-73007. 269p. 1994. 43.50 (0-88033-281-6, 384, Pub. by East Eur Monographs) Col U Pr.

Neumann, Walter, jt. auth. see Eisenbud, David.

Neumann, Waltraud M. Die Stellung des Gottesbeweises in Augustins "De Libero Arbitrio" (GER.). xvi, 145p. 1986. write for info. (3-487-07765-5) G Olms Pubs.

Neumann, William L. America Encounters Japan: From Perry to MacArthur. LC 63-17667. (Goucher College Ser.). 365p. 1963. reprint ed. pap. 113.20 (0-608-04049-5, 206478500011) Bks Demand.

Neumark, Alexander, jt. auth. see Baer, Avi.

Neumark, David. Geschichte der Judischen Philosophie des Mittelalters, 3 vols., Set. Katz, Steven, ed. LC 79-7149. (Jewish Philosophy, Mysticism & History of Ideas Ser.). 1980. reprint ed. lib. bdg. 132.95 (0-405-12279-9) Ayer.

— Geschichte der Judischen Philosophie des Mittelalters, 3 vols., Vol. 1. Katz, Steven, ed. LC 79-7149. (Jewish Philosophy, Mysticism & History of Ideas Ser.). 1980. reprint ed. lib. bdg. 44.95 (0-405-12280-2) Ayer.

— Geschichte der Judischen Philosophie des Mittelalters, 3 vols., Vol. 2. Katz, Steven, ed. LC 79-7149. (Jewish Philosophy, Mysticism & History of Ideas Ser.). 1980. reprint ed. lib. bdg. 44.95 (0-405-12281-0) Ayer.

— Geschichte der Judischen Philosophie des Mittelalters, 3 vols., Vol. 2. Katz, Steven, ed. LC 79-7149. (Jewish Philosophy, Mysticism & History of Ideas Ser.). 1980. reprint ed. lib. bdg. 44.95 (0-405-12282-9) Ayer.

*__Neumark, David, ed.__ On the Job: Is Long-Term Employment a Thing of the Past? 608p. 2000. 59.95 (0-87154-618-3) Russell Sage.

Neumayer, Eric. Weak Versus Strong Sustainability: Exploring the Limits of Two Opposing Paradigms. LC 99-15404. 320p. (C). 1999. 95.00 (1-84064-060-X) E Elgar.

N

An Asterisk (*) at the beginning of an entry indicates that the title is appearing for the first time.

Neumayer, Erwin. Lines on Stone: The Prehistoric Rock Art of India. (C). 1993. 54.00 (*81-7304-046-X*, Pub. by Manohar) S Asia.

— Prehistoric Indian Rock Paintings. (Illus.). 1984. 54.00 (*0-19-561387-2*) OUP.

Neumayr, Anton. Dictators in the Mirror of Medicine: Napoleon, Hitler, Stalin. Parent, David J., tr. from GER. LC 95-23605. (Illus.). 462p. 1995. 34.95 (*0-936741-09-0*) Medi-Ed Pr.

— Music & Medicine, 3 vols. Incl. Vol. 1. Haydn, Mozart, Beethoven, Schubert, Notes on Their Lives, Works & Medical Histories. Clarke, Bruce C., tr. from GER. LC 94-21413.Tr. of Musik und Medizin. (Illus.). 448p. 1994. 32.95 (*0-936741-05-8*); Vol. 2. Hummel, Weber, Mendelssohn, Schumann, Brahms, Bruckner, Notes on Their Lives, Works, & Medical Histories. Clarke, Bruce C., tr. from GER. LC 94-21413.Tr. of Musk & Medizin, Am Beispielder Deutschen. (Illus.). 600p. 1995. 34.95 (*0-936741-07-4*); Vol. 3. Chopin, Smetana, Tschaikovsky, Notes on Their Lives, Works, & Medical Histories. Parent, David J., tr. from GER. LC 94-21413. Orig. Title: Musik & Medizin. 1997. 34.95 (*0-936741-08-2*); 102.85 (*0-936741-33-3*) Medi-Ed Pr.

Neumayr, Sharon. American Literature Activities Kit: Ready-to-Use Worksheets for Secondary Students. 256p. 1992. pap. text 24.95 (*0-87628-110-2*) Ctr Appl Res.

— World Literature Activities Kit: Ready-to-Use Worksheets for Secondary Students. LC 94-4282. 336p. 1994. pap. text 27.95 (*0-87628-948-0*) Ctr Appl Res.

***Neumeier, Craig & Schiffer, Michael S.** GURPS Alternate Earths 2. Cambias, James L., ed. 128p. 1999. pap. 19.95 (*1-55634-399-X*, Pub. by S Jackson Games) BookWorld.

Neumeier, Rolf, jt. auth. see Zamir, Jan R.

Neumeister, Michel, jt. photos by see Weiss, Maud B.

Neumeister, Susan M., ed. The World's Columbian Exposition: A Centennial Bibliographic Guide, 26. LC 93-37791. (Bibliographies & Indexes in American History Ser.: No. 26). 480p. 1996. lib. bdg. 89.50 (*0-313-26644-1*, Greenwood Pr) Greenwood.

Neumeyer. Human Venture, Vol. 1. 3rd ed. 144p. 1996. pap. text, student ed. 19.33 (*0-13-232422-9*) P-H.

— Human Venture, Vol. 2. 3rd ed. 1996. pap. text, student ed. 21.80 (*0-13-232489-X*) P-H.

— Out of Many Brief Vol. 1. 1995. pap. text, student ed. 19.33 (*0-13-564808-4*) P-H.

— Study Guide for Out of Many, Vol. 1. 208p. (C). 1993. pap. text, student ed. 19.40 (*0-13-564485-2*) P-H.

— Study Guide to Out of Many, Vol. 2. LC 94-224829. 192p. (C). 1993. pap. text, student ed. 20.40 (*0-13-564501-8*) P-H.

Neumeyer, David & Tepping, Susan. A Guide to Schenkerian Analysis. 160p. (C). 1991. pap. text 26.80 (*0-13-497215-5*) P-H.

Neumeyer, David, tr. see Von Cube, Felix-Eberhard.

Neumeyer, Fritz. The Artless Word: Mies Van Der Roche on the Building Art. Jarzombek, Mark, ed. (Illus.). 416p. 1994. pap. text 30.00 (*0-262-64032-5*) MIT Pr.

Neumeyer, Kathy, ed. see Manfredini, Lou.

Neumeyer, Peter F., ed. Twentieth Century Interpretations of The Castle. 1969. pap. 1.25 (*0-13-120378-9*, Spectrum IN) Macmillan Gen Ref.

Neumeyer, Peter F., tr. see Buchholz, Quinn.

Neumeyer, Peter F., tr. see Buchholz, Quint.

Neumeyer, Susan L. Minnesota Wills & Estate Planning. 400p. 1993. spiral bd. 105.00 (*1-56257-262-8*, MICHIE) LEXIS Pub.

Neumuller, W., comment. Speculum Humanae Salvationis. fac. ed. (Glanzlichter der Buchkunst (Splendor of Book Craft) Ser.: Band 7). (GER., Illus.). 124p. 1997. reprint ed. 98.00 (*3-201-01670-5*, Pub. by Akademische Druck-und) Balogh.

Neumuller, W. & Holter, K., comments. Codex Millenarius. fac. ed. (Codices Selecti A Ser.: Vol. XLV). (GER., Illus.). 700p. 1974. lthr. 1154.00 (*3-201-00902-4*, Pub. by Akademische Druck-und) Balogh.

Neumyer, Marsha M. & Auer, Arthur I., eds. The Noninvasive Vascular Laboratory: Current Issues & Clinical Developments. Date not set. text. write for info. (*0-941022-28-5*) Davies Pubng.

Neumyer, Marsha M. & Thiele, Brian L. Techniques of Abdominal Vascular Sonography. Date not set. text. write for info. (*0-941022-27-7*) Davies Pubng.

Neumyer, Marsha M., et al. Vascular Laboratory Physician's Manual: Indications, Interpretation, & Clinical Decision Making. Date not set. write for info. (*0-941022-29-3*) Davies Pubng.

Neun, Stephen P. & Santerre, Rexford E. Health Economics: Theories, Applications, & Industry Studies. 420p. (C). 1995. text 67.50 (*0-256-15113-X*, Irwn McGrw-H) McGrw-H Hghr Educ.

Neuneck, Gotz, jt. auth. see Muller, Erwin.

Neuner, Arthur J., jt. auth. see Regan, Peter J.

Neuner, G., jt. auth. see Hufeisen, Von B.

Neuner, Gerd, ed. Fertigkeit Lesen. (Fernstudienangebot Ser.). (GER.). (C). 1998. 11.25 (*3-468-49663-X*) Langenscheidt.

— Unterrichtsplanung-von der Lehrwerkslektian zur Deutschstunde. (Fernstudienangebot Ser.). (GER.). (C). Date not set. 12.25 (*3-468-49659-1*) Langenscheidt.

Neuner, Gerd & Desmarets, Peter. Deutsch Konkret. Incl. Deutsch Activ Neu: Arbeitsbuch. 80p. 1983. 9.50 (*3-468-49851-9*); Deutsch Konkret: Lehrbuch. (Illus.). 96p. 1983. pap. text 14.95 (*3-468-49850-0*); Deutsch Konkret Level 1, Tests 1: Ein Lehrwerk Fur Jugendliche. Funk, Hermann. (GER., Illus.). 80p. (YA). 1996. 42.50 (*3-468-49877-2*); Folien. 30 transparencies. 1984. 112.65 (*3-468-84434-4*); Glossar English. 24p. 1984. 5.95 (*3-468-49853-5*); Glossar French. 24p. 1984. 5.95 (*3-468-49854-3*); Resource Pkg. 208p. 49.95 (*3-468-49882-9*); Routinen und Rituale in der Altagskommunikation: Lehrerhandreichungen. 112p. 1984. 11.95 (*3-468-49852-7*); Teacher's Manual. 56p. 1984. 13.25 (*3-468-96747-0*); No. 1B. Deutsch Konkret 1. Funk, Hermann. 144p. text 15.50 (*0-88729-754-4*); write for info. (*0-318-68076-9*) Langenscheidt.

Neuner, Gerd, et al. Deutsch Activ Neu: Lehrbuch, 3 vols., Chapter 1B. (GER.). Date not set. 112.65 (*0-614-10291-X*) Langenscheidt.

— Deutsch Aktiv, Level 1, Level 2. Incl. Lehrbuch. (Illus.). 160p. text 19.25 (*3-468-49900-0*); Arbeitsbuch. 136p. 13.00 (*3-468-49901-9*); Lehrerhandbuch. 141p. 11.25 (*3-468-49902-7*); Glossary-English. 32p. 6.95 (*3-468-49930-2*); Glossary-French. 32p. 6.95 (*3-468-49931-0*); Austrian Supplement. 29p. 4.50 (*3-468-49905-1*); Companion Grammar. 96p. 10.00 (*3-468-49906-X*); Begleitheft zu Cassette 1B. 32p. 13.00 (*3-468-49903-5*); Folien. trans. 112.65 (*3-468-84453-0*); Tests. 33p. 51.95 (*3-468-49909-4*); write for info. (*0-318-56963-9*) Langenscheidt.

— Deutsch Aktiv, Level 2. Incl. Arbeitsbuch. 128p. 14.95 (*3-468-49911-6*); Lehrerhandbuch. 148p. 11.25 (*3-468-49912-4*); Glossary-English. 41p. 5.95 (*3-468-49940-X*); Glossary-French. 41p. 5.95 (*3-468-49941-8*); Companion Grammar. 96p. 9.95 (*3-468-49916-7*); Begleitheft zu Cassette 2B. 39p. 7.95 (*3-468-49913-2*); Folien. trans. 112.65 (*3-468-84463-8*); write for info. (*0-318-56962-0*) Langenscheidt.

— Deutsch Aktiv Neu, 3 vols., Chapter 1-24, Set. (GER., Illus.). 224p. 1996. 33.50 (*3-468-49197-2*) Langenscheidt.

— Deutsch Konkret 1, No. 1B. (GER.). Date not set. lab manual ed. 7.95 (*3-468-49859-4*) Langenscheidt.

— Deutsch Konkret 1, Vol. 1. (GER.). 144p. pap., wbk. ed. 11.50 (*3-468-96746-2*) Langenscheidt.

— Deutsch Konkret 2, No. 2A. (GER.). 128p. 1997. pap., wbk. ed. 12.95 (*3-468-96748-9*) Langenscheidt.

— Paule Puhmanns Paddelboot. 71p. 16.50 (*3-468-49845-4*) Langenscheidt.

— Ubungstypologie zum Kommunikativen Deutschunterricht. 184p. 1981. pap. 26.25 (*3-468-49430-0*) Langenscheidt.

Neuner, Gerd, jt. auth. see Hunfeld, Hans.

Neuner, Gerd, ed. see Albers, H. G. & Bolton, S.

Neuner, Gerd, ed. see Bischof, M. & Kessling, V.

Neuner, Gerd, ed. see Dahlhaus, Barbara.

Neuner, Gerd, ed. see Ehlers, Swantje.

Neuner, Gerd, ed. see Funk, Hermann & Konig, Michael.

Neuner, Gerd, jt. ed. see Kast, Bernd.

Neuner, Gerd, ed. see Muller, B.

Neuner, Gerd, ed. see Wicke, Rainer.

Neuner, Gerhard. Schreiben macht Spass, Heft 2. (GER.). 40p. (J). 1992. pap. text 27.00 (*3-12-675431-7*, Pub. by Klett Edition) Intl Bk Import.

— Schreiben macht Spass, Heft 3. (GER.). 40p. (J). 1993. pap. text 27.00 (*3-12-675432-5*, Pub. by Klett Edition) Intl Bk Import.

— Schreiben macht Spass, Kopiervorlagen, Heft 1. (GER.). 44p. (J). 1991. pap. text 27.00 (*3-12-675430-9*, Pub. by Klett Edition) Intl Bk Import.

Neuner, John. Teacher/Swimmer. (Illus.). 140p. 1998. pap. text 12.95 (*1-889534-22-6*) Jay St Pubs.

Neuner, Josef & Dupuis, J., eds. The Christian Faith: Doctrinal Documents of the Catholic Church. rev. ed. LC 82-22700. 1053p. 1996. 21.95 (*0-8189-0758-4*) Alba.

Neunheuser, Burkhard, ed. see Cast, John & Casel, Odo.

***Neunreither, Karlheinz & Wiener, Antje, eds.** European Integration: Institutional Dynamics & Prospects for Democracy after Amsterdam. LC 99-51896. 400p. 2000. 35.00 (*0-19-829640-1*) OUP.

— European Integration: Institutional Dynamics & Prospects for Democracy after Amsterdam. LC 99-51896. 400p. 2000. 88.00 (*0-19-829641-X*) OUP.

***Neunzert, H. & Siddiqi, Abul H.** Topics in Industrial Mathematics: Case Studies & Related Mathematical Methods. LC 00-33081. (Applied Optimization Ser.). 2000. write for info. (*0-7923-6417-1*) Kluwer Academic.

Neunzert, Helmut, ed. Mathematics in Industry, 2nd European Symposium: Proceedings. (C). 1988. text 195.50 (*90-277-2732-5*) Kluwer Academic.

— Proceedings of the Second Workshop on Road-Vehicle-Systems & Related Mathematics June 20-25, 1987, ISI Torino. (C). 1989. text 171.00 (*0-7923-0243-5*) Kluwer Academic.

Neunzig, H. H. The Moths of America North of Mexico: Fascicle 15.2 Pyraloidea, Pyralidae: Phycitinae: Acrobasis & Allies. Hodges, Ronald W. et al, eds. LC 85-51913. (Illus.). xii, 113p. (Orig.). 1986. pap. text 45.00 (*0-933003-01-3*) Wedge Entomological.

— The Moths of America North of Mexico: Fascicle 15.3-Pyraloidea, Pyralidae Phycitinae (Part) Hodges, Ronald W. et al, eds. LC 90-70020. (Illus.). 165p. (C). 1990. pap. text 55.00 (*0-933003-05-6*) Wedge Entomological.

— The Moths of America North of Mexico: Pyraloidea, Pyralidae, Phycitinae (Part) Hodges, Ronald W., ed. LC 74-169990. (Illus.). 157p. (Orig.). 1997. pap. text 60.00 (*0-933003-08-0*) Wedge Entomological.

Neunzig, Hans A. Dietrich Fischer-Dieskau: A Biography. Whitton, Kenneth S., tr. from GER. LC 97-27573. Orig. Title: Dietrich Fischer-Dieskau: Eine Biographie. (Illus.). 312p. 1998. 29.95 (*1-57467-035-2*, Amadeus Pr) Timber.

Neupaver, Albert J., jt. compiled by see Lall, Chaman.

Neupert, Kent E. & Fry, Joseph N. Cases in Contemporary Strategy Analysis. 480p. (C). 1996. pap. text 37.95 (*1-55786-929-4*) Blackwell Pubs.

Neupert, Kent E., jt. ed. see Grant, Robert M.

Neupert, Ricardo & Goldstein, Sidney. Urbanization & Population Redistribution in Mongolia. LC 94-39475. (Occasional Papers: No. 122). 1994. pap. text. write for info. (*0-86638-166-X*) EW Ctr HI.

Neupert, Richard. The End: Narration & Closure in the Cinema. LC 94-38732. (Contemporary Film & Television Ser.). (Illus.). 216p. (Orig.). 1995. pap. text 19.95 (*0-8143-2525-4*) Wayne St U Pr.

Neupert, Richard, tr. see Aumont, Jacques, et al.

Neupert, Walter & Lill, Roland, eds. Membrane Biogenesis & Protein Targeting. LC 92-24428. (New Comprehensive Biochemistry Ser.: Vol. 22). 344p. 1992. 197.75 (*0-444-89638-4*) Elsevier.

Neurath, Hans. Perspectives in Biochemistry, Vol. 1. LC 89-409. (Illus.). 251p. 1989. pap. text 16.95 (*0-8412-1621-5*, Pub. by Am Chemical) OUP.

Neurath, Maria & Cohen, R. S., eds. Empiricism & Sociology: The Life & Work of Otto Neurath. Foulkes, Paul, tr. LC 72-95889. (Vienna Circle Collection: No. 1). 490p. 1973. pap. text 91.00 (*90-277-0259-4*, D Reidel); lib. bdg. 175.00 (*90-277-0258-6*, D Reidel) Kluwer Academic.

Neurath, Maria, et al. Logical Empiricism at Its Peak: Schlick, Carnap, & Neurath. LC 96-26649. (Science & Philosophy in the Twentieth Century Ser.: Vol. 2). 424p. 1996. reprint ed. text 80.00 (*0-8153-2263-1*) Garland.

Neurath, Maria, ed. see Neurath, Otto.

Neurath, Marie, tr. see Frank, Philipp.

Neurath, Otto. Foundations of the Social Sciences. LC 79-131572. (Foundations of the Unity of Science Ser.: Vol. 2, No. 1). 1993. pap. text 1.95 (*0-226-57591-8*, P410) U Ch Pr.

— Philosophical Papers, 1913-1946. Cohen, Robert S. & Neurath, Maria, eds. 280p. 1983. text 211.50 (*90-277-1483-5*, D Reidel) Kluwer Academic.

Neurath, Otto, et al, eds. Foundations of the Unity of Science: Toward an International Encyclopedia of Unified Science, 1. LC 56-553. (Foundations of the Unity of Science Ser.: Vols. 1 & 2). 1995. lib. bdg. 25.00 (*0-226-57586-1*) U Ch Pr.

— Foundations of the Unity of Science: Toward an International Encyclopedia of Unified Science, 2. LC 56-553. (Foundations of the Unity of Science Ser.: Vols. 1 & 2). 1032p. 1971. lib. bdg. 30.00 (*0-226-57588-8*) U Ch Pr.

Neurath, Otto, et al. Encyclopedia & Unified Science. (Foundations of the Unity of Science Ser.: Vol. 1, No. 1). (Orig.). (C). 1993. pap. text 1.85 (*0-226-57576-4*, P400) U Ch Pr.

Neurath, Otto, ed. see Dewey, John.

Neurath, Paul. From Malthus to the Club of Rome & Back: Problems of Limits to Growth, Population Control, & Migrations. LC 94-8979. (Columbia University Seminars Ser.). 244p. (gr. 13). 1994. text 85.95 (*1-56324-407-1*); pap. text 38.95 (*1-56324-408-X*) M E Sharpe.

Neurenberger, Phil. From Loneliness to Love: A Journey of Spirituality. 128p. 1999. pap. 12.95 (*1-86204-356-6*, Pub. by Element MA) Penguin Putnam.

Neurgaonkar, Ratnakar R., et al, eds. Photorefractive Materials, Vol. 2896. 282p. 1996. 85.00 (*0-8194-2297-5*) SPIE.

Neuringer, Charles & Lettieri, Dan J. Suicidal Women: Their Thinking & Feeling Patterns. LC 81-6294. 250p. 1982. text 26.95 (*0-89876-023-2*) Gardner Pr.

Neuringer, Sheldon. The Carter Administration, Human Rights & the Agony of Cambodia. LC 93-23577. 108p. 1993. 59.95 (*0-7734-9367-0*) E Mellen.

Neuringer, Sheldon M. American Jewry & United States Immigration Policy, 1881-1953. Cordasco, Francesco, ed. LC 80-883. (American Ethnic Groups Ser.). 1981. lib. bdg. 54.95 (*0-405-13444-4*) Ayer.

Neurnberger, Phil. The Quest for Personal Power: Transforming Stress into Strength. 304p. 1997. reprint ed. pap. 14.00 (*0-399-52346-4*, Perigee Bks) Berkley Pub.

Neurootological & Equilibriometric Society Staff, et al. Giddiness & Vestibulo-Spinal Investigations, Combined Audio-Vestibular Investigations, & Experimental Neurootology; Proceedings of the XXIII Scientific Meeting of the Neurootological & Equilibriometric Society Reg. (N.E.S.), Bad Kissingen, 22-24 March 1996, Vol. 100. LC 96-29489. (International Congress Ser.: 1133). 456p. 1997. 192.50 (*0-444-82493-6*) Elsevier.

Neuroth, Rainer. Biosystematik und Evolution Des Polypodium Vulgare-Komplexes (Polypodiaceae; Pteridophyta) (Dissertationes Botanicae Ser.: Band 256). (Illus.). vi, 212p. 1996. pap. 65.00 (*3-443-64168-7*, Pub. by Gebruder Borntraeger) Balogh.

Neusch, Donna R. & Seibenaler, Alan F. The High Performance Enterprise: Reinventing the People Side of Your Business. 400p. 1995. 39.95 (*0-471-13191-1*) Wiley.

Neusch, Donna R. & Siebenaler, Alan F. The High Performance Enterprise. 2nd ed. LC 97-49413. 320p. 1998. 60.00 (*0-471-13283-7*) Wiley.

— The High Performance Enterprise: Reinventing the People Side of Your Business. LC 92-60670. 360p. 1993. 35.00 (*0-939246-29-5*) Wiley.

— The High Performance Enterprise: Reinventing the People Side of Your Business. 2nd ed. 400p. 1995. 35.00 (*0-939246-83-X*) Wiley.

Neuschafer, Anne, jt. ed. see Lope, Hans-Joachim.

Neuschatz, Michael. The Golden Sword: The Coming of Capitalism to the Colorado Mining Frontier, 84. LC 85-27026. (Contributions in American Studies: No. 84). 313p. 1986. 55.00 (*0-313-25104-5*, NGS/, Greenwood Pr) Greenwood.

Neuschel, Sue, jt. auth. see Koss, Barb.

Neuschotz, Nilson. Welcome to Macintosh Multimedia. 1994. pap. 27.95 incl. cd-rom (*1-55828-339-0*, M&T Bks) IDG Bks.

Neuschwander, Cindy. Sir Cumference & the Dragon of Pi: A Math Adventure. LC 99-10185. (Illus.). 32p. (J). 1999. pap. 6.95 (*1-57091-164-9*) Charlesbridge Pub.

— Sir Cumference & the First Round Table: A Math Adventure. LC 97-5820. (Illus.). 32p. (J). (ps up). 1997. pap. 6.95 (*1-57091-152-5*) Charlesbridge Pub.

— Sir Cumference & the First Round Table: A Math Adventure. (Illus.). 32p. (J). (ps-4). 1999. 15.95 (*1-57091-160-6*) Charlesbridge Pub.

***Neuse, Alex.** Jedi Power Battles: Prima's Official Strategy Guide. Prima Temp Authors, ed. (Star Wars). (Illus.). 95p. (YA). 2000. pap. 14.99 (*0-7615-2838-5*) Prima Pub.

— Star Wars Episode I Racer: Official Strategy Guide. LC 99-62516. (Star Wars). (Illus.). 110p. 1999. pap. 14.99 (*0-7615-2193-3*) Prima Pub.

Neuse, Eberhard W. & Rosenberg, Harold. Metallocene Polymers. LC 77-130360. (Reviews in Macromolecular Chemistry Ser.: Vol. 5, Pt. 1). (Illus.). 170p. 1970. reprint ed. pap. 52.70 (*0-608-00006-X*, 205930800007) Bks Demand.

Neuse, Erna K. Der Erzahler in der Deutschen Kurzgeschichte. (GERM Ser.: Vol. 60). (GER.). xii, 94p. 1991. 55.00 (*0-938100-92-0*) Camden Hse.

Neuse, Erna K., ed. Neue Deutsche Prosa. LC 68-30796. (GER., Illus.). (Orig.). (C). 1968. pap. text 12.95 (*0-8290-2383-6*) Irvington.

Neuse, Richard. Chaucer's Dante: Allegory & Epic Theater in "The Canterbury Tales" 332p. 1991. 55.00 (*0-520-07241-3*, Pub. by U CA Pr) Cal Prin Full Svc.

Neuse, Steven M. David E. Lilienthal: The Journey of an American Liberal. LC 95-50237. (Illus.). 432p. (C). 1996. 42.00 (*0-87049-940-8*) U of Tenn Pr.

Neuse, Werner. Geschichte der Erlebten Rede und des Inneren Monologs in der Deutschen Prosa. LC 89-77256. (American University Studies: Germanic Languages & Literature: Ser. I, Vol. 88). (GER.). X, 599p. (C). 1990. text 102.95 (*0-8204-1153-1*) P Lang Pubng.

***Neusel, Mara D.** Inverse Invariant Theory & Steenrod Operations. LC 00-36255. 2000. write for info. (*0-8218-2091-5*) Am Math.

Neuser, Kristina M., jt. auth. see Theodore, Louis.

Neushel, Kristen B. Word of Honor: Interpreting Noble Culture in Sixteenth-Century France. LC 88-47916. 256p. 1989. text 35.00 (*0-8014-2181-0*) Cornell U Pr.

Neushotz, Nilson. Using Director 6 & Lingo for Multimedia Internet Applications. LC 99-55642. 617p. (C). 1999. pap. 56.00 (*0-13-690322-3*) P-H.

Neusius, Phillip D. Archaeological Excavations at the Kruse Bluffbase No. 3 Site, Monroe County, Illinois. LC 85-71910. (Center for Archaeological Investigations Research Paper Ser.: No. 51). (Illus.). x, 95p. 1985. pap. 6.50 (*0-88104-057-6*) Center Archaeol.

Neusner. Comparing Religious Traditions. (Religion Ser.). 2000. pap. text 17.00 (*0-534-53055-9*) Thomson Learn.

— Comparing Religious Traditions, Vol. 2. 2000. pap. text 17.00 (*0-534-53056-7*) Thomson Learn.

— Comparing Religious Traditions, Vol. 3. (Religion). 2000. pap. text 17.00 (*0-534-53057-5*) Thomson Learn.

Neusner, Jacob. The Academic Study of Judaism: Essays & Reflections. LC 82-204699. (Libraries Bibliography: No. 15). 25.00 (*0-87068-431-0*) Ktav.

— The Academic Study of Judaism: Essays & Reflections. (Library of Sephardic History & Thought: No. 3). 25.00 (*0-87068-712-3*) Ktav.

— American Judaism: Adventure in Modernity. reprint ed. pap. 11.95 (*0-87068-681-X*) Ktav.

— Ancient Israel after Catastrophe: The Religious World View of the Mishnah. LC 82-15972. (Richard Lectures). 94p. reprint ed. pap. 30.00 (*0-7837-1771-7*, 204196800001) Bks Demand.

— Ancient Judaism & Modern Category Formation: "Judaism," "Midrash," "Messianism," & Canon in the Past Quarter-Century. LC 85-30416. (Studies in Judaism). 138p. (C). 1986. lib. bdg. 42.00 (*0-8191-5395-8*) U Pr of Amer.

— Androgynous Judaism: Masculine & Feminine in the Dual Torah. LC 93-32291. 216p. 1993. text 30.00 (*0-86554-428-X*, MUP/H342) Mercer Univ Pr.

— Between Time & Eternity: The Essentials of Judaism. 196p. (C). 1975. 35.95 (*0-8221-0160-2*) Wadsworth Pub.

— Canon & Connection: Intertextuality in Judaism. LC 86-26798. (Studies in Judaism). 316p. (Orig.). (C). 1987. pap. text 27.00 (*0-8191-5797-X*) U Pr of Amer.

— Christian Faith & the Bible of Judaism: The Judaic Encounter with Scripture. LC 87-20177. 221p. reprint ed. pap. 68.60 (*0-8357-4366-7*, 203719500007) Bks Demand.

Neusner, Jacob. Classical Judaism: Torah, Learning, Virtue: An Anthology Of the Mishnah, Talmud & Midrash. (Judentum und Umwelt Ser.). 1993. 58.97 (*3-631-45061-3*) P Lang Pubng.

Neusner, Jacob. The Classics of Judaism: A Textbook & Reader. LC 94-12970. 512p. (Orig.). (C). 1995. pap. 34.95 (*0-664-25455-1*) Westminster John Knox.

— Comparing Religions through Law: Judaism & Islam. LC 98-44111. 1999. pap. 27.99 (*0-415-19487-3*) Routledge.

— Comparing Religions Through Law: Judaism & Islam. LC 98-44111. 1999. write for info. (*0-415-19486-5*) Routledge.

— Dictionary of Biblical Judaism, Vol. 1. 1996. 110.00 (*0-02-897288-0*) Macmillan.

— The Economics of the Mishnah: Chicago Studies in the History of Judaism. 200p. 1990. pap. text 18.00 (*0-226-57656-6*); lib. bdg. 34.00 (*0-226-57655-8*) U Ch Pr.

***Neusner, Jacob.** The Emergence of Judaism: Jewish Religion in Response to the Critical Issues of the First Six Centuries. (Studies in Ancient Judaism). 232p. 2000. 47.50 (*0-7618-1639-9*) U Pr of Amer.

Neusner, Jacob. First-Century Judaism in Crisis: Yohanan ben Zakkai & the Renaissance of Torah. 1982. 16.95 (*0-87068-728-X*) Ktav.

— First Principles of Systemic Analysis: The Case of

Judaism Within the History of Religion. LC 87-25235. (Studies in Judaism). 172p. (C). 1988. lib. bdg. 34.00 (*0-8191-6598-0*) U Pr of Amer.

— Four Stages of Rabbinic Judaism. LC 98-44400. 1999. pap. 27.99 (*0-415-19531-4*) Routledge.

***Neusner, Jacob.** Four Stages of Rabbinic Judaism. LC 98-44400. 1999. 85.00 (*0-415-19530-6*) Routledge.

— The Halakhah. (Reference Library of Ancient Judaism : Vol. 2). 380p. 2000. text 125.00 (*90-04-11612-5*) Brill Academic Pubs.

— The Halakhah. (Reference Library of Ancient Judaism : Vol. 3). 428p. 2000. 125.00 (*90-04-11613-3*) Brill Academic Pubs.

— The Halakhah. (Reference Library of Ancient Judaism : Vol. 4). 686p. 2000. 125.00 (*90-04-11614-1*) Brill Academic Pubs.

— The Halakhah. (Reference Library of Ancient Judaism : Vol. 5). 592p. 2000. 125.00 (*90-04-11616-8*) Brill Academic Pubs.

— The Halakhah: An Encyclopaedia of the Law of Judaism. (Reference Library of Ancient Judaism : Vol. 1). 704p. 2000. 125.00 (*90-04-11611-7*) Brill Academic Pubs.

Neusner, Jacob. An Introduction to Judaism: A Textbook & Reader. 448p. (Orig.). 1992. pap. 34.95 (*0-664-25348-2*) Westminster John Knox.

***Neusner, Jacob.** Introduction to Rabbinic Literature. 752p. 1999. pap. 22.95 (*0-385-49751-2*) Doubleday.

Neusner, Jacob. Invitation to Talmud. 1973. 7.95 (*0-06-066098-8*) HarpC.

— Israel & Iran in Talmudic Times: A Political History. (Illus.). 266p. (Orig.). (C). 1987. lib. bdg. 49.50 (*0-8191-5729-5*) U Pr of Amer.

— Israel's Love Affair with God: Song of Songs. LC 93-18503. (Bible of Judaism Library). 152p. 1993. pap. 14.95 (*1-56338-052-8*) Sigler Pr.

— Israel's Politics in Sasanian Iran: Jewish Self-Government in Talmudic Times. (Studies in Judaism). (Illus.). 202p. (Orig.). (C). 1987. pap. text 22.50 (*0-8191-5726-0*) U Pr of Amer.

— Jerusalem & Athens: The Congruity of Talmudic & Classical Philosophy. LC 96-51606. 224p. 1997. 87.50 (*90-04-10698-7*) Brill Academic Pubs.

— The Jewish War Against the Jews: Reflections on Golah, Shoah, & Torah. LC 84-9657. 157p. 1984. 12.95 (*0-88125-050-3*) Ktav.

— Jews & Christians: The Myth of a Common Tradition. LC 90-44866. 176p. (Orig.). (C). 1991. pap. 15.00 (*0-334-02465-X*) TPI PA.

— Judaism: The Classical Statement, the Evidence of the Bavli. LC 85-28875. (Chicago Studies in the History of Judaism). 288p. 1996. 44.50 (*0-226-57620-5*) U Ch Pr.

— Judaism & Christianity in the Age of Constantine: History, Messiah, Israel, & the Initial Confrontation. LC 87-5952. (Chicago Studies in the History of Judaism). xvi, 264p. 1987. 33.00 (*0-226-57652-3*) U Ch Pr.

— Judaism & Its Social Metaphors: Israel in the History of Jewish Thought. 272p. (C). 1989. text 69.95 (*0-521-35471-4*) Cambridge U Pr.

— Judaism & Scripture: The Evidence of Leviticus Rabbah. LC 85-20497. (Chicago Studies in the History of Judaism). 664p. 1998. 60.00 (*0-226-57614-0*) U Ch Pr.

— Judaism & Story: The Evidence of the Fathers According to Rabbi Nathan. LC 91-37130. (Chicago Studies in the History of Judaism). 264p. 1992. 56.50 (*0-226-57630-2*) U Ch Pr.

— Judaism As Philosophy: The Method & Message of the Mishnah. LC 98-46341. 319p. 1999. pap. 18.95 (*0-8018-6160-8*) Johns Hopkins.

— Judaism in Late Antiquity. LC 94-30825. 1995. write for info. (*90-04-11186-7*) Brill Academic Pubs.

— Judaism in Modern Times: An Introduction & Reader. LC 94-29537. 256p. (C). 1995. pap. 29.95 (*1-55786-684-8*) Blackwell Pubs.

— Judaism in Modern Times: An Introduction & Reader. LC 94-29537. 256p. 1995. 58.95 (*1-55786-683-X*) Blackwell Pubs.

— Judaism in Society: The Evidence of the Yerushalmi, Toward the Natural History of a Religion. LC 83-4916. (Chicago Studies in the History of Judaism). 272p. 1984. lib. bdg. 25.00 (*0-226-57616-7*) U Ch Pr.

— Judaism in the Beginning of Christianity. LC 83-48000. 112p. (C). 1984. pap. 13.00 (*0-8006-1750-9*, 1-1750) Augsburg Fortress.

— Judaism Without Christianity: An Introduction to the System of the Mishnah. 1990. pap. 19.95 (*0-88125-333-2*) Ktav.

***Neusner, Jacob.** Judaism's Story of Creation: Scripture, Halakhah, Aggadah. LC 00-39778. (Reference Library of Ancient Judaism). 2000. write for info. (*90-04-11899-3*) Brill Academic Pubs.

Neusner, Jacob. Judaism's Theological Voice: The Melody of the Talmud. LC 94-33405. (Chicago Studies in the History of Judaism). 242p. 1995. pap. text 14.95 (*0-226-57649-3*) U Ch Pr.

— Judaism's Theological Voice: The Melody of the Talmud. LC 94-33405. (Chicago Studies in the History of Judaism). 242p. 1995. lib. bdg. 39.95 (*0-226-57648-5*) U Ch Pr.

— Learn Mishnah. LC 78-5482. (Illus.). (J). (gr. 5-6). 1978. pap. 6.95 (*0-87441-310-9*) Behrman.

— Learn Talmud. (Illus.). (YA). (gr. 9). 1979. pap. 6.95 (*0-87441-292-7*) Behrman.

— The Literature of Formative Judaism: The Midrash Compilations, 2 vols. LC 90-13899. (Origins of Judaism Ser.: Vol. 11). 1072p. 1991. text 45.00 (*0-8240-8182-X*) Garland.

— Meet Our Sages. LC 80-12771. (Illus.). 128p. (J). (gr. 5-8). 1980. pap. text 6.95 (*0-87441-327-3*) Behrman.

— Messiah in Context: Israel's History & Destiny in Formative Judaism. (Studies in Judaism). 288p. (C). reprint ed. lib. bdg. 45.00 (*0-8191-6904-8*) U Pr of Amer.

— Method & Meaning in Ancient Judaism. LC 79-9881. (Brown Judaic Studies: No. 10). 219p. reprint ed. pap. 67.90 (*0-7837-5398-5*, 204516200005) Bks Demand.

— Method & Meaning in Ancient Judaism. LC 80-19449. (Brown Judaic Studies: Third Series). 255p. reprint ed. pap. 79.10 (*0-7837-5425-6*, 204518900005) Bks Demand.

— The Midrash: An Introduction. LC 89-18274. 256p. 1994. reprint ed. pap. text 25.00 (*1-56821-357-3*) Aronson.

— The Mishnah: A New Translation. 1162p. (C). 1991. reprint ed. pap. 35.00 (*0-300-05022-4*) Yale U Pr.

— The Mishnah: An Introduction. LC 88-38460. 256p. 1994. reprint ed. pap. text 25.00 (*1-56821-358-1*) Aronson.

— The Mishnah: Religious Perspectives. LC 99-30517. (Handbook of Oriental Studies). 272p. 1999. 88.50 (*90-04-11492-0*) Brill Academic Pubs.

***Neusner, Jacob.** The Mishnah: Social Perspectives. LC 99-30516. (Handbook of Oriental Studies: Vol. 46). (Illus.). xviii, 270p. 1999. text 94.50 (*90-04-11491-2*) Brill Academic Pubs.

Neusner, Jacob. Mitzvah. (J). (gr. 6-8). pap. 7.95 (*0-317-70156-8*) Behrman.

— Mitzvah: Basic Jewish Ideas. (Ser.). (Orig.). (J). (gr. 6-8). 1981. pap. 6.95 (*0-940646-25-0*) Rossel Bks.

— Mother of the Messiah in Judaism: The Book of Ruth. LC 93-31398. (Bible of Judaism Library). 160p. 1993. pap. 12.00 (*1-56338-061-7*) Sigler Pr.

***Neusner, Jacob.** The Native Category - Formations of the Aggadah: The Later Midrash-Compilations. (Studies in Ancient Judaism : Vol. I). 208/p. 2000. 47.50 (*0-7618-1616-X*) U Pr of Amer.

Neusner, Jacob. Oral Tradition in Judaism: The Case of the Mishnah. LC 87-12056. (Albert Bates Lord Studies in Oral Tradition: Vol. 1). 176p. 1987. text 10.00 (*0-8240-7849-7*, H764) Garland.

— Paradigms in Passage: Patterns of Change in the Contemporary Study of Judaism. (Studies in Judaism). 218p. (C). 1988. lib. bdg. 35.00 (*0-8191-6899-8*) U Pr of Amer.

— The Pharisees: Rabbinic Perspectives. LC 85-5783. (Studies in Ancient Judaism). 300p. (Orig.). 1985. pap. text 19.95 (*0-88125-067-8*) Ktav.

— The Presence of the Past, the Pastness of the Present: History, Time, & Paradigm in Rabbinic Judaism. 1995. 42.00 (*1-883053-22-6*) CDL Pr.

***Neusner, Jacob.** A Rabbi Talks with Jesus. 176p. 2000. pap. 17.95 (*0-7735-2046-5*, Pub. by McG-Queens Univ Pr) CUP Services.

Neusner, Jacob. Rabbinic Judaism: The Documentary History of Its Formative Age 70-600 C. E. 413p. (C). 1994. 42.00 (*1-883053-06-4*) CDL Pr.

— Rabbinic Political Theory: Religion & Politics in the Mishnah. (Chicago Studies in the History of Judaism). 284p. 1991. pap. text 27.00 (*0-226-57651-5*) U Ch Pr.

— Rabbinic Political Theory: Religion & Politics in the Mishnah. (Chicago Studies in the History of Judaism). 288p. 1996. lib. bdg. 57.50 (*0-226-57650-7*) U Ch Pr.

***Neusner, Jacob.** Recovering Judaism: The Universal Dimension of Jewish Religion. LC 00-29358. 2000. 17.00 (*0-8006-3268-0*, Fortress Pr) Augsburg Fortress.

Neusner, Jacob. Religious Study of Judaism: Context, Text, Circumstance, Vol. 3. (Studies in Judaism). 234p. (Orig.). 1987. pap. 22.50 (*0-8191-6048-2*); lib. bdg. 50.00 (*0-8191-6047-4*) U Pr of Amer.

— The Religious Study of Judaism: Description, Analysis & Interpretation. LC 85-30411. (Studies in Judaism: Vol. 1). 188p. (Orig.). (C). 1986. pap. text 20.50 (*0-8191-5394-X*) U Pr of Amer.

— The Religious Study of Judaism: Description, Analysis, Interpretation-The Centrality of Context. LC 85-30411. (Studies in Judaism: Vol. 2). 230p. (Orig.). (C). 1986. pap. text 23.00 (*0-8191-5451-2*); lib. bdg. 50.00 (*0-8191-5450-4*) U Pr of Amer.

— The Religious Study of Judaism Vol. IV: Description, Analysis, Intrepretation: Ideas of History Ethics, Ontology, & Religion in Formative Judaism. LC 85-30411. (Studies in Judaism). 210p. (C). 1988. lib. bdg. 34.00 (*0-8191-7142-5*) U Pr of Amer.

— Scriptures of the Oral Torah: An Anthology of the Sacred Books of Judaism. 256p. 1987. 47.95 (*0-06-066106-2*) Bks Intl VA.

— A Short History of Judaism: Three Meals, Three Epochs. LC 92-7929. 244p. (Orig.). 1992. pap. 20.00 (*0-8006-2552-8*, 1-2552, Fortress Pr) Augsburg Fortress.

— Signposts on the Way of Torah. LC 97-38794. (C). 1998. 38.95 (*0-534-55769-4*) Wadsworth Pub.

— Stranger at Home: "The Holocaust," Zionism, & American Judaism. LC 80-19455. x, 214p. 1993. pap. text 12.95 (*0-226-57629-9*) U Ch Pr.

— Struggle for the Jewish Mind: Debates & Disputes on Judaism Then & Now. (Studies in Judaism). 200p. (Orig.). (C). 1988. lib. bdg. 32.00 (*0-8191-6689-8*) U Pr of Amer.

— The Talmud of the Land of Israel: A Preliminary Translation & Explanation, Rosh Hashanah, Vol. 16. Goldman, Edward A., tr. (Chicago Studies in the History of Judaism). 136p. 1988. lib. bdg. 31.50 (*0-226-57675-2*) U Ch Pr.

— The Talmud of the Land of Israel: A Preliminary Translation & Explanation, Sukkah, Vol. 17. (Chicago Studies in the History of Judaism). 160p. 1988. lib. bdg. 31.50 (*0-226-57676-0*) U Ch Pr.

— The Talmudic Anthropology Vol. I: Torah: Issues of Ethics. LC 95-41291. 299p. 1995. 63.95 (*0-8204-2907-4*) P Lang Pubng.

— The Talmudic Anthropology Vol. II: God: Issues of Theology. LC 95-41291. 325p. 1995. 63.95 (*0-8204-2908-2*) P Lang Pubng.

— The Talmudic Anthropology Vol. III: Israel: Issues of Public Policy. LC 95-41291. 296p. 1995. 63.95 (*0-8204-2909-0*) P Lang Pubng.

— The Theological Grammar of the Oral Torah: Semantics: Models of Analysis, Explanation & Anticipation. (Dowling Studies in the Humanities & Social Sciences: Vol. 3). 498p. 1998. pap. 24.00 (*1-883058-73-2*) Global Pubns.

— The Theological Grammar of the Oral Torah: Syntax: Connections & Constructions. (Dowling Studies in the Humanities & Social Sciences: Vol. 2). 428p. 1998. pap. 24.00 (*1-883058-72-4*) Global Pubns.

— The Theological Grammar of the Oral Torah: Vocabulary: Native Categories. (Dowling Studies in the Humanities & Social Sciences: Vol. 1). 400p. 1998. pap. 24.00 (*1-883058-71-6*) Global Pubns.

***Neusner, Jacob.** The Theology of the Oral Torah: Revealing the Justice of God. 2000. text 49.95 (*0-7735-1802-9*, Pub. by McG-Queens Univ Pr) CUP Services.

Neusner, Jacob. There We Sat Down: Talmudic Judaism in the Making. pap. 11.95 (*0-87068-676-3*) Ktav.

— Torah from Our Sages: Pirke Avot. 1997. reprint ed. pap. 9.95 (*0-940646-36-6*) Behrman.

— The Tosefta, Translated from the Hebrew I. Zeraim: The Order of Seeds. 1986. 59.50 (*0-87068-693-3*) Ktav.

— The Tosefta, Translated from the Hebrew IV. Neziqin: The Order of Damages. 1981. 59.50 (*0-87068-692-5*) Ktav.

— The Tosefta, Translated from the Hebrew Nashim, the Order of Women, Pt. III. 59.50 (*0-87068-684-4*) Ktav.

— The Transformation of Judaism: From Philosophy to Religion. LC 98-46342. 1999. pap. 18.95 (*0-8018-6159-4*) Johns Hopkins.

— Tzedakah: Can Jewish Philanthropy Buy Jewish Survival? LC 97-2339. 1997. pap. 10.00 (*0-8074-0637-6*, 383807) UAHC.

— Understanding Jewish Theology. 1973. pap. 16.95 (*0-87068-215-6*) Ktav.

— Understanding Jewish Theology: From Talmudic to Modern Times. 1973. 25.00 (*0-87068-238-5*) Ktav.

— Uniting the Dual Torah: Sifra & the Problem of the Mishnah. 245p. (C). 1990. text 80.00 (*0-521-38125-8*) Cambridge U Pr.

— Vanquished Nation, Broken Spirit: The Virtues of the Heart in Formative Judaism. 208p. 1987. text 54.95 (*0-521-32832-2*) Cambridge U Pr.

— The Way of Torah: An Introduction to Judaism. 3rd ed. 164p. (C). 1979. pap. write for info. (*0-87872-217-3*) Wadsworth Pub.

— The Way of Torah: An Introduction to Judaism. 4th ed. (Religious Life of Man Ser.). 194p. (C). 1987. pap. write for info. (*0-534-08040-5*) Wadsworth Pub.

— The Way of Torah: An Introduction to Judaism. 5th ed. LC 92-12408. 212p. (C). 1992. mass mkt. 21.75 (*0-534-16938-4*) Wadsworth Pub.

— The Way of Torah: An Introduction to Judaism. 6th ed. LC 96-39049. (The Religious Life in History Ser.). 275p. (C). 1997. 36.95 (*0-534-51568-1*) Wadsworth Pub.

— Who, Where & What Is "Israel"? Zionist Perspectives on Israeli & American Judaism. LC 88-33976. (Studies in Judaism). 176p. (C). 1989. lib. bdg. 35.00 (*0-8191-7360-6*) U Pr of Amer.

— The Wonder-Working Lawyers of Talmudic Bablonia: The Theory & Practice of Judaism in Its Formative Age. LC 87-6161. (Studies in Judaism). (Illus.). 372p. (Orig.). (C). 1987. pap. text 29.00 (*0-8191-6288-4*); lib. bdg. 50.50 (*0-8191-6287-6*) U Pr of Amer.

— World Religions in America: An Introduction. rev. exp. ed. LC 99-30510. 344p. 1999. pap. 18.95 (*0-664-25839-5*) Westminster John Knox.

— Yerushalmi - The Talmud of the Land of Israel: An Introduction. LC 91-19713. 208p. 1993. 30.00 (*0-87668-812-1*) Aronson.

Neusner, Jacob, ed. The Academy & Traditions of Jewish Learning. LC 92-36348. (Judaism in Cold War America, 1945-1990 Ser.: Vol. 9). 344p. 1993. text 25.00 (*0-8153-0081-6*) Garland.

— The Alteration of Orthodoxy. LC 92-37155. (Judaism in Cold War America, 1945-1990 Ser.: Vol. 8). 264p. 1993. text 25.00 (*0-8153-0077-8*) Garland.

— Blackwell Reader in Judaism. (Blackwell Readers Ser.). 400p. 2000. pap. 29.95 (*0-631-20738-4*) Blackwell Pubs.

***Neusner, Jacob, ed.** Blackwell Reader in Judaism. (Blackwell Readers Ser.). 400p. 2000. 64.95 (*0-631-20737-6*) Blackwell Pubs.

Neusner, Jacob, ed. The Challenge of America: Can Judaism Survive in Freedom? LC 92-33631. (Judaism in Cold War America, 1945-1990 Ser.: Vol. 1). 320p. 1993. text 25.00 (*0-8153-0074-3*) Garland.

— The Christian & Judaic Invention of History. 256p. 1991. 44.95 (*1-55540-320-4*, 01 00 55); pap. 29.95 (*1-55540-321-2*) OUP.

— Classical Judaism: Torah, Learning, Virtue: an Anthology of the Mishnah, Talmud, & Midrash. LC 93-3758. (Judentum und Umwelt Ser.: Vol. 38). 254p. 1993. 50.00 (*3-631-45063-X*) P Lang Pubng.

— Conserving Conservative Judaism: Reconstructionist Judaism. LC 92-35453. (Judaism in Cold War America, 1945-1990 Ser.: Vol. 7). 376p. 1993. text 30.00 (*0-8153-0078-6*) Garland.

— Contemporary Judaic Fellowship in Theory & Practice. 1972. 20.00 (*0-87068-187-7*) Ktav.

— Controversies in the Study of Judaic Religion & Theology. LC 90-13895. (Origins of Judaism Ser.: Vol. 4). 330p. 1991. text 20.00 (*0-8240-8175-7*) Garland.

***Neusner, Jacob, ed.** Death & the Afterlife. LC 99-59141. (Pilgrim Library of World Religions Ser.). 176p. 1999. pap. 16.95 (*0-8298-1357-8*) Pilgrim OH.

Neusner, Jacob, ed. Dictionary of Biblical Judaism, 2 vols., 1. 1994. lib. bdg. 62.50 (*0-685-71134-X*) Macmillan.

— Dictionary of Biblical Judaism, 2 vols., 2. 1996. 110.00 (*0-02-897289-9*) Macmillan.

— Dictionary of Biblical Judaism, 2 vols., Set. 1994. text 125.00 (*0-685-59239-1*) Macmillan.

— Evil & Suffering. (Pilgrim Library of World Religions). 176p. 1999. pap. 15.95 (*0-8298-1284-9*) Pilgrim OH.

— Faith Seeking Understanding: The Tasks of Theology in Twenty-First-Century Judaism. (Judaism Transcends Catastrophe: Vol. V). 192p. 1996. text 30.00 (*0-86554-519-7*, MUP/H402) Mercer Univ Pr.

— God. LC 97-210. (Pilgrim Library of World Religions). 176p. (Orig.). 1997. pap. 14.95 (*0-8298-1177-X*) Pilgrim OH.

— History of the Jews in the Second Century of the Common Era. LC 90-13903. (Origins of Judaism Ser.: Vol. 7). 584p. 1991. text 25.00 (*0-8240-8178-1*) Garland.

— History of the Jews in the Second Through Seventh Century of the Common Era, 2 vols. LC 90-13902. (Origins of Judaism Ser.: Vol. 8). 1126p. 1991. text 50.00 (*0-8240-8179-X*) Garland.

— In the Aftermath of the Holocaust. LC 92-35029. (Judaism in Cold War America, 1945-1990 Ser.: Vol. 2). 280p. 1993. text 20.00 (*0-8153-0079-4*) Garland.

— Israel & Zion in American Judaism: The Zionist Fulfillment. LC 92-34800. (Judaism in Cold War America, 1945-1990 Ser.: Vol. 3). 240p. 1993. text 20.00 (*0-8153-0073-5*) Garland.

— Judaism & Christianity: The New Relationship. LC 92-36226. (Judaism in Cold War America, 1945-1990 Ser.: Vol. 4). 224p. 1993. text 20.00 (*0-8153-0075-1*) Garland.

— Judaism in Late Antiquity Vol. 1: The Literary & Archaeological Sources. (Nahe und der Mittlere Osten: No. 16). 268p. 1994. 102.00 (*90-04-10129-2*) Brill Academic Pubs.

— Judaism in Late Antiquity Vol. 2: Historical Syntheses. LC 94-30825. (Handbuch der Orientalistik Ser.: Vol. 17). 340p. 1994. 143.00 (*90-04-10130-6*) Brill Academic Pubs.

— Judaism Transcends Catastrophe Vol. IV: God, Torah & Israel Beyond the Holocaust: Eternal Israel Endures. 192p. 1996. text 30.00 (*0-86554-495-6*, MUP/H389) Mercer Univ Pr.

— Judaism Transcends Catastrophe God, Torah, & Israel Beyond the Holocaust: Faith Renewed: The Judaic Affirmation. 1994. text 30.00 (*0-86554-460-3*, MUP/H365) Mercer Univ Pr.

— The Literature of Formative Judaism: Controversies on the Literature of Formative Judaism. LC 92-13897. (Origins of Judaism Ser.: Vol. 13). 400p. 1991. text 20.00 (*0-8240-8184-6*) Garland.

— The Literature of Formative Judaism: The Talmuds. LC 90-13900. (Origins of Judaism Ser.: Vol. 10). 496p. 1991. text 25.00 (*0-8240-8181-1*) Garland.

— The Literature of Formative Judaism: The Targumim & Other Jewish Writings in Late Antiquity. LC 90-13898. (Origins of Judaism Ser.: Vol. 12). 384p. 1991. text 20.00 (*0-8240-8183-8*) Garland.

***Neusner, Jacob, ed.** The Native Category - Formation of the Aggadah: The Earlier Midrash-Compilations. (Studies in Ancient Judaism : Vol. II). 336p. 2000. 52.50 (*0-7618-1618-6*) U Pr of Amer.

Neusner, Jacob, ed. New Humanities & Academic Disciplines: The Case of Jewish Studies. LC 83-16893. 216p. 1984. reprint ed. pap. 67.00 (*0-7837-9791-5*, 206052000005) Bks Demand.

— Normative Judaism. LC 90-13892. (Origins of Judaism Ser.: Vol. 1). 1592p. 1991. text 70.00 (*0-8240-8172-2*) Garland.

— The Rabbinate in America: Reshaping an Ancient Calling. LC 92-37068. (Judaism in Cold War America, 1945-1990 Ser.: Vol. 10). 256p. 1993. text 20.00 (*0-8153-0082-4*) Garland.

— The Reformation of Reform Judaism. LC 92-33290. (Judaism in Cold War America, 1945-1990 Ser.: Vol. 6). 272p. 1993. text 25.00 (*0-8153-0076-X*) Garland.

— The Religious Renewal of Jewry. LC 92-34799. (Judaism in Cold War America, 1945-1990 Ser.: Vol. 5). 344p. 1993. text 25.00 (*0-8153-0080-8*) Garland.

— Sacred Texts & Authority. LC 98-36235. (Pilgrim Library of World Religions). 176p. (Orig.). 1998. pap. 15.95 (*0-8298-1249-0*) Pilgrim OH.

— The Talmud of the Land of Israel: A Preliminary Translation & Explanation, Vol. 6: Terumot. Avery-Peck, Alan J. & Jaffee, Martin S., trs. (Chicago Studies in the History of Judaism). 582p. 1988. lib. bdg. 90.00 (*0-226-57663-9*) U Ch Pr.

— The Talmud of the Land of Israel: A Preliminary Translation & Explanation- Vol. 25, Gittin. (Chicago Studies in the History of Judaism). 280p. 1985. lib. bdg. 40.00 (*0-226-57684-1*); lib. bdg. 40.00 (*0-226-57683-3*) U Ch Pr.

— The Talmud of the Land of Israel: A Preliminary Translation & Explanation: Vol. 19, Megillah. LC 86-25284. (Chicago Studies in the History of Judaism). x, 200p. (C). 1987. lib. bdg. 35.00 (*0-226-57678-7*); lib. bdg. 45.00 (*0-226-57677-9*) U Ch Pr.

— The Talmud of the Land of Israel: A Preliminary Translation & Explanation, Vol. 2. Brooks, Roger, tr. LC 89-5136. (Chicago Studies in the History of Judaism). 364p. 1990. lib. bdg. 66.00 (*0-226-57659-0*) U Ch Pr.

— The Talmud of the Land of Israel: A Preliminary Translation & Explanation, Vol. 22: Ketubot. (Chicago Studies in the History of Judaism). 420p. 1985. lib. bdg. 59.00 (*0-226-57681-7*) U Ch Pr.

— The Talmud of the Land of Israel: A Preliminary Translation & Explanation, Vol. 22: Ketubot. Zahavy, Tzvee, tr. (Chicago Studies in the History of Judaism). 392p. 1990. lib. bdg. 58.00 (*0-226-57658-2*) U Ch Pr.

— The Talmud of the Land of Israel Vol. 3: Demai. Sarason, Richard S., tr. LC 93-18738. (Chicago Studies in the History of Judaism). 440p. (C). 1993. lib. bdg. 65.00 (*0-226-57660-4*) U Ch Pr.

— The Talmud of the Land of Israel Vol. 5: A Preliminary

N

An Asterisk (*) at the beginning of an entry indicates that the title is appearing for the first time.

Translation & Explanation: Shebiit. Avery-Peck, Alan J., tr. (Chicago Studies in the History of Judaism). 454p. 1991. lib. bdg. 75.00 (*0-226-57662-0*) U Ch Pr.

— The Talmud of the Land of Israel Vol. 8: Maaser Sheni. Brooks, Roger, tr. LC 92-25277. (Chicago Studies in the History of Judaism). (HEB.). 240p. (C). 1993. lib. bdg. 46.50 (*0-226-57665-5*) U Ch Pr.

— The Talmud of the Land of Israel Vol. 9: A Preliminary Translation & Explanation: Hallah. (Chicago Studies in the History of Judaism). 166p. 1991. lib. bdg. 40.50 (*0-226-57666-3*) U Ch Pr.

— The Talmud of the Land of Israel Vol. 13: Yerushalmi Pesahim. Bokser, Baruch M., tr. LC 93-34781. (Chicago Studies in the History of Judaism). 658p. 1995. lib. bdg. 95.00 (*0-226-57672-8*) U Ch Pr.

— The Talmudic Anthology in Three Volumes, 3 vols., Set. LC 95-41291. (Realms of Judaism Ser.: Bd. 52). 299p. 1995. 63.95 (*3-631-47131-9*) P Lang Pubng.

— Understanding American Judaism: Toward the Description of Modern Religion, 2 vols. Incl. Vol.1. Synagogue & the Rabbi. Set pap. 9.95 (*0-686-95149-2*) ADL.

— Women & Families: Women & Families. LC 99-28658. (Pilgrim Library of World Religions). 176p. 1999. pap. 16.95 (*0-8298-1320-9*) Pilgrim OH.

— World Religions in America: An Introduction. 330p. 1996. pap. 12.99 (*0-614-21690-7*, 1336) Kazi Pubns.

— World Religions in America: An Introduction. LC 93-32886. 320p. 1994. pap. 16.00 (*0-664-25300-8*) Westminster John Knox.

Neusner, Jacob, ed. Judaism Transcends Catastrophe Vol. 3: God, Torah & Israel Beyond the Holocaust: The Torah Teaches. 192p. (C). 1995. text 30.00 (*0-86554-492-1*, MUP/H386) Mercer Univ Pr.

Neusner, Jacob, ed. The Talmud of the Land of Israel: A Preliminary Translation & Explanation : Hagigah & Moed Qatan, Vol. 20. LC 85-29037. (Chicago Studies in the History of Judaism). 256p. 1986. lib. bdg. 42.00 (*0-226-57679-5*) U Ch Pr.

— The Talmud of the Land of Israel: A Preliminary Translation & Explanation- Vol. 25, Gittin. (Chicago Studies in the History of Judaism). 256p. 1985. lib. bdg. 37.50 (*0-226-57682-5*) U Ch Pr.

— The Talmud of the Land of Israel: A Preliminary Translation & Explanation, Sheqalim, (Chicago Studies in the History of Judaism: Vol. 15). 190p. 1991. lib. bdg. 42.00 (*0-226-57674-4*) U Ch Pr.

— The Talmud of the Land of Israel: A Preliminary Translation & Explanation-Vol. 26, Qiddushin. 252p. 1984. lib. bdg. 30.00 (*0-226-57688-4*); lib. bdg. 30.00 (*0-226-57689-2*) U Ch Pr.

— The Talmud of the Land of Israel: A Preliminary Translation & Explanation-Vol. 26, Qiddushin. 298p. 1984. lib. bdg. 30.00 (*0-226-57687-6*) U Ch Pr.

— The Talmud of the Land of Israel: A Preliminary Translation & Explanation-Vol. 26, Qiddushin. 278p. 1984 lib. bdg. 30.00 (*0-226-57686-8*) U Ch Pr.

— The Talmud of the Land of Israel: A Preliminary Translation & Explanation-Vol. 30, Baba Batra. 240p. 1982. lib. bdg. 32.50 (*0-226-57693-0*); lib. bdg. 35.00 (*0-226-57694-9*) U Ch Pr.

— The Talmud of the Land of Israel: A Preliminary Translation & Explanation-Vol. 30, Baba Batra. 176p. 1984. lib. bdg. 23.00 (*0-226-57695-7*) U Ch Pr.

— The Talmud of the Land of Israel: A Preliminary Translation & Explanation-Vol. 30, Baba Batra. 224p. 1984. lib. bdg. 30.00 (*0-226-57690-6*) U Ch Pr.

— The Talmud of the Land of Israel: A Preliminary Translation & Explanation-Vol. 30, Baba Batra. 476p. 1984. lib. bdg. 54.00 (*0-226-57691-4*) U Ch Pr.

— The Talmud of the Land of Israel: A Preliminary Translation & Explanation-Vol. 30, Baba Batra. LC 82-17430. Vol. 32. 302p. 1999. lib. bdg. 37.50 (*0-226-57692-2*) U Ch Pr.

— The Talmud of the Land of Israel: Yebamot. LC 86-11406. (Chicago Studies in the History of Judaism). x, 528p. (C). 1987. lib. bdg. 70.00 (*0-226-57680-9*) U Ch Pr.

— The Talmud of the Land of Israel Vol. 10: A Preliminary Translation & Explanation, Orlah & Bikkurim. LC 90-20468. (Chicago Studies in the History of Judaism). 238p. 1991. lib. bdg. 46.00 (*0-226-57667-1*) U Ch Pr.

— The Talmud of the Land of Israel, a Preliminary Translation & Explanation, Vol. 11: Shabbat. LC 90-11100. (Chicago Studies in the History of Judaism). 524p. 1990. lib. bdg. 90.00 (*0-226-57670-1*) U Ch Pr.

— The Talmud of the Land of Israel, a Preliminary Translation & Explanation, Vol. 12: Erubin. LC 90-10963. (Chicago Studies in the History of Judaism). 324p. 1990. lib. bdg. 60.00 (*0-226-57669-8*) U Ch Pr.

Neusner, Jacob, et al, eds. The Encyclopedia of Judaism. LC 99-34729. (Illus.). 1800p. 1998. 300.00 (*0-8264-1178-9*) Continuum.

— Judaisms & Their Messiahs at the Turn of the Christian Era. 320p. 1988. text 80.00 (*0-521-34146-9*); pap. text 24.95 (*0-521-34940-0*) Cambridge U Pr.

— New Perspectives on Ancient Judaism: Religion, Literature, & Society in Ancient Israel, Formative Christianity & Judaism, Vol. II. LC 87-23027. 184p. (C). 1988. lib. bdg. 44.00 (*0-8191-6597-2*) U Pr of Amer.

Neusner, Jacob, intro. The Origins of Judaism: Religion, History, & Literature in Late Antiquity, 13 vols., Set. 1992. 1425.00 (*0-8240-7499-8*) Garland.

Neusner, Jacob, tr. The Talmud of the Land of Israel: A Preliminary Translation & Explanation, Yoma, Vol. 14. (Chicago Studies in the History of Judaism). 254p. 1990. lib. bdg. 48.00 (*0-226-57673-6*) U Ch Pr.

***Neusner, Jacob & Avery-Peck, Alan, eds.** Blackwell Companion to Judaism. (Companions to World Religions Ser.). 576p. 2000. 99.95 (*1-57718-058-5*) Blackwell Pubs.

***Neusner, Jacob & Avery-Peck, Alan J., eds.** Where we Stand Pt. 3: Issues & Debates in Ancient Judaism. . 240p. 1999. 84.00 (*90-04-11282-0*) Brill Academic Pubs.

Neusner, Jacob & Chilton, Bruce. The Intellectual Foundations of Christian & Jewish Discourse: The Philosophy of Religious Argument. LC 97-3402. 200p. (C). 1997. pap. 22.99 (*0-415-15399-9*) Routledge.

— The Intellectual Foundations of Christian & Jewish Discourse: The Philosophy of Religious Argument. LC 97-3402. 200p. (C). 1997. 65.00 (*0-415-15398-0*) Routledge.

— Jewish & Christian Doctrines: Classics Compared. LC 99-10136. 1999. pap. 27.99 (*0-415-17329-9*) Routledge.

— Jewish-Christian Debates: God, Kingdom, Messiah. LC 97-48643. 1998. pap. 24.00 (*0-8006-3109-9*, Fortress Pr) Augsburg Fortress.

— Types of Authority in Formative Christianity & Judaism. LC 98-8112. 1999. 75.00 (*0-415-17325-6*); pap. 24.99 (*0-415-17326-4*) Routledge.

Neusner, Jacob & Chilton, Bruce D. The Body of Faith: Israel & the Church. LC 96-24686. (Christianity & Judaism Ser.). 208p. 1996. pap. 17.00 (*1-56338-157-5*) TPI PA.

— God in the World. LC 97-35414. (Christianity & Judaism Ser.). 192p. (Orig.). 1997. pap. 17.00 (*1-56338-202-4*) TPI PA.

— Revelation: The Torah & the Bible. LC 95-37159. 192p. (Orig.). 1995. pap. 17.00 (*1-56338-124-9*) TPI PA.

Neusner, Jacob & Frerichs, Ernest S., eds. New Perspectives on Ancient Judaism: Judaic & Christian Interpretation of Texts: Contents & Contexts, Vol. 3. 226p. (C). 1987. pap. text 24.00 (*0-8191-6563-8*) U Pr of Amer.

Neusner, Jacob & Green, William S., eds. Dictionary of Judaism in the Biblical Period: 450 B. C. E. to 600 C. E. LC 99-29475. 700p. 1999. reprint ed. text 59.95 (*1-56563-458-6*) Hendrickson MA.

Neusner, Jacob & Jaffee, Martin S., eds. The Talmud of the Land of Israel: A Preliminary Translation & Explanation - Maaserot, Vol. 7. LC 87-5852. (Chicago Studies in the History of Judaism). xii, 288p. (C). 1987. lib. bdg. 30.00 (*0-226-57664-7*) U Ch Pr.

Neusner, Jacob & Neusner, Noam M. Reaffirming Higher Education. LC 99-14816. 158p. 1999. 29.95 (*1-56000-425-8*) Transaction Pubs.

***Neusner, Jacob, et al.** Judaism & Islam in Practice. LC 99-34708. 240p. 2000. pap. 25.99 (*0-415-21674-5*) Routledge.

— Judaism & Islam in Practice: Sourcebook. LC 99-34708. 240p. (C). 1999. text 85.00 (*0-415-21673-7*) Routledge.

Neusner, Jacob, jt. auth. see Avery-Peck, Alan.

Neusner, Jacob, jt. auth. see Chilton, Bruce.

Neusner, Jacob, jt. auth. see Chilton, Bruce D.

Neusner, Jacob, jt. auth. see Greeley, Andrew M.

Neusner, Jacob, jt. auth. see Silverman, Morris.

Neusner, Jacob, ed. see Avery-Peck, Alan J.

Neusner, Jacob, jt. ed. see Chilton, Bruce D.

Neusner, Jacob, ed. see Chilton, Bruce D., et al.

Neusner, Jacob, jt. ed. see Green, William S.

Neusner, Jacob, jt. ed. see Neusner, Noam M.

Neusner, Jacob, tr. see Goodenough, Erwin R.

Neusner, Jacob, tr. see Stemberger, Gunter.

Neusner, Noam M. & Neusner, Jacob, eds. To Grow in Wisdom: An Anthology of Abraham Joshua Heschel. 234p. 1990. 19.95 (*0-8191-7464-5*) Madison Bks UPA.

Neusner, Noam M., jt. auth. see Neusner, Jacob.

Neusner, Suzanne R. Visions of Beauty: Linoleum Prints, Matzah Covers, Stained Glass, Fiber/Quilts, Fiber/Tapestries. (Illus.). 86p. 1998. 90.00 (*1-883058-60-0*) Global Pubns.

Neusom, Daniel. On Earth... As It Is in Heaven. Cecilio, Bob, ed. 190p. 1999. pap. 15.00 (*0-9664226-1-9*) Oneness Pr.

Neuss, Beate, jt. auth. see Grosser, Dieter.

Neuss, Paula, ed. see Skelton, John.

Neustadt, Barbara. Herakles Son of Zeus: The Golden Apples of the Hesperides. (Illus.). 44p. 1997. 30.00 (*0-9616152-3-0*) Pleiades-Studio Graphics.

— The Works of B. Neustadt from 1939-1993. Kipling, Kay, ed. LC 95-74960. (Illus.). 160p. 1996. text 45.00 (*0-9616152-1-4*) Pleiades-Studio Graphics.

***Neustadt, Doniel.** The Weekly Halachah Discussion, 2 vols. 1998. 39.95 (*0-87306-878-5*) Feldheim.

— The Weekly Halachah Discussion, Vol. 1. 1997. 17.95 (*0-87306-834-3*) Feldheim.

— The Weekly Halachah Discussion, Vol. 2. 1998. 19.95 (*0-87306-888-2*) Feldheim.

Neustadt, Egon. The Lamps of Tiffany. LC 78-142102. (Illus.). 224p. 1970. 195.00 (*0-913158-01-1*) Neustadt.

Neustadt, Katherine, jt. auth. see De Monteiro, Longteine.

Neustadt, Kathy. Clambake: A History & Celebration of an American Tradition. LC 91-45599. (Illus.). 240p. 1992. pap. text 17.95 (*0-87023-799-3*); lib. bdg. 40.00 (*0-87023-782-9*) U of Mass Pr.

Neustadt, Lucien W. Optimization: A Theory of Necessary Conditions. LC 76-3010. 439p. 1976. reprint ed. pap. 136.10 (*0-7837-9401-0*, 206014600004) Bks Demand.

Neustadt, Richard E. Presidency & Legislation: The Growth of Central Clearance. (Reprint Series in Social Sciences). (C). 1993. reprint ed. pap. text 5.00 (*0-8290-3230-4*, PS-216) Irvington.

— Presidential Power & the Modern Presidents: The Politics of Leadership from Roosevelt to Reagan. 1989. 22.95 (*0-02-922975-8*) Free Pr.

— Presidential Power & the Modern Presidents: The Politics of Leadership from Roosevelt to Reagan. 1991. pap. 19.95 (*0-02-922796-8*) Free Pr.

— Report to J. F. K. The Skybolt Crisis in Perspective. LC 99-23992. 1999. 25.00 (*0-8014-3622-2*) Cornell U Pr.

Neustadt, Richard E. & May, Ernest R. Thinking in Time: The Uses of History for Decision Makers. 350p. (Orig.). 1988. pap. 15.95 (*0-02-922791-7*) Free Pr.

Neustadt, Richard M. The Birth of Electronic Publishing: Legal & Economic Issues in Telephone, Cable & Over-the-Air Teletext & Videotext. LC 82-6614. (Professional Librarian Ser.). 146p. 1982. 40.00 (*0-86729-030-7*, Hall Reference) Macmillan.

Neustadt, Robert A. (Con)Fusing Signs & Postmodern Positions: Spanish American Performance, Experimental Writing & the Critique of Political Confusion. LC 99-15047. (Latin American Studies: Vol. 15). 232p. 1999. 60.00 (*0-8153-3272-6*) Garland.

Neustaedter, Randall. Homeopathic Pediatrics: Assessment & Case Management. LC 91-37458. 337p. 1991. 39.95 (*1-55643-120-1*) North Atlantic.

— The Vaccine Guide: Making an Informed Choice. 2nd ed. LC 95-48308. Orig. Title: The Immunization Decision. (Illus.). 250p. (Orig.). 1996. pap. 16.95 (*1-55643-215-1*) North Atlantic.

***Neustein, Joshua.** Joshua Neustein: Five Ash Cities. 176p. 2000. 45.00 (*0-89733-488-4*); pap. 29.00 (*0-89733-483-3*) Academy Chi Pubs.

Neustrom, Michael W., et al, eds. Criminal Justice in Louisiana. 3rd ed. 384p. (C). 22.50 (*0-940984-89-X*) Univ LA Lafayette.

Neustupny, J. V. Post-Structural Approaches to Language: Language Theory in a Japanese Context. LC 80-482694. 317p. 1978. reprint ed. pap. 98.30 (*0-608-01255-6*, 206194300001) Bks Demand.

Neususs, Floris M., et al, eds. Experimental Vision: The Evolution of the Photogram since 1919. LC 93-61702. (Illus.). 88p. (Orig.). 1994. pap. 22.95 (*1-879373-73-4*) Roberts Rinehart.

Neut, Hans Van Der, see Van Der Neut, Hans.

Neutens, James & McGuire. Teaching Health Science. 4th ed. (Health Science Ser.). 152p. 1997. pap., teacher ed. 10.00 (*0-7637-0617-5*) Jones & Bartlett.

Neutens, James J. Healthy Sexual Development, Course I. (Discover Ser.). (Illus.). 144p. (J). (gr. 6-8). 1993. 18.95 (*0-7854-0053-2*, 15162); text 7.95 (*0-7854-0052-4*, 15161) Am Guidance.

— Healthy Sexual Development, Course II. (Discover Ser.). (Illus.). 144p. (YA). (gr. 9-12). 1993. 18.95 (*0-7854-0055-9*, 15164); text 7.95 (*0-7854-0054-0*, 15163) Am Guidance.

Neutens, James J. & Rubinson, Laura. Research Teachings in Health Science. 2nd ed. LC 96-30361. 352p. 1996. 77.00 (*0-205-17924-X*) Allyn.

Neutra, Dione, tr. from GER. Richard Neutra: Promise & Fulfillment, 1919-1932: Selections from the Letters & Diaries of Richard & Dione Neutra. LC 85-2245. 264p. 1986. 26.95 (*0-8093-1228-X*) S Ill U Pr.

Neutra, Richard J. Wie Baut Amerika? Vol. 1: Baubucher. (Bauhaus Ser.). 1990. reprint ed. 37.00 (*3-601-00289-2*) Periodicals Srv.

Neutrelle, Dale. Wild Things to Cook. 1974. pap. 5.00 (*0-916552-00-4*) Acoma Bks.

Neuts, Marcel F. Matrix-Geometric Solutions in Stochastic Models: An Algorithmic Approach. LC 80-8872. (Johns Hopkins Series in the Mathematical Sciences: No. 2). 348p. reprint ed. pap. 107.90 (*0-7837-5378-0*, 204514200005) Bks Demand.

— Matrix-Geometric Solutions in Stochastic Models: An Algorithmic Approach. unabridged ed. 332p. 1995. pap. text 9.95 (*0-486-68342-7*) Dover.

Neuts, Marcel F. Structured Stochastic Matrices of M-G-1 Type & Their Applications. (Probability Ser.: Vol. 5). (Illus.). 512p. 1989. text 185.00 (*0-8247-8283-6*) Dekker.

Neutsch, Wolfram. Coordinates. LC 96-24425. xiv, 1365p. (C). 1996. lib. bdg. 248.00 (*3-11-014852-8*) De Gruyter.

Neutze, Grahame M. Economic Policy & the Size of Cities. LC 67-89992. (Illus.). xi, 136p. 1965. 29.50 (*0-678-05190-9*) Kelley.

Neutze, Max. Funding Urban Services: Options for Physical Infrastructure. (Illus.). 288p. 1998. pap. 35.00 (*1-86448-418-7*, Pub. by Allen & Unwin Pty) Paul & Co Pubs.

Neuville, H. Richmond, Jr. Monarch Notes on Dostoyevsky's The Brothers Karamazov. (Orig.). (C). 3.95 (*0-671-00556-1*, Arco) Macmillan Gen Ref.

Neuville, H. Richmond. Space Camp. (J). (gr. 3-6). 1984. per. 1.50 (*0-671-00730-0*, Archway) PB.

Neuville, Maureen B. Living with Attention-Deficit/ Hyperactivity Disorder: Sometimes I Get All Scribbly. 2nd ed. LC 94-41588. 159p. (C). 1995. pap. text 16.00 (*0-89079-667-X*, 6976) PRO-ED.

Neuville, Pierre. Pequeno Diccionario Medico Practico: Small Practical Medical Dictionary. 8th ed. (SPA.). 240p. 1987. pap. 10.95 (*0-7859-4945-3*) Fr & Eur.

***Neuvirth, George.** Out of Hungary: A Memoir. 10p. 2000. pap. 9.95 (*1-891429-07-8*) Armadillo Pubng.

Neuvonen, E. K. Finnish-Spanish-Finnish Dictionary. (FIN & SPA.). 452p. 1980. pap. 59.95 (*0-8288-4698-7*, S37816) Fr & Eur.

Neuweiler, Gerhard. Biology of Bats. Covey, Ellen, tr. (Illus.). 320p. 2000. pap. text 35.00 (*0-19-509951-6*) OUP.

— Biology of Bats. Covey, Ellen, tr. (Illus.). 320p. 2000. text 70.00 (*0-19-509950-8*) OUP.

Neuweiler, Phillip F. Big Game Trails in the Far North. Lapasta, Douglas, ed. (Illus.). 320p. 1990. 35.00 (*0-937708-20-8*) Great Northwest.

***Neuweiler, Phillip F.** Big Game Trails in the Far North. LaPasta, Douglas G., ed. (Illus.). 320p. 2000. 24.95 (*0-937708-16-X*) Great Northwest.

Neuwelt, E. A. Implications of the Blood-Brain Barrier & Its Manipulation: Basic Science Aspects, Vol. 1. (Illus.). 434p. (C). 1989. text 110.00 (*0-306-42628-5*, Kluwer Plenum) Kluwer Academic.

— Implications of the Blood-Brain Barrier & Its Manipulation: Clinical Aspects, Vol. 2. (Illus.). 668p. (C). 1989. text 125.00 (*0-306-42637-4*, Kluwer Plenum) Kluwer Academic.

Neuwelt, E. A., ed. Implications of the Blood - Brain Barrier & Its Manipulation, Vol. 1: Basic Science Aspects, 2 vols. (Illus.). 434p. 1989. 195.00 (*0-318-32869-0*, Kluwer Plenum) Kluwer Academic.

Neuwinder, Hans D. African Ethnobotany: Poisons & Drugs : Chemistry, Pharmacology, Toxicology. LC 96-8524. 1996. mass mkt. 229.95 (*3-8261-0077-8*) Chapman & Hall.

Neuwirt, J. & Ponka, P. Regulation of Hemoglobin Synthesis. 1977. text 85.50 (*90-247-1999-2*) Kluwer Academic.

Neuwirth, Donald & Osborn, John J., Jr. The California Coast: A Traveler's Companion. LC 97-47558. (Illus.). 364p. 1998. pap. 17.95 (*0-88150-395-9*, Pub. by Countryman) Norton.

Neuwirth, Erich. Musical Temperaments. Steblin, R., tr. LC 97-40405. 80p. 1997. pap. 49.95 incl. cd-rom (*3-211-83040-5*) Spr-Verlag.

Neuwirth, Gertrud, ed. see Weber, Max M.

Neuwirth, L. P., ed. see Fox, Ralph H.

Neuwirth, Lee P. Knot Groups. LC 65-14393. (Annals of Mathematics Studies: No. 56). (Illus.). 119p. 1965. reprint ed. pap. 36.90 (*0-608-02518-6*, 206316200004) Bks Demand.

Neuwirth, Lisa, jt. auth. see Diamond, Marilyn.

***Neuwirth, Michael.** The Scoliosis Sourcebook. 304p. 2000. pap. 16.95 (*0-7373-0321-2*, 03212W, Pub. by Lowell Hse) NTC Contemp Pub Co.

Neuwirth, Michael & Osborn, Kevin. The Scoliosis Handbook: A Consultation with a Specialist. LC 95-32801. 89p. 1995. 25.00 (*0-8050-3793-4*) H Holt & Co.

Neuwirth, Rebecca A., tr. see Luhmann, Niklas & Schorr, Karl-Eberhard.

***Neuwirth, Yehoshua.** Halachoth of Educating Children. 1999. 10.95 (*1-58330-385-5*) Feldheim.

Neuwirth, Yehoshua. Shemirath Shabbath, Vol. 2. Grangewood, W., tr. 1989. 21.95 (*0-87306-477-1*); pap. 18.95 (*0-87306-478-X*) Feldheim.

Neuwirth, Yehoshua Y. Shemirath Shabbath, Vol. 1. Grangewood, W., tr. from HEB.Tr. of Shemirath Shabbath Kehilchathah. 360p. 1984. pap. 18.95 (*0-87306-375-9*) Feldheim.

Neuwirth, Yehoshua Y. Shemirath Shabbath, Vol. 3. Grangewood, W., tr.Tr. of Shemirath Shabbath Kehilchathah. 1997. 25.95 (*0-87306-820-3*); pap. 21.95 (*0-87306-821-1*) Feldheim.

Neuzil, Mark & Kovarik, William. Mass Media & Environmental Conflict: America's Green Crusades. LC 96-10051. 372p. 1996. 45.95 (*0-7619-0332-1*); pap. 21.95 (*0-7619-0333-X*) Sage.

Neva, Franklin A. Basic Clinical Parasitology. 6th ed. (Illus.). 400p. 1996. text 46.95 (*0-8385-0624-0*, A0624-5) McGraw.

Nevada Humanities Committee, ed. Western Technological Landscapes. LC 98-213420. (Illus.). 224p. 1998. pap. 14.95 (*1-890591-02-5*) NV Humanities.

Nevada Museum of Art Staff. The Altered Landscape. Pool, Peter E., ed. LC 98-43475. (Illus.). 168p. 1999. 49.95 (*0-87417-330-2*) U of Nev Pr.

Nevada Wildlife Record Book Committee Staff. Nevada Wildlife Record Book. 2nd ed. (Illus.). 346p. 1990. 29.00 (*0-9622467-0-0*) NV WRBC.

— Nevada Wildlife Record Book, 1990. 2nd ed. (Illus.). 250p. 1990. write for info. (*0-318-64890-3*) NV WRBC.

Nevadomski, Stacie, ed. Environmental & Urban Issues. write for info. (*0-318-63044-3*) Fla Atlantic.

Nevaer, Louis E. New Business Opportunities in Latin America: Trade & Investment after the Mexican Meltdown. LC 95-38752. 240p. 1996. 62.95 (*1-56720-023-0*, Quorum Bks) Greenwood.

— Strategies for Business in Mexico: Free Trade & the Emergence of North America, Inc. LC 95-6921. 240p. 1995. 59.95 (*0-89930-882-1*, Quorum Bks) Greenwood.

Nevaer, Louis E. & Deck, Steven A. Corporate Financial Planning & Management in a Deficit Economy. LC 86-25582. 187p. 1987. 59.95 (*0-89930-202-5*, NCF/, Quorum Bks) Greenwood.

— The Management of Corporate Business Units: Portfolio Strategies for Turbulent Times. LC 87-32586. 248p. 1988. 62.95 (*0-89930-284-X*, NVP/, Quorum Bks) Greenwood.

— The Protectionist Threat to Corporate America: The U. S. Trade Deficit & Management Responses. LC 88-39910. 239p. 1989. 62.95 (*0-89930-363-3*, NEW, Quorum Bks) Greenwood.

— Strategic Corporate Alliances: A Study of the Present, a Model for the Future. LC 90-30010. 240p. 1990. 59.95 (*0-89930-361-7*, Quorum Bks) Greenwood.

Nevai, Lucia. Normal. LC 96-47655. 238p. 1997. 17.95 (*1-56512-158-9*, 72158) Algonquin Bks.

Nevai, Paul G. Orthogonal Polynomials. LC 78-32112. (Memoirs of the American Mathematical Society Ser.: No. 213). 185p. 1991. reprint ed. pap. 18.00 (*0-8218-2213-6*, MEMO/18/213) Am Math.

— Orthogonal Polynomials - Theory & Practice: Proceedings of the NATO Advanced Study Institute on "Orthogonal Polynomials & Their Applications" Held in Columbus, Ohio, U. S. A. May 22 - June 3, 1989. (C). 1989. text 255.50 (*0-7923-0569-8*) Kluwer Academic.

Nevala, Steve, jt. auth. see Linsenman, Bob.

Nevalainen, David E., contrib. by. Training Verification for Laboratory Personnel: Approved Guideline (1995) 1995. 85.00 (*1-56238-286-1*, GP21-A) NCCLS.

Nevalainen, David E. & Callery, Marjana F. Quality Systems in the Blood Bank & Laboratory Environment. (Illus.). (C). 1994. pap. text 89.00 (*1-56395-038-3*) Am Assn Blood.

Nevalinna, Olavi. Convergence of Iterations for Linear Equations. LC 93-3187. (Lectures in Mathematics ETH Zurich). vii, 177p. 1993. 34.50 (*0-8176-2865-7*) Birkhauser.

N

An Asterisk (*) at the beginning of an entry indicates that the title is appearing for the first time.

N

Nevanlinna, F., jt. auth. see Nevanlinna, Rolf H.

Nevanlinna, Rolf H. & Nevanlinna, F. Absolute Analysis. Emig, P., tr. from GER. LC 73-75652. (Grundlehren der Mathematischen Wissenschaften Ser.: Vol. 102). (Illus.). 280p. 1973. 79.95 (*0-387-05917-2*) Spr-Verlag.

Nevanlinna, Saara & Taavitsainen, Irma, eds. St. Katherine of Alexandria: The Late Middle English Prose Legend in Southwell Minster MS 7. LC 93-36296. (Illus.). 174p. (C). 1993. 75.00 (*0-85991-391-0*, DS Brewer) Boydell & Brewer.

Nevans, Ronald. Unruly Angels: A Novel. 265p. 1998. pap. 14.95 (*1-879194-23-6*) GLB Pubs.

Nevares, Dora, et al. Delinquency in Puerto Rico: The 1970 Birth Cohort Study, 31. LC 90-32108. (Contributions in Criminology & Penology Ser.: No. 31). 248p. 1990. 62.95 (*0-313-27456-8*, NVD/, Greenwood Pr) Greenwood.

Nevares-Muniz, Dora. Derecho Penal Puertorriqueno: Parte General. 352p. 1983. pap. text 20.00 (*0-914939-00-9*) Instituto Desarrollo.

— Sumario de Derecho Procesal Penal Puertorriqueno. 2nd ed. (SPA.). 296p. 1986. pap. text 20.00 (*0-317-38881-9*); suppl. ed. 10.00 (*0-685-11823-1*) Instituto Desarrollo.

Nevaskar, Balwant S. Capitalists Without Capitalism: The Jains of India & the Quakers of the West, 6. LC 72-98709. (Contributions in Sociology Ser.: No. 6). 252p. 1971. 65.00 (*0-8371-3297-5*, NCA/, Greenwood Pr) Greenwood.

Neve, Brian. Film & Politics in America: A Social Tradition. LC 92-5196. (Studies in Film, Television & the Media Ser.). 192p. (C). (gr. 13). 1992. text 62.95 (*0-415-02619-9*, A7920) Routledge.

— Film & Politics in America: A Social Tradition. LC 92-5196. (Studies in Film, Television & the Media Ser.). (Illus.). 288p. (C). 1992. pap. 24.99 (*0-415-02620-2*, A7924) Routledge.

Neve, D. De & Raad van het Pluralistisch Onderwijs Staff. Pluralism in Education in Europe: Report of the International Conference, Alden Biesen, 18-20 May, 1995. LC 98-230055. 216p. 1997. pap. write for info. (*90-5487-182-2*) VUB Univ Pr.

Neve, Ernest F. Things Seen in Kashmir. (C). 1993. 18.00 (*81-7041-821-6*, Pub. by Anmol) S Asia.

Neve, Herbert, ed. Homeward Journey: Readings in African Studies. LC 93-28433. 340p. (J). 1994. 45.95 (*0-86543-407-7*); pap. 14.95 (*0-86543-408-5*) Africa World.

Neve, Jean, et al, eds. Therapeutic Uses of Trace Elements: Proceedings of the Fifth International Congress Held in Meribel, France, February 4-7, 1996. LC 96-41996. 446p. (C). 1997. text 129.50 (*0-306-45485-8*, Kluwer Plenum) Kluwer Academic.

Neve, Jean & Favier, Alain E., eds. Selenium in Medicine & Biology: Proceedings of the Second International Congress on Trace Elements in Medicine & Biology. xx, 428p. (C). 1989. lib. bdg. 234.65 (*3-11-011770-3*) De Gruyter.

Neve, John. Concordance to the Poetical Works of William Cowper. LC 68-26363. (Studies in Poetry: No. 38). 1969. reprint ed. lib. bdg. 75.00 (*0-8383-0289-0*) M S G Haskell Hse.

— A Concordance to the Poetical Works of William Cowper. (BCL1-PR English Literature Ser.). 504p. 1992. reprint ed. lib. bdg. 99.00 (*0-7812-7340-4*) Rprt Serv.

Neve, Kim A. & Neve, Rachael L., eds. The Dopamine Receptors. (Receptors Ser.). 560p. 1996. 139.00 (*0-89603-433-X*) Humana.

Neve, Michael, jt. ed. see Jay, Mike R.

Neve, P. L. & Van Kappen, O. Moorman, eds. Conservare Jura. 224p. 1988. pap. 27.00 (*90-6544-370-3*) Kluwer Law Intl.

Neve, Rachael L., jt. ed. see Neve, Kim A.

Neve, Richard. The Complete Builder's Guide: A 1726 Dictionary of Builders Terms & Usage. 1969. 45.00 (*0-89979-004-6*) British Am Bks.

Neve, Susan, tr. see Pavon, Francisco G.

Nevel, Bonnie & Harnik, Peter. Railroads Recycled: How Local Initiative & Federal Support Launched the Rails-to-Trails Movement, 1965-1990. 104p. (Orig.). 1990. 12.95 (*0-925794-03-1*) Rails Trails.

Neveldine, Robert B. Bodies at Risk: Unsafe Limits in Romanticism & Postmodernism. LC 97-10555. (SUNY Series in Postmodern Culture). 208p. (Orig.). (C). 1998. text 59.50 (*0-7914-3649-7*); pap. text 19.95 (*0-7914-3650-0*) State U NY Pr.

Neveling, Ulrich. Terminologie de la Documentation. Wersig, Gernot, ed. (ENG, FRE, GER, RUS & SPA.). 274p. 1976. pap. 85.00 (*0-8288-5756-3*, M6529) Fr & Eur.

Nevell, T. P. & Zeronian, S. Haig, eds. Cellulose Chemistry & Its Applications. LC 84-20509. (Chemical Science Ser.). 552p. 1985. text 169.00 (*0-470-20146-0*) P-H.

***Neveln, Bob.** Linux Assembly Language Programming. 350p. 2000. pap. 44.99 incl. cd-rom (*0-13-087940-1*, Prentice Hall) P-H.

Neveloff, Jay A. Developing the Modern Congregate Care/Assisted Living Facility. LC 99-177612. (Tax & Estate Planning Ser.). 320 p. 1999. 99.00 (*0-87224-554-3*) PLI.

Nevelow, Mark, ed. see Baker, Kyle.

Nevelow, Mark, ed. see Messner-Loebs, William F.

Nevels, Lourene A. & Coche, Judith M. Powerful Wisdom: Voices of Distinguished Women Psychotherapists. LC 93-3621. (Social & Behavioral Science Ser.). 190p. 1993. 33.95 (*1-55542-570-4*) Jossey-Bass.

Nevel'son, M. B. & Has'minskii, R. Z. Stochastic Approximation & Recursive Estimation. LC 76-48298. (Translations of Mathematical Monographs: Vol. 47). 244p. 1976. 75.00 (*0-8218-1597-0*, MMONO/47) Am Math.

Nevelson, M. B., et al. Stochastic Approximation & Recursive Estimation. LC 76-48298. (Translations of Mathematical Monographs: No. 47). 244p. 1976. pap. 75.00 (*0-8218-0906-7*) Am Math.

Neven, Damien, et al. Merger in Daylight: The Economics & Politics of European Merger Control. 296p. (C). 1994. pap. 29.95 (*1-898128-01-4*) Brookings.

— Trawling for Minnows: European Competition Policy & Agreements Between Firms. 240p. 1998. 24.95 (*1-898128-34-0*, Pub. by Ctr Econ Policy Res) Brookings.

Neven, Kresic. Karst Water Resources: Evaluation & Protection with Image Library. 1998. 89.95 incl. cd-rom (*1-56670-280-1*, L1280) Lewis Pubs.

Neven, Patrick. The Effect of Tamoxifen on the Uterus in Postmenopausal Breast Cancer Patients. (Acta Biomedica Lovaniensia Ser.). (Illus.). 160p. 1998. pap. 46.50 (*90-6186-895-5*, Pub. by Leuven Univ) Coronet Bks.

Neven, Ruth S. Emotional Milestones from Birth to Adulthood: A Psychodynamic Approach. LC 97-200963. 270p. 1997. pap. write for info. (*1-85302-456-2*, Pub. by Jessica Kingsley) Taylor & Francis.

Neven, Ruth Schmidt. Emotional Milestones: From Birth to Adulthood: A Psychological Approach. 260p. 1996. pap. 22.50 (*0-86431-169-9*, Pub. by Aust Council Educ Res) Stylus Pub VA.

Neverdon-Morton, Cynthia. Afro-American Women of the South & the Advancement of the Race, 1895-1925. LC 88-17481. (Illus.). 288p. 1989. pap. 18.95 (*0-87049-684-0*); text 41.00 (*0-87049-583-6*) U of Tenn Pr.

Nevers, Noel De, see De Nevers, Noel.

Neves, A. C., jt. ed. see Nowak, A. J.

Neves, Claudio, jt. ed. see Magoon, Orville T.

***Neves-e-Castro, M.** Menopause, Hormones & Cancer. (Illus.). 250p. 2001. 65.00 (*1-85070-628-X*) Prthnon Pub.

Neves-e-Castro, M. & Birkhauser, M., eds. Menopause & the Heart. LC 98-32248. (Illus.). 138p. 1999. 78.00 (*1-85070-071-0*) Prthnon Pub.

Neves, E. Maranha Das, see Das Neves, E. Maranha, ed.

Neves, Goncalo. Kompreni: Rakontoj. (ESP.). 56p. 1993. pap. text 3.95 (*1-882251-07-5*) Eldonejo Bero.

Neves, J. Cassiano & Safieha, Nicolas. The Palace & Gardens of Fronteira: 17th & 18th Century Portuguese Style. (Garden Ser.). (POR., Illus.). 142p. 1996. 50.00 (*0-935748-98-9*) M T Train.

Neves, Margaret, tr. see Torres, Antonio.

Neves, Margaret A., tr. see Amado, Jorge.

Neves, Margaret A., tr. see Torres, Antonio.

***Neves, Miguel Santos.** Europe China & the Two Sars. LC 99-86831. 288p. 2000. text 68.00 (*0-312-23207-1*) St Martin.

Neves, Victor, jt. auth. see Jennison, Brian.

***Nevett, Lisa C.** House & Society in the Ancient Greek World. LC 98-38089. 1999. write for info. (*0-05-216439-X*) Cambridge U Pr.

Nevett, Lisa C. House & Society in the Ancient Greek World. (New Studies in Archaeology). (Illus.). 200p. (C). 1999. text 64.95 (*0-521-64349-X*) Cambridge U Pr.

Nevett, T. R. Cases in Advertising Management: Case Analysis Manual. LC 92-7677. xii, 132p. 1992. write for info. (*0-8442-3369-2*, NTC Business Bks) NTC Contemp Pub Co.

Neveu, B. Un Historien a l'Ecole de Port-Royal. Sebastien le Nain de Tillemont 1637-1698. (International Archives of the History of Ideas Ser.: No. 15). 351p. 1966. lib. bdg. 99.50 (*90-247-0191-0*) Kluwer Academic.

Neveu, Jacques. Theorie des Semi-Groupes de Markov. LC 58-9788. (California University Publications in Statistics: Vol. 2, No. 14). 80p. reprint ed. pap. 30.00 (*0-608-30314-3*, 202118500021) Bks Demand.

Neviaser, Donald S. The Inner View: A Look at Life, Love & Human Nature. i, 80p. 1998. vinyl bd. 16.95 (*0-9666123-0-2*) Kanevia.

Neviaser, Robert J., et al. Emergency Orthopaedic Radiology. LC 84-23679. (Illus.). 295p. reprint ed. pap. 91.50 (*0-7837-6241-0*, 204595500010) Bks Demand.

Nevid. The Story of Psychology. Date not set. write for info. (*1-57259-649-X*) Worth.

Nevid, jt. auth. see Rathus.

Nevid, Jeffrey, et al. Health in the New Millennium. (Illus.). (C). 1998. pap. text 38.80 (*1-57259-171-4*) Worth.

— Study Guide to Accompany Health in the New Millennium. (C). 1998. pap. text 12.80 (*1-57259-502-7*) Worth.

Nevid, Jeffrey S. Abnormal Psychology: The Problem of Maladaptive Behavior. 9th ed. (C). 1999. 76.00 (*0-13-084953-7*) P-H.

— Two Hundred & One Things You Should Know about AIDS & Other Sexually Transmitted Diseases. LC 93-185576. (Illus.). 182p. (C). 1993. pap. text 18.00 (*0-205-14873-5*) Allyn.

Nevid, Jeffrey S. & Fichner-Rathus, Lois. Human Sexuality. 2nd ed. 384p. 1995. pap. text, student ed. 27.00 (*0-205-19991-7*) Allyn.

Nevid, Jeffrey S.j. Choices: Sex in the Age of STDs. 2nd ed. LC 97-22388. 292p. 1997. pap. text 26.00 (*0-205-27829-9*) P-H.

Nevidjon, Brenda. Building a Legacy: Voices Oncology Nurses. LC 95-4063. (Nursing Ser.). 464p. 1995. 49.95 (*0-86720-727-2*) Jones & Bartlett.

Nevidjon, Brenda M. & Sowers, Kevin W. Cancer Care: A Nurses' Guide. 448p. pap. text 36.95 (*0-7817-1587-3*) Lppncott W & W.

Nevil, Nevalyn F., et al. Socialization Games for Persons with Disabilities: Structured Group Activities for Social & Interpersonal Development. LC 96-37683. (Illus.). 176p. 1997. text 45.95 (*0-398-06749-X*); pap. text 32.95 (*0-398-06746-5*) C C Thomas.

Nevile, Liddy & Noss, Richard. Proceedings of Logo Mathematics Education Conference. (C). 1992. pap. 70.00 (*0-86431-132-X*, Pub. by Aust Council Educ Res) St Mut.

Nevile, Pran. Lahore: A Sentimental Journey. (C). 1993. 16.00 (*81-7023-253-8*, Pub. by Allied Pubs) S Asia.

***Nevile, Pran.** Rare Glimpses of the Raj. LC 98-901717. xi, 155 p. 1998. write for info. (*81-7039-228-4*) Somaiya Publns.

Nevill, A. M. & Chatterton, M., eds. New Concerete Technologies & Building Design. LC TA0439.N58. 134p. reprint ed. pap. 41.60 (*0-608-30927-3*, 202098300020) Bks Demand.

Nevill, Antonia, tr. see Agulhon, Maurice.

Nevill, Antonia, tr. see David, Jean-Michel.

Nevill, Antonia, tr. see Furet, Francois.

Nevill, Antonia, tr. see Lancel, Serge.

Nevill, Antonia, tr. see Le Glay, Marcel, et al.

Nevill, Antonia, tr. see Richard, Yann.

Nevill, Antonia, tr. see Turcan, Robern.

Nevill, Barry S., ed. Life at the Court of Queen Victoria: Illustrated from the Collection of Lord Edward Pelham-Clinton, Master of the Household with Selections from the Journals of Queen Victoria. (Illus.). 224p. (Orig.). 1997. pap. 26.95 (*0-7509-1481-5*, Pub. by Sutton Pub Ltd) Intl Pubs Mktg.

Nevill, Ted. Scottish Regiments. (Europa Militaria Ser.: Vol. 24). (Illus.). 64p. 1999. pap. 19.95 (*1-86126-186-1*, Pub. by Cro1wood) Motorbooks Intl.

***Nevill, Ted.** Scottish Regiments. (Illus.). 1999. pap. 19.95 (*1-86126-284-1*) Cro1wood.

Nevill, W. The Castell of Pleasure. (EETS, OS Ser.: No. 179). 1972. reprint ed. 36.00 (*0-527-00176-7*) Periodicals Srv.

Neville. Awakened Imagination: Including the Search. 94p. 1993. reprint ed. pap. 8.95 (*0-87516-656-3*) DeVorss.

***Neville.** The China Year. 256p. 1999. pap. 4.95 (*0-06-440407-2*) HarpC Child Bks.

Neville. Concrete Technology. (C). 1987. pap. 49.95 (*0-582-98859-4*, Pub. by Addison-Wesley) Longman.

***Neville.** Immortal Man: A Compilation of Lectures. LC 77-81534. 256p. 1999. pap. 12.95 (*0-87516-723-3*) DeVorss.

Neville. The Law & the Promise. 156p. 1984. reprint ed. pap. 8.95 (*0-87516-532-X*) DeVorss.

— Properties of Concrete. 4th ed. LC 95-31843. 1995. pap. text. write for info. (*0-582-23070-5*, Pub. by Addison-Wesley) Longman.

— The Resurrection. 266p. 1966. pap. 11.95 (*0-87516-076-X*) DeVorss.

— Seedtime & Harvest. 160p. 1985. reprint ed. pap. 8.95 (*0-87516-557-5*) DeVorss.

— Your Faith Is Your Fortune. 1941. pap. 8.95 (*0-87516-078-6*) DeVorss.

Neville, A. C. Biology of Fibrous Composites: Development Beyond the Cell Membrane. (Illus.). 224p. (C). 1993. text 69.95 (*0-521-41051-7*) Cambridge U Pr.

— Symposia of the Royal Entomological Society of London: Insect Ultrastructure. 190p. 1984. 45.00 (*0-7855-0678-0*) St Mut.

Neville, A. G. & Ashe, A. W. Equity Proceedings with Precedents New South Wales. 1981. 102.00 (*0-409-49039-3*, AT, MICHIE) LEXIS Pub.

Neville, A. M., ed. Biochemical & Immunologic Diagnosis of Cancer. (Journal: Tumor Biology: Vol. 8, No. 2-3, 1987). (Illus.). 124p. 1987. pap. 71.50 (*3-8055-4665-3*) S Karger.

Neville, A. M., jt. auth. see Ghali, A.

Neville, A. M., jt. auth. see Ghali, Wagdy R.

Neville, A. M., jt. ed. see Glanville, J.

Neville, Adam M. Properties of Concrete: The Final Edition. 4th ed. LC 97-148152. 844p. 1996. pap. 99.00 (*0-470-23527-6*) Wiley.

Neville, Adam M. & Wainwright, P. High Alumina Cement Concrete. LC 76-354854. 201p. reprint ed. pap. 62.40 (*0-608-30580-4*, 201630200003) Bks Demand.

Neville, Amelia R. The Fantastic City: Memoirs of the Social & Romantic Life of Old San Francisco. LC 75-1863. (Leisure Class in America Ser.). (Illus.). 1975. reprint ed. 29.95 (*0-405-06929-4*) Ayer.

— The Fantastic City San Francisco. 1992. reprint ed. lib. bdg. 75.00 (*0-7812-5069-2*) Rprt Serv.

***Neville, B. & Albright, A. L., eds.** The Management of Spaticity Associated with Cerebral Palsies in Children & Adolescents. (Illus.). 160p. 2000. text. write for info. (*0-9701610-0-X*) Churchill.

Neville, B.G., jt. ed. see Perat, M. Velickovic.

***Neville, Bill.** Beginning Cursive: Modern Handwriting. 32p. (J). 1999. pap. 4.95 (*0-88724-506-4*, CD-0885) Carson-Dellos.

— Beginning Cursive: Traditional Handwriting. 32p. (J). 1999. pap. 4.95 (*0-88724-507-2*, CD-0886) Carson-Dellos.

— Cursive Practice: Modern Handwriting. 32p. (J). 1999. pap. 4.95 (*0-88724-525-0*, CD-0887) Carson-Dellos.

— Cursive Practice: Traditional Handwriting. 32p. (J). 1999. pap. 4.95 (*0-88724-526-9*, CD-0888) Carson-Dellos.

Neville, Brad W., et al. Color Atlas of Clinical Oral Pathology. LC 89-13980. (Illus.). 385p. 1990. text 99.50 (*0-8121-1311-X*) Lppncott W & W.

— Color Atlas of Clinical Oral Pathology. 2nd ed. LC 98-3616. (Illus.). 488p. 1998. 99.95 (*0-683-30208-6*) Lppncott W & W.

— Oral & Maxillofacial Pathology. LC 94-20442. (Illus.). 688p. 1995. text 62.95 (*0-7216-6695-7*, W B Saunders Co) Harcrt Hlth Sci Grp.

Neville, Brian & Goodman, Robert, eds. Congenital Hemiplegia. (Clinics in Developmental Medicine Ser.: Vol. 150). 200p. (C). 2000. text 59.95 (*1-898683-19-0*, Pub. by Mc Keith Pr) Cambridge U Pr.

Neville Brothers. Autobiography. 2000. write for info. (*0-316-26383-4*) Little.

Neville, Charles W. Invariant Subspaces of Hardy Classes on Infinitely Connected Open Surfaces. (Memoirs Ser.: No. 2/160). 151p. 1975. pap. 19.00 (*0-8218-1860-0*, MEMO/2/160) Am Math.

— Invariant Subspaces of Hardy Classes on Infinitely Connected Open Surfaces. LC 75-333144. (American Mathematical Society Ser.: Vol. 160). 161p. 1975. reprint ed. pap. 50.00 (*0-608-07977-4*, 205267200001) Bks Demand.

***Neville, Cynthia.** Violence, Custom & the Law: The Anglo-Scottish Border Lands in the Later Middle Ages. LC 98-202839. 256p. 1998. pap. 30.00 (*0-7486-1073-1*, Pub. by Edinburgh U Pr) Col U Pr.

***Neville, David, et al.** Promoting Positive Parenting of Teenagers. LC 98-19796. (Centre for Fun & Families Ser.). 144p. 1998. pap. 29.95 (*1-85742-417-4*, Pub. by Arena) Ashgate Pub Co.

Neville, Deborah, jt. auth. see Coleman, Bob.

Neville, E. W. Planets in Synastry: Astrological Patterns of Relationships. 276p. 1990. pap. 16.95 (*0-924608-01-3*, Whitford) Schiffer.

— Tarot for Lovers. Lockhart, Julie, ed. LC 87-62096. (Illus.). 252p. 1987. pap. 14.95 (*0-914918-75-3*, Whitford) Schiffer.

Neville, Emily. It's Like This, Cat. (J). 1963. 10.05 (*0-606-01732-1*, Pub. by Turtleback) Demco.

Neville, Emily C. The China Year. LC 90-39899. 256p. (J). (gr. 5-9). 1991. 15.95 (*0-06-024383-X*) HarpC Child Bks.

— It's Like This, Cat. LC 62-21292. (Illus.). 192p. (J). (gr. 4-7). 1963. 15.95 (*0-06-024390-2*) HarpC Child Bks.

— It's Like This, Cat. LC 62-21292. (Illus.). 192p. (YA). (gr. 4-7). 1964. lib. bdg. 15.89 (*0-06-024391-0*) HarpC Child Bks.

— It's Like This, Cat. LC 62-21292. (Trophy Bk.). (Illus.). 192p. (J). (gr. 5-9). 1975. pap. 5.95 (*0-06-440073-5*, HarpTrophy) HarpC Child Bks.

— Newbery Award Library I: It's Like This Cat - Julie of the Wolves - Onion John - Sounder, 4 bks., Set. (J). (gr. 4-6). 1985. pap. 19.80 (*0-06-440162-6*) HarpC Child Bks.

Neville, George. The Argentine Mirror. LC 98-89323. 256p. 1999. pap. 13.99 (*1-56167-487-7*) Am Literary Pr.

Neville, Georgina & Neville, Robert. Family Walks in Oxfordshire. 64p. 1987. 35.00 (*0-905392-21-3*) St Mut.

Neville, Graham. Radical Churchman: Edward Lee Hicks & the New Liberalism. LC 98-26750. 376p. 1999. text 90.00 (*0-19-826977-3*) OUP.

Neville, Graham, ed. The Diaries of Edward Lee Hicks Bishop of Lincoln 1910-1919. (Publications of the Lincoln Record Society: Vol. 82). 303p. 1993. 45.00 (*0-901503-55-X*) Boydell & Brewer.

Neville, Gwen K. The Mother Town: Civic Ritual, Symbols, & Experience in the Borders of Scotland. (Illus.). 176p. 1994. pap. 24.95 (*0-19-509032-2*) OUP.

— The Mother Town: Civic Ritual, Symbols & Experience in the Borders of Scotland. (Illus.). 176p. 1994. text 60.00 (*0-19-508837-9*) OUP.

***Neville-Hadley, Peter.** Beijing - Peking. 2000. pap. 21.95 (*1-86011-933-6*, Pub. by Cadgn Bks) Globe Pequot.

Neville-Hadley, Peter. China: The Silk Route. (Cadogan Guides Ser.). (Illus.). 416p. 1997. pap. text 21.95 (*1-86011-052-5*, Pub. by Cadgn Bks) Macmillan.

Neville, Helen & Halaby, Mona. No-Fault Parenting. LC 82-2525. 484p. 1984. reprint ed. pap. 150.10 (*0-608-02848-7*, 206391400007) Bks Demand.

Neville, Helen & Johnson, Diane C. Temperament Tools: Working with Your Child's Inborn Traits. LC 97-37466. (Illus.). 128p. 1998. pap. 13.95 (*1-884734-34-0*); lib. bdg. 19.95 (*1-884734-35-9*) Parenting Pr.

Neville, Jennifer, jt. auth. see Field-Pickering, Janet.

Neville, Jill. The Love Germ: A Novel. LC 98-24038. 160p. 1998. pap. 12.00 (*1-85984-285-2*, Pub. by Verso) Norton.

Neville, John F. The Press, the Rosenbergs & the Cold War. LC 94-22655. 224p. 1995. 57.95 (*0-275-94995-8*, Praeger Pubs) Greenwood.

Neville, Jonathan. Questions & Answers: Contracts. 2nd rev. ed. (Winning in Law School Ser.). 175p. (Orig.). 1992. pap. text 12.95 (*0-915667-21-5*) Spectra Pub Co.

Neville, Katherine. A Calculated Risk. 1994. mass mkt. 6.99 (*0-345-38682-5*) Ballantine Pub Grp.

— The Eight. 608p. 1990. mass mkt. 6.99 (*0-345-36623-9*) Ballantine Pub Grp.

— Eight. 1998. mass mkt. 6.99 (*0-345-91321-3*) Ballantine Pub Grp.

— Eight Trade. 1997. pap. 12.00 (*0-345-41908-1*) Ballantine Pub Grp.

— The Magic Circle. 1999. mass mkt. 7.99 (*0-345-42313-5*) Ballantine Pub Grp.

Neville, Kathleen. Internal Affairs: The Abuse of Power, Sexual Harassment, & Hypocrisy in the Workplace. 288p. 1999. 24.95 (*0-07-134256-7*) McGraw.

— Yellowbuddy: The Runaway School Bus. (J). (gr. 4-7). 1993. pap. 8.95 (*0-933905-22-X*) Claycomb Pr.

Neville, Kris. The Science Fiction of Kris Neville. Malzberg, Barry N. & Greenberg, Martin H., eds. LC 83-10514. (Alternatives Ser.). 254p. (C). 1984. 21.95 (*0-8093-1112-7*) S Ill U Pr.

Neville, M. C. & Daniel, C. W. The Mammary Gland: Development, Regulation & Function. LC 87-18606. (Illus.). 648p. (C). 1987. text 135.00 (*0-306-42641-2*, Kluwer Plenum) Kluwer Academic.

Neville, Margaret C. & Neifert, Marianne R., eds. Lactation: Physiology, Nutrition & Breast Feeding. LC 83-17652. 482p. 1983. 95.00 (*0-306-41311-6*, Plenum Trade) Perseus Pubng.

Neville, Margaret C., jt. ed. see Jensen, Robert C.

An Asterisk (*) at the beginning of an entry indicates that the title is appearing for the first time.

Neville, Margot. My Bad Boy. large type ed. (Linford Mystery Library). 400p. 1992. pap. 16.99 (*0-7089-7234-9*, Linford) Ulverscroft.

Neville, Mark. Died: Not Yet. (Graphic Works). 36p. 1992. pap. text 2.00 (*0-943123-22-4*) Arjuna Lib Pr.

— The Time Dog. Mycue, Edward, ed. (Took Modern Poetry in English Ser.: No. 16). (Illus.). 32p. (Orig.). 1991. pap. 4.00 (*1-879457-15-6*) Norton Coker Pr.

Neville, Mary, ed. If a Poem Bothers You. (Illus.). 64p. (Orig.). (J). (gr. 2-6). 1991. pap. 3.00 (*0-913678-14-7*) New Day Pr.

***Neville, Pauline.** Peggy. 170p. 1999. pap. write for info. (*1-900850-17-6*) Arcadia Bks.

***Neville, Peter.** Appeasing Hitler. LC 99-37999. (Studies in Diplomacy). 237p. 1999. text 69.95 (*0-312-22850-3*) St Martin.

Neville, Peter. Do Dogs Need Shrinks? What to Do When Man's Best Friend Misbehaves. 288p. 1992. pap. 12.95 (*0-8065-1332-2*, Citadel Pr) Carol Pub Group.

***Neville, Peter.** Dog Owner's Guide: Boxer. (Illus.). 144p. 1999. pap. 12.95 (*0-00-413370-6*, Pub. by HarpC) Trafalgar.

— Dog Owner's Guide: Labrador. (Illus.). 144p. 1999. pap. 12.95 (*0-00-413371-4*, Pub. by HarpC) Trafalgar.

Neville, Peter. Feral Cats in Tunisia. 1984. 30.00 (*0-7855-1127-X*) St Mut.

— France, 1914-69: The Three Republics. (Access to History Ser.). 150p. 1995. pap. 17.00 (*0-340-56561-6*, Pub. by Hodder & Stought Ltd) Lubrecht & Cramer.

— The Holocaust. (Perspectives in History Ser.). (Illus.). 103p. (C). 1999. pap. 11.95 (*0-521-59501-0*) Cambridge U Pr.

— Humane Control of an Urban Cat Colony. 1983. 50.00 (*0-7855-1128-8*) St Mut.

— A Traveller's History of Ireland. 3rd ed. (Traveller's History Ser.). (Illus.). 288p. (Orig.). 1997. pap. 14.95 (*1-56656-259-7*) Interlink Pub.

— Travellers History of Russia & the U. S. S. R. 3rd ed. (Illus.). 336p. 1997. pap. 14.95 (*1-56656-273-2*) Interlink Pub.

Neville, Peter & O'Farrell, Valerie. Manual of Feline Behaviour. Ross, Christopher S., ed. (Illus.). 84p. 1994. pap. text 42.95 (*0-905214-24-2*, Pub. by BSAVA) Iowa St U Pr.

Neville, Peter & Remfry, J. Effect of Neutering on Two Groups of Feral Cats. 1984. 16.00 (*0-7855-2957-8*) St Mut.

Neville, Peter & Tames, Richard. A Traveller's History of Japan. 2nd ed. (Illus.). 304p. 1997. pap. text 14.95 (*1-56656-260-0*) Interlink Pub.

Neville, Peter, et al. The Perfect Kitten. Reader's Digest Editors, ed. LC 97-17994. (Illus.). 160p. 1998. 19.95 (*0-7621-0038-9*, Pub. by RD Assn) Penguin Putnam.

Neville, Peter, jt. auth. see Kagan, Sharon L.

Neville, Peterson & Williams Staff, jt. ed. see Bogard, Lawrence J.

Neville, Richard, jt. ed. see Glanz, Jeffrey.

Neville, Richard C. Solar Energy Conversion: The Solar Cell. 2nd ed. LC 94-39734. 440p. 1995. 181.50 (*0-444-89818-2*) Elsevier.

Neville, Robert, jt. auth. see Neville, Georgina.

Neville, Robert C. The Cosmology of Freedom. LC 95-35771. 385p. (C). 1995. text 59.50 (*0-7914-2757-9*); pap. text 19.95 (*0-7914-2758-7*) State U NY Pr.

— Creativity & God: A Challenge to Process Theology, New Edition. LC 95-39807. 163p. (C). 1995. text 49.50 (*0-7914-2821-4*); pap. text 16.95 (*0-7914-2822-2*) State U NY Pr.

— Eternity & Time's Flow. LC 92-27081. (SUNY Series in Philosophy). 268p. (C). 1993. text 20.50 (*0-7914-1599-6*) State U NY Pr.

— God the Creator: On the Transcendence & Presence of God. LC 90-27103. (Illus.). 320p. (C). 1992. reprint ed. pap. text 18.95 (*0-7914-0844-2*) State U NY Pr.

— The God Who Beckons: Theology in the Form of Sermons. LC 98-48117. 1999. 15.00 (*0-687-08481-4*) Abingdon.

— The Highroad Around Modernism. LC 91-47542. (SUNY Series in Philosophy). 339p. (C). 1992. text 64.50 (*0-7914-1151-6*); pap. text 21.95 (*0-7914-1152-4*) State U NY Pr.

— Normative Cultures. LC 94-33403. 280p. (C). 1995. text 49.50 (*0-7914-2577-0*); pap. text 16.95 (*0-7914-2578-9*) State U NY Pr.

— The Puritan Smile: A Look Toward Moral Reflection. LC 86-30162. 248p. 1987. text 19.50 (*0-88706-542-2*) State U NY Pr.

— Reconstruction of Thinking. LC 81-5347. 350p. (C). 1981. pap. text 19.95 (*0-87395-495-5*) State U NY Pr.

— Recovery of the Measure: Interpretation & Nature. LC 89-11444. 369p. (C). 1989. pap. text 21.95 (*0-7914-0099-9*) State U NY Pr.

— Soldier, Sage, Saint. LC 77-75798. xi, 141p. 1989. reprint ed. pap. 15.00 (*0-8232-1036-7*) Fordham.

— The Tao & the Daimon. LC 82-5888. 281p. (C). 1983. text 59.50 (*0-87395-661-3*); pap. text 19.95 (*0-87395-662-1*) State U NY Pr.

— A Theology Primer. LC 90-19636. 221p. (C). 1991. text 44.50 (*0-7914-0849-3*); pap. text 18.95 (*0-7914-0850-7*) State U NY Pr.

— The Truth of Broken Symbols. LC 95-2363. (SUNY Series in Religious Studies). 320p. (C). 1995. text 59.50 (*0-7914-2741-2*); pap. text 19.95 (*0-7914-2742-0*) State U NY Pr.

Neville, Robert C., ed. New Essays in Metaphysics. LC 86-30011. (SUNY Series in Systematic Philosophy). 321p. (C). 1986. pap. text 20.95 (*0-88706-471-X*) State U NY Pr.

Neville, Robert C., jt. ed. see Kasulis, Thomas P.

Neville, Robert C., ed. & intro. see Delza, Sophia.

***Neville, Robert Cummings.** Boston Confucianism: Portable Tradition in the Late-Modern World. (C). 2000. pap. text 23.95 (*0-7914-4718-9*) State U NY Pr.

— Boston Confucianism: Portable Tradition in the Late-Modern World. (C). 2000. text 71.50 (*0-7914-4717-0*) State U NY Pr.

***Neville, Robert Cummings, ed.** The Human Condition: A Volume in the Comparative Religious Ideas Project. (C). 2000. pap. text 24.95 (*0-7914-4780-4*) State U NY Pr.

— The Human Condition: A Volume in the Comparative Religious Ideas Project. (C). 2000. text 73.50 (*0-7914-4779-0*) State U NY Pr.

— Religious Truth: A Volume in the Comparative Religious Ideas Project. (C). 2000. pap. text 26.95 (*0-7914-4778-2*) State U NY Pr.

— Religious Truth: A Volume in the Comparative Religious Ideas Project. (C). 2000. text 78.50 (*0-7914-4777-4*) State U NY Pr.

— Ultimate Realities: A Volume in the Comparative Religious Ideas Project. (C). 2000. pap. text 24.95 (*0-7914-4776-6*) State U NY Pr.

— Ultimate Realities: A Volume in the Comparative Religious Ideas Project. (C). 2000. text 73.50 (*0-7914-4775-8*) State U NY Pr.

Neville, Robert G., jt. ed. see Benson, John.

Neville-Sington, Pamela. Fanny Trollope: The Life & Adventures of a Clever Woman. 416p. 1998. 29.95 (*0-670-85905-2*, Viking) Viking Penguin.

***Neville, Susan.** Fabrication. 2001. 22.00 (*1-878448-08-0*) MacMurray & Beck.

Neville, Susan. In the House of Blue Lights. LC 97-28953. (Richard Sullivan Prize for Short Fiction Ser.). ix, 169 p. 1998. 35.00 (*0-268-01183-4*); pap. 14.00 (*0-268-01184-2*) U of Notre Dame Pr.

— Indiana Winter. LC 93-40692. 272p. 1994. 29.95 (*0-253-34004-7*); pap. 14.95 (*0-253-20879-3*) Ind U Pr.

— Indiana Winter. 1995. write for info. (*0-253-32953-1*); pap. write for info. (*0-253-21012-7*) Ind U Pr.

— The Invention of Flight. LC 83-24142. (Flannery O'Connor Award for Short Fiction Ser.). 144p. 1984. 19.95 (*0-8203-0706-8*) U of Ga Pr.

***Neville, Susan.** Twilight in Arcadia: Tobacco Farming in Indiana. (Illus.). 100p. 2000. pap. 24.95 (*0-87195-144-4*, Pub. by Ind Hist Soc) Ind U Pr.

Neville, Susan, jt. ed. see Calder, J. Kent.

Neville, Tam L. Journey Cake. LC 97-41141. 88p. (Orig.). 1998. pap. 11.95 (*1-886157-13-8*) BkMk.

Neville, Tove E. Eleven-Headed Avalokitesvara: Chenresigs, Kuan-yin or Kannon Bodhisattva: Its Origin & Iconography. 1999. 79.50 (*81-215-0457-0*, Pub. by M Manoharial) Coronet Bks.

Neville, Victoria Goddard. The Power of Awareness. 124p. 1993. reprint ed. pap. 8.95 (*0-87516-655-5*) DeVorss.

Neville, William. Serve It Up: Volleyball for Life. LC 93-36096. (Illus.). 190p. (C). 1993. pap. 16.95 (*1-55934-110-6*, 1110) Mayfield Pub.

Neville, William J., jt. auth. see United States Volleyball Association Staff.

Neville, Williams. Chronology of the Expanding World, 1492 to 1762. LC 94-30476. 1995. 85.00 (*0-13-326406-8*) S&S Trade.

Nevilles, Renee. The First Book of the Black Goddess. Williams, Tara I., ed. 398p. 1999. pap. write for info. (*0-7392-0082-8*, P02947) Morris Pubng.

Nevills, Jennifer M. Creative Bingo. (Illus.). 94p. (Orig.). 1994. pap. text 9.99 (*0-9655792-1-2*) Don Paul Pub.

— Emotions in Time. (Illus.). vii, 66p. (Orig.). 1996. pap. text 19.99 (*0-9655792-0-4*) Don Paul Pub.

Nevin, Ann I., et al. Collaborative Consultation. 2nd ed. LC 92-42907. (C). 1994. text 38.00 (*0-89079-583-5*, 6598) PRO-ED.

— Models of Curriculum-Based Assessment. 2nd ed. LC 86-17272. (Illus.). 264p. (Orig.). (C). 1996. pap. text 34.00 (*0-89079-629-7*, 7322) PRO-ED.

Nevin, Bruce E. Astrology Inside Out. (Illus.). 320p. 1982. pap. 18.95 (*0-914918-19-2*, Whitford) Schiffer.

***Nevin, David.** Dream West. 928p. 2000. mass mkt. 6.99 (*0-8125-3926-5*) Forge NYC.

— Eagles Cry. 2000. text 24.95 (*0-312-85511-7*) St Martin.

Nevin, David. 1812. 1997. mass mkt. 6.99 (*0-614-27742-6*) Forge NYC.

— 1812. 1997. mass mkt. 6.99 (*0-8125-2471-3*, Pub. by Tor Bks) St Martin.

Nevin, David. 1812. 1997. mass mkt. 8.99 (*0-8125-7150-9*) Tor Bks.

— 1812: A Novel. 442p. 2000. reprint ed. text 25.00 (*0-7881-9050-4*) DIANE Pub.

Nevin, David & Savelle, Isabelle K. John Charles Fremont-the Pathfinder. (Illus.). 12p. 1989. pap. 2.50 (*0-911183-38-8*) Rockland County Hist.

Nevin, Donal, ed. Lion of the Fold: James Larkin. LC 98-231150. (Illus.). 464p. 1998. pap. 19.95 (*0-7171-2779-6*, Pub. by Gill & MacMill) Irish Bks Media.

Nevin, Franklin T. Village of Sewickley, Pennsylvania. (Illus.). 227p. 1997. reprint ed. lib. bdg. 29.00 (*0-8328-7169-9*) Higginson Bk Co.

Nevin, Fred. Business Information Markets, 2002: The Strategic Outlook. 10th ed. (Illus.). 241p. 1998. 2495.00 (*0-88709-115 6*) Simba Info Inc.

Nevin, J. A., jt. ed. see Commons, Michael L.

Nevin, John D. Nevin Genealogica (Some Desc. of Daniel Nevin, Cumberland Valley, Pa., 1770), 2 vols. in 1. 435p. 1995. reprint ed. pap. 65.00 (*0-8328-4453-5*); reprint ed. lib. bdg. 75.00 (*0-8328-4452-7*) Higginson Bk Co.

Nevin, John W. The Anxious Bench: Chambersburg, PA 1844. Kuklick, Bruce, ed. (American Religious Thought of the 18th & 19th Centuries Ser.). 312p. 1987. lib. bdg. 45.00 (*0-8240-6970-6*) Garland.

***Nevin, John Williamson.** The Anxious Bench, Antichrist & The Sermon Catholic Unity. 177p. 2000. pap. 24.00 (*1-57910-429-0*) Wipf & Stock.

— The Mystical Presence. 244p. 2000. pap. 22.00 (*1-57910-348-0*) Wipf & Stock.

Nevin, M. Piano for Adults, Bk. 1. 64p. 1984. pap. 6.95 (*0-7935-0702-2*, 00009295) H Leonard.

Nevin, Pat. Ireland, Where Our Roots Go Deep. LC 87-82207. 320p. 1987. 30.00 (*0-86140-255-3*, Pub. by Smyth); pap. 12.95 (*0-86140-259-6*, Pub. by Smyth) Dufour.

Nevin, Thomas R. Ernst Junger & Germany: Into the Abyss, 1914-1945. LC 96-27326. (Illus.). 312p. 1996. text 24.95 (*0-8223-1879-2*) Duke.

Nevin, Tom. Zamani: African Tales from Long Ago. 1995. pap. 12.95 (*9966-884-29-7*) Jacrnda Wiley.

Nevins, Albert F. Saint Francis of the Seven Seas. LC 95-755666. (Vision Bks.). (Illus.). 130p. (Orig.). (J). (gr. 4-10). 1995. pap. 9.95 (*0-89870-519-3*) Ignatius Pr.

Nevins, Albert J. American Martyrs: From 1542. LC 86-64002. 180p. (Orig.). 1987. pap. 6.95 (*0-87973-488-4*, 488) Our Sunday Visitor.

— Answering a Fundamentalist. LC 90-60644. 144p. (Orig.). 1990. pap. 7.95 (*0-87973-433-7*, 433) Our Sunday Visitor.

— Called to Serve: A Guidebook for Altar Servers. rev. ed. LC 81-82546. 48p. (J). (gr. 4 up). 1981. pap. 15.95 (*0-87973-663-1*, 663) Our Sunday Visitor.

— Catholicism: The Faith of Our Fathers. LC 94-68930. 192p. (Orig.). 1995. pap. 14.95 (*0-87973-650-X*, 650) Our Sunday Visitor.

— Life after Death. LC 83-61888. 156p. (Orig.). 1983. pap. 6.95 (*0-87973-612-7*, 612) Our Sunday Visitor.

— The Life of Jesus Christ. 247p. (Orig.). 1987. pap. 12.95 (*0-87973-500-7*, 500) Our Sunday Visitor.

— Scriptures of Faith: Cornerstone of Catholicism. LC 92-60313. 112p. 1992. pap. 4.95 (*0-87973-480-9*) Our Sunday Visitor.

— Strangers at Your Door: How to Respond to Jehovah's Witnesses, the Mormons, Televangelists, Cults, & More. LC 88-61111. 144p. (Orig.). 1988. pap. 7.95 (*0-87973-496-5*, 496) Our Sunday Visitor.

Nevins, Albert J., ed. see Noll, Archbishop Francis.

Nevins, Allan. American Press Opinion: Washington to Coolidge, A Documentary Record of Editorial Leadership & Criticism, 1785-1927. (BCL1 - U. S. History Ser.). 598p. 1991. reprint ed. lib. bdg. 99.00 (*0-7812-6023-X*) Rprt Serv.

— The American States During & After the Revolution, 1775-1789. (BCL1 - U. S. History Ser.). 728p. 2000. reprint ed. lib. bdg. 109.00 (*0-7812-6134-1*) Rprt Serv.

— American States During & After the Revolution, 1775-1798. LC 68-56552. xviii, 728p. 1969. reprint ed. 57.50 (*0-678-00510-9*) Kelley.

— A Century of Political Cartoons: Caricature in the United States from 1800 to 1900. (BCL1 - U. S. History Ser.). 190p. 1991. reprint ed. lib. bdg. 69.00 (*0-7812-6038-8*) Rprt Serv.

— A Diary of Battle: The Personal Journals of Colonel Charles S. Wainwright, 1861-1865. 1993. 35.00 (*1-879664-15-1*) Stan Clark Military.

— The Emergence of Modern America, 1865-1878. (History - United States Ser.). 446p. 1993. reprint ed. lib. bdg. 99.00 (*0-7812-4906-6*) Rprt Serv.

— The Emergence of Modern America, 1865-1878. LC 77-145207. (Illus.). 1971. reprint ed. 95.00 (*0-403-01127-2*) Scholarly.

— Fremont: Pathmarker of the West. LC 91-40734. (Illus.). xiv, 697p. 1992. reprint ed. pap. 22.00 (*0-8032-8364-4*, Bison Books) U of Nebr Pr.

— Fremont, the World's Greatest Adventurer. 1992. reprint ed. lib. bdg. 75.00 (*0-7812-5070-6*) Rprt Serv.

— History of the Bank of New York & Trust Company, 1784-1934. LC 75-41774. (Companies & Men: Business Enterprises in America Ser.). (Illus.). 1978. reprint ed. 26.95 (*0-405-08088-3*) Ayer.

— History of the U. S. 7th ed. 1989. pap. 6.99 (*0-671-70495-8*) PB.

— James Truslow Adams: Historian of the American Dream. LC 68-16627. (Illus.). 329p. reprint ed. pap. 102.00 (*0-8357-6168-1*, 203445500090) Bks Demand.

— A Pocket History of the U. S. Sacco, Maryanne, ed. 736p. 1992. mass mkt. 7.99 (*0-671-79023-4*) PB.

— The State Universities & Democracy. LC 77-9308. 171p. 1977. reprint ed. lib. bdg. 38.50 (*0-8371-9705-8*, NESU, Greenwood Pr) Greenwood.

Nevins, Allan, ed. Diary of Philip Hone, 1828-1851, 2 vols. LC 77-112559. (Rise of Urban America Ser.). (Illus.). 1970. reprint ed. 57.95 (*0-405-02468-1*) Ayer.

— Letters of Grover Cleveland, 1850-1908. LC 70-123752. (American Public Figures Ser.). 1970. reprint ed. lib. bdg. 75.00 (*0-306-71982-7*) Da Capo.

Nevins, Allan, et al, eds. Civil War Books: A Critical Bibliography, 2 vols. in 1. 326p. 1996. reprint ed. 75.00 (*1-56837-321-X*) Broadfoot.

Nevins, Allan & Commager, Henry S. Breve Historia de Los Estados Unidos (A Pocket History of the Unites States) (SPA) 718p. 1994. 36.99 (*968-16-4256-2*, Pub. by Fondo) Continental Bk.

— A Pocket History of the U. S. (YA). (gr. 10 up). 1991. mass mkt. 4.95 (*0-671-62992-1*) PB.

Nevins, Allan & Hill, Frank E. Ford, 3 vols. Incl. Vol. 1. Times, the Man, the Company. LC 75-41775. 1976. Vol. 2. Expansion & Challenge, 1915-1933. LC 75-41775. 1976. Vol. 3. Decline & Rebirth: 1933-1962. LC 75-41775. 1976. LC 75-41775. (Companies & Men: Business Enterprises in America Ser.). (Illus.). 1976. reprint ed. 154.95 (*0-405-08089-1*) Ayer.

Nevins, Allan & Krout, John A., eds. The Greater City: New York, 1898 to 1948. LC 81-4173. (Illus.). 260p. 1981. reprint ed. lib. bdg. 59.75 (*0-313-23072-2*, NEGC, Greenwood Pr) Greenwood.

Nevins, Allan, ed. see La Follette, Robert M.

Nevins, Allan, ed. see Rhodes, James F.

Nevins, Allan, ed. see Wainwright, Charles S.

Nevins, Christopher B., jt. auth. see Warren, Winthrop D.

Nevins, Dan. Brainbenders. (J). 1996. pap. 2.50 (*0-8167-3140-3*) Troll Communs.

Nevins, Deborah, ed. Grand Central Terminal: City Within the City. LC 82-81177. (Illus.). 148p. (Orig.). 1982. 25.00 (*0-9606892-2-2*) Municipal Art Soc.

Nevins, Deborah & Bogart, Michele. Fauns & Fountains: American Garden Statuary, 1890-1930. LC 85-60160. (Illus.). 80p. (C). 1985. pap. 15.00 (*0-943526-13-2*) Parrish Art.

Nevins, Deborah, et al. Architects' Drawings from the Collection of Barbara Pine. (Illus.). 48p. (Orig.). 1987. pap. 20.00 (*0-941680-05-3*) M&L Block.

Nevins, Edward. Forces of the British Empire - 1914. LC 92-15109. (Illus.). 288p. 1992. 65.00 (*0-918339-18-9*) Vandamere.

Nevins, Elizabeth. Date Tripping with Friends & Lovers: The Fun, Whimsical, Inexpensive, Outrageous, Extravagant, Sensual, Romantic, & Simple Book of Things to Do on a Date. LC 94-92458. (Illus.). 384p. (Orig.). 1995. pap. 9.95 (*0-9643977-0-6*) Sun Tea Bks.

Nevins, Francis M., Jr. Bar-20: The Life of Clarence E. Mulford, Creator of Hopalong Cassidy, with Seven Original Stories Reprinted. LC 92-56670. (Illus.). 264p. 1993. lib. bdg. 37.50 (*0-89950-870-7*) McFarland & Co.

Nevins, Francis M. Commonwealth Avenue. 1997. pap. 14.95 (*0-312-15496-8*) St Martin.

Nevins, Francis M., Jr. Cornell Woolrich: First You Dream, Then You Die. LC 88-40066. 640p. 1988. 19.95 (*0-89296-297-6*, Pub. by Mysterious Pr) Little.

— The Films of Hopalong Cassidy. LC 88-40500. (Illus.). 328p. 1988. pap. 19.95 (*0-936505-09-5*) World Yesterday.

— The Films of The Cisco Kid. LC 98-61613. (Illus.). 240p. 1998. pap. 19.95 (*0-936505-14-1*) World Yesterday.

— Into the Same River Twice. 224p. 1996. 21.00 (*0-7867-0314-8*) Carroll & Graf.

Nevins, Francis M. Joseph H. Lewis: Overview, Interview, & Filmography. LC 98-11493. (Filmmakers Ser.: No. 59). (Illus.). 152p. 1998. 32.50 (*0-8108-3407-3*) Scarecrow.

***Nevins, Francis M.** Paul Landres: A Director's Stories. LC 00-30783. (Filmmakers Ser.). 2000. write for info. (*0-8108-3816-8*) Scarecrow.

Nevins, Francis M., Jr. & Greenberg, Martin H., eds. The Adventures of Henry Turnbuckle: Detective Comedies by Jack Ritchie. LC 86-31372. (Mystery Makers Ser.). 386p. 1987. 31.95 (*0-8093-1397-9*) S Ill U Pr.

— Buffet for Unwelcome Guests: The Best Short Mysteries of Christianna Brand. LC 83-526. (Mystery Makers Ser.). 316p. 1983. 21.95 (*0-8093-1140-2*) S Ill U Pr.

— Exeunt Murderers: The Best Mystery Stories of Anthony Boucher. LC 83-19513. (Mystery Makers Ser.). 320p. 1983. 21.95 (*0-8093-1099-6*) S Ill U Pr.

— Leopold's Way: Detective Stories by Edward D. Hoch. LC 84-27554. (Mystery Makers Ser.). 359p. 1985. 26.95 (*0-8093-1233-6*) S Ill U Pr.

Nevins, Francis M., Jr. & Stanich, Ray. The Sound of Detection: Ellery Queen's Adventures in Radio. LC 85-25462. viii, 109p. 1985. reprint ed. pap. 17.00 (*0-941028-01-1*) Millefleurs.

Nevins, Francis M., Jr., jt. auth. see Greenberg, Martin H.

Nevins, Francis M., Jr., ed. see Hoch, Edward D.

Nevins, Francis M., Jr., ed. see Slesar, Henry.

Nevins, Iris, jt. auth. see Weber, Nancy O.

Nevins, James & Styple, William B. What Death More Glorious: A Biography of General Strong Vincent. (Illus.). 195p. 1997. 21.95 (*1-883926-09-2*) Belle Grv Pub.

Nevins, Mary E. & Chute, Patricia M. Children with Cochlear Implants in Educational Settings. (School-Age Children Ser.). (Illus.). 280p. (Orig.). (C). 1995. pap. text 45.00 (*1-56593-160-2*, 1140) Thomson Learn.

Nevins, Myron & Mellonig, James, eds. Periodontal Therapy Vol. I: Clinical Approaches & Evidence of Success, Vol. 1. LC 97-42610. (Illus.). 412p. 1998. text 178.00 (*0-86715-309-1*) Quint Pub Co.

Nevins, Myron, ed. see Fiorellini, Joseph P.

Nevins, Randi J., jt. auth. see Gorden, William I.

Nevins, Robert. Notebook Progress. 336p. (C). 1995. spiral bd. 44.95 (*0-7872-1011-0*) Kendall-Hunt.

Nevins, W. S., jt. auth. see Webber, C. H.

Nevins, William. Thoughts on Popery. Grob, Gerald N., ed. LC 76-46093. (Anti-Movements in America Ser.). 1977. reprint ed. lib. bdg. 19.95 (*0-405-09966-5*) Ayer.

***Nevinskas, Nancy A. & Pizer, Carol H.** Art in Motion: Early Childhood. (Illus.). 96p. 1999. pap., teacher ed. 11.95 (*1-57690-357-5*, TCM 2357) Tchr Create Mat.

Nevinson, Henry W. Between Two Wars. 1972. 69.95 (*0-87968-725-8*) Gordon Pr.

— Books & Personalities. LC 68-16962. (Essay Index Reprint Ser.). 1977. reprint ed. 20.95 (*0-8369-0738-8*) Ayer.

— Dawn in Russia or Scenes in the Russian Revolution. LC 77-115569. (Russia Observed Ser.). (Illus.). 1971. reprint ed. 25.95 (*0-405-03088-6*) Ayer.

— Essays in Freedom & Rebellion. LC 67-28761. (Essay Index Reprint Ser.). 1977. 19.95 (*0-8369-0739-6*) Ayer.

— Essays, Poems & Tales of Henry Nevinson. Brailsford, Henry, ed. 1977. lib. bdg. 59.95 (*0-8490-1788-2*) Gordon Pr.

— Farewell to America. 1973. 250.00 (*0-87968-103-9*) Gordon Pr.

N

An Asterisk (*) at the beginning of an entry indicates that the title is appearing for the first time.

— Goethe: Man & Poet. LC 77-164619. (Select Bibliographies Reprint Ser.). 1977. reprint ed. 20.95 (*0-8369-5902-7*) Ayer.

— In the Dark Backward. LC 72-111854. (Essay Index Reprint Ser.). 1977. 20.95 (*0-8369-1621-2*) Ayer.

— More Changes, More Chances. 1973. 69.95 (*0-8490-0671-6*) Gordon Pr.

— Running Accompaniments. 1972. 69.95 (*0-8490-0980-4*) Gordon Pr.

— Thomas Hardy. LC 72-2084. (Studies in Thomas Hardy: No. 14). 1972. reprint ed. lib. bdg. 49.00 (*0-8383-1466-X*) M S G Haskell Hse.

— Visions & Memories. 1972. 69.95 (*0-8490-1262-7*) Gordon Pr.

Nevis, Edwin C. Organizational Consulting: A Gestalt Approach. (Gestalt Institute of Cleveland Press Book Ser.). 225p. 1987. pap. 22.50 (*0-88163-249-X*) Analytic Pr.

Nevis, Edwin C., ed. Gestalt Therapy: Perspectives & Applications. (Gestalt Institute of Cleveland Press Book Ser.). 366p. 1992. pap. 29.95 (*0-88163-247-3*) Analytic Pr.

Nevis, Edwin C., et al. Intentional Revolutions: A Seven-Point Strategy for Transforming Organizations. (Business & Management Ser.). 270p. 1996. 32.95 (*0-7879-0240-3*) Jossey-Bass.

Nevis, Joel A. Finnish Particle Clitics & General Clitic Theory. (Linguistics Ser.). 176p. 1988. text 10.00 (*0-8240-5193-9*) Garland.

— FUSAC '88 ACEFO: Proceedings of the Sixth Annual Meeting of the Finno-Ugric Studies Association of Canada. LC 89-34253. 158p. (C). 1989. lib. bdg. 44.50 (*0-8191-7492-0*, Pub. by Finno-Ugric Studies) U Pr of Amer.

Nevis, Joel A., et al, eds. Clitics: A Comprehensive Bibliography 1892-1991. LC 94-27029. (Library & Information Sources in Linguistics: Vol. 22). xxxviii, 274p. 1994. lib. bdg. 69.00 (*1-55619-252-5*) J Benjamins Pubng Co.

Nevis, St. Kitts & Jagdeo, Tirbani P. Caribbean Contraceptive Prevalence Surveys. 1985. write for info. (*0-916683-16-8*) Intl Plan Parent.

Nevisnon, Henry W. Plea of Pan (1901) 212p. 1998. reprint ed. pap. 17.95 (*0-7661-0572-5*) Kessinger Pub.

Nevison, Christopher H., et al. Laboratories for Parallel Programming. LC 93-46893. (Computer Science: Artificial Intelligence Ser.). 352p. (C). 1994. spiral bd. 45.00 (*0-86720-470-2*) Jones & Bartlett.

Nevitt, Amy. Fetal Alcohol Syndrome. rev. ed. (Drug Abuse Prevention Library). (Illus.). 64p. (YA). (gr. 7-12). 1998. lib. bdg. 17.95 (*0-8239-2829-2*) Rosen Group.

Nevitt, Gerald G. Vision for the Local Congregation: God's People on Mission Through Ministry. 210p. 1995. pap. write for info. (*1-887998-01-2*) Ch of God in MI.

Nevitt, Peter, jt. auth. see Fabozzi, Frank J.

Nevitt, Peter K. & Fabozzi, Frank J. Equipment Leasing. 4th ed. (Illus.). 550p. 1999. 150.00 (*1-883249-66-X*) F J Fabozzi.

Nevitt, Peter K., et al. Equipment Leasing for Commercial Bankers. LC 87-5532. (Illus.). 136p. (Orig.). 1987. pap. text 43.00 (*0-936742-37-2*) Robt Morris Assocs.

Nevitte, Neil. The Decline of Deference: Canadian Value Change in Cross-Cultural Perspective. 360p. 1996. pap. 24.95 (*1-55111-031-8*) Broadview Pr.

Nevitte, Neil & Gibbins, Roger. New Elites in Old States: Ideologies in Anglo-American Democracies. (Illus.). 352p. 1991. pap. text 29.95 (*0-19-540803-9*) OUP.

Nevitte, Neil & Kornberg, Allan, eds. Minorities & the Canadian State. 320p. 1994. 24.95 (*0-88962-278-7*); pap. 14.95 (*0-88962-277-9*) Mosaic.

***Nevitte, Neil, et al.** The Unsteady State: The 1997 Canadian Federal Election. (Illus.). 192p. 1999. pap. text 24.95 (*0-19-541466-7*) OUP.

Nevitte, Neil, jt. ed. see Feldman, Elliot J.

Nevius, Blake. American Novel: Sinclair Lewis to the Present. LC 76-103094. (Goldentree Bibliographies Series in Language & Literature). (C). 1970. pap. text 13.95 (*0-88295-524-1*) Harlan Davidson.

Nevius, Blake, ed. see Cooper, James Fenimore.

Nevius, Blake, ed. & intro. see Cooper, James Fenimore.

Nevius, Sandy, jt. auth. see Arnold, Larry.

Nevling, Donna. There Has to Be a Star. 26p. 1998. pap. 6.99 (*1-891635-10-7*) Moore Bks.

Nevo, Baruch, ed. Scientific Aspects of Graphology: A Handbook. (Illus.). 362p. 1987. pap. 44.95 (*0-398-06304-4*) C C Thomas.

— Scientific Aspects of Graphology: A Handbook. (Illus.). 362p. (C). 1987. 59.95 (*0-398-05245-X*) C C Thomas.

***Nevo, Baruch & Breitstein, Stephen.** Psychological & Behavioral Aspects of Diving. LC 98-89160. (Illus.). 192p. 1999. 19.95 (*0-941332-73-X*, B0993) Best Pub Co.

Nevo, David. School-Based Evaluation: A Dialogue for School Improvement. LC 94-46676. 214p. 1995. text 69.25 (*0-08-041942-9*, Pergamon Pr) Elsevier.

Nevo, David & Smilansky, M. The Gifted Disadvantaged: A Ten Year Longitudinal Study of Compensatory Education in Israel. x, 246p. 1979. 79.00 (*0-685-47171-3*) Gordon & Breach.

Nevo, David, jt. auth. see Glasman, Naftaly S.

Nevo, Denise. We Remember: Twenty-Four Members of Kibbutz Megido Testify. Berger, Mira, ed. 336p. 1994. 22.95 (*0-88400-176-8*, Shengold Bks) Schreiber Pub.

Nevo, Eviatar. Mosaic Evolution of Subterranean Mammals: Regression, Progression & Global Convergence. LC 99-10301. (Illus.). 512p. 2000. text 175.00 (*0-19-857572-6*) OUP.

Nevo, Eviatar, jt. auth. see Vasser, Solomon P.

Nevo, Joseph & Pappe, Ilan, eds. Jordan in the Middle East: The Making of a Pivotal State. LC 94-4617. 1994. 52.50 (*0-7146-3454-9*, Pub. by F Cass Pubs) Intl Spec Bk.

Nevo, Ruth. Comic Transformations in Shakespeare. 1981. pap. 13.95 (*0-416-73890-7*, NO.6351) Routledge.

— Shakespeare's Other Language. 160p. 1987. text 39.50 (*0-416-06402-7*) Routledge.

Nevo, Ruth, tr. see Amichai, Yehuda.

Nevsky, Angel, tr. see Scribner, Susan M.

***New.** After the Award. LC 99-44838. (Illus.). 374p. (C). 2000. pap. 39.95 incl. disk (*0-471-33245-3*) Wiley.

New. Dictionary Catalog of the Slavonic Collection. 2nd rev. ed. 1980. 4985.00 (*0-8161-1264-9*, G K Hall & Co) Mac Lib Ref.

— United States Local History Catalog. 1980. 200.00 (*0-8161-1285-1*, G K Hall & Co) Mac Lib Ref.

New & Cormack. Why Did I Do That? (Illus.). (J). 1997. pap. text 19.95 (*0-340-69387-8*, Pub. by Hodder & Stought Ltd) Trafalgar.

New & Rosengarten. Modern Stories in English. 3rd ed. 1991. pap. text. write for info. (*0-7730-5127-9*) Addison-Wes.

New Age Bible Interpretation Staff. New Age Bible Interpretation, Vol. 1. (Illus.). 496p. 1990. reprint ed. lib. bdg. 29.00 (*0-933963-01-7*) New Age Bible.

— New Age Bible Interpretation, Vol. 2. (Illus.). 469p. 1995. reprint ed. lib. bdg. 29.00 (*0-933963-02-5*) New Age Bible.

— New Age Bible Interpretation, Vol. 3. Paelian, Frances, ed. (Illus.). 516p. 1986. reprint ed. text 29.00 (*0-933963-03-3*) New Age Bible.

— New Age Bible Interpretation, Vol. 4. 144p. 1994. reprint ed. pap. 22.00 (*0-933963-04-1*) New Age Bible.

— New Age Bible Interpretation, Vol. 5. 230p. 1992. reprint ed. lib. bdg. 25.00 (*0-933963-05-X*) New Age Bible.

— New Age Bible Interpretation, Vol. 6. (Illus.). 255p. 1992. lib. bdg. 25.00 (*0-933963-06-8*) New Age Bible.

— New Age Bible Interpretation, Vol. 7. (Illus.). 298p. 1988. lib. bdg. 25.00 (*0-933963-07-6*) New Age Bible.

New Age Journal Editors & Miller, Ronald S. As above, So Below: Paths to Spiritual Renewal in Daily Life. LC 91-38673. 346p. (Orig.). 1992. pap. 16.95 (*0-87477-659-7*, Tarcher Putnam) Putnam Pub Group.

***New Age Panel of Experts Staff.** The Complete Idiot's Guide to New Millennium Predictions. (Complete Idiot's Guide Ser.). 400p. 1999. pap. 18.95 (*0-02-863112-9*, Pub. by Macmillan Gen Ref) S&S Trade.

New American Roget's College Thesaurus Editors. The New American Roget's College Thesaurus. 1986. pap. 3.50 (*0-317-47644-0*) NAL.

New Americas Press Staff, ed. A Dream Compels Us: Voices of Salvadoran Women. LC 89-11598. (Illus.). 248p. 1989. 25.00 (*0-89608-369-1*); pap. 11.00 (*0-89608-368-3*) South End Pr.

New, Anne L. Raise More Money for Your Nonprofit Organization: A Guide to Evaluating & Improving Your Fundraising. 55p. (Orig.). 1991. pap. text 14.95 (*0-87954-388-4*) Foundation Ctr.

New Atlantean Press Staff. Vaccine Exemptions: A State-by-State Summary of Legal Exemptions to "Mandatory" Vaccine Laws. 16p. (Orig.). 1995. pap. 10.00 (*1-881217-07-8*) New Atlantean.

New, Bill D., jt. auth. see Wright, D. Franklin.

New Canadian Library Staff. Poets Between the Wars. 198p. 1996. pap. text 7.95 (*0-7710-9475-2*) McCland & Stewart.

— Poets of Contemporary Canada. 144p. 1996. pap. text 7.95 (*0-7710-9506-6*) McCland & Stewart.

New Careers Center, Inc. Staff & Frey, Judith. College Degrees You Can Earn from Home: How to Earn a First-Class Degree Without Attending Class. 181p. 1995. pap. 14.95 (*0-911781-12-9*) Live Oak Pubns.

New, Carl R., jt. auth. see Wolf, Charles, Jr.

New, Caroline. Agency, Health, & Social Survival: The Eco-Politics of Rival Psychologies. LC 96-13394. 192p. 1996. pap. 22.95 (*0-7484-0247-0*, Pub. by Tay Francis Ltd) Taylor & Francis.

— Agency, Health & Social Survival: The Eco-Politics of Rival Psychologies. LC 96-13394. 192p. 1996. 69.95 (*0-7484-0246-2*, Pub. by Tay Francis Ltd) Taylor & Francis.

New, Charles. Life, Wanderings & Labours in Eastern Africa. (Illus.). 529p. 1971. reprint ed. 59.50 (*0-7146-1876-4*, BHA-01876, Pub. by F. Cass Pubs) Intl Spec Bk.

New, Cheryl. Grantseeker's Tool Kit: A Comprehensive Guide to Fine Funding. LC 98-14681. (Nonprofit Law, Finance, & Management Ser.). 272p. 1998. pap. 39.95 incl. disk (*0-471-19303-8*) Wiley.

New, Christopher. Philosophy of Literature: An Introduction. LC 98-39518. 1998. 65.00 (*0-415-14485-X*) Routledge.

— Philosophy of Literature: An Introduction. LC 98-39518. viii, 151p. 1999. pap. write for info. (*0-415-14486-8*) Routledge.

New City Press Editorial Staff, ed. see Lubich, Chiara.

New Combined Bible Dictionary & Concordance Staff. New Combined Bible Dictionary & Concordance. 456p. (YA). (gr. 10). 1973. pap. 6.99 (*0-8010-6680-8*) Baker Bks.

New Connecticut Chapter D.A.R. Staff. Record of the Revolutionary Soldiers Buried in Lake County, with a Partial List of Those in Geauga Co. (Illus.). 94p. 1997. reprint ed. pap. 17.00 (*0-8328-6333-5*) Higginson Bk Co.

New Covent Garden Soup Company Staff, ed. Soup & Beyond: Soup, Beans & Other Things. (Illus.). 192p. 1999. pap. 22.50 (*0-333-75226-0*) Trans-Atl Phila.

New Culture Club Staff, ed. see Ree, Jim.

New, Daniel & Kincaid, Cliff. Michael New: Mercenary... Or American Soldier? 2nd rev. ed. (Illus.). 1999. pap. 19.95 (*0-9666813-2-0*) D New.

New, David S. Daring to Dream Again: Breaking Through Barriers That Hold Us Back, Small Group Leader's Guide. (1994 50-Day Spiritual Adventure Ser.). (Illus.). 52p. (Orig.). 1993. pap. text, student ed. 9.99 (*1-879050-18-8*) Chapel of Air.

New, Derek. Infidelis: A Modern Fable. LC 97-40308. 1997. write for info. (*0-7734-8454-X*) E Mellen.

New Dimensions Foundation Staff, ed. Worlds Beyond: The Everlasting Frontier. LC 78-54345. 320p. 1978. pap. 6.95 (*0-915904-36-5*) And-Or Bks.

New Directions in Physical Education Staff. New Directions in Physical Education, Vol. 1, YN1990. Armstrong, Neil, ed. LC 90-31892. 175p. 1990. reprint ed. pap. 54.30 (*0-608-07115-3*, 206734200001) Bks Demand.

— New Directions in Physical Education, Vol. 2, YN1990. Armstrong, Neil, ed. LC 90-31892. 221p. 1990. reprint ed. pap. 68.60 (*0-608-07116-1*, 206734200002) Bks Demand.

New, Elisa. The Lines's Eye: Poetic Experience, American Sight. LC 98-23450. 1998. 49.95 (*0-674-53462-X*) HUP.

— The Lines's Eye: Poetic Experience, American Sight. LC 98-23450. x, 352p. 1999. text 24.95 (*0-674-53463-8*) HUP.

— The Regenerate Lyric: Theology & Innovation in American Poetry. LC 92-23412. (Cambridge Studies in American Literature & Culture: No. 64). (Illus.). 288p. (C). 1993. text 69.95 (*0-521-43021-6*) Cambridge U Pr.

***New, Elizabeth.** Traitement de Textes. LC 99-46097. (FRE.). 98p. 1999. pap. text 21.00 (*0-13-021066-8*) P-H.

New England Association for Women in Psychology St, ed. Current Feminist Issues in Psychotherapy. LC 82-15721. (Women & Therapy Ser.: Vol. 1, No. 3). 115p. 1983. text 29.95 (*0-86656-206-0*) Haworth Pr.

New England Banking Institute Staff. Bank Operations. 196p. (C). 1990. pap. text 56.00 (*0-536-57797-8*) Pearson Custom.

— Branch Management. 328p. (C). 1991. pap. text 58.00 (*0-536-58058-8*) Pearson Custom.

— Fundamentals of Banking. 2nd ed. 336p. (C). 1991. pap. text 74.00 (*0-536-57950-4*) Pearson Custom.

— Fundamentals of Banking. 4th ed. LC 97-157951. 288p. (C). 1997. pap. text 38.00 (*0-536-00016-6*) Pearson Custom.

New England Deaconess Hospital & Harvard Medical S, et al. The Wellness Book: The Comprehensive Guide to Maintaining Health & Treating Stress-Related Illness. LC 92-39899. (Illus.). 512p. 1993. per. 15.00 (*0-671-79750-6*) S&S Trade.

***New England Genealogy Society Staff.** The New England Historical & Genealogical Register, 1904, Vol. 58. (Illus.). 504p. 1999. reprint ed. pap. 35.50 (*0-7884-1087-3*, NR58) Heritage Bk.

New England Hist. Gen. Soc. Staff. The New England Historical & Genealogical Register, Vol. 35. (Illus.). 419p. 1996. pap. 30.00 (*0-7884-0432-6*, NR35) Heritage Bk.

— The New England Historical & Genealogical Register, Vol. 36. (Illus.). 439p. 1996. pap. 29.50 (*0-7884-0472-5*, NR36) Heritage Bk.

— The New England Historical & Genealogical Register, Vol. 37. (Illus.). 436p. 1996. pap. 29.50 (*0-7884-0473-3*, NR37) Heritage Bk.

— The New England Historical & Genealogical Register, 1886, Vol. XL. 432p. 1996. reprint ed. pap. 29.50 (*0-7884-0539-X*, NR40) Heritage Bk.

— The New England Historical & Genealogical Register, 1887, Vol. XLI. 450p. 1996. reprint ed. pap. 29.50 (*0-7884-0540-3*, NR41) Heritage Bk.

— The New England Register, 1880, Vol. 34. (Illus.). 445p. 1996. pap. 33.00 (*0-7884-0431-8*, NR34) Heritage Bk.

New England Historic Genealogical Soc. Staff. The New England Historical & Genealogical Register, Vol. XLIV, 1890. (Illus.). 472p. 1997. reprint ed. pap. 29.50 (*0-7884-0611-6*, NR44) Heritage Bk.

— The New England Historical & Genealogical Register, Vol. XLV, 1891. (Illus.). 537p. 1997. reprint ed. pap. 29.50 (*0-7884-0610-8*, NR45) Heritage Bk.

New England Historic Genealogical Society Staff. The New England Historical & Genealogical Register, No. LII. 551p. 1998. reprint ed. pap. 40.00 (*0-7884-0916-6*, NR52) Heritage Bk.

— The New England Historical & Genealogical Register, Vol. 42. (Illus.). 432p. 1996. reprint ed. pap. 29.50 (*0-7884-0583-7*, NR42) Heritage Bk.

— The New England Historical & Genealogical Register, Vol. XLIII. 510p. 1996. reprint ed. pap. 29.50 (*0-7884-0584-5*, NR43) Heritage Bk.

— The New England Historical & Genealogical Register, Vol. 46. (Illus.). vii, 518p. 1997. reprint ed. pap. 29.50 (*0-7884-0651-5*, NR46) Heritage Bk.

— The New England Historical & Genealogical Register, Vol. 47. (Illus.). 595p. 1997. reprint ed. pap. 29.50 (*0-7884-0652-3*, NR47) Heritage Bk.

— The New England Historical & Genealogical Register: 1900. 695p. 1998. reprint ed. pap. 46.50 (*0-7884-1029-6*, NR54) Heritage Bk.

***New England Historic Genealogical Society Staff.** The New England Historical & Genealogical Register Vol. LXIII: 1909. 544p. 1999. reprint ed. pap. 36.00 (*0-7884-1344-9*, NR63) Heritage Bk.

New England Historic Genealogical Society Staff. New England Historical Genealogical Register, Vol. LIII. 522p. 1998. reprint ed. pap. 38.00 (*0-7884-0917-4*, NR53) Heritage Bk.

New England Historic Genealogical Society Staff, jt. auth. see Bangs, Jeremy D.

New England Historical & Genealogical Register Sta. Mayflower Source Records: Primary Data Concerning Southeastern Massachusetts, Cape Cod, & the Islands of Nantucket & Martha's Vineyard, from the New England Historical & Genealogical Register. 832p. 1997. reprint ed. 33.50 (*0-8063-1145-2*) Genealog Pub.

New England Historical & Genealogical Society Staf. The Greenlaw Index to the New England Historical Geneological Society. 1981. 260.00 (*0-8161-1335-1*, G K Hall & Co) Mac Lib Ref.

— The New England Historical & Genealogical Register, Vol. VII, 1853. 388p. (Orig.). 1992. reprint ed. pap. text 25.00 (*1-55613-687-0*) Heritage Bk.

— The New England Historical & Genealogical Register, Vol. VIII, 1854. 388p. (Orig.). 1992. reprint ed. pap. text 25.00 (*1-55613-688-9*) Heritage Bk.

— The New England Historical & Genealogical Register, Vol. XVI, 1862. (Illus.). 397p. (Orig.). 1993. reprint ed. pap. text 25.00 (*1-55613-841-5*) Heritage Bk.

— The New England Historical & Genealogical Register, Vol. 24. 451p. (Orig.). 1994. pap. text 25.00 (*0-7884-0071-1*) Heritage Bk.

— The New England Historical & Genealogical Register, 1856, Vol. X. 379p. (Orig.). 1993. reprint ed. pap. text 25.00 (*1-55613-745-1*) Heritage Bk.

— The New England Historical & Genealogical Register, 1857, Vol. XI. xii, 380p. 1993. reprint ed. pap. text 25.00 (*1-55613-777-X*) Heritage Bk.

— The New England Historical & Genealogical Register, 1858, Vol. XII. vi, 379p. 1993. reprint ed. pap. text 25.00 (*1-55613-778-8*) Heritage Bk.

— The New England Historical & Genealogical Register, 1859, Vol. 13. iv, 387p. (Orig.). 1993. pap. 22.00 (*1-55613-813-X*) Heritage Bk.

— The New England Historical & Genealogical Register, 1860, Vol. 14. v, 390p. (Orig.). 1993. reprint ed. pap. text 25.00 (*1-55613-814-8*) Heritage Bk.

— The New England Historical & Genealogical Register, 1861, Vol. 15. (Illus.). 375p. 1993. reprint ed. pap. text 25.00 (*1-55613-840-7*) Heritage Bk.

— The New England Historical & Genealogical Register, 1863, Vol. XVII. (Illus.). 387p. (Orig.). 1994. reprint ed. pap. text 25.00 (*1-55613-937-3*) Heritage Bk.

— The New England Historical & Genealogical Register, 1864, Vol. XVIII. (Illus.). 409p. (Orig.). 1994. reprint ed. pap. text 25.00 (*1-55613-938-1*) Heritage Bk.

— The New England Historical & Genealogical Register, 1867, Vol. 2. 399p. (Orig.). 1994. pap. text 25.00 (*0-7884-0012-6*) Heritage Bk.

— The New England Historical & Genealogical Register, 1873, Vol. 27. 464p. (Orig.). 1995. pap. text 25.00 (*0-7884-0183-1*) Heritage Bk.

— The New England Historical & Genealogical Register, 1876, Vol. 30. 497p. 1995. reprint ed. pap. text 27.50 (*0-7884-0239-0*) Heritage Bk.

— The New England Historical & Genealogical Register, 1877, Vol. 31. 468p. 1995. reprint ed. pap. text 27.50 (*0-7884-0240-4*) Heritage Bk.

— The New England Historical & Genealogical Register, 1878, Vol. 32. 464p. 1995. reprint ed. pap. 27.50 (*0-7884-0292-7*) Heritage Bk.

— The New England Historical & Genealogical Register, 1879, Vol. 33. (Illus.). 460p. 1995. reprint ed. pap. 27.50 (*0-7884-0293-5*) Heritage Bk.

— The New England Historical & Genealogical Register, 1894, Vol. XLVIII. 579p. 1998. reprint ed. pap. 29.50 (*0-7884-0814-3*, NR48) Heritage Bk.

— The New England Historical & Genealogical Register, 1895, Vol. XLIX. 576p. 1998. pap. 29.50 (*0-7884-0815-1*, NR49) Heritage Bk.

— The New England Historical & Genealogical Registry, 1868, Vol. 2. 500p. (Orig.). 1994. pap. text 25.00 (*0-7884-0013-4*) Heritage Bk.

— Vital Records of Tisbury, Massachusetts, to the Year 1850. ii, 244p. 1992. reprint ed. pap. 19.00 (*1-55613-555-6*) Heritage Bk.

New England Historical & Genealogical Society Staf & Lainhart, Ann S. Digging for Genealogical Treasure in New England Town Records. LC 96-848. 1996. 15.00 (*0-88082-053-5*) New Eng Hist.

New England Historical & Genealogical Staff. The New England Historical & Genealogical Register, 1855, Vol. IX. 388p. (Orig.). 1993. reprint ed. pap. text 25.00 (*1-55613-744-3*) Heritage Bk.

***New England Historical Gen. Society Staff.** New England Historical & Genealogical Register, Vol. 61. 552p. 1999. reprint ed. pap. 38.50 (*0-7884-1212-4*, NR61) Heritage Bk.

***New England Historical Genealogical Society Staff.** The New Englad Historical & Genealogical Register, Vol. 65. (Illus.). 537p. 2000. pap. 33.50 (*0-7884-1388-0*, NR65) Heritage Bk.

New England Historical Genealogical Society Staff. The New England Historical & Genealogical Register, Vol. L VII (Illus.). 510p. 1999. reprint ed. pap. 35.00 (*0-7884-1076-8*, NR57) Heritage Bk.

New England Historical Genealogy Society. The New England Historical & Genealogy Register. (Illus.). 542p. 1998. reprint ed. pap. 37.50 (*0-7884-1035-0*, NR55) Heritage Bk.

***New England Historical Society Members.** The New England Historical & Genealogical Register, 1906. (Illus.). 576p. 1999. reprint ed. pap. 39.50 (*0-7884-1191-8*, NR60) Heritage Bk.

New England Historical Society Staff. The New England Historical & Genealogical Register, Vol. 59. 512p. 1999. pap. 36.00 (*0-7884-1139-X*, NR59) Heritage Bk.

***New England History & Genealogical Society Staff.** The New England Historical & Genealogical Register Vol. 62: 1908. 568p. 1999. pap. 39.00 (*0-7884-1313-9*) Heritage Bk.

An Asterisk (*) at the beginning of an entry indicates that the title is appearing for the first time.

New England Jeweler Staff. Illustrated Jewelry Catalog, 1892. unabridged ed. LC 98-28059. (Illus.). 160p. 1998. pap. 12.95 (*0-486-40296-7*) Dover.

New England Press Staff, ed. Vermont Inns & Bed & Breakfast Inns. LC 98-66945. (Illus.). 88p. (Orig.). 1998. pap. 9.95 (*1-881535-29-0*) New Eng Pr VT.

New England Publishing Associates Staff. Advertising for a Small Business Made Simple. LC 95-11876. (Made Simple Bks.). 1996. 12.00 (*0-385-47567-5*) Doubleday.

New England Regional Commission. The New England Regional Plan: An Economic Development Strategy. LC 81-50584. 158p. reprint ed. pap. 49.00 (*0-608-16638-3*, 202753300055) Bks Demand.

New England Science Fiction Association Staff. NESFA Index: Science Fiction Magazines & Original Anthologies 1975. iv, 36p. 1976. pap. 5.00 (*0-915368-04-8*) New Eng SF Assoc.

— The NESFA Index: Science Fiction Magazines & Original Anthologies 1976. iii, 38p. 1977. pap. 5.00 (*0-915368-05-6*) New Eng SF Assoc.

New England Society Of Jungian Analysts Staff. The Analytic Life: Personal & Professional Aspects of Being a Jungian Analyst. 78p. 1988. pap. 11.95 (*0-938434-28-4*) Sigo Pr.

New England Solar Electric, Inc. Staff. Battery Book for Your PV Home. (The PV Home Series Booklets). (Illus.). 25p. (Orig.). 1991. pap. text 8.00 (*1-879523-02-7*) Nw England Solar.

— PV-Generator Hybrid System for Your PV Home. (PV Home Series Booklets). (Illus.). 25p. (Orig.). 1991. pap. text 8.00 (*1-879523-03-5*) Nw England Solar.

— The Solar Electric Independent Home Book. LC 91-71903. (Illus.). 200p. (Orig.). 1998. reprint ed. pap. 16.95 (*1-879523-01-9*) Nw England Solar.

***New England Water Pollution Staff.** That Magnificient Ground Water Connection Vol.TM101: A Resource Book for Grades K-6. (Illus.). 145p. (J). (gr. k-6). 1999. 25.00 (*1-56791-239-7*) Environ Media.

New England Water Works Association Staff. Taking the Bull by the Horns: Adopting a Proactive Approach to Public Relations. 149p. 1991. student ed. 30.00 (*1-881198-00-6*) New Eng Water Wks.

— Treatment Practices of New England Surface Water Supplies. 80p. 1994. 22.50 (*1-881198-01-4*) New Eng Water Wks.

New Explorers Sty Kids Staff. New Explorers Study Bible for Kids: New Living Testament. 19.97 (*0-7852-0729-5*) Nelson.

New Farm Staff, et al. What Really Happens When You Cut Chemicals? Shirley, Christopher & Bowman, Greg, eds. LC 92-41471. 1993. write for info. (*0-913107-16-6*) RDLE INST Bkstre.

New Fourth World Movement Staff, tr. see Wresinski, Joseph.

New Frontiers Staff. Engineering Technical Challenge Brooklyn Bridge. (TP - Technology Education Ser.). (J). (gr. k-12). 1994. pap. 14.95 (*0-8273-6216-1*) S-W Pub.

New, Gregory R., jt. auth. see Davis, Sydney W.

New Hampshire Bicentennial Conference on the Histo. Two Hundred Years of Geology in America: Proceedings of the New Hampshire Bicentennial Conference on the History of Geology. Schneer, Cecil J., ed. LC 78-63149. (Illus.). 399p. reprint ed. pap. 123.70 (*0-8357-7522-4*, 203602900097) Bks Demand.

New Hampshire Retirement System Staff, contrib. by. New Hampshire Public Retirement Laws Annotated, 1998-99. LC 99-172485. v, 112p. 1998. write for info. (*0-327-07116-8*, 28905-10) LEXIS Pub.

New Hampshire State Legislature Staff. Provincial & State Papers, 18 vols., Set. Bouton, Nathaniel & Hammond, I. W., eds. LC 70-173073. reprint ed. 1690.00 (*0-404-07450-2*) AMS Pr.

New Holland Publishing Ltd. Staff. Best of African Wildlife. 1998. 24.95 (*1-86825-450-X*, Pub. by New5 Holland) Sterling.

— Capetown: A Visual Celebration. LC 98-215356. 1998. 22.95 (*1-86872-154-X*, Pub. by New5 Holland) Sterling.

— Feng Shui. LC 99-168455. (Ancient Wisdom for the New Age Ser.). (Illus.). 72p. 1998. 9.95 (*1-85368-979-3*, Pub. by New5 Holland) Sterling.

***New Holland Publishing Ltd. Staff.** Guide to Bed & Breakfast in South Africa. LC 99-160819. (Info Africa Ser.). 216 p. 1999. pap. text 17.95 (*1-86872-158-2*) Stikk Co.

— Guide to guest houses in South Africa. LC 99-160649. (Info Africa Ser.). 171 p. 1999. pap. text 17.95 (*1-86872-159-0*) Stikk Co.

— Guide to Restaurants in South Africa. LC 99-162365. (Info Africa Ser.). 200 p. 1999. pap. text 17.95 (*1-86872-160-4*) Stikk Co.

New Holland Publishing Ltd. Staff. I Ching. (Ancient Wisdom for the New Age Ser.). (Illus.). 72p. 1998. 9.95 (*1-85368-981-5*, Pub. by New5 Holland) Sterling.

— Numerology. LC 99-168287. (Ancient Wisdom for the New Age Ser.). (Illus.). 72p. 1998. 9.95 (*1-85368-983-1*, Pub. by New5 Holland) Sterling.

— Palmistry. LC 99-176195. (Ancient Wisdom for the New Age Ser.). (Illus.). 72p. 1998. 9.95 (*1-85368-977-7*, Pub. by New5 Holland) Sterling.

— Patchwork. (C). 1989. 40.00 (*1-85368-076-1*, Pub. by New5 Holland) St Mut.

***New Holland Publishing Ltd. Staff.** San Francisco & Central California. (Globetrotter Travel Maps Ser.). (Illus.). 1999. pap. 8.95 (*1-85368-794-4*) Sterling.

New Holland Publishing Ltd. Staff. Table Decorating. (C). 1989. 50.00 (*0-7855-4041-5*) St Mut.

***New Holland Publishing Staff.** Algarve. 2nd ed. 2001. pap. 14.95 (*1-85974-417-6*) New5 Holland.

— Andalucia. 2000. pap. 10.95 (*1-85974-312-9*); pap. 8.95 (*1-85974-313-7*); pap. 14.95 (*1-85974-315-3*) New5 Holland.

— Cape Winelands. (Globetrotter Travel Maps Ser.). 2000. pap. 8.95 (*1-85974-492-3*) New5 Holland.

— Crete. 2nd ed. (Globetrotter Travel Guides Ser.). 2001. pap. 10.95 (*1-85974-475-3*); pap. 14.95 (*1-85974-476-1*) New5 Holland.

— Cyprus. (Globetrotter Travel Packs Ser.). 2001. pap. 14.95 (*1-85974-422-2*) New5 Holland.

— Cyprus. 2nd ed. 2001. pap. 10.95 (*1-85974-421-4*) New5 Holland.

— Indonesia. (Globetrotter Travel Packs Ser.). 2000. pap. 14.95 (*1-85974-427-3*) New5 Holland.

— Indonesia. 3rd ed. (Globetrotter Travel Guides Ser.). 2000. pap. 10.95 (*1-85974-425-7*) New5 Holland.

— Kruger National Park. (Globetrotter Travel Packs Ser.). 2000. pap. 14.95 (*1-85974-473-7*) New5 Holland.

— Kruger National Park. 2nd ed. (Globetrotter Travel Maps Ser.). 2000. pap. 8.95 (*1-85974-284-X*) New5 Holland.

— Mauritius. 2nd ed. (Globetrotter Travel Maps Ser.). 2000. pap. 8.95 (*1-85974-416-8*) New5 Holland.

— Mexico. (Globetrotter Travel Guides Ser.). 2000. pap. 10.95 (*1-85974-327-7*); pap. 8.95 (*1-85974-328-5*) New5 Holland.

— Namibia. (Globetrotter Travel Packs Ser.). 2000. pap. 14.95 (*1-85974-248-3*) New5 Holland.

— Namibia. 2nd ed. (Globetrotter Travel Guides Ser.). 2000. pap. 10.95 (*1-85974-200-9*) New5 Holland.

— New York City. 2nd ed. 2001. pap. 14.95 (*1-85974-480-X*) New5 Holland.

— Paris. 2nd ed. (Globetrotter Travel Guides Ser.). 2001. pap. 10.95 (*1-85974-066-9*); pap. 14.95 (*1-85974-483-4*) New5 Holland.

— Phuket. 2nd ed. (Globetrotter Travel Maps Ser.). 2000. pap. 8.95 (*1-85974-205-X*) New5 Holland.

— Prague. 2nd ed. (Globetrotter Travel Guides Ser.). 2000. pap. 10.95 (*1-85974-412-5*) New5 Holland.

— Rome & the Vatican. (Globetrotter Travel Guides Ser.). 2001. pap. 10.95 (*1-85974-485-0*) New5 Holland.

— Sri Lanka. (Globetrotter Travel Maps Ser.). 2000. pap. 8.95 (*1-85368-800-2*); pap. 10.95 (*1-85368-815-0*) New5 Holland.

***New Holland Publishing Staff, ed.** Malta. 2nd ed. (Globetrotter Travel Packs Ser.). (Illus.). 2001. pap. 14.95 (*1-85974-596-2*) New5 Holland.

— Mexico. (Globetrotter Travel Packs Ser.). (Illus.). 2000. pap. 14.95 (*1-85974-330-7*) New5 Holland.

***New Holland Staff.** New York City. 2nd ed. (Globetrotter Travel Guides Ser.). (Illus.). 2001. pap. 10.95 (*1-85974-478-8*) New5 Holland.

***New Holland Staff, ed.** Thailand. (Globetrotter Travel Guides Ser.). (Illus.). 128p. 2000. pap. 10.95 (*1-85974-372-2*) New5 Holland.

***New Hope Charities, Inc. Staff.** De Nuestra Mesa. 222p. 1998. 20.95 (*0-9665197-0-1*, Pub. by New Hope Charits) Wimmer Bks.

New Hope Church Family & Friends Staff. In the Spirit of Christmas: Thanksgiving-Advent-Epiphany: Selections for Daily Use. Daily, Lois, ed. LC 87-26059. (Illus.). 136p. (Orig.). 1987. pap. 8.95 (*0-944741-00-2*) Legacy Hse CA.

New Horizons Equine Education Center Inc. Staff. Dictionary of Equine Terms. LC 96-6759. (Illus.). 304p. 1998. 29.95 (*0-931866-88-X*) Alpine Pubns.

New Horizons Equine Education Center Staff. Dictionary of Equine Terms. LC 96-6759. 304p. 1998. pap. 19.95 (*1-57779-014-6*) Alpine Pubns.

New Horizons Software Inc. Staff. 4 SAT Tests with Hints & Answers: A Student's Preparatory Book. Svenconis, Dan, ed. 220p. (YA). 1999. pap. text 9.95 (*0-9669293-0-6*) New Horizons SW.

— 4 SAT Tests with Hints & Answers Plus CD-ROM: Student's Preparatory Book with CD-ROM for Web Based Tests. (Illus.). 320p. (YA). 1999. pap. 14.95 incl. cd-rom (*0-9669293-2-2*) New Horizons SW.

New Hutchinson Family Singers Office Staff. The Joyce of Music. 32p. 1983. 10.95 incl. audio (*0-252-01083-3*) U of Ill Pr.

New Individualist Review Journal Staff. New Individualist Review. LC 65-35281. 1024p. 1992. pap. 8.50 (*0-86597-065-3*) Liberty Fund.

New Initiatives for Full Employment Staff. Jobs for All: A Plan for the Economic & Social Revitalization of America. LC 95-119750. 112p. (Orig.). 1994. pap. 9.50 (*0-945257-55-4*) Apex Pr.

New International Version of the Bible Staff. Daniel & the Lions. (Stories from the Great Book Ser.). (Orig.). (J). 1986. pap. 4.95 (*0-918789-08-7*) FreeMan Prods.

— The Giant & the Boy. (Stories from the Great Book Ser.). (Illus.). (Orig.). (J). 1986. pap. 4.95 (*0-918789-06-0*) FreeMan Prods.

New International Version of The Bible Staff. The Lost Boy. (Stories from the Great Book Ser.). (Illus.). (Orig.). (J). 1986. pap. 4.95 (*0-918789-07-9*) FreeMan Prods.

New International Version Of The Bible Staff. The Stowaway. (Stories from the Great Book Ser.). (Illus.). (Orig.). (J). 1986. pap. 4.95 (*0-918789-09-5*) FreeMan Prods.

New Jersey Adjutant-General Office Staff. Records of Officers & Men of New Jersey in Wars, 1791-1815. 410p. 1993. reprint ed. pap. 42.50 (*0-8063-0417-0*, 4035) Clearfield Co.

New Jersey Appellate Practice Study Committee. New Jersey Appellate Practice Handbook. 3rd ed. 92p. 1993. ring bd. 65.00 (*0-685-65972-0*) NJ Inst CLE.

New Jersey Association of Legal Secretaries Staff. New Jersey Legal Secretaries Handbook: 1987 Cumulative Supplement. 1987. ring bd. 50.00 (*0-87215-923-X*, 65154-10, MICHIE) LEXIS Pub.

New Jersey Association Of Legal Secretaries Staff. New Jersey Legal Secretary's Handbook. rev. ed. 570p. 1984. spiral bd. 50.00 (*0-87215-721-0*, MICHIE) LEXIS Pub.

— New Jersey Legal Secretary's Handbook. rev. ed. 574p. 1991. ring bd., suppl. ed. 40.00 (*0-87473-859-8*, 65155-10, MICHIE) LEXIS Pub.

New Jersey Conference of Social Work Staff. Negro in New Jersey. LC 74-78772. (Illus.). 116p. 1969. reprint ed. lib. bdg. 57.50 (*0-8371-1411-X*, NNJ&) Greenwood.

***New Jersey Department of State Staff.** New Jersey Index of Wills, Inventories, Etc. In the Office of the Secretary of State Prior to 1901, 3 vols., Set. 1452p. 2000. reprint ed. pap. 125.00 (*0-8063-4968-9*, Pub. by Clearfield Co) ACCESS Pubs Network.

New Jersey. Dept. of Insurance. New Jersey Regulations: Containing Administrative Rules of the New Jersey Insurance Department & Selected Attorney General's Opinions. LC 97-69282. 1997. write for info. (*0-89246-479-8*); write for info. (*0-89246-480-1*); write for info. (*0-89246-481-X*) NILS Pub.

New Jersey Historical Commission, jt. auth. see Karnoutsos, Carmela A.

New Jersey Institute for Continuing Legal Educatio. Criminal Trial Practice (Seminar Materials) 403p. 1988. pap. 55.00 (*0-685-14626-X*) NJ Inst CLE.

— Workers' Compensation Practice: Seminar Materials. 93p. 1992. 35.00 (*0-317-57862-6*) NJ Inst CLE.

New Jersey State Museum Staff, et al. The Hollywood Indian: Stereotypes of Native Americans in Films. LC 98-36661. (Illus.). 80p. (Orig.). 1981. 5.95 (*0-938766-00-7*) NJ State Mus.

New Jersey Supreme Court Committee on Model Jury C. Model Jury Charges - Civil. 4th ed. 813p. 1992. ring bd. 75.00 (*0-685-65971-2*) NJ Inst CLE.

— Model Jury Charges - Criminal. 3rd ed. 658p. 1990. ring bd. 75.00 (*0-939457-03-2*) NJ Inst CLE.

— Model Jury Charges - Criminal. 3rd ed. 658p. 1991. suppl. ed. 39.00 (*0-685-58685-5*) NJ Inst CLE.

— Model Jury Charges - Criminal. 3rd ed. 658p. 1992. suppl. ed. 39.00 (*0-685-58686-3*) NJ Inst CLE.

New Jersey Supreme Court Staff. In the Matter of Karen Quinlan Vol. 1: The Complete Legal Briefs, Court Proceedings, & Decision in the Superior Court of New Jersey. LC 75-42525. 567p. 1975. lib. bdg. 65.00 (*0-313-26920-3*, U6920, Greenwood Pr) Greenwood.

New Jersey Supreme Court Staff, et al. In the Matter of Karen Quinlan Vol. 2: The Complete Briefs, Oral Arguments, & Opinion in the New Jersey Supreme Court, Vol. 2. LC 76-14598. 324p. 1976. lib. bdg. 59.95 (*0-313-26921-1*, U6921, Greenwood Pr) Greenwood.

New Jewish Agency Staff. New Shalom Seders. 1985. pap. 12.95 (*0-915361-22-1*) Lambda Pubs.

New, Joan, ed. see Sterne, Laurence.

New, Joan C. The River Bend. LC 92-82885. (Orig.). 1993. pap. 8.50 (*0-933598-44-0*) NC Wesleyan Pr.

— The River Bend. deluxe limited ed. LC 92-82885. (Orig.). 1993. pap. 17.00 (*0-933598-45-9*) NC Wesleyan Pr.

New, John F., ed. Oliver Cromwell: Pretender, Puritan, Statesman, Paradox? LC 76-23190. (European Problem Studies). 128p. 1977. reprint ed. pap. text 10.50 (*0-03-085178-5*) Krieger.

***New Kids Media Staff.** Nueva Biblia Ilustrada. (SPA., Illus.). (J). 2000. 10.99 (*0-7899-0653-8*) Editorial Unilit.

***New Leaf Press Staff.** Promised Land. (Awsome Adventure Bible Stories Ser.). (Illus.). (J). 2000. pap. 5.99 (*0-89051-327-9*) Master Bks.

— Who is Jesus? Son of God, Son of Man. (Awsome Adventure Bible Stories Ser.). (Illus.). (J). 2000. pap. 5.99 (*0-89051-328-7*) Master Bks.

New Life Clinics Staff. The New Life Journal: A Pathway to Strength & Serenity. 128p. 1998. 14.99 (*0-8407-9702-8*) Nelson.

***New Life Inc. Staff.** New Life Bible: With Salvation Plan. 2000. pap. 4.99 (*0-8297-2405-2*) Vida Pubs.

New Life Inc. Staff, jt. auth. see Prince, Matthew S.

New Life Ministries International Staff, tr. see Clendennen, B. H.

New Line Cinema Staff, ed. see Barstow, Jack.

New Line Cinema Staff, ed. see Chaskin, David.

New Line Cinema Staff, ed. see Craven, Wes & Wagner, Bruce.

New Line Cinema Staff, ed. see Kotzwinkle, William & Helgeland, Brian.

New Line Cinema Staff, ed. see Talalay, Rachel.

New, M. Christopher. Maryland Loyalists in the American Revolution. LC 96-47702. (Illus.). 200p. 1996. 26.95 (*0-87033-495-6*, Tidewtr Pubs) Cornell Maritime.

New Man Magazine Editors. Becoming a New Man: Daily Spiritual Workouts. LC 97-30929. 1997. 14.99 (*0-88419-488-4*) Creation House.

New, Maria I. Pediatric Endocrinology. Pintor, C. et al, eds. (Illus.). 256p. 1993. 242.00 (*0-387-54321-X*) Spr-Verlag.

***New, Maria I., ed.** The Genetics of Endocrine Disorders. 400p. 2000. 99.50 (*0-89603-786-X*) Humana.

New, Maria I. & Levine, Leonore S., eds. Adrenal Diseases in Childhood. (Pediatric & Adolescent Endocrinology Ser.: Vol. 13). (Illus.). viii, 236p. 1984. 143.50 (*3-8055-3777-8*) S Karger.

***New, Maria I., et al.** Diagnosis & Treatment of the Unborn Child. (Illus.). 186p. 1999. 100.00 (*1-928649-00-9*) Idelson Gnocchi Pub.

New, Melvyn. Laurence Sterne As Satirist: A Reading of Tristram Shandy. LC 70-79524. 1969. 29.95 (*0-8130-0278-8*) U Press Fla.

— Telling New Lies: Seven Essays in Fiction, Past & Present. 256p. (C). 1992. 49.95 (*0-8130-1120-5*) U Press Fla.

— Tristram Shandy: A Book for Free Spirits. (Twayne's Masterworks Ser.: No. 132). 125p. 1994. 29.00 (*0-8057-8358-X*) Macmillan.

New, Melvyn, ed. Approaches to Teaching Sterne's Tristram Shandy. LC 88-28977. (Approaches to Teaching World Literature Ser.: No. 20). x, 174p. (Orig.). 1989. pap. 18.00 (*0-87352-516-7*, AP20P); lib. bdg. 37.50 (*0-87352-515-9*, AP20C) Modern Lang.

— The Complete Novels & Selected Writings of Amy Levy, 1861-1889. LC 92-41443. 576p. 1993. 49.95 (*0-8130-1199-X*); pap. 24.95 (*0-8130-1200-7*) U Press Fla.

— Critical Essays on Laurence Sterne. LC 97-34645. 1998. 49.00 (*0-7838-0040-1*) Mac Lib Ref.

New, Melvyn, ed. see Sterne, Laurence.

New Mexico Bureau of Mines & Mineral Resources Sta, et al. Atlas of Major Rocky Mountain Gas Reservoirs. 208p. 1993. 99.75 (*1-883905-00-1*) NM Bureau Mines.

New Mexico. Insurance Dept, et al. New Mexico Regulations: Containing Insurance Department Rules, Selected Attorney General's Opinions, & Advice of the General Counsel. LC 97-67934. (Illus.). 1997. write for info. (*0-89246-476-3*) NILS Pub.

New Mexico Magazine Staff. 100 Years of Filmmaking in New Mexico. Bowman, Jon, ed. LC 98-66406. (Illus.). 140p. 1999. 38.95 (*0-937206-54-7*) New Mexico Mag.

New Mexico Museum of Natural History Foundation St, ed. Chocolate Decadence. 114p. 1996. spiral bd. 9.95 (*0-9641542-1-8*) LPD Pr.

New Mexico Native Plant Protection Advisory Commit. A Handbook of Rare & Endemic Plants of New Mexico. LC 83-16865. 309p. reprint ed. pap. 95.80 (*0-7837-5863-4*, 204558200006) Bks Demand.

New Mexico State University Staff. Lab Manual for Physics 211L, General Physics I, Phys 2131. 158p. (C). 1998. spiral bd. 18.95 (*0-7872-5135-6*) Kendall-Hunt.

— Physics 211L, General Physics I. 158p. (C). 1997. spiral bd., lab manual ed. 13.95 (*0-7872-4168-7*) Kendall-Hunt.

New, Mitya. Switzerland Unwrapped. LC 97-31901. 224p. 1997. text 29.95 (*1-86064-300-0*, Pub. by I B T) St Martin.

New Moon Publishing Incorporated Staff, ed. Friendship. LC 99-24037. (New Moon Ser.). (Illus.). 80p. (J). (gr. 3-8). 1999. pap. 9.99 (*0-517-88581-6*, Pub. by Crown Bks Yng Read); lib. bdg. 16.99 (*0-517-88582-4*, Pub. by Crown Bks Yng Read) Random.

— Sports. LC 99-28712. (New Moon Ser.). (Illus.). 80p. (J). (gr. 3-8). 1999. pap. 9.99 (*0-517-88583-2*, Pub. by Crown Bks Yng Read); lib. bdg. 16.99 (*0-517-88584-0*, Pub. by Crown Bks Yng Read) Random.

***New Moon Staff.** Writing: How to Express Yourself with Passion & Practice. (New Moon Bks.). 96p. 2000. lib. bdg. 16.99 (*0-517-88588-3*, Pub. by Crown Bks Yng Read) Random.

New Museum of Contemporary Art Staff (New York, N. & Akron Art Museum Staff. Dancing at the Louvre: Faith Ringgold's French Collection & Other Story Quilts. Cameron, Dan, ed. LC 97-31079. 168p. (gr. 5 up). 1998. pap. 29.95 (*0-520-21430-7*) U CA Pr.

New Museum of Contemporary Art Staff (New York, N., et al. Dancing at the Louvre: Faith Ringgold's French Collection & Other Story Quilts. Cameron, Dan, ed. LC 97-31079. 168p. 1998. 45.00 (*0-520-21429-3*) Univ of California Angeles Ctr.

New Orleans Academy of Ophthalmology Staff, et al. Peril to the Nerve: Glaucoma & Clinical Neuro-Ophthalmology, Proceedings of the 45th Annual Symposium, New Orleans, La, U. S. A., April 25-28, 1996. LC 97-13859. (Illus.). xiii, 283p. 1998. 94.50 (*90-6299-153-X*) Kugler Pubns.

New Orleans Museum of Art Staff. French Art of four Centuries from the New Orleans Museum of Art. (Illus.). pap. 25.00 (*1-57806-259-4*, Pub. by New Orleans Mus Art) U of Wash Pr.

— Imari: Japanese Porcelain for European Palaces, The Freda & Ralph Lupin Collection. (Illus.). 120p. 1999. pap. 25.00 (*0-89494-060-0*, Pub. by New Orleans Mus Art) U of Wash Pr.

New Orleans Structures Congress, et al. Structural Engineering in the 21st Century: Proceedings of the 1999 New Orleans Structures Congress. LC 99-18131. 1132p. 1999. 110.00 (*0-7844-0421-6*) Am Soc Civil Eng.

New Patent Editors. New Patent Interference Rules. 35.00 (*0-317-29498-9*, #CO3530) Harcourt.

New Readers Press Staff. Flipping Phonics. 1997. pap. text 9.95 (*1-56420-178-3*) New Readers.

New, Rebecca, jt. auth. see Mallory, Bruce.

***New Riders Development Group.** CCNP Examgear. (Examgear Ser.). 50p. 2000. pap. 149.99 incl. cd-rom (*0-7357-0065-6*) New Riders Pub.

New Riders Development Group. MCP Complete + Internet Specialist. 1998. pap. 75.00 (*1-56205-897-5*) New Riders Pub.

***New Riders Development Group.** Red Hat Certified Engineer Training Guide. (Training Guides Ser.). 800p. 2000. 89.95 incl. cd-rom (*0-7357-0941-6*) New Riders Pub.

New Riders Development Group Staff. CCNP/CCDP Trainging Guide: CLSC Exam 640-404. 1999. 49.99 (*0-7357-0056-7*) New Riders Pub.

— CCNP/CCDP Training Guide: ACRC Exam 640-403. 1999. 49.99 (*0-7357-0053-2*) New Riders Pub.

— CCNP/CCDP Training Guide: CMTD Exam 640-405. 1999. 49.99 (*0-7357-0057-5*) New Riders Pub.

— CNE 4 Short Course. LC 96-109799. (Illus.). 816p. (Orig.). 1995. pap. 60.00 incl. cd-rom (*1-56205-513-5*) New Riders Pub.

— Designing Web Animation. LC 96-2752. 320p. 1996. pap. text 39.99 incl. cd-rom (*1-56205-647-6*) New Riders Pub.

— Flying Through the Web. LC 96-143260. (Illus.). 384p. (Orig.). 1996. pap. 35.00 incl. cd-rom (*1-56205-521-6*) New Riders Pub.

N

— Graphics Professionals Powerpack. 1995. pap. 74.99 (1-56205-507-0) New Riders Pub.
— Industrial Strength Internet: Microsoft Internet Studio Programminng. 1997. pap. text 49.99 incl. cd-rom (1-56205-732-4) New Riders Pub.
— Inside ISAPI. LC 97-1238. 608p. 1997. 45.00 (1-56205-650-6) New Riders Pub.
— Inside TCP-IP. LC 94-40855. (Illus.). (Orig.). 1994. pap. 39.99 (1-56205-354-X) New Riders Pub.
— Inside TCP/IP. 2nd ed. (Illus.). 800p. (Orig.). 1995. pap. 40.00 (1-56205-450-3) New Riders Pub.
— Inside the World Wide Web. (Illus.). 1040p. (Orig.). 1995. pap. text 40.00 (1-56205-412-0) New Riders Pub.
— Inside the World Wide Web. 2nd ed. LC 96-199820. 880p. (Orig.). 1996. 39.99 (1-56205-639-5) New Riders Pub.
— Internet Security Professional Reference. 900p. 1996. pap. 60.00 (1-56205-557-7) New Riders Pub.
— Intranet Web Development: Enterprise Alternatives to Client/Server Computing. LC 96-35507. 800p. 1996. pap. text 49.99 incl. cd-rom (1-56205-618-2) New Riders Pub.
— Kai's Power Tools Filters & Effects. (Illus.). 222p. 1995. pap. 45.00 incl. cd-rom (1-56205-480-5) New Riders Pub.
— LAN Server Engineer Certification Handbook. (Illus.). 1536p. (Orig.). 1995. pap. 89.99 (1-56205-406-6) New Riders Pub.
***New Riders Development Group Staff.** LPI Linux Certification Fast Track: Level 1 Basic Administration. (Fast Tracks Ser.). 500p. 2000. pap. 59.95 (0-7357-0942-4) New Riders Pub.
New Riders Development Group Staff. Microsoft Windows NT for Graphics Professionals. (Illus.). 420p. (Orig.). 1996. pap. 35.00 (1-56205-548-8) New Riders Pub.
— NetWare Training Guide: CNA Study Guide. LC 94-34769. (Illus.). 876p. (Orig.). 1994. pap. 50.00 (1-56205-365-5) New Riders Pub.
— New Rider's Official World Wide Web Directory. 1024p. 1995. pap. 29.99 (1-56205-485-6) New Riders Pub.
— New Riders' Official World Wide Web Yellow Pages. 5th ed. 1176p. 1997. 34.99 (1-56205-742-1) New Riders Pub.
— New Riders' Official World Wide Web Yellow Pages: 1996 Edition. (Illus.). 1024p. (Orig.). 1995. pap. 29.99 (1-56205-536-4) New Riders Pub.
— NLW Riders Official Compuserve Yellow Pages. LC 94-37840. 800p. 1994. pap. 29.99 (1-56205-396-5) New Riders Pub.
— Photoshop 3 Filters & Effects. (Illus.). 432p. (Orig.). 1995. pap. text 45.00 (1-56205-448-1) New Riders Pub.
— 3-D Studio Hollywood & Gaming Effects. (Illus.). 272p. (Orig.). 1995. pap. 50.00 incl. cd-rom (1-56205-430-9) New Riders Pub.
— Webmaster's Professional Reference. (Illus.). 1248p. 1996. pap. text 55.00 (1-56205-473-2) New Riders Pub.
— Website Sound. LC 96-46749. 448p. 1996. pap. text 44.99 incl. cd-rom (1-56205-626-3) New Riders Pub.
— Windows NT Server 4 Resource Library. 1996. 119.99 (1-56205-694-8) New Riders Pub.
— Windows NT Server Resource Library. 450p. 1995. pap. 109.00 (1-56205-551-8) New Riders Pub.
New Riders' Development Group Staff. World Wide Web Yellow Pages. 6th ed. 993p. 1997. pap. 34.99 incl. cd-rom (1-56205-785-5) New Riders Pub.
New Riders Development Group Staff & Cheong, Fah-chun. Internet Agents: Robots, Spiders, Fish & Worms. (Illus.). 432p. 1995. pap. 32.00 (1-56205-463-5) New Riders Pub.
New Riders Development Group Staff & Forcade, Tim. The 3D Studio Plug-In Reference. (Illus.). 304p. 1995. pap. text 55.00 (1-56205-431-7) New Riders Pub.
New Riders Development Group Staff, et al. Implementing Internet Security. (Illus.). 400p. (Orig.). 1995. pap. 35.00 (1-56205-471-6) New Riders Pub.
— Inside UNIX. 1130p. 1994. pap. 39.99 incl. disk (1-56205-401-5) New Riders Pub.
New Riders Development Staff. MCSD Training Guide: Wosa I & Wosa II. 1997. 90.00 (1-56205-765-0) New Riders Pub.
— MCSE TestPrep: Windows NT Server 4 Enterprise. LC 98-88512. 1999. pap. 19.99 (0-7357-0009-5) New Riders Pub.
— New Riders Official WWW International Pages. 1997. 34.99 (1-56205-744-8) New Riders Pub.
New Riders Develpoment Staff. Inside MS Wolfpack. 1998. 49.99 (1-56205-776-6) New Riders Pub.
New Riders Publishing Staff. A+ Certification Training Guide. LC 98-84448. 1998. pap. text 49.99 (1-56205-866-5) New Riders Pub.
— Creating Internet Controls with Visual Basic. 450p. 1997. pap. text 39.99 (1-56205-753-7) New Riders Pub.
— Don't Panic! It's Only NetWare. 300p. 1993. pap. 18.95 (1-56205-203-9) New Riders Pub.
— Inside AutoCAD: Release 14. LC 97-11550. 1000p. 1997. pap. text 49.99 (1-56205-755-3) New Riders Pub.
— Inside AutoCAD, Release 13.0 for Windows & NT. 1500p. 1995. 39.99 incl. disk (1-56205-319-1) New Riders Pub.
— Inside JavaScript. LC 96-42687. 650p. 1996. 44.99 (1-56205-593-3) New Riders Pub.
***New Riders Publishing Staff.** Inside 3D Studio MAX 2 Resource Kit. 1998. pap. text 99.99 (1-56205-953-X) New Riders Pub.
New Riders Publishing Staff. Inside 3D Studio Max: Advanced Modeling & Material Editor, Vol. 2. 600p. 1997. pap. text 54.99 incl. cd-rom (1-56205-679-4) New Riders Pub.
— Lotus Notes 4.5 & Domino 4.5: Administrator's Professional Reference. LC 97-17298. 900p. 1997. 69.99 (1-56205-757-X) New Riders Pub.
— MS Internet Studio Expert Techniques. 1996. 50.00 (1-56205-615-8) New Riders Pub.
— New Riders Official Internet Directory. rev. ed. LC 96-174598. 1997. pap. text 29.99 (1-56205-643-3) New Riders Pub.
— New Riders Official World Wide Web Directory, 1997. 1996. pap. text 34.99 incl. cd-rom (1-56205-677-8) New Riders Pub.
— New Riders Reference Guide to AutoCAD Release 12. (Illus.). 577p. (Orig.). 1992. pap. 19.95 (1-56205-058-3) New Riders Pub.
— Novell Intranetware Professional Reference. LC 97-21526. 1000p. 1997. 69.99 incl. cd-rom (1-56205-729-4) New Riders Pub.
— Riding the Internet Highway. 1993. pap. 16.95 (1-56205-192-X) New Riders Pub.
— SQL Server 7 Database Design Study Guide. (MCSE Ser.). 1999. pap. text 19.99 (0-7357-0043-5) New Riders Pub.
— 3D Studio 4: Level 1, Level 1. 1997. pap. text, teacher ed. write for info. (1-56205-542-9) New Riders Pub.
— MCSE Training Guide: Windows NT 4 Exams. LC 97-81214. (MCSE Training Guides). 1998. pap. text 89.99 (1-56205-867-3) New Riders Pub.
New Riders Publishing Staff, contrib. by. Java API Reference: Java, Applet & Java.awt API Packages. LC 96-28598. 416p. 1996. 29.99 (1-56205-598-4) New Riders Pub.
New Riders Publishing Staff, et al. Inside AutoCAD Release 12. LC 92-19826. (Illus.). 1307p. (Orig.). 1992. pap. 37.95 (1-56205-055-9) New Riders Pub.
New Riders Publishing Staff, ed. see Moore, Thomas.
New Riders Staff. DOS/Windows/Win95 Exam. (A+ Fast Track Ser.). 1999. pap. text 19.99 (0-7357-0020-6) New Riders Pub.
— Inside Solaris. 1997. 49.99 (1-56205-809-6) New Riders Pub.
— MCSD Training Guide: Microsoft Access. rev. ed. 1998. 49.99 (1-56205-928-9, New Riders Sftwre) MCP SW Interactive.
— MCSD Training Guide: Solution Architectures. (Training Guides Ser.). 800p. 1999. 74.95 incl. cd-rom (0-7357-0026-5) New Riders Pub.
***New Riders Staff.** MCSE Core Exams Examgear: Exams 70-067, 70-068, 70-073, 70-098, 70-058, Vol. 1. 100p. 1999. 299.99 (0-7357-0863-0) New Riders Pub.
New Riders Staff. MCSE TestPrep Software: Core Exam. 1998. pap. text 69.99 (1-56205-868-1) New Riders Pub.
— MCSE Training Guide: SQL Server 7 Design & Implementation. 1999. pap. 49.99 (0-7357-0004-4) New Riders Pub.
— MCSE Training Guide Internet Specialist Exams. (MCSE Training Guides). 1998. pap. text 99.99 (1-56205-879-7) New Riders Pub.
— MCSETraining Guide: SQL Server 7 Administration. LC 98-83055. 1999. pap. text 49.99 (0-7357-0003-6) New Riders Pub.
— MCSE Fast Track: Windows 98. LC 98-87721. 1998. pap. text 19.99 (0-7357-0016-8) New Riders Pub.
New Riders Staff, et al. Core/Hardware Technology & DOS/Windows Exams: Hardware Exam. LC 98-89487. (A+ Fast Track Ser.). (Illus.). 563p. 1999. pap. 34.99 (0-7357-0028-1) New Riders Pub.
New River Valley Bicycle Club Staff. Cycling the New River Valley. rev. ed. (Illus.). 120p. (Orig.). 1999. pap. 9.95 (0-936015-80-2) Pocahontas Pr.
New Salem Journal Printing Staff, tr. see Diede, Pauline N.
New Sarov Press Staff. Akathist Hymn to the Most Holy Theotokos: In Her Miraculous Icon, "The Inexhaustible Cup" (Illus.). 1998. pap. 5.95 (1-880364-33-6) New Sarov.
***New, Scf Stdy Pckt.** Scofield Study Pocket Bible. 1760p. 1998. 44.99 (0-19-528173-X); 44.99 (0-19-528174-8); 44.99 (0-19-528176-4) OUP.
***New Scofield Reader Staff.** Scofield Study Bible Reader. 1760p. 1998. lthr. 49.99 (0-19-528151-9) OUP.
New Scofield Staff. Bible: New Scofield Supersaver Ed. 1824p. 1998. bond lthr. 39.99 (0-19-527737-6) OUP.
***New Scofield Staff.** Scofield Study Bible. 1998. bond lthr. 76.99 (0-19-528160-8) OUP.
— Scofield Study Bible: Berkshire Leather. 1998. lthr. 86.99 (0-19-528170-5) OUP.
New Scofield Staff, ed. Bible: New Scofield Ed. 1824p. 1998. bond lthr. 69.99 (0-19-527757-0) OUP.
— Bible: New Scofield Ed. 1824p. 1999. 34.99 (0-19-527735-X); 41.99 (0-19-527736-8); bond lthr. 69.99 (0-19-527753-8); bond lthr. 76.99 (0-19-527754-6); bond lthr. 69.99 (0-19-527755-4); bond lthr. 76.99 (0-19-527756-2); lthr. 89.99 (0-19-527733-3); lthr. 89.99 (0-19-527731-7); lthr. 79.99 (0-19-527765-1) OUP.
— Bible: New Scofield Ed. 1824p. 1999. lthr. 96.99 (0-19-527732-5); lthr. 96.99 (0-19-527734-1) OUP.
— Bible: New Scofield Ed. 1824p. 1999. lthr. 100.00 (0-19-527767-8) OUP.
— Bible: New Scofield Supersaver Ed. 1824p. 1998. bond lthr. 39.99 (0-19-527745-7); bond lthr. 39.99 (0-19-527739-2); bond lthr. 39.99 (0-19-527743-0); lthr. 49.99 (0-19-527749-X); lthr. 49.99 (0-19-527747-3) OUP.
— Bible: New Scofield Supersaver Ed. 1824p. 1999. bond lthr. 44.99 (0-19-527740-6); bond lthr. 44.99 (0-19-527742-2); bond lthr. 44.99 (0-19-527744-9); bond lthr. 44.99 (0-19-527738-4); bond lthr. 44.99 (0-19-527746-5); lthr. 54.99 (0-19-527748-1); lthr. 54.99 (0-19-527750-3); lthr. 49.99 (0-19-527769-4); lthr. 54.99 (0-19-527770-8) OUP.
— Bible: New Scofield Supersaver Ed. 1824p. 1999. bond lthr. 39.99 (0-19-527741-4) OUP.
***New Scofield Study Staff.** New Scofield Study Bible. 1760p. 1998. 44.99 (0-19-528144-6) OUP.
***New Scofield Study Staff, ed.** Scofield Study Bible. 1760p. 1998. 86.99 (0-19-528166-7) OUP.
***New Scotland Historical Association Staff.** New Scotland Township: New York. LC 00-101909. (Images of America Ser.). (Illus.). 128p. 2000. pap. 18.99 (0-7385-0420-3) Arcadia Publng.
New Statesman Staff. New Statesmanship. Hyams, E., ed. LC 72-128281. (Essay Index Reprint Ser.). 1977. 23.95 (0-8369-1891-6) Ayer.
***New Strategist Editors.** American Incomes: Demographiecs of Who Has Money. 3rd rev. ed. 404p. 1999. 89.95 (1-885070-24-1) New Strategist.
— The American Marketplace: Demographics & Spending Patterns. 4th rev. ed. (Illus.). 472p. 1999. 89.95 (1-885070-19-5) New Strategist.
— American Men & Women: Demographics of the Sexes. 2000. 89.95 (1-885070-29-2) New Strategist.
New Strategist Editors. Household Spending: Who Spends How Much on What. 5th ed. Orig. Title: The Official Guide to Household Spending. 800p. 1999. 94.95 (1-885070-25-X) New Strategist.
***New Strategist Editors.** Racial & Ethnic Diversity: Asians, Blacks, Hispanics, Native Americans & Whites. 3rd ed. 2000. 94.95 (1-885070-27-6) New Strategist.
New, T. R. Butterfly Conservation. 2nd ed. (Illus.). 260p. 1998. pap. text 27.95 (0-19-554124-3) OUP.
— Invertebrate Surveys for Conservation. (Illus.). 252p. 1998. pap. text 35.00 (0-19-850011-4) OUP.
— Invertebrate Surveys for Conservation. (Illus.). 256p. 1999. text 75.00 (0-19-850012-2) OUP.
New Technology Solutions Staff. Visual Basic 6 Certification Guide. 1998. 59.99 (0-07-134535-3) McGraw.
New, Tim R. Associations Between Insects & Plants. 113p. 1990. pap. 22.95 (0-86840-099-8, Pub. by New South Wales Univ Pr) Intl Spec Bk.
— Biology of Chrysopidae. Canard, M. et al, eds. LC 83-17588. (Entomologica Ser.). 1984. text 192.50 (90-6193-137-1) Kluwer Academic.
— Insect Conservation. (Entomologica Ser.). 1984. text 155.50 (90-6193-507-5) Kluwer Academic.
— Insects As Predators. 178p. 1996. reprint ed. pap. 22.95 (0-86840-276-1, Pub. by New South Wales Univ Pr) Intl Spec Bk.
— An Introduction to Invertebrate Conservation Biology. (Illus.). 206p. 1995. pap. text 35.00 (0-19-854051-5) OUP.
— Introductory Entomology for Australian Students. (Illus.). 196p. pap. 31.95 (0-86840-141-2, Pub. by New South Wales Univ Pr) Intl Spec Bk.
— Name That Insect: A Guide to the Insects of Southeastern Australia. (Illus.). 208p. 1997. pap. text 22.95 (0-19-553782-3) OUP.
— Psocoptera of the Oriental Region - A Review. (Oriental Insects Monographs: No. 6). 1977. pap. 30.00 (1-87711-16-0) Assoc Pubs FL.
New, Tim R. & Collins, N. M. Swallowtail Butterflies: An Action Plan for Their Conservation. (Illus.). 40p. 1991. pap. 21.50 (2-8317-0061-2, Pub. by IUCN) Island Pr.
New, Tim R., et al. Neuroptera, Strepsiptera, Mecoptera, Siphonaptera. (Zoological Catalogue of Australia Ser.: Vol. 28). 230p. 1996. 69.95 (0-643-05801-X, Pub. by CSIRO) Accents Pubns.
New, Timothy & Theischinger, Gunther, eds. Handbuch der Zoologie - Handbook of Zoology: A Natural History of the Phyla of the Animal Kingdom, Band IV - Vol. IV. (ENG & GER.). v, 101p. (C). 1993. lib. bdg. 200.00 (3-11-013566-3) De Gruyter.
New Tokyo Photographers Staff, contrib. by. Deja-vu 18. 130p. 1995. pap. 25.00 (4-309-90338-X) Dist Art Pubs.
New Valaam Monks Staff, ed. Father Gerasim of New Valaam. LC 89-64024. (Acquisition of the Holy Spirit in Russia Ser.). (Illus.). 112p. 1990. pap. 5.00 (0-938635-29-8) St Herman Pr.
New Victoria Publishers Staff, ed. Vicki's Hot Tickets. LC 98-46979. (Illus.). 128p. 1998. pap. 5.95 (0-934678-99-5) New Victoria Pubs.
***New, W. H.** Borderlands: How We Talk about Canada. 128p. 1998. 49.95 (0-7748-0658-3); pap. text 19.95 (0-7748-0659-1) UBC Pr.
— Canadian Writers, 1920-1959. (Dictionary of Literary Biography Ser.: Vol. 68). 400p. 1988. text 155.00 (0-8103-1746-X) Gale.
New, W. H. Dreams of Speech & Violence: The Art of the Short Story in Canada & New Zealand. 302p. 1987. text 35.00 (0-8020-5663-6) U of Toronto Pr.
— A History of Canadian Literature. 380p. 1993. pap. 19.95 (1-56131-040-9, NAB) I R Dee.
— Land Sliding: Imaging Space, Presence, & Power in Canadian Writing. LC 97-170132. (Illus.). 278p. 1997. text 45.00 (0-8020-4119-1, PR9185) U of Toronto Pr.
***New, W. H.** Raucous. 1999. pap. 14.95 (0-88982-175-5, Pub. by Oolichan Bks) Genl Dist Srvs.
New, W. H. Reading Mansfield & Metaphors of Form. 215p. 1999. 55.00 (0-7735-1791-X) McG-Queens Univ Pr.
New, W. H., ed. Canadian Writers since 1960, First Series. (Dictionary of Literary Biography Ser.: Vol. 53). 445p. 1986. text 155.00 (0-8103-1731-1) Gale.
— Canadian Writers since 1960, 2nd Series, Vol. 60. (Dictionary of Literary Biography Ser.). 416p. 1987. text 155.00 (0-8103-1738-9) Gale.
— Dictionary of Literary Biography Vol. 92: Canadian Writers, 1890-1920, Vol. 92. LC 89-48355. (Illus.). 487p. 1990. text 146.00 (0-8103-4572-2) Gale.
New, W. H., ed. Literary History of Canada. 492p. 1990. text 60.00 (0-8020-5685-7) U of Toronto Pr.
— Literary History of Canada. (Literature in English Ser.: Vil. 4). 492p. 1990. pap. 24.95 (0-8020-6610-0) U of Toronto Pr.
New, Warren. Workin' Man. LC 99-207659. 266p. 1998. write for info. (0-9667391-0-8) Blowout Prods.
New Ways to Work Staff, ed. New Policies for Part-Time & Contingent Workers. 67p. 1992. 5.00 (0-685-66556-9, G-006) New Ways Work.
New Ways to Work Staff & Batz, Julie. Work Sharing: An Alternative to Layoffs. rev. ed. 24p. (Orig.). 1991. pap. text 12.00 (0-940173-25-5) New Ways Work.
New, William H. Science Lessons: Poems by W. H. New. 96p. 1996. pap. 14.95 (0-88982-155-0, Pub. by Oolichan Bks) Genl Dist Srvs.
New, William H., ed. Inside The Poem: Essays in Honour of Donald Stephens. 320p. 1993. pap. text 22.00 (0-19-540925-6) OUP.
— Native Writers & Canadian Writing. 352p. 1991. pap. 22.95 (0-7748-0371-1) U of Wash Pr.
New Working Group On New Religious Movments Editor. Sects & New Religious Movements: An Anthology of Texts from the Catholic Church, 1986-1994. LC 96-121349. 78p. (Orig.). 1995. pap. 7.95 (1-57455-023-3) US Catholic.
***New World Communications Staff.** Fox TV One-Tank Trips with Bill Murphy. Krueger, Vicki, ed. (Illus.). 128p. 2000. pap. 9.95 (0-942084-24-1) SeaSide Pub.
New World Foundation Staff. How to Get to Heaven. 100p. (Orig.). 1991. pap. 12.95 (1-879964-01-5) New World TX.
New World Foundation Staff, ed. The Bible II: How to Get to Heaven. 630p. (Orig.). (C). 1991. pap. 24.95 (1-879964-00-7) New World TX.
New World Websters Staff. Webster's New World Pocket Book of Facts, Pocket Ed. Pocket Edition. (Webster's New World Ser.). 448p. 1998. pap. text 6.95 (0-02-862750-4, Webstrs New) Macmillan Gen Ref.
***New York Museum of Modern Art Staff.** Fame. 1999. write for info. (0-8212-2615-0) Little.
New York Academy of Medicine Library Staff. Author Catalog of the Library of the New York Academy of Medicine. 1983. 4910.00 (0-8161-1388-2, G K Hall & Co) Mac Lib Ref.
— Subject Catalog of the Library of the New York Academy of Medicine. 1970. 3695.00 (0-8161-1460-9, G K Hall & Co) Mac Lib Ref.
— Subject Catalog of the Library of the New York Academy of Medicine, Supplement 1. 1980. suppl. ed. 625.00 (0-8161-1273-8, G K Hall & Co) Mac Lib Ref.
New York Academy of Medicine Staff. The End of Life: Guidelines for Health Professionals Concerning Death Certificates, Autopsies & Organ & Tissue Donations. rev. ed. Hirsch, Charles & Messite, Jacqueline, eds. (Illus.). 1994. pap. text 10.00 (0-924143-03-7) NY Acad Med.
— Freud & Contemporary Culture. Galdston, Iago, ed. LC 77-142674. (Essay Index Reprint Ser.). 1977. 13.95 (0-8369-2112-7) Ayer.
— Freud & Contemporary Culture. Galdston, Iago, ed. LC 57-10551. 111p. reprint ed. pap. 34.50 (0-608-11350-6, 205099000069) Bks Demand.
— Frontiers in Medicine. LC 70-142675. (Essay Index Reprint Ser.). 1977. 19.95 (0-8369-2113-5) Ayer.
— Future in Medicine: The March of Medicine, 1949, Laity Lectures, No. 14. LC 74-167391. (Essay Index Reprint Ser.). 1977. reprint ed. 19.95 (0-8369-2465-7) Ayer.
— Illustration Catalog of the Library of New York Academy of Medicine. 3rd ed. 1981. 175.00 (0-8161-1328-9, G K Hall & Co) Mac Lib Ref.
— Landmarks in Medicine. LC 74-142676. (Essay Index Reprint Ser.). 1977. 23.95 (0-8369-2114-3) Ayer.
— March of Medicine Laity Lectures, No. 4. LC 78-142677. (Essay Index Reprint Ser.). 1977. reprint ed. 19.95 (0-8369-2212-3) Ayer.
— March of Medicine Laity Lectures, No. 5. LC 78-142677. (Essay Index Reprint Ser.). 1977. 19.95 (0-8369-2115-1) Ayer.
— March of Medicine Laity Lectures, No. 6. LC 78-142677. (Essay Index Reprint Ser.). 1977. 19.95 (0-8369-2116-X) Ayer.
— March of Medicine Laity Lectures, No. 7. LC 78-142677. (Essay Index Reprint Ser.). 1977. 20.95 (0-8369-2117-8) Ayer.
— March of Medicine Laity Lectures, 1943. LC 78-142677. (Essay Index Reprint Ser.). 1977. reprint ed. 19.95 (0-8369-2466-5) Ayer.
— March of Medicine Laity Lectures, 1944. LC 78-142677. (Essay Index Reprint Ser.). 1977. reprint ed. 17.95 (0-8369-2467-3) Ayer.
— Medicine & Anthropology. Galdston, Iago, ed. LC 71-142678. (Essay Index Reprint Ser.). 1977. 19.95 (0-8369-2118-6) Ayer.
— Medicine & Science. Galdston, Iago, ed. LC 75-142679. (Essay Index Reprint Ser.). 1977. 18.95 (0-8369-2122-4) Ayer.
— Medicine in a Changing Society. Galdston, Iago, ed. LC 70-142680. (Essay Index Reprint Ser.). 1977. 19.95 (0-8369-2123-2) Ayer.
— Medicine in the Postwar World: The March of Medicine, 1947, Laity Lectures, No. 12. LC 78-167392. (Essay Index Reprint Ser.). 1977. reprint ed. 17.95 (0-8369-2468-1) Ayer.
— Medicine Today: The March of Medicine, 1946 (Laity Lectures, No. 11) LC 71-167393. (Essay Index Reprint Ser.). 1977. reprint ed. 19.95 (0-8369-2469-X) Ayer.
— Milestones in Medicine. LC 73-142681. (Essay Index Reprint Ser.). 1977. 21.95 (0-8369-2119-4) Ayer.
— Ministry & Medicine in Human Relations. Galdston, Iago, ed. LC 77-142682. (Essay Index Reprint Ser.). 1977. 19.95 (0-8369-2120-8) Ayer.
— Modern Attitudes in Psychiatry. LC 70-142683. (Essay Index Reprint Ser.). 1977. 19.95 (0-8369-2121-6) Ayer.
— Perspectives in Medicine. LC 75-152204. (Essay Index Reprint Ser.). 1977. 19.95 (0-8369-2813-X) Ayer.

An Asterisk (*) at the beginning of an entry indicates that the title is appearing for the first time.

— Portrait Catalog, 5 vols. 1970. suppl. ed. 175.00 (*0-8161-0733-5*, G K Hall & Co) Mac Lib Ref.

— Portrait Catalog, 5 vols. 1971. suppl. ed. 160.00 (*0-8161-0900-1*, G K Hall & Co) Mac Lib Ref.

— Society & Medicine. Galdston, Iago, ed. LC 74-142684. (Essay Index Reprint Ser.). 1971. 17.95 (*0-8369-2124-0*) Ayer.

New York Academy of Medicine Staff, jt. auth. see De Crombrugghe, Benoit.

New York Academy of Sciences Staff. Immunologic Diseases of the Ear. Bernstein, Joel M. et al, eds. LC 97-42727. (Annals of the New York Academy of Sciences Ser.: Vol. 830). 376p. 1997. pap. 120.00 (*1-57331-101-4*) NY Acad Sci.

New York Academy of Sciences Staff, jt. auth. see Chiorazzi, Nicholas.

New York Academy of Sciences Staff, jt. auth. see Das, Dipak K.

New York Academy of Sciences Staff, jt. auth. see Joseph, James A.

New York Academy of Sciences Staff, jt. auth. see Lohr, J. Matthias.

New York Adjutant-General's Office Staff. New York: Index of Awards on Claims of the Soldiers of the War of 1812. LC 74-75352. 579p. 1994. reprint ed. pap. 42.50 (*0-8063-0258-5*) Clearfield Co.

New York African American Institute, jt. auth. see Veruch Inc.

New York Association for Improving the Condition o. AICP First Annual Reports Investigating Poverty, Nos. 1[00ad]10. LC 77-137179. (Poverty U. S. A. Historical Record Ser.). 1978. reprint ed. 35.95 (*0-405-03117-3*) Ayer.

New York Bar Association Staff. Public Sector Labor & Employment Law: 1995 Supplement. Townley, Rosemary A., ed. 440p. 1995. pap. text 45.00 (*0-942954-77-7*) NYS Bar.

New York Belting Company Staff. Mechanical Rubber Goods Catalogue, 1914. (Illus.). 215p. 1998. reprint ed. pap. text 25.00 (*0-87556-852-1*) Saifer.

New York Book Fair Staff. In Search of Song, Vol. 5. Spiegel, Richard A. & Fisher, Barbara, eds. (Illus.). 40p. (Orig.). (J). (gr. k-9). 1983. pap. 2.00 (*0-934830-30-4*) Ten Penny.

New York Botanical Garden Staff. Reliable Roses. (Serious Gardner Ser.). (Illus.). 1997. pap. 23.00 (*0-614-27226-2*) C Potter.

— Rock Gardens. (Serious Gardner Ser.). (Illus.). 1997. pap. 23.00 (*0-614-27227-0*) C Potter.

— A Walk Through the New York Botanical Garden. 1996. pap. 10.00 (*0-89327-428-3*, 428-3) NY Botanical.

New York Botanical Garden Staff, jt. auth. see Appel, Allan.

New York Botanical Garden Staff, ed. see Bush-Brown, James & Bush-Brown, Louise.

New York City Ballet, jt. auth. see Martins, Peter.

New York City Board of Alderman, Committee on Gene. Preliminary Report of the Committee on General Welfare in the Matter of a Request of the Conference of Organized Labor Relative to Educational Facilities. Meeting of June 26, 1917. LC 73-11924. (Metropolitan America Ser.). 350p. 1974. reprint ed. 28.95 (*0-405-05407-6*) Ayer.

New York City Commission. Report of a Preliminary Scheme of Improvements: Staten Island. LC 73-2910. (Metropolitan America Ser.). 118p. 1974. reprint ed. 11.95 (*0-405-05408-4*) Ayer.

New York City Common Council Staff. Report of the Special Committee of the New York City Board of Aldermen on the New York City Police Department: New York City Common Council Document, Vol. 53. LC 72-154582. (Police in America Ser.). 1971. reprint ed. 26.95 (*0-405-03378-8*) Ayer.

New York City Landmarks Preservation Committee. Guide to New York City Landmarks. LC 92-10790. (Illus.). 256p. 1995. pap. 9.95 (*0-471-14391-X*) Wiley.

— Guide to New York City Landmarks. LC 97-21378. (Illus.). 340p. 1998. pap. 19.95 (*0-471-18289-3*) Wiley.

New York City Museum of Modern Art Max Weber, Retr, et al. Three American Modernist Painters: Max Weber, with an Introduction by Alfred H. Barr, Jr.; Maurice Sterne by H. M. Kallen, with a Note by the Artist; Stuart Davis by James Johnson Sweeney. 1969. reprint ed. 20.95 (*0-405-01528-3*, 15554) Ayer.

New York City Museum of Modern Art Staff. Twenty Centuries of Mexican Art: Viento Siglos de Arte Mexicano, LC 79-169322. (Museum of Modern Art Publications in Reprint). (Illus.). 200p. 1972. reprint ed. 25.95 (*0-405-01580-1*) Ayer.

New York City Museum Of Modern Art Staff & McBride, Henry. Three American Romantic Painters: Burchfield, Stettheimer, Watkins. 1969. 18.95 (*0-405-01538-0*, 15564) Ayer.

New York City Planning Commission. Plan for New York City. Richards, Peter, ed. Incl. Vol. 3. Plan Brooklyn. 1970. pap. text 25.00 (*0-262-64005-8*); Set pap. 24.00 (*0-685-03388-0*) MIT Pr.

New York City 100 Staff. The New York Pop-Up Book: New York City: Historic New York, Celebrating the Century. Salerno, Marie & Gelb, Arthur, eds. (Illus.). 8p. 1999. 39.95 (*0-7893-0374-4*, Pub. by Universe) St Martin.

New York Colony Committee. New York Marriages Previous to 1784. LC 67-30757. 618p. 1999. reprint ed. pap. 45.00 (*0-8063-0259-3*) Clearfield Co.

New York Committee of Fifteen, et al. Prostitution in America: Three Investigations, 1975. Syracuse Moral Survey Committee, ed. Massachusetts Commission for Investigation of Whit, tr. (Social Problems & Social Policy Ser.). 1976. 41.95 (*0-405-07511-1*) Ayer.

New York Committee of Merchants for the Relief of. Anti-Negro Riots in the North, Eighteen Sixty-Three. LC 69-18537. (American Negro: His History & Literature. Series 2). 1969. reprint ed. 19.95 (*0-405-01848-7*) Ayer.

New York Community Service Society Staff, jt. auth. see Northwest Bronx Community & Clergy Coalition Staff.

New York Constitutional Convention Staff. Reports of the Proceedings & Debates of the New York Constitutional Convention, 1821. LC 72-133168. (Law, Politics & History Ser.). 1970. reprint ed. lib. bdg. 85.00 (*0-306-70069-7*) Da Capo.

New York Cooperator Staff. Co-op & Condo Ownership: The Complete Guide for Apartment Buyers, Owners & Boards. Chesler, Vicki, ed. & intro. by. Kovner, Matt, intro. LC 95-69416. 256p. (Orig.). 1995. pap. 19.95 (*0-9646542-0-2*, NY Cooperator) Manhatt Cooperator.

New York Daily News Editors. Amazin' Mets: The Miracle of '69. 256p. 1999. 29.95 (*1-58261-039-8*) Sprts Pubng.

— Joe DiMaggio: An American Icon. 224p. 1999. 29.95 (*1-58261-037-1*) Sprts Pubng.

***New York Daily News Editors.** New York Giants: 75 Years of Football Memories. 200p. 1999. 24.95 (*1-58261-134-3*, Pub. by Sprts Pubng) Partners-West.

— New York Rangers: Millennium Memories. (Illus.). 128p. 2000. 19.95 (*1-58261-147-5*, Pub. by Sports Pub) Partners Pubs Grp.

— Parcells. (Illus.). 304p. 2000. 22.95 (*1-58261-146-7*) Sports Pub.

***New York Daily News Editors, ed.** Big Town, Big Time. 224p. 1998. 39.95 (*1-58261-028-2*) Sprts Pubng.

***New York Daily News Staff.** Amazin' Mets. rev. ed. 210p. 2000. reprint ed. pap. 22.69 (*1-58261-297-8*) Sports Pub.

— Jeter: Hero in Pinstripes. (Illus.). 2000. 24.95 (*1-58261-261-7*) Sports Pub.

— Jets: Broadway's 30-Year Guarantee. 1998. 29.95 (*1-58261-016-9*) Sprts Pubng.

— Joe DiMaggio: An American Icon. (Illus.). 248p. 2000. pap. 22.95 (*1-58261-298-6*) Sports Pub.

— The Justice Story. (Illus.). 256p. 2000. 24.95 (*1-58261-285-4*, Bannon Multimedia) Sports Pub.

— Piazza. (Illus.). 128p. 2000. 24.95 (*1-58261-262-5*) Sports Pub.

***New York Daily News Staff, ed.** The Knicks: New York's 1970 NBA Champion. (Legends Ser.). (Illus.). 128p. 2000. 19.95 (*1-58261-211-0*, Pub. by Sprts Pubng) Partners-West.

— Yankee Stadium: Lasting Images. (Illus.). 160p. 2000. 24.95 (*1-58261-257-9*) Sports Pub.

***New York Daily News Staff & Maeder, Jay, eds.** Big Town Biography. 160p. 1999. 34.95 (*1-58261-238-2*, Pub. by Sprts Pubng) Partners-West.

New York Festivals Staff. New York Festival, Vol. 6. 1998. 59.95 (*0-688-16043-3*, Wm Morrow) Morrow Avon.

— New York Festivals. 3rd ed. 1995. 59.95 (*0-688-14258-3*, Wm Morrow) Morrow Avon.

***New York Festivals Staff & Goldberg, Gerald M.** The New York Festivals: International Advertising Awards 8. (Illus.). 392p. 2000. 69.95 (*0-9655403-4-0*, Pub. by NY Festivals) Watsn-Guptill.

New York Giants. New York Giants. CWC Sports Inc., ed. (NFL Team Yearbooks Ser.). (J). (gr. 1-12). 1998. pap. 9.99 (*1-891613-09-X*) Everett Sports.

New York Gold Staff. Conceptual People Photography, Vol. 10. (Illus.). 200p. 1997. pap. 24.95 (*0-8230-6582-0*) Watsn-Guptill.

— Conceptual Still Life Photography, Vol. 10. (Illus.). 232p. 1997. pap. 24.95 (*0-8230-6580-4*) Watsn-Guptill.

— Gold Book's Eye: Eye on Still Life Photography - Eye on People Photography, 2. (Illus.). 128p. 1995. pap. 22.95 (*0-8230-6386-0*) Watsn-Guptill.

New York Historical Society. Shanties to Skyscrapers: Robert Bracklow's Photographs of Early New York. 1988. write for info. (*0-8212-1622-8*) Little.

New York Historical Society Staff. Collections of the New York Historical Society, 5 vols. in 4. (First Series). reprint ed. 375.00 (*0-404-11070-3*) AMS Pr.

— Colonel Stephen Kemble's Journals & British Army Orders, 1775-1778. Billias, George A., ed. LC 72-8999. (American Revolutionary Ser.). reprint ed. lib. bdg. 38.00 (*0-8398-1355-4*) Irvington.

New York Institute of Finance Staff. After the Trade Is Made - An Operation Training Manual. (Illus.). 224p. 1987. student ed. 24.95 (*0-13-858721-3*) NY Inst Finance.

— Asset Plays: Profiting from Undervalued Stock. 1988. 29.95 (*0-317-03938-5*) NY Inst Finance.

— Futures: A Personal Seminar. (Illus.). 260p. (C). 1989. pap. text 24.95 (*0-13-658196-X*) NY Inst Finance.

New York Institute of Finance Staff. How the Bond Market Works. 288p. (C). 1988. pap. text 15.95 (*0-13-423310-7*) NY Inst Finance.

New York Institute of Finance Staff. Investor's Rights Manual. 1988. pap. 17.95 (*0-13-799099-5*) NY Inst Finance.

— New York Institute of Finance Guide to Investing. LC 87-11323. (Illus.). 320p. (C). 1987. pap. 15.95 (*0-13-620436-8*) NY Inst Finance.

— New York Institute of Finance Guide to Investing. 2nd ed. 320p. (C). 1992. pap. text 19.95 (*0-13-617598-8*) P-H.

— Real Estate Investment Trusts. 320p. 1988. 17.95 (*0-13-763228-2*) NY Inst Finance.

— Securities Analysis: A Personal Seminar. 240p. (C). 1989. pap. text 22.95 (*0-13-658204-4*) NY Inst Finance.

— Technical Analysis: A Personal Seminar. (C). 1989. pap. text 24.95 (*0-13-898370-4*) NY Inst Finance.

New York Jets. New York Jets. CWC Sports Inc., ed. (NFL Team Yearbooks Ser.). (J). (gr. 1-12). 1998. pap. 9.99 (*1-891613-17-0*) Everett Sports.

New York, Kings Country, Grand Jury Staff. A Presentment Concerning the Enforcement of the City of New York of the Laws Against Gambling by the Grand Jury for the Additional Extraordinary Special & Trial Term. LC 73-3844. (Criminal Justice in America Ser.). 1974. reprint ed. 19.95 (*0-405-06148-X*) Ayer.

New York Knicks Staff. Knicks Media Guide, 1993-1994. 1993. per. 8.00 (*0-671-89023-9*) S&S Trade.

New York Landmarks Conservancy Staff. Historic Building Facades: The Manual for Maintenance & Rehabilitation. Foulks, William G., ed. LC 96-36643. 220p. 1997. pap. 39.95 (*0-471-14415-0*) Wiley.

— Repairing Old & Historic Windows: A Manual for Architects & Homeowners. (Illus.). 208p. (Orig.). 1995. pap. 24.95 (*0-471-14418-5*) Wiley.

New York Metropolitan Museum of Art Staff. Tiffany Address Book. (Illus.). 128p. 1991. 19.50 (*0-8212-1878-6*, Pub. by Bulfinch Pr) Little.

New York Microscopical Society Staff. Glossary of Microscopical Terms & Definitions, Vol. 51. 1989. 20.00 (*0-904962-12-1*) Microscope Pubns.

New York-New Jersey Trail Conference Staff. Guide to the Long Path. 4th ed. LC 92-19099. 1996. pap. 9.95 (*1-880775-06-9*) NY-NJ Trail Confer.

— New Jersey Walk Book. LC 98-44411. 1998. 15.95 (*1-880775-05-0*) NY-NJ Trail Confer.

— New York Walk Book. 6th ed. LC 97-35069. 1998. 19.95 (*1-880775-11-5*) NY-NJ Trail Confer.

New York Organ Co. Staff. Vocalian Organ. (Illus.). 25p. 1981. pap. 6.00 (*0-913746-16-9*) Organ Lit.

New York Public Library Staff. Annual Bibliography of Modern Art 1997. 1998. 295.00 (*0-7838-8143-6*) Mac Lib Ref.

— Bibliographic Guide to Art & Architecture 1987. 1384p. 1988. 315.00 (*0-8161-7087-8*, G K Hall & Co) Mac Lib Ref.

— Bibliographic Guide to Art & Architecture 1988. 1175p. 1989. 315.00 (*0-8161-7097-5*, G K Hall & Co) Mac Lib Ref.

— Bibliographic Guide to Art & Architecture 1989. 1992. 370.00 (*0-7838-1002-4*, G K Hall & Co) Mac Lib Ref.

— Bibliographic Guide to Art & Architecture 1990, 2 vols. large type ed. 1335p. 1991. 335.00 (*0-8161-7131-9*, G K Hall & Co) Mac Lib Ref.

— Bibliographic Guide to Art & Architecture 1994 Vol. 1, Vol. 1. 1995. 200.00 (*0-7838-2162-X*, G K Hall & Co) Mac Lib Ref.

— Bibliographic Guide to Art & Architecture 1994 Vol. 2, Vol. 2. 1996. 200.00 (*0-7838-2163-8*, G K Hall & Co) Mac Lib Ref.

— Bibliographic Guide to Art & Architecture 1995. 1996. 410.00 (*0-7838-1305-8*) Macmillan.

— Bibliographic Guide to Black Studies 1998. 1999. 295.00 (*0-7838-0409-1*) Mac Lib Ref.

— Bibliographic Guide to Business & Economics. 1816p. 1994. 600.00 (*0-7838-2069-0*, G K Hall & Co) Mac Lib Ref.

— Bibliographic Guide to Business & Economics 1987. 2256p. 1988. 570.00 (*0-8161-7086-X*, Hall Reference) Macmillan.

— Bibliographic Guide to Business & Economics 1994, Vol. 3. 1995. 220.00 (*0-7838-2168-9*, Hall Reference) Macmillan.

— Bibliographic Guide to Business & Economics 1994 Vol. 1, Vol. 1. (Reference Publications). 1995. 220.00 (*0-7838-2166-2*, G K Hall & Co) Mac Lib Ref.

— Bibliographic Guide to Business & Economics 1994 Vol. 2, Vol. 2. (Reference Publications). 1995. 220.00 (*0-7838-2167-0*, G K Hall & Co) Mac Lib Ref.

— Bibliographic Guide to Business & Economics 1995. 1996. 650.00 (*0-7838-1309-0*) Macmillan.

— Bibliographic Guide to Conference Publications 1987. 1392p. 1988. 315.00 (*0-8161-7096-7*, Hall Reference) Macmillan.

— Bibliographic Guide to Conference Publications 1988. (Bibliographic Guides Ser.). 1235p. 1989. 315.00 (*0-8161-7073-8*, Hall Reference) Macmillan.

— Bibliographic Guide to Conference Publications 1989. 1200p. (C). 1989. 320.00 (*0-8161-7111-4*, Hall Reference) Macmillan.

— Bibliographic Guide to Conference Publications 1993. Incl. Vol. 1. Bibliographic Guide to Conference Publications 1993. 640p. 1994. 170.00 (*0-7838-2074-7*, G K Hall & Co); 1994. 340.00 (*0-7838-2073-9*, G K Hall & Co) Mac Lib Ref.

— Bibliographic Guide to Conference Publications 1993, Vol 2. 1994. 170.00 (*0-7838-2075-5*, G K Hall & Co) Mac Lib Ref.

— Bibliographic Guide to Conference Publications 1995, 2 vols. 1996. 410.00 (*0-7838-1313-9*) Macmillan.

— Bibliographic Guide to Conference Publications 1998. 1999. 545.00 (*0-7838-0196-3*, G K Hall Lrg Type) Mac Lib Ref.

— Bibliographic Guide to Dance 1990. (Bibliographic Guides Ser.). 1150p. 1991. 375.00 (*0-8161-7136-X*, G K Hall & Co) Mac Lib Ref.

— Bibliographic Guide to Dance, 1993, 3 vols., Vol. 3. Incl. Bibliographic Guide to Dance, 1993. 686p. 1994. 160.00 (*0-7838-2077-1*, G K Hall & Co); 1994. 500.00 (*0-7838-2076-3*, G K Hall & Co) Mac Lib Ref.

— Bibliographic Guide to Dance 1994, 3 vols., Set. Incl. Vol. 1. Bibliographic Guide to Dance 1994. 1996. 180.00 (*0-7838-2173-5*, G K Hall & Co); Vol. 2. Bibliographic Guide to Dance 1994. 1996. 180.00 (*0-7838-2174-3*, G K Hall & Co); Vol. 3. Bibliographic Guide to Dance 1994. 1996. 180.00 (*0-7838-2175-1*, G K Hall & Co); 1995. 530.00 (*0-7838-2172-7*, G K Hall & Co) Mac Lib Ref.

— Bibliographic Guide to Dance 1995. 1996. 535.00 (*0-7838-1316-3*) Macmillan.

— Bibliographic Guide to Dance, 1995, Vol. 1. 1996. 190.00 (*0-7838-1317-1*) Mac Lib Ref.

— Bibliographic Guide to Dance, 1995, Vol. 2. 1996. 190.00 (*0-7838-1318-X*) Mac Lib Ref.

— Bibliographic Guide to Dance, 1995, Vol. 3. 1996. 190.00 (*0-7838-1319-8*) Mac Lib Ref.

— Bibliographic Guide to East Asian Studies. 1996. 220.00 (*0-7838-1320-1*) Macmillan.

— Bibliographic Guide to East Asian Studies, 1989. (Monographs). 350p. (C). 1990. 180.00 (*0-8161-7126-2*, G K Hall & Co) Mac Lib Ref.

— Bibliographic Guide to East Asian Studies 1992. 1993. 175.00 (*0-8161-1669-5*, G K Hall & Co) Mac Lib Ref.

— Bibliographic Guide to East Asian Studies, 1993. 432p. 1994. 185.00 (*0-7838-2080-1*, G K Hall & Co) Mac Lib Ref.

— Bibliographic Guide to East Asian Studies 1997. 1998. 295.00 (*0-7838-8160-6*) Mac Lib Ref.

— Bibliographic Guide to Education, 1993. 432p. 1994. 330.00 (*0-7838-2081-X*, G K Hall & Co) Mac Lib Ref.

— Bibliographic Guide to Education, 1994. 1995. 350.00 (*0-7838-2177-8*, G K Hall & Co) Mac Lib Ref.

— Bibliographic Guide to Goverment Publications, 1993 - U. S., 2 vols. 944p. 1994. 520.00 (*0-7838-2086-0*, G K Hall & Co) Mac Lib Ref.

— Bibliographic Guide to Government Publications - Foreign: 1988. 1720p. 1989. 530.00 (*0-8161-7103-3*, Hall Reference) Macmillan.

— Bibliographic Guide to Government Publications - U. S. 1987. 1448p. 1988. 460.00 (*0-8161-7089-4*, Hall Reference) Macmillan.

— Bibliographic Guide to Government Publications - U. S. 1988. 1175p. 1989. 475.00 (*0-8161-7102-5*, Hall Reference) Macmillan.

— Bibliographic Guide to Government Publications-Foreign: 1987. 1808p. 1988. 520.00 (*0-8161-7090-8*, Hall Reference) Macmillan.

— Bibliographic Guide to Government Publications, Foreign, 1994 Vol. 1: Foreign, Vol. 1. 1995. 300.00 (*0-7838-2180-8*, G K Hall & Co) Mac Lib Ref.

— Bibliographic Guide to Government Publications, Foreign, 1994 Vol. 2: Foreign, Vol. 2. 1995. 300.00 (*0-7838-2181-6*, G K Hall & Co) Mac Lib Ref.

— Bibliographic Guide to Government Publications Foreign 1995. 1996. 655.00 (*0-7838-1323-6*) Macmillan.

— Bibliographic Guide to Government Publications Foreign 1998. 1999. 720.00 (*0-7838-0210-2*, G K Hall Lrg Type) Mac Lib Ref.

— Bibliographic Guide to Government Publications, U. S., 1994 Vol. 1: U. S., Vol. 1. 1995. 275.00 (*0-7838-2183-2*, G K Hall & Co) Mac Lib Ref.

— Bibliographic Guide to Government Publications, U. S., 1994 Vol. 2: U. S., Vol. 2. 1997. 290.00 (*0-7838-2184-0*, G K Hall & Co) Mac Lib Ref.

— Bibliographic Guide to Government Publications United States 1995. 1996. 600.00 (*0-7838-1326-0*) Macmillan.

— Bibliographic Guide to Government Publications U.S 1998. 1999. 620.00 (*0-7838-0214-5*, G K Hall Lrg Type) Mac Lib Ref.

— Bibliographic Guide to Government Publications, 1993 - Foriegn. 1664p. 1994. 575.00 (*0-7838-2083-6*, G K Hall & Co) Mac Lib Ref.

— Bibliographic Guide to Latin American Studies, 2 vols. 1668p. 1994. 575.00 (*0-7838-2089-5*, G K Hall & Co) Mac Lib Ref.

— Bibliographic Guide to Latin American Studies 1990. 1992. 560.00 (*0-7838-1003-2*, G K Hall & Co) Mac Lib Ref.

— Bibliographic Guide to Latin American Studies, 1994 Vol. 1, Vol. 1. 1995. 290.00 (*0-7838-2186-7*, G K Hall & Co) Mac Lib Ref.

— Bibliographic Guide to Latin American Studies, 1994 Vol. 2, Vol. 2. 1995. 290.00 (*0-7838-2187-5*, G K Hall & Co) Mac Lib Ref.

— Bibliographic Guide to Law: 1987. 1544p. 1988. 330.00 (*0-8161-7095-9*, Hall Reference) Macmillan.

— Bibliographic Guide to Law 1994 Vol. 1, Vol. 1. 1995. 200.00 (*0-7838-2189-1*, G K Hall & Co) Mac Lib Ref.

— Bibliographic Guide to Law 1994 Vol. 2, Vol. 2. 1995. 200.00 (*0-7838-2190-5*, G K Hall & Co) Mac Lib Ref.

— Bibliographic Guide to Maps & Atlases 1987. 880p. 1988. 315.00 (*0-8161-7085-1*, Hall Reference) Macmillan.

— Bibliographic Guide to Maps & Atlases 1990. (Bibliographic Guides Ser.). 770p. 1991. 315.00 (*0-8161-7143-2*, G K Hall & Co) Mac Lib Ref.

— Bibliographic Guide to Maps & Atlases 1992. 1993. 330.00 (*0-8161-1676-8*, G K Hall & Co) Mac Lib Ref.

— Bibliographic Guide to Maps & Atlases 1993. 535p. 1994. 325.00 (*0-7838-2095-X*, G K Hall & Co) Mac Lib Ref.

— Bibliographic Guide to Microform Publications. (Bibliographic Guides Ser.). 600p. (C). 1990. 265.00 (*0-8161-7129-7*, G K Hall & Co) Mac Lib Ref.

— Bibliographic Guide to Microform Publications. (Bibliographic Guides Ser.). 600p. 1989. 265.00 (*0-8161-7106-8*, Hall Reference) Macmillan.

— Bibliographic Guide to Microform Publications 1992. 1993. 260.00 (*0-8161-1677-6*, G K Hall & Co) Mac Lib Ref.

— Bibliographic Guide to Microform Publications, 1993. 535p. 1994. 275.00 (*0-7838-2096-8*, G K Hall & Co) Mac Lib Ref.

— Bibliographic Guide to Middle Eastern Studies, 1990 Edition. (Bibliographic Guides Ser.). 800p. 1991. 210.00 (*0-8161-7151-3*, G K Hall & Co) Mac Lib Ref.

— Bibliographic Guide to Middle Eastern Studies, 1993. 497p. 1994. 195.00 (*0-7838-2097-6*, G K Hall & Co) Mac Lib Ref.

— Bibliographic Guide to Middle Eastern Studies 1994. 1995. 215.00 (*0-7838-2192-1*, G K Hall & Co) Mac Lib Ref.

N

An Asterisk (*) at the beginning of an entry indicates that the title is appearing for the first time.

— Bibliographic Guide to Music 1987. 752p. 1988. 210.00 (*0-8161-7093-2*, Hall Reference) Macmillan.
— Bibliographic Guide to Music 1992. 1993. 235.00 (*0-8161-1679-2*, G K Hall & Co) Mac Lib Ref.
— Bibliographic Guide to Music 1993. 767p. 1994. 235.00 (*0-7838-2098-4*, G K Hall & Co) Mac Lib Ref.
— Bibliographic Guide to North American History: 1987. 768p. 1988. 290.00 (*0-8161-7092-4*, Hall Reference) Macmillan.
— Bibliographic Guide to North American History: 1989. (C). 1990. 305.00 (*0-8161-7118-1*, Hall Reference) Macmillan.
— Bibliographic Guide to North American History: 1993. 808p. 1994. 330.00 (*0-7838-2099-2*, G K Hall & Co) Mac Lib Ref.
— Bibliographic Guide to North American History 1992. 1993. 315.00 (*0-8161-1680-6*, G K Hall & Co) Mac Lib Ref.
— Bibliographic Guide to North American History 1995. 1996. 365.00 (*0-7838-1338-4*) Macmillan.
— Bibliographic Guide to Psychology. 1996. 225.00 (*0-7838-1339-2*) Macmillan.
— Bibliographic Guide to Psychology: 1987. 152p. 1988. 185.00 (*0-8161-7094-0*, Hall Reference) Macmillan.
— Bibliographic Guide to Psychology: 1989. 150p. 1989. 200.00 (*0-8161-7114-9*, G K Hall & Co) Mac Lib Ref.
— Bibliographic Guide to Psychology: 1993. 224p. 1994. 195.00 (*0-7838-2100-X*, G K Hall & Co) Mac Lib Ref.
— Bibliographic Guide to Psychology 1992. 1993. 195.00 (*0-8161-1681-4*, G K Hall & Co) Mac Lib Ref.
— Bibliographic Guide to Psychology 1994. 1995. 205.00 (*0-7838-2195-6*, G K Hall & Co) Mac Lib Ref.
— Bibliographic Guide to Slavic, Baltic & Eurasian Studies, 1994 Vol. 1, Vol. 1. 1997. 330.00 (*0-7838-2197-2*, G K Hall & Co) Mac Lib Ref.
— Bibliographic Guide to Slavic, Baltic & Eurasian Studies, 1994 Vol. 2, Vol. 2. 1997. 330.00 (*0-7838-2198-0*, G K Hall & Co) Mac Lib Ref.
— Bibliographic Guide to Slavic, Baltic & Eurasian Studies, 1994 Vol. 3, Vol. 3. 1997. 230.00 (*0-7838-2199-9*, G K Hall & Co) Mac Lib Ref.
— Bibliographic Guide to Slavic, Baltic & Eurasian Studies, 1995, Vol. 1. 1996. 240.00 (*0-7838-1341-4*, G K Hall & Co) Mac Lib Ref.
— Bibliographic Guide to Slavic, Baltic & Eurasian Studies, 1995, Vol. 2. 1996. 240.00 (*0-7838-1342-2*, G K Hall & Co) Mac Lib Ref.
— Bibliographic Guide to Slavic, Baltic & Eurasian Studies, 1995, Vol. 3. 1996. 240.00 (*0-7838-1343-0*, G K Hall & Co) Mac Lib Ref.
— Bibliographic Guide to Slavic, Baltic & Eurasians Studies 1995. 1996. 195.00 (*0-7838-1340-6*) Macmillan.
— Bibliographic Guide to Soviet & East European Studies 1979. 1992. 390.00 (*0-7838-1004-0*, G K Hall & Co) Mac Lib Ref.
— Bibliographic Guide to Soviet & East European Studies 1980. 1992. 390.00 (*0-7838-1005-9*, G K Hall & Co) Mac Lib Ref.
— Bibliographic Guide to Soviet & East European Studies 1981. 1992. 390.00 (*0-7838-1006-7*, G K Hall & Co) Mac Lib Ref.
— Bibliographic Guide to Soviet & East European Studies 1982. 1992. 390.00 (*0-7838-1007-5*, G K Hall & Co) Mac Lib Ref.
— Bibliographic Guide to Soviet & East European Studies 1993, Vol 1. 1994. 210.00 (*0-7838-2102-6*, G K Hall & Co) Mac Lib Ref.
— Bibliographic Guide to Technology: 1987. 1080p. 1988. 375.00 (*0-8161-7088-6*, Hall Reference) Macmillan.
— Bibliographic Guide to Technology: 1990, 2 vols., Set. (Bibliographic Guides Ser.). 1020p. 1991. 365.00 (*0-8161-7150-5*, G K Hall & Co) Mac Lib Ref.
— Bibliographic Guide to Technology 1992, Vol. 1. 1993. 200.00 (*0-8161-1724-1*, G K Hall & Co) Mac Lib Ref.
— Bibliographic Guide to Technology, 1994 Vol. 1, Vol. 1. 1997. 190.00 (*0-7838-2201-4*, G K Hall & Co) Mac Lib Ref.
— Bibliographic Guide to Technology, 1994 Vol. 2, Vol. 2. 1995. 190.00 (*0-7838-2202-2*, G K Hall & Co) Mac Lib Ref.
— Bibliographic Guide to Technology 1995. 1996. 390.00 (*0-7838-1344-9*) Macmillan.
— Bibliographic Guide to Technology, 1995, Vol. 1. 1996. 200.00 (*0-7838-1345-7*, G K Hall & Co) Mac Lib Ref.
— Bibliographic Guide to Technology, 1995, Vol. 2. 1996. 200.00 (*0-7838-1346-5*, G K Hall & Co) Mac Lib Ref.
— Bibliographic Guide to the Environment 1992. 1993. 165.00 (*0-8161-1671-7*, G K Hall & Co) Mac Lib Ref.
— Bibliographic Guide to the Environment, 1994. 1995. 195.00 (*0-7838-2178-6*, G K Hall & Co) Mac Lib Ref.
— Bibliographic Guide to the Environment 1995. 1996. 205.00 (*0-7838-1322-8*) Macmillan.
— Bibliographic Guide to the Environment 1997. 1998. 295.00 (*0-7838-8162-2*) Mac Lib Ref.
— Bibliographic Guide to the Environment 1998. 1999. 295.00 (*0-7838-0408-3*) Mac Lib Ref.
— Bibliographic Guide to Theater Arts: 1989. (Bibliographic Guides Ser.). 200p. (C). 1989. 220.00 (*0-8161-7115-7*, Hall Reference) Macmillan.
— Bibliographic Guide to Theatre Arts: 1990. large type ed. 244p. 1991. 205.00 (*0-8161-7149-1*, Hall Reference) Macmillan.
— Bibliographic Guide to Theatre Arts 1992. 1993. 205.00 (*0-8161-1684-9*, G K Hall & Co) Mac Lib Ref.
— Bibliographic Guide to Theatre Arts 1995. 1996. 225.00 (*0-7838-1347-3*) Macmillan.
— Bibliographic Guide to Womens Studies 98, Set. 1999. 449.00 (*0-7838-0405-9*) Mac Lib Ref.
— Bibliographic Guide to Womens Studies 98, Vol. 1. 1999. 222.50 (*0-7838-0406-7*) Mac Lib Ref.
— Bibliographic Guide to Womens Studies 98, Vol. 2. 1999. 222.50 (*0-7838-0407-5*) Mac Lib Ref.
— Bibliogrpahic Guide to Music, 1995. 1996. 275.00 (*0-7838-1337-6*) Macmillan.
— Catalog of Government Publications, Supplement 1974, 2 vols., Set. 1976. 275.00 (*0-8161-0060-8*, G K Hall & Co) Mac Lib Ref.
— Catalog of the Theatre & Drama Collections, 2 pts. Incl. Set. Drama Collection: Author Listing., 6 vols. 1970. 1025.00 (*0-8161-0106-X*, G K Hall & Co); Set. Drama Collection: Listing by Cultural Origin., 6 vols. 1970. 640.00 1970. write for info. (*0-318-52340-X*, G K Hall & Co) Mac Lib Ref.
— Catalog of the Theatre & Drama Collections, Pt. 3. 30 Vols. Non-book Collection. 1976. 4150.00 (*0-8161-1195-2*, G K Hall & Co) Mac Lib Ref.
— Catalog of the Theatre & Drama Collections: First Supplement to Pt. 1, Drama Collection. 1973. 125.00 (*0-8161-0745-9*, G K Hall & Co) Mac Lib Ref.
— Catalog of the Theatre & Drama Collections: Supplement 1974. 1976. 140.00 (*0-8161-0058-6*, G K Hall & Co) Mac Lib Ref.
— Dictionary Catalog of Schomburg Collection Negro Literature Hand History. 1994. 560.00 (*0-7838-2223-5*, G K Hall & Co) Mac Lib Ref.
— Dictionary Catalog of the Albert A. & Henry W. Berg Collection of English & American Literature, First Supplement. 1975. 160.00 (*0-8161-0014-4*, G K Hall & Co) Mac Lib Ref.
— Dictionary Catalog of the Art & Architecture Division, The Research Libraries of The New York Public Library, 30 vols., Set. 1975. 3515.00 (*0-8161-1157-X*, G K Hall & Co) Mac Lib Ref.
— Dictionary Catalog of the Henry W. & Albert A. Berg Collection of English & American Literature, 5 Vols, Set. 1970. 560.00 (*0-8161-0870-6*, G K Hall & Co) Mac Lib Ref.
— Dictionary Catalog of the History of the American Collection, 28 vols. 1994. 2890.00 (*0-7838-2304-5*, G K Hall & Co) Mac Lib Ref.
— Dictionary Catalog of the History of the Americas Collection, First Supplement, 9 vols., Set. 1974. 1130.00 (*0-8161-0771-8*, G K Hall & Co) Mac Lib Ref.
— Dictionary Catalog of the Local History & Genealogy Division. 1974. 1830.00 (*0-8161-1468-4*, G K Hall & Co) Mac Lib Ref.
— Dictionary Catalog of the Manuscript Division. 1970. 180.00 (*0-8161-1450-1*, G K Hall & Co) Mac Lib Ref.
— Dictionary Catalog of the Map Division of the New York Public Library. 1994. 1250.00 (*0-7838-2214-6*, G K Hall & Co) Mac Lib Ref.
— Dictionary Catalog of the Music Collection of the New York Public Library. 1994. 1705.00 (*0-7838-2211-1*, G K Hall & Co) Mac Lib Ref.
— Dictionary Catalog of the Oriental Collection. 1980. 1515.00 (*0-8161-1282-7*, G K Hall & Co) Mac Lib Ref.
— Dictionary Catalog of the Prints Division of the New York Public Library. 1994. 625.00 (*0-7838-2265-0*, G K Hall & Co) Mac Lib Ref.
— Dictionary Catalog of the Rare Book Division, 21 vols, Set. 1971. 2375.00 (*0-8161-0782-3*, G K Hall & Co) Mac Lib Ref.
— Dictionary Catalog of the Research Libraries of the New York Public Library, 1911 to 1971. 1983. 5240.00 (*0-8161-0320-8*, G K Hall & Co) Mac Lib Ref.
— Dictionary Catalog of the Schomburg Collection of Negro Literature & History. 1980. 1045.00 (*0-8161-1259-2*, G K Hall & Co) Mac Lib Ref.
— Dictionary Catalog of the Schomburg Collection of Negro Literature & History, Supplement 1. 1980. suppl. ed. 170.00 (*0-8161-1260-6*, G K Hall & Co) Mac Lib Ref.
— Dictionary Catalog of the Schomburg Collection of Negro Literature & History, Supplement 1974. 1976. 125.00 (*0-8161-0062-4*, G K Hall & Co) Mac Lib Ref.

*__New York Public Library Staff.__ The Folk Music of the Western Hemisphere: A List of References in the New York Public Library, Compiled by Julius Mattfield, Music Division. (LC History-America-E). 74p. 1999. reprint ed. lib. bdg. 69.00 (*0-7812-4290-8*) Rprt Serv.

New York Public Library Staff. The Imprint Catalog in the Rare Book Division, 21 vols., Set. 1979. 2430.00 (*0-8161-0092-6*, G K Hall & Co) Mac Lib Ref.
— Index to Dance Periodicals: 1996. 1997. 215.00 (*0-7838-2032-1*) Mac Lib Ref.
— Index to Dance Periodicals, 1990: Dance Collection of the Performing Arts Research Center at the New York Public Library. annuals 400p. 1991. 135.00 (*0-8161-0523-5*, G K Hall & Co) Mac Lib Ref.
— Index to Dance Periodicals 1992. 1993. 170.00 (*0-8161-0605-3*, G K Hall & Co) Mac Lib Ref.
— Index to Dance Periodicals, 1994. 1996. 185.00 (*0-7838-2148-4*) Macmillan.
— Index to Dance Periodicals, 1995. 1996. 195.00 (*0-7838-1533-6*, G K Hall & Co) Mac Lib Ref.
— The New York Public Library African American Desk Reference. 624p. 1999. 34.95 (*0-471-23924-0*) Wiley.

*__New York Public Library Staff.__ New York Public Library Business Desk Reference. 512p. 1999. pap. 19.95 (*0-471-32835-9*) Wiley.

New York Public Library Staff. The New York Public Library Business Desk Reference: Essential Information for Every Office at Your Fingertips. LC 97-7408. 512p. 1997. 29.95 (*0-471-14442-8*) Wiley.
— The New York Public Library Desk Reference. 2nd ed. LC 93-18299. (Illus.). 944p. 1993. 40.00 (*0-671-85014-8*) Macmillan.
— New York Public Library Desk Reference to the Performing Arts. 1996. 16.95 (*0-02-861447-X*) Macmillan.
— The New York Public Library Performing Arts Desk Reference. (Illus.). 432p. 1994. 35.00 (*0-671-79912-6*) Macmillan.
— The New York Public Library Student's Desk Reference. LC 93-22842. (Illus.). 528p. 1995. 14.95 (*0-02-860418-0*) Macmillan.
— Phic Guide to the Environment, 1993. 392p. 1994. 175.00 (*0-7838-2082-8*, G K Hall & Co) Mac Lib Ref.
— Subject Headings, 5 vols. 1994. 435.00 (*0-7838-2298-7*, G K Hall Lrg Type) Mac Lib Ref.
— Theater Subject Headings. 2nd enl. large type ed. 1994. 175.00 (*0-7838-2319-3*, G K Hall Lrg Type) Mac Lib Ref.

New York Public Library Staff, compiled by. Bibliographic Guide to Dance, 1991, 3 vols., Set. 1800p. 1992. 475.00 (*0-8161-7157-2*, G K Hall & Co) Mac Lib Ref.
— Children's Books, 1911-1986: Favorite Children's Books from the Branch Collections of the New York Public Library. (Illus.). 78p. 1986. 5.00 (*0-87104-689-X*, Branch Libraries) NY Pub Lib.

*__New York Public Library Staff, et al, contrib. by.__ Horse-Drawn Vehicles: Colored Plates from the Hub November 1882-January 1892. (Illus.). 320p. 1999. reprint ed. 100.00 (*1-880499-07-X*); reprint ed. write for info. (*1-880499-08-8*) Carriage Museum.

New York Public Library Staff, ed. Bibliographic Guide to American History 1991. 1992. 315.00 (*0-8161-7166-1*, G K Hall & Co) Mac Lib Ref.
— Bibliographic Guide to Black Studies 1987. 217p. 1988. 150.00 (*0-8161-7053-3*, G K Hall & Co) Mac Lib Ref.
— Bibliographic Guide to Black Studies 1990. 1991. 160.00 (*0-8161-7132-7*, G K Hall & Co) Mac Lib Ref.
— Bibliographic Guide to Black Studies 1991. 545p. 1992. 180.00 (*0-8161-7153-X*, G K Hall & Co) Mac Lib Ref.
— Bibliographic Guide to Black Studies 1992. 1993. 170.00 (*0-8161-1665-2*, G K Hall & Co) Mac Lib Ref.
— Bibliographic Guide to Black Studies 1993. 399p. 1994. 170.00 (*0-7838-2068-2*, G K Hall & Co) Mac Lib Ref.
— Bibliographic Guide to Black Studies 1994. 1995. 190.00 (*0-7838-2164-6*, G K Hall & Co) Mac Lib Ref.
— Bibliographic Guide to Black Studies 1995. 1996. 200.00 (*0-7838-1308-2*, G K Hall & Co) Mac Lib Ref.
— Bibliographic Guide to Black Studies 1996. 1997. 200.00 (*0-7838-1743-6*, G K Hall & Co) Mac Lib Ref.
— Bibliographic Guide to Business & Economics 1988, 3 vols. 1989. 575.00 (*0-8161-7098-3*, G K Hall & Co) Mac Lib Ref.
— Bibliographic Guide to Business & Economics 1995, Vol. 1. 1996. 335.00 (*0-7838-1310-4*, G K Hall & Co) Mac Lib Ref.
— Bibliographic Guide to Business & Economics 1995, Vol. 2. 1996. 335.00 (*0-7838-1311-2*, G K Hall & Co) Mac Lib Ref.
— Bibliographic Guide to Business & Economics 1995, Vol. 3. 1996. 335.00 (*0-7838-1312-0*, G K Hall & Co) Mac Lib Ref.
— Bibliographic Guide to Business & Economics 1996, 3 vols. Incl. Vol. 1. Bibliographic Guide to Business & Economics 1996., 3 vols. 1997. 335.00 (*0-7838-1745-2*, G K Hall & Co); Vol. 2. Bibliographic Guide to Business & Economics 1996. 1997. 335.00 (*0-7838-1746-0*, G K Hall & Co); Vol. 2. Bibliographic Guide to Business & Economics 1996. 1997. 335.00 (*0-7838-1747-9*, G K Hall & Co); 1997. 715.00 (*0-7838-1744-4*, G K Hall & Co) Mac Lib Ref.
— Bibliographic Guide to Conference Publications 1990, 2 vols. 1991. 325.00 (*0-8161-7135-1*, G K Hall & Co) Mac Lib Ref.
— Bibliographic Guide to Conference Publications, 1994, 2 vols., Set. Incl. Vol. 2. Bibliographic Guide to Conference Publications 1994. 1995. 195.00 (*0-7838-2171-9*, G K Hall & Co); 1995. 380.00 (*0-7838-2169-7*, G K Hall & Co) Mac Lib Ref.
— Bibliographic Guide to Education 1991. 1992. 315.00 (*0-8161-7159-9*, G K Hall & Co) Mac Lib Ref.
— Bibliographic Guide to Law: 1991, 2 vols., Vol. 2. 1053p. 1992. 360.00 (*0-8161-7163-7*, G K Hall & Co) Mac Lib Ref.
— Bibliographic Guide to Maps & Atlases 1991. 1992. 330.00 (*0-8161-7164-5*, G K Hall & Co) Mac Lib Ref.
— Bibliographic Guide to Maps & Atlases 1994. 1995. 360.00 (*0-7838-2191-3*, G K Hall & Co) Mac Lib Ref.
— Bibliographic Guide to Music 1994. 1995. 260.00 (*0-7838-2193-X*, G K Hall & Co) Mac Lib Ref.
— Bibliographic Guide to North American History 1994. 1995. 350.00 (*0-7838-2194-8*, G K Hall & Co) Mac Lib Ref.
— Bibliographic Guide to Psychology 1988. 1988. 190.00 (*0-8161-7076-2*, G K Hall & Co) Mac Lib Ref.
— Bibliographic Guide to Psychology 1990. 1991. 185.00 (*0-8161-7147-5*, G K Hall & Co) Mac Lib Ref.
— Bibliographic Guide to Technology 1988, 2 vols. 1989. 375.00 (*0-8161-7109-2*, G K Hall & Co) Mac Lib Ref.
— Bibliographic Guide to Technology 1991, 2 vols. 1992. 310.00 (*0-8161-7171-8*, G K Hall & Co) Mac Lib Ref.
— Big Guide to Middle Eastern Studies 1995. 1996. 225.00 (*0-7838-1336-8*, G K Hall & Co) Mac Lib Ref.
— Dictionary Catalog of Research Libraries of the New York Public Library: 1911 to 1971. 1994. 7460.00 (*0-7838-2207-3*, G K Hall & Co) Mac Lib Ref.
— Index to the Schomburg Clipping File. 176p. 1986. write for info. (*0-89887-035-6*) Chadwyck-Healey.

New York Public Library Staff & Dance Collection Staff. Index to Dance Periodicals: 1991. 525p. 1992. 135.00 (*0-8161-0574-X*, G K Hall & Co) Mac Lib Ref.

New York Public Library Staff & Gioia, Dana. The Hand of the Poet: Poems & Papers in Manuscript. LC 95-50472. (Illus.). 368p. 1997. 40.00 (*0-8478-1958-2*, Pub. by Rizzoli Intl) St Martin.

New York Public Library Staff & Library of Congress Staff. Bibliographic Guide to Art & Architecture 1991, 2 vols., Vol. 2. (Bibliographic Guides Ser.). 960p. 1992. 350.00 (*0-8161-7152-1*, G K Hall & Co) Mac Lib Ref.

New York Public Library Staff & Sonneborne, Liz. The New York Public Library Amazing Native American History: American History: A Book of Answers for Kids. LC 99-22916. 170p. (YA). (gr. 5-9). 1999. pap. 12.95 (*0-471-33204-6*) Wiley.

New York Public Library Staff & University of Texas at Austin Staff. Bibliographic Guide to Latin American Studies: 1987. 2048p. 1988. 545.00 (*0-8161-7083-5*, Hall Reference) Macmillan.

New York Public Library Staff, et al. The New York Public Library Amazing Mythology: A Book of Answers for Kids. LC 99-32203. 192p. (YA). (gr. 5-9). 2000. pap. text 12.95 (*0-471-33205-4*) Wiley.
— The New York Public Library Incredible Earth: A Book of Answers for Kids. LC 96-22112. (Illus.). 192p. 1996. pap. 12.95 (*0-471-14497-5*) Wiley.

New York Public Library Staff, jt. auth. see Columbia University Teachers College OCLC Tapes St.

New York Public Library Staff, jt. auth. see LC Marc Tapes Staff.

New York Public Library Staff, jt. auth. see Library of Congress Staff.

New York Public Library Staff, jt. auth. see University of Texas Staff.

New York Public Library Staff, jt. compiled by see Library of Congress Staff.

New York Road Runner 's Club Staff. New York Road Runners Club Complete Book of Running. 3rd rev. ed. LC 97-23114. 704p. 1997. pap. 18.00 (*0-679-78010-6*) Random Ref & Info.

New York Society for General Semantics Staff, ed. see Daly, T. P.

New York State Bar Association. Environmental Law Index. Gerrard, Michael B. et al, eds. LC 94-65586. 313p. 1994. 50.00 (*0-942954-68-8*) NYS Bar.

New York State Bar Association Staff. Collections & the Enforcement of Money Judgements. Getman, Jack et al, eds. LC 84-60393. 467p. 1996. text 60.00 (*0-942954-05-X*) NYS Bar.
— Corporate Practice Handbook. Merritt, Raymond W. & Ennico, Clifford R., eds. LC 92-61676. 995p. (Orig.). 1992. text 95.00 (*0-942954-55-6*) NYS Bar.
— Federal Civil Practice. LC 89-61058. 1038p. 1990. 95.00 (*0-942954-23-8*) NYS Bar.
— Federal Rules of Civil Procedure: 1993 Amendments. Arenson, Gregory K. & Wise, Robert F., Jr., eds. LC 94-65587. 204p. 1994. pap. text 37.00 (*0-942954-67-X*) NYS Bar.
— The Grand Jury in New York. Gray, Lawrence N., ed. LC 94-65728. 256p. 1994. pap. 44.00 (*0-942954-69-6*) NYS Bar.
— Individual Judges Rules, Procedures & Forms in United States District Courts of the Southern, Eastern, Northern & Western Districts of New York. LC 86-62411. 363p. 1986. 80.00 (*0-942954-13-0*) NYS Bar.
— Medical Malpractice in New York. Devine, Robert, ed. & pref. by. LC 92-63000. 570p. 1993. 90.00 (*0-942954-54-8*) NYS Bar.
— New York Criminal Practice Handbook, 1994 Supplement. Gray, Lawrence N., ed. 229p. 1994. pap. text 40.00 (*0-942954-72-6*) NYS Bar.
— New York Lawyer's Deskbook. LC 89-64413. 1172p. 1990. ring bd. 115.00 (*0-942954-33-5*) NYS Bar.
— New York Lawyer's Formbook. LC 90-50851. 1364p. 1991. ring bd. 115.00 (*0-942954-35-1*) NYS Bar.
— The Partnership Handbook. Merritt, Raymond W. & Helpern, Martin, eds. LC 85-62739. 917p. 1985. 70.00 (*0-942954-09-2*) NYS Bar.
— Pitfalls of Practice. White, Joanne M., ed. LC 93-86813. 348p. (Orig.). 1993. pap. text 45.00 (*0-942954-65-3*) NYS Bar.
— ProForms NYSBA Electronic Legal Forms. 55p. 1994. pap. text 140.00 (*0-942954-71-8*) NYS Bar.
— Real Estate Titles. 2nd ed. Pedowitz, James M., ed. & pref. by. LC 93-86812. (Illus.). 1216p. 1994. text 95.00 (*0-942954-66-1*) NYS Bar.
— The Treatise on New York Environmental Law. Robinson, Nicholas A. & Hopkins, James D., eds. LC 92-53528. 1000p. 1992. 95.00 (*0-685-56517-3*) NYS Bar.

New York State Chamber of Commerce Staff. Papers & Proceedings of the Committee on the Police Problem, City of New York. LC 79-154581. (Police in America Ser.). 1971. reprint ed. 51.95 (*0-405-03364-8*) Ayer.

New York State Commission on Relief for Widowed Mo. Report of the New York State Commission on Relief for Widowed Mothers. LC 74-1696. (Children & Youth Ser.: Vol. 18). 602p. 1974. reprint ed. 48.95 (*0-405-05973-6*) Ayer.

New York State Commission to Investigate Provision. Report of the State Commission to Investigate Provision for the Mentally Deficient. LC 75-17234. (Social Problems & Social Policy Ser.). (Illus.). 1976. reprint ed. 96.95 (*0-405-07503-0*) Ayer.

New York State Committee on State Prisons. Investigation of the New York State Prisons. LC 74-3828. (Criminal Justice in America Ser.). 1974. reprint ed. 87.95 (*0-405-06159-5*) Ayer.

New York State Committee to Review Audio-Visual Co. An Open Courtroom: Cameras in New York Courts. LC 97-16512. xxi, 243p. 1997. 40.00 (*0-8232-1809-0*); pap. 20.00 (*0-8232-1810-4*) Fordham.

New York State Crime Commission. Crime & the Community. LC 74-3820. (Criminal Justice in America Ser.). 1974. reprint ed. 25.95 (*0-405-06158-7*) Ayer.
— Report of the Crime Commission, 1925: Legislative Document Number 23. LC 74-3840. (Mass Violence in America Ser.). 1974. reprint ed. 53.95 (*0-405-06157-9*) Ayer.

N

An Asterisk (*) at the beginning of an entry indicates that the title is appearing for the first time.

New York State Division of Library Development Sta, jt. auth. see New York State Library Staff.

New York State Education Department, Bureau of Adu. Handbook for Teachers of Adult Occupational Education. 96p. 1977. 4.95 (*0-318-15481-1*, SN20) Ctr Educ Trng Employ.

New York State Energy Research & Development Autho, et al. The Electric Industry in Transition. 305p. 1994. pap. 55.00i (*0-910325-58-8*) Public Util.

New York State Historical Association Staff. Proceedings of the New York State Historical Associaton Vol. 6: The Seventh Annual Meeting with the Constitution, By-Laws, & List of Members Including Indian Geographical Names by E. M. Ruttenber. (Illus.). 243p. 1995. reprint ed. pap. text 20.00 (*0-7884-0224-2*) Heritage Bk.

New York State Humane Association Staff. Overpopulation of Cats & Dogs: Causes, Effects, & Prevention. Anchel, Marjorie, ed. LC 90-82350. xx, 260p. 1990. 25.00 (*0-8232-1296-3*) Fordham.

New York State Legislature, Joint Committee Invest, ed. Revolutionary Radicalism: Its History, Purpose & Tactics, 6 vols., Set. 1980. lib. bdg. 1200.00 (*0-8490-3152-4*) Gordon Pr.

New York State Legislature Staff. Town Law, New York State. annuals 350p. 2000. ring bd. 17.95 (*0-930137-41-8*) Looseleaf Law.

— Village Law, New York State. annuals 200p. 2000. ring bd. 15.95 (*0-930137-42-6*) Looseleaf Law.

New York State Library Staff. African American Bibliography: The Arts. 21p. 1990. 2.00 (*0-317-05244-6*) NYS Library.

— Annotated Lists & Indexes of the NYS Assembly & Senate Document Series, 1831-1918, 3 vols., Set. 1992. 50.00 (*0-317-05247-0*) NYS Library.

New York State Library Staff & New York State Division of Library Development Sta. Directory of Library Systems in New York State. 191p. 1993. 8.00 (*0-317-05248-9*) NYS Library.

New York State Museum Staff, jt. auth. see Daniels, Robert A.

New York State of Business Permits Office. The Official Directory of New York State Business Permits. Walters, Ruth S. & OBPRA Staff, eds. 1792p. 1992. pap. 35.00 (*0-942954-51-3*) NYS Bar.

— The Official Directory of New York State Business Permits. Walters, Ruth S. & OBPRA Staff, eds. 1993. 25.00 (*0-942954-60-2*) NYS Bar.

New York State Preservation League Staff. Preservation Directory: A Guide to Programs, Organizations, & Agencies in New York State. rev. ed. (Illus.). 232p. 1989. pap. 15.00 (*0-942000-06-4*) Pres League NYS.

New York State Staff. Fuel Injection Systems Training/ATTP. (Automotive Technology Ser.). 1994. pap. 40.75 (*0-8273-6757-0*) Delmar.

— New York Field Codes, 1850 1865, 5 vols. Incl. Vol. I. Code of Civil Procedure of the State of New York, 1850. LC 97-42137. 1998. reprint ed. Not sold separately (*1-886363-34-X*); Vol. II. Code of Criminal Procedure of the State of New York, 1850. LC 97-42136. 1998. reprint ed. Not sold separately (*1-886363-35-8*); Vol. III. Civil Code of the State of New York, 1865. LC 97-42138. 1998. reprint ed. Not sold separately (*1-886363-38-2*); Vol. IV. Penal Code of the State of New York, 1865. LC 97-42135. 1998. reprint ed. Not sold separately (*1-886363-36-6*); Vol. V. Political Code of the State of New York, 1860. LC 97-38750. 1998. reprint ed. Not sold separately (*1-886363-37-4*); LC 97-38809. 1997. reprint ed. 495.00 (*1-886363-40-4*) Lawbk Exchange.

— System Training: Emission & Performance - ATTP. (Automotive Technology Ser.). 1994. pap. 37.75 (*0-8273-6759-7*) Delmar.

New York State Staff & Matthew Bender Publishers Staff, eds. New York Estate's Surrogate's Court Procedure Act. 1997. write for info. (*0-8205-3496-X*) Bender.

New York State Supreme Court, Appellate Division S. The Investigation of the Magistrated Courts in the First Judicial Department & the Magistrates Thereof, & of Attorneys-at-Law Practicing in Said Courts: Final Report of Samuel Seabury, Referee. LC 74-3842. (Criminal Justice in America Ser.). 1974. reprint ed. 25.95 (*0-405-06160-9*) Ayer.

New York Stock Exchange, Office of the Hearing Boa. Hearing Board Decisions: Index Outline of Procedures. write for info. (*0-318-61975-X*) NYSE Inc.

New York Times Book Review Staff, ed. Books of the Century. LC 98-5477. 384p. 1998. 30.00 (*0-8129-2965-9*, Times Bks) Crown Pub Group.

New York Times Book Review Staff, jt. ed. see McGrath, Charles.

New York Times Information Bank. New York Times Giant Sunday Crossword, Vol. 4. 1994. mass mkt. write for info. (*0-394-59843-1*) Random.

New York Times Staff. The Century in Times Square. 128p. 1999. write for info. (*0-9668659-1-X*, Pub. by NY Times) Publishers Group.

— Champions: The 1998 New York Yankees. (Illus.). 112p. 1998. pap. 14.95 (*0-9668659-0-1*) NY Times.

***New York Times Staff.** Encore! The New York Yankees' 25th World Championship. (Illus.). 112p. 1999. pap. 14.95 (*0-9668659-5-2*, Pub. by NY Times) Publishers Group.

New York Times Staff. Encyclopedia of Film, Vol. 7. Date not set. write for info. (*0-8129-1052-4*, Times Bks) Crown Pub Group.

— Give Us This Day... A Report on the World Food Crisis. LC 75-1038. 1975. 15.95 (*0-405-06644-9*) Ayer.

— If You're Thinking of Living In... All about 115 Great Neighborhoods in & around New York. LC 98-46272. 464p. 1999. pap. 18.00 (*0-8129-2983-7*, Times Bks) Crown Pub Group.

— Introduction to a Good Reading Habit. 36p. 1981. pap. text. write for info. (*0-912853-03-4*) NY Times.

— Israel: The Historical Atlas from Ancient Times to the Modern Nation. (Illus.). 208p. 1997. 45.00 (*0-02-861987-0*) Macmillan.

— The Last Word: The New York Times Book of Obituaries & Farewells: A Celebration of Unusual Lives. Siegel, Marvin, ed. LC 97-11960. 432p. 1997. 25.00 (*0-688-15015-2*, Wm Morrow) Morrow Avon.

— The New York Times Best Crosswords, Vol. 2. Maleska, Eugene T., ed. 64p. 1996. pap. 8.50 (*0-8129-2707-9*, Times Bks) Crown Pub Group.

— The New York Times Crossword Puzzle Omnibus, Vol. 8. 128p. 1996. pap. 11.00 (*0-8129-2759-1*, Times Bks) Crown Pub Group.

— The New York Times Daily Crossword Puzzles, Vol. 43. 80p. 1996. pap. 9.00 (*0-8129-2760-5*, Times Bks) Crown Pub Group.

***New York Times Staff.** The New York Times Guide to New York City 2001. (Illus.). 300p. 2000. pap. 16.95 (*0-9668659-8-7*, Pub. by NY Times) Publishers Group.

— The New York Times on the Sopranos. 176p. 2000. per. 9.95 (*0-7434-0021-6*, Pub. by ibooks) S&S Trade.

New York Times Staff. The New York Times Passover Cookbook: More Than 175 Holiday Recipes from Top Chefs & Writers. Amster, Linda, ed. LC 98-41282. (Illus.). 320p. 1999. 25.00 (*0-688-15590-1*, Wm Morrow) Morrow Avon.

***New York Times Staff.** The New York Times Pocket MBA Series. 1999. pap. 155.40 (*0-86730-810-9*) Lebhar Friedman.

New York Times Staff. The New York Times Reader Philosophy. 1999. pap. 16.00 (*0-13-977497-1*) P-H.

— The New York Times Skillbuilder Crosswords: Three Star Strategiest Level, Vol. 4. 4th ed. 1995. pap. 8.50 (*0-8129-2557-2*, Times Bks) Crown Pub Group.

— The New York Times Skillbuilder Crosswords: Three,Star Strategist Level, Vol. 3. 3rd ed. 1995. pap. 8.50 (*0-8129-2310-3*, Times Bks) Crown Pub Group.

— The New York Times Sports Hall of Fame. 1980. 14.95 (*0-405-13942-X*) Ayer.

— The New York Times Theatre Reviews, 1993-1994, Vol. 28. 568p. 1996. text 180.00 (*0-8153-0644-X*) Garland.

— The New York Times Update, 1979, Set 1. (Great Contemporary Issues Ser.). 1979. 38.95 (*0-405-18421-2*, 1772) Ayer.

— The New York Times Update, 1979, Vol. 2. (Great Contemporary Issues Ser.). 38.95 (*0-405-18422-0*, 1773) Ayer.

— The Newspaper, Its Making & Its Meaning. LC 80-2891. (BCL Ser.: Vols. I & II). reprint ed. 26.00 (*0-404-18069-8*) AMS Pr.

— Page One. 1992. 17.98 (*0-88365-809-7*) Galahad Bks.

***New York Times Staff.** Page One. rev. ed. 416p. 2000. 24.99 (*1-57866-088-2*) Galahad Bks.

New York Times Staff. Page One: The Front Page History of World War II. LC 96-77431. 192p. 1996. 19.98 (*0-88365-962-X*) Galahad Bks.

— Page One: The New York Times, 1995. 1995. 24.98 (*0-88365-906-9*) Galahad Bks.

— Page One: The New York Times, 1997 Edition. (Illus.). 400p. 1997. 24.99 (*1-57866-006-8*) Galahad Bks.

— Page One: 1994 Edition Major Events 1920-1994 As Presented in the New York Times. 1994. 19.98 (*0-88365-884-4*) Galahad Bks.

— Page One: The New York Times: Major Events 1900-1998 as Presented in The New York Times, 1998 Edition. 1998. 24.99 (*1-57866-032-7*) Galahad Bks.

***New York Times Staff.** Scientists at Work. 350p. 2000. pap. 19.95 (*0-07-135882-X*) McGraw.

New York Times Staff. The Curious New Yorker: 329 Fascinating Questions & Surprising Answers about New York City. LC 98-27399. 352p. 1999. pap. 14.00 (*0-8129-3002-9*, Times Bks) Crown Pub Group.

— The Times Atlas of the World. LC 95-33212. (Illus.). 376p. 1995. 100.00 (*0-8129-2604-8*) Random.

— The Times Atlas of the World. 10th ed. 1997. write for info. (*0-8129-2945-4*, Times Bks) Crown Pub Group.

— Traveler's Guide to Art Museum Exhibitions: 2000 Edition. 400p. 1999. pap. 16.95 (*0-8109-6396-5*, Pub. by Abrams) Time Warner.

— United States Vs. Microsoft. (Illus.). 452p. 1999. 14.95 (*0-07-135588-X*) McGraw.

— Update, Set One, 1981. (Great Contemporary Issues Ser.). 55.95 (*0-405-13941-1*) Ayer.

— Update, Set Two, 1980. (Great Contemporary Issues Ser.). 1980. 38.95 (*0-405-13781-8*) Ayer.

New York Times Staff & CBS News Staff. CBS News-The New York Times Election Surveys 1980, 2 vols., I. LC 82-81160. 1982. write for info. (*0-89138-933-4*) ICPSR.

New York Times Staff & Charleston Mercury Staff. The Civil War Extra: From the Pages of the Charleston Mercury & the New York Times. Moehring, Eugene P. & Keylin, Arleen, eds. LC 75-20220. 310p. 1976. 16.95 (*0-405-06662-7*) Ayer.

New York Times Staff & Random House Staff. The New York Times Film Reviews, 1913-1931, No. 1. 787p. 1990. text 165.00 (*0-8240-7575-7*) Garland.

New York Times Staff & Sheehan, Carol S. The Hunter Douglas Guide to Window Decorating: The Complete Reference for Designing Beautiful Window Treatments. 14.95 (*0-9636751-0-9*) G&J USA Pubs.

New York Times Staff, jt. auth. see CBS News Staff.

New York Times Staff, jt. auth. see Prentice-Hall Staff.

New York Transit Museum Staff. I've Been Working on the Subway: The Folklore & Oral History of Transit. (Illus.). 54p. (Orig.). (J). (gr. 5-10). 1991. pap., teacher ed. 5.00 (*0-9637492-9-3*) NY Transit Mus.

New York Turtle & Tortoise Society Staff & WCS Turtle Recovery Program Staff. Proceedings: Conservation, Restoration, & Management of Tortoises & Turtles - An International Conference. Van Abbema, Jim, ed. LC 97-44399. (Illus.). xxiv, 494p. (Orig.). 1997. pap. 40.00 (*0-9659050-0-4*) NY Turtle & Tortoise.

New York University, Burma Research Project Staff, et al. Japanese & Chinese Language Sources on Burma: An Annotated Bibliography. Trager, Frank N., ed. LC 57-13287. (Behavior Science Bibliographies Ser.). 151p. reprint ed. pap. 46.90 (*0-608-11388-3*, 201045300068) Bks Demand.

New York University, Division of General Education. Proceedings of the New York University Conference on Practice & Procedure Under the Immigration & Nationality Act (McCarran-Walter Act) Held on June 13,1953: Proceedings. Sellin, Henry, ed. LC 54-7877. xii, 145p. reprint ed. lib. bdg. 22.50 (*0-8371-7684-0*, NYUP) Greenwood.

New York University Libraries Staff. Fales Library Checklist, 2 vols. Grieder, Theodore, ed. LC 71-122494. 1970. 195.00 (*0-404-07946-6*) AMS Pr.

— Fales Library Checklist: First Supplement. LC 71-122494. 1973. 95.00 (*0-404-11203-X*) AMS Pr.

— Fales Library Checklist: Second Supplement. Grieder, Theodore, ed. LC 77-21906. 1977. 95.00 (*0-404-16025-5*) AMS Pr.

New York University School of Law Staff, ed. Annual Survey of American Law, 1942-1995, 62 vols. LC 46-30523. 1943. lib. bdg. 2367.50 (*0-379-12200-6*) Oceana.

New York University Society Staff. Modern Music & Musicians. 616p. 1991. reprint ed. lib. bdg. 119.00 (*0-7812-9345-6*) Rprt Serv.

— The World's Best Music, 6 vols. 1991. reprint ed. lib. bdg. 540.00 (*0-7812-9365-0*) Rprt Serv.

New York University Staff & Marke, Julius J. A Catalogue of the Law Collection at New York University, 1953. LC 99-19939. 1999. 185.00 (*1-886363-91-9*) Lawbk Exchange.

New York Women's Handbook Group Staff, jt. auth. see ACT-UP - New York Women & AIDS Book Group Staff.

New York Writer's Program Staff. A Maritime History of New York. LC 72-2083. (American History & Americana Ser.: No. 47). 1972. reprint ed. lib. bdg. 75.00 (*0-8383-1460-0*) M S G Haskell Hse.

New Yorker Editors. The New Yorker Book of All-New Cat Cartoons. (Illus.). 112p. 1997. 20.00 (*0-375-40108-3*) Knopf.

New Yorker Magazine Editors. Fifty Five Short Stories from the New Yorker. (BCL1-PS American Literature Ser.). 480p. 1993. reprint ed. lib. bdg. 99.00 (*0-7812-6935-0*) Rprt Serv.

— The New Yorker Book of Cat Cartoons. (Illus.). 1990. 20.00 (*0-394-58795-2*) Knopf.

— The New Yorker Book of Cat Cartoons. LC 90-53070. (Illus.). 112p. 1992. pap. 10.00 (*0-679-74276-X*) Knopf.

— The New Yorker Book of Doctor Cartoons: Mini-Edition. (Illus.). 96p. 1996. pap. 10.00 (*0-679-76573-5*) Knopf.

— The New Yorker Book of Doctor Cartoons & Psychiatrist Cartoons. (Illus.). 96p. 1993. 22.00 (*0-679-43069-5*) Knopf.

— The New Yorker Book of Dog Cartoons. LC 95-21555. (Illus.). 112p. 1995. pap. 10.00 (*0-679-76542-5*) Knopf.

— The New Yorker Book of Lawyer Cartoons. (Illus.). 96p. 1993. 22.00 (*0-679-43068-7*) Knopf.

— The New Yorker Book of Lawyer Cartoons: Mini-Edition. (Illus.). 96p. 1996. pap. 10.00 (*0-679-76574-3*) Knopf.

— The New Yorker Book of War Pieces. LC 75-167394. (Essay Index Reprint Ser.). 1977. reprint ed. 31.95 (*0-8369-2470-3*) Ayer.

— The New Yorker Desk Diary, 1996. 1995. 25.95 (*0-00-221154-8*); 28.95 (*0-00-221155-6*) Harper SF.

New Yorker Magazine Editors, ed. The New Yorker's 75th Anniversary Cartoon Collection. 1999. pap. write for info. (*0-671-03556-8*) S&S Trade.

New Yorker Staff. The New Yorker Book of True Love Cartoons. LC NC1428.N47 1999. 112p. 1999. 20.00 (*0-375-40313-2*) Random.

New Yorker Staff, ed. The New Yorker Book of Literary Cartoons. 1999. pap. write for info. (*0-671-03558-4*) S&S Trade.

New Yorker Staff & Mitchell, Carolyn B. The New Yorker Book of Dog Cartoons. LC 92-70913. (Illus.). 1992. 20.00 (*0-679-41680-3*) Knopf.

New Yorker Staff, et al. Sexy Food for Singles. pap. 12.95 (*0-9700110-0-8*) Sundae Pubns.

New Zealand. Department of Justice: Administration of Community-based Sentences by the Probation Division. LC 95-189415. 50 p. 1992. write for info. (*0-477-02837-3*) Manaaki Whenua.

New Zealand Dept. of Scientific & Industrial Research. New Zealand Framework for Cultural Statistics, 1995. LC 96-131419.Tr. of Te Anga Tatauranga Tikanga-ea-iwi O Aotearoa, 1995.. vi, 115p. 1995. write for info. (*0-478-04422-4*) Manaaki Whenua.

— Rs&t:2010: The Government's Strategy for Research, Science, & Technology to the Year 2010 : Draft for Discussion. LC 97-141700. 42p. 1995. write for info. (*0-478-06112-9*) Manaaki Whenua.

New Zealand Dept. of Scientific & Industrial Research & New Zealand Farm Forestry Association Staff. Indigenous Forestry: Sustainable Management. LC 98-173744. 212 p. 1998. write for info. (*0-478-20041-2*) Manaaki Whenua.

New Zealand Dept. of Scientific & Industrial Research, jt. auth. see New Zealand Petroleum Conference Staff.

New Zealand Education Review Office. Accountability in Action: A Guide to Assurance Audits. LC 98-173466. 24p. 1993. write for info. (*0-478-04904-8*) Manaaki Whenua.

New Zealand Farm Forestry Association Staff, jt. auth. see New Zealand Dept. of Scientific & Industrial Research.

New Zealand Forest Research Institute Staff. Grading Moulding & Shop Lumber for the U. S. Market. LC 95-205764. (Wood Processing Ser.). 26p. 1994. pap. write for info. (*0-477-02127-1*, Pub. by Horticult & Food Res) St Mut.

New Zealand Health Information Service. Suicide Trends in New Zealand, 1974-94. LC 98-145010. 43 p. 1997. write for info. (*0-478-20828-6*) Manaaki Whenua.

New Zealand Institute of Economic Research Staff, jt. auth. see Clough, Peter W.

New Zealand Ministry of Health, jt. auth. see Wilson, Nicholas.

New Zealand Petroleum Conference Staff & New Zealand Dept. of Scientific & Industrial Research. 1996 New Zealand Petroleum Conference Proceedings: Confronting the Issues 1996, an International Perspective. LC 98-210114. 1996. write for info. (*0-478-00312-9*) Manaaki Whenua.

New Zealand Staff. Greenprint: Conservation in New Zealand, 2 vols. LC 97-202002. 1996. write for info. (*0-478-01848-7*, Pub. by Manaaki Whenua) Balogh.

New Zealand Statistical Association Staff, jt. auth. see Forbes, Rebecca.

New Zealand Tourism Board Staff. New Zealand Conservation Estate & International Visitors LC 94-179551. vi, 44 p. 1993. pap. write for info. (*0-478-02150-X*, Pub. by Manaaki Whenua) Balogh.

Newacheck, Paul W. Estimating Medicaid Eligible Pregnant Women & Children Living Below 185 Percent of Poverty: Strategies for Improving State Perinatal Programs. Feinstein, Gerry R., ed. 32p. (Orig.). 1988. pap. text 15.00 (*1-55877-010-0*) Natl Governor.

Newald, Alec. Coevolution: The True Story of 10 Days on an Extraterrestrial Civilization. (Illus.). 210p. 1998. pap. 16.95 (*0-932813-65-8*) Adventures Unltd.

Newall, Christopher. The Art of Lord Leighton. (Illus.). 144p. (C). 1993. reprint ed. pap. 24.95 (*0-7148-2957-9*, Pub. by Phaidon Press) Phaidon Pr.

— Victorian Watercolors. (Illus.). 144p. 1990. text 40.00 (*0-7148-2424-0*) Phaidon Pr.

— Victorian Watercolors. (Illus.). 140p. (C). 1993. reprint ed. pap. 24.95 (*0-7148-2811-4*, Pub. by Phaidon Press) Phaidon Pr.

Newall, George, jt. auth. see Yohe, Tom.

Newall, Venetia. An Egg at Easter: A Folklore Study. LC 72-146724. (Illus.). 448p. 1989. 29.95 (*0-253-31942-0*) Ind U Pr.

***Neward, Ted.** Server Based JAVA Programming. (Illus.). 592p. 2000. pap. 49.95 (*1-884777-71-6*) Manning Pubns.

Newark Beth Israel Medical Center, Dietary Departm. Diet Manual. LC 80-82889. 92p. (Orig.). 1980. pap. 10.00 (*0-937714-00-3*) Newark Beth.

Newark, Elizabeth. Consequence: Or, Whatever Became of Charlotte Lucas. LC 97-92274. (Illus.). 135p. 1997. pap. 12.50 (*0-9659147-0-4*) New Ark Prods.

Newark Museum Junior Museum Staff. Explore Tibet. 32p. 1992. pap. 9.95 (*1-55939-017-4*) Snow Lion Pubns.

Newark, Tim. Brassey's Book of Body Armour. 1999. 32.95 (*1-85753-285-6*, Pub. by Brasseys) Brasseys.

— Brassey's Book of Uniforms. LC 98-204587. (Illus.). 143p. 1998. 34.95 (*1-85753-243-0*, Pub. by Brasseys) Brasseys.

— WarLords: Ancient-Celtic-Medieval. (Illus.). 480p. 1996. 34.95 (*1-85409-349-5*, Pub. by Arms & Armour) Sterling.

— Warlords: Ancient, Celtic, Medieval. (Illus.). 480p. 1998. pap. 19.95 (*1-85409-444-0*, Pub. by Arms & Armour) Sterling.

***Newark, Tim.** Where They Fell: A Walker's Guide to the Battlefields of the World. (Illus.). 160p. 2000. 24.95 (*0-7641-5247-5*) Barron.

Newark, Tim, et al. Brassey's Book of Camouflage. LC 97-42084. (Illus.). 144p. 1998. pap. 16.95 (*1-85753-273-2*, Pub. by Brasseys) Brasseys.

Newark, Tim, jt. auth. see Man, John.

Newark, Tim, ed. see Bull, Stephen B.

Newark, Tim, ed. see Castle, Ian & Knight, Ian.

Newark, Tim, ed. see Smith, Robin.

Newark, Tim, ed. see Sumner, Graham.

Neway, Julie M. Information Specialist As Team Player in the Research Process, 9. LC 85-5488. (New Directions in Librarianship Ser.: No. 9). 194p. 1985. 49.95 (*0-313-24508-8*, NEI/, Greenwood Pr) Greenwood.

Neway, Justin O., ed. Fermentation Process Development of Industrial Organisms. (Bioprocess Technology Ser.: Vol. 4). (Illus.). 344p. 1989. text 160.00 (*0-8247-7917-7*) Dekker.

Newaygo County Bicentennial Committee. White Cloud the First Hundred Years, 1873-1973: White Cloud Area. (Illus.). 166p. 1995. reprint ed. pap. 22.00 (*0-8328-5046-2*); reprint ed. lib. bdg. 29.50 (*0-8328-5045-4*) Higginson Bk Co.

Newaygo County Historical Society Staff, ed. Portrait & Biographical Album of Newatgo County: Containing Portraits & Biographical Sketches of Prominent & Representative Citizens. (Reprinted Without the First 174 Pages Which Contained Biographies of Presidents of the U. S. & Governor of Michigan) (Illus.). 478p. 1995. reprint ed. lib. bdg. 51.00 (*0-8328-5044-6*) Higginson Bk Co.

Newaz, G., et al, eds. Metal Matrix Composites. (Key Engineering Materials Ser.: Vols. 104-107). 928p. 1995. 333.00 (*0-87849-697-1*, Pub. by Trans T Pub) Enfield Pubs NH.

Newaz, Golam M. Advances in Thermoplastic Matrix Composite Materials. LC 89-17634. (Special Technical Publication Ser.: No. STP 1044). (Illus.). 315p. 1989. text 64.00 (*0-8031-1272-6*, STP1044) ASTM.

N

— American Society for Composites: Eight Technical Conference, October 19-21, 1993, Cleveland, Ohio. LC 93-61006. 1150p. 1993. 119.95 (1-56676-103-4) Technomic.

— Composites for the Pressure Vessel Industry. Bees, William J. et al, eds. LC 95-77522. (Proceedings of the 1995 ASME/JSME Pressure Vessels & Piping Conference Ser.: PVP-Vol. 302). 316p. 1995. 120.00 (0-7918-1333-9, H00965) ASME.

***Newaz, Golam M., ed.** Advances in Aerospace Materials & Structures, 1999. LC 99-75418. (AD Ser.: Vol. 58). 187p. 1999. 100.00 (0-7918-1635-4) ASME Pr.

Newaz, Golam M. & Sierakowski, R. L. Damage Tolerance in Advanced Composites. LC 95-60957. 165p. 1995. pap. 99.95 (1-56676-261-8) Technomic.

Newaz, Golam M., jt. ed. see Gibson, Ronald F.

Newball, Harold H., ed. Immunopharmacology of the Lung. LC 83-1799. (Lung Biology in Health & Disease Ser.: No. 19). 540p. reprint ed. pap. 167.40 (0-7837-3346-1, 204330400008) Bks Demand.

Newbattle Abbey Staff. Registrum S. Marie De Neubotle. Innes, Cosmo N., ed. LC 74-173074. (Bannatyne Club, Edinburgh. Publications: No. 89). reprint ed. 52.50 (0-404-52819-8) AMS Pr.

Newbauer, Eric, jt. auth. see Stoneback, Jean C.

Newbegin, Nerida, tr. see Monteverdi, Claudio.

Newbegin, Wade. R. M. Wade & Co. & Family: Four Generations. Bledsoe, Helen W., ed. 112p. (Orig.). 1991. write for info. (0-9630153-0-3) R M Wade.

Newber Library Staff. Checklist of Printed Maps of the Middle West to 1900: Indiana. 1981. 210.00 (0-8161-0347-X) Mac Lib Ref.

— Checklist of Printed Maps of the Middle West to 1900: Iowa. 1981. 210.00 (0-8161-0352-6) Mac Lib Ref.

— Checklist of Printed Maps of the Middle West to 1900: Kansas, Nebraska. 1981. 125.00 (0-8161-0354-2) Mac Lib Ref.

— Checklist of Printed Maps of the Middle West to 1900: Michigan. 1981. 125.00 (0-8161-0349-6) Mac Lib Ref.

— Checklist of Printed Maps of the Middle West to 1900: Minnesota. 1981. 115.00 (0-8161-0351-8) Mac Lib Ref.

— Checklist of Printed Maps of the Middle West to 1900: Missouri. 1981. 115.00 (0-8161-0353-4) Mac Lib Ref.

— Checklist of Printed Maps of the Middle West to 1900: North & South Dakota. 1981. 210.00 (0-8161-0355-0) Mac Lib Ref.

— Checklist of Printed Maps of the Middle West to 1900: Ohio. 1981. 125.00 (0-8161-0346-1) Mac Lib Ref.

Newberg, Andrew B., jt. auth. see D'Aquili, Eugene.

Newberg, Jay & Marcus, Claudio. Target Smart: Database Marketing for the Small Business. LC 96-35404. (Successful Business Library). (Illus.). 194p. 1996. pap. 19.95 (1-55571-384-X) PSI Resch.

Newberg-King, Sara. Dye & Discharge: Playing on Fabric. LC 98-16889. (Love to Quilt Ser.). 56p. 1998. 14.95 (0-89145-895-6, Am Quilters Soc) Collector Bks.

Newberg, Lewis B. Snore or Roar, I've Got the Cure. unabridged ed. (Illus.). 250p. 1997. 31.00 (0-9656368-0-1) Snore or Roar.

Newberg, Paula R. Double Betrayal: Repression & Insurgency in Kashmir. LC 95-31783. 77p. (C). 1995. pap. 9.95 (0-87003-063-9) Carnegie Endow.

— Judging the State: Courts & Constitutional Politics in Pakistan. (South Asian Studies: No. 59). 298p. (C). 1995. text 64.95 (0-521-45289-9) Cambridge U Pr.

Newberg, Paula R., ed. New Directions in Telecommunications Policy, 2 vols., Vol. 2. LC 89-1446. (Duke Press Policy Studies). 346p. 1989. pap. text 29.95 (0-8223-0948-3) Duke.

— New Directions in Telecommunications Policy, 2 vols., Vol. 2: Information Policy & Economic Policy. LC 89-1446. (Duke Press Policy Studies). 346p. 1989. text 69.95 (0-8223-0923-8) Duke.

Newberger, D., jt. auth. see Black, S.

Newberger, Devra. A Full House Family Scrapbook. 40p. (J). (gr. 1-7). 1993. pap. 2.95 (0-590-46640-2, SC12) Scholastic Inc.

— Scary Stories to Drive You Batty. LC 94-21667. (Illus.). 32p. (J). (gr. 2-6). 1994. pap. text 2.95 (0-8167-3534-4) Troll Communs.

Newberger, Edward L. The Button Industry in the United States. LC 98-55546. 1999. pap. 15.00 (1-878282-08-5) St Johann Pr.

Newberger, Eli H. Child Abuse. 1982. 52.95 (0-316-60410-0, Little Brwn Med Div) Lppncott W & W.

— The Men They Will Become: The Nature & Nurture of Male Character. (Merloyd Lawrence Book Ser.). 384p. 1999. 25.00 (0-7382-0113-8, Pub. by Perseus Pubng) HarpC.

***Newberger, Eli H.** The Men They Will Become: The Nature & Nurture of Male Character. 384p. 2000. reprint ed. pap. text 17.00 (0-7382-0363-7, Pub. by Perseus Pubng) HarpC.

Newberger, Joe & Hendricks, Elrod. The Ultimate Baseball Players Yearbook. (Illus.). 96p. (J). (gr. 3-9). 1991. student ed. 12.95 (0-9629307-0-9) Batboy Pr.

Newberger-Speregen, Devra. Hip Hop Till You Drop. abr. ed. (Full House Stephanie Ser.). (J). (gr. 4-7). 1994. mass mkt. 3.99 (0-671-88291-0, Minstrel Bks) PB.

— Phone Call from a Flamingo. (Full House Stephanie Ser.). 128p. (J). (gr. 4-6). 1993. per. 3.99 (0-671-88004-7, Minstrel Bks) PB.

— You Can't Choose Your Family. (Party of Five Ser.: No. 5). 144p. (J). (gr. 3-6). 1997. pap. 3.99 (0-671-01717-9, Minstrel Bks) PB.

Newberne, Paul M., ed. Trace Substances & Health: A Handbook, Pt. 2. LC 75-25167. (Illus.). 187p. reprint ed. pap. 58.00 (0-608-09169-3, 204103700002) Bks Demand.

— Trace Substances & Health, 1976 Pt. 1: A Handbook. LC 75-25167. (Illus.). 412p. reprint ed. pap. 127.80 (0-7837-0705-3, 204103700001) Bks Demand.

Newberry. Computer Concepts: Quicktorial. (DF - Computer Applications Ser.). 1997. 22.95 (0-538-71743-2) S-W Pub.

— Lotus 1-2-3 for Windows 95: Quick Torial. (DF - Computer Applications Ser.). 1998. mass mkt. 22.95 (0-538-67981-6) S-W Pub.

Newberry & CEP Inc., Staff. Corel Presentations 7.0 for Windows 95: Quicktorial. 1997. pap. 22.95 (0-538-67859-3) Thomson Learn.

Newberry, Barbara, jt. auth. see Aiken, David.

Newberry, Benjamin H., et al. A Holistic Conceptualization of Stress & Disease. LC 86-82021. (Stress in Modern Society Ser.: No. 7). 1991. 32.50 (0-404-63258-0) AMS Pr.

Newberry, Betsy. Borland Paradox 7.0 QuickTorial for Windows 95. 200p. 1997. pap., mass mkt. 21.95 incl. disk (0-538-67864-X) S-W Pub.

— Computer Concepts. 200p. 1997. pap., mass mkt. 21.95 incl. disk (0-538-71744-0) S-W Pub.

— Corel Quattro Pro 7.0 QuickTorial for Windows 95. 200p. 1997. pap., mass mkt. 21.95 incl. disk (0-538-67856-9) S-W Pub.

— Designer's Guide to Marketing. LC 97-11259. (Illus.). 144p. 1997. 29.99 (0-89134-809-3, North Lght Bks) F & W Pubns Inc.

— Fresh Ideas in Promotion 2. (Fresh Ideas Ser.). (Illus.). 144p. 1996. 29.99 (0-89134-727-5, North Lght Bks) F & W Pubns Inc.

***Newberry, Betsy.** Fresh Ideas in Promotion 2. (Fresh Ideas Ser.). (Illus.). 144p. 2000. pap. 19.99 (1-58180-056-8, North Lght Bks) F & W Pubns Inc.

Newberry, Betsy. Lotus 1-2-3 97 for Windows 95. (Quicktorial Ser.). 1998. pap. text 21.95 (0-538-68430-5) S-W Pub.

Newberry, Betsy & York, Kate, eds. Fresh Ideas in Limited Budget Design. LC 97-32094. (Fresh Ideas Ser.). (Illus.). 144p. 1998. 29.99 (0-89134-840-9, North Lght Bks) F & W Pubns Inc.

***Newberry, Clare.** Barkis. LC 97-62213. (Newberry Ser.). (Illus.). 32p. (J). (ps-3). 1998. 9.98 (0-7651-9056-7) Smithmark.

— Herbert the Lion. LC 97-62214. (Newberry Ser.). (Illus.). 32p. (J). (ps-3). 1998. 9.98 (0-7651-9057-5) Smithmark.

— Mittens. LC 97-62211. (Newberry Ser.). (Illus.). 32p. (J). (ps-3). 1998. 9.98 (0-7651-9059-1) Smithmark.

— Smudge. LC 97-62212. (Newberry Ser.). (Illus.). 32p. (J). (ps-3). 1998. 9.98 (0-7651-9058-3) Smithmark.

Newberry, Clare T. April's Kittens. LC 40-32442. (Illus.). 40p. (J). (ps-3). 1940. 16.95 (0-06-024400-3) HarpC Child Bks.

***Newberry, Clare Turlay.** Babette. LC 98-75099. (Clare Newberry Classics Ser.). (Illus.). 32p. (J). (ps-3). 1999. 9.98 (0-7651-0950-6) Smithmark.

— Marshmallow. LC 98-75100. (Clare Newberry Classics Ser.). (Illus.). 32p. (J). (ps-3). 1999. 9.98 (0-7651-0951-4) Smithmark.

Newberry, Conrad F., compiled by. Perspectives in Aerospace Design. 1026p. 1991. 79.95 (1-56347-010-1) AIAA.

Newberry, Conrad F., jt. auth. see Wimpress, John K.

***Newberry, David M., et al.** Skills, Drills & Strategies for Strength Training. LC 99-39948. (Teach, Coach & Play Ser.). (Illus.). 2000. pap. 15.00 (1-890871-09-5) Holcomb Hath.

Newberry, David M., jt. ed. see Szekely, Istvan P.

Newberry, Florence O. Cooke. Family of Elizha Cooke. (Illus.). 202p. 1997. reprint ed. pap. 32.00 (0-8328-8034-5); reprint ed. lib. bdg. 42.00 (0-8328-8033-7) Higginson Bk Co.

***Newberry, Ian.** Available for God: A Biblical & Practical Approach to Fasting. 199p. 1998. reprint ed. pap. 12.99 (1-85078-318-7, Pub. by O M Pubng) OM Literature.

Newberry, J. Stuart, ed. see Klein, Chuck.

Newberry, James H., Jr. Legal Aspects of Horse Farm Operations. 2nd ed. (Illus.). vii, 173p. 1995. pap. 43.00 (1-58757-006-8, HM019) Univ of KY.

Newberry, Julia R. Julia Newberry's Diary. (American Biography Ser.). 176p. 1991. reprint ed. lib. bdg. 59.00 (0-7812-8295-0) Rprt Serv.

Newberry, Kevin. Shell's Golf Guide to Greater Houston. 2nd ed. (Illus.). 484p. 1993. pap. 14.95 (1-883369-02-9) Twnty-Frst Media.

Newberry Library, et al. The Hebrew Renaissance. LC 98-154779. (Illus.). 1997. write for info. (0-911028-59-5) Newberry.

Newberry Library Staff. Checklist of Printed Maps of the Middle West to 1900: Illinois. 1981. 125.00 (0-8161-0348-8) Mac Lib Ref.

— Dictionary Catalogue of the History of Printing from the John M. Wing Foundation. 1970. 685.00 (0-8161-1479-X, G K Hall & Co) Mac Lib Ref.

— Dictionary Catalogue of the History of Printing from the John M. Wing Foundation, Second Supplement. 1981. 575.00 (0-8161-0326-7, G K Hall & Co) Mac Lib Ref.

Newberry, Lorene, et al, eds. CEN Review Manual. 2nd rev. ed. (Illus.). 362p. (Orig.). 1996. pap. text 40.00 (0-935890-00-9, C2) Emerg Nurses IL.

Newberry, Lorene & Sheehy, Susan B. Emergency Nursing: Principles & Practice. 4th ed. LC 97-17575. (Illus.). 848p. (C). (gr. 13). 1997. text 59.95 (0-8151-7678-3, 24508) Mosby Inc.

Newberry, P. E. Ancient Egyptian Scarabs. 278p. 1975. pap. 25.00 (0-89005-092-9) Ares.

Newberry, P. F. The Design of an Extendible Graph Editor. (Lecture Notes in Computer Science Ser.: Vol. 704). xv, 184p. 1993. 35.00 (0-387-57090-X) Spr-Verlag.

***Newberry, Paul A.** Ethical Traditions. LC 99-31547. xi, 414p. 1999. pap. text 39.95 (0-7674-0748-2) Mayfield Pub.

Newberry, Paul A. Theories of Ethics. LC 98-17926. vi, 650p. 1998. pap. text 47.95 (1-55934-965-4, 1965) Mayfield Pub.

***Newberry, Robert D.** Space Doctrine for the 21st Century. (Illus.). 68p. (C). 2000. reprint ed. pap. text 20.00 (0-7881-8970-0) DIANE Pub.

— Space Doctrine for the Twenty First Century. 80p. 1998. pap. 11.00 (0-16-061381-7) USGPO.

Newberry, S. Lloyd. Pages of Time: Memoirs of a Southern Sportsman. (Illus.). 350p. 1996. 24.95 (0-9650388-0-7) Spartina Pubng.

Newberry, Sara, ed. see Maguire, Daniel C. & Maguire, Marjorie R.

Newberry, Sheila. A Charm of Finches. large type ed. 416p. 31.99 (0-7089-4038-2) Ulverscroft.

— The Summer Season. 256p. 26.00 (0-7278-5539-5) Severn Hse.

— Tilly's Family. 480p. 2000. 31.99 (0-7505-1471-X) Ulverscroft.

Newberry, Thomas, ed. The Newberry Reference Bible. LC 73-189203. 1112p. 1992. lib. bdg. 49.99 (0-8254-3315-0, Kregel Class); boxed set, bond lthr. 84.99 (0-8254-3298-7, Kregel Class); boxed set, bond lthr. 79.99 (0-8254-3299-5, Kregel Class) Kregel.

***Newberry, Tommy.** Success Is Not an Accident! Change Your Choices. Change Your Life. 1999. pap. text 14.00 (1-886669-09-0) One Percent Club.

Newberry, Tommy. Success Is Not an Accident! Change Your Choices: Change Your Life. (Illus.). 180p. 1997. 22.00 (1-886669-07-4) One Percent Club.

— 366 Days of Wisdom & Inspiration: With America's Success Coach. LC 96-95187. 192p. 1997. 12.00 (1-886669-08-2) One Percent Club.

Newbert, Christopher. Within a Rainbowed Sea. deluxe ed. 224p. 1987. 2250.00 (0-941831-04-3) Beyond Words Pub.

— Within a Rainbowed Sea, Author's Ed. anniversary ed. (EarthSong Collection). (Illus.). 210p. 1986. 95.00 (0-614-19289-7) Beyond Words Pub.

— Within a Rainbowed Sea: Ten Year Anniversary Edition. 2nd anniversary ed. Berry, Paul, ed. LC 94-21962. (Illus.). 224p. 1994. 75.00 (0-941831-99-X); pap. text 39.95 (1-885223-00-5) Beyond Words Pub.

Newbert, Christopher & Wilms, Birgitte. In a Sea of Dreams. LC 94-61043. (Illus.). 204p. 1995. 85.00 (0-9642736-5-9) Fourth Day Pub.

***Newbery, D. M., et al, eds.** Changes & Disturbance in Tropical Rainforest in South-East Asia. 180p. 2000. 32.00 (1-86094-243-1, Pub. by Imperial College) World Scientific Pub.

***Newbery, David M.** Privatization, Restructuring & Regulation of Network Utilities. LC 99-52764. Vol. 2. (Illus.). 475p. 2000. 47.50 (0-262-14068-3) MIT Pr.

Newbery, David M., ed. Taxation & Benefit Reform in Central & Eastern Europe. xvii, 217 p. (C). 1995. pap. 24.95 (1-898128-19-7) Brookings.

Newbery, J. G. Muscle Cars. LC 94-19959. (Illus.). 224p. 1994. 12.99 (1-57145-007-6, Thunder Bay) Advantage Pubs.

Newbery, Lillian. Earth, Wind & Wildlife: The Challenges of Cottage Gardening. LC 99-181161. (Illus.). 120p. 1997. 32.00 (1-55046-205-9, Pub. by Boston Mills) Genl Dist Srvs.

Newbery, P. G., jt. auth. see Wright, A.

Newbery, Tony. Discovering Wales Travelling for Pleasure. 246p. 1994. pap. 23.00 (1-85902-111-5) St Mut.

— Travelling for Pleasure. 246p. 1994. pap. 22.95 (0-8464-4653-7) Beekman Pubs.

Newbigging, Thomas. Fables & Fabulists, Ancient & Modern. LC 76-37799. (Essay Index Reprint Ser.). 1977. reprint ed. 19.95 (0-8369-2615-3) Ayer.

Newbigi. Unfinished Agenda. 1996. 25.90 (0-7152-0679-6, Pub. by St Andrew) St Mut.

Newbigin, Lesslie. Foolishness to the Greeks. 160p. (Orig.). 1988. pap. 13.00 (0-8028-0176-5) Eerdmans.

— Gospel in a Pluralist Society. 255p. 1989. pap. 17.00 (0-8028-0426-8) Eerdmans.

***Newbigin, Lesslie.** The Household of God: Lectures on the Nature of the Church. (Biblical Classics Library: Vol. 41). xiii, 210p. 1998. reprint ed. pap. 5.99 (0-85364-935-9, Pub. by Paternoster Pub) OM Literature.

Newbigin, Lesslie. The Light Has Come: An Exposition of the Fourth Gospel. 281p. 1987. reprint ed. pap. 16.00 (0-8028-1895-1) Eerdmans.

— Mission in Christ's Way: A Gift, a Command, an Assurance. 48p. 1988. pap. 2.95 (0-377-00190-2) Friendship Pr.

— Mission in Christ's Way: Bible Studies. (Mission Ser.: No. 8). 48p. (Orig.). 1987. pap. 2.90 (2-8254-0900-6) Wrld Coun Churches.

— The Open Secret. rev. ed. 192p. 1995. pap. 15.00 (0-8028-0829-8) Eerdmans.

— Proper Confidence: Faith, Doubt, & Certainty in Christian Discipleship. 110p. (Orig.). 1995. pap. 10.00 (0-8028-0856-5) Eerdmans.

***Newbigin, Lesslie.** St. Paul in Limerick: And Other Missionary Journeys He May Have Made. 61p. 1998. pap. text 11.99 (1-900507-69-2, Pub. by Solway) Eisenbrauns.

— Trinitarian Doctrine for Today's Mission. (Biblical Classics Library: Vol. 37). 84p. 1998. reprint ed. mass mkt. 5.99 (0-85364-797-6, Pub. by Paternoster Pub) OM Literature.

Newbigin, Lesslie. Truth & Authority in Modernity. LC 96-13846. (Christian Mission & Modern Culture Ser.). 96p. 1996. pap. 9.00 (1-56338-168-0) TPI PA.

— Unfinished Agenda. 352p. 1993. pap. 60.00 (0-7152-0687-7, Pub. by St Andrew) St Mut.

***Newbigin, Lesslie.** A Walk Through the Bible. 96p. 2000. pap. 9.95 (0-664-22229-3, Pub. by Westminster John Knox) Presbyterian Pub.

Newbigin, Lesslie. A Word in Season. Jackson, Eleanor, ed. 208p. (Orig.). (C). 1994. pap. 15.00 (0-8028-0730-5) Eerdmans.

Newbigin, Lesslie, jt. auth. see Allen, Hubert J.

Newbill, Chris, jt. auth. see Miller, Lynda.

Newble, David I. Handbook for Clinical Teachers. 148p. 1983. text. write for info. (0-85200-728-0) Kluwer Academic.

— A Handbook for Medical Teachers. 2nd ed. 160p. (C). 1987. text 42.50 (0-85200-673-X) Kluwer Academic.

— A Handbook for Medical Teachers. 3rd ed. LC 94-22258. (Illus.). 185p. (C). 1994. text 42.50 (0-7923-8850-X) Kluwer Academic.

Newble, David I. & Cannon, Robert. A Handbook for Teachers in Universities & Colleges. 3rd ed. 176p. 1995. pap. 25.00 (0-7494-1669-6, Kogan Pg Educ) Stylus Pub VA.

***Newble, David I. & Cannon, Robert.** A Handbook for Teachers in Universities & Colleges: A Guide to Improving Teaching Methods. 4th rev. ed. 192p. 2000. pap. 27.50 (0-7494-3181-4, Kogan Pg Educ) Stylus Pub VA.

Newbold, Bruce & Cornell, Brenda. In Our Father's Footsteps. 1998. pap. 16.95 (1-57008-406-8) Bookcraft Inc.

Newbold, Charles E., Jr. The Crucified Ones: Calling Forth the End-Time Remnant. 116p. (Orig.). 1995. pap. 5.00 (0-9647766-0-X) Ingathering Pr.

Newbold, Charles E. In Search of Dad: Calling Forth the Dad Within the Man. LC 96-95019. 198p. (Orig.). 1997. pap. 6.00 (0-9647766-1-8) Ingathering Pr.

Newbold, Charles E. & O'Neil, Mike S. Boundary Power: How I Treat You, How I Let You Treat Me, How I Treat Myself. 182p. (Orig.). 1995. pap. 19.95 (0-9633454-2-7) Sonlight Pub.

— The Church As a Healing Community: Setting up Shop to Deal with the Pain of Life-Controlling Problems. 187p. (Orig.). 1995. pap. 19.95 (0-9633454-1-9) Sonlight Pub.

Newbold, Chris, jt. ed. see Boyd-Barrett, Oliver.

Newbold, Chris A. 30 "Secrets" to Saving Money on Your Auto Insurance. (Illus.). (Orig.). 1995. pap. text 9.95 (0-9646190-0-8) Newbold Ins.

Newbold, Greg. Punishment & Politics: The Maximum Security Prison in New Zealand. 304p. 1989. 45.00 (0-19-558179-2) OUP.

Newbold, H. L. Dr. Newbold's Revolutionary New Discoveries about Weight Loss. 1977. 1.25 (0-89256-014-2, Rawson Assocs) Macmillan.

***Newbold, Heather, ed.** Life Stories: World Renowned Scientists Reflect on Their Lives & the Future of Life on Earth. LC 99-54133. (Illus.). 224p. 2000. 45.00 (0-520-21114-6, Pub. by U CA Pr); pap. 16.95 (0-520-21896-5, Pub. by U CA Pr) Cal Prin Full Svc.

Newbold Jr., Charles Elliott. His Presence in the Midst of You: Calling Forth a Sanctified. LC 98-92767. 76p. 1998. pap. 5.00 (0-9647766-2-6) Ingathering Pr.

Newbold, P., et al. Start Reading with Ann: Short "A" Sound. (Start Reading Ser.: No. A1). 8p. (J). (ps-3). 1986. pap. text 2.99 (1-56422-000-1) Start Reading.

Newbold, Patt & Diebel, Anne. Farm Animals, Hat Patterns & Activities. (Illus.). 46p. (J). (ps-4). 1996. pap. text 9.95 (1-56422-987-4) Start Reading.

— Ocean Animals, Hat Patterns & Activities. (Illus.). 46p. (J). (ps-4). 1996. pap. text 9.95 (1-56422-985-8) Start Reading.

— Paper Hat Tricks Vol. 1: A Big Book of Hat Patterns Holidays, Careers, Characters, & Animals. (Illus.). 36p. (Orig.). 1988. pap. text 15.95 (1-56422-999-8, Paper Hat) Start Reading.

— Paper Hat Tricks Vol. 2: A Big Book of Hat Patterns Farm, Ocean, & Insect Hats. (Illus.). 36p. (Orig.). 1990. pap. text 15.95 (1-56422-998-X, Paper Hat) Start Reading.

— Paper Hat Tricks Vol. 5: A Big Book of Hat Patterns, Circus, Sports, Fun Foods, & Safety First Hats. 39p. (J). (ps-5). 1992. pap. text 15.95 (1-56422-995-5, Paper Hat) Start Reading.

— Zoo Animals Hat Patterns & Activities. (Illus.). 46p. (J). (ps-4). 1996. pap. text 8.95 (1-56422-990-4) Start Reading.

Newbold, Patt, jt. auth. see Diebel, Anne.

Newbold, Paul. Statistics for Business & Economics. 4th ed. LC 94-33610. 867p. 1994. 100.00 (0-13-181595-4) P-H.

Newbold, Paul & Bos, Theodore. Stochastic Parameter Regression Models. (Quantitative Applications in the Social Sciences Ser.: Vol. 51). 1985. 10.95 (0-8039-2425-9) Sage.

Newbold, Peter & Wilson, Martin. Practical Capital Allowances. 220p. 1994. boxed set 88.00 (0-406-03484-2, UK, MICHIE) LEXIS Pub.

Newbold, Robert C. Project Management in the Fast Lane: Applying the Theory of Constraints Management. LC 97-48806. (APICS Series on Constraints Management). 320p. 1998. boxed set 44.95 (1-57444-195-7) St Lucie Pr.

Newbold, S. K., et al, eds. Nursing Informatics: When Caring & Technology Meet. 2nd ed. LC 95-6681. (Computers in Health Care Ser.). (Illus.). 452p. 1995. 49.95 (0-387-94476-1) Spr-Verlag.

Newbold, Will. Client Care & Practice Management in Scotland. 186p. 1995. pap. 33.00 (1-85811-040-8, Pub. by CLT Prof) Gaunt.

Newbolt, Barnaby, jt. auth. see Hollett, Vicki.

Newbolt, Henry. The Island Race. LC 94-24513. (Decadents, Symbolists, Anti-Decadents Ser.). 1995. 48.00 (1-85477-152-3) Continuum.

N

An Asterisk (*) at the beginning of an entry indicates that the title is appearing for the first time.

— Naval Operations, Vol. IV. (Great War Ser.: Vol. 53). (Illus.). 456p. 1996. reprint ed. 49.95 (0-89839-254-3) Battery Pr.
— Naval Operations, Vol. V. (Great War Ser.: Vol. 54). (Illus.). 472p. 1996. reprint ed. 49.95 (0-89839-255-1) Battery Pr.
Newbolt, Henry J. Studies, Green & Gray. LC 68-8485. (Essay Index Reprint Ser.). 1977. reprint ed. 20.95 (0-8369-0740-X) Ayer.
Newbolt, Henry J., compiled by. An English Anthology of Prose-Poetry: Showing the Main Stream of English Literature Through Six Centuries (14th Century-19th Century) LC 75-168785. (Granger Index Reprint Ser.). 1977. reprint ed. 50.95 (0-8369-6305-9) Ayer.
Newbolt, Peter. G. A. Henty, 1832-1902: A Bibliographical Study of His British Editions with Short Accounts of His Publishers, Illustrators, & Designers, & Notes on Production Methods Used for His Books. (Illus.). 650p. 1996. 96.95 (1-85928-208-3, Pub. by Scolar Pr) Ashgate Pub Co.
Newborn, Barbara. Return to Ithaca: A Woman's Triumph over the Disabilities of a Severe Stroke. LC 96-37814. 144p. 1997. pap. 11.95 (1-85230-944-X, Pub. by Element MA) Penguin Putnam.
Newborn, Monroe. Kasparov vs. Deep Blue: Computer Chess Comes of Age. LC 96-24220. (Illus.). 322p. 1996. 29.95 (0-387-94820-1) Spr-Verlag.
Newborn, Sasha, ed. see Bukowski, Charles, et al.
Newborn, Sasha, ed. see Gandhi, Mohandas Karamchand.
Newborn, Sasha, ed. see London, Jack.
Newborn, Sasha, ed. see Whitman, Walt.
Newborn, Sasha, ed. & tr. see Ghalib.
Newborn, Sasha, tr. see Tolstoy, Leo.
Newborn, Sasha, tr. & pref. see Sappho.
Newborn, Tony. Secrets of International Identity Change: New I. D. in Canada, England, Australia & New Zealand. (Illus.). 120p. 1985. pap. 21.00 (0-87364-532-4) Paladin Pr.
Newbould, Brian. Schubert: The Music & the Man. LC 96-49876. (Illus.). 465p. 1997. 39.95 (0-520-21065-4, Pub. by U CA Pr) Cal Prin Full Svc.
— Schubert: The Music & the Man. 480p. 1999. pap. 22.00 (0-520-21957-0, Pub. by U CA Pr) Cal Prin Full Svc.
Newbould, Brian, contrib. by. Franz Schubert: Symphony No. 7 in E, D729: Realization by Brian Newbould. (Illus.). 220p. 1992. 45.00 (0-85958-471-2, Pub. by Univ of Hull Pr) Paul & Co Pubs.
Newbould, Brian, ed. Schubert Studies. LC 98-12585. (Illus.). 277p. 1998. text 96.95 (1-85928-253-9, Pub. by Scolar Pr) Ashgate Pub Co.
Newbould, Gerald D. & Luffman, George A. Successful Business Policies. LC 78-70561. 235p. 1979. 55.00 (0-275-90400-8, C0400, Praeger Pubs) Greenwood.
Newbould, Ian. Whiggery & Reform, 1830-41: The Politics of Government. LC 89-62180. 410p. 1991. 49.50 (0-8047-1759-1) Stanford U Pr.
Newbound, Betty. Blue Ridge Dinnerware. 3rd ed. 1996. pap. 14.95 (0-89145-391-1, 1958) Collector Bks.
— Collector's Encyclopedia of Milk Glass. (Illus.). 224p. 1995. pap. 24.95 (0-89145-626-0) Collector Bks.
— Collector's Encyclopedia of Wall Pockets. (Illus.). 192p. 1995. 19.95 (0-89145-673-2, 4563) Collector Bks.
— Collector's Guide to Blue Ridge Dinnerware. 1994. pap. 19.95 (0-89145-583-3, 3815) Collector Bks.
Newbound, Betty & Newbound, Bill. Collector's Encyclopedia of Blue Ridge Dinnerware, Vol. 2. (Illus.). 224p. 1997. 24.95 (1-57432-005-X, 4932) Collector Bks.
— Collector's Encyclopedia of Figural Planters & Vases: Collector's Encyclopedia. LC 96-209706. (Illus.). 232p. 1996. 19.95 (0-89145-725-9, 4718) Collector Bks.
Newbound, Bill, jt. auth. see Newbound, Betty.
Newbrander, William C. & Asian Development Bank Staff. Private Health Sector Growth in Asia. LC 96-47180. 272p. 1997. 125.00 (0-471-97236-3) Wiley.
Newbrough, Jennie & Greenwood, Carol. Support Group Leaders Guide. 150p. 1993. pap. 12.95 (1-56616-005-7, 572047) Aglow Communs.
Newbrough, John B. & Cardone, David A. Oahspe: A New Bible in the Words of Jehovihand & His Angel Ambassadors. LC 98-92796. (Illus.). xxvii, 923p. 1998. reprint ed. pap. 45.00 (0-9665065-0-2) OAHSPE.
Newbrun, Ernest. Cariology. 3rd ed. (Illus.). 389p. 1989. text 60.00 (0-86715-205-2) Quint Pub Co.
Newbrun, Eva, jt. auth. see Oberlander, H. Peter.
Newburger, Amy E. & Proctor, Pam. Looking Good at Any Age. LC 99-17984. 256p. 1999. 22.95 (0-385-49218-9) Doubleday.
Newburger, Craig. Complex Problem-Solving in Groups. 173p. (C). 1996. pap. text 22.95 (0-89641-294-6) American Pr.
Newburger, Craig, ed. Basic Communication Annual, 1996. 208p. (C). 1996. pap. text 25.00 (0-89641-302-0) American Pr.
Newburger, Craig, ed. Basic Communication Course Annual, 1994. 260p. (C). 1994. pap. text 25.00 (0-89641-227-X) American Pr.
— Basic Communication Course Annual, 1995. 150p. (C). 1995. pap. text 25.00 (0-89641-278-4) American Pr.
Newburger, Eli H. Raising Boys. 1999. write for info. (0-201-33981-1) Addison-Wesley.
***Newburger, Manuel H. & Barron, Barbara M.** 2000 Guide to Fair Debt Collection Practices Law in the U. S. Stewart, John, ed. 905p. 1999. write for info. (1-57987-121-6) Faulkner & Gray.
Newburn. Working with Disaster. 152p. 1993. pap. 28.95 (0-582-10247-2) Ashgate Pub Co.
Newburn, Jewel M., jt. contrib. by see Stevens, Lois P.
Newburn, Tim. Disaster & After: Social Work in the Aftermath of Disaster. 160p. 1993. pap. 29.95 (1-85302-170-9) Taylor & Francis.
— Making a Difference? Social Work after Hillsborough. 1993. pap. 35.00 (0-902789-81-3, Pub. by Natl Inst Soc Work) St Mut.
Newburn, Tim & Stanko, Elizabeth A., eds. Just Boys Doing Business? Men, Masculinities & Crime. 304p. (C). 1995. pap. 24.99 (0-415-09320-1, C0402) Routledge.
Newburn, Tim, jt. auth. see Jones, Trevor.
Newburn, Tim, jt. auth. see Morgan, Rod.
Newbury. Garden Design Made Easy. (Illus.). 208p. 1998. 35.00 (0-7063-7585-8, Pub. by WrLock) Sterling.
Newbury, Anthony. All You Can Eat Diet. (Orig.). 1986. pap. 14.95 (0-9601978-4-2) Health Res Las Vegas.
Newbury, Catharine. The Cohesion of Oppression: Clientship & Ethnicity in Ruanda, 1860-1960. (Illus.). 336p. (C). 1989. text 61.50 (0-231-06256-7) Col U Pr.
— The Cohesion of Oppression: Clientship & Ethnicity in Ruanda, 1860-1960. (Illus.). 336p. (C). 1993. pap. 22.50 (0-231-06257-5) Col U Pr.
Newbury, Colin. British Policy Towards West Africa: Selected Documents, 2 vols., Set. (Modern Revivals in African Studies). 1992. 129.95 (0-7512-0084-0, Pub. by Gregg Revivals) Ashgate Pub Co.
— British Policy Towards West Africa Vol. 1: Selected Documents. 1992. 64.95 (0-7512-0082-4, Pub. by Gregg Revivals) Ashgate Pub Co.
— British Policy Towards West Africa Vol. 2: Selected Documents. 1992. 64.95 (0-7512-0083-2, Pub. by Gregg Revivals) Ashgate Pub Co.
Newbury, Colin W. The Diamond Ring: Business, Politics, & Precious Stones in South Africa, 1867-1945. (Illus.). 448p. 1990. 89.00 (0-19-821775-7) OUP.
— The Western Slave Coast & Its Rulers: European Trade & Administration among the Yoruba & Adja-Speaking Peoples of Southwestern Nigeria, Southern Dahomey & Togo. LC 83-12619. 234p. 1983. reprint ed. lib. bdg. 55.00 (0-313-23967-3, NEWE) Greenwood.
Newbury, D., jt. auth. see Heinrich, K. F.
Newbury, Dale E., et al. Advanced Scanning Electron Microscopy & X-Ray Microanalysis. LC 85-28261. (Illus.). 466p. (C). 1986. text 55.00 (0-306-42140-2, Kluwer Plenum) Kluwer Academic.
Newbury, David. Africa Historiographies: What History for Which Africa? Jewsiewicki, Bogumil, ed. LC 85-8113. (Sage Series on African Modernization & Development: No. 12). 320p. 1986. reprint ed. pap. 99.20 (0-608-01083-9, 205939200001) Bks Demand.
— Kings & Clans: Ijwi Island & the Lake Kivu Rift, 1780-1840. LC 91-28932. (Illus.). 384p. (C). 1992. pap. 19.95 (0-299-12894-6) U of Wis Pr.
Newbury, John S. Man-Machine Systems - Inventions, Models, Devices, Performance & Control: Index of New Information. 160p. 1997. 47.50 (0-7883-1776-8); pap. 44.50 (0-7883-1777-6) ABBE Pubs Assn.
Newbury, Kenneth. Character Word of the Week: Wow LC 99-163844. (Illus.). 32p. (J). 1998. teacher ed. write for info. (1-57279-134-9) YPP.
— Life Skills Handbook. (Illus.). 48p. (YA). (gr. 9-12). 1993. 9.95 (0-7854-0057-5, 15168); text 6.95 (0-7854-0056-7, 15167) Am Guidance.
Newbury, L. E. I Now Start My Life Story. (C). 1989. 22.00 (0-7223-2216-X, Pub. by A H S Ltd) St Mut.
Newbury, Michael. Figuring Authorship in Antebellum America. LC 96-52220. 264p. 1997. 35.00 (0-8047-2858-5) Stanford U Pr.
Newbury, N. R. & Wieman, C. E., eds. Trapping of Neutral Atoms. (Illus.). 134p. (C). 1998. pap. 39.00 (0-917853-88-1) Am Assn Physics.
Newbury, Nathan, et al. Princeton Problems in Physics with Solutions. 336p. 1991. pap. text 19.95 (0-691-02449-9, Pub. by Princeton U Pr) Cal Prin Full Svc.
Newbury, Paul A. A Geography of Agriculture. LC 86-18154. 334p. reprint ed. pap. 103.60 (0-7837-4031-X, 204386000011) Bks Demand.
Newbury, Robert L. Potential Dilution at S&P Super 1500 Companies in 1997. LC 99-174114. 57p. 1998. 95.00 (1-879775-58-1) IRRC Inc DC.
Newbury, Susan L. & Delgado-Gomez, Angel. Spanish Historical Writing about the New World, 1493-1700. LC 95-106283. (Illus.). xiv, 130p. 1994. 50.00 (0-916617-40-8, Pub. by J C Brown) Oak Knoll.
Newbury, Susan L., jt. auth. see Fiering, Norman.
Newbury, Susan L., jt. auth. see Johnson, Julie G.
Newbury, Tim. Garden Design Made Easy. (Illus.). 208p. 1999. pap. 24.95 (0-7063-7832-6, Pub. by WrLock) Sterling.
— 20 Best Garden Designs. LC 97-189037. (Illus.). 128p. 1997. pap. 14.95 (0-7063-7642-0, Pub. by WrLock) Sterling.
***Newbury, Tim.** 20 Best Small Gardens. 96p. 1999. pap. text 14.95 (0-7063-7819-9) Ward & Ward.
Newbury, Tim. The Ultimate Garden Designer. (Illus.). 256p. 1995. 35.00 (0-7063-7335-9, Pub. by WrLock) Sterling.
— The Ultimate Garden Designer. (Illus.). 256p. 1996. pap. 19.95 (0-7063-7486-X, Pub. by WrLock) Sterling.
Newby. Reinforced Concrete up to 1914. 149.95 (0-86078-760-5) Ashgate Pub Co.
Newby & Niemeier, eds. Formability of Metallic Materials, 2,000 A.D. - STP 753. 331p. 1981. 39.50 (0-8031-0742-0, STP753) ASTM.
Newby, Betty A. The Longmont Album: History & Folklore of the St. Vrain Valley. LC 95-25536. 1995. write for info. (0-89865-953-1) Donning Co.
Newby, Bruce W. Electronic Signal Conditioning. LC 93-51084. (Illus.). 304p. 1994. pap. text 39.95 (0-7506-1844-2) Buttrwrth-Heinemann.
— Electronics for Technician Engineers. LC 95-37488. (Illus.). 224p. 1995. pap. text 29.95 (0-7506-2144-3) Buttrwrth-Heinemann.
Newby, Bruce W. & Clayton, George B. Operational Amplifiers. 4th ed. (Illus.). 350p. 2000. text 44.95 (0-7506-0640-1) Buttrwrth-Heinemann.
Newby, Chris. Sales Strategies: The Strategy of Negotiating & Winning at Corporate Sales. 1999. pap. text 24.95 (0-7494-2773-6) Kogan Page Ltd.

Newby, Claude D. Vararies of War: A Chaplain's Continuing Story & Tribute to Combat Enterprises. (Illus.). 260p. (YA). 14.00 (0-9678431-1-1) C D Newby.
Vagaries of War, a first-person non-fiction account of the author's second year in combat, free of artistic license. It focuses on the service, sacrifice & heroics of the enlisted men & small unit leaders, on those who bore the brunt of war upon their bodies & souls & endured the ever-worsening hostility of the "folks back home." It is also a tribute to the soldiers' loved ones that endured the horrors of war vicariously & the disdain of their fellow citizens directly. Vagaries is unique in that it reveals the war & America's faithfully warriors through the eyes of a chaplain. It captures the essence of infantry LRRP (ranger) & serial scout combat in Vietnam, telling the soldiers' story as only a soldier can & provides an intimate look at the anatanomy of the famous 1st Calvary Division Airmobile. Vagaries is for veterans, their loved ones, students & historians even for those critics who blamed the soldier for the war that he dutifully fought on their behalf Vagaries, like It Took Heroes before it, includes an extensive glossary index & photographs; also maps. Available through September 2000. Backorder through Ingram Book 1 (800) 937-8000, or call Tribute Enterprises, 1-(801) 299-1621. ***Publisher Paid Annotation.***

***Newby, Claude D. & Johnson, Lucille. It Took Heroes: A Chaplain's Story & Tribute to Vietnam Veterans & Those Who Wait for Them. 2nd rev. ed. LC 00-19065. (Illus.). xii, 231p. 1998. pap. 13.95 (0-9678431-0-3) C D Newby.**
It Took Heroes, a first-person non-fiction account of the author's second year in combat, free of artistic license, rearrangement of events or creation of composite characters for dramatic or other purposes. Heroes, though tied together by the author's experiences focuses on the service, sacrifice & heroics of the enlisted men & small unit leaders, on those who bore the brunt of war upon their bodies & soul & endured the ever worsening hostility of the "folks back home." It is also a tribute to the soldier's loved ones that endured the horrors of war vicariously & the disdain of their fellow warriors through the eyes of a chaplain. It captures the essence of infantry combat in Vietnam, telling the soldiers' story as only a soldier can. Heroes is for veterans, their loved ones, students & historians & even for those critics who blamed the soldier for the war that he dutifully fought on their behalf. Though written by a chaplain, Heores is not about religious tenets & doctrine. Heroes, the first two books, includes an extensive glossary, index & photographs. Backorder through Ingram Book 1(800) 937-8000, or call Tribute Enterprises, 1 (800) 299-1621. ***Publisher Paid Annotation.***

Newby, Cliff. Canaries. 2nd rev. ed. (Canaries for Pleasure & Profit Ser.). (Illus.). 96p. 1984. pap. 6.95 (0-86622-839-X, PB-102) TFH Pubns.
Newby, David E., jt. auth. see Grubb, Neil R.
Newby, Elizabeth L. Bracera Con Esperanza. 144p. 1992. pap. 9.00 (0-944350-23-2) Friends United.
Newby, Eric. The Last Grain Race. 304p. 1999. pap. 12.95 (0-86442-768-9) Lonely Planet.
***Newby, Eric.** Learning the Ropes: An Apprentice to the Last of the Windjammers. (Illus.). 144p. 1999. 35.00 (0-8129-3252-8, Times Bks) Crown Pub Group.
Newby, Eric. Love & War in the Apennines. (Lonely Planet Journeys (Travel Literature) Ser.). 276p. 1999. pap. 12.95 (0-86442-765-4) Lonely Planet.
— On the Shores of the Mediterranean. 1998. pap. 14.95 (0-86442-621-6) Lonely Planet.
— A Short Walk in the Hindu Kush. (Adventure Library: Vol. 18). (Illus.). 256p. 1999. lib. bdg. 32.50 (1-885283-17-2) Advent Library.
— A Short Walk in the Hindu Kush. 1998. pap. 12.95 (0-86442-604-6) Lonely Planet.
— A Small Place in Italy. (Orig.). 1998. pap. 12.95 (0-86442-605-4) Lonely Planet.
— Something Wholesale: My Life & Times in the Rag Trade. large type ed. 256p. 1991. 19.95 (1-85089-281-4, Pub. by ISIS Lrg Prnt) Transaction Pubs.
Newby, Eric, compiled by. A Book of Travellers' Tales. 576p. 1987. pap. 10.95 (0-14-009567-5, Penguin Bks) Viking Penguin.
Newby, Eric & Newby, Wanda. Round Ireland in Low Gear. 1998. pap. 12.95 (0-86442-627-5) Lonely Planet.
— Slowly down the Ganges. 1998. pap. 14.95 (0-86442-631-3) Lonely Planet.
Newby, Evelyn, ed. The Diary of Joseph Farington: Index. LC 98-16056. 1200p. 1998. 125.00 (0-300-07577-4) Yale U Pr.
Newby-Fraser, Paula & Mora, John. Paula Newby-Fraser's Peak Fitness for Women. LC 94-40070. (Illus.). 232p. (Orig.). 1995. pap. 15.95 (0-87322-672-0, PNEW0672) Human Kinetics.
Newby, Grace, jt. auth. see Albritton, Clarice.
Newby, Gregory B. Directory of Directories on the Internet. (Supplement to Small Computers in Libraries Ser.: No. 33). 175p. 1993. pap. text 29.50 (0-88736-768-2) Mecklermedia.
— The Official Internet World Internet Yellow Pages. 960p. 1995. pap. 39.99 (1-56884-343-7) IDG Bks.
Newby, Gregory B., ed. Handbook of Advanced Library Technology. (Illus.). Date not set. text. write for info. (0-8247-9478-8) Dekker.
Newby, Gregory B., jt. auth. see Peek, Robin P.
Newby, Howard. The National Trust: The Next Hundred Years. 192p. 1996. 39.95 (0-7078-0190-7, Pub. by Natl Trust); pap. 22.95 (0-7078-0231-8, Pub. by Natl Trust) Trafalgar.
Newby, Howard, ed. International Perspectives in Rural Sociology. LC 81-16521. 152p. reprint ed. pap. 47.20 (0-608-08673-8, 206919600003) Bks Demand.
Newby, Howard, et al. Property, Paternalism, & Power: Class & Control in Rural England. LC 78-20301. 432p. reprint ed. pap. 134.00 (0-8357-6797-3, 203547300095) Bks Demand.
Newby, Howard, jt. auth. see Lee, David.
Newby, Howard, jt. ed. see Bell, Colin.
Newby, Howard, jt. ed. see Buttel, Frederick H.
Newby, I. A. Plain Folk in the New South: Social Change & Cultural Persistence, 1880-1915. LC 88-17439. 588p. 1989. text 80.00 (0-8071-1456-1) La State U Pr.
Newby, I. A., ed. Civil War & Reconstruction, 1850-1877. (Literature of History Ser.). (Orig.). (C). 1971. pap. text 14.95 (0-89197-081-9) Irvington.
Newby, Idus A. Jim Crow's Defense: Anti-Negro Thought in America, 1900 to 1930. LC 80-11253. 230p. 1980. reprint ed. lib. bdg. 35.00 (0-313-22353-X, NEJC, Greenwood Pr) Greenwood.
— Jim Crow's Defense: Anti-Negro Thought in America, 1900-1930. LC 65-20297. 246p. reprint ed. pap. 76.30 (0-608-13762-6, 205168400004) Bks Demand.
***Newby, J. D.** Res Gestae Diva Augusti: Text, Translation & a Numismatic Commentary. Miller, M. C. J., ed. (Illus.). 200p. 2000. pap. 20.00 (0-89005-583-1) Ares.
Newby, James R. Gathering the Seekers: Spiritual Growth Through Small Group Ministry. 100p. 1995. pap. 15.95 (1-56699-158-7) Alban Inst.
***Newby, James R.** Sacred Chaos: One Man's Spiritual Journey Through Pain & Loss. 132p. 1999. pap. 12.95 (0-8264-1204-1) Continuum.
Newby, James R. Sacred Chaos & the Quest for Spiritual Intimacy. LC 97-38954. 132p. 1998. 18.95 (0-8264-1080-4) Continuum.
Newby, John R., ed. Source Book on Forming of Steel Sheet: A Discriminative Selection of Outstanding Articles from the Periodical & Reference Literature. LC 76-28176. (American Society for Metals. Engineering Bookshelf Ser.). (Illus.). 399p. reprint ed. pap. 123.70 (0-608-11711-0, 201949800013) Bks Demand.
Newby, Julian. Inside Broadcasting. LC 96-23975. (Career Builders Guide Ser.). 232p. (C). 1997. 80.00 (0-415-15771-4) Routledge.
Newby, Julian, jt. auth. see Barrow, Tony.
Newby, Leroy W., jt. auth. see Armstrong, Robert H.
Newby, Lorraine D. Waukegan Schools: A History in Sketches, 1840's-1990's. Schornick, Lynn, ed. LC 89-52037. (Illus.). 48p. (Orig.). 1989. pap. 10.00 (0-9625103 0-0) Waukegan Pk Dist.
Newby, Martine. Glass. (Handbook Ser.). (Illus.). 80p. 1999. 19.95 (1-85444-124-8, Pub. by Ashmolean Mus) A Schwartz & Co.
***Newby, Martine.** Glass. (Handbook Ser.). (Illus.). 80p. 1999. pap. 12.95 (1-85444-123-X, Pub. by Ashmolean Mus) A Schwartz & Co.
Newby, Martine & Painter, Kenneth, eds. Roman Glass: Two Centuries of Art & Invention. (Illus.). 174p. 1991. pap. 37.50 (0-85431-255-2, Pub. by Soc Antiquaries) David Brown.
Newby, Nicole. Cool Clay. (Illus.). 16p. (Orig.). (J). (gr. 2-9). 1996. pap. 9.95 (0-8167-3870-X, Watermill Pr) Troll Communs.
Newby, P. H. Egypt Story Its Art Its Monuments. 1986. pap. 35.00 (977-424-059-6, Pub. by Am Univ Cairo Pr) Col U Pr.
Newby, Peter, ed. The Mammoth Book of Astounding Word Games. (Mammoth Book Ser.). 512p. 1995. pap. 10.95 (0-7867-0213-3) Carroll & Graf.
Newby, Richard. The Structure of English: A Handbook of English Grammar. 110p. 1987. pap. text 10.95 (0-521-34996-6) Cambridge U Pr.
Newby, Rick. Writing Montana: Literature under the Big Sky. LC 96-77962. (Illus.). 348p. 1996. pap. 19.95 (1-56044-417-7) Falcon Pub Inc.
Newby, Rick, jt. auth. see Gans, Liz.
Newby, Rick, jt. auth. see Grosskopf, Linda A.
Newby, Rick, ed. see Held, Peter & Weiss, Dick.
Newby, Robert. King Midas: With Selected Sentences in American Sign Language. (Awareness & Caring Ser.). (Illus.). 64p. (J). (gr. 1-6). 1990. lib. bdg. 16.95 (1-878363-25-5) Forest Hse.
— King Midas: With Selected Sentences in American Sign Language. LC 90-4908. (Illus.). (J). (gr. 1-5). 1990.

N

An Asterisk (*) at the beginning of an entry indicates that the title is appearing for the first time.

29.95 incl. VHS (0-930323-71-8, 2806, Pub. by K Green Pubns); 38.20 incl. VHS (0-930323-77-7, Pub. by K Green Pubns) Gallaudet Univ Pr.

— Sleeping Beauty: With Selected Sentences in American Sign Language. (Awareness & Caring Ser.). (Illus.). 64p. (J). (gr. k-3). 1992. lib. bdg. 17.95 (1-56674-035-5) Forest Hse.

— Sleeping Beauty: With Selected Sentences in American Sign Language. LC 91-29729. (Illus.). (J). (gr. 1-7). 1992. 29.95 incl. VHS (0-930323-98-X, 2836, Pub. by K Green Pubns); 14.95 (0-930323-97-1, Pub. by K Green Pubns); 38.20 incl. VHS (1-56368-009-2, Pub. by K Green Pubns) Gallaudet Univ Pr.

Newby, Robert, ed. King Midas: With Selected Sentences in American Sign Language. LC 90-4908. (Illus.). 64p. (J). (gr. 1-5). 1990. 14.95 (0-930323-75-0, Pub. by K Green Pubns) Gallaudet Univ Pr.

Newby, T. J. & Stokes, C. R., eds. Local Immune Responses of the GUT. LC 83-26321. 264p. 1984. 129.00 (0-8493-5534-6, QR186, CRC Reprint) Franklin.

***Newby, Timothy J., et al.** Instructional Technology for Teaching & Learning: Designing Instruction, Integrating Computers & Using Media. 2nd ed. LC 99-35614. 313p. 1999. pap. text 59.00 (0-13-914052-2) P-H.

***Newby, Tony.** The Customer Service Pocketbook. 128p. 1999. pap. 8.95 (1-870471-10-5, Pub. by Mngmnt Pocketbks) Stylus Pub VA.

Newby, Tony. Validating Your Training. 136p. (C). 1992. pap. 45.00 (0-7494-0551-1, Pub. by IPM Hse) St Mut.

Newby, Wanda, jt. auth. see Newby, Eric.

Newcastle Architecture Cooperative Staff, jt. auth. see Department of Environment, BDOR Ltd. Staff.

***Newcastle, Margaret C.** Paper Bodies: A Margaret Cavendish Reader. Bowerbank, Sylvia L. & Mendelson, Sara Heller, eds. (Literary Texts Ser.). 340p. 2000. pap. 12.95 (1-55111-173-X) Broadview Pr.

Newcity, Michael A. Taxation in the Soviet Union. LC 85-19359. 406p. 1986. 59.95 (0-275-92005-4, C2005, Praeger Pubs) Greenwood.

Newcom, Josh. The Colorado River. McClurg, Sue, ed. (Layperson's Guide Ser.). (Illus.). 20p. 1998. pap. 5.00 (1-893246-61-2) Water Educ.

— The Delta. rev. ed. McClurg, Sue, ed. (Layperson's Guide Ser.). (Illus.). 20p. 1998. pap. 5.00 (1-893246-62-0) Water Educ.

Newcomb. Cpsm Intro Psycholgl Sci Lml. 5th ed. 1998. pap. text 31.00 (0-07-230699-8) McGraw.

— Enzymes: Catalysts Living Matte, Vol. 1. Date not set. 1.20 (0-7167-9140-4) W H Freeman.

Newcomb, jt. auth. see Bishop, William H.

Newcomb, jt. auth. see Connable.

Newcomb, Annette. The Awesome Almanac: Michigan. LC 92-74709. 1994. 18.43 (0-606-09021-5, Pub. by Turtleback) Demco.

— Awesome Almanacs: Michigan. (J). (gr. 4-12). 1993. pap. 12.95 (1-880190-06-0) B&B Pub.

Newcomb, Anthony. The Madrigal at Ferrara, 1579-1597, 2 vols., Vol. 1. LC 78-573. (Princeton Studies in Music: No. 7). 318p. reprint ed. pap. 98.60 (0-8357-4646-1, 203757700001) Bks Demand.

— The Madrigal at Ferrara, 1579-1597, 2 vols., Vol. 2. LC 78-573. (Princeton Studies in Music: No. 7). 230p. reprint ed. pap. 71.30 (0-8357-4647-X, 203757700002) Bks Demand.

Newcomb, Anthony, ed. The Ricercars of the Bourdeney Codex. (Recent Researches in Music of the Renaissance Ser.: Vol. RRR89). (Illus.). xxii, 139p. 1991. pap. 50.00 (0-89579-264-8) A-R Eds.

Newcomb, Anthony, ed. see Fontanelli, Alfonso.

Newcomb, Benjamin H. Franklin & Galloway: A Political Partnership. LC 72-75205. 344p. reprint ed. pap. 106.70 (0-8357-8136-4, 203384200087) Bks Demand.

— Political Partisanship in the American Middle Colonies, 1700-1776. LC 94-39764. 328p. (C). 1995. text 45.00 (0-8071-1875-3) La State U Pr.

Newcomb, C., tr. see Clauser, C.

Newcomb, C., tr. see Kuehn, Friedrich, et al, eds.

Newcomb, Charles K. The Journals of Charles King Newcomb. Johnson, Judith K., ed. LC 46-3324. (Brown University Studies: 10). 310p. reprint ed. 96.10 (0-608-16594-8, 202752000055) Bks Demand.

Newcomb, David E. Cold Regions Impact on Civil Works: Proceedings. LC 98-38268. 776p. 1998. 89.00 (0-7844-0379-1) Am Soc Civil Eng.

Newcomb, David E., jt. auth. see Stroup-Gardiner, Mary.

Newcomb, Donald L. & Rimler, George W. The Reduction in Force Testament. LC 89-92738. 84p. (Orig.). 1989. pap. text 24.95 (0-9625257-0-7) LACY Pub VA.

Newcomb, Duane G. Small Space, Big Harvest: Turn Your Small Garden into a Vegetable Factory - Naturally. LC 92-39921. 272p. (Orig.). 1993. pap. 14.95 (1-55958-289-8) Prima Pub.

Newcomb, Duane G. & Newcomb, Karen. The Postage Stamp Garden Book. 2nd rev. ed. LC 98-31918. 1999. 12.95 (1-58062-123-6) Adams Media.

— The Postage Stamp Kitchen Garden Book. LC 97-43184. 256p. 1998. 9.95 (1-58062-001-9) Adams Media.

Newcomb, Everett W., Jr. The Creatures Nobody Loves. LC 91-66375. (Illus.). 48p. (J). (gr. 4-6). 1991. pap. 3.95 (0-9627974-3-X) Tabby Hse Bks.

Newcomb, Franc J. Hosteen Klah: Navaho Medicine Man & Sand Painter. LC 64-20759. (Civilization of the American Indian Ser.: No. 73). (Illus.). 227p. 1972. pap. 17.95 (0-8061-1008-2) U of Okla Pr.

Newcomb, Franc J. & Reichard, Gladys A. Sandpaintings of the Navajo Shooting Chant. (Illus.). 32p. 1975. pap. 7.95 (0-486-23141-0) Dover.

Newcomb, Franc Johson. Navaho Folk Tales. LC 90-39570. (Illus.). 203p. 1990. reprint ed. pap. 11.95 (0-8263-1231-4) U of NM Pr.

Newcomb, Geneva R. Please Hold My Hand. (Illus.). 78p. (Orig.). 1989. 9.95 (0-9622762-1-9); pap. 4.95 (0-9622762-0-0) Non-Fictitious.

Newcomb, H. T. The Work of the Interstate Commerce Commission. Bruchey, Stuart, ed. LC 80-1334. (Railroads Ser.). (Illus.). 1981. reprint ed. lib. bdg. 15.95 (0-405-13808-3) Ayer.

Newcomb, Horace, ed. Encyclopedia of Television, 3 vols. LC 97-214692. (Illus.). 2200p. 1997. lib. bdg. 300.00 (1-884964-26-5) Fitzroy Dearborn.

— Television: The Critical View. 5th ed. 656p. (C). 1994. pap. text 29.95 (0-19-508528-0) OUP.

— Television: The Critical View. 6th ed. LC 99-26151. (Illus.). 736p. (C). 2000. pap. text 35.00 (0-19-511927-4) OUP.

Newcomb, Howard R. United States Copper Cents (1816-1857) LC 81-50923. (Illus.). 288p. 1981. reprint ed. lib. bdg. 50.00 (0-88000-127-5) Quarterman.

— United States Copper Cents (1816-1857) (Illus.). 1993. reprint ed. lib. bdg. 60.00 (0-942666-51-8) S J Durst.

Newcomb, J. B. Genealogical Memoir of the Newcomb Family Containing Records of Nearly Every Person of the Name in America from 1635-1874. (Illus.). 600p. 1989. reprint ed. pap. 76.00 (0-8328-0903-9); reprint ed. lib. bdg. 86.00 (0-8328-0902-0) Higginson Bk Co.

Newcomb, Jack. The Ticket: A Fifty-Year Sports Odyssey. Perry, John, ed. LC 96-71357. (Illus.). 248p. 1997. 24.00 (1-887654-25-9) Premium Pr TN.

Newcomb, James W., tr. see Simion, Eugen.

Newcomb, Joan I. John F. Kennedy: An Annotated Bibliography. LC 77-7568. 143p. 1977. 21.00 (0-8108-1042-5) Scarecrow.

Newcomb, John T. Wallace Stevens & Literary Canons. LC 91-31930. 293p. 1992. text 37.50 (0-87805-525-8) U Pr of Miss.

Newcomb, Karen, jt. auth. see Newcomb, Duane G.

***Newcomb, Kerry.** Mad Morgan. LC 00-25936. 288p. 2000. text 24.95 (0-312-26197-7) St Martin.

Newcomb, Kerry. The Red Ripper. LC 99-21752. 288p. 1999. text 23.95 (0-312-20575-9) St Martin.

***Newcomb, Kerry.** The Red Ripper. 352p. 1999. mass mkt. 6.99 (0-312-97153-2) St Martin.

— Texas Anthem. 288p. 2000. pap. 5.99 (0-312-97682-8, St Martins Paperbacks) St Martin.

Newcomb, L. H., et al. Methods of Teaching Agriculture. 2nd ed. 370p. 1993. 39.95 (0-8134-2952-8) Interstate.

Newcomb, Lawrence. Newcomb's Wildflower Guide: An Ingenious New Key System for Quick, Positive Field Identification of Wildflowers, Flowering Shrubs & Vines. (Illus.). 490p. 1989. pap. 19.00 (0-316-60442-9) Little.

Newcomb, Lori, jt. auth. see Fischer, Rusty.

***Newcomb, Mark J.** Cisco IOS Instant Reference. (Cisco IOS Ser.). 2000. pap. 19.99 (0-7821-2733-9) Sybex.

Newcomb, Michael D. Drug Use in the Workplace. LC 87-34921. 265p. 1988. 59.95 (0-86569-182-7, Auburn Hse) Greenwood.

Newcomb, Michael D. & Bentler, Peter M. Consequences of Adolescent Drug Use: Impact on the Lives of Young Adults. LC 87-24061. 285p. 1988. reprint ed. pap. 88.40 (0-608-01527-X, 205957100002) Bks Demand.

Newcomb, Michael D., et al. Sexual Abuse & Consensual Sex: Women's Developmental Patterns & Outcomes. (Illus.). 192p. (C). 1993. text 29.95 (0-8039-4733-X) Sage.

Newcomb, Mildred. The Imagined World of Charles Dickens. LC 88-32682. 243p. 1989. text 52.50 (0-8142-0482-1) Ohio St U Pr.

Newcomb, Norma. Boss Lady. large type ed. (Dales Ser.). 192p. 1994. pap. 18.99 (1-85389-435-4, Dales) Ulverscroft.

— Design by Joan. large type ed. (Linford Romance Library). 256p. 1996. pap. 16.99 (0-7089-7848-7, Linford) Ulverscroft.

— Memo to a Heart. large type ed. (Linford Romance Library). 240p. 1996. pap. 16.99 (0-7089-7833-9, Linford) Ulverscroft.

Newcomb, Peggy C. Popular Annuals of Eastern North America, 1865-1914. LC 84-1674. (Illus.). 208p. (Orig.). 1985. pap. 15.00 (0-88402-138-6) Dumbarton Oaks.

Newcomb, Philip. Reverse Engineering. Wills, Linda, ed. LC 96-26556. 184p. (C). 1996. text 127.00 (0-7923-9756-8) Kluwer Academic.

***Newcomb, Rexford.** Mediterranean Domestic Architecture for the United States. LC 99-40220. (20th Century Ser.). (Illus.). 1999. write for info. (0-926494-13-9) Acanthus Pr.

Newcomb, Rexford. Spanish-Colonial Architecture in the United States. 192p. 1990. pap. 12.95 (0-486-26263-4) Dover.

Newcomb, Richard. Future Resources: Their Geostatistical Appraisal. 179p. 1982. pap. 12.00 (0-937058-13-0) West Va U Pr.

Newcomb, Richard F. U. S. Cruisers. LC 92-61184. (Illus.). 176p. Date not set. 39.95 (1-56311-051-2) Turner Pub KY.

— U. S. Destroyers of the World Wars: History of the "Tin Cans" LC 94-60015. (Illus.). 160p. 1994. 39.95 (1-56311-134-9) Turner Pub KY.

Newcomb, Robert T. Janissa. 1943. 8.00 (0-685-08807-3) Destiny.

Newcomb, Robinson. Mobile Home Parks: An Analysis of Characteristics, Pt. 1. LC 76-167878. (Urban Land Institute, Technical Bulletin Ser.: No. 66). 80p. reprint ed. pap. 30.00 (0-608-14292-1, 201735700007) Bks Demand.

Newcomb, S. B. & Bennett, M. J., eds. Microscopy of Oxidation 2: Proceedings of the 2nd International Conference Held in Selwyn College, University of Cambridge, March 1993. (Illus.). 600p. 1994. 170.00 (0-901716-50-2, Pub. by Inst Materials) Ashgate Pub Co.

Newcomb, S. B. & Little, J. A., eds. Microscopy of Oxidation 3: Proceedings of the 3rd International Conference on the Microscopy of Oxidation. (Illus.). 792p. 1997. 300.00 (1-86125-034-7, Pub. by Inst Materials) Ashgate Pub Co.

Newcomb, Sarah, jt. auth. see Ajemian, Shari.

Newcomb, Simon. The ABC of Finance. (Notable American Authors Ser.). 1999. reprint ed. lib. bdg. 125.00 (0-7812-4617-2) Rprt Serv.

— Astronomy for Everybody. (Notable American Authors Ser.). 1999. reprint ed. lib. bdg. 125.00 (0-7812-4625-3) Rprt Serv.

— Calculus. (Notable American Authors Ser.). 1999. reprint ed. lib. bdg. 125.00 (0-7812-4619-9) Rprt Serv.

— A Critical Examination of Our Political Policy During the Rebellion. (Notable American Authors Ser.). 1999. reprint ed. lib. bdg. 125.00 (0-7812-4614-8) Rprt Serv.

— Elements of Astronomy. (Notable American Authors Ser.). 1999. reprint ed. lib. bdg. 125.00 (0-7812-4622-9) Rprt Serv.

— His Wisdom: The Defender (novel) (Notable American Authors Ser.). 1999. reprint ed. lib. bdg. 125.00 (0-7812-4623-7) Rprt Serv.

— His Wisdom, the Defender. LC 74-16513. (Science Fiction Ser.). (Illus.). 338p. 1975. reprint ed. 28.95 (0-405-06308-3) Ayer.

— Plain Man's Talk on the Labor Question. LC 77-89756. (American Labor, from Conspiracy to Collective Bargaining Ser., No. 1). 195p. 1978. reprint ed. 17.95 (0-405-02143-7) Ayer.

— A Plain Man's Talk on the Labor Question. (Notable American Authors Ser.). 1999. reprint ed. lib. bdg. 125.00 (0-7812-4620-2) Rprt Serv.

— Popular Astronomy. (Notable American Authors Ser.). 1999. reprint ed. lib. bdg. 125.00 (0-7812-4618-0) Rprt Serv.

— Principles of Political Economy. LC 65-26372. (Reprints of Economic Classics Ser.). xvi, 548p. 1966. reprint ed. 57.50 (0-678-00156-1) Kelley.

— Principles of Political Economy. (Notable American Authors Ser.). 1999. reprint ed. lib. bdg. 125.00 (0-7812-4621-0) Rprt Serv.

— Reminiscences of an Astronomer. (Notable American Authors Ser.). 1999. reprint ed. lib. bdg. 125.00 (0-7812-4626-1) Rprt Serv.

— Researches on the Motions of the Moon. (Notable American Authors Ser.). 1999. reprint ed. lib. bdg. 125.00 (0-7812-4615-6) Rprt Serv.

— Side Lights of Astronomy. (Notable American Authors Ser.). 1999. reprint ed. lib. bdg. 125.00 (0-7812-4628-8) Rprt Serv.

— Sperical Astronomy. (Notable American Authors Ser.). 1999. reprint ed. lib. bdg. 125.00 (0-7812-4627-X) Rprt Serv.

— The Stars. (Notable American Authors Ser.). 1999. reprint ed. lib. bdg. 125.00 (0-7812-4624-5) Rprt Serv.

Newcomb, T. P. & Spurr, R. T. A Technical History of the Motorcar. (Illus.). 430p. 1989. 60.00 (0-85274-074-3) IOP Pub.

Newcomb, Theodore M. & Wilson, Everett K., eds. College Peer Groups: Problems & Prospects for Research. LC 65-29033. (Monographs in Social Research: No. 8). 1966. 15.00 (0-202-09002-7) Natl Opinion Res.

Newcomb, Theodore M., jt. auth. see Feldman, Kenneth A.

Newcomb, Thomas J. To Start a Little War: The U. S. S. Kidd: The Taking of Baton Rouge. (Major Kirt Ives Action Adventure Story Ser.). 208p. 1998. per. 10.95 (0-9662548-3-X) New Advent Pub.

— To Start a Little War: The U. S. S. Kidd: The Taking of Baton Rouge. 208p. 1998. pap. 10.95 (0-9662548-0-5) New Advent Pub.

Newcomb, Tim. The Trinity Gene. 330p. (Orig.). 1995. pap. 12.95 (1-878117-07-6) Lagumo Corp.

Newcomb, Tim, jt. auth. see Keiter, Robert S.

Newcomb, V. N. Practical Accounting for Business Studies. LC 82-11103. 380p. reprint ed. pap. 117.80 (0-608-14908-X, 202598400048) Bks Demand.

— Practical Calculations for Business Studies: Problems & Applications for Students in Africa. LC 80-42019. 164p. reprint ed. pap. 50.90 (0-608-15631-0, 203176000076) Bks Demand.

Newcomb, W. W. The Rock Art of Texas Indians. LC 97-147203. (Illus.). 253p. 1996. reprint ed. pap. 34.95 (0-292-74326-2) U of Tex Pr.

Newcomb, W. W., jt. auth. see Kirkland, Forrest.

Newcomb, William W., Jr. The Indians of Texas: From Prehistoric to Modern Times. LC 60-14312. (Texas History Paperbacks Ser.: No. 4). (Illus.). 422p. (C). 1961. pap. 14.95 (0-292-78425-2) U of Tex Pr.

Newcomb, William W., jt. ed. see Davis, Edward M.

Newcombe. Communication & Introduction to Speech. 18.69 (0-205-10304-9) Allyn.

Newcombe, Barbara, jt. auth. see Levine, Stephen.

Newcombe, Barry. Tennis Rules: A Player's Guide. LC 97-183523. (Illus.). 80p. 1997. pap. 10.95 (0-7063-7538-6, Pub. by WrLock) Sterling.

Newcombe, D. G. Henry VIII & the English Reformation. LC 94-39263. (Lancaster Pamphlets Ser.). 80p. (C). 1995. pap. 11.99 (0-415-10728-8) Routledge.

Newcombe, David S. Inherited Biochemical Disorders & Uric Acid Metabolism. LC RC0627.8.N48. 298p. reprint ed. pap. 92.40 (0-608-12367-6, 205207400033) Bks Demand.

Newcombe, David S. & Cathcart, Edgar S., eds. Advances in Acute Phase Reactants & Cytokines, Vol. 1. Date not set. 128.50 (0-7623-0401-4) Jai Pr.

Newcombe, Ellen. Mentoring Programs for New Teachers. 24p. 1988. pap. 5.95 (1-56602-021-2) Research Better.

— Perspectives on Teacher Induction: A Review of the Literature & Promising Program Models. 98p. 1990. pap. 16.95 (1-56602-033-6) Research Better.

Newcombe, Hanna. Design for a Better World. fac. ed. LC 83-15001. (Illus.). 370p. (Orig.). 1983. reprint ed. pap. 114.70 (0-608-00936-9, AU0045500011) Bks Demand.

Newcombe, Jerry. Coming Again. LC 99-15575. 1999. pap. 12.99 (1-56476-769-8, Victor Bks) Chariot Victor.

***Newcombe, Jerry.** Moral of the Story: Timeless Tales To Cherish & Share. (Illus.). 1999. 21.99 (0-8054-2009-6) Broadman.

Newcombe, Jerry & Newcombe, Kirsti. I'll Do It Tomorrow: How to Stop Putting It Off & Get It Done Today. LC 98-50394. (Illus.). 1999. pap. 10.99 (0-8054-1267-0) Broadman.

— A Way of Escape: Experiencing God's Victory over Temptation. LC 99-20474. 192p. 1999. pap. 10.99 (0-8054-1763-X) Broadman.

Newcombe, Jerry, jt. auth. see Kennedy, D. James.

Newcombe, Jude. Literacy at Work: The Workplace Basic Education Project Model of Delivery. 1996. pap. 59.95 (0-7300-1757-5, Pub. by Deakin Univ) St Mut.

Newcombe, Kirsti, jt. auth. see Newcombe, Jerry.

Newcombe, Kristi Sb. Olympic Heroes. LC 97-42696. 32p. (J). (gr. 3-7). 1997. 10.99 (0-7814-3021-6, Chariot Bks) Chariot Victor.

Newcombe, Nora. Chid Development. 8th ed. (C). 1996. pap. text, student ed. 26.25 (0-673-99332-9) Addson-Wesley Educ.

— Child Development. 8th ed. (C). 1998. pap. text 22.00 (0-673-97491-X) Addson-Wesley Educ.

Newcombe, Nora. Child Development. 8th ed. 1997. student ed. 89.66 (0-201-34982-5) S&S Trade.

Newcombe, Nora. Child Development. 8th rev. ed. LC 95-12721. 736p. (C). 1997. 85.00 (0-673-99311-6) Addson-Wesley Educ.

***Newcombe, Nora S. & Huttenlocher, Janellen.** Making Space: The Development of Spatial Representation & Reasoning. LC 99-87408. (Illus.). 280p. 2000. 37.50 (0-262-14069-1) MIT Pr.

Newcombe, P. Judson. Voice & Diction. 2nd ed. (Illus.). 317p. (C). 1991. pap. text 38.95 (0-89892-063-9) Contemp Pub Co of Raleigh.

Newcombe, Tod. The Local Government Guide to Imaging Systems: Planning & Implementation. LC 95-175668. (Special Reports). (Illus.). 120p. 1995. pap. 70.00 (0-87326-097-X) Intl City-Cnty Mgt.

Newcombe, Tod, ed. Solutions for Technology-Sharing Networks, 1988-89. 484p. (Orig.). 1988. pap. 25.00 (1-55657-007-4) Pub Tech Inc.

Newcomber, Joseph M., jt. auth. see Dekker, Edward N.

Newcome, Robert & Newcome, Zita. Little Lion. (Illus.). 32p. (J). (ps-1). 1993. 17.95 (1-85681-181-6, Pub. by Julia MacRae) Trafalgar.

Newcome, Zita. Toddlerobics. LC 95-21062. (Illus.). 32p. (J). (ps-k). 1996. 14.99 (1-56402-809-7) Candlewick Pr.

— Toddlerobics. LC 95-21062. (Illus.). 32p. (J). (ps up). 1997. reprint ed. pap. 5.99 (0-7636-0113-6) Candlewick Pr.

— Toddlerobics: Animal Fun. LC 98-42390. (Illus.). 32p. (J). 1999. text 15.99 (0-7636-0803-3) Candlewick Pr.

Newcome, Zita, jt. auth. see Newcome, Robert.

Newcomer. Governing Los Angeles. 2nd ed. (J). 1994. pap. text 22.00 (0-07-038034-1) McGraw.

Newcomer, C. Armour. Cole's Cavalry: Or, Three Years in the Saddle in the Shenandoah Valley. LC 76-126245. (Select Bibliographies Reprint Ser.). 1977. 16.95 (0-8369-5472-6) Ayer.

Newcomer, Eric, jt. auth. see Bernstein, Phillip A.

Newcomer, Evangeline G. Gossett. The Family of Gossett. (Illus.). 188p. 1997. reprint ed. pap. 27.50 (0-8328-8811-7); reprint ed. lib. bdg. 37.50 (0-8328-8810-9) Higginson Bk Co.

Newcomer, James. Lady Morgan the Novelist. LC 89-43054. 104p. 1990. 26.50 (0-8387-5177-6) Bucknell U Pr.

— Maria Edgeworth. LC 77-125886. (Irish Writers Ser.). 94p. 1975. pap. 1.95 (0-8387-7732-5) Bucknell U Pr.

Newcomer, Joseph M., jt. auth. see Rector, Brent E.

Newcomer, Larry R. Select . . . SQL: The Relational Database Language. 446p. (C). 1991. pap. text 62.00 (0-02-386693-4, Macmillan Coll) P-H.

Newcomer, Mabel. A Century of Higher Education for American Women. LC 75-40214. 1976. reprint ed. 40.00 (0-89201-002-9) Zenger Pub.

— Separation of State & Local Revenues in the United States. LC 68-56675. (Columbia University. Studies in the Social Sciences: No. 180). reprint ed. 27.50 (0-404-51180-5) AMS Pr.

Newcomer, Phyllis L. Understanding & Teaching Emotionally Disturbed Children & Adolescents. 2nd rev. ed. LC 92-33990. 620p. (C). 1993. text 41.00 (0-89079-575-4, 6575) PRO-ED.

Newcomer, Phyllis L., ed. Readings in Emotional Disturbance. LC 93-5040. 313p. 1994. pap. text 19.00 (0-89079-588-6, 6666) PRO-ED.

Newcomer, Robert J. & Benjamin, A. E., eds. Indicators of Chronic Health Conditions: Monitoring Community-Level Delivery Systems. LC 96-42207. (Illus.). 384p. 1997. text 65.00 (0-8018-5491-1); pap. text 24.95 (0-8018-5494-6) Johns Hopkins.

Newcomer, Robert J. & Wilkinson, Anne M., eds. Annual Review of Gerontology & Geriatrics Vol. 16: Focus on Managed Care & Quality Assurance: Integrating Acute & Chronic Care, Vol. 16. (Illus.). 280p. 1996. 54.00 (0-8261-6498-6) Springer Pub.

Newcomer, Roy. A Practical Guide to Inspecting Electrical, No. 5. (Illus.). 91p. 1996. pap. 49.00 (1-928545-04-1) Am Home Inspect.

— A Practical Guide to Inspecting Exteriors, No. 2. (Illus.). 82p. 1996. pap. 49.00 (1-928545-01-7) Am Home Inspect.

An Asterisk (*) at the beginning of an entry indicates that the title is appearing for the first time.

— A Practical Guide to Inspecting Heating & Cooling, No. 6. (Illus.). 150p. 1996. pap. 49.00 (1-928545-05-X) Am Home Inspect.

— A Practical Guide to Inspecting Interiors, Insulation, Ventilation, No. 7. (Illus.). 128p. 1996. pap. 49.00 (1-928545-06-8) Am Home Inspect.

— A Practical Guide to Inspecting Plumbing, No. 4. (Illus.). 95p. 1996. pap. 49.00 (1-928545-03-3) Am Home Inspect.

— A Practical Guide to Inspecting Roofs, No. 3. (Illus.). 85p. 1996. pap. 49.00 (1-928545-02-5) Am Home Inspect.

— A Practical Guide to Inspecting Structure, No. 1. (Illus.). 116p. 1996. pap. 49.00 (1-928545-00-9) Am Home Inspect.

Newcomer, Ruth, jt. ed. see Woolfolk, Doug.

Newdick, Christopher. Who Should We Treat? Law, Patients, & Resources in the NHS. 368p. 1995. text 74.00 (0-19-825924-7); pap. text 28.00 (0-19-825925-5) OUP.

Newdick, Jane. At Home with Herbs. LC 94-20669. (Illus.). 224p. 1994. 29.95 (0-88266-886-2, Storey Pub) Storey Bks.

— Cascade of Flowers. 1995. 9.99 (0-517-14940-0) Random Hse Value.

— Country Flower Style: Creating the Natural Look. (Illus.). 120p. 1994. 24.95 (0-7892-0013-9) Abbeville Pr.

— Herbal Gifts. 1999. 9.99 (1-84100-061-2) Quadrillion Media.

— Victorian Flowercrafts. (Illus.). 128p. 1994. 17.95 (0-87596-603-9) Rodale Pr Inc.

Newdick, Jane & Clark, Maxine. The Provencal Table. (Illus.). 108p. 1998. 24.95 (0-09-182003-0, Pub. by Ebury Pr) Trafalgar.

Newdick, Jane & Levers-Carter, M. The Complete Flower Arranger: Successful Displays with Fresh & Dried Flowers. (Illus.). 192p. 1998. 14.99 (1-85833-309-1) Quadrillion Pubng.

Newdick, Jane & Rutherford, Lyn. The Tuscan Table. (Illus.). 108p. 1998. 24.95 (0-09-181420-0) Ebury Pr.

Newdick, Jane, jt. auth. see Mattock, John.

Newdick, Robert S., jt. ed. see Sutton, William A.

Newdom, Fred A., jt. auth. see Sachs, Jerome.

Newell. Methods & Models in Demography. 224p. 1989. pap. 39.95 (0-471-94729-6) Wiley.

Newell, jt. auth. see Kraemer.

Newell, A. C., ed. see Benjamin, T. B. & Benney, D. J.

Newell, Abraham. A Hillside View of Industrial History: A Study of Industrial Evolution in the Pennine Highlands. LC 73-119540. (Reprints of Economic Classics Ser.). (Illus.). vii, 281p. 1971. reprint ed. 45.00 (0-678-00695-4) Kelley.

Newell, Alan C. Nonlinear Wave Motion. LC 73-19504. (Lectures in Applied Mathematics: No. 15). (Illus.). 237p. reprint ed. pap. 73.50 (0-608-05981-1, 205264700008) Bks Demand.

— Solitons in Mathematics & Physics. LC 84-71051. (CBMS-NSF Regional Conference Ser.: No. 48). xvi, 244p. 1985. pap. text 46.50 (0-89871-196-7) Soc Indus-Appl Math.

Newell, Alan C., jt. auth. see Moloney, Jerome V.

Newell, Alex. The Soliloquies in Hamlet: The Structural Design. LC 89-46410. (Illus.). 192p. 1991. 36.50 (0-8386-3404-4) Fairleigh Dickinson.

Newell, Allen. Unified Theories of Cognition. (Illus.). 544p. 1990. 55.00 (0-674-92099-6) HUP.

— Unified Theories of Cognition. (Illus.). 576p. 1994. pap. 24.95 (0-674-92101-1) HUP.

Newell, Amani. Book Dreams. LC 98-94106. 1999. pap. 8.95 (0-533-12972-9) Vantage.

Newell, Arlo. Blessed Assurance as Revealed in Scripture. 1987. pap. 0.99 (0-87162-480-X, D1550) Warner Pr.

Newell, Arlo F. The Church of God As Revealed in Scripture. 1983. pap. 4.95 (0-87162-269-6, D4775) Warner Pr.

— Receive the Holy Spirit. 1984. pap. 3.95 (0-87162-409-5, D6431) Warner Pr.

Newell, Arlo F., ed. see Byrum, Russell R.

Newell, Arthur. A Knight of the Toilers. LC 74-22799. reprint ed. 39.50 (0-404-58455-1) AMS Pr.

Newell, Bennie. Homeland. 64p. 1997. pap. 8.00 (0-8059-4230-0) Dorrance.

Newell, Bruce, et al. Pocket Guide to Basic Canoeing. (Illus.). 28p. 1994. spiral bd. 12.95 (1-886127-00-X) Greycliff Pub.

Newell, C. F. Application of Queueing Theory. 2nd ed. (Monographs on Statistics & Applied Probability). 220p. 1982. 42.50 (0-412-24500-0, 6620) Chapman & Hall.

Newell, Cam, ed. see Restany, Pierre.

Newell, Carol, ed. see Schraff, Anne.

Newell, Charldean, ed. Effective Local Government Manager. 2nd ed. LC 93-17353. (Municipal Management Ser.). 1993. 39.95 (0-87326-090-2); pap. 32.00 (0-87326-091-0) Intl City-Cnty Mgt.

Newell, Charldean, jt. auth. see Ammons, David N.

Newell, Charldean, jt. auth. see Kraemer, Richard H.

Newell, Chester. History of the Revolution in Texas. LC 72-9462. (Far Western Frontier Ser.). (Illus.). 230p. 1978. reprint ed. 28.95 (0-405-04990-0) Ayer.

Newell, Christopher. The Grosvenor Gallery Exhibitions: Change & Continuity in the Victorian Art World. (Art, Patrons & Public Ser.). (Illus.). 195p. (C). 1995. text 89.95 (0-521-46493-5) Cambridge U Pr.

Newell, Claire, jt. auth. see McDowell, Ian.

Newell, Clarence A. Class Size & Adaptability, Including Observations on Invention: A Study of Selected Elementary School Classes in New Jersey. LC 70-177119. (Columbia University. Teachers College. Contributions to Education Ser.: No. 894). reprint ed. 37.50 (0-404-55894-1) AMS Pr.

— Old Glass Paperweights of Southern New Jersey: An American Folk Art. LC 87-62586. (Illus.). 96p. 1989. pap. 20.00 (0-9619547-0-1) Papier Presse.

Newell, Clayton R. Burma 1942: The United States Army Campaigns of World War 2. 23p. 1994. pap. 1.25 (0-16-042086-5) USGPO.

— Central Pacific: The United States Army Campaigns of World War 2. 23p. 1992. pap. 1.00 (0-16-035880-9) USGPO.

— Historical Dictionary of the Persian Gulf War, 1990-1991. LC 98-18944. (Historical Dictionaries of Wars, Revolutions, & Civil Unrest Ser.: No. 9). (Illus.). 448p. 1998. 65.00 (0-8108-3511-8) Scarecrow.

— Lee vs. McClellan: The First Campaign. (Illus.). 304p. 1996. 24.95 (0-89526-452-8) Regnery Pub.

Newell, Coke. Cow Chips Aren't for Dippin' A Guide to Life in the New Wild West. LC 95-44347. (Illus.). 96p. 1996. pap. 6.95 (0-87905-736-X) Gibbs Smith Pub.

— Dying Words: Colombian Journalists & the Cocaine Warlords. Maxwell, Marilyn C., ed. 192p. (Orig.). 1991. pap. 23.00 (0-9630149-0-0) Red Mesa.

***Newell, Coke.** Latter Days: A Guided Tour Through Six Billion Years of Mormonism. LC 00-27195. (Illus.). 288p. 2000. text 24.95 (0-312-24108-9) St Martin.

Newell, Colin. Methods & Models in Demography. LC 88-45079. 217p. 1990. reprint ed. pap. text 22.95 (0-89862-451-7, 2451) Guilford Pubns.

Newell, D. G., ed. Campylobacter: Progress in Research. (Illus.). 400p. 1982. text 183.00 (0-85200-455-9) Kluwer Academic.

Newell, David. Aspects of Employment Law. 217p. (C). 1990. 78.00 (1-85190-105-1, Pub. by Tolley Pubng) St Mut.

Newell, David, jt. auth. see Hinton, Dennis.

Newell, David W. & Aaslid, Rune. Transcranial Doppler. 288p. 1991. text 182.00 (0-88167-836-8) Lppncott W & W.

Newell, Diane, ed. The Development of the Pacific Salmon-Canning Industry: A Grown Man's Game. (Illus.). 336p. (C). 1989. text 65.00 (0-7735-0717-5, Pub. by McG-Queens Univ Pr) CUP Services.

Newell, Diane & Ommer, Rosemary E., eds. Fishing Places, Fishing People: Traditions & Issues in Canadian Small-Scale Fisheries. (Illus.). 412p. 1998. text 60.00 (0-8020-4116-7); pap. text 24.95 (0-8020-7959-8) U of Toronto Pr.

Newell, Diane G., et al, eds. Campylobacters, Helicobacters & Related Organisms: Proceedings of the 8th International Workshop Held in Winchester, England, July 10-13, 1995. LC 96-38654. 784p. 1997. 175.00 (0-306-45312-6, Kluwer Plenum) Kluwer Academic.

Newell, Dianne. Tangled Webs: Indians & the Law in Canada's Pacific Coast Fisheries. (Illus.). 288p. 1993. text 40.00 (0-8020-0541-0); pap. text 18.95 (0-8020-7746-3) U of Toronto Pr.

***Newell, E. T.** Dated Alexander Coins of Sidon & Ake. (Illus.). 2000. pap. 50.00 (0-915262-78-9) S J Durst.

Newell, E. T. Some Cypriot Alexanders. (Illus.). 1974. pap. 6.00 (0-932106-35-8) S J Durst.

Newell, Edward T. The Coinage of the Eastern Seleucid Mints, from Seleucus I to Antiochus III. (Numismatic Studies: No. 1). (Illus.). 363p. 1978. reprint ed. 40.00 (0-89722-174-5) Am Numismatic.

— Coinage of the Western Seleucid Mints, from Seleucus I to Antiochus III. (Numismatic Studies: No. 4). (Illus.). 552p. 1977. reprint ed. 50.00 (0-89722-183-4) Am Numismatic.

— The Coinages of Demetrius Poliorcetes. (Illus.). 1978. 100.00 (0-916710-36-X) Obol Intl.

— The Dated Alexander Coinage of Sidon & Ake. LC 78-63544. (Yale Oriental Series: Researches: No. 2). reprint ed. 24.50 (0-404-60272-X) AMS Pr.

— The Pre-Imperial Coinage of Roman Antioch. 45p. 1980. reprint ed. pap. 5.00 (0-916710-66-1) Obol Intl.

— Royal Greek Portrait Coins. LC 88-73216. (Illus.). 123p. 2000. reprint ed. pap. 15.00 (0-942666-60-7) S J Durst.

— The Seleucid Mint of Antioch. (Illus.). 1978. 50.00 (0-916710-38-6) Obol Intl.

— Some Cypriote "Alexanders" (Illus.). iii, 29p. 1974. pap. 5.00 (0-916710-14-9) Obol Intl.

— Standard Ptolemaic Silver. LC 80-70056. (Illus.). 1981. reprint ed. pap. 6.00 (0-915262-49-5) S J Durst.

Newell, Elaine. When Your Long-Term Marriage Ends: A Workbook for Divorced Women. LC 94-405. 234p. 1994. pap. 14.95 (0-89390-291-8) Resource Pubns.

Newell, Eric, jt. auth. see Kelly, Laura.

Newell, Frank W. Ophthalmology: Principles & Concepts. 8th ed. (Illus.). 608p. (C). (gr. 13). 1996. text 75.00 (0-8151-7093-9, 27525) Mosby Inc.

***Newell, Fred.** Loyalty.com: Customer Relationship Management in the New Era of Marketing. LC 99-58215. 325p. 2000. 29.95 (0-07-135775-0) McGraw.

Newell, Frederick. The New Rules of Marketing: How to Use One-to-One Relationship Marketing to Be the Leader in Your Industry. LC 97-9622. 1997. 27.95 (0-7863-1228-9, Irwn Prfssnl) McGraw-Hill Prof.

Newell, Frederick H. Water Resources: Present & Future Uses. LC 72-2859. (Use & Abuse of America's Natural Resources Ser.). (Illus.). 350p. 1972. reprint ed. 23.95 (0-405-04523-9) Ayer.

Newell, G. F. The M-M Service System with Ranked Servers in Heavy Traffic. (Lecture Notes in Economics & Mathematical Systems Ser.: Vol. 231). xi, 126p. 1984. 28.00 (0-387-13377-1) Spr-Verlag.

Newell, G. R. & Hong, W. K. The Biology & Prevention of Aerodigestive Tract Cancers. LC 92-21811. (Advances in Experimental Medicine & Biology Ser.: Vol. 320). (Illus.). 184p. (C). 1992. text 85.00 (0-306-44244-2, Kluwer Plenum) Kluwer Academic.

Newell, Gale E. & Kreuze, Jerry G. College Accounting, Vol. 2, Chapters 1-15. 48p. 1989. pap. text 19.95 (0-471-60765-7) Wiley.

— College Accounting, Vol. 3, Chapters 1-27. 276p. 1989. pap. text 16.95 (0-471-61379-7) Wiley.

Newell, Gale E. & Newell, Sydney B. Intro to Microcomputing 2e. 2nd ed. LC 88-26160. 832p. 1989. text 95.95 (0-471-60764-9) Wiley.

Newell, George E. & Durst, Russel K., eds. Exploring Texts: The Role of Discussion & Writing in the Teaching & Learning of Literature. 352p. 1993. text 59.95 (0-926842-24-2) CG Pubs Inc.

Newell, Gordon R. Ships of the Inland Sea: The Story of the Puget Sound Steamboats. 2nd ed. (Illus.). 257p. 1960. 14.95 (0-8323-0039-X) Binford Mort.

Newell, Guy R., ed. Cancer Prevention in Clinical Medicine. fac. ed. LC 83-22994. (Illus.). 271p. pap. 84.10 (0-7837-7220-3, 204707800005) Bks Demand.

Newell, Henry H., jt. auth. see Schwerin, Horace S.

Newell, Herbert M. & Newell, Jeanie P. History of Fayette County Baptist Association. 1968. 15.00 (0-317-13829-4) Banner Pr AL.

Newell, J. D. & Gabrielson, Ira W., eds. Medicine Looks at the Humanities. LC 87-17925. 206p. (Orig.). (C). 1987. lib. bdg. 44.00 (0-8191-6607-3) U Pr of Amer.

***Newell, J. Philip.** The Book of Creation: The Practice of Celtic Spirituality. LC 99-34545. 144p. 1999. pap. 8.95 (0-8091-3899-9) Paulist Pr.

— Celtic Benediction: Morning & Night Prayers. (Illus.). 2000. 16.00 (0-8028-3904-5) Eerdmans.

Newell, J. Philip. Celtic Prayers from Iona. LC 96-48044. (Illus.). 96p. 1997. 11.95 (0-8091-0488-1, 0488-1) Paulist Pr.

— Listening for the Heartbeat of God: A Celtic Spirituality. LC 97-20783. 128p. 1998. pap. 8.95 (0-8091-3759-3, 3759-3) Paulist Pr.

— One Foot in Eden: A Celtic View of the Stages of Life. LC 98-53159. 112p. 1999. pap. 8.95 (0-8091-3869-7) Paulist Pr.

***Newell, J. Philip.** Promptings from Paradise. LC 99-88940. 80p. 2000. pap. 7.95 (0-8091-3935-9) Paulist Pr.

Newell, James, ed. St. James Encyclopedia of Mortgage & Real Estate Finance. 400p. 1991. 55.00 (1-55862-154-7) St James Pr.

Newell, James, tr. see Negri, Antonio.

Newell, James, tr. see Villari, Rosario.

***Newell, James L.** Parties & Democracy in Italy. (Parties & Democracy Ser.). 224p. 2000. pap. 34.95 (1-85521-863-1, Pub. by Ashgate Pub); text 70.95 (1-85521-859-3, Pub. by Ashgate Pub) Ashgate Pub Co.

Newell, Jeanie P., jt. auth. see Newell, Herbert M.

Newell, John, jt. auth. see Calder, Nigel.

Newell, John A., et al. Ingenious Mechanisms for Designers & Inventors, Vol. 4. 4th ed. LC 30-14992. (Illus.). 493p. 1977. 30.00 (0-8311-1032-5) Indus Pr.

Newell, John D., Jr. & Kelsey, Charles A., eds. Digital Imaging in Diagnostic Radiology. fac. ed. LC 90-2231. (Illus.). 173p. 1990. reprint ed. pap. 53.70 (0-7837-7876-7, 204763300007) Bks Demand.

Newell, John D., Jr. & Tarver, Robert D., eds. Thoracic Radiology. LC 92-49207. 192p. 1993. text 108.00 (0-88167-983-6) Lppncott W & W.

Newell, John D., jt. auth. see Lynch, David A.

Newell, John F. Pump Maintenance Handbook for Water & Water Waste Treatment Plants. Date not set. 55.00 (1-56670-099-X, L1099) Lewis Pubs.

Newell, Karl M. & Corcos, Daniel M., eds. Variability & Motor Control. LC 92-33077. (Illus.). 520p. 1993. text 65.00 (0-87322-424-8, BNEW0424) Human Kinetics.

Newell, Karl M. & Molenaar, Peter C., eds. Applications of Nonlinear Dynamics to Developmental Process Modeling. LC 97-3672. 275p. 1997. write for info. (0-8058-2115-5) L Erlbaum Assocs.

Newell, Karl M., ed. see Roberts, Glyn C.

Newell, Karl M., jt. ed. see Sprague, Robert L.

Newell, Keith. Models. LC 98-4529. (Arts & Crafts Skills Ser.). 31p. 1998. lib. bdg. 6.95 (0-516-26451-6) Childrens.

— Models. LC 98-4529. (Arts & Crafts Skills Ser.). (J). 1999. 21.00 (0-516-21205-2) Childrens.

Newell, Kimberly, ed. see Billac, Pete.

Newell, L. Jackson, jt. auth. see McMurrin, Sterling M.

Newell, Lavone. Skagit Valley Fare: A Cookbook Celebrating Bounty & Beauty in the Pacific Northwest. (Illus.). 240p. (Orig.). 1995. pap. 19.95 (0-9615580-5-9) Island Pubs WA.

Newell, Leonard A., jt. ed. see Conrad, C. Eugene.

Newell, Leonard E., jt. auth. see Lamb, Sydney M.

Newell, Leslie, jt. auth. see Schambach, Frank F.

Newell, Linda K. & Avery, Valeen T. Mormon Enigma: Emma Hale Smith. 2nd ed. LC 93-32626. (Illus.). 432p. 1994. 16.95 (0-252-06291-4) U of Ill Pr.

***Newell, Linda King & Talbot, Vivian Linford.** A History of Garfield County. LC 98-61317. (Illus.). 1998. write for info. (0-913738-37-9) Utah St Hist Soc.

Newell, Linda King, et al. A History of Piute County. LC 98-61324. (Illus.). write for info. (0-913738-39-5) Utah St Hist Soc.

Newell, Liz. Why Sarah Ran Away with the Veterinarian. LC 93-27524. 171p. 1994. 22.00 (1-877946-45-1) Permanent Pr.

Newell, Lloyd, tr. Abide with Me: Inspirational Messages from "Music & the Spoken Word" LC 99-10522. 224p. 1999. 19.95 (1-57345-473-7) Deseret Bk.

Newell, Lloyd D. The Divine Connection: Understanding Your Inherent Worth. LC 92-33191. xii, 275p. 1992. 13.95 (0-87579-645-1) Deseret Bk.

— The Divine Connection: Unlocking Your Infinite Potential. LC 97-45963. 1998. pap. 14.95 (1-57345-365-X) Deseret Bk.

— May Peace Be with You: Messages from "The Spoken Word" LC 94-22202. xi, 263p. 1994. 13.95 (0-87579-866-7) Deseret Bk.

Newell, Malcolm. The Cold War. 1995. pap. 17.95 (0-949142-72-7, Pub. by Stirling Pr) Intl Spec Bk.

— 44 Ways to Poison Your Customer. 208p. 1997. pap. 19.95 (0-949142-02-6, Pub. by Stirling Pr) Intl Spec Bk.

— Master Stress. 1995. pap. 17.95 (0-949142-16-6, Pub. by Stirling Pr) Intl Spec Bk.

— More Secrets of Small Business Success. rev. ed. 126p. 1995. pap. 14.95 (0-949142-01-8, Pub. by Stirling Pr) Intl Spec Bk.

— Secrets of Small Business Success. rev. ed. 126p. 1995. pap. 14.95 (0-949142-24-7, Pub. by Stirling Pr) Intl Spec Bk.

— Ten Steps to Financial Health. 139p. 1995. pap. 17.95 (0-949142-32-8, Pub. by Stirling Pr) Intl Spec Bk.

Newell, Malcolm, jt. auth. see Thornton, Lorraine.

Newell, Margaret, jt. auth. see Efurd, Martha.

Newell, Margaret E. From Dependency to Independence: Economic Revolution in Colonial New England. LC 97-50566. (Illus.). 336p. 1998. 39.95 (0-8014-3405-X) Cornell U Pr.

Newell, Marie-Louise, jt. ed. see McIntyre, James.

Newell, Marie-Louise, jt. ed. see Mok, Jacqueline.

Newell, Martin L. A Treatise on the Action of Ejectment: Concurrent Remedies for the Recovery of the Possession of Real Property. cxvii, 935p. 1999. reprint ed. 265.00 (1-56169-521-1) Gaunt.

Newell, Martin L., jt. ed. see De Giovanni, Francisco.

Newell, Maxine. Charlie Steen's Mi Vida. (Illus.). 48p. 1998. pap. 5.95 (0-925685-96-8, 0801) Canyon Country Pubns.

Newell, Maxine & Barnes, Terby. The Untold History of the Grand Staircase - Escalante National Monument. LC 97-78052. (Canyon Country Ser.: Vol. 53). (Illus.). 128p. 1998. pap. 11.00 (0-925685-35-6) Canyon Country Pubns.

***Newell, Micael W.** Preparing for the Project Management Professional (PMP) Certification Exam. 2000. pap. 27.95 (0-8144-7088-2) AMACOM.

Newell, Michael. Using Nursing Case Management to Improve Health Outcomes: Recasting Theory, Tools & Care Delivery. 304p. 52.00 (0-8342-0623-4, 20623) Aspen Pub.

Newell, Michael & Pinardo, Mario. Reinventing Your Nursing Career: A Handbook for Success in the Age of Managed Care. LC 97-30346. 272p. 1997. pap. 21.00 (0-8342-1007-X, 21007) Aspen Pub.

Newell, Mike. Aestiuation. (Illus.). 56p. (Orig.). 1992. pap. 5.00 (1-880977-02-8) Watusi.

Newell, Mindy. The Catwoman: Her Sister's Keeper. O'Neil, Dennis, ed. (Illus.). 104p. 1991. pap. 9.95 (0-930289-97-8) DC Comics.

Newell, Mindy, et al. The Catwoman: Her Sister's Keeper. (Illus.). 1992. reprint ed. mass mkt. 9.99 (0-446-39366-5, Pub. by Warner Bks) Little.

Newell, Neil K. Lovers & Others: A Musical. 1997. pap. 5.00 (1-57514-307-0, 0102) Encore Perform Pub.

Newell, Norman D. Creation & Evolution: Myth or Reality. Anshen, Ruth N., ed. LC 84-17858. (Convergence Ser.). 266p. 1984. pap. 13.95 (0-275-91792-4, B1792, Praeger Pubs) Greenwood.

— Late Paleozoic Pelecypods: Pectinacea & Mytilacea, State Geological Survey of Kansas, Vol. 10. Gould, Stephen Jay, ed. LC 79-8337. (History of Paleontology Ser.). (Illus.). 1980. reprint ed. lib. bdg. 26.95 (0-405-12722-7) Ayer.

Newell, Olive. Tail of the Elephant: The Emigrant Experience on the Trucker Route of the Californial Trail 1844-1852. LC 97-35578. (Illus.). 400p. 1997. 25.00 (0-915641-08-9); pap. 16.50 (0-915641-09-7) Nevada County Hist Society.

Newell, Patrice, jt. auth. see Adams, Phillip.

Newell, Patricia J. Test Yourself Basic Mathmatics. LC 96-47152. (Test Yourself Ser.). 192p. 1996. pap. 11.95 (0-8442-2351-4, 23514, NTC Learningworks) NTC Contemp Pub Co.

Newell, Patricia J. & Lavrack, Kevin R. Elementary Algebra: A Laboratory Workbook. 3rd ed. 112p. (C). 1996. per., wbk. ed., lab manual ed. 13.59 (0-7872-2004-3) Kendall-Hunt.

— Pre-Algebra: A Laboratory Workbook. 3rd ed. 64p. (C). 1996. pap. text, per. 15.95 (0-7872-3471-0, 41347101) Kendall-Hunt.

***Newell, Patrick.** Military Collectibles. LC 99-58093. (Cool Collectibles Ser.). (Illus.). 48p. (J). (gr. 4-7). 2000. pap. 6.95 (0-516-23531-1) Childrens.

— Volunteering to Help Seniors. (Illus.). (YA). 2000. 19.00 (0-516-23399-8) Childrens.

— Volunteering to Help Seniors. (High Interest Bks.). (Illus.). 48p. (J). (gr. 4-7). 2000. pap. 6.95 (0-516-23577-X) Childrens.

Newell, Paul. Japan & the City of London. (Illus.). 180p. (C). 1996. 50.00 (0-485-11501-8, Pub. by Athlone Pr) Humanities.

***Newell, Pete.** Pete Newell's Defensive Basketball: Winning Techniques & Strategies. (Illus.). 220p. 2000. pap. 16.95 (1-58382-043-4) Coaches Choice.

Newell, Pete & Newell, Tom. Basketball Post Play. (Illus.). 144p. (Orig.). 1995. pap. 14.95 (1-57028-030-4, 80304H, Mstrs Pr) NTC Contemp Pub Co.

***Newell, Peter.** Climate for Change: Non-State Actors & the Global Politics of the Greenhouse. LC 99-87673. 256p. (C). 2000. Price not set. (0-521-63250-1) Cambridge U Pr.

Newell, Peter. Hole Book. 1976. 20.95 (0-8488-1440-1) Amereon Ltd.

— The Hole Book. LC 84-52396. (Illus.). 50p. (J). (gr. k-4). 1985. reprint ed. 14.95 (0-8048-1498-8) Tuttle Pubng.

— The Rocket Book. LC 91-3120. 48p. (J). (gr. 4-7). 1992. pap. 3.95 (0-486-26961-2) Dover.

N

An Asterisk (*) at the beginning of an entry indicates that the title is appearing for the first time.

— The Rocket Book. LC 69-12080. (Illus.). 52p. (J). (gr. k-4). 1969. reprint ed. 14.95 (*0-8048-0505-9*) Tuttle Pubng.

— The Slant Book. LC 67-12304. (Illus.). 50p. (J). (gr. k-4). 1967. reprint ed. 16.95 (*0-8048-0532-6*) Tuttle Pubng.

Newell, Peter, jt. auth. see Berkman, Alexander.

Newell, Peter E. Zapata of Mexico. 180p. (Orig.). 1996. 48.99 (*1-55164-073-2*, Pub. by Black Rose); pap. 19.99 (*1-55164-072-4*, Pub. by Black Rose) Consort Bk Sales.

— Zapata of Mexico. (Orig.). 1980. pap. 5.50 (*0-932366-08-2*) Black Thorn Bks.

Newell, Peter S. Topsys & Turvys. (Illus.). 74p. (J). (gr. 3-7). 1964. pap. 3.95 (*0-486-21231-9*) Dover.

— Topsys & Turvys. LC 87-51208. (Illus.). 72p. (J). (gr. k-4). 1988. 12.95 (*0-8048-1551-8*) Tuttle Pubng.

— Topsys & Turvys, No. 2. LC 87-51208. (Illus.). 72p. (J). 1988. 12.95 (*0-8048-1552-6*) Tuttle Pubng.

***Newell, Philip.** Project Studios. LC 99-43615. 224p. 1999. pap. 47.95 (*0-240-51573-0*, Focal) Buttrwrth-Heinemann.

— Recording Spaces. (Illus.). 208p. 2000. pap. 37.95 (*0-240-51627-3*, Focal) Buttrwrth-Heinemann.

Newell, Philip, ed. Recording Spaces. LC 98-158237. (Illus.). 208p. 2000. pap. 37.95 (*0-240-51507-2*, Focal) Buttrwrth-Heinemann.

Newell, Philip R. Studio Monitoring Design: A Personal View. LC 95-35572. (Illus.). 400p. 1995. text 69.95 (*0-240-51407-6*, Focal) Buttrwrth-Heinemann.

Newell, R. A., ed. see British Computer Society Staff.

Newell, R. C. Biology of Intertidal Animals. 781p. 1979. 200.00 (*0-9506920-0-X*) St Mut.

Newell, R. R., et al. An Inquiry into the Ethnic Resolution of Mesolithic Regional Groups: The Study of Their Decorative Ornaments in Time & Space. LC 90-2418. (Illus.). xxxii, 488p. 1990. 173.50 (*90-04-09097-5*) Brill Academic Pubs.

Newell, R. W. Objectivity, Empiricism & Truth. (Studies in Philosophical Psychology). 126p. 27.50 (*0-7102-0897-9*, 08979, Routledge Thoemms) Routledge.

Newell, Ray. The Morris Minor. (Album Ser.: No. 277). (Illus.). 32p. 1998. pap. 6.25 (*0-7478-0149-5*, Pub. by Shire Pubns) Parkwest Pubns.

— Morris Minor. (Illus.). 192p. 1998. 35.95 (*1-86126-133-0*, Pub. by Crolwood) Motorbooks Intl.

— Original Morris Minor: Restorers Guide to All Saloon Tourer/Convertible, Traveller & Light Commercial Models. (Illus.). 126p. 1993. text 35.95 (*1-870979-43-5*, Bay View Bks) MBI Pubg.

Newell, Richard S. Politics of Afghanistan. Park, Richard L., ed. LC 78-176487. (Illus.). 254p. 1972. text 42.50 (*0-8014-0688-9*) Cornell U Pr.

Newell, Robert. Buggy Riddles: Big Book. large type ed. (Little Books & Big Bks.). (Illus.). 16p. (J). (gr. 1-3). 1997. pap. text 29.85 (*0-8215-0985-3*) Sadlier.

Newell, Robert, ed. Developing Your Career in Nursing. LC 95-11758. 1996. 90.00 (*0-304-33226-7*); pap. 25.95 (*0-304-33228-3*) Continuum.

***Newell, Robert & Gournay, Kevin.** Mental Health Nursing: An Evidence-Based Approach. LC 99-34393. 2000. pap. text. write for info. (*0-443-05873-3*) Church.

Newell, Robert H. Avery Glibun: Or Between Two Fires. (Notable American Authors Ser.). 1999. reprint ed. lib. bdg. 125.00 (*0-7812-4631-8*) Rprt Serv.

— The Cloven Foot. (Notable American Authors Ser.). 1999. reprint ed. lib. bdg. 125.00 (*0-7812-4632-6*) Rprt Serv.

— The Orpheus C. Kerr Papers, 3 vols. LC 78-169922. reprint ed. 115.00 (*0-404-03670-8*) AMS Pr.

— The Orpheus C. Kerr Papers. (BCL1-PS American Literature Ser.). 1992. reprint ed. lib. bdg. 79.00 (*0-7812-6805-2*) Rprt Serv.

— The Palace Beautiful & Other Poems. (Notable American Authors Ser.). 1999. reprint ed. lib. bdg. 125.00 (*0-7812-4630-X*) Rprt Serv.

— Smoked Glass. LC 70-171060. reprint ed. 32.50 (*0-404-03663-5*) AMS Pr.

— There Was Once a Man. (Notable American Authors Ser.). 1999. reprint ed. lib. bdg. 125.00 (*0-7812-4634-2*) Rprt Serv.

— Walking Doll: Or, the Asters & Disasters of Society. LC 74-171061. reprint ed. 41.50 (*0-404-03664-3*) AMS Pr.

— The Walking Doll or The Asters & Disasters of Society. (Notable American Authors Ser.). 1999. reprint ed. lib. bdg. 125.00 (*0-7812-4633-4*) Rprt Serv.

Newell, Robery H. The Orpheus C. Kerr Papers. (Notable American Authors Ser.). 1999. reprint ed. lib. bdg. 125.00 (*0-7812-4629-6*) Rprt Serv.

Newell, Stephanie, ed. Writing African Women: Gender, Popular Culture & Literature in West Africa. LC 96-39523. 224p. (C). 1997. text 62.50 (*1-85649-449-7*, Pub. by Zed Books); text 22.50 (*1-85649-450-0*, Pub. by Zed Books) St Martin.

Newell, Steve. Achieving Better Golf: Practical Handbook. 1999. pap. text 10.95 (*0-7548-0006-7*, Lorenz Bks) Anness Pub.

***Newell, Steve.** Complete Golfer: A Celebration of Golf & a Complete Course on How to Play the Game. (Illus.). 256p. 1998. 19.98 (*0-7651-9575-5*) Smithmark.

Newell, Steve. Golf Rules: A Player's Guide. (Illus.). 80p. 1995. pap. 10.95 (*0-7137-2487-0*, Pub. by Blandford Pr) Sterling.

— Lowering Your Handicap. 1999. 12.99 (*1-84100-170-8*) Quadrillion Media.

— Pocket Book of Golf Rules. 1999. pap. text 7.99 (*1-84100-144-9*) Quadrillion Media.

Newell, Steve, jt. auth. see Els, Ernie.

Newell, Susan. The Healthy Organization: Fairness, Ethics, & Effective Management. LC 94-43132. (Essential Business Psychology Ser.). 208p. (C). 1995. pap. 15.95 (*0-415-10327-4*, C0547) Thomson Learn.

— The Healthy Organization: Fairness, Ethics, & Effective Management. LC 94-43132. (Essential Business Psychology Ser.). 208p. (C). (gr. 13). 1995. pap. 43.95 (*0-415-12677-0*, C0546) Thomson Learn.

Newell, Sydney B., jt. auth. see Newell, Gale E.

Newell, T. L. Hear a Million Men Marching, Z. O. S. S. LC 97-90284. 1998. pap. 8.95 (*0-533-12356-9*) Vantage.

Newell, Tom, jt. auth. see Newell, Pete.

Newell, W. R., jt. auth. see Kleinpoppen, H.

***Newell, Waller.** Ruling Passion: The Erotics of Statecraft in Platonic Political Philosophy. LC 99-58566. 288p. 2000. pap. 24.95 (*0-8476-9727-4*); text 70.00 (*0-8476-9726-6*) Rowman.

Newell, Waller, ed. What Is a Man? 3000 Years of Wisdom on the Art of Manly Virtue. LC 99-36304. (Illus.). 752p. 2000. 30.00 (*0-06-039296-7*, ReganBks) HarperTrade.

Newell, Waller R., jt. auth. see Emberley, Peter C.

Newell, William. Basic Sign Communication: Student Materials. 1983. pap. 20.95 (*0-913072-56-7*, SL074) Natl Assn Deaf.

— Basic Sign Communication: Vocabulary. (Basic Sign Communication Ser.). (Illus.). 162p. (Orig.). (C). 1983. pap. text 13.95 (*0-913072-55-9*) Natl Assn Deaf.

Newell, William, jt. auth. see Cagle, Keith M.

Newell, William H. Interdisciplinary Undergraduate Programs: A Directory. LC 85-62972. 1986. 34.95 (*0-9615764-0-5*) Assoc Integ.

— Population Change & Agricultural Development in 19th Century France. Bruchey, Stuart, ed. LC 77-77783. (Dissertations in European Economic History Ser.). (Illus.). 1978. lib. bdg. 29.95 (*0-405-10796-X*) Ayer.

Newell, William H., ed. Ancestors. (World Anthropology Ser.). xvi, 404p. 1976. 56.15 (*3-10-800162-0*) Mouton.

— Japan in Asia, 1942-1945. 132p. (Orig.). 1981. pap. 29.50 (*9971-69-014-4*, Pub. by Sngapore Univ Pr) Coronet Bks.

Newell, William H. & Association for Integrative Studies Staff. Interdisciplinarity: Essays from the Literature. LC 98-71553. 563 P. ;p. 1998. write for info. (*0-87447-608-9*) College Bd.

Newell, William L. The Secular Magi: Marx, Freud, & Nietzsche on Religion. 240p. (C). 1994. pap. text 21.50 (*0-8191-9588-X*) U Pr of Amer.

— Truth Is Our Mask: An Essay on Theological Method. LC 89-39428. 148p. (Orig.). (C). 1990. pap. text 17.00 (*0-8191-7621-4*) U Pr of Amer.

Newell, William M., tr. see Barth, H.

Newell, William R. The Book of the Revelation: Chapter by Chapter. 400p. 1994. pap. 16.99 (*0-8254-3325-8*) Kregel.

— Hebrews: Verse by Verse. LC 94-37701. 512p. 1995. pap. 18.99 (*0-8254-3327-4*, 95-017) Kregel.

— Romanos: Versiculo por Versiculo. Orig. Title: Romans: Verse by Verse. (SPA.). 464p. 1984. pap. 12.99 (*0-8254-1507-1*, Edit Portavoz) Kregel.

— Romans: Verse-by-Verse. LC 94-17883. 592p. 1994. pap. 19.99 (*0-8254-3326-6*) Kregel.

Newell, William W. Games & Songs of American Children. 1998. pap. 9.95 (*0-486-20354-9*) Dover.

— Games & Songs of American Children. 2nd ed. (Illus.). xx, 242p. 1998. reprint ed. pap. 19.95 (*0-8063-1351-X*) Clearfield Co.

— King Arthur & the Round Table: Tales Chiefly after the Old French of Chretien of Troveso with an Account of Arthurian Romance, 2 vols. 1976. lib. bdg. 250.00 (*0-8490-2115-4*) Gordon Pr.

Newendorp, Paul D. Decision Analysis for Petroleum Exploration LC 98-85458. x, 668p. 1996. write for info. (*0-9664401-0-2*) Planning Pr.

Newenhuyse, Elizabeth, ed. Hymns of Devotion & Praise: Words for Worship. LC 98-223701. 96p. 1998. pap. 2.99 (*0-87788-403-X*, H Shaw Pubs) Waterbrook Pr.

Newenhuyse, Elizabeth C. Cooked to Perfection: How to Respond When Life Turns up the Heat. LC 97-26779. 128p. 1997. pap. 8.99 (*0-310-20163-2*) Zondervan.

— God I Know You're Here Somewhere: Finding God in the Clutter of Life. 16p. 1996. pap. 8.99 (*1-55661-512-4*) Bethany Hse.

— I Married You: Celebrating the Romance & the Routine. LC 98-11059. 1998. pap. text 5.99 (*0-87788-613-X*, H Shaw Pubs) Waterbrook Pr.

— Sometimes I Feel Like Running Away. 176p. (Orig.). 1993. pap. 8.99 (*1-55661-317-2*) Bethany Hse.

Newenhuyse, Elizabeth C., ed. Encouragement for Couples: Lifelong Love & Partnership. (Pocketpac Bks.). 80p. (Orig.). 1993. mass mkt. 2.99 (*0-87788-213-4*, H Shaw Pubs) Waterbrook Pr.

— Strength from the Psalms: Verses to Comfort, Uplift, & Challenge. (Pocketpac Bks.). 80p. (Orig.). 1993. mass mkt. 2.99 (*0-87788-799-3*, H Shaw Pubs) Waterbrook Pr.

Newenhuyse, Elizabeth Cody. Encouragement for Teachers. 80p. 1999. pap. 2.99 (*0-87788-220-7*, H Shaw Pubs) Waterbrook Pr.

Newens, Jennifer, ed. The Best 50 Martinis. (Best 50 Ser.). 80p. 1998. pap. 5.95 (*1-55867-217-6*) Bristol Pub Ent CA.

Newens, Jennifer, ed. see Ilies, Algelika.

Newens, Jennifer, ed. see Ilies, Angelika.

Newens, Jennifer, ed. see Marjorie Poore Productions Staff.

Newens, Jennifer, jt. ed. see Poore, Marjorie Productions Staff.

Newens, Jennifer, ed. see Saelzer, Sabine & Dickhaut, Sebastian.

Newens, Jennifer, ed. see Von Cramm, Dagmar.

Newey, Charles & Weaver, Graham. Materials in Action: Principles & Practice. (Illus.). 405p. 1990. pap. text 56.95 (*0-7506-0390-9*) Buttrwrth-Heinemann.

Newey, Deni. Months of the Year Quiet Book. (Illus.). 45p. 1990. pap. 10.98 (*0-88290-363-2*) Horizon Utah.

Newey, Gail, jt. auth. see Rock, Lois.

***Newey, Glen.** The Politics of Toleration: Ethics & Virtue. 224p. 1999. 65.00 (*0-7486-1244-0*, Pub. by Edinburgh U Pr) Col U Pr.

Newey, Judge. Newey: The Official Referees' Courts - Practice & Procedure. 68p. 1988. pap. 38.00 (*0-406-11340-8*, U.K., MICHIE) LEXIS Pub.

Newey, Vincent, ed. Centering the Self: Subjectivity, Society & Reading from Thomas Gray to Thomas Hardy. 291p. 1995. 78.95 (*1-85928-151-6*, Pub. by Scolar Pr) Ashgate Pub Co.

Newey, Vincent & Shaw, Philip, eds. Mortal Pages, Literary Lives: Studies in the Nineteenth-Century Autobiography. (Nineteenth Century Ser.). 250p. 1996. text 78.95 (*1-85928-206-7*, Pub. by Scolar Pr) Ashgate Pub Co.

Newey, Vincent & Thompson, Ann, eds. Literature & Nationalism. 288p. (C). 1991. text 64.00 (*0-389-20954-6*) B&N Imports.

Newey, Vincent, jt. ed. see Beatty, Bernard.

Newfarmer, Richard. Transnational Conglomerates & the Economics of Dependent Development: A Case Study of the International Electrical Oligopoly & Brazils Electrical Industry. Altman, Edward I. & Walter, Ingo I., eds. LC 78-13842. (Contemporary Studies in Economic & Financial Analysis: Vol. 23). 420p. 1980. 78.50 (*0-89232-110-5*) Jai Pr.

Newfarmer, Richard S., ed. From Gunboats to Diplomacy: New U. S. Policies for Latin America. LC 83-16193. 276p. 1984. reprint ed. pap. 85.60 (*0-608-04014-2*, 206475000011) Bks Demand.

Newfeldt. Websters New World Dict 4th Co. 1998. 24.95 (*0-671-84886-0*) PB.

Newfield, Christopher. The Emerson Effect: Individualism & Submission in America. LC 95-23520. 288p. 1995. pap. text 16.95 (*0-226-57700-7*) U Ch Pr.

— The Emerson Effect: Individualism & Submission in America. LC 95-23520. 288p. 1995. lib. bdg. 45.00 (*0-226-57698-1*) U Ch Pr.

Newfield, Christopher, jt. ed. see Gordon, Avery.

Newfield, Dalton. Young Winston, 1874-1898: A Biography Using Stamps. (Educational Ser.: No. 2). (Illus.). 16p. 1990. pap. 5.00 (*0-943879-04-3*) Churchill Ctr.

Newfield, Frank. Creatures: An Alphabet for Adults & Worldly Children. (Illus.). 32p. (YA). (gr. 5 up). 1999. bds. write for info. (*0-88899-333-1*, Pub. by Grolundwood-Douglas) Publishers Group.

Newfield, Marcia. Where Did You Put Your Sleep? LC 83-2785. (Illus.). 32p. (J). (gr. k-4). 1983. lib. bdg. 13.95 (*0-689-50286-9*) McElderry Bks.

Newfield, Nancy L. & Nielsen, Barbara. Hummingbird Gardens: Attracting Nature's Jewels to Your Backyard. Brooks, Cristen, ed. (Illus.). 144p. 1996. 34.95 (*1-881527-88-3*, Chapters Bks); pap. 19.95 (*1-881527-87-5*, Chapters Bks) HM.

Newfield, Phillippa. Neuroanesthesia. 2nd ed. 458p. 1991. pap. text 71.00 (*0-316-60471-2*, Little Brwn Med Div) Lppncott W & W.

Newfield, Phillippa & Cottrell, James E. Handbook of Neuroanesthesia: Clinical & Physiologic Essentials. 437p. 1983. 29.50 (*0-316-60470-4*, Little Brwn Med Div) Lppncott W & W.

Newforth, Patricia, ed. & selected by see Bent, Arthur C.

Newgarden, Albert, ed. The Field Sales Manager: A Manual of Practice. LC 60-12757. (American Management Association, Management Report Ser.: No. 48). 380p. reprint ed. pap. 117.80 (*0-608-13487-2*, 202261400028) Bks Demand.

Newgreen, Don, ed. Epithelial-Mesenchymal Transitions, Pt. II. (Journal Ser.: Vol. 156, No. 3, 1996). (Illus.). 86p. 1997. pap. 91.50 (*3-8055-6435-X*) S Karger.

Newgreen, Don, jt. ed. see Ferguson, M.

***Newhagen, John.** Understanding the Net. 2000. 55.00 (*0-8133-9144-X*, Pub. by Westview) HarpC.

Newhagen, John. Understanding the Network. 25.00 (*0-8133-9145-8*) Westview.

Newhall, Amy W., jt. auth. see O'Bannon, George W.

Newhall, Arthur. Calligraphy. (How to Draw & Paint Ser.). (Illus.). 32p. (Orig.). 1990. pap. 6.95 (*1-56010-064-8*, HT-227) W Foster Pub.

— Calligraphy & Lettering Design. (Artist's Library). (Illus.). 64p. (Orig.). 1990. pap. 7.95 (*1-56010-031-1*, AL15) W Foster Pub.

— Calligraphy Kit. (Illus.). 32p. 1996. pap. text 14.95 (*1-56010-197-0*, K07) W Foster Pub.

Newhall, Barker. The Barker Family of Plymouth Colony & County. (Illus.). 102p. 1988. reprint ed. lib. bdg. 29.00 (*0-8328-0188-7*) Higginson Bk Co.

Newhall, Barker. The Barker Family of Plymouth Colony & County. (Illus.). 102p. 1988. reprint ed. pap. 19.00 (*0-8328-0189-5*) Higginson Bk Co.

Newhall, Beaumont. The Daguerreotype in America. (Illus.). 272p. 1976. reprint ed. pap. 17.95 (*0-486-23322-7*) Dover.

— The History of Photography: From 1839 to the Present Day. 5th rev. ed. (Illus.). 320p. 1982. pap. 32.95 (*0-87070-381-1*, Pub. by Mus of Modern Art) Little.

— Photography & the Book. 1983. pap. 10.00 (*0-89073-066-0*, 290) Boston Public Lib.

— Supreme Instants: The Photography of Edward Weston. 191p. 1986. 50.00 (*0-317-53697-4*) Little.

Newhall, Beaumont, et al. Brett Weston: Master Photographer. Christopher, Carol W., ed. (Illus.). 180p. 1989. 95.00 (*0-9616515-3-9*) Photog West Graphics.

Newhall, Beaumont, ed. & selected by see Davidson, Kathryn & Glassman, Elizabeth.

Newhall, Benjamin F. Sketches of Saugus, Massachusetts. (Illus.). 262p. 1997. reprint ed. pap. 29.50 (*0-8328-7008-0*); reprint ed. lib. bdg. 37.50 (*0-8328-7007-2*) Higginson Bk Co.

Newhall, Charles L. The Adventures of Jack: Or Life on A Wave. 93p. 1981. 12.95 (*0-87770-263-2*) Ye Galleon.

Newhall, Christopher G. & Punongbayan, Raymundo S., eds. Fire & Mud: Eruptions & Lahars of Mount Pinatubo, Philippines. LC 96-33410. (Illus.). 1120p. 1997. 80.00 (*0-295-97585-7*) U of Wash Pr.

Newhall, David S. Clemenceau: A Life at War. LC 90-20994. (Illus.). 724p. 1991. lib. bdg. 139.95 (*0-88946-785-4*) E Mellen.

Newhall, Fales H. & Terry, Milton S. Whedon's Commentary on the Old Testament Vol. 1: Genesis-Exodus. 1987. 25.99 (*0-88019-216-X*) Schmul Pub Co.

Newhall, George N. Sunspots, Dust & Rainfall. LC 87-92277. (Illus.). 208p. (Orig.). (C). 1988. text 10.00 (*0-9619881-0-X*); per. 8.00 (*0-9619881-1-8*) S & G Pub.

Newhall, Guy. Settlement of Estates & Fiduciary Law in Massachusetts, 3 vols. 4th ed. 1992. suppl. ed. 50.00 (*0-317-03269-0*) West Group.

— Settlement of Estates & Fiduciary Law in Massachusetts, 3 vols., Set. 5th ed. LC 94-79126. 125.00 (*0-318-11944-7*) West Group.

Newhall, James R., jt. auth. see Lewis, Alonzo.

Newhall, Nancy. P. H. Emerson: The Fight for Photography As Fine Art. LC 74-76911. (Monographs). (Illus.). 266p. 76.00 (*0-89381-383-4*) Aperture.

Newhall, Nancy, ed. The Daybooks of Edward Weston, 2 vols. in 1, Vol. 1: Mexico; Vol. 2: California. (Illus.). 608p. 1991. pap. 53.00 (*0-89381-445-8*) Aperture.

Newhall, Nancy, jt. auth. see Adams, Ansel.

Newhall, Richard. The Crusades. rev. ed. (Illus.). 64p. (C). 1991. pap. text 2.25 (*1-877891-03-7*) Paperbook Pr Inc.

Newhall, William. Fundamentals of College Math. (Adaptable Courseware Ser.). 1996. suppl. ed. 5.25 (*0-534-49773-X*) Brooks-Cole.

Newham, Cameron. Learning the Bash Shell. 310p. (Orig.). 1995. pap. 27.95 (*1-56592-147-X*) Thomson Learn.

Newham, Cameron & Rosenblatt, Bill. Learning the Bash Shell. 2nd ed. LC 98-132271. 318p. (Orig.). 1998. pap. 29.95 (*1-56592-347-2*) OReilly & Assocs.

Newham, Paul. The Healing Voice. LC 99-15435. 224p. 1999. pap. 16.95 (*1-86204-548-8*, Pub. by Element MA) Penguin Putnam.

— Therapeutic Voicework: Principles & Practice for the Use of Singing As Therapy. LC 98-144494. 600p. 1998. pap. 59.95 (*1-85302-361-2*, Pub. by Jessica Kingsley) Taylor & Francis.

— Using Voice & Movement. 1998. pap. 26.95 (*1-85302-592-5*) Jessica Kingsley.

— Using Voice & Song in Therapy: The Practical Application of Voice Movement Therapy LC 98-50699. 1999. 26.95 (*1-85302-590-9*) Taylor & Francis.

Newhan, Ross. The Anaheim Angels: A Complete History. LC 99-47100. 384p. 2000. pap. 14.95 (*0-7868-8450-9*, Pub. by Hyprn Ppbks) Little.

***Newhardt, David.** Dodge Challenger & Plymouth Barracuda. (Illus.). 96p. 2000. pap. 13.95 (*0-7603-0772-5*, 129801AP, Pub. by MBI Pubg) Motorbooks Intl.

Newhardt, David. Mercury Muscle Cars. LC 99-32415. (Illus.). 128p. 1999. pap. 21.95 (*0-7603-0549-8*, 128062AP) MBI Pubg.

Newhart, Max R. American Battleships: A Pictorial History of BB-1 to BB-71. LC 95-78913. (Illus.). 106p. 1996. pap. 9.95 (*1-57510-004-5*) Pictorial Hist.

Newhaus, Tom. The Informed Baker. 2nd rev. ed. (Illus.). 335p. 1998. pap. text 39.95 (*0-9665117-0-0*) Neuhaus Features.

***Newhauser, Johannes, ed.** Supporting Love: Bert Hellinger's Work with Couples. Beaumont, Colleen, tr. 220p. 2000. 28.95 (*1-891944-49-5*) Zeig Tucker.

***Newhauser, Richard.** The Early History of Greed: The Sin of Avarice in Early Medieval Thought & Literature. (Cambridge Studies in Medieval Literature: No. 41). 262p. 2000. 64.95 (*0-521-38522-9*) Cambridge U Pr.

Newhauser, Richard & Alford, John A., eds. Literature & Religion in the Later Middle Ages: Philological Studies in Honor of Siegfried Wenzel. (Medieval & Renaissance Texts & Studies: Vol. 118). 432p. 1995. 25.00 (*0-86698-172-1*, MR118) MRTS.

Newhnam, Rex E. Away with Arthritis. 1994. 12.50 (*0-533-10814-4*) Vantage.

Newhof Pyle, Susan, ed. A Most Superior Land: Life in the Upper Peninsula of Michigan. 2nd ed. LC 83-620003. (Michigan Heritage Bks.: Vol. 4). (Illus.). 192p. 1987. 24.95 (*0-941912-03-5*) TwoPeninsula Pr.

Newhof, Susan & Pyle, Stephen J. Michigan's Town & Country Inns. 4th ed. LC 97-33944. (Illus.). 280p. 1998. pap. 16.95 (*0-472-08392-9*, 08392) U of Mich Pr.

Newhold, Paul, jt. auth. see Granger, C. W.

***Newhouse, Brian.** A Crossing: A Cyclist's Journey Home. LC 98-16184. 288p. 1998. mass mkt. 14.00 (*0-671-56898-1*, Pocket Books) PB.

***Newhouse, Dave.** The Million Dollar Backfield: The San Francisco 49ers in the 1950s. 250p. (C). 2000. pap. 16.95 (*1-58394-007-3*) Frog Ltd CA.

Newhouse, Dave, jt. auth. see Otto, Jim.

Newhouse, Dora. The Encyclopedia of Homonyms-Sound Alikes: Condensed & Abridged Edition. LC 76-50944. (Illus.). (J). (gr. 6-12). 1978. pap. 6.95 (*0-918050-00-6*) Newhouse Pr.

— How to Become an American Citizen: Amnesty - Legalization - Voter Registration. 8th ed. LC 88-90865. (ENG & SPA., Illus.). 1989. pap. 8.95 (*0-918050-61-8*) Newhouse Pr.

— How to Work or Communicate in a Hotel, Motel or Inn. LC 77-80666.Tr. of Como Trabajar o Comunicar en un Hotel, Motel o Posada. (SPA., Illus.). 1977. pap. 6.95 (*0-918050-47-2*) Newhouse Pr.

— How to Work or Communicate in a Private Home. LC 77-80665.Tr. of Como Trabajar o Comunicar en un Casa Privada. (SPA., Illus.). 1977. pap. 6.95 (*0-918050-48-0*) Newhouse Pr.

An Asterisk (*) at the beginning of an entry indicates that the title is appearing for the first time.

— How to Work or Communicate in a Restaurant or Bar. LC 77-80667.Tr. of Como Trabajar o Comunicar en un Restaurante o Bar. (SPA., Illus.). 1977. pap. 6.95 (*0-918050-49-9*) Newhouse Pr.

— Illustrated Homonyms 'Sound-Alikes' - Homonimos 'Sonidos Identicos' (ENG & SPA., Illus.). 1979. 9.95 (*0-918050-09-X*); pap. 6.95 (*0-918050-27-8*) Newhouse Pr.

Newhouse, Dora. Homonyms Plus. (YA). (gr. 6-12). 1979. 4.95 (*0-918050-44-8*) Newhouse Pr.

— Homonyms Plus - Student Workbook. (YA). (gr. 6-12). 1979. student ed. 6.95 (*0-918050-42-1*) Newhouse Pr.

— Homonyms Plus - Teacher's Edition. (YA). (gr. 6-12). 1979. pap., teacher ed. 6.95 (*0-918050-41-3*) Newhouse Pr.

Newhouse, Dora & Santos, Henrietta. Instructional Study Guide to United States History/Government/Geography. (Illus.). 256p. (Orig.). 1990. pap. text 7.50 (*0-918050-64-2*) Newhouse Pr.

Newhouse, Edward. This Is Your Day. LC 74-2800. (Labor Movement in Fiction & Non-Fiction Ser.). reprint ed. 45.00 (*0-404-58456-X*) AMS Pr.

Newhouse, Elizabeth L., ed. Inventors & Discoverers: Changing Our World. (Illus.). 320p. 1988. 36.95 (*0-87044-752-1*) Natl Geog.

— Inventors & Discoverers: Changing Our World. (Illus.). 320p. 1994. 35.00 (*0-87044-751-3*) Natl Geog.

Newhouse, Elizabeth L., jt. auth. see National Geographic Staff.

Newhouse, Elizabeth L., ed. see McDowell, Bart.

Newhouse, Elizabeth L., ed. see National Geographic Society Book Division Staff.

Newhouse, Elizabeth L., ed. see Scott, John A.

Newhouse, Flower A. The Christward Way. 396p. 1984. pap. 16.00 (*0-910378-19-3*) Christward.

— Disciplines of the Holy Quest. 5th ed. LC 59-15553. (Illus.). 196p. 1959. 16.00 (*0-910378-05-3*) Christward.

— The Drama of Incarnation. 4th ed. 80p. 1948. 12.00 (*0-910378-04-5*) Christward.

— Gateways into Light. 3rd ed. LC 74-75517. 160p. 1974. pap. 12.00 (*0-910378-09-6*) Christward.

— Here Are Your Answers, Vol. I. 3rd ed. LC 49-16192. 248p. 1948. 14.00 (*0-910378-01-0*) Christward.

— Here Are Your Answers, Vol. II. 2nd ed. LC 76-103410. 228p. 1969. 14.00 (*0-910378-06-1*) Christward.

— Here Are Your Answers, Vol. III. Boult, Pamela, ed. LC 82-73083. 222p. 1982. 14.00 (*0-910378-18-5*) Christward.

— The Journey Upward. Bengtson, Athene, ed. LC 78-74955. 191p. (Orig.). 1978. pap. 12.00 (*0-910378 15-0*) Christward.

— The Kingdom of the Shining Ones. 8th ed. 92p. 1955. 16.00 (*0-910378-03-7*) Christward.

— The Meaning & Value of the Sacraments. 2nd ed. LC 77-186123. 123p. 1971. 13.00 (*0-910378-07-X*) Christward.

Newhouse, Flower A. A Measure of Days. LC 85-72907. 63p. 1985. pap. 9.00 (*0-910378-20-7*) Christward.

Newhouse, Flower A. Prayers of a Mystic. LC 86-71083. 102p. (Orig.). 1986. pap. 9.00 (*0-910378-21-5*) Christward.

— Rediscovering the Angels & Natives of Eternity. 8th ed. (Illus.). 156p. 1966. 16.00 (*0-910378-02-9*) Christward.

— The Sacred Heart of Christmas. 2nd ed. Bengtson, Athene, ed. LC 78-74956. (Illus.). 93p. 1978. pap. 10.00 (*0-910378-14-2*) Christward.

— Seven Paths Upward. 8th rev. ed. Bitling, Athene, ed. & illus. by. 68p. 1997. spiral bd. 12.00 (*0-910378-00-2*, TCM Pubns) Christward.

— Songs of Deliverance. LC 72-94582. 263p. 1972. 14.00 (*0-910378-08-8*) Christward.

— These, Too, Shall Be Loved. 2nd ed. LC 76-49246. 104p. 1976. pap. 9.00 (*0-910378-11-8*) Christward.

— Through Lent to Resurrection. Bengtson, Melodie N., ed. LC 77-77088. (Illus.). 72p. 1977. pap. 9.00 (*0-910378-13-4*) Christward.

— Touched by Angels: How Angels Influence Our Daily Lives. LC 98-9680. (Illus.). 165p. 1998. pap. 15.95 (*1-885394-31-4*) Bluestar Communs.

— Travel with Inner Perceptiveness. (Illus.). 112p. (Orig.). 1979. pap. text 9.00 (*0-910378-16-9*) Christward.

Newhouse, Flower A., et al. Insights into Reality. 2nd ed. LC 75-36869. 191p. 1975. pap. 12.00 (*0-910378-10-X*) Christward.

Newhouse, George, jt. auth. see Ezell, Elaine.

Newhouse, J. P. & Culyer, A. J. Handbook of Health Economics. (Handbooks in Economics Ser.: Vol. I). 2000. write for info. (*0-444-82290-9*) Elsevier.

Newhouse, Janette K. Rural & Urban Patterns: An Exploration of How Older Adults Use In-Home Care. LC 94-22166. (Studies on the Elderly in America). (Illus.). 256p. 1995. text 76.00 (*0-8153-1631-3*) Garland.

Newhouse, Jeffrey H. Understanding MRI. 1991. 54.95 (*0-316-60474-7*, Little Brwn Med Div) Lppncott W & W.

***Newhouse, John.** Europe Adrift. 339p. 2000. reprint ed. text 27.00 (*0-7881-6996-3*) DIANE Pub.

Newhouse, John. Europe Adrift: Its Cultural, Social, Political & Economic Confusion after the Cold War. LC 97-2943. 336p. 1997. 27.50 (*0-679-43370-8*) Pantheon.

Newhouse, Joseph P. Free for All? Lessons from the Rand Health Insurance Experiment. (Illus.). 504p. 1996. pap. 24.95 (*0-674-31914-1*) HUP.

***Newhouse, Joseph P., ed.** Structuring Medicare Choices. 123p. 1998. pap. text 15.00 (*1-884902-11-1*) Natl Acad.

Newhouse, Joseph P. & Insurance Experiment Group Staff. Free for All? Lessons from the Rand Health Insurance Experiment. LC 93-1356. (Illus.). 592p. (C). 1994. 57.00 (*0-674-31846-3*) HUP.

Newhouse, Joseph P., ed. see National Bureau of Economic Research Conference on.

Newhouse, Kay. Catch Me: The Journal of a Woman's Surprise. (Illus.). viii, 126p. (Orig.). 1996. pap. 15.00 (*0-9652045-0-2*) Pelle Bks.

Newhouse, M., jt. auth. see Morgenroth, Konrad.

Newhouse, Margaret. Outside the Ivory Tower: A Guide for Academics Considering Alternative Careers. 164p. (Orig.). 1993. pap. 13.00 (*0-943747-08-2*) Harvard OCS.

Newhouse, Margaret L. Cracking the Academia Nut: A Guide to Preparing for Your Academic Career. LC 98-143053. 173p. 1997. pap. 13.00 (*0-943747-18-X*) Harvard OCS.

Newhouse, Michael T. & Barnes, Peter J. Conquering Asthma. 2nd ed. 112p. 1994. pap. 9.95 (*1-896998-01-1*, Empowering Pr) Decker.

Newhouse, Michael T. & Barnes, Peter J. Conquering Asthma: An Illustrated Guide to Understanding & Care for Adults. (Illus.). 112p. (Orig.). 1995. pap. 12.95 (*0-9695171-1-4*) Login Pubs Consort.

Newhouse, Nancy. U. S. History: The Twentieth Century. (Learning Packets - Social Sciences Ser.). (Illus.). 74p. 1996. ring bd. 18.00 (*1-56976-042-X*, 1431-F3) Zephyr Pr AZ.

Newhouse, Neville H. Joseph Conrad. LC 69-16157. (Arco Literary Critiques Ser.). 143 p. 1969. write for info. (*0-668-01888-7*, ARCO) Macmillan.

Newhouse, Sue. Creative Hand Embroidery. (Illus.). 64p. (Orig.). (YA). 1993. pap. 14.95 (*0-85532-727-8*, 727-8, Pub. by Srch Pr) A Schwartz & Co.

— Hand Embroidered Country Scenes. 1997. pap. 19.95 (*0-85532-819-3*, Pub. by Srch Pr) A Schwartz & Co.

Newhouse, Susan M., jt. auth. see Mabee, Carleton.

***Newhouse, Thomas.** The Beat Generation & the Popular Novel in the United States, 1945-1970. (Illus.). 199p. 2000. per. 29.95 (*0-7864-0841-3*) McFarland & Co.

Newhouse, Tom & Routh, David. Ejaculation Control Manual: Extended Lovemaking. 74p. (Orig.). 1992. pap. 7.95 (*0-9625096-1-2*) Starside Pub.

Newhouse, Victoria. Towards a New Museum. LC 98-4584. (Illus.). 1997. pap. 29.95 (*1-885254-60-1*, Pub. by Monacelli Pr) Penguin Putnam.

Newhouse, Wade J. Constitutional Uniformity & Equality in State Taxation, 2 vols. 2nd ed. LC 84-82004. 153p. 1984. lib. bdg. 120.00 (*0-89941-376-5*, 303490) W S Hein.

Newick, Glenn. The Ultimate in Rifle Accuracy. (Illus.). 210p. (Orig.). 1990. pap. 11.95 (*0-88317-159-7*) Stoeger Pub Co.

Newiger, Hans-Joachim. Untersuchungen Zu Gorgias' Schrift Ueber das Nichtseiende. (C). 1973. 89.25 (*3-11-003432-8*) De Gruyter.

***Newing, Angela.** Light, Visible & Invisible & Its Medical Applications. 200p. 1999. 28.00 (*1-86094-164-8*) Imperial College.

Newing, Edward G., jt. ed. see Conrad, Edgar W.

Newing, Francis. First Impressions: Printing the Church Magazine & Other Literature. (C). 1989. 26.00 (*0-9510086-8-4*, Pub. by Jay Bks) St Mut.

Newington, Irene. Presents. LC 95-60782. (Fun to Do Ser.). (Illus.). 32p. (J). (gr. 2 up). 1995. lib. bdg. 15.95 (*1-887238-05-0*) Fitzgerald.

Newitt, jt. ed. see Hintjens, Helen.

Newitt, L. R., et al. IAGA Guide for Magnetic Repeat Station Surveys. (Illus.). 116p. (Orig.). 1996. pap. 25.00 (*0-9650686-1-7*) Intl Assn Geomag.

Newitt, Malyn. A History of Mozambique. LC 96-7477. (Illus.). 400p. 1995. pap. 27.50 (*0-253-34007-1*); text 59.95 (*0-253-34006-3*) Ind U Pr.

Newitt, Malyn D. D. & Bennum, Mervyn, eds. Negotiating Justice: A New Constitution for South Africa. LC 96-140518. 208p. 1995. pap. text 19.95 (*0-85989-459-2*, Pub. by Univ Exeter Pr) Northwestern U Pr.

Newitt, Marilyn D., ed. The First Portuguese Colonial Empire. 112p. 1986. pap. text 19.95 (*0-85989-257-3*, Pub. by Univ Exeter Pr) Northwestern U Pr.

Newitz, Annalee, jt. auth. see Wray, Matt.

Newkirk, David, jt. ed. see Schetgen, Robert.

Newkirk, David P., jt. auth. see Rohde, Ulrich L.

Newkirk, G., ed. see International Astronomical Union Staff.

Newkirk, Ingrid. Free the Animals! The Inside Story of the Animal Liberation Front & Its Founder, "Valerie" LC 91-51222. (Illus.). 224p. (Orig.). 1992. pap. 13.95 (*1-879360-11-X*) Noble Pr.

***Newkirk, Ingrid.** Free the Animals: The Story of the Animal Liberation Front. rev. ed. 2000. pap. 17.00 (*1-930051-22-0*) Lantern Books.

Newkirk, Ingrid. Save the Animals! One Hundred One Easy Things You Can Do. xvi, 192p. 1990. mass mkt. 4.95 (*0-446-39234-0*) Warner Bks.

— 250 Things You Can Do to Make Your Cat Adore You. LC 97-52060. 208p. 1998. per. 11.00 (*0-684-83648-3*, Fireside) S&S Trade Pap.

— You Can Save the Animals: 251 Ways to Stop Thoughtless Cruelty. LC 98-32055. 253p. 1999. pap. 12.95 (*0-7615-1673-5*) Prima Pub.

Newkirk, Ingrid & People for the Ethical Treatment of Animals Staff. Kids Can Save the Animals: 101 Easy Things to Do. 1991. mass mkt. 6.99 (*0-446-39271-5*, Pub. by Warner Bks) Little.

Newkirk, Ingrid, jt. auth. see People for the Ethical Treatment of Animals Staff.

Newkirk, J. B. & Wernick, J. H., eds. Direct Observation of Imperfections in Crystals: Proceedings. LC 61-16633. 629p. reprint ed. pap. 195.00 (*0-608-09953-8*, 200068400038) Bks Demand.

Newkirk, J. B., ed. see International Conference on Structure & Properties.

Newkirk, Jay. Hey Batter! LC 86-82532. 260p. (Orig.). 1987. pap. 7.95 (*0-9617711-0-0*) HR Press.

Newkirk, Lauren, ed. see Schultz, Dave.

Newkirk, Lois G., ed. Hudson: A Survey of Historic Buildings in an Ohio Town. LC 88-8442. (Illus.). 319p. reprint ed. pap. 98.90 (*0-7837-5126-5*, 204485400004) Bks Demand.

Newkirk, Pamela. Within the Veil: Black Journalists, White Media. 2000. 24.95 (*0-8147-5799-5*) NYU Pr.

Newkirk, R. A. The Eriophyid Mites of Alfred Nalepa. (Thomas Say Monographs: Vol. 9). 138p. 1984. 12.50 (*0-938522-22-1*, ESATS9) Entomol Soc.

Newkirk, Robert, Jr., jt. ed. see Anderson, Douglas T.

Newkirk, Sally L. Some Tastes of Home. (Illus.). 480p. 1989. 14.95 (*0-9620596-0-9*) S L Newkirk.

Newkirk, Thomas. Critical Thinking & Writing: Reclaiming the Essay. Harste, Jerome C., ed. & intro. by. LC 89-23515. (Monographs on Teaching Critical Thinking). 56p. (C). 1989. pap. 8.95 (*0-927516-04-7*) ERIC-REC.

— More Than Stories: The Range of Children's Writing. LC 88-26067. (Illus.). 228p. (Orig.). (C). 1989. pap. 29.50 (*0-435-08490-9*, 08490) Heinemann.

— To Compose: Teaching Writing in High School & College. 2nd ed. LC 89-31484. 312p. (C). (gr. 9). 1989. pap. text 28.00 (*0-435-08496-8*, 08496) Heinemann.

Newkirk, Thomas, ed. Nuts & Bolts: A Practical Guide to Teaching College Composition. LC 92-42069. 216p. (C). 1993. pap. text 22.50 (*0-86709-321-8*, 0321, Pub. by Boynton Cook Pubs) Heinemann.

— Workshop 5: The Writing Process Revisited. (Workshops by & for Teachers Ser.). 188p. (C). 1993. pap. text 18.50 (*0-435-08798-3*, 08798) Heinemann.

— Workshop 4: The Teacher As Researcher. (Workshops by & for Teachers Ser.). 187p. (C). (gr. k). 1992. pap. text 17.50 (*0-435-08728-2*, 08728) Heinemann.

Newkirk, Thomas & Atwell, Nancie, eds. Understanding Writing: Ways of Observing, Learning & Teaching. 2nd ed. LC 87-11872. 312p. (Orig.). (C). (gr. k). 1987. reprint ed. pap. text 26.00 (*0-435-08441-0*, 08441) Heinemann.

Newkirk, Thomas & McLure, Patricia. Listening In: Children Talk about Books (& Other Things) 176p. (C). 1993. pap. 14.95 (*0-435-08713-4*, 08713) Heinemann.

Newkirk, Tom, jt. ed. see Tobin, Lad.

Newkirk, Valerie. Fresh Cut Roses from Colombia & Ecuador: An International Trade Investigation. (Illus.). 138p. (Orig.). (C). 1995. pap. text 40.00 (*0-7881-2369-6*) DIANE Pub.

Newkirk, William & Linden, Richard. Managing Emergency Medical Services: Principles & Practices. 272p. 1984. 27.95 (*0-317-58947-4*) P-H.

Newkirk, William L., ed. Occupational Health Services: Practical Strategies for Improving Quality & Controlling Costs. LC 93-26520. 332p. 1993. pap. 56.95 (*1-55648-108-X*, 155400) AHPI.

Newkome, George. Advances in Dendritic Macromolecules, Vol. 4. Date not set. 109.50 (*0-7623-0347-6*) Jai Pr.

Newkome, George R., ed. Advances in Dendritic Macromolecules, Vol. 1. 198p. 1994. 109.50 (*1-55938-696-7*) Jai Pr.

— Advances in Dendritic Macromolecules, Vol. 2. 204p. 1995. 109.50 (*1-55938-939-7*) Jai Pr.

— Advances in Dendritic Macromolecules, Vol. 3. 1996. 109.50 (*0-7623-0069-8*) Jai Pr.

Newkome, George R., et al, eds. Pyridine & Its Derivatives, Vol. 14, Pt. 5. LC 59-103038. (Chemistry of Heterocyclic Compounds, a Series of Monographs: Vol. 14, Pt. 5). 714p. 1984. 635.00 (*0-471-05072-5*, 1-079) Wiley.

Newkome, George R. & Paudler, William W. Contemporary Hetercyclic Chemistry: Syntheses, Reactions & Applications. LC 82-4795. 432p. 1982. 135.00 (*0-471-06279-0*, Wiley-Interscience) Wiley.

Newkome, George R. & Vogtley, F. Dendritic Molecules: Concepts * Synthesis * Perspectives. (Illus.). 262p. 1996. 195.00 (*3-527-29325-6*, Wiley-VCH) Wiley.

Newkumet, Vynola B. & Meredith, Howard L. Hasinai: A Traditional History of the Caddo Confederacy. LC 88-16079. (Illus.). 160p. 1988. 21.95 (*0-89096-312-8*) Tex A&M Univ Pr.

Newland. Haematological Pathology. (C). 1998. text 150.00 (*0-443-04792-8*, W B Saunders Co) Harcrt Hlth Sci Grp.

Newland, Amy. Ukiyo-E. (Illus.). 112p. 1999. pap. 19.95 (*1-57715-069-4*) Knckerbocker.

Newland, Amy & Bongaerts, Jan, eds. German Dictionary of Environmental Technology (Worterbuch Umwelttechnologie), German-English - English-German (Deutsch-Englisch - Englisch-Deutsch) LC 97-21998. (GER & ENG.). 304p. (C). 1997. 140.00 (*0-415-11243-5*) Routledge.

Newland, Chester A. Professional Public Executives. LC 80-81209. (PAR Classics Ser.: No. 1). 222p. reprint ed. pap. 68.90 (*0-8357-4219-9*, 203700400003) Bks Demand.

Newland, D. E. Introduction Random Vibrations Spectral Wavelet Analysis. 3rd ed. LC 93-3888. 477p. (C). 1996. pap. 79.95 (*0-582-21584-6*) Addison-Wesley.

— Mechanical Vibration Analysis & Computation. (C). 1989. 79.95 (*0-582-02744-6*) Longman.

Newland, Dan, jt. auth. see Casad, Joe.

Newland, David H. Mineral Resources of the State of New York. 315p. 1993. reprint ed. lib. bdg. 89.00 (*0-7812-5150-8*) Rprt Serv.

Newland, Ernest T. BLAT Manual. 1971. pap. text 7.50 (*0-252-00886-3*) U of Ill Pr.

Newland, Guy. Appearance & Reality: The Two Truths in Four Buddhist Systems. LC 99-25977. 125p. 1999. pap. 14.95 (*1-55939-131-6*, Pub. by Snow Lion Pubns) Words Distrib.

— The Two Truths: In the Madhyamika Philosophy of the Ge-Luk-Ba Order of Tibetan Buddhism. 320p. 1992. pap. 22.95 (*0-937938-79-3*) Snow Lion Pubns.

— The Two Truths in the Madhyamika Philosophy of the Ge-luk-ba Order of Tibetan Buddhism. 312p. 1992. 39.95 (*0-937938-80-7*) Snow Lion Pubns.

Newland, James R. Pathology: Examination & Board Review. 360p. (C). 1995. pap. text 32.95 (*0-8385-7719-9*, A7719-6, Apple Lange Med) McGraw.

— Pathology: Examination & Board Review. 2nd ed. 1999. pap. 31.95 (*0-8385-8264-8*, Medical Exam) Appleton & Lange.

Newland, James R., ed. see Ishikawa, G.

Newland, John. Primal Instinct. 432p. 1994. mass mkt. 4.50 (*0-8217-4651-0*, Zebra Kensgtn) Kensgtn Pub Corp.

Newland, Joseph N., jt. auth. see Davis, Barbara.

Newland, Joseph N., ed. see Leavens, Ileana B. & Bruce, Chris.

Newland, Kathleen. City Limits: Emerging Constraints on Urban Growth. 1980. pap. write for info. (*0-916468-37-2*) Worldwatch Inst.

— Global Employment & Economic Justice: The Policy Challenge. LC 79-63577. (Worldwatch Papers). 1979. pap. 5.00 (*0-916468-27-5*) Worldwatch Inst.

— Infant Mortality & the Health of Societies. 1981. pap. write for info. (*0-916468-46-1*) Worldwatch Inst.

— International Migration: The Search for Work. LC 79-56318. (Worldwatch Papers). 1979. pap. 5.00 (*0-916468-32-1*) Worldwatch Inst.

— Productivity: The New Economic Context. LC 82-50699. (Worldwatch Papers). 1982. pap. 5.00 (*0-916468-48-8*) Worldwatch Inst.

— Refugees: The New International Politics of Displacement. LC 81-50523. (Worldwatch Papers). 1981. pap. 5.00 (*0-916468-42-9*) Worldwatch Inst.

— U. S. Refugee Policy: Dilemmas & Directions. (International Migration Policy Issues Ser.). 60p. 1995. pap. 8.95 (*0-87003-071-X*) Carnegie Endow.

— Women & Population Growth: Choice Beyond Childbearing. LC 77-91827. (Worldwatch Papers). 1977. pap. 5.00 (*0-916468-15-1*) Worldwatch Inst.

— Women in Politics: A Global Review. 1975. pap. write for info. (*0-916468-02-X*) Worldwatch Inst.

Newland, Kathleen & Soedjatmoko, Kamala C., eds. Transforming Humanity: The Visionary Writings of Soedjatmoko. LC 93-5181. (Library of Management for Development). 224p. 1994. 29.00 (*1-56549-025-8*); pap. 18.95 (*1-56549-026-6*) Kumarian Pr.

Newland, Kathleen & Vitkovskaya, Galina. Strangers in Their Own Land: Migration in Post-Soviet Russia. (International Migration Policy Ser.). 96p. 1999. pap. 10.95 (*0-87003-084-1*) Carnegie Endow.

Newland, Kathleen, jt. ed. see Grant, Rebecca.

Newland, Loren E. Hotel Protection Management Vol. 1: The Innkeeper's Security Guide to Guest Protection & Reasonable Care. Zachow, Betty, ed. (Illus.). 240p. (Orig.). (C). 1997. pap. text 39.95 (*1-886081-00-X*) TNZ Pubs.

Newland, Mary R. The Hebrew Scriptures: The Biblical Story of God's Promise to Israel & Us. LC 90-152729. (Illus.). 264p. (YA). (gr. 10-11). 1990. pap. text 13.90 (*0-88489-231-X*); teacher ed., spiral bd. 18.95 (*0-88489-232-8*) St Marys.

— The Saints & Our Children. 215p. 1995. pap. 12.50 (*0-89555-517-4*) TAN Bks Pubs.

— The Year & Our Children: Planning the Family Activities for Christian Feasts & Seasons. 2nd ed. 192p. 1995. pap. 11.95 (*1-885553-37-4*) Firefly Press.

Newland, Mary Reed. A Popular Guide Through the Old Testament. 280p. 1999. pap. 16.95 (*0-88489-544-0*) St Marys.

Newland, Mary Reed. Written on Our Hearts: The Old Testament Story of God's Love. (Illus.). 304p. (YA). (gr. 10-12). pap. 16.50 (*0-88489-508-4*) St Marys.

***Newland, Matthew Allen.** Of When the Days Ended: A Tale of Epic Fantasy. LC 00-190634. 192p. 2000. 25.00 (*0-7388-1876-3*); pap. 18.00 (*0-7388-1877-1*) Xlibris Corp.

Newland, Roberta L., see Cava, Roberta, pseud.

Newland, Samuel J. Cossacks in the German Army, 1941-1945. 1991. 47.50 (*0-7146-3351-8*, Pub. by F Cass Pubs) Intl Spec Bk.

***Newlands, Anne.** Canadian Art: From Its Beginnings to 2000. (Illus.). 352p. 2000. 85.00 (*1-55209-450-2*) Firefly Bks Ltd.

Newlands, Anne. Emily Carr: An Introduction to Her Life & Art. (Illus.). 64p. 1996. 24.95 (*1-55209-046-9*); pap. 14.95 (*1-55209-045-0*) Firefly Bks Ltd.

Newlands, Anne & National Gallery of Canada Staff. Meet Edgar Degas. LC 88-32035. (Illus.). 32p. (J). (gr. 1 up). 1989. 13.95 (*0-397-32369-7*) HarpC Child Bks.

Newlands, Carole, tr. see Murphy, James J., ed.

Newlands, Carole E. Playing with Time: Ovid & the "Fasti" LC 95-2919. (Studies in Classical Philology: Vol. 55). 256p. 1995. text 45.00 (*0-8014-3080-1*) Cornell U Pr.

Newlands, David, jt. ed. see McCarthy, John.

Newlands, George. God in Christian Perspective. 440p. 54.95 (*0-567-09657-2*, Pub. by T & T Clark); pap. 34.95 (*0-567-29259-2*, Pub. by T & T Clark) Bks Intl VA.

Newlen, Robert R. Writing Resumes That Work: A How-to-Do-It Manual for Librarians. LC 97-51220. 150p. 1998. pap. 39.95 (*1-55570-263-5*); pap. 55.00 (*1-55570-325-9*) Neal-Schuman.

Newlife Staff. Good News Comic, 25 Vols. 1998. pap. 8.99 (*1-56399-094-6*) NewLife Pubns.

Newlin, Algie I. The Battle of New Garden. LC 77-82787. (Illus.). 77p. 1995. reprint ed. pap. 7.50 (*0-942727-26-6*) NC Yrly Pubns Bd.

— Friends "at the Spring" A History of Spring Monthly Meeting. 1984. pap. 7.50 (*0-614-04682-3*) NC Frnds Hist Soc.

Newlin, Claude M. Life & Writings of Hugh Henry Brackenridge (1932) 335p. 1971. 15.00 (*0-911858-20-2*) Appel.

— Philosophy & Religion in Colonial America. LC 68-23317. 212p. 1968. reprint ed. lib. bdg. 59.50 (*0-8371-0184-0*, NEPR, Greenwood Pr) Greenwood.

N

An Asterisk (*) at the beginning of an entry indicates that the title is appearing for the first time.

Newlin, Deborah L. The Tonkawa People: A Tribal History From Earliest Times to 1893. Richardson, Gale, ed. (Museum Journals). (Illus.). 119p. 1982. pap. 5.00 (*0-911618-07-4*) Mus Texas.

Newlin, Dika. Bruckner-Mahler, Schoenberg: Music Book Index. 293p. 1993. reprint ed. lib. bdg. 79.00 (*0-7812-9582-3*) Rprt Serv.

Newlin, Dika, tr. see Leibowitz, Rene.

Newlin, Dika, tr. see Werner, Eric.

Newlin, Gary. Simple Kaleidoscopes: 16 Spectacular Scopes to Make. (Illus.). 112p. (Orig.). (J). 1996. pap. 14.95 (*0-8069-3155-8*) Sterling.

Newlin, George. Everyone in Dickens, 3 vols. LC 95-2453. (Illus.). 2506p. 1995. lib. bdg. 275.00 (*0-313-29580-8*, Greenwood Pr) Greenwood.

Newlin, George. Everyone in Dickens Vol. 2: Plots, People & Publishing Particulars in the Complete, Vol. 2. LC 95-2453. 928p. 1995. lib. bdg. 125.00 (*0-313-29582-4*, Greenwood Pr) Greenwood.

— Understanding a Tale of Two Cities: A Student Casebook to Issues, Sources & Historical Documents. LC 98-4803. (Greenwood Press Literature in Context Ser.). 272p. 1998. 39.95 (*0-313-29939-0*, Greenwood Pr) Greenwood.

— Understanding Great Expectations: A Student Casebook to Issues, Sources & Historical Documents. LC 99-32528. 256p. 2000. 39.95 (*0-313-29940-4*) Greenwood.

Newlin, George, ed. Everyone in Dickens Vol. 1: Plots, People & Publishing Particulars in the Complete, Vol. 1. LC 95-2453. 896p. 1995. lib. bdg. 125.00 (*0-313-29581-6*, Greenwood Pr) Greenwood.

— Everyone in Dickens Vol. 3: Characteristics & Commentaries, Tables & Tabulations: A Taxonomy, Vol. 3. LC 95-2453. 752p. 1995. lib. bdg. 95.00 (*0-313-29583-2*, Greenwood Pr) Greenwood.

Newlin, George, ed. see Dickens, Charles.

Newlin, J. Shipley, Jr., jt. auth. see Frick, Elizabeth.

Newlin, Jeanne T., intro. Our Town on Stage: The Original Promptbook in Fascimile. (Barry & Mary Bingham Series in the Harvard Theatre Collection: No. 1). (Illus.). 96p. 1989. 29.95 (*0-674-64760-2*) HUP.

N

Newlin, John. The World Is Your Market. LC 93-33154. 288p. 1994. 24.95 (*1-55958-439-4*) Prima Pub.

Newlin, Jon, jt. auth. see Bookhardt, D. Eric.

Newlin, Keith. Hardboiled Burlesque: Raymond Chandler's Comic Style. LC 85-25473. (Brownstone Mystery Guides Ser.: Vol. 1). 50p. 1984. reprint ed. pap. 13.00 (*0-941028-03-8*) Millefleurs.

***Newlin, Keith, ed.** American Plays of the New Woman. LC 99-54225. 294p. 2000. pap. 14.95 (*1-56663-299-4*, Pub. by I R Dee); text 27.50 (*1-56663-286-2*, Pub. by I R Dee) Natl Bk Netwk.

Newlin, Keith, ed. Hamlin Garland: A Bibliography, with a Checklist of Unpublished Letters. LC 97-61173. vi, 231p. 1998. 45.00 (*0-87875-497-0*) Whitston Pub.

***Newlin, Keith & Rusch, Frederic E., eds.** The Collected Plays of Theodore Dreiser. LC 99-73842. 200p. 2000. 49.00 (*0-87875-510-1*) Whitston Pub.

Newlin, Keith, ed. see Garland, Hamlin.

Newlin, Lana S. Surviving Sixth Grade. Morey, Cathy, ed. (Illus.). 90p. (J). (gr. 5-7). 1990. 16.95 (*0-9625413-0-3*); pap. 9.95 (*0-9625413-1-1*) Christmans.

Newlin, Nancy L. The Gem of Edenvale: The Historic Hayes Mansion of San Jose, California. LC 94-229186. (Illus.). (Orig.). 1994. pap. 24.95 (*0-9641102-0-2*) Renasci.

Newlin, Paul, jt. ed. see Cushman, Stephen.

Newlin, Richard, ed. Richard Diebenkorn: Works on Paper. LC 86-82665. 293p. 1987. 65.00 (*0-940619-00-8*) Houston Fine Art Pr.

Newlin, Richard, jt. auth. see Adams, Ben Q.

Newling, Donald W., ed. Prostate Cancer: Hormonal Treatment & Treatment of Advanced Disease. (Journal: European Urology: Vol. 26, Suppl. 1, 1994). (Illus.). iv, 34p. 1994. pap. 21.75 (*3-8055-6111-3*) S Karger.

Newlon, Howard, Jr., ed. A Selection of Historic American Papers on Concrete, 1876-1926. LC 76-47294. (American Concrete Institute Publication: SP-52). 342p. reprint ed. pap. 106.10 (*0-608-13001-X*, 202508100042) Bks Demand.

Newlon, Michael. He Came Out a Buckin' A Collection of Cowboy Poetry. (Illus.). 54p. 1998. pap. 10.00 (*1-57502-773-9*, P02130) Morris Pubng.

***Newlon, Sheri A.** Everybody Has a Story: Calvary's Calling. LC 99-93434. (Illus.). vi, 248p. 1999. pap. write for info. (*0-9673619-0-7*, EHS-1) S Newlon.

Newlon, T. Scott, jt. auth. see Grubert, Harry.

Newlove, Donald. First Paragraphs: Inspired Openings for Writers & Readers. 176p. 1995. pap. 9.95 (*0-8050-2597-9*) H Holt & Co.

— Invented Voices. 1995. write for info. (*0-8050-2979-6*); pap. 9.95 (*0-8050-2592-8*) H Holt & Co.

— Painted Paragraphs. 88p. 1995. pap. 9.95 (*0-8050-2591-X*) H Holt & Co.

— Painted Paragraphs: Inspired Description for Writers & Readers. 192p. 1995. 14.95 (*0-8050-2978-8*) H Holt & Co.

Newlove, George H. Consolidated Balance Sheets. LC 82-48380. (Accounting in Transition Ser.). 309p. 1982. text 10.00 (*0-8240-5325-7*) Garland.

Newlove, Jean. Laban for Actors & Dancers: Putting Laban's Movement Theory into Practice: A Step-by-Step Guide. LC 93-40376. 192p. (gr. 13). 1993. pap. 17.99 (*0-87830-044-9*, Thtre Arts Bks) Routledge.

Newlove, John. Apology for Absence... 208p. 1993. pap. write for info. (*0-88984-162-4*) Porcup Quill.

— The Night the Dog Smiled. 80p. (C). 1986. 18.00 (*0-920763-33-2*, Pub. by ECW); pap. 9.00 (*0-920763-31-6*, Pub. by ECW) Genl Dist Srvs.

Newlun, Chester O. Teaching Children to Summarize in Fifth Grade History. LC 75-177120. (Columbia University. Teachers College. Contributions to Education Ser.: No. 404). (C). reprint ed. 37.50 (*0-404-55404-0*) AMS Pr.

Newly, Vincent. Cowper's Poetry: A Critical Study & Reassessment. LC 82-6843. (English Texts & Studies: No. 20). 378p. (C). 1982. text 45.00 (*0-389-20079-4*, N6851) B&N Imports.

Newlyn, Dennis, jt. auth. see Watson, Edward R.

Newlyn, Lucy. Paradise Lost & the Romantic Reader. LC 92-463. (Illus.). 308p. (C). 1993. text 65.00 (*0-19-811277-7*, Clarendon Pr) OUP.

***Newlyn, Lucy.** Reading, Writing & Romanticism: The Anxiety of Influence. 240p. 2000. text 60.00 (*0-19-818710-6*) OUP.

Newman. American Promise. 1997. pap. text, wbk. ed. 11.95 (*0-312-17191-9*) St Martin.

— American Promise Map, Vol. 2. 1997. pap. text, wbk. ed. 11.95 (*0-312-18242-2*) St Martin.

— Biostatistics. 2001. text. write for info. (*0-471-36914-4*) Wiley.

— The Constitution & Its Amendments, Vol. 1. LC 98-8570. 1998. 65.00 (*0-02-864854-4*) S&S Trade.

— The Constitution & Its Amendments, Vol. 2. LC 98-8570. 1998. 65.00 (*0-02-864855-2*) S&S Trade.

— The Constitution & Its Amendments, Vol. 3. 1998. 65.00 (*0-02-864856-0*) S&S Trade.

— The Constitution & Its Amendments, Vol. 4. 1998. 65.00 (*0-02-864857-9*) S&S Trade.

— Development Through Life. 7th ed. LC 98-42025. (Psychology Ser.). 638p. 1998. pap. 75.95 (*0-534-35798-9*) Brooks-Cole.

— Electricity & Electronics: Experiments Manual. (Illus.). (YA). (gr. 6-12). 1999. student ed. 24.54 (*0-02-801257-7*) Glencoe.

— Electricity & Electronics: Instructor's Management System. 1999. teacher ed. 20.00 (*0-02-801256-9*) Glencoe.

— Electricity & Electronics: Mathematics Manual. (Illus.). (gr. 6-12). 1999. student ed. 17.53 (*0-02-801262-3*) Glencoe.

— Electricity & Electronics: Problems & Exercises Manual. (Illus.). (YA). (gr. 6-12). 1999. student ed. 21.20 (*0-02-801259-3*) Glencoe.

— Global Past Map, Vol. 1. Date not set. pap. text, wbk. ed. write for info. (*0-312-19025-5*) St Martin.

— Global Past Map, Vol. 2. Date not set. pap. text, wbk. ed. write for info. (*0-312-19024-7*) St Martin.

— The HBJ Composition: Answer Key. (C). 1992. pap. text 4.50 (*0-03-096771-6*, Pub. by Harcourt Coll Pubs) Harcourt.

— The Holt Composition Workbook. 3rd ed. (C). 1995. pap. text, wbk. ed. 23.50 (*0-15-502528-7*) Harcourt Coll Pubs.

***Newman.** Israel. 2000. 64.95 (*0-8133-2892-6*, Pub. by Westview) HarpC.

Newman. Linear Mathematics. 494p. (C). 1991. pap. text 49.00 (*0-536-57952-0*) Pearson Custom.

— Matzo Ball Moon. 1998. 15.00 (*0-395-71519-9*) Ticknor & Fields.

***Newman.** Neuro-Ophthamology. 2nd ed. 1999. text 97.00 (*0-8385-6697-9*) Appleton & Lange.

— On the Job English Student Book. 1999. pap. 11.50 (*1-56420-147-3*) New Readers.

Newman. Our Global Past. 1998. pap. text, wbk. ed. 6.50 (*0-312-17190-0*) St Martin.

— Plant Physiology. 144p. (C). 1997. write for info. (*0-02-386720-5*, Macmillan Coll) P-H.

— Population Ecotoxicology. text 121.00 (*0-471-98818-9*) Wiley.

— The Prisoner. (J). 1995. pap. 13.95 (*0-689-31363-2*) Atheneum Yung Read.

— Vademecum of Antibiotics: Vadecum de los Antibioticos. (SPA.). 1981. pap. 19.95 (*0-8288-4681-2*, S34979) Fr & Eur.

***Newman.** Yo-Ho-Ho. (J). 2000. pap. 6.95 (*0-552-52843-9*, Pub. by Transworld Publishers Ltd) Trafalgar.

Newman & Martin. Democracy Challenged: Guide to Lecture Launcher. (C). 1997. pap. text 24.00 (*0-673-55378-7*) Addson-Wesley Educ.

Newman, jt. auth. see Ekedahl.

Newman, ed. see HarperCollins Staff.

Newman, ed. see U. S. Postal Service Staff.

Newman & Willen Staff. Retailing. (ITBP Textbooks Ser.). 2001. pap. text 22.99 (*1-86152-533-8*) Thomson Learn.

Newman, A. N. Parliamentary Diary of Sir Edward Knatchbull 1722-30. (Camden Third Ser.). 63.00 (*0-86193-094-0*) David Brown.

Newman, Al. Fibber E. Frog. LC 93-77685. (Illus.). 32p. (J). (ps-3). 1993. reprint ed. 8.95 (*0-89334-213-0*); reprint ed. pap. 3.95 (*0-89334-217-3*) Humanics Ltd.

— Fraid E. Cat. LC 93-77687. (Illus.). 32p. (J). 1993. reprint ed. pap. 3.95 (*0-89334-219-X*) Humanics Ltd.

— Fraid E. Cat. LC 93-77687. (Illus.). 32p. (J). (ps-3). 1993. reprint ed. 8.95 (*0-89334-215-7*) Humanics Ltd.

— Giggle E. Goose. LC 93-77684. (Illus.). 32p. (J). (ps-3). 1993. reprint ed. 8.95 (*0-89334-212-2*); reprint ed. pap. 3.95 (*0-89334-216-5*) Humanics Ltd.

— Grub E. Dog. LC 93-77686. (Illus.). 32p. (J). (ps-3). 1993. reprint ed. 8.95 (*0-89334-214-9*); reprint ed. pap. 3.95 (*0-89334-218-1*) Humanics Ltd.

Newman, Albert H. History of Anti-Pedobaptism: From the Rise of Pedobaptism to A.D. 1609. LC 71-144664. reprint ed. 52.00 (*0-404-04686-X*) AMS Pr.

— A Manual of Church History, 2 vols., Set. 1977. lib. bdg. 250.00 (*0-8490-2205-3*) Gordon Pr.

Newman, Alex. Using Java: Special Edition. 1996. 49.99 incl. cd-rom (*0-614-14450-7*) Macmillan.

Newman, Alexander. Metal Building Systems: Design & Specifications. LC 96-49570. (Illus.). 389p. 1997. 74.95 (*0-07-046379-4*) McGraw.

— Non-Compliance in Winnicott's Words: A Companion to the Writings & Work of D. W. Winnicott. 500p. (C). 1995. text 75.00 (*0-8147-5786-3*) NYU Pr.

***Newman, Alexander.** Structural Renovation of Buildings: Methods, Details & Design Examples. (Illus.). 600p. 2000. 79.95 (*0-07-047162-2*) McGraw.

Newman, Alexander, ed. Non-Compliance in Winnicott's Words: A Companion to the Writings & Work of D. W. Winnicott. 500p. (C). 1995. pap. text 25.00 (*0-8147-5785-5*) NYU Pr.

Newman, Amanda. Women Are from Venus, Men Are from Hell. LC 98-45888. 224p. 1999. pap. 6.95 (*1-58062-124-4*) Adams Media.

Newman, Amy. Camera Lyrica. LC 99-31438. 65p. 1999. pap. 11.95 (*1-882295-24-2*, Pub. by Alice James Bks) SPD-Small Pr Dist.

***Newman, Amy.** Challenging Art: Artforum, 1962-1974. (Illus.). 560p. 2000. 40.00 (*1-56947-207-6*) Soho Press.

Newman, Amy. The Nuremburg Laws. LC 98-27778. (Words That Changed History Ser.). (Illus.). (YA). (gr. 4-12). 1998. lib. bdg. 23.70 (*1-56006-354-8*) Lucent Bks.

— Order, or Disorder. (CSU Poetry Ser.: Vol. XLVIII). 75p. (Orig.). 1995. 15.00 (*1-880834-18-9*); pap. 10.00 (*1-880834-17-0*) Cleveland St Univ Poetry Ctr.

Newman, Amy, ed. see Phelan, Ellen.

Newman, Anabel P. & Beverstock, Caroline. Adult Literacy: Contexts & Challenges. LC 90-38481. 230p. reprint ed. pap. 71.30 (*0-7837-4588-5*, 204430700002) Bks Demand.

Newman, Anabel P. & Metz, Elizabeth. First Reading: Focussed Instruction in Reading for Successful Teaching. Lewis, Warren W., ed. (Orig.). 1996. pap. write for info. (*0-927516-65-9*) ERIC-REC.

Newman, Andrew. The Physical Basis of Predication. (Studies in Philosophy). 285p. (C). 1992. text 69.95 (*0-521-41131-9*) Cambridge U Pr.

***Newman, Andrew J.** The Formative Period of Twelver Shi'ism: Hadith As Discourse Between Qum & Baghdad. 320p. 2000. 85.00 (*0-7007-1277-1*, Pub. by Curzon Pr Ltd) Paul & Co Pubs.

Newman, Andy. The Uncle's Handbook (And Aunt's Too) One Hundred One Things to Do with Kids. 160p. (Orig.). 1993. pap. 8.00 (*0-380-77192-6*, Avon Bks) Morrow Avon.

***Newman, Ann.** Conway: Arkansas. (Images of America Ser.). (Illus.). 128p. 1999. pap. 18.99 (*0-7385-0230-8*) Arcadia Publng.

Newman, Anne & Suk, Julie, eds. Bear Crossings: An Anthology of North American Poets. LC 78-55315. 124p. 1979. pap. 6.95 (*0-917990-08-0*, New South) C & M Online.

Newman, Anny. Die Chronik des Popen von Duklja Kroatische Fassung: Untersuchung zu Schrift und Sprache. (GER., Illus.). 231p. (Orig.). (C). 1988. pap. text 17.95 (*0-317-92494-X*) Intercult Commns.

Newman, Anthony. Bach & the Baroque: European Source Materials from the Baroque & Early Classical Periods with Special Emphasis on the Music of J. S. Bach. 2nd ed. LC 94-5326. 1995. pap. 32.00 (*0-945193-76-9*); lib. bdg. 48.00 (*0-945193-64-5*) Pendragon NY.

Newman, Arnold. The Great British. 1992. pap. 10.00 (*0-226-56680-3*) U Ch Pr.

Newman, Arthur J., ed. In Defense of the American Public School. LC 78-19570. 1979. 32.00 (*0-8211-1307-0*) McCutchan.

— In Defense of the American Public School. LC 78-15699. 192p. 1978. pap. text 21.95 (*0-87073-999-9*) Transaction Pubs.

— In Defense of the American Public School. LC 78-15699. 288p. reprint ed. pap. 89.30 (*0-8357-8917-9*, 203358200086) Bks Demand.

Newman, Aubrey. Follow Me: The Human Element in Leadership. 307p. 1997. reprint ed. text 25.00 (*0-7881-5059-6*) DIANE Pub.

Newman, Aubrey S. Follow Me II: More on the Human Element in Leadership, Vol. II. LC 92-16711. 288p. 1997. pap. 15.95 (*0-89141-613-7*) Presidio Pr.

— Follow Me III: Lessons on the Art & Science of High Command, Vol. III. LC 86-17079. 320p. 1997. pap. 15.95 (*0-89141-614-5*) Presidio Pr.

— Follow Me I: The Human Element in Leadership. LC 71-14363. 336p. 1997. pap. 15.95 (*0-89141-612-9*) Presidio Pr.

Newman, Barbara. Biology Research Activities. Kutscher, Eugene, ed. (Illus.). 1988. teacher ed. write for info. (*0-318-64016-3*); student ed. write for info. (*0-318-64017-1*) Alpha Pub MD.

— From Virile Woman to WomanChrist: Studies in Medieval Religion & Literature. LC 94-37704. (Middle Ages Ser.). (Illus.). 424p. 1995. text 42.50 (*0-8122-3273-9*); pap. text 19.95 (*0-8122-1545-1*) U of Pa Pr.

***Newman, Barbara.** Illustrated Book of Ballet Stories. (Read & Listen Ser.). (Illus.). 64p. (J). 2000. pap. 7.95 (*0-7894-6097-1*, D K Ink) DK Pub Inc.

Newman, Barbara. The Illustrated Book of Ballet Stories: A Musical Introduction to the Classic Ballets. LC 97-15462. (J). (gr. 3-6). 1997. 19.95 incl. audio compact disk (*0-7894-2024-4*); 15.95 (*0-7894-2225-5*, 749705) DK Pub Inc.

— Sadler's Wells Royal Ballet "Swan Lake" (Illus.). 143p. 1983. 29.95 (*0-903102-72-2*, Pub. by Dance Bks) Princeton Bk Co.

— Sister of Wisdom: St. Hildegard's Theology of the Feminine. LC 86-16094. 288p. (C). 1987. pap. 13.95 (*0-520-06615-4*) U CA Pr.

— Sister of Wisdom: St. Hildegard's Theology of the Feminine. 320p. 1997. pap. text 15.95 (*0-520-21162-6*, Pub. by U CA Pr) Cal Prin Full Svc.

— Striking a Balance: Dancers Talk about Dancing. rev. ed. LC 91-44442. (Illus.). 402p. 1992. reprint ed. pap. 17.95 (*0-87910-154-7*) Limelight Edns.

— The Voice of the Living Light: Hildegard of Bingen & Her World. LC 98-14149. 275p. 1998. 48.00 (*0-520-20826-9*, Pub. by U CA Pr); pap. 19.95 (*0-520-21758-6*, Pub. by U CA Pr) Cal Prin Full Svc.

Newman, Barbara, tr. The Life of Juliana of Mont-Cornillon. 2nd rev. ed. (Translations Ser.: Vol. 13). 164p. 1999. pap. 20.00 (*0-920669-13-1*, Pub. by Peregrina Pubng) Cistercian Pubns.

Newman, Barbara & Newman, Philip R. When Kids Go to College: A Parent's Guide to Changing Relationships. LC 91-21700. 166p. 1992. pap. 23.00 (*0-8142-0562-3*) Ohio St U Pr.

Newman, Barbara, ed. & tr. see Hildegard of Bingen, St.

Newman, Barbara, tr. & comment see Saint Hildegard of Bingen.

Newman, Barbara A. & Newman, Philip R. When Kids Go to College: A Parent's Guide to Changing Relationships. LC 91-21700. 202p. reprint ed. pap. 62.70 (*0-608-09862-0*, 206982700006) Bks Demand.

Newman, Barbara M. Development Through Life: A Psychosocial Approach. 5th ed. LC 90-25467. 708p. (C). 1991. text 49.95 (*0-534-15396-8*) Brooks-Cole.

Newman, Barbara M. & Newman, Philip R. Childhood & Adolescence. LC 96-33529. (Psychology Ser.). 656p. (C). 1996. mass mkt. 82.95 (*0-534-13686-9*) Brooks-Cole.

— Development Through Life: A Psychosocial Approach. 4th ed. 628p. (C). 1987. mass mkt. 14.75 (*0-534-10739-7*) Brooks-Cole.

— Development Through Life: A Psychosocial Approach. 4th ed. 628p. (C). 1989. mass mkt. 42.50 (*0-534-10738-9*) Brooks-Cole.

— Development Through Life: A Psychosocial Approach. 6th ed. 763p. 1994. pap. 51.00 (*0-534-23334-1*) Brooks-Cole.

— Development Through Life: A Psychosocial Approach. 6th ed. 1995. mass mkt., teacher ed. write for info. (*0-534-23336-8*) Brooks-Cole.

— Study Guide for Newman & Newman's Childhood & Adolescence. (C). 1996. mass mkt., student ed. 18.25 (*0-534-34520-4*) Brooks-Cole.

Newman, Barbara M., jt. auth. see Newman, Philip R.

Newman, Barclay M. & Nida, Eugene A. A Handbook on Paul's Letter to the Romans. LC 93-39491. (UBS Handbook Ser.). Orig. Title: Translators Handbook on Paul's Letter to the Romans. vii, 325p. 1973. pap. 14.99 (*0-8267-0160-4*, 102680) Untd Bible Soc.

— A Handbook on the Acts of the Apostles. LC 92-40063. (UBS Handbook Ser.). Orig. Title: Translator's Handbook on the Acts of the Apostles. vii, 542p. 1972. pap. 18.99 (*0-8267-0159-0*, 102677) Untd Bible Soc.

— A Handbook on the Gospel of John. LC 92-40060. (UBS Handbook Ser.). Orig. Title: Translator's Handbook on the Gospel of John. viii, 681p. 1980. pap. 23.99 (*0-8267-0158-2*, 102726) Untd Bible Soc.

Newman, Barclay M. & Stine, Philip C. A Handbook on the Gospel of Matthew. LC 92-25802. (UBS Handbook Ser.). Orig. Title: Translator's Handbook on the Gospel of Matthew. x, 911p. 1988. pap. 22.99 (*0-8267-0155-8*, 102725) Untd Bible Soc.

Newman, Barclay M., jt. auth. see Bratcher, Robert G.

Newman, Barnett. Barnett Newman. (Illus.). 336p. 1999. 65.00 (*3-7757-0795-6*, Pub. by Gerd Hatje) Dist Art Pubs.

— Prints of Barnett Newman, 1961-1969. 1997. 50.00 (*3-7757-0609-7*, Pub. by Gerd Hatje) Dist Art Pubs.

Newman, Barry. The Bear's World: Remedy for the Blues. (Illus.). (Orig.). 1994. pap. 9.95 (*0-9642844-4-8*) Chubby Bear.

Newman, Barry, ed. see Peabody, Virginia & Sullivan, Paul.

Newman, Barry M. & Peabody, Virginia S. 1997 Quick Reference to Erisa Compliance. annuals 512p. 1997. pap. 125.00 (*1-56706-363-2*, 63632) Panel Pubs.

— Quick Reference to ERISA Compliance: 1998 Edition. annuals 512p. pap. 125.00 (*1-56706-380-2*, 63802) Panel Pubs.

Newman, Benjamin. Searching for the Figure in the Carpet in the Tales of Henry James: Reflections of an Ordinary Reader. (American University Studies: English Language & Literature: Ser. IV, Vol. 49). 200p. (C). 1987. text 39.00 (*0-8204-0442-X*) P Lang Pubng.

Newman, Bernard. The New Europe. LC 72-4581. (Essay Index Reprint Ser.). 1977. reprint ed. 31.95 (*0-8369-2963-2*) Ayer.

Newman, Bernard H. & Oliverio, Mary E. Business Communications: A Managerial Approach. LC 76-21593. 1976. pap. 4.95 (*0-686-17616-2*) Monong Pub.

Newman, Bertram. Edmund Burke. LC 71-102251. (Select Bibliographies Reprint Ser.). 1977. 30.95 (*0-8369-5136-0*) Ayer.

Newman, Beryl. When Descanso Was Young: Early Settlers & Ranchers Descanso, 1845-1947. (Illus.). 204p. (Orig.). 1994. pap. 12.00 (*0-938711-25-3*) Tecolote Pubns.

Newman, Beth, ed. see Bronte, Charlotte.

Newman, Betsy. Now That You're All Grown up, What Do You Want to Be? A Career Transition Guide. 280p. 1996. pap., per. 21.95 (*0-7872-2250-X*) Kendall-Hunt.

Newman, Betsy & Mara, Joseph. Reading, Writing & TV: A Video Handbook for Teachers. 190p. 1995. pap. 19.00 (*0-917846-33-8*, 95583) Highsmith Pr.

Newman, Betsy, jt. auth. see Newman, Graeme.

Newman, Bill, jt. auth. see Ekedahl, Mike.

Newman, Bob. Common Sense Survival for Outdoor Enthusiasts: Staying Comfortable for 5 Days. (Nuts-N-Bolts Guides Ser.). (Illus.). 32p. 1994. pap. 4.95 (*0-89732-166-9*) Menasha Ridge.

An Asterisk (*) at the beginning of an entry indicates that the title is appearing for the first time.

— The Complete Guide to Fly Fishing Maine: Where, When, & How to Take Maine's Best Fighting Fish. LC 94-14256. (Illus.). 144p. 1994. pap. 13.50 (*0-89272-348-3*, Silver Quill Pr) Down East.

— Complete Guide to Hunting in Maine. LC 96-25749. (Illus.). 144p. (Orig.). 1996. pap. 13.50 (*0-89272-382-3*, Silver Quill Pr) Down East.

— The Complete Guide to Waterfowling in Maine: The Best Locations, Strategies, & Equipment for Bagging Maine's Ducks & Geese. LC 95-36506. (Illus.). 144p. (Orig.). 1995. pap. 13.50 (*0-89272-366-1*, Silver Quill Pr) Down East.

— Inshore Fishing the Carolina Coasts: A Complete Guide to Fishing All Coastal Waters of the Carolinas. Bledsoe, Jerry, ed. LC 94-70668. (Illus.). 151p. 1994. pap. 13.95 (*1-878086-27-8*, Pub. by Down Home NC) Blair.

— Land Navigation for Outdoor Enthusiasts. (Nuts-N-Bolts Guides Ser.). 32p. 1995. pap. 4.95 (*0-89732-178-2*) Menasha Ridge.

— Marine Special Warfare & Elite Unit Tactics. (Illus.). 184p. 1995. pap. 25.00 (*0-87364-845-5*) Paladin Pr.

— North American Fly Fishing. LC 98-10432. (Illus.). 224p. 1998. pap. 15.95 (*0-89732-240-1*) Menasha Ridge.

— Saltwater Angler's Guide to the Florida Keys: Flyfishing & Light Tackle. 2000. pap. 26.95 (*1-885106-74-2*) Wild Adven Pr.

— Successful Landlocked Salmon Fishing. (Illus.). 160p. 1997. pap. text 17.95 (*0-07-046364-6*) McGraw-Hill Prof.

— Survival in the '90's: A Guide for Outdoor Enthusiasts. LC 96-14168. (Illus.). 224p. (Orig.). 1995. pap. 14.95 (*0-89732-191-X*) Menasha Ridge.

— Wilderness Wayfinding: How to Survive in the Wilderness As You Travel. (Illus.). 160p. 1994. pap. 15.00 (*0-87364-760-2*) Paladin Pr.

Newman, Bob. Santa in My Father's Shoes & Other Christmas Stories. 1996. 19.95 (*1-885134-07-X*) Newsday.

Newman, Bob & Brown, Robert K. Guerrillas in the Mist: A Battlefield Guide to Clandestine Warfare. LC 98-125489. (Illus.). 232p. 1997. pap. 22.00 (*0-87364-944-3*) Paladin Pr.

Newman, Bob & Gould, Mike. Saltwater Angler's Guide to the Southeast: Fly Fishing & Light Tackle. (Illus.). 500p. 1999. pap. 26.95 (*1-885106-39-4*) Wild Adven Pr.

Newman, Bob & Knight, Tami. Knots Around the Home. LC 97-4457. (Illus.). 48p. 1997. pap. 6.95 (*0-89732-207-X*) Menasha Ridge.

Newman, Bob, ed. see Kreh, Lefty, et al.

Newman, Bobby. No Virtue in Accident: Behavior Analysis & Utopian Literature. 120p. 1996. pap. 19.95 (*0-9668528-0-X*) Dove & Orca.

— The Reluctant Alliance: Behaviorism & Humanism. LC 92-745. 128p. (C). 1992. 25.95 (*0-87975-727-2*) Prometheus Bks.

***Newman, Bobby.** When Everybody Cares: Case Studies of ABA with People with Autism. 136p. 1999. pap. 18.00 (*0-9668528-1-8*, Pub. by Dove & Orca) BookMasters.

Newman, Boyd & Newman, Linda. Hikes Around Philadelphia. 224p. 1997. 49.95 (*1-56639-529-1*); pap. 14.95 (*1-56639-530-5*) Temple U Pr.

***Newman, Boyd & Newman, Linda A.** Great Hikes in the Poconos & Northeast Pennsylvania. LC 99-49064. 288p. 2000. 19.95 (*0-8117-2773-4*) Stackpole.

Newman, Brian, et al. Transcendent Love: The Fifth Passage of Marriage - Beyond the Thirty-Fifth Anniversary, the Growth Stage That Can Glorify Your Union. LC 92-33182. 1993. 9.99 (*0-8407-4553-2*) Nelson.

Newman, Brian, jt. auth. see Biuso, Joseph.

Newman, Bruce I. Handbook of Political Marketing. LC 99-6226. 1999. write for info. (*0-7619-1109-X*) Sage.

— The Marketing of the President: Political Marketing As Campaign Strategy. LC 93-32450. (C). 1993. text 48.00 (*0-8039-5137-X*); pap. text 21.00 (*0-8039-5138-8*) Sage.

Newman, Bruce I. & Sheth, Jagdish N. A Theory of Political Choice Behavior. LC 86-15152. (Praeger Series in Public & Nonprofit Sector Marketing). 199p. 1987. 52.95 (*0-275-92187-5*, C2187, Praeger Pubs) Greenwood.

Newman, Bruce I. & Sheth, Jagdish N., eds. Political Marketing: Readings & Annotated Bibliography. LC 85-26866. 269p. (Orig.). reprint ed. pap. 83.40 (*0-7837-2494-2*, 204265900005) Bks Demand.

Newman, C. E., et al, eds. Ovarian Cancer: Proceedings of the International Symposium on Ovarian Cancer, 24-25 September 1979, Birmingham. LC 80-40166. (Illus.). 249p. 1980. 50.00 (*0-08-025532-9*, Pergamon Pr) Elsevier.

Newman, C. T. The Newman Report: Interim Report, Eighth Coast Guard District Offshore Operations Liaison Staff, 1 June 1973. 109p. (Orig.). 1985. pap. text 50.85 (*0-934114-67-6*, BK-515) Marine Educ.

***Newman, C. W. & Newman, Rosemary K.** Gamma-Linolenic Acid: What You Need to Know. 48p. 1999. pap. 3.95 (*0-89529-985-2*, Avery) Penguin Putnam.

Newman, Carey C. Paul's Glory - Christology: Tradition & Rhetoric. (Novum Testamentum, Supplements Ser.: Vol. 69). xviii, 305p. 1991. 126.50 (*90-04-09463-6*) Brill Academic Pubs.

***Newman, Carey C., ed.** Jesus & the Restoration of Israel: A Critical Assessment of N. T. Wright's Jesus & the Victory of God. LC 99-36483. 1999. pap. text 22.99 (*0-8308-1587-2*) InterVarsity.

Newman, Carol, ed. see Hildebrand, Verna.

Newman, Carol, ed. see Morton, Ruth.

Newman, Carol M. The Best 50 Sushi Rolls. (Best 50 Ser.). 80p. 1999. pap. 5.95 (*1-55867-231-1*) Bristol Pub Ent CA.

Newman, Carole, jt. auth. see Newman, Isadore.

***Newman, Cathy.** Women Photographers at National Geographic. (Illus.). 232p. 2000. 40.00 (*0-7922-7689-2*) Natl Geog.

Newman, Channa, tr. see Genette, Gerard.

Newman, Charles. A Child's History of America: Some Ribs & Riffs for the Sixties. LC 82-73500. 307p. 1973. 13.95 (*0-89366-245-3*) Ultramarine Pub.

— The Post-Modern Aura: The Act of Fiction in an Age of Inflation. 203p. 1985. reprint ed. 39.95 (*0-8101-0668-X*); reprint ed. pap. 16.95 (*0-8101-0669-8*) Northwestern U Pr.

— There Must Be More to Love Than Death: Three Short Novels. LC 76-17743. 217p. 1976. 12.95 (*0-89366-257-7*) Ultramarine Pub.

— White Jazz. LC 86-46072. 213p. (Orig.). 1984. pap. 7.95 (*0-385-18863-3*) Ultramarine Pub.

Newman, Charles M. Topics in Disordered Systems. LC 97-26435. (Lectures in Mathematics ETH Zurich). 1997. write for info. (*0-8176-5777-0*) Birkhauser.

— Topics in Disordered Systems. LC 97-26435. (Lectures in Mathematics ETH Zurich). 104p. 1997. pap. write for info. (*3-7643-5777-0*) Birkhauser.

Newman, Chris. Essential American Government. 128p. (C). 1995. pap. text 19.95 (*0-7872-1066-8*) Kendall-Hunt.

— Phillip's Dream World: A Coloring Book. (Illus.). 52p. (Orig.). (J). 1992. pap. 5.95 (*0-9635004-3-0*) Flying Heart.

Newman, Chris J., ed. see Minerals, Metals & Materials Society Staff.

Newman, Christopher. Dead End Game. 320p. 1995. mass mkt. 5.99 (*0-425-14564-6*) Berkley Pub.

— Killer. LC 94-32236. 1997. 21.95 (*0-399-14044-1*, G P Putnam) Peng Put Young Read.

— Nineteenth Precinct. 1992. mass mkt. 5.99 (*0-449-14732-0*, GM) Fawcett.

— Precinct Command. 1993. mass mkt. 5.99 (*0-449-14795-9*, GM) Fawcett.

Newman, Claire M. Exploring Probability. pap. 12.95 (*0-86651-334-5*) Seymour Pubns.

Newman, Claire M. & Turkel, Susan. Chance It! Probability Simulation. (C). 1984. pap. 4.00 (*0-89824-056-5*); pap., teacher ed. 5.00 (*0-89824-057-3*) Trillium Pr.

Newman, Claire M., jt. auth. see Artzt, Alice F.

Newman, Claudia, jt. auth. see Hagemann, Bert.

Newman, Clive, jt. ed. see Ryan, Emer.

Newman, Cory F., jt. auth. see Ellis, Thomas E.

Newman, D. & Wilson, K. Models in Plant Physiology & Biochemistry, Vol. 1. LC 87-9363. 160p. 1987. reprint ed. 95.00 (*0-8493-4343-7*, CRC Reprint) Franklin.

— Models in Plant Physiology & Biochemistry, Vol. 2. LC 87-9363. 176p. 1987. reprint ed. 101.00 (*0-8493-4344-5*, CRC Reprint) Franklin.

— Models in Plant Physiology & Biochemistry, Vol. 3. LC 87-9363. 152p. 1987. reprint ed. 91.00 (*0-8493-4345-3*, CRC Reprint) Franklin.

Newman, D. J. Approximation with Rational Functions. LC 79-14971. (CBMS Regional Conference Series in Mathematics: No. 41). 52p. 1979. reprint ed. pap. 19.00 (*0-8218-1691-8*, CBMS/41) Am Math.

— A Problem Seminar. (Problem Books in Mathematics). 113p. 1982. 46.95 (*0-387-90765-3*) Spr-Verlag.

***Newman, D. J. & Ng, Betty, eds.** Crystal Field Handbook. LC 99-52178. (Illus.). 300p. (C). 2000. write for info. (*0-521-59124-4*) Cambridge U Pr.

Newman, D. J., jt. auth. see Bak, J.

Newman, D. J., jt. auth. see MacKeown, P. K.

Newman, D. L., jt. auth. see Van Der Tuin, J. D.

Newman, D. M., jt. ed. see Lingeman, James E.

Newman, Daisy. The Autumn's Brightness. 251p. 1991. pap. 12.00 (*0-944350-18-6*) Friends United.

— Diligence in Love. 252p. 1992. pap. 12.00 (*0-944350-22-4*) Friends United.

— I Take Thee, Serenity. large type ed. LC 94-5392. 470p. 1994. lib. bdg. 21.95 (*0-8161-7492-X*, G K Hall Lrg Type) Mac Lib Ref.

— I Take Thee Serenity. LC 89-11798. 314p. 1989. reprint ed. pap. 12.00 (*0-944350-09-7*) Friends United.

— Indian Summer of the Heart. LC 82-6226. 376p. 1990. pap. 12.00 (*0-944350-15-1*) Friends United.

— A Procession of Friends: Quakers in a America. LC 79-160875. 460p. (C). 1972. pap. 17.00 (*0-913408-59-X*) Friends United.

***Newman-D'Amico, Fran.** Halloween Fun. (Beginners Activity Books Ser.). 1999. pap. text 1.00 (*0-486-40555-9*) Dover.

Newman-D'Amico, Fran. Seashore Fun. (Illus.). 32p. (J). 1998. pap. 1.00 (*0-486-40352-1*) Dover.

***Newman, Dan.** The Dragon Naturally Speaking Guide: Speech Recognition Made Fast & Simple. 2nd ed. 288p. 1999. pap. 19.95 (*0-9670389-7-9*) Waveside Pub.

Newman, Dan, tr. see Maeda, Toshio.

Newman, Daniel. Talk to Your Computer: Speech Recognition Made Easy. (Illus.). 208p. 2000. pap. 14.95 (*0-9670389-3-6*) Waveside Pub.

Newman, Danny. Subscribe Now: Building Arts Audiences Through Dynamic Subscription Promotion. LC 77-81452. xi, 276p. 1977. 12.95 (*0-930452-00-3*) Theatre Comm.

— Subscribe Now: Building Arts Audiences Through Dynamic Subscription Promotion. 3rd ed. LC 77-81452. (Illus.). 300p. (C). 1977. reprint ed. pap. 13.95 (*0-930452-01-1*) Theatre Comm.

Newman, David. David Newman's Movie Quiz Book. Spradlin, Kelly A. & Spradlin, Michael P., eds. 208p. (Orig.). 1993. pap. 12.50 (*1-881892-01-8*) Spradlin & Assocs.

— The Dynamics of Territorial Change: A Political Geography of the Arab-Israeli Conflict. 256p. (C). 2000. text 69.00 (*0-8133-2761-X*); pap. text 24.00 (*0-8133-2762-8*) Westview.

— Population, Settlement, & Conflict: Israel & the West Bank. (Update Ser.). (Illus.). 72p. (C). 1991. pap. text 18.95 (*0-521-40804-0*) Cambridge U Pr.

Newman, David, ed. Boundaries, Territory & Postmodernity. LC 99-22414. 168p. 1999. pap. 24.50 (*0-7146-8033-8*, Pub. by F Cass Pubs) Intl Spec Bk.

***Newman, David, ed.** Boundaries, Territory & Postmodernity. LC 99-22414. 168p. 1999. 49.50 (*0-7146-4973-2*, Pub. by F Cass Pubs) Intl Spec Bk.

Newman, David & Rabushka, Alvin. Hong Kong under Chinese Rule: The First Year. LC 98-29052. (Essays in Public Policy Ser.: No. 90). 1998. pap. 5.00 (*0-8179-5952-1*) Hoover Inst Pr.

Newman, David, et al. Women's Health: Your Guide to a Healthier & Happier Life. LC 97-77581. 479p. 1998. per. 19.95 (*0-9661346-5-6*) Better Hlth.

Newman, David, jt. auth. see Dixon, John.

Newman, David, jt. auth. see Hsieh, John.

Newman, David, jt. auth. see Kliot, Nurit.

Newman, David B. Taxation of Financially Distressed Businesses, 1 vol. LC 93-9101. (Tax Ser.). 1993. 120.00 (*0-685-67256-5*) West Group.

Newman, David J., jt. ed. see Price, Christopher P.

Newman, David M. Sociology: Exploring the Architecture of Everyday Life. 2nd ed. LC 96-45366. 1997. 31.95 (*0-7619-8518-2*) Pine Forge.

— Sociology: Exploring the Architecture of Everyday Life: Readings. 2nd ed. LC 96-45391. 1997. 19.95 (*0-7619-8519-0*) Pine Forge.

— Sociology of Families. LC 98-40130. 1999. write for info. (*0-7619-8514-X*) Pine Forge.

Newman, Deborah. Then God Created Woman: Finding Fulfillment as the Woman God Intended You to Be. LC 97-1429. 1997. pap. 10.99 (*1-56179-533-X*) Focus Family.

Newman, Debra L., compiled by. Black History: A Guide to Civilian Records in the National Archives. LC 84-16597. (Illus.). 379p. 1984. pap. 15.00 (*0-911333-31-2*, 200030); boxed set 25.00 (*0-911333-21-5*, 100030) National Archives & Recs.

Newman, Denis, et al. The Construction Zone: Working for Cognitive Change in School. (Learning in Doing: Social, Cognitive & Computational Perspectives Ser.). (Illus.). 192p. (C). 1989. pap. text 19.95 (*0-521-38942-9*) Cambridge U Pr.

Newman, Denise. The Blood Flower. limited ed. 8p. 1993. pap. 15.00 (*0-9632085-3-5*) Em Pr.

***Newman, Denise.** Human Forest. LC 99-75476. 71p. 2000. pap. 12.95 (*0-9669937-2-1*, Pub. by Apogee) SPD-Small Pr Dist.

Newman, Denise. Why Pear? limited ed. (Illus.). 1996. 25.00 (*0-9632085-9-4*) Em Pr.

Newman, Denise, tr. see Christensen, Inger.

Newman, Diane & Dzurinko, Mary K. The Urinary Incontinence Sourcebook. LC 97-6722. 368p. 1997. 32.00 (*1-56565-648-2*, 06482W, Pub. by Lowell Hse) NTC Contemp Pub Co.

Newman, Diane K. & Jakovac-Smith, Diane A. Geriatric Care Plans. LC 90-9856. 352p. 1990. pap. 32.95 (*0-87434-263-5*) Springhouse Corp.

***Newman, Diane Kaschak.** Urinary Incontinence Sourcebook. (Illus.). 368p. 1999. pap. 19.95 (*0-7373-0261-5*, 02615W) NTC Contemp Pub Co.

Newman, Diann & Hodgetts, Richard. Human Resource Management: Customer Oriented Approach. LC 97-9255. 471p. 1997. 74.00 (*0-13-253675-7*) P-H.

Newman, Diann R. Reflective Teaching. 2nd ed. 1996. pap. text, student ed., wbk. ed. 13.00 (*0-13-459645-5*) P-H.

Newman, Dianna L. & Brown, Robert D. Applied Ethics for Program Evaluation. LC 95-36416. 228p. 1995. 42.00 (*0-8039-5185-X*); pap. 19.95 (*0-8039-5186-8*) Sage.

***Newman, Dolores A.** Papa, How Do You Know? LC 99-91145. (Illus.). 32p. (J). 2000. pap. 9.95 (*0-9676438-0-5*) Sanctuary Pr MI.

Newman, Donald G. & Larock, Bruce E. Engineer-in-Training: Examination Review. 3rd ed. LC 90-12329. 600p. 1991. 110.00 (*0-471-50827-5*) Wiley.

Newman, Donald J. Analytic Number Theory, Vol. 177. LC 97-26431. (Graduate Texts in Mathematics). 100p. (C). 1997. write for info. (*0-387-98308-2*) Spr-Verlag.

Newman, Donald J., ed. James Boswell, Psychological Interpretations. LC 94-43702. 1995. text 45.00 (*0-312-12142-3*) St Martin.

Newman, Donald J., jt. auth. see Anderson, Patrick R.

Newman, Doris. Right Here Lover! Date not set. pap. 12.95 (*1-57532-244-7*) Press-Tige Pub.

Newman, E., et al, eds. Dictionary of Analytical Reagents. 2000p. (gr. 13). 1993. ring bd. 519.95 (*0-412-35150-1*, A9622, Chap & Hall CRC) CRC Pr.

***Newman, E. I.** Applied Ecology: Sustainable Management of Biological Resources. 2nd ed. LC 00-29782. 2000. write for info. (*0-632-04265-6*) Blackwell Sci.

Newman, E. M. Seeing London. 1972. 59.95 (*0-8490-1017-9*) Gordon Pr.

— Seeing Paris. 1972. 59.95 (*0-8490-1018-7*) Gordon Pr.

Newman, Ed. No More Test Anxiety: Effective Steps for Taking Tests & Achieving Better Grades. LC 95-78584. (Illus.). 172p. (Orig.). (YA). (gr. 9 up). 1996. pap. 17.95 (*0-9650930-0-X*) Lrning Skills.

Newman, Edgar L., ed. Historical Dictionary of France from the 1815 Restoration to the Second Empire, 2 vols. LC 85-17728. 1915p. 1987. lib. bdg. 195.00 (*0-313-22751-9*, NDH/) Greenwood.

— Historical Dictionary of France from the 1815 Restoration to the Second Empire, Vol. 1. LC 85-17728. 1915p. 1987. lib. bdg. 125.00 (*0-313-26045-1*, NDH/01) Greenwood.

— Historical Dictionary of France from the 1815 Restoration to the Second Empire, Vol. 2. LC 85-17728. 1915p. 1987. lib. bdg. 125.00 (*0-313-26046-X*, NDH/02) Greenwood.

Newman, Edwin. A Civil Tongue. LC 76-11607. 1976. 9.95 (*0-672-52267-5*, Bobbs) Macmillan.

— Edwin Newman, on Language. 1992. 9.98 (*0-88365-795-3*) Galahad Bks.

— I Must Say. 312p. 1989. mass mkt. 9.95 (*0-446-39099-2*, Pub. by Warner Bks) Little.

— Strictly Speaking: Will America Be the Death of English? LC 74-6525. 224p. 1974. 9.95 (*0-672-51990-9*, Bobbs) Macmillan.

***Newman, Edwin.** Strictly Speaking: Will America Be the Death of English? LC 99-88545. 215p. 2000. 26.95 (*1-56000-442-8*) Transaction Pubs.

Newman, Elizabeth. Gleams of Grace. 1989. pap. 9.95 (*0-938645-19-6*) In His Steps.

Newman, Elizabeth. Instant Replay. Goehner, Amy Lennard, ed. (Illus.). 32p. (J). (gr. 2-8). pap. 3.99 (*1-886749-79-5*) SI For Kids.

Newman, Elizabeth. Mandi & the Fairies. 1992. pap. 9.95 (*0-938645-78-1*) In His Steps.

Newman, Elizabeth L. Security Clearance Law & Procedure. 275p. 1998. pap. 95.00 (*1-878810-47-2*) Dewey Pubns.

Newman, Eric P. Continental Currency of 1776 & Fugio Cent Varieties. (Illus.). 1982. reprint ed. pap. 6.00 (*0-915262-90-8*) S J Durst.

— Early Paper Money of America. 4th ed. LC 76-8365. 488p. 1997. 75.00 (*0-87341-415-2*, EP04) Krause Pubns.

Newman, Eric P., ed. Studies on Money in Early America. LC 76-6790. (Illus.). 222p. reprint ed. pap. 68.90 (*0-7837-6359-X*, 204607100010) Bks Demand.

Newman, Eric P., jt. auth. see Madous, H. Michael.

Newman, Ernest. Elgar. 3rd ed. LC 74-24163. reprint ed. 34.50 (*0-404-13058-5*) AMS Pr.

— Essays from the World of Music. LC 77-17326. (Music Reprint Ser.). (Illus.). 1978. reprint ed. lib. bdg. 29.50 (*0-306-77519-0*) Da Capo.

— Essays from the World of Music, Vol. 1. 1986. 14.95 (*0-7145-3548-6*) Riverrun NY.

— Gluck & the Opera: A Study in Musical History. LC 76-43929. (Music & Theatre in France in the 17th & 18th Centuries Ser.). reprint ed. 45.00 (*0-404-60176-6*) AMS Pr.

— Gluck & the Opera: A Study in Musical History. LC 76-7579. 300p. 1976. reprint ed. lib. bdg. 59.75 (*0-8371-8849-0*, NEGO, Greenwood Pr) Greenwood.

— Gluck & the Opera: A Study in Musical History. 300p. 1990. reprint ed. lib. bdg. 69.00 (*0-7812-9064-3*) Rprt Serv.

— Hugo Wolf. 279p. 1990. reprint ed. lib. bdg. 69.00 (*0-7812-9100-3*) Rprt Serv.

— The Life of Richard Wagner, 4 vols. reprint ed. lib. bdg. 236.00 (*0-685-14824-6*) Rprt Serv.

— The Life of Richard Wagner, Vol. 1. LC 76-22682. reprint ed. pap. 148.00 (*0-608-15758-9*, 2031699) Bks Demand.

— The Man Liszt. (Music Book Index Ser.). 313p. 1992. reprint ed. lib. bdg. 89.00 (*0-7812-9484-3*) Rprt Serv.

— More Essays from the World of Music. 1986. 14.95 (*0-7145-3549-4*) Riverrun NY.

— A Musical Critic's Holiday. 330p. 1990. reprint ed. lib. bdg. 79.00 (*0-7812-9129-1*) Rprt Serv.

— A Musical Motley. LC 76-10332. (Music Reprint Ser.). 1976. lib. bdg. 35.00 (*0-306-70784-5*) Da Capo.

— A Musical Motley. 291p. 1990. reprint ed. lib. bdg. 69.00 (*0-7812-9001-5*) Rprt Serv.

— Musical Studies. LC 68-25297. (Studies in Music: No. 42). 1969. reprint ed. lib. bdg. 75.00 (*0-8383-0309-9*) M S G Haskell Hse.

— Musical Studies: Music Book Index. 319p. 1993. reprint ed. lib. bdg. 89.00 (*0-7812-9706-0*) Rprt Serv.

— Richard Strauss. LC 79-94279. (Select Bibliographies Reprint Ser.). 1977. 21.95 (*0-8369-5053-4*) Ayer.

— Richard Strauss. 144p. 1990. reprint ed. lib. bdg. 59.00 (*0-7812-9092-9*) Rprt Serv.

— Stories of the Great Operas & Their Composers, 3 vols. 1990. reprint ed. lib. bdg. 148.00 (*0-7812-9158-5*) Rprt Serv.

— Stories of the Great Operas & Their Composers, 3 vols., Set. 1988. reprint ed. lib. bdg. 249.00 (*0-7812-0408-9*) Rprt Serv.

— Stories of the Great Operas & Their Composers, 3 vols., Set. reprint ed. 195.00 (*0-403-01632-0*) Scholarly.

— Unconscious Beethoven: An Essay in Musical Psychology. 154p. 1990. reprint ed. lib. bdg. 59.00 (*0-7812-9045-7*) Rprt Serv.

— Wagner As Man & Artist. 1963. 16.50 (*0-8446-2653-8*) Peter Smith.

— The Wagner Operas. 729p. 1991. pap. text 22.95 (*0-691-02716-1*, Pub. by Princeton U Pr) Cal Prin Full Svc.

Newman, Ernest, tr. see Schweitzer, Albert.

Newman, Eva. Going Abroad: A Comprehensive Guide to Answering the Call of Nature Anywhere in the World, from Using the Bidet to the Ubiquitous "Squat" Toilet. LC 97-11367. (Illus.). 144p. 1997. pap. 12.95 (*0-943400-92-9*) Marlor Pr.

***Newman, Eva.** Going Abroad: The Bathroom Survival Guide. 2nd ed. 136p. 2000. pap. 12.95 (*1-892147-03-3*, Pub. by Marlor Pr) IPG Chicago.

Newman, F., jt. auth. see Manza, G.

Newman, F. X., ed. The Meaning of Courtly Love: Papers of the First Annual Conference of the Center for... LC 68-25571. 102p. (C). 1968. text 59.50 (*0-87395-038-0*, Pub. by State U NY Pr) Pegasus Pr.

— The Meaning of Courtly Love: Papers of the First Annual Conference of the Center for Medicine. LC 68-25571. 102p. (C). 1968. pap. text 19.95 (*0-87395-222-7*, Pub. by State U NY Pr) Pegasus Pr.

N

***Newman, Felice.** The Whole Lesbian Sex Book: A Passionate Guide for All of Us. (Illus.). 300p. 1999. pap. 21.95 (*1-57344-088-4*) Cleis Pr.

Newman, Felice, tr. see Galgoczi, Erzsebet.

Newman, Fran & Landsberg, Michele. Children in Crisis. 1993. pap. 14.95 (*0-590-73088-6*) Scholastic Inc.

Newman, Frances. Dead Lovers are Faithful Lovers: A Novel by Frances Newman. LC 93-39195. (Brown Thrasher Bks.). 312p. 1994. reprint ed. pap. 17.95 (*0-8203-1588-5*) U of Ga Pr.

— Frances Newman's Letters. (American Biography Ser.). 372p. 1991. reprint ed. lib. bdg. 90.00 (*0-7812-8296-9*) Rprt Serv.

— The Hard-Boiled Virgin. Hardwick, Elizabeth, ed. LC 76-51674. (Rediscovered Fiction by American Women Ser.). 1977. lib. bdg. 29.95 (*0-405-10052-3*) Ayer.

— The Hard-Boiled Virgin: A Novel by Frances Newman. LC 80-16376. (Brown Thrasher Bks.). 306p. 1993. reprint ed. pap. 17.95 (*0-8203-0526-X*) U of Ga Pr.

Newman, Frances, ed. see Laforgue, Jules.

Newman, Francis W. Regal Rome, an Intro to Roman History. 1952. 20.00 (*0-8196-1556-0*) Biblo.

Newman, Francis X., ed. Social Unrest in the Late Middle Ages: Papers of the Fifteenth Annual Conference of the Center for Medieval & Early Renaissance Studies. LC 85-28420. (Medieval & Renaissance Texts & Studies: Vol. 39). (Illus.). 160p. 1986. 20.00 (*0-86698-071-7*, MR39) MRTS.

Newman, Frank. International Human Rights, 2 vols., set. 2nd ed. 59.00 (*0-87084-395-8*) Anderson Pub Co.

Newman, Frank C. & Weissbrodt, David. International Human Rights: Law, Policy, & Process. 2nd ed. 878p. (C). 1996. 50.00 (*0-87084-370-2*) Anderson Pub Co.

— Selected International Human Rights Instruments & Bibliography for Research on International Human Rights Law. 2nd ed. 304p. (C). 1996. pap. 16.00 (*0-87084-362-1*) Anderson Pub Co.

Newman, Frank C., jt. auth. see Lillich, Richard B.

Newman, Fred. The Myth of Psychology. LC 91-76608. 229p. 1991. pap. 12.95 (*0-9628621-2-6*) Castillo Intl.

— Still on the Corner & Other Postmodern Political Plays by Fred Newman. Friedman, Dan, ed. LC 97-78448. (Illus.). 752p. (C). 1998. pap. 24.95 (*0-9662471-0-8*) Castillo NY.

Newman, Fred & Goldberg, Phyllis. Performance of a Lifetime: A Practical-Philosophical Guide to the Joyous Life. LC 96-83502. 256p. (Orig.). (C). 1996. pap. 11.95 (*0-9628621-7-7*) Castillo Intl.

Newman, Fred & Holzman, Lois. The End of Knowing: And the Rediscovery of Development in the Performance of Conversation. LC 96-52856. 208p. (C). 1997. 80.00 (*0-415-13598-2*); pap. 22.99 (*0-415-13599-0*) Routledge.

— Lev Vygotsky: Revolutionary Scientist. LC 92-28810. (Critical Psychology Ser.). 256p. (C). 1993. pap. 25.99 (*0-415-06442-2*, B0216) Routledge.

— Unscientific Psychology: A Cultural-Performatory Approach to Understanding Human Life. LC 96-2801. 232p. 1996. 59.95 (*0-275-95412-9*, Praeger Pubs) Greenwood.

Newman, Fred, et al. Let's Develop! A Guide to Continuous Personal Growth. LC 94-68612. 272p. 1994. pap. 11.95 (*0-9628621-6-9*) Castillo Intl.

Newman, Frederick L. & Sorenson, James E. Integrated Clinical & Fiscal Management in Mental Health: A Guidebook. Caddy, Glenn R., ed. LC 85-6219. (Developments in Clinical Psychology Ser.). 408p. 1986. text 82.50 (*0-89391-233-6*) Ablx Pub.

Newman, Frederick R. Mouthsounds. LC 80-51513. (Illus.). 128p. 1980. pap. 6.95 (*0-89480-128-7*, 427) Workman Pub.

Newman, G. F. Operation Bad Apple. (Royal Court Writers Ser.). 43p. (C). 1988. pap. 6.95 (*0-413-50270-8*, A0198) Heinemann.

Newman, G. R. & Hobot, J. A. Resin Microscopy & On-Section Immunocytochemistry. LC 93-14253. (Laboratory Ser.). 221p. 1993. 60.95 (*0-387-56429-2*) Spr-Verlag.

Newman, Gail M. Locating the Romantic Subject: Novalis with Winnicott. LC 96-30787. (Kritik: German Literary Theory & Cultural Studies Ser.). 264p. 1997. text 34.95 (*0-8143-2650-1*) Wayne St U Pr.

***Newman, Gavin.** An Unholy Way to Die. 154p. 1999. pap. 14.95 (*0-9532701-3-0*, Pub. by Bulldog Books) Firebird Dist.

Newman, Gene & Tada, Joni Eareckson. All God's Children: Ministry with Disabled Persons. rev. ed. LC 92-28627. 128p. 1993. pap. 12.99 (*0-310-59381-6*) Zondervan.

Newman, Gene, jt. auth. see Newman, Marsha.

Newman, George. Interpreters of Nature: Essays. LC 68-20325. (Essay Index Reprint Ser.). 1977. 20.95 (*0-8369-0741-8*) Ayer.

— 101 Ways to Be a Long-Distance Super-Dad... or Mom, Too! rev. ed. LC 99-94689. (Illus.). 123p. (Orig.). 1999. pap. 9.95 (*0-939894-02-5*) Blossom Valley.

Newman, George Charles, jt. auth. see Person, Ruth J.

Newman, George S., ed. Immigration Options for Doctors. 302p. 1995. 62.00 (*1-878677-77-2*, 53.10) Amer Immi Law Assn.

Newman, Gerald. Britain in the Hanoverian Age, 1714-1837: An Encyclopedia. LC 97-16840. (Illus.). 904p. 1997. text 125.00 (*0-8153-0396-3*, H1481) Garland.

— Happy Birthday, Little League. LC 88-38158. (First Bks.). 64p. (J). (gr. 4-6). 1989. lib. bdg. 22.00 (*0-531-10687-X*) Watts.

— Rise of English Nationalism: A Cultural History, 1740-1830. 294p. 1997. pap. 18.95 (*0-312-17699-6*) St Martin.

Newman, Gerald & Layfield, Eleanor N. PCP. LC 97-484. (Drug Library Ser.). (Illus.). 128p. (YA). (gr. 6 up). 1997. lib. bdg. 20.95 (*0-89490-852-9*) Enslow Pubs.

— Racism: Divided by Color. LC 94-38963. (Multicultural Issues Ser.). (Illus.). 112p. (YA). (gr. 6 up). 1995. lib. bdg. 20.95 (*0-89490-641-0*) Enslow Pubs.

Newman, Gerald & Newman Layfield, Eleanor. Martha Graham: Founder of Modern Dance. LC 98-20410. (Book Report Biography Ser.). (J). 1998. 22.00 (*0-531-11442-2*) Watts.

Newman, Gladys T. & Kroll, William. Olivia. (Illus.). 212p. 1996. text 18.95 (*0-9649532-0-X*, OL 112696-1) G T Newman.

***Newman, Gloria.** My Mommy's Having a Baby. 2nd rev. ed. (Illus.). 20p. (J). (gr. k-3). 2000. pap. 12.95 (*0-9659094-1-7*) Growing Up Great.

Newman, Gordon P. Dictionnaire des Idees dans l'Oeuvre de Marcel Proust. (FRE.). 1968. 59.95 (*0-8288-6634-1*, M-6624) Fr & Eur.

Newman, Graeme. Just & Painful: A Case for the Corporal Punishment of Criminals. 2nd rev. ed. 180p. (C). 1995. pap. text 21.50 (*0-911577-33-5*, Criminal Justice) Willow Tree NY.

— Punishment & Privilege. Groves, W. Byron, ed. LC 86-83030. (Illus.). 180p. 1987. pap. text 22.50 (*0-911577-10-6*, Criminal Justice) Willow Tree NY.

Newman, Graeme, et al, eds. Discovering Criminology: From W. Byron Groves. LC 92-32789. 350p. (C). 1993. text 69.50 (*0-911577-16-5*, Criminal Justice) Willow Tree NY.

— Rational Choice & Situational Crime Prevention: Theoretical Foundations. LC 97-7934. 288p. 1997. text 78.95 (*1-85521-947-6*, Pub. by Ashgate Pub) Ashgate Pub Co.

Newman, Graeme, pref. The Punishment Response. 2nd ed. LC 85-80304. 340p. 1985. reprint ed. pap. text 27.50 (*0-911577-02-5*, Criminal Justice) Willow Tree NY.

Newman, Graeme & Newman, Betsy. Good Food from Australia: A Hippocrene Original Cookbook. 2nd ed. (Original Cookbook Ser.). 188p. 1997. reprint ed. 22.50 (*0-7818-0491-4*) Hippocrene Bks.

Newman, Graeme, jt. auth. see Nalla, Mahesh.

Newman, Graeme, jt. auth. see United Nations Office for Drug Control & Crime Prevention Staff.

Newman, Graeme R., ed. Crime & Deviance: A Comparative Perspective. LC 80-11629. (Sage Annual Reviews of Studies in Deviance: No. 4). 335p. reprint ed. pap. 103.90 (*0-8357-8501-7*, 203477700091) Bks Demand.

Newman, Grant. Teaching Children Music: Fundamentals of Music & Method. 4th ed. 400p. (C). 1994. text. write for info. (*0-697-12540-8*) Brown & Benchmark.

— Teaching Children Music: Fundamentals of Music & Method. 4th ed. 80p. (C). 1995. text, student ed. 23.75 (*0-697-12541-6*) Brown & Benchmark.

Newman, Greg. Sam's Teach Yourself Networking in 24 Hours. LC 97-67498. 425p. 1998. 19.99 (*0-672-31145-3*) Sams.

Newman, Gwen. Perennials: A Southern Celebration of Foods & Flavors. LC 83-81825. vi, 426p. 1984. 14.95 (*0-9612234-0-5*) Perennial Pubns.

Newman, H. B. & Ypsilantis, T. History of Original Ideas & Basic Discoveries in Particle Physics. (NATO ASI Ser.: No. 352). (Illus.). 1018p. (C). 1996. text 234.00 (*0-306-45217-0*, Kluwer Plenum) Kluwer Academic.

Newman, H. Michael. Direct Digital Control of Building Systems: Theory & Practice. (Series of Practical Construction Guides). 264p. 1994. 99.00 (*0-471-51696-1*) Wiley.

Newman, H. Morton, jt. auth. see Blake, Fay M.

Newman, Harold. Effective Language Arts Practices in the Elementary Schools: Selected Readings. LC 75-38951. 894p. reprint ed. pap. 200.00 (*0-608-30293-7*, 201188000079) Bks Demand.

— Extending Reading Horizons. 95p. (Orig.). (C). 1994. pap. text 20.00 (*0-9613577-4-6*) Prestige Educ.

— Extending Reading Horizons: A College Reader. LC 93-40696. 1994. write for info. (*0-9613577-5-4*) Prestige Educ.

— An Illustrated Dictionary of Jewelry. LC 86-51260. (Illus.). 336p. 1994. reprint ed. pap. 29.95 (*0-500-27452-5*, Pub. by Thames Hudson) Norton.

— An Illustrated Dictionary of Silverware. LC 86-51576. (Illus.). 384p. 1987. 39.95 (*0-500-23456-6*, Pub. by Thames Hudson) Norton.

***Newman, Harold.** An Illustrated Dictionary of Silverware. LC 86-51576. (Illus.). 368p. 2000. pap. 29.95 (*0-500-28196-3*, Pub. by Thames Hudson) Norton.

Newman, Harold. Parents & Teachers Ask about Reading. 115p. 1986. pap. text 15.00 (*0-9613577-1-1*) Prestige Educ.

— Reading - Learning - Enjoying: A College Reader. LC 88-19495. 94p. (C). 1988. pap. text 15.00 (*0-9613577-2-X*) Prestige Educ.

— Reading for Understanding & Stimulation: A College Reader. (Orig.). (C). 1990. pap. text. write for info. (*0-9613577-3-8*) Prestige Educ.

— Upgrading Your College Reading: Study Skills. 108p. (Orig.). (C). 1984. pap. 15.00 (*0-9613577-0-3*) Prestige Educ.

— Veilleuses: A Collector's Guide. (Illus.). 176p. 1988. 45.00 (*0-8453-4755-1*, Cornwall Bks) Assoc Univ Prs.

Newman, Harold & Savage, George. An Illustrated Dictionary of Ceramics. LC 85-51073. (Illus.). 320p. 2000. pap. 24.95 (*0-500-27380-4*, Pub. by Thames Hudson) Norton.

***Newman, Harry, Jr.** Turning 21: A Businessman's Poetic Odyssey to the New Century. (Illus.). 200p. 1999. 21.00 (*0-9672058-0-8*) Nine Muses.

Newman, Harry & Davis, Clinton T., eds. Beyond Tradition: Transcripts of the First National Symposium on Non-Traditional Casting. (Illus.). 122p. (Orig.). 1988. pap. 15.00 (*0-927340-00-3*) Non-Traditional.

Newman, Harry W. Anne Arundel Gentry: A Genealogical History of Twenty-Two Pioneers of Anne Arundel County & Their Descendants. 668p. 1995. reprint ed. lib. bdg. 69.50 (*0-8328-4692-9*) Higginson Bk Co.

— Charles County Gentry. (Illus.). 321p. 1997. reprint ed. pap. 30.00 (*0-8063-0486-3*, 4095) Clearfield Co.

— Charles County, Maryland Gentry: Genealogical History of Six Emigrants - Thomas Dent, John Dent, Richard Edelson, John Hanson, George Newman, Humphrey Warren - Who Settled in Charles County, & Their Descedants, Showing Emigrations to the South & West. (Illus.). 321p. 1997. reprint ed. lib. bdg. 39.50 (*0-8328-5950-8*) Higginson Bk Co.

— The Flowering of the Maryland Palatinate: An Intimate & Objective HIstory of the Province of Maryland to the Overthrow of Proprietory Rule in 1654. LC 83-82451. (Illus.). 359p. 1998. reprint ed. pap. 32.50 (*0-8063-1051-0*, Pub. by Clearfield Co) ACCESS Pubs Network.

— Maryland Revolutionary Records: Data Obtained from 3,050 Pension Claims & Bounty Land Applications, Including 1,000 Marriages of Maryland Soldiers & a List of 1,200 Proved Services of Soldiers & Patriots of Other States. LC 67-28367. 155p. 1993. reprint ed. 17.50 (*0-8063-0257-7*) Genealog Pub.

Newman, Harvey K. Southern Hospitality: Tourism & the Growth of Atlanta. 368p. 1999. text 44.95 (*0-8173-0961-6*) U of Ala Pr.

— Southern Hospitality: Tourism & the Growth of Atlanta. LC 98-58014. (Illus.). 368p. 1999. pap. 24.95 (*0-8173-0972-1*) U of Ala Pr.

***Newman, Heather.** PC @ Home. (Illus.). 184p. 1999. pap. 14.95 (*0-937247-31-6*) Detroit Pr.

Newman, Henry W. Acute Alcoholic Intoxication: A Critical Review. x, 207p. 1941. 29.50 (*0-8047-0995-5*) Stanford U Pr.

— Acute Alcoholic Intoxication: A Critical Review. fac. ed. LC 41-28278. 217p. 1941. reprint ed. pap. 30.00 (*0-7837-7919-4*, 204767500008) Bks Demand.

Newman, Herta. Virginia Woolf & Mrs. Brown: Toward a Realism of Uncertainty. LC 96-3370. (Origins of Modernism Ser.: Vol. 03). 168p. 1996. text 40.00 (*0-8240-5172-6*, H1328) Garland.

Newman, Holly. A Grand Gesture. 208p. 1989. mass mkt. 3.50 (*0-446-35043-5*, Pub. by Warner Bks) Little.

— A Lady Follows. LC 98-41785. (Women of the West Ser.). 384p. 1999. 24.95 (*0-312-86871-5*, Pub. by Forge NYC) St Martin.

***Newman, Holly.** Lady Follows. (Women of the West Novels Ser.). 384p. 2000. mass mkt. 6.99 (*0-8125-2407-1*, Pub. by Forge NYC) St Martin.

— Newman American Historical. 2000. text 22.95 (*0-312-86869-3*) St Martin.

Newman, Horatio H., ed. Evolution, Genetics & Eugenics. LC 69-14010. (Illus.). 620p. 1970. reprint ed. lib. bdg. 89.50 (*0-8371-1880-8*, NEEV, Greenwood Pr) Greenwood.

Newman, Isadore. Basic Procedures in Conducting Survey Research. 4th ed. 39p. 1976. pap. text 1.00 (*0-917180-04-6*) I Newman.

Newman, Isadore, ed. Computer-Assisted Instructions. Four Selected Articles & a Cross Referenced, Annotated Bibliography. 141p. 1975. pap. text 4.00 (*0-917180-03-8*) I Newman.

Newman, Isadore & Benz, Carolyn. Multiple Linear Regression: A Workbook, Syllabus, Readings; Problems & Exams. 1979. pap. text 7.25 (*0-917180-07-0*) I Newman.

Newman, Isadore & Benz, Carolyn R. Qualitative-Quantitative Research Methodology: Exploring the Interactive Continuum. LC 97-23117. (Illus.). 176p. (Orig.). 1998. pap. 14.95 (*0-8093-2150-5*) S Ill U Pr.

Newman, Isadore & McNeil, Keith A. Conducting Survey Research in the Social Sciences. LC 98-34837. 103p. (C). 1998. pap. 20.50 (*0-7618-1227-X*) U Pr of Amer.

Newman, Isadore & Newman, Carole. Conceptual Statistics for Beginners. 2nd ed. 298p. (C). 1994. pap. text 29.50 (*0-8191-9420-4*) U Pr of Amer.

— Thirty-Eight, Twenty-Two, Thirty-Six Conceptual Statistics for Beginners. 4th ed. 207p. 1977. pap. text 5.50 (*0-917180-06-2*) I Newman.

Newman, Isadore, et al. An Introduction to the Basic Concepts & Techniques of Measurement & Evaluation. 4th ed. 210p. 1976. reprint ed. pap. text 5.00 (*0-917180-05-4*) I Newman.

— Theses & Dissertations: A Guide to Writing in the Social & Physical Sciences. LC 97-21779. 152p. (C). 1997. 49.00 (*0-7618-0814-0*); pap. 27.50 (*0-7618-0815-9*) U Pr of Amer.

Newman, Isidora. Fairy Flowers. 1976. 22.95 (*0-8488-0596-8*) Amereon Ltd.

Newman, J., jt. auth. see Knight, David C.

Newman, J. C., Jr. & Elber, Wolf, eds. Mechanics of Fatigue Crack Closure, STP 982. LC 88-6303. (Special Technical Publication (STP) Ser.). (Illus.). 650p. 1988. text 105.00 (*0-8031-0996-2*, STP982) ASTM.

Newman, J. C., Jr. & Loss, F. J., eds. Elastic-Plastic Fracture Mechanics Technology, STP 896. LC 85-22965. (Illus.). 185p. 1986. text 30.00 (*0-8031-0449-9*, STP896) ASTM.

Newman, J. C., ed. see Symposium on Advances in Fatigue Crack Closure Measurement & Analysis Staff, et al.

Newman, J. D., ed. The Physiological Control of Mammalian Vocalization. (Illus.). 438p. 1988. 105.00 (*0-306-43003-7*, Plenum Trade) Perseus Pubng.

Newman, J. G., et al. Static SIMS Handbook of Polymer Analysis. LC 90-62564. (Illus.). 200p. (Orig.). 1991. write for info. (*0-9627026-0-9*); pap. write for info. (*0-9627026-1-7*) Perkin-Elmer.

Newman, J. R., jt. auth. see Gates, T. S.

Newman, J. Robert, jt. auth. see Edwards, Ward.

Newman, J. Wilson. The Private Sector. (Credibility of Institutions, Policies & Leadership Ser.: Vol. 6). 140p. (Orig.). 1985. pap. 15.00 (*0-8191-4766-4*) U Pr of Amer.

— The Private Sector. (Credibility of Institutions, Policies & Leadership Ser.: Vol. 6). 140p. (Orig.). 1985. lib. bdg. 39.00 (*0-8191-4765-6*, Pub. by White Miller Center) U Pr of Amer.

***Newman, Jack.** Ultimate Breastfeeding Book of Answers: The Most Comprehensive Problem-Solution Guide to Breastfeeding. (Illus.). 2000. pap. 16.95 (*0-7615-2996-9*) Prima Pub.

***Newman, Jack & Pitman.** Dr. Jack Newman's Guide to Breastfeeding. 256p. 2000. pap. 20.95 (*0-00-638568-0*) HarpC.

Newman, Jacqueline M., ed. Chinese Cuisine & American Palate: The Arts & Science of Chinese Cooking. 120p. (Orig.). pap. 18.95 (*0-930194-99-3*) Ctr Thanatology.

Newman, James A. Making a Living. (Illus.). 120p. (Orig.). (J). (gr. 2-8). 1991. pap. 7.95 (*0-9642980-0-7*) J A Newman.

***Newman, James C., Jr. & Piascik, Robert S., eds.** Fatigue Crack Growth Thresholds, Endurance Limits & Design. LC 99-89527. (STP Ser.: Vol. 1372). (Illus.). 450p. 2000. text 135.00 (*0-8031-2624-7*, STP1372) ASTM.

Newman, James C., Jr., ed. see Reuter, Walter G.

Newman, James L. The Peopling of Africa: A Geographic Interpretation. LC 94-28259. 235p. 1995. 37.00 (*0-300-06003-3*) Yale U Pr.

— The Peopling of Africa: A Geographic Interpretation. 252p. 1997. pap. text 15.00 (*0-300-07280-5*) Yale U Pr.

Newman, James L., jt. ed. see Griffith, Daniel A.

***Newman, James R.** World of Mathematics. (Illus.). (J). 2000. pap. 12.95 (*0-486-41150-8*); pap. 12.95 (*0-486-41151-6*); pap. 12.95 (*0-486-41152-4*); pap. 12.95 (*0-486-41153-2*) Dover.

Newman, James R., jt. auth. see Nagel, Ernest.

Newman, James R., ed. see Clifford, William K.

Newman, James W. Release Your Brakes! 304p. 1993. reprint ed. pap. 14.95 (*0-963898-0-4*) Pace Orgztn.

***Newman, Jane O.** The Intervention of Philology. LC 99-40597. (Studies in the Germanic Languages & Literatures). 304p. 2000. lib. bdg. 45.00 (*0-8078-8122-8*) U of NC Pr.

Newman, Jane O. Pastoral Conventions: Poetry, Language, & Thought in Seventeenth-Century Nuremberg. LC 89-49002. 328p. reprint ed. pap. 101.70 (*0-608-06175-1*, 206650800008) Bks Demand.

Newman, Janet. Shaping Organisational Cultures in Local Government. (Managing Local Government Ser.). 176p. 1996. pap. 42.50 (*0-273-61987-X*) F T P-H.

Newman, Janet, jt. auth. see Clarke, John.

Newman, Janet, jt. ed. see Itzen, Catherine.

Newman, Jay. Competition in Religious Life. LC 89-941106. (Editions SR Ser.: Vol. 11). 245p. (C). 1989. pap. 22.95 (*0-88920-989-8*) W Laurier U Pr.

— Fanatics & Hypocrites. LC 86-9436. 151p. 1986. 32.95 (*0-87975-348-X*) Prometheus Bks.

— Foundations of Religious Tolerance. 192p. 1982. pap. 11.95 (*0-8020-6507-4*); text 30.00 (*0-8020-5591-5*) U of Toronto Pr.

— Inauthentic Culture & Its Philosophical Critics. LC 00-551045. 232p. 1997. text 65.00 (*0-7735-1676-X*, Pub. by McG-Queens Univ Pr); pap. text 22.95 (*0-7735-1691-3*, Pub. by McG-Queens Univ Pr) CUP Services.

— The Journalist in Plato's Cave. LC 88-48022. 208p. 1990. 36.50 (*0-8386-3349-8*) Fairleigh Dickinson.

— Religion & Technology: A Study in the Philosophy of Culture. LC 96-50321. 208p. 1997. 57.95 (*0-275-95865-5*, Praeger Pubs) Greenwood.

— Religion vs. Television: Competitors in Cultural Context. LC 96-10439. (Media & Society Ser.). 168p. 1996. 57.95 (*0-275-95640-7*, Praeger Pubs) Greenwood.

Newman, Jay B., jt. auth. see Goldman, Gary.

Newman, Jean C. Pedro Salinas & His Circumstance. LC 83-10778. (Illus.). 274p. (C). 1984. pap. 11.95 (*0-913480-56-8*) Inter Am U Pr.

Newman, Jeffrey A., et al. Massachusetts Premises Liability: Includes Forms on Disk. LC 97-70630. 618p. 1997. ring bd. 95.00 incl. disk (*1-57589-065-8*, 98-17.05-BK) Mass CLE.

Newman, Jennifer. Exquisite Embroidery. (Milner Craft Ser.). (Illus.). 160p. 1995. pap. 19.95 (*1-86351-154-7*, Pub. by Sally Milner) Sterling.

Newman, Jennifer O. Asia-Pacific Satellite Industry Directory. 2nd ed. 1996. pap., per. 169.00 (*0-614-15319-0*) Phillips Business.

— GPS Directory, Spring '96. 8th ed. 1996. pap., per. 129.00 (*1-881537-48-X*) Phillips Business.

— 1997 Security Industry Buyers Guide. 10th ed. 1996. pap., per. 169.00 (*1-881537-41-2*) Phillips Business.

— 1996 Canadian Electronic Commerce Directory. 1996. pap. 169.00 (*1-881537-49-8*) Phillips Business.

— 1996 Regional Airline Directory. 5th ed. 1996. pap., per. 247.00 (*1-881537-35-8*) Phillips Business.

— 1996 Who's Who in Electronic Commerce. 8th ed. 1996. pap., per. 199.00 (*1-881537-42-0*) Phillips Business.

Newman, Jennifer O., ed. 1996 Cable Industry Directory. 3rd ed. 1996. pap., per. 229.00 (*1-881537-40-4*) Phillips Business.

— 1996 EDI Yellow Pages. 11th ed. 1996. pap., per. 199.00 (*1-881537-36-6*) Phillips Business.

— 1996 International Imaging Source Book. 1996. pap., per. 199.00 (*1-881537-44-7*) Phillips Business.

— 1996 Satellite Industry Directory: Formerly the World Satellite Directory. 18th ed. 1996. pap., per. 257.00 (1-881537-37-4) Phillips Business.

— 1996 Telephone Industry Directory. 10th ed. 1996. pap., per. 249.00 (1-881537-32-3) Phillips Business.

— 1996 Wireless Industry Directory. 7th ed. 1996. pap., per. 249.00 (1-881537-38-2) Phillips Business.

— 1996 World Satellite Almanac: Incorporating the Satellite Systems Handbook. 8th ed. 1996. pap., per. 249.00 (1-881537-39-0) Phillips Business.

***Newman, Jenny, et al, eds.** The Writer's Workbook. 192p. 2000. pap. 16.95 (0-340-76001-X, Pub. by E A); text 55.00 (0-340-75999-2, Pub. by E A) OUP.

Newman, Jeremiah. The Postmodern Church. 157p. 1990. 10.00 (1-85182-064-7) Lumen Christi.

Newman, Jerry. Green Earrings & a Felt Hat. LC 92-29056. (Illus.). 48p. (J). (gr. 1-3). 1995. 14.95 (0-8050-2392-5, Bks Young Read) H Holt & Co.

***Newman, Jerry L., ed.** The Reader's Dictionary. LC 00-91203. 351p. 2000. 11.95 (0-9700398-0-8) Hippogriff.

Newman, Jerry M. & Milkovich, George. CPS - Compensation Chapters 14 & 16. 4th ed. 72p. (C). 1995. text 8.95 (0-256-19897-7, Irwn McGrw-H) McGrw-H Hghr Educ.

***Newman, Jill.** If I Called You a Duck Would You Quack? A Kid's Eye View of Self Esteem: How It Goes Away & How to Get it Back! (Illus.). 16p. (J). (gr. k-5). 1999. pap. 12.95 (0-9674262-0-0) J Newman.

***Newman, Jim.** Cat People. 1999. pap. 10.95 (0-85170-741-6, Pub. by British Film Inst) Ind U Pr.

Newman, Jim. Four Hundred Great R-C Modeling Tips. (Illus.). 74p. 1987. 12.95 (0-911295-05-4) Air Age.

— Four Hundred Great R-C Modeling Tips, Vol. II. LC 92-204234. (Illus.). 74p. 1991. 14.95 (0-911295-17-8) Air Age.

— 401 R/C Tech Tips for Your R/C Car. (Illus.). 71p. 1996. pap. 12.95 (0-911295-11-9) Air Age.

— 402 R/C Control Car Technical Tips. Jeffcoat, Karen, ed. LC 95-161482. (Illus.). 74p. (Orig.). 1994. pap. 12.95 (0-911295-27-5) Air Age.

— 250 Great R/C Marine Tips. (Illus.). 46p. (Orig.). 1996. pap. 12.95 (0-911295-16-X) Air Age.

Newman, Jim & Raymond, Kathleen Z. Workshop Wisdom Dollhouse Crafting Tips from Nutshell News. Kraszewski, Andrea L., ed. (Illus.). 64p. 1992. pap. text 9.95 (0-89778-289-5, 10-7745) Kalmbach.

Newman, Joan, ed. see Kulvinskas, Viktoras.

***Newman, Joanna.** Refugees & the British West Indies During the Nazi Era. (Illus.). 200p. 2000. (0-85303-367-6); pap. (0-85303-374-9) Intl Spec Bk.

Newman, John. Give: A Cognitive Linguistic Study. LC 96-11061. (Cognitive Linguistic Research Ser.: No. 7). xviii, 319p. (C). 1996. lib. bdg. 49.95 (3-11-014894-3) Mouton.

Newman, John. Glamorgan. text 65.00 (0-14-071056-6, Pub. by Pnguin Bks Ltd) Trafalgar.

Newman, John. The Misfit. 228p. 1999. pap. 14.95 (0-7392-0051-8, PO2846) Morris Pubng.

— Old High German Reader. 158p. (Orig.). (C). 1981. pap. text 8.65 (0-89894-012-5) Advocate Pub Group.

— Oswald & the CIA. 608p. 1995. 28.00 (0-7867-0131-5) Carroll & Graf.

— Oswald & the CIA. (Illus.). 627p. 1998. text 28.00 (0-7881-5487-7) DIANE Pub.

***Newman, John.** Scuba Diving & Snorkeling for Dummies. (Illus.). 384p. 1999. pap. 19.99 incl. cd-rom (0-7645-5151-5, Dummies Trade Pr) IDG Bks.

Newman, John. Wisdom for Earthlings: How to Make Better Choices & Take Action in Your Life & in Your Work. 208p. 1996. pap. 16.95 (0-8144-7911-1) AMACOM.

Newman, John, ed. The Linguistics of Giving. LC 97-39855. (Typological Studies in Language: Vol. 36). (ENG & MUL.). xv, 373p. 1998. pap. 34.95 (1-55619-648-2); lib. bdg. 98.00 (1-55619-647-4) J Benjamins Pubng Co.

Newman, John & Hilfinger, Ann. Vietnam War Literature: An Annotated Bibliography of Imaginative Works about Americans Fighting in Vietnam. 2nd ed. LC 88-15747. 299p. 1988. 29.00 (0-8108-2155-9) Scarecrow.

Newman, John, et al. Vietnam War Literature: An Annotated Biliography of Imaginative Works about Americans Fighting in Vietnam. 3rd ed. 1996. 70.00 (0-8108-3184-8) Scarecrow.

Newman, John, jt. auth. see Sands, Trent.

Newman, John D. DeGruchy's Mantle: A Pastoral in Blank Verse. 37p. (Orig.). (YA). (gr. 7-12). 1994. pap. 4.00 (1-57514-218-X, 1112) Encore Perform Pub.

Newman, John E. How to Stay Cool, Calm, & Collected When the Pressure's On: A Stress-Control Plan for Businesspeople. 176p. 1992. pap. 15.95 (0-8144-7765-8) AMACOM.

Newman, John E. & Hinrichs, John R. Performance Evaluation for Professional Personnel. (Studies in Productivity: Highlights of the Literature Ser.: Vol. 14). 48p. 1980. pap. 55.00 (0-89361-021-6) Work in Amer.

— Performance Evaluation for Professional Personnel, Vol. 14. LC 80-20739. (Studies in Productivity, Highlights of the Literature). 1982. pap. 35.00 (0-685-05451-9, Pergamon Pr) Elsevier.

Newman, John Henry. Apologia Pro Vita Sua. Culler, Arthur D., ed. (C). 1956. mass mkt. 13.16 (0-395-05109-6) HM.

Newman, John Henry. Apologia Pro Vita Sua. (C). 1968. pap. text 16.75 (0-393-09766-8) Norton.

— Apologia Pro Vita Sua. 432p. 1993. pap. 10.95 (0-460-87232-X, Everyman's Classic Lib) Tuttle Pubng.

— Apologia Pro Vita Sua. Ker, Ian, ed. & intro. by. 608p. 1995. pap. 15.95 (0-14-043374-0, Penguin Classics) Viking Penguin.

— Apologia Pro Vita Sua: Being a History of His Religious Opinions. Svaglic, Martin J., ed. & intro. by. (Oxford English Texts Ser.). 664p. 1991. 160.00 (0-19-811840-6) OUP.

— The Arians of the Fourth Century. 254p. (Orig.). 1996. pap. 26.00 (0-9653517-2-6) Wipf & Stock.

***Newman, John Henry.** Callista: A Tale of the Third Century. 2nd ed. Hill, Alan G., ed. 416p. 2001. reprint ed. 35.00 (0-268-02260-7, Pub. by U of Notre Dame Pr) Chicago Distribution Ctr.

Newman, John Henry. A Cardinal Newman Prayerbook: Kindly Light. 352p. 1985. pap. 14.95 (0-87193-220-2) Dimension Bks.

— Discourses to Mixed Congregations. 384p. 1995. reprint ed. 24.95 (0-912141-39-5) Roman Cath Bks.

— An Essay in Aid of a Grammar of Assent. Ker, Ian, ed. & intro. by. 480p. 1985. text 94.00 (0-19-812751-0) OUP.

— An Essay in Aid of a Grammar of Assent. LC 78-51523. 1979. reprint ed. pap. text 16.50 (0-268-01000-5) U of Notre Dame Pr.

— An Essay on the Development of Christian Doctrine. LC 89-40021. (Series in the Great Bks.: No. 4). 480p. (C). 1989. pap. text 17.50 (0-268-00921-X) U of Notre Dame Pr.

— Fifteen Sermons Preached Before the University of Oxford Between A.D. 1826 & 1843. LC 96-26441. (Series in the Great Bks.). 392p. (Orig.). (C). 1996. pap. text 14.95 (0-268-00996-1) U of Notre Dame Pr.

— The Idea of a University. LC 99-29539. 1999. pap. text 19.95 (0-89526-400-5, Pub. by Regnery Pub) Natl Bk Netwk.

— The Idea of a University. Turner, Frank M., ed. LC 95-38832. (Rethinking the Western Tradition Ser.). 366p. 1996. 37.00 (0-300-06404-7); pap. 18.00 (0-300-06405-5) Yale U Pr.

— The Idea of a University. Svaglic, Martin J., ed. LC 82-7019. (Series in the Great Bks.). 428p. 1982. reprint ed. pap. text 15.00 (0-268-01150-8) U of Notre Dame Pr.

— The Idea of a University: Defined & Illustrated. O'Connell, Daniel M., ed. 498p. (C). 1987. reprint ed. 15.95 (0-8294-0585-2) Loyola Pr.

— John Henry Newman: Selected Sermons. (Classics of Western Spirituality Ser.). 432p. 1994. 29.95 (0-8091-0465-2); pap. 19.95 (0-8091-3451-9) Paulist Pr.

— The Kingdom Within: Discourses to Mixed Congregations. 1984. pap. 16.95 (0-87193-216-4) Dimension Bks.

— Lead, Kindly Light. Helms, Hal M., ed. LC 87-60611. (Living Library). 208p. 1987. pap. 10.95 (0-941478-78-5, 930-030, Pub. by Paraclete MA) BookWorld.

***Newman, John Henry.** Lectures on the Present Position of Catholics in England. Nash, Andrew, ed. (Works of Cardinal Newman: Vol. 1). 592p. 2000. 40.00 (0-268-01323-3, Pub. by U of Notre Dame Pr) Chicago Distribution Ctr.

Newman, John Henry. The Letters & Diaries of John Henry Cardinal Newman Vol. 1: Ealing, Trinity, Oriel, February 1801 to December 1826. Ker, Ian & Gornall, Thomas, eds. 364p. 1978. text 52.00 (0-19-920102-1) OUP.

— The Letters & Diaries of John Henry Cardinal Newman Vol. 2: Tutor of Oriel, January 1827 to December 1831. Ker, Ian & Gornall, Thomas, eds. 436p. 1979. text 55.00 (0-19-920108-0) OUP.

— The Letters & Diaries of John Henry Cardinal Newman Vol. 3: New Bearings, January 1832 to June 1833. Ker, Ian & Gornall, Thomas, eds. 364p. 1979. text 52.00 (0-19-920109-9) OUP.

— The Letters & Diaries of John Henry Cardinal Newman Vol. 4: The Oxford Movement, July 1833 to December 1834. Ker, Ian & Gornall, Thomas, eds. 428p. 1980. text 55.00 (0-19-920112-9) OUP.

— The Letters & Diaries of John Henry Cardinal Newman Vol. 5: Liberalism in Oxford, January 1835 to December 1836. Gornall, Thomas, ed. 440p. 1981. text 65.00 (0-19-920117-X) OUP.

— The Letters & Diaries of John Henry Cardinal Newman Vol. 6: The Via Media & Froude's Remains, January 1837 to December 1838. Tracey, Gerard, ed. 438p. 1984. text 70.00 (0-19-920141-2) OUP.

— The Letters & Diaries of John Henry Cardinal Newman Vol. 29: The Cardinalate, January 1878-September 1881. Dessain, Charles S. & Gornall, Thomas, eds. 496p. 1976. text 47.00 (0-19-920059-9) OUP.

— The Letters & Diaries of John Henry Cardinal Newman Vol. 30: A Cardinal's Apostolate, October 1881-December 1884. Dessain, Charles S. & Garnall, Thomas, eds. 504p. 1976. text 47.00 (0-19-920060-2) OUP.

— The Letters & Diaries of John Henry Cardinal Newman Vol. 31: The Last Years, January 1885 to August 1890. Dessain, Charles S. & Gornall, Thomas, eds. 458p. 1977. text 52.00 (0-19-920083-1) OUP.

— The Letters & Diaries of John Henry Newman Vol. VIII: Tract 90 & the Jerusalem Bishopric. Tracey, Gerard, ed. 672p. 2000. text 120.00 (0-19-920403-9) OUP.

— Mary the Second Eve. 40p. 1991. reprint ed. pap. 3.00 (0-89555-181-0) TAN Bks Pubs.

— Newman for Everyone: 101 Questions Answered Imaginatively by Newman. Brady, Jules M., ed. LC 96-1267. 170p. (Orig.). 1996. pap. 5.95 (0-8189-0736-3) Alba.

— On Consulting the Faithful in Matters of Doctrine. Coulson, John, ed. LC 62-9877. 128p. 1985. reprint ed. pap. 7.95 (0-934134-51-0) Sheed & Ward WI.

— Parochial & Plain Sermons. 1997. 49.95 (0-89870-638-6) Ignatius Pr.

— The Philosophical Notebook, 2 vols., Set. Sillem, E., ed. Incl. Vol. 1. General Introduction. 257p. 1970. text Vol. 2. Text. v, 218p. 1970. text 1970. 105.00 (0-912116-13-7) Learned Pubns.

— Prayers, Verses & Devotions. LC 88-81571. 766p. 1989. 31.95 (0-89870-217-8) Ignatius Pr.

— A Reason for the Hope Within: Sermons on the Theory of Religious Belief. 368p. 1985. pap. 16.95 (0-87193-219-9) Dimension Bks.

— Roman Catholic Writings on Doctrinal Development. Gaffney, James, tr. & comment by. LC 97-16289. (Orig.). 1997. pap. 15.95 (1-55612-973-4, LL1973) Sheed & Ward WI.

***Newman, John Henry.** Selected Sermons, Prayers & Devotions. Thornton, John F. & Varenne, Susan B., eds. LC BX5133.N4S352 1999. (Spiritual Classics Ser.). 384p. 1999. pap. 12.95 (0-375-70551-1) Vin Bks.

Newman, John Henry. Sermons, 1824-1843 Vol. I: Sermons on the Liturgy & Sacraments & on Christ the Mediator. Murray, Placid, ed. 406p. 1992. text 98.00 (0-19-920088-2) OUP.

— Sermons, 1824-1843 Vol. II: Sermons on Biblical History, Sin & Justification, the Christian Way of Life, & Biblical Theology. Blehl, Vincent F., ed. 494p. 1994. text 95.00 (0-19-920401-2) OUP.

***Newman, John Henry.** Two Essays on Miracles. 412p. 1998. pap. 30.00 (1-57910-186-0) Wipf & Stock.

Newman, John Henry. The Uses of Knowledge: Selections from the Idea of a University. Ward, Leo L., ed. (Crofts Classics). 128p. 1948. pap. text 4.95 (0-88295-063-0) Harlan Davidson.

— Verses on Various Occasions. 1992. 18.95 (0-87193-282-2) Dimension Bks.

— Who Is a Christian? 1985. pap. 16.95 (0-87193-188-5) Dimension Bks.

Newman, John Henry, et al, eds. Tracts for the Times, 6 vols. 1969. lib. bdg. 450.00 (0-404-04710-6) AMS Pr.

Newman, John Henry, jt. auth. see North, Roger.

Newman, John Henry, tr. see Athanasius.

Newman, John Henry, tr. & pref. see Aquinas, Thomas, Saint.

***Newman, John J.** American Naturalization Records, 1790-1990: What They Are & How to Use Them. 2nd rev. ed. LC 98-71939. 127p. 1998. pap. 12.95 (1-877677-91-4, Precision Index) Herit Quest.

Newman, John K. Augustan Propertius - The Recapitulation of a Genre. LC 97-194547. (Spudasmata Ser.: Bd. 63). 560p. 1997. 135.00 (3-487-10298-6) G Olms Pubs.

— The Classical Epic Tradition. LC 85-40766. (Studies in Classics). 576p. 1986. text 35.00 (0-299-10510-5) U of Wis Pr.

Newman, John M. JFK & Vietnam: Deception, Intrigue, & the Struggle for Power. 528p. 1992. 22.95 (0-446-51678-3) Warner Bks.

Newman, John N. Marine Hydrodynamics. 1977. 63.00 (0-262-14026-8) MIT Pr.

***Newman, John Q.** Be Your Own Dick: Private Investigating Made Easy. 2nd ed. 156p. 1999. pap. 14.00 (1-893626-25-3) Breakout Prods Inc.

Newman, John Q. Credit Power! Rebuild Your Credit in 90 Days or Less. LC 95-81309. (Illus.). 164p. (Orig.). 1997. pap. 19.95 (1-56866-131-2) Index Pub Grp.

***Newman, John Q.** The ID Forger: Homemade Birth Certificates & Other Documents Explained. LC 99-67057. 110p. 1999. pap. 15.00 (1-55950-196-0, 61168) Loompanics.

— Identity Theft: The Cybercrime of the Millennium. 106p. 1999. pap. 12.00 (1-55950-195-2, 61163) Loompanics.

Newman, John Q., jt. auth. see Sands, Trent.

Newman, John W. Disciplines of Attention Vol. 26: Buddhist Insight Meditation, the Ignatian Spiritual Exercises, Classical Psychoanalysis. LC 95-44456. (Asian Thought & Culture Ser.). XII, 229p. (C). 1996. text 47.95 (0-8204-2795-0) P Lang Pubng.

Newman, John W. & Birkel, Michael L., eds. The Lamb's War: Essays in Honor of Hugh Barbour. 286p. (Orig.). 1991. pap. write for info. (0-318-68396-2) Earlham Pr.

Newman, John W., jt. ed. see Birkel, Michael L.

***Newman, Jon.** Candles. 2000. 17.98 (1-57145-279-6, Thunder Bay) Advantage Pubs.

***Newman, Joni.** Did He Say "Divorce?" A Jilted Wife's Hope on How to Cope, Living Without That Dope! LC 00-190856. 2000. 25.00 (0-7388-2038-5); pap. 18.00 (0-7388-2039-3) Xlibris Corp.

Newman, Josef. Family Values. 1992. 14.95 incl. disk (1-882833-00-7) Scribe Pr.

Newman, Joseph W. America's Teachers: An Introduction to Education. 2nd ed. LC 93-16924. 355p. (Orig.). (C). 1995. teacher ed. write for info. (0-8013-1424-0, 76491) Longman.

— The Energy Machine of Joseph Newman: An Invention Whose Time Has Come. 4th ed. Soule, Evan R., Jr., ed. (Illus.). 333p. 1986. 38.45 (0-9613835-4-2) J Newman Pub.

— The Energy Machine of Joseph Newman: An Invention Whose Time Has Come. 5th ed. Soule, Evan R., ed. (Illus.). 355p. 1987. 38.45 (0-9613835-5-0) J Newman Pub.

— The Energy Machine of Joseph Newman: An Invention Whose Time Has Come. 7th ed. Soule, Evan R., Jr., ed. & illus. by. LC 84-90652. 1995. text 59.95 (0-9613835-7-7) J Newman Pub.

— The Energy Machine of Joseph Newman: An Invention Whose Time Has Come. 8th ed. Soule, Evan R., Jr., ed. LC 84-90652. (Illus.). 602p. 1998. text 79.95 (0-9613835-8-5) J Newman Pub.

Newman, Judie. The Ballistic Bard: Postcolonial Fictions. LC 95-16018. (An Arnold Publication). 216p. 1995. pap. text 18.95 (0-340-53915-1, Pub. by E A) OUP.

— The Ballistic Bard: Postcolonial Fictions. LC 95-16018. 1995. write for info. (0-340-53914-3, Pub. by E A) Routldge.

— Nadine Gordimer. (Contemporary Writers Ser.). 96p. 1988. pap. text 9.95 (0-415-00660-0) Routledge.

Newman, Judie, ed. see Stowe, Harriet Beecher.

Newman, Judith. Craft of Childrens. (J). 1993. pap. 7.95 (0-590-71449-X) Scholastic Inc.

— The Craft of Children's Writing: A Parent/Teacher Guide to Children's Learning. LC 85-5830. 72p. (Orig.). (C). 1985. pap. 7.95 (0-435-08233-7, 08233) Heinemann.

— Tensions of Teaching: Beyond Tips to Critical Reflection. LC 97-39274. (Practitioners Inquiry Ser.). 1998. 21.95 (0-8077-3736-4) Tchrs Coll.

Newman, Judith M. Interwoven Conversations: Learning & Teaching Through Critical Reflection. 440p. (C). 1998. pap. 24.95 (1-55130-128-8, 301288, Pub. by Can Scholars Pr) Calendar Islands.

Newman, Judith M., ed. Finding Our Own Way: Teachers Exploring Their Assumptions. LC 89-15442. 157p. (Orig.). (C). 1989. pap. 17.95 (0-435-08501-8, 08501) Heinemann.

— Whole Language: Theory in Use. LC 85-17636. 204p. (Orig.). (C). 1985. pap. text 27.00 (0-435-08244-2, 08244) Heinemann.

Newman, K. O., tr. see Von Economo, Constantin.

Newman, Karen. Fashioning Femininity & English Renaissance Drama. LC 90-23374. (Women in Culture & Society Ser.). (Illus.). 202p. 1991. pap. text 13.95 (0-226-57709-0) U Ch Pr.

— Fashioning Femininity & English Renaissance Drama. LC 90-23374. (Women in Culture & Society Ser.). (Illus.). 208p. 1993. lib. bdg. 32.00 (0-226-57708-2) U Ch Pr.

— Fetal Positions: Individualism, Science, Visuality. LC 95-41182. (Writing Science Ser.). 1996. 39.50 (0-8047-2647-7); pap. 16.95 (0-8047-2648-5) Stanford U Pr.

— Shakespeare's Rhetoric of Comic Character: Dramatic Convention in Classical & Renaissance Comedy. 128p. 1985. 18.95 (0-416-37990-7, 9116) Routledge.

Newman, Karen L. & Nollen, Stanley D. Managing Radical Organizational Change. LC 98-9004. 1998. 47.50 (0-7619-0933-8); pap. 23.50 (0-7619-0934-6) Sage.

Newman, Karoline. Century of Lingerie. 1998. 19.99 (0-7858-0836-1) Bk Sales Inc.

Newman, Kate. Dictionary of Ulster Biography. 278p. 1993. pap. 21.00 (0-85389-478-7, Pub. by Inst Irish Studies) Irish Bks Media.

Newman, Katharine D. Never Without a Song: The Years & Songs of Jennie Devlin, 1865-1952. LC 93-6387. (Music in American Life Ser.). (Illus.). 272p. 1994. text 39.95 (0-252-02081-2); pap. text 16.95 (0-252-06371-6) U of Ill Pr.

Newman, Katherine. Law & Economic Organization: A Comparative Study of Preindustrial Societies. LC 83-7169. 276p. 1983. pap. text 19.95 (0-521-28966-1) Cambridge U Pr.

Newman, Katherine, ed. see Newman, Preston.

Newman, Katherine, ed. see Runnells, Robert R.

Newman, Katherine A. Sorority of Survival: Memoirs of a Multiple. (Illus.). 271p. (Orig.). 1996. pap. 23.95 (1-56072-346-7, Nova Kroshka Bks) Nova Sci Pubs.

Newman, Katherine S. Declining Fortunes: The Withering of the American Dream. 288p. 1994. reprint ed. pap. 15.50 (0-465-01594-8, Pub. by Basic) HarpC.

— Falling from Grace: Downward Mobility in the Age of Affluence. LC 98-38119. 340p. 1999. pap. 13.95 (0-520-21842-6, Pub. by U CA Pr) Cal Prin Full Svc.

— Falling from Grace: The Experience of Downward Mobility in the American Middle Class. 304p. 1988. 29.95 (0-02-923121-3) Free Pr.

Newman, Katherine S. No Shame in My Game: The Working Poor in the Inner City. LC 98-38244. 400p. 1999. 27.95 (0-375-40254-3) Knopf.

***Newman, Katherine S.** No Shame in My Game: The Working Poor in the Inner City. 416p. 2000. pap. 15.00 (0-375-70379-9) Vin Bks.

Newman, Kathleen C., ed. see Ives, Katherine J.

Newman, Ken. Southern African Green Guide: Birds of Botswana. (Illus.). 80p. 1999. pap. 17.95 (1-86812-740-0) Menasha Ridge.

— Watching Birds in Southern Africa: Bird Field List. 48p. (Orig.). 1999. pap. 4.95 (1-86812-759-1) Menasha Ridge.

Newman, Ken, et al. Watching Birds in Southern Africa: Confusing Species. LC 99-175313. (Illus.). 128p. 1999. pap. 17.95 (1-86812-751-6) Menasha Ridge.

— Watching Birds in Southern Africa: LBJs (Little Brown Jobs) Made Easy. (Illus.). 96p. 1999. pap. 17.95 (1-86812-750-8) Menasha Ridge.

Newman, Kenneth. Newman's Birds of Southern Africa. LC 96-144471. (Illus.). 1998. 19.95 (1-86812-623-4) Menasha Ridge.

— Newman's Birds of Southern Africa: The Green Edition. (Illus.). 461p. (Orig.). (C). 1996. pap. 39.95 (0-8130-1427-1) U Press Fla.

***Newman, Kenneth.** Newman's Birds Of Southern Africa: 7th Ed., 1. 7th ed. (Illus.). 510p. 1999. pap. 19.95 (1-86812-757-5) Southern Appeal.

Newman, Kenneth, et al. Birds of Malawi: A Supplement to Newman's Birds of Southern Africa. (Illus.). 110p. 1998. pap. 19.95 (1-86812-418-5) Menasha Ridge.

Newman, Kenneth, jt. auth. see Bacal, Howard A.

Newman, Kim. Anno Dracula. 416p. 1994. mass mkt. 5.99 (0-380-72345-X, Avon Bks) Morrow Avon.

***Newman, Kim.** Apocalypse Movies: End of the World Cinema. LC 99-54618. (Illus.). 272p. 2000. pap. 16.95 (0-312-25369-9) St Martin.

Newman, Kim. Bad Dreams. 280p. 1995. mass mkt. 4.95 (0-7867-0227-3) Carroll & Graf.

— Bloody Red Baron. 1997. mass mkt. 5.99 (0-380-72714-5, Avon Bks) Morrow Avon.

— Jago. 536p. 1993. 22.00 (0-88184-868-9) Carroll & Graf.

N

— Judgement of Tears: Anno Dracula 1959. LC 99-186722. 240p. 1998. 22.95 (*0-7867-0558-2*) Carroll & Graf.
— Judgment of Tears: Anno Dracula 1959. 304p. 1999. pap. 12.50 (*0-380-73229-7*, Avon Bks) Morrow Avon.
— The Night Mayor. 202p. 1992. mass mkt. 3.95 (*0-88184-768-2*) Carroll & Graf.
— Original Dr. Shade (& Other Stories) 1998. mass mkt. 48.93 (*0-671-71562-3*) S&S Trade.
— The Quorum. 368p. 1995. mass mkt. 5.95 (*0-7867-0283-4*) Carroll & Graf.
Newman, Kim & Byrne, Eugene. Back in the USSA. 334p. 1997. 29.95 (*0-929480-84-8*) Mark Ziesing.
— Back in the USSA. limited ed. 334p. 1997. 65.00 (*0-929480-85-6*) Mark Ziesing.
Newman, Kim, ed. see British Film Institute Staff.
Newman, Kim, jt. ed. see Jones, Stephen.
Newman-Kuyek, Joan. Fighting for Hope: Organizing to Realize Our Dreams. LC 90-83629. 221p. (Orig.). (C). 1990. 46.99 (*0-921689-87-X*, Pub. by Black Rose); pap. 17.99 (*0-921689-86-1*, Pub. by Black Rose) Consort Bk Sales.
Newman, Larry. The Recorder Fun Book: Recorder Method Book. 2nd rev. ed. (Illus.). 44p. (J). (ps-5). 1997. 4.95 (*0-9664995-0-6*, GNB100) Brass Bell.
Newman, Laura. Make Your Juicer Your Drug Store. LC 66-125414. (Illus.). 192p. 1998. pap. 4.95 (*0-87904-001-7*) Lust.
— 1999 Medical Outcomes & Guidelines Sourcebook: A Progress Report & Resource Guide on Medical Outcomes Research & Practice Guidelines: Developments Data, & Implementation. (Illus.). 1998. pap. 295.00 (*1-57987-084-8*) Faulkner & Gray.
***Newman, Laura, ed.** Medical Outcomes & Guidelines Sourcebook: A Comprehensive Guide to Medical Outcomes Research & Practical Guidelines: Developments, Data & Implementation. (Illus.). 768p. 1999. pap. 295.00 (*1-57987-118-6*) Faulkner & Gray.
Newman, Lawrence. The Covenant of the Holy Innocents. unabridged ed. LC 99-166985. 289p. 1998. pap. 16.95 (*0-9665678-0-3*) Buy Books.
Newman, Lawrence, jt. auth. see Kalter, Albert.
Newman, Lawrence E. The List. (Orig.). Date not set. pap. 6.99 (*0-9650996-0-1*) Newman & Assocs.
Newman, Lawrence G. Texas Corporation Law. 850p. 1994. ring bd. 115.00 (*1-55943-158-X*, MICHIE) LEXIS Pub.
— Texas Corporation Law, No. 1. 850p. 1988. suppl. ed. 40.00 (*0-685-66113-X*, MICHIE) LEXIS Pub.
— Texas Corporation Law, No. 2. 850p. 1990. suppl. ed. 32.50 (*0-685-66114-8*, MICHIE) LEXIS Pub.
— Texas Corporation Law, No. 3. 850p. 1992. suppl. ed. 35.00 (*0-685-70055-0*, MICHIE) LEXIS Pub.
Newman, Lawrence W. & Burrows, Michael. The Practice of International Litigation. 870p. 1993. 125.00 (*1-56425-005-9*) Juris Pubng.
Newman, Lawrence W. & Zaslowsky, David. Litigating International Commercial Disputes. LC 96-18073. 410p. (C). 1996. pap. text 50.00 (*0-314-09367-2*) West Pub.
Newman Layfield, Eleanor, jt. auth. see Newman, Gerald.
Newman, Lea B. A Reader's Guide to the Short Stories of Herman Melville. (Reference Bks.). 344p. 1986. 50.00 (*0-8161-8653-7*, Hall Reference) Macmillan.
Newman, Leonard, ed. Measurement Challenges in Atmospheric Chemistry. LC 92-38528. (Advances in Chemistry Ser.: No. 232). 408p. 1993. text 105.00 (*0-8412-2470-6*, Pub. by Am Chemical) OUP.
***Newman, Leslea.** Cats, Cats, Cats. LC 99-32226. (J). (ps-3). 2001. pap. 17.00 (*0-689-83077-7*) S&S Childrens.
Newman, Leslea. Every Woman's Dream. LC 94-15390. 200p. (Orig.). 1994. pap. 9.95 (*0-934678-62-6*) New Victoria Pubs.
— Fat Chance. 224p. (YA). (gr. 7 up). 1996. pap. 4.99 (*0-698-11406-X*, PapStar) Peng Put Young Read.
Newman, Leslea. Fat Chance. 1996. 10.05 (*0-606-10806-8*, Pub. by Turtleback) Demco.
Newman, Leslea. Girls Will Be Girls: A Novella & Short Stories. LC 99-29477. 248p. 2000. pap. 12.95 (*1-55583-537-6*) Alyson Pubns.
— Good Enough to Eat. LC 86-16228. 272p. (Orig.). 1986. pap. 10.95 (*0-932379-21-4*); lib. bdg. 22.95 (*0-932379-22-2*) Firebrand Bks.
***Newman, Leslea.** Heather Has Two Mommies: Tenth Anniversary Edition. anniversary ed. LC 99-87285. (Illus.). 32p. (J). (ps-3). 2000. 18.95 (*1-55583-570-8*, Pub. by Alyson Pubns) Consort Bk Sales.
— Heather Has Two Mommies: Tenth Anniversary Edition. 10th anniversary ed. LC 99-87285. (Illus.). 32p. (J). (ps-3). 2000. pap. 10.95 (*1-55583-543-0*, Alyson Bks) Alyson Pubns.
Newman, Leslea. In Every Laugh a Tear. 2nd ed. LC 98-22696. 256p. (Orig.). 1998. pap. 11.95 (*0-934678-92-8*) New Victoria Pubs.
— A Letter to Harvey Milk. LC 88-3923. 176p. (Orig.). 1988. pap. 9.95 (*0-932379-43-5*); lib. bdg. 20.95 (*0-932379-44-3*) Firebrand Bks.
— The Little Butch Book. LC 98-27367. (Illus.). 64p. 1998. 10.00 (*0-934678-96-0*) New Victoria Pubs.
— Love Me Like You Mean It. 100p. (Orig.). 1987. reprint ed. pap. 8.95 (*1-878533-14-2*) Pride & Imprints.
— Matzo Ball Moon. LC 95-49577. (Illus.). 32p. (J). (gr. k-3). 1998. 15.00 (*0-395-71530-X*, Clarion Bks) HM.
— My Lover Is a Woman: Contemporary Lesbian Love Poems. 240p. 1996. 18.50 (*0-345-39483-6*) Ballantine Pub Grp.
— My Lover is a Woman: Contemporary Lesbian Love Poems. LC 99-90324. 304p. 1999. pap. 12.00 (*0-345-42114-0*, Ballantine) Ballantine Pub Grp.
— Out of the Closet & Nothing to Wear. LC 97-1369. 232p. (Orig.). 1997. pap. 10.95 (*1-55583-415-9*) Alyson Pubns.
— Remember That. (Illus.). 32p. (J). (gr. k-3). 1996. 14.95 (*0-395-66156-0*, Clarion Bks) HM.
***Newman, Leslea.** Runaway Dreydl. 2000. text 15.95 (*0-8050-6237-8*) St Martin.
Newman, Leslea. Saturday Is Pattyday. LC 93-7014. (Illus.). 24p. (J). (gr. 1-3). 1993. lib. bdg. 14.95 (*0-934678-52-9*) New Victoria Pubs.
— Saturday Is Pattyday. (Illus.). 24p. (J). (ps-5). 1993. pap. 6.95 (*0-934678-51-0*) New Victoria Pubs.
— Saturday Is Pattyday. (Illus.). 24p. (J). pap. 5.95 (*0-88961-181-5*, Pub. by Womens Pr) LPC InBook.
— Secrets. LC 90-31303. 206p. (Orig.). 1990. pap. 8.95 (*0-934678-24-3*) New Victoria Pubs.
— Signs of Love. 220p. 2001. pap. 10.95 (*1-886383-45-6*, Keystone) Pride & Imprints.
— SomeBody to Love: A Guide to Loving the Body You Have. LC 91-34617. 224p. (Orig.). 1991. pap. 10.95 (*1-879427-03-6*) Third Side Pr.
— Still Life with Buddy. 100p. 1997. pap. 9.95 (*1-886383-27-8*) Pride & Imprints.
— Sweet Dark Places: Poetry by Leslea Newman. 110p. 1991. pap. 8.95 (*0-939821-01-X*) Pride & Imprints.
— Too Far Away to Touch. LC 93-30327. (Illus.). 32p. (J). (ps-4). 1995. 14.95 (*0-395-68968-6*, Clarion Bks) HM.
— Too Far Away to Touch. LC 93-30327. (Illus.). 40p. (ps-3). 1998. pap. 5.95 (*0-395-90018-2*, Pub. by Ticknor & Fields) HM.
— Writing from the Heart: Inspirations & Exercises for Women Who Want to Write. (Illus.). 198p. 1993. pap. 14.95 (*0-89594-641-6*) Crossing Pr.
Newman, Leslea, ed. Eating Our Hearts Out: Women & Food. LC 92-33669. (Illus.). 300p. 1993. pap. 12.95 (*0-89594-569-X*) Crossing Pr.
— The Femme Mystique. (Illus.). 350p. (Orig.). 1996. pap. 11.95 (*1-55583-255-5*) Alyson Pubns.
— Pillow Talk: Lesbian Stories Between the Covers. LC 98-5296. 224p. (Orig.). 1998. pap. 12.95 (*1-55583-419-1*) Alyson Pubns.
***Newman, Leslea, ed.** Pillow Talk II: More Lesbian Stories Between the Covers. 2000. pap. 12.95 (*1-55583-519-8*, Pub. by Alyson Pubns) Consort Bk Sales.
Newman, Linda, jt. auth. see Newman, Boyd.
Newman, Linda A. Maintaining Function in Older Adults. LC 95-13936. (Illus.). 141p. 1995. pap. text 29.00 (*0-7506-9568-4*) Buttrwrth-Heinemann.
Newman, Linda A., jt. see Newman, Boyd.
Newman, Linda P., jt. auth. see Ansari, Mary B.
Newman, Lindsay, ed. see Hervouet, Yves.
***Newman, Lisa.** Allergies. LC 99-37387. (Crossing Press Pocket Ser.). 96p. 1999. pap. 6.95 (*1-58091-002-5*) Crossing Pr.
— Arthritis. LC 99-37386. (Crossing Press Pocket Ser.). 96p. 1999. pap. 6.95 (*1-58091-003-3*) Crossing Pr.
— Natural Cat. LC 99-37385. (Crossing Press Pocket Ser.). 96p. 1999. pap. 6.95 (*1-58091-001-7*) Crossing Pr.
— Natural Dog. LC 99-37371. (Crossing Press Pocket Ser.). 96p. 1999. pap. 6.95 (*1-58091-000-9*) Crossing Pr.
— Nutrition. LC 99-37372. (Crossing Press Pocket Ser.). 96p. 1999. pap. 6.95 (*1-58091-004-1*) Crossing Pr.
— Parasites. LC 99-37373. (Crossing Press Pocket Ser.). 96p. 1999. pap. 6.95 (*1-58091-006-8*) Crossing Pr.
— Skin & Coat Care. LC 99-37375. (Crossing Press Pocket Ser.). 96p. 1999. pap. 6.95 (*1-58091-008-4*) Crossing Pr.
— Training Without Trauma. LC 99-37374. (Crossing Press Pocket Ser.). 96p. 1999. pap. 6.95 (*1-58091-007-6*) Crossing Pr.
Newman, Louis. Burn, Yellow Candle, Burn. 1972. write for info. (*0-318-64102-X*) Poets Pr.
— Genesis: The Student's Guide, Pt. 2. pap. 4.95 (*0-8381-0404-5*) USCJE.
— Pebbles & Sand. LC 77-99935. (Illus.). 96p. 1990. pap. 6.00 (*0-912292-12-1*) Smith.
— Teacher's Supplement to Genesis the Student's Guide, Pt. 1. pap. 2.95 (*0-8381-0403-7*) USCJE.
— Tear Down the Walls. 76p. 1973. write for info. (*0-318-64146-1*) Poets Pr.
Newman, Louis E. Past Imperatives: Studies in the History & Theory of Jewish Ethics. LC 97-38798. (Series in Jewish Philosophy). 288p. (C). 1998. text 59.50 (*0-7914-3867-8*); pap. text 19.95 (*0-7914-3868-6*) State U NY Pr.
Newman, Louis E., jt. ed. see Dorff, Elliot N.
Newman, Louis I. A Child's Introduction to Torah. (Orig.). (J). 1995. pap., teacher ed. 14.95 (*0-87441-068-1*) Behrman.
— Jewish Influence on Christian Reform Movements. LC 26-883. (Columbia University. Oriental Studies: No. 23). reprint ed. 45.00 (*0-404-50513-9*) AMS Pr.
Newman, Louis I., ed. see Newman, Shirley.
Newman, Louis I., ed. see Spitz, Samuel.
Newman, Louise. White Women's Rights: The Racial Origins of Feminism in the United States. LC 97-53286. (Illus.). 272p. 1999. pap. 19.95 (*0-19-512466-9*) OUP.
Newman, Louise M. Men's Ideas, Women's Realities: Popular Science, 1870-1915. LC 84-1072. (Athene Ser.). 367p. 1985. pap. 113.80 (*0-7837-8952-1*, 204966400002) Bks Demand.
Newman, Louise M., ed. Men's Ideas, Women's Realities: "Popular Science", Eighteen Seventy to Nineteen Fifteen. (Athene Ser.). 384p. 1984. text 55.00 (*0-08-031930-0*, Pergamon Pr); pap. text 19.95 (*0-08-031929-7*, Pergamon Pr) Elsevier.
Newman, Lowell S., jt. auth. see Rohrbach, Peter T.
Newman, Lucile. Hunger in History: Food Shortage, Poverty & Deprivation. 1995. pap. text 29.95 (*1-55786-628-7*) Blackwell Pubs.
Newman, Lucile F. Women's Medicine: A Cross-Cultural Study of Indigenous Fertility Regulation. 203p. (Orig.). (C). 1995. pap. text 16.00 (*0-8135-2257-9*) Rutgers U Pr.
Newman, Lucille & Vega, Vicki A. The Wonder of Water. (Illus.). 24p. (J). (gr. 2-3). 1997. pap. 3.25 (*0-9636426-2-6*) Windham Pr.
Newman, M. F., et al. Manual of Dipterocarps for Foresters: Borneo Island Light Hardwoods. (Manual Ser.). (Illus.). x, 278p. 1996. pap. 40.00 (*1-872291-76-7*, Pub. by Royal Botanic Edinburgh) Balogh.
— Manual of Dipterocarps for Foresters: Philippines. (Manual Ser.). (Illus.). x, 126p. 1996. pap. 23.00 (*1-872291-61-9*, Pub. by Royal Botanic Edinburgh) Balogh.
— Manual of Dipterocarps for Foresters: Sumatra Light Hardwoods. (Manuals Ser.). (Illus.). x, 158p. 1996. pap. 31.00 (*1-872291-91-0*, Pub. by Royal Botanic Edinburgh) Balogh.
— Manuals of Dipterocarps for Foresters: Singapore. (Illus.). 104p. 1995. pap. 23.00 (*1-872291-31-7*, Pub. by Royal Botanic Edinburgh) Balogh.
Newman, M. H. Elements of the Topology of Plane Sets of Points. (Illus.). vii, 214p. 1999. reprint ed. pap. 6.95 (*0-486-67037-6*) Dover.
Newman, M. T. Indian Skeletal Material from the Central Coast of Peru. (Harvard University Peabody Museum of Archaeology & Ethnology Papers). 1969. reprint ed. pap. 25.00 (*0-527-01270-X*) Periodicals Srv.
***Newman, M. W., intro.** The People's Palace: The Story of the Chicago Cultural Center. (Illus.). 70p. 1999. pap. 14.95 (*0-938903-25-X*) Cty of Chicago.
Newman, Marc. Civil War Knives. LC 99-186259. (Illus.). 120p. 1998. 44.95 (*0-87364-999-0*) Paladin Pr.
***Newman, Marc & McKenney, Thomas L.** Biographical Portraits of 108 Native Americans: Based on History of the Indian Tribes of North America. LC 99-36074. (Illus.). 1999. 12.00 (*1-57281-243-5*) US Games Syst.
Newman, Marc T. A Rhetorical Analysis of Popular American Film. 400p. (C). 1993. pap. text 36.95 (*0-8403-9003-3*) Kendall-Hunt.
Newman, Margaret. Stepfamily Realities: How to Overcome Difficulties & Have a Happy Family. LC 93-86800. 264p. (Orig.). 1994. pap. 15.95 (*1-879237-69-5*) New Harbinger.
Newman, Margaret A. A Developing Discipline: Selected Works of Margaret Newman. LC 94-23657. 1995. pap. 21.95 (*0-88737-638-X*) Natl League Nurse.
— Health as Expanding Consciousness. 2nd ed. 150p. 1994. 21.95 (*0-88737-620-7*, 14-2626) Natl League Nurse.
Newman, Marilyn Stephanie Mercedes. The Comprehensive Catalogue of Duet Literature for Female Voices: Vocal Chamber Duets with Keyboard Accompaniment Composed Between 1820-1995. LC 99-19510. 608p. 1999. 75.00 (*0-8108-3647-5*) Scarecrow.
Newman, Marjorie. Hornpipe's Hunt for Pirate Gold. LC 97-12350. (Gamebook Preschool Puzzles Ser.). (Illus.). 32p. (Orig.). (J). (gr. k-3). 1998. 5.99 (*0-7636-0419-4*) Candlewick Pr.
— Ideas for a Windy Day. LC 99-93021. (Ideas Activity Bks.). (Illus.). 12p. (J). (gr. 1-5). 1999. pap. 5.99 (*0-89051-245-0*) Master Bks.
— Ideas with Water. LC 99-93021. (Ideas Activity Bks.). (Illus.). 12p. (J). (gr. 1-5). 1999. pap. 5.99 (*0-89051-246-9*) Master Bks.
— The Wonderful Journey of Cameron the Cat. LC 96-48668. (Gamebook Preschool Puzzles Ser.). (Illus.). 32p. (Orig.). (J). 1998. 5.99 (*0-7636-0274-4*) Candlewick Pr.
Newman, Mark. Agency of Change: One Hundred Years of the North Central Association of Colleges & Schools. LC 96-28885. (Illus.). 400p. 1996. 40.00 (*0-943549-42-6*, 0943549) Truman St Univ.
— Entrepreneurs of Profits & Pride: From Black-Appeal to Radio Soul. LC 88-5887. 202p. 1988. 57.95 (*0-275-92888-8*, C2888, Praeger Pubs) Greenwood.
***Newman, Mark.** Getting Right with God: Southern Baptists Desegregation, 1945-1995. 2000. 39.95 (*0-8173-1060-6*) U of Ala Pr.
Newman, Mark. Mapping "The American Promise" Historical Geography Workbook, Vol. II. 1997. pap. text, wbk. ed. 1.33 (*0-312-18026-8*) St Martin.
Newman, Mark & Barkema, G. T. Monte Carlo Methods in Statistical Physics. LC 99-213405. (Illus.). 490p. 1999. pap. text 45.00 (*0-19-851797-1*) OUP.
***Newman, Mark & Barkema, G. T.** Monte Carlo Methods in Statistical Physics. LC 99-213405. (Illus.). 490p. 1999. text 98.00 (*0-19-851796-3*) OUP.
Newman, Mark A. Save! Biographies of Greatness in Goalkeeping. (Illus.). 200p. (Orig.). 1993. pap. text 12.95 (*0-9636916-2-7*) Minds Eye Pr.
Newman, Mark J., jt. ed. see Powell, Michael F.
Newman, Mark W. A Little Book of Missionary Reminders. LC 95-154135. 1996. pap. 7.95 (*1-55503-774-7*, 01111884) Covenant Comms.
Newman, Marsha. Fire & Glory: The Millennial Story I. 229p. 1989. 12.95 (*0-9608658-5-3*) Wellspring Utah.
— Fire & Glory: The Millennial Story II. 226p. 1989. 12.95 (*0-9608658-4-5*) Wellspring Utah.
— The Lightning & the Storm. 229p. 1986. 9.95 (*0-9608658-2-9*) Wellspring Utah.
— A Love Beyond Time. 329p. 1987. 14.95 (*0-9608658-3-7*) Wellspring Utah.
— Reflections of Eve & Her Daughters. (Illus.). 1981. 6.95 (*0-9608658-0-2*) Wellspring Utah.
Newman, Marsha & Miller, Barbara. The Jewels of Vicarey Harbor. 208p. (Orig.). (YA). (gr. 11-12). 1993. pap. 5.95 (*0-9608658-8-8*) Wellspring Utah.
Newman, Marsha & Newman, Gene. She Shall Be Called Woman. 1981. pap. write for info. (*0-318-56398-3*) Wellspring Utah.
Newman, Martha G. The Boundaries of Charity: Cistercian Culture & Ecclesiastical Reform, 1098-1180. LC 95-14016. (Figurae - Reading Medieval Culture Ser.). (Illus.). 466p. 1996. 49.50 (*0-8047-2512-8*) Stanford U Pr.
Newman, Mary, jt. auth. see Kacuba, John.
Newman, Mary A., tr. see De Ventos, Xavier R.
***Newman, Matthew.** Brandy. (Galaxy of Superstars Ser.). 2000. 17.95 (*0-7910-5781-X*) Chelsea Hse.
— Brandy. LC 99-462031. (Galaxy of Superstars Ser.). (Illus.). 2000. pap. 9.95 (*0-7910-5782-8*) Chelsea Hse.
— Ricky Martin. (Galaxy of Superstars Ser.). 2000. 17.95 (*0-7910-5771-2*) Chelsea Hse.
— Ricky Martin. LC 99-462030. (Galaxy of Superstars Ser.). (Illus.). 2000. pap. 9.95 (*0-7910-5772-0*) Chelsea Hse.
Newman, Maxwell H. Elements of the Topology Plane Sets of Points. LC 85-12548. 214p. 1985. reprint ed. lib. bdg. 65.00 (*0-313-24956-3*, NETO, Greenwood Pr) Greenwood.
Newman, Michael. The Complete Guide to Everything Romantic: Unique & Creative Ideas. LC 94-20220. 256p. 1995. 15.95 (*0-8065-1547-3*, Citadel Pr) Carol Pub Group.
— Democracy, Sovereignty & the European Community. 224p. 1996. text 59.95 (*0-312-15860-2*) St Martin.
— Epicene Pronouns: The Linguistics of a Precriptive Problem. Horn, Laurence, ed. LC 96-34686. (Linguistics Ser.). 180p. 1996. text 73.00 (*0-8153-2554-1*) Garland.
— Rewriting Conceptual Art. (Illus.). 264p. 2000. pap. 24.95 (*1-86189-052-4*, Pub. by RBL) Consort Bk Sales.
Newman, Michael, jt. ed. see Mazey, Sonia.
Newman, Michael C. Fundamentals of Ecotoxicology. LC 97-48518. (Illus.). 450p. (C). 1998. ring bd. 64.95 (*1-57504-013-1*) CRC Pr.
Newman, Michael C. & Jagoe, Charles H., eds. Ecotoxicology: A Hierarchical Treatment. (Savannah River Series on Environmental Sciences). 432p. 1996. lib. bdg. 85.00 (*1-56670-127-9*, L1127) Lewis Pubs.
Newman, Michael C. & McIntosh, A. Metal Ecotoxicology: Concepts & Applications. (Advances in Trace Substances Research Ser.). 424p. 1991. lib. bdg. 110.00 (*0-87371-411-3*, L411) Lewis Pubs.
Newman, Michael C. & Strojan, Carl L., eds. Risk Assessment: Logic & Measurement. LC 97-46420. (Illus.). 400p. (C). 1998. ring bd. 89.95 (*1-57504-048-4*) CRC Pr.
Newman, Michael E. Computer Applications in Agriculture & Agribusiness. 172p. 1994. pap. text 14.95 (*0-8134-2976-5*) Interstate.
Newman, Michael E. & Wills, Walter J. Agribusiness Management & Entrepreneurship. 3rd ed. LC 93-78223. 443p. 1998. 53.75 (*0-8134-2955-2*, 2955); teacher ed. 12.95 (*0-8134-2956-0*, 2956) Interstate.
Newman, Michael E., jt. auth. see Lee, J. S.
Newman, Michael E., jt. auth. see Lee, Jasper S.
Newman, Michael G. & Kornman, Kenneth G. Antibiotic - Antimicrobial Use in Dental Practice. LC 90-9099. (Illus.). 260p. 1990. pap. text 32.00 (*0-86715-172-2*) Quint Pub Co.
Newman, Michael G., jt. ed. see Nisengard, Russell J.
Newman, Micheal C. Quantitative Methods in Aquatic Ecotoxicology. 448p. 1994. lib. bdg. 95.00 (*0-87371-622-1*, L622) Lewis Pubs.
Newman, Michele, ed. Researching Canadian Markets, Industries & Business Opportunities. 260p. 1997. pap. 275.00 (*1-56365-085-1*) Wash Res.
Newman, Milda, tr. see Greimas, Algirdas J.
Newman, Mildred & Berkowitz, Bernard. How to Be Your Own Best Friend. 1986. mass mkt. 5.99 (*0-345-34239-9*) Ballantine Pub Grp.
Newman, Molly. Shooting Stars. 1988. pap. 5.25 (*0-8222-1023-1*) Dramatists Play.
Newman, Molly & Damashek, Barbara. Quilters. 1986. pap. 6.00 (*0-8222-0928-4*) Dramatists Play.
Newman, Mona. Conflict in Berlin. large type ed. 1996. pap. 18.99 (*1-85389-563-6*, Dales) Ulverscroft.
— The Faithful Heart. large type ed. (Linford Romance Library). 336p. 1996. pap. 16.99 (*0-7089-7899-1*, Linford) Ulverscroft.
— Hills of the Purple Mist. large type ed. (Dales Large Print Ser.). 274p. 1996. pap. 18.99 (*1-85389-605-5*, Dales) Ulverscroft.
***Newman, Mona.** The Hong Kong Triangle. large type ed. 320p. 1998. pap. 20.99 (*1-85389-916-X*) Dales Lrg Prnt.
Newman, Mona. Night of a Thousand Stars. large type ed. 320p. 1987. 27.99 (*0-7089-1628-7*) Ulverscroft.
Newman, Morton. Design & Construction Details of Low Rise Steel Structures. 400p. 1997. text 69.95 (*0-07-046399-9*) McGraw.
— Design & Construction of Wood Framed Buildings. LC 94-33842. 400p. 1995. 59.95 (*0-07-046363-8*) McGraw.
— Standard Handbook of Structural Details for Building Contruction. 2nd ed. LC 92-35654. 750p. 1993. 99.95 (*0-07-046352-2*) McGraw.
Newman, Moshe, jt. auth. see Becher, Mordechai.
Newman, N. A. Muhammad, the Qur'an & Islam. LC 96-78495. 442p. 1996. 39.95 (*0-944788-85-8*); pap. 19.95 (*0-944788-86-6*) IBRI.
Newman, N. A., ed. Early Christian-Muslim Dialogue. LC 93-61140. xvii, 776p. 1994. 65.95 (*0-944788-91-2*) IBRI.
Newman, N. A., ed. see Noldeke, Theodor.
Newman, Nancy. Competence in Cloze: Level D, Science. 56p. 1990. student ed. 4.25 (*0-910307-87-3*) Comp Pr.
— Competence in Cloze: Level F, Social Studies. 54p. 1990. student ed. 4.25 (*0-910307-96-2*) Comp Pr.
Newman, Nancy. Disturbing the Peace. Date not set. mass mkt. write for info. (*0-380-79839-5*) Morrow Avon.
Newman, Nancy, jt. auth. see Miller, Neil.
Newman, Nancy J., jt. auth. see Miller, Neil R.
Newman, Nancy K., ed. see Davis, Charles.
Newman, Nancy M. Neuro-Ophthalmology: A Practical Text. (Illus.). 484p. (C). 1992. pap. text 115.00 (*0-8385-6698-7*, A6698-3, Apple Lange Med) McGraw.
***Newman, Nanette.** Little Book of Kids' Talk. (Illus.). (J). 2000. pap. 4.95 (*0-7407-0473-7*) Andrews & McMeel.

An Asterisk (*) at the beginning of an entry indicates that the title is appearing for the first time.

Newman, Nanette. That Dog! LC 81-43892. (Illus.). 48p. (J). (gr. 1-4). 1983. 11.95 (*0-690-04229-9*); lib. bdg. 10.89 (*0-690-04230-2*) HarpC Child Bks.

Newman, Nick. Wallace & Gromit Anoraknophobia. (Wallace & Gromit Comic Strip Bks.). 1998. 16.95 (*0-8417-2031-2*) Adlers Foreign Bks.

Newman, Oscar. Creating Defensible Space. (Illus.). 123p. (Orig.). (C). 1997. pap. text 40.00 (*0-7881-4528-2*) DIANE Pub.

Newman, P. B. House on the Saco. 1977. pap. 8.95 (*0-87233-038-9*) Bauhan.

— Paula: A Narrative Poem. limited ed. LC 74-25862. (Living Poets' Library). 1975. pap. 2.50 (*0-686-10402-1*) Dragons Teeth.

Newman, P. P. Neurophysiology. (Illus.). 455p. 1980. text 35.00 (*0-88331-165-8*) R B Luce.

Newman, P. R. Atlas of the English Civil War. (Illus.). 144p. 1985. 35.00 (*0-02-906540-2*) Free Pr.

— Atlas of the English Civil War. (Illus.). 128p. (C). 1998. pap. 24.99 (*0-415-19610-8*, D6631) Routledge.

— Atlas of the English Civil War. (Illus.). 128p. (C). (gr. 13). 1998. 75.00 (*0-415-19609-4*, D6627) Routledge.

— Companion to Irish History, 1603-1921: From the Submission of Tyrone to Partition. LC 91-23677. 256p. 1991. reprint ed. pap. 79.40 (*0-608-02867-3*, 206393100007) Bks Demand.

— Companion to the English Civil Wars. LC 90-3114. 215p. 1990. reprint ed. pap. 66.70 (*0-608-02858-4*, 206392200007) Bks Demand.

— The Old Service: Royalist Regimental Colonels & the Civil War, 1642-46. LC 93-14678. (C). 1993. text 59.95 (*0-7190-3752-2*, Pub. by Manchester Univ Pr) St Martin.

Newman, Pamela & Lynch, Alfred F. Behind Closed Doors: A Guide to Successful Meetings. (Illus.). 192p. 1983. 18.50 (*0-13-072025-9*) P-H.

Newman, Patricia E., et al. Callaham's Russian-English Dictionary of Science & Technology. 4th ed. LC 94-37599. (ENG & RUS.). 814p. 1996. 170.00 (*0-471-61139-5*) Wiley.

Newman, Paul. Alternative Dispute Resolution. 224p. 1999. pap. 64.60 (*1-85811-170-6*, Pub. by CLT Prof) Gaunt.

— Construction Litigation Tactics. 206p. 1996. pap. 53.00 (*1-85811-099-8*, Pub. by CLT Prof) Gaunt.

***Newman, Paul.** The Hausa Language: An Encyclopedic Reference Grammar. LC 99-54069. (Language Ser.). 800p. 2000. 80.00 (*0-300-08189-8*) Yale U Pr.

— History of Terror: Fear & Dread Throughout the Ages. (Illus.). 256p. 2000. 32.95 (*0-7509-2008-4*) Sutton Publng.

Newman, Paul. Lost Gods of Albion: The Chalk Hill-Figures of Britain. LC 98-155071. (Illus.). 224p. 1998. 39.95 (*0-7509-1563-3*, Pub. by Sutton Pub Ltd) Intl Pubs Mktg.

***Newman, Paul.** Lost Gods of Albion: The Chalk Hill-Figures of Britain. (Illus.). 224p. 1999. pap. 19.95 (*0-7509-1792-X*, Pub. by Sutton Pub Ltd) Bks Intl VA.

Newman, Paul. Nominal & Verbal Plurality in Chadic. (Publications in African Languages & Linguistics: No. 12). 164p. 1990. pap. 60.00 (*90-6765-499-X*) Mouton.

— Optical Resolution Procedures for Chemical Compounds: Alcohols, Phenols, Thiols, Aldehydes & Ketones, Vol. 3. 738p. 1984. lib. bdg. 57.50 (*0-9601918-4-4*) Optical Resolution.

— Optical Resolution Procedures for Chemical Compounds Vol. 2: Acids, 2 pts. LC 78-61452. 1981. write for info. (*0-9601918-1-X*); write for info. (*0-9601918-2-8*) Optical Resolution.

— Optical Resolution Procedures for Chemical Compounds Vol. 2. Acids, 2 pts., Set. LC 78-61452. 1981. 79.00 (*0-9601918-3-6*) Optical Resolution.

— Optical Resolution Procedures for Chemical Compounds Vol. 4, Pt. 1: Compounds Containing a Sulfur or Selenium Stereocenter. 1611p. 1993. write for info. (*0-9601918-5-2*) Optical Resolution.

— Optical Resolution Procedures for Chemical Compounds Vol. 4, Pt. 2: Compounds Containing a Sulfur or Selenium Stereocenter. 1611p. 1993. write for info. (*0-9601918-6-0*) Optical Resolution.

Newman, Paul, compiled by. Optical Resolution Procedures for Chemical Compounds Vol. 1: Amines & Related Compounds. 1978. 52.50 (*0-9601918-0-1*) Optical Resolution.

Newman, Paul & Botre, Robert D. Current Approaches to African Linguistics, Vol. 5. (Publications in African Languages & Linguistics: No. 8). viii, 266p. 1989. pap. 83.10 (*90-6765-324-1*) Mouton.

Newman, Paul & Hotchner, A. E. The Hole in the Wall Gang Cookbook: Kid-Friendly Recipes for Families to Make Together. LC 98-35511. 128p. 1998. pap. 14.00 (*0-684-84843-0*) Simon & Schuster.

— Newman's Own Cookbook. LC 98-35430. (Illus.). 224p. 1998. 24.50 (*0-684-84832-5*) Simon & Schuster.

Newman, Paul & Newman, Roxana M., eds. Modern Hausa-English Dictionary. 154p. 1988. pap. text 14.95 (*0-19-575303-8*) OUP.

Newman, Paul, jt. auth. see Hibberd, Peter R.

Newman, Paul B., ed. see Kratt, Mary N.

***Newman, Paul F.** You're Not a Person - Just a Birth Chart: The Astrological Cartoon Humour of Paul F. Newman. (Illus.). 1999. pap. 11.00 (*1-902405-07-2*) Wessex Astrologer.

Newman, Penny, jt. auth. see BBC Staff.

Newman, Peter. Miniature Schnauzers Today. LC 97-34517. 176p. 1997. 29.95 (*0-87605-239-1*) Howell Bks.

— Miniature Schnauzers Today. 176p. 1998. 27.95 (*0-87605-275-8*) Macmillan.

— Sustainability & Cities: Overcoming Automobile Dependence. LC 98-42239. (Illus.). 350p. 1998. pap. text 40.00 (*1-55963-660-2*) Island Pr.

Newman, Peter, ed. European Municipal Directory. 8th rev. ed. 950p. 1999. 475.00 (*1-902812-00-X*) Newmedia Pubng.

— The New Palgrave Dictionary of Economics & the Law, 3 vols. 2210p. 1998. 550.00 (*1-56159-215-3*) Groves Dictionaries.

Newman, Peter & Richards, Delphine. Newfoundlands Today. LC 97-34518. 176p. 1997. 29.95 (*0-87605-246-4*) Howell Bks.

Newman, Peter, et al. The New Palgrave Dictionary of Money & Finance, 2 Vols., Set. 2621p. 1992. 595.00 (*1-56159-041-X*) Groves Dictionaries.

Newman, Peter, jt. auth. see Thornley, Andy.

Newman, Peter, ed. see Eatwell, John.

Newman, Peter C. & Lazarus, Eve. Vancouver: The Art of Living Well. LC 96-32967. (Urban Tapestry Ser.). (Illus.). 240p. 1996. 49.95 (*1-881096-34-3*) Towery Pub.

Newman, Peter W. & Kenworthy, Jeffrey R. Cities & Automobile Dependence: A Sourcebook. (Illus.). xviii, 388p. 1989. text 89.95 (*1-85742-103-5*, Pub. by Avebury Technical) Ashgate Pub Co.

Newman, Philip, jt. auth. see Sizer, Richard.

Newman, Philip R. Development Through Life: Study Guide. 6th ed. (Psychology Ser.). 1995. mass mkt., student ed. 17.75 (*0-534-23335-X*) Brooks-Cole.

Newman, Philip R. & Newman, Barbara M. Childhood & Adolescence. 1997. teacher ed. write for info. incl. trans. (*0-534-34521-2*) Brooks-Cole.

Newman, Philip R., jt. auth. see Newman, Barbara.

Newman, Philip R., jt. auth. see Newman, Barbara A.

Newman, Philip R., jt. auth. see Newman, Barbara M.

Newman, Phyllis. Just in Time: Notes from My Life. LC 89-49726. 224p. 1990. reprint ed. pap. 12.95 (*0-87910-138-5*) Limelight Edns.

Newman, Phyllis E. & Craven, Sue. Newman's Conveyancing Practice & Procedure. 214p. (C). 1991. 110.00 (*1-85190-108-6*, Pub. by Tolley Pubng) St Mut.

Newman, Phyllis E., jt. auth. see Gittins, Vera D.

Newman, Preston. The Land Stacks Up. LC 85-90788. 95p. 1985. pap. 4.95 (*0-9619636-0-3*) K Newman.

— The Land Stacks Up. 2nd ed. Newman, Katherine, ed. LC 85-90788. (Appalachian Connection Ser.). (Illus.). 128p. 1993. pap. 5.95 (*0-936015-33-0*) Pocahontas Pr.

Newman, R. C., jt. ed. see Frankel, G. S.

Newman, R. R., ed. Rail Transportation, 1995, Vol. 10. (1995 ASME International Mechanical Engineering Congress & Exposition Ser.: RTD-Vol. 10). 164p. 1995. 56.00 (*0-7918-1744-X*, H01024) ASME.

Newman, Rafael. The Visible God: Staging the History of Money. LC 98-38403. 208p. 1998. 39.00 (*0-7618-1252-0*) U Pr of Amer.

Newman, Ralph, text. The Death of Your Kind & Brave Father. limited ed. 42p. 1996. write for info. (*0-614-24558-3*) Rowan Tree IN.

Newman, Ralph A. Law of Labor Relations. LC 53-10762. viii, 310p. 1953. lib. bdg. 37.50 (*0-89941-615-2*, 501940) W S Hein.

***Newman, Raquel.** Giving Away Your Money: A Personal Guide to Philanthropy. LC 00-33849. 113p. 2000. pap. 14.95 (*1-887563-54-7*, Pub. by Schreiber Pub) Natl Bk Netwk.

Newman, Raymond J. Orthogeriatrics: Comprehensive Orthopedic Care for the Elderly Patient. (Illus.). 224p. 1992. text 150.00 (*0-7506-1371-8*) Buttrwrth-Heinemann.

Newman, Rebecca. Belly Dancer in the Barrel of Oil. LC 84-90336. 1984. 10.00 (*0-87212-177-1*) Libra.

***Newman, Rebecca.** Educating Homeless Children: Witness to a Cataclysm LC 99-33822. 1999. write for info. (*0-8153-3475-3*) Garland.

Newman, Renee. The Diamond Ring Buying Guide. 5th rev. ed. LC 95-48305. (Illus.). 140p. (C). 1996. pap. 14.95 (*0-929975-24-3*) Intl Jewelry Pubns.

— The Diamond Ring Buying Guide: How to Spot Value & Avoid Ripoffs. 4th ed. LC 93-9741. (Illus.). 151p. (C). 1993. pap. 12.95 (*0-929975-20-0*) Intl Jewelry Pubns.

— Diamonds: Fascinating Facts. (Gemstones Ser.). (Illus.). 16p. (C). 1990. 3.95 (*0-929975-01-4*) Intl Jewelry Pubns.

— Gemstone Buying Guide. LC 97-24288. (Illus.). 152p. (Orig.). 1998. pap. 19.95 (*0-929975-25-1*) Intl Jewelry Pubns.

***Newman, Renee.** Gold & Platinum Jewelry Buying Guide: How to Judge, Buy, Test & Care for It. LC 99-58327. 2000. pap. 19.95 (*0-929975-29-4*, Pub. by Intl Jewelry Pubns) Seven Hills Bk.

Newman, Renee. The Gold Jewelry Buying Guide. LC 93-17583. (Illus.). 170p. (Orig.). (C). 1993. pap. 19.95 (*0-929975-19-7*) Intl Jewelry Pubns.

— The Pearl Buying Guide. 2nd ed. LC 93-43758. (Illus.). 188p. (C). 1994. pap. 19.95 (*0-929975-22-7*) Intl Jewelry Pubns.

— Pearl Buying Guide. 3rd ed. LC 98-29627. (Illus.). 156p. 1999. pap. 19.95 (*0-929975-27-8*) Intl Jewelry Pubns.

— The Ruby & Sapphire Buying Guide: How to Spot Value & Ripoffs. 2nd ed. LC 93-9054. (Illus.). 204p. (C). 1994. pap. 19.95 (*0-929975-21-9*) Intl Jewelry Pubns.

***Newman, Renee.** Ruby, Sapphire & Emerald Buying Guide: How to Evaluate, Identify, Select & Care for These Gemstones. LC 99-32785. (Newman Gem & Jewelry Ser.). (Illus.). 164p. 2000. pap. 19.95 (*0-929975-28-6*) Intl Jewelry Pubns.

Newman, Reta, et al. Handbook of Gas Chromatographic Mass Spectral Data of Ignitable Liquids. LC 97-24293. 768p. 1997. boxed set 104.95 (*0-8493-3107-2*) CRC Pr.

***Newman, Richard.** African American Quotations. 504p. 2000. pap. 18.95 (*0-8160-4439-2*, Checkmark) Facts on File.

Newman, Richard. Afro-American Education, 1907-1932: A Bibliographic Index. LC 83-24869. 198p. 1995. 45.00 (*0-931186-05-6*) Lambeth Pr.

— The Complete Guide to College Success: What Every Student Needs to Know. (Illus.). 320p. (C). 1995. text 50.00 (*0-8147-5783-9*); pap. text 18.50 (*0-8147-5784-7*) NYU Pr.

— Distinguished African American Dancers & Choreographers. (Illus.). 344p. 2001. 65.00 (*1-57356-260-2*) Oryx Pr.

Newman, Richard. Everybody Say Freedom: Everything You Need to Know about African-American History. (Illus.). (J). 1996. 18.30 (*0-606-18361-2*) Turtleback.

— The Horse That Screamed. 283p. mass mkt. 4.99 (*1-55197-054-6*) Picasso Publ.

Newman, Richard. Lemuel Haynes: A Bio-Bibliography. LC 83-24877. 160p. 1995. 40.00 (*0-931186-04-8*); 40.00 (*0-03-118604-1*) Carlson Pub.

— The Stone Sculpture of India: A Study of the Materials Used by Indian Sculptors from Ca. 2nd Century B. C. to the 16th Century. (Illus.). 106p. 1984. pap. 14.00 (*0-916724-57-3*) Harvard Art Mus.

— Words Like Freedom: Afro-American Books & Manuscripts in the Henry W. & Albert A. Berg Collection of English & American Literature. (Illus.). 42p. (Orig.). 1989. pap. 10.00 (*0-87104-413-7*) NY Pub Lib.

— Workers & Unions in Bombay, 1918-1929: A Study of Organisation in the Cotton Mills. 1982. pap. 22.00 (*0-686-91580-1*) S Asia.

Newman, Richard, compiled by. African American Quotations. LC 98-8430. 520p. (YA). (gr. 9 up). 1998. 54.95 (*1-57356-118-5*) Oryx Pr.

— Black Access: A Bibliography of Afro-American Bibliographies. LC 83-8537. 249p. 1984. lib. bdg. 55.00 (*0-313-23282-2*, NEB/, Greenwood Pr) Greenwood.

Newman, Richard, ed. Black Preacher to White America: The Collected Writings of Lemuel Haynes, 1774-1833. LC 89-48246. 291p. 1989. 75.00 (*0-926019-24-4*) Carlson Pub.

— Nine Decades of Scholarship. 83p. 1986. pap. 3.00 (*0-87104-288-6*) NY Pub Lib.

— Treasures from the New York Public Library. (Illus.). 134p. (Orig.). 1985. pap. 19.95 (*0-87104-286-X*) NY Pub Lib.

***Newman, Richard, et al, eds.** Pamphlets of Protest: An Anthology of Early African American Protest Literature, 1790-1860. 320p. 2000. 45.00 (*0-415-92443-X*); pap. 22.99 (*0-415-92444-8*) Routledge.

Newman, Richard, intro. The Negro Churchman, 2 vols., Set. 1990. reprint ed. 190.00 (*0-527-66370-0*) Periodicals Srv.

***Newman, Richard & Kirtley, Karen.** Alma Rose: Vienna to Auschwitz. LC 99-36000. (Illus.). 432p. 2000. 29.95 (*1-57467-051-4*, Amadeus Pr) Timber.

Newman, Richard & Sawyer, Marcia. Everybody Say Freedom: Everything You Need to Know about African-American History. LC 95-44431. 320p. 1996. pap. 12.95 (*0-452-27593-8*, Plume) Dutton Plume.

Newman, Richard, jt. auth. see Tomasek, Jaroslav.

Newman, Richard, jt. ed. see Weisenfeld, Judith.

Newman, Richard G. Supplier Price Analysis: A Guide for Purchasing, Accounting, & Financial Analysts. LC 91-33084. 200p. 1992. 57.95 (*0-89930-545-8*, NSR/, Quorum Bks) Greenwood.

Newman, Richard G. & Simkins, Robert J. Capital Equipment Buying Handbook. LC 97-45962. 450p. 1998. 89.95 (*0-8144-0369-7*) AMACOM.

Newman, Richard L. Heads-Up Displays: Designing the Way Ahead. 371p. 1994. 133.95 (*0-291-39811-1*, Pub. by Avebury Technical) Ashgate Pub Co.

— Tort Remedies in Connecticut, 1998 Cumulative Supplement. 150p. 1998. suppl. ed. write for info. (*0-327-00339-1*, 6520411) LEXIS Pub.

***Newman, Richard L.** Tort Remedies in Connecticut, 1999 Cumulative Supplement: Pocketpart. 175p. 1999. suppl. ed. write for info. (*0-327-01155-4*, 6520412) LEXIS Pub.

Newman, Richard L. & Wildstein, Jeffrey S. Tort Remedies in Connecticut. LC 96-76380. 601p. 1996. 95.00 (*1-55834-327-X*, 65203-10, MICHIE) LEXIS Pub.

Newman, Robert. Case of the Baker Street Irregular: A Sherlock Holmes Story. 1978. 10.05 (*0-606-03375-0*, Pub. by Turtleback) Demco.

— The Case of the Baker Street Irregulars. LC 77-15463. 228p. (J). (gr. 3-7). 1984. mass mkt. 4.95 (*0-689-70766-5*) Aladdin.

— The Case of the Baker Street Irregulars. 1994. 19.00 (*0-8446-6762-5*) Peter Smith.

***Newman, Robert.** Disciples of the Buddha: Imagery of the Human & Superhuman Meditation. (Illus.). 168p. 2000. pap. 12.95 (*1-887276-21-1*, Pub. by Cool Grove Pub) LPC Group.

Newman, Robert. Merlin's Mistake. (Illus.). (J). (gr. 5-9). 1990. 16.25 (*0-8446-6187-2*) Peter Smith.

— The Testing of Tertius. (Illus.). (J). (gr. 5-9). 1990. 20.25 (*0-8446-6188-0*) Peter Smith.

Newman, Robert, ed. Pedagogy, Praxis, Ulysses: Using Joyce's Text to Transform the Classroom. LC 95-19276. 280p. (C). 1995. text 44.50 (*0-472-10636-8*, 10636) U of Mich Pr.

Newman, Robert, jt. auth. see Magee, Doug.

***Newman, Robert C.** The Biblical Firmament: Vault or Vapor? LC 00-131905. (Illus.). vi, 90p. 2000. 7.95 (*0-944788-80-7*, N11) IBRI.

Newman, Robert C., ed. The Evidence of Prophecy: Fulfilled Prediction as a Testimony to the Truth of Christianity. LC 88-82536. 150p. 1988. pap. 9.95 (*0-944788-98-X*) IBRI.

Newman, Robert C. & Eckelmann, Herman J., Jr. Genesis One & the Origin of the Earth. LC 77-72526. 158p. 1989. pap. 9.95 (*0-944788-97-1*, N4) IBRI.

Newman, Robert C., et al. What's Darwin Got to Do with It? A Friendly Discussion about Evolution. LC 99-55902. 156p. 1999. pap. 9.99 (*0-8308-2249-6*) InterVarsity.

Newman, Robert C., jt. auth. see Fawcett, Cheryl.

Newman, Robert D. Transgressions of Reading: Narrative Engagement As Exile & Return. LC 92-13546. (Post-Contemporary Interventions Ser.). (Illus.). 192p. 1992. text 49.95 (*0-8223-1280-8*); pap. text 17.95 (*0-8223-1296-4*) Duke.

Newman, Robert D., ed. Centuries' Ends, Narrative Means. 1996. 49.50 (*0-8047-2649-3*); pap. 18.95 (*0-8047-2650-7*) Stanford U Pr.

Newman, Robert D. & Thorton, Weldon, eds. Joyce's Ulysses: The Larger Perspective. LC 86-40399. (Illus.). 312p. 1987. 40.00 (*0-87413-316-5*) U Delaware Pr.

Newman, Robert P. Owen Lattimore & the "Loss" of China. 685p. 1992. 45.00 (*0-520-07388-6*, Pub. by U CA Pr) Cal Prin Full Svc.

— Truman & the Hiroshima Cult. 260p. 1995. 34.95 (*0-87013-403-5*) Mich St U Pr.

***Newman, Roberta L.** Building Relationships with Parents & Families in School-Age Programs: Resources for Staff Training & Program Planning. LC 99-72952. 1999. pap. 16.95 (*0-917505-09-3*) School Age.

Newman, Rochelle. Malleable Matter/Stretchable Space: Interweaving Art, Math & Nature in N-Dimensions. (Illus.). 400p. (C). 2000. text 53.95 (*0-9614504-5-2*) Pythagorean Pr.

Newman, Rochelle & Fowler, Donna M. Space, Structure & Form. 1996. pap. text 40.00 (*0-697-33058-3*) Pythagorean Pr.

Newman, Rochelle, jt. auth. see Boles, Martha.

Newman, Roger C. Murtagh & the Vikings. (Hawthorn Series in Irish History). (Illus.). 96p. (Orig.). (J). (gr. 5-8). 1986. pap. 9.95 (*0-947962-06-9*, Pub. by Childrens Pr) Irish Bks Media.

— Murtagh the Warrior. LC 97-207217. 144p. 1997. pap. 8.95 (*0-947962-98-0*) Dufour.

Newman, Roger K. Hugo Black: A Biography. LC 94-10233. 944p. 1994. 30.00 (*0-679-43180-2*) Pantheon.

— Hugo Black: A Biography. 2nd rev. ed. LC 97-13406. xvi, 741p. 1997. pap. 19.95 (*0-8232-1786-8*) Fordham.

Newman, Roger K., jt. auth. see De Grazia, Edward.

Newman, Ron. HBJ Composition Workbook. 448p. (C). 1992. 25.00 (*0-03-079567-2*) Harcourt Coll Pubs.

Newman, Rosemary K., jt. auth. see Newman, C. W.

Newman, Roxana M. An English-Hausa Dictionary. LC 89-51452. 344p. (C). 1990. 40.00 (*0-300-04702-9*) Yale U Pr.

Newman, Roxana M., jt. ed. see Newman, Paul.

Newman, Roxanna Ma, ed. see O'Meara, Patrick, et al.

Newman, Russell W. A Comparative Analysis of Prehistoric Skeletal Remains from the Lower Sacramento Valley. fac. ed. (Reports of the University of California Archaeological Survey: No. 39). (Illus.). 75p. 1957. reprint ed. pap. 8.75 (*1-55567-356-2*) Coyote Press.

Newman, Ruth. Comforting, Inspiring, Sacred Prayers & Thoughts in Verse. (Orig.). 1997. pap. write for info. (*1-57553-440-1*) Watermrk Pr.

— Poetry & Prose with a Purpose. 1998. pap. write for info. (*1-57553-756-7*) Watermrk Pr.

Newman, Ruth, jt. ed. see Cliver, Dean O.

Newman, Ruth G. & Ketchum, Bradford W., Jr., eds. How to Really Recruit, Motivate & Lead Your Team: Managing People. 1997. pap. 15.95 (*1-880394-15-4*) Thomson Learn.

***Newman-Ryan, Jodell.** Auditory Brain Stem Evoked Potentials. 240p. 2000. pap. 60.00 (*0-205-31982-3*) Allyn.

Newman, S. The Foundations of Helicopter Flight: MR 88. LC 94-181796. 303p. 1994. pap. 75.00 (*0-470-23394-X*) Wiley.

Newman, S., jt. auth. see Mallick, P. K.

Newman, S., ed. see ACS Symposium on Highly Cross-Linked Polymer Networks.

Newman, S. S., jt. auth. see Gayton, A. H.

Newman, Sally. Intergenerational Programs: Past, Present, & Future. LC 97-10289. 1997. pap. 27.95 (*1-56032-421-X*); boxed set 59.95 (*1-56032-420-1*) Hemisp Pub.

Newman, Sally & Brummel, Steven W., eds. Intergenerational Programs: Imperatives, Strategies, Impacts, Trends. LC 89-1775. (Illus.). 258p. 1994. lib. bdg. 49.95 (*0-86656-773-9*) Haworth Pr.

Newman, Sally, jt. auth. see Kramer, Cynthia.

Newman, Sally, ed. see Smith, Thomas B., et al.

Newman, Samuel P. Elements of Political Economy. LC 68-30535. (Reprints of Economic Classics Ser.). xi, 324p. 1973. reprint ed. 45.00 (*0-678-00691-1*) Kelley.

— A Practical System of Rhetoric: or The Principles & Rules of Style. LC 95-31654. 334p. 1995. 50.00 (*0-8201-1496-0*) Schol Facsimiles.

Newman, Sandra J. Federal Policy & the Mobility of Older Homeowners: The Effects of the One-Time Capital Gains Exclusion. LC 84-29745. (Institute for Social Research, Research Report). 98p. (Orig.). reprint ed. pap. 30.40 (*0-7837-5265-2*, 204500300005) Bks Demand.

— The Home Front: Implications of Welfare Reform for Housing Policy. LC 98-48887. 1999. pap. 19.50 (*0-87766-685-7*) Urban Inst.

Newman, Sandra J., ed. The Home Front: Implications of Welfare Reform for Housing Policy. LC 98-48887. 1999. lib. bdg. 49.50 (*0-87766-684-9*) Urban Inst.

— Worlds Apart? Long-Term Care in Australia & the United States. LC 87-29770. (Home Health Care Services Quarterly Ser.: Vol. 8, No. 3). (Illus.). 113p. 1988. text 32.95 (*0-86656-703-8*) Haworth Pr.

N

An Asterisk (*) at the beginning of an entry indicates that the title is appearing for the first time.

Newman, Sandra J. & Owen, Michael S. Residential Displacement in the United States, 1970-1977. LC 82-12101. (Institute for Social Research, Research Report). 106p. reprint ed. pap. 32.90 (*0-608-17272-3*, 202946900060) Bks Demand.

Newman, Sandra J. & Schnare, Ann B. Beyond Bricks & Mortar: Reexamining the Purpose & Effects of Housing Assistance. LC 92-23289. (Urban Institute Report: No. 92-3). 152p. (C). 1992. pap. text 24.00 (*0-87766-585-0*); lib. bdg. 55.00 (*0-87766-584-2*) Urban Inst.

Newman, Sarah. Games & Activities for Pre-School Children with Special Needs: Using Games & Activities to Help Your Pre-School Child with Special Needs. LC 98-45817. 255p. 1999. pap. 19.95 (*1-85302-643-3*) Jessica Kingsley.

Newman, Sarah W., jt. auth. see Gilman, Sid.

Newman, Sasha M., et al. Felix Vallotton. (Illus.). 328p. 1991. 60.00 (*1-55859-312-8*) Abbeville Pr.

— Felix Vallotton. LC 91-66233. 328p. (C). 1991. pap. 40.00 (*0-89467-057-3*) Yale Art Gallery.

Newman, Sasha N., ed. see Weber, Nicholas F.

Newman, Saul. Ethnoregional Conflict in Democracies: Mostly Ballots, Rarely Bullets, 373. LC 95-48357. (Contributions in Political Science Ser.: Vol. 373). 296p. 1996. 65.00 (*0-313-30039-9*, Greenwood Pr) Greenwood.

Newman, Sharan. The Chessboard Queen. LC 97-229295. 320p. 1997. pap. 13.95 (*0-312-86391-8*) St Martin.

***Newman, Sharan.** Crime Through Time III. 352p. 2000. mass mkt. 6.99 (*0-425-17509-X*) Berkley Pub.

— Cursed in the Blood. 2000. mass mkt. 6.99 (*0-8125-9020-1*) Forge NYC.

Newman, Sharan. Cursed in the Blood. LC 98-14608. 352p. 1998. text 23.95 (*0-312-86567-8*) St Martin.

— Death Comes As Epiphany. 320p. 1995. 4.99 (*0-8125-2293-1*, Pub. by Forge NYC) St Martin.

— Death Comes As Epiphany. 320p. 1993. 19.95 (*0-312-85419-6*, Pub. by Tor Bks) St Martin.

— The Devil's Door. 416p. 1995. 4.99 (*0-8125-2295-8*, Pub. by Forge NYC) St Martin.

***Newman, Sharan.** The Difficult Saint. LC 99-26644. 352p. 1999. 23.95 (*0-312-86966-5*, Pub. by Forge NYC) St Martin.

— Difficult Saint. 2000. mass mkt. 6.99 (*0-8125-8433-3*) Tor Bks.

Newman, Sharan. Guinevere. LC 96-23853. 320p. 1996. pap. 13.95 (*0-312-86233-4*) St Martin.

— Guinevere Evermore. LC 98-15415. 288p. 1998. pap. 13.95 (*0-312-86641-0*) St Martin.

— Strong As Death. 1997. mass mkt. 5.99 (*0-8125-3935-4*, Pub. by Forge NYC) St Martin.

***Newman, Sharan.** To Wear White Cross. 352p. 2000. text 22.95 (*0-312-86965-7*) St Martin.

— The Wandering Arm. 1996. mass mkt. 5.99 (*0-8125-5089-7*, Pub. by Forge NYC) St Martin.

***Newman, Sharan.** The Wandering Arm. 2001. pap. write for info. (*0-312-87733-1*, Pub. by Forge NYC) St Martin.

Newman, Sharan, jt. ed. see Monfredo, Miriam G.

Newman, Sharon, jt. auth. see Aug, Bobbie.

Newman, Sharon, jt. auth. see Aug, Bobby.

Newman, Sharon, jt. auth. see Morfreds, Miriam G.

***Newman, Shirlee P.** African Slave Trade. (Illus.). (J). 2000. 24.00 (*0-531-11694-8*) Watts.

— Child Slavery in Modern Times. (Illus.). (J). 2000. 24.00 (*0-531-11696-4*) Watts.

Newman, Shirlee P. The Creek. LC 96-11623. (First Books-Indians of the Americas). 64p. (J). (gr. 4-6). 1996. lib. bdg. 22.00 (*0-531-20236-4*) Watts.

— The Creek. (First Bks.). 64p. (J). (gr. 4-6). 1997. pap. 6.95 (*0-531-15809-8*) Watts.

— The Inuits. LC 93-18370. (First Bks.). (Illus.). 64p. (J). (gr. 4-6). 1993. lib. bdg. 22.00 (*0-531-20073-6*) Watts.

— The Inuits. (First Bks.). (J). (gr. 4-7). 1994. pap. 6.95 (*0-531-15701-6*) Watts.

***Newman, Shirlee P.** Slavery in the United States. (Illus.). (J). 2000. 24.00 (*0-531-11695-6*) Watts.

***Newman, Shirlee Petkin.** Pequots. (Indians of the Americas Library). (Illus.). (YA). 2000. pap. 8.95 (*0-531-16482-9*) Watts.

Newman, Shirlee Petkin. The Pequots in Southern New England: The Fall & Rise of an American Indian Nation. LC 99-13702. 2000. 24.00 (*0-531-20327-1*) Watts.

Newman, Shirley. A Child's Introduction to the Early Prophets. LC 75-14052. (Illus.). 128p. 1975. pap., teacher ed. 14.95 (*0-87441-227-7*) Behrman.

— A Child's Introduction to the Early Prophets. Newman, Louis I., ed. LC 75-14052. (Illus.). 128p. (J). (gr. 3-4). 1975. pap. 8.95 (*0-87441-244-7*) Behrman.

— A Child's Introduction to the Early Prophets, No. 2. LC 75-14052. (Illus.). 128p. (J). (gr. 3-4). 1975. pap., wbk. ed. 3.95 (*0-87441-269-2*) Behrman.

— A Child's Introduction to Torah. Newman, Louis I., ed. (Illus.). 128p. (Orig.). (J). (gr. 2-3). 1995. pap. 8.95 (*0-87441-067-3*) Behrman.

— Introduction to Kings, Later Prophets & Writings, Vol. 3. Rossel, Seymour, ed. (Child's Introduction to Bible Ser.). (Illus.). 160p. (J). (gr. 4-5). 1981. pap., wbk. ed. 4.95 (*0-87441-361-3*); pap. text 8.95 (*0-87441-336-2*) Behrman.

Newman, Shirley, jt. auth. see Rosenberg, Amye.

Newman, Shirley A. We Brought Sinai to San Joaquin: Story of the Jews of Kern County. LC 98-61139. 152p. 1998. text 20.00 (*1-889159-01-8*) BitterSweet CA.

Newman, Simon K. March, 1939: A Study in the Continuity of British Foreign Policy. 264p. 1976. text 55.00 (*0-19-822532-6*) OUP.

Newman, Simon P. Parades & the Politics of the Street: Festive Culture in the Early American Republic. LC 97-5392. (Early American Studies). (Illus.). 296p. 1997. text 39.95 (*0-8122-3399-9*) U of Pa Pr.

***Newman, Simon P.** Parades & the Politics of the Street: Festive Culture in the Early American Republic. 2000. pap. text 19.95 (*0-8122-1724-1*) U of Pa Pr.

Newman-St. John, Judy. Bbile Zone - Where the Bible Comes to Life: Older Elementary. (J). (gr. 4-6). 1998. pap. 19.95 (*0-687-09282-5*) Abingdon.

— In the Beginning. (Great Big Bks.). (Illus.). 16p. (J). (gr. k-1). 1996. pap. 14.95 (*0-687-07068-6*) Abingdon.

Newman-St. John, Judy. In the Beginning: Leader's Guide. (J). (gr. k-1). 1.50 (*0-687-05388-9*) Abingdon.

***Newman, Standford J. & Miller, James V.** Cigar Family: A 100 Year Journey in the Cigar Industry. LC 99-47467. (Illus.). 240p. 1999. 29.50 (*0-8281-1339-4*) Forb Custom Pub.

Newman, Stanley. The Crossword Answer Book. 1998. pap. 17.50 (*0-8129-2972-1*, Times Bks) Crown Pub Group.

— Cryptic Crossword, Vol. 1. Date not set. write for info. (*0-8129-2639-0*, Times Bks) Crown Pub Group.

— Monster Crossword Omnibus. 1998. pap. 17.50 (*0-8129-3059-2*, Times Bks) Crown Pub Group.

— New York Times Beginner Crossword Dictionary. 512p. 1999. 23.00 (*0-8129-3043-6*, Times Bks) Crown Pub Group.

— New York Times Best Diagramless Crosswords, Vol. 1. Vol. 1. 64p. 1995. pap. 8.50 (*0-8129-2608-0*, Times Bks) Crown Pub Group.

— The New York Times Skillbuilder Crosswords Vol. 5: Three-Star Strategist Puzzles. 64p. 1995. pap. 8.50 (*0-8129-2611-0*, Times Bks) Crown Pub Group.

— Plethora of Puzzles. 1995. 75.45 (*0-394-27306-0*) Random.

— Random House Cryptic Crosswords, Vol. 1. Vol. 1. 80p. 1994. pap. 11.00 (*0-8129-6371-7*, Times Bks) Crown Pub Group.

— Random House Cryptic Crosswords, Vol. 2. 2nd ed. Vol. 2. 1995. pap. 12.00 (*0-8129-2562-9*, Times Bks) Crown Pub Group.

— Random House Cryptic Crosswords, Vol. 3. 80p. 1996. pap. 11.00 (*0-8129-2770-2*, Times Bks) Crown Pub Group.

— Random House Cryptic Crosswords, Vol. 4. 1997. pap. 12.00 (*0-8129-2784-2*, Times Bks) Crown Pub Group.

— Random House Cryptic Crosswords, Vol. 5. 5th ed. 1998. pap. 12.50 (*0-8129-2974-8*, Times Bks) Crown Pub Group.

— Random House Lexercise, Vol. 2. 64p. 1997. pap. 8.50 (*0-8129-2765-6*, Times Bks) Crown Pub Group.

— Random House Lexercise Vol. 1: Word Games to Build Your Mental Fitness, Vol. 1. 64p. 1996. pap. 8.50 (*0-8129-2702-8*, Times Bks) Crown Pub Group.

— Random House Masterpiece crosswords. 1998. pap. 9.00 (*0-8129-2941-1*, Times Bks) Crown Pub Group.

***Newman, Stanley.** Random House Monster Crossword Puzzle Omnibus, Vol. 1. 1999. pap. 17.50 (*0-8129-3213-7*, Times Bks) Crown Pub Group.

Newman, Stanley. Random House Sunday Crossword Puzzle, Vol. 4. 1998. pap. 9.00 (*0-8129-3019-3*, Times Bks) Crown Pub Group.

— Random House Sunday Crossword Puzzles: Two, Star Apprentice Level, Vol. 1. Vol. 1. 1995. pap. 9.00 (*0-8129-2554-8*, Times Bks) Crown Pub Group.

— Random House Sunday Crosswords, Vol. 2. Vol. 2. 64p. 1996. pap. 9.00 (*0-8129-2766-4*, Times Bks) Crown Pub Group.

— Random House Sunday Crosswords, Vol. 3. 3rd ed. 1997. pap. 9.00 (*0-8129-2914-4*, Times Bks) Crown Pub Group.

— Random House 10,000 Dollar Crossword Challenge. 1996. pap. 14.00 (*0-8129-2772-9*, Times Bks) Crown Pub Group.

— Random House Ultrahard Crosswords, Vol. 1. Vol. 1. 64p. 1994. pap. 8.50 (*0-8129-6372-5*, Times Bks) Crown Pub Group.

— Random House Ultrahard Crosswords, Vol. 2. 2nd ed. Vol. 2. 1995. pap. 8.50 (*0-8129-2482-7*, Times Bks) Crown Pub Group.

— Random House Ultrahard Crosswords, Vol. 4. 4th ed. Vol. 4. 64p. 1996. pap. 9.00 (*0-8129-2783-4*, Times Bks) Crown Pub Group.

— Random House Ultrahard Omnibus Crossword Puzzles, Vol. 1. 1999. pap. 12.50 (*0-8129-3126-2*, Times Bks) Crown Pub Group.

***Newman, Stanley.** Random House Vacation, Vol. 1. 112p. 2000. pap. 6.95 (*0-8129-3289-7*, Times Bks) Random.

Newman, Stanley. Sport Magazine, Vol. 1. 128p. 1999. pap. 9.95 (*0-8129-3155-6*, Times Bks) Crown Pub Group.

— Washington Post Sunday Crossword Puzzle, Vol. 6. 6th ed. Vol. 6. 64p. 1997. pap. 9.00 (*0-8129-2649-8*, Times Bks) Crown Pub Group.

— Zuni Law: A Field of Values, with an Appendix. Incl. Practical Zuni Orthography. 1954. (HU PMP Ser.). 1954. 32.00 (*0-527-01312-9*) Periodicals Srv.

***Newman, Stanley, ed.** Random House Sunday Crosswords, Vol. 5. 64p. 1999. pap. 9.50 (*0-8129-3163-7*, Times Bks) Crown Pub Group.

Newman, Stanley, ed. Random House Ultrahard Crosswords, Vol. 3. 3rd ed. 64p. 1996. pap. 8.50 (*0-8129-2701-X*, Times Bks) Crown Pub Group.

Newman, Stanley & Stark, Daniel. The Crossword Answer Book. 1200p. 1996. 27.50 (*0-8129-2729-X*, Times Bks) Crown Pub Group.

Newman, Stanley, jt. auth. see Rosen, Mel.

Newman, Stanley, jt. ed. see Maleska, Eugene T.

Newman, Stanley, jt. ed. see Rosen, Mel.

Newman, Stanton, et al. Understanding Rheumatoid Arthritis. LC 95-16023. 256p. (C). 1995. 85.00 (*0-415-10540-4*); pap. 24.99 (*0-415-10541-2*) Routledge.

***Newman, Stanton P. & Harrison, Michael J.G.** The Brain & Cardiac Surgery: Causes of Neurological Complications & Their Prevention. 416p. 1999. text 112.00 (*90-5702-476-4*, Harwood Acad Pubs) Gordon & Breach.

Newman, Stephen. Philosophy & Teacher Education: A Reinterpretation of Donald A. Schon's Epistemology of Reflective Practice. LC LB1707.N49 1999. (Series in Philosophy). 262p. 1999. text 69.95 (*1-84014-891-8*) Ashgate Pub Co.

Newman, Stephen A., ed. Acid & Sour Gas Treating Processes: Latest Data & Methods for Designing & Operating Today's Gas Treating Facilities. LC 84-25339. (Illus.). 832p. 1985. reprint ed. pap. 200.00 (*0-608-04203-X*, 206493800011) Bks Demand.

— Thermodynamics of Aqueous Systems with Industrial Applications. LC 80-16044. (ACS Symposium Ser.: No. 133). 1980. 86.95 (*0-8412-0569-8*); suppl. ed. 14.95 (*0-8412-0590-6*) Am Chemical.

— Thermodynamics of Aqueous Systems with Industrial Applications. LC 80-16044. (ACS Symposium Ser.: No. 133). (Illus.). 783p. 1980. reprint ed. pap. 200.00 (*0-608-03235-2*, 206375400007) Bks Demand.

Newman, Stephen L. Liberalism at Wit's End: The Libertarian Revolt Against the Modern State. LC 84-7108. 192p. 1984. text 37.50 (*0-8014-1747-3*) Cornell U Pr.

***Newman, Steve, et al.** House Plant Tips. (Illus.). 20p. 1999. pap. 4.75 (*1-889143-05-7*, 569A) CO St U Coop.

Newman, Steven A., jt. ed. see Tusa, Ronald J.

Newman, Steven M. Worldwalk. 560p. 1990. mass mkt. 5.95 (*0-380-71150-8*, Avon Bks) Morrow Avon.

Newman, Steven M., jt. ed. see Gordon, Andrew M.

Newman, Steven T., jt. ed. see Case, Keith.

Newman, Stewart A. A Free Church Perspective: A Study in Ecclesiology. 113p. (Orig.). 1986. pap. 8.95 (*0-913029-12-2*) Stevens Bk Pr.

Newman, Stuart A., jt. auth. see Hall, Brian K.

Newman, Susan. Dont Be S. A. D. A Teenage Guide to Handling Stress, Anxiety & Depression. (J). 1991. lib. bdg. 8.95 (*0-671-72611-0*, Julian Messner) Silver Burdett Pr.

— Let's Always Make Love Last: Promises to Make Love Last. LC 94-16788. 194p. (Orig.). 1995. pap. 8.00 (*0-399-51901-7*, Perigee Bks) Berkley Pub.

— Little Things Long Remembered: Making Your Children Feel Special Every Day. LC 92-42897. 1993. 14.00 (*0-517-59302-5*, Crown) Crown Pub Group.

— Little Things Mean A Lot: Creating Happy Memories with Your Granchildren. 128p. 1996. 14.00 (*0-517-70463-3*, Crown) Crown Pub Group.

— Little Things Shared: Lasting Connections Between Family & Friends. LC 97-28721. 1998. 14.00 (*0-517-70821-3*) Crown Pub Group.

— Parenting an Only Child. 256p. 1990. pap. 12.95 (*0-385-24964-0*) Doubleday.

Newman, Susan & King, Janet S. Getting Your Child into College: What Parents Must Know. LC 95-36302. 160p. 1996. pap. 10.95 (*0-312-14107-6*) St Martin.

Newman, Susan B. Literacy in the Television Age. 2nd ed. (Illus.). 232p. 1995. pap. 39.50 (*1-56750-162-1*); text 73.25 (*1-56750-161-3*) Ablx Pub.

Newman, Susan D. With Heart & Hand: The Black Church Working to Save Black Children. LC 94-39334. 96p. 1995. pap. 10.00 (*0-8170-1223-0*) Judson.

Newman, T. C., jt. auth. see Odell, P. L.

Newman, Thomas, jt. auth. see Ostrager, Barry R.

Newman, Thomas E. Electricity & Electronics. LC 94-37494. 1994. 39.95 (*0-02-801253-4*) Glencoe.

Newman, Thomas R. New York Appellate Practice, 2 vols. 1985. ring bd. 365.00 (*0-8205-1519-1*) Bender.

Newman, Thomas R., jt. auth. see Ostrager, Barry R.

Newman, Vicky, jt. auth. see Cumming, Candy.

Newman, Victor. Made-to-Measure Problem-Solving LC 98-163867. xi, 139p. 1998. pap. 26.95 (*0-566-08006-0*) Ashgate Pub Co.

— Problem Solving for Results. 158p. 1995. 61.95 (*0-566-07566-0*, Pub. by Gower) Ashgate Pub Co.

Newman, W. Interactive System Design. 2nd ed. (C). 1999. text. write for info. (*0-201-36049-7*) Addison-Wesley.

Newman, W. A., jt. auth. see Rose, T. K.

Newman, W. S. & Stipcich, S. Nuclear Winter & the New Defense Systems: Problems & Perspectives, the 4th International Seminar on Nuclear War. (Science & Culture Ser.). 532p. 1992. text 123.00 (*981-02-1187-2*) World Scientific Pub.

— SDI, Computer Simulations, New Proposals to Stop the Arms Race: Fifth International Seminar on Nuclear War. (Science & Culture Ser.). 396p. 1992. text 121.00 (*981-02-1188-0*) World Scientific Pub.

— The Technical Basis for Peace: Third International Seminar on Nuclear War. (Science & Culture Ser.). 400p. 1992. text 121.00 (*981-02-1186-4*) World Scientific Pub.

Newman, Walter H., jt. ed. see Abel, Francis L.

Newman, Wilda B., jt. auth. see Mount, Ellis.

Newman, William. Gehennical Fire: The Lives of George Starkey, an American Alchemist in the Scientific Revolution. (Illus.). 320p. 1994. text 57.00 (*0-674-34171-6*, NEWGEH) HUP.

Newman, William & Ekedahl, Michael. New Perspectives on Visual Basic 5.0: Introductory. 10th ed. (New Perspectives Ser.). 376p. (C). 1997. pap. 28.50 (*0-7600-5380-4*) Course Tech.

Newman, William & Ohmann, Sarah. Guide to Sea Kayaking the Eastern Great Lakes: The Best Trips on Lakes Huron, Erie & Ontario. LC 99-25249. (Regional Sea Kayaking Ser.). 1999. text 15.95 (*0-7627-0417-9*) Globe Pequot.

Newman, William A. & Ross, Arnold, eds. Antarctic Cirripedia. LC 74-129339. (Antarctic Research Ser.: Vol. 14). (Illus.). 257p. 1971. 32.00 (*0-87590-114-X*) Am Geophysical.

Newman, William H. Administrative Action. 1972. pap. 32.00 (*0-8464-4364-3*) Beekman Pubs.

— Administrative Action: The Techniques of Organization & Management. 2nd ed. 1963. text 48.00 (*0-13-007195-1*) P-H.

— Birth of a Successful Joint Venture. LC 92-10759. 1992. 22.50 (*0-8191-8724-0*); 48.50 (*0-8191-8723-2*) U Pr of Amer.

Newman, William H. & Lamming, Michael G. Interactive System Design. LC 95-3377. 468p. (C). 1995. 45.94 (*0-201-63162-8*) Addison-Wesley.

Newman, William H., jt. auth. see Yavitz, Boris.

Newman, William I., et al, eds. Nonlinear Dynamics & Predictability of Geophysical Phenomena. IUGG, 1994, Vol. 18. LC 94-20388. (Geophysical Monographs: Vol. 83). 107p. 1994. 28.00 (*0-87590-469-6*) Am Geophysical.

Newman, William L. Geologic Time: The Age of the Earth. 20p. 1991. pap. 1.25 (*0-16-028750-2*) USGPO.

Newman, William L., jt. ed. see Weis, Paul L.

Newman, William M. Charters of St-Fursy of Peronne. LC 75-36479. (Medieval Academy Bks.: No. 85). 1977. 25.00 (*0-910956-59-6*) Medieval Acad.

— Le Domaine Royal Sous les Premiers Capetiens (987-1180) LC 80-2014. reprint ed. 41.50 (*0-404-18581-9*) AMS Pr.

— Interactive Systems Design. text. write for info. (*0-07-046343-3*) McGraw.

— The Kings, the Court & Royal Power in France in the 11th Century. LC 80-2030. reprint ed. 28.00 (*0-404-18582-7*) AMS Pr.

***Newman, William M. & Halvorson, Peter L.** Atlas of American Religion: The Denominational Era, 1776-1990. (Illus.). 176p. 1999. text 49.95 (*0-7425-0345-3*) Rowman.

Newman, William M. & Halvorson, Peter L. Atlas of American Religions: The Denominational Era, 1776-1996. LC 99-6320. 192p. 1999. 49.95 (*0-7619-9057-7*) AltaMira Pr.

— Patterns in Pluralism: A Portrait of American Religion, 1952-1971. LC 79-55177. 1980. pap. 5.00 (*0-914422-10-3*) Glenmary Res Ctr.

Newman, William M., jt. auth. see Halvorson, Peter L.

Newman, William R. The Summa Perfectionis of Pseudo-Geber: A Critical Edition, Translation & Study. LC 91-25350. (CTAI Ser.: No. 35). viii, v, 785p. 1991. 296.00 (*90-04-09464-4*) Brill Academic Pubs.

Newman, William S. Beethoven on Beethoven: Playing His Piano Music His Way. 1991. pap. 16.95 (*0-393-30719-0*) Norton.

— The Pianist's Problems. 4th ed. (Quality Paperbacks Ser.). (Illus.). x, 208p. 1986. reprint ed. pap. 11.95 (*0-306-80269-4*) Da Capo.

— Six Keyboard Sonatas from the Classical Era Score. LC M 0023.N4. 67p. reprint ed. pap. 30.00 (*0-608-10737-9*, 200433600042) Bks Demand.

— The Sonata in the Classic Era. 3rd ed. (C). 1983. text 26.50 (*0-393-95286-X*) Norton.

— The Sonata since Beethoven: The Third & Final Volume of a History of the Sonata Idea. LC 76-80924. 880p. reprint ed. pap. 200.00 (*0-8357-3860-4*, 203659300004) Bks Demand.

Newman, William S., ed. Diabelli Variations: Sixteen Contemporaries of Beethoven on a Waltz Tune. LC M 0027.N4. 31p. reprint ed. pap. 30.00 (*0-608-10730-1*, 200433700042) Bks Demand.

Newmann, Carrie & Ballor, Ginny, eds. Oil of Sweet Almond. 40p. (C). 1997. pap. 3.00 (*1-882294-25-4*) Green Gate.

Newmann, Carrie, jt. ed. see Ballor, Ginny.

Newmann, Dana. Coastal Indians: Ready-to-Use Activities & Materials. LC 96-35340. (Illus.). 224p. 1996. pap., teacher ed. 24.95 (*0-87628-609-0*) Ctr Appl Res.

— The Compleat Teacher's Almanack. (Illus.). 380p. 1997. 9.98 (*1-56731-214-4*, MJF Bks) Fine Comms.

— The Compleat Teacher's Almanack: A Practical Guide to Every Day of the Year. 400p. (C). 1991. pap. text 27.95 (*0-87628-243-5*) P-H.

— Complete Native Americans Resource Library: Ready-to-Use Activities & Materials on Desert Indians, Vol. 1. LC 95-31752. (Illus.). 200p. 1995. pap. text, teacher ed. 24.95 (*0-87628-607-4*) Ctr Appl Res.

— Complete Native Americans Resource Library: Ready-to-Use Activities & Materials on Plains Indians, Vol. 2. LC 95-31752. (Illus.). 200p. 1995. pap. text, teacher ed. 24.95 (*0-87628-608-2*) Ctr Appl Res.

— Early Childhood Almanac. LC 97-37759. (Illus.). 240p. 1997. pap. text 14.95 (*0-87628-112-9*) Ctr Appl Res.

— Woodland Indians: Ready-to-Use Activities & Materials. LC 97-25946. (Illus.). 200p. 1996. pap., teacher ed. 24.95 (*0-87628-610-4*) Ctr Appl Res.

Newmann, Frances. Dead Lovers Are Faithful Lovers. LC 76-51673. (Rediscovered Fiction by American Women Ser.). 1977. lib. bdg. 33.95 (*0-405-10051-5*) Ayer.

Newmann, Fred M. Authentic Achievement: Restructuring Schools for Intellectual Quality. LC 96-25324. 1996. 30.95 (*0-7879-0320-5*) Jossey-Bass.

Newmann, Fred M., ed. Student Engagement & Achievement in American Secondary Schools. LC 92-15727. 240p. (C). 1992. 38.00 (*0-8077-3183-8*); pap. 17.95 (*0-8077-3182-X*) Tchrs Coll.

Newmann, Fred M., jt. auth. see Archbald, Doug A.

Newmann, Joan. Coming of Age. 72p. 1995. pap. 11.95 (*0-85640-487-X*, Pub. by Blackstaff Pr) Dufour.

N

An Asterisk (*) at the beginning of an entry indicates that the title is appearing for the first time.

Newmann, Mikel. Home Groups for Urban Cultures: Biblical Small Group Ministry on Five Continents. LC 98-12297. 198p. 1999. pap. 15.95 (*0-87808-281-6*) William Carey Lib.

Newmarch, Jan. Logic Programming: Prolog & Stream Parallel Languages. 288p. 1991. boxed set 35.00 (*0-13-539842-8*) P-H.

— The X Window System & Motif: A Fast Tract Approach. LC 92-25196. (C). 1992. pap. text 34.00 (*0-201-53931-4*) Addison-Wesley.

Newmarch, Rosa H. The Concert-Goer's Library of Descriptive Notes, 2 Vols. LC 70-160984. (Select Bibliographies Reprint Ser.). 1977. reprint ed. 21.95 (*0-8369-5852-7*) Ayer.

— The Concert Goer's Library of Descriptive Notes. 1990. reprint ed. lib. bdg. 79.00 (*0-7812-9165-8*) Rprt Serv.

— The Music of Czechoslovakia. LC 77-26269. (Music Reprint Ser.: 1978). 1978. reprint ed. lib. bdg. 32.50 (*0-306-77563-8*) Da Capo.

— The Music of Czechoslovakia. (Music Book Index Ser.). 244p. 1992. reprint ed. lib. bdg. 79.00 (*0-7812-9510-6*) Rprt Serv.

— The Russian Opera. LC 72-109807. (Illus.). 403p. 1972. reprint ed. lib. bdg. 79.50 (*0-8371-4298-9*, NERO, Greenwood Pr) Greenwood.

— Tchaikovsky: His Life & Works, with Extracts from His Writings, & the Diary of His Tour Abroad in 1888. LC 68-25298. (Studies in Music: No. 42). 1968. reprint ed. lib. bdg. 75.00 (*0-8383-0310-2*) M S G Haskell Hse.

— Tchaikovsky: His Life & Works, with Extracts from His Writings, & the Diary of His Tour Abroad in 1888. 232p. 1990. reprint ed. lib. bdg. 69.00 (*0-7812-0775-4*, 10093) Rprt Serv.

— Tchaikovsky: His Life & Works with Extracts from His Writings & the Diary of His Tour Abroad in 1888. LC 69-14011. 232p. 1969. reprint ed. lib. bdg. 55.00 (*0-8371-1116-1*, NETC, Greenwood Pr) Greenwood.

Newmark. MINITAB Sup Stat/Prob Mod Life. 5th ed. (C). 1992. pap. text, suppl. ed. 22.00 (*0-03-076299-5*) Harcourt Coll Pubs.

— Statistics & Problems in Modern Life. 6th ed. LC 96-70011. (C). 1996. text 78.00 (*0-03-006393-0*) Harcourt Coll Pubs.

— Statistics & Problems in Modern Life. 6th ed. (C). 1997. pap. text, student ed. 22.00 (*0-03-019487-3*) Harcourt Coll Pubs.

— Stats & Prob Mod Life. 6th ed. 1997. pap. text 33.50 (*0-03-019488-1*) Harcourt Coll Pubs.

— STATS & PROB MODERN LIFE 6/E-S. 6th ed. (C). 1996. pap. text 57.50 (*0-03-020338-4*) Harcourt Coll Pubs.

— TI-83 GRAPH CALC MNL T/A STAT. 6th ed. (C). 1997. pap. text, lab manual ed. 22.00 (*0-03-019489-X*) Harcourt Coll Pubs.

Newmark, Charles S. Major Psychological Assessment Instruments, Vol. I. 430p. 1985. text 97.00 (*0-205-08457-5*, H84577, Longwood Div) Allyn.

Newmark, Charles S., ed. Major Psychological Assessment Instruments. 2nd ed. LC 95-40858. 480p. (C). 1996. 68.00 (*0-205-16869-8*) Allyn.

— MMPI: Clinical & Research Trends. LC 79-17777. (Praeger Special Studies). 464p. 1979. 49.95 (*0-03-048926-1*, Praeger Pubs) Greenwood.

Newmark, Deborah, jt. auth. see King, Trisha.

Newmark, Eileen. Women's Roles: A Cross-Cultural Perspective. 128p. 1981. pap. 10.25 (*0-08-026073-X*, Pergamon Pr) Elsevier.

***Newmark, Gerald.** How to Raise Emotionally Healthy Children: Meeting the Five Critical Needs of Children - And Parents Too! LC 95-70472. Orig. Title: Parents, Expectant Parents, All Persons Concerned with Childcare. 176p. 1999. pap. 11.95 (*0-932767-07-9*) Newmark Mgmt Inst.

Newmark, Harris. Sixty Years in Southern California, 1853-1913. 1992. reprint ed. lib. bdg. 75.00 (*0-7812-5071-4*) Rprt Serv.

— Sixty Years in Southern California, 1853-1913: Containing the Reminiscences of Harris Newmark. Newmark, Maurice H. & Newmark, Marco R., eds. 744p. 1984. 25.00 (*0-87093-186-5*) Dawsons.

Newmark, Irving S., jt. auth. see Newmark, Jerry.

Newmark, Jerry & Newmark, Irving S. Happiness Through Superficiality: The War Against Meaningful Relationships. (Illus.). 176p. (Orig.). 1991. pap. 11.95 (*0-932767-02-8*, NMI Pubs) Newmark Mgmt Inst.

Newmark, Joseph. Essential Business Statistics. (C). 1994. text. write for info. (*0-03-030858-5*) Harcourt Coll Pubs.

— Essentials Business Statistics. (C). 1994. pap. text. write for info. (*0-03-051093-7*) Harcourt Coll Pubs.

— Mathematics As a Second Language. 4th ed. LC 85-30646. (Mathematics Ser.). (C). 1987. text. write for info. (*0-201-05885-5*) Addison-Wesley.

— Mathematics As a Second Language. 4th rev. ed. 1987. 51.75 (*0-201-19297-7*) Addison-Wesley.

— Statistics & Probabilities. 5th ed. (C). 1992. pap. text, student ed. 26.50 (*0-03-076298-7*) Harcourt Coll Pubs.

Newmark, Kevin. Beyond Symbolism: Textual History & the Future of Reading. LC 91-55056. 256p. 1991. text 42.50 (*0-8014-2577-8*) Cornell U Pr.

Newmark, Leonard, et al. Spoken Albanian, 6 cass. LC 79-56549. 348p. 1980. audio 75.00 (*0-87950-007-7*, AFAL10) Spoken Lang Serv.

Newmark, Leonard, et al. Spoken Albanian. LC 79-56549. 348p. 1980. pap. 90.00 incl. audio (*0-87950-008-5*) Spoken Lang Serv.

***Newmark, Leonard D.** Oxford Albanian-English Dictionary. (ALB & ENG.). 1056p. 2000. pap. 27.50 (*0-19-860322-3*) OUP.

Newmark, Leonard D. & Bloomfield, Morton W. Linguistic Introduction to the History of English. LC 79-4563. (Illus.). 414p. 1979. reprint ed. lib. bdg. 52.50 (*0-313-20936-7*, BLLI, Greenwood Pr) Greenwood.

Newmark, Leonard D., et al. Spoken Albanian. LC 79-56549. 348p. 1980. pap. 15.00 (*0-87950-005-0*) Spoken Lang Serv.

— Standard Albanian: A Reference Grammar for Students. LC 81-52125. 368p. 1982. 55.00 (*0-8047-1129-1*) Stanford U Pr.

Newmark, Lucy. The Velveteen Rabbit. (Illus.). 32p. (J). (gr. k up). 1998. pap. 14.95 (*1-886201-11-0*) Nana Banana.

Newmark, Lucy. The Nutcracker. abr. large type ed. (NanaBanana Classics Ser.). 32p. (Orig.). (J). (gr. k up). 1995. 14.95 (*1-886201-06-4*) Nana Banana.

Newmark, Marco R., ed. see Newmark, Harris.

Newmark, Maurice H., ed. see Newmark, Harris.

Newmark, Maxim. A Dictionary of Foreign Words & Phrases. LC 70-88915. 245p. 1969. reprint ed. lib. bdg. 35.00 (*0-8371-2103-5*, NEFW, Greenwood Pr) Greenwood.

Newmark, Maxim, jt. ed. see Kendris, Christopher.

Newmark, Michael E. & Penry, J. Kiffin, eds. Genetics of Epilepsy: A Review. LC 79-53067. 132p. 1980. reprint ed. pap. 41.00 (*0-608-00312-3*, 206102900007) Bks Demand.

Newmark, Nathan M. Selected Papers by Nathan M. Newmark. LC 76-25684. (Civil Engineering Classics). (Illus.). 897p. reprint ed. pap. 200.00 (*0-608-30747-5*, 201953700013) Bks Demand.

Newmark, Nathan M. & Hall, William J. Earthquake Spectra & Design. 103p. 1982. 25.00 (*0-943198-22-4*) Earthquake Eng.

Newmark, Peter. About Translation. (Multilingual Matters Ser.: No. 74). 208p. 1991. 89.00 (*1-85359-118-1*, Pub. by Multilingual Matters); pap. 29.95 (*1-85359-117-3*, Pub. by Multilingual Matters) Taylor & Francis.

— More Paragraphs on Translation. LC 97-51150. 226p. 1998. 59.00 (*1-85359-403-2*); pap. 19.95 (*1-85359-402-4*) Multilingual.

— Paragraphs on Translation. LC 92-42551. 1993. 69.00 (*1-85359-192-0*, Pub. by Multilingual Matters); pap. 24.95 (*1-85359-191-2*, Pub. by Multilingual Matters) Taylor & Francis.

***Newmark, Thomas A. & Schulick, Paul.** Beyond Aspirin: Nature's Answer to Arthritis, Cancer & Alzheimer's Disease. 340p. 2000. pap. 14.95 (*0-934252-82-3*, Pub. by Hohm Pr) SCB Distributors.

***Newmark, Thomas M. & Schulick, Paul.** Herbal COX-2 Inhibition: Nature's Challenge to Arthritis, Cancer & Alzheimer's Disease. 320p. 2000. 24.95 (*1-890772-01-1*, Pub. by Hohm Pr) SCB Distributors.

Newmark, Wade. Newmark's U. K. Asset Management Yearbook, 1997/98. 192p. 1997. boxed set 185.00 (*1-85573-325-0*, Pub. by Woodhead Pubng) Am Educ Systs.

Newmeyer, Frederick J. English Aspectual Verbs. LC 74-77826. (Janua Linguarum, Series Practica: No. 203). (Illus.). 95p. (Orig.). 1975. pap. text 37.70 (*90-279-3392-8*) Mouton.

— Generative Linguistics: A Historical Perspective. LC 94-32379. (History of Linguistic Thought Ser.). 232p. (C). (gr. 13). 1995. 65.00 (*0-415-11553-1*) Routledge.

— Generative Linguistics: Historical Perspective. 232p. (C). 1997. pap. 24.99 (*0-415-17126-1*) Routledge.

— Grammatical Theory: Its Limits & Its Possibilities. LC 83-3549. 208p. 1983. pap. text 12.95 (*0-226-57719-8*); lib. bdg. 25.00 (*0-226-57717-1*) U Ch Pr.

— Language Form & Language Function. LC 98-10471. (Language, Speech & Communication Ser.). (Illus.). 442p. 1998. 40.00 (*0-262-14064-0*) MIT Pr.

***Newmeyer, Frederick J.** Language Form & Language Function. (Language, Speech & Communication Ser.). (Illus.). 448p. (C). 2000. pap. 27.00 (*0-262-64044-9*) MIT Pr.

Newmeyer, Frederick J. Linguistic Theory of America. 2nd ed. (C). 1986. text 89.95 (*0-12-517151-X*); pap. text 49.95 (*0-12-517152-8*) Acad Pr.

— The Politics of Linguistics. LC 86-11225. 192p. (C). 1987. 23.95 (*0-226-57720-1*) U Ch Pr.

— The Politics of Linguistics. viii, 184p. 1988. pap. text 12.00 (*0-226-57722-8*) U Ch Pr.

Newmeyer, Frederick J., ed. Linguistics: Linguistic Theory: Extensions & Implications. (Cambridge Survey Ser.: Vol. 2). 328p. (C). 1989. pap. text 23.95 (*0-521-37581-9*) Cambridge U Pr.

— Linguistics Vol. 3: The Cambridge Survey: Language: Psychological & Biological Aspects. 368p. (C). 1989. pap. text 23.95 (*0-521-37582-7*) Cambridge U Pr.

— Linguistics Vol. 3: The Cambridge Survey: Psychological & Biological Aspects. 366p. 1988. text 69.95 (*0-521-30835-6*) Cambridge U Pr.

— Linguistics Vol. 4: The Cambridge Survey: Language: The Socio-Cultural Context. 304p. (C). 1989. pap. text 25.95 (*0-521-37583-5*) Cambridge U Pr.

— Linguistics Vol. 4: The Cambridge Survey: The Socio-Cultural Context. 304p. 1988. text 69.95 (*0-521-30834-8*) Cambridge U Pr.

Newmeyer, John. August Thirty-Two, Two Thousand: And Other Essays for a New Millennium. LC 94-71771. (Illus.). 172p. 1994. 12.95 (*0-9641233-0-4*) Bright Moon.

Newmeyer, William L. Primary Care of Hand Injuries. LC 78-31444. 310p. reprint ed. pap. 96.10 (*0-8357-3248-7*, 205714400012) Bks Demand.

NewMyer, David A., jt. auth. see Wolfe, Harry P.

Newmyer, Frank, jt. auth. see Schroeder, Roger.

Newmyer, R. Kent. Supreme Court Justice Joseph Story: Statesman of the Old Republic. LC 84-11886. (Studies in Legal History). (Illus.). 508p. reprint ed. pap. 157.50 (*0-7837-6854-0*, 204668300003) Bks Demand.

— Supreme Court under Marshall & Taney. Eisenstadt, A. S. & Franklin, John H., eds. LC 68-29540. (American History Ser.). 192p. (C). 1969. pap. text 11.95 (*0-88295-746-5*) Harlan Davidson.

Newmyer, Stephen T. Herodotus, Bk. 3. (Greek Commentaries Ser.). 174p. (Orig.). (C). 1986. pap. text 8.00 (*0-929524-14-4*) Bryn Mawr Commentaries.

— The Silvae of Statius: Structure & Theme LC 79-317581. (Mnemosyne, Bibliotheca Classica Batava Ser.). 146 p. 1979. write for info. (*90-04-05849-4*) Brill Academic Pubs.

— Statius Silvae (Selections) (Latin Commentaries Ser.). 117p. (Orig.). (C). 1987. pap. text 7.00 (*0-929524-52-7*) Bryn Mawr Commentaries.

Newnam, B. E., et al, eds. Laser Induced Damage in Optical Materials, 1983, Vol. STP 911. 560p. 1986. pap. 60.00 (*0-8031-0930-X*, STP911) ASTM.

— Laser Induced Damage in Optical Materials, 1984, Vol. STP 954. 444p. 1986. pap. 60.00 (*0-8031-0960-1*, STP954) ASTM.

Newnan, Donald G. Civil Engineering, Engineering Economy: Review for the Professional Engineer's Exam. (Illus.). 72p. (Orig.). 1999. pap. 19.95 (*1-57645-048-1*, 481) Engineering.

— Compound Interest Tables. 30p. (Orig.). 1991. pap. text 3.00 (*0-910554-08-0*, 08-0) Engineering.

— Students Quick Study Guide: Engineering Economic Analysis. 7th ed. (Illus.). 312p. (C). 1998. pap. 15.00 (*1-57645-050-3*, 503) Engineering.

Newnan, Donald G., ed. EIT Civil Review. 2nd ed. (Illus.). 170p. (C). 1997. pap. 29.95 (*1-57645-013-9*, 139) Engineering.

— Engineer-in-Training License Review. 15th ed. (Illus.). 800p. (C). 1998. pap. 46.95 (*1-57645-014-7*, 147) Engineering.

— Engineering Economic Analysis Student Pak II: EEA Quick Study Guide Plus Software Diskette for Windows. (Engineering Economic Analysis Ser.). (Illus.). 296p. 1996. pap. text, student ed. 20.25 (*0-910554-96-X*) Engineering.

Newnan, Donald G. & Lavelle, Jerome P. Engineering Economic Analysis, Student Pak I: Includes Text, Quick Study Guide & Windows Diskette. 7th ed. (Illus.). 768p. (C). 1998. text 57.00 (*0-910554-97-8*, 978) Engineering.

— Essentials of Engineering Economic Analysis. (Illus.). 470p. 1998. pap. text 38.25 (*1-57645-028-7*, 287) Engineering.

Newnan, Donald G., ed. see Williams, Alan, et al.

Newnan, Edna S. Michigan Nature Association - In Retrospect: Celebrating 28 Years of Preserving Michigan's Wild & Rare Natural Lands, 1960-1988. Daubendiek, Bertha A., ed. LC 88-62060. (Illus.). 99p. 1989. 29.75 (*0-318-37923-6*) MI Nature Assn.

Newnham, Jack, jt. auth. see Handy, Libby.

Newnham, Nicole, jt. auth. see Lanker, Brian.

Newnham, Richard, ed. German Short Stories. 176p. (Orig.). (gr. 9 up). 1965. pap. 10.95 (*0-14-002040-3*, Penguin Bks) Viking Penguin.

Newnham, Robert E., ed. Applied Crystal Chemistry & Physics. (Transactions of the American Crystallographic Association Ser.: Vol. 11). 117p. 1975. pap. 25.00 (*0-686-47114-8*) Polycrystal Bk Serv.

Newnham, Robert E., et al. Solid State NMR & X-Ray Crystallography: Complementary Tools for Structure Determination: Structure-Property Relationships in Sensors. Moore, M., ed. (Crystallography Reviews Ser.: Vol. 1, No. 4). 88p. 1988. pap. text 90.00 (*2-88124-667-2*) Gordon & Breach.

Newport Art Museum Staff, jt. auth. see Warburton, Eileen.

***Newport, Cris.** Beyond the Mask. 250p. 2000. pap. 12.95 (*1-883573-49-1*) Pride & Imprints.

Newport, Cris. 1001 Nights Exotica: Erotic Stories & Artwork. (Illus.). 200p. 1999. pap. 11.00 (*1-886383-82-0*) Pride & Imprints.

— Queen's Champion: The Legend of Lancelot Retold. (From the Wind Fairytale Ser.). (Illus.). 300p. 1997. pap. 11.95 (*1-886383-20-0*) Pride & Imprints.

— Sparks Might Fly. LC 94-15387. 250p. (Orig.). 1994. pap. 9.95 (*0-934678-61-8*) Pride & Imprints.

— The White Bones of Truth. 2nd ed. 200p. (Orig.). 1996. pap. 10.95 (*1-886383-15-4*) Pride & Imprints.

Newport, Cris, ed. see Wolfe, Chris Anne.

Newport, Dan & Schultz, Joe. Planning a Running Event: A Manual on the Administration of a Successful Running Race. LC GV1061.N4. (Quest for Quality Ser.: No. 2). 50p. reprint ed. pap. 30.00 (*0-7837-1551-X*, 204184400024) Bks Demand.

Newport Harbor Art Museum Staff. Just Before the War: Urban America from 1935 to 1941. (Illus.). 1968. 5.95 (*0-8079-0147-4*); pap. 2.95 (*0-8079-0148-2*) October.

Newport, John P. The Lion & the Lamb. LC 85-29887. 384p. 1986. 14.99 (*0-8054-1324-3*, 4213-24) Broadman.

— The Lion & the Lamb. 1998. pap. text 14.99 (*0-8054-1868-7*) Broadman.

— The New Age Movement & the Biblical Worldview: Conflict & Dialogue. 620p. 1998. pap. 35.00 (*0-8028-4430-8*) Eerdmans.

Newport, John Paul. The Fine Green Line: My Year of Adventure on the Pro-Golf Mini-Tours. LC 99-89271. (Illus.). 288p. 2000. 24.00 (*0-7679-0116-9*) Broadway BDD.

Newport, John R. Avionic Systems Design. LC 94-11904. 352p. 1994. boxed set 104.95 (*0-8493-2465-3*) CRC Pr.

— Fuzzy Rule Based Computer Design. 272p. 1995. boxed set 99.95 (*0-8493-7834-6*, 7834) CRC Pr.

***Newport, Kenneth G. C.** Apocalypse & Millennium: Studies in Biblical Eisegesis. LC 99-51375. (Illus.). 272p. (C). 2000. 54.95 (*0-521-77334-2*) Cambridge U Pr.

— The Sources & Sitz Im Leben of Matthew 23. (JSNT Supplement Ser.: No. 117). 205p. 1995. 57.50 (*1-85075-557-4*, Pub. by Sheffield Acad) CUP Services.

Newport, Slobin & Meier, eds. The Acquisition of American Sign Language. (Crosslinguistic Study of Language Acquisition Ser.: Vol. 1). 80p. 1986. pap. 14.95 (*0-89859-849-4*) L Erlbaum Assocs.

Newquist, H. P. Virtual Reality. LC 95-9900. (J). (gr. 7 up). 1995. 6.95 (*0-590-48408-7*) Scholastic Inc.

***Newquist, H. P.** Yahoo! The Ultimate Desk Reference to the Web. 512p. 2000. pap. 24.95 (*0-06-273737-6*, HarpRes) HarpInfo.

Newquist, H. P., jt. auth. see Prown, Pete.

Newquist, Trini. Phoenix Baby Resource Guide, 1993-1994. (Illus.). 304p. (Orig.). (C). 1993. pap. text 9.95 (*0-9637868-0-6*) AZ Baby Res.

Newrock, Melody. The Trail Guide to Microsoft Network: A Rapid-Reading Reference to Using & Cruising the Microsoft Network Online Service. 272p. (C). 1995. pap. 12.95 (*0-201-48943-0*) Addison-Wesley.

News Currents Editors, ed. Editorial Cartoons by Kids, 1998. (Illus.). 208p. (J). (gr. 2 up). 1998. pap. 10.95 (*1-55933-242-5*) Zino Pr.

— Editorial Cartoons by Kids, 1996. LC 96-3086. (Illus.). 208p. (Orig.). (J). (gr. 2 up). 1996. pap. 10.95 (*1-55933-196-8*) Zino Pr.

— Editorial Cartoons by Kids, 1997. (Illus.). 208p. (J). (gr. 2 up). 1997. pap. 10.95 (*1-55933-213-1*) Zino Pr.

***News Gazette - Champaign Urbana Staff, ed.** A Century in Pictures. (Illus.). 208p. 1999. 29.95 (*1-58261-242-0*, Pub. by Sprts Pubng) Partners-West.

News, M. I. & Levine, L. S. Congenital Adrenal Hyperplasia. (Monographs on Endocrinology: Vol. 26). (Illus.). 100p. 1984. 62.95 (*0-387-12259-1*) Spr-Verlag.

Newsam, Barbara & Newsam, David. Making Money Teaching Music. (Illus.). 240p. (Orig.). 1995. pap. 18.99 (*0-89879-657-1*, Wrtrs Digest Bks) F & W Pubns Inc.

Newsam, Barbara S. Complete Student Assistance Program Handbook: Techniques & Materials for Alcohol-Drug Prevention & Intervention in Grades 7-12. LC 92-22749. (Illus.). 400p. 1992. pap. text 34.95 (*0-87628-878-6*) Ctr Appl Res.

Newsam, David, jt. auth. see Newsam, Barbara.

***Newsday Staff.** Home Town Long Island. (Illus.). 1999. 44.95 (*1-885134-21-5*) Newsday.

Newsday Staff. Long Island: Our Story. (Illus.). 418p. 1998. 44.95 (*1-885134-14-2*) Newsday.

***Newsday Staff.** Long Island the Way We Were. 1999. pap. text 9.95 (*1-885134-23-1*) Newsday.

— Newsday's Year 2000 Business Almanac. 1999. pap. 19.95 (*1-885134-22-3*) Newsday.

Newsday Staff. 1998 Fun Book. (Illus.). 176p. 1998. pap. 4.95 (*1-885134-17-7*) Newsday.

— Rush to Burn: Solving America's Garbage Crisis? LC 89-1939. (Illus.). 269p. 1989. text 30.00 (*1-55963-001-9*); pap. text 17.95 (*1-55963-000-0*) Island Pr.

Newseum Staff & Newton, Eric. Crusaders, Scoundrels, Journalists. LC 00-500004. (Illus.). 416p. 1999. 35.00 (*0-8129-3080-0*, Times Bks) Crown Pub Group.

***Newsham, Bradley.** Take Me with You: A Round-the-World Journey to Invite a Stranger Home. (Illus.). 376p. 2000. 24.00 (*1-885211-51-1*, Footstps) Trvlers Tale.

Newsham, Ian. A Treasury of Irish Stories. LC 95-3009. 160p. (J). (ps-4). 1995. pap. 5.95 (*1-85697-595-9*) LKC.

Newsholme. Biochemistry for the Medical Sciences. 2nd ed. pap. write for info. (*0-471-93165-9*) Wiley.

— Functional Biochemistry. 2nd ed. (C). 2000. text. write for info. (*0-471-98820-0*) Wiley.

Newsholme. Keep on Running 1969. text. write for info. (*0-471-89922-4*) Wiley.

Newsholme, Arthur. The Elements of Vital Statistics. 3rd rev. ed. LC 75-38139. (Demography Ser.). (Illus.). 1976. reprint ed. 31.95 (*0-405-07992-3*) Ayer.

— Evolution of Preventive Medicine. LC 75-23748. reprint ed. 37.50 (*0-404-13354-1*) AMS Pr.

— Public Health & Insurance. LC 78-19270. 1979. 28.95 (*0-405-10617-3*) Ayer.

Newsholme, E. A. & Start, C. Regulation in Metabolism. LC 72-5721. (Illus.). 363p. reprint ed. pap. 112.60 (*0-7837-5205-9*, 204493300005) Bks Demand.

Newsholme, Eric, et al. Keep on Running: The Science of Training & Performance. LC 93-49630. 462p. 1994. pap. 44.00 (*0-471-94314-2*) Wiley.

Newsinger, John. Dangerous Men: Myth, Masculinity & the SAS. 196p. 1997. 49.95 (*0-7453-1216-0*, Pub. by Pluto GBR); pap. 15.95 (*0-7453-1206-3*, Pub. by Pluto GBR) Stylus Pub VA.

— Fenianism in Mid-Victorian Britain. 128p. 1994. pap. 14.95 (*0-7453-0899-6*, Pub. by Pluto GBR) Stylus Pub VA.

Newsinger, John. Fenianism in Mid-Victorian Britain. LC 94-32946. (Socialist History of Britain Ser.). 128p. (C). 1994. 44.95 (*0-7453-0900-3*, Pub. by Pluto GBR) Stylus Pub VA.

***Newsinger, John, ed.** United Irishman: The Autobiography of James Hope. 250p. 2000. pap. 29.95 (*0-85036-496-5*, Pub. by MRLN) Paul & Co Pubs.

Newsom. Charles Dickens. LC 99-46317. 2000. 28.95 (*0-8057-1630-0*) Mac Lib Ref.

— Exercise Book-Public Relations Writing: F. 5th ed. (Mass Communication Ser.). (C). 1997. 17.75 (*0-534-52291-2*) Wadsworth Pub.

— Public Relations Writing. 3rd ed. (Mass Communication Ser.). 1990. mass mkt., teacher ed. write for info. (*0-534-14390-3*) Wadsworth Pub.

— Public Relations Writing Exercises. 3rd ed. (Mass Communication Ser.). 1992. pap., wbk. ed. 8.75 (*0-534-14389-X*) Wadsworth Pub.

N

An Asterisk (*) at the beginning of an entry indicates that the title is appearing for the first time.

***Newsom & Carrell.** Public Relations Writing. 6th ed. (Mass Communication Ser.). (C). 2000. text, wbk. ed. 19.25 (*0-534-55640-X*) Wadsworth Pub.

Newsom, Brad. The Athletics of Voice: A Handbook for Teachers & Students of Singing. Windward, Shirley, ed. (Illus.). 108p. (C). 1995. pap. text 15.00 (*0-9644358-0-2*) NewWind.

Newsom, Carol. Dear Santa: A Christmas Countdown Fun Book. (J). (gr. 1 up). 1998. 16.99 (*0-525-46024-1*, Dutton Child) Peng Put Young Read.

***Newsom, Carol.** The Wizard of Oz. 32p. (J). (ps-1). 1998. 12.99 (*1-929174-02-0*) Oshkosh BGosh.

Newsom, Carol, jt. auth. see Tapp, Kathy Kennedy.

Newsom, Carol A. & Ringe, Sharon H., eds. The Women's Bible Commentary. 384p. 1992. text 34.95 (*0-664-21922-5*) Westminster John Knox.

— Women's Bible Commentary. expanded ed. LC 97-50226. 468p. (Orig.). 1998. pap. 29.95 (*0-664-25781-X*) Westminster John Knox.

Newsom, Carol A., ed. see Charlesworth, James H.

Newsom, Carrell. Public Relations Writing: Form & Style. 6th ed. 2000. pap. text 50.95 (*0-534-55639-6*) Thomson Learn.

Newsom, D. Earl. The Birth of Oklahoma. (Illus.). 178p. (J). (gr. 5-12). 1983. 14.95 (*0-934188-08-4*) Evans Pubns.

— The Cherokee Strip: Its History & Grand Opening. (Oklahoma Legacies Ser.). (Illus.). 208p. (Orig.). 1992. pap. 12.95 (*0-913507-27-X*) New Forums.

— Drumright II (& Shamrock, Pemeta, Oilton & Olive) A Thousand Memories. (Illus.). 288p. 1987. 19.95 (*0-934188-25-4*) Evans Pubns.

***Newsom, D. Earl.** Hilarious History: The Funniest True Stories & Legends of Stillwater & Payne County. (Illus.). 54p. 1999. pap. 7.95 (*1-58107-016-0*, Pub. by New Forums) Booksource.

Newsom, David. David Newsom: The Western Observer, 1805-1882. LC 72-92062. (Illus.). 330p. 1972. pap. 7.95 (*0-87595-040-X*) Oregon Hist.

Newsom, David D. Can Negotiation Be Taught? (Pew Case Studies in International Affairs). 50p. (C). 1992. pap. text 3.50 (*1-56927-448-7*) Geo U Inst Dplmcy.

— Diplomacy & the American Democracy. LC 87-45438. 240p. 1988. 20.00 (*0-253-31816-5*); pap. 9.95 (*0-253-20470-4*, MB-470) Ind U Pr.

***Newsom, David D.** The Imperial Mantle: The United States, Decolonization & the 3rd World. LC 00-40754. 2001. write for info. (*0-253-33834-4*) Ind U Pr.

Newsom, David D. The Public Dimension of Foreign Policy. LC 95-20450. 304p. 1996. 35.00 (*0-253-32960-4*); pap. 16.95 (*0-253-21024-0*) Ind U Pr.

— The Soviet Brigade in Cuba: A Study in Political Diplomacy. LC 86-45943. 138p. 1987. reprint ed. pap. 42.80 (*0-608-01068-5*, 205937600001) Bks Demand.

Newsom, David D., ed. Diplomacy under a Foreign Flag: When Nations Break Relations. LC 89-19983. 144p. (Orig.). 1990. pap. text 3.00 (*0-934742-46-4*) Geo U Inst Dplmcy.

— The Diplomatic Record, 1990-1991. (Diplomatic Record Ser.). (Illus.). 337p. 1992. pap. text 9.00 (*0-934742-66-9*) Geo U Inst Dplmcy.

— The Diplomatic Record, 1989-1990. (Diplomatic Record Ser.). (Illus.). 256p. (Orig.). 1991. pap. text 9.00 (*0-934742-65-0*) Geo U Inst Dplmcy.

— Private Diplomacy with the Soviet Union. LC 86-28926. 166p. (Orig.). (C). 1987. pap. text 14.50 (*0-8191-5821-6*) U Pr of Amer.

Newsom, Doug. Media Writing. Wollert, James A., ed. LC 99-21130. 373p. (C). 1999. pap. text 51.00 (*0-321-01137-6*) Addson-Wesley Educ.

— Public Relations. 4th ed. (Mass Communication Ser.). 1995. pap., suppl. ed. 19.95 (*0-534-25501-9*) Wadsworth Pub.

Newsom, Doug & Carrell, Bob. Public Relations Writing: Form & Style. 2nd ed. 442p. (C). 1986. pap. write for info. (*0-534-06096-X*) Wadsworth Pub.

— Public Relations Writing: Form & Style. 3rd ed. 458p. (C). 1990. pap. 26.95 (*0-534-14388-1*) Wadsworth Pub.

— Public Relations Writing: Form & Style. 4th ed. LC 94-33763. 504p. 1994. mass mkt. 37.95 (*0-534-25500-0*) Wadsworth Pub.

— Public Relations Writing: Form & Style. 5th ed. LC 97-20092. (Mass Communication Ser.). (C). 1997. 50.95 (*0-534-52290-4*) Wadsworth Pub.

Newsom, Doug & Scott, Alan. This Is PR: The Realities of Public Relations. 3rd ed. 518p. (C). 1984. pap. write for info. (*0-534-04287-2*) Wadsworth Pub.

Newsom, Doug & Siegfried, Tom. Writing in Public Relations Practice: Form & Style. 364p. 1981. mass mkt. 14.95 (*0-534-00884-4*) Wadsworth Pub.

Newsom, Doug & Wollert, James A. Media Writing: News for the Mass Media. 437p. (C). 1984. pap. write for info. (*0-534-03969-3*) Wadsworth Pub.

***Newsom, Doug, et al.** This Is P. R. The Realities of Public Relations. 7th ed. LC 99-29237. 600p. 1999. 94.95 (*0-534-55962-X*) Wadsworth Pub.

Newsom, Doug, et al. This Is PR: The Realities of Public Relations. 4th ed. 527p. (C). 1989. pap. write for info. (*0-534-10140-2*) Wadsworth Pub.

— This Is PR: The Realities of Public Relations. 5th ed. LC 92-10718. 615p. (C). 1992. mass mkt. 47.75 (*0-534-17262-8*) Wadsworth Pub.

— This Is PR: The Realities of Public Relations. 6th ed. LC 92-10718. (C). 1995. pap. 60.25 (*0-534-22890-9*) Wadsworth Pub.

Newsom, Doug A. & Carrell, Bob J., eds. Silent Voices. 256p. (Orig.). (C). 1995. pap. text 29.50 (*0-8191-9855-2*) U Pr of Amer.

— Silent Voices. (Illus.). 256p. (Orig.). (C). 1995. lib. bdg. 52.00 (*0-8191-9854-4*) U Pr of Amer.

Newsom, Earl. The Story of Exciting Payne County. (Illus.). 265p. 1997. 29.95 (*0-913507-91-1*) New Forums.

Newsom, Horton E. & Jones, John H., eds. Origin of the Earth. (Illus.). 384p. (C). 1990. text 65.00 (*0-19-506619-7*) OUP.

Newsom, Iris, ed. Performing Arts: Motion Pictures. (Performing Arts Ser.). (Illus.). 269p. 49.00 (*0-8444-0937-5*) Lib Congress.

Newsom, Iris, ed. Performing Arts at the Library of Congress. 167p. 1992. 26.00 (*0-16-036054-4*, 030-001-00136-9) Lib Congress.

Newsom, Lila. Recollections of 91 Years. 1989. pap. 8.75 (*0-89137-116-8*) Quality Pubns.

Newsom, Lisa. Showcase of Interior Design: Southern. 2nd ed. LC 95-41521. 207p. 1996. 39.00 (*1-883065-06-2*) Rockport Vitae Pub.

***Newsom, Marc.** Marc Newsom. 1999. pap. 59.95 (*1-86154-062-0*) Booth-Clibborn.

Newsom, Mary M., jt. ed. see Burke, Edmund R.

Newsom, Robert. Dickens on the Romantic Side of Familiar Things: Bleak House & the Novel Tradition. LC 88-70307. xvi, 173p. (C). 1988. reprint ed. pap. 12.70 (*0-9620150-0-8*) UCSC Dickens Project.

— A Likely Story: Probability & Play in Fiction. 258p. (Orig.). (C). 1988. text 35.00 (*0-8135-1320-0*); pap. text 17.00 (*0-8135-1357-X*) Rutgers U Pr.

Newsom, Robert S., jt. auth. see Glick, Rush G.

Newsom, Ron, jt. ed. see Dressler, Dennis W.

Newsom, Samuel. Japanese Garden Construction. (Illus.). 302p. 1988. reprint ed. 65.00 (*0-938290-10-X*) Apollo.

Newsome. Saunders Medical Assisting Review. Date not set. pap. text write for info. (*0-7216-4331-0*) Harcourt.

Newsome, A. Maria, et al. Bridging the Gaps: An African-American Guide to Health & Self-Empowerment. (Orig.). 1997. pap. 15.00 (*0-927936-92-5*) Vincom Pubng Co.

Newsome, A. R., ed. Records of Emigrants from England & Scotland to North Carolina, 1774-1775. 30p. 1998. pap. 5.00 (*0-86526-134-2*) NC Archives.

Newsome, Albert R., jt. auth. see Lefler, Hugh T.

Newsome, Arden. Cork & Wood Crafts. LC 72-112370. (Illus.). 64p. (J). (gr. k-3). 1985. lib. bdg. 13.95 (*0-87460-229-7*) Lion Bks.

Newsome, Chevelle, jt. auth. see Nimmo, Dan.

Newsome, D. H., ed. Weather Radar Networking: COST 73 Project: Final Report. LC 92-26375. 272p. (C). 1992. text 141.50 (*0-7923-1939-7*) Kluwer Academic.

Newsome, D. H. & Edwards, A. M., eds. Third River Basin Management Conference: Proceedings of a Conference Held in York, 4-8 July 1983 & Incorporating the Workshop on Advances in the Application of Mathematical Modelling to Water Quality Management Held in London, July 11-12 1983. (Illus.). 670p. 1984. pap. 130.00 (*0-08-031505-4*, Pergamon Pr) Elsevier.

Newsome, David. Bishop Westcott & the Platonic Tradition. LC 78-409427. (Bishop Westcott Memorial Lecture Ser.: Vol. 1968). 39p. reprint ed. pap. 25.00 (*0-8357-7279-9*, 2051381) Bks Demand.

— On the Edge of Paradise: A. C. Benson; the Diarist. LC 80-12747. (Illus.). 416p. 1996. 30.00 (*0-226-57742-2*) U Ch Pr.

— On the Edge of Paradise: A. C. Benson, the Diarist. LC 80-12747. (Illus.). 426p. reprint ed. pap. 132.10 (*0-608-09488-9*, 205428900005) Bks Demand.

— The Victorian World Picture. (Illus.). 308p. 1999. pap. text 19.00 (*0-8135-2758-9*) Rutgers U Pr.

— The Victorian World Picture: Perceptions & Introspections in an Age of Change. LC 97-15588. (Illus.). 310p. 1997. 30.00 (*0-8135-2454-7*) Rutgers U Pr.

Newsome, David A., ed. Retinal Dystrophies & Degenerations. LC 84-42913. 398p. 1988. reprint ed. pap. 123.40 (*0-608-04744-9*, 206546500004) Bks Demand.

Newsome, David H. Wilberforces & Henry Manning: The Parting of Friends. LC 67-2. (Illus.). 498p. 1966. 42.50 (*0-674-95280-4*) Belknap Pr.

Newsome, Effie Lee. Wonders: The Best Children's Poems of Effie Lee Newsome. LC 99-62256. (Illus.). 40p. (J). (gr. 1-3). 1999. 14.95 (*1-56397-788-5*) Boyds Mills Pr.

— Wonders: The Best Children's Poems of Effie Lee Newsome. Bishop, R. S., ed. LC 99-62256. (Illus.). 40p. 1999. pap. 8.95 (*1-56397-825-3*) Boyds Mills Pr.

Newsome, Eric. Pass the Bottle: Rum Tales of the West Coast. LC 96-111429. (Illus.). 144p. (Orig.). 1995. pap. 12.95 (*1-55143-044-4*) Orca Bk Pubs.

— Wild, Wacky, Wonderful British Columbia: Answers to Questions You Never Thought to Ask. (Illus.). 144p. 1997. pap. 7.95 (*1-55143-096-7*) Orca Bk Pubs.

Newsome, James D. Exodus. LC 98-38366. (Interpretation Bible Studies). 112p. 1998. pap. 7.95 (*0-664-50020-X*) Geneva Press.

Newsome, James D., Jr. The Hebrew Prophets. LC 84-7601. 252p. (Orig.). 1986. pap. 19.95 (*0-8042-0113-7*) Westminster John Knox.

Newsome, James D., et al. Texts for Preaching: A Lectionary Commentary Based on the NRSV, Year B. LC 93-8023. 704p. 1993. text 33.00 (*0-664-21970-5*) Westminster John Knox.

Newsome, Jill. Shadow. LC 99-13450. (Illus.). 32p. (J). 1999. 15.95 (*0-7894-2631-5*) DK Pub Inc.

Newsome, Lisa. Thinker Task Cards. (Illus.). 128p. 1992. student ed. 12.99 (*0-86653-681-7*, 1415) Good Apple.

Newsome, Michael A. After the Rapture: Poems & Prayers Inspired by God. 1998. pap. write for info. (*1-57553-762-1*) Watermrk Pr.

Newsome, Moses, jt. auth. see Pillari, Vimala.

Newsome, Roy. Brass Roots: A Hundred Years of Brass Bands & Their Music (1836-1936) LC 97-19858. (Illus.). 240p. 1997. text 86.95 (*1-85928-168-0*, Pub. by Ashgate Pub) Ashgate Pub Co.

Newsome, S. L., et al, eds. Design Theory Eighty-Eight. (Illus.). xi, 355p. 1989. 79.95 (*0-387-96976-4*) Spr-Verlag.

Newsome, Tom. First Noel: A Story Light Book. LC 99-168117. (Illus.). 16p. (J). (ps-2). 1998. pap. 7.99 (*0-525-45900-6*, Dutton Child) Peng Put Young Read.

Newsome, Tom. Jolly Old Saint Nicholas. LC 99-168116. 16p. (J). (ps-2). 1998. pap. 7.99 (*0-525-45899-X*, Dutton Child) Peng Put Young Read.

Newson, Adele S. & Strong-Leek, Linda, eds. Winds of Change: The Transforming Voices of Carribean Women Writers & Scholars. LC 96-49833. VIII, 237p. (C). 1998. pap. text 29.95 (*0-8204-3715-8*) P Lang Pubng.

Newson, Adele S., jt. ed. see Lavender, Abraham D.

Newson, D. Earl. Drumright, the Glory Days of a Boom Town. LC 85-70033. (Illus.). 200p. 1985. 19.95 (*0-934188-17-3*) Evans Pubns.

Newson, Herbert H. Medical & Health Practices & Defensive Medicine: New Research Bible of Current Trends. 160p. 1994. 47.50 (*0-7883-0200-0*); pap. 44.50 (*0-7883-0201-9*) ABBE Pubs Assn.

Newson, Janice A., jt. auth. see Currie, Jan.

Newson, Lesley. Devastation! The World's Worst Natural Disasters. LC 98-2567. 160p. 1998. 24.95 (*0-7894-3518-7*) DK Pub Inc.

Newson, Linda A. Indian Survival in Colonial Nicaragua. LC 86-40078. (Civilization of the American Indian Ser.: Vol. 175). (Illus.). 496p. 1987. 42.50 (*0-8061-2008-8*) U of Okla Pr.

— Life & Death in Early Colonial Equador. LC 94-41571. (Civilization of the American Indian Ser.: Vol. 214). (Illus.). 505p. 1995. 47.50 (*0-8061-2697-3*) U of Okla Pr.

Newson, Malcolm. Hydrology & the River Environment. (Illus.). 240p. (C). 1994. 59.95 (*0-19-874156-1*); pap. text 31.95 (*0-19-874157-X*) OUP.

— Land, Water & Development: River Basin Systems & Their Sustainable Management. LC 91-39206. (Natural Environment: Problems & Management Ser.). (Illus.). 384p. (C). (gr. 13). 1992. text 89.95 (*0-415-05711-6*, A7502) Routledge.

Newson, Malcolm D. Land, Water, & Development: Sustainable Management of River Basin Systems. 2nd ed. LC 97-7592. (Illus.). 464p. (C). 1997. 110.00 (*0-415-15506-1*); pap. 32.99 (*0-415-15507-X*) Routledge.

Newson, Mark, jt. auth. see Cook, Vivian J.

Newson, Moses, jt. auth. see Lacy, Sam.

Newson, N. Managing the Human Impact on the Natural Environment Patterns & Processes. 282p. 1993. pap. 325.00 (*81-7089-152-3*, Pub. by Intl Bk Distr) St Mut.

Newson, T. Housing Policy: An International Bibliography. 416p. 1986. text 150.00 (*0-7201-1785-2*) Continuum.

Newson, T. M. Pen Pictures of St. Paul, Minnesota & Biographical Sketches of Old Settlers, Vol. 1. 746p. 1994. reprint ed. lib. bdg. 75.00 (*0-8328-3839-X*) Higginson Bk Co.

Newspaper Features Council Staff, jt. auth. see Nordling, Lee.

Newspaper Marketing Association Staff. Head Chefs Recipes Vol. 3: With Dining Guide. Murray, Floyd, ed. pap. text 14.95 (*0-9629776-2-4*) News Mktg Assocs.

— Headcheese Recipes: From Your Favorite Local Restaurants. (Illus.). 160p. 1989. pap. text 12.95 (*0-9629776-0-8*) News Mktg Assocs.

Newstead, P. E. Algebraic Geometry: Papers Presented for the Europroj Conferences in Catania & Barcelona. LC 98-25609. (Lecture Notes in Pure & Applied Mathematics Ser.). (Illus.). 422p. 1998. pap. text 165.00 (*0-8247-0234-4*) Dekker.

Newstead, Stephen E., et al, eds. Human Assessment: Cognition & Motivation. (C). 1986. lib. bdg. 262.00 (*90-247-3331-6*) Kluwer Academic.

***Newstetter, Wendy, ed.** Design Education: A special Issue of the Journal of the Learning Sciences. 112p. 2000. pap. write for info. (*0-8058-9747-X*) L Erlbaum Assocs.

Newstrom, Harvey. Nutrients Catalog: Vitamins, Minerals, Amino Acids, Macronutrients - Beneficial Use, Helpers, Inhibitors, Food Sources, Intake Recommendations, & Symptoms of over or under Use. LC 92-56671. 558p. 1993. lib. bdg. 75.00 (*0-89950-784-0*) McFarland & Co.

Newstrom, John, et al. The Complete Games Trainers Play, Vol. II. LC 97-44683. Vol. II. (Illus.). 672p. 1998. 110.00 (*0-07-046607-6*) McGraw.

Newstrom, John W. & Bittel, Lester R. Supervision: Managing for Results. 7th ed. LC 95-21324. 1995. pap. 25.00 (*0-02-802491-5*) Glencoe.

Newstrom, John W. & Broad, Mary. Managing Transfer Training: Action-Packed Strategies to Ensure High Payoff from Training Investments. (Illus.). 194p. 1992. pap. 30.00 (*0-201-19274-8*) Addison-Wesley.

Newstrom, John W. & Davis, Keith. Organizational Behavior: Human Behavior at Work. 9th ed. LC 92-22097. (Series in Management). (C). 1993. text 78.25 (*0-07-015603-4*) McGraw.

Newstrom, John W. & Kavis, Keith. Organizational Behavior: Human Behavior at Work. 10th ed. LC 96-25597. 624p. (C). 1996. 84.38 (*0-07-046504-5*) McGraw.

Newstrom, John W. & Scannell, Edward E. The Big Book of Business Games: Icebreakers, Creativity Exercises, & Meeting Energizers. LC 95-44899. 170p. 1995. pap. 17.95 (*0-07-046476-6*) McGraw.

— The Big Book of Presentation Games: Wake-Em-Up Tricks, Icebreakers, & Other Fun Stuff. LC 97-35043. (Illus.). 212p. 1997. pap. 17.95 (*0-07-046501-0*) McGraw.

— The Big Book of Team Building Games: Trust Building Activities, Team Spirit Exercises, & Other Fun Things to Do. LC 97-42110. (Illus.). 238p. 1997. pap. 17.95 (*0-07-046513-4*) McGraw.

— Game Trainers Play. 352p. 1980. pap. 24.95 (*0-07-046408-1*) McGraw.

— Games Trainers Play: Experimental Learning Exercises. (Illus.). 336p. pap. 12.95 (*0-318-13271-0*, N E G T) Am Soc Train & Devel.

— Still More Games Trainers Play. 311p. 1991. pap. 24.95 (*0-07-046427-8*) McGraw.

Newstrom, John W., jt. auth. see Bittel, Lester R.

Newstrom, John W., jt. auth. see Bittle, Lester R.

Newstrom, John W., jt. auth. see Pierce, Jon L.

Newstrom, John W., jt. auth. see Scannell, Edward E.

Newsum, jt. auth. see Afolaian.

Newsum, Gillian. Milton. (Illus.). 96p. 1991. 28.95 (*1-872082-20-3*, Pub. by Kenilworth Pr) Half Halt Pr.

Newsum, H. E. Class Language & Education: Class Struggle & Sociolinguistics in an African Situation. LC 89-81017. 97p. (C). 1989. 24.95 (*0-86543-139-6*); pap. 7.95 (*0-86543-140-X*) Africa World.

Newswatch Book Ltd Staff, ed. see Abasika, Etiese T. Mkpa.

Newth, John T. Tolley's Interest & Penalty Provisions. 350p. 1993. 115.00 (*0-85459-580-5*, Pub. by Tolley Pubng) St Mut.

Newth, Mette. Abduction. 256p. (YA). (gr. 7 up). 1993. pap. 3.95 (*0-374-40009-1*) FS&G.

Newth, Mette. Abduction. (Aerial Fiction Ser.). 1993. 9.05 (*0-606-05100-7*, Pub. by Turtleback) Demco.

Newth, Mette. The Dark Light. Ingwersen, Faith, tr. LC 97-21484. 246p. (YA). (gr. 7-12). 1998. 17.00 (*0-374-31701-1*) FS&G.

***Newth, Mette.** Transformation. LC 99-86323. 208p. (gr. 8-12). 2000. text 16.00 (*0-374-37752-9*) FS&G.

Newth, Michael A. The Songs of Aliscans. LC 91-43662. (Library of Medieval Literature: Vol. 85B). 288p. 1992. text 10.00 (*0-8153-0488-9*, GLML 85B) Garland.

Newth, Michael A., tr. Chanson d'Aspremont: Song of Aspremont. LC 88-31024. (Library of Medieval Literature). 292p. 1989. text 20.00 (*0-8240-5618-3*) Garland.

Newth, Michael A., tr. see de Bar-sur-Aube, Bertrand.

***Newth, Rebecca.** Antonia Quail (Antonia la Codorniz) Horton, James F. & Fernandez, Ines, trs. (ENG & SPA., Illus.). 32p. (J). (gr. k-3). 2000. write for info. (*0-9630310-3-1*) Will Hall.

Newth, Rebecca. Finding the Lamb. LC 82-7929. 80p. 1983. pap. 4.95 (*0-940170-05-1*) Open Bk Pubns.

— Great North Woods. LC 93-81219. 74p. 1994. pap. 12.00 (*0-9630310-1-5*) Will Hall.

— Milk Horses: A Memoir. Estes, Martha, ed. LC 98-85089. 160p. 1998. pap. 12.95 (*0-9664290-0-1*) Lost Creek Pr.

— The Oseberg Skiff. (Illus.). 64p. (Orig.). 1991. pap. 6.95 (*0-9630310-0-7*) Will Hall.

Newton. Bankruptcy, Vol. 2. 6th ed. 900p. (C). 2000. text 165.00 (*0-471-33143-0*) Wiley.

— Bankruptcy & Insolvency Accounting, Vol. 2. 6th ed. 900p. (C). 2000. text 165.00 (*0-471-33142-2*) Wiley.

— Business Continuity Handbook. 410p. 1999. 137.95 (*0-471-98622-4*) Wiley.

— Cyclic Nucleotide Biochemistry. 240p. (Orig.). (C). (gr. 13). 1997. pap. text write for info. (*0-412-26480-3*) Chapman & Hall.

— Ferrari Heritage. pap. 10.95 (*1-85532-774-0*, 861709Q, Pub. by Ospry) Stackpole.

Newton. Finance of Manufacturing Industry in 19th Century. 76.95 (*1-85928-393-4*) Ashgate Pub Co.

Newton. Rope: The Twisted Life & Crimes of Harvey Glatman. 1998. mass mkt. 6.99 (*0-671-01747-0*) S&S Trade.

— Searcher of Hearts: Romans 8. 1997. pap. 12.99 (*1-85792-314-6*, Pub. by Christian Focus) Spring Arbor Dist.

— Wake-up Calls: Classic Cases in Business Ethics. 2nd ed. (Philosophy Ser.). 2001. pap. 22.50 (*0-534-52421-4*) Wadsworth Pub.

***Newton & Dillingham.** 10 Cases In Environmental Ethics. 3rd ed. (Philosophy Ser.). (C). 2000. text 21.00 (*0-534-51182-1*) Wadsworth Pub.

Newton & Ford. Business Ethics. 4th ed. 1996. teacher ed. 14.06 (*0-697-31393-X*, WCB McGr Hill) McGrw-H Hghr Educ.

— Ts:business Ethics Society. 6th ed. 416p. 2000. pap. 18.44 (*0-07-236003-8*) McGraw.

Newton, et al. Networking Spatial Information Systems. 1992. 83.95 (*1-85293-204-X*, Belhaven) Halsted Pr.

Newton, jt. auth. see Winsor.

Newton, A. Human Resources & Business Strategy. (Financial Times Management Briefings Ser.). 1997. pap. 89.50 (*0-273-63251-5*, Pub. by F T P-H) Trans-Atl Phila.

Newton, A. The Human Resources Director: A Changing Role. 1996. pap. 129.00 (*1-85953-021-4*, Pub. by Tech Comm) St Mut.

Newton, A. & Ford, J. E. The Production & Properties of Non-Woven Fabrics. 93p. 1973. 70.00 (*0-7855-7215-5*) St Mut.

Newton, A., jt. auth. see Burnip, M. S.

Newton, A. C., jt. ed. see Leakey, R. R.

Newton, A. P., ed. Select Documents Relating to the Unification of South Africa. 574p. 1968. reprint ed. 59.50 (*0-7146-1777-6*, Pub. by F Cass Pubs) Intl Spec Bk.

Newton, A. R. Logic Synthesis for Integrated Circuit Design, Selected Papers On. 144p. 1987. pap. 39.95 (*0-87942-236-X*, PP02261) Inst Electrical.

Newton, A. Richard, jt. auth. see Saleh, Resve A.

Newton, Adam Z. Facing Black & Jew: Literature As Public Space in Twentieth-Century America. LC 98-39339. (Cultural Margins Ser.: Vol. 8). 260p. (C). 1999. write for info. (*0-521-65106-9*) Cambridge U Pr.

***Newton, Adam Z.** Facing Black & Jew: Literature as Public Space in Twentieth-Century America. LC 98-39339. (Cultural Margins Ser.: Vol. 8). 218p. (C). 1999. pap. 19.95 (*0-521-65870-5*) Cambridge U Pr.

An Asterisk (*) at the beginning of an entry indicates that the title is appearing for the first time.

N

An Asterisk (*) at the beginning of an entry indicates that the title is appearing for the first time.

N

Newton-Hurt, Diana. Elephantastic: A Trunkful of Unforgettable Jokes. (Illus.). 64p. (J). (gr. 2-7). 1995. pap. 3.95 (*1-85697-569-X*) LKC.

Newton, Ian. Population Ecology of Raptors. 1997. text 39.95 (*0-85661-023-2*) Acad Pr.

— Population Limitation in Birds. (Illus.). 624p. 1998. boxed set 79.95 (*0-12-517365-2*) Acad Pr.

— Population Limitation in Birds. (Illus.). 624p. (C). 1998. pap. text 49.95 (*0-12-517366-0*) Acad Pr.

Newton, Ian, ed. Lifetime Reproduction in Birds. (Illus.). 496p. 1992. pap. text 53.00 (*0-12-517371-7*) Acad Pr.

Newton, Ian & Olsen, Penny, eds. Birds of Prey. (Illus.). 240p. 1990. 40.00 (*0-8160-2182-1*) Facts on File.

Newton, J. Extractive Metallurgy. LC 59-14124. 540p. reprint ed. pap. 167.40 (*0-8357-9889-5*, 205526500011) Bks Demand.

Newton, J. H., et al. History of the Pan-Handle: Being Historical Collections of the Counties of Ohio, Brooke, Marshall & Hancock, West Virginia. (Illus.). 540p. 1991. reprint ed. pap. 50.00 (*1-55613-413-4*) Heritage Bk.

Newton, J. H., jt. auth. see Caldwell, J. A.

Newton, J. M., jt. auth. see Hickey, A. E.

Newton, Jack & Teece, Philip. The Guide to Amateur Astronomy. 2nd ed. LC 93-40354. (Illus.). 347p. (C). 1995. 39.95 (*0-521-44492-6*) Cambridge U Pr.

Newton, Jack, jt. auth. see Dickinson, Terence.

Newton, James. Small Business Regulatory Compliance Manual. 450p. 1995. ring bd. 70.00 (*1-888555-05-X*) MGR Pr.

— Uncommon Friends. (Illus.). 384p. (C). 1989. pap. 15.00 (*0-15-692620-2*) Harcourt.

Newton, James J. Managing God's Resources. 100p. (Orig.). 1997. pap. 16.95 (*1-888555-08-4*) MGR Pr.

Newton, James R. Forest Log. LC 78-22515. (Illus.). 32p. (J). (gr. 2-5). 1980. 11.95 (*0-690-04007-5*); lib. bdg. 11.89 (*0-690-04008-3*) HarpC Child Bks.

— The March of the Lemmings. LC 75-42491. (Let's-Read-&-Find-Out Science Bks.). (Illus.). 40p. (J). (gr. k-3). 1976. lib. bdg. 11.89 (*0-690-01085-0*) HarpC Child Bks.

Newton, Jane. Good Morning Dogs! (Illus.). 20p. (Orig.). (J). (ps). 1991. pap. text 4.95 (*0-931571-08-1*) RP Pubng.

Newton, Jane M., compiled by. Breckinridge County, Kentucky Marriage Bonds, 1881-1895, Bks. 15-21. 289p. 1997. pap. 26.00 (*1-889221-38-4*) Ancestral Trails.

Newton, Jane M. & Miller, Wathena K. Meade County, Kentucky, 1880 Census. 239p. 1996. pap. 22.00 (*1-889221-31-7*) Ancestral Trails.

Newton, Jane M., jt. auth. see Miller, Wathena K.

Newton, Janet. Introduction to Sociology: Readings. 136p. (C). 1996. pap. text, spiral bd. 29.95 (*0-7872-0498-6*) Kendall-Hunt.

Newton, Janice. Course Outlines on Women & Politics. 2nd ed. 187p. 1998. pap. 24.95 (*0-88920-331-8*) W Laurier U Pr.

— The Feminist Challenge to the Canadian Left, 1900-1918. (Illus.). 272p. 1995. pap. 24.95 (*0-7735-1291-8*, Pub. by McG-Queens Univ Pr) CUP Services.

— The Feminist Challenge to the Canadian Left, 1900-1918. (Illus.). 272p. 1995. 65.00 (*0-7735-1262-4*, Pub. by McG-Queens Univ Pr) CUP Services.

Newton, Janice, ed. Course Outlines on Women & Politics. 293p. (C). 1993. spiral bd. 20.00 (*0-88920-236-2*) W Laurier U Pr.

Newton, Jean, ed. see Prokop, Richard.

Newton, Jennifer. Preventing Mental Illness. 272p. 1988. text 65.00 (*0-7102-0930-4*, Routledge Thoemms) Routledge.

— Preventing Mental Illness in Practice. 240p. (C). 1997. pap. 24.99 (*0-415-11993-6*, C0607) Routledge.

Newton, Jeremiah & Passalacqua, Francesca, eds. My Face for the World to See: The Diaries of Candy Darling. 1997. 29.95 (*0-614-28045-1*) DAP Assocs.

Newton, Jeremiah & Passalacque, Francesca, eds. My Face for the World to See: The Diaries of Candy Darling. 1997. 29.95 (*0-945367-21-X*) Hardy Marks Pubns.

Newton, Jerry. The Complete Book of Forms for the School Health Professional: Ready-to-Use Forms for the School Health Professional. 480p. 1987. text 34.95 (*0-13-156498-6*) P-H.

Newton, Jerry, et al. New School Health Handbook 1997: A Ready Reference for School Nurses & Educators. 3rd ed. LC 97-7189. 388p. (C). 1997. text 34.95 (*0-13-614652-X*) P-H.

Newton, Jim. Conducting Environmental Audits. 675p. 1994. ring bd. 90.00 (*1-888555-03-3*) MGR Pr.

— Conducting Property Transfer Assessments. 400p. 1995. ring bd. 70.00 (*1-888555-02-5*) MGR Pr.

— Developing an Effective Pollution Prevention Program. 650p. 1995. ring bd. 90.00 (*1-888555-04-1*) MGR Pr.

— Emergency Response Planning. 525p. 1995. ring bd. 80.00 (*1-888555-00-9*) MGR Pr.

— EPA Dictionary of Acronyms, Abbreviations & Definitions. 250p. 1995. ring bd. 60.00 (*1-888555-07-6*) MGR Pr.

— Freedom's Trails. 450p. 1997. 22.95 (*1-888555-10-6*) MGR Pr.

— A Psalms Journal. 65p. (Orig.). 1997. pap. 10.95 (*1-888555-09-2*) MGR Pr.

— RCRA Generator's Compliance Manual. 400p. 1994. ring bd. 70.00 (*1-888555-01-7*) MGR Pr.

— Training for Environmental & Safety Compliance. 300p. 1995. ring bd. 60.00 (*1-888555-06-8*) MGR Pr.

Newton, Joe & Henderson, Joe. Coaching Cross Country Successfully. LC 97-35197. (Illus.). 144p. 1998. pap. 17.95 (*0-88011-701-X*, PNEW0701, YMCA USA) Human Kinetics.

Newton, Joe, jt. auth. see Durkin, John F.

Newton, Joe, jt. auth. see Newton, Willis.

***Newton, John.** Complete Conduct Principles for the 21st Century. unabridged ed. LC 99-57919. 192p. 2000. 19.95 (*0-9673705-7-4*); pap. 9.95 (*0-9673705-8-2*) Nicer Century.

Newton, John. Out of the Depths. LC 80-85340. (Illus.). 160p. 1991. pap. 9.99 (*0-8254-3317-7*, Kregel Class) Kregel.

— Works of John Newton, 6 vols, Set. 1985. reprint ed. 169.99 (*0-85151-460-X*) Banner of Truth.

Newton, John & Bohrer, Dick. John Newton. (Golden Oldies Ser.). 128p. mass mkt. 4.99 (*0-8024-0251-8*, 380) Moody.

Newton, John & Hindmarsh, Bruce. The Life & Spirituality of John Newton. (C). 1998. reprint ed. pap. write for info. (*1-57383-118-2*, Regent Coll Pub) Regent College.

Newton, John, et al. Sacred Solos by Adrienne Tindall Vol. III: 12 Sacred Solos from Poems, Prayers, & Scriptures. Tindall, Adrienne, ed. 50p. (Orig.). 1987. pap., student ed. 25.00 (*1-889079-05-7*) Darcey Pr.

Newton, John H. Latacumba Assignment. 165p. (C). 1989. 60.00 (*0-7223-2300-X*, Pub. by A H S Ltd) St Mut.

Newton, John K., tr. see Ahmad, Jalal A.

Newton-John, Olivia & Hurst, Brian S. A Pig Tale. LC 92-44116. (Illus.). 32p. (J). 1999. per. 5.99 (*0-689-82428-9*) Aladdin.

— A Pig Tale. LC 92-44116. (Illus.). 40p. (J). (ps-1). 1993. pap. 14.00 (*0-671-78778-0*) S&S Bks Yung.

Newton, John R., jt. ed. see Clayton, Stanley G.

Newton, Jon. Profitable Organic Farming. LC 95-24181. 1995. pap. 38.95 (*0-632-03929-9*) Blackwell Sci.

Newton, Joseph F. The Builders: A Story & Study of Freemasonry. 12th ed. (Illus.). 345p. 1995. reprint ed. 19.50 (*0-88053-045-6*, M 301) Macoy Pub.

— Builders: A Story & Study of Masonry. 334p. 1998. reprint ed. pap. 18.95 (*0-7661-0220-3*) Kessinger Pub.

— The Great Light in Masonry. 92p. 1992. reprint ed. pap. 12.95 (*1-56459-046-1*) Kessinger Pub.

— The Men's House: Masonic Papers & Addresses. xx, 241p. 1990. text 12.95 (*0-88053-037-5*, M-86) Macoy Pub.

— Men's House: Masonic Papers & Addresses. 262p. 1998. reprint ed. pap. 17.95 (*0-7661-0211-4*) Kessinger Pub.

— Modern Masonry: A Brief Sketch of the Craft since 1717. 92p. 1992. reprint ed. pap. 12.95 (*1-56459-043-7*) Kessinger Pub.

— Short Talks on Masonry. x, 243p. 1994. reprint ed. pap. 10.00 (*0-88053-036-7*, M-85) Macoy Pub.

— Some Living Masters of the Pulpit: Studies in Religious Personality. LC 71-152203. (Essay Index Reprint Ser.). 1977. reprint ed. 20.95 (*0-8369-2287-5*) Ayer.

— The Three Degrees & Great Symbols of Masonry. 112p. 1992. reprint ed. pap. 12.95 (*1-56459-045-3*) Kessinger Pub.

Newton, Joy. La Chauve-Souris et le Papillon Correspondance Montesquiou-Whistler. 264p. 1993. 60.00 (*0-85261-277-X*, Pub. by Univ of Glasgow) St Mut.

Newton, Judith. Starting Over: Feminism & the Politics of Cultural Critique. LC 94-10225. (Critical Perspectives on Women & Gender Ser.). 232p. 1994. text 44.50 (*0-472-09482-3*, 09482); pap. text 16.95 (*0-472-06482-7*, 06482) U of Mich Pr.

Newton, Judith J., et al, eds. Managing Data: From Vision to Reality. (Proceedings of the Annual DAMA Symposium Ser.: No. 4). (Illus.). 158p. (Orig.). (C). 1992. pap. text 35.00 (*1-56806-070-X*) DIANE Pub.

Newton, Judith J. & Spielman, Frankie E., eds. Data Administration: Management & Practice. (Proceedings of the Annual DAMA Symposium Ser.: No. 1). (Illus.). 130p. (Orig.). (C). 1992. pap. text 35.00 (*1-56806-068-8*) DIANE Pub.

— Data Administration: Standards & Techniques. (Proceedings of the Annual DAMA Symposium Ser.: No. 2). (Illus.). 164p. (Orig.). (C). 1992. pap. text 35.00 (*1-56806-069-6*) DIANE Pub.

Newton, Judith L. Women, Power & Subversion: Social Strategies in British Fiction, 1778-1860. 224p. 1985. pap. text 12.95 (*0-416-41200-9*, 9761) Routledge.

Newton, Judith L. & Rosenfelt, D., eds. Feminist Literary Criticism & Social Change. 250p. (Orig.). 1986. 35.00 (*0-416-38700-4*, 9678); pap. 13.95 (*0-416-38710-1*, 9679) Routledge.

Newton, Judith Sperling. Voluntary Termination of Parental Rights & Adoption: A Practical Handbook for Judges, Lawyers & Human Service Providers. LC 89-71245. 275p. 1990. ring bd. 75.00 (*0-945574-28-2*) State Bar WI.

Newton, Judith V. & Weiss, Carol. A Grand Tradition: The Hoosier Salon Art & Artists, 1925-1990. (Illus.). 500p. 1993. 75.00 (*0-9638360-0-5*) Hoosier Salon.

Newton, Judith V. & Weiss, Carol A. Beyond Realism: The Life & Art of Frederik Grue. LC 95-75355. 144p. 1995. 49.95 (*0-9645261-0-7*) BCL Pr.

Newton, Judy A., jt. auth. see Newton, Michael.

***Newton, Julianne Hickerson.** The Burden of Visual Truth: The Role of Photojournalism in Mediating Reality. LC 00-34769. 2000. pap. write for info. (*0-8058-3376-5*) L Erlbaum Assocs.

***Newton, June, ed.** Helmut Newton's SUMO. (Illus.). 480p. 1999. 1500.00 (*3-8228-6394-7*) Taschen Amer.

Newton, K. & Steeds, W. Motor Vehicle. 11th ed. 880p. 1989. text 79.95 (*0-7506-0407-7*) Buttrwrth-Heinemann.

Newton, K., et al. Motor Vehicle. 9th ed. 1972. 26.50 (*0-592-00070-2*) Transatl Arts.

— The Motor Vehicle. 12th ed. (Illus.). 1016p. 2000. pap. text 74.95 (*0-7506-3763-3*) Buttrwrth-Heinemann.

— The Motor Vehicle. 12th ed. 976p. 1996. 85.00 (*1-56091-898-5*, R-172) Soc Auto Engineers.

Newton, K. C., jt. auth. see Edwards, A. C.

Newton, K. M. Twentieth Century Literary Theory: A Reader. 2nd ed. LC 97-10704. 336p. 1997. text 55.00 (*0-312-17588-4*) St Martin.

Newton, Kathleen J., jt. auth. see Birchler, James A.

Newton, Ken M., ed. Theory into Practice: A Reader in Modern Literary Criticism. LC 92-4348. 256p. 1992. pap. 16.95 (*0-312-07997-4*) St Martin.

Newton, Kenneth. Second City Politics: Democratic Processes & Decision-Making in Birmingham. (Illus.). 1976. 26.95 (*0-19-827197-2*) OUP.

Newton, Kenneth, jt. ed. see Kaase, Max.

Newton-King, Susan. Masters & Servants on the Cape Eastern Frontier, 1760-1803. LC 98-38423. (African Studies: No. 97). (Illus.). 275p. (C). 1999. text 64.95 (*0-521-48153-8*) Cambridge U Pr.

***Newton, Kurt.** The House Spider & Other Strange Visitors. limited num. ed. (Illus.). 93p. 1999. lib. bdg. 25.00 (*1-929653-00-X*, DB-001) Delirium Bks.

Newton, L. E., Jr. & Hausler, R. H., eds. CO2 Corrosion in Oil & Gas Production: Selected Papers, Abstracts, & References. LC 82-60734. 687p. 1984. 10.00 (*0-915567-01-6*) NACE Intl.

Newton, L. E. & Hausler, R. H., eds. CO2 Corrosion in Oil & Gas Production: Selected Papers, Abstracts, & References. 6th ed. LC 82-60734. 687p. 1984. 10.00 (*0-915567-06-7*) NACE Intl.

Newton, Lady. Legh Family of England: The House of Lyme, from Its Foundation to the End of the 18th Century. 423p. 1994. reprint ed. pap. 64.00 (*0-8328-4142-0*); reprint ed. lib. bdg. 74.00 (*0-8328-4141-2*) Higginson Bk Co.

Newton, Laurie. Baby's Peek-A-Boo. (Pudgy Pillow Bks.). (Illus.). 8p. (J). 1989. 4.99 (*0-448-02789-5*, Plat & Munk) Peng Put Young Read.

Newton, Laurie. Baby's Animal Sounds. (Pudgy Pillow Bks.). 8p. (J). (ps). 1989. 4.95 (*0-448-02786-0*, Plat & Munk) Peng Put Young Read.

— Baby's Little Engine That Could. (Pudgy Pillow Bks.). 8p. (J). (ps-3). 1989. 4.99 (*0-448-02785-2*, Plat & Munk) Peng Put Young Read.

— Baby's Mother Goose. (Pudgy Pillow Bks.). 8p. (J). (ps-3). 1989. 4.95 (*0-448-02790-9*, Plat & Munk) Peng Put Young Read.

Newton, Leon T. Psycho-Politics in Government Vol. 1: A Dramatic Dialogue. LC 93-85663. 52p. (Orig.). 1993. pap. 9.95 (*0-915885-02-6*) Playwright MI.

— Psycho-Politics in Government Vol. 2: Theatre Version. rev. ed. 52p. 1993. pap. 15.95 (*0-915885-03-4*) Playwright MI.

Newton, Lewis. Social & Political History of Texas. 1993. reprint ed. lib. bdg. 75.00 (*0-7812-5946-0*) Rprt Serv.

Newton, Lewis W. The Americanization of French Louisiana: A Study of the Process of Adjustment Between French & Anglo-American Population of Louisiana. Cordasco, Francesco, ed. LC 80-884. (American Ethnic Groups Ser.). 1981. lib. bdg. 30.95 (*0-405-13445-2*) Ayer.

Newton, Lisa. Ethics in America Source Reader. 208p. 1988. pap. 41.00 (*0-13-290180-3*) P-H.

— Ethics in America Study Guide. 416p. 1988. pap., student ed. 41.00 (*0-13-290206-0*) P-H.

Newton, Lisa H. & Dillingham, Catherine K. Watersheds: Classic Cases in Environmental Ethics. 249p. 1993. mass mkt. 16.50 (*0-534-21180-1*) Wadsworth Pub.

— Watersheds: Classic Cases in Environmental Ethics. 2nd ed. (Philosophy Ser.). 272p. (C). 1996. 28.95 (*0-534-51181-3*) Wadsworth Pub.

Newton, Lisa H. & Ford, Maureen M. Clashing Views on Controversial Issues in Business Ethics & Society. 5th ed. (Taking Sides Ser.). (Illus.). 416p. 1998. pap. text 13.00 (*0-697-39108-6*, Dshkn McG-Hill) McGrw-H Hghr Educ.

— Taking Sides: Clashing Views on Controversial Issues in Business Ethics. 4th ed. 384p. (C). 1996. text. write for info. (*0-697-31291-7*, WCB McGr Hill) McGrw-H Hghr Educ.

Newton, Lisa H. & Ford, Maureen M., eds. Taking Sides: Clashing Views on Controversial Issues in Business Ethics & Society. 3rd rev. ed. LC 93-50063. (Illus.). 384p. (C). 1994. text 13.95 (*1-56134-247-5*, Dshkn McG-Hill) McGrw-H Hghr Educ.

Newton, Lisa H. & Schmidt, David. Wake up Calls: Classic Cases in Business Ethics. 256p. (C). 1995. pap. 35.95 (*0-534-25338-5*) Wadsworth Pub.

Newton, Lucilda A. Big Peanuts. (J). (ps-3). 1976. pap. 3.25 (*0-915374-17-X*, 17-X) Rapids Christian.

Newton, Lucy, jt. ed. see Kinsey, Sara.

Newton, Lynn D. Coordinating Science Across the Primary School. LC 98-206920. (Subject Leaders Handbks.). 212p. 1998. pap. 23.95 (*0-7507-0688-0*, Falmer Pr) Taylor & Francis.

Newton, Lynn D., ed. Primary Science: The Challenge of the Nineteen Nineties. LC 92-31457. 144p. 1992. 29.95 (*1-85359-176-9*, Pub. by Multilingual Matters) Taylor & Francis.

Newton, M. B., Jr. & Walker, H. Jesse, eds. Environment & Culture. (Illus.). 268p. (C). 1978. pap. text 5.00 (*0-938909-64-9*) Geosci Pubns LSU.

Newton, M. T., et al, eds. Tourism in Spain. (A CAB International Publication). (Illus.). 448p. 1996. text 90.00 (*0-85198-929-2*) OUP.

Newton, Mack & St. George, Michele. A Path to Power: A Master's Guide to Conquering Crisis. LC 99-180128. 181p. 1997. pap. 14.95 (*0-9659821-3-0*) NTKD Pub.

Newton, Marjorie. Southern Cross Saints: The Mormons in Australia. LC 91-8229. (Mormons in the Pacific Ser.). (Illus.). 312p. (Orig.). 1991. pap. 14.95 (*0-939154-49-8*) Inst Polynesian.

Newton, Mark G., ed. Rivers to Skyscrapers: Ethics in Modern American Literature. LC 91-60154. 146p. 1991. pap. 12.95 (*0-945759-02-9*) St Leo Col Pr.

Newton, Merlin O. Armed with the Constitution: Jehovah's Witnesses in Alabama & the U. S. Supreme Court, 1939-1946. LC 94-3993. 240p. 1995. text 29.95 (*0-8173-0736-2*) U of Ala Pr.

Newton, Michael. Abstract Specification of Grammar: Algebraic Specification Language: A Case Study. (Studies in Logic, Language & Information). 176p. (C). 1998. 59.95 (*1-57586-123-2*); pap. 22.95 (*1-57586-122-4*) CSLI.

— Armed & Dangerous: A Writer's Guide to Weapons. (Howdunit Ser.). 186p. 1990. pap. 15.99 (*0-89879-370-X*, Wrtrs Digest Bks) F & W Pubns Inc.

— Bitter Grain: Huey Newton & the Black Panther Party. 240p. (Orig.). 1991. mass mkt. 3.95 (*0-87067-751-9*) Holloway.

— Black Collar Crimes: An Encyclopedia of False Prophets & Unholy Orders. LC 98-86893. 280p. 1998. pap. 18.95 (*1-55950-185-5*, 34092) Loompanics.

Newton, Michael. Cat & Mouse. (Illus.). (J). 1995. mass mkt. 5.99 (*0-671-89738-1*) PB.

Newton, Michael. Cop Killers. LC 98-85396. 346p. 1998. pap. 16.95 (*1-55950-180-4*, 34088) Loompanics.

***Newton, Michael.** Destiny of Souls: New Case Studies of Life Between Lives. 2nd ed. LC 00-28270. (Illus.). 432p. 2000. pap. 14.95 (*1-56718-499-5*) Llewellyn Pubns.

Newton, Michael. The Encyclopedia of Serial Killers: A Study of the Chilling Criminal Phenomenon, from the "Angels of Death" to the "Zodiac" Killer. LC 99-14384. (Illus.). 374p. 1999. 75.00 (*0-8160-3978-X*, Checkmark) Facts on File.

***Newton, Michael.** The Encyclopedia of Serial Killers: A Study of the Chilling Criminal Phenomenon, from the "Angels of Death" to the "Zodiac" Killer. (Illus.). 400p. 2000. pap. 19.95 (*0-8160-3979-8*, Checkmark) Facts on File.

— A Handbook of the Scottish Gaelic World. 292p. 2000. 55.00 (*1-85182-540-1*, Pub. by Four Cts Pr); 29.95 (*1-85182-541-X*, Pub. by Four Cts Pr) Intl Spec Bk.

Newton, Michael. Holy Homicide: An Encyclopedia of Those Who Go with Their God & Kill. 286p. 1998. pap. text 16.95 (*1-55950-164-2*) Loompanics.

— Hunting Humans, Vol. I. 416p. 1992. mass mkt. 5.99 (*0-380-76396-6*, Avon Bks) Morrow Avon.

— Hunting Humans, Vol. 2. 360p. 1993. mass mkt. 5.99 (*0-380-76509-8*, Avon Bks) Morrow Avon.

— Journey of Souls: Case Studies of Life Between Lives. LC 94-15730. (Illus.). 288p. 1999. pap. 12.95 (*1-56718-485-5*) Llewellyn Pubns.

— The King Conspiracy: Unexplained Facts Behind the M. L. K. Murder. 256p. (J). 1991. mass mkt. 3.25 (*0-87067-729-2*) Holloway.

— Raising Hell: An Encyclopedia of Devil Worship & Satanic Crime. 432p. (Orig.). 1993. mass mkt. 5.99 (*0-380-76837-2*, Avon Bks) Morrow Avon.

— Still At Large: A Casebook of 20th Century Serial Killers Who Eluded Justice. LC 98-86892. 328p. 1998. pap. 16.95 (*1-55950-184-7*, 34093) Loompanics.

***Newton, Michael.** Stolen Away: The True Story of California's Most Shocking Kidnap-Murder. 464p. 2000. 6.99 (*0-671-01748-9*, Pocket Star Bks) PB.

Newton, Michael. The Waste Land: The Savage Odyssey of Charles Starkweather & Caril Ann Fugate. 1998. per. 6.99 (*0-671-00198-1*) PB.

Newton, Michael & Newton, Judy A. Terrorism in the United States & Europe, 1800-1959: An Annotated Bibliography. LC 88-21848. 522p. 1988. text 25.00 (*0-8240-5747-3*) Garland.

Newton, Michael, jt. ed. see Sinclair, Marion.

Newton, Michael T. & Donaghy, Peter J. Institutions of Modern Spain: A Political & Economic Guide. 407p. (C). 1997. text 64.95 (*0-521-57348-3*); pap. text 24.95 (*0-521-57508-7*) Cambridge U Pr.

Newton, Mike, jt. auth. see Knowlton, Janice.

Newton, Miller. Adolescence: Guiding Youth Through the Perilous Ordeal. 224p. (C). 1995. 27.00 (*0-393-70194-8*) Norton.

Newton, Miller, jt. auth. see Polson, Beth.

Newton, Milton B. Atlas of Louisiana: A Guide for Students. LC 79-186216. (Miscellaneous Publication: No. 72-1). (Illus.). 200p. 1972. pap. 12.00 (*0-938909-25-8*) Geosci Pubns LSU.

Newton, Milton B., Jr., ed. The Journal of John Landreth, Surveyor: An Expedition to the Gulf Coast November 15, 1818-May 19, 1819. LC 84-73203. (Illus.). 208p. 1985. 30.00 (*0-938909-33-9*) Geosci Pubns LSU.

Newton, N. S. The Highland Clearances. 220p. 1998. pap. 36.00 (*0-85976-466-4*, Pub. by J Donald) St Mut.

Newton, N. S., ed. The Life & Times of Inverness. LC 97-178126. 250p. 1996. pap. 45.00 (*0-85976-442-7*, Pub. by J Donald) St Mut.

***Newton, Nancy A. & Sprengle, Kadi.** A Guide to Home-Based Psychological Services. LC 99-87587. 2000. write for info. (*0-8261-1339-7*) Springer Pub.

Newton, Natika. Foundations of Understanding. LC 96-28754. (Advances in Consciousness Research Ser.: No. 10). x, 211p. 1996. pap. 34.95 (*1-55619-190-1*) J Benjamins Pubng Co.

Newton, Natika, jt. ed. see Ellis, Ralph D.

***Newton, Neill.** Uniqueness Is a Red Striped Zebra: Dare to Break Free... Like a Red Striped Zebra. 352p. 2000. 25.95 (*0-9673381-0-7*, 001, Pub. by Falkirk House) ACCESS Pubs Network.

***Newton, Nick & Minutaglio, Bill.** Locker Room Mojo: True Tales of Superstitions in Sports. LC 99-61075. 114p. (YA). 1999. 32.95 (*0-9670466-4-5*) Middlefork Pr.

***Newton, Norman.** The Listening Threads: The Formal Cosmology of Emanuel Swedenborg. LC 99-59854. 1999. 24.95 (*0-915221-70-5*) Swedenborg Sci Assn.

Newton, Norman T. Design on the Land: The Development of Landscape Architecture. LC 70-134955. (Illus.). 740p. 1971. 55.00 (*0-674-19870-0*) Belknap Pr.

An Asterisk (*) at the beginning of an entry indicates that the title is appearing for the first time.

Newton, P. W. & Bell, M., eds. Population Shift: Mobility & Change in Australia. 496p. 1996. 51.95 (*0-644-36118-2*, Pub. by Aust Gov Pub) Accents Pubns.

Newton, Patricia A. Handbook for a Melatonin Friendly Lifestyle. (Illus.). 91p. (Orig.). 1996. pap. 11.95 (*0-9648012-2-1*, HBK96) NTI Pubns.

Newton, Patti, jt. auth. see Newton, Earle.

*__Newton, Pauline.__ Around San Antonio. (Images of America Ser.). (Illus.). 128p. 1999. pap. 18.99 (*0-7385-0311-8*) Arcadia Publng.

Newton, Peter, et al, eds. Desktop Planning: Microcomputer Applications for Infrastructure & Services Planning & Management. (Illus.). 416p. 1990. 69.95 (*0-340-51945-2*, A4221, Pub. by E A) Routldge.

Newton, Peter A. The County of Oxford: A Catalogue of Medieval Stained Glass. (Illus.). 1980. 198.00 (*0-19-725970-7*) OUP.

Newton, Peter M. Freud: From Youthful Dream to Mid-Life Crisis. 297p. 1994. lib. bdg. 35.00 (*0-89862-293-X*, 2293) Guilford Pubns.

Newton, Peter M., jt. auth. see Lohser, Beate.

Newton, R. G. Inverse Schrodinger Scattering in Three Dimensions. (Texts & Monographs in Physics). 185p. 1989. 49.95 (*0-387-50563-6*) Spr-Verlag.

— Scattering Theory of Waves & Particles. 2nd ed. (Texts & Monographs in Physics). 800p. 1982. 117.95 (*0-387-10950-1*) Spr-Verlag.

Newton, R. P. & Wilson, T. J., eds. Applications of Modern Mass Spectrometry in Plant Science Research. LC 96-17223. (Proceedings of the Phytochemical Society of Europe Ser.: Vol. 40). (Illus.). 256p. 1996. text 145.00 (*0-19-854965-2*, Clarendon Pr) OUP.

Newton, Rae R. Your Statistical Consultant: Answers to Your Data Analysis Questions. 1999. write for info. (*0-8039-5822-6*) Sage.

Newton, Rae R. & Rudestam, Kjell E. Your Statistical Consultant: Answers to Your Data Analysis Questions. LC 98-58135. 336p. 1999. 29.95 (*0-8039-5823-4*) Sage.

Newton, Rae R., jt. auth. see Rudestam, Kjell E.

Newton, Rae R., jt. auth. see Rudestam, Kjell Erik.

Newton, Raymann. Political "ISMS" & the Democratic Mind: A Treatise on the Origin, Nature & Outcome of the Modern Conflict over Political Sovereignty. De Roin, Gene, ed. LC 88-92701. 160p. (Orig.). (C). 1989. pap. text 7.95 (*0-9622647-0-9*) Baron & Roth Pub.

Newton, Rebecca, ed. see LaMorte, Kathy & Lewis, Sharen.

Newton, Richard. Bible Jewels. 147p. 1993. reprint ed. pap. 9.99 (*0-88019-312-3*) Schmul Pub Co.

— Corvette Restoration Guide, 1963-1967. LC 98-34415. (Authentic Restoration Ser.). (Illus.). 256p. 1998. pap. 29.95 (*0-7603-0179-4*, 124517AP) MBI Pubg.

— How to Restore & Modify Your Corvette 1968-1982. LC 95-13977. (Illus.). 256p. 1995. pap. 24.95 (*0-7603-0052-6*) MBI Pubg.

— Illustrated Triumph Buyer's Guide. 2nd ed. (Illus.). 176p. 1994. pap. 17.95 (*0-87938-917-6*) MBI Pubg.

Newton, Richard W., ed. Color Atlas of Pediatric Neurology. LC 94-42132. (Illus.). 256p. (gr. 13). 1995. 86.95 (*0-7234-1879-9*) Mosby Inc.

Newton, Rick M., tr. see Ritsos, Yannis.

Newton, Robert. Eighteenth Century Exeter. 208p. 1984. text 33.95 (*0-85989-255-7*, Pub. by Univ Exeter Pr) Northwestern U Pr.

— Tokyo. LC 92-2498. (Cities at War Ser.). (Illus.). 96p. (YA). (gr. 6 up). 1992. lib. bdg. 18.00 (*0-02-768235-8*, Mac Bks Young Read) S&S Childrens.

Newton, Robert, jt. auth. see Marcell, Rita.

Newton, Robert R. Ancient Astronomical Observations & the Accelerations of the Earth & Moon. LC 70-122011. (Illus.). 329p. reprint ed. 102.00 (*0-8357-9261-1*, 201373000087) Bks Demand.

— The Crime of Claudius Ptolemy. LC 77-4211. 428p. 1977. reprint ed. pap. 132.70 (*0-608-00812-5*, 206160000010) Bks Demand.

— Medieval Chronicles & the Rotation of the Earth. LC 78-39780. 848p. reprint ed. pap. 200.00 (*0-608-30526-X*, 201229100081) Bks Demand.

— The Moon's Acceleration & Its Physical Origins Vol. 1: As Deduced from Solar Eclipses. LC 78-20529. 602p. reprint ed. pap. 186.70 (*0-608-06176-X*, 206650900001) Bks Demand.

— The Moon's Acceleration & Its Physical Origins Vol. 2: As Deduced from General Lunar Observations. LC 78-20529. 333p. reprint ed. pap. 103.30 (*0-608-06177-8*, 206650900002) Bks Demand.

— The Origins of Ptolemy's Astronomical Parameters. (Technical Publications of the Center for Archaeoastronomy: No. 4). (Illus.). 228p. (Orig.). 1982. pap. 12.00 (*0-912025-02-6*) JHU Applied Physics.

— The Origins of Ptolemy's Astronomical Tables. (Technical Publications of the Center for Archaeoastronomy: No. 5). (Illus.). 264p. (Orig.). 1985. pap. 12.00 (*0-912025-03-4*) JHU Applied Physics.

Newton, Roger Chatterton. Brian Boru: King of Ireland. 2nd ed. (Illus.). 224p. 1983. reprint ed. pap. 19.95 (*0-900068-65-5*, Pub. by Anvil Books Ltd) Irish Bks Media.

*__Newton, Roger G.__ Thinking about Physics. LC 99-35807. 198p. 2000. 24.95 (*0-691-00920-1*, Pub. by Princeton U Pr) Cal Prin Full Svc.

Newton, Roger G. The Truth of Science: Physical Theories & Reality. LC 97-9079. (Illus.). 272p. 1997. 27.00 (*0-674-91092-3*) HUP.

*__Newton, Roger G.__ Truth of Science: Physical Theories & Reality. 2000. pap. text 16.95 (*0-674-00181-8*) HUP.

Newton, Roger G. What Makes Nature Tick? LC 93-9507. 269p. 1993. text 27.95 (*0-674-95085-2*) HUP.

— What Makes Nature Tick? (Illus.). 272p. 1994. pap. text 14.95 (*0-674-95082-8*, NEWWHX) HUP.

Newton, Ronald C. German Buenos Aires, 1900-1933: Social Change & Cultural Crisis. LC 77-7206. (Texas Pan-American Ser.). 243p. reprint ed. pap. 75.40 (*0-8357-7752-9*, 203611000002) Bks Demand.

— The Nazi Menace in Argentina, 1931-1947. LC 91-20368. (Illus.). 540p. 1992. 52.50 (*0-8047-1929-2*) Stanford U Pr.

Newton, Roy. A History of the Town of Grand Isle As Told by the People of the Town. 222p. (Orig.). 1991. pap. 16.00 (*0-9624658-1-X*) Landside Pr.

Newton, Roy G. & Davison, Sandra. The Conversation of Glass. 322p. 1996. pap. 49.95 (*0-7506-2448-5*) Buttrwrth-Heinemann.

Newton, Roy M. Seven South: The Adventures & Times of a Small Vermont Restaurant, 1972-1982. (Illus.). 250p. 1985. 14.95 (*0-930721-00-4*) Newton Pub.

Newton, Ruth & Lebowitz, Naomi. Dickens, Manzoni, Zola, & James: The Impossible Romance. 256p. 1990. text 29.95 (*0-8262-0738-3*) U of Mo Pr.

Newton, Sam. The Origins of Beowulf: And Their Pre-Viking Kingdom of East Anglia. (Illus.). 192p. 1999. pap. 24.95 (*0-85991-472-0*) Boydell & Brewer.

— The Origins of Beowulf & the Pre-Viking Kingdom of East Anglia. (Illus.). 192p. (C). 1994. 75.00 (*0-85991-361-9*) Boydell & Brewer.

Newton, Sarah E. Learning to Behave: A Guide to American Conduct Books Before 1900, 28. LC 94-2849. 248p. 1994. lib. bdg. 65.00 (*0-313-26752-9*, Greenwood Pr) Greenwood.

Newton, Scott. Profits of Peace: The Political Economy of Anglo-German Appeasement. LC 95-30149. (Illus.). 226p. (C). 1996. text 60.00 (*0-19-820212-1*, Clarendon Pr) OUP.

Newton, Scott & Porter, Dilwyn. Joseph Chamberlain, 1836-1914: A Bibliography, Vol. 32. LC 93-50544. (Bibliographies & Indexes in World History Ser.: No. 32). 152p. 1994. lib. bdg. 65.00 (*0-313-28290-0*, Greenwood Pr) Greenwood.

Newton, Shane. Protecting a Will. 154p. 1994. 49.00 (*1-86287-142-6*, Pub. by Federation Pr) Gaunt.

Newton, Shirley, jt. auth. see Jones, Ursula.

Newton, Sir Isaac. Correspondence, 4 vols., 4. Turnbull, H. W. & Scott, J. F., eds. 1967. 84.95 (*0-521-05815-5*) Cambridge U Pr.

— The Correspondence of Isaac Newton, Vol. 3, 1688-1694. Turnbull, H. W., ed. LC 59-65134. 465p. reprint ed. pap. 132.60 (*0-608-12498-2*, 2024527) Bks Demand.

— Isaac Newton's Observations on the Prophecies of Daniel & the Apocalypse of St. John. Barnett, S. J., ed. LC 99-13609. (Critical Editions & Translations Ser.: Vol. 2). 340p. 1999. text 99.95 (*0-7734-8155-9*) E Mellen.

— Isaac Newton's Papers & Letters on Natural Philosophy & Related Documents. 2nd ed. Cohen, I. Bernard et al, eds. LC 77-72764. 558p. reprint ed. pap. 173.00 (*0-7837-2236-2*, 205732600004) Bks Demand.

— Isaac Newton's Philosophiae Naturalis Principia Mathematica, 2 vols., Set. Koyre, Alexander et al, eds. LC 75-78515. (Illus.). 964p. 1990. 135.00 (*0-674-66475-2*) HUP.

— Mathematical Papers, 1683-1684, Vol. 5. Whiteside, D. T. et al, eds. LC 65-11203. (Illus.). 649p. 1972. text 235.00 (*0-521-08262-5*) Cambridge U Pr.

— Newton's Philosophy of Nature: Selected Writings. 1970. pap. 16.95 (*0-02-849700-7*) Free Pr.

— Observations upon the Prophecies of Daniel, & the Apocalypse of St. John. LC 91-74116. 323p. 1991. reprint ed. 19.95 (*0-942487-02-8*) Oregon Inst Sci Med.

— Opticks. 532p. 1952. pap. text 12.95 (*0-486-60205-2*) Dover.

— The Principia, 2 vols. in 1, Set. Motte, Andrew, tr. LC 95-6733. (Great Minds Ser.). 465p. 1995. pap. 14.95 (*0-87975-980-1*) Prometheus Bks.

Newton, Sir Isaac. The Principia: Mathematical Principles of Natural Philosophy. Cohen, I. Bernard & Whitman, Anne, trs. from LAT. LC 99-10278. 1025p. 1999. 75.00 (*0-520-08816-6*, Pub. by U CA Pr) Cal Prin Full Svc.

*__Newton, Sir Isaac.__ The Principia: Mathematical Principles of Natural Philosophy. Cohen, I. Bernard & Whitman, Anne, trs. from LAT. LC 99-10278. 1025p. 1999. pap. 35.00 (*0-520-08817-4*, Pub. by U CA Pr) Cal Prin Full Svc.

Newton-Smith, W. H. The Rationality of Science. (International Library of Philosophy). 300p. 1981. pap. 14.95 (*0-7100-0913-5*, Routledge Thoemms) Routledge.

— The Rationality of Science. (International Library of Philosophy). 312p. (C). 1981. pap. 22.99 (*0-415-05877-5*) Routledge.

— The Structure of Time. 274p. 1984. pap. 14.95 (*0-7102-0389-6*, Routledge Thoemms) Routledge.

Newton-Smith, William H., ed. A Companion to Philosophy of Science. LC 99-47598. (Companions to Philosophy Ser.). 600p. 2000. 99.95 (*0-631-17024-3*) Blackwell Pubs.

Newton-Smith, William H., et al. College Clues for the Clueless: God's Word in Your World. (Clues for the Clueless Ser.). (Illus.). 224p. 1999. pap. 8.99 (*1-57748-489-4*) Barbour Pub.

— Dating Clues for the Clueless: God's Word in Your World. (Clues for the Clueless Ser.). 241p. 1999. pap. 8.99 (*1-57748-491-6*) Barbour Pub.

Newton, Stanley. MacKinac Island & Sault Saint Marie. LC 76-4405. 1990. reprint ed. pap. 12.00 (*0-912382-19-8*) Black Letter.

Newton, Stella M. The Dress of the Venetians. 180p. 1988. text 91.95 (*0-85967-735-4*, Pub. by Scolar Pr) Ashgate Pub Co.

*__Newton, Stella M.__ Fashion in the Age of the Black Prince: A Study of the Years, 1340-1365. (Illus.). 163p. 1999. pap. 35.00 (*0-85115-767-X*, Suffolk Records Soc) Boydell & Brewer.

— Staging Muscial. LC 99-31790. (Illus.). 160p. (C). (gr. 13). 1975. pap. 29.95 (*0-87830-108-9*, Thtre Arts Bks) Routledge.

Newton, Steven. German Battle Tactics on the Russian Front, 1941-1945. LC 93-87472. (Illus.). 272p. 1994. 24.95 (*0-88740-582-7*) Schiffer.

Newton, Steven H. The Battle of Seven Pines, May 31 - June 1, 1862. (Virginia Civil War Battles & Leaders Ser.). (Illus.). 147p. 1993. 19.95 (*1-56190-048-6*) H E Howard.

— Joseph E. Johnston & the Defense of Richmond. LC 98-20557. (Modern War Studies). 288p. 1998. 29.95 (*0-7006-0921-0*) U Pr of KS.

*__Newton, Steven H.__ Lost for the Cause: The Confederate Army in 1864. LC 99-67802. (Illus.). 384p. 2000. 29.95 (*1-882810-49-X*) Savas Pub.

Newton, Steven H. Retreat from Leningrad: Army Group North, 1944-1945. LC 95-67621. (Illus.). 320p. 1995. 24.95 (*0-88740-806-0*) Schiffer.

*__Newton, Steven H. & Greene, A. Wilson.__ Breaking the Backbone of the Rebellion: The Final Battles of the Petersburg Campaign. LC 99-67800. (Illus.). 384p. 2000. 34.95 (*1-882810-48-1*) Savas Pub.

Newton, Suzanne. I Will Call It Georgie's Blues. 197p. (YA). (gr. 5-9). 1990. pap. 5.99 (*0-14-034536-1*, PuffinBks) Peng Put Young Read.

— I Will Call It Georgie's Blues: A Novel. (J). 1990. 11.09 (*0-606-04700-X*, Pub. by Turtleback) Demco.

— Purro & the Prattleberries. LC 74-127657. 144p. (J). (gr. 2-6). 1998. pap. 5.00 (*0-9664376-4-0*) Green Ridge Bks.

Newton, T. W. Kinetics of the Oxidation-Reduction Reactions of Uranium, Neptunium, Plutonium, & Americium Ions in Aqueous Solutions. LC 75-22030. (ERDA Critical Review Ser.). 142p. 1975. pap. 11.50 (*0-685-01477-0*, TID-26506); fiche 9.00 (*0-87079-252-0*, TID-26506) DOE.

Newton, Tanist. How to ....Salvage Your Marriage or Survive Your Divorce. LC 86-61005. (Metamorphosis Trilogy Ser.: Vol. 1). 212p. (Orig.). 1988. pap. 12.95 (*0-9616881-0-6*) New Vistas Pub.

Newton, Thomas, ed. see Curio, Augustine.

Newton, Thomas, ed. see Seneca, Lucius Annaeus.

Newton, Thomas, tr. see Gratarolus, Gulielmus.

Newton, Thomas H., et al, eds. Computed Tomography of the Head & Neck. (Modern Neuroradiology Ser.: Vol. 3). (Illus.). 480p. 1988. text 173.00 (*0-88167-392-7*) Lppncott W & W.

Newton, Thomas H. & Bilaniuk, Larissa T. Radiology of the Eye & Orbit. (Modern Neuroradiology Ser.: Vol. 4). 320p. 1990. text 138.00 (*0-88167-662-4*, 2129) Lppncott W & W.

Newton, Thomas H. & Potts, D. Gordon. Advanced Imaging Techniques. (Modern Neuroradiology Ser.: Vol. 2). 348p. 1983. 83.50 (*0-685-38980-4*, CL0002) Lppncott W & W.

Newton, Tim. Managing Stress: Subjectivity & Power in the Workplace. 176p. 1995. text 69.95 (*0-8039-8643-2*); pap. text 21.95 (*0-8039-8644-0*) Sage.

Newton, Tom. How Cars Work. LC 98-96784. (Illus.). 96p. 1999. pap. 17.95 (*0-9668623-0-9*) Black Apple Pr. How Cars Work is a completely illustrated auto mechanics primer describing the 250 most important car parts & how they work. This mini text book includes marvelously simple line drawings & clear language to describe all the automotive systems as well as a glossary, index & a test after each chapter. How Cars Work provides the basic vocabulary & mechanical knowledge to help a reader talk intelligently with mechanics, understand shop manuals & diagnose car problems. Tom Newton guides the reader with a one topic per page format that delivers information in bite size chunks, just right for teenage boys. How Cars Work was the most stolen book at Kennedy High School, in Richmond, California! Teachers like our title & so do librarians, our title is used in many public, high school & middle school libraries. The History channel, "Modern Marvels-2000," Actuality Productions, Inc. is using How Cars Work to train staff for a documentary on automobiles. The Ford Dealership in Roseville, California supplies How Cars Work to customers to help explain repairs. See our unsolicited five star reviews on amazon.com. How Cars Work sells off the shelf. Order: www.howcarswork.com, or Black Apple Press, 1609 Fern Pl., Vallejo, CA 94590. *Publisher Paid Annotation.*

Newton, Velma. Commonwealth Caribbean Legal Literature. 350p. 1987. pap. 35.00 (*976-8001-16-X*) Gaunt.

— Commonwealth Caribbean Legal Literature: 1986-1995. xvi, 243p. 1995. pap., suppl. ed. 30.00 (*976-8083-76-X*) Gaunt.

— Commonwealth Caribbean Legal Systems: A Study of Small Jurisdictions. LC 89-46052. xxv, 325p. 1989. reprint ed. 85.00 (*0-912004-76-2*) Gaunt.

Newton, Verne W. Cambridge Spies: The American Cover-up of the Philby, Burgess, MacLean Scandal. 550p. 1991. 24.95 (*0-8191-8059-9*) Madison Bks UPA.

— The Cambridge Spies: The Untold Story of Maclean, Philby, & Burgess in America. LC 91-7889. 462p. 1993. pap. 14.95 (*1-56833-006-5*) Madison Bks UPA.

Newton, Vernon. Homage to a Cat: As It Were: Logscapes of the Lost Ages. LC 91-66800. (Orig.). 1991. pap. 9.95 (*0-9621570-5-8*) North Lights.

Newton, Vincent, jt. ed. see Morse, Flo.

Newton, Violette, jt. auth. see Appelbee, Evelyn C.

Newton, Violette, jt. auth. see Mercer, Gwen.

Newton, Violette, jt. auth. see Ottenstein, Claire.

Newton, Walter H., jt. auth. see Myers, William S.

Newton, Wayne & Maurice, Dick. Once Before I Go. 320p. 1991. mass mkt. 4.95 (*0-380-71405-1*, Avon Bks) Morrow Avon.

Newton, Wesley P. & Rea, Robert R., eds. Wings of Gold: An Account of Naval Aviation Training in World War II,... LC 86-7013. 352p. 1987. 35.95 (*0-8173-0319-7*) U of Ala Pr.

Newton, Wesley P., jt. auth. see Ennels, Jerome A.

Newton, Wesley P., jt. auth. see McFarland, Stephen L.

*__Newton, Wesley Phillips.__ Montgomery in the Good War: Portrait of a Southern City, 1939-1946. 368p. 2000. text 34.95 (*0-8173-1043-6*) U of Ala Pr.

Newton, William. Death Is for Losers. large type ed. 1991. pap. 16.99 (*0-7089-7003-6*) Ulverscroft.

— Don't Hold Your Breath. large type ed. (Linford Mystery Library). 288p. 1992. pap. 16.99 (*0-7089-7272-1*) Ulverscroft.

— If the Price Is Right. large type ed. 1991. pap. 16.99 (*0-7089-7023-0*) Ulverscroft.

— It Never Comes Easy. large type ed. (Linford Mystery Library). 304p. 1993. pap. 16.99 (*0-7089-7347-7*) Ulverscroft.

— The Night We Get Rich. large type ed. 1990. pap. 16.99 (*0-7089-7000-1*, Linford) Ulverscroft.

— Nothing Is for Free. large type ed. (Linford Mystery Library). 1991. pap. 16.99 (*0-7089-7132-6*) Ulverscroft.

— The Rio Contract. large type ed. 1991. pap. 16.99 (*0-7089-7027-3*) Ulverscroft.

— The Set-Up. large type ed. 1990. pap. 16.99 (*0-7089-6954-2*) Ulverscroft.

— A Slice of the Cake. large type ed. (Linford Mystery Library). 1991. pap. 16.99 (*0-7089-7087-7*) Ulverscroft.

— The Smell of Money. large type ed. 1990. pap. 16.99 (*0-7089-6996-8*) Ulverscroft.

— Someone Has to Take the Fall. large type ed. (Linford Mystery Library). 1991. pap. 16.99 (*0-7089-7083-4*) Ulverscroft.

— The Way to Get Dead. large type ed. (Linford Mystery Library). 1991. pap. 16.99 (*0-7089-7071-0*) Ulverscroft.

— You Can Deal Me In. large type ed. (Linford Mystery Library). 1991. pap. 16.99 (*0-7089-7079-6*) Ulverscroft.

— You Can Go Feet First. large type ed. (Linford Mystery Library). 1991. pap. 16.99 (*0-7089-7067-2*) Ulverscroft.

Newton, William E., et al, eds. Nitrogen Fixation Research Progress. (Current Plant Science & Biotechnology in Agriculture Ser.). 1985. text 329.00 (*90-247-3255-7*) Kluwer Academic.

Newton, William E. & Nyman, C. J., eds. Nitrogen Fixation Vol. 1: Proceedings of the First International Symposium, 1974, Pullman, WA. LC TP0245.N8I61. (Illus.). 319p. reprint ed. pap. 98.90 (*0-608-18347-4*, 203302700001) Bks Demand.

Newton, William E. & Veeger, Ces, eds. Advances in Nitrogen Fixation Research. (Advances in Agricultural Biotechnology Ser.). 1983. text 316.50 (*90-247-2906-8*) Kluwer Academic.

Newton, William M. History of Barnard, with Family Genealogies, 1761-1927, 2 vols., Set. (Illus.). 879p. 1996. reprint ed. lib. bdg. 96.00 (*0-8328-5123-X*) Higginson Bk Co.

Newton, Willis & Newton, Joe. The Newton Boys: Portrait of an Outlaw Gang. LC 93-43267. (Illus.). 332p. 1994. pap. 16.95 (*1-880510-16-2*) State House Pr.

— The Newton Boys: Portrait of an Outlaw Gang. limited ed. LC 93-43267. (Illus.). 332p. 1994. 60.00 (*1-880510-17-0*) State House Pr.

Newtown, Charles. Victorian Designs for the Home. (Illus.). 128p. 1999. boxed set 45.00 (*1-85177-284-7*, Pub. by V&A Ent) Antique Collect.

Newville, Jack. New Engineering Concepts in Community Development. LC 67-28256. (Urban Land Institute, Technical Bulletin Ser.: No. 59). 58p. reprint ed. pap. 30.00 (*0-608-10920-7*, 200577600059) Bks Demand.

Newville, Leslie J., tr. see Callinicos, Constantine.

NewYork Public Library Staff. Dictionary Catalog of the Rare Book Division, Supplement 1. 1981. suppl. ed. 175.00 (*0-8161-1258-4*, G K Hall & Co) Mac Lib Ref.

Nexia International Staff. International Handbook of Corporate & Personal Taxes. 2nd ed. 688p. 1994. pap. 93.95 (*0-412-54540-3*, Chap & Hall NY) Chapman & Hall.

Nexia International Staff. International Handbook of Corporate Governance. 288p. 1998. 49.50 (*0-412-63920-3*) Thomson Learn.

— International Handbook of Financial Reporting. 416p. 1993. pap. 80.95 (*0-412-55690-1*) Thomson Learn.

— The International Handbook of Financial Reporting. 2nd ed. 410p. 1997. pap. 69.00 (*1-86152-242-8*) Thomson Learn.

— Tolley's International Handbook of Corporate & Personal Taxes. 4th ed. 1998. pap. 75.00 (*1-86012-818-1*, IHCP02, Pub. by Tolley Pubng) St Mut.

— Tolley's VAT in Europe. 200p. (C). 1994. 105.00 (*0-85459-849-9*, Pub. by Tolley Pubng) St Mut.

— Tolley's Vat in Europe. 200p. (C). 1994. 105.00 (*0-7855-2645-5*) St Mut.

Nexo, Martin Anderson. Pelle the Conqueror Vol. 2: Apprenticeship. Murray, Steven T. & Nunnally, Tiina, trs. from DAN. LC 89-7837. (Modern Classics Ser.: No. 4).Tr. of Pelle Erobreren. 224p. (Orig.). 1991. 19.95 (*0-940242-49-4*) Fjord Pr.

Next Computer Inc. Staff. Next Development Tools. 1991. pap. text 26.95 (*0-201-58132-9*) Addison-Wesley.

NeXT Computer Inc. Staff. Next Operating System Software. 1991. pap. text 24.95 (*0-201-58131-0*) Addison-Wesley.

An Asterisk (*) at the beginning of an entry indicates that the title is appearing for the first time.

Next Computer Inc. Staff. NeXTstep Database Kit Concepts. LC 93-46024. (Nextstep Developer's Library). 208p. (C). 1994. pap. text 24.95 (*0-201-40741-8*) Addison-Wesley.

— NeXTstep Development Tools: Release 3. 480p. (C). 1992. pap. text 30.95 (*0-201-63249-7*) Addison-Wesley.

— NeXTstep General Reference: Release 3. 1992. pap. 49.95 (*0-201-63248-9*) Addison-Wesley.

— NeXTstep User Interface Guidelines: Release 3. 208p. (C). 1992. pap. text 24.95 (*0-201-63250-0*) Addison-Wesley.

Nexus Network Inc. Staff. Manhattan's First Retail Discount Directory. (Nexusguide Ser.). 1998. pap. 20.00 (*1-892983-00-1*) Nexus Network Inc.

Nexus Special Interests Staff, ed. Control-Line Models. (Planbooks Series 5). (Illus.). 32p. (Orig.). 1995. pap. 13.95 (*1-85486-160-3*, Pub. by Nexus Special Interests) Trans-Atl Phila.

— CO2 Models to Build. (Planbooks Series 1). (Illus.). 32p. (Orig.). 1995. pap. 13.95 (*1-85486-156-5*, Pub. by Nexus Special Interests) Trans-Atl Phila.

— Flying Scale Rubber Models. (Planbooks Series 2). (Illus.). 32p. (Orig.). 1995. pap. 13.95 (*1-85486-157-3*, Pub. by Nexus Special Interests) Trans-Atl Phila.

— Flying Scale Rubber Models, Vol. 2. (Planbooks Series 6). (Illus.). 32p. (Orig.). 1995. pap. 13.95 (*1-85486-161-1*, Pub. by Nexus Special Interests) Trans-Atl Phila.

— Free Flight Power Models. (Planbooks Series 4). (Illus.). 32p. (Orig.). 1995. pap. 13.95 (*1-85486-159-X*, Pub. by Nexus Special Interests) Trans-Atl Phila.

— Model Ships & Boats. (Planbooks Series 3). (Illus.). 32p. (Orig.). 1995. pap. 13.95 (*1-85486-158-1*, Pub. by Nexus Special Interests) Trans-Atl Phila.

— Peanut Scale Models. (Planbooks Series 7). (Illus.). 32p. (Orig.). 1995. pap. 13.95 (*1-85486-162-X*, Pub. by Nexus Special Interests) Trans-Atl Phila.

Ney, Catherine R. Using Literature to Unite the Curriculum Vol. 1: A Teaching Resource for Grades K-2. vii, 118p. (Orig.). 1996. teacher ed., spiral bd. 15.95 (*0-9651236-0-X*) BEM Pub.

— Using Literature to Unite the Curriculum Vol. 2: A Teaching Resource for Grades 3-5. vii, 128p. (Orig.). 1996. teacher ed., spiral bd. 15.95 (*0-9651236-1-8*) BEM Pub.

— Using Literature to Unite the Curriculum Vols. 1 & 2: A Teaching Resource for Grades K-2 & Grades 3-5, Set. xiv, 246p. (Orig.). 1996. teacher ed., spiral bd. 31.90 (*0-9651236-2-6*) BEM Pub.

Ney, Denise M., jt. auth. see Zeman, Frances J.

Ney, George & Fadem, Susan S. Cat Condominiums & Other Feline Furniture. (Illus.). 128p. 1989. 16.95 (*0-525-24709-2*, Dutt) Dutton Plume.

Ney, James W. Transformational Grammar: Essays for the Left Hand. (Edward Sapir Monographs in Language, Culture & Cognition: No. 16). vi, 169p. (Orig.). 1988. pap. 24.00 (*0-933104-26-X*) Jupiter Pr.

Ney, James W., et al. GMAT Time Saver: From the Professors Who Know It Best. 2nd rev. ed. (Illus.). 385p. (C). 1995. pap. 17.95 (*1-881018-10-5*) Grt Lks Pr.

Ney, Marian W. Indian America: A Geography of North America Indians. (Illus.). 56p. 1977. 5.50 (*0-935741-06-2*) Cherokee Pubns.

Ney, P. E., jt. auth. see Athreya, K. B.

Ney, Peter, ed. Advances in Probability & Related Topics, Vol. 2. LC 75-79066. 262p. reprint ed. pap. 81.30 (*0-8357-5178-3*, 202707100002) Bks Demand.

Ney, Peter & Port, Sidney, eds. Advances in Probability & Related Topics, 2 vols., 3. LC 75-79066. 422p. pap. 130.90 (*0-8357-8391-X*, 202707100003) Bks Demand.

— Advances in Probability & Related Topics, 2 vols., Vol. 1. LC 75-79066. 229p. pap. 71.00 (*0-8357-8390-1*, 202707100001) Bks Demand.

Ney, Peter, jt. ed. see Joffe, Anatole.

Ney, Philip G. & Peters, Anna. Ending the Cycle of Abuse: The Stories of Women Abused As Children & the Group Therapy Techniques That Helped Them Heal. LC 94-28150. 272p. 1995. 23.95 (*0-87630-752-7*) Brunner-Mazel.

Ney, Ron E., Jr. Fate & Transport of Organic Chemicals in the Environment: A Practical Guide. 3rd rev. ed. 370p. 1998. pap. text 59.00 (*0-86587-626-6*, 626) Gov Insts.

Ney, Ronald E., Jr. Chemicals: What You Need to Know. 2nd rev. ed. Lantzman-Forbes, Arlene G., ed. LC 96-4517. Orig. Title: Chemicals: Your Guide to Safety. (Illus.). 136p. 1996. pap. 12.95 (*1-57420-053-4*) Chatelaine.

Ney, Steven, jt. auth. see Douglas, Mary.

Ney, Tara, ed. True & False Allegations of Child Sexual Abuse: Assessment & Case Management. LC 94-47941. 400p. 1995. text 45.95 (*0-87630-758-6*) Brunner-Mazel.

Ney, Tara & Gale, Anthony, eds. Smoking & Human Behavior. LC 88-33844. 395p. reprint ed. pap. 122.50 (*0-7837-5874-X*, 204559400006) Bks Demand.

Ney, Tom. The Health-Lovers Guide to Super Seafood: 250 Delicious Ways to Enjoy the Ultimate in Natural Nutrition. 282p. 1995. pap. 15.95 (*0-87596-272-6*) Rodale Pr Inc.

Ney, W. Roger, ed. Particle Counting in Radioactivity Measurements. (ICRU Reports: No. 52). 84p. 1994. pap. text 50.00 (*0-913394-51-3*) Intl Comm Rad Meas.

— Prescribing, Recording & Reporting Photon Beam Therapy. LC 93-3633. (ICRU Reports: No. 50). 18p. (Orig.). 1993. pap. text 60.00 (*0-913394-48-3*) Intl Comm Rad Meas.

— Stopping Powers & Ranges for Protons & Alpha Particles. (ICRU Reports: No. 49). 260p. (Orig.). 1993. pap. text 70.00 (*0-913394-47-5*) Intl Comm Rad Meas.

Ney, W. Roger, ed. see ICRU Staff.

***Neye, Emily.** All about Cats & Kittens. LC 99-35341. (All Aboard Bks.). 32p. 1999. pap. 2.99 (*0-448-42082-1*) Putnam Pub Group.

— Butterflies. (All Aboard Reading Ser.). (Illus.). 32p. (J). (ps-3). 2000. 13.89 (*0-448-42280-8*, G & D); pap. 3.99 (*0-448-41966-1*, G & D) Peng Put Young Read.

— Butterflies: Level 1. (All Aboard Reading Ser.). (Illus.). (J). 2000. 9.44 (*0-606-18464-3*) Turtleback.

Neye, Emily. Calling All Girls! A Superbook of 40 Super Activities. (Illus.). 24p. (gr. k-5). 1999. 19.99 (*0-448-42032-5*, G & D) Peng Put Young Read.

***Neye, Emily.** My First Train Trip. LC 99-37709. (All Aboard Bks.). 32p. 1999. pap. 2.99 (*0-448-41998-X*, G & D) Peng Put Young Read.

Neyen, Auguste. Biographie Luxembourgeoise, 3 vols., Set. lii, 1463p. 1973. reprint ed. write for info. (*3-487-04295-9*) Lubrecht & Cramer.

Neyer, H. J., jt. auth. see Flugge, M.

***Neyer, Jeanie E. & Plotkin, Frederick S.** A Holocaust Portfolio. LC 99-75073. (Illus.). 64p. 1999. 25.00 (*1-877675-32-6*) Midmarch Arts.

Neyer, Maria Amata. Edith Stein: Her Life in Photos & Documents. Stein, Waltraut, tr. from GER. LC 98-6863.Tr. of Edith Stein: Ihr Leben in Dokumenten und Bildern. (Illus.). 84p. 1999. pap. 13.95 (*0-935216-66-9*) ICS Pubns.

***Neyer, Rob & Epstein, Eddie.** Baseball Dynasties: The Greatest Teams of All Time. LC 99-56940. (Illus.). 480p. 2000. 29.95 (*0-393-04894-2*, Norton Paperbks); pap. 17.95 (*0-393-32008-1*, Norton Paperbks) Norton.

Neyfakh, A. A. & Timofeeva, M. Ya. Molecular Biology of Development: Molecular Events & Problems of Regulation. Kolchinsky, A. M., ed. 792p. 1985. 155.00 (*0-306-41333-7*, Plenum Trade) Perseus Pubng.

Neyhart, Charles A., jt. auth. see Kemp.

Neyki, Jozsef & Soltesz, Miklos. Floral Biology of Temperate Zone Fruit Trees & Small Fruits. LC 96-171804. 380p. 1996. pap. 210.00 (*963-05-6896-9*, Pub. by Akade Kiado) St Mut.

Neyland, Charlotte S. Southwest Traveler: A Travelers Guide to Southwest Indian Arts & Crafts. LC 93-121608. (American Traveler Ser.: Vol. 21). (Illus.). 48p. 1992. pap. 5.95 (*1-55838-129-5*) R H Pub.

Neyland, David L. Virtual Combat: A Guide to Distributed Interactive. LC 97-24180. 184p. 1997. pap. 19.95 (*0-8117-3125-1*) Stackpole.

Neyland, James. Booker T. Washington: Educator. (Black American Ser.). (Illus.). 192p. (YA). 1993. mass mkt. 3.95 (*0-87067-599-0*, Melrose Sq) Holloway.

— Crispus Attucks: Patriot. (Black American Ser.). (Illus.). 208p. (YA). 1995. mass mkt. 4.95 (*0-87067-791-8*) Holloway.

— The Dark Lady. 320p. (Orig.). 1994. mass mkt. 3.95 (*0-87067-744-6*) Holloway.

— The Fever: Novel Based on L. A.'s Hillside Strangler Case. 288p. 1994. mass mkt. 3.95 (*0-87067-743-8*) Holloway.

Neyland, James. George Washington Carver: Scientist & Educator. (Black American Ser.). (Illus.). 192p. (YA). 1992. mass mkt. 4.95 (*0-87067-894-9*, Melrose Sq) Holloway.

Neyland, James. A Philip Randolph: Labor Leader. (Black American Ser.). (Illus.). 192p. (YA). 1994. mass mkt. 3.95 (*0-87067-777-2*, Melrose Sq) Holloway.

— W. E. B. Du Bois: Scholar & Actitist. (Black American Ser.). (Illus.). 192p. (YA). 1993. mass mkt. 3.95 (*0-87067-588-5*, Melrose Sq) Holloway.

Neyland, James, told to. Politics, Fat-Cats & Honey-Money Boys: The Mem-Wars of Jerry Sadler. LC 83-63199. 336p. 1984. 15.95 (*0-915677-01-6*) Roundtable Pub.

Neyland, Leedell W. Unquenchable Black Fires. LC 94-76316. 204p. 1994. write for info. (*0-9641539-0-4*); pap. write for info. (*0-9641539-1-2*) Leney Educ.

Neylon, Margaret. Wit & Wisdom. 1993. 70.00 (*1-85594-050-7*) St Mut.

— The Wit & Wisdom of Women: A Thought Book. 160p. (C). 1990. pap. text 35.00 (*1-85594-010-8*) St Mut.

Neyman, Abraham, jt. ed. see Hart, Sergiu.

Neyman, E., jt. auth. see Brainina, Z.

Neyman, Jerry & Pearson, E. K. Joint Statistical Papers. 299p. 1967. lib. bdg. 35.00 (*0-85264-706-9*) Lubrecht & Cramer.

Neyman, Jerzy, ed. The Heritage of Copernicus: Theories: "Pleasing to the Mind" 553p. 1977. pap. text 16.95 (*0-262-64016-3*) MIT Pr.

Neymark, N. Assessing the Economic Value of Anticancer Therapies. LC 97-52408. (Recent Results in Cancer Research Ser.: Vol. 148). 270p. 1998. 109.00 (*3-540-64030-4*) Spr-Verlag.

Neymeyr, Barbara. Aesthetische Autonomie als Abnormitaet: Kritische Analysen zu Schopenhauers Aesthetik im Horizont Seiner Willensmetaphysik. (Quellen und Studien zur Philosophie: Vol. 42). (GER.). x, 430p. (C). 1996. lib. bdg. 185.20 (*3-11-015229-0*) De Gruyter.

Neymeyr, Ulrich. Die Christlichen Lehrer im Zweiten Jahrhundert: Ihre Lehrtatigkeit, ihr Selbstverstandnis und ihre Geschichte. LC 88-29247. (Supplements to Vigiliae Christianae Ser.: Vol. IV). (GER.). 279p. (C). 1989. text 97.00 (*90-04-08773-7*) Brill Academic Pubs.

Neyra, Carlos A. Biochemical Basis Plant Breeding: Carbon Metabolism, Vol. I. 176p. 1985. 106.00 (*0-8493-5741-1*, SB123, CRC Reprint) Franklin.

Neyra, Carlos A., ed. Biochemical Basis of Plant Breeding, Vol. II. 192p. 1986. 96.00 (*0-8493-5742-X*, SB123, CRC Reprint) Franklin.

Neyra, Jose L. Al Paso Del Tiempo (As Time Goes By) (SPA., Illus.). 64p. 1987. pap. 8.99 (*968-16-2640-0*, Pub. by Fondo) Continental Bk.

Neyrey, Jerome H. First & Second Timothy, Titus, James, First Peter, Second Peter, Jude. Karris, Robert J., ed. (Collegeville Bible Commentary - New Testament Ser.: No. 9). 112p. (C). 1983. pap. 4.95 (*0-8146-1309-8*) Liturgical Pr.

— Honor & Shame in the Gospel of Matthew. LC 98-7521. 280p. 1998. pap. 26.00 (*0-664-25643-0*) Westminster John Knox.

— Second Peter, Jude: A New Translation with Introduction & Commentary. LC 92-21142. (Anchor Bible Ser.: Vol. 37C). 304p. 1993. 28.00 (*0-385-41362-9*, Anchor NY) Doubleday.

Neyrey, Jerome H., ed. The Social World of Luke-Acts: Models for Interpretation. LC 91-3333. 436p. 1991. 19.95 (*0-943575-48-6*) Hendrickson MA.

***Neyrey, Jerome H., ed.** The Social World of Luke-Acts: Models for Interpretation. 440p. 1999. pap. 19.95 (*1-56563-512-4*) Hendrickson MA.

Neyrey, Jerome H., jt. auth. see Malina, Bruce J.

Neyrohr, Deborah, jt. auth. see Brothers, Barbara.

***Neysmith, Sheila M.** Critical Issues for Future Social Work Practice with Aging Persons. LC 99-22409. 288p. 1999. pap. 21.50 (*0-231-11339-0*) Col U Pr.

***Neysmith, Sheila M., ed.** Critical Issues for Future Social Work Practice with Aging Persons. LC 99-22409. 288p. 1999. 49.50 (*0-231-11338-2*) Col U Pr.

— Restructuring Caring Labour: Discourse, State Practice, & Everyday Life. 2000. pap. 24.95 (*0-19-541480-2*) OUP.

Nez, Martha M. & Haburay, J. Keitz. Laboratory Manual for General Zoology. 2nd ed. 176p. (C). 1995. spiral bd. 19.95 (*0-8403-8541-2*) Kendall-Hunt.

Nez, Redwing T. Forbidden Talent. LC 95-11087. (Illus.). 32p. (J). (ps-3). 1995. lib. bdg. 14.95 (*0-87358-605-0*, Rising Moon Bks) Northland AZ.

Nezadal, Werner. Unkrautgesellschaften der Getreide und Fruehjahrshackfruchkulturen (Stellarietea Mediae) Im Mediterranen Iberien (La Vegetacion Arvense (Stellarietea Mediae) de los Cultivos de Primavera de Iberia Mediterranea) (Dissertationes Botanicae Ser.: Band 143). (GER., Illus.). iv, 206p. 1989. pap. 83.00 (*3-443-64052-4*, Pub. by Gebruder Borntraeger) Balogh.

***Nezhat, Camran.** Operative Gynecologic Laparoscopy: Principles & Techniques. 2nd ed. LC 99-88759. (Illus.). 352p. 2000. 125.00 (*0-07-105431-6*) McGraw-Hill Prof.

Nezhat, Camran, et al. Modern Surgical Management of Endometriosis. LC 94-19130. (Illus.). 288p. 1995. 129.00 (*0-387-94243-2*) Spr-Verlag.

— Operative Gynecologic Laparoscopy: Principles & Techniques. 352p. 1995. text 125.00 (*0-07-105422-7*) McGraw-Hill HPD.

Nezinska, Emma, tr. see Hudec, Ivan.

Neziroglu, Fugen A. & Yaryura-Tobia, Jose A. Over & over Again: Understanding Obsessive-Compulsive Disorder. rev. ed. LC 97-12122. 240p. 1997. pap. 17.95 (*0-7879-0876-2*) Jossey-Bass.

Neziroglu, Fugen A. & Yaryura-Tobias, Jose A. Obsessive Compulsive Spectrum Disorders (Norton Professional Books) Biobehavioral Treatment & Management. LC 97-8564. 224p. (C). 1997. 29.00 (*0-393-70245-6*) Norton.

Neziroglu, Fugen A., jt. auth. see Yaryura-Tobias, Jose A.

Nezlin, Mikhail V. Physics of Intense Beams in Plasmas. (Plasma Physics Ser.). (Illus.). 344p. 1993. 176.00 (*0-7503-0186-4*) IOP Pub.

Nezlin, Mikhail V. & Snezhkin, E. N. Rossby Vortices, Spiral Structures, Solitons: Astrophysics & Plasma Physics in Shallow Water Experiments. Dobrolavsky, A. & Pletnev, A., trs. LC 93-28898. (Nonlinear Dynamics Ser.). (Illus.). 240p. 1993. 97.95 (*0-387-50115-0*) Spr-Verlag.

Nezlin, Roald S. The Immunoglobulins: Structure & Function. LC 98-4750. (Illus.). 269p. 1998. boxed set 69.95 (*0-12-517970-7*) Acad Pr.

— Structure & Biosynthesis of Antibodies. Haigh, Basil, tr. from RUS. LC 76-30506. (Studies in Soviet Science). (Illus.). 383p. 1977. reprint ed. pap. 118.80 (*0-608-05498-4*, 206596700006) Bks Demand.

Neznansky, Fridrikh. The Prosecution of Economic Crimes in the U. S. S. R., 1954-1984. Michta, Andrew A., ed. (Orig.). 1985. pap. text 75.00 (*1-55831-031-2*) Delphic Associates.

— Zapiski Sledovatelia (Notes of an Investigator) LC 89-61028. (RUS.). 342p. (Orig.). (C). 1990. pap. 16.00 (*0-911971-44-0*) Effect Pub.

Neznek, Mary, jt. ed. see Janger, Michael.

Nezu, Arthur M., et al. Helping Cancer Patients Cope: A Problem-Solving Approach. LC 98-36683. 314p. 1999. 39.95 (*1-55798-533-2*, 431-721A) Am Psychol.

***Nezu, Arthur M., et al.** Practitioner's Guide to Empirically-Based Measures. 362p. 2000. 69.95 (*0-306-46246-X*) Kluwer Academic.

Nezu, Arthur M., et al. Problem-Solving Therapy for Depression: Theory, Research & Clinical Guidelines. LC 88-17287. (Personality Processes Ser.). 274p. 1989. 105.00 (*0-471-62885-9*) Wiley.

Nezu, Arthur M., jt. auth. see D'Zurilla, Thomas J.

Nezu, Christine M., et al. Psychopathology in Persons with Mental Retardation: Clinical Guidelines for Assessment & Treatment. LC 92-61116. 342p. (Orig.). 1992. pap. text 24.95 (*0-87822-328-2*, 4625) Res Press.

Nezu, suo, tr. see Niwamo, Nikkyo.

Nezunan. French-Polish Medical Dictionary. (FRE & POL.). 1990. 150.00 (*0-8288-7273-2*) Fr & Eur.

***Nezval, Vitezslav.** Antilyrik & Other Poems. 136p. 2000. pap. 10.95 (*1-892295-75-X*) Green Integer.

Nezworski, Teresa, jt. ed. see Belsky, Jay.

Nfah-Abbenyi, Juliana M. Gender in African Women's Writing: Identity, Sexuality & Difference. LC 97-13083. 1997. 35.00 (*0-253-33344-X*); pap. 14.95 (*0-253-21149-2*) Ind U Pr.

***Nfah-Abbenyi, Juliana M.** Your Madness, Not Mine: Stories of Cameroon. LC 98-48353. (Monographs in International Studies, Africa). 157p. 1999. pap. 16.95 (*0-89680-206-X*) Ohio U Pr.

***NFL Staff.** NFL 1999 Championship Spec Mkt. 2000. pap. 15.00 (*0-06-107593-0*) HarpC.

NFL Staff. Warren Moon. (NFL Quarterback Club in My Pocket Ser.). (Illus.). 1998. 249.00 (*0-7651-1652-9*) Smithmark.

NFPA Staff. National Electrical Code, 1996. (Electrical Trades Ser.). 1070p. (C). 1995. pap. 51.50 (*0-87765-402-6*, 70-96) Natl Fire Prot.

Ng & Hung. Safety, Reliability & Applications of Emerging Intelligent Control. 240p. 1995. pap. write for info. (*0-08-042374-4*, Pergamon Pr) Elsevier.

Ng, Anne Bjorkquist, see Renkiewicz, Frank & Bjorkquist Ng, Anne, compiled by.

Ng, Anthony, jt. auth. see Wei, William.

Ng, Betty, jt. ed. see Newman, D. J.

Ng, C., ed. Optical Methods for Time & State-Resolved Chemistry. 1992. 20.00 (*0-8194-0784-4*, 1638) SPIE.

Ng, C. S., ed. Frontiers in Reproductive Endocrinology & Infertility. (C). 1988. text 95.50 (*0-7462-0092-7*) Kluwer Academic.

Ng, C. Y., ed. see Franzen, H. F.

Ng, Cecilia. Changing Gender & Class Relations: Women's Work & Lives in Industrializing Malaysia. LC 98-19156. (International Political Economy Ser.). 1999. text 65.00 (*0-312-21789-7*) St Martin.

Ng, Chee H. Queueing Modelling Fundamentals. LC 96-2146. 234p. 1997. 94.95 (*0-471-96819-6*) Wiley.

Ng Chee Yuen, et al, eds. State-Owned Enterprise Reform in Vietnam: Lessons from Asia. (Illus.). 182p. (Orig.). (C). 1997. pap. text 50.00 (*0-7881-3707-7*) DIANE Pub.

***Ng, Cheuk-Yiu.** Photoionization & Photodetachment, Vol. 10. LC 99-57907. (Advanced Series in Physical Chemistry). 1999. 170.00 (*981-02-3892-4*) World Scientific Pub.

Ng, Cheuk-Yiu, ed. Cluster Ions. (Current Topics in Ion Chemistry & Physics Ser.: Vol. 1). 494p. 1993. 360.00 (*0-471-93830-0*) Wiley.

— Vacuum Ultraviolet Photoionization & Photodissociation of Molecules & Clusters. 580p. (C). 1991. pap. 48.00 (*981-02-0431-0*); text 150.00 (*981-02-0430-2*) World Scientific Pub.

Ng, Cheuk-Yiu, et al, eds. Unimolecular & Bimolecular Ion-Molecule Reaction Dynamics. LC 93-46718. (Ion Chemistry & Physics Ser.). 522p. 1994. 360.00 (*0-471-93831-9*) Wiley.

Ng, Cheuk-Yiu & Baer, Michael, eds. State-Selected & State-to-State Ion-Molecule Reaction Dynamics: Experiment, Vol. 82, Pt. 1, Experiment. (Advances in Chemical Physics Ser.: Vol. 82, Pt. 1). 704p. 1992. 280.00 (*0-471-53258-4*) Wiley.

Ng, Cheuk-Yiu, jt. ed. see Baer, Michael.

Ng, Chin-Keong. Trade & Society, the Amoy Network on the China Coast, 1683-1735. LC 84-941296. xxiv, 318 p. 1983. write for info. (*9971-69-069-1*) Corporate Bk Services.

Ng, David, ed. People on the Way: Asian North Americans Discovering Christ, Culture, & Community. 336p. (Orig.). 1996. pap. 18.00 (*0-8170-1242-7*) Judson.

Ng, David & Thomas, Virginia. Children in the Worshipping Community. LC 80-84655. (Illus.). 128p. (Orig.). (C). 1981. pap. 14.95 (*0-8042-1688-6*) Westminster John Knox.

Ng, Donna, ed. see Blakely, Mary Kay.

Ng, Donna, ed. see Brown, Alan.

Ng, Donna, ed. see Goddard, Robert.

Ng, Donna, ed. see Kay, Terry.

Ng, Donna, ed. see Lederer, Richard & Dowis, Richard.

Ng, Donna, ed. see Pelletier, Cathie.

Ng, Donna, ed. see Von Arnim, Elizabeth.

Ng, Donna, ed. see Ward, Robert.

Ng, Donna, ed. see Yoshimoto, Banana.

Ng, Fae M. Bone: A Novel. 208p. (J). 1993. 19.45 (*1-56282-944-0*, Pub. by Hyperion) Time Warner.

Ng, Fae M. Bone: Novel, A. LC 93-37200. 208p. 1994. reprint ed. pap. 12.50 (*0-06-097592-X*, Perennial) HarperTrade.

***Ng, Fae M.** Untitled Fae M. Ng. 2002. 21.95 (*0-7868-6097-9*, Pub. by Hyperion) Little.

Ng, Franklin. Asian American Women & Gender: A Reader. LC 99-29041. (Paperback Ser.). (Illus.). 266p. 1999. reprint ed. pap. 24.95 (*0-8153-3436-2*) Garland.

— Chinese Americans Struggle for Equality. LC 92-7472. (Discrimination Ser.). 112p. (J). 1992. lib. bdg. 18.95 (*0-86593-181-X*) Rourke Corp.

— The Taiwanese Americans. LC 97-37530. (New Americans Ser.). 176p. 1998. 39.95 (*0-313-29762-2*, Greenwood Pr) Greenwood.

Ng, Franklin, ed. Adaptation, Acculturation & Transnational Ties among Asian Americans. LC 98-14134. (Asians in American Life Ser.: Vol. 4). (Illus.). 272p. 1998. 70.00 (*0-8153-2693-9*) Garland.

— The Asian American Encyclopedia, 6 vols. LC 94-33003. (Illus.). 1900p. 1994. lib. bdg. 657.07 (*1-85435-677-1*) Marshall Cavendish.

— Asian American Family Life & Community. LC 98-10881. (Asians in American Life Ser.: Vol. 2). (Illus.). 304p. 1998. 72.00 (*0-8153-2691-2*) Garland.

— Asian American Interethnic Relations & Politics. LC 98-14136. (Asians in American Life Ser.: Vol. 5). (Illus.). 280p. 1998. 70.00 (*0-8153-2694-7*) Garland.

— Asian American Issues Relating to Labor, Economics, & Socioeconomic Status. (Asians in American Life Ser.: Vol. 6). (Illus.). 240p. 1998. 67.00 (*0-8153-2695-5*) Garland.

— Asian American Women & Gender: A Reader, 3. (Asians in American Life Ser.: Vol. 3). (Illus.). 272p. 1998. 75.00 (*0-8153-2692-0*) Garland.

— The History & Immigration of Asian Americans. LC 98-16245. (Asians in American Life Ser.: Series 1). (Illus.). 264p. 1998. 69.00 (*0-8153-2690-4*) Garland.

Ng, Franklin, ed. Asians in American Life: The Peoples of East, Southeast, & South Asia in American Life & Culture, 6 vols. 1998. 450.00 (*0-8153-2689-0*) Garland.

An Asterisk (*) at the beginning of an entry indicates that the title is appearing for the first time.

N

An Asterisk (*) at the beginning of an entry indicates that the title is appearing for the first time.

— Fundamentals of Mathematical Statistics, Vol. II. (Texts in Statistics Ser.). xi, 422p. 1989. 59.95 (*0-387-97020-7*) Spr-Verlag.

Nguyen, H. T. & Walker, E. A First Course in Fuzzy Logic. LC 96-2728. 288p. 1996. boxed set 89.95 (*0-8493-9477-5*) CRC Pr.

Nguyen, Hien D. Rain Melody: Poems by Nguyen Hien Duc. Goforth, Ronald, ed. (Illus.). 111p. (Orig.). 1988. pap. 25.00 (*0-9622682-0-8*) H D Nguyen.

Nguyen-Hong-Nhiem, Lucy & Halpern, Joel M., eds. The Far East Comes Near: Autobiographical Accounts of Southeast Asian Students in America. LC 88-32687. (Illus.). 232p. 1989. 30.00 (*0-87023-671-7*); pap. 16.95 (*0-87023-672-5*) U of Mass Pr.

***Nguyen, Hung T.** First Course in Fuzzy Logic. 2nd ed. LC 99-23550. 300p. 1999. boxed set 74.95 (*0-8493-1659-6*) CRC Pr.

Nguyen, Hung T. & Kreinovich, Vladik. Applications of Continuous Mathematics to Computer Science: A Graduate Course. LC 97-28678. (Theory & Decision Library. Mathematical & Statistical Methods). 432p. 1997. 199.00 (*0-7923-4722-6*) Kluwer Academic.

Nguyen, Hung T. & Prasad, Nadipuram R. Sugeno on Fuzzy Modeling & Control Selected Works. LC 99-19201. 14p. 1999. boxed set 89.95 (*0-8493-2884-5*, 2884) CRC Pr.

Nguyen, Hung T. & Sugeno, Michio. Fuzzy Systems: Modeling & Control. LC 98-19094. (Handbooks of Fuzzy Sets Ser.). 1998. 185.00 (*0-7923-8064-9*) Kluwer Academic.

Nguyen, Hung T., jt. auth. see Bosq, Denis.

Nguyen, Huong. Math for Logical Minds. (Illus.). 382p. (J). (gr. 1-4). 1997. spiral bd. 50.00 (*0-9655937-1-1*) Logical Connect.

Nguyen, Jean-Paul. Drilling: Oil & Gas Field Development Techniques. LC 96-150645. 384p. 1995. pap. 270.00 (*2-7108-0689-4*, Pub. by Edits Technip) Enfield Pubs NH.

Nguyen, Jean-Paul & Gabolde, Gilles. Drilling Data Handbook. 552p. (C). 1991. 550.00 (*2-7108-0601-0*, Pub. by Edits Technip) Enfield Pubs NH.

Nguyen, Jean-Paul, jt. auth. see Gabolde, Gilles.

Nguyen, Jim C., jt. auth. see Curry, Jeffrey.

Nguyen, Joe T., et al. Beanie Babies Spring, 1998 Collector's Guide. rev. ed. (Illus.). 96p. 1998. pap. 8.95 (*1-888914-19-X*) CheckerBee.

— Beanie Babies Summer 1998 Value Guide. 1998. pap. 8.95 (*1-888914-28-9*) CheckerBee.

— Boyds Collection Spring, 1998 Collector's Value Guide. 3rd rev. ed. (Illus.). 192p. 1998. pap. 14.95 (*1-888914-17-3*) CheckerBee.

— Charming Tails Value Guide. (Illus.). 128p. 1998. pap. 13.95 (*1-888914-22-X*) CheckerBee.

— Cherished Teddies, 1998 Collector's Value Guide. 3rd rev. ed. (Illus.). 160p. 1998. pap. 13.95 (*1-888914-15-7*) CheckerBee.

— Department 56 Villages, 1998 Collector's Value Guide. 3rd rev. ed. (Illus.). 208p. 1998. pap. 15.95 (*1-888914-18-1*) CheckerBee.

— Dreamsicles, 1998 Collector's Value Guide. rev. ed. (Illus.). 160p. 1998. pap. 13.95 (*1-888914-12-2*) CheckerBee.

— Hallmark Keepsake Ornaments Value Guide, 1998. 2nd ed. (Illus.). 336p. 1998. pap. 19.95 (*1-888914-21-1*) CheckerBee.

— Harbour Lights 1998 Collector's Value Guide. (Illus.). 128p. 1998. pap. 13.95 (*1-888914-23-8*) CheckerBee.

— Harmony Kingdom 1998 Collector's Value Guide. (Illus.). 128p. 1998. pap. 13.95 (*1-888914-25-4*) CheckerBee.

— Looney Tunes 1998 Collector's Value Guide. 1998. pap. 10.95 (*1-888914-26-2*) CheckerBee.

— Precious Moments Spring Value Guide, 1998. (Illus.). 240p. 1998. pap. 19.95 (*1-888914-11-4*) CheckerBee.

— Snowbabies (Department 56) Value Guide, 1998. 3rd rev. ed. (Illus.). 128p. 1998. pap. 14.95 (*1-888914-24-6*) CheckerBee.

— Swarovski Silver Crystal 1998 Collector's Guide. (Illus.). 160p. 1998. pap. 14.95 (*1-888914-27-0*) CheckerBee.

Nguyen-Khac, U. & Lutz, A. M., eds. Neutral Currents 20 Years Later: Proceedings of the International Conference. LC 95-109334. 500p. 1994. text 109.00 (*981-02-1752-8*) World Scientific Pub.

***Nguyen, Kien.** The Unwanted: A Memoir. 320p. 2001. 24.95 (*0-316-28664-8*) Little.

Nguyen, Kim-Anh. Vietnamese Word Book. LC 93-73560. (ENG & VIE., Illus.). 144p. (J). (gr. k-6). 1994. 19.95 (*1-880188-70-8*); pap. 11.95 (*1-880188-51-1*); pap. 19.95 incl. audio (*1-880188-71-6*) Bess Pr.

Nguyen, L. T. & Pecht, Michael G., eds. Electronic Packaging Reliability. LC 93-93270. 131p. pap. 45.00 (*0-7918-1035-6*) ASME.

Nguyen, Lang. Viet Nam Phat Giao Su Luan, Vol. I. 3rd ed. (VIE.). 466p. 1993. reprint ed. pap. 15.00 (*1-891667-20-3*) La Boi Soc.

— Viet Nam Phat Giao Su Luan, Vol. II. 3rd ed. (VIE.). 286p. 1993. reprint ed. pap. 12.00 (*1-891667-21-1*) La Boi Soc.

— Viet Nam Phat Giao Su Luan, Vol. III. 2nd ed. (VIE.). 490p. 1993. reprint ed. pap. 15.00 (*1-891667-22-X*) La Boi Soc.

Nguyen, Luu T. Plastic-Encapsulated Microelectronics: Materials, Processes, Quality, Reliability & Applications. Pecht, Michael G. et al, eds. 512p. 1995. 200.00 (*0-471-30625-8*) Wiley.

Nguyen, Luu T., jt. auth. see Tong, Ho-Ming.

Nguyen, Mai, ed. see Luong Si Hang.

Nguyen, Mai, ed. see Santos, Star.

Nguyen, Mary-Rose, ed. see Link, Edward P.

Nguyen, Ngoc H., et al, trs. The Le Code: Law in Traditional Vietnam, 3 vols. LC 86-8371. 1038p. 1987. text 175.00 (*0-8214-0630-2*) Ohio U Pr.

Nguyen, Ngoc H. & Young, Stephen B. The Tradition of Human Rights in China & Vietnam. (Lac-Viet Ser.: No. 10). 480p. 1990. pap. 20.00 (*0-685-63100-1*) Yale U SE Asia.

Nguyen, Nguyen X., jt. auth. see Psacharopoulos, George.

Nguyen, P. Essential English-Vietnamese Dictionary. (ENG & VIE.). 316p. 1983. 24.95 (*0-8288-1702-2*, M13014) Fr & Eur.

Nguyen, Phong & Campbell, Patricia S. From Rice Paddies & Temple Yards: Traditional Music of Vietnam. LC 89-52161. (Illus.). 88p. (Orig.). 1996. pap. 20.95 incl. audio compact disk (*0-937203-73-4*) World Music Pr.

— From Rice Paddies & Temple Yards: Traditional Music of Vietnam, Set. LC 89-52161. (Illus.). 88p. (Orig.). (J). (gr. 3 up). 1990. pap. 16.95 incl. audio (*0-937203-34-3*) World Music Pr.

Nguyen, Phong & Miller, Terry. Mother Mountain & Father Sea: Living Musical Traditions of Vietnam. LC 98-6300. (Performance in World Music Ser.: No. 13). 1999. pap. 19.95 (*0-941677-93-1*, Pub. by White Cliffs Media) Words Distrib.

Nguyen, Q. S., ed. Bifurcation & Stability of Dissipative Systems. (CISM International Centre for Mechanical Sciences Ser.: Vol. 327). (Illus.). v, 291p. 1993. 86.95 (*0-387-82437-5*) Spr-Verlag.

Nguyen, Qui Duc. Where the Ashes Are: The Odyssey of a Vietnamese Family. LC 93-25869. 1994. 21.95 (*0-201-63202-0*) Addison-Wesley.

Nguyen, Qui Duc, tr. see Ho Anh Thai.

Nguyen, Quoc K. Norsk - Vietnamesisk Ordbok. (NOR & VIE.). 501p. lib. bdg. 225.00 (*0-7859-3668-8*, 8200067572) Fr & Eur.

***Nguyen, Quoc Son.** Stability & Nonlinear Solid Mechanics. LC 00-43322. (Illus.). 2000. write for info. (*0-471-49288-4*) Wiley.

Nguyen, Rosemary. Literature News: Nine Stories from the Newspaper of the Vietnam Writers Union. (Lac Viet Series, Yale Southeast Asia Studies: Vol. 16). (Illus.). 192p. 1997. pap. 18.00 (*0-938692-65-8*) Yale U SE Asia.

Nguyen, Sam. Ephphatha: The Easiest, Most Rational & Natural Anti-Stuttering Self-Reeducation. LC 99-178559. (Illus.). 48p. 1998. pap. 7.00 (*0-8059-4254-8*) Dorrance.

Nguyen, Sang, jt. auth. see Marcotte, Patrice.

Nguyen, Tai T., ed. History of Buddhism in Vietnam. LC 97-18941. (Cultural Heritage & Contemporary Change Ser.: Vol. 1). 250p. Date not set. pap. 17.50 (*1-56518-098-4*) Coun Res Values.

Nguyen, Talia. The Children's Writing Practice Book. 28p. (Orig.). (J). (ps-8). 1996. pap., wbk. ed. 2.50 (*0-9655943-0-0*) T Nguyen.

***Nguyen, Thach N., et al, eds.** Management of Complex Cardiovascular Problems: The Consultant's Approach. LC 99-36190. (Illus.). 272p. 1999. pap. 45.00 (*0-87993-441-7*) Futura Pub.

Nguyen, Than C. Yellow Leaves: Children of the Rolling Thunder. 76p. (Orig.). 1994. 10.00 (*0-9631569-2-6*) Backyard Pr.

Nguyen, Thanh T. & Weigl, Bruce, trs. from VIE. Poems from Captured Documents: A Bilingual Edition. LC 93-46189. 80p. 1994. pap. 10.95 (*0-87023-922-8*) U of Mass Pr.

Nguyen The, H., jt. ed. see Pescia, G.

Nguyen, Thi T. Fallen Leaves: Memoirs of a Vietnamese Woman from 1940-1975. LC 89-60488. (Lac-Viet Ser.: No. 11). vii, 224p. 1989. pap. 15.00 (*0-938692-39-9*) Yale U SE Asia.

Nguyen, Thu T. Dinh Duong Tri Lieu: Nutrition Therapy. LC 92-62316. (Illus.). 928p. 1993. 59.00 (*0-9635459-0-6*) N X Phuong.

Nguyen, Tri Q. Third-World Development: Aspects of Political Legitimacy & Viability. LC 87-45959. (Illus.). 224p. 1989. 35.00 (*0-8386-3327-7*) Fairleigh Dickinson.

***Nguyen, Trung Hieu.** Presenting ESL Units to New Immigrant Students: Sample Lesson Plans & Activities. LC 99-41131. 1999. pap. write for info. (*0-9662708-2-7*) Nghia Sinh.

Nguyen, Truong, jt. auth. see Strang, Gilbert.

Nguyen, Van C. Viet Nam Chinh Su. 630p. 1992. 20.00 (*0-9635574-0-8*) Alpha Bks VA.

Nguyen, Van C. Vietnam under Communism, 1975-1982. LC 83-10754. (Publication Ser.: No. 285). (Illus.). xvi, 312p. 1983. pap. 9.95 (*0-8179-7852-6*) Hoover Inst Pr.

Nguyen Van Dao, jt. auth. see Mitropolskii, Yu A.

Nguyen Van Duong. Medicinal Plants of Vietnam, Cambodia & Laos. LC 93-92625. 528p. (Orig.). (C). 1993. pap. 31.00 (*0-9637303-1-2*) N Van Duong.

Nguyen, Van Hien, ed. see French-German Conference on Optimization Staff.

Nguyen-Van-Huy, Pierre. Le Devenir et la Conscience Cosmique Chez Saint-Exupery. LC 94-38773. (FRE.). 188p. 1995. text 79.95 (*0-7734-2912-3*) E Mellen.

Nguyen-Van-Khanh, Norbert. The Teacher of His Heart. (Franciscan Pathways Ser.). 253p. 1994. pap. 18.00 (*1-57659-066-6*) Franciscan Inst.

Nguyen, Van T., ed. Geothermal Energy: Resource & Utilization. 52p. 1984. 15.00 (*0-917853-05-9*, IO-5) Am Assn Physics.

Nguyen, Van T., jt. ed. see Ehrlich, Daniel J.

Nguyen Xuan Dung, jt. ed. see Oyen, L. P.

Nguyen, Xuan-Mai, tr. see Luong Si Hang.

Nguyen, Xuan T. Vietnamese Phrasebook. 2nd ed. LC 95-220507. (VIE., Illus.). 176p. 1996. pap. 5.95 (*0-86442-347-0*) Lonely Planet.

Ngwainmbi, Emmanuel K. Communication Efficiency & Rural Development in Africa: The Case of Cameroon. (Illus.). 196p. (Orig.). (C). 1994. pap. text 27.50 (*0-8191-9735-1*); lib. bdg. 49.50 (*0-8191-9734-3*) U Pr of Amer.

— Exporting Communication Technology to Developing Countries: Sociocultural, Economic & Educational Factors. 256p. 1999. 52.00 (*0-7618-1418-3*); pap. 31.50 (*0-7618-1419-1*) U Pr of Amer.

Ngwane, Zolani, jt. auth. see Kaschula, Russell.

Ng'Weno, Fleur. Kenya. (Focus On Ser.). (Illus.). 32p. (YA). (gr. 7-10). 1992. write for info. (*0-237-60194-X*) EVN1 UK.

Ngwenyama, Ojelanki, jt. auth. see IFIP TC8 WG8.2 International Working Conference on New Information Technologies in Organizational Processes: Field Studies & Theoretical Reflections on the Future of Work Staff.

Ngwu, Charles. Sports Doctor, Vol. 1. abr. ed. Nwangwu, Mrchido, ed. (Illus.). 80p. 1997. pap. 5.95 (*0-9656754-0-8*) Concept Cascade.

Nha, I. S., jt. ed. see Leung, K. C.

Nhan, Phan-Thein & Kim, Sangtae. Microstructures in Elastic Media: Principles & Computational Methods. (Illus.). 256p. 1994. text 85.00 (*0-19-509086-1*) OUP.

NHK Overseas Broadcasting Department Staff & Mizutani, Nobuko. NHK's Let's Learn Japanese: A Practical Conversation Guide, Bk. II. Maeda, Jun, ed. (Illus.). 176p. 1993. pap. 15.00 (*4-7700-1784-7*); audio 40.00 (*4-7700-1785-5*) Kodansha.

— NHK's Let's Learn Japanese: A Practical Conversation Guide, Bk. III. Maeda, Jun, ed. (Illus.). 176p. 1994. pap. 15.00 (*4-7700-1786-3*) Kodansha.

— NHK's Let's Learn Japanese: A Practical Conversation Guide, Bk. IV. Maeda, Jun, ed. (Illus.). 176p. 1994. audio 40.00 (*4-7700-1789-8*) Kodansha.

NHK Science & Technical Research Laboratories Staf. High Definition Television: Hi-Vision Technology. LC 92-17071. 1993. text 69.95 (*0-442-00798-1*, VNR) Wiley.

NHL Staff. NHL Official Guide & Record Book, 1998-1999. 1998. pap. text 19.95 (*1-892049-02-3*) Benchmark Press.

NHL Staff, jt. auth. see U. S. A. Hockey Staff.

Nhlapo, Thandabantu, jt. ed. see Eekelaar, John.

Nho Hao, Dinh. Methods for Inverse Heat Conduction Problems. Brosowski, Bruno & Martensen, Erich, eds. (Methoden und Verfahren der Mathematischen Physik Ser.: Vol. 43). (Illus.). ix, 249p. 1998. pap. 45.95 (*3-631-32744-7*) P Lang Pubng.

***NHS Estates Staff.** Fluids Sterilizer Log Book, Pts. 1 & 2. 2000. ring bd. 108.00 (*0-11-322397-8*, Pub. by Statnry Office) Balogh.

— Unwrapped Instrument & Utensil Sterilizer Log Book. 2000. ring bd. 66.00 (*0-11-322400-1*, Pub. by Statnry Office) Balogh.

Nhu-hoa, ed. Flowers of Love: 40 Vietnamese Poets. Thanh-thanh, tr. (ENG & VIE., Illus.). v, 105p. 1998. pap. 12.00 (*0-9665293-2-4*) XAY-DUNG.

Nhuan Xuan Le, tr. see Thanh-Thanh (Nhuan Le X), et al.

Nhuong, Huynh Q. The Land I Lost: Adventures of a Boy in Vietnam. LC 80-8437. (Trophy Bk.). (Illus.). 128p. (J). (gr. 4-7). 1998. pap. 4.95 (*0-06-440183-9*, HarpTrophy) HarpC Child Bks.

— The Land I Lost: Adventures of a Boy in Vietnam. (J). (gr. 4-7). 1996. pap. 19.00 (*0-8446-6586-X*) Peter Smith.

Nhuong, Huynh Q. The Land I Lost: Adventures of a Boy in Vietnam. (J). 1982. 9.60 (*0-606-03245-2*, Pub. by Turtleback) Demco.

Nhuong, Nuynh Q. Land I Lost. (J). 1982. 12.95 (*0-06-024592-1*); lib. bdg. 12.89 (*0-06-024593-X*) HarpC Child Bks.

— The Land I Lost: Adventures of a Boy in Vietnam. LC 80-8437. (Illus.). 128p. (J). (gr. 4-7). 1990. lib. bdg. 15.89 (*0-397-32448-0*) HarpC Child Bks.

Ni Bhrolchain, Muireann, ed. An Banshenchas: The Lore of Women. 256p. 1996. 55.00 (*1-85182-245-3*, Pub. by Four Cts Pr) Intl Spec Bk.

Ni Bhuachalla, Bridog. Kid's Day Out. 196p. 1997. pap. 14.95 (*1-86023-016-4*, Pub. by Martello Bks) Irish Amer Bk.

Ni Chuilleanain, Eilean, ed. see Edgeworth, Maria.

Ni, Daoshing. Crane-Style Chi Gong & Its Therapeutic Effects. (Illus.). 68p. (Orig.). 1984. pap. 10.95 (*0-937064-10-6*) SevenStar Comm.

Ni Dhomhnaill, Nuala. Selected Poems/Rogha Danta. Hartnett, Michael, tr. & intro. by. LC 88-51546. (ENG & IRI.). 159p. (Orig.). 1988. pap. 14.95 (*1-85186-027-4*) Dufour.

Ni Dhomhnaill, Nwala. The Astrakhan Cloak. Muldoon, Paul, tr. from IRI. 103p. 1997. reprint ed. pap. text 10.00 (*0-7881-5094-4*) DIANE Pub.

Ni Dhuibhne, Eilis. The Bray House. (Orig.). (C). 1989. pap. 39.00 (*0-946211-96-5*) St Mut.

Ni Dhuibhne, Eilis, et al. Blackstaff Book of Short Stories. 160p. 1989. pap. 14.95 (*0-85640-399-7*, Pub. by Blackstaff Pr) Dufour.

Ni Dhuibhne, Ellis. The Inland Ice & Other Stories. LC 97-213084. 208p. 1997. pap. 16.95 (*0-85640-596-5*; Pub. by Blackstaff Pr) Dufour.

Ni Dhuibhne, Ellis, ed. Voices on the Wind: Women Poets of the Celtic Twilight. 144p. (Orig.). 1995. pap. 13.95 (*1-874597-23-5*, Pub. by New Island Books) Irish Bks Media.

Ni Eidhin, Deirdre, tr. see Godon, Bernard & Boudreau, Armand, eds.

Ni Ghlinn, Aine. Unshed Tears: Deora Nar Caoineadh. LC 97-117951. 80p. 1997. 24.95 (*1-873790-68-6*); pap. 12.95 (*1-873790-67-8*) Dufour.

Ni, Hu-Ching. Concourse of All Spiritual Paths. LC 92-56897. 184p. (Orig.). 1995. pap. 15.95 (*0-937064-61-0*) SevenStar Comm.

— The Gate to Infinity: Realizing Your Ultimate Potential. LC 93-13692. 1995. pap. 13.95 (*0-937064-68-8*) SevenStar Comm.

Ni, Hua C. The Power of Positive Living: The Opportunity of a Lifetime. (Course for Total Health Ser.). 1996. pap. 8.50 (*0-937064-90-4*) SevenStar Comm.

— The Universal Path of Natural Life. LC 95-36374. (Course for Total Health Ser.). 1996. pap. 9.50 (*0-937064-76-9*) SevenStar Comm.

Ni, Hua-Ching. Ageless Counsel for Modern Life: Profound Commentaries on the I Ching by an Achieved Taoist Master. LC 91-53212. 256p. (Orig.). 1992. pap. 15.95 (*0-937064-50-5*) SevenStar Comm.

— Attaining Unlimited Life: Teachings of Chuang Tzu. LC 88-63990. 467p. (Orig.). 1989. 25.00 (*0-937064-23-8*) SevenStar Comm.

— Book of Changes & the Unchanging Truth. 2nd rev. ed. LC 95-149. (Illus.). 669p. 1995. reprint ed. 35.00 (*0-937064-81-5*) SevenStar Comm.

Ni Hua Ching. Eight Thousand Years of Wisdom: Conversations with Taoist Master Ni, Hua Ching, Bk. 1. LC 83-51082. 248p. (Orig.). (C). 1983. pap. text 18.50 (*0-937064-07-6*) SevenStar Comm.

— Eight Thousand Years of Wisdom: Conversations with Taoist Master Ni, Hua Ching, Bk. 2. LC 83-51082. 248p. (Orig.). 1983. pap. text 12.50 (*0-937064-08-4*) SevenStar Comm.

Ni, Hua-Ching. Enlightenment: Mother of Spiritual Independence: Teachings of Hui Neng. LC 88-63988. 264p. (Orig.). 1989. 22.00 (*0-937064-22-X*) SevenStar Comm.

— Enlightenment: Mother of Spiritual Independence: Teachings of Hui Neng. LC 88-63988. 264p. (Orig.). 1989. pap. 12.50 (*0-937064-19-X*) SevenStar Comm.

— Entering the Tao: Master Ni's Guidance for Self-Cultivation. LC 96-36971. 160p. 1997. pap. 13.00 (*1-57062-161-6*, Pub. by Shambhala Pubns) Random.

— The Esoteric Tao Teh Ching. rev. ed. 192p. (Orig.). 1995. reprint ed. pap. 13.95 (*0-937064-49-1*) SevenStar Comm.

— Essence of Universal Spirituality. LC 90-60962. 282p. (Orig.). 1990. pap. 19.95 (*0-937064-35-1*) SevenStar Comm.

— Eternal Light. LC 90-62782. (Esoteric Teachings of the Tradition of Tao Ser.: Bk. 3). 208p. (Orig.). 1991. pap. 14.95 (*0-937064-38-6*) SevenStar Comm.

— The Gentle Path of Spiritual Progress. rev. ed. LC 90-61066. 288p. 1990. pap. 12.95 (*0-937064-33-5*) SevenStar Comm.

Ni Hua Ching. Guide to Inner Light. LC 90-60825. 168p. 1990. pap. text 12.95 (*0-937064-30-0*) SevenStar Comm.

Ni, Hua-Ching. Guide to Your Total Well-Being. (Self Development Ser.). (Orig.). 1994. pap. 4.00 (*0-937064-78-5*) SevenStar Comm.

— Integral Nutrition. (Healthy Living Ser.). 32p. (Orig.). 1995. pap. 3.00 (*0-937064-84-X*) SevenStar Comm.

— Internal Growth Through Tao. LC 90-60824. 208p. (Orig.). 1991. pap. 13.95 (*0-937064-27-0*) SevenStar Comm.

— The Key to Good Fortune: Refining Your Spirit. 144p. (Orig.). 1991. pap. 12.95 (*0-937064-39-4*) SevenStar Comm.

— Less Stress, More Happiness. (Healthy Living Ser.). 32p. (Orig.). 1994. pap. 3.00 (*0-937064-55-6*) SevenStar Comm.

— The Light of All Stars Illuminates the Way. (Self-Development Ser.). 56p. (Orig.). 1994. pap. 4.00 (*0-937064-80-7*) SevenStar Comm.

— The Mystical Universal Mother: The Teachings of Mother of Yellow Altar. LC 90-60709. 210p. (Orig.). 1992. pap. 14.95 (*0-937064-45-9*) SevenStar Comm.

— Nurture Your Spirits. LC 90-60827. 176p. 1991. pap. 12.95 (*0-937064-32-7*) SevenStar Comm.

— The Power of Natural Healing. LC 90-60823. 232p. (Orig.). 1991. pap. 14.95 (*0-937064-31-9*) SevenStar Comm.

— Progress along the Way: Life, Service & Realization. (Self Development Ser.). (Orig.). 1994. pap. 4.00 (*0-937064-79-3*) SevenStar Comm.

— Quest of Soul. LC 89-64093. (Esoteric Teachings of the Tradition of Tao Ser.: Bk. 2). 152p. (Orig.). 1991. pap. 11.95 (*0-937064-26-2*) SevenStar Comm.

— Self-Reliance & Constructive Change: The Declaration of Spiritual Independence. LC 95-10463. (Course for Total Health Ser.). 1995. pap. 7.00 (*0-937064-85-8*) SevenStar Comm.

— Spiritual Messages of a Buffalo Rider, a Man of Tao. rev. ed. LC 90-60963. 240p. 1990. pap. 12.95 (*0-937064-34-3*) SevenStar Comm.

— Stepping Stones for Spiritual Success. LC 89-64020. 160p. (Orig.). 1990. pap. 12.95 (*0-937064-25-4*) SevenStar Comm.

— The Story of Two Kingdoms. LC 88-93051. (Esoteric Teachings of the Tradition of Tao Ser.: Bk. 1). 122p. 1989. 14.95 (*0-937064-24-6*) SevenStar Comm.

— Strength from Movement: Mastering Chi. LC 93-40503. (Illus.). 256p. (Orig.). 1994. pap. 17.95 (*0-937064-73-4*) SevenStar Comm.

— Tao Teh Ching. Sanchez-Piltz, Mark & Barrero, Olga V., trs. (SPA.). 112p. (Orig.). 1995. pap. 8.95 (*0-937064-92-0*) SevenStar Comm.

— The Taoist Inner View of the Universe & the Immortal Realm. LC 79-92389. (Illus.). 218p. (Orig.). 1979. pap. text 14.95 (*0-937064-02-5*) SevenStar Comm.

— The Time Is Now for a Better Life & a Better World. LC 92-50854. 136p. (Orig.). 1993. pap. 10.95 (*0-937064-63-7*) SevenStar Comm.

— The Way of Integral Life. LC 88-63991. 408p. (Orig.). 1989. 20.00 (*0-937064-21-1*); pap. 14.00 (*0-937064-20-3*) SevenStar Comm.

— The Way, the Truth & the Light. LC 92-50543. 232p. (Orig.). 1994. pap. 14.95 (*0-937064-56-4*) SevenStar Comm.

N

An Asterisk (*) at the beginning of an entry indicates that the title is appearing for the first time.

— Workbook for Spiritual Development of All People. rev. ed. LC 92-13036. 240p. 1992. pap. 14.95 (*0-937064-54-8*) SevenStar Comm.

Ni, Hua-Ching, tr. The Complete Works of Lao Tzu: Tao Teh Ching & Hua Hu Ching. LC 90-62782. 212p. 1997. reprint ed. pap. 13.95 (*0-937064-00-9*) SevenStar Comm.

Ni, Hua-Chung. Heavenly Way. LC 81-50158. (Illus.). 41p. (Orig.). 1981. pap. text 2.50 (*0-937064-03-3*) SevenStar Comm.

***Ni, Liangkang.** Seinsglaube in der Phanomenologie Edmund Husserls. 296p. 1999. 144.00 (*0-7923-5779-5*) Kluwer Academic.

***Ni, Lionel & Znati, Taieb F., eds.** Communication Networks & Distributed Systems Modeling & Simulation (CNDS '97) Held in Phoenix, Arizona - January, 1997. 183p. 1998. pap. 80.00 (*1-56555-108-7*, CNDS-97) Soc Computer Sim.

— Communication Networks & Distributed Systems Modeling & Simulation 1998. 178p. 1998. 40.00 (*1-56555-141-9*) Soc Computer Sim.

— Communication Networks & Distributed Systems Modeling & Simulation 1999: CNDS '99. 216p. 1999. pap. 80.00 (*1-56555-159-1*) Soc Computer Sim.

Ni, Maoshing. The Yellow Emperor's Classic of Medicine: A New Translation of the Neijing Suwen with Commentary. 1995. pap. 19.95 (*1-57062-080-6*, Pub. by Shambhala Pubns) Random.

Ni, Maoshing & McNease, Cathy. The Tao of Nutrition. expanded ed. LC 93-7783. 264p. 1993. pap. 14.95 (*0-937064-66-1*) SevenStar Comm.

Ni, W. M., et al, eds. Nonlinear Diffusion Equations & Their Equilibrium States 1. (Mathematical Sciences Research Institute Publications: Vol. 12). (Illus.). 350p. 1988. 63.95 (*0-387-96771-0*) Spr-Verlag.

— Nonlinear Diffusion Equations & Their Equilibrium States 2. (Mathematical Sciences Research Institute Publications: Vol. 13). (Illus.). 350p. 1988. 63.95 (*0-387-96772-9*) Spr-Verlag.

Ni, Wei-Ming, et al, eds. Degenerate Diffusions: Proceedings of the IMA Workshop "Degenerate Diffusions" Held at the University of Minnesota from May 13-18, 1991. LC 93-10431. (IMA Volumes in Mathematics & Its Applications Ser.: Vol. 47). 1993. 69.95 (*0-387-94068-5*) Spr-Verlag.

Nia-Azariah, Kinshasha, et al. A Year of SCRC: 35 Experiential Workshops for the Classroom: A Manual for the Program Students' Creative Response to Conflict. (Illus.). 119p. 1992. 25.00 (*1-891955-00-4*) Creative Resp.

Niacais & Bollens Staff. Labour Market Programs for the Poor in Europe. 160p. 1995. 68.95 (*1-85972-181-8*) Ashgate Pub Co.

NIAID Staff. Sexually Transmitted Diseases: A Practical Guide. Banis, Robert J., ed. LC 97-62235. (Illus.). 140p. 1997. pap. 16.95 (*1-888725-06-0*) Sci & Human Pr.

Niaki, Shahzad & Broscious, John A. Underground Tank Leak Detection Methods. LC 86-31159. (Pollution Technology Review Ser.: No. 139). (Illus.). 123p. 1987. 36.00 (*0-8155-1117-5*) Noyes.

— Underground Tank Leak Detection Methods: A State-of-the-Art Review. 136p. 1988. 55.95 (*0-89116-098-1*) Hemisp Pub.

Niall, Brenda. Georgiana: A Biography of Georgiana McCrae, Painter, Diarist, Pioneer. LC 94-231656. (Miegunyah Press Ser.: No. 1:18). (Illus.). 368p. 1995. 39.95 (*0-522-84513-4*, Pub. by Melbourne Univ Pr) Paul & Co Pubs.

— Georgiana: A Biography of Georgiana McCrae, Painter, Diarist, Pioneer. 368p. 1997. pap. 24.95 (*0-522-84743-9*, Pub. by Melbourne Univ Pr) Paul & Co Pubs.

— Martin Boyd: A Life. 24p. 1989. reprint ed. pap. 19.95 (*0-522-84400-6*, Pub. by Melbourne Univ Pr) Paul & Co Pubs.

Niall, Brenda & Thompson, John. Oxford Book of Australian Letters. LC 98-198961. 336p. 1999. 35.00 (*0-19-553985-0*) OUP.

Niall, Ian. English Country Traditions. (Hoc Voco Ser.). 80p. 1991. 30.00 (*0-87923-870-4*) Godine.

Niall, Mani. Sweet & Natural Baking: Sugar-Free, Flavorful Recipes from Mani's Bakery. LC 96-100. (Illus.). 132p. 1996. pap. 17.95 (*0-8118-1049-6*) Chronicle Bks.

Niall, Michael. Bad Day at Black Rock. 18.95 (*0-8488-0107-5*) Amereon Ltd.

Nials, Fred, et al. Chacoan Roads in the Southern Periphery: Results of Phase II of the BLM Chaco Roads Project. No. 1. (Illus.). 214p. (Orig.). 1987. pap. write for info. (*0-318-68062-9*) Bureau of Land Mgmt NM.

***Niamir-Fuller, Maryam.** Managing Mobility in African Rangelands: The Legitimization of Transhumance. 240p. 1999. pap. 29.95 (*1-85339-473-4*, Pub. by Intermed Tech) Stylus Pub VA.

Niane, D. T., ed. see UNESCO Staff.

Niang. Pulaar-English - English-Pulaar Standard Dictionary. LC 97-24082. 450p. (Orig.). 1997. pap. 24.95 (*0-7818-0479-5*) Hippocrene Bks.

Niang, Mamadou O. Constraints on Pulaar Phonology. LC 96-45200. 170p. 1997. text 34.50 (*0-7618-0611-3*) U Pr of Amer.

Nias, A. H. Clinical Radiobiology. 2nd ed. (Illus.). 304p. 1989. text 122.00 (*0-443-03340-4*) Church.

— An Introduction to Radiobiology. 2nd ed. LC 97-42811. 400p. 1998. pap. 64.95 (*0-471-97590-7*) Wiley.

Nias, Hilary. The Artificial Self: The Psychology of Hippolyte Taine. (Legenda Ser.). (Orig.). pap. 49.50 (*1-900755-18-1*) E H R C.

Nias, Jennifer. Seeing Anew: Teachers Theories of Action. (C). 1995. pap. 28.00 (*0-7300-0448-1*, Pub. by Deakin Univ) St Mut.

Nias, Jennifer, ed. The Human Nature of Learning: Selections from the Work of M. L. J. Abercrombie. LC 93-13277. 160p. 1993. 123.00 (*0-335-09334-5*); pap. 39.95 (*0-335-09333-7*) OpUniv Pr.

— Teacher Socialisation: The Individual in the System. 151p. (C). 1986. 60.00 (*0-7300-0399-X*, Pub. by Deakin Univ) St Mut.

Nias, Jennifer & Groundwater-Smith, Susan, eds. The Enquiring Teacher. 200p. 1988. 75.00 (*1-85000-295-9*, Falmer Pr); pap. 37.95 (*1-85000-296-7*, Falmer Pr) Taylor & Francis.

Nias, Jennifer & Southworth, Geoff. Whole School Curriculum: Development in the Primary School. 270p. 1992. 85.00 (*0-7507-0064-5*, Falmer Pr); pap. 34.95 (*0-7507-0065-3*, Falmer Pr) Taylor & Francis.

Nias, Jennifer, jt. ed. see Biott, Colin.

Niatum, Duane. The Crooked Beak of Love. 72p. 1999. pap. 8.95 (*0-931122-96-1*) West End.

— Drawings of the Song Animals: New & Selected Poems. 136p. 1991. 18.95 (*0-930100-43-3*); pap. 10.95 (*0-930100-44-1*) Holy Cow.

Niatum, Duane, ed. Harper's Anthology of Twentieth Century Native American Poetry. LC 86-45023. 432p. (Orig.). 1988. pap. 24.00 (*0-06-250666-8*, Pub. by Harper SF) HarpC.

Niazi, A. A. The Betrayal of East Pakistan. LC 98-159476. (Illus.). 354p. (C). 1998. text 29.95 (*0-19-577727-1*) OUP.

Niazi, Amir Abdullah Khan. The Betrayal of East Pakistan. LC 98-905085. xxxi, 321 p. 1998. write for info. (*81-7304-256-X*) Manohar.

Niazi, Kausar. Iqbal & the Third World. 40p. (Orig.). 1988. pap. 3.00 (*1-56744-298-6*) Kazi Pubns.

— Zulfiqar Ali Bhutto of Pakistan: The Last Days. (Illus.). 244p. (C). 1992. text 27.50 (*0-685-56704-4*, Pub. by Vikas) S Asia.

Niazi, Zamir. The Web of Censorship. (Illus.). 256p. 1995. text 26.00 (*0-19-577543-0*) OUP.

Nibb, Stephen R. War, Diplomacy, & Development: The United States & Mexico, 1938-1954. Beezley, William H. & Ewell, Judith, eds. (Latin American Silhouettes Ser.). (Illus.). 320p. 1995. 50.00 (*0-8420-2550-2*) Scholarly Res Inc.

Nibeck, Cecilia. Alaska Shrimp & Crab Recipes. (Cooking in Alaska Ser.). (Illus.). 240p. (Orig.). 1996. spiral bd. 12.95 (*0-9622117-4-5*) AK Anchorage.

— Alaskan Halibut Recipes. (Illus.). 200p. 1989. spiral bd. 12.95 (*0-9622117-0-2*) AK Anchorage.

— Moose & Caribou from Alaska. (Illus.). 182p. 1992. spiral bd. 12.95 (*0-9622117-3-7*) AK Anchorage.

— Salmon Recipes from Alaska. (Illus.). 190p. 1987. spiral bd. 12.95 (*0-9622117-1-0*) AK Anchorage.

Nibeck, Richard G., intro. Learning with Microcomputers: Readings from Instructional Innovator-5. 80p. 1983. pap. 10.95 (*0-89240-042-0*) Assn Ed Comm Tech.

Nibert, David. Hitting the Lottery Jackpot: State Governments & the Taxing of Dreams. 1999. pap. 16.00 (*1-58367-014-9*, Pub. by Monthly Rev) NYU Pr.

***Nibert, David.** Hitting the Lottery Jackpot: State Governments & the Taxing of Dreams. 144p. 1999. 48.00 (*1-58367-013-0*, Pub. by Monthly Rev) NYU Pr.

Niblack, Preston, et al. Increasing the Availability & Effectiveness of Non-U. S. Forces for Peace Operations. 60p. 1996. pap. 15.00 (*0-8330-2371-3*, MR-701) Rand Corp.

Niblack, W., jt. ed. see Jamberdino, A. A.

Nibler, F., et al. High-Frequency Circuit Engineering. (Circuits & Systems Ser.: No. 6). 428p. 1995. boxed set 102.00 (*0-85296-801-9*, CS006) INSPEC Inc.

— High-Frequency Circuits. (I. E. E. Circuits & Systems Ser.: No. 6). 428p. 1995. pap. 48.00 (*0-85296-802-7*, CS006Z) INSPEC Inc.

Niblett, John. Disclosure in Criminal Proceedings. 316p. 1997. pap. 54.00 (*1-85431-598-6*, Pub. by Blackstone Pr) Gaunt.

***Niblett, Robin & Wallace, William.** Rethinking European Order. LC 00-41515. 2000. write for info. (*0-333-91571-2*) Macmillan.

Niblett, William R. Education, the Lost Dimension. LC 73-108845. 150p. 1970. reprint ed. lib. bdg. 55.00 (*0-8371-3735-7*, NIED, Greenwood Pr) Greenwood.

Niblett, William R., ed. Higher Education: Demand & Response. LC 71-110637. (Jossey-Bass Higher Education Ser.). 286p. reprint ed. pap. 88.70 (*0-608-30920-6*, 201382100087) Bks Demand.

Nibley, Hugh. The Ancient State: The Rulers & the Ruled. LC 91-8004. (Collected Works of Hugh Nibley: Vol. 10). 515p. 1991. 26.95 (*0-87579-375-4*) Deseret Bk.

— An Approach to the Book of Mormon. 3rd ed. LC 88-3585. (Collected Works of Hugh Nibley: Vol. 6). xvii, 541p. 1988. 27.95 (*0-87579-138-7*) Deseret Bk.

— Approaching Zion. LC 89-38824. (Collected Works of Hugh Nibley: Vol. 9). 631p. 1989. 24.95 (*0-87579-252-9*) Deseret Bk.

— Brother Brigham Challenges the Saints. Norton, Don E. & Ricks, Shirley S., eds. LC 93-38393. (Collected Works of Hugh Nibley: Vol. 13). xv, 541p. 1994. 23.95 (*0-87579-818-7*) Deseret Bk.

— Enoch the Prophet. LC 86-11437. (Collected Works of Hugh Nibley: Vol. 2). viii, 309p. 1986. 23.95 (*0-87579-047-X*) Deseret Bk.

— Lehi in the Desert & the World of the Jaredites. 9.95 (*0-88494-022-5*) Bookcraft Inc.

— Lehi in the Desert & There Were Jaredites. LC 87-32941. (Collected Works of Hugh Nibley). xviii, 464p. 1988. reprint ed. 26.95 (*0-87579-132-8*) Deseret Bk.

— Mormonism & Early Christianity. LC 87-25291. (Collected Works of Hugh Nibley: Vol. 4). 446p. 1987. 25.95 (*0-87579-127-1*) Deseret Bk.

— Of All Things: Classic Quotations from Hugh Nibley. LC 93-6508. xii, 292p. 1993. pap. 12.95 (*0-87579-678-8*) Deseret Bk.

— Old Testament & Related Studies. LC 85-27544. (Collected Works of Hugh Nibley: Vol. 1). xiv, 290p. 1986. 24.95 (*0-87579-032-1*) Deseret Bk.

— The Prophetic Book of Mormon. LC 88-30986. (Collected Works of Hugh Nibley: Vol. 8). xi, 595p. 1989. 26.95 (*0-87579-179-4*) Deseret Bk.

— Since Cumorah: The Book of Mormon. LC 88-3862. (Collected Works of Hugh Nibley: Vol. 7). xv, 512p. 1988. 25.95 (*0-87579-139-5*) Deseret Bk.

— Temple & Cosmos. LC 91-33320. (Collected Works of Hugh Nibley: Vol. 12). 597p. 1992. 26.95 (*0-87579-523-4*) Deseret Bk.

— Tinkling Cymbals & Sounding Brass: The Art of Telling Tales about Joseph Smith & Brigham Young. LC 91-11539. (Collected Works of Hugh Nibley: Vol. 11). xxii, 741p. 1991. 29.95 (*0-87579-516-1*) Deseret Bk.

— The World & the Prophets: Mormonism & Early Christianity. LC 87-620. (Collected Works of Hugh Nibley: Vol. 3). xii, 333p. 1987. 23.95 (*0-87579-078-X*) Deseret Bk.

***Nibley, Hugh & Gillum, Gary P.** Abraham in Egypt 2nd ed. LC 99-24106. (Collected Works of Hugh Nibley Ser.). 1999. write for info. (*1-57345-527-X*) Deseret Bk.

Nibley, Preston, compiled by. Three Mormon Classics. deluxe ed. 11.95 (*0-88494-049-7*) Bookcraft Inc.

Nibley, Reid, jt. auth. see Anderson, Richard P.

Niblo, Graham & Roller, Martin, eds. Geometric Group Theory, Vol. 1. (London Mathematical Society Lecture Note Ser.: No. 181). (Illus.). 222p. (C). 1993. pap. text 42.95 (*0-521-43529-3*) Cambridge U Pr.

— Geometric Group Theory, Vol. 2. (London Mathematical Society Lecture Note Ser.: No. 182). (Illus.). 303p. (C). 1993. pap. text 42.95 (*0-521-44680-5*) Cambridge U Pr.

***Niblo, Stephen R.** Mexico in the 1940s: Modernity, Politics & Corruption. LC 99-28870. (Latin American Silhouettes Ser.). 1999. 55.00 (*0-8420-2794-7*) Scholarly Res Inc.

Niblock, Tim. Class & Power in Sudan: The Dynamics of Sudanese Politics, 1898-1985. LC 86-23059. 370p. (C). 1987. pap. text 21.95 (*0-88706-481-7*) State U NY Pr.

Niblock, Timothy C. & Murphy, Emma, eds. Economic Liberalization in the Middle East. 288p. (C). 1993. text 69.50 (*1-85043-600-2*, Pub. by I B T) St Martin.

Nic Craith, Mairead, et al. Watching One's Tongue: Aspects of Romance & Celtic Languages. LC 97-219053. (Liverpool Studies in European Regional Cultures Ser.). xii, 260p. 1996. write for info. (*0-85323-621-6*) Liverpool Univ Pr.

Nica, Traian, tr. see Smarandache, Florentin.

Nicaise. Poverty & Human Capital. 67.95 (*1-84014-533-1*) Ashgate Pub Co.

Nicaise, Auguste. A Year in the Desert. 125p. 1980. 19.95 (*0-87770-237-3*) Ye Galleon.

Nicaise, Placide N. Children of the Lily. LC 97-91973. (Illus.). iv, 290p. (Orig.). 1997. pap. 10.00 (*0-9658596-0-6*) Nicaise Publ.

— Requiem for the Lily. LC 99-93081. 320p. 1999. pap. 15.00 (*0-9658596-1-4*) Nicaise Publ.

Nicaise, Serge. Polygonal Interface Problems. LC 93-30137. (Methoden und Verfahren der Mathematischen Physik Ser.: Bd. 39). (Illus.). 250p. 1993. 49.00 (*3-631-46380-4*) P Lang Pubng.

Nicander. The Poems & Poetical Fragments. Connor, W. R., ed. LC 78-18579. (Greek Texts & Commentaries Ser.). (Illus.). 1979. reprint ed. lib. bdg. 23.95 (*0-405-11422-2*) Ayer.

Nicandri, David L. Italians in Washington State. LC 77-81592. (Illus.). 71p. 1978. pap. 6.00 (*0-917048-08-3*) Wash St Hist Soc.

Nicandrus. Nicandri Colophonii Carminum. Bernabe, Albertus, ed. write for info. (*0-318-70986-4*) G Olms Pubs.

Nicarthy, Ginny. Getting Free: You Can End Abuse & Take Back Your Life. 2nd enl. ed. LC 86-3774. (New Leaf Ser.). 352p. (Orig.). 1986. pap. 12.95 (*0-931188-37-7*) Seal Pr WA.

— Getting Free: You Can End Abuse & Take Back Your Life. 3rd rev. ed. LC 89-77263. 352p. (Orig.). 1997. pap. 12.95 (*1-878067-92-3*) Seal Pr WA.

NiCarthy, Ginny. The Ones Who Got Away: Women Who Left Abusive Partners. LC 87-20470. (New Leaf Ser.). 329p. (Orig.). 1987. pap. 12.95 (*0-931188-49-0*) Seal Pr WA.

NiCarthy, Ginny & Davidson, Sue. You Can Be Free: An Easy-to-Read Handbook for Abused Women. (New Leaf Ser.). (Illus.). 120p. (Orig.). 1997. pap. 10.95 (*1-878067-06-0*) Seal Pr WA.

NiCarthy, Ginny, et al. Talking It Out: A Guide to Groups for Abused Women. LC 84-23494. (New Leaf Ser.). 165p. (Orig.). 1984. pap. 12.95 (*0-931188-24-5*) Seal Pr WA.

— You Don't Have to Take It! A Woman's Guide to Confronting Emotional Abuse at Work. LC 93-12873. (New Leaf Ser.). 397p. (Orig.). 1993. pap. 14.95 (*1-878067-35-4*) Seal Pr WA.

Nicas, Andrew J. Induction Theorems for Groups of Homotopy Manifold Structures. LC 82-11546. (Memoirs of the American Mathematical Society Ser.: No. 39/267). 108p. 1982. pap. 16.00 (*0-8218-2267-5*, MEMO/39/267) Am Math.

Nicas, Andrew J. & Shadwick, W. F., eds. Differential Geometry, Global Analysis, & Topology. LC 92-5152. (Conference Proceedings, Canadian Mathematical Society Ser.: Vol. 12). 185p. 1992. pap. 50.00 (*0-8218-6017-8*, CMSAMS/12) Am Math.

***Nicaso, Antonio & Lamothe, Lee.** Global Mafia: The New World Order of Organized Crime. 203p. 2000. reprint ed. text 28.00 (*0-7881-6818-5*) DIANE Pub.

Nicassio, Perry M. & Smith, Timothy W., eds. Managing Chronic Illness: A Biopsychosocial Perspective. LC 95-17909. (Application & Practice in Health Psychology Ser.). 425p. 1995. text 29.95 (*1-55798-300-3*) Am Psychol.

Nicassio, Susan V. Tosca's Rome: The Play & the Opera in Historical Perspective. LC 99-19417. (Illus.). 346p. 2000. lib. bdg. 45.00 (*0-226-57971-9*) U Ch Pr.

Nicastro, Anthony J. Laboratory Astronomy: Experiments & Exercises. 208p. (C). 1989. text. write for info. (*0-697-08475-2*, WCB McGr Hill) McGrw-H Hghr Educ.

***Nicastro, Brent.** Madison. LC 99-32507. (ENG, GER & SPA., Illus.). 112p. 1999. 14.95 (*1-879483-63-7*) Prairie Oak Pr.

Nicastro, D. H., ed. Science & Technology of Building Seals, Sealants, Glazing, & Waterproofing, Vol. 4. 149p. 1995. pap. 48.00 (*0-8031-2008-7*, STP1243) ASTM.

Nicastro, David H., ed. Failure Mechanisms in Building Construction. LC 97-25452. (Illus.). 116p. 1997. pap. text 36.00 (*0-7844-0283-3*, 40283-3) Am Soc Civil Eng.

Nicastro, Nicholas & Bolinger, Paul. The Eighteenth Captain: A Novel of John Paul Jones. LC 99-19233. 312p. 1999. pap. 14.95 (*0-935526-54-4*) McBooks Pr.

Niccol, Andrew, frwd. The Truman Show: The Shooting Script. LC 99-48497. (Shooting Script Ser.). (Illus.). 144p. 1998. pap. 16.95 (*1-55704-367-1*, Pub. by Newmarket) Norton.

Niccolai, Giulia. Substitution: Bilingual Edition. Vangelisti, Paul, tr. 1975. per. 2.50 (*0-88031-020-0*) Invisible-Red Hill.

Niccolai, Giulia, tr. see Spatola, Adriano.

Niccoli, Gabriel. Cupid, Satyr & the Golden Age: Pastoral Dramatic Scences of the Late Renaissance. 246p. (C). 1989. text 36.95 (*0-8204-0783-6*) P Lang Pubng.

Niccoli, Ottavia. Prophecy & People in Renaissance Italy. Cochrane, Lydia G., tr. from ITA. (Illus.). 214p. (C). 1990. pap. text 16.95 (*0-691-00835-3*, Pub. by Princeton U Pr) Cal Prin Full Svc.

Niccoli, Ria. Pembroke Welsh Corgis. (Illus.). 1996. pap. 9.95 (*0-7938-2333-1*, KW176S) TFH Pubns.

***Niccoli, Riccardo.** American Eagles: The Greatest Photographs of the USAF. (Illus.). 2000. 12.99 (*0-7858-1190-7*) Bk Sales Inc.

Niccols, Richard. Beggars Ape. LC 37-5555. 48p. 1980. reprint ed. 50.00 (*0-8201-1178-3*) Schol Facsimiles.

— Expicedium. a Funeral Oration, Upon the Late Deceased Princesse, Elizabeth, Queen of England. LC 71-26332. (English Experience Ser.: No. 172). 24p. 1969. reprint ed. 25.00 (*90-221-0172-X*) Walter J. Johnson.

— Sir Thomas Overbury's Vision (1616) & Other English Sources of Nathaniel Hawthorne's "The Scarlet Letter." LC 57-6417. 224p. 1979. 50.00 (*0-8201-1239-9*) Schol Facsimiles.

Nice. Speaking for Impact: Connecting with Every Audience. 167p. 1998. pap. text 14.95 (*0-205-27025-5*) P-H.

Nice, jt. auth. see Brooksbank.

Nice, Claudia. Creating Textures in Pen & Ink with Watercolor. LC 95-12916. (Illus.). 144p. 1995. 28.99 (*0-89134-595-7*, North Lght Bks) F & W Pubns Inc.

— Drawing in Pen & Ink. LC 96-52947. (First Steps Ser.). (Illus.). 128p. 1997. pap. 18.99 (*0-89134-717-8*, North Lght Bks) F & W Pubns Inc.

— Journey of Memories. 44p. 1986. pap. text 6.50 (*1-56770-166-3*) S Scheewe Pubns.

— Painting Nature in Pen & Ink with Watercolor. LC 98-12672. (Illus.). 128p. 1998. 27.99 (*0-89134-813-1*, North Lght Bks) F & W Pubns Inc.

***Nice, Claudia.** Painting Weathered Buildings in Pen, Ink & Watercolor. LC 99-45766. (Illus.). 144p. 2000. 28.99 (*0-89134-917-0*, North Lght Bks) F & W Pubns Inc.

Nice, Claudia. Scenes from Seasons Past. 96p. 1988. pap. text 10.50 (*1-56770-183-3*) S Scheewe Pubns.

— Sketching Your Favorite Subjects in Pen & Ink. (Illus.). 144p. 1993. 22.99 (*0-89134-472-1*, 30473, North Lght Bks) F & W Pubns Inc.

— A Taste of Summer. 96p. 1990. pap. text 10.50 (*1-56770-223-6*) S Scheewe Pubns.

Nice, David. Peter Ilyich Tchaikovsky. (Classic FM Lifelines Ser.). 112p. 1997. pap. 9.95 (*1-86205-043-0*, Pub. by Pavilion Bks Ltd) Trafalgar.

— Richard Strauss: Illustrated Lives of the Great Composers. (Illustrated Lives of the Great Composers Ser.). (Illus.). 160p. 1996. 17.95 (*0-7119-1686-1*, OP 45038) Omnibus NY.

Nice, David C. Amtrak: The History & Politics of a National Railroad. LC 97-37756. (Explorations in Public Policy Ser.). 119p. 1998. lib. bdg. 39.95 (*1-55587-734-6*) L Rienner.

— Policy Innovation in State Government. LC 93-24017. 182p. (C). 1993. text 54.95 (*0-8138-0658-5*) Iowa St U Pr.

Nice, David C., et al, eds. Government & Politics in the Evergreen State. LC 92-8476. (Illus.). 215p. (C). 1992. 18.95 (*0-87422-085-8*) Wash St U Pr.

Nice, David C. & Fredericksen, Patricia. The Politics of Intergovernmental Relations. 2nd ed. LC 94-15923. 1995. pap. text 32.95 (*0-8304-1357-X*) Thomson Learn.

Nice, Graeme, jt. auth. see Emmett, David.

Nice, James W. Putman's Digital Electronics: Lac Manual. (Illus.). 144p. 1986. pap. text 25.00 (*0-13-212549-8*) P-H.

Nice, Jill. Herbal Remedies: The Complete Guide to Natural Healing. 1996. pap. text 24.95 (*0-7499-1090-9*, Pub. by Piatkus Bks) London Brdge.

— Herbal Remedies for Healing: A Complete A-Z of Ailments & Treatments. (Illus.). 1999. pap. 16.95 (*0-7499-1840-3*, Pub. by Piatkus Bks) London Brdge.

— Jill Nice's Herbal Remedies & Home Comforts. (Illus.). 200p. (Orig.). 1996. pap. text 14.95 (*0-7499-1008-9*, Pub. by Piatkus Bks) London Brdge.

N

*Nice, Jill & Davies, Jill Rosemary. Aloe Vera: A Step-by-Step Guide. (In a Nutshell Ser.). 2000. 7.95 (1-86204-709-X, Pub. by Element MA) Penguin Putnam.

— Healing Herbs: Cranberry: A Step-by-Step Guide. (In a Nutshell Ser.). 2000. 7.95 (1-86204-707-3, Pub. by Element MA) Penguin Putnam.

— Milk Thistle: A Step-by-Step Guide. (In a Nutshell Ser.). 2000. 7.95 (1-86204-710-3, Pub. by Element MA) Penguin Putnam.

Nice, John R. Van, see Boyce, William.

Nice, Richard, tr. see Biardeau, Madeleine.

Nice, Richard, tr. see Bourdieu, Pierre.

Nice, Richard, tr. see Bourdieu, Pierre & Passeron, Jean-Claude.

Nice, Stephen D., jt. auth. see Hunter, Edna J.

***Nice, Terri.** Minute of Angle. (Illus.). 132p. 1999. pap. 11.95 (0-7414-0314-5) Buy Books.

Nice, Vivien E. Mothers & Daughters: The Distortion of a Relationship. 1996. 35.00 (0-333-52528-0, Pub. by Macmillan) St Martin.

Nicecoli, Tresa M. Aspen Embroidery No. 40-1040: An Artistic Expression of Poetry. (Illus.). 98p. 1996. reprint ed. pap. 18.95 (0-9660922-2-8) Wldflower Pr.

Niceforo, Alfredo. Kultur und Fortschritt im Spiegel der Zahlen: Culture & Progress in the Mirror of Figures. Schumann, Eva, tr. from GRE. LC 74-25772. 227p. 1975. reprint ed. 20.95 (0-405-06526-4) Ayer.

Nicel. Human Rights. Date not set. pap. text, teacher ed. 21.95 (0-314-06701-9) West Pub.

— Minnesota Supplement to Street Law. 51st ed. (HA - Social Studies). 1997. pap. 52.95 (0-314-22324-X) S-W Pub.

— Teens, Crime & the Community. 3rd ed. (HA - Social Studies). (C). 1998. mass mkt. 13.50 (0-314-20560-8) West Pub.

Nicell, Joan, ed. see Gyatso, Geshe J.

Nicell, Joan, tr. see Tulku, Gomo.

Nicely, Robert F., Jr., jt. ed. see Blume, Glendon W.

Nicephorus. Nicephori Archiepiscopi Constantinopolitani Opuscula Historica. De Boor, Carl G., ed. LC 75-7311. (Roman History Ser.). (GRE.). 1975. reprint ed. 28.95 (0-405-07193-0) Ayer.

Nicetas. Niceta of Remesiana: Sulpicius Severus, Vincent of Lerins, Prosper of Aquitaine: Grace & Free Will. Walsh, Gerald G. et al, trs. LC 50-5703. (Fathers of the Church Ser.: Vol. 7). 449p. 1970. reprint ed. pap. 139.20 (0-7837-9204-2, 204995400004) Bks Demand.

Nicewander, Merritt. Clean Air Act Permitting: A Guidance Manual. LC 95-3028. 1995. 69.95 (0-87814-441-2) PennWell Bks.

Nicgorski, Walter & Weber, Ronald, eds. An Almost Chosen People: The Moral Aspirations of Americans. LC 76-41343. 170p. reprint ed. pap. 52.70 (0-8357-5325-5, 202206200024) Bks Demand.

Nicgorski, Walter, jt. ed. see Deutsch, Kenneth L.

Nichelason, Margery G. Homeless or Helpless? LC 92-19675. (Pro - Con Ser.). (Illus.). 112p. (YA). (gr. 6 up). 1994. lib. bdg. 21.27 (0-8225-2606-9, Lerner Publctns) Lerner Pub.

— Shoes: Household History. LC 96-37459. 48p. (J). (gr. 3-6). 1997. 22.60 (1-57505-047-1, Carolrhoda) Lerner Pub.

Nichelatti, M. Topics on Diffusion in Emulsions. 152p. 1995. text 48.00 (981-02-1789-7) World Scientific Pub.

***Nichele, Franc.** Cuba. (Illus.). 1999. write for info. (3-8228-6997-X) Taschen Amer.

Nichele, Franc. Cuba. LC 00-299998. (Illus.). 160p. 1999. 19.99 (3-8228-7064-1) Taschen Amer.

Nichelmann, Christoph. Christoph Nichelmann: Clavier Concertos in E Major & A Major. Lee, Douglas A., ed. (Recent Researches in Music of the Classic Era Ser.: RRC6). (Illus.). xii, 113p. 1977. pap. 45.00 (0-89579-095-5, RRC6) A-R Eds.

Nichels, J. Two for the Road. 1988. 39.00 (0-7855-1054-0, Pub. by Regency Pr GBR) St Mut.

Nichels, William G., et al. Understanding Business. 4th ed. LC 95-22442. 1995. text. write for info. (0-256-19074-7, Irwn McGrw-H) McGrw-H Hghr Educ.

Nichelsburg, George W. Jewish Literature Between the Bible & Mishnah. LC 80-16176. 352p. (Orig.). 1981. pap. 27.00 (0-8006-1980-3, 1-1980, Fortress Pr) Augsburg Fortress.

Nichelson, Oliver. Tesla's Fuelless Generator & Wireless Method. v, 48p. (Orig.). 1993. pap. 9.95 (0-9636012-0-2) Twty Frst Cent.

NICHHD Workshop on the Testis Staff. Testicular Development, Structure, & Function. fac. ed. Steinberger, Anna & Steinberger, Emil, eds. LC 78-68530. (Illus.). 556p. pap. 172.40 (0-7837-7249-1, 204705600005) Bks Demand.

Nichil, P. Lexique Francais-Anglais et Anglais-Francais des Termes d'usage Courant En Hydraulique et Pneumatique. (ENG & FRE.). 42p. 1974. pap. 8.95 (0-686-56790-0, M-6426) Fr & Eur.

Nichils, James L. General Fitzhugh Lee: A Biography. (Virginia Civil War Battles & Leaders Ser.). (Illus.). 244p. 1989. 19.95 (0-930919-78-5) H E Howard.

***Nichiporuk, Brian.** Forecasting the Effects of Army XXI Design upon Multinational Force Compatability. (Illus.). vi, 45p. (C). 2000. pap. 6.00 (0-8330-2790-5, DB-279-A) Rand Corp.

— The Security Dynamics of Demographic Factors. (Illus.). xxi, 48p. (C). 1999. pap. 8.00 (0-8330-2780-8, MR1088WFHF/RF/A) Rand Corp.

Nichiporuk, Brian & Builder, Carl H. Information Technologies & the Future of Land Warfare. LC 95-41141. 100p. 1996. pap. text 15.00 (0-8330-2316-0, MR-560-A) Rand Corp.

Nichiren. The Awakening to the Truth. Ehara, N. R. et al, trs. from JPN. LC 83-45457. Orig. Title: Kaimokusho. 1983. reprint ed. 28.50 (0-404-20189-X) AMS Pr.

Nichiren Propagation Center Staff, ed. see Suguro, Shinjo.

Nichlaus, Jack & Bowden, Ken. Jack Nicklaus' Playing Lessons. 143p. 1983. 9.95 (0-671-49557-7) S&S Trade.

***Nichllos, A. J.** Weimar & the Rise of Hitler. 4th ed. 2000. text 59.95 (0-312-23350-7) St Martin.

Nichol. Love: A Book of Remembrances. 134p. pap. 14.95 (0-88922-038-7, Pub. by Talonbks) Genl Dist Srvs.

***Nichol.** Zygal: A Book of Mysteries & Translations. 128p. 2000. pap. 16.00 (1-55245-086-4, Pub. by Coach Hse Bks) SPD-Small Pr Dist.

Nichol, Andrew, jt. auth. see Dummett, Ann.

Nichol, B. P. Art Facts: A Book of Contexts. LC 89-667. (Illus.). 168p. (Orig.). (C). 1990. pap. 15.00 (0-925904-00-7) Chax Pr.

— An H in the Heart: A Reader. Ondaatje, Michael & Bowering, George, eds. 256p. 1994. pap. 19.99 (0-7710-6814-X) McCland & Stewart.

— Once: A Lullaby. (Illus.). 24p. (J). (ps-1). 1996. pap. write for info. (0-88753-105-9) Black Moss.

— Selected Writing: As Elected. LC 81-91050. 144p. 1980. pap. 12.95 (0-88922-176-6) Genl Dist Srvs.

Nichol, B. P., jt. auth. see McCaffery, Steve.

Nichol, Babara. Beethoven Lives Upstairs. LC 93-5774. (Illus.). 48p. (J). (gr. k-3). 1999. pap. 5.95 (0-531-07118-9) Orchard Bks Watts.

Nichol, Barbara. Beethoven Lives Upstairs. LC 93-5774. (Illus.). 48p. (J). (gr. k-3). 1994. 15.95 (0-531-06828-5) Orchard Bks Watts.

— Beethoven Lives Upstairs: Vive Arriba. 1996. pap. text 15.95 (1-56014-619-2) Santillana.

— Biscuits in the Cupboard. (Illus.). 32p. (J). (ps-3). 1999. pap. 6.95 (0-7737-5936-0) Genl Dist Srvs.

— Biscuits in the Cupboard. unabridged ed. LC 98-108606. (Illus.). 32p. (J). (ps-3). 1998. 12.95 (0-7737-3025-7) STDK.

— Dippers. LC 96-61695. (Illus.). 32p. (J). (gr. 4 up). 1997. 15.95 (0-88776-396-0) Tundra Bks.

Nichol, C. R. The Lord's Supper, Prayers, Thanksgiving. 1957. pap. 8.95 (0-915547-62-7) Abilene Christ U.

— Nichol Pocket Bible Encyclopedia. 1984. pap. 2.50 (0-915547-55-4) Abilene Christ U.

— Sound Doctrine, Vol. 1. 1984. pap. 6.95 (0-915547-57-0) Abilene Christ U.

— Sound Doctrine, Vol. 2. 1984. pap. 6.95 (0-915547-58-9) Abilene Christ U.

— Sound Doctrine, Vol. 3. 1984. pap. 6.95 (0-915547-59-7) Abilene Christ U.

— Sound Doctrine, Vol. 5. 1984. pap. 6.95 (0-915547-61-9) Abilene Christ U.

Nichol, Catherine, jt. auth. see Museley, David.

Nichol, Claudia, et al. Scattered: Like Chaff in the Wind. (Illus.). 340p. (Orig.). 1989. pap. 13.95 (0-9623121-0-X) CompuWords.

Nichol, Francis D. The Midnight Cry: A Defense of William Miller & the Millerites. LC 72-8249. reprint ed. 52.00 (0-404-11003-7) AMS Pr.

Nichol, Fred. An Odyssey of a Young Fighter Pilot. LC 96-60146. (Illus.). 236p. 1996. reprint ed. pap. 13.50 (1-882194-18-7) TN Valley Pub.

Nichol, Gene R., jt. auth. see Redish, Martin H.

***Nichol, H. Ernest.** Transposition at Sight for Students of the Organ & Pianoforte. 138p. 2000. reprint ed. lib. bdg. 59.00 (0-7812-9308-1) Rprt Serv.

Nichol, James P. Diplomacy in the Former Soviet Republics. LC 95-3353. 256p. 1995. 62.95 (0-275-95192-8, Praeger Pubs) Greenwood.

Nichol, James W. Sainte-Marie among the Hurons. 80p. 1980. reprint ed. pap. 10.95 (0-88922-147-2, Pub. by Talonbks) Genl Dist Srvs.

Nichol, John. American Literature: An Historical Sketch, 1620-1880. LC 77-39071. (Essay Index Reprint Ser.). 1977. reprint ed. 26.95 (0-8369-2706-0) Ayer.

— Byron. Morley, John, ed. LC 68-58390. (English Men of Letters Ser.). reprint ed. lib. bdg. 27.50 (0-404-51722-6) AMS Pr.

— Thomas Carlyle. Morley, John, ed. LC 68-58391. (English Men of Letters Ser.). reprint ed. lib. bdg. 27.50 (0-404-51723-4) AMS Pr.

Nichol, John, jt. auth. see Macdonald, Chris.

Nichol, Jon. Battle of Agincourt. (Resource Units: Middle Ages, 1066-1485 Ser.). (Illus.). 1974. reprint ed. pap. text 12.95 (0-582-39385-X) Longman.

— The Castle. (Resource Units: Middle Ages, 1066-1485 Ser.). (Illus.). 24p. 1974. pap. text, teacher ed. 12.95 (0-582-39379-5) Longman.

— Edward I Campaigns in Wales & Scotland. (Resource Units: Middle Ages, 1066-1485 Ser.). (Illus.). 24p. 1974. pap. text, teacher ed. 12.95 (0-582-39381-7) Longman.

— The First & Third Crusades, 10 bks., Set. (Resource Units: Middle Ages, 1066-1485 Ser.). (Illus.). 24p. 1974. pap. text, teacher ed. 12.95 (0-582-39377-9) Longman.

— Joan of Arc. (Resource Units: Middle Ages, 1066-1485 Ser.). (Illus.). 24p. 1974. pap. text, teacher ed. 12.95 (0-582-39386-8) Longman.

— King John. (Resource Units: Middle Ages, 1066-1485 Ser.). (Illus.). 24p. 1974. pap. text, teacher ed. 12.95 (0-582-39378-7) Longman.

— Richard Third. (Resource Units: Middle Ages, 1066-1485 Ser.). (Illus.). 24p. 1974. reprint ed. pap. text, teacher ed. 12.95 (0-582-39391-4) Longman.

— Ships & Voyages. (Resource Units, Middle Ages, 1066-1485, Ser.). (Illus.). 24p. 1974. reprint ed. pap. text, teacher ed. 12.95 (0-582-39388-4) Longman.

— The Wars of the Roses. (Resource Units Middle Ages, 1066-1485 Ser.). (Illus.). 24p. 1974. reprint ed. pap., teacher ed. 13.25 (0-582-39390-6) Longman.

Nichol, Lee, jt. auth. see Bohm, David.

Nichol, R. T., tr. see Durer, Albrecht.

Nichol, Richard. Muscle Cars. 1987. 8.98 (0-671-07525-X) S&S Trade.

Nichol, Todd W., ed. see Preus, Herman A.

Nichol, Todd W., tr. see Kierkegaard, Soren.

Nicholai, Frank. Qetun'am Ellallugmi Aquilla.Tr. of Oscar Plays Out in the Rain. (ESK., Illus.). 12p. (J). (gr. k-3). 1998. pap. text 6.00 (1-58084-028-0) Lower Kuskokwim.

***Nicholais, Susan.** Membership Marketing. LC 00-26163. (Core Competencies in Membership Management Ser.). 2000. write for info. (0-88034-164-5) Am Soc Assn Execs.

Nicholaisen, Nancy. Visual Basic for Kids. 1996. pap. write for info. (0-201-68802-6) Addison-Wesley.

Nicholaou, Mary. Cracks: Novel. unabridged ed. LC 99-94617. (Illus.). 52p. 1999. pap. 12.95 (1-890812-04-8) EROS.

— Cynthia. unabridged ed. LC 98-94896. (Illus.). 60p. 1999. pap. 12.95 (1-890812-03-X) EROS.

***Nicholaou, Mary.** Desire: Be My Love. unabridged ed. LC 99-95131. (Illus.). 52p. 1999. pap. 11.95 (1-890812-05-6) EROS.

Nicholaou, Mary. Eros: Phases, & Trials of Love. unabridged ed. LC 97-90604. (Illus.). 82p. (Orig.). 1998. pap. 13.95 (1-890812-00-5) EROS.

— Love Nuances: Twelve Great Love Stories. unabridged ed. LC 97-90865. (Illus.). 54p. 1998. pap. 12.95 (1-890812-01-3) EROS.

— Postmodernism: Postmodernism, Women's Voice & Cupid & Psyche. LC 99-94832. (Illus.). 120p. 1999. pap. 14.95 (1-890812-02-1, Pub. by EROS) Brodart.

Nicholas. How to Allow Peace of Mind. (Silent Music Ser.: Vol. 1). (Illus.). 48p. (Orig.). 1997. pap. 10.00 (0-9649124-2-2) Cygnet Pubng.

— How to Awaken Appreciation. (Silent Music Ser.: Vol. 3). (Illus.). 48p. (Orig.). 1998. pap. 10.00 (0-9649124-4-9) Cygnet Pubng.

— How to Open Lovingkindness. (Silent Music Ser.: Vol. 2). (Illus.). 48p. (Orig.). 1998. pap. 10.00 (0-9649124-3-0) Cygnet Pubng.

— Motivos de Conversacion. 4th ed. 1997. audio 26.88 (0-07-913102-6) McGraw.

— Silent Music, 3 vols., Set. (Illus.). 144p. 1998. pap. 25.00 (0-9649124-1-4) Cygnet Pubng.

Nicholas & Consortium for the Teaching of the Middle Ages Sta. Nicholas of Lyra's Apocalypse Commentary. Krey, Philip D., tr. from LAT. LC 96-52918. (Commentary Ser.). 1997. pap. 10.00 (1-879288-78-8) Medieval Inst.

Nicholas & Kiecker, James G. The Postilla of Nicholas of Lyra on the Song of Songs. LC 98-8884. (Reformation Texts with Translation (1350-1650) Ser.). 1998. 15.00 (0-87462-703-6) Marquette.

Nicholas, Allan. Jesus' Day Off. 32p. (J). (gr. 3-7). 1998. 7.95 (0-385-32620-3) Doubleday.

Nicholas, A. T. The Fist of God. 228p. 1998. pap. 14.99 (0-9666807-0-7) TPR.

Nicholas, Alan, et al. Transforming Families & Communities: Christian Hope in a World of Change. 88p. 1987. pap. 5.00 (0-88028-072-7, 922) Forward Movement.

Nicholas, Angela. 99 Film Scenes for Actors. LC 99-230477. 480p. 1999. mass mkt. 5.99 (0-380-79804-2, Avon Bks) Morrow Avon.

Nicholas, Anna K. American Staffordshire Terriers. (Illus.). 1997. pap. 9.95 (0-7938-2378-1, KW-158S) TFH Pubns.

— Black & Tan Coonhounds. 192p. 1990. 9.95 (0-86622-774-1, KW-190) TFH Pubns.

— The Book of the English Springer Spaniel. (Illus.). 480p. 1983. 39.95 (0-87666-744-2, H-1060) TFH Pubns.

— Book of the German Shepherd Dog. (Illus.). 300p. 1983. 39.95 (0-87666-562-8, H-1062) TFH Pubns.

— Book of the Golden Retriever. (Illus.). 480p. 1983. 39.95 (0-87666-738-8, H-1058) TFH Pubns.

— The Book of the Labrador Retriever. (Illus.). 478p. 1983. 39.95 (0-87666-748-5, H-1059) TFH Pubns.

— The Book of the Rottweiler. (Illus.). 544p. 1981. 29.95 (0-87666-735-3, H-1035) TFH Pubns.

— The Book of the Shetland Sheepdog. (Illus.). 544p. 1984. 39.95 (0-86622-036-4, H-1064) TFH Pubns.

— Book of the West Highland White Terrier. (Illus.). 224p. 1993. 35.95 (0-86622-663-X, TS187) TFH Pubns.

— The Boxer. (Illus.). 288p. 1984. text 24.95 (0-86622-028-3, PS-813) TFH Pubns.

— The Collie. (Illus.). 320p. 1986. 24.95 (0-86622-723-7, PS-825) TFH Pubns.

— A Complete Introduction to Poodles. (Complete Introduction to...Ser.). (Illus.). 128p. (Orig.). 1987. pap. 8.95 (0-86622-380-0, CO-032S) TFH Pubns.

— The Dalmatian. (Illus.). 320p. 1986. 24.95 (0-86622-157-3, PS-823) TFH Pubns.

— Finnish Spitz. (KW Ser.). (Illus.). 192p. 1989. 9.95 (0-86622-783-0, KW-194) TFH Pubns.

— French Bulldogs. 1990. 9.95 (0-86622-767-9, KW-186) TFH Pubns.

— The Great Dane. (Illus.). 319p. (YA). (gr. 7 up). 1988. 24.95 (0-86622-122-0, PS-826) TFH Pubns.

— Guide to Owning a Chow Chow: AKC Rank #26. (Guide to Owning Ser.). (Illus.). 64p. 1995. pap. 6.95 (0-7938-1875-3, RE-325) TFH Pubns.

— Jack Russell Terriers. (Illus.). 1997. pap. 9.95 (0-7938-2379-X, KW-164S) TFH Pubns.

— The Maltese. (Illus.). 288p. 1984. 23.95 (0-87666-569-5, PS-803) TFH Pubns.

— Norfolk Terrier No. 112: AKC Rank. (Rare Breed Ser.). (Illus.). 96p. 1997. 19.95 (0-7938-0761-1, RX-111) TFH Pubns.

— Norwegian Elkhounds. (Illus.). 1997. pap. 9.95 (0-7938-2319-6, KW-110S) TFH Pubns.

— Norwich Terriers. (Illus.). 192p. 1993. 9.95 (0-86622-580-3, KW209) TFH Pubns.

— The Poodle. (Illus.). 288p. 1984. text 24.95 (0-86622-033-X, PS-814) TFH Pubns.

— The Professional's Book of Rottweilers. (TS Ser.). (Illus.). 448p. 1991. lib. bdg. 89.95 (0-86622-625-7, TS-147) TFH Pubns.

— Rottweilers: AKC Rank #2. (Illus.). 1996. pap. 9.95 (0-7938-2323-4, KW-116S) TFH Pubns.

— Shar Pei, AKC Rank No. 25. (KW Dog Ser.). (Illus.). 1996. pap. 9.95 (0-7938-2359-5, KW156S) TFH Pubns.

— The World of Doberman Pinschers. (Illus.). 640p. 1986. 59.95 (0-86622-123-9, H-1082) TFH Pubns.

— The World of Rottweilers. (Illus.). 336p. 1986. 47.95 (0-86622-124-7, H-1083) TFH Pubns.

— The World of the Bichon Frise, AKC Rank No. 32. (Illus.). 256p. 1996. 39.95 (0-7938-0191-5, TS245) TFH Pubns.

— World of the Chinese Shar-pei. (Illus.). 304p. 1992. 89.95 (0-86622-199-9, TS-176) TFH Pubns.

Nicholas, Anna K. & Foy, Marcia. The Beagle. (Illus.). 320p. 1982. text 24.95 (0-86622-042-9, PS-811) TFH Pubns.

— The Dachshund. (Breed Ser.). (Illus.). 320p. 1987. 24.95 (0-86622-158-1, PS-822) TFH Pubns.

Nicholas, Anna K., jt. auth. see Brearley, Joan McD.

Nicholas, Anna K., jt. auth. see Foy, Marcia A.

Nicholas, Anna Katherine. The Staffordshire Terriers: American Staffordshire Terrier & Staffordshire Bull Terrier. (TS Ser.). (Illus.). 256p. 2000. 47.95 (0-86622-637-0, TS-143) TFH Pubns.

***Nicholas, Anna Katherine.** Weimaraners. 1998. pap. text 9.95 (0-7938-2329-3) TFH Pubns.

Nicholas, Anne. The Art of the New Zealand Tattoo. (Illus.). 132p. 1995. pap. 17.95 (0-8065-1603-8, Citadel Pr) Carol Pub Group.

Nicholas, Barry. Historical Introduction to the Study of Roman Law. 3rd ed. LC 74-164452. 554p. reprint ed. pap. 157.90 (0-608-30520-0, 2051465) Bks Demand.

— Introduction to Roman Law. (Clarendon Law Ser.). 298p. 1976. pap. text 32.00 (0-19-876063-9) OUP.

Nicholas, Barry, jt. auth. see Jolowicz, H. F.

Nicholas, Bill, jt. auth. see McManus, Ed.

Nicholas, C., et al, eds. Principles of Document Processing: 3rd International Workshop, PODP '96, Palo Alto, California, U. S. A., September 23, 1996. Selected Papers. (Lecture Notes in Computer Science Ser.: Vol. 1293). xi, 195p. 1997. pap. 43.00 (3-540-63620-X) Spr-Verlag.

Nicholas, C. J. Exploring Geology on the Isle of Arran. LC 98-21345. (Illus.). 192p. (C). 1998. pap. 17.95 (0-521-63555-1) Cambridge U Pr.

Nicholas, Charles. Elephant Book. 24p. 1999. pap. text 5.29 (0-307-13317-6) Gldn Bks Pub Co.

Nicholas, Charles. Banner in the Sky. (Contemporary Motivators Ser.). (J). (gr. 4-12). 1978. pap. text 2.25 (0-88301-301-0) Pendulum Pr.

— God Is My Co-Pilot. LC 78-50959. (Contemporary Motivators Ser.). (J). (gr. 4-12). 1978. pap. text 2.25 (0-88301-302-9) Pendulum Pr.

— Hiroshima. LC 78-50861. (Contemporary Motivators Ser.). (J). (gr. 4-12). 1978. pap. text 2.25 (0-88301-304-5) Pendulum Pr.

— Hot Rod. LC 78-50957. (Contemporary Motivators Ser.). (J). (gr. 4-12). 1978. pap. text 2.25 (0-88301-305-3) Pendulum Pr.

— Just Dial a Number. LC 78-50860. (Contemporary Motivators Ser.). (J). (gr. 4-12). 1978. pap. text 2.25 (0-88301-306-1) Pendulum Pr.

— Lost Horizon. (Contemporary Motivators Ser.). 32p. (Orig.). (J). (gr. 3-5). 1979. pap. text 2.25 (0-88301-309-6) Pendulum Pr.

Nicholas, Charles K. & Mayfield, James, eds. Intelligent Hypertext: Advanced Techniques for the World Wide Web, Vol. 132. LC 97-42023. (Lecture Notes in Computer Science Ser.: Vol. 1326). xiv, 182p. 1997. pap. 37.00 (3-540-63637-4) Spr-Verlag.

***Nicholas, Christopher.** Bears! (Know-It-Alls Ser.). (Illus.). 24p. (J). (ps-3). 2000. mass mkt. 2.79 (0-7681-0210-3, McClanahan Book) Learn Horizon.

Nicholas, Christopher. Bugs! (Know-It-Alls Ser.). (Illus.). 24p. (J). (ps-2). 1998. 2.79 (0-7681-0094-1, McClanahan Book) Learn Horizon.

***Nicholas, Christopher.** On the Farm. (Storyshapes Ser.). 24p. 1999. pap. text 2.25 (0-7681-0134-4, McClanahan Book) Learn Horizon.

Nicholas, Christopher. Snakes! (Know-It-Alls Ser.). (Illus.). 24p. (J). (ps-2). 1999. mass mkt. 2.50 (0-7681-0107-7, McClanahan Book) Learn Horizon.

***Nicholas, Christopher.** Spiders. (Know-It-Alls Ser.). 24p. 1999. pap. 2.79 (0-7681-0128-X, McClanahan Book) Learn Horizon.

Nicholas, Christopher. Wolves! (Know-It-Alls Ser.). (Illus.). 24p. (J). (ps-2). 1999. mass mkt. 2.50 (0-7681-0126-3, McClanahan Book) Learn Horizon.

Nicholas, D. Commodities Futures Trading: A Guide to Information Sources & Computerized Services. 154p. 1985. pap. text 90.00 (0-7201-1703-8) Continuum.

Nicholas, D., compiled by. Peter Matthiessen: A Bibliography, 1951-1979. LC 80-109000. (Illus.). 63p. 1980. 15.00 (0-938364-00-6) Orirana Pr.

Nicholas, D. & Erbach, G. Online Information Sources for Business & Current Affairs: An Evaluation. 320p. 1989. text 130.00 (0-7201-1878-6) Continuum.

Nicholas, D., et al. End-Users of Online Information Systems: An Analysis. 168p. 1988. text 95.00 (0-7201-1995-2) Continuum.

Nicholas, D., jt. ed. see Thijsen, J. M.

Nicholas, Darrel D. Wood Deterioration & Its Prevention by Preservative Treatments. Incl. Vol. 1. Degradation & Protection of Wood. 416p. 1982. pap. text 45.00 (0-8156-2285-6); (Wood Science Ser.: No. 5). (Illus.). (C). 1973. Set pap. text 45.00 (0-8156-2303-8) Syracuse U Pr.

N

An Asterisk (*) at the beginning of an entry indicates that the title is appearing for the first time.

Nicholas, David. The Domestic Life of a Medieval City: Women, Children & the Family in Fourteenth-Century Ghent. LC 84-22011. 271p. 1985. reprint ed. pap. 84.10 (*0-608-02037-0*, 206269000003) Bks Demand.

— Evolution Medieval World: Society, Government & Thought in Europe. 560p. (C). 1995. pap. 31.20 (*0-582-09257-4*, 79267) Longman.

— Evolution Medievl Three Twelve Fifteen Hundred. 560p. (C). 1992. text 58.50 (*0-582-09256-6*, 79266) Longman.

Nicholas, David. Growth Medieval City. LC 96-27185. (History of Urban Society in Europe Ser.). 432p. (C). 1997. pap. 40.06 (*0-582-29906-3*) Addison-Wesley.

Nicholas, David. Growth Medieval City. LC 96-27185. (History of Urban Society in Europe Ser.). (C). 1997. 85.00 (*0-582-29907-1*) Longman.

— In the Time of the Wolf. 172p. (Orig.). 1995. pap. 14.95 (*0-9644375-1-1*) Media Chaos.

— Medieval Flanders. (C). 1992. pap. text 60.95 (*0-582-01679-7*) Addison-Wesley.

— Medieval Flanders. LC 91-45256. 463p. (C). 1995. pap. 52.00 (*0-582-01678-9*, 79365) Longman.

— The Metamorphosis of a Medieval City: Ghent in the Age of the Arteveldes, 1302-1390. LC 86-27276. 381p. 1987. reprint ed. pap. 118.20 (*0-7837-6491-X*, 204658100003) Bks Demand.

— The Middle East: Its Oil, Economies, & Investment Policies: A Guide to Sources of Financial Information. LC 80-28555. 199p. 1981. lib. bdg. 49.95 (*0-313-22986-4*, NME/, Greenwood Pr) Greenwood.

— Trade, Urbanisation & the Family: Studies in the History of Medieval Flanders. (Collected Studies: No. CS531). 350p. 1996. 109.95 (*0-86078-585-8*, Pub. by Variorum) Ashgate Pub Co.

***Nicholas, David.** The Transformation of Europe, 1300-1600. LC 98-51966. (Arnold History of Europe Ser.). 448p. 1999. text 80.00 (*0-340-66207-7*, Pub. by E A); pap. text 24.95 (*0-340-66208-5*, Pub. by E A) OUP.

Nicholas, David. The Van Arteveldes of Ghent: The Varieties of Vendetta & the Hero in History. LC 88-3858. (Illus.). 232p. 1988. 35.00 (*0-8014-2149-7*) Cornell U Pr.

— The Van Arteveldes of Ghent: The Varieties of Vendetta & the Hero in History. LC 88-3858. 232p. reprint ed. pap. 72.00 (*0-608-20930-9*, 207202900003) Bks Demand.

Nicholas, David, jt. ed. see Bachrach, Bernard S.

Nicholas, David H. & Randall, Clyde L. Vaginal Surgery. 4th ed. LC 95-17805. (Illus.). 520p. 1996. 89.00 (*0-683-06491-6*) Lppncott W & W.

Nicholas, David R. Foundations of Biblical Inerrancy. pap. 2.99 (*0-88469-104-7*) BMH Bks.

— What's a Woman to Do in Church? 148p. 1979. 7.99 (*0-88469-123-3*) BMH Bks.

Nicholas, Deborah. Shattered Reflections. 416p. 1995. mass mkt. 4.99 (*0-8217-5076-3*) Kensgtn Pub Corp.

Nicholas, E. D., ed. Exploiting Friction Welding in Production. 80p. 1979. pap. 72.00 (*0-85300-125-1*, Pub. by Woodhead Pubng) Am Educ Systs.

Nicholas, Edward. The Chaplain's Lady: Life & Love At Fort Mackinac. (Illus.). 82p. (Orig.). 1987. pap. 7.00 (*0-911872-56-6*) Mackinac St Hist Pks.

***Nicholas, Edward.** The Chaplain's Lady: Life & Love at Fort Mackinac. (Illus.). 82p. 1999. 11.95 (*0-911872-71-X*) Mackinac St Hist Pks.

Nicholas, Flamel, jt. auth. see Urbigerus, Baro.

Nicholas, Francis S., compiled by. Index to Schoolcraft's "Indian Tribes of the United States" reprint ed. 49.00 (*0-403-03611-9*) Scholarly.

***Nicholas, Frank W.** Introduction to Veterinary Genetics. (Illus.). 336p. 2000. reprint ed. pap. 49.95 (*0-632-05639-8*, Pub. by Blackwell Sci) Iowa St U Pr.

Nicholas, G. P. Holocene Human Ecology in Northeastern North America. LC 88-11113. (Interdisciplinary Contributions to Archaeology Ser.). (Illus.). 340p. (C). 1988. 49.50 (*0-306-42869-5*, Plenum Trade) Perseus Pubng.

Nicholas, Geoff & Duncan, Andy. What Drum. 2nd ed. (Illus.). 113p. 1990. pap. 12.95 (*0-933224-52-4*, T032) Bold Strummer Ltd.

Nicholas, H. Lord Nelson, 1, vol. 4. 1999. pap. text 32.95 (*1-86176-051-5*) CHPG.

— Lord Nelson, 1, vol. 6. 1999. pap. text 32.95 (*1-86176-053-1*) CHPG.

— Lord Nelson, 1, vol. 7. 1999. pap. text 32.95 (*1-86176-054-X*) CHPG.

— Lord Nelson, 1, vol.5. 1999. pap. text 32.95 (*1-86176-052-3*) CHPG.

Nicholas, H. G. British General Election of 1950. (Illus.). 353p. 1968. reprint ed. 35.00 (*0-7146-1568-4*, Pub. by F Cass Pubs) Intl Spec Bk.

— The Nature of American Politics. 2nd ed. 160p. 1986. 29.95 (*0-19-827483-1*); pap. text 14.95 (*0-19-827482-3*) OUP.

— The United Nations As a Political Institution. 5th ed. 272p. 1975. pap. text 22.95 (*0-19-519826-3*) OUP.

— The United States & Britain. LC 74-16681. (United States in the World: Foreign Perspectives). 1993. pap. text 3.25 (*0-226-58003-2*, P758) U Ch Pr.

— The United States & Britain. Iriye, Akira, ed. LC 74-16681. (United States in the World, Foreign Perspectives Ser.). viii, 196p. 1996. lib. bdg. 16.00 (*0-226-58002-4*) U Ch Pr.

Nicholas, H. G., ed. Washington Despatches, 1941 to 1945: Weekly Political Reports from the British Embassy. LC 80-6208. xviii, 718p. (C). 1999. pap. text 24.00 (*0-226-58005-9*) U Ch Pr.

Nicholas, Herbert G. Britain & the U. S. A. LC 63-10195. (Albert Shaw Lectures on Diplomatic History: 1961). 192p. reprint ed. pap. 59.60 (*0-8357-7410-4*, 202072800018) Bks Demand.

Nicholas, Ilene M. The Proto-Elamite Settlement at TUV. Sumner, William M., ed. (University Museum Monographs: Malayan Excavation Reports: No. 69, Report #1). (Illus.). xx, 164p. 1990. text 55.00 (*0-934718-86-5*) U Museum Pubns.

Nicholas, J. F. An Atlas of Models of Crystal Surfaces. 238p. 1965. text 412.00 (*0-677-00580-6*) Gordon & Breach.

Nicholas, J. Karl & Nicholl, James R. Effective Argument: A Writer's Guide with Readings. 2nd ed. LC 97-26818. 431p. 1997. pap. 36.00 (*0-205-27039-5*) P-H.

— Effective Argument: A Writer's Guide with Readings: Examination Copy. 2nd ed. 448p. (C). 1997. pap. text. write for info. (*0-205-27650-4*, T7650-9) Allyn.

***Nicholas, J. Karl & Nicholl, James R.** Models for Effective Writing. 2nd ed. LC 99-14599. 416p. 1999. pap. text 34.00 (*0-205-30292-0*) Allyn.

Nicholas, J. Karl & Nicholl, James R., eds. Models for Effective Writing. LC 93-11808. 1994. write for info. (*0-205-40017-5*) Allyn.

Nicholas, J. Karl, jt. ed. see Farwell, Harold.

Nicholas, J. V. Traceable Temperatures: An Introduction of Temperatures, Measurement & Calibration. 378p. 1994. 185.00 (*0-471-93803-3*) Wiley.

Nicholas, James A., ed. The Lower Extremity & Spine in Sports Medicine. 2nd ed. LC 94-26126. (Illus.). 1808p. (C). (gr. 13). 1994. text 280.00 (*0-8151-6391-6*, 23615) Mosby Inc.

Nicholas, James C. State Regulation: Housing Prices. 140p. 1982. pap. text 12.95 (*0-88285-075-X*) Transaction Pubs.

Nicholas, James C., ed. The Changing Structure of Infrastructure Finance. 98p. 1985. 15.00 (*0-317-01542-7*) Fla Atlantic.

— The Changing Structure of Infrastructure Finance. LC HC0110.C3C45. (Lincoln Institute of Land Policy Monograph: No. 85-5). 112p. 1985. reprint ed. pap. 34.80 (*0-608-02091-5*, 206274400004) Bks Demand.

Nicholas, James C., et al. A Practitioner's Guide to Development Impact Fees. LC 90-80606. (Illus.). 300p. (Orig.). 1991. lib. bdg. 56.00 (*0-918286-70-0*, Planners Press) Am Plan Assn.

Nicholas, James H., Jr., tr. see Kojeve, Alexandre.

Nicholas, Jane. Biblical Foundations for Children. (Illus.). 176p. (J). (gr. k-6). 1999. pap. 17.95 (*1-886973-35-0*) Dove Chr Fel.

— Stumpwork Embroidery: A Collection of Fruits, Flowers, Insects. (Illus.). 216p. 1996. 34.95 (*1-86351-183-0*, Pub. by Sally Milner) Sterling.

— Stumpwork Embroidery Designs & Projects. (Illus.). 160p. 1998. 25.00 (*1-86351-208-X*, Pub. by Sally Milner) Sterling.

Nicholas, Jay. Down to the Sea: The Story of a Little Salmon & His Neighborhood. LC 99-32665. (Illus.). 56p. 1999. pap. 15.00 (*1-58151-036-5*) BookPartners.

— Down to the Sea: The Story of a Little Salmon & His Neighborhood. LC 99-32665. (Illus.). 56p. (ps up). 1999. 35.00 (*1-58151-038-1*, Pub. by BookPartners) Midpt Trade.

***Nicholas, Jeff.** Columbia River Gorge. 1998. pap. 4.95 (*0-939365-86-3*) Panorama Intl.

Nicholas, Jeff. Death Valley National Park. Leach, Nicky, ed. (Visual Interpretation Ser.). (Illus.). 64p. (Orig.). 1994. pap. 9.95 (*0-939365-37-5*) Panorama Intl.

***Nicholas, Jeff.** Glacier-Waterton. (Wish You Were Here Postcard Book Ser.). 1998. pap. 4.95 (*0-939365-84-7*) Panorama Intl.

Nicholas, Jeff. Islands in the Sky: Scenes from the Colorado Plateau. (Wish You Were Here Ser.). (Illus.). 96p. 1991. pap. 14.95 (*0-939365-16-2*) Panorama Intl.

— Islands in the Sky: Scenes from the Colorado Plateau. (Wish You Were Here Postcard Book Ser.). (Illus.). 96p. 1992. 24.95 (*0-939365-19-7*) Panorama Intl.

***Nicholas, Jeff.** Mount Rainier. 1998. pap. (*0-939365-83-9*) Panorama Intl.

Nicholas, Jeff, ed. Arches National Park. (Wish You Were Here Postcard Book Ser.). (Illus.). 32p. (Orig.). 1995. pap. 4.95 (*0-939365-48-0*) Panorama Intl.

— Art on the Rocks. (Wish You Were Here Postcard Book Ser.). (Illus.). 32p. 1993. pap. 4.95 (*0-939365-24-3*) Panorama Intl.

— Bryce Canyon National Park. (Wish You Were Here Postcard Book Ser.). (Illus.). 32p. 1992. pap. 4.95 (*0-939365-06-5*) Panorama Intl.

— Cactus Flowers. (Wish You Were Here Postcard Book Ser.). (Illus.). 32p. (Orig.). 1994. pap. 4.95 (*0-939365-39-1*) Panorama Intl.

— Capitol Reef National Park. (Wish You Were Here Postcard Book Ser.). (Illus.). 32p. (Orig.). 1997. pap. 4.95 (*0-939365-56-1*) Panorama Intl.

— Carlsbad Caverns National Park. (Wish You Were Here Postcard Book Ser.). (Illus.). 32p. (Orig.). 1995. pap. 4.95 (*0-939365-46-4*) Panorama Intl.

— Death Valley National Park. (Wish You Were Here Postcard Book Ser.). (Illus.). 32p. (Orig.). 1994. pap. text 4.95 (*0-939365-40-5*) Panorama Intl.

— Desert Dunes. (Wish You Were Here Postcard Book Ser.). (Illus.). 32p. (Orig.). 1994. pap. 4.95 (*0-939365-41-3*) Panorama Intl.

— Glen Canyon/Lake Powell Recreation Area. (Wish You Were Here Postcard Book Ser.). (Illus.). 32p. 1993. pap. 4.95 (*0-939365-28-6*) Panorama Intl.

— Grand Canyon: The Vault of Heaven. (Illus.). 32p. 1998. 4.95 (*0-939365-96-0*) Panorama Intl.

— Grand Canyon National Park. (Wish You Were Here Postcard Book Ser.). (Illus.). 32p. 1990. pap. 4.95 (*0-939365-11-1*) Panorama Intl.

— Grand Canyon National Park. (Coloring Postcard Bks.). (Illus.). 24p. (J). (gr. k-5). 1999. pap. 4.95 (*1-58071-003-4*) Panorama Intl.

— Grand Canyon National Park, Vol. 2. (Wish You Were Here Postcard Book Ser.). (Illus.). 32p. 1997. pap. 4.95 (*0-939365-55-3*) Panorama Intl.

— Grand Teton National Park. (Wish You Were Here Postcard Book Ser.). (Illus.). 32p. 1990. pap. 4.95 (*0-939365-12-X*) Panorama Intl.

— Mars. (Wish You Were Here Postcard Book Ser.). (Illus.). 20p. 1998. pap. 4.95 (*0-939365-87-1*) Panorama Intl.

— Mesa Verde National Park. (Wish You Were Here Postcard Book Ser.). (Illus.). 32p. 1997. pap. 4.95 (*0-939365-81-2*) Panorama Intl.

***Nicholas, Jeff, ed.** Mesa Verde National Park. (Wish You Were Here Postcard Book Ser.). (Illus.). 32p. 1999. pap. 4.95 (*1-58071-006-9*, Pub. by Panorama Intl) Falcon Pub Inc.

Nicholas, Jeff, ed. Monument Valley Navajo Tribal Park. (Wish You Were Here Postcard Book Ser.). (Illus.). 32p. 1993. pap. 4.95 (*0-939365-27-8*) Panorama Intl.

— Mount St. Helens National Volcanic Monument. (Wish You Were Here Postcard Book Ser.). (Illus.). 32p. 1998. pap. 4.95 (*0-939365-88-X*) Panorama Intl.

— Peaks, Plateaus & Canyons: Colorado Plateau. (Wish You Were Here Postcard Book Ser.). (Illus.). 32p. 1998. 4.95 (*0-939365-95-2*) Panorama Intl.

— Petrified Forest National Park. (Wish You Were Here Postcard Book Ser.). (Illus.). 32p. 1995. pap. 4.95 (*0-939365-47-2*) Panorama Intl.

— Rocky Mountain National Park. (Wish You Were Here Postcard Book Ser.). (Illus.). 32p. (Orig.). 1995. pap. 4.95 (*0-939365-45-6*) Panorama Intl.

— Ruins of the Southwest. (Wish You Were Here Postcard Book Ser.). (Illus.). 32p. 1993. pap. 4.95 (*0-939365-23-5*) Panorama Intl.

— Sequoia & Kings Canyon National Parks. (Wish You Were Here Postcard Book Ser.). (Illus.). 32p. 1993. pap. 4.95 (*0-939365-25-1*) Panorama Intl.

— Wildlife of the Rockies. (Wish You Were Here Postcard Book Ser.). (Illus.). 32p. 1994. pap. 4.95 (*0-939365-35-9*) Panorama Intl.

— Yellowstone National Park. (Wish You Were Here Postcard Book Ser.). (Illus.). 32p. 1992. pap. 4.95 (*0-939365-05-7*) Panorama Intl.

— Yellowstone National Park. (Color Me Postcards Ser.). (Illus.). 24p. (J). (gr. k-5). 1999. pap. 4.95 (*1-58071-005-0*) Panorama Intl.

— Yellowstone Wildlife. (Wish You Were Here Postcard Book Ser.). (Illus.). 32p. 1994. pap. 4.95 (*0-939365-34-0*) Panorama Intl.

***Nicholas, Jeff, ed.** Yosemite National Park. (Coloring Postcard Bks.). (Illus.). 24p. (J). (gr. k-5). 1999. pap. 4.95 (*1-58071-004-2*, Pub. by Panorama Intl) Falcon Pub Inc.

Nicholas, Jeff, ed. Yosemite National Park. 3rd ed. (Wish You Were Here Postcard Book Ser.). (Illus.). 32p. 1992. pap. 4.95 (*0-939365-10-3*) Panorama Intl.

— Zion National Park. rev. ed. (Wish You Were Here Postcard Book Ser.). (Illus.). 32p. 1994. pap. 4.95 (*0-939365-33-2*) Panorama Intl.

Nicholas, Jeff, ed. see Aitchison, Stewart.

Nicholas, Jeff, ed. see Gilmore, Jackie.

Nicholas, Jeff, ed. see Goodin, Mark.

Nicholas, Jeff, ed. see Hucko, Bruce.

Nicholas, Jeff, ed. see Lamb, Susan.

Nicholas, Jeff, ed. see Leach, Nicky.

Nicholas, Jeff, ed. see Points, Larry & Jauck, Andrea.

Nicholas, Jeff, ed. see Robinson, George B.

Nicholas, Jeff, ed. see Warfield, Ron.

Nicholas, Jeff, ed. see Wilson, Jim.

Nicholas, Jeff, ed. see Wilson, Lynn.

Nicholas, Jeff, ed. see Wuerthner, George.

***Nicholas, Jeremy.** Classic FM Good Music Guide. 2000. pap. 24.95 (*0-340-75042-1*, Pub. by Hodder & Stought Ltd) Trafalgar.

Nicholas, Jeremy. Classic FM Guide to Classical Music: The Essential Companion to Composers & Their Music. (Illus.). 384p. 1997. pap. 19.95 (*1-86205-051-1*, Pub. by Pavilion Bks Ltd) Trafalgar.

Nicholas, Jesse C. The J. C. Nichols Chronicle: The Authorized Story of the Man & His Company. LC 94-12824. 336p. 1994. 25.00 (*0-7006-0685-8*) U Pr of KS.

Nicholas, Joe. Language Diversity Surveys As Agents of Change. LC 93-50651. (Multilingual Matters Ser.: No. 102). 176p. 1994. 79.00 (*1-85359-233-1*, Pub. by Multilingual Matters); pap. 34.95 (*1-85359-232-3*, Pub. by Multilingual Matters) Taylor & Francis.

***Nicholas, John.** Managing Projects. 2nd ed. 608p. 2000. 85.33 (*0-13-018328-8*) P-H.

Nicholas, John M. Competitive Manufacturing Management: Continuous Improvement, Lean Production, Customer-Focused Quality. LC 97-27344. 1997. write for info. (*0-256-21727-0*, Irwn Prfssnl) McGraw-Hill Prof.

— Managing Business & Engineering Projects: Concepts & Implementation. LC 89-37577. 496p. 1989. 93.33 (*0-13-551854-7*) P-H.

Nicholas, John M., ed. Images, Perception & Knowledge. (Western Ontario Ser.: No. 8). 318p. 1977. text 155.50 (*90-277-0782-0*, D Reidel) Kluwer Academic.

Nicholas, John R. Oh, What a Lovely War. LC 91-75916. 400p. 1991. pap. 12.95 (*0-9630445-0-8*) Harper Hse.

Nicholas, John S. Goethe, the Layman in Science. (Connecticut Academy of Arts & Sciences Ser., Trans.: Vol. 32). 1933. pap. 39.50 (*0-685-22921-1*) Elliots Bks.

Nicholas, Joseph G. Investing in Hedge Funds. LC 98-45960. (Personal Bookshelf Ser.). (Illus.). 288p. 1999. 26.95 (*1-57660-060-2*, Pub. by Bloomberg NJ) Norton.

Nicholas, Joseph G. Market Neutral Investing: The Essential Strategies. 65.00 (*1-57660-037-8*, Pub. by Bloomberg NJ) Norton.

Nicholas, Karl J. Models for Effective Writing. 2nd ed. (C). 1999. pap. text. write for info. (*0-205-31562-3*) Allyn.

Nicholas, Kristin. Knitting the New Classic. (Illus.). 160p. 1998. 17.95 (*0-8069-3170-1*) Sterling.

— Knitting Today's Classics: 65 Beautiful Sweaters from the Studios of Classic Elite. Dierks, Leslie, ed. LC 97-13162. Orig. Title: Knitting Contemporary Classics. (Illus.). 144p. 1997. 27.95 (*1-887374-36-1*, Pub. by Lark Books) Random.

Nicholas-Lewis, Lolda. How to Get a Green Card: Legal Ways to Stay in the USA. 4th ed. 416p. 1999. pap. 29.95 (*0-87337-531-9*) Nolo com.

Nicholas, Lynn H. The Rape of Europa: The Fate of Europe's Treasures in the Third Reich & the Second World War. 1995. pap. 16.00 (*0-679-75686-8*) Vin Bks.

***Nicholas, M. G.** Joining Processes: Introduction to Brazing & Diffusion Bonding LC 98-70928. xvi, 335 p. 1998. write for info. (*0-412-79360-1*) Chapman & Hall.

Nicholas, Margaret I. Handbook of Reference Sources & Services for Small & Medium-Sized Libraries. 2nd ed. 199p. 1996. pap. text 30.00 (*0-7881-3143-5*) DIANE Pub.

Nicholas, Mary. Mystery of Goodness & the Positive Moral Consequences of Psychotherapy. 288p. (C). 1994. 30.00 (*0-393-70166-2*) Norton.

Nicholas, Mary W. Change in the Context of Group Therapy. LC 84-1718. 272p. 1987. text 40.95 (*0-87630-358-0*) Brunner-Mazel.

Nicholas, Michael S. An Actor's Guide: Your First Year in Hollywood. LC 95-76690. 256p. 1996. pap. 16.95 (*1-880559-34-X*) Allworth Pr.

Nicholas, Michele, jt. auth. see Baron, Nick.

Nicholas, Nancy, ed. see Piercy, Marge.

***Nicholas, Nathan.** The Price of Doubt. LC 00-27028. (International Library of Philosophy). 2000. write for info. (*0-415-23415-8*) Routledge.

Nicholas, Nichelle. Beyond Uhura: Star Trek & Other Memories. 336p. 1995. mass mkt. 5.99 (*1-57297-011-1*) Blvd Books.

Nicholas of Cusa. Nicholas of Cusa: Metaphysical Speculations. Hopkins, Jasper, tr. from LAT. & pref. by. LC 97-72945. xii, 333p. (C). 1998. text 25.00 (*0-938060-47-3*) Banning Pr.

Nicholas, Patty. Fiddlin for Fun Functionally - Piano Accompaniment. 72p. 1994. pap. text 10.95 (*0-87487-679-6*) Summy-Birchard.

— Fiddlin for Fun Functionally - Student Book. 44p. 1994. pap. text 6.95 (*0-87487-678-8*) Summy-Birchard.

— Fiddlin for Fun Functionally - Teacher Book. 56p. 1994. pap. text 7.95 (*0-87487-680-X*) Summy-Birchard.

Nicholas, Paul. The Game of Insurance: How Insurance Is Conducted in California. LC 90-92961. (Illus.). 304p. (Orig.). 1990. pap. 17.95 (*0-9626901-0-4*) Jade Pub Co.

Nicholas, Phoebe O., ed. see American Psychological Association Staff.

Nicholas Prince of Greece. Political Memoirs, 1914-17. LC 72-1274. (Select Bibliographies Reprint Ser.). 1977. reprint ed. 34.95 (*0-8369-6833-6*) Ayer.

Nicholas, Ralph W., jt. auth. see Inden, Ronald B.

Nicholas, Richard L. & Servis, Joseph. Powhatan, Salem & Courtney Henrico Artillery. (Virginia Regimental Histories Ser.). (Illus.). 246p. 1998. 25.00 (*1-56190-104-0*) H E Howard.

Nicholas, Richard L., jt. auth. see Sherwood, W. Cullen.

Nicholas, Robert. Mundo Unido: Lectura y Escritura, Vol. 1. (SPA.). 1995. 21.95 (*0-471-10289-X*) Wiley.

— Mundo Unido Vol. 1: Lectura y Escritura. 420p. 1995. pap. 36.95 (*0-471-58484-3*) Wiley.

Nicholas, Robert J. Fifty Creative Exercises, 2 bks. (YA). (gr. 7 up). 1991. reprint ed. pap. 24.00 (*1-879777-02-9*) Leonardos Work.

— Fifty Creative Exercises, 2 bks., Bk. I. (YA). (gr. 7 up). 1991. reprint ed. pap. 12.95 (*1-879777-00-2*) Leonardos Work.

— Fifty Creative Exercises, 2 bks., Bk. II. (YA). (gr. 7 up). 1991. reprint ed. pap. 12.95 (*1-879777-01-0*) Leonardos Work.

Nicholas, Robert L. & Dominicis, Marbia Canteli. Motivos de Conversacion: Essentials of Spanish. 5th ed. LC 99-23951. 1999. write for info. (*0-07-230923-7*) McGraw.

Nicholas, Robert L. & Dominicis, Maria C. Motivos de Conversacion: Essentials of Spanish. 4th ed. LC 96-37557. (SPA.). 1997. write for info. (*0-07-047089-8*) McGraw.

— Motivos de Conversacion: Essentials of Spanish. 4th ed. LC 96-37557. 448p. (C). 1997. 59.38 (*0-07-047088-X*) McGraw.

— Motivos de Conversacion: Essentials of Spanish. 4th ed. (C). 1997. pap., wbk. ed., lab manual ed. 26.88 (*0-07-047090-1*) McGraw.

***Nicholas, Robert L. & Dominicis, Maria Canteli.** Motivos de Conversacion. 5th ed. (SPA & ENG.). 288p. (C). 1999. pap. 27.81 (*0-07-230918-0*) McGrw-H Hghr Educ.

— Motivos De Conversacion: Essentials of Spanish. 5th ed. LC 99-23951. 1999. write for info. (*0-07-230984-9*) McGrw-H Hghr Educ.

Nicholas, Robert L., et al. En Camino! A Cultural Approach to Beginning Spanish. 4th ed. 576p. (C). 1990. 68.75 (*0-07-046189-9*) McGraw.

— En Camino! A Cultural Approach to Beginning Spanish. 4th ed. (C). 1990. teacher ed., student ed. 214.37 incl. audio (*0-07-540861-9*) McGraw.

— En Camino! A Cultural Approach to Beginning Spanish. 4th ed. (C). 1990. teacher ed. 24.06 (*0-07-540859-7*); pap. text, student ed. 32.19 (*0-07-540856-2*); teacher ed., student ed. 24.06 incl. audio (*0-07-540862-7*) McGraw.

— En Camino! A Cultural Approach to Beginning Spanish. 4th ed. (C). 1990. pap. text 22.50 (*0-07-540860-0*) McGraw.

— Motivos de Conversacion: Essentials of Spanish. 3rd ed. 1991. text 43.00 (*0-07-046708-0*) McGraw.

N

— Motivos de Conversacion: Essentials of Spanish. 3rd ed. (C). 1992. pap. text, wbk. ed., lab manual ed. 21.00 (*0-07-046714-5*) McGraw.

Nicholas, Robert L., jt. auth. see Dominicis, Maria.

Nicholas, Robin. The Cowboy & His Lady. (Silhouette Romance Ser.). 1994. per. 2.75 (*0-373-19017-4*, 5-19017-8) Harlequin Bks.

— The Cowboy & His Lady. 1997. per. 63.00 (*0-373-91017-7*, 5-91017-9) Harlequin Bks.

— Cowboy Dad: Men! (Silhouette Romance Ser.: No. 1327). 1998. per. 3.50 (*0-373-19327-0*, 1-19327-5) Harlequin Bks.

— Engaged to the Doctor. (Romance Ser.). 2000. per. 3.50 (*0-373-19418-8*, 1-19418-2) Silhouette.

— Man, Wife & Little Wonder. 1998. per. 3.50 (*0-373-19301-7*, 1-19301-0) Silhouette.

— La Petite Marieuse. (Horizon Ser.: No. 498). (FRE.). 1999. mass mkt. 3.50 (*0-373-39498-5*, 1-39498-0) Harlequin Bks.

— Wrangler's Wedding. (Romance Ser.). 1996. per. 3.25 (*0-373-19149-9*, 1-19149-3) Silhouette.

Nicholas, Robin A. J., jt. ed. see Miles, Roger J.

Nicholas, Ron, et al. Good Things Come in Small Groups. LC 85-778. 188p. (Orig.). 1985. pap. 11.99 (*0-87784-917-X*, 917) InterVarsity.

Nicholas, Sian. The Echo of War: Home Front Propaganda & the Wartime BBC 1939-1945. LC 95-32668. (Illus.). 240p. (C). 1997. text 79.95 (*0-7190-4608-4*) Manchester Univ Pr.

Nicholas, Stephen, ed. Convict Workers: Reinterpreting Australia's Past. (Studies in Australian History). (Illus.). 256p. (C). 1989. text 64.95 (*0-521-36126-5*) Cambridge U Pr.

Nicholas, Susan C., et al. Rights & Wrongs: Women's Struggle for Legal Equality. 2nd ed. LC 86-2461. (Women's Lives - Women's Work Ser.). 112p. 1986. pap. 9.95 (*0-935312-42-0*) Feminist Pr.

Nicholas, T., ed. see Metallurgical Society of AIME Staff.

Nicholas, Tamalyn. The Raven's Feather. 200p. 1998. pap. 16.95 (*1-892745-14-3*) Petals of Life.

Nicholas, Tawa. Three Centuries of American Music: A Collection of Sacred & Secular Music: Solo Song to 1865, Vol. 1. 400p. (C). 1989. 105.00 (*0-8161-0542-1*, G K Hall & Co) Mac Lib Ref.

Nicholas, Ted. The Complete Guide to Nonprofit Corporations. rev. ed. 248p. 1993. pap. 19.95 (*0-7931-0615-X*, 5615-6601) Dearborn.

— The Corporate Forms Kit. 2nd ed. 176p. 1996. pap. 24.95 incl. disk (*1-57410-057-2*, 56158202) Dearborn.

— How to Form Your Own Corporation Without a Lawyer for under $75.00. 25th anniversary rev. ed. 128p. 1996. 19.95 (*1-57410-023-8*, 5615-0103) Dearborn.

— How to Form Your Own "S" Corp & Avoid Double-Taxation. 2nd ed. LC 99-23050. 208p. 1999. pap. 23.95 (*1-57410-126-9*, 56143902) Dearborn.

— Magic Words That Bring You Riche$ 1998. pap. 19.95 (*1-887741-00-3*) Nicholas Direct.

Nicholas, Ted, ed. Advanced Materials, Development, Characterization Processing, & Mechanical Behavior: Proceedings, ASME International Mechanical Engineering Congress & Exposition, Atlanta, GA, 1996. LC 96-78675. (MD Ser.: Vol. 74). 269p. 1996. pap. 96.00 (*0-7918-1533-1*, TA403) ASME.

Nicholas, Ted & Melvin, Sean P. How to Form Your Own Corporation Without a Lawyer for Under $75.00. 26th ed. LC 99-20575. (Illus.). 263p. 1999. pap. 19.95 (*1-57410-125-0*) Dearborn.

Nicholas, Ted & Shenson, Howard L. The Complete Guide to Consulting Success. 205p. 1992. pap. 29.95 (*0-7931-0492-0*, 56155101) Dearborn.

— The Complete Guide to Consulting Success. 3rd rev. ed. LC 96-36016. 256p. 1997. pap. 29.95 (*1-57410-055-6*, 5615-5102) Dearborn.

Nicholas, Theodore, jt. ed. see Mall, Shankar.

Nicholas, Tom & Terelak, John. The Best of Oil Painting. (Illus.). 144p. 1996. 24.99 (*1-56496-267-9*, Quarry Bks) Rockport Pubs.

Nicholas, Warwick L. The Biology of Free-Living Nematodes. 2nd ed. (Illus.). 1984. 69.00 (*0-19-857587-4*) OUP.

Nicholas, William R., jt. ed. see Bachrach, David J.

Nicholaus, B. & Lowie, P. Think Twice: An Entertaining Collection of Choices. LC 97-97038. 128p. 1998. 10.00 (*0-345-41759-3*) Ballantine Pub Grp.

Nicholaus, B. & Lowrie, P. Have You Ever... LC 99-31404. 1999. 10.00 (*0-345-41760-7*) Ballantine Pub Grp.

***Nicholaus, Bret.** The Conversation Piece 2. 2000. 10.00 (*0-345-43866-3*) Ballantine Pub Grp.

***Nicholaus, Bret & Lowrie, Paul.** The Check Book: 200 Ways to Balance Your Life. LC 99-35384. (Illus.). 176p. 1999. pap. 10.95 (*1-57731-112-4*) New Wrld Lib.

— The Talk of the Tee: A Collection of Questions for Tigers, Hackers & Every Golfer in Between. LC 99-10983. (Illus.). 128p. 1999. 9.95 (*0-7407-0041-3*) Andrews & McMeel.

Nicholaus, Bret, jt. auth. see Lowrie, Paul.

Nicholaus, John. Air Defence Weapons. (Army Library). (Illus.). 48p. (J). (gr. 3-8). 1989. lib. bdg. 23.93 (*0-86592-423-6*) Rourke Enter.

— Army Air Support. (Army Library). (Illus.). 48p. (J). (gr. 3-8). 1989. lib. bdg. 23.93 (*0-86592-421-X*) Rourke Enter.

— Artillery. (Army Library). (Illus.). 48p. (J). (gr. 3-8). 1989. lib. bdg. 23.93 (*0-86592-419-8*) Rourke Enter.

— Main Battle Tanks. (Army Library). (Illus.). 48p. (J). (gr. 3-8). 1989. 13.95 (*0-685-58576-X*) Rourke Corp.

— Main Battle Tanks. (Army Library). (Illus.). 48p. (J). (gr. 3-8). 1989. lib. bdg. 23.93 (*0-86592-420-1*) Rourke Enter.

— Rockets & Missiles. (Army Library). (Illus.). 48p. (J). (gr. 3-8). 1989. lib. bdg. 13.95 (*0-685-58577-8*) Rourke Corp.

— Rockets & Missiles. (Army Library). (Illus.). 48p. (J). (gr. 3-8). 1989. lib. bdg. 23.93 (*0-86592-418-X*) Rourke Enter.

— Tracked Vehicles. (Army Library). (Illus.). 48p. (J). (gr. 3-8). 1989. lib. bdg. 13.95 (*0-685-58579-4*) Rourke Corp.

— Tracked Vehicles. (Army Library). (Illus.). 48p. (J). (gr. 3-8). 1989. lib. bdg. 23.93 (*0-86592-422-8*) Rourke Enter.

Nicholaus, Nick, tr. see Shakespeare, William.

Nichole. Friends. 64p. (Orig.). 1993. pap. 8.95 (*0-9637962-0-8*) Joli Pubng.

Nichole, Brianna. Passion's Bedtime Stories, Vol. 1. 2nd ed. Brott, L. J., ed. 139p. 1999. reprint ed. pap. 13.00 (*0-9670079-0-9*, Pub. by Brianna Nichole) Afrikan Wrld.

***Nicholes, Joseph.** At the Inn: A Christmas Story. large type ed. (Illus.). 68p. 1999. pap. 8.00 (*0-9666266-0-5*) Seedling Press.

Nicholes, Lorie. Angels Round About. Isackson, Darla, ed. 252p. 1998. pap. 13.95 (*0-9664447-1-X*) Stellar Pubg.

Nicholes, Mike. Parts Department-Inventory Management. 6th ed. (Illus.). 505p. (Orig.). student ed. 150.00 (*0-685-10193-2*) Mike Nicholes.

Nicholi, Armand. The Harvard Guide to Psychiatry. 3rd ed. LC 98-41672. (Illus.). 856p. 1999. 75.00 (*0-674-37570-X*) HUP.

Nicholi, Armand M. New Harvard Guide to Psychiatry. LC 87-24115. (Illus.). 864p. 1988. 58.00 (*0-674-61540-9*) Belknap Pr.

Nicholl, Boyd, jt. auth. see Bush, Neil L.

Nicholl, Charles. The Creature in the Map: A Journey to El Dorado. LC 96-45631. 1997. pap. 15.95 (*0-226-58025-3*) U Ch Pr.

— Elizabethan Writers. (Character Sketches Ser.). (Illus.). 64p. 1997. 11.95 (*1-85514-200-7*, Pub. by Natl Port Gall) Antique Collect.

— The Reckoning: The Murder of Christopher Marlowe. LC 95-3004. 424p. 1995. pap. 17.00 (*0-226-58024-5*) U Ch Pr.

***Nicholl, Charles.** Somebody Else. 1998. pap. 17.95 (*0-09-976771-6*, Pub. by Random) Trafalgar.

Nicholl, Charles. Somebody Else: Arthur Rimbaud in Africa, 1880-1891. LC 98-51305. (Illus.). 358p. 1999. pap. 17.00 (*0-226-58029-6*) U Ch Pr.

Nicholl, Christopher. Bishop's University, 1843-1970. (Illus.). 392p. 1994. 55.00 (*0-7735-1176-8*, Pub. by McG-Queens Univ Pr) CUP Services.

Nicholl, Desmond S. An Introduction to Genetic Engineering. (Studies in Biology). (Illus.). 182p. (C). 1994. pap. text 19.95 (*0-521-43634-6*) Cambridge U Pr.

Nicholl, Donald. Holiness. 176p. (Orig.). 1984. 8.95 (*0-8164-2336-9*) Harper SF.

Nicholl, Donald, tr. see Bochenski, Innocentius.

Nicholl, Donald, tr. see Von Balthasar, Hans U.

Nicholl, James R., jt. auth. see Nicholas, J. Karl.

Nicholl, James R., jt. ed. see Nicholas, J. Karl.

Nicholl, Malcolm J., jt. auth. see Rose, Colin.

Nicholl, Matthew. Introduction to Midi-Synthesis. Cavalier, Debbie, ed. (Illus.). 172p. (Orig.). (C). 1993. pap. text 19.95 (*1-57623-729-X*, EL03836) Wrner Bros.

Nicholls. Activities for Developing Supervisory Skills. 1993. 245.95 (*1-85904-002-0*) Ashgate Pub Co.

***Nicholls.** Surgery of the Colon & Rectum. 1999. text. write for info. (*0-443-05962-4*) Church.

Nicholls. Surgery of the Colon & Rectum. 1997. text 235.00 (*0-443-05565-3*, W B Saunders Co) Harcrt Hlth Sci Grp.

Nicholls, ed. Bituminous Surfacings. (Illus.). 320p. 1997. pap. 75.00 (*0-7514-0357-1*) Thomson Learn.

***Nicholls, A. J.** Freedom with Responsibility: The Social Market Economy in Germany, 1918-1963. (Illus.). 440p. 2000. pap. text 24.95 (*0-19-820852-9*) OUP.

— Weimar & the Rise of Hitler. 4th ed. 2000. pap. 25.00 (*0-312-23351-5*) St Martin.

Nicholls, Andrew D. The Jacobean Union: A Reconsideration of British Civil Policies Under the Early Stuarts. 64. LC 98-28287. (Contributions to the Study of World History Ser.: Vol. 64). 224p. 1999. 55.00 (*0-313-30835-7*, Greenwood Pr) Greenwood.

Nicholls, Anne. How to Master Public Speaking: A Practical Handbook for Every Occasion. 3rd ed. 160p. 1995. pap. 19.95 (*1-85703-149-0*, Pub. by How To Bks) Trans-Atl Phila.

— Mastering Public Speaking: How to Prepare & Deliver a Successful Speech or Presentation. 4th ed. 144p. 1998. pap. 144.00 (*1-85703-256-X*, Pub. by How To Bks) Trans-Atl Phila.

***Nicholls, Anthony & Wilson, Iain, eds.** Perioperative Medicine: Managing Surgical Patients with Medical Problems. (Illus.). 400p. 2000. pap. 39.95 (*0-19-262975-1*) OUP.

Nicholls, Anthony J. The Bonn Republic: West German Democracy, 1945-1990. LC 96-38922. (Post War World Ser.). (Illus.). 341p. (C). 1997. pap. 22.26 (*0-582-49230-0*) Longman.

— Weimar & the Rise of Hitler. 3rd ed. LC 90-48823. (Making of the Twentieth Century Ser.). (C). 1991. pap. text 30.95 (*0-312-05713-X*) St Martin.

Nicholls, Bruce J. Contextualization: A Theology of Gospel & Culture. 72p. (C). 1995. reprint ed. pap. 5.95 (*1-57383-052-6*) Regent College.

Nicholls, Bruce J., ed. The Unique Christ in Our Pluralistic World. LC 94-36248. (World Evangelical Fellowship Ser.). 288p. 1995. pap. 14.99 (*0-8010-2013-1*) Baker Bks.

Nicholls, C. S. David Livingstone. (Illus.). 128p. 1998. pap. 9.94 (*0-7509-1591-9*, Pub. by Sutton Pub Ltd) Intl Pubs Mktg.

Nicholls, C. S., ed. Encyclopedia of Biography. LC 97-12316. (Illus.). 960p. 1998. text 80.00 (*0-312-17568-X*) St Martin.

Nicholls, Christine S. Dictionary of National Biography: Missing Persons. 790p. 1993. 115.00 (*0-19-865211-9*) OUP.

Nicholls, Christine S. & Blake, Lord, eds. The Dictionary of National Biography: Tenth Supplement: 1981-1985. 532p. 1990. suppl. ed. 89.00 (*0-19-865210-0*) OUP.

Nicholls, Christine S., ed. see Smith, George.

Nicholls, Christine S., jt. ed. see Thomas, Keith.

Nicholls, Christopher J. & Melmed, Raun D. Succeeding with Difficult Children, 2 bks., 4 cass. (Illus.). 195p. (Orig.). 1994. ring bd. 45.00 incl. audio (*0-9655133-0-0*) Thisisit.

Nicholls, Cliff, ed. Asphalt Surfacings. LC 98-165437. (Illus.). 432p. (C). 1997. pap. 140.00 (*0-419-23110-2*, D5757) Thomson Learn.

Nicholls, D. Proteins, Transmitters & Synapses. (Illus.). 288p. 1994. pap. 49.95 (*0-632-03661-3*, Pub. by Blckwll Scitfc UK) Blackwell Sci.

***Nicholls, David.** Adolf Hitler: A Biographical Companion. (Biographical Companions Ser.). (Illus.). 300p. 2000. 55.00 (*0-87436-965-7*) ABC-CLIO.

Nicholls, David. From Dessalines to Duvalier: Race, Colour & National Independence in Haiti. LC 95-8893. (C). 1995. pap. text 18.95 (*0-8135-2240-4*) Rutgers U Pr.

— From Dessalines to Duvalier: Race, Colour & National Independence in Haiti. rev. ed. LC 95-8893. 400p. (C). 1995. reprint ed. text 49.95 (*0-8135-2239-0*) Rutgers U Pr.

— The Lost Prime Minister: A Life of Sir Charles Dilke. LC 95-6072. 1995. 55.00 (*1-85285-125-2*) Hambledon Press.

***Nicholls, David.** Napoleon: A Biographical Companion. LC 99-22535. (Bibliography Ser.). 352p. 1999. lib. bdg. 55.00 (*0-87436-957-6*) ABC-CLIO.

Nicholls, David, ed. The Cambridge History of American Music. LC 98-3814. (Illus.). 640p. (C). 1999. 90.00 (*0-521-45429-8*) Cambridge U Pr.

***Nicholls, David, ed.** The Whole World of Music: A Henry Cowell Symposium. (Illus.). 260p. 1998. text 59.00 (*90-5755-003-2*, Harwood Acad Pubs); pap. text 24.00 (*90-5755-004-0*, Harwood Acad Pubs) Gordon & Breach.

Nicholls, David & Kerr, Fergus, eds. John Henry Newman: Reason, Rhetoric & Romanticism. 224p. (C). 1991. 31.95 (*0-8093-1758-3*) S Ill U Pr.

***Nicholls, David G.** Conjuring the Folk: Forms of Modernity in African America. LC 99-50557. (Illus.). 192p. (C). 2000. text 39.50 (*0-472-11034-9*, 11034) U of Mich Pr.

Nicholls, David G. & Ferguson, Stuart J. Bioenergetics. 2nd ed. 255p. 1992. pap. text 45.00 (*0-12-518124-8*) Acad Pr.

Nicholls, Delia, jt. auth. see Hatherly, Janelle.

Nicholls, Dorothy D., ed. Gleanings from a Cornish Notebook. (C). 1989. 40.00 (*1-85022-025-5*, Pub. by Dyllansow Truran) St Mut.

Nicholls, Elgiva. Tatting. (Knitting, Crocheting, Tatting Ser.). (Illus.). 144p. 1984. reprint ed. pap. 6.95 (*0-486-24612-4*) Dover.

Nicholls, Elizabeth L., jt. ed. see Callaway, Jack M.

Nicholls, Florence Z. Button Hand Book. 288p. 1994. pap. 29.95 (*0-9629046-1-9*) New Leaf Pubs.

Nicholls, G. Measure for Measure. (Text & Performance Ser.). (Illus.). 96p. (C). 1986. pap. 10.95 (*0-333-34982-2*, Pub. by Macmillan) Humanities.

Nicholls, G. Heaton & Jabavu, Davidson D. The Natives Bills (1935) & Native Views on the Native Bills (1935) (Colin Webb Natal & Zululand Ser.: No. 8). (Illus.). 84p. 1995. pap. 19.00 (*0-86980-913-X*, Pub. by Univ Natal Pr) Intl Spec Bk.

Nicholls, Geoff. The Drum Book: A History of the Rock Drum Kit. (Illus.). 108p. 1997. 24.95 (*0-87930-476-6*) Miller Freeman.

Nicholls, George. A History of the English Poor Law, 3 vols. rev. ed. LC 66-19700. (Reprints of Economic Classics Ser.). 1967. reprint ed. 175.00 (*0-678-00277-0*) Kelley.

— A History of the Scotch Poor Law. LC 67-28455. (Reprints of Economic Classics Ser.). x, 288p. 1967. reprint ed. 45.00 (*0-678-00326-2*) Kelley.

Nicholls, Gill. Collaborative Change in Education. 160p. 1997. pap. 27.50 (*0-7494-2113-4*, Kogan Pg Educ) Stylus Pub VA.

— Learning to Teach: A Handbook for Primary & Secondary School Teachers. 224p. 1999. pap. 32.50 (*0-7494-2865-1*, Pub. by Kogan Page Ltd) Stylus Pub VA.

— Professional Development in Higher Education: New Dimensions & Directions. 160p. 2000. pap. 29.95 (*0-7494-3207-1*, Pub. by Kogan Page Ltd) Stylus Pub VA.

Nicholls, H. R. Advanced Tactile Sensing for Robotics. (Series in Robotics & Automated Systems: No. 5). 312p. 1992. text 81.00 (*981-02-0870-7*) World Scientific Pub.

Nicholls, J. & Glass, Richard. Coloproctology. (Illus.). 244p. 1985. 61.95 (*0-387-15140-0*) Spr-Verlag.

Nicholls, J. & Russell, J. K., eds. Modern Methods of Igneous Petrology: Understanding Magmatic Processes. (Reviews in Mineralogy Ser.: Vol. 24). 1990. per. 24.00 (*0-939950-29-4*) Mineralogical Soc.

Nicholls, J., jt. ed. see Torre, V.

Nicholls, J. E. Z User Workshop, York, 1991: Proceedings of the Sixth Annual Z User Meeting York, 16-17 December 1991. Van Rijsbergen, C. J., ed. (Workshops in Computing Ser.). (Illus.). viii, 403p. 1992. 69.00 (*0-387-19780-X*) Spr-Verlag.

Nicholls, J. E. & Van Rijsbergen, C. J., eds. Z User Workshop: Proceedings of the Fourth Annual Z User Meeting, 15 December 1989, Oxford, U. K. (Workshops in Computing Ser.). (Illus.). 288p. 1990. pap. 59.00 (*0-387-19627-7*) Spr-Verlag.

— Z User Workshop Oxford, 1990: Proceedings of the Annual Meeting, 5th, December 17-18, 1990, U. K. (Workshops in Computing Ser.). ix, 387p. 1991. pap. 59.00 (*0-387-19672-2*) Spr-Verlag.

Nicholls, J. G. Repair & Regeneration of the Nervous System: Berlin, 1981 Proceedings. (Dahlem Workshop Reports: Vol. 24). 411p. 1982. 42.95 (*0-387-11649-4*) Spr-Verlag.

Nicholls, J. R., jt. ed. see Strutt, J. E.

***Nicholls, James & Owen, Susan J., eds.** A Babel of Bottles: Drink, Drinkers & Drinking Places in Literature. 208p. 2000. 55.00 (*1-84127-047-4*, Pub. by Sheffield Acad) CUP Services.

Nicholls, John & Sargent, Malcom. Marketing in Europe. LC 95-83290. (Perspectives on Europe Ser.). 192p. 1996. 72.95 (*1-85972-141-9*, Pub. by Avebry) Ashgate Pub Co.

Nicholls, John & Thorkildsen, Theresa, eds. Reasons for Learning: Expanding the Conversation on Student-Teacher Collaboration. 192p. (C). 1995. text 34.00 (*0-8077-3398-9*); pap. text 16.95 (*0-8077-3397-0*) Tchrs Coll.

Nicholls, John, et al. Beginning Writing. (English, Language & Education Ser.). 128p. 1990. pap. 32.95 (*0-335-09224-1*) OpUniv Pr.

Nicholls, John, jt. auth. see Martin, Peter.

Nicholls, John, jt. ed. see Wells, Gordon.

Nicholls, John E. Structure & Design of Programming Languages. LC 74-12801. (IBM Systems Programming Ser.). (Illus.). 592p. (C). 1975. text. write for info. (*0-201-14454-9*) Addison-Wesley.

Nicholls, John G. The Competitive Ethos & Democratic Education. LC 88-16303. (Illus.). 280p. 1989. 49.95 (*0-674-15417-7*) HUP.

***Nicholls, John G.** From Neuron to Brain: A Cellular & Molecular Approach to the Function of the Nervous System. 4th ed. LC 00-36529. 2000. write for info. (*0-87893-439-1*) Sinauer Assocs.

Nicholls, John G. The Search for Connections: Studies of Regeneration in the Nervous System of the Leech. LC 86-22061. (Magnes Memorial Lectures: Vol. 2). (Illus.). 86p. (Orig.). 1987. pap. text 21.95 (*0-87893-577-0*) Sinauer Assocs.

Nicholls, John G. & Hazzard, Susan P. Education As Adventure: Lessons from the Second Grade. LC 92-36030. 240p. (C). 1993. text 37.00 (*0-8077-3240-0*); pap. text 17.95 (*0-8077-3239-7*) Tchrs Coll.

Nicholls, John G., et al. From Neuron to Brain: A Cellular & Molecular Approach to the Function of the Nervous System. 3rd ed. LC 92-15974. (Illus.). 688p. (C). 1992. text 64.95 (*0-87893-580-0*) Sinauer Assocs.

Nicholls, Josephine H. Bayou Triste: A Story of Louisiana. LC 72-1516. (Black Heritage Library Collection). 1977. reprint ed. 26.95 (*0-8369-9040-4*) Ayer.

Nicholls, Judith, ed. Earthways, Earthwise: Poems on Conservation. (Illus.). 96p. (J). 1998. pap. 11.95 (*0-19-272248-4*) OUP.

— What on Earth? Poems with a Conservation Theme. (Illus.). 132p. (J). (gr. 2 up). 1989. pap. 9.95 (*0-571-15262-7*) Faber & Faber.

Nicholls, Keith. Volleyball. (Skills of the Game Ser.). (Illus.). 120p. 1995. pap. 19.95 (*1-85223-831-3*, Pub. by Crolwood) Trafalgar.

Nicholls, M. G., et al. Legal Studies for South Australia Years 11 & 12. 1989. pap. 31.00 (*0-409-49471-2*, AT, MICHIE) LEXIS Pub.

Nicholls, Mark. A History of the Modern British Isles, 1529-1603: The Two Kingdoms. LC 98-21301. (History of Modern Britain Ser.). (Illus.). 352p. (Orig.). 1999. 59.95 (*0-631-19333-2*); pap. 29.95 (*0-631-19334-0*) Blackwell Pubs.

Nicholls, Maureen. Gold Pan Mining Company & Shops Breckenridge, Colorado. Gilliland, Mary E., ed. LC 94-66385. (Illus.). 64p. (Orig.). 1994. pap. text 13.95 (*0-9641029-0-0*) Quandary Pubng.

Nicholls, Paul. Tolley's Discrimination Law Handbook. 304p. 1991. 66.00 (*0-85459-425-6*, Pub. by Tolley Pubng) St Mut.

Nicholls, Paul & Ball, Paul. Tolley's Discrimination Law Handbook. 400p. 1993. pap. 200.00 (*0-85459-628-3*, Pub. by Tolley Pubng) St Mut.

Nicholls, Paul L., jt. auth. see Evans, Lloyd.

Nicholls, Paul T., jt. ed. see Ensor, Pat.

Nicholls, Peter. Modernisms: A Literary Guide. 1995. pap. 17.95 (*0-520-20103-5*, Pub. by U CA Pr) Cal Prin Full Svc.

— The World of Fantastic Films: An Illustrated Survey. LC 84-10185. (Illus.). 224 p. 1984. 22.95 (*0-396-08382-X*) Putnam Pub Group.

Nicholls, Peter, jt. auth. see Clute, John.

Nicholls, Peter, jt. ed. see Clute, John.

Nicholls, R. V., jt. auth. see Cook, R. M.

Nicholls, R. W., jt. auth. see Armstrong, B. H.

Nicholls, Richard. Corpus Speculorum Etruscorum: Great Britain 2 Cambridge. Swaddling, Judith & Rasmussen, Tom, eds. LC 92-35756. (Illus.). 141p. (C). 1994. text 100.00 (*0-521-43380-0*) Cambridge U Pr.

Nicholls, Richard E. Beginning Hydroponics. rev. ed. LC 89-43022. (Illus.). 128p. 1990. pap. text 9.95 (*0-89471-741-3*) Running Pr.

Nicholls, Richard E., ed. see London, Jack.

Nicholls, Robert. Gardens of Delight: A Pop-Up Anthology of Romantic Verse & Paper Flowers. LC 97-150280. 12p. 1997. 16.95 (*0-8109-3392-6*, Pub. by Abrams) Time Warner.

Nicholls, Robert P., jt. ed. see Ray, Mary H.

Nicholls, Robert W. Old Time Masquerading in the U. S. Virgin Islands. (Illus.). 256p. 1998. pap. 15.00 (*1-886007-09-8*) VI Human Coun.

Nicholls, Roger A. Nietzsche in the Early Work of Thomas Mann. LC 55-9553. (University of California Publications in Social Welfare: Vol. 45). 128p. reprint ed. pap. 39.70 (*0-608-14168-2*, 202125200021) Bks Demand.

Nicholls, Sandra. The Untidy Bride. 72p. 1991. pap. 12.95 (*1-55082-021-4*, Pub. by Quarry Pr) LPC InBook.

Nicholls, Sandra, ed. Vintage 95: The League of Canadian Poets. 104p. 1996. pap. 16.95 (*1-55082-170-9*, Pub. by Quarry Pr) LPC InBook.

— Vintage 93: The League of Canadian Poets. 144p. 1996. pap. 16.95 (*1-55082-122-9*, Pub. by Quarry Pr) LPC InBook.

Nicholls, Sandra & Hoadley-Maidment, Elizabeth. Current Issues in Teaching English As a Second Language to Adults. 160p. 1988. pap. text 14.95 (*0-7131-8450-7*, Pub. by E A) Routldge.

***Nicholls, Stan.** Fade to Black. large type ed. (Illus.). (J). 1998. pap. 16.95 (*0-7540-6016-0*, Galaxy Child Lrg Print) Chivers N Amer.

Nicholls, Sue. Michael Finnegan, Tap Your Chinigin: Developing Music Skills with New Songs from Old Favorites. unabridged ed. (Illus.). (J). (gr. 1-2). 1998. pap. 11.95 (*0-7136-4716-7*, Pub. by A & C Blk) Midpt Trade.

Nicholls, Trevor J., jt. auth. see Norstog, Knut J.

Nicholls, William. Christian Antisemitism: A History of Hate. LC 92-35713. 528p. 1993. 40.00 (*0-87668-398-7*) Aronson.

— Christian Antisemitism: A History of Hate. LC 92-35713. 532p. 1997. pap. 40.00 (*1-56821-519-3*) Aronson.

Nicholls, William, jt. auth. see Kent, Ian.

Nicholls, Willis J. English Law for Business Studies. 3rd ed. LC 74-81551. 437p. reprint ed. pap. 135.50 (*0-608-14471-1*, 202098500020) Bks Demand.

Nicholoson, Daniel. Remembering His Benefit. 48p. 1988. pap. text 2.95 (*0-88144-074-4*) Christian Pub.

Nicholoson, Peter, jt. ed. see Horton, John.

Nicholous, Tom, jt. selected by see Schlemm, Betty Lou.

Nichols. Holt Algebra Two with Trigonometry. 1978. pap. 28.00 (*0-03-018916-0*) Holt R&W.

— Algebra with Trigonometry: 1992. 1992. text, student ed. 54.50 (*0-03-005433-8*) H Holt & Co.

— Childbirth Education. 2nd ed. LC 99-32238. (C). 1999. text 59.00 (*0-7216-8009-7*, W B Saunders Co) Harcrt Hlth Sci Grp.

— Cpsq Intr to Law & Legal Proce. 2nd ed. 1998. pap. text 47.00 (*0-07-229105-2*) McGraw.

— The Drinking Driver in Minnesota, Issue 20. 100p. 1998. ring bd. write for info. (*0-327-00718-4*, 8186617) LEXIS Pub.

— The European Pentarchy. 1972. pap. text 85.50 (*90-247-1110-X*, Pub. by M Nijhoff) Kluwer Academic.

— Geometry 1986. 1991. text 58 25 (*0-03-005407-9*) Holt R&W.

— Geometry 1991. 1991. pap., teacher ed. 80.00 (*0-03-005408-7*) H Holt & Co.

— Hearing Each Other. 1994. 24.95 (*0-02-923135-3*) S&S Trade.

— Holt Algebra with Trigonometry 92. 1992. pap., teacher ed. 86.00 (*0-03-005434-6*) H Holt & Co.

— Holt Algebra 1 1992. 1992. pap., teacher ed. 79.00 (*0-03-005422-2*) H Holt & Co.

— The Innkeeper's Horse. (J). 1988. 11.93 (*0-516-09601-X*) Childrens.

— Intermediate Microeconomics. 7th ed. (C). 1997. 209.50 (*0-03-017924-6*) Harcourt Coll Pubs.

— Math, Grade 3. 85th ed. 1985. text 45.75 (*0-03-064203-5*) Holt R&W.

— Math, Grade 4. 85th ed. 1985. text 45.75 (*0-03-064208-6*) Holt R&W.

— Math, Grade 6. 85th ed. 1985. text 46.50 (*0-03-064216-7*) Holt R&W.

— Math, Grade 7. 85th ed. 1985. text 51.75 (*0-03-064219-1*) Holt R&W.

— Math, Grade 8. 85th ed. 1985. text 51.75 (*0-03-064223-X*, q) Holt R&W.

— Math: Grade 5. 1985. 40.00 (*0-03-064212-4*) Harcourt Schl Pubs.

— Math Consumable, 1985. 1985. pap. 28.75 (*0-03-064206-X*) Harcourt Schl Pubs.

— Math, 1985. 1985. pap. 21.75 (*0-03-064196-9*); pap. 21.75 (*0-03-064199-3*); pap., wbk. ed. 12.75 (*0-03-068827-2*); pap., wbk. ed. 12.75 (*0-03-068841-8*); pap., wbk. ed. 12.75 (*0-03-068854-X*); pap., wbk. ed. 12.75 (*0-03-068868-X*); pap., wbk. ed. 14.75 (*0-03-068881-7*); pap., wbk. ed. 14.75 (*0-03-068892-2*) Harcourt Schl Pubs.

***Nichols.** Moving & Learning. 4th ed. 1999. 50.46 (*0-07-092148-2*) McGraw.

Nichols. Moving & Learning: Test & Lessons Plan Manual, No. 2. 1990. 46.95 (*0-8016-3687-6*) Mosby Inc.

— Moving & Learning Lesson Plan Manual. 2nd ed. 392p. 1990. pap. 18.95 (*0-8016-5802-0*) Mosby Inc.

— Pre Algebra, 1986. 1986. 48.50 (*0-03-001858-7*) Harcourt Schl Pubs.

— Pre-Algebra, 1992. 1992. text, teacher ed. 78.25 (*0-03-047069-2*); text, student ed. 48.50 (*0-03-047068-4*) H Holt & Co.

— Psychological Care in Physical Illness. 2nd ed. 248p. 1993. pap. 41.50 (*1-56593-134-3*, 0446) Singular Publishing.

— Service of Glory. 1998. pap. 17.95 (*0-949535-95-8*) Franciscan U Pr.

Nichols & Pashard. Maine One Hundred Years Ago. (Historical Ser.). (Illus.). 1977. pap. 3.50 (*0-89540-049-9*, SB-049) Sun Pub.

Nichols & Woolson. Old Florida. (Historical Ser.). (Illus.). 1977. pap. 3.50 (*0-89540-054-5*, SB-054) Sun Pub.

Nichols, jt. auth. see Barot, Rohit.

Nichols, jt. auth. see Scala, Bea.

Nichols, A. Light from the East. 1990. pap. 118.00 (*0-7220-5080-1*) St Mut.

Nichols, A., jt. auth. see Phillips, Jeffery D.

Nichols, A. L., ed. Aerosol Particle Size Analysis: Good Calibration Practices. 126p. 1998. 89.95 (*0-85404-452-3*) Spr-Verlag.

— Aerosol Sampling Guidelines. 180p. 1998. 120.00 (*0-85404-457-4*) Spr-Verlag.

Nichols, Aidan. Byzantine Gospel: Maximus the Confessor in Modern Scholarship. 280p. 1993. text 47.95 (*0-567-09651-3*, Pub. by T & T Clark) Bks Intl VA.

— Christendom, Awake: On Reenergising the Church in Culture. LC 99-25714. 250p. 1999. pap. 28.00 (*0-8028-4690-4*) Eerdmans.

— Epiphany: A Theological Introduction to Catholicism. LC 96-35209. 496p. (Orig.). 1996. pap. 34.95 (*0-8146-5504-1*, M Glazier) Liturgical Pr.

— From Newman to Congar. 1995. pap. 29.95 (*0-567-29181-2*, Pub. by T & T Clark) Bks Intl VA.

— A Grammar of Consent: The Existence of God in Christian Tradition. LC 90-50978. (Library of Religious Philosophy: Vol. 6). (C). 1991. text 37.00 (*0-268-01026-9*) U of Notre Dame Pr.

— The Holy Eucharist. 200p. 1991. pap. 15.95 (*0-685-51641-5*, Pub. by Veritas Pubns) St Mut.

— Holy Eucharist. 200p. 1989. pap. 45.00 (*1-85390-182-2*, Pub. by Veritas Pubns) St Mut.

— Holy Order: The Apostolic Ministry from the New Testament to Vatican Two. 200p. (Orig.). 1991. pap. 16.95 (*1-85390-175-X*, Pub. by Veritas Pubns) St Mut.

— Looking at the Liturgy: A Critical View of It's Contemporary Reform. LC 96-83645. 128p. 1996. pap. text 9.95 (*0-89870-592-4*) Ignatius Pr.

***Nichols, Aidan.** No Bloodless Myth: A Guide Through Balthasar's Dramatics. LC 99-51509. 1999. pap. 23.95 (*0-8132-0981-1*) Cath U Pr.

— No Bloodless Myth: A Guide Through Balthasar's Dramatics. LC 99-51509. 2000. 23.95 (*0-8132-0980-3*) Cath U Pr.

Nichols, Aidan. The Panther & the Hind: A Theological History of Angelicanism. 208p. 1993. pap. text 24.95 (*0-567-29232-0*, Pub. by T & T Clark) Bks Intl VA.

— The Shape of Catholic Theology: An Introduction to Its Sources, Principles, & History. 250p. 1991. pap. 19.95 (*0-8146-1909-6*) Liturgical Pr.

— Splendour of Doctrine. 1998. pap. text 19.95 (*1-884660-02-9*) Urbi Et Orbi.

— The Word Has Been Abroad: A Guide Through Balthasar's Aesthetics. 288p. 1998. pap. 23.95 (*0-8132-0925-0*); text 43.95 (*0-8132-0924-2*) Cath U Pr.

Nichols, Aidan, ed. see Ratzinger, Joseph C.

Nichols, Aidan, tr. see Von Balthasar, Hans Urs.

Nichols, Aiden. The Theology of Joseph Ratzinger. 1994. pap. 31.95 (*0-567-29148-0*, Pub. by T & T Clark) Bks Intl VA.

Nichols, Alan, Sr. Letters Home from the Lafayette Flying Corps. Nichols, Nancy A., ed. LC 92-28089. (Illus.). 320p. 1993. 24.95 (*0-9630274-0-9*); pap. 14.95 (*0-9630274-7-6*) J D Huff.

Nichols, Alan H. Higher Ground: A Sacred Mountain Primer. (Illus.). 224p. 1994. pap. 19.95 (*0-9630274-1-7*) J D Huff.

— Journey: A Bicycle Odyssey Through Central Asia. Nichols, Nancy A., ed. (Illus.). 221p. 1991. 22.95 (*0-9630274-2-5*) J D Huff.

Nichols, Alan H. & Nichols, Nancy A. Sacred Mountains of California. (Illus.). 224p. 1994. 35.00 (*0-9630274-3-3*) J D Huff.

Nichols, Albert L. Targeting Economic Incentives for Environmental Protection. (Regulation of Economic Activity Ser.). (Illus.). 207p. 1984. 30.00 (*0-262-14036-5*) MIT Pr.

Nichols, Angie. Backstreet Boys Confidential: The Unofficial Book. 1998. pap. 16.95 (*0-8230-7860-4*, Billboard Bks) Watsn-Guptill.

***Nichols, Angie.** Britney Spears. (Illus.). (J). 2000. pap. 7.95 (*0-8230-7865-5*, Billboard Bks) Watsn-Guptill.

Nichols, Angie. 'N Sync: Get 'n Sync with the Guys. (Illus.). 64p. (YA). (gr. 6-12). 1999. pap. 12.95 (*0-8230-8352-7*, Billboard Bks) Watsn-Guptill.

— 'N Sync Confidential. (Illus.). 1999. pap. 16.95 (*0-8230-8353-5*) Watsn-Guptill.

— 98 (Degree Sign) The Unofficial Book. (Illus.). 64p. 1999. pap. 12.95 (*0-8230-8351-9*) Watsn-Guptill.

Nichols, Angie, jt. auth. see Watson-Guptill Staff.

Nichols, Ann, et al. Stories in Stone: The Buildings of the Saint Teresa Campus Schools. (Illus.). 120p. 1998. pap. write for info. (*0-9667816-2-7*) Winona Print.

Nichols, Ann E. Seeable Signs: The Iconography of the Seven Sacraments, 1350-1544. (Illus.). 496p. (C). 1997. reprint ed. 130.00 (*0-85115-342-9*) Boydell & Brewer.

Nichols, Ann E., jt. ed. see Davidson, Clifford.

Nichols, Anne. Abie's Irish Rose. LC 74-29510. (Modern Jewish Experience Ser.). 1975. reprint ed. 30.95 (*0-405-06736-4*) Ayer.

***Nichols, Anne.** Adult Nurse Practitioner Review Course. 2000. 99.95 (*0-9679170-4-2*) NPeducationcom.

***Nichols, Anne & Gibbs, Michael.** Comprehensive Multimedia Pharmacology Course. 80p. 2000. 99.95 incl. cd-rom (*0-9679170-2-6*) NPeducationcom.

Nichols, Anne, jt. auth. see Gibbs, Michael.

Nichols, Annie. Potatoes. 1998. 24.95 (*0-8478-2077-7*, Pub. by Rizzoli Intl) St Martin.

Nichols, Annie, jt. auth. see Drennan, Mathew.

Nichols, Annye & Nichols, Candi. Baby Memories: A Journal of Your Baby's First Year of Life. (Illus.). 64p. (Orig.). 1997. pap. 12.95 (*0-9654914-0-4*) Nichols & Nichols.

Nichols, B. J. Introduction to NAFTA. Ewert, D. E., ed. 68p. 1994. pap. text 44.50 (*1-883006-14-7*) Intl Busn Pubns.

— NAFTA Documentation & Procedures. 140p. 1994. pap. text 88.00 (*1-883006-11-2*) Intl Busn Pubns.

Nichols, B. J., jt. auth. see Ewert, D. E.

Nichols, Barbara & Leonard, Peter, eds. Gender, Aging & the State. LC 94-71246. 230p. 1994. 48.99 (*1-895431-97-2*, Pub. by Black Rose); pap. 19.99 (*1-895431-96-4*, Pub. by Black Rose) Consort Bk Sales.

Nichols, Barry. Opposite Song Big Book: Black & White Nellie Edge I Can Read & Sing Big Book. (J). (ps-2). 1988. pap. text 21.00 (*0-922053-06-5*) N Edge Res.

Nichols, Belia, jt. auth. see Nichols, Peter.

Nichols, Beverley. Down the Garden Path. (Illus.). 290p. 1986. pap. 29.50 (*1-870673-22-0*, Pub. by Garden Art Pr) Antique Collect.

Nichols, Beverley. Down the Garden Path. 290p. 1986. reprint ed. pap. 29.50 (*1-85149-007-8*) Antique Collect.

— Father Figure. LC 72-185138. 1972. write for info. (*0-434-51203-6*) Buttrwrth-Heinemann.

— Garden Open Tomorrow. LC 76-558876. (Illus.). 269 p. 1968. write for info. (*0-434-51200-1*) Buttrwrth-Heinemann.

— The Gift of a Garden: Or, Some Flowers Remembered. LC 70-882119. 344 p. 1971. write for info. (*0-491-00358-7*) Virgin Bks.

— The Gift of a Home. LC 73-150216. 395 p. (J). 1972. write for info. (*0-491-00703-5*) Virgin Bks.

— Green Grows the City: The Story of a London Garden. 1997. 29.50 (*1-870673-23-9*, Pub. by Garden Art Pr) Antique Collect.

— Laughter on the Stairs. LC 98-7155. (Illus.). 260p. 1998. reprint ed. 24.95 (*0-88192-460-1*) Timber.

— Merry Hall. LC 97-47253. (Illus.). 342p. 1998. reprint ed. 24.95 (*0-88192-417-2*) Timber.

— The Moonflower. LC 74-171256. 224 p. (J). 1973. write for info. (*0-491-01111-3*) Virgin Bks.

— No Man's Street. LC 74-170790. 192 p. (J). 1973. write for info. (*0-491-01121-0*) Virgin Bks.

— Sunlight on the Lawn. LC 98-39846. (Illus.). 273p. 1999. reprint ed. 24.95 (*0-88192-467-9*, Amadeus Pr) Timber.

Nichols, Beverley. The Unforgiving Minute: Some Confessions from Childhood to the Outbreak of the Second World War. LC 79-303380. vii, 311 p. 1978. 5.95 (*0-491-02444-4*) Virgin Bks.

***Nichols, Beverly B.** Bev's Collectibles: A Guide to Building Your Own Valuable Collections. 165p. 2000. pap. 12.95 (*1-887650-20-2*, Pub. by Factor Pr) BookWorld.

Nichols, Beverly J., jt. auth. see Ewert, Donald E.

Nichols, Beverly S. No Magic Wands. LC 98-89887. 365p. 1999. 25.00 (*0-7388-0321-9*); pap. 15.00 (*0-7388-0322-7*) Xlibris Corp.

Nichols, Bill. Blurred Boundaries: Questions of Meaning in Contemporary Culture. LC 94-2205. 208p. 1995. 35.00 (*0-253-34064-0*); pap. 14.95 (*0-253-20900-5*) Ind U Pr.

— Newsreel: Documentary Filmaking on the American Left. Jowett, Garth S., ed. LC 79-6681. (Dissertations on Film Ser.). 313p. 1980. 23.95 (*0-405-12914-9*) Ayer.

— Representing Reality: Issues & Concepts in Documentary. LC 91-2637. (Illus.). 336p. 1992. 39.95 (*0-253-34060-8*); pap. 18.50 (*0-253-20681-2*, MB-681) Ind U Pr.

Nichols, Bill, ed. Movies & Methods, Vol. I. LC 74-22968. 1977. pap. 22.50 (*0-520-03151-2*, Pub. by U CA Pr) Cal Prin Full Svc.

— Movies & Methods, Vol. II. LC 74-22969. 1985. pap. 22.50 (*0-520-05409-1*, Pub. by U CA Pr) Cal Prin Full Svc.

Nichols, Bradford, et al. Pthreads Programming: A Posix Standard for Better Understanding. Oram, Andy, ed. (Illus.). 284p. 1996. reprint ed. pap. 34.95 (*1-56592-115-1*) Thomson Learn.

Nichols, Bridget. Liturgical Hermeneutics: Interpreting Liturgical Rites in Performance. LC 96-4312. 318p. 1996. pap. 57.95 (*0-8204-2987-2*, BX5145) P Lang Pubng.

Nichols Brown, Ann L. Hillsborough Co, NH. Census, 1850, Pt. 3. (Illus.). 406p. (Orig.). 1993. pap. text 33.00 (*1-55613-913-6*) Heritage Bk.

Nichols, Bruce & Loescher, Gilburt D., eds. The Moral Nation: Humanitarianism & U. S. Foreign Policy Today. LC 88-40323. (C). 1990. pap. text 18.50 (*0-268-01398-5*) U of Notre Dame Pr.

Nichols, Buffy, jt. auth. see Nichols, Mark.

Nichols, C., jt. ed. see Nichols, Mary A.

***Nichols, C. Reid, et al.** Recent Advances & Issues in Oceanography. (Frontiers of Science Ser.). (Illus.). 304p. 2001. 55.00 (*1-57356-406-0*) Oryx Pr.

Nichols, C. William. Storytelling the Gospel. LC 99-21211. 112p. 1999. pap. 12.99 (*0-8272-3438-4*, 984624, Pub. by Chalice Pr) Abingdon.

Nichols, Candi, jt. auth. see Nichols, Annye.

Nichols, Carol, jt. auth. see Schinzing, Daniel Lee.

Nichols, Carole. Votes & More for Women: Suffrage & after in Connecticut. LC 83-8405. (Women & History Ser.: No. 5). 92p. 1983. text 29.95 (*0-86656-192-7*) Haworth Pr.

Nichols, Catherine. Calligraphy. (Illus.). 16p. (J). (gr. 4-9). 1998. pap. 8.95 (*0-8167-4967-1*) Troll Communs.

— Kachinas: A Native American Craft Kit. (Illus.). 16p. (Orig.). (J). (gr. 2-7). 1996. pap. 7.95 (*0-8167-4049-6*) Troll Communs.

— Language Expression. Whitfield, Jennifer, ed. (Thinking Skills Library). (Illus.). 104p. (Orig.). (J). (gr. 2-5). 1997. pap. text, teacher ed. 9.95 (*1-56784-705-6*) Newbridge Educ.

Nichols, Cathy, ed. see Packard, Mary.

Nichols, Cathy, ed. see Schwabacker, Martin.

Nichols, Cecil B. Human Growth & Development Study Guide. 256p. 1993. per. 19.95 (*0-8403-8688-5*) Kendall-Hunt.

Nichols, Charlene & Wright, Darlene. Loan Administration in the 90s Vol. 1: Looking Ahead. LC 95-152830. 1994. text 65.00 (*1-880999-21-8*); text 65.00 (*1-880999-29-3*); text 65.00 (*1-880999-20-X*); text 585.00 (*1-880999-30-7*) Loan Admin.

— Loan Administration in the 90s Vol. 2: Looking Ahead. 1994. text 65.00 (*1-880999-22-6*) Loan Admin.

— Loan Administration in the 90s Vol. 3: Looking Ahead. 1994. text 65.00 (*1-880999-23-4*) Loan Admin.

— Loan Administration in the 90s Vol. 4: Looking Ahead. 1994. text 65.00 (*1-880999-24-2*) Loan Admin.

— Loan Administration in the 90s Vol. 5: Looking Ahead. 1994. text 65.00 (*1-880999-25-0*) Loan Admin.

— Loan Administration in the 90s Vol. 6: Looking Ahead. 1994. text 65.00 (*1-880999-26-9*) Loan Admin.

— Loan Administration in the 90s Vol. 7: Looking Ahead. 1994. text 65.00 (*1-880999-27-7*) Loan Admin.

— Loan Administration in the 90s Vol. 8: Looking Ahead. 1994. text 65.00 (*1-880999-28-5*) Loan Admin.

Nichols, Charles S., Jr. & Shaw, Henry I., Jr. Okinawa: Victory in the Pacific. (Elite Unit Ser.: No. 19). (Illus.). 368p. 1989. reprint ed. 39.95 (*0-89839-131-8*) Battery Pr.

Nichols, Charlie W. The Ultra-Fashionable Peerage of America. LC 75-1864. (Leisure Class in America Ser.). 1975. reprint ed. 16.95 (*0-405-06930-8*) Ayer.

Nichols, Chase, jt. auth. see Nichols, Sandra.

Nichols, Chase D., jt. auth. see Nichols, Sandra M.

***Nichols, Chilton.** Isuzu-Amigo/Pick-Ups/Rodeo/Trooper, 1981-96. (Illus.). (C). 1999. pap. 22.95 (*0-8019-9134-X*) Thomson Learn.

Nichols, Christopher P. Dracula: Death of Nosferatu. 40p. 1991. pap. 3.50 (*0-87129-091-X*, D54) Dramatic Pub.

Nichols, Christopher P., et al, contrib. by. Real Life. 29p. (J). (gr. 10-12). 1996. pap. 3.50 (*0-87129-663-2*, R59) Dramatic Pub.

Nichols, Christopher P. & Bentley, Earl. Lamia. 1994. 5.60 (*0-87129-404-4*, L80) Dramatic Pub.

Nichols, Claude A. Moral Education among the North American Indians. LC 75-177112. (Columbia University. Teachers College. Contributions to Education Ser.: No. 427). reprint ed. 37.50 (*0-404-55427-X*) AMS Pr.

Nichols, Clifton M., ed. see Kelly, Richard T.

Nichols, Clive. Photographing Plants & Gardens. (Illus.). 160p. 1998. pap. 19.95 (*0-7153-0715-0*, Pub. by D & C Pub) Sterling.

Nichols, Connie. Federal State Conflicts Involving Tender Offer Regulation. 97p. 1985. pap. text 10.00 (*0-931035-03-1*) IRRC Inc DC.

Nichols, Daniel E. Distance off Tables. LC 43-15657. 253p. reprint ed. pap. 78.50 (*0-7837-4377-7*, 204411700012) Bks Demand.

Nichols, David. Creating a Safe Campus: A Guide for College & University Administrators. LC 96-35578. (Illus.). 188p. 1997. 46.95 (*0-398-06709-0*); pap. 33.95 (*0-398-06710-4*) C C Thomas.

— Our Father. 1999. write for info. (*0-201-57010-6*) Addison-Wesley.

— Reoperative Gynecologic & Obstetrics Surgery. 2nd ed. (Illus.). 464p. (C). (gr. 13). 1997. text 95.00 (*0-8151-6452-1*, 26542) Mosby Inc.

Nichols, David, ed. Monitoring the Marine Environment. LC 78-71806. 224p. 1979. 67.95 (*0-275-90401-6*, C0401, Praeger Pubs) Greenwood.

Nichols, David, et al, eds. Butterworths Scottish Family Law Service. 1995. ring bd. write for info. (*0-406-99881-7*, BSFLASET, MICHIE) LEXIS Pub.

Nichols, David & Pollingue, Mary N. Readings in American Government. 5th ed. 592p. (C). 1995. per. 33.95 (*0-7872-1283-0*, 41128301) Kendall-Hunt.

Nichols, David & Ponturo, Don. Town Full of Heroes: A Comedy. LC 87-402839. 99 p. 1986. write for info. (*0-573-69075-8*) S French Trade.

Nichols, David, et al. Butterworth Scottish Family Law Service. 1994. ring bd. 275.00 (*0-406-01356-X*, UK, MICHIE) LEXIS Pub.

— The Law of Succession in Scotland. pap. text. write for info. (*0-406-42500-0*, UK, MICHIE) LEXIS Pub.

Nichols, David, jt. auth. see Hayes, Eric.

***Nichols, David A.** Lincoln & the Indians. LC 99-37213. 2000. pap. 15.95 (*0-252-06857-2*) U of Ill Pr.

Nichols, David G. Golden Hour: The Handbook of Advanced Pediatric Life Support. 2nd ed. (Illus.). 560p. (C). (gr. 13). 1995. pap. text 37.95 (*0-8151-6394-0*, 24726) Mosby Inc.

Nichols, David G., et al, eds. Critical Heart Disease in Infants & Children. (Illus.). 1104p. (C). (gr. 13). 1995. text 185.00 (*0-8016-6929-4*, 06929) Mosby Inc.

Nichols, David G., jt. ed. see Rogers, Mark C.

Nichols, David H. Gynecologic & Obstetric Surgery. (Illus.). 1200p. (C). (gr. 13). 1993. text 170.00 (*0-8016-6245-1*, 06245) Mosby Inc.

Nichols, David H. & Clarke-Pearson, Daniel L., eds. Gynecologic & Obstetric Surgery. 2nd ed. LC 99-27194. (Illus.). 1300p. (C). 1999. text 159.00 (*0-8151-3670-6*, 31391) Mosby Inc.

Nichols, David H. & Delancey, John O. L., eds. Clinical Problems, Injuries & Complications of Gynecologic & Obstetric Surgery. rev. ed. LC 94-44911. 400p. 1995. 85.00 (*0-683-06497-5*) Lppncott W & W.

Nichols, David H. & Randall, Clyde L. Vaginal Surgery. 3rd ed. (Illus.). 480p. 1989. 89.00 (*0-683-06494-0*) Lppncott W & W.

Nichols, David H. & Sweeney, Patrick J., eds. Ambulatory Gynecology. 2nd ed. 528p. 1994. spiral bd. 76.00 (*0-397-51325-9*) Lppncott W & W.

Nichols, David K. The Myth of the Modern Presidency. 192p. (C). 1994. 35.00 (*0-271-01316-8*); pap. 15.95 (*0-271-01317-6*) Pa St U Pr.

N

Nichols, David P. Upper Extremity Neuroanatomy & Clinical Examination: A Programmed Text. 56p. 1997. spiral bd. 24.00 (*90-5702-530-2*, Harwood Acad Pubs) Gordon & Breach.

Nichols, Dean. Copper Sands & The N. P. M. W. A. R. A. LC 93-71480. (Illus.). 1994. pap. 14.95 (*0-8323-0503-0*) Binford Mort.

— Islands of Experience. 80p. 1972. 12.50 (*0-682-47549-1*) Binford Mort.

— Kid on the River. LC 88-72057. (Illus.). 128p. (Orig.). 1988. pap. 9.95 (*0-8323-0463-8*) Binford Mort.

— A Poet's Sketch of His Biography. 96p. 1979. 12.50 (*0-682-49420-8*) Binford Mort.

— Two Cats for Puerto Rico & a Sailor's Yarns & Observations. LC 93-71481. (Illus.). 1993. pap. 14.95 (*0-8323-0502-2*) Binford Mort.

Nichols, Deborah, ed. & intro. see Adams, Richard C.

Nichols, Deborah L. & Charlton, Thomas H. The Archaeology of City-States: Cross-Cultural Approaches. LC 97-8283. 1997. pap. text 34.95 (*1-56098-722-7*) Smithsonian.

Nichols, Deborah L. & Charlton, Thomas H., eds. The Archaeology of City-States: Cross-Cultural Approaches. LC 97-8283. (Smithsonian Series in Archaeological Inquiry). (Illus.). 448p. 1997. text 60.00 (*1-56098-746-4*) Smithsonian.

Nichols, Deborah L. & Smiley, Francis E., eds. Excavations on Black Mesa, 1982: A Descriptive Report. LC 82-72189. (Center for Archaeological Investigations Research Paper Ser.: No. 39). (Illus.). xxxviii, 856p. (Orig.). 1984. pap. 30.00 incl. fiche (*0-88104-016-9*) Center Archaeol.

Nichols, Derek, ed. see Cunningham, Douette.

Nichols, Diane, ed. & footn. see Rucker, Della.

Nichols, Donald H. Drinking - Driving Litigation: Criminal & Civil - Trial Notebook. LC 85-29890. (Criminal Law Ser.). 1987. ring bd. 115.00 (*0-685-59800-4*) West Group.

— The Drinking Driver in Minnesota, Issue 21. 125p. 1999. ring bd. 115.00 (*0-327-01139-4*, 8186618) LEXIS Pub.

— Drinking-Driving Litigation: Criminal & Civil, 5 vols. (Criminal Law Ser.). 1989. ring bd. 520.00 (*0-685-14562-X*) West Group.

Nichols, Donald H., ed. The Drinking Driver in Minnesota, 1989. 1994. suppl. ed. 35.00 (*0-250-40744-2*, MICHIE) LEXIS Pub.

— The Drinking Driver in Minnesota, 1989. 2nd ed. 400p. 1994. spiral bd. 129.00 (*0-86678-009-2*, MICHIE) LEXIS Pub.

Nichols, Donald H. & Whited, Flem K. Drinking Driving Litigation: Criminal & Civil. 2nd ed. LC 98-39055. 1998. write for info. (*0-8366-1278-7*) West Group.

— Drinking Driving Litigation: Criminal & Civil: Trial Notebook. 2nd ed. LC 98-30383. 1998. write for info. (*0-8366-1267-1*) West Group.

Nichols, Dwight. Freedom from Financial Bondage. 224p. (Orig.). 1995. pap. 9.99 (*0-89274-797-8*, HH-797) Harrison Hse.

— God's Plans for Your Finances. LC 97-50101. 205p. 1998. pap. 12.99 (*0-88368-509-4*) Whitaker Hse.

Nichols, Dwight O. Discover Truth & Be Free. 68p. (Orig.). 1994. pap. 4.95 (*0-9624064-1-4*) New Era Trng.

— Listening to Ourselves: The Key to Everything That Matters. 326p. 1993. 21.95 (*0-9624064-0-6*) New Era Trng.

Nichols, E. J. Issues in Education: A Comparative Analysis. 264p. (C). 1983. pap. 39.00 (*0-7855-2379-0*) St Mut.

Nichols, E. Ray. No Escape from Love. LC 89-285. 1991. 14.95 (*0-87949-312-7*) Ashley Bks.

Nichols, Edd, jt. auth. see West Allen, Stephanie.

Nichols, Edward J. Towards Gettysburg: A Biography of General John F. Reynolds. 276p. 1988. reprint ed. 30.00 (*0-942211-64-2*) Olde Soldier Bks.

Nichols, Edward L. & Howes, H. L. Cathodo-Luminescence & the Luminescence of Incandescent Solids. LC 28-21004. (Carnegie Institution of Washington Publication Ser.: No. 384). 358p. reprint ed. pap. 111.00 (*0-608-30887-0*, 200788200066) Bks Demand.

Nichols, Edwin J., et al. Teaching Mathematics Vol. 1: Culture, Motivation, History & Classroom Management. Ratteray, Oswald M., ed. (Illus.). 48p. (Orig.). 1986. pap. 3.50 (*0-941001-00-8*) Inst Indep Educ.

Nichols, Elizabeth. Tune into Limericks. 1983. 8.50 (*0-913650-05-6*, V092TMBX) Wrner Bros.

Nichols, Elizabeth, jt. ed. see Fulford, Michael.

***Nichols, Elizabeth Gackstetter.** Rediscovering the Language of the Tribe in Modern Venezuelan Poetry: The Poetry of Trafico & Guaire. LC 00-32435. (Latin American Studies: Vol. 8). 220p. 2000. 89.95 (*0-7734-7710-1*) E Mellen.

Nichols, Eugene D. Math, 1985. 1985. pap. 16.75 (*0-03-064192-6*) Harcourt Schl Pubs.

Nichols, Eugene D. & Schwartz, Sharon. Mathematics Dictionary & Handbook. 464p. (J). (gr. 5-10). 1999. text 29.95 (*1-882269-09-8*) N Schwartz Pub.

Nichols, Eve K. Mobilizing Against AIDS. enl. rev. ed. LC 88-30100. (Illus.). 387p. 1989. 40.50 (*0-674-57763-9*); pap. text 12.95 (*0-674-57762-0*) HUP.

Nichols, Eve K. & Institute of Medicine - National Academy of Scienc. Human Gene Therapy. LC 88-574. 264p. 1988. pap. text 14.00 (*0-674-41480-2*) HUP.

Nichols, F. Moms in Touch. 1996. pap. 5.00 (*0-9628244-0-2*) Moms Touch Intl.

— World Geography & the Solar System (1811) 160p. 1998. reprint ed. pap. text 25.00 (*0-87556-868-8*) Saifer.

Nichols, Frances S., ed. Index to Schoolcraft's "Indian Tribes of the United States" (Bureau of American Ethnology Bulletins Ser.). 257p. 1995. lib. bdg. 89.00 (*0-7812-4152-9*) Rprt Serv.

Nichols, Frances S., ed. see Schoolcraft, Henry R.

Nichols, Francine H. Maternal-Newborn Nursing. (C). 1997. text 82.00 (*0-7216-7574-3*, W B Saunders Co) Harcrt Hlth Sci Grp.

— Maternal-Newborn Nursing: Theories. 1997. pap. text, student ed. 17.95 (*0-7216-6258-7*, W B Saunders Co) Harcrt Hlth Sci Grp.

Nichols, Francine H. & Humenick, Sharron S. Childbirth Education: Practice, Research & Theory. (Illus.). 544p. 1988. text 61.95 (*0-7216-2052-3*, W B Saunders Co) Harcrt Hlth Sci Grp.

Nichols, Francine H. & Zwelling, Elaine. Maternal-Newborn Nursing: Theory & Practice. Rader, Ilze, ed. LC 96-15371. 1344p. 1997. text 66.95 (*0-7216-6777-5*, W B Saunders Co) Harcrt Hlth Sci Grp.

— Maternal-Newborn Nursing: Theory & Practice. 1997. teacher ed. write for info. (*0-7216-6249-8*, W B Saunders Co) Harcrt Hlth Sci Grp.

Nichols, Francis M. Britton: The French Text Carefully Revised with an English Translation, Introduction & Notes, Set, Vols. 1 & 2. LC 83-80259. 896p. 1983. reprint ed. lib. bdg. 185.00 (*0-912004-24-X*) Gaunt.

Nichols, Francis M., tr. from LAT. The Marvels of Rome. rev. ed. LC 86-45750. (Historical Travel Ser.). Orig. Title: Mirabilia Urbis Romae. (Illus.). 164p. 1986. pap. 12.50 (*0-934977-02-X*) Italica Pr.

Nichols, Frank. Curves. (J). 1989. pap. 1.99 (*0-85953-049-3*) Childs Play.

— Stencils. (J). 1989. pap. 3.99 (*0-85953-048-5*) Childs Play.

— Tangrams. (J). 1989. pap. 3.99 (*0-85953-050-7*) Childs Play.

Nichols, Frank R. One Brief Moment. LC 97-65341. (Illus.). 160p. 1997. pap. 14.95 (*0-923687-41-6*) Celo Valley Bks.

— Pietro's Girl. LC 95-7905. 192p. (Orig.). 1995. pap. 12.95 (*0-923687-36-X*) Celo Valley Bks.

***Nichols, Frank Reed.** The Knell. LC 99-68654. 160p. 2000. 22.95 (*0-923687-54-8*) Celo Valley Bks.

Nichols, Fred J., ed. An Anthology of Neo-Latin Poetry. LC 78-9944. 746p. reprint ed. pap. 200.00 (*0-8357-8027-9*, 203384300087) Bks Demand.

Nichols, Frederic H., jt. ed. see Cloern, James E.

Nichols, Frederick D. & Bear, James A., Jr. Monticello. LC 67-5861. 86p. reprint ed. pap. 30.00 (*0-7837-2022-X*, 204229700002) Bks Demand.

Nichols, Gary. Healthcare Resource Directory: National Edition. Reed, Mark L., ed. 224p. (Orig.). 1993. pap. 25.00 (*0-933745-13-3*) Med Prod.

— Houston Medical Directory, 1993. 10th ed. Schellhous, Shirley & Reed, Mark L., eds. 850p. 1993. 54.95 (*0-933745-11-7*) Med Prod.

— Houston Medical Directory 1994. 11th ed. Schellhous, Shirley, ed. 750p. 1994. pap. 59.95 (*0-933745-14-1*) Med Prod.

— Houston Referral Directory, 1993. 3rd ed. Schellhous, Shirley & Reed, Mark L., eds. 136p. 1993. 14.95 (*0-933745-12-5*) Med Prod.

— Houston Referral Directory 1994. 4th ed. Schellhous, Shirley, ed. 150p. 1994. pap. 19.95 (*0-933745-15-X*) Med Prod.

Nichols, Gary C. The River Runners' Guide to Utah & Adjacent Areas. LC 86-1688. (Bonneville Bks.). (Illus.). 130p. (Orig.). 1986. pap. 14.95 (*0-87480-254-7*) U of Utah Pr.

Nichols, Gary D. On-Line Process Analyzers. LC 87-30538. 320p. 1988. 149.00 (*0-471-86608-3*) Wiley.

***Nichols, Gary J.** Sedimentology & Stratigraphy. LC 98-7562. (Illus.). 8p. 1999. pap. 51.95 (*0-632-03578-1*) Blackwell Sci.

Nichols, Geoff. Taking the Step up to Supervisor. Miller, Karen M., ed. LC 97-77106. (How-To Book Ser.). 124p. 1997. pap. 12.95 (*1-884926-84-3*, ALWA2) Amer Media.

Nichols, George. George Nichols, Salem Shipmaster & Merchant. LC 74-124245. (Select Bibliographies Reprint Ser.). 1977. reprint ed. 15.95 (*0-8369-5433-5*) Ayer.

— George Nichols, Salem Shipmaster & Merchant: An Autobiography. (American Biography Ser.). 89p. 1991. reprint ed. lib. bdg. 59.00 (*0-7812-8297-7*) Rprt Serv.

Nichols, George E. The Vegetation of Northern Cape Breton Island, Nova Scotia. (Connecticut Academy of Arts & Sciences Ser., Trans.: Vol. 22). 1918. pap. 100.00 (*0-685-22837-1*) Elliots Bks.

Nichols, George N. Focus: Pregnancy & Childbirth Problems in the Workplace. write for info. (*0-318-60956-8*) P-H.

Nichols, George W. Mount Desert, 1872. Jones, William R., ed. (Illus.). 24p. 1995. reprint ed. pap. 2.95 (*0-89646-029-0*) Vistabooks.

— The Story of the Great March. (Illus.). 408p. 1996. pap. 29.00 (*0-7884-0455-5*, N313) Heritage Bk.

— The Story of the Great March. 394p. 1972. reprint ed. 27.95 (*0-87928-031-X*) Corner Hse.

Nichols, Geraldine C., intro. Escribir, Espacio Propio: Laforet, Matute, Moix, Tusquets, Riera y Roig por Sis Mismas. (Literature & Human Rights Ser.: Vol. 7). (SPA.). 244p. (Orig.). 1989. pap. 10.00 (*1-877660-04-3*) IFTSOIL.

Nichols, Geri. A Walking Tour of Historic Roscoe Village. (Illus.). 34p. (Orig.). 1989. pap. 3.50 (*1-880443-03-1*) Roscoe Village.

Nichols, Gill & Gardner, John. Pupils in Transition. LC 98-25926. 128p. (C). (gr. 13). 1999. pap. 24.99 (*0-415-17467-8*, D6051) Routledge.

— Pupils in Transition: Moving Between Key Stages. LC 98-25926. 128p. (C). (gr. 13). 1999. 75.00 (*0-415-17466-X*, D6047) Routledge.

Nichols, Grace. Asana & the Animals. LC 96-30307. (Illus.). 32p. (J). (gr. k-4). 1997. 16.99 (*0-7636-0145-4*) Candlewick Pr.

— A Caribbean Dozen. Agard, John, ed. 1994. 12.99 (*0-7445-2172-6*, Pub. by Oxfam Pub) Stylus Pub VA.

— Come on into My Tropical Garden: Poems for Children. LC 89-36335. (Illus.). 48p. (J). (gr. 2-6). 1990. 10.95 (*0-397-32350-6*); lib. bdg. 10.89 (*0-397-32349-2*) HarpC Child Bks.

Nichols, Gregory G., ed. see Trummel, D. Pauline.

Nichols, H. K. & Simpson, D. ESEC '87. (Lecture Notes in Computer Science Ser.: Vol. 289). xii, 404p. 1987. 45.00 (*0-387-18712-X*) Spr-Verlag.

Nichols, Harold. Map Librarianship. 2nd ed. LC 82-126289. 272p. 1982. reprint ed. pap. 84.40 (*0-608-07776-3*, 206786400010) Bks Demand.

— McCoy Cookie Jars. 1988. 15.95 (*0-9617912-1-7*) Nichols Wrestling.

— McCoy Cookie Jars from the 1st to the Last. 2nd ed. LC 91-68550. (Illus.). 198p. (Orig.). 1992. pap. 18.95 (*0-9617912-2-5*) Nichols Wrestling.

— The Work of the Deacon & Deaconess. (Orig.). 1964. pap. 10.00 (*0-8170-0328-2*) Judson.

Nichols, Harriet, tr. see Goldoni, Carlo.

Nichols, Helen. Healing Love. Weinberger, Jane, ed. LC 93-61192. (Illus.). 200p. (Orig.). 1994. pap. 5.95 (*0-932433-38-3*) Windswept Hse.

Nichols, Herbert L., Jr. Moving the Earth: The Workbook of Excavation. 3rd ed. 1760p. 1988. 99.95 (*0-07-046483-9*) McGraw.

***Nichols, Herbert L., Jr.** Science Blundering: An Outsider's View. 2nd rev. ed. LC 99-68226. (Illus.). 160p. 2000. write for info. (*0-944641-36-9*) Greenwich Pub Group.

Nichols, Herbert L., Jr. & Day, David H. Moving the Earth: The Workbook of Excavation. 4th ed. LC 98-15161. (Illus.). 1400p. 1998. 105.00 (*0-07-046484-7*) McGraw.

Nichols, Holly, ed. see Robbins, Curt.

Nichols, Hugh, ed. see Maclean, Norman F.

Nichols, I. A. History of Iowa Falls, Iowa. (Illus.). 365p. 1993. reprint ed. lib. bdg. 39.50 (*0-8328-2842-4*) Higginson Bk Co.

Nichols, J. Snowflake. LC 89-90662. 64p. (Orig.). (C). 1989. pap. 7.95 (*0-9622423-0-6*) Snowflake Pr.

Nichols, J. G. The Poetry of Ben Jonson. LC 75-7260. x, 177p. 1969. write for info. (*0-389-01010-3*) B&N Imports.

Nichols, J. G., tr. see Leopardi, Giacomo.

Nichols, J. G., tr. see Petrarca, Francesco.

Nichols, J. L. & Crogman, William H. Progress of a Race. LC 69-18552. (American Negro: His History & Literature. Series 2). 1969. reprint ed. 21.95 (*0-405-01883-5*) Ayer.

Nichols, J. T. City of Bridgeton: Its Settlement & Growth, Its Attractions, Its Industries, Its Advantages As a Manufacturing Site. With Illustrations. (Illus.). 79p. 1997. reprint ed. pap. 14.00 (*0-8328-6042-5*) Higginson Bk Co.

Nichols, Jack. The Gay Agenda: Talking Back to the Fundamentalists. LC 96-28085. 228p. 1996. 25.95 (*1-57392-103-3*) Prometheus Bks.

Nichols, James, ed. see Annesley, Samuel.

Nichols, James D., et al. Freedom's End: Conspiracy in Oklahoma. Carroll, Gerald A., ed. (Illus.). 415p. (Orig.). 1997. pap. 16.95 (*0-9660439-0-1*) Freedoms End.

Nichols, James H. & Wright, Colin. From Political Economy to Economics - & Back? 250p. (C). 1991. 24.95 (*1-55815-113-3*) ICS Pr.

Nichols, James H., Jr., tr. & intro. see Plato.

Nichols, James O. Assessment Case Studies: Common Issues in Implementation with Various Campus Approaches to Resolution. LC 95-40856. (Illus.). 224p. 1996. text 30.00 (*0-87586-112-1*) Agathon.

— The Departmental Guide & Record Book for Student Outcomes Assessment & Institutional Effectiveness. 2nd rev. ed. LC 95-44077. (Illus.). 80p. (Orig.). 1996. pap. text 7.50 (*0-87586-114-8*) Agathon.

***Nichols, James O. & Nichols, Karen W.** The Departmental Guide & Record Book for Student Outcomes Assessment & Institutional Effectiveness. rev. ed. 80p. (Orig.). (C). 2000. pap. text 10.00 (*0-87586-129-6*) Agathon.

Nichols, James O., et al. A Practitioner's Handbook for Institutional Effectiveness & Student Outcomes Assessment: Assessment Implementation. 3rd rev. ed. LC 95-40857. (Illus.). 296p. 1996. text 36.00 (*0-87586-113-X*) Agathon.

Nichols, James O., jt. auth. see Nichols, Karen W.

Nichols, James R. Afterwords. 52p. 1986. pap. 4.95 (*0-89697-272-0*) Intl Univ Pr.

— Chemistry of the Farm & the Sea. LC 73-125755. (American Environmental Studies). 1974. reprint ed. 15.95 (*0-405-02681-1*) Ayer.

Nichols, Janet. American Music Makers. (Illus.). 232p. (YA). (gr. 7 up). 1990. 19.95 (*0-8027-6957-8*); lib. bdg. 19.85 (*0-8027-6958-6*) Walker & Co.

— Women Music Makers. 224p. (YA). (gr. 7 up). 1992. 18.95 (*0-8027-8168-3*) Walker & Co.

Nichols, Jeanne M. Leaning over the Edge: Poems. 64p. (Orig.). 1993. pap. 8.50 (*1-56474-058-7*) Fithian Pr.

Nichols, Jeff, jt. auth. see Simons, Jack.

Nichols, Jeff, jt. ed. see Fisk, Josiah.

***Nichols, Jim.** Norfolk & Western Color Guide to Freight & Passenger Equipment. (Illus.). 128p. 2000. 54.95 (*1-58248-038-9*) Morning NJ.

Nichols, Jim. Norfolk & Western in Color, 1945-1964, Vol. 1. LC 96-78484. (Illus.). 128p. 1997. 49.95 (*1-878887-72-6*) Morning NJ.

Nichols, Joan K. Mary Shelley: Frankenstein's Creator - The First Science Fiction Writer. LC 98-27023. (Barnard Biography Ser.: No. 3). (Illus.). 150p. (YA). (gr. 8 up). 1998. pap. 6.95 (*1-57324-087-7*) Conari Press.

— A Matter of Conscience: The Trial of Anne Hutchinson. LC 92-18087. (Stories of America Ser.). (Illus.). 101p. (J). (gr. 2-5). 1992. pap. 4.95 (*0-8114-8073-9*); lib. bdg. 25.68 (*0-8114-7233-7*) Raintree Steck-V.

— New Orleans. LC 88-35915. (Downtown America Ser.). (Illus.). 60p. (J). (gr. 3 up). 1989. lib. bdg. 13.95 (*0-87518-403-0*, Dillon Silver Burdett) Silver Burdett Pr.

— No Room for a Dog. 96p. (Orig.). (J). (gr. 2-4). 1995. pap. 3.50 (*0-380-77973-0*, Avon Bks) Morrow Avon.

Nichols, Jody, et al. Primary Education Thinking Skills 2. (Illus.). 208p. 1998. pap. 18.95 (*1-880505-37-1*, CLC0221) Pieces of Lrning.

Nichols, Johanna. Linguistic Diversity in Space & Time. LC 91-43682. (Illus.). 374p. 1992. 42.50 (*0-226-58056-3*) U Ch Pr.

— Linguistic Diversity in Space & Time. 1999. pap. text 19.00 (*0-226-58057-1*) U Ch Pr.

— Predicate Nominals: A Partial Surface Syntax of Russian. LC 80-16745. (University of California Publications in Social Welfare: No. 97). 415p. reprint ed. pap. 128.70 (*0-608-18190-0*, 203291800081) Bks Demand.

***Nichols, John.** Arizona Cardinals. 3rd rev. ed. (Pro Football Today Ser.). (Illus.). 32p. (YA). (gr. 3-12). 2000. lib. bdg. 22.60 (*1-58341-034-1*, Creat Educ) Creative Co.

— Atlanta Falcons. 3rd rev. ed. (NFL Today Ser.). (Illus.). 32p. (YA). (gr. 3-12). 2000. lib. bdg. 22.60 (*1-58341-035-X*, Creat Educ) Creative Co.

— Baltimore Ravens. 3rd rev. ed. (Pro Football Today Ser.). (Illus.). 32p. (YA). (gr. 3-12). 2000. lib. bdg. 22.60 (*1-58341-036-8*, Creat Educ) Creative Co.

Nichols, John. Big Red: The Nebraska Cornhuskers Story. LC 98-46472. (College Sports Today Ser.). (Illus.). 32p. (YA). (gr. 4 up). 1999. lib. bdg. 21.30 (*0-88682-980-1*, Creat Educ) Creative Co.

— Blue Heaven: The North Carolina Tar Heels Story. LC 98-30933. (College Sports Today Ser.). (Illus.). 32p. (YA). (gr. 4 up). 1999. lib. bdg. 21.30 (*0-88682-994-1*, Creat Educ) Creative Co.

***Nichols, John.** Buffalo Bills. 3rd rev. ed. (Pro Football Today Ser.). (Illus.). 32p. (YA). (gr. 3-12). 2000. lib. bdg. 22.60 (*1-58341-037-6*, Creat Educ) Creative Co.

— Carolina Panthers. 3rd rev. ed. (Pro Football Today Ser.). (Illus.). 32p. (YA). (gr. 3-12). 2000. lib. bdg. 22.60 (*1-58341-038-4*, Creat Educ) Creative Co.

— Chicago Bears. 3rd rev. ed. (Pro Football Today Ser.). (Illus.). 32p. (YA). (gr. 3-12). 2000. lib. bdg. 22.60 (*1-58341-039-2*, Creat Educ) Creative Co.

— Cincinnati Bengals. 3rd rev. ed. (Pro Football Today Ser.). (Illus.). 32p. (YA). (gr. 3-12). 2000. lib. bdg. 22.60 (*1-58341-040-6*, Creat Educ) Creative Co.

Nichols, John. Cleveland Browns. LC 99-41030. (Pro Football Today Ser.). (Illus.). 32p. (J). (gr. 4 up). 2000. lib. bdg. 22.60 (*1-58341-080-5*, Creat Educ) Creative Co.

— Collection of All the Wills, Now Known To Be Extant, Of The Kings & Queens Of E. LC 04-25875. reprint ed. 55.00 (*0-404-04759-9*) AMS Pr.

— Conjugal Bliss: A Comedy of Marital Arts. LC 93-1245. 320p. 1995. 22.50 (*0-8050-2803-X*) H Holt & Co.

***Nichols, John.** Dallas Cowboys. 3rd rev. ed. (Pro Football Today Ser.). (Illus.). 32p. (YA). (gr. 3-12). 2000. lib. bdg. 22.60 (*1-58341-041-4*, Creat Educ) Creative Co.

— Dancing on the Stones: Selected Essays. (Illus.). 259p. 2000. 39.95 (*0-8263-2182-8*); pap. 16.95 (*0-8263-2183-6*) U of NM Pr.

— Denver Broncos. 3rd rev. ed. (Pro Football Today Ser.). (Illus.). 32p. (YA). (gr. 3-12). 2000. lib. bdg. 22.60 (*1-58341-042-2*, Creat Educ) Creative Co.

— Detroit Lions. 3rd rev. ed. (Pro Football Today Ser.). (Illus.). 32p. (YA). (gr. 3-12). 2000. lib. bdg. 22.60 (*1-58341-043-0*, Creat Educ) Creative Co.

Nichols, John. Ghost in the Music. 320p. 1996. reprint ed. pap. 13.00 (*0-393-31536-3*) Norton.

***Nichols, John.** Green Bay Packers. 3rd rev. ed. (Pro Football Today Ser.). (Illus.). 32p. (YA). (gr. 3-12). 2000. lib. bdg. 22.60 (*1-58341-044-9*, Creat Educ) Creative Co.

Nichols, John. The History of the Arizona Diamondbacks. LC 98-48314. (Baseball Ser.). (Illus.). 32p. (YA). (gr. 3-12). 1999. lib. bdg. 21.30 (*0-88682-896-1*, Creat Educ) Creative Co.

— The History of the Charlotte Sting. LC 99-18894. (Women's Pro Basketball Today Ser.). 1999. lib. bdg. 21.30 (*1-58341-008-2*, Creat Educ) Creative Co.

***Nichols, John.** The History of the Cleveland Rockers. LC 99-18892. (Women's Pro Basketball Today Ser.). 1999. lib. bdg. 21.30 (*1-58341-009-0*, Creat Educ) Creative Co.

Nichols, John. The History of the Colorado Rockies. rev. ed. LC 97-46395. (Baseball Ser.). (Illus.). 32p. (YA). (gr. 3 up). 1998. lib. bdg. 21.30 (*0-88682-907-0*, Creat Educ) Creative Co.

— The History of the Florida Marlins. LC 97-46396. (Baseball Ser.). (Illus.). 32p. (YA). (gr. 3 up). 1998. lib. bdg. 21.30 (*0-88682-909-7*, Creat Educ) Creative Co.

— The History of the Tampa Bay Devil Rays. LC 98-50641. (Baseball Ser.). (Illus.). 32p. (YA). (gr. 4 up). 1999. lib. bdg. 21.30 (*0-88682-926-7*, Creat Educ) Creative Co.

— Illustrations of the Manners & Expenses of Ancient Times in England in the 15th, 16th & 17th Centuries. LC 79-173078. reprint ed. 45.00 (*0-404-04688-6*) AMS Pr.

***Nichols, John.** Last Beautiful Days of Autumn: A Memoir. LC 00-25731. (Illus.). 220p. 2000. pap. 14.95 (*1-58096-008-1*) Ancient City Pr.

Nichols, John. Literary Anecdotes of the Eighteenth Century, 9 vols. LC 11-32672. reprint ed. 425.00 (*0-404-04720-3*) AMS Pr.

— The Magic Journey. 546p. 1983. mass mkt. 5.99 (*0-345-31049-7*, Ballantine) Ballantine Pub Grp.

— The Magic Journey. 1996. pap. 12.95 (*0-345-41033-5*) Ballantine Pub Grp.

— The Magic Journey. LC 99-42425. 540p. 2000. pap. 14.00 (*0-8050-6339-0*, Owl) H Holt & Co.

— The Milagro Beanfield War. 640p. 1987. mass mkt. 5.95 (*0-345-34446-4*) Ballantine Pub Grp.

N

— The Milagro Beanfield War. LC 96-96673. 1996. pap. 12.95 (*0-345-41016-5*) Ballantine Pub Grp.
— The Milagro Beanfield War. 464p. 2000. pap. 14.00 (*0-8050-6374-9*, Owl) H Holt & Co.
— The Milagro Beanfield War: Facsimile Anniversary Edition. (Illus.). 484p. 1995. 27.50 (*0-8050-2805-6*) H Holt & Co.
— Minor Lives: A Collection of Biographies. Annotated & with an Introduction on John Nichols & the Antiquarian & Anecdotal Movements of the Late Eighteenth Century. Hart, Edward L., ed. LC 73-131470. 402p. reprint ed. pap. 124.70 (*0-7837-4473-0*, 204418100001) Bks Demand.
— The Nirvana Blues. 608p. 1983. mass mkt. 5.95 (*0-345-30465-9*) Ballantine Pub Grp.
— The Nirvana Blues. 1996. pap. 12.95 (*0-345-41037-8*) Ballantine Pub Grp.
— The Nirvana Blues. LC 99-39457. 540p. 2000. pap. 14.00 (*0-8050-6340-4*, Owl) H Holt & Co.
— Progresses & Public Processions of Queen Elizabeth, 3 vols. LC 03-17051. reprint ed. 435.00 (*0-404-04770-X*) AMS Pr.
— Progresses, Processions & Magnificent Festivities of King James First, His Royal Consort, Family & Court, 4 vols., Set. LC 03-29463. reprint ed. 310.00 (*0-404-04780-7*) AMS Pr.
— Sky's the Limit. 1990. pap. 14.95 (*0-393-30717-4*) Norton.
— Some Account of the Alien Priories, & of Such Lands As They Are Known to Have Possessed in England & Wales, 2 vols. in 1. LC 72-173079. reprint ed. 67.50 (*0-404-04689-4*) AMS Pr.
— Sterile Cuckoo. 224p. 1996. reprint ed. pap. 12.00 (*0-393-31535-5*) Norton.
— The Wizard of Loneliness. 320p. 1994. pap. 13.00 (*0-393-31073-6*) Norton.

Nichols, John, ed. Select Collection of Poems, with Notes Biographical & Historical, 8 vols. LC 11-29585. reprint ed. 380.00 (*0-404-04750-5*) AMS Pr.
— Select Collection of Poems, with Notes Biographical & Historical, 8 vols., Set. 1974. reprint ed. 480.00 (*0-527-67180-0*) Periodicals Srv.

Nichols, John, photos by. On the Mesa. LC 95-15130. (Illus.). 208p. 1995. pap. 12.95 (*0-941270-87-4*) Ancient City Pr.
— On the Mesa. deluxe ed. (Illus.). 208p. 1995. 24.95 (*0-941270-86-6*) Ancient City Pr.

Nichols, John & Gough, Richard. Biblioteca Topographica Britannica, 10 vols. LC 70-138264. reprint ed. 1750.00 (*0-404-04740-8*) AMS Pr.

***Nichols, John & Nelson, Julie.** Pro Football Today, 31 bks. 2000. lib. bdg. 700.60 (*1-58341-064-3*, Creat Educ) Creative Co.

Nichols, John & Nichols, John B. Illustrations of the Literary History of the 18th Century, 8 vols. LC 11-32673. reprint ed. 425.00 (*0-404-04730-0*) AMS Pr.

Nichols, John, jt. auth. see McChesney, Robert W.

Nichols, John A. & Shank, M. Thomas, eds. Hidden Springs (Medieval Religious Women), 2 vols., Set. (Cistercian Studies: Vol. III). 300p. 1995. pap. write for info. (*0-87907-913-4*) Cistercian Pubns.
— Hidden Springs (Medieval Religious Women), 2 vols., Set. (Cistercian Studies: Vol. III/113A & B). 300p. 1995. pap. 50.00 (*0-87907-613-5*) Cistercian Pubns.
— Medieval Religious Women I: Distant Echoes. (Cistercian Studies: No. 71). 299p. (C). 1984. pap. 13.95 (*0-87907-971-1*) Cistercian Pubns.

Nichols, John B. Numerical Proportions of the Sexes at Birth. LC 07-23967. (American Anthropological Association Memoirs Ser.: No. 4). 1906. 25.00 (*0-527-00503-7*) Periodicals Srv.

Nichols, John B., jt. auth. see Nichols, John.

Nichols, John B., jt. auth. see Tillman, Barrett.

Nichols, John D. & Nyholm, Earl. A Concise Dictionary of Minnesota Ojibwe. expanded rev. ed. LC 94-35219. Orig. Title: Ojebwewi-Ikodowinan. (ENG & OJI.). 1994. pap. 9.95 (*0-8166-2428-3*) U of Minn Pr.

Nichols, John D., ed. & tr. see Kegg, Maude.

Nichols, John E. Guide to Hospital Security. 176p. 1983. text 61.95 (*0-566-02359-8*, Pub. by Gower) Ashgate Pub Co.

Nichols, John G., ed. Chronicle of Queen Jane & of Two Years of Queen Mary & Especially of the Rebellion of Sir Thomas Wyat. (Camden Society, London. Publications, First Ser.: No. 48). reprint ed. 47.50 (*0-404-50148-6*) AMS Pr.
— Chronicle of the Grey Friars of London. (Camden Society, London. Publications, First Ser.: No. 53). reprint ed. 32.50 (*0-404-50153-2*) AMS Pr.
— Descriptive Catalogue of the Works of the Camden Society. (Camden Society, London. Publications, First Ser.: No. 80B). reprint ed. 25.00 (*0-404-50208-3*) AMS Pr.
— Medieval Tile Designs. LC 97-44799. (Illus.). 64p. 1998. pap. 6.95 (*0-486-29947-3*) Dover.
— Narrative of the Days of the Reformation. (Camden Society, London. Publications, First Ser.: No. 77). reprint ed. 85.00 (*0-404-50177-X*) AMS Pr.

Nichols, John G. & Bruce, John, eds. Wills from Doctors' Commons. (Camden Society, London. Publications, First Ser.: No. 83). reprint ed. 42.50 (*0-404-50183-4*) AMS Pr.

Nichols, John G., ed. see Machin, Henry.

Nichols, John G., ed. see Turpyn, Richard.

Nichols, John H. A Biblical Humanist. (Orig.). 1989. pap. 30.00 (*0-685-29796-9*) Unitarian Soc WH.
— A Biblical Humanist Companion. 157p. (Orig.). 1989. pap. 30.00 (*0-9624948-0-1*) Unitarian Soc WH.

Nichols, John S., jt. auth. see Soley, Lawrence C.

Nichols, Joseph H. Colonial Ancestors & 20th Century Descendants of Samuel A. Nichols (1787-1866) of Howard Co., MD. LC 97-133586. (Illus.). xvii, 498p. 1996. 30.00 (*0-7884-0559-4*, N314) Heritage Bk.

Nichols, Joseph V. Legends of Loudoun Valley. 117p. 1996. pap. 12.00 (*1-888265-09-4*) Willow Bend.

Nichols, Judith. Growing from Good to Great. 210p. 1995. 40.00 (*1-56625-035-8*) Bonus Books.

Nichols, Judith E. Building Sales with Demographics & Psychographics. 289p. 1992. 29.95 (*0-85013-217-7*) Dartnell Corp.
— Changing Demographics: Fund Raising in the 1990's. 1999. pap. text 40.00 (*1-56625-131-1*) Bonus Books.
— Changing Demographics - Fund Raising in the 1990s. LC 89-64110. 279p. 1990. 40.00 (*0-944496-11-3*) Precept Pr.
— Global Demographics: Fund Raising for a New World. LC 95-34025. 201p. 1995. 40.00 (*1-56625-047-1*) Bonus Books.
— Lenny the Sign Man - Signs of Love: A Keepsake Coloring Book. large type unabridged ed. (Illus.). 17p. (J). (ps-5). 1997. 19.50 (*1-57529-061-8*) Kabel Pubs.
— Lessons from Abroad: Fresh Ideas from Fund-Raising Experts in the United Kingdom. LC 96-48040. (Illus.). 298p. 1997. 40.00 (*1-56625-080-3*) Bonus Books.
— Pinpointing Affluence: Increasing Your Share of Major Donor Dollars. 293p. 1994. 40.00 (*0-944496-40-7*) Precept Pr.
— Targeted Fund Raising: Defining & Refining Your Development Strategy. LC 91-77217. 229p. 1991. 40.00 (*0-944496-29-6*) Precept Pr.

Nichols, Judith L., et al. Women Living with Multiple Sclerosis. 288p. 1999. 23.95 (*0-89793-219-6*, Pub. by Hunter Hse) Publishers Group.

***Nichols, Judith Lynn.** Living Beyond Multiple Sclerosis: A Woman's Guide. 256p. 2000. pap. 14.95 (*0-89793-293-5*) Hunter Hse.

***Nichols, Judith Lynn, et al.** Women Living with Multiple Sclerosis. LC 98-35659. 256p. 1999. pap. 13.95 (*0-89793-218-8*, Pub. by Hunter Hse) Publishers Group.

Nichols, Judy. Teaching in Tough Times: Encouragement for Todays's Teacher. LC 97-25290. 128p. (Orig.). 1997. 11.99 (*0-8010-1146-9*) Baker Bks.

Nichols, Judy & Sears, Lori D. Storytimes for Two-Year Olds. 2nd ed. LC 97-44295. (Illus.). 248p. (J). 1998. 28.00 (*0-8389-0719-9*) ALA.

***Nichols, Julie J. & Gresham, Barrett Lansing. The Body's Map of Consciousness: Physical, Mental & Emotional Bodies, 2 vols., Vol. 1. 100p. 2000. 15.95 (*1-893969-01-0*) None Too Soon.**

This volume brings together for the first time in written form basic Integrated Awareness techniques revealing the means by which the physical structure of the human body yields data about all other levels of consciousness. Integrated Awareness is the name given to an unlimited set of innate human states & skills based on the common elements of consciousness & the structural & energetic laws of the earth plane. This volume includes: * how the physical body reflects, maintains & gives insight into the ways we create our personal & uniquely individual experience of the world; * the interrelation between the body's various types of tissue, movements habitually repeated &/or inhibited & the emotional & mental bodies; * Movement Teams the built-in relationships in movement between body sites not necessarily next to each other, (such as jaw, pelvis & ankles); & * how all of the preceding are related to personal choice & responsibility in healing. Those who already touch the bodies, hearts & minds of others & who wish to will find their understanding of the human condition satisfyingly improved. Order from NoneToo Soon Publishing, 893 South McClleland, Salt Lake City, UT, 84102. 801-363-1747 xt 2. *Publisher Paid Annotation.*

***Nichols, Julie J. & Gresham, Lansing Barrett. Ask Anything & Your Body Will Answer: A Personal Journey Through Integrated Awareness. 112p. 2000. pap. 12.95 (*1-893969-00-2*) None Too Soon.**

Ask Anything & Your Body Will Answer is both a quietly elegant read & an enlightening introduction to Integrated Awareness, a major new healing process for the third millennium. IA teaches that each persons physical body provides perceptible detailed information about all levels of that persons consciousness - emotional, mental, spiritual & more. Students of Integrated Awareness learn through expanded perceptual states, experiential movement & touch processess that they can heal by attending in specific ways to the intricate reciprocal relationship between body, mind & emotion. This book is uniquely formatted allowing the reader to follow Nichols' own personal journey as well as to access the "embodied poetry" of IA floor exercises & structure - based healing. The underlying LA principles & corresponding relationships between the many aspects of human consciousness specifically relevant to the narrative are presented on the facing left hand page. Healers, seekers, investigators of the human spirit & those needing pragmatic tools for self-healing will all find Ask Anything & Your Body Will Answer a lively prelude to the Body's Map of Consciousness, coming in summer 2000. Order from NoneTooSoon Publishing, 893 South McClelland, Salt Lake City, UT 84102 801-363-1747 xt 2. *Publisher Paid Annotation.*

Nichols, Karen, et al. Michael Graves: Buildings & Projects, 1982-1990. LC 89-10615. (Illus.). 352p. (Orig.). 1990. pap. 40.00 (*0-910413-17-7*) Princeton Arch.

***Nichols, Karen W. & Nichols, James O.** The Department Head's Guide to Assessment in Administrative & Educational Support Units. (Illus.). 128p. 2000. pap. text 14.00 (*0-87586-130-X*) Agathon.

Nichols, Karen W., jt. auth. see Nichols, James O.

Nichols, Kate E., compiled by. Leominster, Massachusetts of Today: Over Two Hundred Choice Photographical Views of Its Churches, Public Buildings, Streets, Residences, Factories, Reservoirs, Parks & Other Scenes of Interest. (Illus.). 361p. 1998. reprint ed. lib. bdg. 42.00 (*0-8328-7119-2*) Higginson Bk Co.

Nichols, Kathryn M. Smell It Like It Is: Tales from the Garlic Capital of the World. LC 91-36046. (Illus.). 112p. (Orig.). 1992. pap. 8.95 (*1-56474-008-0*) Fithian Pr.

Nichols, Kathryn M. & Silberling, N. J. Stratigraphy & Depositional History of the Star Peak Group (Triassic), Northwestern Nevada. LC 77-89753. (Geological Society of America, Special Paper: No. 178). (Illus.). 79p. reprint ed. pap. 30.00 (*0-8357-3146-4*, 203940900012) Bks Demand.

Nichols, Keith A. Psychological Care in Physical Illness. LC 84-71617. 204p. 1984. pap. text 21.95 (*0-914783-06-8*) Charles.
— Psychological Care in Physical Illness. 2nd ed. LC 92-49595. 1993. 34.95 (*0-412-43560-8*) Chapman & Hall.

Nichols, Keith A. & Jenkinson, John. Groups & Group Work. 140p. 1990. 23.00 (*0-412-34340-1*, A4404) Chapman & Hall.

Nichols, Ken. Hooked on Traprock: Rock Climbing in Connecticut. Date not set. lib. bdg. 29.95 (*0-8488-1750-8*) Amereon Ltd.
— The Incredible Power of Fear: From Fear to Faith. 160p. 1996. pap. 12.99 (*1-885447-05-1*) Walk Thru the Bible.

Nichols, Kenneth. Inventing Software: The Rise of 'Computer-Related' Patents. LC 97-22355. 184p. 1998. 55.00 (*1-56720-140-7*, Quorum Bks) Greenwood.
— El Temor: Enfermedad de Nuestra Decada. (Serie Guia de Bolsillo - Pocket Guides Ser.).Tr. of Fear: Sickness of Our Decade. (SPA.). 120p. 1990. pap. 2.79 (*1-56063-035-3*, 498061) Editorial Unilit.

Nichols, Kenneth G. Physical Electronics: A Guide to the Study of Paper 344 of the CEI Examinations. LC QC0030.N5. (PPL Study Guide Ser.: No. 4). 52p. reprint ed. pap. 30.00 (*0-608-30914-1*, 201148800080) Bks Demand.

Nichols, Kenneth L., jt. auth. see Halachmi, Arie.

Nichols, Kevin. Cornerstone. (C). 1988. 45.00 (*0-85439-157-6*, Pub. by St Paul Pubns) St Mut.
— Pastoral Catechetics in Action. (C). 1988. 30.00 (*0-85439-144-4*, Pub. by St Paul Pubns) St Mut.
— Voice of the Hidden Waterfall. (C). 1988. 39.00 (*0-85439-178-9*, Pub. by St Paul Pubns) St Mut.

Nichols, Kevin & Cummins, John. Into His Fullness. (C). 1988. 39.00 (*0-85439-171-1*, Pub. by St Paul Pubns) St Mut.

Nichols, K.G. Design Automation of Integrated Circuits. (Electronic Engineering Systems Ser.). Date not set. 70.00 (*0-8493-8991-7*) CRC Pr.

Nichols, Kim, jt. auth. see Nichols, Wendy.

***Nichols, Kurt.** 1,001 Things For Kids on the Internet. (YA). (gr. k-12). 1999. pap. 9.95 (*0-9670123-0-9*) Just Child.

***Nichols, L. Joseph.** Soul As Healer: Lessons in Affirmation, Visualization & Color. (Illus.). 2000. pap. write for info. (*1-56718-487-1*, Pub. by Llewellyn Pubns) Bookpeople.

Nichols, Larry, jt. auth. see Mather, George.

Nichols, Larry, jt. auth. see Robbins, Ray K.

Nichols, Larry A., jt. auth. see Mather, George A.

Nichols, Larry D. Law Enforcement Patrol Operations: Police Systems & Practices. 4th ed. LC 98-67152. (Illus.). 546p. 1998. teacher ed. 45.00 (*0-8211-1311-9*) McCutchan.

***Nichols, Lauren.** Accidental Father. (Intimate Moments Ser.: Vol. 994). 2000. per. 4.50 (*0-373-07994-X*) Silhouette.

Nichols, Lauren. Accidental Heiress. (Intimate Moments Ser.: No. 840). 1998. per. 4.25 (*0-373-07840-4*, 1-07840-1) Silhouette.
— Accidental Hero: Way Out West. 1998. per. 4.25 (*0-373-07893-5*, 1-07893-0) Silhouette.

Nichols, Lawrence T., jt. auth. see Buono, Anthony F.

Nichols, Lawrence W., et al. Toledo Treasures: Selections from the Toledo Museum of Art. LC 95-21385. (Illus.). 192p. 1995. 50.00 (*1-55595-118-X*) Hudson Hills.

Nichols, Lee. Breakthrough on the Color Front. rev. ed. 250p. 1993. 18.00 (*1-57889-076-4*) Passeggiata.

Nichols, Leigh, pseud. Shadowfires. 448p. 1987. pap. 3.95 (*0-380-75216-6*, Avon Bks) Morrow Avon.

***Nichols, Les.** Confessions of a Name Dropper. 2000. 21.95 (*1-56311-533-6*) Turner Pub KY.

Nichols, Lew, jt. auth. see Proulx, E. Annie.

Nichols, Linda. Anatomy & Physiology Laboratory Manual. 278p. (C). 1997. per. 30.95 (*0-7872-2877-X*, 41287701) Kendall-Hunt.

***Nichols, Linda.** Handyman. LC 99-88422. 296p. 2000. 20.00 (*0-385-33437-0*) Delacorte.
— Handyman. 2000. mass mkt. 6.99 (*0-440-23542-1*) Dell.
— Handyman. large type ed. LC 00-25199. 411p. 2000. 28.95 (*0-7862-2503-3*) Thorndike Pr.

Nichols, Linda M., jt. ed. see Crumbley, D. Larry.

Nichols, Lonnie J. God, the Universe & Self. LC 82-74521. 96p. 1983. pap. 4.50 (*0-87516-515-X*) DeVorss.

Nichols, Lourdes. Homestyle Mexican Cooking. LC 97-11509. (Homestyle Cooking Ser.). (Illus.). 208p. 1997. pap. 16.95 (*0-89594-861-3*) Crossing Pr.

Nichols, Lyn. Chef Detective & Friends. Nelson, Mary, ed. 256p. 1999. write for info. (*0-9670476-0-9*) Davon Pr.

Nichols, Lynn, ed. see Dobrin, Lise M.

Nichols, M. Q. White Roots: A Nichols Genealogy. (Illus.). 377p. 1983. 25.00 (*0-9612516-0-3*) M Q Nichols.

Nichols, Madaline W. Gaucho: Cattle Hunter, Cavalryman, Ideal of Romance. LC 68-58423. 161p. (C). 1968. reprint ed. 50.00 (*0-87752-077-1*) Gordian.

Nichols, Margaret I. Selecting & Using a Core-Reference Collection. 2nd ed. 67p. (Orig.). (C). 1995. pap. text 20.00 (*0-7881-2358-0*) DIANE Pub.

Nichols, Margaret I., jt. auth. see Safford, Barbara R.

Nichols, Marie H. Rhetoric & Criticism. LC 63-7958. 161p. 1963. pap. 50.00 (*0-7837-8514-3*, 204932300011) Bks Demand.

Nichols, Marilyn. The Journey Symbol. (Teilhard Studies: No. 18). 1987. pap. 3.50 (*0-89012-054-4*) Am Teilhard.

Nichols, Marion. Encyclopedia of Embroidery Stitches, Including Crewel. LC 72-97816. (Illus.). 219p. (Orig.). 1974. pap. 9.95 (*0-486-22929-7*) Dover.

Nichols, Marion, ed. see Briggs Company, Ltd. Staff.

Nichols, Mark & Nichols, Buffy. A Grassroots Survival Company Cookbook of Recipes, Remedies & Memories from the Great Depression. (Illus.). (Orig.). 1980. pap. 19.95 (*0-685-60296-6*) Grassrts Survival.

Nichols, Mary. A Dangerous Undertaking. large type ed. 350p. 1995. 23.99 (*0-263-14426-7*, Pub. by Mills & Boon) Ulverscroft.

***Nichols, Mary.** Dear Deceiver. 1998. 24.99 (*0-263-15765-2*) Ulvrscrft Audio.
— Jack Chiltern's Wife. 352p. 2000. 26.99 (*0-263-16365-2*, Pub. by Mills & Boon) Ulverscroft.
— Mistress of Madderlea. large type ed. 320p. 1999. 25.99 (*0-263-16151-X*, Pub. by Mills & Boon) Ulverscroft.

Nichols, Mary. The Poacher's Daughter. 384p. 1995. 26.00 (*1-85797-696-7*, Pub. by Orion Pubng Grp) Trafalgar.
— Reminiscences of Edgar Allan Poe. LC 74-4041. (Studies in Poe: No. 23). 1974. lib. bdg. 22.95 (*0-8383-2068-6*) M S G Haskell Hse.
— The Ruby Pendant. large type ed. (Mills & Boon Large Print Ser.). 350p. 1998. 24.99 (*0-263-15458-0*, Pub. by Mills & Boon) Ulverscroft.
— The Stubble Field. 432p. 1993. 25.95 (*1-85797-177-9*) Orion Pubng Grp.
— To Win the Lady. large type ed. 350p. 1996. 23.99 (*0-263-14524-7*, Pub. by Mills & Boon) Ulverscroft.

Nichols, Mary & Young, Stanley. The Amazing L. A. Environment: A Handbook for Change. (Illus.). 147p. (Orig.). 1991. pap. 6.95 (*1-879326-11-6*) Living Planet Pr.

Nichols, Mary A. & Nichols, C., eds. Young Adults & Public Libraries: A Handbook of Materials & Services. LC 97-45649. (The Greenwood Library Management Collection). 296p. 1998. lib. bdg. 75.00 (*0-313-30003-8*, Greenwood Pr) Greenwood.

Nichols, Mary D. & Young, Stanley. The Amazing L. A. Environment: A Handbook for Change. (SPA., Illus.). 147p. (Orig.). pap. 6.95 (*1-879326-17-5*) Living Planet Pr.

Nichols, Mary P. Citizens & Statesmen: A Study of Aristotle's Politics. 288p. 1991. pap. text 23.00 (*0-8476-7703-6*) Rowman.
— Citizens & Statesmen: A Study of Aristotle's Politics. 288p. (C). 1991. text 59.50 (*0-8476-7702-8*) Rowman.
— Reconstructing Woody: Art, Love & Life in the Films of Woody Allen. LC 98-7452. (Illus.). 240p. 1998. 22.95 (*0-8476-8989-1*, PN1998, Pub. by Rowman) Natl Bk Netwk.

Nichols, Mary S. & Engam, Barbara W. Medical-Surgical Nursing Study Guide. (Illus.). 350p. 1987. pap. text 16.95 (*0-8016-3856-9*) Mosby Inc.

Nichols, Maynard. Circulation, Water Quality, & Environmental Resources of Perseverance Bay, St. Thomas. (Illus.). 102p. 1977. 15.00 (*0-318-14612-6*) Isl Resources.
— Virgin Islands Bays: Modeling of Water Quality & Pollution Susceptibility. (Illus.). 92p. 1979. 12.50 (*0-318-14619-3*) Isl Resources.
— Water Sediments & Ecology of the Mangrove Lagoon & Benner Bay, St. Thomas. (Illus.). 159p. 1977. 20.00 (*0-318-14622-3*) Isl Resources.

Nichols, Melissa. Jonah & the Whale. Smith, Terrell, ed. LC 96-31793. (Family Time Bible Stories Ser.). (Illus.). 32p. (J). (ps-2). 1996. write for info. (*0-7835-4637-8*) Time-Life.

Nichols, Michael. The Power of Family Therapy. rev. ed. 464p. (C). 1993. reprint ed. pap. text 29.95 (*0-89876-204-9*, RC488.5.N5345) Gardner Pr.

Nichols, Michael, photos by. Gorilla: The Struggle for Survival in the Virungas. (Illus.). 1992. pap. 29.95 (*0-89381-349-4*) Aperture.
— The Great Apes: Between Two Worlds. deluxe ed. LC 93-2261. (Illus.). 1993. 39.95 (*0-87044-948-6*) Natl Geog.

Nichols, Michael & Goodall, Jane. Brutal Kinship. (Illus.). 128p. 1999. 25.00 (*0-89381-806-2*) Aperture.

Nichols, Michael C. A Puzzle with Four Pieces: The Betrayal, Death & Resurrection of Jesus Christ. (Illus.). vi, 136p. 1997. 19.95 (*0-9662051-0-3*) DayStar Pubns.

N

Nichols, Michael P. Inside Family Therapy: A Case Study in Family Healing. annuals LC 98-14393. 242p. 1998. pap. 38.00 (*0-205-28412-4*) Allyn.

— The Lost Art of Listening: How Learing to Listen Can Improve Relationships. LC 94-38111. (Family Therapy Ser.). 251p. 1995. lib. bdg. 32.95 (*0-89862-267-0*) Guilford Pubns.

— The Lost Art of Listening: How Learning to Listen Can Improve Relationships. LC 94-38111. (Guilford Family Therapy Ser.). 251p. 1996. pap. 15.95 (*1-57230-131-7*) Guilford Pubns.

— No Place to Hide: Facing Shame So We Can Find Self-Respect. LC 95-33135. 366p. 1995. pap. 18.95 (*1-57392-016-9*) Prometheus Bks.

— The Self in the System: Expanding the Limits of Family Therapy. LC 87-13773. 328p. 1987. text 40.95 (*0-87630-472-2*) Brunner-Mazel.

Nichols, Michael P. & Paolino, Thomas J., Jr. Basic Techniques of Psychodynamic Psychotherapy. 337p. (C). 1998. reprint ed. pap. text 22.00 (*0-7881-5610-1*) DIANE Pub.

Nichols, Michael P. & Schwartz, Richard C. Family Therapy. 4th ed. LC 97-9840. 586p. 1997. 79.00 (*0-205-26983-4*) P-H.

***Nichols, Michael P. & Schwartz, Richard C.** Family Therapy: Concepts & Methods. 5th ed. LC 99-86266. 608p. 2000. 66.67 (*0-205-31737-5*) Allyn.

Nichols, Michael P., jt. auth. see Minuchin, Salvador.

Nichols, Mike. Life, & Other Ways to Kill Time. 288p. 1988. 15.95 (*0-8184-0462-0*) Carol Pub Group.

— Real Men Belch Downwind: Modern Etiquette for the Primitive Man. Towle, Mike, ed. (Illus.). 142p. 1993. pap. 6.95 (*1-56530-054-8*) Summit TX.

— The Witches Sabbats: And Other Reflections. (Illus.). 110p. Date not set. pap. 14.95 (*1-885569-09-2*) Solar Crown.

— Women Are from Pluto, Men Are from Uranus: The Big Bang & Other Premature Theories of Love. LC 96-35685. (Illus.). 172p. 1996. 9.99 (*1-56530-224-9*) Summit TX.

Nichols, Mike, photos by. Keepers of the Kingdom: The New American Zoo. LC 95-23922. (Illus.). 132p. 1996. 34.95 (*0-9650308-2-2*) Lickle Pubng.

— Keepers of the Kingdom: The New American Zoo. LC 95-23922. (Illus.). 132p. (J). 1996. pap. 19.95 (*0-9650308-3-0*) Lickle Pubng.

Nichols, N. K. & Owens, D. H., eds. The Mathematics of Control Theory: Based on the Proceedings of a Conference on Control Theory, Organized by the Institute of Mathematics & Its Applications, & Held at the University of Strathclyde in September 1988. LC 92-23022. (Institute of Mathematics & Its Applications Conference Series, New Ser.: New Series 37). (Illus.). 496p. 1992. text 115.00 (*0-19-853640-2*, Clarendon Pr) OUP.

Nichols, N. R. Round - Rounds Genealogy: Descendants of John Round of Swansen MA. (Illus.). 259p. reprint ed. pap. 39.00 (*0-8328-1671-X*); reprint ed. lib. bdg. 49.00 (*0-8328-1670-1*) Higginson Bk Co.

Nichols, Nancy. Reach for the Top: Women & the Changing Facts of Work Life. 256p. 1994. 27.95 (*0-07-103580-X*) McGraw.

Nichols, Nancy, jt. auth. see Sgubin, Marta.

Nichols, Nancy A. San Quentin Prison - Inside the Walls. Delahunty, James T., ed. (Illus.). 68p. (Orig.). 1991. pap. 9.95 (*0-9630115-2-9*) San Quentin Mus.

Nichols, Nancy A., ed. Reach for the Top: Women & the Changing Facts of Work Life. 208p. 1996. pap. 13.95 (*0-87584-739-0*) Harvard Busn.

Nichols, Nancy A., intro. Reach for the Top: Women & the Changing Facts of Work Life. LC 93-34718. (Harvard Business Review Book Ser.). 208p. 1994. 27.95 (*0-87584-507-X*) Harvard Busn.

Nichols, Nancy A., jt. auth. see Nichols, Alan H.

Nichols, Nancy A., ed. see Nichols, Alan, Sr.

Nichols, Nancy A., ed. see Nichols, Alan H.

Nichols, Naomi M. Food Drying at Home. 1978. pap. 5.95 (*0-442-26029-6*, VNR) Wiley.

Nichols, Nichelle. Saturn's Child. 1996. mass mkt. 5.99 (*0-441-00384-2*) Ace Bks.

Nichols, Nick. The Comfort Fairy Story. 24p. (J). (gr. k-4). 1990. 19.95 (*0-9632531-0-7*) N Squared Ent.

Nichols, Nina D. Ariadne's Lives. LC 94-31366. 1995. 36.50 (*0-8386-3582-2*) Fairleigh Dickinson.

Nichols, Nina Da Vinci, see Da Vinci Nichols, Nina.

Nichols, P. W., ed. see Russell, Enid.

Nichols, Pamela. Art of Henna: The Ultimate Body Art Book & Kit. 1999. pap. text 29.95 (*0-916860-13-2*, Pub. by Healthy Planet Prods) Ten Speed Pr.

— The Art of Henna: The Ultimate Henna Body Art Book & Kit. (Healthy Planet Kits Ser.). (Illus.). 128p. 1999. pap. 29.95 (*0-89087-941-9*) Celestial Arts.

Nichols, Pamela & Lester, Teri. Escape to Romance. 1982. mass mkt. 2.50 (*0-451-11879-0*, AE1879, Sig) NAL.

Nichols, Patsie, ed. see Bureau of Deep Mine Safety & Mining & Reclamation.

Nichols, Patsie, ed. see Bureau of Deep Mine Safety, Mining & Reclamation S.

Nichols, Paul. Social Survey Methods: A Guide for Development Workers. 132p. (C). 1991. pap. 14.95 (*0-85598-126-1*, Pub. by Oxfam Pub) Stylus Pub VA.

— Where in the World Did You Come From? (Illus.). 26p. (J). (ps-4). 1993. 17.95 (*1-884507-00-X*) Boyer-Caswell.

Nichols, Paul, et al, eds. The Heritage of Perry County, Alabama. (Heritage of Alabama Ser.: No. 53). (Illus.). 240p. 1998. 55.00 (*1-891647-20-2*) Herit Pub Consult.

Nichols, Paul D., et al, eds. Cognitively Diagnostic Assessment. 480p. 1995. 89.95 (*0-8058-1588-0*); pap. 49.95 (*0-8058-1589-9*) L Erlbaum Assocs.

Nichols, Paul L. & Chen, Ta-Chuan. Minimal Brain Dysfunction: A Prospective Study. LC 80-18739. 352p. 1981. text 69.95 (*0-89859-074-4*) L Erlbaum Assocs.

Nichols, Peter. Joe Egg. LC 68-21264. 96p. 1968. pap. 9.95 (*0-8021-5115-9*, Grove) Grove-Atltic.

— Nichols Plays 1. (Methuen World Dramatists Ser.). 376p. (C). 1991. pap. 17.95 (*0-413-64870-2*, A0560) Heinemann.

Nichols, Peter. Nichols Plays 2. (Methuen World Dramatists Ser.). 498p. (C). 1992. pap. 13.95 (*0-413-65070-7*, A0561) Heinemann.

Nichols, Peter. Passion Play. (Methuen Modern Plays Ser.). 106p. (C). 1981. pap. write for info. (*0-413-47800-9*, A0361, Methuen Drama) Methn.

— A Piece of My Mind. LC 88-116276. (Methuen Modern Plays Ser.). 80p. (C). 1988. pap. 10.95 (*0-413-17360-7*, A0210, Methuen Drama) Methn.

— Sea Change. LC 96-51569. 256p. 1997. 23.95 (*0-670-87179-6*) Viking Penguin.

— Sea Change: Across the Atlantic in a Wooden Boat. 1997. 23.95 (*0-614-28022-2*, Viking) Viking Penguin.

— Sea Change: Alone Across the Atlantic in a Wooden Boat. LC 96-51569. 256p. 1998. pap. 12.95 (*0-14-026413-2*) Penguin Putnam.

***Nichols, Peter.** A Voyage for Madmen. 2001. write for info. (*0-06-019764-1*) HarpC.

— A Voyage for Madmen. 2002. pap. write for info. (*0-06-095703-4*, Perennial) HarperTrade.

Nichols, Peter. Voyage to the North Star. (Illus.). 352p. 1999. 24.00 (*0-7867-0664-3*) Carroll & Graf.

***Nichols, Peter.** Voyage to the North Star. 352p. 2000. reprint ed. pap. 14.00 (*0-7867-0799-2*, Pub. by Carroll & Graf) Publishers Group.

Nichols, Peter & Nichols, Belia. Mastodon Hunters to Mound Builders: North American Archaeology. (Illus.). 112p. (J). (gr. 6-7). 1992. 12.95 (*0-89015-748-0*) Sunbelt Media.

Nichols, Phillip. Homeopathy & the Medical Profession. 250p. 1988. lib. bdg. 57.50 (*0-7099-1836-4*, Pub. by C Helm) Routldge.

***Nichols, Polly.** Clear Thinking: Talking Back to Whispering Shadows, a Psychoeducational Curriculum for Preteens, Teens & Young Adults. LC 99-70181. 1999. write for info. (*0-9649142-2-0*) Riv Lghts.

Nichols, Polly. Clear Thinking - Clearing Dark Thought with New Words & Images: A Program for Teachers & Counseling Professionals. (Illus.). 302p. (Orig.). 1996. pap. text 38.00 (*0-9649142-0-4*) Riv Lghts.

Nichols, Polly & Shaw, Martha. Whispering Shadows: Think Clearly & Claim Your Personal Power. LC 99-701801. write for info. (*0-9649142-1-2*) Riv Lghts.

Nichols, Preston B. & Moon, Peter. Encounter in the Pleiades: An Inside Look at UFOs. (Illus.). 260p. 1996. pap. 19.95 (*0-9631889-3-3*) Sky Bks NY.

— The Montauk Project: Experiments in Time. LC 91-91514. (Illus.). 160p. (Orig.). 1992. pap. 15.95 (*0-9631889-0-9*) Sky Bks NY.

— Montauk Revisited: Adventures in Synchronicity. LC 93-84992. (Illus.). 224p. 1994. pap. 19.95 (*0-9631889-1-7*) Sky Bks NY.

— Pyramids of Montauk No. 3: Explorations in Consciousness. LC 94-69941. (Illus.). 266p. 1995. pap. 19.95 (*0-9631889-2-5*) Sky Bks NY.

Nichols Publishing Staff. Guide to Society Hill Philadelphia. (Illus.). pap. 2.50 (*0-8019-8731-8*) CBM Bk.

Nichols, R. Great Zodiac of Glastonbury. (Orig.). 1993. pap. 6.95 (*1-55818-240-3*) Holmes Pub.

— Improving Effectiveness & Reliability of Non-Destructive Testing. Gardner, W. E., ed. LC 91-40554. (International Series on Materials Evaluation & Nondestructive Testing Ser.: No. 2). (Illus.). 272p. 1992. 118.00 (*0-08-036981-2*, Pub. by Pergamon Repr) Franklin.

— Spanish & Portuguese Gardens. 1976. 59.95 (*0-8490-2646-6*) Gordon Pr.

Nichols, R. W., ed. Acoustic Emission. (Illus.). 121p. 1976. 63.00 (*0-85334-681-X*) Elsevier.

Nichols, R. W., jt. ed. see Liu, Cengdian.

Nichols, Randall K. Classical Cryptography Course, Vol. I. 301p. 1996. pap. 36.80 (*0-89412-263-0*) Aegean Park Pr.

— Classical Cryptography Course, Vol. 2. xii, 452p. 1996. pap. 42.80 (*0-89412-264-9*, C-76) Aegean Park Pr.

***Nichols, Randall K.** Defending Your Digital Assets Against Hackers, Crackers, Spies & Thieves. LC 99-59788. 848p. 1999. pap. 49.99 (*0-07-212285-4*) McGraw.

Nichols, Randall K. & International Computer Security Association Staff. ICSA Guide to Cryptography. LC 98-36563. (Illus.). 832p. 1998. 70.00 incl. cd-rom (*0-07-913759-8*) McGraw.

Nichols, Ray. Treason, Tradition & the Intellectual: Julien Benda & Political Discourse. LC 78-7785. x, 270p. 1979. 29.95 (*0-7006-0175-9*) U Pr of KS.

Nichols, Renee E., ed. see White, Darryl R.

Nichols, Richard. American Sportscars. 10.99 (*1-57215-224-9*, JG2249) World Pubns.

— Classic American Cars. 1992. pap. 19.95 (*0-671-08193-4*) S&S Trade.

***Nichols, Richard.** Robert Hooke & the Royal Society. (Illus.). 148p. 1999. 28.50 (*1-85776-465-X*, Pub. by Book Guild Ltd) Trans-Atl Phila.

Nichols, Richard. A Story to Tell: Traditions of a Tlingit Community. LC 97-9592. (We Are Still Here Ser.). (Illus.). (J). 1997. pap. 8.95 (*0-8225-9807-8*, Lerner Publctns); lib. bdg. 21.27 (*0-8225-2661-1*, Lerner Publctns) Lerner Pub.

Nichols, Richard, jt. auth. see Lorentzen, Bob.

Nichols, Robbie, jt. auth. see Molander, Roger C.

Nichols, Robert. Adventures in the High Wind: Poetic Observations & Other Lore. 144p. (Orig.). (C). 1990. pap. 7.95 (*0-9627615-0-8*) Mntn Muse Pub.

— Arrival. LC 77-1362. (Daily Lives in Nghsi-Altai Ser.: Bk. 1). 1977. pap. 1.95 (*0-8112-0653-X*, NDP437, Pub. by New Directions) Norton.

— Exile. LC 79-15330. (Daily Lives in Nghsi-Altai Ser.: Bk. 4). 1979. pap. 3.95 (*0-8112-0732-3*, NDP485, Pub. by New Directions) Norton.

— The Harditts in Sawna. LC 78-10765. (Daily Lives in Nghsi-Altai Ser.: Bk. 3). 1979. pap. 3.95 (*0-8112-0684-X*, NDP470, Pub. by New Directions) Norton.

— The High Priest of Hallelujah. LC 98-86687. 192p. 1999. pap. 11.95 (*1-56315-196-0*, Pub. by SterlingHse) Natl Bk Netwk.

***Nichols, Robert.** Settling the Frontier: Land, Law & Society, in the Peshawar Valley, 1500-1900. 370p. 2000. text 19.95 (*0-19-579380-3*) OUP.

— Travels in Altai. xii, 230p. 1999. pap. 16.50 (*1-930180-01-2*, 2) Glad Day Bks VT.

Nichols, Robert. Travels in Altai: From the Tetralogy: Daily Lives in Nghsi Altai. Orig. Title: Daily Lives in Nghsi Altai. 252p. 1999. pap. 16.95 (*0-9658903-2-5*) Glad Day Bks VT.

Nichols, Robert A. & Mollard, Patrice, eds. Microscopic Imaging in Experimental Neurobiology. (Neuromethods Ser.). 1999. 99.50 (*0-89603-707-X*) Humana.

Nichols, Robert C., jt. auth. see Loehlin, John C.

Nichols, Robert E. Birds of Algonquin Legend. LC 95-19668. 168p. 1996. text 29.95 (*0-472-10611-2*, 10611) U of Mich Pr.

Nichols, Robert M. Fantastica: Being the Smile of the Sphinx, & Other Tales of Imagination. LC 75-128744. (Short Story Index Reprint Ser.). 1977. 23.95 (*0-8369-3635-3*) Ayer.

Nichols, Robert W., jt. auth. see Folio, M. Rhonda.

Nichols, Robert W., jt. auth. see Folio, Rhonda M.

Nichols, Rod. Successful Network Marketing. Wait, Erin, ed. LC 95-18046. (Successful Business Library). (Illus.). 200p. 1995. pap. 15.95 (*1-55571-350-5*) PSI Resch.

Nichols, Roger. The American Indian, Past & Present. 5th ed. LC 98-27761. 1999. pap. 21.00 (*0-07-046600-9*, McGrw-H College) McGrw-H Hghr Educ.

— Black Hawk & the Warrior's Path. Kraut, Alan M. & Wakelyn, Jon L., eds. (American Biographical History Ser.). 190p. 1992. pap. text 11.95 (*0-88295-884-4*) Harlan Davidson.

— Debussy Remembered. (Illus.). 282p. 1992. 24.95 (*0-931340-41-1*, Amadeus Pr) Timber.

— The Life of Debussy. LC 97-25666. (Musical Lives Ser.). (Illus.). 192p. (C). 1998. pap. 14.95 (*0-521-57887-6*); text 39.95 (*0-521-57026-3*) Cambridge U Pr.

— One Hundred Sheep: Songbook. 12p. (J). (gr. 1-3). 1995. pap. 10.00 (*1-880892-69-3*) Com Sense FL.

***Nichols, Roger.** Ravel Remembered. 240p. 2000. pap. 16.00 (*0-571-14986-3*) Faber & Faber.

Nichols, Roger & Halley, Patrick L. Stephen Long & America Frontier Expedition. LC 78-68878. (Illus.). 280p. 1980. 38.50 (*0-87413-149-9*) U Delaware Pr.

Nichols, Roger & Nichols, Sarah. Greek Everyday Life. McLeish, Kenneth & McLeish, Valerie, eds. (Aspects of Greek Life Ser.). (Illus.). 48p. (YA). (gr. 7-12). 1978. reprint ed. pap. text 9.00 (*0-582-20672-3*, 70819) Longman.

Nichols, Roger, ed. & tr. see Debussy, Claude.

Nichols, Roger, tr. see Halbreich, Harry, et al.

Nichols, Roger, tr. see Livy.

Nichols, Roger, tr. see MacDonald, Hugh, ed.

Nichols, Roger L. The American Indian: Past & Present. 4th ed. 352p. (C). 1991. pap. 26.25 (*0-07-046499-5*) McGraw.

— Indians in the United States & Canada: A Comparative History. LC 97-31596. (Illus.). 393p. 1998. text 65.00 (*0-8032-3341-8*) U of Nebr Pr.

— Indians in the United States & Canada: A Comparative History. LC 97-31596. (Illus.). 393p. 1999. pap. 19.95 (*0-8032-8377-6*) U of Nebr Pr.

Nichols, Roger L., ed. American Frontier & Western Issues: A Historiographical Review, 118. LC 85-30181. (Contributions in American History Ser.: No. 118). 312p. 1986. 57.95 (*0-313-24356-5*, NAF/, Greenwood Pr) Greenwood.

Nichols, Roger L. & Halley, Patrick L. Stephen Long & American Frontier Exploration. LC 94-36696. (Illus.). 280p. 1995. pap. 9.95 (*0-8061-2724-4*) U of Okla Pr.

Nichols, Roger L., ed. see Black Hawk.

***Nichols, Ronald H.** In Custer's Shadow: Major Marcus Reno. (Illus.). 432p. 2000. pap. 14.95 (*0-8061-3281-7*) U of Okla Pr.

Nichols, Ronald H., ed. Reno Court of Inquiry: Proceedings of a Court of Inquiry in the Case of Major Marcus A. Reno. 675p. 1993. reprint ed. pap. 26.50 (*1-892258-01-3*) Custer Bttlefield.

Nichols, Roy C. Doing the Gospel: Local Congregations in Ministry. LC 90-33916. 1990. pap. 9.95 (*0-687-11030-0*) Abingdon.

Nichols, Roy F. Advance Agents of American Destiny. LC 79-25886. 254p. 1980. reprint ed. lib. bdg. 65.00 (*0-313-22123-5*, NIAA, Greenwood Pr) Greenwood.

— Democratic Machine, 1850-1854. LC 68-1159. (Columbia University. Studies in the Social Sciences: No. 248). reprint ed. 20.00 (*0-404-51248-8*) AMS Pr.

— The Disruption of American Democracy. LC 83-45826. 1983. reprint ed. 48.50 (*0-404-20190-3*) AMS Pr.

— The Disruption of American Democracy. LC 48-6344. 648p. 1948. reprint ed. pap. 200.00 (*0-608-03956-X*, 205204300029) Bks Demand.

— Franklin Pierce: Young Hickory of the Granite Hills. Speirs, Katherine E., ed. LC 93-70974. (Signature Ser.). (Illus.). 637p. 1993. reprint ed. 35.00 (*0-945707-06-1*) Amer Political.

Nichols, Sallie. Jung & Tarot: An Archetypal Journey. LC 80-53118. (Illus.). 416p. 1984. reprint ed. pap. 16.95 (*0-87728-515-2*) Weiser.

Nichols, Sandra & Nichols, Chase. College Cheerleading Guide. 2nd ed. Date not set. pap. 12.00 (*0-9656179-1-2*) Coll Cheerleading.

Nichols, Sandra M. & Nichols, Chase D. College Cheerleading Guide. (Orig.). (C). 1996. pap. 12.00 (*0-9656179-0-4*) Coll Cheerleading.

***Nichols, Sarah, et al.** Aluminum by Design. (Illus.). 300p. 2000. 75.00 (*0-8109-6721-9*, Pub. by Abrams) Time Warner.

Nichols, Sarah, jt. auth. see Bieler, Henry G.

Nichols, Sarah, jt. auth. see Nichols, Roger.

Nichols, Sharon E., jt. auth. see Howe, Ann C.

Nichols, Spencer V. The Significance of Anthony Trollope. 1977. lib. bdg. 59.95 (*0-8490-2604-0*) Gordon Pr.

Nichols, Stan, et al. Prairie Primer. (Illus.). 59p. (C). 1999. pap. text 15.00 (*0-7881-7758-3*) DIANE Pub.

Nichols, Stephen. A Chronological History of Key West, Vol. 2. 2nd rev. ed. (Illus.). 72p. 1996. pap. 10.95 (*0-9653885-0-6*) Key West Images.

Nichols, Stephen G. & Wenzel, Siegfried, eds. The Whole Book: Cultural Perspectives on the Medieval Miscellany. 200p. (C). 1996. text 42.50 (*0-472-10696-1*, 10696) U of Mich Pr.

Nichols, Stephen G., jt. ed. see Bloch, R. Howard.

Nichols, Stephen G., Jr., ed. see De Lorris, Guillaume.

Nichols, Stephen G., Jr., jt. ed. see Lyons, John D.

Nichols, Stephen G., Jr., jt. ed. see Robinson, Franklin W.

Nichols, Steve, ed. see Barrett, Gloria.

Nichols, Steven, jt. auth. see Seiter, Charles.

Nichols, Stuart E. & Ostrow, David G., eds. Psychiatric Implications of Acquired Immune Deficiency Syndrome. LC 84-6187. (Clinical Insights Ser.). 151p. reprint ed. pap. 46.90 (*0-8357-7822-3*, 203619500002) Bks Demand.

Nichols, Susan K., pref. Patterns in Practice: Selections from the Journal of Museum Education. LC 91-66484. 391p. (Orig.). 1992. pap. 35.00 (*1-880437-00-7*) Mus Ed Round.

***Nichols, T. N., ed.** What's in a Name? Being a Popular Explanation of Ordinary Christian Names. 128p. 2000. pap. 19.50 (*0-7404-0033-9*) Higginson Bk Co.

Nichols, Tawa. Three Centuries of American Music: A Collection of Sacred & Secular Music: Solo Song, 1866-1910, Vol. 2. 400p. (C). 1989. 105.00 (*0-8161-0543-X*, G K Hall & Co) Mac Lib Ref.

Nichols, Terence. That All May Be One: Hierarchy & Participation in the Church. LC 97-21588. 368p. 1997. pap. 29.95 (*0-8146-5857-1*, M Glazier) Liturgical Pr.

Nichols, Teresa. Student Teaching Handbook. 74p. (C). 1996. 12.95 (*0-7872-3317-X*) Kendall-Hunt.

Nichols, Terri V. Francis: The Knight of Assisi. (Illus.). 61p. (J). (ps-6). 1990. pap. text 2.99 (*0-685-62404-8*) CCC of America.

Nichols, Terri Vorndran, jt. auth. see O'Connell-Roussell, Sheila.

Nichols, Theo. The Sociology of Industrial Injury. LC 96-20534. (Illus.). 256p. 1997. 89.50 (*0-7201-2255-4*) Continuum.

Nichols, Thom. The Boy on the Bicycle. 1999. reprint ed. mass mkt. 6.95 (*1-56333-651-0*, Badboy) Masquerade.

Nichols, Thomas L. A Biography of the Brothers Davenport. LC 75-36912. (Occult Ser.). 1976. reprint ed. 29.95 (*0-405-07969-9*) Ayer.

— Esoteric Anthropology: The Mysteries of Man. LC 75-180585. (Medicine & Society in America Ser.). (Illus.). 350p. 1972. reprint ed. 24.95 (*0-405-03962-X*) Ayer.

— Forty Years of American Life: 1812-1861. 2 vols., Set. (American Biography Ser.). 1991. reprint ed. lib. bdg. 148.00 (*0-7812-8298-5*) Rprt Serv.

— Journal in Jail. LC 71-125709. (American Journalists Ser.). 1978. reprint ed. 24.95 (*0-405-01690-5*) Ayer.

— Marriage: Its History, Character, & Results. LC 78-22161. (Free Love in America Ser.). reprint ed. 36.50 (*0-404-60955-4*) AMS Pr.

— Woman in All Ages & All Nations. 1972. 250.00 (*0-8490-1314-3*) Gordon Pr.

Nichols, Thomas M. Russian Presidency: Society & Politics in the Second Russian Republic. LC 99-29167. 200p. 1999. text 45.00 (*0-312-22357-9*) St Martin.

— The Sacred Cause: Civil-Military Conflict over Soviet National Security, 1917-1992. LC 92-34543. (Cornell Studies in Security Affairs). 280p. 1993. text 37.50 (*0-8014-2774-6*) Cornell U Pr.

Nichols, Tim, ed. see National Institute for Exploration Members.

Nichols, Tom. Tintoretto: Tradition & Identity. 1999. 65.00 (*1-86189-043-5*, Pub. by RBL) Consort Bk Sales.

Nichols, Tom, jt. auth. see Garvey, Dennis.

Nichols, Tom, jt. auth. see Ostroff, Harriet.

***Nichols, Trent W.** Optimal Digestion: New Strategies for Achieving Digestive Health. LC 99-29600. (Illus.). 624p. 1999. pap. 16.00 (*0-380-80498-0*, Avon Bks) Morrow Avon.

Nichols, Trudy & Wolf, Conner. The Flintstones. (Look & Find Ser.). (Illus.). 24p. (J). (gr. k-6). 1996. lib. bdg. 14.95 (*1-56674-122-X*, HTS Bks) Forest Hse.

Nichols, Trudy, jt. auth. see McGill, Nancy L.

Nichols, V. Cars & Trucks Sticker Pad. (Illus.). 32p. (J). (gr. k-6). 1993. reprint ed. pap. 2.95 (*1-879424-16-9*) Nickel Pr.

— Dinosaur Coloring Book. (Illus.). 32p. (Orig.). (J). (gr. k-6). 1993. pap. 2.95 (*1-879424-50-9*) Nickel Pr.

— Flags of the World Sticker Atlas. (Illus.). 32p. (Orig.). (J). (gr. k-6). 1992. pap. 3.95 (*1-879424-22-3*) Nickel Pr.

— Funny Faces Sticker Pad. (Illus.). 32p. (J). (gr. k-6). 1993. reprint ed. pap. 2.95 (*1-879424-31-2*) Nickel Pr.

An Asterisk (*) at the beginning of an entry indicates that the title is appearing for the first time.

— Hunt for Humphrey. (Illus.). 32p. (J). (gr. k-6). 1992. pap. 1.95 (*1-879424-15-0*) Nickel Pr.
— Hunt for Humphrey. Turkow, E., tr. (ENG & SPA., Illus.). 32p. (J). (gr. k-6). 1992. pap. 1.95 (*1-879424-23-1*) Nickel Pr.
— The Incredible Dionsaur Activity Book. (Illus.). 128p. (J). (gr. k-6). pap. 2.95 (*1-879424-64-9*) Nickel Pr.
— Large Print Puzzle Assortment. 384p. (Orig.). 1993. pap. 3.95 (*1-879424-60-6*) Nickel Pr.
— Notebook U. S. Atlas. (Illus.). 16p. 1993. pap. 1.95 (*1-879424-44-4*) Nickel Pr.
— Notebook World Atlas. (Illus.). 16p. (YA). (gr. 5-12). 1993. reprint ed. pap. 1.95 (*1-879424-25-8*) Nickel Pr.
— Student Planner & Assignment Book. 2nd ed. (Illus.). 120p. (YA). (gr. 5-12). 1993. reprint ed. pap. 3.95 (*1-879424-20-7*) Nickel Pr.
— U. S. Map & Sticker Book. (Illus.). 32p. (J). (gr. k-6). 1993. reprint ed. pap. 3.95 (*1-879424-10-X*) Nickel Pr.
— Webster's Dictionary. Kauffman, L., ed. (Illus.). 448p. 1993. reprint ed. pap. 2.99 (*1-879424-00-2*); reprint ed. pap. 1.99 (*1-879424-12-6*) Nickel Pr.
— Webster's Dictionary & Thesaurus. rev. ed. Kaufmann, L., ed. (C). 1991. reprint ed. pap. 7.95 (*1-879424-14-2*) Nickel Pr.
— Webster's English-French Rack Size. (ENG & FRE.). 288p. (Orig.). 1993. pap. 1.99 (*1-879424-57-6*) Nickel Pr.
— Webster's English Spanish Dictionary. (ENG & SPA.). 336p. (Orig.). 1992. pap. 1.99 (*1-879424-11-8*) Nickel Pr.
— Webster's English Spanish Rack Dictionary. (ENG & SPA.). 288p. (Orig.). 1993. pap. 1.99 (*1-879424-58-4*) Nickel Pr.
— Webster's English Spanish Vest Pocket. (ENG & SPA.). 192p. (Orig.). 1992. pap. 1.95 (*1-879424-24-X*) Nickel Pr.
— Webster's Giant Print Dictionary. large type ed. Kauffman, L., ed. 288p. 1993. pap. 2.99 (*1-879424-53-3*) Nickel Pr.
— Webster's Thesaurus. Kauffman, L., ed. 288p. 1993. reprint ed. pap. 1.99 (*1-879424-01-0*) Nickel Pr.
— Webster's Two in One Dictionary & Thesaurus. Kauffman, L., ed. (Illus.). 352p. pap. 1.99 (*1-879424-42-8*) Nickel Pr.
Nichols, V. & Kauffman, L. Webster's Speller. 288p. pap. 1.99 (*1-879424-02-9*) Nickel Pr.
— Webster's Three Piece Box Set. 1024p. (Orig.). 1991. pap. 9.95 (*1-879424-03-7*) Nickel Pr.
— Webster's Vest Pocket Dictionary. 192p. 1992. reprint ed. pap. 1.95 (*1-879424-33-9*) Nickel Pr.
— Webster's Vest Pocket Thesaurus. 192p. 1993. reprint ed. pap. 1.95 (*1-879424-34-7*) Nickel Pr.
***Nichols-Vanderpool, J.** Genealogy of the White Family. fac. ed. 104p. 1999. reprint ed. 28.00 (*0-8328-9919-4*); reprint ed. pap. 18.00 (*0-8328-9920-8*) Higginson Bk Co.
***Nichols, Victoria.** Macedonia'a Secret Army: The IMRO Militia & Volunteer Battalions, 1943-44. (Illus.). 700p. 2000. per. write for info. (*1-891227-21-1*, Axis Europa Bks) Axis Europa.
***Nichols, Victoria & Thompson, Susan.** Silk Stalkings: More Women Write of Murder. 656p. 2000. pap. 22.95 (*1-57886-012-1*, Pub. by Scarecrow) Natl Bk Netwk.
Nichols, Victoria & Thompson, Susan. Silk Stalkings II: More Women Write of Murder. LC 97-24372. 656p. 1998. 49.95 (*0-8108-3393-X*) Scarecrow.
Nichols, Vida. Growth Poles: An Investigation of Their Potential As a Tool for Regional Economic Development. (Discussion Papers: No. 30). 1969. pap. 10.00 (*1-55869-051-4*) Regional Sci Res Inst.
Nichols, Vince. Gift of the Mass. LC 97-60967. 144p. 1997. pap. text 9.95 (*0-89622-740-5*) Twenty-Third.
Nichols, Virginia. How to Show Your Own Dog. 254p. 1970. 17.95 (*0-86622-698-2*, PS-607) TFH Pubns.
Nichols, W. Gary & Boykin, Milton L., eds. Arms Control & Nuclear Weapons: U. S. Policies & the National Interest, 59. LC 86-29429. (Contributions in Military Studies Ser.: No. 59). 147p. 1987. 45.00 (*0-313-25389-7*, NAC/, Greenwood Pr) Greenwood.
Nichols, Wendy & Nichols, Kim. Wonderscience: A Developmentally Appropriate Guide to Hands-on Science for Young Children. LC 90-60081. 60p. (Orig.). (J). (ps-3). 1990. pap. 14.95 (*0-9625907-0-3*) Learning Expo.
***Nichols, Weta.** Oh Lonesome Me. Conrad, Melinda, ed. 1999. 7.99 (*1-893108-08-2*) Neighbrhd Pr Pubng.
Nichols, William C. Marital Therapy: An Integrative Approach. LC 88-11179. (Family Therapy Ser.). 282p. 1988. lib. bdg. 35.00 (*0-89862-102-X*) Guilford Pubns.
— The Narrow Way: Examining Both Heaven & Hell & the Message of Salvation in Jesus Christ. 115p. 1993. pap. 6.50 (*0-9641803-1-6*) Internat Outreach.
— The Rich Man & Lazarus. (Proverbs 22:6 Ser.: No. 1). (Illus.). 40p. (J). (ps-4). 1996. pap. 8.00 (*0-9641803-4-0*) Internat Outreach.
— Treating Adult Survivors of Childhood Sexual Abuse. LC 91-50913. (Practitioner's Resource Ser.). 80p. 1992. pap. 15.45 (*0-943158-68-0*, TASBP, Prof Resc Pr) Pro Resource.
— Treating People in Families: An Integrative Framework. (Family Therapy Ser.). (Illus.). 331p. 1995. lib. bdg. 36.00 (*1-57230-036-1*, 0036) Guilford Pubns.
Nichols, William C., ed. Power & Family Therapy: A Special Issue of Contemporary Family Therapy. 75p. 1988. pap. 14.95 (*0-89885-430-X*, Kluwer Acad Hman Sci) Kluwer Academic.
Nichols, William C. & Everett, Craig A. Systemic Family Therapy: An Integrative Approach. LC 85-17235. (Guilford Family Therapy Ser.). (Illus.). 460p. reprint ed. pap. 142.60 (*0-608-07584-1*, 205989900010) Bks Demand.
***Nichols, William C. & Godolphin, Mary.** The Pilgrim's Progress Primer. large type ed. 104p. 1999. pap. 15.95 (*1-892838-03-6*) Internat Outreach.
Nichols, William C., et al. Handbook of Family Development & Intervention. LC 99-37989. (Series in Couples & Family Dynamics & Treatment). 528p. 2000. text 69.95 (*0-471-29967-7*) Wiley.
Nichols, William C., ed. see Nettleton, Asabel.
Nichols, William G., et al. Understanding Canadian Business: Canadian. 704p. (C). 1994. text 44.25 (*0-256-10800-5*, Irwn McGrw-H) McGrw-H Hghr Educ.
Nichols, William L., ed. see Peterson, Alan H.
Nichols, Wilmer W. & O'Rourke, Michael F. McDonald's Blood Flow in Arteries: Theoretical, Experimental & Clinical Principles. 4th ed. LC 97-21356. (Illus.). 576p. 1997. text 150.00 (*0-340-64614-4*) OUP.
***Nichols, Yuriko.** All Around the Farm - Red Readers: Red Book Kit. 2nd ed. (Learning Language Arts Through Literature Ser.). (Illus.). 46p. (J). 1998. pap. 7.00 (*1-880892-53-7*) Com Sense FL.
Nichols, Yuriko. Bookshelf Collection Fifth-Eighth Graders. 144p. (J). 1994. 15.00 (*1-880892-56-1*) Com Sense FL.
— Common Sense Math for Kindergartners. 11p. 1993. pap. 12.00 (*1-880892-68-5*) Com Sense FL.
***Nichols, Yuriko.** Famous People - Red Readers: Red Book Kit. 2nd ed. (Learning Language Arts Through Literature Ser.). (Illus.). 35p. (J). 1998. pap. 7.00 (*1-880892-73-1*) Com Sense FL.
— Forest Fables - Red Readers: Red Book Kit. 2nd ed. (Learning Language Arts Through Literature Ser.). (Illus.). 36p. (J). 1998. pap. 7.00 (*1-880892-54-5*) Com Sense FL.
Nichols, Yuriko. Long Vowel Readers: Blue Book Kit. (Learning Language Arts Through Literature Ser.). (Illus.). 10p. (J). 1998. pap. 15.00 (*1-880892-58-8*) Com Sense FL.
— Short Vowel Readers: Blue Book Kit. 2nd ed. (Learning Language Arts Through Literature Ser.). (Illus.). 10p. (J). 1998. pap. 15.00 (*1-880892-57-X*) Com Sense FL.
Nicholsen, Shierry W. Exact Imagination, Late Work: On Adorno's Aesthetics. LC 97-9398. (Studies in Contemporary German Social Thought). (Illus.). 272p. 1997. 27.50 (*0-262-14062-4*) MIT Pr.
Nicholsen, Shierry W., ed. see Adorno, Theodor W.
Nicholsen, Shierry W., ed. & tr. see Habermas, Jurgen.
Nicholsen, Shierry W., tr. see Adorno, Theodor W.
Nicholsen, Shierry W., tr. see Habermas, Jurgen.
Nicholsen, Shierry W., tr. see Missac, Pierre.
***Nicholsen, Shierry Weber.** Exact Imagination: Late Work on Adorno's Aesthetics. LC 97-9398. (Studies in Contemporary German Social Thought). (Illus.). 270p. 1999. reprint ed. pap. 16.00 (*0-262-64040-6*) MIT Pr.
Nicholson. Annals of the Famine in Ireland. Murphy, Maureen, ed. 308p. 1997. pap. 32.95 (*1-85594-193-7*, Pub. by Attic Press) Intl Spec Bk.
— Essentials of Pagemaker 4.0. (C). 1992. mass mkt. 9.75 (*0-314-01351-2*) West Pub.
— Intermediate Microeconomics. 8th ed. (C). 1999. pap. text, student ed. Price not set. (*0-03-025918-5*) Harcourt Coll Pubs.
— Introduction to Abstract Algebra. 2nd ed. LC 99-25864. 624p. 1999. 89.95 (*0-471-33109-0*) Wiley.
— Linear Algebra with Applications. 3rd ed. (Mathematics Ser.). 1994. mass mkt., student ed. 27.75 (*0-534-93668-7*) PWS Pubs.
Nicholson. London Museums & Galleries Guide. (Illus.). pap. 12.95 (*0-7028-1752-X*) Brtholomew.
Nicholson. Microeconomic Theory. 7th ed. (C). 1997. pap. text, teacher ed. write for info. (*0-03-024696-2*) Harcourt Coll Pubs.
— Microeconomic Theory. 7th ed. (C). 1997. pap. text, student ed. 31.00 (*0-03-024697-0*, Pub. by Harcourt Coll Pubs) Harcourt.
— Paradox 5 for Windows: Standard Course. (DF - Computer Applications Ser.). (C). 1995. mass mkt. 34.95 (*0-538-71353-4*) S-W Pub.
— Work & Personality. 1996. pap. 49.95 (*0-86377-948-4*) L Erlbaum Assocs.
Nicholson, jt. auth. see Miller.
Nicholson, tr. see Iqbal, Muhammad.
Nicholson, Mervyn. Male Envy: The Logic of Malice in Literature & Culture. LC 99-10347. 249p. 1999. 65.00 (*0-7391-0062-9*) Lxngtn Bks.
Nicholson, Andrew. Kiwi Magic. (Illus.). 160p. 1998. 27.95 (*0-7153-0642-1*, Pub. by D & C Pub) Sterling.
***Nicholson, Andrew, ed.** William Nicholson, Painter: Paintings, Woodcuts, Writings, Photographs. (Illus.). 292p. 2000. 75.00 (*1-900357-00-3*, Pub. by Giles Mare Pubs) Trafalgar.
Nicholson, Andrew, ed. see Byron, George Gordon.
Nicholson, Andrew, jt. ed. see Mitchell, Donald.
Nicholson, Andrew, ed. & intro. see Byron, George Gordon.
Nicholson, Andrew, tr. & intro. see Byron, George Gordon.
Nicholson, Anne & Chorpenning, Charlotte B. The Magic Horn. 69p. 1954. reprint ed. pap. 3.50 (*0-87129-051-0*, M75) Dramatic Pub.
Nicholson, Asenoth. Annals of the Famine in Ireland. Murphy, Maureen, ed. LC 98-167974. 256p. 1998. pap. 19.95 (*1-874675-94-5*, Pub. by Lilliput Pr) Irish Bks Media.
Nicholson, Bebe. When a Believer Marries a Nonbeliever: How to Grow Together in Love, Faith & Joy. 312p. 1997. pap. write for info. (*0-9655127-1-1*) Priority Pub.
— When a Believer Marries a Nonbeliever: How to Grow Together in Love, Faith & Joy. unabridged ed. LC 94-12045. 303p. 1997. 19.95 (*0-9655127-0-3*); pap. 12.95 (*0-9655127-9-7*) Priority Pub.
Nicholson, Bertha M. Meditations on a D Major Scale. LC 87-63035. 1987. pap. 4.00 (*0-87574-276-9*) Pendle Hill.
Nicholson, Brinsley, ed. see Shakespeare, William.
Nicholson, Bronwen, et al. Gauguin & Maori Art. (Illus.). 80p. 1996. pap. 20.00 (*0-908877-69-2*, Pub. by Godwit Pubng) U of Wash Pr.
Nicholson-Brown, Barbara, ed. Human Resource Management in Religiously Affiliated Institutions. 125p. 1991. 20.00 (*0-910402-96-5*) Coll & U Personnel.
Nicholson, Bruce K. Hi, Ho, Come to the Fair: Tales of the New York World's Fair, 1964-1965. LC 89-92227. (Illus.). 224p. (Orig.). 1989. pap. 13.95 (*0-9624426-0-7*) Pelagian Pr.
Nicholson, C. David, ed. Anti-Dementia Agents: Research & Prospects for Therapy. (Neuroscience Perspectives Ser.). (Illus.). 316p. 1994. text 74.00 (*0-12-518055-1*) Acad Pr.
Nicholson, Carol A., ed. Law Library Systems Directory. rev. ed. LC 96-24609. (AALL Publications: No. 53). xxxii, 502p. 1996. ring bd. 67.50 (*0-8377-9326-2*, Rothman) W S Hein.
Nicholson, Carol A., et al, eds. Law Library Systems Directory. LC 93-2893. (American Association of Law Libraries Publications Ser.: No. 44). xix, 332p. 1993. 45.00 (*0-8377-0146-5*, Rothman) W S Hein.
Nicholson, Charles. A Field Guide to Southern Speech. LC 89-14872. 86p. 1989. pap. 7.95 (*0-87483-098-2*) August Hse.
Nicholson, Charles F., jt. auth. see Warnken, Philip F.
Nicholson, Charles L. & Alcorn, Charles L. Educational Applications of the WISC-III: A Handbook of Interpretive Strategies & Remedial Recommendations. 100p. 1994. spiral bd. 44.50 (*0-87424-294-0*, W-294A) Western Psych.
Nicholson, Charles P. Atlas of the Breeding Birds of Tennessee. LC 97-4622. (Illus.). 504p. (C). 1998. text 47.00 (*0-87049-987-4*) U of Tenn Pr.
Nicholson, Claire. Decoupage. (Inspirations Ser.). (Illus.). 96p. 1997. 12.95 (*1-85967-431-3*, Lorenz Bks) Anness Pub.
Nicholson, Clara & Nicholson, Judith, eds. Personalized Care Model for the Elderly. 540p. 1983. pap. text 21.30 (*0-317-00780-7*) Elder.
Nicholson, Colin. Alexander Pope: Essays for the Tercentenary. (Illus.). 280p. 1988. text 30.00 (*0-08-036394-6*, Pub. by Aberdeen U Pr) Macmillan.
— Writing & the Rise of Finance: Capital Satires of the Early Eighteenth Century. (Cambridge Studies in Eighteenth-Century English Literature & Thought: No. 21). 237p. (C). 1994. text 59.95 (*0-521-45323-2*) Cambridge U Pr.
Nicholson, Colin, ed. Iain Crichton Smith: Critical Essays. 224p. 1992. pap. 29.50 (*0-7486-0340-9*, Pub. by Edinburgh U Pr) Col U Pr.
— Under Cover: An Anthology of Contemporary Scottish Writing. 224p. 1994. pap. 15.95 (*1-85158-548-6*, Pub. by Mainstream Pubng) Trafalgar.
Nicholson, Colin & Orr, John, eds. Cinema & Fiction: New Modes of Adapting, 1950-1990. 240p. 1993. 25.00 (*0-7486 0356-5*, Pub. by Edinburgh U Pr) Col U Pr.
Nicholson, Cynthia P. The Earth. unabridged ed. (Starting with Space Ser.). (Illus.). 40p. (J). (gr. 2-6). 1997. 14.95 (*1-55074-314-7*, Pub. by Kids Can Pr) Genl Dist Srvs.
Nicholson, D. & Parsonage, N. G. Computer Simulation & the Statistical Mechanics of Adsorption. 1983. text 182.00 (*0-12-518060-8*) Acad Pr.
Nicholson, D. H. The Mysticism of St. Francis of Assissi. 1977. lib. bdg. 250.00 (*0-8490-2319-X*) Gordon Pr.
Nicholson, D. H. & Lee, A. H., eds. The Oxford Book of English Mystical Verse. LC 96-43195. 648p. 1997. pap. 24.95 (*1-889051-16-0*) Acrpls Bks CO.
— The Oxford Book of English Mystical Verse. LC 96-43195. 648p. 1997. reprint ed. 39.95 (*1-889051-02-0*, I Lvl) Acrpls Bks CO.
Nicholson, Dale, jt. ed. see Friend, Diane.
Nicholson, Dan. From Hippie to Happy. 191p. (Orig.). 1984. pap. write for info. (*0-88144-026-4*, CPS026) Christian Pub.
Nicholson, Darrell. Wild Boars. (Nature Watch Bks.). (Illus.). 48p. (J). (gr. 2-5). 1987. lib. bdg. 14.95 (*0-87614-308-7*, Carolrhoda) Lerner Pub.
Nicholson, David. What You Need to Know Before You Fall in Love. LC 94-40598. 1995. pap. text 10.99 (*0-7852-8143-6*) Nelson.
Nicholson, David & Driscoll, Peter, eds. ABC of Emergency Radiology. (Illus.). 120p. (Orig.). 1995. pap. text 30.00 (*0-7279-0832-4*, Pub. by BMJ Pub) Login Brothers Bk Co.
Nicholson, David, ed. see Papagapitos, Karen.
Nicholson, David, ed. see Papgapitos, Karen.
Nicholson, David D. Aristide: The Story of Roger Landes. LC 93-203642. (Illus.). 227p. (C). 1994. 52.50 (*0-85052-365-6*, Pub. by Leo Cooper) Trans-Atl Phila.
Nicholson, David L. Spread Spectrum Signal Design: LPE & AJ Systems. Kahl, Sandy, ed. LC 87-38218. (Electrical Engineering, Telecommunications, & Signal Processing Ser.). 291p. (C). 1988. pap. text 56.95 (*0-7167-8150-6*) W H Freeman.
Nicholson, Dorothy H. The Henry Family from the British Isles to America & Allied Families. LC 90-62578. (Illus.). 1990. lib. bdg. 65.00 (*0-9627521-1-8*) D H Nicholson.
Nicholson, E. W. The Book of the Prophet Jeremiah: Chapters 26-52. LC 74-80357. (Cambridge Bible Commentary on the New English Bible, New Testament Ser.). 247p. 1975. pap. text 24.95 (*0-521-09867-X*) Cambridge U Pr.
Nicholson, Elva M., jt. auth. see Ramsay, O. Bertrand.
Nicholson, Ernest. The Pentateuch in the Twentieth Century: The Legacy of Julius Wellhausen. 304p. 1998. text 75.00 (*0-19-826958-7*) OUP.
Nicholson, Ernest W. God & His People: Covenant & Theology in the Old Testament. 256p. 1988. reprint ed. pap. text 19.95 (*0-19-826727-4*) OUP.
Nicholson, F. SAS Sex Survival Guide. 1999. pap. 7.95 (*1-85782-205-6*, Pub. by Blake Publng) Seven Hills Bk.
Nicholson, Frances. Married to the SAS. 1997. 25.95 (*0-614-28056-7*) Blake Pub.
Nicholson, Frances, ed. Political & Economic Encyclopedia of Western Europe. 380p. 1990. 85.00 (*1-55862-072-9*) St James Pr.
Nicholson, Frances & East, Roger. From the Six to the Twelve: The Enlargement of the European Communities. (Keesing's International Studies). 298p. 1987. 45.00 (*0-912289-74-0*) St James Pr.
***Nicholson, Frances & Twomey, Patrick, eds.** Current Issues in U. K. Asylum Law & Policy. LC 98-71961. 371p. 1998. text 84.95 (*1-84014-180-8*) Ashgate Pub Co.
Nicholson, Frances & Twomey, Patrick, eds. Refugee Rights & Realities: Evolving International Concepts & Regimes. LC 98-43632. 410p. (C). 1999. 69.95 (*0-521-63282-X*) Cambridge U Pr.
Nicholson, Frank C. Old German Love Songs. 1973. 59.95 (*0-8490-0759-3*) Gordon Pr.
Nicholson, G., jt. ed. see Poste, George H.
Nicholson, G. S., et al. Blood Grouping Reagents: Preparation & Application Methods. (WHO Regional Publications: No. 5). 87p. 1993. pap. text 9.00 (*92-9021-179-2*, 1440005) World Health.
Nicholson, Geoff. Bleeding London. LC 97-10215. 320p. 1997. 23.95 (*0-87951-807-3*, Pub. by Overlook Pr) Penguin Putnam.
— Bleeding London. 320p. 1998. pap. 13.95 (*0-87951-886-3*, Pub. by Overlook Pr) Penguin Putnam.
— Everything & More. LC 99-10238. 256p. 1999. pap. 13.95 (*0-87951-710-7*, Pub. by Overlook Pr) Penguin Putnam.
***Nicholson, Geoff.** Female Ruins. 204p. 2000. 26.95 (*1-58567-036-7*, Pub. by Overlook Pr) Penguin Putnam.
Nicholson, Geoff. Flesh Guitar. LC 98-47731. 236p. 1999. text 23.95 (*0-87951-920-7*, Pub. by Overlook Pr) Penguin Putnam.
***Nicholson, Geoff.** Flesh Guitar. 2000. pap. 13.95 (*1-58567-053-7*, Pub. by Overlook Pr) Penguin Putnam.
Nicholson, Geoff. The Food Chain. 184p. 1994. pap. 12.95 (*0-87951-544-9*, Pub. by Overlook Pr) Penguin Putnam.
— Footsucker. 219p. 1996. 22.95 (*0-87951-680-1*, Pub. by Overlook Pr) Penguin Putnam.
— Footsucker. 219p. 1997. pap. 12.95 (*0-87951-793-X*, Pub. by Overlook Pr) Penguin Putnam.
— Hunters & Gatherers. 215p. 1995. pap. 12.95 (*0-87951-601-1*, Pub. by Overlook Pr) Penguin Putnam.
— Still Life with Volkswagens. 232p. 1995. 21.95 (*0-87951-616-X*, Pub. by Overlook Pr) Penguin Putnam.
— Still Life with Volkswagens. 1995. pap. 12.95 (*0-87951-633-X*, Pub. by Overlook Pr) Penguin Putnam.
— Still Life with Volkswagens. 233p. 1996. pap. 12.95 (*0-87951-694-1*, Pub. by Overlook Pr) Penguin Putnam.
Nicholson, Geoffrey, jt. auth. see Morgan, Cliff.
Nicholson, George A. English Words with Native Roots & with Greek, Latin, or Romance Suffixes. LC 70-173081. (Chicago. University. Linguistic Studies in Germanic: No. 3). reprint ed. 27.50 (*0-404-50283-0*) AMS Pr.
***Nicholson, George A.** George Nicholson's on the Primeval Diet of Man (1801) Vegetarianism & Human Conduct Toward Animals. Preece, Rod, ed. LC 99-42379. (Animal Rights Library: Vol. 7). 232p. 1999. text 89.95 (*0-7734-7947-3*) E Mellen.
Nicholson, Gilbert W. Studies on Tumor Formation. LC 51-3965. (Illus.). 649p. reprint ed. pap. 200.00 (*0-608-14718-4*, 202572000046) Bks Demand.
Nicholson, Graeme. Illustrations of Being: Drawing upon Heidegger & Metaphysics. Milchman, Alan & Rosemberg, Alan, eds. (Contemporary Studies in Philosophy & the Human Sciences Ser.). 312p. (C). 1997. pap. 19.95 (*0-391-04016-2*) Humanities.
— Plato's Phaedrus: The Philosophy of Love. LC 97-46404. (In the History of Philosophy Ser.). 1998. 49.95 (*1-55753-118-8*); pap. 24.95 (*1-55753-119-6*) Purdue U Pr.
Nicholson, Graeme, jt. ed. see Greenspan, Louis.
Nicholson, Graeme, jt. ed. see Misgeld, Dieter.
Nicholson, Guides. Nicholson Children's London. 1996. pap. text 11.95 (*0-7028-2943-9*) Hammond World.
— Nicholson London Guide: The Most Comprehensive Guide to London. 1997. pap. text 12.95 (*0-7028-2743-6*) Hammond World.
Nicholson, H. Interconnected Manufacturing Systems: The Problems of Advanced Manufacturing. (Management of Technology Ser.: No. 13). 160p. 1991. 69.00 (*0-86341-224-6*, MT013) INSPEC Inc.
— Structure of Interconnected Systems. (Control Engineering Ser.: No. 5). (Illus.). 258p. 1978. boxed set 61.00 (*0-901223-69-7*, CE005) INSPEC Inc.
***Nicholson, H. B.** Topiltzin Quetzalcoatl: The Once & Future Lord of the Toltecs. (Mesoamerican Worlds Ser.). (Illus.). 256p. 2000. 49.95 (*0-87081-547-4*); pap. 24.95 (*0-87081-554-7*) Univ Pr Colo.
Nicholson, H. B. & Berger, Rainer. Two Aztec Wood Idols: Iconographic & Chronologic Analysis. LC 68-58701. (Studies in Pre-Columbian Art & Archaeology: No. 5). (Illus.). 28p. 1968. pap. 6.00 (*0-88402-026-6*) Dumbarton Oaks.
Nicholson, H. B. & Keber, Eloise Q., eds. Mixteca - Puebla: Discoveries & Research in Mesoamerican Art & Archaeology. LC 92-70648. (Illus.). 264p. (Orig.). 1994. pap. 55.00 (*0-911437-38-X*) Labyrinthos.
Nicholson, H. B., jt. auth. see Aguilera, Carmen.
Nicholson, Heather. The Loving Stitch: A History of Knitting & Spinning in New Zealand. (Illus.). 320p. 1998. pap. 45.00 (*1-86940-188-3*, Pub. by Auckland Univ) Paul & Co Pubs.

N

An Asterisk (*) at the beginning of an entry indicates that the title is appearing for the first time.

Nicholson, Heather J. & Nicholson, Ralph L. Distant Hunger: Agriculture, Food, & Human Values. LC 78-60761. (Science & Society: Series in Science, Technology, & Human Values: Vol. 3). (Illus.). 240p. 1979. pap. 7.95 (*0-931682-00-2*) Purdue U Pubns.

Nicholson, Helen. The Military Orders Vol. 2: Welfare & Warfare. 412p. 1998. text 101.95 (*0-86078-679-X*, Pub. by Ashgate Pub) Ashgate Pub Co.

— Templars, Hospitallers & Teutonic Knights: Images of the Military Orders, 1128-1291. 208p. 1993. text 59.00 (*0-7185-1411-4*) St Martin.

— Templars, Hospitallers & Teutonic Knights: The Image of the Military Orders, 1128-1291. 224p. 1995. pap. 24.95 (*0-7185-2277-X*) St Martin.

Nicholson, Helen J., et al. Chronicle of the Third Crusade: A Translation of the "Itinerarium Peregrinorum et Gesta Regis Ricardi" LC 97-19537. (Illus.). 424p. 1997. text 74.95 (*1-85928-154-0*, Pub. by Ashgate Pub) Ashgate Pub Co.

Nicholson, Henry A. The Ancient Life-History of the Earth. 1980. 37.95 (*0-405-12723-5*) Ayer.

Nicholson, Holly. Money & You: A Woman's Financial Guide. LC 97-72255. 128p. 1997. 24.95 (*1-882897-14-5*) Lost Coast.

Nicholson, Irene, compiled by. The Conquest of Mexico. 39.00 (*1-56696-050-9*) Jackdaw.

Nicholson, Irene, tr. see Castellanos, Rosario.

Nicholson, J. B., Jr., ed. see Beckon, Madge.

Nicholson, J. B., ed. see Ironside, Henry A.

Nicholson, J. Boyd. Behold the Land. 1996. 24.95 (*1-882701-23-2*) Uplook Min.

— The Watered Garden. (Illus.). 96p. 1994. 21.95 (*1-882701-03-8*) Uplook Min.

Nicholson, J. Boyd, ed. see Bramhall, John W.

Nicholson, J. Boyd, ed. see Martin, John B.

Nicholson, J. Shield. The Effects of Machinery on Wages. LC 72-38263. (Evolution of Capitalism Ser.). 160p. 1972. reprint ed. 18.95 (*0-405-04129-2*) Ayer.

Nicholson, J. V. Forest Flora from Within Bihar & Orissa. 70p. (C). 1981. text 60.00 (*0-89771-615-9*, Pub. by Intl Bk Distr) St Mut.

Nicholson, J. W. The Chemistry of Polymers. 2nd ed. (RSC Paperback Ser.). xii, 190p. (C). 1997. pap. 40.00 (*0-85404-558-9*, 1597) Am Chemical.

Nicholson, James. Growing Markets for Laser Materials & Components. LC 99-175682. 155p. 1998. 2950.00 (*1-56965-468-9*, GB-179R) BCC.

Nicholson, James, contrib. by. Growing Markets for Laser Materials & Components. 159p. 1995. 2750.00 (*1-56965-226-0*, GB-179) BCC.

Nicholson, James, jt. auth. see Lucas, Jane.

Nicholson, James H. & Kenelly, John. Calculator Enhancement for Single Variable Calculus: A Manual of Applications Using the HP-48S & HP-28S Calculators. (Clemson Calculator Enhancement Ser.). 196p. (C). 1992. pap. text 19.00 (*0-03-092728-5*) SCP.

Nicholson, James W. Stories of Dixie. 1966. pap. 10.00 (*0-87511-153-X*) Claitors.

Nicholson, Jeff. Nicholson's Small Press Tirade. (Illus.). 104p. (Orig.). 1994. pap. 7.95 (*1-885047-01-0*) Bad Habit.

— Through the Habitrails. 2nd rev. ed. (Illus.). 144p. (Orig.). 1996. pap. 14.95 (*1-885047-03-7*) Bad Habit.

— Ultra Klutz, Bk. 1. (Illus.). 520p. (Orig.). 1996. pap. 29.95 (*1-885047-02-9*) Bad Habit.

Nicholson, Jerome L. Cost Accounting: Theory & Practice. Brief, Richard P., ed. LC 77-87283. (Development of Contemporary Accounting Thought Ser.). 1978. reprint ed. lib. bdg. 31.95 (*0-405-10911-3*) Ayer.

Nicholson, Jill. Mother & Baby Homes: A Survey of Homes for Unmarried Mothers. 1968. 45.00 (*0-7855-0584-9*, Pub. by Natl Inst Soc Work) St Mut.

Nicholson, Jim, ed. see Rick-Burge, L. Cortney.

Nicholson, JoAnna. Dressing Smart in the New Millennium: 200 Quick Tips for Great Style. LC 99-46636. 216p. 1999. pap. 15.95 (*1-57023-121-4*) Impact VA.

— How to Be Sexy Without Looking Sleazy. 150p. 1995. pap. 6.95 (*1-57023-013-7*) Impact VA.

Nicholson, Joe. Inside Cuba. LC 74-1534. xii, 235p. 1974. write for info. (*0-8362-0574-X*) Andrews & McMeel.

Nicholson, John. Chi-la-pe & the White Buffalo. (Indian Culture Ser.). 44p. (J). (gr. 2-10). 1981. pap. 4.95 (*0-89992-064-0*) Coun India Ed.

— Cicero's Return from Exile: The Orations Post Reditum. LC 92-12191. (Classical Studies: Vol. 4). XIII, 174p. (C). 1993. text 39.95 (*0-8204-1945-1*) P Lang Pubng.

— Cruellest Place on Earth: Stories from Antarctica. (True Stories Ser.). 96p. (J). (gr. 3-8). 1996. pap. text 6.95 (*1-86448-244-3*) IPG Chicago.

— Cruellest Place on Earth: Stories from Antarctica. (True Stories Ser.). (Illus.). 96p. (J). (gr. 3-8). 1996. pap. text 6.95 (*1-86373-766-9*) IPG Chicago.

***Nicholson, John.** Fishing for Islands: Traditional Boats & Seafarers of the Pacific. (Illus.). 40p. 2000. 16.95 (*1-86448-590-6*, Pub. by Allen & Unwin Pty) IPG Chicago.

Nicholson, John. A Home among the Gum Trees: The Story of Australian Houses. LC 98-196425. 40 p. 1997. 21.95 (*1-86448-095-5*) Allen & Unwin Pty.

Nicholson, John. Kimberley Warrior: The Story of Jandamarra. LC 98-204678. (Little Ark Book Ser.). 96p. 1997. write for info. (*1-86373-861-4*, Pub. by Allen & Unwin Pty) Paul & Co Pubs.

Nicholson, John. Men & Women: How Different Are They? (Illus.). 193p. 1984. pap. 14.95 (*0-19-286034-8*) OUP.

— Men & Women: How Different Are They? 2nd ed. LC 92-30066. (Illus.). 240p. 1993. pap. 16.95 (*0-19-286157-3*) OUP.

Nicholson, John B., Jr. Reading & the Art of Librarianship: Selected Essays of John B. Nicholson, Jr. Du Bois, Paul Z. & Keller, Dean H., eds. LC 86-18442. (Collection Management: Vol. 8, Nos. 3-4). 271p. 1986. 8.95 (*0-86656-585-X*) Haworth Pr.

Nicholson, John G. Russian Normative Stress. 176p. 1968. 49.95 (*0-7735-0020-0*, Pub. by McG-Queens Univ Pr) CUP Services.

— Russian Normative Stress Notation. LC 67-31404. 187p. reprint ed. pap. 58.00 (*0-7837-6929-6*, 204675800003) Bks Demand.

Nicholson, John P. Catalogue of the Library of John Page Nicholson Relating to the War of the Rebellion. (Illus.). 1022p. 1995. reprint ed. 95.00 (*1-888262-55-9*) Martino Pubng.

Nicholson, John R. Understanding & Using Pagemaker 5.0. LC 94-11725. (Microcomputing Ser.). 480p. (C). 1994. mass mkt. 26.00 (*0-314-03972-4*) West Pub.

Nicholson, John W. Chemistry of Polymers. 1991. 44.00 (*0-85186-413-9*) CRC Pr.

Nicholson, John W., jt. auth. see Wilson, Alan D.

Nicholson, Jon & Hamilton, Maurice. Pole Position William F1: Behind the Scenes of Williams - Renault F1. LC 97-116801. (Illus.). 216p. 1996. 14.98 (*0-7603-0256-1*) MBI Pubg.

Nicholson, Jon, jt. auth. see Hamilton, Maurice.

***Nicholson, Joseph.** Music God Likes. (Spiritual Discovery Ser.). 112p. 1998. pap., teacher ed. 9.95 (*0-88243-228-1*, 02-0228); pap., student ed. 4.95 (*0-88243-128-5*, 02-0128) Gospel Pub.

Nicholson, Joseph S. The Effects of Machinery on Wages. xi, 143p. 1972. 941.50 (*0-405-04110-1*) Arno Press.

— Strikes & Social Problems. LC 72-4517. (Essay Index Reprint Ser.). 1977. reprint ed. 20.95 (*0-8369-2964-0*) Ayer.

Nicholson, Joseph W., jt. auth. see Mays, Benjamin E.

Nicholson, Joy. The Tribes of Palos Verdes. 224p. 1998. pap. 10.95 (*0-312-19532-X*) St Martin.

Nicholson, Judith, jt. ed. see Nicholson, Clara.

Nicholson, K., et al, eds. Manganese Mineralization. (Geological Society Special Publication Ser.: No. 119). vi, 346p. 1996. 115.00 (*1-897799-74-8*, 360, Pub. by Geol Soc Pub Hse) AAPG.

Nicholson, Karl G. Textbook of Influenza. 1998. 125.00 (*0-632-04803-4*) Blackwell Sci.

Nicholson, Keith. Geothermal Fluids: Chemistry & Exploration Techniques. LC 93-29590. 1993. 111.95 (*0-387-56017-3*) Spr-Verlag.

***Nicholson, Kelly R.** Light on the Horizon: The Joy & Challenge of Real Ideas. 196p. 1999. pap. 19.95 (*0-9668911-0-4*, Pub. by Homeward Bnd) ACCESS Pubs Network.

— The Prospect of Immortality. 400p. 1999. pap. 34.95 (*0-9668911-1-2*, Pub. by Homeward Bnd) ACCESS Pubs Network.

Nicholson, Kenneth E. Power Monitoring & Control Systems: Survey of Practices in Use. Cripe, Helen, ed. (Illus.). 40p. 1997. pap., spiral bd. 89.00 (*0-9643916-3-5*) Integ Tech Res.

Nicholson, Kenneth E., jt. auth. see Becnel, Irwin J., Jr.

Nicholson, Kenyon & Robinson, Charles K. The Flying Gerardos. 1949. pap. 5.25 (*0-8222-0414-2*) Dramatists Play.

Nicholson, Kevin & Dixon, Rob. Law for the Medical Profession. 2nd ed. LC 96-228827. 350p. 1996. pap. text 67.50 (*0-7506-8929-3*) Buttrwrth-Heinemann.

Nicholson, Larry G. Instructor Development Training: A Guide for Security & Law Enforcement. LC 96-27787. 200p. 1996. 44.95 (*0-7506-9717-2*) Buttrwrth-Heinemann.

***Nicholson, Larry G.** Security Investigations: A Professional's Guide. LC 99-45113. 235p. 2000. 39.95 (*0-7506-7147-5*) Buttrwrth-Heinemann.

Nicholson, Larry G., jt. auth. see Glazebrook, Jerome H.

Nicholson, Laurel L., ed. 401 (K) Plans. LC 94-47143. 1995. 65.00 (*0-87179-878-6*) BNA Books.

Nicholson-Lawrence, Pamella. Caught on Video...the Most Embarrassing Moment of Funeral - July 11, 1994. 140p. (Orig.). 1995. pap. 8.99 (*0-9647992-0-0*) Triphena Bks.

Nicholson, Lee. Exit 99: Selected Poems by Lee Nicholson. 1999. pap. write for info. (*0-9642725-2-0*) Ietje Kooi Pr.

Nicholson, Lee A., ed. Farewell to Star Trek: The Next Generation. (Illus.). 128p. 1998. reprint ed. pap. text 8.00 (*0-7881-5970-4*) DIANE Pub.

Nicholson, Lewis E. The Vercelli Book Homilies: Translations from the Anglo-Saxon. 184p. (C). 1991. lib. bdg. 39.50 (*0-8191-8116-1*) U Pr of Amer.

Nicholson, Lewis E., ed. Anthology of Beowulf Criticism. 1963. pap. 17.50 (*0-268-00006-9*) U of Notre Dame Pr.

— An Anthology of Beowulf Criticism. 386p. 1977. 20.95 (*0-8369-2567-X*) Ayer.

Nicholson, Libby & Lau, Yvonne. Creating with Fimo. (Kids Can Crafts Ser.). (Illus.). 48p. (J). (gr. 3-7). 1999. pap. 6.99 (*1-55074-274-4*, Pub. by Kids Can Pr) Genl Dist Srvs.

— Creating with Fimo. unabridged ed. (Kids Can Crafts Ser.). (Illus.). 48p. (J). (gr. 3-7). 1999. 16.99 (*1-55074-310-4*, Pub. by Kids Can Pr) Genl Dist Srvs.

Nicholson, Linda. Monetary Penalties in Scotland. 96p. 1994. pap. 25.00 (*0-11-495176-4*, HM51764, Pub. by Statnry Office) Bernan Associates.

— The Play of Reason: From the Modern to the Postmodern. LC 98-39167. 240p. 1998. 39.95 (*0-8014-3517-X*); pap. 17.95 (*0-8014-8516-9*) Cornell U Pr.

Nicholson, Linda, ed. Feminism - Postmodernism. 360p. (C). 1989. pap. 18.99 (*0-415-90059-X*) Routledge.

— The Second Wave: A Reader in Feminist Theory. 416p. 1997. pap. 23.99 (*0-415-91761-1*) Routledge.

— The Second Wave: A Reader in Feminist Theory. 416p. (C). 1997. 75.00 (*0-415-91760-3*) Routledge.

Nicholson, Linda J., intro. Feminism - Postmodernism. 352p. 1989. 45.00 (*0-415-90058-1*) Routledge.

Nicholson, Linda J. & Seidman, Steven, eds. Social Postmodernism: Beyond Identity Politics. (Cultural & Social Studies). 411p. (C). 1995. pap. text 20.95 (*0-521-47571-6*) Cambridge U Pr.

Nicholson, Linda J., ed. see Butler, Judith.

Nicholson, Lois. Babe Ruth: Sultan of Swat. (Illus.). 170p. (YA). (gr. 7-12). 1995. 17.95 (*0-9625427-1-7*) Goodwood Pr.

— Cal Ripken, Jr. Quiet Hero. 2nd ed. LC 95-25926. (Illus.). 128p. (J). (gr. 4-8). 1995. 13.95 (*0-87033-481-6*, Tidewtr Pubs) Cornell Maritime.

— From Maryland to Cooperstown: Seven Maryland Natives in Baseball's Hall of Fame. LC 98-27250. (Illus.). 144p. (J). (gr. 4-8). 1998. 19.95 (*0-87033-494-8*, Tidewtr Pubs) Cornell Maritime.

— George Washington Carver. (Junior World Biographies). (J). 1994. 10.15 (*0-606-07558-5*) Turtleback.

— Lacrosse. LC 98-13891. (Composite Guide Ser.). (Illus.). 64p. (YA). (gr. 3 up). 1999. lib. bdg. 15.95 (*0-7910-4719-9*) Chelsea Hse.

— Michael Jackson. (Black Americans of Achievement Ser.). (J). 1994. 14.05 (*0-606-07865-7*) Turtleback.

Nicholson, Lois & Wyche, James. Schools & Health: Our Nation's Investment. 350p. 1997. 59.95 (*0-309-05435-4*) Natl Acad Pr.

Nicholson, Lois P. Booker T. Washington - Educator/Activist: A Modern Moses. LC 96-52428. (Junior Black Americans of Achievement Ser.). (Illus.). 80p. (J). (gr. 3-6). 1998. pap. 6.95 (*0-7910-4461-0*) Chelsea Hse.

— Helen Keller: The Humantarian Who Became Deaf & Blind at Nineteen Months. LC 94-37512. (Great Achievers Ser.). (Illus.). 120p. (YA). (gr. 5 up). 1995. lib. bdg. 19.95 (*0-7910-2086-X*) Chelsea Hse.

— Ken Griffey, Jr. LC 97-8916. (Baseball Legends Ser.). (Illus.). 64p. (J). (gr. 3 up). 1997. 15.95 (*0-7910-4377-0*) Chelsea Hse.

— Michael Jackson: Entertainer. Huggins, Nathan I., ed. (Black Americans of Achievement Ser.). (Illus.). 124p. (YA). (gr. 5 up). 1994. lib. bdg. 19.95 (*0-7910-1929-2*) Chelsea Hse.

— Mike Schmidt. LC 94-23612. (Baseball Legends Ser.). (Illus.). 64p. (J). (gr. 3 up). 1995. lib. bdg. 15.95 (*0-7910-2173-4*) Chelsea Hse.

— Nolan Ryan. LC 95-3099. (Baseball Legends Ser.). (Illus.). 64p. (YA). (gr. 3 up). 1995. lib. bdg. 15.95 (*0-7910-2174-2*) Chelsea Hse.

— Oprah Winfrey: Entertainer. Huggins, Nathan I., ed. (Black Americans of Achievement Ser.). (Illus.). 124p. (YA). (gr. 5 up). 1994. lib. bdg. 19.95 (*0-7910-1886-5*) Chelsea Hse.

— Oprah Winfrey: Entertainer. Huggins, Nathan I., ed. (Black Americans of Achievement Ser.). 124p. (YA). (gr. 5 up). 1994. pap. 8.95 (*0-7910-1915-2*) Chelsea Hse.

Nicholson, Lois P. Oprah Winfrey: Entertainer. (Junior Black Americans of Achievement Ser.). (Illus.). 76p. (J). (gr. 1-4). 1997. pap. 4.95 (*0-7910-4460-2*) Chelsea Hse.

Nicholson, Lois P. Oprah Winfrey: Entertainer. LC 96-43736. (Junior Black Americans of Achievement Ser.). (Illus.). 76p. (J). (gr. 4-7). 1997. lib. bdg. 15.95 (*0-7910-2390-7*) Chelsea Hse.

Nicholson-Lord, David. Greening of the Cities. 288p. (C). (gr. 13). 1988. pap. 27.99 (*0-7102-0328-4*, Routledge Thoemms) Routledge.

Nicholson, Loren. Old Picture Postcards: A Historic Journey along California's Central Coast. (California Heritage Ser.: No. 1). (Illus.). 144p. (Orig.). (YA). (gr. 9-12). 1989. pap. 12.95 (*0-9623233-1-4*) CA HPA.

— Rails Across the Ranchos: Centennial Edition of the Southern Pacific Coastal Line Railroad Centennial Years. 2nd ed. (California Heritage Ser.). (Illus.). 208p. (Orig.). reprint ed. pap. 18.95 (*0-9623233-6-5*) CA HPA.

— Romualdo Pacheco's California! The Mexican-American Who Won. (California Heritage Ser.: No. 2). (Illus.). 112p. (Orig.). (YA). (gr. 10-12). 1991. pap. text 12.95 (*0-9623233-2-2*) CA HPA.

Nicholson, Louis. The Internet & Healthcare. 2nd ed. LC 98-48490. 125p. 1999. 35.00 (*1-56793-097-2*) Health Admin Pr.

Nicholson, Louis P. George Washington Carver: Scientist. LC 93-38515. (Illus.). 76p. (J). (gr. 4-7). 1993. lib. bdg. 14.95 (*0-7910-1763-X*) Chelsea Hse.

Nicholson, Louise. Delhi, Agra, & Jaipur. (Asian Guides Ser.). 222p. 1992. pap. 12.95 (*0-8442-9917-0*, Passprt Bks) NTC Contemp Pub Co.

— The Festive Food of India & Pakistan. (Illus.). 60p. 1994. 9.95 (*1-85626-051-8*) Trafalgar.

— Fodor's London Companion: The Complete Guide for the Independent Traveler. 3rd ed. 1993. pap. 17.00 (*0-679-02457-3*) Fodors Travel.

— London. 1989. 16.95 (*0-370-31032-2*) Random.

— London Rediscovered. LC 99-227412. (Illus.). 208p. 1999. 45.00 (*0-7892-0488-6*) Abbeville Pr.

— Look Out London. (Illus.). 48p. (J). (gr. 1-4). 1998. pap. 9.95 (*1-898304-84-X*, Pub. by Bodley Head) Trafalgar.

— Louise Nicholson's India Companion. (Illus.). 352p. 1998. pap. 19.95 (*0-7472-7757-5*, Pub. by Headline Bk Pub) Trafalgar.

Nicholson, M., jt. auth. see Sivertsen, J.

Nicholson, M. Jean, jt. auth. see Hein, Eleanor C.

Nicholson, M. P., ed. Architectural Management. 418p. 1992. 109.95 (*0-442-31598-8*) Chapman & Hall.

— Architectural Management. (Illus.). 400p. (C). 1992. 120.00 (*0-419-17780-9*, E & FN Spon) Routledge.

Nicholson, Marjorie H. Newton Demands the Muse: Newton's "Opticks" & the Eighteenth Century Poets, 2. LC 78-13146. 178p. 1979. reprint ed. lib. bdg. 35.00 (*0-313-21044-6*, NIND, Greenwood Pr) Greenwood.

***Nicholson, Martin.** Towards a Russia of the Regions. (Adelphi Papers). (Illus.). 96p. 2000. pap. 26.95 (*0-19-922474-9*) OUP.

Nicholson, Mary. Separation & Divorce in North Carolina: Answers to the Most Commonly Asked Questions about Your Legal Rights. Bledsoe, Jerry, ed. LC 92-72659. 68p. 1992. pap. 7.95 (*1-878086-16-2*, Pub. by Down Home NC) Blair.

Nicholson, Mary E. & St. Pierre, Richard. Sexuality: A Health Education Perspective. rev. ed. (Illus.). 75p. (C). 1991. teacher ed. write for info. (*0-910251-28-2*) Venture Pub PA.

Nicholson, Mary K. Separation & Divorce in North Carolina: Answers to the Most Commonly Asked Questions about Your Legal Rights. 2nd rev. ed. 76p. 1999. pap. 9.95 (*1-878086-75-8*, Pub. by Down Home NC) Blair.

Nicholson, Matt. Successful Computing for Business. LC 96-35968. (Barron's Business Success Ser.). 1997. pap. 6.95 (*0-7641-0058-0*) Barron.

Nicholson, Mavis. Martha Jane & Me. large type ed. 1993. 39.95 (*0-7066-1014-8*, Pub. by Remploy Pr) St Mut.

— What Did You Do in the War, Mummy? large type ed. (Large Print Ser.). (Illus.). 608p. 1996. 27.99 (*0-7089-3638-5*) Ulverscroft.

Nicholson, Meredith. The House of a Thousand Candles. 1975. lib. bdg. 16.70 (*0-89966-142-4*) Buccaneer Bks.

— The House of a Thousand Candles. LC 85-45892. (Library of Indiana Classics). (Illus.). 392p. 1986. 20.00 (*0-253-32852-7*); pap. 3.25 (*0-253-20381-3*, MB-381) Ind U Pr.

— Provincial American & Other Papers. LC 79-152205. (Essay Index Reprint Ser.). 1977. 20.95 (*0-8369-2211-5*) Ayer.

Nicholson, Michael. Causes & Consequences in International Relations. 256p. 1996. pap. 22.50 (*1-85567-243-X*) Bks Intl VA.

— Causes & Consequences in International Relations: A Conceptual Analysis. LC 95-34976. 256p. 1996. 59.95 (*1-85567-242-1*) St Martin.

— International Relations: A Concise Introduction. LC 98-6792. 1998. text 45.00 (*0-8147-5805-3*); pap. text 16.00 (*0-8147-5806-1*) NYU Pr.

— Rationality & the Analysis of International Conflict. (Studies in International Relations). (Illus.). 276p. (C). 1992. pap. text 24.95 (*0-521-39810-X*) Cambridge U Pr.

Nicholson, Michael. Sarajevo: Natasha's Story. LC 97-226349. (Illus.). 208p. (J). 1997. pap. 9.70 (*0-7868-8234-4*, Pub. by Hyperion) Time Warner.

Nicholson, Michael & Winner, David. Raoul Wallenberg. LC 88-2078. (People Who Have Helped the World Ser.). (Illus.). 68p. (J). (gr. 5-6). 1990. pap. 7.95 (*0-8192-1525-2*) Morehouse Pub.

Nicholson, Michael W. A Theological Analysis & Critique of the Postmodernism Debate: Mapping the Labyrinth. LC 97-33577. 376p. 1997. text 99.95 (*0-7734-2246-3*) E Mellen.

Nicholson, N. & Clemie, C. The Good Interview Guide. (C). 1989. text 35.00 (*0-948032-39-1*, Pub. by Rosters Ltd) St Mut.

— The Right Job for You. (C). 1989. text 29.95 (*0-948032-63-4*, Pub. by Rosters Ltd) St Mut.

***Nicholson, Nigel.** Executive Instinct: Managing Stone Age Minds in the Information Age. 352p. 2000. 25.00 (*0-8129-3197-1*, Times Bks) Crown Pub Group.

Nicholson, Nigel, ed. The Blackwell Encyclopedic Dictionary of Organizational Behavior. (Encyclopedia of Management Ser.). 656p. 1997. 105.95 (*0-631-18781-2*) Blackwell Pubs.

— The Blackwell Encyclopedic Dictionary of Organizational Behavior. 656p. 1998. pap. 36.95 (*0-631-20910-7*) Blackwell Pubs.

Nicholson, Nigel & West, Michael. Managerial Job Change: Men & Women in Transition. (Management & Industrial Relations Ser.: No. 12). (Illus.). 288p. 1988. pap. text 22.95 (*0-521-35744-6*) Cambridge U Pr.

Nicholson, Nigel, et al. The Dynamics of White Collar Unionism: A Study of Local Union Participation. LC 81-66682. (Organizational & Occupational Psychology Ser.). 1981. text 125.00 (*0-12-518020-9*) Acad Pr.

Nicholson, Nigel, jt. auth. see O'Creevey, Mark F.

Nicholson, Norman K. Panchayat Raj, Rural Development & the Political Economy of Village India. (Occasional Paper Ser.: No. 1). 61p. (Orig.). (C). 1973. pap. text 4.95 (*0-86731-014-6*) Cornell CIS RDC.

Nicholson, Norman K. & Khan, Dilawar A. Basic Democracies & Rural Development in Pakistan. (Special Series on Rural Local Government: No. 10). 99p. (Orig.). (C). 1974. pap. text 3.50 (*0-86731-096-0*) Cornell CIS RDC.

Nicholson, Norman K., jt. ed. see Russell, Clifford S.

Nicholson, Paul T. Egyptian Faience & Glass. (Egyptology Ser.: No. 18). (Illus.). 80p. 1989. pap. 10.50 (*0-7478-0195-9*, Pub. by Shire Pubns) Parkwest Pubns.

Nicholson, Paul T. & Shaw, Ian. The Dictionary of Ancient Egypt. (Illus.). 320p. 1995. 49.50 (*0-8109-3225-3*, Pub. by Abrams) Time Warner.

Nicholson, Paul T. & Shaw, Ian, eds. Ancient Egyptian Materials & Technology. LC 98-3434. (Illus.). 728p. (C). 2000. 160.00 (*0-521-45257-0*) Cambridge U Pr.

Nicholson, Paul W. Nuclear Electronics. LC 73-8196. 402p. reprint ed. 124.70 (*0-608-15236-6*, 202667700051) Bks Demand.

***Nicholson, Peggy.** The Baby Bargain: Marriage of Inconvenience, Vol. 929. (Superromance Ser.). 2000. mass mkt. 4.50 (*0-373-70929-3*, 1-70929-4) Harlequin Bks.

Nicholson, Peggy. D . . . Comme Desir. (Amours d'Aujourd'Hui Ser.: Vol. 297). 1998. mass mkt. 4.99 (*0-373-38297-9*, 1-38297-7) Harlequin Bks.

An Asterisk (*) at the beginning of an entry indicates that the title is appearing for the first time.

N

— Don't Mess with Texans, No. 834. (Harlequin Super Romance Ser.). 1999. per. 4.25 (*0-373-70834-3*) Harlequin Bks.
— Her Bodyguard. (Superromance Ser.: No. 874). 1999. per. 4.25 (*0-373-70874-2*, 1-70874-2) Harlequin Bks.
— Pure & Simple. (Romance Ser.). 1993. per. 2.89 (*0-373-03250-1*, 1-03250-7) Harlequin Bks.
— Pure & Simple. large type ed. LC 93-13219. 1993. pap. 13.95 (*1-56054-758-8*) Thorndike Pr.
— The Scent of a Woman. (Superromance Ser.: No. 770). 1998. per. 3.99 (*0-373-70770-3*) Harlequin Bks.
— The Truth about George. (Romance Ser.). 1994. per. 2.99 (*0-373-03322-2*, 1-03322-4); per. 2.99 (*0-373-15568-9*) Harlequin Bks.
— The Twenty-Third Man. 1997. per. 3.99 (*0-373-70740-1*, 1-70740-5) Harlequin Bks.
— You Again. (Harlequin Super Romance Ser.: No. 698). 1996. per. 3.99 (*0-373-70698-7*, 1-70698-5) Harlequin Bks.

Nicholson, Peggy & Warner, John F. The Case of the Furtive Firebug. (Kerry Hill Casecrackers Ser.: No. 1). 120p. (J). (gr. 3-6). 1994. lib. bdg. 13.27 (*0-8225-0709-5*, Lerner Publctns) Lerner Pub.
— The Case of the Lighthouse Ghost. (Kerry Hill Casecrackers Ser.: No. 2). 120p. (J). (gr. 3-6). 1994. lib. bdg. 13.27 (*0-8225-0710-2*, Lerner Publctns) Lerner Pub.
— The Case of the Mysterious Codes. (Kerry Hill Casecrackers Ser.: No. 4). 120p. (J). (gr. 3-6). 1994. lib. bdg. 13.27 (*0-8225-0712-9*, Lerner Publctns) Lerner Pub.
— The Case of the Squeaky Thief. (Kerry Hill Casecrackers Ser.: No. 3). 120p. (J). (gr. 3-6). 1994. lib. bdg. 13.27 (*0-8225-0711-0*, Lerner Publctns) Lerner Pub.

Nicholson, Peter. The Barry Album. (Illus.). 48p. (C). 1987. pap. 13.00 (*0-7855-2237-9*, Pub. by Picton) St Mut.
— Diesel Locomotives in Preservation Vol. 2: Former BR LMSR Loco's. 28p. (C). 1987. pap. 35.00 (*0-7855-2238-7*, Pub. by Picton) St Mut.

Nicholson, Peter. A Dwelling Place. LC 97-160947. 1997. write for info. (*0-908022-12-3*) Wellington Lane Pr.

Nicholson, Peter. The Flying Scotsman Story. 1998. pap. text 22.95 (*0-86093-532-9*, Pub. by Oxford Pubng) Motorbooks Intl.
— New Carpenter's Guide of 1818. (Illus.). 100p. 1993. reprint ed. pap. 40.00 (*0-87556-826-2*) Saifer.

Nicholson, Peter, ed. An Annotated Index to the Commentary on John Gower's Confessio Amantis. (Medieval & Renaissance Texts & Studies: Vol. 62). 608p. 1989. 40.00 (*0-86698-046-6*, MR62) MRTS.
— Gower's "Confessio Amantis" A Critical Anthology. (Publications of the John Gower Society: No. III). 224p. (C) 1991. 75.00 (*0-85991-318-X*) Boydell & Brewer.

Nicholson, Peter, ed. New Edition of the Works of T. H. Green, 5 vols. (Thoemmes Press Idealism Ser.). 2870p. 1997. 625.00 (*1-85506-512-6*) Thoemmes Pr.

Nicholson, Peter & Parker, Janet. The Complete Rhodesian Ridgeback. (Illus.). 160p. 1991. 27.95 (*0-87605-295-2*) Howell Bks.

Nicholson, Peter P., ed. The Collected Works of D. G. Ritchie, 6 vols. (Idealism Ser.). 2275p. 1998. 625.00 (*1-85506-578-9*) Thoemmes Pr.

Nicholson, Philip Yale. Who Do We Think We Are? Race & Nation in the Modern World. LC 99-11650. 248p. (gr. 13). 1999. text 34.95 (*0-7656-0391-8*) M E Sharpe.

Nicholson, Phyllis. Country Bouquet. large type ed. (Isis Large Print Ser.). 1997. 24.95 (*0-7531-5424-2*) T T Beeler.

Nicholson, R. A. The Essence of Sufism. 1984. reprint ed. pap. 3.95 (*0-916411-49-4*, Near Eastern) Holmes Pub.
— Idea of Personality in Sufism. 1992. 14.50 (*1-56744-051-7*) Kazi Pubns.

***Nicholson, R. A. & O'Connor, T. P., eds.** People As an Agent of Environmental Change. (Symposia of the Association for Environmental Archaeology Ser.: Vol. 16). (Illus.). 135p. (C). 2000. pap. 45.00 (*1-84217-002-3*, Pub. by Oxbow Bks) David Brown.

Nicholson, R. A., jt. ed. see LeStrange, G.

Nicholson, R. H. Inside the MCC: A Technical Guide to the Mission Control Center at the Johnson Space Center. (Illus.). 96p. (Orig.). 1991. pap. 9.95 (*1-882123-30-1*) Universal Radio Rsch.

Nicholson, R. I., jt. ed. see Linkens, D. A.

Nicholson, R. N. The Sufi Doctrine of the Perfect Man. 1984. reprint ed. pap. 4.95 (*0-916411-48-6*, Near Eastern) Holmes Pub.

Nicholson, Ralph L., jt. auth. see Nicholson, Heather J.

Nicholson, Ranald. The Edinburgh History of Scotland Vol. 2: The Later Middle Ages. 695p. (C). 1986. pap. 75.00 (*0-901824-84-4*, Pub. by Mercat Pr Bks) St Mut.

Nicholson, Reynold, tr. see Al-Arabi.

Nicholson, Reynold A. Ecstasy in Islam. 1995. pap. 3.95 (*1-55818-298-5*, Near Eastern) Holmes Pub.
— A Literary History of the Arabs. 536p. (C). 1995. pap. 32.50 (*0-7007-0336-5*, Pub. by Curzon Pr Ltd) Paul & Co Pubs.
— A Literary History of the Arabs. LC 96-41815. (The Kegan Paul Arabia Library). 1997. 110.00 (*0-7103-0566-4*, Pub. by Kegan Paul Intl) Col U Pr.
— A Literary History of the Arabs. LC 74-401710. 538p. reprint ed. pap. 153.40 (*0-608-13031-1*, 2024502) Bks Demand.
— The Mystics of Islam. 178p. 1996. pap. 9.95 (*0-614-21323-1*, 1346) Kazi Pubns.
— Rumi: Poet & Mystic. 190p. 1995. pap. 11.95 (*1-85168-096-9*, Pub. by Onewrld Pubns) Penguin Putnam.
— Studies in Islamic Mysticism. LC 94-210303. 288p. (C). 1994. pap. 25.00 (*0-7007-0278-4*) Paul & Co Pubs.
— Tales of Mystic Meaning. 200p. 1995. pap. 11.95 (*1-85168-097-7*, Pub. by Onewrld Pubns) Penguin Putnam.

***Nicholson, Reynold A., ed.** A Rumi Anthology. 2000. pap. 19.95 (*1-85168-251-1*, Pub. by Onewrld Pubns) Element MA.

Nicholson, Reynold A., ed. Selected Poems from the Divani Shamsi Tabriz. Orig. Title: Divan-i Shams-i Tabrizi. 432p. (C). 1994. text 68.00 (*0-7007-0277-6*, Pub. by Curzon Pr Ltd) Paul & Co Pubs.
— Selected Poems from the Divani Shamsi Tabriz. Orig. Title: Divan-i Shams-i Tabrizi. 432p. 1996. pap. 29.95 (*0-7007-0462-0*, Pub. by Curzon Pr Ltd) Paul & Co Pubs.

Nicholson, Reynold A., tr. Tales of Mystic Meaning. 200p. 1996. pap. 11.95 (*0-614-21369-X*, 1459) Kazi Pubns.

Nicholson, Reynold A., ed. & tr. see Jalal al-Din Rumi, Maulana.

Nicholson, Reynold A., tr. see Al-Hujwiri.

Nicholson, Reynold A., tr. see Iqbal, Muhammad.

Nicholson, Reynold A., tr. see Rumi, Jalal Al-Din.

***Nicholson, Reynold Alleyne.** The Mystics of Islam, Vol. 8. LC 99-46556. (Orientalism Ser.). 2000. write for info. (*0-415-20905-6*) Routledge.

Nicholson, Richard C., tr. see Guenon, Rene.

Nicholson, Richard W., et al. Basic Accounting for Lawyers. 5th ed. LC 98-83073. 230p. 1999. 98.00 (*0-8318-0791-1*, B791) Am Law Inst.

Nicholson, Robert. Ancient China. LC 94-44170. (Illus.). 32p. (J). (gr. 4-7). 1994. lib. bdg. 15.95 (*0-7910-2702-3*) Chelsea Hse.
— Ancient China. (Illus.). 32p. (J). (gr. 3-7). 1994. pap. 7.95 (*0-7910-2726-0*) Chelsea Hse.

Nicholson, Robert. Ancient China. (Journey into Civilization Ser.). 1994. 13.15 (*0-606-07191-1*, Pub. by Turtleback) Demco.

Nicholson, Robert. Ancient Egypt. LC 94-44169. (Journey into Civilization Ser.). (Illus.). 32p. (J). (gr. 4-7). 1994. lib. bdg. 15.95 (*0-7910-2704-X*) Chelsea Hse.
— Ancient Egypt. LC 94-44169. (Journey into Civilization Ser.). (Illus.). 32p. (J). (gr. 4-7). 1994. pap. 7.95 (*0-7910-2728-7*) Chelsea Hse.
— Ancient Egypt. (Journey into Civilization Ser.). 1994. 13.15 (*0-606-07192-X*, Pub. by Turtleback) Demco.
— Ancient Greece. LC 93-29442. (Journey into Civilization Ser.). (Illus.). 32p. (J). (gr. 4-7). 1994. 7.95 (*0-7910-2727-9*); lib. bdg. 15.95 (*0-7910-2703-1*) Chelsea Hse.
— Ancient Greece. (Journey into Civilization Ser.). 1994. 13.15 (*0-606-07193-8*, Pub. by Turtleback) Demco.
— The Aztecs. LC 93-29445. (Journey into Civilization Ser.). (Illus.). 32p. (J). (gr. 4-7). 1994. pap. 7.95 (*0-7910-2725-2*); lib. bdg. 15.95 (*0-7910-2701-5*) Chelsea Hse.
— Aztecs. (Journey into Civilization Ser.). 1994. 13.15 (*0-606-07216-0*, Pub. by Turtleback) Demco.
— El Los Sivx. Araluce, Jose R., tr. from ENG. (Raices Ser.). (SPA., Illus.). 32p. (J). 1993. 16.95 (*1-56492-092-5*) Laredo.
— The Maya. LC 94-43691. (Illus.). 32p. (J). (gr. 4-7). 1994. lib. bdg. 15.95 (*0-7910-2705-8*) Chelsea Hse.
— The Maya. LC 94-43691. (Illus.). 32p. (J). (gr. 4-7). 1994. pap. 7.95 (*0-7910-2729-5*) Chelsea Hse.
— Maya. (Journey into Civilization Ser.). (J). 1994. 13.15 (*0-606-07852-5*) Turtleback.
— Mississippi: The Blues Today. LC 98-40012. (Illus.). 192p. (Orig.). 1999. mass mkt. 25.00 (*0-306-80883-8*, Pub. by Da Capo) HarpC.
— The Mongols. LC 94-43701. (Illus.). 32p. (J). (gr. 4-7). 1994. lib. bdg. 15.95 (*0-7910-2706-6*) Chelsea Hse.
— The Mongols. LC 94-43701. (Illus.). 32p. (J). (gr. 4-7). 1994. pap. 7.95 (*0-7910-2730-9*) Chelsea Hse.
— Mongols. (Journey into Civilization Ser.). (J). 1994. 13.15 (*0-606-07879-7*) Turtleback.
— The Sioux. LC 94-42216. (Illus.). 32p. (J). (gr. 4-7). 1994. lib. bdg. 15.95 (*0-7910-2708-2*) Chelsea Hse.
— The Sioux. LC 94-42216. (Illus.). 32p. (J). (gr. 4-7). 1994. pap. 7.95 (*0-7910-2732-5*) Chelsea Hse.
— Sioux. (Journey into Civilization Ser.). (J). 1994. 13.15 (*0-606-08167-4*) Turtleback.
— The Ulysses Guide: Tours Through Joyce's Dublin. 150p. 1989. pap. 9.95 (*0-415-90144-8*, A3315) Routledge.
— The Vikings. LC 93-11956. (Illus.). 32p. (J). (gr. 4-7). 1994. 15.95 (*0-7910-2709-0*) Chelsea Hse.
— The Vikings. LC 93-11956. (Illus.). 32p. (J). (gr. 4-7). 1994. pap. 7.95 (*0-7910-2733-3*) Chelsea Hse.
— Vikings. (Journey into Civilization Ser.). 1994. 13.15 (*0-606-08345-6*, Pub. by Turtleback) Demco.
— The Zulus. LC 94-43700. (Illus.). 32p. (J). (gr. 4-7). 1994. lib. bdg. 15.95 (*0-7910-2710-4*) Chelsea Hse.
— The Zulus. LC 94-43700. (Illus.). 32p. (J). (gr. 4-7). 1994. pap. 7.95 (*0-7910-2734-1*) Chelsea Hse.
— The Zulus. (Journey into Civilization Ser.). (J). 1994. 13.15 (*0-606-08418-5*, Pub. by Turtleback) Demco.

Nicholson, Robert & Watts, Claire. La Antigua China: Hechos, Historias, Actividades. Araluce, Jose R., tr. (Raices Ser.). (SPA., Illus.). 32p. (YA). (gr. 6-10). 1993. 14.95 (*1-56492-093-3*) Laredo.
— El Antiguo Egipto: Hechos - Histoias - Actividades. Araluce, Jose R., tr. (Raices Ser.). (SPA., Illus.). 32p. (J). (gr. 6-10). 1993. 14.95 (*1-56492-094-1*) Laredo.
— Los Aztecas. Araluce, Jose R., tr. from ENG. (Raices Ser.). (SPA., Illus.). 24p. (J). 1993. 14.95 (*1-56492-091-7*) Laredo.

***Nicholson, Robert & Watts, Claire.** Egyptians. (Interfact Ser.). (Illus.). (J). (gr. 2-7). 2000. spiral bd. 14.95 (*1-58728-458-8*) Two Can Pub.
— Los Equipcios. (Interfact Ser.). (SPA., Illus.). (J). (gr. 2-7). 2000. spiral bd. 14.95 (*1-58728-474-X*) Two Can Pub.

Nicholson, Robert & Watts, Claire. Eyptians. LC 98-4401. (Interfact Ser.). (Illus.). 48p. (J). (gr. 2-8). 1997. spiral bd. write for info. incl. cd-rom (*0-7166-7206-5*) World Bk.
— Vikings. LC 98-4322. (Interfact Ser.). (Illus.). 48p. (J). (gr. 2-8). 1997. spiral bd. write for info. incl. cd-rom (*0-7166-7221-9*) World Bk.

Nicholson, Robert, jt. auth. see Watts, Claire.

Nicholson, Robert L. Joscelyn I, Prince of Edessa. LC 78-63352. (Crusades & Military Orders Ser.: Second Series). 120p. reprint ed. 31.50 (*0-404-17025-0*) AMS Pr.
— Tancred: A Study of His Career & Work. LC 79-29847. reprint ed. 29.50 (*0-404-15425-5*) AMS Pr.

Nicholson, Roger S., ed. Temporary Shepherds: Congregational Guidelines for Interim Ministry. 1998. pap. 17.95 (*1-56699-208-7*, AL198) Alban Inst.

Nicholson, Ronald A. Practical Footcare for Nurse Practitioners: A Training Manual & Clinical Handbook. LC 94-66314. (Illus.). 192p. (Orig.). (C). 1994. pap. text 69.95 (*1-885421-01-X*) Practical Footcare.
— Practical Footcare for Physician Assistants: A Training Manual & Clinical Handbook. LC 94-66313. (Illus.). 192p. (Orig.). (C). 1994. pap. text 69.95 (*1-885421-00-1*) Practical Footcare.
— Practical Footcare for Primary Care Physicians: A Training Manual & Clinical Handbook. LC 94-66215. (Illus.). 192p. (Orig.). (C). 1994. pap. text 69.95 (*1-885421-02-8*) Practical Footcare.

Nicholson, Roy S. True Holiness: The Wesleyan-Arminian Emphasis. 1985. pap. 8.99 (*0-88019-195-3*) Schmul Pub Co.

Nicholson, S. Francis. Quaker Money. 290p. (Orig.). 1990. pap. 4.00 (*0-87574-290-4*) Pendle Hill.

***Nicholson, Scott.** Thank You for the Flowers: A Story Collection. 250p. 2000. pap. write for info. (*1-887905-24-5*) Pkway Pubs.

Nicholson, Sheila A., ed. see Humble, Tracy W.

Nicholson, Shirley. Nyman's: The Story of a Sussex Garden. (Illus.). 192p. 1994. pap. 17.95 (*0-7509-0615-4*, Pub. by Sutton Pub Ltd) Intl Pubs Mktg.
— A Victorian Household. LC 98-218836. (History Paperback Ser.). (Illus.). 224p. 1998. pap. 21.95 (*0-7509-1826-8*, Pub. by Sutton Pub Ltd) Intl Pubs Mktg.

Nicholson, Shirley, compiled by. Shamanism. LC 86-40405. 402p. 1996. pap. 15.00 (*0-8356-0617-1*, Quest) Theos Pub Hse.

Nicholson, Shirley, ed. The Goddess Re-Awakening: The Feminine Principle Today. LC 88-40488. 314p. 1989. pap. 10.95 (*0-8356-0642-2*, Quest) Theos Pub Hse.

Nicholson, Shirley & Rosen, Brenda, eds. Gaia's Hidden Life: The Unseen Intelligence of Nature. LC 92-50143. (Illus.). 290p. 1992. pap. 14.00 (*0-8356-0685-6*, Quest) Theos Pub Hse.

Nicholson, Shirley, ed. see Besant, Annie W.

Nicholson-Smith, Donald, tr. see Debord, Guy.

Nicholson-Smith, Donald, tr. see Jappe, Anselm.

Nicholson-Smith, Donald, tr. see Lefebvre, Henri.

Nicholson-Smith, Donald, tr. see Vaneigem, Raoul.

Nicholson, Steve. British Theatre & the Red Peril: The Portrayal of Communism, 1917-1945. (Illus.). 200p. 1999. 80.00 (*0-85989-636-6*) Univ Exeter Pr.

***Nicholson, Steve.** British Theatre & the Red Peril: The Portrayal of Communism, 1917-1945. (Illus.). 200p. 1999. 24.95 (*0-85989-637-4*, Pub. by Univ Exeter Pr) Northwestern U Pr.

Nicholson, Stuart. Billie Holiday. LC 95-16155. (Illus.). 320p. 1995. text 42.50 (*1-55553-248-9*); pap. text 17.95 (*1-55553-303-5*) NE U Pr.
— Ella Fitzgerald: A Biography. LC 93-34359. 334p. 1994. 23.00 (*0-684-19699-9*, Scribners Ref) Mac Lib Ref.
— Ella Fitzgerald: A Biography of the First Lady of Jazz. (Illus.). 368p. 1995. reprint ed. pap. 14.95 (*0-306-80642-8*) Da Capo.
— Jazz: The 1980s Resurgence. 2nd ed. (Illus.). 352p. 1995. pap. 14.95 (*0-306-80612-6*) Da Capo.

***Nicholson, Stuart.** Reminiscing in Tempo: A Portrait of Duke Ellington. LC 99-10873. (Illus.). 560p. 1999. 29.95 (*1-55553-380-9*) NE U Pr.

***Nicholson, Stuart A.** Reminiscing in Tempo: A Portrait of Duke Ellington. (Illus.). 552p. 2000. pap. 17.95 (*1-55553-466-X*) NE U Pr.

Nicholson, Sue. A Day at Greenhill Farm. (Eyewitness Readers). 0032p. (J). (ps-1). 12.95 (*0-7894-4251-5*) DK Pub Inc.
— A Day at Greenhill Farm. LC 97-31285. (Eyewitness Readers). (Illus.). 32p. (J). (ps-1). 1998. pap. 3.95 (*0-7894-2957-8*) DK Pub Inc.

Nicholson, Susan B., jt. auth. see Banneck, Janet A.

Nicholson, Susan T., jt. auth. see Andrews, Charlotte J.

***Nicholson, T. J.** Workshop on Review of Dose Modeling for Demonstration of Compliance with the Radiological Criteria for License Termination: NRC Headquarters Auditorium, Rockville, Maryland. 123p. 1998. per. 10.00 (*0-16-063025-8*) USGPO.

***Nicholson, Thomas.** 15 Months in Sog: A Warrior's Tour. large type ed. (G. K. Hall American History Ser.). 2000. 26.95 (*0-7838-8977-1*, G K Hall Lrg Type) Mac Lib Ref.

***Nicholson, Thomas L.** 15 Months with SOG: A Warrior's Tour. LC 99 90094. 1999. mass mkt. 6.99 (*0-8041-1872-8*) Ivy Books.

Nicholson, Thomas L., jt. ed. see Stein, Eric.

***Nicholson, Tilla.** Your Pregnancy Diary. (Illus.). 112p. 2000. 16.95 (*1-55561-288-1*) Fisher Bks.

Nicholson, Tom, jt. auth. see Thompson, Brian.

Nicholson, Tom, jt. auth. see Thompson, G. Brian.

Nicholson, Vincent D. Cooperation & Coercion as Methods of Social Change. (C). 1934. pap. 4.00 (*0-87574-001-4*) Pendle Hill.

***Nicholson, W.** Goodbye God. 171p. (Orig.). 1998. pap. 10.99 (*1-84030-030-2*) Ambassador Prodns Ltd.

Nicholson, W. Keith. Elementary Linear Algebra W /applic. 2nd ed. (Math). 576p. (C). 1990. mass mkt. 53.25 (*0-534-92189-2*) PWS Pubs.
— Introduction to Abstract Algebra. 640p. 1993. text 71.95 (*0-534-93189-8*) PWS Pubs.
— Linear Algebra with Applications. 3rd ed. LC 93-28879. 1994. mass mkt. 62.50 (*0-534-93666-0*) PWS Pubs.

Nicholson, Walter. Intermediate Microeconomics & Its Applications. 7th ed. 608p. (C). 1997. text 104.00 (*0-03-017918-1*) Dryden Pr.
— Intermediate Microeconomics & Its Applications. 7th ed. 1997. 97.50 (*0-03-019924-7*) Harcourt Coll Pubs.
— Intermediate Microeconomics & Its Applications: Instructor's Manual & Test Bank. 7th ed. 192p. (C). 1996. pap. text, teacher ed. 42.00 (*0-03-017919-X*) Dryden Pr.
— Microeconomic Theory. 7th ed. LC 97-67941. (C). 1997. text 88.50 (*0-03-024474-9*, Pub. by Harcourt Coll Pubs) Harcourt.
— Microeconomic Theory, Test bank. 6th ed. 296p. (C). 1995. teacher ed. write for info. (*0-03-007557-2*) Dryden Pr.
— Test Bank to Accompany Intermediate Microeconomics & Its Application. 6th ed. 97p. (C). 1994. pap. text 40.00 (*0-03-006457-0*) Dryden Pr.
— Understanding Human Communication: Student Resource Manual. 6th ed. 390p. (C). 1996. pap. text, student ed. 23.50 (*0-15-504170-3*, Pub. by Harcourt Coll Pubs) Harcourt.

Nicholson-Ware, Mary F. Visions of Inspiration. (Orig.). 1997. pap. write for info. (*1-57553-429-0*) Watermrk Pr.

Nicholson, Watson. Historical Sources of DeFoe's Journal of the Plague Years. LC 68-54174. (British History Ser.: No. 30). (C). 1969. reprint ed. lib. bdg. 75.00 (*0-8383-0600-4*) M S G Haskell Hse.
— The Struggle for a Free Stage in London. LC 65-27915. 487p. 1972. reprint ed. 24.95 (*0-405-08816-7*, Pub. by Blom Pubns) Ayer.

Nicholson, Wendy. Simon Schuster the First 75 Years: 1924-1999. LC 99-21964. 160p. 1999. write for info. (*0-684-86480-0*) S&S Trade.

Nicholson, William. An Alphabet. LC 75-14747. (Illus.). 1975. reprint ed. 30.00 (*0-915346-02-8*) A Wofsy Fine Arts.
— Exposition of the Catechism. LC 72-173190. (Library of Anglo-Catholic Theology: No. 14). reprint ed. 32.50 (*0-404-52106-1*) AMS Pr.
— Shadowlands. 96p. 1991. pap. 10.95 (*0-452-26732-3*, Plume) Dutton Plume.

***Nicholson, William.** Wind Singer. 256p. 2000. lib. bdg. 18.49 (*0-7868-2494-8*) Hyprn Child.
— The Wind Singer. 256p. (J). 2000. 17.99 (*0-7868-0569-2*, Pub. by Hyprn Child) Time Warner.

Nicholson's Photography Staff, jt. photos by see John Thomas Photography Staff.

Nichter, M. Ethnomedicine, i. 172p. 1990. text 93.00 (*2-88124-470-X*) Gordon & Breach.

Nichter, Mark. Essays on Anthropology & International Health. (C). 1989. pap. text 61.00 (*0-7923-0158-7*); lib. bdg. 196.50 (*0-7923-0005-X*) Kluwer Academic.

Nichter, Mark, ed. Anthropological Approaches to the Study of Ethnomedicine, Vol. 2. LC 92-20369. 260p. 1992. text 85.00 (*2-88124-530-7*); pap. text 36.00 (*2-88124-529-3*) Gordon & Breach.

Nichter, Mark & Nichter, Mimi. Anthropology & International Health: South Asian Case Studies. 384p. 1996. text 35.00 (*2-88449-171-6*); pap. text 15.00 (*2-88449-172-4*) Gordon & Breach.

***Nichter, Mimi.** Fat Talk: What Girls & Their Parents Say about Dieting. LC 99-59521. 251p. 2000. pap. text 22.95 (*0-674-00229-6*) HUP.

Nichter, Mimi, jt. auth. see Nichter, Mark.

Nichter, Rhoda. How to Stop Smoking Once & for All. Hammond, Debbie, ed. LC 79-12134. 1980. 22.95 (*0-87949-173-6*) Ashley Bks.
— Yes, I Do Mind If You Smoke. LC 77-83110. 1978. 22.95 (*0-87949-114-0*) Ashley Bks.

Nichurraighin, Deirbhile, jt. auth. see Odonaill, Eamonn.

Nici Mare, Nancy. Insights for Today: A High-Beginning Reading Skills Text. 2nd ed. LC 98-42661. 1999. pap. text 27.95 (*0-8384-0847-8*) Heinle & Heinle.

Nicieza & Simonson, Louise. Attack from Beyond, 2. 1999. mass mkt. 3.99 (*0-671-01174-X*) PB.

Nicieza, Fabian. Deadpool: The Circle Chase. 96p. 1997. pap. text 12.95 (*0-7851-0259-0*) Marvel Entrprs.
— The Ultimate Amazing X-Men. (Illus.). 96p. 1995. pap. 8.95 (*0-7851-0126-8*) Marvel Entrprs.
— The Ultimate Gambit & the X-Ternals. (Illus.). 96p. 1995. pap. 8.95 (*0-7851-0129-2*) Marvel Entrprs.
— X-Men: Fatal Attractions. (X-Men Ser.). (Illus.). 256p. 1994. pap. 24.95 (*0-7851-0065-2*) Marvel Entrprs.
— X-Men: Legion Quest. (Illus.). 112p. 1996. pap. 8.95 (*0-7851-0179-9*) Marvel Entrprs.
— X-Men Visionaries: The Art of Andy & Adam Kubert. (X-Men Visionaries Ser.). (Illus.). 96p. 1996. pap. text 8.95 (*0-7851-0178-0*) Marvel Entrprs.

Nicieza, Fabian, et al. Lethal Origins the 6 1 Digest. (J). 1997. per. 3.99 (*0-671-01167-7*) PB.
— X-Men: X-Cutioner's Song. (Illus.). 272p. 1994. pap. 24.95 (*0-7851-0025-3*) Marvel Entrprs.
— X-Men - Avengers: Bloodties. (Illus.). 128p. 1995. pap. 15.95 (*0-7851-0103-9*) Marvel Entrprs.

Nicita, Michael & Petrusha, Ronald. The Reader's Guide to Microcomputer Books. LC 84-15451. (Professional Librarian Ser.). 500p. 1984. 35.00 (*0-86729-122-2*, Hall Reference) Macmillan.

Nicjoll, Donald. Holiness. 1989. pap. 11.95 (*0-8091-3113-7*) Paulist Pr.

N

An Asterisk (*) at the beginning of an entry indicates that the title is appearing for the first time.

Nick, Dagmar. Lilith, a Metamorphosis. Partenheimer, Maren & Partenheimer, David, trs. LC 95-34503. 50p. 1995. pap. 10.00 (*0-943549-32-9*) Truman St Univ.

— Numbered Days: Poems by Dagmar Nick. Barnes, Jim, tr. from GER. LC 98-8816.Tr. of Gezahlte Tage. (Illus.). 134p. 1998. 22.00 (*0-943549-54-X*); pap. 15.00 (*0-943549-53-1*) Truman St Univ.

— Summons & Sign. Barnes, Jim, tr. from GER. LC 80-18367. Orig. Title: Zeugnis & Zeichen. (Illus.). 124p. (Orig.). 1980. pap. 100.00 (*0-933428-02-2*) Chariton Review.

Nick, Paul. Ralph Stover State Park. (Classic Rock Climbs Ser.: No. 12). (Illus.). 60p. (Orig.). 1997. pap. 9.95 (*1-57540-037-5*) Falcon Pub Inc.

***Nick, Paul.** Rock Climbing New Jersey. (Illus.). 200p. 2000. pap. 21.95 (*1-56044-790-7*) Falcon Pub Inc.

Nick, Paul & Sloane, Neil J. New Jersey Crags. (Classic Rock Climbs Ser.: No. 5). 1996. pap. 12.95 (*1-57540-032-4*) Falcon Pub Inc.

***Nick, Van der Bijk.** Nine Battles to Stanley. 1999. 36.95 (*0-85052-619-1*) Pen & Sword.

Nickalls, John L. & Penn, William, prefs. The Journal of George Fox. rev. ed. LC 85-80620. 789p. 1985. reprint ed. pap. 14.75 (*0-941308-05-7*) Phila Yrly Mtg RSOF.

Nickalls, R. W. & Ramasubramanian, R. Interfacing the IBM-PC to Medical Equipment: The Art of Serial Communication. (Illus.). 424p. (C). 1995. text 80.00 (*0-521-46280-0*) Cambridge U Pr.

Nickas, Paul. How to Make Money with Puts & Calls: The Smart Way to Unlimited Profits with the Least Amount of Risk. 1993. 39.95 (*0-9634155-3-0*) Sigma Pub Assocs.

Nickas, Paul A. Let's Have a Drink: A Complete Guide to Ethyl Alcohol. Harvey, Katerine, ed. LC 98-55563. (Illus.). 256p. 1999. 29.95 (*0-9634155-0-6*) Sigma Pub Assocs.

Nickau, ed. Ammonii. (GRE.). 1966. 49.50 (*3-322-00906-8*, T1040, Pub. by B G Teubner) U of Mich Pr.

Nickau, Klaus. Untersuchungen zur Textkritischen Methode des Zenodotos von Ephesos. (Untersuchungen zur Antiken Literatur und Geschichte Ser.: Vol. 16). (C). 1977. 103.10 (*3-11-001827-6*) De Gruyter.

Nickel. Pinocchio. (J). Date not set. 4.99 (*0-7214-5404-6*) Nickel Pr.

— Semiconductors & Semimetals Vol. 6: Hydrogen in Semiconductors II. (Illus.). 544p. (C). 1999. 155.00 (*0-12-752170-4*) Acad Pr.

Nickel, Amy J., ed. Roll Forming: Collected Articles & Technical Papers. (Illus.). 125p. (Orig.). (C). 1994. pap. 39.00 (*1-881113-07-8*) Croydon Grp.

Nickel, Amy J., ed. Sheet Metal Cutting: Collected Articles & Technical Papers. (Illus.). 143p. (Orig.). (C). 1994. pap. 33.00 (*1-881113-05-1*) Croydon Grp.

Nickel, Amy J., ed. Tube Fabricating Vol. 2: Collected Articles & Technical Papers. (Illus.). 258p. (Orig.). 1995. pap. 39.00 (*1-881113-09-4*) Croydon Grp.

Nickel, Amy J., ed. see Conner, Gary B.

Nickel, Amy J., ed. see Menhart, John & Lynn, Donald.

Nickel, Amy J., ed. see O'Con, Robert.

Nickel, Barbara. The Gladys Elegies. LC 98-114697. 80p. 1997. pap. 9.95 (*1-55050-112-7*, Pub. by Coteau) Genl Dist Srvs.

— The Secret Wish of Nannerl Mozart. 208p. 1996. pap. 6.95 (*0-929005-89-9*, Pub. by Sec Story Pr) LPC InBook.

Nickel, Catherine, jt. ed. see Gonzalez-del-Valle, Luis T.

Nickel, David J. Acupressure for Athletes. 2nd rev. ed. LC 86-12097. (Illus.). 176p. 1995. pap. 10.95 (*0-8050-0128-X*, Owl) H Holt & Co.

***Nickel, Douglas R.** Carleton Watkins: The Art of Perception. 228p. 1999. 65.00 (*0-8109-4102-3*, Pub. by Abrams) Time Warner.

Nickel, E. H., jt. auth. see Strunz, Hugo.

Nickel, Ernest H. Mineral Reference Manual. 1990. pap. 16.95 (*0-442-00344-7*) Chapman & Hall.

Nickel, Erwin & Fettel, Michael. Vorderer Odenwald Zwischen Darmstadt und Heidelberg. 2nd ed. (Sammlung Geologischer Fuehrer Ser.: Band 65). (GER., Illus.). xvi, 231p. 1985. spiral bd. 25.00 (*3-443-15045-4*, Pub. by Gebruder Borntraeger) Balogh.

Nickel, Friedhelm. Woerterbuch der Umweltechnik. (GER.). 290p. 1990. 95.00 (*0-7859-8483-6*, 3802304217) Fr & Eur.

Nickel, Gerhard, ed. see International Congress of Applied Linguistics Staf.

Nickel, Glenice M. & Moore, Glenice. Bitterroot Backroads, Vol. 2. (Illus.). 70p. 1995. pap. 10.50 (*1-56770-340-2*) S Scheewe Pubns.

***Nickel, Gordon D.** Peaceable Witness among Muslims. 152p. 2000. pap. 14.99 (*0-8361-9105-6*) Herald Pr.

Nickel, Gudrun M. Debtors' Rights. 3rd ed. LC 98-14286. (Legal Survival Guides Ser.). 158p. 1998. pap. 12.95 (*1-57071-342-1*) Sourcebks.

Nickel, Gundrun M. How to Probate an Estate in Florida. 3rd ed. LC 98-3538. (Legal Survival Guides Ser.). 160p. 1998. pap. 24.95 (*1-57071-364-2*) Sourcebks.

Nickel, Heinrich L. Medieval Architecture of Eastern Europe. LC 82-6254. (Illus.). 210p. 1983. 65.00 (*0-8419-0811-7*) Holmes & Meier.

Nickel, Helmut, et al. Studies in European Arms & Armor: The C. Otto von Kienbusch Collection in the Philadelphia Museum of Art. LC 95-47037. (Illus.). 208p. (C). 1992. 49.95 (*0-8122-7963-8*) Phila Mus Art.

***Nickel, James.** Lift up Your Eyes on High: Understanding the Stars. (Illus.). (YA). (gr. 7-12). 1999. pap., teacher ed. 7.95 (*1-930367-38-4*, CLP 69595); pap. text 9.95 (*1-930367-37-6*, CLP 69590) Christian Liberty.

Nickel, Karl & Wohlfahrt, Michael. Tailless Aircraft in Theory & Practice. LC 94-28604. (Education Ser.). Orig. Title: Schwanzlose Flugzeuge. (Illus.). 498p. 1994. 79.95 (*1-56347-094-2*, 94-2) AIAA.

Nickel, Klaus G., ed. Corrosion of Advanced Ceramics Measurement & Modelling: Proceedings of the NATO Advanced Research Workshop, Tubingen, Germany, August 30-September 3, 1993. LC 94-13365. (NATO ASI Series E. Applied Sciences: Vol. 267). 1994. text 298.50 (*0-7923-2838-8*) Kluwer Academic.

Nickel, Mike & Horvath, Cindy. Kay Finch Art Pottery: Her Enchanted World. (Illus.). 176p. 1996. 29.95 (*0-7643-0008-3*) Schiffer.

Nickel, Mildred L., jt. auth. see Wasman, Ann.

Nickel, N. H., et al, eds. Hydrogen in Semiconductors & Metals Vol. 513: Proceedings Materials Research Society Symposium. LC 98-28358. 455p. 1998. text 84.00 (*1-55899-419-X*) Materials Res.

Nickel-Pepin-Donat, B., jt. ed. see Charvosset, H.

***Nickel, Peter.** Plant Microtubules: Potential for Biotechnology. LC 00-24394. 2000. write for info. (*3-540-67105-6*) Spr-Verlag.

Nickel Press Staff. Christian Student Planner. 1995. pap. 5.99 (*1-57122-077-1*) Nickel Pr.

Nickel, R., et al, eds. The Locomotor System of the Domestic Mammals. (Anatomy of the Domestic Animals Ser.: Vol. 1). (Illus.). 520p. 1985. 117.95 (*0-387-91259-2*) Spr-Verlag.

Nickel, R., et al. Anatomy of the Domestic Birds. 1977. 71.00 (*0-387-91134-0*) Spr-Verlag.

***Nickel, Robert E. & Desch, Larry W.** The Physician's Guide to Caring for Children with Disabilities & Chronic Conditions. LC 99-35344. 2000. 125.00 (*1-55766-446-3*) P H Brookes.

***Nickel, Scott.** Barney's Halloween Fun. (Barney Ser.). (Illus.). 84p. (Orig.). (J). (ps-2). 2000. pap. 1.99 (*1-57064-780-1*, 97986) Lyrick Pub.

— Freddi Fish A Whale of A Tale! LC 00-105047. (Humongous Ser.). (Illus.). 24p. (J). (ps-1). 2001. 3.99 (*1-58668-061-7*) Lyrick Studios.

Nickel, Steven. Torso. 264p. 1990. mass mkt. 4.95 (*0-380-70987-2*, Avon Bks) Morrow Avon.

— Torso: The True Story of Eliot Ness & the Search for a Psychopathic Killer. LC 89-792. (Illus.). 232p. 1989. 18.95 (*0-89587-072-X*) Blair.

Nickel, Sue S. Missed Blessings. 1993. 9.95 (*0-9637015-0-9*) Crossover OK.

Nickel, Vernon L. & Botte, Michael J., eds. Orthopaedic Rehabilitation. 2nd ed. (Illus.). 939p. 1992. text 155.00 (*0-443-08726-1*) Church.

Nickell, Daniel B. Forecasting on Your Microcomputer. 1991. 24.95 (*0-8306-6648-6*) McGraw-Hill Prof.

Nickell, Denise. Product of Love: From the Bottom Up. LC 96-61917. 176p. (Orig.). 1997. pap. 12.95 (*1-883893-94-1*) WinePress Pub.

Nickell, Eugenie, jt. auth. see Witherspoon, Del.

***Nickell, Hilary.** Surfing Your Career. (Jobs & Careers Ser.). (Illus.). 176p. 2000. pap. 22.50 (*1-85703-586-0*, Pub. by How To Bks) Midpt Trade.

Nickell, Joe. Ambrose Bierce Is Missing: And Other Historical Mysteries. LC 91-3049. (Illus.). 192p. 1991. 24.00 (*0-8131-1766-6*) U Pr of Ky.

— Camera Clues: A Handbook for Photographic Investigation. LC 94-15623. (Illus.). 248p. 1994. 27.50 (*0-8131-1894-8*) U Pr of Ky.

— Detecting Forgery: Forensic Investigation of Documents. LC 95-35048. (Illus.). 240p. 1996. text 27.50 (*0-8131-1953-7*) U Pr of Ky.

— Entities: Angels, Spirits, Demons & Other Alien Beings. LC 94-44761. (Illus.). 297p. 1995. 25.95 (*0-87975-961-5*) Prometheus Bks.

— Inquest on the Shroud of Turin. 2nd rev. ed. LC 87-61608. (Illus.). 186p. 1987. pap. 19.95 (*0-87975-396-X*) Prometheus Bks.

— Inquest on the Shroud of Turin: Latest Scientific Findings. LC 98-27902. 1998. pap. 19.95 (*1-57392-272-2*) Prometheus Enterprises.

— Looking for a Miracle: Weeping Icons, Relics, Stigmata, Visions & Healing Cures. LC 93-25322. (Illus.). 253p. 1993. 26.95 (*0-87975-840-6*) Prometheus Bks.

— Looking for a Miracle: Weeping Icons, Relics, Stigmata, Visions & Healing Cures. LC 98-43809. (Illus.). 253p. 1999. pap. 17.95 (*1-57392-680-9*) Prometheus Bks.

— The Magic Detectives: Join Them in Solving Strange Mysteries. LC 89-62787. (Young Readers Ser.). (Illus.). 115p. (J). (gr. 4-9). 1989. pap. 9.95 (*0-87975-547-4*) Prometheus Bks.

***Nickell, Joe.** Pen, Ink & Evidence: A Study of Writing & Writing Materials for Penman. LC 99-57973. (Illus.). 240p. 2000. 39.95 (*1-58456-017-7*) Oak Knoll.

Nickell, Joe. Wonder-Workers! How They Perform the Impossible. LC 91-27484. (Young Readers Ser.). (Illus.). 91p. (Orig.). (YA). 1991. pap. 12.95 (*0-87975-688-8*) Prometheus Bks.

Nickell, Joe, ed. Psychic Sleuths: ESP & Sensational Cases. LC 93-43069. (Illus.). 251p. (C). 1994. 26.95 (*0-87975-880-5*) Prometheus Bks.

Nickell, Joe & Fischer, John F. Crime Science: Methods of Forensic Detection. LC 98-30749. (Illus.). 312p. 1998. 25.00 (*0-8131-2091-8*) U Pr of Ky.

— Secrets of the Supernatural: Investigating the World's Occult Mysteries. LC 88-12633. (Illus.). 199p. 1988. 27.95 (*0-87975-461-3*) Prometheus Bks.

— Secrets of the Supernatural: Investigating the World's Occult Mysteries. LC 88-12633. (Illus.). 199p. 1991. pap. 18.95 (*0-87975-685-3*) Prometheus Bks.

Nickell, Joe & Fischer, John F., eds. Mysterious Realms: Probing Paranormal, Historical, & Forensic Enigmas. LC 92-36998. (Illus.). 221p. 1992. 26.95 (*0-87975-765-5*) Prometheus Bks.

Nickell, Joe, jt. auth. see Baker, Robert A.

Nickell, Judy. Enchanted Gardening. (Illus.). 227p. 1992. spiral bd. 25.00 (*0-9632261-3-4*) Canaima Pr.

— A Gardener's Guide to Cataloging Flower & Garden Slides: And Prints, Too. (Illus.). 36p. 1994. pap. 7.00 (*0-9632261-2-6*) Canaima Pr.

Nickell, Louis G. Plant Growth Regulators: Agricultural Uses. (Illus.). 173p. 1981. 70.00 (*0-387-10973-0*) Spr-Verlag.

Nickell, Louis G., ed. Plant Growth Regulating Chemicals, 2 Vols., Vol. 1. LC 82-22832. 288p. 1983. 165.00 (*0-8493-5002-6*, QK745, CRC Reprint) Franklin.

— Plant Growth Regulating Chemicals, 2 Vols., Vol. 2. LC 82-22832. 264p. 1983. 152.00 (*0-8493-5003-4*, QK745, CRC Reprint) Franklin.

Nickell, Molli. Guerrillas of Goodness Handbook: 127 Little Ways You Can Make a Big Difference in the World. LC 94-6241. (Illus.). 1994. pap. 4.95 (*1-56305-561-9*, 3561) Workman Pub.

Nickell, Molli, ed. AIDS: Spirits Share Understanding & Comfort from the "Other" Side. 110p. 1986. 9.95 (*0-938283-99-5*) Spirit Speaks.

— Relationships: Yours-Mine-Ours. (Celebration of Discovery Ser.: Vol. III). (Illus.). 192p. 1989. pap. 12.95 (*0-938283-02-2*) Spirit Speaks.

***Nickell, Nancy L.** Nature's Aphrodisiacs. LC 98-47924. 192p. 1999. pap. 14.95 (*0-89594-890-7*) Crossing Pr.

Nickell, Samila S., ed. see Cook, Harvey A. & Pederson, Duane E.

Nickelodeon Staff. Ren & Stimpy. 1996. per. 14.00 (*0-671-00371-2*) PB.

Nickels. Directory of Marketing Faculty. 1997. pap. text 6.80 (*1-57259-317-2*) Worth.

— Select Chapters Understand Bus Custom. 5th ed. 1999. write for info. (*0-07-235819-X*) McGraw.

— Under. Business Irwin Career Handbook. 4th ed. 1995. 60.25 (*0-256-19363-0*) McGraw.

Nickels & Wood. Marketing Windows Powerpoint. 1997. 109.20 (*1-57259-319-9*) Worth.

Nickels, Cameron C. New England Humor: From the Revolutionary War to the Civil War. LC 93-320. (Illus.). 304p. (C). 1993. text 36.00 (*0-87049-804-5*) U of Tenn Pr.

Nickels, David. 4,000 Great Knock-Knock Jokes. LC 96-79107. 206p. (J). (gr. 2-12). 1998. vinyl bd. 12.50 (*1-886197-26-1*) Joy Books.

— 4,000 Great Knock-Knock Jokes. deluxe ed. LC 96-79107. (Illus.). 248p. (J). (gr. 2-12). 1996. vinyl bd. 29.50 (*1-886197-03-2*) Joy Books.

Nickels, George. The Gypsy Season. LC 80-12821. 1982. 22.95 (*0-87949-187-6*) Ashley Bks.

Nickels, Hamilton. Codemaster: Secrets of Making & Breaking Codes. 144p. 1990. pap. 16.00 (*0-87364-564-2*) Paladin Pr.

— Secrets of Making & Breaking Codes. LC 94-18198. 144p. 1994. 6.95 (*0-8065-1563-5*, Citadel Pr) Carol Pub Group.

Nickels, Luveta. Junk Jeans Recycled. (Illus.). 55p. 1997. 20.00 (*1-928727-01-8*) Get n Even.

Nickels, Lyndsey. Spoken Word Production & Its Breakdown in Aphasia. LC 98-106170. (Illus.). x, 230p. 1997. write for info. (*0-86377-466-0*, Pub. by Psychol Pr) Taylor & Francis.

Nickels, Sue, jt. auth. see Holly, Pat.

Nickels, Tom, et al. Explorations in Macroeconomics. rev. ed. 464p. 1997. pap. text 34.95 (*1-56226-373-0*) CAT Pub.

Nickels, Tracy. Dancing Wheat. 200p. (YA). 1998. pap. 12.95 (*1-928727-00-X*) Get n Even.

— Maiden Wheat. 1999. pap. write for info. (*1-928727-02-6*) Get n Even.

Nickels, Trudy, jt. auth. see Morgan, Colette.

Nickels, William & McHugh, James. Understanding Business. 4th ed. (C). 1996. text 55.95 (*0-256-20282-6*, Irwn McGrw-H) McGrw-H Hghr Educ.

Nickels, William G. Understanding Business. 4th ed. (C). 1996. text, pap. text 11.87 incl. disk (*0-256-19638-9*, Irwn McGrw-H) McGrw-H Hghr Educ.

— Understanding Business. 6th ed. 2001. 56.25 (*0-07-232054-0*) McGraw.

Nickels, William G. & Barrett, Barbara. Understanding Business Study Guide. 4th ed. 344p. (C). 1995. text 20.00 (*0-256-19562-5*, Irwn McGrw-H) McGrw-H Hghr Educ.

Nickels, William G. & McHugh, James M. Understanding Business: Electronic Presentation/Power-Point Slide With 3.50 IBM Disks. 4th ed. (C). 1995. text 24.37 incl. 5.25 ld (*0-256-19384-3*, Irwn McGrw-H) McGrw-H Hghr Educ.

Nickels, William G. & Wood, Marian B. Marketing: Relationships, Quality, & Value. LC 96-60599. 768p. 1996. text 58.20 (*1-57259-144-7*) Worth.

— Marketing: Relationships, Quality, & Value. 1997. pap. text, student ed. 12.80 (*1-57259-311-3*) Worth.

Nickels, William G., et al. Understanding Business. 4th ed. LC 95-22442. 784p. (C). 1995. text 55.95 (*0-256-14054-5*, Irwn McGrw-H); text 39.95 (*0-256-20215-X*, Irwn McGrw-H) McGrw-H Hghr Educ.

— Understanding Business. 5th ed. LC 98-23637. 1998. write for info. (*0-256-21980-X*, Irwn Prfssnl) McGraw-Hill Prof.

***Nickels, William G., et al.** Understanding Business. 5th ed. LC 98-23637. (Illus.). 1999. write for info. (*0-07-365714-X*); write for info. (*0-07-303975-6*) McGrw-H Hghr Educ.

Nickels, William G., et al. Understanding Business: Study Guide & Software Package. 4th ed. (C). 1995. text 55.95 incl. cd-rom (*0-256-21654-1*, Irwn McGrw-H) McGrw-H Hghr Educ.

— Understanding Business Getting & Keeping the Job You Want: A Practical Job Search Handbook. 4th ed. 256p. (C). 1995. text 16.87 (*0-256-19362-2*, Irwn McGrw-H) McGrw-H Hghr Educ.

— Understanding Canadian Business. 2nd ed. 704p. (C). 1997. text 45.95 (*0-256-19444-0*, Irwn McGrw-H) McGrw-H Hghr Educ.

— Understanding Canadian Business: Canadian. (C). 1994. text, student ed. 15.00 (*0-256-10801-3*, Irwn McGrw-H) McGrw-H Hghr Educ.

Nickels, William G., jt. auth. see Ross, Gayle M.

Nickelsburg, George W., Jr., ed. Studies on the Testament of Abraham. LC 76-44205. (Society of Biblical Literature. Septuagint & Cognate Studies: No. 6). 350p. reprint ed. pap. 108.50 (*0-7837-5436-1*, 204520100005) Bks Demand.

Nickelsburg, George W. & Stone, Michael E. Faith & Piety in Early Judaism: Texts & Documents. LC 82-71830. 256p. reprint ed. pap. 79.40 (*0-608-15817-8*, 203125700074) Bks Demand.

— Faith & Piety in Early Judaism: Texts & Documents. LC 91-12033. 256p. (C). 1991. reprint ed. pap. 19.00 (*1-56338-012-9*) TPI PA.

Nickelsburg, Janet. Field Trips: Ecology for Youth Leaders. LC 66-14520. 126p. (C). reprint ed. 39.10 (*0-8357-9048-7*, 201333000086) Bks Demand.

— Nature Activities for Early Childhood. 1976. pap. text 13.85 (*0-201-05097-8*) Addison-Wesley.

***Nickelsen, Leann.** Quick Activities to Build a Very Voluminous Vocabulary. 64p. (J). 1998. pap. 9.95 (*0-590-22179-5*) Scholastic Inc.

Nickelson, Richard & Wedemeyer, Dan, eds. 20th Annual Pacific Telecommunications Council Proceedings: Coping with Convergence. (Illus.). 825p. (C). 1997. pap. 225.00 (*1-880672-13-8*) Pac Telecom.

Nickelson, Richard L. & Wedemeyer, Dan J., eds. PTC'95 Proceedings: Convergence: Closing the Gap. (Orig.). 1994. cd-rom 50.00 (*1-880672-09-X*) Pac Telecom.

— PTC'95 Proceedings: Convergence: Closing the Gap. (Illus.). 740p. (Orig.). 1994. pap. 130.00 (*1-880672-06-5*) Pac Telecom.

— PTC'96 Proceedings: The Information Infrastructure: Users, Resources & Strategies. (Orig.). 1995. cd-rom 50.00 (*1-880672-08-1*) Pac Telecom.

— PTC'96 Proceedings: The Information Infrastructure: Users, Resources & Strategies. (Illus.). 750p. (Orig.). 1995. pap. 130.00 (*1-880672-07-3*) Pac Telecom.

Nickens, Bessie. Walking the Log: Memories of a Southern Childhood. LC 94-10803. (Illus.). 32p. (J). (gr. 2 up). 1994. 14.95 (*0-8478-1794-6*, Pub. by Rizzoli Intl) St Martin.

Nickens, Boure. Boure (Boo-Ray) A Louisiana Card Game. 1972. 6.95 (*1-57980-020-3*) Claitors.

Nickens, C., jt. auth. see Leigh, Janet.

Nickens, Paul R. Johnson Canyon-Pueblo III Transition. (Memoir Ser.: No. 2). 62p. (C). 1981. pap. text 6.00 (*1-888400-00-5*) Colo Archaeol.

Nickens, Paul R., jt. auth. see Williamson, Ray A.

Nickerson. Modern Basics of Programming. (C). 1992. pap. 8.33 (*0-06-501133-3*) HarpC.

Nickerson, Arlene, jt. auth. see Ariel Books Staff.

Nickerson, Barbara. Shakespeare's a Midsummer Night's Dream: A Prose Narrative. LC 96-93039. 70p. (J). 1997. 22.95 (*0-9655702-0-7*) Seventy Fourth St.

Nickerson, Camilla & Wakefield, Neville, eds. Fashion: Photography of the Nineties. (Illus.). 256p. 1998. pap. 29.95 (*3-931141-81-0*, 810252, Pub. by Scalo Pubs) Dist Art Pubs.

— Fashion Now! Fashion Photography of the Nineties. LC 97-159381. (Illus.). 256p. 1996. 59.95 (*3-931141-26-8*, 620051, Pub. by Scalo Pubs) Dist Art Pubs.

Nickerson, Catherine. The Web of Iniquity: Early Detective Fiction by American Writers. LC 98-8397. 1999. 49.95 (*0-8223-2251-X*); pap. 17.95 (*0-8223-2271-4*) Duke.

Nickerson, Catherine L., jt. auth. see Tivnan, Elsa B.

***Nickerson, Dan.** Cako Kit Me Lyo Lok (Introduction to Co-Counseling) Odonkara, Abitimo, tr. from ENG. (ACE., Illus.). 14p. 1999. pap. 1.00 (*1-58429-062-5*) Rational Isl.

Nickerson, Dan. Introduction to Co-Counseling. 1994. pap. 1.00 (*0-913937-93-2*) Rational Isl.

— Introduction to Co-Counseling. 1995. pap. 1.00 (*1-885357-17-6*) Rational Isl.

— Introduction to Co-Counseling. (PER.). 1996. pap. 1.00 (*1-885357-41-9*) Rational Isl.

— Introduction to Co-Counseling. (GRE.). 1996. pap. 1.00 (*1-885357-38-9*) Rational Isl.

— Introduction to Co-Counseling. (HUN.). 1998. pap. 1.00 (*1-885357-60-5*) Rational Isl.

— Introduction to Co-Counseling. Vajda, Ileana, tr. (RUM., Illus.). 10p. 1999. pap. 1.00 (*1-58429-039-0*) Rational Isl.

***Nickerson, Dan.** Introduction to Co-Counseling. Ruzkova, Milena, tr.Tr. of Predstavujeme Vam Svepomocne Vzajemne Poradenstvi (SVP). (CZE., Illus.). 14p. 1999. pap. 1.00 (*1-58429-064-1*) Rational Isl.

***Nickerson, Dan & Jackins, Harvey.** A Welcome to Re-Evaluation Counseling. (JPN.). 19p. 1999. mass mkt. 1.00 (*1-58429-056-0*) Rational Isl.

Nickerson, E. Fundamentals of Structured Cobol with RM/Cobol 85. (C). 1997. 92.00 (*0-06-500171-0*) Addson-Wesley Educ.

Nickerson, Edward A., ed. see Sheridan, Thomas.

Nickerson, Eileen T. The Dissertation Handbook: A Guide to Successful Dissertations. 2nd ed. 152p. (C). 1994. per. 24.95 (*0-8403-8300-2*) Kendall-Hunt.

Nickerson, Eve, jt. auth. see Thomsett, Kay.

Nickerson, Gifford S. Native North Americans in Doctoral Dissertations, 1971-1975: A Classified & Indexed Research Bibliography, No. 1232. 1977. 7.50 (*0-686-19688-0*, Sage Prdcls Pr) Sage.

Nickerson, Jan & Hamilton, Marilyn. Y2K Connections: The Scenario Game Building Community Not Crises. (Illus.). 26p. 1999. pap. 30.00 incl. audio (*0-9673386-0-3*) Y Connect.

An Asterisk (*) at the beginning of an entry indicates that the title is appearing for the first time.

Nickerson, Jane. Jane Nickerson's Florida Cookbook. LC 73-17413. (Illus.). 204p. 1973. 24.95 (*0-8130-0443-8*); pap. 13.95 (*0-8130-0816-6*) U Press Fla.

Nickerson, Jane S. Short History of North Africa. LC 68-54233. 1961. pap. 20.00 (*0-8196-0219-1*) Biblo.

Nickerson, Joshua A. Days to Remember. 1988. pap. 14.95 (*0-317-67586-9*) Chatham His Soc.

Nickerson, Kathy. Once upon a Childhood. (Fresh Perspective Ser.). 30p. 1998. pap. 3.50 (*0-9660886-2-X*) Scribbles & Scribes.

Nickerson, Kathy, jt. auth. see Youngblood, Steve.

Nickerson, Lloyd C., ed. see Barlow, Raymond E. & Kaiser, Joan B.

Nickerson, Lloyd C., ed. see Barlow, Raymond E. & Kaiser, Joan E.

Nickerson, Margaret. Gathering Food. large type ed. (Illus.). 8p. (J). (gr. k-3). 1999. pap. text 14.50 (*1-58084-060-4*) Lower Kuskokwim.

***Nickerson, Margaret.** Katitchirugut Niqinik. large type ed.Tr. of Gathering Food. (ESK., Illus.). 8p. (J). (gr. k-3). 1999. pap. text 14.50 (*1-58084-136-8*) Lower Kuskokwim.

— Katitchiyuanni Niqinik. large type ed.Tr. of Gathering Food. (ESK., Illus.). 8p. (J). (gr. k-3). 1999. pap. text 14.50 (*1-58084-126-0*) Lower Kuskokwim.

Nickerson, Margaret. Neqengnaqler. large type ed.Tr. of Gathering Food. (ESK., Illus.). 8p. (J). (gr. k-3). 1999. pap. text 14.50 (*1-58084-105-8*) Lower Kuskokwim.

— Niginik Katittigaangapta. large type ed.Tr. of Gathering Food. (ESK., Illus.). 8p. (J). (gr. k-3). 1999. pap. text 14.50 (*1-58084-133-3*) Lower Kuskokwim.

— Quyurciyaraq Neqnek. large type ed.Tr. of Gathering Food. (ESK., Illus.). 8p. (J). (gr. k-3). 1999. pap. text 14.50 (*1-58084-061-2*) Lower Kuskokwim.

Nickerson, Marie-Louise, jt. auth. see Fergenson, Laraine.

Nickerson, Nancy K., jt. auth. see Murphy, Linda J.

Nickerson, Norma P. Foundations of Tourism. LC 95-16945. 332p. (C). 1995. 71.00 (*0-13-108119-5*) P-H.

Nickerson, Pat. Managing Multiple Bosses: How to Juggle Priorities, Personalities & Projects - And Make It Look Easy. LC 98-29095. 144p. 1998. pap. 22.95 (*0-8144-7025-4*) AMACOM.

Nickerson, Patricia. Nickerson's Four-Star Management Workshop. 384p. 1988. 39.95 (*0-685-37794-6*) P-H.

Nickerson, Ray, et al. The Teaching of Thinking. 400p. (C). 1985. text 49.95 (*0-89859-539-8*) L Erlbaum Assocs.

Nickerson, Raymond & Zodhiates, Philip. Technology in Education: Looking Toward 2020. 352p. (C). 1988. pap. 36.00 (*0-8058-0297-5*); text 69.95 (*0-8058-0214-2*) L Erlbaum Assocs.

Nickerson, Raymond, ed. see National Research Council Staff.

Nickerson, Raymond S. Looking Ahead: Human Factors Challenges in a Changing World. 456p. 1992. text 89.95 (*0-8058-1150-8*) L Erlbaum Assocs.

— Looking Ahead: Human Factors Challenges in a Changing World. 456p. 1992. pap. 45.00 (*0-8058-1151-6*) L Erlbaum Assocs.

— Reflections on Reasoning. 160p. (C). 1986. 29.95 (*0-89859-762-5*); pap. 18.50 (*0-89859-763-3*) L Erlbaum Assocs.

— Reflections on Reasoning. (C). 1986. teacher ed. write for info. (*0-89859-764-1*) L Erlbaum Assocs.

— Using Computers: Human Factors in Information Systems. 22.50 (*0-317-42856-X*) McGraw.

— Using Computers: Human Factors in Information Systems. 456p. 1987. reprint ed. pap. text 15.95 (*0-262-64022-8*, Bradford Bks) MIT Pr.

Nickerson, Raymond S., ed. Attention & Performance VIII. LC 80-23850. (Attention & Performance Ser.). 864p. 1980. 180.00 (*0-89859-038-8*) L Erlbaum Assocs.

Nickerson, Raymond S., jt. auth. see Durso, Francis T.

Nickerson, Richard P. Genetics Guide & Basics. 430p. (C). 1997. pap. text 44.00 (*0-673-39684-3*) Addson-Wesley Educ.

Nickerson, Robert C. Business & Information Systems. LC 97-41551. 576p. (C). 1998. 83.00 (*0-321-01378-6*, Prentice Hall) P-H.

***Nickerson, Robert C.** Business & Information Systems. 2nd ed. 512p. 2000. 77.33 (*0-13-089496-6*, Prentice Hall) P-H.

— Business & Information Systems Using Intuit's Quickbooks. 1998. pap. text 93.00 (*0-321-04138-0*) Addison-Wesley.

Nickerson, Robert C. Computer Hardware: Module 2. LC 92-37221. (C). 1992. write for info. (*0-06-501698-X*) HarperTrade.

— Computers: Concepts & Application. 2nd ed. (C). 1993. text 55.95 (*0-673-46790-2*) Addson-Wesley Educ.

— Computers: Concepts & Applications for Users. 2nd ed. LC 91-36536. 1992. text 7.25 (*0-673-46678-7*) Addison-Wesley.

— Computers: Concepts & Applications with BASIC. 2nd ed. (C). 1992. write for info. (*0-673-46690-6*) Addson-Wesley Educ.

— Computers & Society: Module 5. LC 92-37224. (C). 1993. write for info. (*0-06-501699-8*) Addson-Wesley Educ.

— Fundamentals of Programming in BASIC. 2nd ed. (C). 1997. 58.00 (*0-673-39040-3*) Addson-Wesley Educ.

— Fundamentals of Structured COBOL. (C). 1987. teacher ed. write for info. (*0-318-61087-6*) Little.

— Fundamentals of Structured COBOL. 2nd ed. (C). 1987. student ed. write for info. (*0-318-61088-4*); trans. write for info. (*0-318-61089-2*); disk. write for info. (*0-318-61090-6*); disk. write for info. (*0-318-61091-4*) Little.

— Information Systems in Business. (C). 1998. pap. text, student ed. write for info. (*0-321-01399-9*) Addson-Wesley Educ.

Nickerson, Robert L., jt. auth. see Whalen, Harold B.

Nickerson, Roy. Lahaina: Royal Capital of Hawaii. Wirtz, Richard, ed. LC 77-94277. (Illus.). 1978. pap. 8.95 (*0-930492-03-X*) Hawaiian Serv.

— Sea Otters: A Natural History & Guide. 1998. pap. 14.95 (*0-8118-1922-1*) Chronicle Bks.

— Sea Otters: A Natural History & Guide. rev. ed. (Illus.). 96p. (C). 1989. pap. 14.95 (*0-87701-567-8*) Chronicle Bks.

Nickerson, S. Harold. Conversations of Silence: A Memoir. LC 94-45897. 226p. (Orig.). 1995. pap. 18.95 (*0-86534-231-8*) Sunstone Pr.

Nickerson, Sara. Martin the Cavebine. LC 88-71369. (Illus.). 28p. (Orig.). (J). (gr. 2-4). 1988. pap. 9.00 (*0-935529-06-3*) Comprehen Health Educ.

— Peter Parrot, Private Eye. LC 88-63800. (Illus.). 43p. (Orig.). (J). (gr. 3-5). 1988. pap. 9.00 (*0-935529-07-1*) Comprehen Health Educ.

Nickerson, Sheila. Disappearance: A Map, a Meditation on Death & Loss in the Hight Latitudes. LC 97-4446. 304p. 1997. pap. 11.00 (*0-15-600498-4*, Harvest Bks) Harcourt.

— Feast of the Animals: An Alaska Bestiary. (Illus.). 68p. (Orig.). 1987. pap. 12.95 (*0-9615529-4-8*) Old Harbor Pr.

— Feast of the Animals Vol. II: An Alaska Bestiary. LC 86-62524. (Illus.). 56p. (Orig.). 1991. pap. 12.95 (*0-9615529-8-0*) Old Harbor Pr.

— In an August Garden. limited ed. 24p. 1997. pap. write for info. (*1-884236-03-0*) Limner Pr.

— In the Compass of Unrest. 34p. (Orig.). 1988. pap. 4.00 (*0-916155-04-8*) Trout Creek.

Nickerson, Sheila. On Why the Quiltmaker Became a Dragon: A Visionary Poem. (Illus.). 59p. 1985. pap. 7.95 (*0-914221-04-3*) Vanessapress.

Nickerson, Sheila B. In Rooms of Falling Rain. LC 76-28466. (Orig.). 1976. pap. 4.00 (*0-914476-59-9*) Thorp Springs.

Nickerson, Stephen R., contrib. by. Early Daoist Scriptures. LC 96-43415. (Daoist Classics Ser.). 520p. 1997. 55.00 (*0-520-20322-4*, Pub. by U CA Pr) Cal Prin Full Svc.

***Nickerson, Thomas.** Loss of the Ship Essex, Sunk by a Whale. LC 00-20147. (Penguin Classics Ser.). 256p. 2000. pap. 12.95 (*0-14-043796-7*) Viking Penguin.

Nickerson, Todd W., jt. auth. see Kristof, David.

Nickerson, Virginia & White, Doreen, eds. The Natural Resources of the Garifuna of Orinoco, Nicaragua. (Illus.). 108p. (Orig.). 1990. pap. 7.00 (*0-9637982-4-3*) Orang-Utan Pr.

Nickerson, Warren S. & Carpenter, Delores B. Land Ho! - 1620: A Seaman's Story of the Mayflower, Her Construction, Her Navigation & Her First Landfall. LC 96-51685. (Illus.). 250p. 1997. pap. 18.95 (*0-87013-465-5*) Mich St U Pr.

Nickeson, David, jt. auth. see Shields, Don W.

Nickl, Peter. Crocodile, Crocodile. Cutler, Ebbitt, tr. Orig. Title: Krokodil, Krokodil. (Illus.). 32p. (J). 1994. pap. 7.95 (*0-940793-32-6*, Crocodile Bks) Interlink Pub.

— The Story of the Kind Wolf. 1994. mass mkt. 5.95 (*0-200-72929-2*) HarpC.

— The Story of the Kind Wolf. LC 82-670149. (Illus.). 32p. (J). (gr. k-3). 1988. pap. 5.95 (*1-55858-058-1*, Pub. by North-South Bks NYC) Chronicle Bks.

Nicklas, John D. Am I Worthy? LC 94-92223. 100p. (Orig.). 1995. pap. 9.00 (*0-9641766-0-2*) Beauty Within.

Nicklas, Michael L. Great Basin: The Story Behind the Scenery. LC 96-75072. (Illus.). 48p. (Orig.). 1996. pap. 7.95 (*0-88714-105-6*) KC Pubns.

— Great Basin: The Story Behind the Scenery. Hosford, Helga, tr. (GER., Illus.). 48p. (Orig.). 1996. pap. 8.95 (*0-88714-808-5*) KC Pubns.

Nicklas, Pascal. The School of Affliction - Gewalt und Empfindsamkeit in Samuel Richardsons "Clarissa" (Anglistische und Amerikanistische Texte und Studien Ser.: Bd. 9). (Illus.). 323p. 1997. 60.00 (*3-487-10300-1*) G Olms Pubs.

Nicklas, Steven D. A General Survey of Coinage in the Roman Empire A. D. 294-408 & Its Relationship to Roman Military Deployment. LC 94-18059. 380p. 1994. text 99.95 (*0-7734-9104-X*) E Mellen.

Nicklaus, Carol. Come Dance with Me. (Sports Ser.). (Illus.). 32p. (J). (ps-1). 1991. pap. 3.95 (*0-671-73507-1*, Silver Pr NJ) Silver Burdett Pr.

— The Go Club. (Sports Ser.). (Illus.). 32p. (J). (ps-1). 1991. pap. 2.95 (*0-671-73505-5*, Silver Pr NJ) Silver Burdett Pr.

***Nicklaus, Carol.** Grover's Own Alphabet. (Big Bird's Favorite Bird Bks.). 12p. 2000. 4.99 (*0-375-80540-0*, Pub. by Random Bks Yng Read) Random.

Nicklaus, Carol. Oscar! Furry Faces. (Illus.). 5p. (J). 1999. 7.99 (*0-679-89489-6*) Random.

— Silver Sports Series, 4 vols., Set. (Illus.). (J). (ps-1). 1991. pap. 11.80 (*0-671-31272-3*, Silver Pr NJ) Silver Burdett Pr.

Nicklaus, Carol. Big Bird. 1999. 7.99 (*0-679-89490-X*) Random.

— Elmo's Wash & Dry. (Magic Bath Bks. Ser.). (J). 1999. 4.99 (*0-375-80128-6*) Random.

— Yo, Ho, Rubber Duckie. (Magic Bath Bks. Ser.). 10p. (J). 1999. 4.99 (*0-679-89427-6*) Random.

Nicklaus, Jack. Golf My Way. 272p. 1998. per. 14.00 (*0-684-85211-X*, Fireside) S&S Trade Pap.

— Jack Nicklaus: My Story. 1998. per. 15.00 (*0-684-83870-2*, Fireside) S&S Trade Pap.

— Jack Nicklaus' Lesson Tee: Let the World's Greatest Golfer Teach You How to Play Your Best Golf. 160p. 1998. per. 15.00 (*0-684-85212-8*, Fireside) S&S Trade Pap.

— Jack Nicklaus Presents Golden Bear Challenge: Official Strategy Guide, 1. LC 99-72267. 1999. pap. text 14.99 (*1-56686-885-8*) Brady Pub.

— My 55 Ways to Lower Your Golf Score. 1998. per. 14.00 (*0-684-84754-X*, Fireside) S&S Trade Pap.

— My Fifty-Five Ways to Lower Your Golf Score. (Illus.). 128p. 1985. pap. 10.00 (*0-671-55395-X*) S&S Trade.

— Play Better Golf, No. 1. 1989. mass mkt. 5.50 (*0-671-68492-2*) PB.

— Play Better Golf: The Short Game & Scoring, Vol. II. 1986. mass mkt. 5.50 (*0-671-63257-4*) PB.

Nicklaus, Jack & Bowden, Ken. Golf My Way. 266p. 1976. pap. 12.00 (*0-671-22278-3*, Fireside) S&S Trade Pap.

— Jack Nicklaus: My Story. LC 97-3824. (Illus.). 505p. 1997. 29.50 (*0-684-83628-9*) S&S Trade.

— Jack Nicklaus' Lesson Tee: 15th Anniversary Edition. 15th ed. (Illus.). 160p. 1992. pap. 13.00 (*0-671-78007-7*, Fireside) S&S Trade Pap.

— My Most Memorable Shots in the Majors: And What You Can Learn from Them. (Illus.). 128p. 1988. 14.95 (*0-8129-1750-2*, Times Bks) Crown Pub Group.

— Play Better Golf: Problems & Answers, Vol. 3. (Orig.). 1990. mass mkt. 4.99 (*0-671-72765-6*) PB.

Nicklaus, Jack, jt. auth. see Walker, D.

Nicklaus, Janice, jt. auth. see Crawford, George.

Nickle, John. The Ant Bully. LC 98-19970. (Illus.). 32p. (J). (ps-2). 1999. 15.95 (*0-590-39591-2*) Scholastic Inc.

***Nickle, John.** TV Rex. LC 99-53214. (Illus.). (J). 2000. write for info. (*0-439-12043-8*) Scholastic Inc.

***Nickle, Keith F.** Preaching in the Gospel of Luke: Proclaiming God's Royal Rule. 352p. 2000. pap. 21.95 (*0-664-50120-6*, Pub. by Westminster John Knox) Presbyterian Pub.

Nickle, Keith F. The Synoptic Gospels: An Introduction. LC 79-92069. (Orig.). 1980. pap. 17.95 (*0-8042-0422-5*) Westminster John Knox.

***Nickle, Keith Fullerton.** Preaching the Gospel of Luke: Proclaiming God's Royal Rule. LC 99-53854. 296p. 2000. pap. text 21.95 (*0-664-22239-0*) Westminster John Knox.

Nickle Press Staff. Designs to Color. Date not set. pap. text 5.99 (*1-57122-163-8*) Nickel Pr.

Nickle, William R., ed. Manual of Agricultural Nematology. (Illus.). 1064p. 1991. text 275.00 (*0-8247-8397-2*) Dekker.

— Plant & Insect Nematodes. fac. ed. LC 84-4937. (Illus.). 943p. 1984. pap. 200.00 (*0-7837-7715-9*, 204747700007) Bks Demand.

***Nicklen, Paul, photos by.** Seasons of the Arctic. LC 00-30103. (Illus.). 128p. 2000. 32.00 (*1-57805-057-X*, Pub. by Sierra) Random.

Nickles, Alfred E. The AS/400 Client/Server Series Bk. 2: Getting Started. 182p. 1995. 99.00 (*1-887519-02-5*) C-S Technol.

— The AS/400 Client/Server Series Bk. 1: Introduction. 130p. 1994. 99.00 (*1-887519-01-7*) C-S Technol.

— The Client/Server Marketing & Technology Report. 344p. 1993. 99.00 (*1-887519-00-9*) C-S Technol.

Nickles, Don, ed. Competitive Change in the Electric Power Industry: The Oklahoma Perspective. (Illus.). 80p. (C). 1999. reprint ed. pap. text 20.00 (*0-7881-8147-5*) DIANE Pub.

***Nickles, Greg.** Argentina the Culture. (Lands, Peoples & Cultures Ser.). (Illus.). 32p. (YA). (gr. 4-9). 2000. pap. 7.95 (*0-86505-326-X*); lib. bdg. 20.60 (*0-86505-246-8*) Crabtree Pub Co.

— Argentina the Land. (Lands, Peoples & Cultures Ser.). (Illus.). 32p. (YA). (gr. 4-9). 2000. pap. 7.95 (*0-86505-324-3*); lib. bdg. 20.60 (*0-86505-244-1*) Crabtree Pub Co.

— Argentina the People. (Lands, Peoples & Cultures Ser.). (Illus.). 32p. (YA). (gr. 4). 2000. pap. 7.95 (*0-86505-325-1*) Crabtree Pub Co.

— Argentina the People. (Lands, Peoples & Cultures Ser.). (Illus.). 32p. (YA). (gr. 4-9). 2000. lib. bdg. 20.60 (*0-86505-245-X*) Crabtree Pub Co.

— France: The Culture. (Lands, Peoples & Cultures Ser.). (Illus.). 32p. (YA). (gr. 4-9). 2000. lib. bdg. 20.60 (*0-86505-243-3*) Crabtree Pub Co.

— France: The Culture. (Lands, Peoples, & Cultures Ser.). (Illus.). (J). 2000. 13.40 (*0-606-18054-0*) Turtleback.

— France the Land. (Lands, Peoples & Cultures Ser.). (Illus.). 32p. (YA). (gr. 4-9). 2000. pap. 7.95 (*0-86505-321-9*); lib. bdg. 20.60 (*0-86505-241-7*) Crabtree Pub Co.

— France the People. (Lands, Peoples & Cultures Ser.). (Illus.). 32p. (YA). (gr. 4-9). 2000. pap. 7.95 (*0-86505-322-7*); lib. bdg. 20.60 (*0-86505-242-5*) Crabtree Pub Co.

— The Hispanics. (We Came to North America Ser.). (Illus.). 32p. (J). (gr. 3-9). 2000. pap. 8.95 (*0-7787-0200-6*); lib. bdg. 21.28 (*0-7787-0186-7*) Crabtree Pub Co.

— Pirates. (Crabapples Ser.). 1996. 11.15 (*0-606-12793-3*, Pub. by Turtleback) Demco.

— Russia the Culture. LC 99-56187. (Lands, Peoples & Cultures Ser.). (Illus.). 32p. (YA). (gr. 4-9). 2000. lib. bdg. 20.60 (*0-86505-240-9*) Crabtree Pub Co.

— Russia the Land. LC 99-56154. (Lands, Peoples & Cultures Ser.). (Illus.). 32p. (YA). (gr. 4-9). 2000. pap. 7.95 (*0-86505-318-9*); lib. bdg. 20.60 (*0-86505-238-7*) Crabtree Pub Co.

— Russia the People. LC 99-56058. (Lands, Peoples & Cultures Ser.). (Illus.). 32p. (YA). (gr. 4-9). 2000. pap. 7.95 (*0-86505-319-7*); lib. bdg. 20.60 (*0-86505-239-5*) Crabtree Pub Co.

***Nickles, Greg & Kalman, Bobbie.** France the Culture. (Lands, Peoples & Cultures Ser.). (Illus.). 32p. (YA). (gr. 4-9). 2000. pap. 7.95 (*0-86505-323-5*) Crabtree Pub Co.

— Russia the Culture. LC 99-56187. (Lands, Peoples, & Cultures Ser.). (Illus.). 32p. (YA). (gr. 4-9). 2000. pap. 7.95 (*0-86505-320-0*) Crabtree Pub Co.

***Nickles, Greg & Walker, Niki.** Canada. LC 99-42688. (Nations of the World Ser.). (Illus.). 128p. (J). (gr. 6-7). 2000. 31.40 (*0-8172-5780-2*) Raintree Steck-V.

Nickles, Greg, jt. auth. see Kalman, Bobbie.

***Nickles, Liz.** All the Time in the World: Love Knows No Limits. 272p. 2000. mass mkt. 6.99 (*0-380-81076-X*, HarpTorch) Morrow Avon.

Nickles, Liz & Asseyev, Tamara. Always Kiss with Your Whiskers: Love Advice from My Cat. (Illus.). 64p. 1991. pap. 6.00 (*0-671-74983-8*) PB.

Nickles, Liz, jt. auth. see Colette, Martine.

Nickles, Liz, jt. auth. see Navratilova, Martina.

Nickles, Sara, ed. Drinking, Smoking, & Screwing: Great Writers on Good Times. LC 94-9336. 224p. 1994. pap. 12.95 (*0-8118-0784-3*) Chronicle Bks.

— Lying, Cheating & Stealing: Great Writers on Getting What You Want When You Want It. LC 97-26165. 224p. 1997. pap. text 12.95 (*0-8118-1820-9*) Chronicle Bks.

***Nickles, Sara, ed.** Wine Memories: Great Writers on the Pleasures of Wine. LC 99-54533. (Illus.). 144p. 2000. 16.95 (*0-8118-2645-7*) Chronicle Bks.

Nickles, Steve H. Lender Liability in Secured Financing: Major Causes & Effective Cures. 4th ed. 456p. 1989. pap. 35.00 (*0-943380-04-9*) PEG MN.

— Negotiable Instruments. 2nd ed. LC 92-47440. (Black Letter Ser.). 574p. (C). 1993. pap. 24.50 incl. disk (*0-314-01979-0*) West Pub.

Nickles, Steve H. & Epstein, David G. Creditors' Rights & Bankruptcy. (Black Letter Ser.). 576p. (C). 1989. reprint ed. pap. 24.50 incl. disk (*0-314-48841-3*) West Pub.

Nickles, Steve H., et al. Teacher's Manual to Accompany Course Materials on Commercial Paper & Modern Payment Systems. (American Casebook Ser.). 146p. 1993. pap. text. write for info. (*0-314-03587-7*) West Pub.

Nickles, Steve H., jt. auth. see Epstein, David G.

Nickles, Steve H., jt. auth. see Speidel, Richard E.

Nickles, Steve M., et al. Modern Commercial Paper: The New Law of Negotiable Instruments (& Related Commercial Paper) LC 94-131558. (American Casebook Ser.). 767p. (C). 1993. 57.50 (*0-314-03240-1*) West Pub.

Nickles, Steven, jt. auth. see Epstein, David.

Nickles, Thomas, ed. Scientific Discovery: Case Studies. (Boston Studies in the Philosophy of Science: No. 60). 404p. 1980. pap. text 62.50 (*90-277-1093-7*, D Reidel); lib. bdg. 93.00 (*90-277-1092-9*, D Reidel) Kluwer Academic.

N

Nickles, Thomas, jt. ed. see Asquith, Peter D.

Nicklin, D. J., jt. ed. see Potter, O. E.

***Nicklin, George.** "Doctors in Peril" How They Cope. 301p. 2000. pap. text. write for info. (*0-940429-23-3*) M B Glass Assocs.

Nicklin, J., et al. Instant Notes in Microbiology. (Instant Notes Ser.). 352p. 1998. pap. 24.95 (*0-387-91559-1*) Spr-Verlag.

Nicklin, Joan. Four Outstanding Black Women Historians in Africa & the U. S. A. LC 95-67257. (African Women Ser.: No. 2). 50p. (Orig.). (C). 1995. pap. text 5.00 (*0-943324-60-7*) Omenana.

— Patterns of Indigeneous Capitalist Formations In Pre-Colonial Africa & North America. LC 95-67260. (African Women Ser.: No. 1). 50p. (Orig.). (C). 1995. pap. text 5.00 (*0-943324-56-4*) Omenana.

Nicklin, Stephen, jt. ed. see Miller, Klara.

Nicklin, Walter. Pieces of the Piedmont, the Puzzle of One Life: A Personal Geography of Virginia's Foothills & America's Historic Heart. unabridged ed. (Illus.). 112p. 1997. pap. 19.95 (*1-885937-06-7*, Virginia Heritage) Casco Commns.

— The Rappahannock River. (Virginia Heritage Publications). 48p. 1994. pap. 5.95 (*1-885937-00-8*) Casco Commns.

***Nickol, Peter.** Learning to Read Music: How to Make Sense of Those Mysterious Symbols. 112p. 2000. pap. 14.95 (*1-85703-390-6*, Pub. by How To Bks) Midpt Trade.

Nickolae, Barbara. Finders, Keepers. large type ed. 1991. 27.99 (*0-7089-2375-5*) Ulverscroft.

— Ties That Bind. large type ed. LC 93-29304. 351p. 1993. lib. bdg. 19.95 (*0-8161-5885-1*, G K Hall Lrg Type) Mac Lib Ref.

Nickolaisen, Robert H. Principles of Machine Design for Engineering & Industrial Technology. (C). 2000. write for info. (*0-13-720632-1*, Macmillan Coll) P-H.

Nickolas, Markos, jt. auth. see Timiadis, Emilianos.

Nickolaus, Martin, tr. see Marx, Karl.

Nickoles, Janet. White Roses. 320p. 1998. mass mkt. 4.99 (*0-8439-4375-0*, Leisure Bks) Dorchester Pub Co.

Nickolls, Brian. Making Character Dolls' Houses in 1-12 Scale. (Illus.). 192p. 1995. 29.95 (*0-7153-0200-0*, Pub. by D & C Pub) Sterling.

***Nickolls, Brian.** Making Character Dolls' Houses in 1/2 Scale. (Illus.). 2000. pap. 19.95 (*0-7153-0854-8*) D & C Pub.

Nickolls, Brian. Making Dolls' Houses in 1/12 Scale. LC 98-137931. (Illus.). 192p. 1996. pap. 19.95 (*0-7153-0480-1*, Pub. by D & C Pub) Sterling.

Nickoloff, Brian J. Dermal Immune System. 352p. 1992. lib. bdg. 189.00 (*0-8493-5941-4*, RL97) CRC Pr.

***Nickoloff, Brian J., ed.** Melanoma Methods & Protocols. 375p. 2000. 99.50 (*0-89603-684-7*) Humana.

Nickoloff, Jac A., ed. Animal Cell Electroporation & Electrofusion Protocols. LC 95-30825. (Methods in Molecular Biology Ser.: Vol. 48). (Illus.). 385p. 1995. 69.50 (*0-89603-304-X*) Humana.

— Electroporation Protocols for Microorganisms. LC 95-14992. (Methods in Molecular Biology Ser.: No. 47). (Illus.). 392p. 1995. 69.50 (*0-89603-310-4*) Humana.

— Plant Cell Electroporation & Electrofusion Protocols. LC 95-358. (Methods in Molecular Biology Ser.: Vol. 55). 220p. 1995. 79.50 (*0-89603-328-7*) Humana.

Nickoloff, Jac A. & Hoekstra, Merl F. DNA Damage & Repair Vol. II: DNA Repair in Higher Eukaryotes. LC 97-28562. (Contemporary Cancer Research Ser.). (Illus.). 656p. 1998. 125.00 (*0-89603-500-X*) Humana.

Nickoloff, Jac A. & Hoekstra, Merl F., eds. DNA Damage & Repair Vol. I: DNA Repair in Prokaryotes & Lower Eukaryotes. LC 97-28562. (Contemporary Cancer Research Ser.). (Illus.). 640p. 1998. 125.00 (*0-89603-356-2*) Humana.

Nickoloff, Jac A., jt. ed. see Hoekstra, Merl F.

Nickoloff, James B., ed. Gustavo Gutierrez: Essential Writings. LC 96-34927. (The Making Of Modern Theology Ser.). 320p. 1996. pap. 22.00 (*0-8006-3409-8*, 1-3409, Fortress Pr) Augsburg Fortress.

Nickols, Kevin, ed. see Stoutt, Glenn R. & Womack, Marvyn.

Nickon, A. The Organic Chemistry Name Game. 1987. 55.00 (*0-08-035549-8*, Pergamon Pr) Elsevier.

Nickrosz, John D., tr. see Heurtelou, Maude.

***Nicks, Dewey, photos by.** Kustom. (Illus.). 160p. 2000. 65.00 (*0-9672366-2-2*, Pub. by Greybull Pr) Dist Art Pubs.

Nicks, J. E. Cooking with Chef Dinosaur. Nicks, Mary, ed. LC 95-182727. (Illus.). 200p. 1995. pap. 11.95 (*0-9642743-6-1*) Jensen Pubng.

— Cost Estimating for Metal Stampers & Fabricators. Boesselager, Amy, ed. (Illus.). 152p. (Orig.). (C). 1993. pap. 33.00 (*1-881113-04-3*) Croydon Grp.

Nicks, Jensen E. BASIC Programming Solutions for Manufacturing. LC 82-137513. (Illus.). 297p. reprint ed. pap. 92.10 (*0-8357-6496-6*, 203586700097) Bks Demand.

Nicks, Mary, ed. see Nicks, J. E.

Nicks, Mel J., jt. auth. see Ortwerth, John.

Nickse, Ruth S., jt. auth. see Quezada, Shelley.

Nickson. Business Communications Made Simple. 200p. Date not set. pap. text 19.95 (*0-7506-2572-4*) Buttrwrth-Heinemann.

— Will Smith, Vol. 1. 160p. 1998. 4.99 (*0-312-96722-5*, Pub. by Tor Bks) St Martin.

Nickson & Siodons. Managing Projects Made Simple. 96p. Date not set. pap. text. write for info. (*0-7506-3471-5*) Buttrwrth-Heinemann.

Nickson, Chris. David Boreanaz. (Illus.). 160p. 1999. mass mkt. 4.99 (*0-312-97361-6*, St Martins Paperbacks) St Martin.

— Denzel Washington. LC 97-111104. 1996. mass mkt. 5.99 (*0-312-96043-3*) St Martin.

— Ewan Mcgregor. LC 99-204496. 256p. 1999. mass mkt. 5.99 (*0-312-96910-4*) St Martin.

— Go, Ricki! LC 95-94908. (Illus.). 216p. (Orig.). 1996. mass mkt. 5.50 (*0-380-78473-4*, Avon Bks) Morrow Avon.

— Lauryn Hill: She's Got That Thing. 2nd ed. LC 99-204511. (Illus.). 224+8p. 1999. mass mkt. 5.99 (*0-312-97210-5*) St Martin.

— Mariah Carey: Her Story. LC 95-9883. 1995. pap. 9.95 (*0-312-13121-6*) St Martin.

— Mariah Carey Revisited. LC 98-23938. 192p. 1998. pap. 11.95 (*0-312-19512-5*, St Martin Griffin) St Martin.

— Matt Damon: An Unauthorized Biography. LC 99-18745. (Illus.). 256p. 1999. pap. 16.95 (*1-58063-072-3*, Pub. by Renaissance) St Martin.

— Melissa Etheridge. LC 96-30621. (Illus.). 160p. 1997. pap. 11.95 (*0-312-15171-3*) St Martin.

— Superhero: A Biography of Christopher Reeve. LC 98-2680. 240p. 1998. text 22.95 (*0-312-19028-X*) St Martin.

— Superhero: An Unauthorized Biography of Christopher Reeve. 232p. 1999. mass mkt. 5.99 (*0-312-96980-5*) St Martin.

— The X-Factor: David Duchovny. LC 96-96459. 192p. 1996. mass mkt. 5.99 (*0-380-78851-9*, Avon Bks) Morrow Avon.

Nickson, Hilda. Now with His Love. large type ed. (Linford Romance Library). 317p. 1984. pap. 16.99 (*0-7089-6027-8*, Linford) Ulverscroft.

Nickson, Jeanne. Shadow of the Condor. 400p. (Orig.). 1994. mass mkt. 4.99 (*0-505-51975-5*, Love Spell) Dorchester Pub Co.

— Tears of the Moon. 464p. 1992. pap. text, mass mkt. 4.50 (*0-8439-3328-3*) Dorchester Pub Co.

Nickson, M. A. The British Library Guide to the Catalogues & Indexes of the Department of Manuscripts. 3rd rev. ed. LC 99-192566. 32p. 1998. write for info. (*0-7123-0660-9*, Pub. by B23tish Library) U of Toronto Pr.

***Nickson, Marilyn.** Teaching & Learning Mathematics: A Teacher's Guide to Recent Research. (Illus.). 2000. 74.95 (*0-304-70618-3*); pap. 31.95 (*0-304-70619-1*) Continuum.

Nickson, Noel, jt. auth. see Picken, Laurence.

Nickson, Noel J., jt. ed. see Picken, Laurence E. R.

Nickson, R. Andrew. Historical Dictionary of Paraguay. 2nd ed. (Latin American Historical Dictionaries Ser.: No. 24). (Illus.). 710p. 1992. 75.00 (*0-8108-2643-7*) Scarecrow.

— Local Government in Latin America. LC 94-43541. 250p. 1995. pap. text 55.00 (*1-55587-366-9*) L Rienner.

— Paraguay. LC 88-143693. (World Bibliographical Ser.: No. 84). 240p. 1988. lib. bdg. 45.00 (*1-85109-028-2*) ABC-CLIO.

***Nickson, R. Andrew.** Paraguay. rev. ed. (World Bibliographical Ser.: Vol. 84). 249p. 1999. 76.00 (*1-85109-320-6*) ABC-CLIO.

Nickul, Karl. The Skolt Lapp Community Suenjelsijd During the Year 1938. LC 77-87728. (Acta Lapponica Ser.: 5). (Illus.). 160p. 1983. reprint ed. 79.50 (*0-404-16504-4*) AMS Pr.

Nickum, James E. Dam Lies & Other Statistics: Taking the Measure of Irrigation in China, 1931-1991. LC 94-44338. (Occasional Papers: Vol. 18). 1995. write for info. (*0-86638-168-6*) EW Ctr HI.

— Water Management Organizations in the People's Republic of China. LC 80-5458. (China Book Project Ser.). (Illus.). 285p. reprint ed. pap. 88.40 (*0-608-18129-3*, 203278300081) Bks Demand.

Nickum, James E., ed. see Fourth Pacific Environmental Conference Staff.

NICL Editors, jt. auth. see Foster, Ramsey.

NICL Staff. Construction & Design Law Digest, July 1998. 85p. 1998. pap. 50.00 (*0-327-00278-6*, 5017415) LEXIS Pub.

— Construction & Design Law Digest, October 1998. 90p. 1998. pap. write for info. (*0-327-00590-4*, 5017715) LEXIS Pub.

NicLeodhas, Sorche. Always Room for One More. LC 65-12881. (Illus.). 32p. (J). (ps-2). 1995. 14.95 (*0-8050-0331-2*, Bks Young Read) H Holt & Co.

Nicod, J., et al, eds. Geomorphology & Geoecology, Karst Vol. 7: Proceedings of the Second International Conference on Geomorphology, Frankfurt/Main, 1989. (Zeitschrift fuer Geomorphologie - Annals of Geomorphology Ser.: Supplementband 85). (Illus.). vi, 144p. 1992. pap. 49.00 (*3-443-21085-6*, Pub. by Gebruder Borntraeger) Balogh.

Nicod, Pascal, jt. auth. see Peterson, Kirk L.

Nicodemi, F., ed. Scientific Highlights in Memory of Leon Van Hove, Napoli, Italy, October 25-26, 1991. LC 93-17108. (Twentieth Century Physics Ser.: Vol. 2). 180p. 1993. text 67.00 (*981-02-1399-9*) World Scientific Pub.

Nicodemi, Olympia. Discrete Math. Date not set. pap. text, student ed. write for info. (*0-314-59201-6*) West Pub.

Nicogossian, Arnauld E. & Pool, Sam L. Space Physiology & Medicine. 4th ed. 600p. text 110.00 (*0-683-30731-2*) Lppncott W & W.

Nicogossian, Arnauld E., et al. Space Physiology & Medicine. 3rd ed. (Illus.). 481p. 1994. text 95.00 (*0-8121-1595-3*) Lppncott W & W.

Nicol, Adelheid A. M. & Pexman, Penny. Presenting Your Findings: A Practical Guide for Creating Tables. LC 99-24966. 157p. 1999. pap. 14.95 (*1-55798-593-6*, 431-621A) Am Psychol.

Nicol, Andrew & Rogers, Heather. Changing Contempt of Court. (C). 1988. 21.00 (*0-901108-92-8*, Pub. by NCCL) St Mut.

Nicol, Ann. Fun Cakes for Special Occasions. (Illus.). 112p. 1997. pap. 15.95 (*1-85368-586-0*, Pub. by New5 Holland) Sterling.

Nicol, Arthur R., ed. Longitudinal Studies in Child Psychology & Psychiatry: Practical Lessons from Research Experience. LC 84-11802. (Wiley Series on Studies in Child Psychiatry). 423p. reprint ed. pap. 131.20 (*0-8357-4945-2*, 203787600009) Bks Demand.

Nicol, Brad. Alaska Resource Guide. large type ed. (Retirement & Relocation Guide Ser.). (Illus.). 350p. Date not set. pap. 24.95 (*1-56559-114-3*) HGI-Over Fifty.

— British Columbia Retirement & Relocation Guide. large type ed. (Retirement & Relocation Guides Ser.). (Illus.). 350p. Date not set. pap. 24.95 (*1-56559-113-5*) HGI-Over Fifty.

Nicol, Brad & Swope, Wendy. Idaho Retirement & Relocation Guide. large type ed. (Retirement & Relocation Guides Ser.). (Illus.). 350p. Date not set. pap. 24.95 (*1-56559-110-0*) HGI-Over Fifty.

Nicol, Bruce. Canterbury Tales Notes. (Cliffs Notes Ser.). 80p. 1964. pap. 4.95 (*0-8220-0292-2*, Cliff) IDG Bks.

— Wind of Chance. 178p. (C). 1989. text 45.00 (*0-946270-98-8*, Pub. by Pentland Pr) St Mut.

Nicol, Charles & Barabtarlo, Gennady, eds. A Small Alpine Form: Studies in Nabokov's Short Fiction. LC 92-22715. 264p. 1992. text 15.00 (*0-8153-0857-4*, H1580) Garland.

Nicol, David & Fujimoto, Richard, eds. Conference on Distributed Simulation, 1990. (Simulation Ser.: Vol. 22, No. 1). 230p. 1990. 50.00 (*0-911801-62-6*, SS22-1) Soc Computer Sim.

***Nicol, David & Pilling, Simon.** Changing Architectural Education: Towards a New Professionalism. LC 00-23887. 2000. pap. write for info. (*0-419-25920-1*, E & FN Spon) Routledge.

Nicol, Davidson, et al, eds. Regionalism & the New International Economic Order: Studies Presented to the UNITAR-CEESTEM Club of Rome Conference at the United Nations. LC 80-23706. (Policy Studies on International Development). 448p. 1981. pap. text 46.00 (*0-08-026331-3*, Pergamon Pr) Elsevier.

Nicol, Donald M. The Byzantine Lady: Ten Portraits, 1250-1500. LC 93-35728. (Illus.). 153p. (C). 1994. text 39.95 (*0-521-45531-6*) Cambridge U Pr.

— The Byzantine Lady: Ten Portraits, 1250-1500. (Canto Book Ser.). (Illus.). 168p. (C). 1996. pap. 10.95 (*0-521-57623-7*) Cambridge U Pr.

— Byzantium & Venice. (Illus.). 479p. (C). 1992. pap. text 29.95 (*0-521-42894-7*) Cambridge U Pr.

— The Immortal Emperor: The Life & Legend of Constantine Palaiologos, Last Emperor of the Romans. (Canto Book Ser.). (Illus.). 164p. (C). 1994. pap. 10.95 (*0-521-46717-9*) Cambridge U Pr.

— The Last Centuries of Byzantium, 1261-1453. 2nd ed. LC 92-46203. (Illus.). 483p. (C). 1993. text 89.95 (*0-521-43384-3*); pap. text 29.95 (*0-521-43991-4*) Cambridge U Pr.

— The Reluctant Emperor: A Biography of John Cantacuzene, Byzantine Emperor & Monk c. 1295-1383. (Illus.). 217p. (C). 1996. text 44.95 (*0-521-55256-7*) Cambridge U Pr.

— Studies in Late Byzantine History & Prosopography. (Collected Studies: No. CS242). (Illus.). 330p. (C). 1986. reprint ed. lib. bdg. 115.95 (*0-86078-190-9*, Pub. by Variorum) Ashgate Pub Co.

Nicol, Donald M., ed. & tr. see Spandounes, Theodore.

Nicol, E. R., compiled by. Common Names of Plants in New Zealand. LC 98-140377. (Landcare Research Science Ser.). 115p. 1997. pap. 29.95 (*0-478-09310-1*, Pub. by Manaaki Whenua) Balogh.

***Nicol, Elisabeth.** 50 Jahre Danach: Psychisches Trauma Aus der Zeit des Deutschen Nationalsozialismus und Dessen Folgen am Beispiel Nordostdeutscher Frauen der Damaligen Zivilbevolkerung. (Europaische Hochschulschriften Ser.: Reihe 6). (GER.). ix, 307p. 1999. 48.95 (*3-631-35175-5*) P Lang Pubng.

Nicol, Eric. Dickens of the Mounted. 296p. 1996. mass mkt. 6.95 (*0-7710-6808-5*) McCland & Stewart.

***Nicol, Eric.** When Nature Calls: Life at a Gulf Island Cottage. 198p. 1999. 28.95 (*1-55017-210-7*) Harbour Pub Co.

Nicol, F., jt. auth. see Rudge, Janet.

Nicol, G. T. Flex: The Lexical Scanner Generator, Edition 103 for Version 2.3.7. 124p. 1993. spiral bd. 20.00 (*1-882114-21-3*) Free Software.

***Nicol, Gloria.** The Complete Book of Candles. 2000. 35.00 (*0-7548-0276-0*) Anness Pub.

— Complete Book of Candles & Candle-making: Creative Ideas for Making, Using & Displaying Cand. 1999. 19.98 (*1-84038-401-8*) Hermes Hse.

Nicol, Gloria. The Linen Cupboard. (Illus.). 80p. 1998. 19.95 (*1-57076-115-9*, Trafalgar Sq Pub) Trafalgar.

— The New Candle Book: Inspirational Ideas for Displaying, Using & Making Candles. (Illus.). 160p. 1995. 30.00 (*1-85967-066-0*, Lorenz Bks) Anness Pub.

— The New Candle Kit. (Illus.). 160p. 1996. 32.50 (*1-85967-166-7*, Lorenz Bks) Anness Pub.

Nicol, Gloria & Evans, Hazel. The Herb Basket: Basil, Bay & Borage. 61p. 1996. write for info. (*1-57215-108-0*) World Pubns.

— The Herb Basket: Lavender, Lovage & Lemongrass. 61p. 1996. write for info. (*1-57215-110-2*) World Pubns.

— The Herb Basket: Marjoram, Mint & Marigold. 61p. 1996. write for info. (*1-57215-109-9*) World Pubns.

— The Herb Basket: Rosemary, Rue & Rose. 61p. 1996. write for info. (*1-57215-111-0*) World Pubns.

— The Herb Basket: Sage, Sorrel & Savory. 61p. 1996. write for info. (*1-57215-113-7*) World Pubns.

— The Herb Basket: Thyme, Tansy & Tarragon. 61p. 1996. write for info. (*1-57215-112-9*) World Pubns.

Nicol, Gloria, jt. auth. see Schneebeli-Morrell, Deborah.

***Nicol, H. Gilbert.** Families of Wanlockhead: A Profile of a Lead Mining Village in 19th Century Scotland. x, 355p. 1999. pap. 25.00 (*0-9672099-0-0*) Locin Pr.

Nicol, Iain G., ed. Schleiermacher & Feminism: Sources, Evaluations, & Responses. LC 92-26504. (Schleiermacher Studies & Translations: Vol. 12). 140p. 1992. text 69.95 (*0-7734-9587-8*) E Mellen.

Nicol, Iain G., tr. see Schleiermacher, Friedrich Daniel Ernst.

Nicol, J. A. The Eyes of Fishes. (Illus.). 328p. 1989. 90.00 (*0-19-857195-X*) OUP.

Nicol, Jim. Golf Resorts: Where to Play in the U. S. A., Canada, Mexico & the Caribbean. 2nd ed. 1998. pap. text 16.95 (*1-55650-815-8*) Hunter NJ.

Nicol, Jodi. Silken Chains. 256p. (Orig.). 1997. mass mkt. 5.95 (*0-352-33143-7*, Pub. by BLA4) London Brdge.

Nicol, Kenneth J., ed. Agricultural Development Planning in Thailand. LC 81-18593. (Illus.). 342p. 1982. reprint ed. pap. 106.10 (*0-608-00024-8*, 206079000006) Bks Demand.

Nicol, Kimberly A., jt. auth. see Workman, Michelle L.

Nicol, M. L. Arabians, from the Camera of Johnny Johnston. (Illus.). v, 84p. 1999. 45.00 (*0-9668521-0-9*) Boldheart Pubns.

Nicol, Maggie, jt. auth. see Dacre, Jane.

Nicol, Margaret. Enemy of the Average. LC 98-13283. 622p. 1997. 25.00 (*1-888310-60-X*) A A Knoll Pubs.

Nicol, Michelle. Ugo Rondinone: Heyday. 1996. 40.00 (*3-9520497-5-1*, Pub. by Memory-Cage) Dist Art Pubs.

Nicol, Mike. Horseman. 1996. pap. 12.00 (*0-679-76039-3*, Evrymans Lib Childs) Knopf.

— On South Africa. 1999. pap. 13.00 (*0-679-78095-5*) Vin Bks.

— This Day & Age. LC 92-53054. 288p. 1995. pap. 11.00 (*0-679-74200-X*) Random.

Nicol, N. Douglas. Standard Catalog of German Coins, 1601-Present. 2nd ed. Bruce, Colin R., 2nd, ed. LC 93-77549. (Illus.). 1064p. 1998. pap. 59.00 (*0-87341-644-9*, GE02) Krause Pubns.

Nicol, Nancy M. & Walker, Stanley, eds. Basic Management for Staff Nurses: A Companion to Practice. 176p. (C). 1991. pap. text 28.00 (*0-412-35520-5*, A5239) Chapman & Hall.

Nicol, Rosemary. Irritable Bowel Syndrome: A Natural Approach. 2nd rev. ed. (The Natural Approach Health Ser.). 256p. (Orig.). 1999. pap. 13.95 (*1-56975-188-9*) Ulysses Pr.

Nicol, Stewart H. A Book of Saints. 142p. 1993. pap. 40.00 (*0-7152-0693-1*) St Mut.

Nicola. Smalltalk. (C). 2000. pap. text 39.00 (*0-13-206145-7*) P-H.

Nicola, Jill, jt. auth. see Coad, Peter.

Nicola, Lisa W. Summer Suns Risin' Date not set. 15.95 (*0-8050-4914-2*, Bks Young Read) H Holt & Co.

Nicola-McLaughlin, Andree, jt. ed. see Braxton, Joanne.

Nicola, Michel. Arabic Key Reader - Thousand & One Nights: (English - Arabic), Bk. 1. (ARA & ENG.). 58p. 1986. pap. 14.95 incl. audio (*0-86685-371-5*) Intl Bk Ctr.

Nicola, Nicos A., ed. Guidebook to Cytokines & Their Receptors. (Illus.). 276p. 1995. pap. text 45.00 (*0-19-859946-3*); bds. 85.00 (*0-19-859947-1*) OUP.

Nicola, Nicos A., et al. Theories of Mimesis. (Literature, Culture, Theory Ser.: No. 12). 200p. (C). 1995. pap. text 19.95 (*0-521-45856-0*) Cambridge U Pr.

Nicola, Nicos A., jt. auth. see Metcalf, Donald.

***Nicola, P. C.** Mainstream Mathematical Economics in the 20th Century. (Illus.). xx, 521p. 2000. 92.00 (*3-540-67084-X*) Spr-Verlag.

Nicola, Pier C. Imperfect General Equilibrium: The Economy As an Evolutionary Process, Individualistic, Discrete, Deterministic. (Lecture Notes in Economics & Mathematical Systems Ser.). 1994. 47.95 (*0-387-58102-2*) Spr-Verlag.

Nicola, S. De, see De Martino, S.

Nicolacopoulos, Pantelis, ed. Greek Studies in the Philosophy & History of Science. 428p. (C). 1990. lib. bdg. 218.00 (*0-7923-0717-8*, Pub. by Kluwer Academic) Kluwer Academic.

Nicolacopoulos, Toula & Vassilacopoulos, George. Hegel & the Logical Structure of Love: An Essay on Sexualities, Family & the Law. LC 98-74632. (Series in Philosophy). 1p. 1999. text 61.95 (*1-85972-657-7*) Ashgate Pub Co.

Nicolae, Petre. CMEA in Theory & Practice. Jones, Steven, ed. 90p. (Orig.). 1984. pap. text 75.00 (*1-55831-032-0*) Delphic Associates.

Nicolaeff, Ariadne, tr. see Arbuzov, Aleksei.

Nicolaeff, Ariadne, tr. see Turgenev, Ivan Sergeevich.

Nicolaenko, B., et al, eds. Nonlinear Systems of Partial Differential Equations in Applied Mathematics, 2 pts., Pt. I. LC 85-15107. (Lectures in Applied Mathematics: Vol. 23). 470p. 1986. text 61.00 (*0-8218-1125-8*, LAM/23.1) Am Math.

— Nonlinear Systems of Partial Differential Equations in Applied Mathematics, 2 pts., Pt. II. LC 85-15107. (Lectures in Applied Mathematics: Vol. 23). 387p. 1986. text 61.00 (*0-8218-1126-6*, LAM/23.2) Am Math.

— Nonlinear Systems of Partial Differential Equations in Applied Mathematics, 2 pts., Set. LC 85-15107. (Lectures in Applied Mathematics: Vol. 23). 858p. 1986. text 101.00 (*0-8218-1123-1*, LAM/23) Am Math.

Nicolaescu, Liviu I. Generalized Symplectic Geometries & the Index of Families of Elliptic Problems. LC 97-12292. (Memoirs of the American Mathematical Society Ser.: Vol. 128, No. 609). 81p. 1997. pap. 36.00 (*0-8218-0621-1*, MEMO/128/609) Am Math.

— Lectures on the Geometry of Manifolds. LC 96-28020. 450p. 1996. write for info. (*981-02-2836-8*) World Scientific Pub.

Nicolai, Christoph F., et al, eds. Bibliothek der Schonen Wissenschaften und der Freyen Kunste, 12 vols. in 6, Set. 1979. reprint ed. write for info. (*3-487-06659-9*) G Olms Pubs.

Nicolai, D. Miles. The Summer the Flowers Had No Scent. (Illus.). (J). 1978. pap. 2.75 (*0-933992-00-9*) Coffee Break.

— The Summer the Flowers Had No Scent. 3rd ed. (Color-A-Story Ser.). (Illus.). 28p. (J). (gr. 3-5). 1977. pap. 2.75 (*0-933992-19-X*) Coffee Break.

Nicolai, Friedrich. Gesammelte Werke. (GER.). 614p. 1997. reprint ed. 145.00 (*3-487-07578-4*) G Olms Pubs.

— Gesammelte Werke Bd. II: Beschreibung der Koeniglichen Residenzstaedte Berlin und Postdamm, 1769. (GER.). 1988. reprint ed. write for info. (*3-487-07579-2*) G Olms Pubs.

— Gesammelte Werke Bd. III: Das Leben und die Meinungen das Herm Magister Sebaldus Nothanker. (GER.). 1988. reprint ed. write for info. (*3-487-07580-6*) G Olms Pubs.

— Gesammelte Werke Bd. V: Versuch Ueber die Beschuldigungen Welche Dem Tempelherrenorden Gemacht Worden. (GER.). 1988. reprint ed. write for info. (*3-487-07582-2*) G Olms Pubs.

— Gesammelte Werke Bd. VI: Nachricht von den Baumeistern, Bildhauern, Kupferstechern, Malern, Stukkateuren, und Andern Kuestlern. (GER.). 1987. reprint ed. write for info. (*3-487-07583-0*) G Olms Pubs.

— Gesammelte Werke Bd. VII: Anekdoten von Koenig Friedrich II. von Preussen, 1788-1792. (GER.). 1985. reprint ed. write for info. (*3-487-07584-9*) G Olms Pubs.

— Gesammelte Werke Bd. VIII: Fragment Ueber Friedrich Den Grossen, 1791-92. (GER.). 1985. reprint ed. write for info. (*3-487-07585-7*) G Olms Pubs.

— Gesammelte Werke Bd. IX: Geschichte Eines Dicken Mannes, 1794. (GER.). 1987. reprint ed. write for info. (*3-487-07586-5*) G Olms Pubs.

— Gesammelte Werke Bd. X: Leben und Meinungen Sempronius Gundibert's, eines Deutschen Philosophen, 1798. x, 587p. 1987. reprint ed. write for info. (*3-487-07587-3*) G Olms Pubs.

— Gesammelte Werke Bd. XI: Philosophische Abhandlungen, 1808. (GER.). xii, 519p. 1991. write for info. (*3-487-07588-1*) G Olms Pubs.

— Gesammelte Werke Bd. XII: Opera Minora I, 1760 - 1788. (GER.). liv, 590p. 1995. reprint ed. write for info. (*3-487-07589-X*) G Olms Pubs.

— Gesammelte Werke Bd. XIII: Opera Minora II, 1789-1792. (GER.). xxxiv, 572p. 1995. reprint ed. write for info. (*3-487-07590-3*) G Olms Pubs.

— Gesammelte Werke Bd. XIV: Opera Minora III, 1797-1810. (GER.). xxxii, 562p. 1995. reprint ed. write for info. (*3-487-07591-1*) G Olms Pubs.

— Gesammelte Werke Bd. XV: Beschreibung Einer Reise Durch Deutschland und die Schweiz Im Jahre, 1781. (GER.). cccxlvi, 5825p. 1994. reprint ed. write for info. (*3-487-07592-X*) G Olms Pubs.

— Gesammelte Werke Bd. XVI: Beschreibung Einer Reise Durch Deutschland und die Schweiz Im Jahre, 1781. (GER.). cccxlvi, 5825p. 1994. reprint ed. write for info. (*3-487-07593-8*) G Olms Pubs.

— Gesammelte Werke Bd. XVII: Beschreibung Einer Reise Durch Deutschland und die Schweiz Im Jahre, 1781. (GER.). cccxlvi, 5825p. 1994. reprint ed. write for info. (*3-487-07594-6*) G Olms Pubs.

An Asterisk (*) at the beginning of an entry indicates that the title is appearing for the first time.

— Gesammelte Werke Bd. XVIII: Beschreibung Einer Reise Durch Deutschland und die Schweiz Im Jahre, 1781. (GER.). cccxlvi, 5825p. 1994. reprint ed. write for info. (*3-487-07595-4*) G Olms Pubs.

— Gesammelte Werke Bd. XIX: Beschreibung Einer Reise Durch Deutschland und die Schweiz Im Jahre, 1781. (GER.). cccxlvi, 5825p. 1994. reprint ed. write for info. (*3-487-07596-2*) G Olms Pubs.

— Gesammelte Werke Bd. XX: Beschreibung Einer Reise Durch Deutschland und die Schweiz Im Jahre, 1781. (GER.). cccxlvi, 5825p. 1994. reprint ed. write for info. (*3-487-09752-4*) G Olms Pubs.

— Gessamelte Werke Bd. XXXI: Leopold Friedrich Guenther von Goeckingk, Friedrich Nicolais Leben und Literarischer Nachlass. (GER.). vi, 207p. 1997. reprint ed. write for info. (*3-487-10154-8*) G Olms Pubs.

Nicolai, Friedrich, ed. Allgemeine Deutsche Bibliothek, 118 vols. reprint ed. write for info. (*0-318-71727-1*) G Olms Pubs.

Nicolai, Friedrich, jt. auth. see Von Thummel, Moritz A.

Nicolai, Friedrich, ed. see Briefe.

Nicolai, J., et al. Birds. (Illus.). 253p. 1994. pap. 14.95 (*0-00-219995-5*, Pub. by HarpC) Trafalgar.

Nicolai, Margaret. Kitaq Goes Ice Fishing. LC 98-17335. (Illus.). 32p. (J). (ps-2). 1998. 15.95 (*0-88240-504-7*, Alaska NW Bks) Gr Arts Ctr Pub.

Nicolai, Marie, jt. auth. see Jones, Loddie.

Nicolai-Mazery, Christiane de, see de Nicolai-Mazery, Christiane.

***Nicolai, Michelle M.** Interlingua World Business Internet Research Guide: The Definitive Guide to World Business Internet Resources. LC 99-67182. 2000. pap. 45.00 (*1-891628-01-1*) Interlingua Pubns.

Nicolai, Michelle M. Multilingual International Trade Term Lexicon: Over 7,000 International Trade Terms Entries in 6 Languages. LC 97-80767. 792p. 1998. 95.00 (*1-891628-00-3*) Interlingua Pubns.

Nicolaides, A., jt. auth. see Belcaro, G.

Nicolaides, Andrew N. & Novo, Salvatore. Advances in Vascular Pathology 1997: Selected Papers from the European Congress of Angiology, 11th Meeting of the European Chapter, EUROCHAP '97, Rome 23-26, October 1997, Vol. 115. LC 97-41394. (International Congress Ser.). 194p. 1997. 158.00 (*0-444-82833-8*) Elsevier.

Nicolaides, Andrew N. & Salmasi, Abdul-Majeed, eds. Diagnosis, Assessment & Management. (Developments in Cardiovascular Medicine Ser.). (C). 1991. text 249.00 (*0-7923-1188-4*) Kluwer Academic.

Nicolaides, Andrew N. & Yao, James S., eds. Investigation of Vascular Disorders. LC 81-6194. (Illus.). 649p. reprint ed. pap. 200.00 (*0-7837-2589-2*, 204275100006) Bks Demand.

Nicolaides, Andrew N., jt. ed. see Salmasi, Abdul-Majeed.

Nicolaides, Anthony. Algebra, No. 111. (C). 1990. pap. 39.95 (*1-872684-13-0*, Pub. by P A S S Pubns) St Mut.

— Analytical Mathematics, No. 11. (C). 1990. pap. 39.95 (*1-872684-14-9*, Pub. by P A S S Pubns) St Mut.

— Calculus, No. 111. (C). 1990. pap. 39.95 (*1-872684-12-2*, Pub. by P A S S Pubns) St Mut.

— Coordinate Geometry. 240p. 1994. 45.00 (*1-872684-04-1*, Pub. by P A S S Pubns) St Mut.

— Electrical & Electronic Principles, No. 11. (C). 1990. pap. 39.95 (*1-872684-10-6*, Pub. by P A S S Pubns) St Mut.

— Integral Calculus & Applications. 432p. 1994. 59.00 (*1-872684-09-2*, Pub. by P A S S Pubns) St Mut.

— Mathematics, No. 11. (C). 1990. pap. 39.95 (*1-872684-11-4*, Pub. by P A S S Pubns) St Mut.

— Pure Mathematics: Algebra. (C). 1990. pap. 39.95 (*1-872684-01-7*, Pub. by P A S S Pubns) St Mut.

— Pure Mathematics: Cartesianand Polar Curve Sketching. (C). 1990. pap. 50.00 (*1-872684-06-8*, Pub. by P A S S Pubns) St Mut.

— Pure Mathematics: Complex Numbers. (C). 1990. pap. 50.00 (*1-872684-00-9*, Pub. by P A S S Pubns) St Mut.

— Pure Mathematics: Differential Calculus & Applications. (C). 1990. pap. 45.00 (*1-872684-08-4*, Pub. by P A S S Pubns) St Mut.

— Pure Mathematics: Trigonometry. (C). 1990. pap. 39.95 (*1-872684-02-5*, Pub. by P A S S Pubns) St Mut.

— Vectors. 224p. (C). 1994. pap. 45.00 (*1-872684-03-3*, Pub. by P A S S Pubns) St Mut.

Nicolaides, C. A., et al, eds. Atoms in Strong Fields. LC 89-48928. (NATO ASI Ser.: Vol. 212). (Illus.). 550p. (C). 1990. text 174.00 (*0-306-43414-8*, Kluwer Plenum) Kluwer Academic.

Nicolaides, Cleanthes A. & Beck, Donald R., eds. Excited States in Quantum Chemistry. (NATO Advanced Study Institutes Series C, Mathematical & Physical Sciences: No. 46). 1978. text 184.00 (*90-277-0961-0*) Kluwer Academic.

Nicolaides, Cleanthes A., jt. ed. see Bitsakis, Eftichios.

***Nicolaides, K. H., et al, eds.** The 11-14 Week Scan: The Diagnosis of Fetal Abnormalities. LC 99-52488. (Diploma in Fetal Medicine Ser.). (Illus.). 250p. 2000. 65.00 (*1-85070-743-X*) Prthnon Pub.

***Nicolaides, K. H. & Rizzo, G.** Placental & Fetal Doppler. LC 00-25526. (Diploma in Fetal Medicine Ser.). (Illus.). 224p. 2000. 65.00 (*1-85070-757-X*) Prthnon Pub.

Nicolaides, K. H., jt. ed. see Snijders, R. J.

Nicolaides, K. H., jt. ed. see Thorpe Beeston, J. G.

Nicolaides, Kimon. Natural Way to Draw: A Working Plan for Art Study, 001. (Illus.). 1975. pap. 8.95 (*0-395-20548-4*) HM.

Nicolaides, Kimon. Natural Way to Draw: A Working Plan for Art Study. 240p. 1990. pap. 15.00 (*0-395-53007-5*) HM.

Nicolaides, Kypros H., jt. ed. see Pilu, Gianluigi.

Nicolaides, L., et al. Food Safety & the Developing World. 1998. pap. 60.00 (*0-85954-493-1*, Pub. by Nat Res Inst) St Mut.

Nicolaides, Lou. Cafe U. S. A. Where to Go for the Best Cup of Joe: Your Ultimate Annual Guide to Massachusetts. 1994. pap. 12.95 (*0-9637060-1-2*) Ludwig CA.

— Cafe U. S. A. Where to Go for the Best Cup of Joe: Your Ultimate Annual Guide to the Coffee State. 1994. pap. 11.95 (*0-9637060-2-0*) Ludwig CA.

Nicolaides, Louis. Caffe' L.A. The Coffeehouse Directory for L.A. County. 1993. pap. 9.95 (*0-9637060-0-4*) Ludwig CA.

— Caffe U. S. A. Ventura, Santa Barbara & Central Coast Edition; Your Ultimate Guide to the Coffee. 1994. pap. 12.95 (*0-9637060-3-9*) Ludwig CA.

Nicolaides, Phedon, ed. Industrial Policy in the European Community: A Necessary Response to Economic Integration? LC 92-41377. 148p. (C). 1993. lib. bdg. 95.50 (*0-7923-2084-0*) Kluwer Academic.

Nicolaides, Roy A. & Walkington, Noel J. Maple: A Comprehensive Introduction. (Illus.). 485p. 1996. text 42.95 (*0-521-56230-9*) Cambridge U Pr.

Nicolaides, Roy A., jt. ed. see Gunzburger, Max D.

Nicolaidis. Cultural Determinants of Corporate Excellence. 59.95 (*1-84014-369-X*) Ashgate Pub Co.

Nicolaidis, Kalypso, jt. ed. see Allison, Graham T.

Nicolaidis, Kalypso, jt. ed. see Bressand, Albert.

Nicolaidis, Michael & Zorian, Yervant. On-Line Testing. LC 98-2694. 1998. 125.00 (*0-7923-8132-7*) Kluwer Academic.

Nicolaidis, Stylianos, ed. New Perspectives on the Treatment of Obesity & Redux: A Comprehensive Overview. LC 96-36686. (Illus.). 150p. 1996. pap. text 36.00 (*0-12-518170-1*) Acad Pr.

Nicolais, Luigi, et al, eds. Polymers in Medicine II: Biomedical & Pharmaceutical Applications. (Polymer Science & Technology Ser.: Vol. 34). 440p. 1986. 105.00 (*0-306-42390-1*, Plenum Trade) Perseus Pubng.

Nicolaisen, Jay. Italian Opera in Transition, 1871-1893. LC 80-22512. (Studies in Musicology: No. 31). 324p. reprint ed. pap. 100.50 (*0-8357-1121-8*, 207022400064) Bks Demand.

Nicolaisen, W. F., ed. Oral Tradition in the Middle Ages: Selected Papers from the 1988 CEMERS Conference. LC 93-14340. (Medieval & Renaissance Texts & Studies: Vol. 112). (Illus.). 240p. 1995. 24.00 (*0-86698-165-9*, MR112) MRTS.

Nicolaison, Ida, jt. auth. see Nicolaison, Johannes.

Nicolaison, Johannes & Nicolaison, Ida. The Pastoral Tuareg: Ecology, Culture, & Society, 2 vols. LC 96-61101. (Carlsberg Nomad Ser.). (Illus.). 800p. 1997. 70.00 (*0-614-22210-9*) Thames Hudson.

Nicolaou, K. C. & Sorensen, E. J. Classics in Total Synthesis. LC 95-51360. 798p. 1996. 135.00 (*3-527-29284-5*, Wiley-VCH); pap. 71.00 (*3-527-29231-4*, Wiley-VCH) Wiley.

Nicolaou, Kyriakos. The Historical Topography of Kition. (Studies in Mediterranean Archaeology: Vol. XLIII). (Illus.). 442p. (Orig.). 1976. pap. 65.00 (*91-85058-64-5*, Pub. by P Astroms) Coronet Bks.

Nicolaou, M. L. & Andreadakis, A. D., eds. The Pollution of the Mediterranean Sea: Selected Proceedings of the International Symposium on Pollution of the Mediterranean Sea, Held in Nicosia, Cyprus, 2-4 November, 1994. (Water Science & Technology Ser.). 368p. 1996. pap. text 109.25 (*0-08-042885-1*, Pergamon Pr) Elsevier.

Nicolaou-Smokoviti, Litsa & Bruyn, Severyn T. International Issues in Social Economy: Studies in the United States & Greece. LC 88-3525. 375p. 1989. 85.00 (*0-275-92518-8*, C2518, Praeger Pubs) Greenwood.

Nicolaou-Smokoviti, Litsa & Szell, Gyorgy, eds. Participation, Organizational Effectiveness & Quality of Work Life in the Year 2000. LC 94-43952. (Illus.). 456p. 1994. pap. 57.95 (*3-631-47924-7*) P Lang Pubng.

Nicolaou, Stephane. Flying Boats & Seaplanes: A History from 1905. LC TL684.N53 1998. (Illus.). 192p. 1998. 39.95 (*0-7603-0621-4*) MBI Pubg.

Nicolas & Rodrigues. Dictionnaire Economique, Juridique. (FRE.). 1998. 350.00 (*0-320-00374-4*) Fr & Eur.

Nicolas, A. The Mid-Oceanic Ridges: Mountains below Sea Level. (Geology, Tectonics, Structural Geology, Oceanographic Science Geochemistry, Volcanology). (Illus.). 192p. 1995. 43.95 (*0-387-57380-1*) Spr-Verlag.

Nicolas, Adolphe. Principles of Rock Deformation. 1987. pap. text 66.00 (*90-277-2369-9*) Kluwer Academic.

Nicolas, Adolphe, jt. auth. see Poirier, Jean-Paul.

Nicolas, D. French-English - English-French Vocabulary of Genetic Engineering & Molelcular Biology. (ENG & FRE.). 100p. 1990. pap. 24.00 (*2-85608-035-9*) IBD Ltd.

Nicolas, Francoise, jt. auth. see Thomsen, Stephen.

Nicolas, G., et al. Wirtschaft - Auf Deutsch: Lehr-/Arbeitsbuch. (GER.). 326p. (C). 1991. pap. text 38.00 (*3-12-675215-2*, Pub. by Klett Edition) Intl Bk Import.

— Wirtschaft - Auf Deutsch: Lehrerhandbuch. (GER.). 168p. (C). 1992. pap. text 26.25 (*3-12-675216-0*, Pub. by Klett Edition) Intl Bk Import.

Nicolas, G., jt. auth. see Macaire, D.

***Nicolas, Harris.** A Treatise on the Law of Adulterine Bastardy with a Report of the Banbury Case & of All Other Cases Bearing upon the Subject, 1 vol. xvi, 588p. 2000. reprint ed. 180.00 (*1-56169-631-5*) Gaunt.

Nicolas, Harris, ed. see Chaucer, Geoffrey.

Nicolas, John F. Complete Cookbook of American Fish & Shellfish. 1990. text 52.95 (*0-442-23504-6*, VNR) Wiley.

Nicolas, John F. The Complete Cookbook of American Fish & Shellfish. 2nd ed. 480p. 1989. 52.95 (*0-471-28886-1*, VNR) Wiley.

Nicolas, John F. The Professional Chef's Art of Garde Manger. 5th ed. LC 92-23801. (Illus.). 286p. 1993. text 49.95 (*0-442-01153-9*, VNR) Wiley.

Nicolas, Jules Emile. Replica. LC 98-83086. 340p. 2000. pap. 17.25 (*0-88739-239-3*) Creat Arts Bk.

Nicolas, S. Dictionnaire Prosopographique: Derniers Maitres Ancien Regime. (FRE.). 1998. 79.95 (*0-320-00261-6*) Fr & Eur.

Nicolau, Alexander. Languages & Compilers for Parallel Computing: 5th International Workshop, New Haven, Connecticut, August 1992. Banerjee, Uptal et al, eds. (Lecture Notes in Computer Science Ser.: Vol. 757). xi, 576p. 1993. 78.00 (*0-387-57502-2*) Spr-Verlag.

Nicolau, Alexander, ed. see Banerjee, Uptal, et al.

Nicolau, C. Experimental Methods in Biophysical Chemistry. LC 72-5720. 703p. reprint ed. 200.00 (*0-8357-9888-7*, 201615500098) Bks Demand.

Nicolau, George, et al. Arbitration, 1997: The Next Fifty Years (50th NAA Proceedings), 2-2-2. Najita, Joyce M., ed. 341p. 1998. 40.00 (*1-57018-093-8*) BNA Books.

***Nicolaus, Knut.** Restoration of Paintings, 1. 1999. 39.95 (*3-89508-922-2*) Konemann.

***Nicolaus, Marty, ed.** Keepers: Voices of Secular Recovery. 224p. 1999. pap. 12.00 (*0-9659429-1-0*) LifeRing Pr.

Nicolaus of Cusa. The Catholic Concordance. Sigmund, Paul E., ed. (Cambridge Texts in the History of Political Thought Ser.). 375p. 1992. text 69.95 (*0-521-40207-7*) Cambridge U Pr.

Nicolaus of Damascus. Nicolaus Damascenus de Plantis: Five Translations. Lulofs, H. J. Drossaart & Poortman, E. L., eds. (Verhandelingen der Koninklijke Nederlandse Akademie van Wetenschappen, Afd. Letterkunde, Nieuwe Reeks Ser.: No. 139). 732p. 103.25 (*0-444-85703-6*) Elsevier.

Nicolay. Fluidized Bed Systems. 1983. text 126.50 (*90-277-1616-1*) Kluwer Academic.

Nicolay, Carol & Barrette, Judith. Assembling Course Materials: A Trainer's Action Guide. 128p. (C). 1992. pap. 39.95 (*0-89397-415-3*) Nichols Pub.

Nicolay, D., jt. ed. see Ouden, Den C.

Nicolay, Helen. Lincoln's Secretary: A Biography of John G. Nicolay. LC 70-138169. (Illus.). 363p. 1971. reprint ed. lib. bdg. 65.00 (*0-8371-5626-2*, NILS, Greenwood Pr) Greenwood.

Nicolay, John G. The Outbreak of Rebellion. (Illus.). 246p. 1995. pap. 12.95 (*0-306-80657-6*) Da Capo.

***Nicolay, John G. & Burlingame, Michael.** With Lincoln in the White House: Letters, Memoranda & Other Writings of John G. Nicolay, 1860-1865. LC 99-86598. 2000. write for info. (*0-8093-2332-X*) S Ill U Pr.

Nicolay, Nicolas De, see De Nicolay, Nicolas.

Nicolay, Theresa F., et al. Gender Roles, Literary Authority & Three American Women Writers: Anne Dudley Brandstreet, Mercy Otis Warren, Margaret Fuller Ossoli, Vol. 9. LC 94-5282. (Age of Revolution & Romanticism Ser.: 9). 176p. (C). 1995. text 42.95 (*0-8204-2560-5*) P Lang Pubng.

Nicolaz, jt. auth. see Jacobson.

Nicole, Christopher. Bloody Sunset. 1994. 22.00 (*0-7278-4614-0*) Severn Hse.

***Nicole, Christopher.** Guns in the Desert. 256p. 1999. 26.00 (*0-7278-2238-1*, Pub. by Severn Hse) Chivers N Amer.

Nicole, Christopher. Iron Ships, Iron Men. 1987. 19.00 (*0-7278-1444-3*) Severn Hse.

— The Last Battle. 352p. 1993. lib. bdg. 20.00 (*0-7278-4454-7*) Severn Hse.

— Prelude to War. 256p. 1999. 26.00 (*0-7278-5416-X*, Pub. by Severn Hse) Chivers N Amer.

Nicole, Christopher. The Quest. 256p. 26.00 (*0-7278-5556-5*) Severn Hse.

Nicole, Christopher. Raging Sea, Searing Sky. 1988. 19.00 (*0-7278-1613-6*) Severn Hse.

— Red Gods. 320p. 1996. 24.00 (*0-7278-4972-7*) Severn Hse.

— The Red Tide. 352p. 1996. 24.00 (*0-7278-4850-X*) Severn Hse.

— Resumption. 352p. 1993. lib. bdg. 20.00 (*0-7278-4398-2*) Severn Hse.

— The Scarlet Generation. (Russian Saga Ser.: No. 5). 320p. 1996. 24.00 (*0-7278-4968-9*) Severn Hse.

— The Sea & the Sand. 1986. 19.00 (*0-7278-1350-1*) Severn Hse.

— The Seeds of Power. 224p. 1995. lib. bdg. 20.00 (*0-7278-4691-4*) Severn Hse.

— Shadows in the Sun. 288p. 1998. 25.00 (*0-7278-5364-3*) Severn Hse.

***Nicole, Christopher.** Shadows in the Sun. large type ed. 448p. 1999. 31.99 (*0-7505-1425-6*, Pub. by Mgna Lrg Print) Ulverscroft.

Nicole, Christopher. The Titans. 352p. 1992. 20.00 (*0-7278-4319-2*) Severn Hse.

— To All Eternity. 1999. 26.00 (*0-7278-5498-4*) Severn Hse.

***Nicole, Christopher.** The Trade. large type ed. 448p. 1998. 29.99 (*0-7505-1333-0*) Mgna Lrg Print.

Nicole, David. The Crusades. (Paper Soldiers of the Middle Ages Ser.: Bk. 1). (J). (gr. 1-9). 1992. pap. 4.95 (*0-88388-096-2*) Bellerophon Bks.

— The Hundred Years War. (Paper Soldiers of the Middle Ages Ser.: Bk. 2). (J). (gr. 1-9). 1992. pap. 3.95 (*0-88388-142-X*) Bellerophon Bks.

***Nicole, David.** Medieval Warfare Source Book: Warfare in Western Christendom. (Illus.). 320p. 2000. reprint ed. 40.00 (*0-7881-9224-8*) DIANE Pub.

Nicole, Eugene, jt. ed. see Caws, Mary A.

Nicole, Jules. Les Scolies Genevoises de l'Iliade, 2 vols. in 1. lxxxiii, 574p. 1966. reprint ed. write for info. (*0-318-70987-2*); reprint ed. write for info. (*0-318-71382-9*) G Olms Pubs.

***Nicole, Karen.** Bible Tells Me About. 1998. pap. text 6.99 (*0-8280-0913-9*) Review & Herald.

— I Like to Talk to God. 1998. pap. text 6.99 (*0-8280-0912-0*) Review & Herald.

Nicole, Pierre. Oeuvres Philosophiques et Morales. xxiii, 475p. 1970. reprint ed. write for info. (*0-318-71383-7*) G Olms Pubs.

Nicole, Pierre, jt. auth. see Arnauld, Antoine.

***Nicole, Robert.** The Word, the Pen & the Pistol: Literature & Power in Tahiti. (C). 2000. text 59.50 (*0-7914-4739-1*) State U NY Pr.

— The Word, the Pen, & the Pistol: Literature & Power in Tahiti. 2000. pap. 19.95 (*0-7914-4740-5*) State U NY Pr.

Nicoleau, Guitele, jt. ed. see Geismar, Kathryn.

***Nicolelis, M. A., ed.** Principals of Neural Ensemble & Distributed Coding in the Central Nervous System. (Progress in Brain Research Ser.). 2000. write for info. (*0-444-50110-X*, Excerpta Medica) Elsevier.

Nicolelis, Miguel. Methods for Simultaneous Neuronal Ensemble Recordings. LC 98-38795. 272p. 1998. boxed set 94.95 (*0-8493-3351-2*) CRC Pr.

Nicolello, Ildo. Complete Pastrywork Techniques. 255p. 1993. pap. 49.95 (*0-470-23353-2*) Wiley.

Nicolello, Ildo & Foote, R. Complete Confectionary Techniques. (Illus.). 148p. 1994. pap. 48.00 (*0-340-58259-6*, Pub. by Hodder & Stought Ltd) Lubrecht & Cramer.

Nicolello, L. G. & Dinsdale, J. Basic Pastrywork Techniques. 2nd ed. 239p. 1993. pap. text 39.95 (*0-470-23349-4*) Halsted Pr.

Nicoles. GED Writing Skills. (YA - Adult Education Ser.). 1995. pap. 10.95 (*0-538-71083-7*); pap., wbk. ed. 6.95 (*0-538-71101-9*) S-W Pub.

Nicoles & Lyons. GED Comprehensive Book. (Adult Education Ser.). 1997. pap. 13.95 (*0-538-71420-4*) S-W Pub.

Nicoles & Schmidt. GED Tests, Posttests. (YA - Adult Education Ser.). 1996. 5.95 (*0-538-71222-8*) S-W Pub.

Nicolescu, Basarab. Science, Meaning & Evolution: The Cosmology of Jacob Boehme. Baker, Rob, tr. from FRE. (Illus.). 231p. 1991. reprint ed. 17.95 (*0-930407-20-2*) Parabola Bks.

Nicolescu, L. J. & Stoka, M. Mathematics for Engineers, Vol. 2. (Illus.). 412p. 1974. text 110.00 (*0-85626-004-5*, Abacus) Gordon & Breach.

Nicolescu, Patricia, jt. ed. see Stevens, Tracy.

Nicolet, A., et al, eds. Boundary Element Technology X. LC 95-68886. (BETECH Ser.: Vol. 10). 248p. 1995. 146.00 (*1-56252-241-8*, 317X) Computational Mech MA.

Nicolet, A. & Belmans, R. Electric & Magnetic Fields: From Numerical Models to Industrial Applications. LC 95-13990. (Illus.). 388p. (C). 1995. 115.00 (*0-306-44991-9*, Plenum Trade) Perseus Pubng.

Nicolet, Art, ed. see Hubbard, Edward L.

Nicolet, Claude. The Sixteenth Myres Memorial Lecture: Financial Documents & Geographical Knowledge in the Roman World. (Myres Memorial Lectures: Vol. 16). 24p. 1997. pap. 9.00 (*0-904920-32-1*, Pub. by Leopards Head Pr) David Brown.

— Space, Geography, & Politics in the Early Roman Empire. (Illus.). 276p. 1991. text 52.50 (*0-472-10096-3*, 10096) U of Mich Pr.

Nicolet-Monnier, Michel & Gheorge, Adrian V. Quantitative Risk Assessment of Hazardous Materials Transport Systems: Rail, Road, Pipelines & Ship. LC 95-49989. (Topics in Safety, Risk, Reliability & Quality Ser.). xviii, 343p. 1996. text 184.00 (*0-7923-3923-1*) Kluwer Academic.

Nicolet-Monnier, Michel & Gheorghe, Adrian V. Integrated Regional Risk Assessment. LC 95-37546. (Environmental Science & Technology Library: Vol. 4). 1995. lib. bdg. 183.00 (*0-7923-3717-4*) Kluwer Academic.

Nicoleta, Lascu D. & Ricks, David A. Global Marketing Management. (C). 1995. 60.00 (*0-02-367761-9*, Macmillan Coll) P-H.

Nicoletta, Julie. The Architecture of the Shakers. LC 94-23258. (Illus.). 176p. 1996. pap. 29.00 (*0-88150-337-1*, Pub. by Countryman) Norton.

— The Architecture of the Shakers. LC 94-23258. (Illus.). 176p. 2000. 35.00 (*0-88150-310-X*, Pub. by Countryman) Norton.

***Nicoletta, Julie.** Buildings of Nevada. (Buildings of the United States Ser.). (Illus.). 320p. 2000. 45.00 (*0-19-514139-3*) OUP.

Nicoletti, B., et al. Human Achondroplasia: A Multidisciplinary Approach. LC 88-25288. (Basic Life Sciences Ser.: Vol. 48). (Illus.). 514p. (C). 1988. text 130.00 (*0-306-43006-1*, Kluwer Plenum) Kluwer Academic.

Nicoletti, Giuseppe. Diccionario de Bacteriologia Humana. (SPA.). 320p. 1989. pap. write for info. (*0-7859-6034-1*, 8440435959) Fr & Eur.

***Nicoletti, John, et al.** Survival-Oriented Kids in a Violent World: A Skills Training Manual for Parents & Other Protectors. 93p. 1998. pap. 18.00 (*0-9673710-3-1*) Nicoletti.

— Violence Goes to School: Lessons Learned from Columbine. 124p. 1999. pap. 24.00 (*0-9673710-2-3*) Nicoletti.

Nicoletti, John, jt. auth. see Zinna, Kelly A.

***Nicoletti, Joseph P. & Forell, Nicholas F.** Nicholas F. Forell. LC 99-54561. (EERI Oral History Ser.). 1999. write for info. (*0-943198-98-4*) Earthquake Eng.

Nicoletto, Paul. Anatomy & Physiology Laboratory Manual. 150p. (C). spiral bd., lab manual ed. 36.95 (*0-7872-6490-3*) Kendall-Hunt.

Nicolie, K. Ndal Sukdu/Gheldzay Sukdu (Crane Story/Moon Story) 18p. 1977. pap. 2.50 (*0-933769-94-6*) Alaska Native.

Nicolin, Pievluigi, ed. Lotus, Vol. 29. 1981. pap. 29.95 (*0-8478-5339-X*) Rizzoli Intl.

Nicolini, C. Structure & Dynamics of Biopolymers. (C). 1987. text 167.00 (*90-247-3527-0*) Kluwer Academic.

— Towards the Biochip. 240p. (C). 1990. text 92.00 (*9971-5-0958-X*) World Scientific Pub.

N

An Asterisk (*) at the beginning of an entry indicates that the title is appearing for the first time.

Nicolini, C., ed. Biophysics of Electron Transfer & Molecular Bioelectronics. LC 98-31320. (Electronics & Biotechnology Advanced (E.L.B.A) Forum: 3). (Illus.). 206p. (C). 1998. text 95.00 (*0-306-46028-9*, Kluwer Plenum) Kluwer Academic.

— Modeling & Analysis in Biomedicine: Proceedings of the 4th Course of the International School of Pure & Applied Biostructure, Erice, Italy, Oct. 18-27,1982. 552p. 1984. 108.00 (*9971-950-81-2*) World Scientific Pub.

Nicolini, Claudio. Biophysics & Cancer. LC 86-4926. (Illus.). 480p. (C). 1986. text 167.00 (*0-306-42122-4*, Kluwer Plenum) Kluwer Academic.

Nicolini, Claudio, ed. Bioscience at the Physical Science Frontier. 270p. 1987. 125.00 (*0-89603-131-4*) Humana.

— From Neural Networks & Biomolecular Engineering to Bioelectronics: Proceedings of the 1993 International Workshop on Electronics & Biotechnology Advances Held on the Isle of Elba, Italy, July 13-16, 1993. LC 95-11436. (Electronics & Biotechnology Advanced (EL.B.A.) Forum Ser.: Vol. 1). (Illus.). 262p. 1995. 95.00 (*0-306-44907-2*, Kluwer Plenum) Kluwer Academic.

— Genome Structure & Function from Chromosomes Characterization to Genes Technology. LC 97-16670. 348p. 1997. text 184.00 (*0-7923-4565-7*) Kluwer Academic.

— Molecular Basis of Human Cancer. (NATO ASI Ser.: Vol. 209). (Illus.). 224p. (C). 1991. text 114.00 (*0-306-44018-0*, Kluwer Plenum) Kluwer Academic.

Nicolini, Claudio & Vakula, Sergei, eds. Molecular Manufacturing, Vol. 2. LC 96-5249. (Electronics & Biotechnology Advanced Forum Ser.: No. 2). (Illus.). 234p. (C). 1996. text 95.00 (*0-306-45284-7*, Kluwer Plenum) Kluwer Academic.

Nicolini, Claudio, jt. ed. see Bradbury, E. Morton.

Nicolini, M. & Zatta, Paolo F. Non-Neuronal Cells in Alzheimer's Disease. 200p. 1995. text 61.00 (*981-02-2092-8*) World Scientific Pub.

Nicolini, Marino, ed. Platinum & Other Metal Coordination Compounds in Cancer Chemotherapy. (Developments in Oncology Ser.). (C). 1988. text 330.00 (*0-89838-358-7*) Kluwer Academic.

Nicolini, Marino, et al, eds. Alzheimer's Disease & Related Disorders. (Advances in the Biosciences Ser.: Vol. 87). 526p. 1993. 190.25 (*0-08-042330-2*, Pergamon Pr) Elsevier.

Nicolini, Marino & Zatta, R. F., eds. Glycobiology & the Brain. LC 93-21168. (Studies in Neuroscience). 304p. 1994. 168.00 (*0-08-042283-7*, Pergamon Pr) Elsevier.

Nicolis, C. & Nicolis, G., eds. Irreversible Phenomena & Dynamical Systems Analysis in Geosciences. 1986. text 267.50 (*90-277-2363-X*) Kluwer Academic.

Nicolis, G. Introduction to Nonlinear Science. (Illus.). 270p. (C). 1995. text 69.95 (*0-521-46228-2*); pap. text 27.95 (*0-521-46782-9*) Cambridge U Pr.

Nicolis, G. & Baras, F., eds. Chemical Instabilities: Applications in Chemistry, Engineering, Geology, & Materials Science. 1983. text 220.00 (*90-277-1705-2*) Kluwer Academic.

Nicolis, G. & Prigogine, Ilya. Self-Organization in Non-Equilibrium Systems: From Dissipative Structures to Order Through Fluctuations. 512p. 1977. 199.00 (*0-471-02401-5*, Wiley-Interscience) Wiley.

Nicolis, G., jt. ed. see Nicolis, C.

Nicolis, J. S. Chaos & Information Processing. 304p. 1991. text 48.00 (*981-02-0076-5*) World Scientific Pub.

— Dynamics of Hierarchical Systems. (Synergetics Ser.: Vol. 25). (Illus.). 415p. 1986. 118.95 (*0-387-13323-2*) Spr-Verlag.

Nicoll. Pocket Guide to Diagnostic Tests. 3rd ed. (Illus.). 500p. (C). 1999. pap. text 19.95 (*0-8385-8135-8*) Appleton & Lange.

Nicoll, ed. The National Gallery Technical Bulletin. (National Gallery Publications: Vol. 19). (Illus.). 96p. 1998. pap. 30.00 (*0-300-07573-1*) Yale U Pr.

Nicoll, A. & Pusey, Edward E. Bibliothecae Bodleianae Codicum Manuscriptorum Catalogi Partis Secundae Volumen Secundum, Arabicos Complectens, 2 vols in 1. (Illus.). viii, 535p. reprint ed. write for info. (*0-318-71539-2*) G Olms Pubs.

Nicoll, Allardyce. Dryden As an Adapter of Shakespeare. LC 78-173083. reprint ed. 20.00 (*0-404-07848-6*) AMS Pr.

— English Theatre: A Short History. LC 75-98861. 252p. 1971. reprint ed. lib. bdg. 35.00 (*0-8371-3133-2*, NIET, Greenwood Pr) Greenwood.

— Film & Theatre. LC 77-169335. (Literature of Cinema, Ser. 2). 272p. 1975. reprint ed. 19.95 (*0-405-03902-6*) Ayer.

— Stuart Masques & the Renaissance Stage. LC 63-23186. (Illus.). 224p. 1972. 30.95 (*0-405-08817-5*, Pub. by Blom Pubns) Ayer.

— Studies in Shakespeare. (BCL1-PR English Literature Ser.). 164p. 1992. reprint ed. lib. bdg. 69.00 (*0-7812-7300-5*) Rprt Serv.

— The Theatre & Dramatic Theory. LC 78-5609. 221p. 1978. reprint ed. lib. bdg. 55.00 (*0-313-20433-0*, NITD, Greenwood Pr) Greenwood.

— The Theory of Drama. LC 66-29422. 1972. reprint ed. 23.95 (*0-405-08818-3*, Pub. by Blom Pubns) Ayer.

— The World of Harlequin: A Critical Study of the Commedia Dell'arte. LC 76-18411. 259p. reprint ed. pap. 73.90 (*0-608-13030-3*, 2024501) Bks Demand.

Nicoll, Allardyce, ed. Chapman's Homer: The Iliad. Chapman, George, tr. LC 98-33505. (Bollinger Ser.). 741p. 1998. pap. 19.95 (*0-691-00236-3*, Pub. by Princeton U Pr) Cal Prin Full Svc.

***Nicoll, Allardyce, ed.** Chapman's Homer: The Odyssey. Chapman, George, tr. from GRE. 741p. 2000. pap. 19.95 (*0-691-04891-6*) Princeton U Pr.

Nicoll, Allardyce, ed. Shakespeare Survey: An Annual Survey of Shakespearian Study & Production, Vol. II. LC 49-1639. 139p. reprint ed. pap. 39.70 (*0-608-14564-5*, 2024944) Bks Demand.

Nicoll, Angus, jt. ed. see Rudd, Peter.

Nicoll, Barb, jt. auth. see Buckland, Wendy.

Nicoll, Diana, et al. Pocket Guide to Diagnostic Tests. 2nd rev. ed. 457p. (C). 1998. pap. 24.95 (*0-8385-8100-5*, A8100-8, Apple Lange Med) McGraw.

Nicoll, Eric H. Small Water Pollution Control Works: Design & Practice. LC 87-22439. (Water & Waste Water Technology Ser.). 432p. 1988. text 105.00 (*0-470-20999-2*) P-H.

Nicoll, Greg. Uncle Compone's Beer Guide: A Downhome Review of Gourmet Beers from Around the World. (Illus.). 52p. (C). 1999. pap. 5.00 (*1-893816-03-6*) Ozark Tri.

Nicoll, Helen. Poems for Seven Year Olds. (J). 1984. pap. 9.95 (*0-14-031489-X*, Pub. by Pnguin Bks Ltd) Trafalgar.

Nicoll, Helen & Pienkowski, Jan. Meg's Car. (Picture Puffin Ser.). 32p. (J). (ps). 1984. pap. 3.50 (*0-14-050259-9*, Penguin Bks) Viking Penguin.

— Meg's Veg. 32p. (J). (ps). 1985. pap. 3.50 (*0-14-050356-0*, PuffinBks) Peng Put Young Read.

Nicoll, Henry J. Landmarks of English Literature. LC 72-3282. (English Literature Ser.: No. 33). (Illus.). 1972. reprint ed. lib. bdg. 75.00 (*0-8383-1500-3*) M S G Haskell Hse.

Nicoll, Jessica & Wilmerding, John. Winslow Homer at the Portland Museum of Art. rev. ed. Orig. Title: Winslow Homer: The Charles Shipman Payson Collection. (Illus.). 48p. 1998. pap. 12.50 (*0-916857-14-X*) Port Mus Art.

Nicoll, Jessica, et al. A Legacy for Maine: The November Collection of Elizabeth B. Noyce. (Illus.). 80p. 1997. pap. 14.95 (*0-916857-11-5*) Port Mus Art.

Nicoll, Jessica E. Quilted for Friends: Delaware Valley Signature Quilts. (Illus.). 40p. 1986. pap. 7.95 (*0-912724-15-3*) Winterthur.

Nicoll, Jessica F. The Allure of the Maine Coast: Robert Henri & His Circle, 1903-1918. Ransom, Susan L., ed. LC 95-69965. (Illus.). 40p. (Orig.). 1995. pap. text 12.50 (*0-916857-07-7*) Port Mus Art.

Nicoll, Jessica F. & Ira Spanierman Gallery Staff. Abraham J. Bogdanove: Painter of Maine. LC 99-173551. (Illus.). 118p. 1997. 45.00 (*0-945936-15-X*) Spanierman Gallery.

Nicoll, John. Diary of Public Transactions & Other Occurrences, Chiefly in Scotland. LC 71-173084. (Bannatyne Club, Edinburgh. Publications: No. 52). reprint ed. 47.50 (*0-404-52762-0*) AMS Pr.

Nicoll, Josephine, tr. see Von Boehn, Max.

Nicoll, Lesie H. Computers in Nursing's Nurses' Guide to the Internet. 2nd ed. LC 97-43982. 240p. 1998. pap. text 29.95 (*0-7817-1435-4*) Lppncott W & W.

Nicoll, Leslie H. Computers in Nursings: Nurses' Guide to the Internet. 3rd ed. 224p. pap. text 29.95 (*0-7817-2459-7*) Lppncott W & W.

Nicoll, Leslie H. Perspectives on Nursing Theory. 3rd ed. LC 96-33075. 736p. 1996. pap. text 36.95 (*0-397-55312-9*) Lppncott W & W.

Nicoll, Lindsey. All Work & No Play. (Longman American Business English Skills Ser.). 1994. pap. text 12.60 (*0-582-08421-0*, Pub. by Addison-Wesley) Longman.

Nicoll, Martin E. & Rathbun, Galen. African Insectivora & Elephant-Shrews: An Action Plan for Their Conservation. (Illus.). 58p. (Orig.). 1990. pap. 16.00 (*2-8317-0020-5*, Pub. by IUCN) Island Pr.

Nicoll, Maud C. Cuyler. Earliest Cuylers in Holland & America & Some of Their Descendants: Researches Establishing a Line from Tydeman Cuyler of Hasselt, 1456. (Illus.). 69p. 1997. reprint ed. pap. 14.00 (*0-8328-8194-5*); reprint ed. lib. bdg. 24.00 (*0-8328-8193-7*) Higginson Bk Co.

Nicoll, Maurice. Psychological Commentaries on the Teaching of Gurdjieff & Ouspensky, No. 1. LC 96-16548. 384p. 1996. reprint ed. 30.00 (*0-87728-899-2*) Weiser.

— Psychological Commentaries on the Teaching of Gurdjieff & Ouspensky, Vol. 2. 416p. 1996. reprint ed. 25.00 (*0-87728-900-X*) Weiser.

— Psychological Commentaries on the Teaching of Gurdjieff & Ouspensky, Vol. 3. 454p. 1996. reprint ed. 25.00 (*0-87728-901-8*) Weiser.

— Psychological Commentaries on the Teaching of Gurdjieff & Ouspensky, Vol. 4. 280p. 1996. reprint ed. 25.00 (*0-87728-902-6*) Weiser.

— Psychological Commentaries on the Teaching of Gurdjieff & Ouspensky, Vol. 5. 264p. 1996. reprint ed. 25.00 (*0-87728-903-4*) Weiser.

— Psychological Commentaries on the Teaching of Gurdjieff & Ouspensky, Vol. 6. 216p. 1996. reprint ed. 25.00 (*0-87728-904-2*) Weiser.

— Psychological Commentaries on the Teachings of Gurdjieff & Ouspensky, Vol. 3. LC 83-25194. 447p. (Orig.). 1984. pap. 24.95 (*0-394-72396-1*, Pub. by Shambhala Pubns) Random.

Nicoll, Maurice. Simple Explanation of Work Ideas. 54p. 1996. pap. text 15.95 (*1-85398-081-1*) Word Enter.

Nicoll, Maurice & Gurdjieff Society of Washington D.C. Staff. Psychological Commentaries on the Teaching of Gurdjieff & Ouspensky, 6 vols. LC 96-16548. 2030p. 1996. 150.00 (*0-87728-910-7*) Weiser.

Nicoll, Mildred R., tr. see Steiner, Rudolf.

Nicoll, Peggy. MTV's Daria: Daria's Database. LC 99-199267. 80p. 1998. per. 14.00 (*0-671-02596-1*, MTV Bks) PB.

Nicoll, W. Robertson. The Problem of 'Edwin Drood' LC 72-1330. (Studies in Dickens: No. 52). 1972. reprint ed. lib. bdg. 75.00 (*0-8383-1442-2*) M S G Haskell Hse.

Nicoll, William & Salmon, Trevor C. Understanding the European Communities. (Illus.). 260p. (C). 1990. pap. 25.50 (*0-86003-709-6*); lib. bdg. 64.50 (*0-389-20912-0*) B&N Imports.

— Understanding the New European Community. 368p. (C). 1994. pap. text 39.95 (*0-13-302241-2*) P-H.

Nicoll, William, jt. auth. see Salmon, Trevor C.

Nicoll, William R. & Wise, Thomas J. Literary Anecdotes of the Nineteenth Century, 2 vols. LC 11-21329. reprint ed. 115.00 (*0-404-04717-3*) AMS Pr.

Nicolle. Aesthetic Rhinoplasty. 1995. text 105.00 (*0-7020-1776-0*, W B Saunders Co) Harcrt Hlth Sci Grp.

— Ottoman Army of Napoleonic War. 1998. 12.95 (*1-85532-697-3*, 847844Q, Pub. by Osprey) Stackpole.

Nicolle, David. The Age of Charlemagne. (Men-at-Arms Ser.: No. 150). (Illus.). 48p. pap. 11.95 (*0-85045-042-X*, 9082, Pub. by Osprey) Stackpole.

— The Age of Tamerlane. (Men-at-Arms Ser.: No. 222). (Illus.). 48p. pap. 12.95 (*0-85045-949-4*, 9180, Pub. by Osprey) Stackpole.

— The Armies of Islam Seventh to Eleventh Centuries. (Men-at-Arms Ser.: No. 125). (Illus.). 48p. 1984. pap. 12.95 (*0-85045-448-4*, 9057, Pub. by Osprey) Stackpole.

— Armies of the Muslim Conquest. (Men-at-Arms Ser.: No. 255). (Illus.). 48p. pap. 11.95 (*1-85532-279-X*, 9226, Pub. by Osprey) Stackpole.

— Armies of the Ottoman Turks 1300-1774. (Men-at-Arms Ser.: No. 140). (Illus.). 48p. pap. 11.95 (*0-85045-511-1*, 9072, Pub. by Osprey) Stackpole.

— Arms & Armour of the Crusading Era: 1050-1350: Western Europe & the Crusader States. LC 98-46532. 1999. 49.95 (*1-85367-347-1*) Stackpole.

***Nicolle, David.** Arms & Armour of the Crusading Era, 1050-1350: Islam, Eastern Europe & Asia. (Illus.). 480p. 1999. 49.95 (*1-85367-369-2*, Pub. by Greenhill Bks) Stackpole.

Nicolle, David. Arthur & the Anglo-Saxon Wars. (Men-at-Arms Ser.: No. 154). (Illus.). 48p. 1984. pap. 11.95 (*0-85045-548-0*, 9086, Pub. by Osprey) Stackpole.

— Attila & the Nomad Hordes. (Elite Ser.: No. 30). (Illus.). 64p. pap. 12.95 (*0-85045-996-6*, 9430, Pub. by Osprey) Stackpole.

***Nicolle, David.** Attila the Hun. (Illus.). 64p. 2000. pap. 14.95 (*1-84176-034-X*) Osprey.

Nicolle, David. The Crusades. (Elite Ser.: No. 19). (Illus.). 64p. pap. 12.95 (*0-85045-854-4*, 9419, Pub. by Osprey) Stackpole.

— El Cid & the Reconquista, 1000-1492. (Men-at-Arms Ser.: No. 200). (Illus.). 48p. pap. 11.95 (*0-85045-840-4*, 9133, Pub. by Osprey) Stackpole.

— Fornovo, 1495. (Campaign Ser.: No. 43). (Illus.). 96p. 1996. pap. 16.95 (*1-85532-522-5*, Pub. by Osprey) Stackpole.

***Nicolle, David.** French Armies of the Hundred Years War. (Men at Arms Ser.: Vol. 337). 2000. pap. 12.95 (*1-85532-710-4*) Osprey.

Nicolle, David. French Medieval Armies 1000-1300. (Men-at-Arms Ser.: No. 231). (Illus.). 48p. pap. 11.95 (*1-85532-127-0*, 9189, Pub. by Osprey) Stackpole.

— Granada, 1481-92. (Campaign Ser.: No. 53). (Illus.). 96p. 1998. pap. 16.95 (*1-85532-740-6*, Pub. by Osprey) Stackpole.

— Gravelotte-St. Privat 1871. (Campaign Ser.: No. 21). (Illus.). 96p. pap. 14.95 (*1-85532-286-2*, 9520, Pub. by Osprey) Stackpole.

— Hattin 1187. (Campaign Ser.: No. 19). (Illus.). 96p. pap. 14.95 (*1-85532-284-6*, 9518, Pub. by Osprey) Stackpole.

— Hungary & the Fall of Eastern Europe 1000-1568. (Men-at-Arms Ser.: No. 195). (Illus.). 48p. pap. 11.95 (*0-85045-833-1*, 9128, Pub. by Osprey) Stackpole.

— Italian Medieval Armies, 1300-1500. (Men-at-Arms Ser.: No. 136). (Illus.). 48p. pap. 11.95 (*0-85045-477-8*, 9068, Pub. by Osprey) Stackpole.

— Italian Militiaman 1260-1392. (Warrior Ser.: Vol. 25). (Illus.). 64p. 1999. pap. text 14.95 (*1-85532-826-7*) Osprey.

— The Janissary. (Elite Ser.). (Illus.). 64p. 1995. pap. 12.95 (*1-85532-413-X*, Pub. by Osprey) Stackpole.

— Knight of Outremer, 1187-1344. (Warrior Ser.: Vol. 18). 64p. pap. 12.95 (*1-85532-555-1*, Pub. by Osprey) Stackpole.

— Lake Peipus 1214. (Campaign Ser.: No. 47). (Illus.). 96p. 1996. pap. 15.95 (*1-85532-553-5*, Pub. by Osprey) Stackpole.

— Lawrence & the Arab Revolts, 1914-1918. (Men-at-Arms Ser.: No. 208). (Illus.). 48p. pap. 11.95 (*0-85045-888-9*, 9141, Pub. by Osprey) Stackpole.

— The Mamluks, 1250-1517. (Men-at-Arms Ser.). (Illus.). 48p. 1993. pap. 11.95 (*1-85532-314-1*, 9230, Pub. by Osprey) Stackpole.

— Medieval Knights. LC 96-61599. 48p. (gr. 3-7). 1997. 19.99 (*0-670-87463-9*) Viking Penguin.

— Medieval Russian Armies 838-1252, 333. 1999. pap. text 12.95 (*1-85532-848-8*) Osprey.

— Medieval Warfare Source Book Vol. 2: Christian Europe & Its Neighbor. (Medieval Warfare Source Book: Vol. II). (Illus.). 320p. 1997. 34.95 (*1-85409-307-X*, Pub. by Arms & Armour) Sterling.

— Moghul India, 1523-1805. (Men-at-Arms Ser.). (Illus.). 48p. 1993. pap. 11.95 (*1-85532-344-3*, 9234, Pub. by Osprey) Stackpole.

— Nicopolis 1396, Vol. 64. 1999. pap. text 17.95 (*1-85532-918-2*) Greenhill Bks.

— The Normans. (Elite Ser.: No. 9). (Illus.). 64p. pap. 12.95 (*0-85045-729-7*, 9408, Pub. by Osprey) Stackpole.

— Normans, Vol. 9. 64p. 1998. pap. 14.95 (*1-85532-944-1*) Osprey.

— The Ottoman Army, 1914-18. (Men-at-Arms Ser.). (Illus.). 48p. 1994. pap. 11.95 (*1-85532-412-1*, 9240, Pub. by Osprey) Stackpole.

— Romano-Byzantine Armies Fourth-Ninth Century. (Men-at-Arms Ser.: No. 247). (Illus.). 48p. pap. 12.95 (*1-85532-224-2*, 9218, Pub. by Osprey) Stackpole.

— Rome's Enemies Vol. 5: The Desert Frontier. (Men-at-Arms Ser.: No. 243). (Illus.). 48p. pap. 11.95 (*1-85532-166-1*, 9203, Pub. by Osprey) Stackpole.

— Saladin & the Saracens Armies of the Middle East, 1100-1300. (Men-at-Arms Ser.: No. 171). (Illus.). 48p. 1986. pap. 11.95 (*0-85045-682-7*, 9103, Pub. by Osprey) Stackpole.

— Saracen Faris, 1100-1250 A. D. (Warrior Ser.). (Illus.). 64p. 1994. pap. 12.95 (*1-85532-453-9*, 9609, Pub. by Osprey) Stackpole.

— The Venetian Empire, 1200-1700. (Men-at-Arms Ser.: No. 210). (Illus.). 48p. pap. 12.95 (*0-85045-899-4*, 9143, Pub. by Osprey) Stackpole.

— Yarmuk 636 AD. (Campaign Ser.). (Illus.). 96p. 1994. pap. 14.95 (*1-85532-414-8*, 9530, Pub. by Osprey) Stackpole.

Nicolle, David & Hook, Adam. Armies of the Caliphates, 862-1098. (Men-at-Arms Ser.). (Illus.). 48p. 1999. pap. 12.95 (*1-85532-770-8*, Pub. by Osprey) Stackpole.

Nicolle, David & Ruggeri, Raffaele. Men at Arms. (Italian Invasion Ser.: No. 309). (Illus.). 48p. 1997. 12.95 (*1-85532-692-2*, Pub. by Osprey) Stackpole.

Nicolle, David, jt. auth. see Nordeen, Lon O.

Nicollian, Edward H. & Brews, John R. MOS (Metal Oxide Semiconductor) Physics & Technology. LC 81-7607. 928p. 1982. 250.00 (*0-471-08500-6*) Wiley.

Nicollier, Alain. Dictionnaire des Mots Suisses de la Langue Francaise. (FRE.). 171p. 1990. pap. 49.95 (*0-7859-8200-0*, 2881150055) Fr & Eur.

— Dictionnaire Encyclopedique Suisse. (FRE.). 1988. write for info. (*0-7859-8199-3*, 2-88115-001-2) Fr & Eur.

Nicolluci, Guy, jt. auth. see Jones, Kent.

Nicolo, F. Robot Control, 1994 (SYROCO '94) A Postscript Volume from the IFAC Symposium, Capri, Italy, 19-21 September 1994. Sciavicco, L. & Bonivento, C., eds. LC 95-5963. 942p. 1995. pap. 120.50 (*0-08-042227-6*, Pergamon Pr) Elsevier.

Nicoloff, Philip L. Emerson on Race & History: An Examination of English Traits. LC 80-2540. 1981. reprint ed. 33.50 (*0-404-19266-1*) AMS Pr.

***Nicolopoulou-Stamati, P., et al.** Health Impacts of Waste Management Policies: Proceedings of the Seminar 'Health Impacts of Waste Policies' Hippocrates Foundation, Kos, Greece, 12-14 November, 1998. LC 00-30656. (Environmental Science & Technology Library). 2000. write for info. (*0-7923-6362-0*) Kluwer Academic.

***Nicolopulos, James.** The Poetics of Empire in the Indies: Prophecy & Imitation in La Araucana & Os Lusbiadas. LC 99-42052. (Series in Romance Literature). 2000. 55.00 (*0-271-01990-5*) Pa St U Pr.

Nicolosi, Alfredo, ed. HIV Epidemiology: Models & Methods. LC 93-30218. 384p. 1993. text 85.00 (*0-7817-0118-X*) Lppncott W & W.

Nicolosi, Joseph. Reparative Therapy of Male Homosexuality: A New Clinical Approach. 1997th ed. LC 97-37093. 384p. 1997. pap. 40.00 (*0-7657-0142-1*) Aronson.

Nicolosi, Lucille, et al. Terminology of Communication Disorders: Speech, Language & Hearing. 4th ed. (Illus.). 384p. 1996. 33.00 (*0-683-06505-X*) Lppncott W & W.

Nicolosi, R. J. & Kris-Etherton, Penny M. Trans Fatty Acids & Coronary Heart Disease Risk. 24p. 1995. pap. 12.50 (*0-944398-67-7*, 398677) ILSI.

***Nicolov, Nicolas, et al, eds.** Recent Advances in Natural Language Processing II: Selected Papers from RANLP'97. LC 99-50325. (Current Issues in Linguistic Theory Ser.: Vol. 189). xii, 422p. 2000. 84.00 (*1-55619-966-X*) J Benjamins Pubng Co.

Nicolov, Nicolas, jt. ed. see Mitkov, Ruslan.

Nicols, Eugene, jt. auth. see Schwartz, Sharon.

Nicols, John. Turning Setbacks into Comebacks. 75p. (Orig.). (C). pap. text 4.99 (*0-940487-15-2*) Jubilee CA.

Nicols, Michel & Gianinazzi-Pearson, Vivienne, eds. Histology, Ultrastructure & Molecular Cytology of Plant-Microorganism Interactions. 272p. (C). 1996. text 125.00 (*0-7923-3886-3*) Kluwer Academic.

Nicols, Virginia S., jt. auth. see Gaudio, Peter E.

Nicolsky, R. Transport Properties of Superconductors Vol. 25: Prog in Hts. 808p. 1990. text 151.00 (*981-02-0211-3*) World Scientific Pub.

Nicolsky, R. & Escudero, R., eds. High Temperature Superconductivity: Proceedings of the Latin American Conference, Rio de Janeiro, Brazil, May 5-6, 1988. (Progress in High Temperature Superconductivity Ser.: Vol. 9). 504p. 1988. pap. 60.00 (*9971-5-0646-7*); text 125.00 (*9971-5-0645-9*) World Scientific Pub.

***Nicolson, Adam, photos by.** Panoramas of England. (Illus.). 160p. 2000. pap. 17.95 (*1-85799-947-9*) Phoenix Hse.

Nicolson, Alexander, ed. Gaelic Proverbs. 510p. pap. 19.95 (*1-874744-14-9*, Pub. by Birlinn Ltd) Dufour.

Nicolson, Alexander & MacLean, Alasdair. A History of Skye. (Illus.). 376p. pap. 35.95 (*0-9516022-7-6*, Pub. by Maclean Pr) Dufour.

Nicolson, C., jt. auth. see Boatswain, T.

***Nicolson, Colin.** The "Infamas Govener" Francis Bernard & the Origins of the American Revolution. (Illus.). 224p. 2000. 50.00 (*1-55553-463-5*) NE U Pr.

Nicolson, Cynthia P. Comets, Asteroids & Meteorites. (Starting with Space Ser.). 40p. (J). (gr. 2-6). 1999. pap. text 6.95 (*1-55074-580-8*) Kids Can Pr.

— The Earth. unabridged ed. (Starting with Space Ser.). (Illus.). 40p. (J). (gr. 2-6). 1999. pap. 6.95 (*1-55074-327-9*, Pub. by Kids Can Pr) Genl Dist Srvs.

— Earthdance: How Volcanoes, Earthquakes, Tidal Waves & Geysers Shake... unabridged ed. (Illus.). 48p. (J). (gr. 3-7). 1994. pap. 9.95 (*1-55074-155-1*, Pub. by Kids Can Pr) Genl Dist Srvs.

An Asterisk (*) at the beginning of an entry indicates that the title is appearing for the first time.

N

— The Planets. (Starting with Space Ser.). (Illus.). 40p. (J). (gr. 3-4). 1998. 1495.00 (*1-55074-512-3*, Pub. by Kids Can Pr) Genl Dist Srvs.

— The Stars. (Starting with Space Ser.). (Illus.). 40p. (J). (gr. 3-4). 1998. pap. 14.95 (*1-55074-524-7*, Pub. by Kids Can Pr) Genl Dist Srvs.

Nicolson, Cynthia P. & Slavin, Bill. Starting with Space: The Earth.Tr. of Destination Univers: La Terre. (FRE., Illus.). 40p. (J). pap. 8.99 (*0-590-16009-5*) Scholastic Inc.

***Nicolson, Cynthia Pratt.** Comets, Asteroids & Meteorites. (Starting with Space Ser.). (Illus.). 40p. (J). (gr. 2-6). 1999. 14.95 (*1-55074-578-6*) Kids Can Pr.

— The Planets. (Starting with Space Ser.). (Illus.). 40p. (J). (gr. 2-6). 1999. pap. text 6.95 (*1-55074-716-9*) Kids Can Pr.

— The Stars. (Starting with Space Ser.). 40p. (J). (gr. 2-6). 1999. pap. text 6.95 (*1-55074-659-6*) Kids Can Pr.

***Nicolson, Cynthia Pratt & Slavin, Bill.** Exploring Space. (Starting with Space Ser.). (Illus.). 32p. (J). (gr. 2-6). 2000. 12.95 (*1-55074-711-8*, Pub. by Kids Can Press); pap. 6.95 (*1-55074-713-4*, Pub. by Kids Can Press) Genl Dist Srvs.

Nicolson, Dan H., et al. Flora of Dominica, Pt. 2: Dicotyledoneae. LC 90-10415. (Smithsonian Contributions to Botany Ser.: No. 77). 278p. reprint ed. pap. 86.20 (*0-8357-2611-8*, 203993100014) Bks Demand.

***Nicolson, Donald & Webb, Julian S.** Professional Legal Ethics: Critical Interrogations. LC 99-48741. 344p. 2000. text 85.00 (*0-19-876471-5*) OUP.

Nicolson, Doula & Ayers, Harry. Adolescent Problems: A Practical Guide for Parents & Teachers. LC 97-195784. 96p. 1997. pap. 24.95 (*1-85346-464-3*, Pub. by David Fulton) Taylor & Francis.

— Individual Counselling Theory & Practice: A Reference Guide. (Resource Materials for Teachers Ser.). 96p. 1995. pap. 21.95 (*1-85346-373-6*, Pub. by David Fulton) Taylor & Francis.

Nicolson, Garth L. & Poste, George H., eds. Dynamic Aspects of Cell Surface Organization. (Cell Surface Reviews Ser.: Vol. 3). 1980. 368.25 (*0-7204-0623-4*) Elsevier.

Nicolson, Garth L., jt. ed. see Moloy, Peter.

***Nicolson, Harold.** Byron: The Last Journey. 260p. 1999. 19.95 (*1-85375-300-9*, Pub. by Prion) Trafalgar.

— Congress of Vienna: A Study in Allied Unity 1812-1822. 2000. pap. text 16.00 (*0-8021-3744-X*, Grove) Grove-Atltic.

Nicolson, Harold. Diplomacy. 3rd ed. LC 88-31994. 168p. (C). 1989. reprint ed. pap. text 12.95 (*0-934742-52-9*) Geo U Inst Dplmcy.

— Good Behavior: Being a Study of Certain Types of Civility. 1990. 16.50 (*0-8446-0822-X*) Peter Smith.

Nicolson, Harold G. Byron, the Last Journey, April 1823-April 1824. (BCL1-PR English Literature Ser.). 288p. 1992. reprint ed. lib. bdg. 79.00 (*0-7812-7481-8*) Rprt Serv.

— Dwight Morrow. LC 75-2657. (Wall Street & the Security Market Ser.). (Illus.). 1975. reprint ed. 39.95 (*0-405-06982-0*) Ayer.

— Dwight Morrow. (History - United States Ser.). 409p. 1993. reprint ed. lib. bdg. 99.00 (*0-7812-4922-8*) Rprt Serv.

— The Evolution of Diplomatic Method: The Chichele Lectures Delivered at Oxford, November, 1953. LC 76-56181. 93p. 1977. reprint ed. lib. bdg. 59.75 (*0-8371-9428-8*, NIDM, Greenwood Pr) Greenwood.

— Paul Verlaine. LC 77-10281. reprint ed. 49.50 (*0-404-16332-7*) AMS Pr.

— Sainte-Beuve. LC 77-20072. (Illus.). 274p. 1978. reprint ed. lib. bdg. 65.00 (*0-313-20013-0*, NISB, Greenwood Pr) Greenwood.

— Small Talk. LC 72-152206. (Essay Index Reprint Ser.). 1977. reprint ed. 19.95 (*0-8369-2420-7*) Ayer.

— Swinburne. (BCL1-PR English Literature Ser.). 207p. 1992. reprint ed. lib. bdg. 79.00 (*0-7812-7706-X*) Rprt Serv.

— Swinburne. LC 70-145208. 1971. reprint ed. 39.00 (*0-403-00807-7*) Scholarly.

— Tennyson: Aspects of His Life. LC 74-145209. 308p. 1925. reprint ed. 15.00 (*0-403-00806-9*) Scholarly.

— Tennyson: Aspects of His Life, Character & Poetry. LC 72-12. (Select Bibliographies Reprint Ser.). 1977. reprint ed. 19.95 (*0-8369-9967-3*) Ayer.

— Tennyson: Aspects of His Life, Character & Poetry. LC 72-2100. (English Literature Ser.: No. 33). 1972. reprint ed. lib. bdg. 75.00 (*0-8383-1458-9*) M S G Haskell Hse.

— Tennyson: Aspects of His Life, Character & Poetry. (BCL1-PR English Literature Ser.). 308p. 1992. reprint ed. lib. bdg. 89.00 (*0-7812-7697-7*) Rprt Serv.

Nicolson, Iain. Unfolding Our Universe. LC 99-17151. (Illus.). 269p. 1999. 39.95 (*0-521-59270-4*) Cambridge U Pr.

Nicolson, Ian. Boat Data Book. 3rd ed. 1996. text 30.00 (*0-07-046522-3*) McGraw.

— Build Your Own Boat: Completing a Bare Hull. (Illus.). 206p. 1996. reprint ed. pap. 19.95 (*1-57409-020-8*) Sheridan.

— Cold-Moulded & Strip-Planked Wood Boatbuilding. (Illus.). 187p. 1991. 39.95 (*0-924486-14-7*) Sheridan.

— A Sail for All Seasons: Cruising & Racing Sail Tips. LC 98-23203. (Illus.). 128p. 1998. pap. 19.95 (*1-57409-047-X*) Sheridan.

— Surveying Small Craft. 3rd ed. (Illus.). 224p. 1994. 29.95 (*0-924486-58-9*) Sheridan.

Nicolson, Malcolm, jt. auth. see Von Humboldt, Alexander.

Nicolson, Marjorie H. Pepys' Diary & the New Science. LC 65-26012. (Illus.). 217p. reprint ed. pap. 67.30 (*0-8357-3139-1*, 203940200012) Bks Demand.

— A Reader's Guide to John Milton. LC 97-32703. 1998. 24.95 (*0-8156-0496-3*) Syracuse U Pr.

Nicolson, Marjorie H., ed. The Conway Letters: The Correspondence of Anne, Viscountess Conway, Henry More & Their Friends: 1642-1684. rev. ed. (Illus.). 622p. 1992. text 110.00 (*0-19-824876-8*) OUP.

Nicolson, Marjorie H., ed. see Conway, Anne.

Nicolson, Marjorie H., ed. see Shadwell, Thomas.

Nicolson, Marjorie Hope. Mountain Gloom & Mountain Glory: The Development of the Aesthetics of the Infinite. LC 96-49189. (Weyerhaeuser Environmental Classics Ser.). 432p. 1997. pap. 17.95 (*0-295-97577-6*) U of Wash Pr.

***Nicolson, Nigel.** Kent. 2000. pap. 17.95 (*1-84188-013-2*) Seven Dials.

Nicolson, Nigel. Portrait of a Marriage: Vita Sackville-West & Harold Nicolson. LC 98-23343. (Illus.). 262p. 1998. pap. 15.00 (*0-226-58357-0*) U Ch Pr.

***Nicolson, Nigel.** Virginia Woolf. (Penguin Lives Ser.). 160p. 2000. 19.95 (*0-670-89443-5*, Viking) Viking Penguin.

Nicolson, Nigel. The World of Jane Austen: Her Houses in Fact & Fiction. (Illus.). 192p. 1997. pap. 19.95 (*0-7538-0017-9*, Pub. by Orion Pubng Grp) Trafalgar.

Nicolson, Nigel & Trautmann, Joanne, eds. The Letters of Virginia Woolf, 1911-1922, Vol. II. LC 76-40422. (Illus.). 672p. 1978. pap. 5.95 (*0-15-650882-6*, Harvest Bks) Harcourt.

— The Letters of Virginia Woolf, 1923-1928, Vol. III. LC 76-40422. (Illus.). 632p. 1980. pap. 5.95 (*0-15-650883-4*, Harvest Bks) Harcourt.

— The Letters of Virginia Woolf, 1929-1931, Vol. IV. LC 76-40422. Vol. IV. 442p. 1981. pap. 10.95 (*0-15-650884-2*, Harvest Bks) Harcourt.

Nicolson, Paula. Gender, Power & Organization: A Psychological Perspective. LC 95-51514. 192p. (C). 1996. 70.00 (*0-415-10402-5*); pap. 22.99 (*0-415-10403-3*) Routledge.

— Post-Natal Depression: Psychology, Science, & the Transition to Motherhood. LC 97-49218. (Women & Psychology Ser.). 160p. (C). 1998. 60.00 (*0-415-16362-5*); pap. 18.99 (*0-415-16363-3*) Routledge.

Nicolson, Paula & Ussher, Jane M., eds. Gender Issues in Clinical Psychology. LC 91-25284. 240p. (C). 1992. pap. 25.99 (*0-415-05486-9*) Routledge.

Nicolson, Robert B. & Davies, Brian F. The Pitcairners. LC 96-225098. (Illus.). 1997. write for info. (*0-908597-28-2*) Pasifika Pr.

Nicolson, Robert B. & Davies, Brian F. The Pitcairners. LC 96-35483. (Pasifika Library). (Illus.). 200p. 1997. pap. 19.95 (*0-8248-1921-7*) UH Pr.

Nicolson, Sheryl A. & Shipstead, Susan G. Thru the Looking Glass. 2nd ed. LC 97-16725. 368p. 1997. pap. text 42.00 (*0-13-651993-8*) P-H.

Nicolson, William. The London Diaries of William Nicolson, Bishop of Carlisle, 1702-1718. Holmes, Geoffrey & Jones, Clyve, eds. (Illus.). 1985. 115.00 (*0-19-822404-4*) OUP.

Nicomachus the Pythagorean. The Manual of Harmonics. Levin, Flora, tr. from GRE. (Illus.). 200p. (Orig.). 1993. pap. 18.00 (*0-933999-43-7*) Phanes Pr.

Nicomede, B. Dictionnaire du Roman Policier. (FRE.). 1998. 19.95 (*0-320-00272-1*) Fr & Eur.

Nicori, Helen, jt. auth. see Olick, Hilda.

Nicori, Sandi. Minguyaq Elitnauryartuq.Tr. of Julie Goes to School. (ESK., Illus.). 8p. (J). (gr. k-3). 1998. pap. text 6.00 (*1-58084-039-6*) Lower Kuskokwim.

***Nicosi, Nic.** Real Pictures, 1979-1999. (Illus.). 104p. 2000. pap. 19.95 (*0-936080-53-1*) Cont Arts Museum.

Nicosia, Francis R. The Third Reich & the Palestine Question. 2nd ed. LC 99-52040. 319p. 1999. pap. 27.95 (*0-7658-0624-X*) Transaction Pubs.

Nicosia, Francis R., ed. Central Zionist Archives, 1933-1945, Jerusalem. LC 89-16915. (Archives of the Holocaust Ser.: Vol. 3). 450p. 1991. text 127.00 (*0-8240-5485-7*) Garland.

— Central Zionist Archives 1939-1945, Jerusalem. LC 89-16915. (Archives of the Holocaust Ser.: Vol. 4). 470p. 1990. reprint ed. text 138.00 (*0-8240-5486-5*) Garland.

Nicosia, Francis R. & Stokes, Lawrence D., eds. Germans Against Nazism: Nonconformity, Opposition & Resistance in the Third Reich. (Illus.). 450p. 1991. 19.50 (*0-85496-688-9*) Berg Pubs.

Nicosia, Francis R., jt. auth. see Niewyk, Donald L.

Nicosia, Gerald. Lunatics, Lovers, Poets, Jet & Bargirls: Poems by Gerald Nicosia. (Illus.). 80p. (Orig.). 1991. pap. text 9.50 (*0-924047-05-4*) Host Pubns.

— Memory Babe: A Critical Biography of Jack Kerouac. LC 93-33457. 1994. 22.50 (*0-520-08569-8*, Pub. by U CA Pr) Cal Prin Full Svc.

Nicosia, Gerald, ed. see Kaufman, Bob.

Nicosia, Gerald, ed. see Kerouac, Jan.

Nicosia, Joan E. & Petro, Jane A. Manual of Burn Care. fac. ed. LC 82-25499. (Illus.). 166p. pap. 51.50 (*0-7837-7288-2*, 204701800005) Bks Demand.

Nicosia, Mary E. & Brandes, Louis G. Can You Believe What You See? Laycock, Mary, ed. (Illus.). 96p. (Orig.). (J). (gr. 5-12). 1988. pap. 13.95 (*0-918932 92-0*, A-2223) Activity Resources.

Nicosia, Sal, jt. auth. see Pfaffle, A. E.

Nicoson, William, et al. Large-Scale Development: Benefits, Constraints, & State & Local Policy Incentives. LC 77-74659. (Management & Control of Growth Ser.). 141p. reprint ed. pap. 43.80 (*0-608-17347-9*, 202980400065) Bks Demand.

Nicot, Philippe C., ed. see Nguyen, Christophe, et al.

Nicot, S. Dictionnaire de la Science Fiction. (FRE.). 1998. 19.95 (*0-320-00269-1*) Fr & Eur.

Nicotera, Anne M. Interpersonal Communication in Friend & Mate Relationships. LC 92-3099. (SUNY Series, Human Communication Processes). 256p. (C). 1993. pap. text 21.95 (*0-7914-1352-7*) State U NY Pr.

— Interpersonal Communication in Friend & Mate Relationships. LC 92-3099. (SUNY Series, Human Communication Processes). 256p. (C). 1993. text 64.50 (*0-7914-1351-9*) State U NY Pr.

— The Mate Relationship: Cross-Cultural Applications of a Rules Theory. LC 97-500. (SUNY Series, Human Communication Processes). 183p. (C). 1997. text 59.50 (*0-7914-3543-1*); pap. text 19.95 (*0-7914-3544-X*) State U NY Pr.

Nicotera, Anne M., ed. Conflict & Organizations: Communicative Processes. LC 94-44925. (SUNY Series, Human Communication Processes). 301p. (C). 1995. text 59.50 (*0-7914-2665-3*); pap. text 21.95 (*0-7914-2666-1*) State U NY Pr.

Nicoteri, jt. auth. see Farrell.

Nicotra, Brooke, jt. auth. see Carter, Rick.

Nicotra-D'Urso, Eduardo, ed. Dizionario Siciliano-Italiano: Sicilian Dialect-Italian Dictionary. (ITA.). 404p. 1992. 48.00 (*0-614-24423-4*) S F Vanni.

Nicotra, Francesco, jt. auth. see Scolastico, Carlo.

Nicozisin, George. The Orthodox Church - A Well-Kept Secret: A Journey Through Church History. 192p. (Orig.). 1997. pap. 11.95 (*1-880971-33-X*) Light&Life Pub Co MN.

— What Every Orthodox Christian Should Know: A Synopsis of Orthodox Christian Teachings. 1992. pap. 5.95 (*0-937032-85-9*) Light&Life Pub Co MN.

Niculescu-Duvaz, I. Wonders Of Technology Volume 1. 1998. 36.50 (*0-07-234211-0*) McGraw.

Niculescu, Mihai, jt. auth. see Eliade, Mircea.

***Niculescu, Silviu I.** Advances in Linear Matrix Inequality Methods in Control. El Ghaoui, Laurent, ed. LC 99-39162. (Advances in Design & Control Ser.: Vol. 2). 1999. pap. 71.50 (*0-89871-438-9*, DC02) Soc Indus-Appl Math.

Niculescu, V. Adam. Wonders of Technology: Physics in Action. 150p. 1997. 66.95 (*0-7872-3805-8*, 41380501) Kendall-Hunt.

Nida, Eugene A. Language Structure & Translation: Essays by Eugene A. Nida. Dil, Anwar S., ed. LC 75-183. (Language Science & National Development Ser.). 300p. 1975. 42.50 (*0-8047-0885-1*) Stanford U Pr.

— Message & Missions: The Communication of the Christian Faith. rev. ed. LC 60-11785. (Illus.). 315p. 1990. pap. text 10.95 (*0-87808-756-7*, WCL756-7) William Carey Lib.

— Synopsis of English Syntax. (Janua Linguarum, Series Practica: No. 19). (Orig.). 1966. pap. text 40.00 (*90-279-2430-9*) Mouton.

— Towards a Science of Translating. (Illus.). 1964. 68.00 (*90-04-02605-3*) Adlers Foreign Bks.

Nida, Eugene A., jt. auth. see Arichea, Daniel C.

Nida, Eugene A., jt. auth. see Bratcher, Robert G.

Nida, Eugene A., jt. auth. see De Waard, Jan.

Nida, Eugene A., jt. auth. see Ellingworth, Paul.

Nida, Eugene A., jt. auth. see Loh, I-Jin.

Nida, Eugene A., jt. auth. see Newman, Barclay M.

***Nida-Rhumelin, Julian & Spohn, Wolfgang.** Rationality, Rules & Structure. LC 00-38457. (Theory & Decision Library). 2000. write for info. (*0-7923-6326-4*, Kluwer Plenum) Kluwer Academic.

Nida-Ruemelin, Julian, ed. Praktische Rationalitaet: Grundlagenprobleme und Ethische Anwendungen Des Rational Choice-Paradigmas. (Perspektiven der Analytischen Philosophie - Perspectives in Analytical Philosophy Ser.: No. 2). (GER.). viii, 458p. 1993. lib. bdg. 167.70 (*3-11-013656-2*) De Gruyter.

Nida-Rumeli, Julian. Economic Rationality & Practical Reason. LC 97-2849. (Theory & Decision Library). 172p. 1997. lib. bdg. 87.00 (*0-7923-4493-6*) Kluwer Academic.

Nida-Rumelin, Julian, ed. Rationality, Realism, Revision Rationalitat, Realismus & Revision. (Illus.). 1010p. 1999. 186.00 (*3-11-016393-4*) De Gruyter.

Nida-Rumelin, Julian & Vossenkuhl, Wilhelm, eds. Ethische und Politische Freiheit. (GER.). 500p. (C). 1997. pap. text 53.80 (*3-11-015697-0*); lib. bdg. 158.00 (*3-11-014271-6*) De Gruyter.

Nidditch, P. H. The Development of Mathematical Logic. (Key Texts Ser.). 96p. 1998. pap. 14.00 (*1-85506-582-7*) Thoemmes Pr.

Nidditch, Peter H., ed. An Essay Concerning Human Understanding. (Clarendon Edition of the Works of John Locke Ser.). (Illus.). 924p. (C). 1979. reprint ed. pap. text 29.95 (*0-19-824595-5*) OUP.

Nidditch, Peter H., ed. see Hume, David.

Nidditch, Peter H., ed. see Locke, John.

Nideffer, Robert M. The Ethics & Practice of Applied Sport Psychology. 1981. pap. 24.95 (*0-685-42270-4*) Mouvement Pubns.

— Psyched to Win. LC 91-38529. 152p. 1992. pap. 14.95 (*0-88011-463-0*, PNID0463) Human Kinetics.

Niderost, Eric, jt. auth. see Henig, Gerald S.

Nidetch, Jean T. Weight Watchers Quick Start Plus Program Cookbook. 1986. pap. 15.95 (*0-452-26477-4*, Plume) Dutton Plume.

— Weight Watchers Quick Success Program Cookbook. (Illus.). 448p. 1990. pap. 10.95 (*0-452-26428-6*, Plume) Dutton Plume.

Nidever, Jack. Eros Lost. 108p. (Orig.). (C). 1997. pap. 12.75 (*0-9647066-3 6*) Wellstone Pr.

Nidhiprabha, Bhanupong, jt. auth. see Warr, Peter G.

Nidich, Randi J., jt. auth. see Nidich, Sanford I.

Nidich, Sanford I. & Nidich, Randi J. Growing up Enlightened: How Maharishi School of the Age of Enlightenment Is Awakening the Creative Genius of Students & Creating Heaven on Earth. LC 90-61520. (Illus.). 250p. (Orig.). 1989. pap. 13.00 (*0-923569-03-0*, C-01) Maharishi U Mgmt Pr.

***Nidiffer, Jana.** Pioneering Deans of Women. LC 99-41290. (Athene Ser.). 208p. 2000. pap. text 26.95 (*0-8077-3914-6*) Tchrs Coll.

— Pioneering Deans of Women: More Than Wise & Pious Matrons. LC 99-41290. (Athene Series in Women's Studies). 208p. 2000. write for info. (*0-8077-3915-4*) Tchrs Coll.

***Nidiffer, Jana & Bashaw, Carolyn Terry, eds.** Women Administrators in Higher Education: Historical & Contemporary Perspectives. (C). 2000. pap. text 18.95 (*0-7914-4818-5*) State U NY Pr.

— Women Administrators in Higher Education: Historical & Contemporary Perspectives. (C). 2001. text 57.50 (*0-7914-4817-7*) State U NY Pr.

Nidiffer, Jana, jt. auth. see Levine, Arthur.

Niditch, B. Z. AM/PM. Date not set. pap. 3.00 (*0-9674487-2-7*) Good SAMAR.

Niditch, B. Z. Exile. Schuler, Ruth W., ed. (Illus.). 16p. (Orig.). 1986. pap. text 3.00 (*0-910083-22-3*) Heritage Trails.

***Niditch, B. Z.** The Inside-Out World of B. Z. Niditch. unabridged ed. Armstrong, R. D., ed. (Little Red Books Ser.). (Illus.). 48p. 1999. pap. 5.00 (*1-929878-11-7*) Lummox.

Niditch, B. Z. Nine Pieces for Theater. Carbone, Joyce, ed. 40p. (Orig.). 1995. pap. 4.95 (*1-878116-42-8*) JVC Bks.

Niditch, B. Z., et al. PlopLop No. 9: An "Antholozine" of Poetry, Prose & Artwork. Clark, John, ed. & illus. by. 50p. (Orig.). 1997. pap. 5.00 (*1-885710-20-8*) Geekspeak Unique.

Niditch, Susan. Ancient Israelite Religion in Historical Perspective. (Illus.). 160p. (C). 1998. pap. text 16.95 (*0-19-509128-0*) OUP.

— Chaos to Cosmos: Studies in Biblical Patterns of Creation. (Studies in Humanities: No. 6). (C). 1985. pap. 14.95 (*0-89130-763-X*, 00 01 06) Duke.

— Folklore & the Hebrew Bible. LC 93-17830. (Guides to Bibical Scholarship Ser.). 128p. 1993. pap. 13.00 (*0-8006-2590-0*, 1-2590, Fortress Pr) Augsburg Fortress.

— Oral World & Written Word: Ancient Israelite Literature. Knight, Douglas A., ed. LC 96-21497. (Library of Ancient Israel). 176p. 1996. 19.00 (*0-664-21946-2*) Westminster John Knox.

***Niditch, Susan.** A Prelude to Biblical Folklore: Underdogs & Tricksters. LC 99-52086. 2000. pap. 15.00 (*0-252-06883-1*) U of Ill Pr.

Niditch, Susan. War in the Hebrew Bible: A Study in the Ethics of Violence. 192p. 1995. pap. text 16.95 (*0-19-509840-4*) OUP.

N

Nidl. Can Someone Please Tell Me Whe. 1984. pap. 17.95 (*0-684-18230-0*, Scribners Ref) Mac Lib Ref.

Nidle, Sheldon & Essene, Virginia. You Are Becoming a Galactic Human. (Orig.). 1995. mass mkt. 11.99 (*0-446 67204-1*) Warner Bks.

Nidzi, Hiam I. My Kitchen to Your Kitchen. (Illus.). 80p. 1998. pap. 16.95 (*0-9664045-0-5*) H I Nidzi.

***Nie, Norman H.** The Changing American Voter. 454p. 1999. 31.95 (*0-7351-0187-6*) Replica Bks.

Nie, Norman H., et al. The Changing American Voter. LC 75-42429. (Illus.). 450p. 1980. 43.50 (*0-674-10830-2*); pap. 19.50 (*0-674-10835-3*) HUP.

— Education & Democratic Citizenship in America. (Illus.). 240p. 1996. pap. text 16.95 (*0-226-58389-9*) U Ch Pr.

— Education & Democratic Citizenship in America. (Illus.). 240p. 1997. lib. bdg. 48.00 (*0-226-58388-0*) U Ch Pr.

— Social Structure & Political Participation: Development Relationships, Pt. I. (Reprint Series in Political Science). (C). 1993. reprint ed. pap. text 5.00 (*0-8290-2748-3*, PS-519) Irvington.

Nie, Norman H., jt. auth. see Verba, Sidney.

Nie, Winter, jt. auth. see Young, Scott T.

Niebanck, Paul L., ed. The Rent Control Debate. LC 85-1181. (Urban & Regional Policy & Development Studies). 160p. reprint ed. pap. 49.60 (*0-7837-2468-3*, 204262100005) Bks Demand.

Niebauer, Abby. Sun Rose. 60p. 1985. pap. 14.00 (*0-930513-01-0*) Blackwells Pr.

Niebel, Benjamin. Motion & Time Study. 10th ed. 727p. 1998. 97.25 (*0-256-19507-2*) McGraw.

Niebel, Benjamin W. Engineering Maintenance Management. 2nd expanded rev. ed. (Industrial Engineering Ser.: Vol. 18). (Illus.). 384p. 1994. text 145.00 (*0-8247-9247-5*) Dekker.

— Motion & Time Study. 9th ed. LC 92-15051. 880p. (C). 1992. text 74.95 (*0-256-09248-6*, Irwn McGrw-H) McGrw-H Hghr Educ.

Niebel, Benjamin W., et al. Modern Wrestling: A Primer for Wrestlers, Parents, & Fans. LC 82-7478. (Illus.). 128p. (Orig.). (C). 1982. pap. text 12.50 (*0-271-00328-6*); lib. bdg. 25.00 (*0-271-00323-5*) Pa St U Pr.

Niebergall, Jane. The Alaska Report. (Teaching Alaska Ser.: No. 4). 123p. (YA). (gr. 4 up). 1994. pap. text, teacher ed. 15.95 (*1-878051-16-4*) Circumpolar Pr.

***Niebergall, Jane.** The Alaska Report. rev. ed. O'Meara, Jan, ed. (Illus.). 76p. (J). (gr. 4-8). 1999. pap. 7.95 (*1-878051-46-6*) Circumpolar Pr.

— Alaska Sled Dogs & Mushers: A Teaching Unit about the Iditarod Race & Other Dog Races. (Illus.). 90p. (YA). (gr. 4-12). 1993. pap. 14.95 (*1-878051-51-2*) Circumpolar Pr.

Niebergall, Jane. Alaska Studies: History, Vol. 2. (Illus.). 165p. (J). (gr. 4-6). 1990. pap. 22.95 (*1-878051-39-3*, CP026) Circumpolar Pr.

— Bears to Barely Bears: A Theme Unit about Alaskan Bears. (Alaskan Teaching Unit Ser.). (Illus.). 71p. (Orig.). (C). 1990. pap., teacher ed. 9.95 (*1-870511-21-2*) Circumpolar Pr.

Niebergall, Jane, ed. Dash the Dog: A Theme Unit. (Illus.). 30p. (J). (gr. 1-8). 1990. pap. 6.95 (1-878051-49-0) Circumpolar Pr.

— Maps, Maps, Maps: A Collection of Alaskan Maps. (Illus.). 113p. 1996. pap. 11.95 (1-878051-48-2) Circumpolar Pr.

Niebergall, Jane, ed. see Hickock, David, et al.

Niebergall, Jane S. Alaskan Whales. (Illus.). 64p. (YA). (gr. 3-11). 1990. pap. 12.95 (1-878051-13-X) Circumpolar Pr.

— Geography of Alaska. (Alaska Studies: Unit 1). 202p. (J). (gr. 4-6). 1989. pap. 34.95 (1-878051-10-5) Circumpolar Pr.

— Interdisciplinary Theme Writing. 70p. 1991. pap. 11.95 (1-878051-08-3) Circumpolar Pr.

— Sam-the-Salmon: A Whole-Language Unit about Alaskan Salmon. (Illus.). 51p. (J). 1996. pap. 6.95 (1-878051-15-6) Circumpolar Pr.

Niebergall, Jane S., ed. Alaska Clip Art. 31p. (J). (gr. k-6). 1991. pap. 6.95 (1-878051-09-1) Circumpolar Pr.

Niebergall, Jane S., ed. see Avery, Orabell, et al.

Nieberl, Helen R. On the Trail: The Adventures of a Middle-Aged Tenderfoot. (Illus.). 104p. 1994. pap. 11.95 (0-9636921-1-9) Pack & Paddle.

Niebes, Joylyn. Children's Pages: A Parent Source Book for North Central Texas. 320p. (Orig.). 1986. pap. 8.95 (0-933547-02-1) Lauren Pubns.

— The Children's Pages: A Parent Source Book for the Dallas Area. 128p. (Orig.). 1985. pap. 8.95 (0-933547-00-5) Lauren Pubns.

Niebla, G. G. La Catastrofe Silenciosa. (SPA.). pap. 14.99 (968-16-3933-2, Pub. by Fondo) Continental Bk.

Niebler, Horst, tr. from GER. German Code of Criminal Procedure. (American Series of Foreign Penal Codes: Vol. 10). xvii, 235p. 1965. 22.50 (0-8377-0030-2, Rothman) W S Hein.

Nieboehr, E., et al. Rare Earths. LC 67-11280. (Structure & Bonding Ser.: Vol. 22). iv, 1p. 1975. 56.95 (0-387-07268-3) Spr-Verlag.

Nieboer, Evert & Nriagu, Jerome O., eds. Nickel & Human Health: Current Perspectives. LC 91-31093. (Advances in Environmental Science & Technology Ser.). 704p. 1992. 235.00 (0-471-50076-3) Wiley.

Nieboer, Evert, jt. ed. see Nriagu, Jerome O.

Nieboer, Laura. Home Care Organizer: A Resource for Families. 94p. 1997. ring bd. 14.95 (1-881782-04-2) State Art.

— My Child's Care. 50p. 1992. 25.00 (1-881782-00-X) State Art.

Nieborak, Stefan. Homo Analogia: Zur Philosophisch-Theologischen Bedeutung der "Analogia Entis" Im Rahmen der Existentiellen Frage Bei Erich Przywara S. J. (1889-1972) (Theologie Im Ubergang Ser.: Bd. 13). (GER.). XVIII, 633p. 1994. 84.95 (3-631-46528-9) P Lang Pubng.

***Niebrand, Chris & Horn.** The Pocket Mentor: A Handbook for Teachers. LC 98-54370. 268p. 1999. 27.50 (0-205-29693-9) Allyn.

Niebrand, Chris, et al. The Pocket Mentor: A Handbook for Teachers. LC 93-145416. xviii, 248 p. 1992. write for info. (0-8251-2123-X) J W Walch.

***Niebrugge, Gail.** Gail Niebrugge's Alaska Wildflowers. 2000. 16.95 (0-945397-89-5) Epicenter Pr.

Niebuhr, Gary W. A Reader's Guide to the Private Eye Novel. LC 93-22212. (Reader's Guides to Mystery Novels Ser.). 323p. 1993. 50.00 (0-8161-1802-7, G K Hall & Co) Mac Lib Ref.

Niebuhr, H. Richard. Christ & Culture. 272p. 1956. pap. 15.00 (0-06-130003-9, TB3, Torch) HarpC.

— Faith on Earth. 123p. 1989. 30.00 (0-300-04315-5) Yale U Pr.

— Faith on Earth: An Inquiry into the Structure of Human Faith. Niebuhr, Richard R., ed. 136p. (C). 1991. reprint ed. pap. 14.00 (0-300-05122-0) Yale U Pr.

— The Kingdom of God in America. LC 88-17328. 247p. 1988. pap. 19.95 (0-8195-6222-X, Wesleyan Univ Pr) U Pr of New Eng.

— Radical Monotheism & Western Culture: With Supplementary Essays. (Library of Theological Ethics). 112p. 1993. pap. 12.00 (0-664-25326-1) Westminster John Knox.

— Theology, History, & Culture: Major Unpublished Writings. Johnson, William S., ed. LC 95-22557. 280p. 1996. 42.00 (0-300-06370-9) Yale U Pr.

Niebuhr, H. Richard, tr. see Troeltsch, Ernst.

Niebuhr, Reinhold. Beyond Tragedy: Essays on the Christian Interpretation of History. LC 76-167397. (Essay Index Reprint Ser.). 1977. reprint ed. 26.95 (0-8369-2437-1) Ayer.

— Children of the Light & Children of the Dark. 1985. pap. 13.50 (0-684-15027-1, Scribners Ref) Mac Lib Ref.

— The Contribution of Religion to Social Work. LC 74-172444. reprint ed. 20.00 (0-404-04708-4) AMS Pr.

— Faith & History: A Comparison of Christian & Modern Views of History. 272p. 1977. 35.00 (0-684-15318-1, Scribners Ref) Mac Lib Ref.

— The Irony of American History. 192p. 1982. 30.00 (0-684-17602-5, Scribners Ref) Mac Lib Ref.

— Leaves from the Notebook of a Tamed Cynic. (American Biography Ser.). 198p. 1991. reprint ed. lib. bdg. 59.00 (0-7812-8299-3) Rprt Serv.

— Leaves from the Notebook of a Tamed Cynic. 152p. 1990. reprint ed. pap. 16.95 (0-664-25164-1) Westminster John Knox.

— Love & Justice: Selections from the Shorter Writings of Reinhold Niebuhr. Robertson, D. B., ed. 1990. 16.50 (0-8446-2659-7) Peter Smith.

— Love & Justice: Selections from the Shorter Writings of Reinhold Niebuhr. Robertson, D. B., ed. (Library of Theological Ethics). 320p. 1992. pap. 16.00 (0-664-25322-9) Westminster John Knox.

— Nature & Destiny Vol. 2: Manual, Vol. 2. 1980. pap. text 18.60 (0-02-387520-8, Macmillan Coll) P-H.

— The Nature & Destiny of Man: A Christian Interpretation, 2 vols. (Library of Theological Ethics). 672p. 1996. pap. 32.00 (0-664-25709-7) Westminster John Knox.

— Reinhold Niebuhr & the Issues of Our Time. Harries, Richard, ed. LC 86-180530. 215p. reprint ed. pap. 66.70 (0-7837-3188-4, 204279200006) Bks Demand.

— The Structure of Nations & Empires: A Study of the Recurring Patterns & Problems of the Political Order in Relation to the Unique Problems of the Nuclear Age. LC 72-128064. xi, 306p. 1977. reprint ed. 39.50 (0-678-02755-2) Kelley.

— The World Crisis & American Responsibility. Lefever, Ernest W., ed. LC 74-10643. 128p. 1974. reprint ed. lib. bdg. 35.00 (0-8371-7649-2, NIWC, Greenwood Pr) Greenwood.

Niebuhr, Reinhold & Heimert, Alan. A Nation So Conceived: Reflections on the History of America from Its Early Visions to Its Present Power. LC 83-10708. 155p. 1983. reprint ed. lib. bdg. 39.75 (0-313-23866-9, NINA, Greenwood Pr) Greenwood.

Niebuhr, Richard H. The Social Sources of Denominationalism. 1984. 23.75 (0-8446-6150-3) Peter Smith.

Niebuhr, Richard R., ed. see Niebuhr, H. Richard.

Niebur, Jay E. & Fell, James E., Jr. Arthur Redman Wilfley: Miner, Inventor, & Entrepreneur. (Illus.). xii, 245p. 1981. pap. 8.95 (0-942576-25-X) CO Hist Soc.

Nieburg, Herbert A. & Fischer, Arlene. Pet Loss: A Thoughful Guide for Adults & Children. LC 96-151056. 176p. 1996. pap. 11.00 (0-06-092678-3) HarpC.

Nieburgs, Herbert E., ed. see International Symposium on Detection & Prevention.

Niebyl, Jennifer R., jt. auth. see Russell, Keith P.

Niebyl, Jennifer R., jt. auth. see Yankowitz, Jerome.

Niebyl, Karl H. Studies in the Classical Theories of Money. LC 70-173795. reprint ed. 20.00 (0-404-04709-2) AMS Pr.

Niechoda, Irene. A Sourcery for Books One & Two of B. P. Nichol's The Martyrology. 214p. (C). 1992. pap. text 25.00 (1-55022-102-7, Pub. by ECW) Genl Dist Srvs.

Niecks, Frederick. Programme Music in the Last Four Centuries. LC 68-25299. (Studies in Music: No. 42). 1969. reprint ed. lib. bdg. 75.00 (0-8383-0311-0) M S G Haskell Hse.

— Programme Music in the Last Four Centuries: A Contribution to the History of Musical Expression. 548p. 1990. reprint ed. lib. bdg. 99.00 (0-7812-9122-4) Rprt Serv.

— Robert Schumann. LC 74-24167. (Dent's International Library of Books on Music). reprint ed. 39.50 (0-404-13065-8) AMS Pr.

Nied, Susanna, tr. see Thomsen, Soren U.

Nieddu, Domenica, tr. see Terruzzi, Giorgio.

Niedecker, Lorine. The Granite Pail: The Selected Poems of Lorine Niedecker. 2nd rev. ed. Corman, Cid, ed. 160p. 1996. pap. 14.50 (0-917788-61-3) Gnomon Pr.

Nieden, Marcel. Organum Deitatis: Die Christologie des Thomas de Vio Cajetan. (Studies in Medieval & Reformation Thought: Vol. 62). (GER.). 288p. 1997. text 99.50 (90-04-10801-7) Brill Academic Pubs.

Niedens, Lyle & Buckner, Steve. Portraits of Excellence: A Heritage of Athletic Achievement at the University of Kansas. (Illus.). 256p. 1998. 39.50 (1-885758-14-6) Quality Sports.

Niedenthal, Michael. Internationaler Handel Und Umweltschutz: Eine Analyse Von Ansatzen Fur eine Okologische Reform der Welthandelsordnung. 170p. 1998. 39.95 (3-631-33963-1) P Lang Pubng.

Niedenthal, Paula M. & Kitayama, Shinobu, eds. The Heart's Eye: Emotional Influences in Perception & Attention. (Illus.). 289p. 1994. text 65.00 (0-12-410560-2) Acad Pr.

Nieder, John & Thompson, Thomas. Forgive & Love Again. 1991. pap. 8.99 (0-89081-934-3) Harvest Hse.

Nieder, Ludwig, tr. see Simmel, Georg.

***Niederehe, Hans-Josef.** Bibliografia Cronologica de la Linguistica, la Gramatica y la Lexicografia del Espanol (BICRES II) Desde el ano 1601 Hasta el ano 1700. LC 99-16871. (Studies in the History of the Language Sciences: Vol. 91). (SPA.). vi, 472p. 1999. 99.00 (1-55619-635-0) J Benjamins Pubng.

Niederehe, Hans-Josef. Bibliografia Cronologica de la Linguistica, la Gramatica y la Lexicografia del Espanol Desde los Principos Hasta el Ano 1600 (BICRES) Scholarly Edition. LC 94-36633. (Studies in the History of the Language Sciences: No. 76). (SPA.). vi, 457p. 1994. 100.00 (1-55619-612-1) J Benjamins Pubng Co.

— In Memoriam Friedrich Diez: Proceedings of the Colloquium for the History of Romance Studies, Trier Oct. 2-4, 1975. Haarmann, Harald, ed. (Studies in the History of Linguistics: No. 9). viii, 508p. 1976. 87.00 (90-272-0900-6) J Benjamins Pubng Co.

Niederehe, Hans-Josef & Koerner, E. F., eds. History & Historiography of Linguistics: Proceedings of the Fourth International Conference on the History of the Language Sciences, Trier, 24-28 August 1987, 2 vols., Set. LC 90-42546. (Studies in the History of the Language Sciences: Vol. 51). 1990. 236.00 (90-272-4534-7) J Benjamins Pubng Co.

— History & Historiography of Linguistics: Proceedings of the Fourth International Conference on the History of the Language Sciences, Trier, 24-28 August 1987, 2 vols., Vol. 2. LC 90-42546. (Studies in the History of the Language Sciences: Vol. 51). x, 452p. 1990. write for info. (90-272-4542-8) J Benjamins Pubng Co.

Niederehe, Hans-Josef & Koerner, E. F. K., eds. History & Historiography of Linguistics: Proceedings of the Fourth International Conference on the History of the Language Sciences, Trier, 24-28 August 1987, 2 vols., Vol. 1. LC 90-42546. (Studies in the History of the Language Sciences: Vol. 51). xii, 394p. 1990. write for info. (90-272-4541-X) J Benjamins Pubng Co.

Niederehe, Hans-Josef & Quilis, Antonio. The History of Linguistics in Spain. LC 86-17314. (Studies in the History of the Language Sciences: No. 34). viii, 360p. 1986. 84.00 (90-272-4517-7) J Benjamins Pubng Co.

***Niederer, Carl.** Cardboard: An Illustrated Fiction. (Illus.). 224p. 1999. 24.50 (0-9676358-0-2) C Niederer.

Niederer, Frances J. Hollins College: An Illustrated History. LC 72-97863. (Illus.). 232p. 1973. reprint ed. pap. 72.00 (0-608-05325-2, 202178900023) Bks Demand.

Niederer, J. A., ed. see Luccio, L. V.

Niedergall, Jane. Primary Alaska. (Teaching Alaska Ser.: Vol. 2). (Illus.). 60p. (J). (ps-3). Date not set. pap., teacher ed. 7.95 (1-878051-17-2, CP061) Circumpolar Pr.

Niederhauser, Hans R. & Frohlich, Margaret. Form Drawing. (Illus.). 57p. (Orig.). (J). 1974. pap. 12.50 (0-318-41110-5) Merc Pr NY.

***Niederhauser, Jurg & Adamzik, Kirsten.** Wissenschaftssprache und Umgangssprache im Kontakt. 1999. 32.95 (3-631-35239-5) P Lang Pubng.

***Niederhauser, Jurg & Szlek, Stanislaw P.** Sprachsplitter und Sprachspiele: Nachdenken uber Sprache und Sprachgebrauch Festschrift fur Willy Sanders. 2000. 41.95 (3-906764-52-4, Pub. by P Lang) P Lang Pubng.

Niederhauser, Warren D. & Meyer, E. Gerald, eds. Legal Rights of Chemists & Engineers. LC 77-9364. (Advances in Chemistry Ser.: No. 161). 1977. 24.95 (0-8412-0357-1); pap. 14.95 (0-8412-0537-X) Am Chemical.

— Legal Rights of Chemists & Engineers. LC 77-9364. (Advances in Chemistry Ser.: Vol. 161). 119p. 1977. reprint ed. pap. 36.90 (0-608-03864-4, 206431100008) Bks Demand.

Niederhellamnn, Annette. Arzt und Heilkunde in den fruhmittelalterlichen Leges: Eine Wort- und Sachkundliche Untersuchung, Vol. 12. 3053p. 1983. 142.35 (3-11-009607-2) De Gruyter.

Niederhofer, Relda E. & Stuckey, Ronald L. Edwin Lincoln Moseley (1865-1948) Naturalist, Scientist, Educator. (Illus.). 320p. 1998. 34.50 (0-9668034-2-6) R L S Creations.

Niederhofer, Ulrike. Die Auseinandersetzung mit dem Expressionismus in der Bildenden Kunst im Wandel der Politischen Realitat der SBZ und der DDR 1945-1989. (Europaische Hochschulschriften, Reihe 28: Bd. 277). (GER., Illus.). 549p. 1996. 95.95 (3-631-30715-2) P Lang Pubng.

Niederhoffer, Arthur, jt. auth. see Bloch, Herbert A.

Niederhoffer, Victor. The Education of a Speculator. LC 96-30765. (Illus.). 444p. 1997. 29.95 (0-471-13747-2) Wiley.

***Niederhoffer, Victor.** Education of a Speculator. 444p. 1998. pap. 18.95 (0-471-24948-3) Wiley.

Niederhube. Imaging for the Surgeon. (C). 1998. text. write for info. (0-443-05629-3) Church.

Niederhuber. Atlas of General Surgery. 1999. pap. text 135.00 (0-8385-0060-9) Appleton & Lange.

Niederhuber, John. Fundamentals of Basic Surgery. (Illus.). 836p. (C). 1999. pap. text 44.95 (0-8385-0509-0, A-0509-8, Apple Lange Med) McGraw.

Niederhuber, John, jt. auth. see Baker, R. Robinson.

***Niederhuber, John E.** Surgery Rotation Value Pak. 1999. 59.95 (0-8385-8818-2, Apple Lange Med) McGraw.

***Niederkorn, K., et al, eds.** European Society of Neurosonology & Cerebral Hemodynamics: 5th Meeting, Graz, Austria, May 2000: Abstracts. (Cerebrovascular Diseases Ser.: Vol. 10, Suppl. 1 (2000)). (Illus.). x, 46p. 2000. pap. 25.25 (3-8055-7109-7) S Karger.

Niederland, William G. & Sholevar, Bahman. The Creative Process: A Psychoanalytic Discussion. LC 82-73946. (Criticism, Literary & Psychoanalytic Ser.). (Illus.). 90p. (Orig.). 1982. pap. 5.95 (0-911323-03-1) Concourse Pr.

Niederle, J. & Fischer, J. Selected Topics in Quantum Field Theory & Mathematical Physics. 468p. (C). 1990. text 144.00 (981-02-0116-8) World Scientific Pub.

Niederle, J., tr. see Maslov, V. P. & Fedoriuk, M. V.

Niederlehner, B. R. & Cairns, John, Jr. Ecological Toxicity Testing: Scale, Complexity, & Relevance. 240p. 1994. lib. bdg. 85.00 (0-87371-599-3, L599) Lewis Pubs.

Niederlinski, A., et al. EFPI - Expert for Process Identification: Software & User's Manual. 1994. text 78.00 (981-02-1272-0) World Scientific Pub.

Niederman, Andrew. Neighborhood Watch. 336p. 2000. per. 6.99 (0-671-02709-3) PB.

***Niederman, Andrew.** Surrogate Child: Move Tie In. 1999. per. 6.99 (0-671-04161-4, Pocket Books) PB.

***Niederman, Derrick.** The Inner Game of Investing: Access the Power of Your Investment Personality. LC HG4515.15.N54 1999. (Wiley Investment Classics Ser.). (Illus.). 198p. 1999. 24.95 (0-471-31479-X) Wiley.

Niederman, Derrick. Inspector Forsooth's Interactive Mysteries. LC 98-39763. (Illus.). 96p. (J). (gr. 3-7). 1998. 14.95 (0-8069-3182-5) Sterling.

***Niederman, Derrick.** Inspector Forsooth's Whodunits. (J). 1999. pap. text 5.95 (0-8069-3199-X) Sterling.

Niederman, Derrick. A Killing on Wall Street: An Investment Mystery. LC 00-28300. 208p. 2000. text 21.95 (0-471-37458-X) Wiley.

— This Is Not Your Father's Stock. 1997. pap. write for info. (0-8129-2862-8, Times Bks) Crown Pub Group.

— This Is Not Your Father's Stockpicking Book. Date not set. write for info. (0-8129-2832-6, Times Bks) Crown Pub Group.

Niederman, Gerald A., jt. auth. see Johnson, Bruce A.

Niederman, Michael S., ed. Respiratory Infections in the Elderly. LC 91-25295. (Illus.). 400p. 1991. reprint ed. pap. 124.00 (0-608-07255-9, 206748200009) Bks Demand.

Niederman, Michael S., et al. Respiratory Infections. 2nd ed. 704p. text 145.00 (0-7817-1902-X) Lppncott W & W.

Niederman, Sharon. Hellish Relish: Sizzling Salsas & Devilish Dips from the Kitchens of New Mexico. (Illus.). 96p. 1999. pap. 16.95 (962-593-529-0) Tuttle Pubng.

— A Quilt of Words: Women's Diaries, Letters, & Original Accounts of Life in the Southwest, 1860-1960. LC 88-81621. (Illus.). 240p. 1988. pap. 11.95 (1-55566-047-9) Johnson Bks.

Niederman, Sharon, ed. Shaking Eve's Tree: Short Stories of Jewish Women. 290p. 1990. pap. 14.95 (0-8276-0369-X) JPS Phila.

Niederman, Sharon & Morgan, Brandt. The Santa Fe & Taos Book: A Complete Guide. 5th rev. ed. LC 99-18186. (Great Destinations Ser.). (Illus.). 320p. 1999. pap. 17.95 (1-58157-009-0) Berkshire Hse.

Niederman, Sharon & Sagan, Miriam, eds. New Mexico Poetry Renaissance. LC 94-12905. (Illus.). 216p. 1994. pap. 14.95 (1-878610-41-4) Red Crane Bks.

Niederman, Sharon, jt. auth. see Brandt, Karen N.

Niedermayer, Oskar & Sinnott, Richard, eds. Public Opinion & International Governance, Vol. 2. (Beliefs in Government Ser.: No. 2). (Illus.). 512p. 1996. text 69.00 (0-19-827958-2) OUP.

— Public Opinion & Internationalized Governance, Vol. 2. (Beliefs in Government Ser.). (Illus.). 508p. 1998. reprint ed. pap. text 35.00 (0-19-829476-X) OUP.

Niedermayer, Walter. Into the Deep Misty Woods of the Ardennes. (Illus.). 170p. (Orig.). (YA). 1990. pap. text 13.50 (0-935648-30-5) Halldin Pub.

— Remagen & Other Rhine Crossings. (Illus.). 67p. 1993. 9.95 (0-935648-45-3) Halldin Pub.

Niedermayr, Walter. Walter Niedermayr: Momentary Resorts. AR/GE Kunst Bozen, ed. (Illus.). 114p. 1999. 50.00 (3-89322-962-0) Edition Cantz.

Niedermeier, Donna. The Virgin Mary Poems. (Illus.). 72p. 1998. pap. 8.00 (0-8059-4180-0) Dorrance.

Niedermeier, Keith E., jt. auth. see Von Eye, Alexander.

Niedermeier, Lynn R. & Vest, Herb D. Wealth: How to Get It, How to Keep It. 160p. 1995. pap. 14.95 (0-8144-7891-3) AMACOM.

Niedermeier, Lynn R., jt. auth. see Vest, Herb D.

Niedermeier, Michael, jt. ed. see Morris-Keitel, Peter.

Niedermeir, Ann M., et al. A New Beginning: An ESL Reader. (Illus.). 128p. (C). 1988. pap. text 20.80 (0-13-611849-6) P-H.

Niedermeyer, Ernest. Epilepsy: Recent View on Its Theory, Diagnosis & Therapy of Epilepsy. (Modern Problems of Pharmacopsychiatry Ser.: Vol. 4). 1970. 90.50 (3-8055-0529-9) S Karger.

Niedermeyer, Ernst & Da Silva, Fernando L., eds. Electroencephalography: Basic Principles, Clinical Applications, & Related Fields. 3rd rev. ed. LC 93-3005. (Illus.). 1189p. 1993. 159.00 (0-683-06511-4) Lppncott W & W.

Niedermeyer, Ernst & Lopes÷aßilva, Fernando. Electroencephalography: Basic Principles, Clinical Applications & Related Fields. 4th ed. LC 97-48637. 1258p. 1998. 189.00 (0-683-30284-1) Lppncott W & W.

Niedermiller-Chaffins, Debra. Network Training Guide: Managing Netware Systems. 3rd ed. LC 94-28058. 800p. 1994. 70.00 incl. disk (1-56205-366-3) New Riders Pub.

— Network Training Guide: Networking Technologies. 3rd ed. LC 94-33319. 1244p. 1994. pap. 70.00 incl. disk (1-56205-363-9) New Riders Pub.

— Novell CNE 4 Study Guide. 1379p. (Orig.). 1995. pap., student ed. 90.00 (1-56205-512-7) New Riders Pub.

Niedernostheide, F. J., ed. Nonlinear Dynamics & Pattern Formation in Semiconductors & Devices. (Proceedings in Physics Ser.: Vol. 79). 272p. 1995. 89.00 (0-387-58833-7) Spr-Verlag.

— Nonlinear Dynamics & Pattern Formation in Semiconductors & Devices: Proceedings of the International Conference, Noorwijkerhout, the Netherlands, July 4-7, 1994. LC 95-2680. (Proceedings in Physics Ser.). xi, 265p. 1995. 97.95 (3-540-58833-7) Spr-Verlag.

Niederquell, Mike, ed. see Wendland, Mike.

Niederreiter, H., jt. auth. see Kuipers, Lauwerens.

Niederreiter, Harald. Random Number Generation & Quasi-Monte Carlo Methods. LC 92-12567. (CBMS-NSF Regional Conference Ser.: No. 63). vi, 241p. 1992. pap. 45.00 (0-89871-295-5) Soc Indus-Appl Math.

Niederreiter, Harald, et al, eds. Monte Carlo & Quasi-Monte Carlo Methods, 1996. LC 97-34133. (Lecture Notes in Statistics Ser.: Vol. 127). 464p. 1997. pap. 44.95 (0-387-98335-X) Spr-Verlag.

Niederreiter, Harald & Shieu, Peter J., eds. Monte Carlo & Quasi-Monte Carlo Methods in Scientific Computing: Proceedings of a Conference at the University of Nevada, Las Vegas, Nevada, USA, June 23-25, 1994. LC 95-37688. (Lecture Notes in Statistics Ser.: Vol. 106). 1995. 54.95 (0-387-94577-6) Spr-Verlag.

***Niederreiter, Harald & Spanier, Jerome, eds.** Monte Carlo & Quasi-Monte Carlo Methods 1998: Proceedings of a Conference at the Claremont Graduate University, Claremont, California, USA, June 22-26, 1998. LC 99-47502. xvi, 472p. 1999. pap. 99.95 (3-540-66176-X) Spr-Verlag.

Niederreiter, Harald, jt. auth. see Lidl, Rudolf.

Niederreiter, Harald, jt. ed. see Cohen, Stephen D.

Niederst, Jennifer. Designing for the Web: Getting Started in a New Medium. LC 97-179470. 1996. pap. 24.95 (1-56592-165-8) Thomson Learn.

— HTML Pocket Reference. Koman, Richard, ed. (Illus.). 100p. 2000. pap. 9.95 (1-56592-579-3) OReilly & Assocs.

***Niederst, Jennifer.** Web Design in a Nutshell. Koman, Richard, ed. (Illus.). 560p. 1999. pap. 19.95 (*1-56592-515-7*) OReilly & Assocs.

Niederwimmer, Kurt. Didache: A Commentary. LC 98-28758. (Hermeneia Ser.). 1998. 52.00 (*0-8006-6027-7*, 1-6027, Fortress Pr) Augsburg Fortress.

— Quaestiones Theologicae. 360p. 1997. text 105.00 (*3-11-015711-X*) De Gruyter.

Niedfeldt, Linda J. Red As in Russia & Measles & Love. LC 92-63029. 128p. (Orig.). 1993. pap. 7.99 (*0-8100-0469-0*, 17N1623) Northwest Pub.

***Niedhart, Gottfried & Broderick, George.** Lieder In Politik und Alltag Des Nationalsozialismus. (GER., Illus.). VI, 288p. 1999. 52.00 (*3-631-33611-X*) P Lang Pubng.

Niedhauk, Charlotte A. Charlotte's Story: A Florida Keys Diary, 1934 & 1935. 2nd rev. ed. Herbert, Mary-Alice, ed. LC 98-39527. (Illus.). 352p. 1999. pap. 17.95 (*0-9619155-4-4*) Laurel & Herbert.

Niednagel, Jonathan P. Your Best Sport: How to Choose & Play It. LC 92-60519. (Illus.). 385p. (Orig.). 1992. pap. 19.95 (*0-916309-01-0*) Laguna Pr.

— Your Key to Sports Success: Using Your Unique Brain Type to Maximize Athletic Performance. LC 92-60519. 408p. 1997. pap. 24.95 (*0-916309-03-7*) Laguna Pr.

Niedner, Marie & Von Reden, Gussi. Knitted Lace. Kliot, Kaethe, ed. & tr. by. from GER. Orig. Title: Kunst-Stricken. (Illus.). 80p. 1993. pap. 12.00 (*0-916896-53-6*) Lacis Pubns.

Niedobitek, Matthias. The Cultural Dimension in EC Law. LC 97-224341. 382p. 1997. 143.00 (*90-411-0685-5*) Kluwer Academic.

Niedrich, Charles. Unlikely Unions: The Angela Nugent Story. 150p. (Orig.). 1996. pap. 15.95 (*1-57502-202-8*, D0834) Morris Pubng.

Niedt, Friederich E. The Musical Guide, Pts. I-III: 1700-1721. Taylor, Irmgard C., ed. & tr. by. Poulin, Pamela L., tr. (Early Music Ser.). (Illus.). 312p. 1989. text 98.00 (*0-19-315251-7*) OUP.

Niedworok, Claudio O. Seafarers: Chronicles of the Suspense & Romance of the Sea. Knight, Tori, ed. (Illus.). 80p. (Orig.). (YA). Date not set. pap. text 11.95 (*1-882133-05-6*) Barefoot Pr.

Niedzialkowski, Stephan & Winslow, Jonathan. Beyond the Word: The World of Mime. LC 93-3164. 140p. 1993. pap. 12.95 (*1-879094-23-1*) Momentum Bks.

Niedzie. Stations of the Cross. 30p. 1992. pap. text 1.50 (*0-8198-6912-0*) Pauline Bks.

Niedzielski, Henri, jt. auth. see Mueller, Theodore.

***Niedzielski, Nancy A. & Preston, Dennis Richard.** Folk Linguistics. LC 99-51346. (Trends in Linguistics Ser.). 1999. write for info. (*3-11-016251-2*) De Gruyter.

Niedzwecki, John M., jt. ed. see Lutes, Loren D.

***Niedzwiecki, Maciej.** Identification of Time-Varying Processes in Signal Processing. LC 00-33019. 2000. write for info. (*0-471-98629-1*) Wiley.

Niedzwiecki, Matthew E., jt. auth. see Chang, Richard Y.

Niefert, Marianne. Dr. Mom's Parenting Guide: Common-Sense Guidance for the Life of Your Child. 288p. 1996. pap. 10.95 (*0-452-26864-8*, Plume) Dutton Plume.

Nieforth, Karl A., jt. auth. see Witczak, Zbigniew J.

Nieh Hua Ling. People, Twentieth Century. 288p. 1990. pap. text 9.00 (*0-9625118-5-4*) World Scientific Pub.

Nieh, Hua-ling, ed. Literature of the Hundred Flowers: Criticism & Polemics, Vol. 1. LC 80-36748. (Modern Asian Literature Ser.). 338p. reprint ed. pap. 104.80 (*0-8357-4274-1*, 203707200001) Bks Demand.

Nieh, Hualing. Mulberry & Peach: Two Women of China. Young, Jane P. & Lappin, Linda, trs. LC 98-12259. 224p. 1998. reprint ed. pap. 12.95 (*1-55861-182-7*) Feminist Pr.

Nieh, Hualing, ed. Literature of the Hundred Flowers, 2 vols. LC 80-36748. (Modern Asian Literature Ser.). 1981. text 58.00 (*0-231-05074-7*) Col U Pr.

— Literature of the Hundred Flowers, 2 vols., Set. LC 80-36748. (Modern Asian Literature Ser.). 1981. text 173.50 (*0-231-05264-2*) Col U Pr.

— Literature of the Hundred Flowers, 2 vols., Vol. II: Poetry & Fiction. LC 80-36748. (Modern Asian Literature Ser.). 618p. 1981. text 110.50 (*0-231-05076-3*) Col U Pr.

Nieh, T. G., et al. Superplasticity in Metals & Ceramics. (Solid State Science Ser.). (Illus.). 287p. (C). 1997. text 80.00 (*0-521-56105-1*) Cambridge U Pr.

Niehans, Jurg. International Monetary Economics. LC 83-124960. 360p. 1986. reprint ed. pap. text 17.95 (*0-8018-3408-2*) Johns Hopkins.

***Niehardt, John G. & Elk, Nicholas Black.** Black Elk Speaks. 21st ed. LC 00-36382. (Illus.). 300p. 2000. 45.00 (*0-8032-1309-3*, Bison Books) U of Nebr Pr.

Niehaus, Carmen. Bread, Rusks, & Muffins. 1999. pap. text 12.95 (*0-7981-3811-4*) Human & Rousseau.

Niehaus, Earl F. Irish in New Orleans, 1800-1860. LC 76-6359. (Irish Americans Ser.). 1976. reprint ed. 28.95 (*0-405-09352-7*) Ayer.

Niehaus, Gregory R., jt. auth. see Harrington, Scott E.

***Niehaus, Isak.** Witchcraft, Power & Politics: Exploring the Occult in the South African Lowveld. (Anthropology, Culture & Society Ser.). 240p. 2000. 69.95 (*0-7453-1563-1*, Pub. by Pluto GBR); pap. 22.50 (*0-7453-1558-5*, Pub. by Pluto GBR) Stylus Pub VA.

Niehaus, Joe. Investigative Forensic Hypnosis. LC 98-22629. 192p. 1998. boxed set 64.95 (*0-8493-8133-9*) CRC Pr.

Niehaus, Joseph. The Sixth Sense: Practical Tips for Everyday Safety. (Illus.). (Orig.). 1990. pap. 11.95 (*0-933025-19-X*) Blue Bird Pub.

Niehaus, Joseph & Sakora, Mary. Hypnosis Unveiled. 82p. (YA). (gr. 7-12). 1994. pap. 6.95 (*1-57515-056-5*) PPI Pubng.

Niehaus, R. J. & Price, K. F. Human Resource Strategies for Organizations in Transition. LC 90-6759. (Illus.). 344p. (C). 1990. 110.00 (*0-306-43506-3*, Plenum Trade) Perseus Pubng.

Niehaus, Richard J. Strategic Human Resource Planning Applications. 248p. 1987. 75.00 (*0-306-42561-0*, Plenum Trade) Perseus Pubng.

Niehaus, Richard J., ed. Human Resource Policy Analysis: Organizational Application. LC 85-6577. 256p. 1985. 49.95 (*0-275-90218-8*, C0218, Praeger Pubs) Greenwood.

Niehaus, Richard J. & Price, K. F., eds. Bottom Line Results from Strategic Human Resource Planning. (Illus.). 328p. (C). 1991. 126.00 (*0-306-44187-X*, Plenum Trade) Perseus Pubng.

— Creating the Competitive Edge Through Human Resource Applications. LC 87-38076. (Illus.). 280p. 1988. 75.00 (*0-306-42827-X*, Plenum Trade) Perseus Pubng.

Niehaus, Theodore F. A Biosystematic Study of the Genus Brodiaea (Amaryllidaceae) LC 77-170326. (University of California Publications in Social Welfare: No. 60). (Illus.). 73p. reprint ed. pap. 30.00 (*0-8357-7259-4*, 203067800069) Bks Demand.

Niehaus, Thomas, et al. Resources for Latin American Jewish Studies: Essays on Using Jewish Reference Sources for the Study of Latin American Jewry; U. S. Library Collections on L. A. Jews; & U. S. Archival Resources for the Study of Jews in L. A. Elkin, Judith L., ed. LC 84-80219. (LAJSA Publication: No. 1). 59p. (Orig.). 1984. pap. text 10.00 (*0-916921-00-X*) Lat Am Jewish Studies.

***Niehausen, William Alan.** A Bird in the Hand: A Tale of Revenge. LC 00-190676. 2000. 25.00 (*0-7388-1605-1*); pap. 18.00 (*0-7388-1606-X*) Xlibris Corp.

***Niehm, Linda S. & Wickliffe, Vanessa.** International Retailing: Instructor's Guide. 57p. 1998. pap., teacher ed. 3.50 (*1-56367-104-2*) Fairchild.

Niehof, Anke, jt. auth. see Pennartz, Paul.

Niehoff, Arthur. An Anthropologist under the Bed. LC 98-94187. 490p. 1999. pap. 14.95 (*0-9643072-5-1*) Hominid Pr.

— On Becoming Human: A Journey of 5,000,000 Years. LC 94-92303. 420p. (Orig.). 1996. pap. 14.95 (*0-9643072-3-5*, GN281) Hominid Pr.

— Takeover: How Euroman Changed the World, 2 vols. LC 96-75697. Orig. Title: The Other Side of History. 231p. (C). 1996. pap. 13.95 (*0-9643072-2-7*) Hominid Pr.

Niehoff, Arthur & Niehoff, Justin. Bicycling for Life. LC 99-97124. (Journaling Ser.: Vols. 1 & 2). (Illus.). 280p. 2000. pap. 13.95 (*0-9643072-7-8*) Hominid Pr.

Niehoff, Arthur H. Another Side of History. LC 89-63072. 1990. 18.95 (*0-87212-233-6*) Libra.

— On Being a Conceptual Animal. LC 97-76969. xv, 313p. 1998. pap. 13.95 (*0-9643072-4-3*) Hominid Pr.

Niehoff, Arthur H., jt. auth. see Arensberg, Conrad M.

Niehoff, Debra. The Biology of Violence: How Understanding the Brain, Behavior, & Environment Can Break the Vicious Circle of Aggression. LC 98-34673. 368p. 1999. 24.50 (*0-684-83132-5*) Free Pr.

Niehoff, Justin, jt. auth. see Niehoff, Arthur.

Niehoff, M. The Figure of Joseph in Post-Biblical Jewish Literature. LC 91-35676. (Arbeiten zur Geschichte des Antiken Judentums & des Urchristentums Ser.: Vol. 16). viii, 180p. 1992. 71.00 (*90-04-09556-X*) Brill Academic Pubs.

***Niehoff, Martina.** Die Von Internationalen Strafgerichtshofen Anwendbaren Normen des Volkerstrafrechts. XXXVII, 165p. 1999. 39.95 (*3-631-34611-5*) P Lang Pubng.

Niehoff, Richard O. Floyd W. Reeves: Innovative Educator & Distinguished Practitioner of the Art of Public Administration. (Illus.). 348p. (C). 1991. lib. bdg. 57.00 (*0-8191-7921-3*) U Pr of Amer.

Niehorster, Leo W. The Royal Hungarian Army, 1920-1945 Vol. I: Organization & History. (Illus.). 318p. 1999. 55.00 (*1-891227-19-X*, Axis Europa Bks) Axis Europa.

Niehr, Herbert. Der Hochste Gott: Alttestamentlicher JHWH-Glaube im Kontext Syrisch-Kanaanaischer Religion des 1.Jahrtausends v. Chr. (Beiheft zur Zeitschrift fuer die Alttestamentliche Wissenschaft Ser.: Band 190). x, 268p. (C). 1990. lib. bdg. 75.40 (*3-11-012342-8*) De Gruyter.

Niehuser, Elke. French Bronze Clocks. (Illus.). 276p. 1999. 89.95 (*0-7643-0943-9*) Schiffer.

Niehuss, Merith. Arbeiterschaft in Krieg und Inflation: Soziale Schichtung und Lage der Arbeiter in Augsburg und Linz 1910-1925. (Veroeffentlichungen der Historischen Kommission zu Berlin, Band 67, Beitraege zu Inflation und Wiederaufbau in Deutschland und Europa 1914-1924: Band 3). (GER.). xiv, 308p. 1985. 89.25 (*3-11-009660-9*) De Gruyter.

Nieiolowska, Katia. Casa Guatemalteca. 248p. 65.00 (*958-9393-71-3*, Pub. by Villegas Ed) Rizzoli Intl.

Niejenhuis, Van, see Van Niejenhuis, ed.

Niejolt, G. Thomas-Lycklama. On the Road for Work: Migratory Workers on the East Coast of the United States. (Ser. on the Development of Societies: Vol. VII). 224p. 1980. lib. bdg. 73.50 (*0-89838-043-X*) Kluwer Academic.

Nieke, M. R., jt. ed. see Driscoll, S. T.

Niekerk, Andre Van, see Cheadle, Halton.

Niekerk, Andre Van, see Le Roux, Pak & Van Niekerk, Andre.

Niekerk, Andre Van, see Cheadle, Halton.

Niekerk, Barend Van, see Van Niekerk, Barend.

Niekisch, E. A., ed. see Burkel, E.

Niekro, Phil & Bird, Tom. Knuckleballs. LC 86-9902. 232p. 1986. 16.95 (*0-88191-042-2*) Freundlich.

Niel, A. The Man in Revolt. 109p. 1973. 4.95 (*0-318-37033-6*) Asia Bk Corp.

Niel, Jean-Francois M. Diccionario de Mitologia Universal, 2 vols. (SPA.). 1266p. 1991. pap. 95.00 (*0-7859-6254-9*, 8476723571) Fr & Eur.

— Diccionario de mitologia Universal, Vol. 1. (SPA.). 1266p. 1991. pap. 95.00 (*0-7859-6489-4*) Fr & Eur.

— Diccionario de Mitologia Universal, Vol. 2. (SPA.). 1266p. 1991. pap. 95.00 (*0-7859-6255-7*, 8476723598) Fr & Eur.

Niel, Tim, jt. auth. see Campbell, Allan.

Nielandt, Klaus. Die Relevanz der Kantischen Ethik Fur Das Theoretische Selbstverstandnis Einer Emanzipierten Padagogik. (Europaische Hochschulschriften Ser.: Reihe 11, Bd. 722). (GER.). 214p. 1997. 42.95 (*3-631-31838-3*) P Lang Pubng.

Nield. Welcome to My World: Psychology 101. 116p. (C). 1998. pap. text 19.60 (*0-536-01174-5*) Pearson Custom.

Nield, D. A. & Bejan, Adrian. Convection in Porous Media. (Illus.). 424p. 1991. 98.95 (*0-387-97651-5*) Spr-Verlag.

Nield, Donald A. & Bejan, Adrian. Convection in Porous Media. 2nd ed. LC 97-48880. (Illus.). 496p. 1998. 95.00 (*0-387-98443-7*) Spr-Verlag.

Nield, Dorothea. Adventures in Patchwork. 84p. 1976. 8.95 (*0-263-05591-4*) Transatl Arts.

Nield-Gehrig, Jill S. Fundamentals of Periodontal Instrumentation. 4th ed. 576p. spiral bd. write for info. (*0-7817-2860-6*) Lppncott W & W.

Nield-Gehrig, Jill S. Periodontal Instrumentation for the Practitioner. LC 98-21882. 459p. 1998. pap. 29.95 (*0-683-30493-3*) Lppncott W & W.

Nield-Gehrig, Jill S. & Houseman, Ginger A. Fundamentals of Periodontal Instrumentation. 3rd ed. LC 95-19095. (Illus.). 521p. 1996. write for info. (*0-683-06516-5*) Lppncott W & W.

Nield, Jill S. & Houseman, Ginger A. Fundamentals of Dental Hygiene Instrumentation. 2nd ed. LC 87-25975. (Illus.). 521p. 1988. pap. text 37.00 (*0-8121-1130-3*) Lppncott W & W.

***Nield, Maureen.** How Different from Us. LC 99-54912. 28p. (YA). (gr. 4-12). 1999. pap. 5.00 (*0-88734-767-3*) Players Pr.

Nield, Rachel. Policing Haiti: Preliminary Assessment of the Civilian Police Force. Washington Office on Latin America Staff, ed. 56p. (Orig.). 1995. pap. text 7.00 (*0-929513-30-4*) WOLA.

Nieli, Russell. Wittgenstein: From Mysticism to Ordinary Language: A Study of Viennese Positivism & the Thought of Ludwig Wittgenstein. LC 86-23144. (SUNY Series in Philosophy). 261p. 1987. text 21.50 (*0-88706-397-7*) State U NY Pr.

Nieli, Russell, ed. Racial Preference & Racial Justice: The New Affirmative Action Controversy. 544p. (C). 1991. 25.95 (*0-89633-147-4*) Ethics & Public Policy.

Niello, J. F., et al. Nuclear Physics: Proceedings of the 15th Workshop. 400p. 1993. text 114.00 (*981-02-1374-3*) World Scientific Pub.

***Nielloud, Franpcoise & Marti-Mestres, Gilberte.** Pharmaceutical Emulsions & Suspensions. LC 99-87827. (Drugs & the Pharmaceutical Sciences Ser.). 2000. 0.00 (*0-8247-0304-9*) Dekker.

Niels Bohr Library Staff. Guide to the Archival Collections in the Niels Bohr Library at the American Institute of Physics. LC 94-28569. (International Catalog of Sources for History of Physics & Allied Science Ser.: Rept. 7). 1995. 140.00 (*1-56396-379-5*) Am Inst Physics.

— Supplement to the Guide to the Archival Collections in the Niels Bohr Library at the American Institute of Physics. LC 98-4919. (International Catalog of Sources for History of Physics & Allied Sciences Ser.). 1998. pap. write for info. (*1-56396-787-1*) Am Inst Physics.

***Niels, Svennevig, et al, eds.** Sustainable Aquaculture: Food for the Future? - Proceedings of the Second International Symposium, Oslo, Norway, 2-5 November 1997. (Illus.). 360p. 1999. 95.00 (*90-5809-097-3*, Pub. by A A Balkema) Ashgate Pub Co.

Nielsen. Adolescence: A Contemporary View. 3rd ed. (C). 1995. pap. text, suppl. ed. 35.50 (*0-15-503548-7*, Pub. by Harcourt Coll Pubs) Harcourt.

— Adolescence: A Contemporary View. 3rd ed. (C). 1995. pap. text, teacher ed. 26.75 (*0-15-503240-2*) Harcourt Coll Pubs.

— Adolescence: A Contemporary View. 3rd ed. (C). 1996. text 68.00 (*0-15-500995-8*, Pub. by Harcourt Coll Pubs) Harcourt.

— Combinatorial Chemistry in Drug Design. (Illus.). 320p. 1998. text 126.95 (*0-7514-0387-3*, Pub. by B Acad & Prof) Routldge.

— Direct Integral Theory. (Lecture Notes in Pure & Applied Mathematics Ser.: Vol. 61). (Illus.). 184p. 1980. pap. text 115.00 (*0-8247-6971-6*) Dekker.

— Hollywood's Other Blacklist. 192p. 1995. 45.00 (*0-85170-508-1*, Pub. by British Film Inst) Ind U Pr.

— Polymer Rheology. (Illus.). 216p. 1977. text 135.00 (*0-8247-7550-3*) Dekker.

— Religions of the World. 3rd ed. 1993. pap. text, teacher ed. 10.00 (*0-312-08079-4*) St Martin.

Nielsen, A. & Belcher, R. Kinetics of Precipitation. LC 64-15738. (International Series of Monographs on Analytical Chemistry: Vol. 18). 1964. 77.00 (*0-08-010735-4*, Pub. by Pergamon Repr) Franklin.

Nielsen, A. L. Stepping Razor. (Orig.). 1997. pap. 10.00 (*0-9619097-9-X*) Edge Bks.

***Nielsen, A. L.** Vext. LC 98 86548. 113p. 1999. pap. 10.00 (*0-9623806-5-2*) SINK Pr.

Nielsen, A. T., jt. ed. see Feuer, H.

Nielsen, Aldon L. Black Chant: Languages of African-American Postmodernism. LC 96-12762. (Studies in American Literature & Culture: No. 105). 308p. (C). 1997. pap. text 19.95 (*0-521-55526-4*) Cambridge U Pr.

— C. L. R. James: A Critical Introduction. LC 96-39332. 1997. pap. 18.00 (*0-87805-973-3*) U Pr of Miss.

— Reading Race: White American Poets & Racial Discourse in the Twentieth Century. LC 88-3942. (South Atlantic Modern Language Association Award Study). 192p. 1990. pap. 17.00 (*0-8203-1273-8*) U of Ga Pr.

— Reading Race in American Poetry: An Area of Act. LC 99-6417. 2000. 18.95 (*0-252-06832-7*) U of Ill Pr.

— Writing Between the Lines: Race & Intertextuality. LC 93-23000. 312p. 1994. 45.00 (*0-8203-1603-2*) U of Ga Pr.

Nielsen, Aldon Lynn. C. L. R. James: A Critical Introduction. LC 96-39332. 224p. 1997. 45.00 (*0-87805-972-5*) U Pr of Miss.

Nielsen, Alfred C. Life in American Denmark. Scott, Franklyn D., ed. LC 78-15843. (Scandinavians in America Ser.). (Illus.). 1979. reprint ed. lib. bdg. 17.95 (*0-405-11655-1*) Ayer.

Nielsen, Alleen Pace, ed. see Paradoxa Staff.

Nielsen, Amie L., jt. ed. see Scarpitti, Frank R.

Nielsen, Anders, ed. see Aika, K.

Nielsen, Andreas L. The Collection & Evaluation of Intelligence for the German Air Force High Command: Karlsruhe Study. (USAF Historical Studies: No. 171). 224p. 1955. reprint ed. pap. text 36.95 (*0-89126-143-5*) MA-AH Pub.

— German Air Force General Staff. LC 68-22551. (German Air Force in World War 2 Ser.). 1968. reprint ed. 19.95 (*0-405-00043-X*) Ayer.

Nielsen, Andreas L. & Kennedy, Edward P. The German Air Force General Staff. (USAF Historical Studies: No. 173). 301p. 1959. reprint ed. pap. text 43.95 (*0-89126-135-4*) MA-AH Pub.

Nielsen, Anne M. Corpus of Cypriote Antiquities: Cypriote Antiquities in the NY Carlsberg Glyptotek, Copenhagen. (Studies in Mediterranean Archaeology: Vol. XX: 8). (Illus.). 45p. (Orig.). 1983. pap. 29.50 (*91-85058-28-9*, Pub. by P Astroms) Coronet Bks.

Nielsen, Arnold T. Nitrocarbons. LC 94-41183. (Organic Nitro Chemistry Ser.). 1995. 115.00 (*1-56081-681-3*, Wiley-VCH) Wiley.

— Nitrocarbons. Feuer, Henry, ed. (Organic Nitro Chemistry Ser.). (Illus.). 190p. 1995. 150.00 (*0-471-18603-1*, Wiley-VCH) Wiley.

Nielsen, Arnold T., jt. ed. see Feuer, Henry.

Nielsen, Arya. Gua Sha: Traditional Technique for Modern Practice. LC 95-7286. 1995. pap. text 43.00 (*0-443-05181-X*) Church.

Nielsen, Ashleea. Dolphin Tribe: Remembering the Human-Dolphin Connection. Patton, Sara, ed. 136p. (Orig.). 1993. pap. 12.95 (*0-9637429-3-0*) Dancing Dolphin.

Nielsen, Axel E. Expanding Archaeology. Skibo, James M. et al, eds. (Illus.). 224p. (C). 1995. text 40.00 (*0-87480-479-5*) U of Utah Pr.

Nielsen, B. K. English-Danish Comprehensive Dictionary. (DAN & ENG.). 1203p. 1994. 210.00 (*0-7859-8756-8*) Fr & Eur.

— English-Danish Dictionary: Engelsk-Dansk Ordbog. (DAN & ENG.). 1981. 195.00 (*0-8288-4651-0*, M1270) Fr & Eur.

Nielsen, Barbara, jt. auth. see Newfield, Nancy L.

Nielsen, Birgit. Living Language: German 2 All the Way. (GER.). 1995. 85.00 incl. cd-rom (*0-517-70216-9*) Crown Pub Group.

— Living Language German All the Way 2: Conversation, Grammar, Culture, Reading, Writing, Business. Schier, Helga & Suffrendini, Ana, eds. LC 95-5241. (Living Language Ser.). 1995. pap. 15.00 (*0-517-88291-4*, Crown) Crown Pub Group.

Nielsen, Brenda. Lotus 1-2-3 Release 4 for Windows. (Illustrated Ser.). (Illus.). 192p. (C). 1994. pap. write for info. incl. disk (*1-56527-169-6*) Course Tech.

Nielsen, Caroline, jt. auth. see Lusardi, Michelle M.

Nielsen, Cindy. In Pictures Glacier: The Continuing Story. LC 93-77022. (Illus.). 48p. (Orig.). 1993. pap. 7.95 (*0-88714-067-X*) KC Pubns.

— In Pictures Glacier: The Continuing Story. Morales, Brigitte, tr. (GER., Illus.). 48p. (Orig.). 1993. pap. 8.95 (*0-88714-723-2*) KC Pubns.

— In Pictures Glacier: The Continuing Story. Le Bras, Yvon, tr. (FRE., Illus.). 48p. (Orig.). 1993. pap. 8.95 (*0-88714-724-0*) KC Pubns.

— In Pictures Glacier: The Continuing Story. Petzinger, Saori, tr. (JPN., Illus.). 48p. (Orig.). 1993. pap. 8.95 (*0-88714-725-9*) KC Pubns.

Nielsen, Claus. Animal Evolution: Interrelationships of the Living Phyla. (Illus.). 478p. 1995. pap. text 49.95 (*0-19-854867-2*) OUP.

Nielsen, Cliff, jt. auth. see Doyon, Stephanie.

Nielsen, Cliff, jt. auth. see Rosen, Sibyl.

Nielsen, Cynthia, jt. auth. see Hayden, Elizabeth W.

Nielsen, D. R., jt. auth. see Stewart, B. A.

Nielsen, Dave. A Christmas Found. (Illus.). 100p. 1996. 12.95 (*0-89036-627-6*); pap. 9.95 (*0-89036-632-2*) Liahona Pub Trust.

Nielsen, David James. A Christmas Found. 12.95 (*1-55517-340-3*) CFI Dist.

Nielsen, David M., ed. Practical Handbook of Ground Water Monitoring. (Illus.). 728p. (C). 1991. boxed set 115.00 (*0-87371-124-6*, L124) Lewis Pubs.

Nielsen, David M. & Johnson, Ivan A., eds. Ground Water & Vadose Zone Monitoring, STP-1053. LC 89-17992. (Illus.). 312p. 1992. text 49.00 (*0-8031-1275-0*, STP1053) ASTM.

Nielsen, David M. & Sara, Martin N., eds. Current Practices in Ground Water & Vadose Zone Investigations. 436p. 1992. 49.00 (*0-614-16826-0*, ASTM6) Am Soc Civil Eng.

N

An Asterisk (*) at the beginning of an entry indicates that the title is appearing for the first time.

Nielsen, Donald A. Three Faces of God: Society, Religion, & the Categories of Totality in the Philosophy of Emile Durkheim. LC 98-24856. (SUNY Series in Religion, Culture & Society). 250p. (C). 1998. text 59.50 (*0-7914-4035-4*); pap. text 19.95 (*0-7914-4036-2*) State U NY Pr.

***Nielsen, Donna B.** Beloved Bridegroom: Finding Christ in Ancient Jewish Marriage & Family Customs. (Illus.). 183p. 1999. pap. text 13.95 (*1-57636-075-X*, Pub. by SunRise Pbl) Origin Bk Sales.

Nielsen, Dorothy & Evans, Claudia. My Child, My Friend. 1991. pap. 4.95 (*1-55503-273-7*, 011813) Covenant Comms.

Nielsen, E. Hoegh. Dansk-Engelsk Ordbog. 4th ed. (DAN & ENG.). 336p. 1983. 49.95 (*0-8288-0528-8*, M1272) Fr & Eur.

— English-Danish. 3rd ed. 275p. 1987. reprint ed. pap. 34.75 (*87-01-95151-3*) IBD Ltd.

Nielsen, E. Schmidt & Edwards, Ed. Checklist of the Lepidoptera of Australia. Rangis, T. V. et al, eds. LC 97-175120. (Monographs on Australian Lepidoptera: No. 4). (Illus.). 529p. 1996. 120.00 incl. cd-rom (*0-643-05028-0*, Pub. by CSIRO) Accents Pubns.

Nielsen, E. Schmidt, jt. auth. see Traugott-Olsen, E.

Nielsen, Ebbe S. & Kristensen, Niels P. Primitive Ghost Moths. (Monographs on Australian Lepidoptera: Vol. 1). (Illus.). 230p. (C). 1989. text 70.00 (*0-643-04999-1*, Pub. by CSIRO) Accents Pubns.

Nielsen, Elaine. Ogallala: A Century on the Trail, Vol. 1. (Illus.). 102p. 1984. 12.95 (*0-9614379-0-1*) Keith County Hist.

Nielsen, Elaine A. Waiting for the Harvest. LC 94-73475. 123p. (Orig.). (YA). (gr. 9-12). 1994. pap. 12.00 (*0-9625040-7-6*, 297-231-X) Legendary Pub.

Nielsen, Elizabeth. Soda Bread on Sunday. LC 97-3111. 1997. 18.95 (*0-944957-69-2*) Rivercross Pub.

— Sweet Geraniums & Soda Bread, Too. LC 99-23222. 262p. 1999. 19.95 (*1-58141-033-6*) Rivercross Pub.

Nielsen Engineering & Research, Inc. Staff. NEAR Conference on Missile Aerodynamics, Monterey, CA, Oct. 31-Nov. 2, 1988: Proceedings. 1989. pap. 65.00 (*0-9620629-1-X*) Nielsen Engineering & Res Inc.

Nielsen, Erik & Nielsen, Hans F. Irregularities in Modern English Vol. 2: NOWELE Suppl. 359p. (Orig.). 1986. pap. 30.00 (*87-7492-566-0*, Pub. by Odense Universitets Forlag) Coronet Bks.

Nielsen, Flemming A. The Tragedy in History: Herodotus & the Deuteronomistic History. LC 98-103667. (JSOT Supplement Ser.: Vol. 251). 251p. 1997. 75.00 (*1-85075-688-0*, Pub. by Sheffield Acad) CUP Services.

Nielsen, Frank. Franko's Maps: 3 Recreational Maps for Mountain Bikers, Hikers & Horseback Rides to Big Bear, Chino Hills State Park & Santa Ana Mountains. (Illus.). 3p. 1997. 9.00 (*1-879415-24-0*) Mtn n Air Bks.

Nielsen, Gary, intro. Borderline & Acting-Out Adolescents: A Developmental Approach. LC 81-20223. (Illus.). 256p. 1983. 35.95 (*0-89885-109-2*, Kluwer Acad Hman Sci) Kluwer Academic.

Nielsen, George R. In Search of a Home: Nineteenth-Century Wendish Immigration. LC 89-31217. (Illus.). 232p. 1989. 24.95 (*0-89096-400-9*) Tex A&M Univ Pr.

Nielsen, Greg. Beyond Pendulum Power: Entering the Energy World. LC 88-70068. (Illus.). 153p. (Orig.). 1988. pap. 11.95 (*0-9619917-0-4*) Conscious Bks.

— MetaBusiness: Creating a New Global Culture. LC 90-86068. (Illus.). 136p. 1991. pap. 9.95 (*0-9619917-2-0*) Conscious Bks.

— Tuning to the Spiritual Frequencies. LC 89-91602. (Illus.). 224p. (Orig.). 1990. pap. 14.95 (*0-9619917-1-2*) Conscious Bks.

Nielsen, Greg & Polansky, Joseph. Pendulum Power. 128p. (Orig.). 1987. pap. 8.95 (*0-89281-157-9*) Inner Tradit.

Nielsen, Gwyn English. Torey the Turkey Goes Skiing. LC 97-94577. (Illus.). 24p. (Orig.). (J). (ps-4). 1998. pap. 10.99 (*0-9660726-0-X*) CGS Inc.

Nielsen, H. A. Where the Passion Is: A Reading of Kierkegaard's Philosophical Fragments. LC 83-6923. 209p. 1983. 39.95 (*0-8130-0742-9*) U Press Fla.

Nielsen, H. Dean & Cummings, William K. Quality Education for All: Community-Oriented Approaches. Beauchamp, Edward, ed. LC 97-1995. (Reference Books in International Education, Vol. 3B, Reference Library of Social Science: Vol. 38). (Illus.). 288p. 1997. text 72.00 (*0-8153-2378-6*, SS1105) Garland.

Nielsen, H. Dean, jt. ed. see Gopinathan, S.

Nielsen, Hanne S., jt. ed. see Nielsen, Inge.

***Nielsen, Hans F.** The Continental Backgrounds of English & Its Insular Development Until 1154. LC 99-218095. (Illus.). 234p. 1998. pap. 34.00 (*87-7838-420-6*, Pub. by Odense Univ) Intl Spec Bk.

Nielsen, Hans F., jt. auth. see Nielsen, Erik.

Nielsen, Hans F., jt. ed. see Juul, Arne.

Nielsen, Harald. Ancient Ophthamological Agents. (Acta Historica Scientiarum Ser.: No. 31). 117p. (Orig.). 1974. pap. 24.00 (*87-7492-108-8*, Pub. by Odense Universitets Forlag) Coronet Bks.

Nielsen Hayden, Patrick, ed. Starlight 1. LC 96-8454. 316p. 1996. 24.95 (*0-312-86214-8*, Pub. by Tor Bks); pap. 13.95 (*0-312-86215-6*, Pub. by Tor Bks) St Martin.

— Starlight 2, 2. LC 98-8266. 320p. 1998. 24.95 (*0-312-86184-2*, Pub. by Tor Bks) St Martin.

***Nielsen Hayden, Patrick, ed.** Starlight 2, 2. 318p. 1999. pap. 14.95 (*0-312-86312-8*, Pub. by Tor Bks) St Martin.

Nielsen Hayden, Patrick, ed. see Nielsen Hayden, Teresa.

Nielsen Hayden, Teresa. Making Book. Nielsen Hayden, Patrick, ed. LC 93-87492. (Boskone Bks.). 160p. 1994. pap. 11.00 (*0-915368-55-2*) New Eng SF Assoc.

Nielsen, Henry. Bad Golf My Way. 144p. 1997. pap. 12.95 (*0-385-48883-1*, Main St Bks) Doubleday.

Nielsen, Holger E., jt. ed. see Graudal, Lars.

Nielsen, Holger T., jt. auth. see Landwehr, Richard.

Nielsen, Ilga, jt. ed. see Barron, Enid M.

Nielsen, Inge. Hellenistic Palaces. Bilde, Per et al, eds. LC 96-128091. (Studies in Hellenistic Civilization: No. 5). (Illus.). 360p. (C). 1995. 40.00 (*87-7288-445-2*, Pub. by Aarhus Univ Pr) David Brown.

***Nielsen, Inge.** Hellenistic Palaces: Tradition & Renewal. (Studies in Hellenistic Civilization: Vol. 5). (Illus.). 360p. 1998. 49.95 (*87-7288-645-5*, Pub. by Aarhus Univ Pr) David Brown.

Nielsen, Inge. Thermae et Balnea: The Architecture & Cultural History of Roman Public Baths, 2 vols., Set. 2nd ed. (Illus.). 412p. (C). 1993. 100.00 (*87-7288-512-2*, Pub. by Aarhus Univ Pr) David Brown.

Nielsen, Inge & Nielsen, Hanne S., eds. Meals in a Social Context: Aspects of the Communal Meal in the Hellenistic & Roman World. LC 99-163706. (Aarhus Studies in Mediterranean Antiquity: Vol. 1). (Illus.). 248p. 1998. 34.95 (*87-7288-697-8*, Pub. by Aarhus Univ Pr) David Brown.

Nielsen, Ingvar. Wooden Toys: Step-by-Step Plans for over 50 Colourful Toys. (Illus.). 80p. 1998. pap. 15.95 (*1-870586-36-0*, D Porteous-Parkwest) Parkwest Pubns.

Nielsen, J. Designing User Interfaces for International Use. (Advances in Human Factors-Ergonomics Ser.: No. 13). 230p. 1990. 171.00 (*0-444-88428-9*) Elsevier.

Nielsen, J. & Villadsen, J. Bioreaction Engineering Principles. (Illus.). 480p. (C). 1994. text 95.00 (*0-306-44688-X*, Kluwer Plenum) Kluwer Academic.

Nielsen, J., jt. ed. see Brown, Chris J.

Nielsen, J. L., ed. Evolution & the Aquatic Ecosystem: Defining Unique Units in Population Conservation. LC 95-83247. (AFS Symposium Ser.: Vol. 17). 435p. 1995. pap. 76.00 (*0-913235-94-6*, 540.17) Am Fisheries Soc.

Nielsen, J. Rud, ed. see Bohr, Niels.

Nielsen, Jack N. Missile Aerodynamics. LC 88-15223. (Illus.). 450p. (C). 1988. reprint ed. text 40.00 (*0-9620629-0-1*) Nielsen Engineering & Res Inc.

Nielsen, Jakob. Designing Web Usability: The Practice of Simplicity. LC 99-63014. (Illus.). 419p. 1999. pap. 45.00 (*1-56205-810-X*) New Riders Pub.

— Multimedia & Hypertext: The Internet & Beyond. LC 94-44429. (Illus.). xiii, 480p. 1995. pap. text 34.00 (*0-12-518408-5*) Morgan Kaufmann.

— Usability Engineering. (Illus.). 362p. 1994. pap. text 32.00 (*0-12-518406-9*) Morgan Kaufmann.

Nielsen, Jakob, ed. Coordinating User Interfaces for Consistency. 144p. 1989. text 52.00 (*0-12-518400-X*) Acad Pr.

Nielsen, Jakob & Kellogg, Wendy. Conceptual Analysis of the Web. 400p. 1999. 49.95 (*1-55860-492-8*) Morgan Kaufmann.

Nielsen, Jakob & Mack, Robert L. Usability. 448p. 1994. 64.99 (*0-471-01877-5*) Wiley.

Nielsen, James F., ed. see American Bankers Association Staff.

Nielsen, James H. Handbook of Federal Drug Law. 2nd ed. LC 91-37918. (Illus.). 225p. 1992. text 34.00 (*0-8121-1439-6*) Lppncott W & W.

Nielsen, Jens E. How to Create Your Own Real-Estate Fortune Using Tax Shelters to Protect Your Profits. 8th ed. 126p. 1996. pap. 17.50 (*1-56150-184-0*) Intl Wealth.

— How to Create Your Own Real-Estate Fortune Using Tax Shelters to Protect Your Profits. 9th ed. 126p. 1998. pap. 17.50 (*1-56150-234-0*) Intl Wealth.

— How to Create Your Own Real Estate Fortune Using Tax Shelters to Protect Your Profits. 10th ed. 126p. 1999. pap. 17.50 (*1-56150-285-5*) Intl Wealth.

***Nielsen, Jens E.** How to Create Your Own Real Estate Fortune Using Tax Shelters to Protect Your Profits. 11th ed. 126p. 2000. pap. 17.50 (*1-56150-345-2*) Intl Wealth.

***Nielsen, Jerri.** Ice Bound: A Doctor's Incredible Battle for Survival at the South Pole. (Illus.). 256p. 2001. 23.95 (*0-7868-6684-5*, Pub. by Talk Miramax Bks) Time Warner.

Nielsen, Joan, jt. auth. see Castle, Timothy J.

Nielsen, John Mark, ed. see Loeffler, Martha.

Nielsen, John T., jt. auth. see Ostler, Neal K.

***Nielsen, John W., ed.** A Frame but No Picture: The Story of a Boy Left in Denmark. Engskow, Ninna & Staermose, Dorte, trs. LC 99-216132. (Illus.). xiv, 63p. 1998. pap. 8.50 (*0-930697-03-0*) Lur Pubns.

— Tante Johanne: Letters of a Danish Immigrant Family, 1887-1910. (Illus.). xii, 118p. 1999. pap. 12.95 (*0-930697-01-4*) Lur Pubns.

Nielsen, John W., ed. see Bansen, Norman C.

Nielsen, John W., jt. ed. see Lund-Jones, Barbara.

Nielsen, Jorgen S. Muslims in Western Europe. (Islamic Surveys Ser.). (Illus.). 192p. 1992. 42.50 (*0-7486-0309-3*, Pub. by Edinburgh U Pr) Col U Pr.

— Muslims in Western Europe. (Islamic Surveys Ser.). 192p. 1992. pap. 17.50 (*0-7486-0364-6*, Pub. by Edinburgh U Pr) Col U Pr.

— Muslims in Western Europe. 2nd ed. 192p. 1995. pap. 17.50 (*0-7486-0617-3*, Pub. by Edinburgh U Pr) Col U Pr.

Nielsen, Jorgen S., ed. Christian-Muslim Frontier: Chaos, Clash or Dialogue? LC 96-61069. 256p. 1998. text 59.50 (*1-86064-099-0*, Pub. by I B T) St Martin.

***Nielsen, Joyce J.** Internet 9 in 1 for Dummies Desk Reference. (For Dummies Ser.). (Illus.). 840p. 2000. pap. 29.99 incl. cd-rom (*0-7645-0676-5*) IDG Bks.

Nielsen, Joyce M. Sex & Gender in Society: Perspectives on Stratification. 2nd ed. 293p. (C). 1990. pap. text 16.95 (*0-88133-456-1*) Waveland Pr.

Nielsen, Jrgen Ulff-Miller, jt. auth. see Hansen.

Nielsen, Jurgen S., jt. ed. see Samir, Samir K.

Nielsen, K. Hvidtfelt. An Ideal Critic: Ciceronian Rhetoric & Contemporary Criticism. LC 96-147003. 154p. 1995. pap. 22.95 (*3-906752-94-1*, Pub. by P Lang) P Lang Pubng.

Nielsen, Kai. Equality & Liberty: A Defense of Radical Egalitarianism. 336p. 1986. 65.00 (*0-8476-6758-8*); pap. 26.95 (*0-8476-7516-5*) Rowman.

— Ethics Without God. rev. ed. LC 89-39720. 207p. (C). 1990. reprint ed. pap. 18.95 (*0-87975-552-0*) Prometheus Bks.

***Nielsen, Kai.** Naturalism & Religion. 350p. 2001. 40.00 (*1-57392-853-4*) Prometheus Bks.

Nielsen, Kai. Naturalism Without Foundations. LC 96-8794. 607p. 1996. 49.95 (*1-57392-076-2*) Prometheus Bks.

— On Transforming Philosophy: A Metaphilosophical Inquiry. 304p. (C). 1995. text 75.00 (*0-8133-0666-3*, Pub. by Westview) HarpC.

— Philosophy & Atheism. LC 84-63084. (Skeptic's Bookshelf Ser.). 231p. 1985. 32.95 (*0-87975-289-0*) Prometheus Bks.

— Why Be Moral? LC 89-3524. 300p. 1989. pap. 21.95 (*0-87975-519-9*) Prometheus Bks.

Nielsen, Kai & Hart, Hendrik. Search for Community in a Withering Tradition. 254p. (C). 1991. pap. text 27.50 (*0-8191-7990-6*); lib. bdg. 48.50 (*0-8191-7989-2*) U Pr of Amer.

Nielsen, Kai & Ware, Robert, eds. Exploitation. LC 97-14605. (Key Concepts in Critical Theory Ser.). 376p. (C). 1996. pap. 22.50 (*0-391-04000-6*) Humanities.

Nielsen, Kai, jt. auth. see Moreland, J. P.

Nielsen, Karen H., jt. ed. see Jensen, Claus K.

Nielsen, Kathy A., jt. auth. see Waller, Gerry H.

Nielsen, Kirsten. Ruth: A Commentary. Broadbridge, Edward, tr. from DAN. LC 96-41719. (The Old Testament Library). 120p. 1997. 20.00 (*0-664-22092-4*) Westminster John Knox.

— Satan - The Prodigal Son? A Family Problem in the Bible. (Biblical Seminar Ser.: Vol. 50). 198p. 1998. pap. 23.75 (*1-85075-820-4*, Pub. by Sheffield Acad) CUP Services.

Nielsen, Kirsten. There Is Hope for a Tree: The Tree as Metaphor in Isaiah. (JSOT Supplement Ser.: No. 65). 301p. 1989. 85.00 (*1-85075-182-X*, Pub. by Sheffield Acad) CUP Services.

Nielsen, Kjeld. Incense in Ancient Israel. (Supplements to Vetus Testamentum Ser.: No. 38). xi, 147p. 1986. 45.50 (*90-04-07702-2*) Brill Academic Pubs.

Nielsen, Klas, jt. ed. see Mendell, Marguerite.

Nielsen, Klaus & Duncan, J. Robert, eds. Animal Brucellosis. 464p. 1990. lib. bdg. 259.00 (*0-8493-5878-7*, SF809) CRC Pr.

Nielsen, Klaus & Johnson, Bjorn, eds. Institutions & Economic Change: New Perspectives on Markets, Firms & Technology. LC 97-30629. 328p. 1998. 95.00 (*1-85898-322-3*) E Elgar.

Nielsen, L., jt. auth. see Kienecke, U.

Nielsen, L. A. Methods of Marking Fish & Shellfish. LC 92-74200. (Special Publication Ser.: No. 23). 208p. 1992. text 48.00 (*0-913235-80-6*, 510.19C) Am Fisheries Soc.

Nielsen, L. A., jt. auth. see Kiencke, Uwe.

***Nielsen, Lars.** Pricing & Hedging of Derivative Securities. (Illus.). 460p. 1999. text 55.00 (*0-19-877619-5*) OUP.

Nielsen, Laura F. Jeremy's Muffler. LC 93-27521. (Illus.). 32p. (J). (ps-2). 1995. 15.00 (*0-689-80319-2*, Bradbury S&S) S&S Childrens.

Nielsen, Lawrence E. Polymer Rheology. LC 77-24187. (Illus.). 217p. Date not set. reprint ed. pap. 67.30 (*0-608-20717-9*, 207181500002) Bks Demand.

— Predicting the Properties of Mixtures: Mixture Rules in Science & Engineering. LC 77-16705. 108p. reprint ed. pap. 33.50 (*0-8357-3501-X*, 203455700090) Bks Demand.

Nielsen, Lawrence E. & Galbreath, Donald S. Oregon's Fading Past. 200p. 1993. pap. 19.95 (*0-89288-240-9*) Maverick.

Nielsen, Lawrence E., jt. ed. see Landel, Robert F.

Nielsen, Lee B. Blast Off! Rocketry for Elementary & Middle School Students. LC 96-43789. 110p. (J). (gr. 4-8). 1997. pap. text 18.00 (*1-56308-438-4*) Teacher Ideas Pr.

Nielsen, Lee Brattland. The Exceptional Child in the Regular Classroom: An Educator's Guide. LC 96-32287. 128p. 1997. pap. 19.95 (*0-8039-6484-6*); lib. bdg. 45.95 (*0-8039-6483-8*) Corwin Pr.

Nielsen, Leon. Chemical Immobilization of Wild & Exotic Animals. LC 98-43258. (Illus.). 400p. (C). 1999. pap. 44.95 (*0-8138-2936-4*) Iowa St U Pr.

Nielsen, Leslie. Leslie Nielsen: The Naked Truth. 1994. pap. 10.00 (*0-671-79578-3*) PB.

— Leslie Nielsen's Stupid Little Golf Book. 144p. 1995. 17.50 (*0-385-47598-5*) Doubleday.

Nielsen, Leslie & Beard, Henry. Bad Golf My Way. 256p. 1996. 19.95 (*0-385-48464-X*) Doubleday.

Nielsen, Leslie J. & De Villiers, Michael. Is Democracy Fair? The Mathematics of Voting & Apportionment. (Illus.). 120p. (YA). (gr. 7-12). 1997. pap. text 14.95 (*1-55953-277-7*) Key Curr Pr.

Nielsen, Leslie M., tr. see Itoh, Mamoru.

Nielsen, Lynn E., ed. see Osen, Mary E.

***Nielsen, M., et al, eds.** Scale-Space Theories in Computer Vision: 2nd International Conference, Scale-Space'99, Corfu, Greece, September 26-27, 1999, Proceedings. LC 99-49731. (Lecture Notes in Computer Science Ser.: Vol. 1682). xii, 532p. 1999. pap. 70.00 (*3-540-66498-X*) Spr-Verlag.

Nielsen, M., et al. Minimizing Gear Noise Excitation. (1985 Fall Technical Meeting: Vol. 85FTM12). 19p. 1985. pap. text 30.00 (*1-55589-105-5*) AGMA.

Nielsen, M., ed. see European Association for Computer Science Logic.

Nielsen, M. A., jt. auth. see Chuang, Isaac l.

Nielsen, Mark T., jt. ed. see Davis, D. Layten.

Nielsen Marketing Research Staff. Category Management: Positioning Your Organization to Win. LC 97-45504. (Illus.). 176p. 1993. 27.95 (*0-8442-3489-3*, NTC Business Bks) NTC Contemp Pub Co.

Nielsen, Marvin. Trains of the Twin Ports Photo Archive: Duluth-Superior in the 1950's. LC 99-71752. (Illus.). 126p. 1999. pap. 29.95 (*1-58388-003-8*, 129095AE, Pub. by Iconografix) Motorbooks Intl.

Nielsen, Mary, ed. see Penner, Mil & Schmidt, Carol.

Nielsen, Mary T., ed. see Osen, Mary E.

Nielsen-McLellan, Karen L. Ginger Bear's Christmas Cookie Mystery. (Illus.). 32p. (J). (ps-1). 1992. 12.95 (*0-9634851-0-5*) Scand Descent.

Nielsen, Mike. Hollywood's Other Blacklist. 192p. 1995. pap. text 18.95 (*0-85170-509-X*, Pub. by British Film Inst) Ind U Pr.

Nielsen, Mogens C. Michigan Butterflies & Skippers No. E2675: A Field Guide & Reference. Johnson, Leslie, ed. LC 99-6307. (Illus.). 252p. 1999. pap. 19.95 (*1-56525-012-5*) MSU Ext.

***Nielsen, Morten S.** Windows 2000 Server Architecture & Planning. 2nd ed. LC 00-43142. (Illus.). 2000. write for info. (*1-57610-607-1*) Coriolis Grp.

***Nielsen, Morten Strunge.** Windows 2000 Professional Advanced Configuration & Implementation. LC 00-27941. (Illus.). 800p. 2000. pap. 49.99 (*1-57610-528-8*) Coriolis Grp.

— Windows 2000 Server Architecture & Design. LC 99-13386. (Illus.). 715p. 1999. pap. 29.99 (*1-57610-436-2*) Coriolis Grp.

Nielsen, M.P. Limit Analysis & Concrete Plasticity. 2nd ed. LC 98-23303. (New Directions in Civil Engineering Ser.). 936p. 1998. boxed set 84.95 (*0-8493-9126-1*) CRC Pr.

Nielsen, Nancy. Teen Alcoholism. LC 90-66. (Overview Ser.). (Illus.). 96p. (J). (gr. 5-8). 1990. lib. bdg. 22.45 (*1-56006-121-9*) Lucent Bks.

Nielsen, Nancy, ed. see Fisher, Gary L., et al.

Nielsen, Nancy J. Carnivorous Plants. (First Bks.). (Illus.). 64p. (J). (gr. 5-8). 1992. pap. 6.95 (*0-531-15644-3*) Watts.

— Reformers & Activists. annot. ed. LC 96-41254. (American Indian Lives Ser.). 128p. (YA). (gr. 5-12). 1997. 19.95 (*0-8160-3440-0*) Facts on File.

Nielsen, Nancy J., ed. see Fisher, Gary L. & Cummings, Rhoda Woods.

Nielsen, Nancy L. Blackberries & Dust. 20p. (Orig.). 1984. pap. 4.00 (*0-914473-01-8*) Stone Man Pr.

— East of the Light. 50p. (Orig.). 1984. pap. 6.95 (*0-914473-02-6*) Stone Man Pr.

Nielsen, Nancy L., jt. auth. see Brooks, Alan.

Nielsen, Nicki J. The Iditarod: Women on the Trail. LC 85-52335. (Illus.). 80p. 1986. pap. 12.00 (*0-9616191-0-4*) Wolfdog Pubns.

Nielsen, Niels. Die Gammafunktion, 2 vols. in 1. Incl. Integrallogarithmus. LC 64-13785. 1965. LC 64-13785. (GER.). 1965. 29.50 (*0-8284-0188-8*) Chelsea Pub.

Nielsen, Niels, jt. auth. see Wiig, Elisabeth H.

Nielsen, Niels C., Jr. Christianity after Communism: Social, Political & Cultural Struggle in Russia. LC 94-29700. 172p. (C). 1994. pap. 59.50 (*0-8133-2365-7*, Pub. by Westview) HarpC.

— Fundamentalism, Mythos, & World Religions. LC 92-37601. 186p. (C). 1993. text 21.50 (*0-7914-1653-4*) State U NY Pr.

Nielsen, Niels C. Revolutions in Eastern Europe: The Religious Roots. LC 91-23592. 183p. 1991. reprint ed. pap. 56.80 (*0-7837-9855-5*, 206058400005) Bks Demand.

Nielsen, Niels Kayser, jt. ed. see Hansen, Jorn.

Nielsen, Ole A. Introduction to Integration & Measure Theory. LC 96-25131. (Canadian Mathematical Society Series & Advanced Texts). 496p. 1997. 89.95 (*0-471-59518-7*, Wiley-Interscience) Wiley.

Nielsen, Ole V., jt. ed. see Jensen, Steen L.

Nielsen, Olevagn, jt. ed. see Jensen, Steen L.

Nielsen, P. Coastal Bottom Boundary Layers & Sediment Transport. 352p. 1994. text 64.00 (*981-02-0472-8*); pap. text 32.00 (*981-02-0473-6*) World Scientific Pub.

Nielsen, Pamela, ed. see Woodroof, F. Aubrey & Woodroof, Nancy.

Nielsen, Peter. Black Man's Place in South Africa. LC 70-109347. 149p. 1970. reprint ed. lib. bdg. 49.50 (*0-8371-3619-9*, NIB&) Greenwood.

— Will of Iron: A Champion's Journey; a Strategy for Fitness. LC 92-27532. (Illus.). 227p. (Orig.). 1992. pap. 14.95 (*1-879094-19-3*) Momentum Bks.

Nielsen, Peter E., ed. Photochemical Probes in Biochemistry. (C). 1989. text 171.00 (*0-7923-0171-4*) Kluwer Academic.

***Nielsen, Peter E. & Egholm, Michael, eds.** Peptic Nucleic Acids: Protocols & Applications. LC 99-494986. 1999. 119.99 (*1-898486-16-6*, Pub. by Horizon Sci) Intl Spec Bk.

Nielsen, Poul, ed. Social Priorities of Civil Society: Speeches by Non-Governmental Organizations at the World Summit for Social Development. 163p. (C). 1998. pap. text 35.00 (*0-7881-7149-6*) DIANE Pub.

***Nielsen, Randall.** Evaluation, Public Performance & Civil Investing. 15p. 1999. pap. text 10.00 (*0-929556-18-6*) Ind Sector.

Nielsen, Richard, jt. auth. see Kohl, Arthur.

Nielsen, Richard O. Sonar Signal Processing. LC 91-3102. (Artech House Acoustics Library). 380p. 1991. reprint ed. pap. 117.80 (*0-608-01418-4*, 206218100002) Bks Demand.

Nielsen, Rick, jt. auth. see Rich, Bill.

Nielsen, Ruth. Contract Law in Denmark. LC 97-47053. 192p. 1998. 71.00 (*90-411-0535-2*) Kluwer Law Intl.

— Employers' Prerogatives: In A European & Nordic Perspective. 1999. 37.00 (*87-16-13280-7*) Mksgaard.

An Asterisk (*) at the beginning of an entry indicates that the title is appearing for the first time.

— Social Dimensions of the European Union. LC 98-106699. 1999. 34.00 (*87-16-13357-9*) Mksgaard.

Nielsen, Ruth & Jorgensen, Kurt, eds. Advances in Industrial Ergonomics & Safety 5. 800p. 1993. 210.00 (*0-7484-0061-3*, Pub. by Tay Francis Ltd) Taylor & Francis.

Nielsen, Sanne, jt. auth. see Haslebo, Gitte.

Nielsen, Shelly. Birthday. LC 96-12761. (Illus.). 32p. (J). (ps-4). 1996. lib. bdg. 13.98 (*1-56239-706-0*) ABDO Pub Co.

— Caring. Wallner, Rosemary, ed. LC 91-73044. (Values Matter Ser.). (J). 1992. lib. bdg. 14.98 (*1-56239-064-3*) ABDO Pub Co.

— Christmas. Wallner, Rosemary, ed. LC 91-73034. (Holiday Celebrations Ser.). (Illus.). 32p. (J). (ps-4). 1992. lib. bdg. 13.98 (*1-56239-067-8*) ABDO Pub Co.

— Father's Day. (Illus.). 32p. (J). (ps-4). 1996. lib. bdg. 13.98 (*1-56239-705-2*) ABDO Pub Co.

— Fun With A - a. LC 92-16038. (J). 1992. lib. bdg. 14.98 (*1-56239-134-8*) ABDO Pub Co.

— Fun with E - e. LC 92-16041. (J). 1992. lib. bdg. 14.98 (*1-56239-135-6*) ABDO Pub Co.

— Fun with I - i. LC 92-16040. (J). 1992. lib. bdg. 14.98 (*1-56239-136-4*) ABDO Pub Co.

— Fun with O - o. LC 92-16039. (J). 1992. lib. bdg. 14.98 (*1-56239-137-2*) ABDO Pub Co.

— Gloria Estefan: International Pop Star. LC 93-26000. (Reaching for the Stars Ser.). (Illus.). 32p. 1993. lib. bdg. 13.98 (*1-56239-226-3*) ABDO Pub Co.

— Hanukkah. Wallner, Rosemary, ed. LC 91-73029. (Holiday Celebrations Ser.). (Illus.). 32p. (J). (ps-4). 1992. lib. bdg. 13.98 (*1-56239-072-4*) ABDO Pub Co.

— I Love Air. LC 93-7597. (Target Earth Ser.). (J). 1993. pap. 7.49 (*1-56239-404-5*) ABDO Pub Co.

— I Love Air. LC 93-7597. (Target Earth Ser.). (Illus.). (J). (ps-7). 1993. lib. bdg. 15.98 (*1-56239-189-5*) ABDO Pub Co.

— I Love Animals. Berg, Julie, ed. LC 93-18955. (Target Earth Ser.). (J). 1993. pap. 7.49 (*1-56239-406-1*) ABDO Pub Co.

— I Love Animals. Berg, Julie, ed. LC 93-18955. (Target Earth Ser.). (Illus.). (J). (ps-7). 1993. 15.98 (*1-56239-191-7*) ABDO Pub Co.

— I Love Dirt. Berg, Julie, ed. LC 93-18956. (Target Earth Ser.). (J). (gr. 3 up). 1993. pap. 7.49 (*1-56239-407-X*) ABDO Pub Co.

— I Love Dirt. Berg, Julie, ed. LC 93-18956. (Target Earth Ser.). (Illus.). (J). (ps-7). 1993. lib. bdg. 15.98 (*1-56239-188-7*) ABDO Pub Co.

— Independence Day. Wallner, Rosemary, ed. LC 91-73030. (Holiday Celebrations Ser.). (Illus.). 32p. (J). (ps-4). 1992. lib. bdg. 13.98 (*1-56239-071-6*) ABDO Pub Co.

— Manners. Wallner, Rosemary, ed. LC 91-73042. (Values Matter Ser.). (J). 1992. lib. bdg. 14.98 (*1-56239-066-X*) ABDO Pub Co.

— Mother's Day. (Illus.). 32p. (J). (ps-4). 1996. lib. bdg. 13.98 (*1-56239-704-4*) ABDO Pub Co.

— Playing Fair. Wallner, Rosemary, ed. LC 92-73043. (Values Matter Ser.). (J). 1992. lib. bdg. 14.98 (*1-56239-065-1*) ABDO Pub Co.

— Self-Esteem. Wallner, Rosemary, ed. LC 91-73047. (Values Matter Ser.). (J). 1992. lib. bdg. 14.98 (*1-56239-061-9*) ABDO Pub Co.

— Sharing. Wallner, Rosemary, ed. LC 91-73045. (Values Matter Ser.). (J). 1992. lib. bdg. 14.98 (*1-56239-063-5*) ABDO Pub Co.

— Star Chasers. (Illus.). 82p. (Orig.). (J). 1995. pap. 12.95 (*0-9650654-0-5*); pap. 39.95 incl. cd-rom (*0-9650654-2-1*) Starborn.

— Star Chasers: Ultimate Bible Edition. (Illus.). 82p. (Orig.). (J). 1995. pap. 49.95 incl. cd-rom (*0-9650651-3-X*) Starborn.

— Telling the Truth. Wallner, Rosemary, ed. LC 91-73046. (Values Matter Ser.). (J). 1992. lib. bdg. 14.98 (*1-56239-062-7*) ABDO Pub Co.

— Trash! Trash! Trash! Berg, Julie, ed. LC 93-18952. (Target Earth Ser.). (J). 1993. pap. 7.49 (*1-56239-408-8*) ABDO Pub Co.

— Trash! Trash! Trash! Berg, Julie, ed. LC 93-18952. (Target Earth Ser.). (Illus.). (J). (ps-7). 1993. lib. bdg. 15.98 (*1-56239-192-5*) ABDO Pub Co.

— Valentine's Day. (Illus.). 32p. (J). (ps-4). 1996. lib. bdg. 13.98 (*1-56239-703-6*) ABDO Pub Co.

Nielsen, Shelly & Berg, Julie. I Love Water. LC 93-18957. (Target Earth Ser.). (J). 1993. pap. 7.49 (*1-56239-405-3*) ABDO Pub Co.

— I Love Water. LC 93-18957. (Target Earth Ser.). (Illus.). (J). (ps-7). 1993. lib. bdg. 15.98 (*1-56239-190-9*) ABDO Pub Co.

— Love Earth: The Beauty Makeover. LC 93-18954. (Target Earth Ser.). (J). 1993. pap. 7.49 (*1-56239-409-6*) ABDO Pub Co.

— Love Earth: The Beauty Makeover. LC 93-18954. (Target Earth Ser.). (Illus.). (J). (ps-7). 1993. lib. bdg. 15.98 (*1-56239-198-4*) ABDO Pub Co.

Nielsen, Stephen. Pak: Speaking for Results. 336p. (C). 1996. 39.95 (*0-7872-2161-9*) Kendall-Hunt.

***Nielsen, Susan B.** Across & Down Through the Book of Mormon: A Novel. 1999. pap. 11.95 (*1-57734-444-8*, 01113844) Covenant Comms.

Nielsen, Susin. Melanie. (Degrassi Book Ser.). 188p. (J). (gr. 6-9). 1995. mass mkt. 4.95 (*1-55028-256-5*); bds. 16.95 (*1-55028-254-9*) Formac Dist Ltd.

— Shane. (Degrassi Book Ser.). 188p. (J). (gr. 6-9). 1995. mass mkt. 4.95 (*1-55028-235-2*); bds. 16.95 (*1-55028-237-9*) Formac Dist Ltd.

— Snake. (Degrassi Book Ser.). 196p. (J). (gr. 6-9). 1995. mass mkt. 4.95 (*1-55028-368-5*); bds. 16.95 (*1-55028-370-7*) Formac Dist Ltd.

— Wheels. (Degrassi Book Ser.). 183p. (J). (gr. 6-9). 1995. mass mkt. 4.95 (*1-55028-360-X*); bds. 16.95 (*1-55028-362-6*) Formac Dist Ltd.

Nielsen, Suzanne S. Food Analysis. 2nd ed. LC 97-44132. 672p. 1998. 69.00 (*0-8342-1203-X*) Aspen Pub.

Nielsen, T. T. Bose Algebras: Complex & Real Wave Representations. (Lecture Notes in Mathematics Ser.: Vol. 1472). v, 132p. 1991. 31.95 (*0-387-54041-5*) Spr-Verlag.

***Nielsen, Thomas.** Inside Fortress Norway - Bjorn West: A Norwegian Guerrilla Base, 1944-1945.Tr. of Bak de Tyske Linjer: Milorg-Basen Bjorn West, 1944-1945. (Illus.). 340p. 2000. pap. 24.95 (*0-89745-245-3*) Sunflower U Pr.

***Nielsen, Thomas & Wigard, Jeroen.** Performance Enhancements in a Frequency Hopping GSM Network. 352p. 2000. 126.00 (*0-7923-7819-9*) Kluwer Academic.

Nielsen, Toth. Pyramid Power. 1977. mass mkt. 2.25 (*0-446-82569-7*, Pub. by Warner Bks) Little.

Nielsen, Veneta L. Familiar As a Sparrow. LC 78-55118. 1978. 4.95 (*0-8425-1072-9*, Friends of the Library) Brigham.

Nielsen, Virginia. Batty Hattie. LC 98-47667. 144p. (YA). (gr. 3-7). 1999. 14.95 (*0-7614-5047-5*) Marshall Cavendish.

— To Love a Pirate. (Historical Ser.). 1993. per. 3.99 (*0-373-28761-5*, 1-28761-4) Harlequin Bks.

Nielsen, Waldemar. The Big Foundations. LC 72-3676. (Twentieth Century Fund Study Ser.). 475p. 1972. reprint ed. text 69.00 (*0-231-03665-5*) Col U Pr.

Nielsen, Waldemar A. The Great Powers & Africa. LC 77-83342. 447p. reprint ed. pap. 138.60 (*0-608-18607-4*, 200294700016) Bks Demand.

— Inside American Philanthropy: The Dramas of Donorship. LC 95-39302. (Illus.). 304p. 1996. 26.95 (*0-8061-2802-X*) U of Okla Pr.

***Nielsen-Wallace, Diane.** Guardians of the Light. (Illus.). 60p. 1999. pap. 10.50 (*1-56770-468-9*) S Scheewe Pubns.

Nielsen, Yvonne V. Verbal Elixirs: Thoughts to Peace of Mind; How to Have Heaven on Earth. 96p. 1991. pap. 16.95 (*0-9630324-0-2*) YV Prods.

Nielson, jt. auth. see Sherwood.

Nielson, Aleene B., jt. auth. see Maker, C. June.

Nielson, Bill. Beacon Small-Group Bible Studies, I & II Thessalonians: The Distinguishing Marks of a Christian. 56p. 1981. pap. 4.99 (*0-8341-0738-4*) Beacon Hill.

Nielson, Bruce, jt. auth. see Lewis, Ian.

***Nielson, Claire.** Snappy Little Bugs. LC 99-210166. (Snappy Pop-Ups Ser.). (Illus.). 20p. (J). (gr. k-1). 1999. 12.95 (*0-7613-1279-X*, Copper Beech Bks) Millbrook Pr.

Nielson, Claire. Spirit of Beardsley: A Celebration. 224p. 1998. 17.99 (*0-517-16084-6*) Random Hse Value.

Nielson, D. & Bishop, R. F., eds. Recent Progress in Many-Body Theories: Proceedings of the 9th International Conference New South Wales, Australia 21-25 July, 1997. 550p. 1998. 108.00 (*981-02-3369-8*) World Scientific Pub.

Nielson, David G. Black Ethos: Northern Urban Negro Life & Thought, 1890-1930, 29. LC 76-47169. (Contributions in Afro-American & African Studies: No. 29). 248p. 1977. 29.95 (*0-8371-9402-4*, NBE/, Greenwood Pr) Greenwood.

Nielson, David M. & Sapa, Martin N., eds. Current Practices in Ground Water & Vabose Zone Investigations. (Special Technical Publication Ser.: STP 1118). (Illus.). 435p. 1992. text 49.00 (*0-8031-1462-1*, STP1180) ASTM.

Nielson, Debra, ed. CorpTech Directory of Technology Companies. 7416p. 1998. 545.00 (*1-57114-014-X*) CorpTech.

Nielson, Denis P., jt. auth. see Chatfield, Michael.

***Nielson, F., et al.** Principles of Program Analysis. LC 99-47677. 450p. 1999. 46.00 (*3-540-65410-0*) Spr-Verlag.

Nielson, Flemming, ed. ML with Concurrency: Design, Analysis, Implementation & Application. LC 96-35926. (Monographs in Computer Science). 255p. 1997. 49.95 (*0-387-94875-9*) Spr-Verlag.

Nielson, Flemming & Nielson, Hanne R. Two-Level Functional Languages. (Tracts in Theoretical Computer Science Ser.: No. 34). (Illus.). 311p. (C). 1992. text 49.95 (*0-521-40384-7*) Cambridge U Pr.

Nielson, Gregory M., et al. Scientific Visualization: Overviews, Methodologies, & Techniques. LC 97-5922. 400p. 1997. 69.00 (*0-8186-7777-5*, BP07777) IEEE Comp Soc.

Nielson, Hanne R., ed. Programming Languages & Systems, ESOP '96: Proceedings of the 6th European Symposium on Programming, Link Oping, Sweden, April 22-24, 1996. (Lecture Notes in Computer Science Ser.: Vol. 1058). 405p. 1996. pap. 68.00 (*3-540-61055-3*) Spr-Verlag.

Nielson, Hanne R., jt. auth. see Nielson, Flemming.

Nielson, Helen, ed. see Moore, Dolores L.

Nielson, J. C. Involute Spline Size Inspection. (1984 Fall Technical Meeting Ser.: Vol. 84FTM3). 12p. 1984. pap. text 30.00 (*1-55589-085-7*) AGMA.

Nielson, Jakob. Jakob Nielsen: Collected Mathematical Papers, 2 Vols., Set. Hansen, Vagn L. & Topsoe, Fleming, eds. (Contemporary Mathematicians Ser.). 1986. 194.50 (*0-8176-3152-6*) Birkhauser.

— Jakob Nielsen: Collected Mathematical Papers, 2 Vols., Vol. 1. Hansen, Vagn L. & Topsoe, Fleming, eds. (Contemporary Mathematicians Ser.). 472p. 1986. 122.00 (*0-8176-3140-2*) Birkhauser.

— Jakob Nielsen: Collected Mathematical Papers, 2 Vols., Vol. 2. Hansen, Vagn L. & Topsoe, Fleming, eds. (Contemporary Mathematicians Ser.). 432p. 1986. 122.00 (*0-8176-3151-8*) Birkhauser.

Nielson, James. Unread Herrings: Thomas Nashe & the Prosaics of the Real. LC 93-31708. (Renaissance & Baroque Studies & Texts: Vol. 11). XI, 224p. 1994. 43.95 (*0-8204-2254-1*) P Lang Pubng.

Nielson, James, tr. see Serres, Michel.

***Nielson, Joan & Ibsen, Gary.** The Great Tomato Book. LC 98-53268. (Illus.). 160p. 1999. pap. 14.95 (*1-58008-048-0*) Ten Speed Pr.

Nielson, John. Geography & World Affairs. 3rd ed. 224p. (C). 1997. spiral bd. 29.95 (*0-7872-3776-0*) Kendall-Hunt.

Nielson, John B. Beacon Small Group Bible Studies, Zehariah-Malachi: Prisoners of Hope. 80p. (Orig.). 1986. pap. 4.99 (*0-8341-1100-4*) Beacon Hill.

Nielson, Jon, ed. see Cole, Terrence.

Nielson, Jonathan M. American Historians in War & Peace: Patriotism, Diplomacy & the Paris Peace Conference 1919 Value Pak, Set. 416p. (C). 1994. 45.95 (*0-8403-9587-6*); per. write for info. (*0-8403-9585-X*) Kendall-Hunt.

— Armed Forces on a Northern Frontier: The Military in Alaska's History, 1867-1987, 74. LC 87-31781. (Contributions in Military Studies Ser.: No. 74). 301p. 1988. 49.95 (*0-313-26030-3*, NAE/, Greenwood Pr) Greenwood.

Nielson, Joyce. 1-2-3 Release 4 for Windows QuickStart. (QuickStart Ser.). 544p. (Orig.). 1993. pap. 9.95 (*0-685-70408-4*) Que.

Nielson, K. Textiles for Today's Interiors. 1991. text. write for info. (*0-442-01202-0*, VNR) Wiley.

Nielson, Karla J. Window Treatments. 448p. 1989. 75.00 (*0-471-28946-9*, VNR) Wiley.

— Window Treatments. (Illus.). 368p. 1989. text 64.95 (*0-442-26809-2*, VNR) Wiley.

Nielson, Karla J. & Taylor, David A. Interiors: An Introduction. 2nd ed. (Illus.). 464p. (C). 1994. text. write for info. (*0-697-12543-2*) Brown & Benchmark.

Nielson, Kathleen V. No One Prepared Me for This. 130p. (Orig.). 1989. pap. 7.95 (*0-317-93837-1*) IHC Home Health.

— No One Prepared Me for This. (Orig.). 1991. pap. 9.95 (*0-9622967-0-8*) IHC Home Health.

Nielson, Kathryn E. God's Creative World. LC 97-140412. (Illus.). 32p. (J). (ps-2). 1996. 6.99 (*0-570-04807-9*, 56-1822) Concordia.

Nielson, Larry. How Would You Like to See the Slides of My Mission? A Tasteful Collection of Missionary Humor. LC 80-82708. (Illus.). 158p. (Orig.). 1980. pap. 8.98 (*0-88290-153-2*, 2040) Horizon Utah.

Nielson, Lavrans. Sacred Art of Lavrans Nielson. 32p. (Orig.). 1992. pap. 24.95 (*1-55612-461-9*) Sheed & Ward WI.

Nielson, Nancy, jt. auth. see Robinson, James.

Nielson, Nancy, ed. see Baum, Joanne.

Nielson, Niels C., Jr., et al. Religions of the World. 3rd ed. LC 92-50025. (Illus.). 536p. (C). 1993. pap. text 60.95 (*0-312-05023-2*) St Martin.

Nielson, Norm. Guns along the Comstock. Turner, Phyllis, ed. 207p. 1994. pap. 6.95 (*0-9625020-4-9*) Tales Nevada.

— Tales of Nevada, Vol. 1. Lonse, Kris, ed. (Illus.). 230p. 1989. pap. 12.95 (*0-9625020-0-6*) Tales Nevada.

— Tales of Nevada!, Vol. 2. Wright, Karen, ed. (Illus.). 300p. 1990. pap. 12.95 (*0-9625020-1-4*) Tales Nevada.

— The West: The Way It Really Was! Nevada. Turner, Phyllis B., ed. 218p. (Orig.). 1994. pap. 12.95 (*0-9625020-3-0*) Tales Nevada.

Nielson, Norma L. Taxes & Employee Benefits in Canada. LC 99-207912. 54p. 1998. 25.00 (*0-89154-528-X*) Intl Found Employ.

Nielson, Norma L., et al. Financial Planning As an Employee Benefit. Brzezinski, Mary Jo, ed. LC 91-76439. 74p. (Orig.). 1992. pap. 15.00 (*0-89154-431-3*) Intl Found Employ.

Nielson, Norman, jt. auth. see Walters, John R.

Nielson, Palle. The Enchanted City. Morch, Dea T. & Doyle, Judith A., eds. Taylor, Alexander, tr. LC 87-71734. (Printworks Ser.). 72p. (Orig.). 1987. pap. 9.95 (*0-915306-75-1*) Curbstone.

Nielson, Parker M. The Dispossessed: Cultural Genocide of the Mixed-Blood Utes, An Advocate's Chronicle. LC 97-53046. (Illus.). x, 384p. 1998. 34.95 (*0-8061-3043-1*) U of Okla Pr.

Nielson, Peter Heine. The Sicilian Accelerated Dragon. 176p. 1998. pap. text 24.95 (*0-7134-7986-8*, Pub. by B T B) Branford.

Nielson, R. LaRell. Petrology, Sedimentology & Stratigraphic Implications of the Rock Canyon Conglomerate, Southwestern Utah. (Miscellaneous Publication Ser.: Vol. 91-7). (Illus.). 65p. 1991. pap. 6.00 (*1-55791-316-1*, MP-91-7) Utah Geological Survey.

Nielson, Scott. A Season with Eagles. LC 90-25444. (Illus.). 96p. 1994. pap. 16.95 (*0-89658-247-7*) Voyageur Pr.

Nielson, Steven P., jt. auth. see Marks, Kenneth E.

Nielson, Thomas P. T'ang Poet-Monk Chiao-Jan. 64p. 1972. pap. 6.00 (*0-939252-01-5*) ASU Ctr Asian.

***Nielson, V.** Work Sciences in Sustainable Agriculture: Proceedings of the 28th Ciosta-Cigrv International Conference. 484p. 1999. 74.00 (*90-74134-67-X*) Wageningen Pers.

Nielson, W. R., et al. Evaluation of Gasification & Novel Thermal Processes: For the Treatment of Municipal Solid Waste. unabridged ed. 1996. spiral bd. 25.00 (*1-890607-15-0*) Biomass Energy.

Nielson, Waldo. Right-of-Way: A Guide to Abandoned Railroads in the United States. rev. ed. (Illus.). 220p. 1992. pap. 19.95 (*0-89288-001-5*) Maverick.

Nielsson, Francis T. Manual of Fertilizer Processing. (Fertilizer Science & Technology Ser.: Vol. 5). (Illus.). 544p. 1986. text 250.00 (*0-8247-7522-8*) Dekker.

Nielsson, Gunnar P. Mediation under Crisis Management Conditions: The U. N. Secretary General & the Falkland - Malvinas Islands Crisis. (Pew Case Studies in International Affairs). 50p. (C). 1994. pap. text 3.50 (*1-56927-127-5*) Geo U Inst Dplmcy.

Nieman, David C. The Exercise Health Connection. LC 97-36227. (Illus.). 328p. 1997. pap. 14.95 (*0-88011-584-X*, BNIE0584) Human Kinetics.

— Exercise Testing & Prescription: A Health-Related Approach. 4th ed. LC 98-10359. xii, 708p. 1998. pap. text 55.95 (*0-7674-0474-2*) Mayfield Pub.

***Nieman, David C. & Pedersen, Bente Klarlund.** Nutrition & Exercise Immunology. LC 00-21954. (Nutrition in Exercise & Sport Ser.). 2000. write for info. (*0-8493-0741-4*) CRC Pr.

Nieman, Donald G. African-Americans & Southern Politics from Redemption to Disfranchisement. LC 93-36874. (African American Life in the Post-Emancipation South Ser.: Vol. 6). 360p. 1994. text 72.00 (*0-8153-1443-4*) Garland.

— Promises to Keep: African Americans & the Constitutional Order, 1776 to Present. (Bicentennial Essays on the Bill of Rights Ser.). (Illus.). 304p. (C). 1991. pap. text 21.95 (*0-19-505561-6*) OUP.

Nieman, Donald G., ed. African Americans & Education in the South, 1865-1900. LC 93-38436. (African American Life in the Post-Emancipation South Ser.: Vol. 10). (Illus.). 464p. 1994. reprint ed. text 85.00 (*0-8153-1447-7*) Garland.

— Freedom, Racism, & Reconstruction: Collected Writings of LaWanda Cox. LC 97-20517. 416p. 1997. text 70.00 (*0-8203-1901-5*) U of Ga Pr.

Nieman, Donald G., ed. Black Southerners & the Law, 1865-1900. LC 93-29263. (African American Life in the Post-Emancipation South Ser.: Vol. 12). 488p. 1994. text 88.00 (*0-8153-1449-3*) Garland.

Nieman, Donald G., intro. African-Americans & Non-Agricultural Labor in the South, 1865-1900. LC 93-37339. (African American Life in the Post-Emancipation South Ser.: Vol. 4). 400p. 1994. text 77.00 (*0-8153-1441-8*) Garland.

— African-Americans & the Emergence of Segregation, 1865-1900. LC 93-29264. (African American Life in the Post-Emancipation South Ser.: Vol. 11). (Illus.). 464p. 1994. text 79.00 (*0-8153-1448-5*) Garland.

— Black Freedom - White Violence, 1865-1900. LC 93-29265. (African American Life in the Post-Emancipation South Ser.: Vol. 7). 408p. 1994. text 83.00 (*0-8153-1444-2*) Garland.

— The Day of the Jubilee: The Civil War Experience of Black Southerners. LC 93-33613. (African American Life in the Post-Emancipation South Ser.: No. 1). (Illus.). 408p. 1994. text 77.00 (*0-8153-1438-8*) Garland.

— The Freedman's Bureau & Black Freedom. LC 93-36877. 424p. 1994. text 83.00 (*0-8153-1439-6*) Garland.

— The Politics of Freedom: African Americans & the Political Process During Reconstruction. LC 93-36875. (Illus.). 432p. 1994. text 83.00 (*0-8153-1442-6*) Garland.

Nieman, Gideon. The Franchise Option: How to Franchise Your Business. 150p. 1999. pap. 25.00 (*0-7021-4371-5*, Pub. by Juta & Co) Intl Spec Bk.

Nieman, H. Pattern Analysis. (Information Sciences Ser.: Vol. 4). (Illus.). 305p. 1981. 47.00 (*0-387-10792-4*) Spr-Verlag.

Nieman, Jean. A World of Travel Tips. (Illus.). 270p. (Orig.). 1982. write for info. (*0-9609388-0-X*) Travel Inter.

Nieman, Lynette, jt. ed. see Halley, Janet E.

Nieman, Nancy D., tr. see Rossetti, Ana & Suntree, Susan.

Nieman, Patricia. Long Days Journey. 1997. pap. write for info. (*1-57553-489-4*) Watermrk Pr.

Nieman, Valerie. Survivors. LC 99-21854. 272p. 2000. 25.00 (*0-9657639-6-X*) Van Neste.

***Nieman, Valerie.** Survivors. 2nd ed. 272p. 2000. reprint ed. 18.00 (*1-929871-02-3*) Van Neste.

Niemand, Jackie. Physical Abuse What Is It? An Informational Book for People Who Are Deaf or Hard of Hearing. (Illus.). 51p. (Orig.). (J). (ps-12). 1994. pap. text 9.00 (*0-9629302-2-9*) Ramsey Found.

Niemand, Jasper, compiled by. Letters That Have Helped Me (1891) 94p. 1998. reprint ed. pap. 12.95 (*0-7661-0571-7*) Kessinger Pub.

Niemand, Jasper, ed. & intro. see Judge, William Q.

Niemann. Special Approach to Regional Guide. LC 99-37675. 2000. text 65.00 (*0-312-22596-2*) St Martin.

Niemann, Art. The Ultimate Lesson: 10 Point Guide on How to Teach Yourself Anything. LC 96-92211. iix, 177p. (Orig.). 1996. pap. 14.95 (*0-9651335-5-9*, SLI Pr) Niemann Ent.

Niemann, Erika H. Love a Journey of Discovery: Selected Poems. LC 99-94714. xvi, 125p. 1999. pap. 10.95 (*0-9670746-0-6*, 1) Close Connects Pubg.

Niemann, Greg. Baja Fever: Journeys into Mexico's Intriguing Peninsula. LC 98-87785. (Illus.). 352p. 1999. pap. 19.50 (*1-879415-19-4*) Mtn n Air Bks.

Niemann, H. Pattern Analysis & Understanding. 2nd ed. (Information Sciences Ser.: Vol. 4). (Illus.). 360p. 1990. 59.95 (*0-387-51378-7*) Spr-Verlag.

Niemann, H., et al, eds. Recent Advances in Speech Understanding & Dialog Systems. (NATO Asi Series F: Vol. 46). (Illus.). x, 521p. 1988. 129.95 (*0-387-19245-X*) Spr-Verlag.

Niemann, H. J., jt. ed. see Kratzig, W. B.

Niemann, H. Michael, et al, eds. Nachdenken Uber Israel, Bibel und Theologie: Festschrift Fur Klaus-Dietrich Schunck Zu Seinem 65. Geburtstag. (Beitrage zur Erforschung des Alten Testaments & Antiken Judentums Ser.: Bd. 37). (GER., Illus.). 498p. 1994. 85.95 (*3-631-47033-9*) P Lang Pubng.

Niemann, Henry. Folk Art in America. 1999. pap. 19.95 (*0-14-023993-6*, Viking) Viking Penguin.

— Rectification: Known-Unknown Birthtimes. 1990. pap. 23.95 (*0-86690-373-9*, 3043-014) Am Fed Astrologers.

Niemann, Linda. On the Rails: A Woman's Journey. 2nd ed. LC 96-45546. Orig. Title: Boomer: Railroad Memoirs. 250p. 1997. reprint ed. pap. 14.95 (*1-57344-064-7*) Cleis Pr.

Niemann, Linda & Bertucci, Lina. Railroad Voices. LC 98-5970. 160p. 1998. 35.00 (*0-8047-3209-4*) Stanford U Pr.

Niemann, Paul J. The Lent, Triduum, & Easter Answer Book: ML Answers the 101 Most Asked Questions. LC 98-39648. (ML Answers the 101 Most-Asked Questions Ser.). 152p. 1998. pap. 29.95 (*0-89390-447-3*) Resource Pubns.

Niemann, Ralf. Hardware Software Co-Design for Data Flow Dominated Embedded Systems. 223p. 1998. 120.00 (*0-7923-8299-4*) Kluwer Academic.

Niemann, Sandy, ed. see Burns, A. August, et al.

Niemann, Walter. Brahms. 492p. 1990. reprint ed. lib. bdg. 89.00 (*0-7812-9054-6*) Rprt Serv.

Niemantsverdriet, J. W. Spectroscopy in Catalysis: An Introduction. LC 93-15537. 288p. 1993. 150.00 (*3-527-28593-8*, Wiley-VCH) Wiley.

Niemantsverdriet, J. W., jt. auth. see Van Santen, R. A.

Niemark, Ju. I. & Fufaev, N. A. Dynamics of Nonholonomic Systems. LC 72-3274. (Translations of Mathematical Monographs: No. 33). 518p. 1972. text 123.00 (*0-8218-1583-0*, MMONO/33) Am Math.

Niemcryk, Steve J., jt. ed. see Bolek, Catherine S.

Niemczyk, E. Ecology & Effectiveness of Aphidophaga. 342p. 1988. 120.00 (*90-5103-018-5*, Pub. by SPB Acad Pub) Balogh.

Niemczynowicz, Janusz, ed. Integrated Water Management in Urban Areas: Searching for New, Realistic Approaches with Respect to the Developing Worlds. (Environmental Research Forum Ser.: Nos. 3-4). (Illus.). 492p. 1996. text 144.00 (*0-87849-736-6*, Pub. by Trans T Pub) Enfield Pubs NH.

Niemeier, jt. ed. see Newby.

Niemeier, Jim. From the Inside Out: A Parole Planning Manual. 144p. (Orig.). 1991. pap. 19.95 (*0-8134-2920-X*) Interstate.

Niemeier, Susanne, et al, eds. The Cultural Context in Business Communication. LC 97-52990. iv, 269p. 1998. 69.00 (*1-55619-530-3*) J Benjamins Pubng Co.

***Niemeier, Susanne & Dirven, Rene, eds.** Evidence for Linguistic Relativity. LC 00-21104. (Current Issues in Linguistic Theory Ser.: Vol. 198). xxii, 240p. 2000. 75.00 (*1-55619-976-7*) J Benjamins Pubng Co.

Niemeier, Susanne & Dirven, Rene, eds. The Language of Emotions: Conceptualization, Expression, & Theoretical Foundation. LC 97-4952. xviii, 337p. 1997. 94.00 (*1-55619-514-1*) J Benjamins Pubng Co.

Niemeier, Utts. Statistics for the Natural & Environmental Sciences. 2001. pap. text 53.00 (*0-534-37054-3*) Thomson Learn.

Niemeijer, J. W. & Te Rijdt, R. J. Eighteenth-Century Watercolors from the Rijksmuseum Printroom, Amsterdam. Hoyle, Michael, tr. LC 93-492. 1993. pap. 24.95 (*0-88397-107-0*) Art Srvc Intl.

Niemela, Pirkko, jt. ed. see Bjorkqvist, Kaj.

Niemer, William T., jt. auth. see Snider, Ray S.

Niemeyer, Carl, ed. & intro. see Carlyle, Thomas.

Niemeyer, Eberhardt V. Revolution at Queretaro: The Mexican Constitutional Convention of 1916-1917. LC 73-20203. (Latin American Monographs: No. 33). 319p. reprint ed. pap. 98.90 (*0-8357-7714-6*, 203607100002) Bks Demand.

Niemeyer, G. & Huber, Charles H. Techniques in Clinical Electrophysiology of Vision. 1982. text 332.00 (*90-6193-727-2*) Kluwer Academic.

Niemeyer, Gerhart. Aftersight & Foresight: Selected Essays. LC 87-33418. 374p. (Orig.) (C). 1988. pap. text 32.00 (*0-8191-6841-6*); lib. bdg. 48.00 (*0-8191-6840-8*) U Pr of Amer.

— Between Nothing & Paradise. LC 97-37674. 238p. 1997. reprint ed. 35.00 (*1-890318-05-1*) St Augustines Pr.

— Within & above Ourselves: Essays in Political Analysis. LC 95-81660. 1997. pap. text 14.95 (*1-882926-11-0*) ISI Books.

***Niemeyer, Gerhart & Henry, Michael.** Law Without Force. 408p. 1999. pap. 29.95 (*0-7658-0640-1*) Transaction Pubs.

Niemeyer, Gerhart, ed. see Voegelin, Eric.

***Niemeyer, J. C. & Truran, J. W., eds.** Type Ia Supernovas: Theory & Cosmology. (Cambridge Contemporary Astrophysics Ser.). (Illus.). 350p. (C). 2000. text 59.95 (*0-521-78036-5*) Cambridge U Pr.

Niemeyer, Juanita. Hobby Ceramist's Guide to Finishing Products: How to Correctly Use Ceramic Decorating & Repairing Media. Bayer, Gregory W., ed. 56p. (Orig.). 1994. pap. 7.99 (*1-879825-14-7*) Jones Publish.

Niemeyer, Louis V. & Auger, Susan J., eds. How to Deal with Unacceptable Behaviors While Promoting Positive Self-Esteem: Success with Children 3 to 5. 228p. (C). 1996. pap. text 21.00 (*0-536-59325-6*) Pearson Custom.

Niemeyer, Lucian. Where Water Meets Land. (Illus.). 96p. (Orig.). 1996. pap. 16.95 (*0-9651966-0-7*) York Graphic.

Niemeyer, Lucian, photos by. Chesapeake Country. (Illus.). 224p. 2000. 37.50 (*1-55859-063-3*) Abbeville Pr.

— Long-Legged Wading Birds of the North American Wetlands. LC 92-28154. (Illus.). 224p. 1993. 49.95 (*0-8117-1889-1*) Stackpole.

— Shenandoah: Daughter of the Stars. LC 94-18981. (Illus.). 224p. 1994. 39.95 (*0-8071-1966-0*) La State U Pr.

Niemeyer, Pat. Core Java Networking. (C). 2001. pap. 49.95 incl. cd-rom (*0-13-761537-X*) P-H.

Niemeyer, Pat & Peck, Jash. Exploring Java. 2nd ed. Loukides, Mike, ed. LC 97-224808. (Illus.). 614p. (Orig.). 1997. reprint ed. pap. 34.95 (*1-56592-271-9*) OReilly & Assocs.

Niemeyer, Pat & Peck, Josh. Exploring Java. Loukides, Mike & Ferguson, Paula, eds. 426p. (Orig.). 1996. pap. 29.95 (*1-56592-184-4*) Thomson Learn.

***Niemeyer, Patrick & Knudsen, Jonathan.** Learning Java. Posner, John & Loukides, Mike, eds. (Illus.). 650p. 2000. pap. 34.95 incl. cd-rom (*1-56592-718-4*) OReilly & Assocs.

Niemeyer, Paul V. & Schuette, Linda M. Maryland Rules Commentary. 610p. 1993. 85.00 (*0-614-06185-7*, MICHIE) LEXIS Pub.

Niemeyer, Ralph W., tr. see De Broglie, Louis.

***Niemeyer, Robert A. & Raskin, Jonathan D., eds.** Constructions of Disorder: Meaning-Making Frameworks for Psychotherapy. LC 99-41598. (Illus.). 373p. 2000. 39.95 (*1-55798-629-0*, 431739A) Am Psychol.

Niemeyer, Suzanne, ed. Money for Performing Artists: A Comprehensive Arts Resource Guide. LC 91-29393. 268p. (Orig.). 1991. pap. 12.00 (*0-915400-96-0*, ACA Bks) Am for the Arts.

— Research Guide to American Historical Biography Vol. 4: Women & Minorities. LC 88-19316. 572p. 1990. lib. bdg. 75.00 (*0-933833-21-0*) Beacham Pub Corp.

Niemeyer, Suzanne & Dilima, Sara N. Chronic Disease Patient Education Manual. LC 97-11530. 1997. 169.00 (*0-8342-0941-1*, 5459) Aspen Pub.

Niemeyer, Suzanne, ed. see Aspen Reference Group Staff.

Niemeyer, Suzanne, jt. ed. see Di Lima, Sara N.

Niemi. Russell Banks. LC 96-50231. 1997. 32.00 (*0-8057-4018-X*, Twyne) Mac Lib Ref.

Niemi, Albert W., Jr. State & Regional Patterns in American Manufacturing, 1860-1900, 10. LC 73-13289. (Contributions in Economics & Economic History Ser.: No. 10). 209p. 1974. 69.50 (*0-8371-7148-2*, NAM, Greenwood Pr) Greenwood.

— U. S. Economic History. 2nd ed. LC 87-10730. (Illus.). 492p. 1987. reprint ed. pap. text 32.00 (*0-8191-6335-X*) U Pr of Amer.

Niemi, Erkki, ed. Stress Determination for Fatigue Analysis of Welded Components. 80p. 1995. pap. 120.00 (*1-85573-213-0*, Pub. by Woodhead Pubng) Am Educ Systs.

Niemi, Ernie & Whitelaw, Ed. Assessing Economic Tradeoffs in Forest Management. (Illus.). 78p. (C). 1999. reprint ed. pap. text 20.00 (*0-7881-7655-2*) DIANE Pub.

Niemi, H., et al, eds. Proceedings of the Third Finnish-Soviet Conference on Probability Theory & Mathematical Statistics. (Frontiers in Pure & Applied Probability Ser.: Vol. 1). 306p. 1994. 175.00 (*90-6764-156-1*) Coronet Bks.

Niemi, John A., ed. Mass Media & Adult Education. LC 73-168491. 128p. 1971. pap. 24.95 (*0-87778-025-0*) Educ Tech Pubns.

Niemi, Judith. Basic Essentials: Women in the Outdoors. 2nd ed. LC 99-36413. (Illus.). 80p. 1999. pap. text 7.95 (*0-7627-0526-4*) Globe Pequot.

Niemi, Judith & Wieser, Barbara, eds. Rivers Running Free: A Century of Women's Canoeing Adventures. LC 92-23108. (Adventura Bks.). (Illus.). 304p. 1997. pap. 16.95 (*1-878067-90-7*) Seal Pr WA.

Niemi, Matt, jt. auth. see Sharp, Mary.

***Niemi, Richard G.** Civic Development of 9th Through 12th Grade Students in the United States: 1996. 93p. 1999. pap. 8.00 (*0-16-063680-9*) USGPO.

Niemi, Richard G. How Family Members Perceive Each Other: Political & Social Attitudes in Two Generations. LC 73-86913. (Illus.). 228p. 1974. 37.50 (*0-300-01698-0*) Yale U Pr.

Niemi, Richard G. & Jennings, M. Kent. Generations & Politics: A Panel Study of Young Adults & Their Parents. LC 80-8555. 440p. reprint ed. pap. 136.40 (*0-608-06340-1*, 206670100008) Bks Demand.

Niemi, Richard G. & Junn, Jane. Civic Education: What Makes Students Learn. LC 97-32807. 224p. 1998. 27.50 (*0-300-07247-3*) Yale U Pr.

Niemi, Richard G. & Weisberg, Herbert F., eds. Classics in Voting Behavior. LC 92-23085. 376p. 1992. text 19.17 (*0-87187-705-8*) Congr Quarterly.

— Controversies in Voting Behavior. 2nd ed. LC 84-9605. (Illus.). 651p. reprint ed. pap. 200.00 (*0-8357-8537-8*, 203484000091) Bks Demand.

Niemi, Richard G. & Wiesberg, Herbert F., eds. Controversies in Voting Behavior. 3rd ed. LC 92-22878. 433p. (YA). (gr. 11). 1992. pap. text 32.95 (*0-87187-706-6*) Congr Quarterly.

Niemi, Richard G., et al. Trends in Public Opinion: A Compendium of Survey Data. LC 89-2213. (Documentary Reference Collections). 344p. 1989. lib. bdg. 85.00 (*0-313-25426-5*, NTP/, Greenwood Pr) Greenwood.

Niemi, Richard G., jt. auth. see Jennings, M. Kent.

Niemi, Richard G., jt. auth. see Stanley, Harold W.

Niemi, Robert, jt. auth. see Gillane, Daniel.

Niemi, Tina, et al, eds. The Dead Sea: The Lake & Its Setting. (Oxford Monographs on Geology & Geophysics: No. 36). (Illus.). 298p. 1997. text 75.00 (*0-19-508703-8*) OUP.

Niemic, Robert J. Mediation & Conference Programs in the Federal Courts of Appeals: A Sourcebook for Judges & Lawyers. 107p. (C). 1999. pap. text 25.00 (*0-7881-4365-4*) DIANE Pub.

Niemiec, Dennis, jt. auth. see Langlos, Ruth.

Niemiec, Paul, et al. Play in Practice: A Systems Approach to Making Good Play Happen. (Source Books on Education). 175p. Date not set. text 30.00 (*0-8153-0217-7*) Garland.

Niemiec, Rich. Oracle DBA: Tips & Techniques. 1999. pap. 39.99 (*0-07-882432-5*) Osborne-McGraw.

Niemiec, Richard J., et al. Oracle Application Server Web Toolkit Reference. 924p. 1998. pap. text 44.99 (*0-07-882433-8*) Osborne-McGraw.

— Oracle Performance Tuning: Tips & Techniques. (Illus.). 894p. 1999. pap. 49.99 (*0-07-882434-6*) Osborne-McGraw.

— Oracle PL/SQL: Tips & Techniques. 942p. 1999. pap. 49.99 (*0-07-882438-9*) McGraw.

Niemiec, Richard P. & Walberg, Herbert J., eds. Evaluating Chicago School Reform. LC 85-644749. (New Directions for Evaluation Ser.: No. PE 59). 110p. (Orig.). 1993. pap. 22.00 (*1-55542-678-6*) Jossey-Bass.

Niemiejer, J. W., et al. How to Construct Reitveld Furniture. (Illus.). 120p. 1996. reprint ed. pap. 29.95 (*90-6868-025-0*, Pub. by Thoth Pubs) Bks Nippan.

Niemier, B. A., et al, eds. Formatibility Topics: Metallic Materials - STP 647. 279p. 1978. 27.75 (*0-8031-0358-1*, STP647) ASTM.

Nieminen, Jarmo, ed. East-West Business Relationships: Establishment & Development. LC 96-13564. 124p. (C). 1996. text 39.95 (*1-56024-747-9*) Haworth Pr.

Nieminen, R. M., et al, eds. Many-Atom Interactions in Solids: Proceedings of the International Workshop, Pajulahti, Finland, June 5-9, 1989. (Proceedings in Physics Ser.: Vol. 48). (Illus.). viii, 319p. 1990. 68.00 (*0-387-52657-9*) Spr-Verlag.

Nieminen, Raija. Voyage to the Island. LC 90-19178. 272p. 1990. 19.95 (*0-930323-62-9*) Gallaudet Univ Pr.

Nieminski, John. John Nieminski: Somewhere a Roscoe. Liebow, Ely & Scott, Art, eds. LC 87-36833. (Brownstone Mystery Guides Ser.: No. 3). 61p. (C). 1987. reprint ed. pap. 13.00 (*0-941028-06-2*) Millefleurs.

Niemira, Michael P. & Kahan, Samuel D. Forecasting Financial & Economics Cycles. 544p. 1994. 59.95 (*0-471-84544-2*) Wiley.

Niemira, Michael P. & Zukowski, Gerald F. Trading the Fundamentals: The Trader's Complete Guide to Interpreting Economic Indicators & Monetary Policy. 300p. 1993. text 37.50 (*1-55738-450-9*, Irwn Prfssnl) McGraw-Hill Prof.

— Trading the Fundamentals: The Trader's Guide to Interpreting Economic Indicators & Monetary Policy. 2nd rev. ed. LC 97-30364. 278p. 1997. 40.00 (*0-7863-1100-2*, Irwn Prfssnl) McGraw-Hill Prof.

Niemitz, Carsten, ed. German Primate Society: 5th International Meeting, Berlin, October 1997 - Abstracts. (Folia Primatologica Ser.: Vol. 69, No. 4). 66p. 1998. pap. 34.00 (*3-8055-6690-5*) S Karger.

Niemoeller, A. F., tr. see D'Hancarville.

Niemoeller, Michael. Stone Made Flesh. Wolverton, Terry, ed. LC 95-68980. 100p. (Orig.). 1995. pap. 9.95 (*0-9629528-2-6*) Silverton Bks.

Niemoller, Martin. Exile in the Fatherland: Martin Niemoller's Letters from Moabit Prison. Locke, Hubert G., ed. Kaemke, Ernst et al, trs. LC 86-491. 182p. (Orig.). reprint ed. pap. 56.50 (*0-608-17882-9*, 203273900080) Bks Demand.

Niemtschek, Franz X. Life of Mozart. 1988. reprint ed. lib. bdg. 49.00 (*0-7812-0253-1*) Rprt Serv.

— Life of Mozart. LC 74-181224. 87p. 1956. reprint ed. 49.00 (*0-403-01751-3*) Scholarly.

Niemtzow, Richard C., ed. Transmembrane Potentials & Characteristics of Immune & Tumor Cells. 176p. 1985. 101.00 (*0-8493-5688-1*, RC267, CRC Reprint) Franklin.

Niemuth, Neal D. Owls for Kids. LC 95-6694. (Wildlife for Kids Ser.). (Illus.). 48p. (Orig.). (J). (gr. 3-7). 1995. pap. 6.95 (*1-55971-475-1*, NorthWord Pr) Creat Pub Intl.

Niemz, Markolf H. Laser-Tissue Interactions: Fundamentals & Applications. LC 96-118. (Illus.). 299p. 1996. text, student ed. 119.00 (*3-540-60363-8*) Spr-Verlag.

Nien, Tung. Setting Out: The Education of Li-Li. O'Connor, Mike, tr. from CHI. LC 97-76162. 139p. 1998. pap. 15.00 (*0-9651413-3-0*) Pleasure Boat.

Nienaber, A. G., jt. auth. see Van der Walt, C.

Nienaber, Christoph A. & Fattori, Rossella. Diagnosis & Treatment of Aortic Diseases. LC 98-49373. (Developments in Cardiovascular Medicine Ser.). 1999. pap. 127.00 (*0-7923-5517-2*) Kluwer Academic.

Nienaber, Christoph A. & Sechtem, Udo, eds. Imaging & Intervention in Cardiology, Vol. 173. LC 95-34054. (Developments in Cardiovascular Medicine Ser.). 548p. (C). 1995. text 313.00 (*0-7923-3649-6*) Kluwer Academic.

Nienaber, Jeanne, jt. auth. see Mazmanian, Daniel A.

Niendorff, John, ed. see Sawyer, Colene.

Niendorff, John S., ed. see Holmes, Ernest.

Niendorff, John S., ed. see Moseley, Naomi & Moseley, Douglas.

Nienhauser, W. H. Liu Tsung-Yuan. (Twayne's World Authors Ser.). (C). 1971. lib. bdg. 20.95 (*0-8057-2538-5*) Irvington.

Nienhauser, W. H., Jr., et al, eds. Critical Essays on Chinese Literature. x, 207p. 1976. text 33.50 (*0-8248-0488-0*) Coronet Bks.

Nienhauser, William H., Jr., et al, eds. The Indiana Companion to Traditional Chinese Literature, Vol. I. LC 83-49511. 1096p. 1985. 95.00 (*0-253-32983-3*) Ind U Pr.

— The Indiana Companion to Traditional Chinese Literature, Vol. II. 576p. 1998. text 59.95 (*0-253-33456-X*) Ind U Pr.

Nienhauser, William H., Jr., ed. see Chien, Ssu-ma.

Nienhauser, William H., Jr., tr. see Levy, Andre.

Nienhueser, Helen & Wolfe, John, Jr. Fifty-Five Ways to the Wilderness in Southcentral Alaska. 4th ed. (Illus.). 176p. 1994. pap. 12.95 (*0-89886-389-9*) Mountaineers.

Nienhuis, Arthur W., jt. ed. see Stamatoyannopoulos, George.

Nienhuis, P. H. New Concepts for Sustainable Management of River Basins. Leuven, R. S. & Ragas, A. M., eds. (Illus.). 400p. 1998. pap. 111.00 (*90-73348-81-1*) Balogh.

Nienhuis, P. H. & Smaal, A. C., eds. The Oosterschelde Estuary: A Case Study of a Changing Ecosystem. LC 94-14882. (Developments in Hydrobiology Ser.: Vol. 97). 624p. (C). 1994. text 403.50 (*0-7923-2817-5*) Kluwer Academic.

Nienhuis, P. N., jt. ed. see Schramm, W.

Nienhuis, Pieter H., jt. ed. see Schramm, Winfried.

Nienhuys-Cheng, S. H. & De Wolf, R. Foundations of Inductive Logic Programming, Vol. 122. Carbonell, J. G. & Siekmann, J., eds. LC 97-16488. (Lecture Notes in Artificial Intelligence Ser.: No. 1228). 250p. 1997. pap. 44.95 (*3-540-62927-0*) Spr-Verlag.

Nienhuys, J., tr. see Comtet, L.

Nienhuys, J. W., tr. see Chaillou, Jacques.

Nienkamp, Jean, ed. see Tenney, Tabitha G.

Nienkemper, Robert C. Fatal Games. 2nd ed. 1998. reprint ed. mass mkt. 7.50 (*1-892614-00-6*, BWP-FG-2) Briarwood VA.

— Fatal Genes. 351p. 1999. pap. 7.50 (*1-892614-15-4*, BWP-FG) Briarwood VA.

Nienkirchen, Charles W. A. B. Simpson & the Pentecostal Movement: A Study in Continuity, Crisis & Change. 162p. 1992. pap. 9.95 (*0-913573-99-X*) Hendrickson MA.

Nienstedt, Vermadel P. & Smith, Lynn. Laugh to Keep from Crying. LC 83-91465. (Illus.). 90p. pap. 5.95 (*0-9613010-0-7*) Nienstedt VP & L Smith.

Nienstedt, W., jt. auth. see Hervonen, A.

Nieper. Niederlandisches Burgerliches Gesetzbuch, Buch 8 Verkehrsmittel und Beforderun, Vol. LETR 13. 1997. 130.00 (*90-411-0388-0*) Kluwer Law Intl.

Nieper, Hans A. The Curious Man: The Life & Works of Dr. Hans Nieper. (Illus.). 188p. 1998. pap. 13.95 (*0-89529-864-3*, Avery) Penguin Putnam.

Niepokuj, Mary. The Development of Verbal Reduplication in Indo-European. (Journal of Indo-European Studies Monograph Ser.: No. 24). 348p. (C). 1997. pap. text 48.00 (*0-941694-60-7*) Inst Study Man.

Niepoth, Burkhard. Der Untaugliche Versuch Beim Unechten Unterlassungsdelikt. (Schriften zum Strafrecht und Strafprozesrecht Ser.: Bd. 16). (GER.). 483p. 1994. 66.95 (*3-631-47053-3*) P Lang Pubng.

Nier, Keith A. The Papers of Thomas A. Edison Vol. 3: Menlo Park: the Early Years April 1876-December 1877. Israel, Paul B. et al, eds. (Illus.). 752p. 1995. text 65.00 (*0-8018-3102-4*) Johns Hopkins.

Nier, M., jt. ed. see Courtot, M. E.

Nier, M. C., ed. Standards for Electronic Imaging Technologies, Devices, & Systems: Proceedings of a Conference Held 1-2 February 1996, San Jose, California. LC 95-49185. (Critical Reviews of Optical Science & Technology Ser.: Vol. CR61). 1996. pap. 70.00 (*0-8194-2016-6*) SPIE.

Nier, Susan & Monastery of Arkashea Staff. The Discovery, Vol. 1. unabridged ed. 548p. (Orig.). 1993. pap. 24.95 (*0-9636142-0-7*, 1001, Pub. by Gldn Scribe) New Leaf Dist.

Nieratka, Ernest B., jt. auth. see Epstein, Ira D.

Nierenberg, Gerald. How to Read a Person Like a Book. 1990. per. 5.99 (*0-671-73557-8*) PB.

Nierenberg, Gerard. How to Give Yourself Good Advice. 1975. 14.95 (*0-936305-01-0*) Nierenberg-Zeif.

Nierenberg, Gerard I. The Art of Negotiating. 1990. student ed. 69.95 incl. audio (*0-924967-00-5*) Intl Ctr Creat Think.

— The Art of Negotiation. unabridged ed. 1989. 12.00 incl. audio (*0-394-29850-0*) Random.

— Do It Right the First Time: A Short Guide to Learning from Your Most Memorable Errors, Mistakes & Blunders. LC 96-2172. 310p. 1996. pap. 14.95 (*0-471-14889-X*) Wiley.

— Meta-Talk. 1981. pap. 4.95 (*0-685-03973-0*) PB.

— You're the Expert: How You Can Solve Problems in Business & in Life. 1991. pap. 8.95 (*0-425-13082-7*) Nierenberg-Zeif.

Nierenberg, J. Backcountry Companion for Denali National Park. (Illus.). 96p. 1995. pap. 8.95 (*0-930931-03-3*) Alaska Natural.

Nierenberg, Judith & Janovic, Florence. The Hospital Experience: A Complete Guide to Understanding & Participating in Your Own Care. LC 78-55658. (Illus.). 1978. 12.95 (*0-672-52372-8*, Bobbs); pap. 9.95 (*0-672-52373-6*, Bobbs) Macmillan.

Nierenberg, William A. Encyclopedia of Enviormental Biology. 1995. text 168.00 (*0-12-226733-8*) Acad Pr.

Nierenberg, William A., ed. Encyclopedia of Earth Systems Science, 1. (Illus.). 3264p. 1991. text 305.00 (*0-12-226722-2*) Acad Pr.

— Encyclopedia of Earth Systems Science, 2. (Illus.). 3264p. 1991. text 305.00 (*0-12-226723-0*) Acad Pr.

— Encyclopedia of Earth Systems Science, 3. (Illus.). 3264p. 1991. text 305.00 (*0-12-226724-9*) Acad Pr.

— Encyclopedia of Earth Systems Science, 4. (Illus.). 3264p. 1991. text 305.00 (*0-12-226725-7*) Acad Pr.

— Encyclopedia of Earth Systems Science, Vols. 1-4. (Illus.). 2629p. 1991. text 1101.00 (*0-12-226719-2*) Acad Pr.

— Encyclopedia of Environmental Biology, 3 vols., Set. (Illus.). 2168p. 1995. text 499.00 (*0-12-226730-3*) Acad Pr.

— Encyclopedia of Environmental Biology, 3 vols., Vol. 1. LC 94-24917. 1160p. 1995. text 168.00 (*0-12-226731-1*) Acad Pr.

— Encyclopedia of Environmental Biology, Vol. 2. LC 94-24917. 1995. text 168.00 (*0-12-226732-X*) Acad Pr.

Nierengarten, Ruth. New Borns, 3 bks., Set. (Illus.). 96p. 1994. boxed set 12.95 (*0-87839-092-8*) North Star.

Nierhaus, K. H., et al. The Translational Apparatus: Structure, Function, Regulation & Evolution. (Illus.). 760p. (C). 1993. text 175.00 (*0-306-44538-7*, Kluwer Plenum) Kluwer Academic.

An Asterisk (*) at the beginning of an entry indicates that the title is appearing for the first time.

Niering, William A. Wetlands. Elliott, Charles, ed. LC 84-48672. (Audubon Society Nature Guides Ser.). (Illus.). 638p. 1985. pap. 19.95 (*0-394-73147-6*) Knopf.

Niering, William A. & Spellenberg, Richard. Familiar Flowers of North America, Eastern Region. (Audubon Society Pocket Guides Ser.). 1987. pap. 4.95 (*0-317-56707-1*) Knopf.

— Familiar Flowers of North America, Western Region. (Audubon Society Pocket Guides Ser.). 1987. pap. 4.95 (*0-317-56709-8*) Knopf.

— Familiar Wildflowers of North America, 6 vols. (Illus.). 192p. 1988. write for info. (*0-318-63230-6*) Knopf.

— Familiar Wildflowers of North America, 6 vols., Set. (Illus.). 192p. 1988. 95.70 (*0-318-36011-X*) Knopf.

Niering, William A., jt. ed. see Dreyer, Glenn D.

Nierman, J. Harris. Preparing Your Research Paper. (Illus.). 23p. (Orig.). (gr. 10 up). 1979. pap. 1.95 (*0-935770-00-3*) Creative Res & Educ.

***Nierman, M. Murray.** Chutzpah: More Than Skin Deep. LC 99-63422. 256p. 1999. pap. 18.95 (*1-56167-550-4*, Five Star Spec Ed) Am Literary Pr.

***Nierman, Murray.** Stuffed Dermatologist with More Than One-Liners. 1999. pap. 9.00 (*0-8059-4942-9*) Dorrance.

Nierman, Rose. Medical Insurance Manual for Dentists: Maximizing Reimbursements. LC 95-25462. (Pennwell Bks.). 1995. 89.95 (*0-87814-459-5*) PennWell Bks.

Nierman, W. C. & Maglott, D. R., eds. ATCC/NIH Repository Catalogue of Human & Mouse DNA Probes & Libraries. 8th ed. 220p. 1995. pap. text. write for info. (*0-930009-56-8*) ATCC.

Nierman, W. C., jt. ed. see Maglott, D. R.

Niermann, Eleanor M., ed. Papers of John L. Lewis: Guide to a Microfilm Edition. (Guides to Historical Resources Ser.). 12p. 1970. pap. 1.00 (*0-87020-182-4*) State Hist Soc Wis.

— Papers of the University Settlement Society of New York City: Guide to a Microfilm Edition. (Guides to Historical Resources Ser.). 1972. pap. 1.00 (*0-87020-183-2*) State Hist Soc Wis.

— The Papers of the University Settlement Society of New York City, 1886-1945: Guide to a Microfilm Edition. 15p. 1972. pap. write for info. (*0-89887-187-5*) Chadwyck-Healey.

Niermann, Johannes. Woerterbuch der DDR Paedagogik. (GER.). 1974. pap. 24.95 (*0-7859-0839-0*, M-7032) Fr & Eur.

Niermeyer, J. F. Mediae Latinitatis Lexicon Minus. LC 92-42558. (ENG, FRE & LAT.). xvi, 1138p. 1993. reprint ed. 209.00 (*90-04-07108-3*) Brill Academic Pubs.

Nierop, H. K. Van, see Van Nierop, H. K.

Nierop, Tom. Systems & Regions in Global Politics: An Empirical Study of Diplomacy, International Organization & Trade 1950-1991. LC 93-46291. (Belhaven Studies in Political Geography). 284p. 1995. 100.00 (*0-471-94942-6*) Wiley.

Nierstrasz, Oscar M., ed. ECOOP '93 - Object-Oriented Programming: Proceedings of the Seventh European Conference Held in Kaiserslautern, Germany, July 26-30, 1993. (Lecture Notes in Computer Science Ser.: Vol. 707). xi, 531p. 1993. 73.95 (*0-387-57120-5*) Spr-Verlag.

Nierstrasz, Oscar M. & Tsichritzis, Dennis. Object-Oriented Software Composition. 362p. 1995. pap. 69.00 (*0-13-220674-9*) P-H.

Nierstrasz, Oscar M., ed. see ESEC/FSE '99 Staff, et al.

Nierstrasz, Oscar M., ed. see Seventh European Conference on Object-Oriented Pro.

Nierstrasz, V. A. Marginal Regeneration. (Illus.). 108p. (Orig.). 1996. pap. 62.50 (*90-407-1237-9*, Pub. by Delft U Pr) Coronet Bks.

***Nies.** Community Health Nursing. 3rd ed. 2001. text. write for info. (*0-7216-9161-7*) Harcourt.

Nies, Barbara J. Finding Ways: Recovering from Rheumatoid Arthritis Through Alternative Medicine. LC 96-92944. 272p. (Orig.). 1997. pap. 19.95 (*0-9653648-6-0*) Synchrony Pub.

Nies, H., jt. auth. see Singer, C.

Nies, James B. Historical, Religious & Economic Texts & Antiquities. LC 78-63522. (Babylonian Inscriptions in the Collection of James B. Nies Ser.: No. 2). reprint ed. 37.50 (*0-404-60132-4*) AMS Pr.

Nies, Judith. Native American History: A Chronology of the Vast Achievements of a Culture & Their Links to World Events. 384p. 1997. pap. 13.95 (*0-345-39350-3*) Ballantine Pub Grp.

Nies, Kevin A. From Priestess to Physician Vol. 2: Biological Scientists. LC 97-172134. (Illus.). 135p. (YA). (gr. 8-12). 1996. pap. text 19.95 (*1-880211-04-1*) Calif Video Inst.

— From Sorceress to Scientist: Biographies of Women Physical Scientists. (Lives of Women Scientists Ser.: Vol. I). (Illus.). 95p. (Orig.). (YA). (gr. 8 up). 1991. pap. 19.95 (*1-880211-01-7*) Calif Video Inst.

Nies, Mary, jt. auth. see Swanson, Janice M.

Nies, Mary, jt. ed. see Swanson, Janice M.

Nies, Nelson L. Health in Stress - Actions, Reactions & the General Adaptation Syndrome: Index of New Information & Bibliography. 150p. 1996. 47.50 (*0-7883-0980-3*); pap. 44.50 (*0-7883-0981-1*) ABBE Pubs Assn.

Niesar, Gerald V., et al. California Limited Liability Company Forms & Practice Manual, 2 vols. LC 94-41019. 940p. 1994. ring bd. 239.90 (*0-9637468-8-X*) Data Trace Pubng.

Nieschlag, E., ed. Hormone Assays in Reproductive Medicine. (Journal: Hormone Research Ser.: Vol. 9, No. 6). (Illus.). 1978. pap. 27.00 (*3-8055-2975-9*) S Karger.

Nieschlag, E., et al, eds. Spermatogenesis - Fertilization Contraception: Molecular, Cellular, & Endocrine Events in Male Reproduction. LC 92-2300. (Schering Foundation Workshop Ser.: Vol. 4). (Illus.). 528p. 1992. 59.00 (*0-387-55436-X*); write for info. (*3-540-55436-X*) Spr-Verlag.

Nieschlag, E. & Behre, H. M. Testosterone: Action, Deficiency, Substitution. 2nd ed. LC 98-13005. 1998. 109.00 (*0-387-64283-8*) Spr-Verlag.

Nieschlag, E. & Behre, H. M., eds. Testosterone: Action, Deficiency, Substitution. 2nd ed. LC 98-13005. (Illus.). 350p. 1998. 109.00 (*3-540-64283-8*) Spr-Verlag.

— Testosterone - Action, Deficiency, Substitution. (Illus.). 352p. 1990. 70.00 (*0-387-52763-X*) Spr-Verlag.

Nieschlag, E., et al. Andrology: Male Reproductive Health & Dysfunction. LC 96-45653. 1997. write for info. (*0-387-61616-0*) Spr-Verlag.

Nieschlag, E., ed. see Brinkworth, M.

Niesen, De Abruno L. The Refining Fire: Herakles & Other Heroes in T. S. Eliot's Works. (American University Studies: English Language & Literature: Ser. IV, Vol. 62). 188p. (C). 1992. text 35.95 (*0-8204-0550-7*) P Lang Pubng.

Niesen, Karen L. & Onaga, Christine. Malawi. LC 95-22633. (Country Guide Series Report from the AACRAO-AID Project). 1998. 22.00 (*0-929851-51-X*) Am Assn Coll Registrars.

— Myanmar (Burma) LC 95-22467. (Oles Country Guide Ser.). 1996. 22.00 (*0-929851-54-4*) Am Assn Coll Registrars.

Niesen, Karen L. & Onaga, Christine Y. 1996 Supplement to the Wisconsin Directory of International Institutions. 64p. 1996. pap. 12.95 (*0-299-15054-2*) U of Wis Pr.

— Wisconsin Directory of International Institutions. 261p. 1994. pap. 25.00 (*0-299-97079-5*) U of Wis Pr.

Niesen, Thomas M. Beachcomber's Guide to California Marine Life. LC 93-29207. (Illus.). 192p. 1994. pap. 16.95 (*0-88415-075-5*, 5075) Gulf Pub.

— Beachcomber's Guide to Marine Life of the Pacific Northwest: Includes Vancouver, Washington, Oregon, & Northern California. LC 97-54. (Illus.). 160p. 1997. pap. 18.95 (*0-88415-132-8*, 5132) Gulf Pub.

— Marine Biology Coloring Book. (Illus.). 224p. 1982. pap. 18.00 (*0-06-460303-2*, CO 303, Harper Ref) HarpC.

Niesewand, Nonie. Contemporary Details. LC 98-30919. (Illus.). 192p. 1999. text 35.00 (*0-8230-0934-3*, Whitney Lib) Watsn-Guptill.

— Converted Spaces. 1998. 50.00 (*1-85029-951-X*, Pub. by Conran Octopus) Antique Collect.

— The Lighting Book. LC 98-41252. (Illus.). 176p. 1999. 35.00 (*0-8230-2775-9*) Watsn-Guptill.

Niesewand, Nonie, jt. auth. see Guild, Tricia.

Niesewand, Nonie, jt. ed. see Mendini, Allesandro.

Nieshtadt, Yakov, ed. Catastrophe in the Opening. (Chess Ser.). (Illus.). 271p. 1980. 25.95 (*0-08-023121-7*, Pergamon Pr); pap. 14.95 (*0-08-024097-6*, Pergamon Pr) Elsevier.

Niesiecki, K. Herbarz Polski, 10 vols., Set. (Illus.). 1979. reprint ed. 800.00 (*0-318-23353-3*) Szwede Slavic.

Niesink, Raymond J. Drugs of Abuse & Addiction: Neurobehavioral Toxicology. LC 98-39869. (Pharmacology & Toxicology Ser.). 1998. 99.95 (*0-8493-7803-6*) CRC Pr.

***Niesink, Raymond J.** Introduction to Neurobehavioral Toxicology: Food & Environment. LC 98-39870. (Pharmacology & Toxicology Ser.). 496p. 1998. boxed set 129.95 (*0-8493-7802-8*) CRC Pr.

***Niesley, Robert C.** Model Jury Instructions for Surety Cases. LC 00-42147. 2000. write for info. (*1-57073-837-8*) Amer Bar Assn.

Niesluchowski, Warren, tr. see Cooke, Lynne, et al.

Niess, Frank. A Hemisphere to Itself: A History of U. S.-Latin-American Relations. LC 89-18272. (C). 1990. pap. 17.50 (*0-86232-867-5*, Pub. by Zed Books); text 55.00 (*0-86232-866-7*, Pub. by Zed Books) St Martin.

Niessen, M. & Peschar, J. International Comparative Research: Problems of Theory Methodology & Organization in East & West. LC 82-16519. 1982. 86.00 (*0-08-027960-0*, Pub. by Pergamon Repr) Franklin.

Niessen, M. & Peschar, J., eds. International Comparative Research: Problems of Theory, Methodology & Organisation in Eastern & Western Europe. (Vienna Centre Ser.: No. 10). (Illus.). 184p. 1982. 47.00 (*0-317-66833-1*, Pergamon Pr) Elsevier.

Niessen, Sandra, jt. ed. see Brydon, Anne.

Niessen, Sandra A. Batak Cloth & Clothing: A Dynamic Indonesian Tradition. (Asia Collection). (Illus.). 148p. 1994. text 49.95 (*967-65-3040-9*) OUP.

Niessen, W. M. Liquid Chromatography-Mass Spectrometry. 2nd ed. LC 98-39466. (Chromatographic Science Ser.). (Illus.). 648p. 1998. text 195.00 (*0-8247-1936-0*) Dekker.

Niessen, W. M. & Voyksner, R. D. Current Practice of Liquid Chromatography-Mass Spectrometry. LC 98-4691. 438p. 1998. 215.75 (*0-444-82938-5*) Elsevier.

Niessen, Walter R. Combustion & Incineration Processes: Applications in Environmental Engineering. 2nd expanded rev. ed. LC 94-29112. (Environmental Science & Pollution Ser.: Vol. 13). (Illus.). 680p. 1994. text 190.00 (*0-8247-9267-X*) Dekker.

Niesser, R., jt. ed. see Hock, B.

Niestle, Axel. German U-Boat Losses During World War II: Details of Destruction. LC 98-5218. (Illus.). 160p. 1998. 27.95 (*1-55750-641-8*) Naval Inst Pr.

***Niestrath, Rebecca A.** Treasured Memories: The Story of Our Baby. (Illus.). 124p. 1999. ring bd. 39.99 (*0-9674740-0-0*) Speranza Pubg.

Nieswand-Verlag Staff. Diary of Jazz: A Perpetual Calendar. 1997. 39.95 (*3-926048-38-7*, Pub. by Nieswand-Verlag) Dist Art Pubs.

Nieswiadomy. Foundations of Nursing Research. 3rd ed. LC 97-37912. 400p. (C). 1997. pap. text 34.95 (*0-8385-2696-9*, A-2696-1) Appleton & Lange.

Nieswiadomy, Michael, jt. auth. see Rubin, Rose M.

Niesz, Anita. Anita Niesz: Photographs. (Illus.). 152p. 1989. pap. 35.00 (*3-7165-0672-9*, Pub. by Benteli Verlag) Dist Art Pubs.

Nietenhoefer, Ken. Fifty Ways to Enrich Your Life, Bk. 1. LC 94-96026. 152p. 1991. pap. 5.00 (*0-9631681-0-X*) Ken Co.

— Fifty Ways to Enrich Your Life, Bk. 2. LC 91-91567. 136p. 1994. pap. 6.00 (*0-9631681-1-8*) Ken Co.

Niethammer, Carolyn. American Indian Cooking: Recipes from the Southwest. LC 99-14817. 224p. 1999. pap. 14.95 (*0-8032-8375-X*) U of Nebr Pr.

— American Indian Food & Lore. LC 73-7681. (Illus.). 191p. 1996. pap. 16.95 (*0-02-010000-0*) Macmillan.

— Daughters of the Earth. 281p. 1977. pap. 16.00 (*0-02-096150-2*) Macmillan.

— Daughters of the Earth. 1995. per. 17.00 (*0-684-82955-X*) S&S Trade.

***Niethammer, Carolyn.** I'll Go & Do More: Annie Dodge Wauneka, Navajo Leader & Activist. (American Indian Lives Ser.). (Illus.). 2001. 29.95 (*0-8032-3345-0*) U of Nebr Pr.

Niethammer, Carolyn J. American Indian Food & Lore. LC 73-7681. 191p. 1974. write for info. (*0-02-588570-7*) Macmillan.

Niethammer, Lutz. Posthistoire: Has History Come to an End? 160p. (C). (gr. 13 up). 1994. pap. 19.00 (*0-86091-697-9*, Pub. by Verso) Norton.

Nietiedt, Thomas. Kommunikationspolitik fur Hochschulen Vol. XVIII: Analyse und Instrumentarium. (Europaische Hochschulschriften: Reihe 5: Bd. 1996). (GER., Illus.). XVIII, 315p. 1996. pap. 57.95 (*3-631-30919-8*) P Lang Pubng.

Nietmann, William F. The Unmaking of God. LC 93-49437. 240p. (Orig.). (C). 1994. pap. text 28.50 (*0-8191-9436-0*); lib. bdg. 49.50 (*0-8191-9435-2*) U Pr of Amer.

Nieto, Amparo Y. Esmorgantes. (Nueva Austral Ser.: Vol. 153). (SPA.). 1991. pap. text 24.95 (*84-239-1953-6*) Elliots Bks.

Nieto, Beatriz C., jt. auth. see Roach, Sally S.

***Nieto, Benigno S.** Los Paraisos Artificiales. 1999. 24.95 (*84-239-7948-2*) Planeta.

Nieto, Benigno S. Los Paraisos Artificiales. LC 97-80164. (Coleccion Caniqui). (SPA.). 496p. 1997. pap. 19.95 (*0-89729-854-3*) Ediciones.

Nieto, Dudley, jt. auth. see Kraig, Bruce.

Nieto-Galan, Augusti, jt. ed. see Fox, Robert.

Nieto, Jose C. Religious Experience & Mysticism: Otherness As Experience of Transcendence. LC 97-10422. 288p. 1997. 57.50 (*0-7618-0765-9*); pap. 34.50 (*0-7618-0766-7*) U Pr of Amer.

— Valdes' Two Catechisms: The Dialogue on Christian Doctrine & the Christian Instruction for Children. 2nd rev. ed. Jones, William B. & Jones, Carol D., eds. (Illus.). 276p. 1993. 25.00 (*0-87291-205-1*) Coronado Pr.

Nieto, Jose R., jt. auth. see DeCandido, Keith R.

Nieto-Manjon, Luis. Diccionario Illustrado de Terminos Taurinos. 3rd ed. (SPA.). 438p. 1991. pap. 65.00 (*0-7859-5751-0*) Fr & Eur.

Nieto, Marcus. Boot Camps: An Alternative Punishment Option for the Criminal Justice System. 50p. 1995. pap. write for info. (*1-58703-036-5*, CRB-95-003) CA St Libry.

— The Changing Role of Probation in California's Criminal Justice System. 70p. 1996. pap. write for info. (*1-58703-050-0*) CA St Libry.

— Community Correction Punishment: An Alternative to Incarceration for Nonviolent Offenders. 23p. 1996. pap. write for info. (*1-58703-052-7*) CA St Libry.

— Concealed Handgun Laws & Public Safety. 13p. 1997. pap. write for info. (*1-58703-067-5*, CRB-97-007) CA St Libry.

— Health Care in California State Prisons. 69p. 1998. pap. write for info. (*1-58703-087-X*, CRB-98-009) CA St Libry.

— Mentallly Ill Offenders in California's Criminal Justice System. 57p. 1999. pap. write for info. (*1-58703-099-3*, CRB-99-002) CA St Libry.

— The 1994 Violent Crime Control & Law Enforcement Act Today. 42p. 1995. pap. write for info. (*1-58703-034-9*, CRB-95-001) CA St Libry.

— Overview of Arbitration in California Managed Health Care Plans, Vol. 5. 13p. 1997. pap. write for info. (*1-58703-072-1*, CRB Note 4) CA St Libry.

— Probation for Adult & Juvenile Offenders: Options for Improved Accountability. 24p. 1998. pap. write for info. (*1-58703-093-4*, CRB-98-014) CA St Libry.

— Public Video Surveillance: Is It an Effective Crime Prevention Tool? 1997. write for info. (*1-58703-062-4*) CA St Libry.

— Security & Crime Prevention Strategies in California Public Schools. 54p. 1999. pap. write for info. (*1-58703-112-4*, CRB-99-012) CA St Libry.

Nieto, Marcus, et al. Firearm Related Violence in California: Incidence & Economic Costs. 41p. 1994. pap. write for info. (*1-58703-032-2*) CA St Libry.

Nieto, Michael M., et al, eds. Science Underground. LC 83-70377. (AIP Conference Proceedings Ser.: No. 96). 446p. 1983. lib. bdg. 38.75 (*0-88318-195-9*) Am Inst Physics.

Nieto, Sonia. Affirming Diversity: The Sociopolitical Context of Multicultural Education. 3rd ed. 412p. (Orig.). (C). 1999. pap. 50.00 (*0-8013-3103-X*) Longman.

— Light in Their Eyes Creating Multicultural Learning Communities. LC 98-51677. 240p. 1999. pap. 22.95 (*0-8077-3782-8*) Tchrs Coll.

— Light in Their Eyes: Creating Multicultural Learning Communities, Vol. #5. LC 98-51677. 5. 240p. 1999. 50.00 (*0-8077-3783-6*) Tchrs Coll.

***Nieto, Sonia.** Puerto Rican Students in U. S. Schools. LC 99-47154. 2000. write for info. (*0-8058-2765-X*) L Erlbaum Assocs.

Nieto, Sonia, jt. ed. see Rivera, Ralph.

Nieto-Vesperinas, M. & Garcia, N., eds. Optics at the Nanometer Scale: Imaging & Storing with Photonic Near Fields. (NATO ASI Ser.: Series E, Vol. 319). 1996. text 180.50 (*0-7923-4020-5*) Kluwer Academic.

Nieto-Vesperinas, M., jt. ed. see Fiddy, M. A.

Nieto, Zoilo C. & Ossa, Pat. The Zoni English System, No. 1. Hansen, Keith W., ed. (Illus.). 148p. 1996. pap. text 15.00 (*0-9658015-0-0*) Zoni Language.

Nieto, Zoilo C., et al. The Zoni English System, Vol. 2. Hansen, Keith W., ed. (Illus.). 146p. 1998. pap. text 20.00 (*0-9658015-2-7*) Zoni Language.

Nietschmann, Bernard. The Unknown War: The Miskito Nation, Nicaragua, & the United States. LC 89-7831. (Focus on Issues Ser.: No. 8). (Illus.). 120p. (Orig.). (C). 1989. pap. text 16.50 (*0-932088-42-2*); lib. bdg. 37.00 (*0-932088-41-4*) Freedom Hse.

Nietupski, Paul K. Labrang: A Tibetan Buddhist Monastery at the Crossroads of Four Civilizations. LC 98-5347. (Illus.). 123p. 1999. pap. 24.95 (*1-55939-090-5*) Snow Lion Pubns.

Nietzel, jt. auth. see Wrightsman.

Nietzel, G. P. & Smith, M. K., eds. Surface-Tension-Driven Flows. LC 93-73260. 88p. pap. 35.00 (*0-7918-1024-0*) ASME.

Nietzel, Michael. Crime & Its Modification: A Social Learning Perspective. LC 78-23984. (General Psychology Ser.: Vol. 77). (Illus.). 1979. pap. 24.00 (*0-08-023877-7*, Pergamon Pr) Elsevier.

***Nietzel, Michael T.** Abnormal Psychology & Study Guide, 2 bks. 1998. text 67.95 (*0-205-28947-9*) Allyn.

Nietzel, Michael T., et al. Abnormal Psychology. LC 96-52617. 764p. 1997. 88.00 (*0-205-14721-6*) Allyn.

— Abnormal Psychology. 1997. pap. text, student ed. 19.00 (*0-205-27327-0*, T7327-4) Allyn.

— Abnormal Psychology. (C). 1997. text, teacher ed. write for info. (*0-205-26281-3*, T6281-4) Allyn.

— Abnormal Psychology: Examination Copy. 784p. (C). 1997. text. write for info. (*0-205-26282-1*, T6282-2) Allyn.

— Introduction to Clinical Psycholgy. 5th ed. LC 97-29348. 646p. 1998. 77.00 (*0-13-269549-9*) P-H.

Nietzel, Michael T., jt. auth. see Baker, Robert.

Nietzel, Michael T., jt. auth. see Wrightsman, Lawrence S.

Nietzke, Ann. Natalie on the Street. 190p. 1994. 24.95 (*0-934971-42-0*); pap. 14.95 (*0-934971-41-2*) Calyx Bks.

— Solo Spinout. LC 95-47335. 196p. 1996. 22.00 (*1-56947-052-9*) Soho Press.

— Windowlight. LC 95-50724. 200p. 1996. 12.00 (*1-56947-060-X*) Soho Press.

Nietzsche, Friedrich Wilhelm. Also Sprach Zarathustra. (Cloth Bound Pocket Ser.). (GER.). 238p. 1998. 7.95 (*3-89508-037-3*, 510025) Konemann.

— Also Sprach Zarathustra. unabridged ed. (World Classic Literature Ser.). (GER.). pap. 7.95 (*3-89507-039-4*, Pub. by Bookking Intl) Distribks Inc.

***Nietzsche, Friedrich Wilhelm.** Antichrist. (Great Books in Philosophy). 111p. 2000. pap. 6.95 (*1-57392-832-1*) Prometheus Bks.

Nietzsche, Friedrich Wilhelm. The Antichrist. LC 70-161338. (Atheist Viewpoint Ser.). 60p. 1972. reprint ed. 9.95 (*0-405-03799-6*) Ayer.

— The Antichrist. LC 70-161338. 60p. 1997. reprint ed. pap. 15.95 (*0-88143-146-X*) Ayer.

— The Antichrist. Mencken, H. L., tr. from GER. 96p. 1999. reprint ed. pap. 6.95 (*1-884365-20-5*) See Sharp Pr.

— The Antichrist. 3rd large type ed. Mencken, H. L., tr. from GER. 182p. 1997. reprint ed. pap. 7.95 (*0-939482-50-9*, 0300, Noontide Pr) Legion Survival.

— The Antichrist & Twilight of the Gods. 1974. 300.00 (*0-87968-210-8*) Gordon Pr.

Nietzsche, Friedrich Wilhelm. Anticristo. 1997. pap. 5.98 (*968-15-0824-6*) Ed Mex.

Nietzsche, Friedrich Wilhelm. Basic Writings of Nietzsche. large type ed. Kaufmann, Walter, ed. & tr. by. LC 92-50233. 864p. 1992. 21.00 (*0-679-60000-0*) Modern Lib NY.

— Beyond Good & Evil. Zimmern, Helen, tr. 1974. lib. bdg. 300.00 (*0-87968-207-8*) Gordon Pr.

— Beyond Good & Evil. Zimmern, Helen, tr. from GER. LC 89-62325. (Great Books in Philosophy). 274p. 1989. reprint ed. pap. text 8.95 (*0-87975-558-X*) Prometheus Bks.

— Beyond Good & Evil. Hollingdale, R. J., tr. 240p. 1990. reprint ed. pap. 11.95 (*0-14-044513-7*, Penguin Classics) Viking Penguin.

— Beyond Good & Evil: Prelude to a Philosophy of the Future. Zimmern, Helen, tr. from GER. LC 97-12411. (Dover Thrift Editions Ser.). (Illus.). 176p. 1997. pap. 1.50 (*0-486-29868-X*) Dover.

— Beyond Good & Evil: Prelude to a Philosophy of the Future. Faber, Marion, ed. & tr. by. LC 98-15016. (Oxford World's Classics Ser.). 230p. 1999. pap. 9.95 (*0-19-283263-8*) OUP.

— Beyond Good & Evil: Prelude to a Philosophy of the Future. Kaufmann, Walter, tr. 1989. pap. 12.00 (*0-679-72465-6*) Vin Bks.

— The Birth of Tragedy. 1974. 300.00 (*0-87968-172-1*) Gordon Pr.

— The Birth of Tragedy. 1967. pap. 10.00 (*0-394-70369-3*) Knopf.

***Nietzsche, Friedrich Wilhelm.** The Birth of Tragedy. Smith, Douglas, ed. (Oxford World's Classics Ser.). 208p. 2000. pap. 8.95 (*0-19-283292-1*) OUP.

N

An Asterisk (*) at the beginning of an entry indicates that the title is appearing for the first time.

Nietzsche, Friedrich Wilhelm. The Birth of Tragedy. Tanner, Michael, ed. Whiteside, Shaun, tr. LC 94-163915. 160p. 1994. pap. 9.95 (*0-14-043339-2*, Penguin Classics) Viking Penguin.

— The Birth of Tragedy. unabridged ed. Fadiman, Clifton, tr. (Thrift Editions Ser.). 96p. 1995. pap. text 1.50 (*0-486-28515-4*) Dover.

— The Birth of Tragedy: And Other Writings. Speirs, Ronald, ed. & tr. by. from GER. Geuss, Raymond, ed. LC 98-35097. (Cambridge Texts in the History of Philosophy Ser.). 203p. (C). 1999. text 37.95 (*0-521-63016-9*); pap. text 10.95 (*0-521-63987-5*) Cambridge U Pr.

— The Birth of Tragedy & the Genealogy of Morals. Golffing, Francis, tr. Incl. Genealogy of Morals. LC 56-7535. 1956. LC 56-7535. 320p. 1956. Set pap. 8.95 (*0-385-09210-5*, A81, Anchor NY) Doubleday.

— Briefwechsel: Kritische Gesamtausgabe, Section 1, Vol. 1. Colli, Giorgio & Montinari, Mazzino, eds. xiv, 452p. (C). 1975. 156.95 (*3-11-005911-8*) De Gruyter.

— Briefwechsel: Kritische Gesamtausgabe, Section 1, Vols. 2 & 3. Incl. Vol. 2. September 1864 - April 1869. 1975. 56.00 (*3-11-006514-2*); Vol. 3. October 1864 - March 1869. 1975. 52.00 (*3-11-006558-4*); (C). 1975. write for info. (*0-318-51616-0*) De Gruyter.

— Le Cas Wagner: Nietzsche Contre Wagner. (FRE.). 1991. pap. 9.95 (*0-7859-3982-2*) Fr & Eur.

— The Case of Wagner. 1974. lib. bdg. 300.00 (*0-87968-203-5*) Gordon Pr.

— Complete Works, 18 vols. 1974. 3500.00 (*0-87968-173-X*) Gordon Pr.

— The Complete Works of Friedrich Nietzsche Vol. 3: Human, All Too Human. Handwerk, Gary, tr. LC 96-31901. 1997. 29.95 (*0-8047-2665-5*) Stanford U Pr.

— The Dawn of Day. Kennedy, J. M., tr. 1974. 300.00 (*0-87968-204-3*) Gordon Pr.

— Early Greek Philosophy & Other Essays. Mugge, Maximilian A., tr. 1974. lib. bdg. 300.00 (*0-87968-174-8*) Gordon Pr.

— Ecce Homo. Hollingdale, R. J., tr. 144p. 1992. pap. 10.95 (*0-14-044515-3*, Penguin Classics) Viking Penguin.

— Ecce Homo (Nietzsche's Autobiography) 1974. 300.00 (*0-87968-211-6*) Gordon Pr.

— The Gay Science. Kauffmann, Walter, tr. 1974. pap. 11.00 (*0-394-71985-9*) Vin Bks.

— Genealogy of Morals & Peoples & Countries. 1974. lib. bdg. 300.00 (*0-87968-208-6*) Gordon Pr.

— Hammer of the Gods: Apocalyptic Texts for the Criminally Insane. Metcalf, Stephen, ed. & tr. by. from GER. 256p. (Orig.). 1996. pap. 14.95 (*1-871592-46-1*) Creation Books.

— Human, All Too Human, 2 vols. Ludovici, Anthony M., tr. 1974. lib. bdg. 600.00 (*0-87968-201-9*) Gordon Pr.

— Human, All Too Human: A Book for Free Spirits. rev. ed. Faber, Marion & Lehmann, Stephen, trs. LC 95-36383. xxxix, 275p. 1996. pap. 14.00 (*0-8032-8368-7*, Bison Books) U of Nebr Pr.

— Index to Nietzsche. Guppy, Robert, ed. Cohn, Paul V., tr. 1974. lib. bdg. 300.00 (*0-87968-212-4*) Gordon Pr.

— Jenseits Von Gut und Boese. (Cloth Bound Pocket Ser.). (GER.). 238p. 1998. 7.95 (*3-89508-038-1*, 510031) Konemann.

— The Joyful Wisdom. Common, Thomas, tr. 1974. lib. bdg. 300.00 (*0-87968-205-1*) Gordon Pr.

— Menschliches, Allzumenschliches. (Cloth Bound Pocket Ser.). (GER.). 238p. 1998. 7.95 (*3-89508-036-5*, 510024) Konemann.

— My Sister & I. Levy, Oscar, tr. from GER. (Illus.). 340p. (C). 1990. reprint ed. pap. 9.95 (*1-878923-01-3*) Amok Bks.

— Nietzsche: A Self-Portrait from His Letters. Fuss, Peter & Shapiro, Henry, eds. LC 73-134953. 208p. reprint ed. pap. 64.50 (*0-8357-9170-X*, 201465500093) Bks Demand.

— Nietzsche: Daybreak: Thoughts on the Prejudices of Morality. Clark, Maudemarie & Leiter, Brian, eds. (Cambridge Texts in the History of Philosophy Ser.). 292p. (C). 1997. text 49.95 (*0-521-59050-7*); pap. text 16.95 (*0-521-59963-6*) Cambridge U Pr.

— Nietzsche: The Great Philosophers. Schacht, Richard, ed. LC 92-38158. 330p. (Orig.). (C). 1993. pap. text 15.60 (*0-02-406681-8*, Macmillan Coll) P-H.

— Nietzsche: Untimely Meditations. Breazeale, Daniel, ed. Hollingdale, R. J., tr. LC 96-37028. (Cambridge Texts in the History of Philosophy Ser.). 328p. (C). 1997. text 49.95 (*0-521-58458-2*); pap. text 15.95 (*0-521-58584-8*) Cambridge U Pr.

— Nietzsche - Human, All Too Human: A Book for Free Spirits. Schacht, Richard, ed. Hollingdale, R. J., tr. LC 96-10969. (Cambridge Texts in the History of Philosophy Ser.). 420p. (C). 1996. pap. text 16.95 (*0-521-56704-1*) Cambridge U Pr.

— Nietzsche - Human, All Too Human: A Book for Free Spirits. Hollingdale, R. J., tr. LC 96-10969. (Cambridge Texts in the History of Philosophy Ser.). 429p. (C). 1996. text 54.95 (*0-521-56200-7*) Cambridge U Pr.

— A Nietzsche Reader. Hollingdale, R. J., ed. & tr. by. from GER. (Classics Ser.). 288p. (Orig.). 1978. pap. 12.95 (*0-14-044329-0*, Penguin Classics) Viking Penguin.

— Nietzsche-Studien, Vol. 4. Montinari, Mazzino, ed. (Internationales Jahrbuch fuer die Nietzsche-Forschung Ser.). (GER.). 1975. 142.35 (*3-11-005844-8*) De Gruyter.

— Nietzsche-Studien, Vol. 6. (C). 1977. 113.85 (*3-11-007166-5*) De Gruyter.

— Nietzsche-Studien, Vol. 7. (Internationales Jahrbuch fuer die Nietzsche-Forschung Ser.). (GER.). 1978. 126.95 (*3-11-007338-2*) De Gruyter.

— Nietzsche-Studien, Vol. 8. (Internationales Jahrbuch fuer die Nietzsche-Forschung Ser.). (GER.). 1979. 150.00 (*3-11-007861-9*) De Gruyter.

— Nietzsche-Studien, Vol. 9. Behler, Ernst et al, eds. (Internationales Jahrbuch fuer die Nietzsche-Forschung Ser.). (GER.). 1980. 157.70 (*3-11-008241-1*) De Gruyter.

— Nietzsche-Studien, Vol. 10-11. (Internationales Jahrbuch fuer die Nietzsche-Forschung Ser.). (GER.). 1982. 215.40 (*3-11-008638-7*) De Gruyter.

— Nietzsche-Studien, Vol. 12. (Internationales Jahrbuch fuer die Nietzsche-Forschung Ser.). (GER.). 1982. 176.95 (*3-11-009507-6*) De Gruyter.

— Nietzsche-Studien, Vol. 13. (Internationales Jahrbuch fuer die Nietzsche-Forschung Ser.). (GER.). 1984. 234.65 (*3-11-009648-X*) De Gruyter.

— Nietzsche-Studien, Vol. 14. (Internationales Jahrbuch fuer die Nietzsche-Forschung Ser.). (GER.). 1985. 153.85 (*3-11-010207-2*) De Gruyter.

— Nietzsche-Studien, Vol. 15. (Internationales Jahrbuch fuer die Nietzsche-Forschung Ser.). (GER.). 1986. 176.95 (*3-11-010540-3*) De Gruyter.

— Nietzsche-Studien, Vol.5. (Internationales Jahrbuch fuer die Nietzsche-Forschung Ser.). (GER.). (C). 1976. 134.65 (*3-11-006656-4*) De Gruyter.

— Nietzsche-Studien: Internationales Jahrbuch fuer die Nietzsche - Forschung, Vol. 2. Montinari, Mazzino et al, eds. (Internationales Jahrbuch fuer die Nietzsche-Forschung Ser.). vi, 368p. (C). 1973. 112.35 (*3-11-004332-7*) De Gruyter.

— Nietzsche-Studien: Internationales Jahrbuch fuer die Nietzsche-Forschung, Vol. 1. Montinari, Mazzino et al, eds. 470p. (C). 1972. 142.35 (*3-11-002224-9*) De Gruyter.

— Nietzsche-Studien: Internationales Jahrbuch fuer die Nietzsche-Forschung, Vol. 3. Montinari, Mazzino et al, eds. (GER.). (C). 1974. 73.10 (*3-11-004726-8*) De Gruyter.

— Nietzsche Werke: Kritische Gesamtausgabe: I.Abteilung, Bd. 1: Nachgelassene Aufzeichnungen Anfang 1852 - Sommer 1858. Figl, Johann, ed. (GER.). xiv, 397p. (C). 1995. lib. bdg. 144.60 (*3-11-013007-6*) De Gruyter.

— Nietzsche Werke: Kritische Gesamtausgabe Sect. 8, Vol. 3: Nachgelassene Fragmente Anfang 1888-Anfang Januar 1889. Colli, Giorgio & Montinari, Mazzino, eds. LC 68-84293. 484p. (C). 1972. 104.65 (*3-11-004192-8*) De Gruyter.

— Nietzsche Werke Sect. 5, Vol. 2: Kritische Gesamtausgabe: Idyllen aus Messina. Die Froehliche Wissenschaft. Nachgelassene Fragmente Fruehjahr 1881 bis Sommer 1882. (GER.). viii, 587p. (C). 1973. 127.70 (*3-11-004476-5*) De Gruyter.

— Nietzsche Werke Sect. 7, Vol. 2: Kritische Gesamtausgabe: Nachgelassene Fragmente Fruehjahr bis Herbst 1884. iv, 324p. (C). 1973. 69.25 (*3-11-004797-7*) De Gruyter.

— Nietzsche Werke Sect. 7, Vol. 3: Kritische Gesamtausgabe: Nachgelassene Fragmente Herbst 1884 bis Herbst 1885. iv, 476p. (C). 1974. 101.55 (*3-11-004983-X*) De Gruyter.

— Nietzsche Werke, Kritische Gesamtausgabe Sect. 3, Vol. 1: Die Geburt der Tragoedie. Unzeitgemaesse Betrachtungen I-III (1872-1874) Colli, Giorgio & Montinari, Mazzino, eds. (GER.). iv, 427p. (C). 1972. 92.35 (*3-11-004294-0*) De Gruyter.

— Nietzsche Werke, Kritische Gesamtausgabe Sect. 3, Vol. 2: Sect. 3, Vol. 2: Nachgelassene Schriften 1870-1873. Colli, Giorgio & Montinari, Mazzino, eds. (GER.). 400p. (C). 1973. 86.15 (*3-11-004312-2*) De Gruyter.

— Nietzsche Werke, Kritische Gesamtausgabe Sect. 5, Vol. 1: Morgenroethe, Nachgelassene Fragmente Anfang 1880 bis Fruehjahr 1881. (GER.). (C). 1971. 150.80 (*3-11-001828-4*) De Gruyter.

— Nietzsche Werke, Kritische Gesamtausgabe Sect. 8, Vol. 1: Nachgelassene Fragmente, Herbst 1885 bis Herbst 1887. Colli, Giorgio & Montinari, Mazzino, eds. (GER.). viii, 360p. (C). 1974. 73.85 (*3-11-004741-1*) De Gruyter.

Nietzsche, Friedrich Wilhelm. Nietzsches Werke: Historisch - Kritische Ausgabe (Macintosh) Brown, Malcolm, ed. (Past Masters Ser.). (C). write for info. incl. cd-rom (*1-57085-079-8*) Intelex.

Nietzsche, Friedrich Wilhelm. On the Advantage & Disadvantage of History for Life. Preuss, Peter, tr. from GER. & intro. by. LC 80-16686. (HPC Classics Ser.). 70p. (C). 1980. pap. text 5.95 (*0-915144-94-8*); lib. bdg. 19.95 (*0-915144-95-6*) Hackett Pub.

— On the Future of Our Educational Institutions & Homer & Classical Philology. 1974. lib. bdg. 300.00 (*0-87968-200-0*) Gordon Pr.

— On the Genealogy of Morality. Clark, Maudemarie & Swenson, Alan, trs. LC 98-37868. (HPC Classics Ser.). (GER.). 192p. (C). 1998. pap. text 9.95 (*0-87220-283-6*) Hackett Pub.

— On the Genealogy of Morality. Clark, Maudmarie & Swenson, Alan, trs. LC 98-37868. (HPC Classics Ser.). (GER.). 192p. (C). 1998. lib. bdg. 34.95 (*0-87220-284-4*) Hackett Pub.

— On the Genealogy of Morality & Other Writings. Ansell-Pearson, Keith & Diethe, Carol, eds. LC 93-41334. (Cambridge Texts in the History of Political Thought Ser.). 243p. (C). 1994. text 44.95 (*0-521-40459-2*); pap. text 12.95 (*0-521-40610-2*) Cambridge U Pr.

— On the Genealogy of Morals. Kaufman, Walter, tr. 1967. 5.95 (*0-394-70401-0*) Vin Bks.

— On the Genealogy of Morals. Kaufmann, Walter, tr. 1989. pap. 12.00 (*0-679-72462-1*) Vin Bks.

— On the Genealogy of Morals: A Polemic, by Way of Clarification & Supplement to My Last Book Beyond Good & Evil. Smith, Douglas, tr. & intro. by. (Oxford World's Classics Ser.). 208p. 1999. pap. 10.95 (*0-19-283617-X*) OUP.

— Philosophical Writings. Grimm, Reinhold & Molina y Vedia, Caroline, eds. LC 81-70120. (German Library). 324p. 1995. 39.50 (*0-8264-0278-X*) Continuum.

— Philosophical Writings. Grimm, Reinhold, ed. LC 81-70120. (German Library). 324p. 1995. pap. 19.95 (*0-8264-0279-8*) Continuum.

— Philosophy & Truth: Selections from Nietzsche's Notebooks of the Early 1870s. Breazeale, Daniel, ed. & tr. by. LC 76-53746. (Humanities Paperback Library). 232p. (C). 1990. pap. 15.95 (*0-391-03671-8*) Humanities.

Nietzsche, Friedrich Wilhelm. Philosophy & Truth: Selections from Nietzsches Notebooks of the Early 1870s. (Humanities Paperback Library). 1990. pap. 16.95 (*1-57392-532-2*) Prometheus Bks.

Nietzsche, Friedrich Wilhelm. Philosophy in the Tragic Age of the Greeks. 117p. 1996. pap. 9.95 (*0-89526-710-1*, Gateway Editions) Regnery Pub.

— The Philosophy of Nietzsche. 1984. pap. 14.95 (*0-452-00699-6*, Mer) NAL.

— The Portable Nietzsche. Kaufmann, Walter, ed. (Portable Library: No. 62). 704p. 1977. pap. 22.99 (*0-14-015062-5*, Penguin Bks) Viking Penguin.

— Saemtliche Briefe: Kritische Studienausgabe in 8 Baenden. Colli, Giorgio & Montinari, Mazzino, eds. 3630p. 1986. pap. 121.55 (*3-11-010963-8*) De Gruyter.

— Saemtliche Werke: Kritische Studierausgabe, 15 vols. (GER.). 8800p. 1980. 199.95 (*3-11-008117-2*) De Gruyter.

— Selected Letters. Levy, Oscar, ed. Ludovici, A. N., tr. from GER. 364p. 1985. reprint ed. pap. 16.95 (*0-948166-01-0*, Pub. by Soho Bk Co) Dufour.

— Selected Letters of Friedrich Nietzsche. Middleton, Christopher, ed. LC 69-20453. 1969. lib. bdg. 15.00 (*0-226-58410-0*) U Ch Pr.

— Selected Letters of Friedrich Nietzsche. LC 96-46577. 388p. 1996. reprint ed. pap. text 18.95 (*0-87220-358-1*); reprint ed. lib. bdg. 39.95 (*0-87220-359-X*) Hackett Pub.

— Der Streit um "Nietzsches Geburt der Tragodie" (Olms Paperbacks Ser.: Bd. 40). 136p. 1989. pap. write for info. (*3-487-02599-X*) G Olms Pubs.

— Thoughts Out of Season, 2 vols. Ludovici, Anthony M., tr. 1974. lib. bdg. 600.00 (*0-87968-202-7*) Gordon Pr.

— Thus Spake Zarathustra. LC 99-13580. 288p. 1999. pap. text 2.00 (*0-486-40663-6*) Dover.

— Thus Spake Zarathustra. Common, Thomas, tr. 1974. lib. bdg. 300.00 (*0-87968-206-X*) Gordon Pr.

— Thus Spake Zarathustra. LC 93-30268. (Great Books in Philosophy). 341p. 1993. pap. 9.95 (*0-87975-861-9*) Prometheus Bks.

— Thus Spake Zarathustra. Kaufmann, Walter, tr. 352p. 1978. pap. 12.95 (*0-14-004748-4*, Penguin Classics) Viking Penguin.

Nietzsche, Friedrich Wilhelm. Thus Spake Zarathustra. (Classics of World Literature Ser.). pap. 5.95 (*1-85326-776-7*, 7767WW, Pub. by Wrdsworth Edits) NTC Contemp Pub Co.

Nietzsche, Friedrich Wilhelm. Thus Spoke Zarathustra. Kauffmann, Walter, tr. 352p. 1961. pap. 12.95 (*0-14-044118-2*, Penguin Classics) Viking Penguin.

— Thus Spoke Zarathustra. Kaufmann, Walter, tr. from GER. & pref. by. LC 95-15383.Tr. of Also Sprach Zarathustra. 364p. 1995. 15.95 (*0-679-60175-9*) Modern Lib NY.

— Twilight of the Idols. Polt, Richard, tr. from GER. LC 96-40331. (Classics Ser.). 128p. 1997. pap. text 7.95 (*0-87220-354-9*); lib. bdg. 29.95 (*0-87220-355-7*) Hackett Pub.

— Twilight of the Idols: Or How to Philosophize with a Hammer. Large, Duncan, tr. & intro. by. LC 97-28215. (Oxford World's Classics Ser.). 166p. 1998. pap. 9.95 (*0-19-283138-0*) OUP.

— The Twilight of the Idols & the Anti-Christ. Hollingdale, R. J., tr. & intro. by. (Classics Ser.). 208p. (Orig.). 1990. pap. 10.95 (*0-14-044514-5*, Penguin Classics) Viking Penguin.

— Unfashionable Observations. Gray, Richard T., tr. from GER. LC 94-6177. (Complete Works of Friedrich Nietzsche: Vol. 2).Tr. of Unzeitgem Asse Betrachtungen. 430p. 1995. 45.00 (*0-8047-2382-6*) Stanford U Pr.

— Unmodern Observations. Arrowsmith, William, ed. 424p. (C). 1990. 52.00 (*0-300-04311-2*) Yale U Pr.

***Nietzsche, Friedrich Wilhelm.** Unpublished Writings from the Period of Unfashionable Observations. Gray, Richard T., tr. from GER. & afterword by by. LC 98-37649. (Complete Works of Friedrich Nietzsche). 515p. 1999. 49.50 (*0-8047-2884-4*) Stanford U Pr.

Nietzsche, Friedrich Wilhelm. The Vision of Nietzsche. Novak, Philip, ed. (Spirit of Philosophy Ser.). 176p. 1996. pap. 10.95 (*1-85230-896-6*, Pub. by Element MA) Penguin Putnam.

— The Will to Power. 1976. 72.95 (*0-8488-1112-7*) Amereon Ltd.

— The Will to Power. Kaufmann, Walter, tr. 1969. pap. 15.00 (*0-394-70437-1*) Vin Bks.

— The Will to Power, 2 vols., Set. Ludovici, Anthony M., tr. 1974. lib. bdg. 600.00 (*0-87968-209-4*) Gordon Pr.

Nietzsche, Friedrich Wilhelm, ed. Nietzsche Werke. Incl. Sect 4, Vol. 1. Richard Wagner in Bayreuth: Unzeitgemaesse Betrachtungen, Nummer 4; Nachgelassene Fragmente, Anfang 1875 bis Fruehjahr, 1876. iv, 366p. 1967. 68.00 (*3-11-005170-2*); Sect. 4, Vol. 2. Menschliches, Allzumenschliches: Band 1; Nachgelassene Fragmente, 1876 bis Winter, 1877-78. Colli, Giorgio & Montinari, Mazzino, eds. (GER.). iv, 586p. 1967. 108.00 (*3-11-005171-0*); Sect 4, Vol. 3. Menschliches, Allzumenschliches: Band 2; Nachgelassene Fragmente, Fruehling, 1878 Bis November, 1879. Colli, Giorgio & Montinari, Mazzino, eds. (GER.). iv, 482p. 1967. 89.35 (*3-11-005172-9*); Sect 4, Vol. 4. Nachbericht Zur Vierten Abteilung: Richard Wagner in Bayreuth; Menschliches, Allzumenschliches, Baende 1 & 2, Nachgelassene Fragmente, 1875-79. Colli, Giorgio & Montinari, Mazzino, eds. (GER., Illus.). viii, 615p. 1969. 118.75 (*3-11-002553-1*); Sect. 6, Vol 1. Also Sprach Zarathustra: Ein Buch fuer Alle und Keinen, 1883-85. Colli, Giorgio & Montinari, Mazzino, eds. (GER.). iv, 410p. 1968. 77.35 (*3-11-005174-5*); Sect. 6, Vol. 2. Jenseits von Gut und Boese - Zur Genealogie der Moral, 1886-1887. Colli, Giorgio & Montinari, Mazzino, eds. (GER.). iv, 436p. 1968. 80.00 (*3-11-005175-3*); Sect. 6, Vol. 3. Fall Wagner; Goetzen-Daemmerung; Nachgelassene Schriften, August, 1888 Bis Anfang Januar, 1889; der Antichrist; Ecce Homo; Dionysius-Dithyramben; Nietzsche Contra Wagner. Colli, Giorgio & Montinari, Mazzino, eds. (GER.). iv, 449p. 1969. 84.00 (*3-11-002554-X*); Sect. 8, Vol. 2. Nachgelassene Fragmente: Herbst, 1887 Bis Maerz, 1888. Colli, Giorgio & Montinari, Mazzino, eds. (GER.). xii, 477p. 1970. 82.70 (*3-11-006393-X*); (GER.). (C). write for info. (*0-318-51631-4*) De Gruyter.

Nietzsche, Friedrich Wilhelm & Hollingdale, R. J. Dithyrambs of Dionysus. 88p. 1984. 21.95 (*0-85646-119-9*, Pub. by Anvil Press) Dufour.

***Nieukirk, Donald L.** Pekin & Tremont, Illinois: In Vintage Postcards. (Postcard History Ser.). (Illus.). 128p. 2000. pap. 18.99 (*0-7385-0705-9*) Arcadia Publng.

Nieuweboer, Adele, jt. auth. see Berkvens-Stevelinck, Christiane.

***Nieuwejaar, Jeanne.** The Gift of Faith: Tending the Spiritual Lives of Children. LC 99-32378. 1999. write for info. (*1-55896-385-5*, Skinner Hse Bks) Unitarian Univ.

Nieuwenhuijze, C. A. Van, see Van Nieuwenhuijze, C. A.

Nieuwenhuijzen, H., jt. ed. see De Jager, C.

Nieuwenhuis. Teamwork in Neurology. 160p. 1993. pap. 46.95 (*1-56593-121-1*, 0433) Singular Publishing.

***Nieuwenhuis, G. J., et al, eds.** Operational Remote Sensing for Sustainable Development: Proceedings of the 18th EARSeL Symposium, Enschede, Netherlands, 11-14 May 1998. (Illus.). 540p. (C). 1999. 115.00 (*90-5809-029-9*, Pub. by A A Balkema) Ashgate Pub Co.

Nieuwenhuis, Paul & Wells, Peter. The Death of Motoring? Car Making & Automobility in the 21st Century. LC 97-9815. 266p. 1998. 100.00 (*0-471-97084-0*) Wiley.

Nieuwenhuis, Tom. Politics & Society in Early Modern Iraq. 1982. lib. bdg. 106.00 (*90-247-2576-3*) Kluwer Academic.

Nieuwenhuizen, Agnes, jt. auth. see Duder, Tessa.

Nieuwenhuizen, C., jt. auth. see Zeelie, J.

Nieuwenhuizen, Cecile. Management of a Small Business. 184p. 1996. pap. 28.00 (*0-7021-3785-5*, Pub. by Juta & Co) Gaunt.

Nieuwenhuizen, John, tr. see Quintana, Anton.

Nieuwenhuizen, O. Van, see Van Nieuwenhuizen, O.

Nieuwenhuizen, Peter Van, see Van Nieuwenhuizen, Peter, ed.

Nieuwenhuys, Olga. Children's Lifeworlds: Gender, Welfare & Labour in the Developing World. LC 93-17607. (Illus.). 304p. (C). 1994. pap. 25.99 (*0-415-09751-7*) Routledge.

— Children's Lifeworlds: Gender, Welfare & Labour in the Developing World. LC 93-17607. (Illus.). 304p. (C). (gr. 13). 1994. 90.00 (*0-415-09750-9*) Routledge.

Nieuwenhuys, R. Chemoarchitecture of the Brain. (Illus.). 256p. 1985. 115.00 (*0-387-15349-7*) Spr-Verlag.

Nieuwenhuys, R., et al. The Central Nervous System of Vertebrates, 3 vols. LC 97-19923. 2200p. 1997. write for info. (*3-540-56013-0*) Spr-Verlag.

— The Human Central Nervous System. 3rd ed. (Illus.). 440p. 1996. 74.95 (*0-387-13441-7*) Spr-Verlag.

Nieuwenhuys, Rob. Mirror of the Indies: A History of Dutch Colonial Literature. Beekman, E. M., ed. Van Rosevelt, Frans, tr. from DUT. LC 82-4755. (Library of the Indies).Tr. of Oost-indische Spiegel. 368p. 1982. text 40.00 (*0-87023-368-8*) U of Mass Pr.

Nieuwenhuys, Robert. Mirror of the Indies: A History of Dutch Colonial Literature.Tr. of Oost-indische Spiegel. 202p. 1999. pap. 22.95 (*962-593-509-6*) Tuttle Pubng.

Nieuwenhuys, Rudolf. Chemoarchitecture of the Brain. 246p. 1985. pap. 110.00 (*3-540-15349-7*) Spr-Verlag.

Nieuwenhuyse, H., jt. ed. see Thijssen, J. H. H.

Nieuwkoop, P. D. & Faber, J., eds. Normal Table of Xenopus Laevis (Daudin) A Systematical & Chronological Survey of the Development from the Fertilized Egg till the End of Metamorphosis. LC 94-11518. (Illus.). 252p. 1994. pap. text 61.00 (*0-8153-1896-0*) Garland.

Nieuwland, D. A., jt. ed. see Buchanan, P. G.

Nieuwolt, Simon. Tropical Climatology: An Introduction to the Climates of the Low Latitudes. LC 76-13454. 217p. reprint ed. pap. 67.30 (*0-608-15786-4*, 203102400073) Bks Demand.

Nieuwolt, Simon & Mcgregor, Glenn R. Tropical Climatology: An Introduction to the Climate of the Low Latitudes. 2nd ed. LC 97-41190. 352p. 1998. pap. 49.95 (*0-471-96611-8*) Wiley.

Nieuwsma, Milton J. Kinderlager: An Oral History of Young Holocaust Survivors. LC 97-34959. (Illus.). 192p. (YA). (gr. 5 up). 1998. 18.95 (*0-8234-1358-6*) Holiday.

Nieuwsma, Virginia H., ed. Our Heart's True Home: Modern Women Find Fulfillment in the Ancient Christian Faith. LC 96-26042. (Orig.). 1996. pap. 12.95 (*1-888212-02-0*) Conciliar Pr.

Nieuwstadt, F. T., ed. Advances in Turbulence. LC 93-7604. (Fluid Mechanics & Its Applications Ser.: Vol. 18). 1993. text 285.50 (*0-7923-2282-7*) Kluwer Academic.

— Flow Visualization & Image Analysis. LC 92-32223. (Fluid Mechanics & Its Applications Ser.: Vol. 14). 1993. text 199.00 (*0-7923-1994-X*) Kluwer Academic.

Nieuwstadt, F. T. & Steketee, J. A., eds. Selected Papers of J. M. Burgers. LC 94-39288. 650p. 1994. text 401.00 (*0-7923-3265-2*) Kluwer Academic.

Nieuwstadt, F. T. & Van Dop, Han, eds. Atmospheric Turbulence & Air Pollution Modelling. rev. ed. 1984. lib. bdg. 49.00 (*0-318-01663-X*) Kluwer Academic.

Nieuwstadt, F. T., jt. ed. see Dijksman, J. F.

N

An Asterisk (*) at the beginning of an entry indicates that the title is appearing for the first time.

N

An Asterisk (*) at the beginning of an entry indicates that the title is appearing for the first time.

Nightingale, Kate, et al. Learning to Care in the Operating Department. 2nd ed. 78p. 1995. pap. 18.95 (*0-340-59492-6*, Pub. by E A) Routldge.
— Learning to Care in the Operating Department. 2nd ed. 112p. 1994. pap. text 18.95 (*1-56593-394-X*, 0816) Singular Publishing.
***Nightingale, Kath.** Taxation: Theory & Practice. 2nd ed. LC 99-42467. 1999. pap. write for info. (*0-273-63832-7*, Finc Times) F T P-H.
Nightingale, Kimberly, et al. A Book about Feeling Angry Vol. 2: Seemor's Flight to Freedom. large type ed. LC 96-92472. (Illus.). 36p. (J). (ps-3). 1998. pap. 14.95 (*0-9635127-1-4*) Emotional Mgmt Educ.
Nightingale, Lois V. My Parents Still Love Me, Even Though They're Getting Divorced: An Interactive Tale for Children. LC 96-92679. (Illus.). 128p. (J). (gr. k-6). 1996. pap. 14.95 (*1-889755-00-1*) Nightngale Rose.
— Overcoming Postpartum Depression: A Doctor's Own Story. 128p. 1998. pap. 10.95 (*1-889755-26-5*) Nightngale Rose.
Nightingale, M. P. & Umrigar, Cyrus J., eds. Quantum Monte Carlo Methods in Physics & Chemistry. LC 98-51578. (NATO ASI Series C). 14p. 1999. write for info. (*0-7923-5551-2*) Kluwer Academic.
Nightingale, Michael. Acupuncture. (Alternative Health Ser.). (Illus.). 128p. (Orig.). 1994. pap. 12.95 (*0-8048-3004-5*) Tuttle Pubng.
— Acupuncture: An Introductory Guide to the Technique & Its Benefits. (Illus.). 122p. 1997. pap. 13.95 (*0-09-181518-5*) Trafalgar.
Nightingale, Pamela. A Medieval Mercantile Community: The Grocers' Company & the Politics & Trade of London. LC 95-12262. 1996. 70.00 (*0-300-06325-3*) Yale U Pr.
— A Medieval Mercantile Community: The Grocers' Company & the Politics & Trade of London, 1000-1485. LC 95-12262. (Illus.). 650p. 1995. reprint ed. pap. 200.00 (*0-608-07840-9*, 205401600010) Bks Demand.
Nightingale, Paul, jt. ed. see Martin, Ben R.
Nightingale, Peggy. Assessing Learning in Universities. LC 98-103943. 320p. 1996. pap. 39.95 (*0-86840-408-X*, Pub. by New South Wales Univ Pr) Intl Spec Bk.
— Journey Through Darkness: The Writing of V. S. Naipaul. LC 86-13231. 255p. (Orig.). 1987. pap. text 29.95 (*0-7022-2016-7*, Pub. by Univ Queensland Pr) Intl Spec Bk.
Nightingale, Peggy, ed. A Sense of Place in the New Literatures in English. 252p. 1986. text 29.95 (*0-7022-1849-9*, Pub. by Univ Queensland Pr) Intl Spec Bk.
Nightingale, Peggy & O'Neil, Mike S., eds. Achieving Quality Learning in Higher Education. LC 94-224138. 220p. 1994. pap. 29.95 (*0-7494-1325-5*, Kogan Pg Educ) Stylus Pub VA.
Nightingale, Rita. Freed for Ever. 191p. 1987. pap. 4.95 (*0-310-55182-X*, 19018P) Zondervan.
— Freed for Life. 255p. 1987. pap. 4.95 (*0-310-55322-9*, 19032P) Zondervan.
***Nightingale, Sandra.** Dear Fairies: A Book of Letters. (Illus.). 16p. (J). (ps-3). 1999. per. 14.95 (*0-689-83121-8*) Litle Simon.
Nightingale, Sandy. Cider Apples. LC 95-49311. (Illus.). 32p. (J). (ps-3). 1996. 15.00 (*0-15-201244-3*) Harcourt.
— A Giraffe on the Moon. LC 91-451. (Illus.). 32p. (J). (ps-1). 1992. 13.95 (*0-15-230950-0*, Harcourt Child Bks) Harcourt.
— Giraffe on the Moon. LC 91-451. (Illus.). 32p. 1996. pap. 6.00 (*0-15-201348-2*) Harcourt.
— I'm a Little Monster. LC 94-18345. (Illus.). 24p. (J). (ps-3). 1995. 15.00 (*0-15-200309-6*) Harcourt.
— The Witch's Spell. (Illus.). 32p. (J). (ps-2). 1998. 19.95 (*0-86264-739-8*, Pub. by Andersen Pr) Trafalgar.
Nightingale Staff. Lost Coast. LC 97-11288. 1997. pap. 11.95 (*0-312-15572-7*) St Martin.
Nightingale, Steven. The Thirteenth Daughter of the Moon. LC 97-15593. 256p. 1997. text 23.95 (*0-312-16911-6*) St Martin.
— Thirteenth Daughter of the Moon. 256p. 1998. pap. 12.95 (*0-312-19528-1*) St Martin.

Nightingale, Suzan & I. C. E. Staff. Electric Bread. 2nd rev. ed. (Illus.). 160p. 1997. pap. 14.95 (*0-9629831-8-7*) Innov Cook Enter.
Innovative Cooking Enterprises set the standard of excellence for bread machine recipe books. Updated with each printing: ELECTRIC BREAD continually embraces the dramatic changes in bread machine technology, offering proven recipes for all sizes of bread machines -- including the new larger capacity models on the market. Filled with sumptuous photography, it also provides the latest guidance on ingredients, terms & troubleshooting. The "secret ingredient" is Innovative Cooking Enterprises' test kitchen, with more than 300 bread machines & over 35,000 loaves of experience. And every ELECTRIC BREAD purchaser gets the added benefit of toll-free access to personalized support & this ever-current information. The hardback ELECTRIC BREAD SECOND EDITION features full page color photographs, water-resistent pages, lay-open design & a gourmet gift box. The paperback version delivers the same text & color photos in a smaller format. Both have an easy, understandable narrative that makes ELECTRIC BREAD as user friendly as the push-button bread machines themselves. And best of all, ELECTRIC BREAD recipes bake a quality loaf in every single bread machine in America today! To order contact: Innovative Cooking Enterprises, P.O. Box 240888, Anchorage, AK 99524-0888; FAX 907-561-1835; or phone 1-800-541-2733. ***Publisher Paid Annotation.***

— Electric Bread: The Best in Bread Maching Making. 2nd rev. ed. (Illus.). 160p. 1997. 29.95 (*0-9629831-7-9*) Innov Cook Enter.
Nightingale, Suzan & I.C.E. Inc. Staff. More Electric Bread. (Illus.). 120p. 1995. 29.95 (*0-9629831-6-0*) Innov Cook Enter.
Nightingale, Tom & Hill, Mike. Birds of Bahrain. 288p. (C). 1995. 135.00 (*0-907151-79-5*, Pub. by IMMEL Pubng) St Mut.
Nightingale, Virginia. Studying Audiences: Shock of the Real. LC 97-137001. 184p. (C). 1996. pap. 22.99 (*0-415-14398-5*) Routledge.
— Studying Audiences: Shock of the Real. LC 97-137001. 184p. (C). (gr. 13). 1996. 75.00 (*0-415-02447-1*) Routledge.
Nightmare, M. Macha, et al. The Pagan Book of Living & Dying: Practical Rituals, Prayers, Blessings & Meditations on Crossing Over. LC 97-26317. (Illus.). 384p. 1997. pap. 18.00 (*0-06-251516-0*, Pub. by Harper SF) HarpC.
Nigl, Alfred J. The Development of Children's Understanding of Space Relations Among Objects: The Coordination of Perspectives Task of Jean Piaget. (European University Studies: Psychology: Ser. 6, Vol. 62). 74p. 1981. 9.00 (*3-261-04872-7*) P Lang Pubng.
Nigmatulin, R. I. Dynamics of Multiphase Media: Revised & Augmented Edition, 2 vols., Set. rev. ed. Friedly, John C., ed. Piterman, Mark A., tr. 1990. 280.00 (*1-56032-207-1*) Hemisp Pub.
— Dynamics of Multiphase Media: Revised & Augmented Edition, Vol. 1. rev. ed. Friedly, John C., ed. Piterman, Mark A., tr. 536p. 1990. 185.00 (*0-89116-316-6*) Hemisp Pub.
— Dynamics of Multiphase Media: Revised & Augmented Edition, Vol. 2. rev. ed. Friedly, John C., ed. Piterman, Mark A., tr. 384p. 1990. 145.00 (*0-89116-328-X*) Hemisp Pub.
Nigon, Donna. Clinical Laboratory Management Handbook. LC 99-27977. (Illus.). 450p. 1999. pap. text 49.00 (*0-07-047182-7*) McGraw-Hill HPD.
Nigon, Donna L. Within Your Reach: A Manual for Developing a Laboratory Outreach Program. LC 97-182347. (Illus.). iv, 99p. 1997. pap. 59.00 (*0-9625414-7-8*) Clinical Lab Mgmnt Assn.
***Nigosian, S. A.** World Religions: A Historical Approach. 3rd ed. 1999. text 49.95 (*0-312-22757-4*) St Martin.
Nigosian, Solomon A. Islam: The Way of Submission. 1987. pap. 12.95 (*0-85030-490-3*, Pub. by Aqn Pr) HarpC.
— World Faiths. 2nd ed. 560p. (Orig.). 1993. pap. text 40.95 (*0-312-08414-5*); pap. text, teacher ed. 5.00 (*0-312-09598-8*) St Martin.
— World Faiths. 2nd ed. 234p. (Orig.). 1994. text 39.95 (*0-312-10274-7*) St Martin.
— World Faiths. 3rd ed. 544p. (Orig.). 1999. pap. text 40.95 (*0-312-15268-X*) St Martin.
— The Zoroastrian Faith: Tradition & Modern Research. 168p. 1993. 60.00 (*0-7735-1133-4*, Pub. by McG-Queens Univ Pr); pap. 19.95 (*0-7735-1144-X*, Pub. by McG-Queens Univ Pr) CUP Services.
Nigrin, Albert. Neural Networks for Pattern Recognition. LC 93-10027. (Illus.). 435p. 1993. 55.00 (*0-262-14054-3*, Bradford Bks) MIT Pr.
Nigrini, Mark, jt. auth. see Robertson, Jack C.
Nigro, A., jt. auth. see D'Agostino, Guido.
***Nigro, Anthony.** Regents High School Mathematics: A Answer Key. 50p. 2000. pap. 4.25 (*0-937820-76-8*) WestSea Pub.
***Nigro, August J.** A Chain of Events: The Death of Friendly Fire of Lt. Laura Piper - A Mother's Account of Government Cover-Up. 2000. 22.95 (*1-57488-231-7*) Brasseys.
Nigro, August J. The Diagonal Line. LC 83-50945. 192p. 1984. 32.50 (*0-941664-02-3*) Susquehanna U Pr.
***Nigro, August J.** The Net of Nemesis: Studies in Tragic Bond-Age. LC 99-54287. 192p. 2000. 35.00 (*1-57591-036-5*) Susquehanna U Pr.
— Wolfsangel: A German City on Trial. 2000. 22.95 (*1-57488-245-7*) Brasseys.
Nigro, Debbie. The Working Mom on the Run Manual: A.K.A. What the Heck Happened to My Life? 220p. 1995. pap. 9.95 (*1-57101-011-4*) MasterMedia Pub.
Nigro, Don. Cincinnati & Other Plays: Monologues for the Theatre. LC 90-103975. 111p. 1989. write for info. (*0-573-62105-5*) S French Trade.
— The Dark Sonnets of the Lady: A Play in Two Acts. LC 92-178198. 149p. 1992. write for info. (*0-573-69312-9*) S French Trade.
— The Great Gromboolian Plain & Other Plays LC 99-195821. 147 p. 1998. write for info. (*0-573-60167-4*) S French Trade.
— Ravenscroft: A Play. LC 93-140578. 100p. 1991. write for info. (*0-573-69274-2*) S French Trade.
Nigro, Don. Robin Hood: A Play. LC 93-208108. 140p. 1987. write for info. (*0-573-69051-0*) S French Trade.
Nigro, Felix A. & Nigro, Lloyd G. The New Public Personnel Administration. 4th ed. LC 92-61962. 328p. (C). 1993. boxed set 50.00 (*0-87581-374-7*, NPPA4) F E Peacock Pubs.
Nigro, Kirsten F. Palabras Mas Que Comunes: Ensayos Sobre el Teatro de Jose Triana. LC 93-85373. (SPA.). 112p. 1994. pap. 32.00 (*0-89295-073-0*) Society Sp & Sp-Am.
Nigro, Kirsten F. & Cypress, Sandra M., eds. Studies in Honor of Frank Dauster. (Homenajes Ser.: Vol. 9). 220p. 1995. 22.50 (*0-936388-66-8*) Juan de la Cuesta.
Nigro, Linea, jt. ed. see Dietz, Kevin C.
Nigro, Linea, ed. see Millhollon, Mary.
***Nigro, Linnea, ed.** Basic Data for MMTA Certification. (Illus.). 250p. (YA). 2000. pap. write for info. (*0-7423-0446-9*) ComputerPREP.
Nigro, Linnea, ed. see Davenhauer, Frank.
Nigro, Lloyd G., ed. Decision Making in the Public Sector. (Public Administration & Public Policy Ser.: Vol. 25). (Illus.). 336p. 1984. text 75.00 (*0-8247-7155-9*) Dekker.
Nigro, Lloyd G., jt. auth. see Nigro, Felix A.
***Nigro, Louis John, Jr.** The New Diplomacy in Italy: American Propaganda & U. S.-Italian Relations, 1917-1919. LC 97-32371. (Studies in Modern European History: Vol. 28). XIV, 153p. (C). 1999. text 44.00 (*0-8204-3942-8*) P Lang Pubng.
Nigro, Natalie & Nigro, Shirley. Companion Guide to Healthy Cooking Vol. 1: A Practical Introduction to Natural Ingredients. LC 96-84097. (Illus.). 256p. (Orig.). 1996. pap. 17.95 (*0-9641731-1-5*) Featherstne Inc.
Nigro, Nicholas J. Confessions of a Lapsed Liberal: I've Seen the Light, No. I. Mannion, James, ed. LC 96-86184. (Illus.). 125p. (Orig.). 1997. pap. 11.00 (*1-887775-41-2*) Cryptic NY.
Nigro, Nicholas J. & Mannion, James. America Off-Line: Reagan to O. J. LC 95-71613. 160p. (Orig.). 1996. pap. 12.95 (*1-887775-01-3*) Cryptic NY.
Nigro, Nicholas J., jt. auth. see Mannion, James.
Nigro, Salvatore S. Pontormo: Paintings. LC 93-31283. (Illus.). 160p. 1994. 75.00 (*0-8109-3727-1*) Abrams.
Nigro, Samuel A. Happy Ending. rev. ed. (Illus.). 574p. 1997. pap. 20.00 (*1-887567-00-3*) CBCCU Amer.
Nigro, Shirley, jt. auth. see Nigro, Natalie.
Nigrosh, Leon I. Claywork: Form & Idea in Ceramics Design. 3rd ed. LC 93-74643. (Illus.). 296p. (YA). (gr. 9-12). 1995. text 37.95 (*0-87192-285-1*) Davis Mass.
— Low Fire: Other Ways to Work in Clay. LC 79-56377. (Illus.). 112p. (YA). (gr. 7-12). 1980. 20.75 (*0-87192-120-0*) Davis Mass.
— Sculpting Clay. (Illus.). 192p. (YA). (gr. 9-12). 1991. 25.95 (*0-87192-236-3*) Davis Mass.
Niguidula, David. Introduction to Programming: A Graphical Approach. (Illus.). 750p. 1994. write for info. (*0-614-32116-6*) Addison-Wesley.
NIH Staff & National Heart, Lung & Blood Institute Staff. The Sixth Report of the Joint National Committee on Prevention, Detection, Evaluation, & Treatment of High Blood Pressure. 6th ed. 78p. (C). 1997. pap. 8.95 (*1-883205-42-5*) Intl Med Pub.
Nihan, James F. The Marxist Empire: Communist Dream - World Nightmare. 322p. 1990. pap. 12.80 (*0-89412-171-5*) Aegean Park Pr.
***Nihan, James F.** World Slavery: A Documented History. 146p. 1999. pap. 28.80 (*0-89412-276-2*, M-28) Aegean Park Pr.
Nihart, Mary Ann, jt. auth. see Boyd, Mary Ann.
Nihelena, Ormazebel M. Diccionaire Basque Pour Tous: Francais-Basque. (BAQ & FRE.). 660p. 1975. pap. 6.95 (*0-7859-6033-3*, 8440082304) Fr & Eur.
Nihin Vogue Staff. Fine Crochet Lace. 2nd ed. (Illus.). 90p. 1982. pap. 17.00 (*0-87040-503-9*) Japan Pubns USA.
Nihon Geijutsu Shuppan Editors. Free Time, Vol. 3. (Illus.). 204p. 1997. pap. 29.95 (*4-89011-355-X*, Pub. by Nihon Geijutsu) Bks Nippan.
Nihon Konkurito Kogaku Kyokai, jt. auth. see Tazawa, Eiichi.
Nihon Seishin Shinkei Gakkai. Signal Transduction in Affective Disorders. Ozawa, H. et al, eds. LC 97-44757. (Illus.). x, 146p. 1997. 99.00 (*4-431-70210-5*) Spr-Verlag.
Nihon Vogue Staff. Basic Embroidery. (Illus.). 1986. pap. 9.00 (*0-87040-650-7*) Japan Pubns USA.
— Basic Lace. (Illus.). 1986. pap. 13.00 (*0-87040-651-5*) Japan Pubns USA.
— Beautiful Lace. LC 81-84803. (Illus.). 82p. 1982. pap. 15.00 (*0-87040-504-7*) Japan Pubns USA.
— The Best Collections of Cross Stitch Design & Handywork. LC 82-81054. (Illus.). 84p. 1982. pap. 12.95 (*0-87040-522-5*) Japan Pubns USA.
— Golden Lace. (Illus.). 90p. (Orig.). 1983. pap. 17.00 (*0-87040-562-4*) Japan Pubns USA.
— Lace for Beginners. (Illus.). 82p. 1984. pap. 13.95 (*0-87040-567-5*) Japan Pubns USA.
— Lovely Cross Stitch Designs. (Illus.). 84p. (Orig.). 1983. pap. 11.95 (*0-87040-529-2*) Japan Pubns USA.
— Mohair Knitting. (Illus.). 80p. (Orig.). 1985. pap. 19.00 (*0-87040-610-8*) Japan Pubns USA.
— Sashiko: Traditional Japanese Quilt Designs. LC 88-80146. (Illus.). 42p. (Orig.). 1988. pap. 11.95 (*0-87040-769-4*) Japan Pubns USA.
— Simple Pineapple Crochet. (Illus.). 74p. 1995. pap. text 17.00 (*0-87040-951-4*) Japan Pubns USA.
— White Sweaters. (Illus.). 61p. (Orig.). 1985. pap. 17.00 (*0-87040-652-3*) Japan Pubns USA.
Nihoul, J. C., jt. auth. see Brasseur, P.
Nihsreyasananda, Swami. Man & His Mind. 343p. pap. 6.95 (*81-7120-643-3*) Vedanta Pr.
Nii-owoo, Ife. A Is for Africa: Looking at Africa Through the Alphabet. LC 90-81575. (Young Reader's Ser.). (Illus.). 32p. (J). (ps-k). 1992. 12.95 (*0-86543-182-5*); pap. 5.95 (*0-86543-183-3*) Africa World.
Niihara, K., et al, eds. High Temperature Ceramic Matrix Composites III: Proceedings of the 3rd International Conference on High Temperature Ceramic Matrix Composites (HT-CMC 3), Osaka, Japan, September 1998. (Key Engineering Materials Ser.: Vols. 164 & 165). (Illus.). 464p. 1998. text 165.00 (*0-87849-818-4*, Pub. by Trans T Pub) Enfield Pubs NH.
— The Science of Engineering Ceramics II: Proceedings of the 2nd International Symposium on the Science of Engineering Ceramics (EnCera '98), Osaka, Japan, September 1998. (Key Engineering Materials Ser.: Vols. 161 to 163). (Illus.). 701p. 1998. text 240.00 (*0-87849-817-6*, Pub. by Trans T Pub) Enfield Pubs NH.
Niihara, Koichi, et al, eds. Materials Processing & Design: Grain-Boundary-Controlled Properties of Fine Ceramics II. (Ceramic Transactions Ser.: Vol. 44). 1994. 88.00 (*0-944904-78-5*, CT044) Am Ceramic.
Niimi. Progress in Microcirculation Research. LC 94-26568. 540p. 1994. 173.00 (*0-08-042503-8*, Pergamon Pr) Elsevier.
Niimi, Hideyuji, et al, eds. Microcirculatory Approach to Asian Traditional Medicine: Strategy for the Scientific Evaluation: Selected Proceedings from the Satellite Symposium of the 2nd Asian Congress for Microcirculation, Beijing, China, 17 August 1995. LC 96-17518. (International Congress Ser.: No. 1117). 206p. 1996. text 139.00 (*0-444-82343-3*, Excerpta Medica) Elsevier.
Niimi, Nankichi. Buying Mittens. LC 98-47513. (Illus.). 40p. (J). (ps-3). 1999. 16.95 (*0-8248-2129-7*, Kolowalu Bk) UH Pr.
Niimura, M., et al, eds. Phacomatosis in Japan: Epidemiology, Clinical Picture & Molecular Biology. (Gann Monograph on Cancer Research Ser.: Vol. 46). (Illus.). viii, 230p. 1999. 243.50 (*3-8055-6838-X*) S Karger.
Niinikoski, J., jt. ed. see Aro, H.
Niiniluoto, I. Critical Scientific Realism. LC 99-32396. (Clarendon Library of Logic & Philosophy). (Illus.). 352p. 2000. 55.00 (*0-19-823833-9*) OUP.
— Is Science Progressive? (Synthese Library: 177). 283p. 1984. text 160.50 (*90-277-1835-0*) Kluwer Academic.
— Truthlikeness. (Synthese Library: Vol. 185). 528p. 1987. text 234.00 (*90-277-2354-0*, D Reidel) Kluwer Academic.
Niiniluoto, I. & Tuomela, Raimo. Theoretical Concepts & Hypothetico-Inductive Inference. LC 73-83567. (Synthese Library: No. 53). 269p. 1973. text 126.50 (*90-277-0343-4*, D Reidel) Kluwer Academic.
Niiniluoto, I., ed. see International Asssociation for Philosophy of Law &.
Niiniluoto, I., ed. see International Congress for Logic, Methodology, & P.
Niino, Masayuki, jt. ed. see Phipps, Claude R.
Niiro, Katsuyuki, jt. ed. see Boenau, A. Bruce.
***Niit.** Access 97: Module 3. (CT Course Instructor Training Ser.). 2000. 8.00 (*0-619-02295-7*) Course Tech.
— Access 2000: Module 1. (C). 1999. text 9.95 (*0-619-01035-5*) Course Tech.
— ACT! 4.0: Module 1. (CT Course Instructor Training Ser.). 2000. 8.00 (*0-619-02293-0*) Course Tech.
— ACT! 4.0: Module 2. (CT Course Instructor Training Ser.). 2000. 8.00 (*0-619-02294-9*) Course Tech.
— Director 7: Module 1. (CT Course Instructor Training Ser.). 2000. 8.00 (*0-619-02302-3*) Course Tech.
— Director 7: Module 2. (CT Course Instructor Training Ser.). 2000. 8.00 (*0-619-02303-1*) Course Tech.
— Excel 97: Module 3. (CT Course Instructor Training Ser.). 2000. 8.00 (*0-619-02296-5*) Course Tech.
— Excel 2000: Module 1. 1999. pap. 9.95 (*0-619-01017-7*) Course Tech.
— Excel 2000: Module 2. 2000. pap. 9.95 (*0-619-01018-5*) Course Tech.
— Freehand 8: Module 1. (CT Course Instructor Training Ser.). 2000. 8.00 (*0-619-02301-5*) Course Tech.
— Frontpage 97: Module 2. (CT Course Instructor Training Ser.). 2000. 8.00 (*0-619-02292-2*) Course Tech.
— Linux: Module 1. (CT Course Instructor Training Ser.). 2000. 8.00 (*0-619-02344-9*) Course Tech.
— Linux: Module 2. (CT Course Instructor Training Ser.). 2000. 8.00 (*0-619-02345-7*) Course Tech.
— Lotus 1-2-3 97: Module 2. 2000. 8.00 (*0-619-02304-X*) Course Tech.
— MAC OS 8.x: Module 2. (CT Course Instructor Training Ser.). 2000. 8.00 (*0-619-02318-X*) Course Tech.
— Outlook 2000: Integration. 2000. 8.00 (*0-619-01418-0*) Course Tech.
— Powerpoint 97: Module 2. (CT Course Instructor Training Ser.). 2000. 8.00 (*0-619-02297-3*) Course Tech.
— Quarkxpress 4.0: Module 1. (CT Course Instructor Training Ser.). 2000. 8.00 (*0-619-02300-7*) Course Tech.
— Understanding Microsoft Networking. (CT Course Instructor Training Ser.). 2000. 8.00 (*0-619-02272-8*) Course Tech.
— Understanding Novell Networking. 2000. 8.00 (*0-619-02271-X*) Course Tech.
— Windows 95: Module 1. 1999. pap. 9.95 (*0-619-01026-6*) Course Tech.
— Word 97: Module 3. (CT Course Instructor Training Ser.). 2000. 8.00 (*0-619-02298-1*) Course Tech.
— Word 2000: Module 1. 1999. pap. 9.95 (*0-619-01008-8*) Thomson Learn.
— Wordperfect 8.0: Module 2. (CT Course Instructor Training Ser.). 2000. 8.00 (*0-619-02299-X*) Course Tech.
Niitsuma, N. Collision Tectonics in the South Fossa Magna, Central Japan, Pt. 2. 100p. 1991. pap. text 237.00 (*2-88124-818-7*) Gordon & Breach.
Niitsuma, N., jt. auth. see Matsuda, T.
Niiya, Brian, ed. see Japanese-American National Museum Staff.
Niizeki. The Role of Crystal Growth for Device Development. (Progress in Crystal Growth & Character Ser.: Vol. 23). Orig. Title: Progress in Crystal Growth & Characterization, Vol. 23. 436p. 1992. 486.50 (*0-08-042045-1*) Elsevier.
Nijboer, Donald. Cockpit: An Illustrated History of World War II Aircraft Interiors. LC 99-200298. (Illus.). 176p. 1998. 39.95 (*1-57427-068-0*) Howell Pr VA.

N

An Asterisk (*) at the beginning of an entry indicates that the title is appearing for the first time.

Nijboer, J. F., et al, eds. Forensic Expertise & the Law of Evidence: Proceedings of the Colloquium, Amsterdam, the Netherlands, August 1992. 204p. pap. 47.00 *(0-444-85777-X*, North Holland) Elsevier.

Nijeholt, Geertje A. & Wieringa, Saskia. Women's Movements & Public Policy in Europe, Latin America, & the Caribbean: The Triangle of Empowerment. Vargas, Virginia & Mohanty, Chandra, eds. LC 97-13518. (Gender, Culture, & Global Politics Ser.: No. 2). 196p. 1997. text 42.00 *(0-8153-2479-0)* Garland.

Nijenhuis, Emmie Te, see Te Nijenhuis, Emmie, ed.

Nijenhuis, K. Thermoreversible Networks: Viscoelastic Properties & Structure of Gels. LC 97-222606. (Advances in Polymer Science Ser.: Vol. 130). (Illus.). 340p. 1997. 220.00 *(3-540-61857-0)* Spr-Verlag.

Nijenhuis, K. T. & Mijs, W. J. The Wiley Polymer Networks Review. LC 97-24361. (Wiley Polymer Networks Group Review Ser.). 574p. 1998. 285.00 *(0-471-97344-0)* Wiley.

Nijenhuis, Willem. Ecclesia Reformata. (Studies on the Reformation: Vol. II). 320p. 1994. 94.00 *(90-04-09465-2*, NLG135) Brill Academic Pubs.

Nijf, Onno M. Van, see Van Nijf, Onno M., ed.

Nijhar, Preeti, jt. auth. see Brogden, Mike.

Nijhar, Saranjit, jt. auth. see Brogden, Mike.

Nijhawan, B. R., ed. Production of Iron, Steel & High Quality Product Mix: Latest Technological Innovations & Processes. LC 92-82923. (Conference Proceedings Ser.). (Illus.). 325p. 1992. reprint ed. pap. 100.80 *(0-608-02636-0*, 206329400004) Bks Demand.

Nijhof, Wim J. & Brandsma, T. F. Bridging the Skills Gap Between Work & Education. LC 99-13935. 1999. write for info. *(0-7923-5653-5)* Kluwer Academic.

Nijhof, Wim J. & Steumer, Jan N., eds. Key Qualifications in Work & Education. LC 97-44702. 276p. 1998. 127.00 *(0-7923-4864-8)* Kluwer Academic.

Nijhoff, F. W., jt. ed. see Clarkson, P. A.

Nijholm, Earl, tr. see Nelson, Kimberly K.

Nijholt, A. Context-Free Grammars: Covers, Normal Forms, & Parsing. (Lecture Notes in Computer Science Ser.: Vol. 93). 253p. 1980. 28.00 *(0-387-10245-0)* Spr-Verlag.

Nijholt, A., ed. Computers & Languages: Theory & Practice - Studies in Computer Science & Artificial Intelligence. 482p. 1988. 140.75 *(0-444-70463-9*, North Holland) Elsevier.

Nijholt, J. L. Design of a Michelson Interferometer for Quantitative Refraction Index Profile Measurements. (Series 01 - Aerodynamics: No. 11). (Illus.). 54p. 1998. pap. 15.95 *(90-407-1574-2*, Pub. by Delft U Pr) Coronet Bks.

Nijhout, H. Frederick. The Development & Evolution of Butterfly Wing Patterns. LC 90-24312. (Series in Comparative Evolutionary Biology). (Illus.). 336p. (C). 1991. pap. text 21.95 *(0-87474-917-4)* Smithsonian.

— The Development & Evolution of Butterfly Wing Patterns. LC 90-24312. (Series in Comparative Evolutionary Biology). (Illus.). 336p. (C). 1991. text 45.00 *(0-87474-921-2)* Smithsonian.

Nijhout, H. Frederik. Insect Hormones. LC 93-42301. 280p. 1994. text 49.50 *(0-691-03466-4*, Pub. by Princeton U Pr); pap. text 19.95 *(0-691-05912-8*, Pub. by Princeton U Pr) Cal Prin Full Svc.

Nijhuis, Jan G., ed. Fetal Behaviour: Developmental & Perinatal Aspects. LC 92-12913. (Illus.). 312p. 1992. 79.95 *(0-19-262089-4)* OUP.

Nijim, Basheer K., ed. American Church Politics & the Middle East. (Monographs: No. 15). 156p. (Orig.). 1982. pap. 6.95 *(0-937694-53-3)* Assn Arab-Amer U Grads.

Nijinksy, Vaslav. The Diary of Vaslav Nijinsky. unexpurgated ed. Acocella, Joan, ed. FitzLyon, Kyril, tr. from RUS. LC 98-37409. (Illus.). 306p. 1999. 30.00 *(0-374-13921-0)* FS&G.

Nijinska, Bronislava. Bronislava Nijinska: Early Memoirs. Nijinska, Irina & Rawlinson, Jean, eds. & trs. by. LC 92-13666. (Illus.). 576p. 1992. pap. text 19.95 *(0-8223-1295-6)* Duke.

Nijinska, Irina, ed. & tr. see Nijinska, Bronislava.

Nijinsky, Romola, ed. see Nijinsky, Vaslav.

***Nijinsky, Vaslav.** The Diary of Vaslav Nijinsky. Acocella, Joan, ed. FitzLyon, Kyril, tr. 2000. pap. write for info. *(0-374-52693-1)* FS&G.

Nijinsky, Vaslav. The Diary of Vaslav Nijinsky. Nijinsky, Romola, ed. (Illus.). 187p. 1968. pap. 14.95 *(0-520-00945-2*, Pub. by U CA Pr) Cal Prin Full Svc.

***Nijinsky, Vaslav.** The Diary of Vaslav Nijinsky. unexpurgated ed. Acocella, Joan, ed. FitzLyon, Kyril, tr. from RUS. (Illus.). 320p. 2000. pap. 15.00 *(0-374-52685-0)* FS&G.

Nijk, Henry, ed. see Ben Meir, Dov B.

Nijkama, Peter & Reggiani, Aura. The Economics of Complex Spatial Systems. LC 98-13470. 1998. write for info. *(0-444-82931-8)* Elsevier.

Nijkamp, F. P. & Parnham, M. J., eds. Principles of Immunopharmacology. LC 99-10441. 450p. 1999. pap. 95.00 *(3-7643-5780-0)* Birkhauser.

Nijkamp, E. P., et al, eds. Mediators in Airway Hyperreactivity. (Agents & Actions Supplements Ser.: Vol. 31). 296p. 1990. 79.50 *(0-8176-2513-5)* Birkhauser.

Nijkamp, Franciscus P. & Parnham, Michael J. Principles of Immunopharmacology. LC 99-10441. 1999. pap. write for info. *(0-8176-5780-0)* Birkhauser.

Nijkamp, H.J., et al, eds. Progress in Plant Cellular & Molecular Biology. (Current Plant Science & Biotechnology in Agriculture Ser.). (C). 1990. lib. bdg. 257.00 *(0-7923-0873-5)* Kluwer Academic.

Nijkamp, P. & Coccossis, H., eds. Sustainable Tourist Development. 224p. 1995. 72.95 *(1-85972-177-X*, Pub. by Avebry) Ashgate Pub Co.

Nijkamp, P., jt. ed. see Coccossis, H.

Nijkamp, Peter. Environmental Policy Analysis: Operational Methods & Models. LC 79-41778. (Illus.). 299p. reprint ed. pap. 92.70 *(0-608-17553-6*, 203053300069) Bks Demand.

— Impact Assessment & Evaluation in Transportation Planning. (Transportation, Research, Economics & Policy Ser.). 284p. (C). 1994. lib. bdg. 136.00 *(0-7923-2648-2)* Kluwer Academic.

— Sustainability of Urban Systems: A Cross-National Evolutionary Analysis of Urban Innovation. 323p. 1990. text 75.95 *(1-85628-094-2*, Pub. by Avebry) Ashgate Pub Co.

Nijkamp, Peter, ed. Environmental Economics, Vol. 2. 1976. pap. text 72.50 *(90-207-0645-4)* Kluwer Academic.

— Europe on the Move. 368p. 1993. 79.95 *(1-85628-547-2*, Pub. by Avebry) Ashgate Pub Co.

— New Borders & Old Barriers in Spatial Development. LC 94-7287. 272p. 1994. 77.95 *(1-85628-906-0*, Pub. by Avebry) Ashgate Pub Co.

Nijkamp, Peter, et al, eds. Information Technology: Social & Spatial Perspectives. (Lecture Notes in Economics & Mathematical Systems Ser.: Vol. 315). vi, 268p. 1988. 38.70 *(0-387-50158-4)* Spr-Verlag.

Nijkamp, Peter & Leitner, Helga, eds. Measuring the Unmeasurable: Analysis of Qualitative Spatial Data. Wrigley, Neil, tr. 1985. lib. bdg. 306.50 *(90-247-3124-0)* Kluwer Academic.

Nijkamp, Peter & Perrels, Adriaan. Sustaining Cities in Europe. 1994. 57.00 *(1-85383-229-4*, Pub. by Escan Pubns); pap. 26.00 *(1-85383-203-0*, Pub. by Escan Pubns) Island Pr.

Nijkamp, Peter & Reggiani, Aura. Interaction, Evolution, & Chaos in Space. LC 92-13515. (Illus.). xii, 276p. 1992. 98.00 *(3-540-55458-0)*; 116.95 *(0-387-55458-0)* Spr-Verlag.

Nijkamp, Peter & Reggiani, Aura, eds. Nonlinear Evolution of Spatial Economic Systems. LC 93-34002. (Illus.). x, 285p. 1993. 119.95 *(0-387-57162-0)* Spr-Verlag.

Nijkamp, Peter & Rietveld, Piet. Cities in Transition: Problems & Policies. (NATO Advanced Study, Behavioral & Social Sciences Ser.: No. 4). 432p. 1981. lib. bdg. 135.00 *(90-286-2641-7)* Kluwer Academic.

Nijkamp, Peter, et al. Euromobile: Transport, Communication & Mobility in Europe: A Cross-National Comparative Overview. 424p. 1990. text 93.95 *(0-566-07150-9*, Pub. by Avebry) Ashgate Pub Co.

— Missing Transport Networks in Europe. 224p. 1994. 78.95 *(1-85628-674-6*, Pub. by Avebry) Ashgate Pub Co.

— Multicriteria Evaluation in Physical Planning. (Contributions to Economic Analysis Ser.: No. 185). 616p. 1990. 125.50 *(0-444-88851-9*, North Holland) Elsevier.

— Multicriteria Evaluation in Physical Planning. (Contributions to Economic Analysis Ser.: Vol. 185). 220p. 1990. 131.50 *(0-444-88124-7)* Elsevier.

— Multidimensional Spatial Data & Decision Analysis. LC 79-40518. (Illus.). 334p. reprint ed. pap. 103.60 *(0-608-17610-9*, 203046000069) Bks Demand.

— Telematics & Transport Behaviour. LC 96-14883. (Advances in Spatial Science Ser.). 227p. 1996. 99.00 *(3-540-60919-9)* Spr-Verlag.

***Nijkamp, Peter, et al.** Transportation Planning & the Future. LC 97-34188. 312p. 1998. 90.00 *(0-471-97408-0)* Wiley.

Nijkamp, Peter, jt. auth. see Beinat, Euro.

Nijkamp, Peter, jt. auth. see Chatterjee, Lata.

Nijkamp, Peter, jt. auth. see Giaoutzi, Maria.

Nijkamp, Peter, jt. auth. see Van Delft, A.

Nijkamp, Peter, jt. auth. see Van Lierop, F. J.

Nijkamp, Peter, jt. ed. see Archibugi, F.

Nijkamp, Peter, ed. see Batty, Michael, et al.

Nijkamp, Peter, jt. ed. see Beuthe, Michel.

Nijkamp, Peter, jt. ed. see Fischer, M. M.

Nijkamp, Peter, jt. ed. see Fischer, Manfred M.

Nijkamp, Peter, jt. ed. see Lakshmanan, T. R.

Nijkamp, Peter, jt. ed. see Mills, E. S.

Nijman, Jan, jt. auth. see Grant, Richard.

Nijman, Jan, jt. ed. see Grant, Richard.

***Nijmeijer, H. & Fossen, T. I., eds.** New Directions in Nonlinear Observer Design Vol. 244. LC 99-12174. (Lecture Notes in Control & Information Sciences Ser.). (Illus.). xx, 532p. 1999. pap. 119.00 *(1-85233-134-8*, Pub. by Spr-Verlag) Spr-Verlag.

Nijmeijer, H. & Schumacher, J. M., eds. Three Decades of Mathematical System Theory. (Lecture Notes in Control & Information Sciences: Vol. 135). (Illus.). vi, 562p. 1989. 103.95 *(0-387-51605-0)* Spr-Verlag.

Nijmeijer, H. & Van der Schaft, A. Nonlinear Dynamical Control Systems. (Illus.). xiii, 467p. (C). 1996. 59.95 *(0-387-97234-X)* Spr-Verlag.

Nijmeijer, H. & Van der Schaft, A. J. Nonlinear Control Systems. LC 98-47481. 1998. pap. write for info. *(0-08-043049-X*, Pergamon Pr) Elsevier.

Nijmeijer, Peter, tr. see Barkan, Stanley H., ed.

***Nijoh, Ambe J.** Urban Planning, Housing & Spatial Structures in Sub-Saharan Africa: Nature, Impact & Development Implications of Exogenous Forces. (SOAS Studies in Development Geography). 287p. 1999. text 69.95 *(0-7546 1094-2*, Pub. by Ashgate Pub) Ashgate Pub Co.

***Nijru, Cyrus & Merna, Tony.** Financing & Managing Infrastructure Projects. 150p. 1998. pap. 170.00 *(962-936-046-2*, Pub. by Asia Law & Practice) Am Educ Systs.

Nijs, E. Breton de. Faded Portraits. Beekman, E. M., ed. Sturtevant, Donald & Sturtevant, Elsje, trs. from DUT. LC 81-19653. (Library of the Indies). Orig. Title: Vergeelde Portretten Uit Een Indisch Familie-Album. 192p. 1982. lib. bdg. 27.50 *(0-87023-363-7)* U of Mass Pr.

Nijs, Johan F., ed. Advanced Silicon & Semiconducting Silicon Alloy-Based Materials & Devices. (Illus.). 488p. 1994. 200.00 *(0-7503-0299-2)* IOP Pub.

Nijs, Loes Den, see Booij, C. J. & Den Nijs, Loes, eds.

Nijssen, Han, jt. auth. see Kullander, Sven O.

Nijura, Miguel. Maribel y la Extrana Familia. (Nueva Austral Ser.: Vol. 123). (SPA.). 1991. pap. text 24.95 *(84-239-1923-4)* Elliots Bks.

Nik-Safiah, N. I., jt. auth. see Pathmanathan, I.

Nikaido, H. Introduction to Sets & Mappings in Modern Economics, 1. 280p. 1999. pap. 115.00 *(0-444-10038-5)* Elsevier.

Nikaido, Hukukane. Monopolistic Competition & Effective Demand. LC 74-25623. (Princeton Studies in Mathematical Economics: No. 6). 158p. reprint ed. pap. 49.00 *(0-8357-6225-4*, 203464800090) Bks Demand.

— Prices, Cycles, & Growth. (Studies in Dynamical Economic Science). (Illus.). 305p. (C). 1996. 42.00 *(0-262-14059-4)* MIT Pr.

***Nikaido, Susan.** Building Better Relationships. (Discipleship Journals: Vol. 7). 2000. pap. text 6.00 *(1-57683-167-1)* NavPress.

Nikam, N. A. Some Concepts of Indian Culture. 212p. 1980. 15.95 *(0-318-36979-6)* Asia Bk Corp.

Nikam, N. A. & McKeon, Richard, eds. The Edicts of Asoka. LC 59-5748. (Midway Reprint Ser.). 96p. 1978. pap. text 14.00 *(0-226-58611-1)* U Ch Pr.

Nikam, Shriram. Destiny of Untouchables in India. 1998. 28.00 *(81-7629-050-5)* Deep & Deep Pubns.

Nikam, T. B. & Khole, V. V. Insect Spiracular Systems. LC 08-828410. 1989. text 59.95 *(0-470-21308-6)* P-H.

***Nikanne, Urpo & Van De Zee, Emile, eds.** Cognitive Interfaces: Constraints on Linking Cognitive Information. 288p. 2000. text 74.00 *(0-19-829961-3)*; pap. text 29.95 *(0-19-829962-1)* OUP.

Nikanne, Urpo, jt. ed. see Homberg, Anders.

Nikas. Neurological & Neurosurgical. Date not set. text. write for info. *(0-7216-6001-0*, W B Saunders Co) Harcrt Hlth Sci Grp.

***Nikayin, Fazlollah.** The Holy Quran: A Proper Poetic Translation. 1120p. 2000. 59.95 *(0-9674732-0-9)* Ultimate Bk.

Nikazy, Eddie M. Abstracts of Death Records for Johnson County, Tennessee, 1908 to 1941. 482p. (Orig.). 1992. pap. 33.00 *(1-55613-665-X)* Heritage Bk.

— Abstracts of Tennessee Death Records for Carter County, 1908-1925. 485p. 1993. pap. text 32.50 *(1-55613-738-9)* Heritage Bk.

— Carter County, Tennessee Death Record Abstracts, 1926-1934. LC 94-187644. 335p. (Orig.). 1994. pap. text 26.00 *(1-55613-953-5)* Heritage Bk.

— Carter County, Tennessee, Marriages, 1871-1920. ix, 322p. (Orig.). 1993. pap. 24.50 *(1-55613-765-6)* Heritage Bk.

— Forgotten Soldiers: History of the 2nd Tennessee Volunteer Infantry Regiment, U. S. A., 1861-1865. (Illus.). xii, 272p. (Orig.). 1996. pap. 22.00 *(0-7884-0571-3*, N349) Heritage Bk.

— Forgotten Soldiers: History of the 4th Tennessee Volunteer Infantry Regiment (U. S. A.) 1863-1865. (Illus.). 160p. (Orig.). 1995. pap. text 16.00 *(0-7884-0241-2)* Heritage Bk.

— Greene County, Tennessee, Death Record Abstracts, 1908-1918, Vol. 1. LC 97-194459. vi, 344p. (Orig.). 1997. pap. 26.00 *(0-7884-0660-4*, N340) Heritage Bk.

— Johnson County, Tennessee, Death Record Abstracts 1908-1943. 389p. 1998. pap. 28.00 *(0-9668208-0-0)* East TN Bks.

— Sullivan County, Tennessee Death Records, 1908-1918. 311p. (Orig.). 1994. pap. text 22.00 *(0-7884-0099-1)* Heritage Bk.

— Sullivan County, Tennessee Death Records, 1919-1925, Vol. 2. 346p. (Orig.). 1995. pap. 26.00 *(0-7884-0290-0)* Heritage Bk.

— Unicoi County, Tennessee, Death Record Abstracts, 1908-1936. LC 98-107771. v, 356p. 1997. pap. 21.00 *(0-7884-0747-3*, N339) Heritage Bk.

— Washington Co., TN: Death Record Abstracts, 1908-1916. 316p. (Orig.). 1994. pap. text 23.00 *(0-7884-0100-9)* Heritage Bk.

Nikbakht, Ehsan. Foreign Loans & Economic Performance: The Experience of the Less Developed Countries. LC 84-8296. 134p. 1984. 55.00 *(0-275-91235-3*, C1235, Praeger Pubs) Greenwood.

Nikbakht, Ehsan & Groppelli, A. A. Finance. 3rd ed. LC 94-28891. (Business Review Ser.). 1995. pap. 13.95 *(0-8120-1916-4)* Barron.

Nike De-Nur, Eliyah, tr. see Ka-Tzetnik, pseud.

Nikel, Casimir M., jt. auth. see Pfeiffer, Guy O.

Nikelly, John C., jt. ed. see Horvath, Csaba.

Nikephoros. Zeitschrift Fur Sport und Kultur Im Altertum, Bd. 1. Decker, Wolfgang et al, eds. 320p. 1988. write for info. *(3-615-00038-2)* G Olms Pubs.

— Zeitschrift Fur Sport und Kultur Im Altertum, Bd. 2. Decker, Wolfgang et al, eds. 330p. 1989. write for info. *(3-615-00058-7)* G Olms Pubs.

— Zeitschrift Fur Sport und Kultur Im Altertum, Bd. 3. Decker, Wolfgang et al, eds. 338p. 1990. write for info. *(3-615-00067-6)* G Olms Pubs.

— Zeitschrift fur Sport und Kultur Im Altertum, Band 4. Decker, Joachim et al, eds. (GER.). 334p. 1991. write for info. *(3-615-00077-3)* G Olms Pubs.

***Nikhil, Rishiyur S.** Implicit Parallel Programming in PH. 400p. 2000. 64.95 *(1-55860-644-0)* Morgan Kaufmann.

Nikhilananda, Swami. Hinduism: Its Meaning for the Liberation of the Spirit. LC 58-6155. 220p. 1992. pap. 12.50 *(0-911206-26-4)* Ramakrishna.

— Holy Mother: Being the Life of Sri Sarada Devi, Wife of Sri Ramakrishna & Helpmate in His Mission. LC 62-13423. (Illus.). 384p. 1962. pap. 15.50 *(0-911206-20-5)* Ramakrishna.

— Man in Search of Immortality: Testimonials from the Hindu Scriptures. LC 68-101793. 112p. 1992. pap. 10.50 *(0-911206-27-2)* Ramakrishna.

— Vivekananda: A Biography. LC 53-7851. (Illus.). 256p. 1989. pap. 15.50 *(0-911206-25-6)* Ramakrishna.

Nikhilananda, Swami, tr. The Bhagavad Gita. LC 44-33674. 404p. 1944. 17.50 *(0-911206-09-4)* Ramakrishna.

— The Bhagavad Gita: Pocket Edition. LC 44-33674. 256p. 1944. 12.50 *(0-911206-10-8)* Ramakrishna.

— Drg Drsya Viveka. 69p. pap. 3.00 *(81-7505-027-6*, Pub. by Advaita Ashrama) Vedanta Pr.

— Gospel of Sri Ramakrishna. abr. ed. LC 58-8948. 640p. 1958. 17.50 *(0-911206-02-7)* Ramakrishna.

— Gospel of Sri Ramakrishna. unabridged ed. LC 58-8948. (Illus.). 1106p. 1942. 35.50 *(0-911206-01-9)* Ramakrishna.

— Mandukopanisad. 5.95 *(81-7505-022-5*, Pub. by Advaita Ashrama) Vedanta Pr.

— Upanishads, Set, 4 vols., Set. LC 49-9558. 1994. 72.00 *(0-911206-14-0)* Ramakrishna.

Nikhilananda, Swami, tr. see Campbell, Joseph, ed.

Nikhilananda, Swami, tr. see Sankara.

Niki, E. & Ong, A. S. Nutrition, Lipids, Health & Disease. 384p. 1995. 95.00 *(0-935315-64-0)* Am Oil Chemists.

Niki, Hiromi & Becker, K. H., eds. The Tropospheric Chemistry of Ozone in the Polar Regions. LC 93-19454. (NATO ASI Series I: Global Environmental Change: Vol. 7). 1993. 237.95 *(0-387-56683-X)* Spr-Verlag.

Niki, K., jt. ed. see Dryhurst, G.

Nikias, Chrysostomos L. & Petropulu, Athina P. Higher Order Spectral Analysis: A Non-Linear Signal Processing Framework. LC 93-28. (Signal Processing Ser.). 528p. (C). 1993. 65.20 *(0-13-678210-8)* P-H.

Nikias, Chrysostomos L. & Shao, Min. Signal Processing with Alpha-Stable Distribution & Applications. LC 95-1482. (Adaptive & Learning Systems for Signal Processing, Communications & Control Ser.). 184p. 1995. 98.95 *(0-471-10647-X*, Wiley-Interscience) Wiley.

Nikibc, Gozard, jt. auth. see Baletibc, Zvonimir.

Nikiel, J. Topologies on Pseudo-Trees & Applications. LC 89-17764. (Memoirs Ser.: Vol. 82/416). 116p. 1989. pap. 21.00 *(0-8218-2479-1*, MEMO/82/416) Am Math.

Nikiel, J., et al. Continuous Images of Arcs & Inverse Limit Methods. LC 93-17171. (Memoirs of the American Mathematical Society Ser.: Vol. 104/498). 80p. 1993. pap. 28.00 *(0-8218-2561-5*, MEMO/104/498) Am Math.

Nikiforoff-Volgin, V. Dorozhnij Posokh.Tr. of A/Staff for the Road. 188p. 1971. reprint ed. pap. 6.00 *(0-317-30421-6)* Holy Trinity.

— Zemlja Imjeninnitsa.Tr. of Feast of the Land. 182p. 1960. reprint ed. pap. 6.00 *(0-317-30418-6)* Holy Trinity.

Nikiforov, A. & Uvarov, V. Special Functions of Mathematical Physics. 500p. 1988. 180.50 *(0-8176-3183-6)* Birkhauser.

Nikiforov, A. F., et al. Classical Orthogonal Polynomials of a Discrete Variable. Glowinski, Roland et al, eds. (Computational Physics Ser.). (Illus.). 368p. 1992. 97.95 *(0-387-51123-7)* Spr-Verlag.

Nikiforowa, Anna. Woerterbuch Wirtschaftsrussisch: German-Russian. (GER & RUS.). 496p. 1993. 105.00 *(0-7859-8380-5*, 3464494063) Fr & Eur.

— Woerterbuch Wirtschaftsrussisch: Russian-German. (GER & RUS.). 496p. 1994. 105.00 *(0-7859-8381-3*, 3464494071) Fr & Eur.

Nikiforuk, Andrew, ed. see Royal Tyrrell Museum of Palaeontology Staff & Budgen, Dennis.

Nikiforuk, Andrew, ed. see Royal Tyrrell Museum of Palaeontology Staff & Wishart, Pat.

Nikiforuk, G., ed. Prevention: Basic & Clinical Aspects. (Understanding Dental Caries (Ltd. Vol.) Ser.: Vol. 2). (Illus.). xiv, 290p. 1985. 50.50 *(3-8055-3905-3)* S Karger.

— Understanding Dental Caries, 2 vols., Vols. 1 & 2. (Illus.). xxviii, 596p. 1985. 101.00 *(3-8055-3906-1)* S Karger.

— Understanding Dental Caries Vol. 1: Etiology & Mechanisms. (Illus.). xiv, 306p. 1985. 50.50 *(3-8055-3864-2)* S Karger.

Nikinmaa, M. Vertebrate Red Blood Cells. (Zoophysiology Ser.: Vol. 28). (Illus.). 300p. 1990. 149.00 *(0-387-51590-9)* Spr-Verlag.

Nikishin, E. M., et al. Rational Approximations & Orthogonality. LC 91-18793. (Translations of Mathematical Monographs: Vol. 92). 221p. 1991. text 90.00 *(0-8218-4545-4*, MMONO/92) Am Math.

Nikitas, Matthew. Grand Finishes for Walls & Floors: Interior House Painting, Wallpapering, & Wood Floor Refinishing. LC 94-31857. (Illus.). 160p. 1994. pap. 16.95 *(1-56440-487-0)* Globe Pequot.

***Nikitas, Matthew.** Grand Finishes for Walls & Floors: Interior House Painting, Wallpapering, & Wood Floor Refinishing. (Illus.). 128p. 2000. pap. 17.95 *(0-312-26331-7)* St Martin.

Nikitin, A. G., jt. auth. see Fushchich, W. I.

Nikitin, E. E. & Umanskii, S. Y. Theory of Slow Atomic Collisions. (Chemical Physics Ser.: Vol. 30). (Illus.). 440p. 1984. 103.95 *(0-387-12414-4)* Spr-Verlag.

Nikitin, E. E., jt. auth. see Kondratiev, V. N.

Nikitin, Eric W. Into the Realm of Oberon: An Introduction to Programming & the Oberon-2 Programming Language. LC 97-22886. 220p. 1997. 39.95 *(0-387-98279-5)* Spr-Verlag.

Nikitin, Evengii. Theory of Thermally Induced Gas Phase Reactions. Schlag, E. W., tr. LC 66-12733. 167p. reprint ed. pap. 51.80 *(0-608-30694-0*, 205096100074) Bks Demand.

Nikitin, P. I. The Fundamentals of Political Economy. 430p. 1983. 35.00 *(0-7855-1219-5*, Pub. by Collets) St Mut.

Nikitin, S. Global Controllability & Stabilization of Nonlinear Systems. (Series on Advances in Mathematics). 284p. 1994. text 61.00 *(981-02-1779-X)* World Scientific Pub.

N

An Asterisk (*) at the beginning of an entry indicates that the title is appearing for the first time.

Nikitin, S. Y., jt. auth. see Akhmanov, S. A.

Nikitin, Yakov. Asymptotic Efficiency of Nonparametric Tests. 292p. (C). 1995. text 54.95 (*0-521-47029-3*) Cambridge U Pr.

Nikitin, Yu P. & Rosental, I. L. Theory of Multiparticle Production Processes. (Studies in High Energy Physics: Vol. 6). xviii, 340p. 1988. 444.00 (*3-7186-4809-1*) Gordon & Breach.

Nikitin, Yu P. & Rozental, I. L. High Energy Physics with Nuclei. xii, 294p. 1986. text 412.00 (*3-7186-0172-9*) Gordon & Breach.

Nikitin, Yu P., et al. Kinematic Methods in High Energy Physics, Vol. 2. (SSRSS Ser.). x, 258p. 1989. text 436.00 (*3-7186-4819-9*) Gordon & Breach.

— Passage of High-Energy Particles Through Matter. Amoretty, S. J., tr. from RUS. (AIP Translation Ser.). (Illus.). 272p. 1989. 79.95 (*0-88318-618-7*) Spr-Verlag.

Nikjoo, Hooshang. Trends in Baha'i Education: Proceedings of the 2nd Symposium on Baha'i Education 1989. 238p. 1990. pap. 16.95 (*1-870987-11-X*) Bahai.

Nikjoo, Hooshang & Vickers, Stephen, eds. Distinctive Aspects of Baha'i Education: Proceedings of the 3rd Symposium of Baha'i Education. 195p. 1993. pap. 17.50 (*1-870989-46-5*) Bahai.

***Nikkah, John.** Our Boys Speak: Adolescent Boys Write About Their Inner Lives. LC 00-26415. 192p. 2000. pap. 12.95 (*0-312-26280-9*) St Martin.

Nikkal, Nancy E. & Mastin, Deborah B. Reps Consultants & Agents. Stevens, Marilyn, ed. (Art Calendar Guide Ser.). 36p. (C). 1999. pap. 9.95 (*0-945388-19-5*) Art Calendar.

***Nikkal, Nancy Egol.** An Art Calendar Guide to College & University Galleries. Steis, Drew, ed. (Art Calendar Guide Ser.). 76p. 1999. pap. 12.95 (*0-945388-22-5*) Art Calendar.

Nikkel, David. Panentheism in Hartshorne & Tillich Vol. 121: A Creative Synthesis. (American University Studies: Series VII). VII, 229p. (C). 1996. text 42.95 (*0-8204-1678-9*) P Lang Pubng.

Nikkila, E., jt. auth. see Mustajoki, A.

Nikkonen, Albina I., jt. ed. see Verkoeyen, C. M.

Niklas, Gerald R. The Making of a Pastoral Person. 2nd expanded rev. ed. LC 96-11427. 229p. (Orig.). 1996. pap. 12.95 (*0-8189-0761-4*) Alba.

Niklas, Gerald R. & Stefanics, Charlotte. Ministry to the Sick. LC 82-4083. 153p. (Orig.). 1982. pap. 7.95 (*0-8189-0429-1*) Alba.

Niklas, Karl J. The Evolutionary Biology of Plants. LC 96-31060. 1997. pap. text 20.00 (*0-226-58083-0*) U Ch Pr.

— The Evolutionary Biology of Plants. LC 96-31060. 1997. lib. bdg. 65.00 (*0-226-58082-2*) U Ch Pr.

— Plant Allometry: The Scaling of Form & Process. LC 94-2418. 412p. 1994. pap. text 24.95 (*0-226-58081-4*); lib. bdg. 62.50 (*0-226-58080-6*) U Ch Pr.

— Plant Biomechanics: An Engineering Approach to Plant Form & Function. (Illus.). 622p. 1992. pap. text 32.95 (*0-226-58631-6*); lib. bdg. 82.50 (*0-226-58630-8*) U Ch Pr.

Niklas, Karl J., ed. Paleobotany, Paleoecology, & Evolution, 2 vols., Set. LC 81-1838. 1981. 95.00 (*0-275-90691-4*, C06910, Praeger Pubs) Greenwood.

— Paleobotany, Paleoecology, & Evolution, 2 vols., Vol. 1. LC 81-1838. 1981. 69.50 (*0-275-90690-6*, C06901, Praeger Pubs) Greenwood.

— Paleobotany, Paleoecology, & Evolution, 2 vols., Vol. 2. LC 81-1838. 1981. 125.00 (*0-275-90689-2*, C06892, Praeger Pubs) Greenwood.

***Niklas, Kurt.** Corner Table: Memories from Hollywood's Colorful Years of Cafe Society. (Illus.). 1,368p. 1999. 29.95 (*1-57098-301-1*, R Rinehart Intl) Roberts Rinehart.

***Niklas, Michael.** Diskurskonstitution in der Franzosischen Barockliteratur: Charles Sorel und Jean Rotrou. 302p. 1999. 51.95 (*3-631-34410-4*) P Lang Pubng.

Niklasson, Karin. Early Prehistoric Burials in Cyprus. (Studies in Mediterranean Archaeology: Vol. XCVI). (Illus.). 295p. (Orig.). 1991. pap. 125.00 (*91-7081-021-4*, Pub. by P Astroms) Coronet Bks.

***Niklasson, Karin H., ed.** Cypriote Archaeology in Goteborg: Papers Presented at a Symposium on Cypriote Archaeology Held in Goteborg 20 May 1998. (Pocket-Book Ser.: Vol. 157). (Illus.). 110p. 1999. 45.00 (*91-7081-146-6*, Pub. by P Astroms) Coronet Bks.

Niklasson, Lars & Boden, Mikael B., eds. Current Trends in Connectionism. 392p. 1995. text 79.95 (*0-8058-1997-5*) L Erlbaum Assocs.

Niklasson, Lars & Hoden, Mikael. Connectionism in a Broad Perspective. 1994. text 46.50 (*0-685-70922-1*) P-H.

Niklasson, Lars F., et al. ICANN 98: Proceedings of the 8th International Conference on Artificial Neural Networks, Skovde, Sweden, 2-4 September 1998. LC 98-28433. (Perspectives in Neural Computing Ser.). 1998. pap. 179.00 (*3-540-76263-9*) Spr-Verlag.

Niklaus, Robert L. To All Peoples: Missions World Book of the Christian & Missionary Alliance. LC 90-81150. (Illus.). 412p. 1990. 29.99 (*0-87509-432-5*) Chr Pubns.

Nikles, D. C., jt. auth. see Burley, J.

Nikles, D. G., et al. Progress & Problems of Genetic Improvement of Tropical Forest Trees, 2 Vols. 1978. 165.00 (*0-85074-020-7*) St Mut.

Nikles, G., jt. auth. see Burley, J.

Nikly, Michelle. The Perfume of Memory. LC 98-33108. (Illus.). 40p. (J). (ps-3). 1999. 16.95 (*0-439-08206-4*, Pub. by Scholastic Inc) Penguin Putnam.

Niko, Nicholas J. Gods of the Universe. LC 95-94055. (Illus.). 400p. 1996. 20.00 (*0-9607228-6-6*) Gods Universe.

Nikoghosian, J., et al. Caete de Gusto Hacia el Otono Con las Matematicas y Ciencias - Fall into Math & Science. (ENG & SPA.). 116p. (J). (gr. k-1). 1988. 16.95 (*1-881431-19-3*, 1401) AIMS Educ Fnd.

Nikogoian, D. N. Handbook of Properties of Optical Materials. LC 97-15136. 614p. 1997. 305.00 (*0-471-97384-X*) Wiley.

Nikol, S. M., ed. Theory & Applications of Differentiable Functions of Several Variables, 14. (Proceedings of the Steklov Institute of Mathematics Ser.: Vol. 194). 265p. 1994. 175.00 (*0-8218-3152-6*, STEKLO/194C) Am Math.

Nikola, Beatrice. Your Birthday in History. LC 98-73835. 288p. 2000. 10.95 (*0-8158-0537-3*) Chris Mass.

Nikola-Lisa, W. La Alegria de Ser Tu y Yo. Canetti, Yanitzia, tr. LC 95-52980. (SPA., Illus.). 32p. (J). (ps-3). 1996. pap. 6.95 (*1-880000-36-9*, Pub. by Lee & Low Bks) Publishers Group.

— La Alegria de Ser Tu y Yo. (SPA.). (J). 1996. 12.15 (*0-606-09520-9*, Pub. by Turtleback) Demco.

***Nikola-Lisa, W.** La Alegria de Ser Tu y Yo, Set. unabridged ed. Canetti, Yanitzia, tr.Tr. of Bein' with You This Way. (SPA.). (J). (gr. k-3). 1999. 24.95 incl. audio (*0-87499-550-7*) Live Oak Media.

Nikola-Lisa, W. La Alegria de Ser Tu y Yo (Bein' with You This Way) Canetti, Yanitzia, tr. LC 95-52980. (SPA., Illus.). 32p. (J). (ps-3). 1996. 14.95 (*1-880000-35-0*) Lee & Low Bks.

— America: My Land, Your Land, Our Land. LC 96-5753. (Illus.). 32p. (J). (gr. 1-2). 1997. 15.95 (*1-880000-37-7*) Lee & Low Bks.

— Bein' with You This Way. LC 93-5164. (Illus.). 32p. (J). (ps-3). 1994. 15.95 (*1-880000-05-9*) Lee & Low Bks.

— Bein' with You This Way. LC 93-5164. (Illus.). 32p. (J). (ps up). 1995. pap. 6.95 (*1-880000-26-1*) Lee & Low Bks.

Nikola-Lisa, W. Bein' with You This Way. 1994. 12.15 (*0-606-08915-2*, Pub. by Turtleback) Demco.

***Nikola-Lisa, W.** Bein' with You This Way. (SPA.). (J). (gr. k-3). 1999. 24.95 incl. audio (*0-87499-546-9*) Live Oak Media.

***Nikola-Lisa, W.** Can You Top That? LC 99-47895. (Illus.). (J). 2000. 15.95 (*1-880000-99-7*) Lee & Low Bks.

Nikola-Lisa, W. No Babies Asleep. LC 93-20589. (Illus.). 32p. (J). (ps-1). 1995. 15.00 (*0-689-31841-3*) Atheneum Yung Read.

— One Hole in the Road. LC 95-41321. (Illus.). 32p. (J). (ps-2). 1995. 15.95 (*0-8050-4285-7*, B Martin BYR) H Holt & Co.

— 1, 2, 3 Thanksgiving! Levine, Abby, ed. LC 90-28638. (Illus.). 32p. (J). (ps-3). 1991. lib. bdg. 14.95 (*0-8075-6109-6*) A Whitman.

— 1, 2, 3 Thanksgiving! LC 90-28638. 1991. 11.15 (*0-606-10117-9*, Pub. by Turtleback) Demco.

— 1, 2, 3 Thanksgiving! LC 90-28638. (Illus.). 32p. (J). (ps-1). 1996. reprint ed. pap. 6.95 (*0-8075-6110-X*) A Whitman.

— Shake D'em Halloween Bones. LC 94-49738. (Illus.). 32p. (J). (ps-3). 1997. 16.00 (*0-395-73095-3*) HM.

***Nikola-Lisa, W.** Shake Dem Halloween Bones. (Illus.). 32p. (J). (ps-3). 2000. pap. 5.95 (*0-618-07034-6*) HM.

Nikola-Lisa, W. Till Year's Good End. LC 95-45822. (Illus.). 32p. (J). (gr. 3-7). 1997. 16.00 (*0-689-80020-7*) Atheneum Yung Read.

***Nikola-Lisa, W. & Moses.** The Year with Grandma Moses. LC 99-40726. (Illus.). 32p. (ps-5). 2000. 16.95 (*0-8050-6243-2*) H Holt & Co.

***Nikola-Lisa, W., et al.** The Dancin' Fox. LC 00-26033. (Illus.). (J). 2000. write for info. (*0-689-82621-4*) Atheneum Yung Read.

Nikola, R. J. Romantic Massage. LC 97-21597. (Illus.). 128p. 1997. 14.95 (*0-8069-9973-X*) Sterling.

Nikola, Tesla. Tesla Nikola - Colorado Springs Notes, 1899-1900. 440p. 35.00 (*0-913022-26-8*) Angriff Pr.

— Tesla Nikola - Complete Patents. 500p. 35.00 (*0-913022-44-6*) Angriff Pr.

— Tesla Nikola - Inventions, Researches & Writings - 1894. 512p. reprint ed. 14.00 (*0-913022-23-3*) Angriff Pr.

Nikola Tesla Museum Staff, ed. Nikola Tesla, 1856-1943: Lectures, Patents, Articles, 2 vols., Set. 1996. reprint ed. 89.50 (*0-7873-0634-7*) Hlth Research.

Nikola Tesla Museum Staff, ed. Nikola Tesla: Colorado Springs Notes (1899-1900) unabridged ed. 437p. 1978. reprint ed. 40.00 (*0-945001-69-X*) GSG & Assocs.

Nikolaev, Alexei, jt. ed. see Console, Rodolfo.

Nikolaev, E. S. & Samarskii, A. A. Numerical Methods for Grid Equations, 2 vols., Set. 744p. 1989. 415.50 (*0-8176-2278-0*) Birkhauser.

— Numerical Methods for Grid Equations, 2 vols., Vol. 1. 242p. 1989. 165.00 (*0-8176-2276-4*) Birkhauser.

— Numerical Methods for Grid Equations, 2 vols., Vol. 2. 502p. 1989. 313.50 (*0-8176-2277-2*) Birkhauser.

Nikolaev, Mikhail. Detdom. Schweitzer, Victoria, ed. LC 84-51670. (RUS.). 150p. (Orig.). 1985. pap. 10.00 (*0-89830-091-6*) Russica Pubs.

Nikolaev, Yu V., ed. Chechen Tragedy: Who Is to Blame. LC 95-47624. (Illus.). 157p. (C). 1996. lib. bdg. 75.00 (*1-56072-298-3*) Nova Sci Pubs.

Nikolaeva, I. A. Eighteen Twelve Borodino Panorama. (RUS., Illus.). 1982. 100.00 (*0-7855-3005-3*) St Mut.

***Nikolaeva, I. A. & Zhuzhoma, E.** Flows on 2-Dimensional Manifolds: An Overview. Dold, A. et al, eds. (Lecture Notes in Mathematics Ser.: Vol. 1705). (Illus.). xix, 294p. 1999. pap. 57.00 (*3-540-66080-1*) Spr-Verlag.

Nikolaeva, P., jt. auth. see Kozhenikov, V.

Nikolaevskii, Boris I. Istoriia Odnogo Predatelia. LC 80-53079. (RUS.). 374p. 1980. reprint ed. pap. 12.00 (*0-89830-026-6*) Russica Pubs.

Nikolaevskij, V. N. Mechanics of Porous & Fractured Media. (Series in Theoretical & Applied Mechanics: Vol. 8). 492p. 1990. text 108.00 (*9971-5-0383-2*) World Scientific Pub.

Nikolaevskiy, Victor N. Geomechanics & Fluidodynamics: With Applications to Reservoir Engineering. (Theory & Applications of Transport in Porous Media Ser.: Vol. 8). 364p. (C). 1996. text 173.50 (*0-7923-3793-X*) Kluwer Academic.

Nikolai. Intermediate Accounting. 8th ed. LC 99-12961. 1999. 107.95 (*0-324-00731-0*) S-W Pub.

— Intermediate Accounting. 8th ed. (SWC-Accounting). 1999. pap., student ed. 18.00 (*0-324-00732-9*) S-W Pub.

***Nikolai.** WP Intermediate Accounting Chapters 12-22, Vol. 2. 8th ed. (SWC-Accounting Ser.). 1999. pap. 19.75 (*0-324-02803-2*) Sth-Wstrn College.

Nikolai, jt. auth. see Bazley.

Nikolai, Babiel, et al, compiled by. Barron's Russian Dictionary. LC 97-72276. 400p. 1997. pap. text 10.95 (*0-8120-9825-0*) Barron.

Nikolai, Loren A. Intermediate Accounting. 6th ed. (AB - Accounting Principles Ser.). (C). 1993. mass mkt., student ed. 22.50 (*0-538-82721-1*) S-W Pub.

— Intermediate Accounting. 7th ed. LC 96-12048. (AC - Intermediate Accounting Ser.). 1996. 75.00 (*0-538-85499-5*) S-W Pub.

— Intermediate Accounting: Working Papers. 7th ed. (AC - Intermediate Accounting Ser.). 1996. mass mkt., student ed. 16.00 (*0-538-85504-5*) S-W Pub.

— Intermediate Accounting: Working Papers, Vol. 1. 7th ed. (AC - Intermediate Accounting Ser.). 1996. wbk. ed. 17.00 (*0-538-85502-9*) S-W Pub.

— Intermediate Accounting: Working Papers, Vol. 2. 7th ed. (AC - Intermediate Accounting Ser.). 1996. wbk. ed. 17.00 (*0-538-85503-7*) S-W Pub.

— Intermediate Accounting - Working Papers, Vol. 2. 6th ed. (AB - Accounting Principles Ser.). (C). 1994. mass mkt., wbk. ed. 17.00 (*0-538-82726-2*) S-W Pub.

— Intermediate Accounting Working Papers, Vol. 1. 6th ed. (AB - Accounting Principles Ser.). (C). 1994. mass mkt., wbk. ed. 17.00 (*0-538-82725-4*) S-W Pub.

Nikolai, Loren A. & Bazley, John D. Intermediate Accounting. 6th ed. (C). 1993. mass mkt. 63.50 (*0-538-82531-6*, AC65FA) S-W Pub.

Nikolai, Loren A., jt. auth. see Cunningham, Billie M.

Nikolai, Robert J. Bioengineering Analysis of Orthodontic Mechanics. LC 84-5712. 493p. reprint ed. pap. 152.90 (*0-7837-2848-4*, 205762400006) Bks Demand.

Nikolaidis, Efstratios & Perakis, Anastassios N. Partially Saturated Ocean Detection: Second Order Process Statistics, PARSAT Computer Program Manual. LC VM0605., (University of Michigan, Dept. of Naval Architecture & Marine Engineering, Report Ser.: No. 291). 73p. reprint ed. pap. 30.00 (*0-608-12936-4*, 202468700038) Bks Demand.

Nikolaidis, Nikos & Pitas, Ioannis. 3-D Image Processing Algorithms. 180p. 2000. 74.95 (*0-471-37736-8*) Wiley.

Nikolajeva, Maria. Children's Literature Comes of Age: Toward a New Aesthetic. LC 95-19560. (Children's Literature & Culture Ser.: Vol. 1). (Illus.). 256p. 1995. text 60.00 (*0-8153-1556-2*, H1816) Garland.

***Nikolajeva, Maria.** From Mythic to Linear: Time in Children's Literature. LC 99-55126. (Illus.). 316p. (J). 1999. 75.00 (*0-8108-3713-7*) Scarecrow.

Nikolajeva, Maria. The Magic Code: The Use of Magical Patterns in Fantasy for Children. (Studies Published by the Swedish Institute for Children's Books). 163p. (Orig.). 1988. pap. 46.00 (*91-22-01200-1*) Coronet Bks.

Nikolajeva, Maria, ed. Aspects & Issues in the History of Children's Literature, 60. LC 94-43041. (Contributions to the Study of World Literature Ser.: Vol. 60). 224p. 1995. 57.95 (*0-313-29614-6*, Greenwood Pr) Greenwood.

Nikolajeva, Maria, ed. see Deakin University Press Staff.

Nikolajewsky, Boris I. Aseff the Spy. (Russian Ser.: Vol. 11). 1969. 25.00 (*0-87569-011-4*) Academic Intl.

Nikolajsen, Inge L., jt. auth. see Nikolajsen, Kirstine.

Nikolajsen, Kirstine & Nikolajsen, Inge L. The DMC Book of Charted Tatting Designs. (Illus.). 48p. 1999. pap. 10.00 (*1-891656-07-4*, LE63) Lacis Pubns.

Nikolaou, Christos & Stephanidis, Constantine. Reserach & Advanced Technology for Digital Libraries: Second European Conference, ECDL '98, Heraklion, Crete, Cyprus, September 21-23, 1998: Proceedings. LC 98-42084. (Lecture Notes in Computer Science: Vol. 151). 1998. pap. 99.00 (*3-540-65101-2*) Spr-Verlag.

Nikolay, Peter. All Colour Wok Cookbook. (Illus.). 64p. 1995. 9.95 (*0-572-01767-7*, Pub. by Foulsham UK) Assoc Pubs Grp.

Nikolayev, G. A. English-Russian Historical Dictionary. 464p. (C). 1995. 40.00 (*0-8285-5145-6*) Firebird NY.

Nikolayev, Philip. Artery Lumen. 37p. 1996. 6.00 (*0-9645516-1-6*) B Matteau.

Nikolelis, Dimitrios P., et al, eds. Biosensors for Direct Monitoring of Environmental Pollutants in Field. LC 97-43087. 381p. 1998. text 227.50 (*0-7923-4867-2*) Kluwer Academic.

Nikolenko, Lada. Francesco Ubertini Called Il Bacchiacca. LC 66-2377. 16.00 (*0-685-71755-0*) J J Augustin.

Nikolic, M. Methods in Subnuclear Physics, Vol. 1. 516p. 1968. 190.00 (*0-677-11950-X*) Gordon & Breach.

Nikolic, M., ed. Kinematics & Multi-Particle Systems. (Documents on Modern Physics Ser.). xii, 314p. (Orig.). 1968. text 349.00 (*0-677-01800-2*) Gordon & Breach.

Nikolic, M., ed. see International School of Elementary Particle Physic.

***Nikolic-Ristanovic, Vesa.** Women, Violence & War: Wartime Victimization of Refugees in the Balkans. 2000. pap. text 22.95 (*963-9116-60-2*) Ctrl Europ Univ.

***Nikolic-Ristanovic, Vesna, ed.** Women, Violence & War: Wartime Victimization of Refugees in the Balkans. 300p. (C). 2000. 49.95 (*963-9116-59-9*) Ctrl Europ Univ.

Nikolic-Zugic, Janko, ed. Intrathymic T-Cell Development. LC 93-41387. (Molecular Biology Intelligence Unit Ser.). 110p. 1994. 99.00 (*1-57059-014-1*, LN9014) Landes Bioscience.

Nikolitsis, Nikos T. The Battle of the Granicus. (Acta Instituti Atheniensis Regni Sueciae Ser.: Series 4, Vol. XXI). (Illus.). 76p. (Orig.). 1974. pap. 23.50 (*91-85086-08-8*, Pub. by P Astroms) Coronet Bks.

Nikolopoulos, Chris. Expert Systems: Introduction to First & Second Generation & Hybrid Knowledge Based Systems. LC 96-50429. (Illus.). 336p. 1997. text 110.00 (*0-8247-9927-5*) Dekker.

Nikolopoulou, Anastasia, jt. ed. see Hays, Michael.

Nikolov, Hristo. Dictionary of Plant Names in Latin, German, English & French. (ENG, FRE, GER & LAT.). 926p. 1996. 295.00 (*0-7859-9529-3*) Fr & Eur.

— Dictionary of Plant Names in Latin, German, English & French. LC 96-229541. vi, 926p. 1996. 111.00 (*3-443-50019-6*, Pub. by Gebruder Borntraeger) Balogh.

Nikolov, Lyubomir. Pagan. Flint, Roland & Tcholakova, Viara, trs. from BUL. LC 92-70687. (Poetry Ser.). 48p. (Orig.). 1992. pap. 11.95 (*0-88748-146-9*) Carnegie-Mellon.

Nikolowa, J., et al. Bulgarich-Deutsches Phraseologisches Worterbuch: Bulgarian-German Phraseology Dictionary. (BUL & GER.). 1088p. 1977. 95.00 (*0-8288-5295-2*, M9833) Fr & Eur.

Nikolowski, W., et al. Kohabitations-und Fertilitaets-Stoerungen: Ein Leitfaden fuer die aerztliche Praxis. (Illus.). 1977. 17.50 (*3-8055-2682-2*) S Karger.

Nikol'skaia, T. L., et al, eds. Kofeinia Razbitykh Serdets: Kollektivnaia Shutochnaia P'esa V Stikhakh Pri Uchastii O. E. Manel'shtama. (Stanford Slavic Studies: Vol. 12).Tr. of Specialists in Russian Literature. (RUS.). 89p. 1997. pap. text 15.00 (*1-57201-029-0*) Berkeley Slavic.

Nikolskaia, Tatiana, ed. see Tufanov, Aleksandr V.

Nikolski, N. K., jt. auth. see Havin, V. P.

Nikolski, N. K., jt. ed. see Havin, V. P.

Nikol'skii, G. V. Special Ichthyology: Israel Program for Scientific Translation. Lengy, J. I. & Krauthamer, Z., trs. (RUS., Illus.). 538p. 1989. reprint ed. 55.00 (*1-55528-162-1*, Pub. by Today Tomorrow) Scholarly Pubns.

Nikolskii, N. K. Topics on Toeplitz Operators & Spectral Function Theory. (Operator Theory Ser.: No. 42). 300p. 1989. 156.00 (*0-8176-2344-2*) Birkhauser.

Nikol'skii, N. K. Treatise on the Shift Operator. Peetre, J., tr. from RUS. LC 84-26869. (Grundlehren der Mathematischen Wissenschaften Ser.: Vol. 273). (Illus.). 504p. 1986. 182.95 (*0-387-15021-8*) Spr-Verlag.

Nikol'skii, N. K., ed. Selected Problems of Weighted Approximation & Spectral Analysis: Proceedings. LC 76-46375. (Proceeding of the Steklov Institute of Mathematics Ser.: No. 120). 276p. 1976. pap. 92.00 (*0-8218-3020-1*, STEKLO/120) Am Math.

— Spectral Theory of Functions & Operators. LC 80-1102. (Proceedings of the Steklov Institute of Mathematics Ser.: No. 130). 233p. 1980. pap. 70.00 (*0-8218-3030-9*, STEKLO/130) Am Math.

— Spectral Theory of Functions & Operators, 1983, Vol. II. LC 80-11102. (Proceedings of the Steklov Institute of Mathematics Ser.: Vol. 155). 176p. 1983. pap. text 75.00 (*0-8218-3072-4*, STEKLOV/155) Am Math.

Nikol'skii, S. M. Approximation of Functions of Several Variables & Embedding Theorems. Danskin, J. M., tr. from RUS. LC 74-4652. (Grundlehren der Mathematischen Wissenschaften Ser.: Vol. 205). 450p. 1975. 97.95 (*0-387-06442-7*) Spr-Verlag.

— Theory & Applications of Differentiable Functions of Several Variables. LC 68-1677. 293p. 1990. pap. 154.00 (*0-8218-3131-3*, STEKLO/181) Am Math.

Nikolskii, S. M., ed. Differential Equations & Function Spaces: Dedicated to the Memory of Academician Sergei Lvovich Sobolev: Collection of Papers. LC 92-30907. 256p. 1992. pap. 163.00 (*0-8218-3146-1*, STEKLO/192) Am Math.

— International Conference on Analytic Methods in Number Theory & Analysis. LC 86-47529. (Steklov Institute of Mathematics Ser.: Vol. 163). 319p. 1986. pap. 137.00 (*0-8218-3090-2*, STEKLO/163) Am Math.

— Theory & Application of Differentiable Functions of Several Variables, 16. (Proceedings of the Steklov Institute of Mathematics Ser.: Vol. 204). 260p. 1994. 189.00 (*0-8218-0276-3*, STEKLO/204C) Am Math.

Nikol'skii, S. M., ed. Theory & Applications of Differentiable Functions of Several Variables. LC 68-1677. (Proceedings of the Steklov Institute of Mathematics Ser.: Vol. 156). 403p. 1974. pap. 115.00 (*0-8218-3017-1*, STEKLO/117) Am Math.

— Theory & Applications of Differentiable Functions of Several Variables. LC 84-24501. (Proceedings of the Steklov Institute of Mathematics Ser.: Vol. 161). 253p. 1985. reprint ed. pap. 80.00 (*0-8218-3083-X*, STEKLO/161) Am Math.

— Theory & Applications of Differentiable Functions of Several Variables: Proceedings. (Proceedings of the Steklov Institute of Mathematics Ser.: No. 77). 212p. 1968. pap. 62.00 (*0-8218-1877-5*, STEKLO/77) Am Math.

— Theory & Applications of Differentiable Functions of Several Variables, II: Proceedings. (Proceedings of the Steklov Institute of Mathematics Ser.: No. 89). 290p. 1968. pap. 92.00 (*0-8218-1889-9*, STEKLO/89) Am Math.

— Theory & Applications of Differentiable Functions of

An Asterisk (*) at the beginning of an entry indicates that the title is appearing for the first time.

Several Variables, III: Proceedings. LC 72-681. (Proceedings of the Steklov Institute of Mathematics Ser.: No. 105). 295p. 1971. pap. 62.00 (*0-8218-9900-7*, STEKLO/105) Am Math.

— Theory & Applications of Differentiable Functions of Several Variables, V: Proceedings. (Proceedings of the Steklov Institute of Mathematics Ser.: No. 131). 252p. 1975. pap. 82.00 (*0-8218-3031-7*, STEKLO/131) Am Math.

— Theory & Applications of Differentiable Functions of Several Variables, VII. LC 68-1677. (Proceedings of the Steklov Institute of Mathematics Ser.: Vol. 150). 336p. 1982. reprint ed. pap. 137.00 (*0-8218-3047-3*, STEKLO/150C) Am Math.

— Theory & Applications of Differentiable Functions of Several Variables, 6. (Proceedings of the Steklov Institute of Mathematics Ser.: No. 140). 312p. 1979. pap. 113.00 (*0-8218-3039-2*, STEKLO/140) Am Math.

Nikol'skij, L. B., jt. auth. see Svejcer, Aleksandr D.

Nikol'skij, N. K., jt. auth. see Khavin, V. P.

Nikol'skij, N. K., ed. see Ashurov, R. R., et al.

Nikol'skij, N. K., jt. ed. see Havin, V. P.

Nikol'skij, N. K., ed. see Lyubich, Y. I.

Nikol'skij, S. M. & Gamkrelidze, R. V., eds. Analysis Three: Spaces of Differentiable Functions. Peetre, J., tr. (Encyclopedia of Mathematical Sciences Ser.: Vol. 26). (RUS., Illus.). 232p. 1990. 118.95 (*0-387-51866-5*) Spr-Verlag.

Nikol'skij, S. M., jt. auth. see Maz'ya, V. G.

Nikol'sku, N. K., jt. ed. see Gurarii, V. P.

Nikonowa, O. N. & Zwilling, M. J. Russian-German Dictionary: Russisch-Deutsches Woerterbuch. 8th ed. (GER & RUS.). 798p. 1982. 75.00 (*0-8288-1239-X*, F60170) Fr & Eur.

Nikos, ed. see Wilson, et al.

Nikos, Cheryl, ed. Concerns of Small Business. 33p. 1992. pap. text 10.00 (*0-89834-125-6*, 0323) US Chamber DC.

Nikos, Cheryl, ed. see U. S. Chamber of Commerce Staff & Fasman, Zachary D.

Nikoshkova, E. V. English-Russian Dictionary of Psychology. 352p. (C). 1998. 28.95 (*0-8285-5495-1*) Firebird NY.

Nikpay, Ali, jt. ed. see Faull, Jonathan.

Niks, Sandra L., et al. Composites Bonding. LC 94-35645. (STP Ser.: Vol. 1227). 120p. 1994. 39.00 (*0-8031-1887-2*, STP1227) ASTM.

Niku-Lari, A. Shot Peening. 1981. pap. 26.00 (*0-08-027600-8*, Pergamon Pr) Elsevier.

— Structural Analysis Systems. 1986. 120.00 (*0-08-032581-5*, Pergamon Pr) Elsevier.

— Structural Analysis Systems, 3 vols., Vol. 2. 1986. 40.00 (*0-08-033436-9*, Pergamon Pr) Elsevier.

— Structural Analysis Systems, 3 vols., Vol. 3. 1986. 40.00 (*0-08-033435-0*, Pergamon Pr); 40.00 (*0-08-033437-7*, Pergamon Pr) Elsevier.

Niku-Lari, A. & Ghosh, S. K., eds. CAD-CAM & FEM in Metal Working. LC 88-19669. (Technology Transfer Handbook Ser.). (Illus.). 300p. 1988. 125.00 (*0-08-035917-5*, Pub. by Pergamon Repr) Franklin.

Niku, Lari A., jt. ed. see Waterhouse, R. B.

Niku, Saeed. Engineering Mechanics: Statics. (Illus.). 232p. (C). 1995. text 21.95 (*0-03-026312-3*) OUP.

Nikulin, M., jt. ed. see Limnios, N.

Nikulin, M. S., jt. auth. see Voinov, Vasilii G.

Nikulin, Michael S., jt. auth. see Greenwood, Priscilla E.

Nikulin, N. & Asvarishch, B. German & Austrian Painting in the Hermitage. (Illus.). 424p. (C). 1986. text 450.00 (*0-7855-5860-8*, Pub. by Collets) St Mut.

Nikulin, Nikolai. The Golden Age of Netherlandish Painting (Fifteenth Century) (ENG & RUS., Illus.). 398p. 1981. 174.00 (*0-7855-0702-7*) St Mut.

Nikulin, V. V. & Shafarevich, I. R. Geometries & Groups. (Soviet Mathematics Ser.). (Illus.). 265p. 1994. 64.95 (*0-387-15281-4*) Spr-Verlag.

Nikulinsky, Philippa. 1998 Wildflower Diary. 1997. pap. 19.95 (*1-86368-194-9*, Pub. by Fremantle Arts) Intl Spec Bk.

***Nikulinsky, Philippa & Hopper, Stephen D.** Life on the Rocks: The Art of Survival. (Illus.). 184p. 1999. pap. 24.95 (*1-86368-258-9*, Pub. by Fremantle Arts) Intl Spec Bk.

Nikuradse, Tamara, ed. African-American Wedding Readings. 192p. 1999. pap. 10.95 (*0-452-28023-0*, Plume) Dutton Plume.

Nikuradse, Tamara & Matthews, Scott. To the Man I Love, Thank You for Being Mine. 160p. (Orig.). 1994. pap. 5.99 (*0-449-90914-X*, Columbine) Fawcett.

Nikuradse, Tamara, jt. auth. see Matthews, Scott.

Nikvlin, Nikolai. Netherlandish Paintings in Soviet Museums. (Illus.). 404p. 1990. text 45.00 (*0-7148-2441-0*) Phaidon Pr.

Nila, M. S. Law of Suspension. 3rd rev. ed. (C). 1994. 62.50 (*81-7012-523-5*, Pub. by Eastern Book) St Mut.

Nilan, Robert A., ed. see International Barley Genetics Symposium Staff.

Nilan, Roxanne, jt. auth. see Davis, Margo.

Niland, D'Arcy. The Shiralee. 250p. 1992. reprint ed. lib. bdg. 31.95 (*0-89966-941-7*) Buccaneer Bks.

Niland, John. A History of Sheep Raising in the Great Divide Basin of Wyoming. 2nd ed. (Illus.). 238p. 1995. 27.95 (*1-878117-04-1*) Lagumo Corp.

Niland, John, et al, eds. The Future of Industrial Relations: Global Change & Challenges. LC 93-48901. 384p. (C). 1994. text 52.00 (*0-8039-5547-2*) Sage.

Niland, John & Clarke, Oliver, eds. Agenda for Change: An International Analysis of Industrial Relations in Transition. 224p. 1991. pap. 24.95 (*0-04-442270-9*, Pub. by Allen & Unwin Pty) Paul & Co Pubs.

Niland, Kurt R. & Armstrong, Scott. The Spirit of the Place Vol. 1: The Emerald-Coast Celebrates Its Finest Restaurants, Chefs, & Cuisine. (Illus.). 154p. 1995. pap. 18.95 (*0-9645334-0-5*) Oracle Pub.

Nilausen, Jesper. APPN Networks. LC 93-50760. (Illus.). 191p. 1994. reprint ed. pap. 59.30 (*0-608-05310-4*, 206584800001) Bks Demand.

Nilcae, Grace S., jt. ed. see Madigan, Mary G.

Nile, David. Edward Elgar. (Classic FM Lifelines Ser.). (Illus.). 112p. 1997. 9.95 (*1-85793-977-8*, Pub. by Pavilion Bks Ltd) Trafalgar.

Nile, Lauren N. Developing Diversity Training for the Workplace: A Guide for Trainers. 4th ed. 220p. 1997. teacher ed., ring bd. 149.95 (*1-885077-40-8*) NMCI Pubns.

***Nile, Lauren N.** Developing Diversity Training for the Workplace: A Guide for Trainers. 6th rev. ed. xvi, 333p. 1999. 149.95 (*1-885077-41-6*) NMCI Pubns.

Nile, Richard. Australian Aborigines. LC 92-17044. (Threatened Cultures Ser.). (Illus.). 48p. (J). (gr. 5-6). 1992. lib. bdg. 24.26 (*0-8114-2303-4*) Raintree Steck-V.

***Nile, Richard.** Threatened Cultures. 1999. pap. 152.82 (*0-8172-9645-X*) Raintree Steck-V.

Nile, Richard, ed. Australian Civilization. 272p. 1995. pap. text 28.00 (*0-19-553504-9*) OUP.

— The Australian Legend & Its Discontents. 2000. pap. 19.95 (*0-7022-2985-7*, Pub. by Univ Queensland Pr) Intl Spec Bk.

Nile, Richard & Clerk, Christian. Cultural Atlas of Australia, New Zealand, & the South Pacific. LC 96-1456. (Illus.). 240p. 1996. 50.00 (*0-8160-3083-9*) Facts on File.

Niles. Federal Civil Procedure. 3rd ed. LC 98-67060. 851p. 1998. ring bd. 115.00 (*0-327-00586-6*, 8045111) LEXIS Pub.

Niles, Ann, ed. CD-ROM Book Index: An International Guide to Full-Text Books on CD-ROM. 207p. 1995. pap. 39.50 (*0-938734-98-9*) Info Today Inc.

Niles, Blair. Rivers of America - The James. lib. bdg. 25.95 (*0-8488-2008-8*) Amereon Ltd.

— Strange Brother. LC 75-12341. (Homosexuality Ser.). 1975. reprint ed. 17.95 (*0-405-07390-9*) Ayer.

***Niles, Bo.** Boutique Restaurant. 2000. 50.00 (*0-86636-788-8*) PBC Intl Inc.

Niles, Bo. Country Living Country Decorating: Achieving the Country Look, Room by Room. Bramson, Ann, ed. LC 88-4112. (Illus.). 256p. 1988. 29.95 (*0-688-08073-1*, Hearst) Hearst Commns.

— Living with Lace. LC 90-34556. (Illus.). 176p. 1990. 35.00 (*1-55670-156-X*) Stewart Tabori & Chang.

— Living with Lace. rev. ed. (Illus.). 176p. 1999. pap. text 20.00 (*1-55670-447-X*) Stewart Tabori & Chang.

— Make Yourself at Home. 192p. 1995. mass mkt. 4.99 (*0-425-14536-0*); mass mkt. 4.99 (*0-425-14539-5*) Berkley Pub.

— Timeless Design. LC 96-49986. 1997. pap. 34.95 (*0-86636-544-3*) PBC Intl Inc.

— Timeless Design. LC 96-49986. 1997. 34.95 (*0-86636-543-5*) PBC Intl Inc.

— White by Design. LC 84-228. (Illus.). 200p. 1984. 40.00 (*0-941434-54-0*); pap. 24.95 (*1-55670-277-9*) Stewart Tabori & Chang.

Niles, Bo & Kate's Paperie Staff. Paperie: The Art of Writing & Wrapping with Paper. LC 98-33664. (Illus.). 192p. 1999. 35.00 (*0-684-84423-0*) S&S Trade.

Niles, Bo & McNiff, Veronica. The Big Cup: A Guide to New York's Coffee Culture. 2nd rev. ed. LC 97-12220. Orig. Title: The New York Book of Coffee & Cake. 128p. 1997. pap. 12.95 (*1-885492-19-7*) City & Co.

— The New York Book of Tea: Where to Take Tea & Buy Tea & Teaware. 2nd rev. ed. LC 97-8247. (Illus.). 128p. 1997. 18.00 (*1-885492-37-5*) City & Co.

Niles, Bo, jt. auth. see MacLachlan, Cheryl.

Niles, Chris. Run Time. 1999. reprint ed. mass mkt. 5.99 (*0-425-17119-1*, Prime Crime) Berkley Pub.

— Spike It. 272p. 1998. pap. 5.99 (*0-425-16565-5*, Prime Crime) Berkley Pub.

Niles, Cornelia D., ed. see Smithsonian Institution, Washington, D. C. Staff.

Niles, Douglas. Advanced Dungeons & Dragons: Complete Thief Manual. 2nd ed. 1990. 20.00 (*0-88038-780-7*, Pub. by TSR Inc) Random.

— A Breach in the Watershed. 448p. (Orig.). 1995. pap. 13.00 (*0-441-00208-0*) Ace Bks.

— A Breach in the Watershed. (Watershed Ser.: No. 1). (Orig.). 1996. pap. 6.99 (*0-441-00349-4*) Ace Bks.

***Niles, Douglas.** Circle at Center. Vol. 1. 400p. 2000. pap. 13.00 (*0-441-00728-7*) Ace Bks.

Niles, Douglas. The Complete Book of Gnomes & Halflings. (Advanced Dungeons & Dragons, Second Edition; Al-Qadim Ser.). (Illus.). 1993. 18.00 (*1-56076-573-9*, Pub. by TSR Inc) Random.

— Cult of the Reptile God. 1982. 5.50 (*0-394-52864-6*) Random.

— Curse of Xanathon, No. 3. 1983. 5.50 (*0-394-53069-1*) Random.

— Darkenheight. (Watershed Trilogy Ser.: No. 2). 416p. 1996. pap. 13.95 (*0-441-00333-8*) Ace Bks.

— The Dragons. (DragonLance Lost Histories Ser.). 1996. pap. 5.99 (*0-7869-0513-1*, Pub. by TSR Inc) Random.

— Horror on the Hill. 1983. 6.00 (*0-394-53345-3*) Random.

— The Kagonesti. (DragonLance Lost Histories Ser.: No. 1). 320p. (Orig.). 1995. pap. 5.99 (*0-7869-0091-1*, Pub. by TSR Inc) Random.

— The Last Thane. (DragonLance Chaos War Ser.). 1998. pap. 5.99 (*0-7869-1172-7*, Pub. by TSR Inc) Random.

— The Rod of Seven Parts. LC 95-62073. 1996. 21.99 (*0-7869-0479-8*, Pub. by TSR Inc) Random.

— Seeds of Chaos. 1998. pap. 13.95 (*0-7869-1198-0*, Pub. by TSR Inc) Random.

— War of Three Waters. (Watershed Trilogy Ser.: Bk. 3). 1997. pap. 14.00 (*0-614-27309-9*) Ace Bks.

— War of Three Waters. (Watershed Trilogy Ser.). 1998. mass mkt. 6.99 (*0-441-00532-2*) Ace Bks.

— The Watershed Trilogy Book: Darkenheight, Vol. 2. (Watershed Trilogy Ser.). 480p. 1997. mass mkt. 6.99 (*0-441-00456-3*) Ace Bks.

— The Watershed Trilogy 3: War of Three Waters, Vol. 3. LC 97-183794. (Watershed Ser.). 384p. 1997. pap. 14.00 (*0-441-00442-3*) Ace Bks.

***Niles, Douglas & Dobson, Michael.** Fox on the Rhine. 416p. 2000. 27.95 (*0-312-86894-4*) Forge NYC.

Niles, Douglas & Miller, Steve. DragonLance Reader's Companion: The Odyssey of Gilthanas. (DragonLance Ser.). (Illus.). 316p. 1999. mass mkt. 6.99 (*0-7869-1446-7*, Pub. by TSR Inc) Random.

Niles, Douglas, jt. auth. see Kirchoff, Mary.

Niles, Edward. Federal Civil Procedure. 3rd ed. 1001p. 1998. ring bd. write for info. (*0-327-00129-1*, 80453-20) LEXIS Pub.

— House Design: Edward Niles. 1998. pap. text 19.95 (*1-86470-006-8*) Images.

Niles, Edward I. California Arbitration Handbook. LC 96-68797. 1996. spiral bd. 120.00 (*1-55834-358-X*, 80294-10, MICHIE) LEXIS Pub.

— Federal Civil Procedure. 2nd ed. 700p. 1994. spiral bd. 95.00 (*1-55943-148-2*, MICHIE) LEXIS Pub.

— Federal Civil Procedure. 3rd ed. LC 98-67060. 1997. write for info. (*1-55834-253-2*) LEXIS Pub.

***Niles, Edward I.** Federal Civil Procedure, Issue 1. 100p. 1999. ring bd. write for info. (*0-327-01665-5*, 8045221) LEXIS Pub.

Niles, Edward I., jt. auth. see Faber, Stuart J.

Niles, Eldredge. The Pattern of Evolution. LC 98-34754. 250p. 1998. text 24.95 (*0-7167-3046-4*) W H Freeman.

Niles, Francis L., jt. auth. see McNally, Margaret Cheney.

Niles, Gayle L. & Snider, Douglas H. Woman's Counsel: A Legal Guide for Women. LC 84-11161. 240p. (Orig.). 1984. pap. 8.50 (*0-912869-04-6*) Arden Pr.

Niles, Grace G. Hoosac Valley: Its Legend & Its History. 584p. 1993. reprint ed. lib. bdg. 99.00 (*0-7812-5191-5*) Rprt Serv.

— The Hoosac Valley - Its Legends & Its History. (Illus.). xxv, 584p. 1997. reprint ed. pap. 39.50 (*0-7884-0686-8*, N350) Heritage Bk.

***Niles, J.** Ballad Book of John Jacob Niles. 2000. pap. 9.95 (*0-486-41094-3*) Dover.

Niles, J. Niles, Songs of John Jacob: Low Voice & Piano. 1993. per. 12.95 (*0-7935-2334-6*) H Leonard.

Niles, J. J. I Wonder As I Wander: A Capella Soprano or Tenor Solo. 8p. 1986. pap. 1.25 (*0-7935-5495-0*, 50300910) H Leonard.

— I Wonder As I Wander: For Handbells. 8p. 1994. pap. 3.95 (*0-7935-5525-6*, 50482212) H Leonard.

— I Wonder As I Wander: Low Voice & Piano in B Flat. 6p. 1986. pap. 3.95 (*0-7935-5349-0*, 50283290) H Leonard.

— I Wonder As I Wonder: High Voice & Piano in E Flat Major. 6p. 1986. pap. 3.95 (*0-7935-5346-6*, 50283300) H Leonard.

Niles, John D. Beowulf: The Poem & Its Tradition. LC 83-4308. 320p. 1983. reprint ed. pap. 99.20 (*0-7837-2304-0*, 205739200004) Bks Demand.

— Homo Narrans: The Poetics & Anthropology of Oral Literature LC 99-10074. 1999. 45.00 (*0-8122-3504-5*) U of Pa Pr.

Niles, John D. & Amodio, Mark, eds. Anglo-Scandinavian England: Norse-English Relations in the Period Before Conquest. LC 88-31728. (Old English Colloquium Ser.: No. 4). 94p. (Orig.). (C). 1989. pap. text 17.00 (*0-8191-7268-5*); lib. bdg. 29.00 (*0-8191-7267-7*) U Pr of Amer.

Niles, John D., jt. ed. see Bjork, Robert E.

Niles, John D., jt. ed. see Frantzen, Allen J.

Niles, John D., tr. see Luthi, Max.

Niles, John J. The Songs of John Jacob Niles: For High Voice & Piano. 104p. 1990. otabind 12.95 (*0-7935-2584-5*, 50481076) H Leonard.

Niles, John J. & Merton, Thomas. The Niles-Merton Songs: Opus 171 & 172. (Illus.). 95p. 1981. spiral bd. 15.95 (*0-916656-16-0*, MF755) Mark Foster Mus.

Niles, John J., jt. auth. see Hall, Bert.

***Niles, John Jacob.** The Ballad Book of John Jacob Niles. (Illus.). 400p. 2000. reprint ed. pap. 30.00 (*0-8131-0987-6*) U Pr of Ky.

Niles, Kathleen M., jt. auth. see Broccolo, Bernadette M.

Niles, Kathryn B. Food Preparation Recipes. LC 55-5964. 372p. reprint ed. pap. 115.40 (*0-8357-9892-5*, 205518700011) Bks Demand.

Niles, Lori, ed. Amazing Science Devotions for Children's Ministry. LC 98-21717. (Illus.). 96p. (J). 1998. per. 14.99 (*0-7644-2105-0*, Vital Ministry) Group Pub.

— Bible Story Games for Preschool. LC 97-52258. (Illus.). 112p. (J). (ps). 1998. per. 15.99 (*0-7644-2059-3*, Vital Ministry) Group Pub.

— Character Builders: Practical Activities for Children's Ministry. LC 98-12122. (Illus.). 112p. (J). 1998. per. 14.99 (*0-7644-2061-5*, Vital Ministry) Group Pub.

— Just-Add-Kids Games for Children's Ministry. LC 98-20200. (Illus.). 112p. (J). 1998. per. 14.99 (*0-7644-2112-3*, Vital Ministry) Group Pub.

— The Ultimate Bible Guide for Children's Ministry: Making the Bible a Kid's Lifelong Friend. LC 98-45392. (Illus.). 96p. (J). (ps-6). 1998. per. 14.99 (*0-7644-2076-3*, Vital Ministry) Group Pub.

Niles, Lori, jt. ed. see Group Publishing Staff.

Niles, Lori H., jt. auth. see Capehart, Jody.

Niles, Lori H., jt. auth. see Sikes, Kim.

Niles, Nathan O. & Haborak, George E. Calculus with Analytic Geometry. 2nd ed. (Illus.). 640p. 1982. text 60.00 (*0-13-112011-5*) P-H.

Niles, Nathaniel. The American Hero: A Sapphick Ode. 1975. 3.00 (*0-89073-039-3*, 103) Boston Public Lib.

***Niles, Nolene.** Rare & Beautiful Treasures. 168p. 2000. 14.99 (*1-56322-071-7*) Hensley Pub.

Niles, Olive S. & Purves, Alan C., eds. Becoming Readers in a Complex Society. LC 83-62344. (National Society for the Study of Education Yearbook Ser.: No. 83). xii, 324p. (C). 1984. lib. bdg. 20.00 (*0-226-60137-4*) U Ch Pr.

Niles, Phillip, ed. see Pelizza, John J.

Niles, Richard. Time-Saving Training for Multisport Athletes: How to Fit Workouts into Workdays. LC 96-31260. (Illus.). 192p. (Orig.). 1997. pap. 16.95 (*0-88011-538-6*, PNIL0538) Human Kinetics.

Niles, Susan A. Callachaca: Style & Status in an Inca Community. LC 87-16782. (Illus.). 264p. 1987. text 32.95 (*0-87745-177-X*) U of Iowa Pr.

— The Dickeyville Grotto: The Vision of Father Mathias Wernerus. LC 96-37975. (Folk Art & Artists Ser.). 1997. pap. 16.95 (*0-87805-996-2*) U Pr of Miss.

— The Shape of Inca History: Narrative & Architecture in an Andean Empire. LC 98-51181. (Illus.). 360p. 1999. text 49.95 (*0-87745-673-9*) U of Iowa Pr.

Niles, W. E. Taxonomic Investigations in the Genera Perityle & Laphamia (Compositae) (Memoirs Ser.: Vol. 21 (1)). (Illus.). 82p. 1970. pap. 10.00 (*0-89327-070-9*) NY Botanical.

Nilges, Richard G. Cycles. LC 80-12889. 1983. pap. 14.95 (*0-87949-182-5*) Ashley Bks.

Nilius, R. & Paquet, K. J., eds. Lebererkrankungen: Praevention, Progressionshemmung, Rehabilitation. (Illus.). viii, 232p. 1995. 143.50 (*3-8055-6171-7*) S Karger.

Nilkanth, H. G., tr. see Desai, Mahadev.

Nill, Annegreth, jt. auth. see Caldwell, John, pseud.

Nill, Kimball R. Glossary of Biotechnology Terms. 2nd ed. LC 97-62206. 225p. 1997. 49.95 (*1-56676-580-3*) Technomic.

Nilles. Teleworking. 1999. pap. text. write for info. (*0-13-905134-1*) P-H.

Nilles, Burgandy & Thiewes, Sam. Beauty & the Beast. (Favorite Fairy Tales Ser.). 24p. (J). (gr. 2-4). 1993. lib. bdg. 11.95 (*1-56674-061-4*, HTS Bks) Forest Hse.

— Goldilocks & the Three Bears. (Favorite Fairy Tales Ser.). 24p. (J). (gr. 2-4). 1993. lib. bdg. 11.95 (*1-56674-063-0*, HTS Bks) Forest Hse.

Nilles, Camilla J. & Winter, Ian J., intros. Rabelais et Montaigne: Chapitres Choisis. LC 91-29802. 596p. 1991. lib. bdg. 119.95 (*0-7734-9704-8*) E Mellen.

***Nilles, Jack.** Managing Telework: Strategies for Managing the Virtual Workforce. LC 98-13509. (Upside Bks.). 352p. 1998. 29.95 (*0-471-29316-4*) Wiley.

Nilles, Jack M. Exploring the World of the Personal Computer. (Illus.). 256p. 1982. 17.95 (*0-13-297572-6*); text 19.39 (*0-685-03857-2*) P-H.

— Making Telecommuting Happen: A Guide for Telemanagers & Telecommuters. 196p. 1994. pap. 25.95 (*0-442-01857-6*, VNR) Wiley.

Nilles, Mary E. In a Large Circle of Relatives: A Genealogical Guide to the Early Community of Rollingstone, Minnesota. (Illus.). 525p. 1989. pap. 30.00 (*0-9616845-1-8*) M E Nilles.

— A Legacy from Luxembourg: A Historical Guide to the Early Settlement of Rollingstone, Minnesota. 154p. (Orig.). 1986. pap. 9.95 (*0-9616845-0-X*) M E Nilles.

Nilles, Myrah J. Fix My Hair Pretty: Hair Designs for Young Girls. (Illus.). 64p. (Orig.). 1985. pap. 6.95 (*0-9613683-0-6*) Nilles Pub.

Nillsen, Rodney Victor. Difference Spaces & Invariant Linear Forms. (Lecture Notes in Mathematics Ser.: Vol. 1586). 1994. write for info. (*3-540-58323-8*) Spr-Verlag.

— Difference Spaces & Invariant Linear Forms. (Lecture Notes in Mathematics Ser.: Vol. 1586). 1994. 35.95 (*0-387-58323-8*) Spr-Verlag.

Nilmani, M., et al, eds. Fifth Australasian-Asian Pacific Conference Aluminum Cast House Technology Theory & Practice: Aluminum Cast House Technology Theory & Practice. LC 97-12379. (Illus.). 420p. 1997. 80.00 (*0-87339-378-3*, 3783) Minerals Metals.

Nilmani, Madhu, ed. Aluminium Cast House Technology: Theory & Practice. LC 93-78760. (Illus.). 427p. 1993. pap. 132.40 (*0-608-04883-6*, 206557500004) Bks Demand.

— Aluminum Cast House Technology - Theory & Practice: Australasian Asian Pacific Conference on Aluminum Cast House Technology (4th) (Illus.). 407p. 1995. 20.00 (*0-87339-298-1*, 2981) Minerals Metals.

Nilmani, Madhu, et al, eds. Pyrometallurgy for Complex Materials & Wastes: International Conference Staged by the G. K. Williams Cooperative Research Centre of the Department of Chemical Engineering, University of Melbourne, Held at the University of Melbourne, Victoria, Australia, June 6-8, 1994. LC 94-76293. 403p. 1994. reprint ed. pap. 125.00 (*0-608-03829-6*, 206279100004) Bks Demand.

Nilmani, Madhu & Lehner, Theo, eds. The Howard Worner International Symposium on Injection in Pyrometallurgy. (Illus.). 478p. 1996. 80.00 (*0-87339-341-4*) Minerals Metals.

Nilne, William, jt. auth. see Lownie, Andrew.

Nilon, Charles H. Bibliography of Bibliographies in American Literature. LC 73-103542. xi, 483p. 1970. write for info. (*0-8352-0259-3*) Bowker.

— Bibliography of Bibliographies in American Literature. LC 73-103542. 495p. reprint ed. pap. 153.50 (*0-8357-7178-4*, 201329900084) Bks Demand.

Nilos. Law of the Sea Document Yearbook. 1900. lib. bdg. write for info. (*0-86010-598-9*) Kluwer Academic.

***NILS Publishing Company.** Maine Related Regulations. LC 98-66834. (Illus.). 1999. write for info. (*0-89246-501-8*) NILS Pub.

N

An Asterisk (*) at the beginning of an entry indicates that the title is appearing for the first time.

…tions. LC 97-76152. 1999. write … NILS Pub.

…ions. LC 97-69597. (Illus.). 1997. …89246-483-6) NILS Pub.

…ed Regulations. LC 98-66244. (Illus.). … for info. (0-89246-499-2) NILS Pub.

…ishing Company, jt. auth. see Arkansas.

…Publishing Company, jt. auth. see Michigan.

…ILS Publishing Company, jt. auth. see Montana.

NILS Publishing Company, jt. auth. see Tennessee.

NILS Publishing Company Staff. Iowa Insurance Laws. LC 97-76486. 1997. ring bd. write for info. (*0-89246-486-0*) NILS Pub.

— Ohio Related Laws to the Insurance Laws, 2 vols. LC 98-67440. 1998. ring bd. write for info. (*0-89246-502-6*) NILS Pub.

Nilsen. Living Language: Reading, Thinking & Writing. LC 98-30375. 490p. 1998. pap. text 37.00 (*0-205-27091-3*) Allyn.

Nilsen, jt. auth. see Albertalli.

Nilsen, Alleen P. & Donelson, Kenneth L. LIterature for Today's Young Adult. 5th ed. LC 95-26604. 640p. (YA). 1997. pap. 74.00 (*0-673-99737-5*) HarpC.

Nilsen, Alf J., jt. auth. see Fossa, Svein A.

Nilsen, Alleen P. Presenting M. E. Kerr. (Twayne's Young Adult Authors Ser.: No. 527). 136p. 1986. 20.95 (*0-8057-8202-8*, Twyne) Mac Lib Ref.

Nilsen, Alleen P., ed. Presenting M. E. Kerr. rev. ed. LC 96-39134. (Young Adult Authors Ser.). 173p. (YA). (gr. 8 up). 1997. 24.95 (*0-8057-9248-1*, Twyne) Mac Lib Ref.

Nilsen, Alleen P. & Donelson, Kenneth L. Lit for Today's Young Adults. 3rd ed. (C). 1989. 56.00 (*0-673-38400-4*) Addson-Wesley Educ.

Nilsen, Alleen Pace & Nilsen, Don L. F. Encyclopedia of 20th-Century American Humor: Patterns, Trends & Connections. LC 99-47257. (Illus.). 384p. 2000. boxed set 67.50 (*1-57356-218-1*) Oryx Pr.

***Nilsen, Angela & Maxwell, Sarah.** Cake Decorator's Bible. 2000. pap. 19.95 (*1-84215-082-0*) Anness Pub.

Nilsen, Angela, jt. auth. see Maxwell, Sarah.

***Nilsen, Anna.** Art Fraud Detective: Spot the Difference, Solve the Crime. (Illus.). 48p. (YA). 2000. 15.95 (*0-7534-5308-8*) LKC.

Nilsen, Anna. Dinosaur Sticker Book. (Illus.). 16p. (J). (ps-k). 1998. pap. 3.99 (*0-7636-0418-6*) Candlewick Pr.

***Nilsen, Anna.** I Can Add: Flip-Card Fun with Adding Games. (I Can Count Ser.). (Illus.). 26p. (YA). (ps-3). 2000. spiral bd. 9.95 (*0-7534-5238-3*, Kingfisher) LKC.

Nilsen, Anna. I Can Count 1 to 10. (Illus.). 23p. (J). (ps-2). 1999. teacher ed. 9.95 (*0-7534-5181-6*) LKC.

— I Can Count 10 to 20. (Illus.). 23p. (J). (ps-2). 1999. teacher ed. 9.95 (*0-7534-5189-1*) LKC.

— I Can Spell--Words with Four Letters. LC 97-39698. 26p. (J). (ps-2). 1998. 9.95 (*0-7534-5125-5*) LKC.

***Nilsen, Anna.** I Can Spell--Words with Three Letters. LC 97-39702. 26p. (J). (ps-2). 1998. 9.95 (*0-7534-5124-7*) LKC.

— I Can Subtract: Flip-Card Fun with Subtracting Games. (I Can Count Ser.). (Illus.). 26p. (YA). (ps-3). 2000. spiral bd. 9.95 (*0-7534-5239-1*, Kingfisher) LKC.

Nilsen, Anna. In the Jungle: A Sticker Book. (Illus.). 16p. (J). 1998. pap. 3.99 (*0-7636-0457-7*) Candlewick Pr.

— Let's All Leap & Jump! (Illus.). 24p. (J). 1999. 10.95 (*1-84089-157-2*) LKC.

***Nilsen, Anna.** Let's All Swim & Dive! (Illus.). 24p. (J). 1999. 10.95 (*1-84089-156-4*) LKC.

— Mousemazia: Am Amazing Dream House Maze. LC 99-52865. (Illus.). 24p. (YA). (gr. 2 up). 2000. 11.99 (*0-7636-1251-0*, Pub. by Candlewick Pr) Penguin Putnam.

Nilsen, Anna. My Favorite Fairy Tales: A Sticker Book. (Illus.). 16p. (J). (ps-1). 1999. pap. text 3.99 (*0-7636-0501-8*) Candlewick Pr.

— On the Farm: A Sticker Book. (Illus.). 16p. (J). 1998. pap. 3.99 (*0-7636-0499-2*) Candlewick Pr.

— People in My Neighborhood Sticker Book. (Illus.). 16p. (J). (ps-k). 1998. pap. 3.99 (*0-7636-0430-5*) Candlewick Pr.

— Terrormazia. LC 95-67535. (Candlewick Gamebooks Ser.). (Illus.). 32p. (J). (gr. 1-4). 1996. reprint ed. pap. 7.99 (*1-56402-865-8*) Candlewick Pr.

— Terrormazia: A Hole New Kind of Maze Game. LC 95-67535. (Illus.). 32p. (J). (gr. k up). 1995. 12.95 (*1-56402-461-X*) Candlewick Pr.

— Under the Sea Sticker Book. (Illus.). 16p. (Orig.). (J). (ps-k). 1998. pap. 3.99 (*0-7636-0434-8*) Candlewick Pr.

— Where Are Percy's Friends? LC 95-72153. (Illus.). 16p. (J). (ps-3). 1996. 7.99 (*0-7636-0017-2*) Candlewick Pr.

— Where Is Percy's Dinner? LC 95-83547. (Illus.). 16p. (J). (ps-3). 1996. 7.99 (*0-7636-0019-9*) Candlewick Pr.

Nilsen, Anna & Axworthy, Anni. Let's All Dig & Burrow! LC 99-161890. (Animals on the Move Ser.). (J). 1998. 10.95 (*1-84089-003-7*) Zero to Ten.

— Let's All Hang & Dangle! LC 98-60346. (Animals on the Move Ser.). (J). 1998. 10.95 (*1-84089-002-9*) Zero to Ten.

Nilsen, Anna, tr. see Farkas, Gyorgy.

Nilsen, B. & Olsen, J., eds. Storage of Gases in Rock Caverns: Proceedings of the International Conference, Trondheim, 26-28 June 1989. 480p. 1989. 201.00 (*90-6191-896-0*, Pub. by A A Balkema) Ashgate Pub Co.

***Nilsen, Barbara.** Week by Week: Plans for Observing & Recording Young Children. 2nd ed. (Illus.). 2000. pap. text. write for info. (*0-7668-1054-2*) Delmar.

Nilsen, Barbara. Week by Week: Plans for Observing & Recording Young Children's Development. LC 96-12008. (Early Childhood Education Ser.). 320p. (C). 1997. mass mkt. 54.95 (*0-8273-7646-4*) Delmar.

Nilsen, Barbara A. Early Education: Observation & Recording. (Early Childhood Education Ser.). (C). 1996. teacher ed. 9.00 (*0-8273-7647-2*) Delmar.

***Nilsen, Beth A.** Burning Down the House, Cooking with Kids. (Illus.). 96p. (J). 2000. pap. 9.95 (*0-9701019-0-2*) T C Pubng.

Nilsen, Clifford L. Managing the Analytical Laboratory: Plain & Simple. 337p. 1996. ring bd. 179.00 (*1-57491-015-9*) Interpharm.

— The QC Laboratory Chemist: Plain & Simple. (Illus.). 275p. 1997. ring bd. 159.00 (*1-57491-053-1*) Interpharm.

Nilsen, Dave. The Backwoods Guide to Computer Lingo. 2nd ed. (Illus.). 80p. 1995. reprint ed. pap. 6.95 (*0-9649972-1-5*) Cowsamungus.

— The Vermonters' Guide to Computer Lingo. (Illus.). 80p. (Orig.). 1995. pap. 6.95 (*0-9649972-0-7*) Cowsamungus.

Nilsen, Diana. Where You Live Counts. 1999. pap. 6.95 (*1-881542-57-2*) Blue Star Prodns.

— Your Pet's Horoscope. LC 98-11167. (Illus.). 192p. (gr. 4-7). 1999. pap. 7.95 (*1-56718-488-X*) Llewellyn Pubns.

Nilsen, Don L. English Adverbials. (Janua Linguarum, Ser. Practica: No. 125). 1972. pap. text 42.35 (*90-279-2146-6*) Mouton.

— Humor in American Literature: A Selected Annotated Bibliography. LC 91-42821. 584p. 1992. text 25.00 (*0-8240-8395-4*, H#1049) Garland.

— Humor in British Literature, from the Middle Ages to the Restoration: A Reference Guide. LC 96-26190. 256p. 1997. lib. bdg. 79.50 (*0-313-29706-1*) Greenwood.

— Humor in Eighteenth & Nineteenth-Century British Literature: A Reference Guide. LC 98-14819. 312p. 1998. lib. bdg. 75.00 (*0-313-29705-3*, Greenwood Pr) Greenwood.

— Humor in Irish Literature: A Reference Guide. LC 95-39489. 248p. 1996. lib. bdg. 67.95 (*0-313-29551-4*, Greenwood Pr) Greenwood.

— Humor Scholarship: A Research Bibliography, 1. LC 92-38989. (Bibliographies & Indexes in Popular Culture Ser.). 416p. 1993. lib. bdg. 65.00 (*0-313-28441-5*, NHS/) Greenwood.

— The Instrumental Case in English: Syntactic & Semantic Considerations. LC 72-94490. (Janua Linguarum, Ser. Minor: No. 156). (Illus.). 187p. 1973. pap. text 43.10 (*90-279-2387-6*) Mouton.

— Toward a Semantic Specification of Deep Case. (Janua Linguarum, Ser. Minor: No. 152). 52p. (Orig.). 1972. text 34.65 (*90-279-2318-3*) Mouton.

***Nilsen, Don L. F.** Humor in Twentieth-Century British Literature: A Reference Guide. LC 99-54482. 576p. 2000. lib. bdg. write for info. (*0-313-29424-0*) Greenwood.

Nilsen, Don L. F., jt. auth. see Nilsen, Alleen Pace.

Nilsen, Erik T. & Orcutt, David M. The Physiology of Plants under Stress Vol. 1: Abiotic Factors, Vol. 1. 2nd ed. LC 96-5443. 704p. 1996. 175.00 (*0-471-03152-6*) Wiley.

Nilsen, Erik T., jt. auth. see Orcutt, David M.

Nilsen, Frances S. & Salter, James L. Amerigo: The Amerigo Vespucci Story. LC 92-93878. (Illus.). 253p. (YA). (gr. 10-12). 1992. 14.95 (*0-9633937-6-6*) Shamrock TN.

Nilsen-Hamilton, Marit, ed. Growth Factors & Signal Transduction in Development. (Modern Cell Biology Ser.: Vol. 14). 244p. 1994. 165.00 (*0-471-30539-1*) Wiley.

***Nilsen, Kim Robert.** The Cohos Trail: The Guidebook to New Hampshire's Great Unknown. (Illus.). 224p. 2000. pap. 17.95 (*0-9637077-7-9*, Pub. by Nicolin Flds) A C Hood.

***Nilsen, Kirsti.** The Impact of Information Policy: Measuring the Effects of the Commercialization of Canadian Government Statistics. LC 99-58738. 2000. write for info. (*1-56750-509-0*) Ablx Pub.

Nilsen, Marit-Jentoft & Trendall, Arthur D. Corpus Vasorum Antiquorum, United States of America, Fascicule 26: The J. Paul Getty Museum, Fascicule 3. LC 88-12781. (Illus.). 50p. 1990. 90.00 (*0-89236-172-7*, Pub. by J P Getty Trust) OUP.

Nilsen, Mary Y. Our Family Shares Advent: Scripture, Prayer, & Activities for Families. (Illus.). 64p. (Orig.). (J). (gr. 1-8). 1981. 7.95 (*0-86683-637-3*, 8129) Harper SF.

— Tending the Family Tree: A Family-Centered, Bible-Based Experience for Church Groups. 80p. (Orig.). 1982. 7.95 (*0-86683-169-X*) Harper SF.

— A Time for Peace: Daily Meditations for Twelve-Step Living. Friedman, R. Cheryl, ed. LC 90-90177. (Illus.). 416p. (Orig.). 1990. pap. 8.95 (*0-9627147-0-4*) Zion Pub.

***Nilsen, Mary Y., et al.** For Everything a Season: 75 Blessings for Daily Life. (Illus.). ix, 81p. 1999. pap. 14.95 (*0-9627147-1-2*) Zion Pub.

Nilsen, Odd. A Bibliography of the Mineral Resources of Tanzania. 92p. 1980. write for info. (*91-7106-173-8*, Pub. by Nordic Africa) Transaction Pubs.

Nilsen, Per. Prince the First Decade: DanceMusicSexRomance. 224p. 1999. pap. 18.95 (*0-946719-23-3*, Pub. by Helter Skelter) Interlink Pub.

Nilsen, Per, jt. ed. see Eagles, Paul F.

Nilsen, Ragnar, ed. Conference on Tools for the Simulation Profession, 1989. 76p. 1989. pap. 20.00 (*0-911801-53-7*, EMC89-1) Soc Computer Sim.

Nilsen, Richard, ed. see Point Foundation Staff.

Nilsen, Robert. Moon Handbooks: South Korea. 2nd ed. (Illus.). 820p. 1997. pap. 19.95 (*1-56691-074-9*, Moon Handbks) Avalon Travel.

Nilsen, Robert, jt. auth. see Bisignani, Joe D.

Nilsen, Sigurd R. Employment Training: Successful Projects Share Common Strategy. (Illus.). 48p. 1997. pap. text 20.00 (*0-7881-4682-3*) DIANE Pub.

Nilsen, Sigurd R. & Sylvia, Wayne. Job Corps: Need for Better Enrollment Guidance & Improved Placement Measures. (Illus.). 76p. (C). 1998. pap. text 20.00 (*0-7881-7554-8*) DIANE Pub.

Nilsen, Sigurd R., et al. U. S. Commission on Civil Rights: Agency Lacks Basic Management Controls. (Illus.). 75p. (C). 1998. pap. text 20.00 (*0-7881-7545-9*) DIANE Pub.

Nilsen, Thomas R. Ethics of Speech Communication. 2nd ed. LC 72-86834. 1974. pap. 3.50 (*0-672-61300-X*, SC10, Bobbs) Macmillan.

Nilsen, Thor Sigurd. British & American English Pronunciation. 267p. 1996. pap. 34.00 (*82-00-22562-3*) Scandnvan Univ Pr.

Nilsen, Tor H., jt. ed. see Ingersoll, Raymond V.

Nilson. Bible Break. 1996. pap. 2.95 (*0-7601-0650-9*) Brentwood Music.

— Design Concrete Structures. 11th ed. 1991. student ed. 23.75 (*0-07-046568-1*) McGraw.

— Pronounciation of Contrast English. 112p. 1987. pap. text 19.93 (*0-13-730938-4*) P-H.

Nilson, Arthur H. Design of Concrete Structures. 11th ed. (C). 1991. text 72.00 (*0-07-046567-3*) McGraw.

— Design of Prestressed Concrete. 2nd ed. 608p. 1987. text 108.95 (*0-471-83072-0*) Wiley.

Nilson, Arthur H. & Darwin, David. Design of Concrete Structures. 3rd ed. LC 96-36814. (McGraw-Hill Series in Construction Engineering & Project Management). (C). 1997. pap. 26.25 (*0-07-046587-8*) McGraw.

— Design of Concrete Structures. 12th ed. LC 96-36814. (McGraw-Hill Series in Construction Engineering & Project Management). 880p. (C). 1997. 95.31 (*0-07-046586-X*) McGraw.

Nilson, Ben. Cathedral Shrines of Medieval England. LC 97-52221. (Illus.). 288p. 1998. 75.00 (*0-85115-540-5*, Boydell Pr) Boydell & Brewer.

Nilson, Carolyn. Games That Drive Change. LC 95-17015. 307p. 1995. pap. 21.95 (*0-07-046589-4*) McGraw.

— How to Manage Training: A Guide to Administration, Design, & Delivery. 275p. 1991. ring bd. 69.95 (*0-8144-1150-9*, 040530) AMACOM.

— How to Manage Training: A Guide to Design & Delivery for High Performance. 2nd ed. LC 97-21498. 304p. 1967. ring bd. 35.00 (*0-8144-1100-2*) AMACOM.

***Nilson, Carolyn.** How to Start a Training Program. LC 99-72539. 240p. 1999. pap. 32.00 (*1-56286-118-2*) Am Soc Train & Devel.

Nilson, Carolyn. More Team Games for Trainers. LC 97-41224. (Illus.). 283p. 1997. pap. 27.95 (*0-07-046590-8*) McGraw.

— The Performance Consulting Toolbook: Tools & Activities for Trainers in a Performance Consulting Role. (ASQ Ser.). (Illus.). 300p. 1998. 128.95 (*0-07-913760-1*); pap. 57.95 (*0-07-047169-X*) McGraw-Hill Prof.

— Team Games for Trainers. LC 93-3369. 352p. 1992. pap. 24.95 (*0-07-046588-6*) McGraw.

***Nilson, Carolyn.** Training & Development Yearbook, 2000. 10th ed. (Illus.). (C). 2000. 79.95 (*0-13-021235-0*) P-H.

Nilson, Carolyn. Training for Non-Trainers: A Do-It-Yourself Guide for Managers. 240p. 1991. pap. 16.95 (*0-8144-7775-5*) AMACOM.

Nilson, Donald E. & Kroenke, David M. Managing Information with Microcomputers: Database Management Systems. Craig, Dorothy P., ed. LC 84-6651. (R BASE Ser.). (Illus.). (Orig.). 1984. 19.95 (*0-916937-00-3*) Microrim.

Nilson, Jeena, jt. auth. see Aslett, Don.

Nilson, Jon. Nothing Beyond the Necessary: Roman Catholicism & the Ecumenical Future. LC 95-11964. 120p. (Orig.). 1995. pap. 7.95 (*0-8091-3576-0*) Paulist Pr.

Nilson, Linda, ed. Natural Disasters & Public Policy. 200p. (Orig.). 1985. pap. 15.00 (*0-918592-75-5*) Pol Studies.

Nilson, Linda B. Teaching at Its Best: A Research-Based Resource for College Instructors. 240p. 1997. 29.95 (*1-882982-20-7*) Anker Pub.

Nilson, Tor H., jt. auth. see Nelson, Carlton H.

Nilson, Torsten H. Competitive Branding: Winning in the Market Place with Value-Added Brands. LC 98-16682. 248p. 1998. 48.50 (*0-471-98457-4*) Wiley.

Nilsson, A., jt. auth. see Onvural, R. O.

Nilsson, A. G., et al, eds. Perspectives on Business Modelling: Understanding & Changing Organizations. LC 99-20541. (Illus.). 360p. 1999. 85.00 (*3-540-65249-3*) Spr-Verlag.

Nilsson, Ake. Groundwater Dams for Small-Scale Water Supply. (Illus.). 64p. 1988. pap. 15.00 (*1-85339-050-X*, Pub. by Intermed Tech) Stylus Pub VA.

Nilsson, Anders, jt. auth. see Abrahamsson, Hans.

Nilsson, Anders N. & Holmen, Mogens. The Aquatic Adephaga (Coleoptera) of Fennoscandia & Denmark. (Fauna Entomologica Scandinavica Ser.: Vol. 32). 192p. 1995. 90.00 (*90-04-10456-9*) Brill Academic Pubs.

Nilsson, Annika. Greenhouse Earth. LC 00-92. (Scientific Committee on Problems of the Environment Ser.). 236p. 1992. pap. 80.00 (*0-471-93628-6*) Wiley.

— Ultraviolet Reflections: Life under a Thinning Ozone Layer. LC 96-11463. 164p. 1996. pap. 54.95 (*0-471-95843-3*) Wiley.

Nilsson, Birgit. La Nilsson: The Autobiography of Birgit Nilsson. unabridged ed. (Great Voices Ser.). 500p. 1997. 42.00 (*1-880909-57-X*) Baskerville.

Nilsson, Dale R. & Sarantokos, Bill. Developing JavaBeans Using VisualAge for Java 2. 2nd ed. LC 99-18993. (Illus.). 448p. 1999. pap. 54.99 incl. cd-rom (*0-471-34534-2*) Wiley.

***Nilsson, Dale R., et al.** Enterprise Development with VisualAge for Java, Version 3. 544p. 2000. pap. 54.99 incl. cd-rom (*0-471-38949-8*) Wiley.

Nilsson, Dex. Discover Why It's Called... 2nd ed. LC 91-65521. (Illus.). 68p. (Orig.). 1995. pap. 5.95 (*0-9629170-2-8*) Twinbrook Comms.

***Nilsson, Dex.** The Names of Washington, D. C. LC 98-90927. (Illus.). 176p. 1999. pap. 14.95 (*0-9629170-5-2*) Twinbrook Comms.

***Nilsson, Eric.** Severance Package: The Novel Your Boss Does Not Want You to Read. 328p. 2000. 24.95 (*0-9677444-0-7*) Third Option.

Nilsson, Erik. Rocky Mountain National Park. 1978. pap. 5.95 (*0-02-499400-6*, Macmillan Coll) P-H.

— Rocky Mountain National Park Trail Guide. LC 78-362. (Illus.). 187p. 1978. pap. 4.95 (*0-89037-098-2*) Anderson World.

Nilsson, Goran. Effects of Bisulphite & the Stability of Adrenaline. (Uppsala Dissertations from the Faculty of Science Ser.: No. 2). (Illus.). vii, 98p. 1986. pap. text 42.50 (*91-554-1888-0*, Pub. by Uppsala Univ Acta Univ Uppsaliensis) Coronet Bks.

Nilsson, Goran E., jt. auth. see Lutz, Peter L.

Nilsson, James W. Electric Circuits. 2nd ed. LC 85-1380. (Electrical Engineering Ser.). 820p. (C). 1985. text. write for info. (*0-201-12695-8*); pap. text, teacher ed. 9.50 (*0-201-12696-6*) Addison-Wesley.

— Electric Circuits. 3rd ed. (Electrical Engineering Ser.). (Illus.). 832p. (C). 1990. text 61.25 (*0-201-17288-7*) Addison-Wesley.

***Nilsson, James W.** Electric Circuits. 6th ed. LC 99-26620. 1030p. (C). 1999. 96.00 (*0-201-43653-1*, Prentice Hall) P-H.

Nilsson, James W. Electric Circuits: WSS Version. 5th ed. (C). 1995. pap. text. write for info. (*0-201-40013-8*) Addison-Wesley.

— Electric Circuits: WSS Version. 5th ed. 1024p. (C). 1996. pap. text. write for info. (*0-201-40100-2*) Addison-Wesley.

— Electric Circuits: State Space Supplement. 5th ed. (C). 1997. pap. text, suppl. ed. write for info. (*0-201-18066-9*) Addison-Wesley.

— Electrical Circuits. 4th ed. (Illus.). 992p. (C). 1993. text 68.33 (*0-201-54987-5*) Addison-Wesley.

— Nilsson Electric Circuits Translation: Translation. 4th ed. (C). 1995. pap. text. write for info. (*0-201-42044-9*) Addison-Wesley.

Nilsson, Jan-Evert, et al, eds. The Internationalization Process: European Firms in Global Competition. LC 96-131442. 224p. 1996. pap. 34.95 (*1-85396-319-4*) Taylor & Francis.

Nilsson, Jenny Lind, jt. auth. see Keillor, Garrison.

Nilsson, Jerker & Host, Viggo. Reseller Assortment Decision Criteria. 181p. (Orig.). 1987. pap. 27.00 (*87-7288-079-1*, Pub. by Aarhus Univ Pr) David Brown.

Nilsson, Jim. Circuitos Electricos. 4th ed. (SPA.). 1008p. (C). 1994. pap. text 30.33 (*0-201-60101-X*) Addison-Wesley.

Nilsson, K. Robert, jt. auth. see Gilbert, Mark F.

Nilsson, Kare & Nilsson, Paasche. Norsk - Spansk Ordbok. (NOR & SPA.). 392p. lib. bdg. 150.00 (*0-7859-3673-4*, 8200075869) Fr & Eur.

Nilsson, Karen B. A Wild Flower by Any Other Name: Sketches of Pioneer Naturalists Who Named Our Western Plants. LC 93-44015. (Illus.). 162p. 1994. pap. 14.95 (*0-939666-76-6*) Yosemite Assn.

Nilsson, L. Anders, jt. auth. see Faegri, Knut.

Nilsson, L. G., ed. Perspectives on Memory Research. 416p. 1979. text 79.95 (*0-89859-483-9*) L Erlbaum Assocs.

Nilsson, L. G. & Archer, Trevor, eds. Perspectives on Learning & Memory. (Comparative Cognition & Neuroscience Ser.). 352p. (C). 1985. 69.95 (*0-89859-628-9*) L Erlbaum Assocs.

Nilsson, L. G., jt. ed. see Archer, T.

Nilsson, Lars-Goran, jt. auth. see Markowitsch, Hans J.

Nilsson, Lena, jt. auth. see Ross, Michael W.

Nilsson, Lennart. Behold Man. LC 73-14087. (Illus.). 1978. 29.95 (*0-316-60751-7*) Little.

— A Child Is Born. 216p. 1986. pap. 19.95 (*0-440-50691-3*) Dell.

— A Child Is Born: The Completely New Edition. (Illus.). 208p. 1990. 29.95 (*0-385-30237-1*) Delacorte.

Nilsson, Lennart & Swanberg, Lena K. How Was I Born? 72p. (J). 1996. pap. 11.95 (*0-440-50767-7*, Dell Trade Pbks) Dell.

Nilsson, Magnus, jt. auth. see Lorentzi, Jakob.

Nilsson, Martin P. Cults, Myths, Oracles, & Politics in Ancient Greece. (Studies in Mediterranean Archaeology & Literature: No. 44). 179p. (Orig.). 1986. pap. 42.50 (*91-86098-43-8*, Pub. by P Astroms) Coronet Bks.

— The Dionysiac Mysteries of the Hellenistic & Roman Age. LC 75-10643. (Ancient Religion & Mythology Ser.). (Illus.). 1980. reprint ed. 18.95 (*0-405-07261-9*) Ayer.

— A History of Greek Religion. Fielden, F. J., tr. from SWE. LC 80-13430. 316p. 1980. reprint ed. lib. bdg. 69.50 (*0-313-22466-8*, NIHG, Greenwood Pr) Greenwood.

— Imperial Rome. (Illus.). 376p. 1974. pap. 30.00 (*0-89005-054-6*) Ares.

— The Minoan-Mycenaean Religion. LC 70-162300. 1950. pap. 25.00 (*0-8196-0273-6*) Biblo.

Nilsson, Mary, jt. auth. see Ferson, Mark.

Nilsson, Mike, jt. auth. see Bays, Harold.

Nilsson, N., jt. auth. see Kleczkowski, B.

Nilsson, N. R., jt. ed. see Lundqvist, S. O.

Nilsson, Nancy M. Very Truly Yours, M. L. A Visit with Mary Lincoln. (Illus.). 36p. (Orig.). 1992. pap. 6.95 (*0-9629170-3-6*) Twinbrook Comms.

Nilsson, Nils A., ed. Boris Pasternak: Essays. 215p. 1977. pap. text 30.00 (*91-22-00086-0*) Coronet Bks.

— Slavic Literatures & Modernism. (Nobel Symposium Ser.: No. 62). 318p. 1986. pap. text 48.50 (*91-7402-180-X*) Coronet Bks.

— Velimir Chlebnikov. (Studies in Russian Literature: No. 20). 150p. (Orig.). 1985. pap. text 35.00 (*91-22-00765-2*) Coronet Bks.

Nilsson, Nils-Ake, ed. Czeslaw Milosz: A Stockholm Conference. 1991. 112p. (Orig.). 1992. pap. 29.00 (*91-7402-231-8*) Coronet Bks.

Nilsson, Nils J. Artificial Intelligence: A New Synthesis. LC 97-47159. 513p. (C). 1998. 59.95 (*1-55860-467-7*) Morgan Kaufmann.

— Principles of Artificial Intelligence. LC 86-2815. (Illus.). 476p. 1980. reprint ed. text 58.95 (*0-934613-10-9*) Morgan Kaufmann.

Nilsson, Nils J. & Genesereth, Michael. Logical Foundations of Artificial Intelligence. LC 87-5461. (Illus.). 406p. 1980. text 63.95 (*0-934613-31-1*) Morgan Kaufmann.

Nilsson, Nils J., et al. Mathematical Foundations of Learning Machines. 1998. pap. text 28.95 (*1-55860-123-6*) Morgan Kaufmann.

Nilsson, Nils J., jt. ed. see Webber, Bonnie L.

Nilsson, Paasche, jt. auth. see Nilsson, Kare.

Nilsson, S., jt. auth. see Ekspong, Gosta.

Nilsson, Stefan & Holmgreen, Susanne. Comparative Physiology & Evolution of the Autonomic Nervous System. LC 93-25356. (Autonomic Nervous System Ser.: Vol. 4). xviii, 376p. 1994. text 126.00 (*3-7186-5137-8*) Gordon & Breach.

Nilsson, Sten, et al. The Forest Resources of the Former U. S. S. R. 408p. (C). 1992. text 85.00 (*1-85070-425-2*) Prthnon Pub.

— Future Forest Resource of Western & Eastern Europe. 496p. (C). 1992. 85.00 (*1-85070-424-4*) Prthnon Pub.

Nilsson, Sten, jt. auth. see Virtanen, Yrjo.

Nilsson, Sven G., jt. auth. see Ragnarsson, Ingemar.

Nilsson, T. K., et al. Clinical Aspects of Fibrinolysis. (Illus.). 187p. 1991. 143.50 (*91-22-01436-5*) Coronet Bks.

Nilsson, Tage A. The Pleistocene. 1983. text 376.50 (*90-277-1466-5*) Kluwer Academic.

Nilsson, Ulf. If You Didn't Have Me. Blecher, Lone T. & Blecher, George, trs. LC 86-21327. (Illus.). 128p. (J). (gr. 4-7). 1987. 15.00 (*0-689-50406-3*) S&S Trade.

Nilsson, W. Achieving Strategic Goals Through Executive Development. LC 86-32201. 1987. text 28.95 (*0-201-12751-2*) Addison-Wesley.

Nilton, Bonder. Kabbalah of Envy: Transforming Hatred, Anger & Other Negative Emotions. Michaels, Julia, tr. LC 97-7928. 224p. 1997. 18.00 (*1-57062-294-9*, Pub. by Shambhala Pubns) Random.

Nilus & Marsden, Victor E., trs. The Protocols of Zion. unabridged ed. 299p. 1934. reprint ed. pap. 12.00 (*0-945001-59-2*) GSG & Assocs.

Nilus of Sinai. Selected Texts on Prayer. 1994. pap. 0.50 (*0-89981-090-X*) Eastern Orthodox.

Nilus, Schema-Hieromonk. Prayers to the Most Holy Theotokos (The Virgin Mary) 1992. pap. 1.00 (*0-89981-134-5*) Eastern Orthodox.

Nily, Gisela, et al. NCLEX: PMIC's Comprehensive Review for the Registered Nurse Licensing Exam. Lynch, Maureen & DiDonato, Adrienne, eds. LC 98-21936. 600p. (Orig.). 1998. pap. text 34.95 (*1-57066-045-X*, ME073) Practice Mgmt Info.

Nim, A., ed. see Cajori, Florian.

Nima, Ramy. The Wrath of Allah: Islamic Revolution & Reaction in Iran. LC 83-230937. v, 170 p. 1983. write for info. (*0-86104-733-8*) Pluto GBR.

Niman, Michael I. People of the Rainbow: A Nomadic Utopia. LC 97-4626. 1997. pap. 18.95 (*0-87049-989-0*) U of Tenn Pr.

— People of the Rainbow: A Nomadic Utopia. LC 97-4626. (Illus.). 360p. 1997. text 50.00 (*0-87049-988-2*) U of Tenn Pr.

Niman, Neil B. Hypermarkets. Date not set. write for info. (*0-679-77013-5*) McKay.

Nimbark, Ashakant, ed. Honeycomb. 1976. pap. 1.95 (*0-917428-01-3*, Dowling College) Global Pubns.

Nimble, Jack B. The Construction & Operation of Clandestine Drug Laboratories. 2nd rev. ed. LC 93-80258. (Illus.). 132p. (C). 1994. pap. 17.95 (*1-55950-108-1*, 85178) Loompanics.

Nimbus Publishing Limited, Staff. A Guide to Whale Watching in the Maritimes. (Illus.). 68p. 1998. 29.95 (*1-55109-207-7*) Nimbus Publ.

Nimersheim, Jack. First Book of Microsoft Windows, No. 3. 1990. pap. 16.95 (*0-672-27334-9*, MICHIE) LEXIS Pub.

— In Plain English: Includes DOS. LC 93-60387. (Illus.). 144p. (Orig.). 1993. pap. 9.95 (*1-56664-029-6*) WorldComm.

— In Plain English: Microsoft Word 6.0. McDonald, Susie et al, eds. LC 95-40402. (Illus.). 142p. 1995. pap. 9.95 (*1-56664-078-4*) WorldComm.

— In Plain English: Microsoft's Windows 95. McDonald, Susie et al, eds. LC 95-37887. (Illus.). 144p. (Orig.). 1995. pap. 9.95 (*1-56664-074-1*) WorldComm.

— In Plain English: Windows 3.1. LC 93-60164. (Illus.). 144p. (Orig.). 1993. pap. 9.95 (*1-56664-007-5*) WorldComm.

Nimeth, Albert J. Grow Old Gracefully. 88p. 1989. reprint ed. pap. 1.95 (*0-8199-0509-7*, Frncscn Herld) Franciscan Pr.

— I Like You, Just Because. LC 79-139971. (Illus.). 112p. (J). (gr. 5 up). 1971. pap. 3.50 (*0-8199-0422-8*, Frncscn Herld) Franciscan Pr.

— In Your Time of Sorrow. 79p. 1976. pap. 0.75 (*0-8199-0566-6*, Frncscn Herld) Franciscan Pr.

— Joy: Nature's Best Remedy. 79p. 1975. pap. 0.75 (*0-8199-0602-6*, Frncscn Herld) Franciscan Pr.

— Of Course I Love You. 126p. 1973. pap. 5.00 (*0-8199-0951-3*, Frncscn Herld) Franciscan Pr.

— Tenderly I Care. 123p. 1977. pap. 5.00 (*0-8199-0952-1*, Frncscn Herld) Franciscan Pr.

— To Listen Is to Heal. 126p. 1984. pap. 5.00 (*0-8199-0950-5*, Frncscn Herld) Franciscan Pr.

Nimetz, Alexandra. Healthy College Cookbook: Quick, Cheap & Easy. LC 98-55398. 1999. pap. text 14.95 (*1-58017-126-5*, Pub. by Storey Bks) Random.

Nimetz, Michael. Humor in Galdos: A Study of the Novelas Contemporaneas. LC 68-13921. (Yale Romanic Studies, Second Ser.: No. 18). 237p. reprint ed. pap. 73.50 (*0-608-14024-4*, 202202400024) Bks Demand.

Nimetz, Michael, tr. see Alas, Leopoldo (Clarin).

Nimi, Hideyuki, ed. Microcirculatory Disorders in the Heart & Brain. xv, 195p. 1991. text 223.00 (*3-7186-5090-8*, Harwood Acad Pubs) Gordon & Breach.

Nimick, Ellen H., et al. Juvenile Court Statistics, 1982. 45p. 1984. 10.00 (*0-318-36228-7*) Natl Juv & Family Ct Judges.

Nimier, Marie. The Giraffe. Feeney, Mary, tr. LC 94-38766. 200p. 1995. 18.00 (*1-56858-026-6*) FWEW.

— Hypnotism Made Easy. Hawkes, Sophie, tr. from FRE. LC 96-13823.Tr. of L'Hypnotisme a la Portee de Tous. 260p. 1996. 18.00 (*1-56858-036-3*) FWEW.

Nimier, Roger. Les Enfants Tristes. (FRE.). 1983. pap. 12.95 (*0-7859-4184-3*) Fr & Eur.

— L' Etrangere. (FRE.). 1980. pap. 10.95 (*0-7859-4137-1*) Fr & Eur.

— Le Grand d'Espagne. (FRE.). 1975. pap. 10.95 (*0-7859-4036-7*) Fr & Eur.

— Le Hussard Bleu. (FRE.). 434p. 1977. pap. 11.95 (*0-7859-4088-X*, 2070369862) Fr & Eur.

Nimis, Erika. Photographes du Mali. (Illus.). 1998. pap. text 14.95 (*2-909571-21-1*, Pub. by Revue Noire) Dist Art Pubs.

Nimis, P. L. & Crovello, T. J., eds. Quantitative Approaches to Phytogeography. (Tasks for Vegetation Science Ser.). (C). 1990. text 285.00 (*0-7923-0795-X*) Kluwer Academic.

Nimis, Stephen A. Narrative Semiotics in the Epic Tradition: The Simile. LC 87-45323. 223p. reprint ed. pap. 69.20 (*0-7837-3722-X*, 205790000009) Bks Demand.

Nimitz, Jonathan S. Experiments in Organic Chemistry. 450p. 1989. boxed set 39.00 (*0-685-27167-6*) P-H.

Nimitz, Jonathan S. Experiments in Organic Chemistry: From Microscale to Macroscale. 512p. 1990. 87.00 (*0-13-295718-3*) P-H.

Nimke, R. W. The Rutland Betterments - Statistics. LC 89-81530. (Rutland Ser.). (Illus.). 192p. (Orig.). 1989. 35.00 (*0-914960-90-3*); pap. 25.00 (*0-914960-77-6*) Academy Bks.

Nimmen, Jane van, see Curtis, Verna P.

Nimmen, Jane van, see Van Nimmen, Jane.

Nimmen, Jane van, see Curtis, Verna P.

Nimmer & Hillinger. Commercial Transactions: Secured Financing, Cases, Materials, & Problems: 1992 Edition. 662p. 1992. text 42.00 (*0-87473-963-2*, 12530-10, MICHIE) LEXIS Pub.

Nimmer, Dave. Lessons on the Journey. 1996. 17.95 (*0-931714-72-9*, Pub. by Nodin Pr) Bookmen Inc.

Nimmer, David. The Journey Goes On. 109p. 1992. pap. 9.95 (*0-931714-49-4*, Pub. by Nodin Pr) Bookmen Inc.

Nimmer, Melville B. Nimmer on Copyright, 6 vols. 1978. ring bd. 1160.00 (*0-8205-1465-9*) Bender.

Nimmer, Melville B., jt. auth. see Marcus, Paul.

Nimmer, Raymond T. Commercial Asset-Based Financing: 1988-1990, 4 vols. annuals suppl. ed. 500.00 (*0-685-24490-3*) West Group.

— Diversion: The Search for Alternative Forms of Prosecution. LC 74-81693. xiv, 119p. Date not set. pap. 20.00 (*0-910058-63-6*, 304810) W S Hein.

— Diversion: The Search for Alternative Forms of Prosecution. LC 74-81693. xiv, 119p. 1986. 20.00 (*0-910058-64-4*, 304810) W S Hein.

— The Law of Computer Technology. 2nd ed. 688p. 1992. 149.50 (*0-7913-1270-4*) Warren Gorham & Lamont.

— The Nature of System Change: Reform Impact in the Criminal Courts. LC 78-67457. xiv, 225p. 1991. reprint ed. 30.00 (*0-89941-574-1*, 304980) W S Hein.

— Omnibus Hearing: An Experiment in Relieving Inefficiency, Unfairness & Judicial Delay. (American Bar Foundation Publications). ix, 125p. 1971. 22.50 (*1-57588-347-3*, 304990) W S Hein.

— Prosecutor Disclosure & Judicial Reform: The Omnibus Hearing in Two Courts. LC 75-13605. vii, 117p. 1986. 25.00 (*0-910058-72-5*, 305010); pap. 20.00 (*0-910058-71-7*, 305010) W S Hein.

— Two Million Unnecessary Arrests: Removing a Social Service Concern from the Criminal Justice System. LC 70-160799. (American Bar Foundation Publications). ix, 202p. 1970. 27.50 (*1-57588-369-4*, 305060); pap. 20.00 (*1-57588-427-5*, 305060) W S Hein.

Nimmer, Raymond T. & American Bar Foundation Staff. The Nature of System Change: Reform Impact in the Criminal Courts. LC 78-67457. xiv, 225p. 1991. reprint ed. pap. 30.00 (*0-910058-93-8*, 304980) W S Hein.

Nimmer, Raymond T., et al. Commercial Transactions: Secured Financing. 2nd ed. (Contemporary Legal Education Ser.). 685p. 1992. 37.00 (*0-87215-963-9*, MICHIE); 37.00 (*0-685-62351-3*, MICHIE) LEXIS Pub.

***Nimmer, Raymond T., et al.** Commercial Transactions: Secured Financing, Cases, Materials, Problems. 2nd ed. 670p. 1999. 46.00 (*0-327-04958-8*, 1253011) LEXIS Pub.

Nimmer, Raymond T., jt. auth. see White, James J.

Nimmer, Ron, jt. auth. see Trantina, Gerry.

Nimmi, Marcel E. Collagen, 4 vols., Set. LC 87-20946. 1988. reprint ed. 669.00 (*0-8493-4600-2*, CRC Reprint) Franklin.

— Collagen: Biochemistry, Biomechanics, Biotechnology, Vol. 2. LC 87-20946. (Collagen Ser.). 336p. 1988. 174.00 (*0-8493-4602-9*, QP552) Franklin.

Nimmi, Marcel E., jt. auth. see Kang, Andrew H.

Nimmo, Andrew P. Bibliographia Trichopterorum Vol. 1: A World Bibliography of Trichoptera (Insecta) with Indexes: 1961-1970. 640p. 1996. pap. 79.95 (*954-642-012-3*) Intl Scholars.

***Nimmo, Beth & Scott, Darrell.** Rachel's Tears: The Spiritual Journey of Columbine Martyr Rachel Scott. 224p. 2000. pap. 12.99 (*0-7852-6848-0*) Nelson.

***Nimmo, Christine M., ed.** Staff Development for Pharmacy Practice. 144p. 2000. pap. text 37.50 (*1-58528-000-3*) Am Soc Hlth-Syst.

Nimmo, Claude. Collins-Robert Gem French Dictionary. 3rd ed. (ENG & FRE.). 630p. 1993. write for info. (*0-7859-7412-1*, 0004589777) Fr & Eur.

Nimmo, Dan, ed. Communication Yearbook,, No. 3. 704p. 1979. 59.95 (*0-87855-341-X*) Transaction Pubs.

— Communication Yearbook, No. 4. 752p. 1980. 59.95 (*0-87855-385-1*) Transaction Pubs.

Nimmo, Dan & Combs, James E. Mediated Political Realities. 2nd ed. 256p. (C). 1990. pap. text 42.00 (*0-8013-0220-X*, 75878) Longman.

— Nightly Horrors: Crisis Coverage in Television Network News. LC 84-10464. 232p. 1985. pap. 17.95 (*0-87049-625-5*) U of Tenn Pr.

— The Political Pundits. LC 91-34491. (Praeger Series in Political Communication). 208p. 1992. 57.95 (*0-275-93541-8*, C3541, Praeger Pubs); pap. 16.95 (*0-275-93545-0*, B3545, Praeger Pubs) Greenwood.

Nimmo, Dan & Mansfield, Michael W., eds. Government & the News Media: Comparative Dimensions. LC 82-73859. 320p. 1982. 14.50 (*0-918954-36-3*); pap. 14.50 (*0-918954-42-8*) Baylor Univ Pr.

Nimmo, Dan & Newsome, Chevelle. Political Commentators in the United States: A Bio-Critical Sourcebook, 1930 to the Present. LC 96-28069. 448p. 1997. lib. bdg. 99.50 (*0-313-29585-9*) Greenwood.

Nimmo, Dan & Sanders, Keith R., eds. Handbook of Political Communication. LC 81-9362. (Illus.). 732p. reprint ed. pap. 200.00 (*0-608-01146-0*, 205944600001) Bks Demand.

Nimmo, Dan, jt. auth. see Smith, Larry D.

Nimmo, Dan, jt. ed. see Swanson, David L.

Nimmo, Dan D. The Political Persuaders: The Techniques of Modern Election Campaigns. 2nd ed. LC 99-13923. 214p. 1999. write for info. (*0-7658-0613-4*) Transaction Pubs.

Nimmo, Derek. Up Mount Everest Without a Paddle. large type ed. 256p. 1989. reprint ed. 19.95 (*1-85089-325-X*, Pub. by ISIS Lrg Prnt) Transaction Pubs.

Nimmo, Dorothy. Testimony to the Grace of God. 1999. pap. 21.00 (*1-85072-129-7*, Pub. by W Sessions) St Mut.

Nimmo, H. Arlo. The Pele Literature: An Annotated Bibliography of the English-Language Literature on Pele, Volcano Goddess of Hawai'i. (Bulletin in Anthropology Ser.: No. 6). 104p. 1992. 15.00 (*0-930897-72-2*) Bishop Mus.

— The Songs of Salanda: And Other Stories of Sulu. LC 93-42674. 1994. pap. write for info. (*0-295-97335-8*) U of Wash Pr.

Nimmo, H. Arlo, jt. ed. see Kaeppler, A. L.

Nimmo, Ian. Edinburgh: The New Town. 200p. (C). 1996. 50.00 (*0-85976-323-4*, Pub. by J Donald) St Mut.

Nimmo, J. Dragon's Child. (J). mass mkt. 7.95 (*0-340-67304-4*, Pub. by Hodder & Stought Ltd) Trafalgar.

Nimmo, Jenny. Branwen. (Legends from Wales Ser.: Vol. 2). (Illus.). (J). (gr. 2-5). 1998. pap. 11.95 (*0-8464-4602-2*) Beekman Pubs.

— The Chestnut Soldier. large type ed. (Lythway Ser.). 312p. (J). (gr. 3-7). 1991. 18.50 (*0-7451-1178-5*, G K Hall Lrg Type) Mac Lib Ref.

***Nimmo, Jenny.** Delilah Alone. large type ed. (Illus.). (J). 1998. pap. 16.95 (*0-7540-6014-4*, Galaxy Child Lrg Print) Chivers N Amer.

Nimmo, Jenny. Griffin's Castle. LC 96-42382. 208p. (J). (gr. 5 up). 1997. 16.95 (*0-531-30006-4*); lib. bdg. 17.99 (*0-531-33006-0*) Orchard Bks Watts.

— Gwion & the Witch. (Illus.). 36p. (J). (gr. 2-5). 1996. pap. 11.95 (*0-8464-4636-7*) Beekman Pubs.

— Orchard of the Crescent Moon. 170p. (J). (gr. 5-9). 1997. pap. 2.95 (*0-8167-2265-X*) Troll Communs.

***Nimmo, Jenny & Howard, Paul.** Esmeralda & the Children Next Door. LC 99-28563. 32p. (J). 2000. 15.00 (*0-618-02902-8*) HM.

Nimmo, John. Identity of the Religions Called Druidical & Hebrew: Demonstrated from the Nature & Objects of Their Worship (1829) 125p. 1996. reprint ed. pap. 11.95 (*1-56459-859-4*) Kessinger Pub.

Nimmo, John, jt. auth. see Jones, Elizabeth.

Nimmo, Joseph, Jr. Report in Regard to the Range & Ranch Cattle Business of the United States. LC 72-2860. (Use & Abuse of America's Natural Resources Ser.). 214p. 1972. reprint ed. 19.95 (*0-405-04524-7*) Ayer.

Nimmo, Paul. Will Shakespeare Save Us! Will Shakespeare Save the King! LC 96-28290. 58p. (J). (gr. k-8). 1996. pap. 12.00 (*0-88734-658-8*) Players Pr.

Nimmo, Walter S. Anaesthesia. 1989. 205.00 (*0-632-02257-4*) CRC Pr.

Nimmo, Walter S. & Prescott, L. F., eds. Novel Drug Delivery & Its Therapeutic Application. LC 89-14662. (Illus.). 383p. 1989. reprint ed. pap. 118.80 (*0-608-02598-4*, 206325600004) Bks Demand.

Nimmo, Walter S. & Rowbotham, D. Anaesthesia, 2 vols. 2nd ed. (Illus.). 2072p. 1994. 295.00 (*0-632-03244-8*) Blackwell Sci.

Nimmo, Walter S. & Tucker. Clinical Measurement in Drug Evaluation. (C). 1991. text 94.95 (*0-8493-7731-5*) CRC Pr.

Nimmo, Walter S. & Tucker, Gregory T., eds. Clinical Measurement in Drug Evaluation. LC 94-40650. 344p. 1995. 235.95 (*0-471-94391-6*) Wiley.

Nimmo, William F. Behind a Curtain of Silence: Japanese in Soviet Custody, 1945-1956, 78. LC 88-5623. (Contributions in Military Studies Ser.: No. 78). (Illus.). 159p. 1988. 49.95 (*0-313-25762-0*, NCS/, Greenwood Pr) Greenwood.

— Japan & Russia: A Re-Evaluation in the Post-Soviet Era, 3. LC 93-11847. (Contributions in Asian Studies: No. 3). 240p. 1994. 55.00 (*0-313-28440-7*, Greenwood Pr) Greenwood.

Nimmo, William F., ed. The Occupation of Japan: Grass Roots Level. 193p. (C). 1992. lib. bdg. 19.25 (*0-9606418-7-4*) Genl D MacArthur Fnd.

— The Occupation of Japan: The Impact of the Korean War. 189p. (C). 1986. lib. bdg. 19.25 (*0-9606418-6-6*) Genl D MacArthur Fnd.

Nimmons, Carol A. The Child-Care Worker Manual. Wren, Jim & Bowman, Suzanne, eds. (Illus.). 28p. 1990. teacher ed. 3.00 (*0-89606-320-8*, 805TK); pap. 9.00 (*0-89606-267-8*, 805) Am Assn Voc Materials.

Nimmons, David, jt. auth. see Rossi, Ernest L.

Nimni. Marxism & Nationalism: The Theoretical Origins of the Political Crisis. (C). pap. 19.95 (*0-7453-0730-2*, Pub. by Pluto GBR) Stylus Pub VA.

Nimni. Marxism & Nationalism: The Theoretical Origins of the Political Crisis. 242p. (C). 54.95 (*0-7453-0358-7*, Pub. by Pluto GBR) Stylus Pub VA.

Nimni, Ephraim J., ed. see Bauer, Otto.

Nimni, Marcel E., ed. Collagen: Biochemistry, Biomechanics, Biotechnology, Vol. I. 384p. 1988. 175.00 (*0-8493-4601-0*, QP552, CRC Reprint) Franklin.

— Collagen: Biochemistry, Biomechanics, Biotechnology, Vol. III. 368p. 1988. 176.00 (*0-8493-4603-7*, QP552, CRC Reprint) Franklin.

Nimni, Marcel E., jt. auth. see Olsen, Bjorn R.

Nimnicht, Nona, jt. ed. see Askew, Judith.

Nimo, Neri. Cocina Yucateca. (SPA.). 1997. pap. text 7.98 (*970-643-078-4*) Selector.

Nimocks, Walter. Milner's Young Men: The Kindergarten in Edwardian Imperial Affairs. LC 68-8588. 248p. reprint ed. pap. 76.90 (*0-608-11980-6*, 202342900033) Bks Demand.

Nimori, Tomoe, et al. Kona Coffee Days. 25p. 1995. spiral bd. 7.50 (*1-881161-13-7*) Japanese Museum.

Nimoy, Leonard. I Am Not Spock. 1997. reprint ed. lib. bdg. 31.95 (*1-56849-691-5*) Buccaneer Bks.

— I Am Spock. (Illus.). 352p. (J). 1995. 24.95 (*0-7868-6182-7*, Pub. by Hyperion) Time Warner.

— I Am Spock. 560p. (J). 1996. mass mkt. 5.99 (*0-7868-8910-1*, Pub. by Hyperion) Time Warner.

— Leonard Nimoy's Primortals Vol. 1, No. 1: Origins. Chambers, James et al, eds. (Illus.). 36p. (Orig.). (YA). pap. 2.25 (*0-9645175-1-5*) Big Enter Inc.

— Leonard Nimoy's Primortals Chronicles, 2 vols. Incl. Vol. II. (Illus.). 144p. 1996. reprint ed. pap. 14.95 (*1-57780-004-4*); Vol. I. (Illus.). 144p. 1996. reprint ed. pap. 14.95 (*1-57780-003-6*); (Primortals Chronicles Ser.). 25.00 (*1-57780-002-8*) Big Enter Inc.

— Vincent. 1985. pap. 5.95 (*0-87129-386-2*, V17) Dramatic Pub.

Nimrod, Carl & Griener, Glenn, eds. Biomedical Ethics & Fetal Therapy. (Calgary Institute for the Humanities Ser.). 122p. (C). 1988. pap. 14.95 (*0-88920-962-6*) W Laurier U Pr.

Nimrod, Dan. Israel's Mistakes Are Never Forgiven : Amidst a Sea of Hatred & Hypocrisy It Is a Miracle That Israel Is Still Alive. LC 99-207763. 1997. write for info. (*0-921401-37-X*) Dawn CAN.

Nimrod, Naomi, jt. auth. see Broner, E. M.

Nims. Westen Wind: Introduction to Poetry. 4th ed. LC 98-32224. 672p. 1999. pap. 35.00 (*0-07-303180-1*) McGraw.

Nims, Cynthia & McKean, Lori. The Northwest Best Places Cookbook: Recipes from the Outstanding Restaurants & Inns of Washington, Oregon, & British Columbia. LC 96-13187. 280p. (Orig.). 1996. pap. 16.95 (*1-57061-075-4*) Sasquatch Bks.

***Nims, Cynthia C. & Dille, Carolyn.** Northern California Best Places Cookbook: Recipes from the Region's Outstanding Restaurants & Inns. LC 99-15349. (Best Places Ser.). 256p. 1999. pap. 19.95 (*1-57061-183-1*) Sasquatch Bks.

***Nims, Debra.** Basics of Industrial Hygiene. LC 98-53835. 376p. 1999. pap. 49.95 (*0-471-29983-9*) Wiley.

Nims, Harry D. Law of Unfair Business Competition: Including Chapters on Trade Secrets & Confidential Business Relations; Unfair Interference with Contracts; Libel & Slander of Articles of Merchandise, Trade Names, & Business Credit & Reputation. LC 97-28833. xlvi, 581p. 1997. reprint ed. 125.00 (*0-8377-2452-X*, Rothman) W S Hein.

Nims, John F. A Local Habitation: Essays on Poetry. (Poets on Poetry Ser.). 320p. 1985. pap. 13.95 (*0-472-06356-1*, 06356) U of Mich Pr.

— Selected Poems. LC 81-19820. (Phoenix Ser.). xii, 160p. 1982. pap. 8.95 (*0-226-58118-7*) U Ch Pr.

— Selected Poems. LC 81-19820. (Phoenix Ser.). xii, 148p. 1993. lib. bdg. 17.00 (*0-226-58117-9*) U Ch Pr.

— The Six-Cornered Snowflake & Other Poems. LC 90-33222. 64p. 1990. 14.95 (*0-8112-1143-6*, Pub. by New Directions) Norton.

— Western Wind: An Introduction to Poetry. 2nd ed. LC 82-16504. xxxi, 639p. 1983. 10.95 (*0-394-33070-6*) Random.

Nims, John F., ed. Sappho to Valery: Poems in Translation. LC 89-38953. 435p. 1990. pap. 24.00 (*1-55728-141-6*) U of Ark Pr.

— Western Wind: An Introduction to Poetry. 3rd ed. 672p. (C). 1992. pap. 35.38 (*0-07-046574-6*) McGraw.

Nims, John F., et al, eds. The Columbia Granger's Index to Poetry. 10th rev. ed. LC 93-39161. 2,078p. 1993. 270.00 (*0-231-08408-0*) Col U Pr.

N

An Asterisk (*) at the beginning of an entry indicates that the title is appearing for the first time.

Nims, John F., tr. Andromache. LC 55-5787. write for info. U Ch Pr.
— The Poems of St. John of the Cross. 3rd ed. LC 79-12943. 160p. 1979. pap. 12.00 (*0-226-40110-3*, P845) U Ch Pr.
Nims, John F., jt. auth. see Buonarroti.
Nims, John F., tr. see Grene, David.
Nims, John F., tr. see St. John of the Cross.
Nims, John Frederick, ed. see Golding, Arthur, et al.
Nims, John Frederick, tr. see di Lodovico Buonarroti Simoni, Michelangelo.
Nims, Margaret R. Down on Cut Meat Creek. 200p. (Orig.). 1996. pap. write for info. (*1-57502-171-4*, PO793) Morris Pubng.
Nims, Marion R., ed. see U. S. Council of National Defense Staff.
Nimsch, Hubertus. A Reference Guide to the Gymnosperms of the World. (Illus.). 180p. 1995. pap. 25.00 (*1-878762-52-4*) Balogh.
Nimse, Gordon. Take What You Want. large type ed. (Dales Mystery Ser.). 422p. 1993. pap. 18.99 (*1-85389-372-2*) Ulverscroft.
Nimtz, August H. Islam & Politics in East Africa: The Sufi Order in Tanzania. LC 80-429. 250p. reprint ed. pap. 77.50 (*0-7837-2933-2*, 205752100006) Bks Demand.
***Nimtz, August H., Jr.** Marx & Engels: Their Contribution to the Democratic Breakthrough. LC 99-53178. (C). 2000. text 71.50 (*0-7914-4489-9*); pap. text 23.95 (*0-7914-4490-2*) State U NY Pr.
Nimtz, Wendy, jt. auth. see Hahn, Lisa.
Nimuendaju, Curt. The Serente. Lowie, Robert H., tr. LC 76-44769. reprint ed. 37.50 (*0-404-15873-0*) AMS Pr.
— The Serente. Lowie, Robert H., ed. & tr. by. (Frederick Webb Hodge Publications: No. 4). (Illus.). xii, 106p. 1967. reprint ed. pap. 5.00 (*0-916561-58-5*) Southwest Mus.
Nimura, Kazuo. The Ashio Riot of 1907: A Social History of Mining in Japan. Gordon, Andrew, ed. & tr. by. from JPN. Boardman, Terry, tr. from JPN. LC 97-24268. (Comparative & International Working Class History Ser.). (Illus.). xviii, 275p. 1997. pap. text 17.95 (*0-8223-2018-5*) Duke.
Nimura, Kazuo & Gordon, Andrew. The Ashio Riot of 1907: A Social History of Mining in Japan. Boardman, Terry, tr. from JPN. LC 97-24268. (Comparative & International Working Class History Ser.). (Illus.). 288p. 1997. lib. bdg. 54.95 (*0-8223-2008-8*) Duke.
Nimz, Horst H., ed. Holzforschung: Supplement Issue in Honor of Guenther Stegmann. (GER.). 158p. (C). 1994. pap. text 242.35 (*3-11-014247-3*, 10-94) De Gruyter.
Nimzowitsc, Aron. My System. 1995. pap. 17.95 (*1-85744-089-7*) S&S Trade.
Nimzowitsch, Aron. Blockade. rev. ed. Platz, Joseph, tr. from GER. (Illus.). 65p. (Orig.). 1983. pap. 6.00 (*0-931462-07-X*) Chess Ent.
— Chess Praxis. Orig. Title: Praxis of My System. (Illus.). 369p. 1962. pap. 10.95 (*0-486-20296-8*) Dover.
— Chess Praxis: Twenty First Century Edition. Artz, Ken, ed. Du Mont, J., tr. 296p. 1993. pap. 17.95 (*1-880673-91-6*) Hays Pub.
— My System. rev. ed. 1979. pap. 18.00 (*0-679-14025-5*) McKay.
Nimzowitsch, Aron & Nimzowitsch, Lou. My System - 21st Century Edition: The Landmark Positional Chess Training Classic in an Easy-to-Study Algebraic. Hays, Lou, ed. 260p. 1993. pap. 17.50 (*1-880673-85-1*) Hays Pub.
Nimzowitsch, Lou, jt. auth. see Nimzowitsch, Aron.
Nin, Anais. Anais Nin Reads: Nin,&Anais. abr. ed. 1993. audio 12.00 (*1-55994-836-1*, DCN 1613) HarperAudio.
Nin, Anais. Children of the Albatross. LC 66-6826. 111p. 1959. pap. 8.95 (*0-8040-0039-5*) Swallow.
— Cities of the Interior, 5 vols. (Illus.). xx, 589p. 1975. pap. 22.95 (*0-8040-0666-0*) Swallow.
— Collages. LC 64-25338. (Illus.). 122p. 1964. pap. 8.95 (*0-8040-0045-X*) Swallow.
— D. H. Lawrence: An Unprofessional Study. LC 64-16109. 110p. (Orig.). 1964. pap. 8.95 (*0-8040-0067-0*) Swallow.
— Delta of Venus. 1991. per. 6.99 (*0-671-74249-3*) PB.
— The Diary of Anais Nin Vol. 1: 1931-1934. 384p. 1969. pap. 12.00 (*0-15-626025-5*) Harcourt.
— The Diary of Anais Nin Vol. 3: 1939-1944. 348p. 1971. pap. 10.95 (*0-15-626027-1*) Harcourt.
— The Diary of Anais Nin Vol. 6: 1955-1966. Stuhlmann, Gunther, ed. & pref. by. LC 77-3599. 432p. 1977. pap. 12.00 (*0-15-626032-8*, Harvest Bks) Harcourt.
— The Early Diary of Anais Nin: 1920-1923, Vol. II. LC 77-20314. (Illus.). 576p. 1983. reprint ed. pap. 15.00 (*0-15-627248-2*, Harvest Bks) Harcourt.
— Fire: From "A Journal of Love" 400p. 1995. 25.00 (*0-15-100088-3*) Harcourt.
— Fire: From "A Journal of Love": The Unexpurgated Diary of Anais Nin, 1934-1937. 448p. 1996. pap. 16.00 (*0-15-600390-2*) Harcourt.
— Fire: 1934-1937. (Illus.). 448p. 1996. boxed set. write for info. (*0-7206-0992-5*, Pub. by P Owen Ltd) Dufour.
— Four-Chambered Heart. LC 66-6825. 187p. 1959. pap. 8.95 (*0-8040-0121-9*) Swallow.
— Henry & June: From the Unexpurgated Diary of Anais. 288p. 1986. 14.95 (*0-15-140003-2*) Harcourt.
— Henry & June: From the Unexpurgated Diary of Anais. 288p. 1990. pap. 13.00 (*0-15-640057-X*) Harcourt.
— House of Incest. LC 61-65487. 72p. 1958. pap. 7.95 (*0-8040-0148-0*) Swallow.
— In Favor of the Sensitive Man & Other Essays. LC 75-38583. 176p. (Orig.). 1976. pap. 10.00 (*0-15-644445-3*, Harvest Bks) Harcourt.
— Incest. (Illus.). 432p. (C). 1993. pap. 15.00 (*0-15-644300-7*) Harcourt.
— Journal, Vol. 2. write for info. (*0-614-20074-1*, Pub. by P Owen Ltd) Dufour.
— Journal, Vol. 3. write for info. (*0-614-20075-X*, Pub. by P Owen Ltd) Dufour.
— Journal, Vol. 5. write for info. (*0-614-20076-8*, Pub. by P Owen Ltd) Dufour.
— Journal, Vol. 6. write for info. (*0-614-20077-6*, Pub. by P Owen Ltd) Dufour.
— Journal, Vol. 7. write for info. (*0-614-20078-4*, Pub. by P Owen Ltd) Dufour.
— Journal of a Wife. write for info. (*0-614-20073-3*, Pub. by P Owen Ltd) Dufour.
— Ladders to Fire. rev. ed. LC 61-66834. (Cities of the Interior Ser.: Vol. 1). 192p. 1995. reprint ed. pap. 9.95 (*0-8040-0181-2*) Swallow.
— Little Birds. 176p. 1990. per. 5.99 (*0-671-68011-0*) PB.
— La Maison de l'Inceste. (POR.). 24.95 incl. audio (*0-318-36212-0*) Fr & Eur.
— The Novel of the Future. LC 86-1895. 212p. 1986. reprint ed. pap. 10.95 (*0-8040-0879-5*) Swallow.
— Seduction of the Minotaur. LC 61-66834. 146p. (Orig.). 1961. pap. 8.95 (*0-8040-0268-1*) Swallow.
— A Spy in the House of Love. LC 66-6833. 140p. 1959. pap. 8.95 (*0-8040-0280-0*) Swallow.
— A Spy in the House of Love. Rubenstein, Julie, ed. 176p. 1994. reprint ed. mass mkt. 5.99 (*0-671-87139-0*) PB.
— Under a Glass Bell. LC 94-32163. 101p. (Orig.). 1995. pap. 8.95 (*0-8040-0302-5*) Swallow.
— Waste of Timelessness: And Other Early Stories. LC 74-28648. viii, 110p. 1994. reprint ed. pap. 9.95 (*0-8040-0981-3*) Swallow.
***Nin, Anais.** White Stains. 1998. mass mkt. 6.95 (*1-56333-609-X*) Masquerade.
Nin, Anais. Winter of Artifice. LC 61-17530. 175p. (Orig.). 1961. pap. 8.95 (*0-8040-0322-X*) Swallow.
Nin, Anais & Miller, Henry. A Literate Passion: Letters of Anais Nin & Henry Miller, 1932-1953. 448p. 1989. pap. 16.00 (*0-15-652791-X*) Harcourt.
Nin, Anais & Pollak, Felix. Arrows of Longing: The Correspondence Between Anais Nin & Felix Pollak, 1952-1976. Mason, Gregory H., ed. LC 97-46482. 243p. 1998. pap. 14.95 (*0-8040-1007-2*); text 34.95 (*0-8040-1006-4*) Swallow.
Nin, Anais, et al. Going Down: Great Writing on Oral Sex. LC 98-35218. 144p. 1998. 12.95 (*0-8118-2245-1*) Chronicle Bks.
Nin, Anais, jt. auth. see Miller, Henry.
Ninacs, William A., jt. ed. see Sherraden, Margaret S.
Ninan, K. N. Edible Oilseeds: Growth, Area Responses & Prospects. (C). 1989. 24.00 (*81-204-0397-5*, Pub. by Oxford IBH) S Asia.
Nincic, Miroslav. Anatomy of Hostility: The U. S.-Soviet Rivalry in Perspective. 292p. (C). 1989. pap. text 32.50 (*0-15-502712-3*, Pub. by Harcourt Coll Pubs) Harcourt.
— The Arms Race: The Political Economy of Military Growth. LC 81-13808. 224p. 1982. 49.95 (*0-275-90869-0*, C0869, Praeger Pubs) Greenwood.
— Democracy & Foreign Policy: The Fall of Political Realism. 200p. 1994. pap. 19.50 (*0-231-07669-X*) Col U Pr.
— Democracy & Foreign Policy: The Fallacy of Political Realism. 224p. 1992. text 46.00 (*0-231-07668-1*) Col U Pr.
Nincic, Miroslav & Lepgold, Joseph, eds. Being Useful: Policy Relevance & International Relations Theory. (Illus.). 352p. (C). text 62.50 (*0-472-11072-1*, 11072); pap. text 27.95 (*0-472-08656-1*, 08656) U of Mich Pr.
Nincic, Miroslav, jt. auth. see Stockholm International Peace Research Institute S.
Nind, Melanie & Hewett, David. Access to Communication: Developing the Basics of Communication with People with Severe Learning Difficulties Through Intensive Interaction. 244p. 1994. pap. 34.00 (*1-85346-206-3*, Pub. by David Fulton) Taylor & Francis.
Ninde, Edward S. The Story of the American Hymn. LC 72-1708. (Illus.). reprint ed. 57.45 (*0-404-09914-9*) AMS Pr.
Nine, Jennifer. Like the English Sun: The Official Story of Bush. (Illus.). 1999. pap. 19.95 (*0-7535-0189-9*) London Brdge.
Nine, Jerry. Cattle Buyers & Cattle Poop by the Pound or by the Scoop. (Illus.). 64p. 1989. pap. write for info. (*0-318-65802-X*) Rocking Nine.
Nine Stories, jt. see Loeb, Lisa.
Nine, William G. & Wilson, Ronald G. The Appomattox Paroles April 9-15, 1865. (Virginia Civil War Battles & Leaders Ser.). (Illus.). 236p. 1989. 19.95 (*0-930919-69-6*) H E Howard.
Ninebrenner, Jan, jt. auth. see Davidson, James.
Nineham, A. & Slack, R. Medical & Veterinary Chemicals, 2 vols., Set. LC 66-28423. 1968. reprint ed. 225.00 (*0-08-011967-0*, Pub. by Pergamon Repr) Franklin.
Nineham, Dennis, ed. see Ziesler, John A.
Nineham, Dennis E., ed. see Houlden, J. L.
Nineham, Dennis E., ed. see Sweet, John.
Ninemeier, Jack D. Food & Beverage Management. 2nd ed. (Illus.). 374p. (C). 1995. pap. write for info. (*0-86612-119-6*) Educ Inst Am Hotel.
— Management of Food & Beverage Operations. 2nd ed. LC 90-36083. (Illus.). 370p. 1995. pap. write for info. (*0-86612-100-5*) Educ Inst Am Hotel.
***Ninemeier, Jack D.** Management of Food & Beverage Operations 3rd ed. LC 99-37315. 1999. write for info. (*0-86612-181-1*) Educ Inst Am Hotel.
Ninemeier, Jack D. Planning & Control for Food & Beverage Operations. 4th ed. LC 97-46737. 424p. 1998. pap. 68.95 (*0-86612-161-7*) Educ Inst Am Hotel.
Ninemeier, Jack D. & Kavanaugh, Raphael R. Hospitality Supervision. 2nd ed. (Illus.). 316p. (C). 1995. pap. write for info. (*0-86612-117-X*) Educ Inst Am Hotel.
Ninemeier, Jack D., jt. auth. see Kavanaugh, Raphael R.
Ninestein, Eleanor H. Introduction to Computer Mathematics. (C). 1987. text 44.66 (*0-673-18205-3*) Addson-Wesley Educ.
— Technical Math with Calculus. (C). 1997. 23.20 (*0-673-46458-X*) Addson-Wesley Educ.
— Technical Mathematics. (C). 1991. student ed. write for info. (*0-318-68849-2*) Addson-Wesley Educ.
Nineteen Ninety-Four United Nations, The. The 1994 United Nations Convention on the Law of the Sea: Basic Documents. LC 94-39925. (Law Specials Ser.: Vol. 8). 1995. pap. text 51.50 (*0-7923-3271-7*, Pub. by M Nijhoff) Kluwer Academic.
Nineteenth Draft Members. Woodfrogs in Chaos: A 19th Draft Anthology. Dinsmore, Danika, ed. (Illus.). 88p. (Orig.). 1996. pap. 7.00 (*1-890051-00-4*) It Plays in Peoria.
Nineth European Symposium on Medieval Logic & Sema. Sophisms in Medieval Logic & Grammar: Acts of the Ninth European Symposium on Medieval Logic & Semantics, Held at St, Andrews, June 1990. Read, Stephen, ed. LC 93-16500. (Nijhoff International Philosophy Ser.: Vol. 48). 440p. (C). 1993. lib. bdg. 241.50 (*0-7923-2196-0*, Pub. by Kluwer Academic) Kluwer Academic.
Ninety-First Psalm Ministries, Phoenix Church Staf. From Lovin' Ovens. Waltz, Nyla & Williams, Gale, eds. (Illus.). 91p. 1995. pap. 12.00 (*0-9647498-0-7*) Words Paradise.
Ninety Niner Home Computer Magazine Editors. The Best of Ninety-Niner, Vol. I. (Illus.). 360p. (Orig.). 1984. pap. 19.95 (*0-933094-11-6*) Waggle Dancer.
Ninfa, Alexander J. & Ballou, David P. Fundamental Laboratory Approaches for Biochemistry & Biotechnology. LC 98-9662. (Illus.). 350p. (C). 1998. pap. text 39.95 (*1-891786-00-8*) Fitzgerald Sci.
Ninfo, Vito & Chung, E. B., eds. Tumors & Tumor-Like Lesions of Soft Tissues. (Contemporary Issues in Surgical Pathology Ser.: Vol. 18). (Illus.). 295p. 1991. text 126.00 (*0-443-08672-9*) Church.
Ning, Cynthia. Chinese Sentence Book: A Copy-Ready Workbook. (CHI & ENG., Illus.). 104p. (Orig.). (J). (gr. 1-8). 1996. pap. 19.95 (*1-57306-050-X*) Bess Pr.
— Communicating in Chinese: Audio Program for Listening & Speaking. (Reading & Writing Ser.). (CHI & ENG.). 284p. (YA). 1994. pap. text, student ed. Price not set. (*0-88710-178-X*) Yale Far Eastern Pubns.
Ning, Cynthia. Communicating in Chinese: Audio Program for Listening & Speaking. (Communicating in Chinese Ser.). 1995. boxed set 59.95 incl. audio (*0-88710-180-1*) Yale Far Eastern Pubns.
Ning, Cynthia. Communicating in Chinese: Listening & Speaking. (Communicating in Chinese Ser.). (CHI.). (Orig.). (C). 1993. pap. text, teacher ed., spiral bd. 24.95 (*0-88710-176-3*) Yale Far Eastern Pubns.
— Communicating in Chinese: Listening & Speaking. (Illus.). (Orig.). 1994. boxed set 46.95 (*0-88710-177-1*) Yale Far Eastern Pubns.
— Communicating in Chinese an Interactive Approach to Beginning Chinese: Student Book Reading & Writing. 284p. (Orig.). 1994. pap. 24.95 (*0-614-31048-2*) Yale Far Eastern Pubns.
— Communicating in Chinese an Interactive Approach to Beginning Chinese: Student's Book for Listening & Speaking. (Illus.). 286p. (Orig.). (YA). 1994. pap., student ed. 24.95 (*0-88710-175-5*) Yale Far Eastern Pubns.
Ning H. Chen. Process Reactor Design. 512p. (C). 1983. teacher ed. write for info. (*0-318-57278-8*, H79049) P-H.
Ning, Jimmy, tr. see Blake, Alice A.
Ning, Li. Animal Biotechnology: Proceedings of the International Conference Beijing, China, 11-14 June, 1997. (Illus.). xiv, 408p. 1997. 126.00 (*7-80003-396-1*) World Scientific Pub.
Ning, Ma. Broad Sworder. Shicong, Liu, tr. 184p. 1993. 6.95 (*0-8351-3134-3*) China Bks.
Ning, Tak H. & Taur, Yuan. Fundamentals of Modern VLSI Devices. LC 98-16162. (Illus.). 480p. (C). 1998. 110.00 (*0-521-55056-4*); pap. 44.95 (*0-521-55959-6*) Cambridge U Pr.
Ning, Zhen-Qiu, jt. auth. see Dewilde, Patrick.
Ninh, Bao. The Sorrow of War: A Novel of North Vietnam. Hao, Phan T., tr. from VIE. 240p. 1996. pap. 12.95 (*1-57322-543-6*, Riverhd Trade) Berkley Pub.
Ninh, Nguyen H., ed. Potential Socioeconomic Effect. (C). 1996. pap. text 34.85 (*0-8133-8860-0*) Westview.
Ninham, B. W., jt. auth. see Barber, M. N.
Ninham, B. W., jt. auth. see Hughes, B. D.
Ninham, Sue, jt. auth. see Latimer, Deborah.
Nini, jt. auth. see Parfitt.
Nini, Y. The Jews of the Yemen, 1800-1914. xii, 256p. 1991. text 77.00 (*3-7186-5041-X*, Harwood Acad Pubs) Gordon & Breach.
Nini, Yehuda. Jews of Yemen. (WVSS on the Middle East Ser.). (C). 1996. pap. text 32.50 (*0-8133-7945-8*) Westview.
Nini, Yehuda, jt. ed. see Parfitt, Tudor.
Nininger, H. H. A Comet Strikes the Earth. rev. ed. (Illus.). 1969. pap. 3.00 (*0-910096-04-X*) Am Meteorite.
Ninio, Moshe, jt. auth. see Vergne, Philippe.
Niniowskyi, W. Ukrainian - English English - Ukrainian Dictionary. 1991. lib. bdg. 29.95 (*0-8288-2634-X*) Fr & Eur.
— Ukrainian-English & English-Ukrainian Dictionary. 680p. 1992. pap. 21.00 (*0-317-05517-8*) Szwede Slavic.
Ninkovich, Frank A. The Diplomacy of Ideas: U. S. Foreign Policy & Cultural Relations, 1938-1950. 264p. 1981. text 57.95 (*0-521-23241-4*) Cambridge U Pr.
— The Diplomacy of Ideas: U. S. Foreign Policy & Cultural Relations, 1938-1950. LC 95-78628. 253p. 1995. pap. 19.95 (*1-879176-23-8*) Imprint Pubns.
— Germany & the United States. rev. ed. (International History Ser.: No. 2). (Illus.). 224p. 1995. 33.00 (*0-8057-7928-0*, Twyne); pap. 20.00 (*0-8057-9223-6*, Twyne) Mac Lib Ref.
— Modernity & Power: A History of the Domino Theory in the Twentieth Century. LC 94-5733. 1994. pap. text 19.95 (*0-226-58651-0*); lib. bdg. 49.95 (*0-226-58650-2*) U Ch Pr.
— U. S. Information Policy & Cultural Diplomacy. Hoepli-Phalon, Nancy L., ed. LC 95-83910. (Headline Ser.: No. 308). (Illus.). 64p. (Orig.). (YA). (gr. 9-12). 1996. pap. text 5.95 (*0-87124-168-4*) Foreign Policy.
***Ninkovich, Frank A.** The United States & Imperialism. 2000. 59.95 (*1-57718-055-0*); pap. 26.95 (*1-57718-056-9*) Blackwell Pubs.
— The Wilsonian Century: U. S. Foreign Policy since 1900. LC 98-14219. 318p. 1999. 27.50 (*0-226-58648-0*) U Ch Pr.
Ninkovich, Thomas. Family Reunion Handbook: A Complete Guide for Reunion Planners. 2nd rev. ed. LC 98-8245. 288p. 1998. pap. 14.95 (*0-9610470-6-2*) Reunion Research.
Ninman, Stefani B. The Malibu Million Dollar Rock. LC 79-53369. (Illus.). 36p. 1979. pap. 4.00 (*0-930422-21-X*) Dennis-Landman.
Ninneman, Eric, ed. see Haroutunian, Virginia.
Ninness, H. A. & Glenn, Sigrid S. Applied Behavior Analysis & School Psychology: A Research Guide to Principles & Procedures. LC 87-29544. 298p. 1988. lib. bdg. 72.95 (*0-313-24267-4*, NBA/, Greenwood Pr) Greenwood.
Ninness, H. A., et al. Assessment & Treatment of Emotional or Behavioral Disorders. LC 93-20502. 192p. 1993. 59.95 (*0-275-94098-5*, C4098, Praeger Pubs) Greenwood.
Ninness, Michael. Adobe Photoshop 5 Web Magic. LC 98-84902. 288p. 1998. pap. 39.99 (*1-56205-913-0*) New Riders Pub.
***Ninness, Michael.** Photoshop Power Shortcuts. 250p. 1999. pap. text 17.99 (*0-7897-2172-4*) Que.
— Photoshop X Power Shortcuts. 350p. 2000. pap. 17.99 (*0-7897-2426-X*) Que.
Nino, Carlos, ed. Rights. (International Library of Essays in Law & Legal Theory). 550p. (C). 1992. lib. bdg. 150.00 (*0-8147-5771-5*) NYU Pr.
Nino, Carlos S. The Constitution of Deliberative Democracy. 272p. 1996. pap. 17.00 (*0-300-07727-0*) Yale U Pr.
— The Constitution of Deliberative Democracy. LC 95-53688. 272p. (C). 1996. 40.00 (*0-300-06748-8*) Yale U Pr.
— Radical Evil on Trial. 224p. 1996. pap. 17.00 (*0-300-07728-9*) Yale U Pr.
— Radical Evil on Trial. LC 95-53689. 224p. (C). 1996. 35.00 (*0-300-06749-6*) Yale U Pr.
Nino, Carmen di, see Di Nino, Carmen.
Nino, Raul. Breathing Light. fac. ed. (Illus.). 48p. (Orig.). 1991. pap. 6.00 (*1-877636-10-X*) March Abrazo.
Ninomiya, H. Flow Analysis Using a PC. 1991. 94.00 (*0-8493-7733-1*, Q) CRC Pr.
Ninomiya, H. & Onishi, K. Flow Analysis Using a PC. 212p. 1991. 83.00 (*1-85312-144-4*) Computational Mech MA.
Ninomiya, H. & Onishi, K. Flow Analysis Using a PC. 212p. 1991. text 83.00 incl. disk (*1-56252-077-6*) Computational Mech MA.
Ninomiya, I. & Naito, T. Photochemical Synthesis. (Best Synthetic Methods Ser.). 350p. 1989. text 132.00 (*0-12-519490-0*) Acad Pr.
— Recent Developments in the Chemistry of Natural Carbon Compounds, Vol. 10. 210p. (C). 1984. 150.00 (*0-7855-6294-X*, Pub. by Collets) St Mut.
***Ninomiya, Joko & Zorensky, Ed.** My Journey in Karate: The Sabaki Way. LC 99-87452. (Illus.). 240p. 2000. pap. 16.95 (*1-58394-017-0*, Pub. by Frog Ltd CA) Publishers Group.
***Ninomiya, Kancho & Zorensky, Ed.** Sabaki Method: Karate in the Inner Circle. LC 98-7063. (Illus.). 150p. 1998. pap. 18.95 (*1-883319-74-9*) Frog Ltd CA.
Ninomiya, Kazuji, tr. see Mori Ogai, pseud.
Ninomiya, M. & Kikkawa, K. Quantum Gravity: Proceedings of the Seventh Nishinomiya-Yuk. 216p. 1993. text 67.00 (*981-02-1460-X*) World Scientific Pub.
Ninomiya, Sontoku. Sage Ninomiya's Evening Talks. Yamagata, Isoh, tr. LC 70-98786. 139p. 1970. reprint ed. lib. bdg. 38.50 (*0-8371-3134-0*, NIEV, Greenwood Pr) Greenwood.
Ninomiya, T., jt. ed. see Yonezawa, F.
Ninomiya, Takamichi & Enright, D. J., eds. The Poetry of Living Japan. LC 78-11863. 104p. 1979. reprint ed. lib. bdg. 49.50 (*0-313-21210-4*, NIPL, Greenwood Pr) Greenwood.
Ninomiya, Yoshifumi, et al, eds. Extracellular Matrix-Cell Interaction: Molecules to Diseases. LC 99-166904. (Illus.). xx, 382p. 1998. 255.75 (*3-8055-6741-3*) S Karger.
Ninommiya, T., jt. ed. see Kuo, K. H.
Ninoyama, Yoshifumi, jt. ed. see Glew, Robert H.
***Nintendo of America Staff.** Official Nintendo Pokemon Stadium Player's Guide. (Illus.). 208p. 2000. pap. 14.95 (*1-930206-01-1*, NES B GD40) Nintendo.
— Official Nintendo Power Perfect Dark Player's Guide. (Illus.). 192p. 2000. pap. 14.95 (*1-930206-02-X*, NES B GD42) Nintendo.
— Official Nintendo Power Pokemon Trading Card Game Player's Guide. (Illus.). 112p. 2000. pap. 14.95 (*1-930206-00-3*, NES B GD44) Nintendo.
Nintendo Staff. Turok: Seeds of Evil, Official Strategy Guide. 1998. pap. 12.99 (*1-57840-989-6*) Acclaim Bks.
Ninth International Conference Staff. Fundamentals of Computation Theory: Proceedings of the 9th International Conference, FCT '93, Szeged, Hungary,

An Asterisk (*) at the beginning of an entry indicates that the title is appearing for the first time.

August 23-27, 1993. Esik, Zoltan, ed. (Lecture Notes in Computer Science Ser.: Vol. 710). ix, 471p. 1993. pap. write for info. (*3-540-57163-9*) Spr-Verlag.

Ninyerola, Alfonso. Jose Maria Sicilia: New Paintings. Bell, Suzanne, ed. Vidal, Africa, tr. from SPA. (Illus.). 36p. 1990. pap. 0.20 (*0-685-32872-4*) Blum Helman.

Niobet, George. Larousse Dictionnaire Analogique. (FRE.). 1992. pap. 59.95 (*0-8288-7857-9*) Fr & Eur.

— Nouveau Larousse Dictionnaire Analogique. (FRE.). 856p. 1980. pap. 31.95 (*0-8288-1942-4*, M14296) Fr & Eur.

Niocaill, Gearoid M., jt. ed. see Monahan, Edward C.

Nioche, Brigitte. What Turns Men On? 224p. (Orig.). 1989. mass mkt. 6.99 (*0-451-16054-1*, Sig) NAL.

Nioclai, Friedrich. Gesammelte Werke Bd. IV: Eyn Feyner Kleyner Almanach Vol Schoenerr Echterr Liblicherr Volckslieder. (GER.). 1985. write for info. (*3-487-07581-4*) G Olms Pubs.

Niomiya, Y. & Chiariglione, L., eds. Signal Processing of HDTV: Proceedings of the International Workshop on HDTV '94, Turin, Italy, October 26-28, 1994. 592p. 1995. text 321.00 (*0-444-82283-6*) Elsevier.

Nion, Beth. Analysis of the Sources: Companion to the Battles of Arthur. (Illus.). 1999. pap. 14.95 (*1-882427-17-3*) Aspasia Inc.

— The Battles of Arthur. (Illus.). 250p. (Orig.). 1999. pap. 14.95 (*1-882427-16-5*, 316-5) Aspasia Inc.

Niordson, F. I. Shell Theory. (Applied Mathematics & Mechanics Ser.: Vol. 29). 408p. 1985. 149.50 (*0-444-87640-5*, North Holland) Elsevier.

Niordson, F. I., ed. see International Union of Theoretical & Applied Mecha.

Niordson, F. I., ed. see Symposium of International Union of Theoretical &.

Niosi, Jorge. The Economy of Canada: Who Controls It? 2nd rev. ed. Williams, Penelope & Ballem, Hugh, trs. from FRE. (Study of Ownership & Control). Orig. Title: Le Controle Financier de Capitalisme Canadien. 179p. 1978. 41.99 (*0-919618-49-9*, Pub. by Black Rose); pap. 12.99 (*0-919618-75-8*, Pub. by Black Rose) Consort Bk Sales.

— Flexible Innovation: Technological Alliances in Canadian Industry. 144p. 1995. text 65.00 (*0-7735-1334-5*) McG-Queens Univ Pr.

Niosi, Jorge, ed. New Technology Policy & Social Innovations in the Firm. LC 94-15090. 1995. 60.00 (*1-85567-259-6*) St Martin.

— Technology & National Competitiveness: Oligopoly, Technological Innovation & International Competition. 304p. (C). 1991. text 65.00 (*0-7735-0827-9*, Pub. by McG-Queens Univ Pr); pap. text 22.95 (*0-7735-0859-7*, Pub. by McG-Queens Univ Pr) CUP Services.

***Niosi, Jorge, et al.** Canada's National System of Innovation. 240p. 2000. 65.00 (*0-7735-2012-0*, Pub. by McG-Queens Univ Pr) CUP Services.

Niosi, Jorge, et al. Flexible Innovation: Technological Alliances in Canadian Industry. LC 96-121629. 144p. (C). 1995. pap. text 22.95 (*0-7735-1335-3*, Pub. by McG-Queens Univ Pr) CUP Services.

Niosi, Jorge, jt. auth. see Bellon, Bertrand.

Nip. Poli Formal Ontology. LC 96-185793. 1996. text 161.50 (*0-7923-4104-X*) Kluwer Academic.

Niparko, John K. Cochlear Implants. 304p. text 99.00 (*0-7817-1782-5*) Lppncott W & W.

***Nipe, George M.** Last Victory in Russia: SS Panzerkorps & Manstein's Kharkov Counter Offensive. (Illus.). 300p. 2000. 59.95 (*0-7643-1186-7*) Schiffer.

Niphuis-Nell, M., ed. Demographic Aspects of the Changing Status of Women in Europe. (Publications of the Netherlands Inter-University Demographic Institute & the Population & Family Study Centre Ser.: Vol. 7). 1978. pap. text 40.50 (*90-207-0714-0*) Kluwer Academic.

Nipkow, T., ed. Rewriting Techniques & Applications: Proceedings of the 9th International Conference, RTA-98, Tsukuba, Japan, March 28-April 1, 1998, Vol. 137. LC 98-6357. (Lecture Notes in Computer Science: Vol. 1379). x, 343p. 1998. pap. 59.00 (*3-540-64301-X*) Spr-Verlag.

Nipkow, Tobias, jt. auth. see Baader, Franz.

Nipkow, Tobias, jt. ed. see Barendregt, Hank.

Nipp, G. L. Quaternary Quadratic Forms: Computer Generated Tables. vii, 155p. 1991. 79.95 (*0-387-97601-9*) Spr-Verlag.

Nipp, Hagen S., jt. auth. see Beall, Pamela Conn.

Nipp, Luitgard. Kapitalausstattung im Landlichen Kleingewerbe in der 2. Halfte Des 19. Jahrunderts. Bruchey, Stuart, ed. LC 80-2818. (Dissertations in European Economic History Ser.).Tr. of Capital Equipment in Bavarian Rural Crafts in the Second Half of the Nineteenth Century. (Illus.). 1981. lib. bdg. 26.95 (*0-405-14002-9*) Ayer.

Nipp, Susan, jt. auth. see Beall, Pamela Conn.

Nipp, Susan H., jt. auth. see Beall, Pamela Conn.

Nipp, Susan Hagen, jt. auth. see Beall, Pamela Conn.

Nippan Book Staff. Fentress Bradburn. (Master Architect Ser.). 1998. 59.95 (*1-875498-86-9*) Bks Nippan.

***Nippan Books Staff.** Costume Play Vol. 3. (Combat Action Pose Collection). (Illus.). 1999. pap. 39.95 (*4-906436-99-4*, Pub. by Ginga Shuppan) Bks Nippan.

— Duet Poses. (Pose File Ser.: Vol. 9). 1998. pap. 49.95 (*4-87199-055-9*, Pub. by Erute-Shuppan) Bks Nippan.

— Nude Vol. 2, Vol. 3. (Combat Action Pose Collection). (Illus.). 1999. pap. 39.95 (*4-906436-97-8*, Pub. by Ginga Shuppan) Bks Nippan.

— Office Buildings. LC 96-152249. (New Concepts in Architecture & Design Ser.). 1996. 85.00 (*4-938812-10-X*, Pub. by Puroto Gyarak) Bks Nippan.

— Sorayama Sexy Robot Poster Book. 1996. pap. 8.99 (*3-89268-037-X*, Pub. by Taschen Benedik) Bks Nippan.

***Nippan Books Staff, NIPPAN.** Combat Action Pose Collection Vol. 1: Battle Suit. (Illus.). 1999. pap. 39.95 (*4-906436-96-X*, Pub. by Ginga Shuppan) Bks Nippan.

Nippel, Wilfried. Public Order in Ancient Rome. (Key Themes in Ancient History Ser.). 173p. (C). 1995. text 59.95 (*0-521-38327-7*) Cambridge U Pr.

— Public Order in Ancient Rome. (Key Themes in Ancient History Ser.). 173p. (C). 1995. pap. text 18.95 (*0-521-38749-3*) Cambridge U Pr.

Nippell, Janet, jt. auth. see Yandell, Ben.

Nipperdey. Germany from Napoleon to Bismarck. (Illus.). (C). text. write for info. (*0-472-10725-9*) U of Mich Pr.

Nipperdey, Karl & Andresen, Georg, eds. Tacitus, Annalen, 2 vols., Bd. I: Ab Excessu Divi Augusti I-IV. (GER.). 466p. 1978. write for info. (*3-296-15751-4*) G Olms Pubs.

— Tacitus, Annalen, 2 vols., Bd. II: Ab Excessu Divi Augusti XI-XVI. (GER.). 347p. 1978. write for info. (*3-296-15752-2*) G Olms Pubs.

Nipperdey, Karl & Witte, Kurt, eds. Nepos, Cornelius. iii, 300p. 1967. write for info. (*3-296-12000-9*) G Olms Pubs.

Nipperdey, Thomas. Germany from Napoleon to Bismarck, 1800-1866. Nolan, Daniel, tr. from GER. LC 95-4498. 760p. 1996. text 69.95 (*0-691-02636-X*, Pub. by Princeton U Pr) Cal Prin Full Svc.

Nippert-Eng, Christena E. Home & Work: Negotiating Boundaries Through Everyday Life. 304p. 1996. pap. 16.95 (*0-226-58146-2*) U Ch Pr.

— Home & Work: Negotiating Boundaries Through Everyday Life. 1996. lib. bdg. 48.00 (*0-226-58145-4*) U Ch Pr.

— Telecommuting Problems. 1995. 19.95 (*0-226-58652-9*) U Ch Pr.

***Nippert, Irmgard, et al, eds.** The New Genetics: From Research into Health Care: Social & Ethical Implications for Users & Providers. LC 99-31137. (Illus.). viii, 185p. 1999. pap. 109.00 (*3-540-65920-X*) Spr-Verlag.

Nippold, Marilyn A. Later Language Development: The School-Age & Adolescent Years. 2nd ed. LC 97-20020. 1998. pap. text 34.00 (*0-89079-725-0*) PRO-ED.

Nippold, Marilyn A., ed. Later Language Development: Ages 9 Through 19. LC 90-52764. 271p. (Orig.). 1988. pap. text 29.00 (*0-89079-304-2*, 1756) PRO-ED.

Nippold, Otfried. The Development of International Law after the World War. Hershey, Amos S., tr. from GER. xv, 241p. 1998. reprint ed. 78.00 (*1-56169-414-2*, 15603) Gaunt.

Nippon Bonsai Association Staff. Classic Bonsai of Japan. Bester, John, tr. from JPN. (Illus.). 188p. 1989. 100.00 (*0-87011-933-8*) Kodansha.

Nippon Dental University Staff. Osseointegrated Implant Manual. (Illus.). 159p. 1994. pap. 150.00 (*1-56386-014-7*, Ishiyaku EuroAmerica) Med Dent Media.

Nippon Shuppan Hanbai Inc Staff, tr. see Kuwayama, Yasaburo, ed.

Nipps, Karen. Naturally Fond of Pictures: American Illustration of the 1840s & 1850s. (Illus.). 30p. 1989. pap. 6.00 (*0-914076-68-X*) Lib Co Phila.

Nips, Nick L. Driver Training. xp. 1976. pap. 4.00 (*0-935350-71-3*) Luna Bisonte.

Nique, Thomas A. & Tu, Harold K., eds. Anesthesia for Facial Plastic Surgery. LC 93-11651. 114p. 1993. 62.00 (*0-86577-445-5*) Thieme Med Pubs.

Niquette, Alan & Niquette, Beth. Building Your Christian Defense System. (Building Bks.). 8p. (Orig.). (YA). 1988. pap. 7.99 (*1-55661-015-7*); pap., teacher ed. 7.99 (*1-55661-016-5*) Bethany Hse.

Niquette, Beth, jt. auth. see Niquette, Alan.

Nir, Dov. Region As a Socio-Environmental System: An Introduction to a Systemic Regional Geography. (C). 1990. lib. bdg. 139.00 (*0-7923-0516-7*) Kluwer Academic.

Nir, Roman. Catalog of the Collection of Dr. Edward & Loda Rozanski at Orchard Lake. LC 98-109325. 1997. write for info. (*0-9649869-5-7*) Orchrd Lake Sch.

— Catalog of the Collection of Dr. Edward & Loda Rozanski at Orchard Lake, Vol. I. LC 98-109325. 1997. write for info. (*0-9649869-6-5*) Orchrd Lake Sch.

— Catalog of the Polish American Archives at Orchard Lake. 1996. write for info. (*0-9649869-1-4*) Orchrd Lake Sch.

— Catalog of the Polish American Archives at Orchard Lake, Vol. I. 1996. write for info. (*0-9649869-2-2*) Orchrd Lake Sch.

— A Guidebook to Polish Archival Collections in the United States. 1997. write for info. (*0-9649869-0-6*) Orchrd Lake Sch.

— Polish American Archives at Orchard Lake Yearbook. 1996. write for info. (*0-9649869-3-0*) Orchrd Lake Sch.

Nir, Yehuda. The Lost Childhood. 256p. 1989. 19.95 (*0-15-158862-7*) Harcourt.

***Nir, Yehuda.** Lost Childhood: A World War II Memoir. LC 99-87444. (Illus.). 240p. (YA). (gr. 7 up). 2000. 15.95 (*0-439-16389-7*) Scholastic Inc.

— The Lost Childhood: A World War II Memoir of a Jewish Boy. LC 99-87444. (Illus.). (J). 2000. pap. write for info. (*0-439-16390-0*) Scholastic Inc.

Niramayananda. Call of the Spirit: Conversion with Swami Akhandananda. 170p. 1987. pap. 2.95 (*0-87481-538-X*, Pub. by Ramakrishna Math) Vedanta Pr.

Niranjan, K., et al, eds. Environmentally Responsible Food Processing. LC 94-28115. 117p. 1994. 75.00 (*0-8169-0651-3*, S-300) Am Inst Chem Eng.

Niranjan, Shiva. Raja Rao, Novelist As Sadhaka. 154p. 1986. 13.50 (*0-8364-1664-3*, Pub. by Popular Prakashan) S Asia.

Niranjana, Tejaswini. Siting Translation: History, Post-Structuralism, & the Colonial Context. LC 91-21487. 216p. 1992. 48.00 (*0-520-07450-5*, Pub. by U CA Pr) Cal Prin Full Svc.

— Siting Translation: History, Post-Structuralism, & the Colonial Context. LC 91-21487. 216p. 1992. pap. 16.95 (*0-520-07451-3*, Pub. by U CA Pr) Cal Prin Full Svc.

Niranjana, Tejaswini, ed. Interrogating Modernity: Culture & Colonialism in India. (C). 1993. 34.00 (*81-7046-109-X*, Pub. by Seagull Bks) S Asia.

Nirash, K. L. & Iqbal, S. M., eds. The Culture of Kashmir. 244p. 1978. 16.95 (*0-318-36980-X*) Asia Bk Corp.

Nirav, Shunyam. Hawaiian Organic Growing Guide: Hawaii's "How-to-Grow-It" Gardening Encyclopedia for the Tropics & Subtropics. 3rd ed. LC 92-60821. (Illus.). 232p. 1996. pap. 16.95 (*0-9633187-0-5*) New Dawn Environ.

Nirdlinger, Charles F. Four Short Plays. LC 79-50027. (One-Act Plays in Reprint Ser.). 1980. reprint ed. 20.00 (*0-8486-2052-6*) Roth Pub Inc.

Nirenberg, David. Communities of Violence: Persecution of Minorities in the Middle Ages. LC 95-33589. 288p. 1996. text 39.50 (*0-691-03375-7*, Pub. by Princeton U Pr); pap. text 16.95 (*0-691-05889-X*, Pub. by Princeton U Pr) Cal Prin Full Svc.

Nirenberg, Ira. Living with Math: Making Healthy Decisions for Yourself & the Earth. LC 96-85805. 208p. 1997. pap. 12.95 (*1-57706-676-6*) Burlington Natl.

Nirenberg, Jackie, ed. see Almaraz, Felix D., Jr., et al.

Nirenberg, Jesse S. Getting Through to People. LC 63-15341. 1986. reprint ed. 10.95 (*0-13-354860-0*, Reward) P-H.

Nirenberg, John. Management Insight, 1989: Annual Planner & Sourcebook. 200p. (Orig.). 1988. pap. 19.95 (*0-945693-00-1*) Mgmt Insight.

— Management Insight, 1990: Annual Planner. 176p. 1989. pap. 14.95 (*0-945693-02-8*) Mgmt Insight.

— Power Tools: A Leader's Guide to the Latest Management Thinking. LC 96-30054. 460p. (C). 1997. pap. text 24.95 (*0-13-745845-2*) P-H.

Nirenberg, L. Lectures on Linear Partial Differential Equations. LC 73-4400. (Regional Conference Series in Mathematics: No. 17). 66p. 1973. reprint ed. pap. 30.00 (*0-608-07824-7*, 205266900011) Bks Demand.

Nirenberg, Louis. Lectures on Linear Partial Differential Equations. LC 73-4400. (CBMS Regional Conference Series in Mathematics: No. 17). 58p. 1973. reprint ed. pap. 16.00 (*0-8218-1667-5*, CBMS/17) Am Math.

Nirenberg, Sue, jt. auth. see Ruedy, Elisabeth.

Nirenberg, Ted D. & Maisto, Stephen A. Developments in the Assessment & Treatment of Addictive Behaviors. Caddy, Glenn R., ed. LC 87-11446. (Developments in Clinical Psychology Ser.: Vol. 5). 400p. 1987. text 82.50 (*0-89391-170-4*) Ablx Pub.

Nirenberg, Ted D., jt. ed. see Gomberg, Edith S.

Nirenberg, Ted D., jt. ed. see Miller, Peter M.

Nirenburg, S., ed. Progress in Machine Translation. LC 92-3503. 334p. 1992. 70.00 (*90-5199-074-X*, Pub. by IOS Pr) IOS Press.

Nirenburg, Sergei, et al. Knowledge-Based Machine Translation. Goodman, Kenneth, ed. 250p. 1991. text 48.95 (*1-55860-128-7*) Morgan Kaufmann.

Nirenburg, Sergei, jt. ed. see Goodman, Kenneth.

Nirgiotis, Nicholas. Thomas Edison. LC 93-37028. (Cornerstones to Freedom Ser.). (Illus.). 32p. (J). (gr. 4-6). 1994. lib. bdg. 19.50 (*0-516-06676-5*) Childrens.

— Volcanoes: Mountains That Blow Their Tops. LC 95-22045. (All Aboard Reading Ser.: Level 2). (Illus.). 48p. (J). (gr. 1-3). 1996. pap. 3.95 (*0-448-41143-1*, G & D) Peng Put Young Read.

Nirgiotis, Nicholas & Nirgiotis, Theodore. No More Dodos: How Zoos Help Endangered Wildlife. LC 95-45972. (J). 1996. 23.95 (*0-8225-2856-8*, Lerner Publctns) Lerner Pub.

Nirgiotis, Theodore, jt. auth. see Nirgiotis, Nicholas.

Nirgun, Ma A., ed. see Osho.

Nirmal, Barry K. CICS Application & System Programming: Tools & Techniques. 559p. 1993. pap. 49.95 (*0-471-58477-0*, GD3934) Wiley.

— MVS - TSO: Mastering CLISTs. 272p. 1993. pap. 49.95 (*0-471-58441-X*, GC3195) Wiley.

— REXX Tools & Techniques. 264p. 1993. pap. 49.95 (*0-471-58559-9*, GD4175) Wiley.

Nirmal, Chiranjivi J. Human Rights in India: Historical, Social & Political Perspectives. (Law in India Ser.). 272p. 2000. text 27.95 (*0-19-564597-9*) OUP.

Nirodbaran. Memorable Contacts with the Mother. 2nd ed. 190p. 1994. pap. 9.95 (*81-900160-8-3*, Pub. by SAA) E-W Cultural Ctr.

— Sri Aurobindo: A Dream-Dialogue with Children. 232p. 1994. pap. 12.95 (*81-900160-6-7*, Pub. by SAA) E-W Cultural Ctr.

— Sri Aurobindo for All Ages. 241p. 1998. pap. 9.95 (*81-7058-202-4*, Pub. by SAA) E-W Cultural Ctr.

— Sri Aurobindo's Humour. 125p. 1994. pap. 7.95 (*81-900160-4-0*, Pub. by SAA) E-W Cultural Ctr.

— Twelve Years with Sri Aurobindo. 3rd ed. 334p. 1996. pap. 7.95 (*81-7058-099-4*, Pub. by SAA) E-W Cultural Ctr.

Nirodbaran, ed. see Aurobindo, Sri.

Nirtaut, Dennis J. Controlling Health Care Costs: An Approach to Maximizing Cost Savings & Efficiencies. (Building Blocks Ser.: Vol. 14). (Illus.). 24p. (Orig.). 1994. pap. 24.95 (*1-57963-017-0*, A0034) Am Compensation.

Nirula, R. High-Yield General Surgery. 220p. 18.95 (*0-683-30691-X*) Lppncott W & W.

— High-Yield Internal Medicine. LC 97-7043. 350p. 1997. pap. 16.95 (*0-683-18044-4*) Lppncott W & W.

Nirvesha, Deva, ed. see Osho.

***Nisam, Horst G. & Nisam, Thorsten G.** Generation Without Ethics? An Informational & Educational Te LC 99-67187. 1999. pap. 20.00 (*1-55605-289-8*) Wyndham Hall.

Nisam, Thorsten G., jt. auth. see Nisam, Horst G.

Nisan, Mordechai. Identity & Civilization: Essays on Judaism, Christianity & Islam. LC 99-11511. 232p. (C). 1998. 51.00 (*0-7618-1355-1*) U Pr of Amer.

***Nisan, Mordechai.** Identity & Civilization: Essays on Judaism, Christianity & Islam. LC 99-11511. 232p. (C). 1999. pap. 32.50 (*0-7618-1356-X*) U Pr of Amer.

— Minorities in the Middle East: A History of Struggle & Self-Expression. LC 91-52512. 312p. 1991. lib. bdg. 45.00 (*0-89950-564-3*) McFarland & Co.

Nisan, Mordechai. Towards a New Israel: The Jewish State & the Arab Question. LC 91-11936. (Studies in Modern Society: No. 24). 1992. 42.50 (*0-404-61631-3*) AMS Pr.

Nisan, Noam, jt. auth. see Kushilevitz, Eyal.

Nisargand, Julie. The Wednesday Girl. limited ed. LC 96-78581. 192p. (Orig.). 1997. pap. 10.00 (*0-9654757-1-9*) Anima Bks CA.

***Nisberg, Edith.** A Garden Carried in the Pocket: A Magic Button to Wall Street. Geiger, Margaret, ed. 45p. 1999. pap. 10.95 (*0-7392-0251-0*, PO3294) Morris Pubng.

Nisbert, Robert G., ed. see Cicero, Marcus Tullius.

Nisbet, Alexander. 1 & 2 Peter. (Geneva Series of Commentaries). 300p. 1995. reprint ed. 25.99 (*0-85151-338-7*) Banner of Truth.

Nisbet, Anne M. The Gourmet's Guide to Northwest Bed & Breakfast Inns. (Northwest Gourmet Guides Ser.). (Illus.). 280p. 1998. pap. 16.95 (*0-9617699-9-8*) Speed Graphics.

Nisbet, B. N., ed. see Hegel, Georg Wilhelm Friedrich.

Nisbet-Brown, Eric, jt. auth. see Cooper, Edwin L.

***Nisbet, Delia Fabbroni-Giannotti.** Heinrich Heine & Giacomo Leopardi: The Rhetoric of Midrash. LC 98-27357. (Studies on Themes & Motifs in Literature: Vol. 47). 168p. (C). 2000. 42.95 (*0-8204-4152-X*) P Lang Pubng.

Nisbet, Euan G. The Young Earth: An Introduction to Archean Geology. 400p. 1987. text 90.00 (*0-04-550045-2*); pap. text 49.95 (*0-04-550049-5*) Routledge.

Nisbet, Evan G. The Geology of the Belingwe Greenstone Belt, Zimbabwe: A Study of the Evolution of Archaean Continental Crust. Bickle, M. J., ed. (Illus.). 242p. 1993. text 123.00 (*90-5410-120-2*, Pub. by A A Balkema) Ashgate Pub Co.

— Komatiites. Arndt, N. T., ed. (Illus.). 544p. 1982. text 150.00 (*0-04-552019-4*) Routledge.

— Leaving Eden: To Protect & Manage the Earth. (Illus.). 378p. (C). 1991. pap. text 21.95 (*0-521-42579-4*) Cambridge U Pr.

— Living Earth: A Short History of Life & Its Home. (Illus.). 238p. (C). 1992. pap. text 25.00 (*0-04-445856-8*, A8183) Routledge.

Nisbet, H. B. & Rawson, Claude, eds. The Cambridge History of Literary Criticism Vol. 4: The Eighteenth Century. (Cambridge History of Literary Criticism Ser.). 970p. (C). 1997. text 125.00 (*0-521-30009-6*) Cambridge U Pr.

Nisbet, H. B., ed. see Hegel, Georg Wilhelm Friedrich.

Nisbet, H. B., tr. see Hegel, Georg Wilhelm Friedrich.

Nisbet, H. B., tr. see Kant, Immanuel.

Nisbet, Jack. Purple Flat Top: In Pursuit of a Place. 196p. (Orig.). 1996. pap. 12.95 (*1-57061-058-4*) Sasquatch Bks.

***Nisbet, Jack.** Singing Grass, Burning Sage. LC 99-16619. (Illus.). 119p. 1999. pap. 19.95 (*1-55868-478-6*) Gr Arts Ctr Pub.

Nisbet, Jack. Sky People. LC 84-61542. (Illus.). 128p. (Orig.). 1984. 12.95 (*0-931849-00-4*); pap. 5.95 (*0-931849-01-2*) Quartzite Bks.

— Sources of the River: Tracking David Thompson Across Western North America. LC 94-6478. (Illus.). 288p. 1995. pap. 14.95 (*1-57061-006-1*) Sasquatch Bks.

Nisbet, James C. Four Years on the Firing Line. (Illus.). 267p. 1992. reprint ed. 35.00 (*0-916107-24-8*) Broadfoot.

Nisbet, James D. Boyhood on a Farm. Beckham, Claire, ed. 157p. 1995. 18.00 (*0-9640139-1-6*) Capital Bks.

— Weathering Stock Market Storms: Learning about Risk Control Timing. (Illus.). 208p. (C). 29.95 (*0-9640139-0-8*) Capital Bks.

— Wheels Up: Memoirs of a Private Pilot. 176p. 1998. text 15.00 (*1-891724-00-2*) New River.

Nisbet, Jan, ed. Natural Supports in School, at Work, & in the Community for People with Severe Disabilities. LC 92-9855. 368p. 1992. pap. text 30.00 (*1-55766-101-4*) P H Brookes.

***Nisbet, Jan & Hagner, David.** Part of the Community: Strategies for Including Everyone. LC 00-21848. 2000. write for info. (*1-55766-456-0*) P H Brookes.

Nisbet, Jim. Small Apt. (Thumbscrew Press Ser.). (Illus.). 68p. (Orig.). 1992. pap. 8.95 (*0-926664-12-3*) Bay Area Ctr Art & Tech.

Nisbet, John. The Impact of Research on Policy & Practice in Education. 96p. 1980. text 17.50 (*0-08-025723-2*, Pergamon Pr) Elsevier.

Nisbet, John & Shucksmith, Janet. Learning Strategies. (Education Bks.). 144p. (C). 1986. text 37.50 (*0-7102-0569-4*, Routledge Thoemms) Routledge.

Nisbet, John, et al. Towards Community Education: An Evaluation of Community Schools. 144p. 1980. 20.00 (*0-08-025735-6*, Pergamon Pr) Elsevier.

***Nisbet, Lee.** Gun Control Debate: You Decide. 2nd ed. 380p. 2000. pap. 19.95 (*1-57392-861-5*) Prometheus Bks.

Nisbet, Lee, ed. The Gun Control Debate: You Decide. LC 90-9138. (Contemporary Issues Ser.). 341p. (Orig.). (C). 1990. pap. 18.95 (*0-87975-618-7*) Prometheus Bks.

N

oks of George Grosz. LC
pap. 24.95
rd Art Mus.
The Busch-Reisinger
oldings. (Illus.). 125p. 1991. pap.
4, 4794) Harvard Art Mus.
cted Papers on Latin Literature. 460p.
65.00 (0-19-814948-4) OUP.

M. & Gurney, W. S. Modelling Fluctuating Populations. LC 81-14668. 393p. reprint ed. pap. 121.90 (0-608-17609-5, 203045900069) Bks Demand.

Nisbet, R. M. & Wood, S. N. Estimation of Mortality Rates in Stage Structured Populations. (Lecture Notes in Biomathematics Ser.). viii, 101p. 1991. 31.95 (0-387-53979-4) Spr-Verlag.

Nisbet, R. M., jt. auth. see Gurney, W. S.

Nisbet, Richard. Capacity of Negroes for Religious & Moral Improvement Considered. LC 73-100295. 207p. 1970. reprint ed. lib. bdg. 49.50 (0-8371-2940-0, NIC&) Greenwood.

Nisbet, Robert A. Conservatism: Dream & Reality. Parkin, Frank, ed. (Concepts in the Social Sciences Ser.). 128p. (Orig.). 1986. 32.50 (0-335-15377-1); pap. 9.99 (0-335-15378-X) OpUniv Pr.

— Emile Durkheim. LC 75-36358. 179p. 1976. reprint ed. lib. bdg. 55.00 (0-8371-8626-9, NIEDU, Greenwood Pr) Greenwood.

— History of the Idea of Progress. LC 93-28738. 380p. (C). 1993. pap. text 24.95 (1-56000-713-3) Transaction Pubs.

— Pieces of Eight. 145p. (C). 1982. pap. 30.00 (0-85088-555-8, Pub. by Gomer Pr) St Mut.

— Prejudices: A Philosophical Dictionary. 336p. 1982. pap. text 9.95 (0-674-70066-X) HUP.

— The Quest for Community: A Study in the Ethics of Order & Freedom. LC 90-32568. 300p. 1990. reprint ed. pap. 21.95 (1-55815-058-7) ICS Pr.

— The Social Group in French Thought. Zuckerman, Harriet & Merton, Robert K., eds. LC 79-9017. (Dissertations on Sociology Ser.). 1980. lib. bdg. 23.95 (0-405-12985-8) Ayer.

— The Sociological Tradition. rev. ed. LC 92-35189. 365p. (C). 1993. pap. text 24.95 (1-56000-667-6) Transaction Pubs.

— Teachers & Scholars: A Memoir of Berkeley in Depression & War. 224p. (C). 1992. 39.95 (1-56000-034-1) Transaction Pubs.

— Tradition & Revolt. LC 98-28938. 320p. 1999. pap. 24.95 (0-7658-0486-7) Transaction Pubs.

***Nisbet, Robert A.** Twilight of Authority. LC 99-34146. 2000. 18.00 (0-86597-211-7); pap. 10.00 (0-86597-212-5) Liberty Fund.

Nisbet, Robert A. & Himmelfard, Gertrude. The Degradation of the Academic Dogma. LC 96-20341. 263p. 1996. pap. text 21.95 (1-56000-915-2) Transaction Pubs.

Nisbet, Robert A., jt. ed. see Merton, Robert K.

Nisbet, Robin G. & Hubbard, Margaret. A Commentary on Horace: Odes, Bk. 1. 498p. 1989. pap. text 35.00 (0-19-814914-X) OUP.

Nisbet, Robin G. & Hubbard, Margaret. A Commentary on Horace: Odes, Bk. II. 372p. 1991. reprint ed. pap. text 32.00 (0-19-814771-6) OUP.

Nisbet, Ulric. Onlie Begetter. LC 70-121234. (Studies in Shakespeare: No. 24). 1970. reprint ed. lib. bdg. 75.00 (0-8383-1095-8) M S G Haskell Hse.

Nisbett, Alec. The Sound Studio. 6th rev. ed. LC 94-24609. (Illus.). 400p. 1995. pap. text 49.95 (0-240-51395-9, Focal) Buttrwrth-Heinemann.

— The Technique of the Sound Studio. 4th ed. (Library of Communication Techniques Ser.). (Illus.). 1983. pap. 29.95 (0-240-51100-X, Focal) Buttrwrth-Heinemann.

— The Use of Microphones. 4th ed. LC 93-6236. (Media Manuals Ser.). 192p. 1994. pap. text 29.95 (0-240-51365-7, Focal) Buttrwrth-Heinemann.

Nisbett, Edward G. & Melilli, Albert S., eds. Steel Forgings: STP 903. LC 86-14066. (Illus.). 610p. 1986. text 59.00 (0-8031-0465-0, STP903) ASTM.

Nisbett, Edward G., ed. see American Society for Testing & Materials Staff.

Nisbett, Edward G., jt. ed. see Melilli, Albert S.

Nisbett, Jean. Beginner's Guide to the Doll's House Hobby. LC 98-106190. (Illus.). 128p. 1997. pap. text 14.95 (1-86108-037-9, Pub. by Guild Master) Sterling.

— The Dolls' House 1/24 Scale: A Complete Introduction. (Illus.). 144p. 1999. pap. 17.95 (1-86108-113-8, Pub. by Guild Master) Sterling.

— The Secrets of the Dolls' House Makers. (Illus.). 200p. 1995. pap. 21.95 (0-946819-54-8) Sterling.

Nisbett, Richard, jt. auth. see Ciochon, Russell L.

Nisbett, Richard E., ed. Rules for Reasoning. LC 92-39042. 424p. 1993. pap. 45.00 (0-8058-1257-1); text 99.95 (0-8058-1256-3) L Erlbaum Assocs.

Nisbett, Richard E. & Cohen, Dov. Culture of Honor: The Psychology of Violence in the South. (New Directions in Social Psychology Ser.). 2p. (C). 1996. pap. 15.95 (0-8133-1993-5, Pub. by Westview) HarpC.

Nisbett, Richard E., jt. auth. see Ross, Lee.

Nischal, Ken K., jt. auth. see Kanski, Jack J.

Nischan, Bodo. Prince, People, & Confession: The Second Reformation in Brandenburg. LC 93-49639. (Illus.). 384p. (C). 1994. text 51.95 (0-8122-3242-9) U of Pa Pr.

Nischik, Reingard, ed. Margaret Atwood: Works & Impact. (Illus.). 272p. 2000. 55.00 (1-57113-139-6, Pub. by Camden Hse) Boydell & Brewer.

Nischik, Reingard, ed. see Mainar, Luis M.

Nise. Systems Engineer. 2nd ed. 880p. 1995. text 100.95 (0-471-36736-2) Wiley.

Nise. Systems Engineer Solution Manual. 2nd abr. ed. 1995. pap. text 25.00 (0-471-36572-6) Wiley.

***Nise, Norman S.** Control Systems Engineering. 2nd ed. 944p. 1998. text 125.95 (0-471-36606-4) Wiley.

Nise, Norman S. Control Systems Engineering. 3rd ed. 850p. (C). 2000. text 85.00 (0-201-33798-3) Addison-Wesley.

***Nise, Norman S.** Control Systems Engineering. 3rd ed. LC 99-49144. 960p. 2000. text 102.95 incl. audio compact disk (0-471-36601-3, Wiley Heyden) Wiley.

— Control Systems Engineering: Solutions Manual. 2nd ed. student ed. write for info. (0-8053-5426-3) Benjamin-Cummings.

Nisen, William G., et al. Marketing Your Software: Strategies for Success. (Illus.). 224p. 1984. pap. 16.95 (0-201-00105-5) Addison-Wesley.

Nisenfeld, A. Eli. Artificial Intelligence Handbook, Vol. 1. LC 89-19914. 248p. 1990. reprint ed. pap. 76.90 (0-608-01355-2, 206209500001) Bks Demand.

— Artificial Intelligence Handbook, Vol. 2. LC 89-19914. 363p. 1989. reprint ed. pap. 112.60 (0-608-01356-0, 206209500002) Bks Demand.

— Centrifugal Compressors: Principles of Operation & Control. LC 82-80223. (Instrument Society of America Monographs: No. 3). 253p. reprint ed. pap. 78.50 (0-7837-5132-X, 204486000004) Bks Demand.

— Industrial Evaporators: Principles of Operation & Control. LC 85-24201. (Instrument Society of America Monographs: No. 9). 255p. 1985. reprint ed. pap. 79.10 (0-608-01359-5, 206209800002) Bks Demand.

Nisenfeld, A. Eli, ed. Batch Control: Practical Guides for Measurement & Control. LC 95-36233. (Practical Guide Ser.). 750p. 1996. 160.00 (1-55617-563-9) ISA.

Nisenfeld, A. Eli & Seemann, Richard C. Distillation Columns. LC 80-85271. (Instrument Society of America Monographs: No. 2). (Illus.). 256p. reprint ed. pap. 79.40 (0-7837-5155-9, 204488400004) Bks Demand.

Nisengard, Russell J. & Newman, Michael G., eds. Oral Microbiology & Immunology. 2nd ed. (Illus.). 512p. 1993. pap. text 54.50 (0-7216-6753-8, W B Saunders Co) Harcrt Hlth Sci Grp.

Nisenholz, jt. auth. see Peterson.

Nisenoff, M. & Weinstock, Harold, eds. Superconducting Electronics. (NATO Asi Series F: Vol. 59). (Illus.). 456p. 1989. 107.95 (0-387-51521-6) Spr-Verlag.

Nisenson, Eric. Ascension: John Coltrane & His Quest. 298p. 1995. reprint ed. pap. 13.95 (0-306-80644-4) Da Capo.

***Nisenson, Eric.** Blue: The Murder of Jazz. LC 99-88606. 272p. 1999. pap. text 16.00 (0-306-80925-7, Pub. by Da Capo) HarpC.

Nisenson, Eric. Blue: The Murder of Jazz. LC 97-20846. 272p. 1997. text 22.95 (0-312-16785-7) St Martin.

***Nisenson, Eric.** Making of Kind of Blue: Miles Davis & His Masterpiece. 2000. 22.95 (0-312-26617-0) St Martin.

— Open Sky. 2000. mass mkt. 14.00 (0-306-80988-5, Pub. by Da Capo) HarpC.

— Open Sky: Sonny Rollins & His World of Improvisation. LC 99-55285. 256p. 2000. text 24.95 (0-312-25330-3) St Martin.

Nisenson, Eric. Round about Midnight: A Portrait of Miles Davis. 2nd ed. (Illus.). 300p. 1996. pap. 13.95 (0-306-80684-3) Da Capo.

Nisetich, Frank, tr. see Callimachus.

Nisetich, Frank J. Pindar & Homer. LC 88-46123. (American Journal of Philology Monographs: No. 4). 128p. 1989. text 24.00 (0-8018-3820-7) Johns Hopkins.

— Pindar's Victory Songs. LC 79-3739. 384p. 1980. pap. text 25.95 (0-8018-2356-0) Johns Hopkins.

Nisetich, Frank J. & Euripides. Orestes. Peck, John, tr. (Greek Tragedy in New Translations Ser.). 128p. 1995. pap. text 7.95 (0-19-509659-2) OUP.

Nisevich, N. I., jt. ed. see Marchuk, Gurii I.

Nish, Ian, ed. The Iwakura Mission to America & Europe: A New Assessment. 224p. 1998. text 45.00 (1-873410-84-0, Pub. by Curzon Pr Ltd) UH Pr.

Nish, Ian H. The Anglo-Japanese Alliance: The Diplomacy of Two Island Empires 1894-1907. 2nd ed. LC 84-18600. 420p. (C). 1985. text 50.00 (0-485-13139-0, Pub. by Athlone Pr) Humanities.

— Britain & Japan: Biographical Portraits, Vol. II. 280p. (C). 1997. text 49.00 (1-873410-62-X, Pub. by Curzon Pr Ltd) UH Pr.

— Japan's Struggle with Internationalism: Japan, China & the League of Nations, 1931-1933. (Illus.). 280p. 1993. 59.95 (0-7103-0437-4, A7316) Routledge.

— Origins Russo Japan War. (Origins of Modern Wars Ser.). 274p. (C). 1989. pap. 39.06 (0-582-49114-2, 73483) Longman.

— Work & Society: Labor & Human Resources in East Asia. LC 97-143399. 244p. (Orig.). 1996. pap. 52.50 (962-209-391-4, Pub. by HK Univ Pr) Coronet Bks.

Nish, Ian H., ed. Anglo-Japanese Alienation, 1919-1952: Papers of the Anglo-Japanese Conference on the History of the Second World War. LC 81-18111. (Cambridge International Studies). 320p. 1982. text 74.95 (0-521-24061-1) Cambridge U Pr.

***Nish, Ian Hill, et al.** The History of Anglo-Japanese Relations. LC 99-55779. 2000. 69.95 (0-312-23032-X) St Martin.

Nish, Wayne & Greaves, Ellen. American Bento. Schwartz, Justin, ed. LC 97-31929. 168p. 1998. 25.00 (0-688-14204-4, Wm Morrow) Morrow Avon.

Nishesh, Gagan N. Three Reasons to Love Tea. 40p. 1999. pap. 10.95 (0-9669958-0-5, 0102) Locus Press.

***Nishi, Dennis.** The Incan Empire. LC 99-45620. (World History Ser.). (Illus.). 128p. (YA). (gr. 6-9). 2000. lib. bdg. 23.70 (1-56006-538-9) Lucent Bks.

Nishi, Dennis. Life During the Great Depression. LC 97-33030. (Way People Live Ser.). (Illus.). (YA). (gr. 5 up). 1997. lib. bdg. 22.45 (1-56006-381-5) Lucent Bks.

***Nishi, Dennis.** Weapons of War (WWII) LC 99-53209. (American War Library). (Illus.). 144p. (YA). (gr. 6-9). 2000. lib. bdg. 18.96 (1-56006-584-2) Lucent Bks.

Nishi, Kazuo & Hozumi, Kazuo. What Is Japanese Architecture? A Survey of Traditional Japanese Architecture. (International Ser.). (Illus.). 144p. 1996. pap. 28.00 (4-7700-1992-0, Pub. by Kodansha Int) OUP.

Nishi, Keiko. Love Song. (Illus.). 208p. 1998. pap. text 15.95 (1-56931-255-9, Viz Comics) Viz Commns Inc.

Nishi, M., et al, eds. Gastric Cancer. LC 93-31369. 1994. 304.00 (0-387-70127-3) Spr-Verlag.

Nishi, Masao, ed. see Campbell, John H.

***Nishi, S. & Imai, K., eds.** From Tumor Biology to Clinical Oncology: 27th Meeting of the International Society for Oncodevelopmental Biologyand Medicine, ISOBM 1999, Kyoto, October 1999:Abstracts. (Tumor Biology Ser.: Vol. 20). (Illus.). ii, 116p. 1999. pap. 34.00 (3-8055-6991-2) S Karger.

Nishida, A., ed. Magnetospheric Plasma Physics. 364p. 1982. text 191.50 (90-277-1345-6) Kluwer Academic.

Nishida, A., et al, eds. New Perspectives on the Earth's Magnetotail. LC 98-38668. (Geophysical Monograph Ser.: Vol. 105). 341p. 1998. 70.00 (0-87590-088-7) Am Geophysical.

Nishida, Gordon M. & Tenorio, JoAnn M. What Bit Me? Identifying Hawai'i's Stinging & Biting Insects & Their Kin. LC 92-33673. (Illus.). 80p. (Orig.). 1993. pap. 11.95 (0-8248-1492-4) UH Pr.

Nishida, Gordon M., jt. auth. see Tenorio, JoAnn M.

Nishida, Hiroko. Japanese Porcelains from Burghley House. LC 86-80691. (Illus.). 284p. 1986. 50.00 (0-913304-24-7) Japan Soc.

Nishida, Hiroshi, jt. ed. see Grooters, Ronald K.

Nishida Kitaro. Art & Morality. Dilworth, David A. & Viglielmo, Valdo H., trs. LC 72-92067. 228p. reprint ed. pap. 65.00 (0-8357-6026-X, 2034642) Bks Demand.

— An Inquiry into the Good. Abe, Masao & Ives, Christopher, trs. from JPN. 218p. (C). 1992. reprint ed. pap. 15.00 (0-300-05233-2) Yale U Pr.

— Intelligibility & the Philosophy of Nothingness. Schinzinger, Robert, tr. from JPN. LC 72-12319. (Illus.). 251p. 1973. reprint ed. lib. bdg. 35.00 (0-8371-6689-6, NIIP, Greenwood Pr) Greenwood.

— Last Writings: Nothingness & the Religious Worldview. Dilworth, David A., tr. LC 86-30931. 176p. 1987. pap. text 16.00 (0-8248-1554-8) UH Pr.

— A Study of God, 10 vols., Set. Viglielmo, V. H., tr. (Documentary Reference Collections). 1988. 395.00 (0-318-35982-0, CMJ/, Greenwood Pr) Greenwood.

— A Study of God, 10 vols., Vol. 2. Viglielmo, V. H., tr. (Documentary Reference Collections). 217p. 1988. lib. bdg. 45.00 (0-313-26560-7, CMJ02, Greenwood Pr) Greenwood.

Nishida, Koji, jt. auth. see Goto, Shiro.

Nishida, Ryoko. Pokemon Origami. (Illus.). 80p. (J). (gr. 4-7). 1999. pap. 8.95 (1-56931-391-1, Pub. by Viz Commns Inc) Publishers Group.

***Nishida, Ryoko.** Pokemon Origami, Vol.2. (Illus.). 80p. (ps-3). 2000. pap. 8.95 (1-56931-415-2, Pub. by Viz Commns Inc) Publishers Group.

Nishida, S. Analysis, Design & Evaluation of Man-Machine Systems: Proceedings from the 7th IFAC/IFIP/IFORS/IEA Symposium, Kyoyo, Japan, 16-18 September 1998. LC 99-57320. 1999. pap. write for info. (0-08-043032-5, Pergamon Pr) Elsevier.

Nishida, T., ed. Corneal Healing Responses to Injuries & Refractive Surgeries. (Illus.). 1998. 43.00 (90-6299-157-2) Kugler Pubns.

Nishida, Tina Y., jt. ed. see Nakanishi, Donald T.

Nishida, Toshisada, ed. The Chimpanzees of the Mahale Mountains: Sexual & Life History Strategies. (Illus.). 336p. 1990. 69.50 (0-86008-462-0, Pub. by U of Tokyo) Col U Pr.

***Nishida, Toyoaki.** Dynamic Knowledge Interaction. LC 00-23087. (International Series on Computational Intelligence). 2000. write for info. (0-8493-0314-1) CRC Pr.

— Dynamic Knowledge Interaction. (International Series on Computational Intelligence). 296p. 2000. boxed set 89.95 (0-8493-0113-0) CRC Pr.

Nishidate, Kazume, jt. auth. see Gaylord, Richard J.

Nishigauchi, Taisuke. Quantification in the Theory of Grammar. (C). 1990. pap. text 64.50 (0-7923-0644-9); lib. bdg. 98.00 (0-7923-0643-0) Kluwer Academic.

Nishigomi, George, jt. auth. see Houghton, Steve.

Nishigomi, George, jt. auth. see Houghton, Steven.

Nishiguchi, Toshihiro. Strategic Industrial Sourcing: The Japanese Advantage. LC 92-13254. (Illus.). 352p. 1994. text 55.00 (0-19-507109-3) OUP.

Nishiguchi, Toshihiro, ed. Managing Product Development. (Illus.). 320p. 1996. text 60.00 (0-19-507438-6) OUP.

Nishiguchi, Toshihiro, jt. auth. see Nonaka, Ikujiro.

Nishihara, Hiroshi, et al. Optical Integrated Circuits. 454p. 1989. 55.00 (0-07-046092-2) McGraw.

Nishihara, M., jt. ed. see Inoue, H.

Nishihara, Masashi. East Asian Security & the Trilateral Countries. (Triangle Papers: Vol. 30). 1985. 6.00 (0-8147-5759-6) Trilateral Comm.

Nishihara, Masashi, jt. ed. see Harrison, Selig S.

Nishihara, Masashi, jt. ed. see Morley, James W.

Nishijima, Gudo & Bailey, Jeffrey. To Meet the Real Dragon. 2nd ed. 215p. 1992. pap. 10.95 (0-9523002-0-6) Windbell Pubns.

Nishijima, Gudo & Bailey, Jeffrey A. To Meet the Real Dragon: Seeking the Truth in a World of Chaos. LC 85-100097. 226p. 1984. write for info. (0-87040-594-2) Japan Pubns USA.

Nishijima, Gudo & Cross, Chodo, trs. from JPN. Master Dogen's Shobogenzo, Bk. 1. LC 94-220964. 358p. 1994. pap. 20.00 (0-9523002-1-4) Windbell Pubns.

— Master Dogen's Shobogenzo, Bk. 2. 400p. 1996. pap. 20.00 (0-9523002-2-2) Windbell Pubns.

— Master Dogen's Shobogenzo, Bk. 3. 350p. 1997. pap. 20.00 (0-9523002-3-0) Windbell Pubns.

— Master Dogen's Shobogenzo, Bk. 4. 1999. pap. 25.00 (0-9523002-4-9) Windbell Pubns.

Nishijima, K. Fields & Particles: Field Theory & Dispersion Relations. 4th ed. 465p. (C). 1969. pap. text 33.56 (0-8053-7399-3) Addison-Wesley.

Nishijima, K., jt. auth. see Eguchi, T.

Nishijima, K., jt. ed. see Eguchi, T.

Nishijima, Satoshi, et al, eds. Computerization & Networking of Material Databases: STP 1311, Vol. 5. 2nd ed. (Illus.). 315p. 1997. pap. text 99.00 (0-8031-2419-8, STP1311) ASTM.

Nishijima, Shoji, ed. see Smith, Peter H.

***Nishikawa, Gayle T., ed.** Rice Cooker's Companion: Japanese American Good & Stories. (Illus.). 192p. 2000. pap. 20.00 (1-881506-09-6) Natl Japnse Am HS.

Nishikawa, K. Plasma Physics - Basic Theory with Fusion Applications. Ecker, G. et al, eds. (Atoms & Plasmas Ser.: Vol. 8). (Illus.). 320p. 1990. 69.00 (0-387-52481-9) Spr-Verlag.

Nishikawa, K. & Wakatani, M. Plasma Physics: Basic Theory with Fusion Applications. 2nd rev. ed. LC 93-36463. 340p. 1994. 59.00 (0-387-56854-9) Spr-Verlag.

Nishikawa, Kiisa C., ed. Evolution of Neural Ontogenies: the Ontogeny & Phylogeny of Invertebrate & Vertebrate Nervous Systems: Symposium on 'The Mechanism of Evolutionary Change in Neural Systems', Vancouver, December 1992. (Brain, Behavior & Evolution Ser.: Vol. 50, No. 1, 1997). (Illus.). 60p. 1997. pap. 62.75 (3-8055-6540-2) S Karger.

***Nishikawa, Kyoji & Wakatani, M.** Plasma Physics: Basic Theory with Fusion Applications. 3rd ed. LC 99-39641. (Series in Atoms, Molecular, Optical & Plasma Physics: Vol. 8). (Illus.). 335p. 2000. 89.95 (3-540-65285-X) Spr-Verlag.

Nishikawa, Kyotaro, et al. The Great Age of Japanese Buddhist Sculpture, AD 600-1300. LC 82-82805. (Illus.). 152p. (Orig.). 1982. pap. 24.95 (0-912804-08-4) Kimbell Art.

Nishikawa, S. & Schoen, R., eds. Lectures on Geometric Variational Problems. 154p. 1996. pap. 39.00 (4-431-70152-4) Spr-Verlag.

Nishikawa, T., et al, eds. Tricontinental Symposium on Autoimmune Skin Diseases, Proceedings, Kyodai Kaikan, Kyoto - Japan, November 1, 1993. (Journal: Dermatologica: Vol. 189, Suppl. 1, 1994). (Illus.). xii, 138p. 1994. pap. 62.75 (3-8055-5993-3) S Karger.

Nishikawa, Y. & Kaya, Y., eds. Energy Systems, Management & Economics: Selected Papers from the IFAC-IFORS-IAEE Symposium, Tokyo, Japan, 25-27 October 1989. (IFAC Symposia Ser.: No. 9014). 480p. 1990. 197.75 (0-08-037021-7, Pergamon Pr) Elsevier.

Nishikida, Koichi, et al. Selected Applications of Modern FT-IR Techniques. 280p. 1995. text 110.00 (2-88449-073-6) Gordon & Breach.

Nishimo, Akiyo, ed. Two Hundred Fifty Essential Kanji for Everyday Use. (Illus.). 232p. 1993. pap. 19.95 (0-8048-1911-4) Tuttle Pubng.

Nishimoto, A., jt. auth. see Tabuchi, K.

Nishimoto, Katsuyuki. Fractional Calculus: Integrations & Differentiations of Arbitrary Order, Vol. 1. xiii, 195p. (C). 1984. write for info. (0-936285-06-0, JPY8200, Pub. by Descartes) NACE Intl.

— Fractional Calculus: Integrations & Differentiations of Arbitrary Order, Vol. 2. xiv, 189p. (C). 1987. write for info. (0-936285-07-9, JPY9200, Pub. by Descartes) NACE Intl.

— Fractional Calculus: Integrations & Differentiations of Arbitrary Order, Vol. 3. (C). 1989. write for info. (0-318-64057-0, Pub. by Descartes) NACE Intl.

Nishimoto, Keiske. Japanese Fairy Tales, Vol. 1. (Illus.). 32p. (J). (gr. k-3). 1999. reprint ed. 12.95 (0-89346-845-2) Heian Intl.

— Japanese Fairy Tales, Vol. 2. (Illus.). 32p. (J). 1999. 12.95 (0-89346-849-5) Heian Intl.

***Nishimoto, Keisuke, ed.** Haiku Picturebook for Children. (Illus.). 32p. (J). (gr. 3 up). 1999. 13.95 (0-89346-916-5) Heian Intl.

Nishimoto, Richard S. Inside an American Concentration Camp: Japanese American Resistance at Poston, Arizona. Hirabayashi, Lane R., ed. LC 95-21635. (Illus.). 262p. 1995. pap. 19.95 (0-8165-1563-8) U of Ariz Pr.

Nishimura, Eshin, jt. auth. see Sato, Giei.

Nishimura, H. How to Conquer Air Pollution: A Japanese Experience. (Studies in Environmental Science: Vol. 38). 300p. 1990. 161.25 (0-444-88537-4, SES 38) Elsevier.

Nishimura, J. & Yamawaki, K., eds. Perspectives of Strong Coupling Gauge Theories: Proceedings of the 1996 International Workshop, Nagoya, Japan, 13-16 November 1996. 450p. 1997. 84.00 (981-02-3187-3) World Scientific Pub.

Nishimura, Kimiko, tr. see Hidenobu Jinnai.

Nishimura, Kiyohiko G. Imperfect Competition, Differential Information, & Microfoundations of Macroeconomics. (Illus.). 248p. 1992. 45.00 (0-19-828617-1) OUP.

— Imperfect Competition, Differential Information, & Microfoundations of Macroeconomics. (Illus.). 240p. 1996. pap. text 29.95 (0-19-829039-X) OUP.

Nishimura, Mari. The Twentieth-Century Composer Speaks: An Index of Interviews. LC 93-29548. (Reference Books in Music: No. 28). xxxii, 189p. 1993. 39.50 (0-914913-29-8, Fallen Lef Pr) Scarecrow.

Nishimura, Masao, tr. see Pearson, Richard J., et al, eds.

Nishimura, Miwa. Japanese/English Code-Switching: Syntax & Pragmatics. LC 95-39569. (Berkeley Insights in Linguistics & Semiotics Ser.: No. 24). (Illus.). XIV, 176p. (C). 1997. text 43.95 (0-8204-3076-5) P Lang Pubng.

Nishimura, N., jt. ed. see Kobayashi, Shoshichi.

An Asterisk (*) at the beginning of an entry indicates that the title is appearing for the first time.

Nishimura, T., ed. Automatic Control in Aerospace: Selected Papers from the IFAC Symposium, Tsukuba, Japan, 17-21 July 1989. LC 90-31776. (IFAC Proceedings Ser.: No. 9006). (Illus.). 296p. 1990. 158.25 (*0-08-037027-6*, Pergamon Pr) Elsevier.

Nishimura, Tsutomu. The Words Book, Roman, Nepali English-Japanese & Japanese-English Nepali. (ENG, JPN & NEP.). 1991. 25.00 (*0-7855-0292-0*, Pub. by Ratna Pustak Bhandar) St Mut.

Nishimura, Tsutomu, ed. The Words Book (Roman) Nepali-English Japanese & Japanese-English Nepali. (C). 1984. 75.00 (*0-89771-086-X*, Pub. by Ratna Pustak Bhandar) St Mut.

Nishimura, Yoshifumi, jt. ed. see Kyogoku, Yoshimasa.

Nishimura, Yoshihisa. Bakudan Sensei. (Illus.). 100p. 1982. pap. 2.95 (*0-933704-43-7*) Dawn Pr.

Nishimura, Yuko. Gender, Kinship & Property Rights: Nagarattar Womanhood in South India. LC 98-902980. (Gender Studies). (Illus.). 358p. 1998. text 28.00 (*0-19-564273-2*) OUP.

Nishinaga, T., et al. Advances in the Understanding of Crystal Growth Mechanisms. LC 96-51028. 610p. 1997. 118.75 (*0-444-82504-5*) Elsevier.

***Nishinari, K., ed.** Physical Chemistry & Industrial Application of Gellan Gum. (Progress in Colloid & Polymer Science Ser.: Vol. 114). (Illus.). 200p. 2000. 89.95 (*3-540-66389-4*) Spr-Verlag.

Nishinari, K. & Doi, E. Food Hydrocolloids: Structure, Properties & Functions. LC 93-44786. (Illus.). 524p. (C). 1994. text 135.00 (*0-306-44594-8*, Kluwer Plenum) Kluwer Academic.

***Nishinari, Katsuyoshi.** Hydrocolloids. LC 99-88289. 980p. 2000. 380.50 (*0-444-50178-9*) Elsevier.

Nishino, Kozo. Breath of Life: Using the Power of Ki for Maximum Vitality. LC 97-36104. 1997. 25.00 (*4-7700-2022-8*, Pub. by Kodansha Intl) OUP.

Nishinuma, Y. & Espesser, R. UNIX - First Contact. Mariani, J. A., ed. Stewart, M. J., tr. from FRE. (Computer Science Ser.). (Illus.). 258p. (C). 1988. pap. text 30.00 (*0-333-43624-5*) Scholium Intl.

***Nishio, Motohiro, et al.** The CH Interaction: Evidence, Nature & Consequences. LC 97-41114. (Methods in Stereochemical Analysis Ser.). 232p. 1998. 98.95 (*0-471-25290-5*, Wiley-VCH) Wiley.

Nishio, S., et al, eds. Advanced Multimedia Content Processing: First International Conference, AMCP'98, Osaka, Japan, November 9-11, 1998, Proceedings. LC 99-14934. (Lecture Notes in Computer Science Ser.: Vol. 1554). xiv, 454p. 1999. pap. 73.00 (*3-540-65762-2*) Spr-Verlag.

Nishio, Shojiro & Yonezawa, Akinori, eds. Object Technologies for Advanced Software: First JSSST International Symposium, Kanazawa, Japan, November 4-6, 1993: Proceedings. LC 93-32466. (Lecture Notes in Computer Science Ser.: Vol. 742). 1993. 79.95 (*0-387-57342-9*) Spr-Verlag.

Nishio, T., jt. auth. see Osaki, Shunji.

Nishio, Yvonne. Longman ESL Literacy. 256p. 1991. teacher ed. 29.95 (*0-8013-0579-9*, 78505) Longman.

Nishio, Yvonne W. Longman ESL Literacy. 2nd ed. LC 97-46997. 192p. 1998. pap. text, student ed. 17.64 (*0-201-35182-X*) Addison-Wesley.

Nishioka. Tuftsin: Biochemistry, Immunology & Clinical Prospects. 1995. 177.95 (*0-8493-6701-8*) CRC Pr.

Nishioka-Evans, Vicki, et al. Functional Living Skills for Adolescents & Adults with Mild & Moderate Disabilities: Budgeting Skills. 80p. 1988. pap. text 13.00 (*0-944232-03-5*) Teaching Res.

Nishioka, H., jt. ed. see Seligman, T. H.

Nishioka, Hayward. Judo Heart & Soul. Date not set. mass mkt. 16.95 (*0-89750-137-3*, 469) Ohara Pubns.

Nishioka, Hayward & West, James R. The Judo Textbook. LC 78-65737. (Japanese Arts Ser.). (Illus.). 1979. pap. 16.95 (*0-89750-063-6*, 210) Ohara Pubns.

Nishioka, Judy R., ed. see Fourth Pacific Environmental Conference Staff.

Nishioka, K., et al. Viral Hepatitis & Liver Disease. 824p. 1994. 280.00 (*0-387-70132-X*) Spr-Verlag.

Nishioka, Kenji. Polyamines in Cancer: Basic Mechanisms & Clinical Approaches. LC 96-15935. (Medical Intelligence Unit Ser.). 278p. 1996. 99.00 (*1-57059-346-9*) Landes Bioscience.

Nishioka, Kumiko. Mahler Functions & Transcendence. LC 96-33383. (Lecture Notes in Mathematics Ser.: Vol. 153). 185p. 1996. pap. 35.00 (*3-540-61472-9*) Spr-Verlag.

Nishioka, M., et al, eds. Autoimmune Hepatitis. 358p. 1994. 201.25 (*0-444-88196-4*) Elsevier.

Nishioka, Rodger Y. Rooted in Love: 52 Meditations & Stories for Youth Ministry Leaders. Burdick, Faye, ed. LC 97-28445. (Roots of Youth Ministry Ser.). 144p. (Orig.). 1997. pap. 8.95 (*1-57895-010-4*) Curriculm Presbytrn KY.

— Sowing the Seeds. Burdick, Faye, ed. LC 98-6760. (Roots of Youth Ministry Ser.). 1998. 8.95 (*1-57895-013-9*) Bridge Resources.

Nishioka, Roger, et al. The Roots of Who We Are. unabridged ed. Burdick, Faye, ed. LC 97-218423. (Roots of Youth Ministry Ser.). 77p. (Orig.). 1997. pap. 10.95 (*1-57895-007-4*, Bridge Res) Curriculm Presbytrn KY.

Nishioka, Shuzo & Harasawa, Hideo. Global Warming: The Potential Impact on Japan. LC 98-25967. 1998. 119.00 (*4-431-70236-9*) Spr-Verlag.

Nishioka, T., et al, eds. Dynamic Fracture, Failure, & Deformation. (Proceedings of the 1995 ASME/JSME Pressure Vessels & Piping Conference Ser.: PVP-Vol. 300). 204p. 1995. 110.00 (*0-7918-1331-2*, H00963) ASME.

Nishioka, Takashi, jt. ed. see Yoshiji Matsumoto.

Nishisato, Shizuhiko. Analysis of Categorical Data: Dual Scaling & Its Applications. LC 81-116307. (Mathematical Expositions Ser.: No. 24). 290p. reprint ed. pap. 89.90 (*0-8357-8023-6*, 203401200088) Bks Demand.

— Elements of Dual Scaling: An Introduction to Practical Data Analysis. 400p. 1994. text 79.95 (*0-8058-1209-1*) L Erlbaum Assocs.

Nishitani Keiji. Nishida Kitaro. Seisaku, Yamamoto & Heisig, James W., trs. from JPN. (Nanzan Studies in Religion & Culture: No. 15). 200p. 1991. 35.00 (*0-520-07364-9*, Pub. by U CA Pr) Cal Prin Full Svc.

— Religion & Nothingness. Van Bragt, Jan, tr. from JPN. LC 81-4084. (Nanzan Studies in Religion & Culture: No. 1). 366p. 1982. pap. 16.95 (*0-520-04946-2*, Pub. by U CA Pr) Cal Prin Full Svc.

Nishitani Keiji. The Self-Overcoming of Nihilism. Parkes, Graham & Setsuko Aihara, trs. from JPN. LC 90-31631. (SUNY Series in Modern Japanese Philosophy). 240p. (C). 1990. text 69.50 (*0-7914-0437-4*); pap. text 23.95 (*0-7914-0438-2*) State U NY Pr.

***Nishitani, Kosuke.** Niebuhr, Hromadka, Troeltsch & Barth: The Significance of Theology of History of Christian Social Ethics. LC 98-30468. (American University Studies, VII: Vol. 209). XVII, 400p. (C). 1999. text 64.00 (*0-8204-4188-0*) P Lang Pubng.

Nishitani, T., jt. auth. see Kajitani, K.

Nishitani, Takao, et al, eds. VLSI Video - Image Signal Processing. LC 93-12673. 176p. (C). 1993. text 157.50 (*0-7923-9342-2*) Kluwer Academic.

Nishitani, Takao, jt. ed. see Parhi, Keshab K.

Nishiura, E. Schaum's Outline of Mathematics for Nurses. 224p. (C). 1986. pap. 12.95 (*0-07-046100-7*) McGraw.

Nishiura, Elizabeth, ed. American Battle Monuments: A Guide to Battlefields & Cemeteries of the United States Armed Forces. (Illus.). 450p. 1989. 74.00 (*1-55888-812-8*) Omnigraphics Inc.

Nishiura, T., jt. auth. see Aarts, J. M.

Nishiyama, Chiaki & Leube, Kurt R., eds. The Essence of Hayek. (Publication Ser.: No. 301). 419p. (C). 1984. 34.95 (*0-8179-8011-3*); pap. text 22.95 (*0-8179-8012-1*) Hoover Inst Pr.

Nishiyama, Hidetaka & Brown. Karate. 18.95 (*0-685-22002-8*) Wehman.

Nishiyama, Hidetaka & Brown, Richard C. Karate: Art of Empty-Hand Fighting. (Illus.). 246p. (YA). (gr. 9 up). 1991. pap. 21.95 (*0-8048-1668-9*) Tuttle Pubng.

Nishiyama, Kazuno. Hotel Japanese: Practical Japanese for the Hotel Industry. (JPN., Illus.). 144p. 1993. pap. 12.95 (*0-8048-1917-3*) Tuttle Pubng.

Nishiyama, Kazuo. Doing Business with Japan: Successful Strategies for Intercultural Communication. LC 99-30350. 216p. 1999. pap. text 25.00 (*0-8248-2127-0*) UH Pr.

— Japan - U. S. Business Communication. 180p. 1995. per. 27.95 (*0-7872-0446-3*) Kendall-Hunt.

— Welcoming the Japanese Visitor: Insights, Tips, Tactics. LC 95-46072. (Illus.). 224p. (C). 1996. pap. 14.95 (*0-8248-1759-1*, Kolowalu Bk) UH Pr.

Nishiyama, Matsunosuke. Edo Culture: Daily Life & Diversions in Urban Japan, 1600-1868. Groemer, Gerald, tr. from JPN. LC 96-9710. (Illus.). 1997. text 49.00 (*0-8248-1736-2*) UH Pr.

— Edo Culture: Daily Life & Diversions in Urban Japan, 1600-1868. Groemer, Gerald, tr. from JPN. LC 96-9710. (Illus.). 1997. pap. text 21.95 (*0-8248-1850-4*) UH Pr.

Nishiyama, Shigeo, et al. Atlas of Regional Dermatology. (Illus.). 472p. 1998. write for info. (*1-85317-410-6*) Martin Dunitz.

Nishiyama, T., et al, eds. Proceedings of the 29th International Geological Congress Pt. A: Metamorphic Reactions; Sandstone Petrology; Evaporite & Desert Environment. (Illus.). 316p. 1994. 140.00 (*90 6764-173-1*, Pub. by VSP) Coronet Bks.

Nishiyama, Yuriko. Harlem Beat, No. 1 1999. mass mkt. 9.95 (*1-892213-04-4*, 48241872, Mixx Special Edtns) Mixx Enter Inc.

***Nishiyama, Yuriko.** Harlem Beat, Vol. 7. 2000. pap. 9.95 (*1-892213-58-3*) Talisman Hse.

Nishiyama, Yuriko. Harlem Beat 3. (Illus.). 192p. (J). (gr. 4 up). 2000. mass mkt. 9.95 (*1-892213-23-0*, Pocket Mixx) Mixx Enter Inc.

***Nishiyama, Yuriko.** Harlem Beat 2. (Illus.). 192p. (J). (gr. 4 up). 1999. mass mkt. 9.95 (*1-892213-17-6*, Pocket Mixx) Mixx Enter Inc.

Nishizawa, Junichi, jt. auth. see Suto, Ken.

Nishizawa, Ryue, jt. auth. see Sejima, Kazuyo.

Nishizawa, Tetsuo, tr. see Moran, Patrick R., ed.

Nishizawa, Toshie & Uitto, Juha. The Fragile Tropics of Latin America: Sustainable Mangement of Changing Environment. 336p. 35.00 (*92-808-0877-X*, UNUP-788) UN.

Nishizawa, Y. & Smogorzewski, M. New Actions of Parathyroid Hormone. (Journal: Mineral & Electrolyte Metabolism Ser.: Vol. 21, Nos. 1-3, 1995). (Illus.). 244p. 1995. pap. 129.75 (*3-8055-6195-4*) S Karger.

Nishizeki, T., jt. ed. see Saito, N.

Nishizuka, Yasutomi, et al, eds. The Biology & Medicine of Signal Transduction. LC 88-646597. (Advances in Second Messenger & Phosphoprotein Research Ser.: Vol. 24). 784p. 1990. reprint ed. pap. 200.00 (*0-608-03436-3*, 206413700024) Bks Demand.

Nishuilleabhain, Aine, jt. auth. see Noam, Eli M.

Nisiroccia, Daniella, jt. auth. see Lee, Judith A.

Nisitani, H., ed. Computational & Experimental Fracture Mechanics. 448p. 1994. 166.00 (*1-85312-278-5*) Computational Mech MA.

Nisitani, H., ed. Computational & Experimental Fracture Mechanics. LC 93-74382. (Topics in Engineering Ser.: Vol. 16). 448p. 1994. 166.00 (*1-56252-202-7*, 2785) Computational Mech MA.

Nisitani, N., et al, eds. Localized Damage IV: Computer Aided Assessment & Control. 965p. 1996. teacher ed., suppl. ed. 357.00 (*1-85312-397-8*, 3978) Computational Mech MA.

Niskanen, Ansi, et al. Tree Plantations in the Philippines & Thailand: Economic, Social & Environmental Evaluation. LC 97-188600. (Research for Action Ser.). x, 51p. 1996. 0.00 (*952-9520-44-1*) UN.

Niskanen, William A. Bureaucracy & Public Economics. (John Locke Ser.). (Illus.). 320p. 1994. 90.00 (*1-85898-019-4*) E Elgar.

Niskanen, William A., Jr. Bureaucracy & Public Economics. LC 94-15926. (John Locke Ser.). (Illus.). 320p. (C). 1996. pap. 30.00 (*1-85898-041-0*) E Elgar.

— Policy Analysis & Public Choice: Selected Papers by William A. Niskanen. LC 97-29956. (John Locke Ser.). 448p. 1998. 100.00 (*1-85898-702-4*) E Elgar.

Niskanen, William A., jt. auth. see Litan, Robert E.

***Nisker, Wes.** Buddha's Nature: Who We Really Are & Why This Matters. 256p. 2000. reprint ed. pap. 15.95 (*0-553-37999-2*) Bantam.

Nisker, Wes. Crazy Wisdom. rev. ed. LC 98-35477. (Illus.). 240p. 1998. pap. 15.95 (*1-58008-040-5*) Ten Speed Pr.

Nisker, Wes C. If You Don't Like the News, Go Out & Make Some of Your Own. LC 94-26664. 248p. 1994. pap. 14.95 (*0-89815-626-2*) Ten Speed Pr.

Nisley, Edward. The Embedded PC's ISA Bus: Firmware, Gadgets & Practical Tricks. LC 97-12572. (Illus.). 300p. (Orig.). 1997. pap. 39.95 (*1-57398-017-X*) Annabooks.

Nisley, Omer. The End of the Rainbow. LC 97-60961. (Illus.). 144p. 1997. mass mkt. 9.95 (*0-9659370-0-3*) CPA Books.

Nisly, Paul W. Sweeping up the Heart: A Father's Lament for His Daughter. LC 92-4565. 88p. 1992. pap. 8.95 (*1-56148-069-X*) Good Bks PA.

— Why Suffering? 16p. 1980. pap. text 2.99 (*0-8361-1914-2*) Herald Pr.

Niso Staff. American National Standard for Standard Address Number for the Publishing Industry. LC 93-149. (National Information Standards Ser.). 18p. (C). 1993. pap. 20.00 (*0-88738-933-3*) Transaction Pubs.

NISO Staff. Computerized Book Ordering, No. Z39.49, 1992. 50p. 1993. pap. 50.00 (*0-88738-942-2*) Transaction Pubs.

— Criteria for Price Indexes for Printed Library Materials, Z39.20 1999. LC 99-21579. 9p. 1999. 45.00 (*1-880124-46-7*) NISO.

— Electronic Manuscript Preparation & Markup. (National Information Standards Ser.: No. Z39.59-1988). 96p. (C). 1991. pap. 75.00 (*0-88738-945-7*) Transaction Pubs.

Nisolle, M. & Donnez, J. Peritoneal, Ovarian & Recto-Vaginal Endometriosis: The Identification of Three Separate Diseases. (Illus.). 190p. 1996. pap. 48.00 (*1-85070-941-6*) Prthnon Pub.

Nison, Steve. Beyond Candlesticks: More Japanese Charting Techniques. LC 94-4290. 296p. 1994. 69.95 (*0-471-00720-X*) Wiley.

— Japanese Candlestick: Charting Techniques. 315p. (C). 1991. text 75.00 (*0-13-931650-7*) P-H.

Nisonger, Thomas E. Collection Evaluation in Academic Libraries: A Guide & Annotated Bibliography. LC 92-11037. xix, 271p. 1992. lib. bdg. 45.00 (*0-87287-925-9*) Libs Unl.

— Management of Serials in Libraries. LC 98-28879. (Illus.). 440p. 1998. 70.00 (*1-56308-213-6*) Libs Unl.

Nisonoff, Alfred, jt. ed. see Greene, Mark I.

Nispen, Frans K. Van, see Peters, B. Guy & Van Nispen, Frans K., eds.

Nisperos, Christopher, jt. auth. see Hicks, Roger.

Niss, Michael. Workers' Compensation in Oklahoma: Administrative Inventory. LC 98-5949. 128p. 1998. 35.00 (*0-935149-73-2*, WC-98-2) Workers Comp Res Inst.

***Niss, Michael & Barth, Peter.** Permanent Partial Disability Benefits: Interstate Differences in Approach. LC 99-26093. 1999. 50.00 (*0-935149-79-1*, WC-99-2) Workers Comp Res Inst.

Niss, Mogens, ed. Cases of Assessment in Mathematics Education: An ICMI Study. LC 92-41538. (Diverse Ser.). 226p. (C). 1993. lib. bdg. 138.00 (*0-7923-2089-1*) Kluwer Academic.

— Investigations into Assessment in Mathematics Education. LC 92-41132. (ICMI Study Ser.). 1993. lib. bdg. 146.50 (*0-7923-2095-6*) Kluwer Academic.

Nissan, Alfred H. Lectures of Fiber Science in Paper. LC TS1120.N5. (Pulp & Paper Technology Ser.: No. 4). (Illus.). 163p. reprint ed. pap. 50.60 (*0-8357-8206-9*, 203395400087) Bks Demand.

Nissan, Ephraim & Schmidt, Klaus. From Information to Knowledge. 420p. (Orig.). 1994. pap. text 37.95 (*1-871516-50-1*, Pub. by Intellect) Cromland.

Nissan Motor Company Staff. Business Japanese: A Guide to Communicating in Japanese. (ENG & JPN.). 300p. 1988. pap. 39.95 (*0-8288-0992-5*, M 900) Fr & Eur.

Nissanice, Nimmal. Introductory Logic & Sets for Computer Scientists. LC 98-28534. (Illus.). 352p. (C). 1998. pap. text 43.00 (*0-201-17957-1*) Addison-Wesley.

Nissanka, H. S. Buddhist Psychotherapy: An Eastern Therapeutical Approach to Mental Problems. 1993. 27.50 (*0-7069-6883-2*, Pub. by Vikas) S Asia.

— Buddist Psychotherapy: An Eastern Approach to Mental Problems. (C). 1995. 24.00 (*0-7069-9003-X*, Pub. by Vikas) S Asia.

— International Relations & Geopolitics. 1997. 28.00 (*81-259-0234-1*, Pub. by Vikas) S Asia.

— Maha Bodhi Tree in Anuradhapura, Sri Lanka: The Oldest Historical Tree in the World. (C). 1994. 32.00 (*0-7069-7063-2*, Pub. by Vikas) S Asia.

Nissanke, Machiko & Hewitt, Adrian, eds. Overcoming Economic Crisis in Developing Countries: Policies for Recovery & Development. 288p. 1994. 59.00 (*1-85567-152-2*, Pub. by P P Pubs) Cassell & Continuum.

Nissanke, Machiko, jt. auth. see Aryeetey, Ernest.

***Nissanke, N.** Formal Specification: Techniques & Applications. LC 99-36324. xx, 300p. 1999. pap. 49.95 (*1-85233-002-3*, Pub. by Spr-Verlag) Spr-Verlag.

Nissanke, Nimal. Logic for Computer Science. 1997. pap. text 14.95 (*3-540-76072-5*) Spr-Verlag.

Nissanke, Nimal. Real Time Systems: An Introduction. 228p. 1997. pap. 42.00 (*0-13-651274-7*) P-H.

***Nissel, Muriel.** Married to the Amadeus: Life with a String Quartet. (Illus.). 184p. 2000. pap. 22.95 (*1-900357-12-7*, Pub. by Giles Mare Pubs) Trafalgar.

***Nissen, Axel.** Bret Harte: Prince & Pauper. LC 99-48552. (Illus.). 360p. 2000. 28.00 (*1-57806-253-5*) U Pr of Miss.

Nissen, Bruce. Fighting for Jobs: Case Studies of Labor-Community Coalitions Confronting Plant Closings. LC 94-34608. (SUNY Series in the Sociology of Work). 215p. (C). 1995. text 49.50 (*0-7914-2567-3*); pap. text 16.95 (*0-7914-2568-1*) State U NY Pr.

— Which Direction for Organized Labor? Essays on Organizing Outreach & Internal Transformations. LC 98-24151. 1998. pap. text 28.95 (*0-8143-2779-6*, Great Lks Bks) Wayne St U Pr.

***Nissen, Bruce, ed.** Unions & Workplace Reorganization. LC 97-15001. 224p. 1999. pap. 17.95 (*0-8143-2885-7*) Wayne St U Pr.

Nissen, Bruce, jt. ed. see Craypo, Charles.

Nissen, Bruce, jt. ed. see Larson, Simeon.

***Nissen, C., ed.** Is There a Cure for Aplastic Anaemia? In Memoriam Bruno Speck (1934-1998) (Acta Haematologica Ser.: Vol. 103, No. 1). (Illus.). 66p. 2000. pap. 25.25 (*3-8055-7040-6*) S Karger.

Nissen, Christopher. Ethics of Retribution in the Decameron & the Late Medieval Italian Novella: Beyond the Circle. LC 93-20916. 156p. 1993. text 69.95 (*0-7734-9835-4*) E Mellen.

Nissen, Georg N. Biographie W. A. Mozarts. (Olms Paperbacks Ser.: Vol. 37). 1991. pap. write for info. (*3-487-00548-6*); 3.5 hd. write for info. (*3-487-06076-0*) G Olms Pubs.

Nissen, Graig, jt. auth. see Hanson, Bob.

Nissen, H., et al. Information Systems Research: Contemporary Approaches & Emergent Trends. 754p. 1991. 201.25 (*0-444-89029-7*) Elsevier.

Nissen, Hans J. The Early History of the Ancient Near East, 9000-2000 B.C. Lutzeier, Elizabeth & Northcott, Kenneth J., trs. LC 87-25530. (Illus.). xiv, 230p. 1990. pap. text 21.95 (*0-226-58658-8*) U Ch Pr.

— The Early History of the Ancient Near East, 9000-2000 B.C. Lutzeier, Elizabeth & Northcott, Kenneth J., trs. (Illus.). 230p. 1996. 42.50 (*0-226-58656-1*) U Ch Pr.

Nissen, Hans J., et al. Archaic Bookkeeping: Early Writing & Techniques of the Economic Administration of the Ancient Near East. Larsen, Paul, tr. from GER. LC 93-909.Tr. of Fruhe Schrift und Techniken der Wirtschaftsverwaltung im alten Vorderen Orient: Informationsspeicherung und Verarbeitung vor 5000 Jahren. (Illus.). 184p. 1993. 34.95 (*0-226-58659-6*) U Ch Pr.

Nissen, Heinrich. Italische Landeskunde, 2 vols., Set. Finley, Moses, ed. LC 79-4997. (Ancient Economic History Ser.). (GER.). 1979. reprint ed. lib. bdg. 143.95 (*0-405-12383-3*) Ayer.

— Italische Landeskunde, Vol. 1. 1979. 47.95 (*0-405-12385-X*) Ayer.

— Italische Landeskunde, 2 vols., Vol. 2. Finley, Moses, ed. LC 79-4997. (Ancient Economic History Ser.). (GER.). 1979. reprint ed. 47.95 (*0-405-12488-0*) Ayer.

— Italische Landeskunde, Vol. 2, Pt. 1. 1979. 47.95 (*0-405-12386-8*) Ayer.

— Kritische untersuchungen uber die Quellen der Vierten und Funften Dekade des Livius. LC 75-7332. (Roman History Ser.). (GER.). 1975. reprint ed. 29.95 (*0-405-07109-4*) Ayer.

Nissen, Henrik S., ed. Scandinavia During the Second World War. Munch-Petersen, Thomas, tr. LC 82-2779. (Nordic Ser.: No. 9). 417p. reprint ed. pap. 129.30 (*0-7837-2932-4*, 205752200006) Bks Demand.

***Nissen, Johannes.** New Testament & Mission: Historical & Hermeneutical Perspectives. 199p. 1999. pap. 35.95 (*3-631-34500-3*) P Lang Pubng.

— New Testament & Mission: Historical & Hermeneutical Perspectives. LC 99-48713. 199p. (C). 1999. pap. 35.95 (*0-8204-4309-3*) P Lang Pubng.

***Nissen, Johannes & Pedersen, Sigfred, eds.** New Readings in John: Literary & Theological Perspectives Essays from the Scandinavian Conference on the Fourth Gospel in Aarhus 1997. (JSNTS Ser.: Vol. 182). 289p. 1999. 85.00 (*1-85075-974-X*, Pub. by Sheffield Acad) CUP Services.

Nissen, Lowell. Teleological Language in the Life Sciences. LC 97-7424. 192p. 1997. 52.50 (*0-8476-8693-0*); pap. 21.95 (*0-8476-8694-9*) Rowman.

Nissen, Mrs. Carl, ed. Index to the New Jersey Genesis, 1953-1971. 172p. 1973. 16.00 (*0-913478-03-2*) Hermosa.

***Nissen, Thisbe.** Out of the Girls' Room & into the Night. LC 00-38991. 208p. 2000. pap. 12.00 (*0-385-72053-X*, Anchor NY) Doubleday.

Nissen, Thisbe. Out of the Girls' Room & into the Night. LC 99-16672. (John Simmons Short Fiction Award Ser.). 250p. 1999. pap. 19.95 (*0-87745-691-7*) U of Iowa Pr.

Nissen, Volker, jt. auth. see Biethahn, Jorg.

Nissenbaum, Helen, jt. ed. see Johnson, Deborah G.

Nissenbaum, Stephen. The Battle for Christmas. 400p. 1996. 30.00 (*0-679-41223-9*) McKay.

— The Battle for Christmas. 381p. 1997. pap. 16.00 (*0-679-74038-4*) McKay.

— Sex, Diet & Debility in Jacksonian America: Sylvester Graham & Health Reform. 198p. (C). 1989. reprint ed. text 21.50 (*0-534-10915-2*) Wadsworth Pub.

— Sex, Diet & Debility in Jacksonian America: Sylvester Graham & Health Reform, 4. LC 79-8280. (Contributions in Medical History Ser.: No. 4). 198p. 1980. 49.95 (*0-313-21415-8*, NSY/, Greenwood Pr) Greenwood.

Nissenbaum, Stephen, jt. auth. see Boyer, Paul.

Nissenbaum, Stephen, jt. ed. see Boyer, Paul.

Nissenbaum, Stephen, ed. see Hawthorne, Nathaniel.

Nissenbaum, Stephen W. Christmas in Early New England, 1620-1820: Puritanism, Popular Culture, & the Printed Word. (Illus.). 85p. 1997. reprint ed. pap. 15.00 (*0-944026-72-9*) Oak Knoll.

Nissenberg, Sandra K. How Should I Feed My Child: From Pregnancy to Preschool. 192p. 1993. pap. 12.95 (*0-471-34737-X*) Wiley.

Nissenberg, David. The Law of Commercial Trucking: Damages to Persons & Property. LC 94-77560. 1000p. 1994. 105.00 (*1-55834-165-X*, 65200-10, MICHIE) LEXIS Pub.

Nissenberg, David N. The Law of Commercial Trucking: Damages to Persons & Property, 2 vols. 2nd ed. LC 98-87770. 1157 p. 1998. 127.00 (*0-327-00350-2*, 6520011) LEXIS Pub.

— The Law of Commercial Trucking: Damages to Persons & Property, Vol. 1. 2nd ed. LC 98-87770. 650p. 1998. write for info. (*0-327-00348-0*, 6520510) LEXIS Pub.

— The Law of Commercial Trucking: Damages to Persons & Property, Vol. 2. 2nd ed. LC 98-87770. 650p. 1998. write for info. (*0-327-00349-9*, 6520610) LEXIS Pub.

Nissenberg, Heather, jt. auth. see Nissenberg, Sandra K.

Nissenberg, Sandra K. The Healthy Start Kids Cookbook: Fun & Healthful Recipes That Kids Can Make Themselves. 200p. 1994. pap. 9.95 (*0-471-34733-7*) Wiley.

Nissenberg, Sandra K. Healthy Start Kids' Cookbook: Fun & Healthful Rrecipes That Kids Can Make Themselves. 192p. 1994. pap. 9.95 (*1-56561-054-7*) Wiley.

— How Should I Feed My Child: From Pregnancy to Preschool. 192p. 1993. pap. 12.95 (*1-56561-035-0*) Wiley.

N

***Nissenberg, Sandra K.** I Made It Myself! Mud Cups, Pizza Puffs & over 100 Other Fun & Healthy Recipes for Kids to Make. 144p. 1998. pap. 13.95 (*0-471-34740-X*) Wiley.

Nissenberg, Sandra K. Quick Meals for Healthy Kids & Busy Parents: Wholesome Family Meals in 30 Minutes or Less. (Illus.). 256p. 1995. pap. 14.95 (*0-471-34698-5*) Wiley.

***Nissenberg, Sandra K. & Nissenberg, Heather.** I Made It Myself! Mud Cups, Pizza Puffs & over 100 Other Fun & Healthy Recipes for Kids to Make. LC 98-230254. 144p. (J). 1998. 13.95 (*1-56561-151-9*) Wiley.

Nissenberg, Sandra K. & Pearl, Barbara N. Brown Bag Success: Making Healthy Lunches Your Kids Won't Trade. LC 98-231232. 112p. (Orig.). 1997. pap. 9.95 (*1-56561-123-3*) Wiley.

Nissenberg, Sandra K. & Pearl, Barbara N. Brown Bag Success: Making Healthy Lunches Your Kids Won't Trade. 112p. (Orig.). 1997. pap. 9.95 (*0-471-34664-0*) Wiley.

Nissenberg, Sandra K., et al. Quick Meals for Healthly Kids & Busy Parents: Wholesome Family Recipes in 30 Minutes or Less. 256p. 1995. pap. 12.95 (*1-56561-064-4*) Wiley.

Nissenboim, Sylvia & Vroman, Christine. Interactions by Design: The Positive Interactions Program for Persons with Alzheimer's Disease & Related Disorders. rev. ed. LC 89-85538. (Series in Nonprofit Management). 100p. 1989. pap. 27.95 (*0-9621846-1-6*) Geri-Active.

— The Positive Interactions Program of Activities for Persons with Alzheimer's Disease. LC 97-29098. 152p. 1997. pap. 28.95 (*1-878812-40-8*) Hlth Prof Pr.

Nissenson. Macoy's Star Songs. 48p. 1966. reprint ed. pap. 1.00 (*0-88053-311-0*, S301) Macoy Pub.

Nissenson, Allen. Clinical Dialysis. 3rd ed. 1005p. (C). 1996. pap. text 250.00 (*0-8385-1379-4*, A1379-5, Apple Lange Med) McGraw.

Nissenson, Hugh. My Own Ground. LC 97-21602. (Library of Modern Jewish Literature). 180p. 1997. pap. 17.95 (*0-8156-0485-8*) Syracuse U Pr.

***Nissenson, Hugh.** The Tree of Life. LC 99-88926. ixx, 208p. 2000. reprint ed. pap. 14.95 (*0-9664913-2-7*, Pub. by Paul Dry Bks) IPG Chicago.

***Nissenson, Marilyn & Jonas, Susan.** Jeweled Bugs & Butterflies. LC 99-36663. 120p. 2000. 29.95 (*0-8109-3523-6*, Pub. by Abrams) Time Warner.

Nissenson, Marilyn & Jonas, Susan. The Ubiquitous Pig. (Illus.). 136p. 1996. pap. 17.98 (*0-8109-8155-6*, Pub. by Abrams) Time Warner.

Nissenson, Marilyn, jt. auth. see Jonas, Susan.

Nissenson, Robert A. & Draper, M. W., eds. Parathyroid Hormone. (Journal: Mineral & Electrolyte Metabolism Ser.: Vol. 8, No. 3-4). (Illus.). vi, 124p. 1982. pap. 68.00 (*3-8055-3550-3*) S Karger.

Nissenson, Robert A., jt. auth. see Halloran, Bernard P.

Nissenson, S. G. The Patroon's Domain. 416p. 1993. reprint ed. lib. bdg. 99.00 (*0-7812-5192-3*) Rprt Serv.

Nisset-Raidon, Lucques, jt. auth. see Cassagne, Jean-Marie.

Nissi Wang, jt. ed. see Jirui Chen.

Nissim-Momigliano, Luciana. Continuity & Change in Psychoanalysis: Letters from Milan. 192p. 1992. pap. text 15.00 (*1-85575-009-0*, Pub. by H Karnac Bks Ltd) Other Pr LLC.

Nissim-Momigliano, Luciana & Robutti, Andreina. Shared Experience: The Psychoanalytic Dialogue. 272p. 1992. pap. text 32.00 (*1-85575-034-1*, Pub. by H Karnac Bks Ltd) Other Pr LLC.

Nissim, Perahyah B. Perush Rabbenu Perahyah Ben Nissim Al Masskheth Shabbath. Hirschfeld, Boruch, ed. (HEB.). 339p. (C). 1988. 14.00 (*1-881255-04-2*) OFEQ Inst.

Nissim, Rina. Natural Healing in Gynecology: A Manual for Women. 220p. 1986. pap. 9.95 (*0-86358-069-6*, Pub. by Pandora) Harper SF.

Nissim, Roger. Land Administration & Practice in Hong Kong. 188p. 1998. pap. 29.50 (*962-209-459-7*, Pub. by HK Univ Pr) Coronet Bks.

Nissim, Yves I. & Rosencher, Emmanuel, eds. Heterostructures on Silicon: One Step Further with Silicon. (C). 1989. text 234.50 (*0-7923-0124-2*) Kluwer Academic.

***Nissinen, Marja.** Latvia's Transition to a Market Economy: Political Determinants of Economic Reform Policy. LC 98-40719. 300p. 1999. text 65.00 (*0-312-21989-X*) St Martin.

Nissinen, Martti. Homoeroticism in the Biblical World: A Historical Perspective. Stjedna, Kirsi, tr. 224p. 1998. 24.00 (*0-8006-2985-X*, 1-2895) Augsburg Fortress.

***Nissinen, Martti.** References to Prophecy in Neo-Assyrian Sources. (State Archives of Assyria Studies: Vol. 7). x, 194p. (Orig.). 1998. pap. text 35.00 (*951-45-8079-6*, Pub. by Neo-Assyrian Text) Eisenbrauns.

***Nissinen, Sheryl.** The Conscious Bride: Women Unveil Their True Feelings about Getting Hitched. 160p. 2000. pap. 12.95 (*1-57224-213-2*, Pub. by New Harbinger) Publishers Group.

Nissiotis, N. Interpreting Orthodoxy. 1980. pap. 5.95 (*0-937032-23-9*) Light&Life Pub Co MN.

Nissley, D. Lowell. Where Do All the Memories Go? My Life Story & Extended Family Influences. (Illus.). 126p. 1998. pap. 14.50 (*0-9666379-0-9*) Nussli Haus.

***Nissley, D. Lowell.** Where Do All the Memories Go? My Life Story & Extended Family Influences, 1921-1997. LC 99-191111. (Illus.). 1998. write for info. (*0-09-666379-0*) Trafalgar.

Nissley, Denny. Fear No Evil: The Story of Denny Nissley & Christ in Action. LC 99-26637. 150p. 1999. pap. text 11.99 (*0-87788-260-6*, H Shaw Pubs) Waterbrook Pr.

Nissley, Julia. How to Probate an Estate, California. 9th ed. LC 97-13004. (Self-Help Law Ser.). 416p. 1997. pap. text 34.95 (*0-87337-386-3*) Nolo com.

Nissley, Julia P. How to Probate an Estate. 10th ed. LC 98-6787. 416p. 1998. pap. 34.95 (*0-87337-475-4*) Nolo com.

***Nissley, Julia P.** How to Probate an Estate. 11th ed. LC 99-40107. 2000. 39.95 (*0-87337-561-0*) Nolo com.

Nissman, David & Hagen, Ed. Law of Confessions. 2nd ed. LC 94-67910. 1994. 120.00 (*0-685-59837-3*) West Group.

Nist. Study Skills. LC 99-31659. 394p. (C). 1999. pap. text 34.00 (*0-205-28856-1*, Longwood Div) Allyn.

Nist, John. Style in English. LC 72-77824. 1969. pap. 1.75 (*0-672-60904-5*, CR18, Bobbs) Macmillan.

Nist, Sherrie & Simpson, Michele L. Developing Vocabulary Concepts for College Thinking, 2 Vols. 2nd ed. (C). 1997. pap. text, teacher ed. 11.96 (*0-669-41851-X*) HM Trade Div.

Nist, Sherrie & Simpson, Michele L. Developing Vocabulary Concepts for College Thinking. 2nd ed. 400p. (C). 1997. pap. text 35.96 (*0-669-41835-8*); pap. text, teacher ed. 37.16 (*0-669-41850-1*) HM Trade Div.

Nist, Sherrie L. & Diehl, William A. Developing Textbook Thinking: Strategies for Success in College. 3rd ed. (C). 1994. text, teacher ed. 37.96 (*0-669-29780-1*); pap. text 36.76 (*0-669-29779-8*) HM Trade Div.

Nist, Sherrie L. & Mohr, Carole. Improving Vocabulary Skills. 2nd ed. 192p. 1996. pap. text 7.90 (*0-944210-33-3*) Townsend NJ.

— Improving Vocabulary Skills, Short Version. 2nd ed. 132p. 1996. pap. text 7.40 (*0-944210-34-1*) Townsend NJ.

Nist, Sherrie L. & Simpson, Michele L. Developing Textbook Fluency: Active Reading & Studying in the Content Areas. (C). 1996. text, teacher ed. 37.16 (*0-669-28034-8*); pap. text 35.96 (*0-669-28033-X*) HM Trade Div.

— Developing Vocabulary Concepts for College Thinking. 416p. (C). 1993. pap. text 35.96 (*0-669-27914-5*); teacher ed. 2.66 (*0-669-27916-1*) HM Trade Div.

Nist, Sherrie L., et al. Advancing Vocabulary Skills. 2nd ed. 192p. 1996. pap. text 10.97 (*0-944210-36-8*) Townsend NJ.

Nista, Leila, jt. auth. see Anderson, Maxwell L.

Nista, Leila, jt. ed. see Anderson, Maxwell L.

Nister, Ernest. Farm Yard Friends. (Nister Minis Ser.). (Illus.). 5p. (J). (ps up). 4.95 (*1-888443-59-6*) Intervisual Bks.

— Playtime Surprises: An Antique Moving Picture Book. LC 84-16579. (Illus.). 12p. (J). (gr. k up). 1985. 13.95 (*0-399-21214-0*, Philomel) Peng Put Young Read.

— Rainbow Round-a-Bout. LC 91-77799. (Illus.). 10p. (J). 1993. 7.95 (*1-56397-088-0*) Boyds Mills Pr.

***Nisters, Thomas.** Aristotle on Courage. (Studia Philosophica et Historica: Vol. 26). 111p. 2000. pap. 26.95 (*0-8204-4719-6*) P Lang Pubng.

Nistico, Giuseppe, et al, eds. Neurotransmitters, Seizures, & Epilepsy III. LC 86-13104. 527p. 1986. reprint ed. pap. 163.40 (*0-608-00397-2*, 206111100007) Bks Demand.

Nistico, Giuseppe & Bolis, Liana, eds. Progress in Nonmammalian Brain Research, 3 Vols., III. 1983. 146.00 (*0-8493-6352-7*, CRC Reprint) Franklin.

— Progress in Nonmammalian Brain Research, 3 Vols., Vol. I. 208p. 1983. 114.00 (*0-8493-6350-0*, QP376, CRC Reprint) Franklin.

— Progress in Nonmammalian Brain Research, 3 Vols., Vol. II. 240p. 1983. 135.00 (*0-8493-6351-9*, CRC Reprint) Franklin.

Nistral-Moret, Benjamin, ed. Esclavos Profugos Y Cimarrones Puerto Rico 1770-1870. LC 84-20885. (SPA., Illus.). 287p. 1984. text 10.50 (*0-8477-0885-3*) U of PR Pr.

Nisula, Dasha C., ed. Leading Contemporary Poets: An International Anthology. (Illus.). (Orig.). 1997. pap. 23.00 (*0-9657851-0-6*) Poetry Intl.

NISW Information Service Staff. A Guide to the Wagner Report. (C). 1988. 23.00 (*0-7855-0094-4*, Pub. by Natl Inst Soc Work) St Mut.

— Social Work Update. (C). 1988. 90.00 (*0-7855-3739-2*, Pub. by Natl Inst Soc Work) St Mut.

NISW Staff. Assessment & Care Co-Ordination. 1993. 105.00 (*1-873153-13-9*, Pub. by Natl Inst Soc Work) St Mut.

— Community Care in Context. 1992. 90.00 (*0-7855-2688-9*, Pub. by Natl Inst Soc Work) St Mut.

— The Wagner Report Vol. 1: Report of the Independent Review of Residential Care, 1988: A Positive Choice (Report & Recommendations) (C). 1988. 59.00 (*0-7855-3730-9*, Pub. by Natl Inst Soc Work) St Mut.

NISW Staff, ed. The Wagner Report Vol. 11: Report of the Independent Review of Residential Care: The Research Reviewed (Background Information) (C). 1988. 75.00 (*0-7855-3729-5*, Pub. by Natl Inst Soc Work) St Mut.

Niswander, Adam. The Charm: A Southwestern Supernatural Thriller. LC 93-26241. 288p. 1993. lib. bdg. 21.95 (*0-9626148-1-5*) Integra Pr.

— Repository. 408p. 1999. pap. 14.00 (*1-892065-08-8*) Meisha Merlin.

— The Sand Dwellers. (Shaman Cycle Ser.: No. 4). 261p. 1998. 27.00 (*1-878252-29-1*) Fedogan & Bremer.

— The Serpent Slayers: A Southwestern Supernatural Thriller. LC 94-1284. (Shaman Cycle Ser.: Bk. 2). 320p. 1994. lib. bdg. 21.95 (*0-9626148-2-3*) Integra Pr.

Niswander, Kenneth R. Manual of Obstetrics: Diagnosis & Therapy. 3rd ed. 1987. spiral bd. 22.50 (*0-316-61139-5*, Little Brwn Med Div) Lppncott W & W.

— Manual of Obstetrics Asia, No. 3. 1987. 10.95 (*0-316-61135-2*, Little Brwn Med Div) Lppncott W & W.

— Manual of Obstetrics Asia, No. 4. 1991. 10.95 (*0-316-61171-9*, Little Brwn Med Div) Lppncott W & W.

— Manual of Obstetrics ISE, No. 3. 1987. 15.95 (*0-316-61136-0*, Little Brwn Med Div) Lppncott W & W.

— Obstetrics: Essentials of Clinical Practice. 2nd ed. 379p. 1981. 34.95 (*0-316-61147-6*, Little Brwn Med Div) Lppncott W & W.

Niswander, Kenneth R. & Evans, Authur T., eds. Manual of Obstetrics: Diagnosis & Therapy. 5th ed. 538p. 1995. spiral bd. 32.95 (*0-316-61172-7*, Little Brwn Med Div) Lppncott W & W.

Niswander, Kenneth R., jt. auth. see Evans, Arthur T.

Niswonger, Dennis, jt. auth. see Colker, Jay.

Niswonger, Richard L. New Testament History. 368p. 1988. 19.95 (*0-310-31200-0*, 18436) Zondervan.

— New Testament History. (History - New Testament Studies). 336p. 1992. pap. 19.99 (*0-310-31201-9*) Zondervan.

NITB Staff. Where to Eat in Northern Ireland, 1997. (Northern Ireland Tourist Board Ser.). (Illus.). 200p. (Orig.). 1997. pap. 7.95 (*1-86193-010-0*, Pub. by JARR UK) Seven Hills Bk.

— Where to Stay in Northern Ireland, 1997. (Northern Ireland Tourist Board Ser.). (Illus.). 264p. (Orig.). 1997. pap. 8.95 (*1-86193-015-1*, Pub. by JARR UK) Seven Hills Bk.

Nitchie, Edward B. Lip Reading Made Easy. 1998. pap. text 10.00 (*0-9666932-8-0*) Breakout Prods Inc.

Nitchie, Elizabeth. Mary Shelley, Author of Frankenstein. LC 72-100233. 255p. 1970. reprint ed. lib. bdg. 59.50 (*0-8371-3689-X*, NIMS, Greenwood Pr) Greenwood.

— Reverend Colonel Finch. LC 40-33650. reprint ed. 20.00 (*0-404-04777-7*) AMS Pr.

— Vergil & the English Poets. LC 19-9760. reprint ed. 20.00 (*0-404-04778-5*) AMS Pr.

Nitchie, George W. Human Values in the Poetry of Robert Frost: A Study of a Poet's Convictions. LC 60-10813. 256p. reprint ed. pap. 79.40 (*0-608-11979-2*, 202343000033) Bks Demand.

— Human Values in the Poetry of Robert Frost: A Study of a Poet's Convictions. LC 78-4612. 242p. 1978. reprint ed. 50.00 (*0-87752-199-9*) Gordian.

— Marianne Moore: An Introduction to the Poetry. LC 79-96998. (Introduction to Twentieth Century American Poetry Ser.). 205p. 1972. pap. text 23.00 (*0-231-08312-2*) Col U Pr.

Nitchman, Karoleigh K. Karoleigh's Finger-Lickin' Lip-Smackin' Quick-Fixin' Snackin' Book. (Illus.). 108p. 1995. spiral bd. 15.95 (*1-883962-02-1*) Kristalex Pr.

— Whistlin' Dixie: A Tale of the South. 191p. (Orig.). 1993. pap. 12.95 (*1-883962-01-3*) Kristalex Pr.

Nitchman, Paul, ed. Blacks in Ohio, 1880, Vol. 8. 1996. per. 17.50 (*0-935057-86-2*) OH Genealogical.

— Blacks in Ohio, 1880, Vol. 9. 1996. per. 17.50 (*0-935057-84-6*) OH Genealogical.

— Blacks in Ohio, 1880, Vol. 10. 1996. per. 17.50 (*0-935057-85-4*) OH Genealogical.

Nite, Norm N. Rock On, Vol. 2. (J). 1978. 18.95 (*0-690-01196-2*) HarpC Child Bks.

Nitecki, Alicia. Recovered Land. LC 94-41650. (Illus.). 128p. 1995. 19.95 (*0-87023-976-7*) U of Mass Pr.

Nitecki, Andre, jt. ed. see Arnold, Stephen.

Nitecki, D. V., jt. auth. see Nitecki, M. H.

Nitecki, D. V., jt. ed. see Nitecki, M. N.

Nitecki, Doris V., jt. ed. see Nitecki, Matthew H.

Nitecki, M. H. & Nitecki, D. V. Origins of Anatomically Modern Humans. (Interdisciplinary Contributions to Archaeology Ser.). (Illus.). 356p. (C). 1994. 52.50 (*0-306-44675-8*, Plenum Trade) Perseus Pubng.

Nitecki, M. N. & Nitecki, D. V., eds. The Evolution of Human Hunting. LC 87-34302. (Illus.). 472p. 1988. 95.00 (*0-306-42821-0*, Plenum Trade) Perseus Pubng.

Nitecki, Matthew H. Evolutionary Innovations. LC 90-10990. (Illus.). 314p. 1990. lib. bdg. 54.00 (*0-226-58694-4*) U Ch Pr.

— Evolutionary Innovations. LC 90-10990. (Illus.). 330p. 1996. pap. text 22.00 (*0-226-58695-2*) U Ch Pr.

Nitecki, Matthew H., ed. Biochemical Aspects of Evolutionary Biology. LC 82-70746. (Chicago Original Paperback Ser.). 334p. 1995. pap. text 20.50 (*0-226-58684-7*) U Ch Pr.

— Coevolution. LC 83-47773. 382p. 1994. pap. text 18.95 (*0-226-58687-1*) U Ch Pr.

— Coevolution. LC 83-47773. 382p. 2000. lib. bdg. 30.00 (*0-226-58686-3*) U Ch Pr.

— Evolutionary Progress. LC 88-20835. (Illus.). 362p. 1989. lib. bdg. 51.00 (*0-226-58692-8*) U Ch Pr.

— Evolutionary Progress. LC 88-20835. (Illus.). 362p. 1996. pap. text 21.95 (*0-226-58693-6*) U Ch Pr.

— Extinctions. LC 84-40253. (Illus.). 340p. 1993. pap. text 16.00 (*0-226-58690-1*) U Ch Pr.

Nitecki, Matthew H. & Kitchell, Jennifer A. Evolution of Animal Behavior: Paleontological & Field Approaches. (Illus.). 224p. 1986. text 55.00 (*0-19-504006-6*) OUP.

Nitecki, Matthew H. & Nitecki, Doris V., eds. Evolutionary Ethics. LC 92-47270. (SUNY Series in Philosophy & Biology). 368p. (C). 1993. pap. text 21.95 (*0-7914-1500-7*) State U NY Pr.

— Evolutionary Ethics. LC 92-47270. (SUNY Series in Philosophy & Biology). 368p. (C). 1993. text 64.50 (*0-7914-1499-X*) State U NY Pr.

— History & Evolution. LC 92-724. (SUNY Series in Philosophy & Biology). 269p. (C). 1992. text 59.50 (*0-7914-1211-3*); pap. text 19.95 (*0-7914-1212-1*) State U NY Pr.

Nitecki, Matthew H., jt. ed. see Hoffman, Antoni.

Nitecki, Z. H., jt. auth. see Devaney, R. L.

Nitecki, Zbigniew, jt. auth. see Misiurewicz, Michael.

Nitecki, Zbigniew H., jt. auth. see Guterman, Martin M.

Nitecki, Zibigniew H., et al. Global Structural Stability of Flows on Open Surfaces. LC 81-22941. (Memoirs Ser.: No. 37/261). 109p. 1983. reprint ed. pap. 19.00 (*0-8218-2261-6*, MEMO/37/261) Am Math.

Nitenberg, G., jt. auth. see Mason, J.

Nithy, S. R. & Goldschen, Stuart. Expedition of the Americas. 1996. pap. 14.95 (*0-614-97658-8*) North Star Pr.

Nitka, Arthur & Kulbach, Joanna E. The Recorder Guide. (Illus.). 128p. pap. 15.95 (*0-8256-0020-0*, OK63743, Oak) Music Sales.

Nitka, David, II. Allergic Reactions. 91p. 1994. pap. 7.00 (*0-9641196-0-9*) Champion Bks.

***Nitka, Margaret Dooley.** Voices of Grief: A Journey of Healing from the Loss of a Loved One. 1999. pap. 14.00 (*0-9658137-7-0*) Woven Word.

Nitken, Karen, ed. see Rodengen, Jeffrey L.

Nitkin, Karen, ed. see Rodengen, Jeffrey L.

Nitkina, N. V. Guide to Bibliographies of Russian Periodicals & Serials Publications, 1728-1985. 2nd ed. Mikheeva, G. V., ed. 387p. (C). 1993. text 295.00 (*1-56072-059-X*) Nova Sci Pubs.

***Nitko, Anthony J.** Educational Assessment of Students. 3rd ed. LC 00-23012. (Illus.). 2001. write for info. (*0-13-013708-1*) P-H.

— Educational Assessments Students. 2nd ed. 487p. (C). 1996. student ed. 77.00 (*0-02-387651-4*, Macmillan Coll) P-H.

Nitobe, Inazo O. Bushido: The Soul of Japan. 228p. 1994. pap. 8.95 (*0-8048-1961-0*) Tuttle Pubng.

— Bushido, The Warrior's Code. Lucas, Charles, ed. LC 75-21718. (History & Philosophy Ser.). (Illus.). 1975. pap. text 9.95 (*0-89750-031-8*, 303) Ohara Pubns.

— The Intercourse Between the U. S. & Japan: An Historical Sketch. LC 78-64252. (Johns Hopkins University. Studies in the Social Sciences. Thirtieth Ser. 1912: 8). reprint ed. 32.50 (*0-404-61356-X*) AMS Pr.

Nitobe, Inazo, pseud. The Intercourse Between the U. S. & Japan: An Historical Sketch. LC 72-82102. (Japan Library). 1973. reprint ed. lib. bdg. 24.00 (*0-8420-1397-0*) Scholarly Res Inc.

***Nitorig.** Oink to Ointment. (Illus.). 246p. 1999. pap. 17.95 (*0-9678955-0-2*) Antiok Onitar.

Nitsch, J., jt. ed. see Winter, C. J.

Nitsch, Manfred, ed. see Kiefer, Manfred.

Nitsch, Manfred, ed. see Ruhle, Ilonka.

Nitsch, Roger M., et al, eds. Alzheimer's Disease: Amyloid Precursor Proteins, Signal Transduction, & Neuronal Transplantation. LC 93-26927. (Annals Ser.: Vol. 695). 339p. 1993. 100.00 (*0-89766-853-7*); pap. 100.00 (*0-89766-854-5*) NY Acad Sci.

Nitsch, Sherry. The Euclidean Woman. LC 88-28753. 54p. 1988. pap. text 3.00 (*0-943123-10-0*) Arjuna Lib Pr.

Nitsch, Thomas O., ed. On the Condition of Labor & the Social Question One Hundred Years Later: Commemorating the One Hundredth Anniversary of Rerum Novarum, & the Fiftieth Anniversary of the Association for Social Economics. LC 94-17918. (Toronto Studies in Theology: Vol. 69). 626p. 1994. text 129.95 (*0-7734-9069-8*) E Mellen.

Nitsch, Twylah. Creature Teachers: A Guide to the Spirit Animals of the Native American Tradition. LC 97-17939. (Illus.). 104p. 1997. pap. 14.95 (*0-8264-1023-5*) Continuum.

Nitsch, Twylah H. Creature Totems: Nature Teacher Medicine. Rinebold, Albert F., ed. (Illus.). 130p. (Orig.). 1991. pap. 16.00 (*0-9626135-1-7*) Aware Tribe.

An Asterisk (*) at the beginning of an entry indicates that the title is appearing for the first time.

Nitsch, Twylah H. & Sams, Jamie. Other Council Fires Were Here Before Ours: A Classic Native American Creation Story As Retold by a Seneca Elder & Her Granddaughter. LC 90-55307. (Illus.). 160p. (Orig.). 1991. pap. 17.00 (*0-06-250763-X*, Pub. by Harper SF) HarpC.

Nitsche, J. Dictionary of Aluminum Production. (ENG, FRE, GER & SPA.). 1992. 98.00 (*0-7859-9740-7*) Fr & Eur.

— Dictionary of Aluminum Production English-French-German-Spanish: Glossary of Technical Terms English-French-German-Spanish. (ENG, FRE & GER.). 361p. 1992. pap. 98.00 (*3-87017-182-0*, Pub. by Aluminium Verlag) IBD Ltd.

Nitsche, J., jt. auth. see Lang, G.

Nitsche, J. C., jt. ed. see Davis, H. T.

Nitsche, Johannes C. Introduction to Minimal Surfaces, Vol. 1. (Illus.). 592p. 1989. text 189.95 (*0-521-24427-7*) Cambridge U Pr.

Nitsche, Michael. Polygraph Dictionary for the Graphic Arts: English - German - Italian - French. 642p. (C). 128.00 (*0-911126-09-0*, 1-245) Perfect Graphic.

— Polygraph Dictionary of the Graphic Arts. (ENG & GER.). 327p. 1987. 125.00 (*0-8288-7916-8*) Fr & Eur.

Nitsche, Michael & Trondt, Leonhard. Polygraph Dictionary of the Graphic Arts. (ENG & GER.). 334p. 1987. 95.00 (*0-8288-0691-8*, M 15136) Fr & Eur.

— Polygraph Dictionary of the Graphic Arts: German-English, English-German. 6th rev. ed. 339p. 1995. 65.00 (*0-911126-08-2*, 1-158) Perfect Graphic.

Nitschke, A. Historia Universal. Mann, Golo et al, eds. (SPA., Illus.). 1989. pap. 1595.00 (*84-239-4409-3*) Elliots Bks.

Nitschke, Camela. Christmas Ribbonry. LC 98-16656. (Illus.). 144p. 1998. pap. 29.95 (*1-56477-228-4*, DB345, PasTimes) Martingale & Co.

— A Passion for Ribbonry. (Illus.). 144p. 1998. pap. 29.95 (*1-56477-211-X*, DB327, PasTimes) Martingale & Co.

***Nitschke, Camela.** Wedding Ribbonry. LC 99-47875. (Illus.). 96p. 2000. pap. 24.95 (*1-56477-244-6*, PasTimes) Martingale & Co.

Nitschke, Diana L., et al, eds. The Seventh National Space Symposium Proceedings Report. (Illus.). 224p. 1991. pap. 50.00 (*0-9616962-5-7*) US Space Found.

Nitschke, Diane L., et al, eds. The 6th National Space Symposium Proceedings Report. (Illus.). 198p. 1990. pap. 50.00 (*0-9616962-4-9*) US Space Found.

Nitschke, Gunter. From Shinto to Ando: Studies in the Anthropology & Architecture of Japan. 144p. 1993. pap. 30.00 (*1-85490-289-X*, Pub. by Wiley) Wiley.

***Nitschke, Gunter.** Japanese Gardens. 1999. 24.99 (*3-8228-7633-X*) Benedikt Taschen.

***Nitschke, Gunther.** Japanese Gardens. 1999. 24.99 (*3-8228-7573-2*) Taschen Amer.

Nitschke, Wolf. Volkssouveranitat Oder Monarchisches Prinzip? (Illus.). 262p. 1995. 46.95 (*3-631-48228-0*) P Lang Pubng.

Nitsun, Morris. The Anti-Group: Destructive Forces in the Group & Their Creative Potential. 2nd ed. LC 95-35988. (International Library of Group Psychotherapy & Group Process Ser.). 336p. (C). 1996. 85.00 (*0-415-10210-3*); pap. 29.99 (*0-415-10211-1*) Routledge.

Nitta, Jiro. Death March on Mount Hakkoda. Westerhoven, James, tr. from JPN. LC 91-24157. (Rock Spring Collection). 204p. (Orig.). 1991. pap. 10.95 (*0-9628137-2-9*, Rock Spring Collect) Stone Bridge Pr.

Nitta, Y. & Tatematsu, H., eds. Japanese Phenomenology: Phenomenology as the Transcultural Philosophical Approach. (Analecta Husserliana Ser.: No. VIII). 302p. 1978. text 135.00 (*90-277-0924-6*) Kluwer Academic.

Nitti, Francesco S. Catholic Socialism. 1976. lib. bdg. 69.95 (*0-8490-1586-3*) Gordon Pr.

— Population & the Social System. LC 75-38140. (Demography Ser.). (Illus.). 1976. reprint ed. 19.95 (*0-405-07993-1*) Ayer.

Nitti, John J. 501 Portuguese Verbs. (POR.). 1995. pap. text 13.95 (*0-8120-9034-9*) Barron.

Nitti, Victor W. Practical Urodynamics. Donley, Stephanie, ed. LC 97-37848. (Illus.). 352p. (C). 1998. text 115.00 (*0-7216-3806-6*, W B Saunders Co) Harcrt Hlth Sci Grp.

Nittrouer, C. A. & Demaster, D. J., eds. Sedimentary Processes on the Amazon Continental Shelf. (Illus.). 336p. 1987. 39.50 (*0-08-033928-X*, Pergamon Pr) Elsevier.

Nittve, L., et al, contrib. by. Gary Hill: In Light of the Other. 1993. pap. 50.00 (*1-85437-129-0*, Pub. by Museum Modern Art) St Mut.

Nittve, Lars. Walter De Maria. Pincus-Witten, Robert & Wingate, Ealan, eds. (Five-Seven-Nine Ser.). (Illus.). 46p. 1992. pap. 30.00 (*1-880154-01-3*) Gagosian Gallery.

***Nityanawda, Mahamandaleshwar Swami.** Simply Being Vol. 1: The Essence of the Spiritual Path. Campbell, Gregory & Cable, Kimberly, eds. 120p. 1999. pap. 9.95 (*0-9675317-0-5*) Shanti.

Nityaswarupannda, Swami, tr. see Astavakra.

Nityo, Prabodh, ed. see Osho.

Nitz. Intro to Chemistry. 6th ed. 1998. pap. text, lab manual ed. 25.00 (*0 697-79541-9*) McGraw.

Nitz, Dwight V., jt. auth. see Brown, Herbert O.

Nitz, Kristen W., jt. auth. see Jensen, Julie.

Nitz, Kristin W. Fundamental Softball. LC 96-34258. (Fundamental Sports Ser.). (Illus.). (J). 1997. lib. bdg. 21.27 (*0-8225-3460-6*, Lerner Publctns) Lerner Pub.

***Nitz, Kristin Wolden.** Softball. LC 99-47671. (Play-by-Play Ser.). (Illus.). 80p. (YA). (gr. 6-9). 2000. pap. 7.95 (*0-8225-9875-2*, First Ave Edns) Lerner Pub.

Nitz, Lawrence H. Business Analysis & Graphics with Lotus 1-2-3. (Illus.). 176p. 1985. pap. 32.95 (*0-13-091604-8*) P-H.

— Business Analysis & Graphics with Lotus 1-2-3. write for info. (*0-318-59621-0*) S&S Trade.

Nitz, Tim, ed. Sapatq'ayn: Twentieth Century Nez Perce Artists. LC 91-62472. 60p. 1991. 20.00 (*0-917652-95-9*) Confluence Pr.

Nitzan, Bilhah. Qumran Prayer & Poetry. (Biblical Encyclopaedia Library: No. XIV). 453p. 1996. pap. text 50.00 (*965-342-669-9*, Pub. by Bialik) Eisenbrauns.

Nitzan, Bilhah, et al, eds. Qumran Cave 4 XX: Poetical & Liturgical Texts, Part 2. (Discoveries in the Judaean Desert Ser.: XXIX). (Illus.). 496p. 2000. 150.00 (*0-19-827005-4*) OUP.

Nitzan, Menachem, ed. The Influence of Maternal Hormones on the Fetus & Newborn. (Pediatric & Adolescent Endocrinology Ser.: Vol. 5). (Illus.). 1979. pap. 86.25 (*3-8055-2902-3*) S Karger.

Nitzberg, Esther M. Hippocrates' Handmaidens: Women Married to Physicians. LC 90-41946. (Women Ser.: Vol. 4). 238p. 1991. pap. 22.95 (*0-918393-81-7*, Harrington Park) Haworth Pr.

— Hippocrates' Handmaidens: Women Married to Physicians. LC 90-41947. (Women Ser.: Vol. 4). 238p. 1991. text 59.95 (*0-86656-880-8*) Haworth Pr.

Nitzberg, M. & Mumford, D. Filtering, Segmentation & Depth. Goos, G. & Hartmanis, J., eds. (Lecture Notes in Computer Science Ser.: Vol. 662). 151p. 1993. 35.00 (*0-387-56484-5*) Spr-Verlag.

Nitzberg, M., et al. Filtering, Segmentation, & Depth. LC 93-2797. (Lecture Notes in Computer Science Ser.: Vol. 662). 1993. write for info. (*3-540-56484-5*) Spr-Verlag.

Nitzberg, Ramon. Adaptive Signal Processing for Radar. LC 91-29576. (Artech House Radar Library). (Illus.). 328p. 1992. reprint ed. pap. 93.50 (*0-608-00570-3*, 2061453) Bks Demand.

— Radar Signal Processing & Adaptive Systems. LC 99-22870. (Radar Library). 449p. 1999. 119.00 (*1-58053-034-6*) Artech Hse.

Nitzberg, Richard S., jt. ed. see Geller, Peter L.

Nitze, William A. Arthurian Romance & Modern Poetry & Music. LC 76-122995. (Arthurian Legend & Literature Ser.: No. 1). (C). 1970. reprint ed. lib. bdg. 59.00 (*0-8383-1128-8*) M S G Haskell Hse.

***Nitzel, Scott.** A Man & a Map. 380p. 2000. pap. 14.95 (*0-9679618-0-7*) October Turtles.

Nitzsch, Karl W. Die Romische Annalistik. xii, 355p. 1974. reprint ed. write for info. (*3-487-05190-7*) G Olms Pubs.

Nitzsch, Paul F. Worterbuch der Alten Geographie. Hopfner, J. G., ed. (GER.). xxviii, 648p. 1983. reprint ed. write for info. (*3-487-06958-X*) G Olms Pubs.

Nitzsche, Jane C. The Genius Figure in Antiquity & the Middle Ages. LC 74-17206. 201p. 1975. text 52.00 (*0-231-03852-6*) Col U Pr.

Niu, Alan K., jt. ed. see Lin, Yu-Chong.

Niu, Xiaodong. Education East & West: The Influence of Mao Zedong & John Dewey. LC 94-7854. 195p. 1994. 64.95 (*1-883255-57-0*); pap. 44.95 (*1-883255-56-2*) Intl Scholars.

— Policy Education & Inequalities in Communist China since 1949. 122p. (C). 1992. lib. bdg. 35.00 (*0-8191-8335-0*) U Pr of Amer.

Niv. Revelation. (Life Applications Bible Studies). 90p. Date not set. 5.99 (*0-8423-3407-6*) Tyndale Hse.

Niv, Amittai & Bar-On, Dan. The Dilemma of Size from a System Learning Perspective Vol. 6: The Case of the Kibbutz. Levy, Judith A., ed. LC 92-6580. (Contemporary Studies in Applied Behavioral Science: Vol. 6). 258p. 1988. 73.25 (*1-55938-101-9*) Jai Pr.

Niva, George D., jt. auth. see Baughman, W. Henry.

Nivardus, Magister. Ysengrimus. Sypher, F. J. & Sypher, Eleanor, trs. from LAT. (Illus.). 280p. 1980. 95.00 (*0-317-00052-7*) F Sypher.

Nivat, M., et al, eds. Foundations of System Specification & Computation Structures: 1st International Conference, FoSSaCS'98, Held As Part of the Joint European Conferences on Theory & Practice of Software, ETAPS'98, Lisbon, Portugal, March 28-April 4, 1998, Proceedings, Vol. 137. LC 98-14855. (Lecture Notes in Computer Science: Vol. 1378). x, 289p. 1998. pap. 49.00 (*3-540-64300-1*) Spr-Verlag.

Nivat, M., jt. ed. see Wirsing, M.

Nivat, Maurice, et al, eds. Algebraic Methodology & Software Technology (AMAST '91) Proceedings of the Second International Conference on Algebraic Methodology & Software Technology, Iowa City, U. S. A. 22-25 May 1991. LC 92-33753. (Workshops in Computing Ser.). 1993. 89.95 (*0-387-19797-4*) Spr-Verlag.

— Parallel Image Analysis: Theory & Applications. LC 96-141279. (Series in Machine Perception & Artificial Intelligence: Vol. 19). 280p. 1995. text 68.00 (*981-02-2476-1*, R-PB2947) World Scientific Pub.

Nivat, Maurice & Perrin, D., eds. Automata on Infinite Words. (Lecture Notes in Computer Science Ser.: Vol. 192). (ENG & FRE.). iii, 216p. 1985. 30.00 (*0-387-15641-0*) Spr-Verlag.

Nivat, Maurice & Podelski, Andreas, eds. Tree Automata & Languages. LC 92-17937. (Studies in Computer Science & Artificial Intelligence: Vol. 10). 486p. 1992. 161.50 (*0-444-89026-2*, North Holland) Elsevier.

Nivat, Maurice, et al. Algebraic Methodology & Software Technology (AMAST '91) Proceedings of the Third International Conference on Algebraic Methodology & Software Technology. LC 93-38672. (Workshops in Computing Ser.). 1994. 85.95 (*0-387-19852-0*) Spr-Verlag.

— Parallel Image Processing. (Series on Machine Perception). 268p. 1992. text 45.00 (*981-02-1120-1*) World Scientific Pub.

Nivat, Maurice, jt. ed. see Alagar, V. S.

Nivat, Maurice, jt. ed. see Dauchet, M.

Nivatvongs, Santhat, jt. auth. see Gordon, Philip H.

Nivedita. Complete Works of Sister Nivedita, 5 vols., Set. Noble, Margaret, ed. Incl. Vol. 1. Our Master & His Message, the Master As I Saw Him, Kali the Mother, Lectures & Articles. 10.95 (*0-87481-112-0*); Vol. 2. Web of Indian Life, an Indian Study on Love & Death, Studies from an Eastern Home, Lectures & Articles. 10.95 (*0-87481-113-9*); Vol. 3. Indian Art, Cradle Tales of Hinduism, Religion & Dharma. 1967. 10.95 (*0-87481-114-7*); Vol. 4. Footfalls of Indian History, Bodh-Gaya, Civic Ideal & Indian Nationality, Hints on National Education in India. 10.95 (*0-87481-115-5*); Vol. 5. Lectures & Writings. 10.95 (*0-87481-226-7*); 1967. 54.75 (*0-87481-216-X*) Vedanta Pr.

— Letters of Sister Nivedita. 1982. 25.00 (*0-87481-228-3*, Pub. by Advaita Ashrama) Vedanta Pr.

— Notes of Some Wanderings. 3.00 (*0-87481-185-6*) Vedanta Pr.

Nivedita, Sister, jt. auth. see Noble, Margaret.

Nivedita, Sr., jt. auth. see Coomaraswamy, Ananda K.

Nivelle, Armand. Fruehromantische Dichtungstheorie. (C). 1970. 76.15 (*3-11-002703-8*) De Gruyter.

Niven. The Best of All Possible Wars. 1998. per. 6.99 (*0-671-87879-4*, Pocket Books) PB.

— Calculus Introductory Appr 2nd. 2nd ed. (Math). 1966. 11.25 (*0-534-06032-3*) Brooks-Cole.

— Thornton Wilder: A Biography. Date not set. 37.50 (*0-8050-5695-5*) H Holt & Co.

Niven, jt. auth. see Hennings.

Niven, Alastair & Schmidt, Michael, eds. Enigmas & Arrivals: An Anthology of Commonwealth Writing. LC 97-216851. 220p. 1997. pap. 18.95 (*1-85754-314-9*, Pub. by Carcanet Pr) Paul & Co Pubs.

***Niven, Bill & Clarke, David, eds.** Christoph Hein. 170p. 2000. 29.95 (*0-7083-1650-6*, Pub. by U Wales Pr); pap. 16.95 (*0-7083-1614-X*, Pub. by U Wales Pr) Paul & Co Pubs.

***Niven, Bill & Thomaneck, Jurgen.** Dividing & Uniting Germany. LC 00-32319. (Making of the Contemporary World Ser.). 2000. pap. write for info. (*0-415-18329-4*) Routledge.

Niven, Bruce M. The Mountain Kingdom: Portraits of Nepal & the Gurkhas. (Illus.). 96p. (Orig.). 1991. pap. 18.95 (*0-911977-07-4*) Seven Hills Bk.

— Special Men, Special War: Portraits of the SAS & Dhofar. (Illus.). 76p. 1992. 21.95 (*0-911977-10-4*) Seven Hills Bk.

Niven, Catherine A. & Carroll, Douglas, eds. The Health Psychology of Women. LC 92-49332. 214p. 1993. text 51.00 (*3-7186-5335-4*); pap. text 27.00 (*3-7186-5336-2*) Gordon & Breach.

Niven, Catherine A. & Walker, Anne, eds. Conception, Pregnancy & Birth, Vol. 2. LC 96-13554. (Reproductive Psychology Ser.). 192p. 1996. pap. text 36.50 (*0-7506-2250-4*) Buttrwrth-Heinemann.

***Niven, Christine.** Auckland. (Illus.). 170p. 2000. pap. 14.95 (*1-86450-092-1*) Lonely Planet.

Niven, Christine. Lonely Planet Sri Lanka. 2nd ed. (FRE.). 1997. 22.95 (*2-84070-056-5*) Lonely Planet.

— Lonely Planet Sri Lanka. 6th ed. (Illus.). 282p. 1996. pap. 14.95 (*0-86442-476-0*) Lonely Planet.

***Niven, Christine.** Sri Lanka. 7th ed. (Illus.). 304p. 1999. pap. 16.95 (*0-86442-720-4*) Lonely Planet.

***Niven, Christine, et al.** India. 8th ed. (Illus.). 1216p. 1999. pap. 25.95 (*0-86442-687-9*) Lonely Planet.

Niven, Christine, et al. Lonely Planet South India. (Illus.). 696p. 1998. pap. 24.95 (*0-86442-594-5*) Lonely Planet.

Niven, David. The Missing Majority: The Recruitment of Women As State Legislative Candidates. LC 97-26173. 208p. 1998. 59.95 (*0-275-96073-0*, Praeger Pubs) Greenwood.

***Niven, David.** The 100 Simple Secrets of Happy People: What Scientists Have Learned & How You Can Use It. LC 99-87647. 224p. 2000. pap. 9.95 (*0-06-251650-7*, Pub. by Harper SF) HarpC.

Niven, David, jt. auth. see Hilbert, Robert.

Niven, David, jt. auth. see Zilber, Jeremy.

Niven, Ivan. Irrational Numbers. (Carus Mathematical Monograph: No. 11). 164p. 1956. text 25.00 (*0-88385-011-7*, CAM-11) Math Assn.

— The Mathematics of Choice. LC 65-17470. (New Mathematical Library: No. 15). 202p. 1965. pap. text 18.50 (*0-88385-615-8*, NML-15) Math Assn.

— Numbers: Rational & Irrational. LC 61-6226. (New Mathematical Library: No. 1). 140p. 1961. pap. text 20.95 (*0-88385-601-8*, NML-01) Math Assn.

Niven, Ivan, et al. An Introduction to the Theory of Numbers. 5th ed. LC 90-13013. 544p. 1991. text 95.95 (*0-471-62546-9*) Wiley.

Niven, Jennifer. The Ice Master: The Doomed 1913 Voyage of the Karluk & the Miraculous Rescue of Her Survivors. 288p. 2001. 24.95 (*0-7868-6529-6*, Pub. by Hyperion) Time Warner.

Niven, John. Coming of the Civil War, 1837-1861. Eisenstadt, A. S. & Franklin, John H., eds. (American History Ser.). 192p. (C). 1990. pap. text 11.95 (*0-88295-861-5*) Harlan Davidson.

— Gideon Welles: Lincoln's Secretary of Navy. LC 73-82671. (Illus.). 696p. 1994. pap. 17.95 (*0-8071-1912-1*) La State U Pr.

— John C. Calhoun & the Price of Union: A Biography. LC 88-11775. (Southern Biography Ser.). 392p. (C). 1993. pap. 18.95 (*0-8071-1858-3*) La State U Pr.

***Niven, John.** Martin Van Buren: The Romantic Age of American Politics. Speirs, Katherine, ed. (Signature Ser.). (Illus.). 715p. 2000. reprint ed. 37.50 (*0-945707-25-8*) Amer Political.

Niven, John. Niven: The Family of Niven, with Biographical Sketches & the Voyages, Letters & Diaries of Capt. John Niven. 252p. 1992. reprint ed. pap. 37.00 (*0-8328-2395-3*); reprint ed. lib. bdg. 47.00 (*0-8328-2394-5*) Higginson Bk Co.

— Salmon P. Chase: A Study in Paradox. (Illus.). 576p. 1995. 39.95 (*0-19-504653-6*) OUP.

Niven, John, et al, eds. The Salmon P. Chase Papers Vol. 1: Journals, 1829-1872. LC 93-16217. (Illus.). 880p. 1993. text 55.00 (*0-87338-472-5*) Kent St U Pr.

— The Salmon P. Chase Papers Vol. 2: Correspondence, 1823-1857. LC 94-16217. (Illus.). 520p. 1995. text 45.00 (*0-87338-508-X*) Kent St U Pr.

— The Salmon P. Chase Papers Vol. 3: Correspondence, 1858 - March, 1863. LC 93-16217. (Illus.). 492p. 1996. 45.00 (*0-87338-532-2*) Kent St U Pr.

— The Salmon P. Chase Papers Vol. 4: Correspondence, April 1863-1864. LC 97-931621. (Illus.). 503p. 1997. 45.00 (*0-87338-567-5*) Kent St U Pr.

— The Salmon P. Chase Papers Vol. 5. LC 93-16217. (Correspondence, 1865-1873: Vol. 5). (Illus.). 432p. 1998. text 45.00 (*0-87338-618-3*) Kent St U Pr.

Niven, Larry. Beowulf's Children. 1996. mass mkt. 6.99 (*0-8125-2496-9*, Pub. by Tor Bks) St Martin.

— The Best of All Possible Wars: The Best of the Man-Kzin Wars. 1998. pap. 62.91 (*0-671-71327-2*) Baen Bks.

— Choosing Names. (Man-Kzin Wars Ser.: Vol. VIII). 288p. 1998. mass mkt. 6.99 (*0-671-87888-3*) Baen Bks.

— Crashlander. 1994. mass mkt. 5.99 (*0-345-38168-8*, Del Rey) Ballantine Pub Grp.

— Destiny's Road. LC 96-53197. 352p. 1997. text 24.95 (*0-312-85122-7*) St Martin.

— Destiny's Road. 1998. mass mkt. 6.99 (*0-8125-1106-9*, Pub. by Tor Bks) St Martin.

— Flatlander: The Collected Tales of Gil "The Arm" Hamilton. 1995. mass mkt. 5.99 (*0-345-39480-1*, Del Rey) Ballantine Pub Grp.

Niven, Larry. Gripping Hand. (Illus.). (J). 1993. 12.34 (*0-606-18371-X*) Turtleback.

Niven, Larry. The Magic Goes Away. 224p. 1985. mass mkt. 4.99 (*0-441-51554-1*) Ace Bks.

— The Man-Kzin Wars V. 336p. 1992. mass mkt. 5.99 (*0-671-72137-2*) Baen Bks.

— N-Space. 704p. 1991. mass mkt. 5.99 (*0-8125-1001-1*, Pub. by Tor Bks) St Martin.

— Neutron Star. 1986. mass mkt. 5.99 (*0-345-33694-1*, Del Rey) Ballantine Pub Grp.

— Niven's Laws. 108p. 1984. 12.00 (*0-913896-24-1*) Owlswick Pr.

— Playgrounds of the Mind. 704p. 1992. mass mkt. 5.99 (*0-8125-1695-8*, Pub. by Tor Bks) St Martin.

— Protector. 224p. (Orig.). 1987. mass mkt. 5.99 (*0-345-35312-9*, Del Rey) Ballantine Pub Grp.

— Rainbow Mars. LC 98-41613. 320p. 1999. 24.95 (*0-312-86777-8*, Pub. by Tor Bks) St Martin.

***Niven, Larry.** Rainbow Mars. 384p. 2000. mass mkt. 6.99 (*0-8125-6678-5*) Tor Bks.

Niven, Larry. Ringworld. 352p. 1985. mass mkt. 5.99 (*0-345-33392-6*, Del Rey) Ballantine Pub Grp.

— The Ringworld Engineers. 368p. 1985. mass mkt. 6.99 (*0-345-33430-2*, Del Rey) Ballantine Pub Grp.

— The Ringworld Engineers. 1997. pap. 11.00 (*0-345-41841-7*, Del Rey) Ballantine Pub Grp.

— The Ringworld Throne. 1997. mass mkt. 6.99 (*0-345-41296-6*, Del Rey) Ballantine Pub Grp.

— Three Books of Known Space. 608p. 1996. pap. 12.95 (*0-345-40448-3*) Ballantine Pub Grp.

— A World Out of Time. 1986. mass mkt. 5.99 (*0-345-33696-8*, Del Rey) Ballantine Pub Grp.

Niven, Larry, creator. The Man-Kzin Wars VII. 352p. 1995. mass mkt. 5.99 (*0-671-87670-8*) Baen Bks.

— The Man-Kzin Wars VI. 416p. (Orig.). 1994. mass mkt. 5.99 (*0-671-87607-4*) Baen Bks.

Niven, Larry, ed. The Magic May Return. 256p. 1983. mass mkt. 4.99 (*0-441-51549-5*) Ace Bks.

Niven, Larry & Barnes, Steven. Achilles' Choice. 256p. 1992. mass mkt. 4.99 (*0-8125-1083-6*, Pub. by Tor Bks) St Martin.

— The Descent of Anansi. 1991. pap. 3.95 (*0-8125-1292-8*, Pub. by Tor Bks) St Martin.

— Dream Park. 448p. 1982. mass mkt. 5.99 (*0-441-16730-6*) Ace Bks.

— Dream Park II: The Barsoom Project. 1989. mass mkt. 5.50 (*0-441-16712-8*) Ace Bks.

***Niven, Larry & Barnes, Steven.** Saturn's Race. 320p. 2000. 24.95 (*0-312-86726-3*, Pub. by Tor Bks) St Martin.

Niven, Larry & Byrne, John. Green Lantern: Ganthet's Tale. O'Neil, Dennis, ed. (Illus.). 64p. 1992. pap. 5.95 (*1-56389-026-7*, Pub. by DC Comics) Time Warner.

Niven, Larry & Pournelle, J. Footfall. 1997. pap. 12.00 (*0-345-41842-5*, Del Rey) Ballantine Pub Grp.

Niven, Larry & Pournelle, Jerry. The Burning City. LC 99-57479. 544p. 2000. 24.95 (*0-671-03660-2*, PB Hardcover) PB.

— Footfall. (Military Science Fiction Promotion Ser.). 608p. 1986. mass mkt. 6.99 (*0-345-32344-0*, Del Rey) Ballantine Pub Grp.

— The Gripping Hand. 432p. 1994. per. 6.99 (*0-671-79574-0*) PB.

— The Legacy of Heorot. Stern, Dave, ed. 400p. 1989. mass mkt. 6.99 (*0-671-69532-0*) PB.

— Lucifer's Hammer. 640p. 1985. mass mkt. 5.95 (*0-449-20813-3*, Crest) Fawcett.

— The Mote in God's Eye. Stern, Dave, ed. 592p. 1991. per. 6.99 (*0-671-74192-6*) PB.

— Oath of Fealty. Stern, Dave, ed. 1984. per. 5.99 (*0-671-53227-8*) PB.

Niven, Larry, et al. Beowulf's Children. 384p. 1995. 23.95 (*0-312-85522-2*) Tor Bks.

— Fallen Angels. 384p. (Orig.). 1991. per. 5.99 (*0-671-72052-X*) Baen Bks.

— The Man-Kzin Wars. 304p. 1991. reprint ed. per. 6.99 (*0-671-72076-7*) Baen Bks.

N

— The Man-Kzin Wars III. 320p. 1990. mass mkt. 5.99 (0-671-72008-2) Baen Bks.

— The Man-Kzin Wars II. 320p. 1990. mass mkt. 5.99 (0-671-72036-8) Baen Bks.

Niven, Larry, jt. auth. see Gerrold, David.

Niven, Marian. The Altar & the Crown. LC 73-175112. (Seekers Ser.: Pt. I). 413p. 1971. 10.00 (0-8164-0099-7) Univ South Pr.

— A Doctor of Souls. LC 77-80171. (Seekers Ser.: Pt. III). 356p. 1977. 10.00 (0-8164-0098-9) Univ South Pr.

— The Inheritors. LC 77-80170. (Seekers Ser.: Pt. II). 252p. 1977. 10.00 (0-8164-0097-0) Univ South Pr.

— Melody Unheard. 296p. 1980. 10.00 (0-8164-9217-4) Univ South Pr.

Niven, Mary M. Personnel Management, 1913-1963: The Growth of Personnel Management & the Development of the Institute. 174p. (C). 1978. 50.00 (0-85292-199-3) St Mut.

Niven, Neil. Health Psychology. 396p. 1989. pap. text 26.00 (0-443-03665-9) Church.

— Health Psychology: An Introduction for Nurses & Other Health Care Professionals. 2nd ed. LC 94-8465. 1994. pap. text 26.95 (0-443-04810-X) Church.

***Niven, Neil.** Health Psychology for Health Care Professionals. 3rd ed. LC 99-31875. 2000. write for info. (0-443-05989-6) Church.

Niven, Penelope. Carl Sandburg: A Biography. (Illus.). 864p. 1994. text 19.95 (0-252-02115-0) U of Ill Pr.

Niven, Penelope, jt. auth. see Jones, James E.

***Niven, Penelope E.** Old Salem Official Guidebook. 3rd rev. ed. Wright, Cornelia B., ed. LC 99-39890. (Illus.). 128p. 1999. pap. 8.00 (1-879704-07-2) Old Salem NC.

Niven, RGN, BSc, PhD, Catherine A. & Walker, Anne, eds. Infancy & Parenthood, Vol. 3. LC 98-16256. (Reproductive Psychology Ser.). 320p. 1998. pap. text 35.00 (0-7506-2442-6) Buttrwrth-Heinemann.

Niven, William, jt. auth. see Jones, James E.

Nivens, Beatryce. Success Strategies. 1999. pap. 24.95 (0-525-94062-6) NAL.

— Success Strategies for African-Americans: A Guide to Creating Personal & Professional Achievement. LC 97-49893. 288p. 1998. pap. 13.95 (0-452-27524-5, Plume) Dutton Plume.

Nivens, Shelba S. Abingdon's Easter Drama Collection. 48p. 1996. pap. 5.95 (0-614-18852-0) Abingdon.

Niver, Kemp. Motion Pictures from the Library of Congress Paper Print Collection 1894-1912. 424p. 1997. 200.00 (0-913616-34-6) Hollywd Film Arch.

Nivin, Septimus E. Evans: Genealogy of the Evans, Nivin & Allied Families. 2nd ed. 270p. 1997. reprint ed. pap. 42.00 (0-8328-8506-1); reprint ed. lib. bdg. 52.00 (0-8328-8505-3) Higginson Bk Co.

***Nivin, Septimus E.** Regional Innovation Potential. 172p. 2000. 59.95 (0-7546-1008-X) Ashgate Pub Co.

Nivison, David S. The Life & Thought of Chang Hseuh-ch'eng (1738-1801) ix, 336p. 1966. 47.50 (0-8047-0230-6) Stanford U Pr.

— The Ways of Confucianism: Investigations in Chinese Philosophy. Van Norden, Bryan, ed. LC 96-39050. 354p. 1996. 36.95 (0-8126-9339-6) Open Court.

Nivison, David S. & Wright, Arthur F., eds. Confucianism in Action. LC 59-7433. xiv, 390p. 1959. 52.50 (0-8047-0554-2) Stanford U Pr.

Nivola, Claire A. Elisabeth. LC 96-23877. 32p. (J). (ps-3). 1997. 16.00 (0-374-32085-3) FS&G.

***Nivola, Pietro S.** Laws of the Landscape: How Policies Shape Cities in Europe & America LC 98-58140. 1999. 14.95 (0-8157-6081-7) Brookings.

Nivola, Pietro S. The Politics of Energy Conservation. LC 85-48265. 294p. 1986. 34.95 (0-8157-6088-4); pap. 14.95 (0-8157-6087-6) Brookings.

— Regulating Unfair Trade. 284p. (C). 1993. 34.95 (0-8157-6090-6); pap. 14.95 (0-8157-6089-2) Brookings.

Nivola, Pietro S., ed. Comparative Disadvantages? Social Regulations & the Global Economy. LC 97-21003. 368p. 1997. text 49.95 (0-8157-6086-8); pap. text 19.95 (0-8157-6085-X) Brookings.

Nivola, Pietro S. & Crandall, Robert W. The Extra Mile: Rethinking Energy Policy for Automotive Transportation. 180p. (C). 1995. 34.95 (0-8157-6092-2); pap. 14.95 (0-8157-6091-4) Brookings.

Nivola, Pietro S. & Rosenbloom, David H., eds. Classic Readings in American Politics. 2nd ed. LC 88-63045. 524p. (C). 1989. pap. text 34.95 (0-312-02014-7) St Martin.

Nivrith, George. Out of Hungary. 1999. pap. text 11.95 (1-57558-033-0) Hearthstone OK.

Niwa, Fumio. Buddha Tree. Strong, Kenneth, tr. from JPN. 1966. 25.00 (0-7206-1125-3) Dufour.

— Buddha Tree. LC 74-15259. 380p. 1971. pap. 12.95 (0-8048-0995-X) Tuttle Pubng.

***Niwa, Fumio.** The Buddha Tree. Strong, Kenneth, tr. 384p. 2000. pap. 12.95 (0-8048-3254-4) Tuttle Pubng.

Niwa, S., et al, eds. Biomechanics in Orthopedics. LC 92-49957. 1993. write for info. (4-431-70108-7); write for info. (3-540-70108-7); 181.00 (0-387-70108-7) Spr-Verlag.

— Reconstruction of the Knee Joint, Vol. XII. (Illus.). 420p. 1997. 198.00 (4-431-70170-2) Spr-Verlag.

Niwamo, Nikkyo. A Buddhist Approach to Peace. Nezu, sdo, tr. from JPN. (Illus.). 162p. 1977. 12.95 (4-333-00308-3, Pub. by Kosei Pub Co) Tuttle Pubng.

Niwano, Nichiko. The Inward Path. 168p. (Orig.). 1990. pap. 5.95 (4-333-01422-0, Pub. by Kosei Pub Co) Tuttle Pubng.

— Modern Meditations: A Buddhist Sampler. 152p. 1992. pap. 5.95 (4-333-01477-8, Pub. by Kosei Pub Co) Tuttle Pubng.

— My Father, My Teacher: A Spiritual Journey. Gage, Richard L., tr. from JPN. 144p. (Orig.). 1982. pap. 5.95 (4-333-01095-0, Pub. by Kosei Pub Co) Tuttle Pubng.

Niwano, Nikkyo. A Guide to the Threefold Lotus Sutra. Langston, Eugene, tr. from JPN. Orig. Title: Hokke-Sambu-Kyo-Nyumon. 168p. 1981. pap. 5.95 (4-333-01025-X, Pub. by Kosei Pub Co) Tuttle Pubng.

— Invisible Eyelashes. 175p. 1995. pap. 6.95 (4-333-01681-9, Pub. by Kosei Pub Co) Tuttle Pubng.

— Lifetime Beginner: An Autobiography. Gage, Richard L., tr. from JPN. LC 79-374242. Orig. Title: Shoshin Issho & Niwano Nikkyo Jiden. (Illus.). 300p. 1990. 19.95 (4-333-00336-9, Pub. by Kosei Pub Co) Tuttle Pubng.

— The Richer Life. Gage, Richard L., tr. from JPN. Orig. Title: Ningen Rashiku Ikiru. 138p. 1979. pap. 4.95 (4-333-00351-2, Pub. by Kosei Pub Co) Tuttle Pubng.

— Shakyamuni Buddha: A Narrative Biography. rev. ed. Miyasaka, Kojiro, tr. from JPN. LC 80-154779. Orig. Title: Bukkyo No Inochi Hokekyo. (Illus.). 128p. 1980. pap. 4.95 (4-333-01001-2, Pub. by Kosei Pub Co) Tuttle Pubng.

— Thw Wholesome Family Life. Alexander, Joy, tr. from JPN. Orig. Title: Ningen o Sodateru Kokoro. 182p. 1982. pap. 6.95 (4-333-01026-8, Pub. by Kosei Pub Co) Tuttle Pubng.

Niwano, Nikkyo, jt. auth. see Gage, Richard L.

Niwinski, Andrzej. Studies on the Illustrated Theban Funerary Papyri of the 11th & 10th Centuries B.C. (Orbis Biblicus et Orientalis Ser.: Vol. 86). 402p. 1989. text 90.50 (3-7278-0613-3, Pub. by Presses Univ Fribourg) Eisenbrauns.

Nix & Schmidt, eds. Heronis Alexandrini Vol. II: Mechanica et Catoptrica (Die Mechanik, Die Katoptrik) (GER & GRE.). 1976. reprint ed. 53.50 (3-519-01414-9, T1414, Pub. by B G Teubner) U of Mich Pr.

Nix, Alvin C. The Inside Scoop on Buying & Leasing Vehicles. 49p. 1998. pap. 9.95 (0-8059-4514-8) Dorrance.

***Nix, Charlie.** Skills, Drills & Strategies for Basketball. Pellett, Tracy L. et al, eds. LC 99-53051. (Teach, Coach, Play Ser.). (Illus.). 176p. (C). 2000. pap. 15.50 (1-890871-11-7) Holcomb Hath.

Nix, Don & Spiro, Rand J., eds. Cognition, Education, & Multimedia: Exploring Ideas in High Technology. 232p. 1990. 55.00 (0-8058-0036-0) L Erlbaum Assocs.

Nix, Eileen, jt. auth. see Anderson, Alan H.

Nix, Elizabeth. Why Don't You . . . 701 Ways to Jumpstart Your Life. 1996. mass mkt. 5.50 (0-380-78671-0, Avon Bks) Morrow Avon.

Nix, Evett D. Oklahombres, Particularly the Wilder Ones. LC 92-37966. xxxiv, 316p. 1993. pap. 12.95 (0-8032-8366-0, Bison Books) U of Nebr Pr.

***Nix, Garth.** Castle. (Seventh Tower Ser.: No. 2). (Illus.). (J). (gr. 3-6). 2000. pap. 4.99 (0-439-17683-2) Scholastic Inc.

Nix, Garth. Daughter of the Clayr. (Illus.). 320p. (YA). (gr. 7 up). 2001. 15.95 (0-06-027823-4); lib. bdg. 15.89 (0-06-027824-2) HarpC Child Bks.

***Nix, Garth.** The Fall. (Seventh Tower Ser.: No. 1). 190p. (J). (gr. 4-7). 2000. pap. 5.99 (0-439-17682-4) Scholastic Inc.

Nix, Garth. The Ragwitch. 320p. (J). 1995. 3.99 (0-8125-3506-5, Pub. by Tor Bks) St Martin.

— Sabriel. LC 96-1295. 304p. (YA). (gr. 7 up). 1996. 16.95 (0-06-027322-4) HarpC Child Bks.

— Sabriel. LC 96-1295. (Trophy Bk.). 496p. (J). (gr. 7-12). 1997. reprint ed. pap. 5.95 (0-06-447183-7, HarpTrophy) HarpC Child Bks.

— Shade's Children. LC 97-3841. 352p. (J). (gr. 12 up). 1998. pap. 5.95 (0-06-447196-9) HarpC.

— Shade's Children. LC 97-3841. (Illus.). 320p. (J). (gr. 12 up). 1997. 16.95 (0-06-027324-0) HarpC Child Bks.

— Shade's Children. LC 97-3841. (Illus.). 288p. (J). (gr. 1-4). 1997. lib. bdg. 15.89 (0-06-027325-9) HarpC Child Bks.

Nix, Garth. X Files: Calusari, No. 1. (X-Files Ser.: Vol. 2). 112p. (YA). (gr. 7 up). 1997. pap. 4.50 (0-06-447171-3, HarpTrophy) HarpC Child Bks.

Nix, H. A. & Elliott, M. A., eds. Managing Aquatic Ecosystems. 174p. (C). 1975. text 100.00 (0-909436-01-0, Pub. by Surrey Beatty & Sons) St Mut.

Nix, Jacob. The Sioux Uprising in Minnesota, 1862: Jacob Nix's Eyewitness History. Tolzmann, Don H., ed. & tr. by. from GER. Steinhauser, Gretchen et al, trs. from GER. LC 94-214625. (ENG & GER., Illus.). xxii, 165p. 1994. reprint ed. pap. text 12.80 (1-880788-02-0) MKGAC & IGHS.

Nix, Jan. The Book of Southwest Cooking. (Illus.). 120p. 1993. pap. 12.95 (1-55788-074-3, HP Books) Berkley Pub.

Nix, Janeth J. & Smith, Margaret A. Zinfandel Cookbook: Food to Go with California's Heritage Wine. Braasch, Barbara J., ed. LC 94-60979. (Illus.). 112p. (Orig.). 1994. pap. 14.95 (0-9642901-0-3) Toyon Hill Pr.

Nix, John, et al. Land & Estate Management. 225p. (C). 1981. text 190.00 (1-85341-038-1, Pub. by Surrey Beatty & Sons) St Mut.

Nix, Kelley, tr. see Bernard, David K.

Nix, Mike. Make Money at Home: 101 Home Based Business Ideas. 160p. (Orig.). 1995. pap. text 9.95 (0-9646277-0-1) B&T Prodns.

Nix, Neeleke, ed. see Parker-Fairbanks, Dixie, et al.

Nix, Nelleke. 1940-1945 Remembered: Translated from My Diary & Retold. (Illus.). 40p. 1992. 300.00 (1-881067-01-7); teacher ed. 60.00 (1-881067-04-1); pap. 200.00 (1-881067-00-9); lib. bdg. 200.00 (1-881067-03-3); 280.00 (1-881067-02-5) N Nelleke Studio.

— Papua New Guinea: Where She Invented Bow & Arrow. (Illus.). 116p. 1996. 260.00 (1-881067-06-8); lib. bdg. 200.00 (1-881067-07-6) N Nelleke Studio.

Nix, Nelleke & Tsoek. Tsoek: Earthy Writings by a Four-Paw. (Illus.). 50p. 1996. 95.00 (1-881067-10-6); pap. 95.00 (1-881067-09-2) N Nelleke Studio.

Nix, Rebekah, jt. auth. see Parker, Sue.

Nix-Rice, Nancy. Looking Good: Wardrobe Planning & Personal Style Development. (Illus.). 160p. 1996. pap. text 19.95 (0-935278-42-7) Palmer-Pletsch.

***Nix, S. M.** Women at the Podium. 432p. 2000. 25.00 (0-380-80286-4, HarpRes) HarpInfo.

Nix, Simon, jt. auth. see Raby, Philip.

Nix, Stephan J., ed. see Symposium on Monitoring, Modeling, & Mediating Wat.

Nix, Stephen J. Urban Storm Modeling & Stimulation. 224p. 1994. lib. bdg. 85.00 (0-87371-527-6, L527) Lewis Pubs.

Nix, W. D., et al, eds. Thin Films: Stresses & Mechanical Properties III. (Symposium Proceedings Ser.: Vol. 239). 723p. 1992. text 17.50 (1-55899-133-6) Materials Res.

Nix, William, jt. auth. see Geisler, Norman L.

Nix, William E., jt. auth. see Geisler, Norman L.

Nix, William H. Character Works. LC 99-28284. 176p. 1999. pap. 10.99 (0-8054-1653-6) Broadman.

— Transforming Your Workplace for Christ. LC 96-51759. 224p. (Orig.). 1997. pap. 12.99 (0-8054-6290-2) Broadman.

***Nixon.** Dynamics of International Relations. (Political Science Ser.). (C). 2002. text 42.00 (0-534-52357-9) Wadsworth Pub.

Nixon. Spinal Cord Injury: A Guide to Functional Outcomes in Physical Therapy Management. LC 84-18474. (Illus.). 251p. (C). 1985. 64.00 (0-89443-552-3) Aspen Pub.

— Spinal Stenosis. 416p. 1991. text 150.00 (0-7131-4525-0) Routledge.

Nixon, Alan J. Equine Fracture Repair. LC 94-32748. (Illus.). 352p. 1995. text 104.00 (0-7216-6754-6, W B Saunders Co) Harcrt Hlth Sci Grp.

Nixon, Anthony. The Three English Brothers: Sir T. Sheley His Travels, Sir A. Sherley His Ambassage to the Christian Princes, Master R. Sheley His Wars Against the Turkes. LC 72-26473. (English Experience Ser.: No. 270). 80p. 1970. reprint ed. 30.00 (90-221-0270-X) Walter J Johnson.

Nixon, Barbara B. Behind the Question: Listen for Success in Job Interviews. (Illus.). 64p. 1995. 18.95 (0-614-05150-9); 18.95 (0-614-05418-4) SPECTRA Inc.

Nixon, Bebe, jt. auth. see Nixon, Nicholas.

Nixon, Bruce. Sunlight & Shadows: The Art of Roland Petersen, 1953-1990. (Illus.). 48p. 1991. pap. 20.00 (0-8150-0017-0) Wittenborn Art.

Nixon, Bruce & Hopps, Walter. Hassel Smith. Resler, Nancy D. & Natsoulas, John, eds. 108p. 1997. 35.00 (1-881572-91-9) J Natsoulas.

Nixon, C. E., tr. from LAT. Pacatus: Panegyric to the Emperor Theodosius. (Translated Texts for Historians Ser.). 128p. (Orig.). 1992. reprint ed. pap. text 15.95 (0-85323-076-5, Pub. by Liverpool Univ Pr) U of Pa Pr.

Nixon, C. E. & Rodgers, Barbara S. In Praise of Later Roman Emperors: The Panegyrici Latini: Introduction, Translation, & Historical Commentary with the Latin Text of R.A.B. Mynors. LC 93-27872. (Transformation of the Classical Heritage Ser.: Vol. 21). (ENG.). 1994. 80.00 (0-520-08326-1, Pub. by U CA Pr) Cal Prin Full Svc.

Nixon, Carol T. & Northrup, Denine A., eds. Evaluating Mental Health Services: How Do Programs for Children "Work" in the Real World? LC 96-35681. (Children's Mental Health Services Annual Ser.: Vol. 3). 312p. 1997. 29.00 (0-7619-0795-5) Sage.

— Evaluating Mental Health Services: How Do Programs "Work" in the Real World? LC 96-35681. (Children's Mental Health Services Annual Ser.: Vol. 3). 312p. 1997. pap. 12.99 (0-7619-0796-3) Sage.

Nixon, Carol T., jt. auth. see Heflinger, Craig A.

Nixon, Chris. Racing Silver Arrows: Mercedes-Benz vs. Auto Union, 1934-1939. (Illus.). 362p. 1997. 75.00 (0-85184-055-8, Pub. by Transport Bookman) Motorbooks Intl.

Nixon, Chris, jt. auth. see Klemantaski, Louis.

***Nixon, Cornelia.** Angels Go Naked: A Novel in Stories. LC 99-57278. 300p. 2000. text 24.00 (1-58243-062-4, Pub. by Counterpt DC) HarpC.

Nixon, D., ed. Unsteady Transonic Aerodynamics. (PAAS Ser.: Vol. 120). 385p. 1989. 69.95 (0-930403-52-5, V-120) AIAA.

Nixon, Daniel W. The Cancer Recovery Eating Plan: The Right Foods to Help Fuel Your Recovery. LC 97-188693. 1996. pap. 15.00 (0-8129-2590-4, Times Bks) Crown Pub Group.

— Chemoprevention of Cancer. 144p. 1994. lib. bdg. 110.00 (0-8493-6850-2, 6850) CRC Pr.

Nixon, David. The Year of the Locust. 140p. (Orig.). 1980. pap. 8.99 (0-8341-0675-2) Beacon Hill.

Nixon, David, ed. Transonic Aerodynamics. LC 82-4027. (PAAS Ser.: Vol. 81). (Illus.). 669p. 1982. 79.95 (0-915928-65-5) AIAA.

***Nixon, David J.** The Vineyard Central Househchurch Guidebook: By Dave Nixon & the House Churches of Vineyard Central. Davis, John J., ed. 78p. 1999. 2.00 (0-9673764-0-8, HC1) Vineyard Christian.

Nixon, Debra A., see Debra Ann, pseud.

Nixon, Dennis W. Marine & Coastal Law: Cases & Materials. LC 93-30986. 392p. 1994. text 69.50 (0-275-93763-1, Praeger Pubs) Greenwood.

Nixon, Don W., jt. auth. see Gaddy, C. Welton.

Nixon, Donald W., jt. auth. see Gaddy, C. Welton.

Nixon, E. Anna. On the Cutting Edge: The Story of a Surgeon & His Family who Served Country Folk to Kings in Four Nations. LC 87-72972. (Illus.). 325p. 1987. pap. 11.95 (0-913342-61-0) Barclay Pr.

Nixon, Edgar B., ed. Franklin D. Roosevelt & Conservation, 1911-1945, 2 vols., Set. LC 72-2861. (Use & Abuse of America's Natural Resources Ser.). 1342p. 1972. reprint ed. 85.95 (0-405-04525-5) Ayer.

— Franklin D. Roosevelt & Conservation, 1911-1945, 2 vols., Vol. 1. LC 72-2861. (Use & Abuse of America's Natural Resources Ser.). 1342p. 1972. reprint ed. 39.95 (0-405-04526-3) Ayer.

— Franklin D. Roosevelt & Conservation, 1911-1945, 2 vols., Vol. 2. LC 72-2861. (Use & Abuse of America's Natural Resources Ser.). 1342p. 1972. reprint ed. 44.95 (0-405-04527-1) Ayer.

Nixon, Edgar B., ed. see Roosevelt, Franklin D.

Nixon, Edwina, ed. see Ellaraino & Sanders, Bernice A.

Nixon, Elray S. Trees, Shrubs & Woody Vines of East Texas. 2nd rev. ed. (Illus.). x, 240p. Date not set. 42.95 (0-934115-01-X) Cunningham Productions.

Nixon, Frank, intro. Japan Quality Control Circles: Quality Control Circle Case Studies. 3rd ed. (Illus.). 208p. 1984. pap. text 19.75 (92-833-1022-5, 310225) Productivity Inc.

Nixon, Graham T. The Geology of Iztaccihuatl Volcano & Adjacent Areas of the Sierra Nevada & Valley of Mexico. LC 88-30879. (Geological Society of America Ser.: Vol. 219). (Illus.). 96p. 1989. reprint ed. pap. 30.00 (0-608-07745-3, 206783300010) Bks Demand.

Nixon, Hargrave, Devons & Doyle Staff. New York Environmental Law Handbook. 5th ed. LC 98-120602. 317p. 1999. pap. text 95.00 (0-86587-653-3) Gov Insts.

Nixon, Herman C. Lower Piedmont Country. LC 78-142685. (Essay Index Reprint Ser.). 1977. 20.95 (0-8369-2064-3) Ayer.

— Lower Piedmont Country: The Uplands of the Deep South. LC 83-24164. (Library of Alabama Classics). (Illus.). 296p. 1980. reprint ed. pap. 19.95 (0-8173-0214-X) U of Ala Pr.

Nixon, Howard. The History of Decorated Bookbinding in England. Foot, Mirjam M., ed. (Lyell Lectures). (Illus.). 136p. 1992. 75.00 (0-19-818182-5) OUP.

Nixon, Howard L., II. Mainstreaming & the American Dream: Sociological Perspectives on Parental Coping with Blind & Visually Impaired Children. LC 91-6866. 256p. 1992. pap. 34.95 (0-89128-191-6) Am Foun Blind.

Nixon, Howard L., III. Sport & Social Organization. LC 75-31742. (Studies in Sociology). 64p. 1976. pap. text. write for info. (0-672-61337-9) Macmillan.

Nixon, Howard L. Sport & the American Dream. LC 82-83943. (Illus.). 264p. reprint ed. pap. 81.90 (0-608-07105-6, 206733200009) Bks Demand.

Nixon, Howard L., II & Frey, James H. A Sociology of Sport. LC 95-15353. 363p. 1995. 57.95 (0-534-24762-8) Wadsworth Pub.

Nixon, J. Ashley, jt. auth. see Harrop, D. Owen.

Nixon, J. H. Underwater Repair Technology: Ninth Annual North American Welding Research Conference. 200p. 2000. boxed set 135.00 (1-85573-239-4, Pub. by Woodhead Pubng) Am Educ Systs.

Nixon, J. R., ed. see International Symposium on Microencapsulation (2nd.

Nixon, James F., jt. auth. see James, Frederic.

Nixon, Jason, jt. auth. see Volkwein, Ann.

Nixon, Jean L. Beware of the Pirate Ghost. LC 95-83884. (Adventures Casebusters Ser.: No. 7). (Illus.). 96p. (J). (gr. 4-7). 1996. pap. 3.95 (0-7868-4080-3, Pub. by Disney Pr) Little.

— A Deadly Game of Magic. LC 99-955088. 160p. (YA). (gr. 7 up). 1985. mass mkt. 4.99 (0-440-92102-3, LLL BDD) BDD Bks Young Read.

— A Deadly Game of Magic. LC 83-8379. 148p. (YA). (gr. 7 up). 1983. 13.95 (0-15-222954-X, Harcourt Child Bks) Harcourt.

Nixon, Joan Lowery. Aggie's Home. LC 97-47760. (Orphan Train Ser.). (Illus.). 128p. (J). (gr. 2-6). 1998. 9.95 (0-385-32295-X, Delacorte Pr Bks) BDD Bks Young Read.

***Nixon, Joan Lowery.** Aggie's Home. (Orphan Train Ser.). 128p. 2000. pap. 4.50 (0-440-41312-5, YB BDD) BDD Bks Young Read.

Nixon, Joan Lowery. And Maggie Makes Three. LC 85-16389. 128p. (J). (gr. 3-7). 1986. 12.95 (0-15-250355-2, Harcourt Child Bks) Harcourt.

— Backstage with a Ghost. LC 94-71793. (Disney Adventures: No. 3). (Illus.). 96p. (J). (gr. 2-4). 1995. 13.95 (0-7868-3048-4, Pub. by Disney Pr) Little.

— Backstage with a Ghost. LC 94-71793. (Disney Adventures: No. 3). (J). (gr. 2-4). 1995. 9.05 (0-606-09129-7, Pub. by Turtleback) Demco.

— Bait for a Burglar. LC 96-72038. (Disney Adventures: No. 12). 96p. (J). (gr. 2-4). 1997. pap. 3.95 (0-7868-4089-7, Pub. by Disney Pr) Little.

— Before You Were Born. LC 79-91741. (Illus.). 40p. (J). (ps up). 1980. pap. 7.95 (0-87973-343-8) Our Sunday Visitor.

— Beware the Pirate Ghost. LC 95-83884. (Disney Adventures: No. 7). (J). (gr. 2-4). 1996. 9.05 (0-606-09133-5, Pub. by Turtleback) Demco.

— Candidate for Murder. 1991. 9.09 (0-606-00815-2, Pub. by Turtleback) Demco.

— Candidate for Murder. large type ed. LC 93-42058. 1994. pap. 15.95 (0-7862-0142-8) Thorndike Pr.

Nixon, Joan Lowery. Catch a Crooked Clown. (Disney Adventures: No. 8). (J). (gr. 2-4). 1996. 9.05 (0-606-10768-1, Pub. by Turtleback) Demco.

Nixon, Joan Lowery. Caught in the Act. No. 2. 160p. (YA). 1996. mass mkt. 4.50 (0-440-22678-3) BDD Bks Young Read.

— Caught in the Act. (Orphan Train Quartet Ser.). (J). 1996. 9.60 (0-606-04184-2, Pub. by Turtleback) Demco.

— Check in to Danger. LC 94-71794. (Disney Adventures: No. 4). (J). (gr. 2-4). 1995. 9.15 (0-606-09130-0, Pub. by Turtleback) Demco.

— Circle of Love. LC 96-44950. (Orphan Train Ser.: No. 7). 176p. (J). (gr. 2 up). 1997. 15.95 (0-385-32280-1, Delacorte Pr Bks) BDD Bks Young Read.

An Asterisk (*) at the beginning of an entry indicates that the title is appearing for the first time.

— Circle of Love. 176p. (YA). 1998. mass mkt. 4.50 *(0-440-22731-3)* BDD Bks Young Read.

— Circle of Love. (Orphan Train Ser.). 1998. 9.60 *(0-606-13276-7,* Pub. by Turtleback) Demco.

— A Dangerous Promise. (Orphan Train Adventures Ser.). (J). 1996. 9.09 *(0-606-08511-4,* Pub. by Turtleback) Demco.

— A Dangerous Promise: The Orphan Train Adventures. 160p. (YA). (gr. 5 up). 1995. mass mkt. 4.99 *(0-440-21965-5,* LLL BDD) BDD Bks Young Read.

— The Dark & Deadly Pool. 192p. (YA). (gr. 6 up). 1989. mass mkt. 4.50 *(0-440-20348-1,* LLL BDD) BDD Bks Young Read.

— The Dark & Deadly Pool. (J). 1993. mass mkt. 3.99 *(0-440-90036-0)* Dell.

— The Dark & Deadly Pool. (Laurel-Leaf Suspense Ser.). (J). 1987. 9.60 *(0-606-04194-X,* Pub. by Turtleback) Demco.

***Nixon, Joan Lowery.** David's Search. (Orphan Train Ser.: Vol. 4). (Illus.). 144p. (J). (gr. 2-6). 2000. pap. 4.50 *(0-440-41315-X,* Yearling) BDD Bks Young Read.

Nixon, Joan Lowery. David's Search. LC 98-3281. (Orphan Train Children Ser.: No. 4). 144p. (J). (gr. 2-8). 1998. 9.95 *(0-385-32296-8)* Delacorte.

— Don't Scream. 176p. (YA). (gr. 7 up). 1997. mass mkt. 4.50 *(0-440-22710-0)* BDD Bks Young Read.

— Don't Scream. 1997. 9.60 *(0-606-12919-7,* Pub. by Turtleback) Demco.

***Nixon, Joan Lowery.** The Eileen Book. (YA). 2001. mass mkt. *(0-385-32759-5)* BDD Bks Young Read.

Nixon, Joan Lowery. A Family Apart. 176p. (YA). 1995. mass mkt. 4.50 *(0-440-22676-7)* BDD Bks Young Read.

— A Family Apart. (J). 1996. mass mkt. 5.99 *(0-440-91116-8)* BDD Bks Young Read.

— A Family Apart. 176p. (J). 1997. mass mkt. 4.50 *(0-440-91309-8)* BDD Bks Young Read.

— Family Apart. (Orphan Train Adventures Ser.). (J). 1996. 9.60 *(0-606-04092-7,* Pub. by Turtleback) Demco.

Nixon, Joan Lowery. Fear Stalks Grizzly Hill. (Disney Adventures: No. 9). (J). (gr. 2-4). 1996. 9.05 *(0-606-10769-X,* Pub. by Turtleback) Demco.

Nixon, Joan Lowery. The Ghosts of Now. 192p. (YA). (gr. 7 up). 1986. mass mkt. 4.99 *(0-440-93115-0,* LLL BDD) BDD Bks Young Read.

— Ghosts of Now. (J). 1986. 9.09 *(0-606-02390-9,* Pub. by Turtleback) Demco.

***Nixon, Joan Lowery.** Gus & Gertie & the Missing Pearl. (Illus.). (J). 2000. 14.95 *(1-58717-022-1)* SeaStar.

Nixon, Joan Lowery. The Happy Birthday Mystery. Ann, Fay, ed. LC 79-18362. (First Read-Alone Mysteries Ser.). (Illus.). 32p. (J). (gr. 1-3). 1980. lib. bdg. 8.95 *(0-8075-3150-2)* A Whitman

— The Haunting. LC 97-32658. 192p. (YA). (gr. 7-12). 1998. 15.95 *(0-385-32247-X)* Doubleday.

***Nixon, Joan Lowery.** Haunting. 192p. (gr. 8-12). 2000. mass mkt. 4.99 *(0-440-22008-4,* LE) Dell.

Nixon, Joan Lowery. The House Has Eyes. LC 95-83383. (Disney Adventures: No. 5). 96p. (J). (gr. 2-4). 1996. pap. 3.95 *(0-7868-4078-1,* Pub. by Disney Pr) Little.

— The House Has Eyes. LC 49-208200. (Disney Adventures: No. 5). (J). (gr. 2-4). 1996. 9.05 *(0-606-09131-9,* Pub. by Turtleback) Demco.

— If You Were a Writer. (J). 1995. mass mkt. 5.99 *(0-689-71900-0)* Aladdin.

— If You Were a Writer. LC 88-402. (Illus.). 32p. (J). (gr. k-3). 1988. lib. bdg. 15.00 *(0-02-768210-2,* Mac Bks Young Read) S&S Childrens.

— If You Were a Writer. 1995. 10.15 *(0-606-07697-2,* Pub. by Turtleback) Demco.

— In the Face of Danger. Vol. 3. 160p. (J). (gr. 4-7). 1996. mass mkt. 4.50 *(0-440-22705-4)* BDD Bks Young Read.

— In the Face of Danger. (Orphan Train Quartet Ser.). (J). 1988. 9.60 *(0-606-01526-4,* Pub. by Turtleback) Demco.

— The Internet Escapade. LC 96-70875. (Disney Adventures: No. 11). 96p. (J). (gr. 2-4). 1997. pap. 3.95 *(0-7868-4088-9,* Pub. by Disney Pr) Time Warner.

— The Island of Dangerous Dreams. 192p. (Orig.). (YA). (gr. k-12). 1989. mass mkt. 4.50 *(0-440-20258-2,* LLL BDD) BDD Bks Young Read.

— Island of Dangerous Dreams. (Laurel-Leaf Suspense Ser.). (J). 1989. 9.09 *(0-606-04115-X,* Pub. by Turtleback) Demco.

— Keeping Secrets. (J). 1996. 20.95 *(0-385-30994-5)* BDD Bks Young Read.

— Keeping Secrets. (Orphan Train Adventures Ser.: No. 6). 176p. (YA). (gr. 5). 1996. mass mkt. 4.50 *(0-440-21992-2)* Dell.

— Keeping Secrets. (Orphan Train Adventures Ser.). 1996. 9.60 *(0-606-08789-3,* Pub. by Turtleback) Demco.

— The Kidnapping of Christina Lattimore. 192p. (YA). (gr. 7 up). 1992. mass mkt. 4.99 *(0-440-94520-8,* LLL BDD) BDD Bks Young Read.

— The Kidnapping of Christina Lattimore. (Laurel-Leaf Bks.). 1980. 9.09 *(0-606-01208-7,* Pub. by Turtleback) Demco.

— Land of Dreams. (J). 1994. mass mkt. 4.99 *(0-440-91013-7)* BDD Bks Young Read.

Nixon, Joan Lowery. Land of Dreams. (Ellis Island Ser.). 1994. 9.09 *(0-606-07160-1,* Pub. by Turtleback) Demco.

Nixon, Joan Lowery. Land of Hope. (Ellis Island Ser.: No. 1). 176p. (YA). (gr. 7 up). 1993. mass mkt. 4.50 *(0-440-21597-8)* Dell.

— Land of Hope. (Ellis Island Ser.). (J). 1992. 9.09 *(0-606-05265-8,* Pub. by Turtleback) Demco.

Nixon, Joan Lowery. Land of Promise. LC 92-28591. (Ellis Island Ser.). 1993. 9.09 *(0-606-06359-5,* Pub. by Turtleback) Demco.

Nixon, Joan Lowery. The Legend of Deadman's Mine. LC 94-71792. (Disney Adventures: No. 2). (Illus.). 96p. (J). (gr. 2-4). 1995. 13.95 *(0-7868-3047-6,* Pub. by Disney Pr) Little.

— The Legend of Deadman's Mine. LC 94-71792. (Disney Adventures: No. 2). (J). (gr. 2-4). 1995. 9.15 *(0-606-09128-9,* Pub. by Turtleback) Demco.

— Lucy's Wish. LC 97-21529. (Orphan Train Ser.: No. 1). (Illus.). 128p. (J). (gr. 4-6). 1998. 9.95 *(0-385-32293-3,* Delacorte Pr Bks) BDD Bks Young Read.

— Lucy's Wish. (Orphan Train Ser.: No. 1). (J). 1999. pap. 4.50 *(0-440-41306-0)* BDD Bks Young Read.

— Maggie Forevermore. LC 86-20135. 112p. (J). (gr. 3-7). 1987. 13.95 *(0-15-250345-5)* Harcourt.

— Maggie, Too. LC 84-19766. 101p. (J). (gr. 3-7). 1985. 11.95 *(0-15-250350-1,* Harcourt Child Bks) Harcourt.

— Murdered My Sweet. 208p. (YA). 1998. mass mkt. 4.50 *(0-440-22005-X)* BDD Bks Young Read.

— Murdered My Sweet. LC 96-43431. 176p. (J). (gr. 7). 1997. 15.95 *(0-385-32245-3)* Delacorte.

***Nixon, Joan Lowery.** Murdered My Sweet. 1998. pap. 11.70 *(0-613-10217-7)* Econo-Clad Bks.

Nixon, Joan Lowery. The Name of the Game Was Murder. 192p. (YA). (gr. 7 up). 1994. mass mkt. 4.99 *(0-440-21916-7)* Dell.

Nixon, Joan Lowery. The Name of the Game Was Murder. (J). 1993. 9.09 *(0-606-07048-6,* Pub. by Turtleback) Demco.

Nixon, Joan Lowery. The Name of the Game Was Murder. large type ed. LC 93-20596. 247p. (J). 1993. 16.95 *(1-56054-775-8)* Thorndike Pr.

***Nixon, Joan Lowery.** Nancy's Story, 1765. (Colonial Williamsburg Ser.). (YA). 2000. 9.95 *(0-385-32679-3)* Delacorte.

— Nobody's There. LC 99-55106. (Illus.). 192p. (YA). (gr. 4-7). 2000. 15.95 *(0-385-32567-3,* Delacorte Pr Bks) BDD Bks Young Read.

— The Orphan Train Adventures, 6 bks. large type ed. Incl. Caught in the Act. large type ed. LC 99-89431. (J). (gr. 4 up). 1999. lib. bdg. 21.27 *(0-8368-2639-6)*; Dangerous Promise. large type ed. LC 99-55938. (J). (gr. 4). 1999. lib. bdg. 21.27 *(0-8368-2642-6)*; Family Apart. large type ed. LC 99-55932. (J). (gr. 4 up). 1999. lib. bdg. 21.27 *(0-8368-2638-8)*; In the Face of Danger. large type ed. LC 99-55933. (J). 1999. lib. bdg. 21.27 *(0-8368-2640-X)*; Keeping Secrets. large type ed. LC 99-55931. (J). 1999. lib. bdg. 21.27 *(0-8368-2643-4)*; Place to Belong. large type ed. LC 99-55934. (J). 1999. lib. bdg. 21.27 *(0-8368-2641-8)*; (J). (gr. 4 up). 1999. Set lib. bdg. 127.62 *(0-8368-2637-X)* Gareth Stevens Inc.

Nixon, Joan Lowery. Other Side of Dark. (Laurel-Leaf Suspense Ser.). 192p. (YA). (gr. 7-12). 1987. mass mkt. 4.50 *(0-440-96638-8,* LLL BDD) BDD Bks Young Read.

— Other Side of Dark. (YA). 1992. 8.84 *(0-606-03631-8,* Pub. by Turtleback) Demco.

— A Place to Belong. (Orphan Train Ser.: No. 4). 160p. (J). 1996. mass mkt. 4.50 *(0-440-22696-1)* BDD Bks Young Read.

— A Place to Belong. (Orphan Train Quartet Ser.). (J). 1996. 9.60 *(0-606-04516-3,* Pub. by Turtleback) Demco.

— Sabotage on the Set. LC 96-86050. (Disney Adventures: No. 10). (Illus.). 96p. (J). (gr. 2-4). 1996. pap. 3.95 *(0-7868-4087-0,* Pub. by Disney Pr) Little.

— Sabotage on the Set. (Disney Adventures: No. 10). (J). (gr. 2-4). 1996. 9.05 *(0-606-10767-3,* Pub. by Turtleback) Demco.

— The Seance. 176p. (YA). (gr. 7 up). 1981. mass mkt. 4.50 *(0-440-97937-4,* LLL BDD) BDD Bks Young Read.

— The Seance. (Laurel-Leaf Suspense Ser.). (J). 1980. 9.60 *(0-606-00351-7,* Pub. by Turtleback) Demco.

— Search for the Shadowman. LC 96-5740. 160p. (J). (gr. 3-7). 1996. 15.95 *(0-385-32203-8)* Delacorte.

— Search for the Shadowman. (J). 1998. 9.60 *(0-606-13083-7,* Pub. by Turtleback) Demco.

— Search for the Shadowman. 160p. (J). (gr. 3-7). 1998. reprint ed. pap. 4.50 *(0-440-41128-9,* YB BDD) BDD Bks Young Read.

Nixon, Joan Lowery. Secret of the Time Capsule. LC 95-83601. (Disney Adventures: No. 6). (J). (gr. 2-4). 1996. 9.05 *(0-606-09132-7,* Pub. by Turtleback) Demco.

— Secret, Silent Screams. (J). 1988. 9.09 *(0-606-02358-5,* Pub. by Turtleback) Demco.

Nixon, Joan Lowery. Secret Silent Screams. 192p. (YA). (gr. k-8). 1989. mass mkt. 4.50 *(0-440-20539-5,* LLL BDD) BDD Bks Young Read.

— Shadowmaker. (J). 1995. mass mkt. 4.99 *(0-440-91056-0)* BDD Bks Young Read.

— Shadowmaker. 208p. (YA). (gr. 7 up). 1995. mass mkt. 4.99 *(0-440-21942-6)* Dell.

— Shadowmaker. 1995. 9.60 *(0-606-08150-X)* Turtleback.

— The Specter. 192p. (YA). 1993. mass mkt. 3.99 *(0-440-97740-1)* Dell.

Nixon, Joan Lowery. Specter. (J). 1982. 9.09 *(0-606-02902-8,* Pub. by Turtleback) Demco.

Nixon, Joan Lowery. Spirit Seeker. (J). 1995. mass mkt. 21.95 *(0-385-31007-2)* BDD Bks Young Read.

— Spirit Seeker. 208p. (J). (gr. 6 up). 1997. mass mkt. 4.99 *(0-440-22685-6,* LLL BDD) BDD Bks Young Read.

— Spirit Seeker. (J). 1997. 9.09 *(0-606-11874-8,* Pub. by Turtleback) Demco.

— The Stalker. 192p. (YA). (gr. 7 up). 1987. mass mkt. 4.50 *(0-440-97753-3,* LLL BDD) BDD Bks Young Read.

— The Statue Walks at Night. (Disney Adventures: No. 1). (J). (gr. 2-4). 1995. 9.05 *(0-606-09127-0,* Pub. by Turtleback) Demco.

— The Weekend Was Murder. 208p. (YA). 1994. mass mkt. 3.99 *(0-440-21901-9)* Dell.

— The Weekend Was Murder. 1992. 9.09 *(0-606-06085-5,* Pub. by Turtleback) Demco.

— The Weekend Was Murder. large type ed. 225p. 1993. reprint ed. lib. bdg. 15.95 *(1-56054-598-4)* Thorndike Pr.

— Whispers from the Dead. 192p. (YA). 1991. mass mkt. 4.50 *(0-440-20809-2,* LLL BDD) BDD Bks Young Read.

Nixon, Joan Lowery. Whispers from the Dead. (Laurel-Leaf Suspense Ser.). 1989. 9.09 *(0-606-04846-4,* Pub. by Turtleback) Demco.

Nixon, Joan Lowery. Who Are You? LC 98-43000. 192p. (YA). 1999. 15.95 *(0-385-32566-5)* BDD Bks Young Read.

***Nixon, Joan Lowery.** Who Are You. (Illus.). 192p. (YA). 2001. mass mkt. 4.99 *(0-440-22757-7)* Dell.

Nixon, Joan Lowery. Will's Choice. LC 97-27139. (Orphan Train Ser.: No. 2). (Illus.). 128p. (J). (gr. 4-6). 1998. 9.95 *(0-385-32294-1,* Delacorte Pr Bks) BDD Bks Young Read.

— Will's Choice. (Orphan Train Ser.: No. 2). (J). 1999. pap. 4.50 *(0-440-41309-5)* BDD Bks Young Read.

***Nixon, Joan Lowery.** Will's Story 1771. 2001. mass mkt. 9.95 *(0-385-32682-3,* Pub. by Random Bks Yng Read) Random.

Nixon, Joan Lowery & Brush, Kathleen Nixon. Champagne at Risk. (Thumbprint Mysteries Ser.). 128p. (J). (gr. 1). 1999. pap. 5.95 *(0-8092-0671-4,* 067060) NTC Contemp Pub Co.

— Champagne at the Murder. LC 99-189237. (Thumbprint Mysteries Ser.). 128p. 1999. pap. 5.95 *(0-8092-0670-6,* 067060) NTC Contemp Pub Co.

***Nixon, Joan Lowery & Brush, Kathleen Nixon.** Champagne with a Corpse. (Thumbprint Mysteries Ser.). 128p. 1999. pap. 5.95 *(0-8092-0672-2,* 067220) NTC Contemp Pub Co.

***Nixon, Joan Lowery & De Groat, Diane.** Gus & Gertie & the Missing Pearl. LC 00-22564. (Illus.). (J). 2000. lib. bdg. write for info. *(1-58717-023-X)* SeaStar.

Nixon, Joan R. Candidate for Murder. 224p. (YA). 1992. mass mkt. 4.50 *(0-440-21212-X)* Dell.

Nixon, Jon, et al. Encouraging Learning: Towards a Theory of the Learning School. 152p. 1995. 108.95 *(0-335-19088-X)*; pap. 29.95 *(0-335-19087-1)* Taylor & Francis.

Nixon, Judith M. Hotel & Restaurant Industries: A Bibliography & Sourcebook. 2nd ed. LC 93-10578. 1993. 44.95 *(0-931682-35-5)* Purdue U Pubns.

Nixon, Judith M. & Hawbaker, A. Craig, eds. Industry & Company Information: Illustrated Search Strategy & Sources. (Library Research Guides Ser.: No. 10). 184p. 1996. reprint ed. pap. 25.00 *(0-87650-287-7)* Pierian.

Nixon, Lois L., jt. auth. see Wear, Delese.

Nixon, Marianne R. Basset Hound. 1999. 29.95 *(1-85279-094-6)* TFH Pubns.

Nixon, Martin, jt. ed. see Coventry, Lucinda.

Nixon, Mary S. Rainbows & Butterflies. 1991. pap. 9.95 *(0-938645-49-8)* In His Steps.

Nixon, Matt, jt. auth. see Griffin, John.

Nixon, Mignon, jt. ed. see Buskirk, Martha.

***Nixon, Nicholas.** Brown Sisters. (Museum of Modern Art Bks.). 64p. 1999. 29.95 *(0-8109-6200-4,* Pub. by Abrams) Time Warner.

Nixon, Nicholas & Nixon, Bebe. People with AIDS. (Imago Mundi Ser.). (Illus.). 168p. 1991. pap. 25.00 *(0-87923-886-0)* Godine.

Nixon, Nicholas, jt. auth. see Coles, Robert.

Nixon, Nicholas, jt. auth. see Galassi, Peter.

Nixon, Nick. Winds of Retribution. LC 85-3858. 1987. 12.95 *(0-87949-250-3)* Ashley Bks.

Nixon, P., ed. Transputer & Occam Developments. LC 95-75772. (Transputer & Occam Engineering Ser.). 69.50 *(90-5199-222-X)* IOS Press.

Nixon, P., tr. Amphitryon, Vol. I. (Loeb Classical Library: No. 60). 15.50 *(0-674-99067-6)* HUP.

— Casina, Vol. II. (Loeb Classical Library: No. 61). 15.50 *(0-674-99068-4)* HUP.

— Little Carthaginian, Vol. IV. (Loeb Classical Library: No. 260). 15.50 *(0-674-99286-5)* HUP.

— Merchant, Vol. III. (Loeb Classical Library: No. 163). 15.50 *(0-674-99181-8)* HUP.

***Nixon, Paddy, et al, eds.** Managing Interactions in Smart Environments: 1st International Workshop on Managing Interactions in Smart Environments (MANSE'99), Dublin, December 1999. LC 99-58033. (Illus.). 265p. 2000. 84.95 *(1-85233-228-X)* Spr-Verlag.

Nixon, Pat I. Pat Nixon of Texas: Autobiography of a Doctor. Lang, Herbert H., ed. LC 78-65575. 248p. 1979. 18.95 *(0-89096-072-0)* Tex A&M Univ Pr.

***Nixon, Paul.** Waratah. 2nd ed. 1998. pap. 16.95 *(0-86417-878-6,* Pub. by Kangaroo Pr) Seven Hills Bk.

***Nixon, Paul G.** Representations of Education in Literature. LC 00-41567. 2000. write for info. *(0-7734-7707-1)* E Mellen.

Nixon, Peter H., ed. Mantle Xenoliths. fac. ed. LC 86-15705. (Illus.). 895p. 1994. pap. 200.00 *(0-7837-7663-2,* 204741600007) Bks Demand.

Nixon, Phyllis J. A Glossary of Virginia Words. (Publications of the American Dialect Society: No. 5). 46p. 1946. pap. 4.50 *(0-8173-0605-6)* U of Ala Pr.

Nixon, Regina, jt. auth. see Hill, Robert B.

***Nixon, Richard.** In the Arena. 1999. pap. 9.98 *(0-671-04443-5)* PB.

Nixon, Richard G. Roadmap to Riches: Your Personal Guidebook for the Lazy Man's Way to Riches. 144p. 1995. student ed. 12.95 *(1-884337-15-5)* F P Pubng.

Nixon, Richard G. & Karbo, Joe. The Lazy Man's Way to Riches: How to Have Everything in the World You Really Want. rev. ed. LC 93-41887. (Illus.). 318p. 1995. pap. 20.00 *(1-884337-11-2)* F P Pubng.

Nixon, Richard G., ed. see Karbo, Joe.

Nixon, Richard M. In the Arena. Rubenstein, Julie, ed. 488p. 1991. reprint ed. pap. 6.99 *(0-671-72934-9)* PB.

— Leaders. 1994. lib. bdg. 24.95 *(1-56849-497-1)* Buccaneer Bks.

— Memoirs. 1994. lib. bdg. 39.95 *(1-56849-498-X)* Buccaneer Bks.

— 1999: The Global Challenges We Face in the Next Decade. 1988. 100.00 *(0-671-65992-8)* S&S Trade.

— Nixon Tapes: Submission of Recorded Presidential Conversations to the Committee on the Judiciary of the House of Representatives. 1308p. 1974. reprint ed. 45.00 *(1-57588-342-2,* 200830) W S Hein.

— Nixon's Ten Commandments of Statecraft: His Guiding Principles of Leadership & Negotiation. LC 97-17420. 1997. 19.50 *(0-684-83795-1)* S&S Trade.

— No More Vietnams. 240p. 1986. reprint ed. mass mkt. 4.99 *(0-380-70119-7,* Avon Bks) Morrow Avon.

— Real Peace - No More Vietnams. (Richard Nixon Library). 1990. pap. 12.95 *(0-671-70620-9,* Touchstone) S&S Trade Pap.

— The Real War. (Richard Nixon Library). (Orig.). 1990. pap. 12.95 *(0-671-70617-9,* Touchstone) S&S Trade Pap.

— RN: The Memoirs of Richard Nixon. (Richard Nixon Library). 1136p. 1990. per. 23.00 *(0-671-70741-8,* Touchstone) S&S Trade Pap.

— Six Crises. 1990. pap. 12.95 *(0-671-70619-5)* S&S Trade.

***Nixon, Rob.** Dreambirds: The Natural History of a Fantasy. LC 99-88357. 304p. 2000. text 23.00 *(0-312-24540-8,* Picador USA) St Martin.

Nixon, Rob. Homelands, Harlem, & Hollywood: South African Culture & the World Beyond. LC 93-47906. 320p. (C). (gr. 13). 1994. pap. 20.99 *(0-415-90861-2)* Routledge.

Nixon, Robert, jt. auth. see Brown-Nixon, Candace.

Nixon, Ron, jt. photos by see McGee, Warren.

Nixon, Sean. Hard Looks: Masculinities, Spectatorship & Contemporary Consumption. LC 96-21862. 256p. 1996. pap. 19.95 *(0-312-16333-9)*; text 59.95 *(0-312-16332-0)* St Martin.

***Nixon, Shelley.** From Where I Sit: Making My Way with Cerebral Palsy. (Illus.). (J). 1999. 10.34 *(0-606-18549-6)* Turtleback.

— From Where I Sit Vol. 1: Making My Way with Cerebral Palsy. 144p. (YA). (gr. 7-12). 1999. mass mkt. 4.99 *(0-590-39584-X)* Scholastic Inc.

Nixon, Stuart, et al. DeadBase, Jr. The Portable Guide to Grateful Dead Songlists. (Illus.). 288p. 1995. 16.00 *(0-685-34694-3)* DeadBase.

— DeadBase Nine: The Complete Guide to Grateful Dead Songlists. (Illus.). 576p. 1996. pap. 34.00 *(1-877657-18-2)*; lib. bdg. 42.00 *(1-877657-19-0)* DeadBase.

— DeadBase '93: The Annual Edition of the Complete Guide to Grateful Dead Songlists. (Illus.). 240p. (Orig.). 1994. pap. 14.00 *(1-877657-14-X)* DeadBase.

— DeadBase '88: The Annual Edition of the Complete Guide to Grateful Dead Songlists. (Illus.). 128p. (Orig.). 1989. pap. 12.00 *(1-877657-02-6)* DeadBase.

— DeadBase '89: The Annual Edition of the Complete Guide to Grateful Dead Songlists. (Illus.). 192p. (Orig.). 1990. pap. 14.00 *(1-877657-04-2)* DeadBase.

— DeadBase '90: The Annual Edition of the Complete Guide to Grateful Dead Songlists. (Illus.). 224p. (Orig.). 1991. pap. 14.00 *(1-877657-06-9)* DeadBase.

— DeadBase '91: The Annual Edition of the Complete Guide to Grateful Dead Songlists. (Illus.). 208p. (Orig.). 1992. pap. 14.00 *(1-877657-08-5)* DeadBase.

— DeadBase '92: The Annual Edition of the Complete Guide to Grateful Dead Songlists. (Illus.). 208p. (Orig.). 1993. pap. 14.00 *(1-877657-11-5)* DeadBase.

Nixon, Thomas C. Angelic Encounter. unabridged ed. 80p. Date not set. pap. write for info. *(0-9650982-2-2)* Elmira Pr.

Nixon, Toni. New Treatment of Alcohol & Substance Abuse in Akhter Absen's Eidetic Image Therapy. 308p. 1997. pap. 25.00 *(0-913412-39-2)* Brandon Hse.

Nixon, W. A., et al, eds. Offshore Mechanics & Arctic Engineering, 1993 Vol. 4: Arctic-Polar Technology. LC 82-70515. 219p. 1993. pap. 57.50 *(0-7918-0786-X,* G00680) ASME.

Nixon, Wilfred A. Improved Cutting Edges for Ice Removal. 98p. (C). 1993. pap. text 15.00 *(0-309-05605-5,* SHRP-H-346) SHRP.

Nixon, Wilfred A., et al, eds. Arctic/Polar Symposium Vol. 4: Arctic/Polar Symposium. LC 82-70515. (1995 Offshore Mechanics & Arctic Engineering Conference Ser.: Vol. IV). 300p. 1995. 120.00 *(0-7918-1310-X,* H00942) ASME.

Nixon, William. Strategic Compromise. 400p. 1990. 19.95 *(1-55972-026-3,* Birch Ln Pr) Carol Pub Group.

Nixon, William H., jt. auth. see Roth, William V., Jr.

Nixons. Hard Looks: Masculinities, Spectatorship & Contemporary Consumption. LC 96-21862. 241p. 1997. 49.95 *(1-85728-556-5,* 85565, Pub. by UCL Pr Ltd) Taylor & Francis.

Nixson, Frederick I. & Colman, David. Economics of Change in Less Developed Countries. 2nd ed. LC 84-24361. 320p. 1986. 58.50 *(0-389-20548-6,* 08109) B&N Imports.

Nixson, Frederick I. & Cook, Paul, eds. The Move to the Market: Trade & Industry Policy Reform in Transitional Economies. 250p. 1995. text 79.95 *(0-312-12404-X)* St Martin.

Niyama, Eisuke. Physical Metallurgy of Cast Iron IV. Ohira, Goro et al, eds. (Conference Proceedings Ser.: Vol. PMC4). 1990. text 17.50 *(1-55899-090-9)* Materials Res.

Niyargikar, Rao, ed. see American Society of Civil Engineers Staff.

Niyazov, Shlomohai, jt. auth. see Kimyagarov, Amnun.

Niyogi, K. K., jt. ed. see Singh, K. P.

Niyogi, Partha. The Informational Complexity of Learning: Perspectives on Neural Networks & Generative Grammar. LC 97-42280. 248p. 1997. text 108.00 *(0-7923-8081-9)* Kluwer Academic.

N

An Asterisk (*) at the beginning of an entry indicates that the title is appearing for the first time.

Nizam-Ud-Din-Wani. Muslim Rule in Kashmir: 1554 A. D. to 1586 A. D. (C). 1993. 30.00 (*81-7041-831-3*, Pub. by Anmol) S Asia.

***Nizamani, Haider K.** The Roots of Rhetoric: Politics of Nuclear Weapons in India & Pakistan. LC 00-25463. 176p. 2000. 60.00 (*0-275-96877-4*, C6877, Praeger Pubs) Greenwood.

***Nizameddin, Talal.** Russia & The Middle East: Towards A New Foreign Policy. LC 99-14834. 2000. text 49.95 (*0-312-22538-5*) St Martin.

Nizami. The Story of Layla & Majnun. 2nd ed. Gelpke, R., tr. from PER. 177p. 1998. reprint ed. pap. 14.00 (*0-930872-52-5*, 1204P) Omega Pubns NY.

Nizami, Ganjavi. Haft Paykar: A Medieval Persian Romance. Meisami, Julie S., ed. & tr. by. (Illus.). 362p. 1995. pap. 11.95 (*0-19-283184-4*) OUP.

— Layla & Majnun. Turner, Colin, tr. 270p. 1997. 15.95 (*1-85782-161-0*, Pub. by Blake Publng) Seven Hills Bk.

Nizami, Khaliq A. Royalty in Medieval India. LC 97-904131. (C). 1997. 32.50 (*81-215-0733-2*, Pub. by M Manoharial) Coronet Bks.

Nizami, N. Story of Layla & Majnun. Gelpke, R., tr. 192p. 1996. pap. 14.00 (*0-614-21351-7*, 1426) Kazi Pubns.

— Story of Layla & Majnun. Gelpke, r., tr. 192p. 1996. pap. 14.00 (*0-614-21656-7*, 1426) Kazi Pubns.

Nizami, Nizam. The Sikandar Nama: E Bara, or Book of Alexander the Great Written AD 1200. Clarke, H. Wilberforce, tr. 857p. reprint ed. text 67.50 (*0-685-13397-4*) Coronet Bks.

Nizamuddin, Mohammed. Contribution to the Marine Algae of Libya Dictyotales. (Bibliotheca Phycologica Ser.: No. 54). (Illus.). 120p. 1982. pap. text 32.00 (*3-7682-1305-6*) Lubrecht & Cramer.

Nizan, Paul. Aden, Arabie. Pinkham, Joan, tr. 159p. 1987. pap. text 18.00 (*0-231-06357-1*) Col U Pr.

— Antoine Bloye: A Novel. LC 72-92034. 255p. reprint ed. pap. 79.10 (*0-7837-3897-8*, 204374500010) Bks Demand.

— La Conspiration. (FRE.). 1973. pap. 11.95 (*0-7859-4023-5*) Fr & Eur.

— The Trojan Horse. 1975. reprint ed. 35.00 (*0-86527-317-0*) Fertig.

N

Nizel, Abraham E. & Papas. Nutrition in Clinical Dentistry. 3rd ed. 400p. 1989. pap. text 48.50 (*0-7216-2423-5*, W B Saunders Co) Harcrt Hlth Sci Grp.

Nizer, Louis. My Life in Court. 1993. reprint ed. lib. bdg. 35.95 (*1-56849-145-X*) Buccaneer Bks.

— New Courts of Industry: Self-Regulation under the Motion Picture Code, Including an Analysis of the Code. LC 70-160243. (Moving Pictures Ser.). 344p. 1971. reprint ed. lib. bdg. 41.95 (*0-89198-044-X*) Ozer.

Nizetic, B. Z., et al, eds. Scientific Approaches to Health & Health Care. 186p. 1986. pap. text 15.00 (*92-890-1032-0*, 1340030) World Health.

Nizetich, Andre. Teaching Hair Coloring: A Step-by-Step Guide to Building Props. LC 92-35110. (Career Development Ser.). 1992. pap. 21.95 (*1-56253-072-0*) Thomson Learn.

Nizhny, Vladimir. Lessons with Eisenstein. LC 78-27394. (Quality Paperbacks Ser.). 1979. reprint ed. pap. 9.95 (*0-306-80100-0*) Da Capo.

Nizich, Sharon V., et al. National Air Pollutant Emission Trends, 1990-1995. (Illus.). 64p. (C). 1998. pap. text 20.00 (*0-7881-7438-X*) DIANE Pub.

Niziol, J., jt. auth. see Piszczek, K.

Niznik, Hyman B. Dopamine Receptors & Transporters, Pharmacology, Structure & Function: Pharmacology, Structure & Function. LC 93-42705. (Illus.). 704p. 1994. text 235.00 (*0-8247-9158-4*) Dekker.

Niznik, Jozef T. & Sanders, John. Debating the Future of Philosophy: Habermas, Rorty & Kolakowski. LC 96-20680. 160p. 1996. 55.00 (*0-275-95715-2*, Praeger Pubs) Greenwood.

Niznik, Jozef T. & Sanders, John, eds. Debating the State of Philosophy: Habermas, Rorty & Kolakowski. LC 96-20680. 160p. 1996. pap. 18.95 (*0-275-95835-3*, Praeger Pubs) Greenwood.

Nizri, Osnath, ed. see Pollack, Aharon.

Nizzoli, F., et al, eds. Dynamical Phenomena at Surfaces, Intersurfaces & Superlattices. (Surface Sciences Ser.: Vol. 3). (Illus.). 350p. 1985. 78.95 (*0-387-15505-8*) Spr-Verlag.

Njaka, E. N. Igbo Political Culture. LC 73-80120. (Studies in Political Culture & National Integration). 187p. reprint ed. pap. 58.00 (*0-8357-9460-1*, 201607700097) Bks Demand.

Njama, Karari, jt. auth. see Barnett, Donald L.

Njegos, Petar Petrovic. The Mountain Wreath. Mihailovich, Vasa D., ed. & tr. by. LC 86-21998. xix, 220p. 1986. pap. 22.50 (*1-884445-18-7*) C Schlacks Pub.

***Njeh, Christopher F., ed.** Quantitative Ultrasound: Assessment of Osteoporosis & Bone Status. 420p. 1999. 125.00 (*1-85317-679-6*, Pub. by Martin Dunitz) Blackwell Sci.

Njeng, Pierre Yves. Vacation in the Village. LC 99-61827. 32p. (J). (ps-2). 1999. 14.95 (*1-56397-768-0*) Boyds Mills Pr.

— Vacation in the Village. LC 99-61827. (Illus.). 32p. (J). (ps-3). 1999. pap. 6.95 (*1-56397-823-7*) Boyds Mills Pr.

***Njeri, Itabari.** Shadowed Feats: Untold Story. 2000. text (*0-374-26185-7*) FS&G.

Njogu, A. R., jt. auth. see Tukei, P. M.

Njoh, Ambe J. Interorganizational Relations & Effectiveness in Planning & Administration in Developing Countries: Towards a Strategy for Improving the Performance of Development Policy Organizations. LC 97-28279. 192p. 1997. text 79.95 (*0-7734-8587-2*) E Mellen.

Njoku, John E. An Allegorical Story of the Restoration of African Democracy: The Strong Versus the Weak. LC 94-25202. (Illus.). 162p. 1995. text 79.95 (*0-7734-8973-8*) E Mellen.

— The Dawn of African Women. LC 77-154067. 96p. reprint ed. pap. 30.00 (*0-608-13974-2*, 205558800029) Bks Demand.

— Short Stories of the Traditional People of Nigeria: African Folks, Back Home. LC 91-38739. (Studies in African Literature: Vol. 7). 172p. 1992. lib. bdg. 79.95 (*0-7734-9631-9*) E Mellen.

— Traditionalism vs. Modernism at Death: Allegorical Tales of Africa. LC 88-14075. (African Studies: Vol. 11). 150p. 1989. lib. bdg. 69.95 (*0-88946-188-0*) E Mellen.

Njoku, John E. Eberegbulam, see Eberegbulam Njoku, John E.

Njoku, Onwuka N. Mbundu. LC 96-32811. (Heritage Library of African Peoples: Set 3). (Illus.). 64p. (YA). (gr. 7-12). 1997. lib. bdg. 16.95 (*0-8239-2004-6*, D2004-6) Rosen Group.

Njoku, Scholastica I. Dog What? (Ngozi of Africa Ser.: No. 2). (Illus.). 49p. (J). (gr. k up). 1989. per. 6.95 (*0-9617833-1-1*) S I NJOKU.

— The Miracle of a Christmas Doll. (Ngozi of Africa Ser.: No. 1). (Illus.). 29p. (J). (gr. k up). 1986. per. 5.95 (*0-9617833-0-3*) S I NJOKU.

***Njoku, Scholastica I.** You Can Write Poems: Just Play with Words. 80p. (J). (gr. 3-7). 1999. 15.00 (*1-57532-213-7*) Press-Tige Pub.

Njolstad, Olav, jt. ed. see Gjelstad, Jorn.

Njolstad, Olav, jt. ed. see Gleditsch, Nils P.

Njozi, Hamza M. The Sources of the Quaran. 96p. 1991. pap. write for info. (*1-882837-29-0*) W A M Y Intl.

NK Lawn & Garden Co. Staff. Beautiful Roses. (NK Lawn & Garden Step-by-Step Visual Guides Ser.). (Illus.). 80p. (Orig.). 1992. pap. 6.95 (*0-380-76663-9*, Avon Bks) Morrow Avon.

— Beautiful Roses. (Step-by-Step Visual Guide Ser.). 80p. (Orig.). 1991. pap. 7.95 (*1-880281-01-5*) NK Lawn & Garden.

— Caring for Lawns. (NK Lawn & Garden Step-by-Step Visual Guides Ser.). (Illus.). 80p. (Orig.). 1992. pap. 6.95 (*0-380-76664-7*, Avon Bks) Morrow Avon.

— Caring for Lawns. 80p. (Orig.). 1991. pap. 7.95 (*1-880281-04-X*) NK Lawn & Garden.

— Garden Fresh Vegetables. (NK Lawn & Garden Step-by-Step Visual Guides Ser.). (Illus.). 80p. 1992. pap. 6.95 (*0-380-76662-0*, Avon Bks) Morrow Avon.

— Garden Fresh Vegetables. (Step-by-Step Visual Guide Ser.). 80p. 1991. pap. 7.95 (*1-880281-00-7*) NK Lawn & Garden.

— Improving Garden Soils. (NK Lawn & Garden Step-by-Step Visual Guides Ser.). (Illus.). 80p. 1992. pap. 6.95 (*0-380-76666-3*, Avon Bks) Morrow Avon.

— Improving Garden Soils. (Step-by-Step Visual Guide Ser.). 80p. 1991. pap. 7.95 (*1-880281-03-1*) NK Lawn & Garden.

— My First Garden Book. (NK Lawn & Garden Step-by-Step Visual Guides Ser.). (Illus.). 80p. (J). 1992. pap. 6.95 (*0-380-76667-1*, Avon Bks) Morrow Avon.

— My First Garden Book. (Step-by-Step Visual Guide Ser.). 80p. 1991. pap. 7.95 (*1-880281-05-8*) NK Lawn & Garden.

— Planning Landscapes. (Step-by-Step Visual Guide Ser.). 80p. 1991. pap. 7.95 (*1-880281-02-3*) NK Lawn & Garden.

Nkabinde, A.C., jt. auth. see Hlongwane, J.B.

Nkabinde, Zandile P. An Analysis of Educational Challenges in the New South Africa. LC 96-51717. 290p. (C). 1997. 57.50 (*0-7618-0657-1*); pap. 36.50 (*0-7618-0658-X*) U Pr of Amer.

Nkemdirim, Bernard. Social Change & Political Violence in Colonial Nigeria. 160p. (C). 1990. 35.00 (*0-7223-0693-8*, Pub. by A H S Ltd) St Mut.

Nkemnji, John Fonjia, jt. ed. see Achankeng, Fuankem.

Nketia, J. H. African Music in Ghana. LC 63-8873. (Northwestern University, Evanston, Ill. African Studies: No. 11). (Illus.). 158p. reprint ed. pap. 49.00 (*0-8357-5237-2*, 201671600004) Bks Demand.

Nketia, J. H. & Dje Dje, Jacqueline C., eds. Selected Reports in Ethnomusicology: Studies in African Music, Vol. V. LC 76-640181. (Illus.). xx, 387p. (Orig.). 1984. pap. text 18.95 incl. audio (*0-88287-017-3*) UCLA Dept Ethnom.

Nketia, Joseph H. The Music of Africa. (Illus.). 278p. (C). 1974. pap. text 18.75 (*0-393-09249-6*) Norton.

Nkimba, Hussein K., tr. see Hutchinson, Hanna.

Nkomo, Mokubung. Student Culture & Activism in Black South African Universities: The Roots of Resistance, 78. LC 84-3819. (Contributions in Afro-American & African Studies: No. 78). (Illus.). 209p. 1984. 55.00 (*0-313-24357-3*, NSC/) Greenwood.

Nkomo, Mokubung, ed. Pedagogy of Domination: Toward a Democratic Education in South Africa. LC 90-80152. 460p. (C). 1990. 49.95 (*0-86543-153-1*); pap. 16.95 (*0-86543-154-X*) Africa World.

Nkomo, Stella, jt. auth. see Oches, Norm.

Nkomo, Stella M., et al. Applications in Human Resource Management. 2nd ed. 256p. (C). 1992. pap. 30.75 (*0-534-92959-1*) S-W Pub.

***Nkomo, Stella M., et al.** Applications in Human Resource Management. 4th ed. LC 99-23370. 310p. 1999. pap. 36.95 (*0-324-00711-6*) Sth-Wstrn College.

Nkomo, Stella M., et al. Applications in Human Resource Management: Cases, Exercises, & Skill Builders. 3rd ed. LC 95-9035. 1995. mass mkt. 27.95 (*0-538-85337-9*) S-W Pub.

Nkongho, Ngozi O. Favorite Iboe Stories: A Family Tradition. LC 96-60592. (J). (ps up). 1997. write for info. (*0-923950-16-8*) Tucker IL.

Nkosi, Lewis. Tasks & Masks: Themes & Styles of African Literature. LC 82-107343. 212p. reprint ed. pap. 65.80 (*0-608-18744-5*, 203035000068) Bks Demand.

Nkosi, Nicholas, jt. auth. see Wilkes, Arnett.

Nkotsoe, Mmantho, jt. auth. see Bozzoli, Belinda.

Nkrumah, Kwame. Consciencism: Philosophy & the Ideology for Decolonization. LC 65-11834. 122p. 1970. reprint ed. pap. 10.00 (*0-85345-136-2*, Pub. by Monthly Rev) NYU Pr.

NKS-Factory Magazine Staff, ed. Poka-Yoke: Improving Product Quality by Preventing Defects. LC 88-62593. (Illus.). 295p. 1989. 65.00 (*0-915299-31-3*) Productivity Inc.

***Nkwocha, Oguchi H.** God, by Man. LC 88-90335. 2000. 8.95 (*0-533-08228-5*) Vantage.

Nkwocha, Oguchi H. Ruminations. LC 88-90126. 1997. 7.95 (*0-533-08006-1*) Vantage.

— Stirring the Dreamer. 52p. 1993. 8.95 (*0-533-07984-5*) Vantage.

NLA (Potter) Staff. Stabilization of Pavement Subgrades & Base Courses with Lime. 256p. 1995. 39.95 (*0-8403-9632-5*) Kendall-Hunt.

NLG Central America Task Force Staff. The Illegality of U. S. Intervention: Central America & Caribbean Litigation. 2.00 (*0-685-14988-9*) Natl Lawyers Guild.

NLG Civil Liberties Committee. Counterintelligence: A Documentary Look at America's Secret Police. 1979. 5.00 (*0-685-14938-2*) Natl Lawyers Guild.

NLG Delegation to Nicaragua Committee. Freedom of Expression in Nicaragua. 52p. 1985. 4.00 (*0-685-14986-2*); 2.50 (*0-685-14987-0*) Natl Lawyers Guild.

NLG Labor Law Center Staff. Forming a Union: A Worker's Guide. 1980. 2.75 (*0-685-14946-3*) Natl Lawyers Guild.

NLN Council of Associate Degree Programs Staff. Educational Outcomes of Associate Degree Nursing Programs. 10p. 1990. 5.95 (*0-88737-495-6*, 23-2348) Natl League Nurse.

NLN Council of Diploma Programs Staff. Role & Competencies of Graduates of Diploma Programs in Nursing. 2nd ed. 4p. 1989. 5.95 (*0-88737-474-3*, 16-1735) Natl League Nurse.

***NLN Research Division Staff.** Nursing Datasource 1998. (Illus.). 64p. (C). 1999. pap. text 41.25 (*0-7637-1113-6*) JB Pubns.

— Nursing Datasource 1998, Vol. 2. (Illus.). 64p. (C). 1999. pap. text 41.25 (*0-7637-1114-4*) JB Pubns.

— Nursing Datasource 1998, Vol. 3. (Illus.). 64p. (C). 1999. pap. text 41.25 (*0-7637-1115-2*) JB Pubns.

— State Approved LPN Programs 1999. (Illus.). 160p. (C). 1999. pap. text 41.25 (*0-7637-1139-X*) JB Pubns.

***NLN Staff.** Nurse Educators, 1997: Findings from the RN & LPN Faculty Census. (Illus.). 72p. (C). 1999. pap. text 32.50 (*0-7637-1011-3*) JB Pubns.

— Nursing Datasource. (Illus.). 48p. (C). 1998. pap. text 42.50 (*0-7637-0939-5*) JB Pubns.

— Nursing Datasource 1997, Vol. 3. (Illus.). (C). 1999. pap. text 41.25 (*0-7637-0940-9*) JB Pubns.

NLN Staff, ed. Indices of Quality in Long-Term Care: Research & Practice. 192p. 1989. 5.95 (*0-88737-454-9*) Natl League Nurse.

NLN Staff, jt. auth. see Johnson, Ruth W.

NLN Staff, jt. auth. see McDonald, Mary.

NLN Staff, jt. auth. see Munhall, Patricia L.

NLN Staff, jt. auth. see Parse, Rosemarie Rizzo.

NLN Staff, jt. auth. see Torres, Sara.

NLN Staff, jt. auth. see Watson, Jean.

NLNAC Staff. Directory of Accredited Nursing Programs, 1997. 192p. 1997. 30.00 (*0-88737-750-5*, 18-7505, NLN Pr) Natl League Nurse.

— Interpretive Guidelines for Standards & Criteria for Associate Degree Programs in Nursing, 1997. 1997. 7.95 (*0-88737-767-X*, 23-767-X, NLN Pr) Natl League Nurse.

— Interpretive Guidelines for Standards & Criteria for Baccalaureate & Higher Degree Programs in Nursing, 1997. 1997. 7.95 (*0-88737-766-1*, 15-7661, NLN Pr) Natl League Nurse.

— Interpretive Guidelines for Standards & Criteria for Diploma Programs in Nursing, 1997. 1997. 7.95 (*0-88737-768-8*, 16-7688, NLN Pr) Natl League Nurse.

— Interpretive Guidelines for Standards & Criteria for Practical Nursing Programs, 1997. 1997. 7.95 (*0-88737-769-6*, 38-7696, NLN Pr) Natl League Nurse.

— The National League for Nursing Accrediting Commission Accreditation Manual for Post-Secondary, Baccalaureate & Higher Degree Programs in Nursing, 1997. 100p. 1997. 13.95 (*0-88737-754-8*, 18-7548, NLN Pr) Natl League Nurse.

NM Magazine Staff & Cameron, Sheila M. More of the Best from New Mexico Kitchens. King, Scottie, ed. LC 82-62076. (Illus.). 164p. 1983. pap. 9.95 (*0-937206-02-4*) New Mexico Mag.

Nm. Mod. Art Tokyo Staff. Japanese Menu Cookbook. 1996. pap. 23.95 (*4-07-972275-3*) Shufu No.

N.M.B.C. (Pisula) Staff. Selling to Corporate America. LC 96-157547. 272p. 1996. pap. text, per. 155.00 (*0-7872-1831-6*) Kendall-Hunt.

NMBC Staff. Rational Minority Business Council Directory of Minority & Women Owned Business. 144p. 1996. pap. text 125.00 (*0-7872-2101-5*) Kendall-Hunt.

NMSI Trading Ltd. Staff, jt. auth. see Smithsonian Institution Staff.

NMSU (Geological Department) Staff. Geology. 96p. (C). 1996. spiral bd., lab manual ed. 24.95 (*0-8403-9371-7*) Kendall-Hunt.

NMSU Geographics Applications Research Laboratory. Border Atlas New Mexico-Chihuahua. 28p. (Orig.). (C). 1993. pap. text 10.00 (*0-937795-17-8*) Waste-Mgmt Educ.

Nmungwun, Aaron F. Video Recording Technology: Its Impact on Media & Home Entertainment. (Communication Ser.). 304p. (C). 1989. pap. 36.50 (*0-8058-0622-9*); text 69.95 (*0-8058-0360-2*) L Erlbaum Assocs.

Nnadi-Okolo, Eucharia E., ed. Handbook on Human Resources Management for Health Care Professionals. LC 96-44092. 200p. (Orig.). (C). 1997. pap. text 17.95 (*0-88258-195-3*, OKHHP) Howard U Pr.

Nnadozie, Emmanuel, jt. auth. see Azevedo, Mario.

Nnadozie, Emmanuel A. African Culture & American Business in Africa: How to Strategically Manage Cultural Differences in African Business. LC 97-73858. 117p. 1998. pap. 19.95 (*0-9658867-4-3*, HF3132) Afrimax.

Nnadozie, Emmanuel U. Oil & Socioeconomic Crisis in Nigeria: A Regional Perspective to the Nigerian Disease & the Rural Sector. LC 95-40212. 208p. 1996. text 49.95 (*0-7734-4240-5*) E Mellen.

Nnaemeka, Obioma. Marginality: Speech Writing & the African Woman Writer. (Opening Out: Feminism for Today Ser.). 256p. (C). 1999. write for info. (*0-415-06811-8*); pap. write for info. (*0-415-06812-6*) Routledge.

— Sisterhood, Feminisms & Power: From Africa to the Diaspora. LC 97-19965. 532p. 1997. 84.95 (*0-86543-438-7*) Africa World.

Nnaemeka, Obioma, ed. The Politics of Mothering: Womanhood, Identity & Resistance in African Literature. LC 96-20491. (Opening Out: Feminism for Today Ser.). (Illus.). 256p. (C). 1997. 75.00 (*0-415-13789-6*); pap. 22.99 (*0-415-13790-X*) Routledge.

— Sisterhood, Feminisms & Power: From Africa to the Diaspora. LC 97-19965. 532p. 1995. pap. 29.95 (*0-86543-439-5*) Africa World.

Nnaji, Bartholomew O. Theory of Automatic Robot Assembly & Programming. LC 92-30586. 1992. write for info. (*0-442-31663-1*) Chapman & Hall.

Nnaji, Bartholomew O., ed. Advanced Sensor & Control-System Interface, Vol. 2911. 152p. 1996. 56.00 (*0-8194-2313-0*) SPIE.

Nnaji, Bartholomew O. & Wang, Anbo, eds. Sensors & Controls for Advanced Manufacturing, Vol. 3201. 222p. 1998. 69.00 (*0-8194-2633-4*) SPIE.

Nnaji, Bartholomew O., jt. auth. see Badiru, Adedeji B.

Nnamani, Amuluche G. The Paradox of a Suffering God: On the Classical, Modern-Western & Third World Struggles to Harmonise the Incompatible Attributes of the Trinitarian God. (Studies in the Intercultural History of Christianity: Vol. 95). 428p. 1995. pap. 69.95 (*3-631-49032-1*) P Lang Pubng.

— The Paradox of a Suffering God: On the Classical, Modern-Western & Third World Struggles to Harmonise the Incompatible Attributes of the Trinitarian God. LC 95-40439. (Studien zur Interkulturellen Geschichte des Christentums, 0170-9240, Studies in the Intercultural History of Christianity: Bd. 95). 428p. 1995. pap. 69.95 (*0-8204-2935-X*) P Lang Pubng.

N'Namdi, George, ed. see Joans, Ted, et al.

Nnamdi, Reginal. Offenbarung und Geschichte: Zur Hermeneutischen Bestimmung der Theologie Wolfhart Pannenbergs. (Wurzburger Studien Zur Fundamentaltheologie Ser.: Bd. 13). (GER.). 473p. 1993. 68.80 (*3-631-44559-8*) P Lang Pubng.

Nnochiri, Enyinnaya. Textbook of Imported Diseases. (Illus.). 1980. text 49.50 (*0-19-261192-5*) OUP.

Nnoli. Introduction to Politics. 1986. pap. text. write for info. (*0-582-64709-6*, Pub. by Addison-Wesley) Longman.

Nnoli, Okwudiba. Ethnicity & Development in Nigeria. (Research in Ethnic Relations Ser.). 320p. 1995. 82.95 (*1-85972-115-X*, Pub. by Avebry) Ashgate Pub Co.

— Self Reliance & Foreign Policy in Tanzania. LC 73-91415. (Studies in East African Society & History). 1977. text 21.50 (*0-88357-014-9*); pap. text 8.95 (*0-88357-039-4*) NOK Pubs.

Nnolim, Charles E., ed. The Role of Education in Contemporary Africa. LC 88-9931. 133p. (Orig.). 1988. pap. 9.95 (*0-943852-53-6*) Prof World Peace.

Nnorom, Columba A. American Churches & Southern Africa: Rhetoric & Reality. LC 96-35235. 204p. 1996. 39.50 (*0-7618-0567-2*) U Pr of Amer.

Nnoromele, Salome C. Life among the Ibo Women of Nigeria. LC 97-45172. (Other America Ser.). (Illus.). (J). (gr. 9 up). 1997. lib. bdg. 22.45 (*1-56006-344-0*) Lucent Bks.

— Somalia. LC 99-36772. (Overview Ser.). (Illus.). 144p. (YA). (gr. 6-9). 2000. lib. bdg. 23.70 (*1-56006-396-3*) Lucent Bks.

***No, Hana Kaiga.** Sha-Girl '97. (Illus.). 208p. 1999. 29.95 (*4-89011-379-7*, Pub. by Nihon Geijutsu) Bks Nippan.

No, Hana Kaiga, ed. Sha-girl '98. (Illus.). 208p. 1999. 29.95 (*4-89011-388-6*, Pub. by Nihon Geijutsu) Bks Nippan.

No, Yongkyoon & Libucha, Mark, eds. ESCOL '90: Proceedings of the Seventh Eastern States Conference on Linguistics. (Illus.). 363p. (Orig.). (C). 1991. pap. 10.00 (*0-685-48582-X*); lib. bdg. 12.00 (*1-878594-07-9*) OSU Dept Linguistics.

Noachtar, Soheyi, jt. auth. see Luders, Hans O.

Noachtar, Soheyl, jt. auth. see Luders, Hans O.

Noack, Ludwig. Philosophie Geschichtliches Lexikon. 2nd ed. (GER.). 1968. 195.00 (*0-8288-6658-9*, M-7585) Fr & Eur.

Noack, Mary L. Pain to Peace, a Journey. LC 96-85569. 1996. mass mkt., spiral bd. 12.95 (*1-889131-00-8*) CasAnanda.

Noack, Peter, et al, eds. Psychological Responses to Social Change: Human Development in Changing Environments. (Prevention & Intervention in Childhood & Adolescence Ser.: No. 18). 264p. (C). 1994. lib. bdg. 64.95 (*3-11-014343-7*) De Gruyter.

Noack, Ruth K. Cadenza. 30p. 1991. 14.95 incl. VHS (*0-942229-04-5*); spiral bd. 4.95 (*0-942229-03-7*) Video Album.

Noack, Wolfgang. X-SAR Picture Book: Radar Scanning of the Earth. 200p. 1998. 59.00 (*3-540-59441-8*) Spr-Verlag.

Noad, Frederick. The New Guitar Songbook. 160p. 1997. pap. 16.95 (*0-8256-1309-4*, FN 10032) Music Sales.
— Playing the Guitar. 3rd ed. (Illus.). 196p. 1997. pap. 16.95 (*0-8256-1308-6*, FN 10040) Music Sales.
***Noad, Frederick.** Solo Guitar Playing, Bk. 2. 3rd ed. 159p. 1999. pap. text 27.95 (*0-8256-1798-7*, AM949465) Music Sales.
Noad, Frederick. Solo Guitar Playing II. 160p. 1997. pap. 16.95 (*0-8256-1307-8*, FN 10008) Music Sales.
Noad, Frederick M. The Baroque Guitar. (Illus.). 128p. 1974. pap. 19.95 (*0-8256-9951-7*, AM35890) Music Sales.
— The Classical Guitar. (Illus.). (Orig.). 1976. pap. 19.95 (*0-8256-9952-5*, AM35908) Music Sales.
— First Book for the Guitar, Pt. 1. 64p. 1986. pap. 7.95 (*0-7935-5515-9*, 50334370) H Leonard.
— First Book for the Guitar: Complete Text. 200p. 1986. per. 15.95 (*0-7935-5522-1*, 50336760) H Leonard.
— First Book for the Guitar Pt. 2: G. Schirmer. 68p. 1986. pap. 7.95 (*0-7935-5189-7*, 50334520) H Leonard.
— First Book for the Guitar Pt. 3: G. Schirmer. 1986. pap. 5.95 (*0-7935-5558-2*, 50335160) H Leonard.
— Popular Elizabethan Tunes for Recorder & Guitar. (Ensemble Ser.). (Illus.). 1977. pap. 9.95 (*0-8256-9963-0*, AY15133, Ariel) Music Sales.
— The Renaissance Guitar. (Illus.). 104p. 1974. pap. 19.95 (*0-8256-9950-9*, AM35882) Music Sales.
Noad, Frederick M., ed. One Hundred Graded Classical Guitar Studies. (Illus.). 176p. 1985. pap. 21.95 (*0-7119-0612-2*, AM38597) Music Sales.
Noad, Frederick M., selected by. The Romantic Guitar. LC 89-752495. (Illus.). 128p. 1974. pap. 19.95 (*0-8256-2415-0*, AM38993) Music Sales.
Noad, Timothy. Calligraphy. (Illus.). 104p. 1995. write for info. (*1-57215-189-7*) World Pubns.
Noah, Belinda. The Black Seminoles: The Little-Known Story of the First Seminoles. 1995. pap. 9.95 (*0-9647644-0-7*) B Noah Prods.
Noah, Catherine A., ed. see Wyatt, Steve M.
Noah, Harold J. Financing Soviet Schools. LC 66-29416. 318p. reprint ed. pap. 98.60 (*0-8357-9600-0*, 201694500005) Bks Demand.
Noah, Harold J., jt. auth. see Eckstein, Max A.
Noah, Harold J., jt. ed. see Eckstein, Max A.
Noah, M., tr. from HEB. Book of Jasher. LC 87-72939. 272p. (C). 1988. reprint ed. pap. 10.00 (*0-934666-25-3*) Artisan Pubs.
***Noah, Mordecai M.** Book of Jasher. 292p. 1999. pap. 60.00 (*1-57074-442-4*) Greyden Pr.
Noah, N. D. Communicable Disease Epidemiology & Control. LC 97-26054. 274p. 1998. 137.50 (*0-471-97273-8*) Wiley.
Noah, Robert. All the Right Answers. 320p. 1988. 17.95 (*0-15-104779-0*) Harcourt.
— The Man Who Stole the Mona Lisa. LC 97-36510. 1998. text 22.95 (*0-312-16916-7*) St Martin.
Noah's Ark Staff. Month by Month: Language Enrichment Activities for Early Learning. (Illus.). 299p. 1989. pap. text 59.00 (*0-7616-7582-5*) Commun Skill.
Noak, Elsa, ed. Meditations on Marriage: Translated from Hermann Oeser's Original. (C). 1989. pap. 21.00 (*0-900657-98-7*, Pub. by W Sessions) St Mut.
Noakes. Raymond Radiguet. (Coll. Poetes d'aujourd'hui). pap. 14.95 (*0-685-37076-3*) Fr & Eur.
— War & the British. (Illus.). 256p. 1997. text 59.50 (*1-86064-306-X*, Pub. by I B T) St Martin.
Noakes, ed. The Civilian in War. (Illus.). 207p. 1992. pap. 16.95 (*0-85989-357-X*, Pub. by Univ Exeter Pr) Northwestern U Pr.
Noakes, Aubrey. Sportsmen in a Landscape. LC 72-134122. (Essay Index Reprint Ser.). 1977. 26.95 (*0-8369-2005-8*) Ayer.
Noakes, David E. Fertility & Obstetrics in Cattle. 2nd ed. LC 96-43821. (Library of Veterinary Practice). (Illus.). 1997. pap. 41.95 (*0-632-04083-1*, Pub. by Blckwell Science) Iowa St U Pr.
— Veterinary Reproduction & Obstetrics. 7th ed. 1995. text 82.95 (*0-7020-1785-X*, W B Saunders Co) Harcrt Hlth Sci Grp.
Noakes, David L. & Ward, J. A., eds. Ecology & Ethology of Fishes. (Developments in Environmental Biology of Fishes Ser.: No. 1). 144p. 1981. 34.00 (*90-6193-896-1*) Kluwer Academic.
Noakes, J. E., et al, eds. Liquid Scintillation Spectrometry, 1992. LC 93-36422. 483p. 1993. 10.00 (*0-9638314-0-2*) Radiocarbon.
Noakes, Jeremy, ed. Government, Party & People in Nazi Germany. 108p. 1980. pap. text 9.00 (*0-85989-112-7*, Pub. by Univ Exeter Pr) Northwestern U Pr.
— Nazism, 1919-1945 - A Documentary Reader Vol. 1: The Rise to Power 1919-1934. rev. ed. 220p. 1998. pap. text 15.95 (*0-85989-598-X*, Pub. by Univ Exeter Pr) Northwestern U Pr.
Noakes, Jeremy & Pridham, Geoffrey, eds. Nazism, Foreign Policy, War & Racial Extermination, 1919-1945. (Illus.). 640p. 1995. pap. text 18.95 (*0-85989-474-6*, Pub. by Univ Exeter Pr) Northwestern U Pr.
— Nazism, State, Economy & Society, 1933-39: A Documentary Reader. 430p. 1995. pap. text 15.95 (*0-85989-461-4*, Pub. by Univ Exeter Pr) Northwestern U Pr.
— Nazism, the Rise to Power: A Documentary Reader. 193p. 1995. pap. text 12.95 (*0-85989-472-X*, Pub. by Univ Exeter Pr) Northwestern U Pr.
Noakes, Jeremy, jt. ed. see Andrew, Christopher.
Noakes, Keith. The Fiberglass Manual. (Illus.). 128p. 1998. 29.95 (*1-85915-088-8*, Pub. by Windrow & Green) Motorbooks Intl.
— Successful Composite Techniques: A Practical Introduction to the Use of Modern Composite Materials. 3rd ed. (Illus.). 176p. 1999. pap. 34.95 (*1-85532-886-0*, 128258AE) Motorbooks Intl.
Noakes, Patrick & Golding, Jon. Tolley's Inheritance Tax, 1995-1996. 270p. 1995. 195.00 (*1-86012-009-1*, Pub. by Tolley Pubng) St Mut.
Noakes, Patrick & Mackley-Smith, Gary B. Tolley's Capital Allowances, 1995-96. 550p. 1995. 250.00 (*0-7855-2692-7*, Pub. by Tolley Pubng) St Mut.
— Tolley's Capital Gains Tax, 1995-96. 650p. 1995. 195.00 (*1-86012-010-5*, Pub. by Tolley Pubng) St Mut.
Noakes, Patrick & Savory, Stephen. Tolley's Capital Gains Tax, 1993-94. 470p. 1993. 81.00 (*0-85459-772-7*, Pub. by Tolley Pubng) St Mut.
— Tolley's Inheritance Tax, 1993-1994. 260p. 1993. 72.00 (*0-85459-773-5*, Pub. by Tolley Pubng) St Mut.
Noakes, Patrick, et al. Tolley's Capital Allowances, 1993-94. 440p. 1993. 140.00 (*0-85459-783-2*, Pub. by Tolley Pubng) St Mut.
Noakes, Sara, et al. Developing Child Protection Practice. 80p. 1998. pap., spiral bd. 25.50 (*1-900990-28-8*, Pub. by Natl Childrens Bur) Paul & Co Pubs.
Noakes, Susan. Timely Reading: Between Exegesis & Interpretation. LC 87-47862. 288p. 1988. 39.95 (*0-8014-2144-6*) Cornell U Pr.
— Timely Reading: Between Exegesis & Interpretation. LC 87-47862. 269p. reprint ed. pap. 83.40 (*0-608-20931-7*, 207203000003) Bks Demand.
Noakes, Susan, jt. ed. see Koelb, Clayton.
Noakes, Timothy D. Lore of Running. 3rd ed. LC 90-29001. (Illus.). 832p. 1991. pap. 22.95 (*0-88011-438-X*, PNOA0438) Human Kinetics.
Noakes, Timothy D. & Granger, Stephen. Running Injuries: How to Prevent & Overcome Them. 2nd ed. (Illus.). 176p. 1996. pap. 29.50 (*0-19-571384-2*) OUP.
— Running Your Best. (Illus.). 240p. 1995. pap. (*0-19-570956-X*) OUP.
Noakes, Tony, jt. auth. see James, Paul.
Noaks, Lesley, et al, eds. Contemporary Issues in Criminology. 262p. 1995. pap. 28.00 (*0-7083-1297-7*) Paul & Co Pubs.
Noall, Cyril. Cornish Mine Disasters. (C). 1989. 100.00 (*1-85022-032-8*, Pub. by Dyllansow Truran) St Mut.
— The St. Ives Mining District, Vol. 1. (C). 1989. 50.00 (*0-907566-33-2*, Pub. by Dyllansow Truran) St Mut.
— The Saint. Ives Mining District, Vol. 11. Payton, Philip, ed. (C). 1993. 39.00 (*1-85022-067-0*, Pub. by Dyllansow Truran) St Mut.
Noall, Gyril. Early Lifeboats. (C). 1990. pap. 40.00 (*0-85025-317-9*, Pub. by Tor Mark Pr) St Mut.
— Fishermen. (C). 1989. pap. 24.95 (*0-85025-314-4*, Pub. by Tor Mark Pr) St Mut.
Noam, E., ed. Private Networks Public Objectives. 464p. 1996. text 140.75 (*0-444-82549-5*, North Holland) Elsevier.
Noam, Eli. Telecommunications in Europe. (Communication & Society Ser.). (Illus.). 536p. 1992. text 75.00 (*0-19-507052-6*, 819) OUP.
Noam, Eli, ed. Telecommunications in Latin America. LC 96-36073. 304p. 1998. text 65.00 (*0-19-510200-2*) OUP.
— Telecommunications in Western Asia. LC 96-36944. (Illus.). 272p. 1997. text 55.00 (*0-19-510202-9*) OUP.
Noam, Eli M. Egalitarianism & the Generation of Inequality. (Illus.). 568p. 1991. reprint ed. pap. text 32.00 (*0-19-828390-3*, 10227) OUP.
***Noam, Eli M.** Interconnecting the Network of Networks. (Illus.). 375p. (C). 2001. 45.00 (*0-262-14072-1*) MIT Pr.
Noam, Eli M. Television in Europe. (Communication & Society Ser.). (Illus.). 408p. (C). 1992. text 58.00 (*0-19-506942-0*) OUP.
Noam, Eli M., ed. Asymmetric Deregulation: The Dynamics of Telecommunication Policy in Europe. 272p. 1994. text 73.25 (*0-89391-696-X*) Ablx Pub.
— Globalism & Localism in Telecommunications. 1996. write for info. (*0-614-17913-0*, North Holland) Elsevier.
— Telecommunications in Africa. LC 96-36158. (Illus.). 320p. 1999. 75.00 (*0-19-510201-0*) OUP.
— Telecommunications Regulation Today & Tomorrow. 1984. 45.00 (*0-15-004294-9*) Harcourt.
— Video Media Competition: Regulation, Economics & Technology. LC 85-435. (Columbia Studies in Business, Government & Society). 416p. 1985. text 75.00 (*0-231-06134-X*) Col U Pr.
Noam, Eli M., et al, eds. International Market in Film & Television Programs. (Communication & Information Science Ser.). 224p. (C). 1993. pap. 39.50 (*0-89391-953-5*) Ablx Pub.
— International Market in Film & Television Programs. (Communication & Information Science Ser.). 224p. (C). 1993. text 73.25 (*0-89391-545-9*) Ablx Pub.
— Services in Transition: The Impact of Information Technology on the Service Sector. LC 86-7918. 240p. 1986. text 34.95 (*0-88730-092-8*, HarpBusn) HarpInfo.
— Telecommunications in the Pacific Basin: An Evolutionary Approach. LC 92-46617. (Communication & Society Ser.). (Illus.). 544p. 1994. text 65.00 (*0-19-508421-7*) OUP.
Noam, Eli M. & Nishuilleabhain, Aine. Private Networks Public Objectives. LC 96-9496. 465p. 1996. 140.75 (*0-444-82516-9*) Elsevier.
Noam, Eli M. & Pogorel, Gerard. Asymmetric Deregulation: The Dynamics of Telecommunication Policy in Europe. LC 93-43433. 272p. 1994. pap. 39.50 (*1-56750-003-X*) Ablx Pub.
Noam, Eli M. & Wolfson, Alex J. Globalism & Localism in Telecommunications. LC 96-47843. 432p. 1997. 140.75 (*0-444-82382-4*) Elsevier.
Noam, Gil G. & Borst, Sophie, eds. Children, Youth, & Suicide: Developmental Perspectives. LC 85-644581. (New Directions for Child Development Ser.: No. CD 64). 121p. (Orig.). 1994. pap. 25.00 (*0-7879-9960-1*) Jossey-Bass.
Noam, Gil G. & Fischer, Kurt, eds. Development & Vulnerability in Close Relationships. (Jean Piaget Symposia Ser.). 368p. 1996. text 69.95 (*0-8058-1369-1*) L Erlbaum Assocs.
Noam, Gil G. & Wren, Thomas E., eds. The Moral Self: Building a Better Paradigm. LC 92-21501. (Illus.). 412p. (C). 1993. 46.50 (*0-262-14052-7*) MIT Pr.
Noam, Rachel. The View from Above. 200p. (C). 1993. 16.95 (*1-56062-178-8*) CIS Comm.
***Noan, Frank Vinh.** Vietnam, My Love. LC 99-91232. 182p. 1999. pap. 19.95 (*1-892183-17-X*, Lukeion) DTTN.
Noaro, Pierre, et al. Dictionnaire Italien D'Aujourd'Hui. (FRE.). 1993. write for info. (*0-7859-7872-0*, 2-266-02936-3) Fr & Eur.
Noback, C. R. & Harting, J. K. Spinal Cord (Spinal Medulla) Primatologia, Vol. 2, Pt. 2. Hofer, H. et al, eds. (Illus.). 1971. pap. 39.25 (*3-8055-1205-8*) S Karger.
Noback, C. R. & Montagna, W., eds. The Primate Brain. LC 73-95612. (Advances in Primatology Ser.: Vol. 1). 334p. reprint ed. pap. 103.60 (*0-608-12430-3*, 205569200030) Bks Demand.
Noback, Charles R., et al. The Human Nervous System: Introduction & Review. 4th ed. LC 90-5882. (Illus.). 448p. 1991. text 39.00 (*0-8121-1343-8*) Lppncott W & W.
— The Human Nervous System: Introduction & Review. 5th ed. LC 95-10315. (Illus.). 432p. 1996. 37.50 (*0-683-06538-6*) Lppncott W & W.
Nobar, Charles, tr. see Carotenuto, Aldo.
Nobari, Nuchine, ed. Books & Periodicals Online: A Directory of Online Publications, 1997, 2 vols. 2005p. 1997. pap. 350.00 (*0-9630277-3-5*) Lib Tech Alliance.
— Books & Periodicals Online, 1999. rev. ed. 2000p. 1999. 365.00 (*0-9630277-5-1*) Lib Tech Alliance.
Nobay, A. R., jt. ed. see Johnson, Harry G.
Nobbe, C. F., ed. see Ptolemy, Claudius.
Nobbe, George. North Briton: A Study in Political Propaganda. LC 39-24192. reprint ed. 20.00 (*0-404-04779-3*) AMS Pr.
Nobbman, Dale V. Christmas Music Companion Fact Book: The Chronological History of Christmas Hymns, Carols & Songs. (Illus.). 86p. 1998. 12.95 (*1-57424-067-6*) Centerstream Pub.
Nobbs, Alanna. Ancient History in a Modern University: Egypt, Greece & Rome, Vol. 1. (Illus.). 328p. 45.00 (*0-8028-3840-5*) Eerdmans.
Nobbs, Alanna, ed. Ancient History in a Modern University: Early Christianity & Late Antiquity, 2. (Illus.). 504p. 1998. 55.00 (*0-8028-3841-3*) Eerdmans.
***Nobbs, David.** The Better World of Reginald Perrin. large type unabridged ed. 386p. 1999. 25.95 (*0-7531 5506-0*, 155060, Pub. by ISIS Lrg Prnt) ISIS Pub.
Nobbs, David. The Fall & Rise of Reginald Perrin. large type unabridged ed. 368p. 1998. 24.95 (*0-7531-5504-4*, 155044) ISIS Pub.
***Nobbs, David.** The Legacy of Reginald Perrin. large type unabridged ed. 336p. 1999. 25.95 (*0-7531-5507-9*, 155079, Pub. by ISIS Lrg Prnt) ISIS Pub.
— The Return of Reginald Perrin. large type unabridged ed. 342p. 1999. 26.95 (*0-7531-5505-2*, 155052, Pub. by ISIS Lrg Prnt) ISIS Pub.
Nobbs, Jack. Economic Problems of the 1970s. LC 71-135099. (Commonwealth & International Library). xii, 274p. 1971. write for info. (*0-08-016283-5*, Pergamon Pr) Elsevier.
— Social Economics. 3rd ed. LC 80-42247. 1981. write for info. (*0-07-084643-X*) McGraw.
Nobbs, Jack & Hopkins, Ian. Economics: A Core Text. 4th ed. LC 94-34367. 1994. write for info. (*0-07-707916-7*) McGraw.
Nobel. Timelines. (C). Date not set. pap. 2.76 (*0-395-90328-9*) HM.
— Western Civilization. (C). 1993. pap. text 49.16 (*0-395-55122-6*) HM.
— Western Civilization, Vol. 2. (C). 1993. pap. text 49.16 (*0-395-55123-4*) HM.
Nobel, Agnes. Educating Through Art: The Steiner School Approach. LC 95-128890. 1996. pap. text 26.95 (*0-86315-187-6*, Pub. by Floris Bks) Gryphon Hse.
Nobel, Albert. Medizinisches Sachwoeterbuch: German-English-French-Latin. (ENG, FRE & GER.). 846p. 1987. 150.00 (*0-7859-6961-6*) Fr & Eur.
Nobel, Albert, jt. auth. see Veillon, E.
Nobel, Cascell, jt. auth. see Farrell, H. Clyde.
Nobel, D. & Powell, T., eds. Electrophysiology of Single Cardiac Cells. 252p. 1987. text 116.00 (*0-12-520040-4*) Acad Pr.
Nobel, Erika D., et al. Soviet Defense Decision-Making: An Integrated View, Vol. I. (Illus.). 200p. (Orig.). 1989. pap. text 125.00 (*1-55831-101-7*) Delphic Associates.
Nobel, Erika D., ed. see Ash, Ehiel, et al.
Nobel, Erika D., ed. see Kruglikov, Alexander.
Nobel, Erika D., ed. see Lusnikov, Aleksey.
Nobel, Erika D., ed. see Ryaboy, Vladislav.
Nobel, Park S. Environmental Biology of Agaves & Cacti. (Illus.). 288p. 1988. text 85.00 (*0-521-34322-4*) Cambridge U Pr.
— Physicochemical & Environmental Plant Physiology. 2nd ed. LC 98-88525. (Illus.). 512p. 1999. 59.95 (*0-12-520025-0*) Acad Pr.
— Physiochemical & Environmental Plant Physiology. 635p. (C). 1991. pap. text 48.00 (*0-12-520021-8*) Acad Pr.
— Remarkable Agaves & Cacti. (Illus.). 180p. 1994. pap. text 30.00 (*0-19-508415-2*) OUP.
Nobel, Park S., jt. auth. see Gibson, Arthur C.
Nobel, Peter. Refugee Law in the Sudan: With the Refugee Conventions & the Regulation of Asylum Act of 1974. (Research Report Ser.: No. 64). 56p. 1982. write for info. (*91-7106-209-2*, Pub. by Nordic Africa) Transaction Pubs.
Nobel, Peter, ed. Meeting of the OAU-Secretariat & Voluntary Agencies in African Refugees, Arusha, March 1983. 36p. 1983. write for info. (*91-7106-215-7*, Pub. by Nordic Africa) Transaction Pubs.
— Refugees & Development in Africa. (Scandinavian Institute of African Studies: No. 19). 121p. 1987. 42.00 (*91-7106-272-6*, Pub. by Nordisk Afrikainstitutet) Coronet Bks.
— Reunion du Secretariat de l'OAU et des Agences Benevoles sur les Refuges, Arusha, Mars 1983. 31p. 1983. write for info. (*91-7106-221-1*, Pub. by Nordic Africa) Transaction Pubs.
Nobel, Peter, jt. ed. see Melander, Goran.
Nobel, Sylvia. Deadly Sanctuary. Lebowitz, Max, ed. LC 97-75426. (Illus.). iii, 360p. 1998. pap. 15.95 (*0-9661105-7-9*) Nite Owl Bks.
— The Devil's Cradle. large type ed. Williams, Jerry, ed. (Kendall O'Dell Mystery Ser.). (Illus.). 445p. 1999. pap. 17.95 (*0-9661105-8-7*) Nite Owl Bks.
Nobel Symposium Staff. Substance P. Von Euler, Ulf S. & Pernow, Bengt, eds. LC 76-52600. (Illus.). 358p. reprint ed. pap. 111.00 (*0-7837-7103-7*, 204693200004) Bks Demand.
***Nobel Symposium Staff, et al.** Museums of Modern Science: Nobel Symposium 112. LC 00-29680. 2000. write for info. (*0-88135-299-3*) Watson Pub Intl.
Nobel Symposium 84 Staff. Early Life on Earth. Bengtson, Stefan, ed. LC 94-3822. 656p. 1994. 55.00 (*0-231-08088-3*) Col U Pr.
Nobel, W. N., compiled by. Calendars of Huntingdonshire Wills: 1479-1652. (British Record Society Index Library: Vol. 42). 1972. reprint ed. pap. 25.00 (*0-8115-1487-0*) Periodicals Srv.
Nobels, Virginia, ed. see Conner, Tom.
Nobeoka, Ketaro, jt. auth. see Cusumano, Michael.
Nober, E. Harris, jt. auth. see Seymour, Charlena M.
Nobers, Mary A., ed. Violence & Weapons Possession in Pennsylvania's Schools Annual Report: 1995-96 School School Year. (Illus.). 120p. (C). 1998. pap. text 25.00 (*0-7881-4948-2*) DIANE Pub.
Nobes. Introduction to Financial Accounting. 4th ed. (ITBP Textbooks Ser.). 1997. pap. 18.99 (*1-86152-165-0*) Thomson Learn.
Nobes, C. W., jt. ed. see Parker, R. H.
***Nobes, Christopher.** International Accounting & Comparative Financial Reporting: Selected Essays. LC 99-21907. 256p. 1999. 90.00 (*1-85898-974-4*) E Elgar.
Nobes, Christopher. Introduction to Financial Accounting. 4th ed. LC 97-11081. 1997. mass mkt. 26.95 (*0-415-14120-6*) Routledge.
***Nobes, Christopher & Parker, R. H.** Comparative International Accounting. 6th ed. LC 00-21450. 2000. 77.00 (*0-273-64602-8*) F T P H.
Nobes, Christopher, jt. auth. see James, Simon R.
Nobes, Christopher W. Comparative International Accounting. 5th ed. LC 97-32381. 564p. 1998. pap. 81.00 (*0-13-736463-6*) P-H.
— Interpreting U. S. Financial Statements - Towards 1992. 216p. 1993. 120.00 (*0-406-51170-5*, MICHIE) LEXIS Pub.
— Introduction to Financial Accounting. 3rd ed. (Illus.). 224p. (C). 1992. pap. 24.95 (*0-415-08778-3*, B0107) Thomson Learn.
Nobes, Christopher W., ed. International Accounting: General Issues & Classification. LC 96-2508. (Library of International Accounting: Vol. 1). 384p. 1996. 195.00 (*1-85898-148-4*) E Elgar.
— International Harmonization of Accounting. LC 95-2503. (Library of International Accounting: Vol. 4). 448p. 1996. 200.00 (*1-85898-147-6*) E Elgar.
Nobes, Christopher W. & James, Sinmmon. The Economics of Taxation: Principles, Policy, & Practice. 5th ed. LC 95-46376. 1996. 35.85 (*0-13-240904-6*) P-H.
Nobes, Christopher W., et al. The Development of Accounting in an International Context: A Festschrift in Honour of R. H. Parker. LC 96-37762. 280p. (C). 1997. 85.00 (*0-415-15528-2*) Routledge.
Nobhan, G. P., jt. auth. see Tuxill, J.
Nobile, Nancy. The School of Days: Heinrich Von Kleist & the Traumas of Education. LC 98-55435. (Kritik Ser.). 1999. 39.95 (*0-8143-2823-7*) Wayne St U Pr.
Nobile, Peter, jt. auth. see Richards, Ann.
Nobile, Robert. Guide to Employee Handbooks, 1992: An Annual. 1993. per. 158.00 (*0-7913-1045-0*) Warren Gorham & Lamont.
Nobilt, George, ed. see Corbett, H. Dickson & Wilson, Bruce L.
Nobis, Norbert, et al, frwds. Marc Chagall - Arabian Nights: Four Tales from 1001 Arabian Nights. (Illus.). 176p. 1995. 60.00 (*3-7913-0842-4*, Pub. by Prestel) te Neues.
***Nobisso, Josephine.** Forest Fires: Run for Your Life! LC 00-21620. 2000. write for info. (*1-57255-802-4*) Mondo Pubng.
— Forest Fires: Run for Your Life! 48p. (J). (gr. 2-5). 2000. pap. 5.95 (*1-57255-793-1*) Mondo Pubng.
Nobisso, Josephine. Grandma's Scrapbook. LC 91-23309. (Illus.). (J). 1991. 12.95 (*0-671-74976-5*, Green Tiger S&S) S&S Childrens.
***Nobisso, Josephine.** Grandma's Scrapbook. 2nd rev. ed. (Illus.). 32p. 2000. pap. 8.50 (*0-940112-05-1*) Gingerbread Hse.
— Grandma's Scrapbook. 2nd rev. ed. LC 99-75394. (Illus.). 32p. 2000. reprint ed. 16.95 (*0-940112-02-7*) Gingerbread Hse.

N

An Asterisk (*) at the beginning of an entry indicates that the title is appearing for the first time.

— Grandpa Loved. LC 99-75393. (Illus.). 32p. 2000. pap. 8.50 (*0-940112-04-3*) Gingerbread Hse.
— Grandpa Loved. 2nd rev. ed. LC 99-75393. (Illus.). 32p. 2000. reprint ed. 16.95 (*0-940112-01-9*) Gingerbread Hse.
Nobisso, Josephine. Hot-Cha-Cha! LC 97-62298. (Illus.). 32p. (J). (gr. k-4). 1998. 15.95 (*1-890817-00-7*, Pub. by Winslow Pr) Publishers Group.
***Nobisso, Josephine.** Shh! the Whale Is Smiling. LC 99-96976. (Illus.). 32p. (J). 2000. pap. 8.50 (*0-940112-06-X*) Gingerbread Hse.
— Shh! The Whale Is Smiling. 2nd rev. ed. LC 99-96976. (Illus.). 32p. (J). (ps-3). 2000. reprint ed. 16.95 (*0-940112-03-5*) Gingerbread Hse.
***Nobisso, Josephine & Coalson, Glo.** The Yawn. LC 00-39953. (Illus.). (J). 2001. lib. bdg. write for info. (*0-531-33319-1*) Orchard Bks Watts.
Noble. Biophysics Progression, ser. vol. 36. (Progress in Biophysics & Molecular Biology Ser.). 1980. pap. 23.00 (*0-08-026055-1*, 1, Pergamon Pr) Elsevier.
— Physiology of Exercise & Sport, No. 2. (Illus.). 608p. 1991. 37.95 (*0-8016-3342-7*) Mosby Inc.
— Psychosocial Approach to Alcoholism. (Substance & Alcohol Actions & Misuse). 1984. pap. 20.00 (*0-08-031611-5*, Pergamon Pr) Elsevier.
***Noble.** Thrust. 1999. pap. 14.95 (*0-553-81208-4*, Pub. by Transworld Publishers Ltd) Trafalgar.
Noble. Western Civilization Brief 1998. pap. text, student ed. 12.57 (*0-395-88555-8*) HM.
— Western Civilization Since 1300, 2 vols. 2nd ed. (C). 1997. pap. text 50.76 (*0-395-87058-5*) HM.
Noble, jt. auth. see McGrath.
Noble, Verda. Snow Cherries. 170p. 1999. pap. 11.95 (*0-7392-0063-1*, P02894) Morris Pubng.
Noble & Associates - Tyson Foods, Inc. Staff. Tastes of the Times: Great Chicken Recipes from Foodservice Kitchens Across America. Bernard, Melanie, ed. LC 98-61123. (Illus.). 272p. 1998. 49.95 (*0-9665996-0-8*) Tyson Foods.
Noble, A. Biophysics Progression: Some Physical, Mathematical & Logical Aspects, Vol. 37, No. 1. LC 50-11295. (Illus.). 48p. 1981. pap. 28.00 (*0-08-027133-2*, Pergamon Pr) Elsevier.
Noble, A., ed. From the Clyde to California: Robert Louis Stevenson's Emigrant Journey. (Illus.). xi, 291p. 1985. text 25.00 (*0-08-032423-1*, R140, K150, P110, Pub. by Aberdeen U Pr) Macmillan.
Noble, Aaron, intro. Flag: Nineteen Ninety Annual Exhibition. (Illus.). 28p. (Orig.). 1990. pap. write for info. (*0-930495-09-8*) San Fran Art Inst.
Noble, Aileen. Get off the Karmic Wheel: With Conscious Ascension & Rejuvenation. 176p. 1993. reprint ed. pap. text 11.95 (*0-9638102-0-0*) Lght Transform.
Noble, Alexandra. Estorick Collection of Modern Italian Art. 1999. 45.00 (*88-422-0767-5*) Dist Art Pubs.
Noble, Alfredo D. From Me to You with Love. 42p. (Orig.). 1991. pap. 6.50 (*0-9622849-0-4*) Papito.
— I Will Not Have You Ignorant. Noble, Jean E. et al, eds. (Illus.). 70p. (Orig.). 1992. text 8.95 (*0-9622849-8-X*) Papito.
— A Message to a Black Man. 52p. (Orig.). (C). 1992. pap. 5.95 (*0-9622849-2-0*) Papito.
— A Message to a Black Woman. Patterson, Victoria & Boulware, Chris, eds. 80p. 1998. pap. 8.95 (*0-9622849-7-1*) Papito.
— Poemas para Todas Ocasiones. Ortiz, William, tr. (SPA.). 46p. 1998. pap. 7.95 (*1-887653-02-3*) Papito.
— Poems for All Occasions. 42p. (Orig.). 1991. pap. 5.70 (*0-9622849-3-9*) Papito.
— Poems for All Occasions. rev. ed. Noble, Jean et al, eds. 72p. (Orig.). (YA). 1998. reprint ed. pap. 8.95 (*1-887653-06-6*) Papito.
— These Are My Favorite Things. rev. ed. 56p. (C). 1992. pap. 5.95 (*0-9622849-5-5*) Papito.
— 31 Days of Prayers. Noble, Jean E. & Boulware, Chris, eds. 89p. 1997. pap. text 10.95 (*1-887653-00-7*); pap. text, spiral bd. 10.95 (*1-887653-04-X*) Papito.
Noble, Allen G. An Ethnic Geography of Early Utica, New York: Time, Space & Community. LC 99-20053. (Studies in Geography: Vol. 1). (Illus.). 120p. 1999. text 59.95 (*0-7734-8046-3*) E Mellen.
— Wood, Brick, & Stone: The North American Settlement Landscape: Barns & Farm Structures, Vol. 2. LC 83-24110. (Illus.). 192p. 1984. pap. 18.95 (*0-87023-518-4*) U of Mass Pr.
Noble, Allen G., ed. To Build in a New Land: Ethnic Landscapes in North America. LC 91-20753. (Creating the North American Landscape Ser.). (Illus.). 512p. 1992. text 68.00 (*0-8018-4188-7*) Johns Hopkins.
Noble, Allen G., et al, eds. Regional Development & Planning for the 21st Century: New Priorities, New Philosophies. LC 98-72805. 396p. 1998. text 72.95 (*1-84014-800-4*, Pub. by Ashgate Pub) Ashgate Pub Co.
Noble, Allen G. & Cleek, Richard K. The Old Barn Book: A Field Guide to North American Barns & Other Farm Structures. (Illus.). 222p. 1996. 32.95 (*0-8135-2172-6*) Rutgers U Pr.
— The Old Barn Book: A Field Guide to North American Barns & Other Farm Structures. LC 94-41300. (Illus.). xii, 222p. (C). 1996. pap. 17.95 (*0-8135-2173-4*) Rutgers U Pr.
***Noble, Allen G. & Costa, Frank J., eds.** Preserving the Legacy: Concepts in Support of Sustainability. LC 98-45368. 256p. 1999. 60.00 (*0-7391-0015-7*) Lxngtn Bks.
Noble, Allen G. & Wilhelm, Hubert G., eds. Barns of the Midwest. LC 94-44659. (Illus.). 307p. 1995. pap. 25.00 (*0-8214-1116-0*) Ohio U Pr.
***Noble, Andrea.** Tina Modotti: Photography & the Body. LC 00-9607. (Illus.). 2001. write for info. (*0-8263-2254-9*) U of NM Pr.
***Noble, Andrew & Hogg, Patrick Scott, eds.** The Canongate Burns. 2000. pap. 15.00 (*0-86241-994-8*, Pub. by Canongate Books) Interlink Pub.
***Noble, Arienne.** Making Babies. 2001. write for info. (*0-688-17644-5*, Wm Morrow) Morrow Avon.
Noble, Art. Expressions for Her. vi, 22p. 1996. 5.00 (*0-9653085-0-2*) Noble House.
— It's O. K. to Be Human: A Cookbook of Entrees & Poetry Sandwiches on Eclectic Humanity. rev. ed. LC 96-92208. (Illus.). vii, 163p. 1996. spiral bd. 16.95 (*0-9653085-4-5*) Noble House.
Noble, Barbara. Your Editor Will Love You! Tips for Broadcasters & Writers. LC 98-92119. (Illus.). 90p. (Orig.). 1999. spiral bd. 22.00 (*0-933829-16-7*) Ponce Pr.
Noble, Ben. Methods Based on the Wiener-Hopf Technique for the Solution of Partial Differential Equations. 2nd ed. LC 88-70741. x, 246p. (C). 1988. text 19.95 (*0-8284-0332-5*, 332) Chelsea Pub.
Noble, Ben & Daniel, James W. Applied Linear Algebra. 3rd ed. (Illus.). 500p. (C). 1988. 93.33 (*0-13-041260-0*) P-H.
Noble, Bruce & Robertson, Robert. Perceived Exertion. LC 96-374. (Illus.). 336p. 1996. text 34.00 (*0-88011-508-4*, BNOB0508) Human Kinetics.
***Noble, Bruce & Simmons, Ian.** Complications of Cataract Surgery: A Primer. (Illus.). 128p. 2000. 80.00 (*0-7506-4799-X*) Buttrwrth-Heinemann.
— Damaged Eye - The Anerior Segment Reconstruction. (Illus.). 192p. 2000. 135.00 (*0-7506-4573-3*) Buttrwrth-Heinemann.
Noble, C. A., ed. Gedenkschrift for Victor Poznanski. (European University Studies: German Language & Literature: Ser. 1, Vol. 330). 178p. 1981. pap. 32.00 (*3-261-04713-5*) P Lang Pubng.
Noble, Carol R. & Khmeleva, Galina. Gossamer Webs: The History & Techniques of Orenburg Lace Shawls. LC 98-36138. (Illus.). 144p. 1999. pap. 21.95 (*1-883010-41-1*) Interweave.
Noble, Charles. Liberalism at Work: The Rise & Fall of OSHA. (Labor & Social Change Ser.). (Illus.). 304p. 1989. pap. 19.95 (*0-87722-665-2*) Temple U Pr.
— Welfare As We Knew It: A Political History of the American Welfare State. LC 97-23704. 224p. 1997. pap. 19.95 (*0-19-511337-3*) OUP.
***Noble, Christina.** Mama Tina. large type unabridged ed. 1999. 25.95 (*0-7531-5709-8*, 157098, Pub. by ISIS Lrg Prnt) ISIS Pub.
Noble, Claudia, ed. see Wanner, Donna T.
***Noble, Colin & Bradford, Wendy.** Getting It Right for Boys & Girls. LC 99-16267. 280p. 2000. write for info. (*0-415-20885-8*) Routledge.
Noble, Corwin K. The Executive Protection Manual: An Encyclopedia on Techniques, Procedures, Forms, Surveys & Checklists for Top Quality Executive & Dignitary Protection. 173p. (Orig.). 1997. pap. text 45.00 (*0-918487-09-9*) Thomas Investigative.
Noble, D. Progress in Biophysics & Molecular Biology, Vol. 34. 1979. 76.00 (*0-08-024858-6*, Pergamon Pr) Elsevier.
— Progress in Biophysics & Molecular Biology, Vol. 45. LC 50-11295. (Illus.). 256p. 1986. 102.00 (*0-08-033225-0*, Pub. by PPL) Elsevier.
Noble, D. & Blundell, T. L. Progress in Biophysics & Molecular Biology, Vol. 36, Nos. 1-3 Complete. (Illus.). 130p. 1981. 83.00 (*0-08-028394-2*, Pergamon Pr) Elsevier.
— Progress in Biophysics & Molecular Biology, Vol. 44. (Illus.). 288p. 1985. 110.00 (*0-08-033210-2*, Pub. by PPL) Elsevier.
Noble, D. & Blundell, T. L., eds. Progress in Biophysics & Molecular Biology, Vol. 35. (Illus.). 206p. 1981. 76.00 (*0-08-027122-7*, Pergamon Pr) Elsevier.
— Progress in Biophysics & Molecular Biology, Vol. 37. (Illus.). 229p. 1982. 95.00 (*0-08-029120-1*, Pergamon Pr) Elsevier.
— Progress in Biophysics & Molecular Biology, Vol. 38. (Illus.). 210p. 1982. 94.00 (*0-08-029683-1*, Pergamon Pr) Elsevier.
— Progress in Biophysics & Molecular Biology, Vol. 39. (Illus.). 230p. 1983. 86.00 (*0-08-030015-4*, Pergamon Pr) Elsevier.
— Progress in Biophysics & Molecular Biology, Vol. 41. (Illus.). 260p. 1983. 99.00 (*0-08-031020-6*, Pergamon Pr) Elsevier.
— Progress in Biophysics & Molecular Biology, Vol. 42. LC 50-11295. (Illus.). 202p. 1984. 99.00 (*0-08-031691-3*, Pergamon Pr) Elsevier.
— Progress in Biophysics & Molecular Biology, Vol. 43. (Illus.). 268p. 1985. 110.00 (*0-08-032324-3*, Pergamon Pr) Elsevier.
Noble, Daniel. Elements of Psychological Medicine. LC 78-72815. (Brainedness, Handedness, & Mental Abilities Ser.). reprint ed. 45.00 (*0-404-60885-X*) AMS Pr.
— The Human Mind in Its Relations with the Brain & Nervous System. LC 78-72817. (Brainedness, Handedness, & Mental Abilities Ser.). reprint ed. 37.50 (*0-404-60886-8*) AMS Pr.
Noble, David. Gallery of Best Resumes for Two Year Degrees: A Special Collection of Quality Resumes by Professional Resume Writers. 392p. (Orig.). 1996. pap. 16.95 (*1-56370-239-8*, J2398) JIST Works.
Noble, David & Course, Charles. Spreadsheets for Agriculture. 259p. (Orig.). 1993. pap. text 59.95 (*0-470-22067-8*) Halsted Pr.
Noble, David & Course, Charles, eds. Spreadsheets for Agriculture. LC 92-41099. (Orig.). 1993. pap. text. write for info. (*0-582-05389-7*) Longman.
Noble, David, ed. see Nestor, Sarah & Robertson, Edna E.
Noble, David F. America by Design: Science, Technology, & the Rise of Corporate Capitalism. 384p. (Orig.). 1979. pap. text 12.95 (*0-19-502618-7*) OUP.
***Noble, David F.** Expert Resumes for Computer Occupations. 2000. pap. 16.95 (*1-56370-798-5*) JIST Works.
— Expert Resumes for Education Majors: A Gallery of Quality Resumes by Professional Resume Writers. 2001. pap. 16.95 (*1-56370-799-3*) JIST Works.
— Expert Resumes for People Returning to Work. 2000. pap. 16.95 (*1-56370-797-7*) JIST Works.
Noble, David F. Forces of Production: A Social History of Industrial Automation. (Illus.). 432p. 1986. pap. text 24.95 (*0-19-504046-5*) OUP.
— Gallery of Best Cover Letters. Noble, Virginia D., ed. LC 99-41503. (Illus.). 424p. 1999. pap. 18.95 (*1-56370-551-6*, J5516) Park Ave.
— Gallery of Best Resumes: A Collection of Quality Resumes by Professional Resume Writers. LC 94-26608. 400p. (Orig.). 1994. pap. 16.95 (*1-56370-144-8*, GBR) JIST Works.
***Noble, David F.** Gallery of Best Resumes for People Without a Four-Year Degree: A Special Collection of Quality Resumes. (Illus.). 2000. pap. 16.95 (*1-56370-736-5*) JIST Works.
— Professional Resumes for Accounting, Tax, Finance & Law: A Special Gallery of Quality Resumes by Professional Resume Writers. Noble, Virginia D., ed. LC 99-43465. 416p. 1999. pap. 19.95 (*1-56370-605-9*, J6059) Park Ave.
Noble, David F. Professional Resumes for Executives, Managers & Other Administrators: A New Gallery of Best Resumes by Professional Resume Writers. LC 98-20676. 624p. 1998. pap. 19.95 (*1-56370-483-8*, J4838) JIST Works.
***Noble, David F.** Professional Resumes for Tax & Accounting Occupations. LC 99-40714. (Illus.). 2000. pap. write for info. (*1-56370-604-0*) JIST Works.
Noble, David F. Progress Without People - In Defense of Luddism. 156p. (C). 1993. pap. 15.00 (*0-88286-218-9*) C H Kerr.
— The Religion of Technology: The Divinity of Man & the Spirit of Invention. 288p. 1999. pap. 14.95 (*0-14-027916-4*) Penguin Putnam.
— Using WordPerfect in Your Job Search. 454p. (Orig.). 1995. pap. 19.95 (*1-56370-177-4*, J1774) JIST Works.
— A World Without Women: The Christian Clerical Culture of Western Science. LC 92-44613. 352p. (C). 1993. pap. text 12.95 (*0-19-508435-7*) OUP.
***Noble, David G.** Contaminants in Canadian Seabirds. (Illus.). 75p. (C). 2000. reprint ed. pap. text 25.00 (*0-7881-8733-3*) DIANE Pub.
Noble, David G. 101 Questions about Ancient Indians of the Southwest. LC 98-25115. (Illus.). 32p. (J). (gr. 1-6). 1998. pap. 9.95 (*1-877856-87-8*) SW Pks Mnmts.
Noble, David G., ed. The Hohokam: Ancient People of the Desert. (Illus.). 90p. 1991. pap. 13.95 (*0-933452-29-2*) Schol Am Res.
— Houses Beneath the Rock: The Anasazi of Canyon de Chelly & Navajo National Monument. 2nd ed. LC 91-78069. Orig. Title: Tse Ya Kin. (Illus.). 56p. (J). 1993. reprint ed. pap. 7.95 (*0-941270-72-6*) Ancient City Pr.
— New Light on Chaco Canyon. LC 84-10506. (Exploration Ser.). (Illus.). 108p. 1984. pap. 14.95 (*0-933452-10-1*) Schol Am Res.
— Pecos Ruins: Geology, Archaeology, History, & Prehistory. 2nd ed. LC 92-55032. (Illus.). 32p. (C). 1993. reprint ed. pap. 6.95 (*0-941270-76-9*) Ancient City Pr.
— Salinas: Archaeology, History, Prehistory. 2nd ed. LC 92-55035. (Illus.). 40p. (C). 1993. reprint ed. pap. 7.95 (*0-941270-78-5*) Ancient City Pr.
— Wupatki & Walnut Canyon: New Perspectives on History, Prehistory & Rock Art. 2nd ed. LC 92-55034. (Illus.). 48p. (C). 1993. reprint ed. pap. 7.95 (*0-941270-75-0*) Ancient City Pr.
Noble, David G. & Woodbury, Richard B., eds. Zuni & El Morro: Past & Present. 2nd ed. LC 92-55033. (Illus.). 40p. (C). 1993. reprint ed. pap. 7.95 (*0-941270-77-7*) Ancient City Pr.
Noble, David G., ed. see Levine, Francis, et al.
Noble, David Grant. Ancient Ruins of the Southwest: An Archaeological Guide. 2nd rev. ed. LC 80-83016. (Illus.). 230p. 2000. pap. 15.95 (*0-87358-530-5*) Northland AZ.
— Pueblos Villages Forts & Trails: A Guide to New Mexico's Past. LC 93-42192. (Coyote Bks.). 346p. (C). 1994. pap. 13.95 (*0-8263-1485-6*) U of NM Pr.
Noble, David W. The End of American History: Democracy, Capitalism, & the Metaphor of Two Worlds in Anglo-American Historical Writing, 1880-1980. LC 85-1077. 177p. 1985. pap. 14.95 (*0-8166-1416-4*) U of Minn Pr.
— Historians Against History: The Frontier Thesis & the National Covenant in American Historical Writing since 1830. LC 65-22811. 205p. reprint ed. pap. 63.60 (*0-8357-8898-9*, 203327600085) Bks Demand.
— The Paradox of Progressive Thought. LC 58-8765. 282p. reprint ed. pap. 87.50 (*0-8357-8979-9*, 203327700085) Bks Demand.
Noble, David W., jt. auth. see Carroll, Peter.
Noble, Denis. The Initiation of the Heartbeat. 2nd ed. (Illus.). 200p. 1980. pap. text 11.95 (*0-19-857178-X*) OUP.
Noble, Denis & Earm, Yung E., eds. Ionic Channels & Effect of Taurine on the Heart: Proceedings of the International Symposium on Cardiac Ion Channels & Effects of Taurine on the Heart, Seoul, Korea, 1992. LC 93-9516. (Developments in Cardiovascular Medicine Ser.: Vol. 141). 192p. (C). 1993. text 127.00 (*0-7923-2199-5*) Kluwer Academic.
Noble, Dennis E. Game: A One-Act Play. (Illus.). 37p. 1972. pap. 3.25 (*0-88680-062-5*) I E Clark.
— Game: Director's Script. (Illus.). 37p. 1972. pap. 10.00 (*0-88680-063-3*) I E Clark.
Noble, Dennis L. Forgotten Warriors: Combat Art from Vietnam. LC 91-44451. 224p. 1992. 37.95 (*0-275-93868-9*, C3868, Praeger Pubs) Greenwood.
— Lifeboat Sailors: Disasters, Rescues & the Perilous Future of the Coast Guard's Small Boat Stations. 2000. 27.95 (*1-57488-200-7*) Brasseys.
— Lighthouses & Keepers: The U. S. Lighthouse Service & Its Legacy. LC 97-20882. (Illus.). 272p. 1997. 34.95 (*1-55750-638-8*) Naval Inst Pr.
— That Others Might Live: The U. S. Life-Saving Service, 1878-1915. LC 93-37539. (Illus.). 198p. 1994. 29.95 (*1-55750-627-2*) Naval Inst Pr.
Noble, Dennis L. & O'Brien, Mike. U. S. Life-Saving Service 1889-1915, U. S. Coast Guard Service 1915-1989. (Illus.). 24p. (Orig.). (YA). (gr. 8 up). 1989. reprint ed. pap. text 2.00 (*0-935549-12-9*) MI City Hist.
***Noble, Diane.** Blossom & the Nettle, Vol. 2. LC 00-35931. (California Chronicles Ser.: Vol. 2). 400p. 2000. pap. 11.95 (*1-57856-090-X*) Waterbrook Pr.
— Distant Bells. LC 99-37047. 450p. 1999. pap. 11.99 (*1-57673-400-5*) Multnomah Pubs.
Noble, Diane. It's Time: Explore Your Dream & Discover Your Gifts. LC 95-12361. 208p. (Orig.). (gr. 10). 1995. pap. 10.99 (*0-8010-5155-X*) Baker Bks.
— Tangled Vines. LC 97-52098. 400p. 1998. pap. 11.99 (*1-57673-219-3*) Multnomah Pubs.
***Noble, Diane.** The Veil: A Novel. LC 98-229707. 400p. 1998. pap. 11.95 (*1-57856-014-4*) Waterbrook Pr.
Noble, Diane. When the Far Hills Bloom. LC 99-22462. (California Chronicles Ser.: Vol. 1). 384p. 1999. pap. 11.95 (*1-57856-140-X*) Waterbrook Pr.
Noble, Donald E. Like Only Yesterday: The Memoirs of Donald E. Noble Chief Executive Officer Emeritus Rubbermaid Inc. LC 96-42180. 262p. (Orig.). 1996. pap. 12.95 (*1-888683-15-5*) Wooster Bk.
Noble, Donald R., ed. The Steinbeck Question: New Essays in Criticism. LC 91-75026. x, 278p. 1993. 29.50 (*0-87875-424-5*) Whitston Pub.
Noble, Douglas, jt. auth. see Glebbeek, Caesar.
Noble, Douglas, jt. auth. see Kensek, Karen M.
Noble, Douglas E. & Kenser, Karen M. Software for Architects: The Guide to Computer Applications for the Architecture Profession. (Illus.). 472p. (Orig.). pap. 50.00 (*1-882352-00-9*) Ctr Architect Tech.
Noble, E. Myron. General Procedures & Catalog of the Middle Atlantic Regional Gospel Music Festival. LC 90-23335. (Illus.). 60p. (Orig.). 1991. pap. 4.95 (*1-877971-04-9*) Mid Atl Reg Pr.
— The Gospel of Music: A Key to Understanding a Major Chord of Ministry. LC 85-63559. 159p. (Orig.). 1986. pap. 4.95 (*0-9616056-1-8*) Mid Atl Reg Pr.
— Twentieth Annual Middle Atlantic Regional Gospel Music Festival Journal, 1992. 25p. (Orig.). 1993. pap. 5.00 (*1-877971-06-5*) Mid Atl Reg Pr.
— The Vision & the Mission: Selected Papers Presented at the 11th Annual Middle Atlantic Regional Gospel Ministries Conference in Nassau, Bahamas (1997) Noble, Shiren T., ed. LC 98-134883. 102p. (Orig.). 1997. pap. 11.95 (*1-877971-19-7*) Mid Atl Reg Pr.
Noble, E. Myron, ed. Constitution & Bylaws & General Procedures of the National Youth Convention of the Apostolic Faith Churches of God, Inc. LC 89-14602. 56p. (Orig.). 1989. pap. 3.95 (*0-9616056-8-5*) Mid Atl Reg Pr.
Noble, E. Myron, intro. Like As of Fire: Newspapers from the Azusa Street World Wide Revival, 1906-1909. 68p. (Orig.). 1994. reprint ed. pap. 16.95 (*1-877971-10-3*) Mid Atl Reg Pr.
Noble, E. Myron & Taylor, Evelyn M. Set My Spirit Free: Expressions of Pentecost. large type ed. Payne, Wardell J., tr. & intro. by. 95p. (Orig.). 1995. pap. text 9.95 (*1-877971-18-9*) Mid Atl Reg Pr.
***Noble, E. Myron, et al.** Witness Bold to Craving Souls: Leadership Conference Papers & Evangelistic Reports of 13th Annual Session - Middle Atlantic Regional Gospel Ministries in India (March 1999) 39p. 2000. pap. 9.95 (*1-877971-21-9*) Mid Atl Reg Pr.
Noble, E. Myron, ed. see Hawkins, M. Elizabeth.
Noble, Elin. Dyes & Paints: A Hands-On Guide to Coloring Fabric. Lowe, Melissa, ed. LC 97-27637. (Illus.). 161p. 1998. pap. 34.95 (*1-56477-103-2*, B219, Fiber Studio Pr) Martingale & Co.
Noble, Elizabeth. Essential Exercises for the Childbearing Year: A Guide to Health & Comfort Before & After Your Baby Is Born. 4th rev. ed. (Illus.). 277p. 1995. pap. 16.95 (*0-9641183-1-9*) New Life Images.
— Having Twins: A Parent's Guide to Pregnancy, Birth & Early Childhood. 2nd ed. 430p. 1991. pap. 18.00 (*0-395-49338-2*) HM.
— Having Your Baby by Donor Insemination: A Complete Resource Guide. 352p. 1988. pap. 15.95 (*0-395-45395-X*) HM.
Noble, Elizabeth & Sorger, Leo. The Joy of Being a Boy. 15p. (J). (gr. k up). 1994. pap. 4.95 (*0-9641183-0-0*) New Life Images.
Noble, Emily. A Method for the Millions. 38p. 1996. reprint ed. spiral bd. 9.00 (*0-7873-0635-5*) Hlth Research.
***Noble, Frances Khirallah.** The Situe Stories. LC 00-30779. (Arab American Writings). 200p. 2000. 22.95 (*0-8156-0657-5*) Syracuse U Pr.
Noble, G. Bernard. Christian A. Herter. LC 73-122753. (American Secretaries of State & Their Diplomacy, New Ser. 1925-1961: Vol. 18). 1970. 60.50 (*0-8154-0341-0*) Cooper Sq.
Noble, Gail, jt. auth. see Morton, Mark.
Noble, George. Hazardous Waste & the Public Works Official. (High Tech Waste Management Ser.). (Illus.). 63p. (Orig.). 1984. pap. text 10.00 (*0-917084-50-0*) Am Public Works.
Noble, Gil. Black Is the Color of My TV Tube. 1991. pap. 9.95 (*0-8184-0538-4*) Carol Pub Group.

An Asterisk (*) at the beginning of an entry indicates that the title is appearing for the first time.

Noble, Gilbert W., ed. The Official Catalog of U. S. Bureau Precancels. 64th ed. 1983. 6.00 (*0-685-53039-6*) G W Noble.

***Noble, Ginny.** Sams Teach Yourself E-Homework Today: Using the Internet to Get Help on School Projects, Reports. (Illus.). 300p. 2000. pap. 17.99 (*0-672-31979-9*) Sams.

Noble, Glen. Frontier Steamboat Town. LC 89-62356. (Illus.). 257p. 1989. pap. 9.95 (*0-934904-35-9*) J & L Lee.

— John Brown & the Jim Lane Trail. (Illus.). 1977. 13.00 (*0-931068-11-8*) Purcells.

Noble, Grant. Children in Front of the Small Screen. LC 75-15432. (Communication & Society Ser.: No. 5). 256p. reprint ed. pap. 79.40 (*0-7837-1116-6*, 204164600022) Bks Demand.

— The Trader's Edge: Cashing in on the Winning Strategies of Floor Traders, Commercials & Market Traders. 225p. 1994. text 34.95 (*1-55738-599-8*, Irwn Prfssnl) McGraw-Hill Prof.

Noble, Gregory W. Collective Action in East Asia: How Ruling Parties Shape Industrial Policy. Katzenstein, Peter J., ed. LC 98-36834. (Studies in Political Economy). (Illus.). 256p. 1998. 37.50 (*0-8014-3177-8*) Cornell U Pr.

— Flying Apart? Japanese-American Negotiations over the FSX Fighter Plane. LC 92-73489. (Policy Papers in International Affairs: No. 41). 66p. (Orig.). 1992. pap. text 7.25 (*0-87725-541-5*) U of Cal IAS.

***Noble, Gregory W. & Ravenhill, John, eds.** The Asian Financial Crisis & the Architecture of Global Finance. (Cambridge Asia-Pacific Studies). (Illus.). 320p. (C). 2000. Price not set. (*0-521-79091-3*); pap. text Price not set. (*0-521-79422-6*) Cambridge U Pr.

***Noble, Harry P., Jr.** Texas Trailblazers: San Augustine Pioneers. 296p. 1999. 24.95 (*1-878096-52-4*, Epigram Pr) Best E TX Pubs.

Noble, Holcomb B. Next: The Coming Era in Medicine, Vol. 1. 1988. pap. 9.95 (*0-316-61134-4*, Little Brwn Med Div) Lppncott W & W.

Noble, Holcomb B., ed. Next: The Coming Era in Science. 192p. 1988. pap. 9.95 (*0-316-61133-6*) Little.

Noble, I. R., jt. ed. see Purdie, P. W.

Noble, Ian. Language & Narration in Celine's Writings: The Challenge of Disorder. LC 86-7188. 196p. (C). 1987. text 55.00 (*0-391-03402-2*) Humanities.

Noble, J. World Wide Navigation. (C). 1987. 175.00 (*0-85174-528-8*) St Mut.

***Noble, J., et al.** Prototype-Based Object-Oriented Programming: Concepts, Languages & Applications. LC 98-50712. 324p. 1999. pap. 59.95 (*981-4021-25-3*) Spr-Verlag.

Noble, J. C. & Bradstock, R. A., eds. Mediterranean Landscapes in Australia: Mallee Ecosystems & Their Management. 1989. 70.00 (*0-643-04985-1*, Pub. by CSIRO) Accents Pubns.

***Noble, James.** Patterns for Memory Challenged Systems. (C). 2000. pap. text. write for info. (*0-201-59607-5*) Addison-Wesley.

Noble, James & Brooks, Roger. Tax Increment Financing (in Minnesota) (Illus.). 100p. (Orig.). (C). 1997. pap. text 30.00 (*0-7881-4150-3*) DIANE Pub.

***Noble, James A.** Murder by Degrees: A Winnie & Thatch I-95 Mystery. 308p. 2000. pap. 18.00 (*0-7388-2071-7*) Xlibris Corp.

Noble, James P., tr. see Cotillon, Pierre.

Noble, Janet, et al. New American Plays 2. LC 91-32100. 291p. (C). 1992. pap. 15.95 (*0-435-08605-7*, 08605) Heinemann.

Noble, Janet, ed. see Breeden, Terri & Egan, Emalie.

Noble, Jean, ed. see Noble, Alfredo D.

Noble, Jean, ed. see Patterson, Victoria.

Noble, Jean E., jt. ed. see Boolware, Chris.

Noble, Jean E., ed. see Noble, Alfredo D.

Noble, Jeremy. St. Petersburg - A Century of Russian Ballet: Book of Days, 2000. LC 99-90177. (Illus.). 136p. 1999. 24.99 (*1-928563-00-7*); pap. 19.99 (*1-928563-01-5*) Fndt Russian Ballet.

Noble, Jerry. Holding the Harvest Manual. 1992. 34.99 (*0-685-55397-3*, 872099); pap., student ed. 4.95 (*0-685-55398-1*, 872195) Pathway Pr.

Noble, Jim. Swimming Games & Activities Fun Ideas for Individuals, Partners & Groups for Children. 1999. pap. text 12.95 (*0-7136-5204-7*) A & C Blk.

Noble, Jim, jt. auth. see Austin, George.

Noble, Joan Russell, ed. Recollections of Virginia Woolf by Her Contemporaries. LC 94-13782. 208p. 1994. reprint ed. pap. text 16.95 (*0-8214-1105-5*) Ohio U Pr.

Noble, John. Lonely Planet Mexico City. 256p. 1998. pap. 14.95 (*0-86442-499-X*) Lonely Planet.

***Noble, John.** Lonely Planet Mexico City. 2nd ed. (Travel Guides Ser.). (Illus.). 224p. 2000. pap. 14.95 (*1-86450-087-5*) Lonely Planet.

Noble, John. Primary Care. 1987. 142.00 (*0-316-61150-6*, Little Brwn Med Div) Lppncott W & W.

— Swanson's Family Practice Review. 4th rev. ed. (Illus.). 2045p. 2000. text. write for info. (*0-323-00914-X*, Pub. by Mosby) Saunders.

— Textbook of Primary Care Medicine. 2nd ed. (Illus.). 2050p. (C). (gr. 13). 1995. text 99.95 (*0-8016-7841-2*, 07841) Mosby Inc.

Noble, John, ed. Textbook of General Medicine & Primary Care. 2320p. 1987. text 85.00 (*0-317-53603-6*, Little Brwn Med Div) Lppncott W & W.

Noble, John & Forsyth, Susan. Lonely Planet Etats Baltes et Kaliningrad. 11th ed. (FRE., Illus.). 300p. 1994. 23.95 (*2-84070-019-0*) Lonely Planet.

Noble, John, et al. Lonely Planet Estonia, Latvia & Lithvonia. LC 98-118689. (Illus.). 464p. 1997. pap. 19.95 (*0-86442-416-7*) Lonely Planet.

— Lonely Planet Mexico. 6th ed. (Illus.). 976p. 1998. pap. 19.95 (*0-86442-429-9*) Lonely Planet.

— Lonely Planet Spain. (Illus.). 800p. 1997. pap. 19.95 (*0-86442-474-4*) Lonely Planet.

***Noble, John, et al.** Mexico. 7th ed. 2000. reprint ed. pap. 24.99 (*1-86450-089-1*) Lonely Planet.

Noble, John, jt. auth. see Forsyth, Susan.

Noble, John D. Rare & Lovely Dolls. (Illus.). 128p. 2000. 29.95 (*0-87588-527-6*) Hobby Hse.

***Noble, John D.** Selected Writings of John Darcy Noble: Favorite Articles from Dolls Magazine, 1982-1995. 1999. 24.95 (*0-942620-26-7*) Portfolio Pr.

Noble, John H. I Was a Slave in Russia. 1957. 16.95 (*0-8159-5800-5*) Devin.

***Noble, John H., Jr.** A Legacy of Failure: The Inability of the Federal-State Vocational Rehabilitation System to Serve People with Sevre Mental Illnesses. (Illus.). 125p. (C). 2000. reprint ed. pap. text 20.00 (*0-7881-8667-1*) DIANE Pub.

Noble, John H., et al. Emergency Medical Services: Behavioral & Planning Perspectives. LC 73-9940. 595p. 1973. 59.95 (*0-87705-117-8*, Kluwer Acad Hman Sci) Kluwer Academic.

Noble, Joseph A. From Cab to Caboose: Fifty Years of Railroading. LC 64-11327. (Illus.). 281p. reprint ed. pap. 87.20 (*0-608-11722-6*, 201624300002) Bks Demand.

Noble, Judith. Hispanic Way: Aspects of Behavior, Attitudes, & Customs in the Spanish-Speaking World. 1991. 15.05 (*0-606-04696-8*, Pub. by Turtleback) Demco.

Noble, Judith & Lacasa, Jaime. Complete Handbook of Spanish Verbs. (SPA., Illus.). 360p. 1994. 19.95 (*0-8442-7633-2*, 76332, Natl Textbk Co) NTC Contemp Pub Co.

— The Hispanic Way. LC 90-61551. (The...Way Ser.). (Illus.). 114p. 1990. pap. 10.95 (*0-8442-7389-9*, 73899, Passprt Bks) NTC Contemp Pub Co.

***Noble, Judith & Lacasa, Jaime.** Introduction to Quechua: Language of the Andes. (QUE.). 240p. 1999. pap. 31.88 incl. audio (*0-8442-7206-X*, 7206X, Natl Textbk Co) NTC Contemp Pub Co.

Noble, Judy A. How to Manage Your Own Rental Property: The Easy Way. 121p. 1995. pap. 24.95 (*0-9647366-0-8*) Stars End Pubng.

Noble, Judy A., ed. see Goldsmith, Jeff.

Noble, Julian V. Scientific Forth: A Modern Language for Scientific Computing. (Illus.). 330p. (Orig.). (C). 1992. mass mkt. 39.95 (*0-9632775-0-2*) Mechum Banks.

Noble, Kate. The Blue Elephant. (Zoo Stories Ser.). (Illus.). 32p. (J). (ps-4). 1995. 14.95 (*0-9631798-3-7*) Silver Seahorse.

— Bubble Gum. (Africa Stories Ser.). (Illus.). 32p. (J). (ps-4). 1995. 14.95 (*0-9631798-0-2*) Silver Seahorse.

— The Dragon of Navy Pier. LC 96-187963. (Illus.). 32p. (J). (ps-4). 1996. 15.95 (*0-9631798-5-3*) Silver Seahorse.

— Oh Look, It's a Nosserus. (Africa Stories Ser.). (Illus.). 32p. (J). (ps-4). 1995. 14.95 (*0-9631798-2-9*) Silver Seahorse.

— Pamela's Plan. (Zoo Stories Ser.). (Illus.). 32p. (J). (ps-4). 15.95 (*0-9631798-4-5*) Salmon Run.

Noble, Kathleen. College Mathematics with Business Applications. 7th annot. ed. 1996. teacher ed. 61.84 (*0-02-803382-5*) Glencoe.

Noble, Kathleen N. & Belden, Kim. College Mathematics with Business Applications. 7th rev. ed. LC 95-38760. Orig. Title: Mathematics for Business. 1995. write for info. (*0-02-803376-0*) Glencoe.

Noble, Keith A. Changing Doctoral Degrees: An International Perspective. LC 93-14603. 128p. 1993. 101.95 (*0-335-19213-0*) OpUniv Pr.

Noble, Keith A., ed. The International Education Quotations Encyclopedia. LC 94-36312. 400p. 1995. 102.95 (*0-335-19394-3*) OpUniv Pr.

Noble, Konrad. Primal Destiny. Tomak, Judith et al, eds. LC 96-68531. 525p. 1999. 42.50 (*0-9654156-0-0*, 101) Nobless Oblige.

Noble, Lela G. Philippine Policy Toward Sabah: A Claim to Independence. (Monographs: No. 33). viii, 267p. 1977. 24.00 (*0-8165-0598-5*) Assn Asian Studies.

Noble, Lela G., jt. ed. see Silliman, G. Sidney.

Noble, Louis. Course of Empire, Voyage of Life, & Other Pictures of Thomas Cole. 415p. 1993. reprint ed. lib. bdg. 99.00 (*0-7812-5281-4*) Rprt Serv.

Noble, Louis L. The Life & Works of Thomas Cole. Vesell, Elliot S., ed. LC 64-22725. 401p. reprint ed. pap. 124.40 (*0-608-11213-5*, 200164400002) Bks Demand.

— The Life & Works of Thomas Cole. Vesell, Elliot S., ed. LC 97-15713. (Illus.). 400p. 1997. reprint ed. pap. 21.95 (*1-883789-13-3*) Blk Dome Pr.

***Noble, M.** Secret Garden. (Little Activity Bks.). (J). 2000. pap. 1.00 (*0-486-40984-8*) Dover.

Noble, M. I., jt. ed. see Ter Keurs, H. E.

Noble, Margaret & Nivedita, Sister. Kali the Mother. 101p. 1985. pap. 2.95 (*81-7505-040-3*, Pub. by Advaita Ashrama) Vedanta Pr.

Noble, Margaret, ed. see Nivedita.

Noble, Marguerite. Filaree: A Novel of an American Life. LC 98-28599. (Zia Bks.). 243p. 1985. pap. 12.95 (*0-8263-0825-2*) U of NM Pr.

***Noble, Marianne.** The Masochistic Pleasures of Sentimental Literature. LC 99-48831. 240p. 2000. text 55.00 (*0-691-00936-8*, Pub. by Princeton U Pr); pap. text 18.95 (*0-691-00937-6*, Pub. by Princeton U Pr) Cal Prin Full Svc.

Noble, Mark I., jt. ed. see Drake-Holland, Angela J.

Noble, Martha L. Statutory Agricultural Liens: Rapid Finder Charts. 174p. 1993. lib. bdg. 35.00 (*1-882461-01-0*) Natl Ctr Agricult LR&I.

Noble, Martin. Ewan McGregor. 1999. 5.95 (*0-7894-4667-7*) DK Pub Inc.

— Leonardo Dicaprio: Unofficial Biography. LC 99-172617. 1998. pap. 5.99 (*0-7894-4405-4*) DK Pub Inc.

Noble, Marty. Alice in Wonderland Stained Glass Coloring Book. (Illus.). 8p. (J). 1998. pap. 1.00 (*0-486-40305-X*) Dover.

— Alice in Wonderland Sticker Activity Book. (J). 1998. pap. 1.00 (*0-486-40314-9*) Dover.

— Angel Oranments Stained Glass Coloring Book. (Illus.). (J). pap. 1.00 (*0-486-40257-6*) Dover.

— Angels & Cherubs Iron-On Transfer Patterns. 48p. 3.95 (*0-486-29231-2*) Dover.

— Angels Stained Glass Coloring Book. (Illus.). pap. 3.95 (*0-486-28991-5*) Dover.

— Baby Girl. 1998. pap. text 1.00 (*0-486-40323-8*) Dover.

— Beauty & the Beast Stained Glass Coloring Book. (Illus.). (J). pap. 1.00 (*0-486-29340-8*) Dover.

— Christmas Ornaments Stained Glass Coloring Book. (Illus.). (J). pap. 1.00 (*0-486-40246-0*) Dover.

— Cinderella. 1998. pap. 1.00 (*0-486-40321-1*) Dover.

— Cinderella Stained Glass Coloring Book. (Dover Little Activity Bks.). 1999. pap. 1.00 (*0-486-40497-8*) Dover.

***Noble, Marty.** Create Your Own Ballet Sticker Cards. (Illus.). (J). 1999. pap. 1.00 (*0-486-40751-9*) Dover.

— Create Your Own Friendship Sticker Cards. (Illus.). 1999. pap. 1.00 (*0-486-40752-7*) Dover.

Noble, Marty. Easter Ornaments Stained Glass Coloring Book. (Illus.). 8p. (J). 1998. pap. 1.00 (*0-486-40304-1*) Dover.

— Emerald Isle Sticker Activity Book. (J). 1998. pap. text 1.00 (*0-486-40315-7*) Dover.

— Fairies & Elves. (Illus.). 32p. (J). pap. 1.00 (*0-486-40050-6*) Dover.

Noble, Marty. Fairies & Elves Iron-On Transfer Patterns. 48p. 3.95 (*0-486-40092-1*) Dover.

Noble, Marty. Fairies Stained Glass Coloring Book. (Illus.). (J). pap. 1.00 (*0-486-40247-9*) Dover.

***Noble, Marty.** Fairyland Sticker Activity Book. (Illus.). (J). 1998. pap. 1.00 (*0-486-40051-4*) Dover.

— Fantasy Fashions. (Illus.). 16p. (J). (ps-3). 2000. pap. 4.99 (*0-448-42170-4*, G & D) Peng Put Young Read.

— Flower Fairies Activity Book. 1999. pap. text 1.00 (*0-486-40495-1*) Dover.

— Fun with Bugs Stencils. (Little Activity Bks.). (Illus.). (J). 1999. pap. 1.00 (*0-486-40759-4*) Dover.

— Fun with Nutcracker Stencils. (Little Activity Bks.). (J). 1999. pap. 1.00 (*0-486-40524-9*) Dover.

— Fun with Rain Forest Animals Stencils. (Illus.). (J). 1999. pap. 1.00 (*0-486-40760-8*) Dover.

— Goldilocks & the Three Bears Sticker Storybook. (Illus.). (J). 1997. pap. 1.00 (*0-486-29906-6*) Dover.

— Happy Chanukah. (Little Activity Bks.). (Illus.). (J). 2000. pap. 1.00 (*0-486-40987-2*) Dover.

— Ice Skaters. (Little Activity Bks.). (Illus.). (J). 1999. pap. text 1.00 (*0-486-40511-7*) Dover.

Noble, Marty. Invisible Angels Magic Picture Book. (Illus.). 32p. (J). 1999. pap. text 1.00 (*0-486-40330-0*) Dover.

***Noble, Marty.** Invisible Irish Magic Picture Book. (Illus.). (J). 1999. pap. 1.00 (*0-486-40765-9*) Dover.

Noble, Marty. Invisible Mythological Creatures Magic Picture Book. (J). pap. 1.00 (*0-486-40119-7*) Dover.

***Noble, Marty.** Invisible Nutcracker Magic Picture Book. (Little Activity Bks.). (Illus.). (J). 1999. pap. 1.00 (*0-486-40531-1*) Dover.

— Invisible Rain Forest Animals Magic Picture Book. (Illus.). (J). 1999. pap. 1.00 (*0-486-40766-7*) Dover.

— Invisible Wild Animals Magic Picture Book. (Illus.). (J). 1999. pap. 1.00 (*0-486-40767-5*) Dover.

Noble, Marty. Japanese Geishas Stained Glass Coloring Book. (Illus.). 1998. pap. 4.50 (*0-486-40366-1*) Dover.

***Noble, Marty.** Legend of Sleepy Hollow Stained Glass Coloring Book. (Little Activity Bks.). (Illus.). (J). 2000. pap. 1.00 (*0-486-40971-6*) Dover.

Noble, Marty. The Little Mermaid Stained Glass Coloring Book. (Illus.). (J). pap. 1.00 (*0-486-29341-6*) Dover.

Noble, Marty. Little Red Riding Hood Sticker Storybook. (Illus.). (J). 1997. pap. 1.00 (*0-486-29908-2*) Dover.

— Merry Christmas. (Little Activity Bks.). (Illus.). (J). 2000. pap. 1.00 (*0-486-40986-4*) Dover.

Noble, Marty. Mike Piazza: Mike & the Mets. Rains, Rob, ed. (Super Star Ser.). 96p. (J). 1999. pap. 4.95 (*1-58261-051-7*) Sprts Pubng.

— Mythological Creatures Iron-On Transfer Patterns. (Illus.). 48p. 1998. pap. 3.95 (*0-486-40093-X*) Dover.

***Noble, Marty.** The Nutcracker. (Little Activity Bks.). (Illus.). (J). 1999. pap. 1.00 (*0-486-40516-8*) Dover.

— Pioneer Life Sticker Picture. (Illus.). (J). 1999. pap. 4.50 (*0-486-40586-9*) Dover.

Noble, Marty. Rapunzel: Full-Color Sturdy Book. LC 96-2948. (Little Activity Bks.). (Illus.). 12p. (J). 1996. pap. 1.00 (*0-486-29390-4*) Dover.

— Ready-to-Use Angel Illustrations. (Illus.). 64p. 1997. pap. text 5.95 (*0-486-29763-2*) Dover.

***Noble, Marty.** Thumbelina Sticker Storybook. (Illus.). (J). 1998. pap. 1.00 (*0-486-40082-4*) Dover.

Noble, Marty. Ugly Duckling Sticker Storybook. (Illus.). 16p. (Orig.). (J). 1997. pap. text 1.00 (*0-486-29728-4*) Dover.

Noble, Marty & Bianco, Margery W. Velveteen Rabbit. LC 97-19551. (Sturdy Storybks.). (Illus.). 12p. (J). (gr. 2). 1997. pap. 1.00 (*0-486-29916-3*) Dover.

Noble, Marty, jt. auth. see Stroebe, Clara.

Noble, Mary. You Can Grow Cattleya Orchids. 2nd ed. LC 90-92175. (Illus.). 100p. 1997. reprint ed. pap. 12.95 (*0-913928-07-0*) McQuerry Orchid.

— You Can Grow Orchids. 5th rev. ed. LC 87-90685. (Illus.). 128p. 1999. reprint ed. pap. 12.95 (*0-913928-06-2*) McQuerry Orchid.

— You Can Grow Phalaenopsis Orchids. 2nd rev. ed. LC 90-92175. (Illus.). 102p. 1998. reprint ed. pap. 12.95 (*0-913928-08-9*) McQuerry Orchid.

Noble, Mary T., tr. see Fesch, Jacques.

Noble, Mary T., tr. see Milot, Jean-Rene.

Noble, Mary T., tr. see Pinckaers, Servais.

Noble, Maurine. Basic Quiltmaking Techniques for Machine Applique. LC 98-28905. (Your First Quilt Book Ser.). (Illus.). 80p. 1998. pap. 14.95 (*1-56477-241-1*, B353, Pub. by Martingale & Co) F & W Pubns Inc.

Noble, Maurine. Machine Quilting Made Easy. Reikes, Ursula G., ed. (Joy of Quilting Ser.). (Illus.). 56p. 1994. pap. 12.95 (*1-56477-074-5*, B200) Martingale & Co.

Noble, Maurine & Hendricks, Elizabeth. Machine Quilting with Decorative Threads. Reikes, Ursula, ed. LC 97-44178. (Illus.). 88p. 1998. pap. 21.95 (*1-56477-216-0*, B333, That Patchwrk Pl) Martingale & Co.

Noble, Michael A., jt. auth. see Borchardt, Kenneth A.

***Noble, Michael T.** Organizational Mastery with Integrated Management Systems: Controlling the Dragon. 500p. 2000. 79.95 (*0-471-38928-5*) Wiley.

Noble, Mike. Luna Bella Luna: A Portrait of Vesale, Italy. Rosso, Alba, tr. (Illus.). 100p. 1997. 100.00 (*0-9657333-0-0*); pap. 40.00 (*0-9657333-1-9*) P Elledge Photo.

Noble, Miranda M. The Magical Enchantress's Test of Virtue: An Exciting 66 Fairy Tale Journey. deluxe ed. LC 97-69820. (Illus.). 200p. (J). (gr. 2-12). 1998. vinyl bd. 23.50 (*1-886197-22-9*) Joy Books.

Noble, Nathaniel N. Love Me, I'm a Criminal: or How to Get Away with Murder. Costa, Gwen, ed. 1990. pap. 14.95 (*0-87949-356-9*) Ashley Bks.

— Love Me, I'm a Criminal: or How to Get Away with Murder. 1996. pap. 19.95 (*0-614-20719-3*) Rainbow Bks.

Noble, Nicholas, jt. auth. see Tomsett, Eric.

Noble, P. B. & Levine, M. D. Computer Assisted Analyses of Cell Locomotion & Chemotaxis. 152p. 1986. 92.00 (*0-8493-6342-X*, QH647, CRC Reprint) Franklin.

Noble, Park S., jt. auth. see Gibson, Arthur C.

Noble, Patricia, ed. Technology, the Environment, & Social Change: Papers of the 38th Annual Meeting of the Seminar on the Acquisition of Latin American Library Materials. 467p. (Orig.). (C). 1995. pap. 55.00 (*0-917617-49-5*) SALALM.

Noble, Paul, jt. auth. see Cooper, Paulette.

Noble, Paul R. The Canonical Approach: A Critical Reconstruction of the Hermeneutics of Brevard S. Childs. LC 95-25291. (Biblical Interpretation Ser.: Vol. 16). 1995. 117.00 (*90-04-10151-9*) Brill Academic Pubs.

Noble, Pete & Peterson, James A. Coaching Football's Split 4-4 Defense. LC 96-72472. (Art & Science of Coaching Ser.). (Illus.). 145p. (Orig.). 1997. pap. 16.95 (*1-57167-091-2*) Coaches Choice.

Noble, Peter. Alfred Hitchcock. (Film Ser.). 1979. lib. bdg. 250.00 (*0-8490-2862-0*) Gordon Pr.

— Anthony Asquith. (Film Ser.). 1979. lib. bdg. 6.95 (*0-8490-2866-3*) Gordon Pr.

— The Cinema & the Negro: Nineteen Five to Nineteen Forty-Eight. (Film Ser.). 1980. lib. bdg. 69.95 (*0-8490-3093-5*) Gordon Pr.

***Noble, Peter.** Hebert: Les Fous de Bassan. 72p. 1999. pap. 35.00 (*0-85261-470-5*, Pub. by U of Glasgow) St Mut.

Noble, Peter. Hollywood Scapegoat: The Biography of Erich Von Stroheim. LC 70-169352. (Arno Press Cinema Program Ser.). (Illus.). 250p. 1975. reprint ed. 20.95 (*0-405-03922-0*) Ayer.

— Negro in Films. LC 72-124022. (Literature of Cinema, Ser. 1). 1978. reprint ed. 32.95 (*0-405-01629-8*) Ayer.

Noble, Philip D. Fool of the Kingdom: How to Be an Effective Clown Minister. Wray, Rhonda, ed. LC 96-12723. 208p. (Orig.). 1996. pap. 12.95 (*1-56608-023-1*, B202) Meriwether Pub.

Noble Press Staff. Soulful Travel. 400p. 1997. pap. text 15.95 (*1-879360-42-X*) Noble Pr.

Noble, R. & Brummett, R. E. Aquaculture for African Smallholders. (ICLARM Technical Reports: No. 46). 69p. 1995. per. write for info. (*971-8709-66-5*, Pub. by ICLARM) Intl Spec Bk.

Noble, Reginald, ed. see National Research Council Staff.

Noble, Richard. Language, Subjectivity, & Freedom in Rousseau's Moral Philosophy. LC 91-10201. (Political Theory & Political Philosophy Ser.). 256p. 1991. text 10.00 (*0-8153-0136-7*) Garland.

Noble, Richard, ed. see Lillo, George.

Noble, Richard B. Rhythmic Breathing Plus Olfactory Nerve Influence on Respiration. 143p. 1996. reprint ed. pap. 12.50 (*0-7873-1026-3*) Hlth Research.

— Rhythmic Breathing Plus Olfactory Nerve Influence on Respiration (1908) 165p. 1996. reprint ed. pap. 11.95 (*1-56459-835-7*) Kessinger Pub.

— Rhythmic Breathings & Olfactory Nerve Influence on Respiration. 1991. lib. bdg. 79.95 (*0-8490-4958-X*) Gordon Pr.

Noble, Richard D. & Stern, S. A., eds. Membrane Separations Technology: Principles & Applications. (Membrane Science & Technology Ser.: Vol. 2). 738p. 1995. 389.50 (*0-444-81633-X*) Elsevier.

Noble, Richard D. & Way, J. Douglas, eds. Liquid Membranes: Theory & Applications. LC 87-18684. (Symposium Ser.: No. 347). (Illus.). ix, 223p. 1987. 54.95 (*0-8412-1407-7*) Am Chemical.

— Liquid Membranes: Theory & Applications. LC 87-18684. (ACS Symposium Ser.: Vol. 347). 208p. 1987. reprint ed. pap. 64.50 (*0-608-03870-9*, 206431700008) Bks Demand.

Noble, Robert D. Continuing Incorporation: Workbook 4. (Welcome in Ser.). 88p. (Orig.). 1987. 10.00 (*0-944687-04-0*) Gather Family Inst.

— Discovery Weekend: Workbook 4. 7th ed. (Reach Out Ser.). (Illus.). 79p. (Orig.). 1994. pap. 20.00 (*0-944687-16-4*) Gather Family Inst.

— The Facts: Workbook 1. (Reach Out Ser.). 74p. (Orig.). 1987. 10.00 (*0-944687-06-7*) Gather Family Inst.

N

An Asterisk (*) at the beginning of an entry indicates that the title is appearing for the first time.

— Identify the Fish: Workbook 2. (Reach Out Ser.). (Illus.). 55p. (Orig.). 1987. 10.00 (0-944687-07-5) Gather Family Inst.

— In the Footsteps of John: The Book of Revelation. 49p. (Orig.). 1994. pap. 10.00 (0-944687-15-6) Gather Family Inst.

— Intentional Caring: Workbook 2. (Welcome in Ser.). (Illus.). 57p. (Orig.). 1987. 10.00 (0-944687-02-4) Gather Family Inst.

— Job Descriptions. 2nd rev. ed. (Leadership Workbooks). 75p. (Orig.). 1991. pap., wbk. ed. 15.00 (0-944687-17-2) Gather Family Inst.

— Ministries Weekend. rev. ed. 138p. (Orig.). 1993. pap., student ed. 20.00 (0-944687-13-X) Gather Family Inst.

— Organizing for Growth. 51p. 1987. 10.00 (0-944687-10-5) Gather Family Inst.

— Prepare the Bait: Workbook 3. (Reach Out Ser.). 64p. (Orig.). 1987. 10.00 (0-944687-08-3) Gather Family Inst.

— Shepherding: Workbook 3. (Welcome in Ser.). 68p. (Orig.). 1987. 10.00 (0-944687-03-2) Gather Family Inst.

— Spiritual Gifts: Your Portion of Christ's Bounty, Workbook 1. 4th ed. (Welcome in Ser.). 61p. (Orig.). 1985. pap. 10.00 (0-944687-01-6) Gather Family Inst.

— A Study of St. Paul's Letter to the Galatians: The Christian Emancipation Proclamation. 83p. (Orig.). 1993. pap. 10.00 (0-944687-14-8) Gather Family Inst.

***Noble, Roy.** Roy Noble's Wales. (Illus.). 192p. 2000. pap. 25.00 (1-900477-05-X, Pub. by U Wales Pr) Paul & Co Pubs.

— Roy Noble's Welsh Nicknames. 72p. 2000. pap. 9.95 (1-900477-04-1, Pub. by U Wales Pr) Paul & Co Pubs.

Noble, Rudolf E. CD's: A New Concept in Dieting. 100p. 1989. pap. 9.95 (1-885078-03-X) Noble Enter.

— The Soup Diet. 80p. 1993. pap. 9.95 (1-885078-04-8) Noble Enter.

Noble, Sandy. Mel Gibson. LC 97-26960. (Superstars of Film Ser.). (Illus.). 48p. (YA). (gr. 5 up). 1999. lib. bdg. 15.95 (0-7910-4643-5) Chelsea Hse.

Noble, Sara. Feng Shui in Singapore. 128p. 1996. pap. 13.95 (981-218-021-4) Heian Intl.

Noble, Sara P., ed. Managing People: One Hundred One Proven Ideas for Making You & Your People More Productive. 191p. (Orig.). 1992. text 24.95 (1-880394-04-9) Inc Pub MA.

Noble, Sara P., ed. Managing People: One Hundred One Proven Ideas for Making You & Your People More Productive. 191p. (Orig.). 1997. pap. 11.50 (1-880394-02-2) Thomson Learn.

Noble, Sharon L., jt. ed. see McDowell, Gary L.

***Noble, Sheilagh.** More! (Illus.). 24p. (J). 2000. 9.95 (1-84089-127-0, Pub. by Zero to Ten) IPG Chicago.

Noble, Shiren T. Journey Through the Scriptures: Bible Games & Quizzes for Youth & Adults. 30p. (Orig.). Date not set. pap. text 5.95 (1-877971-07-3) Mid Atl Reg Pr.

Noble, Shiren T., ed. see Noble, E. Myron.

Noble-Smith, Dorothy. Oh, Shenandoah. (Illus.). 336p. 1995. pap. 15.95 (1-57087-078-0) Prof Pr NC.

— Recollections: The People of the Blue Ridge Remember. 96p. 1995. 12.95 (1-57087-162-0) Prof Pr NC.

Noble, Stephanie. Tapping the Wisdom Within: A Guide to Joyous Living. LC 93-79753. 240p. (Orig.). 1994. pap. 10.95 (0-9638088-3-4) Inside Out Bks.

Noble, Stuart G. Forty Years of Public Schools in Mississippi: With Special Reference to the Education of the Negro. LC 73-177109. (Columbia University. Teachers College. Contributions to Education Ser.: No. 94). reprint ed. 37.50 (0-404-55094-0) AMS Pr.

— History of American Education. rev. ed. LC 76-92304. 552p. 1970. reprint ed. lib. bdg. 75.00 (0-8371-2408-5, NOAE, Greenwood Pr) Greenwood.

Noble Sullivan, Patricia, et al. Toefl: Everything You Need to Score High on the Toefl: 2000 Edition. 2000th ed. (Arco TOEFL:). (Illus.). 437p. 1999. pap. 12.95 (0-02-863219-2, Arc) IDG Bks.

Noble, Thomas A., ed. see Eliot, George, pseud.

***Noble, Thomas F.** Letters of St. Boniface. (Foundations of Social Work Knowledge Ser.). 2000. 45.00 (0-231-12092-3); pap. text 16.50 (0-231-12093-1) Col U Pr.

Noble, Thomas F. Western Civilization. (C). Date not set. pap., teacher ed., suppl. ed. 49.16 (0-395-69143-5); text, teacher ed., suppl. ed. 67.96 (0-395-69141-9) HM.

— Western Civilization. (C). 1994. pap., teacher ed. 7.96 (0-395-68838-8) HM.

— Western Civilization. (C). 1994. pap. text, student ed. 19.96 (0-395-55128-5); pap. text, student ed. 19.96 (0-395-55127-7) HM.

— Western Civilization Complete. LC 93-78655. (C). 1994. text 67.96 (0-395-55121-8) HM.

Noble, Thomas F. & Contreni, John J., eds. Religion, Culture & Society in the Early Middle Ages. LC 87-5709. (Studies in Medieval Culture: No. 23). 1987. pap. 15.95 (0-918720-84-2); boxed set 32.95 (0-918720-83-4) Medieval Inst.

Noble, Thomas F., et al. Western Civilization Vol. C: The Continuing Experiment: 1815 to Present. 446p. (C). 1994. pap. text 43.96 (0-395-55126-9) HM.

— Western Civilization Vol. A: The Continuing Experiment: To 1500. 544p. (C). 1994. pap. text 43.96 (0-395-55124-2) HM.

— Western Civilization Vol. B: The Continuing Experiment: 1300 to 1815. 382p. (C). 1994. pap. text 43.96 (0-395-55125-0) HM.

***Noble, Trevor.** Social Theory & Social Change. LC 99-86156. 2000. pap. 18.95 (0-312-23329-9); text 59.50 (0-312-23328-0) St Martin.

Noble, Trinka Hakes. Apple Tree Christmas. LC 84-1901. (J). 1984. 11.19 (0-606-03978-3, Pub. by Turtleback) Demco.

— The Day Jimmy's Boa Ate the Wash. LC 80-15098. (Pied Piper Bks.). (Illus.). 32p. (J). (ps-3). 1980. 15.99 (0-8037-1723-7, Dial Yng Read) Peng Put Young Read.

— The Day Jimmy's Boa Ate the Wash. (Illus.). 32p. (J). (ps-3). 1992. pap. 5.99 (0-14-054623-5, PuffinBks) Peng Put Young Read.

— The Day Jimmy's Boa Ate the Wash. (J). 1980. 11.19 (0-606-03377-7, Pub. by Turtleback) Demco.

— Jimmy's Boa & the Big Splash Birthday Bash. LC 88-10933. (Illus.). 32p. (J). (ps-3). 1989. 15.99 (0-8037-0539-5, Dial Yng Read) Peng Put Young Read.

— Jimmy's Boa & the Big Splash Birthday Bash. (Picture Puffin Ser.). (Illus.). (J). 1989. 10.19 (0-606-05892-3, Pub. by Turtleback) Demco.

— Jimmy's Boa Bounces Back. (Illus.). 32p. (J). (ps-3). 1992. pap. 5.99 (0-14-054654-5, PuffinBks) Peng Put Young Read.

Noble, Trinka Hakes. Jimmy's Boa Bounces Back. (J). 1987. 10.19 (0-606-02248-1, Pub. by Turtleback) Demco.

Noble, Trinka Hakes. Meanwhile Back at the Ranch. (Illus.). 32p. (J). (ps-3). 1992. pap. 5.99 (0-14-054564-6, PuffinBks) Peng Put Young Read.

Noble, Trinka Hakes. Meanwhile Back at the Ranch. (Reading Rainbow Bks.). (J). 1987. 11.19 (0-606-01722-4, Pub. by Turtleback) Demco.

Noble, Trudy V. God Answers Children's Prayers Too. LC 85-217377. (Illus.). 30p. (J). (ps-4). 1990. write for info. (0-9620133-0-7) Joy Deliverance.

Noble, Valerie A., ed. see Pitcher, Emma B.

Noble, Vicki. Making Ritual with Motherpeace Cards: Multicultural, Woman-Centered Practices for Spiritual Growth. LC 98-3527. (Illus.). 224p. 1998. pap. 14.00 (0-609-80208-9) Harmony Bks.

— Motherpeace: A Way to the Goddess Through Myth, Art & Tarot. LC 82-47752. (Illus.). 288p. 1994. reprint ed. pap. 19.00 (0-06-251085-1, Pub. by Harper SF) HarpC.

— Shakti Woman: Feeling Our Fire, Healing Our World. LC 89-45959. 272p. 1991. pap. 18.00 (0-06-250667-6, Pub. by Harper SF) HarpC.

Noble, Vicki & Tenney, Jonathan. Motherpeace Tarot Playbook. LC 86-1510. (Illus.). 207p. 1986. pap. 21.00 (0-914728-53-9) Wingbow Pr.

Noble, Virginia D., ed. see Noble, David F.

Noble, W. C., ed. The Skin Microflora & Microbial Skin Disease. (Illus.). 402p. (C). 1993. text 110.00 (0-521-40198-4) Cambridge U Pr.

Noble, Weston, jt. auth. see Nesheim, Paul.

Noble, William. Bookbanning in America: Who Bans Books? - & Why. LC 90-3413. 352p. 1992. reprint ed. pap. 14.95 (0-8397-1081-X) Eriksson.

— Conflict, Action & Suspense. (Elements of Fiction Writing Ser.). 185p. 1999. pap. 12.00 (0-89879-907-4, Wrtrs Digest Bks) F & W Pubns Inc.

— Make That Scene: A Writer's Guide to Setting, Mood & Atmosphere. 224p. 1988. 17.95 (0-8397-5708-5, Pub. by Eriksson) IPG Chicago.

— Self-Assessment of Hearing & Related Functions. 1998. pap. text 47.95 (1-86156-092-3) Whurr Pub.

— Three Rules for Writing a Novel: A Writer's Guide to Story Development. abr. ed. LC 97-18127. 384p. 1997. pap. 17.95 (0-8397-8050-8) Eriksson.

***Noble, William.** Writing Dramatic Nonfiction. 192p. 2000. 22.95 (0-8397-8645-X, Pub. by Eriksson) IPG Chicago.

Noble, William & Davidson, Iain. Human Evolution, Language & Mind: A Psychological & Archaeological Inquiry. (Illus.). 286p. (C). 1996. pap. text 23.95 (0-521-57635-0) Cambridge U Pr.

Noble, William, jt. auth. see Whitehill, Angela.

Noble, William J. Le, see Le Noble, William J.

Nobleman, Louis R. Second-Hand Dreams. (Illus.). (J). (gr. k-6). 1993. pap. 9.95 (1-56883-010-6) Colonial Pr AL.

Nobleman, Marc T., jt. auth. see Moseley, Leslie.

***Nobleman, Marc Tyler.** Felix Explores Our World: An Activity Book. 288p. (J). 1999. pap. text 8.95 (0-7892-0596-3) Abbeville Pr.

Nobleman, Roberta. Fifty Projects for Creative Dramatics. 2nd rev. ed. 34p. 1980. pap. 4.95 (0-932720-22-6) New Plays Inc.

— Mime & Masks. (Illus.). 151p. 1979. pap. 8.95 (0-932720-46-3); write for info. (0-932720-47-1) New Plays Inc.

Nobles, Anita K. Dinner Will Be Ready in a Minute: Quick & Easy, So-You-Can-Relax Recipes. 128p. (Orig.). 1994. pap. 12.95 (1-882626-22-X) Impress Ink.

— Dinner Will Be Ready in a Minute: Quick & Easy, So-You-Can-Relax Recipes, Set. (Cookin' Bks.). (Illus.). 128p. (Orig.). 1994. pap. 19.95 (1-882626-25-7) Impress Ink.

— Hey Mom...I'll Cook Dinner: Recipes That Turn a Kid into the Family Chef. 128p. (Orig.). 1994. pap. 12.95 (1-882626-21-4) Impress Ink.

— Hey Mom...I'll Cook Dinner: Recipes That Turn a Kid into the Family Chef, Set. (Cookin' Bks.). (Illus.). 128p. (Orig.). 1994. pap. 19.95 (1-882626-26-5) Impress Ink.

— A Mother's Kiss. 144p. 1993. pap. 4.95 (1-882626-13-3) Impress Ink.

— Windows to the Soul. 384p. 1992. pap. 7.95 (1-882626-10-9) Impress Ink.

Nobles, Charles. Diana Collecting on a Princess. (Illus.). 112p. 1999. pap. 14.95 (0-87588-543-8) Hobby Hse.

***Nobles, Edward.** The Bluestone Walk. 112p. 2000. pap. 14.00 (0-89255-247-6, Pub. by Persea Bks) Norton.

Nobles, Edward. Through One Tear: Poems. LC 96-50262. 80p. 1997. 22.00 (0-89255-227-1) Persea Bks.

— Through One Tear: Poems. 1998. pap. 12.00 (0-89255-238-7) Persea Bks.

***Nobles, Graham, photos by.** England, the Nature of the Land. (Illus.). 120p. 2000. 29.95 (1-84107-002-5, Pub. by Colin Baxter Ltd) Voyageur Pr.

Nobles, Gregory H. American Frontiers. LC 96-9784. 288p. 1997. 25.00 (0-8090-2471-3) Hill & Wang.

— American Frontiers: Cultural Encounters & Continental Conquest. (Illus.). 304p. 1998. pap. 13.00 (0-8090-1602-8) Hill & Wang.

Nobles, Gregory H., jt. auth. see Henretta, James A.

Nobles, James. Early Retirement Incentives: State of Minnesota Public Employees. (Illus.). 98p. (C). 1998. reprint ed. pap. text 20.00 (0-7881-4209-7) DIANE Pub.

— Guardians Ad Litem: State of Minnesota. (Illus.). 94p. (C). 1998. reprint ed. pap. text 20.00 (0-7881-4211-9) DIANE Pub.

— Health Care Administrative Costs: State of Minnesota. (Illus.). 96p. 1998. reprint ed. pap. text 20.00 (0-7881-4210-0) DIANE Pub.

Nobles, Joan S. Run with the Horses. LC 97-27208. 178p. 1998. pap. 14.95 (0-87565-181-X) Tex Christian.

***Nobles, Melissa.** Shades of Citizenship: Race & the Census in Modern Politics. LC 00-26707. 2000. write for info. (0-8047-4013-5) Stanford U Pr.

Nobles, Pat, ed. & illus. see Rail, Axel.

Nobles, Richard. Pensions, Employment, & the Law. (Monographs on Labour Law). 282p. 1993. text 59.00 (0-19-825448-2) OUP.

***Nobles, Robin & O'Neill, Susan.** Streetwise Maximize Web Site Traffic: Build Web Site Traffic Fast & Free by Optimizing Search Engine Placement. (Illus.). 352p. 2000. pap. 19.95 (1-58062-369-7) Adams Media.

Nobles, Wade W. African Psychology: Toward its Reclamation, Reascension & Revitalization. 134p. 1986. 10.00 (0-939205-02-5) Blk Fam Inst Pub.

— Africanity & the Black Family: The Development of a Theoretical Model. 116p. 1985. 10.00 (0-939205-01-7) Blk Fam Inst Pub.

Nobles, Wade W. & Goddard, Lawford L. Understanding the Black Family: A Guide for Scholarship & Research. 137p. 1984. 10.00 (0-939205-00-9) Blk Fam Inst Pub.

Nobles, Wade W., et al. African-American Families: Issues, Insights & Directions. 1987. 10.00 (0-939205-04-1) Blk Fam Inst Pub.

— The Km Ebit Husia: Authoritative Utterances of Exceptional Insights for the Black Family. 201p. 1985. 15.00 (0-939205-03-3) Blk Fam Inst Pub.

Noblet, Martine, jt. auth. see Braguet, Anne.

Noblet, Martine, jt. auth. see Deltenre, Chantal.

***Noblit, George W.** Particularities: Collected Essays on Ethnography & Education. LC 97-17054. (Counterpoints Ser.: Vol. 44). VII, 224p. (C). 1999. pap. text 29.95 (0-8204-3674-7, 36747) P Lang Pubng.

Noblit, George W. & Dempsey, Van O. The Social Construction of Virtue: The Moral Life of Schools. LC 95-39477. 192p. (C). 1996. pap. text 18.95 (0-7914-3080-4) State U NY Pr.

Noblit, George W. & Hare, R. Dwight. Meta-Ethnography: Synthesizing Qualitative Studies. (Qualitative Research Methods Ser.: Vol. 11). 96p. (C). 1988. text 24.00 (0-8039-3022-4); pap. text 10.50 (0-8039-3023-2) Sage.

Noblit, George W. & Pink, William. Continuity & Contradiction: The Futures of the Sociology of Education. LC 95-8715. (Understanding Education & Policy Ser.). 416p. (C). 1995. pap. text 29.95 (1-881303-68-3) Hampton Pr NJ.

Noblit, George W. & Pink, William T., eds. Continuity & Contradiction: The Futures of the Sociology of Education. LC 97-8715. (Understanding Education & Policy Ser.). 416p. (C). 1995. text 79.50 (1-881303-67-5) Hampton Pr NJ.

— Schooling in Social Context: Qualitative Studies. LC 86-10890. 352p. (C). 1987. text 73.25 (0-89391-326-X) Ablx Pub.

Noblit, George W. & Tesconi, Charles A. Good Schools: The Policy Environment Perspective. LC 95-10003. (Understanding Education & Policy Ser.). 172p. (C). 1995. text 46.50 (1-57273-024-2) Hampton Pr NJ.

Noblit, George W., et al. The Social Construction of Virtue: The Moral Life of Schools. LC 95-39477. 192p. (C). 1996. text 57.50 (0-7914-3079-0) State U NY Pr.

Noblit, George W., ed. see Corson, David.

Noblit, George W., ed. see Fox, Thomas.

Noblit, George W., ed. see Kanpol, Barry.

Noblit, George W., ed. see Miron, Louis.

Noblit, George W., ed. see Tesconi, Charles A.

***Noblit, Richard L.** Questions & Answers of the Bible. 2000. pap. 5.95 (0-9702230-0-5) R L Noblit.

Noblitt. Atajo-tech Sheet. (C). 1996. pap. 1.00 (0-8384-6977-9) Heinle & Heinle.

Noblitt. Systeme-D: Short Course. (C). pap. text. write for info. (0-8384-1618-7) Thomson Learn.

— Systeme-D Two Point One: User's Manual. (C). 1994. pap. text 17.25 (0-8384-5417-8) Thomson Learn.

Noblitt, James R. & Perskin, Pamela S. Cult & Ritual Abuse: Its History, Anthropology, & Recent Discovery. LC 95-2492. 248p. 1995. 59.95 (0-275-95281-9, Praeger Pubs) Greenwood.

— Cult & Ritual Abuse: Its History, Anthropology & Recent Discovery in Contemporary America. rev. ed. LC 99-22108. 288p. 2000. 62.50 (0-275-96664-X, C6664, Praeger Pubs) Greenwood.

Noblitt, James Randall & Perkins, Pamela Sue. Cult & Ritual Abuse: Its History, Anthropology & Recent Discovery in Contemporary America. rev. ed. LC 99-22108. 288p. 2000. pap. 24.95 (0-275-96665-8, Praeger Pubs) Greenwood.

Noblitt, James S. Atajo 1.0. (College Spanish Ser.). (SPA.). 1995. pap. 13.95 (0-8384-5739-8) Heinle & Heinle.

— Atajo 1.0. (College Spanish Ser.). (SPA.). (C). 1995. mass mkt., suppl. ed. 6.95 (0-8384-6359-2) Heinle & Heinle.

Noblitt, James S. & Dominguez. User Manual Dos - Atajo 1.1. 2nd ed. (College Spanish). (SPA.). (C). 1995. suppl. ed. 12.95 (0-8384-6360-6) Heinle & Heinle.

Noblitt, James S. & Kossuth, Karen C. Quelle 1.0. (College German Ser.). (GER.). (C). 1996. mass mkt., suppl. ed. 18.95 incl. 3.5 hd, 5.25 hd, 3.5 ld (0-8384-5458-5) Heinle & Heinle.

Noblitt, Loren W., jt. auth. see Turner Publishing Company Staff.

Noblitt, Mary J. Learning Activities for Business Report Writing. 96p. 1986. pap. text 16.50 (0-471-82931-5) P-H.

Noblitt, Philip T. A Mansion in the Mountains: The Story of Moses & Bertha Cone & Their Blowing Rock Mansion. LC 96-6277. (Illus.). 225p. 1996. pap. 14.95 (1-887905-02-2) Pkway Pubs.

Noblitt, Tony M., jt. auth. see Gabrilska, Warren.

Nobo, Jorge L. Whitehead's Metaphysics of Extension & Solidarity. LC 85-25040. 437p. (Orig.). (C). 1986. pap. text 24.95 (0-88706-262-8) State U NY Pr.

N.O.B.O. Staff, ed. Black Prison Movements/U. S. A. Date not set. pap. 14.95 (0-86543-489-1) Africa World.

NOBO Staff, ed. Black Prison Movements/U. S. A. 199p. 1995. 45.95 (0-86543-488-3) Africa World.

N.O.B.O. Staff, ed. Malcolm X: The Man in Context. 200p. Date not set. 14.95 (0-86543-495-6) Africa World.

***Nobrega.** Going Global. 256p. 2000. 29.95 (0-471-32695-X) Wiley.

Nobrega, E., ed. see Food & Beverage Instrumentation Symposium Staff.

Nobrega, Jose N., jt. auth. see Gaito, John.

Nobs, Malcolm A., jt. auth. see Hiesey, William M.

Nobuhiko, Maruyama, jt. auth. see Hayao, Ishimura.

Nobuka, Yuzuru, tr. see Takahashi, Masanobu.

***Nobus, Dany.** Jacques Lacan & the Freudian Practice of Psychoanalysis. LC 00-25501. (Makers of Modern Psychotherapy Ser.). 2000. pap. write for info. (0-415-17962-9) Routledge.

***Nobus, Dany, ed.** Key Concepts in Lacanian Psychotherapy. LC 99-17394. 240p. 1999. reprint ed. pap. 22.00 (1-892746-14-X, 4614X) Other Pr LLC.

Noce, C., et al. Superconductivity & Strongly Correlated Electron Systems. 448p. 1994. text 124.00 (981-02-2038-3) World Scientific Pub.

Noceda, Joaquin Garcia De La, see Garcia de La Noceda, Joaquin.

Nocedal, Jorge & Wright, Stephen J. Numerical Optimization. LC 99-13263. (Series in Operations Research). 600p. 1999. 64.95 (0-387-98793-2) Spr-Verlag.

Nocek, James E. Hoof Care for Dairy Cattle. 2nd rev. ed. (Illus.). 39p. (Orig.). (C). 1996. pap. text 4.50 (0-932147-28-3, Hoards Dairyman) Hoard & Sons Co.

Nocella, Luisa, jt. auth. see Jamozik, Adam.

Nocent, Adrian. The Liturgical Year, 4 vols., Set. 1977. pap. 40.00 (0-8146-0971-6) Liturgical Pr.

— The Liturgical Year Vol. 1: Advent, Christmas, Epiphany, Sundays 2-8 in Ordinary Time. 446p. 1977. pap. 10.00 (0-8146-0962-7) Liturgical Pr.

— The Liturgical Year Vol. 2: Lent & Holy Week. 251p. (C). 1977. pap. 10.00 (0-8146-0963-5) Liturgical Pr.

— The Liturgical Year Vol. 3: Paschal Triduum, Easter Season, & Solemnities of the Lord. 326p. (C). 1977. pap. 10.00 (0-8146-0964-3) Liturgical Pr.

— The Liturgical Year Vol. 4: Sundays Nine to Thirty-Four in Ordinary Time. 406p. (C). 1977. pap. 10.00 (0-8146-0965-1) Liturgical Pr.

Nocent, Adrien. A Rereading of the Renewed Liturgy. Misrahi, Mary M., tr. LC 94-7253. (ENG & FRE.). 152p. (Orig.). 1994. pap. write for info. (0-8146-2299-2, Liturg Pr Bks) Liturgical Pr.

***Nocenti, Ann.** X-Men: Prisoner X. (Illus.). 304p. 1998. mass mkt. 6.99 (0-425-16493-4) Berkley Pub.

Nocentini, Alberta. Pasta al Dente: Recipes from All the Regions of Italy. LC 86-22268. (Illus.). 1989. 24.95 (0-87949-264-3) Ashley Bks.

Nocera, Daniel G., jt. ed. see Wishart, James F.

Nocerino, Kathryn. Candles in the Daylight. (Illus.). 46p. 1985. pap. 5.00 (0-942292-03-0) Warthog Pr.

— Death of the Plankton Bar & Grill. 85p. 1987. pap. 5.00 (0-89823-092-6) New Rivers Pr.

Nocetti, D. Fabian & Fleming, Peter J. Parallel Processing in Digital Control. Grimble, Michael J. & Johnson, M., eds. LC 92-21882. (Advances in Industrial Control Ser.). (Illus.). xiv, 146p. 1992. 76.95 (0-387-19728-1) Spr-Verlag.

Nochimson, Martha P. No End to Her: Soap Opera & the Female Subject. 1993. 48.00 (0-520-07763-6, Pub. by U CA Pr); pap. 16.95 (0-520-07771-7, Pub. by U CA Pr) Cal Prin Full Svc.

— The Passion of David Lynch: Wild at Heart in Hollywood. LC 97-7732. (Illus.). 296p. 1997. 40.00 (0-292-75566-X); pap. 19.95 (0-292-75565-1) U of Tex Pr.

Nochimson, Richard, jt. ed. see Bushnell, Rebecca W.

***Nochlin, Linda.** Mary Frank: Encounters. (Illus.). 120p. 2000. 34.95 (0-8109-6723-5, Pub. by Abrams) Time Warner.

Nochlin, Linda. Mathis at Colmar: A Visual Confrontation. LC 63-2298. (Illus.). 1963. 5.00 (0-87376-002-6) Red Dust.

Nochlin, Linda. Politics of Vision. LC 89-45055. (Illus.). 224p. 1991. pap. 24.00 (0-06-430187-7, Icon Edns) HarpC.

Nochlin, Linda. Realism. 1972. pap. 12.95 (0-14-013222-8) Viking Penguin.

— Representing Women. LC 98-61187. (Interplay Ser.). (Illus.). 272p. 1999. pap. 24.95 (0-500-28098-3, Pub. by Thames Hudson) Norton.

Nochlin, Linda. Women, Art, & Power. LC 88-45118. 1989. pap. 22.00 (0-06-430183-4, Icon Edns) HarpC.

N

An Asterisk (*) at the beginning of an entry indicates that the title is appearing for the first time.

Noe, Raymond A., et al. Readings in Human Resource Management. 2nd ed. LC 96-39077. 704p. (C). 1996. text 46.25 (*0-256-25865-1*, Irwn McGrw-H) McGrw-H Hghr Educ.

Noe, Robert M., III, jt. auth. see Mondy, R. Wayne.

Noe, Sydney P. Massachusetts Silver Coinage. LC 88-72077. (Illus.). 210p. 1990. 35.00 (*0-942666-56-9*) S J Durst.

Noe, Sydney P. & Johnston, Ann. The Coinage of Metapontum. (Numismatic Notes & Monographs: Nos. 32 & 47). (Illus.). 165p. 1983. reprint ed. 32.00 (*0-89722-202-4*) Am Numismatic.

Noe, Sydney P., jt. auth. see Kleiner, Fred S.

Noe, Tom. Into the Lion's Den. 190p. (Orig.). 1995. pap. 11.95 (*0-937779-29-6*) Greenlawn Pr.

Noe, Tom, ed. see Redwood, Ray.

Noe, Virgilio. Prayers to Mary. Buono, Anthony M., ed.Tr. of Preghiere a Maria. 96p. 1988. pap. 3.95 (*0-89942-210-1*, 210/04) Catholic Bk Pub.

***Noe, Winfried.** Das Indiansche Horoskop. LC 98-30847. (Illus.). 128p. 1998. 10.95 (*0-8069-4234-7*) Sterling.

Noebel, David A. Understanding the Times. LC 94-29314. 1994. 36.99 (*1-56507-268-5*) Harvest Hse.

— Understanding the Times: The Religious Worldviews of Our Day & the Search for Truth. abr. ed. 1995. pap. write for info. (*0-936163-22-4*) Summit Pr CO.

Noebel, David A., et al. Clergy in the Classroom: The Religion of Secular Humanism. 1995. pap. write for info. (*0-936163-27-5*) Summit Pr CO.

Noebels, Jeffrey L., jt. ed. see Kellaway, Peter.

Noecker, Marshall. He Went East & He Done Good. LC 99-90341. (Illus.). 248p. 1999. 24.95 (*0-9671663-0-6*) Sanborn Pr.

Noegel, Scott B. Janus Parallelism in the Book of Job. (JSOTS Ser.: No. 223). 223p. 1996. 65.00 (*1-85075-624-4*, Pub. by Sheffield Acad) CUP Services.

***Noegel, Scott B.** Puns & Pundits: Word Play in the Hebrew Bible & Ancient Near Eastern Literature. LC 99-53810. 350p. 2000. 50.00 (*1-883053-49-8*) CDL Pr.

Noehbauer, Hans F. Munich: City of the Arts. (Illus.). 348p. 1994. boxed set 150.00 (*1-55859-865-0*) Abbeville Pr.

***Noehren, Robert.** An Organist's Reader: Essays. LC 99-13271. 1999. write for info. (*0-89990-086-0*) Harmonie.

Noehrenberg, Peter C., jt. auth. see Allen, Patrick D.

Noehring, Jeanne. For Hearts That Had Hopes & Dreams. Boggs, Marlene, ed. (Illus.). 18p. 1997. 29.95 (*0-9664111-0-2*) Buttrfly Crssng.

***Noel, Angela.** Awaken Me. large type ed. 288p. 1999. pap. 20.99 (*1-85389-926-7*, Dales) Ulverscroft.

— Promise Me. large type ed. 320p. 1999. pap. 20.99 (*1-85389-925-9*, Dales) Ulverscroft.

— Remember Me. 256p. 1999. 20.99 (*1-85389-927-5*) Ulverscroft.

Noel, Ann, jt. auth. see Frazee, David.

Noel, Ann, jt. ed. see Williams, Emmett.

Noel, Anthony. Terracotta: Pots with Style. LC 97-46791. (Illus.). 128p. 1998. 30.00 (*1-57959-005-5*, SOMA) BB&T Inc.

Noel-Baker, Philip J. The Private Manufacture of Armaments. 1990. 15.75 (*0-8446-4593-1*) Peter Smith.

— The Private Manufacture of Armaments. LC 78-145399. 1972. reprint ed. pap. 9.95 (*0-486-22736-7*) Dover.

Noel-Bentley, Peter. Earle Birney: An Annotated Bibliography. 116p. (C). 1983. pap. 9.00 (*0-920763-50-2*, Pub. by ECW) Genl Dist Srvs.

Noel, Bernard. The Castle of Communion. Buck, Paul, tr. from FRE.Tr. of Le Chateau De Cene. 140p. 1993. reprint ed. pap. 14.99 (*0-947757-29-5*, Pub. by Atlas Pr) Serpents Tail.

— Dictionnaire de la Commune, Vol. 1. (FRE.). 1978. pap. 9.95 (*0-8288-5177-8*, M6428) Fr & Eur.

— Magritte. (Illus.). 1995. pap. 12.00 (*0-517-88414-3*) Random.

Noel, Bernard, et al, texts. Opalka. LC 97-138747. (Illus.). 128p. 1996. pap. 23.50 (*2-906571-57-1*, 620803, Pub. by Editions Dis Voir) Dist Art Pubs.

Noel, Brook. Back to Basics: 101 Ideas for Strengthening Our Children & Our Families. 1999. pap. 13.95 (*1-891400-48-7*) Champion Pr.

— Shadows of a Vagabond. LC 97-76842. 120p. 1998. pap. 12.00 (*1-891400-06-1*) Champion Pr.

***Noel, Brook & Blair, Pamela D.** I Wasn't Ready to Say Goodbye: Surviving, Coping & Healing after the Death of a Loved One. 304p. 2000. pap. 14.95 (*1-891400-27-4*) Champion Pr.

Noel, Brook & Klein, Art. The Single Parent Resource. LC 97-76841. 282p. 1998. pap. 13.95 (*1-891400-44-4*) Champion Pr.

Noel, Carol. Get It? Got It. Good! A Guide for Teenagers, Vol. 1. LC 96-67556. (Illus.). 192p. (Orig.). (J). (ps-12). 1996. pap. 7.95 (*0-9649479-0-0*) Serious Busn MI.

Noel, Christian, Le, see Le Noel, Christian.

Noel, Christopher. Rumpelstiltskin. LC 92-4592. (We All Have Tales Ser.). (Illus.). 40p. (J). (gr. k up). 1993. 19.95 incl. audio (*0-88708-280-7*, Rabbit Ears); 14.95 (*0-88708-279-3*, Rabbit Ears) Litle Simon.

— Rumpelstiltskin. (Illus.). 40p. (J). (gr. k-3). 1995. 19.95 incl. audio (*0-689-80061-4*) S&S Trade.

Noel, Daniel C. Paths to the Power of Myth: Joseph Campbell & the Study of Religion. 228p. 1994. pap. 12.95 (*0-8245-1389-4*) Crossroad NY.

— The Soul of Shamanism: Western Fantasies, Imaginal Realities. 252p. 1997. reprint ed. pap. 17.95 (*0-8264-1081-2*) Continuum.

Noel, Darby, jt. auth. see Noel, Darcy.

Noel, Darcy & Noel, Darby. Sweet Dreams & Goodnight Stories. LC 99-62034. 365p. 1999. 25.00 (*0-7388-0396-0*); pap. 15.00 (*0-7388-0397-9*) Xlibris Corp.

Noel, David. Nuteeriat. 200p. 1989. pap., per. 5.00 (*0-9593205-4-7*) Bonsall Pub.

Noel, Diana. Five to Seven. 2.95 (*0-86072-032-2*, Pub. by Quartet) Charles River Bks.

Noel, Dirk, ed. see Simon-Vandenbergen, Anne-Marie, et al.

Noel, Francoise. The Christie Seigneuries: Estate Management & Settlement in the Upper Richelieu Valley, 1760-1854. (Illus.). 248p. 1992. 60.00 (*0-7735-0876-7*, Pub. by McG-Queens Univ Pr) CUP Services.

Noel, Gary J., et al. Pediatric Infectious Diseases: A Comprehensive Guide to the Subspecialty. LC 96-31925. (Illus.). 336p. 1997. text 65.00 (*0-8018-5563-2*); pap. text 28.95 (*0-8018-5564-0*) Johns Hopkins.

Noel, Gerard E. The Great Lock-Out of, 1926. LC 76-372463. 263p. reprint ed. pap. 81.60 (*0-608-14385-5*, 201938100011) Bks Demand.

***Noel, Gilbert.** Le Conseil de l'Europe et l'Agriculture. (Euroclio Ser.: Vol. 14). x, 254p. 1999. 39.95 (*3-906762-92-0*, Pub. by P Lang) P Lang Pubng.

Noel, Gilbert. France, Allemagne et "Europe Verte" (Euroclio Ser.). (FRE.). 217p. 1995. 36.95 (*3-906751-65-1*, Pub. by P Lang) P Lang Pubng.

Noel Hume, Audrey. Food. LC 78-4683. (Archaeology Ser.: No. 9). (Illus.). 68p. 1978. pap. 5.95 (*0-87935-045-8*) Colonial Williamsburg.

Noel Hume, Ivor. Digging for Carter's Grove. LC 73-88326. (Archaeology Ser.: No. 8). (Illus.). 61p. (Orig.). 1974. pap. 5.95 (*0-87935-016-4*) Colonial Williamsburg.

— Discoveries in Martin's Hundred. rev. ed. LC 83-1951. (Archaeology Ser.: No. 10). (Illus.). 64p. (Orig.). 1987. pap. 5.95 (*0-87935-069-5*) Colonial Williamsburg.

Noel-Hume, Ivor. Here Lies Virginia: An Archaeologists View of Colonial Life & History. (Illus.). 384p. (C). 1994. reprint ed. pap. 18.95 (*0-8139-1528-7*) U Pr of Va.

Noel Hume, Ivor. Martin's Hundred. rev. ed. 400p. 1991. pap. text 17.50 (*0-8139-1323-3*) U Pr of Va.

Noel-Hume, Ivor. The Virginia Adventure: Roanoke to James Towne: An Archaeological & Historical Odyssey. LC 97-16651. (Virginia Bookshelf Ser.). (Illus.). 519p. 1997. pap. 19.95 (*0-8139-1758-1*) U Pr of Va.

Noel, J. The Golden Scarabs & Other Tales. LC 94-70215. (Illus.). 1994. pap. 8.95 (*0-930422-15-5*) Dennis-Landman.

— My Name Is Selah. (Illus.). 22p. 1994. pap. 4.95 (*0-930422-19-8*) Dennis-Landman.

— The Secret of the Seraphims & Other Poems. (Illus.). 28p. pap. 4.95 (*0-930422-16-3*) Dennis-Landman.

***Noel, James.** Nuclear Waste: Further Actions Needed to Increase the Use of Innovative Cleanup Technologies. 65p. (C). 1999. pap. text 20.00 (*0-7881-8274-9*) DIANE Pub.

Noel, James, jt. auth. see Dotlich, David.

Noel, Jan. Canada Dry: Temperance Crusades Before Confederation. (Illus.). 296p. 1994. text 50.00 (*0-8020-0552-7*); pap. text 19.95 (*0-8020-6976-2*) U of Toronto Pr.

Noel, Jana. Developing Multicultural Educators. LC 99-44780. 208p. (C). 1999. pap. text 40.33 (*0-8013-2056-9*) Longman.

***Noel, Jana.** Sources: Notable Selections in Multicultural Education. 400p. 1999. pap. 20.94 (*0-07-233330-8*) McGraw-H Hghr Educ.

Noel, Jesse, ed. The Consultant Directory. 4th rev. ed. 950p. 1999. 325.00 (*0-939712-10-5*) Money Mkt.

— Directory of Registered Investment Advisors. rev. ed. 2200p. 1999. 415.00 (*0-939712-08-3*) Money Mkt.

— Directory of Tax-Exempt Organizations. 7th rev. ed. 1170p. 1999. 450.00 (*0-939712-09-1*) Money Mkt.

Noel, John. Foundations. (Illus.). 38p. 1995. mass mkt. 2.00 (*1-888616-45-8*) Noel Grp.

— Foundations, Vol. II. (Illus.). 38p. 1996. pap. 2.00 (*1-888616-00-8*) Noel Grp.

— Foundations III. (Illus.). 42p. 1997. pap. 2.00 (*1-888616-01-6*) Noel Grp.

Noel, John V., Jr., ed. Knight's Modern Seamanship. 18th ed. 800p. 1989. text 92.95 (*0-442-26983-8*, VNR) Wiley.

Noel, John V., et al, eds. Knight's Modern Seamanship. 8th ed. 800p. 1988. 110.00 (*0-471-28948-5*, VNR) Wiley.

Noel, John V., Jr. & Beach, Edward L. Naval Terms Dictionary. 5th ed. LC 88-18657. 336p. 1988. text 24.95 (*0-87021-571-X*) Naval Inst Pr.

Noel, Karen G. Cut & Color Flannel Board Stories, Bk. 1. (Teacher Aid Ser.). 1985. 9.95 (*0-513-01787-9*) Denison.

— Cut & Color Flannel Board Stories, Bk. 2. (Teacher Aid Ser.). 1985. 9.95 (*0-513-01788-7*) Denison.

— Cut & Color Flannel Board Stories, Bk. 3. (Teacher Aid Ser.). 1985. 9.95 (*0-513-01789-5*) Denison.

Noel, Lee, Jr. PageMaker 3 Solutions. (Illus.). (Orig.). 1989. pap. 18.95 (*0-929307-06-2*) GP Pubns.

Noel, Leon & Leon, Marynel. Dictionnaire Marabout des Mots Croises. (FRE.). 508p. 1993. pap. 17.95 (*0-7859-5632-8*, 2501018850) Fr & Eur.

Noel, Lisa, jt. auth. see Kider, Mitchel.

Noel, Lise. Intolerance: The Parameters of Oppression. Bennett, Arnold, tr. LC 93-90589. 288p. (C). 1994. pap. text 19.95 (*0-7735-1187-3*, Pub. by McG-Queens Univ Pr) CUP Services.

— Intolerance: The Parameters of Oppression. Bennett, Arnold, tr. LC 93-90589. 288p. (C). 1994. 65.00 (*0-7735-1160-1*, Pub. by McG-Queens Univ Pr) CUP Services.

Noel, Michael D., ed. Church-Planting Voices. LC 99-163430. 1998. mass mkt. 5.99 (*0-87509-801-0*) Chr Pubns.

Noel, Michel, jt. auth. see Borish, Michael S.

***Noel, N. A.** I Am Wherever You Are. (Illus.). 40p. 2000. 23.95 (*0-9652531-4-7*) Noel Studio.

Noel, N. A. Joy in Simplicity: An Artistic & Poetic Journey into Amish Country, Featuring Original Art by N. A. Nohel. LC 97-95061. (Illus.). 112p. 1998. 49.95 (*0-9652531-2-0*) Noel Studio.

Noel, N. A. & Sisson, John W. On Earth as It Is in Heaven. (Illus.). 32p. (J). (gr. k-8). 1999. 19.95 (*0-9652531-3-9*) Noel Studio.

Noel, Nancy, jt. auth. see Noel, Reuben.

Noel, Octave. Histoire du Commerce du Monde Depuis les Temps les Plus Recules, 3 vols. 1990. reprint ed. 300.00 (*0-8115-3872-9*) Periodicals Srv.

Noel, P. Technologie de la Pierre de Taille. (FRE.). 376p. 1968. 49.95 (*0-686-56777-3*, M-6429) Fr & Eur.

Noel, Reuben & Noel, Nancy. Saigon for a Song: The True Story of a Vietnam Gig to Remember. LC 87-16244. (Illus.). 264p. (Orig.). 1987. pap. 6.95 (*0-943247-02-0*) UCS Press.

Noel, Roden B. Life of Lord Byron. LC 72-990. reprint ed. 21.50 (*0-404-07436-7*) AMS Pr.

Noel, Roger. Joufroi de Poitiers: Traduction Critique. (Studies in the Humanities: Literature-Politics-Society: Vol. 7). 219p. (C). 1987. text 36.50 (*0-8204-0376-8*) P Lang Pubng.

Noel, Roger, jt. auth. see Danner, Horace G.

Noel, Ruth S. The Languages of Tolkien's Middle-Earth. 001. 224p. 1980. pap. 14.00 (*0-395-29130-5*) HM.

— The Mythology of Middle-earth. LC 78-303237. 198p. 1977. write for info. (*0-500-01187-7*) Thames Hudson.

Noel, S. J. Patrons, Clients, Brokers: Ontario Society & Politics, 1791-1896. 328p. 1990. pap. 19.95 (*0-8020-6774-3*); text 45.00 (*0-8020-5858-2*) U of Toronto Pr.

Noel, Sidney, ed. The Revolutionaries at Queen's Park: Ontario's Political Merry-Go-Round. LC 98-101382. (Illus.). 224p. 1997. pap. 19.95 (*1-55028-546-7*, Pub. by J Lorimer); bds. 34.95 (*1-55028-547-5*, Pub. by J Lorimer) Formac Dist Ltd.

Noel, Susan. Autobiography in Words. (Illus.). 29p. 1998. pap. 5.95 (*0-9666328-1-8*) CUZ Ed.

Noel, Thomas J. Buildings of Colorado. LC 97-12674. (Buildings of the United States Ser.). (Illus.). 688p. 1997. 45.00 (*0-19-509076-4*) OUP.

— The City & the Saloon: Denver, 1858-1916. (Illus.). 168p. 1996. pap. 19.95 (*0-87081-426-5*) Univ Pr Colo.

— Colorado: A Liquid History & Tavern Guide to the Highest State. LC 98-49390. (Illus.). 254p. 1999. pap. 18.95 (*1-55591-260-5*) Fulcrum Pub.

— Denver Landmarks & Historic Districts: A Pictorial Guide. LC 96-24062. (Illus.). 184p. 1996. 34.95 (*0-87081-427-3*) Univ Pr Colo.

— Mile High City: An Illustrated History of Denver. Parks, Lori, ed. LC 97-71126. (Illus.). 550p. 1997. 49.95 (*1-886483-10-8*) Heritge Media.

Noel, Thomas J. & Corson, Dan W. Boulder County: An Illustrated History. Parks, Lori, ed. LC 98-73493. (Illus.). 350p. 1999. 49.95 (*1-886483-26-4*) Heritge Media.

***Noel, Thomas J. & Hansen, William J.** Montclair Neighborhood. (Illus.). 112p. 1999. pap. 9.95 (*0-914248-24-3*) Hist Denver.

Noel, Thomas J. & Smith, Duane A. Colorado: The Highest State. LC 95-2813. 324p. (J). 1995. text 32.50 (*0-87081-373-0*) Univ Pr Colo.

Noel, Thomas J., et al. Colorado Givers: A History of Philanthropic Heroes. LC 98-45566. (Illus.). 129p. 1998. 24.95 (*0-87081-532-6*) Univ Pr Colo.

Noel, Thomas J., jt. auth. see Leonard, Stephen J.

***Noel, Thomas Jacob.** Mile High City: An Illustrated History of Denver. 2nd rev. ed. Parks, Lori M., ed. (Illus.). 200p. 2000. pap. 29.95 (*1-886483-43-4*, Pub. by Heritge Media) Sunbelt Pubns.

Noel, Thomas S. & Norgren, Barbara J. Denver the City Beautiful & Its Architects, 1893 to 1941. (Illus.). 256p. 1993. reprint ed. pap. 17.95 (*0-914628-22-4*) Hist Denver.

Noel, William. The Harley Psalter. (Studies in Palaeography & Codicology: No. 4). (Illus.). 249p. (C). 1996. text 69.95 (*0-521-46495-1*) Cambridge U Pr.

Noeli, T., jt. auth. see Schoen, T.

***Noelker, Colette A.** Cancer! If I'd Only known. LC 99-73024. 115p. 1999. pap. 8.95 (*1-890622-84-2*) Leathers Pub.

Noell, Chuck & Wood, Gary. We Are All POWs. LC 75-13032. 96p. reprint ed. pap. 30.00 (*0-608-16830-0*, 202683900052) Bks Demand.

Noell, Wilma. Christian Meditations. pap. 1.95 (*0-317-05928-9*) Crusade Pubs.

Noelle, Christine. State & Tribe in Nineteenth-Century Afghanistan: The Reign of Amir Dost Muhammad Khan 1826-1863. 380p. 1997. 75.00 (*0-7007-0629-1*, Pub. by Curzon Pr Ltd) Paul & Co Pubs.

Noelle-Neumann, Elisabeth. The Spiral of Silence: Public Opinion - Our Social Skin. LC 83-18204. (Illus.). 212p. 1984. 20.00 (*0-226-58932-3*) U Ch Pr.

— The Spiral of Silence: Public Opinion - Our Social Skin. LC 83-18204. (Illus.). 212p. 1995. pap. text 16.95 (*0-226-58933-1*) U Ch Pr.

— The Spiral of Silence: Public Opinion, Our Social Skin. 2nd ed. LC 93-15484. (ENG & GER.). 304p. 1993. pap. text 14.95 (*0-226-58936-6*) U Ch Pr.

— The Spiral of Silence: Public Opinion, Our Social Skin. 2nd ed. LC 93-15484. (ENG & GER.). 304p. 1998. lib. bdg. 44.00 (*0-226-58935-8*) U Ch Pr.

Noelle-Neumann, Elisabeth, ed. Allensbacher Jahrbuch der Demoskopie, 1993-1997 (Allensbacher Yearbook of Survey Research, 1993-1997) 750p. 1997. write for info. (*3-598-20719-0*) K G Saur Verlag.

— The Germans: Public Opinions Polls, 1967-1980. rev. ed. LC 81-1075. (Illus.). 516p. 1981. lib. bdg. 59.95 (*0-313-22490-0*, NEG/, Greenwood Pr) Greenwood.

Noelle-Neumann, Elisabeth & Neumann, Erich P., eds. The Germans: Public Opinion Polls 1947-1966. Finan, Gerard, tr. from GER. LC 81-1478. (Illus.). 630p. 1981. reprint ed. lib. bdg. 89.50 (*0-313-22611-3*, NEGE5, Greenwood Pr) Greenwood.

Noels, A., et al. Metal Promoted Selectivity in Organic Synthesis. (C). 1900. text 234.00 (*0-7923-1184-1*) Kluwer Academic.

Noemer, Fred E. Halftone Photography. 8th enl. rev. ed. (Illus.). 194p. (C). 29.50 (*0-911126-05-8*) Perfect Graphic.

Noepel, Penny. Fast Healthy Way with Vegetables. 1989. pap. 2.95 (*0-88266-521-9*) Storey Bks.

Noer, David M. Breaking Free: A Prescription for Personal & Organizational Change. 304p. 1996. 25.00 (*0-7879-0267-5*) Jossey-Bass.

— Healing the Wounds: Overcoming the Trauma of Layoffs & Revitalizing Downsized Organizations. LC 93-13407. (Management Ser.). 276p. 1993. 29.50 (*1-55542-560-7*) Jossey-Bass.

— Healing the Wounds: Overcoming the Trauma of Layoffs & Revitalizing Downsized Organizations. LC 93-13407. (Management Ser.). 288p. 1995. mass mkt. 18.00 (*1-55542-708-1*) Jossey-Bass.

Noer, H. Rolf. Navigator's Pocket Calculator Handbook. LC 82-74136. (Illus.). 173p. (Orig.). reprint ed. pap. 53.70 (*0-7837-1212-X*, 204174400023) Bks Demand.

Noer, John H. ChokePoints: Maritime Economic Concerns in Southeast Asia. Gregory, David, ed. (Illus.). 99p. (Orig.). (C). 1997. pap. text 30.00 (*0-7881-4025-6*) DIANE Pub.

Noer, Richard J., jt. auth. see Casper, Barry M.

Noer, Thomas J. Briton, Boer & Yankee: The United States & South Africa, 1870-1914. LC 78-16749. 206p. reprint ed. pap. 63.90 (*0-7837-0296-5*, 204061700018) Bks Demand.

— Cold War & Black Liberation: The United States & White Rule in Africa, 1948-1968. LC 84-19665. 288p. 1985. text 30.00 (*0-8262-0458-9*) U of Mo Pr.

Noerper. Opportunities in Dental Care Careers. (Opportunities In . . . Ser.). (Illus.). 160p. pap. 11.95 (*0-8442-8576-5*, 85765, VGM Career) NTC Contemp Pub Co.

— Opportunities in Dental Care Careers. (Illus.). 160p. 1992. 14.95 (*0-8442-8575-7*, 85757, VGM Career) NTC Contemp Pub Co.

Noerper, Norman N. Data Processing. (Opportunities In . . . Ser.). 160p. pap. 12.95 (*0-8442-8638-9*, 297IODP, VGM Career) NTC Contemp Pub Co.

— Opportunities in Data Processing. (Illus.). 160p. 1989. 14.95 (*0-8442-8637-0*, VGM Career) NTC Contemp Pub Co.

— Opportunities in Data Processing. (Illus.). 148p. 1995. pap. 10.95 (*0-8442-6226-9*, VGM Career) NTC Contemp Pub Co.

Noeter, Herman, jt. auth. see Noether, D.

Noeth, Louise Ann. Bonneville Salt Flats. LC 99-28378. (Illus.). 156p. 1999. text 39.95 (*0-7603-0605-2*, 128923AP, Pub. by MBI Pubg) Motorbooks Intl.

***Noeth, Winfried.** Intimate Astrology: Better Love & Sex Through the Zodiac. LC 99-43500. 120p. 1999. pap. text 9.95 (*0-8069-5942-8*) Sterling.

Noeth, Winfried, ed. Semiotics of the Media: State of the Art, Projects, & Perspectives. LC 97-16398. (Approaches to Semiotics Ser.: Vol. 127). 850p. 1997. lib. bdg. 275.00 (*3-11-015537-0*) Mouton.

Noethe, Sheryl, jt. auth. see Collom, Jack.

***Noethen, Otto.** What a Wonderful World. (GER & ENG.). 140p. 2000. pap. 13.95 (*1-57532-247-1*) Press-Tige Pub.

Noether, D. & Noeter, Herman. Encyclopedic Dictionary of Chemical Technology. 297p. 1993. 59.50 (*0-89573-329-3*, Wiley-VCH) Wiley.

Noether, D. & Noether, H. Encyclopedic Dictionary of Chemical Technology. Ep. 1992. 110.00 (*0-471-18694-5*) Wiley.

Noether, Emiliana P. As Others Saw Us: Italian Views on the United States During the Nineteenth Century. (Transactions Ser.: Vol. 50, Pt. 2). 31p. 1990. pap. 10.50 (*1-878508-01-6*) CT Acad Arts & Sciences.

Noether, Emiliana P., ed. The American Constitution As a Symbol & Reality for Italy. LC 89-14041. (Studies in American History: Vol. 4). 250p. 1989. lib. bdg. 89.95 (*0-88946-095-7*) E Mellen.

Noether, Emiliana P., ed. see Lavigna, Claire.

Noether, Emmy. Collected Papers. 776p. 1983. 165.00 (*0-387-11504-8*) Spr-Verlag.

Noether, G. E. Introduction to Statistics: The Nonparametric Way. (Texts in Statistics Ser.). (Illus.). 488p. 1990. 72.95 (*0-387-97284-6*) Spr-Verlag.

Noether, H., jt. auth. see Noether, D.

***Noever, P., ed.** Oswald Oberhuber: Written Pictures, up Until Now. (Illus.). 157p. 1999. pap. 36.00 (*3-211-83352-8*) Spr-Verlag.

Noever, P., ed. Philip Johnson: Turning Point. (Illus.). 72p. 1997. pap. 28.00 (*3-211-82958-X*, Pub. by Birkhauser) Princeton Arch.

Noever, Peter. Chris Burden: Beyond the Limits: Machines & Models, Powertime Distance. 1996. pap. text 49.95 (*3-89322-835-7*, Pub. by Edition Cantz) Dist Art Pubs.

***Noever, Peter.** Jannis Kounellis. (Illus.). 160p. 2000. 35.00 (*3-7757-0864-2*) Gerd Hatje.

— Visionary Clients for New Architecture. (Illus.). 2000. pap. 25.00 (*3-7913-2296-6*) Prestel Pub NY.

Noever, Peter, ed. The Havana Project: Architecture Again. (Illus.). 184p. 1995. pap. 25.95 (*3-7913-1600-1*, Pub. by Prestel) te Neues.

— Josef Hoffmann Designs: MAK-Austrian Museum of Applied Arts. (Illus.). 230p. 1997. pap. text 29.95 (*3-7913-1370-3*, Pub. by Prestel) te Neues.

— MAK-Austrian Museum of Applied Arts, Vienna. (Museum Guides Ser.). (Illus.). 176p. (Orig.). 1996. pap. 14.95 (*3-7913-1472-6*, Pub. by Prestel) te Neues.

Noever, Peter, et al, eds. Aleksandr M. Rodchenko & Varvara F. Stepanova: The Future Is Our Only Goal. (Illus.). 260p. 1991. 35.00 (*3-7913-1134-4*, Pub. by Prestel) te Neues.

An Asterisk (*) at the beginning of an entry indicates that the title is appearing for the first time.

— Architecture in Transition: Between Deconstruction & New Modernism. (Illus.). 160p. (C). 1991. pap. 25.95 (*3-7913-1136-0*, Pub. by Prestel) te Neues.

— The End of Architecture? Documents & Manifestos. (Illus.). 136p. (Orig.). 1993. pap. 25.95 (*3-7913-1263-4*, Pub. by Prestel) te Neues.

— Josef Hoffmann Designs: MAK/Austrian Museum of Applied Arts. (Illus.). 331p. 1992. 65.00 (*3-7913-1229-4*, Pub. by Prestel) te Neues.

Noever, Peter, ed. see Schindler, R. M.

Noey, Christopher & Temos, Janet. Art of India from the Williams College Museum of Art. LC 93-41492. (Illus.). 136p. (Orig.). 1994. pap. 35.00 (*0-913697-18-4*) Williams Art.

Nof, Shimon Y., ed. Handbook of Industrial Robotics. LC 92-3435. 1376p. (C). 1992. reprint ed. lib. bdg. 175.00 (*0-89464-722-9*) Krieger.

— Handbook of Industrial Robotics. 2nd ed. LC 98-8017. 1378p. 1999. 150.00 incl. cd-rom (*0-471-17783-0*) Wiley.

— Integration: Information & Collaboration Models Based on the NATO Advanced Research Workshop, Il Ciocco, Italy, June 6-11, 1993. LC 94-1386. (NATO Advanced Study Institutes Series E, Applied Sciences: Vol. 259). 484p. (C). 1994. text 267.50 (*0-7923-2753-5*) Kluwer Academic.

Nof, Shimon Y. & Moodie, C. L., eds. Advanced Information Technologies for Industrial Material Systems. (NATO Asi Series F: Vol. 53). x, 710p. 1989. 143.95 (*0-387-50905-4*) Spr-Verlag.

Nof, Shimon Y., jt. auth. see Dorf, Richard C.

Nof, Shimon Y., jt. ed. see Dorf, Richard C.

Nofal, Maria B. Absentee Entrepreneurship & the Dynamics of the Motor Vehicle Industry in Argentina. LC 87-15159. 288p. 1989. 79.50 (*0-275-92607-9*, C2607, Praeger Pubs) Greenwood.

Noffke, Susan E. & Stevenson, Robert B. Educational Action Research: Becoming Practically Critical. 240p. (C). 1995. text 46.00 (*0-8077-3441-1*); pap. text 21.95 (*0-8077-3440-3*) Tchrs Coll.

Noffke, Suzanne, ed. Catherine of Siena: The Dialogue. LC 79-56755. (Classics of Western Spirituality Ser.). 416p. 1980. pap. 22.95 (*0-8091-2233-2*) Paulist Pr.

Noffke, Suzanne, jt. auth. see Catherine.

Noffs, David. The Wool Curtain: An Essay on Australia & its Politics. 15p. Date not set. pap. 2.95 (*0-929875-18-4*) Noffs Assocs.

Noffs, David & Noffs, Laurie. Harold: Revista. rev. ed. (SPA., Illus.). 24p. (J). 1991. student ed. 2.50 (*0-929875-11-7*) Noffs Assocs.

Noffs, Laurie, jt. auth. see Noffs, David.

Noffs, Ted. Humanology. 32p. (Orig.). 1988. pap. 3.95 (*0-929875-00-1*) Noffs Assocs.

Noffsinger, Carol. Associational Woman's Missionary Union Guide. Edwards, Judith, ed. 44p. 1995. pap. text 3.95 (*1-56309-123-2*, W953139) Womans Mission Union.

Noffsinger, James P. World War I Aviation: A Bibliography of Books in English, French, German, & Italian. rev. ed. LC 95-37995. (FRE & GER.). 576p. 1996. 98.00 (*0-8108-3085-X*) Scarecrow.

— World War I Aviation Books in English: An Annotated Bibliography. LC 86-26109. (Illus.). 331p. 1987. 34.50 (*0-8108-1951-1*) Scarecrow.

Noffsinger, John S. A Program for Higher Education in the Church of the Brethren. LC 78-177711. (Columbia University. Teachers College. Contributions to Education Ser.: No. 172). (C). reprint ed. 37.50 (*0-404-55172-6*) AMS Pr.

Nofi, Albert A. The Alamo & the Texas War of Independence: Heroes, Myths & History. LC 93-33619. (Illus.). 234p. 1994. reprint ed. pap. 13.95 (*0-306-80563-4*) Da Capo.

— Civil War Journal. 1995. 6.98 (*0-88394-090-6*) Promntory Pr.

— The Civil War Notebook. (Illus.). 160p. 1992. pap. 8.95 (*0-938289-23-3*, 289233) Combined Pub.

— A Civil War Treasury: Being a Miscellany of Arms & Artillery Facts & Figures, Legends & Lore, Etc. (Illus.). 432p. 1992. 24.95 (*0-938289-12-8*, 289128) Combined Pub.

— A Civil War Treasury: Being a Miscellany of Arms & Artillery, Facts & Figures, Legends & Lore, Muses & Minstrels, Personalities & People. LC 94-31227. 431p. 1995. 15.95 (*0-306-80622-3*) Da Capo.

***Nofi, Albert A.** The Combined Publishing Guide to American Military History. 2000. 29.95 (*1-58097-040-0*) Combined Pub.

Nofi, Albert A. Gettysburg July 1. 3rd rev. ed. LC 97-15383. (Illus.). 256p. 1995. 34.95 (*0-938289-81-0*, 289810) Combined Pub.

— Marine Corps Book of Lists: A Definitive Compendium of Marine Corps Facts, Feats & Traditions. LC 97-16681. (Illus.). 240p. 1998. pap. 14.95 (*0-938289-89-6*, 289896) Combined Pub.

***Nofi, Albert A.** Spies in the Civil war. LC 99-52501. (Untold History of the Civil War Ser.). (Illus.). 64p. (YA). (gr. 3 up). 1999. 17.95 (*0-7910-5427-6*) Chelsea Hse.

— The Underground Railroad & the Civil War. LC 99-52499. (Illus.). 64p. 1999. 19.95 (*0-7910-5434-9*) Chelsea Hse.

Nofi, Albert A. The War Against Hitler: Military Strategy in the West. 274p. 1994. pap. 15.95 (*0-938289-49-7*, 289497) Combined Pub.

— Waterloo Campaign: June 1815. 1998. pap. 18.95 (*0-938289-98-5*, 289985) Combined Pub.

Nofi, Albert A., ed. Opening Guns: Fort Sumter to Fredericksburg. (Eyewitness History of the Civil War Ser.). 439p. 1994. pap. 16.95 (*0-938289-41-1*, 289411) Combined Pub.

Nofi, Albert A. & Kiraly, Bela K., eds. The Boer War & Military Reform. write for info. (*0-318-60326-8*) Brooklyn Coll Pr.

Nofi, Albert A. & Martin, David G. The Gettysburg Campaign: June-July, 1863. rev. ed. LC 97-15383. (Illus.). 256p. 1997. pap. 16.95 (*0-938289-83-7*, 289837) Combined Pub.

Nofi, Albert A., jt. auth. see Dunnigan, James F.

Nofi, Albert A., jt. ed. see Kiraly, Bela K.

Nofsinger, Mary M. Children & Adjustment to Divorce: An Annotated Bibliography. LC 89-16986. 298p. 1990. text 50.00 (*0-8240-4297-2*) Garland.

Nofsinger, Ray & Hargrove, Jim. Pigeons & Doves. LC 92-12948. (New True Books Ser.). (Illus.). 48p. (J). (ps-3). 1992. lib. bdg. 21.00 (*0-516-02196-6*) Childrens.

Nofsinger, Robert E. Everyday Conversation. (Interpersonal CommTexts Ser.: Vol. 1). 192p. 1990. 44.00 (*0-8039-3309-6*); pap. 19.95 (*0-8039-3310-X*) Sage.

***Nofsinger, Robert E.** Everyday Conversation. 180p. (C). 1999. pap. 17.95 (*1-57766-079-X*) Waveland Pr.

Noftzger, Richard L., Jr., jt. ed. see Guthrie, David S.

Nofz, Michael P. Sociology & You: An Applied Approach. 3rd ed. (Illus.). 454p. (Orig.). (C). 1995. pap. text 28.95 (*0-87563-574-1*) Stipes.

Nofziger, Ed. Animal Cartoons. (How to Draw & Paint Ser.). (Illus.). 32p. (Orig.). 1989. pap. 6.95 (*0-929261-53-4*, HT134) W Foster Pub.

Nofziger, Edward. Mrs. Fox & Mrs. Stork. 19p. (Orig.). (J). (gr. k-12). 1993. pap. 2.95 (*0-922852-21-9*) Another Lang Pr.

Nofziger, Harold H. And It Was Good. LC 93-19336. 36p. (J). (ps-1). 1993. 12.99 (*0-8361-3634-9*) Herald Pr.

Nofziger, Lyn. Nofziger. LC 92-15908. 352p. 1992. 21.95 (*0-89526-513-3*) Regnery Pub.

— Tackett. (Tackett Trilogy Ser.). 1998. 19.95 (*0-915463-80-6*) Jameson Bks.

— Tackett. 214p. 2000. pap. text 10.95 (*0-915463-85-7*) Jameson Bks.

— Tackett. LC 93-8244. 192p. 1993. 16.95 (*0-89526-495-1*) Regnery Pub.

— Tackett & the Indian. LC 97-49588. (Tackett Ser.: Vol. 4). 208p. 1998. 19.95 (*0-915463-75-X*, Frontier Libr) Jameson Bks.

— Tackett & the Saloon Keeper. 1998. 19.95 (*0-915463-82-2*) Jameson Bks.

— Tackett & the Saloon Keeper. 1994. 16.95 (*0-89526-480-3*) Regnery Pub.

— Tackett & the Teacher. (Ground Source Chronicles Ser.). 1998. pap. 19.95 (*0-915463-81-4*) Jameson Bks.

— Tackett & the Teacher. LC 93-45949. 192p. 1994. 16.95 (*0-89526-488-9*) Regnery Pub.

***Nofziger, Lyn.** Unbridled Joy: The Verse of Joy Skilmer. LC 99-76226. 112p. 2000. pap. 14.00 (*0-940847-13-2*) MND Publish.

Nofziger, Margaret. Cooperative Method of Natural Birth Control. 4th ed. LC 91-33429. (Illus.). 112p. 1992. pap. 7.95 (*0-913990-84-1*) Book Pub Co.

— Signs of Fertility. 2nd rev. ed. LC 98-66831. (Illus.). 100p. (Orig.). 1998. pap. 7.95 (*0-940847-08-6*) MND Publish.

— Signs of Fertility: The Personal Science of Natural Birth Control. LC 86-90578. (Illus.). 100p. (Orig.). 1988. pap. 6.95 (*0-940847-07-8*) MND Publish.

***Noga, Edward J.** Fish Disease: Diagnosis & Treatment. LC 99-58466. 378p. 1999. 99.95 (*0-8138-2558-X*) Iowa St U Pr.

Nogales, Ana. Book of Love. 304p. 1999. reprint ed. pap. 13.00 (*0-7679-0119-3*) Broadway BDD.

Nogales, Ana & Belloti, Lauren G. Amor, Intimidad y Sexo. (SPA.). 304p. 1998. pap. 14.00 (*0-7679-0120-7*) Broadway BDD.

Nogales, Francisco, ed. The Human Yolk Sac & Yolk Sac Tumors. LC 92-18512. 1993. 327.00 (*0-387-56031-9*) Spr-Verlag.

Nogales, Patti D. Metaphorically Speaking. LC 98-54375. (Lecture Notes Ser.: Vol. 93). 256p. (C). 1999. text 59.95 (*1-57586-159-3*); pap. text 22.95 (*1-57586-158-5*) CSLI.

Nogales, Rafael De, see De Nogales, Rafael.

Nogalski, James. Literary Precursors to the Book of Twelve. (Beiheft zur Zeitschrift fuer die Alttestamentliche Wissenschaft Ser.: Vol. 217). x, 301p. (C). 1993. lib. bdg. 106.15 (*3-11-013702-X*) De Gruyter.

— Redactional Process in the Book of the Twelve. LC 93-37633. (Beiheft zur Zeitschrift fuer die Alttestamentliche Wissenschaft Ser.: Vol. 218). xi, 300p. (C). 1993. lib. bdg. 106.15 (*3-11-013767-4*) De Gruyter.

***Nogalski, James & Sweeney, Marvin A.** Reading & Hearing the Book of the Twelve. LC 00-30813. (Symposium Ser.). 2000. pap. write for info. (*0-88414-021-0*) Soc Biblical Lit.

Nogalski, James D., tr. see Gunkel, Hermann & Begrich, Joachim.

Nogalski, James D., tr. see Steck, Odil Hannes.

***Nogami, Sanami.** Resultativkonstruktionen im Deutschen und Japanischen. 2000. 42.95 (*3-631-36011-8*) P Lang Pubng.

Nogami, Toyoaki, ed. Dynamic Response of Pile Foundations: Experiment, Analysis & Observation. 192p. 1987. 22.00 (*0-87262-591-5*) Am Soc Civil Eng.

— Observation & Modeling in Numerical Analysis & Model Tests in Dynamic Soil-Structure Interaction: Proceedings of Sessions Held in Conjunction with Geo-Logan, Logan, UT, July 16-17. LC 97-19515. (Geotechnical Special Publication Ser.). 152p. 1997. 22.00 (*0-7844-0252-3*) Am Soc Civil Eng.

Nogar, Raymond J. Lord of the Absurd. LC 98-23394. 160p. 1998. reprint ed. pap. 12.00 (*0-268-01320-9*) U of Notre Dame Pr.

Noge, H., jt. auth. see Sakaki, H.

Nogee, Joseph L., ed. Soviet Politics: Russia after Brezhnev. LC 84-26289. 238p. 1985. 55.00 (*0-275-90148-3*, C0148, Praeger Pubs) Greenwood.

Nogee, Joseph L. & Donaldson, Robert H. Soviet Foreign Policy since World War II. (Policy Studies on International Politics). 300p. 1981. text 43.00 (*0-08-025997-9*, Pergamon Pr); pap. text 12.00 (*0-08-025996-0*, Pergamon Pr) Elsevier.

— Soviet Foreign Policy since World War II. 2nd ed. 400p. 1984. text 47.00 (*0-08-030152-5*, Pergamon Pr); pap. text 13.95 (*0-08-030151-7*, Pergamon Pr) Elsevier.

— Soviet Foreign Policy Since World War II. 3rd ed. 350p. 1988. text. write for info. (*0-08-035885-3*, Pergamon Pr) Elsevier.

Nogee, Joseph L. & Mitchell, R. Judson. Russian Politics: The Struggle for a New Order. LC 96-14435. 200p. (C). 1996. pap. text 39.06 (*0-02-388062-7*, Macmillan Coll) P-H.

Nogee, Joseph L. & Spanier, John W. Peace Impossible - War Unlikely: The Cold War Between the United States & the Soviet Union. (C). 1988. pap. text 21.00 (*0-673-39783-1*) Addson-Wesley Educ.

Nogee, Joseph L., jt. auth. see Donaldson, Robert H.

Nogg, Sharon M. A Whale Watcher's Cookbook: Views from the Galley. (Illus.). 224p. 1990. reprint ed. pap. 11.95 (*0-939644-66-5*) Actors Etc.

Noggle. Physical Chemistry. 3rd ed. 416p. (C). 1997. pap. text, student ed. 37.00 (*0-673-52343-8*) Addson-Wesley Educ.

Noggle, Anne. A Dance with Death: Soviet Airwomen in World War II. LC 94-1301. (Illus.). 336p. 1994. 32.95 (*0-89096-601-X*) Tex A&M Univ Pr.

— For God, Country, & the Thrill of It: Women Airforce Service Pilots in World War II. LC 89-20382. (Charles & Elizabeth Prothro Texas Photography Ser.: No. 1). (Illus.). 176p. 1990. 29.95 (*0-89096-401-7*) Tex A&M Univ Pr.

Noggle, Burl. Fleming Lectures, 1937-1990: A Historiographical Essay. LC 92-11948. 104p. (C). 1992. text 19.95 (*0-8071-1780-3*) La State U Pr.

— Teapot Dome: Oil & Politics in the 1920's. LC 80-15396. (Illus.). 234p. 1980. reprint ed. lib. bdg. 59.75 (*0-313-22601-6*, NOTD, Greenwood Pr) Greenwood.

Noggle, Dillard & Jeffries, Carolyn. Dillsboro. LC 86-82646. 187p. (Orig.). 1986. pap. 10.00 (*0-931889-05-7*) Epistemology Pubs.

Noggle, Joseph H. Physical Chemistry. 3rd ed. LC 95-10742. 1035p. (C). 1997. 115.00 (*0-673-52341-1*) Addson-Wesley Educ.

— Physical Chemistry Using Mathcad. LC 97-163201. (Illus.). 274, xp. 1997. pap. text 20.00 (*0-9655849-0-9*) Pike Creek Pub.

— Quickbasic Programming for Scientists & Engineers. 400p. 1992. boxed set 68.95 (*0-8493-4434-4*, QA76) CRC Pr.

Nogle, Alfredo D. The Deaconess Manual. Bowlware, Chris et al, eds. 101p. 1999. pap. text 15.95 (*1-887653-08-2*) Papito.

Nogosek, Robert J. The Enneagram Journey to New Life: Who Am I? What Do I Stand For? 1995. 24.95 (*0-87193-287-3*) Dimension Bks.

— Nine Portraits of Jesus: Discovering Jesus Through the Enneagram. 1987. pap. 14.95 (*0-87193-260-1*) Dimension Bks.

Nogowski, John. Bob Dylan: A Descriptive, Critical Discography & Filmography, 1961-1994. LC 94-27330. 208p. 1995. pap. 36.50 (*0-89950-785-9*) McFarland & Co.

Nogradi, M. Stereoselective Synthesis: A Practical Approach. 2nd rev. ed. LC 97-165615. (Illus.). 387p. 1994. pap. 72.95 (*3-527-29243-8*, Wiley-VCH) Wiley.

Nogrady, T., et al. Guides to the Identification of Microinvertebrates of the Continental Waters of the World Vol. 8: Rotifera: The Notommatidae of the Scaridiidae. Dumont, H. J., ed. (Illus.). iv, 228p. 1995. pap. 75.00 (*90-5103-103-3*, Pub. by SPB Acad Pub) Balogh.

Nogrady, Thomas. Medicinal Chemistry: A Biochemical Approach. 2nd ed. (Illus.). 542p. 1988. pap. text 49.95 (*0-19-505369-9*) OUP.

Nogrady, Thomas, et al, eds. Guides to the Identification of Microinvertebrates of the Continental Waters of the World Vol. 4: Rotifera1, Biology, Ecology & Systematics. (Illus.). vii, 142p. 1993. pap. 50.00 (*90-5103-080-0*, Pub. by SPB Acad Pub) Balogh.

Nograsek, Andrea. Ascomyceten Auf Gefuegpflanzen der Polsterseggenrasen in Den Ostalpen. (Bibliotheca Mycologica: Vol. 133). (GER., Illus.). vi, 278p. 1990. 71.00 (*3-443-59034-9*, Pub. by Gebruder Borntraeger) Balogh.

Noguchi, J. & Ochiai, T. Geometric Function Theory in Several Complex Variables. LC 90-546. (Translations of Mathematical Monographs: Vol. 80). 282p. 1990. pap. 49.00 (*0-8218-4533-0*, MMONO/80) Am Math.

Noguchi, J. & Ohsawa, T., eds. Prospects in Complex Geometry: Proceedings of the 25th Taniguchi International Symposium Held in Katata, & the Conference held in Kyoto, July 31-August 9, 1989. (Lecture Notes in Mathematics Ser.: Vol. 1468). vii, 421p. 1991. 62.95 (*0-387-54053-9*) Spr-Verlag.

Noguchi, Junjireo, et al. Prospects in Complex Geometry: Proceedings of the 25th Taniguchi International Symposium Held in Katata & the Conference Held in Kyoto, July 31-August 9, 1989. LC 91-202464. 421p. 1991. write for info. (*3-540-54053-9*) Spr-Verlag.

Noguchi, Junjiro, tr. Introduction to Complex Analysis. LC 97-14392. (Translations of Mathematical Monographs: Vol. Noguchi2). 254p. 1997. text 99.00 (*0-8218-0377-8*) Am Math.

Noguchi, Kaku C. Flowers of the Secret Garden: The Final Episode of the Korean Dynasty of Lee. Briggs, Everett F., tr. from JPN. LC 85-91557.Tr. of Hien No Hana. 222p. 1999. pap. write for info. (*0-9615976-0-7*) E F Briggs.

— Rajagriha: A Tale of Gautama Buddha. (C). 1992. 15.00 (*81-7023-359-3*, Pub. by Allied Pubs) S Asia.

Noguchi, Masao, pref. Taro Ashihara: Program & Style. (I Talenti Ser.). (FRE, ITA & KOR., Illus.). 100p. 1997. pap. write for info. (*88-7838-037-7*) Rockport Pubs.

Noguchi, Rei R. Grammar & the Teaching of Writing Limits & Possibilities. 140p. 1991. pap. 12.95 (*0-8141-1874-7*) NCTE.

Noguchi, Rick. The Ocean Inside Kenji Takezo. LC 96-10143. (Poetry Ser.). 75p. 1996. pap. 10.95 (*0-8229-5613-6*); text 24.95 (*0-8229-3959-2*) U of Pittsburgh Pr.

— The Wave He Caught. (Orig.). 1995. pap. 6.00 (*0-9628094-7-0*) Pearl Edit.

Noguchi, S. & Umeo, H., eds. Transputer - Occam Japan Four: Proceedings of the Fourth T-O International Conference, June 4-5, 1992, Tokyo, Japan. LC 92-53262. (Transputer & Occam Engineering Ser.: Vol. 27). 278p. (gr. 12). 1992. pap. 105.00 (*90-5199-093-6*) IOS Press.

Noguchi, S. & Yamamoto, M., eds. Transputer - Occam Japan Five: Proceedings of the 5th Transputer - Occam International Conference 10-11 June 1993, Osaka, Japan. LC 92-63412. (Transputer & Occam Engineering Ser.: Vol. 35). 266p. (gr. 12). 1993. pap. 105.00 (*90-5199-125-8*, Pub. by IOS Pr) IOS Press.

Noguchi, S., et al. Transputer - Occam Japan 6: Proceedings of the 6th International Conference Jun 14-17, 1993, Tokyo, Japan. LC 94-77314. (Transputer & Occam Engineering Ser.: Vol. 39). 330p. (YA). (gr. 12). 1994. pap. 99.00 (*90-5199-174-6*) IOS Press.

Noguchi, Shiro, jt. ed. see Clark, Orlo H.

Noguchi, Yukio & Poterba, James M., eds. Housing Markets in the United States & Japan. LC 93-48441. 278p. (C). 1994. lib. bdg. 40.00 (*0-226-59015-1*) U Ch Pr.

Noguchi, Yukio & Wise, David A., eds. Aging in the United States & Japan: Economic Trends. LC 94-14101. (National Bureau of Economic Research Conference Report Ser.). (Illus.). 214p. 1994. 39.95 (*0-226-59018-6*) U Ch Pr.

Noguchi, Yukio & Yamamura, Kozo, eds. U. S.-Japan Macroeconomic Relations: Interactions & Interdependence in the 1980s. 320p. 1996. text 50.00 (*0-295-97551-2*) U of Wash Pr.

Nogueira, Crespo. Glossary of Basic Archival & Library Conservation Terms. 155p. 1988. lib. bdg. 95.00 (*0-8288-3398-2*, F41072) Fr & Eur.

Nogueira, J. & Turover, G. Diccionario Ruso-Espanol. deluxe ed.Tr. of Russian-Spanish Dictionary. (RUS & SPA.). 956p. 1979. 39.95 (*0-8288-4781-9*, S33593) Fr & Eur.

Noguer More, Jesus. Diccionario Enciclopedico de la Vida Sexual, 5 vols., Set. (SPA.). 792p. 1974. 250.00 (*0-8288-5987-6*, S50029) Fr & Eur.

Noguera. Urban Education. 1998. pap. text 27.00 (*0-205-18937-7*) Allyn.

Noguera, Claudine. Physics & Chemistry at Oxid Surfaces. (Illus.). 238p. (C). 1996. text 69.95 (*0-521-47214-8*) Cambridge U Pr.

Noguera, Pedro. The Imperatives of Power: Political Change & the Social Basis of Regime Support in Grenada from 1951-1991. (American University Studies XXI: Vol. 15). VIII, 302p. (C). 1997. text 48.95 (*0-8204-3095-1*) P Lang Pubng.

Nogueras, Amber. Eres Tu una Oveja Herida?Tr. of Are You a Wounded Lamb?. (SPA.). 229p. 1994. pap. 6.99 (*1-56063-734-X*, 550070) Editorial Unilit.

Noguere, Suzanne. Whirling Round the Sun. LC 96-76462. (Poetry Ser.). (Illus.). 96p. (Orig.). 1996. pap. 12.00 (*1-877675-22-9*) Midmarch Arts.

Noguez, Xavier. Documentos Guadalupanos. (SPA.). pap. 13.99 (*968-16-4206-6*, Pub. by Fondo) Continental Bk.

Noguez, Xavier, et al, contrib. by. The Huexotzinco Codex: El Codice de Huexotzinco: An Exact Facsimile of the 1531 Huexotzinco Codex in the Harkness Colleciotn, Manuscript Division, of the Library of Congress, Washington, D. C. LC 95-35990. (SPA.). 1995. write for info. (*0-8444-0887-5*) Lib Congress.

Noguiera, Carmen C., ed. Glossary of Basic Archival & Library Conservation Terms. (ICA Handbook Ser.: Vol. 4). (ENG, FRE, GER, ITA & RUS.). 151p. 1988. lib. bdg. 37.50 (*3-598-20276-8*) K G Saur Verlag.

Noh, Chin-hwa. Healthful Korean Cooking: Meats & Poultry, 3 vols., Vol. 1. LC 85-80450. 76p. 1998. 16.95 (*0-930878-46-9*) Hollym Intl.

— Low-Fat Korean Cooking: Fish, Shellfish & Vegetables, 3 vols., Vol. 2. LC 85-80451. (Illus.). 64p. 1997. 16.98 (*0-930878-47-7*) Hollym Intl.

— Practical Korean Cooking. (Illus.). 192p. 1998. 46.95 (*0-930878-37-X*) Hollym Intl.

— Traditional Korean Cooking: Snacks & Basic Side Dishes, 3 vols., Vol. 3. (Illus.). 64p. 1997. 16.95 (*0-930878-48-5*) Hollym Intl.

***Noh, Eun-Ju.** Metarepresentation: A Relevance-Theory Approach. LC 00-23580. (Pragmatics & Beyond New Ser.: Vol. 69). xii, 236p. 2000. 75.00 (*1-55619-947-3*) J Benjamins Pubng Co.

Nohara, Chuck. Patchwork Bags. (Illus.). 96p. (Orig.). 1989. pap. 18.95 (*0-87040-820-8*) Japan Pubns USA.

— Useful Patchwork Gifts. (Illus.). 96p. (Orig.). 1993. pap. 22.00 (*0-87040-907-7*) Japan Pubns USA.

Nohbauer, Hans F. Ludwig II, Vol. II. 1998. pap. 9.99 (*3-8228-7430-2*) Taschen Amer.

Nohda, Nobuhiko, jt. ed. see Reys, Robert E.

N

Nohel, Emile & European Commission. Working Together: The Institutions of the European Community & Union. LC 98-196060. 50p. 1996. write for info. (*92-828-0294-9*, Pub. by Comm Europ Commun) Bernan Associates.

Nohel, J. A. & Sattinger, D. H., eds. Selected Papers of Norman Levinson, 2 vols. Incl. Selected Papers of Norman Levin, 1997. LC 97-38621. (Illus.). 550p. 1997. 175.00 (*0-8176-3862-8*); Vol. 2. 1997. LC 97-38621. 450p. 1997. 175.00 (*0-8176-3979-9*); 180.00 (*0-8176-3978-0*) Spr-Verlag.

Nohel, John A., jt. auth. see Brauer, Fred.

Noher, Ursula R. & Garcia, F. O. Librarian's Puzzle: MARC-CIP-ISBN-ISSN-RLIN. 2nd ed. 130p. 1993. 15.00 (*0-929928-15-6*) Fog Pubns.

***Nohilly, Eamonn A.** Quarterback Your Investment Plan: The Basics for Beginners. 300p. 2001. pap. 19.95 (*0-9676249-9-1*) Personal Finance.

Nohl, Herman. Introduccion a la Etica. (Breviarios Ser.). (SPA.). pap. 7.99 (*968-16-0998-0*, Pub. by Fondo) Continental Bk.

Nohl, Louis. Life of Haydn. 1889. reprint ed. 49.00 (*0-403-00343-1*) Scholarly.

— Life of Mozart. Lalor, John J., tr. LC 82-1593. (Music Reprint Ser.). (GER., Illus.). 236p. 1982. reprint ed. lib. bdg. 29.50 (*0-306-76171-8*) Da Capo.

Nohl, Ludwig. Life of Haydn. 7th ed. Upton, George P., tr. LC 73-173796. reprint ed. 37.50 (*0-404-04786-6*) AMS Pr.

Nohlen, Dieter, et al, eds. Elections in Africa: A Data Handbook. LC 99-15993. (Illus.). 1,000p. 1999. text 140.00 (*0-19-829645-2*) OUP.

Nohlen, Klaus & Radt, Wolfgang. Kapikaya: Ein Felsheiligtum Bei Pergamon. (Altertumer Von Pergamon Ser.: Vol. 12). (Illus.). (C). 1978. 107.70 (*3-11-006710-2*) De Gruyter.

Nohmberg, James. Like unto Moses: The Constituting of an Interruption. LC 94-18785. (Indiana Studies in Biblical Literature). 368p. 1995. text 39.95 (*0-253-34090-X*) Ind U Pr.

Nohmeier, Martina. Agenten in Globalen Informationsraumen. (Illus.). 252p. 1998. 45.95 (*3-631-33812-0*) P Lang Pubng.

Nohowel, Shelley. Portraits of Unique Homes, Vol. 1. Goodwin, Richard A., ed. (Illus.). 224p. 1992. 90.00 (*1-56333-000-8*) Masquerade.

— Portraits of Unique Homes Vol. 2: A Luxury Perspective. Goodwin, Richard A., ed. (Illus.). 208p. 1993. 90.00 (*1-56333-998-6*) Masquerade.

***Nohria, Nitin.** The Portable MBA Desk Reference: An Essential Business Companion. 2nd ed. LC 98-3767. (Portable MBA Ser.). 680p. 1998. 35.00 (*0-471-24530-5*) Wiley.

Nohria, Nitin & Eccles, Robert G., eds. Networks & Organizations: Structure, Form & Action. LC 92-11442. 560p. 1994. pap. 27.95 (*0-87584-578-9*) Harvard Busn.

Nohria, Nitin & Ghoshal, Sumantra. The Differentiated Network: Organizing Multinational Corporations for Value Creation. LC 96-48257. (Jossey-Bass Business & Management Ser.). 256p. 1997. 34.95 (*0-7879-0331-0*) Jossey-Bass.

Nohria, Nitin, jt. auth. see Beer, Michael.

Nohria, Nitin, jt. auth. see Champy, James.

Nohria, Nitin, jt. ed. see Champy, James.

Nohria, Nitin, jt. ed. see Eccles, Robert G.

Nohring, F. Worterbuch Medizin, French to German. (FRE & GER.). 800p. 1994. 295.00 (*0-320-00587-9*) Fr & Eur.

Nohring, Fritz-Jurgen. English/German Dictionary of Medicine & Veterinary Medicine. 3rd ed. (ENG & GER.). 750p. 1996. 295.00 (*0-7859-9345-2*) Fr & Eur.

— German/English Dictionary of Medicine & Veterinary Medicine. (ENG & GER.). 850p. 1997. 295.00 (*0-7859-9346-0*) Fr & Eur.

— Routledge Langenscheidt German Dictionary of Medicine, Vol. 2. 3rd ed. LC 97-43142. (Routledge Bilingual Specialist Dictionaries Ser.). (GER.). 904p. (C). 1998. 115.00 (*0-415-17337-X*) Routledge.

Nohring, Fritz-Jurgen, ed. Routledge Langenscheidt German Dictionary of Medicine: Germanenglish, Vol. 1. 2nd ed. LC 97-43142. (Routledge Bilingual Specialist Dictionaries Ser.). (GER.). 975p. (C). 1998. 115.00 (*0-415-17130-X*) Routledge.

Nohring, Jurgen. Dictionary of Medicine, German & English. (ENG & GER.). 848p. 1987. 195.00 (*0-8288-0572-5*, M1735) Fr & Eur.

— English & German Dictionary of Medicine. 2nd ed. (ENG & GER.). 708p. 1986. 195.00 (*0-8288-0571-7*, M 14674) Fr & Eur.

Nohrnberg, Peter C. The Book the Poet Makes: Collection & Re-Collection in W. B. Yeats's The Tower & Robert Lowell's Life Studies. LC 95-8401. (The LeBaron Russell Briggs Prize, Honors Essay in English, 1993 Ser.: Vol. 1993). 102p. (Orig.). (C). 1995. pap. text 11.75 (*0-674-07867-5*) HUP.

Noice, Helga, jt. auth. see Noice, Tony.

Noice, Karen, jt. auth. see Ogle, Gini.

Noice, Marshall, jt. auth. see Long, David.

Noice, Tony & Noice, Helga. The Nature of Expertise in Professional Acting: A Cognitive View. LC 97-12571. 200p. 1997. 45.00 (*0-8058-2169-4*); pap. write for info. (*0-8058-2170-8*) L Erlbaum Assocs.

Noij, I. G., et al. Modeling Nutrient & Moisture Cycling in Tropical Forests. (Tropenbos Technical Ser.: No. 4). (Illus.). 195p. 1993. pap. 40.00 (*90-5113-016-3*, Pub. by Backhuys Pubs) Balogh.

Noike, T., et al, eds. Anaerobic Digestion VIII: Selected Proceedings of the 8th IAWQ International Conference on Anaerobic Digestion, Held in Sendai, Japan, 25-29 May 1997. 552p. 1997. pap. write for info. (*0-08-043374-X*) Elsevier.

Noin, Daniel & White, Paul. Paris. LC 97-206195. (World Cities Ser.). 302p. 1997. 110.00 (*0-471-94944-2*) Wiley.

Noin, Daniel, jt. ed. see Clarke, John I.

Noire, Ludwig. Logos, Ursprung und Wesen der Begriffe. (Documenta Semiotica Ser.: Bd. 1). (GER.). 362p. 1989. reprint ed. write for info. (*3-487-09259-X*) G Olms Pubs.

Noiriel, Gerard. The French Melting Pot: Immigration, Citizenship, & National Identity. De Laforcade, Geoffroy, tr. (Contradictions of Modernity Ser.: Vol. 5). (Illus.). (C). 1996. pap. 22.95 (*0-8166-2420-8*); text 57.95 (*0-8166-2419-4*) U of Minn Pr.

— Workers in French Society in the 19th & 20th Centuries. McPhail, Helen, tr. from FRE. LC 89-35885. 288p. 1990. 19.50 (*0-85496-610-2*) Berg Pubs.

Noiriel, Gerard, jt. ed. see Horowitz, Donald L.

Noiset, Marie-Therese, tr. see Badian, Seydou.

***Noiseux, Donald, ed.** Our Vine of Sharing Recipes. (Illus.). 175p. 1999. spiral bd. 15.00 (*1-929486-04-9*) SonRises Bk Pubg.

Noiseux, Ronald A., jt. auth. see Glass, Robert L.

Noivo, Edite. Inside Ethnic Families: Three Generations of Portuguese-Canadians. pap. 22.95 (*0-7735-1869-X*) McG-Queens Univ Pr.

— Inside Ethnic Families: Three Generations of Portuguese-Canadians. LC 99-208025. 176p. 1997. text 49.95 (*0-7735-1643-3*, Pub. by McG-Queens Univ Pr) CUP Services.

Noizet, Georges, jt. ed. see Mehler, Jacques A.

Noizet, Yvonne, tr. see Mehler, Jacques A. & Noizet, Georges, eds.

Nojd, Ruben. English-Swedish Dictionary. (ENG & SWE.). 39.50 (*0-87557-083-6*) Saphrograph.

— Swedish-French, French-Swedish Dictionary: Svensk-Fransk-Svensk Ordbok. (FRE & SWE.). 450p. 1986. 49.95 (*0-8288-1681-6*, F57114) Fr & Eur.

Nojd, Ruben & Angstrom, M. Swedish-English Dictionary. (ENG & SWE.). 39.50 (*0-87557-082-8*) Saphrograph.

***Nojer, Stephen M. & Andrews, Jean F.** Critical Pedagogy in Deaf Education: Bilingual Methodology & Staff Development (Year 2) 1999. pap. write for info. (*1-9668769-1-1*) NM School Deaf.

Noji, Eric K. Manual of Toxicologic Emergencies. 1989. 99.95 (*0-685-25523-9*) Mosby Inc.

Noji, Eric K., ed. The Public Health Consequences of Disasters. (Illus.). 488p. 1996. text 59.95 (*0-19-509570-7*) OUP.

Nokel, K. Temporally Distributed Symptoms in Technical Diagnosis. Siekmann, Joerg H., ed. (Lecture Notes in Artificial Intelligence Ser.: Vol. 517). ix, 164p. 1991. 31.00 (*0-387-54316-3*) Spr-Verlag.

Nokes, David. Jane Austen: A Life. LC 97-24768. (Illus.). 512p. 1997. text 35.00 (*0-374-11326-2*) FS&G.

— Jane Austen: A Life. LC 98-15785. 592p. 1998. pap. 19.95 (*0-520-21606-7*, Pub. by U CA Pr) Cal Prin Full Svc.

— John Gay, a Profession of Friendship: A Critical Biography. (Illus.). 578p. 1995. 45.00 (*0-19-812971-8*) OUP.

— Jonathan Swift, a Hypocrite Reversed: A Critical Biography. (Illus.). 448p. 1986. text 35.00 (*0-19-812834-7*) OUP.

Nokes, Garry J., ed. LaSalle Banks Guide, 1998-99: Major Publicly Held Corporations & Financial Institutions Headquartered in Illinois. 34th rev. ed. LC 86-640098. (Scholl Corporate Guides Ser.). Orig. Title: First Chicago NBD Guide. 352p. 1998. pap. 29.95 (*0-912519-20-7*) Scholl.

— LaSalle Banks Guide, 1997-98: Major Publicly Held Corporations & Financial Institutions Headquartered in Illinois. 33rd rev. ed. LC 86-640098. (Corporate Guides Ser.). Orig. Title: First Chicago NBD Guide. 352p. 1997. pap. 29.95 (*0-912519-19-3*) Scholl.

Nokes, J. Richard. Almost a Hero: The Voyages of John Meares, R. N. to China, Hawaii & the Northwest Coast. LC 98-30762. 200p. 1998. 35.00 (*0-87422-155-2*) Wash St U Pr.

— Almost a Hero: The Voyages of John Meares, R. N. to China, Hawaii & the Northwest Coast. LC 98-30762. 200p. 1998. pap. 19.95 (*0-87422-158-7*) Wash St U Pr.

— Columbia's River: The Voyages of Robert Gray, 1787-1793. (Illus.). 352p. 1991. pap. 24.95 (*0-917048-68-7*) Wash St Hist Soc.

***Nokes, Jill.** How to Grow Native Plants of Texas & the Southwest. LC 00-44352. 2001. pap. write for info. (*0-292-75573-2*) U Pr of Amer.

Nokes, Kathleen M., ed. HIV-AIDS & the Older Adult. 264p. 1996. 59.95 (*1-56032-429-5*); pap. 29.95 (*1-56032-430-9*) Hemisp Pub.

Nokes, L. D. M. Introduction to Medical Electronics Appliance. (Electrical Engineering Ser.). 1995. pap. text 54.95 (*0-340-61457-9*, VNR) Wiley.

***Nokes, Sebastian.** Taking Control of IT Costs: A Business Managers Guide. (Illus.). 272p. 2000. pap. 40.00 (*0-273-64943-4*) F T P-H.

Nokleberg, ed. Alaskan Geological & Geophysical Transect. (IGC Field Trip Guidebooks Ser.). 136p. 1989. 28.00 (*0-87590-653-2*, T104) Am Geophysical.

Nol, Sally. Watch Where You Go!Tr. of Attention Ou Tu Vas!. (FRE., Illus.). (J). pap. 5.99 (*0-590-24231-8*) Scholastic Inc.

Nola, Antonio Di, see Di Nola, Antonio.

Nola, Robert, ed. Foucault. LC 98-21412. 120p. 1998. 49.50 (*0-7146-4915-5*, Pub. by F Cass Pubs); pap. 19.50 (*0-7146-4469-2*, Pub. by F Cass Pubs) Intl Spec Bk.

— Relativism & Realism in Science. 312p. (C). 1988. lib. bdg. 168.50 (*90-277-2647-7*, Pub. by Kluwer Academic) Kluwer Academic.

***Nola, Robert & Sankey, Howard.** After Popper, Kuhn & Feyerabend: Recent Issues in Theories of Scientific Method. LC 99-52368. (Australasian Studies in History & Philosophy of Science). 388p. 1999. 156.00 (*0-7923-6032-X*) Kluwer Academic.

Nolan. Abnormal Psychology. LC 97-68714. 1998. text 18.44 (*0-07-289545-4*) McGraw.

— Cps Human Societies. 1998. 18.25 (*0-07-233023-6*) McGraw.

— Creative Destruction. 272p. 1995. 29.95 (*0-07-103583-4*) McGraw.

— Fundamentals of Air Traffic. (Aviation Ser.). 1990. text, teacher ed. write for info. (*0-534-12247-7*) Wadsworth Pub.

— Fundamentals of Air Traffic Control. 3rd ed. (Aviation Ser.). 1999. pap. 73.95 (*0-534-56795-9*) Wadsworth Pub.

— Fundamentals of College Physics. 1992. teacher ed. 13.75 (*0-697-14404-6*, WCB McGr Hill); teacher ed. 13.75 (*0-697-17201-5*, WCB McGr Hill) McGrw-H Hghr Educ.

— Fundamentals of College Physics. 2nd ed. 1994. student ed. 20.25 (*0-697-26704-0*) McGraw.

— Fundamentals of College Physics. 2nd ed. 1994. 16.50 (*0-697-26724-5*, WCB McGr Hill) McGrw-H Hghr Educ.

— Gale Directory of Databases Vol. 1: Online Databases. 1998. 249.00 (*0-8103-5755-0*, GML00198-101816) Visible Ink Pr.

Nolan & Sedley, Stephen. The Making & Remaking of the British Constitution. LC 98-151840. (Law in Its Social Setting Ser.). 142p. 1997. pap. 44.00 (*1-85431-704-0*, Pub. by Blackstone Pr) Gaunt.

Nolan, jt. auth. see Lee, E.

Nolan, jt. auth. see Mackintosh.

Nolan, jt. auth. see Street, Brian.

Nolan, Alan T. The Iron Brigade: A Military History. LC 93-28908. (Illus.). 432p. 1994. 35.00 (*0-253-34102-7*); pap. 19.95 (*0-253-20863-7*) Ind U Pr.

— Lee Considered: General Robert E. Lee & Civil War History. LC 90-48296. xii, 231p. (C). 1991. 29.95 (*0-8078-1956-5*) U of NC Pr.

— Lee Considered: General Robert E. Lee & Civil War History. 243p. (C). 1996. pap. 16.95 (*0-8078-4587-6*) U of NC Pr.

***Nolan, Alan T.** "Rally, Once Again!" Selected Civil War Writings of Alan T. Nolan. LC 99-89974. 2000. write for info. (*0-945612-71-0*) Madison Hse.

Nolan, Alan T. & Eggleston Vipond, Sharon, eds. Giants in Their Tall Black Hats: Essays on the Iron Brigade. LC 98-23926. (Illus.). 320p. 1998. 27.95 (*0-253-33457-8*) Ind U Pr.

Nolan, Alan T., jt. auth. see Gallagher, Gary W.

Nolan, Albert. God in South Africa: The Challenge of the Gospel. LC 88-21737. 255p. reprint ed. pap. 79.10 (*0-7837-0523-9*, 204084700018) Bks Demand.

— Jesus Before Christianity. LC 78-6708. 168p. (Orig.). reprint ed. pap. 52.10 (*0-7837-5515-5*, 204528500005) Bks Demand.

— Jesus Before Christianity. rev. ed. LC 92-5604. 142p. (Orig.). 1992. pap. 12.00 (*0-88344-832-7*) Orbis Bks.

Nolan, Anne C., ed. see Whitmore, Marilyn P.

Nolan, Barbara. The Gothic Visionary Perspective. LC 76-56241. 311p. 1977. reprint ed. pap. 96.50 (*0-7837-9402-9*, 206014700004) Bks Demand.

Nolan, Barbara E. The Political Theory of Beatrice Webb. LC 87-12592. (Studies in Social History: No. 7). 1988. 47.50 (*0-404-61607-0*) AMS Pr.

Nolan, Brian. Tarnished Brass. rev. ed. (Illus.). 272p. 1997. mass mkt. 8.99 (*0-7704-2767-7*) Bantam.

Nolan, Brian & Turbat, Vincent. Cost Recovery in Public Health Services in Sub-Saharan Africa. LC 95-14406. (EDI Technical Materials Ser.). 114p. 1995. pap. 22.00 (*0-8213-3240-6*, 13240) World Bank.

Nolan, Brian & Whelan, Christopher T. Resources, Deprivation & Poverty. LC 95-47230. (Illus.). 272p. 1996. text 65.00 (*0-19-828785-2*, Clarendon Pr) OUP.

Nolan, Bryan. Data Analysis: An Introduction. Leigh, Sue, ed. (Illus.). 240p. (C). 1994. pap. text 29.95 (*0-7456-1146-X*) Blackwell Pubs.

— Data Analysis: An Introduction. Leigh, Sue, ed. (Illus.). 240p. (C). 1994. text 68.95 (*0-7456-1145-1*) Blackwell Pubs.

Nolan, Carson Y. & Kederis, Cleves J. Perceptual Factors in Braille Word Recognition. LC 79-9310. (American Foundation for the Blind Research Ser.: No. 20). 192p. reprint ed. pap. 59.60 (*0-7837-0224-8*, 204053200017) Bks Demand.

Nolan, Cathal J. Ethics & Statecraft: The Moral Dimension of International Affairs. LC 95-22978. 256p. 1995. pap. 22.95 (*0-275-95382-3*, Praeger Pubs) Greenwood.

— Principled Diplomacy: Security & Rights in U. S. Foreign Policy, 313. LC 92-30006. (Contributions in Political Science Ser.: No. 313). 312p. 1993. 65.00 (*0-313-28006-1*, NPD/, Greenwood Pr) Greenwood.

Nolan, Cathal J., ed. Ethics & Statecraft: The Moral Dimension of International Affairs, 362. LC 95-22978. (Contributions in Political Science Ser.: Vol. 362). 256p. 1995. 69.50 (*0-313-29642-1*, Greenwood Pr) Greenwood.

— Notable U. S. Ambassadors since 1775: A Biographical Dictionary. LC 96-50291. 448p. 1997. lib. bdg. 95.00 (*0-313-29195-0*, Greenwood Pr) Greenwood.

Nolan, Cathal J., jt. ed. see Hodge, Carl C.

Nolan, Charles J., Jr. Aaron Burr & the American Literary Imagination, 45. LC 79-8291. (Contributions in American Studies: No. 45). 210p. 1980. 55.00 (*0-313-21256-2*, NAB/, Greenwood Pr) Greenwood.

***Nolan, Christopher.** The Banyan Tree. 384p. 2000. 25.95 (*1-55970-511-6*, Pub. by Arcade Pub Inc) Time Warner.

— The Banyan Tree. large type unabridged ed. 2000. 26.95 (*0-7531-6104-4*, 161044, Pub. by ISIS Lrg Prnt) ISIS Pub.

— The Banyon Tree. 2000. reprint ed. 14.00 (*0-385-72068-8*, Anchor NY) Doubleday.

Nolan, Christopher. Dam-Burst of Dreams. LC 81-9669. 144p. 1988. pap. 9.95 (*0-8214-0912-3*) Ohio U Pr.

***Nolan, Christopher.** Under the Eye of the Clock. 2000. pap. text 13.95 (*1-55970-512-4*, Pub. by Arcade Pub Inc) Time Warner.

***Nolan, Christopher W.** Managing the Reference Collection. LC 98-37178. 200p. 1998. 32.00 (*0-8389-0748-2*) ALA.

***Nolan, Colleen.** What I Like About You. 2000. 14.99 (*1-929125-14-3*, Pub. by Loyal Pubng) BookWorld.

***Nolan, D. J. & Speed, T. P.** Stat Labs: Learning Theory Through Applications. Casella, G. et al, eds. LC 99-57464. (Springer Texts in Statistics Ser.). (Illus.). 336p. 2000. pap. 39.95 (*0-387-98974-9*) Spr-Verlag.

Nolan, D. J., jt. ed. see Gourtsoyiannis, N. C.

Nolan, Daniel, tr. see Nipperdey, Thomas.

Nolan, David. The Houses of St. Augustine. LC 94-41776. (Illus.). 112p. 1995. 27.95 (*1-56164-069-7*); pap. 16.95 (*1-56164-075-1*) Pineapple Pr.

Nolan, Deborah, ed. Women in Mathematics: Scaling the Heights. LC 97-74342. (MAA Notes Ser.). 146p. 1997. pap. 29.95 (*0-88385-156-3*, NTE-46/JR) Math Assn.

Nolan, Denis. Medjugorje: A Time for Truth & a Time for Action. 1993. pap. text 2.00 (*1-882972-05-8*, 3061) Queenship Pub.

Nolan, Dennis. Androcles & the Lion. LC 95-47578. (Illus.). 32p. (J). (gr. 1-5). 1997. 15.00 (*0-15-203355-6*) Harcourt.

— Dinosaur Dream. LC 93-48409. (Illus.). 32p. (J). (gr. k-3). 1994. mass mkt. 5.99 (*0-689-71832-2*) Aladdin.

— Dinosaur Dream. LC 89-78208. (Illus.). 32p. (J). (ps-2). 1990. lib. bdg. 16.00 (*0-02-768145-9*, Mac Bks Young Read) S&S Childrens.

Nolan, Dennis. Dinosaur Dream. LC 93-48409. 1994. 11.19 (*0-606-06323-4*, Pub. by Turtleback) Demco.

— Encyclopedia of Fire Protection. LC 99-88963. (Illus.). 2000. pap. text 44.95 (*0-7668-0869-6*) Delmar.

Nolan, Dennis. Wolf Child. LC 88-35955. (Illus.). 40p. (J). (gr. 1-5). 1989. mass mkt. 16.00 (*0-02-768141-6*, Mac Bks Young Read) S&S Childrens.

Nolan, Dennis. The Blessing of the Lord: Stories from the Old & New Testaments. LC 96-11402. 160p. (J). (gr. 3). 1997. 20.00 (*0-8028-3789-1*, Eerdmans Bks) Eerdmans.

— William Shakespeare's A Midsummer Night's Dream. LC 94-12600. 48p. (gr. 4-7). 1996. 16.99 (*0-8037-1784-9*, Dial Yng Read) Peng Put Young Read.

Nolan, Dennis, jt. auth. see Dodson, Bryan.

Nolan, Dennis P. Application of HAZOP & What-If Safety Reviews to the Petroleum, Petro-Chemical & Chemical Industries. LC 94-4889. (Illus.). 127p. 1994. 98.00 (*0-8155-1353-4*) Noyes.

— Fire Fighting Pumping Systems at Industrial Facilities. LC 97-44016. (Illus.). 223p. 1998. 98.00 (*0-8155-1428-X*) Noyes.

— Handbook of Fire & Explosion Protection Engineering Principles for Oil, Gas, Chemical, & Related Facilities. LC 96-10908. 291p. 1996. 64.00 (*0-8155-1394-1*) Noyes.

Nolan, Dennis R. Labor & Employment Arbitration in a Nutshell. LC 98-10054. (Paralegal). 425p. 1998. pap. text 15.00 (*0-314-21160-8*) West Pub.

— Labor Arbitration Law & Practice in a Nutshell. LC 79-4316. (Nutshell Ser.). 358p. (C). 1979. reprint ed. pap. text 15.00 (*0-8299-2032-3*) West Pub.

Nolan, Dennis R., ed. The Australian Labour Law Reforms: Australia & New Zealand at the End of the Twentieth Century. LC 98-212528. 257p. 1998. pap. 50.00 (*1-86287-276-7*, Pub. by Federation Pr) Gaunt.

Nolan, Dennis R., jt. auth. see Cooper, Laura J.

Nolan, Donald J. Regents College: The Early Years. LC 98-14919. 1998. write for info. (*1-57864-030-X*) Donning Co.

Nolan, Edward P. Cry Out & Write: A Feminine Poetics of Revelation. LC 84-8595. 192p. (C). 1994. 22.50 (*0-8264-0684-X*) Continuum.

— Now Through a Glass Darkly: Specular Images of Being & Knowing from Virgil to Chaucer. 364p. 1991. text 47.50 (*0-472-10170-6*, 10170) U of Mich Pr.

Nolan, Edward W. Frank Palmer-Scenic Photographer. 32p. 1987. pap. 7.95 (*0-910524-05-X*) Eastern Wash.

— A Guide to the Manuscript Collections in the Eastern Washington State Historical Society. 180p. 1987. pap. 9.95 (*0-910524-06-8*) Eastern Wash.

— A Night of Terror, Devastation, Suffering & Awful Woe: The Spokane Fire of 1889. 64p. 1989. pap. 10.95 (*0-910524-12-2*) Eastern Wash.

Nolan, Finbarr & Duffy, Martin. Seventh Son of a Seventh Son: The Life Story of a Healer. (Illus.). 192p. 1993. 19.95 (*1-85158-414-5*, Pub. by Mainstream Pubng) Trafalgar.

Nolan, Frederick. Bad Blood: The Life & Times of the Horrel Brothers. LC 94-27503. (Illus.). 212p. 1994. 25.95 (*0-935269-16-9*, Barbed Wire Pr) Western Pubns.

***Nolan, Frederick.** West of Billy the Kid. 368p. 1999. pap. text 22.95 (*0-8061-3104-7*) U of Okla Pr.

Nolan, Frederick W. The Sound of Their Music: The Story of Rodgers & Hammerstein. LC 78-313105. 272p. 1978. write for info. (*0-460-04315-3*) J M Dent & Sons.

Nolan, Frederick W., jt. auth. see Garrett, Pat F.

Nolan, Fredrick. Lorenz Hart: A Poet on Broadway. (Illus.). 416p. 1995. pap. 15.95 (*0-19-510289-4*) OUP.

Nolan, Godfrey. Decompiling Java. 358p. 1998. pap. 44.95 incl. cd-rom (*0-07-913767-9*) McGraw.

Nolan, Graham, jt. auth. see Dixon, Chuck.

Nolan-Haley, Jacqueline M. Alternative Dispute Resolution in a Nutshell. (Nutshell Ser.). 298p. (C). 1992. pap. 21.00 (*0-314-00781-4*) West Pub.

Nolan, Han. Dancing on the Edge. LC 96-52152. 244p. (J). (gr. 7). 1997. 16.00 (*0-15-201648-1*, Harcourt Child Bks) Harcourt.

— Dancing on the Edge. LC 98-28618. 256p. (J). (gr. 7 up). 1999. pap. 4.99 (*0-14-130203-8*, PuffinBks) Peng Put Young Read.

An Asterisk (*) at the beginning of an entry indicates that the title is appearing for the first time.

— Face in Every Window. LC 99-14230. 272p. (J). 1999. 16.00 (*0-15-201915-4*, Harcourt Child Bks) Harcourt.

— If I Should Die Before I Wake. LC 93-30720. 288p. (YA). (gr. 7 up). 1994. 18.00 (*0-15-238040-X*, Harcourt Child Bks) Harcourt.

— If I Should Die Before I Wake. LC 93-30720. 228p. (YA). (gr. 7 up). 1996. pap. 6.00 (*0-15-238041-8*, Harcourt Child Bks) Harcourt.

— Send Me down a Miracle. LC 95-38169. 256p. (YA). (gr. 7 up). 1996. 13.00 (*0-15-200979-5*); pap. 6.00 (*0-15-200978-7*) Harcourt.

Nolan, Helen. How Much, How Many, How Far, How Heavy, How Long, How Tall Is 1,000? (Illus.). 32p. (J). (gr. k-4). 1995. 14.95 (*1-55074-164-0*, Pub. by Kids Can Pr) Genl Dist Srvs.

Nolan, Hugh J., ed. Pastoral Letters of the United States Catholic Bishops, 1792-1940, Vol. I. 489p. 1984. pap. 24.95 (*1-55586-880-0*) US Catholic.

— Pastoral Letters of the United States Catholic Bishops, 1941-1961, Vol. II. 273p. 1984. pap. 24.95 (*1-55586-885-1*) US Catholic.

— Pastoral Letters of the United States Catholic Bishops, 1962-1974, Vol. III. 511p. 1984. pap. 24.95 (*1-55586-870-3*) US Catholic.

— Pastoral Letters of the United States Catholic Bishops, 1975-1983, Vol. IV. 617p. 1984. pap. 24.95 (*1-55586-875-4*) US Catholic.

— Pastoral Letters of the United States Catholic Bishops, 1983-1988, Vol. V. 797p. 1989. 39.95 (*1-55586-200-4*) US Catholic.

***Nolan, Iris.** Bells for Caroline. large type ed. 384p. 1999. 31.99 (*0-7089-4162-1*) Ulverscroft.

Nolan, J. Bennett. Early Narratives of Berks County, Pennsylvania. (Illus.). 189p. 1997. reprint ed. lib. bdg. 25.00 (*0-8328-7158-3*) Higginson Bk Co.

Nolan, Jack & Fandray, Dayton. Mind Tuning: Likely or Not? Drolet, Cindy et al, eds. (Mind Tuning Ser.). 46p. (Orig.). (YA). 1996. pap. text 14.95 (*1-883315-17-4*, 8303) Imaginart Intl.

Nolan, Jack & Fardray, Dayton. Mind Tuning: Suggest & Guess. large type ed. Rule, Michael, ed. (Mind Tuning Ser.). 56p. (Orig.). 1995. pap. text 14.95 (*1-883315-11-5*, 8302) Imaginart Intl.

Nolan, Jack, jt. auth. see Fandray, Dayton.

Nolan, James. Face to Face: Men & Women Talk Freely about Their Plastic Surgery. LC 96-79213. 120p. 1998. pap. 14.95 (*1-885221-44-4*) BookPartners.

— Poet-Chief: The Native American Poetics of Walt Whitman & Pablo Neruda. LC 93-2379. 270p. 1994. 16.95 (*0-8263-1484-8*) U of NM Pr.

Nolan, James & Lipkin, David P. Coronary Care Manual: A Practical Guide to the Management of Acute Cardiac Problems & Their Subsequent Follow-Up. LC 92-49665. (Pocket Medical Reference Ser.). (Illus.). 134p. 1993. 25.95 (*0-19-262315-X*) OUP.

— Coronary Care Manual: A Practical Guide to the Management of Acute Cardiac Problems & Their Subsequent Follow-Up. LC 92-49665. (Pocket Medical Reference Ser.). (Illus.). 260p. 1993. pap. text 27.50 (*0-19-262314-1*) OUP.

Nolan, James, et al. Australia Business: The Portable Guide to Doing Business with Australia. LC 96-16357. (Country Business Guide Ser.). (Illus.). 328p. (Orig.). 1996. pap. 24.95 (*1-885073-03-8*) Wrld Trade Pr.

— U. S. A. Business: The Portable Encyclopedia for Doing Business with the United States. LC 95-7680. (Country Business Guide Ser.). 507p. (Orig.). 1995. pap. 24.95 (*1-885073-01-1*) Wrld Trade Pr.

Nolan, James, tr. see De Biedma, Jaime G.

Nolan, James, tr. see Neruda, Pablo.

Nolan, James B. Lafayette in America Day by Day. LC 72-1709. reprint ed. 38.50 (*0-404-52427-3*) AMS Pr.

Nolan, James F., jt. auth. see Levin, James.

Nolan, James L., tr. see Osorio, Lizaraza J.

Nolan, James L. The Therapeutic State. LC 97-21234. 395p. 1998. text 45.00 (*0-8147-5790-1*); pap. text 19.00 (*0-8147-5791-X*) NYU Pr.

Nolan, James L., Jr., ed. The American Culture Wars: Current Contests & Future Prospects. 264p. 1996. pap. text 15.00 (*0-8139-1697-6*) U Pr of Va.

***Nolan, James L., Jr. & Meister, Denise.** Teachers & Educational Change: The Lived Experience of Secondary School Restructuring. LC 00-26563. (C). 2000. pap. text 19.95 (*0-7914-4700-6*) State U NY Pr.

— Teachers & Educational Change: The Lived Experience of Secondary School Restructuring. LC 00-26563. (C). 2000. text 59.50 (*0-7914-4699-9*) State U NY Pr.

Nolan, James L., et al. Argentina Business: The Portable Encyclopedia for Doing Business with Argentina. LC 95-18706. (Country Business Guide Ser.). (Illus.). 372p. (Orig.). 1995. pap. 24.95 (*1-885073-04-6*) Wrld Trade Pr.

— Mexico Business: The Portable Encyclopedia for Doing Business with Mexico. LC 94-15696. (Country Business Guide Ser.). 488p. 1994. pap. 24.95 (*0-9631864-0-X*) Wrld Trade Pr.

Nolan, James S., jt. ed. see Monahan, Kathleen N.

Nolan, Jana. Mind Power. 120p. 1997. pap. 12.95 (*0-944851-10-X*) Earth Star.

— The Old Henderson Mine. LC 97-61443. 1997. pap. 11.95 (*0-944851-11-8*) Earth Star.

— Sounds of Fear. 200p. 1998. pap. 11.95 (*0-944851-13-4*) Earth Star.

Nolan, Jane, jt. ed. see Weintraut, Linda.

Nolan, Jane T. What's So Funny about Getting Old? LC 94-25971. (Illus.). 1994. pap. 7.00 (*0-88166-223-2*, 0671511521) Meadowbrook.

Nolan, Janet A. Ourselves Alone: Women's Emigration from Ireland, 1885-1920. LC 89-35145. 152p. 1989. text 20.00 (*0-8131-1684-8*) U Pr of Ky.

Nolan, Janne E. An Elusive Consensus: Nuclear Weapons & American Security after the Cold War. LC 99-6374. 1999. 36.95 (*0-8157-6102-3*); pap. 14.95 (*0-8157-6101-5*) Brookings.

— Trappings of Power: Ballistic Missiles in the Third World. 209p. 1991. 32.95 (*0-8157-6096-5*); pap. 12.95 (*0-8157-6095-7*) Brookings.

Nolan, Janne E., ed. Global Engagement: Cooperation & Security in the 21st Century. 623p. (C). 1994. 52.95 (*0-8157-6098-1*); pap. 24.95 (*0-8157-6097-3*) Brookings.

Nolan, Janne E., jt. auth. see Blechman, Barry M.

Nolan, Jim. Moonshine. 86p. 1992. pap. 12.95 (*1-85235-096-2*) Dufour.

Nolan, John, ed. see Collis, Harry.

Nolan, John A., III. Confidential: How to Uncover Your Competitor's Top Business Secrets Legally & Quickly--& Protect Your Own. LC 99-26034. 384p. 1999. 26.00 (*0-06-661984-X*) HarpC.

Nolan, John S. Sir John Norreys & the Elizabethan Military World. LC 98-185138. (Illus.). 288p. 1998. 70.00 (*0-85989-548-3*, Pub. by Univ Exeter Pr) Northwestern U Pr.

***Nolan, Joseph.** Prayer for the Planet. 128p. 2000. pap. 14.95 (*0-88347-464-6*, 661-239) T More.

Nolan, Joseph. They Shall Be Comforted: For Those Who Grieve & Hope:Reflection, Readings, Prayers Rituals. LC 99-70801. 140p. 1999. pap. 9.95 (*0-89622-978-5*) Twenty-Third.

Nolan, Joseph, jt. auth. see Noonan, Joseph.

Nolan, Joseph R. Trial Practice Cases & Materials. LC 80-29182. (American Casebook Ser.). 518p. (C). 1981. 50.50 (*0-8299-2129-X*) West Pub.

***Nolan, Joseph T.** Let the Earth Rejoice! Prayers for Life, Prayers for Love. 128p. 2000. pap. 14.95 (*0-88347-466-2*, Pub. by T More) BookWorld.

Nolan, Joseph T. The World, the Church, & Preaching: The Best of Good News Commentary. 142p. (Orig.). 1996. pap. 19.95 (*0-940169-13-4*) Liturgical Pubns.

Nolan, Julie. Taking the Stairs: A Journal of Healing & Self Discovery. 197p. 1997. pap. 13.95 (*0-9659073-0-9*) Carousel Prodns.

***Nolan, Kathy.** Let's Learn Numbers. (J). (ps-3). 1999. write for info. (*1-929343-02-7*) Peer Tutor Pr.

Nolan, Keith W. The Battle for Hue Tet, 1968. LC 83-22962. (Illus.). 204p. 1996. pap. 14.00 (*0-89141-592-0*) Presidio Pr.

— The Battle for Saigon: Tet 1968. 1996. mass mkt. 6.99 (*0-671-52287-6*) PB.

— Sappers in the Wire. 1996. per. 5.99 (*0-671-00254-6*) PB.

— Sappers in the Wire: The Life & Death of Firebase Mary Ann. LC 95-12215. (Texas A&M University Military History Ser.: No. 45). (Illus.). 240p. (C). 1995. 24.95 (*0-89096-654-0*) Tex A&M Univ Pr.

Nolan, Keith William. Death Valley: The Summer Offensive, I Corps, August 1969. 352p. 1999. pap. 18.95 (*0-89141-665-X*) Presidio Pr.

— Into Cambodia. (Illus.). 496p. 1999. pap. 18.95 (*0-89141-673-0*, Pub. by Presidio Pr) Natl Bk Netwk.

***Nolan, Keith William.** Ripcord: Screaming Eagles under Siege, Vietnam 1970. (Illus.). 368p. 2000. 29.95 (*0-89141-642-0*) Presidio Pr.

Nolan, Keith William, jt. auth. see Birdwell, Dwight W.

Nolan, Ken. Masonry & Concrete Construction. rev. ed. LC 97-43739. (Illus.). 304p. (Orig.). 1998. pap. 28.50 (*1-57218-044-7*) Craftsman.

Nolan, Kevin M. Beyond Fear & Pride. LC 96-31413. (Open Door Bks.). 40p. (Orig.). 1996. pap. 1.95 (*1-56212-212-6*) CRC Pubns.

Nolan, Leslie, ed. The Modern Metropolis: Artists' Images of New York from the Museum of the City of New York. (Illus.). 48p. (Orig.). 1993. pap. 9.95 (*1-56584-066-6*, Pub. by New Press NY) Norton.

Nolan, Leslie & O'Connor, Francis V. Creative Lives: New York Paintings & Photographs by Maurice & Lee Sievan. LC 97-12581. (Illus.). 96p. 1997. pap. 25.00 (*0-910961-08-5*) Mus City NY.

Nolan, Leta A. The History of Spink County, SD Area. (Illus.). 481p. 1989. 55.00 (*0-88107-152-8*) Curtis Media.

Nolan, Lewis. Nolan-Miller Family History. LC 97-73438. (Illus.). write for info. (*0-89308-701-7*) Southern Hist Pr.

Nolan, Lucy A. The Lizard Man of Crabtree County. LC 98-47938. (Illus.). 32p. (J). (gr. k-3). 1999. 15.95 (*0-7614-5049-1*, Cav Child Bks) Marshall Cavendish.

Nolan, Madeena B. The Other Side of the Wall. 1973. 3.50 (*0-87129-397-8*, O21) Dramatic Pub.

Nolan, Maggi. Champagne... & Real Pain: Celebrities in Paris in the Fifties. (Illus.). 336p. 1998. pap. 19.95 (*0-88962-665-0*) Mosaic.

Nolan, Marie T. & Agustine, Sharon M., eds. Transplantation Nursing. LC 94-31323. 425p. (C). 1995. 59.95 (*0-8385-8989-8*, A8989-4, Apple Lange Med) McGraw.

Nolan, Mark. The Instant Marketing Plan: How to Create a Money Grabbing Marketing Plan in Just One Day. 2nd ed. LC 98-18940. 186p. (Orig.). 1998. pap. 15.95 (*0-940673-57-6*) Puma Pub Co.

Nolan, Mark, ed. & pref. see Allen, James.

Nolan, Mary. Learning Success Kit. 272p. 1995. ring bd. 49.95 (*0-7872-0577-X*) Kendall-Hunt.

— Visions of Modernity: American Business & the Modernization of Germany. LC 93-20943. 336p. 1994. pap. text 24.95 (*0-19-508875-1*) OUP.

— Visions of Modernity: Fordism & Economic Reform in the Weimar Republic. LC 93-20943. 336p. 1994. text 70.00 (*0-19-507021-6*) OUP.

— Your Childbirth Class: A Comprehensive, Parent-Centered Guide to Birth Options. LC 98-12054. (National Childbirth Trust Guide Ser.). (Illus.). 240p. 1998. pap. 12.95 (*1-55561-127-3*) Fisher Bks.

Nolan, Mary L. & Nolan, Sidney. Christian Pilgrimage in Modern Western Europe. LC 88-14364. (Studies in Religion). (Illus.). xxii, 422p. (C). 1992. reprint ed. pap. 19.95 (*0-8078-4389-X*) U of NC Pr.

Nolan, Melanie, jt. ed. see Daley, Caroline.

Nolan, Michael. Aquinas' Philosophy of Man & Woman. rev. ed. 192p. 1998. boxed set 55.00 (*1-85182-157-0*, Pub. by Four Cts Pr) Intl Spec Bk.

— Smileage: Fun for the Highway Hypnotized. LC 97-6312. 192p. (Orig.). 1997. pap. 8.95 (*1-888952-43-1*) Cumberland Hse.

Nolan, Michael & Grant, Gordon, eds. Regular Respite: An Evaluation of a Shoptial Rota Bed Scheme for Elderly People. 312p. (C). 1992. 75.00 (*0-86242-115-2*, Pub. by Age Concern Eng) St Mut.

Nolan, Michael, ed. see Rowley, William & Heywood, Thomas.

***Nolan, Michael F.** Glimpse of Golden Mountain. Frances, Dee, ed. 1999. pap. 10.00 (*1-885519-19-2*) DDDD Pubns.

Nolan, Michael F. Introduction to the Neurologic Examination. (Illus.). 224p. (C). 1995. pap. text 23.95 (*0-8036-0017-8*) Davis Co.

Nolan, Michael J. PageMaker 5.0 Expert Techniques (Macintosh Edition) (Illus.). 208p. 1993. 34.95 (*1-56830-017-4*) Hayden.

Nolan, Michael J., jt. auth. see LeWinter, Renee.

Nolan, Michael S. Fundamentals of Air Traffic Control. 560p. (C). 1990. pap. 40.95 (*0-534-12246-9*) Wadsworth Pub.

— Fundamentals of Air Traffic Control. 2nd ed. 558p. 1993. pap. 47.00 (*0-534-23058-X*) Wadsworth Pub.

Nolan, Mike. Understanding Family Care: A Multi-Dimensional Model of Caring & Coping. LC 96-20513. 192p. 1996. pap. 27.95 (*0-335-19573-3*) OpUniv Pr.

Nolan, Mike, jt. auth. see Keady, John.

Nolan, P., et al, eds. Applications of Artificial Intelligence in Engineering XIII. LC 99-203398. (Software Studies: No. 1). 200p. 1998. 312.00 incl. cd-rom (*1-85312-596-2*, 5962) Computational Mech MA.

Nolan, Pat, tr. see Soupault, Philippe.

Nolan, Patricia, jt. auth. see Pearson, Mark.

Nolan, Patricia A., jt. auth. see Nolan, Patrick.

Nolan, Patrick & Lenski, Gerhard E. Human Societies: An Introduction to Macrosociology. 8th ed. LC 98-18510. 496p. 1998. 68.13 (*0-07-289132-7*) McGraw.

Nolan, Patrick & Nolan, Patricia A. Against the Odds: The True Story of Michele, A Cancer Survivor. 256p. 1995. per. 14.95 (*1-887170-05-7*) Alchemy Pub.

Nolan, Paul T. Folk Tale Plays Round the World. LC 82-14188. (J). (ps-12). 1982. pap. 15.00 (*0-8238-0253-1*) Kalmbach.

Nolan, Paula R. Zucchini at It's Best: 200 Delicious Ways to Use Zucchini. (Illus.). 90p. (Orig.). 1995. pap. 9.95 (*0-9647464-0-9*) P Nolan.

***Nolan, Peggy.** The Spy Who Came in from the Sea. LC 99-32933. 129p. (J). (gr. 4-8). 2000. 14.95 (*1-56164-186-3*) Pineapple Pr.

Nolan, Peter. State & Market in the Chinese Economy: Essays on Controversial Issues LC 93-198434. (Studies in Economic & Social Theory). xii, 338 p. 1993. write for info. (*0-333-55238-5*) Macmillan.

Nolan, Peter & Fureng, D., eds. Market Forces in China: Competition & Small Business: The Wenzhou Debate. LC 89-70608. (Illus.). 208p. (C). 1997. pap. 19.95 (*0-86232-833-0*, Pub. by St Martin); text 49.95 (*0-86232-832-2*, Pub. by St Martin) St Martin.

Nolan, Peter, jt. ed. see Ha-Joon, Chang.

Nolan, Peter J. Fundamentals of College Physics. 1088p. (C). 1992. text, student ed. 23.75 (*0-697-12238-7*, WCB McGr Hill) McGrw-H Hghr Educ.

— Fundamentals of College Physics. 1088p. (C). 1992. text. write for info. (*0-697-12145-3*, WCB McGr Hill) McGrw-H Hghr Educ.

— Fundamentals of College Physics, 2 vols. 2nd ed. 18p. (C). 1994. text, student ed. write for info. (*0-697-25811-4*, WCB McGr Hill) McGrw-H Hghr Educ.

— Fundamentals of College Physics. 2nd ed. (C). 1995. student ed., ring bd. write for info. (*0-697-29570-2*, WCB McGr Hill) McGrw-H Hghr Educ.

— Fundamentals of College Physics, 2 vols., Set. 2nd ed. LC 94-70898. 1136p. (C). 1995. text. write for info. (*0-697-23138-0*, WCB McGr Hill) McGrw-H Hghr Educ.

— Fundamentals of College Physics, Vol. I. 2nd ed. (C). 1995. text, student ed. write for info. (*0-697-29571-0*, WCB McGr Hill) McGrw-H Hghr Educ.

— Fundamentals of College Physics, Vol. II. 2nd ed. 616p. (C). 1994. text. write for info. (*0-697-24393-1*, WCB McGr Hill) McGrw-H Hghr Educ.

Nolan, Peter J. & Bigliani, Raymond. Experiments in Physics. 2nd ed. 416p. (C). 1994. text. write for info. (*0-697-24225-0*, WCB McGr Hill) McGrw-H Hghr Educ.

Nolan, Phil. The Pop-Up Buck Rogers: Strange Adventures in the Spider Ship. LC 94-71381. (Illus.). 24p. (J). (gr. 4-7). 1994. 14.95 (*1-55709-236-2*) Applewood.

***Nolan, Ray.** Hang-Rope at Harmony. large type ed. 272p. 1999. pap. 18.99 (*0-7089-5541-X*, Linford) Ulverscroft.

— Satan's Saddlemate. large type ed. 280p. 1999. pap. 18.99 (*0-7089-5553-3*, Linford) Ulverscroft.

— Trouble in Twilight. 248p. 2000. 18.99 (*0-7089-5709-9*) Ulverscroft.

Nolan, Riall. Development Anthropology. 224p. (C). 2001. pap. 37.50 (*0-8133-0983-2*); pap. text 19.95 (*0-8133-0984-0*) Westview.

Nolan, Riall W. Building the Global Village. 1999. pap. 10.95 (*0-452-27523-7*, Plume) Dutton Plume.

— Communicating & Adapting Across Cultures: Living & Working in the Global Village: Living & Working in the Global Village. LC 98-44202. 216p. 1999. 55.00 (*0-89789-660-2*, Bergin & Garvey) Greenwood.

Nolan, Richard J., Jr. MBA Golf: The Book for MBAs Who Love Golf. (Illus.). ix, 150p. (Orig.). (C). 1996. pap. 16.95 (*0-9653401-0-4*) MBA Golf.

Nolan, Richard L. & Croson, David C. Creative Destruction: A Six-Stage Process for Transforming the Organization. 272p. 1995. 29.95 (*0-87584-498-7*) Harvard Busn.

Nolan, Richard L., jt. ed. see Bradley, Stephen P.

Nolan, Richard T. & Kirkpatrick, Frank G. Living Issues in Ethics. 388p. (C). 1982. 34.50 (*0-534-01140-3*) Wadsworth Pub.

Nolan, Rick, intro. International Electronics Packaging Conference Proceedings, 1993. (Conference Proceedings Ser.: Vol. 13). (Illus.). (Orig.). 1993. pap. text 84.95 (*1-880433-15-X*) Intl Elect Pack.

Nolan, Rita. Cognitive Practices: Human Language & Human Knowledge. 200p. 1994. pap. 26.95 (*0-631-18974-2*) Blackwell Pubs.

Nolan-Rosager, Sharon, ed. see Behling, Thomas A.

Nolan, Sidney, jt. auth. see Nolan, Mary L.

***Nolan, Simon.** As Good As It Gets. 2000. pap. 12.00 (*0-7043-8108-7*, Pub. by Quartet) Interlink Pub.

Nolan, Thomas E. Primary Care for the Obstetrician & Gynecologist. LC 95-46498. (Illus.). 349p. 1996. pap. 59.95 (*0-471-12279-3*) Wiley.

Nolan, Thomas J., Jr. Retire Easy! A Blueprint for Building Personal Wealth. (Illus.). 1984. 16.95 (*0-13-778952-1*, Busn); pap. 7.95 (*0-13-778945-9*, Busn) P-H.

Nolan, Thomas L., Jr. Aging Smarter. (Illus.). 156p. (Orig.). 1991. pap. 12.95 (*0-9630727-0-6*) Spring Brook.

Nolan, Thomas W. & Institute for Healthcare Improvement Staff. Reducing Delays & Waiting Times Throughout the Healthcare System. LC 96-79933. (Breakthrough Series Guide). 187 p. 1996. 49.95 (*1-890070-00-9*) Inst for Hlthcare.

Nolan, Tim. Plays about Presidents. 128p. (J). 1997. pap. 16.95 (*0-590-48195-9*) Scholastic Inc.

Nolan, Timothy. Read-Aloud Plays: Civil War; Five Short Plays for the Classroom with Backround Information. 1999. pap. text 10.95 (*0-590-02897-9*) Scholastic Inc.

Nolan, Timothy M., et al. Applied Strategic Planning: The Consultant's Kit. LC 92-8097. (Illus.). 555p. 1992. ring bd. 495.00 (*0-88390-310-5*, Pfffr & Co) Jossey-Bass.

— Plan or Die! 10 Keys to Organizational Success. Padgett, JoAnn, ed. LC 92-51082. (Illus.). 178p. 1993. 29.95 (*0-88390-377-6*, Pfffr & Co); pap. 19.95 (*0-89384-207-9*, Pfffr & Co) Jossey-Bass.

Nolan, Tom. Ross Macdonald: A Biography. LC 98-48225. (Illus.). 496p. 1999. 31.50 (*0-684-81217-7*) Scribner.

Nolan, Val, Jr. Ecology & Behavior of the Prairie Warbler Dendroica Discolor. 595p. 1978. 45.00 (*0-943610-26-5*) Am Ornithologists.

Nolan, Val, Jr., et al, eds. Current Ornithology, Vol. 14. (Illus.). 286p. (C). 1998. 107.00 (*0-306-45739-3*, Plenum Trade) Perseus Pubng.

Nolan, Val, Jr. & Ketterson, Ellen, eds. Current Ornithology, Vol. 13. (Illus.). 376p. (C). 1997. text 89.50 (*0-306-45473-4*, Kluwer Plenum) Kluwer Academic.

Nolan, Virginia E. & Ursin, Edmund, eds. Understanding Enterprise Liability: Rethinking Tort Reform for the 21st Century. LC 94-2881. 272p. (C). 1994. text 69.95 (*1-56639-230-6*) Temple U Pr.

Nolan, W. C. Cemetery Inscriptions of Union Parish, Louisiana, Vol. I. 190p. (Orig.). 1988. pap. 16.00 (*1-57088-020-4*) J&W Ent.

— Cemetery Inscriptions of Union Parish, Louisiana, Vol. II. 192p. (Orig.). 1988. pap. 16.00 (*1-57088-021-2*) J&W Ent.

— Cemetery Inscriptions of Union Parish, Louisiana, Vol. III. 200p. (Orig.). 1988. pap. 16.00 (*1-57088-022-0*) J&W Ent.

— Cemetery Inscriptions of Union Parish, Louisiana, Vol. IV. 188p. (Orig.). 1988. pap. 16.00 (*1-57088-023-9*) J&W Ent.

Nolan, William. Fassadinin: Land, Settlement, & Society in Southeast Ireland, 1600-1850 LC 80-450021. xvi, 259p. 1979. write for info. (*0-906602-00-9*) Geography Pubns.

Nolan, William, et al, eds. Donegal: History & Society. LC 96-102534. (County History & Society Ser.). (Illus.). 920p. 1995. pap. 79.95 (*0-906602-45-9*, Pub. by Geography Pubns) Irish Bks Media.

Nolan, William & Hannigan, Ken, eds. Wicklow: History & Society. LC 95-122256. (County History & Society Ser.). (Illus.). 1005p. 1994. pap. 79.95 (*0-906602-30-0*, Pub. by Geography Pubns) Irish Bks Media.

Nolan, William & McGrath, Thomas, eds. Tipperary: History & Society. (Illus.). 493p. 1997. reprint ed. 79.95 (*0-906602-03-3*, Pub. by Geography Pubns) Irish Bks Media.

Nolan, William & O'Neill, Timothy P. Offaly: History & Society. LC 99-165696. (County History & Society Ser.). (Illus.). xxxvi, 1000p. 1998. 85.00 (*0-906602-90-4*, Pub. by Geography Pubns) Irish Bks Media.

Nolan, William & Power, Thomas P., eds. Waterford: History & Society. (County History & Society Ser.). (Illus.). 754p. 1992. pap. 79.95 (*0-906602-20-3*, Pub. by Geography Pubns) Irish Bks Media.

Nolan, William & Simms, Anngret. Irish Towns: A Guide to Sources. LC 98-167370. 249 p. 1998. write for info. (*0-906602-26-2*) Geography Pubns.

Nolan, William & Simms, Anngret, eds. Irish Towns: A Guide to Sources. (Illus.). 249p. 1998. pap. 19.95 (*0-906602-31-9*, Pub. by Geography Pubns) Irish Bks Media.

***Nolan, William F.** California Sorcery: A Group Celebration. 1998. 40.00 (*1-881475-70-0*) Cemetery Dance.

Nolan, William F. Helltracks. 256p. (Orig.). 1991. mass mkt. 4.50 (*0-380-75746-X*, Avon Bks) Morrow Avon.

N

— Legends & Lovers: Fourteen Profiles. LC 88-36791. (Borgo Bioviews Ser.: No. 4). 152p. (C). 1997. reprint ed. pap. 19.00 (*0-89370-440-7*) Millefleurs.
— Logan's Run. Amereon Ltd. Staff, ed. 1985. 18.95 (*0-8488-0103-2*) Amereon Ltd.
— Look Out for Space. 192p. (Orig.). 1985. pap. 4.95 (*0-930330-20-X*) Intl Polygonics.
— Marble Orchard. 224p. 1995. 20.95 (*0-312-14011-8*) St Martin.
— Max Brand: Western Giant the Life & Times of Frederick Schiller Faust. 175p. 1986. pap. 10.95 (*0-87972-292-4*) Bowling Green Univ Popular Press.
— Max Brand: Western Giant the Life & Times of Frederick Schiller Faust. LC 86-70192. 175p. 1986. 22.95 (*0-87972-291-6*) Bowling Green Univ Popular Press.
— Phil Hill: Yankee Champion: First American to Win the Driving Championship of the World. 2nd rev. ed. LC 96-32029. (Illus.). 280p. 1996. 39.50 (*1-888978-10-4*) Brown Fox Bks.
— Sharks Never Sleep. LC 98-19396. 288p. 1998. text 22.95 (*0-312-19331-9*) St Martin.
— Space for Hire. 200p. 1985. reprint ed. pap. 4.95 (*0-930330-19-6*) Intl Polygonics.
— Things Beyond Midnight. Cover, Arthur B., ed. Date not set. pap. write for info. (*1-893475-25-5*) Alexander Pubg.
— Three for Space. 1992. 19.95 (*0-936071-32-X*); pap. 9.95 (*0-936071-33-8*) Gryphon Pubns.
— The Work of Charles Beaumont: An Annotated Bibliography & Guide. 2nd ed. Clarke, Boden, ed. LC 90-15043. (Bibliographies of Modern Authors Ser.: No. 6). 92p. 1990. pap. 17.00 (*0-8095-1517-2*) Millefleurs.
Nolan, William F., ed. Max Brand's Best Western Stories, Vol. II. 192p. 1986. mass mkt. 2.95 (*0-446-34170-3*, Pub. by Warner Bks) Little.
Nolan, William F. & Johnson, George C. Logan's Run. 1976. 18.95 (*0-8488-0102-4*) Amereon Ltd.
— Logan's Run. 160p. 1992. reprint ed. lib. bdg. 25.95 (*0-89966-896-8*) Buccaneer Bks.
Nolan-Woods, Enid, jt. auth. see Broukal, Milada.
Nolan, Yvette, et al. Beyond the Pale: Dramatic Writing from First Nations: Writers of Colour. LC 97-105322. 240p. 1997. pap. text 19.95 (*0-88754-542-4*, Pub. by Playwrights) Consort Bk Sales.
***Noland.** The Lessons of Aloha: Stories of the Human Spirit. LC 99-75822. (Illus.). xvi, 128p. 1999. pap. 18.95 (*0-9631154-8-0*) Watermark.
— Sigmund Freud Revisited. LC 99-29542. 1999. 32.00 (*0-8057-1684-X*, Twyne) Mac Lib Ref.
Noland, Carrie. Poetry at Stake: Lyric Aesthetics & the Challenge of Technology. 280p. 55.00 (*0-691-00416-1*, Pub. by Princeton U Pr) Cal Prin Full Svc.
Noland, Carrie. Poetry at Stake: Lyric Aesthetics & the Challenge of Technology. LC 99-25333. (Illus.). 280p. 1999. 19.95 (*0-691-00417-X*, Pub. by Princeton U Pr) Cal Prin Full Svc.
***Noland, David.** Outside Adventure Travel: Trekking. 224p. 2000. reprint ed. pap. 21.00 (*0-393-32072-3*) Norton.
Noland, David. Travels along the Edge: From Crossing the Sahara to Bicycling Through Vietnam - Ultimate Adventures for the Modern Nomad. LC 97-11594. 1997. pap. 14.00 (*0-679-76344-9*) Random.
Noland, Dianne A. & Bolin, Kirsten. Perennials for the Landscape. LC 99-71696. (Illus.). 216p. 1998. pap. 31.25 (*0-8134-3149-2*, 3149) Interstate.
Noland, J., jt. auth. see Noland, Mimi.
Noland, Jane, ed. see Wolter, Dwight L.
Noland, Jane T. A Day at a Time: Daily Reflections for Recovering People. 384p. (Orig.). reprint ed. pap. 10.00 (*1-56838-036-4*) Hazelden.
— What's So Funny about Getting Old? LC 94-25971. (Illus.). 128p. 1994. 7.00 (*0-671-51152-1*) S&S Trade.
Noland, Joe. A Little Greatness. LC 98-73190. 223p. 1998. pap. 6.00 (*0-9657601-4-6*, Crest Books) SANP.
***Noland, Joe.** No Limits Together - Vision 7007. Flagg, Deborah, ed. 242p. 2000. text. write for info. (*0-9675393-1-5*); pap. text. write for info. (*0-9675393-0-7*) Duden.
Noland, Karen L. Friends of the Menehune. (J). 9.95 (*0-9643674-0-8*) Kaukini Ranch.
Noland, Marcus. Pacific Basin Developing Countries: Prospects for the Future. fac. ed. LC 90-25083. 248p. 1990. reprint ed. pap. 76.90 (*0-7837-8295-0*, 204907700009) Bks Demand.

Noland, Marcus & Institute for International Economics Staff. Economic Integration of Korean Peninsula. LC 97-41152. (Special Report Ser.). 1998. pap. 16.95 (0-88132-255-5) Inst Intl Eco.
The North Korean economy cannot sustain its population. Absent fundamental economic reforms, it will never be able to do so. Hence, North Korea will require sizable external support for the foreseeable future. South Korea, China, Japan & the United States have been willing to provide this support because they fear a collapse in the North, or even worse, a lashing out that would unleash war on the peninsula & put millions of people in Asia in jeopardy - including thousands of US troops stationed in South Korea & Japan.The status quo is thus closer to extortion than charity. In this volume, a diverse group of contributors analyze prospective developments on the Korean peninsula. The authors address the three broad strategic possibilities of war, collapse & gradual adjustment. Four immediate policy issues are then considered: the current economic conditions & policies in the North, the food crisis, the nuclear energy/nuclear weapons issue & the possibility of large-scale refugee flows. Finally, the volume considers several longer-run issues concerning the inevitable integration of the peninsula: the potential relevance of the German experience, the costs & benefits of economic unification between North & South Korea & the possible role of the international financial institutions in funding the new arrangement. The volume concludes with recommendations for policymakers,especially in the United States & South Korea, from the preceding analyses. *Publisher Paid Annotation.*

Noland, Marcus, jt. auth. see Bergsten, C. Fred.
Noland, Mimi & Noland, J. Young Winners' Way. 1996. pap. 3.25 (*0-89638-069-6*) Hazelden.
Noland, Richard W., ed. see Lesser, Simon O.
Noland, Rory. Nurturing Your Soul. LC 99-18211. 2000. pap. 14.99 (*0-310-22471-3*) Zondervan.
Noland, Thomas, jt. auth. see Robinson, Leonard, Jr.
Noland, Wayland E., ed. Organic Syntheses: Collective Volumes, Vol. 6, Vols. 50-59. (Organic Synthesis Ser.). 1232p. 1988. 135.00 (*0-471-85243-0*) Wiley.
Noland, Wayland E., ed. see Gilman, H.
Noland, Wayland E., jt. ed. see Horning, E. C.
Noland, Wayland E., ed. see Rabjohn, N.
Noland, William E. & Bakke, E. Wight. Workers Wanted: Study of Employers' Hiring Policies, Preferences, & Practices in New Haven & Charlotte. Stein, Leon, ed. LC 77-70521. (Illus.). 1977. reprint ed. lib. bdg. 23.95 (*0-405-10189-9*) Ayer.
Nolasco-Carrandi, Guadalupe, tr. see Thompson-Peters, Flossie E.
Nolasco, Domingo F. Three Tombs & Other Stories. 97p. (Orig.). (C). 1992. pap. 6.75 (*971-10-0325-2*, Pub. by New Day Pub) Cellar.
Nolasco, J. B. FEU Class '61 Yearbook: Medical Alumni. Chua, Philip S., ed. LC 94-94310. (Illus.). 153p. 1994. 65.00 (*0-9641472-4-6*) P S Chua.
Nolasco, J. B., jt. auth. see Chua, Philip S.
Nolasco, Pete. Making It Easy... Southwest Desserts. 1998. pap. text 18.95 (*1-55622-650-0*, Rep of TX Pr) Wordware Pub.
Nolasco, Rob. American Wow! Level 2: American Window on the World. (Illus.). 1993. pap. text, teacher ed. 6.95 (*0-19-434549-1*) OUP.
Nolasco, Rob & Arthur, Lois. Conversation. Maley, Alan, ed. (Illus.). 160p. 1987. pap. text 13.95 (*0-19-437096-8*) OUP.
***Nolbay, E. M.** America Gonnif. LC 99-91457. 337p. 1999. 25.00 (*0-7388-0812-1*); pap. 18.00 (*0-7388-0813-X*) Xlibris Corp.
Nold, Chip, et al. The Insiders' Guide to Louisville, Kentucky. 2nd ed. (Insiders' Guide Travel Ser.). (Illus.). 343p. 1997. pap. 15.95 (*1-57380-043-0*, The Insiders Guide) Falcon Pub Inc.
Nold, John. Willing Victims. 64p. 1987. 9.95 (*0-920806-89-9*, Pub. by Penumbra Pr) U of Toronto Pr.
Nold, Robert. Penstemons. LC 98-51574. (Illus.). 307p. 1999. 29.95 (*0-88192-429-6*) Timber.
Nolde, Eduard. Reise Nach Innerarabien, Kurdistan und Armenien, 1892. (Illus.). xvi, 272p. reprint ed. write for info. (*0-318-71542-2*) G Olms Pubs.
Nolde, John. Ezra Pound & China. (Ezra Pound Scholarship Ser.). 1996. pap. 12.95 (*0-943373-32-8*) Natl Poet Foun.
Noldeke, T. Sketches from Eastern History. 292p. 1985. 220.00 (*1-85077-065-4*, Pub. by Darf Pubs Ltd) St Mut.
Noldeke, Theodor. Beitrage Zur Kenntnis der Poesie der Alten Araber. xxiv, 244p. 1967. reprint ed. write for info. (*0-318-71540-6*) G Olms Pubs.
— Geschichte des Qorans, 3 vols. in 1. xxxi, 837p. 1981. reprint ed. write for info. (*0-318-71541-4*) G Olms Pubs.
— Orientalische Skizzen. (GER.). ix, 304p. 1974. reprint ed. 65.00 (*3-487-05207-5*) G Olms Pubs.
— The Quran: An Introductory Essay. Newman, N. A., ed. 40p. 1992. pap. 5.95 (*0-944788-93-9*) IBRI.
Noldge, G., et al. Cholangiography after Orthotopic Liver Transplantation. LC 95-46876. 104p. 1995. pap. 75.00 (*3-540-60491-X*) Spr-Verlag.
Nole, Joseph P., II. West Orange. LC 98-86554. (Images of America Ser.). (Illus.). 128p. 1998. pap. 16.99 (*0-7524-1293-0*) Arcadia Publng.
***Nolen.** Plantzilla. 2002. write for info. (*0-15-202412-3*) Harcourt.
Nolen & Hoeksema. Abnormal Psychology. 256p. 1997. pap. 22.50 (*0-697-25271-X*) McGraw.
Nolen, Anita L. & Coutts, Mary C., eds. International Directory of Bioethics Organizations. 1993. pap. 20.00 (*1-883913-11-X*) Geo U Kennedy Inst.
***Nolen, Anne C. & Whitmore, Marilyn P., eds.** Instruction & Training for Enhanced Reference Service Using Hands-On Active Learning Techniques: Major Topics & Their Reference Resources. LC 98-66459. (Active Learning Ser.: No. 3). 220p. 1999. pap. 45.00 incl. disk (*0-9652711-4-5*) Lib Instruct.
Nolen, Ben M. & Narramore, Robert E. Rivers & Rapids. rev. ed. (Illus.). lib. bdg. 19.95 (*0-9632403-9-0*) Overview Pr.
Nolen, Ben M. & Narramore, Robert E. Rivers & Rapids: A Very Complete Canoeing, Rafting & Fishing Guide to the Streams & Rivers of Texas, Arkansas & Oklahoma, Vol. 8. (Illus.). 144p. (Orig.). 1992. pap. 13.95 (*0-9632403-8-2*) Rivers & Rapids.
***Nolen, Billy James.** Parents, Teens & Drugs. LC 99-91298. 168p. 2000. pap. 14.95 (*1-56167-575-X*) Am Literary Pr.
Nolen, Claude H. The Negro's Image in the South: The Anatomy of White Supremacy. LC 67-17843. 252p. reprint ed. 78.20 (*0-8357-9792-9*, 20110710074) Bks Demand.
Nolen, Evelyn T., jt. ed. see Boles, John B.
Nolen-Harold, Jerdine. Big Jabe. LC 99-38001. (Illus.). 32p. (YA). (ps-3). 2000. 15.89 (*0-688-13663-X*) Morrow Avon.
***Nolen-Harold, Jerdine.** In My Momma's Kitchen. LC 93-37433. (Illus.). 32p. (J). (ps up). 1999. 15.95 (*0-688-12760-6*, Wm Morrow); 15.89 (*0-688-12761-4*) Morrow Avon.
Nolen, Herman C., jt. auth. see Beckman, Theodore N.
Nolen-Hoeksema. Abnormal Psychology. 1997. 66.25 (*0-07-561315-8*) McGraw.
Nolen-Hoeksema, Susan. Abnormal Psychology. LC 97-16976. 736p. (C). 1997. text. write for info. (*0-697-23118-6*, WCB McGr Hill) McGrw-H Hghr Educ.
— Abnormal Psychology. 2nd ed. 2000. 50.25 (*0-697-36193-4*) McGraw.
***Nolen-Hoeksema, Susan.** Abnormal Psychology. 2nd ed. LC 00-37982. 2001. pap. write for info. (*0-07-235799-1*) McGraw.
Nolen-Hoeksema, Susan. Sex Differences in Depression. LC 89-27303. 270p. 1990. 42.50 (*0-8047-1640-4*) Stanford U Pr.
— Sex Differences in Depression. 270p. (C). 1993. pap. 14.95 (*0-8047-2180-7*) Stanford U Pr.
Nolen-Hoeksema, Susan & Hoeksema. Abnormal Psychology. 2nd ed. 2000. pap. text 13.80 (*0-697-36197-7*) McGraw.
Nolen-Hoeksema, Susan & Larson, Judith. Coping with Loss. LC 98-35307. 300p. 1998. 29.95 (*0-8058-2139-2*); pap. write for info. (*0-8058-2140-6*) L Erlbaum Assocs.
Nolen, James. Computer-Automated Process Planning for World-Class Manufacturing. (Manufacturing Engineering & Materials Processing Ser.: Vol. 29). (Illus.). 448p. 1989. text 165.00 (*0-8247-7918-5*) Dekker.
Nolen, Jerdine. Big Jabe. LC 99-38001. (Illus.). 32p. (J). (gr. 1-4). 2000. 15.95 (*0-688-13662-1*) HarpC.
— Harvey Potter's Balloon Farm. LC 91-38129. (J). (ps-3). 1994. 16.00 (*0-688-07887-7*); lib. bdg. 15.93 (*0-688-07888-5*) Lothrop.
***Nolen, Jerdine.** Harvey Potter's Balloon Farm. 32p. (J). (ps up). 1998. mass mkt. 5.95 (*0-688-15845-5*, Wm Morrow) Morrow Avon.
Nolen, Jerdine. Harvey Potter's Balloon Farm. (J). 1998. 10.15 (*0-606-13100-0*, Pub. by Turtleback) Demco.
***Nolen, Jerdine.** Hewitt Anderson's Big Life. LC 98-14039. 2002. write for info. (*0-15-201669-4*) Harcourt.
Nolen, Jerdine. Irene's Wish. LC 98-31427. (J). 2000. 20.01 (*0-15-202024-1*) Harcourt.
— Max & Jax in Second Grade. LC 98-5544. (Easy Reader Ser.). (Illus.). (J). 2000. 14.00 (*0-15-201668-6*) Harcourt.
— Max & Jax in Second Grade. 2002. write for info. (*0-15-201672-4*) Harcourt.
— Raising Dragons. LC 95-43307. (Illus.). 32p. (J). (ps-3). 1998. 16.00 (*0-15-201288-5*) Harcourt.
***Nolen, Jerdine & Tilley, Debbie.** Lauren McGill's Pickle Musem. LC 00-9577. (Illus.). (J). 2003. write for info. (*0-15-202279-1*, Pub. by Harcourt) Harcourt.
Nolen, Roland D. Beyond Performance: What Employees REALLY Need to Know to Climb the Success Ladder. LC 99-60318. (Illus.). 168p. 1999. 20.00 (*0-9647697-5-1*) New Persp IL.
Nolen, William A. The Making of a Surgeon. 269p. 1990. reprint ed. pap. 16.00 (*0-922811-46-6*, Pub. by Mid-List) SPD-Small Pr Dist.
Nolen, William A. The Making of a Surgeon. 2nd ed. 288p. 1990. reprint ed. 17.95 (*0-922811-05-9*) Mid-List.
Nolen, William A., et al. Refractory Depression: Current Strategies & Future Directions. LC 93-49532. 252p. 1994. 230.00 (*0-471-94315-0*) Wiley.
Noles, Bj. Cookbook for a Career Mother. (Illus.). 180p. 1983. pap. 8.95 (*0-9613684-0-3*) B J Noles.
Noles, Gwendolyn & Parker, Martha. Test Preparation Guide for Life & Health Insurance Underwriting. 107p. pap. 24.00 (*1-57974-024-3*, Pub. by Life Office) PBD Inc.
Nolet, Andree, jt. auth. see Campbell, Carmen.
Nolet, Guust, ed. Seismic Tomography: With Applications in Global Seismology & Exploration Geophysics. (C). 1987. pap. text 87.00 (*90-277-2583-7*); lib. bdg. 156.50 (*90-277-2521-7*) Kluwer Academic.
***Nolet, Victor & McLaughlin, Margaret J.** Accessing the General Curriculum: Making It Happen for Students with Disabilities. 184p. 2000. pap. 32.95 (*0-7619-7670-1*); lib. bdg. 69.95 (*0-7619-7669-8*) Corwin Pr.
Noley, Homer. First White Frost: Native Americans & United Methodism. 276p. 1991. pap. 8.97 (*0-687-13051-4*) Abingdon.
Nolf, D. Otolithi Piscium. (Handbook of Paleoichthyology: Vol. 10). (Illus.). 145p. 1985. pap. text 128.70 (*3-437-30399-6*) Lubrecht & Cramer.
Nolf, D. & Stringer, G. L. Bulletins of American Paleontology Vol. 102, No. 340: Neogene Paleontology in the Northern Dominican Republic, 14. Otoliths of Teleostean Fishes. 1992. 23.00 (*0-87710-424-7*) Paleo Res.
Nolf, Nancy, jt. auth. see Yohannan, Kohle.
Nolf, Pam, ed. see Kaiser, Hal.
Nolfi. Basics Legal Research. 1992. 11.00 (*0-02-800286-5*) Glencoe.
Nolfi, Edward A. Basic Wills, Trusts, & Estates. LC 94-13452. (Legal Studies). 1994. 30.00 (*0-02-801338-7*) Glencoe.
Nolfi, Edward A. & Tepper, Pamela R. Basic Legal Research & Writing. LC 92-25750. (Legal Studies). 1992. 45.00 (*0-02-801276-3*) Glencoe.
Nolfi, Kristine. My Experience with Living Food. 23p. 1994. reprint ed. spiral bd. 10.00 (*0-7873-1034-4*) Hlth Research.
— Raw Food Treatment of Cancer & Other Diseases. 8p. 1996. reprint ed. spiral bd. 10.00 (*0-7873-1028-X*) Hlth Research.
***Nolfi, Stefano & Floreano, Dario.** Evolutionary Robotics: The Biology, Intelligence & Technology of Self-Organizing Machines. LC 00-28172. (Intelligent Robotics & Autonomous Agents Ser.). (Illus.). 384p. 2000. 50.00 (*0-262-14070-5*, Bradford Bks) MIT Pr.
***Nolfi Torok, Tricia, et al.** Advising Student Governments: Models for Practice & Strategies for Success. (Illus.). 127p. (C). 2000. pap. text 25.00 (*1-890271-02-0*) Natl Assn Camp.
Nolfo, Ennio Di, see Di Nolfo, Ennio, ed.
Nolfo-Wheeler, Amy A. All God's Creatures Go to Heaven. LC 96-68622. (Illus.). 24p. (J). (ps-12). 1996. 19.95 (*0-9652531-0-4*) Noel Studio.
Nolhac, Pierre de, jt. auth. see Du Bellay, Joachim.
Nolin, Mary Jo. National Household Education Survey: An Overview of the National Household Education Survey. LC 97-191495. 34p. 1997. pap. 4.25 (*0-16-049076-6*) USGPO.
— Student Participation in Community Service Activity: National Household Education Survey. LC 97-171801. 52p. 1997. pap. 5.00 (*0-16-049044-8*) USGPO.
— Use of Cognitive Laboratories & Recorded Interviews in the National Household Education Survey. 40p. 1996. pap. 4.00 (*0-16-048830-3*) USGPO.
Nolk, Brian, ed. Fourth International Ferro Alloys Conference Proceedings. 288p. (Orig.). 1985. pap. text. write for info. (*0-913333-05-0*) Metal Bulletin.
— Titanium & Superalloys II: Battling the Economics Elements. 188p. 1984. pap. text. write for info. (*0-913333-04-2*) Metal Bulletin.
Noll, A. Michael. Highway of Dreams: A Critical View along the Information Superhighway. LC 96-41620. (LEA's Telecommunications Ser.). 190p. 1996. text 49.95 (*0-8058-2557-6*); pap. text 24.50 (*0-8058-2558-4*) L Erlbaum Assocs.
— Introduction to Telecommunication Electronics. 2nd ed. LC 95-19091. 246p. 1995. pap. 56.00 (*0-89006-828-3*) Artech Hse.
— Introduction to Telephones & Telephone Systems. 190p. 1986. pap. text 35.00 (*0-89006-203-X*) Artech Hse.
— Introduction to Telephones & Telephone Systems. 3rd ed. LC 99-10309. (Telecommunications Library). 280p. 1999. 55.00 (*1-58053-000-1*) Artech Hse.
Noll, Anna C. Earthly Delights: Garden Imagery in Contemporary Art. LC 88-81964. (Illus.). 46p. (Orig.). 1988. pap. 10.00 (*0-917185-01-3*) Fort Wayne.
— A Point of View: Twentieth-Century Art from a Long Island Collection. LC 90-84052. (Illus.). 48p. (Orig.). 1990. pap. text 9.95 (*1-879195-05-4*) Heckscher Mus.
Noll, Archbishop Francis. Father Smith Instructs Jackson. rev. ed. Nevins, Albert J., ed. LC 75-628. 295p. 1975. pap. 8.95 (*0-87973-864-2*) Our Sunday Visitor.
Noll, Bink. The House: Poems. fac. ed. LC 84-12590. 64p. 1984. reprint ed. pap. 30.00 (*0-7837-7812-0*, 204756800007) Bks Demand.
Noll, Chuck, intro. Football Legends, 18 bks. (Illus.). (J). (gr. 3 up). 1995. lib. bdg. 269.10 (*0-7910-2450-4*) Chelsea Hse.
Noll, David. The Age of Dinosaurs. (Arts & Letters Ser.). 44p. 1993. pap. text 3.95 (*1-883515-00-9*) Computer Support.
Noll, Ed. Backyard Birds: Feeders & Photography. 1999. pap. 11.95 (*1-892896-35-4*) Buy Books.
Noll, Edward M. Easy-Up Antennas for Radio Listeners & Hams. 2nd ed. (Illus.). 163p. (Orig.). 1991. reprint ed. pap. 16.95 (*1-891237-10-1*, MFJ-38) MFJ Ent.
— FET Principles. 2nd ed. (Illus.). 160p. 1975. reprint ed. pap. 16.95 (*1-891237-02-0*, MFJ-3504) MFJ Ent.
— Ham Radio Communications Circuit Files. 2nd ed. (Illus.). 89p. 1991. reprint ed. pap. 9.95 (*1-891237-11-X*, MFJ-37) MFJ Ent.
— 73 Dipole Antennas. (Illus.). 158p. 1992. pap. 12.95 (*1-891237-06-3*, MFJ-3302) MFJ Ent.
— 73 Vertical Beam Antennas. 2nd ed. 160p. 1992. reprint ed. pap. 12.95 (*1-891237-05-5*, MFJ-3303) MFJ Ent.
— Shortwave Listener's Guide. (Illus.). 56p. 1991. pap. 9.95 (*1-891237-12-8*, MFJ-36) MFJ Ent.
— Solid State QRP Project. (Illus.). 127p. 1992. pap. 12.95 (*1-891237-03-9*, MFJ-3502) MFJ Ent.
Noll, Greg & Gabbard, Andrea. Da Bull: Life over the Edge. 2nd ed. (Illus.). 200p. 1992. reprint ed. pap. 16.95 (*1-55643-143-0*) North Atlantic.
Noll, Greg, et al. Hazardous Materials: Managing the Incident. (Illus.). 206p. (C). 1988. 19.00 (*0-945316-02-X*) IFSTA.
Noll, Greg G., et al. Hazardous Materials: Managing the Incident. (Illus.). 206p. (C). 1994. student ed. 35.00 (*0-945316-01-1*) IFSTA.
Noll, Gregory G., et al. Hazardous Materials Emergencies Involving Intermodal Containers: Guidelines & Procedures. (Illus.). 108p. 1996. pap. text 17.00 (*0-87939-126-X*, 35924) IFSTA.
Noll, J. G. They Came in Ships Hotel Altantico. Treece, David, tr. 144p. 1997. pap. 16.95 (*1-899460-65-9*, Pub. by Boulevard-Babel) Paul & Co Pubs.
Noll, James. Taking Sides: Clashing Views on Controversial Educational Issues. 9th ed. (C). 1997. text. write for info. (*0-697-37534-X*) Brown & Benchmark.
Noll, James W. Clashing Views on Controversial Educational Issues. 10th ed. (Taking Sides Ser.). (Illus.). 400p. 1999. pap. text 13.00 (*0-07-303183-6*, Dshkn McG-Hill) McGrw-H Hghr Educ.

N

An Asterisk (*) at the beginning of an entry indicates that the title is appearing for the first time.

Noll, James W., ed. Taking Sides: Clashing Views on Controversial Educational Issues. 8th ed. LC 94-47628. (Illus.). 400p. (C). 1995. text 13.95 (*1-56134-330-7*, Dshkn McG-Hill) McGrw-H Hghr Educ.

Noll, James W. & Kelly, Sam P. Foundations of Education in America: An Anthology of Major Thoughts & Significant Actions. LC 76-95838. 531p. reprint ed. pap. 164.70 (*0-7837-3951-6*, 204378000011) Bks Demand.

Noll, Joyce E. Company of Prophets: African American Psychics, Healers & Visionaries. LC 91-26482. (Illus.). 272p. (Orig.). 1999. pap. 12.95 (*0-87542-583-6*) Llewellyn Pubns.

Noll, K. L. The Faces of David. (JSOTS Ser.: Vol. 242). 204p. 1997. 57.50 (*1-85075-659-7*, Pub. by Sheffield Acad) CUP Services.

Noll, Kathy. Taking the Bully by the Horns: Children's Version of Best-selling book Nasty People. Carter, Jay, ed. (Illus.). 80p. (J). (gr. 4-9). 1998. pap. 9.95 (*0-937004-11-1*) Unicorn PA.

Noll, Kathy, jt. auth. see Carter, Jay.

Noll, Keith S., et al, eds. The Collision of Comet Shoemaker-Levy 9 & Jupiter. (Space Telescope Science Institute Symposium Ser.: No. 9). (Illus.). 387p. (C). 1996. text 74.95 (*0-521-56192-2*) Cambridge U Pr.

Noll, Kenneth E. Adsorption Technology for Air & Water Pollution Control. (Illus.). 376p. 1991. lib. bdg. 119.00 (*0-87371-340-0*, L340) Lewis Pubs.

— Fundamentals of Air Quality Systems: Design of Air Pollution Control Devices. LC 98-27184. (Illus.). xii, 611p. 1999. 94.95 (*1-883767-25-3*) Am Acad Environ.

Noll, Kirk, jt. auth. see Franco.

***Noll, Mark.** Protestants in America. (Religion in American Life Ser.). (Illus.). 144p. (YA). 2000. text 22.00 (*0-19-511034-X*) OUP.

Noll, Mark A. Adding Cross to Crown: The Political Significance of Christ's Passion. LC 96-22613. 96p. (gr. 10). 1996. pap. 9.99 (*0-8010-5731-0*) Baker Bks.

— Between Faith & Criticism: Evangelicals, Scholarship & the Bible in America. 272p. (C). 1986. reprint ed. pap. 26.95 (*1-57383-098-4*, Regent Coll Pub) Regent College.

— Christians & the American Revolution. LC 77-23354. 195p. reprint ed. pap. 60.50 (*0-8357-9125-4*, 201604200097) Bks Demand.

— Confessions & Catechisms of the Reformation. 232p. (Orig.). (C). 1997. reprint ed. pap. 22.95 (*1-57383-099-2*, Regent Coll Pub) Regent College.

— History of Christianity in the United States & Canada. (Illus.). 592p. 1992. pap. 32.00 (*0-8028-0651-1*) Eerdmans.

— Princeton & the Republic, 1768-1822: The Search for a Christian Enlightenment in the Era of Samuel Stanhope Smith. LC 88-39309. 356p. 1989. reprint ed. pap. 110.40 (*0-608-02942-4*, 206400800008) Bks Demand.

— The Scandal of the Evangelical Mind. 283p. 1995. pap. 18.00 (*0-8028-4180-5*) Eerdmans.

— Seasons of Grace. LC 97-19619. 96p. 1997. pap. 10.99 (*0-8010-5777-9*) Baker Bks.

— Turning Points: Decisive Moments in the History of Christianity. LC 97-29873. (Illus.). 336p. 1997. pap. 17.99 (*0-8010-5778-7*) Baker Bks.

Noll, Mark A., ed. Charles Hodge: The Way of Life & Selected Writings, Vol. 7. (Sources of American Spirituality Ser.). 288p. 1987. 14.95 (*0-8091-0392-3*) Paulist Pr.

— Religion & American Politics: From the Colonial Period to the 1980s. (Illus.). 416p. (C). 1989. pap. text 25.95 (*0-19-505881-X*) OUP.

Noll, Mark A., et al, eds. Evangelicalism: Comparative Studies of Popular Protestantism of North America & the British Isles & Beyond, 1700-1900. LC 92-46303. (Religion in America Ser.). 448p. 1994. text 32.95 (*0-19-508362-8*) OUP.

***Noll, Mark A. & Livingstone, David N., eds.** Evolution, Science & Scripture. LC 99-58773. 352p. (YA). (gr. 13 up). 2000. pap. 21.99 (*0-8010-2217-7*) Baker Bks.

***Noll, Mark A. & Thiemann, Ronald F., eds.** Where Shall My Wond'ring Soul Begin? The Landscape of Evangelical Piety & Thought. LC 00-27982. 96p. 2000. pap. 10.00 (*0-8028-4639-4*) Eerdmans.

Noll, Mark A. & Wells, David F., eds. Christian Faith & Practice in the Modern World: Theology from an Evangelical Point of View. LC 88-3635. 357p. reprint ed. pap. 110.70 (*0-7837-3197-3*, 204280200006) Bks Demand.

Noll, Mark A., et al. The Search for Christian America. 208p. 1989. reprint ed. pap. 17.95 (*0-939443-15-5*) Helmers Howard Pub.

Noll, Mark A., ed. see Dorsett, Lyle W.

Noll, Mark A., jt. ed. see Eskridge, Larry.

Noll, Mark A., jt. ed. see Lundin, Roger.

Noll, Mark A., jt. ed. see Rawlyk, George A.

Noll, Mark A., ed. see Stout, Harry S.

Noll, Martina A. Zur Situation des Deutschen als Fremdsprache in Chile: Dargestellt an Einer Untersuchung Erwachsener Fremdsprachenlernerinnen und -Lerner. (Werkstattreihe Deutsch als Fremdsprache Ser.: Band 60). (GER.). 370p. 1998. pap. 56.95 (*3-631-32901-6*) P Lang Pubng.

Noll, Paul. Structured COBOL Methods: How to Design, Code & Test Your Programs So They're Easier to Debug, Document, & Maintain. LC 97-4306. (Illus.). 208p. 1997. pap. 25.00 (*0-911625-94-1*) M Murach & Assoc.

Noll, Paul, jt. auth. see Murach, Mike.

Noll, Peter. In the Face of Death. 254p. 1990. 19.95 (*0-685-31397-2*) Viking Penguin.

Noll, Ray R. Christian Ministerial Priesthood: A Search for Its Beginnings in the Primary Documents of the Apostolic Fathers. 406p. 1993. 64.95 (*1-883255-07-4*) Intl Scholars.

***Noll, Ray R.** Sacraments: A New Understanding for a New Generation. 208p. 1999. pap. 24.95 (*0-89622-993-9*) Twenty-Third.

Noll, Ray Robert. Christian Ministerial Priesthood: A Search for Its Beginnings in the Primary Documents of the Apostolic Fathers. 406p. 1994. pap. 59.95 (*1-883255-00-7*) Intl Scholars.

Noll, Rhona S., jt. auth. see Beeler, Ronald.

Noll, Rhona S., jt. auth. see Nanney, J. Louis.

Noll, Richard. The Amaranth Genes. 1998. 24.00 (*0-375-50040-5*) Random.

***Noll, Richard.** The Encyclopedia of Schizophrenia & Other Psychotic Disorders. 2nd ed. LC 99-44166. 384p. 2000. 60.00 (*0-8160-4070-2*) Facts on File.

Noll, Richard. Encyclopedia of Schizophrenia & Psychotic Disorders. 368p. 1992. lib. bdg. 50.00 (*0-8160-2240-2*) Facts on File.

— The Jung Cult. LC 97-9823. 1997. per. 14.00 (*0-684-83423-5*) S&S Trade.

— The Jung Cult: Origins of a Charismatic Movement. LC 94-4831. 408p. 1994. text 35.00 (*0-691-03724-8*, Pub. by Princeton U Pr) Cal Prin Full Svc.

***Noll, Richard.** When Catholics Die: Eternal Life or Eternal Damnation? 208p. 1999. pap. 9.99 (*0-937422-46-0*, 1041, Olive Pr SC) Midnight Call.

Noll, Richard & Turkington, Carol. Encyclopedia of Memory & Memory Disorders. LC 94-1590. 280p. 1994. 45.00 (*0-8160-2610-6*) Facts on File.

Noll, Robert Thomas, adapted by. Oliver Twist. 85p. Date not set. pap. 5.60 (*0-87129-990-9*, O61) Dramatic Pub.

***Noll, Roger G.** The Economics & Politics of the Slowdown in Regulatory Reform. 43p. 1999. pap. 9.95 (*0-8447-7139-2*, Pub. by Am Enterprise) Pub Resources Inc.

Noll, Roger G. Reforming Regulation: An Evaluation of the Ash Council Proposals. LC 75-179326. (Studies in the Regulation of Economic Activity). 116p. 1971. pap. 8.95 (*0-8157-6107-4*) Brookings.

Noll, Roger G. & Price, Monroe E., eds. A Communications Cornucopia: Markle Foundation Essays on Information Policy. LC 97-45380. 595p. 1998. text 59.95 (*0-8157-6116-3*); pap. text 24.95 (*0-8157-6115-5*) Brookings.

Noll, Roger G. & Zimbalist, Andrew, eds. Sports, Jobs & Taxes: The Economic Impact of Sports Teams & Facilities. LC 97-33764. 525p. 1997. 49.95 (*0-8157-6110-4*); pap. 22.95 (*0-8157-6111-2*) Brookings.

Noll, Roger G., et al. Economic Aspects of Television Regulation. LC 73-1086. (Studies in the Regulation of Economic Activity). 342p. 1973. 32.95 (*0-8157-6108-2*); pap. 12.95 (*0-8157-6109-0*) Brookings.

Noll, Roger G., jt. ed. see Cain, Bruce E.

Noll, Roger G., jt. ed. see Cohen, Linda R.

***Noll, Ryhn.** Skateboard Retrospective: Collectors Guide. (Illus.). 192p. 2000. 39.95 (*0-7643-1122-0*) Schiffer.

Noll, Sally. Surprise! LC 96-36979. (Illus.). 24p. (J). (ps up). 1997. 15.00 (*0-688-15170-1*, Grenwillow Bks); lib. bdg. 14.93 (*0-688-15171-X*, Grenwillow Bks) HarpC Child Bks.

— Watch Where You Go. (Picture Puffin Ser.). (Illus.). (J). 1993. 9.19 (*0-606-02972-9*, Pub. by Turtleback) Demco.

Noll, Stephen F. Angels of Light, Powers of Darkness: Thinking Biblically about Angels, Satan & Principalities. LC 98-24694. 256p. 1998. pap. 19.99 (*0-8308-1504-X*, 1504) InterVarsity.

Noll, Steven. Feeble-Minded in Our Midst: Institutions for the Mentally Retarded in the South, 1900-1940. LC 94-49527. 1995. pap. text 18.95 (*0-8078-4531-0*); lib. bdg. 49.95 (*0-8078-2220-5*) U of NC Pr.

Noll, Terrie. The Encyclopedia of Joint Making. (Illus.). 144p. 1997. 22.99 (*1-55870-449-3*, Betrwy Bks) F & W Pubns Inc.

— The Encyclopedia of Jointmaking. LC 98-185258. 144 p. 1998. write for info. (*1-86108-070-0*) Guild Master.

Noll, Victor H., et al. Introduction to Educational Measurement. 4th ed. LC 89-5504. (Illus.). 560p. (C). 1989. reprint ed. pap. text 49.50 (*0-8191-7411-4*) U Pr of Amer.

Noll, Walter. Finite-Dimensional Spaces: Algebra, Geometry & Analysis, Vol I. (C). pap. text 98.50 (*90-247-3582-3*) Kluwer Academic.

Nolla, Eduardo, ed. Liberty, Equality, Democracy. 216p. (C). 1992. text 50.00 (*0-8147-5774-X*) NYU Pr.

— Liberty, Equality, Democracy. 216p. (C). 1996. pap. text 20.00 (*0-8147-5778-2*) NYU Pr.

Nolla, Olga. El Castillo de la Memoria. (SPA.). 1996. pap. 16.95 (*0-679-77298-7*) Vin Bks.

— Dulcehombre Prohibido. 150p. 1994. pap. write for info. (*1-56758-052-1*) Edit Cultl.

***Nolla, Olga.** El Manuscrito de Miramar. (SPA.). 211p. 2000. pap. 14.95 (*968-19-0455-9*) Aguilar.

Nolla, Olga. La Segunda Hija. 94p. 1993. 11.95 (*0-8477-0176-X*) U of PR Pr.

Nollan, Valerie, tr. & intro. see Soloukhin, Vladimir.

Nolland. Luke 19-24. (Word Biblical Commentary Ser.: Vol. 35C). 1993. 29.99 (*0-8499-1072-2*) Word Pub.

Nolland, John. Luke 9:21-18, Vol.35c. (Biblical Commentary Ser.: Vol. 35B). 1993. 29.99 (*0-8499-0254-1*) Word Pub.

— Luke 1:1-9:20. (Biblical Commentary Ser.: Vol. 35A). 1993. 29.99 (*0-8499-0234-7*) Word Pub.

Nolle, Johannes. Nundinas Instituere et Habere. (Subsidia Epigraphica Ser.). 172p. 1982. write for info. (*3-487-07259-9*) G Olms Pubs.

Nolle, Richard. Astrology Software Buyer's Guide. 44p. 1986. 8.00 (*0-86690-322-4*) Am Fed Astrologers.

— Chiron: New Planet in the Horoscope. LC 83-70810. 159p. 1983. 16.00 (*0-86690-236-8*, N2281-014) Am Fed Astrologers.

— Critical Astrology: Investigating the Cosmic Connection. LC 80-68779. 204p. 1980. 15.00 (*0-86690-144-2*, N1356-014) Am Fed Astrologers.

— Interpreting Astrology: New Techniques & Perspectives. LC 85-71460. 134p. 1986. 15.00 (*0-86690-292-9*, N2647-014) Am Fed Astrologers.

Nolledo, Wilfrido D. But for the Lovers. LC 94-9184. 325p. 1994. reprint ed. pap. 12.95 (*1-56478-067-8*) Dalkey Arch.

Nollen, Scott A. Boris Karloff: A Critical Account of His Screen, Stage, Radio, Television & Recording Work. LC 90-53515. (Illus.). 487p. 1991. lib. bdg. 48.50 (*0-89950-580-5*) McFarland & Co.

— The Boys: The Cinematic World of Laurel & Hardy. LC 89-42742. (Illus.). 167p. 1989. lib. bdg. 29.95 (*0-89950-383-7*) McFarland & Co.

— Robert Louis Stevenson: Life, Literature & the Silver Screen. LC 94-17785. (Illus.). 480p. 1994. lib. bdg. 58.50 (*0-89950-788-3*) McFarland & Co.

— Robin Hood: A Cinematic History of the English Outlaw & His Scottish Counterparts. LC 99-26060. 269p. 1999. lib. bdg. 36.50 (*0-7864-0643-7*) McFarland & Co.

— Sir Arthur Conan Doyle at the Cinema: A Critical Study of the Film Adaptations. LC 96-32550. (Illus.). 327p. 1996. lib. bdg. 48.50 (*0-7864-0269-5*) McFarland & Co.

Nollen, Scott Allen. Boris Karloff: A Gentleman's Life. (Illus.). 320p. 1999. pap. 20.00 (*1-887664-23-8*) Midnght Marquee Pr.

Nollen, Stanley D. New Patterns of Work. (Studies in Productivity: Highlights of the Literature Ser.: Vol. 7). 59p. 55.00 (*0-08-029488-X*, PS7) Work in Amer.

Nollen, Stanley D., jt. auth. see Axel, Helen.

Nollen, Stanley D., jt. auth. see Newman, Karen L.

Nollen, Tim. Culture Shock! Czech Republic. LC 96-77209. (Culture Shock Ser.). 1997. pap. 12.95 (*1-55868-303-8*) Gr Arts Ctr Pub.

Nollen, Tim. Prague & the Czech Republic. 1996. pap. 19.95 (*1-895907-92-6*) ITMP Pub.

Nollendorfs, Cora L., ed. Christian Essellen's "Babylon" (German Life & Civilization Ser.: Vol. 19). XXXVII, 184p. (C). 1996. text 45.95 (*0-8204-3045-5*) P Lang Pubng.

Nollendorfs, Valters, jt. ed. see Lohnes, Walter F.

Noller, Megan. One Grain of Sand. 20p. 1995. pap. 3.95 (*1-883869-16-1*) Gldn Gate Natl Parks Assoc.

Noller, Patricia. Nonverbal Communication & Marital Interaction. (International Series in Experimental Social Psychology: Vol. 9). (Illus.). 250p. 1984. text 104.00 (*0-08-027927-9*, CRC Reprint) Franklin.

Noller, Patricia & Fitzpatrick, MaryAnn. Communication in Family Relationships. LC 92-33046. 355p. (C). 1992. pap. text 44.00 (*0-13-301748-6*) P-H.

Noller, Patricia & Fitzpatrick, MaryAnn, eds. Perspectives on Marital Interaction. (Monographs in the Social Psychology of Language). 1988. 99.00 (*0-905028-91-0*, Pub. by Multilingual Matters); pap. 44.95 (*0-905028-90-2*, Pub. by Multilingual Matters) Taylor & Francis.

***Noller, Patricia, et al.** Personal Relationships Across the Lifespan. LC 00-40311. (International Series in Social Psychology). (C). 2000. write for info. (*0-415-18648-X*) Routledge.

Noller, Patricia, jt. auth. see Feeney, Judith.

Noller, Ruth B. Guide to Creative Action. 1981. 18.95 (*0-684-14888-9*, Scribners Ref) Mac Lib Ref.

Noller, Ruth B. & Frey, Barbara R. Mentoring: An Annotated Bibliography. 80p. (Orig.). 1983. pap. 18.95 (*0-943456-01-0*) Bearly Ltd.

Noller, William O. & Taylor, Kenneth N. My First Bible Words: A Kid's Devotional. LC 97-27171. (Illus.). (J). 1998. 10.99 (*0-8423-4399-7*) Tyndale Hse.

Nollet, L. Food Analysis by HPLC. (Food Science & Technology Ser.: 52). (Illus.). 768p. 1992. text 250.00 (*0-8247-8623-8*) Dekker.

Nollet, Leo M., ed. Handbook of Food Analysis, 2 vols., Set. LC 96-17851. (Food Science & Technology Ser.: Vol. 77). 1088p. 1996. 390.00 (*0-8247-9684-5*) Dekker.

— Handbook of Food Analysis, Vol. 1. LC 96-17851. (Food Science & Technology Ser.: Vol. 77). (Illus.). 1112p. 1996. text 450.00 (*0-8247-9682-9*) Dekker.

***Nollet, Leo M. L.** Food Analysis by HPLC. 2nd rev. ed. LC 00-28051. (Food Science & Technology Ser.). 2000. write for info. (*0-8247-8460-X*) Dekker.

— Handbook of Water Analysis. LC 00-37684. (Food Science & Technology Ser.). 2000. pap. write for info. (*0-8247-8433-2*) Dekker.

Nolletti, Arthur, Jr., ed. The Films of Fred Zinnemann: Critical Perspectives. LC 98-43754. (SUNY Series, Cultural Studies in Cinema/Video). (Illus.). 286p. (C). 1999. pap. text 19.95 (*0-7914-4226-8*) State U NY Pr.

— The Films of Fred Zinnemann: Critical Perspectives. LC 98-43754. (SUNY Series, Cultural Studies in Cinema/Video). 288p. (C). 1999. text 59.50 (*0-7914-4225-X*) State U NY Pr.

Nolletti, Arthur, Jr. & Desser, David, eds. Reframing Japanese Cinema: Authorship, Genre, History. LC 91-33659. (Illus.). 384p. 1992. pap. 18.95 (*0-253-20723-1*, MB-723) Ind U Pr.

Nolling, Wilhelm. Monetary Policy in Europe after Maastricht. LC 93-7294. (ENG & GER.). 1993. text 45.00 (*0-312-09952-5*) St Martin.

Nollius, Henry. The Chymist's Key: The True Doctrine of Corruption & Generation, in Ten Brief Aphorisms Illustrated with the Pure Light of Nature. Vaughan, Henry, tr. from LAT. 1991. reprint ed. pap. 6.95 (*1-55818-187-3*) Holmes Pub.

— Hermetic Physic: or, The Right Way to Preserve & to Restore Health. Holmes, J. D., ed. Vaughan, Henry & Vaughan, Thomas, trs. from LAT. 1995. reprint ed. pap. text 8.95 (*1-55818-273-X*) Holmes Pub.

Nollkaemper, Andre. The Legal Regime for Transboundary Water Pollution: Between Discretion & Constraint. LC 93-31558. (International Environmental Law & Policy Ser.). 408p. (C). 1993. lib. bdg. 149.00 (*0-7923-2476-5*) Kluwer Academic.

Nollman. Whales & Humans. Date not set. pap. 13.95 (*0-8050-5524-X*) H Holt & Co.

Nollman, Jim. The Charged Border: Where Whales & Humans Meet. LC 98-39470. 288p. 1999. 27.50 (*0-8050-5523-1*) H Holt & Co.

— Whales & Dolphins. 1995. 30.00 (*0-8050-4575-9*) H Holt & Co.

— Why We Garden. 1995. write for info. (*0-8050-2719-X*) H Holt & Co.

— Why We Garden: Cultivating a Sense of Place. 320p. 1995. pap. 14.00 (*0-8050-4561-9*, Owl) H Holt & Co.

Nolloth, H. E., ed. see Thoresby, John.

Nolly, Larry. Drum Tuning. 2nd ed. 24p. 1988. pap. text 12.95 (*0-9644658-1-7*) Drumstix Pub.

Nolo Press Editors. Fed up with the Legal System? What's Wrong & How to Fix It. 2nd rev. ed. LC 94-974. 1994. pap. 9.95 (*0-87337-242-5*) Nolo com.

***Nolo Staff Editors.** Small Business Legal Pro 4.0. 1999. 89.95 (*0-87337-541-6*) Nolo com.

Nolo Staff Editors & Legal Star Communications Staff. Legal Research Made Easy: A Roadmap Through the Law Library Maze. 336p. 1996. pap., student ed. 89.95 incl. VHS (*0-87337-138-0*) Nolo com.

Nolon, John. Common Walls-Private Homes: Multiresidential Design. 196p. 1990. 42.00 (*0-07-016819-9*) McGraw.

Nolon, John R. Primer for Local Officials & Citizens: Local Land Use Law & Practice in New York. 80p. 1998. pap. 16.95 (*0-9668221-2-9*) Pace Univ Land Use.

— Well Grounded: Shaping the Destiny of the Empire State Land Use Law & Practice. 450p. 1998. pap. 29.95 (*0-9668221-0-2*) Pace Univ Land Use.

Nolon, John R., ed. see Mohnach, Mary Beth E. & Ryan, Kathryn.

Nolosco, Marynita A. Physician Heal Thyself: Medical Practitioner of Eighteenth-Century New York. LC 94-13012. (American University Studies, Series IX: History: Vol. 170). 1994. write for info. (*0-8204-2580-X*) P Lang Pubng.

N

Nolph, K. D., jt. ed. see Mactier, R. A.

Nolph, Karl D., ed. Peritoneal Dialysis. 2nd ed. 1985. text 326.50 (*0-89838-685-3*) Kluwer Academic.

— Peritoneal Dialysis. 3rd ed. (C). 1988. text 315.00 (*0-89838-406-0*) Kluwer Academic.

Nolph, Karl D., jt. ed. see Gokal, Ram.

Nolst-Trenite, G. J., ed. Rhinoplasty: A Practical Guide to Functional & Aesthetic Surgery of the Nose. (Illus.). xi, 298p. 1998. 257.00 (*90-6299-164-5*) Kugler Pubns.

Nolt, Joanne S., ed. see Chitra Publications Staff.

Nolt, John, et al. Logic. 2nd ed. LC 98-28482. (Schaum's Outline Ser.). (Illus.). 280p. 1998. pap. 15.95 (*0-07-046649-1*) McGraw.

— What Have We Done? The Foundation for Global Sustainability's State of the Bioregion Report for the Upper Tennessee River Valley & Southern Appalachian Mountains. LC 97-60066. 320p. (Orig.). 1997. pap. 19.95 (*0-9644659-2-2*) Earth Knows Publ.

Nolt, John E. Informal Logic: Possible Worlds & Imagination. (C). 1983. pap. text, teacher ed. 15.93 (*0-07-046862-1*) McGraw.

— Informal Logic: Possible Worlds & Imagination. 352p. (C). 1984. 55.94 (*0-07-046861-3*) McGraw.

Nolt, John E. Logics. LC 96-32646. (Philosophy Ser.). (Illus.). 480p. (C). 1996. 69.95 (*0-534-50640-2*) Wadsworth Pub.

Nolt, M. Chester. How to Survive as a Principal: The Legal Dimension. LC 83-62499. 256p. (C). 1983. pap. 17.95 (*0-931028-42-6*) Precept Pr.

Nolt, Steven M. A History of the Amish. LC 92-29684. 317p. 1992. 9.95 (*1-56148-072-X*) Good Bks PA.

Nolt, Steven M., jt. auth. see Kraybill, Donald B.

Nolte, Bernd. Engpabfaktoren der Innovation & Innovationsinfrastruktur: Eine Theoretische & Empirische Analyse fur Landliche Wirtschaftsraume in Baden-Wurttemberg. (GER., Illus.). xxii, 380p. 1996. 63.95 (*3-631-49589-7*) P Lang Pubng.

Nolte, Carl & Brown, John, eds. Walk with Jesus - Lenten Resources Kit. 1997. 24.99 (*0-8100-0804-1*) Northwest Pub.

Nolte, Claude B. Optimum Pipe Size Selection. (Illus.). 304p. (C). 1978. 60.00 (*0-87849-024-8*, Pub. by Trans T Pub) Enfield Pubs NH.

Nolte, David D., ed. Photorefractive Effects & Materials. LC 95-11662. (International Series in Engineering & Computer Science). 504p. (C). 1995. text 181.50 (*0-7923-9560-3*) Kluwer Academic.

Nolte, Dorothy L. Children Learn What They Live. LC 97-49243. (Illus.). 160p. 1997. pap. 7.95 (*0-7611-0919-6*) Workman Pub.

Nolte, Dorothy L., jt. auth. see Harris, Rachel.

***Nolte, Dorothy Law & Harris, Rachel.** Com Inculcar Valores a Sus Hijos: Los Ninos Aprenden Lo Que Viven.Tr. of Parenting to Inspire Values: Children Learn What They Live. (SPA.). 208p. 1999. pap. 12.95 (*0-553-06104-6*) Bantam.

Nolte, Eckhard, ed. see Beck-Kapphan, Cornelia.

Nolte, Ewald V., ed. see Bach, Johann Sebastian.

Nolte, Gilbert, tr. see Coan, Alphonso.

Nolte, John. The Human Brain. 4th ed. (Illus.). 224p. (C). (gr. 13). 1998. pap. text, student ed. 21.95 (*0-8151-8993-1*, 29043) Mosby Inc.

— The Human Brain: An Introduction to Its Functional Anatomy. 4th ed. LC 98-17069. (Illus.). 704p. (C). (gr. 13). 1998. pap. text 43.95 (*0-8151-8911-7*, 29042) Mosby Inc.

Nolte, John & Angevine, Jay B. The Human Brain in Photographs & Diagrams. (Illus.). 208p. (C). (gr. 13). 1995. spiral bd. 36.00 (*0-8016-8125-1*, 08125) Mosby Inc.

***Nolte, John & Angevine, Jay B., Jr.** The Human Brain in Photographs & Diagrams. 2nd ed. (Illus.). 220p. 2000. text. write for info. (*0-323-01126-8*) Mosby Inc.

Nolte, Kristi, ed. The New York Agent: Get the Agent You Need & the Career You Want. 4th ed. 300p. 1995. 17.95 (*1-878355-03-1*) Sweden Pr.

Nolte, Kristi, ed. see Callan, K.

Nolte, L. P., ed. CAOS - Computer-Assisted Orthopedic Surgery. LC 98-3828. (Illus.). 290p. 1999. text 49.00 (*0-88937-168-7*) Hogrefe & Huber Pubs.

Nolte, Larry, jt. auth. see Long, Cathryn.

Nolte, Lawrence W., jt. auth. see Wilcox, Dennis L.

Nolte, Oliver, jt. ed. see Mueller, Erwin.

Nolte, Reginald G. Thunder Monsters over Europe: A History of the 405th Fighter Group in WWII. (Illus.). 160p. 1986. pap. 18.95 (*0-89745-075-2*) Sunflower U Pr.

Nolte, Vincent. Fifty Years in Both Hemispheres: or Reminiscences of the Life of a Former Merchant. LC 75-37903. (Select Bibliographies Reprint Ser.). 1977. reprint ed. 29.95 (*0-8369-6741-0*) Ayer.

Nolte, William, jt. auth. see Wilsted, Thomas.

Nolte, William H., ed. H. L. Mencken's Smart Set Criticism. LC 87-23248. 349p. 1987. reprint ed. pap. 10.95 (*0-89526-790-X*) Regnery Pub.

Noltemeier, H., ed. Computational Geometry & Its Applications. (Lecture Notes in Computer Science Ser.: Vol. 333). vi, 252p. 1988. 36.00 (*0-387-50335-8*) Spr-Verlag.

— Graphtheoretic Concepts in Computer Science: Proceedings. (Lecture Notes in Computer Science Ser.: Vol. 100). 403p. 1981. 37.00 (*0-387-10291-4*) Spr-Verlag.

Noltemeier, H., jt. ed. see Bieri, H.

Noltensmeier, Lucille. A Country Almanac. (Illus.). 160p. 1982. 10.50 (*0-943782-00-7*, Pantagraph Bks); pap. 5.00 (*0-943782-01-5*, Pantagraph Bks) Evergreen Comm.

***Nolter.** Gold Fever. 2000. 11.95 (*962-217-636-4*) Norton.

Nolti, H. J. Flora of Bhutan Vol. 3, Pt. 1: Including Liliaceae & Iridaceae. vi, 456p. 1994. pap. 55.00 (*1-872291-11-2*, Pub. by Royal Botanic Edinburgh) Balogh.

***Noltie, H. J.** Indian Botanical Drawings, 1793-1868. (Illus.). 100p. 1999. pap. 40.00 (*1-872291-23-6*, Pub. by Royal Botanic Edinburgh) Balogh.

***Noltie, Marilyn J.** Pour Applesauce in the Jars. (J). (gr. k-3). 1999. pap. 5.95 (*0-533-13161-8*) Vantage.

Nolting. Study Skills Workbook. pap. text, wbk. ed. 14.97 (*0-395-98225-1*) HM.

Nolting, Anne. Dear Future People. 168p. (YA). (gr. 7 up). 1996. pap. 9.99 (*0-88092-287-7*) Royal Fireworks.

***Nolting, Anne.** Rysaland. 370p. 2000. pap. 14.95 (*1-891929-48-8*) Four Seasons.

Nolting, Frederick. From Trust to Tragedy: The Political Memoirs of Frederick Nolting, Kennedy's Ambassador to Diem's Vietnam. LC 88-15397. 177p. 1988. 55.00 (*0-275-93080-7*, C3080, Praeger Pubs); pap. 12.95 (*0-275-93106-4*, B3106, Praeger Pubs) Greenwood.

Nolting, H. P. & Ulrich, R., eds. Integrated Optics. (Optical Sciences Ser.: Vol. 48). (Illus.). x, 242p. 1985. text (*0-387-15537-6*) Spr-Verlag.

Nolting, Karen S., jt. auth. see Latimer, Jonathan P.

Nolting, Mark. Africa's Top Wildlife Countries: With Mauritius & Seychelles. 4th rev. ed. LC 97-77317. (Illus.). 608p. 1997. pap. text 18.95 (*0-939895-07-2*) Global Travel Pubs.

Nolting, Mark W. African Safari: The Complete Travel Guide to 10 Top Game Viewing Countries. LC 87-8481. (Illus.). 256p. (Orig.). 1987. pap. 15.95 (*0-939895-00-5*) Global Travel Pubs.

***Nolting, Mark W.** African Safari Journal. 4th ed. (Illus.). 288p. 2000. pap. 16.95 (*0-939895-08-0*) Global Travel Pubs.

Nolting, Mark W. Travel Journal: Africa. (Illus.). 160p. (Orig.). 1988. pap. 12.95 (*0-939895-01-3*) Global Travel Pubs.

— Travel Journal: Africa. 3rd deluxe ed. 192p. (Orig.). 1994. pap. 12.95 (*0-939895-06-4*) Global Travel Pubs.

Nolting, Paul. Math & Students with Learning Disabilities: A Practice Guide to Course Substitution. 120p. 1993. pap. 19.95 (*0-940287-24-2*) Acad Success Pr.

— Math Study Skills Workbook: Your Guide to Reducing Test Anxiety & Improving Study Strategies. 112p. 1998. pap., wbk. ed. 9.95 (*0-940287-28-5*) Acad Success Pr.

Nolting, Paul D. Math & the Learning Disabled Student: A Practical Guide for Accommodations. 1991. pap. 14.95 (*0-940287-23-4*) Acad Success Pr.

— Winning at Math: Your Guide to Learning Mathematics Through Successful Study Skills. 3rd expanded rev. ed. LC 96-37939. 356p. (C). 1997. pap. text 18.95 (*0-940287-26-9*) Acad Success Pr.

Nolting, S. & Fegler, K. Medical Mycology. 210p. 1987. pap. 29.40 (*0-387-17606-3*) Spr-Verlag.

Nolting, S. & Korting, H. C., eds. Onychomycoses. (Illus.). x, 126p. 1990. 29.95 (*0-387-52132-1*) Spr-Verlag.

Noltingk, B. E. Instrumentation Reference Book. 2nd ed. (Illus.). 1120p. 1994. 225.00 (*0-7506-0906-0*) Buttrwrth-Heinemann.

Noltingk, B. E., ed. Instrumentation Reference Book. 2nd ed. LC 95-1813. 1000p. 1995. text 235.00 (*0-7506-2056-0*) Buttrwrth-Heinemann.

Nolutshungu, Sam C. Limits of Anarchy: Intervention & State Formation in Chad. 392p. (C). 1996. text 39.50 (*0-8139-1628-3*) U Pr of Va.

Nolutshungu, Sam C., ed. Margins of Insecurity: Minorities & International Security. 328p. 1996. pap. 24.95 (*1-878822-75-6*) Univ Rochester Pr.

— Margins of Insecurity: Minorities & International Security. LC 95-51461. 328p. (C). 1996. 60.00 (*1-878822-63-2*) Univ Rochester Pr.

Noma, Chikako, ed. see Bruna, Dick.

Noma, Chikako, ed. see Momotani, Yoshihide.

Noma, Chikako, ed. see Yamada, Amy.

Noma Research Department Staff. Le Livre Monidal de la Famille Patronyme (Belgium) (FRE., Illus.). 95p. 1998. text 45.00 (*1-885808-17-8*); pap. text 40.00 (*1-885808-18-6*) Numa Corp.

Noma, Seiroku. Arts of Japan, 2 vols., Vol. I: Ancient & Medieval. Rosenfield, John, tr. LC 65-19186. (Illus.). 308p. 1978. pap. 39.00 (*0-87011-335-6*) Kodansha.

— Arts of Japan, 2 vols., Vol. II: Late Medieval to Modern. Rosenfield, John, tr. LC 65-19186. (Illus.). 332p. 1978. pap. 38.00 (*0-87011-336-4*) Kodansha.

***Nomachi, Kazuyoshi.** Bless Ethiopia. LC 98-46906. 1998. 39.95 (*962-217-518-X*, Pub. by China Guides) Norton.

— The Nile. LC 98-46908. 1998. 34.95 (*962-217-543-0*, Pub. by China Guides) Norton.

Nomachi, Kazuyoshi. Tibet. LC 97-3533. 198p. 1997. 55.00 (*1-57062-256-6*, Pub. by Shambhala Pubns) Random.

Nomachi, M. & Ajimura, S., eds. Proceedings from the Second International Data Acquisition Workshop on Networked Data Acquisition Systems (DAS 96) 320p. 1997. text 68.00 (*981-02-3198-9*) World Scientific Pub.

Nomad, Ali. Cosmic Consciousness. 310p. 1997. pap. 25.00 (*0-89540-282-3*, SB-282) Sun Pub.

— Cosmic Consciousness: The Man-God Whom We Await. 310p. 1996. reprint ed. spiral bd. 18.00 (*0-7873-0636-3*) Hlth Research.

— Cosmic Consciousness: The Man-God Whom We Await (1913) 315p. 1996. reprint ed. pap. 24.95 (*1-56459-896-9*) Kessinger Pub.

***Nomad Communications Staff.** Coaching Youth Soccer. LC 99-30450. 160p. 1999. pap. 14.95 (*0-07-134608-2*) McGraw.

Nomad Communications Staff, jt. auth. see Wilson, Mathew.

Nomad, Max. Rebels & Renegades. LC 68-20326. (Essay Index Reprint Ser.). 1977. 23.95 (*0-8369-0745-0*) Ayer.

Noman, Omar. Economic & Social Progress in Asia: Why Pakistan Did Not Become a Tiger. LC 97-930756. (The Jubilee Ser.). (Illus.). 338p. 1998. text 35.00 (*0-19-577781-6*) OUP.

— Economic Development & Environmental Policy. LC 95-23645. 220p. 1995. 110.00 (*0-7103-0516-8*, Pub. by Kegan Paul Intl) Col U Pr.

— Pakistan: Political & Economic History since 1947. 238p. 1996. pap. 15.95 (*0-614-21497-1*, 940); pap. 15.95 (*0-614-21696-6*, 940) Kazi Pubns.

— Pakistan: Political & Economic History Since 1947. 285p. 1990. pap. 15.95 (*0-7103-0389-0*, A4718) Routledge.

— The Political & Economic Development of Pakistan. 260p. 1988. lib. bdg. 55.00 (*0-7103-0211-8*) Routledge.

— Pride & Passion: An Exhilarating Half Century of Cricket in Pakistan. LC 98-931026. (The Jubilee Ser.). (Illus.). 438p. 1999. 26.00 (*0-19-577831-6*) OUP.

Nomandeau, Pierre, tr. see Shelton, Herbert M.

***Nomani.** Tantrika. 2000. 25.00 (*0-06-251713-9*); pap. 14.00 (*0-06-251714-7*) HarpC.

Nomani, Farhad, jt. ed. see Behdad, Sohrab.

Nomani, M. M. Meaning & Message of the Traditions, 2 vols., Set. 1990. 45.00 (*1-56744-132-7*) Kazi Pubns.

Nomberg-Przytyk, Sara. Auschwitz: True Tales from a Grotesque Land. Pfefferkorn, Eli & Hirsch, David, eds. Hirsch, Roslyn, tr. LC 84-17386. xii, 185p. 1985. pap. 15.95 (*0-8078-4160-9*) U of NC Pr.

Nomenology Project Staff. The Hidden Truth of Your Name: A Complete Guide to First Names & What They Say About the Real You. LC 98-29795. 1999. pap. 24.95 (*0-345-42266-X*) Ballantine Pub Grp.

Nomikos, Eugenia V. & North, Robert C. International Crisis: The Outbreak of World War I. LC 76-381852. 355p. reprint ed. pap. 110.10 (*0-7837-2626-0*, 204297600006) Bks Demand.

Nomis, Leo & Cull, Brian. The Desert Hawks. 208p. 1998. 29.95 (*1-898697-82-5*, Pub. by Grub St) Seven Hills Bk.

Nomizu, Katsumi. Selected Papers on Harmonic Analysis, Groups, & Invariants. LC 97-27740. (American Mathematical Society Translations Ser.). 143p. 1997. text 59.00 (*0-8218-0840-0*) Am Math.

— Selected Papers on Number Theory, Algebraic Geometry & Differential Equations. LC 94-26691. (Translations Ser.: Series 2, Vol. 160). 154p. 1994. text 75.00 (*0-8218-7511-6*, TRANS2/160) Am Math.

Nomizu, Katsumi, ed. Selected Papers on Analysis, Probability & Statistics. LC 94-23002. (Translations Ser.: Series 2, Vol. 161). 151p. 1994. text 75.00 (*0-8218-7512-4*, TRANS2/161) Am Math.

— Selected Papers on Number Theory & Algebraic Geometry. LC 95-39031. (American Mathematical Society Translations Ser.: Series 2, Vol. 172). 91p. 1996. text 42.00 (*0-8218-0445-6*, TRANS2/172) Am Math.

Nomizu, Katsumi & Sasaki, Takeshi. Affine Differential Geometry: Geometry of Affine Immersions. LC 93-46712. (Cambridge Tracts in Mathematics Ser.: Vol. 111). (Illus.). 277p. (C). 1995. text 52.95 (*0-521-44177-3*) Cambridge U Pr.

Nomizu, Katsumi, jt. auth. see Kobayashi, Shoshichi.

Nomizu, Katsumi, tr. see Ise, M., et al.

Nomizu, Katsumi, tr. see Ueno, Kenji.

Nomland, Gladys A. Bear River Ethnography. fac. ed. Lowie, Robert H. et al, eds. (University of California Publications: No. 2:2). 43p. (C). 1938. reprint ed. pap. 4.69 (*1-55567-121-7*) Coyote Press.

— Sinkyone Notes. (University of California Publication in American Archaeology & Ethnology Ser.: Vol. 36:2). 35p. (C). 1935. pap. text 4.06 (*1-55567-739-8*) Coyote Press.

Nomoto, K., ed. Atmospheric Diagnostics of Stellar Evolution: Chemical Peculiarity, Mass Loss, & Explosion. (Lecture Notes in Physics Ser.: Vol. 305). xiv, 468p. 1988. 64.95 (*0-387-19478-9*) Spr-Verlag.

Nomura. Let's Write Japanese in Japanese, Custom Pub. 2nd ed. (C). 1994. pap. 31.88 (*0-07-047075-8*) McGraw.

Nomura, Gail M., et al, eds. Frontiers of Asian American Studies: Writing, Research, & Commentary. (Association for Asian American Studies Ser.). 341p. 1989. pap. 20.00 (*0-87422-063-7*) Wash St U Pr.

Nomura, H., et al, eds. Structure, Fluctuation, & Relaxation in Solutions. 452p. 1996. 324.25 (*0-444-82384-0*) Elsevier.

Nomura, J. Virtual Reality Techniques in Commercial & Industrial Applications. Date not set. write for info. (*0-8247-9941-0*) Dekker.

Nomura, M., et al, eds. Ribosomes. LC 74-83791. (Cold Spring Harbor Monographs). 942p. Date not set. reprint ed. pap. 200.00 (*0-608-20711-X*, 207180900002) Bks Demand.

Nomura, Masami, jt. auth. see Berggren, Christian.

Nomura, Noriko S. I Am Shintoist, 8 vols., Set. LC 96-6979. (Religions of the World Ser.). (Illus.). 24p. (J). (gr. k-4). 1996. lib. bdg. 15.93 (*0-8239-2380-0*, PowerKids) Rosen Group.

Nomura, Patricia, ed. see Mitchell, Daniel J., et al.

Nomura, T. & Kunobo, S. Physics with High-Intensity Hadron Accelerators: Eighteenth Ins. International Symposium. 516p. 1990. text 130.00 (*981-02-0261-X*) World Scientific Pub.

Nomura, Takaaki. Grandpa's Town. Stinchecum, Amanda M., tr. from JPN. (Illus.). 32p. (J). (ps-3). 1991. 13.95 (*0-916291-36-7*) Kane-Miller Bk.

— Grandpa's Town. Stinchecum, Amanda M., tr. from JPN. (Illus.). 32p. (J). (ps-3). 1995. pap. 7.95 (*0-916291-57-X*) Kane-Miller Bk.

Nomura, Takeo & Furusawa, Shimpei. Essentials of Microscopic Hematology. (Illus.). 120p. 1991. pap. 43.50 (*0-89640-205-3*) Igaku-Shoin.

Nomura, Takeo, ed. see International Symposium on Myelodyspastic Syndromes Staff.

Nomura, Tatsuji, et al. ICLAS Manual for Genetic Monitoring of Inbred Mice. 200p. 1985. pap. 39.50 (*0-86008-366-7*, Pub. by U of Tokyo) Col U Pr.

Nomura, Y. Otological Significance of the Round Window. (Advances in OtoRhinoLaryngology Ser.: Vol. 33). (Illus.). x, 162p. 1984. 100.00 (*3-8055-3806-5*) S Karger.

Nomura, Y., jt. ed. see Segawa, M.

***Nomura, Yoshiko.** Lifelong Integrated Education as a Creator of the Future. 222p. 1999. pap. 29.95 (*1-85856-154-X*, Trentham Bks) Stylus Pub VA.

Non Gwynn Press Staff. Personal Name Asteroids. 16p. 1990. pap. 4.00 (*0-917086-93-7*) ACS Pubns.

Non-Traditional Study Commission. Diversity by Design. LC 73-3772. (Jossey-Bass Higher Education Ser.). 208p. reprint ed. pap. 64.50 (*0-608-12992-5*, 202387500034) Bks Demand.

***Nonaka, Ikujiro & Nishiguchi, Toshihiro.** Knowledge Emergence. (Illus.). 352p. 2000. 35.00 incl. reel tape (*0-19-513063-4*) OUP.

Nonaka, Ikujiro & Takeuchi, Hiro. The Knowledge-Creating Company: How Japanese Companies Create the Dynamics of Innovation. (Illus.). 304p. 1995. 27.50 (*0-19-509269-4*) OUP.

Nonaka, T., jt. auth. see Kubo, A.

Nonas, Elisabeth. Staying Home. LC 93-41449. 320p. 1994. pap. 10.95 (*1-56280-076-0*) Naiad Pr.

Nonas, Elisabeth, jt. auth. see LeVay, Simon.

Nonas, Elisabeth, jt. auth. see Levay, Simon.

Nonas, Michela, tr. see Gimenez, Juan & Dal Pra, Roberto.

Nonat, A. & Mutin, J. C., eds. Hydration & Setting of Cements: Proceedings of the International Rilem Workshop. (Rilem Proceedings Ser.). (Illus.). 448p. 1993. mass mkt. 139.95 (*0-419-17760-4*, E & FN Spon) Routledge.

None. Just Babies Calendar. 1997. per. 9.99 (*0-373-15289-2*) S&S Trade.

— Writers Notebook Win. 1997. 220.51 (*0-673-19778-6*) Pearson Custom.

None, Dean R. The New Roget's Thesaurus in Dictionary Form. 1992. pap. 5.99 (*0-425-12714-1*) Berkley Pub.

None Given. Dodge D-50/Plymouth Arrow Pickups 1979-93. (Automobile Repair Manuals Ser.). (Illus.). pap. 17.95 (*1-56392-085-9*, MBI 101453AM) Haynes Manuals.

— Haynes Isuzu Pick-Ups & Trooper, 1981-1993. 1993. pap. 17.95 (*1-56392-033-6*) Haynes Manuals.

Nonell, Juan B., jt. auth. see Collins, George R.

Nones, Eric J. Angela's Wings. LC 94-30321. (Illus.). 32p. (J). (ps-3). 1995. 16.00 (*0-374-30331-2*) FS&G.

— Canary Prince. LC 90-55384. 32p. (J). (gr. 2 up). 1991. 16.00 (*0-374-31029-7*) FS&G.

Nonestied, M. East Brunswick. (Images of America Ser.). 1997. pap. 16.99 (*0-7524-0579-9*) Arcadia Publng.

Nonet, Philippe. Administrative Justice: Advocacy & Change in a Government Agency. LC 68-58126. 248p. 1969. 34.95 (*0-87154-627-2*) Russell Sage.

***Nonet, Philippe, et al.** Law & Society in Transition. 130p. 2000. pap. 24.95 (*0-7658-0642-8*) Transaction Pubs.

Nonferrous Metals Society of China Staff, ed. Metallurgy & Materials of Tungsten, Titanium, Rare Earths & Antimony: Proceedings of the 1st International Conference, Changsha, China, 5-8 November 1988. (International Academic Publishers Ser.). (Illus.). 1200p. 1989. 400.00 (*0-08-037202-3*, Pergamon Pr) Elsevier.

Nong, Phua-Xing. Selected Essays by Teochew Chinese in Singapore & Malaysia. 208p. 1993. pap. text 9.00 (*1-879771-05-5*) Global Pub NJ.

Nongard, Paul & Nongard, Richard K. The Step-Spouse: Phantom Relationships with Real Impact. 180p. (Orig.). 1997. pap. 15.95 (*0-9655979-3-8*, SS-03) Peachtree Prof.

Nongard, Paula S., jt. auth. see Nongard, Richard K.

Nongard, Richard K. Last Words: Parting Thoughts & Last Meals from Death Row. unabridged ed. (Illus.). 72p. (Orig.). 1997. pap. 9.95 (*0-9655979-2-X*, 02-97) Peachtree Prof.

Nongard, Richard K. & Nongard, Paula S. Evil Stands Alone: Identifying Those with No Excuse. unabridged ed. LC 96-93015. 132p. (Orig.). 1997. pap. 12.95 (*0-9655979-0-3*, 7217-01) Peachtree Prof.

— The Perfect-Victim Factor: Taking Control of Destructive Personality Traits. LC 97-91576. 120p. (Orig.). 1997. pap. 12.95 (*0-9655979-1-1*, BO2PVF) Peachtree Prof.

Nongard, Richard K., jt. auth. see Nongard, Paul.

Nonhebel, G. & Berry, M. Chemical Engineering in Practice. LC 73-77793. (Wykeham Science Ser.: No. 28). 196p. (C). 1973. pap. 18.00 (*0-8448-1336-2*, Crane Russak) Taylor & Francis.

Nonhebel, Gordon, ed. Gas Purification Processes for Air Pollution Control. 2nd ed. LC 72-193815. (Illus.). 713p. reprint ed. pap. 200.00 (*0-608-14712-5*, 202571500046) Bks Demand.

Nonhof, C. J. Material Processing with ND-Lasers. 259p. 1997. pap. 268.00 (*0-901150-23-1*) St Mut.

Nonica, Datta. Forming an Identity: A Social History of the Jats. LC 99-937584. (Illus.). 240p. 1999. text 26.95 (*0-19-564719-X*) OUP.

Nonini, Donald M. British Colonial Rule & the Resistance of the Malay Peasantry, 1900-1957. (Monograph Ser. - Yale University Southeast Asia Studies: No. 38). 350p. 1992. 30.00 (*0-938692-48-8*); pap. 17.00 (*0-938692-47-X*) Yale U SE Asia.

Nonino, Carlo, jt. auth. see Comini, Gianni.

Nonkin, Lesley J. I Wish My Parents Understood: The Nonkin-Teenage Relationships Survey of Female Relationships. 304p. 1985. 14.95 (*0-317-18014-2*) Freundlich.

***Nonnekes, Paul.** Three Moments of Love in Leonard Cohen & Bruce Cockburn. (Illus.). 192p. 2000. pap. 19.99 (*1-55164-176-3*) Black Rose.

Nonneman, A. J., jt. auth. see Woodruff, M. L.

Nonneman, Gerd. Development Administration & Aid in the Middle East. 240p. (C). 1988. lib. bdg. 47.50 (*0-415-00104-8*) Routledge.

— Development, Administration & Aid in the Middle East. LC 88-12206. (Illus.). 213p. reprint ed. pap. 66.10 (*0-608-20366-1*, 207161900002) Bks Demand.

— Muslim Communities in the New Europe. 1998. pap. text 19.95 (*0-86372-223-7*, Pub. by Garnet-Ithaca) LPC InBook.

Nonneman, Gerd, ed. Political & Economic Liberalization: Dynamics & Linkages in Comparative Perspective. 332p. 1996. lib. bdg. 59.95 (*1-55587-639-0*, 87-639-0) L Rienner.

Nonnenkamp, Donna. Chemistry. 1994. 4.95 (*1-55708-430-0*, MCR766) McDonald Pub Co.

Nonnenmacher, F. F., et al, eds. Fractals in Biology & Medicine. LC 93-44016. 1994. 73.50 (*0-8176-2989-0*) Birkhauser.

Nonnos. Dionysiaca, 3 vols., 1. (Loeb Classical Library: No. 344, 354, 356). 566p. 1940. 19.95 (*0-674-99379-9*) HUP.

— Dionysiaca, 3 vols., 2. (Loeb Classical Library: No. 344, 354, 356). 560p. 1940. 19.95 (*0-674-99391-8*) HUP.

— Dionysiaca, 3 vols., 3. (Loeb Classical Library: No. 344, 354, 356). 530p. 1940. 19.95 (*0-674-99393-4*) HUP.

Nonogaki, Saburo & Ueno, Takumi. Microlithography Fundamentals in Semiconductor Devices & Fabrication Technology. LC 98-4222. (Illus.). 336p. 1998. text 135.00 (*0-8247-9951-8*) Dekker.

Nonte, George C. The Home Guide to Cartridge Conversions. rev. ed. 24.95 (*0-88227-005-2*) Gun Room.

Nonte, George C., Jr. Pistolsmithing. LC 74-10783. (Illus.). 560p. 1974. 29.95 (*0-8117-1265-6*) Stackpole.

Nonte, J. Supercollider: Proceedings of the Fourth International Industrial Symposium on the Super Collider, Held March 4-6, 1992, in Atlanta, Georgia, Vol. 4. LC 92-30221. (Illus.). 1276p. (C). 1992. 215.00 (*0-306-44254-X*, Plenum Trade) Perseus Pubng.

Nonte, John, ed. Supercollider 3. (Illus.). 1196p. (C). 1991. text 258.00 (*0-306-44037-7*, Kluwer Plenum) Kluwer Academic.

Nonweiler, Terence R. Computational Mathematics: An Introduction to Numerical Approximation. LC 83-12224. (Mathematics & Its Applications Ser.: I-176). 431p. 1984. text 76.95 (*0-470-27472-7*) P-H.

Nony, D., jt. auth. see Girault, O.

Nony, Daniele & Andre, Alain. Literature Francaise: Histoire et Anthologie. (FRE., Illus.). 464p. (C). 1987. text 19.95 (*2-218-00976-5*, U0976, Pub. by Edns Didier) Hatier Pub.

Nood, Melvin. Rinones, Su Cura Natural. (SPA.). 1997. pap. text 3.98 (*968-15-0537-9*) Ed Mex.

Nooger & Neville Staff, jt. auth. see Valkenburgh, Van.

Nooijen, Toos S. Freedom's Clothesline: Dutch Citizens During World War II. (Illus.). 238p. (Orig.). 1995. pap. text 16.95 (*1-888042-01-X*) Good Readng.

Noojin, Randy. You Can't Trust the Male. 1991. pap. 3.50 (*0-87129-059-6*, Y18) Dramatic Pub.

Nool, Richard. Mysteria, Jung & the Ancient Mysteries: Extracts from the Collected Works of C. G. Jung. LC 94-34815. (C). 1994. pap. 14.95 (*0-691-03647-0*, Pub. by Princeton U Pr) Cal Prin Full Svc.

Noomen, Willem, jt. ed. see Van Dijk, Hans.

Noomin, Diane, ed. see Lay, Carol & Brown, M. K.

N

An Asterisk (*) at the beginning of an entry indicates that the title is appearing for the first time.

*Noon, Alfred. The History of Ludlow Massachusetts: With Biographical Sketches of Leading Citizens, Reminiscences, Genealogies, Farm Histories & an Account of the Centennial Celebration, June 17, 1874. 2nd ed. (Illus.). 592p. 1999. (0-7884-1215-9, N555) Heritage Bk.

Noon, Alfred. The History of Ludlow, with Biographical Sketches of Leading Citizens, Reminiscences, Genealogies, Etc. 2nd rev. ed. (Illus.). 592p. 1989. reprint ed. lib. bdg. 63.00 (0-8328-0839-3, MA0214) Higginson Bk Co.

Noon, E. Personal Privacy Protection Guide: A Practical Guide to Protecting Your Privacy. LC 97-75677. (Illus.). 1998. pap. 6.95 (0-9661641-0-5) ONOne Inc.

*Noon, J. Mitchell. Counselling & Helping Carers. 1999. pap. 34.00 (1-85433-272-4) Brit Psychol Soc.

*Noon, Jack. The Bassing of New Hampshire: How Black Bass Came to the Granite State. LC 99-32435. (Illus.). 206p. 1999. pap. 20.00 (0-9642213-9-X) Moose Cntry.

Noon, Jack. The Big Fish of Barston Falls. (Illus.). 289p. (C). 1995. 24.00 (0-9642213-2-2) Moose Cntry.

*Noon, Jack. Muster Days at Muster Field Farm: New Hampshire's Muster Day Tradition, 1787-1850. (Illus.). xii, 121p. 2000. 20.00 (0-9677202-0-6) Muster Fld Frm Mus.

Noon, Jack. Old Sam's Thunder. unabridged ed. LC 98-6203. (Illus.). 328p. (YA). 1998. pap. 16.00 (0-9642213-6-5) Moose Cntry.

*Noon, Jack. Up Moosilauke. LC 99-55819. (Illus.). 215p. 2000. pap. 16.00 (1-893863-00-X) Moose Cntry.

Noon, Jack, ed. see Averill, Robert W.

Noon, Jeff. Automated Alice. limited ed. Date not set. write for info. (0-517-70721-7, Crown) Crown Pub Group.

— Pixel Juice. 1998. 29.95 (0-385-40859-5, DD Bks Yng Read) BDD Bks Young Read.

Noon, Jen, ed. see Chall, Jeanne S. & Popp, Helen M.

Noon, Jen, ed. see Chall, Jeanne S. & Roswell, Florence G.

Noon, Jennifer, ed. see Levine, Melvin D.

Noon, Patrick J. English Portrait Drawings & Miniatures. LC 79-63448. (Illus.). 152p. (Orig.). 1979. pap. 10.00 (0-930606-15-9) Yale Ctr Brit Art.

— The Human Form Divine: William Blake from the Paul Mellon Collection. LC 97-60263. (Illus.). 76p. 1997. 35.00 (0-300-07174-4) Yale U Pr.

— Richard Parkes Bonington: On the Pleasure of Painting. LC 91-65083. (Illus.). 311p. 1991. pap. 39.95 (0-930606-67-1) Yale Ctr Brit Art.

Noon, Patrick J., et al. The Human Form Divine: William Blake from the Paul Mellon Collection. LC 97-60263. (Illus.). 1997. write for info. (0-930606-81-7) Yale Ctr Brit Art.

Noon, Patrick J., jt. auth. see Warner, Timothy.

Noon, Randall K. Engineering Analysis of Fires & Explosions. LC 95-3187. 296p. 1995. boxed set 84.95 (0-8493-8107-X, 8107) CRC Pr.

— Engineering Analysis of Vehicular Accidents. LC 93-48723. 256p. 1994. boxed set 83.95 (0-8493-8104-5) CRC Pr.

*Noon, Randall K. Forensic Engineering Investigation. LC 00-44457. 2000. write for info. (0-8493-0911-5) CRC Pr.

Noon, Randall K. Introduction to Forensic Engineering. 224p. 1992. boxed set 83.95 (0-8493-8102-9, TA219) CRC Pr.

Noon, Shereen. Heal Yourself: A Step-by-Step Guide to Self-Healing Through Affirmations. 154p. (Orig.). 1990. pap. 9.95 (0-9624690-0-9) Welcome Home.

Noon, Steve, jt. illus. see Hincks, Gary.

Noona, Carol, jt. auth. see Noona, Walter.

Noona, Carol, jt. ed. see Noona, Walter.

Noona, Walter & Noona, Carol. Improv! Bass Patterns & Progressions, Vol. 2: Basic Concepts in Improvisation. (Illus.). 64p. (Orig.). 1992. pap. 8.95 (0-89328-108-5, KM16) Lorenz Corp.

— Improv! Blues & Rock Styles, Vol. 3: Basic Concepts in Improvisation. (Illus.). 64p. (Orig.). 1992. pap. 8.95 (0-89328-106-9, KM21) Lorenz Corp.

— Improv! Follow the Lead, Vol. 1: Basic Concepts in Improvisation. (Illus.). 64p. (Orig.). 1992. pap. 8.95 (0-89328-107-7, KM9) Lorenz Corp.

— New Horizons Vol. 1: Piano Course for Busy Adults. 96p. (Orig.). 1992. pap. 8.95 (0-89328-109-3, KM152) Lorenz Corp.

— New Horizons Vol. 2: Piano Course for Busy Adults. 96p. (Orig.). 1992. pap. 8.95 (0-89328-111-5, KM153) Lorenz Corp.

— The Video Pianist, Bk. 1. 48p. 1987. pap. 4.95 (0-89328-100-X, KM121) Lorenz Corp.

Noona, Walter & Noona, Carol, eds. Easy Classics, Piano. 96p. (Orig.). 1989. pap. 9.95 (0-89328-110-7, KK437) Lorenz Corp.

Noonan, Ed. Noisy Soil: Selected Poems from the Collected Works 1980-1998. 80p. (Orig.). 1999. pap. 12.00 (0-9668216-0-2) Bedrock Edns.

Noonan, B., jt. auth. see Ferenbach, M.

Noonan, Barry C. Index to Green Bay Newspapers, 1833-1840. 62p. (Orig.). 1987. pap. 8.00 (0-910255-48-2) Wisconsin Gen.

— Index to the Gospel Herald Published at Voree, Racine County, Wisconsin, January 1846-June 6, 1850. 38p. (Orig.). 1988. pap. 8.00 (0-910255-50-4) Wisconsin Gen.

Noonan, Chris. Sales Management: The Complete Marketeer's Guide. (C). 1986. text 49.95 (0-04-658254-1) Routledge.

Noonan, Chris, jt. auth. see Miller, George.

*Noonan, Christine. Cim Handbook of Export Marketing. 1999. pap. 49.95 (0-7506-4346-3) Butterworth-Heinemann Ltd.

*Noonan, D. Castles & Ancient Monum of Scotland. (Golf World Guides Ser.). (Illus.). 192p. 2000. pap. 19.95 (1-85410-677-5, Pub. by Aurum Pr) London Brdge.

Noonan, Damien. Castle & Ancient Monuments of England: A County-by-County Guide to More than 350 Historic Sites. 1999. pap. text 19.95 (1-85410-621-X) London Brdge.

Noonan, David C. & Curtis, James T. Groundwater Remediation & Petroleum: A Guide for Underground Storage Tanks. (Illus.). 250p. 1990. lib. bdg. 99.95 (0-87371-217-X, L217) Lewis Pubs.

Noonan, Diana. Donkeys. LC 93-28998. (Voyages Ser.). (Illus.). (J). 1994. 4.25 (0-383-03741-7) SRA McGraw.

— Fat Cat Tompkin. LC 92-34273. (Voyages Ser.). (Illus.). (J). 1993. 3.75 (0-383-03623-2) SRA McGraw.

— The Shepherd Who Planted a Forest. LC 93-11828. (Illus.). (J). 1994. write for info. (0-383-03774-3) SRA McGraw.

— Shooting It Straight. LC 93-21248. (J). 1994. 4.25 (0-383-03731-X) SRA McGraw.

Noonan, Diane. Houses That Move. LC 92-27085. (Illus.). (J). 1993. 14.00 (0-383-03574-0) SRA McGraw.

Noonan, Douglas S., jt. auth. see Baden, John.

Noonan, Douglas S., jt. ed. see Baden, John A.

Noonan, G. Classification, Cladistics, & Natural History of Native North American Harpalus Latreille. (Thomas Say Monographs: Vol. 13). 310p. 1991. 25.00 (0-938522-35-3, ESATS13) Entomol Soc.

Noonan, Gary P., et al, eds. A Guide to Respiratory Protection for the Asbestos Abatement Industry. (Illus.). 183p. (C). 1997. reprint ed. pap. text 40.00 (0-7881-4156-2) DIANE Pub.

Noonan, George. Fixed Stars & Judical Astrology. 1990. pap. 19.00 (0-86690-376-3, 3028-014) Am Fed Astrologers.

— Spherical Astronomy for Astrologers. 64p. 1974. 7.00 (0-86690-134-5, N1357-014) Am Fed Astrologers.

Noonan, Gregory J. New Brewing Lager Beer: The Most Comprehensive Book for Home- & Microbrewers. (Illus.). 387p. 1996. pap. 14.95 (0-937381-46-2) Brewers Pubns.

— Scotch Ale. (Classic Beer Style Ser.). (Illus.). 197p. 1993. pap. 11.95 (0-937381-35-7) Brewers Pubns.

Noonan, Gregory J., et al. Seven Barrel Brewery Brewers' Handbook. 307p. (Orig.). 1996. pap. text 9.95 (1-887167-00-5) G W Kent.

Noonan, Harol W., ed. Personal Identity. LC 92-29002. (International Research Library of Philosophy). 560p. 1993. 184.95 (1-85521-299-4, Pub. by Dartmth Pub) Ashgate Pub Co.

Noonan, Harold W. Objects & Identity: An Examination of the Relative Identity Thesis & Its Consequences. (Melbourne International Philosophy Ser.: Vol. 6). 192p. 1980. text 126.50 (90-247-2292-6) Kluwer Academic.

— Personal Identity. (Problems of Philosophy Series: Their Past & Present). 304p. 1989. 55.00 (0-415-03365-9, A3246) Routledge.

— Personal Identity. (Problems of Philosophy Series: Their Past & Present). 304p. (C). 1991. pap. 17.95 (0-415-07047-3, A6284) Routledge.

*Noonan, Harold W. Routledge Philosophy Guidebook to Hume on Knowledge. LC 99-14365. 1999. pap. 14.99 (0-415-15047-7) Routledge.

— Routledge Philosophy Guidebook to Hume on Knowledge. 296p. (C). 1999. text 60.00 (0-415-15046-9) Routledge.

Noonan, Harold W., ed. Identity. (International Research Library of Philosophy). 478p. 1993. 163.95 (1-85521-294-3, Pub. by Dartmth Pub) Ashgate Pub Co.

Noonan, Hugh & Gasnick, Roy. Francis of Assisi: The Song Goes On. (Illus.). 48p. 1987. pap. 4.95 (0-86716-250-3, B2503) St Anthony Mess Pr.

Noonan, Janet & Calvert, Jacquelyn. Berries for the Queen. LC 92-32336. 32p. (J). (ps-2). 1994. 8.99 (0-7814-0903-9, Chariot Bks) Chariot Victor.

Noonan, Joe. Baile de Dinosaurios. Palacios, Argentina, tr. (Spanish Whole Language Big Bks.).Tr. of Dinosaur Dance. (SPA., Illus.). 16p. (Orig.). (J). (ps-2). 1995. pap. 14.95 (1-56784-074-4) Newbridge Educ.

— Dinosaur Dance. (Whole-Language Big Bks.). (Illus.). 16p. (Orig.). (J). (ps-2). 1994. pap. 16.95 (1-56784-073-6) Newbridge Educ.

Noonan, John F. A Critic & His Wife. LC 97-28469. 72p. 1997. pap. write for info. (1-55783-325-7) Applause Theatre Bk Pubs.

Noonan, John R. The Singing Bird Will Come: An AIDS Journal. Noonan, Mary R., ed. LC 96-54910. (Illus.). 150p. (Orig.). 1997. pap. 10.95 (0-9641725-4-2) Canticle Press.

Noonan, John T., Jr. The Balanced Budget: The States Call for a Convention. 1984. reprint ed. pap. 2.50 (0-911415-06-8) Natl Taxpayers Union Found.

— Contraception: A History of Its Treatment by the Catholic Theologians & Canonists. 592p. 1986. 45.00 (0-674-16853-4) HUP.

The Lustre of Our Country: The American Experience of Religious Freedom. LC 97 49327. 430p. 1998. 35.00 (0-520-20997-4, Pub. by U CA Pr) Cal Prin Full Svc.

*Noonan, John T. The Lustre of Our Country: The American Experience of Religious Freedom. LC 97-49327. 436p. 2000. pap. text 17.95 (0-520-22491-4) U CA Pr.

Noonan, John T. Power to Dissolve: Lawyers & Marriages in the Courts of the Roman Curia. LC 75-116044. 510p. reprint ed. pap. 158.10 (0-7837-3959-1, 204378800011) Bks Demand.

Noonan, John T., et al, eds. The Morality of Abortion: Legal & Historical Perspectives. LC 70-129118. 296p. reprint ed. pap. 91.80 (0-7837-2305-9, 205739300004) Bks Demand.

Noonan, John T., Jr., et al, eds. The Role & Responsibility of the Moral Philosopher: Proceedings, Vol. 56. LC 81-69068. 214p. 1982. pap. 20.00 (0-918090-16-4) Am Cath Philo.

Noonan, John T., Jr. & Painter, Richard W. The Lawyer: Personal & Professional Responsibility. LC 97-7143. (University Casebook Ser.). 866p. 1997. text. write for info. (1-56662-477-0) Foundation Pr.

— Professional & Personal Responsibilities of the Lawyer. (University Casebook Ser.). 171p. (C). 1997. pap. text. write for info. (1-56662-577-7) Foundation Pr.

Noonan, John T., Jr. & Winston, Kenneth I., eds. The Responsible Judge: Readings in Judicial Ethics. LC 92-31841. 416p. 1993. 79.50 (0-275-94022-5, C4022, Praeger Pubs); pap. 39.95 (0-275-94023-3, B4023, Praeger Pubs) Greenwood.

Noonan, Joseph & Nolan, Joseph. Gospel Bites: Illustrated Wisdom for Lectionary Cycles A, B, & C. LC 92-23076. (Illus.). 200p. (Orig.). (C). 1992. pap. 10.95 (0-89390-239-X) Resource Pubns.

*Noonan, Julia. Bath Day. (Puppy & Me Ser.). (Illus.). 20p. (J). (ps-1). 2000. pap. 6.99 (0-439-11492-6, Cartwheel) Scholastic Inc.

— Breakfast Time. (Puppy & Me Ser.). (Illus.). 20p. (J). (ps-1). 2000. 6.99 (0-439-11490-X, Cartwheel) Scholastic Inc.

— Going to the Corner. (Puppy & Me Ser.). (Illus.). 20p. (J). (ps-1). 2000. bds. 6.99 (0-439-17323-X) Scholastic Inc.

— Hare & Rabbit: Friends Forever. LC 99-44273. (Hello Reader! Ser.). (Illus.). 40p. (J). (gr. 1-3). 2000. pap. 3.99 (0-439-08753-8) Scholastic Inc.

— Hare & Rabbit: Friends Forever. (Illus.). (J). 2000. 9.44 (0-606-18556-9) Turtleback.

Noonan, Julia, jt. auth. see Krauss, Ruth.

Noonan, Margaret E. Influence of Summer Vacation on the Abilities of Fifth & Sixth Grade Children. LC 71-177111. (Columbia University. Teachers College. Contributions to Education Ser.: No. 204). reprint ed. 37.50 (0-404-55204-8) AMS Pr.

Noonan, Mary R., ed. see Noonan, John R.

Noonan, Maryellen, jt. auth. see Goldstein, Eda G.

Noonan, Meg, jt. auth. see Kiley, Deborah S.

Noonan, Melvin A. They Never Came Back: How to Lose Patients. LC 98-96363. (Illus.). 96p. 1998. 12.95 (0-9665934-0-5) Timbritom.

Noonan, Michael. A Different Drummer: The Story of E. J. Banfield, the Beachcomber of Dunk Island. LC 86-16027. (Illus.). 237p. 1987. pap. 16.95 (0-7022-2027-2, Pub. by Univ Queensland Pr) Intl Spec Bk.

— A Grammar of Lango. LC 92-5911. (Mouton Grammar Library: No. 7). xvi, 352p. (C). 1992. lib. bdg. 175.40 (3-11-012992-2) Mouton.

— In with the Tide: Memoirs of a Storyteller. 320p. 1996. pap 24.95 (0-7022-2710-2, Pub. by Univ Queensland Pr) Intl Spec Bk.

Noonan, Michael, ed. The Gentle Art of Beachcombing: A Collection of Writings by E. J. Banfield. 1989. pap. 16.95 (0-7022-2061-2, Pub. by Univ Queensland Pr) Intl Spec Bk.

*Noonan, Michael, et al. Chantyal Dictionary & Texts. LC 98-43669. (Trends in Linguistics Ser.). x, 616p. 1999. 186.00 (3-11-016240-7) De Gruyter.

Noonan, Michael, jt. ed. see Downing, Pamela.

Noonan, Michael P. Cabs I: Switched Access - An Introduction: Carrier Access Billing. LC 73-85629. (Specialized Ser.). (Illus.). 128p. 1996. pap., per. 65.00 (1-56016-048-9) ABC TeleTraining.

— Cabs III: Special Access: Carrier Access Billing. LC 73-85629. (Specialized Ser.). (Illus.). 171p. 1997. pap., spiral bd. 80.00 (1-56016-052-7) ABC TeleTraining.

— Cabs II: Switched Access-Rates & Invoices: Carrier Access Billing. LC 73-85629. (Specialized Ser.). (Illus.). 247p. 1996. pap., spiral bd. 75.00 (1-56016-049-7) ABC TeleTraining.

*Noonan, Nell. Meditations for Church School Teachers. 96p. 2001. pap. 6.95 (0-8192-1861-8) Morehouse Pub.

Noonan, Norma, jt. ed. see Rule, Wilma.

Noonan, Patrick F., jt. auth. see Diamond, Henry L.

*Noonan, Paula. The Write Strategy. 3rd ed. 300p. (C). 1999. spiral bd. 39.95 (0-7872-5858-X, 41585801) Kendall-Hunt.

*Noonan, Peggy. The Case Against Hillary Clinton. (Illus.). 208p. 2000. 24.00 (0-06-039340-8, ReganBks) HarperTrade.

Noonan, Peggy. Great Days. 1995. write for info. (0-614-15510-X) Random.

*Noonan, Peggy. On Speaking Well. LC 97-32537. 224p. 1999. pap. 13.00 (0-06-098740-5, ReganBks) HarperTrade.

— Ronald Reagan. 1999. write for info. (0-670-88235-6) Viking Penguin.

— Simply Speaking: How to Communicate Your Ideas with Style, Substance & Clarity. 212p. 1999. text 23.00 (0-7881-6775-8) DIANE Pub.

— Simply Speaking: Noonan,&Peggy, Set. unabridged ed. 1998. audio 18.00 (0-694-51889-1, 395603, Pub. by HarperAudio) Lndmrk Audiobks.

Noonan, R. A. Beware the Claw! (Monsterville Ser.: 5). (J). (gr. 3-7). 1996. pap. 3.99 (0 614-15782-X) Aladdin.

— Enter at Your Own Risk. LC 95-3173. 155p. (J). (gr. 4-5). 1995. mass mkt. 3.95 (0-689-71863-2, Mac Bks Young Read) S&S Childrens.

— Monsterville. LC 95-25850. (Monsterville USA Ser.: Vol. 6). (Illus.). 144p. (J). (gr. 3-7). 1996. pap. 3.99 (0-689-71868-3) Aladdin.

— Monsterville U. S. A., Vol 7. LC 95-52865. (J). 1996. pap. 3.99 (0-689-71869-1) Aladdin.

— New Grrrl in Town. (Monsterville Ser.). (J). (gr. 3-7). 1996. pap. 3.99 (0-614-15783-8) Aladdin.

— Wild Ghost Chase. (Monsterville Ser.). (J). (gr. 3-7). 1996. pap. 3.95 (0-614-15781-1) Aladdin.

Noonan, Rosalind. Sarah: Don't Say You Love Me. (Party of Five Ser.: No. 5). (J). (gr. 3-6). 1998. pap. 4.50 (0-671-02452-3, Minstrel Bks) PB.

*Noonan, Rosalind. Turning Seventeen: Any Guy You Want, No. 1. LC 00-100949. (Turning Seventeen Ser.: No. 1). 208p. (YA). (gr. 7 up). 2000. mass mkt. 4.95 (0-06-447237-X, HarpTrophy) HarpC Child Bks.

Noonan, Roz & Stine, Megan. Julia: Everything Changes. (Party of Five Ser.: No. 2). (J). (gr. 3-6). 1997. pap. 3.99 (0-671-01721-7) PB.

Noonan, Thomas, jt. ed. see Batalden, Steven K.

Noonan, Thomas E. Cat's Whiskers. Rockwell, Jeanne, ed. (Illus.). 125p. write for info. (0-9602934-1-8) Noon Rock.

Noonan, Thomas E., jt. ed. see Rockwell, Jeanne.

Noonan, Thomas F. The Islamic World, Russia & the Vikings, 750-900. (Variorum Collected Studies: Vol. 595). 350p. 1998. 99.95 (0-86078-657-9, HF3625.N66, Pub. by Ashgate Pub) Ashgate Pub Co.

Noone & Alexander. Cases & Materials on Terrorism, Three Nations' Response, Vol. ISO 7. LC 97-11350. 1997. 217.00 (90-411-0278-7) Kluwer Law Intl.

Noone, Donald J. Creative Problem Solving. 2nd ed. LC 98-6239. (Barron's Business Success Ser.). 96p. 1998. pap. 6.95 (0-7641-0403-9) Barron.

Noone, James A., ed. see Thole, Marsha L. & Ault, Frank W.

Noone, Joanne & Vonfrolio, Laura G. Critical Care Examination Review. 3rd ed. 415p. 1995. per. 24.95 (0-9627246-9-6) Power NY.

— Emergency Nursing Examination Review. 3rd ed. 486p. 1996. per. 24.95 (0-9627246-7-X) Power NY.

Noone, John. The Man Behind the Iron Mask, Vol. 1. 320p. 1994. pap. 16.95 (0-312-12345-0) St Martin.

Noone, John J. Challenge. LC 98-86523. 432p. 1998. text 26.95 (1-56167-421-4) Am Literary Pr.

Noone, Judith. The Same Fate As the Poor. rev. ed. LC 95-20271. 175p. 1995. pap. 13.00 (1-57075-031-9) Orbis Bks.

Noone, Leslie J. The Ability to Risk: Reading Skills for Beginning Students of ESL. (Illus.). 176p. (C). 1995. pap. text 25.40 (0-13-000357-3) P-H.

Noone, Michael. Mediation. MacFarland, Julie, ed. LC 97-101313. (Essential Legal Skills Ser.). 150p. 1996. pap. 22.00 (1-85941-202-5, Pub. by Cavendish Pubng) Gaunt.

— Music & Musicians in the Escorial Liturgy under the Habsburgs, 1563-1700, Vol. 9. LC 97-41721. (Eastman Studies in Music). (Illus.). 416p. 1998. 100.00 (1-878822-71-3) Univ Rochester Pr.

Noone, Michael, et al. Remedies: Commentary & Materials. 2nd ed. 1993. pap. 96.00 (0-455-21158-2, Pub. by LawBk Co) Gaunt.

Noone, Michael, jt. auth. see Kercher, Bruce.

Noone, Oliver. Caddywhacked! LC 97-220746. (Looney Tunes Pop-up Bks.). (Illus.). 10p. (J). (ps-k). 1997. bds. 7.98 (0-7853-2180-2, PIL19) Pubns Intl Ltd.

— Looney Tunes Spooky Stories. LC 97-214310. (Looney Tunes Song & Sound Bks.). (Illus.). 24p. (J). (ps-2). 1997. 14.98 (0-7853-2366-X, PI24) Pubns Intl Ltd.

— Pity the Puddy-Tat. LC 97-220742. (Looney Tunes Pop-up Bks.). (Illus.). 10p. (J). (ps-k). 1997. bds. 7.98 (0-7853-2181-0, PIL20) Pubns Intl Ltd.

— Space Case. LC 97-220738. (Looney Tunes Pop-up Bks.). (Illus.). 10p. (J). (ps-k). 1997. bds. 7.98 (0-7853-2183-7, PIL21) Pubns Intl Ltd.

— Teacher's Pest. LC 97-220714. (Looney Tunes Pop-up Bks.). (Illus.). 10p. (J). (ps-k). 1997. bds. 7.98 (0-7853-2182-9, PIL18) Pubns Intl Ltd.

Noone, Richard W. 5/5/2000: Ice: The Ultimate Disaster. 400p. 1997. pap. 16.00 (0-609-80067-1) Crown.

— 5/5/2000: Ice: The Ultimate Disaster. 400p. 1997. pap. 16.00 (0-614-28098-2) Crown Pub Group.

Noone, Steve, jt. auth. see Milne, Derek.

*Noonen, Tom. Pelicans Belly Can. (Illus.). 38p. (J). (ps-3). 1999. 14.95 (1-893385-04-3) Little Leaf.

Noor, A. K., ed. Buckling & Postbuckling of Composite Structures: 1994 International Mechanical Engineering Congress & Exposition, Chicago, Illinois - November 6-11, 1994. (AD - PVP Ser.: Vol. 41, Vol. 293). 140p. 1994. 60.00 (0-7918-1443-2, G00938) ASME.

— Impact of New Computing Systems on Computational Mechanics. 176p. 1983. pap. text 34.00 (0-317-02625-9, H00275) ASME.

Noor, A. K. & Dwoyer, D. L., eds. Computational Structural Mechanics & Fluid Dynamics: Advances & Trends - Papers Presented at the Symposium Held in Washington DC, U. S. A., 17-19 October 1988. (Computers & Structures Ser.). 448p. 1988. 125.00 (0-08-037197-3, Pergamon Pr) Elsevier.

Noor, A. K. & Housner, J. M., eds. Advances & Trends in Structural & Solid Mechanics: Proceedings of the Symposium, Washington D.C., October 4-7, 1982. 587p. 1983. 180.00 (0-08-029990-3, Pergamon Pr) Elsevier.

Noor, A. K. & McComb, H. G., Jr. Trends in Computerized Structural Analysis & Synthesis, Vol. 10, No. 1-2. 1978. 83.00 (0-08-023261-2) Elsevier.

— Trends in Computerized Structural Analysis & Synthesis, Vol. 10, No. 1-2. 1981. pap. 91.00 (0-08-028707-7, Pergamon Pr) Elsevier.

Noor, A. K. & Needleman, A., eds. Computational Material Modeling: 1994 International Mechanical Engineering Congress & Exposition, Chicago, Illinois - November 6-11, 1994. (AD - PVP Ser.: Vol. 42, Vol. 294). 320p. 1994. 90.00 (0-7918-1444-0, G00939) ASME.

N

Noor, A. K. & Reifsnider, K. L., eds. Durability & Damage Tolerance: 1994 International Mechanical Engineering Congress & Exposition, Chicago, Illinois - November 6-11, 1994. (AD Ser.: Vol. 43). 352p. 1994. 96.00 (*0-7918-1445-9*, G00940) ASME.

Noor, A. K. & Venneri, Samuel L., eds. Flight Vehicle Materials, Structures, & Dynamics Vol. 5: Structural Dynamics & Aeroelasticity. LC 92-170509. 524p. 1993. 105.00 (*0-7918-0663-4*, I00326) ASME.

Noor, Ahmed K., ed. Structures Technology: Historical Perspective & Evaluation. LC 98-5292. (Illus.). 528p. 1998. text 64.95 (*1-56347-116-7*) AIAA.

Noor, Ahmed K. & Venneri, Samuel L., eds. Flight-Vehicle Materials, Structures & Dynamics: Assessment & Future Directions, New & Projected Aeronautical & Space Systems, Design Concepts, & Loads. LC 92-52644. 553p. 1994. 100.00 (*0-7918-0659-6*) ASME.

— Flight-Vehicle Materials, Structures, & Dynamics Vol. 6: Assessment & Future Directions: Computational Structures Technology. LC 92-52644. 187p. 1995. 100.00 (*0-7918-0664-2*, 100327) ASME.

— Future Aeronautical & Space Systems. 579p. 1997. 114.95 (*1-56347-188-4*) AIAA.

Noor Al-Deen, Hana S. Cross-Cultural Communication & Aging in the United States. LC 97-6306. 1997. write for info. (*0-8058-2294-1*); pap. write for info. (*0-8058-2295-X*) L Erlbaum Assocs.

Noor, Asghar. System Design with the MC68020, MC68030 & MC68040 32-Bit Microprocessors. LC 92-12923. 587p. 1994. text 59.95 (*0-442-31886-3*, VNR) Wiley.

Noor, F. A. & Boswell, L. F., eds. Small Scale Modelling of Concrete Structures. (Illus.). 352p. (C). (gr. 13). 1992. text 150.00 (*1-85166-671-0*) Elsevier Applied Sci.

***Noorani, A. G.** Constitutional Questions in India: The President, Parliament & the States. (Law in India Ser.). 280p. 2000. text 19.95 (*0-19-564952-4*) OUP.

Noorani, A. G. Indian Affairs: The Constitutional Dimension. 424p. 1990. text 45.00 (*81-220-0198-X*, Pub. by Konark Pubs Pvt Ltd) Advent Bks Div.

— Indian Affairs: The Political Dimension. 400p. 1990. text 45.00 (*81-220-0199-8*, Pub. by Konark Pubs Pvt Ltd) Advent Bks Div.

— Indian Affairs, the Constitutional Dimension. (C). 1990. 100.00 (*0-89771-201-3*) St Mut.

— The Presidential System: The Indian Debate. 136p. (C). 1989. 25.00 (*0-8039-9610-1*) Sage.

Noorani, A. G., ed. The Gulf Wars: Documents & Analysis. xxxvi, 402p. 1992. text 45.00 (*81-220-0250-1*, Pub. by Konark Pubs Pvt Ltd) Advent Bks Div.

Noorbergen, Rene. Secrets of the Lost Races. LC 77-76883. (Illus.). 1977. write for info. (*0-672-52289-6*) Macmillan.

— Treasures of the Lost Races. LC 82-4209. 1982. 13.95 (*0-672-52696-4*, Bobbs) Macmillan.

Noord, Barbara B. Van, see Van Noord, Barbara B.

Noordam, D. Identification of Plant Viruses: Methods & Experiments. 207p. 1990. 120.00 (*81-7089-118-3*, Pub. by Intl Bk Distr) St Mut.

Noordegraaf, Jan, et al, eds. The History of Linguistics in the Low Countries. LC 92-6410. (Studies in the History of the Language Sciences: No. 64). vi, 400p. 1992. 89.00 (*1-55619-359-9*) J Benjamins Pubng Co.

Noordegraaf, Leo, jt. auth. see Dijstelberge, Paul.

Noordeloos, M. E. Entoloma in North America: The Species Described by L. R. Helser, A. H. Smith & S. J. Mazzer. (Cryptogamic Studies: Vol. 2). (Illus.). 164p. 1988. pap. 50.70 (*3-457-30506-4*) Lubrecht & Cramer.

Noordeloos, Machiel E. Entoloma (Agaricales) in Europe: Synopsis & Keys to All Species & a Monograph of the Subgenera Trichopilus, Inocephalus, Alboleptonia, Leptonia, Paraleptonia & Omphaliopsis. (Nova Hedwigia, Beihefte/Supplementary Issues Ser.: Beih 91). (Illus.). vi, 419p. 1988. pap. text 165.00 (*3-443-51013-2*, Pub. by Gebruder Borntraeger) Balogh.

— Entoloma in North America. (Cryptogamie Studies: Vol. 2). 164p. 1988. pap. text 70.00 (*0-89574-276-4*, Pub. by Gustav Fischer) Balogh.

Noorden, Susan Van, see Polak, Julia & Van Noorden, Susan.

Noordenbos, Greta, jt. auth. see Vandereycken, Walter.

Noordergraaf, Abraham, et al. Ballistocardiography & Cardiac Performance. LC 67-27246. 156p. 1967. 10.50 (*0-87527-062-X*) Green.

Noordhuis, Klaas T. The Complete Book of Gardening: A Comprehensive Guide to Planting, Growing, & Maintaining Your Garden. 480p. 1995. 29.98 (*1-56799-193-9*, MetroBooks) M Friedman Pub Grp Inc.

— The Garden Plants Encyclopedia. Tomlinson, David, ed. LC 97-932268. (Illus.). 320p. 1998. pap. 19.95 (*1-55209-206-2*) Firefly Bks Ltd.

Noordhuis, Klaas T. & Benvie, Sam. Bulbs & Tubers: The Complete Guide to Flowers from Bulbs. (Illus.). 144p. 1998. 19.95 (*1-55209-202-X*) Firefly Bks Ltd.

Noordman, L. G. Inferring from Language. (Language & Communiction Ser.: Vol. 4). (Illus.). 1979. 34.95 (*0-387-09386-9*) Spr-Verlag.

Noordman-Vonk, W. Retrieval from Semantic Memory. (Language & Communication Ser.: Vol. 5). (Illus.). 1979. 24.95 (*0-387-09219-6*) Spr-Verlag.

Noordraven, G. Die Fiduzia im Romischen Recht. (Studia Amstelodamensia Studies in Ancient Law & Society: Vol. 37). (GER.). 394p. 1999. 98.00 (*90-5063-062-6*, Pub. by Gieben) J Benjamins Pubng Co.

Noordtzij, A. Bible Student's Commentary: Leviticus. (Bible Student's Commentary Ser.). 288p. 1983. 19.95 (*0-310-45090-X*, 11757) Zondervan.

— Bible Student's Commentary: Numbers. (Bible Student's Commentary Ser.). 1983. 19.95 (*0-310-43980-9*, 11758) Zondervan.

Noordung, Herman. The Problem with Space Travel: The Rocket Motor. Stuhlinger, Ernst et al, eds. (Illus.). 149p. (C). 1995. pap. text 35.00 (*0-7881-1849-8*) DIANE Pub.

Noordung, Hermann. Problem of Space Travel: The Rocket Motor. 176p. 1995. per. 13.00 (*0-16-061847-9*) USGPO.

Noordung, Hermann. The Problem with Space Travel: The Rocket Motor. (Illus.). 176p. 1995. pap. text 50.00 (*1-57979-064-X*) DIANE Pub.

Noordzij, Gerrit. Letter Letter. (Illus.). 160p. 2000. pap. 19.95 (*0-88179-175-X*, Pub. by Hartley & Marks) Andrews & McMeel.

***Noordzy, Magdalena, ed.** The Interuniversal Poetry Album. (Illus.). 43p. 1999. ring bd. 14.95 (*0-9647357-4-1*, Pub. by Starseed & Uran) Aquarian Concpts.

Nooren, M. J., jt. ed. see Schouten, M. G.

Noori. Operations Management (Expert) 1995. 30.50 (*0-07-832599-4*) McGraw.

— Productions & Operations Management. 1995. text 75.25 (*0-07-912257-4*) McGraw.

Noori, Andy, jt. auth. see Urieli, Israel.

Noori, Ayatollah Y. Legal & Political Structure of an Islamic State: Implications for Iran & Pakistan. 144p. 1987. 60.00 (*0-946706-31-X*, Pub. by Royston Ltd) St Mut.

Noori, Hamid. Managing the Dynamics of New Technology: Issues in Manufacturing Management. 352p. (C). 1989. text 57.00 (*0-13-551763-X*) P-H.

Noori, Hamid & Anatol, Frank. Decision Inventory Package. viii, 58p. 1989. 190.75 incl. 5.25 hd (*0-444-98710-X*) Elsevier.

Noori, Hamid & Radford, Russell. Production & Operations Management: Total Quality & Responsiveness. LC 94-33821. (C). 1994. pap. text, wbk. ed. 70.25 (*0-07-912037-7*) McGraw.

— Productions & Operations Management: Total Quality & Responsiveness. LC 94-33821. 1994. text 61.75 (*0-07-046923-7*) McGraw.

Noori, Y. Finality of Prophethood. 176p. 1985. 25.00 (*0-946706-19-0*, Pub. by Royston Ltd) St Mut.

— Islamic Government & the Revolution in Iran. 1985. 75.00 (*0-946706-25-5*, Pub. by Royston Ltd) St Mut.

Nooriala, Esmail, tr. see Mirzadahgi, Shukuh.

Noorlun, Lyle J. I Can-Can. 131p. (YA). (gr. 9 up). 1989. 16.95 incl. audio (*1-877616-00-1*) Wholeness Intl.

Noorman, Klaas J. & Uiterkamp, Ton S., eds. Green Households? Domestic Consumers, the Environment & Sustainability. 192p. 1997. 80.00 (*1-85383-481-5*, Pub. by Escan Pubns); pap. 32.00 (*1-85383-482-3*, Pub. by Escan Pubns) Island Pr.

Noort, Stanley Van den, see Van den Noort, Stanley, ed.

Noort, Van. An Introduction to Dental Materials. 240p. 1994. text 37.50 (*0-7234-1963-9*) Mosby Inc.

Nooruddin, Allamah. The Holy Quran: An English Translation. 2nd deluxe ed. Mannan, Abdul & Omer, Amatul Rahma, trs. 839p. 1997. pap. 20.00 (*0-9632067-0-2*) Noor Found.

Noory, Samuel. Dictionary of Pronunciation. 4th ed. LC 81-66273. 512p. 1982. 19.95 (*0-8453-4722-5*, Cornwall Bks) Assoc Univ Prs.

Nooshin, H. Formex Configuration Processing in Structural Engineering. (Illus.). xi, 276p. 1985. mass mkt. 105.50 (*0-85334-315-2*) Elsevier.

Noot, Jan Van Der, see Van Der Noot, Jan.

Noot, Jurrien, jt. auth. see Polmar, Norman.

***Nooteboom.** All Souls. 2001. write for info. (*0-15-100566-4*) Harcourt.

***Nooteboom, B.** Inter-Firm Alliances: Analysis & Design. LC 99-200364. x, 239 p. 1999. pap. write for info. (*0-415-18154-2*) Routledge.

— Inter-Firm Alliances: Analysis & Design. LC 99-200364. (Illus.). 1999. write for info. (*0-415-18153-4*) Routledge.

Nooteboom, Bart, jt. auth. see de Jong, Gjalt.

Nooteboom, Bart, jt. ed. see Saviotti, Paolo.

Nooteboom, Cees. Following Story. 128p. 1994. 14.95 (*0-15-100098-0*) Harcourt.

— The Following Story. Rilke, Ina, tr. from DUT. LC 95-19627. 128p. 1996. reprint ed. pap. 11.00 (*0-15-600254-X*) Harcourt.

— Rituals: A Novel. Dixon, Adrienne, tr. 160p. 1996. pap. 11.00 (*0-15-600394-5*, Harvest Bks) Harcourt.

— Rituals: A Novel. Dixon, Adrienne, tr. from DUT. LC 82-17278. vi, 145p. 1983. 16.95 (*0-8071-1081-7*) La State U Pr.

***Nooteboom, Cees.** Roads to Santiago. 2000. pap. 15.00 (*0-15-601158-1*) Harcourt.

Nooteboom, Cees. Roads to Santiago: Detours & Riddles in the Lands & History of Spain. Rilke, Ina, tr. from DUT. (Illus.). 360p. 1997. 25.00 (*0-15-100197-9*) Harcourt.

— A Song of Truth & Semblance. Dixon, Adrienne, tr. from DUT. LC 84-848. Orig. Title: Een Liedvan schijn en wezen. 83p. 1984. 12.95 (*0-8071-1176-7*) La State U Pr.

***Nooteboom, H. P.** Davalliaceae: A Family of Old World (Sub)Tropical Ferns. 2000. cd-rom 49.95 (*3-540-14818-3*) Spr-Verlag.

Nooter, M. & Roberts, Allen F. Luba. LC 96-31073. (Heritage Library of African Peoples). (Illus.). 64p. (YA). (gr. 7-12). 1996. lib. bdg. 16.95 (*0-8239-2002-X*) Rosen Group.

Nooter, Mary H., et al, eds. Secrecy: African Art That Conceals & Reveals. LC 92-38495. (Illus.). 256p. 1993. 75.00 (*3-7913-1230-8*, Pub. by Prestel) te Neues.

Nooter, Nancy I., jt. auth. see Nooter, Robert.

Nooter, Robert & Nooter, Nancy I. The Art of Collecting African Art. Vogel, Susan M., ed. LC 88-7253. (Illus.). 64p. (Orig.). (C). 1988. pap. text 14.50 (*0-9614587-9-8*) Museum African.

Nooy, G. C. & Nederlands Instituut Voor Internationale Betrekkin. Cooperative Security, the OSCE & Its Code of Conduct. LC 96-48859. (Nijhoff Law Specials Ser.). 1997. pap. write for info. (*90-411-0316-3*) Kluwer Law Intl.

Nopar, Charles, tr. see Martinelli, Maria C.

***Nopens, Horst W.** Die rechtliche Ausgestaltung der Apartheid. 2000. 34.95 (*3-631-35283-2*) P Lang Pubng.

Nophlin, Barbara, ed. Fun with Math Resource Kit. 1988. teacher ed. 299.00 (*0-88076-137-7*, 17246) Kaplan Pr.

— Manipulative Resource I. 1988. student ed. 99.50 (*0-88076-128-8*, 15645) Kaplan Pr.

— Manipulative Resource II. 1988. student ed. 175.50 (*0-88076-129-6*, 15646) Kaplan Pr.

Noponen, Helzi, et al, eds. Trading Industries, Trading Regions: International Trade, American Industry & Regional Economic Development. LC 93-19475. (Perspectives on Economic Change Ser.). 290p. 1993. pap. text 20.95 (*0-89862-753-2*) Guilford Pubns.

Noppen, Ina Van, see Van Noppen, Ina.

Noppen, Jean-Pierre Van, see Van Noppen, Jean-Pierre.

Noppen, John Van, see Van Noppen, Ina & Van Noppen, John.

Noppen, Luc. One of the Most Beautiful Chapels in the Land. (Illus.). 52p. 1988. pap. 16.95 (*0-88884-576-6*, Pub. by Natl Gallery) U Ch Pr.

Nora, James. The Upstart Spring. LC 89-3111. 352p. 1989. 16.95 (*0-922811-00-8*) Mid-List.

Nora, James J. The New Whole Heart Book. 2nd ed. (Illus.). 350p. 1989. reprint ed. 18.95 (*0-922811-02-4*); reprint ed. pap. 10.95 (*0-922811-03-2*) Mid-List.

Nora, James J., et al. Cardiovascular Diseases: Genetics, Epidemiology & Prevention. (Oxford Monographs on Medical Genetics: No. 22). (Illus.). 208p. 1991. text 39.95 (*0-19-506032-6*, 2924) OUP.

— Medical Genetics: Principles & Practice. 4th ed. LC 93-19984. (Illus.). 420p. 1994. 42.50 (*0-8121-1663-1*) Lppncott W & W.

Nora, James J., jt. auth. see Fraser, F. Clarke.

Nora, Paul F., ed. Professional Liability-Risk Management: A Manual for Surgeons. 240p. 1991. pap. text. write for info. (*0-9620370-8-7*) Am Coll Surgeons.

Nora, Paul F. & American College of Surgeons Staff. Professional Liability-Risk Management: A Manual for Surgeons. 2nd ed. LC 96-35880. 1997. pap. write for info. (*1-880696-08-8*) Am Coll Surgeons.

Nora, Pierre. Memory of France, Vol. 1. 1996. 35.00 (*0-226-59132-8*) U Ch Pr.

— The Places of Memory, Vol. 2. 1996. 39.95 (*0-226-59133-6*) U Ch Pr.

— The Places of Memory, Vol. 3. 1996. 39.95 (*0-226-59134-4*) U Ch Pr.

— The Places of Memory, Vol. 4. 1996. 39.95 (*0-226-59135-2*) U Ch Pr.

Nora, Pierre. Realms of Memory Vol. 2: Traditions. 576p. (C). 1997. 39.50 (*0-231-10634-3*) Col U Pr.

— Realms of Memory Vol. III: The Construction of the French Past, Symbols. (Realms of Memory Ser.). (Illus.). 688p. 1998. 39.50 (*0-231-10926-1*) Col U Pr.

Noraas, Margaret. Math Activities for Preschool. 93p. (J). (ps). pap. text 12.95 (*0-9637985-0-2*) Penguin Family.

***Norac, Carl.** Hello, Sweetie Pie. LC 99-32204. (Illus.). 24p. (J). (gr. k-1). 2000. 10.95 (*0-385-32733-1*) BDD Bks Young Read.

Norac, Carl. I Love to Cuddle. LC 98-25646. (Illus.). 32p. (J). (ps-1). 1999. 9.95 (*0-385-32646-7*) BDD Bks Young Read.

— I Love You So Much. LC 96-49647. (Illus.). 32p. (J). (ps-1). 1998. 9.95 (*0-385-32512-6*, DD Bks Yng Read) BDD Bks Young Read.

Norang, N., jt. auth. see Goldstein, G.

***Norausky, Patrick.** The Customer & Supplier Innovation Team: Guidebook. LC 99-462076. 2000. write for info. (*0-87389-479-0*) ASQ Qual Pr.

Noravtov, Yu A., ed. see Galperin, A. M. & Zaytsev, V. S.

Norback, Craig T. Human Resource Yearbook, 1989. 750p. 1989. 79.95 (*0-318-41473-2*) P-H.

— The Human Resources Yearbook. 720p. 1987. text 75.00 (*0-13-446378-1*) P-H.

— VGM's Careers Encyclopedia. 3rd ed. LC 90-50726. 502p. (YA). (gr. 7 up). 1995. 39.95 (*0-8442-8692-3*, VGM Career) NTC Contemp Pub Co.

— VGM's Handbook of Business & Management Careers. 1993. pap. 12.95 (*0-8442-8683-4*, VGM Career) NTC Contemp Pub Co.

— VGM's Handbook of Scientific & Technical Careers. 1993. pap. 12.95 (*0-8442-8684-2*, VGM Career) NTC Contemp Pub Co.

Norback, Craig T., jt. auth. see Burrill, Steven G.

Norback, Craig T., jt. auth. see Norback, Peter.

Norback, Peter & Norback, Craig T. The Must Words: The Six Thousand Most Important Words for a Successful & Profitable Vocabulary. 312p. 1983. pap. 12.95 (*0-07-047141-X*) McGraw.

Norbeck, Edward. Changing Japan. 2nd ed. (Illus.). 108p. 1984. reprint ed. pap. text 10.50 (*0-88133-076-0*) Waveland Pr.

— Country to City: The Urbanization of a Japanese Hamlet. LC 77-14737. 381p. reprint ed. pap. 118.20 (*0-8357-3272-X*, 203949300013) Bks Demand.

— Religion in Human Life: Anthropological Views. 74p. (C). 1988. reprint ed. pap. text 8.50 (*0-88133-354-9*) Waveland Pr.

Norbeck, Edward, jt. ed. see Jennings, Jesse D.

Norbeck, Edward, ed. see Rice University Staff.

Norbeck, Jane, jt. auth. see Fitzpatrick, Joyce.

Norbeck, Jane, jt. ed. see Fitzpatrick, Joyce J.

Norbeck, Jane S., et al, eds. Caring & Community: Concepts & Models for Service Learning in Nursing. (Service-Learning in the Disciplines Ser.). 208p. 1998. pap. 28.50 (*1-56377-009-1*, SLI0DS) Am Assn Higher Ed.

Norbeck, Joseph M. Hydrogen Fuel for Surface Transportation. LC 96-38602. 1996. 89.00 (*1-56091-684-2*, R-160) Soc Auto Engineers.

Norbeck, Oscar E. Book of Authentic Indian Life Crafts. rev. ed. LC 74-81910. (Illus.). 260p. 1974. 10.95 (*0-87874-012-0*) Galloway.

Norbelie, Barbro A. Oppressive Narrowness: A Study of the Female Community in George Eliot's Early Writings. (Studia Anglistica Upsaliensia Ser.: No. 80). 163p. (Orig.). 1992. pap. 45.00 (*91-554-2982-3*) Coronet Bks.

Norbelle, Bernard, tr. see Hedin, Sven A.

Norberg, Arthur L., et al. Transforming Computer Technology: Information Processing for the Pentagon, 1962-1986. LC 95-23820. (Studies in the History of Technology). 384p. (C). 1996. text 49.95 (*0-8018-5152-1*) Johns Hopkins.

Norberg, Dag. Syntaktische Forscshungen auf dem Gebiet des Spatlateins. (Universitets Arsskrift Ser.: No. 9). 283p. 1990. reprint ed. write for info. (*3-487-09347-2*) G Olms Pubs.

Norberg, Eric G. Radio Programming: Tactics & Strategy. 208p. 1996. pap. 31.95 (*0-240-80234-9*, Focal) Buttrwrth-Heinemann.

Norberg, Fran, jt. ed. see Ashworth, Sam.

Norberg-Hodge, Helena. Ancient Futures: Learning from Ladakh. LC 91-13868. (Illus.). 224p. 1992. reprint ed. pap. 12.00 (*0-87156-643-5*, Pub. by Sierra) Random.

Norberg, Inga. Good Food from Sweden. 192p. 1996. reprint ed. pap. 10.95 (*0-7818-0486-8*) Hippocrene Bks.

Norberg, Jeanne, ed. see Norberg, John.

Norberg, John. A Force for Change: The Class of 1950. 1995. 24.95 (*0-931682-54-1*) Purdue U Pubns.

— Hail Purdue: A Century of Music at Purdue University. Dunscomb, J. Richard & Norberg, Jeanne, eds. LC 86-72652. 240p. 1987. lib. bdg. 40.95 (*0-9617991-0-2*) All Amer Band Club.

Norberg, Jon. Academic Sportfolio. Gallup, Beth, ed. (Elementary Ser.). (Illus.). 1200p. (J). (gr. 3-6). 1987. 495.00 (*0-685-24265-X*) Acad Sportfolio.

— Academic Sportfolio: Excuse Notes Are No Excuse. Pranzo, Donard, ed. (Elementary Ser.). (Illus.). (J). (gr. 3-6). 1987. 50.00 (*0-924086-00-9*) Acad Sportfolio.

Norberg, Kathryn, jt. auth. see Melzer, Sara E.

Norberg, Kathryn, jt. ed. see Hoffman, Philip T.

Norberg, Robert N., ed. see Nance, Paul J.

Norberg-Schulz, Christian. Architecture Presence. 1997. 45.00 (*1-885254-47-4*) Monacelli Pr.

— Genius Loci: Towards a Phenomenology of Architecture. LC 79-56612. (Illus.). 216p. 1991. pap. 27.50 (*0-8478-0287-6*, Pub. by Rizzoli Intl) St Martin.

— Intentions in Architecture. (Illus.). 1968. pap. text 16.00 (*0-262-64002-3*) MIT Pr.

— Nightlands: Nordic Building. McQuillan, Thomas, tr. (Illus.). 240p. 1996. 40.00 (*0-262-14057-8*) MIT Pr.

— Nightlands: Nordic Building. (Illus.). 240p. 1997. reprint ed. pap. text 18.50 (*0-262-64036-8*) MIT Pr.

Norberg, Tilda. Threadbear: A Story of Christian Healing for Adult Survivors of Sexual Abuse. (Illus.). 120p. 1997. pap. 12.00 (*0-9658707-0-7*) Penn Hse Pr.

Norberg, Tilda & Webber, Robert D. Stretch Out Your Hand: Exploring Healing Prayer. LC 98-20638. 144p. 1999. 10.00 (*0-8358-0872-6*) Upper Room Bks.

Norberg, U. Vertebrate Flight. (Zoophysiology Ser.: Vol. 27). (Illus.). 305p. 1990. 227.95 (*0-387-51370-1*) Spr-Verlag.

Norberg, Viveca Halldin, see Halldin Norberg, Viveca.

Norberry, J., et al, eds. HIV/AIDS & Prisons. (Australian Institute Conference Proceedings Ser.: Vol. 4). 300p. 1991. pap. 25.00 (*0-642-16202-6*, Pub. by Aust Inst Criminology) Advent Bks Div.

Norbet, Gregory. Morning Prayer Evening Prayer: Chants, Songs & Prayers. (Illus.). 70p. 1996. pap. 8.95 (*0-915531-53-4*, 10118) OR Catholic.

***Norbet, Gregory.** Morning Prayer Evening Prayer Vol. 2: Chants, Songs & Prayers. (Illus.). 69p. 1998. pap. 8.95 incl. audio (*0-915531-91-7*, 10637) OR Catholic.

Norbie, Donald L. Baptism: The Church's Troubled Water. 1984. pap. 3.00 (*0-937396-64-8*) Walterick Pubs.

— Danny, a Life Cut Short. 1994. pap. text 6.00 (*0-937396-97-4*) Walterick Pubs.

— Divorce & the Bible. 1971. pap. 3.25 (*0-937396-12-5*) Walterick Pubs.

— First Timothy: Timeless Truths for Today's Church. 1991. pap. 6.00 (*0-937396-85-0*) Walterick Pubs.

— The Lord's Supper: The Church's Love Feast. 1986. pap. 3.00 (*0-937396-67-2*) Walterick Pubs.

— New Testament Church Organization. 1977. pap. 6.00 (*0-937396-28-1*) Walterick Pubs.

— Second Timothy & Titus. 1992. pap. 7.00 (*0-937396-90-7*) Walterick Pubs.

Norbrook, David. The Penguin Book of Renaissance Verse, 1509-1659. Woudhuysen, H. R., ed. 960p. 1993. pap. 23.95 (*0-14-042346-X*, Penguin Classics) Viking Penguin.

— Poetry & Politics in the English Renaissance. 280p. 1984. 32.50 (*0-7100-9778-6*, Routledge Thoemms) Routledge.

Norbrook, David. Writing the English Republic: Poetry, Rhetoric & Politics, 1627-1660. LC 98-3856. 540p. (C). 1999. 69.95 (*0-521-63275-7*) Cambridge U Pr.

***Norbrook, David.** Writing the English Republic: Poetry, Rhetoric & Politics, 1627-1660. 510p. (C). 2000. 24.95 (*0-521-78569-3*) Cambridge U Pr.

Norbrook, David, ed. see Hutchinson, Lucy.

Norbrook, Dominique. Getting to Know France. 2nd ed. (Getting to Know Ser.). (Illus.). 48p. (J). 1989. 9.95 (*0-8442-1410-8*, 14108, Passprt Bks) NTC Contemp Pub Co.

Norbu, Chogyal N. The Crystal & the Way of Light: Sutra, Tantra & Dzogchen. Shane, John, ed. & compiled by. (Illus.). 215p. 1999. pap. 16.95 (*1-55939-135-9*) Snow Lion Pubns.

Norbu, Chogyal N. & Clemente, Adriano. The Supreme Source: The Kunjed Gyalpo, The Fundamental Tantra of Dzogchen Semde. Lukianowicz, Andrew, tr. from TIB. LC 99-30399.Tr. of La Suprema Sorgente (Italian). (ITA., Illus.). 300p. 1999. pap. 19.95 (*1-55939-120-0*) Snow Lion Pubns.

N

An Asterisk (*) at the beginning of an entry indicates that the title is appearing for the first time.

Norbu, Dawa. China's Tibet Policy. (Durham East Asia Ser.). 260p. (C). 1998. text 45.00 (*0-7007-0474-4*, Pub. by Curzon Pr Ltd) UH Pr.

— Tibet. LC 97-913834. 1998. 19.95 (*81-7437-094-3*) Heian Intl.

***Norbu, Dawa.** Tibet: The Road Ahead. 416p. 2000. pap. 13.95 (*0-7126-7063-7*, Pub. by Rider) Trafalgar.

***Norbu, Jamyang.** Sherlock Holmes: The Missing Years. 2001. 23.95 (*1-58234-132-X*) Bloomsbury Pubg.

Norbu, Jamyang. Warriors of Tibet: The Story of Aten & the Khampas' Fight for the Freedom of Their Country. (Tibet Book - Yellow Ser.). 152p. 1986. pap. 12.95 (*0-86171-050-9*) Wisdom MA.

***Norbu, Kalsang, et al.** Modern Oral Amdo Tibetan: A Language Primer. LC 99-47833. (Studies in Linguistics & Semiotics: Vol. 5). 324p. 2000. text 99.95 (*0-7734-7895-7*) E Mellen.

Norbu, Namkhai. Dream Yoga & the Practice of Natural Light. Katz, Michael, ed. LC 92-16147. 128p. 1992. pap. 12.95 (*1-55939-007-7*) Snow Lion Pubns.

— Dzog Chen & Zen. Lipman, Kennard, ed. (Illus.). 48p. (Orig.). 1987. pap. 5.00 (*0-931892-08-2*) B Dolphin Pub.

— Dzogchen: The Self-Perfected State. Clemente, Adriano, ed. Shane, John, tr. (Illus.). 152p. 1996. reprint ed. pap. 12.95 (*1-55939-057-3*) Snow Lion Pubns.

— Mirror: Advice on the Presence of Awareness. LC 96-36348. 80p. 1995. pap. text 9.95 (*1-886449-10-4*) Barrytown Ltd.

Norbu, Thinley. Magic Dance: The Display of the Self-Nature of the Five Wisdom Dakinis. LC 98-20349. (Orig.). 1998. pap. 14.00 (*0-87773-885-8*, Pub. by Shambhala Pubns) Random.

— The Small Golden Key. Anderson, Lisa, tr. LC 92-56459. 120p. 1993. reprint ed. pap. 11.00 (*0-87773-856-4*, Pub. by Shambhala Pubns) Random.

Norbu, Thinley. Welcoming Flowers: Across the Cleansed Threshhold of Hope. 1997. pap. 12.00 (*0-9607000-5-6*) Jewel Pub Hse.

Norbu, Thubten J. Tibet Is My Country: Autobiography of Thubten Jigme Norbu, Brother of the Dalai Lama, as Told to Heinrich Harrer. Fitzgerald, Edward, tr. from GER. (Tibet Book - Yellow Ser.). 276p. 1986. pap. 16.95 (*0-86171-045-2*) Wisdom MA.

Norburn, C. S. & Norburn, Russell. A New Monetary System. 1979. lib. bdg. 59.95 (*0-8490-2977-5*) Gordon Pr.

Norburn, Russell, jt. auth. see Norburn, C. S.

Norbury, Betty. Fine Craftsmanship in Wood. LC 90-6336. (Illus.). 192p. 1990. 39.95 (*0-941936-18-X*) Linden Pub Fresno.

***Norbury, Betty.** Furniture for the 21st Century. (Illus.). 192p. 2000. 39.95 (*0-670-89169-X*, Viking) Viking Penguin.

Norbury, Ian. Carving Facial Expressions. LC 97-36116. (Illus.). 64p. 1997. pap. 14.95 (*0-941936-43-0*) Linden Pub Fresno.

— Fundamentals of Figure Carving. LC 93-31545. (Illus.). 160p. 1993. reprint ed. 31.95 (*0-941936-26-0*) Linden Pub Fresno.

— Projects for Creative Woodcarving. LC 94-32689. (Illus.). 187p. 1994. reprint ed. pap. 19.95 (*0-941936-30-9*) Linden Pub Fresno.

— Relief Woodcarving & Lettering. LC 88-2257. 157p. 1988. reprint ed. pap. 18.95 (*0-941936-11-2*) Linden Pub Fresno.

— Techniques of Creative Wood Carving. 2nd ed. LC 94-5579. 160p. 1994. reprint ed. pap. 19.95 (*0-941936-29-5*) Linden Pub Fresno.

Norbury, J. K. Word Formation in the Noun & Adjective. LC 67-10258. (Studies in the Modern Russian Language: No. 13). 135p. reprint ed. pap. 38.50 (*0-608-13032-X*, 2024503) Bks Demand.

Norbury, James. Traditional Knitting Patterns from Scandinavia, the British Isles, France, Italy & Other European Countries. LC 73-79490. (Illus.). 240p. 1973. reprint ed. pap. 9.95 (*0-486-21013-8*) Dover.

Norbury, Paul & Bownas, Geoffrey. Business in Japan: A Guide to Japanese Business Practice & Procedure. 2nd rev. ed. 226p. 1985. 100.00 (*0-7855-0763-9*, Pub. by P Norbury Pubns Ltd) St Mut.

Norbury, Paul, jt. auth. see Hobday, Peter.

Norby, Claudia, ed. see Tessmer, Kathryn.

Norby, Lisa. Kidnapped. (Bullseye Step into Classics Ser.). 1994. 9.09 (*0-606-09513-6*, Pub. by Turtleback) Demco.

— Treasure Island. (Bullseye Step into Classics Ser.). 1993. 9.09 (*0-606-09989-1*, Pub. by Turtleback) Demco.

— Two by Two Romance: Just the Way You Are, No. 10. 192p. 1984. mass mkt. 1.95 (*0-446-32032-3*, Pub. by Warner Bks) Little.

Norby, Monica, ed. see Holmes, Roger & Buchanan, Rita.

Norbye, Jan P. The Metalcaster's Bible. (Illus.). 434p. 1980. 15.95 (*0-8306-9970-8*); pap. 19.95 (*0-8306-1173-8*, 1173) McGraw-Hill Prof.

Norbygaard, Elisabeth, jt. ed. see Kristensen, Knud.

Norch, Daniel J. De, see De Norch, Daniel J.

Norcia, Katherine. The Kingdom of God Is Ours: An Interpretation of Life. (Illus.). 184p. 1997. 17.00 (*0-8059-4277-7*) Dorrance.

Norcliffe, David. Islam: Faith & Practice. LC 99-10478. (Sussex Religious Beliefs & Practices Library). 224p. 1999. pap. write for info. (*1-898723-86-9*, Pub. by Sussex Acad Pr) Intl Spec Bk.

Norcliffe, Glen & Van Der Plas, Rob, eds. Cycle History 9: Proceedings, 9th International Cycling History Conference. LC 99-70807. (Cycling Resources Ser.). (Illus.). 176p. 1999. 45.00 (*1-892495-04-X*, 504X) Van der Plas.

Norcliffe, Glen B., jt. auth. see Freeman, Donald B.

***Norco, Jay E. & Schroder, Thomas.** Environmental Health & Safety Issues. rev. ed. O'Doughda, Linda, ed. (Illus.). 648p. 1999. teacher ed., ring bd. 100.00 (*1-928594-06-9*); student ed., ring bd. 100.00 (*1-928594-05-0*) BOMI Inst.

Norcom, Stanley. Grindstone: An Island World Remembered. Hein, Norvin, ed. 219p. 1995. pap. 17.95 (*0-9641529-0-8*, TX-3604788) R Edwards Pub.

Norconk, Marilyn A., et al, eds. Adaptive Radiations of Neotropical Primates: Proceedings of Conference on Neotropical Primates: Setting the Future Research Agenda Held in Washington, D. C., February 26-27, 1995. LC 96-41929. 568p. (C). 1997. 135.00 (*0-306-45399-1*, Kluwer Plenum) Kluwer Academic.

Norcross, jt. auth. see Prochaska.

Norcross, Alastair, jt. ed. see Steinbock, Bonnie.

Norcross, Carl. Townhouses & Condominiums: Residents' Likes & Dislikes; A Special Report. LC 73-82886. (Illus.). 111p. reprint ed. pap. 34.50 (*0-8357-3192-8*, 203946400012) Bks Demand.

Norcross, Carl & Hyson, John. Apartment Communities: The Next Big Market; A Survey of Who Rents & Why. LC 68-57114. (Urban Land Institute, Technical Bulletin Ser.: No. 61). 83p. reprint ed. pap. 30.00 (*0-8357-5653-X*, 202324400032) Bks Demand.

Norcross, John C. & Goldfried, Marvin R., eds. Handbook of Psychotherapy Integration. LC 92-52740. 416p. 1992. 59.00 (*0-465-02879-9*, Pub. by Basic) HarpC.

***Norcross, John C., et al.** Authoritative Guide to Self-Help Resources in Mental Health. 432p. 2000. text 39.95 (*1-57230-506-1*, C0506); pap. text 23.95 (*1-57230-580-0*, C0580) Guilford Pubns.

Norcross, John C., jt. auth. see Prochaska, James O.

Norcross, Paul D. Dining at the Master's Table: Learning to Hear the Voice of the Lord. LC 99-93178. 220p. 1999. pap. 12.00 (*0-9671353-0-3*) Kingdom Presence.

Nord, Barry M. Florida Stock Image Directory. (Illus.). 80p. (Orig.). 1993. pap. 49.95 (*0-935656-07-3*) Nords Studio.

— One Hundred Years of Citrus: A Glimpse of Citrus. (Illus.). 64p. (Orig.). 1993. VHS 29.95 (*0-935656-08-1*) Nords Studio.

— One Hundred Years of Citrus: A Glimpse of Citrus, Set. (Illus.). 64p. (Orig.). 1993. pap. 29.95 incl. VHS (*0-935656-04-9*) Nords Studio.

Nord, Barry M. & Nord, Elaine. Etching & Sandblasting of Glass. (Illus.). 80p. 1980. 10.95 (*0-935656-01-4*, 101 B) Nords Studio.

Nord, Barry M., jt. auth. see Nord, E. Laine.

Nord, Barry M., jt. auth. see Nord, Elaine.

Nord, Barry M., ed. see Cottrell, Clayton.

Nord, Bruce. Mexican Social Policy: Affordability, Conflict & Progress. LC 93-42083. 296p. (C). 1994. pap. text 39.00 (*0-8191-9418-2*) U Pr of Amer.

— Mexico City's Alternative Futures. 218p. (C). 1995. lib. bdg. 29.50 (*0-7618-0172-3*) U Pr of Amer.

Nord, Christine W., et al. Fathers' Involvement in Their Children's Schools. (Illus.). 160p. (C). 1999. reprint ed. pap. text 30.00 (*0-7881-7746-X*) DIANE Pub.

Nord, Christine W., jt. auth. see Zill, Nicholas.

Nord, Christine Winquist. Fathers' Involvement in Their Children's Schools. 182p. 1997. pap. 16.00 (*0-16-063645-0*) USGPO.

Nord, David. Multiple AIDS-Related Loss: A Handbook for Understanding & Surviving a Perpetual Fall. LC 96-53419. (Series in Death, Dying & Bereavement Ser.). 1997. pap. 29.95 (*1-56032-582-8*); boxed set 64.95 (*1-56032-581-X*) Taylor & Francis.

Nord, David P. Free Grace, Free Books, Free Riders: The Economics of Religious Publishing in Early Nineteenth-Century America. (James Russell Wiggins Lecture in the History of the Book Ser.: Vol. 13). (Illus.). 32p. 1997. reprint ed. pap. 7.50 (*0-944026-74-5*) Am Antiquarian.

— A Guide to Stonefield. (Illus.). 59p. 1977. pap. 1.50 (*0-87020-176-X*) State Hist Soc Wis.

Nord, Deborah E. The Apprenticeship of Beatrice Webb. LC 83-18235. 304p. 1985. lib. bdg. 35.00 (*0-87023-427-7*) U of Mass Pr.

— Walking the Victorian Streets: Women, Representation, & the City. (Illus.). 280p. 1995. pap. text 17.95 (*0-8014-8291-7*) Cornell U Pr.

Nord, Dennis. Career Keys Student Handbook, Education 164. 2nd ed. 74p. (C). 1997. per. 16.95 (*0-7872-3721-3*, 41372101) Kendall-Hunt.

Nord, E. Laine & Nord, Barry M. Etching & Sandblasting of Glass. (Illus.). 80p. 1980. pap. 6.95 (*0-685-01090-2*) Nords Studio.

Nord, Elaine & Nord, Barry M. Glass Etching-Pattern Book I: Fruit, Flowers & Birds. (Illus.). 50p. (Orig.). 1981. pap. 3.95 (*0-935656-02-2*, 101C) Nords Studio.

— Glass Etching-Pattern Book II: Wildlife, Alphabets, Geometrics. (Illus.). 50p. (Orig.). 1981. pap. 3.95 (*0-935656-03-0*, 101D) Nords Studio.

Nord, Elaine, jt. auth. see Nord, Barry M.

***Nord, Erik.** Cost-Value Analysis in Health Care: Making Sense Out of QALYs. (Studies in Philosophy & Public Policy). (Illus.). 176p. (C). 1999. 54.95 (*0-521-64308-2*); pap. 18.95 (*0-521-64434-8*) Cambridge U Pr.

Nord, Gennie, ed. Surviving the Western State of Mind. (Illus.). 178p. (Orig.). 1997. pap. 15.00 (*1-889367-06-0*) Up the Creek.

Nord, Gennie, ed. Montana Writers' Daybook. (Illus.). 172p. (Orig.). 1995. pap. 12.95 (*1-889367-03-6*) Up the Creek.

Nord, Gennie, ed. see Hoffman, Joan.

Nord, H. Juergen & Brady, Patrick G., eds. Critical Care Gastroenterology. LC 82-12924. (Illus.). 376p. reprint ed. pap. 116.60 (*0-7837-2556-6*, 204271500006) Bks Demand.

Nord, H. Juergen, ed. see Raskin, Nord.

Nord, Nancy A., jt. auth. see Minor, William H.

***Nord, Philip.** Impressionists & Politics: Art & Democracy in the Nineteenth Century. LC 99-47640. (Historical Connections Ser.). (Illus.). 2000. pap. 21.99 (*0-415-07715-X*) Routledge.

Nord, Philip. Republican Moment: The Struggle for Democracy in Nineteenth-Century France. 1998. pap. text 19.95 (*0-674-76272-X*) HUP.

Nord, Philip, jt. ed. see Bermeo, Nancy.

***Nord, Philip G.** Impressionists & Politics: Art & Democracy in Nineteenth Century. LC 99-47640. (Historical Connections Ser.). 144p. (C). 2000. text 65.00 (*0-415-20695-2*) Routledge.

Nord, Philip G. Paris Shopkeepers & the Politics of Resentment. LC 85-42695. 559p. 1986. reprint ed. pap. 173.30 (*0-7837-9403-7*, 206014800004) Bks Demand.

— The Republican Moment: Struggles for Democracy in Nineteenth-Century France. LC 95-10445. (Illus.). 352p. 1995. 56.00 (*0-674-76271-1*) HUP.

— The Republican Moment: Struggles for Democracy in Nineteenth-Century France. (Illus.). 352p. (C). 1995. text 49.95 (*0-614-07251-4*) HUP.

Nord, Robert. Software Architectures: A Practical Guide for Software Designers. LC 99-43579. 400p. (C). 1999. 44.95 (*0-201-32571-3*) Addison-Wesley.

Nord, Warren & Haynes, Charles. Taking Religion Seriously Across the Curriculum. LC 98-8560. 221p. 1998. pap. 18.95 (*0-87120-318-9*, 198190) ASCD.

Nord, Warren A. Religion & American Education: Rethinking a National Dilemma. LC 94-4589. (H. Eugene & Lillian Youngs Lehman Ser.). 502p. 1994. pap. 24.95 (*0-8078-4478-0*); text 59.95 (*0-8078-2165-9*) U of NC Pr.

— Religious Literacy, Textbooks, & Religious Neutrality. (Occasional Papers in Religion & Ethics: No. 1). 1990. 8.00 (*1-881678-41-5*) CSEE.

Nord World Staff, ed. Winter Safety Handbook. 1975. pap. 2.95 (*0-02-499880-X*, Macmillan Coll) P-H.

Nordahl, John E. Travelling: 3 Months on the NBA Road. (Illus.). 304p. 1995. 14.95 (*0-02-860438-5*) Macmillan.

Nordahl, Per. Weaving the Ethnic Fabric: Social Networks among Swedish-American Radicals in Chicago 1890-1940. LC 95-130413. (Illus.). 260p. (Orig.). 1994. pap. 62.50 (*91-7174-955-1*) Coronet Bks.

***Nordal, Gudrun.** Ethics & Action in Thirteenth-Century Iceland. (Viking Collection: Vol. 11). 369p. 1999. 36.99 (*87-7838-419-2*, Pub. by Odense Universitets Forlag) Intl Spec Bk.

Nordal, I., et al. Flora of Tropical East Africa: Anthericaceae. Polhill, R. M., ed. 68p. 1997. pap. 18.00 (*90-6191-376-4*, Pub. by A A Balkema) Ashgate Pub Co.

Nordan, Frances M. Queen of Darkness. 168p. (Orig.). 1993. pap. 9.95 (*1-880365-10-3*) Prof Pr NC.

Nordan, Lee. Practical Atlas of Refractive Surgery. 300p. 1997. text 130.00 (*0-397-51641-X*) Lppncott W & W.

Nordan, Lewis. The All-Girl Football Team. (Contemporaries Ser.). 1989. pap. 5.95 (*0-394-75701-7*) Vin Bks.

***Nordan, Lewis.** Boy with Loaded Gun. LC 99-33339. 290p. 2000. 23.95 (*1-56512-199-6*) Algonquin Bks.

Nordan, Lewis. Delta Land. LC 99-22285. (Author & Artist Ser.). (Illus.). 112p. 1999. 35.00 (*1-57806-177-6*) U Pr of Miss.

— Lightning Song. LC 96-54157. 308p. 1997. 18.95 (*1-56512-084-1*, 72084) Algonquin Bks.

— Lightning Song. 1998. 10.95 (*1-56512-220-8*) Algonquin Bks.

— Music of the Swamp. 210p. 1991. 15.95 (*0-945575-76-9*) Algonquin Bks.

— Music of the Swamp. (Front Porch PB Ser.). 210p. 1992. pap. 7.95 (*1-56512-016-7*) Algonquin Bks.

— The Sharpshooter Blues. (Front Porch Paperback Ser.). 308p. 1997. pap. 11.95 (*1-56512-182-1*, 72182) Algonquin Bks.

— The Sharpshooter Blues: A Novel. LC 95-15306. 300p. 1995. 17.95 (*1-56512-083-3*, 72083) Algonquin Bks.

— Sugar among the Freaks: Selected Stories by Lewis Nordan. (Front Porch PB Ser.). 312p. (Orig.). 1996. pap. 10.95 (*1-56512-131-7*, 72131) Algonquin Bks.

— Welcome to the Arrow-Catcher Fair. (Vintage Contemporaries Ser.). 1989. pap. 6.95 (*0-679-72164-9*) Vin Bks.

— Wolf Whistle: A Novel. LC 93-1011. 294p. 1993. 16.95 (*1-56512-028-0*) Algonquin Bks.

— Wolf Whistle: A Novel. 308p. 1995. pap. 9.95 (*1-56512-110-4*) Algonquin Bks.

Nordau, Max. The Conventional Lies of Our Civilization. LC 74-29511. (Modern Jewish Experience Ser.). (ENG.). 1975. reprint ed. 34.95 (*0-405-06737-2*) Ayer.

— Degeneration. LC 93-8474. xxxvi, 566p. 1993. pap. 18.00 (*0-8032-8367-9*, Bison Books) U of Nebr Pr.

— Morals & the Evolution of Man. 1976. lib. bdg. 250.00 (*0-8490-2280-0*) Gordon Pr.

***Nordbeck, Elizabeth C.** Consolidation & Expansion. (Living Theological Heritage of the United Church of Christ Ser.: Vol. 4). 1999. 60.00 (*0-8298-1110-9*) Pilgrim OH.

Nordbeck, Elizabeth C. & Zuck, Lowell H., eds. Consolidation & Expansion. (Living Theological Heritage Ser.: Vol. 4). 768p. (C). 1999. 75.00 (*0-8298-1358-6*) Pilgrim OH.

Nordberg, Bengt, ed. The Sociolinguistics of Urbanization: The Case of the Nordic Countries. (Sociolinguistics & Language Contact Ser.: Vol. 7). viii, 290p. (C). 1994. lib. bdg. 129.25 (*3-11-011184-5*, 97-94) De Gruyter.

***Nordberg, Bette.** Serenity Bay. 320p. 2000. pap. 10.99 (*0-7642-2396-8*) Bethany Hse.

Nordberg, Beverly, jt. auth. see Stewig, John W.

Nordberg, Erik & Winblad, Uno. Urban Environmental Health & Hygiene in Sub-Saharan Africa. LC 95-200662. (Current African Issues Ser.: No. 18). 26p. 1994. 6.95 (*91-7106-364-1*, Pub. by Nordic Africa) Transaction Pubs.

Nordberg, G. F., et al, eds. Cadmium in the Human Environment: Toxicity & Carcinogenicity. (IARC Scientific Publications: No. 118). (Illus.). 482p. 1993. pap. text 125.00 (*92-832-2118-4*) OUP.

Nordberg, H., jt. ed. see Krauss, G.

Nordberg, Ken. Do-It-Yourself Black Bear Baiting & Hunting. O'Donnell, M. C. et al, eds. 160p. (Orig.). 1990. pap. 8.95 (*1-886422-50-8*) Shingle Creek.

— Whitetail Hunter's Almanac. annuals 9th ed. O'Donnell, Jennifer J., ed. (Illus.). 160p. (Orig.). 1997. pap. 9.95 (*1-886422-09-5*) Shingle Creek.

— Whitetail Hunter's Almanac: An Introduction to Whitetail Hunting. 150p. 1988. pap. 8.95 (*1-886422-01-X*) Shingle Creek.

— Whitetail Hunter's Almanac: An Introduction to Whitetail Hunting. 2nd ed. 153p. 1989. pap. 8.95 (*1-886422-02-8*) Shingle Creek.

— Whitetail Hunter's Almanac: An Introduction to Whitetail Hunting. 3rd ed. 151p. 1990. pap. 8.95 (*1-886422-03-6*) Shingle Creek.

— Whitetail Hunter's Almanac: An Introduction to Whitetail Hunting. 4th ed. 147p. 1991. pap. 8.95 (*1-886422-04-4*) Shingle Creek.

— Whitetail Hunter's Almanac: An Introduction to Whitetail Hunting. 5th ed. 166p. 1992. pap. 8.95 (*1-886422-05-2*) Shingle Creek.

— Whitetail Hunter's Almanac: An Introduction to Whitetail Hunting. 6th ed. 186p. 1993. pap. 8.95 (*1-886422-06-0*) Shingle Creek.

— Whitetail Hunter's Almanac: First-Seventh Edition. 7th ed. (Illus.). (Orig.). 1994. pap. 62.65 (*1-886422-00-1*) Shingle Creek.

Nordberg, Ken & O'Donnell, Jennifer J. Whitetail Hunter's Almanac: An Introduction to Whitetail Hunting. 7th ed. O'Donnell, M. C. et al, eds. (Illus.). 150p. 1994. pap. 8.95 (*1-886422-07-9*) Shingle Creek.

***Nordberg, M. & Verbeke, Alain.** The Strategic Management of High Technology Contracts: The Case of Cern: Competence Based & Transaction Cost Perspectives. LC 99-29392. (Technology, Innovation, Entrepreneurship & Competitive Strategy Ser.). 194p. 1999. write for info. (*0-08-043575-0*, Pergamon Pr) Elsevier.

Nordberg, Marion, jt. auth. see Jenkins, Lee.

Nordbrandt, Henrik. Selected Poems. 2nd ed. Taylor, Alexander, tr. LC 78-1047. (Illus.). 88p. 1978. pap. 9.95 (*0-915306-33-6*) Curbstone.

Nordbring, F. & Burman, L. G., eds. Urinary Tract Infections. (Illus.). 151p. (Orig.). 1981. pap. text 42.50 (*91-22-00455-6*) Coronet Bks.

Nordbruch, Claus. Uber die Pflicht Eine Analyse des Werks Von Siegfried Lenz. (Germanistische Texte und Studien: Vol. 53). (GER.). 250p. 1996. write for info. (*3-487-10078-9*) G Olms Pubs.

Nordby, Beth D. Love - & Other Things. 1992. 14.95 (*0-533-10026-7*) Vantage.

Nordby, Gene M., jt. auth. see Andersen, Paul.

Nordby, Jon J. Basic Ethics for Forensic Scientists. 2000. 29.95 (*0-8493-8121-5*) CRC Pr.

— Dead Reckoning: The Art of Forensic Detection. LC 99-40308. 304p. 1999. per. 49.95 (*0-8493-8122-3*) CRC Pr.

Nordby, Judith. Mongolia. LC 93-247427. (World Bibliographical Ser.). 226p. 1993. lib. bdg. 73.00 (*1-85109-129-7*) ABC-CLIO.

Nordby, Marsha. Leningrad. (Soviet Guides Ser.). (Illus.). 160p. 1994. pap. 14.95 (*0-8442-9678-3*, Passprt Bks) NTC Contemp Pub Co.

— Moscow. (Soviet Guides Ser.). (Illus.). 256p. 1991. pap. 15.95 (*0-8442-9675-9*, Passprt Bks) NTC Contemp Pub Co.

— Moscow & Leningrad. large type ed. (Guidebook Ser.). (Illus.). 1991. pap. 9.95 (*962-217-117-6*) L A Michaux.

Nordby, Steven, tr. see Christensen, Lars S.

Nordby, Vernon J., jt. auth. see Hall, Calvin S.

Nordbye, Masha. Moscow & St. Petersburg. (Odyssey Passport Ser.). (Illus.). 592p. 1999. pap. 24.95 (*962-217-611-9*) Norton.

Norde, Karen, et al, eds. Acquiring Water for Energy: Institutional Aspects. LC 81-69876. 1982. 30.00 (*0-918334-42-X*) WRP.

Nordeen, Lon O. & Nicolle, David. Phoenix over the Nile: A History of Egyptian Air Power, 1932-1994. LC 95-30047. (Illus.). 368p. 1996. 55.00 (*1-56098-626-3*) Smithsonian.

Nordell, John R., Jr. The Undetected Enemy: French & American Miscalculations at Dien Bien Phu, 1953. LC 94-37073. (Military History Ser.: No. 39). (Illus.). 224p. 1995. 29.95 (*0-89096-645-1*) Tex A&M Univ Pr.

Norden, Bengt, jt. auth. see Rodger, Alison.

Norden, C. Christopher. A Comparative Rhetoric of the Contemporary Indigenous Novel. LC 93-47433. (Comparative Cultures & Literatures Ser.: Vol. 6). 1994. write for info. (*0-8204-2441-2*) P Lang Pubng.

Norden, Carl & Gillespie. Infections in Bones & Joints. (Illus.). 400p. 1994. 99.95 (*0-86542-273-7*) Blackwell Sci.

Norden, Deborah, ed. see Gutman, Marta, et al.

Norden, Deborah L. Military Rebellion in Argentina: Between Coups & Consolidation. LC 95-32285. (Illus.). vii, 240p. (C). 1996. text 45.00 (*0-8032-3339-6*); pap. text 25.00 (*0-8032-8369-5*, Bison Books) U of Nebr Pr.

Norden, Denis, jt. auth. see Muir, Frank.

Norden, Eduard. Aus Altromischen Priesterbuchern. LC 75-10644. (Ancient Religion & Mythology Ser.). (GER.). 1976. reprint ed. 25.95 (*0-405-07019-5*) Ayer.

N

Norden, Greg. Landscapes under the Luggage Rack: Great Paintings of Britain. 1997. 50.00 (*0-9529602-0-6*, Pub. by Aidan Ellis Pub) Antique Collect.

Norden, Heinz, tr. see Ritter, Gerhard A.

Norden, Heinz, tr. see Schumpeter, Joseph Alois.

Norden, Hermann. White & Black in East Africa. LC 74-15074. reprint ed. 49.50 (*0-404-12124-1*) AMS Pr.

Norden, Hugo. The Technique of Canon. 1982. pap. 19.95 (*0-8283-1839-5*) Branden Bks.

Norden, J. T. The Best Investment. (Illus.). 102p. (Orig.). 1995. pap. write for info. (*1-57579-003-3*) Pine Hill Pr.

Norden, Jan. Yugoslavia, East Europe & the Fourth International: The Evolution of Pabloist Liquidation. Prometheus Research Library Staff, ed. (Prometheus Research Ser.: No. 4). 70p. 1993. 6.00 (*0-9633828-2-9*) Spartacist Pub.

Norden, John. England: An Intended Guide, for English Travailers. LC 79-84125. (English Experience Ser.: No. 944). 84p. 1979. reprint ed. lib. bdg. 20.00 (*90-221-0944-5*) Walter J Johnson.

— John Norden's Manuscript Maps of Cornwall & Its Nine Hundreds. 104p. 1974. text 50.00 (*0-900771-35-6*, Pub. by Univ Exeter Pr) Northwestern U Pr.

— A Pensive Mans Practise. LC 77-171776. (English Experience Ser.: No. 401). 192p. 1971. reprint ed. 35.00 (*90-221-0401-X*) Walter J Johnson.

— Speculi Britanniae: The Description of Hartfordshire. LC 74-171778. (English Experience Ser.: No. 403). 38p. 1971. reprint ed. 20.00 (*90-221-0403-6*) Walter J Johnson.

— Speculi Britanniae Pars. Ellis, Henry, ed. (Camden Society, London. Publications, First Ser.: No. 9). reprint ed. 30.00 (*0-404-50109-5*) AMS Pr.

— Speculum Britanniae: The First Parte, a Description of Middlesex. LC 70-171777. (English Experience Ser.: No. 402). 58p. 1971. reprint ed. 20.00 (*90-221-0402-8*) Walter J Johnson.

— The Surveiors Dialogue... for All Men to Peruse, That Have to Do with the Revenues of Land, or the Manurance, Use or Occupation. Third Time Imprinted & Enlarged. LC 79-84126. (English Experience Ser.: No. 945). 280p. 1979. reprint ed. lib. bdg. 26.00 (*90-221-0945-3*) Walter J Johnson.

Norden, K. Elis. Electronic Weighing: Fundamentals & Applications. LC 93-25908. (Illus.). 193p. 1993. pap. 59.90 (*0-608-04994-8*, 206561200004) Bks Demand.

— Handbook of Electronic Weighing. LC 98-229735. 488p. 1998. pap. 225.00 (*3-527-29568-2*) Wiley.

Norden, Linda & Morgan, Murray. Chihuly: Baskets. 148p. 1997. 50.00 (*1-57684-003-4*) Portland Pr.

— Chihuly: Baskets. Johnson, Diana, ed. (Illus.). 148p. (C). 1997. pap. 25.00 (*0-9608382-0-1*) Portland Pr.

Norden, Martin F. The Cinema of Isolation: A History of Physical Disability in the Movies. LC 93-44547. (Illus.). 375p. (C). 1994. pap. 16.95 (*0-8135-2104-1*); text 48.00 (*0-8135-2103-3*) Rutgers U Pr.

— The Cinema of Isolation: A History of Physical Disability in the Movies. (Illus.). 384p. 1999. reprint ed. text 30.00 (*0-7881-6275-6*) DIANE Pub.

— John Barrymore: A Bio-Bibliography, 68. LC 95-23020. (Bio-Bibliographies in the Performing Arts Ser.: Vol. 68). 328p. 1995. lib. bdg. 65.00 (*0-313-29268-X*, Greenwood Pr) Greenwood.

Norden, Mary. Beautiful Ribbons: Stylish Ideas for Your Home. LC 97-77955. (Illus.). 152p. 1999. 17.95 (*0-7624-0362-4*) Running Pr.

***Norden, Mary.** Christmas Details. 2000. 16.00 (*0-688-17429-9*, HarpRes) HarpInfo.

Norden, Mary. Decorative Embroidery: More Than 50 Creative Projects & Design Variations for the Home. LC 96-48235. (Illus.). 144p. 1997. 24.95 (*0-89577-933-1*, Pub. by RD Assn) Penguin Putnam.

— Ethnic Needlepoint: Designs from Asia, Africa & the Americas. (Illus.). 160p. 1993. 35.00 (*0-8230-1605-6*) Watsn-Guptill.

— Gift Wraps, Baskets, & Bows. (Illus.). 112p. 1995. 19.95 (*0-7892-0079-1*) Abbeville Pr.

***Norden, Mary.** Modern Country: A New Approach to Country Style. (Illus.). 144p. 2000. 29.95 (*1-57076-139-6*) Trafalgar.

Norden, Michael J. Beyond Prozac: Antidotes for Modern Times. LC 95-16745. 272p. 1995. 23.00 (*0-06-039151-0*) HarperTrade.

— Beyond Prozac: Brain-Toxic Lifestyles, Natural Antidotes & New Generation Antidepressants. 288p. 1996. pap. 14.00 (*0-06-098707-3*) HarpC.

Norden, Nora. Sentenced to Live. 280p. (Orig.). 1986. pap. 7.00 (*0-934145-47-4*) Airborne Pr.

Norden, Peter. Madam Kitty. 1978. mass mkt. 1.50 (*0-345-28191-8*) Ballantine Pub Grp.

Norden, Rudolph. Each Day with Jesus. deluxe large type ed. LC 99-38523. 384p. 1999. 14.99 (*0-570-05359-5*) Concordia.

Norden, Rudolph F. Each Day with Jesus: Daily Devotions Through the Year. 384p. 1994. pap. 14.99 (*0-570-04655-6*, 12-3240) Concordia.

— Symbols & Their Meaning. 64p. 1985. pap. 4.99 (*0-570-03949-5*, 12-2883) Concordia.

— With Jesus Every Day: Daily Devotions Through the Year. LC 12-3336. 384p. Date not set. pap. 14.99 (*0-570-04987-3*, 12-3336) Concordia.

***Norden, Rudolph F.** Year in the Word: Reflections from Portals of Prayer, Vol. 1. 400p. 1999. 14.99 (*0-570-05232-7*) Concordia.

Norden, Rudolph F., ed. The Best of Portals of Prayer. 400p. 1990. 19.99 (*0-570-03083-8*, 06-1198) Concordia.

Nordenberg, Mark A., et al. Modern Pennsylvania Civil Practice, 2 vols. LC 85-71932. 775p. 1998. ring bd. 150.00 (*1-887024-36-0*) Bisel Co.

Nordenfalk, Carl. Celtic & Anglo-Saxon Painting. LC 76-16443. (Illus.). 127p. 1977. pap. 20.95 (*0-8076-0826-2*) Braziller.

Nordenfalk, Carl, comment. Vergilius Augusteus. fac. ed. (Codices Selecti A Ser.: Vol. LVI). (ENG & GER., Illus.). 14p. 1976. lthr. 142.00 (*3-201-00969-5*, Pub. by Akademische Druck-und) Balogh.

***Nordenfelt, Lennart.** Action, Ability & Health - Essays in the Philosphy of Action & Welfare. 192p. 2000. 90.00 (*0-7923-6206-3*) Kluwer Academic.

Nordenfelt, Lennart. On Crime, Punishment & Psychiatric Care: An Introduction to Swedish Philosophy of Criminal Law & Forensic Psychiatry. 87p. (Orig.). 1992. pap. 36.00 (*91-22-01487-X*) Coronet Bks.

— On the Nature of Health. (C). 1987. text 127.50 (*1-55608-032-8*) Kluwer Academic.

— On the Nature of Health: An Action-Theoretic Approach. 244p. 1995. pap. text 50.50 (*0-7923-3470-1*, Pub. by Kluwer Academic) Kluwer Academic.

— Quality of Life, Health & Happiness. 186p. 1993. 61.95 (*1-85628-553-7*, Pub. by Avebry) Ashgate Pub Co.

Nordenfelt, Lennart & Lindahl, Ingemar B., eds. Health, Disease, & Causal Explanations in Medicine. 286p. 1984. text 109.00 (*90-277-1660-9*, D Reidel) Kluwer Academic.

Nordenfelt, Lennart & Tengland, Per-Anders, eds. The Goals & Limits of Medicine. 239p. (Orig.). 1996. pap. 47.50 (*91-22-01713-5*) Coronet Bks.

Nordenskiold, Erik. The History of Biology. 1988. reprint ed. lib. bdg. 89.00 (*0-7812-0380-5*) Rprt Serv.

— The History of Biology: A Survey. 1935. reprint ed. 85.00 (*0-403-01788-2*) Scholarly.

Nordenskiold, Erland. Comparative Ethnographical Studies, 10 vols., Set. reprint ed. write for info. (*0-404-15140-X*) AMS Pr.

— The Copper & Bronze Ages in South America. LC 75-46057. (Comparative Ethnographical Studies: Vol. 4). reprint ed. 55.00 (*0-404-15144-2*) AMS Pr.

— Deductions Suggested by the Geographical Distribution of Some Post-Columbian Words Used by the Indians of South America. LC 75-46058. (Comparative Ethnographical Studies: Vol. 5). 1977. reprint ed. 61.50 (*0-404-15145-0*) AMS Pr.

— An Ethno-Geographical Analysis of the Material Culture of Two Indian Tribes in the Gran Chaco. LC 75-46054. (Comparative Ethnographical Studies: Vol. 1). reprint ed. 55.00 (*0-404-15141-8*) AMS Pr.

— The Ethnography of South America Seen from Mojos in Bolivia. LC 75-46056. (Comparative Ethnographical Studies: Vol. 3). reprint ed. 55.00 (*0-404-15143-4*) AMS Pr.

— An Historical & Ethnological Survey of the Cuna Indians. LC 75-46064. (Comparative Ethnographical Studies: Vol. 10). reprint ed. 92.50 (*0-404-15150-7*) AMS Pr.

— Modifications in Indian Culture Through Inventions & Loans. LC 75-46062. (Comparative Ethnographical Studies: Vol. 8). reprint ed. 55.00 (*0-404-15148-5*) AMS Pr.

— Origin of the Indian Civilizations in South America. LC 75-46063. (Comparative Ethnographical Studies: Vol. 9). reprint ed. 55.00 (*0-404-15149-3*) AMS Pr.

— Picture-Writings & Other Documents by Nele, Paramount Chief of the Cuna Indians, & Ruben Perez Kantule, His Secretary, 2 pts. in 1 vol. LC 75-46061. (Comparative Ethnographical Studies: Vol. 7). reprint ed. 55.00 (*0-404-15147-7*) AMS Pr.

— The Secret of the Peruvian Quipus, 2 pts. in 1 vol. LC 75-46059. (Comparative Ethnographical Studies: Vol. 6). reprint ed. 55.00 (*0-404-15146-9*) AMS Pr.

Nordenskiold, Gustaf E. The Cliff Dwellers of the Mesa Verde, Southwestern Colorado: Their Pottery & Implements. Morgan, D. Lloyd, tr. from SWE. LC 72-5006. (Antiquities of the New World Ser.: Vol. 12). (Illus.). reprint ed. 97.50 (*0-404-57312-6*) AMS Pr.

— From the Far West. Valeri, Renee, tr. from SWE. LC 92-83788. 90p. (Orig.). Date not set. pap. write for info. (*0-937062-20-0*) Mesa Verde Museum.

— Letters of Gustaf Nordenskiold & Articles from Ymer & the Photographic Times. Diamon, Irving L. & Olson, Daniel M., eds. (Illus.). 99p. (Orig.). 1991. pap. 9.95 (*0-937062-16-2*) Mesa Verde Museum.

Nordensson, Stew, jt. auth. see Kelley, Lydia.

Nordenstam, Garry L., jt. auth. see Larson, Steven B.

Nordenstam, Garry L., jt. auth. see Otto, Joseph.

Nordenstam, Garry L., jt. auth. see Otto, Joseph C.

Nordenstam, Tore, jt. ed. see Johannessen, Kjell S.

Nordenstreng, Kaarle. Mass Media Declaration of UNESCO. LC 83-25818. (Communication & Information Science Ser.). 496p. (C). 1984. text 82.50 (*0-89391-077-5*) Ablx Pub.

***Nordenstreng, Kaarle & Griffin, Michael, eds.** International Media Monitoring. LC 99-22901. (Communication Ser.). 464p. (C). 1999. 95.00 (*1-57273-183-4*); pap. 35.00 (*1-57273-184-2*) Hampton Pr NJ.

Nordenstreng, Kaarle & Schiller, Herbert I. Beyond National Sovereignty: International Communications in the 1990s. Dervin, Brenda, ed. (Communication & Information Science Ser.). 496p. (C). 1993. pap. 42.50 (*0-89391-960-8*) Ablx Pub.

Nordenstreng, Kaarle & Schiller, Herbert I., eds. Beyond National Sovereignty: International Communications in the 1990s. (Communication & Information Science Ser.). 496p. (C). 1993. text 82.50 (*0-89391-959-4*) Ablx Pub.

Nordfors, Jill. Needle Lace & Needleweaving: A New Look at Traditional Stitches. (Illus.). 160p. 1992. reprint ed. pap. 16.95 (*1-879504-00-6*, 400-6) A Schwartz & Co.

Nordgaard, M. A. An Historical Survey of Algebraic Methods of Approximating the Roots of Numerical Higher Equations up to the Year 1819. LC 76-177107. (Columbia University. Teachers College. Contributions to Education Ser.: No. 123). reprint ed. 37.50 (*0-404-55123-8*) AMS Pr.

Nordgaarden, Carol. Create a Culture. (Illus.). 120p. (YA). (gr. 5-8). 1995. pap. 9.95 (*0-88160-240-X*, LW335) Learning Wks.

Nordgren, Anders. Evolutionary Thinking: An Analysis of Rationality, Morality & Religion from an Evolutionary Perspective. (Studia Philosophoae Religionis: No. 17). 244p. (Orig.). 1994. pap. 52.50 (*91-22-01615-5*) Coronet Bks.

Nordgren, Anders, et al, eds. Altruism, Society, Health Care. (Studies in Bioethics & Research Ethics Ser.: Vol. 3). 90p. 1998. pap. 33.50 (*91-554-4151-3*) Coronet Bks.

Nordgren, Mary J., jt. auth. see Pepper, Robert C.

Nordgren, Roger K. Staffing Commercial Credit Functions: A Survey. Smith, Daphne & Geehr, Shelley W., eds. (Illus.). 64p. (Orig.). 1994. pap. text 58.00 (*1-57070-008-7*, 32191) Robt Morris Assocs.

Nordh, Katarina. Aspects of Ancient Egyptian Curses & Blessings: Conceptual Background & Transmission. (Uppsala Studies in Ancient Mediterranean & Near Eastern Civilizations: No. 26). xi, 232 p. (Orig.). 1996. pap. 52.50 (*91-554-3811-3*) Coronet Bks.

Nordhaug, Odd. Human Capital in Organizations: Competence, Training, & Learning. (Illus.). 278p. 1994. 36.00 (*82-00-21807-4*) Scandnvan Univ Pr.

Nordhaus, Jean. A Bracelet of Lies. LC 86-51532. (Series Eleven). 82p. 1987. pap. 7.00 (*0-931846-31-5*) Wash Writers Pub.

— My Life in Hiding. (QRL Poetry Bks.: Vol. XXX). 1991. 20.00 (*0-614-06432-5*) Quarterly Rev.

Nordhaus, Jean, et al. The Other Side of the Hill: Poems by the Capitol Hill Poetry Group. Comitz, Cindy, ed. 100p. (Orig.). 1996. pap. 10.00 (*0-938572-18-0*) Bunny Crocodile.

Nordhaus, William B., jt. auth. see Samuelson, Paul Anthony.

Nordhaus, William D. The Efficient Use of Energy Resources. LC 79-64225. (Cowles Foundation for Research in Economics at Yale University. Monograph Ser.: No. 26). 186p. reprint ed. pap. 57.70 (*0-7837-4546-X*, 208033400005) Bks Demand.

— Managing the Global Commons: The Economics of Climate Change. LC 94-3992. (Illus.). 223p. 1994. 35.00 (*0-262-14055-1*) MIT Pr.

— The Swedish Nuclear Dilemma: Energy & the Environment. LC 97-19258. (Illus.). 167p. 1997. 45.00 (*0-915707-84-5*) Resources Future.

Nordhaus, William D., ed. Economics & Policy Issues in Climate Change. LC 98-27128. (Illus.). 324p. 1998. 50.00 (*0-915707-95-0*) Resources Future.

***Nordhaus, William D. & Boyer, Joseph.** Warming the World: Economic Models of Global Warming. LC 00-29230. (Illus.). 264p. (C). 2000. 35.00 (*0-262-14071-3*) MIT Pr.

Nordhaus, William D. & Tobin, James. Economic Research - Retrospect & Prospect Vol. 5: Economic Growth. (General Ser.: No. 96). 112p. 1972. reprint ed. 29.20 (*0-87014-254-2*) Natl Bur Econ Res.

Nordhaus, William D., jt. auth. see Samuelson, Paul Anthony.

Nordhaus, William D., ed. see National Research Council Staff.

Nordhausen, Elizabeth. Practical & Cost Saving Tips for Parents of Infants & Toddlers. 1994. pap. 1.99 (*0-614-15343-3*) Dageforde Pub.

Nordhauser, Fred M. & Olson, Wayne P., eds. Sterilization of Drugs & Devices: Technologies for the 21st Century. LC 98-176740. (Illus.). 552p. 1998. 239.00 (*1-57491-060-4*) Interpharm.

Nordheim, Eckhard Von, see Von Nordheim, Eckhard.

Nordhielm, Curt. Reflecting His Image. LC 90-80689. 160p. (Orig.). (C). 1990. pap. 5.99 (*0-89900-357-5*) College Pr Pub.

— Reflecting His Image: Leader's Guide. 32p. (Orig.). 1991. pap. text 2.99 (*0-89900-365-6*) College Pr Pub.

Nordhjem, Bent. What Fiction Means: An Inquiry into the Nature of Fiction with a Study of Three Comic Novels. (University of Copenhagen Dept of English Ser.: No. 15). 144p. (Orig.). 1987. pap. 45.00 (*87-88648-22-2*) Coronet Bks.

Nordhoff & Hall. No More Gas. 1999. write for info. (*0-316-88839-7*) Little.

Nordhoff, et al. Massachusetts One Hundred Years Ago: The Southeast. (Historical Ser.). (Illus.). 1976. pap. 3.50 (*0-89540-018-9*, SB-018) Sun Pub.

***Nordhoff C & Hall J. N.** Mutiny on the Bounty. 1998. pap. 14.95 (*0-316-19012-8*, Back Bay) Little.

Nordhoff, Charles. America for Free Working Men. (Notable American Authors Ser.). 1999. reprint ed. lib. bdg. 125.00 (*0-7812-4641-5*) Rprt Serv.

— American Utopias. LC 93-27262. (American Classics Ser.). (Illus.). 448p. 1993. reprint ed. pap. 14.95 (*0-936399-53-8*) Berkshire Hse.

— C. P. R. R. The Central Pacific Railroad. Jones, William R., ed. & intro. by. (Illus.). 48p. (Orig.). 1996. pap. 4.95 (*0-89646-090-8*) Vistabooks.

— California for Travellers & Settlers. (Illus.). 255p. 1992. reprint ed. pap. 7.95 (*0-89815-418-9*) Ten Speed Pr.

— Cape Cod, & All Along Shore: Stories. LC 72-116964. (Short Story Index Reprint Ser.). 1977. 19.95 (*0-8369-3468-7*) Ayer.

— Communistic Societies in the United States. (Notable American Authors Ser.). 1999. reprint ed. lib. bdg. 125.00 (*0-7812-4642-3*) Rprt Serv.

— Communistic Societies of the United States: From Personal Visit & Observation. (Illus.). 439p. 1966. pap. 11.95 (*0-486-21580-6*) Dover.

— The Communistic Societies of the United States from Personal Visit & Observation. (Illus.). 439p. 1978. reprint ed. 31.95 (*0-87928-092-1*) Corner Hse.

— The Cotton States in the Spring & Summer of 1875. (Notable American Authors Ser.). 1999. reprint ed. lib. bdg. 125.00 (*0-7812-4644-X*) Rprt Serv.

— The Freedom of South Carolina. (Notable American Authors Ser.). 1999. reprint ed. lib. bdg. 125.00 (*0-7812-4640-7*) Rprt Serv.

— God & the Future Life. (Notable American Authors Ser.). 1999. reprint ed. lib. bdg. 125.00 (*0-7812-4645-8*) Rprt Serv.

— Hawaii-Nei: 1873. Apple, Russell A., ed. (Illus.). 40p. 1977. reprint ed. pap. 2.00 (*0-89646-030-4*) Vistabooks.

— Hawaii-Nei, the Kingdom of Hawaii: One Hundred Years Ago. (Historical Ser.). (Illus.). 1976. pap. 3.50 (*0-89540-035-9*, SB-035) Sun Pub.

— The Lighthouses of the United States in 1874. Jones, William R., ed. & intro. by. LC 92-18576. (Illus.). 64p. 1981. pap. 6.95 (*0-89646-086-X*) Vistabooks.

— Man-of-War Life. LC 85-4935. (Classics of Naval Literature Ser.). 290p. 1985. reprint ed. 32.95 (*0-87021-349-0*) Naval Inst Pr.

— Man-of-War Life. (Notable American Authors Ser.). 1999. reprint ed. lib. bdg. 125.00 (*0-7812-4635-0*) Rprt Serv.

— The Merchant Vessel. (Notable American Authors Ser.). 1999. reprint ed. lib. bdg. 125.00 (*0-7812-4636-9*) Rprt Serv.

— Mutiny on the Bounty. (J). 1989. 20.05 (*0-606-12854-9*, Pub. by Turtleback) Demco.

— Nordhoff's West Coast. (Pacific Basin Ser.). 1998. pap. 31.00 (*0-7103-0257-6*, Pub. by Kegan Paul Intl) Col U Pr.

— Northern California, Oregon & the Sandwich Islands. (Illus.). 256p. 1992. reprint ed. pap. 7.95 (*0-89815-419-7*) Ten Speed Pr.

— Politics of Young Americans. (Notable American Authors Ser.). 1999. reprint ed. lib. bdg. 125.00 (*0-7812-4643-1*) Rprt Serv.

— Secession Is Rebellion. (Notable American Authors Ser.). 1999. reprint ed. lib. bdg. 125.00 (*0-7812-4639-3*) Rprt Serv.

— Stories of the Island World. (Notable American Authors Ser.). 1999. reprint ed. lib. bdg. 125.00 (*0-7812-4638-5*) Rprt Serv.

— Whaling & Fishing. (Notable American Authors Ser.). 1999. reprint ed. lib. bdg. 125.00 (*0-7812-4637-7*) Rprt Serv.

***Nordhoff, Charles & Hall, James.** The Bounty Trilogy. 1998. mass mkt. 21.95 (*0-316-19009-8*) Little.

Nordhoff, Charles & Hall, James N. The Bounty Trilogy. 691p. 1985. pap. 21.95 (*0-316-61166-2*) Little.

— Falcons of France: A Tale of Youth & the Air. Gilbert, James B., ed. LC 79-7290. (Flight: Its First Seventy-Five Years Ser.). (Illus.). 1980. reprint ed. lib. bdg. 33.95 (*0-405-12198-9*) Ayer.

— Mutiny on the Bounty. (Illus.). 379p. 1989. pap. 14.95 (*0-316-61168-9*) Little.

Nordhoff, Charles & Hall, James N. Mutiny on the Bounty LC 84-672646. viii, 416p. 1982. write for info. (*0-86220-511-5*, Pub. by Chivers Pr) Chivers N Amer.

Nordhoff, Charles & Hall, James N. Pitcairn's Island. Date not set. lib. bdg. 23.95 (*0-8488-2153-X*) Amereon Ltd.

Nordhoff, Grace, ed. Inside Looking Out: Mental Hospitals Are Overflowing with People Searching for Freedom & Community. (Illus.). 64p. (Orig.). 1989. pap. 5.00 (*0-943810-42-6*) Southern Exposure.

Nordhoff, Larry S. Whiplash: Mechanisms & Management. LC 92-49445. 608p. 1992. 64.95 (*0-8016-6821-2*) Mosby Inc.

Nordhoff, Lawrence. Motor Vehicle Collision Injuries: Mechanisms, Diagnosis & Management. 391p. 1995. 72.00 (*0-8342-0727-3*) Aspen Pub.

Nordholt, Henk S. The Spell of Power: A History of Balinese Politics, 1650-1940. LC 97-121352. (Verhandelingen Ser.: Vol. 170). (Illus.). 389p. 1997. pap. 44.00 (*90-6718-090-4*, Pub. by KITLV Pr) Cellar.

— State, Village, & Ritual in Bali: An Historical Perspective. (Comparative Asian Studies: No. 6). 58p. (Orig.). 1992. pap. text 14.50 (*90-5383-023-5*, Pub. by VU Univ Pr) Paul & Co Pubs.

Nordholt, Henk S., ed. Outward Appearances: Dressing State & Society in Indonesia. LC 98-120168. (Proceedings Ser.: Vol. 4). (Illus.). 378p. 1998. pap. 37.00 (*90-6718-118-8*, Pub. by KITLV Pr) Cellar.

Nordholt, Nico S. & Visser, Leontine E. Social Science in Southeast Asia: From Particularism to Universalism, Vol. 17. 140p. 1996. pap. 15.00 (*90-5383-427-3*, Pub. by VUB Univ Pr) Paul & Co Pubs.

Nordholz, Petra, jt. auth. see Grabinski, Hartmut.

Nordhues, Robin, ed. see Evans, Harry.

Nordhues, Robin, ed. see Mitchell, James R.

Nordhues, Robin, ed. see Monaco, James & Monaco, Jeannette.

Nordhuff, Charles. Mutiny on the Bounty. 1976. 26.95 (*0-8488-0597-6*) Amereon Ltd.

Nordhuff, Charles & Hall, J. Norman. Men Against the Sea. 20.95 (*0-89190-564-2*) Amereon Ltd.

Nordhuff, Charles & Hall, James N. Falcons of France. 21.95 (*0-89190-232-5*) Amereon Ltd.

— The Hurricane. 22.95 (*0-88411-451-1*) Amereon Ltd.

Nordhus, Inger Hilde, et al, eds. Clinical Geropsychology. LC 98-14132. 371p. 1998. 39.95 (*1-55798-519-7*) Am Psychol.

Nordiander, David J., tr. see Khlevniuk, Oleg V.

Nordic Committee of Senior Officials & Nordic Council of Ministers Staff. Food Safety after Nuclear Accidents: A Nordic Model for National Response: Report from a Group of Experts Appointed by the Nordic Committee of Senior Officials for Food Policy (HAK-LIVS), Nordic

An Asterisk (*) at the beginning of an entry indicates that the title is appearing for the first time.

Council of Ministers. LC 95-135789. (NORD Ser.). 46p. 1992. 13.00 (92-9120-097-2, Pub. by Nordic Coun Minsters) Bernan Associates.

Nordic Council of Ministers Staff, ed. Transport Between the Nordic Countries & the New Eastern Europe. 100p. (Orig.). 1991. pap. 36.00 (91-7996-388-9) Coronet Bks.

— Yearbook of Nordic Statistics, 1992. 428p. (Orig.). 1992. pap. 72.50 (91-7996-411-7) Coronet Bks.

Nordic Council of Ministers Staff, jt. auth. see Nordic Committee of Senior Officials.

Nordic World Editors. Snow Camping. LC 74-16796. (Illus.). 128p. 1974. pap. 3.50 (0-89037-042-7) Anderson World.

— Winter Safety Handbook. LC 74-16794. (Illus.). 96p. 1975. pap. 2.95 (0-89037-044-3) Anderson World.

Nordica, Lillian. Hints to Singers. unabridged ed. LC 98-12584. 96p. 1998. pap. 4.95 (0-486-40094-8) Dover.

Nordin, Albert A., jt. auth. see Alder, William H.

Nordin, B. E., ed. Calcium in Human Biology. (Illus.). 481p. 1988. 60.00 (3-540-17475-3, 174753) Spr-Verlag.

— Calcium in Human Biology. (ILSI Human Nutrition Reviews Ser.). (Illus.). 481p. 1988. 60.00 (0-387-17475-3) Spr-Verlag.

Nordin, Carl S. We Were Next to Nothing: An American POW's Account of Japanese Prison Camps & Deliverance in World War II. LC 96-39692. 264p. 1997. lib. bdg. 29.95 (0-7864-0274-1) McFarland & Co.

Nordin, Dennis S. The New Deal's Black Congressman: A Life of Arthur Wergs Mitchell. LC 97-4478. (Illus.). 336p. 1997. spiral bd. 39.95 (0-8262-1102-X) U of Mo Pr.

Nordin, Julee & Johnson, Pat. Australian Dreamings. Fiore, Jenny, ed. (YA). (gr. 5-12). 1996. teacher ed. 89.95 incl. VHS (0-945666-56-X) Crizmac.

Nordin, Margareta & Frankel, Victor H. Basic Biomechanics of the Musculoskeletal System. 2nd ed. LC 89-2455. (Illus.). 323p. 1989. pap. text 45.00 (0-8121-1227-X) Lppncott W & W.

Nordin, Margareta & Frankel, Victor H. Basic Biomechanics of the Musculoskeletal System. 3rd ed. 450p. 47.00 (0-683-30247-7) Lppncott W & W.

Nordin, Margareta, ed. see Andersson, Gunnar B. J., et al.

***Nordin, Rhonda Kruse.** After the Baby: Making Sense of Marriage after Childbirth. LC 99-56432. 256p. 2000. pap. 14.95 (0-87833-168-9) Taylor Pub.

Nordin, Richard. The Early Hasselblad Cameras. (Illus.). 100p. 1991. write for info. (1-879561-20-4); pap. 19.95 (1-879561-19-0) Hist Camera Pubns.

Nordin, Richard, et al. Command Concepts: A Theory Derived from the Practice of Command & Control. LC 96-39019. (Illus.). xxi, 144p. (C). 1999. pap. 15.00 (0-8330-2450-7, MR-775-OSD) Rand Corp.

Nordine, Ken. Colors. LC 97-23073. (Illus.). 32p. (J). 2000. 16.00 (0-15-201584-1, Harcourt Child Bks) Harcourt.

Nordine, Ray & Vettrus, Linda. Parenting with C. A. R. E. Credibility, Assertiveness, Responsibility, Esteem-Building. 128p. Date not set. pap. 9.95 (1-929293-02-X) Whole Child Institute.

Nordius, Janina. I Am Myself Alone: Solitude & Transcendence in John Cowper Powys. LC 97-185359. (Gothenburg Studies in English: Vol. 67). 244p. 1997. pap. 67.50 (91-7346-304-3, Pub. by Almqvist Wiksell) Coronet Bks.

Nordland, Eva, jt. ed. see Reardon, Betty A.

Nordland, Gerald. Burgoyne Diller: The Early Geometric Work. (Illus.). 56p. 1990. pap. 20.00 (0-8150-0009-X) Wittenborn Art.

Richard Diebenkorn. LC 87-42688. (Illus.). 248p. 1993. 75.00 (0-8478-0870-X, Pub. by Rizzoli Intl) St Martin.

— Ynez Johnston. LC 95-80817. (Illus.). 120p. 1996. 40.00 (0-9628514-9-3) Grassfield Pr.

Nordland, Gerald, et al. Twentieth Century American Drawings. LC 97-78049. (Illus.). 224p. 1998. pap. 39.95 (1-886438-00-5) Grassfield Pr.

Nordland, Gerald, ed. see Wright, Frank Lloyd.

Nordland, John, II. Heroes, 2 vols., Set. (Illus.). 96p. (Orig.). 1992. pap. 9.90 (1-883611-00-8) Blckbird Comics.

— Heroes, 2 vols., Vol. 1. (Illus.). 96p. (Orig.). 1992. pap. 4.95 (1-883611-01-6) Blckbird Comics.

— Heroes, Vol. II. (Illus.). 96p. (Orig.). pap. 4.95 (1-883611-02-4) Blckbird Comics.

Nordlander, D. For God & Tsar: A Brief History of Russian America. (Illus.). 28p. 1995. pap. 3.95 (0-930931-15-7) Alaska Natural.

Nordlander, David J., tr. see Khlevniuk, Oleg V.

Nordlander, Ingegerd. Real Estate Transfer Deeds in Novgorod, 1609-1616: Text & Commentary. (Stockholm Slavic Studies: No. 18). 171p. (Orig.). 1987. pap. text 30.00 (91-22-00857-8) Coronet Bks.

Nordlander, Johan. Towards a Semantics of Linguistic Time: Exploring Some Basic Time Concepts with Special Reference to English & Krio. (Umea Studies in the Humanities: No. 134) 196p. 1997. pap. 52.50 (91-7191-261-4, Pub. by Almqvist Wiksell) Coronet Bks.

Nordlicht, Lillian. Cover Your Eyes & Run. (Illus.). (J). (gr. 1-6). 1995. pap 6.50 (0-87602-344-8) Anchorage.

Nordlicht, Scott M., et al. Why Me? Approaching Coronary Heart Disease, Cardiac Catheterization & Treatment Options from a Position of Strength. Taylor, Rebecca, ed. LC 97-68232. (Illus.). 92p. 1997. pap. 12.95 (0-9657611-1-8) Nrthrn Lghts.

Nordling, JoAnne. Taking Charge: Caring & Discipline That Works - At Home & at School. 3rd rev. ed. Orig. Title: Taking Charge: A Parent & Teacher Guide to Loving Discipline. (Illus.). 300p. 1999. pap. 14.95 (1-889531-03-0) Sibyl Pubns.

Nordling, Lee & Newspaper Features Council Staff. Your Career in the Comics. (Illus.). 304p. 1995. pap. 9.95 (0-8362-0748-3) Andrews & McMeel.

Nordlinger, B. & Jaeck, D., eds. Surgical Treatment of Hepatic Metastases of Colorectal Diseases: Report of the 94th French Congress of Surgery. (Monographs of the French Surgical Association). 140p. 1993. 100.00 (0-387-55142-5) Spr-Verlag.

Nordlinger, Eric A. Conflict Regulation in Divided Societies. (Harvard Studies in International Affairs: No. 29). 154p. 1984. reprint ed. pap. text 19.00 (0-8191-4043-0) U Pr of Amer.

— Isolationism Reconfigured: American Foreign Policy for a New Century. 352p. 1995. pap. text 17.95 (0-691-02921-0, Pub. by Princeton U Pr) Cal Prin Full Svc.

— Isolationism Reconfigured: American Foreign Policy for a New Century. LC 94-43137. 352p. 1995. text 45.00 (0-691-04327-2, Pub. by Princeton U Pr) Cal Prin Full Svc.

— On the Autonomy of the Democratic State. LC 81-1683. (Center for International Affairs Ser.). (Illus.). 247p. 1981. 37.95 (0-674-63407-1) HUP.

— On the Autonomy of the Democratic State. (Center for International Affairs Ser.). (Illus.). 247p. 1981. pap. 13.95 (0-674-63409-8) HUP.

Nordlinger, Rachel. Constructive Case: Evidence from Australian Languages. LC 98-5742. (Dissertations in Linguistics Ser.). 196p. (C). 1998. pap. 22.95 (1-57586-134-8) CSLI.

— Constructive Case: Evidence from Australian Languages. LC 98-5742. (Dissertations in Linguistics Ser.: Vol. 14). 196p. (C). 1998. text 59.95 (1-57586-135-6) CSLI.

Nordloh, David, ed. see Howells, William Dean.

Nordloh, David J. American Literary Scholarship: An Annual 1994. 500p. 1996. text 60.00 (0-8223-1810-5) Duke.

Nordloh, David J., ed. American Literary Scholarship: An Annual, 1989. LC 65-19450. 523p. 1991. text 60.00 (0-8223-1139-9) Duke.

— American Literary Scholarship: An Annual, 1991. LC 65-19450. 540p. 1993. text 60.00 (0-8223-1315-4) Duke.

— American Literary Scholarship: An Annual, 1992. LC 65-19450. 500p. 1994. text 60.00 (0-8223-1480-0) Duke.

— American Literary Scholarship, 1986. LC 65-19450. xvii, 522p. (C). 1988. text 60.00 (0-8223-0802-9) Duke.

Nordlund, James J., et al, eds. The Pigmentary System: Physiology & Pathophysiology. LC 97-28806. (Illus.). 1106p. 1998. text 225.00 (0-19-509861-7) OUP.

Nordlund, James J., jt. auth. see Hann, Seung-Kyung.

***Nordlund, Les.** Dust: A Pishon-Euphrates Journey. LC 99-63244. 272p. 1999. pap. 12.95 (1-57921-186-0) Assoc Comm Servs.

Nordlund, Willis J. The Quest for a Living Wage: The History of the Federal Minimum Wage Program. 48. LC 95-48354. (Contributions in Labor Studies: Vol. 48). 304p. 1997. 65.00 (0-313-26412-0, Greenwood Pr) Greenwood.

— Silent Skies: The Air Traffic Controllers' Strike. LC 97-38545. 224p. 1998. 49.95 (0-275-96188-5, Praeger Pubs) Greenwood.

Nordman, Eric, ed. Regulatory Re-Engineering of Commercial Lines Insurance. 26p. 1998. pap. 25.00i (0-89382-575-1, CDR-OP) Nat Assn Insurance.

Nordman, Marianne, jt. auth. see Lauren, Christer.

Nordman, Marianne, jt. ed. see Lauren, Christer.

Nordmann, Alfred, ed. see Wittgenstein, Ludwig Josef Johann.

Nordmann, Martha. Cooking on Your Own: For Newlyweds, College Students or Anyone Who Is. (Illus.). 97p. 1992. spiral bd. 8.50 (1-882835-24-7) STA-Kris.

Nordmann, P. I. Tahiti. 1972. 250.00 (0-8490-1175-2) Gordon Pr.

Nordmann, Yves. Zwischen Leben und Tod: Aspekte der Judischen Medizinethik. 121p. 1999. 30.95 (3-906760-94-4, Pub. by P Lang Pubng) P Lang Pubng.

Nordmeyer, U., et al, eds. Anesthesiologische und Intensivmedizinische Aspekte in der Kinderheilkunde. (Beitraege zur Intensiv und Notfallmedizin Ser.: Vol. 6). (Illus.). xi, 208p. 1987. 61.75 (3-8055-4589-4) S Karger.

— Grenzbereiche der Anaesthesie und Intensivmedizin. (Beitraege zur Intensiv und Notfallmedizin Ser.: Vol. 7). (GER., Illus.). viii, 190p. 1991. pap. 50.50 (3-8055-5413-3) S Karger.

Nordness, Lee. Jack Earl: The Genesis & Triumphant Survival of an Underground Ohio Artist. LC 85-61064. (Illus.). 352p. (Orig.). 1985. pap. 29.95 (0-937486-03-5) Perimeter Pr.

Nordness, Lee, ed. The Council House. LC 80-82639. (Illus.). 230p. (C). 1980. 39.00 (0-937486-01-9) Perimeter Pr.

Nordoff, Paul & Robbins, Clive. Music Therapy in Special Education. 2nd rev. ed. (Illus.). 272p. 1983. pap. 17.50 (0-918812-22-4, ST 035) MMB Music.

Nordon, Robert, jt. ed. see Schindhelm, Klaus.

Nordoy, A., ed. Blood Vessel Wall Interactions in Thrombogenesis. (Haemostasis Ser.: Vol. 8, Nos. 3-5). 1979. pap. 68.00 (3-8055-0117-X) S Karger.

Nordoy, A., ed. see Inserm-International Symposium Staff.

Nordquist. Progressions. pap. text. write for info. (0-312-08415-3) St Martin.

Nordquist, D. L. & Nordquist, G. E. Twana Twined Basketry. (Illus.). 100p. (Orig.). (C). 1983. pap. 19.95 (0-916552-27-6) Acoma Bks.

Nordquist, G. E., jt. auth. see Nordquist, D. L.

Nordquist, Gullog C. Middle Helladic Village: Asine in the Argolid. (Uppsala Studies in Ancient Mediterranean & Near Eastern Civilizations: No. 16). (Illus.). 195p. (Orig.). 1987. pap. text 45.00 (91-554-1971-2, Pub. by Uppsala Univ Acta Univ Uppsaliensis) Coronet Bks.

Nordquist, Gullog C., jt. ed. see Hagg, Robin.

Nordquist, Joan. Feminist Theory: Women of Color: A Bibliography. (Social Theory: A Bibliographic Ser.: No. 40). 72p. (Orig.). (C). 1995. pap. 20.00 (0-937855-79-0) Ref Rsch Serv.

— Jacques Derrida II: A Bibliography. LC 95-230983. (Social Theory: A Bibliographic Ser.: No. 37). 76p. (Orig.). 1995. pap. 20.00 (0-937855-73-1) Ref Rsch Serv.

— Julia Kristeva Vol. II: A Bibliography. (Social Theory: A Bibliographic Ser.: No. 39). 72p. (Orig.). (C). 1995. pap. 20.00 (0-937855-77-4) Ref Rsch Serv.

— Native Americans: Social, Economic & Political Aspects - A Bibliography. LC 99-196376. (Contemporary Social Issues: Vol. 50). 72p. 1998. pap. 20.00 (0-937855-98-7) Ref Rsch Serv.

— Postcolonial Theory: A Bibliography. (Social Theory: Vol. 50). 72p. 1998. pap. 20.00 (0-937855-99-5) Ref Rsch Serv.

— Recent Immigration from Latin America: Social, Economic & Political Aspects: A Bibliography. (Contemporary Social Issues: A Bibliographic Ser.: No. 37). 76p. 1995. pap. 20.00 (0-937855-72-3) Ref Rsch Serv.

— Simone Weil: A Bibliography. (Social Theory: A Bibliographic Ser.: No. 38). 72p. (C). 1995. pap. 20.00 (0-937855-75-8) Ref Rsch Serv.

Nordquist, Joan, compiled by. Glasnost: The Soviet Union Today: A Bibliography. (Contemporary Social Issues: A Bibliographic Ser.: No. 13). 60p. 1989. pap. 20.00 (0-937855-25-1) Ref Rsch Serv.

— Hannah Arendt: A Bibliography. (Social Theory: A Bibliographic Ser.: No. 14). 60p. (Orig.). (C). 1989. pap. 20.00 (0-937855-26-X) Ref Rsch Serv.

— International Debt & the Third World: A Bibliography. (Contemporary Social Issues: A Bibliographic Ser.: No. 14). 60p. 1989. pap. 20.00 (0-937855-27-8) Ref Rsch Serv.

— Max Weber: A Bibliography. (Social Theory: A Bibliographic Ser.: No. 13). 60p. (Orig.). 1989. pap. 20.00 (0-937855-24-3) Ref Rsch Serv.

Nordquist, Joan, ed. Affirmative Action No. 41: A Bibliography. (Contemporary Social Issues: A Bibliography Ser.: No. 41). (Orig.). 1996. pap. 20.00 (0-937855-80-4) Ref Rsch Serv.

— The African American Woman: Social & Economic Conditions: A Bibliography. (Contemporary Social Issues: A Bibliographic Ser.: No. 32). 64p. (Orig.). 1993. pap. 20.00 (0-937855-62-6) Ref Rsch Serv.

— African Americans: Social & Economic Conditions: A Bibliography. (Contemporary Social Issues: A Bibliographic Ser.: No. 27). 68p. (Orig.). (C). 1992. pap. 20.00 (0-937855-52-9) Ref Rsch Serv.

— AIDS: Political, Social, International Aspects: A Bibliography. (Contemporary Social Issues: A Bibliographic Ser.: No. 10). 60p. (Orig.). 1988. pap. 20.00 (0-937855-19-7) Ref Rsch Serv.

— Anarchism: Contemporary Theories: A Bibliography. (Social Theory: Vol. 54). 72p. 1999. pap. 20.00 (1-892068-07-9) Ref Rsch Serv.

— Animal Rights: A Bibliography. (Contemporary Social Issues: A Bibliographic Ser.: No. 21). 60p. (Orig.). (C). 1991. pap. 20.00 (0-937855-40-5) Ref Rsch Serv.

— Antonio Gramsci: A Bibliography. (Social Theory: A Bibliographic Ser.: No. 7). 50p. 1987. pap. 20.00 (0-937855-12-X) Ref Rsch Serv.

Asian Americans No. 42: Social, Economic & Political Aspects: A Bibliography. (Contemporary Social Issues: A Bibliography Ser.: No. 42). (Orig.). 1996. pap. 20.00 (0-937855-82-0) Ref Rsch Serv.

— Biotechnology & Society: A Bibliography. (Contemporary Social Issues: A Bibliographic Ser.: No. 8). 60p. (Orig.). 1987. pap. 20.00 (0-937855-15-4) Ref Rsch Serv.

***Nordquist, Joan, ed.** Cancer & the Environment: A Bibliography. (Contemporary Social Issues: Vol. 53). 72p. 1999. pap. 20.00 (1-892068-04-4) Ref Rsch Serv.

Nordquist, Joan, ed. Claude Levi-Strauss: A Bibliography. (Social Theory: A Bibliographic Ser.: No. 6). 1987. pap. 20.00 (0-937855-10-3) Ref Rsch Serv.

— Comparable Worth: A Bibliography. (Contemporary Social Issues: A Bibliographic Ser.: No. 2). 1986. pap. 20.00 (0-937855-03-0) Ref Rsch Serv.

— Current Central American-U. S. Relations: A Bibliography. (Contemporary Social Issues: A Bibliographic Ser.: No. 5). 50p. 1987. pap. 20.00 (0-937855-09-X) Ref Rsch Serv.

— Deconstructionism: A Bibliography. (Social Theory: A Bibliographic Ser.: No. 26). 68p. (Orig.). 1992. pap. 20.00 (0-937855-51-0) Ref Rsch Serv.

— Domestic Violence: A Bibliography. (Contemporary Social Issues: A Bibliographic Ser.: No. 4). 50p. 1986. pap. 20.00 (0-937855-07-3) Ref Rsch Serv.

— Eating Disorders: Feminist, Historical, Cultural, Psychological Aspects: A Bibliography. (Contemporary Social Issues: A Bibliographic Ser.: No. 15). 60p. (C). 1989. pap. 20.00 (0-937855-29-4) Ref Rsch Serv.

— The Elderly in America: A Bibliography. (Contemporary Social Issues: A Bibliographic Ser.: No. 23). 60p. (Orig.). (C). 1991. pap. 20.00 (0-937855-44-8) Ref Rsch Serv.

— Environment II: Clean Air: A Bibliography. (Contemporary Social Issues: A Bibliographic Ser.: No. 31). 64p. (Orig.). 1993. pap. 20.00 (0-937855-60-X) Ref Rsch Serv.

— The Environment One: Clean Water: A Bibliography. (Contemporary Social Issues: A Bibliographic Ser.: No. 28). 68p. (Orig.). (C). 1992. pap. 20.00 (0-937855-54-5) Ref Rsch Serv.

— Environmental Issues in the Third World: A Bibliography. (Contemporary Social Issues: A Bibliographic Ser.: No. 22). 60p. (Orig.). (C). 1991. pap. 20.00 (0-937855-42-1) Ref Rsch Serv.

— Environmental Racism & the Environmental Justice Movement: A Bibliography. (Contemporary Social Issues: A Bibliography Ser.: No. 39). 72p. (Orig.). (C). 1995. pap. 20.00 (0-937855-76-6) Ref Rsch Serv.

— Ernst Bloch: A Bibliography. (Social Theory: A Bibliographic Ser.: No. 19). 64p. (Orig.). (C). 1990. pap. 20.00 (0-937855-37-5) Ref Rsch Serv.

— Felix Guattari & Gilles Deleuze: A Bibliography. (Contemporary Social Issues: A Bibliographic Ser.: No. 26). 68p. (Orig.). 1992. pap. 20.00 (0-937855-49-9) Ref Rsch Serv.

— Feminism & Post Modernism No. 41: A Bibliography. (Social Theory: A Bibliographic Ser.: No. 41). (Orig.). 1996. pap. 20.00 (0-937855-81-2) Ref Rsch Serv.

— Feminism Worldwide No. 44: A Bibliography. (Contemporary Social Issues: A Bibliography Ser.: No. 44). (Orig.). 1996. pap. 20.00 (0-937855-86-3) Ref Rsch Serv.

— Feminist Literary Theory: A Bibliography. (Social Theory: Vol. 52). 72p. 1998. pap. 20.00 (1-892068-03-6) Ref Rsch Serv.

— The Feminist Movement: A Bibliography. (Contemporary Social Issues: A Bibliographic Ser.: No. 24). 60p. (Orig.). (C). 1991. pap. 20.00 (0-937855-46-4) Ref Rsch Serv.

— Feminist Theory: A Bibliography. (Social Theory: A Bibliographic Ser.: No. 28). 68p. (Orig.). (C). 1992. pap. 20.00 (0-937855-55-3) Ref Rsch Serv.

— The Feminization of Poverty: A Bibliography. (Contemporary Social Issues: A Bibliographic Ser.: No. 6). 1987. pap. 20.00 (0-937855-11-1) Ref Rsch Serv.

— Food Pollution: A Bibliography. (Contemporary Social Issues: A Bibliographic Ser.: No. 20). 64p. (C). 1990. pap. 20.00 (0-937855-38-3) Ref Rsch Serv.

— French Feminist Theory: Luce Irigaray & Helene Cixous: A Bibliography. (Social Theory: No. 20). 64p. (Orig.). (C). 1990. pap. 20.00 (0-937855-39-1) Ref Rsch Serv.

— French Feminist Theory II: Michele le Doeuff, Monique Wittig, Catherine Clement: A Bibliography. (Social Theory: A Bibliographic Ser.: No. 31). 64p. 1993. pap. 20.00 (0-937855-61-8) Ref Rsch Serv.

— French Feminist Theory III No. 44: Luce Irigaray & Helene Cixous: A Bibliography. (Social Theory: A Bibliographic Ser.: No. 44). (Orig.). 1996. pap. 20.00 (0-937855-87-1) Ref Rsch Serv.

***Nordquist, Joan, ed.** Gay & Lesbian Families: A Bibliography. (Contemporary Social Issues: Vol. 57). 72p. 2000. pap. 20.00 (1-892068-12-5) Ref Rsch Serv.

Nordquist, Joan, ed. Georg Lukacs: A Bibliography. (Social Theory: A Bibliographic Ser.: No. 11). 60p. 1988. pap. 20.00 (0-937855-20-0) Ref Rsch Serv.

***Nordquist, Joan, ed.** Global Warming: A Bibliography. (Contemporary Social Issues: Vol. 55). 72p. 1999. pap. 20.00 (1-892068-08-7) Ref Rsch Serv.

Nordquist, Joan, ed. The Greenhouse Effect: A Bibliography. (Contemporary Social Issues: A Bibliographic Ser.: No. 18). (Orig.). (C). 1990. pap. 20.00 (0-937855-34-0) Ref Rsch Serv.

— Hans-Georg Gadamer: A Bibliography. (Social Theory: Vol. 51). 72p. 1998. pap. 20.00 (1-892068-01-X) Ref Rsch Serv.

— Herbert Marcuse: A Bibliography. (Social Theory: A Bibliographic Ser.: No. 9). 60p. (Orig.). 1988. pap. 20.00 (0-937855-16-2) Ref Rsch Serv.

— The Homeless in America: A Bibliography. (Contemporary Social Issues: A Bibliographic Ser.: No. 12). 60p. (Orig.). 1988. pap. 20.00 (0-937855-23-5) Ref Rsch Serv.

***Nordquist, Joan, ed.** The International Monetary Fund's Harmful Development Policies in the Third World: A Bibliography. (Contemporary Social Issues: Vol. 54). 72p. 1999. pap. 20.00 (1-892068-06-0) Ref Rsch Serv.

Nordquist, Joan, ed. Investment & Social Responsibility: South Africa - A Bibliography. (Contemporary Social Issues: A Bibliographic Ser.: No. 1). 1986. pap. 20.00 (0-937855-01-4) Ref Rsch Serv.

— Jacques Derrida: A Bibliography. (Social Theory: A Bibliographic Ser.: No. 3). 1986. pap. 20.00 (0-937855-02-2) Ref Rsch Serv.

— Jacques Lacan: A Bibliography. (Social Theory: A Bibliographic Ser.: No. 5). 50p. 1987. pap. 20.00 (0-937855-08-1) Ref Rsch Serv.

— Jean Baudrillard: A Bibliography. (Social Theory: A Bibliographic Ser.: No. 24). 60p. (Orig.). (C). 1991. pap. 20.00 (0-937855-47-2) Ref Rsch Serv.

— Jean-Francois Lyotard: A Bibliography. (Social Theory: A Bibliographic Ser.: No. 21). 60p. (Orig.). (C). 1991. pap. 20.00 (0-937855-41-3) Ref Rsch Serv.

— Jean-Paul Sartre: A Bibliography. (Social Theory: A Bibliographic Ser.: No. 29). 64p. (Orig.). 1993. pap. 20.00 (0-937855-57-X) Ref Rsch Serv.

— Julia Kristeva: A Bibliography. (Social Theory: A Bibliographic Ser.: No. 16). 60p. (Orig.). (C). 1989. pap. 20.00 (0-937855-30-8) Ref Rsch Serv.

— Jurgen Habermas: A Bibliography. (Social Theory: A Bibliographic Ser.: No. 1). 1986. pap. 20.00 (0-937855-00-6) Ref Rsch Serv.

— Jurgen Habermas: A Bibliography. (Social Theory: A Bibliographic Ser.: No. 22). 60p. (C). 1991. pap. 20.00 (0-937855-43-X) Ref Rsch Serv.

— Jurgen Habermas (III) A Bibliography. LC 99-219850. (Social Theory: Vol. 49). 72p. 1998. pap. 20.00 (0-937855-97-9) Ref Rsch Serv.

N

An Asterisk (*) at the beginning of an entry indicates that the title is appearing for the first time.

— Labor Abuses in the Global Economy: Women & Children: A Bibliography. (Contemporary Social Issues: Vol. 51). 72p. 1998. pap. 20.00 (*1-892068-00-1*) Ref Rsch Serv.

— Latinas in the United States: Social, Economic, & Political Aspects: A Bibliography. LC 96-199935. (Contemporary Social Issues: A Bibliography Ser.: No. 40). 72p. (Orig.). (C). 1995. pap. 20.00 (*0-937855-78-2*) Ref Rsch Serv.

— Latinos in the United States: Social Economic & Political Aspects: A Bibliography. (Contemporary Social Issues: A Bibliographic Ser.: No. 34). 72p. (C). 1994. pap. 20.00 (*0-937855-66-9*) Ref Rsch Serv.

— Louis Althusser: A Bibliography. (Social Theory: A Bibliographic Ser.: No. 3). 50p. 1986. pap. 20.00 (*0-937855-04-9*) Ref Rsch Serv.

— Martin Heidegger: A Bibliography. (Social Theory: A Bibliographic Ser.: No. 17). 64p. (Orig.). (C). 1990. pap. 20.00 (*0-937855-33-2*) Ref Rsch Serv.

— Martin Heidegger No. 42: A Bibliography. (Social Theory: A Bibliographic Ser.: No. 42). (Orig.). 1996. pap. 20.00 (*0-937855-83-9*) Ref Rsch Serv.

***Nordquist, Joan, ed.** Marxism & Ecology: A Bibliography. (Social Theory: Vol. 56). 1999. pap. 20.00 (*1-892068-11-7*) Ref Rsch Serv.

— Maurice Merleau-Ponty: A Bibliography. (Social Theory: Vol. 57). 72p. 2000. pap. 20.00 (*1-892068-13-3*) Ref Rsch Serv.

Nordquist, Joan, ed. Max Horkheimer: A Bibliography. (Social Theory: A Bibliographic Ser.: No. 18). 64p. (Orig.). (C). 1990. pap. 20.00 (*0-937855-35-9*) Ref Rsch Serv.

— Michel Foucault: A Bibliography. (Social Theory: A Bibliographic Ser.: No. 4). 50p. 1986. pap. 20.00 (*0-937855-06-5*) Ref Rsch Serv.

— Michel Foucault Two: A Bibliography. (Social Theory: A Bibliographic Ser.: No. 27). 68p. (Orig.). (C). 1992. pap. 20.00 (*0-937855-53-7*) Ref Rsch Serv.

— Mikhail Bakhtin: A Bibliography. (Social Theory: A Bibliographic Ser.: No. 12). 60p. (Orig.). 1988. pap. 20.00 (*0-937855-22-7*) Ref Rsch Serv.

— Mikhail Bakhtin Two: A Bibliography. (Social Theory: A Bibliographic Ser.: No. 32). 64p. (Orig.). 1993. pap. 20.00 (*0-937855-63-4*) Ref Rsch Serv.

— The Multicultural Education Debate in the University: A Bibliography. (Contemporary Social Issues: A Bibliographic Ser.: No. 25). 68p. (Orig.). 1992. pap. 20.00 (*0-937855-48-0*) Ref Rsch Serv.

— Multinational Corporations & the Environment: A Bibliography. LC 95-230996. (Contemporary Social Issues: A Bibliographic Ser.: No. 36). 72p. (C). 1994. pap. 20.00 (*0-937855-70-7*) Ref Rsch Serv.

— NAFTA & GATT No. 43: Environmental & Economic Issues: A Bibliography. (Contemporary Social Issues: A Bibliography Ser.: No. 43). (Orig.). 1996. pap. 20.00 (*0-937855-84-7*) Ref Rsch Serv.

***Nordquist, Joan, ed.** The Native American Women - Social, Economic & Political Aspects: A Bibliography. (Contemporary Social Issues: Vol. 56). 72p. 1999. pap. 20.00 (*1-892068-10-9*) Ref Rsch Serv.

— Paul Ricoeur: A Bibliography. (Social Theory: Vol. 53). 72p. 1999. pap. 20.00 (*1-892068-05-2*) Ref Rsch Serv.

Nordquist, Joan, ed. Pornography & Censorship: A Bibliography. (Contemporary Social Issues: A Bibliographic Ser.: No. 7). 50p. 1987. pap. 20.00 (*0-937855-13-8*) Ref Rsch Serv.

***Nordquist, Joan, ed.** Postcolonial Theory II - Literature & the Arts: A Bibliography. (Social Theory: Vol. 55). 72p. 1999. pap. 20.00 (*1-892068-09-5*) Ref Rsch Serv.

— The Privatization of Public Education - Charter School & Vouchers: A Bibliography. (Contemporary Social Issues: Vol. 58). 72p. 2000. pap. 20.00 (*1-892068-14-1*) Ref Rsch Serv.

Nordquist, Joan, ed. Radical Ecological Theory: A Bibliography. (Social Theory: A Bibliographic Ser.: No. 30). 64p. (Orig.). 1993. pap. 20.00 (*0-937855-59-6*) Ref Rsch Serv.

— Rape: A Bibliography. (Contemporary Social Issues: A Bibliographic Ser.: No. 19). 64p. (Orig.). (C). 1990. pap. 20.00 (*0-937855-36-7*) Ref Rsch Serv.

— Reproductive Rights: A Bibliography. (Contemporary Social Issues: A Bibliographic Ser.: No. 9). 60p. 1988. pap. 20.00 (*0-937855-17-0*) Ref Rsch Serv.

— Rosa Luxemberg & Emma Goldman No. 43: A Bibliography. (Social Theory: A Bibliographic Ser.: No. 43). (Orig.). 1996. pap. 20.00 (*0-937855-85-5*) Ref Rsch Serv.

— Simone de Beauvoir: A Bibliography. (Social Theory: A Bibliographic Ser.: No. 23). 60p. (Orig.). (C). 1991. pap. 20.00 (*0-937855-45-6*) Ref Rsch Serv.

— Substance Abuse I: Drug Abuse: A Bibliography. (Contemporary Social Issues: A Bibliographic Ser.: No. 16). 64p. (C). 1989. pap. 20.00 (*0-937855-31-6*) Ref Rsch Serv.

— Substance Abuse II: Alcohol Abuse: A Bibliography. (Contemporary Social Issues: A Bibliographic Ser.: No. 17). 60p. (Orig.). 1990. pap. 20.00 (*0-937855-32-4*) Ref Rsch Serv.

— Talcott Parsons: A Bibliography. (Social Theory: A Bibliographic Ser.: No. 8). 60p. (Orig.). 1987. pap. 20.00 (*0-937855-14-6*) Ref Rsch Serv.

— Theodor Adorno: A Bibliography. (Social Theory: A Bibliographic Ser.: No. 10). 60p. (Orig.). 1988. pap. 20.00 (*0-937855-18-9*) Ref Rsch Serv.

— The Third World Worker in the Multinational Corporation: A Bibliography. (Contemporary Social Issues: A Bibliographic Ser.: No. 30). 64p. (Orig.). 1993. pap. 20.00 (*0-937855-58-8*) Ref Rsch Serv.

— Toxic Waste: A Bibliography. (Contemporary Social Issues: A Bibliographic Ser.: No. 11). 60p. (Orig.). 1988. pap. 20.00 (*0-937855-21-9*) Ref Rsch Serv.

— University Research: Social & Political Implications: A Bibliography. (Contemporary Social Issues: A Bibliographic Ser.: No. 3). 1986. pap. 20.00 (*0-937855-05-7*) Ref Rsch Serv.

— Violence Against Women: A Bibliography. (Contemporary Social Issues: A Bibliographic Ser.: No. 26). 68p. (Orig.). 1992. pap. 20.00 (*0-937855-50-2*) Ref Rsch Serv.

— Violence Against Women: International Aspects - A Bibliography. LC 98-226820. (Contemporary Social Issues: Vol. 49). 72p. 1998. pap. 20.00 (*0-937855-96-0*) Ref Rsch Serv.

— Violence in American Society: A Bibliography. (Contemporary Social Issues: A Bibliographic Ser.: No. 33). 72p. (C). 1994. pap. 20.00 (*0-937855-64-2*) Ref Rsch Serv.

— Walter Benjamin: A Bibliography. (Social Theory: A Bibliographic Ser.: No. 15). 60p. (C). 1989. pap. 20.00 (*0-937855-28-6*) Ref Rsch Serv.

— Women & Aging: A Bibliography. LC 96-171076. (Contemporary Social Issues: A Bibliographic Ser.: No. 35). 72p. (C). 1994. pap. 20.00 (*0-937855-68-5*) Ref Rsch Serv.

— Women & AIDS: A Bibliography. (Contemporary Social Issues: A Bibliographic Ser.: No. 29). 64p. (Orig.). 1993. pap. 20.00 (*0-937855-56-1*) Ref Rsch Serv.

— Women & Cyberspace: Gender Issues: A Bibliography. (Contemporary Social Issues: Vol. 52). 72p. 1998. pap. 20.00 (*1-892068-02-8*) Ref Rsch Serv.

— Women in the United States: Economic Conditions: A Bibliography. LC 96-126492. (Contemporary Social Issues: A Bibliography Ser.: No. 38). 72p. (Orig.). (C). 1995. pap. 20.00 (*0-937855-74-X*) Ref Rsch Serv.

Nordquist, Joan, ed. The Asian American Woman: Social, Economic & Political Conditions: A Bibliography. LC 98-184496. (Contemporary Social Issues: Vol. 48). 72p. (Orig.). 1997. pap. 20.00 (*0-937855-94-4*) Ref Rsch Serv.

— The Disabled: Social, Economic & Political Conditions: A Bibliography. LC 98-132828. (Contemporary Social Issues: Vol. 47). 72p. (Orig.). 1997. pap. 20.00 (*0-937855-92-8*) Ref Rsch Serv.

— Emmanuel Levinas: A Bibliography. (Social Theory: Vol. 45). 72p. (Orig.). 1997. pap. 20.00 (*0-937855-89-8*) Ref Rsch Serv.

— Hannah Arendt II: A Bibliography. (Social Theory: Vol. 46). 72p. 1997. pap. 20.00 (*0-937855-91-X*) Ref Rsch Serv.

— The Health Care Crisis in the United States: A Bibliography. LC 98-110993. (Contemporary Social Issues: Vol. 46). 72p. (Orig.). 1997. pap. 20.00 (*0-937855-90-1*) Ref Rsch Serv.

— Pierre Bourdieu: A Bibliography. (Social Theory: Vol. 47). 72p. (Orig.). 1997. pap. 20.00 (*0-937855-93-6*) Ref Rsch Serv.

— Queer Theory: A Bibliography. (Social Theory: Vol. 48). 72p. (Orig.). 1997. pap. 20.00 (*0-937855-95-2*) Ref Rsch Serv.

— Race, Crime & the Criminal Justice System: A Bibliography. LC 97-206906. (Contemporary Social Issues: Vol. 45). 72p. (Orig.). 1997. pap. 20.00 (*0-937855-88-X*) Ref Rsch Serv.

Nordquist, Kay. Dark Gods. Costa, Gwen, ed. LC 90-21747. 166p. (Orig.). 1992. pap. 13.95 (*0-87949-322-4*) Ashley Bks.

Nordquist, M. & Park, C. H., eds. The Reports of the United States Delegation to the Third United Nations Conference on the Law of the Sea. (Law of the Sea Occasional Papers: No. 33). 689p. 1983. 16.00 (*0-911189-07-6*) Law Sea Inst.

Nordquist, Myron, jt. auth. see Simmonds, Kenneth R.

Nordquist, Myron H. Security Flashpoints: Oil, Islands, Sea Access, & Military Confrontation. LC 99-167100. 480p. 1998. 154.00 (*90-411-1056-9*) Kluwer Law Intl.

Nordquist, Myron H., ed. United Nations Convention on the Law of the Sea, 1982. 1985. lib. bdg. 233.00 (*90-247-3145-3*) Kluwer Academic.

— United Nations Convention on the Law of the Sea, 1982: A Commentary Volume II Article 1 to 85 Annexes I & II Final Act, Annex II. 1088p. (C). 1993. lib. bdg. 250.50 (*0-7923-2471-4*) Kluwer Academic.

— United Nations Convention on the Law of the Sea, 1982 Vol. IV: A Commentary, Articles 192 to 278 Final Act, Annex VI. (C). 1990. lib. bdg. 271.00 (*0-7923-0764-X*) Kluwer Academic.

***Nordquist, Myron H. & Moore, John N.** Current Maritime Issues & the International Maritime Organization. LC 99-52370. 1999. 150.00 (*90-411-1293-6*) Kluwer Law Intl.

Nordquist, Myron H. & Moore, John N., eds. Entry into Force of the Law of the Sea Convention. (Rhodes Papers: Vol. 1). 1995. lib. bdg. 99.50 (*90-411-0099-7*, Pub. by M Nijhoff) Kluwer Academic.

Nordquist, Myron H., et al. Oceans Policy: New Institutions, Challenges & Opportunities. LC 99-22756. 1999. 147.00 (*90-411-1182-4*) Kluwer Law Intl.

Nordquist, Richard F. Passages. 3rd ed. 1995. pap. text, teacher ed. 5.00 (*0-312-10118-X*) St Martin.

— Passages. 3rd ed. 1995. pap. text, teacher ed. 27.50 (*0-312-10119-8*) St Martin.

— Passages. 4th ed. 2000. pap. text. write for info. (*0-312-15389-9*) St Martin.

— Passages: A Beginning Writer's Guide. 3rd ed. 476p. 1995. pap. text 43.95 (*0-312-10117-1*) St Martin.

Nordsieck, Reinhard. Recht und Gesetz: In Theologischer, Philosophischer und Juristischer Perspektive. (Europaische Hochschulschriften Ser.: Reihe 2, Bd. 1074). (GER.). 165p. 1991. 32.80 (*3-631-43671-8*) P Lang Pubng.

Nordskog, John E. Social Reform in Norway. LC 72-13001. 184p. 1973. reprint ed. lib. bdg. 35.00 (*0-8371-6736-1*, NOSR, Greenwood Pr) Greenwood.

Nordstedt, C. F. Index Desmidiacearum Citationibus Locupletissimus Atque Bibliographia & Suppl. 1978. lib. bdg. 160.00 (*3-7682-1171-1*) Lubrecht & Cramer.

Nordstein, S. The Genus Crepidotus (Basidiomycotina, Agaricales) 1990. (Synopsis Fungorum Ser.: No. 2). 1990. pap. text 32.50 (*82-90724-02-0*, Pub. by Fungi-Flora) Lubrecht & Cramer.

Nordstokke, Kjell. Council & Context in Leonardo Boff's Ecclesiology: The Rebirth of the Church among the Poor. MacNeill, Brian, tr. LC 96-31330. (Studies in Religion & Society: Vol. 35). 320p. 1997. text 99.95 (*0-7734-8784-0*) E Mellen.

Nordstrom, Alison. Archives & Archetypes: Photographs by Barbara Norfleet. (Illus.). 90p. 1997. pap. text 54.00 (*1-887040-20-X*) SE Mus Photo.

— FreshWork II. 1998. 12.00 (*1-887040-25-0*) SE Mus Photo.

— Some Things. (Illus.). 16p. 1997. pap. text 8.00 (*1-887040-21-8*) SE Mus Photo.

— This Way to the Crypt. 1998. 18.00 (*1-887040-24-2*) SE Mus Photo.

Nordstrom, Alison D. Architectonic Illusion: Photographs by Beatrice Helg. (Illus.). 68p. 1994. pap. text 20.00 (*1-887040-09-9*) SE Mus Photo.

— Black Totems. (Illus.). 47p. 1995. pap. text 14.00 (*1-887040-15-3*) SE Mus Photo.

— Faces Photographed: The Photographic Portrait. 12p. 1992. pap. text 3.00 (*1-887040-00-5*) SE Mus Photo.

— Fresh Work. (Illus.). 24p. 1996. pap. 14.00 (*1-887040-18-8*) SE Mus Photo.

— Latino America: Photographs by Cecilia Arboleda. 12p. 1993. pap. text 12.00 (*1-887040-05-6*) SE Mus Photo.

— Nervous Landscapes. 28p. 1994. pap. text 12.00 (*1-887040-07-2*) SE Mus Photo.

— Reverberations: Diptychs & Triptychs from the Southeast Museum of Photography. (Illus.). 16p. 1995. pap. text 12.00 (*1-887040-12-9*) SE Mus Photo.

— Three Exhibitions: Photography: 3 Exhibitions. 12p. 1994. pap. text 12.00 (*1-887040-08-0*) SE Mus Photo.

— Victims of Paradox: Photographs by Wallace Wilson. 55p. 1993. pap. text 12.00 (*1-887040-03-X*) SE Mus Photo.

Nordstrom, Alison D. & Blantom, Casey. Telling Our Own Stories: Florida's Family Photographs. (Illus.). 32p. 1997. pap. text 8.00 (*1-887040-22-6*) SE Mus Photo.

Nordstrom, Alison D. & Ely, Deborah. Patterns of Connection: Photography by Leah King-Smith. 24p. 1992. pap. text 12.00 (*1-887040-02-1*) SE Mus Photo.

Nordstrom, Alison D. & Flax, Carol. Some M(Other) Stories, a Parenthetical Tale. 32p. 1995. pap. text 18.00 (*1-887040-11-0*) SE Mus Photo.

Nordstrom, Alison D., jt. auth. see West, Patricia.

Nordstrom, Allison D., jt. auth. see Zeller, Bob.

Nordstrom, Bengt, et al. Programming in Martin-Lof's Type Theory: An Introduction. (International Series of Monographs on Computer Science: No. 7). 232p. 1990. 55.00 (*0-19-853814-6*) OUP.

***Nordstrom, Byron J.** Scandinavia since 1500. LC 99-89029. 2000. pap. write for info. (*0-8166-2099-7*) U of Minn Pr.

— Scandinavia since 1500. LC 99-89029. 2000. 29.95 (*0-8166-2098-9*) U of Minn Pr.

Nordstrom, Byron J., ed. Dictionary of Scandinavian History. LC 83-25204. (Illus.). 724p. 1986. lib. bdg. 99.50 (*0-313-22887-6*, NCH/, Greenwood Pr) Greenwood.

Nordstrom, Carolyn. A Different Kind of War Story. LC 97-15034. (C). (gr. 13). 1997. text 39.95 (*0-8122-3406-5*); pap. text 18.50 (*0-8122-1621-0*) U of Pa Pr.

Nordstrom, Carolyn & Martin, Joanne M., eds. Paths to Domination, Resistance, & Terror. (C). 1992. pap. 17.95 (*0-520-07316-9*, Pub. by U CA Pr) Cal Prin Full Svc.

— Paths to Domination, Resistance, & Terror. (C). 1992. 55.00 (*0-520-07315-0*, Pub. by U CA Pr) Cal Prin Full Svc.

Nordstrom, Carolyn & Robben, Antonius C., eds. Fieldwork under Fire: Contemporary Studies of Violence & Survival. LC 95-6235. (Illus.). 310p. 1995. 48.00 (*0-520-08993-6*, Pub. by U CA Pr); pap. 16.95 (*0-520-08994-4*, Pub. by U CA Pr) Cal Prin Full Svc.

Nordstrom, David. The Complete Booger Book. Carle, Cliff, ed. (Illus.). 96p. 1996. pap. 4.99 (*0-918259-80-0*) CCC Pubns.

Nordstrom, David L., et al, eds. Epidemiology of Farm-Related Injuries: Bibliography with Abstracts. 205p. (C). 1996. reprint ed. pap. text 40.00 (*0-7881-3560-0*) DIANE Pub.

Nordstrom, Folke. Goya, Saturn & Melancholy: Studies in the Art of Goya. (Illus.). 239p. 1962. text 46.50 (*0-685-14723-1*) Coronet Bks.

Nordstrom, Jerry. The Voices of Christmas: Readers' Theater for Advent. (Orig.). 1996. pap. 3.75 (*0-7880-0837-4*) CSS OH.

Nordstrom, Judy. Concord & Lexington. LC 92-23392. (Places in American History Ser.). (Illus.). 72p. (J). (gr. 4 up). 1993. lib. bdg. 14.95 (*0-87518-567-3*, Dillon Silver Burdett) Silver Burdett Pr.

Nordstrom, K. F. Beaches & Dunes of Developed Coasts. LC 99-13766. (Illus.). 280p. 2000. 74.95 (*0-521-47013-7*) Cambridge U Pr.

Nordstrom, Karl, et al. Living with the New Jersey Shore. LC 85-25251. (Living with the Shore Ser.). (Illus.). 208p. (Orig.). 1986. pap. 17.95 (*0-8223-0698-0*); text 39.95 (*0-8223-0543-7*) Duke.

***Nordstrom, Kjell.** Funky Business: Talent Makes Capital Dance. 256p. 2000. pap. 25.00 (*0-273-64591-9*) F T P H.

Nordstrom, Lars. Making It Home: Memoir - Diary - Countrylife. LC 97-1278. (Illus.). 150p. 1997. pap. 15.00 (*0-915986-27-2*) Prescott St Pr.

— Sweden. LC 89-81616. (Illus.). 160p. 1990. 39.95 (*1-55868-023-3*) Gr Arts Ctr Pub.

— Theodore Roethke, William Stafford, & Gary Snyder: The Ecological Metaphor as Transformed Regionalism. (Studia Anglistica Upsaliensia Ser.: No. 67). 197p. (Orig.). 1989. pap. 42.50 (*91-554-2338-8*) Coronet Bks.

Nordstrom, Lars, tr. see Aggestam, Rolf.

Nordstrom, Louis, ed. see Senzaki, Nyogen, et al.

Nordstrom, Lyle. The Bandora: Its Music & Sources. LC 92-19946. (Detroit Studies in Music Bibliography: No. 66). 1992. 30.00 (*0-89990-060-7*) Harmonie Park Pr.

Nordstrom, O., ed. The Dynamics of Vehicles on Roads & on Tracks: Proceedings Ninth IAVSD-Symposium. (Vehicle System Dynamics Ser.: Vol. 15). xii, 656p. 1986. pap. 61.00 (*90-265-0710-0*) Swets.

Nordstrom, Olaf. The Essential Book of Boat Drinks: And Assorted Frozen Concoltions. LC 96-70316. (Illus.). 164p. 1998. 10.00 (*1-883684-15-5*) Peninsula MA.

***Nordstrom, Olaf.** The Margaritaville Cookbook. (Illus.). 288p. 2000. pap. 18.00 (*1-883684-22-6*, Margaritaville Bks) Peninsula MA.

Nordstrom, Oscar L., jt. auth. see Ander, O. Fritiof.

Nordstrom, Robert J. & Clovis, Albert L. Problems & Materials on Commercial Paper. 458p. 1981. reprint ed. write for info. (*0-318-57520-5*) West Pub.

***Nordstrom, Robert J. & De Groot, Wim A., eds.** Optical On-Line Industrial Process Monitoring. 1999. pap. text 50.00 (*0-8194-3452-3*) SPIE.

***Nordstrom, Robert J., et al.** Nordstrom on Sales & Leases of Goods 2nd ed. LC 99-36569. 1999. boxed set 175.00 (*0-7355-0684-1*) Panel Pubs.

Nordstrom, Rolf E. Tissue Expansion. LC 96-6179. (Illus.). 288p. 1996. text 105.00 (*0-7506-9711-3*) Buttrwrth-Heinemann.

Nordstrom, Ursula. Secret Language. 167p. (J). (gr. 3-5). pap. 4.95 (*0-8072-1425-6*) Listening Lib.

— Secret Language. 1972. 10.05 (*0-606-12508-6*, Pub. by Turtleback) Demco.

Nordstrom, Ursula. The Secret Language. LC 60-7701. (Illus.). 192p. (J). (gr. 3-5). 1960. lib. bdg. 12.89 (*0-06-024576-X*) HarpC Child Bks.

— The Secret Language. LC 60-7701. (Trophy Bk.). (Illus.). 176p. (J). (gr. 3-5). 1972. pap. 4.95 (*0-06-440022-0*, HarpTrophy) HarpC Child Bks.

Nordstrom, Ursula, jt. auth. see Marcus, Leonard S.

Nordstrown, Kirk & Munoz, James L. Geochemical Thermodynamics. 2nd ed. LC 93-23633. (Illus.). 574p. 1994. 69.95 (*0-86542-274-5*) Blackwell Sci.

***Nordt, Lee.** Geography: Course Manual. 1999. pap. text 19.75 (*1-56870-355-4*) RonJon Pub.

Nordvik, H., jt. ed. see Fischer, L.

***Nordyke, Eleanor C., ed.** Pacific Images: Views From Captain Cook's Third Voyage. (Illus.). 176p. 1999. text 45.00 (*0-945048-04-1*) UH Pr.

Nordyke, James W. International Finance & New York. Bruchey, Stuart & Bruchey, Eleanor, eds. LC 76-5024. (American Business Abroad Ser.). 1976. 28.95 (*0-405-09291-1*) Ayer.

Nordyke, Lewis. Cattle Empire: The Fabulous Story of the 3,000,000 Acre XIT. Wilkins, Mira, ed. LC 76-29745. (European Business Ser.). (Illus.). 1977. reprint ed. lib. bdg. 26.95 (*0-405-09762-X*) Ayer.

Nordyke, Robert D. Humorous Interpretation: The Text. 74p. 1998. pap. text 24.00 (*1-889510-36-X*) Chmpionship Debate.

***Nored, Ronald E.** Reweaving the Fabric: How Congregations & Communities Can Come Together to Build Their Neighborhood. LC 98-54368. 1999. pap. text 15.95 (*1-881320-50-2*) Black Belt Communs.

Noreen, Eric. Computer-Intensive Methods for Testing Hypotheses: An Introduction. LC 89-30193. 240p. 1989. pap. 109.95 (*0-471-61136-0*) Wiley.

Noreen, Eric, jt. auth. see Garrison, Ray H.

Noreen, Eric W., et al. The Theory of Constraints & Its Implications for Management Accounting. LC 96-128531. 1995. pap. 25.00 (*0-88427-116-1*) North River.

Noreen, Eric W., jt. auth. see Garrison, Ray H.

Noreen, George W. Your First Finch. (YF Ser.). (Illus.). 32p. (Orig.). (YA). 1991. pap. 2.29 (*0-86622-062-3*, YF-106) TFH Pubns.

Noreen, Sarah P. Public Street Illumination in Washington, D. C. An Illustrated History, Vol. M2. 1975. 5.00 (*1-888028-01-7*) GWU Ctr WAS.

Norell, Donna M. Colette: An Annotated Primary & Secondary Bibliography. LC 92-26827. (Illus.). 584p. 1992. text 20.00 (*0-8240-6620-0*, H805) Garland.

Norell, Mark & Dingus, Lowell. Dinosaur Eggs: The Story of the Oviraptor. LC 98-7859. (Illus.). 42p. (YA). (gr. 5-9). 1999. 17.95 (*0-385-32558-4*) Doubleday.

***Norell, Mark A., et al.** Discovering Dinosaurs: Evolution, Extinction, & the Lessons of Pre-History. expanded ed. LC 99-53335. (Illus.). 240p. 2000. pap. 24.95 (*0-520-22501-5*, Pub. by U CA Pr) Cal Prin Full Svc.

Norell, Mark A., et al. Discovering Dinosaurs: Evolution, Extinction, & the Lessons of Pre-History. (Illus.). 204p. 1999. reprint ed. text 35.00 (*0-7881-6465-1*) DIANE Pub.

Norell, Mark A., jt. auth. see Dingus, Lowell.

Norell, Pia. Native-Speaker Reactions to Swedish Pronunciation Errors in English. (Stockholm Studies in English: No. LXXXIX). 181p. (Orig.). 1991. pap. 49.00 (*91-22-01435-7*) Coronet Bks.

Norell, Staffan E. Epidemiology. (Illus.). 328p. 1995. text, wbk. ed. 49.95 (*0-19-507490-4*); pap. text, wbk. ed. 26.50 (*0-19-507491-2*) OUP.

— A Short Course in Epidemiology. 208p. 1991. pap. text 43.00 (*0-88167-842-2*, 2325) Lppncott W & W.

Norell, Staffen E., jt. auth. see Rothman, Kenneth J.

An Asterisk (*) at the beginning of an entry indicates that the title is appearing for the first time.

Norelli-Bachelet, Patrizia. The Gnostic Circle: A Synthesis in the Harmonies of the Cosmos. 2nd ed. (Illus.). 309p. 1994. pap. text 18.00 (*0-87728-411-3*) Aeon Bks.

— The Hidden Manna. 385p. 1976. text 18.00 (*0-945747-99-3*) Aeon Bks.

— The Magical Carousel & Commentaries. (Illus.). 153p. 1979. text 27.00 (*0-945747-30-6*) Aeon Bks.

— The New Way: A Study in the Rise & Establishment of a Gnostic Society, Vols. 1 & 2. (Illus.). 601p. (Orig.). 1981. pap. text 36.00 (*0-945747-06-3*) Aeon Bks.

— The Tenth Day of Victory: An Initiation & Beyond. 300p. (Orig.). Date not set. pap. 18.00 (*0-945747-33-0*) Aeon Bks.

— Time & Imperishability: Essays on the Capricorn Hieroglyph. LC 98-905517. 210p. (Orig.). 1997. pap. 12.00 (*0-945747-90-X*) Aeon Bks.

Norelli, Martina R. East Meets West: Chen Chi Watercolors. 88p. 1989. pap. 10.00 (*1-882650-02-6*) Colmbs Mus GA.

Norelli, Martina R. & Weinke, Jane M. Naturally Drawn: Drawings from the Collection. (Illus.). 48p. (Orig.). 1992. pap. 5.00 (*0-945529-06-6*) Le Yawkey.

Norelli, Martina R., jt. auth. see Harris, Neil.

***Norem.** Defensive Pessimism. 2000. 25.00 (*0-465-05138-3*, Pub. by Basic); pap. 14.00 (*0-465-05139-1*, Pub. by Basic) HarpC.

Norem, Julie K., jt. auth. see Clinchy, Blythe.

***Noren, Allen.** Storm: A Motorcycle Journey of Love, Endurance & Transformation. (Footsteps Ser.). (Illus.). 340p. 2000. write for info. (*1-885211-45-7*, Pub. by Trvlers Tale) Publishers Group.

Noren, Anders. Ski Minnesota: A Cross Country Skier's Guide to Trails Within Sixty Miles of the Twin Cities. (Illus.). 160p. 1995. pap. 10.95 (*0-931714-65-6*, Pub. by Nodin Pr) Bookmen Inc.

Noren, Carol M. What Happens Sunday Morning? A Layperson's Guide to Worship. 112p. (Orig.). 1992. pap. 10.95 (*0-664-25227-3*) Westminster John Knox.

— The Woman in the Pulpit. 176p. (Orig.). 1992. pap. 14.95 (*0-687-45893-5*) Abingdon.

Noren, James H., jt. auth. see Firth, Noel E.

Norena, Carlos G. Juan Luis Vives. (International Archives of the History of Ideas Ser.: No. 34). 334p. 1970. lib. bdg. 99.50 (*90-247-5008-3*, Pub. by M Nijhoff) Kluwer Academic.

— Juan Luis Vives & the Emotions. LC 88-36811. (Philosophical Explorations Ser.). 288p. (C). 1989. text 36.95 (*0-8093-1539-4*) S Ill U Pr.

— Studies in Spanish Renaissance Thought. (International Archives of the History of Ideas Ser.: No. 82). 286p. 1975. lib. bdg. 148.50 (*90-247-1727-2*, Pub. by M Nijhoff) Kluwer Academic.

— A Vives Bibliography. LC 89-78313. (Studies in Renaissance Literature: Vol. 5). 88p. 1990. lib. bdg. 49.95 (*0-88946-148-1*) E Mellen.

Norena, Carlos G., tr. see Vives, Juan L.

***Norenberg, David D.** Essay Questions: Toward a Philosophy of Life Based on Clifford's Dictum. LC 00-190663. 108p. 2000. 25.00 (*0-7388-1534-9*); pap. 18.00 (*0-7388-1535-7*) Xlibris Corp.

Noreng, Oystein. The Oil Industry & Government Strategy in the North Sea. LC 80-81590. 1980. 22.00 (*0-918714-02-8*) Intl Res Ctr Energy.

Noreng, Ystein. Oil & Islam: Social & Economic Issues. LC 97-16413. (Petro Research Series in Petroleum Economics & Politics). 352p. 1997. 135.00 (*0-471-97153-7*) Wiley.

Noresta, Anthony, ed. see Burgis, Donald.

Norevik, Bjarne, jt. auth. see Hjulstad, Havard.

Norfleet, Barbara. Looking at Death. (Imago Mundi Ser.). (Illus.) 144p. 1993. 40.00 (*0-87923-964-6*) Godine.

Norfleet, Barbara P. The Illusion of Orderly Progress. LC 98-38187. 1999. pap. write for info. (*0-375-70531-7*) Knopf.

— The Illusion of Orderly Progress. LC 98-38187. (Illus.). 96p. 1999. 20.00 (*0-375-40558-5*) Knopf.

— The Illusion of Orderly Progress. 1999. write for info. (*0-375-70530-9*) Random.

***Norfolk, Bobby & Norfolk, Sherry.** The Moral of the Story: Folktales for Character Development. LC 99-13190. 175p. 1999. pap. 14.95 (*0-87483-555-0*) August Hse.

Norfolk, Bobby & Norfolk, Sherry. The Moral of the Story: Folktales for Character Development. LC 99-13190. 175p. 1999. 24.95 (*0-87483-542-9*) August Hse.

Norfolk, E. C. Norfolk: Taxation Treatment of Interest. 2nd ed. 272p. 1992. boxed set 133.00 (*0-406-00285-1*, MICHIE) LEXIS Pub.

— Norfolk: Taxation Treatment of Interest. 3rd ed. 1997. write for info. (*0-406-89073-0*, NTTI3, MICHIE) LEXIS Pub.

Norfolk, Elizabeth, ed. Miller's International Antiques Price Guide 2000: Professional Handbook. (Miller's International Antiques Price Guide Ser.). (Illus.). 808p. 1998. 35.00 (*1-84000-060-0*, Pub. by Millers Pubns) Antique Collect.

— Miller's International Antiques Price Guide 2000. (Illus.). 808p. 1999. 35.00 (*1-84000-230-1*, Pub. by Millers Pubns) Antique Collect.

Norfolk, Lawrence. The Pope's Rhinoceros. LC 97-23401. 592p. 1997. 15.00 (*0-8050-5475-8*, Owl) H Holt & Co.

Norfolk, Sherry, jt. auth. see Norfolk, Bobby.

Norfolk, Sherry, jt. auth. see Norfolk, Bobby.

Norfolk, William. Caramba's Revenge: A Comedy. LC 98-232333. 76 p. 1998. pap. write for info. (*0-573-01771-9*) French.

Norgaard. Composing Knowledge. 2000. pap. text. write for info. (*0-312-15313-9*) St Martin.

Norgaard, Corine T. Fundamentals of Management Accounting. 2nd ed. (C). 1977. student ed. 6.50 (*0-256-01948-7*, Irwn McGrw-H) McGrw-H Hghr Educ.

— Fundamentals of Management Accounting. 3rd ed. (C). 1981. student ed., per. 9.95 (*0-256-02455-3*, Irwn McGrw-H) McGrw-H Hghr Educ.

Norgaard, Lasse. Uganda - En Ny Chans? 87p. 1989. write for info. (*91-7106-288-2*, Pub. by Nordic Africa) Transaction Pubs.

***Norgaard, Magnus, et al.** Neural Networks for Modelling & Control of Dynamic Systems: A Practitioner's Handbook. LC 99-49801. (Advanced Textbooks in Control & Signal Processing Ser.). (Illus.). xiv, 246p. 2000. pap. 46.00 (*1-85233-227-1*) Spr-Verlag.

***Norgaard, Martin.** Greatest Stars of Bluegrass Music for Fiddle. 72p. 1999. pap. 12.95 (*0-7866-3559-2*, 97050) Mel Bay.

***Norgaard, Ole.** Economic Institutions & Democratic Reform: A Comparative Analysis of Post-Communist Countries. LC 00-35350. (Economies & Societies in Transition Ser.). 272p. 2000. 90.00 (*1-84064-401-X*) E Elgar.

Norgaard, Ole, et al. The Baltic States after Independence. 2nd ed. LC 99-13202. (Studies of Communism in Transition). 256p. 1999. 90.00 (*1-85898-837-3*) E Elgar.

Norgaard, Richard B. Development Betrayed: The End of Progress & a Co-Evolutionary Revisioning of the Future. 336p. (C). 1994. pap. 27.99 (*0-415-06862-2*) Routledge.

Norgaard, Rolf. Ideas in Action: A Guide to Critical Thinking & Writing. 336p. (C). 1997. pap. text 36.93 (*0-673-46404-0*) Addson-Wesley Educ.

Norgan, N. G., ed. Physical Activity & Health. (Society for the Study of Human Biology Symposium Ser.: No. 34). (Illus.). 263p. (C). 1993. text 74.95 (*0-521-41551-9*) Cambridge U Pr.

Norgard-Sorensen, Jens. Coherence Theory: The Case of Russian. LC 92-10456. (Trends in Linguistics, Studies & Monographs: Vol. 63). x, 222p. (C). 1992. lib. bdg. 83.10 (*3-11-012911-6*) Mouton.

Norgate, Edward, et al. Miniatura: or The Art of Limning. LC 96-43520. 304p. 1997. 65.00 (*0-300-06913-8*) Yale U Pr.

Norgate, Kate. England under the Angevin Kings, 2 vols. Set. LC 68-25255. (British History Ser.: No. 30). 1969. reprint ed. lib. bdg. 150.00 (*0-8383-0184-3*) M S G Haskell Hse.

— John Lackland. LC 71-110740. reprint ed. 45.00 (*0-404-00614-0*) AMS Pr.

Norgate, LeGrys G. The Life of Sir Walter Scott. LC 74-30271. (Sir Walter Scott Ser.: No. 73). 1974. lib. bdg. 75.00 (*0-8383-1927-0*) M S G Haskell Hse.

Norgate, Sheila. Storm Clouds over Party Shoes: Etiquette Problems for Girls. (Illus.). 96p. 1997. pap. 16.95 (*0-88974-080-1*, Pub. by Press Gang Pubs) LPC InBook.

Norgauer, J., jt. ed. see Kownatzki, E.

Norgauer, Johannes, jt. auth. see Kownatzki, Eckhard.

***Norgerg, Tilda & Webber, Robert.** Stretch Our Your Hand: Leader's Guide. 48p. 1999. pap., teacher ed. 4.95 (*0-8358-0871-8*, UR871) Upper Room Bks.

Norget, Judy, ed. see Bialostok, Steve.

Norget, Judy, ed. see Keil, Wayne & Blais, Gil.

Norget, Judy, ed. see Sheanh, Gerry.

Norgren, Barbara J., jt. auth. see Noel, Thomas S.

Norgren, Jill. The Cherokee Cases: The Confrontation of Law & Politics. LC 95-13761. 212p. (C). 1995. pap. 18.13 (*0-07-047191-6*) McGraw.

Norgren, Jill & Davis, Edward, compiled by. Preliminary Index of Shah-Nameh Illustrations. 1969. pap. text 5.00 (*0-932098-02-9*) UM Ctr MENAS.

Norgren, Jill & Nanda, Serena. American Cultural Pluralism & the Law. 2nd ed. LC 95-37643. 320p. 1996. 69.50 (*0-275-94855-2*, Praeger Pubs); pap. 23.95 (*0-275-94858-7*, Praeger Pubs) Greenwood.

Norgren, Jill, jt. auth. see Shattuck, Petra T.

Norgren, William A., ed. Ecumenism of the Possible: Witness, Theology & the Future Church. 340p. (Orig.). 1994. pap. 10.00 (*0-88028-156-1*, 1280) Forward Movement.

Norgren, William A. & Rusch, William G. Toward Full Communion & Concordat of Agreement: Lutheran-Episcopal Dialogue III. LC 91-12472. 120p. (Orig.). 1992. pap. 5.99 (*0-8066-2578-3*, 9-2578, Augsburg) Augsburg Fortress.

Norgren, William A. & Rusch, William G., eds. Toward Full Communion & Concordat of Agreement. (Lutheran-Episcopal Dialogue Ser.: No. III). 120p. (Orig.). 1991. pap. 4.95 (*0-88028-119-7*, 1119) Forward Movement.

Norguet, F., ed. Fonctions de Plusieurs Variables Complexes. (Lecture Notes in Mathematics Ser.: Vol. 1188). vii, 301p. 1986. 53.95 (*0-387-16460-X*) Spr-Verlag.

Norheim & McGill. Communicating Interpersonally for Love, Money, & Meaning. 2nd ed. 370p. (C). 1997. per. 41.95 (*0-7872-3951-8*, 41395101) Kendall-Hunt.

Norheim, Carol & McGill, L. Jerome. Communicating Interpersonally. 328p. (C). 1996. pap. text, per. 33.95 (*0-7872-0354-8*) Kendall-Hunt.

Nori, Don. The Angel & the Judgment. LC 96-203751. 190p. 1996. pap. 11.99 (*1-56043-154-7*) Destiny Image.

— His Manifest Presence: Moving from David's Tabernacle to Solomon's Temple. 182p. (Orig.). 1988. pap. 10.99 (*0-914903-48-9*) Destiny Image.

— His Manifest Presence: Moving from David's Tabernacle to Solomon's Temple. (SPA.). 168p. (Orig.). 1992. pap. 10.99 (*1-56043-079-6*) Destiny Image.

— No More Sour Grapes. 1999. pap. 12.99 (*0-7684-2037-7*) Destiny Image.

— The Power of Brokenness. LC 97-170080. 168p. 1997. pap. 10.99 (*1-56043-178-4*) Destiny Image.

— Secrets of the Most Holy Place. 182p. (Orig.). 1992. pap. 10.99 (*1-56043-076-1*) Destiny Image.

Nori, Donald F. How to Find God's Love. 108p. (Orig.). 1987. pap. 6.99 (*0-914903-28-4*) Destiny Image.

— How to Find God's Love. (SPA.). 144p. (Orig.). 1990. pap. 6.99 (*1-56043-024-9*) Destiny Image.

Nori, K. V., ed. Foundations of Software Technology & Theoretical Computer Science. (Lecture Notes in Computer Science Ser.: Vol. 287). ix, 540p. 1987. 53.00 (*0-387-18625-5*) Spr-Verlag.

Nori, K. V. & Kumar, S., eds. Foundations of Software Technology & Theoretical Computer Science. (Lecture Notes in Computer Science Ser.: Vol. 338). ix, 520p. 1988. 53.00 (*0-387-50517-2*) Spr-Verlag.

Nori, K. V. & Madhavan, C. E., eds. Foundations of Software Technology & Theoretical Computer Science: Proceedings of the Tenth Conference Bangalore, India, December 17-19, 1990. (Lecture Notes in Computer Science Ser.: Vol. 472). x, 420p. 1990. 42.00 (*0-387-53487-3*) Spr-Verlag.

Norian, Nicole A. & Michaud, Paul J. A Continuous Quality Improvement Approach to Discipline. 1995. 20.00 (*1-878240-42-0*) Coll & U Personnel.

Norian, Todd, jt. ed. see Levitt, JoAnn.

Norich, Anita. The Homeless Imagination in the Fiction of Israel Joshua Singer. LC 90-27480. (Jewish Literature & Culture Ser.). (Illus.). 164p. 1992. 32.00 (*0-253-34109-4*) Ind U Pr.

Norick, Sylvester. Outdoor Life in the Menominee Forest. 154p. 1979. 3.95 (*0-8199-0767-7*, Frncscn Herld) Franciscan Pr.

Noricks, Michael L. Dime, Constanza. 142p. 1984. pap. 6.50 (*0-88334-180-8*) Longman.

Norie, E. W. The Official Account of Military Operations in China 1900-1901. (Victorian War Ser.: No. 3). (Illus.). 510p. 1995. reprint ed. 59.95 (*0-89839-215-2*) Battery Pr.

Norie, Imray L. & Wilson Ltd. Staff. Charlie's Charts of Costa Rica. 100p. 1991. pap. 150.00 (*0-9691412-8-9*, Pub. by Laurie Norie & Wilson Ltd) St Mut.

Norie, Imray L. & Wilson, Ltd., Staff. The Upper Reaches of the River Medway. (C). 1980. 25.00 (*0-85288-113-4*, Pub. by Laurie Norie & Wilson Ltd) St Mut.

Norie, Imray L. & Wilson Ltd. Staff, eds. South & West Coasts of Ireland Sailing Directions: Irish Cruising Club. 340p. 1999. 150.00 (*0-9501717-7-8*, Pub. by Irish Cruising Club Pubns Ltd) St Mut.

Norie, Imray L., jt. auth. see Wilson Limited Staff.

Norie, Imray L., jt. auth. see Wilson Ltd. Staff.

Norie, Imray L., jt. ed. see Wilson Ltd. Staff.

Noriega, Bienvenido M., Jr. Soltero. Tinio, Roland S., tr. (ENG & TAG., Illus.). 159p. (Orig.). 1985. pap. 15.00 (*971-10-0252-3*, Pub. by New Day Pub) Cellar.

Noriega, Carlos. Espejo de lluvia. (Aqui y Ahora Ser.). 57p. 1996. pap. 6.95 (*0-8477-0262-6*) U of PR Pr.

***Noriega, Chon.** Shot in America: Television, the State, & the Rise of Chicano Cinema. LC 99-88112. 2000. pap. 19.95 (*0-8166-2931-5*) U of Minn Pr.

Noriega, Chon, jt. auth. see Power, Kevin.

Noriega, Chon A. From the West: Chicano Narrative Photography. 21p. (Orig.). 1995. teacher ed. write for info. (*0-614-24038-7*) Mexican Museum.

***Noriega, Chon A.** Shot in America: Television, the State & the Rise of Chicano Cinema. LC 99-88112. (Illus.). 2000. 49.95 (*0-8166-2930-7*) U of Minn Pr.

— Visible Nations: Latin American Cinema & Video. (Illus.). 2000. 49.95 (*0-8166-3347-9*); pap. 19.95 (*0-8166-3348-7*) U of Minn Pr.

***Noriega, Chon A., ed.** The Chicano Studies Reader: An Anthology of Aztlan 1970-2000. (Aztlan Anthology Ser.: Vol. 2). 300p. 2000. pap. 19.95 (*0-89551-097-9*) UCLA Chicano Studies.

Noriega, Chon A., ed. Chicanos & Film: Representation & Resistance. (Illus.). 416p. (C). 1992. pap. 19.95 (*0-8166-2218-3*) U of Minn Pr.

***Noriega, Chon A., ed.** The Future of Latino Independent Media: A NALIP Sourcebook. 150p. 2000. pap. 16.95 (*0-89551-096-0*) UCLA Chicano Studies.

Noriega, Chon A. & Gonzalez, Jennifer. From the West: Chicano Narrative Photography. LC 96-166023. (Illus.). 87p. (Orig.). 1995. 19.95 (*1-880508-04-4*) Mexican Museum.

Noriega, Chon A. & Lopez, Ana M., eds. The Ethnic Eye: Latino Media Arts. LC 95-44107. 289p. 1996. pap. 19.95 (*0-8166-2675-8*); text 47.95 (*0-8166-2674-X*) U of Minn Pr.

Noriega, Chon A., ed. see Gamboa, Harry, Jr.

Noriega-Crespo, Alberto, jt. ed. see Wallerstein, George.

Noriega, Dienvenido, Jr. Bongbong at Kris Batang Pro. (Illus.). 340p. (Orig.). 1987. pap. 17.50 (*971-10-0264-7*, Pub. by New Day Pub) Cellar.

Noriega, Ed, jt. auth. see Holtzschue, Linda.

Noriega, Edward, jt. auth. see Holtzschue, Linda.

Noriega, Irma S., jt. auth. see Kimble, Socorro M.

Noriega-Muro, Antonio E. Nonstationarity & Structural Breaks in Economic Time Series: Asymptotic Theory & Monte Carlo Simulations. 268p. 1993. 72.95 (*1-85628-580-4*, Pub. by Avebry) Ashgate Pub Co.

Noriega, P., et al, eds. Agent Mediated Electric Commerce: First International Workshop on Agent-Mediated Electronic Trading, AMET-98, Minneapolis, MN, USA, May 10th, 1998, Selected Papers. LC 99-30630. (Lecture Notes in Artificial Intelligence Ser.: Vol. 1571). ix, 207p. 1999. pap. 45.00 (*3-540-65955-2*) Spr-Verlag.

Noriega, Pender B., jt. auth. see Defranco, Agnes L.

Noriega, Violeta A. Philippine Food Adventures for Children. (Illus.). (Orig.). (J). (gr. 1-9). 1996. pap. 15.95 (*0-9636557-3-6*) Paperworks.

— Philippine Recipes Made Easy, Vol. 1. LC 93-84175. (Illus.). (Orig.). 1993. pap. text 12.95 (*0-9636557-0-1*) Paperworks.

Norihiko Kikumura. Shinran: His Life & Thought. LC 70-172538. 192p. (C). 1972. 12.95 (*0-685-65548-2*) Nembutsu Pr.

Norimatsu, Patricia. Funny Facelift: Facial Exercises for a Fast Facelift. rev. ed. LC 81-83602. Orig. Title: Facemetrics. (Illus.). 46p. 1983. 19.50 (*0-9606890-4-4*) Morris Pub.

Norin, N. V. The Extended Stochastic Integral in Linear Spaces with Differentiable Measures. LC 96-16453. 250p. 1996. write for info. (*981-02-2568-7*) World Scientific Pub.

Norinaga, Motoori. Kojiki-Den, Bk. 1. Wehmeyer, Ann, tr. (Cornell East Asia Ser.: Vol. 87). 270p. (C). 1997. 23.80 (*1-885445-57-1*, CEAS 87); pap. 14.45 (*1-885445-87-3*, CEAS 87) Cornell East Asia Pgm.

Norindr, Panivong. Phantasmatic Indochina: French Colonial Ideology in Architecture, Film, & Literature. LC 95-50856. (Asia-Pacific Ser.). 240p. 1996. pap. text 16.95 (*0-8223-1787-7*); lib. bdg. 44.95 (*0-8223-1778-8*) Duke.

Noring, Nina J., jt. auth. see Glennon, John P.

Norins, A. L., ed. Diapering & Infant Skin Care: Journal, Pediatrician, Supplement 1, 1987, Vol. 14. (Illus.). iv, 52p. 1987. pap. 19.25 (*3-8055-4615-7*) S Karger.

Norins, Leslie C. & Norins, Rainey. The Doctor's 30-Day Cholesterol Blitz. LC 96-213590. 350p. 1996. 12.95 (*1-888266-00-7*) Adv Hlth Inst.

Norins, Rainey, jt. auth. see Norins, Leslie C.

Noris, Michael, tr. see Siro.

***Noriss, Andrew.** Aquila. 1999. pap. 29.95 (*0-7540-6213-9*) Chivers N Amer.

Norita, Masao, et al. Extrageniculostriate Mechanisms Underlying Visually-Guided Orientation Behavior. LC 96-41410. (Progress in Brain Research Ser.). 462p. 1996. 237.50 (*0-444-82347-6*) Elsevier.

Norkin, Cynthia C. & Levangie, Pamela K. Joint Structure & Function: A Comprehensive Analysis. 2nd ed. LC 91-42518. (Illus.). 512p. 1992. 43.55 (*0-8036-6577-6*) Davis Co.

Norkin, Cynthia C. & White, Joyce. Measurement of Joint Motion: A Guide to Goniometry. 2nd ed. (Illus.). 241p. 1994. text 24.95 (*0-8036-6579-2*) Davis Co.

Norkin, Cynthia C., et al. Measurement of Joint Motion. 2nd ed. (CHI., Illus.). 272p. 1996. write for info. (*962-356-018-4*) Lppncott W & W.

Norkin, Cynthia C., jt. auth. see Levangie, Pamela K.

Norkin, S. B. Differential Equations of the Second Order with Retarded Argument: Some Problems of the Theory of Vibrations of Systems with Retardation. Grimm, L. & Schmitt, K., trs. LC 70-37627. (Translations of Mathematical Monographs: Vol. 31). 285p. 1972. text 55.00 (*0-8218-1581-4*, MMONO/31) Am Math.

Norkin, Sam. Sam Norkin: Drawings - Stories. LC 94-29122. 350p. 1994. pap. 29.95 (*0-435-08642-1*, 08642) Heinemann.

Norko, Damon. The Glue Factory. 64p. (Orig.). pap. 6.00 (*0-916156-88-5*) Cherry Valley.

Norkunas, Martha K. The Politics of Public Memory: Tourism, History, & Ethnicity in Monterey, California. LC 92-42168. (SUNY Series in Oral & Public History). 123p. (C). 1993. text 57.50 (*0-7914-1483-3*); pap. text 19.95 (*0-7914-1484-1*) State U NY Pr.

Norkunas, Martha K., jt. ed. see Blatt, Martin H.

Norland, Emmalou, jt. auth. see Heimlich, Joe E.

Norland, Howard B. Drama in Early Tudor Britain, 1485-1558. LC 94-12253. xxix, 394p. 1995. text 53.00 (*0-8032-3337-X*) U of Nebr Pr.

Norland, Howard B., ed. see Swinburne, Algernon Charles.

Norlander-Case, Kay A., jt. auth. see Case, Charles W.

Norlen, Art. Death of a Proud Union: The 1960 Bunker Hill Strike. (Illus.). xv, 146p. 1992. 15.00 (*0-9656215-0-2*); pap. 12.00 (*0-9656215-1-0*) Tamarack Pub.

Norlen, Paul, tr. see Lagercrantz, Rose & Lagercrantz, Samuel.

Norlen, Sherron. Entomologist's Dreambook. (Illus.). 48p. 1998. 95.00 (*0-9665810-0-8*); pap. 10.00 (*0-9665810-1-6*) Protean Pr CA.

Norlie, Olaf M. History of the Norwegian People in America. LC 72-1251. (American History & Americana Ser.: No. 47). 1972. reprint ed. lib. bdg. 75.00 (*0-8383-1436-8*) M S G Haskell Hse.

***Norlie, Olaf Morgan.** History of the Norwegian People in America. (Illus.). 602p. 1999. reprint ed. pap. 41.00 (*0-7884-1278-7*, N564) Heritage Bk.

Norlin, Bill. The Business of Woodwork. 326p. 1992. text 75.00 (*0-9635117-7-7*) Woodwork Pr.

Norlin, Dennis A., et al. A Directory of Adaptive Technologies to Aid Library Patrons & Staff with Disabilities. LC 94-36089. (LITA Monographs Ser.: No. 5). 1994. 14.00 (*0-8389-7754-5*) ALA.

Norlin, George. Fascism & Citizenship. LC 70-180419. (Weil Lectures on American Citizenship). reprint ed. 21.50 (*0-404-56194-2*) AMS Pr.

— Integrity in Education, & Other Papers. LC 74-177964. (Essay Index Reprint Ser.). 1977. reprint ed. 20.95 (*0-8369-2568-8*) Ayer.

— Things in the Saddle. LC 74-80393. (Essay Index Reprint Ser.). 1977. 20.95 (*0-8369-1047-8*) Ayer.

Norlin, George, tr. Orations, 3 vols., 1. (Loeb Classical Library: No. 209, 229, 373). 466p. 1928. 18.95 (*0-674-99231-8*) HUP.

Norlin, John W., ed. see Silverman, Thomas N.

Norlin, Julia M., et al. Human Behavior & the Social Environment: Social Systems Theory. 3rd ed. LC 96-10706. 448p. 1996. 82.00 (*0-205-15929-X*) Allyn.

Norling, Bernard. The Intrepid Guerillas of North Luzon. LC 99-17356. (Illus.). 304p. 1999. 25.00 (*0-8131-2118-3*) U Pr of Ky.

— Towards a Better Understanding of History. LC 60-15676. 157p. 1960. pap. 9.50 (*0-268-00284-3*) U of Notre Dame Pr.

N

An Asterisk (*) at the beginning of an entry indicates that the title is appearing for the first time.

Norling, Bernard & Poinsatte, Charles. Understanding History Through the American Experience. LC 76-637. 208p. 1976. pap. 9.50 (0-268-01911-8) U of Notre Dame Pr.

Norling, Bernard, jt. auth. see Hunt, Ray C.

Norling, Bernard, jt. auth. see Lapham, Robert.

Norling, Bernard, jt. auth. see Rinderle, Walter.

Norling, Donna S. Patty's Journey: From Orphanage to Adoption & Reunion. 208p. 1996. 17.95 (0-8166-2866-1) U of Minn Pr.

— Patty's Journey: From Orphanage to Adoption & Reunion. 1998. pap. text 14.95 (0-8166-2867-X) U of Minn Pr.

Norling, Ernest. Perspective. (How to Draw & Paint Ser.). (Illus.). 32p. (Orig.). 1989. pap. 6.95 (1-56010-013-3, HT029) W Foster Pub.

— Perspective Made Easy. LC 99-10310. (Illus.). 224p. 1999. pap. text 7.95 (0-486-40473-0) Dover.

***Norling, Lisa.** Captain Ahab Had a Wife: New England Women & the Whalefishery, 1720-1870. LC 99-88026. (Gender & American Culture Ser.). 352p. 2000. write for info. (0-8078-2561-1) U of NC Pr.

— Captain Ahab Had a Wife: New England Women & the Whalefishery, 1720-1870. LC 99-88026. (Gender & American Culture Ser.). 352p. 2000. pap. 19.95 (0-8078-4870-0) U of NC Pr.

Norling, Lisa, jt. ed. see Creighton, Margaret.

Norling, Thomas B. Auxiliary Tip Party Marking Devices. (ABC Pocket Guide for the Field Ser.). (Illus.). 56p. (Orig.). (C). 1985. pap. 7.95 (1-56016-036-5) ABC TeleTraining.

— Precise Tone Plan for End Offices. (ABC Pocket Guide for the Field Ser.). (Illus.). 40p. 1996. pap. 7.95 (1-56016-033-0) ABC TeleTraining.

— Principles of Party Line Station Identification. (ABC Pocket Guide for the Field Ser.). (Illus.). 36p. 1982. pap. 7.95 (1-56016-034-9) ABC TeleTraining.

Norlund, Irene, et al, eds. Vietnam in a Changing World. LC 96-157035. (SIAS Studies in Asian Topics: No. 17). 320p. (C). 1996. text 49.00 (0-7007-0300-4, Pub. by Curzon Pr Ltd); pap. text 24.95 (0-7007-0291-1, Pub. by Curzon Pr Ltd) UH Pr.

Norma, et al. Advanced Design & Technology. 2nd ed. 1995. text. write for info. (0-582-24406-4, Pub. by Addison-Wesley) Longman.

Normal, Henry. Nude Modelling for the Afterlife. 64p. 1994. pap. 12.95 (1-85224-279-5, Pub. by Bloodaxe Bks) Dufour.

***Norman.** The Crane Who Had to Be Flattered. 2003. write for info. (0-15-201982-0) Harcourt.

Norman. Introduction to Linear Algebra. (C). 1995. text. write for info. (0-201-60210-5) Addison-Wesley.

— Laboratory Manual for Introduction to Psychology, Custom Pub. (C). 1993. pap. text 7.25 (0-07-047216-5) McGraw.

— Mental Health Care of Elderly People. LC 96-25834. 1996. pap. text 54.00 (0-443-05173-9) Church.

— Norman Linear Alg Prelim Ed. 1994. pap. text. write for info. (0-201-44316-3) Addison-Wesley.

— Process Modelling & Computer Aided Design in Chemical Engineering. 93.00 (0-471-93870-X); pap. 37.00 (0-471-96761-0) Wiley.

— To Heal the Earth Leader's Guide. 1994. pap., teacher ed. 2.00 (0-8358-0719-3) Upper Room Bks.

— We Mean Business. 1993. pap. text, student ed. write for info. (0-582-09905-6, Pub. by Addison-Wesley) Longman.

— We Mean Business. rev. ed. 1993. pap. text, wbk. ed. write for info. (0-582-22582-5, Pub. by Addison-Wesley) Longman.

— We're in Business. Date not set. pap. text, student ed. write for info. (0-582-74872-0, Pub. by Addison-Wesley); pap. text, wbk. ed. write for info. (0-582-74871-2, Pub. by Addison-Wesley) Longman.

Norman, ed. Themistii, Vol. II. (GRE.). 1971. 47.50 (3-322-00202-0, T1850, Pub. by B G Teubner) U of Mich Pr.

— Themistii, Vol. III. (GRE.). 1974. 32.50 (3-322-00884-3, T1844, Pub. by B G Teubner) U of Mich Pr.

Norman & Sherwood. Logic & Proof. 206p. (C). 1991. pap. text 45.00 (0-536-58089-8) Pearson Custom.

Norman & Steiner, David L. PDQ Statistics. 1986. 13.95 (0-8016-3840-2) Mosby Inc.

Norman, jt. auth. see Gerson.

Norman, jt. auth. see Gilbert.

Norman, A. F., ed. Libanius: Autobiography & Selected Letters, 2 vols., Vol. I. (Loeb Classical Library: Nos. 478 & 479). 478p. 1993. 19.95 (0-674-99527-9) HUP.

— Libanius: Autobiography & Selected Letters, 2 vols., Vol. 2. (Loeb Classical Library: Nos. 478 & 479). 479p. 1993. 19.95 (0-674-99528-7) HUP.

Norman, A. G., ed. Advances in Agronomy, Vols. 1-24. Incl. Vol. 13. 1961. 75.00 (0-12-000713-4); write for info. (0-318-50155-4) Acad Pr.

Norman, A. Jesse, ed. see Farrell, Martha P. & Farrell, James D.

Norman, A. V. The Rapier & Small-Sword, 1460-1820. (Illus.). 464p. 1980. 46.95 (0-405-13089-9) Ayer.

— The Wallace Collection Catalogue of Ceramics I: Pottery, Maiolica, Faience, Stoneware. (Illus.). 450p. 1976. pap. 19.95 (0-900785-06-3, Pub. by Wallace Collect) Antique Collect.

Norman, A. Vesey. The Medieval Soldier. LC 72-175833. (Medieval Life Ser.). x, 278p. 1971. write for info. (0-213-76447-4) Art Barker.

Norman, A. Vesey & Wilson, G. M. Treasures from the Tower of London: Arms & Armour. LC 83-163369. 131p. 1982. write for info. (0-85368-541-X) Arms & Armour.

Norman, A. W., et al, eds. Vitamin D: Chemical, Biochemical & Clinical Endocrinology of Calcium Metabolism. (Illus.). 1288p. 1982. text 257.70 (3-11-008864-9) De Gruyter.

— Vitamin D: Gene Regulation, Structure-Function Analysis & Clinical Application Proceedings of the 8th Workshop on Vitamin D, Paris, France, July 5-10, 1991. (Illus.). xxxviii, 995p. (C). 1991. lib. bdg. 300.00 (3-11-012638-9, 261-91) De Gruyter.

— Vitamin D - Chemical, Biochemical & Clinical Update: Proceedings of the 6th Workshop on Vitamin D, Italy, March 1985. (Illus.). xxxxiii, 1249p. 1985. 307.70 (0-89925-066-1); 307.70 (3-11-010181-5) De Gruyter.

— Vitamin D - Molecular, Cellular, & Clinical Endocrinology: Proceedings of the Seventh Workshop on Vitamin D, Rancho Mirage, CA, U. S. A., April 1988. xl, 1072p. (C). 1988. lib. bdg. 300.00 (3-11-011477-1) De Gruyter.

Norman, Adrian R., jt. auth. see Martin, James.

***Norman, Al.** Slam-Dunking Wal-Mart! How You Can Stop Superstore Sprawl in Your Hometown. 1999. 29.95 (0-9624808-6-X) Raphel Mktg.

Norman, Albert. The Brittle Middle East: A Political & Internationally Legal Evaluation of Iran & the United States of America, 1979-1980. 190p. 1981. 8.80 (0-318-00824-6) A Norman.

— The Falkland Islands Vol. 4: The 1700's: the Imperial Century. 1993. write for info. (0-614-28542-9) A Norman.

— The Falkland Islands, Their Kinship Isles, the Antarctic Hemisphere & the Freedom of the 2 Great Oceans Vol. 3: Discovery & Diplomacy, Law & War: The 19th Century, to the End of the 20th Century's First World War, 1918 & Vital Principles-Interests of the United States of America & the United Kingdom in the Falklands-Antarctic Regions. 496p. 1989. 31.00 (0-317-03765-X) A Norman.

— The Falkland Islands, Their Kinship Isles, the Antarctic Hemisphere, & the Freedom of the 2 Great Oceans, Vol. 2: Discovery & Diplomacy, Law & War. 672p. 1988. 33.00 (0-317-01605-9) A Norman.

— Operation Overlord, Design & Reality: The Allied Invasion of Western Europe. LC 73-100252. 230p. 1970. reprint ed. lib. bdg. 35.00 (0-8371-2985-0, NOOO, Greenwood Pr) Greenwood.

Norman, Alexander, jt. auth. see Dalai Lama XIV.

Norman, Alfred L. Informational Society: An Economic Theory of Discovery, Invention, & Innovation. LC 92-34667. 1992. lib. bdg. 115.50 (0-7923-9303-1) Kluwer Academic.

Norman, Amy W., ed. see Mitchell, William R., Jr.

Norman, Andrew. Heavy Duty Truck Systems. 2nd ed. (Automotive Technology Ser.). 1995. text 34.00 (0-8273-7844-0) Delmar.

Norman, Andrew & Scharff, Robert. Heavy Duty Truck Systems. 2nd ed. (Automotive Technology Ser.). 912p. 1995. mass mkt. 102.95 (0-8273-6391-5) Delmar.

Norman, Andrew, et al. Diesel Technology: Fundamentals, Service & Repair. LC 94-1439. (Illus.). 350p. 1997. text 45.00 (1-56637-014-0) Goodheart.

***Norman, Andrew, et al.** Diesel Technology: Fundamentals, Service, Repair. LC 00-28759. (Illus.). 2000. write for info. (1-56637-733-1) Goodheart.

Norman, Andrew, jt. auth. see Korejwo.

Norman, Ann E. Rapid ECG Interpretation: A Self-Teaching Manual. 1991. text 24.00 (0-07-105302-6) McGraw-Hill HPD.

— Twelve Lead ECG Interpretation: A Self-Teaching Manual. (Illus.). 300p. 1992. text 24.00 (0-07-105396-4) McGraw-Hill HPD.

Norman, Anne, jt. auth. see Harrington, Cheryl C.

Norman, Anne, jt. auth. see Harrington, Chevy C.

Norman, Anthony W. Vitamin D - A Pluripotent Steroid Hormone: Structional Studies, Molecular Endocrinology & Clinical Applications: Proceedings of the Ninth Workshop on Vitamin D, Orlando, Florida (U. S. A.), May 28-June 2, 1994. LC 94-35262. 1007p. (C). 1994. lib. bdg. 361.55 (3-11-014157-4) De Gruyter.

Norman, Anthony W., ed. Vitamin D: Molecular Biology & Clinical Nutrition. LC 80-14327. (Basic & Clinical Nutrition Ser.: No. 2). 818p. reprint ed. pap. 200.00 (0-7837-3342-9, 204330000008) Bks Demand.

Norman, Anthony W., et al, eds. Vitamin D Chemical, Biology & Clinical Applications. (Vitamin D Ser.). (Illus.). 1020p. (C). 1997. write for info. (1-891168-00-2) U CA Riverside.

***Norman, Anthony W. & Bishop, June, eds.** Vitamin D Endocrine System: Structural, Biological, Genetic & Clinical Aspects. (Vitamin D Ser.). (Illus.). 1050p. (C). 2000. write for info. (1-891168-04-5) U CA Riverside.

Norman, Anthony W. & Litwack, Gerald. The Hormones. 2nd ed. LC 97-80235. (Illus.). 558p. 1997. text 79.95 (0-12-521441-3) Acad Pr.

Norman, Barbara. Engraving & Decorating Glass: Methods & Techniques. (Illus.). 192p. 1987. reprint ed. pap. 8.95 (0-486-25304-X) Dover.

Norman, Barry. The Butterfly Tattoo. LC 96-12753. 445p. 1996. write for info. (0-7451-5384-4) Thorndike Pr.

— The Movie Greats LC 81-148525. 319 P. :p. 1981. write for info. (0-340-25972-8, Pub. by Hodder & Stought Ltd) Trafalgar.

Norman, Barry. The One Hundred Best Films of the Century. LC 93-2520. (Illus.). 280p. 1993. pap. 16.95 (0-8065-1426-4, Citadel Pr) Carol Pub Group.

***Norman, Barry.** 100 Best Films of the Century. (Illus.). 276p. 1999. 29.95 (0-7528-1777-9, Pub. by Orion Media) Trafalgar.

Norman, Bethany. Windows 3.1 for Beginners. (Quicksteps to Learning Ser.). (Illus.). 198p. 1992. spiral bd. 22.95 (1-56951-000-8) Sftware Trng.

Norman, Bill. Failed to Return: The Yorkshire Memorial to the Bomber Squadrons of #4 Group RAF & #6 (RCAF), 1939-1945. (Illus.). 207p. 1995. 29.95 (0-85052-474-1, Pub. by Leo Cooper) Trans-Atl Phila.

Norman, Bill, ed. see Mast, Coleen K.

Norman, Bob, ed. see Norman, Victor.

Norman, C. A., et al, eds. Stellar Populations. (Space Telescope Science Institute Symposium Ser.: No. 1). 256p. 1987. text 69.95 (0-521-33380-6) Cambridge U Pr.

Norman, C. W. Undergraduate Algebra: A First Course. 400p. 1986. 49.95 (0-19-853249-0) OUP.

Norman, Cecil O. Conversations with Elvis. LC 98-89513. 375p. 1998. text 25.00 (0-7388-0219-0); pap. text 15.00 (0-7388-0220-4) Xlibris Corp.

Norman, Cecilia. The Book of Grilling & Barbecuing. (Book of...Ser.). (Illus.). 120p. (Orig.). 1989. pap. 12.00 (0-89586-790-7, HP Books) Berkley Pub.

— Veg & 2 Veg. (Illus.). 160p. (Orig.). 1992. pap. 11.95 (0-563-36358-4, BBC-Parkwest) Parkwest Pubns.

Norman, Cecilia, jt. auth. see Timperley, Carol.

Norman, Charles. Christopher Marlowe: The Muse's Darling. LC 70-142471. 1971. 7.50 (0-672-51406-0, Bobbs) Macmillan.

— Portents of the Air. LC 77-187009. 64p. 1973. 5.95 (0-672-51407-9, Bobbs) Macmillan.

Norman, Charles J., ed. see Paine, Thomas.

Norman, Chris, ed. see Coale, Phil.

Norman, Colin. The God That Limps: Science & Technology in the Eighties. 1982. pap. 8.95 (0-393-30026-9) Norton.

Norman, Colin. Knowledge & Power: The Global Research & Development Budget. LC 79-65904. (Worldwatch Papers). 1979. pap. 4.00 (0-916468-30-5) Worldwatch Inst.

— Microelectronics at Work: Productivity & Jobs in the World Economy. 1980. pap. write for info. (0-916468-38-0) Worldwatch Inst.

— Soft Technologies, Hard Choices. 1978. pap. write for info. (0-916468-20-8) Worldwatch Inst.

Norman, Colleen. A Family to Cherish. 1994. per. 3.50 (0-373-09894-4, 5-09894-2) Harlequin Bks.

Norman, Corrie. Humanist Taste & Franciscan Values: Cornelio Musso & Catholic Preaching in Sixteenth-Century Italy. LC 97-26042. (Renaissance & Baroque: Vol. 24). 188p. (C). 1998. text 43.95 (0-8204-3871-5) P Lang Pubng.

***Norman, David.** Dinosaur! (Eyewitness Books). (Illus.). (J). (gr. 4-8). 2000. 19.99 (0-7894-6562-0) DK Pub Inc.

— Dinosaur! (Eyewitness Books). (J). (gr. 4-7). 2000. 15.95 (0-7894-5808-X) DK Pub Inc.

Norman, David. Dinosaur! LC 95-19199. (Illus.). 288p. 1995. 8.95 (0-02-860434-2) Macmillan.

— Dinosaurios. (SPA.). 1995. 18.95 (84-372-3720-3) Santillana.

— Dinosaurs. (Spotter's Guides Ser.). (Illus.). 64p. (YA). (gr. 8-12). 1985. lib. bdg. 12.95 (0-88110-988-6, Usborne) EDC.

— The Frontier Rakers. (Orig.). 1981. mass mkt. 2.75 (0-89083-859-3, Zebra Kensgtn) Kensgtn Pub Corp.

— Frontier Rakers, No. 5. (Montana Pass Ser.). (Orig.). 1982. mass mkt. 2.95 (0-89083-954-9, Zebra Kensgtn) Kensgtn Pub Corp.

— Frontier Rakers No. 3: Gold Fever. 1981. mass mkt. 2.95 (0-89083-903-4, Zebra Kensgtn) Kensgtn Pub Corp.

— Networks for Small Businesses. (Popular Applications Ser.). 160p. (Orig.). 1995. pap. 15.95 incl. disk (1-55622-455-9) Wordware Pub.

— Prehistoric Life: The Rise of the Vertebrates. (Illus.). 248p. (J). 1994. 30.00 (0-671-79940-1) P-H.

— Silver City. (Frontier Rakers Ser.: No. 4). (Orig.). 1982. mass mkt. 2.95 (0-89083-921-2, Zebra Kensgtn) Kensgtn Pub Corp.

— When Dinosaurs Ruled the Earth. (J). 1985. 6.98 (0-671-07522-5) S&S Trade.

Norman, David, ed. Dinosaurs Sticker Book. (Spotter's Guides Sticker Bks.). (Illus.). 32p. (J). (gr. 2 up). 1999. pap. 7.95 (0-7460-3350-8, Usborne) EDC.

— The Humongous Book of Dinosaurs, Incl. 3-D Glasses. LC 97-398. (Illus.). 1256p. (J). (gr. 4-7). 1997. pap. 34.95 (1-55670-596-4) Stewart Tabori & Chang.

Norman, David & Douglas, Malcolm. Farming Systems Development & Soil Conservation. (Farm Systems Management Ser.: No. 7). 180p. 1994. pap. 16.00 (92-5-103448-6, F34486, Pub. by FAO) Bernan Associates.

Norman, David & Miller, Angela. Dinosaur! LC 88-27167. (Eyewitness Books). (Illus.). 64p. (YA). (gr. 5 up). 1989. 19.00 (0-394-82253-6, Pub. by Knopf Bks Yng Read) Random.

— Dinosaur! LC 88-27167. (Eyewitness Books). (Illus.). 64p. (YA). (gr. 5 up). 1989. lib. bdg. 20.99 (0-394-92253-0, Pub. by Knopf Bks Yng Read) Random.

Norman, David, jt. ed. see Brant-Zawadzki, Michael.

Norman, Dean C., jt. auth. see Yoshikawa, Thomas T.

Norman, Dean C., jt. ed. see Yoshikawa, Thomas T.

***Norman, Diana.** Blood Royal. large type ed. 480p. 1999. 31.99 (0-7089-9054-1) Ulverscroft.

Norman, Diana. The Morning Gift. large type ed. 544p. 1987. 11.50 (0-7089-1629-5) Ulverscroft.

— Road from Singapore. large type ed. 1974. 27.99 (0-85456-287-7) Ulverscroft.

***Norman, Diana.** Siena & the Virgin: Art & Politics in a Late Medieval City State. LC 99-25442. (Illus.). 256p. 1999. 60.00 (0-300-08006-9) Yale U Pr.

Norman, Diana. Siena, Florence, & Padua: Art, Society, & Religion, 1280-1400, Vol. 1. LC 94-25653. Vol. 1. 1995. pap. 30.00 (0-300-06125-0) Yale U Pr.

— Siena, Florence, & Padua: Art, Society, & Religion, 1280-1400, Vol. 2. LC 94-25653. (Case Studies: Vol. 2). 1995. pap. 30.00 (0-300-06127-7) Yale U Pr.

— Terrible Beauty: A Life of Constance Markievicz. 320p. 1988. pap. 12.95 (1-85371-007-5) Dufour.

Norman, Diana, ed. Siena, Florence, & Padua Vol. II: Art, Society, & Religion, 1280-1400, Vol. II. LC 94-25653. 1996. 60.00 (0-300-06126-9) Yale U Pr.

— Sienna, Florence & Padua: Art, Society & Religion 1280-1400, Vol. 1. LC 94-25653. Vol. 1. 1995. 60.00 (0-300-06124-2) Yale U Pr.

Norman, Donald. Things That Make Us Smart: Defending Human Attributes in the Age of the Machine. 304p. 1994. pap. 17.00 (0-201-62695-0) Addison-Wesley.

Norman, Donald A. The Design of Everyday Things. 272p. 1990. pap. 15.95 (0-385-26774-6) Doubleday.

— The Design of Everyday Things. (Illus.). 274p. 1998. pap. text 15.95 (0-262-64037-6) MIT Pr.

— The Invisible Computer: Why Good Products Can Fail, the Personal Computer Is So Complex, & Information Appliances Are the Solution. LC 98-18841. (Illus.). 315p. 1998. 25.00 (0-262-14065-9) MIT Pr.

— The Invisible Computer: Why Good Products Can Fail, the Personal Computer Is So Complex, & Information Appliances Are the Solution. (Illus.). 320p. 1999. reprint ed. pap. 13.95 (0-262-64041-4) MIT Pr.

— The Psychology of Everyday Things. LC 87-47782. (Illus.). 288p. 1930. 26.00 (0-465-06709-3, Pub. by Basic) HarpC.

— Turn Signals Are the Facial Expressions of Automobiles. (Illus.). 224p. 1993. pap. 14.00 (0-201-62236-X) Addison-Wesley.

— Turn Signals Are the Facial Expressions of Automobiles: Notes of a Technology Watcher. (Illus.). 1992. 21.95 (0-201-58124-8) Addison-Wesley.

Norman, Donald A., ed. Perspectives on Cognitive Science. LC 80-21343. 315p. reprint ed. pap. 97.70 (0-7837-0201-9, 204049700017) Bks Demand.

Norman, Donald A. & Draper, Stephen. User Centered System Design. (New Perspectives on Human-Computer Interaction Ser.). 544p. (C). 1986. pap. 49.95 (0-89859-872-9) L Erlbaum Assocs.

Norman, Dorothy. Alfred Stieglitz. 2nd ed. (Masters of Photography Ser.). (Illus.). 96p. 1997. reprint ed. 18.95 (0-89381-745-7) Aperture.

— Alfred Stieglitz: An American Seer. 1990. pap. 25.95 (0-89381-425-3) Aperture.

— Alfred Stieglitz: An American Seer. 1991. 44.95 (0-89381-429-6) Aperture.

Norman, Dorothy, compiled by. Alfred Stieglitz. (Masters of Photography Ser.: Vol. 6). (Illus.). 1989. pap. 23.95 (0-89381-309-5) Aperture.

Norman, Douglas J., et al. Primer on Transplantation. LC 97-50158. (Illus.). xxii, 586p. 1997. text 120.00 (0-9660150-0-2) ASTP.

Norman, Dwayne, ed. Your Beginning with God. 31p. 1982. pap. 1.95 (0-88144-063-9) Christian Pub.

Norman, E. B., ed. Particle Astrophysics: Forefront Experimental Issues. 388p. (C). 1989. pap. 40.00 (9971-5-0869-9); text 108.00 (9971-5-0835-4) World Scientific Pub.

Norman, E. Herbert. Ando Shoeki & the Anatomy of Japanese Feudalism. LC 79-52922. 340p. 1979. reprint ed. lib. bdg. 79.50 (0-313-27034-1, U7034, Greenwood Pr) Greenwood.

— Feudal Background of Japanese Politics... in Preliminary Draft Form. LC 75-30127. (Institute of Pacific Relations Ser.). reprint ed. 49.50 (0-404-59548-0) AMS Pr.

— Japan's Emergence As a Modern State. LC 72-9092. 254p. 1973. reprint ed. lib. bdg. 48.50 (0-8371-6573-3, NOJE, Greenwood Pr) Greenwood.

— Soldier & Peasant in Japan: The Origins of Conscription. LC 77-4281. (Illus.). 76p. 1977. lib. bdg. 45.00 (0-8371-9597-7, NOSP, Greenwood Pr) Greenwood.

— Soldier & Peasant in Japan: The Origins of Conscription. LC 75-33572. (Institute of Pacific Relations Ser.). reprint ed. 29.50 (0-404-59549-9) AMS Pr.

Norman, E. M. Flora of Ecuador No. 176: Buddlejaceae. (Opera Botanica Series B). 23p. 1982. pap. 15.00 (91-86344-03-X, Pub. by Coun Nordic Pubs) Balogh.

Norman, Edward. Christianity in the Southern Hemisphere: The Churches in Latin America & South Africa. 1981. text 45.00 (0-19-821127-9) OUP.

— Roman Catholicism in England from the Elizabethan Settlement to the Second Vatican Council. (Opus Ser.). 160p. 1986. pap. 11.95 (0-19-281935-6) OUP.

Norman, Edward, jt. auth. see Utley, T. E.

Norman, Edward R., et al. Ethics & Nuclear Arms: European & American Perspectives. LC 85-10304. 1985. pap. 13.50 (0-89633-095-8) Ethics & Public Policy.

Norman, Elaine. Drug-Free Youth: A Compendium for Prevention Specialists. LC 96-32670. (Garland Reference Library of Social Science). (Illus.). 208p. 1997. pap. text 19.95 (0-8153-2047-7) Garland.

***Norman, Elaine.** Resiliency Enhancement: Putting the Strengths Perspective into Social Work Practice. LC 00-22727. (Illus.). 2000. write for info. (0-231-11801-5) Col U Pr.

Norman, Elaine & Fordham University Staff, eds. Drug-Free Youth: A Compendium for Prevention Specialists. LC 96-32670. (Garland Reference Library of Social Science). (Illus.). 208p. 1997. text 43.00 (0-8153-2048-5) Garland.

Norman, Elizabeth. Women at War: The Story of Fifty Military Nurses Who Served in Vietnam. LC 90-34487. (Studies in Health, Illness, & Caregiving). (Illus.). 238p. (Orig.). (C). 1990. pap. 16.95 (0-8122-1317-3) U of Pa Pr.

Norman, Elizabeth M. We Band of Angels: The Untold Story of American Nurses Trapped on Bataan by the Japanese. LC 98-45998. 384p. 1999. 26.95 (0-375-50245-9) Random.

*Norman, Elizabeth M. We Band of Angels: The Untold Story of American Nurses Trapped on Bataan by the Japanese. (Illus.). 384p. 2000. reprint ed. per. 13.95 (0-671-78718-7, PB Trade Paper) PB.
Norman, Ernest L. The Anthenium. (Illus.). 143p. 1964. 9.00 (0-932642-13-6) Unarius Acad Sci.
— Cosmic Continuum. 2nd ed. (Illus.). 166p. 1960. 16.00 (0-932642-17-9) Unarius Acad Sci.
— The Elysium. (Illus.). 71p. 1956. 9.00 (0-932642-14-4) Unarius Acad Sci.
*Norman, Ernest L. Infinite Concept of Cosmic Creation. (Illus.). 1998. 50.00 (0-935097-41-4) Unarius Acad Sci.
Norman, Ernest L. Infinite Perspectus. 443p. 1962. 24.00 (0-932642-06-3) Unarius Acad Sci.
— The Little Red Box. (Illus.). 138p. 1968. 7.00 (0-932642-16-0); pap. 5.00 (0-932642-47-0) Unarius Acad Sci.
— Tempus Interludium, Vol. 1. (Illus.). 290p. 1978. 16.00 (0-932642-09-8) Unarius Acad Sci.
— Tempus Interludium, Vol. 2. Norman, Ruth E., ed. 224p. 1982. 16.00 (0-932642-48-9) Unarius Acad Sci.
— Tempus Invictus. rev. ed. (Illus.). 496p. 1968. 18.00 (0-932642-08-X) Unarius Acad Sci.
— Tempus Procedium. (Illus.). 480p. 1968. 18.00 (0-932642-07-1) Unarius Acad Sci.
*Norman, Ernest L. The Truth about Mars: An Eyewitness Account. 176p. 1998. 22.00 (0-935097-39-2) Unarius Acad Sci.
Norman, Ernest L. The Voice of Eros, Vol. 2. 2nd ed. (Pulse of Creation Ser.). (Illus.). 260p. 1962. 20.00 (0-932642-01-2) Unarius Acad Sci.
— The Voice of Hermes. 2nd ed. (Pulse of Creation Ser.: Vol. 3). (Illus.). 259p. 1962. 20.00 (0-932642-02-0) Unarius Acad Sci.
— The Voice of Muse, Unarius, Elysium, Vol. 5. (Pulse of Creation Ser.). (Illus.). 265p. 1964. 20.00 (0-932642-04-7) Unarius Acad Sci.
— The Voice of Orion, Vol. 4. (Pulse of Creation Ser.). (Illus.). 232p. 1961. 20.00 (0-932642-03-9) Unarius Acad Sci.
— The Voice of Venus. 7th ed. (Pulse of Creation Ser.: Vol. 1). (Illus.). 197p. 1995. 20.00 (0-932642-00-4) Unarius Acad Sci.
Norman, Ernest L., ed. The Voice of Venus. 7th ed. (Pulse of Creation Ser.: Vol. 1). (Illus.). 197p. 1995. pap. 15.00 (0-935097-33-3) Unarius Acad Sci.
Norman, Felicia. What's a Group to Do? (C). 1998. pap. text 34.00 (0-12-785027-9) Acad Pr.
— What's a Group to Do. 1998. 34.00 (0-7616-3400-2) Commun Skill.
Norman, Floyd. Faster! Cheaper! The Flip Side to the Art of Animation. (Illus.). 128p. (Orig.). 1992. pap. 12.95 (0-942909-02-X) Get Animated.
Norman, Floyd E. Afro-Classic Folk Tales Bk. 1: A Rattlesnake Tale. Stewart, Lyn, ed. (Illus.). 28p. (Orig.). (J). (gr. 4-7). 1992. pap. 9.95 (1-881368-00-9) Vignette.
— Afro-Classic Folk Tales Bk. 4: High John. Stewart, Lyn, ed. (Illus.). 28p. (Orig.). (J). (gr. 4-7). 1992. pap. 9.95 (1-881368-21-1) Vignette.
Norman, Floyd E., jt. auth. see Sullivan, Leo.
Norman, Fred. Where Is Joey Garcia? Griggs Anthology. annuals unabridged ed. Griggs, Richard, ed. LC 97-25074. (Illus.). 108p. (C). 1997. 11.00 (0-922530-05-X) Tantalus Bks.
Norman, Fred, jt. ed. see Griggs, Rick.
Norman, Fred, ed. see Perry, J. Mitchell & Griggs, Richard E.
Norman, G. SAA & Applications Development. 120p. 1991. 245.00 (1-85617-125-6, Pub. by Elsvr Adv Tech) Elsevier.
Norman, Geoffrey. Blue Chipper. 240p. 1994. mass mkt. 4.99 (0-380-71911-8, Avon Bks) Morrow Avon.
— Bouncing Back. McCarthy, Paul, ed. 256p. 1992. reprint ed. mass mkt. 4.99 (0-671-74635-9) PB.
— Deep End. 256p. 1995. mass mkt. 4.99 (0-380-71912-6, Avon Bks) Morrow Avon.
— Deep End. large type ed. LC 94-16394. 431p. 1994. lib. bdg. 21.95 (0-7862-0241-6) Thorndike Pr.
— Sweetwater Ranch. large type ed. 464p. 31.50 (0-7089-3671-7) Ulverscroft.
*Norman, Geoffrey. Two for the Summit: My Daughter, the Mountains & Me. 2000. 22.95 (0-525-94494-X) NAL.
Norman, Geoffrey, jt. auth. see Edgeworth, Anthony.
Norman, Geoffrey, jt. auth. see Perkins, Leigh.
Norman, Geoffrey, jt. auth. see Ralphs, Lady.
*Norman, Geoffrey R. & Streiner, David L. Biostatistics: The Bare Essentials. (Illus.). 260p. 1998. pap. 36.95 (1-55009-085-2) DEKR.
Norman, Geoffrey R. & Streiner, David L. Biostatistics: The Bare Essentials. LC 92-48446. 1993. write for info. (0-8016-2186-0) Mosby Inc.
*Norman, Geoffrey R. & Streiner, David L. PDQ Statistics. 2nd ed. (Illus.). 188p. 1999. pap. 19.95 (1-55009-076-3) DEKR.
Norman, Geoffrey R., jt. auth. see Streiner, David L.
Norman, George. Economies of Scale, Transport Costs, & Location. (Studies in Applied Regional Science: Vol. 16). 1979. lib. bdg. 73.50 (0-89838-017-0) Kluwer Academic.
*Norman, George, ed. The Economics of Price Discrimination. LC 99-38283. (International Library of Critical Writings in Economics). 574p. 1999. write for info. (1-84064-233-5) E Elgar.
*Norman, George & Thisse, Jacques-Francois, eds. Market Structure & Competition Policy: Game-Theoretic Approaches. (Illus.). 300p. 2001. write for info. (0-521-78333-X) Cambridge U Pr.
Norman, George, jt. auth. see Flanagan, Roger.
Norman, George, ed. see Flanagan, Roger.
Norman, George, jt. ed. see Gee, J. M.
Norman, George, jt. ed. see Greenhut, Melvin L.
Norman, George, jt. ed. see Thisse, Jacques-Francois.
Norman, Geraldine. The Hermitage: The Biography of a Great Museum. LC 97-39655. 386p. 1991. 35.00 (0-88064-190-8) Fromm Intl Pub.
Norman, Geraldine, ed. see Marius.
Norman, Gertrude & Shrifte, Mirian L., eds. Letters of Composers: An Anthology, 1603-1945. LC 78-11483. 422p. 1979. reprint ed. lib. bdg. 79.50 (0-313-20664-3, NOLC, Greenwood Pr) Greenwood.
Norman, Greg & Harmon, Claude, Jr. Advanced Golf. LC 96-219415. (Illus.). 208p. 1996. pap. 19.95 (1-885203-34-9) Jrny Editions.
Norman, Greg & Peper, George. Greg Norman's Instant Lessons: One Hundred Ways to Shave Strokes off Your Golf Game. LC 92-30381. (Illus.). 1993. 25.00 (0-671-74943-9) S&S Trade.
— Greg Norman's Instant Lessons: One Hundred Ways to Shave Strokes off Your Golf Game. LC 92-30381. 224p. 1994. pap. 15.00 (0-671-88425-5, Fireside) S&S Trade Pap.
Norman, Gurney. Divine Right's Trip: A Novel of the Counterculture. 2nd ed. LC 90-80306. 320p. 1990. reprint ed. pap. 15.00 (0-917788-42-7) Gnomon Pr.
— Kinfolks: The Wilgus Stories. LC 77-82064. 1989. pap. 12.50 (0-917788-10-9) Gnomon Pr.
Norman, H. C., ed. see Dhammapadatthakatha.
Norman, H. E. Patents Law. (European Community Law Ser.). (C). 1997. text 90.00 (0-485-70015-8) Humanities.
Norman, Hans, jt. auth. see Dahlgren, Stellan.
Norman, Hans, jt. ed. see Runblom, Harald.
Norman, Helen, jt. auth. see Annand, Ruth.
Norman, Henry W. Delhi. (Illus.). 400p. (C). 1987. reprint ed. 44.00 (0-8364-2142-6, Pub. by Gian Publng Hse) S Asia.
Norman, Hilary. Fascination. 464p. 1993. mass mkt. 5.99 (0-451-40378-9, Onyx) NAL.
*Norman, Hilary. The Key to Susanna. 357p. 1999. reprint ed. text 24.00 (0-7881-6612-3) DIANE Pub.
Norman, Hilary. Laura. 1995. mass mkt. 5.99 (0-451-18012-7, Sig) NAL.
Norman, Hope J. Louisiana Entertains. 1981. 12.95 (0-9603758-0-5) Rapides Symphony.
Norman, Hope J. & Simon, Louise A., eds. Louisiana Entertains: Featured As "A Best Cookbook" by Town & Country Magazine. LC 83-60953. (Illus.). 312p. (Orig.). 1983. pap. 11.95 (0-9603758-1-3) Rapides Symphony.
Norman, Howard. The Bird Artist: A Novel. LC 94-70542. 320p. 1994. text 20.00 (0-374-11330-0) FS&G.
— The Bird Artist: A Novel. large type ed. LC 95-3156. (Large Print Bks.). 1995. pap. 19.95 (1-56895-094-2) Wheeler Pub.
— The Bird Artist: A Novel. 7th ed. LC 95-5216. 289p. 1995. pap. 13.00 (0-312-13027-9, Picador USA) St Martin.
— The Girl Who Dreamed Only Geese: And Other Tales of the Far North. LC 96-20880. (Illus.). 147p. (YA). (gr. 5 up). 1997. 22.00 (0-15-230979-9) Harcourt.
— The Museum Guard. LC 98-8413. 310p. 1998. 23.00 (0-374-21649-5) FS&G.
— The Museum Guard. LC 99-34701. 320p. 1999. pap. 14.00 (0-312-20427-2) St Martin.
— The Northern Lights. 240p. 1988. pap. 10.00 (0-671-65877-8, WSP) PB.
— Northern Tales. 343p. 1998. pap. 16.00 (0-375-70267-9) Random.
*Norman, Howard. Trickster & the Fainting Birds. (Illus.). 96p. (J). (ps-3). 2000. 29.98 (0-7398-1363-3) Raintree Steck-V.
Norman, Howard & Shore, Jane, eds. Ploughshares Winter, 1997-98. 234p. 1997. pap. 9.95 (0-933277-21-0) Ploughshares.
Norman, Howard, ed. see Strauss, Susan.
Norman, Howard, tr. see Akutagawa, Ryunosuke.
Norman, Howard A. Trickster & the Fainting Birds. LC 97-9457. (Illus.). 82p. (YA). (gr. 1 up). 1999. 20.00 (0-15-200888-8, Gulliver Bks) Harcourt.
Norman, I. A., jt. auth. see Clontz, J.
Norman, J. C. Tropical Vegetable Crops. (C). 1992. text 70.00 (0-7223-2595-9, Pub. by A H S Ltd) St Mut.
Norman, J. R. History of Fishes. 1998. 64.00 (81-87067-18-7) Asiatic Pub Hse.
Norman, Jack, jt. auth. see Goldberg, Seymour.
Norman, Jackie D. Chinaberry Songs. unabridged ed. 112p. 1998. 10.00 (1-886364-10-9) J D Norman.
Norman, James. Gallstones & Their Treatment: A Guide for Patients. Carey, Larry, ed. (Surgical Ser.). (Illus.). 24p. (Orig.). 1995. pap. 2.95 (1-885274-21-1) Health InfoNet Inc.
— Murder, Chop Chop. 1997. reprint ed. pap. 13.00 (0-915230-16-X) Rue Morgue.
— The Obsidian Mirror. LC 77-72806. (Illus.). (Orig.). 1977. pap. 12.50 (0-914140-03-5) Carpenter Pr.
Norman, Jan. What No One Ever Tells You about Starting Your Own Business: Real Life Start-Up Advice from 101 Successful Entrepreneurs. LC 98-30479. 221p. 1999. pap. 17.95 (1-57410-112-9, 56146101) Dearborn.
Norman, Jane & Beazley, Frank. The Adventures of Tick-i-ty Ted: The Search for the Peanut Butter King. unabridged ed. LC 93-84311. (Tick-i-ty Ted Adventure Ser.). 24p. (J). (ps-3). 1993. pap. 4.95 incl. audio (1-883585-00-7) Pixanne Ent.
— Big Purr to the Rescue. 24p. (J). (ps-3). 1993. pap. write for info. (1-883585-11-2) Pixanne Ent.
— The Case of the Missing Shoes. 24p. (J). (ps-3). 1993. pap. write for info. (1-883585-07-4) Pixanne Ent.
— It's Raining Vegetables! 24p. (J). (ps-3). 1993. pap. write for info. (1-883585-08-2) Pixanne Ent.
— Maxi's Big Adventure. 24p. (J). (ps-3). 1993. pap. write for info. (1-883585-04-X) Pixanne Ent.
— The Mumble Mystery. 24p. (J). (ps-3). 1993. pap. write for info. (1-883585-12-0) Pixanne Ent.
— The Mysterious Light. 24p. (J). (ps-3). 1993. pap. write for info. (1-883585-05-8) Pixanne Ent.
— The Mystery of the Flying Elephants. 24p. (J). (ps-3). 1993. pap. write for info. (1-883585-02-3) Pixanne Ent.
— The Night the Moon Fell. 24p. (J). (ps-3). 1993. pap. write for info. (1-883585-06-6) Pixanne Ent.
— The Tale of the Tickle Bug. 24p. (J). (ps-3). 1993. pap. write for info. (1-883585-03-1) Pixanne Ent.
— Tick-i-ty Ted Joins the Circus. (Adventures of Tick-i-ty Ted Ser.). 24p. (J). (ps-3). 1993. pap. write for info. (1-883585-01-5) Pixanne Ent.
— Tick-i-ty Ted Meets the Rude Rabbits. (Adventures of Tick-i-ty Ted Ser.). 24p. (J). (ps-3). 1993. pap. write for info. (1-883585-09-0) Pixanne Ent.
— The Voice from Nowhere. 24p. (J). (ps-3). 1993. pap. write for info. (1-883585-10-4) Pixanne Ent.
— Who Lives There? 24p. (J). (ps-3). 1993. pap. write for info. (1-883585-13-9) Pixanne Ent.
Norman, Jean & Sylvan, Richard, eds. Directions in Relevant Logic. (Reason & Argument Ser.: No. 1). 466p. 1989. lib. bdg. 239.50 (0-7923-0386-5, Pub. by Kluwer Academic) Kluwer Academic.
Norman, Jeffrey. Laughing Together & Other Ironies. (Illus.). 56p. (Orig.). 1991. pap. write for info. (0-9628082-0-2) EyeDea Bks.
— Objects from a Romance. (Illus.). 56p. (Orig.). 1991. pap. write for info. (0-9628082-1-0) EyeDea Bks.
Norman, Jennifer. Memory, Baa, Moo, Cock-a-doodle-doo. 1995. pap. 12.99 (0-85953-706-4) Childs Play.
Norman, Jennifer L. & Horton, Edward R. Adult Day Care Therapeutic Activity Manual: A Continuous Quality Improvement Approach. 176p. 1996. ring bd. 49.00 (0-8342-0805-9, 20805) Aspen Pub.
Norman, Jeremy M., ed. Morton's Medical Bibliography. 5th ed. 1046p. 1991. text 159.95 (0-85967-897-0, Pub. by Scolar Pr) Ashgate Pub Co.
Norman, Jerry. Chinese. (Cambridge Language Surveys Ser.). (Illus.). 304p. 1988. text 80.00 (0-521-22809-3); pap. text 28.95 (0-521-29653-6) Cambridge U Pr.
Norman, Jesse, ed. & frwd. see Barford, Charlotte, et al.
Norman, Jill. Bantam Library of the Culinary Arts, 4 vols. 1989. boxed set 23.80 (0-553-30491-7) Bantam.
— The Complete Book of Spices: A Practical Guide to Spices & Aromatic Seeds. LC 90-50371. (Illus.). 160p. 1991. 25.00 (0-670-83437-8, Viking Studio) Studio Bks.
— The Complete Book of Spices: A Practical Guide to Spices & Aromatic Seeds. (Illus.). 160p. 1995. pap. 14.95 (0-14-023804-2, Viking Studio) Studio Bks.
— Ice Creams & Sorbets: Frozen Delicacies to Please the Eye & Palate. (Illus.). 41p. 1998. text 7.00 (0-7881-5499-0) DIANE Pub.
Norman, Jill & Alvarez, Maria V. Penguin Spanish Phrase Book. 288p. 1988. pap. 7.00 (0-14-009936-0, Penguin Bks) Viking Penguin.
Norman, Jill & De Figuerdo, Antonio. Penguin Portuguese Phrase Book. 2nd ed. 288p. 1988. reprint ed. pap. 7.95 (0-14-009937-9, Penguin Bks) Viking Penguin.
Norman, Jill & Giorgetti, Pietro. Penguin Italian Phrase Book. 272p. 1988. pap. 7.00 (0-14-009938-7, Penguin Bks) Viking Penguin.
Norman, Jill & Hitchin, Ute. Penguin German Phrase Book. 272p. (Orig.). 1988. pap. 7.00 (0-14-009940-9, Penguin Bks) Viking Penguin.
Norman, Jill & Orteu, Henri. Penguin French Phrase Book. 320p. (Orig.). 1988. pap. 7.00 (0-14-009942-5, Penguin Bks) Viking Penguin.
Norman, Jill, jt. auth. see Hall, Magda.
Norman, Jim. Circle of Fear. 512p. 1993. mass mkt. 4.50 (1-55817-721-3, Pinncle Kensgtn) Kensgtn Pub Corp.
Norman, Jim Van, see Carpenter, Tom J. & Van Norman, Jim.
Norman, John. Assassins of Gor. 1997. mass mkt. 6.95 (1-56333-538-7) Masquerade.
— Captive of Gor. 1997. mass mkt. 6.95 (1-56333-581-6) Masquerade.
— Fire Officer's Handbook of Tactics. 2nd ed. LC 98-10917. 1998. 48.75 (0-912212-72-1) Fire Eng.
— Fire Officer's Handbook of Tactics Study Guide. 1992. 14.95 (0-912212-28-4) Fire Eng.
— Gor Promotion. Incl. Outlaw of Gor. 1984. pap. 3.95 (0-345-32394-7); Priest-Kings of Gor. 1980. mass mkt. 3.95 (0-345-29539-0); Raiders of Gor. 1985. pap. 3.95 (0-345-33109-5); 1973. Set pap. 2.50 (0-686-76992-9) Ballantine Pub Grp.
— Hunters of Gor. 1998. reprint ed. mass mkt. 6.95 (1-56333-592-1) Masquerade.
— Imaginitive Sex. (Orig.). 1997. mass mkt. 7.95 (1-56333-561-1, Rhinoceros) Masquerade.
— Marauders of Gor. 1998. reprint ed. mass mkt. 6.95 (1-56333-662-6, Masquerade SF) Masquerade.
— Nomads of Gor. 1997. mass mkt. 6.95 (1-56333-527-1, Masquerade SF) Masquerade.
— Outlaw of Gor. (Gor Ser.). 1997. reprint ed. mass mkt. 6.95 (1-56333-487-9, Masquerade SF) Masquerade.
— Priest-Kings of Gor. (Gor Ser.). 1996. mass mkt. 6.95 (1-56333-488-7) Masquerade.
— Raiders of Gor. 1997. mass mkt. 6.95 (1-56333-558-1) Masquerade.
— Tansman of Gor. 1997. mass mkt. 6.95 (1-56333-486-0, Masquerade SF) Masquerade.
— Tribesman of Gor. 1998. mass mkt. 6.95 (1-56333-677-4, Masquerade SF) Masquerade.
Norman, John E. De Burgh, see De Burgh Norman, John E., ed.
Norman, John L., Jr., jt. ed. see Day, Christopher W.
Norman, John M., jt. auth. see Campbell, Gaylon S.
Norman, John P. Law & Practice of the Copyright, Registration & Provisional Registration of Designs: And the Copyright & Registration of Sculpture; with Practical Directions: The Remedies, Pleadings & Evidence in Cases of Piracy; with an Appendix of Tables of Fees, Statutes, & the Rules of the Board of Trade. LC 96-834. xii, 186p. 1996. reprint ed. 35.00 (0-8377-2451-1, Rothman) W S Hein.
Norman, Judith, tr. see Zizek, Slavoj & Von Schelling, F. W.
Norman, K. R. Collected Papers, Vol. I. 271p. (C). 1990. 39.00 (0-86013-295-1, Pub. by Pali Text) Elsevier.
— Collected Papers, Vol. II. 271p. 1991. 39.00 (0-86013-296-X) Wisdom MA.
— Collected Papers, Vol. III. 271p. 1992. 39.00 (0-86013-299-4) Wisdom MA.
— Collected Papers, Vol. IV. 271p. 1993. 39.00 (0-86013-306-0) Wisdom MA.
Norman, K. R., ed. Pali Text Society Journal, Vol. 16. 185p. (C). 1992. 35.50 (0-86013-304-4) Wisdom MA.
— Pali Text Society Journal, Vol. 17. 224p. (C). 1992. 35.50 (0-86013-305-2) Wisdom MA.
— Pali Text Society Journal, Vol. 18. 185p. (C). 1993. 35.50 (0-86013-307-9) Wisdom MA.
— Pali Text Society Journal, Vol. 19. 224p. (C). 1993. 35.50 (0-86013-309-5) Wisdom MA.
— Pali Text Society Journal, Vol. 20. 240p. (C). 1994. 35.50 (0-86013-314-1) Wisdom MA.
Norman, K. R, tr. from PLI. Elder's Verses, 2 vols., 1. (C). 1971. 39.00 (0-86013-029-0) Wisdom MA.
— Elder's Verses, 2 vols., 2. (C). 1971. 39.00 (0-86013-031-2) Wisdom MA.
— Elder's Verses, 2 vols., Set. (C). 1971. 74.80 (0-86013-259-5, Pub. by Pali Text) Elsevier.
Norman, K. R., tr. from PLI. The Group of Discourses (Sutta-Nipata), Vol. II. 450p. (C). 1992. 56.00 (0-86013-303-6) Wisdom MA.
Norman, K. R., ed. see Geiger, Wilhelm.
Norman, K. R., jt. tr. see Davids, C. A.
Norman, Katherine, ed. A Poetry of Reality: Composing with Recorded Sound. (Contemporary Music Review Ser.). 179p. 1997. pap. text 30.00 incl. audio compact disk (3-7186-5932-8, Harwood Acad Pubs) Gordon & Breach.
Norman, Ken. Essential Bonsai: The Definitive Handbook for Creating & Growing Your Own Bonsai. 1998. 12.95 (1-85967-621-9, Lorenz Bks) Anness Pub.
Norman, L. C. Mathland: The Expert Version. (Illus.). 80p. (J). 1994. pap. 8.50 (0-521-46802-7) Cambridge U Pr.
— Mathland: The Novice Version. (Illus.). 88p. (J). 1994. pap. 8.50 (0-521-46801-9) Cambridge U Pr.
Norman L. Peterson Memorial Symposium on Oxidation. Oxidation of Metals & Associated Mass Transport: Proceedings of a Symposium Sponsored Jointly by the Metallurgical Society of AIME & the MSD-ASM Atomic Transport Activity Held at the TMS-AIME Fall Meeting in Orlando, Florida, October, 6-7, 1986 & Dedicated to the Memory of Norman L. Peterson. Dayananda, M. A. et al, eds. LC 87-14192. 353p. reprint ed. pap. 109.50 (0-7837-2208-7, 205245800004) Bks Demand.
Norman, Larry F. Public Mirror: Moliere & the Social Commerce of Depiction. LC 99-32926. 216p. 1999. pap. text 16.00 (0-226-59152-2) U Ch Pr.
— Public Mirror: Moliere & the Social Commerce of Depiction. LC 99-32926. 216p. 1999. lib. bdg. 40.00 (0-226-59151-4) U Ch Pr.
Norman, Laura & Cowan, Thomas. Feet First: A Guide to Foot Reflexology. (Illus.). 336p. 1988. pap. 14.00 (0-671-63412-7, Fireside) S&S Trade Pap.
Norman, Liane E. Hammer of Justice: Molly Rush & the Plowshares Eight. LC 89-61406. (Illus.). 280p. 1989. 24.95 (0-9622766-9-3); pap. 12.95 (0-9622766-8-5) Pittsburgh Peace.
Norman, Lillian. Climb a Lonely Hill. 1992. pap. text. write for info. (0-17-556536-8) Addison-Wesley.
Norman, Lisanne. Dark Nadir. 576p. 1999. mass mkt. 6.99 (0-88677-829-8, Pub. by DAW Bks) Penguin Putnam.
— Fire Margin. 1996. pap. 6.99 (0-88677-718-6, Pub. by DAW Bks) Penguin Putnam.
— Fortune's Wheel. 656p. (Orig.). 1995. mass mkt. 5.99 (0-88677-675-9, Pub. by DAW Bks) Penguin Putnam.
— Razor's Edge. 656p. 1997. pap. 6.99 (0-88677-766-6, Pub. by DAW Bks) Penguin Putnam.
*Norman, Lisanne. Stronghold Rising: A Sholan Alliance Novel. 608p. 2000. mass mkt. 6.99 (0-88677-898-0, Pub. by DAW Bks) Penguin Putnam.
Norman, Lisanne. Turning Point. 256p. (Orig.). 1993. mass mkt. 5.99 (0-88677-575-2, Pub. by DAW Bks) Penguin Putnam.
Norman, Louise. God's Power Versus Satan's Power: Christian Life Lessons. (BMC Teaching Bks.). (Illus.). 64p. (Orig.). (J). (gr. 1-8). 1985. pap. text 12.50 (0-86508-062-3) BCM Pubn.
— Here I Am! 150p. (J). 1996. pap. 14.95 (0-9647583-5-0) Fed Servs.
*Norman, Marc & Stoppard, Tom. Shakespeare in Love: A Screenplay. LC 99-19109. (Illus.). 169p. 1999. pap. 10.95 (0-7868-8485-1, Pub. by Hyperion) Time Warner.
Norman, Margaret G., et al. Congenital Malformations of the Brain: Pathological, Embryological, Clinical, Radiological & Genetic Aspects. (Illus.). 472p. 1995. text 98.50 (0-19-506245-0) OUP.
Norman, Marjorie & Evans, Peter, compiled by. China: A Cultural Heritage. 39.00 (1-56696-011-8) Jackdaw.
Norman, Marsha. Four Plays. LC 88-12362. 240p. (C). 1988. reprint ed. pap. 10.95 (0-930452-84-4) Theatre Comm.
— Getting Out. 1979. pap. 5.25 (0-8222-0439-8) Dramatists Play.
— The Holdup. 1987. pap. 5.25 (0-8222-0524-6) Dramatists Play.

N

An Asterisk (*) at the beginning of an entry indicates that the title is appearing for the first time.

— Marsha Norman Vol. 1: Collected Plays. LC 97-7665. (Contemporary American Playwrights Ser.). 336p. (Orig.). 1997. pap. 19.95 (*1-57525-029-2*) Smith & Kraus.
— 'Night, Mother. 1983. pap. 5.25 (*0-8222-0821-0*) Dramatists Play.
— 'Night, Mother. 92p. 1983. pap. 9.00 (*0-374-52138-7*) FS&G.
— The Secret Garden. LC 92-2562. 120p. 1992. 22.95 (*1-55936-048-8*) Theatre Comm.
— The Secret Garden. LC 92-2562. 120p. 1992. reprint ed. pap. 9.95 (*1-55936-047-X*) Theatre Comm.
— Third & Oak, the Laundromat. 1980. pap. 3.25 (*0-8222-1132-7*) Dramatists Play.
— Third & Oak, the Pool Hall. 1985. pap. 3.25 (*0-8222-1133-5*) Dramatists Play.
— Traveler in the Dark. 1988. pap. 5.25 (*0-8222-1168-8*) Dramatists Play.
Norman, Marty. 101 Uses for a Dead Angel. LC 95-8867. 1995. pap. 6.99 (*0-312-13227-1*) St Martin.
Norman, Mary A. The Texas Economy since World War II. (Texas History Ser.). (Illus.). 38p. (Orig.). 1983. pap. text 9.95 (*0-89641-126-5*) American Pr.
Norman, Matthew W. Colonel Burton's Spiller & Burr Revolver: An Untimely Venture in Confederate Small Arms Manufacturing. (Illus.). 144p. 1996. 22.95 (*0-86554-531-6*, MUP/H406) Mercer Univ Pr.
***Norman, Michael.** Greater Share of Honor. 2000. text 30.00 (*0-8050-6162-2*) St Martin.
Norman, Michael. Historic Haunted America. 1996. mass mkt. 7.99 (*0-8125-6436-7*, Pub. by Tor Bks) St Martin.
Norman, Michael & Edwards, Tim. Micro-Computers in Personnel. 128p. (C). 1984. 75.00 (*0-85292-337-6*) St Mut.
Norman, Michael, jt. auth. see Bourexis, Patricia.
Norman, Michael, jt. auth. see Scott, Beth.
Norman, Michael E., ed. see Pediatric Nephrology International Symposium Staff.
***Norman, Michael J.** Above, down, Inside & Out: Unleashing Your Spiritual Giant Within. 2nd rev. ed. LC 99-97286. (Illus.). 110p. 2000. 14.95 (*0-9676816-0-X*) Abundance Prosperity.
Norman, Michael J. Annual Cropping Systems in the Tropics: An Introduction. LC 79-10625. (Illus.). 288p. reprint ed. pap. 89.30 (*0-7837-4924-4*, 204459000004) Bks Demand.
Norman, Michael L., jt. ed. see Winkler, Karl-Heinz A.
Norman, Mick. Angels from Hell. 368p. (Orig.). 1996. pap. 16.95 (*1-871592-43-7*) Creation Books.
Norman, N. A. Consecration to the Immaculate Heart of Mary: According to the Spirit of St. Louis De-Montfort's True Devotion to Mary. LC 88-50839. 68p. 1988. reprint ed. pap. 2.00 (*0-89555-342-2*) TAN Bks Pubs.
***Norman, N. C.** Chemistry of Arsenic, Antimony & Bismuth. LC 97-77012. (Illus.). 384p. (Orig.). 1998. pap. write for info. (*0-7514-0389-X*) Kluwer Academic.
Norman, N. C. Periodicity & the s- & p-Block Elements. LC 97-12676. (Oxford Chemistry Primers: No. 51). (Illus.). 96p. (C). 1997. pap. text 12.95 (*0-19-855961-5*) OUP.
Norman, N. Philip, jt. auth. see Rorty, James.
Norman, Naomi. Picture Perfect Patchwork. (Illus.). 88p. 1996. pap. text 8.95 (*0-486-29469-2*) Dover.
Norman, Nicholas C. Periodicity & the p-Block Elements. LC 93-37708. (Oxford Chemistry Primers Ser.: Vol. 16). (Illus.). 96p. (C). 1994. pap. text 12.95 (*0-19-855763-9*) OUP.
Norman, P. S., ed. Pathology & Physiology of Allergic Reactions. (Journal: International Archives of Allergy & Applied Immunology: Vol. 77, No. 1-2). (Illus.). 280p. 1985. pap. 101.00 (*3-8055-4056-6*) S Karger.
Norman, Paul, jt. ed. see Connor, Mark.
Norman, Penny. I Can Become an Electro Wiz: Electricity. (Illus.). 40p. (J). (gr. k up). 1995. pap. text, student ed. 19.95 (*1-886978-00-X*) Norman & Globus.
— I Can Become an Electro Wiz: Magnetism. (Illus.). 40p. (J). (gr. k up). 1995. pap., student ed. 19.95 (*1-886978-01-8*) Norman & Globus.
Norman, Philip. Rave On: The Biography of Buddy Holly. (Illus.). 336p. 1997. per. 12.00 (*0-684-83560-6*, Fireside) S&S Trade Pap.
— Shout! (Illus.). 560p. 1983. mass mkt. 4.95 (*0-446-32255-5*, Pub. by Warner Bks) Little.
— Shout. 448p. 1996. per. 13.00 (*0-684-83067-1*) S&S Trade.
— Shout! The Beatles in Their Generation. (Illus.). 414p. 1995. 9.98 (*1-56731-087-7*, MJF Bks) Fine Comms.
Norman, Philip, jt. auth. see Rorty, James.
Norman, Philip A., jt. auth. see Handscombe, Richard S.
Norman, Phillip. Cats. (Infatuation Ser.). 1998. 12.95 (*1-897954-84-0*, Pub. by Mus Quilts Pub) Sterling.
Norman, Randolph. AIDS: Blunt Talk on How to Avoid It. 32p. 1985. pap. 5.95 (*0-86668-057-8*) ARCsoft.
Norman, Remington. The Great Domaines of Burgundy: A Guide to the Finest Wine Producers of the Cote D'Or. (Illus.). 288p. 1995. 40.00 (*0-8050-2463-8*) H Holt & Co.
— The Great Domaines of Burgundy: A Guide to the Finest Wines of the Cote d'or. 2nd rev. ed. (Illus.). 288p. 1995. 45.00 (*0-8050-4680-1*) H Holt & Co.
— Rhone Renaissance: The Finest Rhone & Rhone-Style Wines from France & the New World. large type ed. LC 95-61878. (Illus.). 386p. 1997. 50.00 (*0-932664-95-4*, 6848) Wine Appreciation.
Norman, Rex A. The 1837 Sketchbook of the Western Fur Trade: An Examination of the Artwork of Alfred Jacob Miller. (Illus.). 36p. 1996. pap. 7.95 (*1-880655-06-3*) Scurlock Pub.
Norman, Richard. Ethics & the Market. LC 99-72337. (Society for Applied Philosophy Ser.). 196p. 1999. 65.95 (*1-84014-980-9*, Pub. by Ashgate Pub) Ashgate Pub Co.
— Ethics, Killing & War. 266p. (C). 1995. text 54.95 (*0-521-45539-1*) Cambridge U Pr.
— Hegel's Phenomenology: A Philosophical Introduction. (Modern Revivals in Philosophy Ser.). 140p. 1992. 48.95 (*0-7512-0015-8*, Pub. by Gregg Revivals) Ashgate Pub Co.
— The Moral Philosophers: An Introduction to Ethics. 2nd ed. 240p. (C). 1998. text 44.00 (*0-19-875217-2*); pap. text 21.95 (*0-19-875216-4*) OUP.
— Studies in Equality. LC 96-14677. 288p. 1996. 66.95 (*1-85972-220-2*, Pub. by Avebry) Ashgate Pub Co.
Norman, Richard & Sayers, Sean. Hegel, Marx, & Dialectic: A Debate. (Modern Revivals in Philosophy Ser.). 196p. 1993. 52.95 (*0-7512-0219-3*, Pub. by Gregg Revivals) Ashgate Pub Co.
Norman, Rick. Cross Body Block. LC 95-71611. 220p. (Orig.). 1996. pap. 9.95 (*1-56883-060-2*) Colonial Pr AL.
— Fielder's Choice. 196p. 1992. pap. 9.95 (*0-87483-204-7*) August Hse.
— Fielder's Choice. 1992. 15.05 (*0-606-12284-2*, Pub. by Turtleback) Demco.
Norman, Rick J., jt. auth. see Holliday, James S., Jr.
Norman, Robert, tr. The Safeguard of Sailors: or Great Rutter. LC 76-57412. (English Experience Ser.: No. 827). 1977. reprint ed. lib. bdg. 30.00 (*90-221-0827-9*) Walter J Johnson.
Norman, Robert A. A Dermatologist's Little Instruction Book. 100p. 1999. pap. 10.00 (*1-57626-126-3*) Quality Med Pub.
***Norman, Robert A.** A Doctor's Little Instruction Book. 65 p. 2000. pap. 9.95 (*1-891576-00-3*) North Shore Pr.
Norman, Robert A. The Fax of Life: Jokes, Quotes & Assorted Wisdom. (Illus.). 80p. (Orig.). 1994. pap. 7.95 (*0-9637802-1-2*) North Shore Pr.
— Gaspar Returns. 213p. 1998. pap. 14.95 (*0-9637802-9-8*) North Shore Pr.
***Norman, Robert A.** Geriatric Dermatology: Chronic Care & Rehabilitation. (Illus.). 300p. 2001. 79.00 (*1-85070-311-6*) Prthnon Pub.
Norman, Robert A. Limericks of Maryland. 31p. (Orig.). 1995. pap. 3.95 (*0-9637802-4-7*) North Shore Pr.
— Limericks of Massachusetts. (Illus.). 25p. 1996. pap. 4.95 (*0-9637802-7-1*) North Shore Pr.
— Limericks of Michigan. 31p. (Orig.). 1995. pap. 3.95 (*0-9637802-5-5*) North Shore Pr.
— Limericks of Ohio. (Illus.). 25p. 1996. pap. 4.95 (*0-9637802-6-3*) North Shore Pr.
— Mother Nature, Father Time: Tales of Medicine. 190p. 1998. pap. 14.95 (*1-891576-05-4*) North Shore Pr.
— Take Two Aspirin & See Yourself in the Morning. 2nd ed. 218p. (Orig.). 1997. pap. 16.95 (*0-9637802-8-X*) North Shore Pr.
— Tennis - Volleys of the Mind. (Illus.). 27p. 1995. pap. 4.95 (*0-9637802-2-0*) North Shore Pr.
***Norman, Robert A.** To Life! Stories & Quotes for a Healthy, Happy & Spiritual Life. 140p. 1999. pap. 10.00 (*1-891576-02-X*) North Shore Pr.
Norman, Robert A., ed. Dermatopoetics: Poetry. LC 99-475294. (Illus.). 60p. 1998. pap. 9.95 (*0-9637802-0-4*) North Shore Pr.
Norman, Robert I. & Lodwick, David. Medical Cell Biology Made Memorable. LC 98-46714. 1999. write for info. (*0-443-06135-1*, W B Saunders Co) Harcrt Hlth Sci Grp.
Norman Rockwell Museum Staff. Norman Rockwell: A Centennial Celebration. (Illus.). 120p. 1993. 15.98 (*0-7924-5761-7*, Thunder Bay) Advantage Pubs.
— Norman Rockwell: A Pop-Up Art Experience. (Illus.). 1999. pap. 18.95 (*0-7893-0366-3*, Pub. by Universe) St Martin.
— Norman Rockwell: The Artist & His Work. LC 95-13523. 120p. 1995. 12.95 (*1-56799-209-9*, Friedman-Fairfax) M Friedman Pub Grp Inc.
Norman, Ron. Investigating English Language: Language & Literature. (Illus.). 192p. 1998. pap. 42.50 (*0-7487-3194-6*, Pub. by S Thornes Pubs) Trans-Atl Phila.
Norman, Ronald J. Object-Oriented Systems Analysis & Design. LC 95-36248. (Series in Information Management Ser.). 430p. (C). 1996. text 99.00 (*0-13-122946-X*) P-H.
Norman, Rosemarie Van, see Van Norman, Rosemarie.
Norman, Ruth. Unarius a Biographical History, Vol. 2. (Illus.). 387p. 1985. 17.00 (*0-932642-58-6*) Unarius Acad Sci.
— Your Encounter with Life, Death, Immortality. 6th unabridged ed. LC 89-90108. (Illus.). 71p. (Orig.). 1990. pap. 6.00 (*0-932642-43-8*) Unarius Acad Sci.
Norman, Ruth E. Biography of an Archangel: The Accomplishments of Uriel. (Illus.). 373p. 1989. 25.00 (*0-935097-19-8*) Unarius Acad Sci.
— Bridge to Heaven. 2nd ed. (Illus.). 534p. 1974. 18.00 (*0-932642-10-1*) Unarius Acad Sci.
— The Celebration of the Millenium: Crystal Mountains Cities. (Tesla Speaks Ser.: Vol. VI). (Illus.). 93p. 1974. pap. 6.00 (*0-932642-27-6*) Unarius Acad Sci.
— Countdown to Space Fleet Landing. (Tesla Speaks Ser.: Vol. VII). (Illus.). 186p. 1974. pap. 8.00 (*0-932642-28-4*) Unarius Acad Sci.
— The Decline & Destruction of the Orion Empire, Vol. 1. 2nd ed. (Illus.). 380p. (Orig.). 1983. pap. 9.00 (*0-932642-50-0*) Unarius Acad Sci.
— Decline & Destruction of the Orion Empire, Vol. 2. 369p. 1981. pap. 9.00 (*0-932642-54-3*) Unarius Acad Sci.
— Decline & Destruction of the Orion Empire, Vol. 3. 375p. 1983. pap. 9.00 (*0-932642-55-1*) Unarius Acad Sci.
— The Epic. 2nd ed. (Tesla Speaks Ser.: No. 13). (Illus.). 290p. 1988. 18.00 (*0-932642-36-5*) Unarius Acad Sci.
— Exploring the Universe with Starship Voyager. (Illus.). 533p. (C). 1986. 22.00 (*0-932642-83-7*) Unarius Acad Sci.
— The Grand Design of Life for Man, Vol. 1. 500p. (C). 1984. 18.00 (*0-932642-81-0*) Unarius Acad Sci.
— Have You Lived on Other Worlds Before, 2 vols., 2. (Illus.). 292p. 1980. pap. 9.00 (*0-932642-60-8*) Unarius Acad Sci.
— History of the Universe, Vol. 1. 444p. (Orig.). (C). 1981. 17.00 (*0-932642-71-3*) Unarius Acad Sci.
— History of the Universe, Vol. 2. (Illus.). 450p. (Orig.). (C). 1982. 17.00 (*0-932642-72-1*) Unarius Acad Sci.
— History of the Universe, Vol. 3. (Illus.). 419p. (Orig.). (C). 1983. 17.00 (*0-932642-73-X*) Unarius Acad Sci.
— Interdimensional Physics: The Mind & the Universe. (Illus.). 320p. (C). 1989. 36.00 (*0-935097-15-5*) Unarius Acad Sci.
— The Keys to the Universe & the Mind. 2nd unabridged ed. (Tesla Speaks Ser.: Vol. 11). (Illus.). 382p. 1984. 16.00 (*0-932642-34-9*) Unarius Acad Sci.
— Man - The Regenerative Evolutionary Spirit. 345p. (C). 1988. 18.00 (*0-932642-95-0*) Unarius Acad Sci.
— Mars Underground Cities Discovered. (Tesla Speaks Ser.: Vol. 12). (Illus.). 344p. 1977. 14.00 (*0-932642-35-7*) Unarius Acad Sci.
— The Masters Speak. (Tesla Speaks Ser.: Vol. 8, Pt. 1). (Illus.). 320p. 1975. 16.00 (*0-932642-30-6*) Unarius Acad Sci.
— My Two Thousand Year Psychic Memory As Mary of Bethany: 13th Disciple to Jesus of Nazareth. 2nd ed. (Illus.). 74p. 1988. 6.00 (*0-932642-32-2*) Unarius Acad Sci.
— New Hope!!! There Is New Hope for the Drug & Alcohol Abuser - You Too Can Be Healed! (Illus.). 48p. (Orig.). (C). 1984. pap. 4.00 (*0-932642-96-9*) Unarius Acad Sci.
— Preparation for the Landing. (Illus.). 493p. 1987. 22.00 (*0-935097-07-4*) Unarius Acad Sci.
— Preview for the Spacecraft Landing on Earth 2001 A. D. (Illus.). 139p. 1987. pap. 10.00 (*0-935097-06-6*) Unarius Acad Sci.
— The Proof of the Truth of Past Life Therapy. 212p. 1988. 11.00 (*0-935097-13-9*) Unarius Acad Sci.
— The Rainbow Bridge to the Inner Worlds. (Illus.). 391p. (C). 1985. 18.00 (*0-932642-87-X*) Unarius Acad Sci.
— Ramu of Lemuria Speaks. (Illus.). 431p. 1988. 20.00 (*0-935097-08-2*) Unarius Acad Sci.
— Tesla Speaks: Philosophers. (Tesla Speaks Ser.: Vol. 2). 478p. 1973. 18.00 (*0-932642-21-7*) Unarius Acad Sci.
— Testimonials by Unarius Students. 2nd unabridged ed. (Illus.). 145p. (Orig.). 1987. pap. 8.00 (*0-932642-99-3*) Unarius Acad Sci.
— Thirty-Two Earth Worlds Speak to Planet Earth. (Tesla Speaks Ser.: Vol. 4, Pt. 1). (Illus.). 621p. 1974. 17.00 (*0-932642-23-3*) Unarius Acad Sci.
— Thirty-Two Earth Worlds Speak to Planet Earth. (Tesla Speaks Ser.: Vol. 4, Pt. 3). (Illus.). 410p. 1974. 17.00 (*0-932642-25-X*) Unarius Acad Sci.
— Thwarted: Effort to Destroy the Unarius Mission. 404p. (Orig.). (C). 1984. pap. 9.00 (*0-932642-89-6*) Unarius Acad Sci.
— Touched by Light. LC 97-60335. (Illus.). 150p. (Orig.). 1997. pap. 15.00 (*0-935097-37-6*) Unarius Acad Sci.
— Twenty-Five Planets Speak to Planet Earth. (Tesla Speaks Ser.: Vol. V). (Illus.). 298p. 1975. 12.00 (*0-932642-26-8*); pap. 8.00 (*0-932642-45-4*) Unarius Acad Sci.
— Unarius a Biographical History, Vol. 1. (Illus.). 406p. 1985. 17.00 (*0-932642-57-8*) Unarius Acad Sci.
— The Visitations: A Saga of Gods & Men, Vol. I. (Illus.). 572p. 1987. 80.00 (*0-932642-84-5*) Unarius Acad Sci.
— Whispers of Love on Wings of Light. (Tesla Speaks Ser.: No. 10). (Illus.). 241p. 1975. 17.00 (*0-932642-33-0*); pap. 12.00 (*0-932642-44-6*) Unarius Acad Sci.
Norman, Ruth E., intro. Glowing Moments. 170p. (Orig.). 1982. pap. 7.00 (*0-932642-76-4*) Unarius Acad Sci.
***Norman, Ruth E. & Spaegal, Vaughn.** Conclave of Light Beings. 2nd ed. (Illus.). 547p. 1999. reprint ed. pap. 18.00 (*0-935097-35-X*) Unarius Acad Sci.
Norman, Ruth E. & Spaegal, Vaughn. Who Is the Mona Lisa? (Illus.). 88p. 1973. pap. 5.00 (*0-932642-18-7*) Unarius Acad Sci.
Norman, Ruth E. & Spaegel, Charles. Principles & Practice of Past Life Therapy, Vol. 1. 3rd ed. (Illus.). 414p. 1991. 20.00 (*0-932642-79-9*) Unarius Acad Sci.
— Return to Atlantis, Vol. 1. 2nd ed. (Illus.). 323p. 1992. reprint ed. 25.00 (*0-932642-51-9*) Unarius Acad Sci.
— Return to Atlantis, Vol. 3, Pt. 1. (Illus.). 254p. (C). 1982. pap. 10.00 (*0-932642-53-5*) Unarius Acad Sci.
— Return to Atlantis, Vol. 3, Pt. 2. (Illus.). 334p. 1983. pap. 10.00 (*0-932642-74-8*) Unarius Acad Sci.
— Return to Atlantis, Vol. 4. 244p. 1987. pap. 10.00 (*0-932642-70-5*) Unarius Acad Sci.
Norman, Ruth E., et al. By Their Fruits: Shall They Be Known, 1. (Illus.). 408p. 1978. pap. 8.00 (*0-932642-41-1*) Unarius Acad Sci.
— By Their Fruits: Shall They Be Known, 2. (Illus.). 373p. 1978. pap. 8.00 (*0-932642-42-X*) Unarius Acad Sci.
— Lemuria Rising, 1. (Illus.). 199p. 1976. pap. 7.00 (*0-932642-37-3*) Unarius Acad Sci.
— Lemuria Rising, 2. (Illus.). 372p. 1976. pap. 9.00 (*0-932642-38-1*) Unarius Acad Sci.
— Lemuria Rising, 4. 1977. pap. 9.00 (*0-932642-40-3*) Unarius Acad Sci.
— The Masters Speak. (Tesla Speaks Ser.: Vol. 8, Pt. 2). (Illus.). 285p. 1976. 16.00 (*0-932642-29-2*) Unarius Acad Sci.
— Return to Jerusalem. (Illus.). 286p. (Orig.). 1983. pap. 10.00 (*0-932642-78-0*) Unarius Acad Sci.
Norman, Ruth E., jt. auth. see Spaegel, Charles.
Norman, Ruth E., jt. auth. see Swanson, Jeff.
Norman, Ruth E., ed. see Dallison, Dennis.
Norman, Ruth E., ed. see Norman, Ernest L.
Norman, Sandra J. & Andes, Karrie K. Vintage Cookbooks & Advertising Leaflets. LC 98-85481. 160p. 1998. pap. 29.95 (*0-7643-0621-9*) Schiffer.
***Norman, Seth.** Fly Fisher's Guide to Cromes of Passion: More Sedition from the Master of Meander. 2000. 24.95 (*1-58574-135-3*) Lyon Press.
Norman, Seth. Flyfisher's Guide to Northern California. rev. ed. LC 96-61538. (Illus.). 320p. 1997. pap. 26.95 (*1-885106-36-X*) Wild Adven Pr.
— Meanderings of a Fly Fisherman. LC 96-60840. 234p. 1996. 29.95 (*1-885106-34-3*) Wild Adven Pr.
— Meanderings of a Fly Fisherman. limited ed. LC 96-60840. 1996. lthr. 95.00 (*1-885106-35-1*) Wild Adven Pr.
Norman, Sheila M. Make It Happen! Spiritual Principles for Christian Achievement. 220p. (Orig.). 1997. pap. 12.95 (*0-9657718-0-6*) Joy Pubns CA.
Norman, Sue K., jt. auth. see Vincent, Steven.
Norman, Sylva. Flight of the Skylark: The Development of Shelley's Reputation. LC 54-5932. (Illus.). 338p. reprint ed. 104.80 (*0-8357-9726-0*, 201099600073) Bks Demand.
Norman, Sylva, ed. Contemporary Essays: Nineteen Thirty-Three. LC 68-29235. (Essay Index Reprint Ser.). 1977. reprint ed. 19.95 (*0-8369-0746-9*) Ayer.
Norman, Teresa. The African-American Baby Name Book. LC 98-124014. 288p. 1998. pap. 12.00 (*0-425-15939-6*) Berkley Pub.
— Names Through the Ages. (Orig.). 1999. pap. 15.00 (*0-425-16877-8*) Berkley Pub.
— A World of Baby Names. 592p. 1996. pap. 14.95 (*0-399-51948-3*, Perigee Bks) Berkley Pub.
Norman, Terry L. Just Tell the Truth: Questions Families Ask When Gay Married Men Come Out. 175p. 1998. pap. 14.95 (*0-9664796-0-2*) Prehension Pubns.
Norman, Theodore A., jt. auth. see Wu, C. Thomas.
Norman, Tracey, jt. auth. see Eaton, Timothy A.
Norman, Trevor R., jt. ed. see Burrows, Graham D.
Norman, Trude S. One Word at a Time. 256p. 1998. pap. 16.95 (*1-889734-01-2*) Cock-a-Hoop.
Norman, V. D., jt. auth. see Dixit, Avinash K.
Norman, Van. Raven - Johnson: Understanding Biology Test Bank. 512p. 1991. pap. 100.00 (*0-8016-4692-8*) Mosby Inc.
Norman, Victor. Victor Norman - A Life in Music - A Lifetime of Learning: An Autobiography. deluxe ed. Norman, Bob, ed. 176p. 1999. pap. 17.95 (*0-9673239-0-8*) Baybery Desg Co LLC.
Norman, W. H., tr. see Akutagawa, Ryunosuke.
Norman, W. J. Taking Freedom Too Seriously? An Essay on Analytic & Post-Analytic Political Philosophy. LC 91-9677. (Political Theory & Political Philosophy Ser.). 200p. 1991. text 10.00 (*0-8153-0137-5*) Garland.
Norman, Wallace, jt. auth. see Chadwick, Annie.
***Norman, Wayne.** Expressions: The Poetic Voice of Wayne Norman. LC 00-90599. (Illus.). 62p. 2000. pap. 12.98 (*1-930449-00-3*) Shoelace Pubng.
Norman, Wayne, jt. ed. see Kymlicka, Will.
Norman, William A. L. A. T. A Multiple Murder Story. LC 95-90074. 270p. 1998. 16.95 (*0-533-11459-4*) Vantage.
Norman, Winifred L. & Patterson, Lily. Lewis Latimer: Scientist. Huggins, Nathan I., ed. LC 93-185. (Black Americans of Achievement Ser.). (Illus.). 124p. (J). (gr. 5 up). 1994. lib. bdg. 19.95 (*0-7910-1977-2*) Chelsea Hse.
Normand, C. & Weber, A. Social Health Insurance: A Guidebook for Planning. vii, 136p. 1994. pap. text 12.60 (*0-614-08025-8*, 1930057) World Health.
Normand-Cyrot, D., ed. Perspectives in Control: Theory & Applications. (Illus.). 370p. 1998. 90.00 (*1-85233-042-2*) Spr-Verlag.
Normand, Eugene, ed. see Maimon, Sam B.
Normand, Jacques, ed. see Institute of Medicine Staff.
Normand, Jacques, ed. see National Research Council, Institute of Medicine.
Normand, Laura. The Day the Computers Broke Down. LC 95-43978. (Publish-a-Book Ser.). (Illus.). (J). (gr. 1-6). 1992. lib. bdg. 22.83 (*0-8172-4426-3*) Raintree Steck-V.
— The Day the Computers Broke Down. (Publish-a-Book Ser.). (Illus.). 28p. (J). (gr. k-7). 1997. pap. 5.95 (*0-8172-7213-5*) Raintree Steck-V.
Normand, Lawrence & Roberts, Gareth, eds. Witchcraft in Early Modern Scotland: King James' Demonology & the North Berwick Witches. (Illus.). 300p. 1998. pap. text 26.95 (*0-85989-388-X*) Univ Exeter Pr.
Normandale College, English Composition Dept. Staf, ed. see Stephens, Ted.
Normandi, Carol Emery & Roark, Laurelee. It's Not about Food: Change Your Mind, Change Your Life, End Your Obsession with Food & Weight. 240p. 1999. pap. 13.95 (*0-399-52502-5*, Perigee Bks) Berkley Pub.
***Normandi, Carol Emery & Roark, Laurelee.** It's Not about Food: Change Your Mind, Change Your Life, End Your Obsession with Food & Weight. 216p. 2000. reprint ed. 22.00 (*0-7881-9268-X*) DIANE Pub.
Normandi, Jimmy. Finding Gold Nuggets II. Kruesi, Robbie, ed. 80p. (Orig.). 1996. pap. text 9.95 (*1-882279-06-9*) Whites Elect.
Normandin, Christine, ed. see Lelooska, Chief.
Normann, Bob Von, see Von Normann, Bob.
Normann, Francine & Gorman, Maureen. How to Create, Prepare & Deliver Business Presentations. 164p. 1987. ring bd. 50.95 (*1-55645-438-4*, 438) Busn Legal Reports.
Normann, H. & Mensch, Hermann. Politisches Konversations-Lexikon. (GER.). iv, 336p. 1979. reprint ed. write for info. (*3-487-06854-0*) G Olms Pubs.

An Asterisk (*) at the beginning of an entry indicates that the title is appearing for the first time.

Normann, Richard. Management for Growth. LC 77-2839. (Wiley-Interscience Publications). 216p. reprint ed. pap. 67.00 (*0-7837-1888-8*, 204208900001) Bks Demand.

— Service Management: Strategy & Leadership in Service Business. 2nd ed. LC 90-43731. 202p. 1991. 115.00 (*0-471-92885-2*) Wiley.

Normann, Richard & Ramirez, Rafael. Designing Interactive Strategy: From Value Chain to Value Constellation. LC 94-7850. 180p. 1994. 109.95 (*0-471-95086-6*) Wiley.

Normann, Richard, jt. auth. see Wikstrom, Solveig.

Normann, Richard, jt. ed. see Wikstrom, Solveig.

Normann, Richard A. Principles of Bioinstrumentation. LC 88-5893. 576p. 1988. text 99.95 (*0-471-60514-X*) Wiley.

Normann, Richard A. & Ramirez, Rafael. Designing Interactive Strategy: From Value Chain to Value Constellation. LC 98-232697. (Illus.). 184p. 1998. pap. 54.95 (*0-471-98607-0*) Wiley.

Normann, Roderick De, see De Normann, Roderick.

Normano, J. F. The Struggle for South America: Economy & Ideology. 1977. lib. bdg. 59.95 (*0-8490-3067-6*) Gordon Pr.

Normano, Joao F. Brazil: A Study of Economic Types. LC 67-29551. 1935. 30.00 (*0-8196-0208-6*) Biblo.

— The Japanese in South America: An Introductory Survey with Special Reference to Peru. LC 75-30075. (Institute of Pacific Relations Ser.). reprint ed. 29.50 (*0-404-59550-2*) AMS Pr.

Normansell, D. E. The Principles & Practice of Diagnostic Immunology. 149p. 1994. 89.95 (*0-471-18566-3*, Wiley-VCH) Wiley.

Normansell, David E. The Principles & Practice of Diagnostic Immunology. LC 94-3583. (Analytical Techniques in Clinical Chemistry & Laboratory Medicine Ser.). 1994. 60.00 (*1-56081-534-5*, Wiley-VCH) Wiley.

Normansell, David E., jt. auth. see Folds, James D.

Normantoe, T., jt. auth. see Klepsch, E.

Normanton, Helena, ed. Trial of Alfred Arthur Rouse, No. 1. 2nd ed. (Notable British Trials Ser.). xlviii, 316p. 1995. reprint ed. 110.00 (*1-56169-177-1*) Gaunt.

***Normark, Don.** Chavez Ravine, 1949: A Los Angeles Story. LC 99-18240. 144p. 1999. 29.95 (*0-8118-2534-5*) Chronicle Bks.

Norment, Christopher. In the North of Our Lives: A Year in the Wilderness of Northern Canada. LC 89-50873. (Illus.). 264p. 1989. 21.95 (*0-89272-269-X*) Down East.

Norment, Lisa. Once upon a Time in Junior High. 128p. (J). (gr. 4-6). 1994. pap. 2.95 (*0-590-45287-8*) Scholastic Inc.

Normile, Christine, ed. see Comer, Lauren.

Normile, Dwight. Gymnastics. (How to Play the All-Star Way Ser.). (J). 1997. pap. text 5.95 (*0-8172-6855-3*) Raintree Steck-V.

Normile, Dwight. GymnasToons. LC 98-90553. (Illus.). 100p. 1998. pap. 11.95 (*0-9666104-0-7*) P Ziert Assocs.

Normile, Patti. Following Francis of Assisi: A Spirituality for Daily Living. 128p. (Orig.). 1996. pap. 7.95 (*0-86716-240-6*, B2406) St Anthony Mess Pr.

***Normile, Patti.** To Live as Francis Lived: A Guide for Secular Franciscans. 2000. pap. 12.95 (*0-86716-396-8*) St Anthony Mess Pr.

Normile, Patti. Visiting the Sick: A Guide for Parish Ministers. 139p. 1992. pap. 6.95 (*0-86716-150-7*) St Anthony Mess Pr.

Norminton, E. J., jt. auth. see Kreyszig, Erwin.

Normore, C. Late Medieval Philosophy. 1999. pap. 60.00 (*0-8133-2461-0*); pap. 24.00 (*0-8133-2462-9*) Westview.

Nornang, Ngawang, jt. ed. see Goldstein, Melvyn C.

Nornes, Abe Mark & Yukio, Fukushima, eds. Dialogue of Violence: Filmmaking in World War II's Pacific Theater, Vol. 1. LC 92-40162. (Studies in Film & Video). 292p. 1994. pap. text 20.00 (*3-7186-0562-7*) Gordon & Breach.

Noro, K. & Brown, O., Jr., eds. Human Factors in Organizational Design & Management, No. 3: Proceedings of the 3rd International Symposium, Kyoto, Japan, 18-21 July, 1990. 514p. 1990. 178.50 (*0-444-88784-9*, North Holland) Elsevier.

Noro, Kageyu, ed. Productivity in Japan. (Ergonomics Special Issue Ser.: Vol. 28, No. 6). 1985. pap. 23.00 (*0-85066-986-3*) Taylor & Francis.

— Quality Control in Japan. (Ergonomics Special Issue Ser.: Vol. 27, No. 7). 102p. 1984. pap. 20.00 (*0-85066-992-8*) Taylor & Francis.

— The Science of Seating. 250p. 1994. 99.00 (*0-85066-802-6*, Pub. by Tay Francis Ltd) Taylor & Francis.

Noro, Kageyu, jt. ed. see Imada, A.

Noronha, Durval. Legal Dictionary. (ENG & POR.). 510p. 1993. 175.00 (*0-7859-9549-8*); 195.00 incl. audio compact disk (*0-7859-9550-1*) Fr & Eur.

Noronha, Ligia, jt. auth. see Warhurst, Alyson.

Noronha, Shonan. Careers in Communications. 2nd ed. LC 98-30397. (Professional Careers Ser.). 200p. 1998. 17.95 (*0-8442-6317-6*, 63176, VGM Career); pap. 13.95 (*0-8442-6318-4*, 63184, VGM Career) NTC Contemp Pub Co.

— Opportunities in Television & Video Careers. LC 97-48584. (Opportunities in...Ser.). (Illus.). 160p. 1998. 14.95 (*0-8442-2308-5*, 23085, VGM Career); pap. 11.95 (*0-8442-2309-3*, 23093, VGM Career) NTC Contemp Pub Co.

Noronha, Shonan F. Careers in Communications. 208p. 1993. pap. 12.95 (*0-8442-6116-5*, VGM Career) NTC Contemp Pub Co.

— Careers in Communications. LC 93-25152. (VGM Professional Careers Ser.). (Illus.). 150p. 1993. 17.95 (*0-8442-4182-2*, VGM Career); pap. 13.95 (*0-8442-4183-0*, VGM Career) NTC Contemp Pub Co.

— Careers in Communications. 208p. 1995. text 16.95 (*0-8442-6115-7*, VGM Career) NTC Contemp Pub Co.

— Opportunities in Technical Communications. LC 93-20679. (Opportunities in...Ser.). 1995. 13.95 (*0-8442-4074-5*, VGM Career); pap. 10.95 (*0-8442-4075-3*, VGM Career) NTC Contemp Pub Co.

— Opportunities in Television & Video Careers. (VGM Career Planner Ser.). (Illus.). 160p. 1992. 13.95 (*0-8442-6491-1*, VGM Career) NTC Contemp Pub Co.

— Opportunities in Television & Video Careers. (VGM Career Planner Ser.). (Illus.). 160p. 1993. pap. 10.95 (*0-8442-6493-8*, VGM Career) NTC Contemp Pub Co.

— Television & Video. (Opportunities In . . . Ser.). (Illus.). 160p. pap. 12.95 (*0-8442-4091-5*, 297OITV&V, VGM Career) NTC Contemp Pub Co.

— Television & Video. (Opportunities in...Ser.). (Illus.). 128p. 1993. pap. 7.95 (*0-8442-8682-6*, VGM Career) NTC Contemp Pub Co.

Noronha, Shonan F., et al. Television & Video. (Opportunities in...Ser.). (Illus.). 160p. 1995. 14.95 (*0-8442-4090-7*) NTC Contemp Pub Co.

Norpoth, Helmut. Confidence Regained: Economics, Mrs. Thatcher, & the British Voter. 248p. (C). 1992. text 49.50 (*0-472-10333-4*, 10333) U of Mich Pr.

Norpoth, Helmut, et al, eds. Economics & Politics: The Calculus of Support. 304p. (C). 1991. text 49.50 (*0-472-10186-2*, 10186) U of Mich Pr.

Norpoth, Helmut, jt. auth. see Iversen, Gudmund R.

Norquay, Glenda. Hear the Call: An Anthology of Writings from the Women's Suffrage Campaign. LC 94-43134. 1995. text 79.95 (*0-7190-3975-4*) Manchester Univ Pr.

***Norquay, Glenda.** R. L. Stevenson on Fiction: An Anthology of Literary & Critical Essays. LC 99-488297. 224p. 1999. pap. 23.00 (*0-7486-0777-3*, Pub. by Edinburgh U Pr) Col U Pr.

Norquay, Paul, jt. auth. see Lawrence, Trevor.

Norquist, Ellwood W. We Are One: A Challenge to Traditional Christianity. 176p. 1995. pap. 14.95 (*0-9646995-2-4*) CC Publng.

Norquist, Enerst. Our Paradise: A GI's War Diary. LC 88-61934. (Illus.). 385p. 1989. 19.95 (*0-9606240-9-0*) Pearl-Win.

Norquist, Grover G. Rock the House. Jones, Gordon & Gee, Charles G., eds. 468p. 1995. 25.00 (*0-06-457860-7*) VYTIS Pub.

— Rock the House. rev. unabridged ed. VYTIS Publishing Company Staff, ed. LC 95-60040. (Illus.). 460p. 1995. pap. 9.65 (*0-9645786-0-3*) VYTIS Pub.

Norquist, John O. The Wealth of Cities: Revitalizing the Centers of American Life. 256p. 1999. pap. text 16.00 (*0-7382-0134-0*, Pub. by Perseus Pubng) HarpC.

Norquist, Richard. A Typically Atypical Day. 1985. pap. 3.50 (*0-87129 184-3*, T60) Dramatic Pub.

Norquist, Warren E., jt. auth. see Elderkin, Kenton W.

Norr, A. K., ed. Adaptive, Multilevel, & Hierarchical Computational Strategies. (AMD Ser.: Vol. 157). 157p. 1992. 72.50 (*0-7918-1134-4*, G00778) ASME.

Norr, Dieter, jt. auth. see De Robertis, Francesco M.

Norr, Martin. The Taxation of Corporations & Shareholders. 226p. 1982. 42.00 (*90-6544-015-1*) Kluwer Academic.

Norr, Rita & Tumbarello, Audrey. The Literate Puzzler. LC 94-19668. (Illus.). 128p. 1994. pap. 5.95 (*0-8069-0706-1*) Sterling.

Norrander, Barbara. Super Tuesday: Regional Politics & Presidential Primaries. LC 91-31263. (Illus.). 248p. 1992. text 29.95 (*0-8131-1773-9*) U Pr of Ky.

— Understanding Public Opinion. LC 96-23904. 331p. (YA). 1997. pap. 26.95 (*1-56802-156-9*); text 39.95 (*1-56802-153-4*) Congr Quarterly.

Norrbom, Allen L., jt. auth. see Aluja, Martin.

Norrbom, C. E. Mobility & Transport for Elderly & Disabled Persons, Vol. 13. (Transportation Studies). xv, 1152p. 1991. text 638.00 (*2-88124-763-6*) Gordon & Breach.

Norrby, Erling, ed. Immunochemistry of AIDS. (Chemical Immunology Ser.: Vol. 56). (Illus.). x, 168p. 1993. 161.75 (*3-8055-5655-1*) S Karger.

Norrby, Erling, et al, eds. Vaccines, '94: Modern Approaches to New Vaccines Including Prevention of AIDS. LC QR0189.V27. (Vaccines Ser.: Vol. 94). 423p. 1994. reprint ed. pap. 131.20 (*0-608-00717-X*, 206149100009) Bks Demand.

Norrby, S. R., ed. New Antiviral Strategies. (Frontiers of Infectious Diseases Ser.). (Illus.). 288p. 1989. pap. text 53.00 (*0-443-04166-0*) Church.

— New Insights into the Clinical Profile of Norfloxacin: Journal: European Urology, Vol. 17, Suppl. 1. (Illus.). iv, 52p. 1990. pap. 17.50 (*3-8055-5198-3*) S Karger.

Norreklit, Lennart. Concepts: Their Nature & Significance for Metaphysics & Epistemology. (Odense Studies in Philosophy: No. 2). 226p. (Orig.). 1973. pap. 27.50 (*87-7492-079-0*, Pub. by Odense Universitets Forlag) Coronet Bks.

***Norrell, Julia J., et al.** Myth, Memory & Imagination: Universal Themes in the Life & Culture of the South. (Illus.). 84p. 1999. pap. 20.00 (*0-938983-13-X*) U of SC Pr.

Norrell, Robert J. The Alabama Journey: State History & Geography. LC 98-225188. (Illus.). 299p. (J). (gr. 4). 1998. 39.95 (*1-882700-02-3*) Yellowhammer.

— The Alabama Story: State History & Geography. (Illus.). 304p. (J). (gr. 4). 1993. 22.95 (*1-882700-00-7*) Yellowhammer.

— James Bowron: The Autobiography of a New South Industrialist. LC 91-9847. 319p. 1991. reprint ed. pap. 98.90 (*0-608-02070-2*, 206272300003) Bks Demand.

— A Promising Field: Engineering at Alabama, 1837-1987. LC 89-37626. (Illus.). 278p. reprint ed. pap. 86.20 (*0-608-09237-1*, 205274100005) Bks Demand.

— Reaping the Whirlwind: The Civil Rights Movement in Tuskegee. LC 98-29257. (Illus.). 280p. 1998. pap. 16.95 (*0-8078-4740-2*) U of NC Pr.

— We Want Jobs! A Story of the Great Depression. LC 92-18082. (Stories of America Ser.). (Illus.). 40p. (J). (gr. 2-5). 1992. pap. 5.95 (*0-8114-8069-0*); lib. bdg. 25.68 (*0-8114-7229-9*) Raintree Steck-V.

Norrell, Stephen A., jt. auth. see Messley, Karen.

Norretranders, Tor. Mark the World. 400p. 1999. pap. 14.95 (*0-14-023012-2*, PuffinBks) Peng Put Young Read.

— Mark World. Sydenham, Jonathan, tr. LC 97-39580. 400p. 1999. text 27.95 (*0-7139-9182-8*) Viking Penguin.

— User Illusion: Cutting Consciousness Down to Size. 400p. 1998. 29.95 (*0-670-87579-1*, Viking) Viking Penguin.

Norrgard, Julia M., jt. auth. see Norrgard, Lee E.

Norrgard, Lee E. & DeMars, Jo. Making End-of-Life Decisions. LC 92-28781. (Choices & Challenges Ser.). 200p. 1992. lib. bdg. 45.00 (*0-87436-613-5*) ABC-CLIO.

Norrgard, Lee E. & Norrgard, Julia M. Consumer Fraud: A Reference Handbook. LC 98-42276. (Contemporary World Issues Ser.). 352p. 1998. lib. bdg. 45.00 (*0-87436-991-6*) ABC-CLIO.

***Norri, Marja-Riitta.** Finland: 20th Century Architecture. (Illus.). 2000. 100.00 (*3-7913-2294-X*) Prestel Pub NY.

Norrick, Neal R. Conversational Joking: Forms & Functions of Humor in Everyday Talk. LC 92-19471. 192p. 1993. 35.00 (*0-253-34111-6*) Ind U Pr.

***Norrick, Neal R.** Conversational Narrative: Storytelling in Everyday Talk. LC 00-40333. (Amsterdam Studies in the Theory & History of Linguistic Science). 2000. write for info. (*1-55619-981-3*) J Benjamins Pubng Co.

Norrick, Neal R. How Proverbs Mean: Semantic Studies in English Proverbs. (Trends in Linguistics Ser.: No. 27). xii, 228p. 1985. 65.40 (*0-89925-037-8*) Mouton.

— Semiotic Principles in Semantic Theory. (Current Issues in Linguistic Theory Ser.: No. 20). xiii, 252p. 1981. 59.00 (*90-272-3513-9*) J Benjamins Pubng Co.

***Norrie, Alan.** Punishment, Responsibility & Justice: A Relational Critique. (Oxford Monographs on Criminal Law & Justice). 256p. 2000. text 65.00 (*0-19-825956-5*) OUP.

Norrie, Alan, ed. Closure or Critique: New Directions in Legal Theory. (Edinburgh Law & Society Ser.). 256p. 1994. 60.00 (*0-7486-0445-6*, Pub. by Edinburgh U Pr) Col U Pr.

Norrie, Alan W. Law, Ideology & Punishment: Historical Critique of the Liberal Ideal of Criminal Justice. 244p. (C). 1990. lib. bdg. 108.00 (*0-7923-1013-6*, Pub. by Kluwer Academic) Kluwer Academic.

Norrie, Douglas H., jt. ed. see Six, H. W.

Norrie, Ian. Next Time Round in Provence: The Vaucluse & the Bouchers-du-Rhone. LC 97-125767. (Illus.). 224p. (Orig.). 1996. pap. text 14.95 (*1-85410-239-7*, Pub. by Aurum Pr) London Brdge.

— Next Time Round in the Dordogne. (Illus.). 208p. (Orig.). 1997. pap. text 14.95 (*1-85410-394-6*, Pub. by Aurum Pr) London Brdge.

— Next Time Round in Tuscany. 1998. pap. 17.95 (*1-85410-541-8*, Pub. by Aurum Pr) London Brdge.

Norrie, Kenneth M. Family Planning & the Law. 220p. 1991. text 78.95 (*1-85521-035-5*, Pub. by Dartmth Pub) Ashgate Pub Co.

***Norrie, M.** Dear Boy, Dear Girl. 1998. text 35.00 (*0-09-479190-2*, Pub. by Constable & Co) Trafalgar.

Norrington, A. L. Blackwell's Eighteen Seventy-Nine to Nineteen Seventy-Nine. (Illus.). 191p. 1983. 20.00 (*0-946344-00-0*, Pub. by B H Blackwell) NA Blackwell.

Norrington, A. L., ed. see Clough, Arthur H.

Norrington, David C. To Preach or Not to Preach: The Church's Urgent Question. xiv, 129p. 1996. reprint ed. pap. 14.99 (*0-85364-697-X*, Pub. by Paternoster Pub) OM Literature.

Norrington, Robert. Sketching Harbours & Boats. LC 00-500552. (Illus.). 48p. 1999. pap. 9.95 (*0-304-35117-2*, Pub. by Cassell) Cassell.

Norrington, Ruth, ed. My Dearest Minette: Letters Between Charles II & His Sister. LC 96-224077. (Illus.). 240p. 1996. 39.95 (*0-7206-0991-7*, Pub. by P Owen Ltd) Dufour.

Norris. The Adventures of Antar: An Early Arab Epic Approaches to Arabic. 1980. 42.00 (*0-85668-161-X*, Pub. by Aris & Phillips) David Brown.

— Computer Math Basic Programming. 31.50 (*0-669-12392-7*) HTH.

— Crafts for Young Children. (Illus.). 80p. (J). (ps-1). 1997. pap., teacher ed. 7.95 (*1-55799-620-2*, 720) Evan-Moor Edu Pubs.

— Customer Oriented Selling. (General Business & Business Education Ser.). 1995. pap. 13.00 (*0-8273-6256-0*) Delmar.

— Daily Language Review 1. (Illus.). 112p. (J). (gr. 1-2). 1998. pap., teacher ed. 14.95 (*1-55799-655-5*, 579) Evan-Moor Edu Pubs.

***Norris.** E-Business Essentials. 312p. 2000. pap. 54.95 (*0-471-85203-1*) Wiley.

Norris. Eve. 1999. write for info. (*0-316-88888-5*) Little.

— Fifty Little Stories to Read. (Illus.). 112p. (J). (ps-1). 1998. pap., teacher ed. 14.95 (*1-55799-668-7*, 743) Evan-Moor Edu Pubs.

— Folk Art Around the World. (Illus.). 80p. (J). (gr. 1-6). 1997. pap., teacher ed. 7.95 (*1-55799-621-0*, 721) Evan-Moor Edu Pubs.

— Following Directions. (Illus.). 112p. (J). (ps-1). 1998. pap., teacher ed. 14.95 (*1-55799-663-6*, 738) Evan-Moor Edu Pubs.

— Grammar & Punctuation. (Illus.). 88p. (J). (gr. 1-2). 1997. pap., teacher ed. 14.95 (*1-55799-598-2*, 479) Evan-Moor Edu Pubs.

— How to Use Logs & Journals Across the Curriculum. (Illus.). 64p. (J). (gr. 1-6). 1997. pap., teacher ed. 6.95 (*1-55799-602-4*, 577) Evan-Moor Edu Pubs.

— Important Firsts. (Illus.). 64p. (J). (gr. k-2). 1997. pap., teacher ed. 11.95 (*1-55799-634-2*, 645) Evan-Moor Edu Pubs.

Norris. Information Technology text. write for info. (*0-471-49044-X*) Wiley.

Norris. Keeping Healthy (Science) (Illus.). 32p. (J). (ps-1). 1997. pap., teacher ed. 2.95 (*1-55799-498-6*, 4100) Evan-Moor Edu Pubs.

— Learning with Nursery Rhymes. (Illus.). 112p. (J). (ps-1). 1998. pap., teacher ed. 14.95 (*1-55799-666-0*, 741) Evan-Moor Edu Pubs.

— Nature's Ecosystems. (Illus.). 32p. (J). (gr. 4-6). 1997. pap., teacher ed. 2.95 (*1-55799-523-0*, 4125) Evan-Moor Edu Pubs.

— New Idols of the Cave: On the Limits of Anti-Realism. LC 96-46264. 1997. 69.95 (*0-7190-5092-8*, Pub. by Manchester Univ Pr) St Martin.

— Obstetric Anesthesia. (Illus.). 600p. 1993. text 99.00 (*0-397-51115-9*) Lppncott W & W.

— Phonemic Awareness. (Illus.). 112p. (J). (ps-1). 1998. pap., teacher ed. 14.95 (*1-55799-665-2*, 740) Evan-Moor Edu Pubs.

— Read & Understand Stories & Activities. (Illus.). 144p. (J). (gr. k). 1997. pap., teacher ed. 12.95 (*1-55799-626-1*, 637) Evan-Moor Edu Pubs.

— Read & Understand Stories & Activities. (Illus.). 144p. (J). (gr. 1-2). 1997. pap., teacher ed. 12.95 (*1-55799-627-X*, 638) Evan-Moor Edu Pubs.

— Saving the Earth. (Illus.). 64p. (J). (gr. k-2). 1997. pap., teacher ed. 11.95 (*1-55799-632-6*, 643) Evan-Moor Edu Pubs.

— Taking Responsibility. (Illus.). 64p. (J). (gr. k-2). 1997. pap., teacher ed. 11.95 (*1-55799-633-4*, 644) Evan-Moor Edu Pubs.

— Thinking Skills. (Illus.). 88p. (J). (gr. 1-2). 1997. pap., teacher ed. 14.95 (*1-55799-636-9*, 482) Evan-Moor Edu Pubs.

— Total Area Network Design. LC 99-37649. 348p. 2000. 69.95 (*0-471-85195-7*) Wiley.

— Women & Politics: Harpercollins Political Pamphleteer. (Political Pampheleteer Ser.). (C). 1997. pap. text 7.86 (*0-673-99779-0*) Addson-Wesley Educ.

— Writing Fabulous Sentences & Paragraphs. (Illus.). 112p. (J). (gr. 4-6). 1997. pap., teacher ed. 9.95 (*1-55799-601-6*, 575) Evan-Moor Edu Pubs.

Norris & Davis. Fun with Air & Water. (Illus.). 32p. (J). (ps-1). 1996. pap., teacher ed. 2.95 (*1-55799-494-3*, 4096) Evan-Moor Edu Pubs.

— Learning about Building. (Illus.). 48p. (J). (ps-1). 1995. pap., teacher ed. 5.95 (*1-55799-395-5*, 850) Evan-Moor Edu Pubs.

— Learning about Changes. (Illus.). 48p. (J). (ps-1). 1995. pap., teacher ed. 5.95 (*1-55799-397-1*, 852) Evan-Moor Edu Pubs.

— Learning about Light & Shadow. (Illus.). 48p. (J). (ps-1). 1995. pap., teacher ed. 5.95 (*1-55799-396-3*, 851) Evan-Moor Edu Pubs.

— Learning about Movement. (Illus.). 48p. (J). (ps-1). 1995. pap., teacher ed. 5.95 (*1-55799-394-7*, 849) Evan-Moor Edu Pubs.

— My Community. (Illus.). 48p. (J). (gr. 1-3). 1996. pap., teacher ed. 9.95 (*1-55799-566-4*, 552) Evan-Moor Edu Pubs.

— Native Americans. (Illus.). 48p. (J). (gr. 1-3). 1996. pap., teacher ed. 9.95 (*1-55799-575-3*, 561) Evan-Moor Edu Pubs.

Norris & Evans. Holidays & Celebrations. (How to Make Books with Children Ser.). (Illus.). 160p. (J). (gr. 1-6). 1997. pap., teacher ed. 16.95 (*1-55799-605-9*, 578) Evan-Moor Edu Pubs.

— Learning about Air. (Illus.). 48p. (J). (ps-1). 1995. pap., teacher ed. 5.95 (*1-55799-392-0*, 847) Evan-Moor Edu Pubs.

— Learning about Machines. (Illus.). 48p. (J). (ps-1). 1995. pap., teacher ed. 5.95 (*1-55799-393-9*, 848) Evan-Moor Edu Pubs.

— Literature & Writing Connections. (How to Make Books with Children Ser.). (Illus.). 160p. (J). (gr. 1-6). Date not set. pap., teacher ed. 16.95 (*1-55799-578-8*, 777) Evan-Moor Edu Pubs.

— Read a Book - Make a Book. (How to Make Books with Children Ser.). (Illus.). 160p. (J). (gr. 1-6). 1997. pap., teacher ed. 16.95 (*1-55799-579-6*, 778) Evan-Moor Edu Pubs.

Norris & Lorseyedi. Seasons Through the Year. (Illus.). 48p. (J). (ps-1). 1996. pap., teacher ed. 9.95 (*1-55799-562-1*, 548) Evan-Moor Edu Pubs.

Norris & McMahon. Helping Hands. (Illus.). 48p. (J). (ps-1). 1996. pap., teacher ed. 9.95 (*1-55799-561-3*, 547) Evan-Moor Edu Pubs.

— My Neighborhood. (Illus.). 48p. (J). (ps-1). 1996. pap., teacher ed. 9.95 (*1-55799-560-5*, 546) Evan-Moor Edu Pubs.

Norris & Supancich. The World Is Our Neighborhood. (Illus.). 48p. (J). (gr. 1-3). 1996. pap., teacher ed. 9.95 (*1-55799-563-X*, 549) Evan-Moor Edu Pubs.

Norris, et al. Habitats - Pond & Stream. (Illus.). 48p. (J). (gr. 1-3). 1996. pap., teacher ed. 9.95 (*1-55799-568-0*, 554) Evan-Moor Edu Pubs.

— How to Do Science Fair Projects. (Illus.). 32p. (J). (gr. 4-6). 1996. pap., teacher ed. 2.95 (*1-55799-526-5*, 4128) Evan-Moor Edu Pubs.

— Methods in Microbiology Vol. 29: Automation. 500p. (C). 1998. 99.95 (*0-12-521527-4*) Acad Pr.

Norris, jt. auth. see Moore.

Norris, Ann. On the Go. LC 90-33842. (Illus.). 32p. (J). 1990. 16.00 (*0-688-06336-5*) Lothrop.

Norris, Anne & Douglas, Caroline. Driving. (Illus.). 1990. pap. 21.00 (*0-85131-368-X*, Pub. by J A Allen) St Mut.

— Driving. (Allen Photographic Guides Ser.: No. 18). (Illus.). 24p. 2000. pap. 10.95 (*0-85131-726-X*, Pub. by J A Allen) Trafalgar.
— Harnessing Up. (Allen Photographic Guides Ser.). (Illus.). 24p. 2000. pap. 10.95 (*0-85131-657-3*, Pub. by J A Allen) Trafalgar.

Norris, Anne, jt. auth. see Pethick, Nancy.

Norris, Annette, jt. auth. see Berry, Ron.

Norris, Anthony C. Computational Chemistry: An Introduction to Numerical Methods. LC 80-41691. 468p. reprint ed. pap. 145.10 (*0-7837-4767-5*, 204452100003) Bks Demand.

Norris, Bob. Check Six! 384p. 1998. mass mkt. 5.99 (*0-06-101353-6*, Harp PBks) HarpC.
— Fly-Off. 352p. 1999. mass mkt. 6.99 (*0-06-101354-4*) HarpC.
— Technical Interview Series. Dean, Becky et al, eds. 46p. 1998. reprint ed. pap. 14.95 (*1-891726-12-9*) Aviation Info.

Norris, Bob & Mortensen, Danny. The Airline Career & Interview Manual. 8th large type rev. ed. (Illus.). 160p. 1998. pap. 27.95 (*0-942397-21-5*) Buckeye Aviat Bk.

Norris, C. C. William Empson & the Philosophy of Literary Criticism. 222p. (C). 1978. text 36.50 (*0-485-11175-6*, Pub. by Athlone Pr) Humanities.

Norris, Carol. OJT Personnel Clerk Resource Materials. 2nd ed. (Gregg Office Job Training Program Ser.). (Illus.). 112p. 1981. text 9.96 (*0-07-047225-4*) McGraw.
— OJT Personnel Clerk Training Manual. 2nd ed. (Gregg Office Job Training Program Ser.). (Illus.). 56p. (gr. 11-12). 1981. pap. text 7.56 (*0-07-047226-2*) McGraw.

Norris, Carolyn B. Island of Silence. 4th ed. LC 83-71342. 238p. 1983. pap. 6.00 (*0-933076-04-5*) Alinda Pr.
— Signs Unseen, Sounds Unheard. 3rd ed. 173p. 1991. 5.00 (*0-933076-02-9*) Alinda Pr.

***Norris, Catherine J.** Magnetic Miracles: Your Guide to the Use of Magnetics for Radiant Health. (Illus.). 192p. 2000. pap. 14.99 (*0-9678931-0-0*) Energy Essentials.

Norris, Charles C. Eastern Upland Shooting. deluxe limited ed. (Illus.). 432p. 1989. lthr. 49.00 (*0-924357-05-3*, 11250-B) Countrysport Pr.

Norris, Charles E., ed. see Cole, Deborah & Demoss, Daniel.

Norris, Charles G. Salt: Or, the Education of Griffith Adams. A Novel. LC 80-25152. (Lost American Fiction Ser.). 394p. 1981. reprint ed. 21.95 (*0-8093-1011-2*) S Ill U Pr.

Norris, Charles Head. Elementary Structural Analysis: Instructor's Manual to Accompany. 4th ed. (C). 1991. pap. text 23.43 (*0-07-065934-6*) McGraw.

Norris, Charles W. & Waibel-Owen, Jeanne B. Know Your Body: A Family Guide to Sexuality & Fertility. LC 82-60666. (Illus.). 87p. (gr. 6 up). 1982. pap. text 5.95 (*0-87973-658-5*, 658) Our Sunday Visitor.

Norris, Christopher. Abdominal Training. (Illus.). 128p. 1997. pap. write for info. (*0-7136-4585-7*, Pub. by A & C Blk) Midpt Trade.
— Against Relativism: Philosophy of Science, Deconstruction, & Critical Theory. LC 97-4300. 350p. (C). 1997. text 68.95 (*0-631-19864-4*); pap. text 26.95 (*0-631-19865-2*) Blackwell Pubs.
— The Contest of Faculties: Deconstruction, Philosophy & Theory. (Orig.). 1985. 35.00 (*0-416-39930-4*, 9598); pap. 13.95 (*0-416-39940-1*, 9599) Routledge.
— Deconstruction: Theory & Practice. LC 81-22422. 200p. 1982. pap. 13.95 (*0-416-32070-8*, NO. 3660) Routledge.
— Deconstruction: Theory & Practice. 2nd rev. ed. (New Accents Ser.). 190p. (C). 1991. pap. 18.99 (*0-415-06174-1*, A5676) Routledge.
— Deconstruction & the Interests of Theory. LC 88-40546. (Oklahoma Project for Discourse & Theory Ser.: Vol. 4). 256p. (C). 1992. pap. text 15.95 (*0-8061-2388-5*) U of Okla Pr.
— The Deconstructive Turn: Essays in the Rhetoric of Philosophy. LC 83-22141. 201p. 1984. pap. 12.95 (*0-416-36140-4*, NO. 4063) Routledge.
— Derrida. LC 87-22922. 272p. 1988. pap. 16.50 (*0-674-19824-7*) HUP.
— Jerusalem. (Great Cities Ser.). (Illus.). 96p. 1999. 20.00 (*1-85995-558-4*) Parkstone Pr.

***Norris, Christopher.** Minding the Gap: Epistemology & Philosophy of Science in the Two Traditions. LC 99-86484. 368p. 2000. 39.95 (*1-55849-255-0*) U of Mass Pr.

Norris, Christopher. Paul de Man: Deconstruction & the Critique of Aesthetic Ideology. LC 87-31375. 200p. 1988. pap. text 13.95 (*0-416-01971-4*) Routledge.
— Paul de Man: Deconstruction & the Critique of Aesthetic Ideology. 1988. pap. 14.95 (*0-415-90080-8*) Routledge.

***Norris, Christopher.** Quantum Theory & the Flight from Realism: Philosophical Responses to Quantum Mechanics. LC 99-38146. (Critical Realism--Interventions Ser.). 280p. 1999. pap. 25.99 (*0-415-22322-9*) Routledge.
— Quantum Theory & the Flight from Realism: Philosophical Responses to Quantum Mechanics. LC 99-38146. 280p. (C). 2000. text 85.00 (*0-415-22321-0*) Routledge.

Norris, Christopher. Reclaiming Truth: Contribution to a Critique of Cultural Relativism. LC 96-15885. (Post-Contemporary Interventions Ser.). 272p. 1996. text 49.95 (*0-8223-1882-2*); pap. text 17.95 (*0-8223-1872-5*) Duke.
— Reclaiming Truth: Contribution to a Critique of Cultural Relativism. 244p. 1996. pap. 12.99 (*0-85315-815-0*, Pub. by Lawrence & Wishart) NYU Pr.
— Resources of Realism: Prospect for 'Post-Analytic' Philosophy. LC 97-6416. (Language, Discourse, Society Ser.). 272p. 1997. text 65.00 (*0-312-17551-5*) St Martin.
— Uncritical Theory: Postmodernism, Intellectuals, & the Gulf War. LC 92-12147. 224p. 1992. 30.00 (*0-87023-817-5*); pap. 14.95 (*0-87023-818-3*) U of Mass Pr.
— What's Wrong with Postmodernism: Critical Theory & the Ends of Philosophy. LC 90-38438. (Parallax). 256p. 1991. text 48.50 (*0-8018-4136-4*); pap. text 16.95 (*0-8018-4137-2*) Johns Hopkins.

Norris, Christopher & Benjamin, Andrew. What Is Deconstruction? (Academy Editions Ser.). (Illus.). 56p. 1989. pap. 16.00 (*0-312-02711-7*) St Martin.

Norris, Christopher & Benjamin, Andrew. What Is Deconstruction? (What Is? Ser.). (Illus.). 57p. 1988. pap. 16.00 (*0-85670-961-1*) Wiley.

Norris, Christopher & Mapp, Nigel, eds. William Empson: The Critical Achievement. 329p. (C). 1993. text 64.95 (*0-521-35386-6*) Cambridge U Pr.

***Norris, Christopher M.** Back Stability. LC 99-89545. (Illus.). 256p. 2000. 34.00 (*0-7360-0081-X*) Human Kinetics.
— Complete Guide to Stretching. 1999. pap. 14.95 (*0-7136-4956-9*) A & C Blk.

Norris, Christopher M. Flexibility: Principles & Practice. pap. write for info. (*0-7136-4037-5*, 93303, Pub. by A & C Blk) Midpt Trade.
— Weight Traning. pap. write for info. (*0-7136-3771-4*, 92982, Pub. by A & C Blk) Midpt Trade.

Norris, Chuck. The Secret Power Within: Zen Solutions to Real Problems. LC 96-31801. 192p. 1997. pap. 13.95 (*0-553-06908-X*) Broadway BDD.
— Winning Tournament Karate. Cocoran, John, ed. LC 75-5497. (Japanese Arts Ser.). (Illus.). 1975. pap. text 14.95 (*0-89750-016-4*, 121) Ohara Pubns.

Norris, Clive, et al, eds. CCTV, Surveillance & Social Control. LC 98-71458. 287p. 1998. text 69.95 (*1-84014-126-3*, Pub. by Ashgate Pub) Ashgate Pub Co.

Norris, Clive & Armstrong, Gary. The Maximum Surveillance Society. 224p. 1999. pap. 19.50 (*1-85973-226-7*, Pub. by Berg Pubs) NYU Pr.

***Norris, Clive & Armstrong, Gary.** The Maximum Surveillance Society: The Rise of CCTV. 224p. 1999. 55.00 (*1-85973-221-6*, Pub. by Berg Pubs) NYU Pr.

Norris, Crystal. The Chocolate War: A Study Guide. (Novel-Ties Ser.). (gr. 7-10). 1987. pap. text, teacher ed., student ed. 15.95 (*0-88122-108-2*) Lrn Links.
— The Dark Is Rising: A Study Guide. (Novel-Ties Ser.). (J). (gr. 6-8). 1988. pap. text, teacher ed., student ed. 15.95 (*0-88122-110-4*) Lrn Links.
— A Day No Pigs Would Die: A Study Guide. (Novel-Ties Ser.). (J). (gr. 6-8). 1987. pap. text, teacher ed., student ed. 15.95 (*0-88122-111-2*) Lrn Links.
— Flowers for Algernon: A Study Guide. (Novel-Ties Ser.). (YA). (gr. 9-12). 1985. pap. text, teacher ed. 15.95 (*0-88122-115-5*) Lrn Links.
— Great Expectations: A Study Guide. (Novel-Ties Ser.). (YA). (gr. 9-12). 1987. pap. text, teacher ed. 15.95 (*0-88122-116-3*) Lrn Links.
— I Am the Cheese - Study Guide. Friedland, Joyce & Kessler, Rikki, eds. (Novel-Ties Ser.). (J). (gr. 6-8). 1993. pap. text 15.95 (*0-88122-101-5*) Lrn Links.
— Julie of the Wolves - Study Guide. Friedland, Joyce & Kessler, Rikki, eds. (Novel-Ties Ser.). (J). (gr. 4-6). 1993. pap. text 15.95 (*0-88122-099-X*) Lrn Links.
— Julius Caesar - Study Guide. Friedland, Joyce & Kessler, Rikki, eds. (Novel-Ties Ser.). (YA). (gr. 9-12). 1993. pap. text 15.95 (*0-88122-102-3*) Lrn Links.
— The Light in the Forest - Study Guide. Friedland, Joyce & Kessler, Rikki, eds. (Novel-Ties Ser.). (J). (gr. 6-8). 1993. pap. text 15.95 (*0-88122-117-1*) Lrn Links.
— One Flew over the Cuckoo's Nest. Friedland, Joyce & Kessler, Rikki, eds. (Novel-Ties Ser.). (YA). (gr. 9-12). 1993. pap. text, student ed. 15.95 (*0-88122-121-X*) Lrn Links.
— Ordinary People - Study Guide. Friedland, Joyce & Kessler, Rikki, eds. (Novel-Ties Ser.). (YA). (gr. 9-12). 1993. pap. text 15.95 (*0-88122-122-8*) Lrn Links.
— Shane. Friedland, Joyce & Kessler, Rikki, eds. (Novel-Ties Ser.). (YA). (gr. 9-12). 1993. pap. text, student ed. 15.95 (*0-88122-129-5*) Lrn Links.

Norris, Curt. Ghosts I Have Known. 154p. pap. 5.95 (*0-9628738-5-3*) Jones Riv Pr.
— Ghosts I Have Known: And Other True Tales of Suspense. 160p. 1998. pap. 9.95 (*1-58066-006-1*, Covered Brdge Pr) Douglas Charles Ltd.
— Little-Known Mysteries of New England: True Crime Stories from the Past. Johnson, Doris M., ed. LC 92-70661. (Illus.). 160p. (Orig.). 1992. pap. 10.00 (*0-9628738-1-0*) Jones Riv Pr.
— Mr. Spooner's in the Well: And Other Massachusetts Mysteries. LC 97-24785. 160p. (Orig.). 1997. pap. 12.95 (*0-924771-90-9*, Covered Brdge Pr) Douglas Charles Ltd.
— Tale of the Talking Potato: And More Connecticut Mysteries. 160p. 2000. pap. 12.95 (*0-924771-89-5*, Covered Brdge Pr) Douglas Charles Ltd.

Norris, D. A. Immune Mechanisms in Cutaneous Disease. 2nd rev. ed. (Illus.). Date not set. text. write for info. (*0-8247-9498-2*) Dekker.

Norris, D. O. & Jones, R. E. Hormones & Reproduction in Fishes, Amphibians & Reptiles. LC 87-6944. (Illus.). 590p. (C). 1987. text 140.00 (*0-306-42551-3*, Kluwer Plenum) Kluwer Academic.

Norris, Dan. Violence Against Social Workers. 144p. 1990. 34.95 (*1-85302-041-9*) Taylor & Francis.

***Norris, David.** Introducing Joyce. (Illus.). 176p. 2000. pap. 11.95 (*1-84046-119-5*) Totem Bks.

Norris, David. Teach Yourself Serbo-Croat. (ENG & SER.). 1993. pap. 18.95 (*0-7859-1062-X*, 0-340-568038); pap. 29.95 incl. audio (*0-7859-1063-8*, 0-340-568046) Fr & Eur.
— Teach Yourself Serbo-Croat: A Complete Course for Beginners. (CRO., Illus.). 272p. 1995. pap. 14.95 (*0-8442-3826-0*, Teach Yrslf) NTC Contemp Pub Co.

Norris, David. Teach Yourself Serbo-Croat Complete Course. 272p. 1995. 27.95 incl. audio (*0-8442-3872-4*, Teach Yrslf) NTC Contemp Pub Co.

Norris, David, jt. ed. see Beja, Morris.

Norris, David A. In the Wake of the Balkan Myth. LC 99-11217. 182p. 1999. text 69.95 (*0-312-22175-4*) St Martin.
— Plan to Be Spiritual: The Wonderful Blessing of God's Direction & God's Power. (Illus.). 31p. 1987. pap. 1.95 (*0-943177-05-7*) Heartland Pr.

Norris, David A., ed. Immune Mechanisms in Cutaneous Disease. (Immunology Ser.: Vol. 46). (Illus.). 848p. 1989. text 260.00 (*0-8247-7919-3*) Dekker.

Norris, David O. Vertebrate Endocrinology. 2nd ed. LC 84-19425. 517p. reprint ed. pap. 160.30 (*0-7837-2734-8*, 204311400006) Bks Demand.

Norris, David O., ed. Vertebrate Endocrinology. 3rd ed. (Illus.). 634p. (C). 1996. text 69.95 (*0-12-521670-X*) Acad Pr.

Norris, Dean. Guitar Scale Theory. 28p. 1997. 8.95 (*0-9626973-0-3*, DN 10000) Taxi Design.

Norris, Dean M. Advanced Scale Improvisation. 76p. 1991. 14.95 (*0-9631368-0-1*) Devin Pubns.
— Guitar Chord Studies. (Illus.). 63p. 1992. pap. write for info. (*0-9631368-1-X*) Devin Pubns.

Norris, Deborah. Clinical Research Coordinator Handbook. 2nd ed. (Illus.). 74p. 2000. pap. 34.95 (*0-937548-43-X*) Plexus Pub.

Norris, Deborrah. Glossary of Lay Language Synonyms for Common Terms Used in Informed Consent Documents for Clinical Studies: A Handbook for Clinical Researchers. 69p. 1996. pap. 39.95 (*0-9631310-3-6*) Plexus Pub.

Norris, Debra, jt. auth. see Zunker, Vernon G.

Norris, Dennis. Get a Grant: Yes You Can! 1998. mass mkt. 8.95 (*0-590-96387-2*) Scholastic Inc.

Norris, Donald F. Microcomputers & Local Government: A Handbook (Instructor's Manual) (Illus.). 174p. (Orig.). 1984. pap. 12.50 (*1-55719-012-7*) U NE CPAR.
— Microcomputers & Local Government: A Handbook (Participant's Manual) 108p. (Orig.). 1984. pap. 8.00 (*1-55719-028-3*) U NE CPAR.

Norris, Donald F. & DiMartino, David R. Computers & Small Local Governments: A Survey of Computing in the Plains & Mountain States. 62p. (Orig.). 1983. pap. 4.50 (*1-55719-029-1*) U NE CPAR.

Norris, Donald F. & Thompson, Lyke. The Politics of Welfare Reform. 215p. 1995. text 52.00 (*0-8039-5700-9*); pap. text 25.50 (*0-8039-5701-7*) Sage.

Norris, Donald M. Market-Driven Management: Lessons Learned from 20 Successful Associations. 154p. (Orig.). 1990. pap. 45.00 (*0-88034-044-4*) Am Soc Assn Execs.

***Norris, Donald M.** Revolutionary Strategy for the Knowledge Age. (Illus.). 46p. 1998. pap. 25.00 (*0-9601608-8-4*) Soc Coll & Univ Planning.

Norris, Donald M. & Lofton, Marie C. Winning with Diversity: A Practical Handbook for Creating Inclusive Meetings Events, & Organizations. LC 94-43566. 157p. 1994. 22.95 (*0-88034-093-2*) Am Soc Assn Execs.

***Norris, Donald M. & Malloch, Theodore R.** Unleashing the Power of Perpetual Learning. (Illus.). 46p. 1998. pap. 25.00 (*0-9601608-7-6*) Soc Coll & Univ Planning.

Norris, Donald M. & Poulton, Nick L. A Guide for New Planners. rev. ed. (Illus.). 102p. (C). 1991. pap. text 35.00 (*0-9601608-2-5*) Soc Coll & Univ Planning.

Norris, Donald M. & Poulton, Susan E. Creating a Knowledge - Age Vision for Your Community College. (Illus.). 22p. 1997. pap. 15.00 (*0-87117-308-5*, 1410) Comm Coll Pr Am Assn Comm Coll.

Norris, Donald M., jt. auth. see Dolence, Michael G.

Norris, Donald N., jt. auth. see American Society of Association Executives Staff.

Norris, Dorothy E. & Shiner, Reva P. Keynotes to Modern Dance. LC 69-15426. (Illus.). 237p. (C). reprint ed. 73.50 (*0-8357-9053-3*, 201731600007) Bks Demand.

Norris, Dorry B. The Sage Cottage Herb Garden Cookbook: Celebrations, Recipes, & Herb Gardening Tips for Every Month of the Year. 2nd ed. LC 95-15669. (Illus.). 348p. (Orig.). 1995. pap. 14.95 (*1-56440-727-6*) Globe Pequot.

Norris, Dwight E. Property Management. (Illus.). 512p. (C). 1998. pap. text 39.95 (*0-934772-09-6*) Ashley Crown Systems Inc.

Norris, Edwin, ed. The Ancient Cornish Drama, 2 vols., Set. LC 68-56530. 1005p. 1972. reprint ed. 60.95 (*0-405-08819-1*, Pub. by Blom Pubns) Ayer.
— The Ancient Cornish Drama, 2 vols., Vol. 1. LC 68-56530. 1972. reprint ed. 30.95 (*0-405-08820-5*, Pub. by Blom Pubns) Ayer.
— The Ancient Cornish Drama, 2 vols., Vol. 2. LC 68-56530. 1972. reprint ed. 30.95 (*0-405-08821-3*, Pub. by Blom Pubns) Ayer.

Norris, Eleanor, ed. see Norris, Norman L.

Norris, Emilie, jt. auth. see Nisbet, Peter.

Norris, F. Responsibilities of the Novelist & Other Literary Essays. LC 68-26364. (Studies in Fiction: No. 34). 1969. reprint ed. lib. bdg. 75.00 (*0-8383-0269-6*) M S G Haskell Hse.

Norris, Floyd & Bockelmann, Christine. The New York Times Century of Business. (Illus.). 336p. 1999. 29.95 (*0-07-135589-8*) McGraw.

Norris, Forbes H., jt. auth. see Mitsumoto, Hiroshi.

Norris, Frank. The Argonaut Manuscript: Limited Edition of Frank Norris's Works, 10 vols., Set. (BCL1-PS American Literature Ser.). 1992. reprint ed. lib. bdg. 900.00 (*0-7812-6806-0*) Rprt Serv.
— The Best Short Stories of Frank Norris. LC 98-71892. 180p. (Orig.). 1998. pap. 11.95 (*0-9655309-1-4*) Ironweed Pr.
— Blix. LC 74-95150. reprint ed. 37.50 (*0-404-04787-4*) AMS Pr.
— Blix. (BCL1-PS American Literature Ser.). 339p. 1992. reprint ed. lib. bdg. 90.00 (*0-7812-6807-9*) Rprt Serv.
— Deal in Wheat. LC 77-173797. (Illus.). reprint ed. 21.50 (*0-404-04788-2*) AMS Pr.
— A Deal in Wheat: And Other Stories of the New & Old West. (BCL1-PS American Literature Ser.). 272p. 1992. reprint ed. lib. bdg. 79.00 (*0-7812-6808-7*) Rprt Serv.
— A Deal in Wheat & Other Stories of New & Old West. 272p. 1977. 15.95 (*0-8369-3410-5*) Ayer.
— Deal in Wheat & Other Stories of the New & Old West. LC 74-131788. (Illus.). 1971. reprint ed. 16.00 (*0-403-00675-9*) Scholarly.
— Frank Norris of the Wave Stories & Sketches from the San Francisco. 1988. reprint ed. lib. bdg. 59.00 (*0-7812-0040-7*) Rprt Serv.
— A Man's Woman. LC 71-108125. 1970. reprint ed. 35.00 (*0-404-04789-0*) AMS Pr.
— A Man's Woman. (BCL1-PS American Literature Ser.). 286p. 1992. reprint ed. lib. bdg. 79.00 (*0-7812-6810-9*) Rprt Serv.
— McTeague. 1976. lib. bdg. 18.95 (*0-89968-071-2*, Lghtyr Pr) Buccaneer Bks.
— McTeague. Collins, Carvel, ed. 343p. (C). 1950. pap. text 25.00 (*0-03-009250-7*, Pub. by Harcourt Coll Pubs) Harcourt.
— McTeague. unabridged ed. 201p. 1997. reprint ed. pap. 14.95 (*1-57002-056-6*) Univ Publng Hse.
— McTeague: A Story of California. LC 72-184736. 1971. lib. bdg. 20.00 (*0-8376-0406-0*) Bentley Pubs.
— McTeague: A Story of San Francisco. LC 96-26012. 1996. 17.50 (*0-679-60238-0*) Fodors Travel.
— McTeague: A Story of San Francisco. 1964. mass mkt. 6.95 (*0-451-52421-7*, Sig Classics) NAL.

Norris, Frank. McTeague: A Story of San Francisco. Pizer, Donald, ed. LC 77-479. (C). 1978. pap. text 14.00 (*0-393-09136-8*) Norton.

Norris, Frank. McTeague: A Story of San Francisco. Loving, Jerome, ed. & intro. by. 372p. 1996. pap. 9.95 (*0-19-282356-6*) OUP.
— McTeague: A Story of San Francisco. LC 72-184736. 1981. 12.05 (*0-606-03855-8*, Pub. by Turtleback) Demco.
— McTeague: A Story of San Francisco. Starr, Kevin, ed. & intro. by. 496p. 1994. pap. 10.95 (*0-14-018769-3*, Penguin Classics) Viking Penguin.

***Norris, Frank.** Mcteague: A Story of San Francisco. Loving, Jerome, ed. (Oxford World's Classics Ser.). 388p. 2000. pap. 10.95 (*0-19-284059-2*) OUP.

Norris, Frank. McTeague: A Story of San Francisco. (BCL1-PS American Literature Ser.). 442p. 1992. reprint ed. lib. bdg. 99.00 (*0-7812-6809-5*) Rprt Serv.
— McTeague: A Story of San Francisco: an Authoritative Text, Contexts, Criticism. 2nd ed. Pizer, Donald, ed. LC 96-16305. (Critical Editions Ser.). (C). 1996. pap. text 12.50 (*0-393-97013-2*) Norton.
— Moran of the Lady Letty: A Story of Adventure off the California Coast. LC 70-104533. 297p. 1979. reprint ed. lib. bdg. 11.50 (*0-8398-1351-1*) Irvington.
— Moran of the Lady Letty: A Story of Adventure off the California Coast. (BCL1-PS American Literature Ser.). 293p. 1992. reprint ed. pap. text 59.00 (*0-685-51393-9*); reprint ed. lib. bdg. 79.00 (*0-7812-6811-7*) Rprt Serv.
— Moran of the Lady Letty, a Story of Adventure off the California Coast. LC 75-144665. 293p. 1971. reprint ed. 29.50 (*0-404-04790-4*) AMS Pr.
— Novels & Essays: Vandover & the Brute; McTeague; The Octopus; Essays. Pizer, Donald, ed. LC 85-23133. 1232p. 1986. 35.00 (*0-940450-40-2*, Pub. by Library of America) Penguin Putnam.
— The Octopus. 1976. lib. bdg. 25.95 (*0-89968-070-4*, Lghtyr Pr) Buccaneer Bks.
— The Octopus: A Story of California. 496p. 1994. pap. 14.95 (*0-14-018770-7*, Penguin Classics) Viking Penguin.
— The Octopus: A Story of California. (BCL1-PS American Literature Ser.). 361p. 1992. reprint ed. lib. bdg. 89.00 (*0-7812-6812-5*) Rprt Serv.
— The Pit. 1976. lib. bdg. 19.95 (*0-89968-069-0*, Lghtyr Pr) Buccaneer Bks.
— Pit: A Story of Chicago. lib. bdg. 27.95 (*0-8488-1886-5*) Amereon Ltd.
— The Pit: A Story of Chicago. 496p. 1994. pap. 13.95 (*0-14-018758-8*, Penguin Classics) Viking Penguin.
— The Pit: A Story of Chicago. LC 70-184738. 432p. 1971. reprint ed. lib. bdg. 22.00 (*0-8376-0407-9*) Bentley Pubs.
— The Pit: A Story of Chicago. (BCL1-PS American Literature Ser.). 421p. 1992. reprint ed. lib. bdg. 99.00 (*0-7812-6813-3*) Rprt Serv.
— Vandover & the Brute. (BCL1-PS American Literature Ser.). 354p. 1992. reprint ed. lib. bdg. 89.00 (*0-7812-6814-1*) Rprt Serv.

Norris, Frank, jt. auth. see Neufeld, David.

Norris, Frank, ed. see Morseth, Michele.

Norris, G. M., jt. ed. see Townsend, Frank C.

Norris, Geoffrey, jt. auth. see Threltall, Robert.

Norris, George W. Fighting Liberal: The Autobiography of George W. Norris. LC 83-45829. reprint ed. 36.50 (*0-404-20194-6*) AMS Pr.
— Fighting Liberal: The Autobiography of George W. Norris. LC 91-3928. (Illus.). xxx, 419p. 1992. reprint ed. pap. 14.95 (*0-8032-8365-2*, Bison Books) U of Nebr Pr.
— Fighting Liberal, the Autobiography of George W. Norris. (History - United States Ser.). 419p. 1993. reprint ed. lib. bdg. 99.00 (*0-7812-4807-8*) Rprt Serv.

Norris, Gloria, ed. The Seasons of Women: An Anthology. 480p. 1995. 29.95 (*0-393-03860-2*) Norton.

***Norris, Grant, et al.** E-Business & ERP: Transforming the Enterprise. 320p. 2000. 49.95 (*0-471-39208-1*) Wiley.

N

Norris, Grant, et al. SAP: An Executive's Comprehensive Guide. LC 97-51809. 304p. 1998. 67.95 (*0-471-24992-0*) Wiley.

Norris, Gregory L. Ghost Kisses: Gothic Gay Romance Stories. 160p. (Orig.). 1994. pap. 12.95 (*0-943595-52-5*) Leyland Pubns.

Norris, Gregory L., ed. see Tillman, David.

Norris, Gunilla. Being Home: A Book of Meditations. (Illus.). 96p. 1991. 16.00 (*0-517-58159-0*) Bell T.

— Learning from the Angel. LC 85-80140. 62p. (Orig.). 1985. per. 5.00 (*0-916418-59-6*) Lotus.

***Norris, Guy & Wagner, Mark.** Airbus Jetliners. LC 99-29415. (Enthusiast Color Ser.). (Illus.). 96p. 1999. pap. 13.95 (*0-7603-0677-X*, Pub. by MBI Pubg) Motorbooks Intl.

Norris, Guy & Wagner, Mark. Boeing. LC 98-24792. (Illus.). 192p. 1998. 29.95 (*0-7603-0497-1*) Motorbooks Intl.

— Boeing 747: Design & Development since 1969. LC 97-25441. (Airliner History Ser.). (Illus.). 128p. 1997. pap. 16.95 (*0-7603-0280-4*) MBI Pubg.

— Douglas Jetliners. LC 98-53250. (Enthusiast Color Ser.). (Illus.). 96p. 1999. pap. 13.95 (*0-7603-0676-1*) MBI Pubg.

— Great Jetliners. LC 97-19420. (Illus.). 128p. 1997. 15.98 (*0-7603-0373-8*) MBI Pubg.

***Norris, Guy & Wagner, Mark.** Modern Boeing Jetliners. LC 99-29418. (Illus.). 176p. 1999. 19.98 (*0-7603-0717-2*, Pub. by MBI Pubg) Motorbooks Intl.

Norris, Guy & Wagner, Mark R. Boeing Jetliners. LC 96-14084. (Enthusiast Color Ser.). (Illus.). 96p. 1996. pap. 13.95 (*0-7603-0034-8*) MBI Pubg.

— Boeing 777. (Enthusiast Color Ser.). (Illus.). 96p. 1996. pap. 13.95 (*0-7603-0091-7*) MBI Pubg.

Norris, H. T. The Arab Conquest of the Western Sahara. 309p. 1986. 45.00 (*0-86685-596-3*, LDL5963, Pub. by Librairie du Liban) Intl Bk Ctr.

— The Berbers in Arabic Literature. 280p. 1982. 45.00 (*0-86685-594-7*, LDL5947, Pub. by Librairie du Liban) Intl Bk Ctr.

— Sufi Mystics of the Niger Desert: Sidi Mahmud & the Hermits of Air. (Illus.). 216p. 1990. 65.00 (*0-19-826538-7*) OUP.

Norris, H. Thomas, ed. Pathology of the Colon, Small Intestine & Anus. 2nd ed. (Contemporary Issues in Surgical Pathology Ser.: Vol. 17). (Illus.). 414p. 1991. text 126.00 (*0-443-08729-6*) Church.

Norris, Harold. You Are This Nation. LC 75-27812. 160p. 1976. 7.50 (*0-8187-0020-3*) Harlo Press.

Norris, Harry. Accounting Theory: An Outline of Its Structure with a New Introduction by the Author. Brief, Richard P., ed. LC 80-1512. (Dimensions of Accounting Theory & Practice Ser.). 1980. reprint ed. lib. bdg. 17.95 (*0-405-13537-8*) Ayer.

— Islam in the Balkans: Religion & Society Between Europe & the Arab World. LC 93-1637. 326p. 1994. text 39.95 (*0-87249-977-4*) U of SC Pr.

Norris, Helen. Burning Glass, Stories. LC 91-10557. 192p. 1992. 19.95 (*0-8071-1790-0*) La State U Pr.

— The Christmas Wife: Stories. LC 84-24080. (Illinois Short Fiction Ser.). 144p. 1988. 11.95 (*0-252-06041-5*) U of Ill Pr.

— More Than 7 Watchmen. 144p. 1985. 3.95 (*0-310-45470-0*, 9359) Zondervan.

***Norris, Helen.** One Day in the Life of a Born Again Loser & Other Stories. LC 99-6957. 224p. 2000. 24.95 (*0-8173-1029-0*) U of Ala Pr.

Norris, Helen. Walk with the Sickle Moon. Black, Hillel, ed. 176p. 1989. 15.95 (*1-55972-001-8*, Birch Ln Pr) Carol Pub Group.

— Walk with the Sickle Moon. 1991. mass mkt. 4.95 (*0-446-35971-8*, Pub. by Warner Bks) Little.

— Water into Wine: Stories. LC 87-34289. (Illinois Short Fiction Ser.). 160p. 1988. 14.95 (*0-252-01540-1*) U of Ill Pr.

Norris, Henry H. The Principles of the Jesuits: Developed in a Collection of Extracts from Their Own Authors to Which Are Prefixed a Brief Account of the Origin of the Order & a Sketch of Its Institute. 300p. 1992. reprint ed. pap. 21.00 (*1-56459-292-8*) Kessinger Pub.

Norris, Herbert. Ancient European Costume & Fashion. LC 99-42697. (Illus.). 336p. 1999. pap. text 14.95 (*0-486-40723-3*) Dover.

***Norris, Herbert.** Medieval Costume & Fashion. LC 98-49856. 528p. 1999. pap. text 17.95 (*0-486-40486-2*) Dover.

Norris, Herbert. Tudor Costume & Fashion. LC 97-19413. (Illus.). 904p. pap. 24.95 (*0-486-29845-0*) Dover.

Norris, Herbert & Curtis, Oswald. Nineteenth-Century Costume & Fashion. unabridged ed. LC 98-9926. (Illus.). 248p. 1998. pap. 12.95 (*0-486-40292-4*) Dover.

Norris, Hoke, ed. We Dissent. LC 73-6210. 211p. 1973. reprint ed. lib. bdg. 59.50 (*0-8371-6889-9*, NOWD, Greenwood Pr) Greenwood.

Norris, Ian. Automobile Year No. 42: 1994-95. (Illus.). 280p. 1995. 49.95 (*2-88324-035-3*, Pub. by Editions JR) Motorbooks Intl.

— Automobile Year No. 44: 1996-97. (Illus.). 276p. 1997. 49.95 (*2-88324-043-4*, Pub. by J R Piccard) Motorbooks Intl.

— Automobile Year 1998-1999, 46. (Automobile Year Ser.). 272p. 1999. 54.95 (*2-88324-054-X*) Motorbooks Intl.

***Norris, Ian.** Automobile Year 1999-2000. 47th ed. (Illus.). 2000. 54.95 (*2-88324-057-4*) J R Piccard.

Norris, J. Markov Chains. LC 96-31570. (Cambridge Series in Statistical & Probabilistic Mathematics: No. 2). 253p. 1997. text 49.95 (*0-521-48181-3*) Cambridge U Pr.

— Markov Chains. (Series in Statistical & Probabilistic Mathematics: Vol. 2). (Illus.). 253p. (C). 1998. pap. text 24.95 (*0-521-63396-6*) Cambridge U Pr.

Norris, J. W. & Hachinski, Vladimir C., eds. Prevention of Stroke. (Illus.). 280p. 1991. 159.00 (*0-387-97442-3*) Spr-Verlag.

Norris, Jack. Voyager - The World Flight: The Official Log, Flight Analysis & Narrative Explanation of the Record Around the World Flight of the Voyager Aircraft. LC 88-90609. (Illus.). 72p. (Orig.). 1988. pap. 12.95 (*0-9620239-0-6*) J Norris.

Norris, James. Aladdin & the Wonderful Lamp. (J). 1940. 6.00 (*0-87602-102-X*) Anchorage.

— Robin Hood. (J). (gr. 1-9). 1952. 6.00 (*0-87602-191-7*) Anchorage.

Norris, James D. Advertising & the Transformation of American Society, 1865-1920, 110. LC 90-2760. 224p. 1990. 55.00 (*0-313-26801-0*, Greenwood Pr) Greenwood.

— R. G. Dun & Co., 1841 to 1900: The Development of Credit-Reporting in the Nineteenth Century, 20. LC 77-95359. (Contributions in Economics & Economic History Ser.: No. 20). (Illus.). 206p. 1978. 57.95 (*0-313-20326-1*, NDC/) Greenwood.

Norris, James D. & Shaffer, Arthur H., eds. Politics & Patronage in the Gilded Age: The Correspondence of James A. Garfield & Charles E. Henry. LC 70-629850. (Illus.). 304p. 1970. 15.00 (*0-87020-107-7*) State Hist Soc Wis.

Norris, James R., jt. auth. see Deisenhofer, Johann.

Norris, Jane, ed. Daughters of the Elderly: Building Partnerships in Caregiving. LC 87-46246. 236p. (Orig.). 1988. pap. 14.95 (*0-253-20484-4*, MB-484) Ind U Pr.

***Norris, Jane E.** The Exciting Adventures of Grandma & Grandpa's Grandchildren. (J). (ps-1). 1999. pap. 5.95 (*0-533-12993-1*) Vantage.

Norris, Jane E. & Norris, Lee G. Written in Water: The Life of Benjamin Harrison Eaton. LC 90-9497. (Illus.). 311p. (C). 1990. text 29.95 (*0-8040-0934-1*) Swallow.

Norris, Jeannie, ed. see Porter, Hugh J. & Houser, Lynn.

Norris, Jeffrey A. Corporate Affirmative Action Practices & the Civil Rights Act of 1991. 35p. 1992. pap. 10.00 (*0-614-06153-9*, 2038-PP-4040) EPF.

Norris, Jeffrey A. & Perkins, Salvador T. Developing Effective Affirmative Action Plans. 5th ed. 1995. 125.00 (*0-916559-46-7*, 2017-TM-4045) EPF.

Norris, Jeffrey A. & Shershin, Michael J., Jr. How to Take a Case Before the NLRB. 6th ed. LC 92-16017. 943p. 1992. trans. 175.00 (*0-87179-750-X*, 0750) BNA Books.

Norris, Jeffrey A., jt. auth. see Holmes, William F.

Norris, Jeffrey A., jt. auth. see Williams, Robert E.

Norris, Jeremy. The Russian Piano Concerto Vol. I: The Nineteenth Century. LC 93-11565. (Russian Music Studies). 244p. 1994. 35.00 (*0-253-34112-4*) Ind U Pr.

Norris, Jerrie. Presenting Rosa Guy. (United States Authors Ser.: No. 543). 112p. 1988. 20.95 (*0-8057-8207-9*, TUSAS 543, Twyne) Mac Lib Ref.

Norris, Jill. Activities Using the World Wide Web: Grades 1-5. Evans, Marilyn, ed. (Teaching & Learning with the Computer Ser.: Vol. 6). (Illus.). 80p. 1998. pap., teacher ed. 16.95 (*1-55799-678-4*, 066) Evan-Moor Edu Pubs.

— Alphabet Activities on the Computer: Grades K-1. Evans, Marilyn, ed. (Teaching & Learning with the Computer Ser.: Vol. 2). (Illus.). 80p. 1998. pap., teacher ed. 16.95 (*1-55799-674-1*, 062) Evan-Moor Edu Pubs.

— Author Activities on the Computer: Grades 1-3. Evans, Marilyn, ed. (Teaching & Learning with the Computer Ser.: Vol. 5). (Illus.). 80p. 1998. pap., teacher ed. 16.95 (*1-55799-677-6*, 065) Evan-Moor Edu Pubs.

— Beginning to Read Directions. (Real-Life Reading Activities Ser.). (Illus.). 64p. (J). (gr. k-1). 1996. pap., teacher ed. 7.95 (*1-55799-586-9*, 563) Evan-Moor Edu Pubs.

***Norris, Jill.** Contemporary Cursive: Daily Handwriting Practice: K-6+ Evans, Marilyn, ed. (Daily Handwriting Practice Ser.). (Illus.). 112p. 2000. pap., teacher ed. 14.95 (*1-55799-756-X*, 793) Evan-Moor Edu Pubs.

— Daily Math Practice, Grade 5. Evans, Marilyn, ed. (Daily Math Practice Ser.: Vol. 5). 112p. 1999. pap., teacher ed. 14.95 (*1-55799-745-4*, 754) Evan-Moor Edu Pubs.

— Daily Math Practice, Grade 1. Evans, Marilyn, ed. (Daily Math Practice Ser.: Vol. 1). (Illus.). 112p. 1999. pap., teacher ed. 14.95 (*1-55799-741-1*, 750) Evan-Moor Edu Pubs.

— Daily Summer Activities, Moving from Fourth to Fifth Grade. Evans, Marilyn, ed. (Daily Summer Activities Ser.). (Illus.). 160p. 2000. pap. 14.95 (*1-55799-769-1*, 1031) Evan-Moor Edu Pubs.

— Daily Summer Activities, Moving from Preschool to Kindergarten. Evans, Marilyn, ed. (Daily Summer Activities Ser.). (Illus.). 160p. 2000. pap. 14.95 (*1-55799-764-0*, 1026) Evan-Moor Edu Pubs.

Norris, Jill. Early Math Activities on the Computer: Grades K-1. Evans, Marilyn, ed. (Teaching & Learning with the Computer Ser.: Vol. 1). (Illus.). 80p. 1998. pap., teacher ed. 16.95 (*1-55799-673-3*, 061) Evan-Moor Edu Pubs.

***Norris, Jill.** Fairy Tales & Folktales: Read & Understand: Grade 1-2. Evans, Marilyn, ed. (Read & Understand Ser.). (Illus.). 144p. 2000. pap., teacher ed. 12.95 (*1-55799-749-7*, 756) Evan-Moor Edu Pubs.

— Guided Report Writing: Grade 3-6. Evans, Marilyn, ed. (Illus.). 96p. 1999. pap., teacher ed. 10.95 (*1-55799-732-2*, 732) Evan-Moor Edu Pubs.

— Keeping Healthy. Evans, Joy, ed. (Science Ser.). (Illus.). 32p. (J). (ps-1). Date not set. pap., wbk. ed. 2.50 (*1-58610-115-3*) Learn Horizon.

Norris, Jill. Math Activities on the Computer: Grades 1-3. Evans, Marilyn, ed. (Teaching & Learning with the Computer Ser.: Vol. 3). (Illus.). 80p. 1998. pap., teacher ed. 16.95 (*1-55799-675-X*, 063) Evan-Moor Edu Pubs.

***Norris, Jill.** Modern Manuscript: Daily Handwriting Practice: K-6+ Evans, Marilyn, ed. (Daily Handwriting Practice Ser.). (Illus.). 112p. 2000. pap., teacher ed. 14.95 (*1-55799-755-1*, 792) Evan-Moor Edu Pubs.

— More Read & Understand Stories & Activities, Grade 1. Evans, Marilyn, ed. (Read & Understand Ser.: Vol. 5). (Illus.). 144p. 1999. pap., teacher ed. 12.95 (*1-55799-737-3*, 745) Evan-Moor Edu Pubs.

— Play & Learn with Your Five Year Old. Evans, Marilyn, ed. (Play & Learn Ser.: Vol. 5). (Illus.). 80p. (J). (ps-k). 1999. pap. 9.95 (*1-55799-721-7*, 4504) Evan-Moor Edu Pubs.

— Play & Learn with Your Four Year Old. Evans, Marilyn, ed. (Play & Learn Ser.: Vol. 4). (Illus.). 80p. (J). (ps). 1999. pap. 9.95 (*1-55799-720-9*, 4503) Evan-Moor Edu Pubs.

— Play & Learn with Your One Year Old. Evans, Marilyn, ed. (Play & Learn Ser.: Vol. 1). (Illus.). 80p. (J). (ps). 1999. pap. 9.95 (*1-55799-717-9*, 4500) Evan-Moor Edu Pubs.

— Play & Learn with Your Six Year Old. Evans, Marilyn, ed. (Play & Learn Ser.: Vol. 6). (Illus.). 80p. (J). (gr. k-1). 1999. pap. 9.95 (*1-55799-722-5*, 4505) Evan-Moor Edu Pubs.

— Play & Learn with Your Three Year Old. Evans, Marilyn, ed. (Play & Learn Ser.: Vol. 3). (Illus.). 80p. (J). (ps). 1999. pap. 9.95 (*1-55799-719-5*, 4502) Evan-Moor Edu Pubs.

— Play & Learn with Your Two Year Old. Evans, Marilyn, ed. (Play & Learn Ser.: Vol. 2). (Illus.). 80p. (J). (ps). 1999. pap. 9.95 (*1-55799-718-7*, 4501) Evan-Moor Edu Pubs.

Norris, Jill. Reading & Writing Activities on the Computer: Grades 1-3. Evans, Marilyn, ed. (Teaching & Learning with the Computer Ser.: Vol. 4). (Illus.). 80p. 1998. pap., teacher ed. 16.95 (*1-55799-676-8*, 064) Evan-Moor Edu Pubs.

— Reading at the Supermarket. (Real-Life Reading Activities Ser.). (Illus.). 64p. (J). (gr. 2-3). 1996. pap., teacher ed. 7.95 (*1-55799-592-3*, 569) Evan-Moor Edu Pubs.

— Reading What's In the Mailbox. (Real-Life Reading Activities Ser.). (Illus.). 64p. (J). (gr. k-1). 1996. pap., teacher ed. 7.95 (*1-55799-587-7*, 564) Evan-Moor Edu Pubs.

— Reading While You Shop. (Real-Life Reading Activities Ser.). (Illus.). 64p. (J). (gr. k-1). 1996. pap., teacher ed. 7.95 (*1-55799-588-5*, 565) Evan-Moor Edu Pubs.

***Norris, Jill.** Tall Tales: Read & Understand: Grade 1. Evans, Marilyn, ed. (Read & Understand Ser.). (Illus.). 144p. 2000. pap., teacher ed. 12.95 (*1-55799-751-9*, 758) Evan-Moor Edu Pubs.

— Traditional Cursive: Daily Handwriting Practice: K-6+ Evans, Marilyn, ed. (Daily Handwriting Practice Ser.). (Illus.). 112p. 2000. pap., teacher ed. 14.95 (*1-55799-754-3*, 791) Evan-Moor Edu Pubs.

— Traditional Manuscript: Daily Handwriting Practice: K-6+ Evans, Marilyn, ed. (Daily Handwriting Practice Ser.). (Illus.). 112p. 2000. pap., teacher ed. 14.95 (*1-55799-753-5*, 790) Evan-Moor Edu Pubs.

— What Is in the Sky? Evans, Joy, ed. (Science Ser.). (Illus.). 33p. (J). (ps-1). Date not set. pap., wbk. ed. 2.50 (*1-58610-112-9*) Learn Horizon.

***Norris, Jill & Evans, Marilyn.** Reading Comprehension - Grades 4-6: Great Practice for Standardized Tests. Moore, Jo Ellen, ed. (Learn on the Go Practice Bks.). (Illus.). 64p. (J). (gr. 4-6). 1998. pap., wbk. ed. 2.25 (*1-58610-011-4*, Learn on the Go) Learn Horizon.

Norris, Jill & Tavares, Nalene C. How to Do Science Fair Projects. Evans, Marilyn, ed. (Science Ser.). (Illus.). 32p. (J). (gr. 4-6). Date not set. pap., wbk. ed. 2.50 (*1-58610-127-7*) Learn Horizon.

Norris, Jill, jt. auth. see Liddington, Jill.

Norris, Jill, jt. auth. see Sage, Kathy.

Norris, Jill, jt. auth. see White, Tekla.

Norris, Jill, ed. see Spero, Daniel J.

***Norris, Jim.** After the Year Eighty: The Demise of Franciscan Power in Spanish New Mexico. LC 00-8468. 2000. 39.95 (*0-8263-2211-5*) U of NM Pr.

Norris, Jim. 1879-1886 Customers of Whitcher & Pearson Los Alamos, California Blacksmiths. (Illus.). 38p. 1997. pap. 5.00 (*0-933380-53-4*) Olive Pr Pubns.

— Historical Santa Ynez Valley Coloring Book. 35p. 1989. pap. 6.00 (*0-933380-49-6*) Olive Pr Pubns.

— Tour of Los Alamos Historic District. (Illus.). 36p. 1996. pap. 3.00 (*0-933380-52-6*) Olive Pr Pubns.

Norris, Jim & Norris, Lynne. Urho Saari: Olympian. LC 88-19538. (Illus.). 200p. (Orig.). 1988. 25.00 (*0-933380-35-6*) Olive Pr Pubns.

Norris, Joan, et al, eds. Mental Health Psychiatric Nursing: A Continuum of Care. 1989. pap. text, teacher ed. 12.95 (*0-8273-4325-6*); 12.95 (*0-8273-4326-4*) Delmar.

Norris, Joan, et al. Psychiatric Mental Health Nursing. 1989. text 49.95 (*0-8273-4324-8*) Delmar.

Norris, Joan, ed. see Berger, Suzanne E.

Norris, Joan D. & Forsberg, Barbara. New England. LC 93-49006. (American Food Library). 48p. (J). (gr. 3-6). 1994. lib. bdg. 22.60 (*0-86625-510-9*) Rourke Pubns.

Norris, Joan E. Among Generations: The Cycle of Adult Relationships. LC 93-5972. 200p. (C). 1993. pap. 16.95 (*0-7167-2207-0*) W H Freeman.

— Among Generations: The Cycle of Adult Relationships. LC 93-5972. 200p. (C). 1993. text 28.95 (*0-7167-2206-2*) W H Freeman.

Norris, Joan E., jt. auth. see Pratt, Michael W.

Norris, Joann. Children's Museums: An American Guidebook. LC 97-42194. (Illus.). 223p. 1998. 32.50 (*0-7864-0443-4*) McFarland & Co.

Norris, Joann, jt. auth. see Norris, John.

Norris, Joann, jt. auth. see Norris, John R.

Norris, Joel. Arthur Shawcross: The Genesee River Killer. 1992. audio 5.99 (*1-55817-592-X*, Pinncle Kensgtn) Kensgtn Pub Corp.

— Henry Lee Lucas Shocking True. 1991. mass mkt. 4.95 (*0-8217-3530-6*, Zebra Kensgtn) Kensgtn Pub Corp.

— Horn of the Goat. 1999. mass mkt. 5.99 (*0-671-79515-5*) PB.

— Serial Killers: The Growing Menace. 272p. 1989. pap. 12.95 (*0-385-26328-7*, Anchor NY) Doubleday.

***Norris, Joel & McCammon, Laura.** Learning to Teach Drama: A Case Narrative Approach. LC 99-87989. 186p. 2000. pap. text 22.00 (*0-325-00228-2*, Pub. by Boynton Cook Pubs) Heinemann.

Norris, John. Anti-Tank Weapons. Marchington, James, ed. (Brassey's Modern Military Equipment Ser.). 1996. 28.95 (*1-85753-177-9*, Pub. by Brasseys) Brasseys.

— Artillery: An Illustrated History. (Illus.). 256p. 2000. 36.00 (*0-7509-2185-4*) Sutton Pub Ltd.

— An Essay Towards the Theory of the Ideal or Intelligible World, 2 vols. in 1. (Lockeana Ser.). xvi, 1026p. 1974. reprint ed. 154.70 (*3-487-05223-7*) G Olms Pubs.

— Historic Nelson: The Early Years. (Illus.). 320p. 1996. pap. text 36.95 (*0-88982-150-X*, Pub. by Oolichan Bks) Genl Dist Srvs.

Norris, John & Norris, Joann. Amusement Parks: An American Guidebook. 2nd ed. LC 93-27805. (Illus.). 168p. 1994. pap. 32.50 (*0-89950-789-1*) McFarland & Co.

Norris, John, jt. auth. see Brandes, Donna.

Norris, John, jt. auth. see Fowler, Will.

Norris, John A. Assault Rifles, Rifles & Combat Shotguns: Including Sniping Rifles. Marchington, James, ed. LC 97-33241. (Modern Military Equipment Ser.). (Illus.). 117p. 1997. 29.95 (*1-85753-214-7*, Pub. by Brasseys) Brasseys.

Norris, John F. Sales Primers: Selling Parables by the Staff of Norris & Company. (Illus.). 72p. 1998. 39.95 (*0-9667987-0-8*) J F Norris.

Norris, John M., et al. Designing Second Language Performance Assessments. (Technical Report Ser.: No. 18). 248p. 1998. pap. text 20.00 (*0-8248-2109-2*) UH Pr.

Norris, John R., ed. Methods in Microbiology, Vol. 18. (Serial Publication Ser.). 1985. text 157.00 (*0-12-521518-5*) Acad Pr.

Norris, John R., et al, eds. Methods in Microbiology Vol. 23: Techniques for the Study of Mycorrhiza. (Illus.). 480p. 1991. text 125.00 (*0-12-521523-1*) Acad Pr.

— Methods in Microbiology Vol. 24: Techniques for the Study of Mycorrhiza. (Illus.). 450p. 1992. text 125.00 (*0-12-521524-X*) Acad Pr.

Norris, John R. & Bergan, T. Methods in Microbiology, Vol. 13. LC 68-57745. 1980. text 209.00 (*0-12-521513-4*) Acad Pr.

Norris, John R. & Bergen, T., eds. Methods in Microbiology, 10. 1979. 80.00 (*0-12-521510-X*) Acad Pr.

— Methods in Microbiology, Vol. 11. 1979. text 209.00 (*0-12-521511-8*) Acad Pr.

Norris, John R. & Norris, Joann. The Historic Railroad: A Guide to Museums, Depots & Excursions in the United States. LC 95-40179. (Illus.). 221p. 1996. pap. 32.50 (*0-7864-0040-4*) McFarland & Co.

Norris, John R. & Ribbons, D. W., eds. Methods in Microbiology, Vol. 12. 1979. text 209.00 (*0-12-521512-6*) Acad Pr.

Norris, John R., et al. Methods in Microbiology, 14. 1984. text 157.00 (*0-12-521514-2*) Acad Pr.

— Methods in Microbiology, 15. 1984. text 157.00 (*0-12-521515-0*) Acad Pr.

— Methods in Microbiology, 16. 1985. text 157.00 (*0-12-521516-9*) Acad Pr.

Norris, John R., jt. ed. see Mayer, Frank.

Norris, Johnny. Learn to Play Acoustic Chord Riffs. 48p. 1996. pap. 24.95 incl. cd-rom (*0-7119-3302-2*, AM90239) Music Sales.

***Norris, Johnny.** Start Playing: Rock Guitar Licks. 32p. 2000. pap. text 9.95 incl. audio compact disk (*0-8256-1785-5*, AM962412) Music Sales.

Norris, Joseph E. The Ministry to the Divorced. (Ministry Ser.). 64p. 1990. pap. 1.95 (*0-8146-1923-1*) Liturgical Pr.

Norris, Joye A. & Baker, Susan S. Maximizing Paraprofessional Potential. LC 98-17871. (Professional Practices in Adult Education & Human Resource Development Ser.). (Illus.). 144p. (C). 1999. text 24.50 (*1-57524-027-0*) Krieger.

Norris, Joye A. & Kennington, Paddy A. Developing Literacy Programs for Homeless Adults. 128p. (Orig.). (C). 1992. 17.50 (*0-89464-679-6*); pap. 16.00 (*0-89464-794-6*) Krieger.

Norris, Juli. I Love You, Kate. LC 99-60638. 156p. 2000. pap. 13.95 (*0-88739-257-1*) Creat Arts Bk.

Norris, June, ed. Dentist's Drug Handbook. 608p. (Orig.). 1998. 34.95 (*0-87434-890-0*) Springhouse Corp.

Norris, June, ed. see Springhouse Publishing Company Staff.

Norris, June, jt. ed. see Springhouse Publishing Company Staff.

Norris, K. Hands Full of Living. 1976. 17.95 (*0-89190-303-8*) Amereon Ltd.

Norris, K. P., jt. auth. see Waterhouse, D. F.

Norris, Karen & Norris, Ralph. Northwest Carving Traditions. LC 98-53343. (Illus.). 3p. 1999. 59.95 (*0-7643-0799-1*) Schiffer.

Norris, Kathleen. Amazing Grace: A Vocabulary of Faith. large type ed. LC 98-25579. 1998. pap. 25.95 (*0-7838-0298-6*, G K Hall & Co) Mac Lib Ref.

— Amazing Grace: A Vocabulary of Faith. 384p. 1999. reprint ed. pap. 12.95 (*1-57322-721-8*, Riverhd Trade) Berkley Pub.

— Baker's Dozen. LC 71-130068. (Short Story Index Reprint Ser.). 1977. 20.95 (*0-8369-3649-3*) Ayer.

— The Beloved Woman. (Collected Works of Kathleen Norris). 359p. 1999. reprint ed. lib. bdg. 98.00 (*1-58201-802-2*) Classic Bks.

— The Callahans & the Murphys. (Collected Works of Kathleen Norris). 381p. 1999. reprint ed. lib. bdg. 98.00 (*1-58201-803-0*) Classic Bks.

— Certain People of Importance. (Collected Works of Kathleen Norris). 486p. 1999. reprint ed. lib. bdg. 108.00 (1-58201-792-1) Classic Bks.
— The Cloister Walk. large type ed. 1996. 24.95 (0-7838-1887-4, G K Hall Lrg Type) Mac Lib Ref.
— The Cloister Walk. large type ed. 532p. 1997. pap. 22.95 (0-7838-1973-0, G K Hall Lrg Type) Mac Lib Ref.
— The Cloister Walk. LC 96-863. 416p. 1997. reprint ed. pap. 12.95 (1-57322-584-3, Riverhd Trade) Berkley Pub.
— Dakota: A Spiritual Geography. 224p. 1994. pap. 13.00 (0-395-71091-X) HM.
— Dakota: A Spiritual Geography. LC 92-30820. 192p. 1993. 19.95 (0-395-63320-6, Pub. by Ticknor & Fields) HM.
— Harriet & the Piper. (Collected Works of Kathleen Norris). 341p. 1999. reprint ed. lib. bdg. 98.00 (1-58201-793-X) Classic Bks.
— The Heart of Rachael. (Collected Works of Kathleen Norris). 408p. 1999. reprint ed. lib. bdg. 108.00 (1-58201-804-9) Classic Bks.
— Josselyn's Wife. (Collected Works of Kathleen Norris). 301p. 1999. reprint ed. lib. bdg. 98.00 (1-58201-794-8) Classic Bks.
— Little Girls in Church. LC 94-44508. (Poetry Ser.). 80p. 1995. text 24.95 (0-8229-3875-8) U of Pittsburgh Pr.
— Little Girls in Church. 80p. 1995. pap. 10.95 (0-8229-5556-3) U of Pittsburgh Pr.
— Lucretia Lombard. (Collected Works of Kathleen Norris). 316p. 1999. reprint ed. lib. bdg. 98.00 (1-58201-795-6) Classic Bks.
— Margaret Yorke. reprint ed. lib. bdg. 17.95 (0-89190-307-0, Rivercity Pr) Amereon Ltd.
— Martie, the Unconquered. (Collected Works of Kathleen Norris). 376p. 1999. reprint ed. lib. bdg. 98.00 (1-58201-796-4) Classic Bks.
— Meditations on Mary. (Illus.). 112p. 1999. 19.95 (0-670-88820-6) Viking Penguin.
— Mother. reprint ed. lib. bdg. 17.95 (0-89190-308-9, Rivercity Pr) Amereon Ltd.
— Mother: A Story. (Collected Works of Kathleen Norris). 172p. 1999. reprint ed. lib. bdg. 88.00 (1-58201-797-2) Classic Bks.
— Mother, a Story. LC 70-137319. reprint ed. 27.50 (0-404-04792-0) AMS Pr.
— Mystery House. reprint ed. lib. bdg. 17.95 (0-89190-309-7, Rivercity Pr) Amereon Ltd.
— Poor, Dear Margaret Kirby & Other Stories. (Collected Works of Kathleen Norris). 393p. 1999. reprint ed. lib. bdg. 98.00 (1-58201-798-0) Classic Bks.
— The Psalms. LC 97-19048. 432p. 1997. pap. 12.95 (1-57322-647-5, Riverhd Trade) Berkley Pub.
— The Quotidian Mysteries: Laundry, Liturgy & "Women's Work" LC 98-9949. 104p. 1998. pap. 5.95 (0-8091-3801-8) Paulist Pr.
— The Rich Mrs. Burgoyne. (Collected Works of Kathleen Norris). 297p. 1999. reprint ed. lib. bdg. 88.00 (1-58201-805-7) Classic Bks.
— Rose of the World. (Collected Works of Kathleen Norris). 423p. 1999. reprint ed. lib. bdg. 108.00 (1-58201-799-9) Classic Bks.
— Saturday's Child. (Collected Works of Kathleen Norris). 531p. 1999. reprint ed. lib. bdg. 118.00 (1-58201-800-6) Classic Bks.
— Sisters. (Collected Works of Kathleen Norris). 342p. 1999. reprint ed. lib. bdg. 98.00 (1-58201-801-4) Classic Bks.
— The Treasure. (Collected Works of Kathleen Norris). 186p. 1999. reprint ed. lib. bdg. 88.00 (1-58201-806-5) Classic Bks.
— Undertow. (Collected Works of Kathleen Norris). 248p. 1999. reprint ed. lib. bdg. 88.00 (1-58201-807-3) Classic Bks.
— The Year of Common Things. (Chapbook Ser.: No. 3). 28p. (Orig.). 1998. pap. 4.00 (0-933573-10-3) Wayland Pr.

Norris, Kathleen T. Mother. 176p. 1995. pap. 9.95 (1-887548-01-7) St Michael NC.

Norris, Kathleen Thompson. Angel in the House. 1976. 17.95 (0-89190-301-1) Amereon Ltd.
— Come Back to Me, Beloved. 1976. 17.95 (0-89190-302-X) Amereon Ltd.
— High Holiday. 1976. 17.95 (0-89190-304-6) Amereon Ltd.
— Maiden Voyage. 1976. 17.95 (0-89190-305-4) Amereon Ltd.

Norris, Keith & Wooden, Mark. The Changing Australian Labour Market. LC 97-165682. (Commission Paper / Economic Planning Advisory Commission). vi, 145 p. 1996. write for info. (0-644-46497-6) AGPS Pr.

Norris, Ken. Alphabet of Desire. 70p. (C). 1991. pap. 12.00 (1-55022-148-5, Pub. by ECW) Genl Dist Srvs.
— Autokinesis. 1980. pap. 3.50 (0-916696-12-X) Cross Country.
— Islands. 128p. 1986. pap. 12.95 (0-919627-05-6, Pub. by Quarry Pr) LPC InBook.
— The Music. LC 96-118788. 104p. 1995. pap. 12.00 (1-55022-260-0, Pub. by ECW) Genl Dist Srvs.
— Report on the 2nd Half of the Twentieth Century. 1977. pap. 1.50 (0-916696-05-7) Cross Country.
— Report on the 2nd Half of the Twentieth Century. 96p. 1988. pap. 8.00 (0-919349-84-6) Guernica Editions.
— To Sleep, to Love. 64p. pap. 5.00 (0-919349-13-7) Guernica Editions.
— Under the Skin. 24p. 1976. pap. 1.00 (0-916696-00-6) Cross Country.
— Whirlwinds, Vol. 1. 92p. pap. 5.00 (0-919349-41-2) Guernica Editions.

Norris, Ken & Hilderley, Bob, eds. Poets '88: The New Generation. 160p. 1988. pap. 12.95 (0-919627-88-9, Pub. by Quarry Pr) LPC InBook.

Norris, Kenneth S. Dolphin Days: The Life & Times of the Spinner Dolphin. 1991. 21.95 (0-393-02945-X) Norton.
— Dolphin Days: The Life & Times of the Spinner Dolphin. (Illus.). 336p. 1993. reprint ed. pap. 10.00 (0-380-71965-7, Avon Bks) Morrow Avon.
— The Hawaiian Spinner Dolphin. LC 93-38911. 1994. 48.00 (0-520-08208-7, Pub. by U CA Pr) Cal Prin Full Svc.

Norris, Kenneth S., jt. ed. see Pryor, Karen.

Norris, Kerstin. Say It in Swedish. LC 72-94755. 1979. pap. 3.95 (0-486-20812-5) Dover.

Norris, L. David, et al. William H. Emory: Soldier-Scientist. LC 98-19729. 1998. pap. write for info. (0-8165-1912-9) U of Ariz Pr.
— William H. Emory: Soldier-Scientist. LC 98-19729. (Illus.). 380p. 1998. 29.95 (0-8165-1911-0) U of Ariz Pr.

***Norris, Lawrence, ed.** What You Ought to Know about Living Trusts. 3rd ed. (Client Care Ser.). 32p. 1999. pap. 7.50 (0-8080-0358-5) CCH INC.

Norris, Lawrence, ed. see Austen, Rolf.

Norris, Lawrence, ed. see Kess, Sidney & Weltman, Barbara E.

Norris, Lawrence, ed. see Wisdom, John.

Norris, Lawrence M., ed. see Hackney, Jeffrey A. & Johnson, Linda M.

Norris, Lawrence M., ed. see Johnson, Linda M. & Hackney, Jeffrey A.

Norris, Lawrence M., ed. see Meldman, Robert E. & Sideman, Richard J.

Norris, Lawrence M., ed. see Smith, Ephraim P. & Fenn, Christopher J.

Norris, Lawrence M., ed. see Wisdom, John C.

Norris, Lee G., jt. auth. see Norris, Jane E.

Norris, Leslie. Albert & the Angels. LC 98-36184. (Illus.). 48p. (J). 2000. 17.00 (0-374-30192-1) FS&G.
— Collected Poems. 260p. 1996. pap. 19.95 (1-85411-132-9, Pub. by Seren Bks) Dufour.
— Collected Stories. 260p. 1996. pap. 19.95 (1-85411-133-7, Pub. by Seren Bks) Dufour.
— The Girl from Cardigan. 200p. 1988. 25.00 (0-907476-95-3, Pub. by Seren Bks) Dufour.
— Glyn Jones. 94p. 1998. pap. 12.95 (0-7083-1410-4, Pub. by Univ Wales Pr) Paul & Co Pubs.
— Islands off Maine. deluxe ed. (Illus.). 1977. boxed set 75.00 (0-930954-16-5) Tidal Pr.

Norris, Leslie, tr. see Rilke, Rainer Maria.

Norris, Linda, jt. auth. see Ice, Joyce.

Norris, Lucy L., jt. auth. see Hitchcock, Michael.

Norris, Lynne. Be Careful What You Dream (It Might Come True) LC 84-29619. 200p. (Orig.). 1985. pap. 7.95 (0-933380-43-7) Olive Pr Pubns.
— Can a Woman Over Forty? LC 79-12587. 1979. 10.95 (0-933380-41-0); pap. 5.95 (0-933380-47-X) Olive Pr Pubns.

Norris, Lynne, ed. Smut: American Sex Slang: Over Four Thousand Five Hundred Entries. LC 92-26396. (Illus.). 254p. 1993. 12.00 (0-933380-22-4); lib. bdg. 14.00 (0-933380-23-2) Olive Pr Pubns.

Norris, Lynne, jt. auth. see Norris, Jim.

Norris, M. K. & House, Mary A. Organ & Tissue Transplantation: Nursing Care from Procurement Through Rehabilitation. LC 90-14141. 346p. (C). 1991. 39.95 (0-8036-6587-3) Davis Co.

Norris, M. W. Local Government in Peninsular Malaysia. 132p. 1980. text 43.95 (0-566-00283-3) Ashgate Pub Co.

Norris, Malcolm, jt. auth. see Badham, Sally.

Norris, Margaret. Integration of Special Hospital Patients into the Community. LC 84-13733. 180p. 1984. text 67.95 (0-566-00728-2, Pub. by Avebry) Ashgate Pub Co.

Norris, Margot. Beasts of the Modern Imagination: Darwin, Nietzsche, Kafka, Ernst & Lawrence. LC 84-21320. (Illus.). 279p. reprint ed. pap. 86.50 (0-7837-4778-0, 204453300003) Bks Demand.
— The Decentered Universe of Finnegans Wake: A Structuralist Analysis. LC 76-25507. 159p. reprint ed. pap. 49.30 (0-8357-8089-9, 203411600088) Bks Demand.
— Joyce's Web: The Social Unraveling of Modernism. LC 92-15209. (Literary Modernism Ser.). 255p. 1992. 35.00 (0-292-76537-1) U of Tex Pr.

***Norris, Margot.** Writing War in the Twentieth Century. 320p. 2000. 59.50 (0-8139-1991-6); pap. 19.50 (0-8139-1992-4) U Pr of Va.

***Norris, Margot, ed.** A Companion To James Joyce Ulysses, Vol. 1. LC 97-74966. 288p. 1998. pap. text 11.95 (0-312-11598-9) St Martin.

Norris, Marjorie. A Leaven of Ladies: A History of the Calgary Local Council of Women. LC 95-224737. (Illus.). 288p. (Orig.). 1995. pap. write for info. (1-55059-123-1) Detselig Ents.

***Norris, Mark.** Communications Technology Explained. 272p. 2000. pap. text 54.95 (0-471-98625-9) Wiley.
— Component-Based Network System Engineering. (Illus.). 1999. 89.00 (1-58053-008-7) Artech Hse.

Norris, Mark. Deep Blue. 1999. mass mkt. 5.95 (0-563-55571-8) BBC Worldwide.
— Survival in the Software Jungle. LC 95-33001. 256p. 1995. 27.00 (0-89006-831-3) Artech Hse.
— Total Area of Computing: A Distributed Approach. LC 97-140272. 328p. (C). 1996. pap. 39.95 (0-201-87738-4) Addison-Wesley.
— Understanding Networking Technology. LC 96-26606. 243p. 1996. 19.00 (0-89006-879-8) Artech Hse.
— Understanding Networking Technology: Concepts, Terms & Trends. 2nd ed. LC 99-26560. (Artech House Telecommunications Library). 328p. 1999. 65.00 (0-89006-998-0) Artech Hse.

Norris, Mark, jt. auth. see Frost, A.

Norris, Mark C. Handbook of Obstetric Anesthesia. 350p. pap. text 125.00 (0-7817-1859-7) Lppncott W & W.
— Obstetric Anesthesia. 2nd ed. LC 98-27543. 750p. 1998. text 125.00 (0-7817-1017-0) Lppncott W & W.

Norris, Martin. Rolling Thunder: The Harley-Davidson Legend. 1999. pap. text 12.99 (0-7858-1083-8) Bk Sales Inc.

Norris, Martin J. The Law of Maritime Personal Injuries, 2 vols., Set. 4th ed. LC 90-61399. 1990. 215.00 (0-685-59891-8) West Group.
— Law of Seamen, 3 vols., Set. 4th ed. LC 84-52821. 1985. 370.00 (0-685-59890-X) West Group.

Norris, Mary, jt. auth. see Wagner, Chris.

***Norris, Michael E.** Reinventing the Administrative State. 304p. 2000. 47.50 (0-7618-1620-8) U Pr of Amer.

***Norris, Michael K. & Goodhead, Giles.** Consultants News' Career Guide to the Top Consulting Firms. Cooper, Marshall, ed. 150p. 1999. pap. 29.95 (1-885922-60-4, Pub. by Kennedy Info) Baker & Taylor.

Norris, Mikki, et al. Shattered Lives: Portraits from America's Drug War. (Illus.). 128p. 1998. pap. 19.95 (0-9639754-3-9) Creat Express.

Norris, Miles. Cheffy Baby's Low Fat Gourmet Secrets: Cut the Fat, Not the Flavor. Chaney, Linda, ed. 120p. (Orig.). 1995. pap. text. write for info. (0-9645697-0-1); pap. text. write for info. incl. VHS (0-9645697-2-8) Madison Direct.

Norris, Miranda & Shelton, Pauline. Oman Adorned: A Portrait in Silver. (Illus.). 368p. 1997. 200.00 (1-898888-04-3, Pub. by Art Bks Intl) Partners Pubs Grp.

Norris, Miriam & Spaulding, Patricia J. Blindness in Children. LC 57-6983. 195p. reprint ed. pap. 60.50 (0-8357-7322-1, 202013900016) Bks Demand.

Norris, Neal A., ed. Community College Futures: From Rhetoric to Reality. 229p. (Orig.). 1989. pap. 24.95 (0-913507-09-1) New Forums.

Norris, Norman L. The Magic of the Mountains: Memories from California's Sequoia National Forest, 1919-1926. Norris, Eleanor, ed. LC 98-96795. (Illus.). 183p. 1998. pap. 20.00 (0-9667922-0-3) Tule Rvr Cntry.

Norris, Norval, jt. ed. see Tonry, Michael H.

Norris, O. J. Legends of Journeys. (Illus.). 32p. 1988. 16.95 (0-521-32181-6) Cambridge U Pr.

Norris, P. About Honey: Nature's Elixir for Health. 1982. pap. 2.95 (0-87904-043-2) Lust.

Norris, Pamela. Eve: A Biography. LC 99-34540. Orig. Title: Story of Eve. (Illus.). 496p. 1999. 29.95 (0-8147-5812-6) NYU Pr.

***Norris, Pamela.** The Story of Eve. (Illus.). 496p. 1999. 37.50 (0-330-33699-1, Pub. by Picador) Trans-Atl Phila.

Norris, Pamela, ed. The Brontes. (Everyman's Poetry Ser.). 1997. pap. 3.50 (0-460-87864-6, Everyman's Classic Lib) Tuttle Pubng.

Norris, Pamela, ed. see Austen, Jane.

Norris, Pamela, ed. see Hardy, Thomas.

Norris, Pamela (Ed). Sound the Deep Waters: U.K. Edition Only. 1991. write for info. (0-316-88876-1) Little.

***Norris, Pat Wastell.** High Seas, High Risk: The Story of the Sudburys. (Illus.). 250p. 1999. 28.95 (1-55017-208-5) Harbour Pub Co.

Norris, Patrick. History by Design. 96p. 1984. pap. 8.00 (0-935260-02-1) Tex Assn Mus.

Norris, Patrick, et al. A Primer for Health Care Ethics: Essays for a Pluralistic Society. LC 94-11005. 255p. 1994. pap. 19.95 (0-87840-562-3) Georgetown U Pr.

Norris Pattie, Steven. For Fathers of Sons. LC 95-184187. 1995. 8.95 (0-8378-8828-X) Gibson.

Norris, Peter. Arthur Henry Knighton-Hammond. LC 95-82208. (Illus.). 1996. 49.95 (0-7188-2824-0, Lutterworth-Parkwest) Parkwest Pubns.

Norris, Philip A., ed. see Schnorrenberg, John.

Norris, Phillip E. The Job Doctor: Good Advice on Getting a Good Job. LC 90-4881. (Illus.). 106p. (Orig.). 1990. pap. 5.95 (0-942784-43-X, JD) JIST Works.

***Norris, Pippa.** Britain Votes, 1997. (Illus.). 264p. 1998. pap. text 22.95 (0-19-922322-X) OUP.

Norris, Pippa. British By-Elections: The Volatile Electorate. (Illus.). 278p. 1990. text 75.00 (0-19-827330-4) OUP.
— Electoral Change since 1945: Since 1945. LC 96-24899. (Making Contemporary Britain Ser.). (Illus.). 256p. (C). 1996. pap. 25.95 (0-631-16716-1) Blackwell Pubs.
— Politics & the Press: The News Media & Its Influences. LC 97-3827. 336p. 1997. pap. 59.95 (1-55587-681-1) L Rienner.
— Politics & the Press: The News Media & Its Influences. LC 97-3827. 336p. 1997. 58.00 (1-55587-670-6) L Rienner.

***Norris, Pippa.** A Virtuous Circle: Political Communications in Postindustrial Societies. (Communication, Society & Politics Ser.). (Illus.). 352p. (C). 2000. 54.95 (0-521-79015-8); pap. 19.95 (0-521-79364-5) Cambridge U Pr.
— Women in Politics. (Illus.). 244p. 1996. pap. text 22.95 (0-19-922275-4) OUP.

Norris, Pippa, ed. Critical Citizens: Global Support for Democratic Governance. LC 98-40751. (Illus.). 320p. 1999. text 65.00 (0-19-829479-4); pap. text 19.95 (0-19-829568-5) OUP.
— Elections & Voting Behaviour: New Challenges, New Perspectives. (International Library of Comparative Government). 542p. 1998. 162.95 (1-85521-802-X, JF1001.E35, Pub. by Ashgate Pub) Ashgate Pub Co.
— Passages to Power: Legislative Recruitment in Advanced Democracies. 275p. (C). 1997. text 59.95 (0-521-59099-X); pap. text 22.95 (0-521-59908-3) Cambridge U Pr.
— Women, Media & Politics. (Illus.). 288p. (C). 1996. pap. 23.95 (0-19-510567-2) OUP.

Norris, Pippa & Lovenduski, Joni. Political Representation & Recruitment: Gender, Race & Class in the British Parliament. (Illus.). 334p. (C). 1995. pap. text 21.95 (0-521-46961-9) Cambridge U Pr.

Norris, Pippa, jt. ed. see Lovenduski, Joni.

Norris, R. C., jt. auth. see Meeske, Milan D.

Norris, Ralph, jt. auth. see Norris, Karen.

Norris, Randall. Women of Coal. (Illus.). 136p. 1996. 24.95 (0-8131-1993-6) U Pr of Ky.

***Norris, Richard.** Meteorite! The Last Days of the Dinosaurs. (Turnstone Ocean Explorer Ser.). 64p. (YA). (gr. 5-9). 1999. pap. 8.95 (0-7398-1241-6) Raintree Steck-V.
— Meteorite! The Last Days of the Dinosaurs. LC 99-27285. (Turnstone Ocean Explorer Bks.). 64p. (YA). (gr. 6-8). 2000. 27.11 (0-7398-1240-8) Raintree Steck-V.
— Musician's Survival Manual: A Guide to Preventing & Treating Injuries in Instrumentalists. 1993. pap. text 19.95 (0-918812-74-7) MMB Music.

Norris, Richard A., Jr. & Rusch, William G., eds. The Christological Controversy. LC 79-8890. (Sources of Early Christian Thought Ser.). 176p. 1980. pap. 17.00 (0-8006-1411-9, 1-1411, Fortress Pr) Augsburg Fortress.

Norris, Robert. Memoirs of the Reign of Bossa Ahadee King of Dahomey: An Inland Country of Guiney. (Illus.). 186p. 1968. 45.00 (0-7146-1840-3, Pub. by F Cass Pubs) Intl Spec Bk.
— The People's Will. 80p. (Orig.). 1989. pap. 16.95 (0-317-93473-2) Peoples Birmingham.
— A Power of Attorney Handbook. 80p. (Orig.). 1989. pap. 15.95 (0-317-93474-0) Peoples Birmingham.
— You Decide: A Power of Attorney Handbook. 80p. (Orig.). 1989. pap. 15.95 (0-317-93747-2) Peoples Birmingham.

Norris, Robert D., et al. Handbook of Bioremediation. LC 93-21172. 272p. 1993. lib. bdg. 85.00 (1-56670-074-4, L1074) Lewis Pubs.
— In-Situ Bioremediation of Ground Water & Geological Material: A Review of Technologies. (Illus.). 200p. (Orig.). (C). 1995. pap. text 40.00 (0-7881-2250-9) DIANE Pub.

Norris, Robert S., jt. auth. see Arkin, William M.

Norris, Ronald V. & Sullivan, Colleen. PMS: Pre-Menstrual Syndrome. 50p. 1987. mass mkt. 4.95 (0-425-10332-3) Berkley Pub.

Norris, Rosalie N. & Powell, Janet C. Easy-to-Chew & Easy-on-Salt. LC 81-65460. 176p. 1982. 10.95 (0-8453-4718-7, Cornwall Bks) Assoc Univ Prs.

Norris, Rosalie N., ed. & tr. see Salomone-Marino, Salvatore.

Norris, Ross. The Lords Last Call. LC 98-73707. 287p. 1998. pap. 12.95 (1-883697-19-0) Hara Pub.

Norris, Ruby T. The Theory of Consumer's Demand. rev. ed. LC 75-39261. (Getting & Spending: The Consumer's Dilemma Ser.). (Illus.). 1976. reprint ed. 23.95 (0-405-08034-4) Ayer.

Norris, Russell B. Creation, Cosmology, & the Cosmic Christ. (Teilhard Studies: No. 31). 1995. pap. 3.50 (0-89012-077-3) Am Teilhard.

Norris, Sarah, ed. see Johnson, Joe B.

Norris, Stephen P. The Generalizability of Critical Thinking: Multiple Perspectives on an Educational Ideal. 248p. (C). 1992. text 45.00 (0-8077-3173-0); pap. text 22.95 (0-8077-3172-2) Tchrs Coll.

Norris, Stephen P. & Phillips, Linda M., eds. Foundations of Literacy Policy in Canada. 278p. (C). 1990. pap. text 19.95 (1-55059-020-0) Temeron Bks.

Norris, Thomas. Only Life Gives Life: Revelation, Theology & Christian Living According to Cardinal Newman. 256p. 1996. 74.95 (1-85607-220-7, Pub. by Columba Press); pap. 54.95 (1-85607-141-3, Pub. by Columba Press) Intl Scholars.

Norris, Thomas, jt. ed. see McGregor, Bede.

Norris, Tom R., ed. see American Academy of Orthopaedic Surgeons Staff.

Norris, W. Sonny. How to Tame a One-Eyed Monster: Basic 35mm Photography Course, 2 bks., Bk. 1. (Illus.). 102p. (Orig.). 1988. pap. 24.95 (0-9619555-0-3) Son-Ora Photo.
— How to Tame a One-Eyed Monster: Basic 35mm Photography Course, 2 bks., Bk. 2. (Illus.). 48p. (Orig.). 1988. pap. 24.95 (0-9619555-1-1) Son-Ora Photo.

Norris, Wayne B. The Big Book of Photocopier Humor: A Treasury of High-Tech Grafitti, Left-Brain Witticisms, & Generic Humor. LC 84-90667. (Illus.). 256p. (Orig.). 1984. reprint ed. pap. 8.96 (0-685-10088-X) Norris Assocs Pr.

Norris, William E. & Strain, Jeris E., eds. Charles Carpenter Fries: His Oral Approach for Teaching & Learning Foreign Languages. fac. ed. LC 88-33465. (Illus.). 77p. 1989. reprint ed. pap. 30.00 (0-7837-7783-3, 204753800007) Bks Demand.

Norrise, Bobbe. Easy Yoga for Busy People, Vol. 1. Major, Devorah, ed. (Illus.). 72p. 1997. spiral bd., wbk. ed. 16.95 (0-9660218-1-9) Tot Hlth Inst.

Norrisey, Marie C., jt. auth. see Michael, Chester P.

Norrish, Peter. New Tragedy & Comedy in France, 1945-1970. LC 87-11571. 192p. (C). 1988. text 50.00 (0-389-20746-2, N8305) B&N Imports.

Norrish, Peter, ed. see Adamov, Arthur & Fernando, Arrabal.

Norriss, Norma G. Impersonal Intimacy: The Story of an Adolescent's Psychotherapy As Viewed by Both the Patient & the Therapist. LC 97-92519. iv, 247p. 1997. pap. 10.95 (0-9660066-0-7) Sahuaro Pr.

Norry, M. J., et al, eds. Protoplasts Poster Proceedings 1983. (Experientia Supplementa Ser.: Vol. 45). 388p. (C). 1983. pap. text 93.95 (3-7643-1513-X) Birkhauser.
— Protoplasts Poster Proceedings 1983, Vol. 46. (Experientia Supplementa Ser.: Vol. 45). 388p. (C). 1983. 70.95 (3-7643-1514-8) Birkhauser.

Norse, Elliott A. Ancient Forests of the Pacific Northwest. LC 89-20029. (Illus.). 325p. (C). 1989. pap. 25.00 (1-55963-016-7); text 40.00 (1-55963-017-5) Island Pr.

N

An Asterisk (*) at the beginning of an entry indicates that the title is appearing for the first time.

Norse, Elliott A., ed. Global Marine Biological Diversity: A Strategy for Building Conversation Into Decision Making. LC 93-25350. 350p. 1993. text 58.00 (*1-55963-255-0*); pap. text 32.00 (*1-55963-256-9*) Island Pr.

Norse, Harold. Beat Hotel. (Illus.). 78p. (C). 1983. 25.00 (*0-317-11746-7*); pap. 6.95 (*0-912377-00-3*) Atticus Pr.

— Karma Circuit. (Illus.). 70p. (Orig.). 1973. pap. 6.00 (*0-915572-04-4*) Panjandrum.

— Mysteries of Magritte. (Orig.). (C). 1984. pap. 5.00 (*0-912377-07-0*) Atticus Pr.

— Mysteries of Magritte. limited ed. (Orig.). (C). 1984. 15.00 (*0-912377-06-2*) Atticus Pr.

— Sniffing Keyholes. (Chapbook Ser.). (Illus.). 9p. 1998. pap. 10.00 (*0-9652505-7-1*) Synaesthesia.

Norse, Harold & Williams, William Carlos. The American Idiom: A Correspondence. (Illus.). 176p. (C). 1991. 21.95 (*0-944378-80-3*) Bright Tyger Pr.

Norse, Harold & Williams, William Carlos. The American Idiom: A Correspondence. (Illus.). 176p. (Orig.). (C). 1991. pap. 10.95 (*0-944378-79-X*) Bright Tyger Pr.

Norse, Harold, tr. see Belli, G. G.

Norseng, Kay M., jt. ed. see Ingwersen, Faith.

Norseng, Mary Kay. Dagny - The Woman/Myth: Dagny Juel Przybyszewska, the Woman & the Myth. LC 90-30147. (Samuel & Althea Stroum Bks.). (Illus.). 240p. 1991. pap. 24.95 (*0-295-96999-7*) U of Wash Pr.

Norsgaard, E. Jaediker. Butterflies for Kids. LC 95-36453. (Wildlife for Kids Ser.). (Illus.). 48p. (J). (gr. 3-7). 1996. pap. 6.95 (*1-55971-546-4*, NorthWord Pr) Creat Pub Intl.

Norsic, Donald. To Save Russia. Charles, Rodney & Pasco, Elizabeth, eds. LC 97-65714. (Illus.). 440p. (YA). 1998. pap. 16.95 (*1-887472-35-5*) Sunstar Pubng.

Norskog, Howard L. Beyond a Sleeping Prairie. 40p. (Orig.). 1994. pap. 6.00 (*0-9625171-3-5*) H L Norskog.

— High Country Ballads. 40p. (Orig.). 1994. pap. 6.00 (*0-9625171-5-1*) H L Norskog.

— High Country Ballads: Cowboy Poetry. (DNA Ser.). 80p. (Orig.). (YA). (gr. 8 up). 1988. pap. 6.99 (*0-685-30409-4*) H L Norskog.

— Lonesome, Old Camp Fires. 40p. 1994. pap. 6.00 (*0-9625171-6-X*) H L Norskog.

— Mountains of Thunder. 35p. (Orig.). 1994. pap. 6.00 (*0-685-71206-0*) H L Norskog.

— Sing Me a Mountain. 35p. (Orig.). 1994. pap. 6.00 (*0-9625171-1-9*) H L Norskog.

— Under a Far Away Star. 40p. (Orig.). 1994. pap. 6.00 (*0-9625171-4-3*) H L Norskog.

— Where Wild Rivers Run. 40p. (Orig.). pap. 6.00 (*0-9625171-7-8*) H L Norskog.

— Yesterdays Trails. 35p. (Orig.). 1994. pap. 6.00 (*0-9625171-0-0*) H L Norskog.

— Yesterdays Trails: Cowboy Poetry. (DNA Ser.). 49p. (YA). (gr. 8 up). 1989. pap. 6.99 (*0-685-30410-8*) H L Norskog.

Norst, Marlene J. Ferdinand Bauer: The Australian Natural History Drawings. (Art in Natural History Ser.: Vol. 1). (Illus.). 120p. 1993. pap. 20.00 (*0-11-310037-X*) Statnry Office.

Norstedt, Johann A. Thomas MacDonagh, a Critical Biography. LC 78-31320. 187p. 1980. reprint ed. pap. 58.00 (*0-608-04238-2*, 206499400012) Bks Demand.

Norstedt, Marilyn L., jt. ed. see McMillan, Gail.

Norstein, J., jt. ed. see Soreide, O.

Norstog, Knut J. & Nicholls, Trevor J. The Biology of the Cycads. LC 96-48889. (Comstock Bks.). (Illus.). 504p. 1996. text 145.00 (*0-8014-3033-X*, Comstock Pub) Cornell U Pr.

Norstrom, Alison D. Proofreading At The Computer:10 Hour Series. LC 99-14154. 76p. 1999. 16.95 (*0-538 68974-2*) Thomson Learn.

***Norstrom, Barbara & Cole, Mary V.** Proofreading at the Computer. 80p. 1999. pap. 19.95 (*0-538-68925-0*) Sth-Wstrn College.

Norstrom, Lars, jt. tr. see Salisbury, Ralph.

Norstrom Ridaeus, Barbro. 100 Vagar Till Afrika: En Introduktion Till Modern Afrikansk Skonlitteratur. 168p. 1995. write for info. (*91-7106-368-4*, Pub. by Nordic Africa) Transaction Pubs.

Norstrom, Wanda. An American Artist in Africa, 1937: Sketch Book & Diary. (Illus.). 112p. (Orig.). 1991. pap. 19.00 (*0-9630357-0-3*) P Shedding.

Norsworthy, Alex, ed. FRI Prospect Research Resource Directory, Vol. 2. 2nd ed. 491p. 1991. 85.00 (*0-930807-24-3*, 600311) Fund Raising.

— The Nonprofit Computer Sourcebook: The Professional's Guide to Products, Services & Information Sources for Computer Systems. 91st ed. 355p. 1990. 75.00 (*0-914756-97-4*, 600087) Taft Group.

Norsworthy, Elaine, jt. auth. see Lambert, Eddie.

Norsworthy, Gary D. Current Feline Practice. (Illus.). 725p. 1993. text 99.00 (*0-397-51204-X*) Lppncott W & W.

— The Feline Patient: Essentials of Diagnosis & Treatment. LC 97-13122. 350p. 1998. write for info. (*0-683-06556-4*) Lppncott W & W.

Norsworthy, J. R. & Jang, S. L. Empirical Measurement & Analysis of Productivity & Technological Change: Applications in High-Technology & Service Industries. LC 92-36913. (Contributions to Economic Analysis Ser.: No. 211). 318p. 1992. 98.50 (*0-444-89002-5*, North Holland) Elsevier.

Norsworthy, J. R., jt. auth. see Pitt, Ivan L.

Norsworthy, John R. & Tsai, Diana H. Macroeconomic Policy as Implicit Industrial Policy: Its Industry & Enterprise Effects. LC 97-38536. 280p. 1997. 126.50 (*0-7923-8075-4*) Kluwer Academic.

Norsworthy, Kent & Barry, Tom. Nicaragua: A Country Guide. 2nd ed. 226p. 1990. pap. 9.95 (*0-911213-29-5*) Interhemisp Res Ctr.

Norsworthy, Kent, jt. ed. see Pasch, Grete.

Norsworthy, Steven R., et al, eds. Delta-Sigma Data Converters: Theory, Design, & Simulation. LC 96-14774. 512p. 1996. 89.95 (*0-7803-1045-4*, PC3954) Inst Electrical.

***Nortell, Bruce.** Rimed Recipes: Cooking In Seven Sages. LC 99-96401. 240p. 2000. 15.00 (*0-9674812-0-1*) Lendtroninc.

Norten, Ellen. Neem: India's Miraculous Healing Plant. LC 99-49948. (Illus.). 96p. 2000. pap. 9.95 (*0-89281-837-9*) Inner Tradit.

Norten, Enrique & Gomez-Pimiento, Bernardo. Ten Arquitectos. LC 98-7125. (Work in Progress Ser.). 224p. 1998. pap. text 35.00 (*1-885254-91-1*, Pub. by Monacelli Pr) Penguin Putnam.

***North.** Key to Latin Prose Composition. 1999. pap. 12.95 (*0-941051-92-7*) Focus Pub-R Pullins.

North. Simeon North: First Official Pistol Maker of the United States. reprint ed. 15.95 (*0-88227-001-X*) Gun Room.

— Work & the Eye. 288p. 1993. pap. text 50.00 (*0-7506-4045-6*) Buttrwrth-Heinemann.

North & Hillard, eds. Latin Prose Composition. LC 96-137203. (LAT.). 310p. (Orig.). (C). 1988. pap. 20.00 (*0-86516-308-1*) Bolchazy-Carducci.

North, jt. auth. see Crowley.

***North, A.** Perils of Pauline Peach. 1998. mass mkt. 6.95 (*0-7472-5776-0*, Pub. by Headline Bk Pub) Trafalgar.

— The Taming of Tracie Trix. 1998. mass mkt. 6.95 (*0-7472-5777-9*, Pub. by Headline Bk Pub) Trafalgar.

North, Adrian, jt. ed. see Hargreaves, David.

North, Alan. One Hundred One Atari Computer Programming Tips & Tricks. 128p. (Orig.). 1982. pap. 8.95 (*0-86668-022-5*) ARCsoft.

— Thirty-One New Atari Computer Programs for Home, School & Office. (Illus.). 96p. (Orig.). 1982. pap. 8.95 (*0-86668-018-7*) ARCsoft.

North American Association of Wardens & Superintendents. A View from the Trenches: A Manual for Wardens by Wardens. 200p. 1999. pap. 27.50 (*1-56991-114-2*, 407) Am Correctional.

North American Bear Co., Inc. Staff. A Charmed Life by Muffy Vander Bear. (Illus.). 32p. (J). (ps-6). 1998. 14.95 (*0-9665277-0-4*) North Am Bear.

North American Bear Company Inc. Staff, jt. auth. see Vanderbear, Muffy.

North American Geosynthetics Soc. Staff. Geosynthetics '97 Conference Proceedings, 2 vols. Intl. Geosynthetics Soc., Industrial Fabrics Assn., ed. (Illus.). 1140p. 1997. pap. text 97.00 (*0-935803-06-8*) Indus Fabrics.

North American Geosynthetics Society Staff, ed. Geosynthetics 1995 Conference Proceedings. (Illus.). 1350p. 1995. pap. text 95.00 (*0-935803-03-3*) Indus Fabrics.

North American Hunting Club, jt. auth. see Vail, Mike.

North American Man-Boy Love Association Staff. A Witchhunt Foiled: The FBI vs. NAMBLA. LC 85-72763. (Illus.). 93p. (Orig.). 1985. pap. 5.95 (*0-9615497-0-X*) N Am Man-Boy.

North American Manufacturing Research Conference (. North American Manufacturing Research Conference Proceedings: May 27-29, 1987, Lehigh University, Bethlehem, PA. LC 76-646280. (SME Manufacturing Technology Review Ser.: No. 2). (Illus.). 702p. reprint ed. pap. 200.00 (*0-8357-6507-5*, 203587800097) Bks Demand.

— North American Manufacturing Research Conference Proceedings: May 28-30, 1986, University of Minnesota, Minneapolis, MN - Organized by the University of Minnesota Department of Mechanical Engineering, Minneapolis, MN. LC 76-646280. (Manufacturing Technology Review Ser.: No. 1). (Illus.). 684p. reprint ed. pap. 200.00 (*0-8357-6475-3*, 203584600097) Bks Demand.

— North American Manufacturing Research Conference Proceedings, May 19-22, 1985, University of California-Berkeley, Berkeley, CA. LC 76-646280. (Manufacturing Engineering Transactions Ser.: No. 13). (Illus.). 602p. 1985. reprint ed. pap. 186.70 (*0-8357-6505-9*, 203587600097) Bks Demand.

— Transactions of the North American Manufacturing Research Institution of SME 1989: Papers Presented at NAMRC XVII, May 24-26, 1989, Ohio State University, Columbus, OH. LC 89-60331. (Illus.). 396p. 1989. reprint ed. pap. 122.80 (*0-7837-9726-5*, 206045700005) Bks Demand.

North American Manufacturing Reserach Conference (. North American Manufacturing Research Conference Proceedings, May 24-26, 1983, University of Wisconsin-Madison, Madison, WI. 2nd ed. LC 76-646280. (Manufacturing Engineering Transactions Ser.: No. 11). (Illus.). 504p. 1983. reprint ed. pap. 156.30 (*0-7837-8192-X*, 204789700008) Bks Demand.

North American Meat Processors Association Staff. The Meat Buyers Guide. (Illus.). 218p. (Orig.). (C). 1991. reprint ed. pap. text 49.00 (*1-878154-00-1*) N Am Meat Process.

North American Metalworking Research Conference St. North American Metalworking Research Conference: Proceedings, 7th, May 13-16, 1979, University of Michigan, Ann Arbor, MI. LC 79-63779. (Manufacturing Engineering Transactions Ser.: No. 7). (Illus.). 389p. reprint ed. pap. 120.60 (*0-608-18100-5*, 203216700078) Bks Demand.

North American Nursing Diagnosis Association Staff. Classification of Nursing Diagnoses: Proceedings of the Eleventh Conference. LeMone, Priscilla & Rantz, Marilyn J., eds. LC 95-25622. 1995. write for info. (*0-910478-54-6*) Cum Index Nursing.

— NANDA Nursing Diagnoses: Definitions & Classifications, 1995-1996. rev. ed. 124p. (C). 1995. pap. 11.00 (*0-9637042-1-4*) N Am Nursing.

North American Prairie Conference Staff. Prairie Peninsula Proceedings, Sixth, Ohio State University, Columbus, Ohio, August 12-17, 1978: In the "Shadow" of Transeau. Stuckey, Ronald L. & Reese, Karen J., eds. LC 81-82059. (Biological Notes Ser.: No. 15). (Illus.). 1981. pap. text 15.00 (*0-86727-090-X*) Ohio Bio Survey.

North American Publishing Company Staff. World Guide to Packaging, 1997: International Edition. 828p. 1998. pap. 375.00 (*0-912920-97-1*) North Am Pub Co.

North American Rapid Excavation & Tunneling Confer. North American Rapid Evacuation & Tunneling: Proceedings of the Conference, 2nd, San Francisco, CA, June 24-27, 2 vols., 1. LC 74-84644. 968p. reprint ed. pap. 200.00 (*0-608-11783-8*, 200513000050) Bks Demand.

— North American Rapid Evacuation & Tunneling: Proceedings of the Conference, 2nd, San Francisco, CA, June 24-27, 2 vols., 2. LC 74-84644. 807p. reprint ed. pap. 200.00 (*0-608-11784-6*, 200513000051) Bks Demand.

— Proceedings, 1972, Vol. 1. Lane, Kenneth S. & Garfield, Larry A., eds. LC 72-86918. (Illus.). 852p. reprint ed. pap. 200.00 (*0-7837-7867-8*, 200906500072) Bks Demand.

— Proceedings, 1972, Vol. 2. Lane, Kenneth S. & Garfield, Larry A., eds. LC 72-86918. (Illus.). 830p. reprint ed. pap. 200.00 (*0-7837-7868-6*, 200906500073) Bks Demand.

North American Rock Gardening Society Staff. Rock Garden Plants of North America: An Anthology from the Bulletin of the North American Rock Garden Society. McGary, Jane, ed. LC 95-23104. (Illus.). 504p. 1996. 49.95 (*0-88192-343-5*) Timber.

North American Society for the Psychology of Sport. Psychology of Motor Behavior & Sport, 1976, Vol. 1. Christina, Robert W. & Landers, Daniel M., eds. LC 78-641529. 296p. 1977. reprint ed. pap. 91.80 (*0-608-10450-7*, 202952800001) Bks Demand.

— Psychology of Motor Behavior & Sport, 1976, Vol. 2. Christina, Robert W. & Landers, Daniel M., eds. LC 78-641529. 283p. 1977. reprint ed. pap. 87.80 (*0-608-10451-5*, 202952800002) Bks Demand.

North American Society for the Psychology of Sport & Physical Activity Staff. Psychology of Motor Behavior & Sport, 1979. Nadeau, Claude H., ed. LC 78-641529. 760p. 1980. reprint ed. pap. 200.00 (*0-608-10453-1*, 202953000061) Bks Demand.

— Psychology of Motor Behavior & Sport, 1980. Roberts, Glyn C. & Landers, Daniel M., eds. LC 78-641529. 220p. 1981. reprint ed. pap. 68.20 (*0-608-10454-X*, 202953300061) Bks Demand.

North American Spine Society Staff & Fardon, David F., eds. Disorders of the Spine: A Coding System for Diagnoses. LC 91-71142. 132p. (Orig.). 1991. text 30.00 (*1-56053-014-6*) Hanley & Belfus.

North American Strawberry Growers Association Staff. Strawberry Eats & Treats: The Guide to Enjoying Strawberries. LC 96-71975. (Illus.). 112p. 1997. pap. 12.95 (*0-942495-62-4*) Palmer Pubns Inc.

North American Symposium on Family Practice Staff. The Many Dimensions of Family Practice. LC 80-14847. 340p. 1983. 45.00 (*0-87668-427-4*) Aronson.

***North American Transportation Management Institute Staff.** Motor Fleet Safety Supervision: Principals & Practices. 1998. pap. 25.00 (*0-88711-390-7*) Am Trucking Assns.

North, Anthony. Descent into Crime: Britian's Century of Lawlessness 1650-1750. 26.95 (*1-902809-10-6*, Pub. by Allison & Busby) Intl Pubs Mktg.

North, Anthony. Paranormal. (Illus.). 272p. 1998. 16.95 (*0-7137-2715-2*, Pub. by Blandford Pr) Sterling.

— The Paranormal: A Guide to the Unexplained. (Illus.). 294p. 1996. 24.95 (*0-7137-2615-6*, Pub. by Blandford Pr) Sterling.

— Pewter. 1999. 65.00 (*1-85177-223-5*) V&A Ent.

— The Supernatural: A Guide to Mysticism & the Occult. (Illus.). 224p. 1998. 27.95 (*0-7137-2728-4*) Sterling.

North, Arielle, ed. see Franzwa, Gregory M.

North, Arthur A. Supreme Court: Judicial Process & Judicial Politics. LC 66-17855. (Orig.). 1966. pap. text 11.95 (*0-89197-435-0*) Irvington.

North, Arthur W. The Founders & the Founding of Walton, New York. (Illus.). 68p. 1996. reprint ed. pap. 12.00 (*1-887530-02-9*) RSG Pub.

North Atlantic Treaty Organization, jt. auth. see Jennings, Keith R.

North Atlantic Treaty Organization, Advisory Group. Ethnic Variables in Human Factors Engineering: Based on Papers Presented at a Symposium on "National & Cultural Variables in Human Factors Engineering," Held in Oosterbeek, The Netherlands, 19-23 June 1972. Chapanis, Alphonse, ed. LC 74-24393. (Illus.). 312p. 1975. reprint ed. pap. 96.80 (*0-608-04058-4*, 206479400011) Bks Demand.

North Atlantic Treaty Organization Staff. Decadal Climate Variability: Dynamics & Predictability. Anderson, D. L. & Willebrand, J., eds. LC 96-27903. (NATO ASI Ser.: Global Environmental Change). 504p. 1996. 229.50 (*3-540-61459-1*) Spr-Verlag.

— Gravity Wave Processes Vol. VIII: Their Parameterization in Global Climate Models. Hamilton, Kevin, ed. LC 96-37587. (NATO ASI Series I: Vol. 50). 414p. 1997. 197.00 (*3-540-62036-2*) Spr-Verlag.

— Masses of Fundamental Particles: Cargese 1996: Proceedings of a NATO ASI Held in Cargese, France, August 5-17, 1996. Levy, Maurice et al, eds. LC 97-31221. (NATO ASI Ser.: Vol. 363). 404p. (C). 1997. text 125.00 (*0-306-45694-X*, Kluwer Plenum) Kluwer Academic.

— Sea-Dumped Chemical Weapons - Aspects, Problems & Solutions: Proceedings of the NATO Advanced Research Workshop on 'Sea-Dumped Chemical Munitions', Kaliningrad (Moscow Region), Russia, Jan. 12-15. Kaffka, Alexander V., ed. LC 96-18909. (NATO Advanced Science Institutes). 184p. (C). 1996. text 110.50 (*0-7923-4090-6*) Kluwer Academic.

— Spectroscopy & Dynamics of Collective Excitations in Solids: Proceedings of a NATO ASI & an International School of Atomic & Molecular Spectroscopy Workshop on Spectroscopy & Dynamics of Collective Excitation in Solids Held in Erice, Italy, June 1-July 1, 1995. Di Bartolo, Baldassare, ed. LC 96-47008. (NATO ASI Ser.: Vol. 356). 516p. (C). 1997. text 135.00 (*0-306-45390-8*) Plenum.

North Atlantic Treaty Organization Staff, et al. Air Pollution Modeling & Its Application. Gryning, Sven-Erik & Schiermeier, Francis A., eds. LC 96-28437. (NATO - Challenges of Modern Society Ser.: Vol. 21). (Illus.). 722p. (C). 1996. 191.00 (*0-306-45381-9*, Vol. XI, Plenum Trade) Perseus Pubng.

— The Aral Sea Basin. Micklin, Philip P. & Williams, W. D., eds. LC 96-32764. (NATO ASI Ser.; Environment). 186p. 1996. 89.50 (*3-540-61494-X*) Spr-Verlag.

— Chemical Exchange Between the Atmosphere & Polar Snow. LC 96-21625. (NATO ASI Ser.). 676p. 1996. 316.00 (*3-540-61280-7*) Spr-Verlag.

— Neurobiology: Ionic Channels, Neurons & the Brain. Torre, Vincent & Conti, Franco, eds. LC 96-29397. (NATO ASI Series A: Vol. 289). (Illus.). 404p. (C). 1997. text 150.00 (*0-306-45480-7*) Plenum.

North Atlantic Treaty Organization Staff, jt. auth. see Derouane, E. G.

North Atlantic Treaty Organization Staff, jt. auth. see Diaz, J. I.

North Atlantic Treaty Organization Staff, jt. auth. see Fortier, Suzanne.

North Atlantic Treaty Organization Staff, jt. auth. see Jordan, Michael I.

North Atlantic Treaty Organization Staff, jt. auth. see Kanellis, A. K.

North Atlantic Treaty Organization Staff, jt. auth. see Kossowsky, Ram.

North Atlantic Treaty Organization Staff, jt. auth. see Wierzbicki, Jacek G.

North, Audrey. Australia's Fan Heritage. 70p. (C). 1990. 85.00 (*0-86439-001-7*, Pub. by Boolarong Pubns) St Mut.

North, B. Ourselves. Date not set. 5.99 (*1-871676-04-5*, Pub. by Christian Focus) Spring Arbor Dist.

— Welcome Home. 1995. 5.99 (*1-871676-03-7*, Pub. by Christian Focus) Spring Arbor Dist.

North, B. H., ed. Light Transit Systems: Proceedings of the Symposium on the Potential of Light Transit Systems in British Cities, Nottingham, England, March 14-15, 1990. 282p. 1990. 10.00 (*0-7277-1590-9*) Am Soc Civil Eng.

North, Barbara & Crittenden, Penelope. Anti-Stress Workbook. (Illus.). 79p. (Orig.). 1980. pap. 4.95 (*0-938480-00-6*) Healthworks.

North, Barbara, tr. see Duverger, Maurice.

North, Barbara A., jt. auth. see Headley, Barbara J.

North Berwick Priory Staff. Carte Monialium De Northberwic. Innes, Cosmo N., ed. LC 74-173799. (Bannatyne Club, Edinburgh. Publications: No. 84). reprint ed. 37.50 (*0-404-52809-0*) AMS Pr.

North, Bill. The Prints of John S. DeMartelly, 1903-1979. Bandes, Susan J. & Mayers, Bonney, eds. (Illus.). 96p. (Orig.). 1997. pap. 18.00 (*1-879147-14-9*) Kresge Art Mus.

North, Bill, et al. Rural America: Prints from the Collection of Steven Schmidt. (Illus.). (Orig.). 1993. pap. 11.95 (*0-913689-37-8*) Spencer Muse Art.

***North, Brownlow.** A Great Gulf Fixed. 125p. 1999. reprint ed. pap. 6.99 (*0-85151-765-X*) Banner of Truth.

North, Brownlow. The Rich Man & Lazarus. 1979. pap. 4.99 (*0-85151-121-X*) Banner of Truth.

— El Ricoy Lazaro: The Rich Man & Lazarus. (ENG & SPA.). 118p. 1997. reprint ed. pap. 4.50 (*0-85151-420-0*) Banner of Truth.

North, C. P. & Prosser, D. J., eds. Characterization of Fluvial & Aeolian Reservoirs. (Geological Society Special Publications: No. 73). (Illus.). 450p. 1993. 108.00 (*0-903317-90-7*, 287, Pub. by Geol Soc Pub Hse) AAPG.

North, Carol. My First Backpack. (Illus.). 24p. (Orig.). (J). (ps-1). 1996. pap. 2.25 (*1-56293-909-2*, McClanahan Book) Learn Horizon.

North, Carol S. Welcome, Silence: My Triumph over Schizophrenia. 240p. 1989. reprint ed. mass mkt. 4.99 (*0-380-70627-X*, Avon Bks) Morrow Avon.

North, Carol S., et al. Multiple Personalites, Multiple Disorders: Psychiatric Classification & Media Influence. LC 92-49904. (Oxford Psychiatry Ser.: No. 1). (Illus.). 296p. (C). 1993. text 45.00 (*0-19-508095-5*) OUP.

North Carolina Adjutant, General's Office Staff & Toler, Maurice S. Muster Rolls of the Soldiers of the War of 1812 Detached from the Militia of North Carolina in 1812 & 1814: Detached from the Militia of North Carolina in 1812 & 1814. With an Added Index. LC 76-20239. 193p. 1998. reprint ed. pap. 22.50 (*0-8063-0728-5*) Clearfield Co.

North Carolina Bar Association Foundation Staff & Blalock, Steven F. Social Security Disability Claims. 1983. write for info. (*0-318-58303-8*) NC Bar Found.

North Carolina Biotechnology Center Staff, jt. auth. see Kennedy, Kathleen E.

North Carolina Board of Science Staff, jt. auth. see National Research Council Staff.

North Carolina. Dept. of Insurance. North Carolina Regulations: Containing Insurance Department Regulations, Bulletins & Directives, & Selected Attorney General's Opinions. LC 97-67932. 1997. write for info. (*0-89246-474-7*) NILS Pub.

N

An Asterisk (*) at the beginning of an entry indicates that the title is appearing for the first time.

North Carolina General Assembly Staff. Colonial Records of North Carolina, 1662-1776, 10 vols. Saunders, William L., ed. LC 72-130612. reprint ed. 1800.00 (*0-404-05590-7*) AMS Pr.
— Index to Colonial & State Records of North Carolina, 1662-1790, 4 vols. Weeks, Stephen B., ed. LC 72-1797. reprint ed. 700.00 (*0-404-07487-1*) AMS Pr.
— State Records of North Carolina, 1777-1790, 16 vols. Clark, Walter, ed. LC 72-1798. reprint ed. 2880.00 (*0-404-07470-7*) AMS Pr.
North Carolina Local Government Performance Measur. Performance & Cost Data Phase I: City Services. 108p. (C). 1997. pap. text 15.00 (*1-56011-337-5*, 97.18A) Institute Government.
— Performance & Cost Data Phase II: County Services. 115p. 1998. pap. text 15.00 (*1-56011-340-5*, 97.18B) Institute Government.
***North Carolina Local Government Staff, prod.** Final Report on City Services for Fiscal Year 1998-99: Performance & Cost Data, February 2000. (C). 2000. pap. 15.00 (*1-56011-368-5*) Institute Government.
— Final Report on County Services for Fiscal Year 1998-99: Performance & Cost Data, February 2000. (C). 2000. pap. 15.00 (*1-56011-372-3*) Institute Government.
North Carolina Local Government Staff, prod. Performance & Cost Data Phase III City Services: Medium & Smaller Cities. 1999. pap. 15.00 (*1-56011-355-3*) Institute Government.
— Performance & Cost Data Phase III County Services: Medium & Smaller Counties. 1999. pap. 15.00 (*1-56011-356-1*) Institute Government.
North Carolina Museum of Art Staff, ed. E. L. Kirchner, German Expressionist: A Loan Exhibition. LC 59-2148. (Illus.). 1958. pap. 1.50 (*0-88259-002-2*) NCMA.
North Carolina Museum of Art Staff, et al. The Store of Joys: Writers Celebrate the North Carolina Museum of Art's Fiftieth Anniversary. LC 97-7004. 1997. write for info. (*0-89587-207-2*) Blair.
North Carolina Museum of Art Staff, jt. auth. see Ferguson, Herman W.
North Carolina School of Science & Mathematics, De. Contemporary Calculus Through Applications. 1995. write for info. (*0-614-01932-X*) Janson Pubns.
— Contemporary Precalculus Through Applications: Answer Key. (Illus.). 231p. 1992. pap. 12.95 (*0-939765-55-1*, G149) Janson Pubns.
— Contemporary Precalculus Through Applications: Assessment Resource. 126p. 1993. pap. 19.95 (*0-939765-58-6*, G150) Janson Pubns.
— Contemporary Precalculus Through Applications: Instructor's Guide. 143p. 1993. pap. 19.95 (*0-939765-57-8*, G152) Janson Pubns.
— Contemporary Precalculus Through Applications: Supplementary Resource. 79p. 1993. pap. 19.95 (*0-939765-60-8*, G160) Janson Pubns.
North Carolina School of Science & Mathematics, De, et al. Contemporary Precalculus Through Applications: Functions, Data Analysis & Matrices. (Illus.). 344p. 1992. text 38.50 (*0-939765-54-3*, G148) Janson Pubns.
North Carolina State Staff. Biology 100. 112p. (C). 1997. spiral bd., lab manual ed. 20.95 (*0-7872-4211-X*) Kendall-Hunt.
North Carolina State University Staff. Survey & Evaluation of Factors Affecting Heat Transfer Performance & Cost of Steam Condensers. 93p. 1967. 13.95 (*0-317-34551-6*, 104) Intl Copper.
***North Carolina University Staff.** Biology 111 Lab Manual. 150p. (C). 2000. spiral bd. 29.95 (*0-7872-7191-8*) Kendall-Hunt.
— Biology 112 Lab Manual. 210p. (C). 2000. spiral bd. 32.95 (*0-7872-7192-6*) Kendall-Hunt.
— Biology 105 Lab Manual. 125p. (C). 2000. spiral bd. 29.95 (*0-7872-7190-X*) Kendall-Hunt.
— General Chemistry Lab Manual. 3rd ed. 135p. (C). 2000. 14.95 (*0-7872-7274-4*) Kendall-Hunt.
— Introductory Chemistry: Lab Manual. 3rd ed. 118p. (C). 2000. 12.95 (*0-7872-7283-3*) Kendall-Hunt.
North Carolina Wildlife Resources Commission Staff. North Carolina Wild Places: A Closer Look. Earley, Lawrence S., ed. LC 92-81998. (Illus.). 82p. (Orig.). (J). (gr. 2-6). 1994. pap. 10.00 (*0-9628949-1-5*) NC Wildlife.
***North, Carolyn.** Crop Circles: Hoax or Happening? (Fringe Ser.: Vol. 2). (Illus.). 96p. 2000. pap. 7.95 (*1-57951-019-1*, Pub. by Ronin Pub) Publishers Group.
North, Carolyn. Death: The Experience of a Lifetime. LC 96-40274. (Fringe Ser.). 1997. 3.95 (*1-889059-06-4*) Regent Pr.
— The Experience of a Lifetime: Living Fully, Dying Consciously. (Illus.). 257p. 1998. pap. 17.95 (*1-56937-218-7*) Amber Lotus.
— Seven Movements, One Song. 325p. (Orig.). 1991. pap. 14.95 (*0-916147-17-7*) Regent Pr.
North, Catharine M. The History of Berlin, Connecticut. 294p. 1988. reprint ed. lib. bdg. 38.00 (*0-8328-6537-0*, CT0001) Higginson Bk Co.
North Central Regional Center for Rural Developmen. Communities Left Behind: Alternatives for Development. LC 74-11286. 161p. reprint ed. pap. 50.00 (*0-608-15337-0*, 202962200061) Bks Demand.
— Rural Industrialization: Problems & Potentials. LC 73-20027. 163p. reprint ed. pap. 50.60 (*0-608-15237-4*, 202916400059) Bks Demand.
North, Charles. Leap Year. (Illus.). 7.00 (*0-686-65482-X*); pap. 3.50 (*0-686-65483-8*) Kulchur Foun.
— New & Selected Poems. (Sun & Moon Classics Ser.: No. 102). 205p. 1998. pap. 13.00 (*1-55713-265-8*, Pub. by Sun & Moon CA) Consort Bk Sales.
— No Other Way: Selected Prose. LC 97-46108. 176p. 1998. 22.00 (*1-882413-53-9*); pap. 13.50 (*1-882413-52-0*) Hanging Loose.
— The Year of the Olive Oil. 1989. 15.00 (*0-914610-67-8*); pap. 8.00 (*0-914610-66-X*) Hanging Loose.
North, Charles & Schuyler, James, eds. Broadway Two: A Poets' & Painters' Anthology. 1989. 25.00 (*0-914610-71-6*); pap. 15.00 (*0-914610-70-8*) Hanging Loose.
North Country Press Staff. Maine Animals. (Maine Nature Ser.). 64p. 1997. pap. text 4.50 (*0-945980-25-6*) Nrth Country Pr.
— Maine Rivers. (Maine Nature Ser.). 64p. 1997. pap. text 4.50 (*0-945980-12-4*) Nrth Country Pr.
North, D. C. & Thomas, R. P. The Rise of the Western World: A New Economic History. LC 73-77258. (Illus.). 179p. 1976. pap. text 19.95 (*0-521-29099-6*) Cambridge U Pr.
***North Dakota.** North Dakota Related Laws to the Insurance Laws. LC 97-76070. 1999. write for info. (*0-89246-491-7*) NILS Pub.
North Dakota Council on the Arts, jt. auth. see Geist, Troyd A.
North, Darian. Bone Deep. 1996. mass mkt. 6.99 (*0-451-18550-1*, Sig) NAL.
North, Darian. Criminal Seduction. 560p. 1994. mass mkt. 6.99 (*0-451-18022-4*, Sig) NAL.
North, Darian. Violation. large type ed. LC 98-31481. 1999. 30.00 (*0-7862-1719-7*) Thorndike Pr.
— Violation. 448p. 1999. reprint ed. mass mkt. 6.99 (*0-451-17915-3*, Sig) NAL.
***North, David.** After the Slaughter: Political Lessons of the Balkan War. (SEP Pamphlet Ser.: Vol. 12). 39p. 1999. pap. 3.00 (*1-875639-35-7*) Mehring Bks.
— Anti-Semitism, Fascism & the Holocaust: A Critical Review of Daniel Goldhagen's Hitler's Willing Executioners. 1997. 2.00 (*0-929087-75-5*) Mehring Bks.
North, David. Forbidden Region. (Time Warriors Ser.: Vol. 2). 1991. per. 3.50 (*0-373-63602-4*) Harlequin Bks.
— Fuse Point. (Time Warriors Ser.: No. 6). 1991. per. 3.50 (*0-373-63601-6*) Harlequin Bks.
— Gerry Healy & His Place in the History of the Fourth International. (Illus.). 117p. 1991. pap. 11.95 (*0-929087-58-5*) Mehring Bks.
— Guardian Strikes. (Time Warriors Ser.: Vol. 3). 1991. per. 3.50 (*0-373-63603-2*) Harlequin Bks.
— The Heritage We Defend: A Contribution to the History of the Fourth International. 539p. 1988. pap. 21.95 (*0-929087-00-3*) Mehring Bks.
— In Defense of the Russian Revolution: A Reply to the Post-Soviet School of Historical Falsification. (Illus.). 53p. (Orig.). 1995. pap. 3.95 (*0-929087-72-0*) Mehring Bks.
— Leon Trotsky & the Fate of Socialism in the 20th Century: A Reply to Professor Eric Hobsbawm. (SEP Lecture Ser.). 56p. 1998. 5.00 (*1-875639-22-5*, Pub. by Mehring Bks) Mehring Bks.
— Marxism & the Trade Unions. (SEP Lecture Ser.). 38p. 1998. pap. 5.00 (*1-875639-29-2*) Mehring Bks.
— Perestroika Versus Socialism: Stalinism & the Restoration of Capitalism in the U. S. S. R. 80p. (Orig.). (C). 1989. pap. 7.95 (*0-929087-39-9*) Mehring Bks.
— Reform & Revolution in the Epoch of Imperialism. (SEP Lecture Ser.). 38p. 1998. pap. 5.00 (*1-875639-28-4*) Mehring Bks.
— Socialism, Historical Truth & the Crisis of Political Thought in the United States. 46p. (Orig.). 1996. pap. 3.50 (*0-929087-73-9*) Mehring Bks.
***North, David.** A Tribute to Tom Henehan, 1951-1977. 20p. 1998. pap. 2.00 (*0-929087-78-X*) Mehring Bks.
— A Tribute to Vadim Z. Rogovin, 1937-1998: Historian of the Socialist Opposition to Stalinism. 42p. 1999. pap. 5.00 (*0-929087-50-X*) Mehring Bks.
North, David. Trotskyism vs. Stalinism. 33p. 1987. pap. 1.50 (*0-929087-20-8*) Mehring Bks.
North, David. Trotskyism Was the Revolutionary Alternative to Stalinism: A Reply to the Historical Falsifiers. (Illus.). 1996. 3.00 (*1-873045-72-7*, Pub. by Mehring Bks) Mehring Bks.
North, David. The U. S. S. R. & Socialism: The Trotskyist Perspective. 41p. 1989. pap. 3.00 (*0-929087-45-3*) Mehring Bks.
— The Workers League & the Founding of the Socialist Equality Party. 37p. 1996. pap. 2.00 (*0-929087-74-7*) Mehring Bks.
North, David S. Soothing the Establishment: The Impact of Foreign-Born Scientists & Engineers on America. LC 95-3988. 192p. (C). 1995. lib. bdg. 34.00 (*0-8191-9887-0*) U Pr of Amer.
North, Dexter. John North of Farmington, Connecticut & His Descendants. 322p. 1999. pap. 26.50 (*0-7884-1195-0*, N568) Heritage Bk.
North, Diane M. Samuel Peter Heintzelman & the Sonora Exploring & Mining Company. LC 79-15307. 248p. 1980. 33.95 (*0-8165-0679-5*) U of Ariz Pr.
North, Dick. The Lost Patrol: The Mounties' Yukon Tragedy. (Illus.). 160p. 1995. reprint ed. pap. 9.95 (*1-895714-70-2*) Raincoast Bk.
— The Mad Trapper of Rat River. (Illus.). 144p. 1991. pap. 5.95 (*0-7736-7307-5*) Genl Dist Srvs.
North, Douglass. Washington Whitewater: The Thirty-Four Best Whitewater Rivers. rev. ed. LC 91-39562. (Illus.). 304p. 1992. pap. 18.95 (*0-89886-327-9*) Mountaineers.
North, Douglass C. Understanding the Process of Economic Change. (Occasional Paper Ser.: No. 106). 27p. 1999. pap. 11.95 (*0-255-36422-9*, Pub. by Inst Economic Affairs) Coronet Bks.
North, Douglass Cecil. Institutions, Institutional Change & Economic Performance. (Political Economy of Institutions & Decisions Ser.). 159p. (C). 1990. text 49.95 (*0-521-39416-3*); pap. text 14.95 (*0-521-39734-0*) Cambridge U Pr.
— Structure & Change in Economic History. (C). 1982. pap. text 13.25 (*0-393-95241-X*) Norton.
North, Douglass Cecil & World Institute for Development Economics Research. The Contribution of the New Institutional Economics to An Understanding of the Transition Problem. LC 98-122312. (Wider Annual Lectures). 18p. 1997. write for info. (*952-9520-54-9*) UN.
North, Douglass Cecil, jt. auth. see Davis, Lance.
North, E. Lee. The 55 West: A Guide to the State's Counties. rev. ed. (Illus.). 118p. (Orig.). 1997. 20.00 (*0-937058-38-6*) West Va U Pr.
— Fifty-Five West Virginias. 2nd rev. ed. 117p. 1997. pap. 19.95 (*0-937058-21-1*) West Va U Pr.
North, E. Lee & Wyman, Jane M. Chris, the Rhode Island Wonder Dog. (Illus.). 180p. 1993. spiral bd. 16.95 (*0-9665746-0-5*) Jane Wyman.
North East London Polytechnic, London, England Sta. The Psychology Readings Catalogue of the North East London Polytechnic, London, England, 2 vols, Set. 1976. 180.00 (*0-8161-1179-0*, G K Hall & Co) Mac Lib Ref.
North East Weld County Book Committee. History of North East Weld County, Colorado. (Illus.). 336p. 1986. 50.00 (*0-88107-064-5*) Curtis Media.
North, Elizabeth. Ancient Enemies. 240p. 1986. reprint ed. pap. 7.95 (*0-89733-214-8*) Academy Chi Pubs.
— Enough Blue Sky. 190p. 1985. 20.00 (*0-89733-150-8*) Academy Chi Pubs.
— Everything in the Garden. 200p. 1984. 20.00 (*0-89733-114-1*) Academy Chi Pubs.
— Pelican Rising. 232p. 1978. reprint ed. pap. 7.95 (*0-915864-93-2*) Academy Chi Pubs.
— Pelican Rising. 232p. 1979. reprint ed. 20.00 (*0-915864-94-0*) Academy Chi Pubs.
North, F. K. Petroleum Geology. (Illus.). 620p. (C). (gr. 13). pap. text 69.50 (*0-412-53830-X*, Chap & Hall NY) Chapman & Hall.
— Petroleum Geology. (Illus.). 750p. 1985. text 95.00 (*0-04-553003-3*); pap. text 59.95 (*0-04-553004-1*) Routledge.
North, Freddie. Getting Started. LC 97-39106. (How to Play Bridge Ser.). (Illus.). 96p. 1998. pap. 8.95 (*0-8442-2563-0*) NTC Contemp Pub Co.
— Plan Your Defense. Sowter, Tony, ed. LC 98-39176. (How to Play Bridge Ser.). (Illus.). 96p. 1998. pap. 8.95 (*0-8442-0079-4*, 00794, Natl Textbk Co) NTC Contemp Pub Co.
North, Gary. Backward, Christian Soldiers? 290p. 1984. pap. 5.95 (*0-930464-01-X*) Inst Christian.
— Baptized Patriarchalism: The Cult of the Family. 77p. (Orig.). 1994. pap. 6.95 (*0-930464-71-0*) Inst Christian.
— The Coase Theorum: A Study in Economic Epistemology. LC 91-40767. 128p. 1992. 25.00 (*0-930464-61-3*) Inst Christian.
— Conspiracy: A Biblical View. 2nd ed. LC 96-24984. 1996. 14.95 (*0-930462-11-4*, Dominion) Am Bur Eco Res.
— Crossed Fingers: How the Liberals Captured the Presbyterian Church. LC 95-194. 1096p. 1996. 34.95 (*0-930464-74-5*) Inst Christian.
— Dominion & Common Grace. 295p. 1987. pap. 8.95 (*0-930464-09-5*) Inst Christian.
— The Dominion Covenant: Genesis. 512p. 1987. reprint ed. 19.95 (*0-930464-03-6*) Inst Christian.
— Entrega Icondicional: Programa de Dios para la Victoria. Howden, Paul, tr. from ENG. (SPA.). 312p. 1990. pap. 6.95 (*0-930464-34-6*) Inst Christian.
— Heredaran la Tierra: Esquemas Biblicos para la Economia Politica. Howden, Paul, tr. from ENG. (SPA.). 261p. 1990. pap. 5.95 (*0-930464-26-5*) Inst Christian.
— The Hoax of Higher Criticism. 72p. 1989. pap. 3.95 (*0-930464-30-3*) Inst Christian.
— Is the World Running Down? Crisis in the Christian Worldview. 345p. 1988. 19.95 (*0-930464-13-3*) Inst Christian.
— The Judeo-Christian Tradition: A Guide for the Perplexed. LC 89-48350. 204p. 1990. 14.95 (*0-930464-28-1*) Inst Christian.
— Leviticus: An Economic Commentary. LC 94-37832. 792p. 1994. 29.95 (*0-930464-72-9*) Inst Christian.
— Liberando la Tierra: Regeneracion O Revolucion? Howden, Paul, tr. from ENG. (SPA.). 254p. 1989. pap. 5.95 (*0-930464-31-1*) Inst Christian.
— Lone Gunners for Jesus: Letters to Paul J. Hill. LC 94-37301. 47p. 1994. pap. 3.95 (*0-930464-73-7*) Inst Christian.
— Marx's Religion of Revolution: Regeneration Through Chaos. 280p. 1989. pap. 8.95 (*0-930464-15-X*) Inst Christian.
— Millennialism & Social Theory. LC 90-47609. 393p. 1990. 14.95 (*0-930464-49-4*) Inst Christian.
— Moses & Pharaoh: Dominion Religion vs. Power Religion. 426p. (C). 1985. pap. text 12.50 (*0-930464-05-2*) Inst Christian.
— Political Polytheism: The Myth of Pluralism. LC 89-27431. 771p. 1989. 22.50 (*0-930464-32-X*) Inst Christian.
— Puritan Economic Experiments. 65p. (Orig.). 1989. pap. 5.95 (*0-930464-14-1*) Inst Christian.
— Rapture Fever: Why Dispensationalism is Paralyzed. LC 93-444. 246p. 1993. student ed. 25.00 (*0-930464-67-2*); pap. 12.95 (*0-930464-65-6*) Inst Christian.
— La Religion Revolucionaria de Marx: La Regeneracion por Medio del Caos. Howden, Paul & Gonzalez, Jose L., trs. from ENG. (SPA.). 292p. 1990. pap. 6.95 (*0-930464-37-0*) Inst Christian.
— Salvation Through Inflation: The Economics of Social Credit. LC 93-18285. 300p. 1993. student ed. 25.00 (*0-930464-66-4*); pap. 12.95 (*0-930464-64-8*) Inst Christian.
— Sanctions & Dominion: An Economic Commentary on Numbers. LC 96-9229. 399p. 1996. 19.95 (*0-930464-76-1*) Inst Christian.
— Seventy-Five Bible Questions Your Instructors Pray You Won't Ask. 3rd ed. LC 96-28357. 238p. (Orig.). (C). 1996. pap. 5.95 (*0-930462-03-3*) Inst Christian.
— The Sinai Strategy: Economics & the Ten Commandments. 368p. (Orig.). 1986. pap. 12.50 (*0-930464-07-9*) Inst Christian.
— Tithing & the Church. LC 93-47685. 1994. 25.00 (*0-930464-69-9*); pap. 9.95 (*0-930464-70-2*) Inst Christian.
— Tools of Dominion: The Case Laws of Exodus. LC 90-4054. 1296p. 1990. 29.95 (*0-930464-10-9*) Inst Christian.
— Unconditional Surrender: God's Program for Victory. 417p. 1994. reprint ed. pap. 5.95 (*0-930464-12-5*) Inst Christian.
— Unholy Spirits: Occultism & New Age Humanism. LC 94-20710. 426p. (Orig.). 1994. reprint ed. pap. 12.95 (*0-930462-53-X*) Inst Christian.
— Victim's Rights: The Biblical View of Civil Justice. LC 90-44629. 316p. 1990. 14.95 (*0-930464-17-6*) Inst Christian.
— Was Calvin a Theonomist? 20p. (Orig.). 1990. pap. 1.00 (*0-930464-36-2*) Inst Christian.
— Westminster's Confession: The Abandonment of Van Til's Legacy. LC 91-7200. 385p. 1991. 14.95 (*0-930464-54-0*) Inst Christian.
North, Gary, jt. auth. see DeMar, Gary.
North, Gary, jt. auth. see Robinson, Arthur.
North, Gerald. Advanced Amateur Astronomy. 1991. text 60.00 (*0-7486-0253-4*, Pub. by Edinburgh U Pr) Col U Pr.
— Advanced Amateur Astronomy. 2nd ed. LC 96-51100. (Illus.). 414p. (C). 1997. pap. 24.95 (*0-521-57430-7*); text 69.95 (*0-521-57407-2*) Cambridge U Pr.
— Astronomy Explained. LC 97-3761. 352p. 1997. pap. text 24.95 (*3-540-76136-5*) Spr-Verlag.
***North, Gerald.** Observing the Moon: The Modern Astronomer's Guide. LC QB581.N67 2000. (Illus.). 356p. 2000. 39.95 (*0-521-62274-3*) Cambridge U Pr.
North, Gerald R., et al, eds. The Impact of Global Warming on Texas. LC 94-15147. (HARC Global Change Studies). (Illus.). 248p. 1995. 29.95 (*0-292-75555-4*) U of Tex Pr.
North, Gerald R., jt. auth. see Crowley, Thomas J.
North, Hailey. Bedroom Eyes. 384p. 1998. mass mkt. 5.99 (*0-380-79895-6*, Avon Bks) Morrow Avon.
***North, Hailey.** Perfect Match. 384p. 2000. mass mkt. 5.99 (*0-380-81306-8*) Morrow Avon.
— Pillow Talk. LC 98-94823. 384p. 1999. mass mkt. 5.99 (*0-380-80519-7*, Avon Bks) Morrow Avon.
***North, Helen F. & North, Mary C.** The West of Ireland: A Megalithic Primer. LC 99-40741. (Columban Celtic Ser.). 1999. pap. write for info. (*0-941638-03-0*) Iona Phila.
North, Holly. Dr. Malone, I Presume? large type ed. 291p. 1994. 27.99 (*0-7505-0633-4*, Pub. by Mgna Lrg Print) Ulverscroft.
— The Invisible Doctor. large type ed. (Magna Romance Ser.). 230p. 1992. 27.99 (*0-7505-0394-7*) Ulverscroft.
— Nurse at Large. large type ed. 245p. 1992. 27.99 (*0-7505-0323-8*, Pub. by Mgna Lrg Print) Ulverscroft.
— Sister Slater's Secret. large type ed. 271p. 1993. 27.99 (*0-7505-0433-1*) Ulverscroft.
North Iowa Writers Club Staff. Patches of Iowa. Wagner, Catherine et al, eds. 152p. 1988. 6.75 (*0-317-91216-X*) N Iowa Writers.
North, Ira. Balance: A Tried & Tested Formula for Church Growth. 2nd rev. ed. (Classics Ser.: Vol. 1). 154p. 1998. reprint ed. pap. 9.99 (*0-89225-270-7*, G52707) Gospel Advocate.
— Marching to Zion: A Collection of Ira North's Sermons. 1995. pap. 10.99 (*0-89225-454-8*) Gospel Advocate.
North, J. D. Chaucer's Universe. (Illus.). 640p. (C). 1988. 155.00 (*0-19-812668-9*) OUP.
— Measure of the Universe: A History of Modern Cosmology. 480p. 1990. pap. 12.95 (*0-486-66517-8*) Dover.
— Stars, Minds & Fate: Essays on Ancient & Medieval Cosmology. 460p. 1989. 60.00 (*0-907628-94-X*) Hambledon Press.
— The Universal Frame: Historical Essays in Astronomy. 400p. 1989. 60.00 (*0-907628-95-8*) Hambledon Press.
North, J. D. & Klein, P. W., eds. Science & Culture under William & Mary. (Mededelingen der Koninklijke Nederlandse Akademie van Wetenschappen, Afd. Letterkunde Ser.: No. 55(2)). 48p. 1992. pap. text 17.50 (*0-444-85748-6*) Elsevier.
North, J. J. The Coinages of Edward I & II. 1968. pap. 6.00 (*0-685-51543-5*) S J Durst.
— English Hammered Coinage, Vol. I. LC 91-226083. 1994. 85.00 (*0-907605-45-1*) S J Durst.
— English Hammered Coinage, Vol. II. LC 91-226083. 1991. 80.00 (*0-907605-34-6*) S J Durst.
North, Jack. Arnold Schwarzenegger. LC 93-40891. (Taking Part Ser.). (J). 1994. lib. bdg. write for info. (*0-87518-638-6*, Dillon Silver Burdett) Silver Burdett Pr.
— Arnold Schwarzenegger. LC 93-40891. (Taking Part Ser.). 72p. (J). (gr. 3). 1994. pap. 7.95 (*0-382-24726-4*, Dillon Silver Burdett) Silver Burdett Pr.
North, Jacquelyne. Perfume, Cologne & Scent Bottles. LC 86-61205. (Illus.). 243p. 1986. 69.95 (*0-88740-072-8*) Schiffer.
— Perfume, Cologne & Scent Bottles. 3rd rev. ed. (Illus.). 244p. 1999. 69.95 (*0-7643-0714-2*) Schiffer.
North, James. A History of the Church: From Pentecost to Present. rev. ed. 1991. pap. text 19.99 (*0-89900-371-0*) College Pr Pub.
North, James B., jt. auth. see Callen, Barry L.
North, James W. History of Augusta: From Earliest Settlement to the Present Time (1870), with Notes on the Plymouth Company & Settlements on the Kennebec,

N

An Asterisk (*) at the beginning of an entry indicates that the title is appearing for the first time.

with Biographical Sketches & Genealogical Register. (Illus.). 990p. 1997. reprint ed. lib. bdg. 99.00 (0-8328-5807-2) Higginson Bk Co.
— History of Augusta, Maine. LC 81-80137. 1120p. 1981. reprint ed. 60.00 (0-89725-020-6, 1195) Picton Pr.
— Index to the History of Augusta, Maine. 59p. 1981. pap. 10.00 (0-89725-157-1, 1492) Picton Pr.
North, Jeffrey. The J. J. North Collection: Edwardian English Silver Coins, 1279-1351. (Sylloge of Coins of the British Isles British Academy Ser.: Vol. 39). (Illus.). 286p. 1989. 74.00 (0-19-726075-6) OUP.
North, Joanna, jt. ed. see Enright, Robert D.
North, John. Astronomy & Cosmology. 1995. 35.00 (0-393-03656-1); pap. 18.95 (0-393-31193-7) Norton.
— The Purples. 120p. 1999. pap. 7.95 (1-891929-16-X) Four Seasons.
— Sherlock Holmes & the Arabian Princess. 124p. 1991. 25.00 (0-86025-270-1, Pub. by I Henry Pubns) Empire Pub Srvs.
— Sherlock Holmes & the German Nanny. 144p. 1991. 25.00 (0-86025-273-6, Pub. by I Henry Pubns) Empire Pub Srvs.
— Stonehenge: A New Interpretation of Prehistoric Man & the Cosmos. (Illus.). 609p. 1999. text 35.00 (0-7881-6071-0) DIANE Pub.
— Stonehenge: Prehistoric Man & the Cosmos. LC 97-31439. (Illus.). 656p. 1997. 34.50 (0-684-84512-1) Free Pr.
***North, John, ed.** Napoleon Options: Alternative Decisions of the Napoleonic Wars. 208p. 2000. 34.95 (1-85367-388-9, Pub. by Greenhill Bks) Stackpole.
North, John, jt. ed. see Beard, Mary.
North, John, jt. ed. see Sellers, Peter.
North, Joseph. The New Masses: An Anthology of the Rebel Thirties. LC 77-93268. (Illus.). 352p. 1980. pap. 2.25 (0-7178-0355-4) Intl Pubs Co.
— No Men Are Strangers. LC 58-11504. 300p. 1976. pap. 2.25 (0-7178-0462-3) Intl Pubs Co.
— Socialist Cuba: As Seen by a U. S. Communist Delegation. 1970. pap. 0.60 (0-87898-073-3) New Outlook.
— What Everyone Should Know about the U. S. S. R. An Eyewitness Report of a Three-Year Visit. 1976. pap. 0.50 (0-87898-121-7) New Outlook.
North, Joseph, et al. Gus Hall: The Man & the Message. 1970. pap. 0.50 (0-87898-060-1) New Outlook.
North, Joseph H. The Early Development of the Motion Picture, 1887-1909. LC 72-558. (Dissertations on Film Ser.). 316p. 1974. reprint ed. 21.95 (0-405-04101-2) Ayer.
North, Julian & Blackburn, Robert, eds. Quality Business: Quality Issues & Smaller Firms. LC 98-133987. 224p. (C). 1998. 90.00 (0-415-14608-9) Routledge.
North, Julian M. De Quincey Reviewed: Thomas de Quincey's Critical Reception, 1821-1994. LC 96-46387. (LCENG Ser.). viii, 172p. (C). 1997. 55.00 (1-57113-072-1) Camden Hse.
North, Julie, jt. auth. see Ruehrwein, Dick.
North, K. Environmental Business Management: An Introduction. (Management Development Ser.: No. 30). v, 194p. (Orig.). 1992. pap. 24.75 (92-2-107289-4) Intl Labour Office.
North, Kate. Land of My Dreams. large type ed. 464p. 31.99 (0-7089-4027-7) Ulverscroft.
North, Kathryn. Neurofibromatosis Type 1 in Childhood. LC 97-181243. (International Review of Child Neurology Ser.). (Illus.). 142p. (C). 1997. 47.95 (1-898683-13-1, Pub. by Mc Keith Pr) Cambridge U Pr.
North, Ken. The Complete Guide to JAVA: Database Programming JDBC, ODBC & SQL. LC 97-41802. 416p. 1997. pap. 44.95 incl. cd-rom (0-07-913286-3) McGraw.
— Database Magic with Activex. 480p. 1998. pap. text 44.99 (0-13-647199-4) P-H.
— Database Magic with Ken North's Cyber Classroom. (C). Date not set. 65.95 (0-13-647116-1, Macmillan Coll) P-H.
— Windows Multi-DBMS Programming: Using C Plus Plus, Visual BASIC, ODBC & Tools for DBMS Projects. LC 94-27650. 757p. 1995. pap. text 59.95 incl. cd-rom (0-471-01676-4) Wiley.
North, Kenda. Kenda North. (Min Gallery Series of Contemporary American & Japanese Photography). (Illus.). 84p. 1989. pap. 44.95 (4-906265-21-9) Aperture.
North, Kenneth E. Criminal Tax Fraud, Vol. 1. 3rd ed. LC 98-89367. 2000p. 1998. write for info. (0-327-00831-8, 6465212) LEXIS Pub.
— Criminal Tax Fraud, Vol. 1, 2, 3 & 4. 3rd ed. LC 98-89367. 2000p. 1998. write for info. (0-327-00830-X, 6465512) LEXIS Pub.
— Criminal Tax Fraud, Vol. 2. 3rd ed. LC 98-89367. 2000p. 1998. write for info. (0-327-00832-6, 6465312) LEXIS Pub.
— Criminal Tax Fraud, Vol. 3. 3rd ed. LC 98-89367. 2000p. 1998. write for info. (0-327-00833-4, 6465412) LEXIS Pub.
— Criminal Tax Fraud, Vol. 4. 3rd ed. LC 98-89367. 2000p. 1998. write for info. (0-327-00834-2, 6465612) LEXIS Pub.
— Criminal Tax Fraud (Tables, Index), Vol. 5. LC 98-89367. 1999. write for info. (0-327-01058-4) LEXIS Pub.
North, Klaus. Environmental Business Management. LC 98-198975. (Management Development Ser.: Vol. 30). 200p. 1997. pap. 31.50 (92-2-109516-9) Intl Labour Office.
— Localizing Global Production: Know-How Transfer in International Manufacturing. LC 97-181070. (Management Development Ser.: Vol. 33). 191p. 1997. pap. 27.00 (92-2-109512-6) Intl Labour Office.
North, Larry. Larry North's Slimdown for Life. LC 98-67476. (Illus.). 263p. 1999. 24.00 (1-57566-403-8) Kensgtn Pub Corp.
***North, Larry.** Larry North's Slimdown for Life: The Real Diet for Real People. 2000. pap. 14.00 (1-57566-497-6, Knsington) Kensgtn Pub Corp.
North, Larry. Living Lean: The Larry North Program. LC 96-46973. (Illus.). 259p. 1997. pap. 12.95 (0-684-83700-5, Fireside) S&S Trade Pap.
North Light Books Editors. Art Fun! LC 97-1934. (Art & Activities for Kids Ser.). (Illus.). 216p. (J). (gr. 1-6). 1997. pap. 19.99 (0-89134-833-6, North Lght Bks) F & W Pubns Inc.
— Craft Fun! LC 97-370. (Art & Activities for Kids Ser.). (Illus.). 216p. (J). (gr. 1-6). 1997. pap. 19.99 (0-89134-834-4, North Lght Bks) F & W Pubns Inc.
***North, Liisa & Simmons, Alan.** Journeys of Fear: Refugee Return & National Transformation in Guatemala. 368p. 1999. 60.00 (0-7735-1861-4) McG-Queens Univ Pr.
***North, Liisa L.** Journeys of Fear: Refugee Return & National Transformation in Guatemala. 352p. 2000. pap. 22.95 (0-7735-1862-2, Pub. by McG-Queens Univ Pr) CUP Services.
North, Lucy, tr. see Kono, Taeko.
North, Luther H. Man of the Plains: Recollections of Luther North, 1856-1882. Danker, Donald F., ed. LC 61-6409. (Pioneer Heritage Ser.: No. 4). 371p. reprint ed. pap. 115.10 (0-7837-7045-6, 204685600004) Bks Demand.
North, M. Principles & Applications of Stereochemistry. 192p. 1998. pap. text 42.50 (0-7487-3994-7) St Mut.
North, M. A. & Hillard, A. E. Greek Prose Composition. 272p. (C). 1989. pap. text 15.95 (0-89341-564-2, Longwood Academic) Hollowbrook.
***North, M. A. & Hillard, A. E.** Greek Prose Composition. (Classical Reprints Ser.). 272p. (C). 1999. reprint ed. pap. text 20.95 (0-941051-89-7) Focus Pub-R Pullins.
North, M. A. & Hillard, A. E. Key to Greek Prose Composition. 109p. 1990. pap. text 12.50 (0-89341-733-5, Longwood Academic) Hollowbrook.
***North, M. A. & Hillard, A. E.** Key to Greek Prose Composition: Answer Key. (Classical Reprints Ser.). 120p. (C). 1999. reprint ed. pap. text 17.95 (0-941051-90-0) Focus Pub-R Pullins.
North, M. A. & Hillard, A. E. Key to Latin Prose Composition. 113p. 1990. reprint ed. pap. text 12.50 (0-89341-623-1, Longwood Academic) Hollowbrook.
— Latin Prose Composition. (Classical Reprints Ser.). 320p. (Orig.). (C). 1999. reprint ed. pap. text 20.95 (0-941051-91-9) Focus Pub-R Pullins.
North, M. A. & Hillard, A. E. Latin Prose Composition. LC 89-2646. 300p. (Orig.). 1989. reprint ed. pap. text 15.95 (0-89341-568-5, Longwood Academic) Hollowbrook.
North, Mack O. Commercial Chicken Production. 1990. text 79.95 (0-442-31881-2) Chapman & Hall.
North Manhattan Health Action Group & CSS & Center for Health & Human Services. Washington Heights-Inwood Neighborhoods: Assessment of Health Care Needs-Appendices. 175p. (Orig.). 1984. pap. text 15.00 (0-88156-055-3) Comm Serv Soc NY.
North Manhattan Health Action Group Report Staff & CCS Center for Health & Human Services Staff. Washington Heights-Inwood Neighborhood: Assessment of Health Care Needs. 129p. (Orig.). 1984. pap. text 12.00 (0-88156-054-5) Comm Serv Soc NY.
North, Margie. To Chase a Dream. 418p. (YA). (gr. 8-12). 1989. 14.95 (0-934188-26-2) Evans Pubns.
North, Margot. Fiesta of the Heart. large type ed. (Linford Romance Library). 224p. 1995. pap. 16.99 (0-7089-7720-0, Linford) Ulverscroft.
North, Marianne. Recollections of a Happy Life: Being the Autobiography of Marianne North, Vol. 1. Morgan, Susan, ed. LC 93-12326. 400p. 1993. reprint ed. text 60.00 (0-8139-1469-8); reprint ed. pap. text 19.50 (0-8139-1470-1) U Pr of Va.
North, Mark. Act of Treason: The Role of J. Edgar Hoover in the Assassination of President Kennedy. 672p. 1992. pap. 13.95 (0-88184-877-8) Carroll & Graf.
North, Mary C., jt. auth. see North, Helen F.
North, Max M. How to Build Skills for Research LC 98-91756. 1998. write for info. (1-880930-11-0) IPI Pr.
North, Max M., et al. Virtual Reality Therapy: An Innovative Paradigm. Pyle, Trussell & Wilson, Anne, eds. LC 96-94811. (Illus.). 232p. (Orig.). (C). 1996. pap. 26.00 (1-880930-08-0) IPI Pr.
***North, Merry.** Let's Get to Work. (Giant Flap Bks.). (Illus.). 10p. (J). (ps-k). 1999. bds. write for info. (1-57584-345-5, Pub. by Rdrs Digest) Random.
— My Neighborhood. (Giant Flap Bks.). (Illus.). 10p. (J). (ps-k). 1999. bds. write for info. (1-57584-346-3, Pub. by Rdrs Digest) Random.
North, Michael. Art & Commerce in the Dutch Golden Age: A Social History of Seventeenth-Century Netherlandish Painting. LC 96-46135. 192p. 1997. 35.00 (0-300-05894-2) Yale U Pr.
***North, Michael.** Art & Commerce in the Dutch Golden Age: A Social History of Seventeenth-Century Netherlandish Painting. LC 96-46135. (Illus.). 192p. 1999. 14.00 (0-300-08131-6) Yale U Pr.
North, Michael. The Dialect of Modernism: Race, Language, & Twentieth Century Literature. (Race & American Culture Ser.). (Illus.). 272p. 1998. reprint ed. pap. 19.95 (0-19-512291-7) OUP.
— The Final Sculpture: Public Monuments & Modern Poets. LC 84-17011. (Illus.). 264p. (C). 1985. text 42.50 (0-8014-1725-2) Cornell U Pr.
— From the North Sea to the Baltic: Essays in Commercial Monetary & Agrarian History, 1500-1800. (Collected Studies: No. CS548). 320p. 1996. 101.95 (0-86078-600-5, Pub. by Variorum) Ashgate Pub Co.
— Henry Green & the Writing of His Generation. LC 84-3534. 234p. reprint ed. pap. 72.60 (0-8357-3132-4, 203939500012) Bks Demand.
— The Political Aesthetic of Yeats, Eliot & Pound. 249p. (C). 1992. text 64.95 (0-521-41432-6) Cambridge U Pr.
— Reading 1922: A Return to the Scene of the Modern. (Illus.). 288p. 1999. 35.00 (0-19-512720-X) OUP.
North, Michael, jt. ed. see Ormrod, David.
North, Nigel. Continuo Playing on the Lute, Archlute & Theorbo: A Comprehensive Guide for Performers. LC 86-46028. (Music Scholarship & Performance Ser.). (Illus.). 321p. 1987. 59.95 (0-253-31415-1) Ind U Pr.
North, Norma Robinson, see Robinson North, Norma.
North, Oliver S. Mineral Exploration, Mining, & Processing Patents, 1979. fac. ed. LC 80-66760. (Illus.). 143p. 1980. reprint ed. pap. 44.40 (0-7837-7850-3, 204760900007) Bks Demand.
— Mineral Exploration, Mining, & Processing Patents, 1980. fac. ed. LC 66-23725. (Illus.). 141p. 1982. reprint ed. pap. 43.80 (0-7837-7851-1, 204761000007) Bks Demand.
North, P. M. & Fawcett, J. J., eds. Cheshire & North: Private International Law. 12th ed. 1040p. 1992. pap. 68.00 (0-406-53081-5, UK, MICHIE) LEXIS Pub.
North, P. M., jt. auth. see Morris, J. H.
North, P. M., jt. contrib. by see Pearce, S. C.
North, P. M., jt. ed. see Morgan, B. J.
North, Patsy, jt. auth. see Bullock, Patrick.
North, Percy. Bernhard Gutmann: An American Impressionist. LC 95-15263. (Illus.). 192p. 1996. 85.00 (1-55859-611-9) Abbeville Pr.
North, Peter. Essays in Private International Law. 292p. 1993. text 75.00 (0-19-825826-7) OUP.
***North, Peter.** Success Secrets to Maximize Business in Britian. 2000. pap. 12.95 (1-55868-481-6) Gr Arts Ctr Pub.
North, Peter & Toews, Bea. Culture Shock: Succeed in Business: Australia. LC 98-84831. (Culture Shock! Ser.). 1998. pap. 12.95 (1-55868-414-X) Gr Arts Ctr Pub.
***North, Peter & Toews, Bea.** Success Secrets to Maximize Business in Australia. (Culture Shock! Ser.). 2000. pap. 12.95 (1-55868-539-1) Gr Arts Ctr Pub.
North, Peter M. Private International Law Problems in Common Law Jurisdictions. LC 92-18236. 1993. lib. bdg. 104.50 (0-7923-1845-5) Kluwer Academic.
North, Ph. M., jt. ed. see Lebreton, J. D.
North, Philip M., jt. auth. see Castle, Win M.
North, R. A. Cleaning Professional Kitchens. 1986. 75.00 (0-7855-1792-8, Pub. by Cresta Pub) St Mut.
— Kitchen Cleaning Manual. 1987. 40.00 (0-7855-1797-9, Pub. by Cresta Pub) St Mut.
— Kitchen Cleaning Manuals, 5 vols., Set. 1986. 90.00 (0-7855-1798-7, Pub. by Cresta Pub) St Mut.
North, R. Alan, ed. Handbook of Receptors - Channels. 368p. 1994. boxed set 156.95 (0-8493-8322-6) CRC Pr.
North, Rachel V. Work & the Eye. LC 92-22606. 240p. 1994. 79.50 (0-19-262282-X); pap. 41.50 (0-19-261885-7) OUP.
***North, Rachel V.** Work & the Eye. 2nd ed. (Illus.). 240p. 2001. pap. text 49.50 (0-7506-4172-X) Buttrwrth-Heinemann.
North, Ralph, ed. see Bresell, Ronald & Ben-Zikri, Abdul.
North, Ray. Ants. (Illus.). 128p. 1996. pap. 19.95 (1-873580-25-8, Pub. by Whittet Bks) Diamond Farm Bk.
North, Raymond. Night Came to the Farms of the Great Plains. LC 91-71312. 286p. 1991. pap. 17.50 (0-911311-29-7) Acres USA.
North, Richard. Heathen Gods in Old English Literature. LC 96-40353. (Studies in Anglo-Saxon England: Vol. 22). 390p. (C). 1998. text 74.95 (0-521-55183-8) Cambridge U Pr.
North, Richard, ed. The Haustlong of Thjodolf of Hvin. LC 96-172146. 1996. 22.95 (1-874312-20-6, Pub. by Hisarlik Pr) Intl Spec Bk.
North, Richard & Hofstra, Tette, eds. Latin Culture & Medieval Germanic Europe: Proceedings from the First Germania Latina Conference Held at the University of Groningen, 26 May 1989. LC 95-103216. (Mediaevalia Groningana Ser.: No. 11). 128p. 1992. pap. 34.00 (90-6980-059-4, Pub. by Egbert Forsten) Hodlder & Stoughton.
North, Richard, et al. Spinal Cord Stimulation. (Illus.). 280p. 1997. text 110.00 (0-7817-0270-4) Lppncott W & W.
North, Richard B., jt. ed. see Levy, Robert M.
***North, Richard D.** Fur & Freedom: In Defence of the Fur Trade. (Studies on the Environment Ser.: No. 16). 100p. 2000. pap. 18.95 (0-255-36486-5, Pub. by Inst Economic Affairs) Coronet Bks.
North, Richard D. Life on a Modern Planet: A Manifesto for Progress. LC 94-28599. 304p. 1995. 35.00 (0-7190-4566-5, Pub. by Manchester Univ Pr); pap. write for info. (0-7190-4567-3, Pub. by Manchester Univ Pr) St Martin.
North, Rick. Young Astronauts, No. 2. (J). 1990. mass mkt. 2.95 (0-8217-3173-4, Zebra Kensgtn) Kensgtn Pub Corp.
North, Robert, tr. see Duverger, Maurice.
North, Robert C. Moscow & Chinese Communists. 2nd ed. viii, 310p. 1963. pap. 15.95 (0-8047-0454-6) Stanford U Pr.
North, Robert C., jt. auth. see Doolin, Dennis J.
North, Robert C., jt. auth. see Nomikos, Eugenia V.
North, Robert J., jt. ed. see Steinman, Ralph.
North, Roche, ed. The Light of Nature. 1985. lib. bdg. 247.50 (90-247-3165-8) Kluwer Academic.
North, Roger. Memoirs of Musick. Rimbault, Edward F., ed. LC 74-24169. reprint ed. 25.00 (0-404 13073-9) AMS Pr.
North, Roger & Newman, John Henry. Of Building: Roger North's Writings on Architects. Colvin, Howard, ed. (Illus.). 1981. 59.00 (0-19-817325-3) OUP.
North, Roger, jt. auth. see Chan, Mary.
North, Ronald M., et al, eds. Unified River Basin Management: Proceedings of a Symposium Held in Gatlinburg, Tennessee, May 4-7, 1980. LC 81-69176. (American Water Resources Association Technical Publication Ser.: No. TPS-81-3). (Illus.). 666p. reprint ed. pap. 200.00 (0-8357-3163-4, 203942600012) Bks Demand.
North, S. N. History & Present Conditions of Newspapers. 446p. 1977. reprint ed. lib. bdg. 40.00 (0-930342-50-X, 301100) W S Hein.
— Marriage Laws in the United States, 1887-1906. Allen, Desmond W., ed. 91p. 1994. pap. 14.95 (0-941765-89-X) Arkansas Res.
***North Shore Writers' Workshop Staff.** Between the Sounds. LC 00-90111. (Illus.). x, 62p. 2000. pap. 10.95 (0-9702506-0-6) North Shore.
***North-South Books Staff.** Bologna Annual Fiction 2000. (Illus.). 224p. 2000. pap. 45.00 (0-7358-1271-3) North-South Bks NYC.
— Bologna Annual Non-Fiction 2000. (Illus.). 232p. 2000. pap. 45.00 (0-7358-1272-1) North-South Bks NYC.
North-South Books Staff. Little Polar Bear Journal. (J). 1998. 8.95 (1-55858-909-0, Pub. by North-South Bks NYC) Chronicle Bks.
North, Stafford. Armageddon Again? A Reply to Hal Lindsey. rev. ed. 124p. (Orig.). 1991. pap. 4.95 (0-9631138-0-1) Landmark Bks.
— Handbook on Church Doctrines. 4th ed. 174p. (Orig.). 1990. pap. write for info. (0-9631138-1-X) Landmark Bks.
North State Cooperative Library System Advisory Bo, compiled by. Resources Directory for Special Libraries: 1995/1996 Edition. rev. ed. 113p. 1996. ring bd. 13.00 (1-891367-02-1) North State Coop.
North State Cooperative Library System Advisory Bo & McNally, Deirdre, compiled by. Directory of Public & Academic Libraries in the North State Cooperative Library System: 1993 Edition. rev. ed. 58p. 1993. ring bd. 7.00 (1-891367-10-2) North State Coop.
North State Cooperative Library System Staff, compiled by. Personnel Manual: 1994 Edition. rev. ed. 72p. 1994. ring bd. 9.00 (1-891367-04-8) North State Coop.
— System Advisory Board Manual. rev. ed. 149p. 1998. ring bd. 18.00 (1-891367-07-2) North State Coop.
North State Cooperative Library System Staff & Coronado, Shirleigh, compiled by. Interlibrary Loan & Interlibrary Reference Manual: 1995 Edition. rev. ed. 93p. 1995. ring bd. 11.00 (1-891367-00-5) North State Coop.
North State Cooperative Library System Staff & Kirks, James H., Jr., compiled by. System Advisory Board Manual: July 1997 Edition. rev. ed. 149p. 1997. ring bd. 18.00 (1-891367-05-6) North State Coop.
North State Cooperative Library System Staff & McElroy, Tom, compiled by. Listen-In Catalog: A Guide to the Audio Cassette & Compact Disc Service of the North State Cooperative Library System, 1996 Edition. rev. ed. 447p. 1996. ring bd. 52.00 (1-891367-01-3) North State Coop.
— Listen-In Catalog: A Guide to the Audio Cassette & Compact Disc Service of the North State Cooperative Library System, 1998 Edition. rev. ed. 507p. 1998. ring bd. 60.00 (1-891367-08-0) North State Coop.
North State Cooperative Library System Video Cente, compiled by. VHS Videocassette Catalog: 1997 Edition. rev. ed. 663p. 1997. ring bd. 77.00 (1-891367-03-X) North State Coop.
— VHS Videocassette Catalog: 1999 Edition. rev. ed. 810p. 1999. ring bd. 89.00 (1-891367-06-4) North State Coop.
North, Stephen M. The Making of Knowledge in Composition: Portrait of an Emerging Field. LC 87-5141. 403p. (C). 1987. pap. text 27.50 (0-86709-151-7, 0151, Pub. by Boynton Cook Pubs) Heinemann.
***North, Stephen M. & Chepaitis, Barbara.** Refiguring the Ph.D. in English Studies: Writing, Doctoral Education & Suny-Albany's Fusion-Based Curriculum. LC 99-51593. (Refiguring English Studies). 1999. pap. write for info. (0-8141-3977-9) NCTE.
North, Sterling. Abe Lincoln: Log Cabin to White House. LC 87-4654. (Landmark Ser.: No. 61). (Illus.). 160p. (J). (gr. 5-9). 1987. pap. 5.99 (0-394-89179-1, Pub. by Random Bks Yng Read) Random.
North, Sterling. Abe Lincoln: Log Cabin to White House. 1987. 11.09 (0-606-12866-2, Pub. by Turtleback) Demco.
— Racal. 189p. (YA). pap. 4.99 (0-8072-1513-9) Listening Lib.
North, Sterling. Rascal. (Illus.). (J). (gr. 5). 1995. 9.32 (0-395-73253-0) HM.
— Rascal. (Illus.). 192p. (J). (ps up). 1990. pap. 4.99 incl. audio (0-14-034445-4, PuffinBks) Peng Put Young Read.
— Rascal. (J). 1990. 9.09 (0-606-02954-0, Pub. by Turtleback) Demco.
***North, Sterling.** Rascal, Class Set. unabridged ed. (YA). 1998. 100.70 incl. audio (0-7887-2541-6, 46711) Recorded Bks.
— Rascal, Homework Set. unabridged ed. (YA). (gr. 7). 1998. 43.24 incl. audio (0-7887-2236-0, 40720) Recorded Bks.
North, Sterling. Rascal: A Memoir of a Better Era. LC 63-13882. (Illus.). (J). (gr. 4 up). 1984. 15.99 (0-525-18839-8, Dutton Child) Peng Put Young Read.
— Rascal, Mi Tremendo Mapache - Rascal. Vol. 9. (SPA.). (gr. 4-7). 1996. pap. text 7.95 (84-279-3109-3) Lectorum Pubns.
— The Wolfling. (Illus.). 224p. (J). (gr. 5-9). 1992. pap. 4.99 (0-14-036166-9, PuffinBks) Peng Put Young Read.
— The Wolfling. (J). (gr. 5-9). 1996. 18.75 (0-8446-6894-X) Peter Smith.

N

North, Steven. Graph Drawing: Symposium on Graph Drawing, GD '96, Berkeley, California, U. S. A., September 18-20, 1996: Proceedings, Vol. 119. LC 96-53985. (Lecture Notes in Computer Science Ser.). 1997. pap. 67.00 (*3-540-62495-3*) Spr-Verlag.

North Suburban Bethel Sisterhood Staff. Tradition in the Kitchen Two: The Authentic Guide to Kosher Cooking. Frost, Eenie, ed. (Illus.). 328p. 1993. 19.95 (*0-9635594-0-0*) N Suburban BES.

North Sunflower Academy Staff. Pick of the Crop. 2nd ed. (Illus.). 18.95 (*0-9664025-0-2*) Sthborough Grdnrs.

North Sunflower PTA Staff. Pick of the Crop Vol. 2: Favorites from the Mississippi Delta. 2nd ed. (Illus.). 320p. 1998. 18.95 (*0-9666954-0-2*) North Sunflower Academy.

North, Susan, jt. auth. see Grimaldi, Fulvio.

North, Susan, jt. auth. see Hart, Avril.

North, Suzanne. Seeing Is Deceiving. (Phoebe Fairfax Mystery Ser.). 336p. 1997. pap. text 6.99 (*0-7710-6806-9*) McCland & Stewart.

— Seeing Is Deceiving: A Phoebe Fairfax Mystery. 336p. 1996. 25.99 (*0-7710-6805-0*) McCland & Stewart.

North, T. H., jt. ed. see Olson, D. L.

North, Terrell. How to Turn Your Newspapers into Cash. 42p. 1984. pap. 11.95 (*0-915665-05-0*) Premier Publishers.

North, Thomas, ed. see Plutarch.

North, Thomas J. Losing Liberty Judicially: Prohibitory & Kindred Laws Examined. xiv, 252p. 1981. reprint ed. 36.00 (*0-8377-0907-5*, Rothman) W S Hein.

North, Thomas J., et al. Modern French Legal Philosophy. Scott & Chamberlin, Joseph P., trs. (Modern Legal Philosophy Ser.: Vol. 7). lxvi, 578p. 1969. reprint ed. 47.50 (*0-8377-2126-1*, Rothman) W S Hein.

North, Tony, jt. auth. see Bailey, Mike.

North, Tony, ed. see Bull, Stephen.

North, Tracy, jt. auth. see Enciso, Carmen E.

North Tyneside Social Services Home Managers Staff. The Home Manager As Trainer: An Approach to Foundation Training. Payne, Chris & Graham, Norma, eds. 1994. 74.00 (*0-902789-88-0*, Pub. by Natl Inst Soc Work) St Mut.

North Valley Press Staff, ed. & intro. see Darnell, Yolanda.

North, W., et al. Laser Inspected Gear Geometry. (Technical Papers: Vol. P239.15). 10p. 1981. pap. text 30.00 (*1-55589-311-2*) AGMA.

North, W. R. Chinese Themes in American Verse. 1973. 59.95 (*0-87968-857-2*) Gordon Pr.

North, Walter, jt. ed. see Pryor, Timothy R.

North, William. Baron Von Steuben: Major General Continental Army. Sleeman, G. Martin, ed. 32p. 1990. pap. 3.95 (*0-932052-52-5*) North Country.

Northall, G. F. Folk-Phrases of Four Counties: Gloucester, Staffordshire, Warwickshire & Worshestershire: Gathered from Unpublished Manuscripts & Oral Tradition. (English Dialect Society Publications: No. 73). 1969. reprint ed. pap. 15.00 (*0-8115-0491-3*) Periodicals Srv.

Northall, G. T. A Warwickshire Word-Book Comprising Obsolescent & Dialect Words, Colloquialisms, Etc. (English Dialect Society Publications: No. 79). 1974. reprint ed. pap. 35.00 (*0-8115-0497-2*) Periodicals Srv.

Northam, Bruce & Olsen, Brad. In Search of Adventure: A Wild Travel Anthology. LC 98-92915. (In Search of Adventure Ser.: No. 1). (Illus.). 465p. 1999. pap. 17.95 (*1-888729-03-1*, 420-2) Cnsrtm Cllctive Cnscnss.

Northam, Bruce T. The Frugal Globetrotter: Your Guide to World Adventure Bargains. (Illus.). 208p. (Orig.). 1996. pap. 16.95 (*1-55591-249-4*) Fulcrum Pub.

Northam, John, tr. see Ibsen, Henrik.

Northam, Mark. Film & Television Composer's Resource Guide. 248p. 1998. spiral bd. 34.95 (*0-7935-9561-4*) H Leonard.

Northam, Ray M. Urban Geography. 2nd ed. LC 78-12335. (Illus.). 524p. reprint ed. pap. 162.50 (*0-7837-3496-4*, 205782900008) Bks Demand.

Northan, Irene. The Hollander's Daughter. large type ed. (Linford Romance Library). 384p. 1992. pap. 16.99 (*0-7089-7134-2*) Ulverscroft.

— The Incomparable Lydia. large type ed. (Linford Romance Library). 304p. 1996. pap. 16.99 (*0-7089-7928-9*) Ulverscroft.

— Miss Astbury & Milordo. large type ed. (Linford Romance Library). 304p. 1996. pap. 16.99 (*0-7089-7973-4*) Ulverscroft.

***Northan, Irene.** Phyllida. large type ed. 360p. 1999. 31.99 (*0-7089-4125-7*, Linford) Ulverscroft.

Northan, Irene. The Tinner's Bride. large type ed. (Large Print Ser.). 320p. 1996. 27.99 (*0-7089-3639-3*) Ulverscroft.

— A Treacherous Season. large type ed. (Large Print Ser.). 288p. 1996. 27.99 (*0-7089-3558-3*) Ulverscroft.

Northard, Jackie, jt. auth. see Lee, Julie.

***Northborough Historical Society Staff.** Northborough. (Images of America Ser.). (Illus.). 128p. 2000. pap. 18.99 (*0-7385-0423-8*) Arcadia Publng.

Northbourne. Looking Back on Progress. 1996. pap. 17.95 (*0-614-21232-4*, 735) Kazi Pubns.

— Looking Back on Progress. 2nd ed. Wetmore, James R., ed. & frwd. by. (Perennial Wisdom Ser.). 122p. 1995. reprint ed. pap. text 16.95 (*0-900588-03-9*) S Perennis.

Northbourne, tr. see Guenon, Rene.

Northbourne, Lord, tr. see Burckhardt, Titus.

Northbrooke, John. Treatise Against Dicing, Dancing, Plays & Interludes. LC 77-149667. reprint ed. 29.50 (*0-404-04793-9*) AMS Pr.

Northcon 98 Staff. Northcon 98: Conference Proceedings, Washington State Convention Center, Seattle, Washington, Occober 21-23, 1998. LC 98-86795. iv, 254 p. 1998. pap. write for info. (*0-7803-5077-4*) IEEE Standards.

Northcon/93 & IEEE, Oregon Section. Northcon/93: Conference Record, Oregon Convention Center, Portland, Oregon, October 12-14, 1993. LC 94-184712. iv, 263 p. 1993. write for info. (*0-7803-9973-0*) IEEE Standards.

Northcote, Hugh. Christianity & Sex Problems. 2nd ed. LC 72-9668. reprint ed. 72.50 (*0-404-57486-6*) AMS Pr.

Northcote, John H. From Sailor to Professional Hunter: The Autobiography of John Northcote. limited ed. LC 97-60382. (Illus.). 414p. 1997. 125.00 (*1-882458-17-6*) Trophy Rm Bks.

Northcote, Sydney. The Songs of Henri Duparc: Music Book Index. 122p. 1993. reprint ed. lib. bdg. 69.00 (*0-7812-9595-5*) Rprt Serv.

Northcote, T. G., jt. ed. see Comin, F. A.

Northcott, Bayan, ed. see Keller, Hans.

***Northcott, Bea & Helm, Janette.** Untapped Options: Building Links Between Marketing & Human Resources to Achieve Organizational Goals in Health Care. 2000. 49.95 (*1-55648-279-5*) AHPI.

— Untapped Options: Building Links Between Marketing & Human Resources to Achieve Organizational Goals in Health Care. 2000. 49.95 (*0-7879-5537-X*) Jossey-Bass.

Northcott, Cecil. South Seas Sailor: The Story of John Williams & His Ships. (J). 1979. 3.95 (*0-87508-622-5*) Chr Lit.

Northcott, Clarence H. Australian Social Development. LC 68-56676. (Columbia University. Studies in the Social Sciences: No. 189). reprint ed. 29.50 (*0-404-51189-9*) AMS Pr.

Northcott, Deryl. Capital Investment Decision-making. 1992. write for info. (*1-86152-458-7*, Pub. by ITBP) Thomson Learn.

Northcott, Herbert C. Aging in Alberta: Rhetoric & Reality. 2nd ed. 128p. (Orig.). (C). 1997. pap. text. write for info. (*1-55059-135-5*) Detselig Ents.

Northcott, Herbert C. & Milliken, Jane. Aging in British Columbia. LC 98-231657. 150p. (Orig.). 1997. pap. write for info. (*1-55059-139-8*) Detselig Ents.

Northcott, Jim. Britain in Europe in 2010. LC 96-131173. 371p. (C). 1995. pap. 22.95 (*0-85374-645-1*, Pub. by Pol Studies Inst) Brookings.

Northcott, Kenneth J., ed. see Lenz, J. M.

Northcott, Kenneth J., ed. see Lessing, Gotthold Ephraim.

Northcott, Kenneth J., ed. see Schiller, Friedrich.

Northcott, Kenneth J., tr. see Bernhard, Thomas.

Northcott, Kenneth J., tr. see Braunfels, Wolfgang.

Northcott, Kenneth J., tr. see Hauser, Arnold.

Northcott, Kenneth J., tr. see Nissen, Hans J.

Northcott, Kenneth J., tr. see Unseld, Siegfried.

Northcott, Kenneth J., tr. see Von Hallberg, Robert.

Northcott, Kenneth J., tr. & intro. see Lessing, Gotthold Ephraim.

Northcott, Leslie. Molybdenum. LC 57-228. (Metallurgy of the Rarer Metals Ser.: No. 5). 234p. reprint ed. pap. 72.60 (*0-608-15059-2*, 202576000046) Bks Demand.

Northcott, Michael, ed. Urban Theology: A Reader. LC 98-203724. 384p. 1998. pap. 29.95 (*0-304-70265-X*) Continuum.

Northcott, Michael S. The Environment & Christian Ethics. (New Studies in Christian Ethics: No. 10). 395p. (C). 1996. pap. text 22.95 (*0-521-57631-8*) Cambridge U Pr.

Northcraft, Gregory B. & Neale, Margaret A. Organizational Behavior: A Management Challenge. 2nd ed. LC 97-72827. 726p. (C). 1994. text 68.00 (*0-03-074611-6*) Dryden Pr.

Northcraft, Gregory B., jt. auth. see Pinkley, Robin.

Northcroft, G. J. Sketches of Summerland: Nassau & the Bahama Islands. 1976. lib. bdg. 59.95 (*0-8490-2614-8*) Gordon Pr.

Northcroft, Meg, jt. auth. see Donovan, Alvin G., III.

Northcut, Allan, ed. see Knauff, Thomas L.

Northcut, Debbie, ed. see Knauff, Thomas L.

Northcut, Terry B. & Heller, Nina R., eds. Cognitive-Behavioral Techniques for Psychodynamic Therapy. LC 98-21443. 1998. 50.00 (*0-7657-0181-2*) Aronson.

Northcutt, Cecilia A. Successful Career Women: Their Professional & Personal Characteristics, 120. LC 90-38415. (Contributions in Women's Studies: No. 120). 144p. 1991. 39.95 (*0-313-27256-5*, NPY, Greenwood Pr) Greenwood.

Northcutt, John D., et al. Between Demonstration & Imagination: Essays in the History of Science & Philosophy Presented to John D. North. LC 99-24783. (Studies in Intellectual History). 428p. 1999. 117.50 (*90-04-11468-8*) Brill Academic Pubs.

Northcutt, Kay B. Praying by Heart: Prayers for Personal Devotion & Public Worship. LC 98-35075. 144p. 1998. pap. 12.95 (*0-8298-1285-7*) Pilgrim OH.

Northcutt, Marjorie. Matilda's Bloomers: Prairie School Stories. Williams, Sue, ed. LC 93-61048. (Illus.). 112p. (Orig.). 1994. pap. 9.95 (*1-882420-09-8*) Hearth KS.

Northcutt, R. G., ed. Comparative Neurobiology: Problems for a New Decade: 1st Annual Karger Workshop - Journal: Brain, Behavior & Evolution, Vol. 36, Nos. 2 & 3, 1990. 104p. 1990. pap. 130.50 (*3-8055-5319-6*) S Karger.

Northcutt, R. G. & Bemis, W. E. Cranial Nerves of the Coelacanth, Latimeria Chalumnae - Osteichtyes: Sarcoterygii: Actinistia-Comparisons with Other Cranista: Actinistia - Comparisons with Other Craniata. (Journal: Reprint of Brain, Behavior & Evolution: Vol. 42, Suppl. 1, 1993). (Illus.). x, 76p. 1993. 81.00 (*3-8055-5802-3*) S Karger.

Northcutt, Stephen. Network Intrusion Detection: An Analyst's Handbook. (Illus.). 267p. 1999. pap. 39.99 (*0-7357-0868-1*) New Riders Pub.

Northcutt, Vicki. Performance Tuning Microsoft Networks. 2nd rev. ed. (Illus.). 70p. 1998. pap. 20.00 (*0-9668334-1-4*) Intelligentsia.

— Phurst One. 1998. pap. write for info. (*1-58235-009-4*) Watermrk Pr.

— Plano: An Illustrated Chronicle. Fairchild, Lori, ed. (Illus.). 128p. 1999. 39.95 (*0-9654999-5-2*) Hist Pub Network.

Northcutt, Vicki & Perica, Esther. Persuasive Public Relations for Libraries. LC 83-15473. xii, 199 p. 1983. 15.00 (*0-8389-3284-3*) ALA.

Northcutt, Wayne. Mitterrand: A Political Biography. LC 91-29986. 416p. 1992. 42.95 (*0-8419-1295-5*) Holmes & Meier.

— The Regions of France: A Reference Guide to History & Culture. LC 96-5806. 344p. 1997. 55.00 (*0-313-29223-X*, Greenwood Pr) Greenwood.

Northcutt, Wayne, ed. Historical Dictionary of the French Fourth & Fifth Republics, 1946-1990. LC 91-17387. 552p. 1992. lib. bdg. 99.50 (*0-313-26356-6*, NDF, Greenwood Pr) Greenwood.

***Northcutt, Wendy.** The Darwin Awards: Evolution in Action. 256p. 2000. 16.95 (*0-525-94572-5*) NAL.

Northeast Drama Institute Staff. Full-Color Designs from Chinese Opera Costumes. (Illus.). 48p. 1980. reprint ed. pap. 8.95 (*0-486-23979-9*) Dover.

Northeast Foundation for Children Staff. Off to a Good Start: Launching the School Year. LC 97-68711. (Responsive Classroom Ser.: No. 1). (Illus.). 70p. (Orig.). 1997. pap. 8.50 (*0-9618636-6-8*) NE Found Child.

Northeast Foundation for Children Staff, compiled by. 16 Songs Kids Love to Sing. LC 98-66593. 38p. (J). (gr. k-8). 1998. pap. 22.95 incl. cd-rom (*0-9618636-9-2*) NE Found Child.

Northeast Foundation for Children Staff, contrib. by. 16 Songs Kids Love to Sing. LC 98-66593. 38p. (J). (gr. k-8). 1998. pap. 17.95 incl. audio (*0-9618636-8-4*) NE Found Child.

Northeast-Midwest Institute Staff. Education Incorporated: School-Business Cooperation for Economic Growth. LC 87-32591. 218p. 1988. 59.95 (*0-89930-282-3*, MUE/, Quorum Bks) Greenwood.

Northeast Missouri State University Staff. In Pursuit of Degrees with Integrity: A Value-Added Approach to Undergraduate Assessment. 95p. (Orig.). 1984. pap. text 17.50 (*0-88044-106-2*) AASCU Press.

Northeast Regional Agricultural Engineering Servic, jt. auth. see Wells, G. D.

Northeastern State University Staff. Mentoring Program Internship Handbook: The Mentoring Experience in Teacher Education. 2nd ed. 72p. (C). 1997. per. 25.95 (*0-7872-4564-X*, 41456401) Kendall-Hunt.

***Northeastern State University Staff, ed.** Seminary Leaves Revised. 360p. 2000. pap. text 31.00 (*0-536-02644-0*) P-H.

Northeastern University Center for Labor Market St, jt. auth. see Children's Defense Fund Staff.

Northeastern Women's Geoscientists Conference Staf. Women in Geology: Proceedings of the Northeastern Women's Geoscientists Conference, First. Halsey, S. D. et al, eds. LC 76-21580. (Illus.). 1976. pap. 2.00 (*0-915492-02-4*) Ash Lad Pr.

Northedge, Alastair. Excavations at 'Ana Vol. 1: Qala Island Iraq Archaeological Reports. (Illus.). 192p. 1989. pap. 75.00 (*0-85668-425-2*, Pub. by Aris & Phillips) David Brown.

Northedge, Alastair, et al. Studies on Roman & Islamic Amman Vol. I: The Excavations of Mrs. C-M Bennett & Other Investigations: History, Site & Architecture, Vol. 1. (British Academy Monographs in Archaeology). (Illus.). 232p. 1993. text 135.00 (*0-19-727002-6*) OUP.

Northedge, F. S. & Donelan, M. D. International Disputes: The Political Aspects. 1971. 35.00 (*0-900362-36-7*) St Mut.

Northen, Helen. Clinical Social Work Knowledge & Skills. 2nd ed. 360p. 1994. 44.00 (*0-231-10110-4*); pap. text, teacher ed. write for info. (*0-231-10107-4*) Col U Pr.

— Social Work with Groups. LC 69-19462. (C). 1969. text 46.00 (*0-231-02965-9*) Col U Pr.

— Social Work with Groups. 2nd ed. 452p. 1988. text 44.00 (*0-231-06744-5*) Col U Pr.

Northen, Helen, jt. auth. see Ell, Kathleen.

Northen, Helen, jt. auth. see Roberts, Robert W.

Northen, Henry T. & Northen, Rebecca T. Greenhouse Gardening. 2nd ed. LC 75-190208. (Illus.). 396p. reprint ed. 122.80 (*0-8357-9900-X*, 205511800008) Bks Demand.

Northen, Rebecca T. Miniature Orchids & How to Grow Them. enl. rev. ed. LC 95-36243. (Illus.). 192p. 1996. reprint ed. pap. 14.95 (*0-486-28920-6*) Dover.

— Orchids As Houseplants. rev. ed. (Illus.). 160p. 1976. reprint ed. pap. 4.95 (*0-486-23261-1*) Dover.

Northen, Rebecca T., jt. auth. see Northen, Henry T.

Northen, William J., ed. Men of Mark in Georgia: A Complete & Elaborate History of the State from Its Settlement to the Present Time, Vols. 1-7. Incl. Vol. 1. LC 74-2193. 1974. 30.00 (*0-87152-176-8*); Vol. 3. LC 74-2193. 1974. 30.00 (*0-87152-178-4*); Vol. 4. LC 74-2193. 1974. 30.00 (*0-87152-179-2*); Vol. 5. LC 74-2193. 1974. 30.00 (*0-87152-180-6*); Vol. 6. LC 74-2193. 1974. 30.00 (*0-87152-181-4*); Vol. 7. LC 74-2193. 1974. 30.00 (*0-87152-182-2*); LC 74-2193. (Illus.). 3952p. 1974. reprint ed. 197.75 (*0-87152-331-0*) Reprint.

Northern Cartographic Staff. The Atlas of New Hampshire Trout Ponds. 2nd ed. (Illus.). 164p. 1994. pap. 14.95 (*0-944187-33-1*) N Cartographic.

Northern Ireland Comptroller & Auditor General & Great Britain, Foreign Office Historical Section. Towards Better Practice in the Management of Education & Library Board Transport Services: Report. LC 98-209091. 46 p. 1997. 25.00 (*0-10-255298-3*, Pub. by Statnry Office) Bernan Associates.

Northern Ireland Comptroller & Auditor General & Great Britain, Northern Ireland Audit Office Staff. The Training & Employment Agency: Evaluation of Performance: Report by the Comptroller & Auditor General for Northern Ireland. LC 98-122707. xiv, 46p. 1998. 19.00 (*0-10-257298-4*, Pub. by Statnry Office) Bernan Associates.

***Northern Ireland. Comptroller and Auditor General.** Northern Ireland Health & Personal Social Services: Controls to Prevent & Detect Fraud in Family Practitioner Service Payments : Report. LC 98-203521. 1998. write for info. (*0-10-251898-X*) Statnry Office.

***Northern Ireland. Comptroller and Auditor General & Great Britain. Northern Ireland Audit Office.** The Administration of Disability Living Allowance by the Social Security Agency: Report. LC 98-117851. 1998. write for info. (*0-10-257198-8*) Statnry Office.

— Department of Education, Northern Ireland: Provision of Initial Teacher Training. LC 98-124968. (Illus.). 1998. write for info. (*0-10-257398-0*) Statnry Office.

— Financial Skills in Northern Ireland Departments: Report. LC 97-215449. 1997. write for info. (*0-10-256397-7*) Statnry Office.

— Privatisation of Belfast International Airport: Report by the Comptroller & Auditor General for Northern Ireland. LC 98-122786. (Illus.). 1997. write for info. (*0-10-257598-3*) Statnry Office.

Northern Ireland. Comptroller and Auditor General, jt. auth. see Great Britain. Northern Ireland Audit Office.

Northern Ireland Staff & Great Britain. Financial Control in Voluntary Grammar & Grant-Maintained Integrated Schools in Northern Ireland: Report. LC 98-209026. 51 p. 1997. 25.00 (*0-10-255998-8*, Pub. by Statnry Office) Bernan Associates.

Northern Ireland Staff & Great Britain, Parliament Staff. Disability: An Assessment of the Implications of Physical & Sensory Disability in a Northern Ireland Context, Together with Supporting Research Papers. LC 98-169285. vii, 296 p. 1994. 45.00 (*0-10-127402-5*, Pub. by Statnry Office) Bernan Associates.

Northern Ireland Tourist Board Staff. Where to Stay - Ireland Self Catering Guide. (Where to Stay Ser.). 1998. pap. 8.95 (*0-9528915-5-7*, Pub. by JARR UK) Seven Hills Bk.

Northern, Jerry. Hearing in Children. 5th ed. 500p. 56.95 (*0-683-30764-9*) Lppncott W & W.

Northern, Jerry L., ed. Hearing Disorders. 3rd ed. LC 95-35294. 384p. 1995. 75.00 (*0-205-15226-0*) Allyn.

Northern, Jerry L. & Downs, Marion P. Hearing in Children. 4th ed. (Illus.). 432p. 1991. 50.00 (*0-683-06574-2*) Lppncott W & W.

Northern, Jerry L., jt. auth. see Hayes, Deborah.

Northern, Jerry L., ed. see Wood, Raymond P.

Northern Lights Consulting Staff. Sybase SQL Server 11 DBA Survival Guide. 2nd ed. LC 95-72924. 656p. 1996. 49.99 incl. cd-rom (*0-672-30888-6*) Sams.

— Sybase SQL Server 11 Unleashed. LC 95-72919. 1152p. 1996. pap. 59.99 incl. cd-rom (*0-672-30909-2*) Sams.

Northern Neonatal Network Staff, compiled by. Neonatal Formulary. 199p. 1996. pap. text 31.00 (*0-7279-1030-2*, Pub. by BMJ Pub) Login Brothers Bk Co.

Northern Nevada Writing Project Teacher Researcher. Team Teaching. LC 96-27862. 120p. (Orig.). (C). 1996. pap. text 12.50 (*1-57110-040-7*) Stenhse Pubs.

Northern Pacific Railroad Staff. The Pacific Northwest: Oregon & Washington Territory. (Shorey Historical Ser.). 32p. 1975. reprint ed. pap. 10.00 (*0-8466-0229-6*) Shoreys Bkstore.

Northern, Penny B., jt. ed. see Wall, C. Edward.

Northern, Rebecca T. Home Orchid Growing. 4th ed. 384p. 1990. 50.00 (*0-671-76327-X*) S&S Trade.

***Northern Sea Route User Conference Staff & Ragner, Claes Lykke.** The 21st Century--Turning Point for the Northern Sea Route? Conference Proceedings of the Northern Sea Route User Conference, Oslo, 18-20 November 1999. LC 00-33070. 2000. write for info. (*0-7923-6365-5*) Kluwer Academic.

Northern, Tamara. Expressions of Cameroon Art: The Franklin Collection. LC 86-61839. (Illus.). 80p. 1986. pap. 19.95 (*0-295-96985-7*) U of Wash Pr.

Northern, Tamara & Brown, Wendi-Starr. To Image & to See: Crow Indian Photographs by Edward S. Curtis & Richard Throssel, 1905-1910. LC 93-8625. (Illus.). 1993. 6.00 (*0-944722-14-8*) Hood Mus Art.

Northern Virginia Community College Staff, jt. auth. see JIST Works, Inc. Staff.

Northey, Margot. The Haunted Wilderness: The Gothic & Grotesque in Canadian Fiction. LC 76-23329. 139p. reprint ed. pap. 43.10 (*0-8357-8164-X*, 203400700088) Bks Demand.

— William Kirby & His Works. (Canadian Author Studies). 26p. (C). 1989. pap. text 9.95 (*1-55022-048-9*, Pub. by ECW) Genl Dist Srvs.

***Northey, Margot & Knight, David B.** Making Sense in Geography & Environmental Studies: A Student's Guide to Research, Writing, & Style. 2nd ed. (Illus.). 224p. 2000. pap. 13.95 (*0-19-541527-2*) OUP.

Northey, Margot & Procter, Margaret. Writer's Choice: A Portable Guide to Student Writing. (C). 1950. 22.67 (*0-13-440017-8*, Macmillan Coll) P-H.

Northey, Margot, jt. auth. see Fischer, Ann.

Northey, Neil W. The Bluebirds & Their Neighbors. (Illus.). 160p. 1998. pap. 6.95 (*1-881545-80-6*) Angelas Bkshelf.

— The Mallords & Their Neighbors. (Illus.). 181p. 1998. pap. 6.95 (*1-881545-82-2*) Angelas Bkshelf.

An Asterisk (*) at the beginning of an entry indicates that the title is appearing for the first time.

— Old Homestead Tales, Set 4. (Illus.). 1998. pap. 27.80 (*1-881545-89-X*) Angelas Bkshelf.
— Paddletail the Beaver & His Neighbors. (Illus.). 182p. 1998. pap. 6.95 (*1-881545-84-9*) Angelas Bkshelf.
— Wild Animals of Africa. 1998. pap. text 6.95 (*1-881545-88-1*) Angelas Bkshelf.
— Wild Creatures in Winter. (Illus.). 188p. 1998. pap. 6.95 (*1-881545-86-5*) Angelas Bkshelf.
Northey, Patrick & Southway, Nigel. Cycle Time Management: The Fast Track to Time-Based Productivity Improvement. LC 92-32449. 1993. 30.00 (*1-56327-015-3*) Productivity Inc.
Northey, William B. The Land of the Gurkhas. LC 78-179229. (Illus.). reprint ed. 54.00 (*0-404-54856-3*) AMS Pr.
Northfield, Jeffrey, jt. auth. see Loughran, J. John.
Northfield, T. C., ed. Bile Acids in Health & Disease. (C). 1988. text 156.00 (*0-7462-0076-5*) Kluwer Academic.
— Helicobacter Pylori: Pathophysiology, Epidemiology, & Management. LC 93-38532. 1993. text 89.00 (*0-7923-8825-9*) Kluwer Academic.
Northington. The Botanical World. 1994. teacher ed. 14.06 (*0-697-23488-6*) McGraw.
— The Botanical World. 2nd ed. 1995. 109.37 (*0-697-27051-3*, WCB McGr Hill) McGrw-H Hghr Educ.
— Botanical World. 2nd ed. 1995. teacher ed. 10.93 (*0-697-24280-3*, WCB McGr Hill) McGrw-H Hghr Educ.
— Botanical World with Art Study Workbook. 2nd ed. 1995. student ed., wbk. ed. 53.25 (*0-697-29211-8*, WCB McGr Hill) McGrw-H Hghr Educ.
***Northington, David, et al.** The Botanical World Laboratory Manual. 2nd ed. (C). 1999. pap. 33.44 (*0-07-239046-8*) McGrw-H Hghr Educ.
Northington, David K. The Botanical World. 3rd ed. 1999. pap. text 45.00 (*0-697-34562-9*); pap. text 23.00 (*0-697-34564-5*) McGraw.
— Systematic Studies of the Genus Pyrrhopappus (Compositae, Cichorieae) (Special Publications: No. 6). 38p. 1974. pap. 2.00 (*0-89672-031-4*) Tex Tech Univ Pr.
Northington, David K. & Schneider, Edward L. The Botanical World: Art Study Workbook. 2nd ed. LC 95-76844. 128p. (C). 1995. per. 66.70 (*0-697-24279-X*, WCB McGr Hill) McGrw-H Hghr Educ.
Northington, David K., et al. Art Study Workbook: The Botanical World. 2nd ed. xvi, 480p. (C). 1995. text. write for info. (*0-697-27050-5*, WCB McGr Hill) McGrw-H Hghr Educ.
— Art Study Workbook: The Botanical World. 2nd ed. 192p. (C). 1995. text, student ed. write for info. (*0-697-24281-1*, WCB McGr Hill) McGrw-H Hghr Educ.
— The Botanical World. 2nd ed. 1995. lab manual ed. 9.68 (*0-697-29722-5*) McGraw.
Northington, Marshall. Managing the Family Business: Mixing Family & Business Productively. Paris, Janis, ed. LC 92-54372. (Small Business & Entrepreneurship Ser.). 162p. (Orig.). 1993. pap. 15.95 (*1-56052-174-0*) Crisp Pubns.
Northland Childrens Books. Grandmother Spider Brings the Sun Notecards. 1999. pap. text 9.95 (*0-87358-645-X*) Northland Pr.
Northland Publishing Staff, ed. Jack & the Giant/Cowboy Billy. (J). 1998. pap. 15.95 (*0-87358-696-4*, Rising Moon Bks) Northland AZ.
Northland School Division No. 61 Staff. Navajo Rug Stik-Withit Notecubes: Red & Black Rug Design. 1995. 12.00 (*0-87358-620-4*) Northland AZ.
Northman, Phillip. Great Gatsby Notes. (Cliffs Notes Ser.). 56p. 1964. pap. 4.95 (*0-8220-0560-3*, Cliff) IDG Bks.
Northmore, David. Lifting the Lid: A Guide to Investigative Research. LC 95-32339. 1996. 65.00 (*0-304-33109-0*) LPC InBook.
— Lifting the Lid: A Guide to Investigative Research. LC 95-32339. 1996. pap. 16.95 (*0-304-33113-9*) LPC InBook.
Northorp, Bruce L., jt. auth. see Holmes, W. Leslie.
Northouse. Health Communication: Strategies for Health Professionals. 3rd ed. LC 97-14846. 340p. (C). 1997. pap. text 36.95 (*0-8385-3680-8*, A-3680-4) Appleton & Lange.
Northouse, Cameron. Americans Doing Business in Japan: A Resource Book. LC 92-27061. 1992. 21.95 (*0-935061-48-7*) Contemp Res.
— Ishmael Reed: An Interview. LC 93-36204. (Glen Cove Interviews Ser.). 1993. 10.00 (*0-935061-53-3*) Contemp Res.
Northouse, Cameron, ed. Concept: An Anthology of Contemporary Writing. (Orig.). 1979. pap. 9.95 (*0-89683-014-4*) New London Pr.
Northouse, Peter G. Leadership: Theory & Practice. LC 96-45796. 274p. 1997. 48.00 (*0-8039-5768-8*) Sage.
— Leadership: Theory & Practice. 256p. (C). 1997. 48.00 (*0-614-25349-7*, 57689); pap. 22.95 (*0-8039-5769-6*, 57696) Sage.
Northover, John M. Modern Coloproctology: Surgical Grand Rounds from St. Mark's Hospital. 208p. 1993. text 45.00 (*0-340-55258-1*, Pub. by E A) OUP.
Northover, John M. & Kettner, Joel D. Bowel Cancer: The Facts. LC 92-12443. 1992. pap. 10.50 (*0-19-262207-2*) OUP.
Northrop, Albert W., et al. Decedents' Estates in Maryland, 1999 Cumulative Supplement. 165p. 1999. write for info. (*0-327-01056-8*, 6518213) LEXIS Pub.
Northrop, Albert W., jt. auth. see Schmuhl, Robert A.
Northrop, Christi M. Skiing with Kids. LC 76-18486. (Illus.). 160p. (Orig.). 1976. pap. 8.95 (*0-85699-136-8*) Chatham Pr.
Northrop, Claire. Around the World in Eighteen Plays: Folktale Scripts for the Classroom. (Illus.). 84p. 1994. pap., teacher ed. 14.00 (*1-895411-72-6*) Peguis Pubs Ltd.
Northrop, Douglas T., jt. auth. see Chiesa, Giulietto.
Northrop, F. S. The Logic of the Sciences & the Humanities. LC 83-60576. xiv, 402p. 1983. reprint ed. pap. 17.00 (*0-918024-31-5*) Ox Bow.
— The Meeting of East & West: An Inquiry Concerning World Understanding. LC 79-89839. (Illus.). xxii, 531p. 1979. reprint ed. pap. 22.00 (*0-918024-11-0*) Ox Bow.
— The Prolegomena to a Nineteen Eighty-Five Philosophiae Naturalis Principia Mathematica. LC 84-27350. xvi, 73p. 1986. 30.00 (*0-918024-35-8*) Ox Bow.
— Science & First Principles. LC 79-89840. 1979. reprint ed. 32.00 (*0-918024-08-0*) Ox Bow.
— The Taming of the Nations: A Study of the Cultural Bases of International Policy. LC 86-28587. xvi, 362p. (C). 1987. reprint ed. 30.00 (*0-918024-45-5*); reprint ed. pap. 16.00 (*0-918024-46-3*) Ox Bow.
Northrop, Filmer S. The Logic of the Sciences & the Humanities. LC 78-21524. 402p. 1979. reprint ed. lib. bdg. 35.00 (*0-313-21161-2*, NOLS, Greenwood Pr) Greenwood.
Northrop, Henry D. College of Life or Practical Self Educator. LC 71-79014. (Black Heritage Library Collection). (Illus.). 1977. 54.95 (*0-8369-8638-5*) Ayer.
Northrop, Jo. Country Matters. (Illus.). 208p. 1994. 21.95 (*1-55591-150-1*) Fulcrum Pub.
Northrop, Marie E. Spanish Mexican Families of Early California, 1769-1850, Vol. 1. 2nd ed. (Illus.). 421p. 1999. 30.00 (*0-9617773-0-3*) S CA Geneal Soc.
Northrop, Michael, ed. see Deutsch, Richard.
Northrop, Michael, ed. see Schwarz, Alan.
Northrop, Mildred B. Control Policies of the Reichsbank, 1924-1933. LC 68-58613. (Columbia University. Studies in the Social Sciences: No. 436). reprint ed. 32.50 (*0-404-51436-7*) AMS Pr.
***Northrop Moore, Jerrold.** F. L. Griggs, 1876-1938: The Architecture of Dreams. LC 99-38294. (Illus.). 308p. 2000. text 120.00 (*0-19-817407-1*) OUP.
Northrop, N. B. Pioneer History of Medina County. (Illus.). 224p. 1997. reprint ed. lib. bdg. 29.50 (*0-8328-6344-0*) Higginson Bk Co.
— Pioneer History of Medina County, Ohio. 236p. 1999. reprint ed. pap. 21.00 (*0-7884-1184-5*, N569) Heritage Bk.
Northrop, Nancy. ABCs for the Child With-in. (Illus.). 30p. 1993. pap. 5.95 (*0-9627894-2-9*) LNR Pubns.
***Northrop, Nancy.** ELFIS the Earthworm. (Illus.). 32p. 1999. 6.95 (*0-9627894-4-5*) LNR Pubns.
Northrop, Nancy. Mystari. (Illus.). 16p. (J). 1991. spiral bd. 5.95 (*0-9627894-1-0*) LNR Pubns.
— Watch Out for My Nest. (Illus.). 44p. (Orig.). (J). (gr. 1-5). 1994. pap. 5.95 (*0-9627894-3-7*) LNR Pubns.
***Northrop, Robert B.** Endogenous & Exogenous Regulation & Control of Physiological Systems LC 99-40282. 472p. 1999. boxed set 79.95 (*0-8493-9694-8*, Chap & Hall CRC) CRC Pr.
Northrop, Robert B. Introduction to Instrumentation & Measurements. LC 97-2462. (Electronic Engineering Systems Ser.). 544p. 1997. lib. bdg. 89.95 (*0-8493-7898-2*) CRC Pr.
Northrop, S. A., ed. Albuquerque Country. (Guidebook Ser.: No. 12). (Illus.). 199p. 1961. 7.00 (*1-58546-042-7*) NMex Geol Soc.
— History of New Mexico Geological Society, 1947-1968. (Special Publications: No. 2). 78p. 1969. pap. 2.00 (*1-58546-001-X*) NMex Geol Soc.
Northrop, S. A. & Read, C. B., eds. Taos-Raton-Spanish Peaks Country: New Mexico & Colorado. (Guidebook Ser.: No. 17). (Illus.). 128p. 1966. reprint ed. pap. 20.00 (*1-58546-047-8*) NMex Geol Soc.
Northrop, S. A., jt. ed. see Elston, W. E.
Northrop, S. A., jt. ed. see Woodward, L. A.
Northrop, Sandy & Hess, Steven. Drawn & Quartered: The History of American Political Cartoons. (Illus.). 164p. 1996. 29.95 (*1-880216-39-6*, Elliott Clark) Black Belt Communs.
Northrop, Stuart A. Minerals of New Mexico. rev. ed. 1959. 34.95 (*0-8263-0079-0*) U of NM Pr.
— Minerals of New Mexico. 3rd ed. LC 95-25171. (Illus.). 356p. 1996. 34.95 (*0-8263-1662-X*) U of NM Pr.
Northrop, Susan. Seance. 272p. 1995. mass mkt. 6.50 (*0-440-22176-5*) Dell.
Northrop, Susan & McLoughlin, Kate. Seance: A Guide for Living. LC 94-17689. 208p. 1994. text 18.00 (*0-9641509-0-5*) Allian Pubng.
— The Seance: Healing Messages from Beyond. 1995. mass mkt. 5.99 (*0-614-15542-8*) Dell.
Northrup, jt. auth. see LeGarde.
Northrup, A. J. Early Records of the First Presbyterian Church of Syracuse, New York from the Date of Its Establishment in 1826 to 1850 (with Marriages & Baptisms) (Illus.). 53p. 1997. reprint ed. pap. 11.00 (*0-8328-7148-6*) Higginson Bk Co.
— Fifty Fallen Stars. Williams, Bonnie, ed. LC 98-92023. (Illus.). 304p. 1998. pap. 19.95 (*0-9667486-0-3*) A J Northrup.
— Northrup-Northrop Genealogy; a Record of the Known Descendants of Joseph Northrup, One of the Original Settlers of Milford, Connecticut, in 1639. (Illus.). 473p. 1989. reprint ed. pap. 71.00 (*0-8328-0907-1*); reprint ed. lib. bdg. 79.00 (*0-8328-0906-3*) Higginson Bk Co.
Northrup, Anthony. NT Network Plumbing: Routers, Proxies & Web Services. LC QA76.76.O63N673 1998. 624p. 1998. pap. 39.99 (*0-7645-3209-X*) IDG Bks.
Northrup, Bill, jt. auth. see Mollica, Tony.
Northrup, Bruce E., jt. ed. see Garfin, Steven R.
Northrup, Charles J. Programming with UNIX Threads. LC 95-35799. 416p. 1996. pap. 44.99 (*0-471-13751-0*) Wiley.
Northrup, Christiane. Women's Bodies, Women's Wisdom: Creating Physical & Emotional Health & Healing. 1996. mass mkt. 20.95 (*0-553-85091-1*) Bantam.
— Women's Bodies, Women's Wisdom: Creating Physical & Emotional Health & Healing. rev. ed. 944p. 1998. 35.00 (*0-553-11033-0*); pap. 17.95 (*0-553-37953-4*) Bantam.
***Northrup, Christiane.** Your Diet, Your Health. 1999. 29.95 (*0-945923-45-7*) J Wilson & Assocs.
Northrup, Curt. Los Angeles Survival Guide. LC 92-74429. (City Survival Guides Ser.). 156p. 1992. pap. 10.00 (*0-9634720-0-3*) Arkobaleno.
— New York Survival Guide. LC 93-71212. (City Survival Guides Ser.). 170p. (Orig.). (C). 1993. pap. 7.95 (*0-9634720-1-1*) Arkobaleno.
Northrup, David. The Atlantic Slave Trade. (Problems in World History Ser.). 221p. (C). 1994. pap. text 20.36 (*0-669-33145-7*) HM Trade Div.
— Indentured Labor in the Age of Imperialism, 1834-1922. (Studies in Comparative World History). (Illus.). 200p. (C). 1995. text 54.95 (*0-521-48047-7*); pap. text 17.95 (*0-521-48519-3*) Cambridge U Pr.
Northrup, Denine A., jt. ed. see Nixon, Carol T.
Northrup, Gordon, ed. Applied Research in Residential Treatment. LC 94-24683. 99p. 1995. 29.95 (*1-56024-687-1*) Haworth Pr.
Northrup, Gordon, intro. The Management of Sexuality in Residential Treatment. LC 93-41273. (Residential Treatment for Children & Youth Ser.). (Illus.). 150p. 1994. lib. bdg. 39.95 (*1-56024-483-6*) Haworth Pr.
— Managing the Residential Treatment Center in Troubled Times. LC 94-17286. (Residential Treatment for Children & Youth Ser.). 111p. 1994. 39.95 (*1-56024-676-6*) Haworth Pr.
Northrup, Gordon & Garfinkel, Barry, eds. Adolescent Suicide: Recognition, Treatment & Prevention. LC 89-19773. (Residential Treatment for Children & Youth Ser.: Vol. 7, No. 1). (Illus.). 116p. 1994. text 39.95 (*0-86656-949-9*) Haworth Pr.
Northrup, Herbert R. Black & Other Minority Participation in the All Voluntary Navy & Marine Corps. LC 78-72037. (Pennsylvania University, Wharton School of Finance & Commerce, Industrial Research Unit Study Ser.: No. 57). 265p. reprint ed. pap. 82.20 (*0-8357-7283-7*, 201121200073) Bks Demand.
— The Changing Role of Women in Research & Development. LC 88-81113. (Manpower & Human Resources Studies: No. 11A). 78p. 1988. pap. 20.00 (*0-89546-072-6*) U PA Ctr Hum Res.
— Construction Union Tactics to Regain Jobs & Public Policy. (Labor Relations & Public Policy Ser.: Vol. 36). 250p. 1998. 42.50 (*1-891496-09-3*) J M Olin.
***Northrup, Herbert R.** The Great Paper Strike: International Paper, the Paperworkers, the Corporate Campaign & the "Peace Treaty" (Labor Relations & Public Policy Ser.: Vol. L37). 200p. 2000. pap. 30.00 (*1-891496-18-2*) J M Olin.
Northrup, Herbert R. Open Shop Construction Revisited. LC 84-48502. (Major Industrial Research Unit Studies: No. 62). 674p. 1984. 38.00 (*0-89546-047-5*) U PA Ctr Hum Res.
***Northrup, Herbert R. & Clinch, Richard P.** The Impact of Union-Management Relations on Industrial Employment: The Case of Briggs & Stratton Corp. in Milwaukee. (Labor Relations & Public Policy Ser.: Vol. L38). 175p. 2000. pap. 30.00 (*1-891496-17-4*) J M Olin.
Northrup, Herbert R. & Larson, John A. The Impact of the AT&T-EEO Consent Decree. LC 79-128190. (Labor Relations & Public Policy Ser.: No. 20). 270p. reprint ed. pap. 83.70 (*0-608-14859-8*, 202591200047) Bks Demand.
Northrup, Herbert R. & Malin, Margot E. Personnel Policies for Engineers & Scientists: An Analysis of Major Corporate Practice. LC 85-60642. (Manpower & Human Resources Studies: Vol. 11). 331p. 1985. 30.00 (*0-89546-053-X*) U PA Ctr Hum Res.
Northrup, Herbert R. & Rowan, Richard L. The International Transport Workers' Federation & Flag of Convenience Shipping. (Multinational Industrial Relations Ser.: No. 7c). 251p. (Orig.). 1983. pap. text 20.00 (*0-89546-042-4*) U PA Ctr Hum Res.
— Multinational Collective Bargaining Attempts: The Record, the Cases, & the Prospects. (Multinational Industrial Relations Ser.: No. 6). 580p. 1979. 27.50 (*0-89546-016-5*) U PA Ctr Hum Res.
Northrup, Herbert R. & Rowan, Richard L., eds. Employee Relations & Regulation in the '80s: Proceedings of a Conference. LC 81-84823. (Labor Relations & Public Policy Ser.: No. 22). 482p. reprint ed. pap. 149.50 (*0-8357-3154-5*, 203941700012) Bks Demand.
Northrup, Herbert R. & Thornton, Amie D. The Federal Government As Employer: The Federal Labor Relations Authority & the PATCO Challenge. LC 87-82880. (Labor Relations & Public Policy Ser.: No. 32). 152p. 1988. pap. 20.00 (*0-89546-068-8*) U PA Ctr Hum Res.
Northrup, Herbert R., et al. Doublebreasted Operations & Pre-Hire Agreements in Construction: The Facts & the Law: A Supplement to Open Shop Construction Revisited. LC 87-81475. (Major Industrial Research Unit Ser.: No. 62a). (Illus.). 136p. reprint ed. pap. 42.20 (*0-7837-4334-3*, 204404500012) Bks Demand.
— Government Protection of Employees Involved in Mergers & Acquisitions. LC 88-81112. (Labor Relations & Public Policy Ser.: No. 34). 676p. 1989. pap. 45.00 (*0-89546-070-X*) U PA Ctr Hum Res.
— The Impact of OSHA: A Study of the Effects of the Occupational Safety & Health Act on Three Key Industries - Aerospace, Chemicals, & Textiles. LC 77-95129. (Labor Relations & Public Policy Ser.: No. 17). 592p. reprint ed. pap. 183.60 (*0-608-14855-5*, 202591100047) Bks Demand.
— Negro Employment in Land & Air Transport: A Study of Racial Policies in the Railroad, Airline, Trucking, & Urban Transit Industries. LC 70-161216. (Studies of Negro Employment: Vol. 5). 687p. reprint ed. pap. 200.00 (*0-8357-3156-1*, 203941900012) Bks Demand.
— The Objective Selection of Supervisors: A Study of Informal Industry Practice & Two Models for Improved Supervisor Selection. LC 78-61998. (Manpower & Human Resources Studies: No. 8). 247p. 1978. 22.50 (*0-89546-006-8*) U PA Ctr Hum Res.
Northrup, Herbert R., jt. auth. see Bloom, Gordon F.
Northrup, Herbert R., jt. auth. see Rowan, Richard L.
Northrup, Herbert R., jt. frwd. see Diss-Greis, Theresa.
Northrup, Herbert R., jt. frwd. see Perry, Charles R.
Northrup, James P. Old Age, Handicapped & Vietnam-Era Antidiscrimination. rev. ed. LC 80-53990. (Labor Relations & Public Policy Ser.: No. 14). 280p. reprint ed. pap. 86.80 (*0-608-14865-2*, 202591400047) Bks Demand.
Northrup, Jean. Remarriage & All Those Kids. 7.95 (*1-55517-028-5*) CFI Dist.
Northrup, Jim. The Rez Road Follies: Canoes, Casinos, Computers, & Birch Bark Baskets. LC 97-36078. 228p. 1997. 20.00 (*1-56836-205-6*) Kodansha.
— The Rez Road Follies: Canoes, Casinos, Computers, & Birch Bark Baskets. LC 99-30701. 256p. 1999. pap. 14.95 (*0-8166-3495-5*, Pub. by U of Minn Pr) Chicago Distribution Ctr.
Northrup, L. W. Encounters with Angels. 123p. 1988. pap. 8.99 (*0-8423-0765-6*) Tyndale Hse.
Northrup, Lesley. Women & Religious Ritual. 205p. 1993. pap. 14.95 (*1-56929-008-3*, Pastoral Press) OR Catholic.
Northrup, Lesley, jt. auth. see Marshall, Paul.
Northrup, Mary. American Computer Pioneers. LC 97-24155. (Collective Biographies Ser.). (Illus.). 112p. (YA). (gr. 6 up). 1998. lib. bdg. 20.95 (*0-7660-1053-8*) Enslow Pubs.
Northsun, Nila. A Snake in Her Mouth: Poems, 1974-96. 80p. (Orig.). 1997. pap. 8.95 (*0-931122-87-2*) West End.
Northsun, Nila & Sagel, Jim. Small Bones, Little Eyes. Robertson, Kirk, ed. (Windriver Ser.). 72p. (Orig.). (C). 1982. pap. 5.00 (*0-916918-17-3*) Duck Down.
***Northup, James E., et al.** Drifting to an Unknown Future: The Civil War Letters of James E. Northup & Samuel W. Northup. (The Prairie Plains Ser. : 7). (Illus.). 120p. 2000. 24.95 (*0-931170-74-5*); 14.95 (*0-931170-73-7*) Ctr Western Studies.
Northup, Arthur. Scenario of the Savior As Sovereign: The Book of Revelation As a Christian World View & Philosophy of History. 345p. 1991. pap. 11.95 (*1-881909-18-2*) Advent Christ Gen Conf.
Northup, Bill, jt. auth. see Mollica, Anthony S.
Northup, Bill, jt. auth. see Mollica, Tony.
Northup, Clark S. Representative Phi Beta Kappa Orations: Second Series. (BCL1-PS American Literature Ser.). 553p. 1992. reprint ed. lib. bdg. 99.00 (*0-7812-6658-0*) Rprt Serv.
Northup, Clark S., ed. Representative Phi Beta Kappa Orations, Series 1. 2nd ed. reprint ed. 45.00 (*0-404-04795-5*) AMS Pr.
— Representative Phi Beta Kappa Orations, Series 2. LC 74-173800. reprint ed. 45.00 (*0-404-04796-3*) AMS Pr.
Northup, Diana E., et al. A Guide to Speleological Literature of the English Language, 1794-1996. LC 98-10758. 539p. 1998. 34.95 (*0-939748-51-7*); pap. 24.95 (*0-939748-52-5*) Cave Bks MO.
Northup, George T. Introduction to Spanish Literature. 3rd enl. ed. Adams, Nelson B., ed. LC 60-8727. 1993. pap. text 9.95 (*0-226-59443-2*, P419) U Ch Pr.
— An Introduction to Spanish Literature. 3rd rev. ed. LC 60-8127. 542p. reprint ed. pap. 168.10 (*0-608-09027-1*, 206966200005) Bks Demand.
Northup, Harry E. The Ragged Vertical. 264p. (Orig.). 1996. pap. 15.00 (*0-9649240-0-5*) Cahuenga Pr.
Northup, Jim. Walking the Rez Road. LC 92-4418. 176p. 1993. 15.95 (*0-89658-181-0*) Voyageur Pr.
— Walking the Rez Road. LC 92-4418. 176p. 1995. pap. text 12.00 (*0-89658-321-X*) Voyageur Pr.
Northup, Lesley A. The Eighteen Ninety-Two Book of Common Prayer. LC 93-17882. (Toronto Studies in Theology: Vol. 65). 1993. text. write for info. (*0-7734-9322-0*) E Mellen.
Northup, Leslie A. Ritualizing Women: Patterns of Spirituality. LC 97-31512. 176p. (Orig.). 1997. pap. 13.95 (*0-8298-1213-X*) Pilgrim OH.
Northup, Mary E., jt. auth. see Rodekohr, Mark E.
***Northup, Solomon.** Twelve Years a Slave. LC 99-89488. 2000. pap. 8.95 (*0-486-41143-5*) Dover.
Northup, Solomon. Twelve Years a Slave. Eakin, Sue & Logsdon, Joseph, eds. LC 68-13454. (Library of Southern Civilization). (Illus.). xxxviii, 274p. 1968. pap. text 14.95 (*0-8071-0150-8*) La State U Pr.
— Twelve Years a Slave: Excerpts from the Narrative of Solomon Northup. abr. ed. Lucas, Alice, ed. (Illus.). 48p. (Orig.). (J). (gr. 5-12). 1991. pap. text 7.00 (*0-936434-39-2*, Pub. by Zellerbach Fam Fund) Intl Spec Bk.
Northway, Della, tr. see Yarber, Yvonne & Madison, Curt, eds.
Northwest Bronx Community & Clergy Coalition Staff & New York Community Service Society Staff. Lenders & Landlords: A Guide to Tenant Organizing in Financially Distressed Housing. (Illus.). 73p. (Orig.). 1996. mass mkt. 10.00 (*0-88156-172-X*) Comm Serv Soc NY.
Northwest Environment Watch Staff, jt. auth. see Ryan, John C.

N

An Asterisk (*) at the beginning of an entry indicates that the title is appearing for the first time.

***Northwest Historical Association Staff.** Memoirs of Allegheny County Pennsylvania: Personal & Genealogical Portraits, 2 vols. (Illus.). 1096p. 1999. reprint ed. pap. 67.50 (0-7884-1105-5, N567) Heritage Bk.

Northwest Home Designing, Inc. Staff. The Designment Review 1987. Lord, Todd, ed. LC 86-62347. (Illus.). 40p. 1986. pap. 8.00 (0-936909-02-1) Northwest Home.

— Designment Review, 1988. Lord, Todd, ed. LC 86-657614. (Illus.). 40p. pap. 8.00 (0-936909-04-8) Northwest Home.

Northwest Home Designing Inc. Staff. Designment Review 1990. Lord, Todd, ed. LC 86-657614. (Pacific Rim Edition Ser.). (JPN., Illus.). 40p. (Orig.). (C). 1990. pap. 8.00 (0-936909-07-2) Northwest Home.

Northwest Institute for Psycholinguistic Studies Staff, jt. auth. see Worthley, William J.

Northwest Matrix Staff, ed. see Barton, Lois.

Northwest Montana Historical Society Staff, jt. auth. see Mckay, Kathryn L.

Northwest Publishers Consortium Staff. Northwest Journal: Mountain Cover. 1996. pap. 10.95 (1-882877-07-1) Panoply Pr.

Northwest Regional Educational Laboratory Staff. Advertising Techniques & Consumer Fraud. (Lifeworks Ser.). (Illus.). 1980. text 13.96 (0-07-047308-0) McGraw.

— Buying a House, Buying a Mobile Home. (Illus.). 1980. text 13.96 (0-07-047302-1) McGraw.

— Buying & Caring for Your Car & Insurance for Your Life, Health & Possessions. (Lifeworks Ser.). (Illus.). 1980. text 13.96 (0-07-047307-2) McGraw.

— Comparison Shopping & Caring for Your Personal Possessions. (Lifeworks Ser.). (Illus.). 1980. text 13.96 (0-07-047309-9) McGraw.

— Moving on & Getting Utilities & Saving Energy. (Illus.). 1980. text 13.96 (0-07-047303-X) McGraw.

— Ordering from Catalogs & Dining Out. (Lifeworks Ser.). (Illus.). 1980. text 13.96 (0-07-047305-6) McGraw.

— Understanding Contracts & Legal Documents & Understanding Criminal Law. (Lifeworks Ser.). (Illus.). 1980. text 13.96 (0-07-060913-6) McGraw.

— Using Credit & Banking Services & Understanding Income Tax. (Lifeworks Ser.). (Illus.). 1980. text 13.96 (0-07-047306-4) McGraw.

Northwest Seafood Consultant Staff. The Professional Seafood Demonstrator's Handbook. Lane, Jay, ed. (How-To Ser.). (Illus.). 80p. 1988. pap. text 5.00 (0-934363-06-4) Lance Pubns.

Northwest Seafood Consultant Staff, et al. The Professional Seafood Demonstrator's Handbook. rev. ed. (Illus.). 48p. (Orig.). 1989. pap. text 5.95 (0-934363-07-2) Lance Pubns.

Northwest U Staff & Organos, Minnie, eds. Catalog of the Dental School Library, 8 vols., Set. 1978. 950.00 (0-8161-0239-2, G K Hall & Co) Mac Lib Ref.

Northwest Underground Explorations Staff. Discovering Washington's Historic Mines Vol. 1: The West Central Cascade Mountains. LC 97-50097. (Illus.). 230p. 1997. pap. 24.95 (0-9647521-2-3) Oso Pubng.

Northwestern Learning Center Staff. Preparation for the MCAT: The Medical College Admission Test, Bklet. B. 80p. 1997. pap. 15.00 (1-884083-97-8) Maval Pub.

Northwestern Learning Center Staff, jt. auth. see Eptekar, Johan.

Northwestern Publishing House Staff. Planning Christian Worship, Ser. A. LC 95-69080. 130p. 1995. pap. 14.99 (0-8100-0569-7, 03N3007) Northwest Pub.

— Planning Christian Worship, Ser. B. LC 93-86632. 160p. 1993. pap. 14.99 (0-8100-0509-3, 03N3008) Northwest Pub.

— This We Believe. rev. ed. 36p. 1999. pap. 1.50 (0-8100-0983-8) Northwest Pub.

Northwestern Publishing House Staff, ed. Wels Yearbook 1999 - Wisconsin Ev. Lutheran Synod. 250p. 1998. pap. text 13.25 (0-8100-0896-3) Northwest Pub.

Northwestern University (Evanston Ill.) Staff, jt. auth. see Martin, Gary J.

Northwestern University, School of Commerce Staff. The Ethical Problems of Modern Advertising. Assael, Henry, ed. LC 78-288. (Century of Marketing Ser.). 1979. reprint ed. lib. bdg. 17.95 (0-405-11169-X) Ayer.

Northwestern University Staff. Catalog of the Transportation Center Library, Northwestern University. 1972. 1020.00 (0-8161-0185-X, G K Hall & Co); 1360.00 (0-8161-0924-9, G K Hall & Co) Mac Lib Ref.

— Catalog of the Transportation Center Library, Northwestern University, 12 vols., Set. 1972. lib. bdg. write for info. (0-685-01569-6, G K Hall & Co) Mac Lib Ref.

Northwestern University Traffic Institute Staff. Civil Liability & the Police. LC 83-114221. (Know the Law Ser.: No. 202). 1987. 12.00 (0-685-07053-0) Traffic Inst.

Northwood, Arthur, Jr., jt. auth. see Rapport, Leonard.

Northwood, S., jt. auth. see Sekunda, Nicholas V.

NorthWord Press Staff. Nature's Tranquility. LC 99-21046. (Illus.). 64p. 1999. text 9.95 (1-55971-711-4, NorthWord Pr) Creat Pub Intl.

Nortier, J. W. Adjunctive Medical Therapy of Acromegalic Patients. (Clinical Research Ser.: No. 2). x, 91p. (Orig.). (C). 1984. pap. text 23.10 (3-11-013365-2) Mouton.

Nortier, Jacomine. Dutch-Moroccan Code Switching among Moroccans in the Netherlands. xiv, 237p. (Orig.). (C). 1990. pap. text 57.70 (3-11-013102-1) Mouton.

Nortmann, Ulrich. Deontische Logik Ohne Paradoxien Semantik Und Logik Des Normativen. (Introductiones Ser.). (GER.). 200p. (C). 1989. 50.00 (3-88405-067-2) Philosophia Pr.

— Modale Syllogismen, Moegliche Welten, Essentialismus: Eine Analyse Der Aristotelischen Modallogik. (Perspektiven der Analytischen Philosophie - Perspectives in Analytical Philosophy Ser.: No. 9). (GER.). x, 427p. (C). 1996. lib. bdg. 192.60 (3-11-014660-6) De Gruyter.

Norton. The Bare Essentials. (C). 1995. pap. text 26.50 (0-15-504433-8) Harcourt Coll Pubs.

— Cosmetic Merchandising & Marketing. (General Business & Business Education Ser.). 1995. teacher ed. 10.50 (0-8273-6113-0); text 42.25 (0-8273-6112-2) Delmar.

— Design of Machinery. 1992. student ed. 27.50 (0-07-047827-9) McGraw.

— Emerging Financial Markets & Secured Transactions, Vol. IEDL 6. LC 98-162773. 1997. 229.00 (90-411-0675-8) Kluwer Law Intl.

— Human Geography Test. 1992. write for info. (0-19-540963-9) OUP.

— India & South Asia. 1993. 14.25 (1-56134-113-4) McGraw.

— Inside the IBM PC & PS 2: Tandy Version. 3rd ed. 1990. pap. 24.95 (0-13-471780-5) P-H.

— Movie World Underworld. 1995. write for info. (0-393-08793-X) Norton.

— Multicultural Children's Literature. 2000. pap. text 19.98 (0-13-243122-X) P-H.

— New Norton Guides: Borland C++ 1991. pap. 5.00 incl. 3.5 hd (0-13-625054-8) Macmillan USA.

— New Norton Guides: Engine. 1990. pap. 34.95 (0-13-617358-6) P-H.

— New Norton Guides: Turbo Pascal 6.0. 1991. pap. 5.00 incl. 3.5 hd (0-13-625062-9) Macmillan USA.

— People & Nations, 3 vols. 3rd ed. (C). Date not set. pap. text, teacher ed., suppl. ed. write for info. (0-395-57401-3) HM.

— People & Nations, 3 vols. 3rd ed. (C). 1991. pap. text, teacher ed. 3.16 (0-395-56302-X) HM.

— Peter Norton's WordPerfect On-Line Guide. 1989. pap. 5.00 incl. 3.5 hd (0-13-660861-2) Macmillan USA.

Norton. Stand Deliver. 1989. mass mkt. write for info. (0-8125-4758-6) Tor Bks.

Norton. Technology & Design for Learning. LC 97-73102. (C). 1997. pap. text 36.00 (0-15-503087-6, Pub. by Harcourt Coll Pubs) Harcourt.

— Yearbook International Financial 1999. 1997. lib. bdg. write for info. (90-411-0717-7) Kluwer Law Intl.

Norton & Stuntz, Daniel E. Descriptive Catalog of Hemerocallis Clones, 1893-1948. 100p. 1949. 10.00 (0-930653-02-5) Intl Bulb Soc.

Norton, et al. A People & a Nation, 3 vols. 3rd ed. (C). 1990. pap. text 4.76 (0-395-52982-4) HM.

— A People & a Nation, 3 vols. 3rd ed. (C). 1990. pap. text 4.76 (0-395-52981-6) HM.

Norton, jt. auth. see Holzner, Steven.

Norton, jt. auth. see Schneider.

Norton & Norton, et al. Language Arts Activites for Children. 4th ed. LC 98-33598. 432p. 1998. pap. text 37.00 (0-13-913005-5) P-H.

Norton, A. Banning. A History of Knox Co., Ohio 1779-1862. (Illus.). 424p. 1993. reprint ed. lib. bdg. 45.00 (0-8328-2998-6) Higginson Bk Co.

Norton, Alan. International Handbook of Local & Regional Government: A Comparative Analysis of Advanced Democracies. 576p. 1994. 160.00 (1-85278-005-3) E Elgar.

Norton, Andre. Breed to Come. 1999. mass mkt. 4.99 (0-451-45266-6, Onyx) NAL.

***Norton, Andre.** Brother to Shadows. 320p. 1999. mass mkt. 5.99 (0-380-77096-2, Avon Bks) Morrow Avon.

Norton, Andre. Brother to Shadows. LC 93-13971. 2000. 20.00 (0-380-97229-8, Avon Bks) Morrow Avon.

— Dare to Go A-Hunting. (Illus.). 256p. 1990. pap. 3.95 (0-8125-4712-8, Pub. by Tor Bks) St Martin.

***Norton, Andre.** Echoes in Time. 2000. mass mkt. 5.99 (0-8125-5274-1, Pub. by Tor Bks) St Martin.

Norton, Andre. Elvenblood. (Half-Blood Ser.: Bk. 2). 1996. mass mkt. 5.99 (0-8125-6319-0, Pub. by Tor Bks) St Martin.

— Flight in Yiktor. (Illus.). 256p. 1990. reprint ed. pap. 3.95 (0-8125-1008-9, Pub. by Tor Bks) St Martin.

— Forerunner. (Illus.). 256p. 1991. pap. 3.95 (0-8125-1364-9, Pub. by Tor Bks) St Martin.

— Fur Magic. (Illus.). 1992. 30.00 (1-880418-20-7); 65.00 (1-880418-19-3) D M Grant.

— Garan the Eternal. 1972. 6.50 (0-686-02511-3) Fantasy Pub Co.

— Hands of Lyr. 1994. 22.00 (0-688-13417-3, Wm Morrow) Morrow Avon.

— Imperial Lady. 1990. pap. 3.95 (0-8125-0722-3, Pub. by Tor Bks) St Martin.

— Key Out of Time. 188p. 1978. 25.00 (0-89366-186-4) Ultramarine Pub.

— The Mark of the Cat. 1993. mass mkt. 4.99 (0-441-51971-7) Ace Bks.

— Mirror of Destiny. LC 94-32818. 400p. 1995. 22.00 (0-688-13988-4, Avon Bks) Morrow Avon.

— Mirror of Destiny. 400p. 1996. mass mkt. 6.50 (0-380-77976-5, Avon Bks) Morrow Avon.

***Norton, Andre.** Mirror of Destiny. 2000. 22.00 (0-380-97249-2) Morrow Avon.

Norton, Andre. The Monster's Legacy. LC 95-80677. (Dragonflight Ser.: No. 11). (Illus.). 160p. (YA). (gr. 7 up). 1996. 17.00 (0-689-80731-7) Atheneum Yung Read.

— Moon Called. (Illus.). (Orig.). 1991. mass mkt. 3.99 (0-8125-1533-1, Pub. by Tor Bks) St Martin.

— Quest Across Time. 1999. mass mkt. 4.99 (0-451-45262-3, Onyx) NAL.

— Ralestone Luck. 256p. 1988. pap. 2.95 (0-8125-4754-3, Pub. by Tor Bks) St Martin.

— Redline the Stars. 304p. 1994. mass mkt. 4.99 (0-8125-1986-8, Pub. by Tor Bks) St Martin.

— Scent of Magic. LC 98-18173. 368p. 1998. mass mkt. 23.00 (0-380-97687-0, Eos) Morrow Avon.

***Norton, Andre.** Scent of Magic. LC 98-18173. 384p. (YA). (gr. 8 up). 1999. mass mkt. 6.50 (0-380-78416-5, Avon Bks) Morrow Avon.

Norton, Andre. Voodoo Planet. (Solar Queen Ser.: No. 3). 1983. pap. 2.75 (0-441-78196-9) Ace Bks.

— The Warding of Witch World. (Secrets of the Witch World Ser.: Vol. 3). 608p. 1998. mass mkt. 6.50 (0-446-60369-4, Pub. by Warner Bks) Little.

— Wheel of Stars. (Orig.). 1991. mass mkt. 3.99 (0-8125-1678-8, Pub. by Tor Bks) St Martin.

***Norton, Andre.** Wind in the Stone. LC 99-36104. 288p. 1999. 23.00 (0-380-97602-1, Avon Bks) Morrow Avon.

— Wind in the Stone. 352p. 2000. mass mkt. 6.50 (0-380-79556-6) Morrow Avon.

Norton, Andre. Wizards' Worlds. 1990. mass mkt. 4.95 (0-8125-4750-0, Pub. by Tor Bks) St Martin.

— Wraiths of Time. 256p. 1992. mass mkt. 3.99 (0-8125-4752-7, Pub. by Tor Bks) St Martin.

Norton, Andre, ed. Catfantastic IV. 1996. mass mkt. 5.99 (0-88677-711-9, Pub. by DAW Bks) Penguin Putnam.

— Grand Masters' Choice. 1991. mass mkt. 3.99 (0-8125-0619-7, Pub. by Tor Bks) St Martin.

— Moon Mirror. 1989. pap. 4.99 (0-8125-0303-1, Pub. by Tor Bks) St Martin.

Norton, Andre & Adams, Robert. Magic in Ithkar I. 320p. 1988. pap. 3.95 (0-8125-4715-2) Tor Bks.

— Magic in Ithkar III, No. 3. (Illus.). 320p. 1989. pap. 3.95 (0-8125-4709-8) Tor Bks.

Norton, Andre & Crispin, A. C. Gryphon's Eyrie. 256p. 1992. mass mkt. 4.99 (0-8125-3169-8, Pub. by Tor Bks) St Martin.

— Songsmith. 304p. 1992. 19.95 (0-312-85123-5, Pub. by Tor Bks) St Martin.

— Songsmith. 304p. 1993. mass mkt. 4.99 (0-8125-1107-7, Pub. by Tor Bks) St Martin.

Norton, Andre & Greenberg, Martin H., eds. Catfantastic. 320p. (Orig.). 1989. mass mkt. 5.99 (0-88677-355-5, Pub. by DAW Bks) Penguin Putnam.

— Catfantastic V. 320p. 1999. mass mkt. 6.99 (0-88677-847-6, Pub. by DAW Bks) Penguin Putnam.

— Catfantastic II. 320p. (Orig.). 1991. mass mkt. 5.99 (0-88677-461-6, Pub. by DAW Bks) Penguin Putnam.

— Catfantastic III. 320p. (Orig.). 1994. mass mkt. 4.99 (0-88677-591-4, Pub. by DAW Bks) Penguin Putnam.

Norton, Andre & Griffin, P. M. Fire Hand. 288p. 1995. 4.99 (0-8125-1984-1, Pub. by Tor Bks) St Martin.

— Storms of Victory. (Witch World: The Turning Ser.: Vol. 1). 1992. mass mkt. 4.99 (0-8125-1109-3, Pub. by Tor Bks) St Martin.

Norton, Andre & Hogarth, Grace A. Sneeze on Sunday. 256p. 1992. reprint ed. mass mkt. 4.99 (0-8125-1697-4, Pub. by Tor Bks) St Martin.

Norton, Andre & Lackey, Mercedes. The Elvenbane. 576p. 1995. 5.99 (0-8125-1175-1, Pub. by Tor Bks) St Martin.

— Elvenblood. 352p. 1996. mass mkt. 5.99 (0-614-08675-2) Tor Bks.

Norton, Andre & McConchie, Lyn. Ciara's Song: A Chronicle of Witch World. 256p. 1998. mass mkt. 6.50 (0-446-60644-8, Pub. by Warner Bks) Little.

— The Key of the Keplian. 304p. 1995. reprint ed. mass mkt. 5.99 (0-446-60220-5, Pub. by Warner Bks) Little.

Norton, Andre & Miller, Phyllis. House of Shadows. 256p. 1985. reprint ed. pap. 2.95 (0-8125-4743-8, Pub. by Tor Bks) St Martin.

Norton, Andre & Schaub, Mary H. The Magestone. (Secrets of the Witch World Ser.: Vol. 2). 288p. (Orig.). 1996. reprint ed. mass mkt. 5.99 (0-446-60222-1, Pub. by Warner Bks) Little.

Norton, Andre & Shwartz, Susan. Empire of the Eagle. 416p. 1995. 5.99 (0-8125-1393-2, Pub. by Tor Bks) St Martin.

Norton, Andre & Smith, Sherwood. Derelict for Trade. 1998. mass mkt. 5.99 (0-8125-5272-5, Pub. by Tor Bks) St Martin.

— Echoes in Time. LC 99-36342. 288p. 1999. 23.95 (0-312-85921-X, Pub. by Tor Bks) St Martin.

— A Mind for Trade. (Solar Queen Ser.). 1998. mass mkt. 5.99 (0-8125-5273-3, Pub. by Tor Bks) St Martin.

— A Mind for Trade. large type ed. LC 97-52119. 1998. 23.95 (0-7838-8432-X, G K Hall & Co) Mac Lib Ref.

Norton, Andre, et al. Flight of Vengeance. 384p. 1994. mass mkt. 4.99 (0-8125-0706-1, Pub. by Tor Bks) St Martin.

— On the Wings of Magic: Witch World. (Turning Ser.: Bk. 3). 416p. 1995. mass mkt. 5.99 (0-8125-0828-9, Pub. by Tor Bks) St Martin.

Norton, Andre, jt. auth. see Bloch, Robert.

Norton, Andre, jt. auth. see Edghill, Rosemary.

Norton, Andre, jt. auth. see Miller, Sasha.

Norton, Andre, jt. ed. see Adams, Robert.

Norton, Andre, jt. ed. see Greenberg, Martin H.

Norton, Ann V. Paradoxical Feminism: The Novels of Rebecca West. 112p. 1999. 74.95 (1-57309-392-0) Intl Scholars.

Norton, Ann W. Gods, Saints & Demons: The Sacred Art of India & Tibet. (Illus.). 24p. 1989. 5.00 (0-918386-40-3) W Benton Mus.

Norton, Anne. Alternative Americas: A Reading of Antebellum Political Culture. LC 86-6987. (Illus.). x, 364p. (C). 1994. 24.95 (0-226-59510-2) U Ch Pr.

— Reflections on Political Identity. (Johns Hopkins Series in Constitutional Thought). 224p. (C). 1993. reprint ed. pap. text 14.95 (0-8018-4728-1) Johns Hopkins.

— Republic of Signs: Liberal Theory & American Popular Culture. LC 92-36749. 208p. (C). 1993. pap. text 12.95 (0-226-59513-7); lib. bdg. 34.00 (0-226-59512-9) U Ch Pr.

Norton, Anthony R. Drift. Axelrod, David B., ed. (Student Chapbook Ser.). (Illus.). 24p. 1987. pap. 10.00 (0-925062-18-9) Writers Ink Pr.

Norton, Arthur J., tr. see Bryk, Felix.

Norton, Arthur O. Readings in the History of Education: Mediaeval Universities. LC 78-173801. reprint ed. 34.50 (0-404-04797-1) AMS Pr.

Norton, Arthur O., ed. First State Normal School in America: The Journals of Cyrus Pierce & Mary Swift. LC 76-89213. (American Education: Its Men, Institutions, & Ideas. Series 1). 1975. reprint ed. 29.95 (0-405-01452-X) Ayer.

Norton, Augustus R. Amal & the Shi'a: Struggle for the Soul of Lebanon. (Modern Middle East Ser.: No. 13). (Illus.). 264p. 1987. pap. 12.95 (0-292-73040-3) U of Tex Pr.

— Civil Society in the Middle East. LC 94-33780. (Social, Economic, & Political Studies of the Middle East: 50). xi, 328p. 1994. 117.00 (90-04-10037-7) Brill Academic Pubs.

Norton, Augustus R., ed. Civil Society in the Middle East, Vol. II. (Social, Economic & Political Studies of the Middle East: No. 50-2). xxviii, 353p. 1995. 117.00 (90-04-10039-3) Brill Academic Pubs.

— Civil Society in the Middle East, Vol. 2. (Social, Economic & Political Studies of the Middle East: No. 2). (Illus.). 432p. 1996. pap. 36.00 (90-04-10469-0) Brill Academic Pubs.

Norton, Augustus R. & Muslih, Muhammad Y. Political Tides in the Arab World. Hoepli, Nancy L., ed. LC 91-78231. (Headline Ser.: No. 296). (Illus.). 72p. (Orig.). 1992. pap. 5.95 (0-87124-142-0, 296) Foreign Policy.

Norton, Augustus R. & Weiss, Thomas G. U. N. Peacekeepers: Soldiers with a Difference. LC 90-82248. (Headline Ser.: No. 292). 64p. 1990. pap. 5.95 (0-87124-133-1) Foreign Policy.

Norton, Augustus R., jt. ed. see Greenberger, Martin H.

Norton, B. Efficient Use of Energy in Buildings, No. 11. (C). 1989. 110.00 (0-7855-4204-3, Pub. by Interntl Solar Energy Soc) St Mut.

— Efficient Use of Energy in Buildings (2nd UK-ISES Conference) (C46) 75p. (C). 1986. 120.00 (0-7855-3806-2, Pub. by Interntl Solar Energy Soc) St Mut.

— Linguistic Framework & Ontology. 1977. 51.55 (3-10-800283-X) Mouton.

— Solar Energy Technology. (Illus.). xvi, 279p. 1991. 130.00 (0-387-19583-1) Spr-Verlag.

Norton, B. & Lockhart-Ball, H. Daylighting Buildings. (C). 1989. 125.00 (0-7855-4212-4, Pub. by Interntl Solar Energy Soc) St Mut.

Norton, Bettina A. Around the Square: An Architectural Hunt in the Environs of Harvard Square. (Neighborhood Trivia Hunt Ser.). (Illus.). 80p. (Orig.). 1992. pap. 11.95 (0-938357-08-5) BAN Pub Boston.

— Neighborhood Trivia Hunt for Boston's Back Bay. (Neighborhood Trivia Hunt Ser.). (Illus.). 36p. (Orig.). 1985. pap. 4.95 (0-938357-01-8) BAN Pub Boston.

— Neighborhood Trivia Hunt for Boston's Beacon Hill. (Neighborhood Trivia Hunt Ser.). (Illus.). 36p. (Orig.). 1985. pap. 4.95 (0-938357-00-X) BAN Pub Boston.

— Neighborhood Trivia Hunt for Boston's Downtown. (Neighborhood Trivia Hunt Ser.). (Illus.). 40p. (Orig.). 1986. pap. 5.95 (0-938357-03-4) BAN Pub Boston.

— Neighborhood Trivia Hunt for Concord, Massachusetts. (Neighborhood Trivia Hunt Ser.). (Illus.). 20p. (J). (gr. 7-12). 1985. pap. 4.95 (0-938357-02-6) BAN Pub Boston.

— Neighborhood Trivia Hunt for New Haven, Connecticut. (Illus.). 36p. (Orig.). 1986. pap. 4.95 (0-938357-04-2) BAN Pub Boston.

— Neighborhood Trivia Hunt for Providence, R. I. (Illus.). 36p. (Orig.). 1987. pap. 4.95 (0-938357-06-9) BAN Pub Boston.

— Neighborhood Trivia Hunt for Salem, Massachusetts. (Illus.). 36p. (Orig.). 1986. pap. 4.95 (0-938357-05-0) BAN Pub Boston.

— Neighborhood Trivia Hunt on the Salem Heritage Trail for Boys & Girls. (Neighborhood Trivia Hunt Ser.). (Illus.). 16p. (Orig.). 1986. pap. 1.50 (0-938357-07-7) BAN Pub Boston.

— Prints at the Essex Institute. Farnam, Anne & Tolles, Bryant F., Jr., eds. LC 78-19448. (E.I. Museum Booklet Ser.). (Illus.). 1978. pap. 5.95 (0-88389-069-0, PEMP193, Essx Institute) Peabody Essex Mus.

Norton, Bob. Charging for Library & Information Services. LC 88-34825. (Viewpoints in Library & Information Science: No. 1). 48p. reprint ed. pap. 30.00 (0-608-09588-5, 205439000006) Bks Demand.

— The Quality Classroom Manager. LC 95-22715. 138p. 1995. 28.95 (0-89503-131-0) Baywood Pub.

Norton, Bob & Smith, Cathy. Understanding the Virtual Organization. LC 97-24746. (Barron's Business Success Ser.). 96p. 1998. pap. 6.95 (0-7641-0305-9) Barron.

Norton, Bob & Smith, Cathy A. Understanding Business on the Internet. LC 96-32473. (Barron's Business Success Ser.). 1997. pap. 6.95 (0-7641-0069-6) Barron.

***Norton, Bonham.** Booke of Common Prayer. 1999. pap. 39.00 (1-58329-006-0) Lazarus Minist.

***Norton, Bonny.** Identity & Language Learning: Social Processes & Educational Practice. LC 99-86879. (Language in Social Life Ser.). 173p. 2000. pap. 0.00 (0-582-38224-6) Addison-Wesley.

Norton, Boyd. The Art of Outdoor Photography: Techniques for the Advanced Amateur & Professional. LC 92-35905. (Illus.). 152p. 1993. 35.00 (0-89658-159-4) Voyageur Pr.

— The Art of Outdoor Photography: Techniques for the Advanced Amateur & Professional. LC 92-35905. (Illus.). 152p. 1997. pap. 21.95 (0-89658-346-5) Voyageur Pr.

— Backroads of Colorado. 2nd ed. LC 95-7222. (Illus.). 192p. 1995. pap. 19.95 (0-89658-316-3) Voyageur Pr.

Norton, Boyd, photos by. Baikal: Sacred Sea of Siberia. LC 92-3057. (Illus.). 1995. pap. 18.00 (0-87156-358-4, Pub. by Sierra) Random.

N

Norton, Bret. Kama Sutra: The Erotic Essence of India. (Illus.). 144p. 1999. pap. 14.95 (*965-494-089-2*) Astrolog Pub.

Norton, Bruce H. Force Recon Diary, 1969. 1991. mass mkt. 5.99 (*0-8041-0671-1*) Ivy Books.

— Force Recon Diary, 1970. 1992. mass mkt. 5.99 (*0-8041-0806-4*) Ivy Books.

Norton, Bruce H. Stingray. (Illus.). 256p. 2000. mass mkt. 6.99 (*0-8041-1026-3*) Ivy Books.

Norton, Bruce H. & Jacques, Maurice J. Sergeant Major, U. S. Marine. 1995. mass mkt. 5.99 (*0-8041-1030-1*) Ivy Books.

Norton, Bruce H. & Maffioli, Len. Grown Grey in War: The Len Maffioli Story. LC 96-95499. 1997. mass mkt. 5.99 (*0-8041-1599-0*) Ivy Books.

Norton, Bruce H. & Maffioli, Leonard J. Grown Gray in War: The Len Maffioli Story. LC 96-32350. (Illus.). 328p. 1996. 31.95 (*1-55750-643-4*) Naval Inst Pr.

Norton, Bryan G. On the Inherent Danger of Undervaluing Species. (Working Papers on the Preservation of Species). 1988. 2.50 (*0-318-33312-0*, PS3) IPPP.

— Toward Unity among Environmentalists. (Illus.). 304p. 1994. reprint ed. pap. text 24.95 (*0-19-509397-6*) OUP.

— Why Preserve Natural Variety? 1987. 35.00 (*0-317-05526-7*); pap. 13.95 (*0-317-05216-0*) IPPP.

— Why Preserve Natural Variety? Cohen, Marshall, ed. (Cambridge Studies in Philosophy & Public Policy). 295p. (C). 1988. text 45.00 (*0-691-07762-2*) IPPP.

— Why Preserve Natural Variety? Cohen, Marshall, ed. (Studies in Moral, Political, & Legal Philosophy). 295p. (C). 1988. pap. text 18.95 (*0-691-02507-X*, Pub. by Princeton U Pr) Cal Prin Full Svc.

Norton, Bryan G., ed. The Preservation of Species: The Value of Biological Diversity. 1986. 45.00 (*0-317-05211-X*); pap. 16.95 (*0-317-05212-8*) IPPP.

— The Preservation of Species: The Value of Biological Diversity. LC 85-42696. 272p. 1986. text 45.00 (*0-691-08389-4*) IPPP.

— The Preservation of Species: The Value of Biological Diversity. LC 85-42696. 318p. 1986. reprint ed. pap. 98.60 (*0-608-04591-8*, 206536100003) Bks Demand.

Norton, Bryan G., et al, eds. Ethics on the Ark: Zoos, Animal Welfare, & Wildlife Conservation. (Zoo & Aquarium Biology & Conservation Ser.). 330p. 1996. pap. 17.95 (*1-56098-689-1*) Smithsonian.

Norton, Byron E., jt. auth. see Norton, Carol C.

Norton, Camille, jt. ed. see Robinson, Lou.

Norton, Carla. Disturbed Ground. 440p. 1995. mass mkt. 5.50 (*0-380-71188-5*, Avon Bks) Morrow Avon.

Norton, Carla, jt. auth. see McGuire, Christine.

Norton, Carol C. & Norton, Byron E. Reaching Children Through Play Therapy: An Experential Approach. LC 97-1139. (Illus.). 378p. (Orig.). 1997. pap. text 19.95 (*0-9644849-4-3*) Pendleton Clay.

Norton, Carol V. Tapestry Crochet. 1991. pap. 17.95 (*0-932394-15-9*) Dos Tejedoras.

Norton, Caroline Sheridan. Caroline Norton's Defense: English Laws for Women in the 19th Century. 208p. 1982. 17.95 (*0-915864-87-8*); pap. 8.95 (*0-915864-88-6*) Academy Chi Pubs.

— The Letters of Caroline Norton to Lord Melbourne. Hoge, James O. & Olney, Clarke, eds. LC 74-12344. (Illus.). 200p. reprint ed. pap. 62.00 (*0-608-09687-3*, 206980200006) Bks Demand.

— Lost & Saved. LC 88-32738. 536p. 1989. 75.00 (*0-8201-1434-0*) Schol Facsimiles.

— Selected Writings of Caroline Norton. LC 78-18828. 1000p. 1978. 100.00 (*0-8201-1312-3*) Schol Facsimiles.

— A Voice from the Factories, 1836. LC 93-46507. (Revolution & Romanticism, 1789-1834 Ser.). 1994. 35.00 (*1 85477-169-8*) Continuum.

Norton, Catherine S. Life Metaphors: Stories of Ordinary Survival. LC 88-17549. 256p. (C). 1989. text 31.95 (*0-8093-1427-4*) S Ill U Pr.

Norton, Charles E. Historical Studies of Church-Building in the Middle Ages. LC 78-95072. (Select Bibliographies Reprint Ser.). 1977. 24.95 (*0-8369-5072-0*) Ayer.

— Letters of Charles Eliot Norton with Biographical Comment, 2 vols. Norton, Sara & Howe, M. A., eds. LC 76-148817. reprint ed. 125.00 (*0-404-04800-5*) AMS Pr.

Norton, Charles E., ed. Two Notebooks of Thomas Carlyle: From 23rd March 1822 to 16th May 1832. 317p. 1972. reprint ed. 15.00 (*0-911858-21-0*) Appel.

Norton, Charles E., ed. see Carlyle, Thomas.

Norton, Charles E., ed. see Lowell, James Russell.

Norton, Charles H. Pilgrim. 136p. (Orig.). 1993. pap. 9.95 (*1-880451-04-2*) Rainbows End.

***Norton, Charlotte O. & Jamison, Lynette J.** A Team Approach to the Aquatic Continuum of Care. (Illus.). 184p. 2000. pap. 24.95 (*0-7506-7168-8*) Buttrwrth-Heinemann.

Norton, Christine B., ed. see CGI Staff.

Norton, Colleen K., jt. auth. see Kesten, Karen S.

Norton, Curtis, jt. auth. see Porter, Gary.

Norton, Cynthia F. Microbiology. LC 80-23350. (Life Sciences Ser.). (Illus.). 850p. (C). 1981. teacher ed. write for info. (*0-201-05308-X*); text. write for info. (*0-201-05304-7*); student ed. write for info. (*0-201-05307-1*) Addison-Wesley.

— Microbiology. 2nd ed. LC 85-3909. 800p. (C). 1986. student ed. 16.25 (*0-201-11037-7*) Addison-Wesley.

— Trans Microbiology. 2nd ed. LC 85-3909. 800p. (C). 1986. trans. 150.00 (*0-201-11038-5*) Addison-Wesley.

Norton, D. Early History of Port Moody. Bryce, Herb, ed. 184p. (Orig.). 1987. pap. 12.95 (*0-88839-197-8*) Hancock House.

— Hospitals & the Long-Stay Patient. 1967. pap. 64.00 (*0-08-011052-5*, Pub. by Pergamon Repr) Franklin.

Norton, D. C., jt. auth. see Weston, R.

***Norton, D. P., et al, eds.** Substrate Engineering--Paving the Way to Epitaxy Vol. 587: Materials Research Society Symposium Proceedings. 2000. text 90.00 (*1-55899-495-5*) Materials Res.

Norton, Daniel A. Writing Windows Device Drivers. 448p. 1991. pap. text 34.95 (*0-201-57795-X*) Addison-Wesley.

— Writing Windows Device Drivers. 2nd ed. (C). 1996. pap. text. write for info. (*0-201-62486-9*) Addison-Wesley.

Norton, Daniel S. & Rushton, Peters. Classical Myths in English Literature. LC 70-92305. 444p. 1969. reprint ed. lib. bdg. 41.50 (*0-8371-2440-9*, NOCM, Greenwood Pr) Greenwood.

Norton, David. History of the Bible As Literature, Vol. 1: From the Beginnings to Jerome, Vol. 1. 393p. (C). 1993. text 85.00 (*0-521-33398-9*) Cambridge U Pr.

— History of the Bible As Literature, Vol. 2: From 1700 to the Present Day. 505p. (C). 1993. text 85.00 (*0-521-33399-7*) Cambridge U Pr.

***Norton, David.** A History of the English Bible as Literature. LC 99-16897. (History of the Bible as Literature Ser.). (Illus.). 486p. (C). 2000. write for info. (*0-521-77140-4*); pap. 29.95 (*0-521-77807-7*) Cambridge U Pr.

Norton, David. Sketches of the Town of Old Town, Penobscot Co., from Its Earliest Settlement to 1879, with Biographical Sketches. (Illus.). 152p. 1997. reprint ed. pap. 19.50 (*0-8328-5883-8*) Higginson Bk Co.

Norton, David, et al, eds. Advanced Laser Processing of Materials - Fundamentals & Applications: Materials Research Society Symposium Proceedings. (MRS Symposium Proceedings Ser.: Vol. 397). 674p. 1996. 75.00 (*1-55899-300-2*, 397) Materials Res.

Norton, David F., ed. The Cambridge Companion to Hume. LC 92-47406. (Companions to Philosophy Ser.). 416p. (C). 1993. text 69.95 (*0-521-38273-4*); pap. text 22.95 (*0-521-38710-8*) Cambridge U Pr.

Norton, David Fate, ed. see Hume, David.

Norton, David L. Democracy & Moral Development: A Politics of Virtue. LC 90-37723. 198p. 1991. 40.00 (*0-520-07067-4*, Pub. by U CA Pr) Cal Prin Full Svc.

— Democracy & Moral Development: A Politics of Virtue. LC 90-37723. 198p. 1995. pap. 15.95 (*0-520-20348-8*, Pub. by U CA Pr) Cal Prin Full Svc.

— Imagination, Understanding, & the Virtue of Liberality. LC 95-38510. 128p. (C). 1996. pap. text 19.95 (*0-8476-8128-9*); lib. bdg. 48.50 (*0-8476-8127-0*) Rowman.

Norton, David L. & Kille, Mary F., eds. Philosophies of Love. (Helix Bks.: No. 376). 296p. (C). 1983. reprint ed. pap. 20.00 (*0-8226-0376-4*) Littlefield.

Norton, David P., jt. auth. see Kaplan, Robert S.

Norton, Delores G. Dual Perspective: Inclusion of Ethnic Minority Content in the Social Work Curriculum. 1978. 3.85 (*0-685-21303 X*, 78-380-06) Coun Soc Wk Ed.

Norton, Don E., jt. auth. see Welch, John W.

Norton, Don E., ed. see Nibley, Hugh.

Norton, Donald J. Larry: A Biography of Lawrence D. Bell. LC 80-27791. (Illus.). 280p. 1981. text 37.95 (*0-88229-615-9*) Burnham Inc.

Norton, Donna, ed. & illus. see Diamond, Melvin.

Norton, Donna E. The Effective Teaching of Language Arts. 5th ed. LC 96-6404. 590p. 1996. text 74.00 (*0-13-507195-X*, Merrill Pub Co) Macmillan.

— The Impact of Literature-Based Reading. (Illus.). 464p. (Orig.). (C). 1992. pap. text 26.25 (*0-675-21369-X*, Merrill Coll) P-H.

— Through the Eyes of a Child: An Introduction to Children's Literature. 5th ed. LC 97-39057. 834p. 1998. 72.00 (*0-13-667973-0*, Merrill Coll) P-H.

Norton, Doreen M. The Palomino Horse. limited ed. (Illus.). 265p. 1996. reprint ed. 45.00 (*0-87505-419-6*) Borden.

Norton, E. C. The House, 1916. 250p. 1999. pap. 17.95 (*0-9667883-4-6*) Ravensyard.

Norton, E. W., ed. see Gorin, Jules, Club Staff.

***Norton, Edgar.** Find a Value Creation Approach. 2002. pap. 64.50 (*0-324-02031-7*) Thomson Learn.

Norton, Edgar, et al. Instructor's Manual-Test Bank to Accompany Investments. 4th ed. 656p. (C). 1995. pap. text, teacher ed. 47.75 (*0-03-001022-5*) Dryden Pr.

Norton, Edgar A., jt. auth. see Reilly, Frank K.

Norton, Elliot. Broadway Down East. 1978. 10.00 (*0-89073-055-5*, 197) Boston Public Lib.

Norton, Eric. Sparks Fly. (Orig.). 1997. mass mkt. 6.95 (*1-56333-551-4*, Badboy) Masquerade.

Norton, F. H. Elements of Ceramics. (Illus.). 319p. (C). 1991. reprint ed. 97.00 (*1-878907-28-X*) TechBooks.

— Refractories. 4th ed. LC 67-20660. (Illus.). 462p. (C). 1985. reprint ed. text 138.00 (*1-878907-06-9*, RAN) TechBooks.

Norton-Ford, Julian D., jt. auth. see Kendall, Philip C.

Norton, Frances. A Victorian Cup of Tea: A Guide to Victorian Entertaining. 90p. (Orig.). 1997. per. 13.95 (*0-9632938-0-X*) F M Norton.

Norton, Frederick J. Printing in Spain, 1501-1520: With a Note on the Early Editions of the "Celestina" LC 65-19156. (Sandars Lectures in Bibliography: 1963). 242p. reprint ed. pap. 69.00 (*0-608-11343-3*, 2022464) Bks Demand.

Norton, Gale. A Constitutional Convention to Achieve Term Limits: What Happens When the States Apply for a Convention. (Issue Paper #8-97 Ser.). 15p. 1997. pap. text 8.00 (*1-57655-160-1*) Independ Inst.

Norton, Gale, et al. Hard Questions for the "Vision Colorado" Task Force. 11p. 1988. pap. text 8.00 (*1-57655-114-8*) Independ Inst.

Norton, Gale, jt. auth. see Schwiff, Steve.

***Norton, George.** West Pacific. (Illus.). 40p. 1999. pap. 8.00 (*0-8059-4781-7*) Dorrance.

Norton, George P. Textile Manufacturers' Bookkeeping for the Counting House, Mill & Warehouse. 3rd ed. LC 75-18478. (History of Accounting Ser.). 1979. reprint ed. 25.95 (*0-405-07560-X*) Ayer.

Norton, George W. Introduction to the Economics of Agricultural Development. (C). 1993. text 44.50 (*0-07-047922-4*) McGraw.

Norton, Gerard J. & Pisano, Stephen, eds. Tradition of the Text: Studies Offered to Dominque Barthelemy in Celebration of His 70th Birthday. (Orbis Biblicus et Orientalis Ser.: Vol. 109). 310p. 1991. text 66.00 (*3-7278-0761-X*, Pub. by Presses Univ Fribourg) Eisenbrauns.

Norton, Gilbert F. Biology of Hagfish & Lamprey (Cyclostomes) Index of New Information & Research Reference Book. 150p. 1996. 47.50 (*0-7883-1210-3*); pap. 44.50 (*0-7883-1211-1*) ABBE Pubs Assn.

***Norton, Gloria & Gallagher, Pat.** The Written Conversation Handbook: A Jump Start Toward Literacy. 2000. pap. text 9.00 (*0-325-00287-8*) Heinemann.

Norton, Gregory. There Ain't No Justice - Just Us. LC 98-85963. 340p. 1998. pap. 15.00 (*0-935243-04-6*) Xlibris Corp.

— There Ain't No Justice - Just Us. LC 98-85963. 325p. 1998. 25.00 (*0-7388-0004-X*) Xlibris Corp.

Norton-Griffiths, M., jt. auth. see Sinclair, A. R.

Norton-Griffiths, M., jt. ed. see Sinclair, A. R.

Norton, Harry N. Handbook of Transducers. 480p. (C). 1989. text 56.20 (*0-13-382599-X*) P-H.

— Sensor & Transducer Selection Guide. 252p. 1990. 272.25 (*0-946395-80-2*, Pub. by Elsvr Adv Tech) Elsevier.

Norton, Herman A. Religion in Tennessee, 1777-1945. LC 81-1562. (Tennessee Three Star Ser.). (Illus.). 136p. 1981. pap. 7.00 (*0-87049-318-3*) U of Tenn Pr.

Norton, Holbrook & Ryffel, Henry H. Mathematics at Work. 3rd ed. (Illus.). 624p. 1990. pap. text 20.95 (*0-8311-3029-6*) Indus Pr.

***Norton Institute on Bankruptcy Law Staff, ed.** 1999 Update & Review: Bankruptcy Litigation & Bankruptcy Law. 550p. 1999. ring bd. 250.00 (*1-887617-69-8*) St Bart Pr Ltd.

Norton, J. B., jt. auth. see Brayton, Isabella.

Norton, J. H. The Giant Clam: An Anatomical & Histological Atlas. 142p. 1992. pap. 144.00 (*1-86320-066-5*, Pub. by ACIAR) St Mut.

Norton, J. J., ed. International Banking Regulation & Supervision: Change & Transformation in the 1990s. (International Banking & Finance Law Ser.). 440p. (C). 1994. lib. bdg. 158.00 (*1-85333-998-9*, Pub. by Graham & Trotman) Kluwer Academic.

Norton, J. J., et al, eds. International Banking Regulation & Supervision: Change & Transformation in the 1990s. LC 94-2887. (International Banking & Finance Law Ser.). 1994. write for info. (*1-85333-989-X*, Pub. by M Nijhoff) Kluwer Academic.

Norton, J. J. & Cheng, Chia-Jui, eds. International Banking Operations & Practices: Current Developments. LC 94-2886. (International Banking & Finance Law Ser.). 320p. (C). 1994. lib. bdg. 123.50 (*1-85333-997-0*, Pub. by Graham & Trotman) Kluwer Academic.

Norton, J. P. An Introduction to Identification. 1986. text 83.00 (*0-12-521730-7*) Acad Pr.

Norton, J. Renae & Fox, Ronald E. The Change Equation: Capitalizing on Diversity for Effective Organizational Change. LC 97-4934. 263p. 1997. 24.95 (*1-55798-388-7*, 431-7800) Am Psychol.

Norton, J. T., et al. Freedom's Gift: or Sentiments of the Free. LC 71-83914. (Black Heritage Library Collection). 1977. 13.95 (*0-8369-8575-3*) Ayer.

Norton, James. Global Studies: India & South Asia. 2nd ed. 256p. (C). 1995. text 13.95 (*1-56134-379-X*, Dshkn McG-Hill) McGrw-H Hghr Educ.

***Norton, James.** India & South Asia. 4th ed. (Global Studies). (C). 1999. pap., student ed. 18.75 (*0-07-024954-7*) McGrw-H Hghr Educ.

Norton, James. Oregon Main Street: A Rephotographic History. 100p. 1994. pap. 19.95 (*0-87595-256-9*) Oregon Hist.

— Winning Japan for Jesus. 200p. 1988. pap. 9.95 (*0-933704-66-6*) Dawn Pr.

Norton, James H.K. Global Studies: India & South Asia. 3rd ed. 224p. (C). 1997. text. write for info. (*0-697-37424-6*) Brown & Benchmark.

Norton, James J., jt. auth. see Lewis, David.

Norton, Jane E. Guide to National & Provincial Directories. (Royal Historical Society Guides & Handbooks Ser.: No. 5): 299p. 21.50 (*0-86193-102-5*) David Brown.

Norton, Janet. The Book of Me. large type rev. ed. (Illus.). 61p. 1997. pap. 19.95 (*1-892297-02-7*, 002) A M Janor.

Norton, Janet L. Rubber Stamper's World Project Bk. 1: "Fast, Easy & Elegant" large type rev. ed. (Illus.). 81p. 1997. pap. 29.95 (*1-892297-01-9*, 001) A M Janor.

Norton, Jed. Corrigan's Range. large type ed. (Linford Western Library). 240p. 1988. pap. 16.99 (*0-7089-6607-1*, Linford) Ulverscroft.

***Norton, Jeffrey A., et al, eds.** Surgery: Basic Science & Clinical Evidence. (Illus.). 2500p. 2000. 119.00 (*0-387-98447-X*) Spr-Verlag.

Norton, Jeni F., jt. auth. see Reckner, Jerald H.

Norton, Jenny. Our Garden Book: The Garden Planner & Record Keeper. 142p. 1988. 14.95 (*0-948751-01-0*) Interlink Pub.

Norton, Joan. The Contracted Marriage. large type ed. 1994. 27.99 (*0-7089-3154-5*) Ulverscroft.

Norton, Jody. Narcissus Sous Rature: Male Subjectivity in Contemporary American Poetry. LC 99-24089. (Illus.). 256p. 2000. 43.50 (*0-8387-5356-6*) Bucknell U Pr.

Norton, Joe, ed. see Green, Dusty.

Norton, John. Abel Being Dead, Yet Speaketh. LC 78-8184. 1978. reprint ed. 50.00 (*0-8201-1310-7*) Schol Facsimiles.

— Building with Earth: A Handbook. 2nd ed. 80p. 1997. pap. 19.50 (*1-85339-337-1*, Pub. by Intermed Tech) Stylus Pub VA.

— The Light at the End of the Bog. 2nd ed. 48p. reprint ed. pap. 8.50 (*0-685-61094-2*) Black Star.

***Norton, John.** Re: Marriage. 80p. 1999. pap. (*0-9607630-4-X*, Pub. by Black Star) SPD-Small Pr Dist.

— Re: Marriage. iv, 80p. 2000. 10.00 (*0-9607630-5-8*, Pub. by Black Star) SPD-Small Pr Dist.

Norton, John, tr. see Walter, E. & Pronzato, L.

Norton, John B. The Rebellion in India: How to Prevent Another. (C). 1988. reprint ed. 35.00 (*81-7013-059-X*, Pub. by Navarang) S Asia.

Norton, John D., jt. ed. see Earman, John.

Norton, John F. & Wittemore, Joel. History of Fitzwilliam, from 1752 to 1887, with a Genealogical Record of Many Fitzwilliam Families. (Illus.). 829p. 1995. reprint ed. lib. bdg. 85.00 (*0-8328-4624-4*) Higginson Bk Co.

Norton, John J. Jonathan Hale Farm: A Chronicle of the Cuyahoga Valley. 160p. 1991. reprint ed. pap. 12.95 (*0-911704-02-7*) Western Res.

Norton, Joseph A., ed. Commercial Loan Documentation Guide, 2 vols. 1988. ring bd. 210.00 (*0-8205-2069-1*) Bender.

Norton, Joseph J. Devising International Bank Supervisory Standards. LC 95-1060. (International Banking & Finance Law Ser.: International Banking & Finance Regulation Ser.: Vol. 3). 1995. lib. bdg. 119.00 (*1-85966-185-8*, Pub. by M Nijhoff) Kluwer Academic.

— Lender Liability Law, 2 vols. 1989. ring bd. 195.00 (*0-8205-1488-8*, 488) Bender.

***Norton, Joseph J.** Yearbook of International Financial & Economic Law 1998. 680p. 2000. 225.00 (*90-411-9772-9*) Kluwer Law Intl.

Norton, Joseph J., ed. Bank Regulation & Supervision in the 1990s. 178p. 1991. 115.00 (*1-85044-382-3*) LLP.

— Banks: Fraud & Crime. 286p. 1994. 120.00 (*1-85044-575-3*) LLP.

— Cross Border Electronic Banking. 330p. 1995. 110.00 (*1-85044-848-5*) LLP.

— International Finance in the 1990s: Global Challenges & Opportunities. LC 92-32847. 1993. pap. 35.95 (*0-631-18876-2*) Blackwell Pubs.

— Public International Law & the Future World Order: Liber Amicorum in Honor of A. J. Thomas, Jr. LC 87-4688. (Illus.). xxxii, 583p. 1987. 65.00 (*0-8377-2510-0*, Rothman) W S Hein.

Norton, Joseph J., et al, eds. International Asset Securitisation. 300p. 1995. 100.00 (*1-85044-854-X*) LLP.

— NAFTA & Beyond: A New Framework for Doing Business in the Americas. LC 95-165428. (International Economic Development Law Ser.). 704p. 1995. lib. bdg. 237.00 (*0-7923-3239-3*, KDZ944) Kluwer Academic.

Norton, Joseph J. & Andenas, Mads. Emerging Financial Markets & the Role of International Financial Organizations. LC 96-18495. (International Economic Development Law Ser.: Vol. 4). 539p. 1996. lib. bdg. 183.00 (*90-411 0909-9*) Kluwer Academic.

Norton, Joseph J., et al. Commercial Finance Guide, 2 vols. 1990. ring bd. 210.00 (*0-8205-2070-5*, 395) Bender.

Norton, Joseph J., jt. auth. see Aguirre, Ernesto.

Norton, Joseph Jude, jt. auth. see Horn, Norbert.

Norton, Joy. Furusato: Issa's Journey Home. (Illus.). 176p. 1987. pap. 10.00 (*0-933704-58-5*) Dawn Pr.

Norton, Judith A., compiled by. New England Planters in the Maritime Provinces of Canada, 1759-1800: Bibliography of Sources. 512p. 1992. text 125.00 (*0-8020-2840-3*) U of Toronto Pr.

Norton, Karl K. Numbers with Small Prime Factors & the Least Kth Power Non-Residue. LC 52-42839. (Memoirs Ser.: No. 1/106). 106p. 1971. pap. 16.00 (*0-8218-1806-6*, MEMO/1/106) Am Math.

— Numbers with Small Prime Factors & the Least kth Power Non-Residue. LC 52-42839. (American Mathematical Society Ser.: No. 106). 110p. reprint ed. pap. 34.10 (*0-608-09213-4*, 205271700005) Bks Demand.

Norton, Kay. Normand Lockwood: His Life & Music. LC 93-16889. (Composers of North America Ser.: No. 11). (Illus.). 545p. 1993. 62.50 (*0-8108-2683-6*) Scarecrow.

***Norton, Ken & Terrill, Marshall.** Ken Norton: Going the Distance. (Illus.). 256p. 2000. 22.95 (*1-58261-225-0*) Sports Pub.

Norton, Kevin & Olds, Tim, eds. Anthropometrica: A Textbook of Body Measurement for Sports & Health Courses. 1996. pap. 44.95 (*0-86840-223-0*, Pub. by New South Wales Univ Pr) Intl Spec Bk.

Norton, Kevin, jt. auth. see Olds, Timothy.

Norton, Kingsley & Smith, Samuel P. Problems with Patients: Managing Complicated Transactions. (Illus.). 192p. (C). 1994. text 69.95 (*0-521-43043-7*); pap. text 27.95 (*0-521-43628-1*) Cambridge U Pr.

Norton, Kingsley, jt. auth. see Smith, Sam.

Norton-Kyshe, James W. Dictionary of Legal Quotations. 1972. 300.00 (*0-8490-0037-8*) Gordon Pr.

— Dictionary of Legal Quotations. xxi, 344p. 1984. reprint ed. 47.50 (*0-89941-375-7*, 303500) W S Hein.

Norton, L. & Schnare, H. Aahahaanaaq. (ESK.). 26p. 1974. pap. 2.50 (*0-933769-55-5*) Alaska Native.

Norton, L. B., jt. auth. see Anderson, Debby.

Norton, L. Charnette. Keep It Hot! Keep It Cold! The Selection of a Patient Trax Rethermatization System for Cook Chill. 75p. 1996. 29.00 (*0-9644447-5-5*) Norton Grp.

Norton, L. Charnette, jt. auth. see Hofmeister, Linda R.

Norton, L. Charnette, jt. auth. see Puckett, Ruby P.

***Norton, Laura P.** Peter Cottontail & the Great Mitten Hunt. LC 98-83006. (J). 1999. write for info. (*0-307-16007-6*, Goldn Books) Gldn Bks Pub Co.

Norton, Lawrence, et al. Surgical Decision Making. 3rd ed. (Illus.). 368p. 1992. text 95.00 (*0-7216-6598-5*, W B Saunders Co) Harcrt Hlth Sci Grp.

Norton, Leslie. Leonide Massine: A Bio-Bibliography. Stahl, Joan, ed. (Garland Library of Dance). 250p. Date not set. text 37.50 (*0-8153-1733-6*) Garland.

Norton, Lisa D. Hawk Flies Above. (Illus.). 240p. 1997. pap. 12.00 (*0-312-16861-6*) St Martin.

Norton, LoraBeth, ed. see Anderson, Debby.

Norton, LoraBeth, ed. see Dockrey, Emily & Dockrey, Karen.

Norton, LoraBeth, ed. see Littleton, Mark R.

Norton, LoraBeth, ed. see Matthews, Beth, et al.

Norton, LoraBeth, ed. see McEwan, Elaine K.

Norton, LoraBeth, ed. see Tada, Joni Eareckson & Jensen, Steve.

Norton, Lorraine. The California Real Estate Consultant. (Series in California Real Estate). 560p. (C). 1998. pap. 26.40 (*0-13-378837-7*) P-H.

Norton, Louis A. & Burstone, Charles J., eds. The Biology of Tooth Movement. 384p. 1988. lib. bdg. 259.00 (*0-8493-4733-5*, QP88) CRC Pr.

***Norton, Louis Arthur.** Joshua Barney: Hero of the Revolution & 1812. (Illus.). 248p. 2000. 32.95 (*1-55750-490-3*) Naval Inst Pr.

Norton, Louis R. Sailors' Folk-Art under Glass: A Story of Ships-in-Bottles. (Illus.). 32p. (Orig.). 1995. pap. 3.95 (*0-9626162-8-1*) Old Salt Box.

***Norton, Lucy, ed.** Memoirs: Duc de Saint-Simon. (Lost Treasures Ser.: Vol. 1). 560p. 2000. pap. 19.95 (*1-85375-352-1*, Pub. by Prion) Trafalgar.

— Memoirs: Duc de Saint-Simon. (Lost Treasures Ser.: Vol. 2). 560p. 2000. pap. 19.95 (*1-85375-353-X*, Pub. by Prion) Trafalgar.

— Memoirs: Duc de Saint-Simon. (Lost Treasures Ser.: Vol. 3). 560p. 2000. pap. 19.95 (*1-85375-354-8*, Pub. by Prion) Trafalgar.

Norton, Lucy, tr. see Delacroix, Eugene.

Norton, M. D., tr. see Blume, Friedrich.

Norton, M. D., tr. see Rilke, Rainer Maria.

Norton, M. G., jt. auth. see Suryanarayana, C.

Norton, M. Herter, tr. see Blume, Friedrich.

Norton, M. Herter, tr. see Haushofer, Albrecht.

Norton, M. Ruth. A Canal for All Seasons: The Romance of Ohio's Canal Era. (Illus.). 85p. (Orig.). pap. 4.00 (*1-880443-07-4*) Roscoe Village.

— A Fine Poor Man's Country: The Life of Ohio's Early Craftsmen. (Illus.). 85p. (Orig.). 1991. pap. 3.95 (*1-880443-04-X*) Roscoe Village.

— Why Is It Called Whitewoman Street? Roscoe's Pre-Canal History. (Illus.). 80p. (Orig.). 1992. pap. 4.00 (*1-880443-06-6*) Roscoe Village.

Norton, M. Scott & Kelly, Larry K. Resource Allocation: Managing Money & People. LC 97-4940. (Illus.). 160p. 1997. 29.95 (*1-883001-35-8*) Eye On Educ.

Norton, M. Scott, jt. auth. see Webb, L. Dean.

Norton, Marcia M., jt. auth. see Lester, Paula E.

Norton, Margaret, et al. Student Planned Acquisition of Required Knowledge. Langdon, Danny G., ed. LC 79-23442. (Instructional Design Library). 104p. 1980. 27.95 (*0-87778-155-9*) Educ Tech Pubns.

Norton, Margaret C. Illinois Census Returns, 1820. 466p. 1996. reprint ed. pap. 36.00 (*0-8063-0262-3*, 4165) Clearfield Co.

Norton, Mark, contrib. by. Living Words of Jesus. LC 97-215931. 1997. pap. 2.99 (*0-8423-3249-9*) Tyndale Hse.

Norton, Mark R., jt. ed. see Brown, Robert K.

Norton, Mark R., ed. see Petersen, William J. & Petersen, Randy.

Norton, Martin L., ed. Atlas of the Difficult Airway. 2nd ed. (Illus.). 256p. (C). (gr. 13). 1996. text 110.00 (*0-8151-6433-5*, 24216) Mosby Inc.

Norton, Martin L., et al, eds. High Intensity Care: Medical, Administrative, & Legal Issues. (Health Care Administration Ser.). 346p. 1988. 77.00 (*0-8342-0001-5*) Aspen Pub.

Norton, Mary. Are All the Giants Dead? LC 78-6622. (Illus.). 123p. (J). (gr. 3-7). 1978. pap. 9.95 (*0-15-607888-0*, Voyager Bks) Harcourt.

— Are All the Giants Dead? LC 97-151682. (Illus.). 128p. 1997. pap. 7.00 (*0-15-201523-X*, Harcourt Child Bks) Harcourt.

— Are All the Giants Dead? 1997. 12.10 (*0-606-13147-7*, Pub. by Turtleback) Demco.

— Bed-Knob & Broomstick. LC 89-38863. (Illus.). 189p. (J). (gr. 3-7). 1990. pap. 6.00 (*0-15-206231-9*, Odyssey) Harcourt.

***Norton, Mary.** Bed-Knob & Broomstick. LC 99-89153. (Illus.). 240p. (J). (gr. 4-7). 2000. 17.00 (*0-15-202450-6*, Harcourt Child Bks) Harcourt.

Norton, Mary. Bed-Knob & Broomstick. (J). 1990. 11.10 (*0-606-02277-5*, Pub. by Turtleback) Demco.

— Bedknob & Broomstick. large type ed. (Illus.). 296p. (J). (gr. 3-7). 1989. lib. bdg. 14.95 (*0-8161-4786-8*, G K Hall Lrg Type) Mac Lib Ref.

— The Borrowers. LC 53-7870. (Borrowers Ser.). (Illus.). 180p. (J). (gr. 3-7). 1953. 17.00 (*0-15-209987-5*, Harcourt Child Bks) Harcourt.

— The Borrowers. LC 86-4645. (Borrowers Ser.). (Illus.). 180p. (J). (gr. 3-7). 1989. pap. 6.00 (*0-15-209990-5*, Odyssey) Harcourt.

— The Borrowers. (Borrowers Ser.). (Illus.). 180p. (J). (gr. 3-7). 1993. pap. 6.00 (*0-15-200086-0*) Harcourt.

Norton, Mary. The Borrowers. (J). 1981. 11.10 (*0-606-02413-1*, Pub. by Turtleback) Demco.

Norton, Mary. The Borrowers Afield. LC 55-11011. (Borrowers Ser.). (Illus.). 215p. (J). (gr. 3-7). 1955. 17.00 (*0-15-210166-7*, Harcourt Child Bks) Harcourt.

— The Borrowers Afield. LC 89-39891. (Borrowers Ser.). (Illus.). 215p. (J). (gr. 3-7). 1990. pap. 6.00 (*0-15-210535-2*, Odyssey) Harcourt.

— The Borrowers Afield. (Borrowers Ser.). (J). (gr. 3-7). 1983. 11.10 (*0-606-02414-X*, Pub. by Turtleback) Demco.

— The Borrowers Afloat. LC 59-5630. (Borrowers Ser.). (Illus.). 191p. (J). (gr. 3-7). 1959. 16.00 (*0-15-210345-7*, Harcourt Child Bks) Harcourt.

— The Borrowers Afloat. LC 89-39890. (Borrowers Ser.). (Illus.). 191p. (J). (gr. 3-7). 1990. pap. 6.00 (*0-15-210534-4*, Odyssey) Harcourt.

— The Borrowers Afloat. (Borrowers Ser.). (J). (gr. 3-7). 1987. 11.10 (*0-606-02417-4*, Pub. by Turtleback) Demco.

— The Borrowers Aloft. (Borrowers Ser.). (J). (gr. 3-7). 1961. 11.10 (*0-606-02416-6*, Pub. by Turtleback) Demco.

— The Borrowers Aloft. LC 61-11751. (Borrowers Ser.). (Illus.). 192p. (J). (gr. 3-7). 1961. reprint ed. 17.00 (*0-15-210524-7*, Harcourt Child Bks) Harcourt.

— The Borrowers Aloft. LC 89-24641. (Borrowers Ser.). (Illus.). 192p. (J). (gr. 3-7). 1990. reprint ed. pap. 6.00 (*0-15-210533-6*, Odyssey) Harcourt.

— The Borrowers Avenged. LC 90-36246. (Borrowers Ser.). (Illus.). 304p. (J). (gr. 3-7). 1982. 17.00 (*0-15-210530-1*) Harcourt.

— The Borrowers Avenged. LC 90-36246. (Borrowers Ser.). (Illus.). 304p. (J). (gr. 3-7). 1990. pap. 6.00 (*0-15-210532-8*, Odyssey) Harcourt.

— The Borrowers Avenged. (Borrowers Ser.). (J). (gr. 3-7). 1982. 11.10 (*0-606-03322-X*, Pub. by Turtleback) Demco.

— The Complete Borrowers. LC 97-6327. 1997. 20.00 (*0-15-201573-6*); pap. 15.00 (*0-15-201571-X*) Harcourt.

— A People & a Nation: A History of the United States, 4 vols. 4th ed. (C). 1993. 65.16 (*0-395-69773-5*) HM.

— Poor Stainless. LC 70-140781. (Borrowers Ser.). (Illus.). 32p. (J). (gr. 3-7). 1985. 7.95 (*0-15-263221-2*, Harcourt Child Bks) Harcourt.

***Norton, Mary & Blegvad, Erik.** Bed-Knob & Broomstick. LC 99-89153. 240p. (J). (gr. 4-7). 2000. pap. 6.00 (*0-15-202456-5*, Harcourt Child Bks) Harcourt.

Norton, Mary B. Founding Mothers & Fathers. LC 95-43791. 496p. 1996. 35.00 (*0-679-42965-4*) Knopf.

— Founding Mothers & Fathers: Gendered Power & the Forming of American Society. 496p. 1998. text 35.00 (*0-7881-5781-7*) DIANE Pub.

— Founding Mothers & Fathers: Gendered Power & the Forming of American Society. 1997. pap. 17.00 (*0-679-74977-2*) Vin Bks.

— Liberty's Daughters: The Revolutionary Experience of American Women, 1750-1800. LC 96-12247. (Illus.). 400p. 1996. pap. text 16.95 (*0-8014-8347-6*) Cornell U Pr.

Norton, Mary B., ed. American Historical Association's Guide to Historical Literature, 2 vols., Set. 3rd ed. 2064p. 1995. text 225.00 (*0-19-505727-9*) OUP.

Norton, Mary B. & Alexander, Ruth M. Major Problems in American Women's History: Documents & Essays. 2nd ed. 530p. (C). 1996. pap. text 29.16 (*0-669-35390-6*) HM Trade Div.

Norton, Mary B., et al. Norton A People in A Nation with Atlas, 4 vols., 2. 5th ed. Price not set. (*0-395-78884-6*) HM.

Norton, Mary B., et al. A People & a Nation: A History of the United States: Instructor's Resource Manual with Video Guide, 4 vols. 4th ed. (C). 1993. text 5.16 (*0-395-67822-6*) HM.

— A People & a Nation Vol. I: A History of the United States, Brief Edition, 4 vols. 4th ed. (C). 1995. pap. text, student ed. 19.56 (*0-395-74571-3*) HM.

— A People & a Nation Vol. 1: A History of the United States, Brief Edition: To 1877, 4 vols. 4th ed. 324p. (C). 1995. pap. text 28.76 (*0-395-74569-1*) HM.

— A People & a Nation Vol. I: A History of the United States: To 1877. 4 vols. 4th ed. 464p. (C). 1993. pap. text 48.76 (*0-395-69774-3*) HM.

— A People & a Nation Vol. II: A History of the United States. 2nd ed. LC 85-60316. 1072p. 1985. trans. 84.76 (*0-685-12000-7*); disk. write for info. (*0-318-60190-7*) HM.

— A People & a Nation Vol. II: A History of the United States, 4 vols. 4th ed. (C). 1994. pap. text, student ed. 21.96 (*0-395-67820-X*); pap. text, student ed. 21.96 (*0-395-67821-8*) HM.

— A People & a Nation Vol. II: A History of the United States, 1. 2nd ed. LC 85-60316. 1072p. 1985. 27.16 (*0-685-11998-X*) HM.

— A People & a Nation Vol. II: A History of the United States, 2. 2nd ed. LC 85-60316. 1072p. 1985. text 27.16 (*0-685-11999-8*) HM.

— A People & a Nation Vol. II: A History of the United States, Brief Edition, 4 vols. 4th ed. (C). 1995. pap. text, student ed. 19.56 (*0-395-74572-1*) HM.

— A People & a Nation Vol. 2: A History of the United States, Brief Edition: Since 1865, 4 vols. 4th ed. 375p. (C). 1995. pap. text 28.76 (*0-395-74570-5*) HM.

Norton, Mary B., jt. ed. see Groneman, Carol.

Norton, Mary J., ed. see Hume, David.

Norton, MaryJane P. Children Worship! 128p. 1997. pap. 21.95 (*0-88177-223-2*, DR223) Discipleship Res.

— Teaching Young Children: A Guide for Teachers & Leaders. (Children Ministry Ser.). 64p. 1997. pap. 9.95 (*0-88177-229-1*, DR229) Discipleship Res.

***Norton, Matt.** Fallout 2: Official Strategies & Secrets. LC 98-87284. 352p. 1998. pap. text 19.99 (*0-7821-2415-1*) Sybex.

***Norton, Matthew J.** Baldur's Gate: Tales of the Sword Coast. 176p. 1999. pap. 14.99 (*0-7821-2622-7*) Sybex.

— Baldur's Gate: Ultimate Strategy Guide for Playstation. 128p. 2000. pap. 14.99 (*0-7821-2671-5*) Sybex.

***Norton, Melanie J., ed.** Introductory Concepts in Information Science. 2000. 39.50 (*1-57387-087-0*) Info Today Inc.

Norton, Michael. Dental Implants: A Guide for the General Practitioner. (Illus.). 148p. 1995. text 68.00 (*1-85097-037-8*) Quint Pub Co.

— Directory of Social Change: Community. 1988. 40.00 (*0-7045-0285-2*) St Mut.

— Directory of Social Change: Education & Play. 1988. 40.00 (*0-7045-0291-7*) St Mut.

***Norton, Michael & Culshaw, Murray.** Getting Started in Fundraising. LC 00-42217. 2000. pap. write for info. (*0-7619-9443-2*) Sage.

Norton, Michael & Hedgecoe, Adam. The European Union & Research: EU Framework Programmes & National Priorities. LC 98-146619. 73p. 1996. write for info. (*1-897941-26-9*) Parl Ofc Sci.

Norton, Michael, jt. auth. see Corbett, Margery.

Norton, Michael J. Spells of Fury: Building Games in Windows 95. 672p. (Orig.). 1996. pap. 49.99 incl. cd-rom (*1-57169-067-0*) Sams.

Norton, Michael P. Fundamentals of Noise & Vibration Analysis for Engineers. (Illus.). 640p. (C). 1990. pap. text 69.95 (*0-521-34941-9*) Cambridge U Pr.

Norton, Miriam. The Kitten Who Thought He Was a Mouse. LC 98-84182. (Family Storytime Ser.: No. 6). (Illus.). 32p. (J). (ps-k). 1998. 9.95 (*0-307-10219-X*, 10219, Goldn Books) Gldn Bks Pub Co.

— Kitten Who Thought He Was a Mouse. (J). 1996. 11.19 (*0-606-11538-2*, Pub. by Turtleback) Demco.

Norton, Mortimer, ed. Angling Success, by Leading Outdoor Writers. LC 67-30224. (Essay Index Reprint Ser.). 1977. 23.95 (*0-8369-0747-7*) Ayer.

Norton, N. P., jt. auth. see Ewing, John S.

***Norton, N. S. & Peutrell, Jane M.** Paediatric Anaesthesia & Critical Care in the District Hospital. (Illus.). 226p. 2000. pap. text 50.00 (*0-7506-4302-1*) Buttrwrth-Heinemann.

Norton, Natascha. Belize. (Cadogan Guides Ser.). (Illus.). 224p. 1997. pap. 14.95 (*1-86011-087-8*, Pub. by Cadgn Bks) Globe Pequot.

— Guatemala & Belize. 2nd ed. (Cadogan Guides Ser.). 1997. pap. text 16.95 (*1-86011-017-7*, Pub. by Cadgn Bks) Macmillan.

Norton, O. Richard. Rocks from Space: Meteorites & Meteorite Hunters. 2nd rev. ed. Ort, Kathleen & Carey, Jennifer, eds. LC 97-51574. (Illus.). 467p. 1998. pap. 30.00 (*0-87842-373-7*) Mountain Pr.

Norton, Oliver W. The Attack & Defense of Little Round Top, Gettysburg, July 2, 1863. (Illus.). 350p. 1992. reprint ed. 25.00 (*1-879664-07-0*); reprint ed. pap. 17.95 (*1-879664-08-9*) Stan Clark Military. "The writer was a private soldier at Gettysburg, & on service at General Vincent's headquarters as a bugler. His account of this particular engagement shows that Vincent took his brigade to Round Top without either orders from Warren or Barnes & fixed his own position..."--New York Times. "It seems to us that this book is conclusive; a most important addition to the records of the fighting at Gettysburg."--The Boston Herald. "This is an attempt to describe more fully & accurately than had heretofore been done that part of the battle fought on one corner of the field where more than in any other place, the fate of the contests between the two armies was decided."--Army & Navy Journal. "It is an example of the sort of book about the Civil War of which more ought to be written. It carefully examines the accepted accounts of the fight & compares them with one another & with all the official reports of the occurrence, both Union & Confederate."--The Evening Mail. "No one will ever write a history of the Battle of Gettysburg again without referring to your book. It is all together admirable, a model for such a book."--Cyrus Townsend Brady. Order from: Stan Clark Military Books, 915 Fairview Ave., Gettysburg, PA 17325; Phone: 717-337-1728; Fax: 717-337-0581. *Publisher Paid Annotation.*

Norton, Penny. Earth Watch: A Fact Finder Book. (Illus.). 48p. (J). (gr. 7-9). 1992. 14.95 (*0-563-34407-5*, BBC-Parkwest); pap. 8.95 (*0-563-34408-3*, BBC-Parkwest) Parkwest Pubns.

***Norton, Peter.** Access 2000 Programming. (Peter Norton (Sams) Ser.). 1999. pap. 34.99 (*0-672-31760-5*) Sams.

— Complete Guide to Windows 2000 Professional. LC 99-64729. 944p. 2000. pap. 39.99 (*0-672-31778-8*) Sams.

Norton, Peter. Inside the PC: Upgrading & Repairing PC's, Complete Guide to Windows 95. 1998. pap. 64.99 (*0-672-31269-7*) Sams.

— Intro to Computing Fund. LC 94-24444. 1995. write for info. (*0-02-802875-9*) Glencoe.

— Peter Norton's Advanced DOS 5.0. 1991. pap. 39.95 (*0-13-529652-8*) Brady Pub.

— Peter Norton's Assembly Language Book for the IBM PC. 2nd rev. ed. 512p. 1989. pap. 24.95 (*0-13-662453-7*) Brady Pub.

— Peter Norton's BASIC On-Line Guide. (Programming Ser.). 1989. pap. 49.95 (*0-13-662677-7*) Brady Pub.

— Peter Norton's Complete Guide to DOS 6.22. 6th ed. (Illus.). 1150p. (Orig.). 1994. 29.99 (*0-672-30614-X*) Sams.

— Peter Norton's Complete Guide to Linux. (Peter Norton (Sams) Ser.). 650p. 1999. pap. text 29.99 (*0-672-31573-4*) Sams.

***Norton, Peter.** Peter Norton's Complete Guide to Network Security. 800p. 1999. pap. 39.99 (*0-672-31691-9*) Sams.

— Peter Norton's Complete Guide to TCP/IP. 1999. pap. 29.99 (*0-672-31695-1*) Sams.

Norton, Peter. Peter Norton's Complete Guide to Windows NT Workstation. LC 95-72348. 936p. 1996. 39.99 (*0-672-30901-7*) Sams.

— Peter Norton's Complete Guide to Windows NT Workstation 4. 2nd ed. LC 98-85651. 1998. pap. 29.99 (*0-672-31373-1*) Sams.

***Norton, Peter.** Peter Norton's Complete Guide to Windows 98. 2nd ed. 800p. 1999. pap. text 29.99 (*0-672-31693-5*) Sams.

Norton, Peter. Peter Norton's Complete Guide to Windows 98. 3rd ed. LC 97-69209. 672p. 1998. 29.99 (*0-672-31230-1*) Sams.

— Peter Norton's Computing Essentials. 3rd ed. LC 98-39586. 1998. 18.00 (*0-02-804394-4*) Glencoe.

— Peter Norton's Computing Fundamentals. LC 96-32936. 1996. 30.95 (*0-02-804337-5*) Glencoe.

— Peter Norton's Computing Fundamentals. 3rd ed. LC 99-166725. xxxi, 461 p. 1999. write for info. (*0-02-804395-2*) Glencoe.

— Peter Norton's Computing Fundamentals. 3rd ed. LC 98-39530. 1998. 300.00 (*0-02-804410-X*) Glencoe.

***Norton, Peter.** Peter Norton's Computing Fundamentals. 4th ed. LC 00-34044. (Illus.). 2000. write for info. (*0-07-822723-2*) Glencoe.

Norton, Peter. Peter Norton's DOS Guide. 744p. 1994. 24.95 (*1-56686-136-5*) Sams.

***Norton, Peter.** Peter Norton's Essential Concepts. 4th ed. LC 00-34101. (Illus.). 2000. write for info. (*0-07-822728-3*) Glencoe.

Norton, Peter. Peter Norton's Guide to Delphi 2. LC 95-72346. 816p. 1996. 49.99 incl. disk (*0-672-30898-3*) Sams.

— Peter Norton's Guide to Java: Premier Title. LC 96-67206. 912p. 1996. 39.99 (*1-57521-088-6*) Sams.

— Peter Norton's Guide to Linux. 800p. 1997. 39.99 (*0-672-31141-0*) Macmillan.

— Peter Norton's Guide to Visual Basic 6. LC 96-72394. 600p. 1998. 29.99 (*0-672-31054-6*) Sams.

— Peter Norton's Guide to Visual C++ 6. 1000p. 1999. 34.99 (*0-672-31053-8*) Sams.

— Peter Norton's Guide to Windows X.0. 640p. 1995. pap. 30.00 (*0-679-75588-8*) Random.

— Peter Norton's Inside the PC. 6th ed. 654p. 1995. 35.00 (*0-672-30624-7*) Sams.

— Peter Norton's Inside the Sun 486i & 386i. 1990. pap. 29.95 (*0-13-661612-7*) P-H.

— Peter Norton's Introduction to Computers. LC 93-46202. 1994. pap. 34.95 (*0-02-801318-2*) Glencoe.

— Peter Norton's Introduction to Computers. LC 93-46202. 1994. write for info. (*0-02-801331-X*) Glencoe.

— Peter Norton's Introduction to Computers. 2nd ed. LC 96-32939. 1996. write for info. (*0-02-804325-1*) Glencoe.

— Peter Norton's Introduction to Computers. 3rd ed. LC 98-39587. 1998. 34.00 (*0-02-804386-3*) Glencoe.

***Norton, Peter.** Peter Norton's Introduction to Computers. 3rd ed. LC 99-474353. (Illus.). 1999. write for info. (*0-02-804389-8*); write for info. (*0-02-804412-6*) Glencoe.

— Peter Norton's Introduction to Computers. 4th ed. LC 00-34045. (Illus.). 2000. write for info. (*0-07-821058-5*) Glencoe.

Norton, Peter. Peter Norton's Introduction to Computers: Essential Concepts. LC 94-10091. 1994. 36.25 (*0-02-802902-X*) Glencoe.

— Peter Norton's Introduction to Computers: Essential Concepts. 2nd ed. LC 96-29222. 1996. write for info. (*0-02-804332-4*) Glencoe.

— Peter Norton's Introduction to Computers: With Microsoft Works for Windows. LC 94-25920. 1994. write for info. (*0-02-802896-1*) Glencoe.

— Peter Norton's OS-2 On-Line Guide. (Productivity Ser.). 1989. pap. 49.95 (*0-13-662693-9*) Brady Pub.

Norton, Peter & Alvernaz, Bill. Peter Norton's PC Resource. (Illus.). 400p. 1987. pap. 19.95 (*0-685-18872-8*) P-H.

Norton, Peter & Andersen, Virginia. Peter Norton's Guide to Access 97 Programming. 624p. 1997. 35.00 (*0-672-31050-3*) Sams.

Norton, Peter & Desmond, Michael. Peter Norton's Guide to Upgrading & Repairing PCs: Premier Edition. LC 97-67495. 704p. 1997. pap. 29.99 (*0-672-31140-2*) Sams.

— Peter Norton's Upgrading & Repairing PCs. 2nd ed. LC 98-87673. 700p. 1999. pap. 29.99 (*0-672-31483-5*) Sams.

Norton, Peter & John, Goodman. Peter Norton's Inside the PC. 8th ed. (Peter Norton (Sams) Ser.). 816p. 1999. pap. 29.99 (*0-672-31532-7*) Sams.

Norton, Peter & McGregor, Rob. Peter Norton's Guide to Windows 95/NT 4 Programming with MFC. LC 95-72339. 1200p. 1996. 49.99 (*0-672-30900-9*) Sams.

Norton, Peter & Mueller, John. Peter Norton's Complete Guide to Windows 95. 2nd ed. LC 96-71999. 1124p. 1997. pap. 35.00 (*0-672-31040-6*) Sams.

— Peter Norton's Complete Guide to Windows 95: Primer Edition. 2nd ed. 1997. pap. 35.00 (*0-614-28485-6*, Sams Sftwre) MCP SW Interactive.

N

An Asterisk (*) at the beginning of an entry indicates that the title is appearing for the first time.

Norton, Peter, et al. Peter Norton's Complete Guide To Microsoft Office 2000. LC 97-67998. (Peter Norton (Sams) Ser.). (Illus.). 792p. 1999. pap. 29.99 (*0-672-31174-7*) Sams.
— Peter Norton's Inside the PC. 7th ed. LC 96-72009. 752p. 1997. 29.99 (*0-672-31041-4*) Sams.
Norton, Peter G., et al, eds. Primary Care Research: Traditional & Innovative Approaches. LC 90-21954. (Research Methods for Primary Care Ser.: No. 1). (Illus.). 253p. 1991. pap. 78.50 (*0-608-05070-9*, 206562500005) Bks Demand.
— Primary Care Research: Traditional & Innovative Approaches. (Research Methods for Primary Care Ser.: Vol. 1). (Illus.). 272p. (C). 1990. text 58.00 (*0-8039-3870-5*); pap. text 26.00 (*0-8039-3871-3*) Sage.
Norton, Peter G., ed. see Peace, Sheila M.
Norton, Philip. British Polity. 3rd ed. LC 93-14317. 432p. (C). 1993. pap. text 47.00 (*0-8013-1169-1*, 79663) Longman.
— The British Polity. 4th ed. (C). 2000. pap. text. write for info. (*0-8013-1844-0*) Longman.
— Dissension in the House of Commons: 1974-1979. (Illus.). 560p. (C). 1980. text 98.00 (*0-19-827430-0*) OUP.
Norton, Philip, ed. The Conservative Party. LC 95-50139. 256p. (C). 1996. pap. text 29.95 (*0-13-374653-4*) P-H.
Norton, Philip, ed. Legislatures. (Oxford Readings in Politics & Government Ser.). (Illus.). 352p. 1990. 65.00 (*0-19-827582-X*) OUP.
— Legislatures & Legislators. LC 97-39112. (International Library of Politics & Comparative Government). 571p. 1998. text 162.95 (*1-85521-357-5*, Pub. by Ashgate Pub) Ashgate Pub Co.
— National Parliaments & the European Union. LC 95-24867. (Journal of Legislative Studies). 204p. 1995. 45.00 (*0-7146-4691-1*, Pub. by F Cass Pubs) Intl Spec Bk.
— National Parliaments & the European Union. 204p. (C). 1997. pap. 19.50 (*0-7146-4330-0*, Pub. by F Cass Pubs) Intl Spec Bk.
***Norton, Philip, ed.** Parliaments & Citizens in Western Europe. 200p. 1999. 52.50 (*0-7146-4835-3*); pap. 22.50 (*0-7146-4387-4*) F Cass Pubs.
Norton, Philip, ed. Parliaments & Governments in Western Europe. LC 98-16206. (Parliaments in Contemporary Western Europe Ser.). 232p. 1998. 52.50 (*0-7146-4833-7*, Pub. by F Cass Pubs); pap. 22.50 (*0-7146-4385-8*, Pub. by F Cass Pubs) Intl Spec Bk.
***Norton, Philip, ed.** Parliaments & Pressure Groups in Western Europe. 200p. 1999. pap. 22.50 (*0-7146-4386-6*, Pub. by F Cass Pubs) Intl Spec Bk.
— Parliaments & Pressure Groups in Western Europe: Philip Norton, the Lord Norton of Louth. 181p. 1999. 52.50 (*0-7146-4834-5*, Pub. by F Cass Pubs) Intl Spec Bk.
Norton, Philip, ed. Parliaments in Western Europe. 2nd ed. 176p. (C). 1996. pap. text 19.50 (*0-7146-4331-9*, Pub. by F Cass Pubs) Intl Spec Bk.
Norton, Philip & Wood, David M. Back from Westminster: British Members of Parliament & Their Constituents. LC 93-14766. (Comparative Legislative Studies). 192p. 1993. 29.95 (*0-8131-1834-4*) U Pr of Ky.
Norton, Philip, jt. ed. see Ahmed, Nizam.
Norton, Philip, jt. ed. see Ahmed, Nizam.
Norton, Philip, jt. ed. see Franklin, Mark N.
Norton, Philip, jt. ed. see Olson, David M.
Norton, Phillip. British Polity. 2nd ed. LC 83-19952. 429p. (C). 1991. pap. text 23.95 (*0-8013-0123-8*, 75787) Longman.
Norton, Phillip, ed. New Directions in British Politics? Essays on the Evolving Constitution. 208p. 1991. text 80.00 (*1-85278-350-8*) E Elgar.
***Norton, R. D.** Creating the New Economy: The Entrepreneur & the U. S. Resurgence. LC 00-42695. 2000. write for info. (*1-84064-448-6*) E Elgar.
Norton, R. D. Research in Urban Economics, Vol. 12. 1999. 78.50 (*0-7623-0572-X*) Jai Pr.
Norton, R. D., ed. Research in Urban Economics Vol. 11: Regional Resilence & Defense-Conversion in the United States. 1997. 78.50 (*0-7623-0149-X*) Jai Pr.
Norton, R. L. Design of Machinery. (C). 1991. text 77.25 (*0-07-909702-2*) McGraw.
Norton, R. W., Art Gallery Staff. America the Beautiful: A Bicentennial Exhibition. LC 75-28257. (Illus.). 40p. 1975. pap. 3.50 (*0-913060-07-0*) Norton Art.
— The American Porcelain Tradition. LC 72-82888. (Illus.). 1972. pap. 3.00 (*0-9600182-8-X*) Norton Art.
— American Sculpture: A Tenth Anniversary Exhibition. LC 76-50425. (Illus.). 1976. pap. 3.50 (*0-913060-11-9*) Norton Art.
— American Silver & Pressed Glass. LC 67-24712. (Illus.). 1967. pap. 3.50 (*0-9600182-0-4*) Norton Art.
— Artistry in Arms: The Art of Gunsmithing & Gun Engraving. LC 75-164699. (Illus.). 1971. pap. 2.50 (*0-9600182-4-7*) Norton Art.
— Artistry in Silver: An Exhibition of Sculpture by Charles M. Russell. LC 78-17945. (Illus.). 1970. pap. 1.00 (*0-9600182-1-2*) Norton Art.
— Bob Timberlake: Paintings & Watercolors. LC 74-5029. (Contemporary Realists Ser.). (Illus.). 1974. pap. 3.50 (*0-913060-04-6*) Norton Art.
— Carolyn Wyeth: A Retrospective Exhibition. LC 75-43579. (Contemporary Realists Ser.). (Illus.). 1976. pap. 2.50 (*0-913060-08-9*) Norton Art.
— Charles M. Russell, 1864-1926: Paintings & Sculpture in the R. W. Norton Art Gallery Collection. LC 78-7115. (Illus.). 1980. pap. 8.50 (*0-913060-15-1*) Norton Art.
— E. C. Prudhomme: Master Gun Engraver. LC 73-78704. (Illus.). 32p. 1973. pap. 3.00 (*0-913060-01-1*) Norton Art.
— Felix Kelly. LC 77-732. (Contemporary Realists Ser.). (Illus.). 1977. pap. 4.50 (*0-913060-12-7*) Norton Art.
— Felix Kelly: A Romantic Realist. LC 72-78863. (Contemporary Realists Ser.). (Illus.). 1972. pap. 2.50 (*0-9600182-7-1*) Norton Art.
— Frederic Remington, Eighteen Sixty-One to Nineteen Hundred Nine: Paintings, Drawings & Sculpture. LC 78-7114. (Illus.). 1979. pap. 8.00 (*0-913060-14-3*) Norton Art.
— John Chumley's Rural America. LC 76-187913. (Contemporary Realists Ser.). (Illus.). 1972. pap. 3.50 (*0-913060-00-3*) Norton Art.
— John McClusky: A Retrospective Exhibition. LC 74-14946. (Contemporary Realists Ser.). (Illus.). 1974. pap. 5.50 (*0-913060-05-4*) Norton Art.
— Medallic Art of the United States, 1800-1972. LC 72-187912. (Illus.). 1972. pap. 3.00 (*0-9600182-9-8*) Norton Art.
— The Old West in Miniature: Sculptures by Don Polland. LC 74-24491. 1974. pap. 2.50 (*0-913060-06-2*) Norton Art.
— The Old West Pictorialized by Joe Ruiz Grandee. LC 79-171014. (Contemporary Realists Ser.). (Illus.). 1971. pap. 1.50 (*0-9600182-5-5*) Norton Art.
— Portrait Miniatures in Early American History, 1750-1840: 1750-1840. LC 76-11634. 1976. pap. 3.50 (*0-913060-09-7*) Norton Art.
— Realism in Retrospect: The Works of James Peter Cost. LC 75-164700. (Contemporary Realists Ser.). (Illus.). 1971. pap. 3.50 (*0-9600182-3-9*) Norton Art.
— Robert William Addison: A Retrospective Exhibition. LC 73-155783. (Contemporary Realists Ser.). (Illus.). 1971. pap. 1.00 (*0-9600182-2-0*) Norton Art.
— Roses in Porcelain by Jean du Tilleux. LC 73-81397. (Illus.). 16p. 1973. pap. 3.50 (*0-913060-02-X*) Norton Art.
— Samuel Kirk & Son: American Silver Craftsmen since Eighteen Fifteen. (Illus.). 32p. 1971. pap. 1.00 (*0-913060-17-8*) Norton Art.
— The Seasonal Transitions of Richard Earl Thompson. LC 82-12437. (Illus.). 76p. 1982. pap. 10.00 (*0-913060-20-8*) Norton Art.
— Stow Wengenroth, Artist-Lithographer: A Retrospective Exhibition. LC 76-26456. (Contemporary Realists Ser.). (Illus.). 1976. pap. 3.00 (*0-913060-10-0*) Norton Art.
— Will Hinds: Artist of the Deep South. LC 79-187911. (Contemporary Realists Ser.). (Illus.). 1972. pap. 2.00 (*0-9600182-6-3*) Norton Art.
— The Works of E. L. Henry: Recollections of a Time Gone By. (Illus.). 56p. 1987. pap. 12.00 (*0-913060-26-7*) Norton Art.
Norton, Ralph G. Investing for Income: A Bond Mutual Fund Approach to High-Return, Low-Risk Profits. LC 98-48173. (Illus.). 202p. 1999. pap. 19.95 (*0-07-134295-8*) McGraw.
Norton, Ralph G., ed. see IBC Publishing Inc. Staff.
Norton, Richard. Tonality in Western Culture: A Critical & Historical Perspective. LC 83-43030. (Illus.). 336p. 1984. 35.00 (*0-271-00359-6*) Pa St U Pr.
Norton, Richard C. Chronology of American Musical Theater, 3 vols. 2016p. 2000. text 225.00 (*0-19-508888-3*) OUP.
Norton, Richard J., jt. ed. see Ricketts, R. Allan.
Norton, Richard L., jt. auth. see Jackman, Sidney D.
Norton, Richard L., jt. auth. see Maddox, George T.
Norton, Richard L., jt. auth. see Webb, W. L.
Norton, Richard L., ed. see Younger, Thomas C., et al.
***Norton, Rictor.** Gothic Readings: The First Wave, 1764-1840. 2000. 99.95 (*0-7185-0216-7*) Leicester U Pr.
— Gothic Readings: The First Wave, 1764-1840. 2000. pap. 29.95 (*0-7185-0217-5*) Leicester U Pr.
Norton, Rictor. Mistress of Udolpho: The Life of Ann Radcliffe. LC 98-8412. 1998. 75.00 (*0-7185-0201-9*); pap. 19.95 (*0-7185-0202-7*) Bks Intl VA.
— The Myth of the Modern Homosexual: Queer History & the Search for Cultural Unity. LC 97-7785. 1997. 69.95 (*0-304-33891-5*); pap. 19.95 (*0-304-33892-3*) Continuum.
Norton, Rictor, ed. My Dear Boy: Gay Love Letters Through the Centuries. LC 97-28335. (Illus.). 288p. 1998. 50.00 (*0-943595-70-3*); pap. 15.95 (*0-943595-71-1*) Leyland Pubns.
Norton, Rictor H. The Homosexual Literary Tradition. 432p. 1974. 250.00 (*0-87700-204-5*) Revisionist Pr.
Norton, Robert. Communicator Style: Theory, Applications, & Measures. LC 83-13720. (Sage Series in Interpersonal Communication: No. 1). (Illus.). 320p. reprint ed. pap. 99.20 (*0-8357-4837-5*, 203777400009) Bks Demand.
— The Gunner: Shewing the Whole Practise of Artillerie, No. 617. LC 73-6155. 1973. reprint ed. 70.00 (*90-221-0617-9*) Walter J Johnson.
— The Willow in the Tempest. 324p. (Orig.). 1990. pap. 15.00 (*0-918980-13-5*) St Alban Pr.
Norton, Robert & Brenders, David. Communication & Consequences: Laws of Interaction. (LEA's Communication Ser.). 272p. 1995. pap. 29.95 (*0-8058-2034-5*); text 59.95 (*0-8058-2033-7*) L Erlbaum Assocs.
Norton, Robert, jt. auth. see Tyler John, Martha.
Norton, Robert, jt. compiled by see Wharton, Edith.
Norton, Robert E. The Beautiful Soul: Aesthetic Morality in the Eighteenth Century. 336p. 1995. text 37.50 (*0-8014-3050-X*) Cornell U Pr.
— Herder's Aesthetics & the European Enlightenment. LC 90-55759. (Illus.). 280p. 1991. text 42.50 (*0-8014-2530-1*) Cornell U Pr.
Norton, Robert E. & Belcher, James O. A Guide to Linkages Between Vocational Education & Organized Labor In The United States. 162p. 1984. 12.00 (*0-318-17786-2*, RD252) Ctr Educ Trng Employ.
Norton, Robert E. & Harrington, Lois G. Administrator Competency Study. 114p. 1987. 10.50 (*0-318-35277-X*, RD 268) Ctr Educ Trng Employ.
Norton, Robert F., et al. A Treatise on Deeds. LC 81-83533. 854p. 1981. reprint ed. 180.00 (*0-912004-17-7*) Gaunt.
Norton, Robert L. Design of Machinery: An Introduction to the Synthesis & Analysis of Mechanisms & Machines. 1992. text. write for info. (*0-07-047799-X*) McGraw.
— Design of Machinery: An Introduction to the Synthesis & Analysis of Mechanisms & Machines. 2nd ed. LC 98-2770. (Series in Mechanical Engineering). 1998. 32.25 (*0-07-048395-7*) McGraw.
***Norton, Robert L.** Design of Machinery: An Introduction to the Synthesis & Analysis of Mechanisms & Machines. 2nd ed. LC 00-32898. 2001. write for info. (*0-07-237960-X*) McGraw.
— Machine Design: An Integrated Approach. 2nd ed. 875p. 2000. 110.00 (*0-13-017706-7*) P-H.
Norton, Robert L. & Leck, Charles F. An Annotated Checklist of Birds of the U. S. Virgin Islands. (Illus.). 35p. 1986. pap. text 6.95 (*0-916611-01-9*) Antilles Pr.
Norton, Roger D. & Leopoldo, Solis M., eds. The Book of CHAC: Programming Studies for Mexican Agriculture. LC 80-29366. (World Bank Research Publications). 622p. reprint ed. pap. 192.90 (*0-7837-5386-1*, 204515000005) Bks Demand.
Norton, Rosaleen. Three Macabre Stories. Richmond, Keith, ed. (Illus.). 48p. 1996. 45.00 (*0-930126-50-5*) Typographeum.
Norton Rose M5 Group Staff, et al. Developing Transparent, Efficient, & Effective Procurement Processes for Power Infrastructure in APEC Member Economies: A Comparative Study Report. LC 98-945506. 1997. 0.00 (*981-00-9230-X*) Miscell Pubs.
Norton Rose M5 Group Staff, jt. ed. see Boyle, A.
Norton, Roy A., jt. ed. see Alberti, Gerd.
Norton, Rudolph F. Hosea: Critic & Comforter for Today. LC 96-157731. (God's Word for Today Ser.). 1996. pap. 5.50 (*0-570-09544-1*, 20-2652) Concordia.
Norton, Russell. Stereoviews Illustrated: Fifty Early American, Vol. I. LC 94-92191. (Illus.). 64p. (Orig.). 1994. pap. 18.95 (*0-9641653-0-9*) Stereoviews.
Norton, S. A., et al, eds. Acidic Precipitation. (Advances in Environmental Science Ser.: Vol. 4). (Illus.). xiv, 293p. 1989. 248.00 (*0-387-97026-6*, 2939) Spr-Verlag.
***Norton, Sally.** Essential Beauty: Instant Make-up. 64p. 2000. pap. 6.95 (*1-84215-136-3*) Anness Pub.
— Essential Beauty: Skincare. 64p. 2000. pap. 6.95 (*1-84215-135-5*) Anness Pub.
Norton, Sara, ed. see Norton, Charles E.
Norton, Sarah, et al. The Bare Essentials: English Writing Skills. 299p. (C). 1983. pap. text 22.00 (*0-03-059821-4*) Harcourt Coll Pubs.
***Norton, Scott M.** Finance: A Value Creation Approach. 2002. pap. 39.00 (*0-324-02025-2*); pap., student ed. 30.00 (*0-324-02033-3*) Thomson Learn.
Norton, Shana. Water's for Fighting: The Edwards Aquifer Dilemma. (Working Paper Ser.). 34p. 1994. pap. 5.50 (*0-89940-557-6*) LBJ Sch Pub Aff.
Norton-Smith, John. A Reader's Guide to Hart Crane's White Buildings. LC 93-18842. 164p. 1993. 79.95 (*0-7734-9257-7*) E Mellen.
Norton-Smith, John. Bodleian Library Manuscript Fairfax 16. (Medieval Manuscripts Ser.). 1979. 288.95 (*0-85967-513-0*, Pub. by Scolar Pr) Ashgate Pub Co.
Norton Staff. Business Admin & Economics. pap. text 0.00 (*0-393-09866-4*) Norton.
— Golden Monkey. 0.00 (*0-393-08715-8*) Norton.
— On Existential Psychotherapy. 0.00 (*0-393-01725-7*) Norton.
— Substance Abuse Management Module: Skills Illustration Videotape. 1999. VHS 0.00 (*0-393-70318-5*) Norton.
Norton Staff & Morgan, Robert P. Twentieth-Century Music. (Introduction to Music History Ser.). 554p. (C). 1991. text 47.25 (*0-393-95272-X*) Norton.
***Norton, Stephen A. & Fernandez, Ivan J.** The Bear Brook Watershed in Maine: A Paired Watershed Experiment: The First Decade (1987-1997) LC 99-30204. 1999. write for info. (*0-7923-5628-4*) Kluwer Academic.
***Norton, Stephen G.** Mom, Can I Play Football? An Introspective View of the Game for Parents & Coaches. (Illus.). 180p. 1999. pap. 15.95 (*0-9673456-0-X*) Sideline Pr.
Norton, Stephen L. Devils Tower: The Story Behind the Scenery. LC 91-60036. (Illus.). 48p. (Orig.). 1991. pap. 7.95 (*0-88714-051-3*) KC Pubns.
— Devils Tower: The Story Behind the Scenery. Morales, Brigitte, tr. (GER., Illus.). 48p. (Orig.). 1992. pap. 8.95 (*0-88714-712-7*) KC Pubns.
Norton, Susan J. & Kemp, David T. Otoacoustic Emissions: Theory Application & Techniques. 300p. 1998. 34.95 (*1-56593-270-6*, 0592) Singular Publishing.
Norton, Suza. Yoga for People over Fifty: Exercise Without Exhaustion. LC 76-18445. 1977. 15.95 (*0-8159-7404-3*) Devin.
Norton, T. W. & Dovers, S. R., eds. Ecology & Sustainability of Southern Temperate Ecosystems. LC 95-175789. 1994. pap. 39.95 (*0-643-05691-2*, Pub. by CSIRO) Accents Pubns.
Norton-Taylor, Richard. The Accountability of the Security Services. (C). 1988. 21.00 (*0-900137-31-2*, Pub. by NCCL) St Mut.
— Nuremberg. LC 97-182455. (Nick Hern Bks.). 96p. 1997. pap. 14.95 (*1-85459-332-3*, Pub. by N Hern Bks) Theatre Comm.
***Norton-Taylor, Richard, ed.** Colour of Justice. 1999. pap. 10.95 (*1-84002-107-1*, Pub. by Theatre Comm) Consort Bk Sales.
Norton, Thomas. Gorboduc: or Ferrex & Porres. Cauthen, Irby B., Jr. et al, eds. LC 74-88095. (Regents Renaissance Drama Ser.). 118p. reprint ed. pap. 36.60 (*0-608-16038-5*, 203313900084) Bks Demand.
— Thomas Norton's the Ordinal of Alchemy. Reidy, John, ed. (OS 272 Ser.). (Illus.). 1975. 22.00 (*0-19-722274-9*) OUP.
Norton, Thomas & Sackville, Thomas. Ferrex & Porrex. LC 78-133732. (Tudor Facsimile Texts. Old English Plays Ser.: No. 32). reprint ed. 59.50 (*0-404-53332-9*) AMS Pr.
Norton, Thomas E. The Fur Trade in Colonial New York, 1686-1776. LC 73-2047. 255p. 1974. reprint ed. pap. 79.10 (*0-608-01916-X*, 206256800003) Bks Demand.
Norton, Thomas J., jt. ed. see Kalat, James W.
Norton, Thomas L. Trade Union Policies in the Massachusetts Shoe Industry. LC 78-76630. (Columbia University. Studies in the Social Sciences: No. 372). reprint ed. 27.50 (*0-404-51372-7*) AMS Pr.
***Norton, Thomas T., et al.** Fundamentals of Visual Psychphysics. (Illus.). 256p. 2000. 55.00 (*0-7506-9935-3*) Buttrwrth-Heinemann.
Norton, Tina P. Always a Lady. 86p. 1997. pap. 10.00 (*1-57502-665-1*, PO1885) Morris Pubng.
Norton, Tom A., et al. The Hanging Tree & Other Clocks. 2nd ed. Uphoff, Joseph A., Jr., ed. (Illus.). 32p. 1986. pap. text 2.00 (*0-943123-02-X*) Arjuna Lib Pr.
***Norton, Trevor.** Stars Beneath the Sea: The Pioneers of Diving. (Illus.). 288p. 2000. 25.00 (*0-7867-0750-X*, Pub. by Carroll & Graf) Publishers Group.
Norton, Virgil J., jt. auth. see Saila, Saul B.
Norton, W. T., et al, eds. Centennial History of Madison County & Its People, 1812 to 1912, 2 vols. (Illus.). 1208p. 1997. reprint ed. lib. bdg. 125.00 (*0-8328-5765-3*) Higginson Bk Co.
Norton, W. W., jt. ed. see Modlin, Charles E.
Norton-Wayne, L., jt. auth. see Browne, A.
Norton, Wilbert H., jt. auth. see Engel, James F.
***Norton, William.** Cultural Geography: Themes, Concepts, Analyses. (Illus.). 512p. (C). 2000. pap. text 32.95 (*0-19-541307-5*) OUP.
Norton, William. Explorations in the Understanding of Landscape: A Cultural Geography, 77. LC 88-21340. (Contributions in Sociology Ser.: No. 77). 213p. 1989. 55.00 (*0-313-26494-5*, NEX/, Greenwood Pr) Greenwood.
— Human Geography. 3rd ed. (Illus.). 427p. (C). 1998. pap. text 47.95 (*0-19-541316-4*) OUP.
Norton, William L., Jr., et al. Annual Survey of Bankruptcy. LC 93-71459. 1979. 145.00 (*0-685-59826-8*) West Group.
— Norton Banker Forms, 2 vols., Set. LC 81-10028. 1992. ring bd. 195.00 (*0-685-59825-X*) West Group.
— Norton Bankruptcy Code & Rules, 2 vols. LC 81-10028. 1981. pap. 99.75 (*0-685-44923-8*) West Group.
— Norton Bankruptcy Law & Practice, 11 vols. 2nd ed. LC 93-71471. 1993. ring bd. 975.00 (*0-317-11808-0*) West Group.
Norton, William T., ed. Oligodendroglia. (Advances in Neurochemistry Ser.: Vol. 5). 338p. 1984. 95.00 (*0-306-41547-X*, Plenum Trade) Perseus Pubng.
Norton, Yuri E. Dear Uncle Dave. (Illus.). 40p. (Orig.). (J). (gr. 1 up). 1993. pap. 13.95 (*0-9622808-4-4*) S&T Waring.
Nortung, Sandra. Voice from the Forest. LC 99-90439. (Illus.). 32p. (J). (gr. k-6). 1999. 11.95 (*1-892885-50-6*) Daring Child Pr.
***Nortung, Sandra.** Watching over You. LC 99-64529. (Illus.). 32p. (J). (gr. k-5). 2000. 11.95 (*1-892885-51-4*) Daring Child Pr.
Nortwick, Thomas Van, see Van Nortwick, Thomas.
Nortwick, Thomas Van, see Hallett, Judith P. & Van Nortwick, Thomas, eds.
Nortwick, Thomas Van, see Van Nortwick, Thomas.
Noru, Namkhai & Library of Tibetan Works & Archives Staff. Journey among the Tibetan Nomads: An Account of a Remote Civilization. LC 99-931534. 88p. 1997. write for info. (*81-86470-10-7*) S Asia.
Norup, Kim. The Corporate Entrepreneur: How to Create Business Success. (Illus.). 176p. 1998. 21.95 (*1-890256-42-0*, 3502) Geodex Intl.
Norup, Kim & Norup, Willy. Life Beyond Time Management: How High Achievers Balance & Succeed in a Rapidly Changing World. (Illus.). 176p. 1997. 21.95 (*1-890256-32-3*, 3501) Geodex Intl.
Norup, Willy, jt. auth. see Norup, Kim.
***Norusis.** Spss 9.0 Guide to Data Analysis. (C). 1999. pap. text 58.00 incl. disk (*0-13-020399-8*) P-H.
Norusis, Marija J. SPSS - PC Plus Advanced Statistics, Version 5.0. LC 92-85165. 592p. 1992. pap. 21.95 (*0-923967-68-0*) SPSS Inc.
— SPSS - PC Plus Base System User's Guide, Version 5.0. LC 92-85164. 800p. 1992. pap. 29.95 (*0-923967-66-4*) SPSS Inc.
— SPSS - PC Plus Professional Statistics, Version 5.0. LC 92-85163. 272p. (Orig.). 1992. pap. 21.95 (*0-923967-67-2*) SPSS Inc.
— SPSS - PC Plus Studentware for Business. SPSS Inc. Staff, ed. LC 91-62550. 604p. (Orig.). 1991. pap. text 44.95 incl. disk (*0-923967-30-3*); pap. text 44.95 incl. disk (*0-923967-31-1*) SPSS Inc.
— SPSS - PC Plus Studentware Plus. rev. ed. LC 91-62551. 483p. 1991. pap. text 39.95 incl. disk (*0-923967-28-1*); pap. text 39.95 incl. disk (*0-923967-29-X*) SPSS Inc.
— SPSS 8.0 Guide to Data Analysis. LC 98-229114. 563p. 1998. pap. 58.00 (*0-13-687484-3*, Pub. by P-H) S&S Trade.
— SPSS for Windows: Advanced Statistics Release 5. LC 92-85019. 400p. (Orig.). pap. 24.95 (*0-923967-56-7*) SPSS Inc.
— SPSS for Windows: Base System User's Guide, Release 5.0. SPSS Inc. Staff, ed. LC 91-68310. 768p. 1992. pap. 32.95 (*0-923967-49-4*) SPSS Inc.

N

— The SPSS Guide to Data Analysis for Release 4. SPSS Inc. Staff, ed. LC 90-63465. (Illus.). 470p. 1991. pap. text 16.95 (*0-923967-08-7*) SPSS Inc.
— The SPSS Guide to Data Analysis for SPSS-X. rev. ed. SPSS Inc. Staff, ed. LC 87-60776. (Illus.). 448p. (C). 1988. pap. text 16.95 (*0-918469-42-2*) SPSS Inc.
— SPSS-PC Plus Studentware. SPSS Inc. Staff, ed. LC 88-80965. 416p. (Orig.). (C). 1988. pap. text 34.95 (*0-918469-73-2*) SPSS Inc.
— SPSS 7.5 Guide to Data Analysis. LC 97-66250. 497p. (C). 1997. pap. 58.00 (*0-13-656877-7*) P-H.
— SPSS-X Advanced Statistics Guide. 2nd ed. SPSS Inc. Staff, ed. LC 88-61671. 544p. 1988. pap. text 19.95 (*0-918469-81-3*) SPSS Inc.
— SPSS-X Introductory Statistics Guide for SPSS-X Release 3. rev. ed. LC 87-62352. 384p. (C). 1988. pap. text 16.95 (*0-918469-54-6*) SPSS Inc.

Norusis, Marija J. & SPSS Inc. Staff. SPSS for Windows: Professional Statistics User's Guide, Release 5.0. LC 91-68311. 400p. pap. 24.95 (*0-923967-50-8*) SPSS Inc.

Norusis, Marija J., jt. auth. see SPSS Inc. Staff.

Norvaisa, R., jt. auth. see Dudley, R. M.

Norval, Aletta J. Deconstructing Apartheid Discourse. 385p. (C). 1996. 65.00 (*1-85984-989-X*, Pub. by Verso) Norton.

Norval, Aletta J., jt. auth. see Howarth, David R.

Norval, Arletta J. Deconstructing Apartheid Discourse. LC 95-47511. 385p. (C). 1996. pap. 23.00 (*1-85984-125-2*, Pub. by Verso) Norton.

***Norval-Kruger, Liezel & Fraser, Craig.** Country Chic: A Fresh Look at Contemporary Country Decor. LC 00-31790. 2000. write for info. (*1-58663-062-8*) M Friedman Pub Grp Inc.

Norval, Morgan. Death in the Desert: The Namibian Tragedy. LC 89-62602. (Illus.). 364p. 1989. 24.95 (*0-944273-03-3*) Selous Found Pr.
— Inside the ANC, Vol. I: The Evolution of a Terrorist Organization. 2nd ed. Kvederas, Robert, ed. LC 90-63074. (Illus.). 263p. 1991. 21.95 (*0-944273-07-6*) Selous Found Pr.
— Politics by Other Means: The ANC's War on South Africa. Krederas, Robert, ed. 350p. 1993. 25.00 (*0-944273-11-4*) Selous Found Pr.
— Red Star over Southern Africa. LC 87-51366. 220p. 1988. 18.95 (*0-944273-00-9*); pap. 5.95 (*0-944273-02-5*) Selous Found Pr.
— Triumph of Disorder: Islamic Fundamentalism, the New Face of War. LC 98-45855. 314p. 1998. 25.95 (*0-9651213-1-3*) Sligo Pr.

Norval, Morgan, ed. The Militia in Twentieth Century America: A Symposium. 252p. (Orig.). 1985. pap. 9.95 (*0-317-19795-9*) Gun Ownrs Fund.

Norval, Morsan, jt. auth. see Aker, Frank.

Norval, R. A., et al. The Epidemiology of Theileriosis in Africa. (Illus.). 481p. 1991. text 104.00 (*0-12-521740-4*) Acad Pr.

Norvell, Anthony. Astrology, Romance, You & the Stars. 1979. pap. 10.00 (*0-87980-011-9*) Wilshire.

Norvell, Candyce. Los Angeles Retirement & Relocation Guide. large type ed. (Retirement & Relocation Guides Ser.). (Illus.). 350p. Date not set. pap. 24.95 (*1-56559-116-X*) HGI-Over Fifty.

Norvell, Candyce, jt. auth. see Bledsoe, Karen E.

Norvell, Candyce, jt. auth. see Schraff, Anne.

Norvell, Douglas G., jt. auth. see Branson, Robert E.

Norvell, Edward P. Southport. 224p. (Orig.). 1997. pap. 12.95 (*1-884570-68-2*) Research Triangle.

Norvell, Nancy & Belles, Dale. Stress Management Training: A Group Leader's Guide. LC 89-62711. 96p. 1990. pap. 17.45 (*0-943158-33-8*, SM-GBP) Pro Resource.

Norvelle, Don. Fluid Power Technology. LC 93-46736. 672p. (C). 1994. mass mkt. 53.50 (*0-314-01218-4*) West Pub.

Norvelle, F. D. Electrohydraulic Control Systems. LC 99-53027. (Illus.). 285p. (C). 1999. 93.00 (*0-13-716359-2*, Macmillan Coll) P-H.

Norvelle, Joan. Introduction to Fund Accounting. 5th ed. LC 92-84109. (Illus.). 264p. 1997. reprint ed. pap. 49.95 (*0-9656936-0-0*, Book 012A) Res Info Assocs.

Norvelle, Joan W., jt. auth. see Nossen, Richard A.

Norvig, Gerda S. Dark Figures in the Desired Country: Blake's Illustrations to the Pilgrim's Progress. 304p. 1993. 75.00 (*0-520-04471-1*, Pub. by U CA Pr) Cal Prin Full Svc.

Norvig, Peter. Paradigms of Artificial Intelligence Programming: Case Studies in Common LISP. LC 91-39187. 946p. 1992. pap. text 54.95 (*1-55860-191-0*, QA76.6) Morgan Kaufmann.

Norvig, Peter, jt. auth. see Russell, Stuart J.

Norville, Barbara. Writing the Modern Mystery. 224p. 1992. pap. 14.99 (*0-89879-523-0*, Wrtrs Digest Bks) F & W Pubns Inc.

Norville, Deborah. Back on Track: How to Straighten Out Your Life When It Throws You a Curve. LC 97-9586. 256p. 1997. 23.00 (*0-684-83260-7*) S&S Trade.

Norville, Deborah. Back on Track: How to Straighten Out Your Life When It Throws You a Curve. abr. ed. 1997. audio 17.00 (*0-671-57902-9*) S&S Audio.
— I Don't Want to Sleep Tonight. 12p. (J). 1999. 12.99 (*0-307-10609-8*) Gldn Bks Pub Co.

Norville, Mary A. Drug Dosages & Solutions: A Workbook. 3rd ed. LC 93-41308. (Illus.). 320p. (C). 1994. pap. text 29.95 (*0-8385-1613-0*, A1613-7) Appleton & Lange.

Norville, Warren. Celestial Navigation - Step-by-Step. 2nd ed. (Illus.). 264p. (C). 1994. pap. text 30.00 (*1-879778-20-3*, BK-203) Marine Educ.

Norvin, W., ed. Olympiodorus Philosophus, In Platonis Gorgiam Commentaria. 250p. 1966. reprint ed. write for info. (*0-318-70988-0*) G Olms Pubs.

Norwak, Mary. Book of Crepes & Omelets. Thiesen, Jan, ed. LC 87-17602. (Book of...Ser.). 120p. (Orig.). 1989. pap. 12.00 (*0-89586-669-2*, HP Books) Berkley Pub.
— Book of Preserves: Jams, Chutneys, Pickles, Jellies. Aaron, Patricia J., ed. (Book of...Ser.). 128p. (Orig.). 1988. pap. 12.00 (*0-89586-507-6*, HP Books) Berkley Pub.
— Cakes & Cookies. 1986. 4.98 (*0-671-07752-X*) S&S Trade.
— Chocolate Chocolate: 185 Seductive Recipes for the Uncontrollable Chocoholic LC 98-219717. 128p. 1997. write for info. (*0-304-34991-7*) Continuum.
— Cooking with Fruit. 1960. 7.95 (*0-685-20569-X*) Transatl Arts.
— Microwave Meals in Minutes. (Getting It Right Ser.). 1995. pap. 3.95 (*0-572-01764-2*, Pub. by Foulsham UK) Assoc Pubs Grp.
— WI Book of Cakes. 1992. pap. 8.95 (*1-85391-351-0*) Sterling.

Norwalk, Jay. Descendants of Betfield Sawyer of Hill, N. H. (Illus.). 110p. 1995. 35.00 (*1-892446-03-0*) Axion Pr.
— Descendants of Nicholas Barth of Strasbourg. LC 98-74157. (Illus.). 120p. 1998. 35.00 (*1-892446-05-7*) Axion Pr.

***Norwalk, Jay.** Descendants of Nicholas Barth of Strasbourg. 120p. 1999. 29.50 (*0-8328-9885-6*) Higginson Bk Co.
— Descendants of the Salvo Family of Sant'agata Dimilitello, Sicily. LC 98-74158. 88p. 1999. 35.00 (*1-892446-04-9*) Axion Pr.
— The Gargiulo Family of Capri: And Related Genealogies of Vuotto, Lembo & DeMartino Families. (Illus.). 320p. 1999. 55.00 (*1-892446-06-5*) Axion Pr.

Norwalk, Jay. Genealogy of Johan Jost Zimmerman, 1721-1787: And Related Families: Roth, Yagg, Schlunegger, Bratton, Cochlin, Elliott, Campbell, McCullough. (Illus.). 700p. 1998. 35.00 (*1-892446-00-6*) Axion Pr.
— Johan Jost Zimmerman & Related Genealogies. 1999. pap. 97.00 (*0-8328-9830-9*) Higginson Bk Co.
— Johan Jost Zimmerman & Related Genealogies of Roth, Yaggy, Schlunegger, Bratton, Cochlin, Elliott, Campbell & McCullough. 664p. 1999. 107.00 (*0-8328-9829-5*) Higginson Bk Co.
— Paternal Ancestry of Alexandra Leah Aschheim Feld: Genealogy of the Norwalk, Eilenberg, Heilperin, Gutman & Kronenberg. LC 97-70572. (Illus.). 170p. 1997. 35.00 (*1-892446-02-2*) Axion Pr.

***Norwalk, Jay.** Paternal Ancestry of Alexandra Leah Aschheim Feld: The Genealogy of the Norwalk, Eilenberg, Heilperin, Gutman. 128p. 1999. 31.00 (*0-8328-9883-X*) Higginson Bk Co.

Norwalk, Mary. Microwave Recipes. (Getting It Right Ser.). 1994. pap. 9.95 (*0-572-01773-1*, Pub. by W Foulsham) Trans-Atl Phila.

Norwalk, Rosemary. Dearest Ones: A True World War II Love Story. LC 98-33652. 288p. 1999. 24.95 (*0-471-32049-8*) Wiley.

***Norwalk, Rosemary.** Dearest Ones: A True World War II Love Story. 288p. 2000. pap. 15.95 (*0-471-37946-8*) Wiley.

Norway, Mary-Louise & Norway, Arthur Hamilton. The Sinn Fein Rebellion as They Saw It. LC 98-53977. (Illus.). 124p. 1999. reprint ed. 24.50 (*0-7165-2664-6*, Pub. by Irish Acad Pr) Intl Spec Bk.

Norway, Arthur Hamilton, jt. auth. see Norway, Mary-Louise.

Norway, Nevil S. The Breaking Wave. 22.95 (*0-405-18913-3*) Ayer.

Norwegian-American Historical Association. Norwegian-American Studies, Vol. 24, 1970. LC 87-657088. (Illus.). 311p. reprint ed. pap. 96.50 (*0-608-10411-6*, 204038500024) Bks Demand.
— Norwegian-American Studies, Vol. 30. LC 87-657088. 352p. reprint ed. pap. 109.20 (*0-7837-0108-X*, 204038500030) Bks Demand.
— Norwegian-American Studies & Records, Vol. 14. LC 26-145503. 273p. reprint ed. pap. 84.70 (*0-608-15445-8*, 202929200014) Bks Demand.

Norwegian-American Historical Association, jt. auth. see Lovoll, Odd Sverre.

Norwegian-American Historical Association Staff. Studies & Records, 1926, Vol. 1. LC 87-657087. (Illus.). 195p. reprint ed. pap. 60.50 (*0-7837-1650-8*, 204194800001) Bks Demand.

Norwegian Institute of Technology Staff. North Sea Oil & Gas Reservoirs. (C). 1987. lib. bdg. 281.00 (*0-86010-865-1*, Pub. by Graham & Trotman) Kluwer Academic.

Norwegian Petroleum Directorate Staff. Act Relating to Petroleum Activities. 1997. pap. 75.00 (*82-7257-536-1*, Pub. by Oljedirektoratet) St Mut.
— Act Relating to Worker Protection & Working Environment Etc. 1997. pap. 75.00 (*82-7257-544-2*, Pub. by Oljedirektoratet) St Mut.
— Acts, Regulations & Provisions for the Petroleum Activities 1997, Bk. 1. 1997. pap. 700.00 (*82-7257-508-6*, Pub. by Oljedirektoratet) St Mut.
— Acts, Regulations & Provisions for the Petroleum Activities 1997, Bk. 2. 1997. pap. 800.00 (*82-7257-509-4*, Pub. by Oljedirektoratet) St Mut.
— Annual Report 1990. 144p. 1991. pap. 250.00 (*82-7257-329-6*, Pub. by Oljedirektoratet) St Mut.
— Annual Report 1995. 164p. 1996. pap. 250.00 (*82-7257-489-6*, Pub. by Oljedirektoratet) St Mut.
— Annual Report 1994. 186p. 1995. pap. 250.00 (*82-7257-458-6*, Pub. by Oljedirektoratet) St Mut.
— Annual Report 1991. 151p. 1992. pap. 250.00 (*82-7257-347-4*, Pub. by Oljedirektoratet) St Mut.
— Annual Report 1996. 163p. 1997. pap. 250.00 (*82-7257-526-4*, Pub. by Oljedirektoratet) St Mut.
— Annual Report 1993. 168p. 1994. pap. 250.00 (*82-7257-424-1*, Pub. by Oljedirektoratet) St Mut.
— Annual Report 1992. 162p. 1993. pap. 250.00 (*82-7257-388-1*, Pub. by Oljedirektoratet) St Mut.
— The Arrangement of Regulatory Supervision Relating to Safety & the Working Environment in the Petroleum Activities. 1998. pap. 60.00 (*82-7257-479-9*, Pub. by Oljedirektoratet) St Mut.
— Bulletin 8 Pt. 11: Structural Elements of the Norwegian Continental Shelf: The Norwegian Sea Region. 1995. pap. 200.00 (*82-7257-452-7*, Pub. by Oljedirektoratet) St Mut.
— Bulletin 5: A Revised Cretaceous & Tertiary Lithostratigraphic Nomenclature for the Norwegian North Sea. 60p. 1989. pap. 200.00 (*82-7257-295-8*, Pub. by Oljedirektoratet) St Mut.
— Bulletin 4: A Lithostratigraphic Scheme for the Mesozoic & Cenozoic Succession Offshore Mid- & Northern Norway. 65p. 1988. pap. 200.00 (*82-7257-241-9*, Pub. by Oljedirektoratet) St Mut.
— Bulletin 7: Geostandard, a Geological Standard for Use Within the Petroleum Industry. 1992. pap. 200.00 (*82-7257-377-6*, Pub. by Oljedirektoratet) St Mut.
— Bulletin 6: Structural Elements of the Norwegian Continental Shelf. 1990. pap. 200.00 (*82-7257-304-0*, Pub. by Oljedirektoratet) St Mut.
— Bulletin 3: A Revised Triassic & Jurassic Lithostratigraphic Nomenclature for the Norwegian North Sea. 1984. pap. 200.00 (*82-7257-155-2*, Pub. by Oljedirektoratet) St Mut.
— Bulletin 2: Palynology-Micropalentology: Laboratories, Equipment & Methods. 151p. 1983. pap. 200.00 (*82-7257-132-3*, Pub. by Oljedirektoratet) St Mut.
— Classification of Petroleum Resources on the Norwegian Continental Shelf. 1997. pap. 75.00 (*82-7257-534-5*, Pub. by Oljedirektoratet) St Mut.
— Deep Water Drilling Project Phase II, Vols. I-IV. 1996. pap. 6000.00 (*82-7257-446-2*, Pub. by Oljedirektoratet) St Mut.
— Description & Classification of Chalks. 147p. 1996. pap. 600.00 (*82-7257-491-8*, Pub. by Oljedirektoratet) St Mut.
— Development Wells. 1998. pap. 300.00 (*82-7257-421-7*, Pub. by Oljedirektoratet) St Mut.
— Discoveries on the Norwegian Continental Shelf. 1997. pap. 100.00 (*82-7257-514-0*, Pub. by Oljedirektoratet) St Mut.
— Geology & Petroleum Resources in the Barnets Sea. 1996. pap. 75.00 (*82-7257-504-3*, Pub. by Oljedirektoratet) St Mut.
— Health Examination of Divers-Fitness to Dive-Decompression Use of Oxygen: Conference Papers. 110p. 1988. pap. 100.00 (*82-7257-265-6*, Pub. by Oljedirektoratet) St Mut.
— Interfaces in Legislation Applicable to the Norwegian Continental Shelf. 70p. 1998. pap. 60.00 (*82-7257-510-8*, Pub. by Oljedirektoratet) St Mut.
— Interim Jet Fire Test for Determining the Effectiveness of Passive Fire Protection Materials. 1993. pap. 60.00 (*82-7257-401-2*, Pub. by Oljedirektoratet) St Mut.
— Jet Fire Resistance Test of Passive Fire Protection Materials. 1997. pap. 75.00 (*82-7257-516-7*, Pub. by Oljedirektoratet) St Mut.
— Licenses, Areas, Area-Coordinates, Exploration Wells. 1998. pap. 1000.00 (*82-7257-429-2*, Pub. by Oljedirektoratet) St Mut.
— Norwegian Petroleum Directorate Seismic Data Packages Jan Mayen, North Sea, Norwegian Sea & Barents Sea. 320p. 1993. pap. 150.00 (*82-7257-384-9*, Pub. by Oljedirektoratet) St Mut.
— Orientation Relating to Exploration & Exploration Drilling for Petroleum Deposits on Svalbard. 1998. pap. text 60.00 (*82-7257-376-8*, Pub. by Oljedirektoratet) St Mut.
— Petroleum Resources on the Norwegian Continental Shelf. 1997. pap. 75.00 (*82-7257-512-4*, Pub. by Oljedirektoratet) St Mut.
— Profit Project Summary Reports. Reservoir Characterization near Well Flow. 355p. 1995. pap. 250.00 (*82-7257-443-8*, Pub. by Oljedirektoratet) St Mut.
— Provisional Regulations Relating to Littering & Pollution Caused by Petroleum Activities on the Norwegian Continental Shelf. 1998. pap. 75.00 (*82-7257-037-8*, Pub. by Oljedirektoratet) St Mut.
— Provisions Relating to Digital Transmission of Geological & Reservoir Technical Data in Connection with the Final Report. 72p. 1998. pap. 100.00 (*82-7257-476-4*, Pub. by Oljedirektoratet) St Mut.
— Regulations Laid Down by Royal Decree. 1998. pap. 75.00 (*82-7257-541-8*, Pub. by Oljedirektoratet) St Mut.
— Regulations Relating to Drilling & Well Activities & Geological Data Collected in the Petroleum Activities with Guidelines. 1998. pap. 125.00 (*82-7257-492-6*, Pub. by Oljedirektoratet) St Mut.
— Regulations Relating to Electrical Installations in the Petroleum Activities with Guidelines. 1998. pap. 75.00 (*82-7257-486-1*, Pub. by Oljedirektoratet) St Mut.
— Regulations Relating to Emergency Preparedness in the Petroleum Activities with Guidelines. 1998. pap. 75.00 (*82-7257-503-5*, Pub. by Oljedirektoratet) St Mut.
— Regulations Relating to Explosion & Fire Protection of Installation in the Petroleum Activities with Guidelines. 1998. pap. 75.00 (*82-7257-502-7*, Pub. by Oljedirektoratet) St Mut.
— Regulations Relating to Fiscal Measurement of Oil & Gas Etc. with Guidelines. 1998. pap. 75.00 (*82-7257-437-3*, Pub. by Oljedirektoratet) St Mut.
— Regulations Relating to Fishery Expert on Board Seismic Vessels on the Norwegian Continental Shelf with Guidelines. 1998. pap. 75.00 (*82-7257-339-3*, Pub. by Oljedirektoratet) St Mut.
— Regulations Relating to Implementation & Use of Risk Analyses in the Petroleum Activities with Guidelines. 1998. pap. 75.00 (*82-7257-314-8*, Pub. by Oljedirektoratet) St Mut.
— Regulations Relating to Lifting Appliances & Lifting Gear in the Petroleum Activities with Guidelines. 1998. pap. 75.00 (*82-7257-494-2*, Pub. by Oljedirektoratet) St Mut.
— Regulations Relating to Loadbearing Structures in the Petroleum Activities. 1998. pap. 185.00 (*82-7257-500-0*, Pub. by Oljedirektoratet) St Mut.
— Regulations Relating to Management Systems for Compliance with Statutory Requirements in Relations to Safety, Working Environment & Protection of the External Environment in the Petroleum Activities. 1998. pap. 75.00 (*82-7257-542-6*, Pub. by Oljedirektoratet) St Mut.
— Regulations Relating to Manned Underwater Operations in the Petroleum Activities with Guidelines. 1998. pap. 125.00 (*82-7257-475-6*, Pub. by Oljedirektoratet) St Mut.
— Regulations Relating to Marking of Installations in the Petroleum Activities with Guidelines. 1998. pap. 75.00 (*82-7257-495-0*, Pub. by Oljedirektoratet) St Mut.
— Regulations Relating to Measurement of Fuel & Flare Gas for Calculation of Co2 Tax in the Petroleum Activities with Guidelines. 1998. pap. 75.00 (*82-7257-469-1*, Pub. by Oljedirektoratet) St Mut.
— Regulations Relating to Pipeline Systems in the Petroleum Activities with Guidelines. 1998. pap. 75.00 (*82-7257-501-9*, Pub. by Oljedirektoratet) St Mut.
— Regulations Relating to Process & Auxiliary Facilities in the Petroleum Activities with Guidelines. 1998. pap. 75.00 (*82-7257-493-4*, Pub. by Oljedirektoratet) St Mut.
— Regulations Relating to Refund of Expense for Supervision with Safety, Working Environment & Resource Management in the Petroleum Activities. 1998. pap. 75.00 (*82-7257-543-4*, Pub. by Oljedirektoratet) St Mut.
— Regulations Relating to Safe Practice in Exploration & Exploration Drilling for Petroleum Deposits on Svalbard. 1998. pap. 75.00 (*82-7257-256-7*, Pub. by Oljedirektoratet) St Mut.
— Regulations Relating to Safety & Communication Systems on Installations in the Petroleum Activities with Guidelines. 1998. pap. 75.00 (*82-7257-460-8*, Pub. by Oljedirektoratet) St Mut.
— Regulations Relating to Safety Delegates & Working Environment Committees. 1996. pap. 75.00 (*82-7257-483-7*, Pub. by Oljedirektoratet) St Mut.
— Regulations Relating to Safety in Petroleum Activities. 1998. pap. 75.00 (*82-7257-539-6*, Pub. by Oljedirektoratet) St Mut.
— Regulations Relating to Safety Zones Etc. with Comments. 1998. pap. 75.00 (*82-7257-240-0*, Pub. by Oljedirektoratet) St Mut.
— Regulations Relating to Systematic Follow-Up of the Working Environment in the Petroleum Activities with Guidelines. 1998. pap. 125.00 (*82-7257-471-3*, Pub. by Oljedirektoratet) St Mut.
— Regulations Relating to the Collection of Environmental Data Etc. with Guidelines. 1998. pap. 75.00 (*82-7257-496-9*, Pub. by Oljedirektoratet) St Mut.
— Regulations Relating to the Petroleum Register. 1998. pap. 75.00 (*82-7257-538-8*, Pub. by Oljedirektoratet) St Mut.
— Regulations Relating to Worker Protection & Working Environment in the Petroleum Activities with Guidelines. 1998. pap. 75.00 (*82-7257-468-3*, Pub. by Oljedirektoratet) St Mut.
— Regulatory Supervisory Activities with the Safety Etc. in the Petroleum Activities on the Norwegian Continental Shelf. 1998. pap. 75.00 (*82-7257-187-0*, Pub. by Oljedirektoratet) St Mut.
— Released Seismic Surveys. 1992. pap. 2200.00 (*82-7257-363-6*, Pub. by Oljedirektoratet) St Mut.
— Report from the Dive Database DSYS 1996. 1997. pap. 60.00 (*82-7257-524-8*, Pub. by Oljedirektoratet) St Mut.
— Report No. 7, Waves at Tromsoflaket 1980. 155p. 1981. pap. 150.00 (*82-7257-069-6*, Pub. by Oljedirektoratet) St Mut.
— Report No. 8, Intermediate Summary Report. Results of Measurements from 1976-1981. 435p. 1983. pap. 250.00 (*82-7257-126-9*, Pub. by Oljedirektoratet) St Mut.
— Report No. 5, Waves at Tromsoflaket 1978 & 1979. 291p. 1981. pap. 150.00 (*82-7257-054-8*, Pub. by Oljedirektoratet) St Mut.
— Report No. 4, Waves & Currents at Tromsoflaket 1978 & 1979. 164p. 1981. pap. 150.00 (*82-7257-052-1*, Pub. by Oljedirektoratet) St Mut.
— Report No. 9, Current Data 1980-1983, Wave Data 1981-1983. 1985. pap. 250.00 (*82-7257-181-1*, Pub. by Oljedirektoratet) St Mut.
— Report No. 6, Waves at Tromsoflaket 1976 & 1977. 191p. 1981. pap. 150.00 (*82-7257-055-6*, Pub. by Oljedirektoratet) St Mut.
— Report No. 10, Current Data 1984, Wave Data 1984. 286p. 1986. pap. 250.00 (*82-7257-205-2*, Pub. by Oljedirektoratet) St Mut.
— Report No. 3, Waves & Currents at Tromsoflaket Sept. 1976. 93p. 1978. pap. 150.00 (*82-7257-008-4*, Pub. by Oljedirektoratet) St Mut.
— Ruth-A Norwegian Research Program on Improved Oil Recovery-Program Summary. 446p. 1996. pap. 250.00 (*82-7257-484-5*, Pub. by Oljedirektoratet) St Mut.
— Safety Notices from the Norwegian Petroleum Directorate. 1989. pap. 100.00 (*82-7257-296-6*, Pub. by Oljedirektoratet) St Mut.

— Shallow Gas Seminar-August 27-28, 1987. 380p. 1987. pap. 100.00 (*82-7257-238-9*, Pub. by Oljedirektoratet) St Mut.

— Well Data Summary Sheets, Vol. 5. 1980. pap. 100.00 (*82-7257-033-5*, Pub. by Oljedirektoratet) St Mut.

— Well Data Summary Sheets, Vol. 6. 1981. pap. 100.00 (*82-7257-050-5*, Pub. by Oljedirektoratet) St Mut.

— Well Data Summary Sheets, Vol. 7. 1982. pap. 100.00 (*82-7257-080-7*, Pub. by Oljedirektoratet) St Mut.

— Well Data Summary Sheets, Vol. 8. 1984. pap. 100.00 (*82-7257-114-5*, Pub. by Oljedirektoratet) St Mut.

— Well Data Summary Sheets, Vol. 9. 1985. pap. 250.00 (*82-7257-159-5*, Pub. by Oljedirektoratet) St Mut.

— Well Data Summary Sheets, Vol. 10. 1985. pap. 100.00 (*82-7257-171-4*, Pub. by Oljedirektoratet) St Mut.

— Well Data Summary Sheets, Vol. 11. 1986. pap. 1000.00 (*82-7257-198-6*, Pub. by Oljedirektoratet) St Mut.

— Well Data Summary Sheets, Vol. 12. 1987. pap. 1200.00 (*82-7257-219-2*, Pub. by Oljedirektoratet) St Mut.

— Well Data Summary Sheets, Vol. 13. 1988. pap. 1600.00 (*82-7257-249-4*, Pub. by Oljedirektoratet) St Mut.

— Well Data Summary Sheets, Vol. 15. 1990. pap. 2000.00 (*82-7257-300-8*, Pub. by Oljedirektoratet) St Mut.

— Well Data Summary Sheets, Vol. 16. 1992. pap. 2400.00 (*82-7257-338-5*, Pub. by Oljedirektoratet) St Mut.

— Well Data Summary Sheets, Vol. 17. 1992. pap. 2600.00 (*82-7257-359-8*, Pub. by Oljedirektoratet) St Mut.

— Well Data Summary Sheets, Vol. 18. 1993. pap. 3000.00 (*82-7257-371-7*, Pub. by Oljedirektoratet) St Mut.

— Well Data Summary Sheets, Vol. 19. 1994. pap. 3000.00 (*82-7257-402-0*, Pub. by Oljedirektoratet) St Mut.

— Well Data Summary Sheets, Vol. 20. 1995. pap. 3000.00 (*82-7257-438-1*, Pub. by Oljedirektoratet) St Mut.

— Well Data Summary Sheets, Vols. 1-4. 231p. 1979. pap. 400.00 (*82-7257-012-2*, Pub. by Oljedirektoratet) St Mut.

Norwegian Petroleum Directorate Staff, jt. auth. see Ministry of Local Government Staff.

Norwegian Petroleum Society (NPF) Staff, ed. Habitat of Hydrocarbons on the Norwegian Continental Shelf. (C). 1986. lib. bdg. 281.00 (*0-86010-833-3*, Pub. by Graham & Trotman) Kluwer Academic.

Norwegian Petroleum Society Staff. Geology of the European Countries, 4 vols., Set. Incl. Vol. 1. Geology of the European Countries: Austria, Federal Republic of Germany, Ireland, the Netherlands, Switzerland, United Kingdom. 500p. 1980. lib. bdg. 163.00 (*0-86010-261-0*); Vol. 2. Geology of the European Countries: Denmark, Finland, Iceland, Norway, Sweden. 500p. 1980. lib. bdg. 163.00 (*0-86010-262-9*); Vol. 4. Geologie des Pays Europeens: France, Belgique, Luxembourg. (FRE.). 620p. 1980. lib. bdg. 163.00 (*2-04-011122-0*); (ENG & FRE.). 444p. 1987. Set text 652.00 (*0-86010-919-4*) Kluwer Academic.

— The Petroleum Geology of the North European. 444p. 1984. lib. bdg. 192.50 (*0-86010-486-9*) G & T Inc.

Norwich. A History Of Venice. 1989. 14.95 (*0-07-558706-8*) McGraw.

***Norwich.** Journey of the Pink Dolphins. 2001. pap. 16.00 (*0-7432-0026-8*, Touchstone) S&S Trade Pap.

Norwich. Twelve Days of Christmas. LC 99-204505. (Illus.). 32p. 1999. text 9.95 (*0-312-20163-X*) St Martin.

***Norwich, Brahm.** Education & Psychology in Interaction: Working with Uncertainty in Interconnected Fields. LC 99-44824. 2000. 90.00 (*0-415-22431-4*) Routledge.

Norwich, John Julius. Byzantium: The Apogee, Vol. 2. 1992. 45.00 (*0-394-53779-3*) Knopf.

— Byzantium: The Decline & Fall. (Illus.). 512p. 1995. 45.00 (*0-679-41650-1*) Knopf.

— Byzantium: The Decline & Fall. 1996. 35.00 (*0-614-12878-1*) Knopf.

— Byzantium: The Early Centuries, Vol. 1. 1989. 45.00 (*0-394-53778-5*) Knopf.

— A History of Venice. 1989. pap. 25.00 (*0-679-72197-5*) Vin Bks.

***Norwich, John Julius.** The Normans in Sicily: The Magnificent Story of the Other Norman Conquest. (Illus.). 793p. 2000. pap. 35.00 (*0-14-015212-1*, Pub. by Pnguin Bks Ltd) Trafalgar.

Norwich, John Julius. Shakespeare's Kings: The Great Plays & the History of England in the Middle Ages: 1337-1485. LC 99-58271. (Illus.). 432p. 2000. 29.50 (*0-684-81434-X*) Scribner.

— A Short History of Byzantium. abr. ed. 1998. pap. 17.00 (*0-679-77269-3*) McKay.

— A Short History of Byzantium: Based on the Great Three-Volume Work. abr. ed. LC 96-44458. 1997. 40.00 (*0-679-45088-2*) McKay.

Norwich, John Julius, ed. The Embassy to Constantinople: And Other Works. 224p. 1993. pap. 10.95 (*0-460-87235-4*, Everyman's Classic Lib) Tuttle Pubng.

— Great Architecture of the World. (Quality Paperbacks Ser.). (Illus.). 288p. 1991. reprint ed. pap. 29.50 (*0-306-80436-0*) Da Capo.

Norwich, John Julius, jt. auth. see Miles, Christopher.

Norwich, Julian. I Promise You a Crown. Hazzard, David, ed. (Rekindling the Inner Fire Ser.: Vol. 8). 16p. 1995. pap. 8.99 (*1-55661-606-6*) Bethany Hse.

Norwich, Kenneth H. Information, Sensation, & Perception. LC 93-16692. 326p. 1993. text 49.95 (*0-12-521890-7*) Acad Pr.

***Norwich, William.** Learning to Drive. 224p. 1998. pap. 12.95 (*0-7472-5584-9*, Pub. by Headline Bk Pub) Trafalgar.

Norwick, Kenneth P. & Chasen, Jerry S. The Rights of Authors, Artists, & Other Creative People: The Basic ACLU Guide to Author & Artist Rights. 2nd rev. ed. LC 91-23721. (ACLU Handbook Ser.). 293p. 1992. pap. 9.95 (*0-8093-1773-7*) S Ill U Pr.

Norwin, W., ed. Olympiodorus Philosophus, In Platonis Phaedonem Commentaria. xi, 272p. 1987. reprint ed. write for info. (*0-318-70989-9*) G Olms Pubs.

Norwine, Jim. Climate & Human Ecology. LC 78-52975. (Illus.). 1978. pap. 9.95 (*0-918464-19-6*) D Armstrong.

— A Postmodernist Tao: A Guide to Apprehending Ways of Meaning in Pathless Lands. Winans, Linda F., ed. LC 92-40602. 172p. (Orig.). (C). 1993. pap. text 21.50 (*0-8191-8993-6*); lib. bdg. 46.00 (*0-8191-8992-8*) U Pr of Amer.

Norwine, Jim, et al, eds. The Changing Climate of Texas: Predictability & Implications for the Future. 355p. (C). 1995. pap. 25.00 (*0-9645710-0-5*) TX A&M CGMS.

Norwine, Jim & Gonzalez, Alfonso, eds. The Third World: States of Mind & Being. (Illus.). 320p. 1988. text 55.00 (*0-04-910106-4*) Routledge.

***Norwine, Jim & Smith, Jonathan M., eds.** Worldview Flux: Perplexed Values among Postmodern Peoples. 280p. 2000. 60.00 (*0-7391-0138-2*) Lxngtn Bks.

Norwine, Jim, jt. ed. see Gonzalez, Alfonso.

Norwood, jt. auth. see Guthrie.

Norwood, Ann E., jt. ed. see Ursano, Robert J.

Norwood, Audrianne. Like Mama Used to Say. LC 92-96895. (Illus.). 208p. (C). 1992. pap. 9.00 (*1-882338-05-7*) Via God Pub.

— Like Mama Used to Say. LC 92-96895. (Illus.). 208p. (C). 1998. 16.00 (*1-882338-13-8*) Via God Pub.

***Norwood, Ben.** Plenum. Robbins, James M., ed. LC 99-72886. 80p. 1999. pap. 10.00 (*0-9657687-5-9*) Sulphur River.

Norwood, Bev, jt. auth. see Sommers, Robert.

Norwood, Bev, ed. see Dennis, Larry.

Norwood, Bev, ed. see Dorman, Larry.

Norwood, Bev, ed. see Green, Bob, et al.

Norwood, Bev, ed. see Hopkins, John.

Norwood, Bev, ed. see Mizell, Hubert.

Norwood, Bev, ed. see Nuhn, Gary.

Norwood, Bev, ed. see Parascenzo, Marino.

Norwood, Bev, ed. see Rosaforte, Tim, et al.

Norwood, Bev, ed. see Sommers, Robert.

Norwood, D. Chess Puzzles. (Usborne Guides Ser.). (Illus.). 64p. (J). (gr. 5-9). 1992. pap. text 7.95 (*0-7460-0950-X*) EDC.

— Chess Puzzles. (Chess Guides Ser.). (Illus.). 64p. (J). (gr. 5 up). 1999. lib. bdg. 15.95 (*0-88110-464-7*) EDC.

Norwood, David. Chess Puzzles. 1995. pap. 14.00 (*0-8050-4226-1*) H Holt & Co.

— Vishy Anand. 1995. pap. 17.00 (*0-8050-4223-7*, Pub. by Batsford Chess) H Holt & Co.

— Winning with Modern. (Batsford Chess Library). 1995. pap. write for info. (*0-8050-3281-9*) H Holt & Co.

Norwood, David, et al. Children's Tour of Red Stick City. 32p. (J). (gr. 1-6). 1980. pap. text 2.00 (*0-9608282-2-2*) YWCO.

Norwood-Fontbonne Home & School Association Staff. Philadelphia Homestyle Cookbook. Wimmer Brothers Books Staff, ed. (Illus.). 288p. 1985. 12.95 (*0-9614938-0-1*) Norwood-Fontbonne.

Norwood, Frederick A. The Reformation Refugees As an Economic Force. LC 83-45668. reprint ed. 39.50 (*0-404-19818-X*) AMS Pr.

— The Story of American Methodism. 1974. pap. 16.50 (*0-687-39641-7*) Abingdon.

Norwood, Gilbert. Essays on Euripidean Drama. LC 53-11243. (Scholarly Reprint Ser.). 197p. reprint ed. pap. 61.10 (*0-608-13753-7*, 205547800022) Bks Demand.

Norwood, Gus. Washington Grangers Celebrate a Century: History, Fraternal Organization (100th Anniversary), Agriculture. LC 88-50556. (Illus.). (Orig.). 1988. 7.95 (*0-929612-01-9*); pap. 4.95 (*0-929612-02-7*) WA State Grange.

Norwood, James, tr. see Body, Jacques.

Norwood, Janet L. Organizing to Count: Change in the Federal Statistical System. 150p. (C). 1995. pap. text 25.50 (*0-87766-635-0*); lib. bdg. 48.50 (*0-87766-634-2*) Urban Inst.

Norwood, Janet L., ed. see NRC Staff.

Norwood, Janet W. & People's Medical Society Staff. Understanding Diabetes. LC 98-50750. 214p. 1999. pap. 14.95 (*0-02-862437-8*, Pub. by Macmillan) S&S Trade.

Norwood, Janet Worsley, jt. auth. see Inlander, Charles B.

Norwood, Jesse W. The Person of the Holy Spirit & His Works. 104p. 1998. pap. 12.95 (*1-888398-20-5*, Lightfall Pub) WJC Designs.

— Repentance - The Link to Revival: He Will Come to Us Like the Rain. 74p. 1998. pap. 9.95 (*1-888398-19-1*, Lightfall Pub) WJC Designs.

Norwood, John. John Norwood's American Railroads. LC 94-72883. (Illus.). 204p. 1996. pap. 29.95 (*0-911581-38-3*) Heimburger Hse Pub.

— John Norwood's Western Cookbook. LC 85-82339. 76p. 1986. pap. 9.95 (*0-911581-06-5*) Heimburger Hse Pub.

Norwood, John B. Rio Grande Memories. LC 91-71587. (Illus.). 192p. 1991. 41.95 (*0-911581-21-9*) Heimburger Hse Pub.

— Rio Grande Narrow Gauge. Heimburger, Donald J. & Heimburger, Marilyn M., eds. LC 82-84384. (Illus.). 312p. 1983. 44.95 (*0-911581-00-6*) Heimburger Hse Pub.

— Rio Grande Narrow Gauge Recollections. Heimburger, Donald J. & Heimburger, Marilyn M., eds. LC 86-81505. (Illus.). 272p. 1986. 41.95 (*0-911581-07-3*) Heimburger Hse Pub.

Norwood, John H. The Schism in the Methodist Episcopal Church, 1844: A Study of Slavery & Ecclesiastical Politics. LC 76-10284. (Perspectives in American History Ser.: No. 33). 255p. 1976. reprint ed. lib. bdg. 37.50 (*0-87991-357-6*) Porcupine Pr.

Norwood, Ken & Smith, Kathleen. Rebuilding Community in America: Housing for Ecological Living, Personal Empowerment, & the New Extended Family. LC 94-92061. (Illus.). 432p. 1995. pap. 24.50 (*0-9641346-2-4*) Shared Liv Res.

Norwood, Michael. I'm Not Crying. 195p. 1998. pap. 10.00 (*0-9666297-0-1*) L Everett Publ.

Norwood, Michael R. I Have a Gift for You. (Wealthy Soul Ser.). 1999. pap. 12.95 (*0-911649-03-4*) Global Pub GA.

— The 9 Insights of the Wealthy Soul. 1999. pap. write for info. (*0-911649-02-6*) Global Pub GA.

— Taking Stock: A Soul's Journey Through Life, Death & the World of Investment. unabridged ed. (Illus.). 272p. (Orig.). 1998. pap. 12.95 (*0-911649-01-8*) Global Pub GA.

Norwood, O'Tar T. & Shiell, Richard C. Hair Transplant Surgery. 2nd ed. (Illus.). 356p. (C). 1984. 79.95 (*0-398-04946-7*) C C Thomas.

***Norwood, Pam Z.** Confluence: A Living Literary Legacy of the Rock River Valley. Swanberg, Christine, ed. 120p. 2000. pap. text 10.00 (*0-9700276-0-5*) Rockford Lit.

Norwood, Peggy & Stabler, Jan. Oops, Your Manners Are Showing: A Study Course for Ages 8 & Up. 2nd rev. ed. (Illus.). 132p. (J). (gr. 2-9). 1997. pap. text, teacher ed. 14.95 (*0-9660287-1-6*); pap. text, wbk. ed. 11.95 (*0-9660287-0-8*) Oops Grp.

— Oops, Your Manners Are Showing: Lessons for Ages 4 to 7. LC 98-148278. (Illus.). 88p. (J). (ps-2). 1998. pap. text 9.95 (*0-9660287-2-4*) Oops Grp.

Norwood, Richard. Fortification, or Architecture Military. LC 72-6019. (English Experience Ser.: No. 545). 1973. reprint ed. 25.00 (*90-221-0545-8*) Walter J Johnson.

— The Sea-Mans Practice. LC 74-28877. (English Experience Ser.: No. 755). 1975. reprint ed. 30.00 (*90-221-0755-8*) Walter J Johnson.

— Trigonometrie: or The Doctrine of Triangles, 2 pts. LC 78-171779. (English Experience Ser.: No. 404). 362p. 1971. reprint ed. 75.00 (*90-221-0404-4*) Walter J Johnson.

Norwood, Richard H., et al. A Cultural Resource Overview of the Eureka, Saline, Panamint & Darwin Region, East Central, California. (Illus.). 256p. (C). 1980. reprint ed. pap. text 26.88 (*1-55567-404-6*) Coyote Press.

Norwood, Rick, ed. see Foster, Hal.

Norwood, Robin. Daily Meditations for Women Who Love Too Much. LC 97-10244. (Illus.). 384p. 1997. 12.95 (*0-87477-876-X*, Tarcher Putnam) Putnam Pub Group.

— Letters from Women Who Love Too Much. 1989. mass mkt. 6.50 (*0-671-73342-7*) PB.

— Why . . . A Guide to Answering Life's Toughest Questions. LC 97-27796. 250p. 1997. pap. 12.95 (*1-55874-522-X*) Health Comm.

— Women Who Love Too Much: When You Keep Wishing & Hoping He'll Change. 308p. 1990. per. 6.99 (*0-671-73341-9*) PB.

Norwood, Seth W. Sketches of Brooks History. (Illus.). 454p. 1995. reprint ed. lib. bdg. 46.50 (*0-8328-4666-X*) Higginson Bk Co.

Norwood, Stephen H. Labor's Flaming Youth: Telephone Operators & Worker Militancy, 1878-1923. (Working Class in American History Women in American History Ser.). (Illus.). 360p. 1990. text 34.95 (*0-252-01633-5*) U of Ill Pr.

— Labor's Flaming Youth: Telephone Operators & Worker Militancy, 1878-1923. (Working Class in American History - Women in American History Ser.). (Illus.). 360p. 1991. pap. text 16.95 (*0-252-06225-6*) U of Ill Pr.

Norwood, Susan. Nurses as Consultants: Essential Concepts & Processes. LC 97-22981. 336p. 1997. pap. text 41.00 (*0-8053-5427-1*, Prentice Hall) P-H.

Norwood, Susan L. Research Strategies for Nurses in Advanced Practice. LC 99-26913. 512p. (C). 1999. 45.95 (*0-8385-8406-3*) Appleton & Lange.

Norwood, Sybil. The Traveler's World: A Dictionary of Industry & Destination Literacy. LC 95-16338. 238p. (C). 1995. pap. text 20.80 (*0-13-228651-3*) P-H.

Norwood, Tom, et al, eds. North American Airline Handbook. (Illus.). 256p. (Orig.). 1997. pap. 19.95 (*0-9653993-1-1*) Airways Intnl.

***Norwood, Tom & Wegg, John.** North American Airlines Handbook. 2nd rev. ed. (Illus.). 248p. 1999. pap. 19.95 (*0-9653993-5-4*, A-19) Airways Intnl.

Norwood, Tom W. Deregulation Knockouts: Round One. Wegg, John, ed. (Illus.). 120p. 1996. 24.95 (*0-9653993-0-3*) Airways Intnl.

Norwood, Vera. Made from This Earth: American Women & Nature. LC 92-22562. (Gender & American Culture Ser.). (Illus.). xxiv, 368p. (C). 1993. 49.95 (*0-8078-2062-8*); pap. 19.95 (*0-8078-4396-2*) U of NC Pr.

Norwood, Vera & Monk, Janice. The Desert Is No Lady: Southwestern Landscapes in Women's Writing & Art. LC 96-35492. (Illus.). 281p. 1997. pap. 19.95 (*0-8165-1649-9*) U of Ariz Pr.

Norwood, Victor G. Drums along the Amazon. large type ed. (Non-Fiction Ser.). 1974. 27.99 (*0-85456-269-9*) Ulverscroft.

Norwood, William F. Medical Education in the U. S. Before the Civil War. LC 72-165726. (American Education, Ser, No. 2). 1975. reprint ed. 30.95 (*0-405-03714-7*) Ayer.

Norwood, William L., jt. ed. see Jacobs, Marshall L.

Norworth, Jack. Take Me Out to the Ballgame. LC 91-18555. (Illus.). 40p. (J). 1999. per. 5.99 (*0-689-82433-5*) Aladdin.

— Take Me Out to the Ballgame. LC 91-18555. (Illus.). 40p. (J). (ps up). 1992. lib. bdg. 16.00 (*0-02-735991-3*, Four Winds Pr) S&S Childrens.

Norworthy, Kent. Inside Honduras. 2nd ed. (Illus.). 208p. 1994. pap. 11.95 (*0-911213-49-X*) Interhemisp Res Ctr.

Nosakhere, Moyenda. The Path Toward Liberation: Understanding the Need for Polygamy in the African-American Community. 110p. (Orig.). 1991. pap. 9.95 (*0-9626613-0-9*) New Nation Bks.

Nosal, Denise, ed. Houston Women: From Suffrage to City Hall. (Illus.). 85p. (Orig.). 1987. pap. text 15.00 (*0-939903-02-4*) LWV Houston Ed Fund.

Nosanchuk, Terry, jt. auth. see Erickson, Bonnie.

Nosay, G., jt. auth. see Nakamura, T.

Nosco, Michelle, ed. see Youngs, Robert J.

Nosco, Peter. Confucianism & Tokugawa Culture. LC 96-27834. 1996. pap. text 18.00 (*0-8248-1865-2*) UH Pr.

— Remembering Paradise: Nativism & Nostalgia in Eighteenth-Century Japan. (Harvard-Yenching Institute Monographs: No. 31). 280p. 1990. 30.00 (*0-674-76007-7*) HUP.

Nosco, Peter, ed. Japanese Identity Vol. II: Cultural Analysis. LC 96-46565. (Publications of the Center for Japan Studies at Teikyo Loretto Heights University: Vol. I). 275p. (Orig.). 1997. pap. text 15.00 (*0-9650254-1-1*) Teikyo Loretto.

Nose, Hiroshi, et al, eds. The 1997 Nagano Symposium on Sports Sciences. LC 98-71207. 646p. 1998. text 75.00 (*1-884125-71-9*) Cooper Pubng.

***Nose, Hiroshi & Gisolfi, Carl V., eds.** Exercise, Nutrition & Environmental Stress. 450p. 2000. text 60.00 (*1-884125-74-3*) Cooper Pubng.

***Nose, Michiko Rico.** Japan Modern: New Ideas for Contemporary Living. (Illus.). 224p. 2000. 45.00 (*962-593-495-2*) Tuttle Pubng.

Nose, Yukihiko, et al, eds. Plasmapheresis: Therapeutic Applications & New Techniques. fac. ed. LC 82-42896. (Illus.). 462p. pap. 143.30 (*0-7837-7187-8*, 204711200005) Bks Demand.

Nosee, Reed F., jt. auth. see Cooperrider, Allen.

Nosek, Jorg. Regulation Spezifischer Gene in der Cephalosporin C Biosynthese Von Acremonium Chrysogenum. (Bibliotheca Mycologica Ser.: Vol. 167). (Illus.). 116p. 1997. 47.20 (*3-443-59069-1*, Pub. by Gebruder Borntraeger) Balogh.

Nosek, Kathleen. Dyslexia in Adults: Taking Charge of Your Life. LC 96-29589. 216p. (Orig.). 1997. pap. 12.95 (*0-87833-948-5*) Taylor Pub.

— The Dyslexic Scholar: Helping Your Child Achieve Academic Success. LC 94-45423. 184p. 1995. pap. 11.95 (*0-87833-882-9*) Taylor Pub.

Nosh Brothers Staff. Entertaining with the Nosh Brothers. (Illus.). 192p. (Orig.). 1997. pap. 32.50 (*0-333-71608-6*, Pub. by Macmillan) Trans-Atl Phila.

***Nosher, John L.** Interventional Radiology: A Multimedia Approach. (Illus.). 352p. 2000. 195.00 incl. cd-rom (*0-632-04404-7*) Blackwell Sci.

Noshpitz, Joseph D. Handbook of Child & Adolescent Psychiatry, Vols. 5-7. 1800p. 1998. 495.00 (*0-471-19329-1*) Wiley.

Noshpitz, Joseph D., ed. Handbook of Child & Adolescent Psychiatry, 4 Vol. Set, 4 vols., Vol. 4. 2828p. 1997. 700.00 (*0-471-17640 0*) Wiley.

***Noshpitz, Joseph D., ed.** Handbook of Child & Adolescent Psychiatry, 7 vols. Incl. Adolescence. Flaherty, Lois T. & Sarles, Richard M., eds. 480p. 1997. 165.00 (*0-471-55076-0*); Grade-School Child. Kernberg, Paulina F. & Bemporad, Jules R., eds. LC 96-17210. 720p. 1997. 165.00 (*0-471-55075-2*); Infancy & Preschoolers. LC 96-17210. 624p. 1997. 165.00 (*0-471-55079-5*); Varieties of Development. Alessi, Norman E., ed. 704p. 1997. 165.00 (*0-471-55078-7*); Vol. 5, Clinical Assessment and Intervention Plann. Clinical Assessment & Intervention Planning. Harrison, Saul & Eth, Spencer, eds. 848p. 1998. 175.00 (*0-471-19330-5*); Vol. 6, Basic Psychiatric Science and Treatment. Basic Psychiatric Science & Treatment. Alessi, Norman. 640p. 1998. 175.00 (*0-471-19331-3*); Vol. 7, Advances and New Directions. Advances & New Directions. Adams, Paul L. & Bleiberg, Efrain, eds. 581p. 1998. 175.00 (*0-471-19332-1*); (Child & Adolescent Mental Health Ser.). 4300p. 1998. 1155.00 (*0-471-19328-3*) Wiley.

Noshpitz, Joseph D. & Coddington, R. Dean. Stressors & the Adjustment Disorders. LC 89-25065. (Series on Personality Processes). 693p. 1990. 195.00 (*0-471-62186-2*) Wiley.

Noshpitz, Joseph D. & King, Robert. Pathways of Growth: Essentials of Child Psychiatry, 1999 Edition, 2 vols., Vol. 1: Introduction to Child Psychiatry. 99th ed. LC 90-12693. 453p. 1991. 150.00 (*0-471-09917-1*) Wiley.

Nosis, George J. Visionary Thinking. LC 86-70664. 120p. 6.95 (*0-910977-02-X*) Avenue Pub.

Nosis, George J., jt. auth. see Pitrone, Jean M.

Noske, Barbara. Beyond Boundaries: Humans & Other Animals. 256p. 1996. 52.99 (*1-55164-079-1*, Pub. by Black Rose); pap. 23.99 (*1-55164-078-3*, Pub. by Black Rose) Consort Bk Sales.

Noske, Frits. French Song from Berlioz to Duparc. 454p. 1988. reprint ed. pap. 14.95 (*0-486-25554-9*) Dover.

— The Signifier & the Signified. 1977. lib. bdg. 214.50 (*90-247-1995-X*) Kluwer Academic.

Noske, Rainer. Die Sprachphilosophie Hilary Putnams. (Europaische Hochschulschriften Ser.: Reihe 20, Bd. 524). (GER.). 90p. 1996. 29.95 (*3-631-31036-6*) P Lang Pubng.

Noskin, Gary A., ed. Management of Infectious Complications in Cancer Patients. LC 98-16254. (Cancer Treatment & Research Ser.). 312p. 1998. 295.00 (*0-7923-8150-5*) Kluwer Academic.

Nosko, Michael G. Animal Models in the Neurosciences. 2000. 99.95 (*0-8493-7683-1*) CRC Pr.

Noskova, Nina I., jt. auth. see Chow, Gan-Moog, Gan-Moog.

Noskowitz, Jack. Mayn Folk Vol. 2: Beyz.Tr. of My People. (YID., Illus.). 190p. (YA). (gr. 4-11). 1994. pap. 10.00 (*1-877909-62-9*) Jwsh Bk Ctr Wrkmns Cir.

N

An Asterisk (*) at the beginning of an entry indicates that the title is appearing for the first time.

Noskowitz, Jack. Mayn Folk ALEF.Tr. of My People. 167p. 1962. pap. 10.00 (*0-318-22121-7*) Jwsh Bk Ctr Wrkmns Cir.

***Nosner, Ellen Susanna.** Clearview: America's Course. LC 00-133049. (Illus.). 160p. 2000. 27.99 (*0-9677000-1-9*); pap. 18.99 (*0-9677000-2-7*) Foxsong.

Noson, Dennis, jt. ed. see Ando, Yoichi.

Noson, Linda L., jt. auth. see Perbix, Todd W.

Noson of Breslov. The Fiftieth Gate: Likutey Tefilot (Prayers 1-20), Vol. 1. Greenbaum, Avraham, tr. from HEB. & intro. by. 609p. 1993. pap. 13.00 (*0-930213-67-X*) Breslov Res Inst.

Nosov, V. R. & Kolmanovski, Vladimir B. Stability of Functional Differential Equations. 1986. pap. text 73.00 (*0-12-417941-X*) Acad Pr.

Nosov, V. R., et al. Mathematical Theory of Control Systems Design. LC 95-20901. (Mathematics & Its Applications Ser.: Vol. 341). 1996. text 309.00 (*0-7923-3724-7*) Kluwer Academic.

Nosov, Vladimir A. Ultrasonics in the Chemical Industry. LC 64-23248. (Soviet Progress in Applied Ultrasonics Ser.: Vol. 2). 171p. reprint ed. pap. 53.10 (*0-608-11377-8*, 202069200018) Bks Demand.

Nosova, L. & Basu, Prabir. Tables of Thomson Functions: Their First Derivatives. LC 61-12445. (Mathematical Tables Ser.). 1961. 191.00 (*0-08-009518-6*, Pub. by Pergamon Repr) Franklin.

Nosrati, Farhad D. & Ghalili, Jesse. What the Heck Is Golf. (What the Heck Is . . . Ser.). Date not set. 3.99 (*0-9660787-9-9*) Crystal Media.

— What the Heck Is Internet. (What the Heck Is . . . Ser.). Date not set. 3.99 (*0-9660787-8-0*) Crystal Media.

— What the Heck Is Internet with "CD" (What the Heck Is . . . Ser.). Date not set. pap. text 4.99 (*0-9660787-3-X*) Crystal Media.

Noss, Alfred & Havernick, Walter. Die Munzen und Medaillen von Koln. (GER.). 1652p. 1975. reprint ed. write for info. (*3-487-05331-4*) G Olms Pubs.

Noss, David S. A History of the World's Religion. 10th ed. LC 98-19235. 642p. (C). 1999. 67.00 (*0-13-010532-5*) P-H.

Noss, David S. & Noss, John B. History Worlds Religions. 9th ed. LC 93-3732. 705p. (C). 1993. text 67.00 (*0-02-388471-1*, Macmillan Coll) P-H.

Noss, John B., jt. auth. see Noss, David S.

Noss, Luther. Paul Hindemith in the United States. LC 88-10694. (Music in American Life Ser.). (Illus.). 248p. 1989. text 27.95 (*0-252-01563-0*) U of Ill Pr.

Noss, Philip, ed. see Ali, Mushin J.

Noss, Philip A., ed. Grafting Old Rootstock: Studies in Culture & Religion of the Chamba, Duru, Fula & Gbaya of Cameroun. LC 81-51153. (International Museum of Cultures Publications: No. 14). (Illus.). 246p. (Orig.). 1982. pap. 10.00 (*0-88312-165-4*) S I L Intl.

Noss, Philip A., jt. auth. see Omanson, Roger L.

Noss, Reed F. The Science of Conservation Planning: Habitat Conservation under the Endangered Species Act. LC 97-34520. 272p. 1997. pap. text 25.00 (*1-55963-567-3*) Island Pr.

Noss, Reed F. & O'Connell, Michael A. The Science of Conservation Planning: Habitat Conservation Under the Endangered Species Act. LC 97-34520. 272p. 1997. text 40.00 (*1-55963-566-5*) Island Pr.

Noss, Reed F., jt. auth. see Cooperrider, Allen.

Noss, Richard & Hoyles, Celia. Windows on Mathematical Meanings: Learning Cultures & Computers. LC 96-17822. (Mathematics & Its Applications, Soviet Ser.: Vol. 17). 275p. (C). 1996. lib. bdg. 130.00 (*0-7923-4073-6*) Kluwer Academic.

Noss, Richard, et al. Cambodian (Khmer) Intensive Course. (Intensive Cassette Ser.). 449p. 1998. spiral bd. 225.00 incl. audio (*1-58214-000-6*) Mltilingl Bks.

Noss, Richard, jt. auth. see Nevile, Liddy.

Noss, Richard, jt. ed. see Dowling, Paul.

Noss, Richard, jt. ed. see Hoyles, Celia.

Noss, Richard R. Heavens His Handiwork. (Illus.). 55p. 1962. 2.50 (*0-910840-09-1*) Kingdom.

— Heavens His Handiwork. (Illus.). 55p. 1962. pap. 1.50 (*0-910840-08-3*) Kingdom.

Nossack, Hans E. An Offering for the Dead. Neugroschel, Joachim, tr. from GER. LC 90-85935. 150p. 1992. 19.00 (*0-941419-29-0*, Eridanos Library) Marsilio Pubs.

Nossal, G. J., jt. auth. see Coppel, R.

Nossal, K. Patterns of World Politics. 1999. pap. text 39.95 (*0-13-907478-3*) P-H.

Nossal, Kim R. Rain Dancing: Sanctions in Canadian & Australian Foreign Policy. 324p. 1994. text 60.00 (*0-8020-0472-5*); pap. text 21.95 (*0-8020-7571-1*) U of Toronto Pr.

Nossal, Ralph & Lecar, Harold. Introduction to Cell Physics. (Illus.). 387p. (C). 1991. 54.95 (*0-201-19560-7*) Addison-Wesley.

Nossal, Ralph, et al. Proceedings of Static & Dynamic Light Scattering in Medicine & Biology: 21-22 January 1993, Los Angeles, California. LC 93-83352. (SPIE Proceedings Ser.). ix, 366p. 1993. write for info. (*0-8194-1111-6*) SPIE.

Nossaman, Allen. Many More Mountains, Vol. 2. (Illus.). 352p. 1993. 39.00 (*0-913582-57-3*) Sundance.

— Many More Mountains Vol. 3: Rails into Silverton. (Illus.). 352p. 1998. 39.00 (*0-913582-64-6*, 0258) Sundance.

Nosse, Larry & Friberg, Deborah. Management Principles for Physical Therapists. (Illus.). 336p. 1991. 47.00 (*0-683-06576-9*) Lppncott W & W.

Nosse, Larry J., et al. Managerial & Supervisory Principles for Physical Therapists. LC 98-29592. 370p. 1998. 49.95 (*0-683-30254-X*) Lppncott W & W.

Nosseir, Aida I. Arabic Books Published in Egypt in the Nineteenth Century. 1991. text 50.00 (*977-424-214-9*, Pub. by Am Univ Cairo Pr) Col U Pr.

Nossen, Richard A. & Norvelle, Joan W. The Detection, Investigation, & Prosecution of Financial Crimes. 2nd ed. (Illus.). 200p. (Orig.). 1993. pap. text 30.00 (*0-9623645-4-1*) Thoth Bks.

***Nossiff, Rosemary.** Before Roe: Abortion Policy in the States. 216p. 2000. 69.50 (*1-56639-809-6*); pap. 21.95 (*1-56639-810-X*) Temple U Pr.

Nossing, Anne F. Heine in Italia nel Secolo Decimonono. (ITA.). 1948. pap. 7.50 (*0-913298-60-3*) S F Vanni.

Nossiter, Adam. Of Long Memory: Mississippi & the Murder of Medgar Evers. LC 94-45. 303p. 1994. 22.00 (*0-201-60844-8*) Addison-Wesley.

— Of Long Memory: Mississippi & the Murder of Medgar Evers. 320p. 1995. pap. 12.00 (*0-201-48339-4*) Addison-Wesley.

Nossiter, Bernard D. Britain: A Future that Works LC 79-300651. 224p. 1978. write for info. (*0-233-97038-X*) Andre Deutsch.

— The Global Struggle for More: Third World Conflicts with Rich Nations. LC 86-45762. 272p. 1988. 20.00 (*0-318-32651-5*, Icon Edns) HarpC.

Nossiter, Josh. Using Corel WordPerfect Seven. LC 95-72574. 488p. 1995. 24.99 (*0-7897-0141-3*) Que.

Nossiter, Josh C. Using Excel 5 for Windows. (Illus.). 360p. (Orig.). 1995. 19.99 (*0-7897-0288-6*) Que.

— Using Excel for Windows 95. (Illus.). 427p. (Orig.). 1995. 19.99 (*0-7897-0111-1*) Que.

Nossiter, Joshua C., jt. auth. see Maloney, Eric.

Nossiter, T. J. Marxist State Government in India: Politics, Economics & Society. 250p. 1992. 49.00 (*0-86187-456-0*, Pub. by P P Pubs) Cassell & Continuum.

— Marxist State Government in India: Politics, Economics & Society. (Marxist Regimes Ser.). 250p. 1992. pap. 17.50 (*0-86187-457-9*) St Martin.

Nossiter, T. J., jt. ed. see Blumler, Jay G.

Nossman, Walter L. & Wyatt, Joseph L. Trust Administration & Taxation, 4 vols. 1966. ring bd. 830.00 (*0-8205-1470-5*) Bender.

Nossum, R. T., ed. Advanced Topics in Artificial Intelligence. (Lecture Notes in Artificial Intelligence Ser.: Vol. 345). vii, 233p. 1989. 34.00 (*0-387-50676-4*) Spr-Verlag.

***Nostbakken, Faith.** Understanding Othello: A Student Casebook to Issues, Sources & Historical Documents. LC 00-22334. (Greenwood Press "Literature in Context" Ser.). 225p. 2000. 40.00 (*0-313-30986-8*, GR0986, Greenwood Pr) Greenwood.

Nostbakken, Faith & Shakespeare, William. Understanding Macbeth: A Student Casebook to Issues, Sources & Historical Documents. LC 96-35013. (Literature in Context Ser.). 256p. 1997. 39.95 (*0-313-29630-8*) Greenwood.

Nostlinger, Christine. Die Ilse Ist Weg. 103p. 1991. 6.95 (*3-468-49720-2*) Langenscheidt.

Nostradamus. Preguntale a Nostradamus Por Tus Suenos. 1997. pap. text 14.98 (*968-855-234-8*) J H Surovek.

Nostradamus & Cheetham, Erika. The Prophecies of Nostradamus. LC 74-155828. 426p. 1973. write for info. (*0-85435-152-3*) C W Daniel.

Nostrand, Albert D. Van, see Van Nostrand, Albert D., ed.

Nostrand, Carol A. A Handbook for Improving Your Diet. (Illus.). 363p. 1985. pap. write for info. (*0-9614721-0-3*) Eatongude Pr.

Nostrand, Catharine H. Van, see Van Nostrand, Catharine H.

Nostrand, J. F. Van, see Cohen, R. A.

Nostrand, J. F. Van, see Cohen, R. A. & Van Nostrand, J. F.

Nostrand, J. F. Van, see Cohen, R. A.

Nostrand, Joan F. Van, see Van Nostrand, Joan F.

Nostrand, Joan F. Van, see Cohen, Robin A.

Nostrand, R. Van, see Van Nostrand, R., ed.

Nostrand, Randy Van, see Clayton, Lawrence & Van Nostrand, Randy.

Nostrand, Richard L. The Hispano Homeland. LC 91-50867. (Illus.). 296p. 1996. pap. text 13.95 (*0-8061-2889-5*) U of Okla Pr.

Nostrand, Richard L. & Hilliard, Sam B., eds. The American South. LC 88-81746. (Geoscience & Man Ser.: Vol. 25). (Illus.). 174p. (Orig.). (C). 1988. pap. text 25.00 (*0-938909-60-6*) Geosci Pubns LSU.

Nostredame. Les Perles ou les Larmes de la Saincte Magdeleine. Corum, ed. (Exeter French Texts Ser.: Vol. 58). (FRE.). 64p. Date not set. pap. text 19.95 (*0-85989-207-7*, Pub. by Univ Exeter Pr) Northwestern U Pr.

Nostredame, Jehan D. Les Vies des Plus Celebres et Anciens Poetes Provencaux. 258p. 1971. reprint ed. write for info. (*0-318-71936-3*) G Olms Pubs.

Nostwich, T. D., ed. see Dreiser, Theodore.

Nostwich, T. D., ed. & intro. see Dreiser, Theodore.

Nosu, Kiyoshi. Optical FDM Network Technologies. LC 97-8687. (Optoelectronics Engineering Ser.). 184p. 1997. 83.00 (*0-89006-769-4*) Artech Hse.

Noswat, Erd, pseud. Maws. (Illus.). 36p. 1976. pap. 1.50 (*0-939748-11-8*) Cave Bks MO.

Nosworthy, Brent. With Musket, Cannon & Sword: Battle Tactics of Napoleon & His Enemies. LC 96-6161. (Illus.). 528p. 1996. 35.00 (*1-885119-27-5*) Sarpedon.

Nosworthy, J. M., ed. see Shakespeare, William.

Noszlopy, George. Public Sculpture of Birmingham. Beach, Jeremy, ed. (Public Sculpture of Britain Ser.: Vol. 2). (Illus.). 256p. 1998. 58.95 (*0-85323-682-8*, Pub. by Liverpool Univ Pr); pap. 25.95 (*0-85323-692-5*, Pub. by Liverpool Univ Pr) Intl Spec Bk.

Not Famous. Letters to My Government: Dear, Dear Government . . . (Illus.). 165p. (Orig.). 1998. lib. bdg. 12.95 (*0-9662733-0-3*) Goldy Pub.

Nota, Antonella & Lamers, Henny J., eds. Luminous Blue Variables: Massive Stars in Transition: Proceedings of a Workshop Held in Kona, Hawaii, October 6-12, 1996. (ASP Conference Series Proceedings: Vol. 120). 404p. 1997. 34.00 (*1-886733-40-6*) Astron Soc Pacific.

Nota, John H. Max Scheler: The Man & His Work. 213p. 1983. 5.95 (*0-8199-0852-5*, Frncscn Herld) Franciscan Pr.

Notaise, J. French-English Dictionary of Multimedia Terminology. 2nd ed. (ENG & FRE.). 903p. 1996. pap. 130.00 (*2-12-465027-0*, Pub. by AFNOR) IBD Ltd.

— French/English Dictionary of Multimedia Terminology. (ENG & FRE.). 1996. 130.00 (*0-7859-9684-2*) Fr & Eur.

Notar, Ellen E. Solving the Puzzle: Teaching & Learning with Adults. LC 93-51500. (Illus.). 1994. pap. text 12.95 (*0-944957-20-X*) Rivercross Pub.

Notari, Robert E. Biopharmaceutics & Clinical Pharmacokinetics: An Introduction. 4th rev. ed. (Illus.). 440p. 1986. text 55.00 (*0-8247-7523-6*) Dekker.

Notari-Syverson, Angela, et al. Ladders to Literacy: A Preschool Activity Book. LC 97-37862. 376p. 1998. 49.95 (*1-55766-317-3*) P H Brookes.

Notarianni, Barbara. Solar System Grades 5-8. Pedigo, Patricia & DeSanti, Roger, eds. (Kelley Wingate Ser.). 105p. (J). (gr. 5-8). 1996. pap. text 10.95 (*0-88724-446-7*, CD-3728) Carson-Dellos.

— Solar System Grades 2-4. Pedigo, Patricia & DeSanti, Roger, eds. (Kelley Wingate Ser.). 132p. (J). (gr. 2-4). 1996. pap. text 10.95 (*0-88724-445-9*, CD-3727) Carson-Dellos.

Notarius. Bed & Breakfast. 4th ed. pap. text. write for info. (*0-471-37399-0*) Wiley.

Notarius, Barbara & Brewer, Gail S. Open Your Own Bed & Breakfast. 3rd rev. enl. ed. LC 95-23952. 336p. 1996. pap. 17.95 (*0-471-13044-3*) Wiley.

Notarius, Clifford. We Can Work It Out: How to Solve Conflicts, Save Your Marriage & Strenjthen Your Love for Each Other. Markman, Howard, ed. LC 94-14009. 336p. (Orig.). 1994. pap. 13.95 (*0-399-52137-2*) Berkley Pub.

Notaro, Anthony T., jt. auth. see Smolin, Ronald P.

Notbohm, Brent, jt. ed. see Friedman, Lester D.

Notch, Lisa. Paint a Victorian Holiday. (Illus.). 1994. pap. 6.95 (*1-883675-01-4*, 101) J Shaw Studio.

— Paint a Victorian Memory, Vol. 1. (Illus.). 1992. pap. 5.95 (*0-941284-91-3*, 91) J Shaw Studio.

— Tolin' along Memory Lane. (Illus.). 1997. pap. 7.95 (*1-883675-18-9*, 118) J Shaw Studio.

— Tolin' down Victorian Lane. (Illus.). 1995. pap. 7.95 (*1-883675-07-3*, 107) J Shaw Studio.

Notcutt, L. A. & Latham, G. C. The African & the Cinema. 1976. lib. bdg. 69.95 (*0-8490-1403-4*) Gordon Pr.

Notcutt, H. Clement. An Interpretation of Keats's Endymion. LC 65-15889. 84p. (C). 1964. lib. bdg. 75.00 (*0-8383-0601-2*) M S G Haskell Hse.

Notcutt, Michael. Thai Scene. 1995. pap. 12.95 (*0-85449-224-0*) LPC InBook.

Note Chism, Nancy Van, see Van Note Chism, Nancy.

Note, Tatia Van, see Johnson, Douglas & Van Note, Tatia.

Noteboom, Cees. In the Dutch Mountains. Dixon, Adrienne, tr. from DUT. LC 96-37991. 144p. 1997. pap. 11.00 (*0-15-600402-X*) Harcourt.

Notehelfer, F. G. American Samurai: Captain L. L. Janes & Japan. LC 84-42896. 401p. 1985. reprint ed. pap. 124.40 (*0-608-06475-0*, 206677200009) Bks Demand.

Notehelfer, F. G., ed. see Hall, Francis.

Notehelfer, F. G., ed. & anno. see Hall, Francis.

Notelovitz, Morris. Estrogen: Yes or No? 1993. mass mkt. 4.50 (*0-312-95105-1*) St Martin.

***Notelovitz, Morris.** Osteoporosis: Prevention, Diagnosis & Management. 3rd rev. ed. 244p. 1999. pap. text 19.95 (*1-884735-50-9*) Prof Comms.

Notelovitz, Morris & Tonnessen, Diana. Menopause & Midlife Health. 3rd ed. 528p. 1994. pap. 17.95 (*0-312-11314-5*) St Martin.

Notelowitz, Morris, et al. Stand Tall! Every Woman's Guide to Preventing & Treating Osteoporosis. 2nd rev. ed. LC 97-43586. (Illus.). 240p. 1998. 24.95 (*0-937404-38-1*) Triad Pub FL.

Notely, David, ed. A Little Book of Humorous Quotations. (Little Book Ser.). 1998. 7.00 (*0-7117-0983-1*, Pub. by JARR UK) Seven Hills Bk.

Noter, Raphael. Dictionnaire des Synonymes: Repertoire des Mots Francais Usuels Ayant un Sens Sembable, Analogue ou Approche. 140th ed. (FRE.). 283p. 1992. pap. 28.95 (*0-7859-7746-5*, 2130442404) Fr & Eur.

Noterman, Julie. Bloodletting. LC 96-211569. 80p. (Orig.). 1995. pap. 9.95 (*0-9645666-0-5*) Eco Cult Perspect.

***Notermans, Ton.** Money, Markets & the State: Social Democratic Economic Policies since 1918. LC 99-24406. (Cambridge Studies in Comparative Politics). (Illus.). 328p. (C). 2000. 59.95 (*0-521-63339-7*) Cambridge U Pr.

Notermans, Ton, jt. ed. see Forsyth, Douglas J.

Notes, Akwesasne, ed. Basic Call to Consciousness. rev. ed. LC 91-16048. (Illus.). 120p. 1991. 7.95 (*0-913990-23-X*) Book Pub Co.

***Notes, Akwesasne, tr.** Kaianerekowa Hotinonsionne /The Great Law of Peace of the Longhouse People. rev. ed. (Illus.). 60p. 1999. pap. 10.00 (*0-9625175-7-7*) Oyate.

***Notess, Greg R.** Government Information on the Internet 1999. 3rd ed. 800p. 2000. pap. 39.50 (*0-89059-247-0*) Bernan Pr.

Notess, Greg R. Internet Access Providers: An International Resource Directory. 350p. 1994. pap. 30.00 (*0-88736-933-2*) Mecklermedia.

Notestein, Lucy L. Wooster of the Middle West. 1993. reprint ed. lib. bdg. 89.00 (*0-7812-5394-2*) Rprt Serv.

Notestein, Wallace. English Folk. LC 72-99643. (Essay Index Reprint Ser.). 1977. 30.95 (*0-8369-1475-9*) Ayer.

— The House of Commons, Sixteen Hundred Four to Sixteen Hundred Ten. LC 72-118733. 612p. reprint ed. pap. 189.80 (*0-8357-8170-4*, 203384400087) Bks Demand.

— The Scot in History. LC 76-104225. 371p. 1970. reprint ed. lib. bdg. 65.00 (*0-8371-3342-4*, NOSH, Greenwood Pr) Greenwood.

***Notestine, Kerry E.** Fundamentals of Employment Law. 2nd ed. American Bar Association Staff, ed. LC 00-20124. 2000. write for info. (*1-57073-806-8*) Amer Bar Assn.

Notevitz, M. & Van Keep, P. A., eds. The Climacteric in Perspective. 1986. text 392.50 (*0-85200-919-4*) Kluwer Academic.

Notgrass, Ray. How Is Jesus Good News? 156p. 1992. pap. 7.95 (*0-945441-12-6*) Res Pubns AR.

Noth, Albrecht & Conrad, Lawrence I. The Early Arabic Historical Tradition: A Source-Critical Study. 2nd rev. ed. Bonner, Michael, tr. LC 94-6798. (Studies in Late Antiquity & Early Islam: No. 3). xii, 248p. 1994. 27.50 (*0-87850-082-0*) Darwin Pr.

Noth, Martin. The Chronicler's History. (JSOT Supplement Ser.: No. 50). 200p. 1987. 57.50 (*1-85075-043-2*, Pub. by Sheffield Acad) CUP Services.

Noth, Martin. The Deuteronomistic History. 153p. (C). 1990. 12.50 (*0-905774-30-2*, Pub. by Sheffield Acad) CUP Services.

— The Deuteronomistic History. 2nd ed. (Journal for the Study of the Old Testament Supplement Ser.: Vol. 15). 168p. 1981. pap. 19.95 (*1-85075-287-7*, Pub. by Sheffield Acad) CUP Services.

Noth, Martin & Anderson, Bernhard W. History of Pentateuchal Traditions. LC 80-24937. (Scholars Press Reproductions Ser.). (C). 1981. 22.00 (*0-89130-446-0*, 00-07-05) Duke.

Noth, Paul. Live & Learn for Better Health about the Fountain of Youth. (Illus.). 40p. 1999. pap. 7.50 (*0-8059-4712-4*) Dorrance.

Noth, Winfried. Handbook of Semiotics. LC 89-45199. (Advances in Semiotics Ser.). (Illus.). 588p. 1990. text 59.95 (*0-253-34120-5*) Ind U Pr.

— Handbook of Semiotics. LC 89-45199. (Advances in Semiotics Ser.). (Illus.). 588p. 1995. pap. 29.95 (*0-253-20959-5*) Ind U Pr.

Noth, Winfried, ed. Origins of Semiosis: Sign Evolution in Nature & Culture. LC 94-21517. (Approaches to Semiotics Ser.: Vol. 116). x, 480p. 1994. 198.50 (*3-11-014196-5*) Mouton.

Nothdurft, Ivan H. Reflections on That Other America. LC 95-95357. 120p. (Orig.). 1996. pap. 8.00 (*0-934426-66-X*) NAPSAC Reprods.

Nothdurft, Milton H. Between Two Worlds. 1985. 9.00 (*0-9615415-0-4*) Mtn Valley Pub.

Nothdurft, Werner. Schlichtung Bd. 2: Konfliktstoff: Gespraechsanalyse der Konfliktbearbeitung in Schlichtungsgespraechen. (Schriften Des Instituts Fuer Deutsche Sprache: Vol. 5.2). (GER.). vi, 195p. (C). 1996. lib. bdg. 91.45 (*3-11-013623-6*) De Gruyter.

Nothdurft, Werner, ed. Schlichtung Vol. 1: Streit Schlichten - Gespraechsanalytische Untersuchungen Zu Institutionellen Formen Konsensueller Konfliktregelung. (Schriften des Instituts fuer Deutsche Sprache: Vol. 5.1). (GER.). viii, 431p. 1996. lib. bdg. 158.50 (*3-11-013508-6*) De Gruyter.

Nothdurft, William E. Going Global: How Europe Helps Small Firms Export. LC 92-22243. 118p. 1992. 28.95 (*0-8157-6204-6*); pap. 10.95 (*0-8157-6203-8*) Brookings.

— Going to Market: The New Aggressiveness in State Domestic Agricultural Marketing. 6.00 (*0-934842-52-3*) CSPA.

— Renewing America: Natural Resource Assets & State Economic Development. Dyer, Barbara, ed. LC 84-9190. 190p. 1984. 16.95 (*0-934842-32-9*) CSPA.

— SchoolWorks: Reinventing Public Schools to Create the Workforce for the Future. 104p. 1990. pap. 9.95 (*0-8157-6201-1*) Brookings.

Nothdurft, William E., jt. auth. see Conway, Carol.

Notheisz, Ferenc, jt. auth. see Smith, Gerard V.

Nothern Ireland Tourist Board Staff. Where to Eat - Northern Ireland. (Where To Eat Ser.). 1998. pap. text 7.95 (*1-86193-090-9*, Pub. by JARR UK) Seven Hills Bk.

— Where to Stay - Northern Ireland. (Where to Stay Ser.). 1998. pap. 8.95 (*1-86193-085-2*, Pub. by JARR UK) Seven Hills Bk.

Nothiger, Andreas. World History Chart. 48p. 1991. pap. 19.95 (*0-14-051270-5*) Viking Penguin.

***Nothnagel, Juliana.** My Very Own Bible for Toddlers. 1999. 14.95 (*0-86997-635-4*) Lux Verbi.

Nothnagle, Alan L. Building the East German Myth: Historical Mythology & Youth Propaganda in the German Democratic Republic, 1945-1989. LC 98-58051. (Social History, Popular Culture, & Politics in Germany Ser.). 224p. 1999. text 44.50 (*0-472-10946-4*, 10946) U of Mich Pr.

Nothnagle, John. Pierre Crignon: Poete et Navigateur: Oeuvres en Prose et en Vers. LC 90-70299. (FRE., Illus.). 133p. 1990. lib. bdg. 27.95 (*0-917786-80-7*) Summa Pubns.

Nothnagle, John, tr. & intro. see D'Aubigne, Agrippa.

***Nothof, Anne, ed.** Sharon Pollock. (Writers Ser.: No. 1). 150p. 2000. pap. 10.00 (*1-55071-108-3*, , Pub. by Guernica Editions) Paul & Co Pubs.

Nothof, Anne, et al. Ethnicities: Plays from the New West. (Prairie Play Ser.). (Orig.). (J). (gr. 3-7). 1999. pap. 15.00 (*1-896300-03-0*) NeWest Pubs.

Notholt, A. J. & Jarvis, I., eds. Phosphorite Research & Development. (Geological Society Special Publications: No. 52). (Illus.). 326p. 1990. 48.00 (*0-903317-53-2*, 254, Pub. by Geol Soc Pub Hse) AAPG.

***Nothomb, Amalie.** Loving Sabotage. Wilson, Andrew, tr. from FRE. 2000. 21.95 (*0-8112-1459-1*, Pub. by New Directions) Norton.

An Asterisk (*) at the beginning of an entry indicates that the title is appearing for the first time.

Nothomb, Amelie. The Stranger Next Door. Volk, Carol, tr. LC 97-24566.Tr. of Les Catilinaires. 192p. 1998. 20.00 (*0-8050-4841-3*) H Holt & Co.

Nothstein, Gary Z. Toxic Torts: Litigation of Hazardous Substance Cases. LC 83-27128. (Trial Practice Ser.). 776p. 1984. text 95.00 (*0-07-047454-0*) Shepards.

Nothstein, I. O., ed. Selected Documents Dealing with the Organization of the First Congregations & the First Conferences of the Augustana Synod & Their Growth until 1860, Pt. 1. (Augustana Historical Society Publications: No. 10). 195p. 1944. pap. 3.00 (*0-910184-10-0*) Augustana.

— Selected Documents Dealing with the Organization of the First Congregations & the First Conferences of the Augustana Synod & Their Growth until 1860, Pt. 2. (Augustana Historical Society Publications: Vol. 11). 167p. 1946. pap. 3.00 (*0-910184-11-9*) Augustana.

Nothstein, Ira O., ed. The Planting of the Swedish Church in America: Graduation Dissertation of Tobias Eric Biorck. LC 43-18182. (Augustana College Library Publications: No. 19). 39p. 1943. pap. 4.00 (*0-910182-14-0*) Augustana Coll.

Nothstine, William. Influencing Others: A Handbook to Persuasive Strategies. Crisp, Michael G., ed. LC 88-92734. (Fifty-Minute Ser.). (Illus.). 74p. 1989. pap. 10.95 (*0-931961-84-X*) Crisp Pubns.

Nothstine, William L., jt. auth. see Cooper, Martha D.

Nothwehr, Dawn M. Mutuality: A Formal Norm for Christian Social Ethics. LC 97-2614. 224p. 1997. 74.95 (*1-57309-158-8*, Cath Scholar Pr); pap. 54.95 (*1-57309-157-X*, Cath Scholar Pr) Intl Scholars.

Notini, Anja. Made in Sweden: Art Handicrafts Design. (Illus.). 185p. 1988. 45.00 (*0-88736-300-8*) Mecklermedia.

Notini, S., tr. see Celli, L., ed.

Notis, M. D., et al, eds. Cross-Craft & Cultural Interactions in Ceramics. (Ceramics & Civilization Ser.: Vol. 4). 390p. 1989. (*0-916094-48-0*) Am Ceramic.

Notker, jt. auth. see Einhard.

Notker der Deutsche von St. Gallen Staff. De Categorie: Boethius' Bearbeitung von Aristoteles' Schrift "Kategorie", 2 vols., Set. Firchow, Evelyn S. & Hotchkiss, Richard, eds. (GER.). xxvi, 1243p. (C). 1996. lib. bdg. 503.70 (*3-11-014762-9*) De Gruyter.

Notkin, Boris. Good Morning, Moscow. (Grace A. Tanner Lecture in Human Values Ser.). 17p. 1991. 7.50 (*0-910153-08-6*) E T Woolf.

Notkin, Debbie. Flying Cups & Saucers: Gender Exploration in Science Fiction & Fantasy. 1998. 40.00 (*0-9629066-9-7*) Edgewood Pr.

— Flying Cups & Saucers: Gender Explorations in Science Fiction & Fantasy. LC 99-175515. 1998. pap. text 18.00 (*0 9629066-8-9*) Edgewood Pr.

Notkin, Debbie, jt. auth. see DeChancie, John.

Notkin, Debbie, jt. auth. see Edison, Laurie T.

Notkin, Lenore. El Autobus Magico Se Queda Plantado; Un Libro Sobre La Fotosintesis. 1997. 8.19 (*0-606-11292-8*, Pub. by Turtleback) Demco.

Notkins, A. L., jt. ed. see Oldstone, M. B.

Notkins, A. L., jt. ed. see Oldstone, Michael B.

***Notkola, Veijo.** Fertility, Mortality & Migration in Subsaharan Africa. LC 99-48174. 1999. text 69.95 (*0-312-22661-6*) St Martin.

Notley, Alice. Alice Notley. 1988. pap. 5.00 (*0-944521-13-4*) Dia Ctr Arts.

— Alice Ordered Me to Be Made. LC 76-26060. 1976. pap. 2.50 (*0-685-99370-1*) Yellow Pr.

— At Night the States. LC 87-51506. (Illus.). 78p. (Orig.). 1988. pap. 6.95 (*0-916328-18-X*) Yellow Pr.

— Close to Me & Closer... (The Language of Heaven) & Desamere. LC 94-80136. 139p. 1995. 10.50 (*1-882022-26-2*) O Bks.

— The Descent of Alette. LC 95-32698. 151p. 1996. pap. 14.95 (*0-14-058764-0*, Penguin Bks) Viking Penguin.

— Margaret & Dusty. LC 84-27472. (Illus.). 80p. (Orig.). 1985. pap. 8.95 (*0-918273-08-0*) Coffee Hse.

— Mysteries of Small Houses. LC 97-42195. (Penguin Poets Ser.). 160p. 1998. pap. 14.95 (*0-14-058896-5*) Viking Penguin.

— Selected Poems of Alice Notley. LC 93-30099. 144p. (Orig.). 1993. pap. 11.95 (*1-883689-02-3*); lib. bdg. 32.95 (*1-883689-03-1*) Talisman Hse.

— Waltzing Matilda. 7.00 (*0-317-17176-3*); pap. 3.50 (*0-317-17177-1*) Kulchur Foun.

Notley, David, ed. A Little Book of Naughty Quotations. (Little Book Ser.). 1998. 7.00 (*0-7117-0982-3*, Pub. by JARR UK) Seven Hills Bk.

— A Little Book of Wisdom. (Little Book Ser.). 1998. 7.00 (*0-7117-0985-8*, Pub. by JARR UK) Seven Hills Bk.

— A Little Book of Wit. (Little Book Ser.). 1998. 7.00 (*0-7117-0984-X*, Pub. by JARR UK) Seven Hills Bk.

— William Shakespeare Quotations. (Little Book Ser.). 1998. 7.00 (*0-7117-0978-5*, Pub. by JARR UK) Seven Hills Bk.

— Winston Churchill Quotations. (Little Book Ser.). 1998. 7.00 (*0-7117-0980-7*, Pub. by JARR UK) Seven Hills Bk.

Notley, Larry V. Fly Leaders & Knots. LC 98-164413. (Illus.). 64p. 1998. per. 7.95 (*1-57188-121-2*) F Amato Pubns.

Notley, Larry V. Guide to Fly Fishing Knots. (Illus.). 32p. pap. 4.95 (*1-57188-183-2*) F Amato Pubns.

***Notley, Raymond.** Miller's Popular Glass of the 19th & 20th Centuries. (Illus.). 64p. 2000. pap. 9.95 (*1-84000-188-7*, Pub. by Millers Pubns) Antique Collect.

Notley, Raymond. Pressed Flint Glass. (Album Ser.: No. 162). (Illus.). 32p. 1999. pap. 5.25 (*0-85263-782-9*, Pub. by Shire Pubns) Parkwest Pubns.

***Notley, Thelma.** China Bound. Turrentine, Jan, ed. 192p. 1999. pap. 9.99 (*1-56309-741-9*) Womans Mission Union.

Notman, Malkah T. & Nadelson, Carol C., eds. The Woman Patient Vol. 1: Sexual & Reproductive Aspects of Women's Health Care. (Women in Context Ser.). (Illus.). 376p. 1978. 47.50 (*0-306-31151-8*, Plenum Trade) Perseus Pubng.

— The Woman Patient Vol. 3: Aggressions, Adaptations, & Psychotherapy. LC 82-5325. (Women in Context Ser.). 326p. 1982. 45.00 (*0-306-40859-7*, Plenum Trade) Perseus Pubng.

— Women & Men: New Perspectives on Gender Differences. LC 90-548. (Issues in Psychiatry Ser.). 144p. 1991. pap. text 12.95 (*0-88048-136-6*, 8136) Am Psychiatric.

Noto, Cosimo. Ideal City. LC 70-154454. (Utopian Literature Ser.). 1976. reprint ed. 33.95 (*0-405-03536-5*) Ayer.

Noto, John. Psycho-Motor Breathscapes. unabridged ed. 74p. (Orig.). 1996. pap. 7.95 (*0-9654877-0-9*) Vatic Hum Pr.

***Noto, John.** Simulcast Yearning. 83p. 1999. pap. 9.00 (*1-877655-32-5*, Pub. by Wordcraft Oregon) SPD-Small Pr Dist.

Notomi, Noburu. The Unity of Plato's Sophist: Between the Sophist & the Philosopher. LC 98-4060. (Cambridge Classical Studies). 365p. (C). 1999. text 64.95 (*0-521-63259-5*) Cambridge U Pr.

Noton, Bryan R., ed. Composite Materials in Engineering Design: Proceedings of the Sixth St. Louis Symposium Held on 11-12 May, 1972. LC 73-84938. 737p. reprint ed. pap. 200.00 (*0-608-14344-8*, 205195300017) Bks Demand.

Noton, Bryan R., ed. see Metallurgical Society of AIME Staff.

Noton, Maxwell. Spacecraft Navigation & Guidance. LC 97-53165. (Advances in Industrial Control Ser.). (Illus.). xiv, 186p. 1998. 64.95 (*3-540-76248-5*) Spr-Verlag.

Notovitch, Nicolas. The Unknown Life of Jesus Christ. 2nd rev. ed. Leonardo, Bianca, ed. LC 96-23833. (Illus.). 56p. 1996. pap. 10.00 (*0-9602850-1-6*) Tree Life Pubns.

Notovitch, Nicolas & Loranger, Alexina, trs. The Unknown Life of Jesus Christ. 66p. 1996. reprint ed. spiral bd. 9.00 (*0-7873-0637-1*) Hlth Research.

Notovitch, Nicolas T. The Unknown Life of Jesus Christ. 1973. 250.00 (*0-87968-073-3*) Gordon Pr.

Notre Dame Conference on Population Staff. Family & Fertility: Proceedings of the Notre Dame Conference on Population, 5th, University of Notre Dame, 1966. Liu, William T., ed. LC 68-6934. 287p. reprint ed. pap. 89.00 (*0-608-15044-4*, 202594300047) Bks Demand.

Notrik, Paul, pseud. Intraneural Injections for Rheumatoid Arthritis & Osteoarthritis & the Control of Pain in Arthritis in the Knee. LC 84-61283. 97p. (Orig.). 1984. pap. 9.95 (*0-931150-14-0*) Arthritis Trust.

Notrog, Bryna. It's Raining Whisper. (Illus.). 48p. (J). 1998. lib. bdg. 17.95 (*0-9652479-1-0*) Zipper Pr.

— The Little Wooden Table. LC 97-201489. (Illus.). 48p. (J). 1997. lib. bdg. 14.95 (*0-9652479-0-2*) Zipper Pr.

Nott, jt. auth. see Morris.

Nott, C. S., ed. A. R. Orage's Commentaries on All & Everything. 136p. 1999. reprint ed. 16.00 (*0-89756-015-9*) Two Rivers.

Nott, C. S., tr. see Attar, Farid Al-Din.

Nott, George F., ed. see Howard, Henry & Wyatt, Thomas.

Nott, J. C. & Gliddon, George R. Types of Mankind: or Ethnological Researches. LC 76-89386. (Black Heritage Library Collection). (Illus.). 1977. 54.95 (*0-8369-8639-3*) Ayer.

***Nott, Kenneth H. & Vedhara, Kav.** Psychosocial & Biomedical Interactions in HIV Infection. (Biobehavioural Perspectives on Health & Disease Prevention Ser.: Vol. 2). 288p. 2000. 58.00 (*90-5823-037-6*, Harwood Acad Pubs) Gordon & Breach.

***Nott, Robert.** Last of the Cowboy Heroes: The Westerns of Randolph Scott, Joel McCrea & Audie Murphy. LC 99-58785. (Illus.). 205p. 2000. 32.50 (*0-7864-0762-X*) McFarland & Co.

Nott, Susan, jt. auth. see Morgan, Peter.

Nott, Susan, jt. auth. see Morris, Anne.

Nott, Valerie. Great Disasters. (What Happened Next? Ser.). (Illus.). 48p. (J). (gr. 5-8). 1995. lib. bdg. 23.60 (*0-531-14360-0*) Watts.

— Great Disasters. (What Happened Next? Ser.). 40p. (J). 1997. pap. 6.95 (*0-531-15298-7*) Watts.

***Nottage, Cindy & Morse, Virginia.** IIM: Independent Investigation Method Teacher Manual. rev. ed. 228p. 2000. teacher ed. 34.95 (*1-57652-008-0*) Active Lrng NH.

— Iim: Independent Investigation Method Teacher Manual. rev. ed. (Illus.). 228p. 1999. text, teacher ed. 34.95 (*1-57652-006-4*) Active Lrng NH.

Nottage, James & Carlson, George. George Carlson: Dignity in Art. 1993. pap. 24.95 (*1-882880-00-5*) Autry Mus Wstrn.

Nottage, James H. Saddlemaker to the Stars: The Leather & Silver Art of Edward H. Bohlin. LC 96-78955. (Illus.). 228p. (Orig.). 1996. 60.00 (*0-295-97605-5*) U of Wash Pr.

Nottage, Jane. Ferrari: The Inside Story of the Battle for the Championship. LC 98-3190. (Illus.). 224p. 1998. 39.95 (*0-7603-0447-5*) MBI Pubg.

Nottage, Luke R., jt. auth. see Baum, Harald.

***Nottage, Lynn.** Crumbs from the Table of Joy. 1998. pap. 5.25 (*0-8222-1572-1*) Dramatists Play.

Nottage, Lynn. Mud, River, Stone. 1998. pap. 5.25 (*0-8222-1660-4*) Dramatists Play.

Nottage, W. H. The Calculation & Measurement of Inductance & Capacity: A Handbook for Experimenting with Tesla Coils & Radio. 1991. lib. bdg. 88.95 (*0-8490-4928-8*) Gordon Pr.

Nottale, L. Fractal Space-Time & Microphysics: Towards a Theory of Scale Relativity. 300p. 1993. text 61.00 (*981-02-0878-2*) World Scientific Pub.

Notten, P. H., et al. Etching of III-V Semiconductors. 356p. 1991. 231.00 (*0-946395-84-5*, Pub. by Elsvr Adv Tech) Elsevier.

Notter, Harley. Postwar Foreign Policy Preparation, 1939-1945. (History - United States Ser.). 726p. 1993. reprint ed. lib. bdg. 109.00 (*0-7812-4920-1*) Rprt Serv.

Notter, Lucille E. & Hott, Jacqueline R. Essentials of Nursing Research. 5th rev. ed. LC 93-38407. (Illus.). 224p. 1994. pap. text 27.95 (*0-8261-1598-5*) Springer Pub.

***Notter, Robert H.** Lung Surfactants: Basic Science & Clinical Applications. LC 00-31583. (Lung Biology in Health & Disease Ser.). 2000. write for info. (*0-8247-0401-0*) Dekker.

Notterman, J. M. & Drewry, H. N. Psychology & Education: Parallel & Interactive Approaches. LC 93-1257. (Illus.). 292p. (C). 1993. 42.50 (*0-306-44364-3*, Plenum Trade) Perseus Pubng.

Notterman, Joseph M., ed. The Evolution of Psychology: Fifty Years of the American Psychologist. LC 97-37081. 783p. 1997. 39.95 (*1-55798-473-5*) Am Psychol.

— The Evolution of Psychology: Fifty Years of the American Psychologist. LC 97-37081. 783p. 1998. pap. 34.95 (*1-55798-484-0*) Am Psychol.

Notthingham, Joanne. An Introduction to Teaching the Profession of Teaching. 110p. (C). 1997. per. 33.95 (*0-7872-4169-5*, 41416901) Kendall-Hunt.

Nottingham. Eat Your Genes: How Genetically Modified Food Is Entering Our Diet, Vol. 1. LC 98-18260. 208p. 1998. text 17.95 (*1-85649-578-7*) Zed Books.

— The Technique of Bobbin Lace. LC 96-103092. (Illus.). 192p. pap. 16.95 (*0-486-29205-3*) Dover.

Nottingham Andragogy Group Staff. Towards a Developmental Theory of Andragogy. (C). 1986. 35.00 (*0-7855-7011-X*, Pub. by Univ Nottingham) St Mut.

— Towards a Developmental Theory of Andragogy. (C). 1988. text 40.00 (*0-7855-3179-3*, Pub. by Univ Nottingham) St Mut.

Nottingham Andragogy Group Staff, ed. Towards a Developmental Theory of Andragogy. (C). 1986. reprint ed. 25.00 (*0-7855-6561-2*, Pub. by Univ Nottingham) St Mut.

Nottingham, Carolyn W. & Hannah, Evelyn. Early History of Upson County, Georgia. 1982. reprint ed. 40.00 (*0-89308-029-2*) Southern Hist Pr.

Nottingham, Chris. Pursuit of Serenity: Havelock Ellis & the New Politics. 1999. pap. 29.95 (*90-5356-386-5*, Pub. by Amsterdam U Pr) U of Mich Pr.

Nottingham, Ed. It's Not As Bad As It Seems. LC 92-75828. (Illus.). 186p. 1993. pap. 12.95 (*0-916693-16-3*) Castle Bks.

Nottingham, Elizabeth K. Methodism & the Frontier: Indiana Proving Ground. LC 41-19465. reprint ed. 20.00 (*0-404-04798-X*) AMS Pr.

Nottingham, Judith, jt. auth. see Cookson, John.

Nottingham, Pamela. Bucks Point Lace-Making. 1985. 18.50 (*0-7134-2234-3*) Robin & Russ.

Nottingham, Stratton. Accomack (Virginia) Land Causes, 1728-1825. 178p. 1990. reprint ed. pap. 17.50 (*1-55613-280-8*) Heritage Bk.

— Certificates & Rights, Accomack County, Virginia, 1663-1709. LC 77-76846. 91p. 1997. reprint ed. pap. 12.00 (*0-8063-0773-0*, Pub. by Clearfield Co) ACCESS Pubs Network.

***Nottingham, Stratton.** Land Causes, Accomack County, Virginia, 1727-1826. LC 98-75214. 183 p. 1999. reprint ed. 28.50 (*0-8063-1588-1*) Genealog Pub.

Nottingham, Stratton. The Marriage License Bonds of Accomack County, Virginia from 1774 to 1806. 49p. 1997. reprint ed. pap. 9.00 (*0-8063-0263-1*, 4180) Clearfield Co.

— The Marriage License Bonds of Lancaster County, Virginia, from 1701 to 1848. 106p. 1996. reprint ed. pap. 13.50 (*0-8063-4638-8*, 9282) Clearfield Co.

— The Marriage License Bonds of Westmoreland County, Virginia from 1786 to 1850 97p. 1995. reprint ed. pap. 12.00 (*0-8063-0651-3*, 4195) Clearfield Co.

— Marriages of Mecklenburg County, Virginia, from 1765 to 1810. 71p. 1996. reprint ed. pap. 10.00 (*0-8063-4639-6*, 9283) Clearfield Co.

***Nottingham, Stratton.** Wills & Administrations, Accomack County, Virginia, 1663-1826, 2 vols. in 1. LC 98-75213. 1999. reprint ed. 45.00 (*0-8063-1589-X*) Genealog Pub.

Nottingham, Stratton, ed. Wills & Administrations of Accomack County, Virginia, 1663-1800. 563p. 1991. reprint ed. pap. 32.50 (*1-55613-405-3*) Heritage Bk.

Nottingham, Suzanne & Fedel, Frank. Fitness In-Line Skating. LC 96-48336. (Fitness Spectrum Ser.). (Illus.). 176p. 1997. pap. 15.95 (*0-87322-982-7*, PNOT0982) Human Kinetics.

Nottingham, Ted. Winning Chess Piece by Piece. LC 98-48171. (Illus.). 128p. 1998. 17.95 (*0-8069-9955-1*) Sterling.

***Nottingham, Ted.** Winning Chess Piece by Piece. (Illus.). 2000. pap. 10.95 (*0-8069-9970-5*) Sterling.

Nottingham, Ted. Winning Chess Tactics. LC 99-20300. 1999. 17.95 (*0-8069-9956-X*) Sterling.

Nottingham, Ted, et al. Chess for Children. LC 93-24832. (Illus.). 128p. (J). (gr. 3 up). 1993. 16.95 (*0-8069-0452-6*) Sterling.

— Chess for Children. (Illus.). 128p. (J). 1996. pap. 9.95 (*0-8069-0453 4*) Sterling.

— Chess for Children Gift Pack. (Illus.). 128p. (J). 1996. pap. 17.95 (*0-8069-8177-6*) Sterling.

Nottingham, Theodore J. The Color of the Wind: Fables for a New Age. LC 98-91565. (Illus.). 107p. 1999. pap. 12.95 (*0-9664960-0-0*, Pub. by Nottingham Pubg) ACCESS Pubs Network.

***Nottingham, Theodore J.** The Holy Man's War. (Mystic Isle Legends Ser.: Bk. 1). 400p. 2000. pap. 12.95 (*0-9664960-2-7*, Pub. by Nottingham Pubg) ACCESS Pubs Network.

Nottingham, Theodore J. The Tribulation. (Messiah Chronicles Ser.: Bk. 2). 368p. 1999. pap. 12.95 (*0-9664960-1-9*, Pub. by Nottingham Pubg) ACCESS Pubs Network.

Nottingham, William J., tr. see Clevenot, Michel.

Nottle, Trevor. Gardens of the Sun. (Illus.). 208p. 1996. 29.95 (*0-88192-365-6*) Timber.

— Growing Old-Fashioned Roses. 2nd ed. (Growing Ser.). (Illus.). 88p. 1995. pap. 13.95 (*0-86417-641-4*) Seven Hills Bk.

— New Cottage Garden. 1998. pap. 14.95 (*0-86417-901-4*, Pub. by Kangaroo Pr) Seven Hills Bk.

— Old Fashioned Gardens. (Illus.). 192p. 1993. 29.95 (*0-86417-436-5*, Pub. by Kangaroo Pr) Seven Hills Bk.

***Nottonson, Ira N.** Before You Go into Business Read This. LC 99-10747. 280p. 1999. pap. 17.95 (*1-55571-481-1*) PSI Resch.

Nottonson, Ira N. Secrets to Buying & Selling a Business. 3rd ed. LC 99-41578. 300p. 1999. pap. text 24.95 (*1-55571-489-7*, Oasis Pr) PSI Resch.

Nottridge, Rhoda. Additives. LC 92-33083. (J). (gr. 2-5). 1993. lib. bdg. 19.93 (*0-87614-794-5*, Carolrhoda) Lerner Pub.

— Care for Your Body. LC 92-13917. (Staying Healthy Ser.). (Illus.). 32p. (J). (gr. 6). 1993. lib. bdg. 13.95 (*0-89686-787-0*, Crstwood Hse) Silver Burdett Pr.

— Fats. LC 92-26758. (Food Facts Ser.). (Illus.). (J). (gr. 2-5). 1993. lib. bdg. 19.93 (*0-87614-779-1*, Carolrhoda) Lerner Pub.

— Sugars. LC 92-21414. (Food Facts Ser.). (Illus.). 32p. (J). (gr. 2-5). 1993. lib. bdg. 14.95 (*0-87614-796-1*, Carolrhoda) Lerner Pub.

— Vitamins. LC 92-21415. (J). (gr. 2-5). 1993. lib. bdg. 14.95 (*0-87614-795-3*, Carolrhoda) Lerner Pub.

Nottridge, Robin E., jt. auth. see Marston, John.

Notturno, M. A., ed. Perspectives on Psychologism. LC 89-9849. (Brill's Studies in Epistemology, Psychology & Psychiatry). 504p. 1989. text 167.50 (*90-04-09182-3*) Brill Academic Pubs.

Notturno, Mark A. Objectivity, Rationality & the Third Realm: Justification & the Grounds of Psychologism: A Study of Frege & Popper. (Nijhoff International Philosophy Ser.: No. 16). 268p. 1985. pap. text 46.00 (*90-247-3129-1*); lib. bdg. 127.50 (*90-247-2956-4*) Kluwer Academic.

***Notturno, Mark A.** Science & the Open Society: In Defense of Reason & the Freedom of Thought. LC 99-462316. 2000. pap. 23.95 (*963-9116-70-X*) Ctrl Europ Univ.

— Science & the Open Society: The Future of Karl Popper's Philosophy. LC 99-462316. 300p. (C). 2000. 49.95 (*963-9116-69-6*) Ctrl Europ Univ.

***Nottvedt, A., ed.** Dynamics of the Norwegian Margin. (Special Publication Ser.: No. 167). 448p. 2000. 158.00 (*1-86239-056-8*, Pub. by Geol Soc Pub Hse) AAPG.

Notzing, A. Von Schrenck, see Von Schrenck Notzing, A.

Notzing, Baron V. Phenomena of Materialisation. 340p. 1996. reprint ed. spiral bd. 31.00 (*0-7873-0638-X*) Hlth Research.

Notzon, Francis C. Proceedings of the International Collaborative Effort on Perinatal & Infant Mortality, Vol. III. (Illus.). 325p. (Orig.). (C). 1994. pap. text 50.00 (*0-7881-1432-8*) DIANE Pub.

Notzon, Mark. The Noise of Reason: Scepticism & the Art of Rochester. Lee, Don Y., ed. LC 84-81310. 83p. (C). 1984. 36.50 (*0-939758-09-1*) Eastern Pr.

— The Noise of Reason: Scepticism & the Art of Rochester. rev. ed. Lee, Don Y., ed. LC 92-72327. 170p. (C). 1992. 39.50 (*0-939758-23-7*) Eastern Pr.

***Noubary, Reza.** Statistical Methods for Earthquake Hazard Assessment & Risk Analysis. LC 99-54557. 242p. 2000. lib. bdg. 79.00 (*1-56072-770-5*) Nova Sci Pubs.

Noud, Keith. Courses for Horses. 159p. (C). 1990. pap. 60.00 (*0-7316-7935-0*, Pub. by Boolarong Pubns) St Mut.

Nouet, Noel. The Shogun's City: A History of Tokyo. Mills, John & Mills, Michele, trs. 160p. (C). 1989. text 35.00 (*0-904404-62-5*, Pub. by Curzon Pr Ltd) UH Pr.

— The Shogun's City: A History of Tokyo. Mills, John & Mills, Michele, trs. 160p. (C). 1996. text 35.00 (*0-904404-61-7*, Pub. by Curzon Pr Ltd) UH Pr.

Noufi, Rommel. Photovolatic Advanced Research & Development. (AIP Conference Proceedings Ser.: No. 268). 560p. 1992. 125.00 (*1-56396-056-7*) Am Inst Physics.

Noufi, Rommel & Ullah, Harin S., eds. NREL Photovoltaic Program Review, 12th Proceedings. LC 94-70748. (AIP Conference Proceedings Ser.: No. 306). 624p. 1994. text 150.00 (*1-56396-315-9*) Am Inst Physics.

Noufi, Rommel, jt. ed. see McConnell, R. D.

Nougayrol, Pierre, et al. Dictionnaire Elementaire Creole Haitien-Francais. Bentolila, Alain, ed. (FRE.). 511p. 1976. 69.95 (*0-8288-5649-4*, M6430) Fr & Eur.

Nouguier, Evariste. Dictionnaire d'Argot. 2nd ed. (FRE.). 167p. 1993. pap. 32.95 (*0-7859-8197-7*, 2877710173) Fr & Eur.

Nouhuys, Tabitta Van, see Van Nouhuys, Tabitta.

Nouick, Jane, ed. see Huth, Bill.

Noun, Bertic. Georg Brandes. LC 76-2718. (Twayne's World Authors Ser.). 208p. (C). 1976. lib. bdg. 20.95 (*0-8057-6232-9*) Irvington.

Noun, Louise. Iowa Women in the WPA. LC 99-47065. (Illus.). 176p. 1999. 24.95 (*0-8138-2647-0*) Iowa St U Pr.

Noun, Louise & Danoff, I. Michael. Agnes Weinrich. 30p. 1997. pap. 10.00 (*1-879003-19-8*) Edmundson.

Noun, Louise R. Journey to Autonomy: A Memoir. LC 90-4187. (Illus.). 152p. 1990. 21.95 (*0-8138-1899-0*) Iowa St U Pr.

N

— Journey to Autonomy: A Memoir. LC 95-25532. (Iowa Heritage Collection). (Illus.). 158p. 1996. pap. 14.95 (*0-8138-2358-7*) Iowa St U Pr.

— Strong-Minded Women: The Emergence of the Woman-Suffrage Movement in Iowa. LC 86-18597. (Iowa Heritage Collection). (Illus.). 322p. 1986. reprint ed. pap. 9.95 (*0-8138-1724-2*) Iowa St U Pr.

— Three Berlin Artists of the Weimar Era: Hannah Hoch, Kathe Kollowitz, Jeanne Mammen. LC 94-71498. (Illus.). 48p. 1993. pap. 20.00 (*1-879003-10-4*) Edmundson.

Noun, Louise R., ed. More Strong-Minded Women: Iowa Feminists Tell Their Stories. LC 92-23124. (Illus.). 317p. reprint ed. pap. 98.30 (*0-608-08904-4*, 206953900004) Bks Demand.

Noun, Louise R., jt. auth. see Demetrion, James T.

Nouokov, Anna, ed. see Adams, Dennis, et al.

Nour-Al-Din Al-Salihi. Die Neuere Musik Agyptens und Muhammad Abdu'l-Wahhab: Eine Musikethnologische Untersuchung. (Europaische Hochschulschriften Ser.: Reihe 36, Bd. 180). 215p. 1998. pap. 37.95 (*3-631-33032-4*) P Lang Pubng.

Nour, Jabbour A. Arabe-Francais Dictionnaire. (ARA & FRE.). 1129p. 1983. 45.00 (*0-86685-334-0*, LDL3340, Pub. by Librairie du Liban) Intl Bk Ctr.

Nour, Jabbour A., jt. auth. see Abdel, Jabbour.

Nourallah, Riad. The Messenger: A Verse Narrative in Fifteen Parts. LC 98-35467. 60p. 1998. pap. 12.00 (*1-883053-34-X*) Univ Pr MD.

***Nourbakhsh, H. P.** Analysis of Spent Fuel Heatup Following Loss of Water in a Spent Fuel Pool: Manual for the Computer Code Sharp, Draft Report for Comment. 88p. 1998. pap. 7.50 (*0-16-062920-9*) USGPO.

Nourbakhsh, Illah, ed. Planning with Incomplete Information for Robot Problems: Papers from the 1996 Spring Symposium. (Technical Reports). (Illus.). 143p. 1996. spiral bd. 25.00 (*1-57735-006-5*) AAAI Pr.

Nourbakhsh, Illah R. Interleaving Planning & Execution for Autonomous Robots, Vol. 385. LC 96-44526. (Kluwer International Series in Engineering & Computer Science). 168p. (C). 1996. text 106.50 (*0-7923-9828-9*) Kluwer Academic.

N

Nouri, Fereidoun K., ed. see Obolensky, Serge, et al.

Nourie, Alan & Nourie, Barbara, eds. American Mass-Market Magazines. LC 89-17084. (Historical Guides to the World's Periodicals & Newspapers Ser.). 624p. 1990. lib. bdg. 105.00 (*0-313-25254-8*, NMM/, Greenwood Pr) Greenwood.

Nourie, Barbara, jt. ed. see Nourie, Alan.

Nourissier, Francois. Lettre a Mon Chien. (FRE.). 1976. pap. 8.95 (*0-7859-4068-5*) Fr & Eur.

Nourmand, Tony. Film Posters of the 60s: The Essential Movies of the Decade. (Illus.). 128p. 1999. pap. text 22.95 (*0-87951-934-7*, Pub. by Overlook Pr) Penguin Putnam.

Nourmand, Tony & Marsh, Graham, eds. Film Posters of the 70s: The Essential Movies of the Decade. LC 98-16618. (Illus.). 128p. 1998. 35.00 (*0-87951-904-5*, Pub. by Overlook Pr) Penguin Putnam.

— Film Posters of the 70s: The Essential Movies of the Decade. 128p. 1999. pap. 22.95 (*0-87951-730-1*, Pub. by Overlook Pr) Penguin Putnam.

— Film Posters of the 60s: The Essential Movies of the Decade. LC 97-27374. (Reel Poster Gallery Collection). 127p. 1998. 27.50 (*0-87951-851-0*, Pub. by Overlook Pr) Penguin Putnam.

Nourmand, Tony, jt. ed. see Wolff, Mark H.

Nourrigat, Jean, jt. auth. see Helffer, Bernard.

Nourse, Alan E. The Virus Invaders. Mathews, V., ed. LC 91-36650. (Venture Bks.). (Illus.). 112p. (YA). (gr. 9-12). 1992. lib. bdg. 24.00 (*0-531-12511-4*) Watts.

Nourse, Alan E., jt. auth. see Phelps, Janice K.

Nourse, Carol, jt. auth. see Nourse, Hugh O.

Nourse, Dick, et al. Salt Lake City: The Right Place. LC 98-34799. (Urban Tapestry Ser.). (Illus.). 1998. 44.95 (*1-881096-58-0*) Towery Pub.

Nourse, Edwin G. Price Making in a Democracy. LC 75-39262. (Getting & Spending: The Consumer's Dilemma Ser.). 1976. reprint ed. 46.95 (*0-405-08035-2*) Ayer.

Nourse, Edwin G. & Drury, Horace B. Industrial Price Policies & Economic Progress. (Brookings Institution Reprint Ser.). (Illus.). reprint ed. lib. bdg. 42.50 (*0-697-00177-6*) Irvington.

Nourse, Edwin G., et al. America's Capacity to Produce. (Brookings Institution Reprint Ser.). (Illus.). reprint ed. lib. bdg. 39.00 (*0-697-00176-8*) Irvington.

Nourse, Henry S. The Military Annals of Lancaster, 1740-1865: Including Lists of Soldiers Serving in the Colonial & Revolutionary Wars. 402p. 1989. reprint ed. lib. bdg. 42.50 (*0-8328-0834-2*, MA0021) Higginson Bk Co.

***Nourse, Hugh O. & Nourse, Carol.** Wildflowers of Georgia: A Photographic Celebration of Their Beauty & Diversity. LC 99-16493. (Illus.). 2000. 29.95 (*0-8203-2179-6*) U of Ga Pr.

Nourse, Jennifer W. Conceiving Spirits: Birth Rituals & Contested Identities among the Lauje' of Indonesia. LC 99-19368. (Series in Ethnographic Inquiry). (Illus.). 320p. 1999. 45.00 (*1-56098-875-4*); pap. 19.95 (*1-56098-850-9*) Smithsonian.

Nourse, Joan T. Monarch Notes on Cather's My Antonia & Other Works. (Orig.). (C). 3.50 (*0-671-00604-5*, Arco) Macmillan Gen Ref.

— Monarch Notes on Miller's Crucible & View from the Bridge. (Orig.). (C). 3.95 (*0-671-00687-8*, Arco) Macmillan Gen Ref.

Nourse, Jonathan, jt. auth. see Berry, David.

Nourse, Joseph, jt. auth. see Fitzgerald, Oscar P.

Nourse, Kenneth A. How to Write Your College Application Essay. LC 92-37909. (Opportunities in...Ser.). (Illus.). 120p. 1994. pap. 12.95 (*0-8442-4169-5*, 41695, VGM Career) NTC Contemp Pub Co.

— Write Your College Application Essay. LC 97-30116. (Here's How Ser.). (Illus.). 128p. 1997. pap. 12.95 (*0-8442-2477-4*, 24774, NTC Learningworks) NTC Contemp Pub Co.

Nourse, Marsha B., jt. auth. see Spofford, Charles B.

Nouryeh, Christopher. Translation & Critical Study of Ten Pre-Islamic Odes: Traces in the Sand. LC 93-26256. 264p. 1993. text 89.95 (*0-7734-9319-0*) E Mellen.

Nouse, C. Dale. The International Marine Log Book. (Illus.). 224p. 1997. 22.95 (*0-07-048237-3*) McGraw.

Nousiainen, Jaakko. The Finnish Political System. Hodgson, John H., tr. LC 76-120320. 464p. reprint ed. pap. 143.90 (*0-7837-2306-7*, 205739400004) Bks Demand.

Noussias, Sotirios J. Man's Questions - God's Answers. LC 96-85003. 240p. (Orig.). 1997. per. 12.95 (*0-9652284-0-1*) Flower Pub.

Noussitou, F. M., et al. Leprosy in Children. 1976. pap. text 8.10 (*92-4-154053-2*, 1150095) World Health.

Nouveau. Pages Complementaires. Pakenham, ed. (Exeter French Texts Ser.: Vol. 49). (FRE.). 144p. Date not set. pap. text 19.95 (*0-85989-178-X*, Pub. by Univ Exeter Pr) Northwestern U Pr.

Nouveau, Germain. Germain Nouveau's Symbolist Poetry, 1851-1920: Valentines. Groves, Gerald, tr. LC 88-36513. (Studies in French Literature: Vol. 1). 416p. 1990. lib. bdg. 109.95 (*0-88946-573-8*) E Mellen.

Nouveau, Germain, ed. see De Lautreamont, Isidore.

Nouvel, Jean. Jean Nouvel: Architecture & Design, 1976-1995. Bosoni, Giampiero, ed. (Illus.). 96p. 1999. 19.95 (*88-8118-211-4*, Pub. by Skira IT) Abbeville Pr.

***Nouvel, Jean.** Jean Nouvel: Concert Hall Konzertsaal Salle De Concert Luzern. LC 98-49153. 1999. pap. write for info. (*0-8176-5995-1*) Birkhauser.

Nouvel, Jean. Present & Futures: Architecture in Cities. 1997. 52.00 (*84-89698-01-5*, Pub. by Actar) Dist Art Pubs.

Nouvel, Jean & Jodard, Paul, eds. The International Design Yearbook 10, Vol. 10. (International Design Yearbooks Ser.). (Illus.). 240p. 1995. 65.00 (*0-7892-0015-5*) Abbeville Pr.

***Nouvel-Kammerer, Odile, ed.** French Scenic Wallpaper, 1790-1865. (Illus.). 2000. 95.00 (*2-08-013684-4*, Pub. by Flammarion) Abbeville Pr.

Nouvel, Marcel. Bilingual Dictionary of International Telecommunications, Vol. 1: Antenna Theory. (ENG & FRE.). 128p. 1983. 49.95 (*0-8288-9448-5*) Fr & Eur.

Nouvel, Walter W., jt. auth. see Haskell, Arnold.

Nouvet, Claire, ed. see Yale French Studies Staff.

Nouwen, Henri J. M. Adam: God's Beloved. LC 97-35829. 128p. 1997. 16.00 (*1-57075-133-1*) Orbis Bks.

— Behold the Beauty of the Lord: Praying with Icons. LC 86-72698. (Illus.). 80p. 1987. pap. 11.95 (*0-87793-356-1*) Ave Maria.

— Bread for the Journey. LC 96-23679. 1997. pap. 12.00 (*0-06-066359-6*) Harper SF.

— Bread for the Journey: A Daybook of Wisdom & Faith. LC 96-23679. 416p. 1996. 20.00 (*0-06-066376-6*, Pub. by Harper SF) HarpC.

— Can You Drink the Cup? LC 96-24924. (Illus.). 112p. 1996. pap. 9.95 (*0-87793-581-5*) Ave Maria.

***Nouwen, Henri J. M.** Clowning in Rome. 128p. 2000. pap. 9.95 (*0-385-49999-X*) Doubleday.

Nouwen, Henri J. M. Creative Ministry. LC 73-139050. 144p. 1991. pap. 11.95 (*0-385-12616-6*, Image Bks) Doubleday.

— A Cry for Mercy: Prayers from the Genesee. LC 93-38555. 125p. (Orig.). 1994. reprint ed. pap. 10.50 (*0-88344-961-7*) Orbis Bks.

— From Resentment to Gratitude. (Synthesis Ser.). 1976. 1.95 (*0-685-77512-7*, Frncscn Herld) Franciscan Pr.

— The Genesee Diary: Report from a Trappist Monastery. LC 80-23632. 224p. 1981. pap. 10.95 (*0-385-17446-2*, Image Bks) Doubleday.

— The Genesee Diary: Report from a Trappist Monastery. large type ed. (Large Print Inspirational Ser.). 1985. pap. 12.95 (*0-8027-2500-7*) Walker & Co.

— Gracias! A Latin American Journal. 188p. 1993. reprint ed. pap. 12.00 (*0-88344-851-3*) Orbis Bks.

— Heart Speaks to Heart: Three Prayers to Jesus. LC 88-71851. 64p. 1989. pap. 6.95 (*0-87793-388-X*) Ave Maria.

— Henri Nouwen. Garvey, John, ed. (Modern Spirituality Ser.). 96p. 1990. pap. 4.95 (*0-87243-169-X*) Templegate.

— In Memoriam. LC 79-56690. 64p. 1980. pap. 6.95 (*0-87793-197-6*) Ave Maria.

— In the Name of Jesus: Reflections on Christian Leadership. 2nd ed. 81p. 1989. reprint ed. pap. 8.95 (*0-8245-1259-6*) Crossroad NY.

— The Inner Voice of Love: A Journey Through Anguish to Freedom. 144p. 1996. 18.95 (*0-385-48589-1*) Doubleday.

— The Inner Voice of Love: A Journey Through Anguish to Freedom. 144p. 1999. pap. 9.95 (*0-385-48348-1*) Doubleday.

— Intimacy - Reissue. LC 80-8906. 160p. 1998. reprint ed. pap. 13.00 (*0-06-066323-5*, RD359, Pub. by Harper SF) HarpC.

— Jesus & Mary: Finding Our Sacred Center. 66p. 1993. pap. 4.95 (*0-86716-189-2*) St Anthony Mess Pr.

— Letter of Consolation, A - Reissue. LC 81-48212. 96p. 1998. pap. 11.00 (*0-06-066314-6*, Pub. by Harper SF) HarpC.

— Letters to Marc about Jesus. 96p. 1988. 16.00 (*0-06-066315-4*, Pub. by Harper SF) HarpC.

— Letters to Marc About Jesus: Living a Spiritual Life in a Material World. 96p. 1998. pap. 10.00 (*0-06-066367-7*, Pub. by Harper SF) HarpC.

— Life of the Beloved: Spiritual Living in a Secular World. 120p. 1992. 14.95 (*0-8245-1184-0*) Crossroad NY.

— Lifesigns: Intimacy, Fecundity & Ecstasy in Christian Perspective. 128p. 1989. pap. 9.95 (*0-385-23628-X*) Doubleday.

— Living Reminder, The - Reissue: Service & Prayer in Memory of Jesus Christ. LC BV4011.6.N68 1998. 80p. 1998. reprint ed. pap. 10.00 (*0-86683-915-1*, Pub. by Harper SF) HarpC.

— Making All Things New. large type ed. 96p. 1986. pap. 7.95 (*0-8027-2560-0*) Walker & Co.

— Making All Things New - Reissue. LC 80-8897. 96p. 1998. 16.00 (*0-06-066326-X*, Pub. by Harper SF) HarpC.

— Ministry & Spirituality: Reaching Out, Creativity Ministry. LC 96-84430. 240p. 1996. 29.00 (*0-8264-0910-5*) Continuum.

— The Only Necessary Thing: Living a Prayerful Life. Greer, Wendy, ed. & compiled by by. LC 99-43205. 160p. 1999. 18.95 (*0-8245-1833-0*) Crossroad NY.

— Our Greatest Gift: A Meditation on Dying & Caring. LC 93-34310. 144p. 1995. pap. 11.00 (*0-06-066355-3*, Pub. by Harper SF) HarpC.

— Out of Solitude: Three Meditations on the Christian Life. (Illus.). 64p. 1974. pap. 6.95 (*0-87793-072-4*) Ave Maria.

— The Path of Freedom. 32p. 1994. pap. 3.95 (*0-8245-2001-7*) Crossroad NY.

— The Path of Power. 32p. 1994. pap. 3.95 (*0-8245-2003-3*) Crossroad NY.

— Reaching Out: The Three Movements of the Spiritual Life. LC 86-2901. (Illus.). 160p. 1986. pap. 10.95 (*0-385-23682-4*, Image Bks) Doubleday.

— The Return of the Prodigal Son: A Story of Homecoming. (Illus.). 160p. 1994. pap. 16.00 (*0-385-47307-9*) Doubleday.

— The Road to Daybreak. 240p. 1990. pap. 11.95 (*0-385-41607-5*) Doubleday.

— The Road to Peace: Writings on Peace & Justice. Dear, John, ed. LC 97-44940. 200p. (Orig.). 1998. pap. 18.00 (*1-57075-180-3*) Orbis Bks.

— Sabbatical Journey: The Diary of His Final Year. LC 98-26746. 240p. 1998. 19.95 (*0-8245-1708-3*, Crsrd) Crossroad NY.

***Nouwen, Henri J. M.** Sabbatical Journey: The Diary of His Final Year. 240p. 2000. pap. 16.95 (*0-8245-1878-0*, Pub. by Crossroad NY) Natl Bk Netwk.

Nouwen, Henri J. M. Spiritual Journals: Genesee Diary, Gracias!, the Road to Daybreak. LC 96-71389. 288p. 1997. 29.00 (*0-8264-1010-3*) Continuum.

— Thomas Merton: Contemplative Critic. LC 90-47991. 168p. 1991. reprint ed. pap. 9.95 (*0-89243-508-9*, Liguori Triumph) Liguori Pubns.

— Walk with Jesus: Stations of the Cross. LC 89-27875. (Illus.). 1990. pap. 11.50 (*0-88344-666-9*) Orbis Bks.

— The Way of the Heart. (Epiphany Bks.). 1985. mass mkt. 5.99 (*0-345-32959-7*) Ballantine Pub Grp.

— The Way of the Heart: Desert Spirituality & Contemporary Ministry. 96p. 1991. pap. 10.00 (*0-06-066330-8*, Pub. by Harper SF) HarpC.

— With Burning Hearts: A Meditation on the Eucharist. LC 94-14622. 96p. 1998. reprint ed. pap. 10.00 (*1-57075-116-1*) Orbis Bks.

— With Burning Hearts: A Meditation on the Eucharistic Life. LC 94-14622. 96p. 1994. 29.95 incl. VHS (*0-88344-984-6*) Orbis Bks.

— With Open Hands. 1987. mass mkt. 4.99 (*0-345-35299-8*) Ballantine Pub Grp.

— With Open Hands. large type rev. ed. LC 94-79358. 96p. 1995. pap. 9.95 (*0-8027-2694-1*) Walker & Co.

— With Open Hands. rev. ed. LC 94-79358. (Illus.). 136p. 1995. pap. 10.95 (*0-87793-545-9*) Ave Maria.

— The Wounded Healer: Ministry in Contemporary Society. LC 72-186312. 128p. 1979. pap. 10.95 (*0-385-14803-8*, Image Bks) Doubleday.

Nouwen, Henri J. M. & Gaffney, Walter J. Aging: The Fulfillment of Life. LC 74-1773. 160p. 1976. pap. 10.95 (*0-385-00918-6*, Image Bks) Doubleday.

Noux, O'Neil De, see De Noux, O'Neil.

NOVA (Young) Staff. Responding to Communities in Crisis: The Training Manual of the Crisis Response Team. LC 95-115028. 336p. 1996. spiral bd. 50.00 (*0-8403-9461-6*) Kendall-Hunt.

***Nova, Craig.** Brook Trout & the Writing Life. LC 99-30595. 1999. 20.00 (*1-55821-974-9*) Lyons Pr.

Nova, Craig. The Universal Donor. LC 96-37997. 288p. 1997. 23.00 (*0-395-70938-5*) HM.

— The Universal Donor. LC 96-37997. 256p. 1998. pap. 13.00 (*0-393-31845-1*, Norton Paperbks) Norton.

Nova, Curie. The Sight of the Lord. LC 99-62360. 224p. 2000. pap. 14.95 (*0-88739-273-3*) Creat Arts Bk.

Nova Law Staff. African-American Cemeteries & Their History of Choctaw County, Alabama. (Illus.). 113p. (Orig.). 1993. pap. text 29.95 (*1-882804-01-5*) Legacy Pub AL.

— African-American Genealogy: Workbook for Beginners. 2nd ed. (Illus.). 113p. 1993. 19.95 (*1-882804-02-3*) Legacy Pub AL.

— African-American Genealogy Workbook: Finding Your Roots. 3rd ed. (Illus.). 118p. 1992. wbk. ed. 17.95 (*1-882804-03-1*) Legacy Pub AL.

— African-American Genealogy Workbook for Beginners: Tracing Your Ancestry Historically & Genetically. 75p. 1992. wbk. ed. 10.95 (*1-882804-00-7*) Legacy Pub AL.

Nova, Lily, ed. see Kirk, Margaret.

Nova, Lily, ed. see Sams, Margaret, et al.

Nova Scotia Conference on Early Identification of. Nova Scotia Conference on Early Identification of Hearing Loss, Halifax, Nova Scotia, September 9-11, 1974. Mencher, Georges T., ed. 1976. 42.75 (*3-8055-2296-7*) S Karger.

Novac, Ana. Beautiful Days of My Youth. 15.95 (*0-8050-5340-9*) St Martin.

Novac, L., jt. auth. see Szantay, C. S.

Novacek, Michael. Dinosaurs of the Flaming Cliffs. (Illus.). 384p. 1997. pap. 14.95 (*0-385-47775-9*, Anchor NY) Doubleday.

***Novacek, Michael.** Travels with Tyrannosaurus. 2001. text. write for info. (*0-374-27880-6*) FS&G.

***Novacek, Michael, ed.** The Biodiversity Crisis: Losing What Counts. LC 99-54732. (Illus.). 256p. 2000. pap. 19.95 (*1-56584-570-6*, Pub. by New Press NY) Norton.

Novacek, Michael J. & Wheeler, Quentin, eds. Extinction & Phylogeny. (Illus.). 269p. 1992. text 58.50 (*0-231-07438-7*) Col U Pr.

***Novacek, Sandy.** Friends.Link: A Manual of the Friends of Michigan Libraries. 153p. 1999. pap. 20.00 (*0-9632341-9-6*) Whitefoord.

Novack, Barbara, jt. auth. see Ross, George E.

Novack, Cynthia J. Sharing the Dance: Contact Improvisation & American Culture. LC 89-40534. (New Directions in Anthropological Writing Ser.). (Illus.). 272p. (Orig.). 1990. pap. text 19.95 (*0-299-12444-4*) U of Wis Pr.

Novack, George. Democracy & Revolution. LC 74-143807. 286p. 1971. reprint ed. lib. bdg. 50.00 (*0-87348-192-5*) Pathfinder NY.

— Democracy & Revolution. LC 74-143807. 286p. 1971. reprint ed. pap. 18.95 (*0-87348-191-7*) Pathfinder NY.

— Empiricism & Its Evolution: A Marxist View. LC 68-59426. 164p. 1969. reprint ed. pap. 13.95 (*0-87348-020-1*); reprint ed. lib. bdg. 40.00 (*0-87348-021-X*) Pathfinder NY.

— Genocide Against the Indians. 46p. 1970. reprint ed. pap. 4.00 (*0-87348-160-7*) Pathfinder NY.

— How Can the Jews Survive: A Socialist Answer to Zionism. 22p. 1969. reprint ed. pap. 2.50 (*0-87348-090-2*) Pathfinder NY.

— Humanism & Socialism. LC 73-77559. 159p. 1973. reprint ed. pap. 13.95 (*0-87348-309-X*); reprint ed. lib. bdg. 40.00 (*0-87348-308-1*) Pathfinder NY.

— Introduction to the Logic of Marxism. 5th rev. ed. LC 76-87909. 144p. 1969. reprint ed. lib. bdg. 40.00 (*0-87348-019-8*) Pathfinder NY.

— Introduction to the Logic of Marxism. 5th rev. ed. LC 76-87909. 144p. 1969. reprint ed. pap. 12.95 (*0-87348-018-X*) Pathfinder NY.

— The Long View of History. 3rd ed. 46p. 1979. reprint ed. pap. 3.50 (*0-87348-428-2*) Pathfinder NY.

— The Origins of Materialism: The Evolution of a Scientific View of the World. rev. ed. LC 76-160511. 300p. 1965. reprint ed. pap. 19.95 (*0-87348-022-8*) Pathfinder NY.

— Polemics in Marxist Philosophy. LC 77-70457. 344p. 1978. pap. 19.95 (*0-87348-820-2*) Pathfinder NY.

— Polemics in Marxist Philosophy. LC 77-70457. 344p. 1978. reprint ed. lib. bdg. 55.00 (*0-913460-63-X*) Pathfinder NY.

— Pragmatism Versus Marxism: An Appraisal of John Dewey's Philosophy. LC 75-10032. 320p. 1975. reprint ed. lib. bdg. 55.00 (*0-87348-452-5*) Pathfinder NY.

— Pragmatism Versus Marxism: An Appraisal of John Dewey's Philosophy. LC 75-10032. 320p. 1975. reprint ed. pap. 19.95 (*0-87348-453-3*) Pathfinder NY.

— Revolutionary Dynamics of Women's Liberation. 1973. reprint ed. pap. 2.00 (*0-87348-120-8*) Pathfinder NY.

— Understanding History: Marxist Essays. 3rd ed. LC 75-186684. 210p. 1980. reprint ed. pap. 15.95 (*0-87348-605-6*); reprint ed. lib. bdg. 50.00 (*0-87348-606-4*) Pathfinder NY.

Novack, George, ed. America's Revolutionary Heritage. rev. ed. LC 76-12292. 399p. 1976. reprint ed. pap. 21.95 (*0-87348-465-7*) Pathfinder NY.

— America's Revolutionary Heritage. rev. ed. LC 76-12292. 1993. reprint ed. lib. bdg. 60.00 (*0-87348-464-9*) Pathfinder NY.

Novack, George, jt. auth. see Mandel, Ernest.

Novack, Janet L. The ISO 9000 Documentation Toolkit: 1994 Revised ISO 9001 Standard. LC 94-31190. 1994. 90.00 (*0-13-199374-7*) P-H.

— ISO9000 DOCUMTATN 94 REV. 2nd ed. 368p. (C). 1994. 90.00 incl. disk (*0-13-199373-9*) P-H.

— ISO 9000 Quality Manual Developer. LC 95-13584. (C). 1995. pap. text 63.00 incl. disk (*0-13-215477-3*) Prntice Hall Bks.

Novack, M., jt. auth. see Korites, Bernard J.

Novack, Miriam S. The Bar-Bat Mitzvah Autograph Book. LC 93-13991. 128p. 1994. 20.00 (*1-56821-069-8*) Aronson.

Novacky, A. J. Computers & Networks. 2nd ed. 1998. 21.00 (*0-07-234140-8*) McGraw.

Novacky, A. J., jt. auth. see Goodman, R. N.

Novaco, Raymond W. Anger Treatment for Offenders. text. write for info. (*0-471-49153-5*); pap. text. write for info. (*0-471-49154-3*) Wiley.

Novaes de Mota, Clarice. Jurema's Children in the Forest of Spirits: Healing & Ritual among Two Brazilian Indigenous Groups. LC 97-186685. 128p. 1997. pap. 28.50 (*1-85339-402-5*, Pub. by Intermed Tech) Stylus Pub VA.

Novaes, Sylvia C. Play of Mirrors: The Representation of Self Mirrored in the Other. Burbridge, Izabel M., tr. from SPA. LC 97-13918. (Translations from Latin America Ser.). (Illus.). 192p. 1997. pap. 14.95 (*0-292-71196-4*) U of Tex Pr.

Novak. Hydraulic Structures. 1995. pap. 65.00 (*0-419-20070-3*) Routledge.

— Jazzbo Goes to School, Vol. 1. LC 98-32070. 32p. (J). 1999. lib. bdg. 13.49 (*0-7868-2339-9*, Pub. by Hyprn Child) Little.

— Lewis Mumford. 1998. 23.95 (*0-8057-4548-3*, Twyne) Mac Lib Ref.

An Asterisk (*) at the beginning of an entry indicates that the title is appearing for the first time.

— Liberation South, Liberation North. 100p. (Orig.). 1981. pap. 13.25 (*0-8447-3464-0*) Am Enterprise.

— Maternal & Child Nursing. 9th ed. LC 99-10442. 1999. text 45.95 (*0-323-00322-2*) Mosby Inc.

— One Hundred Fourth Congress. 1997. 25.00 (*0-02-874082-3*) Macmillan.

— Taking Glasnost Seriously: Toward an Open Soviet Union. LC 87-34895. 50p. 1988. pap. 9.75 (*0-8447-3642-2*) Am Enterprise.

— This Hemisphere of Liberty: A Philosophy of the Americas. 100p. 1990. pap. 12.95 (*0-8447-3736-4*) Am Enterprise.

— Toward a Theology of the Corporation. rev. ed. 50p. (C). 1991. pap. 7.25 (*0-8447-3744-5*) Am Enterprise.

— William Congreve. 1971. 13.50 (*0-8057-1116-3*, Twyne) Mac Lib Ref.

Novak, ed. Introduction to Sociology. (C). 2000. text. write for info. (*0-321-01366-2*); pap. text, student ed. write for info. (*0-321-01367-0*) Addson-Wesley Educ.

Novak & Ireland. Hillcrest Medical Center. 5th ed. 208p. 1998. teacher ed. 25.95 (*0-7668-0324-4*) Delmar.

— Hillcrest Medical Center. 5th ed. LC 98-16973. (Allied Health Ser.). 272p. (C). 1998. pap. 52.95 (*0-7668-0322-8*) Delmar.

Novak, et al. Illinois Zoning - Eminent Domain & Land Use Manual. LC 97-76491. 708p. 1997. text 105.00 (*1-55834-712-7*, 62570-10, MICHIE) LEXIS Pub.

Novak, A. Czech Literature. Harkins, W. E., ed. Kussi, Peter, tr. (Joint Committee on Eastern Europe Publication Ser.: No. 4). 1986. 15.00 (*0-930042-64-6*) Mich Slavic Pubns.

Novak, Adolph. Store Planning & Design. LC 76-56649. (Illus.). 1977. pap. 28.95 (*0-86730-514-2*) Lebhar Friedman.

Novak, Alys. Governing Policies Manual for Medical Practices. 464p. (Orig.). 1996. pap. 148.50 (*1-56829-079-9*, 4929) Med Group Mgmt.

Novak, Alys, jt. auth. see Price, Courtney.

Novak, Alys, ed. see Kaiser, Leland R.

Novak, Arne. Czech Literature. Harkins, W. E., ed. (Joint Committee on Eastern Europe Publication Ser.: No. 4). 1976. 15.00 (*0-930042-20-4*) Mich Slavic Pubns.

Novak, Barbara. Alice's Neck. 288p. 1987. 17.95 (*0-89919-539-3*, Pub. by Ticknor & Fields) HM.

Novak, Barbara. American Painting of the 19th Century. LC 79-2093. (Icon Editions Ser.). (Illus.). 1979. reprint ed. pap. 29.00 (*0-06-430099-4*, IN99, Icon Edns) HarpC.

Novak, Barbara. The Ape & the Whale: An Interplay Between Charles Darwin & Herman Melville in Their Own Words. LC 94-77616. (Illus.). 96p. (Orig.). 1994. pap. 12.95 (*0-943972-33-7*) Homestead WY.

— Nature & Culture: American Landscape & Painting, 1825-1875. rev. ed. (Illus.). 476p. 1995. pap. 27.50 (*0-19-510188-X*) OUP.

— Nineteenth-Century American Painting: The Thyssen-Bornemisza Collection. (Illus.). 332p. 1991. 39.98 (*0-89660-026-2*, Artabras) Abbeville Pr.

— On Distant Shores. LC 94-71401. 40p. (Orig.). 1994. pap. text. write for info. (*1-885206-01-1*, Iliad Pr) Cader Pubng.

Novak, Barbara & Eaton, Timothy A. Martin Johnson Heade: A Survey: 1840-1900. LC 96-61842. (Illus.). 80p. 1996. 39.95 (*0-9655819-0-X*); pap. 29.00 (*0-9655819-1-8*) Eaton Fine Art.

Novak, Barbara, jt. auth. see Kahn, Wolf.

Novak, Bill, jt. auth. see Sylvia, Claire.

Novak, Bogdan C. Trieste, 1941-1954: The Ethnic, Political & Ideological Struggle. LC 73-96068. 546p. 1996. lib. bdg. 25.00 (*0-226-59621-4*) U Ch Pr.

***Novak, Brenda.** Baby Business. (Superromance Ser.). 2000. mass mkt. 4.50 (*0-373-70955-2*, 1709559) Harlequin Bks.

— Expectations. (Superromance Ser.: Vol. 899). 2000. mass mkt. 4.50 (*0-373-70899-8*) Harlequin Bks.

— Of Noble Birth. 416p. 1999. mass mkt. 5.99 (*0-06-109859-0*) HarpC.

— Snow Baby. (Superromance Ser.: Vol. 939). 2000. mass mkt. 4.50 (*0-373-70939-0*, 1-70939-3) Harlequin Bks.

Novak, Bruce M., jt. auth. see Boffa, Lisa Saunders.

Novak, Carole, ed. see Kemp, Jerrold E.

Novak, Carole, ed. see Thayer, Yvonne V. & Shortt, Thomas L.

Novak, Christopher, jt. auth. see Platzer, Michaela D.

***Novak, Dagmar.** Dubious Glory: The Two World Wars & the Canadian Novel. LC 99-30009. (Studies of World Literature in English: Vol. 9). 184p. (C). 2000. text 50.95 (*0-8204-4549-5*) P Lang Pubng.

Novak, Dan & Weinberger, Paula. Computer Applications: Programming with SeeLogo: Course Code 194-6. Doheny, Catherine & Schroeder, Bonnie, eds. (Illus.). 36p. (J). (gr. 8). 1989. reprint ed. pap. text 5.95 (*0-917531-58-2*) CES Compu-Tech.

— Programming with SeeLogo: Lab Pack. Doheny, Catherine & Schroeder, Bonnie, eds. (Illus.). teacher ed., student ed. 149.95 incl. disk (*1-56177-051-5*, L194-6) CES Compu-Tech.

Novak, Dan, jt. auth. see Weinberger, Paula.

***Novak, David.** Covenantal Rights: A Study in Jewish Political Theory. LC 99-32287. (New Forum Bks.). 240p. 2000. 29.95 (*0-691-02680-7*, Pub. by Princeton U Pr) Cal Prin Full Svc.

Novak, David. The Election of Israel: The Idea of the Chosen People. 303p. (C). 1995. text 59.95 (*0-521-41690-6*) Cambridge U Pr.

— The Image of the Non-Jew in Judaism: An Historical & Constructive Study of the Noahide Laws. LC 83-21989. (Toronto Studies in Theology: Vol. 14). 500p. 1984. lib. bdg. 109.95 (*0-88946-759-5*) E Mellen.

Novak, David. Itsy-Bitsy Spider's Heroic Climb & Other Stories. unabridged ed. (American Storytelling Ser.). (J). (ps-3). 1994. 12.00 incl. audio (*0-87483-346-9*) August Hse.

Novak, David. Jewish-Christian Dialogue: A Jewish Justification. 208p. 1992. pap. text 19.95 (*0-19-507273-1*) OUP.

— Law & Theology in Judaism. 1974. 25.00 (*0-87068-245-8*) Ktav.

— Letter from Dad/Letter from Mom. (Illus.). 32p. 1994. pap. 6.95 (*0-9625261-7-7*) Medlicott Pr.

— Natural Law in Judaism. LC 97-50609. 208p. (C). 1998. text 54.95 (*0-521-63170-X*) Cambridge U Pr.

***Novak, David.** Sonnets. LC 99-85861. 140p. 2000. pap. 14.95 (*0-9675429-4-4*) Non Fit.

Novak, David, ed. Leo Strauss & Judaism: Jerusalem & Athens Revisited. 208p. (C). 1996. pap. text 23.95 (*0-8476-8147-5*); lib. bdg. 55.50 (*0-8476-8146-7*) Rowman.

Novak, David & Samuelson, Norbert M., eds. Creation & the End of Days - Judaism & Scientific Cosmology: Proceedings of the 1984 Meeting of the Academy for Jewish Philosophy. LC 86-19062. 336p. (Orig.). 1986. 52.00 (*0-8191-5524-1*) U Pr of Amer.

Novak, David, jt. auth. see MacCashill, Libby.

Novak, David, ed. see Cummings, Delano.

Novak, David, jt. ed. see Novak, Marian.

Novak, David W. Basic Mathematics. 3rd ed. 680p. (C). 1991. pap. text 49.56 (*0-669-24691-3*); pap. text, student ed. 20.36 (*0-669-24693-X*); teacher ed. 2.66 (*0-669-24692-1*); teacher ed. 2.76 (*0-669-24694-8*); 2.66 (*0-669-24696-4*) HM Trade Div.

— Developmental Mathematics. 2nd ed. 947p. (C). 1988. 280.36 (*0-669-27651-0*) HM Trade Div.

Novak, Deborah, jt. auth. see Novak, Elaine A.

Novak, Derry, jt. ed. see Romke, Adam.

Novak, Devi, ed. see Walters, J. Donald.

Novak, Donald & Doggett, Thomas. Just in Time Business Development Planner. 164p. 1996. 95.00 (*1-57740-052-6*, ILW056) Intl LrningWrk.

***Novak, Dori E.** HELP! It's an Indoor Recess Day. LC 99-50873. (One-Off Ser.). (Illus.). 128p. 2000. pap. 27.95 (*0-7619-7528-4*); lib. bdg. 61.95 (*0-7619-7527-6*) Corwin Pr.

Novak, Dori E. & Strohmer, Joanne C. You Don't Have to Dread Cafeteria Duty: A Guide to Surviving Lunchroom, Recess, Bus, & "Other Duties As Assigned" LC 98-9027. (One-Off Ser.). 104p. 1998. 55.95 (*0-8039-6734-9*, 82701); pap. 24.95 (*0-8039-6735-7*, 82702) Corwin Pr.

Novak, E. Deterministic & Stochastic Error Bounds in Numerical Analysis. (Lecture Notes in Mathematics Ser.: Vol. 1349). 115p. 1988. 30.95 (*0-387-50368-4*) Spr-Verlag.

Novak, Elaine A. Performing in Musicals. 304p. 1988. 28.00 (*0-02-871731-7*, Schirmer Books) Mac Lib Ref.

Novak, Elaine A. & Novak, Deborah. Staging Musical Theatre: A Complete Guide for Directors, Choreographers & Producers. LC 96-18158. (Illus.). 192p. 1996. pap. 19.99 (*1-55870-407-8*, Betrwy Bks) F & W Pubns Inc.

***Novak, Elaine Adams.** Staging Shakespearean Theatre. 192p. 2000. pap. 19.99 (*1-55870-517-1*, Betrwy Bks) F & W Pubns Inc.

Novak, Estelle G. The Shape of a Pear: Poems. 112p. (Orig.). 1996. pap. 9.95 (*1-56474-147-8*) Fithian Pr.

Novak, F. Surgical Gynecologic Techniques. 422p. 1978. text 112.00 (*1-57235-025-3*) Piccin Nuova.

Novak, Gary. Developmental Psychology: Dynamical Systems & Behavior Analysis. (Illus.). 339p. (C). 1996. text 39.95 (*1-878978-25-X*) Context Pr.

Novak, Giles & Dandsberg, Randall H., eds. Astrophysics from Antarctica. LC 98-71241. (Conference Series Proceedings: Vol. 141). 388p. 1998. 52.00 (*1-886733-61-9*) Astron Soc Pacific.

Novak, Glenn, ed. Mailboxes. LC 97-23280. (Illus.). 136p. (Orig.). 1997. pap. 14.95 (*0-88266-970-2*) Storey Bks.

***Novak, Gregor, et al.** Just-in-Time Teaching. Blending Active Learning with Web Technology. 188p. (C). 1999. pap. text 24.20 (*0-13-085034-9*) P-H.

Novak, J., ed. Convergence Structures, Nineteen Eighty-Four. 2545p. (C). 1985. 100.00 (*0-7855-4992-7*, Pub. by Collets) St Mut.

Novak, J., jt. auth. see Karger, A.

Novak, James. The Wisconsin Father's Guide to Divorce & Custody. LC 96-8258. 264p. (Orig.). 1996. pap. 18.95 (*1-879483-31-9*) Prairie Oak Pr.

Novak, James J. Bangladesh: Reflections on the Water. LC 92-41794. (Essential Asia Ser.). 260p. 1993. 29.95 (*0-253-34121-3*) Ind U Pr.

Novak, Jan. Commies, Crooks, Gypsies, Spooks, & Poets: Thirteen Books of Prague in the Year of the Great Lice Epidemic. LC 95-2977. 202p. 1995. 22.00 (*1-883642-09-4*) Steerforth Pr.

— Schola Cantans. 1997. pap. 30.00 incl. audio (*0-86516-404-5*) Bolchazy-Carducci.

— Schola Cantans. 52p. 1997. pap. 15.00 (*0-86516-358-8*) Bolchazy-Carducci.

— Schola Cantans. 24p. 1997. pap. 20.00 incl. audio (*0-86516-357-X*) Bolchazy-Carducci.

Novak, Jana, jt. auth. see Novak, Michael.

Novak, Janice. Posture, Get It Straight! 1999. pap. 11.95 (*0-399-52548-3*, Perigee Bks) Berkley Pub.

Novak, Janice S. Posture, Get It Straight! LC 98-51991. 192p. 1999. pap. 11.95 (*0-399-52500-9*) Berkley Pub.

Novak, Jeannie & Markiewicz, Pete. Creating Internet Entertainment. LC 96-35810. 454p. 1996. pap. text 39.95 incl. cd-rom (*0-471-16073-3*) Wiley.

— Internet World Guide to Maintaining & Updating: Dynamic Web Sites. LC 97-38093. 365p. 1998. pap. 29.99 (*0-471-24273-X*) Wiley.

***Novak, Jeannie & Markiewicz, Pete.** Web Developer.com Guide to Producing Live Webcasts. LC 98-34422. 368p. 1998. pap. 34.99 (*0-471-29409-8*) Wiley.

Novak, Joe, et al, eds. Obituary Dates from the Denni Hlasatel, 1891-1899. 22p. (Orig.). 1995. pap. 3.00 (*1-881125-18-1*) Chi Geneal Soc.

— Obituary Dates from the Denni Hlasatel, 1930-1939. 105p. (Orig.). 1995. pap. 4.00 (*1-881125-15-7*) Chi Geneal Soc.

— Obituary Dates from the Denni Hlasatel, 1940-1949. 130p. (Orig.). 1995. pap. 4.00 (*1-881125-19-X*) Chi Geneal Soc.

Novak, John, ed. Democratic Teacher Education: Programs, Processes, Problems, & Prospects. LC 93-26763. (SUNY Series, Democracy & Education). 262p. (C). 1994. text 64.50 (*0-7914-1927-4*); pap. text 21.95 (*0-7914-1928-2*) State U NY Pr.

Novak, John, jt. auth. see Berry, Fred.

Novak, John, tr. see Erbelding, Dietrich, ed.

Novak, John J. How to Meditate. (Illus.). 119p. 1991. pap. 7.95 (*1-56589-716-1*, BHTM) Crystal Clarity.

Novak, John M., ed. Advancing Invitational Thinking. 260p. 1992. pap. text 15.95 (*1-880192-02-0*) Caddo Gap Pr.

Novak, John M., jt. auth. see Purkey, William W.

Novak, Josef. Domino Murders. 150p. (Orig.). 1997. pap. 14.95 (*1-882833-03-1*) Scribe Pr.

Novak, Josef F. & McMaster, James H., eds. Frontiers of Osteosarcoma Research. LC 92-49083. (Illus.). 592p. 1993. 138.00 (*0-88937-113-X*) Hogrefe & Huber Pubs.

Novak, Josef P. Quantitative Analysis by Gas Chromatography. 2nd ed. (Chromatographic Science Ser.: Vol. 41). (Illus.). 360p. 1987. text 175.00 (*0-8247-7818-9*) Dekker.

Novak, Joseph D. Improvement of Biology Teaching. LC 75-77822. (C). 1970. pap. write for info. (*0-672-60635-6*, Bobbs) Macmillan.

— Learning, Creating, & Using Knowledge: Concept Maps As Tools to Understand & Facilitate the Process in Schools & Corporations. LC 97-33965. 288p. 1998. write for info. (*0-8058-2625-4*); pap. write for info. (*0-8058-2626-2*) L Erlbaum Assocs.

Novak, Joseph D. & Gowin, D. Bob. Learning How to Learn. (Illus.). 150p. 1984. pap. text 16.95 (*0-521-31926-9*) Cambridge U Pr.

Novak, Josip & Spencer, David. Hrvatski Orlovi: Paratroopers of the Independent State of Croatia, 1941-1945. (Illus.). 70p. 1997. 22.00 (*1-891227-13-0*, Axis Europa Bks) Axis Europa.

Novak, Jozef & Schlachetzki, Andreas, eds. Heterostructure Epitaxy & Devices. LC 96-11761. (NATO ASI Series C: Vol. 11). 1996. text 195.00 (*0-7923-4018-3*) Kluwer Academic.

Novak, Jr., Frank G., Jr., ed. Lewis Mumford & Patrick Geddes: The Correspondence. LC 94-41551. (Illus.). 408p. (C). (gr. 13). 1995. 75.00 (*0-415-11906-5*) Routledge.

***Novak, Julie C. & Broom, Betty L.** Ingalls & Salerno's Maternal & Child Health Nursing. 7th ed. (Illus.). 364p. 1999. student ed. write for info. (*0-323-00325-7*) Mosby Inc.

Novak, Julie C. & Broom, Betty L. Ingalls & Salerno's Maternal & Child Health Nursing. 8th ed. teacher ed., suppl. ed. write for info. (*0-8151-6432-7*) Mosby Inc.

***Novak, Julie C. & Broom, Betty L.** Ingalls & Salerno's Maternal & Child Health Nursing, Includes Testbank. 9th ed. 1999. teacher ed. write for info. (*0-323-00323-0*) Mosby Inc.

***Novak, Karen.** Five Mile House. 288p. 2000. 23.95 (*1-58234-096-X*) Bloomsbury Pubg.

Novak, Kate & Grubb, Jeff. Finder's Bane. (Forgotten Realms Novel Ser.). 1997. pap. 5.99 (*0-7869-0658-8*, Pub. by TSR Inc) Random.

— Tymora's Luck. 1998. pap. 5.99 (*0-7869-0726-6*, Pub. by TSR Inc) Random.

Novak, Kurt, ed. Adolf von Harnack Als Zeitgenosse: Reden und Schriften Aus Den Jahren des Kaiserreichs und Der Weimarer Republik Teil 1: Der Theologie und Historiker Teil 2: Der Wissenschaftsorganisator und Gelehrtpolitiker. (GER.). (C). 1995. lib. bdg. 353.85 (*3-11-013799-2*) De Gruyter.

Novak, L. & Gibbons, A. Hybrid Graph Theory & Network Analysis. LC 98-29505. (Cambridge Tracts in Theoretical Computer Science Ser.: No. 49). (Illus.). 220p. (C). 1998. 49.95 (*0-521-46117-0*) Cambridge U Pr.

Novak, L., jt. ed. see Dvorak, J.

Novak, Lajos, jt. auth. see Poppe, Laszlo.

Novak, M. Democracy & Mediating Structures: A Theological Inquiry. 200p. 1979. 34.00 (*0-8447-2175-1*); pap. 12.50 (*0-8447-2176-X*) Am Enterprise.

Novak, M. & Cooper. The Corporation: A Theological Inquiry. 180p. 1981. 34.00 (*0-8447-2203-0*); pap. 18.75 (*0-8447-2204-9*) Am Enterprise.

Novak, M. & Jackson. Latin America: Dependency or Interdependence? 200p. 1985. 34.00 (*0-8447-2258-8*) Am Enterprise.

Novak, M. & Pelikan, E., eds. Theoretical Aspects of Neurocomputing. 300p. (C). 1991. text 118.00 (*981-02-0549-X*) World Scientific Pub.

Novak, M. M. Fractals & Beyond: Complexity in the Sciences. (Nonlinear Science Ser.). 400p. 1998. 86.00 (*981-02-3593-3*) World Scientific Pub.

— Modula-2 in Science & Engineering. 1990. write for info. (*0-07-707200-6*) Gregg-McGraw.

Novak, M. M. & Dewey, T. G., eds. Fractal Frontiers: Fractals in the Natural & Applied Sciences, Denver, Colorado, 8-11 April 1997. LC 97-172194. 500p. 1997. 86.00 (*981-02-3155-5*) World Scientific Pub.

Novak, Marian & Novak, David, eds. Stonewall: Memories from the Ranks & Other Places. (Illus.). 247p. 1998. pap. 14.00 (*0-9651858-2-6*) Signal Tree.

Novak, Marian, ed. see Cummings, Delano.

Novak, Mark. Issues in Aging. LC 96-13466. 560p. (C). 1997. pap. text 67.00 (*0-673-99900-9*) Addson-Wesley Educ.

Novak, Mary A. & Ireland, Patricia A. Hillcrest Medical Center: Beginning Medical Transcription Course. 4th ed. 240p. 1995. pap., teacher ed. write for info. incl. disk (*0-538-71210-4*) S-W Pub.

Novak, Mary H. & Schmalensee, Richard. The Impact of Climate Change Policy on Consumers: Can Tradable Permits Reduce the Cost? LC 98-210006. (Monograph Series on Tax, Regulatory, & Environmental Policies & U. S. Economic Growth). (Illus.). 88p. 1998. pap. 25.00 (*1-884032-07-9*) Am Coun Capital.

***Novak, Mary H., et al.** The Kyoto Commitments: Can Nations Meet Them with the Help of Technology? (Monograph Series on Tax, Trade & Environmental Policies). (Illus.). 228p. 2000. pap. 25.00 (*1-884032-10-9*) Am Coun Capital.

Novak, Matt. Elmer Blunt's Open House. LC 91-38424. (Illus.). 24p. (J). (ps-1). 1996. pap. 5.95 (*0-531-07074-3*) Orchard Bks Watts.

— Elmer Blunt's Open House. LC 91-38424. 1996. 11.15 (*0-606-09238-2*, Pub. by Turtleback) Demco.

— Gertie & Gumbo. LC 94-45913. (Illus.). 32p. (J). (ps-3). 1996. 15.95 (*0-531-09478-2*) Orchard Bks Watts.

***Novak, Matt.** Jazzbo, Vol. 3. 32p. (J). 2001. 12.99 (*0-7868-0591-9*, Pub. by Hyperion) Time Warner.

— Jazzbo, Vol. 4. 32p. (J). 2002. 12.99 (*0-7868-0592-7*, Pub. by Hyperion) Time Warner.

Novak, Matt. Jazzbo & Googy. LC 99-28507. Vol. 2. (Illus.). 32p. (J). (ps-k). 2000. 14.99 (*0-7868-0388-6*, Pub. by Hyprn Child) Time Warner.

— Jazzbo & Googy, Vol. 2. LC 99-28507. (Illus.). (J). 2000. lib. bdg. 15.49 (*0-7868-2340-2*, Pub. by Hyprn Child) Time Warner.

— Jazzbo Goes to School, Vol. 21. LC 98-32070. Vol. 1, (Illus.). 32p. (J). (ps-k). 1999. 12.99 (*0-7868-0387-8*, Pub. by Hyprn Child) Time Warner.

***Novak, Matt.** Jazzbo #3. 32p. (J). 2001. lib. bdg. 13.49 (*0-7868-2507-3*, Pub. by Hyperion) Little.

— Jazzbo #4. (J). 2002. lib. bdg. 13.49 (*0-7868-2508-1*, Pub. by Hyperion) Little.

Novak, Matt. The Last Christmas Present. LC 92-44513. (Illus.). 32p. (J). (ps-1). 1993. 15.95 (*0-531-05495-0*) Orchard Bks Watts.

***Novak, Matt.** Little Wolf, Big Wolf. LC PZ7.N867Li 2000. (I Can Read Bks.). (Illus.). 48p. (J). (gr. 1-3). 2000. 14.95 (*0-06-027486-7*); lib. bdg. 14.89 (*0-06-027487-5*) HarpC.

— Little Wolf, Big Wolf. (I Can Read Bks.). (J). (gr. 1-3). 2001. pap. write for info. (*0-06-444230-6*, HarpTrophy) HarpC Child Bks.

Novak, Matt. Mouse TV. LC 93-49399. (Illus.). 32p. (J). (ps-1). 1994. 16.95 (*0-531-06856-0*); lib. bdg. 17.99 (*0-531-08706-9*) Orchard Bks Watts.

— Mouse TV. LC 93-49399. (Illus.). 32p. (J). (ps-1). 1998. pap. 6.95 (*0-531-07099-9*) Orchard Bks Watts.

— Newt. LC 95-13286. (I Can Read Bks.). (Illus.). 48p. (J). (gr. 1-3). 1996. lib. bdg. 15.89 (*0-06-024502-6*) HarpC Child Bks.

— Newt. (I Can Read Bks.). (Illus.). 48p. (J). (gr. 1-3). 1997. pap. 3.95 (*0-06-444236-5*, HarpTrophy) HarpC Child Bks.

Novak, Matt. Newt. (I Can Read Bks.). (J). (gr. 1-3). 1997. 8.95 (*0-606-11681-8*, Pub. by Turtleback) Demco.

— No Zombies Allowed. LC 00-37125. (Illus.). 2001. write for info. (*0-689-84130-2*) Atheneum Yung Read.

Novak, Matt. The Pillow War. LC 96-53864. (Illus.). 32p. (J). (ps-1). 1998. pap. 15.95 (*0-531-30048-X*); lib. bdg. 16.99 (*0-531-33048-6*) Orchard Bks Watts.

— The Robobots. LC 98-7374. (Illus.). (J). (ps-2). 1999. 15.95 (*0-7894-2566-1*, D K Ink) DK Pub Inc.

Novak, Maximillian E. Realism, Myth, & History in Defoe's Fiction. LC 82-11141. 199p. reprint ed. pap. 61.70 (*0-7837-2087-4*, 204236300004) Bks Demand.

Novak, Maximillian E., ed. The Works of John Dryden Vol. XIII: Plays: All for Love Oedipus, Troilus & Cressida. 1985. 80.00 (*0-520-02127-4*, Pub. by U CA Pr) Cal Prin Full Svc.

Novak, Maximillian E., intro. The Merry-Thought: or The Glass-Window & Bog House Miscellany, Pts. II, III, & IV. 2nd ed. LC 92-24240. (Augustan Reprints Ser.: Nos. 221-222). 1983. reprint ed. 21.50 (*0-404-70221-X*) AMS Pr.

***Novak, Maximillian E. & Mellor, Anne Kostelanetz, eds.** Passionate Encounters in a Time of Sensibility. LC 99-55925. 280p. 2000. 45.00 (*0-87413-703-9*) U Delaware Pr.

Novak, Maximillian E., jt. auth. see Defoe, Daniel.

Novak, Maximillian E., jt. ed. see Dudley, Edward J.

Novak, Maximillian E., ed. see Southerne, Thomas.

Novak, Maxmilliam E., jt. ed. see Guffey, George R.

Novak, Melinda A. & Petto, Andrew J., eds. Through the Looking Glass: Issues of Psychological Well-Being in Captive Nonhuman Primates. 285p. 1991. text 19.95 (*1-55798-087-X*) Am Psychol.

Novak, Michael. Awakening from Nihilism: Why Truth Matters. (IEA Health & Welfare Unit Ser.: No. 4). 30p. 1995. pap. 8.95 (*0-255-36358-3*, Pub. by Inst Economic Affairs) Coronet Bks.

— Belief & Unbelief: The Context of Self-Knowledge. 3rd ed. 250p. (C). 1994. pap. 24.95 (*1-56000-741-9*) Transaction Pubs.

— Business as a Calling: Work & the Examined Life. LC 96-482. 224p. 1996. 22.00 (*0-684-82748-4*) Free Pr.

— Business as a Calling: Work & the Examined Life. 1996. 22.50 (*0-02-874089-0*) Free Pr.

— Capitalism & Socialism: A Theological Inquiry. 180p. 1988. 38.50 (*0-8447-2153-0*); pap. 19.50 (*0-8447-2154-9*) Am Enterprise.

— The Catholic Ethic & the Spirit of Capitalism. 336p. 1993. 27.95 (*0-02-923235-X*) Free Pr.

— Catholic Social Thought & Liberal Institutions: Freedom with Justice. 2nd ed. 292p. 1989. pap. text 21.95 (*0-88738-763-2*) Transaction Pubs.
— Choosing Presidents: Symbols of Political Leadership. 2nd ed. 402p. (C). 1991. pap. text 24.95 (*1-56000-567-X*) Transaction Pubs.
— Confession of a Catholic. LC 85-20367. 232p. 1986. reprint ed. pap. text 24.00 (*0-8191-5023-1*) U Pr of Amer.
— Cultivating Liberty: Writings on Moral Ecology. Anderson, Brian C., ed. 256p. 1998. pap. 24.95 (*0-8476-8690-6*) Rowman.
— The Experience of Nothingness. LC 97-49872. 160p. 1998. pap. 21.95 (*1-56000-988-8*) Transaction Pubs.
— The Fire of Invention: Civil Society & the Future of the Corporation. LC 97-18755. 192p. 1997. 30.00 (*0-8476-8664-7*, Pub. by Rowman) Natl Bk Netwk.
— The Fire of Invention: Civil Society & the Future of the Corporation. 192p. 1999. pap. 12.95 (*0-8476-8665-5*, Pub. by Rowman) Natl Bk Netwk.
— The Fire of Invention, the Fuel of Interest: On Intellectual Property. LC 97-105657. (Pfizer Lecture Ser.). 51p. 1996. pap. 9.95 (*0-8447-7081-7*) Am Enterprise.
— Free Persons & the Common Good. 175p. 1988. 14.95 (*0-8191-6499-2*) U Pr of Amer.
— The Future of the Corporation. LC 97-105688. (Pfizer Lecture Ser.). 51p. 1996. pap. 9.95 (*0-8447-7080-9*) Am Enterprise.
***Novak, Michael.** God's Country: Taking the Declaration Seriously: The 1999 Francis Boyer Lecture. 42p. 2000. pap. 9.95 (*0-8447-7145-7*, Pub. by Am Enterprise) Pub Resources Inc.
Novak, Michael. The Guns of Lattimer. LC 95-50669. 303p. 1996. reprint ed. pap. text 24.95 (*1-56000-764-8*) Transaction Pubs.
— Human Rights & the New Realism: Strategic Thinking in a New Age. LC 86-7660. (Perspectives on Freedom Ser.). 1986. pap. 10.25 (*0-932088-08-2*) Freedom Hse.
— The Joy of Sports. rev. ed. LC 93-8815. 1993. pap. 17.95 (*1-56833-009-X*) Madison Bks UPA.
— On Corporate Governance. LC 97-174722. (Pfizer Lecture Ser.). 51p. 1997. pap. 9.95 (*0-8447-7082-5*) Am Enterprise.
— On Cultivating Liberty: Reflections on Moral Ecology. Anderson, Brian C., ed. 256p. 1999. 24.95 (*0-8476-9405-4*, Pub. by Rowman) Natl Bk Netwk.
— On Cultivating Liberty: Writings on Moral Ecology. 1999. 63.00 (*0-8476-8689-2*) Rowman.
— The Spirit of Democratic Capitalism. LC 90-48169. 448p. 1991. pap. 16.95 (*0-8191-7823-3*) Madison Bks UPA.
— This Hemisphere of Liberty: A Philosophy of the Americas. 150p. 1990. 24.75 (*0-8447-3735-6*, AEI Pr) Am Enterprise.
— Unmeltable Ethnics: Politics & Culture in American Life. 2nd ed. 512p. (C). 1996. pap. text 21.95 (*1-56000-773-7*) Transaction Pubs.
— Will It Literate? Questions about Liberation Theology. 330p. (C). 1991. reprint ed. pap. 17.95 (*0-8191-8060-2*) Madison Bks UPA.
***Novak, Michael, et al, eds.** A Free Society Reader: Principles for the New Millennium. 224p. 2000. 65.00 (*0-7391-0143-9*); pap. 22.95 (*0-7391-0144-7*) Lxngtn Bks.
Novak, Michael, et al, trs. A World Without Welfare: A Family Research Council Symposium. 165p. (Orig.). 1997. pap. 10.00 (*1-55872-001-4*, BK013) Fam Res Council.
Novak, Michael & Novak, Jana. Tell Me Why: A Father Answers His Daughter's Questions about God. LC 98-214447. 320p. 1998. 24.00 (*0-671-01885-X*, Pocket Books) PB.
— Tell Me Why: A Father Answers His Daughter's Questions about God. 336p. 1999. per. 14.00 (*0-671-01886-8*, Pocket Books) PB.
Novak, Michael, et al. Philanthropy: Four Views. 100p. (Orig.). 1988. 32.95 (*0-912051-20-5*); pap. 21.95 (*0-912051-21-3*) Transaction Pubs.
Novak, Michael, ed. see Berger, Peter L. & Neuhaus, Richard J.
Novak, Michael P. A Story to Tell. LC 90-39896. 72p. 1990. 9.50 (*0-933532-75-X*) BkMk.
Novak, Michael P., jt. ed. see Gillman, Richard.
Novak, Miroslav M., ed. Fractal Reviews in the Natural & Applied Sciences: Proceedings IFIP Working Conference on Fractals in the Natural & Applied Sciences. 3rd ed. 380p. (gr. 13). 1995. ring bd. 175.00 (*0-412-71020-X*, Chap & Hall CRC) CRC Pr.
— Fractals in the Natural & Applied Sciences: Proceedings of the Second IFIP Working Conference on Fractals in the Natural & Applied Sciences, London, U. K., 7-10 September 1993. LC 93-48196. (IFIP Transactions A: Computer Science & Technology Ser.: Vol. A-41). 464p. 1994. pap. 152.50 (*0-444-81628-3*, North Holland) Elsevier.
***Novak, Miroslav M., ed.** Paradigms of Complexity: Fractals & Structures in the Sciences. 400p. 2000. 98.00 (*981-02-4292-1*) World Scientific Pub.
Novak, Nancy. Ultimate Russian: Basic-Intermediate. unabridged ed. 1998. 75.00 incl. audio (*0-517-70004-2*) Liv Lang.
Novak, P. World's Wisdom. 440p. 1996. 8.98 (*0-7858-0718-7*) Bk Sales Inc.
Novak, P., ed. Developments in Hydraulic Engineering, Vol. 3. (Illus.). 332p. 1986. mass mkt. 128.50 (*0-85334-375-6*) Elsevier.
Novak, Pamela K., jt. auth. see Ditchey, Karen M.
Novak, Paul M. A Baker's Dozen of Daily Breads & More. 2nd ed. LC 91-90205. 64p. (Orig.). 1991. pap. 11.95 (*0-9622472-2-7*) Only Connect.
Novak, Peter. Division of Consciousness: The Secret Afterlife of the Human Psyche. 264p. 1997. pap. 14.95 (*1-57174-053-8*) Hampton Roads Pub Co.
— Mental Symbols: A Defence of the Classical Theory of Mind. LC 96-49054. (Studies in Cognitive Systems COGS: Vol. 19). 238p. (C). 1997. text 117.50 (*0-7923-4370-0*) Kluwer Academic.
Novak, Philip. The World's Wisdom: Sacred Texts of the World's Religions. LC 93-43995. 448p. 1995. pap. 15.00 (*0-06-066342-1*, Pub. by T & T Clark) HarpC.
Novak, Philip, ed. see Nietzsche, Friedrich Wilhelm.
Novak, R., et al, eds. Proceedings of the Symposium on Contamination Control & Defect Reduction in Semiconductor Manufacturing II. LC 93-70066. (Proceedings Ser.: Vol. 94-03). 346p. 1994. 43.00 (*1-56677-065-3*) Electrochem Soc.
Novak, R. E., et al, eds. Cleaning Technology in Semiconductor Device Manufacturing V. (Proceedings Ser.: Vol. 97-35). 650p. 1998. 92.00 (*1-56677-188-9*) Electrochem Soc.
Novak, R. E., jt. ed. see Ruzyllo, J.
Novak, R. Elizabeth, tr. see Wilson, Paul, ed.
Novak, Ralph M., Jr., jt. auth. see Locke, William H., Jr.
Novak, Richard. Moorhaven Fair. 16p. (Orig.). 1994. pap. 3.00 (*0-9640168-0-X*) Pirate Writings.
Novak, Richard E., ed. see International Symposium on Cleaning Technology in.
Novak, Robert. At the Splinter House. 1971. 4.00 (*0-685-67928-4*) Windless Orchard.
— Disappearing Like a Snowman. 1973. 4.00 (*0-686-16136-X*) Windless Orchard.
— The Hemingway Poems. 1973. 4.00 (*0-685-72802-1*) Windless Orchard.
— High Afternoon. rev. ed. 1978. 4.00 (*0-685-67943-8*) Windless Orchard.
— King Tut in America. 1988. 4.00 (*0-685-25018-0*) Windless Orchard.
— Machines for Loving. 1973. 4.00 (*0-686-16137-8*) Windless Orchard.
— Shoes. 1975. 4.00 (*0-685-67937-3*) Windless Orchard.
— Sleeping with Sylvia Plath. 1983. 4.00 (*0-686-43216-9*) Windless Orchard.
— Things to Do in Fort Wayne. 1973. 4.00 (*0-685-67934-9*) Windless Orchard.
— The Woman in the Red Skirt. 1971. 4.00 (*0-685-67925-X*) Windless Orchard.
Novak, Robert, ed. Haiku from the Windless Orchard 1970-1978. 1978. 4.00 (*0-685-67940-3*) Windless Orchard.
Novak, Robert D. Completing the Revolution: A Vision for Victory in 2000. LC 99-58482. 256p. 2000. 24.00 (*0-684-82746-8*) Free Pr.
Novak, Sandy, ed. see Tuttle, Tom.
Novak, Slobodan. Gold, Frankincense & Myrrh. Hawkesworth, C., tr. from CRO. (Croatian Literature Ser.: Vol. 4). (Illus.). 244p. (Orig.). 1991. pap. 19.95 (*0-948259-88-4*, Pub. by Forest Bks) Dufour.
Novak, Steven J. The Rights of Youth: American Colleges & Student Revolt, 1798-1815. LC 76-43109. (Illus.). 230p. reprint ed. pap. 71.30 (*0-7837-5939-8*, 204573800007) Bks Demand.
Novak, Susan, ed. see Wilkerson, Ted & Wilkerson, Evelyn.
Novak, Suzanne M. Clip Art for Parish Life. 160p. 1998. pap. 30.00 (*1-56854-086-8*, ARTLIF) Liturgy Tr Pubns.
Novak, Thomas, ed. see Conference on the Use of Computers in the Coal Ind.
Novak, V. The Alternative Mathematical Model of Linguistic Semantics & Pragmatics. (IFSR International Series on Systems Science: Vol. 8). (Illus.). 220p. (C). 1992. 75.00 (*0-306-44269-8*, Plenum Trade) Perseus Pubng.
Novak, Vilem, et al, eds. Fuzzy Approach to Reasoning & Decision Making. LC 91-24675. (Theory & Decision Library: Vol. 8). 220p. 1992. text 158.50 (*0-7923-1358-5*) Kluwer Academic.
Novak, W. David. Intermediate Algebra. 2nd ed. 668p. (C). 1987. pap. text 49.56 (*0-669-12227-0*); pap. text, student ed. 20.36 (*0-669-12229-7*); teacher ed. 2.66 (*0-669-12228-9*); 2.76 (*0-669-12230-0*) HM Trade Div.
— Introductory Algebra. 2nd ed. 586p. (C). 1987. pap. text 49.56 (*0-669-12231-9*); pap. text, student ed. 20.36 (*0-669-12233-5*); teacher ed. 2.66 (*0-669-12232-7*); 2.76 (*0-669-12234-3*) HM Trade Div.
Novak, Walt. The Haole Substitute. LC 93-41290. 160p. (Orig.). 1994. pap. 12.95 (*1-879384-19-1*) Cypress Hse.
Novak, William & Waldoks, Moshe. The Big Book of Jewish Humor. LC 81-47234. (Illus.). 336p. 1990. pap. 21.00 (*0-06-090917-X*, CN 917, Perennial) HarperTrade.
Novak, William, jt. auth. see Barrows, Sydney B.
Novak, William, jt. auth. see Iacocca, Lee.
Novak, William, jt. auth. see Johnson, Earvin "Magic".
Novak, William, jt. auth. see Reagan, Nancy.
Novak, William, jt. auth. see Sylvia, Claire.
Novak, William J. The People's Welfare: Law & Regulation in Nineteenth-Century America. 416p. (C). 1996. pap. text 19.95 (*0-8078-4611-2*); lib. bdg. 59.95 (*0-8078-2292-2*) U of NC Pr.
Novak, William J., jt. auth. see McPartland, Joseph F.
Novakovich, Josip. Apricots from Chernobyl. LC 93-35921. 224p. (Orig.). 1995. pap. 12.95 (*1-55597-212-8*) Graywolf.
— Fiction Writer's Workshop. 256p. 1995. 17.99 (*1-884910-03-3*, Story Press) F & W Pubns Inc.
— Fiction Writer's Workshop. 256p. 1998. pap. 15.99 (*1-884910-39-4*, Story Press) F & W Pubns Inc.
— Salvation & Other Disasters. LC 97-80084. 216p. 1998. pap. 12.95 (*1-55597-271-3*) Graywolf.
***Novakovich, Josip.** Stories in the Stepmother Tongue. 256p. 2000. pap. 17.00 (*1-893996-04-2*) White Pine.
Novakovich, Josip. Writing Fiction Step by Step. LC 98-7333. 288p. 1998. pap. 17.99 (*1-884910-35-1*, Story Press) F & W Pubns Inc.
— Yolk. LC 95-77951. 224p. (Orig.). 1995. pap. 12.95 (*1-55597-229-2*) Graywolf.
Novakshonoff, Varlaam, tr. see Khrapovitsky, Antony.
Novakshonoff, Varlaarm, tr. God's Fools. 91p. Date not set. pap. 6.50 (*1-879038-48-X*, 9017) Synaxis Pr.
— Kievcaves-Paterikon. 68p. Date not set. pap. 5.00 (*1-879038-47-1*, 9016) Synaxis Pr.
Novalis. Henry Von Ofterdingen: A Novel. Hilty, Palmer, tr. from GER. 169p. (C). 1990. reprint ed. pap. text 8.95 (*0-88133-574-6*) Waveland Pr.
— Hymns to the Night. 3rd rev. ed. LC 87-34706. 55p. 1988. pap. 5.95 (*0-914232-90-8*) McPherson & Co.
Novalis, George. The Binding Spell. 224p. (Orig.). 1990. 17.95 (*0-9621858-2-5*); pap. 9.95 (*0-9621858-3-3*) Tintagel Assocs.
Novalis, Peter N., et al. Clinical Manual of Supportive Psychotherapy. 362p. 1993. spiral bd. 48.50 (*0-88048-403-9*, 8403) Am Psychiatric.
Novalis Staff, jt. auth. see Wood Lake Books Staff.
Novalis, Susann. Access 97 Macro & VBA Handbook. LC 96-71017. 1104p. 1997. pap. text 54.99 incl. disk (*0-7821-1977-8*) Sybex.
— Access 2000 VBA Handbook. 2nd ed. 880p. 1999. 49.99 (*0-7821-2324-4*) Sybex.
***Novara, Joe.** From My Side of the Fence: From a Horsehusbands Point of View. LC 00-101726. (Illus.). 96p. 2000. pap. 9.95 (*0-9671978-8-0*) Syncopated Pr.
Novaresio, Paolo. The Explorers: From the Ancient World to the Present. (Illus.). 312p. 1986. 60.00 (*1-55670-495-X*) Stewart Tabori & Chang.
Novarina, Valere. The Theater of the Ears. Weiss, Allen S., tr. from FRE. (Sun & Moon Classics Ser.: No. 85). 200p. 1996. pap. 13.95 (*1-55713-251-8*) Sun & Moon CA.
***Novartis staff.** Gramacidin & Related Ion Channel-Forming Peptides - No. 225. 284p. 1999. 125.00 (*0-471-98846-4*) Wiley.
— Novartis Foundation Symposium. LC 98-46843. 296p. 1999. 128.00 (*0-471-98259-8*) Wiley.
Novartis staff. Novartis Foundation Symposium. LC 99-204533. 292p. (C). 1999. 128.00 (*0-471-98540-6*) Wiley.
— Novartis Foundation Symposium. LC 99-32328. 290p. 1999. 125.00 (*0-471-98815-4*) Wiley.
— Novartis Foundation Symposium. 528p. 2000. text 125.00 (*0-471-97978-3*) Wiley.
— Novartis Foundation Symposium 227. LC 99-57033. 280p. 2000. 125.00 (*0-471-99918-0*) Wiley.
— Novartis Foundation Symposium 229. 300p. 2000. text 125.00 (*0-471-62744-5*) Wiley.
***Novartis staff.** Transport & Trafficking in the Malaria-Infected Erthrocyte. LC 99-39806. (Novartis Foundation Symposium Ser.). 304p. 1999. 125.00 (*0-471-99893-1*) Wiley.
***Novartis staff & Hall, Brian.** Homology. 266p. 1999. 128.00 (*0-471-98493-0*) Wiley.
Novas Calvo, Lino, tr. see Faulkner, William.
Novas, Himilce. La Buena Mesa: La Autentica Cocina Latinoamerica en los Estados Unidos. (SPA.). 400p. 1997. 27.50 (*0-679-44803-9*) Knopf.
— Everything You Need to Know about Latino History. LC 98-4354. 1998. pap. 13.95 (*0-452-27991-7*, Plume) Dutton Plume.
— The Hispanic 100: A Ranking of the Latino Men & Women Who Have Most Influenced American Thought & Culture. (Illus.). 556p. Date not set. 24.95 (*0-8065-1651-8*, Citadel Pr) Carol Pub Group.
— Mangos, Bananas & Coconuts: A Cuban Love Story. LC 95-37661. 168p. 1996. 9.95 (*1-55885-092-9*) Arte Publico.
— Passport Spain: Your Pocket Guide to Spanish Business, Customs & Etiquette. Szerlip, Barbara, ed. LC 96-52741. (Passport to the World Ser.). (Illus.). 96p. (Orig.). 1997. pap. 6.95 (*1-885073-35-6*) Wrld Trade Pr.
Novas, Himilce & Silva, Rosemary. Latin American Cooking Across the U. S. A. LC 97-74754. 352p. 1997. 27.50 (*0-679-44408-4*) Knopf.
— Remembering Selena: A Tribute in Pictures & Words. LC 95-38834.Tr. of Recordando a Selena: Un Tributo en Palabras y Fotos. (ENG & SPA., Illus.). 128p. 1995. pap. 9.95 (*0-312-14160-2*, St Martin Griffin) St Martin.
Novas, Himilce, jt. auth. see Cao, Lan.
Novas, Maria J. San Juan De, see De La Soledad, Rosalia & San Juan De Novas, Maria J.
Novaskshonoff, Varlaarm. Creation of the World: For Young People. (Illus.). 27p. (YA). (gr. 7-12). Date not set. pap. 3.00 (*1-879038-44-7*, 9012) Synaxis Pr.
Novatny, Fritz & Dobai, Johannes. Gustav Klimt: Catalogue Raisonne of the Paintings. (GER., Illus.). 424p. 1975. 600.00 (*1-55660-052-6*) A Wofsy Fine Arts.
Novatt, Jedd, frwd. Robert DeNiro, Sr. Paintings. (Illus.). 32p. 1997. pap. write for info. (*1-58821-029-4*) Salander OReilly.
***Novbak, Vilbem, et al.** Mathematical Principles of Fuzzy Logic. LC 99-37210. (International Series in Engineering & Computer Science). 1999. write for info. (*0-7923-8595-0*) Kluwer Academic.
Nove, A. & McKay, S. War Pensions Agency Customer Satisfaction Survey, 1994. (DSS Research Report Ser.). 1995. (*0-11-762358-X*) Bernan Associates.
Nove, Alec. The Economics of Feasible Socialism Revisited. 2nd rev. ed. 272p. (C). 1992. pap. 29.99 (*0-04-446015-5*, A8227) Routledge.
— Glasnost' in Action: Cultural Renaissance in Russia. 256p. (C). (gr. 13). 1989. text 74.95 (*0-04-445340-X*) Routledge.
— Marxism & "Really Existing Socialism" (Fundamentals of Pure & Applied Economics Ser.: Vol. 8). viii, 56p. 1986. pap. text 35.00 (*3-7186-0330-6*) Gordon & Breach.
— Political Economy & Soviet Socialism. pap. text 14.95 (*0-04-335037-2*) Routledge.
— Socialism, Economics & Development. 280p. (C). 1986. text 37.95 (*0-04-335054-2*); pap. text 16.95 (*0-04-335055-0*) Routledge.
— The Soviet Economic System. 3rd ed. 420p. (C). 1986. pap. text 25.00 (*0-04-497025-0*) Routledge.
— Stalinism & After: The Road to Gorbachev. 3rd ed. LC 92-36715. 224p. (C). 1988. pap. 20.99 (*0-04-445112-1*) Routledge.
— Stalinism & After: The Road to Gorbachev. 3rd ed. LC 92-36715. 1992. 19.95 (*0-415-09445-3*) Routledge.
Nove, Alec & Thatcher, Ian, eds. Markets & Socialism. (International Library of Critical Writings in Economics: Vol. 39). 584p. 1994. 240.00 (*1-85278-842-9*) E Elgar.
Nove, Alec & Thatcher, Ian D. Alec Nove on Communist & Post-Communist Countries: Previously Unpublished Writings. LC 98-17086. 288p. 1998. pap. 90.00 (*1-85898-862-4*) E Elgar.
— Alec Nove on Economic Theory: Previously Unpublished Writings. LC 98-17086. 224p. 1998. 85.00 (*1-85898-829-2*) E Elgar.
Noveck, Simon, ed. Creators of Jewish Experience in the Modern World. (Jewish History Ser.: Vol. II). 1985. pap. 12.00 (*0-910250-05-7*) Bnai Brith Intl.
Novel Units, Inc. Staff. Belle Prater's Boy. 40p. 1998. 9.95 (*1-58130-557-5*, NU5575) Novel Units.
Novell. Advance Skills, Quattro Pro, for Windows. 1997. pap. 30.00 (*0-538-65467-8*) Thomson Learn.
Novell Staff. WordPerfect 3.1-3.5 Mac: Official Coursework. (DF - Computer Applications Ser.). 1995. mass mkt. 29.95 (*0-538-66321-9*) S-W Pub.
Novell Staff, jt. auth. see Hughes, Jeffrey F.
Novelli, Barbara A., et al. Bats Incredible. (J). (gr. 2-4). 1993. 16.95 (*1-881431-41-X*, 1125) AIMS Educ Fnd.
— Cycles of Knowing & Growing. Cordel, Betty, ed. (Illus.). 155p. (J). (gr. 1-3). 1998. pap., teacher ed., wbk. ed. 16.95 (*1-881431-65-7*, 1108) AIMS Educ Fnd.
Novelli, G. P., ed. Oxygen-Free Radicals in Shock. (Illus.). xii, 248p. 1986. 139.25 (*3-8055-4233-X*) S Karger.
Novelli, Jean Christophe & Keating, Sheila. Your Place or Mine? LC 99-462695. (Illus.). 160p. 1999. 35.00 (*0-609-60436-8*) Random Hse Value.
***Novelli, Joan.** Birthdays: Dozens of Instant & Irresistible Ideas & Activities from Teachers Across the Country. (Fresh & Fun Ser.). (Illus.). 32p. 2000. pap. 8.95 (*0-439-05185-1*) Scholastic Inc.
— Fresh & Fun - Valentine's Day: Dozens of Instant & Irresistable Ideas & Activities from Tea. (Fresh & Fun Ser.). (Illus.). 32p. (J). (gr. k-2). 2000. pap. text 12.99 (*0-439-05011-1*) Scholastic Inc.
— Hands-On Homework Pages. (Illus.). 80p. (J). 2000. pap. 11.95 (*0-439-04385-9*) Scholastic Inc.
— Instant Send-Home Letters: 50 Reproducible Letters - Filled with Tips, Strategies & Easy Activities. (Illus.). 80p. 2000. pap. 11.95 (*0-439-10618-4*) Scholastic Inc.
Novelli, Joan. Interactive Bulletin Boards: September to June. 1998. pap. 10.95 (*0-590-18739-2*) Scholastic Inc.
***Novelli, Joan.** Irresistible ABC's: 50 Easy, Fun, Multi-Sensory Activities to Help All Kids Explore & Learn. (Illus.). 48p. 2000. pap. text 8.95 (*0-590-04930-5*) Scholastic Inc.
— Irresistible 1, 2, 3s: 50 Easy, Fun, Multi-Sensory Activities to Help All Kids Explore & Learn. (Illus.). 48p. (J). 2000. pap. 8.95 (*0-439-04095-7*) Scholastic Inc.
Novelli, Joan. Phonics Make-&-Take Manipulatives: Dozens of Reproducible Patterns & Activities That Make Le, 1 vol. 64p. 1999. pap. 9.95 (*0-590-86716-4*) Scholastic Inc.
— Using Caldecotts Across the Curriculum: Reading & Writing Mini-Lessons, Math & Science Spin-Offs, Unique Art Activities, & More! 112p. (J). (gr. k-3). 1998. pap. 12.95 (*0-590-11033-0*) Scholastic Inc.
***Novelli, Joan & Meagher, Judy.** Interactive Bulletin Boards: Math. 80p. 1998. mass mkt. 10.95 (*0-590-21965-0*) Scholastic Inc.
Novelli, L., jt. ed. see Mattavelli, L.
Novellinc. Printing In Integrated Netware Environment. (DF - Computer Applications Ser.). (C). 1998. pap. 80.95 (*0-538-68263-9*) S-W Pub.
Novelline, Robert A. & Squire, Lucy F. Living Anatomy: A Working Atlas Using Computed Tomography, Magnetic Resonance & Angiography Images. LC 86-80893. (Illus.). 117p. (Orig.). 1986. pap. text 39.95 (*0-932883-03-6*) Hanley & Belfus.
— Squire's Fundamentals of Radiology. 5th ed. LC 96-36574. (Illus.). 640p. 1997. 72.50 (*0-674-83339-2*) HUP.
Novelline, Robert A., jt. auth. see Squire.
Novelline, Robert A., jt. auth. see Squire, Lucy F.
Novellino, Peter. Advanced Electronic Tune Up. 1984. student ed. 7.00 (*0-8064-0179-6*, 464) Bergwall.
— The Alternator Explained. LC 80-730752. 1980. student ed. 7.00 (*0-8064-0143-5*, 439) Bergwall.
— The Automatic Transmission. LC 77-731115. 1978. student ed. 7.00 (*0-8064-0115-X*, 425) Bergwall.
— The Automotive Air Conditioner. LC 81-730758. 1981. student ed. 7.00 (*0-8064-0149-4*, 442) Bergwall.
— Automotive Clutch Assembly. LC 76-731515. 1976. student ed. 7.00 (*0-8064-0089-7*, 412) Bergwall.
— Automotive Pollution Control. LC 81-730757. (C). 1982. student ed. 7.00 (*0-8064-0157-5*, 447) Bergwall.
— Basic Automotive Jobs Explained. 1980. student ed. 7.00 (*0-8064-0159-1*, 448) Bergwall.
— Electronic Ignition Tune Up. 1983. student ed. 6.00 (*0-8064-0175-3*, 462) Bergwall.
— Electronic Wheel Balancing. 1985. student ed. 7.00 (*0-8064-0161-3*, 449) Bergwall.

N

An Asterisk (*) at the beginning of an entry indicates that the title is appearing for the first time.

— Front Wheel Drive: Transaxle Overhaul. 1984. wbk. ed. 7.00 (*0-8064-0177-X*, 463) Bergwall.
— How to Balance Wheels. LC 76-732022. 1977. student ed. 7.00 (*0-8064-0099-4*, 417) Bergwall.
— How to Overhaul a Carburetor. LC 76-732026. 1977. student ed. 7.00 (*0-8064-0107-9*, 421) Bergwall.
— How to Overhaul a 400 Turbo Hydramatic Transmission. LC 80-730404. 1979. student ed. 7.00 (*0-8064-0133-8*, 434) Bergwall.
— How to Overhaul an Engine. LC 75-735762. 1975. student ed. 7.00 (*0-8064-0085-4*, 410) Bergwall.
— How to Use a Valve & Valve Seat Refacer. LC 76-732029. 1977. student ed. 7.00 (*0-8064-0103-6*, 419) Bergwall.
— How to Use Auto Precision Tools. LC 76-732030. 1977. student ed. 7.00 (*0-8064-0105-2*, 420) Bergwall.
— The Ignition System Explained. LC 73-733984. 1973. student ed. 7.00 (*0-8064-0067-6*, 401) Bergwall.
— Light Beam Alignment. LC 81-730690. 1982. student ed. 7.00 (*0-8064-0155-9*, 446) Bergwall.
— The Operation of the Fuel System. LC 74-734388. 1974. student ed. 7.00 (*0-8064-0079-X*, 407) Bergwall.
— The Problems of the Fuel System. LC 74-734385. 1974. student ed. 7.00 (*0-8064-0081-1*, 408) Bergwall.
— Problems of the Internal Combustion Engine. LC 75-733226. 1975. student ed. 7.00 (*0-8064-0083-8*, 409) Bergwall.
— Problems of the 400 Turbo Hydramatic Transmission Explained. LC 80-730755. 1981. student ed. 7.00 (*0-8064-0139-7*, 437) Bergwall.
— Troubleshooting Electrical Components. (Orig.). 1983. student ed. 7.00 (*0-8064-0173-7*, 461) Bergwall.

Novello, Antonia C. & Soto-Torres, Lydia E., eds. Surgeon General's National Workshop: Implementation Strategies for Improving Hispanic-Latino Health. (Illus.). 36p. (Orig.). (C). 1994. pap. text 20.00 (*0-7881-1518-9*) DIANE Pub.

Novello, David, jt. auth. see Martineau, Robert J.

Novello, Don. Citizen Lazlo! The Lazlo Letters, Vol. 2. LC 92-5483. (Illus.). 160p. 1992. pap. 7.95 (*1-56305-182-6*, 3182) Workman Pub.
— The Lazlo Letters. LC 92-7832. (Illus.). 160p. 1992. pap. 7.95 (*1-56305-285-7*, 3285) Workman Pub.

***Novello, John.** The Contemporary Keyboardist. rev. expanded ed. 576p. 2000. otabind 49.95 (*0-634-01091-3*) H Leonard.
— The Contemporary Keyboardist: Stylistic Etudes. 128p. 2000. per. 26.95 incl. audio compact disk (*0-634-01092-1*) H Leonard.

Novello, John A. The Contemporary Keyboardist. (Illus.). 551p. (Orig.). 1985. pap. 50.00 (*0-9614966-0-6*) Source Prods.

***Novello, Joseph R.** The Myth of More: And Other Lifetraps That Sabotage the Happiness You Deserve. 2001. pap. 16.95 (*0-8091-3941-3*) Paulist Pr.

Novello, Joseph R. What to Do until the Grownup Arrives: The Art & Science of Raising Teenagers. LC 91-18659. (Illus.). 360p. 1993. 24.50 (*0-88937-040-0*) Hogrefe & Huber Pubs.

Novello, Joseph R., ed. The Short Course in Adolescent Psychiatry. LC 93-74373. 288p. 1994. pap. 45.00 (*1-56821-195-3*) Aronson.

Novello, M., ed. Cosmology & Gravitation: Proceedings of the Fifth Brazilian School of Cosmology & Gravitation, Rio de Janeiro, Brazil 20-31 July 1987. 624p. 1988. text 98.00 (*9971-5-0430-8*) World Scientific Pub.
— Relativity & Gravitation (SILARG 6) Proceedings of the Sixth Latin-American Symposium on Relativity & Gravity. 380p. (C). 1988. text 121.00 (*9971-5-0436-7*) World Scientific Pub.

Novello, M., et al. Cosmology & Gravitation: Proceedings of the 6th Brazilian Sch 1993. text 103.00 (*981-02-0123-0*) World Scientific Pub.

Novello, Mary K. For All the Wrong Reasons: The Story Behind Government Schools. LC 98-8115. 170p. 1998. 49.00 (*0-7618-1189-3*); pap. 29.00 (*0-7618-1190-7*) U Pr of Amer.

Novello, Raymond. Web Storefront Construction Kit. 456p. 1999. 39.99 (*0-7897-1265-2*) Que.

Novelly, Maria C. Theatre Games for Young Performers: Improvisations & Exercises for Developing Acting Skills. Pijanowski, Kathy & Zapel, Arthur L., eds. LC 85-60572. (Illus.). 160p. (J). (gr. 6-10). 1985. pap. 16.95 (*0-916260-31-3*, B188) Meriwether Pub.

November, Harry J. Reflections of a Romantic: Visions in Verse. 2nd ed. 1998. pap. write for info. (*1-57553-950-0*) Watermrk Pr.

Novembre, A. E., ed. Advances in Resist Technology & Processing IX. 1992. 86.00 (*0-8194-0827-1*, 1672) SPIE.

Nover, Elizabeth Z. The Hebrew Primer: Reading Workbook. (Hebrew Primer Ser.). 60p. (J). (gr. 4-7). 1995. pap. 3.95 (*0-87441-433-4*) Behrman.
— My Land of Israel. (Illus.). 32p. (Orig.). (J). (gr. k-2). 1987. pap. 4.95 (*0-87441-447-4*) Behrman.

Nover, Lutz. Heat Shock Response. (Illus.). 866p. 1991. lib. bdg. 259.00 (*0-8493-4912-5*, QP552) CRC Pr.
— Plant Promoters & Transcription Factors. LC 93-29266. (Results & Problems in Cell Differentiation Ser.: Vol. 20). 1994. 198.00 (*0-387-57288-0*) Spr-Verlag.

Nover, Lutz, et al, eds. Heat Shock & Other Stress Responses in Plants. (Results & Problems in Cell Differentiation Ser.: Vol. 16). (Illus.). 168p. 1990. 71.95 (*0-387-51837-1*) Spr-Verlag.

***Nover, Peter, ed.** The Great Good Place? A Collection of Essays on American & British College Mystery Novels. xiii, 224p. 1999. pap. 42.95 (*3-631-34619-0*) P Lang Pubng.
— The Great Good Place? A Collection of Essays on American & British College Mystery Novels. LC PS374.D4G74 1999. xiii, 224p. (C). 1999. pap. text 42.95 (*0-8204-4324-7*) P Lang Pubng.

Noverr, Douglas A., ed. Film Studies: Introductory Courses Interdisciplinary & Cultural Courses, Courses about Directors & Film & Literature: Selected Course Outlines & Reading Lists. (Selected Course Outlines & Reading Lists from American Colleges & Universities Ser.). 300p. (Orig.). (C). 1989. pap. text 16.95 (*1-55876-001-6*) Wiener Pubs Inc.

Noverr, Douglas A. & Ziewacz, Lawrence E. The Games They Played: Sports in American History, 1865-1980. LC 83-5647. (Illus.). 432p. 1983. pap. text 30.95 (*0-88229-819-4*) Burnham Inc.

Noverr, Douglas A., jt. ed. see Lunde, Erik S.

Noverr, Douglas A., ed. see Whitman, Walt.

Noverre, Jean-Georges. Lettres sur la Danse, et sur les Ballets. fac. ed. (Monuments of Music & Music Literature in Facsimile, II Ser.: Vol. 47). (Illus.). 1967. lib. bdg. 35.00 (*0-8450-2247-4*) Broude.
— The Works of Monsieur Noverre, Translated from the French, 3 vols., Set. LC 76-43930. reprint ed. 185.00 (*0-404-60110-3*) AMS Pr.

Novey. Alternative Medicine. 1999. 39.95 (*0-323-00755-4*) Mosby Inc.

Novey, Don. Rapid Access Guide to the Physical Examination. 2nd ed. LC 98-3979. 1998. spiral bd. 29.95 (*0-323-00128-9*) Mosby Inc.

Novey, Donald W., et al. The Guide to Heart Sounds: Normal & Abnormal. 104p. 1988. audio 62.95 (*0-8493-0153-X*, RC683) CRC Pr.

Novey, Jack. The Cold Blue Sky: A B-17 Gunner in World War Two. (Illus.). 208p. 1997. 24.95 (*1-57427-066-4*) Howell Pr VA.

Novey, Samuel. The Second Look: The Reconstruction of Personal History in Psychiatry & Psychoanalysis. Chicago Institute for Psychoanalysis Staff, ed. LC 85-10884. (Classics in Psychoanalysis Monograph: No. 3). xiv, 162p. 1986. reprint ed. 30.00 (*0-8236-6022-2*, 06022) Intl Univs Pr.

Novey, Theodore B. An Advanced Reference Guide to the Transactional Analysis Literature. 80p. 1987. pap. 12.00 (*0-9617020-1-X*) TA Assocs.

Novice, Fred M., et al. Handbook of Genetic Skin Disorders. LC 93-25389. (Illus.). 704p. 1994. text 115.00 (*0-7216-3803-1*, W B Saunders Co) Harcrt Hlth Sci Grp.

Novich, Max M. & Taylor, Buddy. Training & Conditioning of Athletes. 2nd ed. LC 82-17988. (Illus.). 335p. reprint ed. pap. 103.90 (*0-8357-7651-4*, 205697700096) Bks Demand.

Novichkov, N. N. & Pimenov, G. S. English - Russian Military Dictionary of Radioelectronic, Laser & Infrared Engineering. (ENG & RUS.). 639p. (C). 1984. 29.95 (*0-8285-5326-2*) Firebird NY.

Novichkov, N. N., et al. English - Russian Dictionary of Antimissile & Antisatellite Defense. (ENG & RUS.). 592p. (C). 1989. 31.95 (*0-8285-5316-5*) Firebird NY.

Novichkov, N. N., jt. auth. see Murashkevich, A. M.

Novichkov, N. N., jt. auth. see Pimenoz.

Novick. Molecular Biology of the Staphylococci. 639p. 1990. 220.00 (*0-471-18784-4*) Wiley.

Novick. Plasmids. Date not set. 1.20 (*0-7167-9273-7*) W H Freeman.
— Renal Vascular Disease. 1995. text 107.00 (*0-7020-1814-7*, W B Saunders Co) Harcrt Hlth Sci Grp.

***Novick, et al.** Public Health Administration. 2000. 79.00 (*0-8342-1751-1*) Aspen Pub.

Novick, Adam. Harmonics for Electric Bass. (Illus.). 80p. (Orig.). 1985. pap. 16.95 (*0-8256-9943-6*, AM33473) Music Sales.

Novick, Amy R., jt. contrib. by see Plotkin, Norman C.

Novick, Amy R., jt. ed. see Goldblum, Jane.

Novick, Amy R., jt. ed. see Tapia-Ruano, Carlina.

Novick, Andrew, jt. ed. see Bukowski, Ronald M.

Novick, Andrew, jt. ed. see Resnick, Martin I.

Novick, Andrew C., et al. Stewart's Operative Urology, 2 vols., Set. 2nd ed. (Illus.). 908p. 1989 225.00 (*0-683-06589-0*) Lppncott W & W.

Novick, Barbara Z. & Arnold, Maureen M. Why Is My Child Having Trouble at School? A Parent's Guide to Learning Disabilities. LC 95-13772. 272p. 1995. pap. 13.95 (*0-87477-817-4*, Tarcher Putnam) Putnam Pub Group.

Novick, David, ed. Program Budgeting: Program Analysis & the Federal Budget. 2nd ed. LC 68-1604. (Rand Corporation Research Studies). (Illus.). 406p. 1967. 38.50 (*0-674-71350-8*) HUP.

Novick, David, et al. Wartime Production Controls. LC 76-5795. (FDR & the Era of the New Deal Ser.). 1976. reprint ed. lib. bdg. 49.50 (*0-306-70818-3*) Da Capo.

Novick, Harold J. Selling Through Independent Reps. 2nd ed. LC 93-20716. 372p. 1993. 69.95 (*0-8144-5146-2*) AMACOM.

***Novick, Harold J.** Selling Through Independent Reps. 3rd ed. LC 99-57938. (Illus.). 352p. 1999. 75.00 (*0-8144-0522-3*) AMACOM.

Novick, Jack & Kelly, Kerry K. Fearful Symmetry: The Development & Treatment of Sadomasochism. LC 95-31774. 432p. 1995. 45.00 (*1-56821-652-1*) Aronson.

Novick, Jeremy. In a League of Their Own: The Maverick Managers. (Illus.). 190p. 1996. 34.95 (*1-85158-780-2*, Pub. by Mainstream Pubng) Trafalgar.

Novick, Julius, ed. see Shaw, George Bernard.

Novick, Laurie B., jt. auth. see Andrews, Laurie J.

Novick, Lee & Cantley, Charles. Bull Shoals Lake: An Archeological Survey. (Illus.). 94p. 1979. pap. 2.00 (*1-56349-028-5*, RR16) AR Archaeol.

Novick, Lloyd F., et al. Public Health Leaders Tell Their Stories. LC 97-15629. 168p. 1997. 35.00 (*0-8342-0961-6*) Aspen Pub.

Novick, Michael. White Lies, White Power: The Fight Against White Supremacy & Reactionary Violence. Bates, Greg, ed. 330p. (C). 1995. lib. bdg. 29.95 (*1-56751-051-5*) Common Courage.
— White Lies, White Power: The Fight Against White Supremacy & Reactionary Violence. Bates, Greg, ed. 330p. (C). 1995. pap. 16.95 (*1-56751-050-7*) Common Courage.

Novick, Nelson L. You Can Do Something about Your Allergies. 256p. 1995. mass mkt. 5.99 (*0-553-57267-9*) Bantam.
— You Can Look Younger at Any Age. LC 95-24962. 1995. 14.95 (*0-8050-3970-8*) H Holt & Co.
— You Can Look Younger at Any Age. LC 95-24962. (J). 1995. 15.98 (*0-8050-3871-X*) H Holt & Co.
— You Can Look Younger at Any Age: A Leading Dermatologist's Guide. 89p. 1995. pap. 14.95 (*0-8050-3971-6*, Owl) H Holt & Co.

Novick, Patricia M., jt. auth. see Brawdy, Brian P.

Novick, Peter. The Holocaust in American Life. LC 99-20074. 320p. 1999. 27.00 (*0-395-84009-0*) HM.

***Novick, Peter.** The Holocaust in American Life. 384p. 2000. pap. 15.00 (*0-618-08232-8*, Mariner Bks) HM.

Novick, Peter. That Noble Dream: The Objectivity Question & the American Historical Profession. (Ideas in Context Ser.). 670p. 1988. text 85.00 (*0-521-34328-3*); pap. text 19.95 (*0-521-35745-4*) Cambridge U Pr.

Novick, Rebecca. Fundamentals of Tibetan Buddhism. LC 98-49025. 216p. 1999. pap. 12.95 (*0-89594-953-9*) Crossing Pr.

Novick, Richard, ed. Molecular Biology of the Staphylococci. 639p. 1991. lib. bdg. 160.00 (*1-56081-032-7*, Wiley-VCH) Wiley.

Novick, Richard, jt. ed. see Levy, Stuart B.

Novick, Richard J., jt. auth. see Lewis, James F.

Novick, Robert, ed. Thirty Years of Parity Nonconservation: A Symposium Honoring T. D. Lee. 220p. 1987. 54.00 (*0-8176-3375-8*) Birkhauser.

Novick, Robert & Novick, Varda U. Impulse Survey of Focus Facilities 1995. 250p. 1995. pap. 65.00 (*1-884301-02-9*) Impulse Res.

Novick, Robert & Novick, Varda U., eds. Impulse Survey of Focus Facilities, 1999. 1999. pap. 80.00 (*1-884301-06-1*) Impulse Res.
— Impulse Survey of Focus Facilities, 1997. 290p. 1997. pap. 75.00 (*1-884301-04-5*) Impulse Res.
— Impulse Survey of Focus Facilities, 1998. 290p. 1998. pap. 80.00 (*1-884301-05-3*) Impulse Res.

***Novick, Robert & Novick, Varda Ullman, eds.** Impulse Survey of Focus Facilities, 2000. 310p. 2000. pap. 80.00 (*1-884301-07-X*) Impulse Res.

Novick, Robert & Novick, Verda U., eds. Impulse Survey of Focus Facilities 1992. 129p. 1992. pap. 35.00 (*1-884301-00-2*) Impulse Res.
— Impulse Survey of Focus Facilities 1993. 232p. 1993. pap. 50.00 (*1-884301-01-0*) Impulse Res.

Novick, Sheldon M. The Life of Henry James. write for info. (*0-679-45023-8*) Fodors Travel.

Novick, Sheldon M., ed. see Holmes, Oliver W.

Novick, Shimshon, jt. auth. see Lunetta, Vincent N.

Novick, Varda U., jt. auth. see Novick, Robert.

Novick, Varda U., jt. ed. see Novick, Robert.

Novick, Varda Ullman, jt. ed. see Novick, Robert.

Novick, Verda U., jt. ed. see Novick, Robert.

Novick, Verda U., jt. ed. see Novik, Robert.

Novick, William J., Jr., contrib. by. Development of In Vitro Susceptibility Testing Criteria & Quality Control Parameters: Approved Guideline (1994), Vol. 10. 1994. 95.00 (*1-56238-101-6*, M23-A) NCCLS.

Novick, William M., jt. auth. see Kerrigan, Joseph J.

Noviello. Statistics. pap. text 29.00 (*0-471-37821-6*) Wiley.

Noviello. Statistics. (C). 1998. pap. text 28.00 (*0-471-32097-8*) Wiley.

Novik, Mary & Creeley, Robert, frwds. Robert Creeley: An Inventory, 1945-1970. LC 72-96943. (Serif Series: Bibliographies & Checklists: No. 28). 228p. 1973. reprint ed. pap. 70.70 (*0-8357-5578-9*, 203520500093) Bks Demand.

Novik, Robert & Novick, Verda U., eds. Impulse Survey to Focus Facilities 1996. 260p. 1996. pap. 70.00 (*1-884301-03-7*) Impulse Res.

Novik, Ylda, ed. Tchaikovsky/Album for the Young, Opus 39. (Masterwork Edition Ser.). 64p. 1976. pap. 9.50 (*0-7390-0363-1*, 485) Alfred Pub.

Novikov & Krichever, eds. Reviews in Mathematics & Mathematical Physics Vol. 10, No.1: Multidimensional Monge Ampere Equation, Vol. 10. (Reviews in Mathematics & Mathematical Physics Ser.). 102p. 1995. pap. text 39.00 (*3-7186-5831-3*) Gordon & Breach.

Novikov, A. A. & Shiryaev, A. N., eds. Statistics & Control of Random Processes. (Proceedings of the Steklov Institute of Mathematics Ser.: Vol. 202). 242p. 1995. 189.00 (*0-8218-0411-1*, STEKLO/202C) Am Math.

Novikov, Alexei V., ed. The Geometric Alphabet of Cultural Landscapes. (Geograffity Ser.: Vol. 1, No. 1). (Illus.). 88p. 1993. pap. 16.95 (*0-939923-29-7*) M & W Pub Co.

Novikov, B. K., et al. Nonlinear Underwater Acoustics. LC 87-70336.Tr. of Russian. 272p. 1987. pap. 39.00 (*0-88318-522-9*) Acoustical Soc Am.

Novikov, Denis G. Okno V Ianvare: Stikhi, 1984-1994. LC 95-1982. (RUS.). 102p. 1995. pap. 8.50 (*1-55779-082-5*) Hermitage Pubs.

Novikov, Euvgeny & Bascio, Patrick. Gorbachev & the Collapse of the Soviet Communist Party: The Historical & Theoretical Background. LC 93-24107. (Major Concepts in Politics & Political Theory Ser.: Vol. 4). 238p. (C). 1994. text 32.95 (*0-8204-2287-8*) P Lang Pubng.

Novikov, I. D. & Zel'Dovich, Ya B. Relativistic Astrophysics Vol. 2: The Structure & Evolution of the Universe. Steigman, Gary, ed. Fishbone, Leslie, tr. LC 77-128549. (Illus.). 752p. (C). 1983. reprint ed. lib. bdg. 96.00 (*0-226-97957-1*) U Ch Pr.
— Stars & Relativity. unabridged ed. LC 96-35378. (Illus.). 540p. 1996. reprint ed. pap. text 14.95 (*0-486-69424-0*) Dover.

Novikov, I. D., jt. auth. see Frolov, V. P.

Novikov, I. D., jt. auth. see Zeldovich, Ya B.

Novikov, Igor D. Black Holes & the Universe. (Canto Book Ser.). (Illus.). 186p. (C). 1995. pap. 10.95 (*0-521-55870-0*) Cambridge U Pr.
— The River of Time. LC 97-43010. (Illus.). 298p. (C). 1998. text 49.95 (*0-521-46177-4*) Cambridge U Pr.

Novikov, Igor D. & Frolov, Valery P. Physics of Black Holes. (C). 1989. text 234.50 (*90-277-2685-X*) Kluwer Academic.

Novikov, Igor D., jt. auth. see Semenov, Evgenij.

Novikov, Igor D., jt. auth. see Sharov, Alexander S.

Novikov, M. P. Dictionary of Atheism. (RUS.). 559p. 1983. 39.95 (*0-8288-2316-2*, M15213) Fr & Eur.

Novikov, N. V., ed. XI Airapt: Selected Soviet Papers from the International High Pressure Conference, July 12-17, 1987, Kiev, U. S. S. R.: A Special Issue of the Journal High Pressure Research. ii, 106p. 1989. pap. text 184.00 (*2-88124-727-X*) Gordon & Breach.

Novikov, S., et al. Theory of Solitons: The Inverse Scattering Method. LC 83-21051. (Contemporary Soviet Mathematics Ser.). (Illus.). 288p. (C). 1984. 115.00 (*0-306-10977-8*, Kluwer Plenum) Kluwer Academic.

Novikov, S. P. Mathematical Physics Reviews, Vol. 7. (Soviet Scientific Reviews Ser.: Section C). xiv, 338p. 1988. text 483.00 (*3-7186-0455-8*) Gordon & Breach.
— Solitons & Geometry. (Lezione Fermiane Ser.). 62p. (C). 1995. pap. text 22.95 (*0-521-47196-6*) Cambridge U Pr.

Novikov, S. P., ed. Mathematical Physics Reviews, Vol. 2. (Soviet Scientific Reviews Ser.: Section C). x, 268p. 1981. text 600.00 (*3-7186-0069-2*) Gordon & Breach.
— Mathematical Physics Reviews, Vol. 3. x, 312p. 1982. text 516.00 (*3-7186-0107-9*) Gordon & Breach.
— Mathematical Physics Reviews, Vol. 4. Hamermesh, Morton, tr. from RUS. (Soviet Scientific Reviews Ser.: Section C). x, 280p. 1984. text 552.00 (*3-7186-0146-X*) Gordon & Breach.
— Mathematical Physics Reviews, Vol.1. (Soviet Scientific Reviews Ser.). xiv, 208p. 1980. text 552.00 (*3-7186-0019-6*) Gordon & Breach.
— Mathematical Physics Reviews: Soviet Scientific Reviews, Section C, Vol. 5. xii, 272p. 1985. text 440.00 (*3-7186-0198-2*) Gordon & Breach.
— Mathematical Physics Reviews: Soviet Scientific Reviews, Section C, Vol. 6. HAmermesh, Morton, tr. from RUS. xii, 272p. 1987. text 457.00 (*3-7186-0292-X*) Gordon & Breach.
— Topics in Topology & Mathematical Physics. LC 91-640741. (American Mathematical Society Translations Ser.: Series 2, Vol. 170). 206p. 1995. text 89.00 (*0-8218-0455-3*, TRANS2/170) Am Math.
— Topology & Its Applications: Proceedings of the International Topology Conference, Baku, October 3-8, 1987. LC 93-6106. (Proceedings of the Steklov Institute of Mathematics Ser.: Vol. 193). 250p. 1993. pap. 180.00 (*0-8218-3151-8*, STEKLO/193) Am Math.
— Topology I, Vol. 12. Botvinnik, B. & Burns, R., trs. (Encyclopedia of Mathematical Sciences Ser.). (Illus.). 344p. 1996. 115.00 (*0-387-17007-3*) Spr-Verlag.

Novikov, S. P., et al, eds. Discrete Geometry & Topology: On the 100th Anniversary of the Birth of Boris Nikolaevich Delone: Collection of Papers. LC 92-37675. (Proceedings of the Steklov Institute of Mathematics Ser.: Vol. 196). 193p. 1993. pap. 129.00 (*0-8218-3147-X*, STEKLO/196) Am Math.

Novikov, S. P. & Fomenko, A. T. Basic Elements of Differential Geometry & Topology. (C). 1990. text 268.50 (*0-7923-1009-8*) Kluwer Academic.

Novikov, S. P. & Sinai, Ya G., eds. Integrable Pseudospin Models in Condensed Matter, Vol. 9. (Soviet Scientific Reviews Series, Section D: Biology Reviews: Vol. 9, Pt. 3). 152p. 1993. text 173.00 (*3-7186-5378-8*) Gordon & Breach.

Novikov, S. P., jt. ed. see Arnold, V. I.

Novikov, S. P., jt. ed. see Arnol'd, V. I.

Novikov, S. P., jt. ed. see Buchstaber, V. M.

Novikov, S. P., ed. see Chernikov, A. A., et al.

Novikov, S. P., ed. see Kozlov, Valery V.

Novikov, V. Grain Growth & Control of Microstructure & Texture in Polycrystalline Materials. LC 96-3458. (Materials Science & Technology Ser.). 192p. 1996. boxed set 134.95 (*0-8493-8223-8*) CRC Pr.

Novikov, V. M., ed. Handbook of Fishery Technology, Vol. 1. 2nd enl. rev. ed. (Russian Translation Ser.: No. 3). 504p. 1983. 181.00 (*90-6191-409-4*, Pub. by A A Balkema) Ashgate Pub Co.
— Handbook of Fishery Technology, Vol. 4. Sharma, B. R., tr. from RUS. 506p. (C). 1984. text 181.00 (*90-6191-421-3*, Pub. by A A Balkema) Ashgate Pub Co.

Novikov, V. V., jt. auth. see Privalko, V. P.

Novikov, Valerie. Dictionary of Physics: English, French, German, Russian. (ENG, FRE, GER & RUS.). 546p. 1995. 150.00 (*0-7859-9980-9*) Fr & Eur.

***Novikova, D. P., ed.** High Temperature Vacuum Metallography of Welded Joints, Vol. 10, Part 1. (Welding & Surfacing Reviews Ser.: Vol. 10, Issue 1). 110p. 1998. pap. text 65.00 (*90-5702-356-3*, Harwood Acad Pubs) Gordon & Breach.

Novikova, Liubov A. Blindness & the Electrical Activity of the Brain: Electroencephalographic Studies of the Effects of Sensory Impairment. Jastzembska, Z. S., ed. Sznycer, B. & Zielinski, L., trs. LC 75-155920. (American Foundation for the Blind Research Ser.: No. 23). 359p. reprint ed. pap. 111.30 (*0-7837-0129-2*, 204041300016) Bks Demand.

Novin, D., jt. ed. see Hoebel, B. G.

N

An Asterisk (*) at the beginning of an entry indicates that the title is appearing for the first time.

Novin, Donald, et al, eds. Hunger: Basic Mechanisms & Clinical Implications. LC 75-14563. 510p. 1976. reprint ed. pap. 158.10 (*0-608-00348-4*, 206106400007) Bks Demand.

***Novinger, Tracy.** Intercultural Communication: A Practical Guide. LC 00-36408. (Illus.). 224p. 2001. 35.00 (*0-292-75570-8*); pap. 16.95 (*0-292-75571-6*) U of Tex Pr.

Novis, Constance, ed. see Dempsey, Michael.

Novisky, Ed, ed. The Mercury Labels Vol. IV: The 1969-1991 Era & Classical Recordings, Vol. 4. LC 93-15254. (Discographies Ser.: No. 51). 1993. lib. bdg. 95.00 (*0-313-29034-2*, RMG04, Greenwood Pr) Greenwood.

Novit, Renee Z. Alphabet Aa to Zz. (Kidz & Katz Educational Learning Book Ser.). (Illus.). 16p. (J). (ps). pap. 7.95 (*1-883371-00-7*) Kidz & Katz.

— Counting by Tens & Fives. (Kidz & Katz Educational Learning Book Ser.). (Illus.). 16p. (J). (ps). pap. 7.95 (*1-883371-02-3*) Kidz & Katz.

— Counting One to Twenty. (Kidz & Katz Educational Learning Book Ser.). (Illus.). 16p. (J). (ps). pap. 7.95 (*1-883371-01-5*) Kidz & Katz.

Novitch, Miriam. The Passage of the Barbarians. 176p. 1993. 45.00 (*1-870360-10-9*) St Mut.

Novitchkov, Nicolai, jt. auth. see Goursau, Henri.

Novitski, B. J. Rendering Real & Imagined Buildings: The Art of Computer Modeling from the Palace of Kublai Khan to Le Carbusier's Villas. (Illus.). 192p. 1998. 40.00 (*1-56496-497-3*) Rockport Pubs.

— Rendering Real & Imagined Buildings: The Art of Computer Modeling from the Palace of Kublai Khan to Le Corbusier's Villas. (Illus.). 192p. 1999. 50.00 incl. cd-rom (*1-56496-511-2*) Rockport Pubs.

Novitski, B. J., jt. auth. see Mays, Patrick C.

Novitski, Marya. Auguste Laurent & the Prehistory of Valence. LC 92-23090. (History of Science & Technology Ser.: Vol. 1). 147p. 1992. text 85.00 (*3-7186-5235-8*) Gordon & Breach.

Novitsky, A. Sienitieteelinen Sanasto Suomi-Venaja-Latina. (FIN, LAT & RUS.). 190p. 1984. 29.95 (*0-8288-1250-0*, F22445) Fr & Eur.

Novitsky, Ed, ed. The Mercury Labels, 5 vols., 51. LC 93-15254. 4240p. 1993. lib. bdg. 395.00 (*0-313-27371-5*, RMG/, Greenwood Pr) Greenwood.

— The Mercury Labels Vol. I: The 1945-1956 Era, Vol. 1. LC 93-15254. (Discographies Ser.: No. 51). 832p. 1993. lib. bdg. 95.00 (*0-313-29031-8*, RMG01, Greenwood Pr) Greenwood.

— The Mercury Labels Vol. II: The 1956-1964 Era, Vol. 2. LC 93-15254. (Discographies Ser.: No. 51). 840p. 1993. lib. bdg. 95.00 (*0-313-29032-6*, RMG02, Greenwood Pr) Greenwood.

— The Mercury Labels Vol. III: The 1964-1969 Era, Vol. 3. LC 93-15254. (Discographies Ser.: No. 51). 768p. 1993. lib. bdg. 95.00 (*0-313-29033-4*, RMG03, Greenwood Pr) Greenwood.

— The Mercury Labels Vol. V: Record & Artist Indexes, Vol. 5. LC 93-15254. (Discographies Ser.: No. 51). 912p. 1993. lib. bdg. 95.00 (*0-313-29035-0*, RMG05, Greenwood Pr) Greenwood.

Novitsky, Ed, jt. compiled by see Ruppli, Michel.

Novitt, J. J., jt. auth. see Brown, Robert H.

Novitt-Moreno, Anne. How Your Brain Works. (How It Works Ser.). (Illus.). 192p. (Orig.). 1995. pap. 19.95 (*1-56276-255-9*, Ziff-Davis Pr) Que.

Novitzky, Dimitry, jt. ed. see Cooper, David K.

Novo, G. Diccionario General de Turismo. (SPA.). 19.50 (*0-7859-0917-6*, S-28710) Fr & Eur.

Novo, Salvador. Poesia - Novo (Poetry - Novo) 2nd ed. (SPA.). 180p. 1993. 13.99 (*968-16-4449-2*, Pub. by Fondo) Continental Bk.

— The War of the Fatties & Other Stories from Aztec History. Alderson, Michael, tr. from SPA. 256p. (C). 1993. pap. 14.95 (*0-292-75554-6*); text 37.50 (*0-292-79059-7*) U of Tex Pr.

Novo, Salvatore, jt. auth. see Nicolaides, Andrew N.

Novobatzsky. Depraved English. 2nd ed. LC 99-26421. 1999. text 17.95 (*0-312-20773-5*) St Martin.

Novobiliski, Andrew. Magic Cap Programming. 1996. pap. write for info. (*0-201-40954-2*) Addison-Wesley.

Novobilski, Andrew. Penpoint Programming. LC 92-13076. 400p. (C). 1992. pap. text 26.95 (*0-201-60833-2*) Addison-Wesley.

— Wireless Transport: A Technological Overview. (C). 1996. pap. text. write for info. (*0-201-48405-6*) Addison-Wesley.

Novobilski, Andrew, jt. auth. see Cox, Brad J.

***Novogradac, Michael J.** Building Owners' Income Tax Manual. 1998. spiral bd. 29.95 (*0-9663962-7-8*) Novogradac & Co.

— Community Reinvestment Act Manual. 2000. 59.95 (*0-9663962-3-5*) Novogradac & Co.

Novogradac, Michael J. Foreign Sales Corporation Handbook. 1998. spiral bd. 89.95 (*0-9663962-1-9*) Novogradac & Co.

***Novogradac, Michael J.** GAAP Accounting for the LIHC: Historical Documentation. 1999. spiral bd. 59.95 (*0-9663962-5-1*) Novogradac & Co.

— Historic Rehabilitation Handbook: Documentation. 2000. 59.95 (*0-9663962-4-3*) Novogradac & Co.

Novogradac, Michael J. Low Income Housing Tax-Exempt Bond Handbook. 1998. spiral bd. 89.95 (*0-9663962-0-0*) Novogradac & Co.

***Novogradac, Michael J.** Tax Credit Application Workbook. 2000. ring bd. 79.95 (*0-9663962-6-X*) Novogradac & Co.

Novogradac, Mike J. Tax Credit Property Manager's Reference Manual. 1998. ring bd. 89.95 (*0-9663962-2-7*) Novogradac & Co.

Novokshenov, V. Y., jt. auth. see Its, A. R.

Novoouspensky, Nikolai. Ivan Aivazovsky. (Great Painters Ser.). (Illus.). 172p. 1996. 40.00 (*1-85995-288-7*) Parkstone Pr.

Novosad, Garland S. Touchstone for Public Leadership: A Focus on City Government. (Illus.). 150p. 1988. 15.00 (*0-918464-77-3*) D Armstrong.

Novosad, Nancy. Promise Keepers: Playing God. (Illus.). 250p. 1999. 24.95 (*1-57392-700-7*) Prometheus Bks.

***Novosel, Gary.** MCSE TCP/IP Exam Cram. 3rd ed. (Illus.). 2000. pap. text. write for info. (*1-57610-677-2*) Coriolis Grp.

Novosel, Gary, et al. MCSE TCP/IP Exam Cram. LC 99-26464. (Exam Cram (Coriolis' Certification Insider Press) Ser.). (Illus.). 426p. 1999. pap. 29.99 (*1-57610-476-1*) Coriolis Grp.

Novosel, Michael J. Dustoff: The Memoir of an Army Aviator. LC 99-35143. (Illus.). 352p. 1999. 29.95 (*0-89141-698-6*) Presidio Pr.

Novoselskia, I. N., et al. Master Drawings from the Hermitage & Pushkin Museums. LC 98-27216. 1998. 45.00 (*0-87598-125-9*) Pierpont Morgan.

Novoshilov, K. V., jt. ed. see Fadeev, Iu. N.

Novosti Press Editors. The Armenian Earthquake Disaster. LC 89-38352. (Illus.). 243p. 1989. pap. 29.95 (*0-943071-12-7*) Sphinx Pr.

— Soviet Almanac. LC 80-7938. (Illus.). 228p. 1981. pap. 10.95 (*0-15-683923-7*, Harvest Bks) Harcourt.

***Novotni, Michele & Petersen, Randy.** What Does Everybody Know That I Don't? Social Skills Help for Adults with Attention Deficit/Hyperactivity Disorder (AD/HD) LC 99-45492. (Illus.). 314p. 1999. pap. 14.95 (*1-886941-34-3*, Pub. by Spec Pr FL) Partners Pubs Grp.

Novotny, A. J., jt. ed. see Nash, C. E.

Novotny, Ann. Alice's World: The Life & Photography of an American Original: Alice Austen, 1866-1952. LC 76-18489. (Illus.). (J). (gr. 7-9). 1976. 24.95 (*0-85699-128-7*) Chatham Pr.

Novotny, Ann, ed. see Special Libraries Association Staff.

Novotny, Bruce. Tales from an Endless Summer: A Novel of the Beach. 208p. 1996. pap. 12.00 (*0-945582-31-5*) Down the Shore Pub.

Novotny, D. W. & Lipo, T. A. Vector Control & Dynamics of AC Drives, Vol. 41. LC 97-126143. (Monographs in Electrical & Electronic Engineering). (Illus.). 454p. 1996. text 90.00 (*0-19-856439-2*) OUP.

Novotny, Donald, jt. auth. see Schmitz, Norbert L.

Novotny, Eva. Lernen und Realitatsverlust in der Schule. 190p. 1996. 38.95 (*3-631-49752-0*) P Lang Pubng.

Novotny, Frantisek. The Posthumous Life of Plato. Svoboda, Ludvik & Barton, J. L., eds. Fabryova, Jana, tr. 664p. 1978. lib. bdg. 296.00 (*90-247-2060-5*, Pub. by M Nijhoff) Kluwer Academic.

Novotny, Fritz. Painting & Sculpture in Europe: 1780-1880. (Pelican History of Art Ser.). (Illus.). 483p. (C). 1988. reprint ed. pap. 25.00 (*0-300-05321-5*) Yale U Pr.

Novotny, Fritz, et al. The Great Impressionists. (Illus.). 144p. 1997. 50.00 (*3-7913-1450-5*, Pub. by Prestel) te Neues.

Novotny, George, jt. auth. see Huhtala, Jon.

Novotny, Jeanne, jt. auth. see Schoolcraft, Victoria.

Novotny, Josef L. English-German Dictionary of American Verbs-Idioms: English-Deutsches Woerterbuch Amerikanischer Zeitwort-Idiome. (ENG & GER.). 464p. 1980. 150.00 (*0-8288-1436-8*, M15480) Fr & Eur.

Novotny, Pamela P. The Joy of Twins & Multiple Births. 1994. pap. 16.00 (*0-517-88071-7*) Crown Pub Group.

Novotny, Pamela P., jt. auth. see Atkinson, Holly.

***Novotny, Patrick.** Where We Live, Work & Play: The Environmental Justice Movement & the Struggle for a New Environmentalism. LC 99-86115. (Praeger Series in Transformational Politics & Political Science). 172p. 2000. 57.00 (*0-275-96026-9*, C6026, Praeger Pubs) Greenwood.

Novotny, Vladimir, ed. Political, Institutional & Fiscal Alternatives for Nonpoint Pollution Abatement Programs: Proceedings of a Conference Held in Milwaukee, Wisconsin, December 7-9, 1987. LC 88-61504. 210p. 1988. reprint ed. pap. 65.10 (*0-608-04196-3*, 206493100011) Bks Demand.

Novotny, Vladimir & Olem, Harvey. Water Quality: Prevention, Identification, & Management of Diffuse Pollution. (Environmental Engineering Ser.). 1072p. 1993. 140.00 (*0-471-28413-0*, VNR) Wiley.

Novotny, Vladimir & Olem, Harvey. Water Quality & Diffuse Pollution. 1056p. 1994. text 98.95 (*0-442-00559-8*, VNR) Wiley.

Novotny, Vladimir & Somlyody, Laszlo, eds. Remediation & Management of Degraded River Basins with Emphasis on Central & Eastern Europe: With Emphasis on Central & Eastern Europe, Vol. XI. (NATO ASI Ser, Partnership Sub-Series 2: Vol. 3). (Illus.). 529p. 1995. 264.95 (*3-540-60115-5*) Spr-Verlag.

Novotny, Vladimir, ed. see Symposium on Nonpoint Pollution: Policy, Economy,.

Novouspensky, N. The Russian Museum, Leningrad. 193p. 1975. 50.00 (*0-7855-0705-1*, Pub. by Collets) St Mut.

Novouspensky, Nikolai. Paul Cezanne: Unknown Horizons. (Great Painters Ser.). (Illus.). 176p. 1996. 40.00 (*1-85995-191-0*) Parkstone Pr.

Novozhilov, H. M. Fundamental Metallurgy of Gas-Shielded ARC Welding. x, 400p. 1988. text 358.00 (*2-88124-666-4*) Gordon & Breach.

Novozhilov, I. Fractional Analysis: Methods of Motion Decomposition. (Illus.). 216p. 1997. write for info. (*3-7643-3889-X*) Birkhauser.

Novozhilov, I. V. Fractional Analysis: Methods & Motion Decomposition. LC 96-49997. (Illus.). 231p. 1997. 59.95 (*0-8176-3889-X*) Birkhauser.

Novozhilov, K. V., ed. Microbiological Methods for Biological Control of Pests of Agricultural Crops. Nair, Indira, tr. from RUS. (Russian Translation Ser.: Vol. 51). (Illus.). 91p. (C). 1987. text 71.00 (*90-6191-493-0*, Pub. by A A Balkema) Ashgate Pub Co.

Novozhilov, V. & Lusher, J. Theory of Elasticity. LC 60-14992. 1961. 201.00 (*0-08-009523-2*, Pub. by Pergamon Repr) Franklin.

Novozhilov, V. V. Foundations of the Nonlinear Theory of Elasticity. LC 98-43889. 1999. text 8.95 (*0-486-40684-9*) Dover.

Novrup, Svend. Checkmate. 160p. 1990. pap. write for info. (*0-08-037790-4*, Pub. by CHES) Macmillan.

Novshek, William. Mathematics for Economists. LC 93-16696. (Economic Theory, Econometrics & Mathematical Economics Ser.). (Illus.). 308p. 1993. text 69.95 (*0-12-522575-X*) Acad Pr.

Novy. Transforming Shakespeare. LC 98-37271. 272p. 1999. text 45.00 (*0-312-21472-3*) St Martin.

Novy, Lubomir & Gabriel, Jiri, eds. Czech Philosophy in the Twentieth Century. LC 93-5986. (Cultural Heritage & Contemporary Change Series IVA: Vol. 4).Tr. of Kapitoly z Dejin Ceske Filozofie 20 Stoleti. 1993. 45.00 (*1-56518-028-3*); pap. 17.50 (*1-56518-029-1*) Coun Res Values.

Novy, Marianne. Love's Argument: Gender Relations in Shakespeare. LC 84-3553. 249p. 1984. reprint ed. pap. 77.20 (*0-7837-9031-7*, 204978200003) Bks Demand.

— Women's Re-Visions of Shakespeare. 272p. 1990. pap. text 15.95 (*0-252-06114-4*) U of Ill Pr.

Novy, Marianne, ed. Cross-Cultural Performances: Differences in Women's Re-visions of Shakespeare. LC 92-44535. 280p. 1993. text 49.95 (*0-252-02017-0*); pap. text 18.95 (*0-252-06323-6*) U of Ill Pr.

Novy, Marianne L. Engaging with Shakespeare: Responses of George Eliot & Other Women Novelists. LC 93-4158. 286p. 1998. reprint ed. pap. text 17.95 (*0-87745-650-X*) U of Iowa Pr.

***Novy, Marianne L., ed.** Imagining Adoption: Essays on Literature & Culture. (Illus.). 312p. (C). 2000. text 47.50 (*0-472-11181-7*, 11181) U of Mich Pr.

NOW Legal Defense & Education Fund Staff, jt. auth. see Assn. for Union Democracy Women's Project Staff.

***Now Magazine Staff.** Now City Guide to Toronto: The Insider's Handbook. (Illus.). 256p. 1999. pap. 15.95 (*0-7710-6818-2*) McCland & Stewart.

Now You're Talking Staff. Now You're Talking: French in No Time. 2nd ed. (Now You're Talking! Ser.). (FRE & ENG.). 48p. 1992. pap. 13.95 incl. audio (*0-8120-7880-2*) Barron.

Nowack, H. & Lutjering, G. Fatigue '96: Proceedings of the 6th International Fatigue Congress. 2116p. 1996. pap. text 431.50 (*0-08-042268-3*, Pergamon Pr) Elsevier.

Nowacki, H., et al, eds. Computational Geometry for Ships. LC 94-46516. 252p. 1995. text 53.00 (*981-02-2139-8*) World Scientific Pub.

— Neutrabas: A Neutral Product Definition Database for Large Multifunctional Systems. (Research Reports ESPRIT: Project 2010, Vol. 1). 214p. 1996. pap. 43.00 (*3-540-59300-4*) Spr-Verlag.

Nowacki, Louis J., jt. auth. see Vigo, Tyrone L.

Nowacki, Louis J., jt. ed. see Vigo, Tyrone L.

Nowacki, Wojoiech K. Theory of Asymmetrical Elasticity. 2nd ed. 1986. 178.00 (*0-08-027584-2*, Pub. by Pergamon Repr) Franklin.

Nowacki, Wojoiech K., ed. see CISM (International Center for Mechanical Sciences.

Nowaczy, Ronald H. Introduction Statistics for Behavioral Research. 544p. (C). 1988. text. write for info. (*0-03-004043-4*) Harcourt Coll Pubs.

Nowaczyk, Ronald H., jt. auth. see Jahnke, John C.

Nowak. Essentials of Pathophysiology: Concepts & Applications for Health Care Professionals. 3rd ed. 2002. 68.74 (*0-07-027255-7*) McGraw.

— International Human Rights. 1993. pap. text 77.50 (*90-6544-725-3*) Kluwer Academic.

— Pathophysiology. 1994. teacher ed. 14.06 (*0-697-17438-7*) McGraw.

Nowak & Handford. Essentials of Pathophysiology: Concepts & Applications of Healing. 1994. trans. 10.93 (*0-697-26625-7*) McGrw-H Hghr Educ.

Nowak, A. J. & Neves, A. C., eds. The Multiple Reciprocity Boundary Element Method. 256p. 1994. 110.00 (*1-85312-277-7*) Computational Mech MA.

Nowak, A. J. & Neves, A. C., eds. The Multiple Reciprocity Boundary Element Method. LC 93-74381. (Computational Engineering Ser.). 256p. 1994. 110.00 (*1-56252-201-9*, 2777) Computational Mech MA.

Nowak, A. J., jt. auth. see Kurpisz, K.

Nowak, A. J., jt. ed. see Wrobel, L. C.

Nowak, Andrzej & Vallacher, Robin R. Dynamical Social Psychology. LC 98-30200. 318p. 1998. lib. bdg. 42.00 (*1-57230-353-0*) Guilford Pubns.

Nowak, Andrzej S. Bridge Structures. (C). 1997. pap. text 81.00 (*0-13-520966-8*) P-H.

— Making Buildings Safer for People During Hurricanes, Earthquakes, & Fires. 200p. (C). (gr. 13). 1990. text 57.95 (*0-442-26473-9*) Chapman & Hall.

Nowak, Andrzej S., ed. Bridge Evaluation, Repair & Rehabilitation. (C). 1990. text 304.50 (*0-7923-0999-5*) Kluwer Academic.

— Modeling Human Error in Structural Design & Construction. (Workshop Proceedings Ser.). 200p. 1986. 28.00 (*0-87262-558-3*) Am Soc Civil Eng.

***Nowak, Andrzej S. & Collins, Kevin R.** Reliability of Structures. LC 99-26732. 2000. write for info. (*0-07-048163-6*) McGrw-H Hghr Educ.

Nowak, Arlene, ed. see Faison, Delphine P.

Nowak, Barbara. Cook It Right! The Comprehensive Source for Substitutions, Equivalents & Cooking Tips. LC 93-86735. 192p. 1994. pap. text 22.95 (*0-9627756-8-1*) Sandcastle Pub.

***Nowak, Barbara & Wichman, Beverly.** The Saucy Sisters Best Places to Eat in Nashville. 128p. 2000. pap. 9.95 (*0-9658399-1-5*) Saucy Sisters.

Nowak, Barbara & Wichman, Beverly. The Saucy Sisters Insider's Guide to the Best Places to Eat in Nashville. 110p. (Orig.). 1997. pap. 9.95 (*0-9658399-0-7*) Saucy Sisters.

Nowak, Bernd. Untersuchungen Zur Vegetation Ostliguriens (Italian) (Dissertationes Botanicae Ser.: Band 111). (GER., Illus.). vii, 259p. 1987. pap. 77.00 (*3-443-64023-0*, Pub. by Gebruder Borntraeger) Balogh.

Nowak, Ed & Yanosey, Robert J. New York Central Color Photography of Ed Nowak, Bk. I. LC 91-67986. (Illus.). 128p. 1992. 45.00 (*1-878887-09-2*) Morning NJ.

— New York Central Color Photography of Ed Nowak, Bk. II. LC 91-67986. (Illus.). 128p. 1992. 49.95 (*1-878887-17-3*) Morning NJ.

— New York Central Color Photography of Ed Nowak, Bk. 3. LC 91-67986. (Illus.). 128p. 1993. 49.95 (*1-878887-24-6*) Morning NJ.

Nowak, Elke. Transforming the Images: Ergativity & Transitivity in Inuktitut (Eskimo) LC 96-15691. (Empirical Approaches to Language Typology Ser.: Vol. 15). xii, 312p. (C). 1996. lib. bdg. 168.90 (*3-11-014980-X*) Mouton.

Nowak, G. A. Cosmetic Preparations, Vol. 1. Alexander, Philip, tr. from GER.Tr. of Die Kosmetischen Praparate, Band 1. (Illus.). 352p. 1985. 125.00 (*3-87846-118-6*) Micelle Pr.

Nowak, H. Revision der Laubmoosgattung Mitthyridium (Mitten) Robinson Fuer Oreanien (Calymperaceae) (Bryophytorum Bibliotheca Ser.: No. 20). (GER., Illus.). 1981. lib. bdg. 48.00 (*3-7682-1236-X*) Lubrecht & Cramer.

Nowak-Handford. Essential Pathophysiology: Concepts & Applications. 2nd ed. LC 98-6339. 1998. 63.00 (*0-697-25205-1*, Dshkn McG-Hill) McGrw-H Hghr Educ.

Nowak, Jan. Courier from Warsaw. LC 82-8599. (Illus.). 479p. reprint ed. pap. 148.50 (*0-608-16066-0*, 203319800084) Bks Demand.

Nowak, Jan, ed. Marketing in Central & Eastern Europe. LC 97-762. (Journal of East-West Business Monograph Ser.: Vol. 3, No. 1). 101p. (C). 1997. 29.95 (*0-7890-0039-3*, Intl Busn Pr) Haworth Pr.

Nowak, Janie B. The Forty-Seven Hundred: The Story of the Mount Sinai Hospital School of Nursing. LC 81-5202. (Illus.). 160p. 1981. 15.00 (*0-914016-79-2*) Phoenix Pub.

***Nowak, Jeff, ed.** Birds & Blooms Backyard Projects. LC 99-74411. (Illus.). 178p. 1999. 29.99 (*0-89821-264-2*) Reiman Pubns.

Nowak, Jerzy & Zajac, Marek, eds. Tenth Polish-Czech-Slovak Optical Conference Vol. 3320: Wave & Quantum Aspects of Contemporary Optics. LC 98-145674. 330p. 1998. 69.00 (*0-8194-2761-6*) SPIE.

Nowak, John E. & Rotunda, Ronald D. Constitutional Law. 5th ed. LC 95-23766. (Hornbook Ser.). 1428p. (C). 1995. 49.50 (*0-314-06175-4*) West Pub.

— Treatise on Constitutional Law: Substance & Procedure, 1. 2nd ed. (Practice Ser.: Vols. 1-3). 1992. text. write for info. (*0-314-00803-9*) West Pub.

— Treatise on Constitutional Law: Substance & Procedure, 2. 2nd ed. (Practice Ser.: Vols. 1-3). 1992. text. write for info. (*0-314-00804-7*) West Pub.

— Treatise on Constitutional Law: Substance & Procedure, 3. 2nd ed. (Practice Ser.: Vols. 1-3). 1992. text. write for info. (*0-314-00805-5*) West Pub.

Nowak, John F. Jasiu: or Lumpy Oatmeal & Burnt Toast. 80p. (Orig.). 1995. pap. 7.95 (*0-9644883-0-2*) Ottawa St Pr.

Nowak, John M. Sobriety Amen: Growth Beyond the Initial Spiritual Experience. LC 98-92022. iv, 250p. 1998. pap. 14.95 (*0-9666037-0-2*) Prov Two.

Nowak, Karl F. Versailles. Thomas, Norman M. & Dickes, E. W., trs. LC 76-175705. (Select Bibliographies Reprint Ser.). 1977. reprint ed. 21.95 (*0-8369-6620-1*) Ayer.

— Versailles. Thomas, Norman F. & Dickes, E. W., trs. from FRE. LC 76-175705. (Select Bibliographies Reprint Ser.). 284p. reprint ed. lib. bdg. 17.50 (*0-8290-0822-5*) Irvington.

***Nowak, Kathleen.** Service with Honor. 250p. 2002. pap. 12.95 (*1-57532-278-1*, Pub. by Press-Tige Pub) Baker & Taylor.

***Nowak, Kathleen A.** Sonador. 400p. 2002. pap. 12.95 (*1-57532-277-3*) Press-Tige Pub.

Nowak, Laura S. Monetary Policy & Investment Opportunities. LC 92-18366. 232p. 1993. 59.95 (*0-89930-611-X*, NIO, Quorum Bks) Greenwood.

Nowak, Leszek. Power & Civil Society: Toward a Dynamic Theory of Real Socialism, 271. LC 90-47324. (Contributions in Political Science Ser.: No. 271). 248p. 1991. 59.95 (*0-313-27505-X*, NDP/, Greenwood Pr) Greenwood.

— Property & Power. 1983. pap. text 79.50 (*90-277-1595-5*); lib. bdg. 152.00 (*90-277-1351-0*) Kluwer Academic.

— The Structure of Idealization: Towards a Systematic Interpretation of the Marxian Idea of Science. (Synthese Library: No. 139). 288p. 1979. text 106.00 (*90-277-1014-7*, D Reidel) Kluwer Academic.

Nowak, M. A., et al. Chiral Nuclear Dynamics. LC 96-16455. 400p. 1996. text 74.00 (*981-02-1000-0*) World Scientific Pub.

Nowak, M. T., jt. auth. see Kaczor, W. J.

Nowak, Margaret C. Two Who Were There: A Biography of Stanley Nowak. LC 88-39057. (Illus.). 276p. 1989. 39.95 (*0-8143-1883-5*); pap. 19.95 (*0-8143-1878-9*) Wayne St U Pr.

N

An Asterisk (*) at the beginning of an entry indicates that the title is appearing for the first time.

***Nowak, Mark.** Revenants. 160p. 2000. pap. 14.95 (*1-56689-107-8*, Pub. by Coffee Hse) Consort Bk Sales.

Nowak, Mark, ed. see Enslin, Theodore.

Nowak, Mark, jt. ed. see Glancy, Diane.

***Nowak, Norman Jay.** I Buy Low: How to Succeed in the Stock Market, Set. 2000. write for info. incl. audio (*0-9700029-0-4*) Millionaire.

Nowak, Patrick, et al. Coalition Navy. Marciniszyn, Alex et al, eds. (Rifts Sourcebook Ser.: Vol. 4). (Illus.). 128p. (Orig.). (YA). (gr. 8 up). 1997. pap. 12.95 (*1-57457-003-X*, 828) Palladium Bks.

Nowak, Patrick, jt. auth. see Siembieda, Kevin.

Nowak, Phil, jt. auth. see Jatich, Alida M.

Nowak, Ronald M. Walker's Bats of the World. LC 94-30262. (Illus.). 287p. 1995. pap. 19.95 (*0-8018-4986-1*) Johns Hopkins.

— Walker's Mammals of the World, 2 vols. 5th rev. ed. LC 91-27011. (Illus.). 1732p. 1991. 95.00 (*0-8018-3970-X*) Johns Hopkins.

— Walker's Mammals of the World, 2 vols. 6th ed. LC 98-23686. (Illus.). 2160p. 1999. 99.95 (*0-8018-5789-9*) Johns Hopkins.

— Walker's Primates of the World. LC 99-28958. (Illus.). 272p. 1999. pap. 19.95 (*0-8018-6251-5*) Johns Hopkins.

Nowak-Solinski, Witold. Krysia. 132p. 1988. 50.00 (*0-85335-242-9*, Pub. by Stuart Titles Ltd) St Mut.

Nowak, Stanley J., Jr. Institutional Structures & Human Values: Making Choices. (Academic Edition Ser.). 100p. (C). 1994. student ed. 75.00 (*1-885886-10-1*) Eikon PA.

— Institutional Structures & Human Values: Making Choices. (Professional Edition Ser.). 100p. 1994. student ed. 300.00 (*1-885886-11-X*); student ed. 115.00 (*1-885886-16-0*) Eikon PA.

Nowak, Stefan. Methodology of Sociological Research, 2 vols, Vol. 1. Lepa, Maria O., tr. (Synthese Library: No. 82). 521p. 1977. text 155.50 (*90-277-0486-4*, D Reidel) Kluwer Academic.

— Understanding & Prediction Essays in the Methodology of Social & Behavioral Theories. LC 75-44179. (Synthese Library: No. 94). 507p. 1976. lib. bdg. 158.50 (*90-277-0558-5*, D Reidel) Kluwer Academic.

Nowak, Thaddeus S., Jr., jt. ed. see Robertson, James T.

Nowak, Thomas J. & Handford, A. Gordon. Essentials of Pathophysiology: Concepts & Applications for Health Care Professionals. 688p. (C). 1994. text. write for info. (*0-697-13314-1*, WCB McGr Hill) McGrw-H Hghr Educ.

Nowak, W. S. The Marketing of Shellfish. 1978. 50.00 (*0-7855-6937-5*) St Mut.

Nowakowska, Maria. Language of Motivation & Language of Actions. LC 72-94491. (Janua Linguarum, Ser. Major: No. 67). (Illus.). 272p. 1973. text 67.70 (*90-279-2385-X*) Mouton.

— Theories of Research. (Systems Inquiry Ser.). 580p. (Orig.). 1984. pap. text 30.50 (*0-914105-20-5*) Intersystems Pubns.

***Nowakowski, Antoni & Chachulski, Bogdan, eds.** Optoelectronic & Electronic Sensors III. 248p. 1999. pap. text 72.00 (*0-8194-3204-0*) SPIE.

Nowakowski, Jacek. Pleasing Polish Recipes. 160p. 1989. spiral bd. 6.95 (*0-941016-63-3*) Penfield.

Nowakowski, Jacek, ed. Polish Touches: Recipes & Traditions. 1996. pap. 12.95 (*1-57216-016-0*) Penfield.

Nowakowski, Jeri. A Handbook of Educational Variables: A Guide to Evaluation. 1984. lib. bdg. 83.50 (*0-89838-161-4*) Kluwer Academic.

Nowakowski, Jeri, ed. The Client Perspective on Evaluation. LC 85-644749. (New Directions for Program Evaluation Ser.: No. PE 36). 1987. 19.00 (*1-55542-942-4*) Jossey-Bass.

Nowakowski, John B. Vegetarian Magic: At the Regency House Spa. (Illus.). 272p. (Orig.). 1996. pap. 19.95 (*0-9654045-0-1*) JBN Prods.

— Vegetarian Magic at the Regency House Spa. LC 00-37853. 2000. pap. write for info. (*1-57067-100-1*) Book Pub Co.

Nowakowski, R., ed. Games of No Chance. (Mathematical Sciences Research Institute Publications: No. 29). 549p. (C). 1998. pap. text 29.95 (*0-521-64652-9*) Cambridge U Pr.

— Games of No Chance: Combinatorial Games at MSRI, 1994. LC 97-100006. (Mathematical Sciences Research Institute Publications: No. 29). (Illus.). 549p. (C). 1996. text 54.95 (*0-521-57411-0*) Cambridge U Pr.

Nowakowski, Richard S., jt. ed. see Levinson, Steven W.

Nowakowski, Rodney W. Primary Low Vision Care. LC 94-8438. 300p. (C). 1995. pap. text 75.00 (*0-8385-7980-9*, A7980-4, Apple Lange Med) McGraw.

Nowarra, Heinz J. Blohm & Voss Bv 138. Cox, Don, tr. from GER. LC 97-219905. 48p. 1997. pap. 9.95 (*0-7643-0296-5*) Schiffer.

— Blohm & Voss Bv 222. Cox, Don, tr. from GER. LC 97-219987. 48p. 1997. pap. 9.95 (*0-7643-0295-7*) Schiffer.

— Dornier DO 335 - "Pfeil" Aircraft. LC 89-84180. (Illus.). 48p. 1989. pap. 9.95 (*0-88740-189-9*) Schiffer.

— Fiesler Fi 156 Storch. LC 97-219962. 48p. 1997. pap. 9.95 (*0-7643-0299-X*) Schiffer.

— The Flying Pencil: Dornier DO 17-215. LC 90-60475. (Illus.). 48p. 1990. pap. 9.95 (*0-88740-236-4*) Schiffer.

— The Focke-Wulf FW 190: Fighters, Bombers, Ground Attack Aircraft. Cable, James C., tr. from GER. LC 91-62744. (Illus.). 48p. 1991. pap. 9.95 (*0-88740-354-9*) Schiffer.

— Focke-Wulf FW 190-Tal 52: Aircraft & Legend. (Illus.). 160p. 1989. pap. 19.95 (*0-85429-881-9*) Haynes Manuals.

— Fokker Dr. 1 in Action. (Aircraft in Action Ser.). (Illus.). 50p. 1989. pap. 9.95 (*0-89747-229-2*, 1098) Squad Sig Pubns.

— The Fokker Dr.1 & D VII in WWI. Cox, Don, tr. from GER. LC 91-62743. (Illus.). 48p. 1991. pap. 9.95 (*0-88740-353-0*) Schiffer.

— German Airships - Parseval - Schutte - Lanz - Zeppelin. LC 89-63353. (Illus.). 52p. 1989. pap. 9.95 (*0-88740-199-6*) Schiffer.

— German Gliders in WW II. Force, Edward, tr. from GER. LC 91-62747. (Illus.). 48p. 1991. pap. 9.95 (*0-88740-358-1*) Schiffer.

— German Guided Missles. Cox, Don, tr. (Illus.). 48p. (Orig.). 1993. pap. 9.95 (*0-88740-475-8*) Schiffer.

— German Helicopters, 1928-1945. LC 90-62988. (Illus.). 48p. 1991. pap. 9.95 (*0-88740-289-5*) Schiffer.

— German U-Boat Type VII - Grey Ghosts of the Sea. Force, Edward, tr. from GER. (Illus.). 48p. 1992. pap. 9.95 (*0-88740-409-X*) Schiffer.

— German "UHU" - He219 Aircraft. LC 89-84179. (Illus.). 48p. 1989. pap. 9.95 (*0-88740-188-0*) Schiffer.

— Heinkel HE 162. Carle, James, tr. (Illus.). 48p. (Orig.). 1993. pap. 9.95 (*0-88740-478-2*) Schiffer.

— Junkers JU 52. (Illus.). 48p. 1993. pap. 9.95 (*0-88740-523-1*) Schiffer.

— Junkers Ju 290, Ju 390, Etc. Cox, Don, tr. from GER. LC 97-219900. 48p. 1997. pap. 9.95 (*0-7643-0297-3*) Schiffer.

— Messerschmitt Bf 109. LC 91-60857. (German Aircraft of WWII Ser.). (Illus.). 48p. 1991. pap. 9.95 (*0-88740-311-5*) Schiffer.

— Russian Fighter Aircraft, 1920-1941. Cox, Don, tr. from GER. LC 97-219895. 48p. 1997. pap. 9.95 (*0-7643-0294-9*) Schiffer.

Nowatzki, E. A., jt. auth. see Karafiath, L. L.

Nowatzki, Richard J. Memoirs of a Navy Major. (Illus.). 256p. (Orig.). 1995. pap. 10.95 (*0-9645284-0-1*) R J Nowatzki.

Nowell, Alexander. A Catechisme, or First Instruction & Learning of Christian Religion. LC 74-23570. 185p. 1975. reprint ed. lib. bdg. 50.00 (*0-8201-1143-0*) Schol Facsimiles.

Nowell, D., jt. auth. see Hills, D. A.

Nowell, Elizabeth. Letters of Thomas Wolfe. (Hudson River Editions Ser.). 1984. 52.00 (*0-684-18269-6*, Scribners Ref) Mac Lib Ref.

— Thomas Wolfe: A Biography. LC 72-7507. 456p. 1973. reprint ed. lib. bdg. 38.50 (*0-8371-6519-9*, NOTW, Greenwood Pr) Greenwood.

Nowell, Eppler. Sky Scanner. 2nd ed. (Illus.). 17p. (Orig.). 1980. pap. text 4.95 (*0-9611454-0-4*) E Nowell.

Nowell, Gregory P. Mercantile States & the World Oil Cartel, 1900-1939. LC 93-38020. (Cornell Studies in Political Economy). (Illus.). 344p. (C). 1994. text 47.50 (*0-8014-2878-5*) Cornell U Pr.

Nowell, Irene. Jonah, Tobit, Judith. (Collegeville Bible Commentary - Old Testament Ser.). 94p. 1986. pap. 4.95 (*0-8146-1482-5*) Liturgical Pr.

— Sing a New Song: The Psalms in the Sunday Lectionary. 320p. 1993. pap. 19.95 (*0-8146-2043-4*, Liturg Pr Bks) Liturgical Pr.

— Women in the Old Testament. LC 97-2358. 216p. (Orig.). 1997. pap. text 7.95 (*0-8146-2411-1*, Liturg Pr Bks) Liturgical Pr.

Nowell, Iris. Hot Breakfast for Sparrows: My Life with Harold Town. (Illus.). 272p. 1992. 26.95 (*0-7737-2645-4*) Genl Dist Srvs.

Nowell, John. A Hearing. Bickford, Gail H., ed. 307p. 1997. spiral bd. write for info. (*0-945069-07-3*) Freedom Pr Assocs.

Nowell, Kristin, jt. ed. see Jackson, Peter.

Nowell, Lisa H., et al. Pesticides in Bed Sediments & Aquatic Biota in Streams: Distribution, Trends, & Governing Factors. Gilliom, Robert J., ed. (Pesticides in the Hydrologic System Ser.). 400p. (C). 1997. text 59.95 (*1-57504-007-7*) CRC Pr.

Nowell, Richard C. & Marshak, Laura E., eds. Understanding Deafness & the Rehabilitation Process. LC 93-50768. 304p. (C). 1994. 70.00 (*0-205-15628-2*) Allyn.

Nowell, Robert, tr. see Haag, Herbert.

Nowell, Roger. Skipper: A Fisherman's Tale. 1995. 24.95 (*0-563-36755-5*, BBC-Parkwest) Parkwest Pubns.

Nowell-Smith, Geoffrey. L' Avventura. LC 98-130861. (BFI Film Classics). (Illus.). 80p. 1998. pap. 10.95 (*0-85170-534-0*, Pub. by British Film Inst) Ind U Pr.

Nowell-Smith, Geoffrey, ed. The Oxford History of World Cinema. (Illus.). 846p. 1996. 55.00 (*0-19-811257-2*) OUP.

— The Oxford History of World Cinema. (Illus.). 846p. 1999. reprint ed. pap. 27.50 (*0-19-874242-8*) OUP.

Nowell-Smith, Geoffrey & Wollen, Tana, eds. After the Wall. (European Media Monograph: No. 1). (Illus.). 96p. 1992. pap. 9.95 (*0-85170-296-1*, Pub. by British Film Inst) Ind U Pr.

Nowell-Smith, Geoffrey, ed. see Gramsci, Antonio.

Nowell-Smith, Geoffry & Ricci, Stephen, eds. Hollywood & Europe: Economics, Culture, National Identity, 1945-95. LC 98-211614. 240p. 1998. 60.00 (*0-85170-596-0*); pap. 23.95 (*0-85170-597-9*) Ind U Pr.

Nowell-Smith, Simon. Legend of the Master. (BCL1-PS American Literature Ser.). 176p. 1993. reprint ed. lib. bdg. 69.00 (*0-7812-6980-6*) Rprt Serv.

Nowell-Smith, Simon, jt. auth. see Plomer, William.

Nowell-Usticke, G. W. Rembrandt's Etchings: States & Values. LC 87-80028. (Illus.). 379p. 1988. reprint ed. lib. bdg. 60.00 (*0-87817-300-5*) Hacker.

Nowell, Vernon L. Fur Rendezvous Remembered, No. 1. (Illus.). 92p. (Orig.). 1991. pap. 9.95 (*0-9628955-0-4*) Blue Star Vid.

Nowels, William C., jt. auth. see Bova, Joyce.

Nower, Joyce. Year of the Fires & Other Poems. LC 81-70725. 83p. 1983. pap. 4.75 (*0-9600856-2-9*) Ctr Womens Studies.

Nowick, Arthur S. Crystal Properties via Group Theory. (Illus.). 244p. (C). 1996. text 80.00 (*0-521-41945-X*) Cambridge U Pr.

Nowicka-Jankowska, T., et al. Comprehensive Analytical Chemistry: Analytical Visible & Ultraviolet Spectrometry. (Wilson & Wilson's Comprehensive Analytical Chemistry Ser.: Vol. 19). 690p. 1986. 442.75 (*0-444-42371-0*) Elsevier.

Nowicki, Cynthia R. Mentoring the Stars: A Mentorship Program for New Board Members. 325p. 1998. spiral bd. write for info. (*0-9655310-2-3*) Jannetti Pubns.

Nowicki, Dariusz. Gold Medal Mental Workout for Combat Sports: Boxing, Fencing, Judo, Karate, Kickboxing, Taekwondo, & Wrestling. 2nd rev. ed. (Illus.). 122p. 1997. pap. 59.95 incl. audio (*0-940149-07-9*) Stadion Pub.

Nowicki, Dolores A. First Steps in Ritual. 1990. pap. 10.95 (*0-85030-874-7*, Pub. by Aqrn Pr) Harper SF.

— Inner Landscapes: A Journey Into Awareness by Pathworking. 1990. pap. 10.95 (*0-85030-623-X*, Pub. by Aqrn Pr) HarpC.

— Sacred Cord Meditations. 1990. pap. 10.95 (*0-85030-907-7*, Pub. by Aqrn Pr) Harper SF.

Nowicki, Edward J. Supervisory Survival: A Practical Guide for the Professional Survival of New, Experienced, & Aspiring Law Enforcement Supervisors. LC 93-4274. 1993. pap. 17.95 (*1-879411-23-7*) Perf Dimensions Pub.

— Total Survival: A Comprehensive Guide for the Physical, Psychological, Emotional, & Professional Survival of Law Enforcement Officers. LC 92-85340. 1993. pap. 24.95 (*1-879411-18-0*) Perf Dimensions Pub.

— True Blue: True Stories about Real Cops. LC 91-66414. 280p. (Orig.). 1992. pap. 14.95 (*1-879411-15-6*) Perf Dimensions Pub.

Nowicki, Edward J. & Ramsey, Dennis A. Street Weapons: An Identification Manual for Improvised, Unconventional, Unusual, Homemade, Disguised & Exotic Personal Weapons. LC 90-92207. (Illus.). 272p. (Orig.). 1991. pap. 19.95 (*1-879411-11-3*) Perf Dimensions Pub.

Nowicki, J. R. Digital Circuits. (Electrical Engineering Ser.). 1991. pap. 36.50 (*0-7131-3641-3*, VNR) Wiley.

Nowicki, Joseph J. & Meehan, Kerry F. Interdisciplinary Strategies for English & Social Studies Classrooms: Toward Collaborative Middle & Secondary Teaching. LC 96-1235. 207p. (C). 1996. pap. text 33.00 (*0-205-19839-2*) Allyn.

Nowicki, Joseph J., jt. auth. see Meehan, Kerry F.

Nowicki, Maciej. Environment in Poland: Issues & Solutions. 191p. (C). 1993. text 134.50 (*0-7923-2269-X*) Kluwer Academic.

Nowicki, Michael. The Financial Management of Hospitals & Healthcare Organizations. LC 98-36556. 300p. 1998. 52.00 (*1-56793-092-1*) Health Admin Pr.

Nowicki, Ron. Warsaw: The Cabaret Years. LC 92-16660. (Illus.). 288p. 1992. 30.00 (*1-56279-030-7*) Mercury Hse Inc.

Nowicki, Stephen, Jr. & Duke, Marshall. Helping the Child Who Doesn't Fit In: Clinical Psychologists Decipher the Hidden Dimensions of Social Rejection. (Illus.). 192p. (Orig.). 1992. pap. 14.95 (*1-56145-025-1*) Peachtree Pubs.

Nowicki, Tim. Awake to Wildlife: The Complete Naturalist's Great Lakes Wildlife Almanac. 192p. 1994. pap. 11.95 (*1-881139-08-5*) Glovebox Guidebks.

Nowik, William, ed. see Patsula, Peter J.

Nowill, Paul H. Productivity & the Technological Change in Electric Power Generating Plants. Bruchey, Stuart, ed. LC 78-22703. (Energy in the American Economy Ser.). (Illus.). 1979. lib. bdg. 19.95 (*0-405-12005-2*) Ayer.

Nowinski, J. L. Applications of Functional Analysis in Engineering. LC 81-5213. (Mathematical Concepts & Methods in Science & Engineering Ser.: Vol. 22). 320p. 1981. 65.00 (*0-306-40693-4*, Plenum Trade) Perseus Pubng.

Nowinski, Joseph. Clinical Research Guide for Therapists Treating Individuals with Alcohol Abuse & Dependence: Twelve Step Facilitation Therapy Manual, Vol. 1. 133p. 1996. per. 14.00 (*0-16-061513-5*) USGPO.

Nowinski, Joseph. Family Recovery & Substance Abuse: A Twelve-Step Guide for Treatment. LC 98-25422. 216p. 1998. 36.00 (*0-7619-1110-3*); pap. 15.99 (*0-7619-1111-1*) Sage.

Nowinski, Joseph & Baker, Stuart. The Twelve-Step Facilitation Handbook: A Systematic Approach to Early Recovery from Alcoholism & Addiction. LC 97-37746. 1998. pap. 22.95 (*0-7879-4049-6*) Jossey-Bass.

Nowinski, Joseph, et al. Twelve Step Facilitation Therapy Manual: A Clinical Research Guide for Therapists Treating Individuals with Alcohol Abuse & Dependence. 123p. (Orig.). (C). 1995. pap. text 35.00 (*0-7881-2463-3*) DIANE Pub.

Nowinski, Joseph K. Becoming Satisfied: A Man's Guide to Sexual Fulfillment. 1980. 12.95 (*0-13-073031-9*, Spectrum IN) Macmillan Gen Ref.

— Lifelong Love Affair. 1989. pap. 7.95 (*0-393-30621-6*) Norton.

— Substance Abuse in Adolescents & Young Adults: A Guide to Treatment. (C). 1990. 29.95 (*0-393-70097-6*) Norton.

Nowinski, Judith. Baron Dominique Vivant Denon, 1747-1825: Hedonist & Scholar in a Period of Transition. LC 78-86651. (Illus.). 280p. 1975. 27.50 (*0-8386-7470-4*) Fairleigh Dickinson.

Nowitschkowa, A. L., jt. auth. see Scharow, W. A.

Nowitz, Marilyn, jt. auth. see Caserta, Carmen.

Nowk, Andrzej S., jt. ed. see Vallacher, Robin R.

Nowka, Richard H., jt. auth. see Leibson, David J.

Nowka, Richard H., jt. auth. see Liebson, David J.

Nowlan, Alden. Early Poems. (Illus.). 183p. 1983. pap. 10.95 (*0-86492-001-6*, Pub. by Goose Ln Edits) Genl Dist Srvs.

— An Exchange of Gifts: Poems New & Selected. 284p. 1985. 14.95 (*0-7725-1525-5*) Genl Dist Srvs.

— Miracle at Indian River. 132p. 1982. pap. 8.95 (*0-7720-1402-7*) Genl Dist Srvs.

— The Wanton Troopers. 171p. 1988. 18.95 (*0-86492-079-2*, Pub. by Goose Ln Edits); pap. 10.95 (*0-86492-083-0*, Pub. by Goose Ln Edits) Genl Dist Srvs.

Nowlan, Alden. What Happened When He Went to the Store for Bread? Poems. Smith, Thomas R., ed. LC 93-14682. 1993. pap. 10.00 (*1-883070-00-7*) Nineties Pr.

Nowlan, Alden. Will Ye Let the Mummers In? 164p. 1984. 14.95 (*0-7720-1451-5*); 8.95 (*0-7720-1407-8*) Genl Dist Srvs.

Nowlan, Alden & Learning, Walter. Frankenstein: The Play. LC 77-370615. 181p. 1976. write for info. (*0-7720-1058-7*) Irwin Publ.

***Nowlan, Gwendolyn L., ed.** A Dictionary of Quotations & Proverbs about Cats & Dogs. (Illus.). 232p. 2000. 38.50 (*0-7864-0801-4*) McFarland & Co.

Nowlan, Gwendolyn L., jt. ed. see Nowlan, Robert A.

Nowlan, Gwendolyn W., jt. auth. see Nowlan, Robert A.

***Nowlan, James D.** The Itinerant: A Heartland Story. (Illus.). 256p. 2000. pap. 15.95 (*0-9634395-6-1*) Conversation Pr.

Nowlan, James D., jt. auth. see Gove, Samuel K.

Nowlan, Kevin B. & O'Connell, Maurice R., eds. Daniel O'Connell: Portrait of a Radical. LC 85-80412. 120p. 1985. 24.95 (*0-8232-1140-1*) Fordham.

Nowlan, Phil & Calkins, Dick. Buck Rogers in the 25th Century. 32p. (J). 1994. pap. 4.95 (*0-9647830-0-2*) EKTEK.

Nowlan, Robert A. Born This Day: A Book of Birthdays & Quotations of Prominent People Through the Centuries. LC 96-4189. 263p. 1996. lib. bdg. 39.95 (*0-7864-0166-4*) McFarland & Co.

***Nowlan, Robert A. & Nowlan, Gwendolyn L., eds.** A Dictionary of Quotations about Communication. 347p. 2000. 49.95 (*0-7864-0767-0*) McFarland & Co.

Nowlan, Robert A. & Nowlan, Gwendolyn W. Cinema Sequels & Remakes, 1903-1987. LC 88-42640. (Illus.). 966p. 1988. lib. bdg. 95.00 (*0-89950-314-4*) McFarland & Co.

— An Encyclopedia of Film Festivals. LC 88-13152. (Foundations in Library & Information Science: Vol. 23). 380p. 1989. 78.50 (*0-89232-734-0*) Jai Pr.

— Film Quotations: 11,000 Lines Spoken on Screen, Arranged by Subject, & Indexed. LC 92-56673. (Illus.). 763p. 1994. lib. bdg. 75.00 (*0-89950-786-7*) McFarland & Co.

— The Films of the Eighties: A Complete, Qualitative Filmography to over 3400 Feature-Length English Language Films, Theatrical & Video-Only, Released Between Janaury 1, 1980, & December 31, 1989. LC 90-53516. 868p. 1991. lib. bdg. 85.00 (*0-89950-560-0*) McFarland & Co.

— The Name Is Familiar: Who Played Who in the Movies. 1016p. 1993. pap. text 99.95 (*1-55570-054-3*) Neal-Schuman.

Nowlen, Kevin, ed. Governments, Ethnic Group & Political Representations. (Comparative Studies on Governments & Non-Dominant Ethnic Groups in Europe (1850-1940)). 400p. (C). 1993. text 85.00 (*0-8147-5766-9*) NYU Pr.

Nowlen, Philip. A New Approach to Continuing Education for Business & the Professions. (ACE-Oryx Series on Higher Education). 304p. 1987. 31.95 (*0-02-922740-2*) Free Pr.

Nowles, William, jt. auth. see Bova, Joyce.

Nowlin, Barry, jt. ed. see Franklin, Tom.

Nowlin, Bill & Ross, Mike. Fenway Saved. (Illus.). 192p. 1999. 29.95 (*1-58382-020-5*) Sports Masters.

***Nowlin, Bill, et al.** Fenway Saved. (Illus.). 2000. pap. 19.95 (*1-58382-065-5*) Sports Pub.

Nowlin, Bill, jt. auth. see Prime, Jim.

Nowlin, David V. & Stupak, Ronald J. War As an Instrument of Policy: Past, Present, & Future. LC 97-25301. 744p. (C). 1998. 52.00 (*0-7618-0843-4*); pap. 29.50 (*0-7618-0844-2*) U Pr of Amer.

Nowlin, James E. Nowlin - Stone Genealogy: Record of the Descendants of James Nowlin, Who Came to Pittsylvania County, Virginia, from Ireland about 1700; Also a Record of the Descendants of George Stone & of James Hoskin Stone Who Was born in Pittsylvania County in 1778. (Illus.). 548p. 1993. reprint ed. pap. 82.00 (*0-8328-3727-X*); reprint ed. lib. bdg. 92.00 (*0-8328-3726-1*) Higginson Bk Co.

Nowlin, James E. & Blackburn, J. Vernon. Humanism & Environmentalism Vol. 24: Philosophical Perspectives in Counseling. LC 93-44078. (American University Studies XIV: Education: Ser. XIV, Vol. 24). 178p. (C). 1995. 41.95 (*0-8204-1109-4*) P Lang Pubng.

Nowlin, Jerry L. Construction Financing to Build Your Own Home. LC 90-92261. 70p. (Orig.). 1990. pap. 19.95 (*0-9628643-0-7*) J L Nowlin.

Nowlin, Sterling. September Monthly Activities. (Monthly Activities Ser.). (Illus.). 80p. (J). (gr. 1-3). 1996. pap., wbk. ed. 9.95 (*1-55734-151-6*) Tchr Create Mat.

Nowlin, Susan S., jt. auth. see Sterling.

Nowlin, Susan S., jt. auth. see Sterling, Mary E.

Nowlin, William F. Negro in American National Politics. LC 71-173802. reprint ed. 20.00 (*0-404-00204-8*) AMS Pr.

Nowlin, William G., Jr., ed. see Berkman, Alexander.

Nowlin, William G., Jr., ed. see Maximoff, Gregory P.

Nowlis, Elizabeth A., jt. auth. see Ellis, Albert.

Nowlis, Vincent. Companionship Preference & Dominance in the Social Interaction of Young Chimpanzees. (Comparative Psychology Monographs). 1941. pap. 25.00 (*0-527-24920-3*) Periodicals Srv.

Nowman, Daniel S. Placido Domingo's Tales from the Opera. (Illus.). 186p. 1998. text 23.00 (*0-7881-5699-3*) DIANE Pub.

N

Nown, Graham, jt. auth. see Wells, Chris.

Nown, Sylvana. Baby Names & Star Signs. (Family Matters Ser.). (Illus.). 96p. (Orig.). 1990. pap. 4.95 (*0-7063-6801-0*, Pub. by WrLock) Sterling.

Nownes, Laura. Grandmother's Flower Garden. LC 90-42336. (Classic Quilt Ser.). (Illus.). 20p. 1990. pap. 6.95 (*0-8442-2614-9*, Quilt Dgst Pr) NTC Contemp Pub Co.

— Log Cabin. LC 90-41882. (Classic Quilt Ser.). (Illus.). 20p. 1990. pap. 6.95 (*0-8442-2612-2*, Quilt Dgst Pr) NTC Contemp Pub Co.

— Star of Bethlehem. LC 90-41883. (Classic Quilt Ser.). (Illus.). 20p. 1990. pap. 6.95 (*0-8442-2613-0*, Quilt Dgst Pr) NTC Contemp Pub Co.

Nownes, Laura & McClun, Diana. Say It with Quilts. Kuhn, Barbara K., ed. LC 96-38606. (Illus.). 144p. 1997. 29.95 (*1-57120-023-1*, 10147) C & T Pub.

Nownes, Laura, jt. auth. see McClun, Diana.

Nownes, Laura, jt. auth. see McClun, Dians.

Nowosad, Frank. Ciccimarra: A Biography. LC 88-31037. (Illus.). 253p. 1988. 24.95 (*0-940537-04-4*) Fuller Tech.

Nowotny, A. Basic Exercises in Immunochemistry: A Laboratory Manual. 2nd ed. LC 79-14029. (Illus.). 1979. pap. 39.00 (*0-387-09453-9*) Spr-Verlag.

Nowotny, Alois, ed. Beneficial Effects of Endotoxins. LC 83-2256. 596p. 1983. 125.00 (*0-306-41147-4*, Plenum Trade) Perseus Pubng.

— Biomembranes Vol. 11: Pathological Membranes. LC 82-22343. 494p. 1983. 110.00 (*0-306-41065-6*, Plenum Trade) Perseus Pubng.

Nowotny, Franz A., jt. ed. see Jones, Larry W.

Nowotny, Helga & Felt, Ulrike. After the Breakthrough: The Emergence of High-Temperature Superconductivity As a Research Field. (Illus.). 220p. (C). 1997. text 52.95 (*0-521-56124-8*) Cambridge U Pr.

Nowotny, Helga & Rose, Hilary, eds. Countermovements in the Sciences. (Sociology of the Sciences Yearbook Ser.: No. 3). 1979. pap. text 66.50 (*90-277-0972-6*) Kluwer Academic.

Nowotny, Helga & Taschwer, Klaus, eds. The Sociology of the Sciences, 2 vols., Set. LC 95-48335. (International Library of Critical Writings in Economics: Vol. 8). 1152p. 1996. 390.00 (*1-85278-911-5*) E Elgar.

N

***Nowotny, Helga, et al.** Rethinking Science. 2001. 59.95 (*0-7456-2607-6*, Pub. by Polity Pr); pap. 27.95 (*0-7456-2608-4*, Pub. by Polity Pr) Blackwell Pubs.

Nowotny, Helga, jt. ed. see Mendelsohn, Everett I.

Nowotny, J., ed. Diffusion in Solids & High Temperature Oxidations of Metals. 446p. 1992. text 183.00 (*0-87849-626-2*, Pub. by Trans T Pub) Enfield Pubs NH.

— Electronic Ceramic Materials. 568p. 1992. text 183.00 (*0-87849-627-0*, Pub. by Trans T Pub) Enfield Pubs NH.

— Interface Segregation & Related Processes in Materials. 460p. 1991. text 200.00 (*0-87849-620-3*, Pub. by Trans T Pub) Enfield Pubs NH.

Nowotny, J. & International Workshop on Interfaces of Ceramic Ma, eds. Science of Ceramic Interfaces II. LC 94-43582. (Materials Science Monographs: Vol. 81). 706p. 1995. 243.25 (*0-444-81666-6*) Elsevier.

Nowotny, J. & Sorrell, C. C., eds. Electrical Properties of Oxide Materials. (Key Engineering Materials Ser.: Vols. 125 & 126). (Illus.). 436p. (C). 1997. 184.00 (*0-87849-746-3*, Pub. by Trans T Pub) Enfield Pubs NH.

Nowotny, J. & Weppner, W., eds. Non-Stoichiometric Compounds. (C). 1989. text 287.50 (*0-7923-0225-7*) Kluwer Academic.

Nowotny, J., jt. ed. see Dutour, L. C.

Nowotny, Janusz, jt. ed. see Smart, Roger C.

Nowotny, K. A., comment. Codex Borbonicus. fac. ed. (Codices Selecti C Ser.: Vol. XLIV). (ENG, FRE, GER & SPA.). 38p. 1974. lthr. 556.00 (*3-201-00901-6*, Pub. by Akademische Druck-und) Balogh.

— Codices Becker I-II. fac. ed. (Codices Selecti C Ser.: Vol. IV). (Illus.). 1961. lthr. 142.00 (*3-201-00756-0*, Pub. by Akademische Druck-und) Balogh.

Nowotny, K. A., intro. Codex Cospi. fac. ed. (Codices Selecti C Ser.: Vol. XVIII). (Illus.). 32p. 1968. lthr. 214.00 (*3-201-00762-5*, Pub. by Akademische Druck-und) Balogh.

Nowotny, Karl. Messages from a Doctor in the Fourth Dimension. 128p. (C). 1990. 50.00 (*0-7212-0895-9*, Pub. by Regency Pr GBR) St Mut.

Nowotny, Karl A., comment. Codex Borgia. fac. ed. (Codices Selecti C Ser.: Vol. LVIII). (ENG, FRE & SPA., Illus.). 52p. 1976. lthr. 556.00 (*3-201-00964-4*, Pub. by Akademische Druck-und) Balogh.

Nowotny, Kenneth & Smith, David B., eds. Public Utility Regulation. (C). 1989. lib. bdg. 100.50 (*0-7923-9019-9*) Kluwer Academic.

***Nowottny, Marianne.** Nowottny: Shells & Corridors. (Illus.). 74p. 1998. pap. 10.00 (*0-9677326-1-1*) Abaton Bk.

Nowottny, Winifred. The Language Poets Use. 2nd ed. 225p. (C). 1965. pap. 14.95 (*0-485-12009-7*, Pub. by Athlone Pr) Humanities.

Nowra, Louis. Cosi. 2nd rev. ed. (Currency Plays Ser.). (Illus.). xx, 90p. 1994. pap. 16.95 (*0-86819-403-4*, Pub. by Currency Pr) Accents Pubns.

Nowra, Louis. Cosi: The Screenplay. 116p. (C). 1996. pap. text 16.95 (*0-86819-475-1*, Pub. by Currency Pr) Accents Pubns.

Nowra, Louis. The Golden Age. 105p. 1990. pap. 5.60 (*0-87129-015-4*, G49) Dramatic Pub.

Nowry, Laurence. Man of Mana: Marius Barbeau, a Biography. abr. ed. LC 96-134745. (Illus.). 448p. 1998. 27.95 (*1-55021-100-5*, Pub. by NC Ltd) U of Toronto Pr.

Nowshadi, Farshad. Managing Netware & Windows 95. 2nd ed. LC 98-29668. 504p. (C). 1999. pap. text 46.88 (*0-201-17784-6*) Addison-Wesley.

Nowzad, Bahram. The IMF & Its Critics. LC 82-958. (Essays in International Finance Ser.: No. 146). 34p. reprint ed. pap. 30.00 (*0-608-14558-0*, 202474900038) Bks Demand.

***Noy, David.** Foreigners at Rome: Citizens & Strangers. (Illus.). 360p. (C). 2000. lib. bdg. 49.50 (*0-7156-2952-2*, Pub. by Classical Pr) David Brown.

Noy, David. Jewish Inscriptions of Western Europe: The City of Rome, Vol. 2. 592p. (C). 1995. text 135.00 (*0-521-44202-8*) Cambridge U Pr.

— Jewish Inscriptions of Western Europe Vol. 1: Italy (Excluding the City of Rome), Spain & Gaul. (Illus.). 407p. (C). 1993. text 110.00 (*0-521-44201-X*) Cambridge U Pr.

Noy, Dov. Studies in Jewish Folklore. 1981. 25.00 (*0-87068-802-2*) Ktav.

Noy, Dov, ed. Folktales of Israel. Baharav, Gene, tr. LC 63-16721. (Folktales of the World Ser.). 1969. pap. text 7.95 (*0-226-59720-2*, FW8) U Ch Pr.

Noy, Dov & Ben-Amos, Dan, eds. Folktales of Israel. Baharav, Gene, tr. LC 63-16721. (Folktales of the World Ser.). 245p. reprint ed. pap. 76.00 (*0-608-09489-7*, 205429000005) Bks Demand.

Noy, Edward A. Building Surveys & Reports. 339p. 1990. 53.00 (*0-614-16813-9*, BSP130) Am Soc Civil Eng.

Noy, Gary. Distant Horizon: Historical Documents & Readings on the Nineteenth Century. LC 98-30643. 1999. pap. 22.00 (*0-8032-8371-7*) U of Nebr Pr.

Noy, William. Principal Grounds & Maxims with an Analysis of the Laws of England. 3rd ed. xxvii, 219p. 1980. reprint ed. 37.00 (*0-8377-0906-7*, Rothman) W S Hein.

Noy, Y. Ian, ed. Ergonomics & Safety of Intelligent Driver Interfaces. LC 97-17943. (Human Factors in Transportation Ser.). (Illus.). 440p. 1996. 89.95 (*0-8058-1955-X*); pap. 45.00 (*0-8058-1956-8*) L Erlbaum Assocs.

Noya, Juan E. Las Palmas Ya No Son Verdes: Analisis y Testimonios de la Tragedia Cubana. LC 85-80134. (Coleccion Cuba y sus Jueces). (SPA., Illus.). 93p. (Orig.). 1985. pap. 9.95 (*0-89729-368-1*) Ediciones.

***Noya, Manuel S., ed.** Marsilius of Inghen. 336p. 1999. 109.00 (*90-04-11312-6*) Brill Academic Pubs.

***Noya, Manuel S., et al, eds.** Marsilius of Inghen. (Studies in the History of Christian Thought). 344p. 1999. 126.50 (*90-04-11224-3*) Brill Academic Pubs.

Noya, Manuel Santos, see Santos Noya, Manuel.

Noyan, I. C. & Cohen, J. B. Residual Stress. (Materials Research & Engineering Ser.). (Illus.). 300p. 1987. 105.95 (*0-387-96378-2*) Spr-Verlag.

Noyce, Gaylord. Church Meetings That Work. LC 94-78332. (Church Leader's Core Library). 80p. 1994. pap. 10.25 (*1-56699-132-3*, AL153) Alban Inst.

— Why Can't I Believe? LC 99-38105. 1999. pap. 15.99 (*0-8272-4241-7*) Chalice Pr.

Noyce, Richard. Contemporary Graphic Art in Poland. (Illus.). 232p. 1997. text 55.00 (*90-5703-481-6*) Gordon & Breach.

— Contemporary Painting in Poland. LC 96-120854. (Illus.). 240p. 1995. text 60.00 (*976-8097-97-3*, Pub. by IPG Chicago) Gordon & Breach.

Noyce, Vera. Emerald Lotus: A Collection of Poetry & Prose. 60p. 1998. pap. 9.95 (*1-887747-18-4*) Legendary Pub.

Noye, B. J. Computational Techniques for Differential Equations. (North-Holland Mathematical Library: Vol. 83). 1991. 134.50 (*0-685-50935-4*) Elsevier.

Noye, B. J., jt. ed. see Hogarth, W. L.

Noye, Dominique. Dictionnaire Foulfoulde-Francais. (FRE.). 1989. 150.00 (*0-7859-7925-5*, 2-7053-0484-3) Fr & Eur.

Noye, John. Computational Techniques & Applications: CTAC 97. 1998. 135.00 (*981-02-3519-4*) World Scientific Pub.

— Sea Level Changes & Their Effects: International Ocean & Atmosphere Pacific Conference. (Ocean Engineering Ser.). 1999. 64.00 (*981-02-3618-2*) World Scientific Pub.

Noye, John, ed. Modelling Coastal Sea Processes: Proceedings of the International Ocean & Atmosphere Pacific Conference. 390p. 1999. 68.00 (*981-02-3556-9*) World Scientific Pub.

Noyed, Robert B., jt. auth. see Klingel, Cynthia Fitterer.

Noyelle, Thierry J. New Technologies & Services: Impacts on Cities & Jobs. (Urban Studies: No. 5). 55p. (Orig.). 1986. pap. text 6.00 (*0-913749-03-6*) U MD Urban Stud.

Noyer, Alain-Pierre. Dictionnaire des Chanteurs Francophones de 1900 a nos Jours. (FRE.). 210p. 1989. pap. 59.95 (*0-7859-8082-2*, 2853192091) Fr & Eur.

Noyer, Albert. The Saint's Day Deaths. LC 98-83260. 360p. 2000. pap. 17.25 (*0-88739-252-0*) Creat Arts Bk.

***Noyer, Jennifer.** The Legacy: Bill Evans Reaching Out from the Regional Southwest. (Choreography & Dance Archives Ser.: Vol. 2). (Illus.). 112p. 1999. pap. text 49.00 incl. VHS (*90-5755-115-2*, Harwood Acad Pubs); pap. text 49.00 incl. VHS (*90-5755-118-7*, Harwood Acad Pubs) Gordon & Breach.

Noyer, Paul Du, see Du Noyer, Paul.

Noyer, Rolf. Features, Positions & Affixes in Autonomous Morphological Structure. rev. ed. LC 96-53528. (Outstanding Dissertations in Linguistics Ser.). (Illus.). 428p. 1997. text 98.00 (*0-8153-2759-5*) Garland.

Noyes. Principles & Positioning for MRI. (Allied Health Ser.). (C). 2001. pap. 49.95 (*0-7668-1204-9*) Delmar.

— Principles & Positioning for MRI-Exam Review. (Allied Health Ser.). (C). 2001. pap. 24.95 (*0-7668-1205-7*) Delmar.

— Principles & Positioning For Ultrasound. (C). 2002. pap. 45.00 (*0-7668-1304-5*) Delmar.

— Ruff's Bone. 1994. 23.75 (*1-57135-107-8*) Living Bks.

Noyes, Alexander D. Forty Years of American Finance. Bruchey, Stuart, ed. LC 80-1163. (Rise of Commercial Banking Ser.). 1981. reprint ed. lib. bdg. 41.95 (*0-405-13672-2*) Ayer.

Noyes, Alfred. The Highwayman. 2nd ed. (Illus.). 32p. (YA). 1999. pap. 10.95 (*0-19-272370-7*) OUP.

— The Last Voyage Bk. 3: Torch-Bearers. LC 70-167477. (Granger Index Reprint Ser.). 1977. reprint ed. 18.95 (*0-8369-6282-6*) Ayer.

— Opalescent Parrot: Essays. (Essay Index Reprint Ser.). 1977. 20.95 (*0-8369-0748-5*) Ayer.

— Pageant of Letters. LC 68-22935. (Essay Index Reprint Ser.). 1977. reprint ed. 23.95 (*0-8369-0749-3*) Ayer.

— Watchers of the Sky. 1988. reprint ed. lib. bdg. 59.00 (*0-7812-0390-2*) Rprt Serv.

— Watchers of the Sky. LC 72-131790. 1971. reprint ed. 29.00 (*0-403-00677-5*) Scholarly.

— William Morris. LC 72-39201. (Select Bibliographies Reprint Ser.). 1977. reprint ed. 15.95 (*0-8369-6803-4*) Ayer.

— William Morris. LC 70-173176. 164p. 1972. reprint ed. 17.95 (*0-405-08822-1*, Pub. by Blom Pubns) Ayer.

Noyes, Alice. Around Hooksett. (Images of America Ser.). 1999. pap. 16.99 (*0-7524-0836-4*) Arcadia Publng.

Noyes, Alice D. Metallak, His Legacy. Jordan Assocs. Staff, ed. & illus. by. 266p. 1988. 18.95 (*0-685-25278-7*) A D Noyes.

Noyes, Alva. Story of Ajax. LC 67-6837. (Studies in European Literature: No. 56). (C). 1970. lib. bdg. 75.00 (*0-8383-1109-1*) M S G Haskell Hse.

Noyes Anderson, Susan D. Awaken Your Spiritual Power: (The Fairy Godmother Isn't Coming!) LC 99-94228. 184p. (Orig.). 1999. pap. 12.95 (*0-9670525-0-5*, 1000, Pub. by Karisma Pr) Granite UT.

Noyes, Benjamin L., tr. Vital Records of Deer Isle, Maine Prior to 1867. 252p. 1997. pap. 29.50 (*0-89725-329-9*, 1851) Picton Pr.

Noyes, Beppie. Mosby, the Kennedy Center Cat: A True Story Made Legend. 2nd ed. (Illus.). 130p. (J). (gr. 5-9). 1998. reprint ed. 14.95 (*0-9637688-8-3*) Vacation Spot.

Noyes, C. P. Noyes-Gilman Ancestry: Being a Series of Sketches with a Chart of the Ancestry of Charles Phelps Noyes & Emily H. (Gilman) Noyes, His Wife. (Illus.). 478p. 1989. reprint ed. pap. 72.00 (*0-8328-0909-8*); reprint ed. lib. bdg. 80.00 (*0-8328-0908-X*) Higginson Bk Co.

Noyes, Charlene, jt. auth. see Mellon, Steve.

Noyes, Claudia M., jt. auth. see Lundblad, Roger L.

Noyes, David. History of Norway: Comprising a Minute Account of Its First Settlement...Interspersed with Historical Sketches, Narrative & Anecdote. (Illus.). 215p. 1997. reprint ed. lib. bdg. 29.00 (*0-8328-5880-3*) Higginson Bk Co.

***Noyes, Deborah.** It's Vladimir! LC 00-26173. (Illus.). (J). 2000. write for info. (*0-7614-5071-8*) Marshall Cavendish.

Noyes, Diane D. & Mellody, Peggy. Beauty & Cancer: Looking & Feeling Your Best. LC 92-14254. (Illus.). 192p. 1992. pap. 12.95 (*0-87833-809-8*) Taylor Pub.

Noyes, Dorothy. Uses of Tradition: Arts of Italian Americans in Philadelphia. (Illus.). 80p. (C). 1991. pap. 12.95 (*0-9644937-3-X*) Phila Folklore.

— Uses of Tradition: Arts of Italian Americans in Philadelphia. (Illus.). 79p. 1997. reprint ed. pap. text 30.00 (*0-7881-3771-9*) DIANE Pub.

Noyes, E. The Story of Milan. (Mediaeval Towns Ser.: Vol. 20). 1974. reprint ed. 65.00 (*0-8115-0862-5*) Periodicals Srv.

Noyes, Edward S., ed. Readings in the Modern Essay. LC 70-121494. (Essay Index Reprint Ser.). 1977. 36.95 (*0-8369-2008-2*) Ayer.

Noyes, Edward S., ed. see Smollett, Tobias George.

Noyes, Eliot F. Organic Design in Home Furnishings. LC 70-86424. (Museum of Modern Art Publications in Reprint). (Illus.). 1969. reprint ed. 10.95 (*0-405-01540-2*) Ayer.

Noyes, Florence, tr. see Krasinski, Zygmunt.

Noyes, Frederick B. Noyes' Oral Histology & Embryology. 7th rev. ed. Schour, Isaac, ed. LC 53-9573. 448p. reprint ed. pap. 138.90 (*0-608-14006-6*, 205544200023) Bks Demand.

Noyes, George R., ed. see Krasinski, Zygmunt.

Noyes, George R., ed. see Ostrovsky, Alexander.

Noyes, George R., tr. see Asch, Sholem.

Noyes, George R., tr. see Gogol, Nikolai Vasilevich.

Noyes, George R., tr. see Zielinski, Thaddeus.

Noyes, George W., ed. Religious Experience of John Humphrey Noyes. 1923. 39.95 (*0-8156-8060-0*) Syracuse U Pr.

Noyes, George W., ed. see Noyes, John H.

Noyes, Gertrude E., jt. auth. see Starnes, De Witt T.

***Noyes, H. F.** Favorite Haiku, Vol. 3. 64p. 2000. pap. 10.00 (*0-9657818-4-4*) Red Moon Pr.

— Favorite Haiku, Vol. 4. 64p. 2001. pap. 10.00 (*1-893959-09-0*) Red Moon Pr.

— Favorite Haiku: Short Essays on the Shortest Poems, 4 vols., Vol. 2. (Illus.). 64p. 1999. 10.00 (*0-9657818-3-6*, Pnd Frog) Red Moon Pr.

Noyes, H. F. Favorite Haiku Vol. 1: Brief Essays on Ordinary Moments. (Favorite Haiku Ser.). 64p. 1998. pap. 10.00 (*0-9657818-2-8*, Pnd Frog) Red Moon Pr.

Noyes, Harriette E. Records of Hampstead, New Hampshire. 60p. 1984. pap. 6.50 (*0-912606-23-1*) Hunterdon Hse.

***Noyes, Harriette Eliza.** A Memorial History of Hampstead New Hampshire Vol. 2: Congregation Church 1752-1902. (Illus.). 844p. 1999. reprint ed. pap. 54.50 (*0-7884-1312-0*) Heritage Bk.

— A Memorial of the Town of Hampstead New Hampshire. (Illus.). 658p. 1999. reprint ed. pap. 43.50 (*0-7884-1295-7*, N591) Heritage Bk.

Noyes, Henry. China Born: Adventures of a Maverick Bookman. LC 89-60880. 224p. (Orig.). 1989. reprint ed. 19.95 (*0-8351-2198-4*); reprint ed. pap. 12.95 (*0-8351-2199-2*) China Bks.

— China Born: Memoirs of a Westerner. 224p. 1989. 32.00 (*0-7206-0748-5*, Pub. by P Owen Ltd) Dufour.

— Valley of the Sun: Selected Poems. (Illus.). 117p. (Orig.). 1993. pap. 9.95 (*0-915117-13-4*) Freedom Voices Pubns.

Noyes, Henry S., jt. auth. see Noyes, Shana Connell.

Noyes, J. Chalcidoidea Catalogue: Windows Version. (World Biodiversity Database Ser.). 298.00p. 1998. 298.00 incl. cd-rom (*3-540-14675-X*) Spr-Verlag.

Noyes, J. M. & Baber, C. User-Centered Design of Systems. LC 99-17688. (Applied Computing Ser.). (Illus.). xiv, 226p. 1999. pap. 39.95 (*3-540-76007-5*) Spr-Verlag.

Noyes, James H., jt. ed. see Ahrari, Mohammed E.

Noyes, James L. Artificial Intelligence with Common LISP: Fundamentals of Symbolic & Numeric Processing. (Computer Science Ser.). 542p. (C). Date not set. pap., teacher ed. 10.00 (*0-669-19474-3*) Jones & Bartlett.

— Artificial Intelligence with Common LISP: Fundamentals of Symbolic & Numeric Processing. (Computer Science Ser.). 542p. (C). 1992. 60.00 (*0-669-19473-5*) Jones & Bartlett.

***Noyes, Janet M.** Interface Technology The Leading Edge. LC 99-18037. (Industrial Control, Computers & Communications Ser.). 1998. 110.00 (*0-86380-233-8*) Research Studies Pr Ltd.

Noyes, Janet M., jt. ed. see Baber, Christopher.

Noyes, John E. The United Nations at 50: Proposals for Improving Its Effectiveness. LC 97-175251. 288p. 1997. pap. 40.00 (*1-57073-365-1*, 521-0113, ABA Intl Law) Amer Bar Assn.

Noyes, John E., ed. see Ely, Susan H. & Plimpton, Elizabeth B.

Noyes, John E., ed. see Janis, Mark W.

Noyes, John H. Berean. LC 74-83431. (Religion in America, Ser. 1). 1974. reprint ed. 35.95 (*0-405-00256-4*) Ayer.

— The Berean. (Notable American Authors Ser.). 1999. reprint ed. lib. bdg. 125.00 (*0-7812-4646-6*) Rprt Serv.

— Bible Communism. (Notable American Authors Ser.). 1999. reprint ed. lib. bdg. 125.00 (*0-7812-4647-4*) Rprt Serv.

— History of American Socialisms. (Notable American Authors Ser.). 1999. reprint ed. lib. bdg. 125.00 (*0-7812-4649-0*) Rprt Serv.

— Home Talks. (Notable American Authors Ser.). 1999. reprint ed. lib. bdg. 125.00 (*0-7812-4651-2*) Rprt Serv.

— Home Talks, Vol. 1. Barron, Alfred & Miller, George N., eds. LC 72-2974. reprint ed. 57.50 (*0-404-10738-9*) AMS Pr.

— Male Continence. 1975. 250.00 (*0-87968-231-0*) Gordon Pr.

— Male Continence, 4 vols. in 1. Incl. Dixon & His Copyists, a Criticism of the Accounts of the Oneida Community in "New America," "Spiritual Wives," & Kindred Publications. 2nd ed. LC 72-2975. Essay on Scientific Propagation. LC 72-2975. Salvation from Sin, the End of Christian Faith. LC 72-2975. LC 72-2975. reprint ed. 37.50 (*0-404-10739-7*) AMS Pr.

— Male Continence. (Notable American Authors Ser.). 1999. reprint ed. lib. bdg. 125.00 (*0-7812-4648-2*) Rprt Serv.

— Mutual Criticism. 128p. 1975. reprint ed. pap. 17.95 (*0-8156-2170-1*) Syracuse U Pr.

— Religious Experience of John Humphrey Noyes, Founder of the Oneida Community. Noyes, George W., ed. (Select Bibliographies Reprint Ser.). 1977. reprint ed. 29.95 (*0-8369-5750-4*) Ayer.

— Salvation from Sin. 1972. 59.95 (*0-8490-0990-1*) Gordon Pr.

— Scientific Propagation. (Notable American Authors Ser.). 1999. reprint ed. lib. bdg. 125.00 (*0-7812-4650-4*) Rprt Serv.

Noyes, John K. Colonial Space: Spatiality, Subjectivity & Society in the Colonial Discourse of German South West Africa 1884-1916, Vol. 4. (Studies in Anthropology & History). 320p. 1991. text 87.00 (*3-7186-5167-X*, Harwood Acad Pubs) Gordon & Breach.

— The Mastery of Submission: Inventions of Masochism. LC 96-51035. (Cornell Studies in the History of Psychiatry). (Illus.). 256p. 1997. text 29.95 (*0-8014-3345-2*) Cornell U Pr.

Noyes, John K., ed. Acta Germanica: German Studies in Africa in Verbindung Mit Walter Koppe, Carlotta von Maltzan und Gunther Pakendorf, (Jahrbuch des Germanistenverbandes Im Sudlichen Afrika Ser.: Bd. 24/1996). 220p. 1997. 42.95 (*3-631-32247-X*) P Lang Pubng.

***Noyes, John K., et al.** Kultur Sprache Macht: Festschrift fur Peter Horn. 2000. 52.95 (*3-631-35875-X*) P Lang Pubng.

Noyes, John S. & Hayat, M. Oriental Mealybug Parasitoids of the Anagyrini. (Illus.). 560p. 1994. text 150.00 (*0-85198-895-4*) OUP.

Noyes, Katherine H., jt. auth. see Ellis, Susan J.

Noyes, Lawrence. The Enlightenment Intensive: The Dyad Communication Method for Self-Realization. LC 98-18358. 250p. 1998. pap. 16.95 (*1-883319-73-0*) North Atlantic.

***Noyes, Lin E.** Caregiving at a Glance: Finger Tip Help for Families Taking Care of People with Alzheimers. rev. ed. 28p. 2000. pap. write for info. (*0-9678646-0-7*) Family Respte.

Noyes, Mary W. Everybody's Mucked Up (Or They Used to Be) Observations from the Lunatic Fringe. LC 95-90266. 88p. 1995. 16.95 (*1-887361-01-4*) Wolf Wise Pub.

— Eyes of Wolf: The Journal of Marc Wolf of North Staf. LC 95-90267. 121p. 1995. 18.95 (*1-887361-00-6*) Wolf Wise Pub.

An Asterisk (*) at the beginning of an entry indicates that the title is appearing for the first time.

Noyes, Nick. Easy Composters You Can Build. LC 95-30708. (Storey Publishing Bulletin Ser.: No. A-139). 1995. pap. 2.95 (*0-88266-350-X*, Storey Pub) Storey Bks.

Noyes, Pierrepont B. My Father's House. 312p. 1993. reprint ed. lib. bdg. 89.00 (*0-7812-5312-8*) Rprt Serv.

— My Father's House: An Oneida Boyhood. (American Biography Ser.). 312p. 1991. reprint ed. lib. bdg. 79.00 (*0-7812-8300-0*) Rprt Serv.

Noyes, Richard, ed. Now the Synthesis: Capitalism, Socialism & the New Social Contract. 247p. 1991. 36.00 (*0-8419-1300-5*) Holmes & Meier.

Noyes, Richard, jt. auth. see Lichter, Robert.

Noyes, Richard E., jt. auth. see Lichter, S. Robert.

Noyes, Robert. Chemical Weapons Destruction & Explosive Waste/Unexploded Ordnance Remediation. LC 96-29056. 235p. 1996. 98.00 (*0-8155-1406-9*) Noyes.

— Nuclear Waste Cleanup Technology & Opportunities. LC 95-22674. (Illus.). 456p. 1995. 129.00 (*0-8155-1381-X*) Noyes.

Noyes, Robert, ed. Handbook of Leak, Spill & Accidental Release Prevention Techniques. LC 92-5376. (Illus.). 487p. 1992. 109.00 (*0-8155-1296-1*) Noyes.

— Handbook of Pollution Control Processes. LC 91-27950. (Illus.). 758p. 1992. 127.00 (*0-8155-1290-2*) Noyes.

— Pollution Prevention Technology Handbook. LC 92-32508. (Illus.). 683p. 1993. 145.00 (*0-8155-1311-9*) Noyes.

— Unit Operations in Environmental Engineering. LC 94-1324. (Illus.). 498p. 1994. 129.00 (*0-8155-1343-7*) Noyes.

Noyes, Robert G. Ben Jonson on the English Stage, 1660-1776. LC 65-27916. (Illus.). 361p. 1972. 23.95 (*0-405-08823-X*, Pub. by Blom Pubns) Ayer.

— Ben Jonson on the English Stage, 1660-1776. (BCL1-PR English Literature Ser.). 351p. 1992. reprint ed. lib. bdg. 89.00 (*0-7812-7258-0*) Rprt Serv.

Noyes, Robert W. The Sun, Our Star. LC 82-11733. (Harvard Books on Astronomy). (Illus.). 271p. reprint ed. pap. 84.10 (*0-7837-3861-7*, 204368300010) Bks Demand.

Noyes, Russell. William Wordsworth. (Twayne's English Authors Ser.). 184p. 1991. 32.00 (*0-8057-7002-X*, TEAS 118) Macmillan.

— Wordsworth & the Art of Landscape. LC 72-6864. (Studies in Wordsworth: No. 29). 1972. reprint ed. lib. bdg. 75.00 (*0-8383-1660-3*) M S G Haskell Hse.

Noyes, Russell, ed. English Romantic Poetry & Prose. 1360p. 1956. text 52.95 (*0-19-501007-8*) OUP.

Noyes, Russell, Jr. & Hoehn-Saric, Rudolf. The Anxiety Disorders. LC 97-42566. (Illus.). 350p. (C). 1998. text 74.95 (*0-521-55207-9*) Cambridge U Pr.

***Noyes, Shana Connell & Noyes, Henry S.** Acing Your First Year of Law School: The Ten Steps to Success You Won't Learn in Class. LC 99-13986. 1999. write for info. (*0-8377-0913-X*); pap. 12.95 (*0-8377-0912-1*, 323050, Rothman) W S Hein.

Noyes, Stanley. Beyond the Mountains. 1979. 7.25 (*0-941490-00-9*) Solo Pr.

— Los Comanches: The Horse People, 1751-1845. (Illus.). 393p. 1993. reprint ed. pap. 16.95 (*0-8263-1548-8*) U of NM Pr.

Noyes, Stanley & Gelo, Daniel J. Comanches in the New West, 1895-1908: Historic Photographs. LC 98-22004. (Jack & Doris Smothers Series in Texas History, Life, & Culture). 120p. 1999. 24.95 (*0-292-75568-6*) U of Tex Pr.

Noyes, Sybil, et al. Genealogical Dictionary of Maine & New Hampshire, 5 pts. in 1. LC 79-88099. 795p. 1996. reprint ed. 40.00 (*0-8063-0502-9*, 4245) Genealog Pub.

Noyes, William A. Advances in Photochemistry, Vol. 11: 1979. LC 63-13592. (Illus.). 552p. pap. 171.20 (*0-8357-5176-7*, 205645600011) Bks Demand.

Noyle, Linda J. Pianists on Playing: Interviews with 12 Concert Pianists. LC 86-29810. (Illus.). 187p. 1987. 24.00 (*0-8108-1953-8*) Scarecrow.

Noyola, Robert. Out of the Grave. 1997. 10.00 (*0-9656116-0-4*) Stonegate Pr.

Noyori, Kimiharu, et al. Ophthalmic Laser Therapy. (Illus.). 289p. 1992. 170.00 (*0-89640-199-5*) Igaku-Shoin.

Noyori, Ryoji. Asymmetric Catalysis in Organic Synthesis. LC 93-3884. (Baker Lectures). 400p. 1994. 79.95 (*0-471-57267-5*) Wiley.

***Noys, Benjamin.** Georges Bataille: A Critical Introduction. LC 00-24889. (Modern European Thinkers Ser.). 192p. 2000. 59.95 (*0-7453-1592-5*, Pub. by Pluto GBR); pap. 17.95 (*0-7453-1587-9*, Pub. by Pluto GBR) Stylus Pub VA.

Noz, Marilyn E. & Kim, Y. S., eds. Special Relativity & Quantum Theory: A Collection of Papers on the Poincare Group. (C). 1988. text 237.50 (*90-277-2799-6*) Kluwer Academic.

Noz, Marilyn E., jt. auth. see Kim, Y. S.

Noz, Marilyn E., jt. auth. see Macguire, G. Q.

Noz, Marilyn E., jt. auth. see Maguire, Gerald Q., Jr.

Nozaka, Akiyuki. The Pornographers. Gallagher, Michael, tr. 312p. 1991. pap. 9.95 (*0-8048-1378-7*) Tuttle Pubng.

Nozaki, H., ed. Current Trends in Organic Synthesis: Proceedings of the Fourth International Conference on Organic Synthesis, Tokyo, Japan, August 22-27, 1982. LC 82-22445. (IUPAC Symposium Ser.). (Illus.). 442p. 1983. 199.00 (*0-08-029217-8*, Pub. by Pergamon Repr) Franklin.

***Nozawa, Randall, et al.** Inside Dentistry: Everything You Need to Know Before Your Next Dental Visit. Strand, Laurel, ed. (Illus.). 208p. 2000. pap. 14.95 (*0-9679932-0-2*, Pub. by Isa Mira) Elfin Cove Pr.

Nozdrev, V. F. Applications of Ultrasonics to Molecular Physics. (Illus.). 542p. 1963. 353.00 (*0-685-01944-6*) Gordon & Breach.

Nozelle, Shirley. The Cow Is in the Kitchen, the Cat Is on the Shelf. LC 96-30212. (Illus.). 32p. (J). (ps-1). 2000. 15.00 (*0-395-78627-4*, Clarion Bks) HM.

Nozette, Stewart & Kuhn, Robert L., eds. Commercializing SDI Technologies. LC 87-18333. 262p. 1987. 59.95 (*0-275-92332-0*, C2332, Praeger Pubs) Greenwood.

Nozick, jt. auth. see Patt.

Nozick, Betsy & Henry, Tricia. The Mystique of Entertaining in Texas. LC 97-6987. (Illus.). 232p. 1997. 21.95 (*1-57168-074-8*) Sunbelt Media.

Nozick, Martin. Miguel de Unamuno: The Agony of Belief. LC 81-47966. 238p. 1982. reprint ed. pap. 73.80 (*0-608-02510-0*, 206315400004) Bks Demand.

Nozick, Martin, jt. ed. see Patt, Beatrice.

Nozick, Martin, tr. see Unamuno, Miguel de.

Nozick, Robert. Agricultural Growth & Japanese Economic Development. Smitka, Michael, ed. LC 98-9410. (Japanese Economic History 1600-1960 Ser.: Vol. 7). (Illus.). 368p. 1998. 85.00 (*0-8153-2711-0*) Garland.

— Anarchy, State & Utopia. LC 73-91081. 384p. 1977. pap. 20.00 (*0-465-09720-0*, Pub. by Basic) HarpC.

— The Emergence of Logical Empiricism: From 1900 to the Vienna Circle. LC 95-26648. (Science & Philosophy in the Twentieth Century Ser.: Vol. 1). 432p. 1996. reprint ed. text 85.00 (*0-8153-2262-3*) Garland.

— The Examined Life: Philosophical Meditations. 320p. 1990. pap. 12.00 (*0-671-72501-7*, Touchstone) S&S Trade Pap.

— Historical Demography & Labor Markets in Prewar Japan. Smitka, Michael, ed. LC 98-9507. (Japanese Economic History 1600-1960 Ser.: Vol. 3). (Illus.). 248p. 1998. 70.00 (*0-8153-2707-2*) Garland.

— The Interwar Economy of Japan: Colonialism, Depression, & Recovery, 1910-1940. Smitka, Michael, ed. LC 98-9494. (Japanese Economic History 1600-1960 Ser.: Vol. 2). (Illus.). 320p. 1998. reprint ed. 80.00 (*0-8153-2706-4*) Garland.

— The Japanese Economy in the Tokugawa Era, 1600-1868. Smitka, Michael, ed. LC 98-9411. (Japanese Economic History 1600-1960 Ser.: Vol. 6). (Illus.). 384p. 1998. 85.00 (*0-8153-2710-2*) Garland.

— Japanese Prewar Growth: Lessons for Development Theory?, 1. Smitka, Michael, ed. LC 98-9495. (Japanese Economic History 1600-1960 Ser.: Vol. 1). (Illus.). 280p. 1998. reprint ed. 80.00 (*0-8153-2705-6*) Garland.

— Japan's Economic Ascent: International Trade, Growth, & Postwar Reconstruction. Smitka, Michael, ed. LC 98-9407. (Japanese Economic History 1600-1960 Ser.: Vol. 5). (Illus.). 376p. 1998. 85.00 (*0-8153-2709-9*) Garland.

— The Nature of Rationality. 232p. 1993. text 42.50 (*0-691-07424-0*, Pub. by Princeton U Pr); pap. text 13.95 (*0-691-02096-5*, Pub. by Princeton U Pr) Cal Prin Full Svc.

— Philosophical Explanations. LC 81-1369. 777p. 1981. 42.50 (*0-674-66448-5*) Belknap Pr.

— Philosophical Explanations. 777p. 1983. pap. text 22.00 (*0-674-66479-5*) Belknap Pr.

— Socratic Puzzles. LC 96-39221. (Illus.). 416p. 1997. 35.00 (*0-674-81653-6*) HUP.

— Socratic Puzzles. (Illus.). 400p. 1999. pap. 19.95 (*0-674-81654-4*) HUP.

— The Textile Industry & the Rise of the Japanese Economy. Smitka, Michael, ed. LC 98-9408. (Japanese Economic History 1600-1960 Ser.: Vol. 4). (Illus.). 392p. 1998. 85.00 (*0-8153-2708-0*) Garland.

Nozick, Robert, jt. ed. see Brewer, Scott.

Nozick, Robert, jt. ed. see Dominguez, Jorge I.

Nozieres. Nozieres Thry Quan Liq. pap. (*0-201-40841-4*) Addison-Wesley.

Nozieres, P. Interacting Fermi Systems. (Advanced Book Classics Ser.). 1997. pap. text 35.45 (*0-201-09474-6*) Addison-Wesley.

Nozieres, Philippe. Theory of Interacting Fermi System. Hone, D., tr. LC 97-43055. 1997. pap. 32.53 (*0-201-32824-0*) Addison-Wesley.

Nozieres, Philippe & Pines, David. Theory of Quantum Liquids, Vol. 1&2. 576p. 1999. pap. text 49.00 (*0-7382-0229-0*, Pub. by Perseus Pubng) HarpC.

Nozieres, Philippe, jt. auth. see Pines, David.

Nozik, Arthur J., ed. Photoeffects at Semiconductor-Electrolyte Interfaces. LC 80-27773. (Symposium Ser.: No. 146). 1981. 49.95 (*0-8412-0604-X*) Am Chemical.

— Photoeffects at Semiconductor-Electrolyte Interfaces. LC 80-27773. (ACS Symposium Ser.: No. 146). (Illus.). 426p. 1981. reprint ed. pap. 132.10 (*0-608-03275-1*, 206379300007) Bks Demand.

Nozik, Robert A., jt. auth. see Smith, Ronald E.

Nozinski, Michael J. Outrage at Lincheng: China Enters the Twentieth Century. LC 89-80780. (Illus.). 243p. 1990. 19.95 (*0-944435-07-6*) Glenbridge Pub.

Nozoe, Tetsuo. Seventy Years in Organic Chemistry. Seeman, Jeffrey I., ed. LC 90-876. (Profiles, Pathways, & Dreams Ser.). (Illus.). 267p. 1991. text 36.00 (*0-8412-1769-6*, Pub. by Am Chemical) OUP.

Nozolino, Paulo. Penumbra: The Shadow of Destiny in the Arabic World. (Illus.). 112p. 39.95 (*3-931141-32-2*, 620352, Pub. by Scalo Pubs) Dist Art Pubs.

NP-Chilton Editors. ATV Handbook. (Illus.). 400p. (C). 1999. pap. 22.95 (*0-8019-9123-4*) Thomson Learn.

— Electric Cooling Fans & Accessory Drive Belts: 1995-1999. (Illus.). (C). 1999. pap. 34.95 (*0-8019-9126-9*, Pub. by NP-Chilton) Natl Bk Netwk.

— Powertrain Codes & Oxygen Sensors: 1990-1999. (Illus.). (C). 1999. pap. 34.95 (*0-8019-9127-7*) Thomson Learn.

— Ford - Contour/Mystique/Cougar, 1995-99. (Total Car Care Ser.). (Illus.). (C). 1999. pap. 22.95 (*0-8019-9105-6*) Thomson Learn.

— Ford - Crown Victoria/Grand Marquis, 1989-98. (Total Car Care Ser.). (C). 2000. pap. 22.95 (*0-8019-8960-4*) NP-Chilton.

— GM - Blazer/Jimmy/Typhoon/Bravada, 1983-93. (Total Car Care Ser.). (C). 1999. pap. 22.95 (*0-8019-9110-2*) Thomson Learn.

— GM - Celebrity/Century/Ciera/6000, 1982-96. (Total Car Care Ser.). (Illus.). (C). 1999. pap. 22.95 (*0-8019-9108-0*) Thomson Learn.

— GM - Corvette, 1984-96. (Total Car Care Ser.). (C). 1999. pap. 22.95 (*0-8019-9103-X*) Thomson Learn.

— GM - Full-Size Trucks, 1988-98. LC 98-74837. (Total Car Care Ser.). (C). 1999. pap. 22.95 (*0-8019-9102-1*) Thomson Learn.

— GM - GrandAm/Achieva/Calais/Skylark/Somerset, 1985-98. (Total Car Care Ser.). (Illus.). 552p. (C). 2000. pap. 22.95 (*0-8019-9106-4*) NP-Chilton.

— GM-Cavalier/Cimarron/Firenza/Skyhawk/Sunbird/Sunfire, 1982-94. (Total Car Care Ser.). (Illus.). (C). 1999. pap. 22.95 (*0-8019-9113-7*) Thomson Learn.

***NP-Chilton Editors.** GM-S10/Sonoma/Blazer/Jimmy/Bravada/Hombre, 1994-99. LC 99-72297. (Total Car Care Ser.). (Illus.). (C). 1999. pap. 22.95 (*0-8019-9111-0*) Thomson Learn.

NP-Chilton Editors. Honda - 4-Stroke Outboard, All Engines, 1988-98. (Illus.). 352p. (C). 2000. pap. 34.95 (*0-89330-048-9*) Seloc.

— Isuzu - Trooper/Pick-Ups/Rodeo/Amigo, 1992-99. (Total Car Care Ser.). (Illus.). (C). 2000. pap. 22.95 (*0-8019-9112-9*) Thomson Learn.

— Jeep - Wagoneer/Commanche/Cherokee, 1984-98. (Total Car Care Ser.). (C). 1999. pap. 22.95 (*0-8019-9107-2*) Thomson Learn.

— Specifications & Maintenance Intervals: 1995-1999. (Illus.). (C). 1999. pap. 34.95 (*0-8019-9128-5*) Thomson Learn.

— Timing Belts, 1995-99. LC 98-74941. (Illus.). (C). 1999. pap. 24.95 (*0-8019-9125-0*) Thomson Learn.

— Yamaha - 2-Stroke Outboards, All Engines, 1992-98. (Illus.). (C). 1999. pap. 34.95 (*0-89330-047-0*) Thomson Learn.

— Yanmar - Inboards, 1975-1998. (Illus.). (C). 1999. pap. 34.95 (*0-89330-049-7*) Thomson Learn.

NPC (Randell) National Press Club Staff. The Greatest National Press Club Speakers, Vol. 1. LC 95-78049. 200p. 1995. 34.95 (*0-7872-1005-6*) Kendall-Hunt.

NPC Staff & IUCN Staff. EIA Guidelines for the Forestry Sector. 1995. pap. 21.00 (*0-7855-7391-7*, Pub. by Ratna Pustak Bhandar) St Mut.

***NPC Staff & IUCN Staff.** Report on the End of the Project Workshop of the National Conservation Strategy Implementation Project. 1998. pap. 22.00 (*0-7855-7630-4*) St Mut.

NPD Group Staff. Consumer Research Study on Book Purchasing, 1998. (Illus.). 175p. 1999. pap. 295.00 (*0-940016-75-3*) Bk Indus Study.

NPS Staff. The Hopewell Coloring Book. rev. ed. (Illus.). 24p. (J). (gr. k-5). 1998. reprint ed. pap. 1.95 (*1-888213-30-2*) Eastern National.

— Jr. Ranger Booklet - Minute Man National Historical Park. (Illus.). 16p. 1999. pap., wbk. ed. 1.50 (*1-888213-35-3*) Eastern National.

— Russian Bishop's House. (Illus.). 16p. 1995. pap. 2.95 (*0-614-04305-0*) Alaska Natural.

NPS Staff, ed. see Gilmore, Jackie.

NPS Staff, ed. see Hayden, Bill & Freillich, Jerry.

NPS Staff, ed. see Salts, Bobbi.

NRA Staff. Nepal District Profile: A District-Wise Socio-Techno-Economic Profit along with a Comprehensive National Profit of Nepal, 1997. 1997. pap. 267.00 (*0-7855-7440-9*, Pub. by Ratna Pustak Bhandar) St Mut.

— Who's Who Nepal. (C). 1992. 240.00 (*0-7855-0220-3*, Pub. by Ratna Pustak Bhandar) St Mut.

***NRAES Staff.** Workforce Management for Farms & Horticultural Businesses: Finding, Training & Keeping Good Employees: Workshop Handouts. 66p. 1999. pap. text 12.00 (*0-935817-44-1*, 122) NRAES.

***NRAES Staff, ed.** CA Storage: Meeting the Market Requirements: Proceedings from the CA Storage: Meeting the Market Requirements Workshop, Cornell University, Ithaca, New York, August 18, 1999. LC 99-48022. (NRAES Ser.: Vol. 136). 82p. 1999. pap. text 16.00 (*0-935817-48-4*) NRAES.

— Engineering Aspects of Intensive Aquaculture: Proceedings from the Aquaculture Symposium, Cornell University, Ithaca, NY, April 4-6, 1991. 348p. 1991. pap. text 38.00 (*0-935817-28-X*, 49) NRAES.

NRAES Staff, ed. see Agriculture Natural Resource Staff.

NRC, Advisory Committee, Office of the Internation. Careers in Science & Technology: An International Perspective. 194p. (Orig.). 1996. pap. text 35.00 (*0-309-05427-3*) Natl Acad Pr.

NRC, Committee on Decontamination & Decommissionin. Affordable Cleanup? Opportunities for Cost Reduction in the Decontamination & Decommissioning of the Nation's Uranium Enrichment Facilities. LC 96-67092. xiv, 309p. (Orig.). 1996. pap. text 39.00 (*0-309-05438-9*) Natl Acad Pr.

NRC, Committee on Evaluation of 1950s Air Force Hu. The Arctic Aeromedical Laboratory's Thyroid Function Study: A Radiological Risk & Ethical Analysis. 116p. (Orig.). 1996. pap. text 34.00 (*0-309-05428-1*) Natl Acad Pr.

NRC, Committee on Occupational Health & Safety of. Occupational Health & Safety in the Care & Use of Research Animals. LC 97-4794. 250p. (Orig.). 1997. pap. text 39.95 (*0-309-05299-8*) Natl Acad Pr.

NRC, Committee on the Future of the Colleges of Ag. Colleges of Agriculture at the Land Grant Universities: Public Service & Public Policy, Vol. 2. 140p. (Orig.). 1996. pap. text 34.95 (*0-309-05433-8*) Natl Acad Pr.

NRC, Possible Effects of Electromagnetic Fields on. Possible Health Effects of Exposure to Residential Electric & Magnetic Fields. LC 96-51230. 384p. 1997. text 39.95 (*0-309-05447-8*) Natl Acad Pr.

NRC Staff. The Bureau of Transportation Statistics: Priorities for the Future. Citro, Constance F. & Norwood, Janet L., eds. LC 97-204025. 160p. 1997. pap. text 35.00 (*0-309-06404-X*) Natl Acad Pr.

Nremmam, Joseph. The Great White Shark. (American Museum of Natural Book & Diorama Ser.). (Illus.). 64p. 1996. pap. 10.95 (*0-7611-0451-8*, 10451) Workman Pub.

NREP Board Members Staff. Official Review Guide Book for National Registry of Environmental Manager's Examination. 515p. 1989. 49.95 (*0-925760-29-3*) SciTech Pubs.

NRF Staff. Retail Industry Indicators. 85p. 1997. pap. 35.00 (*0-614-30167-X*) Nat Retail Fed.

Nrgaard, Ole, et al, eds. The European Community in World Politics. LC 93-5588. 1993. 49.00 (*1-85567-147-6*) St Martin.

Nrgard, Jurgen S., et al. Development with Sustainable Use of Electricity. LC 98-29277. (NATO Science Ser.). 12p. 1998. write for info. (*0-7923-5217-3*) Kluwer Academic.

NRI Staff. The Desert Locust Pocket Book. 2nd ed. 1990. pap. 25.00 (*0-85954-276-9*, Pub. by Nat Res Inst) St Mut.

Nriagu, Jerome O. Cadmium in the Environment: Ecological Cycling, Pt. I. LC 79-25087. 696p. 1980. 120.00 (*0-471-06455-6*) Krieger.

— Cadmium in the Environment: Health Effects, Pt. II. (Environmental Science & Technology Ser.). 920p. 1986. reprint ed. 158.00 (*0-471-05884-X*) Krieger.

— Copper in the Environment. (Environmental Science & Technology Texts & Monographs Ser.: Pt. 1). 1980. 94.00 (*0-471-04778-3*) Krieger.

— Copper in the Environment: Zinc in the Environment. (Environmental Science & Technology Texts & Monographs Ser.: Pt. 2). 494p. 1986. reprint ed. 105.00 (*0-471-05889-0*) Krieger.

Nriagu, Jerome O., ed. Environmental Impacts of Smelters. LC 83-21761. (Advances in Environmental Science & Technology Ser.: 2-010). 608p. 1984. 245.00 (*0-471-88043-4*) Wiley.

— Gaseous Pollutants: Characterization & Cycling. LC 91-14369. (Environmental Science & Technology Ser.: No. 1121). 560p. 1992. 195.00 (*0-471-54898-7*) Wiley.

— Nickel in the Environment, Pt. 1. LC 80-16600. (Environmental Science & Technology Ser.). 848p. 1980. 140.00 (*0-471-05885-8*) Krieger.

***Nriagu, Jerome O., ed.** Thallium in the Environment, 30. LC 97-14871. (Advances in Environmental Science & Technology Ser.). 284p. 1998. 120.00 (*0-471-17755-5*) Wiley.

— Vanadium in the Environment, 2 vols., 29. (Advances in Environmental Science & Technology Ser.). 844p. 1998. 175.00 (*0-471-24907-6*) Wiley.

Nriagu, Jerome O., ed. Vanadium in the Environment: Health Effects, Vol. 2. (Advances in Environmental Science & Technology Ser.: Vol. 31). 403p. 1998. 99.00 (*0-471-17776-8*) Wiley.

— Vanadium in the Environment, Pt. 1, Chemistry & Biochemistry, Pt. 1. LC 97-14872. (Advances in Environmental Science & Technology Ser.). 410p. 1998. 99.00 (*0-471-17778-4*) Wiley.

Nriagu, Jerome O. & Lakshminarayana, J. S., eds. Aquatic Toxicology & Water Quality Management. LC 88-7282. (Advances in Environmental Science & Technology Ser.). 292p. 1989. 175.00 (*0-471-61551-X*) Wiley.

Nriagu, Jerome O. & Moore, P. B., eds. Phosphate Minerals. (Illus.). 470p. 1984. 190.95 (*0-387-12757-7*) Spr-Verlag.

Nriagu, Jerome O. & Nieboer, Evert, eds. Chromium in the Natural & Human Environments. LC 87-27303. (Advances in Environmental Science & Technology Ser.). 571p. 1988. 150.00 (*0-471-85643-6*) Wiley.

Nriagu, Jerome O. & Simmons, Milagros S., eds. Environmental Oxidants. (Advances in Environmental Science & Technology Ser.: Vol. 28). 630p. 1994 120.00 (*0-471-57928-9*) Wiley.

— Food Contamination from Environmental Sources. LC 89-5671. (Environmental Science & Technology Ser.). 785p. 1990. 315.00 (*0-471-50891-8*) Wiley.

Nriagu, Jerome O. & Sprague, John B., eds. Cadmium in the Aquatic Environment. (Advances in Environmental Science & Technology Ser.). 288p. 1987. 175.00 (*0-471-85884-6*) Wiley.

Nriagu, Jerome O., jt. ed. see Nieboer, Evert.

NRMC Staff, jt. ed. see NEBSS Staff.

NRP Staff. 3D Studio 4 for Level 1. 1996. wbk. ed. 30.00 (*1-56205-539-9*) New Riders Pub.

NRP 20 (Switzerland) Staff, jt. auth. see Pfiffner, Othmar A.

NRTC Staff. NRTC Programme Guide. (Competent Retail Manager Ser.). 1992. pap. text 34.00 (*0-08-042095-8*) Elsevier.

NS Dar Lucretia Council Committee. Arlington Treasured Recipes. 608p. 1975. 17.95 (*0-9674473-0-5*, Pub. by NSDA Rev) Wimmer Bks.

NSA of Australia Staff. Local Spiritual Assembly Handbook. 3rd ed. LC 98-104111. 451p. 1996. pap. 24.95 (*0-909991-78-2*) Bahai.

N.S.A.I. Equity Committee Staff. The Essential Songwriter's Contract Handbook. 120p. (Orig.). (C). 1994. pap. 12.95 (*1-886092-00-1*) Nashville Songwrit.

Nsamenang, A. Bame. Human Development in Cultural Context: A Third World Perspective. (Cross-Cultural Research & Methodology Ser.: Vol. 16). 320p. (C). 1992. text 52.00 (*0-8039-4636-8*) Sage.

NSBA Council of School Attorney Members Staff. School Reform: The Legal Challenges of Change. 150p. 1996. pap. 30.00 (*0-88364-202-6*, 06-158) Natl Sch Boards.

NSBA Council of School Attorneys Members. Child Abuse: Legal Issues for Schools. 194p. (Orig.). 1994. pap. 25.00 (*0-88364-184-4*, 06-148) Natl Sch Boards.
— Environmental Law: Fundamentals for Schools. 36p. (Orig.). 1995. pap. 15.00 (*0-88364-194-1*, 06-151) Natl Sch Boards.
— Legal Guidelines for Curbing School Violence. 162p. 1995. pap. 30.00 (*0-88364-195-X*, 06-152) Natl Sch Boards.
— Legal Handbook on School Athletics. 120p. 1997. pap. text 35.00 (*0-88364-206-9*, 06-160) Natl Sch Boards.
— 1999 School Law in Review. 160p. 1999. pap. 35.00 (*0-88364-223-9*, 06-168) Natl Sch Boards.
— Protect the Future of Your School District Client. 800p. 1995. pap. 200.00 (*0-88364-191-7*, 06-149) Natl Sch Boards.
— Religion, Education, & the U. S. Constitution. 198p. (Orig.). 1994. reprint ed. pap. 25.00 (*0-88364-183-6*, 06-147) Natl Sch Boards.
— School Law in Review, 1998. 176p. 1998. pap. 35.00 (*0-88364-215-8*, 06-165) Natl Sch Boards.
— School Law in Review, 1995. (Orig.). 1995. pap. 35.00 (*0-88364-193-3*, 06-150) Natl Sch Boards.
— School Law in Review, 1997. 146p. 1997. pap. text 35.00 (*0-88364-208-5*, 06-191) Natl Sch Boards.
— School Law in Review, 1996. 160p. (Orig.). 1996. pap. 35.00 (*0-88364-201-8*, 06-157) Natl Sch Boards.

***NSBA Council of School Attorneys Members.** School Law in Review 2000. 190p. 2000. pap. 35.00 (*0-88364-233-6*, 06-174, Pub. by Natl Sch Boards) PMDS-AACRAO.

NSBA Council of School Attorneys Members. Selecting & Working with a School Attorney: A Guide for School Boards. 142p. 1997. pap. text 35.00 (*0-88364-209-3*, 06-162) Natl Sch Boards.

***NSBA Council of School Attorneys Members.** Student to Student Sexual Harassment: A Legal Guide for Schools. 2nd rev. ed. 2000. pap. 35.00 (*0-88364-235-2*, Pub. by Natl Sch Boards) PMDS-AACRAO.

NSBA Council of School Attorneys Members. Termination of School Employees: Legal Issues & Techniques. 316p. 1997. pap. text 35.00 (*0-88364-210-7*, 06-163) Natl Sch Boards.

NSBA Council of School Attorneys Staff. A School Law Retreat: October 17-18, 1997 Phoenix, AZ. 600p. 1997. pap., wbk. ed. 200.00 (*0-88364-213-1*, 06-164) Natl Sch Boards.

NSC Staff, jt. auth. see AHA, American Society for Healthcare Materials Man.

NSDAR Youghiogheny Glades Chapter Staff. Maryland's Garrett County Graves. LC 87-50355. (Illus.). 488p. 1987. 29.00 (*0-9618240-0-X*) N S D A R.

Nsekela, Amon J., ed. Southern Africa: Toward Economic Liberation. 274p. 1981. 35.00 (*0-86036-154-3*) St Mut.
— Toward Economic Liberation: Southern Africa. (Illus.). 294p. 1981. text 48.00 (*0-8476-4741-2*) Rowman.

NSELA Staff, jt. auth. see NSSA (Roy) Staff.

Nseyo, Unyime, et al. Urology for Primary Care Physicians. Donley, Stephanie, ed. LC 98-40584. (Illus.). 365p. (C). 1999. text. write for info. (*0-7216-7148-9*, W B Saunders Co) Harcrt Hlth Sci Grp.

***NSF-CBMS Conference on Spectral Problems in Geometry & Arithmetic Staff & Branson, Thomas.** Spectral Problems in Geometry & Arithmetic: NSF-CBMS Conference on Spectral Problems in Geometry & Arithmetic, August 18-22, 1997, University of Iowa. LC 99-29632. (Contemporary Mathematics Bks.). 1999. write for info. (*0-8218-0940-7*) Am Math.

NSF-CBMS Regional Conference in Mathematics on Euler Products & Eisenstein Series Staff, et al. Automorphic Forms, Automorphic Representations & Arithmetic: NSF-CBMS Regional Conference in Mathematics on Euler Products & Eisenstein Series, May 20-24, 1996, Texas Christian University. LC 99-28916. (Symposia in Pure Mathematics Ser.). 1999. write for info. (*0-8218-1051-0*) Am Math.

NSF Design & Manufacturing Systems Conference Staf. Proceedings of the 1993 NSF Design & Manufacturing Systems Conference: The University of North Carolina at Charlotte, Mechanical Engineering & Engineering Science Department, Precision Engineering Laboratory, Charlotte, North Carolina, January 6-8, 1993, Vol. I. LC 92-64413. (Illus.). 981p. 1993. reprint ed. pap. 200.00 (*0-7837-9728-1*, 206045900001) Bks Demand.
— Proceedings of the 1993 NSF Design & Manufacturing Systems Conference: The University of North Carolina at Charlotte, Mechanical Engineering & Engineering Science Department, Precision Engineering Laboratory, Charlotte, North Carolina, January 6-8, 1993, Vol. II. LC 92-64413. (Illus.). 972p. 1993. reprint ed. pap. 200.00 (*0-7837-9729-X*, 206045900002) Bks Demand.

NSF Science & Technology Center in Discrete Mathem. African Americans in Mathematics: Second Conference for African-American Researchers in the Mathematical Sciences, June 26-28, 1996. Dean, Nathaniel, ed. LC 97-21748. (DIMACS: Series in Discrete Mathematics & Theoretical Computer Science: Vol. 34). 205p. 1997. text 49.00 (*0-8218-0678-5*) Am Math.
— Satisfiability Problem: Theory & Applications. Du Dingzhu et al, eds. LC 97-25448. (DIMACS: Series in Discrete Mathematics & Theoretical Computer Science: Vol. PARDALOS4). 720p. 1997. text 149.00 (*0-8218-0479-0*) Am Math.

NSF Science & Technology Center in Discrete Mathem & DIMACS Staff. Logic & Random Structures: DIMACS Workshop, November 5-7, 1995. Boppana, Ravi B. & Lynch, James F., eds. LC 97-10666. (DIMACS: Series in Descrete Mathematics & Theoretical Computer Science: Vol. 33). 130p. 1997. text 29.00 (*0-8218-0578-9*) Am Math.

NSF Science & Technology Center in Discrete Mathem, jt. auth. see DIMACS (Group) Staff.

Nsibande, jt. auth. see Forster.

Nsouli, Mona A., jt. compiled by see Meho, Lokman I.

Nsouli, Saleh M., et al. The Path to Convertibility & Growth: The Tunisian Experience. LC 93-45034. (Occasional Papers: No. 109). 1993. pap. 15.00 (*1-55775-357-1*) Intl Monetary.
— Resilience & Growth Through Sustained Adjustment: The Moroccan Experience. LC 94-44348. (Occasional Paper Ser.: No. 117). 130p. 1995. pap. 15.00 (*1-55775-422-5*) Intl Monetary.

Nsouli, Saleh M., jt. auth. see Zulu, Justin B.

NSPS Construction Standards Survey Committee Staff. Manual on Construction Layout. 40p. 1993. pap. 20.00 (*0-614-06108-3*, S309) Am Congrs Survey.

NSSA (Roy) Staff & NSELA Staff. Local Leadership for Science Education Reform. 208p. 1995. pap. text, per. 13.95 (*0-8403-9947-2*) Kendall-Hunt.

NSSTE Staff. The Sales Manager's Guide to Training & Developing Your Team. 216p. 1993. text 25.00 (*0-7863-0300-X*, Irwn Prfssnl) McGraw-Hill Prof.

NSU (Collins) Staff. Mentoring Program. 88p. (C). 1995. pap. text 21.95 (*0-8403-8465-3*) Kendall-Hunt.

Nsync. Inside Nsynic. 144p. 1999. 45.00 (*0-7893-0385-X*, Pub. by Universe) St Martin.

Nsync, et al. Nside Nsync. LC 99-71280. (Illus.). 144p. (gr. 4-7). 1999. pap. 25.00 (*0-7893-0380-9*, Pub. by Universe) St Martin.

NT Inovation Staff. Invitation New Testament: With Psalms & Proverbs. LC 98-61550. 1999. pap. text 5.99 (*0-310-90202-9*) Zondervan.

Ntalaja, Nzongola. Class Struggles & National Liberation in Africa. LC 82-81279. 175p. (Orig.). (C). 1982. pap. 6.95 (*0-943324-00-9*) Omenana.
— The Development of a Marxist Perspective in Africa. Omenana Collective Research Group Staff, ed. (Etudes et Analyses Marxistes en Afrique Ser.). 24p. (Orig.). (C). 1985. reprint ed. pap. 3.00 (*0-686-88663-1*) Omenana.

Ntantu, I., jt. auth. see McCoy, R. A.

Ntara, Samuel Y. Headman's Enterprise: An Unexpected Page in Central African History. Young, T. Cullen, tr. & pref. by. (B. E. Ser.: No. 102). 1949. 25.00 (*0-8115-3034-5*) Periodicals Srv.

Ntara, Samuel Y. Man of Africa. Young, T. Cullen, tr. from NYA. (B. E. Ser.: No. 101). 1934. 25.00 (*0-8115-3033-7*) Periodicals Srv.

NTB Staff. Activity Breaks 1997. (Where to Stay Ser.). (Illus.). 180p. (Orig.). 1997. pap. 16.95 (*0-86143-201-0*, Pub. by JARR UK) Seven Hills Bk.

***NTC Contemporary Publishing Staff.** Vox English & Spanish Learners Dictionary. (SPA & ENG.). 1392p. 2000. pap. 15.95 (*0-658-00188-4*, 001884) NTC Contemp Pub Co.

***NTC Contemporary Publishing Staff, ed.** Literature of Asia. LC 98-44317. (Traditions in World Literature Ser.). 1998. write for info. (*0-8442-1157-5*); pap. write for info. (*0-8442-1158-3*) NTC Contemp Pub Co.

NTC Publishing Group Editors, ed. Vox New College Spanish-English Dictionary. (SPA & ENG., Illus.). 1536p. 1995. 19.95 (*0-8442-7998-6*, 79986, Natl Textbk Co) NTC Contemp Pub Co.

NTC Publishing Group Staff. Austalia. (Passport Essential Guide Ser.). 128p. 1998. pap. 8.95 (*0-8442-0131-6*, Passprt Bks) NTC Contemp Pub Co.
— Bali & Lombok. (Passport Essential Guide Ser.). (Illus.). 128p. 1998. pap. 8.95 (*0-8442-0114-6*, 01146, Passprt Bks) NTC Contemp Pub Co.
— California. (Passport Essential Guide Ser.). 128p. 1998. pap. 8.95 (*0-8442-0116-2*, 01162, Passprt Bks) NTC Contemp Pub Co.

***NTC Publishing Group Staff.** Common American Phrases in Everyday Contexts. 2000. pap. 30.00 (*0-658-00127-2*, 001272); audio compact disk 20.00 (*0-658-00158-2*, 001582) NTC Contemp Pub Co.

NTC Publishing Group Staff. Costa Del Sol. (Passport Essential Guide Ser.). 128p. 1998. pap. 8.95 (*0-8442-0130-8*, 01308, Passprt Bks) NTC Contemp Pub Co.
— Cyprus. (Passport Essential Guide Ser.). (Illus.). 128p. 1998. pap. 8.95 (*0-8442-0139-1*, 01391, Passprt Bks) NTC Contemp Pub Co.

***NTC Publishing Group Staff.** Drive-In French for Kids: Songs & Games for On-the-Go Children. (Drive-In Audio Packs for Kids Ser.). (FRE & ENG., Illus.). 32p. (J). 2000. pap. 9.95 incl. audio (*0-658-00868-4*, 008684) NTC Contemp Pub Co.
— French Thematic Vocabulary Guide. (Thematic Vocabulary Guides Ser.). (FRE., Illus.). 192p. 2000. pap. 8.95 (*0-658-00871-4*, 008714) NTC Contemp Pub Co.

NTC Publishing Group Staff. Germany, Austria, & Switzerland: The All-in-One Travel & Language Guide. LC 98-51066. (Get Around in . . . Ser.). (GER., Illus.). 128p. 1998. pap. 18.95 incl. audio (*0-8442-0163-4*, 01634) NTC Contemp Pub Co.
— Gran Canaria. (Passport Essential Guide Ser.). 128p. 1998. pap. 8.95 (*0-8442-0119-7*, 01197, Passprt Bks) NTC Contemp Pub Co.
— Hungary. (Passport Essential Guide Ser.). (Illus.). 128p. 1998. pap. 8.95 (*0-8442-0137-5*, 01375, Passprt Bks) NTC Contemp Pub Co.
— Ireland. (Passport Essential Guide Ser.). 128p. 1998. pap. 8.95 (*0-8442-0138-3*, 01383, Passprt Bks) NTC Contemp Pub Co.
— Italy: The All-in-One Travel & Language Guide. (Get Around in . . . Ser.). (ITA., Illus.). 128p. 1998. pap. 17.95 incl. audio (*0-8442-0165-0*, 01650) NTC Contemp Pub Co.
— Kenya. (Passport Essential Guide Ser.). (Illus.). 128p. 1998. pap. 8.95 (*0-8442-0117-0*, 01170, Passprt Bks) NTC Contemp Pub Co.
— Klett's Modern German & English Dictionary. 3rd ed. LC 98-12961. (ENG & GER.). 1408p. 1998. 29.95 (*0-8442-2870-2*) NTC Contemp Pub Co.
— The Lover's Dictionary: How to Be Amorous in Five Delectable Languages. 2nd ed. (ENG, FRE, GER, ITA & SPA., Illus.). 128p. 1994. pap. 5.95 (*0-8442-9097-1*, Natl Textbk Co) NTC Contemp Pub Co.
— Mainland Greece. (Passport Essential Guide Ser.). (Illus.). 128p. 1998. pap. 8.95 (*0-8442-0136-7*, 01367, Passprt Bks) NTC Contemp Pub Co.
— Mexico & Central America: The All-in-One Travel & Language Guide. (Get Around in . . . Ser.). (SPA., Illus.). 128p. 1998. pap. 17.95 incl. audio (*0-8442-0161-8*, 01618) NTC Contemp Pub Co.
— Morocco. (Passport Essential Guide Ser.). 128p. 1998. pap. 8.95 (*0-8442-0128-6*, 01286, Passprt Bks) NTC Contemp Pub Co.
— New York. (Passport Essential Guide Ser.). 128p. 1998. pap. 8.95 (*0-8442-0124-3*, Passprt Bks) NTC Contemp Pub Co.
— New Zealand. (Passport Essential Guide Ser.). (Illus.). 128p. 1998. pap. 8.95 (*0-8442-0129-4*, 01294, Passprt Bks) NTC Contemp Pub Co.

***NTC Publishing Group Staff.** NTC's American English Learner's Dictionary. 2000. pap. 45.00 (*0-658-00131-0*, 001310); pap. 30.00 (*0-658-00156-6*, 001566) NTC Contemp Pub Co.
— NTC's American Idioms Dictionary. 2000. pap. 30.00 (*0-658-00130-2*, 001302); audio compact disk 20.00 (*0-658-00160-4*, 001604) NTC Contemp Pub Co.

NTC Publishing Group Staff. NTC's Compact Dutch & English Dictionary: The Most Practical & Convenient Dutch & English Dictionary. (DUT & ENG.). 584p. 1999. pap. 19.95 (*0-8442-0101-4*, 01014, Natl Textbk Co) NTC Contemp Pub Co.
— NTC's Compact Finnish & English Dictionary. LC 98-26853. (ENG & FIN.). 800p. 1998. 27.95 (*0-8442-0147-2*, 01472) NTC Contemp Pub Co.
— NTC's Compact Finnish & English Dictionary: The Most Practical & Convenient Finnish & English Dictionary. (FIN & ENG.). 800p. 1999. pap. 21.95 (*0-8442-0325-4*, 03254, Natl Textbk Co) NTC Contemp Pub Co.

***NTC Publishing Group Staff.** NTC's Dictionary of American Slang & Colloquial Expressions. 2000. pap. 30.00 (*0-658-00087-X*, 00087X); audio compact disk 20.00 (*0-658-00157-4*, 001574) NTC Contemp Pub Co.
— NTC's Dictionary of Phrasal Verbs & Other Idiomatic Verbal Phrases. 2000. pap. 30.00 (*0-658-00090-X*, 00090X); audio compact disk 20.00 (*0-658-00159-0*, 001590) NTC Contemp Pub Co.
— NTC's EFL Bookshelf. 2000. cd-rom 50.00 (*0-658-00161-2*, 001612) NTC Contemp Pub Co.

NTC Publishing Group Staff. Orlando & Disney World. (Passport Essential Guide Ser.). 128p. 1998. pap. 8.95 (*0-8442-0135-9*, 01359, Passprt Bks) NTC Contemp Pub Co.
— Paris. (Passport Essential Guide Ser.). 128p. 1998. pap. 8.95 (*0-8442-0133-2*, Passprt Bks) NTC Contemp Pub Co.
— Portugal. (Passport Essential Guide Ser.). (Illus.). 128p. 1998. pap. 8.95 (*0-8442-0125-1*, 01251, Passprt Bks) NTC Contemp Pub Co.
— Prague. (Passport Essential Guide Ser.). (Illus.). 128p. 1998. pap. 8.95 (*0-8442-0134-0*, 01340, Passprt Bks) NTC Contemp Pub Co.
— Provence & the Cote d'Azur. (Passport Essential Guide Ser.). (Illus.). 128p. 1998. pap. 8.95 (*0-8442-0113-8*, 01138, Passprt Bks) NTC Contemp Pub Co.
— Rome. (Passport Essential Guide Ser.). (Illus.). 128p. 1998. pap. 8.95 (*0-8442-0127-8*, 01278, Passprt Bks) NTC Contemp Pub Co.

***NTC Publishing Group Staff.** SDrine-In Spanish for Kids: Songs & Games for On-the-Go Children. (Drive-In Audio Packs for Kids Ser.). (ENG & SPA., Illus.). 32p. (J). 2000. pap. 9.95 incl. audio (*0-658-00862-5*, 008625) NTC Contemp Pub Co.
— Spanish Thematic Vocabulary Guide. (Thematic Vocabulary Guides Ser.). (SPA.). 192p. 2000. pap. 8.95 (*0-658-00872-2*, 008722) NTC Contemp Pub Co.

NTC Publishing Group Staff. Tuscany & Florence. (Passport Essential Guide Ser.). (Illus.). 128p. 1998. pap. 8.95 (*0-8442-0123-5*, 01235, Passprt Bks) NTC Contemp Pub Co.

***NTC Publishing Group Staff.** The Ultimate French Review & Practice: Mastering French Grammar for Confident Communication. LC 99-42641. (Ultimate Grammar Review & Practice Ser.). 448p. 1999. pap. 12.95 (*0-658-00074-8*, 000748) NTC Contemp Pub Co.

NTC Publishing Group Staff. Vox English & Spanish Learner's Dictionary. LC 98-8398. (SPA & ENG.). 1392p. 1998. 34.95 (*0-8442-7094-6*, 70946, Natl Textbk Co) NTC Contemp Pub Co.
— Vox Spanish & English Student Dictionary: The Most Practical & Instructive Spanish & English Dictionary. (Vox Ser.). (ENG & SPA.). 672p. 1999. 14.95 (*0-8442-2554-1*); pap. 10.95 (*0-8442-2438-3*, 24383) NTC Contemp Pub Co.

NTC Publishing Group Staff, ed. NTC's Compact Dutch & English Dictionary: The Most Practical & Concise Dutch & English Dictionary. LC 97-48917. (DUT., Illus.). 592p. 1998. 24.95 (*0-8442-8351-7*) NTC Contemp Pub Co.

NTC Publishing Group Staff, jt. auth. see Spears, Richard A.

***NTC Publishing Group Staff, Publishing Group.** Diccionario de Primaria de la Lengua Espanola: A Simple & Comprehensive Illustrated Spanish Dictionary. (SPA.). 992p. 1999. 19.95 (*0-658-00066-7*, 000667, NTC Business Bks) NTC Contemp Pub Co.

NTC Publishing Staff. BBC French Phrase Book. (BBC Phrase Bks.). (Illus.). 302p. 1994. pap. 5.95 (*0-8442-9224-9*, 92249) NTC Contemp Pub Co.
— BBC German Phrase Book. (BBC Phrase Bks.). (Illus.). 288p. 1994. pap. 5.95 (*0-8442-9225-7*, 92257) NTC Contemp Pub Co.
— BBC Italian Phrase Book. (BBC Phrase Bks.). (Illus.). 288p. 1994. pap. 5.95 (*0-8442-9227-3*, 92273) NTC Contemp Pub Co.
— BBC Spanish Phrase Book. (BBC Phrase Bks.). (Illus.). 286p. 1994. pap. 5.95 (*0-8442-9234-6*, 92346) NTC Contemp Pub Co.
— Dictionary of British Social History. (Reference Library). 1998. pap. 6.95 (*1-85326-378-8*, 3788WW, Pub. by Wrdsworth Edits) NTC Contemp Pub Co.
— Essential Singapore. (Essential Travel Guides Ser.). 128p. 1997. pap. text 7.95 (*0-8442-4811-8*, 48118, Passprt Bks) NTC Contemp Pub Co.

Ntc Publishing Staff. Indonesia: The All-in-One Travel & Language Guide. (Get Around in . . . Ser.). (IND., Illus.). 128p. 1998. pap. 19.95 incl. audio (*0-8442-0157-X*, 0157X) NTC Contemp Pub Co.

NTC Publishing Staff. Israel. (Passport Essential Guide Ser.). (Illus.). 128p. 1999. pap. text 8.95 (*0-8442-0088-3*, 00883, Passprt Bks) NTC Contemp Pub Co.
— Japan. (Essential Travel Guides Ser.). 128p. 1999. pap. 8.95 (*0-8442-4975-0*, 49750, Passprt Bks) NTC Contemp Pub Co.
— London. (Passport Essential Guide Ser.). (Illus.). 128p. 1999. pap. 8.95 (*0-8442-0089-1*, 00891, Passprt Bks) NTC Contemp Pub Co.
— Mexico. (Passport Essential Guide Ser.). 128p. 1999. pap. text 8.95 (*0-8442-0086-7*, 00867, Passprt Bks) NTC Contemp Pub Co.
— Portugal: The All-in-One Travel & Language Guide. (Get Around in . . . Ser.). (POR., Illus.). 128p. 1998. pap. 19.95 incl. audio (*0-8442-0174-X*, 0174X) NTC Contemp Pub Co.
— Vox Diccionario Compacto Espanol & Ingles. 2nd ed. LC 98-16232. (ENG & SPA., Illus.). 302p. 1996. pap. 8.95 (*0-8442-7991-9*, 79919) NTC Contemp Pub Co.
— Vox Diccionario para la Ensenanza de la Lengua Espanola: A Learner's Dictionary of Spanish. (ENG & SPA.). 1280p. 1998. 34.95 (*0-8442-7096-2*, 70962, Natl Textbk Co) NTC Contemp Pub Co.

***NTC/Contemporary Publishing Group Staff.** Klett's Modern German & English Dictionary: Includes Both Traditional & Reformed German Spelling. 3rd ed. (Klett's Ser.). (Illus.). 1408p. 1999. pap. 26.95 (*0-8442-2874-5*) NTC Contemp Pub Co.

nternational Symposium on Gas Chromatography Staff. Gas Chromatography, 1964: Proceedings of the International Symposium, 5th, Brighton, 1964. Goldup, A., ed. LC QD0271.. 398p. reprint ed. pap. 123.40 (*0-608-13896-7*, 202368500033) Bks Demand.

Nthunya, Mpho M. & Kendall, K. Limakatso. Singing Away the Hunger: The Autobiography of an African Woman. LC 97-18778. 220p. 1997. 35.00 (*0-253-33352-0*); pap. 12.95 (*0-253-21162-X*) Ind U Pr.

Ntiamoa-Baidu, Yaa & United Nations Food & Agriculture Organization Staff. Wildlife & Food Security in Africa. LC 98-210562. (Conservation Guide Ser.). vii, 109p. 1997. 14.00 (*92-5-104103-2*, Pub. by FAO) Bernan Associates.

Ntiri, Daphne W. Blossoming Trends. (C). 1994. pap. 7.00 (*0-911557-06-7*) Bedford Publishers.

Ntiri, Daphne W., ed. Consonance & Continuity in Poetry: Detroit Black Writers. (Illus.). 146p. (Orig.). 1988. pap. text 7.00 (*0-911557-01-6*) Bedford Publishers.
— One Is Not a Woman, One Becomes: The African Woman in a Transitional Society. (Illus.). 143p. (Orig.). 1988. reprint ed. pap. text 15.00 (*0-911557-02-4*) Bedford Publishers.

NTIS Staff. Laser Gyroscopes: September 70 - January 90. 1990. 85.00 (*0-614-18521-1*, 135P25) Info Gatekeepers.
— Ultrasonic Transducers: January 70 - February 90. 1990. 85.00 (*0-614-18506-8*, 135P43) Info Gatekeepers.

NTL Institute for Applied Behavioral Science Staff. Reading Book for Human Relations. 8th ed. (Illus.). vii, 450p. 1999. 55.00 (*0-9610392-7-2*) NTL Inst.

Ntuen, Celestine A., ed. see Park, Eui H.

Ntumy, Michael A., ed. South Pacific Islands Legal Systems. LC 92-41464. 720p. (C). 1993. text 75.00 (*0-8248-1438-X*) UH Pr.

Nu, Roland. Early Japanese Painted Crockery & Sculpture. (JPN., Illus.). 200p. 1993. reprint ed. pap. 50.00 (*0-87556-818-1*) Saifer.

NuAge Survival Publishing Editors. How to Prepare for an Earthquake Made Easy: A Planning Workbook for Personal Earthquake Preparedness for California Residents & Visitors. (Illus.). 64p. 1989. 10.00 (*0-9622924-0-0*) NuAge Survival.

Nuala Ni Dhomhnaill. The Astrakhan Cloak. Muldoon, Paul, tr. from IRI. LC 92-51047. 112p. 1993. 15.95 (*0-916390-55-1*) Wake Forest.

Nualart, D., jt. auth. see Barlow, M. T.

Nualart, D., jt. auth. see Carmona, R. A.

Nualart, David. The Malliavin Calculus & Related Topics. LC 94-48195. (Probability & Its Applications Ser.). 1995. 54.95 (*0-387-94432-X*) Spr-Verlag.

Nualart, David & Sole, Marta S., eds. Barcelona Seminar on Stochastic Analysis: St. Feliu de Guixols, 1991. LC 92-45002. (Progress in Probability Ser.: Vol. 32). x, 234p. 1993. 81.50 (*0-8176-2833-9*) Birkhauser.

Nuallain, Sean O. Stone Circles in Ireland. LC 95-164225. (Irish Treasures Ser.). (Illus.). 48p. (Orig.). 1995. pap. 8.95 (*0-946172-45-5*, Pub. by Town Hse) Roberts Rinehart.

***Nuallain, Sean O. & Dublin City University, Dublin City.** Search for Mind: The Third Millenium Mind. 384p. 2000. pap. text 44.95 (*1-84150-021-6*, Pub. by Intellect) Intl Spec Bk.

Nuara, Leonard T. What Lawyers Need to Know about the Internet: Powerful Strategies & Practical Uses. LC 98-106643. (Patents, Copyrights, Trademarks, & Literary Property Course Handbook Ser.). 176p. 1997. 129.00 (*0-87224-399-0*) PLI.

An Asterisk (*) at the beginning of an entry indicates that the title is appearing for the first time.

***Nuara, Leonard T. & Practising Law Institute Staff.** What Lawyers Need to Know about the Internet: Powerful Strategies & Practical Uses. LC 98-207495. (Patents, Copyrights, Trademarks & Literary Property Course Handbook Ser.). 216 p. 1998. 129.00 (*0-87224-474-1*) PLI.

Nuba, Hannah, et al, eds. Children's Literature: Developing Good Readers. LC 98-25543. (Source Books on Education: Vol. 51). 208p. 1998. 55.00 (*0-8153-2395-6*, SS1113) Garland.

— Resources for Early Childhood: A Handbook. LC 93-5044. 576p. 1994. text 40.00 (*0-8240-7395-9*, SS680) Garland.

***Nubar, Pierre.** Blind Fate. 2000. pap. 11.95 (*0-533-13277-0*) Vantage.

Nuber, Achim. Mehrstimmigkeit und Desintegration: Studien Zu Narration und Geschichte in Morikes Maler Nolten. (GER.). 278p. 1997. 54.95 (*3-631-31346-2*) P Lang Pubng.

Nuberg, Matt. REALbasic: The Definitive Guide. O'Reilly, Tim, ed. (O'Reilly Programming Ser.). (Illus.). 686p. 1999. pap. 29.95 (*1-56592-657-9*) OReilly & Assocs.

Nucci, Deborah, jt. auth. see Saunders, Jefferson.

Nucci, Deborah, jt. auth. see Saunders, Jefferson C.

Nucci, Larry P., ed. Moral Development & Character Education: A Dialogue. LC 88-63921. (National Society for the Study of Education Publication Ser.). 200p. 1989. 31.75 (*0-8211-1308-9*) McCutchan.

***Nucci, Larry P., et al.** Culture, Thought & Development. LC 00-42207. (Jean Piaget Symposium Ser.). 2000. write for info. (*0-8058-3009-X*) L Erlbaum Assocs.

Nucci, N. L., et al, eds. Developments in River Basin Management: Proceedings of an IAWPRC Conference Held in Sao Paulo, Brazil, 13-15 August, 1986. LC 82-645900. (Water Science & Technology Ser.: Vol. 19). (Illus.). 2288p. 1988. pap. 71.75 (*0-08-035593-5*, Pergamon Pr) Elsevier.

***Nuccio, Linda.** A Different Kind of Child. LC 00-90926. (J). (gr. 1-3). 2000. pap. 7.95 (*0-533-13537-0*) Vantage.

Nuccio, Richard A. What's Wrong, Who's Right in Central America? 2nd ed. 170p. 1989. pap. 14.95 (*0-8419-1177-0*) Holmes & Meier.

— What's Wrong, Who's Right in Central America: A Citizen's Guide. LC 85-31093. (Illus.). 154p. reprint ed. pap. 47.80 (*0-608-16042-3*, 203316800084) Bks Demand.

Nuccitelli, R., et al, eds. Mechanisms of Egg Activation. (Bodega Marine Laboratory Marine Science Ser.). (Illus.). 322p. 1989. 95.00 (*0-306-43245-5*, Plenum Trade) Perseus Pubng.

Nuccitelli, Richard, ed. Methods in Cell Biology: A Practical Guide to the Study of CA2Plus in Living Cells, Vol. 40. (Illus.). 368p. 1994. spiral bd. 52.00 (*0-12-522810-4*) Acad Pr.

Nuccitelli, Richard, ed. Methods in Cell Biology, Vol. 40: A Practical Guide to the Study of CA2Plus in Living Cells. (Illus.). 368p. 1994. text 104.00 (*0-12-564141-9*) Acad Pr.

NUCEA Staff & National University Continuing Education Associati. The Foundation of American Distance Education: A Century of Collegiate Correspondence Study. 336p. 1991. pap. text 24.95 (*0-8403-7101-2*) Kendall-Hunt.

Nucete, Leopoldo M. Democracia Economica. (SPA., Illus.). vi, 215p. (Orig.). 1996. pap. 15.00 (*0-9652798-0-4*, 001-001, AEME) Ediciones Disenos.

Nuchelmans, G. Dilemmatic Arguments: Towards a History of Their Logic & Rhetoric. (Verhandelingen der Koninklijke Nederlandse Akademie van Wetenschappen, Afd. Letterkunde, Nieuwe Reeks Ser.: No. 145). 152p. pap. 47.00 (*0-444-85730-3*) Elsevier.

— Geulincx Containment Theory of Logic. (Mededelingen der Koninklijke Nederlandse Akademie van Wetenschappen, Afd. Letterkunde Ser.: No. 51(8)). 58p. pap. 40.00 (*0-444-85698-6*) Elsevier.

— Judgment & Proposition: From Descartes to Kant. (Verhandelingen der Koninklijke Nederlandse Akademie van Wetenschappen, Afd. Letterkunde, Nieuwe Reeks Ser.: No. 118). 296p. pap. 56.25 (*0-444-85571-8*) Elsevier.

— Late-Scholastic & Humanist Theories of the Propostion. (Verhandelingen der Koninklijke Nederlandse Akademie van Wetenschappen, Afd. Letterkunde, Nieuwe Reeks Ser.: No. 103). 238p. pap. 50.00 (*0-7204-8468-5*) Elsevier.

Nuchelmans, G., ed. Secundum/Tertium Adiacens Vicissitudes of a Logical Distinction. (Verhandelingen der Koninklijke Nederlandse Akademie van Wetenschappen, Afd. Letterkunde, Nieuwe Reeks Ser.). 56p. 1992. pap. text 20.00 (*0-444-85762-1*) Elsevier.

Nuchelmans, Gabriel. Studies on the History of Logic & Semantics, 12th-17th Centuries. Bos, E. P., ed. LC 96-9296. (Collected Studies: No. CS560). 352p. 1996. 117.95 (*0-86078-618-8*, Pub. by Variorum) Ashgate Pub Co.

Nuchelmans, Gabriel. Theories of the Proposition: Ancient & Medieval Conceptions of the Bearers of Truth & Falsity. 8. LC 72-93495. ix, 309 p. 1973. write for info. (*0-7204-6188-X*) Elsevier.

Nucho, Aina O. The Psychocybernetic Model of Art Therapy. (Illus.). 248p. 1987. 51.95 (*0-398-05339-1*); pap. 35.95 (*0-398-06646-9*) C C Thomas.

— Spontaneous Creative Imagery: Problem-Solving & Life-Enhancing Skills. LC 95-20397. (Illus.). 174p. 1995. pap. 27.95 (*0-398-06550-0*); text 44.95 (*0-398-06549-7*) C C Thomas.

— Stress Management: The Quest for Zest. (Illus.). 194p. 1988. pap. text 24.95 (*0-398-06645-0*) C C Thomas.

— Stress Management: The Quest for Zest. (Illus.). 194p. (C). 1988. text 38.95 (*0-398-05478-9*) C C Thomas.

Nucho, Leslie S., ed. Education in the Arab World, Vol. 1. 737p. (Orig.). 1993. pap. 50.00 (*0-913957-12-7*) AMIDEAST.

Nucho, Leslie S., ed. see Amideast Publications Staff.

Nuchols, M. L. & Tucker, Wayne C. Life Support System Design Diving & Hyperbaric Application. 308p. (C). 1996. text 43.00 (*0-536-59616-6*) Pearson Custom.

Nucius, Nicander. The Second Book of the Travels of Nicander Nucius of Corcyra. Cramer, J. A., tr. (Camden Society, London. Publications, First Ser.: No. 17). reprint ed. 38.50 (*0-404-50117-6*) AMS Pr.

Nuckles, Douglas B. Baltimore & Ohio E-Unit Diesel Passenger Locomotives. (Illus.). 78p. 1996. pap. 15.95 (*1-883089-06-9*) TLC VA.

Nuckles, Vernon V. Biology of Venomous Sea Snakes (Hydrophidae) Index of New Information Teaching, Clinics & Research. 150p. 1998. 47.50 (*0-7883-1352-5*); pap. 44.50 (*0-7883-1353-3*) ABBE Pubs Assn.

Nuckolls, Benjamin F. Goodykoontz Family: Extract "Pioneer Settlers of Grayson County, Virginia" 16p. 1994. reprint ed. pap. 5.00 (*0-8328-4170-6*) Higginson Bk Co.

— Hale Family: Extract "Pioneer Settlers of Grayson County, Virginia" 36p. 1994. reprint ed. pap. 7.00 (*0-8328-4169-2*) Higginson Bk Co.

— Nuckolls Family: Extract "Pioneer Settlers of Grayson County, Virginia" 32p. 1994. reprint ed. pap. 6.50 (*0-8328-4168-4*) Higginson Bk Co.

Nuckolls, Charles W. The Cultural Dialectics of Knowledge & Desire. LC 96-18175. (New Directions in Anthropological Writing Ser.). (Illus.). 350p. 1996. pap. 24.95 (*0-299-15124-7*) U of Wis Pr.

— The Cultural Dialectics of Knowledge & Desire. LC 96-18175. (New Directions in Anthropological Writing Ser.). (Illus.). 350p. 1996. 60.00 (*0-299-15120-4*) U of Wis Pr.

— Culture: A Problem That Cannot Be Solved. LC 98-6856. 1998. 55.00 (*0-299-15890-X*); pap. 22.95 (*0-299-15894-2*) U of Wis Pr.

Nuckolls, Charles W., ed. Siblings in South Asia: Brothers & Sisters in Cultural Context. LC 92-30076. (Culture & Human Development Ser.). 247p. 1993. lib. bdg. 30.00 (*0-89862-146-1*) Guilford Pubns.

Nuckolls, James L., jt. auth. see Gordon, Gary.

Nuckolls, Janis B. Sounds Like Life: Sound-Symbolic Grammar, Performance & Cognition in Pastaza Quechua. (Oxford Studies in Anthropological Linguistics). (Illus.). 312p. 1996. text 75.00 (*0-19-508985-5*) OUP.

Nuckols, C. C. Children in Pain: Helping Chronically Addicted Adolescents. 224p. 1992. pap. 12.95 (*0-8306-3768-0*, 4096) McGraw-Hill Prof.

— Goodbye to the White Lady: Cocaine Addiction & Recovery. 154p. 1992. 17.95 (*0-8306-3388-X*); pap. 7.95 (*0-8306-3385-5*) McGraw-Hill Prof.

Nuckols, Cardwell C., jt. auth. see Chickering, Bill.

Nuckols, Frank J. The Ghost, the Gold & the Whippoorwill LC 97-67644. (Illus.). 157p. (J). (gr. 4-6). 1998. pap. 8.95 (*0-943864-91-7*) Davenport.

Nuckols, Marshall L., ed. see American Society of Mechanical Engineers Staff.

Nuckols, Maureen, jt. auth. see Flood, Nancy.

***Nuclear & Plasma Science Society Staff.** IEEE Radiation Effects Data Workshop, 1999. Institute of Electrical & Electronics Engineers, Inc. Staff, ed. LC 99-63072. 194p. 1999. pap. write for info. (*0-7803-5660-8*, 99TH8463) IEEE Standards.

***Nuclear Energy Agency Staff, contrib. by.** Reform of Civil Nuclear Liability: Budapest Symposium 1999. 680p. 2000. pap. 129.00 (*92-64-05885-0*, 66-2000-08-3-P, Pub. by Org for Econ) OECD.

Nuclear Instruments & Detectors Committee of the I, ed. IEEE Standard 960-1989: Revision of IEEE Standard 960-1986 with IEEE Standard 1177-1989. (IEEE Standard Fastbus Modular High-Speed Data Acquisition & Control System & IEEE Fastbus Standard Routines Ser.). (Illus.). 352p. (Orig.). 1990. pap. 54.00 (*1-55937-026-2*) IEEE Standards.

Nuclear Medicine Annual Staff. Nuclear Medicine Annual, 1988. Freeman, Leonard M. & Weissmann, Heidi S., eds. LC 80-645231. 352p. 1988. reprint ed. pap. 109.20 (*0-608-04720-1*, 206544100004) Bks Demand.

— Nuclear Medicine Annual, 1994. Freeman, Leonard M., ed. LC 80-645231. 304p. 1994. reprint ed. pap. 94.30 (*0-608-04729-5*, 206545000004) Bks Demand.

— Nuclear Medicine Annual 1995. Freeman, Leonard M., ed. LC 80-645231. (Illus.). 298p. reprint ed. pap. 92.40 (*0-608-09643-1*, 205441900001) Bks Demand.

— Nuclear Medicine Annual 1996. Freeman, Leonard M., ed. LC 80-645231. 304p. reprint ed. pap. 94.30 (*0-608-09736-5*, 206989900007) Bks Demand.

Nudds, J. R., ed. Directory of British Geological Museums. (Illus.). vii, 142p. 1994. 25.00 (*1-897799-08-X*, 225, Pub. by Geol Soc Pub Hse) AAPG.

Nudds, J. R. & Pettitt, C. W., eds. Value & Valuation of Natural Science Collections. 230p. 1996. 92.00 (*1-897799-76-4*, 239, Pub. by Geol Soc Pub Hse) AAPG.

Nudel, Eva, jt. auth. see Nudel, Michael.

Nudel, Ida. A Hand in the Darkness: The Autobiography of a Refusenik. Hoffman, Stefani, tr. 336p. 1991. reprint ed. mass mkt. 13.99 (*0-446-39325-8*, Pub. by Warner Bks) Little.

***Nudel, Michael & Nudel, Eva.** Health by Bio-Energy & Mind: Everything You Need to Develop Your Ability to Feel & Assess Human Energy & Perform Energy Healing. (Illus.). 152p. 2000. pap. 16.00 (*0-9677514-0-3*) Bio-Energy System.

— 21st Century's New Chakra Healing: The Revolutionary Method of Healing That Will Make You Healthy & Balanced. (Illus.). 155p. 2000. pap. 16.00 (*0-9677514-1-1*) Bio-Energy System.

Nudell, Mayer & Antokol, Norm. No One a Neutral: Political Hostage-Taking in the Modern World. LC 90-60358. 256p. 1990. pap. 12.95 (*0-939427-78-8*, 09052); boxed set 19.95 (*0-939427-59-1*, 09051) Alpha Pubns OH.

***Nudell, Mayer & Antokol, Norman.** The Handbook for Effetive Emergency & Crisis Management. LC 87-45997. (Illus.). 192p. 1999. reprint ed. 35.00 (*0-9677492-0-4*) M Nudell.

Nudel'Man, A. A., jt. auth. see Krein, M. G.

***Nudelman, Barry M.** Federal Taxation of Estates, Gifts & Trusts. 6th ed. LC 99-64846. 796p. 1999. text 172.50 (*0-8318-0794-6*, B794) Am Law Inst.

Nudelman, Barry M. & Blumenthal, Max E. Federal Taxation of Estates, Gifts & Trusts. 5th ed. LC 95-76586. 884p. 1995. text 70.00 (*0-8318-0632-X*, B632) Am Law Inst.

Nudelman, Dorothea & Willingham, David. Healing the Blues: A Personal Account by a Patient & Her Therapist. LC 98-102904. 202p. 1997. pap. 12.95 (*1-885987-10-2*, ME082, Health Info Pr) Practice Mgmt Info.

Nudelman, Dorothea & Willingham, David, eds. Healing the Blues: Drug-Free Psychotherapy of Depression. LC 94-12688. 235p. 1994. 22.00 (*0-940168-31-6*) Boxwood.

Nudelman, Edward D. Jessie Wilcox Smith: American Illustrator. LC 89-48273. (Illus.). 144p. 1990. 39.95 (*0-88289-786-1*) Pelican.

Nudelman, Jerrold. Steps in Composition Custom Chicago State 586p. (C). 1994. text 48.00 (*0-536-58553-9*) Pearson Custom.

Nudelman, Jerrold, jt. auth. see Troyka, Lynn.

***Nudelman, Pamela.** Secret Handbook for Perpetually Paralyzed Procrastinating Pack Rats Anonymous. 1999. pap. 17.95 (*0-9666656-0-0*) Panacea.

Nudelman, Phil. Dear Colleague: A Collection of Letters, Speeches & Commentaries. 1998. 25.00 (*0-89716-770-8*, Peanut Btr Pubng) Elton-Wolf Pub.

Nudelman, S., ed. see NATO Advanced Study Institute Staff.

Nudelman, Sol, ed. Photoelectronic Imaging Devices, 2 vols. Incl. Devices & Their Evaluation. Biberman, L. M., des. LC 74-120029. 584p. 1971. 125.00 (*0-306-37082-4*, Kluwer Plenum); Physical Processes & Methods of Analysis. Biberman, L. M., ed. LC 74-120029. 430p. 1971. 115.00 (*0-306-37081-6*, Kluwer Plenum); LC 74-120029. (Optical Physics & Engineering Ser.). 1971. write for info. (*0-318-55334-1*, Plenum Trade) Perseus Pubng.

***Nuding, Anton.** Schuler Beurteilen Durch Beobachtung: Entwicklung eines Beobachtungsbogens zur Gewinnung Schulrelevanter Diagnostischer Informationen. (Europaische Hochschulschriften: Reihe 11, Padagogik Ser.). 227p. 1999. 37.95 (*3-631-35159-3*) P Lang Pubng.

Nuding, M. N., ed. see Speart, Jessica.

Nudler, Oscar, jt. ed. see Lutz, Mark A.

Nudo, Sal. Nevermind: Its Only Rock of Ages. 40p. 1999. pap. 8.00 (*0-8059-4662-4*) Dorrance.

Nudson, Teny. All Through the Night. (Illus.). 36p. (Orig.). 1990. pap. 14.95 (*0-935133-38-0*) CKE Pubns.

— Dimensions of Christmas. (Illus.). 36p. 1989. pap. 14.95 (*0-935133-33-X*) CKE Pubns.

Nudson, Teny, jt. auth. see Kyle, Carolyn.

Nuebeck, Kenneth J. & Neubeck, Mary A. Social Problems. 4th ed. LC 96-22208. 646p. (C). 1996. pap. 50.31 (*0-07-046372-7*) McGraw.

Nuechterlein, Anne M. Improving Your Multiple Staff Ministry: How to Work Together More Effectively. LC 89-30879. 160p. (Orig.). 1989. pap. 14.99 (*0-8066-2422-1*, 9-2422) Augsburg Fortress.

***Nuechterlein, Donald E.** America Recommitted: A Superpower Assesses Its Role in a Turbulent World. 2nd rev. ed. 320p. (C). 2000. pap. 19.00 (*0-8131-9005-3*) U Pr of Ky.

Nuechterlein, Donald E. America Recommitted: United States National Interests in a Restructured World. LC 91-163. 280p. 1991. 30.00 (*0-8131-1746-1*) U Pr of Ky.

— A Cold War Odyssey. LC 97-11349. 296p. (C). 1997. 29.95 (*0-8131-2027-6*) U Pr of Ky.

— United States National Interests in a Changing World. LC 73-77255. 215p. reprint ed. pap. 66.70 (*0-8357-8595-5*, 203496900091) Bks Demand.

Nuegroschel, Joachim, tr. see Kafka, Franz.

Nuelle, Helen S. Land Where Our Fathers Died. large type ed. (Linford Mystery Library). 384p. 1992. pap. 16.99 (*0-7089-7230-6*) Ulverscroft.

Nueman, Donald, jt. auth. see Mayesky, Mary E.

Nueman, Mark & Payne, Michael, eds. Self, Sign, & Symbol. LC 86-47606. (Bucknell Review Ser.: Vol. 30, No. 2). 184p. 1987. 22.00 (*0-8387-5108-3*) Bucknell U Pr.

Nueno, Pedro. Corporate Turnaround: A Practical Guide to Business Survival. 176p. 1993. text 29.95 (*0-89397-398-X*) Nichols Pub.

Nuermberger, Ruth K. Free Produce Movement. LC 73-110135. (Duke University. Trinity College Historical Society. Historical Papers: No. 25). reprint ed. 30.00 (*0-404-51775-7*) AMS Pr.

Nuernberg, Susan M. The Critical Response to Jack London, 19. LC 95-15448. (Critical Responses in Arts & Letters Ser.: No. 19). 336p. 1995. lib. bdg. 65.00 (*0-313-28927-1*, Greenwood Pr) Greenwood.

Nuernberger, Phil. Freedom from Stress: A Holistic Approach. LC 80-80542. (Illus.). 261p. (C). 1981. pap. 14.95 (*0-89389-064-2*) Himalayan Inst.

Nuese, Charles J. Building the Right Things Right: A New Model for Product & Technology Development. LC 95-14651. 230p. 1995. 29.95 (*0-527-76300-4*) Productivity Inc.

— Building the Right Things Right: A New Model for Product Technology Development. (Illus.). 264p. 1995. 29.95 (*0-8144-0302-6*) AMACOM.

Nueslein, Robert. Deadly Dreams with Ghostly Encounters. 224p. 1999. pap. 12.95 (*1-56167-510-5*) Am Literary Pr.

Nuesse, C. Joseph. The Catholic University of America: A Centennial History. LC 89-29649. 508p. 1990. 39.95 (*0-8132-0722-3*); pap. 19.95 (*0-8132-0736-3*) Cath U Pr.

Nuessel, Frank. The Image of Older Adults in the Media: An Annotated Bibliography, 18. LC 92-24259. (Bibliographies & Indexes in Gerontology Ser.: No. 18). 224p. 1992. lib. bdg. 55.00 (*0-313-28018-5*, NIA, Greenwood Pr) Greenwood.

— The Study of Names: A Guide to the Principles & Topics. LC 92-5424. 176p. 1992. lib. bdg. 55.00 (*0-313-28356-7*, NSM, Greenwood Pr) Greenwood.

Nuetem, J. M. Van, see Van Nuetem, J. M., ed.

***Nuetzel, Sandra.** Seasons of Grace. LC 99-96686. 2000. pap. 8.95 (*0-533-13312-2*) Vantage.

Nueva Cronica Staff, ed. see Fox, Lucia.

Nuez Caballero, Sebastian De La, see De la Nuez Caballero, Sebastian, ed.

Nuez, Manuel De La, see De La Nuez, Manuel.

Nufer, Peter & Mulligan, Shelia. The Medicine Wheel: Earth Astrology. LC 96-231979. 204p. 1980. per. 11.00 (*0-671-76420-9*) P-H.

Nuffield Canadian Seminar Staff. Post-Secondary Education in a Technological Society. McLeod, Thomas H., ed. LC 73-79099. (ENG & FRE., Illus.). 259p. reprint ed. pap. 80.30 (*0-7837-6895-8*, 204672500003) Bks Demand.

Nuffield, Edward W. The Pacific Northwest. 288p. (Orig.). 1990. pap. 16.95 (*0-88839-236-2*) Hancock House.

— With The West In Her Eyes. 152p. (YA). (gr. 3 up). pap. write for info. (*0-920534-44-9*) Hyperion Pr.

***Nugayev, Rinat M.** Reconstruction of Mature Theory Change: A Theory-Change Model. LC 99-36556. 199p. (C). 1999. pap. text 37.95 (*0-8204-3627-5*) P Lang Pubng.

Nugel, Bernfried, ed. Now More Than Ever: Proceedings, Aldous Huxley Centenary Symposium, University of Munster, 1994. LC 96-33951. (Illus.). XV, 379p. 1996. 63.95 (*0-8204-2963-5*, PR6015) P Lang Pubng.

Nugent, jt. auth. see Bromfield.

Nugent, jt. auth. see Hudson.

Nugent, B. A., ed. see Divitis, Antonius.

Nugent, Barb, et al. 101 Ways to Be an Earth Angel. 112p. 1995. text 18.00 (*1-885499-20-5*) Angelight.

Nugent, Beth. Live Girls. 1997. pap. 12.00 (*0-679-74424-X*) Vin Bks.

Nugent, Charles & Croal, Melva. Turner Watercolors from Manchester. (Illus.). 128p. (Orig.). 1996. pap. 24.95 (*1-882507-05-3*) Trust Mus Exhib.

Nugent, Christopher. Masks of Satan: The Demonic in History. 216p. 1984. 22.50 (*0-89860-128-2*) Eastview.

— Mysticism, Death, & Dying. LC 93-50159. (SUNY Series in Western Esoteric Traditions). 127p. (C). 1994. text 16.50 (*0-7914-2205-4*) State U NY Pr.

Nugent, Daniel. Rural Revolt in Mexico: U. S. Intervention & the Domain of Subaltern Politics. 2nd ed. LC 97-36951. 1998. write for info. (*0-8223-2086-X*); pap. write for info. (*0-8223 2113-0*) Duke.

— Spent Cartridges of Revolution: An Anthropological History of Namiquipa, Chihuahua. LC 93-15997. (Illus.). 242p. 1993. pap. text 15.95 (*0-226-60742-9*) U Ch Pr.

— Spent Cartridges of Revolution: An Anthropological History of Namiquipa, Chihuahua. LC 93-15997. (Illus.). 244p. 1993. lib. bdg. 39.95 (*0-226-60741-0*) U Ch Pr.

Nugent, Daniel, jt. ed. see Joseph, Gilbert M.

Nugent, David. Modernity at the Edge of Empire: State, Individual & Nation in the Northern Peruvian Andes, 1885-1935. LC 96-49742. 1997. write for info. (*0-8047-2782-1*); pap. write for info. (*0-8047-2958-1*) Stanford U Pr.

Nugent, Donald. Ecumenism in the Age of the Reformation: The Colloquy of Poissy. LC 73-80026. (Historical Studies: No. 89). 296p. 1974. 20.00 (*0-674-23725-0*) HUP.

Nugent, Ed, ed. see Ebert, Sandi N.

Nugent, Elizabeth. The Case of Capital Intrigue. (Nancy Drew Mystery Stories Ser.: No. 142). (J). (gr. 3-6). 1998. per. 3.99 (*0-671-00751-3*, Minstrel Bks) PB.

Nugent, Elizabeth & Keene, Carolyn. Mystery on Maui. (Nancy Drew Mystery Stories Ser.: No. 143). 147p. (J). (gr. 3-6). 1998. per. 3.99 (*0-671-00753-X*, Minstrel Bks) PB.

***Nugent, Frances.** Northern Lights. large type ed. 360p. 2000. 31.99 (*0-7089-4173-7*) Ulverscroft.

Nugent, Frank A. Profession of Counseling. 3rd ed. LC 99-32596. (Illus.). 506p. (C). 1999. 59.00 (*0-13-260944-4*, Macmillan Coll) P-H.

Nugent, Gabriel M. Employment Discrimination Based on Sexual Orientation. LC 98-85892. (Legal Research Guides Ser.: Vol. 30). xi, 68p. 1998. 46.00 (*1-57588-445-3*, 311760) W S Hein.

Nugent-Head, Andrew. Energy for a More Dynamic Living: A Set Often Qi Gong Exercises. 32p. pap. 8.00 (*1-888179-54-6*) Assn For Tradit.

Nugent-Head, Andrew, jt. auth. see Wang Jin Huai.

Nugent-Head, Andrew, tr. see Peiqi, Xie.

Nugent, I., et al. Key Topics in Orthopaedic Surgery. 300p. (Orig.). 1994. pap. 52.50 (*1-872748-33-3*, Pub. by Bios Sci) Coronet Bks.

Nugent, J. Kevin, et al, eds. Biology, Culture & Infant Development. LC 88-26059. (Cultural Context of Infancy Ser.: Vol. 1). 416p. 1989. text 78.50 (*0-89391-190-9*) Ablx Pub.

Nugent, J. Kevin, jt. ed. see Brazelton, T. Berry.

Nugent, Jeffrey B. Economic Integration in Central America: Empirical Investigations. LC 74-6832. (Illus.). 226p. reprint ed. pap. 70.10 (*0-608-10689-5*, 202072900018) Bks Demand.

Nugent, JoAnne. Handbook of Dual Diagnosis, Vol. 1. 2nd rev. ed. 150p. 1997. pap. 27.95 (*0-9662099-0-7*) Mariah Manage.

***Nugent, Julian L., Jr.** Lose Three, Win One. 96p. 1999. pap. 10.00 (*0-8059-4785-X*) Dorrance.

Nugent, Kathy, ed. see Rebrovich, Victor E.

Nugent, Kevin, et al, eds. Multicultural & Interdisciplinary Approaches to Parent-Infant Relations. (Cultural Context of Infancy Ser.: Vol. 2). 384p. (C). 1991. text 78.50 (*0-89391-627-7*) Ablx Pub.

Nugent, Madeline P. Praying with Anthony of Padua. (Companions for the Journey Ser.). (Illus.). 120p. 1996. pap. 7.95 (*0-88489-397-9*) St Marys.

— Saint Anthony: Words of Fire, Life of Light. LC 95-23131. 416p. 1995. pap. 13.95 (*0-8198-6984-8*) Pauline Bks.

***Nugent, Neill.** At the Heart of the Union: Studies of the European Commission. 2nd ed. LC 99-59236. 2000. 22.95 (*0-312-23233-0*) St Martin.

— The European Commission. LC 00-40436. 2000. write for info. (*0-333-58743-X*) St Martin.

Nugent, Neill. The Government & Politics of the European Community. rev. ed. LC 91-14311. 448p. 1991. pap. text 23.95 (*0-8223-1193-3*) Duke.

— The Government & Politics of the European Community. 2nd rev. ed. LC 91-14311. 448p. 1991. lib. bdg. 52.95 (*0-8223-1184-4*) Duke.

— The Government & Politics of the European Union. 3rd ed. LC 94-17236. 496p. 1994. text 59.95 (*0-8223-1506-8*); pap. text 23.95 (*0-8223-1517-3*) Duke.

***Nugent, Neill.** The Government & Politics of the European Union. 4th ed. LC 98-55980. 480p. 1999. 64.95 (*0-8223-2207-2*) Duke.

Nugent, Neill. Government & Politics of the European Union. 4th ed. LC 98-55980. 480p. 1999. pap. 22.95 (*0-8223-2223-4*) Duke.

Nugent, Neill, ed. The European Union, 2 vols., Set. LC 96-19707. (International Library of Politics & Comparative Government). 996p. 1997. text 282.95 (*1-85521-685-X*, Pub. by Dartmth Pub) Ashgate Pub Co.

— European Union Annual Review of Activities 1996. (Journal of Common Market Studies). 208p. 1997. pap. 33.95 (*0-631-20760-0*) Blackwell Pubs.

— The European Union 1995. (Journal of Common Market Studies). 192p. 1996. pap. text 35.95 (*0-631-20264-1*) Blackwell Pubs.

Nugent, Neill & O'Donnell, Rory, eds. The European Business Environment. LC 94-28903. 1994. text 59.95 (*0-312-12351-5*) St Martin.

Nugent, Nell M. Cavaliers & Pioneers: Abstracts of Virginia Land Patents & Grants, 1695-1732, No. 1. LC 80-141230. iii, 18p. 1980. 4.95 (*0-88490-088-6*) Library of VA.

— Cavaliers & Pioneers: Abstracts of Virginia Land Patents & Grants, 1695-1732, Vol. 2. LC 34-42407. xi, 609p. 1992. reprint ed. text 30.00 (*0-88490-009-6*, F225 N842) Library of VA.

— Cavaliers & Pioneers: Abstracts of Virginia Land Patents & Grants, 1695-1732, Vol. 3. LC 34-42407. ix, 578p. 1979. 30.00 (*0-88490-083-5*) Library of VA.

Nugent, Nell M., contrib. by. Cavaliers & Pioneers Vol. 1: Abstracts of Virginia Land Patents & Grants, 1623-1666, 1. LC 92-27183. xxxv, 767p. 1992. reprint ed. text 30.00 (*0-88490-174-2*, F225 N842) Library of VA.

— Cavaliers & Pioneers Vol. 1: Abstracts of Virginia Land Patents & Grants, 1623-1666, Set. LC 92-27183. xxxv, 767p. 1992. reprint ed. 75.00 (*0-88490-175-0*) Library of VA.

Nugent, Patricia M. & Vitale, Barbara A. Test Success: Test-Taking Techniques for Beginning Nursing Students. 3rd ed. (Illus.). 378p. 2000. pap. text 24.95 (*0-8036-0524-2*) Davis Co.

Nugent, Patricia M., jt. auth. see Vitale, Barbara A.

Nugent, Paul. Big Men, Small Boys & Politics in Ghana: Power, Ideology & the Burden of History, 1982-1994. LC 95-12503. 256p. 1995. 110.00 (*1-85567-373-8*) Bks Intl VA.

Nugent, Paul & Asiwaju, A. I., eds. African Boundaries: Barriers, Conduits & Opportunities. 256p. 1996. 110.00 (*1-85567-372-X*) Bks Intl VA.

Nugent, Robert. Paul Elvard. LC 74-4132. (Twayne's World Authors Ser.). (C). 1974. lib. bdg. 20.95 (*0-8057-2299-8*) Irvington.

— Prayer Journey for Persons with AIDS. 49p. 1990. pap. text 3.95 (*0-86716-127-2*) St Anthony Mess Pr.

Nugent, Robert & Gramick, Jeannine. Building Bridges: Gay & Lesbian Reality & the Catholic Church. LC 91-67051. 240p. 1992. pap. 12.95 (*0-89622-503-8*) Twenty-Third.

Nugent, Robert, tr. see De Sponde, Jean.

Nugent, Robert, jt. tr. see Lunardi, Egidio.

Nugent, Robert, tr. see Matute, Ana M.

Nugent, Stephen. Big Mouth: The Amazon Speaks. (Illus.). 258p. 1994. 19.95 (*1-56313-443-8*); pap. 12.95 (*1-56313-722-4*) BrownTrout Pubs Inc.

Nugent, Stephen, jt. auth. see Shore, Cris.

Nugent, Stephen L. Amazonian Caboclo Society: An Essay on Invisibility & Peasant Economy. (Explorations in Anthropology Ser.). (Illus.). 278p. 1993. 25.00 (*0-85496-756-7*, Pub. by Berg Pubs) NYU Pr.

***Nugent, Ted.** God, Guns & Rock & Roll. 288p. 2000. 24.95 (*0-89526-279-7*) Regnery Pub.

Nugent, Thomas, tr. see Burlamaqui, Jean-Jaques.

Nugent, Thomas, tr. see Condillac, Etienne Bonnot de.

Nugent, Thomas, tr. see De Secondat, Charles L.

Nugent, Walter. Crossings: The Great Transatlantic Migrations, 1870-1914. LC 92-7156. (Illus.). 256p. 1992. text 35.00 (*0-253-34140-X*) Ind U Pr.

Nugent, Walter. Crossings: The Great Transatlantic Migrations, 1870-1914. LC 92-7156. (Illus.). 256p. 1995. pap. 17.95 (*0-253-20953-6*) Ind U Pr.

***Nugent, Walter & Ridge, Martin, eds.** The American West: The Reader. LC 99-19404. 1999. text. write for info. (*0-253-33530-2*) Ind U Pr.

Nugent, Walter & Ridge, Martin, eds. The American West: The Reader. LC 99-19404. 1999. pap. 19.95 (*0-253-21290-1*) Ind U Pr.

***Nugent, Walter & Walter, T. K.** Into the West: The Story of Its People. LC 99-18957. 493p. 1999. 35.00 (*0-679-45479-9*) Knopf.

Nugent, Walter T. Tolerant Populists: Kansas Populism & Nativism. LC 63-13069. 268p. reprint ed. 83.10 (*0-8357-9659-0*, 201576100003) Bks Demand.

Nugent, Ward J. Prejudice: Index of Modern Information with Bibliography. LC 88-47787. 150p. (Orig.). 1988. 47.50 (*0-88164-902-3*); pap. 44.50 (*0-88164-903-1*) ABBE Pubs Assn.

Nugent, Wendi M. Handbook of Polysomnographic Technology. (Illus.). 256p. 1998. text 50.00 (*0-7506-9513-7*) Buttrwrth-Heinemann.

Nugent, Wendy W. Fantastic Fresno Fun Book: An Educational Activity Book for Kids. (Illus.). 32p. (J). (ps-6). 1998. 6.95 (*0-9666581-0-8*) Clover Pubns.

Nugent, William A. & Mayer, James M. Metal Ligand Multiple Bonds. LC 88-233. 334p. 1988. 140.00 (*0-471-85440-9*) Wiley.

***Nuggard, Scott, ed.** Swing Guitar Essentials. LC 99-26412. (Acoustic Guitar Magazine's Private Lessons Ser.). 80p. 1999. pap. 19.95 (*1-890490-18-0*) String Letter.

Nugter, A. C. Transborder Flow of Personal Data Within the EC. (Computer - Law Ser.: Vol. 6). 456p. 1990. pap. 94.00 (*90-6544-513-7*) Kluwer Law Intl.

Nugues, E., et al. Practical Manual for the Piano & Harmonium Tuner: A Treatise on the Tuning & Repair of These Instruments. (Illus.). vi, 146p. 1913. pap. text 20.00 (*0-913746-30-4*) Organ Lit.

***Nugurney, Anna.** Sustainable Transportation Networks. LC 99-59384. 304p. 2000. 95.00 (*1-84064-357-9*) E Elgar.

***Nuhfer, Shirley.** Reflections. 1999. pap. write for info. (*1-58235-271-2*) Watermrk Pr.

Nuhfer, Shirley A. From Heart 'n Home. 1998. pap. write for info. (*1-58235-047-7*) Watermrk Pr.

— Just Me. 1998. pap. write for info. (*1-57553-768-0*) Watermrk Pr.

Nuhn, Gary. Eighty Ninth U. S. Open. Norwood, Bev, ed. (Illus.). 64p. 1989. 15.00 (*0-9615344-7-8*) Intl Merc OH.

— Ninetieth U. S. Open. Norwood, Bev, ed. (Illus.). 64p. 1990. 15.00 (*1-878843-00-1*) Intl Merc OH.

Nuhn, Roger, ed. New Braunfels, Comal County, Texas: A Pictorial History. LC 93-35505. 1993. write for info. (*0-89865-879-9*) Donning Co.

Nuijts, R. M. Ocular Toxicity of Intraoperatively Used Drugs & Solutions. (Illus.). 150p. 1995. text 46.00 (*90-6299-141-6*, Pub. by Kugler) Kugler Pubns.

Nuiry, Octavio. The 1999 National Hispanic Media Directory Pt. 3: Latin American Media. Whisler, Kirk, ed. (Marketing Guidepost Ser.). 220p. 1998. pap. 95.00 (*1-889379-10-7*) WPR Pubng.

Nuiry, Octavio, jt. auth. see Whisler, Kirk.

Nuiry, Octavio, jt. ed. see Whisler, Kirk.

Nuis, Hermine J. Van, see Van Nuis, Hermine J.

Nuitter, C. & Thoinan, E. Les Origines de l'Opera Francais. LC 77-4106. (Music Reprint Ser.). 1977. reprint ed. lib. bdg. 42.50 (*0-306-70895-7*) Da Capo.

Nujkamp, Peter, jt. auth. see Cappellin, Riccardo.

Nujssbaumer, H., ed. see Livio, Mario, et al.

Nukayis, Ventris. Last Days? Spiritual Reality & Physical Illusions. 272p. (Orig.). 1991. pap. 9.95 (*1-56266-149-3*) Anwol.

***Nukem, Duke.** Duke Nukem Zero Hour Official Strategy Guide. 1999. pap. 12.95 (*1-56893-940-X*) GT Interactive Software.

Nukewatch Staff. Nuclear Heartland: A Guide to the One Thousand Missile Silos of the United States. Day, Samuel H., Jr., ed. (Illus.). 96p. (Orig.). (C). 1988. pap. 10.00 (*0-942046-01-3*) Prog Found.

— Prisoners on Purpose: A Peacemaker's Guide to Jails & Prisons. Day, Samuel H., Jr., ed. (Illus.). 145p. (Orig.). (C). 1989. pap. 5.00 (*0-942046-02-1*) Prog Found.

***Nukunya, G. K.** Kinship & Marriage among the Anlo Ewe. LC 98-45323. (London School of Economics: No. 37). 217p. 1999. 29.95 (*0-485-19637-9*, Pub. by Athlone Pr) Humanities.

Nuland, Sherwin B. Doctors: The Biography of Medicine. 1995. pap. 16.00 (*0-679-76009-1*) Vin Bks.

— How We Die: Reflections on Life's Final Chapter. 1995. pap. 14.00 (*0-679-74244-1*) Vin Bks.

— How We Live. 432p. 1998. pap. 14.00 (*0-679-78140-4*) Vin Bks.

***Nuland, Sherwin B.** Leonardo da Vinci: A Penguin Life. (Illus.). 2000. 19.95 (*0-670-89391-9*, Viking) Viking Penguin.

— The Mysteries Within: A Surgeon Reflects on Medical Myths. LC 99-88659. 288p. 2000. 24.00 (*0-684-85486-4*) S&S Trade.

Nuland, Sherwin B. The Wisdom of the Body. LC 96-45113. 416p. 1997. 5.99 (*0-679-44407-6*) Knopf.

Nuland, Victoria, jt. contrib. by see Lugar, Richard.

Null. Cooking with Spirit of Love. LC 99-36858. 256p. 1999. pap. 14.95 (*0-312-20639-9*) St Martin.

***Null, Ashley.** Thomas Cranmer's Doctrine of Repentance: Renewing the Power to Love. (Illus.). 300p. 2001. text 74.00 (*0-19-827021-6*) OUP.

Null, Casey, jt. auth. see Sima, Patti.

Null, Cheryl J. & Gad, Carol L. The Barnyard Buddies. (Illus.). 32p. (J). (gr. 2-6). 1989. pap. 5.95 (*1-880171-00-7*) Stardom.

— The Barnyard Buddies in Circus Champions. (Illus.). 36p. (J). (gr. 2-6). 1990. pap. 5.95 (*1-880171-01-5*) Stardom.

— The Barnyard Buddies in Finders Keepers. (Illus.). 36p. (J). (gr. 2-6). 1992. pap. 5.95 (*1-880171-04-X*) Stardom.

Null, Gary. Allergies & Weight Control, Set. unabridged ed. 1995. 16.95 incl. audio (*1-879323-21-4*) Sound Horizons AV.

Null, Gary. Be Kind to Yourself: Explorations into Self-Empowerment. (Illus.). 240p. 1995. pap. text 12.95 (*0-7867-0269-9*) Carroll & Graf.

— Black Hollywood: From Nineteen Seventy to Today. LC 92-37551. 1993. pap. 16.95 (*0-8065-1216-4*) Carol Pub Group.

— Choosing Joy. LC 98-15304. 304p. 1998. pap. 12.95 (*0-7867-0522-1*) Carroll & Graf.

— Clinician's Handbook of Natural Healing: The First Comprehensive Guide to Scientific Peer Review. LC 97-75439. 880p. 1998. 60.00 (*1-57566-284-1*) Kensgtn Pub Corp.

***Null, Gary.** Complete Encyclopedia of Natural Healing. 2000. pap. 20.00 (*1-57566-719-3*, Knsington) Kensgtn Pub Corp.

Null, Gary. The Complete Encyclopedia of Natural Healing: A Comprehensive A-Z Listing of Common & Chronic Illnesses & Their Proven Natural Treatments. LC 97-73471. 612p. 1998. 35.00 (*1-57566-258-2*, Knsington) Kensgtn Pub Corp.

— The Complete Guide to Health & Nutrition: A Source Book for a Healthier Life. 608p. 1986. pap. 21.95 (*0-440-50612-3*, Dell Trade Pbks) Dell.

— The Complete Guide to Sensible Eating. 3rd ed. LC 97-22206. (Illus.). 352p. 1998. pap. 16.95 (*1-888363-61-4*) Seven Stories.

***Null, Gary.** The Food-Mood-Body Connection: Nutrition-Based Approaches to Mental Health. 512p. 2000. 35.00 (*1-58322-031-3*) Seven Stories.

— Gary Null's Guide to a Joyful & Healthy Life. 848p. 2000. 28.00 (*0-7867-0712-7*) Carroll & Graf.

— Gary Null's Ultimate Anti-Aging Program. Campbell, Ann, ed. LC 99-34050. (Illus.). 528p. 1999. pap. 17.50 (*0-7679-0436-2*) Broadway BDD.

— Gary Nulls Ultimate Lifetime Diet. 2000. reprint ed. pap. 17.50 (*0-7679-0474-5*) Broadway BDD.

— Gary Null's Ultimate Lifetime Diet: A Revolutionary All-Natural Program for Losing Weight & Building a Healthy Body, Vol. 1. LC 99-48028. 720p. 1999. 30.00 (*0-7679-0473-7*) Broadway BDD.

Null, Gary. Get Healthy Now! with Gary Null: A Complete Guide to Prevention, Treatment & Healthy Living. McDonald, Amy, ed. LC 98-55547. 1088p. 1999. 39.95 (*1-888363-97-5*, Pub. by Seven Stories) Publishers Group.

***Null, Gary.** Get Healthy Now! with Gary Null: A Complete Guide to Prevention, Treatment & Healthy Living. 1152p. 2001. reprint ed. pap. 29.95 (*1-58322-042-9*) Seven Stories.

Null, Gary. Healing Everything with Magnets. 224p. 1998. pap. 11.95 (*0-7867-0530-2*) Carroll & Graf.

— Healing Your Body Naturally: Alternative Treatments to Illness. 3rd rev. ed. LC 96-39683. (Illus.). 336p. 1997. pap. 16.95 (*1-888363-46-0*) Seven Stories.

***Null, Gary.** How to Live Forever: The Ultimate Anti-Aging, 1. LC 98-75068. 1999. 29.95 (*1-57566-409-7*) Kensgtn Pub Corp.

— How to Strengthen the Immune System, Set. 141p. 1995. 16.95 incl. audio (*1-879323-22-2*) Sound Horizons AV.

Null, Gary. The International Vegetarian Cookbook. 256p. 1998. 16.00 (*0-02-862327-4*) Macmillan.

— The New Vegetarian Cookbook. 250p. 1980. pap. 13.95 (*0-02-010040-X*) Macmillan.

— The New Vegetarian Cookbook. 1987. pap. 15.95 (*0-02-590890-1*) Macmillan.

— New Vegetarian Cookbook. 1998. pap. text 9.99 (*1-57866-014-9*) Promntory Pr.

— No More Allergies: Identifying & Eliminating Allergies & Sensitivity Reactions to Everything in Your Environment. LC 92-50149. 1992. pap. 14.00 (*0-679-74310-3*) Villard Books.

— Nutrition & the Mind. LC 94-46982. 303p. (Orig.). 1995. pap. 14.95 (*1-888363-24-X*) Seven Stories.

Null, Gary. Reversing the Aging Process Naturally: A Practical Guide for the Prevention of Pre-Mature Aging. abr. ed. 1996. 16.95 incl. audio (*0-9644002-0-0*) Common Mode Hrmnic Wave.

Null, Gary. Secrets of the Sacred White Buffalo: Native American Healing Remedies, Rites, & Rituals. LC 98-14522. (Illus.). 320p. (C). 1997. pap. 15.00 (*0-7352-0008-4*) PH Pr.

— Ultimate Training: Gary's Null's Complete Guide to Eating Right, Exercising & Living Longer. LC 92-44033. 1993. pap. 12.95 (*0-312-08796-9*) St Martin.

— The Vegetarian Handbook. rev. ed. 304p. 1996. pap. 13.95 (*0-312-14441-5*) St Martin.

— Weapon of Denial: Air Power & the Battle for New Guinea. 32p. 1995. pap. 2.00 (*0-16-048422-7*) USGPO.

— Who Are You, Really? Understanding Your Life's Energy. LC 96-19282. 144p. 1996. pap. 9.95 (*0-7867-0326-1*) Carroll & Graf.

— The Woman's Encyclopedia of Natural Healing: The New Healing Techniques of over 100 Leading Alternative Practitioners. LC 96-28291. 416p. (Orig.). 1996. pap. 19.95 (*1-888363-35-5*) Seven Stories.

Null, Gary & Feldman, Martin. Good Food, Good Mood. 208p. 1991. pap. 11.95 (*0-312-06985-5*) St Martin.

— Reverse the Aging Process Naturally: How to Build the Immune System with Antioxidants, the Supernutrients of the Nineties. LC 92-56703. (Gary Null Health Library). 1993. pap. 12.95 (*0-679-74509-2*) Villard Books.

Null, Gary & Null, Shelly. The Joy of Juicing Recipe Guide: Creative Cooking with Your Juicer. LC 92-10462. 240p. pap. 10.95 (*0-89529-592-X*, Avery) Penguin Putnam.

Null, Gary & Null, Sherry. Vegetarian Cooking for Good Health. 274p. 1999. 9.99 (*1-57866-050-5*) Galahad Bks.

Null, Gary & Robins, Howard. How to Keep Your Feet & Legs Healthy for a Lifetime: The Complete Guide to Foot & Leg Care. LC 89-71438. (Illus.). 288p. (Orig.). 1990. pap. 14.95 (*1-888363-30-4*) Seven Stories.

Null, Gary & Seaman, Barbara. For Women Only! Your Guide to Health Empowerment. LC 99-39822. 1573p. 2000. 49.95 (*1-58322-015-1*, Pub. by Seven Stories) Publishers Group.

Null, Gary, jt. auth. see Watts.

Null, Kathleen. How to Give a Presentation. (How to Ser.). 48p. (J). (gr. 2-6). 1997. pap. 7.95 (*1-57690-325-7*) Tchr Create Mat.

— How to Make a Book Report. (How to Ser.). (Illus.). 48p. (J). (gr. 2-6). 1998. pap., teacher ed. 7.95 (*1-57690-327-3*, TCM2327) Tchr Create Mat.

— How to Punctuate & Capitalize. (How to Ser.). 48p. (J). (gr. 2-6). 1997. pap. 7.95 (*1-57690-329-X*) Tchr Create Mat.

— How to Write a Paragraph. (How to Ser.). 48p. (J). (gr. 2-6). 1997. pap. 7.95 (*1-57690-330-3*) Tchr Create Mat.

— How to Write a Poem. (How to Ser.). 48p. (J). (gr. 2-6). 1997. pap. 7.95 (*1-57690-331-1*) Tchr Create Mat.

— How to Write a Research Report. (How to Ser.). 48p. (J). (gr. 2-6). 1997. pap. 7.95 (*1-57690-332-X*) Tchr Create Mat.

— How to Write a Sentence. (How to Ser.). 48p. (J). (gr. 2-6). 1997. pap. 7.95 (*1-57690-326-5*) Tchr Create Mat.

— How to Write a Story. (How to Ser.). 48p. (J). (gr. 2-6). 1997. pap. 7.95 (*1-57690-328-1*) Tchr Create Mat.

— Learning Center Activities for Writing. 80p. (J). (gr. k-2). 1997. pap. 9.95 (*1-57690-075-4*) Tchr Create Mat.

Null, Kathleen C. I Used to Think People My Age Were Old. 1995. pap. 7.95 (*0-88494-984-2*) Bookcraft Inc.

***Null, Kathleen Christopher.** How to Write a Paragraph. Wally, Barbara M., ed. (Illus.). 48p. (J). (gr. 1-3). 1999. pap., teacher ed. 7.95 (*1-57690-494-6*, TCM2494) Tchr Create Mat.

— How to Write a Paragraph. Wally, Barbara M., ed. (Illus.). 48p. (YA). (gr. 6-8). 1999. pap., teacher ed. 7.95 (*1-57690-490-3*, TCM2490) Tchr Create Mat.

— How to Write a Sentence. Cook, David, ed. 48p. (J). (gr. 1-3). 1999. pap., teacher ed. 7.95 (*1-57690-498-9*, TCM2498) Tchr Create Mat.

— How to Write a Story. Guckian, Mary Ellen, ed. (Illus.). 48p. (J). (gr. 1-3). 1999. pap., teacher ed. 7.95 (*1-57690-495-4*, TCM2495) Tchr Create Mat.

Null, Kathleen Christopher, jt. auth. see Teacher Created Materials Staff.

***Null, Lucinda K.** Billy, the Bear Hugger. (Illus.). 12p. (J). (ps-2). 1999. pap. 4.00 (*0-9671500-0-0*) Heartfelt MO.

Null, Ralph. The Florist's Guide to Successful Weddings. Hilton, Pat, ed. (Illus.). 130p. 1988. write for info. (*0-9620684-0-3*) Teleflora.

Null, Ralph, jt. auth. see Hampton, Bob.

Null, Roberta L. & Cherry, Kenneth F. Universal Design: Creative Solutions for ADA Compliance. LC 95-23842. (Illus.). 325p. 1996. 69.95 (*0-912045-86-8*) Prof Pubns CA.

Null, Shelly, jt. auth. see Null, Gary.

Null, Sherry, jt. auth. see Null, Gary.

Nulman, Louis. What Is Chanukah? A Programmed Text. 1997. pap. 3.25 (*0-914131-73-7*, A360) Torah Umesorah.

— What Is Kosher? A Programmed Text. 1997. pap. 3.50 (*0-914131-74-5*, A370) Torah Umesorah.

Nulman, Macy. Encyclopedia of Jewish Prayer: Ashkenazic & Sephardic Rites. LC 92-33637. 464p. 1996. pap. 40.00 (*1-56821-885-0*) Aronson.

— The Encyclopedia of the Sayings of the Jewish People. LC 96-51944. 384p. 1997. 45.00 (*0-7657-5980-2*) Aronson.

Nulman, Marilyn, ed. see Hagerty, Kevin D.

Nulman, Philip R. Just Say Yes! Extreme Customer Service: How to Give It, How to Get It! LC 99-46846. 192p. 1999. pap. 14.99 (*1-56414-420-8*) Career Pr Inc.

— Start up Marketing: An Entrepreneur's Guide to Launching, Advertising, Marketing &... LC 96-28856. 288p. (Orig.). 1996. pap. 16.99 (*1-56414-256-6*) Career Pr Inc.

Nulsen, R. O., Jr., et al. Compete! 4th ed. 130p. (C). 1994. text, pap. text 32.95 incl. 3.5 hd (*0-256-14711-6*, Irwn McGrw-H) McGrw-H Hghr Educ.

Nulty, Leslie. The Green Revolution in West Pakistan: Implications of Technological Change. LC 73-170471. (Special Studies in International Economics & Development). 1972. 32.50 (*0-89197-779-1*) Irvington.

Nulty, William H. Confederate Florida: The Road to Olustee. LC 89-33849. 288p. 1994. pap. text 19.95 (*0-8173-0748-6*) U of Ala Pr.

Num, Dummy. The Wizard of 4th Street, Vol. 1. 1989. mass mkt. 3.95 (*0-445-77054-6*, Pub. by Warner Bks) Little.

Num, Dummy. Wizard of White. 1989. mass mkt. 3.95 (*0-445-77055-4*, Pub. by Warner Bks) Little.

Numa Research Department Staff. El Gran Libro de los XXXX en el Mundo (Argentina) (SPA., Illus.). 95p. 1998. 54.95 (*1-885808-19-4*); pap. 44.95 (*1-885808-20-8*) Numa Corp.

— Het Wereldwijde Boek Van de Familienamen. 95p. 1994. 51.00 (*1-885808-05-4*); pap. text 46.00 (*1-885808-06-2*) Numa Corp.

— Il Libro Mondiale di Cognomi. 95p. 1994. 54.00 (*1-885808-11-9*); pap. text 48.00 (*1-885808-12-7*) Numa Corp.

— El Libro Mundial de los Apellidos Familiares. 95p. 1994. 54.00 (*1-885808-09-7*); pap. text 48.00 (*1-885808-10-0*) Numa Corp.

— Le Livre Mondial de la Famille Patronyme. 95p. 1994. 52.00 (*1-885808-07-0*); pap. text 46.00 (*1-885808-08-9*) Numa Corp.

An Asterisk (*) at the beginning of an entry indicates that the title is appearing for the first time.

— Das Weltbuch fur Familiennamen. 95p. 1994. 53.00 (*1-885808-03-8*); pap. text 46.00 (*1-885808-04-6*) Numa Corp.
— Wielka Ksiega Rodzinky (Poland) (POL., Illus.). 95p. 1998. text 154.00 (*1-885808-21-6*); pap. text 136.50 (*1-885808-22-4*) Numa Corp.
— The World Book of Family Surnames. 95p. 1994. 40.00 (*1-885808-00-3*); pap. text 30.00 (*1-885808-01-1*) Numa Corp.
Numan. Atlas 3, Bk. 3. 1995. text, teacher ed. 28.00 (*0-8384-4095-9*) Heinle & Heinle.
Numan, jt. auth. see Malins.
Numan, David. Atlas 1, No. 1. annot. ed. (Global ESL/ELT Ser.). (J). 1995. mass mkt., teacher ed. 26.00 (*0-8384-4093-2*) Heinle & Heinle.
Nu'man, Muhammad A. What Every American Should Know about Islam & the Muslims. 74p. (Orig.). 1985. pap. 5.00 (*0-933821-04-2*) New Mind Prod.
Nu'Man, Muhammad A. & Nu'man, Muhammad A. Muslim Names & Their Meanings. 20p. (Orig.). reprint ed. pap. 2.50 (*0-933821-02-6*) New Mind Prod.
Nu'Man, Muhammad A., jt. auth. see Akbar, Na'im.
Nu'man, Muhammad A., jt. auth. see El-Amin, Mustafa.
Nu'man, Muhammad A., jt. auth. see Nu'Man, Muhammad A.
Numan, Philips. Miracles Lately Wrought by the Intercession of the Glorious Virgin Marie at Mont-Aigu. LC 76-370285. (English Recusant Literature, 1558-1640 Ser.). 298 p. 1975. write for info. (*0-85967-231-X*) Scolar Pr.
***Numan, R., ed.** The Behavioral Neuroscience of the Septal Region. LC 99-30295. (Illus.). 416p. 1999. 89.00 (*0-387-98879-3*) Spr-Verlag.
Numani, Allama S. Al-Faruq: Life of Umar the Great. Khan, Mawlana Z., tr. 700p. 1996. 10.50 (*0-614-21704-0*, 292) Kazi Pubns.
— Al-Faruq Vol. I: Life of Umar the Great. Khan, Mawlana Z., tr. 700p. 1996. 10.50 (*0-614-21703-2*, 291) Kazi Pubns.
Numani, Shibli. Umar the Great, Vol. II. Saleem, M., tr. 200p. (YA). (gr. 7-12). 1985. 14.50 (*1-56744-407-5*) Kazi Pubns.
Numano, Fujio & Ross, Russel, eds. Atherosclerosis Vol. 811: Recent Advances in Atherosclerosis Research. LC 97-10469. 550p. 1997. 160.00 (*1-57331-022-0*) NY Acad Sci.
***Numano, Fujio, et al.** Atherosclerosis V: The 5th Saratoga International Conference. LC 00-36154. 2000. write for info. (*1-57331-247-9*) NY Acad Sci.
Numano, Fujio, ed. see Saratoga International Conference on Atheroscleros.
Numano, Fujio National Conference on Atheroscleros & Ross, Russell. Atherosclerosis IV: Recent Advances in Atherosclerosis Research. LC 97-10469. (Annals of the New York Academy of Sciences Ser.). 1997. pap. 160.00 (*1-57331-023-9*) NY Acad Sci.
Numata, Bo. Mac Graphics: A Basic Design Workshop. (Illus.). 144p. 1995. pap. 39.95 (*4-7661-0830-2*, Pub. by Graphic-Sha) Bks Nippan.
Numata Center Buddhist Translation & Research Staff. A Comprehensive Commentary on the Prajnaparamita Hrdaya Sutra. Sengaku, Mayeda & Inada, Kenneth, eds. Shih, Heng-Ching, tr. (BDK English Tripitaka Ser.). 175p. 2000. 35.00 (*1-886439-11-7*) Numata Ctr.
— Kaimokusho or Liberation from Blindness. Sengaku, Mayeda & Inada, Kenneth, eds. Murano, Senchu, tr. (BDK English Tripitaka Ser.). 150p. 2000. 35.00 (*1-886439-12-5*) Numata Ctr.
— The Scripture on the Explication of Underlying Meaning. Sengaku, Mayeda & Inada, Kenneth, eds. Keenan, John, tr. from CHI. (BDK English Tripitaka Ser.). 200p. 2000. 35.00 (*1-886439-10-9*) Numata Ctr.
Numata Center for Buddhist Translation & Research. The Biographical Scripture of King Asoka. Rongxi, Li, tr from CHI. & intro. by. LC 92-82067. (BDK English Tripitaka Ser.: Vol. 76-II). 203p. (C). 1993. text 30.00 (*0-9625618-4-3*) Numata Ctr.
— A Biography of the Tripitaka Master of the Great Ci'en Monastery of the Great Tang Dynasty. Rongxi, Li, tr. from CHI. & intro. by. LC 94-73928. (BDK English Tripitaka Ser.: Vol. 77). 385p. (C). 1995. text 35.00 (*1-886439-00-1*) Numata Ctr.
— The Blue Cliff Record. Sengaku, Mayeda & Inada, Kenneth, eds. Cleary, Thomas, tr. from CHI. LC 94-68462. (BDK English Tripitaka Ser.: Vol. 75). 456p. (C). 1998. text 45.00 (*0-9625618-8-6*) Numata Ctr.
— Buddhist Monastic Traditions of Southern Asia. Sengaku, Mayeda & Inada, Kenneth, eds. Li, Rongxi, tr. from CHI. (BDK English Tripitaka Ser.: No. 93-I). 225p. (C). 2000. text 35.00 (*1-886439-09-5*) Numata Ctr.
— The Essentials of the Eight Traditions - The Candle of the Latter Dharma. Pruden, Leo M. & Rhodes, Robert, trs. from JPN. LC 94-66379. (BDK English Tripitaka Ser.: Vols. 107-I & III). 190p. (C). 1994. 30.00 (*0-9625618-7-8*) Numata Ctr.
— The Essentials of the Vinaya Tradition - The Collected Teachings of the Tendai Lotus School. Shoyu, Hanayama et al, eds. Pruden, Leo M. & Swanson, Paul L., trs. from JPN. LC 94-68461. (BDK English Tripitaka 97-I, II Ser.: Vol. 97-I & II). 330p. (C). 1996. 35.00 (*0-9625618-9-4*) Numata Ctr.
— The Great Tang Dynasty Record of the Western Regions. Yampolsky, Philip et al, eds. Rongxi, Li, tr. from CHI. & intro. by. LC 96-69942. (BDK English Tripitaka Ser.: Vol. 79). 425p. (C). 1997. 45.00 (*1-886439-02-8*) Numata Ctr.
— The Lotus Sutra. Tsugunari, Kubo & Akira, Yuyama, trs. from CHI. LC 91-60119. (BDK English Tripitaka Ser.: Vol. 13-I). 363p. (C). 1993. text 35.00 (*0-9625618-0-0*) Numata Ctr.
— The Pratyutpanna Samadhi Sutra/The Surangama Samadhi Sutra. Sengaku, Mayeda & Inada, Kenneth, eds. Harrison, Paul & McRae, John, trs. from CHI. LC 97-69169. (BDK English Tripitaka Ser.: Vol. 25-II, III). 288p. (C). 1998. text 35.00 (*1-886439-06-0*) Numata Ctr.
— The Scriptural Text. Sengaku, Mayeda & Inada, Kenneth, eds. Willemen, Charles, tr. from CHI. (BDK English Tripitaka Ser.: No. 10-II). 250p. (C). 2000. text 35.00 (*1-886439-08-7*) Numata Ctr.
— Senchaku Hongan Nembutsu Shu: A Collection of Passages on the Nembutsu Chosen in the Original Vow. Sengaku, Mayeda et al, eds. Augustine, Morris J. & Tessho, Kondo, trs. from JPN. LC 97-69168. (BDK English Tripitaka Ser.: Vol. 104-II). 176p. (C). 1998. text 35.00 (*1-886439-05-2*) Numata Ctr.
— The Storehouse of Sundry Valuables. Willemen, Charles, tr. from CHI. & intro. by. LC 92-82068. (BDK English Tripitaka Ser.: Vol. 10-I). 275p. (C). 1995. text 35.00 (*0-9625618-3-5*) Numata Ctr.
— Summary of the Great Vehicle. Keenan, John P., tr. from CHI. & intro. by. LC 92-82069. (BDK English Tripitaka Ser.: Vol. 46-III). 147p. (C). 1992. text 25.00 (*0-9625618-6-X*) Numata Ctr.
— The Sutra on Upasaka Precepts. Shih, Heng-Ching, tr. from CHI. & intro. by. LC 91-60120. (BDK English Tripitaka Ser.: Vol. 45-II). 224p. (C). 1994. text 30.00 (*0-9625618-5-1*) Numata Ctr.
— Tannisho - Passages Deploring Deviations of Faith; Rennyo Shonin Ofumi; The Letters of Rennyo. Sengaku, Mayeda & Yampolsky, Philip, eds. Shojun, Bando et al, trs. from JPN. LC 95-73152. (BDK English Tripitaka Ser.: Vols. 105-II & 106-I). 261p. (C). 1996. 30.00 (*1-886439-03-6*) Numata Ctr.
***Numata Center for Buddhist Translation & Research.** Three Chan Classics: The Recorded Sayings of Linji; Wumen's Gate; Faith-Mind Maxim. Sengaku, Mayeda & Inada, Kenneth, eds. Cleary, J. C. & Osamu, Yoshida, trs. from CHI. LC 97-69167. (BDK English Tripitaka Ser.: Vol. 74-I, II, III). 136p. (C). 1999. text 35.00 (*1-886439-07-9*) Numata Ctr.
Numata Center for Buddhist Translation & Research. The Three Pure Land Sutras: The Larger Sutra on Amitayus; The Sutra on Contemplation of Amitayus; The Smaller Sutra on Amitayus. Shoyu, Hanayama et al, eds. Hisao Inagaki, tr. from CHI. & pref. by. LC 94-73930. (BDK English Tripitaka Ser.: Vol. 12-II, III, & IV). 173p. (C). 1995. 30.00 (*1-886439-01-X*) Numata Ctr.
— Three Texts on Consciousness Only: The Demonstration of Consciousness Only; The Thirty Verses on Consciousness Only; & The Treatise in Twenty Verses on Consciousness Only. Sengaku, Mayeda et al, eds. Cook, Francis, tr. from CHI. & intro. by. LC 96-69942. (BDK English Tripitaka Ser.: Vol. 60-I, II, III). 460p. (C). 1999. 45.00 (*1-886439-04-4*) Numata Ctr.
Numata, Makoto. Ecological Studies in Japanese Grasslands: With Special Reference to the IBP Area: Productivity of Terrestrial Communities. LC 79-304576. (JIBP Synthesis Ser.: No. 13). 287p. 1975. reprint ed. pap. 89.00 (*0-608-01590-3*, 206200900001) Bks Demand.
— Studies in Conservation of Natural Terrestrial Ecosystems in Japan, Pt. 1. LC 77-360040. (JIBP Synthesis Ser.: No. 8-9). 167p. 1975. reprint ed. pap. 51.80 (*0-608-01588-1*, 206200800001) Bks Demand.
Numata, Makoto, ed. Ecology of Grasslands & Bamboolands in the World. 1980. text 155.50 (*90-6193-601-2*) Kluwer Academic.
Numata, Makoto, jt. auth. see Holzner, W.
Numbers, Ronald L. Almost Persuaded: American Physicians & Compulsory Health Insurance, 1912-1920. LC 77-17254. (Henry E. Sigerist Supplements to the Bulletin of the History of Medicine, New Ser.: No. 1). 173p. reprint ed. pap. 53.70 (*0-7837-6425-1*, 204642300012) Bks Demand.
— The Creationists. LC 93-15804. 458p. 1993. pap. 17.95 (*0-520-08393-8*, Pub. by U CA Pr) Cal Prin Full Svc.
— Darwinism Comes to America. LC 98-16212. (Illus.). 288p. 1998. 39.95 (*0-674-19311-3*); pap. 18.95 (*0-674-19312-1*) HUP.
— Prophetess of Health: Ellen G. White & the Origins of Seventh-Day Adventist Health Reform. LC 91-22807. Orig. Title: Prophetess of Health. (Illus.). 408p. (C). 1992. reprint ed. pap. text 19.95 (*0-87049-713-8*); reprint ed. lib. bdg. 49.95 (*0-87049-712-X*) U of Tenn Pr.
Numbers, Ronald L., ed. The Antievolution Works of Arthur I. Brown. LC 94-45074. (Creationism in Twentieth-Century America Ser.: Vol. 3). 224p. 1995. text 66.00 (*0-8153-1804-9*) Garland.
— Compulsory Health Insurance: The Continuing American Debate, 11. LC 82-6145. (Contributions in Medical History Ser.: No. 11). 172p. 1982. 49.95 (*0-313-23436-1*, NHI/, Greenwood Pr) Greenwood.
— Early Creationist Journals. LC 94-45522. (Creationism in Twentieth-Century America Ser.: Vol. 9). 650p. 1995. text 116.00 (*0-8153-1810-3*) Garland.
— The Early Writings of Harold W. Clark & Frank Lewis Marsh. LC 94-45067. (Creationism in Twentieth-Century America Ser.: Vol. 8). 560p. 1995. text 106.00 (*0-8153-1809-X*) Garland.
— Selected Works of George McCready Price. LC 94-45071. (Creationism in Twentieth-Century America Ser.: Vol. 7). 512p. 1995. text 88.00 (*0-8153-1808-1*) Garland.
Numbers, Ronald L. & Amundsen, Darrel W., eds. Caring & Curing: Health & Medicine in the Western Religious Traditions. LC 97-28500. 601p. 1998. reprint ed. pap. text 19.95 (*0-8018-5796-1*) Johns Hopkins.
Numbers, Ronald L. & Leavitt, Judith W. Wisconsin Medicine: Historical Perspectives. LC 80-52297. (Illus.). 224p. 1981. 19.95 (*0-299-08430-2*) U of Wis Pr.
Numbers, Ronald L. & Rosenberg, Charles E. The Scientific Enterprise in America: Readings from Isis. LC 95-47657. 320p. (C). 1996. pap. text 17.95 (*0-226-60838-7*) U Ch Pr.
Numbers, Ronald L. & Rosenberg, Charles E., eds. The Scientific Enterprise in America: Readings from Isis. LC 95-47657. (C). 1996. lib. bdg. 35.00 (*0-226-60837-9*) U Ch Pr.
Numbers, Ronald L. & Savitt, Todd L., eds. Science & Medicine in the Old South. fac. ed. LC 88-32648. (Illus.). 382p. 1989. reprint ed. pap. 118.50 (*0-7837-7768-X*, 204752400007) Bks Demand.
Numbers, Ronald L. & Stenhouse, John, eds. Disseminating Darwinism: The Role of Place, Race, Religion & Gender. LC 98-32167. 310p. (C). 1999. 54.95 (*0-521-62071-6*) Cambridge U Pr.
Numbers, Ronald L., jt. ed. see Leavitt, Judith W.
Numbers, Ronald L., jt. ed. see Lindberg, David C.
Numbers, Ronald L., ed. & intro. see Patterson, Alexander, et al.
Numerical Algorithmns Group Staff. NAG FORTRAN Library Manual Mark 9. 1981. 35.00 (*0-317-52218-3*, Pub. by Numer Algo) Princeton Bk Co.
Numerical Algorithms Group. NAG Graphical Supplement Mark 2. 1985. 25.20 (*0-317-52231-0*, Pub. by Numer Algo) Princeton Bk Co.
Numerical Algorithms Group Staff. NAG FORTRAN PC50 Handbook - Release 1. 324p. 1983. 30.00 (*0-317-52225-6*, Pub. by Numer Algo) Princeton Bk Co.
Numerical Algorithms Group Staff. NAG FORTRAN PC50 Handbook - Release 1. 2nd ed. 324p. 1984. 30.00 (*0-317-52226-4*, Pub. by Numer Algo) Princeton Bk Co.
Numerical Algorithms Group Staff. NAG Graphical Supplement Mark 1. 1981. 40.00 (*0-317-52228-0*, Pub. by Numer Algo) Princeton Bk Co.
Numeroff. Easter Egg Designs. (J). 7.95 (*0-694-01419-2*) HarpC Child Bks.
Numeroff. If You Give a Moose a Matzoh. (J). Date not set. pap. write for info. (*0-06-443558-X*) HarpC Child Bks.
— If You Give a Moose a Matzoh. 32p. (J). (ps-2). Date not set. 15.95 (*0-06-028328-9*); lib. bdg. 15.89 (*0-06-028329-7*) HarpC Child Bks.
Numeroff. If You Give a Moose a Cookie: Mini Book. 32p. 1994. 3.95 (*0-694-00589-4*) HarpC Child Bks.
Numeroff. If You Give Cat a Cupcake. 32p. (J). (ps-2). 1999. lib. bdg. 15.89 (*0-06-026684-8*) HarpC Child Bks.
Numeroff, Barney, jt. auth. see Numeroff, Laura.
Numeroff, Laura. The Best Mouse Cookie Board Book. (Illus.). 24p. (J). (ps-k). 1999. 6.95 (*0-694-01270-X*, HarpFestival) HarpC Child Bks.
— The Chicken Sisters. LC 96-30297. (Illus.). 32p. (J). (ps-3). 1999. pap. 5.95 (*0-06-443520-2*, HarpTrophy) HarpC Child Bks.
Numeroff, Laura. Chimps Don't Wear Glasses. LC 94-20320. (Illus.). 32p. (J). (ps-3). 1995. pap. 14.00 (*0-689-80150-5*) S&S Bks Yung.
Numeroff, Laura. Chimps Don't Wear Glasses. LC 94-20320. (Illus.). 32p. (J). (ps-3). 1998. per. 5.99 (*0-689-82030-5*) S&S Childrens.
— If You Give a Mouse a Cookie Book & Tape. (Illus.). 32p. (J). (ps-3). 1994. 11.95 incl. audio, digital audio (*0-694-00630-0*) HarpC Child Bks.
— If You Give a Pig a Pancake (Spanish edition) Si le das un panqueque a una cerdita. Mlawer, Teresa, tr. LC 98-41511. (SPA., Illus.). 32p. (J). (ps-2). 1999. 15.95 (*0-06-028316-5*) HarpC Child Bks.
***Numeroff, Laura.** If You Take a Mouse to the Movies. (Illus.). (J). 2000. pap. 251.10 (*0-694-01484-2*) HarpC Child Bks.
Numeroff, Laura. Monster Munchies. LC 97-48559. (J). 1998. lib. bdg. 11.99 (*0-679-99163-8*, Pub. by Random Bks Yng Read) Random.
— Monster Munchies. LC 97-48559. 48p. (J). (gr. k-3). 1998. 7.99 (*0-679 89163-3*, Pub. by Random Bks Yng Read) Random.
— Parents Can Be Different. LC 99-22575. (J). (ps-3). 2000. 14.00 (*0-689-80552-7*) S&S Bks Yung.
— What Mommies Do Best/What Daddies Do Best. LC 96-44375. (Illus.). 32p. (J). (ps-3). 1998. 13.00 (*0-689-80577-2*) S&S Bks Yung.
— Why a Disguise? LC 93-19025. (Illus.). 32p. (J). (ps-3). 1996. 14.00 (*0-689-80513-6*) S&S Bks Yung.
— Why a Disguise? LC 83-19025. (Illus.). 32p. (J). (ps-1). 1999. pap. 5.99 (*0-689-82530-7*, 076714005990) S&S Childrens.
***Numeroff, Laura & Numeroff, Barney.** Two for Stew. 32p. (J). 1999. per. 5.99 (*0-689-82944-2*) Aladdin.
Numeroff, Laura & Saltzberg, Barney. Two for Stew. (Illus.). 32p. (J). (ps-3). 1996. 15.00 (*0-689-80571-3*) S&S Childrens.
Numeroff, Laura J. The Chicken Sisters. LC 96-30297. (Laura Geringer Bks.). (Illus.). 32p. (J). (ps-2). 1997. 14.95 (*0-06-026679-1*); lib. bdg. 14.89 (*0-06-026680-5*) HarpC Child Bks.
— Dogs Don't Wear Sneakers. LC 92-27007. (Illus.). 40p. (J). (ps-1). 1993. 15.00 (*0-671-79525-2*) S&S Bks Yung.
— Dogs Don't Wear Sneakers. 40p. 1996. per. 5.99 (*0-689-80874-7*) S&S Bks Yung.
— Fathers & Mothers. (J). 1995. 15.95 (*0-8050-2056-X*) H Holt & Co.
— If You Give a Moose a Muffin. LC 91-2207. (Illus.). 32p. (J). 1994. pap. 5.95 (*0-06-443398-6*) HarpC.
— If You Give a Moose a Muffin. LC 91-2207. (Laura Geringer Bks.). (Illus.). 32p. (J). (ps-3). 1991. 15.95 (*0-06-024405-4*); lib. bdg. 15.89 (*0-06-024406-2*) HarpC Child Bks.
— If You Give a Moose a Muffin Big Book. LC 91-2207. (Trophy Picture Bk.). (Illus.). 32p. (J). (ps-2). 1994. pap. 21.95 (*0-06-443366-8*, HarpTrophy) HarpC Child Bks.
— If You Give a Moose a Muffin Mini Book & Tape. unabridged ed. 32p. (J). (ps-2). 1997. 11.95 incl. audio (*0-694-70092-4*) HarperAudio.
— If You Give a Moose a Muffin (Spanish edition) Si le das un panecillo a un alce. Mlawer, Teresa, tr. LC 94-37255. (SPA., Illus.). 32p. (J). (ps-3). 1995. 16.95 (*0-06-025440-8*, HpArco Iris) HarpC Child Bks.
— If You Give a Mouse a Cookie. LC 84-48343. (Illus.). 32p. (J). (ps-2). 2000. 14.95 (*0-06-024586-7*) HarpC Child Bks.
— If You Give a Mouse a Cookie. large type ed. (J). (ps-2). 1993. 19.95 (*0-590-71885-1*) Scholastic Inc.
— If You Give a Mouse a Cookie Big Book. LC 84-48343. (Trophy Big Bk.). (Illus.). 32p. (J). (ps-2). 1996. pap. 21.95 (*0-06-443409-5*, HarpTrophy) HarpC Child Bks.
— If You Give a Mouse a Cookie Box & Doll. LC 91-46093. (Illus.). 32p. (J). (ps-3). 1992. 17.95 (*0-694-00416-2*, HarpFestival) HarpC Child Bks.
— If You Give a Mouse a Cookie (Spanish edition) Si le das una galletita a un raton. Mlawer, Teresa, tr. LC 94-37254. (SPA., Illus.). 32p. (J). (ps-3). 1995. 15.95 (*0-06-025438-6*, HpArco Iris) HarpC Child Bks.
— Mouse Cookies: 10 Easy-to-Make Cookie Recipes. LC 95-238087. (Illus.). 32p. (J). (gr. 2-4). 1995. spiral bd., boxed set 13.95 (*0-694-00633-5*, HarpFestival) HarpC Child Bks.
— Sometimes I Wonder If Poodles Like Noodles. LC 96-44988. 32p. (J). 1999. 14.00 (*0-689-80563-2*) S&S Childrens.
— Why a Disguise? LC 93-19025. (Illus.). (J). 1995. pap. 14.00 (*0-671-87006-8*) S&S Bks Yung.
Numeroff, Laura J. & Bond, Felicia. If You Give a Mouse a Cookie. (FRE.). (J). 1996. 13.99 incl. audio (*0-590-16044-3*) Scholastic Inc.
— If You Give a Mouse a Cookie, Big Bk. large type ed. (FRE.). (J). 29.99 (*0-590-71930-0*) Scholastic Inc.
Numeroff, Laura Joffe. Chimps Don't Wear Glasses. LC 94-20320. 1998. pap. 14.00 (*0-671-87007-6*) S&S Trade.
— Dogs Don't Wear Sneakers. 1996. 11.19 (*0-606-10789-4*, Pub. by Turtleback) Demco.
Numeroff, Laura Joffe. If You Give a Bear a Brownie. 32p. (J). (ps-2). 15.95 (*0-06-027571-5*); lib. bdg. 15.89 (*0-06-027572-3*) HarpC Child Bks.
— If You Give A Bear A Brownie: Book & Doll. (Illus.). (J). 19.95 (*0-694-01423-0*) HarpC.
— If You Give a Bear a Brownie Recipes. (Illus.). 32p. (J). 12.95 (*0-06-028559-1*) HarpC.
— If You Give A Cat A Cupcake: Book & Doll. (Illus.). (J). 19.95 (*0-694-01431-1*) HarpC.
— If You Give A Cat A Cupcake Recipes. (Illus.). 32p. (J). 12.95 (*0-06-028560-5*) HarpC.
— If You Give a Moose a Muffin. (Illus.). (J). 1994. 11.30 (*0-606-18696-4*) Turtleback.
— If You Give A Moose A Muffin: Board Book. (Illus.). (J). 6.95 (*0-694-01426-5*) HarpC.
— If You Give A Moose A Muffin: Book & Doll. (Illus.). (J). 19.95 (*0-694-01421-4*) HarpC.
— If You Give A Moose A Muffin Recipe Book. (Illus.). 32p. (J). 12.95 (*0-06-028562-1*) HarpC.
— If You Give A Mouse A Cookie. LC 84-48343. (Illus.). 32p. (J). (ps-2). write for info. (*0-06-443166-5*) HarpC.
Numeroff, Laura Joffe. If You Give a Mouse a Cookie. LC 84-48343. (Illus.). 32p. (J). (ps-3). 2000. lib. bdg. 14.89 (*0-06-024587-5*) HarpC Child Bks.
— If You Give a Pig a Pancake. LC 97-36832. (Illus.). 32p. (J). (ps-2). 1998. 15.95 (*0-06-026686-4*, Perennial); lib. bdg. 14.89 (*0-06-026687-2*, Perennial) HarperTrade.
Numeroff, Laura Joffe. If You Give A Pig A Pancake: Board Book. (Illus.). (J). 6.95 (*0-694-01430-3*) HarpC.
— If You Give a Pig a Pancake big Book. LC 97-36832. (Illus.). 32p. (J). (ps-2). 2000. pap. 21.95 (*0-06-443663-2*, HarpTrophy) HarpC Child Bks.
Numeroff, Laura Joffe. If You Give a Pig a Pancake Mini Book & Doll. (Illus.). (J). (ps-2). 1999. 17.95 (*0-694-01299-8*) HarpC Child Bks.
— If You Give a Pig a Pancake Mini Book & Tape. (Illus.). (J). (ps-2). 1999. 11.95 incl. reel tape (*0-694-70100-9*, HarpFestival) HarpC Child Bks.
Numeroff, Laura Joffe. If You Give A Pig A Pumpkin: Book & Doll. (Illus.). 19.95 (*0-694-01432-X*) HarpC.
— If You Take a Mouse to the Movies. (J). Date not set. write for info. (*0-06-029388-8*) HarpC Child Bks.
Numeroff, Laura Joffe. If You Take a Mouse to the Movies. LC 99-27258. (Illus.). 40p. (J). (ps-2). 2000. 15.95 (*0-06-027867-6*); lib. bdg. 15.89 (*0-06-027868-4*) HarpC Child Bks.
Numeroff, Laura Joffe. If You Take A Mouse to the Movies: Book & Doll. (Illus.). (J). 19.95 (*0-694-01427-3*) HarpC.
— If You Take a Mouse to the Movies Kit. (J). Date not set. write for info. (*0-06-029314-4*) HarpC Child Bks.
— If You Take a Mouse to the Movies Mini Doll Ornament. (J). 2000. 9.95 (*0-694-01531-8*, HarpFestival) HarpC Child Bks.
— Moose Sticker Book. (Illus.). (J). 7.95 (*0-694-01425-7*) HarpC.
— Moose Stroller Songs. (Illus.). (J). 9.95 (*0-694-01424-9*) HarpC.
— Mouse House Sticker Book. (J). 7.95 (*0-694-01422-2*) HarpC.
— Mouse Stroller Songs. (J). 9.95 (*0-694-01420-6*) HarpC.
— Mouse's Family Album. 32p. (J). 10.95 (*0-06-028561-3*, L Geringer) HarpC Child Bks.
— Pig Pancakes. (Illus.). 32p. (J). (ps-2). 12.95 (*0-06-028563-X*) HarpC Child Bks.
— Pig Stroller Songs. (Illus.). (J). 10.95 (*0-694-01428-1*) HarpC.
Numes, Maxine. Backtrack: A Novel by Maxine Nunes on the Screenplay. 1989. pap. 3.95 (*0-671-67893-0*) PB.

N

An Asterisk (*) at the beginning of an entry indicates that the title is appearing for the first time.

Numez, J. & Dupont, J. E., eds. Hormones & Cell Regulation European Symposium, 11th. (Colloquim Ser.: Vol. 153). 248p. (Orig.). 1987. pap. 63.00 (*2-85598-324-X*) S M P F Inc.

Numina. Casebriefs-Evidence, Version 4.1. 1998. 27.95 (*0-15-900198-6*) Harcourt.

— Casebriefs-Remedies, Version 4.1. 1998. 27.95 (*0-15-900202-8*) Harcourt.

Nummedal, Dag, ed. see Price, William A.

Nummedal, Susan G., jt. ed. see Halpern, Diane F.

Nummi, Gerald E. & White, Janet A. I'm Going to See What Has Happened. LC 97-90088. (Illus.). 54p. (Orig.). 1997. pap., spiral bd. 10.95 (*0-9657174-0-2*) J White.

Nummikoski, Marita. A Communicative Approach to Russian Language, Life, & Culture: Troika. 1996. text 34.95 (*0-471-13805-3*) Wiley.

Nummikoski, Marita. Troika: A Communicative Approach to Russian Language, Life, & Culture. LC 95-46413. 640p. 1996. text 86.95 (*0-471-30945-1*) Wiley.

Numn, John & Burgess, Graham. The New Classical King's Indian. 320p. (Orig.). 1997. pap. 26.95 (*1-879479-48-6*) ICE WA.

Numrich, Carol. Consider the Issues: Advanced Listening & Critical Thinking Skills. 2nd ed. LC 94-33391. 176p. 1995. pap. text 17.59 (*0-201-82529-5*) Addison-Wesley.

— Raise the Issues: An Integrated Approach to Critical Thinking. LC 93-33842. 1994. audio 37.95 (*0-8013-1015-6*) Longman.

— Raise the Issues: An Integrated Approach to Critical Thinking. LC 93-33842. 1994. pap. text 22.64 (*0-8013-1014-8*) Longman.

Numrich, Carol & National Public Radio Staff. Face the Issues: Intermediate Listening & Critical Thinking Skills. 2nd ed. LC 96-28064. 1996. pap. text 17.59 (*0-201-84672-1*) Addison-Wesley.

Numrich, Charles H. Passion Play. 1983. 5.25 (*0-89536-601-0*, 1627) CSS OH.

***Numrich, Paul D.** Old Wisdom in the New World: Americanization in Two Immigrant Theravada Buddhist Temples. (Illus.). 208p. 1999. pap. text 14.00 (*1-57233-063-5*) U of Tenn Pr.

Numrich, Robert W., ed. Supercomputer Applications. 316p. 1985. 85.00 (*0-306-42013-9*, Plenum Trade) Perseus Pubng.

Numrick, Carol. Face the Issues: Intermediate Listening & Critical Thinking Skills, 2 cass., Set. (Orig.). 1990. audio 38.00 (*0-8013-0301-X*, 75951) Longman.

Nun, Pamela Gerrish, jt. auth. see Marsh, Jan.

Nunamaker, J. A. Rose Genealogy, Including Descendants of Israel Rose, Pioneer of Washington & Oregon, with Additions & Corrections. (Illus.). 71p. 1993. reprint ed. pap. 16.00 (*0-8328-3779-2*); reprint ed. lib. bdg. 26.00 (*0-8328-3778-4*) Higginson Bk Co.

***Nunan.** Go for It!, Bk. 1. (J). 2000. 5.00 (*0-8384-1194-0*); 5.00 (*0-8384-1195-9*) Heinle & Heinle.

— Go For It!, Bk. 2. (J). 2000. 5.00 (*0-8384-1196-7*); 5.00 (*0-8384-1197-5*) Heinle & Heinle.

— Go for It!, Bk. 3. (J). 2000. 5.00 (*0-8384-1198-3*); 5.00 (*0-8384-1199-1*) Heinle & Heinle.

— Go for It!, Bk. 4. (J). 2000. 5.00 (*0-8384-1200-9*); 5.00 (*0-8384-1201-7*) Heinle & Heinle.

Nunan. Go for It, Tests & Games Resource Book 2. (Adult ESL Ser.). (J). 1999. pap. 25.00 (*0-8384-7972-3*) Heinle & Heinle.

— Language Teaching Methodology. 301p. (C). 1991. 25.25 (*0-13-521469-6*, Macmillan Coll) P-H.

***Nunan.** Speak Out: Book 1. 1999. pap. 22.95 (*0-534-83560-0*); pap., teacher ed. 18.75 (*0-534-83561-9*) Thomson Learn.

— Speak Out Book 2. 1999. pap. 22.95 (*0-534-83563-5*); pap., teacher ed. 18.75 (*0-534-83564-3*) Thomson Learn.

— Speak Out Book 3: Student Text. 1999. pap. 22.95 (*0-534-83567-8*) Thomson Learn.

Nunan, David. Atlas: Learning-Centered Communication, Bk. 1. (J). 1994. mass mkt. 18.95 (*0-8384-4085-1*) Heinle & Heinle.

— Atlas: Learning-Centered Communication, Bk. 1. (J). 1996. mass mkt., wbk. ed. 8.95 (*0-8384-4089-4*) Heinle & Heinle.

— Atlas 1. (Global ESL/ELT Ser.). (J). 1994. suppl. ed. 18.95 incl. audio (*0-8384-4097-5*) Heinle & Heinle.

— Atlas 2. (Global ESL/ELT Ser.). Date not set. wbk. ed. 2.95 incl. audio (*0-614-10349-5*) Heinle & Heinle.

— Atlas 2. (Global ESL/ELT Ser.). (J). 1994. suppl. ed. 18.00 incl. audio (*0-8384-4098-3*) Heinle & Heinle.

— Atlas 2, Bk. 2. (Global ESL/ELT Ser.). (J). 1994. mass mkt. 18.95 (*0-8384-4086-X*) Heinle & Heinle.

— Atlas 2, Bk. 2. (Global ESL/ELT Ser.). (J). 1996. mass mkt., wbk. ed. 8.95 (*0-8384-4090-8*) Heinle & Heinle.

— Atlas 2, No. 2. annot. ed. (Global ESL/ELT Ser.). (J). 1995. mass mkt., teacher ed. 26.00 (*0-8384-4094-0*) Heinle & Heinle.

— Atlas 3. (Global ESL/ELT Ser.). (J). 1994. suppl. ed. 17.95 incl. audio (*0-8384-4099-1*); wbk. ed. 4.95 incl. audio (*0-8384-5500-X*) Heinle & Heinle.

— Atlas 3, Bk. 3. (Global ESL/ELT Ser.). (J). 1994. mass mkt., wbk. ed. 8.95 (*0-8384-4091-6*) Heinle & Heinle.

— Atlas 4. (Global ESL/ELT Ser.). (J). 1995. suppl. ed. 18.00 incl. audio (*0-8384-4100-9*) Heinle & Heinle.

— Atlas 4, Bk. 4. (Global ESL/ELT Ser.). (J). 1995. mass mkt. 18.95 (*0-8384-4088-6*) Heinle & Heinle.

— Atlas 4, Bk. 4. (Global ESL/ELT Ser.). (J). 1995. mass mkt., wbk. ed. 8.95 (*0-8384-4092-4*) Heinle & Heinle.

— Atlas 4, No. 4. annot. ed. (Global ESL/ELT Ser.). (J). 1995. mass mkt., teacher ed. 26.00 (*0-8384-4096-7*) Heinle & Heinle.

— Compass, Bk. 1. (Global ESL/ELT Ser.). (J). 1998. pap. 16.95 (*0-8384-6773-3*) Wadsworth Pub.

— Compass, Bk. 1. (Global ESL/ELT Ser.). (J). 1998. pap., teacher ed. 4.95 (*0-8384-6775-X*); pap., wbk. ed. 7.95 (*0-8384-6774-1*) Wadsworth Pub.

— Compass, Bk. 2. (Global ESL/ELT Ser.). (J). 1998. pap. 16.95 (*0-8384-6777-6*) Wadsworth Pub.

— Compass, Bk. 2. (Global ESL/ELT Ser.). (J). 1998. pap., wbk. ed. 7.95 (*0-8384-6778-4*) Wadsworth Pub.

— Compass, Bk. 2. (Global ESL/ELT Ser.). (J). 1999. pap., teacher ed. 4.95 (*0-8384-6779-2*) Wadsworth Pub.

— Compass, Bk. 3. (Global ESL/ELT Ser.). (J). 1999. pap. 7.95 (*0-8384-6782-2*, Newbury) Heinle & Heinle.

— Compass, Bk. 3. (Global ESL/ELT Ser.). (J). 1999. pap., teacher ed. 4.95 (*0-8384-6783-0*) Heinle & Heinle.

— Compass, Bk. 3. (Global ESL/ELT Ser.). (J). 1999. pap. 16.95 (*0-8384-6781-4*) Wadsworth Pub.

— Compass, Bk. 4. (Global ESL/ELT Ser.). (J). 1999. pap., wbk. ed. 7.95 (*0-8384-6786-5*) Heinle & Heinle.

— Compass, Bk. 4. (Global ESL/ELT Ser.). (J). 1999. pap., teacher ed. 4.95 (*0-8384-6787-3*) Wadsworth Pub.

— Compass Book 4. (Global ESL/ELT Ser.). (J). 1999. pap. 16.95 (*0-8384-6785-7*) Heinle & Heinle.

— Designing Tasks for the Communicative Classroom. (Cambridge Language Teaching Library). (Illus.). 224p. (C). 1989. pap. text 20.95 (*0-521-37915-6*) Cambridge U Pr.

— EFL Series, Bk. 2. (Global ESL/ELT Ser.). (J). 1997. mass mkt. 18.95 (*0-8384-4087-8*) Heinle & Heinle.

— Geos Atlas A. (Global ESL). (J). 1995. mass mkt. 13.95 (*0-8384-6540-4*) Heinle & Heinle.

— Geos Atlas B. (Global ESL). (J). 1995. mass mkt. 13.95 (*0-8384-6546-3*) Heinle & Heinle.

— The Learner-Centered Curriculum. (Cambridge Applied Linguistics Ser.). (Illus.). 208p. 1988. pap. text 19.95 (*0-521-35843-4*) Cambridge U Pr.

— Listen In, Bk. 1. 1998. teacher ed. 18.75 (*0-8384-7653-8*) Heinle & Heinle.

Nunan, David. Listen In, Bk. 2. 96p. pap. 20.95 (*0-534-83537-6*, Pub. by Heinle & Heinle) Thomson Learn.

Nunan, David. Research Methods in Language Learning. (Cambridge Language Teaching Library). (Illus.). 261p. (C). 1992. pap. text 22.95 (*0-521-42968-4*) Cambridge U Pr.

— Research Methods in Language Learning. (Cambridge Language Teaching Library). (Illus.). 261p. (C). 1992. text 59.95 (*0-521-41937-9*) Cambridge U Pr.

— Second Language Teaching & Learning. 1998. pap. text 24.95 (*0-8384-0838-9*) Heinle & Heinle.

— Syllabus Design. Widdowson, H. G. & Candlin, C. N., eds. (Illus.). 176p. 1988. pap. text 14.95 (*0-19-437139-5*) OUP.

Nunan, David, ed. Collaborative Language Learning & Teaching. (Cambridge Language Teaching Library). 280p. (C). 1992. text 54.95 (*0-521-41687-6*); pap. text 20.95 (*0-521-42701-0*) Cambridge U Pr.

Nunan, David & Lamb, Clarice. The Self-Directed Teacher: Managing the Learning Process. (Language Education Ser.). (Illus.). 310p. (C). 1996. text 59.95 (*0-521-49716-7*); pap. text 22.95 (*0-521-49773-6*) Cambridge U Pr.

Nunan, David & Miller, Linsday, eds. New Ways in Teaching Listening. 290p. 1995. pap. 24.95 (*0-939791-58-7*) Tchrs Eng Spkrs.

Nunan, David & Wenger, Christine A. Listen In, Bk. 1. 96p. pap. 20.95 (*0-534-83536-8*, Pub. by Heinle & Heinle) Thomson Learn.

Nunan, David, jt. ed. see Bailey, Kathleen M.

Nunan, David, jt. ed. see Richards, Jack C.

Nunan, J. Carlton, jt. auth. see Masterson, Thomas R.

Nunberg, Barbara. Managing the Civil Service: The Lessons of Reform in Industrial Countries. LC 93-23872. (Discussion Paper Ser.: Vol. 204). 62p. 1995. pap. 22.00 (*0-8213-2498-5*, 12498) World Bank.

— The State after Communism: Administrative Transitions in Central & Eastern Europe. LC 98-39052. 286p. 1998. pap. 35.00 (*0-8213-4205-3*, 14205) World Bank.

Nunberg, Barbara, jt. auth. see Nellis, John R.

Nunberg, Barbara, jt. ed. see Lindauer, David L.

Nunberg, Barbara, jt. ed. see Lindauer, David.

Nunberg, Geoffrey. The Linguistics of Punctuation. LC 90-1411. (CSLI Lecture Notes Ser.: No. 18). 160p. (C). 1990. 59.95 (*0-937073-47-4*); pap. 17.95 (*0-937073-46-6*) CSLI.

Nunberg, Geoffrey, ed. The Future of the Book. LC 95-45441. (Illus.). 250p. (C). 1996. pap. 15.95 (*0-520-20451-4*, Pub. by U CA Pr) Cal Prin Full Svc.

Nunberg, Herman. Curiosity. LC 58-9230. (New York Psychoanalytic Institute Freud Anniversary Lecture Ser.). 88p. 1961. 27.50 (*0-8236-1100-0*) Intl Univs Pr.

— Practice & Theory of Psychoanalysis, 2 vols., Vol. 1. 218p. 1961. 32.50 (*0-8236-4220-8*) Intl Univs Pr.

— Practice & Theory of Psychoanalysis, Vol. 2. 219p. 1961. 32.50 (*0-8236-4240-2*) Intl Univs Pr.

— Principles of Psychoanalysis: Their Application to the Neuroses. LC 55-11549. 382p. (Orig.). 1969. reprint ed. 57.50 (*0-8236-4300-X*); reprint ed. pap. 24.95 (*0-8236-8198-X*, 24300) Intl Univs Pr.

Nunberg, Herman & Federn, Ernst, eds. Minutes of the Vienna Psychoanalytic Society, 4 vols. Incl. Vol. 1. 1906-1908. LC 62-15591. 1963. text 70.00 (*0-8236-3380-2*); Vol. 2. 1908-1910. LC 62-15591. 1963. text 70.00 (*0-8236-3400-0*); Vol. 3. 1910-1911. LC 62-15591. 1963. text 70.00 (*0-8236-3401-9*); Vol. 4. 1912-1918. LC 62-15591. 1963. text 70.00 (*0-8236-3402-7*); LC 62-15591. 1963. text. write for info. (*0-318-53692-7*) Intl Univs Pr.

Nunberg, Margarete, tr. see Meyer, Joachim E.

Nunemacher, Greg. LAN Primer: An Introduction to Local Area Networks. 2nd ed. 300p. (Orig.). 1995. pap. 26.95 (*1-55851-287-X*, M&T Bks) IDG Bks.

— LAN Primer: The Best Introduction to Networking Fundamentals. 3rd ed. (Illus.). 372p. 1999. reprint ed. pap. text 20.00 (*0-7881-6504-6*) DIANE Pub.

— Point of Care Testing. (Market Research Reports: No. 430). (Illus.). 91p. 1994. 795.00 (*0-614-09925-0*) Theta Corp.

— Powerbuilder for Xbase Programmers. abr. ed. 1995. pap. 39.95 incl. disk (*1-55851-453-8*, M&T Bks) IDG Bks.

Nunemaker, Carolyn H. Downtown Spokane Images, 1930-1949. LC 97-92779. (Illus.). 148p. 1997. pap. 19.95 (*0-9661391-0-0*) C Nunemaker.

Nunes, jt. auth. see Fazio.

Nunes, Ana, jt. auth. see Llibre, Jaume.

Nunes-Atabaki, Sara, jt. auth. see Nunes, Shiho S.

Nunes, C. Dicionario de Bolso Russo-Portuguese. (POR & RUS.). 376p. 1976. 9.95 (*0-8288-5627-3*, M9062) Fr & Eur.

***Nunes Correia, Francisco, ed.** Water Resources Management in Europe: Institutions, Issues & Dilemmas, 2 vols. (Illus.). 1112p. 1998. text 206.00 (*90-5410-438-4*) Ashgate Pub Co.

Nunes de Barros, Leliane, et al, eds. Knowledge Engineering & Acquisition for Planning - Bridging Theory & Practice: Papers from the 1998 AIPS Workshop. (Technical Reports). (Illus.). 122p. 1998. spiral bd. 25.00 (*1-57735-056-1*) AAAI Pr.

***Nunes, John.** Voices from the City: Issues & Images of Urban Preaching. LC 99-23474. 144p. 1999. 13.00 (*0-570-05375-7*) Concordia.

Nunes, Lygia B. My Friend the Painter. Pontiero, Giovanni, tr. from POR. LC 90-46043. 96p. (J). (gr. 3-7). 1991. 13.95 (*0-15-256340-7*) Harcourt.

— My Friend the Painter. Pontiero, Giovanni, tr. LC 90-46043. (Illus.). 96p. (J). (gr. 3-7). 1995. pap. 5.00 (*0-15-200872-1*) Harcourt.

Nunes, Maria L. Becoming True to Ourselves: Cultural Decolonization & National Identity in the Literature of the Portuguese-Speaking World, 22. LC 87-8390. (Contributions to the Study of World Literature Ser.: No. 22). 113p. 1987. 45.00 (*0-313-25726-4*, NLS/) Greenwood.

— The Craft of an Absolute Winner: Characterization & Narratology in the Novels of Machado de Assis, 71. LC 82-11717. (Contributions in Afro-American & African Studies: No. 71). 158p. 1983. 47.95 (*0-313-23631-3*, NCW/) Greenwood.

— A Portuguese Colonial in America: Belmira Nunes Lopes: The Autobiography of a Cape Verdean-American. Miller, Yvette E., ed. LC 82-6569. 224p. 1982. 25.00 (*0-935480-08-0*); pap. 11.95 (*0-935480-07-2*) Lat Am Lit Rev Pr.

Nunes, Maxine, jt. auth. see Griner, Thomas.

Nunes, Morris A. Operational Cash Flow Management & Control. 256p. 1982. 34.95 (*0-13-637470-0*) P-H.

***Nunes, Rachel.** A Greater Love. 192p. 2000. pap. 12.95 (*0-9675174-6-X*) Truebekon.

Nunes, Rachel A. Ariana: A Gift Most Precious. LC 97-18033. 1997. pap. 11.95 (*1-57734-129-5*, 01112929) Covenant Comms.

***Nunes, Rachel A.** Ariana: A Glimpse of Eternity. LC 98-53345. 1999. pap. 13.95 (*1-57734-436-7*, 01113828) Covenant Comms.

Nunes, Rachel A. Ariana: A New Beginning. LC 97-50173. 1998. pap. 11.95 (*1-57734-258-5*, 01113305) Covenant Comms.

— Ariana: The Making of a Queen. LC 96-44061. 1996. pap. 10.95 (*1-57734-025-6*, 01112481) Covenant Comms.

***Nunes, Rachel A.** Tomorrow & Always. LC 00-43049. 2000. write for info. (*1-57734-718-8*) Covenant Comms.

***Nunes, Rachel Ann.** Framed for Love: A Novel. LC 99-32236. 1999. pap. 13.95 (*1-57734-474-X*, 01113984) Covenant Comms.

— Love on the Run: A Novel. LC 99-88762. 2000. write for info. (*1-57734-604-1*) Covenant Comms.

Nunes, Rachel Ann. Love to the Highest Bidder. LC 98-24031. 1998. pap. 12.95 (*1-57734-278-X*, 01113429) Covenant Comms.

***Nunes, Rachel Ann.** To Love & to Promise: A Novel. LC 99-43534. 1999. pap. 13.95 (*1-57734-536-3*, 01114328) Covenant Comms.

Nunes, Shiho S. & Nunes-Atabaki, Sara. The Shishu Ladies of Hilo: Japanese Embroidery in Hawai'i. LC 99-20722. (Extraordinary Lives Ser.). (Illus.). 168p. 1999. 50.00 (*0-8248-2128-9*); pap. 24.95 (*0-8248-2235-8*) UH Pr.

Nunes, Susan. A Small Obligation & Other Stories of Hilo. LC 82-72555. (Bamboo Ridge Ser.: No. 16). 88p. (Orig.). 1982. pap. 8.00 (*0-910043-00-0*) Bamboo Ridge Pr.

— To Find the Way. LC 91-31334. (Illus.). 48p. (J). (gr. 4-8). 1992. 12.95 (*0-8248-1376-6*, Kolowalu Bk) UH Pr.

Nunes, Susan M. The Last Dragon. LC 93-30631. (Illus.). 32p. (J). 1995. 15.00 (*0-395-67020-9*, Clarion Bks) HM.

— The Last Dragon. (Illus.). 32p. 1997. pap. 6.95 (*0-395-84517-3*, Clarion Bks) HM.

Nunes, Susan Miho. The Last Dragon. (J). 1997. 11.15 (*0-606-11548-X*, Pub. by Turtleback) Demco.

Nunes, Terezhina & Bryant, Peter. Children Doing Mathematics. (Understanding Children's Worlds Ser.). (Illus.). 288p. (C). 1996. 70.95 (*0-631-18471-6*); pap. 27.95 (*0-631-18472-4*) Blackwell Pubs.

Nunes, Terezhina, et al. Street Mathematics & School Mathematics. LC 92-23183. (Learning in Doing: Social, Cognitive & Computational Perspectives Ser.). (Illus.). 180p. (C). 1993. pap. text 18.95 (*0-521-38813-9*) Cambridge U Pr.

***Nunes, Terezinha.** Learning to Read: An Integrated View from Research & Practice. LC 99-41411. (Neuropsychology & Cognition Ser.). 404p. 1999. 215.00 (*0-7923-5513-X*) Kluwer Academic.

***Nunes, Terezinha, ed.** Learning to Read: An Integrated View from Research & Practice. (Neuropsychology & Cognition Ser.). 404p. 1999. pap. 60.00 (*0-7923-5992-5*, Kluwer Acad) Kluwer Academic.

Nunes, Terezinha & Bryant, Peter. Learning & Teaching Mathematics: An International Perspective. LC 97-202039. (Illus.). xiv, 443p. 1997. write for info. (*0-86377-454-7*, Pub. by Psychol Pr) Taylor & Francis.

Nunes-Vais, Al. Vacation Time Sharing: Is It Right for You? (Illus.). 1983. pap. 9.95 (*0-910793-02-6*) Marlborough Pr.

Nunes, Warren. Jazz Guitar Chord Bible, Vol. 1. (Orig.). 1982. pap. 12.95 (*0-89898-167-0*, F1839JGX) Wrner Bros.

— Jazz Guitar Chord Bible, Vol. 2. (Orig.). 1982. pap. 12.00 (*0-89898-168-9*, F1840JGX) Wrner Bros.

***Nunes, Warren.** Three in One Book-CD Set. 56p. 1998. pap. 17.95 incl. cd-rom (*0-7866-3520-7*, 97013BCD) Mel Bay.

Nunes, Warren, ed. Jazz Guitar Chord Bible. 190p. (Orig.). 1979. pap. 9.95 (*0-89705-049-5*) Almo Pubns.

Nunez, Ana R. Algunas Fuentes para el Servicio de Referencia en Materia Legal Cubana. (SPA.). 1975. pap. 2.00 (*0-89729-147-6*) Ediciones.

— Antologia de Poesia Infantil. LC 85-81795. (Coleccion Antologias). (SPA.). 180p. (Orig.). (J). (gr. 3-12). 1985. pap. 9.95 (*0-89729-369-X*) Ediciones.

— Escamas del Caribe: Haikus de Cuba. (SPA.). 1971. pap. 9.00 (*0-89729-060-7*) Ediciones.

— Homenaje a Dulce Maria Loynaz: Premio Cervantes, 1993. LC 92-75732. (Coleccion Clasicos Cubanos). (SPA.). 415p. (Orig.). 1993. pap. 29.95 (*0-89729-669-9*) Ediciones.

— Poesia en Exodo: Antologia de Poesias Cubanas del Exilio 1959-1969. (SPA.). 1970. pap. 12.00 (*0-89729-006-2*) Ediciones.

— Sol de un Solo Dia. LC 92-75884. (Coleccion Espejo de Paciencia). (SPA.). 93p. (Orig.). 1993. pap. 9.95 (*0-89729-658-3*) Ediciones.

— Viaje al Casabe. (SPA.). 1970. pap. 5.00 (*0-89729-056-9*) Ediciones.

— Uno Y Veinte Golpes Por America. LC 90-82805. (Coleccion Espejo de Paciencia). (SPA.). 48p. (Orig.). 1991. pap. 9.00 (*0-89729-571-4*) Ediciones.

Nunez, Ana R., ed. see Gomez de Avellaneda, Gertrudis.

Nunez, Angel. Let Me Live Again. 1998. pap. 10.99 (*1-56043-310-8*, Treasure Hse) Destiny Image.

Nunez, Anne-Marie, et al. First-Generation Students: Undergraduates Whose Parents Never Enrolled in Postsecondary Education. LC 98-166445. (Education Department Publication NCES 98 Ser.: Vol. 082). 99p. 1998. pap. 9.50 (*0-16-049614-4*) USGPO.

Nunez, Benjamin. Dictionary of Afro-Latin American Civilization. LC 79-7731. (Illus.). 525p. 1980. lib. bdg. 75.00 (*0-313-21138-8*, NAL/, Greenwood Pr) Greenwood.

— Dictionary of Portuguese-African Civilization Vol. 1: From Discovery to Independence, 2 vols. 1060p. 1996. 220.00 (*1-873836-70-8*, Pub. by H Zell Pubs) Seven Hills Bk.

— Dictionary of Portuguese-African Civilization Vol. 2: Biographies: From Ancient Kings to Presidents. 478p. 1996. 110.00 (*1-873836-65-1*) Bowker-Saur.

Nunez Cabeza de Vaca, Alvar. Adventures in the Unknown Interior of America. Covey, Cyclone, tr. from SPA. LC 82-21897. 160p. (C). 1983. pap. 9.95 (*0-8263-0656-X*) U of NM Pr.

— The Journey of Alvar Nunez Cabeza de Vaca & His Companions from Florida to the Pacific, 1528-1536. Bandelier, Adolf F., ed. Bandelier, Fanny, tr. LC 72-2822. (American Explorers Ser.). reprint ed. 52.50 (*0-404-54915-2*) AMS Pr.

Nunez Cabeza de Vaca, Alvar, jt. auth. see Johnston, Lisa J.

Nunez-Cedeno, Rafael A. & Morales-Front, Alfonso. Fonologia Generativa Contemporanea de la Lengua Espanola. LC 98-13261. (SPA.). 344p. 1999. 65.00 (*0-87840-693-X*); pap. 34.95 (*0-87840-694-8*) Georgetown U Pr.

Nunez, Celia H., jt. auth. see Perkins, Michael C.

***Nunez, Cesar Guillen.** Macao Streets. LC 99-31642. (Illus.). 148p. 1999. text 45.00 (*0-19-587766-7*) OUP.

Nunez, Claudia C., tr. see Dodge, Diane T. & Colker, Laura J.

Nunez, Claudia Caicedo, tr. see Dodge, Diane Trister & Heroman, Cate.

Nunez de Villavicencio, Maruxa De, see De Nunez de Villavicencio, Maruxa.

Nunez del Arco, Jose, ed. Politicas de Ajuste y Pobreza: Falsos Dilemas, Verdaderos Problemas. (SPA.). 243p. 1994. pap. text 18.50 (*0-940602-88-1*) IADB.

Nunez, Diego Rivera, see Obon de Castro, Concepcion & Rivera Nunez, Diego.

Nunez, E. A. Hacia una Misionologia Evangelical Latino.Tr. of Making an Evangelical Latin Mission. 9.99 (*0-7899-0441-1*, 498657) Editorial Unilit.

Nunez, Eithne A. Miracles Galore. 1998. pap. 9.99 (*1-873796-67-6*) Review & Herald.

Nunez, Elizabeth. Beyond the Limbo Silence. LC 98-36375. 320p. 1998. pap. 12.00 (*1-58005-013-1*) Seal Pr WA.

***Nunez, Elizabeth.** Bruised Hibiscus: A Novel. LC 99-86362. 300p. 2000. 24.95 (*1-58005-036-0*) Seal Pr WA.

Nunez, Elizabeth & Greene, Brenda M., eds. Defining Ourselves: Black Writers in the 90s. LC 98-43060. X, 250p. (C). 1999. pap. text 32.95 (*0-8204-4261-5*) P Lang Pubng.

Nunez, Emilio A. La Biblia y la Sanidad Divina. (SPA.). 80p. 1976. mass mkt. 3.99 (*0-8254-1514-4*, Edit Portavoz) Kregel.

— Desafios Pastorales. (SPA.). 144p. 1999. pap. 6.99 (*0-8254-1515-2*, Edit Portavoz) Kregel.

An Asterisk (*) at the beginning of an entry indicates that the title is appearing for the first time.

Nunez, Emilio A. & Taylor, William D. Crisis & Hope in Latin America: An Evangelical Perspective. rev. ed. (Illus.). 528p. 1996. pap. text 15.95 (*0-87808-766-4*, WCL766-4) William Carey Lib.

Nunez, Guillermo. Libros de Poemas. LC 78-1444. (UPREX, Poesia Ser.: No. 53). (SPA.). 231p. 1978. pap. 1.50 (*0-8477-3225-8*) U of PR Pr.

Nunez-Harrell, Elizabeth. When Rocks Dance. 320p. 1992. pap. 10.00 (*0-345-38068-1*) One Wrld.

Nunez-Harrell, Elizabeth, et al. Native Landscapes: An Anthology of Caribbean Short Stories. Clarke, Velta J., ed. 131p. (Orig.). (YA). (gr. 7-12). 1989. pap. 7.50 (*1-878433-03-2*) Caribbean Diaspora Pr.

Nunez, Henry J. Bring Your Own Restaurant Guide. (Orig.). 1992. pap. 9.95 (*0-9634741-0-3*) Phoenix Comns.

— Bring Your Own Restaurant Guide. 2nd enl. rev. ed. (Orig.). 1993. pap. 9.95 (*0-9634741-1-1*) Phoenix Comns.

Nunez, Huberto, jt. auth. see Babson, Steve.

Nunez, Javier F., ed. see Alberti.

Nunez Jimenez, Antonio. The Journey of the Havana Cigar. (Illus.). 124p. 1995. 29.95 (*0-7938-0592-9*, XY-200) TFH Pubns.

Nunez, Luis. Relationships, You - Me - And the Others. 160p. 1994. pap. 8.95 (*0-9640457-0-2*) Cerebral Impact.

Nunez, Luis M. Santeria: A Practical Guide to Afro-Caribbean Magic. LC 92-24219. 164p. (Orig.). 1995. pap. 16.00 (*0-88214-349-2*) Spring Pubns.

***Nunez, Manuel & Ferriz-Mas, Antonio, eds.** Stellar Dynamos: Nonlinearity & Chaotic Flows. (Conference Series Proceedings: Vol. 178). 213p. 1999. text 52.00 (*1-58381-002-1*) Astron Soc Pacific.

Nunez, Margaret L., tr. see Baines, John.

Nunez-Melendez, Esteban. Plantas Medicinales de Puerto Rico: Folklore y Fundamentos Cientificos. 2nd abr. rev. ed. LC 82-17321. (SPA., Illus.). xii, 498p. 1989. pap. 22.95 (*0-8477-2328-3*) U of PR Pr.

Nunez, Nemours H. Chien Negre: A Tale of the Vaudoux. LC 72-4645. (Black Heritage Library Collection). 1977. reprint ed. 29.95 (*0-8369-9116-8*) Ayer.

Nunez, Nicolas. Anthropocosmic Theatre: Rite in the Dynamics of Theatre. Middleton, Deborah, ed. Fitzsimons, Ronan, tr. (Contemporary Theatre Studies: Vol. 13). 160p. 1996. text 51.00 (*3-7186-5710-4*, ECU38, Harwood Acad Pubs); pap. text 17.00 (*3-7186-5711-2*, ECU18, Harwood Acad Pubs) Gordon & Breach.

Nunez, Paul L. Neocortical Dynamics & Human EEG Rhythms. (Illus.). 728p. 1995. text 98.50 (*0-19-505728-7*) OUP.

***Nunez, Pedro.** Conozca Primerso Su Fe Catolica. LC 97-75566. (SPA.). 352p. 1998. pap. 9.95 (*0-7648-0155-4*, Libros Liguori) Liguori Pubns.

Nunez-Portuondo, Ricardo. Cuba: La Otra Imagen. LC 94-92123. (SPA.). 232p. (Orig.). 1994. pap. 19.95 (*0-9641879-9-X*) Cultural Pub.

— Cuban Refugee Program: The Early Years, 1959 - 1965. LC 94-92122. 135p. (Orig.). 1995. pap. 16.50 (*0-9641879-7-3*) Cultural Pub.

— General Emilio Nunez: Un Procer Cubano. (SPA., Illus.). 70p. (Orig.). 1994. pap. 6.00 (*0-9641879-8-1*) Cultural Pub.

***Nunez, Rafael.** Reclaiming Cognition: The Primacy of Action, Intention & Emotion. xx, 284p. 2000. pap. 24.95 (*0-907845-06-1*, Pub. by Imprint Acad) Philos Document.

Nunez, Rafael, jt. auth. see Lakoff, George.

Nunez, Ralph D. Our Wish Activity Book. (Illus.). 12p. (J). (ps-3). 1998. wbk. ed. 1.95 (*0-9641784-3-5*) Homes Homeless.

Nunez, Ralph Da Costa, see Da Costa Nunez, Ralph.

Nunez, Raquel, tr. see Hume, Maggie.

Nunez, Raul. The Lonely Hearts Club. Emery, Ed, tr. from SPA. (Masks Ser.). 160p. (Orig.). 1990. pap. 10.95 (*1-85242-137-1*) Serpents Tail.

Nunez, Samuel. The Vision of Daniel 8: Interpretations from 1700-1800. (Andrews University Seminary Doctoral Dissertation Ser.: Vol. 14). 462p. (Orig.). 1989. pap. 19.99 (*0-943872-95-2*) Andrews Univ Pr.

Nunez, Sandra & Marx, Trish. And Justice for All: The Legal Rights of Young People. LC 96-40523. (Illus.). 176p. (YA). (gr. 7 up). 1997. lib. bdg. 22.40 (*0-7613-0068-6*) Millbrook Pr.

Nunez, Sigrid. A Feather on the Breath of God: Novel, A. 192p. 1996. pap. 11.00 (*0-06-092684-8*) HarpC.

***Nunez, Sigrid.** Scenery of Farewell. 2002. text (*0-374-25430-3*) FS&G.

Nunez, Victor Leon, see Leon Nunez, Victor.

Nunez-Wormack, Elsa, jt. auth. see Astone, Barbara.

Nunge, Richard J. Flow Through Porous Media. LC 78-146798. 248p. 1970. 15.95 (*0-8412-0111-0*) Am Chemical.

Nungesser, Lon G. Heros, Hopes, Heartbreak. 1999. text. write for info. (*0-312-37187-X*) St Martin.

— Homosexual Acts, Actors & Identities. LC 83-13826. 215p. 1983. 57.95 (*0-275-91052-0*, C1052, Praeger Pubs) Greenwood.

— One Day at a Time: A Personal Guide to Coping with a Terminal Diagnosis. 1988. write for info. (*0-318-61942-3*) St Martin.

Nungezer, Edwin. A Dictionary of Actors. LC 75-173803. reprint ed. 27.50 (*0-404-04806-4*) AMS Pr.

— Dictionary of Actors & of Other Persons Associated with the Public Representation of Plays in England Before 1642. LC 68-57633. 437p. 1969. reprint ed. lib. bdg. 75.00 (*0-8371-0593-5*, NUDI, Greenwood Pr) Greenwood.

Nunhead, Nancy. Renoir. 1992. 5.98 (*1-55521-765-6*) Bk Sales Inc.

Nunhofer, Nicholas, tr. see Reuveni, Amnon.

Nunis & Knill, Harry. Tales of Mexican California. (YA). (gr. 7-12). 1995. pap. 8.95 (*0-88388-161-6*) Bellerophon Bks.

Nunis, Doyce, Jr., intro. The Bidwell-Bartleson Party, 1841 California Emigrant Adventure: The Documents & Memoirs of the Overland Pioneers. LC 88-51900. (Illus.). 300p. 1991. 19.95 (*0-934136-32-7*) Good Life.

Nunis, Doyce B., Jr. Great Doctors. (Illus.). 64p. (Orig.). (J). (gr. 8). 1991. pap. 3.95 (*0-88388-144-6*) Bellerophon Bks.

Nunis, Doyce B., Jr., ed. The 1769 Transit of Venus: The Baja California Observations of Jean-Baptiste Chappe d'Auteroche, Vicente de Doz, & Joaquin Velazquez Cardenas de Leon. Donahue, James et al, trs. from FRE. LC 82-3548. (Baja California Travels Ser.: No. 46). (Illus.). 185p. 1982. 60.00 (*0-938644-18-1*) Nat Hist Mus.

— Southern California Local History: A Gathering of the Writings of W. W. Robinson. LC 93-78012. (Illus.). 520p. 1993. 45.00 (*0-914421-10-7*) Hist Soc So CA.

— Southern California's Spanish Heritage: An Anthology. LC 92-74172. (Illus.). 550p. 1992. 90.00 (*0-914421-08-5*) Hist Soc So CA.

— Woman in the Life of Southern California: An Anthology. LC 95-81833. (Illus.). 450p. 1996. 50.00 (*0-914421-16-6*) Hist Soc So CA.

Nunis, Doyce B., Jr. & Lothrop, Gloria R., eds. A Guide to the History of California. LC 88-15488. 321p. 1989. lib. bdg. 79.50 (*0-313-24970-9*, NGC/, Greenwood Pr) Greenwood.

Nunis, Doyce B., Jr., ed. see Robinson, W. W.

Nunis, Doyce B., Jr., ed. see Taylor, Raymond G.

Nunley. Cultural Landscape. 6th ed. 1998. pap. text, student ed. 23.60 (*0-13-080180-1*) P-H.

***Nunley, Ann.** Inner Counselor. 1999. pap. write for info. (*1-58501-018-9*) CeShore Pubg.

— Inner Counselor, 1. 1999. pap. 39.95 (*1-58501-011-1*) CeShore Pubg.

***Nunley, Debbie & Elliot, Karen Jane.** A Taste of Pennsylvania History: A Guide to Historic Eateries & Their Recipes. 285p. 2000. pap. 16.95 (*0-89587-193-9*) Blair.

Nunley, Elma P., jt. auth. see Averill, James R.

Nunley, John W. Moving with the Face of the Devil: Art & Politics in Urban West Africa. LC 85-16455. (Illus.). 312p. 1987. text 29.95 (*0-252-01015-9*) U of Ill Pr.

Nunley, John W. & McCarty, Cara. Masks: Faces of Culture. LC 98-53973. (Illus.). 344p. 1999. 60.00 (*0-8109-4379-4*, Pub. by Abrams) Time Warner.

***Nunley, John W. & McCarty, Cara.** Masks: Faces of Culture. (Illus.). 280p. 1999. pap. 39.95 (*0-89178-078-5*) St Louis Art Mus.

Nunley, Kenneth D. A Half Bubble Off. 180p. 1996. pap. 10.00 (*0-9652468-0-9*) K D Nunley.

***Nunley, Lovie.** Glutton for Punishment. 2000. pap. 6.95 (*0-533-13200-2*) Vantage.

***Nunley, Michael & Rambo, Karl.** Peoples of the World: A Reader for Cultural Anthropology. 166p. (C). 1999. per. 36.95 (*0-7872-6400-8*, 41640001) Kendall-Hunt.

Nunley, Richard, ed. The Berkshire Reader: Writings from New England's Secluded Paradise. LC 92-33106. (Illus.). 540p. 1992. 29.95 (*0-936399-33-3*) Berkshire Hse.

Nunley, Richard, ed. The Berkshire Reader: Writings from New England's Secluded Paradise. LC 92-33106. (Illus.). 544p. 1995. reprint ed. pap. 16.95 (*0-936399-63-5*) Berkshire Hse.

Nunley, William & Bechtel. Infrared Optoelectronics: Devices & Applications. (Optical Engineering Ser.: Vol. 12). (Illus.). 288p. 1987. text 140.00 (*0-8247-7586-4*) Dekker.

Nunn. Environmental Change in the Pacific Basin. LC 98-47323. 372p. 1999. 195.00 (*0-471-94945-0*) Wiley.

Nunn, Abigail. The Land of Tuppitry: An Adventure in Imagination. (Illus.). 96p. (J). (gr. 2-4). 1989. reprint ed. pap. 4.95 (*0-9620765-3-8*) Victory Press.

Nunn, Adrian D., ed. Radiopharmaceuticals: Chemistry & Pharmacology. LC 92-18394. (Drugs & the Pharmaceutical Sciences Ser.: Vol. 55). (Illus.). 460p. 1992. text 199.00 (*0-8247-8624-6*) Dekker.

Nunn, Becky & Gallaher, Janet. Inspiring Tranquility: Stress Management & Learning Styles in the Inclusive Classroom. (Inspired Classroom Ser.). 112p. 1997. pap. 12.95 (*0-614-30867-4*, 2952-6) NEA.

Nunn, Bill. Eye of the Eagle: The Outdoor Photography of Don Wooldridge. LC 81-83818. (Illus.). 128p. 1982. 20.00 (*0-913504-71-8*); pap. 12.95 (*0-913504-72-6*) Lowell Pr.

— Wrestling with Special Ed: Recollections by Bill Nunn (Written Without Assistance) of His Trials & His Triumphs As a Learning-Disabled Student. Sharkey, Corinne, ed. & illus. by. LC 94-93958. 352p. (Orig.). 1994. 15.00 (*0-9644490-0-5*) Bill Nunn.

Nunn, C. F. Foreign Immigrants in Early Bourbon Mexico: Seventeen Hundred to Seventeen Sixty. LC 78-1159. (Cambridge Latin American Studies: No. 31). 256p. 1979. text 89.95 (*0-521-22051-3*) Cambridge U Pr.

Nunn, Chris. Awareness: What It Is, What It Does. LC 95-13966. 176p. (C). 1995. pap. 20.99 (*0-415-13227-4*) Routledge.

Nunn, Clyde Z., et al. Tolerance for Nonconformity. LC 77-82920. (Jossey-Bass Social & Behavioral Science Ser.). 230p. reprint ed. pap. 71.30 (*0-608-18061-0*, 205220100058) Bks Demand.

Nunn, Curtis. Marguerite Clark: America's Darling of Broadway & the Silent Screen. LC 81-4178. (Illus.). 188p. 1981. pap. 15.00 (*0-912646-69-1*) Tex Christian.

Nunn, D. M., ed. The Dyeing of Synthetic-Polymer & Acetate Fibres. 1979. pap. 49.00 (*0-901956-35-X*, Pub. by Textile Inst) St Mut.

Nunn, Eric. Books, Books, Everywhere: A Browser's Guide to Bookstores & Libraries in Seattle & Bellevue. LC 93-93613. 68p. 1993. 6.95 (*0-9637281-0-5*) E Nunn Res.

Nunn, Frederick M. The Time of the Generals: Latin American Professional Militarism in World Perspective. LC 91-39896. xvi, 340p. 1992. text 60.00 (*0-8032-3334-5*) U of Nebr Pr.

— Yesterday's Soldiers: European Military Professionalism in South America, 1890-1940. LC 82-6961. xiv, 365p. 1983. text 60.00 (*0-8032-3305-1*) U of Nebr Pr.

Nunn, Frederick M., ed. see Lastarria, Jose Victorino.

Nunn, G. Raymond. Canada & Asia: A Guide to Archive & Manuscript Sources in Canada, 2 vols., Set. LC 98-3227. (Asian/Pacific Studies). 1320p. 1998. 250.00 (*0-7201-2110-8*) Continuum.

Nunn, Geoffrey, jt. auth. see Baum, Jan A.

Nunn, George E. The Geographical Conceptions of Colombus: A Critical Consideration of Four Problems. LC 72-8429. (Select Bibliographies Reprint Ser.). 1977. reprint ed. 20.95 (*0-8369-6984-7*) Ayer.

— The Geographical Conceptions of Columbus: A Critical Consideration of Four Problems. LC 92-71996. (Illus.). 195p. 1992. 15.00 (*1-879281-06-6*); pap. 8.00 (*1-879281-08-2*) G Meir Lib.

— Geographical Conceptions of Columbus: A Critical Consideration of Four Problems. (Select Bibliographies Reprint Ser.). reprint ed. lib. bdg. 26.50 (*0-8290-0847-0*) Irvington.

Nunn, Godfrey R. Canada & Asia: Guide to Archive & Manuscript Sources in Canada. LC 98-3227. 671p. 1998. write for info. (*0-7201-2372-0*) Continuum.

— Canada & Asia: Guide to Archive & Manuscript Sources in Canada. LC 98-3227. 1304 p. 1999. write for info. (*0-7201-2373-9*) Continuum.

Nunn, H. Jack. Managing for Profits: Lumber Yard Management in the Decades Ahead. 87p. 1995. pap. 150.00 (*0-9645680-0-4*) CTBMA.

Nunn, J. F. Nunn's Applied Respiratory Physiology. 4th ed. (Illus.). 608p. 1999. text 100.00 (*0-7506-1336-X*) Buttrwrth-Heinemann.

Nunn, J. F., jt. auth. see Lumb, Andrew.

Nunn, Jack H. The Soviet First Strike Threat: The U. S. Perspective. LC 82-344. 292p. 1982. 59.95 (*0-275-90871-2*, C0871, Praeger Pubs) Greenwood.

***Nunn, Joan.** Fashion in Costume, 1200-2000. rev. ed. LC 99-47516. (Illus.). 288p. 2000. pap. 19.95 (*1-56663-279-X*, Pub. by I R Dee) Natl Bk Netwk.

Nunn, John. Beating the Sicillian 3. 1995. pap. 22.50 (*0-8050-4227-X*) H Holt & Co.

— The Classical King's Indian. 96p. 1990. pap. 14.95 (*0-02-035540-8*) Macmillan.

— The Complete Najdorf. LC 96-78267. (New American Batsford Chess Library). 304p. (Orig.). 1997. pap. 26.95 (*1-879479-45-1*) ICE WA.

— John Nunns Best Games. LC 94-72762. 1995. pap. 26.95 (*0-8050-3899-X*, Pub. by Batsford Chess) H Holt & Co.

— John Nunn's Chess Puzzle Book. 1998. pap. text 17.95 (*1-901983-08-0*) Gambit.

***Nunn, John.** Learn Chess. 2000. pap. 9.95 (*1-901983-30-7*, Pub. by Gambit) BHB Intl.

Nunn, John. The Main Line King's Indian. 288p. 1996. pap. 29.00 (*0-87447-719-0*) H Holt & Co.

— New Ideas in the Four Knights. (Batsford Chess Library). 128p. 1993. pap. 16.95 (*0-8050-2629-0*, Owl) H Holt & Co.

— New Ideas in the Pirc Defence. 144p. 1995. pap. 16.95 (*0-8050-2939-7*, Pub. by Batsford Chess) H Holt & Co.

***Nunn, John.** 101 Brilliant Chess Miniatures. (Illus.). 176p. 2000. pap. 19.95 (*1-901983-16-1*, Pub. by Gambit) BHB Intl.

Nunn, John. Secrets of Grandmaster Chess. 2nd rev. ed. LC 97-71875. (New American Batsford Chess Library). 288p. 1997. pap. 26.95 (*1-879479-54-0*) ICE WA.

— Secrets of Minor-Piece Endings. 1995. pap. 27.50 (*0-8050-4228-8*, Pub. by Batsford Chess) H Holt & Co.

— Secrets of Pawnless Endings. (Batsford Chess Library). 1995. pap. 26.95 (*0-8050-3285-1*) H Holt & Co.

— Secrets of Rook Endings. (Illus.). 336p. 1999. pap. 19.95 (*1-901983-18-8*, Pub. by Gambit) BHB Intl.

— Secrets of Rook Endings. (Batsford Chess Library). 320p. 1993. pap. 26.95 (*0-8050-2640-1*, Owl) H Holt & Co.

— Tactical Chess Endings: Improve Your Chess by Unlocking the Secrets of the Endgame. 1998. pap. text 22.95 (*0-7134-5937-9*, Pub. by B T B) Branford.

— The Ultimate Pirc. (Illus.). 240p. 1998. pap. text 24.95 (*0-7134-8221-4*, Pub. by B T B) Branford.

Nunn, John, jt. auth. see Keres, Paul.

Nunn, John, ed. see Euwe, Max.

Nunn, John F. Ancient Egyptian Medicine. LC 95-39770. (Illus.). 240p. 1996. 39.95 (*0-8061-2831-3*) U of Okla Pr.

Nunn, Julia. Laboratory Psychology: A Beginner's Guide. (Cognitive Psychology Ser.). 1998. 54.95 (*0-86377-710-4*, Pub. by Psychol Pr); pap. 22.95 (*0-86377-711-2*, Pub. by Psychol Pr) Taylor & Francis.

Nunn, June H., jt. auth. see Rugg-Gunn, Andrew J.

Nunn, Kem. The Dogs of Winter. 1998. per. 14.00 (*0-671-79334-9*, PB Trade Paper) PB.

— The Dogs of Winter. LC 96-51556. 400p. 1997. 23.50 (*0-684-82647-X*) S&S Trade.

***Nunn, Kem.** Pomona Queen. 236p. 2000. pap. 12.95 (*1-56858-176-9*, Pub. by FWEW) Publishers Group.

Nunn, Kem. Pomona Queen. Sacco, Maryanne, ed. 240p. 1993. reprint ed. mass mkt. 10.00 (*0-671-79877-4*, WSP) PB.

***Nunn, Kem.** Tapping the Source. 300p. 2000. reprint ed. pap. 14.95 (*1-56858-162-9*, Pub. by FWEW) Publishers Group.

Nunn, Maxine, tr. see Hass, Amira.

Nunn, Michael W. Teach Someone to Read! An Effective How-to Method for Basic Reading & Literacy Programs. (Orig.). 1986. pap. text 12.00 (*0-910609-13-6*) Gifted Educ Pr.

Nunn, Nancy, jt. auth. see Brett, Jai.

Nunn, Pamela G. Problem Pictures: Women & Men in Victorian Painting. (Illus.). 224p. 1996. 69.95 (*1-85928-152-4*, Pub. by Scolar Pr) Ashgate Pub Co.

Nunn, Patrick. Oceanic Islands. LC 92-28002. (Natural Environment Ser.). 360p. 1994. pap. 50.95 (*0-631-18967-X*) Blackwell Pubs.

Nunn, Patrick D. Keimami Sa Vakila Na Liga Ni Kalou: Feeling the Hand of God: Human & Nonhuman Impacts on Pacific Island Environments. rev. ed. LC 92-27305. (Occasional Papers: No. 13). 1992. write for info. (*0-86638-154-6*) EW Ctr HI.

Nunn, R. Asia & Oceania: A Guide to Archival & Manuscript Sources in the United States, 5 vols., Set. 1985. text 999.00 (*0-7201-1713-5*) Continuum.

Nunn, Rebecca O., jt. auth. see Gallaher, Janet O.

Nunn, Robert G. Water Treatment Essentials for Boiler Plant Operation. LC 96-47395. (Illus.). 225p. 1996. 49.00 (*0-07-048219-5*) McGraw.

Nunn, Robert H. Intermediate Fluid Mechanics. (Illus.). 225p. (C). 1989. text 70.95 (*0-89116-647-5*) Hemisp Pub.

— Intermediate Fluid Mechanics. (Illus.). 225p. (C). 1989. write for info. (*0-89116-020-5*) Hemisp Pub.

Nunn, Robert R. & Geary, Edward J. The Yourcenar Collection: A Descriptive Catalogue. (Illus.). 1984. pap. 6.00 (*0-916606-07-4*) Bowdoin Coll.

Nunn, Ron & Marten, Kay. Adventures in Indian Cooking. (Illus.). 61p. (Orig.). 1990. pap. text 5.95 (*0-936731-10-9*) Devel Self Rel.

Nunn, Sam. Critical Defense Choices. Gulliver, Hal, ed. LC 82-63197. (Papers on International Issues: No. 4). 19p. (Orig.). 1983. pap. text 5.00 (*0-935082-03-4*) Southern Ctr Intl Stud.

Nunn, Sam, et al. The CSIS Strengthening of America Commission First Report. 182p. (C). 1992. pap. text 20.00 (*0-89206-211-8*) CSIS.

***Nunn, Sam, et al.** The Geopolitics of Energy in the 21st Century. LC 00-29493. (Panel Reports). 2000. write for info. (*0-89206-370-X*) CSIS.

— Managing the Nuclear Materials Threat: A Report of the CSIS Nuclear Materials Management Project. LC 99-88665. (Panel Report Ser.). 118p. 1999. 24.95 (*0-89206-359-9*) CSIS.

Nunn, T. Percy. Anthropomorphism & Physics. 1977. lib. bdg. 59.95 (*0-8490-1438-7*) Gordon Pr.

Nunn, Tamara. Celebrate ABC's: A Learning Center Approach. LC 98-148299. 400p. (J). (gr. 1-3). 1997. pap. 24.95 (*1-57690-034-7*) Tchr Create Mat.

— The Farmer Didn't Wake Up, Vol. 4351. (Fun & Fantasy Ser.). (Illus.). 16p. (J). (ps-1). 1997. pap. 2.75 (*1-57471-248-9*, 4351) Creat Teach Pr.

— Mi Direccion Global (My Global Address), Vol. 4099. Williams, Rozanne L., ed. Mallernee, Nora, tr. (Learn to Read Social Studies). (SPA., Illus.). 16p. (J). (ps-1). 1997. pap. 2.75 (*1-57471-286-1*, 4099) Creat Teach Pr.

— My Global Address, Vol. 2927. Williams, Rozanne L., ed. (Social Studies Learn to Read Ser.). (Illus.). 16p. (J). (ps-2). 1996. pap. 2.75 (*1-57471-132-6*, 3927) Creat Teach Pr.

— My Global Address, Vol. 3971. Williams, Rozanne L., ed. (Social Studies Big Bks.). (Illus.). 16p. (J). (ps-2). 1997. pap. 12.98 (*1-57471-178-4*, 3970) Creat Teach Pr.

— The Three R's: Respect, Rights & Responsibility. (Illus.). 144p. 1995. pap., teacher ed. 14.95 (*1-55734-623-2*) Tchr Create Mat.

Nunn, Tammy. This Is the Way, Vol. 4150. Graves, Kimberlee, ed. (Science Ser.). (Illus.). 16p. (J). (gr. k-1). 1997. pap. 2.75 (*1-57471-313-2*, 4150) Creat Teach Pr.

Nunn, William C. Escape from Reconstruction. LC 74-9977. (Illus.). 140p. 1974. reprint ed. lib. bdg. 35.00 (*0-8371-7611-5*, NUER, Greenwood Pr) Greenwood.

— Somervell: Story of a Texas County. LC 75-39912. 267p. reprint ed. pap. 82.80 (*0-7837-1240-5*, 204137700020) Bks Demand.

Nunnally, et al. Financial Management: A Practical Approach. 496p. (C). 1997. pap. text 50.95 (*0-7872-4280-2*, 41428001) Kendall-Hunt.

Nunnally, Bennie & Plath, Anthony D. Cases in Finance. 2nd ed. LC 96-217690. 288p. (C). 1996. text 28.95 (*0-256-15385-X*, Irwn McGrw-H) McGrw-H Hghr Educ.

Nunnally, Bennie, Jr. & Plath, Anthony D. CPS Cases in Finance, Custom Edition. 212p. (C). 1995. 22.95 (*0-256-21567-7*, Irwn McGrw-H) McGrw-H Hghr Educ.

Nunnally, Bennie, jt. ed. see Plath, Tony.

Nunnally, Bennie H. & Kester, George. Financial Management: A Practical Approach. 336p. (C). 1994. per. 28.95 (*0-8403-9514-0*) Kendall-Hunt.

Nunnally, Bennie H. & Kester, George. Financial Management: A Practical Approach. 2nd ed. 336p. (C). 1997. per. 35.95 (*0-7872-3626-8*) Kendall-Hunt.

Nunnally, Bennie H., Jr., et al. Corporate Lease Analysis: A Guide to Concepts & Evaluation. LC 90-45147. 256p. 1991. 65.00 (*0-89930-513-X*, NCC, Quorum Bks) Greenwood.

Nunnally, Elam & Moy, Caryl. Communication Basics for Human Service Professionals. (Human Services Guides Ser.: Vol. 56). 172p. (C). 1989. pap. text 18.95 (*0-8039-3118-2*) Sage.

Nunnally, Elam, et al. Connecting Instructor Manual. 256p. 1989. ring bd. 65.00 (*0-917340-17-5*) Interpersonal Comm.

— Connecting Skills Workbook. 210p. (Orig.). 1989. pap. text, student ed. 16.00 (*0-917340-16-7*) Interpersonal Comm.

— Connecting with Self & Others. 312p. (Orig.). 1988. pap. text 16.00 (*0-917340-15-9*) Interpersonal Comm.

N

An Asterisk (*) at the beginning of an entry indicates that the title is appearing for the first time.

— Talking & Listening Together: Couple Communication One. (Illus.). 160p. (C). 1991. pap. 16.00 (*0-917340-18-3*) Interpersonal Comm.

Nunnally, Elam W., et al, eds. Mental Illness, Delinquency, Addictions, & Neglect. LC 89-13473. (Families in Trouble Ser.: No. 4). 266p. 1988. reprint ed. pap. 82.50 (*0-608-01182-7*, 205948000001) Bks Demand.

— Troubled Relationships. LC 88-6539. (Families in Trouble Ser.: No. 3). 288p. 1988. reprint ed. pap. 89.30 (*0-608-01511-3*, 205955500002) Bks Demand.

Nunnally, Jim C. & Bernstein, Ira H. Psychometric Theory. 3rd ed. LC 93-22756. (Series in Social Psychology). 736p. (C). 1994. 101.88 (*0-07-047849-X*) McGraw.

***Nunnally, S. W.** Construction Methods & Management. 5th ed. LC 00-39179. (Illus.). 2001. write for info. (*0-13-085962-1*) Aspen Law.

— Managing Construction Equipment. 2nd ed. LC 99-27056. (Illus.). 399p. 1999. 75.00 (*0-13-901216-8*) P-H.

Nunnally, Stephens W. Construction Methods & Management. 4th ed. LC 96-46691. (Illus.). 567p. 1997. 76.00 (*0-13-570367-0*) P-H.

Nunnally, Thomas M., jt. auth. see Caplan, Suzanne.

Nunnally, Tiina. Fate of Ravens: A Margit Andersson Mystery. LC 98-6627. (Suspense Ser.: Vol. 2). 220p. 1998. pap. 12.00 (*0-940242-80-X*) Fjord Pr.

— Runemaker. LC 96-28795. (Suspense Ser.: No. 1). 213p. (Orig.). 1996. pap. 12.00 (*0-940242-77-X*) Fjord Pr.

Nunnally, Tiina, tr. see Bang, Herman.

Nunnally, Tiina, tr. see Davidsen, Leif.

Nunnally, Tiina, tr. see Ditlevsen, Tove.

Nunnally, Tiina, tr. see Hamsun, Knut.

Nunnally, Tiina, tr. see Heinesen, William.

Nunnally, Tiina, tr. see Jacobsen, Jens Peter.

Nunnally, Tiina, tr. see Mankell, Henning.

Nunnally, Tiina, tr. see Nexo, Martin Anderson.

Nunnally, Tiina, tr. see Rifbjerg, Klaus.

Nunnally, Tiina, tr. see Sorensen, Villy.

Nunnally, Tiina, tr. see Ullmann, Linn.

Nunnally, Tiina, tr. & notes see Undset, Sigrid.

Nunnally, Tina, tr. see Kopperud, Gunnar.

Nunnally, Tina, tr. see Undset, Sigrid.

Nunnelee, Janice, jt. ed. see Morgan, Linda K.

Nunneley, Faithe S. Thrums. Bress, Seymour, ed. (Illus.). 149p. 1991. pap. 14.95 (*0-9620543-3-X*) Flower Valley Pr.

Nunneley, Paul, jt. auth. see Emchowicz, Antoni.

***Nunneley, Peg.** The Biodynamic Philosophy & Treatment of Psychosomatic Conditions. (Biodynamic Psychology & Psychotherapy Ser.: Vol. 1). 159p. 2000. pap. text 29.95 (*0-8204-4608-4*) P Lang Pubng.

Nunnelley, Jeanette C. Behavior Guidance for 3-4 Year Old Children. rev. ed. (Illus.). 21p. (C). 1995. pap. 6.00 (*0-942388-19-4*) So Early Chldhood Assn.

Nunnelley, L. L. & Arnoldssen, T. C. Noise in Digital Magnetic Recording. 250p. 1994. text 74.00 (*981-02-0865-0*); pap. text 48.00 (*981-02-1025-6*) World Scientific Pub.

Nunnelley, William A. Bull Connor. LC 89-78196. 240p. 1990. pap. 21.95 (*0-8173-0495-9*) U of Ala Pr.

Nunnery. Songs, Rhymes & Fingerplays: Language through Action & Rhyming. 1993. 49.00 (*0-7616-7969-3*) Commun Skill.

Nunnery, Michael Y., jt. auth. see Kimbrough, Ralph B.

Nunnery, Rose K. Advancing Your Career: Concepts of Professional Nursing. LC 96-29493. (Illus.). 424p. 1997. pap. 36.95 (*0-8036-0235-9*) Davis Co.

Nunney, M. J. Light & Heavy Vehicle Technology. 2nd ed. (Illus.). 528p. 1992. pap. text 59.95 (*0-7506-0477-8*) Buttrwrth-Heinemann.

— Light & Heavy Vehicle Technology. 3rd ed. LC 98-232660. (Illus.). 672p. 2000. pap. text 39.95 (*0-7506-3827-3*) Buttrwrth-Heinemann.

Nunno, T. J., et al. Toxic Waste Minimization in the Printed Circuit Board Industry. LC 88-22630. (Pollution Technology Review Ser.: No. 162). (Illus.). 162p. 1989. 69.00 (*0-8155-1183-3*) Noyes.

Nunno, Thomas, et al. International Technologies for Hazardous Waste Site Cleanup. LC 90-30223. (Pollution Technology Review Ser.: No. 183). (Illus.). 283p. 1990. 45.00 (*0-8155-1238-4*) Noyes.

Nuno, Daniel. Enciclopedia de Poesia Evangelica: Encyclopedia of Evangelical Poetry. 5th ed. (SPA.). 365p. 1983. 19.95 (*0-7859-5054-0*); pap. 19.95 (*0-8288-5220-0*, S50573) Fr & Eur.

Nuno, Jose P., jt. tr. see Sullivan, Gianna T.

Nuno, Juan Gaya, see Gaya Nuno, Juan.

Nunokawa, Jeff. The Afterlife of Property: Domestic Security & the Victorian Novel. LC 93-30912. 160p. 1994. text 29.50 (*0-691-03320-X*, Pub. by Princeton U Pr) Cal Prin Full Svc.

***Nunoz, Pilar.** Campo Libre Vol. 2: La Vida Initima - Students Books. Thacker, Mike, ed. (SPA., Illus.). 82p. (C). 1999. pap., student ed. 20.00 (*0-85668-688-3*, Pub. by Aris & Phillips) David Brown.

Nunrich, C. Consider Issues. (Illus.). 1989. 58.52 incl. audio (*0-8013-0137-8*, 75801) Longman.

— Consider the Issues: Developing Listening & Critical Thinking Skills. (Illus.). 1989. pap. text 17.59 (*0-582-90749-7*, 75257) Longman.

Nuns of the Monastery of St. Clare, Balsbach, Germ, et al. The Celebration of the Eucharist: The Church's Festival of Love. Smith, David, tr. 1983. pap. 4.00 (*0-8199-0866-5*, Frncscn Herld) Franciscan Pr.

Nuns of the Visitation Staff, tr. see St. Francis de Sales.

Nunz, Gregory J. Electronics in Our World: A Survey. LC 70-146682. (Illus.). 1972. 39.00 (*0-13-252288-8*) P-H.

Nunzio, Mario R. Di, see Di Nunzio, Mario R.

Nunzio, Rollo R. Jews, Judaism & the Holocaust: Index of New Information & Current Results of Conditions, Analysis & Progress. 170p. 1995. 47.50 (*0-7883-0686-3*); pap. 44.50 (*0-7883-0687-1*) ABBE Pubs Assn.

Nuotio-Antar, Vappu S., jt. auth. see Antar, Basil N.

Nuovo, Gerard J. Cytopathology of the Lower Female Genital Tract: An Integrated Approach. LC 93-9608. (Illus.). 520p. 1994. 165.00 (*0-683-06595-5*) Lppncott W & W.

— PCR in Situ Hybridization: Protocols & Applications. 3rd ed. LC 96-25449. 512p. 1996. text 97.00 (*0-397-58749-X*) Lppncott W & W.

Nuovo, Gerard J., jt. auth. see Crum, Christopher P.

Nuovo, Victor. Visionary Science: A Translation of Tillich's "On the Idea of a Theology of Culture" with an Interpretive Essay. LC 87-26352. 196p. 1987. 29.95 (*0-8143-1940-8*) Wayne St U Pr.

Nuovo, Victor, ed. The Collected Works of Edmund Law, 6 vols. 1870p. 1997. 850.00 (*1-85506-516-9*) Thoemmes Pr.

— John Locke & Christianity No. 16: Contemporary Responses to the Reasonableness of Christianity. 250p. 1997. 75.00 (*1-85506-539-8*); pap. 24.00 (*1-85506-540-1*) Thoemmes Pr.

Nuovo, Victor, tr. see Tillich, Paul Johannes.

Nuquist, Reidun D., compiled by. Index to News & Notes & Vermont History News, 1949-1989, Vols. 1-40. 185p. 1993. pap. 34.95 (*0-934720-39-8*) VT Hist Soc.

— Vermont History Index: The Proceedings of the Vermont Historical Society, 1953-1977, Vols. 21-45. 268p. 1979. pap. 3.75 (*0-934720-20-7*) VT Hist Soc.

— Vermont History Index: The Proceedings of the Vermont Historical Society, 1978-1987, Vols. 46-55. 136p. 1991. pap. 24.95 (*0-934720-34-7*) VT Hist Soc.

Nur, Amos & Wang, Zhijing, eds. Seismic & Acoustic Velocities in Reservoir Rocks Vol. 1: Experimental Studies. (Geophysics Reprint Ser.: No. 10). 420p. (Orig.). 1989. pap. 45.00 (*0-931830-70-2*, 184A) Soc Expl Geophys.

Nur, Amos, jt. ed. see Wang, Zhijing.

Nur, Muhammad, tr. see Kashifi, Samal A.

Nur, Muhammad, tr. see Rauf, A.

NurAhmed, Steven. Love Garden Colors Poetry. 1992. pap. text. write for info. (*0-9629532-2-9*) Black Angels.

Nurbakhsh, Ali-Reza, tr. see Nurbakhsh, Javad & Lewisehn, Leonard.

Nurbakhsh, Javad. Discourses on the Sufi Path. LC 96-8009. 120p. 1996. 24.95 (*0-933546-58-0*) KNP.

— Dogs: From a Sufi Point of View. Graham, Terry, tr. (Illus.). 100p. 1989. pap. 7.95 (*0-933546-39-4*) KNP.

— The Great Satan 'Eblis' Johnston, Neil et al, trs. 103p. 1986. pap. 7.95 (*0-933546-23-8*) KNP.

— In the Paradise of the Sufis. LC 79-83588. 126p. 1979. pap. 8.95 (*0-933546-01-7*) KNP.

— In the Paradise of the Sufis. 126p. 1996. pap. 8.95 (*0-614-21290-1*) Kazi Pubns.

— In the Tavern of Ruin: Seven Essays on Sufism. LC 78-102838. 135p. (Orig.). 1978. pap. 9.95 (*0-933546-00-9*) KNP.

— Jesus in the Eyes of the Sufis. 131p. 1983. pap. 8.95 (*0-933546-21-1*) KNP.

— Jesus in the Eyes of the Sufis. 132p. 1996. pap. 8.95 (*0-614-21295-2*, 670) Kazi Pubns.

— Masters of the Path: A History of the Nimatulahi Sufi Order. 2nd ed. LC 80-80902. (Illus.). 130p. 1980. pap. 8.95 (*0-933546-03-3*) KNP.

— Psychology of Sufism. 1993. 22.95 (*0-933646-49-6*) Aries Pr.

— Psychology of Sufism. 142p. 1996. 22.95 (*0-614-21557-9*, 1020) Kazi Pubns.

— The Psychology of Sufism. 141p. 1992. 20.00 (*0-933546-49-1*) KNP.

— Spiritual Poverty in Sufism. Lewishon, Leonard, tr. 15p. 1984. pap. 8.95 (*0-933546-11-4*) KNP.

— Spiritual Poverty in Sufism. 150p. 1996. pap. 8.95 (*0-614-21348-7*, 1161) Kazi Pubns.

— Sufi Symbolism Vol. I: The Nurbakhsh Encyclopedia of Sufi Symbolism. Graham, Terry et al, trs. 228p. 1986. 24.95 (*0-933546-12-2*) KNP.

— Sufi Symbolism Vol. II: The Nurbakhsh Encyclopedia of Sufi Terminology: Love, Lover, Beloved, Allusion & Metaphors. Graham, Terry, tr. 193p. 1987. 24.95 (*0-933546-31-9*) KNP.

— Sufi Symbolism Vol. III: The Nurbakhsh Encyclopedia of Sufi Terminology: Religions Terminology. Graham, Terry et al, trs. 263p. 1988. 24.95 (*0-933546-35-1*) KNP.

— Sufi Symbolism Vol. IV: The Nurbakhsh Encyclopedia of Sufi Terminology: the Symbolism of the Natural World. Lewisohn, Leonard & Graham, Terry, trs. 199p. 1990. 25.00 (*0-933546-40-8*) KNP.

— Sufi Symbolism Vol. V: The Nurbakhsh Encyclopedia of Sufi Terminology: Veils, & Clothing, Government, Economics & Commerce, Medicine & Healing. Graham, Terry, tr. 194p. 1991. 25.00 (*0-933546-45-9*) KNP.

— Sufi Symbolism Vol. VI: The Nurbakhsh Encyclopedia of Sufi Terminology: Titles & Epithets. 141p. 1992. 25.00 (*0-933546-48-3*) KNP.

— Sufi Symbolism Vol. VII: The Nurbakhsh Encyclopedia of Sufi Terminology: Comtemplative Disciplines. Graham, Terry et al, trs. 207p. 1993. 25.00 (*0-933546-52-1*) KNP.

— Sufi Symbolism Vol. VIII: The Nurbakhsh Encyclopedia of Sufi Terminology: Inspirations, Revelations, Lights. Graham, Terry et al, trs. 168p. 1995. 25.00 (*0-933546-53-X*) KNP.

— Sufi Symbolism Vol. IX: The Narbakhsh Encyclopedia of Sufi Terminology: Spiritual Faculties, Spiritual Organs, Knowledge, Wisdom & Perfection. 181p. 1995. 25.00 (*0-933546-55-6*) KNP.

— Sufi Symbolism Vol. X: The Nurbakhsh Encyclopedia of Sufi Terminology: Spiritual State & Mystical Stations, Vol. XI. Graham, Terry, tr. 151p. 1996. 25.00 (*0-933546-56-4*) KNP.

— Sufi Symbolism Vol. XI: The Nurbakhsh Encyclopedia of Sufi Symbolism. 166p. 1997. 25.00 (*0-933546-59-9*) KNP.

Nurbakhsh, Javad. Sufi Symbolism Vol. XII: The Nurbakhsh Encyclopedia of Sufi Terminology - Spiritual States & Mystical Stations. Graham, Terry, tr. 203p. 1997. 25.00 (*0-933546-65-3*) KNP.

Nurbakhsh, Javad. Sufi Symbolism Vol. XIII: The Nurbakhsh Encyclopedia of Sufi Terminology - Spiritual States & Mystical Stations. Graham, Terry, tr. 208p. 1998. 25.00 (*0-933546-66-1*) KNP.

— Sufi Women. 202p. 1996. pap. 12.95 (*0-614-21362-2*, 1190) Kazi Pubns.

— Sufi Women. rev. ed. Lewisohn, Leonard, tr. (Illus.). 263p. 1983. pap. 11.95 (*0-933546-42-4*) KNP.

— Sufism No. 1: Meaning, Knowledge & Unity. Wilson, Peter & Chiltick, William, trs. from PER. 111p. (Orig.). 1991. pap. 9.95 (*0-933546-05-X*) KNP.

— Sufism No. 2: Fear & Hope, Contractions & Expansion, Gathering & Dispersion. Chittick, William C., tr. from PER. 126p. (Orig.). 1982. pap. 9.95 (*0-933546-07-6*) KNP.

— Sufism No. 3: Submission, Contentment, Absence, Presence, Intimacy, Awe, Tranquility, Serenity. Lewisohn, Leonard & Graham, Terry, trs. 133p. 1985. pap. 9.95 (*0-933546-19-X*) KNP.

— Sufism No. 4: Repentance, Abstinence, Renunciation, Wariness, Humility, Humbleness, Sincerity. 166p. 1988. pap. 9.95 (*0-933546-33-5*) KNP.

— Sufism No. 5: Gratitude, Patience, Trust-in-God, Aspiration, Veracity, Zeal, Valour, Altruism, Shame. Graham, Terry et al, trs. 158p. 1991. pap. 9.95 (*0-933546-43-2*) KNP.

— Traditions of the Prophet, Vol. 2. Lewisohn, Leonard & Graham, Terry, trs. (ARA, ENG & PER.). 96p. 1983. pap. 8.95 (*0-933546-10-6*) KNP.

— The Truths of Love: Sufi Poetry. Lewisohn, Leonard, tr. (ENG & PER.). 110p. 1982. pap. 8.95 (*0-933546-08-4*) KNP.

***Nurbakhsh, Javad & Graham, Terry.** Sufi Symbolism: The Nubakhsh Encyclopedia of Sufi Terminology - Metaphysical & Philosophical Terms: Unity of Being & Degrees of Multiplicity. 196p. 1999. write for info. (*0-933546-67-X*) KNP.

Nurbakhsh, Javad & Lewisehn, Leonard. Traditions of the Prophet, Vol. 1. Rothschild, Jeffrey et al, eds. Nurbakhsh, Ali-Reza, tr. (ARA, ENG & PER.). 101p. 1981. reprint ed. pap. 8.95 (*0-933546-06-8*) KNP.

Nurcombe, Barry & Gallagher, Rollin M. The Clinical Process in Psychiatry: Diagnosis & Management Planning. (Illus.). 768p. 1986. pap. text 49.95 (*0-521-28928-9*) Cambridge U Pr.

Nurcombe, Barry & Partlett, David F. Child Mental Health & the Law. LC 93-50557. 1994. 39.95 (*0-02-923245-7*) Free Pr.

Nurcombe, Valerie. Information Sources in Official Publications. LC 96-29867. 1997. 95.00 (*1-85739-151-9*) Bowker-Saur.

Nurcombe, Valerie, ed. Information Sources in Architecture & Construction. 2nd ed. LC 95-43214. 489p. 1995. 110.00 (*1-85739-094-6*) Bowker-Saur.

Nurcombe, Valerie J. International Real Estate Valuation, Investment & Development: A Select Bibliography, 7. LC 87-14906. (Bibliographies & Indexes in Economics & Economic History Ser.: No. 7). 205p. 1987. lib. bdg. 65.00 (*0-313-26082-6*, NRE/, Greenwood Pr) Greenwood.

Nuremberg War Trials Staff. Trial of the Major War Criminals Before the International Military Tribunal, 44 vols. LC 70-145536. reprint ed. write for info. (*0-404-53650-6*) AMS Pr.

Nurenberger, M. J. The Scared & the Doomed: The Jewish Establishment vs. the Six Million. (Illus.). 350p. 1994. 24.95 (*0-88962-290-6*); pap. 14.95 (*0-88962-289-2*) Mosaic.

Nurge, Ethel, ed. The Modern Sioux: Social Systems & Reservation Culture. LC 71-88089. 368p. reprint ed. pap. 114.10 (*0-608-17171-9*, 202787900056) Bks Demand.

Nurick. Interpersonal Relationships in Management. 2nd ed. 1998. 29.00 (*0-07-229937-1*) McGraw.

Nurick, A. Interpersonal Relations in Management (Custom Pub) (C). 1994. pap. text 23.00 (*0-07-048148-2*) McGraw.

Nurick, Aaron J. Participation in Organizational Change: The TVA Experiment. LC 84-26652. 255p. 1985. 59.95 (*0-275-90149-1*, C0149, Praeger Pubs) Greenwood.

Nuriddin, J. & El Hadi, S. The Last Poets: Vibes from the Scribes Selected Poems. LC 91-78312. 92p. 1992. reprint ed. 24.95 (*0-86543-316-X*); reprint ed. pap. 9.95 (*0-86543-317-8*) Africa World.

Nuridsany, Claude & Perennou, Marie. The Metamorphosis of Flowers. Lifson, Ben, tr. from FRE. LC 97-45862. (Illus.). 136p. 1998. 39.95 (*0-8109-3625-9*, Pub. by Abrams) Time Warner.

Nurissany, Claude, et al. Microcosmos: The Invisible World of Insects. (Illus.). 160p. 1997. 35.00 (*1-55670-555-7*) Stewart Tabori & Chang.

Nurius, Paula S. Education & Research for Empowerment Practice. 312p. (Orig.). 1994. pap. 18.50 (*0-935035-03-6*) U WA Ctr Pol Rsch.

Nurius, Paula S., jt. auth. see Franklin, Cynthia.

Nurkse, D. Leaving Xaia. LC 98-75586. 77p. 2000. pap. 13.95 (*1-884800-26-2*, Pub. by Four Way Bks) SPD-Small Pr Dist.

— Shadow Wars. 1988. pap. 7.00 (*0-914610-53-8*) Hanging Loose.

— Voices over Water. LC 96-86009. (Encore Ser.). 98p. 1996. pap. 12.95 (*1-884800-18-1*) Four Way Bks.

Nurkse, Dennis. Shadow Wars. 1988. 15.00 (*0-914610-54-6*) Hanging Loose.

— Staggered Lights. 1990. pap. 12.00 (*0-937669-42-3*) Owl Creek Pr.

Nurkse, Dennis & Castelle, Kay. In the Spirit of Peace: A Global Introduction to Children's Rights. (Illus.). 72p. (Orig.). (gr. 5-10). 1990. pap. text 7.95 (*0-943965-14-4*) DCI USA.

Nurkse, Dennis & Castelle, Kay, eds. Children's Rights: Crisis & Challenge: A Global Report on the Situation of Children in View of the U. N. Convention on the Rights of the Child. 384p. (Orig.). 1990. pap. 25.00 (*0-943965-13-6*) DCI USA.

***Nurmann, Britta & Schulze.** Vikings Recreated in Color: Europa Militaria Special #6. 96p. 2000. pap. 22.95 (*1-86126-289-2*, Pub. by Crolwood) Motorbooks Intl.

Nurmela, T. Finnish-French Dictionary. (FIN & FRE.). 683p. 95.00 (*0-7859-0914-1*, M-9651) Fr & Eur.

Nurmi, Hannu. Comparing Voting Systems. (C). 1987. lib. bdg. 122.00 (*90-277-2600-0*) Kluwer Academic.

— Rational Behaviour & the Design of Institutions: Concepts, Theories & Models. LC 97-39590. 224p. 1998. 80.00 (*1-85898-804-7*) E Elgar.

***Nurmi, Hannu.** Voting Paradoxes & How to Deal with Them. LC 99-12502. (Illus.). x, 153p. 1999. 54.95 (*3-540-66236-7*) Spr-Verlag.

Nurmi, Jari-Erik. Adolescents, Culture & Conflicts: Growing up in Contemporary Europe. Michigan State University Staff, ed. LC 97-43496. (Michigan State University Series on Children, Youth, & Families: Vol. 3). 256p. 1998. text 55.00 (*0-8153-2389-1*, SS1112) Garland.

Nurmi, Kari E., jt. auth. see Lehtinen, Ritva.

Nurmi, Lasse A., jt. auth. see Williams, Mary Beth.

Nurmi, Martin K. Blake's Marriage of Heaven & Hell. LC 72-6067. (Studies in Blake: No. 3). 1972. reprint ed. lib. bdg. 75.00 (*0-8383-1599-2*) M S G Haskell Hse.

Nurmi, Martin K., jt. auth. see Bentley, Gerald E.

Nurmi, Raimo W. & Darling, John R. International Management Leadership: The Primary Competitive Advantage. LC 97-2108. (Illus.). 224p. (C). 1997. 49.95 (*0-7890-0090-3*, Intl Busn Pr) Haworth Pr.

Nurmi, Raimo W. & Darling, John R. International Management Leadership: The Primary Competitive Advantage. LC 97-2108. (Illus.). 224p. (C). 1997. pap. 24.95 (*0-7890-0260-4*, Intl Busn Pr) Haworth Pr.

Nurmi, Ruth. A Plain & Easy Introduction to the Harpsichord. LC 86-1875. 262p. 1986. reprint ed. 31.00 (*0-8108-1886-8*) Scarecrow.

Nurminen, Mika. Wild West Country Dancing. LC 95-3836. (Illus.). 128p. 1995. pap. 20.00 (*0-88734-652-9*) Players Pr.

***Nurnberg, Gabriele.** Das Unterrichtsgesprach Als Textsorte und Methode: Klarung des Begriffs, Entwicklung und Erprobung eines Kommunikationstheoretisch-Didaktischen Modells zur Analyse von Unterrichtsgesprachen. (Europaische Hochschulschriften Ser.: Reihe 11). (GER.). 275p. 1999. 45.95 (*3-631-35128-3*) P Lang Pubng.

Nurnberg, H. W., ed. Electroanalytical Chemistry. LC 73-15061. (Advances in Analytical Chemistry & Instrumentation Ser.: No. 10). 621p. 1974. reprint ed. pap. 192.60 (*0-608-04785-6*, 203043000069) Bks Demand.

— Pollutants & Their Ecotoxicological Significance. LC 84-7540. (Wiley-Interscience Publications). (Illus.). 529p. reprint ed. pap. 164.00 (*0-7837-3413-1*, 204338000008) Bks Demand.

Nurnberg, H. W., ed. see West, T. S.

Nurnberg, Maxwell & Rosenblum, Morris. How to Build a Better Vocabulary. 384p. 1989. reprint ed. mass mkt. 4.50 (*0-446-31506-0*, Pub. by Warner Bks) Little.

— What to Name Your Baby: From Adam to Zoe. 2nd ed. 352p. 1984. pap. 6.95 (*0-02-081010-5*) Macmillan.

Nurnberger. Beyond Marx & Market. 1999. text 65.00 (*1-85649-647-3*, Pub. by Zed Books); text 22.50 (*1-85649-648-1*, Pub. by Zed Books) St Martin.

— Prosperity, Poverty, & Pollution: The Emergence of Global Economic Responsibility. LC 98-32145. 480p. 1999. pap. 27.50 (*1-85649-731-3*) St Martin.

Nurnberger, Fred, jt. ed. see Traber, Chris.

Nurnberger, G. Approximation by Spline Functions. (Illus.). xi, 243p. 1989. 84.95 (*0-387-51618-2*, 3491) Spr-Verlag.

Nurnberger, G., et al. Multivariate Approximation & Splines. LC 97-37814. (International Series of Numerical Mathematics). 1997. write for info. (*0-8176-5654-5*) Birkhauser.

Nurnberger, Gunter, jt. auth. see Meinardus, Gunter.

Nurnberger, John I. & Berrettini. Psychiatric Genetics. (Illus.). 256p. 1997. text 45.00 (*0-412-53580-7*, E & FN Spon) Routledge.

Nurnberger, Lisa, jt. ed. see Lethcoe, Nancy.

Nurnberger, M. W., et al. Analysis of a Log-Periodic Folded Slot Antenna Array on Planar & Cylindrical Platforms. fac. ed. LC TK6590.A6. (University of Michigan Report: No. 031169-1-T). 61p. 1994. pap. 30.00 (*0-7837-7697-7*, 204745400007) Bks Demand.

Nurnberger, Marianne. Dance Is the Language of the Gods. LC 99-938127. 250p. 1998. pap. 27.50 (*90-5383-579-2*, Pub. by VU Univ Pr) Paul & Co Pubs.

Nurnberger, Ralph D., jt. ed. see Abshire, David M.

Nurnberger, Ulf, ed. Stainless Steel in Concrete: State of the Art Report. (European Federation of Corrosion Publications Ser.: No. 18). 48p. 1996. pap. 20.00 (*1-86125-008-8*, Pub. by Inst Materials) Ashgate Pub Co.

Nurock, Max, jt. ed. see Boasson, Charles.

***Nurosi, Aki & Shulman, Mark.** Colorful Illusions: Tricks to Fool Your Eyes. 2000. 19.95 (*0-8069-2997-9*) Sterling.

***Nurre, Joseph H. & Corner, Brian R., eds.** Three-Dimensional Image Capture & Applications II. 262p. 1999. pap. text 72.00 (*0-8194-3111-7*) SPIE.

Nurre, Joseph H., jt. ed. see Ellson, Richard N.

Nurse, Shirley, ed. see Mwalimu.

***Nurse, A. Rodney.** Family Assessment: Effective Uses of Personality Tests with Couples & Families. LC 98-37415. (Series in Couples & Family Dynamics & Treatment). 324p. 1999. 65.00 (*0-471-15397-4*) Wiley.

Nurse, Charlie. Argentina Handbook. LC 97-78491. (Footprint Handbooks Ser.). 528p. 1998. 21.95 (*0-8442-4946-7*, 49467, Natl Textbk Co) NTC Contemp Pub Co.

***Nurse, Charlie.** Argentina Handbook. 2nd ed. (Footprint Handbooks Ser.). (Illus.). 2000. pap. 19.95 (*0-658-01082-4*, Passprt Bks) NTC Contemp Pub Co.

Nurse, Charlie. Chile Handbook. (Illus.). 400p. 1997. 16.95 (*0-8442-4917-3*) NTC Contemp Pub Co.

— Chile Handbook. 2nd ed. (Footprint Handbooks Ser.). 496p. 1999. pap. 19.95 (*0-8442-2127-9*, 21279) NTC Contemp Pub Co.

Nurse, Derek & Hinnebusch, Thomas J. Swahili & Sabaki: A Linguistic History. LC 93-4560. (Problems in Linguistics Ser.: Vol. 121). 1993. 95.00 (*0-520-09775-0*, Pub. by U CA Pr) Cal Prin Full Svc.

Nurse, Derek, jt. auth. see Heine, Bernd.

Nurse, Derek, jt. auth. see Spear, Thomas G.

Nurse, Derek, jt. ed. see Heine, Bernd.

Nurse, G. T. & Jenkins, T. Health & the Hunter-Gatherer. (Monographs in Human Genetics: Vol. 8). 1976. 44.50 (*3-8055-2401-3*) S Karger.

Nurse, Keith. Torments Ancient & Modern: An Anglo-Welsh Experience. 55p. 1997. pap. 8.95 (*1-85756-234-8*, Pub. by Janus Pubng) Paul & Co Pubs.

Nurse, Lawrence A. Trade Unionism & Industrial Relations in the Commonwealth Caribbean: History, Contemporary Practice & Prospect, 40. LC 91-38212. (Contributions in Legal Studies: No. 40). 168p. 1992. 47.95 (*0-313-28380-X*, NTU, Greenwood Pr) Greenwood.

Nurse, Milton, ed. Foundry Directory & Register of Forgas Europe. 16th ed. 371p. 1991. 110.00 (*0-947671-44-7*) Metal Bulletin.

Nurse, Milton C. & Serjeantson, Richard M., eds. Metallurgical Plantmakers of the World. 3rd ed. 494p. 1989. 167.00 (*0-947671-18-8*) Metal Bulletin.

Nurse, Paul & Streiblova, Eva, eds. The Microbial Cell Cycle. 304p. 1984. 164.00 (*0-8493-5574-5*, QR73, CRC Reprint) Franklin.

Nurse, Peter H., ed. see Corneille, Pierre.

Nursey-Bray, Paul, et al. Anarchist Thinkers & Thought: An Annotated Bibliography, 17. LC 91-33407. (Bibliographies & Indexes in Law & Political Science Ser.: No. 17). 304p. 1992. lib. bdg. 65.00 (*0-313-27592-0*, NBR, Greenwood Pr) Greenwood.

Nursey-Bray, Paul, jt. auth. see Ahluwalia, Pal.

Nursey-Bray, Rosemary. The Little Mermaid: Director's Script. (Illus.). 56p. 1982. pap. 15.00 (*0-88680-114-1*) I E Clark.

— The Little Mermaid: 2-Act Dramatization. (Illus.). 56p. 1982. pap. 4.00 (*0-88680-113-3*) I E Clark.

— Through the Looking Glass & What Alice Found There: Playscript. (J). (ps up). 1988. 6.50 (*0-87602-276-X*) Anchorage.

Nursi, Said. Divine Destiny & Man's Free Will. 36p. 1993. pap. 3.95 (*975-7388-02-5*) Fountain Pub.

— Epitomes of Light. 522p. 1999. pap. 11.95 (*975-7388-61-0*) Fountain Pub.

— The Letters, Vol. 1. 281p. 1993. pap. 8.95 (*0-9521497-2-9*) Fountain Pub.

— The Letters, Vol. 2. 330p. 1993. pap. 8.95 (*975-7388-44-0*) Fountain Pub.

— The Spirit & the Angels. 64p. 1993. 3.95 (*975-7388-01-7*) Fountain Pub.

— The Words, Vol. 1. 188p. 1993. pap. 5.95 (*0-9521497-3-7*) Fountain Pub.

— The Words, Vol. 1. 498p. 1998. pap. 11.95 (*975-7388-31-9*) Fountain Pub.

— The Words, Vol. 2. 442p. 1998. pap. 11.95 (*975-7388-33-5*) Fountain Pub.

Nursing Home Task Force National Hospice Organizat. Nursing Home Task Force Report. LC 99-181747. 88p. 1998. write for info. (*0-931207-56-8*) Natl Hospice.

Nursing Staff of Lucile Salter Packard Children's. Family First Aid: Owies, Boo-Boos & All Other Things That Really Happen. (Illus.). 60p. (J). 1997. spiral bd. 12.95 (*1-57054-128-0*) Klutz.

Nursten, Jean, jt. ed. see Berg, Ian.

Nuru, Saka & Ryan, J. G. Nigeria-Australia Collaborative Agricultural Research. 146p. 1985. pap. 60.00 (*0-949511-07-2*) St Mut.

Nuryanti, jt. auth. see Hitchcock.

Nus, Jeff, ed. see Burpee, L. L.

Nusairi, Osman, tr. see El-Saadawi, Nawal.

Nusbaum, Barry D., et al. The Integrated Ibm Suites for Windows Nt: A Powerful Package. LC 99-161522. 469p. 1998. write for info. (*0-7384-0004-1*) IBM Cary NC.

Nusbaum, D. D., jt. auth. see Zehren, Vincent.

Nusbaum, Ellen, jt. auth. see Fodale, Victoria.

Nusbaum, Howard C., jt. ed. see Goodman, Judith.

***Nusbaum, Robert A.** Once in a Lifetime: A World War II Memoir. (World War II Memoir Ser.: Vol. 54). (Illus.). 116p. 1999. 34.95 (*1-57638-171-4*, 54-H); pap. 24.95 (*1-57638-170-6*, 54-S) Merriam Pr.

Nusbaum, Rosemary. The City Different & the Palace: A History of a Famous Santa Fe Landmark. LC 78-17591. (Illus.). 1978. pap. 6.95 (*0-913270-79-2*) Sunstone Pr.

— Tierra Dulce: The Jesse Nusbaum Papers. LC 80-18365. (Illus.). 128p. 1980. pap. 7.95 (*0-913270-83-0*) Sunstone Pr.

Nusbaumer, Jacques A. Services in the Global Market. (C). 1987. lib. bdg. 95.50 (*0-89838-198-3*) Kluwer Academic.

Nusberg, Charlotte, et al. Innovative Aging Programs Abroad: Implications for the United States, 2. LC 83-10811. (Contributions to the Study of Aging Ser.: No. 2). (Illus.). 260p. 1984. 67.95 (*0-313-23684-4*, NPE/, Greenwood Pr) Greenwood.

Nuschke, Marie K. The Dam That Could Not Break. (Illus.). 50p. 1961. pap. 3.75 (*0-939542-05-6*) Leader Pub Co Inc.

Nuseibeh, Said. The Dome of the Rock. LC 96-13260. (Illus.). 180p. 1996. 60.00 (*0-8478-1942-6*, Pub. by Rizzoli Intl) St Martin.

Nusmann, Ernst. Take a Break - Everybody Needs One: Call to Worship. LC 96-38670. 130p. (Orig.). 1997. pap. 17.75 (*0-7880-0846-3*) CSS OH.

Nusom, Lynn. Authentic Southwestern Cooking. LC 98-52130. 1999. 7.95 (*1-877856-89-4*) SW Pks Mnmts.

— Christmas in Arizona: Recipes, Traditions & Folklore for the Holiday Season. Parker, Steve, tr. LC 92-32251. (Illus.). 128p. 1992. ring bd. 9.95 (*0-914846-65-5*) Golden West Pub.

— Christmas in New Mexico: Recipes, Traditions & Folklore for the Holiday Season. LC 91-34113. (Illus.). 144p. (Orig.). 1991. pap. 8.95 (*0-914846-59-0*) Golden West Pub.

— The Hatch Chile Cookbook: Hot & Spicy Recipes Featuring the World's Finest Chile Peppers. (Illus.). 220p. 1994. 15.95 (*1-884374-03-4*) Border Bks.

— New Mexico Cook Book. LC 90-3391. 144p. (Orig.). 1990. ring bd. 5.95 (*0-914846-48-5*) Golden West Pub.

— The Sizzling Southwestern Cookbook. LC 94-35379. 224p. 1995. 25.00 (*1-56565-210-X*) Lowell Hse.

— The Tequila Cook Book. LC 93-21428. 128p. 1993. ring bd. 7.95 (*0-914846-89-2*) Golden West Pub.

Nuss, A. M. Export for Marketing French. (ENG & FRE.). 96p. 1979. pap. 17.95 (*0-8288-5456-4*, M9208) Fr & Eur.

Nuss, Calvin E. Her Golden Door. LC 85-15333. 163p. 1991. pap. 10.00 (*0-9615278-0-3*) Am Hist Soc Ger.

— Memories Humor of a Second Generation Volga American. 1993. pap. 7.50 (*0-614-23856-0*) Am Hist Soc Ger.

Nuss, Ingo. Zur Oekologie der Porlinge, II: Die Entwicklungsmorphologie der Fruchtkoerper und Ihre Beeinflussung Durch Klimatische und Andere Faktoren. (Bibliotheca Mycologica: Vol. 105). (GER., Illus.). 456p. 1986. 106.00 (*3-443-59006-3*, Pub. by Gebruder Borntraeger) Balogh.

Nuss, Martin & Bowers, John, eds. Ultrafast Electronics & Optoelectronics. LC 97-65312. (Trends in Optics & Photonics Ser.: Vol. 13). (Illus.). 302p. 1997. pap. 55.00 (*1-55752-486-6*) Optical Soc.

Nuss, Shirley, et al. Women in the World of Work: Statistical Analysis & Projections to the Year 2000. (Women, Work & Development Ser.: No. 18). x, 132p. (Orig.). 1989. pap. 18.00 (*92-2-106507-3*) Intl Labour Office.

Nussbaum. Citizens of the World: A Classical Defense of Radical Reform in Higher Education. 1995. 22.95 (*0-02-923247-3*) S&S Trade.

— My World Is Not Flat. 1993. 12.95 (*1-55550-895-2*, Pub. by Universe) St Martin.

Nussbaum, Alan J. Head & Horn in Indo-European. (Studies in Indo-European Language & Culture NF: Vol. 2). xiii, 305p. 1986. 146.15 (*3-11-010449-0*) De Gruyter.

Nussbaum, Allen. Optical System Design. LC 97-43430. 224p. (C). 1997. 84.00 (*0-13-901042-4*) P-H.

Nussbaum, Chaim. The Essence of Teshuvah: A Path to Repentance. LC 93-1226. 208p. 1994. 30.00 (*1-56821-025-6*) Aronson.

Nussbaum, D., jt. ed. see Greer, W. R., Jr.

Nussbaum, David, jt. auth. see Young, Mary A.

Nussbaum, Debra. There's a Hearing Impaired Child in My Class: A Learning Packet about Hearing Loss for Public School Teachers. Mahshie, Shawn, ed. (Into the Mainstream Ser.). 44p. 1998. pap. text, teacher ed. 17.95 (*0-88095-204-0*) Gallaudet U Pre Coll.

Nussbaum, Elaine. Recovery from Cancer: A Personal Story of Sickness & Health. LC 92-3385. 192p. (Orig.). 1992. pap. 9.95 (*0-89529-504-0*, Avery) Penguin Putnam.

Nussbaum, Eric, jt. auth. see Cologni, Franco.

Nussbaum, Felicity & Brown, Laura, eds. The New 18th Century: Theory, Politics, English Literature. 325p. 1987. 35.00 (*0-416-01631-6*, 1191); pap. 13.95 (*0-416-01641-3*, 1196) Routledge.

Nussbaum, Felicity, jt. ed. see Deutsch, Helen.

Nussbaum, Felicity A. The Autobiographical Subject: Gender & Ideology in Eighteenth-Century England. LC 89-32587. 288p. 1989. text 48.00 (*0-8018-3825-8*) Johns Hopkins.

— The Autobiographical Subject: Gender & Ideology in Eighteenth-Century England. 288p. 1995. reprint ed. pap. text 16.95 (*0-8018-5237-4*) Johns Hopkins.

— Torrid Zones: Maternity, Sexuality & Empire in Eighteenth Century English Narratives. LC 95-11801. (Parallax). (Illus.). 248p. 1995. text 48.00 (*0-8018-5074-6*); pap. text 16.95 (*0-8018-5075-4*) Johns Hopkins.

Nussbaum, Felicity A., intro. Satires on Women. LC 92-24348. (Augustan Reprints Ser.: No. 180). 1976. reprint ed. 14.50 (*0-404-70180-9*, PR1195) AMS Pr.

Nussbaum, Frederick L. Commercial Policy in the French Revolution: A Study of the Career of G. J. A. Ducher. LC 79-111782. reprint ed. 57.50 (*0-404-04807-2*) AMS Pr.

— A History of the Economic Institutions of Modern Europe: An Introduction to "Der Moderne Kapitalismus" of Werner Sombart. LC 67-29494. (Reprints of Economic Classics Ser.). (Illus.). xvi, 448p. 1968. reprint ed. 49.50 (*0-678-00348-3*) Kelley.

Nussbaum, G. Homer's Metre. 44p. 1986. pap. 12.95 (*0-86292-172-4*, Pub. by Brist Class Pr) Focus Pub-R Pullins.

— Virgil's Metre. 104p. 1986. pap. text 12.95 (*0-86292-173-2*, Pub. by Brist Class Pr) Focus Pub-R Pullins.

Nussbaum, Gilbert H., ed. Physical Aspects of Hyperthermia: Proceedings of the AAPM Summer School Held at Dartmouth College, Hanover, New Hampshire, August 3-7, 1981. (American Association of Physicists in Medicine Symposium Ser.: No. 8). 650p. 1982. 50.00 (*0-88318-414-1*, Pub. by Am Inst Physics) Med Physics Pub.

Nussbaum, Harriet, jt. auth. see Gilletz, Norene.

Nussbaum, Jack. Punch Line Rhyme. LC 92-96976. (Illus.). 102p. 1992. 13.50 (*0-9636110-0-3*); pap. 9.50 (*0-9636110-1-1*) Nut Tree Ent.

***Nussbaum, Jon F.** Communication & Aging. 2nd ed. LC 99-45143. 2000. pap. write for info. (*0-8058-3332-3*) L Erlbaum Assocs.

Nussbaum, Jon F. & Coupland, Justine, eds. Handbook of Communication & Aging Research. (Communication Ser.). 536p. 1995. text 89.95 (*0-8058-1453-1*) L Erlbaum Assocs.

Nussbaum, Jon F., jt. auth. see Coupland, Nikolas.

Nussbaum, Jon F., jt. auth. see Williams, Angela.

Nussbaum, Jon F., jt. ed. see Hummert, Mary L.

Nussbaum, Kathy. Preparing the Children: Information & Ideas for Families Facing Terminal Illness & Death. (Illus.). iv, 65p. 1998. pap. 8.95 (*0-9665496-0-0*) Gifts Hope Trst.

***Nussbaum, Martha.** Plato's Republic: The Good Society & the Deformation of Desire. LC 97-4414. (Bradley Lecture Ser.). 30p. 1998. pap. 5.00 (*0-8444-0951-0*) Lib Congress.

Nussbaum, Martha & Glover, Jonathon, eds. Women, Culture, & Development: A Study of Human Capabilities. (WIDER Studies in Development Economics). (Illus.). 492p. 1996. text 95.00 (*0-19-828917-0*); pap. text 22.00 (*0-19-828964-2*) OUP.

Nussbaum, Martha, jt. auth. see Plato.

Nussbaum, Martha C. Cultivating Humanity: A Classical Defense of Reform in Liberal Education. LC 96-53190. 352p. 1997. 26.00 (*0-674-17948-X*) HUP.

— Cultivating Humanity: A Classical Defense of Reform in Liberal Education. 352p. 1998. pap. 15.95 (*0-674-17949-8*) HUP.

— The Fragility of Goodness: Luck & Ethics in Greek Tragedy & Philosophy. 576p. 1986. pap. text 34.95 (*0-521-27702-7*) Cambridge U Pr.

***Nussbaum, Martha C.** The Fragility of Goodness: Luck & Ethics in Greek Tragedy & Philosophy. 544p. (C). 2001. pap. text Price not set. (*0-521-79472-2*) Cambridge U Pr.

— The Fragility of Goodness: Luck & Ethics in Greek Tragedy & Philosophy. rev. ed. 544p. (C). 2001. text 90.00 (*0-521-79126-X*) Cambridge U Pr.

Nussbaum, Martha C. Love's Knowledge: Essays on Philosophy & Literature. 432p. 1992. pap. text 22.00 (*0-19-507485-8*) OUP.

— Poetic Justice: The Literary Imagination & Public Life. 128p. 1997. pap. 14.00 (*0-8070-4109-2*) Beacon Pr.

— Sex & Social Justice. LC 97-50576. 488p. 1999. 35.00 (*0-19-511032-3*) OUP.

— The Therapy of Desire: Theory & Practice in Hellenistic Ethics. LC 93-6417. 464p. 1994. text 49.50 (*0-691-03342-0*, Pub. by Princeton U Pr) Cal Prin Full Svc.

— The Therapy of Desire: Theory & Practice in Hellenistic Ethics. 572p. (C). 1994. pap. text 17.95 (*0-691-00052-2*, Pub. by Princeton U Pr) Cal Prin Full Svc.

***Nussbaum, Martha C.** Women & Human Development: The Capabilities Approach. (Seeley Lectures). 328p. 2000. 24.95 (*0-521-66086-6*) Cambridge U Pr.

Nussbaum, Martha C. & Rorty, Amelie O., eds. Essays on Aristotle's De Anima. 462p. 1995. reprint ed. pap. text 26.00 (*0-19-823600-X*) OUP.

Nussbaum, Martha C. & Sen, Amartya K., eds. The Quality of Life. (WIDER Studies in Development Economics). (Illus.). 480p. 1993. pap. text 29.95 (*0-19-828797-6*) OUP.

Nussbaum, Martha C. & Sunstein, Cass, eds. Clones & Clones: Facts & Fantasies about Human Cloning. LC 97-51781. 288p. 1998. 26.95 (*0-393-04648-6*) Norton.

Nussbaum, Martha C. & Sunstein, Cass R. Clones & Clones: Facts & Fantasies about Human Cloning. 352p. 1999. pap. 14.95 (*0-393-32001-4*, Norton Paperbks) Norton.

Nussbaum, Martha C., et al. For Love of Country: Debating the Limits of Patriotism. Cohen, Joshua, ed. 208p. (Orig.). 1996. pap. 15.00 (*0-8070-4313-3*) Beacon Pr.

Nussbaum, Martha C., jt. ed. see Estlund, David M.

Nussbaum, Martha C., jt. ed. see Olyan, Saul M.

Nussbaum, Melissa M. Bible Stories for the Forty Days. LC 97-70097. (Illus.). 96p. (Orig.). (J). (ps-6). 1997. pap. 15.00 (*1-56854-179-1*, ARKBK) Liturgy Tr Pubns.

— I Will Arise This Day. LC 96-20695. (Illus.). 154p. (Orig.). 1996. pap. 10.00 (*1-56854-135-X*, ARISE) Liturgy Tr Pubns.

— I Will Lie down This Night. LC 95-11973. (Illus.). 152p. 1995. pap. 10.00 (*1-56854-085-X*, NPRAY) Liturgy Tr Pubns.

Nussbaum, Nancy & Bigler, Erin D. Identification & Treatment of Attention Deficit Disorder. Coleman, Maggie, ed. (Child Guidance Mental Health Ser.). 69p. 1990. pap. text 9.00 (*0-89079-263-1*, 1506) PRO-ED.

***Nussbaum, Norbert.** German Gothic Church Architecture. LC 99-87079. (Illus.). 240p. 2000. 60.00 (*0-300-08321-1*) Yale U Pr.

Nussbaum, P. D., ed. Handbook of Neuropsychology & Aging. LC 97-12001. (Critical Issues in Neuropsychology Ser.). (Illus.). 580p. (C). 1997. 85.00 (*0-306-45460-2*, Plenum Trade) Perseus Pubng.

Nussbaum, Paul D., jt. ed. see Snyder, Peter J.

Nussbaum, R. Hilbert's Projective Metric & Iterated Nonlinear Maps. LC 88-16693. (Memoirs Ser.: No. 75/391). 137p. 1988. pap. 22.00 (*0-8218-2454-6*, MEMO/75/391) Am Math.

— Iterated Nonlinear Maps & Hilbert's Projective Metric. LC 89-6590. (Memoirs Ser.: No. 79/401). 118p. 1989. pap. 20.00 (*0-8218-2465-1*, MEMO/79/401) Am Math.

Nussbaum, Roger & Peitgen, Heinz-Otto. Special & Spurious Solutions of X(T) Equals -aF(X(T-1)), Vol. 310. LC 84-14568. (Memoirs of the American Mathematical Society Ser.: No. 51/310). 129p. 1984. pap. 21.00 (*0-8218-2311-6*, MEMO/51/310) Am Math.

Nussbaum, Roger D. Differential-Delay Equations with Two Time Lags. LC 78-16320. (Memoirs of the American Mathematical Society Ser.: No. 205). 77p. 1978. reprint ed. pap. 30.00 (*0-7837-2035-1*, 204230200003) Bks Demand.

***Nussbaum, Roger D.** Generalizations of the Perron-Frobenius Theorem for Nonlinear Maps. LC 98-53118. 1999. write for info. (*0-8218-0969-5*) Am Math.

Nussbaum, Ronald A., et al. Amphibians & Reptiles of the Pacific Northwest. LC 82-60202. (Northwest Naturalist Ser.). (Illus.). 332p. 1983. pap. 24.95 (*0-89301-086-3*) U of Idaho Pr.

Nussbaum Soumerai, Eve & Schulz, Carol D. Daily Life During the Holocaust. LC 98-5272. (Daily Life Through History Ser.). 344p. 1998. 45.00 (*0-313-30202-2*) Greenwood.

Nussbaumer, H. Fast Fourier Transform & Convolution Algorithms. 2nd ed. (Information Sciences Ser.). (Illus.). 280p. 1990. 53.95 (*0-387-11825-X*) Spr-Verlag.

Nussbaumer, Henri. Computer Communication Systems, Vol. 2, Principles, Design, Protocols, 2 vols., Vol. 2, Principles, Design, Protocols. LC 89-24871. 268p. 1990. 300.00 (*0-471-92495-4*) Wiley.

Nussbaumer, Henri. Computer Communications Systems: Data Circuits, Error Detection, Data Links, 2 vols., Vol. 1, Data Circuits, Error Detection, Data Links. LC 89-24871. 282p. 1990. 300.00 (*0-471-92379-6*) Wiley.

Nussberger, J., ed. see Von Mutius, A.

Nussbaum, J. F., ed. Life-Span Communication: Normative Processes. (Communication Textbook Ser.). 392p. 1989. 79.95 (*0-8058-0195-2*) L Erlbaum Assocs.

Nussdorfer, Laurie. Civic Politics in the Rome of Urban VIII. (Illus.). 296p. 1992. text 52.50 (*0-691-03182-7*, Pub. by Princeton U Pr) Cal Prin Full Svc.

***Nusse, Andrea.** Palestine for the Muslims: The Ideology of Hamas. 204p. 1998. text 42.00 (*90-5702-333-4*, Harwood Acad Pubs); pap. text 22.00 (*90-5702-334-2*, Harwood Acad Pubs) Gordon & Breach.

Nusse, Helen E. Dynamics: Numerical Explorations. (Illus.). 484p. 1994. 60.95 (*0-387-94334-X*) Spr-Verlag.

Nusse, Helena E. & Yorke, James A. Dynamics: Numerical Explorations, Vol. 101. 2nd ed. LC 97-26972. (Applied Mathematical Sciences Ser.). 484p. 1997. 59.95 (*0-387-98264-7*) Spr-Verlag.

Nusseibeh, Sari. Jerusalem. (Occasional Papers). iv, 13p. 1995. pap. 2.95 (*1-929218-09-5*, 1) Georgetwn U Ctr Muslim.

Nusseibeh, Sari, jt. auth. see Moshe, Ma'oz.

Nussel, Edward, jt. auth. see Kretovics, Joseph.

Nussel, F. E., jt. ed. see Leparsky, E.

Nussenblatt, R. B., et al. Uveitis Scoring System. 20p. 1991. 20.00 (*0-387-54957-9*) Spr-Verlag.

Nussenblatt, Robert B., et al, eds. Advances in Ocular Immunology & Immunopathology of the Eye: Proceedings of the Sixth International Symposium on the Immunology & Immunopathology of the Eye, Bethesda, U. S. A. LC 94-35302. (International Congress Ser.). 496p. 1995. 240.25 (*0-444-81742-5*) Elsevier.

Nussenblatt, Robert B., et al. Uveitis: Fundamentals & Clinical Practice. 2nd ed. (Illus.). 432p. (C). (gr. 13). 1995. text 118.00 (*0-8151-6446-7*, 23708) Mosby Inc.

Nussenblatt, Robert B., jt. auth. see Tabbara, Khalid F.

Nussenzveig, H. M. Diffraction Effects in Semiclassical Light Scattering. (Montroll Memorial Lecture Series in Mathematical Physics). (Illus.). 252p. (C). 1992. text 74.95 (*0-521-38318-8*) Cambridge U Pr.

— Introduction to Quantum Optics. LC 72-80356. (Documents on Modern Physics Ser.). xiv, 264p. 1973. pap. text 332.00 (*0-677-03900-X*) Gordon & Breach.

Nusser, Alden. French Fries up Your Nose: 208 Ways to Annoy People. LC 95-6192. 96p. (Orig.). (J). (gr. 3-7). 1995. pap. 3.50 (*0-380-77913-7*, Avon Bks) Morrow Avon.

Nusser, Richard. Walking after Midnight. 432p. 1990. mass mkt. 3.95 (*0-380-70939-2*, Avon Bks) Morrow Avon.

Nussey, Dora, tr. see Male, Emile.

Nussey, Kent. In Christ There Is No East or West. 208p. 1993. pap. 11.95 (*1-55082-046-X*, Pub. by Quarry Pr) LPC InBook.

— The War in Heaven. LC 97-160340. 192p. 1997. pap. 13.99 (*1-895837-42-1*) Insomniac.

***Nussle, Jim, ed.** Budgetary Treatment of Emergencies: Congressional Hearing. (Illus.). 162p. (C). 1999. reprint ed. pap. text 35.00 (*0-7881-8443-1*) DIANE Pub.

***Nusslein-Vollhard, C. & Kratzschmar, J., eds.** Of Fish, Fly, Worm & Man: Lessons from Developmental Biology for Human Gene Function & Disease. LC 99-56995. (Ernst Schering Research Foundation Workshop Ser.: Vol. 29). (Illus.). 260p. 2000. 76.95 (*3-540-66324-X*) Spr-Verlag.

N

Nustad, Harry L. & Wesner, Terry H. Elementary Algebra with Applications. 4th ed. 567p. (C). 1995. text. write for info. (*0-697-23323-5*, WCB McGr Hill) McGraw-H Hghr Educ.

— Essentials of Technical Mathematics. 800p. (C). 1983. text 48.75 (*0-697-08551-1*, WCB McGr Hill); text, student ed. 25.00 (*0-697-08552-X*, WCB McGr Hill) McGraw-H Hghr Educ.

— Intermediate Algebra with Applications. 4th ed. 672p. (C). 1995. text. write for info. (*0-697-23324-3*, WCB McGr Hill) McGrw-H Hghr Educ.

— Principles of Elementary Algebra with Applications. 2nd ed. 640p. (C). 1991. text 50.00 (*0-697-01351-0*, WCB McGr Hill); text, student ed. 18.75 (*0-697-11083-4*, WCB McGr Hill) McGrw-H Hghr Educ.

— Principles of Intermediate Algebra with Applications. 2nd ed. 736p. (C). 1991. text 51.25 (*0-697-01338-3*, WCB McGr Hill) McGrw-H Hghr Educ.

Nustad, Harry L., et al. Principles of Intermediate Algebra with Applications. 2nd ed. 304p. (C). 1991. text, student ed. 18.75 (*0-697-11084-2*, WCB McGr Hill) McGrw-H Hghr Educ.

Nustad, Harry L., jt. auth. see Wesner, Terry H.

Nusum, Lynn. Billy the Kid Cook Book. 112p. 1998. ring bd. 7.95 (*1-885590-32-6*) Golden West Pub.

Nutall, Deirdre, jt. ed. see Muirithe, Diarmuid O.

***Nutbeam, Don & Harris, Elizabeth.** Theory in a Nutshell: A Guide to Health Promotion Theory. (Illus.). 80p. 1999. Price not set. (*0-07-470821-X*) McGraw.

Nutbourne, Anthony W. & Martin, Ralph R. Differential Geometry Applied to Curve & Surface Design Vol. 1: Foundations. LC 87-32765. 330p. 1988. text 120.00 (*0-470-21036-2*) P-H.

Nutbrown, Cathy, ed. Respectful Educators - Capable Learners: Young Children's Rights & Early Education. 176p. 1996. pap. 24.95 (*1-85396-304-6*, Pub. by P Chapman) Taylor & Francis.

Nute, Carol L. Common Sense to Retailing. (Illus.). 90p. 1995. pap. 9.95 (*0-9645328-0-8*) Retail Pr.

Nute, Donald. Topics in Conditional Logic. (Philosophical Studies in Philosophy: No. 20). 168p. 1980. text 99.50 (*90-277-1049-X*, D Reidel) Kluwer Academic.

Nute, Donald, jt. auth. see Covington, Michael A.

Nute, Grace L. Caesars of the Wilderness: Medard Chouart, Sieur des Groseilliers & Pierre Esprit Radisson, 1618-1710. LC 78-811. (Publications of the Minnesota Historical Society). 428p. reprint ed. pap. 132.70 (*0-8357-3319-X*, 203954300013) Bks Demand.

— Lake Superior. (American Lakes Ser.). lib. bdg. 26.95 (*0-8488-2009-6*) Amereon Ltd.

— Rainy River Country: A Brief History of the Region Bordering Minnesota & Ontario. LC 71-96385. (Publications of the Minnesota Historical Society). 193p. reprint ed. pap. 59.90 (*0-8357-3314-9*, 203953800013) Bks Demand.

— The Voyageur. LC 55-12180. xi, 289p. 1987. reprint ed. pap. 8.95 (*0-87351-213-8*) Minn Hist.

— The Voyageur's Highway: Minnesota's Border Lake Land. LC 65-63529. (Illus.). xv, 113p. 1941. pap. 7.95 (*0-87351-006-2*) Minn Hist.

Nute, Grace Lee. Caesars of the Wilderness: Medard Chouart, Sieur des Groesilliers & Pierre Espirt Radisson, 1618-1710. Wilkins, Mira, ed. LC 76-29750. (European Business Ser.). (Illus.). 1977. reprint ed. lib. bdg. 35.95 (*0-405-09766-2*) Ayer.

***Nute, Grace Lee.** Lake Superior. LC 00-20940. (Fesler-Lampert Minnesota Heritage Bks.). (Illus.). 408p. 2000. pap. 15.95 (*0-8166-3581-1*) U of Minn Pr.

Nute, Kevin. Frank Lloyd Wright & Japan. (Illus.). 244p. 1994. text 66.95 (*0-442-30908-2*, VNR) Wiley.

— Frank Lloyd Wright & Japan: The Role of Traditional Japanese Art & Architecture in the Work of Frank Lloyd Wright. (Architecture Ser.). 244p. 1993. 66.95 (*0-471-28966-3*, VNR) Wiley.

Nuthmann, J. Hobs with Carbide Inserts for Machining of Large Gears. (1984 Fall Technical Meeting Ser.: Vol. 84FTM7). 20p. 1984. pap. text 30.00 (*1-55589-089-X*) AGMA.

Nuti, D. M. V. K. Dmitriev. (Modern Revivals in Economics Ser.). 231p. 1992. 61.95 (*0-7512-0095-6*, Pub. by Gregg Pub) Ashgate Pub Co.

Nuti, Marco. Emissions from Two-Stroke Engines. LC 98-22186. 284p. 1998. 69.00 (*0-7680-0215-X*, R-223) Soc Auto Engineers.

Nutini, Hugo G. Essays on Mexican Kinship. Carrasco, Pedro & Taggart, James M., eds. LC 75-9124. (Pitt Latin American Ser.). 268p. pap. 83.10 (*0-608-12652-7*, 202544200043) Bks Demand.

— San Bernardino Contla: Marriage & Family Structure in a Tlaxcalan Municipio. LC 68-21632. 436p. 1968. reprint ed. pap. 135.20 (*0-608-03994-2*, 206473000011) Bks Demand.

— Todos Santos in Rural Tlaxcala: A Syncretic, Expressive, & Symbolic Analysis of the Cult of the Dead. LC 87-15173. (SPA.). 492p. 1988. reprint ed. pap. 152.60 (*0-7837-9404-5*, 206014900004) Bks Demand.

— The Wages of Conquest: The Mexican Aristocracy in the Context of Western Aristocracies. 464p. 1995. text 69.50 (*0-472-10484-5*, 10484) U of Mich Pr.

Nutini, Hugo G. & Bell, Betty. Ritual Kinship Vol. 2: Ideological & Structural Integration of the Compadrazgo System in Rural Tlaxcala. LC 79-3225. 520p. 1980. reprint ed. pap. 161.20 (*0-7837-9296-4*, 206003500002) Bks Demand.

Nutini, Hugo G. & Roberts, John M. Bloodsucking Witchcraft: An Epistemological Study of Anthropomorphic Supernaturalism in Rural Tlaxcala. LC 92-34513. 475p. 1993. 44.95 (*0-8165-1197-7*) U of Ariz Pr.

Nutkins, Terry & Corwin, Marshall. Pets. (Illus.). 48p. (J). (gr. 7-9). 1992. pap. 8.95 (*0-563-34524-1*, BBC-Parkwest) Parkwest Pubns.

Nutku, Yavuz, et al. Conformal Field Theory: New Non-Perturbative Methods in String & Field Theory. 352p. 2000. text 65.00 (*0-7382-0204-5*, Pub. by Perseus Pubng) HarpC.

Nutley, Joyce. Advanced Service Techniques. 192p. 1993. pap. 54.95 (*0-470-23354-0*) Wiley.

Nutley, Stephen D. Unconventional & Community Transport in the U. K., Vol. 14. (Transportation Studies). xvi, 430p. 1990. text 176.00 (*2-88124-764-4*) Gordon & Breach.

Nutman, P. S., ed. Symbiotic Nitrogen Fixation in Plants. LC 75-2732. (International Biological Programme Ser.: No. 7). (Illus.). 612p. 1976. text 155.00 (*0-521-20645-6*) Cambridge U Pr.

Nutman, Thomas B., ed. Lymphatic Filariasis. 250p. 1998. pap. text 16.00 (*1-86094-059-5*) World Scientific Pub.

Nutrinfo Corporation Staff. What's in It? The Busy Cook's Diet & Nutrition Guide to...Chef Paul Prudhomme's Louisiana Kitchen. LC 91-62643. (Orig.). 1991. pap. text 4.95 (*1-56503-012-5*) Nutrinfo.

— What's in It? The Busy Cook's Diet & Nutrition Guide to...Crockery Cookery. LC 91-62644. (Orig.). 1991. pap. text 4.95 (*1-56503-013-3*) Nutrinfo.

— What's in It? The Busy Cook's Diet & Nutrition Guide to...the Classic Italian Cookbook. LC 91-62635. (Orig.). 1991. pap. text 4.95 (*1-56503-004-4*) Nutrinfo.

— What's in It? The Busy Cook's Diet & Nutrition Guide to...the Cooks with Wine. LC 91-62634. (Orig.). 1991. pap. text 4.95 (*1-56503-003-6*) Nutrinfo.

— What's in It? The Busy Cook's Diet & Nutrition Guide to...the Enchanted Broccoli Forest Cookbook. LC 91-62640. (Orig.). 1991. pap. text 4.95 (*1-56503-009-5*) Nutrinfo.

— What's in It? The Busy Cook's Diet & Nutrition Guide to...the Fannie Farmer Cookbook. LC 91-62632. (Orig.). 1991. pap. text 4.95 (*1-56503-001-X*) Nutrinfo.

— What's in It? The Busy Cook's Diet & Nutrition Guide to...the Frugal Gourmet. LC 91-62631. (Orig.). 1991. pap. text 4.95 (*1-56503-000-1*) Nutrinfo.

— What's in It? The Busy Cook's Diet & Nutrition Guide to...the Microwave Gourmet Cookbook. LC 91-62642. (Orig.). 1991. pap. text 4.95 (*1-56503-011-7*) Nutrinfo.

— What's in It? The Busy Cook's Diet & Nutrition Guide to...the Moosewood Cookbook. LC 91-62636. (Orig.). 1991. pap. text 4.95 (*1-56503-005-2*) Nutrinfo.

— What's in It? The Busy Cook's Diet & Nutrition Guide to...the New Basics Cookbook. LC 91-62633. (Orig.). 1991. pap. text 4.95 (*1-56503-002-8*) Nutrinfo.

— What's in It? The Busy Cook's Diet & Nutrition Guide to...the New York Times Cookbook. LC 91-62638. (Orig.). 1991. pap. text 4.95 (*1-56503-007-9*) Nutrinfo.

— What's in It? The Busy Cook's Diet & Nutrition Guide to...the New York Times 60 Minute Gourmet Cookbook. LC 91-62637. (Orig.). 1991. pap. text 4.95 (*1-56503-006-0*) Nutrinfo.

— What's in It? The Busy Cook's Diet & Nutrition Guide to...the Silver Palate Cookbook. LC 91-62639. (Orig.). 1991. pap. text 4.95 (*1-56503-008-7*) Nutrinfo.

— What's in It? The Busy Cook's Diet & Nutrition Guide to...the Silver Palate Goodtimes Cookbook. LC 91-62641. (Orig.). 1991. pap. text 4.95 (*1-56503-010-9*) Nutrinfo.

— What's in It? The Busy Cook's Diet & Nutrition Guide to...the Way to Cook Cookbook. LC 91-62804. (Orig.). 1991. pap. text 4.95 (*1-56503-014-1*) Nutrinfo.

Nutrition Conference for Feed Manufacturers Staff, et al. Recent Advances in Animal Nutrition, 1977: Proceedings of the Nutrition Conference for Feed Manufacturers, 11th, University of Nottingham, 1977. LC 77-30256. (Studies in the Agricultural & Food Sciences). 214p. reprint ed. pap. 66.40 (*0-608-14832-6*, 202573800046) Bks Demand.

Nutrition Education Center Staff, ed. see Gerwick, Clara L.

Nutrition Foundation Staff, jt. auth. see Journal of Nutrition Staff.

Nutt, A. The Fairy Mythology of Shakespeare. LC 68-24913. (Studies in Shakespeare: No. 24). 1969. reprint ed. lib. bdg. 75.00 (*0-8383-0929-1*) M S G Haskell Hse.

Nutt, Alex. Mountain Biking Georgia. LC 98-40717. (Illus.). 256p. 1998. pap. 12.95 (*1-56044-647-1*) Falcon Pub Inc.

Nutt, Alfred T. Cuchulainn, the Irish Achilles. LC 70-139171. (Popular Studies in Mythology, Romance & Folklore: No. 8). reprint ed. 27.50 (*0-404-53508-9*) AMS Pr.

— The Fairy Mythology of Shakespeare. LC 71-139169. (Popular Studies in Mythology, Romance & Folklore: No. 6). reprint ed. 27.50 (*0-404-53506-2*) AMS Pr.

— The Fairy Mythology of Shakespeare. (BCL1-PR English Literature Ser.). 40p. 1992. reprint ed. lib. bdg. 59.00 (*0-7812-7305-6*) Rprt Serv.

— Influence of Celtic Upon Medieval Romance. LC 73-139164. (Popular Studies in Mythology, Romance & Folklore: No. 1). reprint ed. 27.50 (*0-404-53501-1*) AMS Pr.

— Legends of the Holy Grail. LC 78-139176. (Popular Studies in Mythology, Romance & Folklore: No. 14). reprint ed. 12.50 (*0-404-53514-3*) AMS Pr.

— Ossian & Ossianic Literature. LC 70-139166. (Popular Studies in Mythology, Romance & Folklore: No. 3). reprint ed. 27.50 (*0-404-53503-8*) AMS Pr.

Nutt, Alfred T., ed. see MacInnes, Duncan.

Nutt, Barbara. Country Applique. LC 98-145486. (Illus.). 80p. 1998. 14.95 (*1-86351-212-8*, Pub. by Sally Milner) Sterling.

Nutt, C. Descendants of George Puffer of Braintree, Mass, 1639-1915. (Illus.). 376p. 1993. reprint ed. pap. 48.50 (*0-8328-3050-X*); reprint ed. lib. bdg. 58.50 (*0-8328-3049-6*) Higginson Bk Co.

Nutt, Chas., jt. auth. see Roe, Alfred S.

Nutt, David J., jt. auth. see Briley, M.

Nutt, Frances D., ed. An Arizona Alibi: The Desert Humor of Dick Wick Hall Sr. LC 90-91497. 569p. 1990. 29.50 (*0-910973-01-6*) Arrowhead AZ.

***Nutt, Gary.** Kernel Projects for Linux. 240p. 2000. pap. 30.00 (*0-201-61243-7*) Pearson Educ.

Nutt, Gary. Operating System Projects for Windows NT. LC 98-46037. 256p. (C). 1998. pap. text 38.00 (*0-201-47708-4*) Addison-Wesley.

— Operating System Projects for Windows NT. 250p. (C). 1999. pap. text. write for info. incl. cd-rom (*0-201-47707-6*) Addison-Wesley.

***Nutt, Gary.** Operating Systems: A Modern Perspective. 2nd ed. 611p. (C). 1999. 69.00 (*0-201-61251-8*) Addison-Wesley.

Nutt, Jimm, jt. contrib. by see Yood, James.

Nutt, Joe. John Donne: The Poems. LC 99-20922. (Analysing Texts Ser.). 1999. pap. 19.95 (*0-312-22523-7*) St Martin.

***Nutt, Joe.** John Donne: The Poems. LC 99-20922. 224p. 1999. text 55.00 (*0-312-22522-9*) St Martin.

Nutt, Joe. Kernels: Haiku & Senryu, 1968-1989. (Illus.). 100p. (Orig.). 1989. pap. 11.00 (*0-9623063-0-4*) Nutt Studio.

Nutt, John W. Fragments of a Samaritan Targum. viii, 256p. 1979. reprint ed. 37.70 (*3-487-06927-X*) G Olms Pubs.

***Nutt-Kofoth, Rudiger.** Letzte Gaben von Annette von Droste-Hulshoff 1860: Zum Editionsphilologischen Umgang Mit einer Fruhen Nachla & Beta; Edition eine Exemplarische Untersuchung Mit Dem Faksimiledruck der Letzten Gaben Als Beigabe. (Arbeiten Zur Editionswissenschaft Ser.). 910p. 1999. 120.95 (*3-906763-46-3*) P Lang.

Nutt, Michael, jt. auth. see Rostron, Jack.

Nutt, Paul C. Making Tough Decisions: Tactics for Improving Managerial Decision Making. LC 88-46079. (Management-Leadership & Management Development Ser.). 648p. 1989. text 48.95 (*1-55542-138-5*) Jossey-Bass.

— Managing Planned Change. (Illus.). 576p. (C). 1991. teacher ed. write for info. (*0-318-69331-3*) Macmillan.

Nutt, Paul C. & Backoff, Robert W. Strategic Management of Public & Third Sector Organizations: A Handbook for Leaders. LC 91-16608. (Public Administration Ser.). 510p. 1992. 41.95 (*1-55542-386-8*) Jossey-Bass.

Nutt-Powell, Thomas E. Manufactured Homes: Making Sense of a Housing Opportunity. LC 81-14846. 219p. 1982. 62.95 (*0-86569-086-3*, Auburn Hse) Greenwood.

Nutt, Rick L. Toward Peacemaking: Presbyterians in the South & National Security, 1945-1983. LC 94-4828. 192p. 1994. pap. text 19.95 (*0-8173-0759-1*) U of Ala Pr.

— The Whole Gospel for the Whole World: Sherwood Eddy & American Protestant Mission. LC 97-46349. (C). 1997. text 39.95 (*0-86554-566-9*, MUP/H424) Mercer Univ Pr.

Nutt, Sharon. Now Faith: If It Be Thy Will. 32p. 1999. pap. 4.95 (*0-9640801-2-5*, 8012-5) Jireh Pubns.

Nutt, Tim & Bale, Chris. Hong Kong: A Moment in Time. LC 97-222347. (C). 1997. 50.00 (*962-201-772-X*, Pub. by Chinese Univ) U of Mich Pr.

Nutt, Willie G. Embracing the Vision: How to Receive from God. (Illus.). 268p. (Orig.). 2000. pap. 13.50 (*0-9640801-1-7*, 8011-7) Jireh Pubns.

— The Warrior: Being More Than a Conqueror. 1999. pap., student ed., wbk. ed. 8.95 (*0-9640801-5-X*, 8015-0) Jireh Pubns.

— The Warrior: Being More Than a Conqueror. 1999. pap. 18.95 (*0-9640801-4-1*, 8014-1) Jireh Pubns.

— The Warrior: Being More Than a Conqueror, Answers Booklet. 1999. pap. 4.95 (*0-9640801-6-8*, 8016-8) Jireh Pubns.

Nutta, Joyce, jt. auth. see Feyten, Carine M.

Nuttal, Mark. Arctic Homeland: Kinship, Community, & Development in Northwest Greenland. (Anthropological Horizons Ser.: No. 2). (Illus.). 256p. 1992. text 50.00 (*0-8020-2886-1*); pap. text 19.95 (*0-8020-7391-3*) U of Toronto Pr.

Nuttall, A. D. The Alternative Trinity: Gnostic Heresy in Marlowe, Milton, & Blake. (Illus.). 296p. 1998. text 75.00 (*0-19-818462-X*) OUP.

— A New Mimesis: Shakespeare & the Representation of Reality. 232p. (C). 1985. pap. 12.95 (*0-416-35870-5*, 3947) Routledge.

— Openings: Narrative Beginnings from the Epic to the Novel. 266p. 1992. text 65.00 (*0-19-811741-8*) OUP.

— Pope's Essay on Man. LC 83-22298. (Unwin Critical Library). 250p. (C). 1984. text 55.00 (*0-04-800017-5*) Routledge.

— Timon of Athens. (Critical Introductions to Shakespeare Ser.). 150p. 1989. pap. 17.00 (*0-8057-8715-1*) Macmillan.

— Why Does Tragedy Give Pleasure? LC 95-40530. 120p. 1996. text 39.95 (*0-19-818371-2*, Clarendon Pr) OUP.

***Nuttall, Anthony.** It Adds Up to Trouble. large type ed. 272p. 1999. pap. 20.99 (*1-85389-906-2*) Ulverscroft.

Nuttall, Brian. Algarve, Travel & Property Guide. (Illus.). 192p. (Orig.). 1990. pap. 19.95 (*1-85365-177-X*, Pub. by McCarta) Seven Hills Bk.

Nuttall, C. GNVQ Advanced Financial Planning & Monitoring. 200p. 1995. pap. 59.95 (*1-85805-114-2*, Pub. by DP Publns) St Mut.

Nuttall, Christine. Teaching Reading Skills in a Foreign Language. 282p. 1996. pap. text 29.50 (*0-435-24057-9*) Heinemann.

Nuttall, David. Good Lawyer Bad Lawyer. 253p. 1993. pap. 19.95 (*0-88839-315-6*) Hancock House.

— Mooching Sub: The Salmon Fisherman's Bible. (Illus.). 180p. 1980. pap. 16.95 (*0-88839-097-1*) Hancock House.

Nuttall, Desmond L., jt. ed. see Riley, Katheryn A.

Nuttall, Ena V., et al, eds. Assessing & Screening Preschoolers: Psychological & Educational Dimensions. 2nd ed. LC 98-25701. 466p. (C). 1998. 75.00 (*0-205-26676-2*, Longwood Div) Allyn.

Nuttall, Floyd H. Memoirs in a Country Churchyard: A Tobacconman's Plea: Clean up Tobacco Row. LC 96-34852. 288p. 1996. 24.95 (*1-55618-159-0*) Brunswick Pub.

— The Rebel Redhead: Misfit on Madison Avenue. LC 98-38936. 450p. 1999. 24.95 (*1-55618-175-2*) Brunswick Pub.

Nuttall, Geoffrey. Christian Pacifism in History. 1971. pap. 1.25 (*0-912018-13-5*) World Without War.

Nuttall, Geoffrey F. The Holy Spirit in Puritan Faith & Experience. 224p. 1992. pap. text 15.00 (*0-226-60941-3*) U Ch Pr.

— Studies in Christian Enthusiasm. (C). 1948. pap. 7.00 (*0-87574-041-3*) Pendle Hill.

— To the Refreshing of the Children of Light. (C). 1959. pap. 4.00 (*0-87574-101-0*) Pendle Hill.

Nuttall, Geoffrey F., jt. auth. see Keeble, N. H.

Nuttall, Graeme, jt. auth. see Nelson-Jones, John.

Nuttall, Graeme, jt. auth. see Nelson-Jones, Rodney.

Nuttall, Jeff. Performance Art: Memoirs, Vol. I. (Orig.). 1986. pap. 11.95 (*0-7145-3788-8*) Riverrun NY.

— Performance Art: Scripts, Vol. II. (Orig.). 1986. pap. 11.95 (*0-7145-3789-6*) Riverrun NY.

Nuttall, Jon. Moral Questions: An Introduction to Ethics. LC 92-19117. 240p. 1993. 58.95 (*0-7456-1039-0*); pap. 22.95 (*0-7456-1040-4*) Blackwell Pubs.

Nuttall, Leonard J. Progress in Adjusting Differences of Amount of Educational Opportunity Offered Under the County Unit Systems of Maryland & Utah. LC 72-177122. (Columbia University. Teachers College. Contributions to Education Ser.: No. 43). reprint ed. 37.50 (*0-404-55431-8*) AMS Pr.

Nuttall, Mark. Protecting the Arctic: Indigenous Peoples & Cultural Survival. (Studies in Environmental Anthropology: Vol. 3). 204p. 1998. text 42.00 (*90-5702-354-7*, Harwood Acad Pubs); pap. text 22.00 (*90-5702-355-5*, Harwood Acad Pubs) Gordon & Breach.

Nuttall, Mark, jt. auth. see Jedrej, Charles.

Nuttall, Neil & Hawkins, Andy. Thoughs Like an Ocean: Teachers' Book: Notes & Prompt Sheet. (Illus.). 40p. (YA). (gr. 4 up). 1998. pap. 14.95 (*0-8464-4935-8*) Beekman Pubs.

Nuttall, Neil, jt. ed. see Hawkins, Andy.

Nuttall Ornithological Club Staff. Bulletin of the Nuttall Ornithological Club: A Quarterly Journal of Ornithology, 8 vols., Set. LC 73-17834. (Natural Sciences in America Ser.). (Illus.). 1826p. 1974. reprint ed. 134.95 (*0-405-05754-7*) Ayer.

— Bulletin of the Nuttall Ornithological Club: A Quarterly Journal of Ornithology, 8 vols., Vol. 1. LC 73-17834. (Natural Sciences in America Ser.). (Illus.). 1826p. 1974. reprint ed. 45.95 (*0-405-05755-5*) Ayer.

— Bulletin of the Nuttall Ornithological Club: A Quarterly Journal of Ornithology, 8 vols., Vol. 2. LC 73-17834. (Natural Sciences in America Ser.). (Illus.). 1826p. 1974. reprint ed. 45.95 (*0-405-05756-3*) Ayer.

— Bulletin of the Nuttall Ornithological Club: A Quarterly Journal of Ornithology, 8 vols., Vol. 3. LC 73-17834. (Natural Sciences in America Ser.). (Illus.). 1826p. 1974. reprint ed. 44.95 (*0-405-05757-1*) Ayer.

Nuttall, P. Austin, ed. see Fuller, Thomas.

Nuttall, R. Preston. Warriors of the Triple Chevron: A Story of the American Civil War. LC 99-93055. 450p. 1999. 29.95 (*0-9670496-0-1*) R P Nuttall.

Nuttall, Ronald, jt. auth. see Jackson, Helene.

Nuttall, Sarah & Coetzee, Carli, eds. Negotiating the Past: The Making of Memory in South Africa. LC DT1776.N44 1998. (Illus.). 314p. 1998. pap. text 19.95 (*0-19-571503-9*) OUP.

Nuttall, Sarah & Gunner, Liz, eds. Text, Theory, Space: Postcolonial Representations & Identity. 280p. (C). 1996. 85.00 (*0-415-12407-7*); pap. 27.99 (*0-415-12408-5*) Routledge.

***Nuttall, Simon J.** European Foreign Policy. 280p. 2000. text 55.00 (*0-19-829336-4*) OUP.

Nuttall, Simon J. European Political Co-Operation. 350p. 1992. text 75.00 (*0-19-827318-5*) OUP.

Nuttall, Thomas. A Manual of the Ornithology of the United States & Canada, 2 vols., Set. LC 73-17833. (Natural Sciences in America Ser.). 1332p. 1974. reprint ed. 96.95 (*0-405-05751-2*) Ayer.

— A Manual of the Ornithology of the United States & Canada, 2 vols., Vol. 1. LC 73-17833. (Natural Sciences in America Ser.). 1332p. 1974. reprint ed. 48.95 (*0-405-05752-0*) Ayer.

— A Manual of the Ornithology of the United States & Canada, 2 vols., Vol. 2. LC 73-17833. (Natural Sciences in America Ser.). 1332p. 1974. reprint ed. 48.95 (*0-405-05753-9*) Ayer.

Nuttall, Thomas & Lottinville, Savoie. A Journal of Travels into the Arkansas Territory During the Year 1819. LC 98-55991. (Classics Ser.). 1999. pap. 22.00 (*1-55728-561-6*) U of Ark Pr.

Nuttall, Zelia. Atlatl or Spear-Thrower of the Ancient Mexicans. (HU PMP Ser.: Vol. 1, No. 3). 1972. pap. 25.00 (*0-527-01185-1*) Periodicals Srv.

— Fundamental Principles of Old & New World Civilization. (HU PMP Ser.: Vol. 2). 65.00 (*0-527-01190-8*) Periodicals Srv.

— Official Reports on the Towns of Tequizistlan, Tepechpan, Acolman, & San Juan Teotihuacan, Sent to His Majesty Philip Second & the Council of the Indies in 1580. (HU PMP Ser.: Vol. 11, No. 2). 1926. pap. 25.00 (*0-527-01219-X*) Periodicals Srv.

— Standard or Head-Dress? (HU PMP Ser.). 1888. 25.00 (*0-527-01183-5*) Periodicals Srv.

Nuttall, Zelia, ed. The Codex Nuttall. LC 74-83057. (Illus.). 96p. 1998. reprint ed. pap. 12.95 (0-486-23168-2) Dover.

Nutter, Carolyn N. The Resume Workbook: A Personal Career File for Job Applications. 5th ed. LC 77-17412. 128p. 1978. 9.95 (0-910328-00-5) Sulzburger & Graham Pub.

Nutter, David. Selecting a Developer. McClean, Mary, ed. 20p. (Orig.). 1983. pap. 13.00 (0-317-04834-1) Natl Coun Econ Dev.

Nutter, David, ed. see Vecchi, Orazio.

Nutter, G. Warren. Growth of Government in the West. LC 78-1674. (AEI Studies: No. 185). (Illus.). 104p. reprint ed. pap. 32.30 (0-8357-4486-8, 203733800008) Bks Demand.

— Political Economy & Freedom: A Collection of Essays. Nutter, Jane C., ed. LC 82-48106. (Illus.). 328p. 1983. 14.00 (0-86597-024-6); pap. 5.50 (0-86597-025-4) Liberty Fund.

— Some Observations on Soviet Industrial Growth. (Occasional Papers: No. 55). 20p. 1957. reprint ed. 20.00 (0-87014-369-7) Natl Bur Econ Res.

Nutter, G. Warren, et al. Growth of Industrial Production in the Soviet Union. (General Ser.: No. 75). 735p. 1962. reprint ed. 160.00 (0-87014-074-4) Natl Bur Econ Res.

Nutter, Jane C., ed. see Nutter, G. Warren.

***Nutter, Jeanne D.** Delaware. (Black America Ser.). (Illus.). 128p. 1999. pap. 18.99 (0-7385-0327-4) Arcadia Publng.

— Growing up Black in New Castle County, Delaware. (Voices of America Ser.). 128p. 2000. pap. 18.99 (0-7385-0622-2) Arcadia Publng.

***Nutter, John Jacob.** The CIA's Black OPS: Covert Action, Foreign Policy, & Democracy. LC 99-40404. 350p. 1999. 26.95 (1-57392-742-2) Prometheus Bks.

Nutter, John W. Reflections on the Rubaiyat. 204p. (Orig.). 1996. pap. write for info. (1-883938-34-1) Dry Bones Pr.

Nutter, Judy. Stepping Stones. Vol. 1. (Illus.). 44p. 1980. pap. 6.50 (1-56770-121-3) S Scheewe Pubns.

***Nutter, Kathleen B.** The Necessity of Organization: Mary Kenney O'Sullivan & Trade Unionism for Women, 1892-1919. rev. ed. LC 99-35081. (Studies in the History of American Labor). 232p. 1999. 59.00 (0-8153-3505-9) Garland.

Nutter, Robert S. Economics. Phil, M., ed. 340p. (C). 1991. pap. 60.00 (1-85352-927-3, Pub. by HLT Pubns) St Mut.

Nutter, Ronald. A Dream of Peace: Art & Death in the Fiction of John Gardner. LC 96-22420. (Modern American Literature Ser.: Vol. 9). X, 236p. (C). 1998. text 47.95 (0-8204-3368-3) P Lang Pubng.

Nutter, W. Yarn Production & Properties. 110p. 1971. 95.00 (0-7855-7238-4) St Mut.

***Nuttgens, Patrick.** The Art of Learning: A Personal Journey Through the World of Education. (Illus.). 163p. 2000. 27.50 (1-85776-463-3, Pub. by Book Guild Ltd) Trans-Atl Phila.

Nuttgens, Patrick J. The Story of Architecture. (Illus.). 288p. (C). 1983. pap. text 36.95 (0-13-850131-9) P-H.

— The Story of Architecture. 2nd ed. (Illus.). 352p. 1997. pap. 24.95 (0-7148-3616-8, Pub. by Phaidon Press) Phaidon Pr.

— Understanding Modern Architecture. 220p. 1990. text 45.00 (0-04-500040-9) Routledge.

Nuttgenx, Patrick J. The Story of Architecture. 2nd ed. (Illus.). 200p. 1997. 39.95 (0-7148-3615-X, Pub. by Phaidon Press) Phaidon Pr.

Nuttin, J. M. The Illusion of Attitude Change: Towards a Response Contagion Theory of Persuasion. 243p. (Orig.). 1975. pap. 39.50 (90-6186-227-2, Pub. by Leuven Univ) Coronet Bks.

— Motivation, Planning & Action: A Relational Theory of Behavior Dynamics. 259p. (Orig.). 1984. pap. 52.50 (90-6186-154-3, Pub. by Leuven Univ) Coronet Bks.

Nuttin, J. M., jt. auth. see Lens, W.

Nuttin, Joseph R. Future Time Perspective & Motivation: Theory & Research Method. (Louvain Psychology Ser.: Studia Psychologica). 238p. 1985. 49.95 (0-89859-611-4) L Erlbaum Assocs.

Nuttin, Joseph R., et al. Motivation, Planning & Action: A Relational Theory of Behavior Dynamics. 264p. 1984. text 49.95 (0-89859-332-8) L Erlbaum Assocs.

Nutting, Brian, jt. ed. see Duncan, Philip D.

***Nutting, Cherie.** Yesterday's Perfume: An Intimate Memoir of Paul Bowles. (Illus.). 240p. 2000. 75.00 (0-609-60573-9) C Potter.

Nutting, George L. & Nutting, Ruth E. Cathedrals of the Deep. 163p. (Orig.). 1996. pap. 5.95 (0-9612266-4-1) Numard Bks.

— Chapa's Spring. 268p. (Orig.). 1994. pap. text 6.95 (0-9612266-3-3) Numard Bks.

Nutting, J., jt. ed. see Viswanathan, R.

Nutting, Jack, jt. ed. see Viswanathan, R.

Nutting, Jeri. Capitalization & Punctuation. (Basic Skills Ser.). (Illus.). 32p. (J). (gr. 2). 1997. pap. text 4.95 (0-88724-408-4, CD-2108) Carson-Dellos.

— Capitalization & Punctuation. (Basic Skills Ser.). (Illus.). 32p. (J). (gr. 3). 1997. pap. text 4.95 (0-88724-413-0, CD-2113) Carson-Dellos.

Nutting, Paul A. Community-Oriented Primary Care: From Principle to Practice. LC 90-12627. 572p. 1990. reprint ed. pap. 22.50 (0-8263-1230-6) U of NM Pr.

Nutting, Ruth E., jt. auth. see Nutting, George L.

***Nutting, Stephanie.** Le Tragique dans le Theatre Quebecois et Canadien-Francais, 1950-1989. LC 99-86705. (Canadian Studies: Vol. 23). (FRE.). 196p. 2000. text 79.95 (0-7734-7802-7) E Mellen.

Nutting, Teresa. Traveler's French Dictionary. 1993. pap. 6.95 (0-8050-2909-5) H Holt & Co.

Nutting, Teresa & Marcy, Michel. Cortina - Holt Traveler's French Dictionary: English-French - French-English. LC 93-3672. 1993. pap. 6.95 (0-8327-0722-8) Cortina.

Nutting, Wallace. Furniture Treasury, 2 vols., Vol. 3. unabridged ed. (Illus.). 560p. 1949. 50.00 (0-02-591040-X) Macmillan.

— Furniture Treasury, 2 vols., Vols. 1 & 2 in 1. unabridged ed. (Illus.). 1536p. 1954. 100.00 (0-02-590980-0, Pub. by Macmillan) S&S Trade.

— New York Beautiful. 305p. 1993. reprint ed. lib. bdg. 89.00 (0-7812-5131-1) Rprt Serv.

— Wallace Nutting: Supreme Edition, General Catalog. LC 77-608284. 160p. 1978. pap. 10.95 (0-916838-09-9) Schiffer.

— The Wallace Nutting Expansible Catalog. Ivankovich, Michael, ed. LC 87-70415. (Illus.). 175p. (Orig.). 1987. reprint ed. pap. 12.95 (0-9615843-3-5) Diamond Pr PA.

— Wallace Nutting's Biography. 1976. 24.95 (0-8488-0599-2) Amereon Ltd.

Nutting, William B. Mammalian Diseases & Arachnids, Vol. II. LC 83-20998. 304p. 1984. 165.00 (0-8493-6563-5, RA641, CRC Reprint) Franklin.

Nutting, William B., ed. Mammalian Diseases & Arachnids, Vol. I. LC 83-20998. 288p. 1984. 163.00 (0-8493-6562-7, RA641, CRC Reprint) Franklin.

***Nuttle, Jim.** If I Were... A Book of Make-Believe. (J). 1999. reprint ed. 5.95 (1-892374-24-2) Weldon Owen.

— The Ways I Play. 16p. (J). 1999. 5.95 (1-892374-18-8) Weldon Owen.

Nuttli, Otto. Effects of Earthquakes in the Central United States. (Earthquake Ser.: No. 8). (Illus.). 50p. (Orig.). 1993. reprint ed. pap. 9.95 (0-934426-50-3, Gutenberg-Richter) NAPSAC Reprods.

Nutton, Vivian. From Democedes to Harvey: Studies in the History of Medicine. (Collected Studies: No. CS277). (Illus.). 332p. (C). 1990. reprint ed. text 115.95 (0-86078-225-5, Pub. by Variorum) Ashgate Pub Co.

Nutz, Patricia A., jt. auth. see Albanese, Joseph A.

Nutzinger, H. G. & Backhaus, J., eds. Codetermination. (Illus.). 320p. 1989. 99.00 (0-387-50648-9) Spr-Verlag.

Nuutinen, Olli. Finnish/Danish/Finnish Dictionary. (DAN & FIN.). 580p. 1991. 105.00 (0-320-00096-6) Fr & Eur.

Nuventures Consultants, Inc. Staff. America's Changing Workforce: About You, Your Job & Your Changing Work Environment. McNamara, Ellen, ed. 270p. (Orig.). 1990. pap. 12.95 (0-9625632-1-8) NUVENTURES Pub.

***Nuwer, Hank.** High School Hazing: When Rites Become Wrongs LC 99-33768. 2000. 25.00 (0-531-11682-4) Watts.

Nuwer, Hank. The Legend of Jesse Owens. LC 96-51188. (Impact Biograpies Ser.). 176p. (YA). (gr. 5-9). 1997. lib. bdg. 24.00 (0-531-11356-6) Watts.

***Nuwer, Hank.** Wrongs of Passage: Fraternities, Sororities, Hazing, & Binge Drinking. LC 99-14864. (Illus.). 336p. 1999. 27.95 (0-253-33596-5) Ind U Pr.

Nuwer, Marc R. Evoked Potential Monitoring in the Operating Room. (Illus.). 256p. 1986. text 58.00 (0-88167-230-0) Lppncott W & W.

Nuxoll, Elizabeth, ed. see Morris, Robert.

Nuxoll, Elizabeth M. & Gallagher, Mary A., eds. The Papers of Robert Morris, 1781-1784, Vol. 8. (Illus.). 1032p. 1996. text 100.00 (0-8229-3886-3) U of Pittsburgh Pr.

Nuys, Laura B. Van, see Van Nuys, Laura B.

Nuyts, Jan, et al, eds. Layers & Levels of Representation in Language Theory: A Functional View. LC 90-33948. (Pragmatics & Beyond New Ser.: No. 13). xii, 348p. 1990. 71.00 (1-55619-279-7) J Benjamins Pubng Co.

Nuyts, Jan & De Schutter, Georges, eds. Getting One's Words into Line: On Word Order & Functional Grammar. (Functional Grammar Ser.). xiv, 218p. (Orig.). (C). 1987. pap. 46.45 (90-6765-349-7) Mouton.

Nuyts, Jan & Pederson, Eric, eds. Language & Conceptualization. LC 96-8776. (Language, Culture & Cognition Ser.: No. 1). (Illus.). 289p. (C). 1997. text 59.95 (0-521-55303-2) Cambridge U Pr.

***Nuyts, Jan & Pederson, Eric, eds.** Language & Conceptualization. (Language, Culture & Cognition Ser.: No. 1). (Illus.). 290p. (C). 2000. pap. 24.95 (0-521-77481-0) Cambridge U Pr.

Nuyts, Jan & Verschueren, Jef, compiled by. A Comprehensive Bibliography of Pragmatics, 4 vols., Set. LC 87-20824. xi, 2197p. 1987. 354.00 (90-272-2031-X) J Benjamins Pubng Co.

Nuzum, C. The Life of Faith. 95p. 1956. pap. 4.50 (0-88243-539-6, 02-0539) Gospel Pub.

Nuzzi, Debra. Pocket Herbal Reference Guide. (Crossing Press Pocket Ser.). (Illus.). 144p. (Orig.). 1992. pap. 6.95 (0-89594-568-1) Crossing Pr.

Nuzzi, Ronald. Gifts of the Spirit: Multiple Intelligences in Religious Education. 2nd ed. 64p. 1999. pap. 12.00 (1-55833-181-6) Natl Cath Educ.

Nuzzo, Elizabeth A., jt. auth. see Nuzzo, Raymond G.

***Nuzzo, Raymond G. & Nuzzo, Elizabeth A.** Behold a Time of Passing. LC 00-190638. 139p. 2000. 25.00 (0-7388-1882-8); pap. 18.00 (0-7388-1883-6) Xlibris Corp.

***Nuzzolo, Deborah.** Dolphin Discovery: Bottlenose Dolphin Training & Interaction. Wolf, Joy L. & Wlodarski, Loran, eds. (Education Department Publications). (Illus.). 72p. (YA). (gr. 4-12). 1999. pap. 8.00 (1-893698-03-3) SeaWorld Inc.

Nuzzolo, Luccio & Vellucci, Augusto. Tissue Culture Techniques. LC 67-26015. (Illus.). 258p. 1983. 37.50 (0-87527-117-0) Green.

NVision Grafix Inc. Staff & Hripko, Thomas. Official Tour Guide to Holusion Art. (Illus.). 40p. 1994. 24.95 (0-9640923-1-X) NVision Grafix.

NW Bed & Breakfast Reservation Service Staff, ed. West Coast Town & Country B & B's U. S. A. & Canada: Directory of Homes & Inns. 6th ed. (Illus.). 150p. (C). 1989. per. 9.50 (0-945796-01-3) NW Bed Breakfast.

Nwabueze, B. O. Constitutionalism in the Emergent States. LC 72-14221. 320p. 1973. 39.50 (0-8386-1365-9) Fairleigh Dickinson.

Nwabueze, Benjamin O. Nigeria's Presidential Constitution: The Second Experiment in Constitutional Democracy. LC 84-19438. 502p. 1985. pap. 155.70 (0-608-05252-3, 206579000001) Bks Demand.

Nwabueze, Emeka. Heroes of Conscience. LC 98-92284. 72p. (C). 1999. pap. 9.95 (0-7392-0046-1) Morris Pubng.

Nwabugwu, Frank. Antalo the Antelope, B-era the Bear, C-esto the Cheetah, D-opicooko the Deer. (Bed Time Stories Ser.). 18p. (J). 1992. write for info. (1-881687-04-X); teacher ed. write for info. (1-881687-07-4); pap. write for info. (1-881687-06-6); lib. bdg. write for info. (1-881687-05-8) F Nwabugwu.

— Sparo: The Wild & Crazy Pretty Dog. 2nd ed. 26p. (J). (gr. 2-8). 1993. write for info. (1-881687-08-2) F Nwabugwu.

Nwachuku, Daisy, jt. ed. see Ma Mpolo, Jean M.

Nwachukwu, P. Akujuobi. Towards an Igbo Literary Standard. 200p. 1983. pap. 19.50 (0-7103-0045-X) Routledge.

Nwachukwu, Richard O. The Agony: The Untold Tale of the Nigerian Society. 118p. (Orig.). 1987. pap. 6.95 (0-941823-00-8) Good Hope Enterp.

— The Dark & Bright Continent: Africa in the Changing World. LC 89-80209. 344p. 1989. 17.95 (0-941823-02-4); pap. 9.25 (0-941823-01-6) Good Hope Enterp.

Nwaelele, O. Dan. Your Company Safety & Health Manual: Programs, Policies & Procedures for Preventing Accidents & Injuries in the Workplace. LC 97-39524. (Illus.). 438p. 1997. pap. text 79.00 (0-86587-590-1) Gov Insts.

Nwaezeigwe, Nwankwo T. Ngoni. LC 96-22945. (Heritage Library of African Peoples: Set 3). (Illus.). 64p. (YA). (gr. 7-12). 1996. lib. bdg. 16.95 (0-8239-2006-2, D2006-2) Rosen Group.

Nwafor, Azinna. Frelimo & Socialism in Mozambique. Omenana Collective Research Group Staff, ed. (Etudes et Analyses Marxistes en Afrique Ser.). 45p. (Orig.). (C). pap. 3.00 (0-686-88661-5) Omenana.

— Revolution & Socialism in Ethiopia. Omenana Collective Research Group Staff, ed. (Etudes et Analyses Marxistes en Afrique Ser.). 55p. (Orig.). (C). 1987. reprint ed. pap. 3.00 (0-686-88660-7) Omenana.

Nwagboso, Christopher O. Advanced Vehicles & Infrastructure Systems: Computer Applications, Control & Automation. LC 96-27886. 522p. 1997. 210.00 (0-471-95645-7) Wiley.

— Road Vehicle Automation II: Towards Systems Integration: ROVA '95 International: Proceedings of the 2nd International Conference, Held at Vehicle Systems Research Centre, School of Engineering, Bolton Institute, Bolton, U. K., 11th-13th September, 1995. LC 96-31746. 640p. 1998. 240.00 (0-471-96726-2) Wiley.

Nwaigbo, Ferdinand. Church As a Communion - An African Christian Perspective: Theology of the Local Church in the Light of the Second Vatican Council. LC 97-123585. (Bamberger Theologische Studien: Vol. 3). 434p. 1996. pap. 69.95 (3-631-49853-5) P Lang Pubng.

— Church As a Communion - An African Christian Perspective: Theology of the Local Church in the Light of the Second Vatican Council. (Bamberger Theologische Studien: Vol. 3). 434p. 1996. pap. 69.95 (0-8204-2980-5) P Lang Pubng.

Nwana, Hyacinth S. Mathematical Intelligent Learning Environments. 272p. (Orig.). 1993. pap. text 29.95 (1-871516-29-3, Pub. by Intellect) Cromland.

Nwana, Hyacinth S. & Azarmi, Nadar. Software Agents & Soft Computing: Toward Enhancing Machine Intelligence: Concepts & Applications. LC 97-878. (Lecture Notes in Artificial Intelligence Ser.: Vol. 119). 298p. 1997. 39.95 (3-540-62560-7) Spr-Verlag.

Nwangu, Peter, ed. Concepts & Strategies in New Drug Development, 4. LC 83-19248. (Clinical Pharmacology & Therapeutics Ser.). 265p. 1983. 65.00 (0-275-91406-2, C1406, Praeger Pubs) Greenwood.

Nwangwu, Mrchido, ed. see Ngwu, Charles.

Nwankwo, Josephat O. Ethical Challenges of Authority in a Pluralistic Society: The Nigerian Example. (European University Studies: Vol. 648). (Illus.). 209p. (C). 1998. pap. text 37.95 (0-8204-3608-9) P Lang Pubng.

Nwankwo, Josephat Okanumee. Ethical Challenges of Authority in a Pluralistic Society: The Nigerian Example. (European University Studies: Vol. 648). 209p. 1998. pap. 37.95 (3-631-33562-8) P Lang Pubng.

Nwanna, Gladson I. Americans Traveling Abroad: What You Should Know Before You Go. 2nd ed. (International Traveler's Guide Ser.). 630p. (Orig.). 1996. pap. 39.99 (0-9623820-7-8) Wld Trvl Inst.

— Do's & Don'ts Around the World - A Country Guide to Cultural & Social Taboos & Etiquette - Africa. LC 97-19166. (Do's & Don'ts Around the World: A Country Guide to Cultural & Social Taboos & Etiquette Ser.). 445p. 1998. pap. 34.99 (1-890605-04-2) Wld Trvl Inst.

— Do's & Don'ts Around the World - A Country Guide to Cultural & Social Taboos & Etiquette - Asia. LC 97-17211. (Do's & Don'ts Around the World: A Country Guide to Cultural & Social Taboos & Etiquette Ser.). 260p. 1998. pap. 24.99 (1-890605-01-8) Wld Trvl Inst.

— Do's & Don'ts Around the World - A Country Guide to Cultural & Social Taboos & Etiquette - Europe. LC 97-19643. (Do's & Don'ts Around the World: A Country Guide to Cultural & Social Taboos & Etiquette Ser.). 320p. 1997. pap. 29.99 (1-890605-00-X) Wld Trvl Inst.

— Do's & Don'ts Around the World - A Country Guide to Cultural & Social Taboos & Etiquette - Middle East. LC 97-17205. (Do's & Don'ts Around the World: A Country Guide to Cultural & Social Taboos & Etiquette Ser.). 120p. 1998. pap. 12.99 (1-890605-05-0) Wld Trvl Inst.

— Do's & Don'ts Around the World - A Country Guide to Cultural & Social Taboos & Etiquette - Oceania & Japan. LC 97-17207. (Do's & Don'ts Around the World: A Country Guide to Cultural & Social Taboos & Etiquette Ser.). 180p. (Orig.). 1998. pap. 15.99 (1-890605-07-7) Wld Trvl Inst.

— Do's & Don'ts Around the World - A Country Guide to Cultural & Social Taboos & Etiquette - Russia & the Independent States. LC 97-19167. (Do's & Don'ts Around the World: A Country Guide to Cultural & Social Taboos & Etiquette Ser.). 120p. 1998. pap. 12.99 (1-890605-06-9) Wld Trvl Inst.

— Do's & Don'ts Around the World - A Country Guide to Cultural & Social Taboos & Etiquette - South America. LC 97-19644. (Do's & Don'ts Around the World: A Country Guide to Cultural & Social Taboos & Etiquette Ser.). 230p. 1997. pap. 19.99 (1-890605-03-4) Wld Trvl Inst.

— Do's & Don'ts Around the World - A Country Guide to Cultural & Social Taboos & Etiquette - The Caribbean. LC 97-20454. (Do's & Don'ts Around the World: A Country Guide to Cultural & Social Taboos & Etiquette Ser.). 230p. 1998. pap. 19.99 (1-890605-02-6) Wld Trvl Inst.

— Do's & Don'ts Around the World - A Country Guide to Cultural & Social Taboos & Etiquette - U. S. A., Canada & Australia. LC 97-19165. (Do's & Don'ts Around the World: A Country Guide to Cultural & Social Taboos & Etiquette Ser.). 75p. 1998. pap. 12.99 (1-890605-08-5) Wld Trvl Inst.

— Practical Tips for Americans Traveling Abroad: Ignore Them at Your Own Risk. LC 97-19149. 255p. (Orig.). 1998. pap. 19.99 (1-890605-09-3) Wld Trvl Inst.

Nwanunibu, C. O. Malinke, 14 vols. (Heritage Library of African Peoples). (Illus.). 64p. (YA). (gr. 7-12). 1996. lib. bdg. 16.95 (0-8239-1979-X) Rosen Group.

— Soninke, 14 vols. Bond, George, ed. LC 94-45813. (Heritage Library of African Peoples: Set 2). (Illus.). 64p. (YA). (gr. 7-12). 1996. lib. bdg. 16.95 (0-8239-1978-1) Rosen Group.

Nwanze, K. F., jt. auth. see Harris, K. M.

Nwaogwugwu, Josiah. 125 African Parables & Wise Sayings. LC 99-173641. (Illus.). 1998. pap. 20.00 (1-886094-78-0) Chicago Spectrum.

Nwapa, Flora. Efuru. (African Writers Ser.). 221p. (C). 1966. pap. 8.95 (0-435-90026-9, 90026) Heinemann.

— Never Again. 90p. 1992. 24.95 (0-86543-318-6); pap. 9.95 (0-86543-319-4) Africa World.

— One Is Enough. 157p. 1992. 24.95 (0-86543-322-4); pap. 9.95 (0-86543-323-2) Africa World.

— This Is Lagos & Other Stories. 140p. 1992. 24.95 (0-86543-320-8); pap. 9.95 (0-86543-321-6) Africa World.

— Wives at War & Other Stories. 125p. 1992. 24.95 (0-86543-327-5); pap. 9.95 (0-86543-328-3) Africa World.

— Women Are Different. 144p. 1992. 24.95 (0-86543-325-9); pap. 9.95 (0-86543-326-7) Africa World.

Nwariaku, Fiemu & Thal, Erwin R., eds. The Parkland Trauma Handbook, 2. 2nd ed. LC 98-54476. (Illus.). 544p. (C). (gr. 13). 1999. pap. text 36.95 (0-8151-2618-2, 31645) Mosby Inc.

Nwauwa, Apollos O. Imperialism, Academe & Nationalism: Britain & University Education for Africans. LC 96-21116. 272p. (C). 1997. 49.50 (0-7146-4668-7, Pub. by F Cass Pubs) Intl Spec Bk.

***NWECT Staff.** Programming for Web Authors. (C). 1999. pap. text 81.00 (0-03-029284-0, Pub. by Harcourt Coll Pubs) Harcourt.

Nweke, Ken M. Information Seeking & Veterinary Medical Scientists (HVMS) in Africa: Case Study from Borno State, Nigeria. 30p. 1992. 5.00 (0-941934-59-4) Indiana Africa.

Nwenmely, Hubisi. Language Reclamation: French-Creole Language Teaching in the U. K. & the Caribbean. 160p. 1995. 49.00 (1-85359-299-4, Pub. by Multilingual Matters) Taylor & Francis.

Nwoga, Donatus I. Critical Perspectives on Christopher Okigo LC 80 53349. (Critical Perspectives Ser.). 367 p. 1984. write for info. (0-89741-258-3) Gila River.

Nwoga, Donatus I., ed. Critical Perspectives on Christopher Okigbo. LC 80-53349. (Critical Perspectives Ser.). (Illus.). 367p. (C). 1985. 35.00 (0-89410-258-3, Three Contnts); pap. 16.00 (0-89410-259-1, Three Contnts) L Rienner.

Nwokah, Osita D. Mechanical Systems Design Handbook Modeling Measurement & Control. (Electrical Engineering Handbks.). 1999. 110.00 (0-8493-8596-2, 8596) CRC Pr.

Nwomonoh, Jonathan, ed. Education & Development in Africa: A Contemporary Survey. LC 98-13510. (Distinguished Education Ser.). 378p. (C). 1998. 70.00 (1-57309-011-5, U Pr W Africa); pap. 50.00 (1-57309-010-7, U Pr W Africa) Intl Scholars.

Nwosu, Eugene. Cut Your Own Firewood: The Ultimate Power to Succeed. 160p. 1998. pap. 15.95 (1-898256-36-5, Pub. by Collins Press) Dufour.

Nwosu, Kingsley C., et al, eds. Multimedia Database Systems: Design & Implementation Strategies. LC 96-1595. (Illus.). 400p. (C). 1996. text 131.00 (0-7923-9712-6) Kluwer Academic.

Nwosu, Peter, et al, eds. Communication & the Transformation of Society: A Developing Region's Perspectives. LC 95-10746. 474p. (C). 1995. lib. bdg. 58.50 (0-8191-9961-3) U Pr of Amer.

***Nwoye, Joseph.** Multi-Cultural Education: Insight on Policies & Pratices in Selected Schools. 92p. (C). 1999. per. 41.95 (0-7872-6499-7, 41649901) Kendall-Hunt.

NWPA Executive Staff, ed. see Ayim, Martin A.

Nwuga, Vincent C. Manual Treatment of Back Pain. LC 84-3965. 224p. (C). 1986. lib. bdg. 23.50 (0-89874-753-8) Krieger.

N

Nwulia, Moses D. Britain & Slavery in East Africa. LC 75-25756. (Illus.). 244p. (Orig.). 1975. 25.00 (*0-914478-11-7*, Three Contnts); pap. 12.00 (*0-914478-12-5*, Three Contnts) L Rienner.

— The History of Slavery in Mauritius & the Seychelles, 1810-1875. LC 79-15363. 248p. 1981. 33.50 (*0-8386-2398-0*) Fairleigh Dickinson.

Nwuneli, O. & Opubor, A., eds. The Development & Growth of the Film Industry in Nigeria. (Illus.). 114p. 1980. 19.95 (*0-89388-220-8*); pap. 11.95 (*0-685-59744-X*) Okpaku Communications.

Nwuneli, Onuira E., ed. Communication & Human Needs in Africa. 99p. 1989. pap. 8.95 (*0-940738-13-9*) Lamplight Edits.

NWWA Staff. The Handbook of Suggested Practices for the Design & Installation of Ground Water Monitoring Wells. 380p. 1989. 43.75 (*1-56034-061-4*, T479) Natl Grnd Water.

— U. S. Cities & Towns: Source of Water Supply. 26p. 1989. 6.25 (*1-56034-055-X*, K500) Natl Grnd Water.

Nxumalo, Thandiwe & Cioran, Samuel D. Funda Isizulu/Learn Zulu! LC 97-189702. (ZUL.). 1997. 89.95 incl. audio, disk (*0-7021-4124-0*, Pub. by Juta & Co) Intl Spec Bk.

Ny, Linda. Vocation Counselling. 1989. pap. text 21.40 (*0-13-945676-7*) P-H.

NY State School Board Staff. Disciplining School Employees. LC 94-231823. 136p. 1994. pap. 37.50 (*1-56452-047-1*) NY Boards Assoc.

— Fiscal Management: Handbook for School Board Members. LC 98-135754. 81p. 1997. pap. 22.50 (*1-56452-052-8*) NY Boards Assoc.

***Nyad, Diana.** Boss of Me: The Keyshawn Johnson Story. unabridged ed. 70p. (YA). 1999. pap. 5.95 (*1-885478-66-6*, Pub. by Genesis Press) BookWorld.

Nyakatura, J. W. Anatomy of an African Kingdom: A History of Bunyoro-Kitara. LC 73-91729. 282p. 1973. text 19.95 (*0-88357-025-4*) NOK Pubs.

Nyala, Hannah. Point Last Seen: A Woman Tracker's Story of Domestic Violence & Personal Triumph. LC 96-18397. 176p. 1998. pap. 11.95 (*0-14-027463-4*) Viking Penguin.

Nyamndi, George. The West African Village Novel, Vol. 8. (European University Studies: Ser. 27). XII, 241p. 1983. pap. 37.00 (*3-261-05077-2*) P Lang Pubng.

Nyamongo, Issac K., jt. auth. see Kau, Samvit S.

Nyan, T. Metalinguistic Operators with Reference to French. 169p. (C). 1998. pap. text 30.95 (*0-8204-3416-7*) P Lang Pubng.

Nyana, U. The Vipassana Dipani: or The Manual of Insight. LC 78-70107. reprint ed. 22.00 (*0-404-17357-8*) AMS Pr.

***Nyanaponika & Bodhi.** The Vision of Dhamma: Buddhist Writings of Nyanaponika Thera. 2nd enl. ed. LC 99-53425. 368p. 2000. 17.00 (*1-928706-03-7*) Vipassana Res Pubns.

***Nyanasobhano, Bhikkhu.** Landscapes of Wonder: Discovering Buddhist Dhamma in the World Around Us. LC 98-17767. 208p. 1998. pap. 14.95 (*0-86171-142-4*) Wisdom MA.

Nyanasobhano, Bhikkhu. Two Dialogues on Dhamma. 64p. 1989. 2.40 (*955-24-0057-0*, Pub. by Buddhist Pub Soc) Vipassana Res Pubns.

Nyanatiloka. Buddhist Dictionary. LC 77-87508. reprint ed. 27.50 (*0-404-16846-9*) AMS Pr.

Nyandoro, Gideon, jt. ed. see Nyangoni, Christopher.

Nyang Oro, Julius E. The State & Capitalist Development in Africa: Declining Political Economies. LC 88-34030. 189p. 1989. 49.95 (*0-275-93120-X*, C3120, Praeger Pubs) Greenwood.

Nyang, Sulayman. Islam in the United States of America. 1999. pap. 14.95 (*1-871031-69-9*) Abjad Bk.

Nyang, Sulayman S. Islam, Christianity & African Identity. LC 84-72247. 106p. (Orig.). 1985. pap. 6.95 (*0-915597-05-5*) Amana Bks.

— Islam, Christianity & African Identity. 128p. (Orig.). 2000. pap. 12.95 (*0-614-21669-9*, 575) Kazi Pubns.

Nyang, Sulayman S., jt. ed. see Olupona, Jacob K.

Nyangoni, Christopher & Nyandoro, Gideon, eds. Zimbabwe Independence Movements: Select Documents. LC 79-51834. 456p. 1979. text 46.00 (*0-06-495222-3*, N6621) B&N Imports.

Nyangoni, Wellington W. Africa in the United Nations System. LC 81-72033. 288p. 1985. 46.50 (*0-8386-3118-5*) Fairleigh Dickinson.

Nyang'oro, Julius E. & Shaw, Timothy M., eds. Beyond Structural Adjustment in Africa: The Political Economy of Sustainable & Democratic Development. LC 91-47087. 192p. 1992. 55.00 (*0-275-94221-X*, C4221, Praeger Pubs) Greenwood.

Nyankanzi, Edward L. Genocide: Rwanda & Burundi. LC 97-773. 250p. 1997. 29.95 (*0-87047-105-8*) Schenkman Bks Inc.

Nyantakyi, Kaayire. The Ancestral Sacrifice. LC 98-148926. 1998. pap. 9.95 (*1-886094-79-9*) Chicago Spectrum.

Nyasaland Economic Symposium Staff. Economic Development in Africa: Proceedings of the Nyasaland Economic Symposium held in Blantyre, 18 to 28 July, 1962. Jackson, Edward F., ed. LC 77-1786. vii, 368p. 1965. 45.00 (*0-678-06258-7*) Kelley.

Nyatanga, Lovemore, et al. Good Practice in the Accreditation of Prior Learning. LC 98-206583. vi, 144 p. 1998. write for info. (*0-304-34651-9*) Continuum.

Nyatetu-Waigwa, Wangari W. The Liminal Novel: Studies in the Francophone-African Novel As Bildungsroman. LC 93-470. (American University Studies XVIII: Vol. 6). 134p. (C). 1997. 32.95 (*0-8204-2168-5*) P Lang Pubng.

Nyazee, Imran, tr. see Rushd, Ibn.

Nyazee, Imran A. Theories of Islamic Law. 344p. (C). 1995. text 21.95 (*0-934905-66-5*) Kazi Pubns.

Nybakken. The Diversity of Invertebrates. 2nd ed. 2002. 38.00 (*0-07-012202-4*) McGraw.

Nybakken, Elizabeth I., ed. The Centinel: Warnings of a Revolution. LC 77-92570. 240p. 1980. 25.00 (*0-87413-141-3*) U Delaware Pr.

Nybakken, Elizabeth I., jt. ed. see Hawes, Joseph M.

Nybakken, James W. The Diversity of the Invertebrates. LC 95-79008. 328p. (C). 1995. text, lab manual ed. write for info. (*0-697-15120-4*, WCB McGr Hill) McGrw-H Hghr Educ.

— Marine Biology: An Ecological Approach. 446p. (C). 1982. write for info. (*0-06-364800-8*) Addson-Wesley Educ.

— Marine Biology: An Ecological Approach. 4th ed. LC 96-645. 446p. (C). 1997. 73.00 (*0-673-99451-1*) Addson-Wesley Educ.

Nybakken, James W. & McClintock, James. The Diversity of Invertebrates: A Laboratory Manual Gulf of Mexico Version. LC 96-83888. 320p. (C). 1996. text. write for info. (*0-697-15123-9*, WCB McGr Hill) McGrw-H Hghr Educ.

Nybakken, Oscar E. Greek & Latin in Scientific Terminology. LC 59-5992. (ENG, GRE & LAT.). 322p. 1985. pap. text 29.95 (*0-8138-0721-2*) Iowa St U Pr.

***Nyberg.** Monasticism in North-Western Europe, 800-1200. 2000. 70.95 (*1-85928-212-1*) Ashgate Pub Co.

***Nyberg, Albert & Rozelle, Scott.** Accelerating China's Rural Transformation. LC 99-43474. 152p. 1999. 30.00 (*0-8213-4576-1*, 14576) World Bank.

Nyberg, Amy K. Seal of Approval: The History of the Comics Code. LC 97-21789. (Studies in Popular Culture Ser.). 256p. 1998. 45.00 (*0-87805-974-1*); pap. 18.00 (*0-87805-975-X*) U Pr of Miss.

Nyberg, Ben & Clift, G. W. Britain 101. (Illus.). 170p. (Orig.). 1989. pap. 8.95 (*0-9624608-0-X*) Island Pk Bks.

Nyberg, Carl O., jt. auth. see Bailey, Joanne I.

Nyberg, Cheryl & Boast. Subject Compilations of State Laws, 1979-1983 (1984) 1984. 75.00 (*0-313-23335-7*) Boast-Nyberg.

Nyberg, Cheryl R. Subject Compilations of State Laws: An Annotated Bibliography. 1997. 126.50 (*1-889194-00-X*) Boast-Nyberg.

— Subject Compilations of State Laws, 1983-1985: An Annotated Bibliography. LC 85-73774. 595p. 1986. text 81.50 (*0-9616293-0-4*) Boast-Nyberg.

— Subject Compilations of State Laws, 1985-1988: An Annotated Bibliography. LC 88-93062. 544p. 1989. 86.50 (*0-9616293-1-2*) Boast-Nyberg.

— Subject Compilations of State Laws, 1988-1990: An Annotated Bibliography. 542p. 1991. 101.50 (*0-9616293-2-0*) Boast-Nyberg.

— Subject Compilations of State Laws, 1990-1991: An Annotated Bibliography. 290p. 1992. 106.50 (*0-9616293-4-7*) Boast-Nyberg.

Nyberg, Cheryl R., et al. Laboratory Animal Welfare: A Guide to Reference Tools, Legal Materials, Organizations & Federal Agencies. LC 95-116433. 391p. 1994. 105.00 (*0-9616293-9-8*) Boast-Nyberg.

Nyberg, D. A., jt. auth. see Holzgreve, W.

Nyberg, David. The Varnished Truth: Truth Telling & Deceiving in Ordinary Life. LC 92-20637. 254p. (C). 1993. 24.95 (*0-226-61051-9*) U Ch Pr.

— The Varnished Truth: Truth Telling & Deceiving in Ordinary Life. 256p. 1994. pap. 12.95 (*0-226-61052-7*) U Ch Pr.

Nyberg, David A. Ultrasound of Fetal Anomalies. 1995. text 710.00 (*1-56815-017-2*, 10027) Mosby Inc.

Nyberg, F., et al, eds. Neuropeptides in the Spinal Cord. LC 93-11042. (Progress in Brain Research Ser.: Vol. 104). (Illus.). 438p. 1995. 194.50 (*0-444-81719-0*) Elsevier.

Nyberg, J. Brian, et al. Integrated Management of Timber & Deer: Coastal Forests of British Columbia & Alaska. (Illus.). 72p. 1997. reprint ed. 14.20 (*0-89904-658-4*, Wildlife Resrch Grp); reprint ed. pap. 8.20 (*0-89904-659-2*, Wildlife Resrch Grp) Crumb Elbow Pub.

Nyberg, Jan J. A Caring Approach in Nursing Administration. LC 97-49688. (Illus.). 288p. 1998. 34.95 (*0-87081-478-8*) Univ Pr Colo.

Nyberg, Joan. A Rustling of Wings: An Angelic Guide to the Twin Cities. 2nd ed. LC 94-90051. (Illus.). 194p. (Orig.). 1994. pap. 15.95 (*0-9640578-2-4*) Wingtip Pr.

Nyberg, Judy. Charts for Children: Print Awareness Activities for Young Children. 176p. (Orig.). 1995. pap., teacher ed. 12.95 (*0-673-36176-4*, GoodYrBooks) Addson-Wesley Educ.

— Just Pretend! Creating Dramatic Play Centers with Young Children. (Illus.). 104p. (Orig.). 1994. pap. 8.95 (*0-673-36116-0*, GoodYrBooks) Addson-Wesley Educ.

— Storybook Phonics: Fun-to-Do Initial-Letter Phonics Activities for Home or School. (Illus.). 176p. (J). (ps-2). 1997. pap. 11.95 (*0-673-36398-8*, GoodYrBooks) Addson-Wesley Educ.

Nyberg, K., et al, eds. Advances in Cryptology - EUROCRYPT '98: International Conference on the Theory & Application of Cryptographic Techniques, Espoo, Finland, May 31-June 4, 1998, Proceedings. (Lecture Notes in Computer Science Ser.: Vol. 1403). x, 607p. 1998. pap. 69.00 (*3-540-64518-7*) Spr-Verlag.

Nyberg, K., jt. ed. see Lindner, G.

Nyberg, Klas, jt. auth. see Eberson, Lennart.

Nyberg, Lennart. The Shakespearean Ideal: Shakespeare Production & the Modern Theatre in Britain. 144p. (Orig.). 1988. pap. 40.00 (*91-554-2275-6*, Pub. by Uppsala Univ Acta Univ Uppsaliensis) Coronet Bks.

Nyberg, Morgan. El Dorado Shuffle. LC 98-184358. 331p. 1999. pap. text 15.95 (*1-896951-06-6*, Pub. by Cormor Bks) Genl Dist Srvs.

Nyberg, O. Impact Use of Expert Systems on Marginal Field Development. 1989. 135.00 (*90-6314-502-0*, Pub. by Lorne & MacLean Marine) St Mut.

Nyberg, O., ed. Impact Use of Expert Systems on Marginal Field Development. (C). 1989. 110.00 (*0-89771-740-6*, Pub. by Lorne & MacLean Marine) St Mut.

Nyberg, Sidney L. The Chosen People. LC 74-29512. (Modern Jewish Experience Ser.). 1975. reprint ed. 33.95 (*0-405-06738-0*) Ayer.

Nyberg, Sten. Honesty, Vanity & Corporate Equity: Four Microeconomic Essays. (Industrial Institute for Economic & Social Research Report Ser.). 73p. (Orig.). 1993. pap. 52.50 (*91-7204-418-7*) Coronet Bks.

Nyberg, Tim, et al. Warning Label Book. LC 98-24108. 128p. 1998. pap. 8.95 (*0-312-19534-6*) St Martin.

Nyberg, Tim, jt. auth. see Berg, Jim.

Nyberg, Tim, jt. auth. see Green, Joey.

***Nyberg, Tore & Bekker-Nielsen, Hans, eds.** Mediaeval Scandinavia 13. 300p. 2000. 35.75 (*87-7838-453-2*, Pub. by Odense Universitets Forlag) Intl Spec Bk.

Nyberg, Tore, et al. History & Heroic Tale: A Symposium. 242p. (Orig.). 1985. pap. text 53.00 (*87-7492-534-2*) Coronet Bks.

Nyblom, Kare, jt. auth. see Jervall, Sverre.

Nybom, Thorsten, jt. ed. see Trow, Martin A.

Nyborg, Helmuth. Hormones, Sex & Society: The Science of Physicology. LC 94-8640. (Human Evolution, Behavior & Intelligence Ser.). 256p. 1994. 65.00 (*0-275-94608-8*, Praeger Pubs) Greenwood.

Nyborg, Helmuth, ed. The Scientific Study of Human Nature: Tribute to Hans J. Eysenck at Eighty. LC 97-15771. 360p. 1997. 82.00 (*0-08-042787-1*, Pergamon Pr) Elsevier.

Nyborg, R. L. Brush Plating on Video. (Illus.). 75p. 1995. pap. 35.00 incl. VHS (*1-57002-060-4*) Univ Publng Hse.

— Buffing & Polishing Metal on Video. (Illus.). 75p. 1995. pap. 26.00 incl. VHS (*1-57002-062-0*) Univ Publng Hse.

***Nyborg, R. L.** The Case Against Evolution. 125p. 1999. pap. 10.95 (*1-57002-118-X*) Univ Publng Hse.

Nyborg, R. L. Hard Chrome Plating on Video. (Illus.). 75p. 1995. pap. 45.00 incl. VHS (*1-57002-064-7*) Univ Publng Hse.

— Plastic Injection Molding Made Easy. unabridged ed. (Illus.). 95p. 1991. pap. 22.00 (*1-57002-074-4*) Univ Publng Hse.

— Plating Aluminum on Video. (Illus.). 75p. 1995. pap. 45.00 incl. VHS (*1-57002-063-9*) Univ Publng Hse.

— Plating Plastic on Video. (Illus.). 75p. 1995. pap. 26.95 incl. VHS (*1-57002-065-5*) Univ Publng Hse.

— Pot Metal Plating on Video. (Illus.). 75p. 1995. pap. 35.00 incl. VHS (*1-57002-061-2*) Univ Publng Hse.

— Powder Coating Made Easy. 101p. 1992. pap. 14.95 (*1-57002-079-5*) Univ Publng Hse.

Nyborg, Randell. Analyzing Financial Statements Made Easy. (Illus.). 182p. 1994. ring bd. 21.00 (*1-57002-069-8*) Univ Publng Hse.

— How I Built a 4-Bedroom House for $10,000 & How You Can Save Big on Your New House. (Illus.). 130p. 1998. pap. 9.95 (*1-57002-087-6*) Univ Publng Hse.

Nyborg, Randell L. Electroplating Fundamentals on Video. (Illus.). 75p. (C). 1990. pap. 35.00 incl. VHS (*1-877767-04-2*) Univ Publng Hse.

— Hobbyist Electroplating Made Easy. (Illus.). 73p. (Orig.). (C). 1988. pap. 11.50 (*1-877767-00-X*) Univ Publng Hse.

— How to Repair Your Copy Machine. (Illus.). 1994. pap. 14.95 (*1-877767-84-0*) Univ Publng Hse.

— How to Start & Operate a Limousine Service. (Illus.). 85p. 1990. ring bd. 45.00 (*1-877767-14-X*) Univ Publng Hse.

— How to Start & Operate an Electroplating Shop. (Illus.). 150p. (Orig.). (C). 1988. pap. 31.00 (*1-877767-03-4*) Univ Publng Hse.

Nyburg, Sidney L. The Chosen People. Sarna, Jonathan D., ed. (Masterworks of Modern Jewish Writing Ser.). 373p. (C). 1986. reprint ed. pap. 9.95 (*0-910129-47-9*) Wiener Pubs Inc.

Nyce, Ben. Satyajit Ray: A Study of His Films. LC 88-6620. 223p. 1988. 55.00 (*0-275-92666-4*, C2666, Praeger Pubs) Greenwood.

Nyce, Dorothy Y. Jesus' Clear Call to Justice. LC 90-43599. (Peace & Justice Ser.: Vol. 11). 96p. (Orig.). 1990. pap. 6.99 (*0-8361-3533-4*) Herald Pr.

— To See Each Other's Good. (Illus.). 148p. (Orig.). 1996. pap. write for info. (*1-57579-016-5*) Pine Hill Pr.

Nychka, D., et al, eds. Case Studies in Environmental Statistics. LC 98-16281. (Lecture Notes in Statistics Ser.: Vol. 132). 192p. 1998. pap. 39.95 (*0-387-98478-X*) Spr-Verlag.

Nycz, jt. auth. see Collins1.

Nyczek, Tadeusz, ed. see Karasek, Krzysztof, et al.

Nydahl, Hannah, tr. see Nydahl, Ole.

Nydahl, John E., jt. auth. see Silver, Howard A.

Nydahl, John E., jt. auth. see Silver, Howard F.

Nydahl, Lama O., jt. auth. see Nydahl, Ole.

Nydahl, Ole. Basic Dharma: An Introduction to the Nature of Mind. Clemens, Paul M., ed. 32p. 1988. pap. 5.00 (*0-931892-17-1*) B Dolphin Pub.

— Entering the Diamond Way: Tibetan Buddhism Meets the West. 2nd ed. LC 85-73182. (Illus.). 240p. (Orig.). 1998. pap. 14.95 (*0-931892-03-1*) B Dolphin Pub.

— Mahamudra: Boundless Joy & Freedom. Nydahl, Hannah, tr. from TIB. LC 91-26450. (Illus.). 96p. (Orig.). 1991. pap. 9.95 (*0-931892-69-4*) B Dolphin Pub.

— Ngondro: The Four Foundational Practices of Tibetan Buddhism. (Illus.). 96p. (Orig.). 1990. pap. 9.95 (*0-931892-23-6*) B Dolphin Pub.

— Riding the Tiger: Twenty Years on the Road: The Risks & Joys of Bringing Tibetan Buddhism to the West. Aronoff, Carol A., ed. LC 92-6605. (Illus.). 512p. (Orig.). 1992. pap. 17.95 (*0-931892-67-8*) B Dolphin Pub.

— Teachings on the Nature of Mind. (Illus.). 40p. (Orig.). 1993. pap. 5.00 (*0-931892-58-9*) B Dolphin Pub.

Nydahl, Ole & Aronoff, Carol. Practical Buddhism: The Kagyu Path. 48p. (Orig.). 1989. pap. 5.00 (*0-931892-63-5*) B Dolphin Pub.

Nydahl, Ole & Nydahl, Lama O. The Way Things Are: A Living Approach to Buddhism for Today's World. LC 96-35059. (Illus.). 96p. (Orig.). 1996. pap. 10.00 (*0-931892-38-4*) B Dolphin Pub.

Nydegger, Joanne E. Dad. 1998. pap. write for info. (*1-57553-937-3*) Watermrk Pr.

— Meandering. 1998. pap. write for info. (*1-57553-875-X*) Watermrk Pr.

Nydegger, U. E., ed. Immunochemotherapy: A Guide to Intravenous Immunoglobulin Therapy. LC 81-68971. 1982. text 136.00 (*0-12-523280-2*) Acad Pr.

— Therapeutic Hemapheresis in the 1990s. (Current Studies in Hematology & Blood Transfusion: No. 57). (Illus.). viii, 282p. 1990. 232.25 (*3-8055-5166-5*) S Karger.

Nydegger, U. E. & Morell, A. Clinical Use of Intravenous Immunoglobulins. 1986. text 121.00 (*0-12-523282-9*) Acad Pr.

Nydegger, U. E., jt. ed. see Starsia, Z.

Nydell, Margaret K. Arabic Dialect Identification Course. 223p. 1993. pap. text 59.95 incl. audio (*0-9628410-9-9*) DLS VA.

— From Modern Standard Arabic to the Egyptian Dialect: Answer Key to Supplement. 61p. (Orig.). 1993. pap. text 9.95 (*1-886737-01-0*, DLSP-001K, DLS Pr) DLS VA.

— From Modern Standard Arabic to the Egyptian Dialect: Classroom Activity Supplement. 103p. (Orig.). 1993. pap. text 19.95 (*1-886737-00-2*, DLSP-001S, DLS Pr) DLS VA.

— From Modern Standard Arabic to the Egyptian Dialect, Conversion Course. 526p. 1993. pap. text 39.95 (*0-9628410-2-1*) DLS VA.

— From Modern Standard Arabic to the Gulf Dialects: Answer Key to Supplement. 75p. (Orig.). 1991. pap. text 9.95 (*1-886737-04-5*, DLSP-006K, DLS Pr) DLS VA.

— From Modern Standard Arabic to the Gulf Dialects: Classroom Activity Supplement. 141p. (Orig.). 1991. pap. text 19.95 (*1-886737-03-7*, DLSP-006S, DLS Pr) DLS VA.

— From Modern Standard Arabic to the Gulf Dialects, Conversion Course. 335p. 1991. pap. text 39.95 (*0-9628410-4-8*) DLS VA.

— From Modern Standard Arabic to the Iraqi Dialect: Answer Key to Supplement. 69p. (Orig.). 1991. pap. text 9.95 (*1-886737-07-X*, DLSP-005K, DLS Pr) DLS VA.

— From Modern Standard Arabic to the Iraqi Dialect: Classroom Activity Supplement. 124p. (Orig.). 1991. pap. text 19.95 (*1-886737-06-1*, DLSP-005S, DLS Pr) DLS VA.

— From Modern Standard Arabic to the Iraqi Dialect, Conversion Course. 324p. 1991. pap. text 39.95 (*0-9628410-5-6*) DLS VA.

— From Modern Standard Arabic to the Levantine Dialects: Answer Key to Supplement. 62p. (Orig.). 1992. pap. text 9.95 (*1-886737-10-X*, DLSP-002K, DLS Pr) DLS VA.

— From Modern Standard Arabic to the Levantine Dialects: Classroom Activity Supplement. 141p. (Orig.). 1992. pap. text 19.95 (*1-886737-09-6*, DLSP-002S, DLS Pr) DLS VA.

— From Modern Standard Arabic to the Levantine Dialects, Conversion Course. 392p. 1992. pap. text 39.95 (*0-9628410-3-X*) DLS VA.

— From Modern Standard Arabic to the Maghrebi Dialects, (Libyan & Tunisian), Conversion Course. 405p. 1993. pap. text 39.95 (*0-9628410-7-2*) DLS VA.

— From Modern Standard Arabic to the Maghrebi Dialects, (Moroccan & Algerian), Conversion Course. 420p. 1992. pap. text 39.95 (*0-9628410-6-4*) DLS VA.

— From Modern Standard Arabic to the Meghrebi Dialects (Libyan & Tunisian) Answer Key to Supplement. 54p. (Orig.). 1993. pap. text 9.95 (*1-886737-13-4*, DLSP-004K, DLS Pr) DLS VA.

— From Modern Standard Arabic to the Meghrebi Dialects (Libyan & Tunisian) Classroom Activity Supplement. 147p. (Orig.). 1993. pap. text 19.95 (*1-886737-12-6*, DLSP-004S, DLS Pr) DLS VA.

— From Modern Standard Arabic to the Meghrebi Dialects (Moroccan & Algerian) Answer Key to Supplement. 59p. (Orig.). 1992. pap. text 9.95 (*1-886737-16-9*, DLSP-003K, DLS Pr) DLS VA.

— From Modern Standard Arabic to the Meghrebi Dialects (Moroccan & Algerian) Classroom Activity Supplement. 157p. (Orig.). 1992. pap. text 19.95 (*1-886737-15-0*, DLSP-003S, DLS Pr) DLS VA.

— Introduction to Colloquial Arabic. 328p. 1994. pap. text 25.00 (*0-9628410-8-0*) DLS VA.

— Understanding Arabs: A Guide for Westerners. 2nd rev. ed. LC 96-9363. (InterAct Ser.). 192p. 1997. pap. text 17.95 (*1-877864-46-3*) Intercult Pr.

Nydell, Margaret K., jt. auth. see Ryding, Karin C.

Nydell, Margerat K. Military Phrasebook for Iraqi Arabic. 72p. 1990. pap. text 9.95 (*0-9628410-0-5*) DLS Inc.

Nyden, Philip. Steel Workers Rank & File. LC 83-22462. 166p. 1984. 45.00 (*0-275-91236-1*, C1236, Praeger Pubs) Greenwood.

Nyden, Philip & Wiewel, Wim. Challenging Uneven Development: An Urban Agenda for the 1990s. LC 90-45221. 275p. (C). 1991. text 37.00 (*0-8135-1658-7*); pap. text 17.00 (*0-8135-1659-5*) Rutgers U Pr.

Nyden, Philip W. Building Community: Social Science in Action. LC 96-45369. 1997. pap. 29.95 (*0-8039-9093-6*) Pine Forge.

Nydia P. De Villarreal, M. L., jt. auth. see Hoyos de Martens, Veronica.

Nye. Come with Me. (J). 1999. mass mkt. 17.00 (*0-689-81232-9*) S&S Childrens.

***Nye.** The Man From Wells Fargo: Breyfogel's Gold. 1998. 20.00 (*0-7862-0990-9*) Mac Lib Ref.

Nye. Myth Abroad. 1993. 4.50 (*0-446-77755-2*) Warner Bks.

N

An Asterisk (*) at the beginning of an entry indicates that the title is appearing for the first time.

— Mythology 101. 1993. 4.95 (*0-446-77754-4*) Warner Bks.

*Nye. Racers: The Legends of Formula One, 1948-1968. (Illus.). 192p. 2000. 39.95 (*0-7603-0790-3*, Pub. by MBI Pubg) Motorbooks Intl.

Nye. This Same Sky. 1998. pap. 8.99 (*0-87628-342-3*) Ctr Appl Res.

— Understanding International Conflict. 3rd ed. LC 99-23196. 244p. (C). 1999. pap. text 32.86 (*0-321-03327-2*) Addison-Wesley.

Nye, Adrian. X Protocol Reference Manual: Volume 0 for Xii, Release 6. 4th ed. 458p. 1995. pap. 34.95 (*1-56592-083-X*) Thomson Learn.

— XLib Programming Manual: For R4-R5, Vol. 1. 3rd ed. (X Window System Ser.). (Illus.). 824p. 1992. pap. 34.95 (*1-56592-002-3*) Thomson Learn.

— XLib Reference Manual: For R4-R5, Vol. 2. 3rd ed. (X Window System Ser.). 1138p. 1992. pap. 34.95 (*1-56592-006-6*) Thomson Learn.

Nye, Adrian, ed. Programmer's Supplement for Release 6 of the Window System. (Illus.). 452p. 1995. pap. 29.95 (*1-56592-089-9*) Thomson Learn.

— The X Resource, Issue 6: A Practical Journal of the X Window System Series. (X Window System Ser.). (Illus.). 234p. (Orig.). 1993. pap. 14.95 (*1-56592-021-X*) Thomson Learn.

Nye, Adrian & O'Reilly, Tim. X Toolkit Intrinsics Programming Manual: For X11 Release 5 - Motif Edition, Vol. 4M. 2nd ed. (X Window System Ser.). (Illus.). 714p. 1992. pap. 34.95 (*1-56592-013-9*) Thomson Learn.

Nye, Adrian, ed. see Oualline, Steve.

Nye, Alan R. How to Stop Paying High Property Taxes in Maine: A Step-by-Step Guide to Reducing Your Tax Bills. 150p. 1991. pap. 19.95 (*0-9631045-0-0*) Portland Pub.

Nye, Alfred, Jr. Understanding & Managing Your Anger & Aggression: A Book to Help Prevent the Damage Anger Causes You & Your Relationships. LC 92-75756. (Illus.). 253p. (Orig.). 1993. pap. 14.95 (*0-9635613-5-9*) BCA Pub.

Nye, Alvan C. American Colonial Furniture in Scaled Drawings. 1983. 16.00 (*0-8446-6009-4*) Peter Smith.

Nye, Andrea. Feminist Theory & the Philosophies of Man. 244p. (C). 1989. pap. 18.99 (*0-415-90204-5*, A3889) Routledge.

— Philosophia: The Thought of Rosa Luxemburg, Simone Weil, & Hannah Arendt. LC 93-10223. 256p. (C). 1994. pap. 19.99 (*0-415-90831-0*, B2303) Routledge.

— Philosophy: Discipline Analysis, Vol. 7L. (Women in the Curriculum Ser.). 22p. (Orig.). 1997. pap. 7.00 (*1-885303-23-8*) Towson St Univ.

— Philosophy & Feminism at the Border. (Impact of Feminism on the Arts & Sciences Ser.). 180p. 1995. 33.00 (*0-8057-9763-7*, Twyne); pap. 20.00 (*0-8057-9778-5*, Twyne) Mac Lib Ref.

— Philosophy of Language: The Big Questions. LC 97-45209. (Philosophy Ser.). 500p. 1998. 62.95 (*0-631-20601-9*); pap. 29.95 (*0-631-20602-7*) Blackwell Pubs.

— The Princess & the Philosopher: Letters of Elisabeth of the Palatine to Rene Descartes. 208p. 1999. pap. 18.95 (*0-8476-9265-5*) Rowman.

— The Princess & the Philosopher: Letters of Elisabeth of the Palatine to Rene Descartes. LC 98-44821. 208p. 1999. text 57.95 (*0-8476-9264-7*) Rowman.

— Words of Power: A Feminist Reading of the History of Logic. 256p. (C). 1990. pap. 19.99 (*0-415-90200-2*, A3705) Routledge.

Nye, Bill. The Best of Bill Nye's Humor. Hasley, Louis, ed. (Masterworks of Literature Ser.). 1972. 19.95 (*0-8084-0343-5*); pap. 15.95 (*0-8084-0344-3*) NCUP.

— Dill Nye, His Own Life Story. LC 78-124246. (Select Bibliographies Reprint Ser.). 1977. reprint ed. 24.95 (*0-8369-5434-3*) Ayer.

***Nye, Bill.** Bill Nye the Science Guy: Consider the Following, a Way Cool Set of Science Questions, Answers & Ideas to Ponder. (Illus.). 112p. (J). 2000. pap. 10.99 (*0-7868-1443-8*, Pub. by Hyprn Child) Time Warner.

Nye, Bill. Bill Nye the Science Guy's Big Blast of Science. (Illus.). 176p. (YA). 1993. pap. 15.00 (*0-201-60864-2*) Addison-Wesley.

— Bill Nye the Science Guy's Big Blue Ocean. 48p. (J). 1999. lib. bdg. 16.49 (*0-7868-5063-9*, Pub. by Disney Pr) Little.

— Bill Nye the Science Guy's Big Blue Ocean. LC 98-33744. (Illus.). 96p. (J). (gr. 2-5). 1999. pap. 15.99 (*0-7868-4221-0*, Pub. by Disney Pr) Time Warner.

***Nye, Bill.** Bill Nye the Science Guy's Consider the Following. (Illus.). (J). 2000. 13.30 (*0-606-18254-3*) Turtleback.

— Bill Nye the Science Guy's Dinosaur Book. 48p. (J). 2000. 15.99 (*0-7868-0542-0*, Pub. by Hyperion) Time Warner.

— Bill Nye the Science Guy's Human Body Book. 48p. (J). 2000. 12.99 (*0-7868-0543-9*, Pub. by Hyperion); lib. bdg. 13.49 (*0-7868-2473-5*, Pub. by Hyperion) Little.

— Bill Nye the Science Guy's Space Book. 48p. (J). (gr. 2-5). 2001. 15.99 (*0-7868-0613-3*, Pub. by Hyperion), lib. bdg. 16.49 (*0-7868-2526-X*, Pub. by Hyperion) Little.

— The Science Guy's Big Blast of Science. 48p. (J). 2000. lib. bdg. 16.49 (*0-7868-2472-7*, Pub. by Disney Pr) Little.

Nye, Bill & Saunders, Ian G. Bill Nye the Science Guy: Consider the Following, a Way Cool Set of Science Questions, Answers, & Ideas to Ponder. LC 95-68629. (Illus.). 112p. (J). (gr. 4-7). 1995. 13.89 (*0-7868-5035-3*, Pub. by Disney Pr) Time Warner.

Nye, C., et al. Assessing the Communication Skills of American Indian Job Applicants During the Interview Process. 92p. 1993. pap. text. write for info. (*1-888557-22-2*, 100035) No Ariz Univ.

Nye, Chad. Review Course for the N. E. S. P. A. large type ed. LC 97-41312. (Illus.). 208p. 1998. pap. 148.95 (*1-56593-741-4*, 1440) Thomson Learn.

Nye, Chris. MS DOS 6.2 by Example. 1994. pap. text 19.95 (*1-86398-035-0*) Prima Pub.

Nye, D. E., jt. ed. see Gidley, M.

Nye, D. F., ed. see Best, Frank E. & Nye, G. S.

***Nye, Dagmar.** Sixty Odd Years: An Alaskan's Selected Reminiscences. LC 99-60555. (Illus.). 288p. 1999. pap. 14.95 (*1-888125-41-1*) Publ Consult.

Nye, David. Alternative Staffing Strategies. LC 87-35857. 219p. 1988. reprint ed. pap. 67.90 (*0-608-00695-5*, 206146600009) Bks Demand.

— Narratives & Spaces: Technology & the Construction of American Culture. LC 97-28777. (Illus.). 224p. 1998. 47.50 (*0-231-11196-7*) Col U Pr.

— Narratives & Spaces: Technology & the Construction of American Culture. LC 97-28777. (Illus.). 224p. 1998. pap. 18.50 (*0-231-11197-5*) Col U Pr.

Nye, David E. American Technological Sublime. LC 94-19273. 384p. 1994. 37.50 (*0-262-14056-X*) MIT Pr.

— American Technological Sublime. (Illus.). 384p. 1996. reprint ed. pap. text 20.00 (*0-262-64034-1*) MIT Pr.

— Christopher Columbus in Philately. (Illus.). 32p. 1992. pap. 6.00 (*0-935991-16-6*) Am Topical Assn.

— Consuming Power: A Social History of American Energies. LC 97-24832. (Illus.). 345p. 1997. 27.50 (*0-262-14063-2*) MIT Pr.

— Consuming Power: A Social History of American Energies. 1999. pap. text 15.00 (*0-262-64038-4*) MIT Pr.

— Electrifying America: Social Meanings of a New Technology. (Illus.). 496p. 1990. 45.00 (*0-262-14048-9*) MIT Pr.

— Electrifying America: Social Meanings of New Technology. (Illus.). 496p. 1992. reprint ed. pap. text 24.00 (*0-262-64030-9*) MIT Pr.

— Image Worlds: Corporate Identities at General Electric, 1890-1930. (Illus.). 250p. 1985. 27.50 (*0-262-14038-1*) MIT Pr.

— Narratives & Spaces: Technology & the Construction of American Culture. (Cultural Studies Ser.). (Illus.). 224p. 1998. 70.00 (*0-85989-555-6*, Pub. by Univ Exeter Pr); pap. 22.00 (*0-85989-556-4*) Univ Exeter Pr.

Nye, David E., ed. Technologies of Landscape: From Reaping to Recycling. LC 99-16762. (Illus.). 280p. 2000. 50.00 (*1-55849-228-3*); pap. 16.95 (*1-55849-229-1*) U of Mass Pr.

Nye, David E. & Thomsen, Christen K., eds. American Studies in Transition: Essays. 234p. (Orig.). 1985. pap. text 43.50 (*87-7492-532-6*) Coronet Bks.

***Nye, Doug.** Cooper Cars: World Champions. (Illus.). 400p. 2000. 39.95 (*1-85532-919-0*, 129672AE) Ospry.

— Racers: The Legends of Formula One, 1948-1968. (Illus.). 192p. 1999. 39.95 (*1-902655-01-X*, Pub. by Queensgate Pubns) Motorbooks Intl.

Nye, Doug. The Single-Seat Lotus: Formula One & Indy Cars LC 78-61840. 200p. 1978. write for info. (*0-930880-02-1*) NewPrt Pr.

— The Story of Lotus, 1961-1971: Growth of a Legend. LC 70-190263. 288 p. 1972. write for info. (*0-8376-0051-0*) Bentley Pubs.

Nye, Doug & Goddard, Geoff. Classic Racers: The Post War Front Engined G.P. Cars. (Illus.). 144p. 1991. 34.95 (*0-85429-775-8*, Pub. by GT Foulis) Haynes Manuals.

Nye, Doug, jt. auth. see Falconer, Richard.

Nye, E. R. & Gibson, M. E. Ronald Ross: Malariologist & Polymath, a Biography. LC 96-8835. (Illus.). 352p. 1997. text 59.95 (*0-312-16296-0*) St Martin.

Nye, E. R. & Gibson, Mary E. Ronald Ross: Malariologist & Polymath: A Biography LC 96-8835. xii, 316p. 1997. write for info. (*0-333-62551-X*, Pub. by Macmillan) St Martin.

Nye, Edgar W. Baled Hay. (Notable American Authors Ser.). 1999. reprint ed. lib. bdg. 125.00 (*0-7812-4654-7*) Rprt Serv.

— Bill Nye: His Own Life Story. (BCL1-PS American Literature Ser.). 412p. 1992. reprint ed. lib. bdg. 99.00 (*0-7812-6815-X*) Rprt Serv.

— Bill Nye & Boomerang. (Notable American Authors Ser.). 1999. reprint ed. lib. bdg. 125.00 (*0-7812-4652-0*) Rprt Serv.

— Bill Nye & Boomerang. LC 70-166823. 1971. reprint ed. 29.00 (*0-403-01449-2*) Scholarly.

— Bill Nye's Blossom Rock. (Notable American Authors Ser.). 1999. reprint ed. lib. bdg. 125.00 (*0-7812-4655-5*) Rprt Serv.

— Bill Nye's Chestnuts Old & New. (Notable American Authors Ser.). 1999. reprint ed. lib. bdg. 125.00 (*0-7812-4658-X*) Rprt Serv.

— Bill Nye's History of England from the Druids to the Reign of Henry. (Notable American Authors Ser.). 1999. reprint ed. lib. bdg. 125.00 (*0-7812-4661-X*) Rprt Serv.

— Bill Nye's History of the United States. LC 75-96891. (Illus.). reprint ed. lib. bdg. 25.00 (*0-8398-1352-X*) Irvington.

— Bill Nye's History of the United States. (Notable American Authors Ser.). 1999. reprint ed. lib. bdg. 125.00 (*0-7812-4660-1*) Rprt Serv.

— Forty Liars & Other Lies. (Notable American Authors Ser.). 1999. reprint ed. lib. bdg. 125.00 (*0-7812-4653-9*) Rprt Serv.

— Fun, Wit, & Poetry (With J. W. Riley) (Notable American Authors Ser.). 1999. reprint ed. lib. bdg. 125.00 (*0-7812-4659-8*) Rprt Serv.

— The Guest at Ludlow. (Notable American Authors Ser.). 1999. reprint ed. lib. bdg. 125.00 (*0-7812-4662-8*) Rprt Serv.

— Nye & Riley's Railway Guide (With J. W. Riley) (Notable American Authors Ser.). 1999. reprint ed. lib. bdg. 125.00 (*0-7812-4657-1*) Rprt Serv.

— Thinks. LC 74-104534. 181p. reprint ed. lib. bdg. 31.00 (*0-8398-1354-6*) Irvington.

— Thinks. 181p. (C). 1986. reprint ed. pap. text 6.95 (*0-8290-2041-1*) Irvington.

— Thinks & Remarks by Bill Nye. (Notable American Authors Ser.). 1999. reprint ed. lib. bdg. 125.00 (*0-7812-4656-3*) Rprt Serv.

Nye, Edgar W. & Nye, Frank W. Bill Nye: His Own Life Story. LC 70-145216. (Illus.). 1971. reprint ed. 24.00 (*0-403-01133-7*) Scholarly.

Nye, F. Ivan. Family Relationships & Delinquent Behavior. LC 73-8562. 168p. 1973. reprint ed. lib. bdg. 38.50 (*0-8371-6967-4*, NYFR, Greenwood Pr) Greenwood.

Nye, Francis, et al. The Employed Mother in America. LC 76-4503. (Illus.). 406p. 1976. reprint ed. lib. bdg. 49.50 (*0-8371-8784-2*, NYEM, Greenwood Pr) Greenwood.

Nye, Frank W., jt. auth. see Nye, Edgar W.

Nye, Fred J., jt. auth. see Beeching, Nick J.

Nye, G. S. Biographical Sketches & Records of the Ezra Olin Family. 441p. 1989. reprint ed. pap. 68.50 (*0-8328-0921-7*); reprint ed. lib. bdg. 78.50 (*0-8328-0920-9*) Higginson Bk Co.

Nye, G. S., jt. auth. see Best, Frank E.

Nye, George A. Old Wine in New Skins: Calls to Worship & Other Worship Resources. LC 93-38001. 168p. 1994. pap. 9.75 (*1-55673-824-2*, 9422) CSS OH.

Nye, Gideon. The Rationale of the China Question. LC 72-79834. (China Library). 1972. reprint ed. lib. bdg. 14.00 (*0-8420-1374-1*) Scholarly Res Inc.

Nye, Heidi. Traditional Chinese Medicine: Ancient Wisdom for a Modern World. (Good Health Guides Ser.). 48p. 1998. pap. 3.95 (*0-87983-898-1*, 38981K, Keats Publng) NTC Contemp Pub Co.

***Nye, J. F.** Natural Focusing & Fine Structure of Light: Caustics & Wave Dislocations. LC 99-11442. 8p. 1999. 50.00 (*0-7503-0610-6*) IOP Pub.

Nye, J. F. Physical Properties of Crystals: Their Representation by Tensors & Matrices. (Illus.). 352p. 1985. pap. text 45.00 (*0-19-851165-5*) OUP.

Nye, J. Michael, ed. see Marketing Consultants International Inc. Staff.

Nye, Jim. Aftershock: Poems & Prose from the Vietnam War. LC 91-372302. 80p. (Orig.). 1991. pap. 8.95 (*0-938317-14-8*) Cinco Puntos.

Nye, Jody L. Medicine Show. 272p. (Orig.). 1994. mass mkt. 4.99 (*0-441-00085-1*) Ace Bks.

— The Ship Errant. 416p. 1996. 21.00 (*0-671-87754-2*) Baen Bks.

— The Ship Errant. (Brain/Brawn Ser.). 1997. per. 6.99 (*0-671-87854-9*) Baen Bks.

— Taylor's Ark. 288p. (Orig.). 1993. mass mkt. 5.99 (*0-441-79974-4*) Ace Bks

— Waking in Dreamland. 1998. per. 5.99 (*0-671-87875-1*) Baen Bks.

Nye, Jody L., ed. Don't Forget Your Spacesuit, Dear. 1996. mass mkt. 5.99 (*0-671-87732-1*) Baen Bks.

Nye, Jody L. & McCaffrey, Anne. The Dragonlover's Guide to Pern. 2nd ed. LC 97-92989. 1997. pap. 15.00 (*0-345-41274-5*, Del Rey) Ballantine Pub Grp.

Nye, Jody L., jt. auth. see McCaffrey, Anne.

Nye, Jody L., ed. see McCaffrey, Anne.

***Nye, Jody Lynn.** Applied Mythology. 600p. 2000. pap. 20.00 (*1-892065-21-5*) Meisha Merlin.

— The Grand Tour. (Illus.). 480p. 2000. mass mkt. 6.99 (*0-671-57883-9*) Baen Bks.

Nye, Jody Lynn. School of Light. 1999. mass mkt. 6.99 (*0-671-57816-2*) S&S Trade.

Nye, Jody Lynn, jt. auth. see Anthony, Piers.

Nye, John. Between the Rivers: A History of United Methodism in Iowa. LC 86-80106. (Illus.). 350p. 1986. 12.95 (*0-9616298-0-0*); pap. 10.95 (*0-9616298-1-9*) IA Conf Com Arch.

Nye, Joseph S., Jr. Ethics & Foreign Policy. 38p. (Orig.). 1985. pap. text 10.50 (*0-8191-5844-5*) U Pr of Amer.

— Nuclear Ethics. 130p. 1988. pap. 12.95 (*0-02-923091-8*) Free Pr.

Nye, Joseph S. Pan-Africanism & East African Integration. LC 65-22063. 327p. reprint ed. pap. 101.40 (*0-7837-3845-5*, 204366700010) Bks Demand.

— Peace in Parts: Integration & Conflict in Regional Organization. LC 87-10480. (Illus.). 224p. (Orig.). (C). 1987. reprint ed. lib. bdg. 46.00 (*0-8191-6393-7*) U Pr of Amer.

Nye, Joseph S., ed. The Making of America's Soviet Policy. LC 83-51295. 379p. 1984. pap. 117.50 (*0-7837-8651-4*, 208231400009) Bks Demand.

Nye, Joseph S., Jr., et al, eds. Fateful Visions: Avoiding Nuclear Catastrophe. 288p. 1988. text 34.95 (*0-88730-272-6*, HarpBusn) HarpInfo.

— Fateful Visions: Avoiding Nuclear Catastrophe. 288p. 1989. pap. text 18.95 (*0-88730-325-0*, HarpBusn) HarpInfo.

— Why People Don't Trust Government. LC 97-20363. (Illus.). 288p. 1997. 39.95 (*0-674-94056-3*); pap. 19.50 (*0-674-94057-1*) HUP.

Nye, Joseph S., Jr. & Rowe, David M., eds. Harness the Rising Sun: An American Strategy for Managing Japan's Rise as a Global Power. LC 93-10863. 240p. 1993. 54.00 (*0-8191-9168-X*); pap. 26.50 (*0-8191-9169-8*) U Pr of Amer.

Nye, Joseph S., Jr. & Schear, James A., eds. On the Defensive? The Future of SDI. LC 88-17342. (Aspen Strategy Group Reports). 222p. (Orig.). (C). 1989. pap. text 20.00 (*0-8191-7021-6*) U Pr of Amer.

Nye, Joseph S., Jr. & Shear, James A., eds. Seeking Stability in Space: Anti-Satelite Weapons & the Evolving Space Regime. LC 87-21619. (Illus.). 184p. (Orig.). (C). 1988. pap. text 19.50 (*0-8191-6422-4*) U Pr of Amer.

Nye, Joseph S. & Smith, Roger K., eds. After the Storm: Lessons from the Gulf War. 426p. 1992. 24.95 (*0-8191-8529-9*) Madison Bks UPA.

— After the Storm: Lessons from the Gulf War. 426p. 1993. pap. 14.95 (*1-56833-015-4*) Madison Bks UPA.

Nye, Joseph S., Jr., et al. Global Cooperation after the Cold War: A Reassessment of Trilateralism. (Triangle Papers: Vol. 41). 1991. 6.00 (*0-930503-67-8*) Trilateral Comm.

Nye, Joseph S., Jr., jt. auth. see Kamarck, Elaine C.

Nye, Joseph S., jt. auth. see Keohane, Robert O., Jr.

Nye, Joseph S., jt. ed. see Hunington, Samuel P.

Nye, Joseph S., Jr., jt. ed. see Keohane, Robert O.

Nye, Judith L. & Brower, Aaron M., eds. What's Social about Social Cognition? Social Cognition Research in Small Groups. 428p. (C). 1996. 37.00 (*0-8039-7204-0*); pap. 17.99 (*0-8039-7205-9*) Sage.

Nye, Julie. Scout. Jordan, Suzette, ed. (Light Line Ser.). 178p. (Orig.). (J). 1987. pap. 6.49 (*0-89084-413-5*, 032839) Bob Jones Univ.

Nye, K. E. & Parkin, J. M. HIV & AIDS. (Medical Perspectives Ser.). 160p. (Orig.). 1994. pap. 44.50 (*1-872748-96-1*, Pub. by Bios Sci) Coronet Bks.

Nye, Kemp B. Ripshin. LC 92-33504. 1992. pap. 12.00 (*0-930095-13-8*) Signal Bks.

— Ripshin. LC 93-42266. 1993. 16.00 (*0-930095-17-0*) Signal Bks.

Nye, Malory. A Place for Our Gods: The Construction of an Edinburgh Hindu Temple Community. (SOAS London Studies on South Asia: No. 8). 220p. (C). 1995. text 45.00 (*0-7007-0356-X*, Pub. by Curzon Pr Ltd) UH Pr.

Nye, Mary J. Before Big Science: The Pursuit of Modern Chemistry & Physics, 1800-1940. (History of Science & Society Ser.: No. 1). 282p. 1996. 32.95 (*0-8057-9512-X*, Twayne) Mac Lib Ref.

— From Chemical Philosophy to Theoretical Chemistry: Dynamics of Matter & Dynamics of Disciplines, 1800-1950. LC 92-43114. 1993. 60.00 (*0-520-08210-9*, Pub. by U CA Pr) Cal Prin Full Svc.

Nye, Mary J., et al, eds. The Invention of Physical Science: Intersections of Mathematics, Theology, & Natural Philosophy since the Seventeenth Century: Essays in Honor of Erwin N. Hiebert. LC 92-12520. (Boston Studies in the Philosophy of Science: Vol. 139). 288p. (C). 1992. lib. bdg. 175.00 (*0-7923-1753-X*, Pub. by Kluwer Academic) Kluwer Academic.

Nye, Mary Jo. Before Big Science: The Pursuit of Modern Chemistry & Physics, 1800-1940. 1999. pap. text 16.95 (*0-674-06382-1*) HUP.

***Nye, Nancy & Schramm, Richard.** Building Higher Education-Community Development Corporation Partnerships. (Illus.). 76p. (C). 2000. pap. text 20.00 (*0-7567-0025-6*) DIANE Pub.

Nye, Naomi S. Benito's Dream Bottle. LC 93-45675. (Illus.). 32p. (J). (ps-2). 1995. text 15.00 (*0-02-768167-9*) S&S Bks Yung.

— Fuel. LC 97-74819. (American Poets Continuum Ser.: Vol. 47). 65p. 1998. pap. 12.50 (*1-880238-63-2*) BOA Edns.

— Never in a Hurry: Essays on People & Places. LC 95-41778. (Illus.). 270p. 1996. pap. 16.95 (*1-57003-082-0*) U of SC Pr.

— Red Suitcase. (American Poets Continuum Ser.: No. 29). 90p. 1994. 20.00 (*1-880238-14-4*) BOA Edns.

— Red Suitcase. LC 94-78069. (American Poets Continuum Ser.: No. 29). 90p. 1998. pap. 12.50 (*1-880238-15-2*, Pub. by BOA Edns) Consort Bk Sales.

— Sitti's Secrets. (J). 1997. mass mkt. 5.99 (*0-689-81706-1*) Aladdin.

— Sitti's Secrets. (J). 1998. pap. 5.99 (*0-87628-371-7*) Ctr Appl Res.

— Sitti's Secrets. LC 93-19742. (Illus.). 32p. (J). (ps-3). 1994. mass mkt. 16.00 (*0-02-768460-1*, Four Winds Pr) S&S Childrens.

Nye, Naomi S. This Same Sky: A Collection of Poems from Around the World. LC 92-11617. (Illus.). 208p. (YA). (gr. 5 up). 1992. pap. 17.00 (*0-02-768440-7*, Four Winds Pr) S&S Childrens.

Nye, Naomi S. Words under the Words: Selected Poems. LC 94-43072. 160p. (Orig.). 1995. pap. 13.95 (*0-933377-29-0*); lib. bdg. 22.95 (*0-933377-32-0*) Eighth Mount Pr.

— Yellow Glove. LC 86-21534. 86p. 1986. pap. 8.00 (*0-932576-42-7*) Breitenbush Bks.

Nye, Naomi S., ed. The Space Between Our Footsteps: Poems & Paintings from the Middle East. LC 97-18622. 144p. (J). 1998. per. 19.95 (*0-689-81233-7*) S&S Childrens.

Nye, Naomi S., selected by. This Same Sky. (Illus.). 232p. (YA). (gr. 5 up). 1996. mass mkt. 6.99 (*0-689-80630-2*) Aladdin.

Nye, Naomi S. & Janeczko, Paul B. I Feel a Little Jumpy Around You: A Book of Her Poems & His Poems Collected in Pairs. 256p. (YA). (gr. 7 up). 1996. mass mkt. 18.00 (*0-689-80518-7*) S&S Childrens.

Nye, Naomi S., jt. auth. see Janeczko, Paul B.

Nye, Naomi S., tr. see Al-Maghut, Muhammad.

Nye, Naomi Shihab. Baby Radar. (J). 2001. 15.95 (*0-688-15948-6*, Grenwillow Bks) HarpC Child Bks.

— Come with Me. LC 99-34164. (Illus.). 40p. (J). (gr. k-3). 2000. 15.89 (*0-688-15947-8*, Grenwillow Bks) HarpC Child Bks.

— Come with Me: Poems for a Journey. LC 99-34164. (Illus.). 40p. (J). (gr. k-3). 2000. 15.95 (*0-688-15946-X*, Grenwillow Bks) HarpC Child Bks.

— Habibi. LC 97-10943. 272p. (J). (gr. 5 up). 1999. per. 4.50 (*0-689-82523-4*) Aladdin.

— Habibi. LC 97-10943. 272p. (YA). (gr. 5 up). 1997. per. 16.00 (*0-689-80149-1*) S&S Childrens.

— Lullaby Raft. LC 96-22425. (Illus.). 32p. (J). (ps-1). 1997. 16.00 (*0-689-80521-7*) S&S Trade.

— Sitti's Secrets. (J). 1997. 11.19 (*0-606-13029-2*, Pub. by Turtleback) Demco.

— This Same Sky: A Collection of Poems from Around the World. 1996. 14.09 (*0-606-09965-4*, Pub. by Turtleback) Demco.

— The Tree Is Older Than You Are: A Bilingual Gathering of Poems & Stories from Mexico with Paintings. (Illus.). 112p. (J). 1998. per. 12.00 (*0-689-82087-9*) Aladdin.

***Nye, Naomi Shihab.** The Tree Is Older Than You Are: A Bilingual Gathering of Poems & Stories from Mexico with Paintings. (J). 1998. 17.10 (*0-606-13867-6*, Pub. by Turtleback) Demco.

— What Have You Lost? (J). 2001. pap. 6.95 (*0-380-73307-2*) Morrow Avon.

***Nye, Naomi Shihab, ed.** What Have You Lost. LC 98-26674. (Illus.). 224p. (J). (gr. 7-12). 1999. 18.95 (*0-688-16184-7*, Grenwillow Bks) HarpC Child Bks.

Nye, Naomi Shihab, selected by. The Tree Is Older Than You Are: A Bilingual Gathering of Poems & Stories from Mexico with Paintings by Mexican Artists. LC 95-1565. (Illus.). 112p. (J). (gr. 3 up). 1995. per. 19.95 (*0-689-80297-8*) S&S Bks Yung.

Nye, Nelson. Iron Hand. large type ed. (Dales Western Ser.). 265p. 1993. pap. 18.99 (*1-85389-342-0*) Ulverscroft.

— The Lonely Grass. large type ed. LC 93-25506. 290p. 1993. lib. bdg. 15.95 (*0-8161-5837-1*, G K Hall Lrg Type) Mac Lib Ref.

— Maverick Marshall. 1978. mass mkt. 1.75 (*0-451-08356-3*, E8356, Sig) NAL.

— Maverick Marshall. large type ed. 1991. 8.95 (*1-55504-588-X*, 2127) Chivers N Amer.

— Not Grass Alone. large type ed. LC 95-11095. (Nightingale Ser.). 237p. 1995. pap. 17.95 (*0-7838-1384-8*, G K Hall Lrg Type) Mac Lib Ref.

— The Palominas Pistolero & Smoke Wagon Kid. 1978. mass mkt. 1.95 (*0-89083-418-0*, Zebra Kensgtn) Kensgtn Pub Corp.

— The Parson of Gunbarrel Basin. large type ed. LC 93-43546. (General Ser.). 281p. 1994. lib. bdg. 17.95 (*0-8161-5923-8*, G K Hall Lrg Type) Mac Lib Ref.

— The Shootin' Sheriff & The Bandit of Bloody Run. (Two-in One Western Ser.). 1979. mass mkt. 1.95 (*0-89083-444-X*, Zebra Kensgtn) Kensgtn Pub Corp.

— The Texas Gun - Gringo. 320p. 1995. pap. text, mass mkt. 4.99 (*0-8439-3822-6*) Dorchester Pub Co.

— Trigger Talk. large type ed. LC 92-30141. (Nightingale Ser.). 224p. 1993. lib. bdg. 14.95 (*0-8161-5631-X*, G K Hall Lrg Type) Mac Lib Ref.

***Nye, Nelson.** The White Chip. 288p. 1999. mass mkt. 4.50 (*0-8439-4473-0*, Leisure Bks) Dorchester Pub Co.

Nye, Nelson. Wild Horse Shorty. large type ed. 1990. pap. 5.00 (*0-7451-1291-9*, Pub. by Chivers N Amer) Chivers N Amer.

— The Wolf That Rode. 224p. (Orig.). 1980. mass mkt. 1.95 (*0-89083-612-4*, Zebra Kensgtn) Kensgtn Pub Corp.

***Nye, Nelson C.** Quick-Trigger Country. large type ed. LC 99-89091. (Thorndike Western Ser.). 2000. 22.95 (*0-7862-2423-1*) Thorndike Pr.

Nye, Nelson C. Speed & the Quarter Horse: A Payload of Sprinters. LC 73-140120. 374p. 1973. reprint ed. pap. 116.00 (*0-7837-7136-3*, 205916300004) Bks Demand.

— Strawberry Roan. LC 81-12649. 297 p. 1982. write for info. (*0-89340-368-7*) Chivers N Amer.

***Nye, Nelson C.** Trouble at Quinn's Crossing. large type ed. LC 00-21439. 2000. pap. 23.95 (*0-7838-9005-2*, G K Hall Lrg Type) Mac Lib Ref.

Nye, Nelson C. The White Chip. large type ed. LC 95-42024. (Five-Star Western Ser.). 1997. 20.00 (*0-7838-1542-5*) Thorndike Pr.

— The White Chip. large type ed. 317p. 1997. 17.95 (*0-7862-0902-X*) Thorndike Pr.

— The White Chip: A Western Story. (Five-Star Western Ser.). 220p. 1996. 16.95 (*0-7862-0565-2*) Thorndike Pr.

Nye, O. B. Bulletins of American Paleontology: Generic Revision & Skeletal Morphology of Some Cerioporoid Cyclostomes, Vol. 69. 1976. 25.00 (*0-87710-298-8*) Paleo Res.

Nye, P. H., jt. auth. see Tinker, Peter B.

***Nye, Penny.** Batter Up! (Bookmates Ser.). (Illus.). 16p. (J). (ps-5). 1999. pap. 12.00 (*1-890703-14-1*) Penny Laine.

Nye, Penny. Gymnastics. (Illus.). 16p. (Orig.). (J). (ps-4). 1997. pap. 12.00 (*1-890703-06-0*) Penny Laine.

— I Love to Dance. (Illus.). 16p. (Orig.). (J). (ps-4). 1997. pap. 12.00 (*1-890703-04-4*) Penny Laine.

— Kindergarten. (Illus.). 16p. (Orig.). (J). (ps-1). 1997. pap. 12.00 (*1-890703-00-1*) Penny Laine.

***Nye, Penny.** Music. (Bookmates Ser.). (Illus.). 15p. (J). (ps-3). 2000. pap. 12.00 (*1-890703-19-2*, Bkmates) Penny Laine.

Nye, Penny. My Cat. (Illus.). (J). (ps-5). 1999. pap. 12.00 (*1-890703-16-8*, Bkmates) Penny Laine.

— My Christmas Memories. (Illus.). 15p. (J). 1998. pap. 12.00 (*1-890703-13-3*, Bkmates) Penny Laine.

— My Dog. (Illus.). (J). (ps-5). 1999. pap. 12.00 (*1-890703-17-6*, Bkmates) Penny Laine.

***Nye, Penny.** My Family. (Bookmates Ser.). (Illus.). 15p. (J). (ps). 2000. pap. 12.00 (*1-890703-18-4*, Bkmates) Penny Laine.

Nye, Penny. My Grandparents. (Illus.). 16p. (Orig.). (J). (ps-4). 1997. pap. 12.00 (*1-890703-05-2*) Penny Laine.

— My Vacation. (Illus.). 16p. (J). (ps-5). 1997. pap. 12.00 (*1-890703-09-5*) Penny Laine.

— Preschool. (Illus.). 16p. (J). (ps). 1997. pap. 12.00 (*1-890703-08-7*) Penny Laine.

— Soccer. (Illus.). 16p. (Orig.). (J). (ps-4). 1997. pap. 12.00 (*1-890703-07-9*) Penny Laine.

— Wow, I'm a Big Brother! (Illus.). 16p. (Orig.). (J). (ps-4). 1997. pap. 12.00 (*1-890703-02-8*) Penny Laine.

— Wow, I'm a Big Sister! (Illus.). 16p. (Orig.). (J). (ps-4). 1997. pap. 12.00 (*1-890703-03-6*) Penny Laine.

Nye, Peter. Hearts of Lions: The Story of American Bicycle Racing. (Illus.). 1989. pap. 14.00 (*0-393-30576-7*) Norton.

Nye, R. Lynn. Implementing Frame Relay & ATM in IBM System Environments. (Computer Communications Ser.). (Illus.). 352p. 1997. pap. text 55.00 (*0-07-048231-4*) McGraw.

Nye, Risa. Road Scholar: An Investigative Journal for the College-Bound Student. (Illus.). 90p. (Orig.). (YA). (gr. 10-12). 1996. pap. 10.00 (*0-9657203-0-6*) No Flak.

Nye, Robert. Beowulf: A New Telling. 1968. 9.60 (*0-606-02034-9*, Pub. by Turtleback) Demco.

— The Late Mr. Shakespeare. LC 98-50763. 400p. (YA). 1999. 25.95 (*1-55970-469-1*, Pub. by Arcade Pub Inc) Time Warner.

***Nye, Robert.** The Late Mr. Shakespeare. 416p. 2000. pap. 13.95 (*0-14-028952-6*) Viking Penguin.

— Mrs. Shakespeare: The Complete Works. 2000. 23.95 (*1-55970-552-3*, Pub. by Arcade Pub Inc) Time Warner.

Nye, Robert, ed. William Barnes (1801-1886) Selected Poems. pap. write for info. (*0-85635-032-X*, Pub. by Carcanet Pr) Paul & Co Pubs.

Nye, Robert, ed. & intro. see Jackson, Laura R.

Nye, Robert, ed. & intro. see Riding, Laura.

Nye, Robert A. Crime, Madness & Politics in Modern France: The Medical Concept of National Decline. LC 83-43087. 386p. 1984. reprint ed. pap. 119.70 (*0-608-04640-X*, 206532700003) Bks Demand.

— Masculinity & Male Codes of Honor in Modern France. LC 98-6520. 336p. 1998. pap. 17.95 (*0-520-21510-9*, Pub. by U CA Pr) Cal Prin Full Svc.

***Nye, Robert A.** Sexuality. LC 98-31709. (Oxford Readers Ser.). 522p. (C). 1999. pap. text 22.95 (*0-19-288019-5*) OUP.

Nye, Robert D. The Legacy of B. F. Skinner: Concepts & Perspectives, Controversies & Misunderstandings. LC 91-21644. 145p. (C). 1991. pap. 18.25 (*0-534-16944-9*) Brooks-Cole.

— Three Psychologies. 6th ed. LC 99-23747. (Psychology Ser.). 181p. 1999. pap. text 22.95 (*0-534-36845-X*) Brooks-Cole.

Nye, Robert D. Three Psychologies: Perspectives from Freud, Skinner & Rogers. 2nd ed. LC 80-25716. 170p. (Orig.). (C). 1981. mass mkt. 13.25 (*0-8185-0438-2*) Brooks-Cole.

— Three Psychologies: Perspectives from Freud, Skinner & Rogers. 3rd ed. LC 86-9663. (Psychology Ser.). 162p. (Orig.). (C). 1986. pap. 16.00 (*0-534-06528-7*) Brooks-Cole.

— Three Psychologies: Perspectives from Freud, Skinner, & Rogers. 5th ed. LC 94-42256. 192p. 1995. mass mkt. 14.00 (*0-534-26616-9*) Brooks-Cole.

Nye, Robert E. Beowulf. 112p. (YA). (gr. 5 up). 1982. mass mkt. 4.99 (*0-440-90560-5*, LLL BDD) BDD Bks Young Read.

Nye, Robert E. & Bergethon, Bjonnar. Basic Music. 6th ed. (Illus.). 256p. (C). 1987. pap. text 35.20 (*0-13-065681-X*) P-H.

Nye, Roger H. The Challenge of Command: Reading for Military Excellence. LC 85-30614. (West Point Military History Ser.). 200p. pap. 9.95 (*0-89529-280-7*, Avery) Penguin Putnam.

— The Patton Mind: The Professional Development of an Extraordinary Leader. LC 92-10490. (Illus.). 224p. pap. 12.95 (*0-89529-428-1*, Avery) Penguin Putnam.

Nye, Russel B., jt. auth. see McAvoy, Thomas T.

Nye, Russel B., ed. see Bancroft, George.

Nye, Russel B., ed. see Franklin, Benjamin.

Nye, Russell. A Simulation Analysis of Capital Structure in a Property Insurance Firm. (C). 1975. 10.50 (*0-256-04607-7*, Irwn McGrw-H) McGrw-H Hghr Educ.

Nye, Sandra G. Employee Assistance Law Answer Book. 452p. 1991. reprint ed. text 89.00 (*1-878375-12-1*) Panel Pubs.

***Nye, Sandra G.** Employee Assistance Law Desk Book LC 98-182203. 1998. write for info. (*0-9662862-0-0*) EAPA.

Nye, Sandra G. & Kaiser, Laura B. Employee Assistance Law Answer Book: 1992 Supplement. 250p. 1991. pap. text 49.00 (*1-878375-54-7*) Panel Pubs.

Nye, Sheridan, et al, eds. Assaults on Convention: Essays on Lesbian Transgression. LC 96-160018. (Women on Women Ser.). (Illus.). 224p. 1997. pap. 21.95 (*0-304-32883-9*) Continuum.

Nye, W. F., ed. see International Symposium on Boron Staff.

Nye, Wilbur, jt. auth. see Stackpole, Edward J.

Nye, Wilbur S. Bad Medicine & Good: Tales of the Kiowas. LC 97-19221. (Illus.). xxiv, 289p. 1997. pap. 15.95 (*0-8061-2965-4*) U of Okla Pr.

— Carbine & Lance: The Story of Old Fort Sill. enl. rev. ed. LC 79-13137. (Illus.). 448p. 1983. pap. 19.95 (*0-8061-1856-3*) U of Okla Pr.

— Here Come the Rebels. (Illus.). 412p. 1988. 25.00 (*0-89029-080-6*); pap. 14.95 (*0-89029-780-0*) Morningside Bkshop.

— Plains Indian Raiders: The Final Phases of Warfare from the Arkansas to the Red River. LC 67-24624. (Illus.). 438p. 1984. pap. 21.95 (*0-8061-1175-5*) U of Okla Pr.

Nye, Wilbur S., jt. auth. see Betzinez, Jason.

Nyeayavijaya & Bhogilal Leherchand Institute of Indology. Jaina Philosophy & Religion. LC 98-905186. (Blii Ser.). xxv, 469 p. 1998. write for info. (*81-208-1490-8*, Pub. by Motilal Bnarsidass) S Asia.

Nyeko, Balam. Uganda. 2nd rev. ed. LC 96-229095. (World Bibliographical Ser.). 398p. 1996. lib. bdg. 102.00 (*1-85109-243-9*) ABC-CLIO.

Nyeko, Balam, compiled by. Swaziland. 2nd rev. ed. (World Bibliographical Ser.: Vol. 24). 276p. 1995. lib. bdg. 64.50 (*1-85109-226-9*) ABC-CLIO.

Nyeko, Balam, jt. auth. see Denoon, Donald.

Nyeko, Balem. Swaziland. (World Bibliographical Ser.: No. 24). 135p. 1983. lib. bdg. 45.00 (*0-903450-35-6*) ABC-CLIO.

Nyeland, Preben. Maxi, the Ultimate Racing Experience. 1990. 50.00 (*0-393-03340-6*) Norton.

Nyembezi, C. L. Learn Zulu. (ENG & ZUL.). 264p. 1990. pap. 15.95 (*0-7859-7521-7*) Fr & Eur.

— Learn Zulu. 5th ed. (ZUL.). 264p. 1990. reprint ed. pap. 12.75 (*0-7960-0237-1*) IBD Ltd.

— Zulu-English, English-Zulu Dictionary. 2nd ed. (ENG & ZUL.). 519p. 1988. pap. 19.95 (*0-7859-7523-3*) Fr & Eur.

— Zulu Proverbs. rev. ed. (ENG & ZUL.). 1963. pap. 18.95 (*0-7859-7522-5*) Fr & Eur.

— Zulu Proverbs. rev. ed. 1963. 12.50 (*0-7960-0230-4*) IBD Ltd.

Nyemchek, John P., jt. auth. see Shell, Niel.

Nyenhuis, G. El Dios Que Adoramos.Tr. of God We Adore. (SPA.). 9.99 (*0-7899-0253-2*, 491045) Editorial Unilit.

Nyer, Evan. Groundwater & Soil Remediation: Practical Methods. LC 98-2874. (Illus.). 250p. 1998. ring bd. 59.95 (*1-57504-088-3*) CRC Pr.

— Practical Techniques for Groundwater & Soil Remediation. 224p. 1992. lib. bdg. 85.00 (*0-87371-731-7*, L731) Lewis Pubs.

Nyer, Evan, et al. In situ Treatment Technology. LC 95-49907. 352p. 1996. lib. bdg. 85.00 (*0-87371-995-6*, L995) Lewis Pubs.

Nyer, Evan K. Groundwater Treatment Technology. 2nd ed. 306p. 1992. 99.00 (*0-471-28414-9*, VNR) Wiley.

Nyer, Evan K. Groundwater Treatment Technology. 2nd ed. (Illus.). 320p. 1992. text 70.95 (*0-442-00562-8*, VNR) Wiley.

Nyer, Genie. Mexico Embraces the "Third Age" (Working Paper Ser.: No. 77). 32p. (C). 1994. pap. 5.50 (*0-89940-571-1*) LBJ Sch Pub Aff.

Nyer, Saul. Escape: A 21,000 Mile Exodus from the 1917 Russian Revolution. LC 97-61823. (Illus.). 400p. (Orig.). 1998. pap. 14.95 (*0-9622726-4-7*) Thomas CA.

Nyerges, Anton N., tr. Poems of Endre Ady. (Illus.). 500p. 1987. reprint ed. lib. bdg. 58.50 (*0-8191-6568-9*) U Pr of Amer.

***Nyerges, Christopher.** Guide to Wild Foods & Useful Plants. LC 98-49812. (Illus.). 256p. 1999. pap. 14.95 (*1-55652-344-0*) Chicago Review.

Nyerges, Endre, ed. The Ecology of Practice: Studies of Food Crop Production in Sub-Saharan West Africa. (Food & Nutrition in History & Anthropology Ser.). 250p. 1997. text 34.00 (*90-5699-573-1*); pap. text 18.00 (*90-5699-574-X*) Gordon & Breach.

Nyerges, Timothy L., ed. Cognitive Aspects of Human-Computer Interaction for Geographic Information Systems: Proceedings of the NATO Advanced Research Workshop, Palma de Mallorca, Spain, March 20-25, 1994. (NATO ASI Series D). 448p. (C). 1995. lib. bdg. 232.00 (*0-7923-3595-3*) Kluwer Academic.

Nyeste, Zoltan. Recsk - Emberek az Embertelensegben (Recsk Man in Inhumanity) LC 82-82973. (Tanuk Korukrol Ser.). (Illus.). 80p. 1982. pap. 6.00 (*0-910539-00-6*) Hungarian Alumni.

Nyffenegger, Eugen. Cristan der Kuchimaister, Nuewe Casus Monasterii Sancti Galli: Edition & Sprachgeschichtliche Einordnung. (Quellen und Forschungen zur Sprach und Kulturgeschichte der Germanischen Voelker: NF Bd. 60). (GER.). (C). 1974. 153.85 (*3-11-004098-0*) De Gruyter.

Nygaard, Anita. Earthclock. 1977. reprint ed. pap. 4.95 (*0-8065-0567-2*, Citadel Pr) Carol Pub Group.

Nygaard, Elizabeth. Snake Alley Band. LC 97-15544. (Illus.). 32p. (J). (ps-3). 1998. 15.95 (*0-385-32323-9*, DD Bks Yng Read) BDD Bks Young Read.

— Snake Alley Band. 32p. 1999. pap. 5.99 (*0-440-41352-4*) BDD Bks Young Read.

Nygaard, Ingrid, jt. auth. see Linder, Marc.

Nygaard, K., jt. ed. see Gjessing, S.

Nygaard, Kimberly. Jorunn's Saga: A Journey of the Spirit. 1999. pap. 12.95 (*1-884570-93-3*) Research Triangle.

***Nygaard, Kimberly.** Jorunn's Saga: A Journey of the Spirit. 1999. pap. 12.95 (*0-9673419-0-6*) Runes-in-Time.

Nygaard, Linda. City Smart: Portland. 2nd rev. ed. (City Smart Ser.). (Illus.). 224p. 1998. pap. text 14.95 (*1-56261-412-6*, City Smart) Avalon Travel.

Nygaard, Niels, et al, eds. The Handbook of Financial Mathematics. (Irwin Library of Investment & Finance). (Illus.). 350p. 1998. 60.00 (*0-07-047129-0*) McGraw.

Nygaard, Oddvar F. & Upton, Arthur C., eds. Anticarcinogenesis & Radiation Protection 2. (Illus.). 488p. (C). 1992. text 174.00 (*0-306-44056-3*, Kluwer Plenum) Kluwer Academic.

Nygaard, Peter. Juan Manuel Fangio Photo Album: World Champion Driver. (Illus.). 112p. 1999. pap. 19.95 (*1-58388-008-9*, Pub. by Iconografix) Motorbooks Intl.

— Mario Andretti Photo Album. (World Champion Driver Ser.). (Illus.). 112p. 1999. pap. 19.95 (*1-58388-009-7*, Pub. by Iconografix) Motorbooks Intl.

— Williams 1969-1998 Photo Album: 30 Years of Grand Prix Racing. LC 98-75270. (Photo Album Ser.). (Illus.). 112p. (Orig.). 1999. pap. 19.95 (*1-58388-000-3*, 128259AE) Iconografix.

***Nygaard, Scott.** Scott Nygaard - Dreamer's Waltz. 88p. 1998. pap. 31.95 (*0-7866-3366-2*, 96666CDP) Mel Bay.

***Nygaard, Scott, ed.** Acoustic Guitar Accompaniment Basics. 64p. 1999. pap. 14.95 (*1-890490-11-3*) String Letter.

— Alternate Tunings Guitar Essentials. 64p. 2000. pap. 19.95 (*1-890490-24-5*) String Letter.

— Flatpicking Guitar Masterpieces: CD Songbook. 64p. 2000. pap. 16.95 (*1-890490-30-X*) String Letter.

— Lead & Melody Basics. 64p. 2000. pap. 14.95 (*1-890490-19-9*) String Letter.

Nygaard, Scott, et al. Acoustic Guitar's Private Lessons: Flatpicking Guitar Essentials, No. 979. LC 98-47113. Vol. 979. 96p. 1998. pap. 19.95 (*1-890490-07-5*) String Letter.

Nygaard, William. The Price of Free Speech. 84p. (C). 1996. pap. 9.00 (*82-00-22749-9*, Pub. by Scand Univ Pr) IBD Ltd.

***Nygard, Bonnie & Hopper, Bonnie.** Gotta Minute? The Ultimate Guide of One-Minute Workouts for Anyone, Anywhere, Anytime. LC 99-67464. (Illus.). 90p. 2000. pap. 9.95 (*1-885003-37-4*, Pub. by R D Reed Pubs) Midpt Trade.

Nygard, Roald & Gjesme, Torgrim, eds. Advances in Motivation. 294p. (C). 1997. text 41.00 (*82-00-22642-5*) Scandnvan Univ Pr.

Nygard, Thomas, jt. ed. see Riess, Peter.

Nygard, Thomas A., ed. Clyde Aspevig. (Illus.). 36p. 1994. pap. 25.00 (*0-9620327-4-3*) Nygard Pub.

Nygh, Justice. Conflict of Laws in Australia. 5th ed. 1991. 126.00 (*0-409-30816-1*, AT, MICHIE) LEXIS Pub.

Nygh, P. Conflict of Laws in Australia. 6th ed. (Butterworths Australia Ser.). 680p. 1994. write for info. (*0-409-30782-3*, MICHIE) LEXIS Pub.

Nygh, Peter. Autonomy in International Contracts. LC 98-37657. (Oxford Monographs in Private International Law). 318p. 1999. text 105.00 (*0-19-826270-1*) OUP.

— Choice of Forum & Laws in International Commercial Arbitration. LC 97-37990. (Forum Internationale Ser.: No. 24). 40p. 1997. pap. 31.00 (*90-411-0492-5*) Kluwer Academic.

Nygh, Peter, jt. ed. see McLachlan, Campbell.

Nygren, Anders. Agape & Eros. Watson, Philip S., tr. from SWE. LC 81-22019. 768p. 1982. reprint ed. pap. text 19.95 (*0-226-61078-0*) U Ch Pr.

Nygren, Carolyn. Starting off Right in Law School. LC 97-12484. 128p. (C). 1997. pap. 12.50 (*0-89089-877-4*) Carolina Acad Pr.

Nygren, Carolyn J. Starting off Right in Civil Procedure. 1998. pap. 12.50 (*0-89089-875-8*) Carolina Acad Pr.

— Starting off Right in Contracts. LC 98-85311. 112p. 1998. pap. 12.50 (*0-89089-880-4*) Carolina Acad Pr.

— Starting off Right in Property. LC 98-85313. 88p. 1998. pap. 12.50 (*0-89089-876-6*) Carolina Acad Pr.

— Starting off Right in Torts. LC 98-85315. 104p. 1998. pap. 12.50 (*0-89089-879-0*) Carolina Acad Pr.

Nygren, David J. & Ukeritis, Miriam D. The Future of Religious Orders in the United States: Transformation & Commitment. LC 93-19088. 344p. 1993. 69.50 (*0-275-94665-7*, C4665, Praeger Pubs) Greenwood.

Nygren, Edward J., intro. Isaac Cruikshank & the Politics of Parody: Watercolors in the Huntington Collection. LC 94-2794. (Illus.). 162p. (Orig.). 1994. pap. 19.95 (*0-87328-147-0*) Huntington Lib.

Nygren, Edward J. & Marzo, Peter C. Of Time & Place: American Figurative Art from the Corcoran Gallery. (Illus.). 208p. 1981. pap. 16.95 (*0-86528-010-X*) SITES.

Nygren, J., jt. auth. see Jones, Bob, Jr.

Nygren, Malcolm. The Lord of the Four Seasons. 144p. (Orig.). 1986. pap. 7.95 (*0-9617890-1-8*) Doxology Lane.

Nyhan, Barry, jt. ed. see Docherty, Peter.

Nyhan, Elizabeth F. Treasury of Patchwork Borders: 92 Foolproof Tricks. 64p. 1991. pap. 4.95 (*0-486-26183-2*) Dover.

— Treasury of Patchwork Quilt Sets. LC 94-17258. 64p. 1994. 3.95 (*0-486-28148-5*) Dover.

Nyhan, Michael, et al. A Snapshot View of Communication Patterns: The New Hampshire Division of Vocational Rehabilitation. 67p. 1982. 7.50 (*0-318-19197-0*, R-55) Inst Future.

Nyhan, Michael J., jt. ed. see Cater, Douglass.

Nyhan, Pat, et al. Let the Good Times Roll! A Guide to Cajun & Zydeco Music. LC 97-90429. (Illus.). 232p. 1998. pap. 16.95 (*0-9658232-0-2*) Upbeat Bks.

Nyhan, W. L., et al, eds. Purine & Pyrimidine Metabolism in Man V, 2 Vols., Set. LC 85-32557. (Advances in Experimental Medicine & Biology Ser.: Vol. 195). 1986. 195.00 (*0-685-13929-8*, Plenum Trade) Perseus Pubng.

— Purine & Pyrimidine Metabolism in Man V, 2 vols., Vol. 1. LC 85-32557. (Advances in Experimental Medicine & Biology Ser.: Vol. 195). 634p. 1986. 120.00 (*0-306-42230-1*, Plenum Trade) Perseus Pubng.

— Purine & Pyrimidine Metabolism in Man V, 2 vols., Vol. 2. LC 85-32557. (Advances in Experimental Medicine & Biology Ser.: Vol. 195). 720p. 1986. 125.00 (*0-306-42231-X*, Plenum Trade) Perseus Pubng.

Nyhan, William L., ed. Heritable Disorders of Amino Acid Metabolism: Patterns of Clinical Expression & Genetic Variation. LC 74-6255. 783p. reprint ed. pap. 200.00 (*0-608-30285-6*, 201257800082) Bks Demand.

Nyhan, William L. & Ozand, Pinar T. Atlas of Metabolic Diseases. (Illus.). 688p. 1999. text 165.00 (*0-412-47960-5*, Pub. by E A) OUP.

Nyhan, William L. & Sakati, Nadia. Diagnostic Recognition of Genetic Disease. LC 86-21132. 766p. reprint ed. pap. 200.00 (*0-7837-2735-6*, 204311500006) Bks Demand.

Nyhart, Lynn K. Before Biology: Animal Morphology & the German Universities, 1800-1900. LC 95-3227. (Science & Its Conceptual Foundations Ser.). 428p. 1995. pap. text 27.50 (*0-226-61088-8*); lib. bdg. 75.00 (*0-226-61086-1*) U Ch Pr.

Nyhart, Nina. French for Soldiers. LC 86-72478. 72p. (Orig.). (C). 1987. 6.95 (*0-914086-70-7*); pap. 9.95 (*0-914086-71-5*) Alice James Bks.

Nyhart, Nina & Lockwood, Margo. Openers & Temper. LC 78-74232. 88p. 1979. pap. 3.95 (*0-914086-26-X*) Alice James Bks.

Nyhoff. Dat Str Pro Des SM. 1999. write for info. (*0-02-388727-3*) P-H.

— Dat Str Pro Des Turb. LC 98-48724. 700p. 1999. 71.33 (*0-02-388725-7*) P-H.

Nyhoff, John E., jt. auth. see Labuszewski, John W.

Nyhoff, Larry & Lee, Sanford. Data Structures & Program Design in Pascal. 2nd ed. (Illus.). 752p. (C). 1991. 49.60 (*0-02-369465-3*, Macmillan Coll) P-H.

— FORTRAN 90 for Engineers & Scientists. LC 96-17843. 1071p. (C). 1996. pap. 68.00 (*0-13-519729-5*) P-H.

— FORTRAN 77 & Numerical Methods. LC 94-7462. 740p. (C). 1995. pap. 78.00 (*0-02-388741-9*, Macmillan Coll) P-H.

***Nyhoff, Larry & Lee, Sanford.** Introduction to Fortran 90. 2nd ed. 390p. (C). 1999. pap. 34.67 (*0-13-013146-6*) P-H.

Nyhoff, Larry, et al. C++ An Introduction to Computing. (Illus.). 900p. (C). 1994. teacher ed. write for info. (*0-318-72461-8*) Macmillan.

Nyhoff, Larry, jt. auth. see Lee, Sanford.

Nyholm, Earl, jt. auth. see Nichols, John D.

Nyholm, N. & Neergard, Jacobsen B., eds. Hazard Assessment & Control of Environmental Contaminants in Water: Selected Proceedings of the 2nd IAWQ International Specialized Conference on Hazard Assessment & Control of Environmental Contaminants in Water, Held in Lyngby, Denmark, 29-30 June 1995. (Water Science & Technology 33 Ser.). 360p. pap. 128.00 (*0-08-042897-5*, Pergamon Pr) Elsevier.

Nyholt, David H. The Complete Natural Health Encyclopedia: Natural Treatments for the World's 350 Most Common Ailments. 2nd ed. (Illus.). 398p. pap. 17.95 (*0-921202-07-5*, Pub. by Gloh) BookWorld.

Nyhuis, Allen W. The Zoo Book: A Guide to America's Best. LC 93-46925. (Illus.). 288p. (Orig.). 1994. pap. 14.95 (*0-917120-13-2*) Carousel Pr.

Nyhuis, Philip, et al. Niagara Attracting the World. LC 97-16127. 288p. 1997. 45.00 (*1-885352-58-1*); pap. write for info. (*1-885352-59-X*) Community Comm.

Nyhus, Lloyd M. Surgery Annual 1984, Vol. 16. LC 69-18093. (Illus.). 432p. (C). 1984. pap. text 95.00 (*0-8385-8722-4*, A8722-9, Apple Lange Med) McGraw.

— Surgery Annual 1983, Vol. 15. (Illus.). 416p. (C). 1983. pap. text 95.00 (*0-8385-8721-6*, A8721-1, Apple Lange Med) McGraw.

— Surgery Annual 1982, Vol. 14. (Illus.). (C). 1982. pap. text 95.00 (*0-8385-8719-4*, A8719-5, Apple Lange Med) McGraw.

— Surgery Annual, 1993, Vol. 25, Pt. 1. (Illus.). 272p. (C). 1992. text 90.00 (*0-8385-8798-4*, A8798-9) Appleton & Lange.

— Surgery Annual 1992, Vol. 24, Pt. 2. (Illus.). 272p. (C). 1992. pap. text 95.00 (*0-8385-8748-8*, A8748-4, Apple Lange Med) McGraw.

Nyhus, Lloyd M., et al, eds. Mastery of Surgery, 2 vols. 3rd ed. (Illus.). 2400p. 1996. text 285.00 (*0-316-61746-6*) Lppncott W & W.

Nyhus, Lloyd M. & Baker, Robert. Mastery of Surgery, 2 vols., Set. 1540p. 1984. 240.00 (*0-316-61742-3*, Little Brwn Med Div) Lppncott W & W.

Nyhus, Lloyd M. & Condon, Robert E. Hernia. 4th ed. (Illus.). 800p. (C). 1994. text 159.00 (*0-397-51286-4*, Lippnctt) Lppncott W & W.

***Nyhus, Lloyd M., et al.** Abdominal Pain: A Guide to Rapid Diagnosis. (Illus.). 273p. (C). 2000. reprint ed. pap. text 20.00 (*0-7881-9270-1*) DIANE Pub.

Nyhus, Lloyd M., et al. Mastery of Surgery. 3rd ed. LC 96-9115. 1996. write for info. (*0-316-61751-2*, Little Brwn Med Div) Lppncott W & W.

Nyhus, Lloyd M., jt. auth. see Barrett, John.

Nyhus, Lloyd M., jt. auth. see Condon, Robert E.

Nyhus, Lloyd M., jt. ed. see Condon, Robert E.

Nyhus, Paul L., tr. see Oberman, Heiko A.

Nyif, jt. auth. see Nenner.

Nyil. Netherland Yearbook International Law. 1995. lib. bdg. 130.00 (*0-7923-3308-X*) Kluwer Academic.

— Netherlands Yearbook International Law. 1990. lib. bdg. 97.50 (*90-247-3481-9*, Pub. by M Nijhoff); lib. bdg. 104.50 (*90-247-3638-2*, Pub. by M Nijhoff) Kluwer Academic.

Nyilas, Jozsef. The World Economy & Its Main Developmental Tendencies. 1982. lib. bdg. 171.00 (*90-247-2650-6*) Kluwer Academic.

Nyingma Centers Art Projects Staff. How to Frame a Thanka: A Guide to Displaying Sacred Art & Constructing Traditional Cloth Mountings. (Illus.). 16p. 1989. pap. 4.95 (*0-89800-203-6*) Dharma Pub.

Nyingpo, Namkhai, jt. auth. see Changchub, Gyalwa.

Nyingpo, Namkhay. Mother of Knowledge: The Enlightenment of Ye-shes Mtsho-Rgyal. Tulku, Tarthang, tr. LC 83-23208. (Translation Ser.: Vol. 12). Orig. Title: Tibetan. (Illus.). 250p. 1983. 35.00 (*0-913546-90-9*); pap. 19.95 (*0-913546-91-7*) Dharma Pub.

Nyiri, Alan. Acadia National Park: Maine's Intimate Parkland. (Illus.). 80p. 1986. pap. 12.95 (*0-89272-219-3*) Down East.

— Images of Cornell. Rhodes, Frank H. T., ed. & intro. by. (Illus.). 40p. (Orig.). 1999. pap. 17.95 (*0-9671311-0-3*) Cornell Campus.

Nyiri, Alan, photos by. Cape Cod. LC 91-77669. (Illus.). 112p. 1992. 29.95 (*0-89272-303-3*) Down East.

Nyiri, J., jt. auth. see Gribov, V. D.

Nyiri, J. C. Tradition & Individuality: Essays. (Synthese Library). 192p. (C). 1992. lib. bdg. 123.00 (*0-7923-1566-9*, Pub. by Kluwer Academic) Kluwer Academic.

Nyiri, J. C., ed. Karl Wittgenstein: Politico-Economic Writings. (Viennese Heritage Ser.: No. 1). (GER.). xl, 240p. 1984. reprint ed. 62.00 (*90-272-3882-0*) J Benjamins Pubng Co.

— Politico-Economic Writings. (Viennese Heritage Ser.: No. 1). (GER.). xl, 240p. 1984. reprint ed. pap. 22.95 (*90-272-3881-2*) J Benjamins Pubng Co.

Nyiri, J. C., et al, eds. Austrian Philosophy Studies & Texts. (Philosophia Resources Library). 200p. 1981. lib. bdg. 59.00 (*3-88405-004-4*) Philosophia Pr.

Nyiri, J. C. & Smith, Barry, eds. Practical Knowledge, Tradition & Technique. 224p. 1987. lib. bdg. 62.50 (*0-7099-4477-2*, Pub. by C Helm) Routldge.

Nyiri, J. C., ed. & intro. see Masaryk, Thomas G.

Nyiri, Janos. Battlefields & Playgrounds. Brandon, William, tr. from HUN. LC 95-5389. 536p. 1995. text 25.00 (*0-374-10918-4*) FS&G.

— Battlefields & Playgrounds. Brandon, William, tr. from HUN. LC 96-29909. (Tauber Institute Ser.: No. 23). 544p. 1997. reprint ed. pap. 19.95 (*0-87451-801-6*) U Pr of New Eng.

Nyiri, Nicolas. The United Nations' Search for a Definition of Aggression. (American University Studies: Political Science: Ser. X, Vol. 22). VIII, 412p. (C). 1989. text 53.95 (*0-8204-0869-7*) P Lang Pubng.

***Nyiri, Pal.** New Chinese Migrants in Europe: The Case of the Chinese Community in Hungary. (Research in Migration & Ethnic Relations Ser.). 150p. 1999. text 65.95 (*0-7546-1154-X*, Pub. by Ashgate Pub) Ashgate Pub Co.

Nyiri, Tamas. Theologie in Ost und West: Karl Rahners Beitrag. Neufeld, Karl H., ed. (Europaische Hochschulschriften Ser.: Reihe 23, Bd. 570). (GER.). 202p. 1996. 42.95 (*3-631-49348-7*) P Lang Pubng.

Nyirjesy, Istvan. Prevention & Detection of Gynecologic & Breast Cancer. 150p. 1994. pap. text. write for info. (*0-9642179-0-2*) Intl Fnd Gynecol.

Nyirkos, I. Finnish-Hungarian-Finnish Dictionary (Suomi-Unkari-Suomi) (FIN & HUN.). 712p. 1979. pap. 79.95 (*0-8288-4800-9*, M9642) Fr & Eur.

Nyirkos, Istvan. Finnish/Hungarian/Finnish Dictionary. (FIN & HUN.). 786p. 1996. 59.95 (*0-320-00100-8*) Fr & Eur.

Nyiroe, L., ed. Literature & Its Interpretation. (De Proprietatibus Litterarum, Ser. Minor: No. 24). 1979. pap. text 40.00 (*90-279-3387-1*) Mouton.

Nyiszli, Miklos. Auschwitz: A Doctor's Eyewitness Account. Kramer, Tibere & Seaver, Richard, trs. 240p. (C). 1993. reprint ed. pap. 11.45 (*1-55970-202-8*, Pub. by Arcade Pub Inc) Time Warner.

Nyjam, Ronald J. Adoptees Come of Age: Living Within Two Familes. LC 99-26278. (Counseling & Pastoral Theology Ser.). 176p. 1999. pap. 20.95 (*0-664-25671-6*) Geneva Press.

***Nykamp, Melinda.** The Customer Differential: The Complete Guide to Implementing Customer Relationship Management. 2000. 25.00 (*0-8144-0622-X*) AMACOM.

Nykanen, Lalli & Suomalainen, Heikki. Aroma of Beer, Wine & Distilled Alcoholic Beverages. 1983. text 226.00 (*90-277-1553-X*) Kluwer Academic.

Nykanen, Marita & Williams, Esther, trs. from FIN. The Faith We Hold: Archbishop Paul. LC 80-10404. 96p. 1980. pap. 7.95 (*0-913836-63-X*) St Vladimirs.

Nykanen, Mark. Hush. LC 97-37120. 304p. 1998. text 23.95 (*0-312-18051-9*) St Martin.

— Hush. 336p. 1999. mass mkt. 6.99 (*0-312-96852-3*) St Martin.

Nykiel, Connie. After the Loss of Your Baby: For Teen Mothers. rev. ed. LC 95-908. (Illus.). 19p. (Orig.). (YA). (gr. 7 up). 1995. pap. 3.50 (*1-888231-00-9*) For Teen Moms.

— Despues de la Perdida de Tu Bebe: Para Madres Adolecentes. Dodge, Grethel, tr. (Illus.). 19p. (Orig.). (YA). (gr. 7 up). 1995. pap. 3.50 (*1-888231-01-7*) For Teen Moms.

— No One Told Me I Could Cry: A Teen's Guide to Hope & Healing after Abortion. LC 95-90855. (Illus.). 85p. (Orig.). (YA). (gr. 7 up). 1997. pap. 8.00 (*1-888231-03-3*) For Teen Moms.

— What It Takes: A Survival Guide for Young & Teen Dads-to-Be. LC 95-90854. (Illus.). 80p. (Orig.). (YA). (gr. 7 up). 1995. pap. 5.00 (*1-888231-02-5*) For Teen Moms.

Nykiel, Ronald A. Marketing in the Hospitality Industry. 3rd ed. LC 96-30823. (Illus.). 308p. 1996. pap. write for info. (*0-86612-143-9*) Educ Inst Am Hotel.

Nykiel, Ronald A. & Jascolt, Elizabeth. Marketing Your City, U. S. A. A Guide to Developing a Strategic Tourism Marketing Plan. LC 98-17980. (Illus.). 112p. 1998. pap. text 19.95 (*0-7890-0592-1*); lib. bdg. 29.95 (*0-7890-0591-3*) Haworth Pr.

Nykl, A. R. Hispano-Arabic Poetry & Its Relations with the Old Provencal Troubadours. 1986. reprint ed. 10.00 (*0-87535-057-7*) Hispanic Soc.

Nykor, Lynda M., jt. auth. see Musson, Patricia.

Nykorowitsch, P., ed. Return Passage of Multi-Stage Turbomachinery. 66p. 1983. pap. text 8.00 (*0-317-02644-5*, G00225) ASME.

Nykrog, Per. L' Amour et la Rose: Le Grand Dessein de Jean de Meun. LC 85-73552. (Harvard Studies in Romance Languages: No. 41). (FRE.). 100p. (Orig.). 1986. pap. 10.00 (*0-940940-41-8*) Harvard U Romance Lang & Lit.

— La Recherche du Don Perdu: Points de Repere dans le Roman de Marcel Proust. LC 85-73551. (Harvard Studies in Romance Languages: No. 42). (FRE.). 100p. (Orig.). 1986. pap. 10.00 (*0-940940-42-6*) Harvard U Romance Lang & Lit.

Nyks-Corkum, R., jt. auth. see Gelderman-Curtis, C.

Nyks, R. J. Packing by the Book: How to Pack - What to Pack. Barns, R. & Krijgsman, E., eds. (Illus.). 250p. 1997. pap. 17.95 (*0-9657337-0-X*) Inside Info.

Nylan, Michael. The Elemental Changes - The Ancient Chinese Companion to the I Ching: The T'ai Hsuan Ching of Master Yang Hsiung: Text & Commentaries Translated by Michael Nylan. LC 93-15594. (SUNY Series in Chinese Philosophy & Culture). 391p. (C). 1994. pap. text 21.95 (*0-7914-1628-3*) State U NY Pr.

Nyland, Chris. Reduced Worktime & the Management of Production. (Illus.). 240p. (C). 1989. text 59.95 (*0-521-34547-2*) Cambridge U Pr.

Nyland, Chris, jt. ed. see Beilharz, Peter.

Nyland, Ralph D. Siviculture: Concepts & Applications. (Illus.). 608p. (C). 1996. 76.56 (*0-07-056999-1*) McGraw.

Nyland, Thomas G. & Mattoon, John S. Veterinary Diagnostic Ultrasound. 512p. 1995. text 88.00 (*0-7216-2745-5*, W B Saunders Co) Harcrt Hlth Sci Grp.

Nylander, Jane C. For Historic Buildings: A Guide to Selecting Reproduction: Fabrics. 4th rev. ed. LC 90-44185. (Historic Interiors Ser.). (Illus.). 304p. 1995. pap. 19.95 (*0-471-14379-0*) Wiley.

— Our Own Snug Fireside: Images of the New England Home, 1760-1860. (Illus.). 330p. 1994. pap. 20.00 (*0-300-05953-1*) Yale U Pr.

Nylander, Jane C., et al. Windows on the Past: Four Centuries of New England Life. LC 99-49516. (Illus.). 208p. 2000. 45.00 (*0-8212-2483-2*, Pub. by Bulfinch Pr) Little.

Nylander, Lucy, ed. see McKenna, Theresa.

Nylander, Richard C. For Historic Buildings: A Guide to Selecting Reproduction: Wall Papers, Vol. 4. rev. ed. LC 95-48332. (Historic Interiors Ser.). (Illus.). 264p. 1995. pap. 19.95 (*0-471-14431-2*) Wiley.

Nylander, Richard C., jt. auth. see Curtis, Nancy.

Nylander, Wiliam. Lichenological Papers 1863-1868 with Addenda Nova Ad Lichenographiam Europaeam 1865-1887, 3 vols. Ahti, Teuvo, ed. & pref. by. (Collected Lichenological Papers: Vol. 2). (GER.). 850p. 1990. reprint ed. 200.00 (*3-443-50014-5*, Pub. by Gebruder Borntraeger) Balogh.

Nylander, William. Collected Lichenological Papers Vol. 4: Papers 1888-1900. Ahti, Teuvi, ed. 826p. 1967. reprint ed. lib. bdg. 90.00 (*3-7682-0434-0*) Lubrecht & Cramer.

— Collected Lichenological Papers Vol. 5: Synopsis Methodica Lichenum 1958-69 & G. Lindau's Index Nominum Nylanderi Synopsis Lichenum 1907- Ahti, Teuvi, ed. (LAT.). 556p. 1967. reprint ed. lib. bdg. 90.00 (*3-7682-0435-9*) Lubrecht & Cramer.

— Collected Lichenological Papers Vol. 6: Prodromus Lichenographiae Galliae et Algeriae 1857; Lichenes Scandinaviae 1861; Lichenes Lapponiae Orientalis 1862. Ahti, Teuvi, ed. (LAT.). 636p. 1967. lib. bdg. 90.00 (*3-7682-0436-7*) Lubrecht & Cramer.

— Introduction & Lichenological Papers, 1852-1862, Vol. 1. Ahti, Teuvo, ed. & pref. by. (Collected Lichenological Papers). xlvi, 732p. 1990. reprint ed. 200.00 (*3-443-50013-7*, Pub. by Balogh) Balogh.

— Lichenological Papers, 1869-1887, 3 vols. Ahti, Teuvo, ed. & pref. by. (Collected Lichenological Papers: Vol. 3). (GER.). 560p. 1990. reprint ed. 200.00 (*3-443-50015 3*, Pub. by Gebruder Borntraeger) Balogh.

Nylen, Robert A., ed. see Oddie, Tasker L.

Nylen, William R. United States-Grenada Relations, 1979-1983: American Foreign Policy Towards a "Backyard" Revolution. (Pew Case Studies in International Affairs). 50p. (C). 1988. pap. text 3.50 (*1-56927-306-5*) Geo U Inst Dplmcy.

Nylund, Arabella W. Oriental Learning & Western Knowledge: The Encounter of Educational Traditions in Bengal 1781-1835. (Uppsala Studies in Education: No. 38). 186p. (Orig.). 1991. pap. 39.00 (*91-554-2778-2*) Coronet Bks.

***Nylund, David.** Treating Huckleberry Finn: A Competency-Based Approach for Treating Children Diagnosed with ADHD. LC 00-8176. 2000. 39.95 (*0-7879-5229-X*) Jossey-Bass.

Nylund, David, jt. ed. see Smith, Craig.

Nylund, Eric S. Dry Water. LC 96-25670. 320p. 1997. pap. 12.50 (*0-380-78542-0*, Avon Bks); mass mkt. 23.00 (*0-380-97474-6*, Avon Bks) Morrow Avon.

— Dry Water. 352p. 1998. reprint ed. mass mkt. 3.99 (*0-380-79614-7*, Avon Bks) Morrow Avon.

— A Game of Universe. 1997. mass mkt. 5.50 (*0-614-20497-6*, Avon Bks); mass mkt. 5.50 (*0-380-78541-2*, Avon Bks) Morrow Avon.

— A Signal Shattered. LC 99-25054. 384p. 1999. 23.00 (*0-380-97514-9*, Avon Bks) Morrow Avon.

***Nylund, Eric S.** A Signal Shattered. 384p. 2000. mass mkt. 6.99 (*0-380-79294-X*) Morrow Avon.

Nylund, Eric S. Signal to Noise. 390p. 1999. mass mkt. 6.99 (*0-380-79292-3*, Avon Bks) Morrow Avon.

Nyman, Anders & Svensson, Borje. Boys: Sexual Abuse & Treatment. LC 97-196483. 176p. 1997. pap. 26.95 (*1-85302-491-0*, Pub. by Jessica Kingsley) Taylor & Francis.

Nyman, Andra, ed. Instructional Methods for the Artroom. 50p. (Orig.). 1996. pap. text 20.00 (*0-937652-93-8*, 261) Natl Art Ed.

Nyman, C. J., et al. Problems For Gen Chem & Quan A. 4th ed. LC 79-24489. 352p. 1980. pap. 40.95 (*0-471-05299-X*) Wiley.

Nyman, C. J., jt. ed. see Newton, William E.

Nyman, Elizabeth & Leer, Jeff. Gagiwdul.at: Brought Forth to Reconfirm the Legacy of a Taku River Tlingit Clan. LC 93-17399. (Illus.). xxxii, 285p. 1993. pap. 26.95 (*1-55500-048-7*) Alaska Native.

Nyman, Heikki, ed. see Wittgenstein, Ludwig Josef Johann.

Nyman, Jopi. Hard-Boiled Fiction & Dark Romanticism. LC 98-5233. (Studien Zur Englischen und Amerikanischen Literatur: Vol. 19). 144p. (C). 1998. pap. text 28.95 (*0-8204-3546-5*) P Lang Pubng.

Nyman, Keith O. Re-Entry: How to Turn Your Military Experience into Civilian Success. 2nd rev. ed. LC 89-28850. (Illus.). 192p. 1990. pap. 13.95 (*0-8117-2317-8*) Stackpole.

— Selecting Business Partners for Success. LC 91-65740. 96p. (Orig.). 1991. pap. 12.95 (*0-9605826-1-4*) Staff Recrters.

Nyman, Lee R. Making Manufacturing Cells Work. 387p. 1994. 60.00 (*0-07-047977-1*) McGraw.

Nyman, Lee R., ed. Making Manufacturing Cells Work. (Illus.). 388p. 1992. 75.00 (*0-87263-419-1*) SME.

Nyman, Mattias. Photoshop in 4 Colors. 2nd ed. (Illus.). 80p. (C). 1995. pap. text 22.95 (*0-201-88424-0*) Peachpit Pr.

Nyman, Michael. Experimental Music: Cage & Beyond. 2nd ed. LC 98-31731. (Music in the Twentieth Century Ser.). (Illus.). 210p. 1999. 54.95 (*0-521-65297-9*); pap. 19.95 (*0-521-65383-5*) Cambridge U Pr.

— Michael Nyman Film Music for Piano Solo. 47p. 1998. pap. 19.95 (*0-7119-6722-9*, CH61400) Music Sales.

— Revisiting the Piano. 23p. 1998. pap. 9.95 (*0-7119-6884-5*, CH 61441, Pub. by Strathmore Music) Music Sales.

Nyman, Monte S. Great Are the Words of Isaiah. 1993. pap. 8.95 (*0-88494-910-9*) Bookcraft Inc.

Nyman, Monte S. & Tate, Charles D., Jr., eds. The Book of Mormon Vol. 6: Alma, the Testimony of the Word. 1992. 11.95 (*0-88494-841-2*) Bookcraft Inc.

Nyman, Monte S., ed. see B. Y. U. Religious Studies Center Staff.

Nyman, Monte S., ed. see BYU Religious Studies Center Staff.

Nyman, Monte S., jt. ed. see Tate, Charles D.

Nyman, Richmond C., jt. auth. see Smith, Elliot D.

Nymeyer, Robert. Carlsbad, Caves & a Camera. LC 78-6650. (Illus.). 318p. (Orig.). 1993. pap. 11.95 (*0-939748-36-3*) Cave Bks MO.

Nyomarkay, Istvan, jt. auth. see Hadrovics, Laszlo.

Nyomarkay, Joseph. Charisma & Factionalism in the Nazi Party. LC 67-21015. 165p. reprint ed. pap. 51.20 (*0-608-15971-9*, 203327800084) Bks Demand.

Nyoongah, Mudrooroo. Aboriginal Mythology: An Encyclopedia of Myth & Legend. (Illus.). 208p. 1995. pap. 16.00 (*1-85538-306-3*, Pub. by Aqrn Pr) Harper SF.

Nyotumba, Godfrey. Mongoose & Mouse. (J). (ps-3). 1995. pap. text 4.95 (*9966-884-39-4*) Jacaranda.

— Nguchiro Na Panyae. LC 95-981889. 1995. pap. text 4.95 (*9966-884-51-3*) Nocturnal Sun.

Nyp, Gary, jt. auth. see Amernic, Jerry.

NYPL Staff. Bibliographic Guide to Art & Architecture, Set, vols. 2. 1995. 395.00 (*0-7838-2161-1*) Mac Lib Ref.

Nyquist (CIDR) Staff. Preparing the Professoriate of Tomorrow to Teach: Selected Readings in TA Training. 480p. (C). 1990. per. 52.95 (*0-8403-6374-5*) Kendall-Hunt.

Nyquist, Edwin R., jt. ed. see Yocum, Ronald H.

Nyquist, Henrik, ed. see Nyquist, Pelle.

Nyquist, James F. & Kuhatschek, Jack. Leading Bible Discussions. rev. ed. (LifeGuide Bible Studies). 64p. 1985. pap., wbk. ed. 4.99 (*0-8308-1000-5*, 1000) InterVarsity.

***Nyquist, Jeff.** Origins of the Fourth World War. 280p. 1999. pap. 14.99 (*1-58275-010-6*, Pub. by Black Forest Pr) Epic Bk Promo.

***Nyquist, Jeffrey R.** Origins of the Fourth World War. 254p. 1998. pap. 15.00 (*1-58538-004-0*) Prophecy Club.

Nyquist, Jeffrey R. Origins of the Fourth World War: And the Coming Wars of Mass Destruction. unabridged ed. vi, 254p. 1998. pap. 20.00 (*0-9666877-0-1*) J Nyquist.

Nyquist, Jody D., et al, eds. Teaching Assistant Training in the 1990s. LC 85-644763. (New Directions for Teaching & Learning Ser.: No. TL 39). 1989. 22.00 (*1-55542-858-4*) Jossey-Bass.

Nyquist, Jody D. & Wulff, Donald H. Working with Graduate Assistants. LC 95-32508. 176p. 1995. 38.00 (*0-8039-5313-5*); pap. 17.95 (*0-8039-5314-3*) Sage.

***Nyquist, John R. & Martin, Robert.** Director 8 & Lingo Bible. LC 00-39634. 1000p. 2000. pap. 49.99 (*0-7645-3486-6*) IDG Bks.

Nyquist, Joy. Travel Light: How to Go Anywhere in the World with Only One Suitcase. LC 97-67146. 196p. 2000. per. 17.95 (*1-879899-02-7*) Newjoy Pr.

***Nyquist, Kate.** Who's Who in the Coral Reef. (Illus.). 32p. (J). (ps-2). 2000. 12.95 (*1-878244-34-5*) Monterey Bay Aquarium.

Nyquist, Mary, jt. ed. see Ferguson, Margaret.

Nyquist, Ola. Juvenile Justice: A Comparative Study with Special Reference to the Swedish Child Welfare Board & the California Juvenile Court Systems, Vol. 12--12. LC 74-17590. (Cambridge Studies in Criminology: Vol. 12). (Illus.). 302p. 1974. reprint ed. lib. bdg. 75.00 (*0-8371-7835-5*, NYJJ) Greenwood.

***Nyquist, Pelle.** Don't Diet! The Book: Eat Right. Nyquist, Henrik, ed. Zackrisson, Bo, tr. (Illus.). 114p. 1999. 14.99 (*0-9677602-0-8*) Dont Diet.

Nyquist, Richard A. Electronic Handbook of Infrared & Raman Spectra of Inorganic Compounds & Organic Salts. 85p. 1998. 3000.00 (*0-12-444560-8*) Acad Pr.

***Nyquist, Richard A.** IR & Raman Spectra. 432p. 2000. 125.00 (*0-12-523355-8*) Acad Pr.

Nyquist, Richard A., et al, eds. Infrared Raman Spectral Analysis of Inorganic Compounds, 4 vols. (Illus.). 1184p. 1996. boxed set 2500.00 (*0-12-523444-9*) Acad Pr.

— Infrared Raman Spectral Analysis of Inorganic Compounds, Vol. 1: Infrared Spectra of Inorganic Compounds. (Illus.). 1971. text 263.00 (*0-12-523450-3*) Acad Pr.

— Infrared Raman Spectral Analysis of Inorganic Compounds, Vol. 3: Raman Spectra Charts. (Illus.). 1996. text 250.00 (*0-12-523446-5*) Acad Pr.

N

An Asterisk (*) at the beginning of an entry indicates that the title is appearing for the first time.

— Infrared Raman Spectral Analysis of Inorganic Compounds, Vol. 4: Infrared Spectra Charts. (Illus.). 1996. text 250.00 (*0-12-523447-3*) Acad Pr.

— Infrared Raman Spectral Analysis of Inorganic Compunds & Organic Salts, Vol. 2: Text & Explanations. (Illus.). 1996. text 250.00 (*0-12-523445-7*) Acad Pr.

Nyr. Random Multifractals. 1994. pap. 69.95 (*0-582-25381-0*) Longman.

Nyre, G. F., jt. ed. see Rose, Clare.

Nyren, Eve A., tr. from CHI. The Bonds of Matrimony Hsing - Shih Yin - Yuan Chuan Vol. 1: A Seventeenth - Century Chinese Novel. LC 94-37609. (Chinese Studies: Vol. 1).Tr. of Hsing shih yin yuan chuan. (CHI.). 312p. 1995. text 99.95 (*0-7734-9033-7*) E Mellen.

Nyrnberger, G., ed. see Walz, Guido.

Nyrop, K. The Kiss & Its History. 1973. 250.00 (*0-87968-330-9*) Gordon Pr.

Nys, Barbara S. Filip de, see Filip de Nys, Barbara S.

NYS Department of Motor Vehicles, Division of Vehi. Fuel Injection Systems Training, New York State Edition. LC 92-24673. 1992. pap. 44.95 (*0-8273-5586-6*) Delmar.

NYS Ed. Dept. Staff. Teaching Writing to Adults. 1990. text 175.00 (*0-8273-4510-0*) S-W Pub.

Nys, Ernest, ed. Franciscus de Victoria de Indis et de Ivre Belli Reflectiones, Vol. 1. Bate, John P., tr. LC 95-77197. (Classics in International Law Reprint Ser.: No.7, Vol.1). (ENG & LAT.). 100, 457p. 1995. reprint ed. 115.00 (*0-89941-951-8*, 310140) W S Hein.

Nys, Herman. Edical Law in Belgium. 152p. 1998. text 90.00 (*90-411-0522-0*) Kluwer Law Intl.

Nys, Herman, ed. Medical Law. (International Encyclopedia of Laws Ser.). 1993. ring bd. 115.00 (*0-685-58994-3*) Kluwer Law Intl.

Nys, Herman, ed. Medical Law, 2 vols. (International Encyclopedia of Laws Ser.). 1994. ring bd. 351.00 (*90-6544-943-4*) Kluwer Law Intl.

NYS Task Force on Life & the Law Staff. Assisted Reproductive Technologies: Analysis & Recommendations for Public Policy. 474p. 1998. pap. 12.00 (*1-881268-03-9*) NYS Task Force.

— When Death Is Sought: Assisted Suicide & Euthanasia in the Medical Context. 234p. 1994. pap. 9.00 (*1-881268-01-2*) NYS Task Force.

Nyschens, Ian. Months of the Sun. (Illus.). 420p. 1998. 100.00 (*1-57157-045-4*) Safari Pr.

Nysenholc, Adolphe, ed. Charlie Chaplin: His Reflection in Modern Times. LC 91-25247. (Approaches to Semiotics Ser.: No. 101). xvi, 412p. (C). 1991. lib. bdg. 121.55 (*3-11-012600-1*) Mouton.

Nyson, Violet W. The Sad Little Cottage. (Illus.). 32p. (Orig.). (J). (ps-4). 1996. pap. 5.95 (*1-888828-05-6*) Anchor Pubing.

Nysrtand, Martin, et al, eds. Opening Dialogue: Understanding the Dynamics of Language & Learning in the English Classroom. LC 96-32840. (Language & Literacy Ser.: Vol. 29). 160p. (C). 1996. text 44.00 (*0-8077-3574-4*); pap. text 19.95 (*0-8077-3573-6*) Tchrs Coll.

Nyssa, Gregor Von, see Von Nyssa, Gregor.

Nyssen, Hubert. Lexique du Marketing. (FRE.). 86p. 1971. pap. 7.50 (*0-686-57064-2*, M-6435) Fr & Eur.

Nyssenus, Gregorius. Oratio Catechetica: Opera Dogmatica Minora, Pars 4. Muhlenberg, E., ed. (Gregorii Nysseni Opera Ser.: Nos. 3 & 4). (GRE.). 216p. 1996. 73.00 (*90-04-10348-1*) Brill Academic Pubs.

Nystedt, Karen, ed. Point of Fracture: Voices of Heinous Crime Survivors. (Illus.). 164p. 1998. per. 29.95 (*0-9662909-0-9*) A Zuckerman.

Nystom, Fred & Nystrom, Mardi M. Special Places: For the Discerning Traveler. 6th ed. Demisco, Brandy K., ed. 312p. 1994. pap. 16.95 (*0-936777-03-6*) Special Pl.

Nystom, Lars-Erik, jt. ed. see Sofer, Gail K.

Nystrand, Martin. The Structure of Written Communication: Studies in Reciprocity Between Writers & Readers. 1986. text 64.95 (*0-12-523482-1*) Acad Pr.

Nystrand, Martin, ed. What Writers Know: The Language Process & Structure of Written Discourse. 1981. text 64.95 (*0-12-523480-5*) Acad Pr.

Nystrom. Que Es un Cristiano?Tr. of What Is a Christian?. (SPA.). 29p. (J). write for info. (*0-614-27127-4*) Editorial Unilit.

Nystrom, Bengt. Rorstrand Porcelain: Art Nouveau Masterpieces. (Illus.). 192p. 1996. 80.00 (*1-55859-844-8*) Abbeville Pr.

Nystrom, Bengt, jt. ed. see Hult, Jan.

Nystrom, Bradley & Spyridakis, Stylianos V. Ancient Rome. 48p. 1995. text, student ed. write for info. (*0-7872-0398-X*) Kendall-Hunt.

— Ancient Rome, Set. 2nd ed. 320p. 1995. pap. text 36.95 (*0-7872-0399-8*, 41039901) Kendall-Hunt.

Nystrom, Bradley, jt. auth. see Spyridakis, Stylianos V.

Nystrom, Bradley P., tr. The Song of Eros: Ancient Greek Love Poems. LC 90-35758. (Illus.). 120p. (C). 1991. 17.95 (*0-8093-1640-4*) S Ill U Pr.

Nystrom, Bradley P., jt. ed. see Spyridakis, Stylianos V.

Nystrom, Brian. Ordinary People - Extraordinary Marriages: Reclaiming God's Original Design. Jensen, Debbie, ed. (Illus.). 200p. 1997. 18.95 (*0-9655512-5-3*) Life Res Am.

Nystrom, C. Que Es un Cristiano?Tr. of What Is a Christian?. (SPA.). 29p. (J). 1995. 2.99 (*1-56063-782-X*, 490459) Editorial Unilit.

— Que Pasa Cuando Morimos?Tr. of What Happens When We Die?. (SPA.). 29p. (J). 1995. 2.99 (*1-56063-781-1*, 490458) Editorial Unilit.

Nystrom, Carolyn. Angels & Me. (Children's Bible Basics Ser.). (Illus.). (J). (ps-3). 6.99 (*0-8024-7863-8*, 573) Moody.

— Basic Beliefs: A Woman's Workshop on the Christian Faith. (Woman's Workshop Ser.). 124p. 1983. pap. 4.99 (*0-310-41971-9*, 11277P) Zondervan.

— Behold Your Christ: A Woman's Workshop on Jesus. (Woman's Workshop Ser.). 128p. (Orig.). 1985. pap. 4.50 (*0-310-41981-6*, 11284P) Zondervan.

— Characters & Kings: A Woman's Workshop on the History of Israel, 2 pts. (Woman's Workshop Ser.). 240p. (Orig.). 1985. pap. 2.99 (*0-310-41881-X*, 11279P); pap. 2.99 (*0-310-41871-2*, 11283P) Zondervan.

***Nystrom, Carolyn.** Children's Bible Basics: Questions Kids Ask about Belief. (Illus.). (J). 2000. 14.99 (*0-8024-7914-6*) Moody.

Nystrom, Carolyn. Courage, Esther! LC 99-207786. (Follow the Leader Stories Ser.). (Illus.). 32p. (J). 1998. 7.99 (*0-8024-2206-3*) Moody.

— Emma Says Goodbye: A Chlid's Guide to Bereavement. 48p. (J). (gr. 4-7). 1994. pap. 4.99 (*0-7459-2924-9*) Lion USA.

— Finding Contentment. (Christian Character Bible Studies). 64p. (Orig.). 1992. pap., wbk. ed. 4.99 (*0-8308-1145-1*, 1145) InterVarsity.

— 1 & 2 Peter & Jude: Compass for a Dark Road. (LifeGuide Bible Studies). 64p. (Orig.). 1992. pap., wbk. ed. 4.99 (*0-8308-1019-6*, 1019) InterVarsity.

— Forgive, Joseph! LC 99-193365. (Follow the Leader Stories Ser.). (Illus.). 32p. (J). 1998. 7.99 (*0-8024-2207-1*) Moody.

— Friendship: Growing Side by Side. (LifeGuide Bible Studies). 64p. (Orig.). 1996. pap., wbk. ed. 4.99 (*0-8308-1076-5*, 1076) InterVarsity.

— Growing Jesus' Way. (Children's Bible Basics Ser.). (J). (ps-3). 6.99 (*0-8024-7860-3*, 574) Moody.

— The Holy Spirit in Me. (Children's Bible Basics Ser.). (J). (ps-3). 6.99 (*0-8024-7858-1*, 576) Moody.

***Nystrom, Carolyn.** Integrity: Living the Truth. (LifeGuide Bible Studies). 64p. 2000. pap. 4.99 (*0-8308-3052-9*) InterVarsity.

Nystrom, Carolyn. Jenny & Grandpa: A Child's Guide to Growing Older. 48p. (J). (gr. 4-7). 1994. pap. 4.99 (*0-7459-2922-2*) Lion USA.

— Jesus Is No Secret. (Children's Bible Basics Ser.). (Illus.). (J). 6.99 (*0-8024-7865-4*, 575) Moody.

— Jonah & Ruth: A Friend for the Journey. 96p. 1995. pap. 4.99 (*1-56476-363-3*, 6-3363, Victor Bks) Chariot Victor.

— Knowing Scripture. (Discipleship Ser.). 64p. 1992. mass mkt. 5.99 (*0-310-54721-0*) Zondervan.

— Living in the World. (Christian Character Bible Studies). 64p. (Orig.). 1992. pap., wbk. ed. 4.99 (*0-8308-1144-3*, 1144) InterVarsity.

— Loving God. (Christian Character Bible Studies). 64p. (Orig.). 1992. pap., wbk. ed. 4.99 (*0-8308-1141-9*, 1141) InterVarsity.

— Loving One Another. (Christian Character Bible Studies). 64p. (Orig.). 1992. pap., wbk. ed. 4.99 (*0-8308-1142-7*, 1142) InterVarsity.

— Loving the World. (Christian Character Bible Studies). 64p. (Orig.). 1992. pap., wbk. ed. 4.99 (*0-8308-1143-5*, 1143) InterVarsity.

— Mario's Big Question: A Child's Guide to Adoption. 48p. (J). (gr. 4-7). 1994. pap. 4.99 (*0-7459-2923-0*) Lion USA.

— Mike's Lonely Summer: A Child's Guide to Divorce. 48p. (J). (gr. 4-7). 1994. pap. 4.99 (*0-7459-2925-7*) Lion USA.

— New Testament Characters. (LifeGuide Bible Studies). 64p. (Orig.). 1993. pap., wbk. ed. 4.99 (*0-8308-1069-2*, 1069) InterVarsity.

— Old Testament Kings. (LifeGuide Bible Studies). 64p. (Orig.). 1993. pap., wbk. ed. 4.99 (*0-8308-1070-6*, 1070) InterVarsity.

— Run, Elijah! (Follow the Leader Stories Ser.). (Illus.). 32p. (J). 1998. 7.99 (*0-8024-2205-5*) Moody.

— Sharing Your Faith. (Discipleship Ser.). 64p. 1992. pap. 5.99 (*0-310-54741-5*) Zondervan.

— What Happens When We Die? (Children's Bible Basics Ser.). (Illus.). 32p. (J). (ps-2). 6.99 (*0-8024-7855-7*, 577) Moody.

— What Is a Christian? (Children's Bible Basics Ser.). (J). 6.99 (*0-8024-7854-9*, 578) Moody.

— What Is Prayer. (Children's Bible Basics Ser.). (J). 6.99 (*0-8024-7859-X*, 579) Moody.

— What Is the Bible? (Children's Bible Basics Ser.). 32p. (J). (ps-2). 6.99 (*0-8024-7864-6*, 580) Moody.

— When Jesus Comes Back. (Children's Bible Basics Ser.). (J). (ps-3). 6.99 (*0-8024-7861-1*, 581) Moody.

— Who Is God? (Children's Bible Basics Ser.). 30p. (J). 6.99 (*0-8024-7857-3*, 582) Moody.

— Who Is Jesus? (Children's Bible Basics Ser.). 30p. (J). 6.99 (*0-8024-7856-5*, 583) Moody.

— Who Is Jesus? A Woman's Workshop on Mark. (Woman's Workshop Ser.). 144p. 1987. pap. 5.99 (*0-310-42001-6*, 11289P) Zondervan.

— Why Do I Do Things Wrong? (Children's Bible Basics Ser.). 32p. (J). (ps-2). 6.99 (*0-8024-7862-X*, 584) Moody.

— A Woman's Workshop on Romans - Leader's Manual. 112p. (Orig.). 1981. pap. 3.99 (*0-310-41911-5*, 11274P) Zondervan.

— A Workshop on the Book of John. 144p. (Orig.). 1989. pap. 6.99 (*0-310-41841-0*) Zondervan.

— You, Jonah! LC 99-207782. (Follow the Leader Stories Ser.). (Illus.). 32p. (J). 1998. 7.99 (*0-8024-2204-7*) Moody.

Nystrom, Carolyn, et al. Christian Character Bible Studies Series, 8 vols., Set. (Orig.). 1992. pap., wbk. ed. 39.92 (*0-8308-1140-0*, 1140) InterVarsity.

Nystrom, Carolyn, jt. auth. see Munger, Robert B.

Nystrom, Carolyn, jt. auth. see Packer, J. I.

Nystrom, Christer & Alderborn, Goran, eds. Pharmaceutical Powder Compaction Technology. (Drugs & the Pharmaceutical Sciences Ser.: Vol. 71). (Illus.). 624p. 1995. text 195.00 (*0-8247-9376-5*) Dekker.

Nystrom, Debra. A Quarter Turn. LC 90-26317. 65p. 1991. text 14.95 (*1-878818-02-3*, Pub. by Sheep Meadow); pap. text 12.95 (*1-878818-00-7*, Pub. by Sheep Meadow) U Pr of New Eng.

Nystrom, Dennis C. Occupation & Career Education Legislation. LC 79-12548. pap. 3.40 (*0-672-97133-X*, Bobbs); pap. 10.50 (*0-685-00789-8*, Bobbs) Macmillan.

Nystrom, Dennis C., et al. Instructional Methods in Occupational Education. LC 76-43204. 1977. 15.95 (*0-672-97111-9*, Bobbs) Macmillan.

Nystrom, Derek, ed. see Rorty, Richard McKay.

Nystrom, Harry. Creativity & Innovation. LC 78-8594. (Illus.). 135p. reprint ed. pap. 41.90 (*0-8357-6636-5*, 203528900094) Bks Demand.

***Nystrom, Jennifer.** Favorite Bible Children: Grades 1 & 2. (Illus.). 96p. (gr. 1-2). 1999. pap. 11.95 (*1-885358-77-6*) Rainbow CA.

— Favorite Bible Children: Grades 3 & 4. (Illus.). 96p. (gr. 3-4). 1999. pap. 11.95 (*1-885358-78-4*) Rainbow CA.

Nystrom, Karl R. State D Coaching Course: Workbook. (Illus.). 50p. (Orig.). (C). 1989. pap. 3.50 (*1-879397-03-X*) Kanvi.

— State D Soccer Coaching Course: Instructor's Manual. 51p. (Orig.). (C). 1989. pap. 3.50 (*1-879397-02-1*) Kanvi.

Nystrom, Karl R., tr. see Fotbollforbundet, Svenska.

Nystrom, Lars-Erik & Sofer, Gail K. Process Chromatography: A Guide to Validation. (Illus.). 800p. 1991. text 48.00 (*0-12-654267-8*) Acad Pr.

Nystrom, Mardi M., jt. auth. see Nystom, Fred.

Nystrom, Paul C. & Starbuck, William H., eds. Handbook of Organizational Design, 2 vols., Set. (Illus.). 582p. 1981. text 75.00 (*0-19-520233-3*) OUP.

Nystrom, Paul H. Economic Principles of Consumption. LC 75-39263. (Getting & Spending: The Consumer's Dilemma Ser.). (Illus.). 1976. reprint ed. 48.95 (*0-405-08036-0*) Ayer.

— Economics of Retailing. Assael, Henry, ed. LC 78-246. (Century of Marketing Ser.). (Illus.). 1979. reprint ed. lib. bdg. 41.95 (*0-405-11180-0*) Ayer.

Nystrom Staff. Desk Atlas. 176p. (C). 1995. per. write for info. (*0-697-29728-4*, WCB McGr Hill) McGrw-H Hghr Educ.

Nystuen, John D., jt. auth. see Arlinghaus, Sandra L.

Nystul. Introduction to Counseling: An Art & Science Perspective. LC 98-45118. 494p. (C). 1999. 71.00 (*0-205-26827-7*, Pub. by P-H) S&S Trade.

***Nystul, Bryan.** Lostech: The Mechwarrior Equipment Guide, Vol. 172. (Mech Warrior Ser.). (Illus.). 2000. pap. 20.00 (*1-55560-399-8*) FASA Corp.

— Maximum Tech. rev. ed. (Battletech Ser.). 1999. pap. 15.00 (*1-55560-381-5*) FASA Corp.

Nystul, Michael S. The Art & Science of Counseling & Psychotherapy. 459p. (C). 1992. pap. text 65.00 (*0-675-21212-X*, Merrill Coll) P-H.

Nyswtrom, Bradley & Spyridakis, Stylianos V. Ancient Rome. 272p. 1995. pap. text, per. write for info. (*0-7872-0397-1*) Kendall-Hunt.

Nythus, Lloyd M., ed. Surgery Annual 1992, Vol. 24, Pt. 1. 258p. (C). 1991. pap. text 95.00 (*0-8385-8745-3*, A8745-0, Apple Lange Med) McGraw.

Nyumen, Sanzen & Sogon, Omori. Introduction to Zen Training. (Illus.). 310p. 1996. 110.00 (*0-7103-0534-6*, Pub. by Kegan Paul Intl) Col U Pr.

Nyvall, Robert. Field Crop Diseases. 3rd ed. LC 99-18995. (Illus.). 1054p. 1999. text 129.95 (*0-8138-2079-0*) Iowa St U Pr.

Nyvlt, Jaroslav. Design of Crystallizers. 192p. 1992. lib. bdg. 110.00 (*0-8493-5072-7*, TP156) CRC Pr.

Nyvlt, Jaroslav & Ulrich, Joachim. Admixtures in Crystallization. LC 95-30316. 391p. 1995. 250.00 (*3-527-28739-6*, Wiley-VCH) Wiley.

Nyweide, David. Plum Lake: Visits to the North Woods. Kirsch, J. Allen, ed. 96p. (YA). 1999. pap. 9.95 (*1-878569-59-7*) Badger Bks Inc.

Nywening, Willy. Sister Stories: Daily Inspiration from the Lives of Ruth & Esther. LC 96-18732. 85p. 1997. pap. 7.95 (*1-56212-248-7*, 1701-0630) CRC Pubns.

***Nywer, Hank.** High School Hazing: When Rites Become Wrongs. 2000. pap. 8.95 (*0-531-16465-9*) Watts.

Nywering, Willy. So You've Been Asked to Lead a Small Group. 8p. 1998. mass mkt. 1.25 (*1-56212-379-3*, 2270-0120) CRC Pubns.

***Nyyssonen, Heino.** Presence of the Past in Politics: '1956' after 1956 in Hungary. 311p. 1999. pap. 27.50 (*951-39-0547-0*, Pub. by SoPhi Academic) Intl Spec Bk.

Nyznyk, Darryl. The Third Term. LC 97-66088. 354p. 1997. 24.95 (*0-9656513-4-7*) Cross Dove.

Nzambi, Philippe D. Proverbes Bibliques et Proverbes Kongo: Etude Comparative de Proverbia 25-29 et de Quelques Proverbes Kongo. (Religionswissenschaft Ser.: Bd. 5). (FRE.). 767p. 1992. 107.80 (*3-631-44827-9*) P Lang Pubng.

Nzegwu, Nkiru, ed. Contemporary Textures: Multidimensonality in Nigerian Art. LC 98-88223. (Illus.). (C). 1999. pap. text 24.95 (*1-892627-01-9*) Bing Univ ISSA.

— Issues in Contemporary African Art. LC 98-88222. (Illus.). 218p. (C). 1998. pap. text 17.50 (*1-892627-00-0*) Bing Univ ISSA.

Nzenza-Shand, Sekai. Songs to an African Sunset: A Zimbabwean Story. (Illus.). 270p. 1997. pap. 10.95 (*0-86442-472-8*) Lonely Planet.

Nzongola-Ntalaja, Georges. Crisis in Zaire: Myths & Realities. 335p. (C). 1988. 45.00 (*0-86543-023-3*); pap. 11.95 (*0-86543-024-1*) Africa World.

***Nzongola-Ntalaja, Georges.** From Zaire to the Democratic Republic of the Congo. LC 98-203025. (Current African Issues Ser.). 18p. 1999. pap. write for info. (*91-7106-424-9*) Nordic Africa.

Nzongola-Ntalaja, Georges, ed. Conflict in the Horn of Africa. 1991. pap. 15.00 (*0-918456-65-7*) African Studies Assn.

Nzongola-Ntalaja, Georges, et al. The State & Democracy in Africa. LC 98-10466. 244p. 1998. 79.95 (*0-86543-637-1*); pap. 21.95 (*0-86543-638-X*) Africa World.

Nzunda, Matembo S. & Ross, Kenneth R. Church, Law & Political Transition in Malawi, 1992-94. LC 95-981425. 170p. 1996. pap. 39.95 (*0-86922-602-9*, U Pr W Africa) Intl Scholars.

O

O., Bill. How It Works: Practical Suggestions on Working Twelve Steps. Laughlin, Bonnie, ed. 31p. (Orig.). 1995. pap. text 3.95 (*0-9649729-4-8*) Recov House.

O Cannain, Tomas. A Lifetime of Notes: The Memoirs of Tomas O Canainn. 128p. 1996. pap. 13.95 (*1-898256-11-X*, Pub. by Collins Press) Irish Bks Media.

O. Ciarain, S. Farewell to Mayo. Date not set. pap. 12.95 (*1-873748-00-0*) Dufour.

***O Conaola, Dara.** Night Ructions: Selected Short Stories. 58p. 2000. pap. 7.95 (*1-900693-15-1*, Pub. by Clo Iar-Chonnachta) Dufour.

O Dalaigh, Brian. Ennis in the 18th Century: Portrait of an Urban Community. 64p. 1995. pap. 9.95 (*0-7165-2571-2*, Pub. by Irish Acad Pr) Intl Spec Bk.

O Dochartaigh, Fionnbarra. Ulster's White Negroes. 136p. (Orig.). 1994. pap. 8.95 (*1-873176-67-8*, AK Pr San Fran) AK Pr Dist.

***O Grada, Cormac.** Black '47 & Beyond: The Great Irish Famine in History, Economics & Memory. (Economic History of the Western World Ser.). (Illus.). 272p. 2000. pap. 17.95 (*0-691-07015-6*, Pub. by Princeton U Pr) Cal Prin Full Svc.

***O heithir, Breandan & O heithir, Ruairi, eds.** An Aran Reader. 312p. 1999. pap. 19.95 (*1-901866-28-9*, Pub. by Lilliput Pr) Dufour.

O heithir, Ruairi, jt. ed. see O heithir, Breandan.

O. Henry Society of Arts & Sciences, contrib. by. Prize Stories 1919: The O. Henry Memorial Award. (BCL1-PS American Literature Ser.). 1992. reprint ed. lib. bdg. 79.00 (*0-7812-6656-4*) Rprt Serv.

O., Jack. Dealing with Depression in 12 Step Recovery. LC 90-14047. (Fellow Travelers Ser.). 72p. (Orig.). pap. 4.95 (*0-934125-13-9*) Hazelden.

O, Jaime E. Rodriguez, see Rodriguez O, Jaime E.

O., Jesse. American Railroad Hobo: The Travels of Wade Hampton Fullbright - A Collection of Short Stories. Thornton, Mike, ed. LC 96-79000. (Illus.). 199p. 1997. 19.95 (*1-889982-00-8*) Ballngton Bks.

O., Paul. There's More to Quitting Drinking Than Quitting Drinking. 1995. pap. 14.95 (*0-9644887-4-4*) Sabrina Pub.

O, Peter. Serenity's Prayer: Asking for Recovery. LC 97-77034. 160p. 1997. pap. 12.95 (*0-9660003-0-7*) E Riv-Saratoga.

O, Ron, tr. & photos by see B, Rick E.

O, Ying-Lie, et al, eds. Shape in Picture: Mathematical Description of Shape in Grey-Level Images. LC 93-48570. (NATO ASI Series F; Computer & Systems Sciences Ser.: Vol. 126). x, 676p. 1994. 172.95 (*0-387-57578-2*) Spr-Verlag.

O Yong-su, jt. auth. see Tong-ni, Kim.

Oae, S. & Ohno, A. Handbook of Synthetic Organic Chemistry. (Illus.). Date not set. text. write for info. (*0-8247-9528-8*, 9528-8) Dekker.

Oae, Shigeru. Organic Sulphur Chemistry: Biochemical Aspects. 288p. 1992. lib. bdg. 199.00 (*0-8493-4740-8*, QP535) CRC Pr.

Oae, Shigeru & Doi, Joyce T. Organic Sulfur Chemistry: Structure & Mechanism. (Illus.). 288p. 1991. lib. bdg. 225.00 (*0-8493-4739-4*, QD412) CRC Pr.

Oae, Shigeru & Furukawa, Naomichi. Sulfilimines & Related Derivatives. LC 83-12220. (ACS Monograph Ser.: No. 179). (Illus.). 352p. 1983. reprint ed. pap. 109.20 (*0-608-04360-5*, 206514100001) Bks Demand.

Oae, Shigeru & Furukawa, Naomichi, eds. Sulfilimines & Related Derivatives. LC 83-12220. (ACS Monograph: No. 179). 340p. 1983. lib. bdg. 92.95 (*0-8412-0705-4*) Am Chemical.

Oak Associates Staff. Business Savvy. 160p. 1995. pap. 11.95 (*4-89684-244-8*, Pub. by Yohan Pubns) Weatherhill.

— Getting Acquainted. 160p. 1995. pap. 11.95 (*4-89684-243-X*, Pub. by Yohan Pubns) Weatherhill.

Oak General Secretariat Staff. Aplicacoes da Teoria de Grupos Na Espectroscopia de Raman e do Infravermelho. (Serie de Fisica Monografia: No. 14). 102p. 1980. pap. text 3.50 (*0-8270-1126-1*) OAS.

Oak, Henry L. A Visit to the Missions of Southern California in February & March 1874. Axe, Ruth F. et al, eds. LC 81-52830. (Frederick Webb Hodge Publications: No. 11). (Illus.). 87p. 1981. 20.00 (*0-916561-66-6*) Southwest Mus.

Oak, Jacquelyn, et al. Face to Face: M. W. Hopkins & Noah North. LC 88-63535. (Illus.). (Orig.). (C). 1989. pap. 34.95 (*0-9621107-7-9*) Mus Our Natl Hertge.

Oak, P. N. Tajmahal: The True Story. Orig. Title: The Tajmahal is a Temple Palace. (Illus.). 336p. (Orig.). 1989. pap. 10.95 (*0-9611614-4-2*) A Ghosh.

An Asterisk (*) at the beginning of an entry indicates that the title is appearing for the first time.

Oak Park Historic Preservation Commission Staff. Ridgeland Revealed: Guide to the Architecture of the Ridgeland-Oak Park Historic District. Sanderson, Arlene, ed. (Illus.). 110p. (Orig.). 1993. pap. 7.95 (0-9616915-1-4) Vil Oak Pk.

Oak, Purushottam N. Islamic Havoc in Indian History. (Illus.). 390p. 1996. pap. 15.95 (1-880628-06-6) A Ghosh.

Oak, Suman, tr. see Joshi, Tarkteerth L.

Oakason, Lori, ed. see Sloan, Colleen.

Oakason, Lori, ed. see Sloan, Colleen & Taylor, Ross.

Oakden, David. Witches & Warlocks. LC 82-10140. (Tales of the Supernatural Ser.). 48 p. 1982. write for info. (0-86625-205-3) Rourke Pubns.

Oakeley, Hilda D. Greek Ethical Thought: From Homer to the Stoics. LC 76-152999. (Select Bibliographies Reprint Ser.). 1977. reprint ed. 20.95 (0-8369-5751-2) Ayer.

Oakeley, Hilda D., ed. Greek Ethical Thought: From Homer to the Stoics. LC 79-173804. (Library of Greek Thought: No. 5). reprint ed. 27.50 (0-404-07804-4) AMS Pr.

Oakely, I. T. & O'Neill, L. J., eds. Language, Logic & Causation: Philosophical Writings of Professor Douglas Gasking. 256p. 1997. pap. 24.95 (0-522-84756-0, Pub. by Melbourne Univ Pr) Paul & Co Pubs.

Oakerson, Ronald J. Governing Local Public Economies: Creating the Civic Metropolis. 2nd rev. ed. LC 99-10992. (Illus.). 175p. (C). 1999. pap. 15.95 (1-55815-512-0) ICS Pr.

Oakes, A. J. Fire Insurance Risks & Claims: A Guide for Construction Professionals. 206p. 1997. pap. 59.95 (0-632-04017-3) Blackwell Sci.

— Ornamental Grasses & Grasslike Plants. LC 92-42440. 624p. (C). 1993. reprint ed. lib. bdg. 79.50 (0-89464-826-8) Krieger.

Oakes, Baile. Sculpting With the Environment. (Illus.). 256p. 1995. text 66.95 (0-442-01642-5, VNR) Wiley.

Oakes, Baile, ed. Sculpting with the Environment: A Natural Dialogue. (Landscape Architecture Ser.). 252p. 1995. 66.95 (0-471-28583-8, VNR) Wiley.

Oakes, Camille C. Well Your Children Teach: The Wisdom of Innocence. 220p. 1998. pap. 14.95 (1-891569-20-1, 00020598) Pura Vida.

Oakes, Claudia M. On Final Approach: The Women Airforce Service Pilots of World War II. LC 90-82246. (Illus.). 710p. 1991. 39.95 (0-9626267-0-8) Falconer Pub.

— United States Women in Aviation, 1930-1939. LC 85-600019. (Illus.). 84p. (Orig.). 1991. pap. 13.95 (0-87474-380-X) Smithsonian.

— United States Women in Aviation, 1930-1939. LC 85-600019. (Smithsonian Studies in Air & Science: No. 6). 74p. (Orig.). reprint ed. pap. 30.00 (0-608-14838-5, 202617500048) Bks Demand.

Oakes, D. O., jt. auth. see Cox, D. R.

Oakes, Dana. Clinical Practitioners Pocket Guide to Respiratory Care. 4th ed. (Illus.). 320p. 1996. ring bd. 19.95 (0-932887-12-0) Health Ed Pubns.

— Hemodynamic Monitoring: A Bedside Reference Manual. (Illus.). 320p. 1995. ring bd. 19.95 (0-932887-07-4) Health Ed Pubns.

— Hemodynamic Monitoring Study Guide. 98p. 1995. 10.95 (0-932887-10-4) Health Ed Pubns.

— Neonatal/Pediatric Respiratory Care: A Critical Care Pocket Guide. 3rd ed. (Illus.). 320p. 1996. ring bd. 19.95 (0-932887-08-2) Health Ed Pubns.

***Oakes, David A.** Science & Destabilization in the Modern American Gothic: Lovecraft, Matheson & King, 92. LC 99-58884. (Contributions to the Study of Science Fiction & Fantasy Ser.: Vol. 92). 160p. 2000. 49.95 (0-313-31188-9, Greenwood Pr) Greenwood.

***Oakes, Dean & Schwartz, John.** Standard Guide to Small Size U. S. Paper Money: 1928 to Date. 3rd ed. LC 93-80100. (Illus.). 352p. 1999. pap. 24.95 (0-87341-751-8) Krause Pubns.

Oakes, Dennis, jt. auth. see Ferrie, Eddie.

Oakes, Donald T. & Scott, Walter H., eds. A Pride of Palaces: Lenox Summer Cottages, 1883-1933. LC 81-82277. Orig. Title: The Summer Cottages of Edwin Hale Lincoln. (Illus.). 84p. (Orig.). 1981. pap. 15.00 (0-685-04621-4, Lenox Lib Assn) SnO Pubns.

Oakes, Donald T., ed. see Irving, Washington.

Oakes, Douglas. Illustrated History of South Africa: The Real Story. 1989. 26.95 (0-318-41851-7) Random.

Oakes, Edward T. Pattern of Redemption: The Theology of Hans Urs von Balthasar. LC 78-134827. 336p. 1997. pap. 24.95 (0-8264-1011-1) Continuum.

Oakes, Edward T., ed. German Essays on Religion. (German Library: Vol. 54). 324p. 1994. 19.95 (0-8264-0734-X) Continuum.

Oakes, Edward T., tr. see Von Balthasar, Hans U.

***Oakes, Elizabeth.** Encyclopedia of World Scientists. (Illus.). 400p. 2000. 75.00 (0-8160-4130-X) Facts on File.

***Oakes, Elizabeth & Olmsted, Jane, eds.** Writing Who We Are: Poems by Kentucky Feminists. 114p. 1999. pap. 10.00 (0-9676782-0-X) West KY U.

Oakes, Elizabeth H. Career Exploration on the Internet. LC 97-32859. 208p. 1998. 15.95 (0-89434-240-1) Ferguson.

— Ferguson's Guide to Apprenticeship Programs. 2nd ed. LC 98-24511. 1998. 89.95 (0-89434-243-6) Ferguson.

— Free & Inexpensive Career Materials: A Resource Directory. 2nd ed. LC 97-26157. 1998. 19.95 (0-89434-221-5) Ferguson.

***Oakes, Elizabeth H. & Bradford, John, eds.** Resources for People with Disabilities: A National Directory, 2 vols. LC 98-9663. 1026p. 1998. 89.95 (0-89434-242-8) Ferguson.

Oakes, George W. Turn Left at the Pub: 22 Walking Tours Through the British Countryside. 4th rev. ed. LC 97-26831. 1995. pap. 14.95 (0-8050-3860-4) H Holt & Co.

Oakes, Ginger. Precious Promises. 32p. 1987. pap. 4.95 (0-929510-01-1) Lewis & Stanley.

***Oakes, Guy.** Collaboration, Reputation & Ethics in American Academic Life: Hans H. Gerth & C. Wright Mill. LC 98-58091. 208p. 1999. 34.95 (0-252-02484-2) U of Ill Pr.

Oakes, Guy. The Imaginary War: Civil Defense & American Cold War Culture. LC 93-46098. (Illus.). 208p. 1995. text 45.00 (0-19-509027-6) OUP.

— The Soul of the Salesman: The Moral Ethos of Personal Sales. LC 90-31350. 128p. (C). 1990. pap. 12.50 (0-391-03683-1); text 35.00 (0-391-03682-3) Humanities.

— Weber & Rickert: Concept Formation in the Social Sciences. (Studies in Contemporary German Social Thought). 200p. 1990. reprint ed. pap. text 12.00 (0-262-65037-1) MIT Pr.

Oakes, Guy, ed. & tr. see Rickert, Heinrich.

Oakes, Guy, tr. see Schmitt, Carl.

Oakes, Guy, tr. see Weber, Max M.

Oakes, James. The Ruling Race: A History of American Slaveholders. LC 97-40417. 328p. 1998. pap. 14.95 (0-393-31705-6) Norton.

— Slavery & Freedom: An Interpretation of the Old South. 264p. 1998. pap. 13.95 (0-393-31766-8) Norton.

Oakes, Jeannie. Becoming Good American Schools: The Struggle for Civic Virtue in Education Reform. LC 99-50416. 285p. 1999. 28.95 (0-7879-4023-2) Jossey-Bass.

— Keeping Track: How Schools Structure Inequality. LC 84-20931. 284p. 1986. pap. 17.00 (0-300-03725-2) Yale U Pr.

Oakes, Jeannie & Lipton, Martin. Making the Best of Schools: A Handbook for Parents, Teachers, & Policymakers. LC 89-39035. 336p. (C). 1990. 37.00 (0-300-04650-2) Yale U Pr.

— Making the Best of Schools: A Handbook for Parents, Teachers, & Policymakers. 336p. (C). 1991. reprint ed. pap. 15.00 (0-300-05123-9) Yale U Pr.

Oakes, Jeannie & Quartz, Karen H., eds. Creating New Educational Communities. 287p. 1995. 29.00 (0-226-60166-8) U Ch Pr.

Oakes, Jeannie, et al. Educational Matchmaking: Academic & Vocational Tracking in Comprehensive High Schools. LC 92-15270. 1992. pap. text 10.00 (0-8330-1244-4, R-4189-NCRVE/UB) Rand Corp.

Oakes, Jeannie, jt. ed. see Sirotnik, Kenneth A.

Oakes, Jill & Riewe, Rick. Spirit of Siberia: Traditional Native Life, Clothing & Footwear. (Illus.). 224p. 1998. 45.00 (1-56098-801-0) Smithsonian.

Oakes, John. Is There a God? Questions about Science & the Bible. Jacoby, Doug et al, eds. 164p. 1999. pap. 10.95 (0-9653469-9-4) GCI Books.

Oakes, John G., ed. In the Realms of the Unreal: "Insane" Writings. LC 90-27390. 254p. 1991. pap. 14.95 (0-941423-52-2) FWEW.

Oakes, John W. Action Amiga: Computer Graphics Animation & Video Production Manual. LC 88-26158. (Illus.). 140p. (Orig.). (C). 1989. pap. text 19.50 (0-8191-7209-X) U Pr of Amer.

Oakes, Len. Prophetic Charisma: The Psychology of Revolutionary Religious Personalities. LC 97-20929. xiii, 246p. 1997. pap. 19.95 (0-8156-0398-3) Syracuse U Pr.

— Prophetic Charisma: The Psychology of Revolutionary Religious Personalities. 192p. 1997. 39.95 (0-8156-2700-9) Syracuse U Pr.

Oakes, M., jt. auth. see King, J. E.

Oakes, Mary L. & Harris-Oakes, Mary L. Motivating Ideas for Teachers, Parents & Students. rev. ed. (Illus.). 20p. 1976. pap. 3.50 (0-9622843-0-0) Oakes & Assocs.

***Oakes, Mary P.** Angels of Mercy: An Eyewitness Account of Civil War & Yellow Fever. LC 98-70216. xv, 112 p. 1998. pap. 16.00 (1-885938-12-8) Cathdrl Fndtn Pr.

***Oakes, Maud.** Las dos Cruces de Todos Santos. (SPA.). 200p. 2000. pap. 12.95 (1-886502-33-1) Yax Te Found.

Oakes, Maud, jt. auth. see Henderson, Joseph L.

Oakes, Maud, jt. auth. see King, J. E.

Oakes, Meredith. The Editing Process. (Oberon Bks.). 74p. 1997. pap. 12.95 (1-870259-46-7) Theatre Comm.

— Faith. 72p. 1998. pap. 12.95 (1-870259-80-7, Pub. by Theatre Comm) Consort Bk Sales.

— The Neighbor. (Oberon Bks.). 64p. 1997. pap. 12.95 (1-870259-31-9) Theatre Comm.

Oakes, Michael. Statistical Inference. LC 90-2834. 185p. (Orig.). (C). 1990. pap. text 24.00 (0-917227-04-2) Epidemiology.

— Statistics for Corpus Linguistics. LC 98-210316. 256p. 1998. 68.00 (0-7486-1032-4, Pub. by Edinburgh U Pr) Col U Pr.

— Statistics for Corpus Linguistics. LC 98-210316. 272p. 1998. pap. 25.00 (0-7486-0817-6, Pub. by Edinburgh U Pr) Col U Pr.

Oakes, Michael & Wells, Jennifer. Remember Me Always LC 92-102771. 51p. 1991. write for info. (0-573-69218-1) S French Trade.

Oakes, Penelope J., et al. Stereotyping & Social Reality. (Illus.). 272p. 1994. pap. 27.95 (0-631-18872-X) Blackwell Pubs.

Oakes, Philip. Shopping for Women. 256p. 1994. 24.95 (0-233-98861-0, Pub. by Andre Deutsch) Trafalgar.

Oakes, Philip, ed. The Film Addicts Archive: Poetry & Prose of the Cinema. 212p. 1966. 25.00 (0-8464-1190-3) Beekman Pubs.

Oakes, R. A., ed. Genealogical & Family History of the County of Jefferson: A Record of Her People & the Phenomenal Growth of Her Agricultural & Mechanical Industries, 2 vols. (Illus.). 1349p. 1997. reprint ed. lib. bdg. 150.00 (0-8328-5459-X) Higginson Bk Co.

Oakes, Richard T. Ancient Laws & Institutes of Ireland: Introduction to Senchus Mor, & Laws of Distress As Contained in the Harleian Manuscripts. LC 83-82325. xvi, 4p. 1983. reprint ed. lib. bdg. 45.00 (0-89941-293-9, 303020) W S Hein.

Oakes, Sandy, ed. see Lovejoy, Carol.

Oakes, Sherry D., jt. auth. see Kirkham, Robert M.

Oakes, Tim. Tourism & Modernity in China. LC 98-227279. (Studies in China in Transition: No. 7). (Illus.). 4p. (C). (gr. 13). 1998. 85.00 (0-415-18850-4, D6341) Routledge.

***Oakes, William C.** Engineering Your Future with CD-ROM. 2nd ed. 2000. pap. 39.95 incl. cd-rom (1-881018-34-2) Grt Lks Pr.

Oakes, William C. The Falconer's Apprentice: A Guide to Training the Passage Red-Tailed Hawk. rev. ed. (Illus.). 118p. 1994. pap. text 11.95 (1-885054-01-7) Eaglewing Pubng.

Oakes, William C., et al. Engineering Your Future: An Introduction to Engineering. 425p. 1999. pap. 39.95 (1-881018-26-1) Grt Lks Pr.

***Oakeshott, Ewart.** The Archaeology of Weapons: Arms & Armour from Prehistory to the Age of Chivalry. (Illus.). 359p. 1999. pap. 45.00 (0-85115-738-6) Boydell & Brewer.

— European Weapons & Armour: From the Renaissance to the Industrial Revolution. (Illus.). 312p. 2000. 45.00 (0-85115-789-0) Boydell & Brewer.

— Knight & His Armor, 2nd Edition. 2nd ed. LC 99-26158. 1999. pap. text 13.95 (0-8023-1329-9) Dufour.

Oakeshott, Ewart. Records of the Medieval Sword. (Illus.). 320p. 1998. pap. 55.00 (0-85115-566-9, Boydell Pr) Boydell & Brewer.

— The Sword in the Age of Chivalry. (Illus.). 204p. 1998. pap. 35.00 (0-85115-715-7) Boydell & Brewer.

Oakeshott, Gordon B. California's Changing Landscapes. 2nd ed. (Illus.). 379p. (C). 1978. 97.50 (0-07-047584-9) McGraw.

Oakeshott, J. & Whitten, M. J., eds. Molecular Approaches to Fundamental & Applied Entomology. (Experimental Entomology Ser.). (Illus.). 488p. 1992. 238.00 (0-387-97814-3) Spr-Verlag.

Oakeshott, Michael. Experience & Its Modes. (Cambridge Paperback Library). 367p. 1986. pap. text 35.95 (0-521-31179-9) Cambridge U Pr.

— Morality & Politics in Modern Europe: The Harvard Lectures, 1958. Letwin, Shirley R., ed. LC 93-24981. 192p. 1993. 32.00 (0-300-05644-3) Yale U Pr.

— On History & Other Essays. LC 99-32045. 1999. pap. 12.00 (0-86597-267-2) Liberty Fund.

***Oakeshott, Michael.** On History & Other Essays. LC 99-32045. 1999. 20.00 (0-86597-266-4) Liberty Fund.

Oakeshott, Michael. On Human Conduct. 340p. 1991. reprint ed. pap. text 29.95 (0-19-827758-X) OUP.

— The Politics of Faith & the Politics of Scepticism. Fuller, Timothy, ed. LC 96-3852. (Selected Writings of Michael Oakeshott Ser.). 139p. 1996. 30.00 (0-300-06625-2) Yale U Pr.

— Rationalism in Politics & Other Essays. LC 91-6951. 584p. (Orig.). 1991. pap. 7.50 (0-86597-095-5); text 21.00 (0-86597-094-7) Liberty Fund.

— Religion, Politics, & the Moral Life. Fuller, Timothy, ed. LC 93-1607. 160p. 1993. 32.00 (0-300-05643-5) Yale U Pr.

Oakeshott, R. Ewart. The Archaeology of Weapons: Arms & Armour from Prehistory to the Age of Chivalry. unabridged ed. LC 96-8921. (Illus.). 382p. 1996. reprint ed. pap. text 10.95 (0-486-29288-6) Dover.

— A Knight & His Armor. 2nd ed. 128p. 1999. pap. 13.95 (0-8023-1296-9) Dufour.

— A Knight & His Castle. 2nd ed. (Illus.). 128p. (J). 1997. pap. 12.95 (0-8023-1294-2) Dufour.

— A Knight & His Horse. 2nd rev. ed. LC 98-32049. (Illus.). 123p. (J). 1999. pap. 13.95 (0-8023-1297-7) Dufour.

— A Knight & His Weapons. 2nd ed. LC 97-36071. 124p. 1997. pap. 12.95 (0-8023-1299-3) Dufour.

— A Knight in Battle. LC 98-197618. (Illus.). 144p. 1998. pap. 13.95 (0-8023-1322-1) Dufour.

Oakeshott, Walter F. Founded upon the Seas. LC 72-10845. (Essay Index Reprint Ser.). 1977. reprint ed. 24.95 (0-8369-7233-3) Ayer.

Oakey, Ray & Mukhtar, Syeda-Masooda, eds. New Technology-Based Firms in the 1990s, Vol. III. 240p. 1997. pap. 89.00 (1-85396-369-0, Pub. by P Chapman) Taylor & Francis.

Oakey, Raymond P. High-Technology New Firms: Variable Barriers to Growth. 144p. 1995. text 49.95 (1-85396-239-2, Pub. by P Chapman) Taylor & Francis.

— New Technology-Based Firms in the 1990s, Vol. II. 208p. 1996. pap. 85.00 (1-85396-343-7, Pub. by P Chapman) Taylor & Francis.

Oakey, Raymond P., ed. New Technology-Based Firms in the 1990s. LC 95-113964. 256p. 1994. 75.00 (1-85396-274-0, Pub. by P Chapman) Taylor & Francis.

Oakey, Raymond P., et al. The Management of Innovation in High Technology Small Firms: Innovation & Regional Development in Britain & the United States. LC 88-11448. 224p. 1988. 55.00 (0-89930-399-4, OMI/, Quorum Bks) Greenwood.

— New Firms in the Biotechnology Industry: Their Contribution to Innovation & Growth. 224p. 1990. text 49.00 (0-86187-126-X) St Martin.

***Oakey, Raymond P., et al.** New Technology-Based Firms in the 1990's. 320p. 1999. 90.00 (0-08-042761-8, Pergamon Pr) Elsevier.

Oakey, Virginia, jt. auth. see Nash, Constance.

OakGrove, Artemis. Dangerous Thoughts: Erotic Short Stories. 191p. 1998. pap. 11.95 (0-9663155-1-0) One Rogue Pr.

— File Not Found. 198p. 1998. pap. 11.95 (0-9663155-0-2) One Rogue Pr.

— Led Astray. LC 94-8012. 280p. (Orig.). 1994. pap. 9.95 (1-885084-00-5) Tickerwick.

— Nighthawk. 1998. mass mkt. 6.95 (1-56333-634-0, Rosebud) Masquerade.

— Throne of Council Vol. 3: The Throne Trilogy. 148p. 1991. reprint ed. pap. 8.95 (1-55583-308-X) Alyson Pubns.

— Undercover: An Erotic Tale of Crime & Betrayal. 187p. 1998. pap. 11.95 (0-9663155-2-9) One Rogue Pr.

— Warclouds. 1998. mass mkt. 6.95 (1-56333-643-X, Rosebud) Masquerade.

Oakgrove, Collins, tr. see McIntyre, Sally.

Oakham Historical Society Staff. Oakham. LC 98-88256. (Images of America Ser.). (Illus.). 1998. pap. 16.99 (0-7524-1391-0) Arcadia Publng.

Oakham, Nandy. Journalism: Don't Bury the Lead. 1996. pap. 50.00 (0-949823-60-0, Pub. by Deakin Univ) St Mut.

Oakham, Ronald, ed. One at the Table: The Reception of Baptized Christians. 159p. (Orig.). 1996. pap. text 11.00 (1-56854-070-1, ONETBL) Liturgy Tr Pubns.

Oakhill, Jane & Beard, Roger, eds. Reading Development & the Teaching of Reading: A Psychological Perspective. LC 99-10517. 288p. 1999. 59.95 (0-631-20681-7); pap., wbk. ed. 29.95 (0-631-20682-5) Blackwell Pubs.

Oakhill, Jane & Garnham, Alan. Becoming a Skilled Reader. (Illus.). 240p. 1988. pap. text 26.95 (0-631-15776-X) Blackwell Pubs.

Oakhill, Jane & Garnham, Alan, eds. Mental Models in Cognitive Science: Essays in Honour of Phil Johnson-Laird. 352p. 1996. 51.00 (0-86377-448-2) L Erlbaum Assocs.

Oakhill, Jane, jt. auth. see Garnham, Alan.

Oakhill, Jane, jt. ed. see Cornoldi, Cesare.

Oakie, Jack. Jack Oakie's Double Takes. LC 79-12432. (Illus.). 240p. (Orig.). 1980. pap. 10.95 (0-89407-019-3) Strawberry Hill.

Oakie, Jack & Oakie, Victoria H. When the Line Is Straight: Jack Oakie's Comedy in Motion Pictures. LC 96-20391. (Illus.). 128p. 1997. 13.95 (0-89407-140-8, 1408) Strawberry Hill.

Oakie, Victoria H. Jack Oakie's Oakridge: A Cultural Heritage Monument. (Illus.). 128p. 1990. pap. 14.95 (0-89407-102-5) Strawberry Hill.

Oakie, Victoria H., compiled by. Dear Jack: Hollywood Birthday Reminiscences to Jack Oakie. (Illus.). 144p. 1994. pap. 9.95 (0-89407-113-0) Strawberry Hill.

Oakie, Victoria H., jt. auth. see Oakie, Jack.

Oakland & Morris. Pocket Guide to TQM. 96p. 1998. pap. text 16.95 (0-7506-3986-5) Buttrwrth-Heinemann.

Oakland, Dennis. Your Planetary Personality: Everything You Need to Make Sense of Your Horoscope. LC 91-47574. (Modern Astrology Library). 580p. 1999. pap. 24.95 (0-87542-594-1) Llewellyn Pubns.

Oakland, Don. Northern Lites: A Brave New Wildwoods. (Illus.). 240p. (Orig.). 1990. pap. 7.95 (0-9615242-2-7) Oak Pr.

— Wildwoods Dad. (Illus.). 220p. (Orig.). (YA). (gr. 5 up). 1987. pap. 6.95 (0-9615242-1-9) Oak Pr.

Oakland, John. British Civilization: An Introduction. 272p. 1989. pap. 12.95 (0-415-00670-8, A2673) Routledge.

— British Civilization: An Introduction. 2nd ed. LC 94-36499. (Illus.). 240p. (C). 1994. pap. 16.95 (0-415-06475-9, A6944) Routledge.

— British Civilization: An Introduction. 4th ed. LC 97-52948. (Illus.). 384p. (C). 1998. pap. 22.99 (0-415-16569-5) Routledge.

— A Dictionary of British Institutions: A Student's Guide. LC 92-38180. (Illus.). 176p. 1993. pap., student ed. write for info. (0-415-07110-0) Routledge.

— Total Quality Management. 2nd ed. 316p. (C). 1993. 37.95 (0-89397-386-6) Nichols Pub.

Oakland, John & Morris, Peter. TQM: A Pictorial Guide for Managers. LC 97-139282. 96p. 1997. pap. text 26.95 (0-7506-2324-1) Buttrwrth-Heinemann.

Oakland, John, jt. auth. see Dale, Barrie.

Oakland, John, jt. auth. see Mauk, David.

Oakland, John S. Statistical Process Control. 3rd ed. (Illus.). 352p. 1999. pap. text 56.95 (0-7506-2464-7) Buttrwrth-Heinemann.

— Total Quality Management. 2nd ed. LC 92-40747. 464p. 2000. text 74.95 (0-7506-0993-1) Buttrwrth-Heinemann.

Oakland, John S. & Followell, Roy F. Statistical Process Control. 2nd ed. (Illus.). 431p. 1990. text 79.95 (0-434-91484-3) Buttrwrth-Heinemann.

Oakland, John S. & Porter, Les. Total Quality Management: Student Edition with Cases. 448p. 1995. pap. 42.95 (0-7506-2124-9, Focal) Buttrwrth-Heinemann.

Oakland Museum Staff. Celebrating a Collection, The Work of Dorothea Lange, Documentary Photographer. LC 78-60388. (Local History Studies: Vol. 25). 1978. pap. 9.97 (0-614-14411-6) CA History Ctr.

Oakland Raiders Staff. Oakland Raiders. CWC Sports Inc., ed. (NFL Team Yearbooks Ser.). (J). (gr. 1-12). 1998. pap. 9.99 (1-891613-18-9) Everett Sports.

Oakland, Roger. New Wine or Old Deception. 2nd rev. ed. 117p. 1995. reprint ed. pap. 4.99 (0-936728-62-0) Word for Today.

— When New Wine Makes a Man Divine: True Revival or Last Days Deception? Carder, Paul, ed. LC 97-90481. 160p. Date not set. pap. 6.00 (0-9637797-5-3) Understand Times.

O

— Witness to This Generation: Creation Evangelism for the Last Days. LaRue, Jan, ed. 170p. 1997. pap. write for info. (*0-9637797-3-7*) Understand Times.

Oakland, Roger & Wooding, Dan. Let There Be Light. 176p. 1993. pap. write for info. (*0-9637797-0-2*) Understand Times.

Oakland, Roger, jt. auth. see McMahon, T. A.

Oakland, Sam. Manhattan Woman. unabridged ed. LC 98-75117. 116p. 1999. pap. 15.00 (*0-9658601-2-4*) Sweetbriar Co.

Oakland, Susan, jt. auth. see Ostell, Alistair.

Oakland, T. & Saigh, Philip A., eds. International Perspectives on Psychology in the Schools. (School Psychology Ser.). 296p. 1989. 59.95 (*0-8058-0110-3*) L Erlbaum Assocs.

Oakland, Thomas & Hambleton, Ronald K., eds. International Perspectives on Academic Assessment. LC 94-38711. (Evaluation in Education & Human Services Ser.). 248p. (C). 1995. lib. bdg. 109.00 (*0-7923-9525-5*) Kluwer Academic.

Oakland, Thomas P. & Terry, Edwin J., Jr. Divorced Fathers: Reconstructing a Quality Life. (Illus.). 201p. 1983. 32.95 (*0-89885-101-7*, Kluwer Acad Hman Sci) Kluwer Academic.

Oaklander, L. Nathan. Temporal Relations & Temporal Becoming: A Defense of a Russellian Theory of Time. 250p. (Orig.). (C). 1984. pap. text 22.50 (*0-8191-4150-X*); lib. bdg. 48.00 (*0-8191-4149-6*) U Pr of Amer.

Oaklander, L. Nathan, ed. Existentialist Philosophy: An Introduction. 2nd ed. LC 95-12632. 402p. 1995. pap. text 42.00 (*0-13-373861-2*) P-H.

Oaklander, L. Nathan & Smith, Quentin. The New Theory of Time. LC 93-47500. 400p. 1994. 45.00 (*0-300-05796-2*) Yale U Pr.

— Time Change & Freedom: An Introduction to Metaphysics. (Illus.). 224p. (C). 1995. pap. 20.99 (*0-415-10249-9*, B7018) Routledge.

— Time Change & Freedom: An Introduction to Metaphysics. LC 94-34474. (Illus.). 224p. (C). (gr. 13). 1995. 75.00 (*0-415-10248-0*, B7014) Routledge.

Oaklander, Violet. Windows to Our Children: A Gestalt Therapy Approach to Children & Adolescents. (Illus.). 352p. 1989. reprint ed. pap. 22.00 (*0-939266-06-7*) Gestalt Journal.

Oakleaf, David, ed. Love in Excess or the Fatal Enquiry: Eliza Haywood. (Literary Texts Ser.). 240p. 1994. pap. 12.95 (*1-55111-016-4*) Broadview Pr.

Oakley. Conservation & Restoration of Ceramics. 252p. 1996. pap. 62.95 (*0-7506-3219-4*) Buttrwrth-Heinemann.

— Manual of Trauma Resuscitation, Anaesthesia & Intensive Care. (Illus.). 320p. (C). 1997. text. write for info. (*0-412-61850-8*, Chap & Hall NY) Chapman & Hall.

— Politics of Welfare State. LC 94-12566. 224p. 1994. 65.00 (*1-85728-205-1*, Pub. by UCL Pr Ltd); pap. 24.95 (*1-85728-206-X*, Pub. by UCL Pr Ltd) Taylor & Francis.

Oakley, A. J. Parker & Mellows: The Modern Law of Trusts. 6th ed. 1994. pap. 44.00 (*0-421-48750-X*, Pub. by Sweet & Maxwll) Gaunt.

Oakley, A. J., ed. Trends in Contemporary Trust Law. 380p. 1997. text 85.00 (*0-19-826286-8*) OUP.

Oakley, Allen. The Foundations of Austrian Economics from Menger to Mises: A Critico-Historical Retrospective of Subjectivism. LC 97-12120. 272p. 1997. 95.00 (*1-85898-308-8*) E Elgar.

— The Making of Marx's Critical Theory: A Bibliographical Analysis. LC 83-9732. 143p. (Orig.). 1983. pap. 9.95 (*0-7100-9570-8*, Routledge Thoemms) Routledge.

— The Revival of Modern Austrian Economics: A Critical Assessment of Its Subjectivist Origins. LC 98-42886. 240p. 1999. 90.00 (*1-85898-540-4*) E Elgar.

Oakley, Ann. Essays on Women, Medicine & Health. 256p. 1993. 76.50 (*0-7486-0441-3*, Pub. by Edinburgh U Pr); pap. 25.00 (*0-7486-0450-2*, Pub. by Edinburgh U Pr) Col U Pr.

***Oakley, Ann.** Experiments in Knowing: Gender & Method in the Social Sciences. (Illus.). 2000. 30.00 (*1-56584-620-6*, Pub. by New Press NY) Norton.

Oakley, Ann. Who's Afraid of Feminism? 1997. 30.00 (*1-56584-384-3*, Pub. by New Press NY) Norton.

Oakley, Ann & Houd, Susanne. Helpers in Childbirth: Midwifery Today. 217p. 1990. 59.95 (*1-56032-036-2*) Taylor & Francis.

Oakley, Ann & Mitchell, Juliet, eds. Who's Afraid of Feminism? 320p. 1997. pap. 15.95 (*1-56584-385-1*, Pub. by New Press NY) Norton.

Oakley, Barbara A. Hair of the Dog: Tales from Aboard a Russian Trawler. (Illus.). 196p. 1996. 35.00 (*0-87422-134-X*); pap. 19.95 (*0-87422-135-8*) Wash St U Pr.

Oakley, Barry. Scribbling in the Dark. LC 85-14090. 160p. 1993. reprint ed. pap. text 14.95 (*0-7022-2524-X*, Pub. by Univ Queensland Pr) Intl Spec Bk.

Oakley, Ben. Windsurfing: The Skills of the Game. (Illus.). 128p. 1994. pap. 19.95 (*1-85223-830-5*, Pub. by Crolwood) Trafalgar.

Oakley, Bruce & Schafer, Rollie. Neuroanatomy: Dissection of the Sheep Brain. (Illus.). 32p. (C). 1980. pap. text 7.95 (*0-472-08691-X*, 08691) U of Mich Pr.

Oakley, Burks, II. Circuittutor: By TutorWare. 50p. (C). 1992. cd-rom 26.67 (*0-201-52615-8*) Addison-Wesley.

— Circut 1.0 Windows Tutwr. (Illus.). 64p. (C). 1993. pap. text 20.00 (*0-201-51370-6*) Addison-Wesley.

Oakley, Celia, ed. Heart Disease in Pregnancy. 442p. 1996. text 120.00 (*0-7279-1065-5*, 340300360, Pub. by BMJ Pub) Login Brothers Bk Co.

Oakley, Charles A. Men at Work. Stein, Leon, ed. LC 77-70522. (Illus.). 1977. reprint ed. lib. bdg. 33.95 (*0-405-10190-2*) Ayer.

***Oakley, Chris.** What Is a Group? A New Look at Theory in Practice. LC 99-44128. 1999. pap. write for info. (*1-892746-41-7*) Other Pr LLC.

Oakley, David, jt. auth. see Furnham, Adrian.

Oakley, David A., ed. Brain & Mind. LC 84-29604. (Psychology in Progress Ser.). 320p. 1985. pap. 14.95 (*0-416-31630-1*, 9627) Routledge.

Oakley, Derek. The Falklands Military Machine. 192p. (C). 1991. 95.00 (*0-946771-24-3*) St Mut.

Oakley, Don. The Adventure of Christian Fast. LC 88-8001. (Illus.). 279p. (Orig.). (YA). (gr. 9 up). 1989. 12.95 (*0-9619465-1-2*); pap. 8.95 (*0-9619465-2-0*) Eyrie Pr.

— The Creston Creeper. LC 87-82574. 1988. 16.95 (*0-9619465-0-4*) Eyrie Pr.

***Oakley, Don.** Slow Burn: The Great American Antismoking Scam (& Why It Will Fail) LC 98-55531. 600p. 1999. pap. 15.95 (*0-9619465-3-9*) Eyrie Pr.

Oakley, Ed & Krug, Doug. Enlightened Leadership. 272p. 1994. per. 12.00 (*0-671-86675-3*) S&S Trade.

— Enlightened Leadership: Getting to the Heart of Change. (Illus.). 256p. 1993. 22.00 (*0-671-86674-5*) S&S Trade.

Oakley, Frances. Understanding the ABCs of Alzheimer's Disease: A Guide for Caregivers. (Illus.). 20p. (Orig.). 1993. pap. text 6.00 (*0-910317-94-1*) Am Occup Therapy.

Oakley, Francis. The Medieval Experience. (Medieval Academy Reprints for Teaching Ser.). 240p. 1988. reprint ed. pap. text 12.95 (*0-8020-6707-7*) U of Toronto Pr.

— Omnipotence, Covenant & Order: An Excursion in the History of Ideas from Abelard to Leibniz. LC 83-45945. 166p. 1984. text 32.50 (*0-8014-1631-0*) Cornell U Pr.

***Oakley, Francis.** Politics & Eternity: Studies in the History of Medieval & Early Modern Political Thought. LC 99-29170. (Studies in the History of Christian Thought). 384p. 1999. 103.00 (*90-04-11327-4*) Brill Academic Pubs.

Oakley, Francis. The Western Church in the Later Middle Ages. LC 79-7621. 346p. (C). 1985. text 47.50 (*0-8014-1208-0*); pap. text 16.95 (*0-8014-9347-1*) Cornell U Pr.

***Oakley, G.** Humphrey Hits the Jackpot. (Illus.). (J). 1998. text 22.95 (*0-340-67079-7*, Pub. by Hodder & Stought Ltd) Trafalgar.

Oakley, Gilbert. Gain the Power of Positive Thought: The Key to Success. 128p. 1997. pap. text 12.95 (*0-572-02336-7*, Pub. by W Foulsham) Trans-Atl Phila.

— Old Moore's Dream Book. 96p. 1995. pap. 9.95 (*0-572-01345-0*, Pub. by Foulsham UK) Assoc Pubs Grp.

— Power of Positive Thought: The Key to Attainment. 148p. 1995. pap. 7.95 (*0-572-01536-4*, Pub. by Foulsham UK) Assoc Pubs Grp.

— The Power of Self-Hypnosis: The Key to Confidence. 144p. (Orig.). 1989. pap. text 14.95 (*0-572-01135-0*, Pub. by W Foulsham) Trans-Atl Phila.

Oakley, Giles. The Devil's Music: A History of the Blues. 2nd ed. LC 96-52633. (Illus.). 306p. 1997. pap. 14.95 (*0-306-80743-2*) Da Capo.

Oakley, Graham. The Church Mice & the Ring. LC 91-45273. (Illus.). 32p. (J). (ps up). 1992. 14.95 (*0-689-31790-5*) Atheneum Yung Read.

— Hetty & Harriet. LC 81-8024. (Illus.). 32p. (J). (gr. k-3). 1982. text 13.95 (*0-689-30888-4*) Atheneum Yung Read.

Oakley, I. Cooper. Comte de St. Germain: The Secret of Kings. 284p. 1985. reprint ed. pap. 21.00 (*0-7873-1265-7*) Hlth Research.

Oakley, J. Ronald. Baseball's Last Golden Age, 1946-1960: The National Pastime in a Time of Glory & Change. LC 93-40432. 384p. 1994. pap. 29.95 (*0-89950-851-0*) McFarland & Co.

— God's Country: America in the Fifties. LC 85-25316. 1990. pap. 10.95 (*0-942637-24-0*, Dembner NY) Barricade Bks.

Oakley, J. Ted. You Sold Your Company: Envisioning the Changes : Emotions, Investments, Future Expectations. LC 97-72363. 143 p. 1998. write for info. (*0-9656287-4-4*) Keysar Pub.

Oakley, Joe, ed. Baptisms Bk. 4: A Study of the Elementary Principles of Christ. (First Principles Ser.). 1990. student ed. 5.00 (*0-923968-04-0*) Shady Grove Ch Pubns.

— Baptisms Bk. 4: A Study of the Elementary Principles of Christ, Set. (First Principles Ser.). 1990. 6.00 (*0-318-49990-8*) Shady Grove Ch Pubns.

— Faith: A Study of the Elementary Principles of Christ, Bk. 3. (First Principles Ser.). (Orig.). 1990. pap., student ed. 5.00 (*0-923968-03-2*) Shady Grove Ch Pubns.

— Faith: A Study of the Elementary Principles of Christ, Set. (First Principles Ser.). (Orig.). 1990. 6.00 (*0-318-50020-5*) Shady Grove Ch Pubns.

— Laying on of Hands: A Study of the Elementary Principles of Christ, Bk. 5. (First Principles Ser.). (Orig.). 1990. pap. 6.00 (*0-318-50021-3*); pap. text, student ed. 5.00 (*0-923968-05-9*) Shady Grove Ch Pubns.

— Repentance, Bk. 2: A Study of the Elementary Principles of Christ. (First Principles Ser.). 1990. student ed. 6.00 (*0-685-45027-9*); student ed. 6.00 (*0-923968-02-4*); pap. 6.00 (*0-685-32619-5*); 6.00 (*0-318-49989-4*) Shady Grove Ch Pubns.

— Vision, 7 vols. (First Principles Ser.: Vol. 1). 1989. 28.00 (*0-923968-00-8*); student ed. 6.00 (*0-923968-01-6*) Shady Grove Ch Pubns.

Oakley, John & Perschbacher, Rex R. Civil Procedure. Goldenberg, Norman S. & Tenen, Peter, eds. (Law Outlines Ser.). 300p. (Orig.). 1996. pap. text. write for info. (*0-87457-179-0*, 5040) Casenotes Pub.

Oakley, John B., jt. auth. see Wright, Charles A.

Oakley, John B., ed. see Wright, Charles A.

Oakley, John H., et al, eds. Athenian Potters & Painters: The Conference Proceedings, LC 97-174389. (Monographs in Archaeology: Vol. 67). (Illus.). 543p. 1996. lib. bdg. 86.00 (*1-900188-12-0*, Pub. by Oxbow Bks) David Brown.

Oakley, John H. & Sinos, Rebecca H. The Wedding in Ancient Athens. LC 93-17881. (Studies in Classics). (Illus.). 170p. reprint ed. pap. 52.70 (*0-608-20463-3*, 207171500002) Bks Demand.

Oakley, John W., jt. auth. see Rotroff, Susan I.

***Oakley, June Peterson.** The Charlottesville Collection Vol. 2: Recipes from Jefferson Country. LC 99-96974. 304p. 1999. 24.95 (*1-57427-107-5*) Howell Pr VA.

Oakley, June Peterson, ed. The Charlottesville Collection: Traditional Recipes for Today's Lifestyles. (Illus.). 221p. 1994. write for info. (*0-9641731-0-7*) Featherstne Inc.

***Oakley, Ken.** A History of Bluegrass in New York & Northeastern Pennsylvania. Ripic, Carol S., ed. LC 99-478485. (Illus.). 192p. 1999. pap. 14.00 (*0-9661351-1-3*) K & C Pub.

Oakley, Kenneth H. & Ripic, Carol S. The Rooney Fest: A History. (Illus.). ix, 160p. 1997. pap. 15.00 (*0-9661351-0-5*) K & C Pub.

Oakley, Kenneth P. Man, the Tool-Maker. 6th ed. LC 50-13440. viii, 102p. 1992. reprint ed. pap. text 1.95 (*0-226-61270-8*, P20) U Ch Pr.

Oakley, Linda D. Mental Health in Primary Care. LC 97-118473. 480p. (C). (gr. 13). 1996. pap. text 31.95 (*0-8151-7310-5*, 28195) Mosby Inc.

Oakley, Lucy, et al. A Brush with Shakespeare: The Bard in Painting, 1780-1910. LC 85-29669. (Illus.). 140p. 1985. pap. 18.00 (*0-89280-024-0*) Montgomery Mus.

Oakley, Mark. Sharks & Other Fish. (Information Ser.). (Illus.). 32p. (J). 1997. text 3.50 (*0-7214-1746-9*, Ladybrd) Penguin Putnam.

Oakley, Meredith L. On the Make: The Rise of Bill Clinton. LC 94-10787. (Illus.). 368p. 1994. 24.95 (*0-89526-493-5*) Regnery Pub.

— On the Make: The Rise of Bill Clinton. (Illus.). 591p. 1996. pap. 16.95 (*0-89526-719-5*) Regnery Pub.

Oakley, Michael, tr. see Thomas, a Kempis.

Oakley, Myrna. Oregon: Off the Beaten Path: A Guide to Unique Places. 4th ed. LC 99-33142. (Off the Beaten Path Ser.). (Illus.). 224p. 1999. pap. text 12.95 (*0-7627-0405-5*) Globe Pequot.

— Recommended Bed & Breakfasts Pacific Northwest. LC 99-18083. (Recommended Bed & Breakfasts Ser.). (Illus.). 282p. 1999. pap. 16.95 (*0-7627-0331-8*) Globe Pequot.

Oakley, Obadiah. Expedition to Oregon. 17p. 1967. reprint ed. pap. 4.95 (*0-87770-067-2*) Ye Galleon.

Oakley, P. Community Involvement in Health Development: An Examination of the Critical Issues. 81p. 1989. 16.00 (*92-4-156126-2*) World Health.

Oakley, Peter & Marsden, David. Approaches to Participation in Rural Development. (WEP Study). x, 91p. (Orig.). 1990. reprint ed. pap. 15.75 (*92-2-103594-8*) Intl Labour Office.

Oakley, Peter & Marsden, David, eds. Evaluating Social Development Projects. (Illus.). 144p. (C). 1990. 39.95 (*0-85598-146-6*, Pub. by Oxfam Pub); pap. 14.95 (*0-85598-147-4*, Pub. by Oxfam Pub) Stylus Pub VA.

Oakley, Peter, et al. Projects with People: The Practice of Participation in Rural Development. xv, 284p. 1991. pap. 29.25 (*92-2-107282-7*) Intl Labour Office.

Oakley, R. J. The Case of Lima Barreto & Realism in the Brazilian "Belle Epoque" LC 98-13280. 228p. 1998. text 89.95 (*0-7734-8493-0*) E Mellen.

Oakley, Ray. New Technology-Based Firms in the 1990s, Vol. IV. 1998. 79.95 (*1-85396-386-0*, Pub. by P Chapman) P H Brookes.

Oakley, Ray, et al. The Diffusion of New Process Technologies in Hungary. LC 92-28351. 1993. 59.00 (*0-86187-062-X*) St Martin.

Oakley, Robert. Copyright & Preservation: A Serious Problem in Need of a Thoughtful Solution. 58p. 1990. pap. 15.00 (*1-887334-04-1*) Coun Lib & Info.

Oakley, Robert, jt. auth. see Hirsch, John.

***Oakley, Robert B.** Policing the New World Disorder: Peace Operations & Public Security. 587p. 1998. per. 27.00 (*0-16-061216-0*) USGPO.

***Oakley, Robert B., et al, eds.** Policing the New World Disorder: Peace Operations & Public Security. 573p. 1999. pap. text 45.00 (*0-7881-8114-9*) DIANE Pub.

Oakley, Robert B., et al. Policing the New World Disorder: Peace Operations & Public Security. LC 97-43986. 587p. 1998. pap., per. 27.00 (*1-57906-006-4*) Natl Defense.

Oakley, Robert B., jt. auth. see Rasmussen, J. Lewis.

Oakley, Robert B., ed. see Wurmser, David & Beargdyke, Nancy.

Oakley, Robin. The Political Year 1971. LC 72-185984. v, 314 p. 1971. write for info. (*0-273-36124-4*, Pub. by F T P-H) Natl Bk Netwk.

Oakley, Robin & Rose, Peter. The Political Year 1970. LC 78-855312. v, 250 p. 1970. write for info. (*0-273-31529-3*, Pub. by F T P-H) Natl Bk Netwk.

Oakley, S. P. The Hill-Forts of the Samnites. (Monographs: Vol. 10). (Illus.). 164p. 1995. pap. 60.00 (*0-904152-28-6*, Pub. by British Schl Rome) David Brown.

Oakley, Stephen. A Commentary on Livy, Vol. II, Bks. 7-8. 880p. 1998. 165.00 (*0-19-815226-4*) OUP.

Oakley, Stephen, ed. see Livy.

Oakley, Stewart P., jt. auth. see Thomas, Alastair H.

Oakley, Thomas P. English Penitential Discipline & Anglo-Saxon Law in Their Joint Influence. LC 71-82243. (Columbia University. Studies in the Social Sciences: No. 242). reprint ed. 27.50 (*0-404-51242-9*) AMS Pr.

***Oakley, W. S.** Physics - The Big Problem - Solve!: or Merging QED & General Relativity. LC 99-98155. 2000. pap. 8.95 (*0-533-13451-X*) Vantage.

Oakley, Wayne. Piano Keys & White Paper. 64p. 1993. pap. 12.95 (*1-55082-091-5*, Pub. by Quarry Pr) LPC InBook.

***Oakley, William P.** An Exegesis of the Revelation. Finley, S. Faithe, ed. 196p. (C). 1999. pap. 10.00 (*0-9665424-2-8*) Mst Design.

Oakman. Lab Notebook. 3rd ed. (C). 1998. pap. text 11.50 (*0-471-32404-3*) Wiley.

Oakman, C. D., et al, eds. Cores from the Northwest European Hydrocarbon Province. (Illus.). 240p. 1997. 184.00 (*1-86239-002-9*, Pub. by Geol Soc Pub Hse) AAPG.

Oakman, Douglas E. Jesus & the Economic Questions of His Day. LC 86-23518. (Studies in the Bible & Early Christianity: Vol. 8). 312p. 1986. lib. bdg. 99.95 (*0-88946-608-4*) E Mellen.

Oakman, Harry. What Flowers When. 1995. pap. 29.95 (*0-7022-2839-7*, Pub. by Univ Queensland Pr) Intl Spec Bk.

Oakman, Robert L. The Computer Triangle: Hardware, Software, People. 1995. 64.00 (*0-471-09219-3*) Wiley.

Oakman, Robert L. The Computer Triangle: Hardware, Software, People. 2nd ed. LC 96-41136. 360p. 1996. pap. 65.95 (*0-471-16965-X*) Wiley.

Oaks. Teaching to Change the World. LC 98-36582. 432p. 1998. pap. 30.63 (*0-07-109381-8*) McGraw.

Oaks, Dallin D. Linguistics at Work: A Reader of Applications. LC 97-70417. 768p. (C). 1997. pap. text 36.50 (*0-15-503532-0*, Pub. by Harcourt Coll Pubs) Harcourt.

Oaks, Dallin H. The Lord's Way. LC 91-30610. x, 259p. 1991. 17.95 (*0-87579-578-1*) Deseret Bk.

— The Lord's Way. LC 91-30610. x, 259p. 1995. pap. 9.95 (*0-87579-960-4*) Deseret Bk.

— Pure in Heart. 1988. 14.95 (*0-88494-650-9*) Bookcraft Inc.

Oaks, Dallin H., ed. Wall Between Church & State. LC 63-20897. 1993. pap. text 1.95 (*0-226-61429-8*, P137) U Ch Pr.

Oaks, Dallin H. & Hill, Marvin S. Carthage Conspiracy: The Trial of the Accused Assassins of Joseph Smith. LC 78-1733. 262p. 1979. pap. text 12.95 (*0-252-00762-X*) U of Ill Pr.

Oaks, Elizabeth. Exploring Tech Careers. 2nd ed. LC 98-29296. 1998. 89.95 (*0-89434-244-4*) Ferguson.

***Oaks, Laury.** Smoking & Pregnancy: The Politics of Fetal Protection. LC 00-39036. (Illus.). 256p. 2001. text 52.00 (*0-8135-2887-9*); pap. text 22.00 (*0-8135-2888-7*) Rutgers U Pr.

Oaks, Marian. Love Lessons. 480p. 1992. mass mkt. 4.50 (*0-8217-3959-X*, Zebra Kensgtn) Kensgtn Pub Corp.

— To Love Again. 1992. mass mkt. 4.50 (*0-8217-3668-X*, Zebra Kensgtn) Kensgtn Pub Corp.

— To Love Again. large type ed. LC 93-26491. 467p. 1993. lib. bdg. 17.95 (*0-7862-0019-7*) Thorndike Pr.

Oaks, Martha, jt. auth. see Ferguson, Charles B.

Oaks, Scott. Java Security. 474p. 1998. reprint ed. pap. 34.95 (*1-56592-403-7*) OReilly & Assocs.

Oaks, Scott & Wong, Henry. Java Threads. Loukides, Mike, ed. LC 97-131876. (Illus.). 268p. 1996. pap. 29.95 (*1-56592-216-6*) Thomson Learn.

***Oaks, Scott & Wong, Henry.** Java Threads. 2nd ed. Loukides, Mike, ed. (Illus.). 336p. 1999. pap. 34.95 (*1-56592-418-5*) OReilly & Assocs.

— Jini in a Nutshell. Loukides, Mike, ed. (Illus.). 250p. 2000. pap. 29.95 (*1-56592-759-1*) OReilly & Assocs.

Oaks, Stanley C., Jr., ed. see Institute of Medicine Staff.

Oaksey, John, jt. auth. see Kidd, Jane.

Oaksford, M. & Chater, N., eds. Rational Models of Cognition. (Illus.). 496p. 1999. text 115.00 (*0-19-852415-3*) OUP.

Oaksford, Michael & Brown, Gordon, eds. Neurodynamics & Psychology. (Illus.). 400p. 1994. text 79.95 (*0-12-523515-1*) Acad Pr.

Oaksholt, Les. Essential Elements of Quantitative Methods. 120p. 1994. pap. 70.00 (*1-85805-098-7*, Pub. by DP Publns) St Mut.

Oakshott, Les. Business Modelling & Simulation. 246p. (Orig.). 1997. pap. 62.50 (*0-273-61251-4*, Pub. by Pitman Pub) Trans-Atl Phila.

— Essential Elements of Business Statistics. 160p. 1994. pap. 59.95 (*1-85805-104-5*, Pub. by DP Publns) St Mut.

Oakshott, Walter. The Two Winchester Bibles. (Illus.). 1981. 395.00 (*0-19-818235-X*) OUP.

***Oakstone Legal & Business Publishing, Inc. Staff.** Higher Education Law in America. LC 00-55074. 2000. pap. write for info. (*0-939675-95-1*) Data Res MN.

Oakum, Peter. Growing Marijuana in New England. rev. ed. (Illus.). 1977. pap. 10.00 (*0-89166-008-9*) Cobblesmith.

Oamek, George E. Economic & Environmental Impacts of Interstate Water Transfers in the Colorado River Basin, Vol. 90-M3. (Illus.). xiv, 197p. (Orig.). 1990. pap. text 15.00 (*0-936911-02-6*) Ctr Agri & Rural Dev.

Oana, Katherine. Bobby Bear & the Blizzard. LC 80-82950. (Bobby Bear Ser.). (Illus.). 32p. (J). (ps-1). 1981. lib. bdg. 9.95 (*0-87783-151-3*) Oddo.

— Bobby Bear Goes to the Beach. LC 80-82951. (Bobby Bear Ser.). (Illus.). 32p. (J). (ps-1). 1981. lib. bdg. 9.95 (*0-87783-153-X*) Oddo.

— Chirpy Chipmunk. LC 88-51854. (Fables for Today Ser.). (Illus.). 16p. (Orig.). (J). (ps). 1989. pap. 5.52 (*0-914127-08-X*) Univ Class.

— Kippy Koala. Cooper, William, ed. LC 85-51823. (Fables for Today Ser.). (Illus.). 16p. (Orig.). (J). (ps up). 1985. pap. text 2.95 (*0-914127-21-7*) Univ Class.

— Learning the Words of Color. Baird, Tate, ed. LC 86-50866. (Illus.). 32p. (Orig.). (J). (ps-1). 1986. pap. 2.95 (*0-914127-79-9*) Univ Class.

— Lori Lamb. Baird, Tate, ed. (Fables for Today Ser.). (Illus.). 16p. (Orig.). (J). (ps). 1989. pap. 5.52 (*0-914127-09-8*) Univ Class.

— Minnie Muskrat. Baird, Tate, ed. LC 88-51856. (Fables for Today Ser.). (Illus.). 16p. (Orig.). (J). (ps). 1989. pap. 5.52 (*0-914127-10-1*) Univ Class.

An Asterisk (*) at the beginning of an entry indicates that the title is appearing for the first time.

— Spacebear Lands on Earth. Baird, Tate, ed. (Illus.). 16p. (Orig.). (J). (ps up). 1988. pap. 2.95 (*0-914127-26-8*) Univ Class.

— The Sporting Way to Reading Comprehension. Cooper, William H., ed. LC 84-51195. (Illus.). 68p. (Orig.). (J). (gr. 3-8). 1984. pap. 4.95 (*0-914127-17-9*) Univ Class.

— Timmy Tiger & the Butterfly Net. LC 80-82954. (Timmy Tiger Ser.). (Illus.). 32p. (J). (ps-4). 1981. lib. bdg. 9.95 (*0-87783-160-2*) Oddo.

— Timmy Tiger & the Masked Bandit. LC 80-82955. (Timmy Tiger Ser.). (Illus.). 32p. (J). (ps-4). 1981. lib. bdg. 9.95 (*0-87783-161-0*) Oddo.

— Zippy Zebra, Vol. IV. Baird, Tate, ed. LC 88-51853. (Fables for Today Ser.). (Illus.). 16p. (Orig.). (J). (ps). 1989. pap. 5.52 (*0-914127-11-X*) Univ Class.

Oana, Katy D. The Little Dog Who Wouldn't Be. LC 77-18351. (Illus.). 32p. (J). (gr. 2-4). 1978. lib. bdg. 9.95 (*0-87783-150-5*) Oddo.

— Robbie & the Raggedy Scarecrow. LC 77-18349. (Sound Ser.). (Illus.). 32p. (J). (gr. 2-4). 1978. lib. bdg. 9.95 (*0-87783-154-8*) Oddo.

— Robbie & the Raggedy Scarecrow. LC 77-18349. (Illus.). (J). (gr. k-2). 1978. lib. bdg. 5.95 (*0-89508-065-6*) Rainbow Bks.

— Shasta & the Shebang Machine. LC 77-18350. (Sound Ser.). (Illus.). 32p. (J). (gr. 2-4). 1978. lib. bdg. 9.95 (*0-87783-152-1*) Oddo.

— Shasta & the Shebang Machine. LC 77-18350. (Illus.). (J). (gr. k-2). 1978. lib. bdg. 5.95 (*0-89508-066-4*) Rainbow Bks.

Oancia, Sandra. Remember: Helen's Story. LC 98-166395. (Illus.). 120p. (Orig.). 1997. pap. write for info. (*1-55059-145-2*) Detselig Ents.

Oanh, Nguyen X. & Grub, Phillip D. Vietnam: The New Investment Frontier in Southeast Asia. 148p. 1992. pap. 18.50 (*981-210-023-7*, Pub. by Times Academic) Intl Spec Bk.

Oar, Ross. Christmas Heirloom Patterns for Woodcarving, Vol. I. (Illus.). (Orig.). 1996. reprint ed. pap. 9.95 (*0-9649796-0-8*) Wst Falls Woodcarving.

— Christmas Heirloom Patterns for Woodcarving, Vol. II. (Illus.). 32p. (Orig.). 1997. pap. 12.00 (*0-9649796-1-6*) Wst Falls Woodcarving.

— Folk & Figure Wood Carving. 52p. 1999. pap. 14.95 (*1-56523-105-8*) Fox Chapel Pub.

Oard, Beverly, jt. auth. see Oard, Michael.

Oard, Doug, jt. ed. see Hull, David.

Oard, Michael. The Weather Book: Wonders of Creation. 82p. 1997. boxed set 15.95 (*0-89051-211-6*, WEABOO) Master Bks.

Oard, Michael & Oard, Beverly. Life in the Great Ice Age. LC 93-77826. 72p. 1998. boxed set 13.95 (*0-89051-167-5*, LIGRIC) Master Bks.

Oard, Michael J. Ancient Ice Ages or Gigantic Submarine Landslides? Howe, George F., ed. (Creation Research Society Technical Monograph Ser.: No. 6). (Illus.). 130p. (Orig.). (C). 1997. pap. 21.00 (*0-940384-18-3*) Creation Research.

***Oarr, Chris.** The Expo: SPX 99. 200p. 2000. pap. 5.00 (*0-9670566-3-2*) Westhampton Hse.

OAS General Secretariat, Bureau of Legal Affairs Staff. Tratados Sobre el Canal de Panama Suscritos Entre la Republica de Panama y los Estados Unidos de America. (Serie Sobre Tratados: No. 57 & 57a). 157p. (C). 1979. text 9.00 (*0-685-03626-X*) OAS.

OAS General Secretariat, Bureau of Legal Affairs Staff, ed. Status of Inter-American Treaties & Conventions. rev. ed. (Treaty Ser.: No. 5). 53p. (C). text 5.00 (*0-8270-1147-4*) OAS.

OAS General Secretariat, Department of Cultural Affairs Staff, tr. see Oquli, Ramon & Melendez, Carlos.

OAS General Secretariat, Department of Scientific Research Staff. Actividad Optica, Dispersion Rotatoria Optica y Dicroismo Circular en Quimica Organica. 2nd ed. (Serie de Quimica: Monografia No. 11). (SPA.). 70p. (C). 1981. pap. 3.50 (*0-8270-1418-X*) OAS.

— Bacteriofagos. 2nd rev. ed. (Serie de Biologia: No. 12). (SPA., Illus.). 102p. (C). 1980. pap. 2.00 (*0-8270-1301-9*) OAS.

— Catalogo de Informes y Documentos Tecnicos de la OEA: Suplemento 1978. (SG Ser. A: No. III.1). 81p. 1981. pap. text 4.00 (*0-8270-1300-0*) OAS.

— Cinetica de Disolucion de Medicamentos. (Serie de Quimica: Monografia No. 24). (SPA.). 102p. (C). 1981. pap. 3.50 (*0-8270-1391-4*) OAS.

— Fisica Cuantica. rev. ed. (Monografias Cientificas (Scientific Monographs)). 62p. (Orig.). (C). 1980. reprint ed. 2.00 (*0-8270-1100-8*) OAS.

— La OEA y la Evolucion del Sistema Interamericano. 50p. (C). 1982. pap. 5.00 (*0-685-05518-3*) OAS.

— Principios Generales de Microbiologia: Serie de Biologia No. 7. 2nd ed. (Serie de Biologia: No. 7). 143p. (C). 1980. text 3.50 (*0-8270-1097-4*) OAS.

— Semiconductors. 2nd ed. (Serie de Fisica (Monograph on Physics): No. 6). 63p. (C). 1980. reprint ed. text 3.50 (*0-8270-1068-0*) OAS.

— A Vida da Celula. (Serie de Biologia: No. 5). (Illus.). 117p. (Orig.). (C). reprint ed. 3.50 (*0-8270-1141-5*) OAS.

OAS General Secretariat, Department of Scientific Research Staff, ed. Boletin Estadistico de la OEA. 207p. (C). 4.00 (*0-686-68291-2*) OAS.

OAS General Secretariat, Department of Scientific Research Staff, ed. see O'Brien, Horacio H.

OAS General Secretariat for Juridical Affairs Staff. Anuario Juridico Interamericano, 1980. 339p. 1981. text 50.00 (*0-8270-1399-X*) OAS.

— Convencao Interamericana Sobre Extradicao. (Serie Sobre Tratados: No. 60). (POR.). 16p. 1981. pap. 2.00 (*0-8270-1331-0*) OAS.

— Convencion Interamericana Sobre Extradiction. (Serie Sobre Tratados: No. 60). (SPA.). 16p. (C). 1981. pap. 2.00 (*0-8270-1328-0*) OAS.

— Convention Interamericaine Sur L'extradition. (Serie Sur les Traites: No. 60). (FRE.). 16p. (C). 1981. pap. 2.00 (*0-8270-1330-2*) OAS.

— Inter-American Convention on Extradition. (Treaty Ser.: No. 60). 16p. (C). 1981. pap. 2.00 (*0-8270-1329-9*) OAS.

— Sistema Interamericano a Treaves de Tratados, Convenciones y Otros Documentos Vol. I: Asuntos Juridicos Politicos. (Sistema Interamericano Ser.). 1040p. (C). 1981. text 60.00 (*0-8270-1426-0*) OAS.

OAS General Secretariat for Legal Affairs Staff. Relacion de Acuerdos Bilaterales: OEA Ser. B-II 1, 1949-1980. (Serie Sobre Tratados: No. 59). (ENG, FRE, POR & SPA.). 74p. (C). 1980. 4.00 (*0-8270-1283-7*) OAS.

— A Statement of the Laws of Honduras in Matters Affecting Business. 4th ed. 292p. (C). 1981. pap. text 10.00 (*0-8270-1421-X*) OAS.

OAS General Secretariat for Management Staff. Documentos Oficiales de la Organizacion de los Estados Americanos Lista General de Documentos, Volumen XX: OEA Ser.Z I. 1. Enero-Diciembre de 1979. (SPA.). 144p. (C). 1980. lib. bdg. 9.00 (*0-8270-1289-6*) OAS.

OAS General Secretariat, Inter-American Commission. Annual Report of the Inter-American Commission on Human Rights, 1979-1980. OAS Staff, tr. (Inter-American Commission on Human Rights Ser.). 153p. (C). 1980. lib. bdg. 6.00 (*0-8270-1285-3*) OAS.

— Annual Report of the Inter-American Commission on Human Rights, 1980-1981. (OEA Ser.: L/V/II.53 Doc. 9, Rev. 1). (SPA.). 130p. (C). 1981. pap. 5.00 (*0-686-81338-3*) OAS.

— La Convencion Americana Sobre Derechos Humanos. (Human Rights Ser.). 248p. 1980. 9.00 (*0-8270-1222-5*) OAS.

— Informe Sobre la Situacion de los Derechos Humanos en Haiti. (Human Rights Ser.). 77p. (C). 1980. text 5.00 (*0-8270-1095-8*) OAS.

— Informe Sobre la Situacion de los Derechos Humanos en la Republica de Bolivia. (OEA Ser.: L/V/II.53 Doc. 16, Rev. 2). (SPA.). 115p. (C). 1981. pap. 5.00 (*0-8270-1423-6*) OAS.

— Informe Sobre la Situacion de los Derechos Humanos en la Republica de Colombia. (OEA Ser.: L/V/II 53 Doc. 22, 30 Junio 1981). 222p. 1981. pap. text 9.00 (*0-8270-1372-8*) OAS.

— Informe Sobre la Situacion de los Derechos Humanos en la Republica de Guatemala. 132p. (C). 1981. pap. 6.00 (*0-8270-1422-8*) OAS.

— Informe Sobre la Situacion de los Derechos Humanos en la Republica de Nicaragua. (OEA Ser.: L/V/II.53 Doc. 25. 30 Junio 1981). 168p. 1981. pap. 7.00 (*0-8270-1369-8*) OAS.

— Report on the Situation of Human Rights in the Republic of Bolivia. (SPA.). 117p. (C). 1981. pap. 5.00 (*0-685-03625-5*) OAS.

— Report on the Situation of Human Rights in the Republic of Colombia. (SPA.). 222p. (C). 1981. pap. 8.00 (*0-8270-1374-4*) OAS.

— Report on the Situation of Human Rights in the Republic of Guatemala. (OAS Ser.: L/V/II.53 Doc 21, Rev. 3). (SPA.). 133p. (C). 1981. pap. 6.00 (*0-8270-1428-7*) OAS.

— Report on the Situation of Human Rights in the Republic of Nicaragua. (SPA.). 171p. (C). 1981. pap. 7.00 (*0-8270-1373-6*) OAS.

— Work Accomplished by the Inter-American Juridical Committee During Its Regular Meeting: Held from August 4-29, 1980. (OFA Ser.: No. Q-IV CJI-43). 129p. 1981. pap. text 10.00 (*0-8270-1363-9*) OAS.

OAS General Secretariat of Development & Codification Staff. Recomendaciones e Informes, 1981, Vol. XIII. (Comite Juridico Interamericano Ser.). 125p. (C). 1981. pap. 8.00 (*0-8270-1441-4*) OAS.

OAS General Secretariat Staff. Boletin Estadistico de la OEA: Enero-Junio 1980, Vol. 2, Nos. 1-2. 221p. 1980. pap. text 4.00 (*0-686-69867-3*) OAS.

— Boletin Estadistico de la OEA: Vol. 2, No. 3 Julio-Septiembre 1980. (SPA.). 212p. (C). 1980. pap. write for info. (*0-318-54727-9*) OAS.

— Cromatografia Liquida Alta Presion: Monografia, No. 10. (Serie de Quimica). (SPA., Illus.). 72p. (C). 1980. reprint ed. pap. 3.50 (*0-8270-1229-2*) OAS.

— La Educacion, No. 83. (POR & SPA.). 152p. (C). 1980. pap. 4.00 (*0-686-74519-1*) OAS.

— Guia de las Fuentes en Hispanoamerica Para el Estudio de la Administracion Virreinal Espanola en Mexico y en el Peru 1535- 1700. 523p. 1980. pap. 15.00 (*0-8270-1091-5*) OAS.

— Introduccion a la Electroquinica. (Serie de Quimica: No. 22). (SPA., Illus.). 136p. (C). 1980. pap. 3.50 (*0-8270-1220-9*) OAS.

— Recomendaciones e Informes del Comite Jurico Interamericano Documetos, 1974-1977, Vol. 2. 675p. (C). 1981. 50.00 (*0-8270-1284-5*) OAS.

— Revista Interamericana de Bibliografia, Vol. XXX, No. 4, 1980. (POR & SPA.). 150p. (C). 1980. pap. 2.00 (*0-686-74520-5*) OAS.

— Revista Interamericana de Bibliografia, Vol. 31, No. 1. (FRE, POR & SPA.). 196p. (C). 1981. pap. 3.00 (*0-686-75080-2*) OAS.

— Revista Interamericana de Bibliografia: (Inter-American Review of Bibliography), Vol. XXX, No. 3. (ENG & SPA.). 116p. 1980. pap. text 2.00 (*0-686-69868-1*) OAS.

— Tratados y Convenciones Interamerianos. (Serie Sobre Tratados: No. 9). 303p. (C). 1980. 15.00 (*0-685-03627-8*) OAS.

— Los Virus. (Serie de Biologia: No. 8). 72p. (Orig.). (C). 1980. reprint ed. pap. text 3.50 (*0-8270-1169-5*) OAS.

— Vocabulario Vial. (ENG, FRE, POR & SPA.). 368p. 1979. text 15.00 (*0-8270-1332-9*) OAS.

OAS General Secretariat Staff, ed. see Butilerrez-Vasquez, J. M.

OAS Staff. Inter-American Yearbook on Human Rights 1995, Vol. 259. 992p. 1998. text 313.50 (*90-411-0534-4*) Kluwer Law Intl.

OAS Staff, tr. see OAS General Secretariat, Inter-American Commission.

Oasis. Morning Glory. 96p. 1996. otabind 19.95 (*0-7935-6288-0*) H Leonard.

— Play Guitar With Oasis. (Guitar Jammin Ser.). Date not set. pap. text 19.95 incl. audio compact disk (*0-7935-6873-0*) H Leonard.

— What's the Story, Morning Glory? 64p. 1996. otabind 14.95 (*0-7935-6419-0*) H Leonard.

Oasis Press Editors. SmartStart Your Illinois Business. LC 98-6055. (Illus.). 340p. 1998. pap. 19.95 (*1-55571-441-2*, SSILP, Oasis Pr) PSI Resch.

***Oasis Press Editors.** SmartStart Your Minnesota Business. LC 98-50169. (Illus.). 1999. pap. write for info. (*1-55517-470-1*) CFI Dist.

Oasis Press Editors. SmartStart Your Nebraska Business. LC 98-50167. (Smartstart Ser.). (Illus.). 340p. 1999. pap. 19.95 (*1-55571-471-4*, Oasis Pr) PSI Resch.

— SmartStart Your Nevada Business. LC 99-10593. 350p. 2000. pap. text 19.95 (*1-55571-473-0*) PSI Resch.

— SmartStart Your New Hampshire Business. LC 98-29471. 350p. 1998. 19.95 (*1-55571-452-8*, SSNHP, Oasis Pr) PSI Resch.

— SmartStart Your New Mexico Business. LC 98-29469. 300p. 1998. 19.95 (*1-55571-451-X*, SSNMP, Oasis Pr) PSI Resch.

— SmartStart Your Oklahoma Business. LC 99-34840. 340p. 1999. pap. 19.95 (*1-55571-472-2*) PSI Resch.

Oasis Press Editors & PSI Research Staff. SmartStart Your Arkansas Business. LC 98-6049. (Illus.). 340p. 1998. pap. 19.95 (*1-55571-437-4*, SSARP, Oasis Pr) PSI Resch.

— SmartStart Your California Business. LC 97-29826. (Illus.). 380p. 1997. pap. 19.95 (*1-55571-416-1*, Oasis Pr) PSI Resch.

— SmartStart Your Connecticut Business. LC 98-6056. (Illus.). 340p. 1998. pap. 19.95 (*1-55571-438-2*, SSCTP, Oasis Pr) PSI Resch.

— SmartStart Your Florida Business. LC 97-29832. (Illus.). 342p. 1997. pap. 19.95 (*1-55571-415-3*, Oasis Pr) PSI Resch.

— SmartStart Your Georgia Business. LC 97-52652. (Illus.). 340p. 1997. pap. 19.95 (*1-55571-423-4*, Oasis Pr) PSI Resch.

— SmartStart Your Hawaii Business. LC 98-6054. (Illus.). 340p. 1998. pap. 19.95 (*1-55571-440-4*, SSHIP, Oasis Pr) PSI Resch.

— SmartStart Your Indiana Business. LC 98-15389. (Illus.). 340p. 1998. pap. 19.95 (*1-55571-442-0*, SSINP, Oasis Pr) PSI Resch.

— SmartStart Your Iowa Business. LC 98-29470. 340p. 1998. pap. 19.95 (*1-55571-454-4*, SSIAP, Oasis Pr) PSI Resch.

— SmartStart Your Kentucky Business. LC 97-29828. (Illus.). 360p. 1997. pap. 19.95 (*1-55571-407-2*, Oasis Pr) PSI Resch.

— SmartStart Your Maryland Business. LC 97-52646. (Illus.). 372p. 1998. pap. 19.95 (*1-55571-424-2*, Oasis Pr) PSI Resch.

— SmartStart Your Massachusetts Business. LC 97-36430. (Illus.). 360p. 1997. pap. 19.95 (*1-55571-408-0*, Oasis Pr) PSI Resch.

— SmartStart Your Michigan Business. LC 98-6051. (Illus.). 340p. 1998. pap. 19.95 (*1-55571-443-9*, SSMIP, Oasis Pr) PSI Resch.

— SmartStart Your Missouri Business. LC 98-29472. 340p. 1998. pap. 19.95 (*1 55571-453-6*, SSMOP, Oasis Pr) PSI Resch.

— SmartStart Your New Jersey Business. LC 97-29830. (Illus.). 356p. 1997. pap. 19.95 (*1-55571-419-6*, Oasis Pr) PSI Resch.

— SmartStart Your New York Business. LC 97-29833. (Illus.). 360p. 1997. pap. 19.95 (*1-55571-414-5*, Oasis Pr) PSI Resch.

— SmartStart Your North Carolina Business. LC 97-29829. (Illus.). 360p. 1997. pap. 19.95 (*1-55571-410-2*, Oasis Pr) PSI Resch.

— SmartStart Your Ohio Business. LC 98-6048. (Illus.). 340p. 1998. pap. 19.95 (*1-55571-447-1*, SSOHP, Oasis Pr) PSI Resch.

— SmartStart Your Oregon Business. LC 97-52649. (Illus.). 372p. 1998. pap. 19.95 (*1-55571-425-0*, Oasis Pr) PSI Resch.

— SmartStart Your Pennsylvania Business. LC 97-52650. (Illus.). 372p. 1998. pap. 19.95 (*1-55571-426-9*, Oasis Pr) PSI Resch.

— SmartStart Your Tennessee Business. LC 98-6050. (Illus.). 340p. 1998. pap. 19.95 (*1-55571-444-7*, SSTNP, Oasis Pr) PSI Resch.

— SmartStart Your Texas Business. LC 97-36435. (Illus.). 368p. 1997. pap. 19.95 (*1-55571-417-X*, Oasis Pr) PSI Resch.

— SmartStart Your Virginia Business. LC 97-52651. (Illus.). 372p. 1998. pap. 19.95 (*1-55571-427-7*, Oasis Pr) PSI Resch.

— SmartStart Your Washington Business. LC 97-29827. (Illus.). 364p. 1997. pap. 19.95 (*1-55571-418-8*, Oasis Pr) PSI Resch.

— SmartStart Your Washington, D. C. Business. LC 98-6053. (Illus.). 340p. 1998. pap. 19.95 (*1-55571-439-0*, SSDCP, Oasis Pr) PSI Resch.

Oasis Press Editors & PSI Research Staff, eds. SmartStart Your South Carolina Business. LC 98-29468. 350p. 2000. pap. 19.95 (*1-55571-450-1*, SSSCP, Pub. by PSI Resch) Midpt Trade.

***Oasis Press Staff, ed.** SmartStart Your Mississippi Business. 350p. 2000. pap. 19.95 (*1-55571-535-4*, Pub. by PSI Resch) Midpt Trade.

Oasis Press Staff, ed. SmartStart Your South Dakota Business. 350p. 2000. pap. 19.95 (*1-55571-474-9*, Pub. by PSI Resch) Midpt Trade.

— SmartStart Your Vermont Business. LC 99-10592. 350p. 2000. pap. 19.95 (*1-55571-476-5*, SSVTP, Pub. by PSI Resch) Midpt Trade.

***Oasis Press Staff, ed.** SmartStart Your Wyoming Business. LC 00-38507. 350p. 2000. pap. 19.95 (*1-55571-534-6*, Pub. by PSI Resch) Midpt Trade.

***Oasis Press/PSI Research Staff.** Smartstart Your Delaware Business. LC 00-41691. 2000. pap. write for info. (*1-55571-536-2*, Oasis Pr) PSI Resch.

— Smartstart Your Rhode Island Business. LC 00-41690. 2000. write for info. (*1-55571-544-3*, Oasis Pr) PSI Resch.

— SmartStart Your Utah Business. LC HD62.5.S623952 2000. 340p. 2000. pap. 19.95 (*1-55571-475-7*, Oasis Pr) PSI Resch.

Oaten, Edward F. European Travellers in India, (C). 1991. reprint ed. 16.00 (*81-206-0710-4*, Pub. by Asian Educ Servs) S Asia.

— European Travellers in India During the 15th, 16th & 17th Centuries. LC 75-137279. reprint ed. 42.50 (*0-404-04808-0*) AMS Pr.

Oates. Foundations of Child Development. 1995. pap. text 33.95 (*0-631-19426-6*) Blackwell Pubs.

— Legal Practice Book. 944p. 1993. 15.00 (*0-316-62197-8*) Little.

— Personnages. (C). 1995. pap., teacher ed., suppl. ed. 11.96 (*0-395-67104-3*) HM.

— Personnages. (C). 1995. pap., wbk. ed., lab manual ed. 24.76 (*0-395-67103-5*) HM.

— Portrait of America, 6 vols. 6th ed. LC 94-76537. (C). 1994. pap. text 31.56 (*0-395-70887-7*) HM.

Oates, jt. auth. see Burns.

Oates, A. S. Around Helston in the Old Days. (C). 1989. text 35.00 (*0-907566-46-4*, Pub. by Dyllansow Truran) St Mut.

Oates, Anthony S., et al, eds. Materials Reliability in Microelectronics V: Materials Research Society Symposium Proceedings. (MRS Symposium Proceedings Ser.: Vol. 391). 523p. 1995. text 82.00 (*1-55899-294-4*, 391) Materials Res.

Oates, Anthony S., et al. Reliability For Logic & Memory Technologies. 1999. 400.00 (*0-7803-5303-X*) IEEE Standards.

***Oates, Bob.** Football in America: Game of the Century. 1999. 19.95 (*1-885758-16-2*) Quality Sports.

Oates, Christine. Truro City Trail. (C). 1989. 40.00 (*0-907566-16-2*, Pub. by Dyllansow Truran) St Mut.

Oates, Dan, ed. The Hanging Rock Rebel: Lieutenant John Blue's War in West Virginia & the Shenandoah Valley. LC 93-39320. (Illus.). 324p. 1994. 24.95 (*0-942597-62-1*, Burd St Pr) White Mane Pub.

Oates, David. Earth Rising: Ecological Belief in An Age of Science. LC 88-25468. 264p. 1989. 27.95 (*0-87071-358-2*); pap. 17.95 (*0-87071-357-4*) Oreg St U Pr.

— Music Reading for Guitar. 160p. 1998. otabind 16.95 (*0-7935-8188-5*) H Leonard.

— Night of the Potato. (Chapbook Ser.: No. 3). 56p. 1994. pap. 5.00 (*1-885912-00-5*) Sows Ear Pr.

— Peace in Exile: Poems. 1992. pap. 12.95 (*0-9617481-9-2*); audio 10.00 (*1-882291-50-6*) Oyster River Pr.

Oates, David, et al. Excavations at Tell Brak Vol. 1: The Mitanni & Old Babylonian Periods. (Monographs Ser.). (Illus.). xxii, 296p. 1998. 80.00 (*0-9519420-5-0*, Pub. by McDonald Inst) David Brown.

Oates, Gisele C., jt. auth. see Jackson, Nicky A.

Oates, Gordon C. Aerothermodynamics of Gas Turbine & Rocket Propulsion. 3rd enl. rev. ed. LC 97-51303. 452p. 1998. 69.95 (*1-56347-241-4*) AIAA.

— Aerothermodynamics of Gas Turbines & Rocket Propulsion. enl. rev. ed. (Education Ser.). 450p. 1988. 61.95 (*0-930403-34-7*, 34-7) AIAA.

— Aircraft Propulsion Systems Technology & Design. (Educ Ser.). 1989. 57.95 (*0-930403-24-X*, 24-X) AIAA.

Oates, Gordon C., ed. Aerothermodynamics of Aircraft Engine Components. LC 85-13355. (Education Ser.). (Illus.). 551p. 1985. 57.95 (*0-915928-97-3*, 97-3) AIAA.

Oates, J. A. M. Lime & Limestone: Chemistry & Technology, Production & Uses. 474p. 1998. 298.00 (*3-527-29527-5*) Wiley.

***Oates, J. C. T.** A Catalogue of the Fifteenth-Century Printed Books in the University Library, Cambridge. xiv, 898p. 1999. reprint ed. 100.00 (*1-57898-153-0*) Martino Pubng.

Oates, Joan C. Babylon. (Ancient Peoples & Places Ser.). (Illus.). 1986. pap. 15.95 (*0-500-27384-7*, Pub. by Thames Hudson) Norton.

— Phoenix Bird Chinaware, Bk. 1. (Illus.). 110p. 1989. reprint ed. pap. 15.00 (*0-9617047-0-5*) J Oates.

— Phoenix Bird Chinaware, Bk. 2. (Illus.). 112p. 1985. pap. 14.95 (*0-9617047-1-3*) J Oates.

— Phoenix Bird Chinaware, Bk. 3. (Illus.). 96p. 1986. reprint ed. pap. 14.50 (*0-9617047-2-1*) J Oates.

— Phoenix Bird Chinaware, Bk. 4. (Illus.). 100p. 1989. pap. 15.00 (*0-9617047-3-X*) J Oates.

Oates, John. The Teaching of Tennyson. LC 72-3619. (Studies in Tennyson: No. 27). 1972. reprint ed. lib. bdg. 75.00 (*0-8383-1583-6*) M S G Haskell Hse.

Oates, John, jt. ed. see Davies, Glyn.

O

Oates, John A., ed. Prostaglandins & the Cardiovascular System. LC 82-15035. (Advances in Prostaglandin, Thromboxane, & Leukotriene Research Ser.: No. 10). (Illus.). 400p. 1982. reprint ed. pap. 124.00 (*0-7837-9638-2*, 206039100005) Bks Demand.

Oates, John F. Myth & Reality in the Rain Forest: How Conservation Strategies are Failing in West Africa. LC 99-20220. 340p. 1999. 50.00 (*0-520-21782-9*, Pub. by U CA Pr) Cal Prin Full Svc.

— Myth & Reality in the Rain Forest: How Conservation Strategies Are Failing in West Africa. LC 99-20220. 340p. 1999. pap. 19.95 (*0-520-22252-0*, Pub. by U CA Pr) Cal Prin Full Svc.

Oates, John F., et al. Checklist of Editions of Greek Papyri & Ostraca. LC 85-2027. (Bulletin of the American Society of Papyrologists Supplements Ser.: No. 4). 74p. reprint ed. pap. 30.00 (*0-7837-5420-5*, 204518400005) Bks Demand.

— Yale Papyri in the Beinecke Rare Book & Manuscript Library, Vol. 1. LC 75-81535. (American Studies in Papyrology: No. 2). 320p. reprint ed. pap. 99.20 (*0-7837-5485-X*, 204525000001) Bks Demand.

Oates-Johnson, Mary. President: America's Leader. 48p. (gr. 1-4). 1996. pap. text 5.95 (*0-8114-5580-7*) Raintree Steck-V.

Oates, Joyce Carol. American Gothic Tales. 1999. pap. 24.95 (*0-525-94037-5*) NAL.

— Assignation. 221p. (C). 1998. 16.95 (*0-88001-200-5*) HarpC.

— The Assignation: Stories. LC 89-45126. 208p. 1996. reprint ed. pap. 12.00 (*0-88001-440-7*) HarpC.

— Because It Is Bitter & Because It Is My Heart. 416p. 1991. pap. 13.95 (*0-452-26581-9*, Plume) Dutton Plume.

— Bellefleur. 1991. pap. 17.95 (*0-452-26794-3*, Plume) Dutton Plume.

— Black Water. 160p. 1993. pap. 11.95 (*0-452-26986-5*, Plume) Dutton Plume.

***Oates, Joyce Carol.** Blonde: A Novel. 752p. 2000. 27.50 (*0-06-019607-6*, Ecco Press) HarperTrade.

— Broke Heart Blues. 2000. pap. 13.95 (*0-452-28034-6*, Plume) Dutton Plume.

Oates, Joyce Carol. Broke Heart Blues. LC 98-51570. 369p. 1999. 24.95 (*0-525-94451-6*, Dutton) NAL.

***Oates, Joyce Carol.** The Collector of Hearts. large type ed. LC 98-56292. 1999. pap. 30.00 (*0-7862-1859-2*) Thorndike Pr.

Oates, Joyce Carol. The Collector of Hearts: New Tales of the Grotesque. 323p. 1999. pap. 12.95 (*0-452-28024-9*, Plume) Dutton Plume.

— Come Meet Muffin. LC 97-43453. (Illus.). 32p. (J). (gr. k-3). 1998. 18.00 (*0-88001-556-X*) HarpC.

— Crossing the Border. 1978. mass mkt. 2.50 (*0-449-23751-6*, Crest) Fawcett.

— Expensive People. LC 89-71059. 244p. 1990. reprint ed. pap. 10.95 (*0-86538-069-4*) Ontario Rev NJ.

— The Fabulous Beasts: Poems. LC 74-27198. (Illus.). xii, 86p. 1975. pap. 6.95 (*0-8071-0285-7*); text 15.95 (*0-8071-0153-2*) La State U Pr.

— First Love: A Gothic Tale. LC 95-36354. (Illus.). 96p. 1996. 18.00 (*0-88001-457-1*) HarpC.

— First Love: A Gothic Tale. (Illus.). 96p. 1997. pap. 9.00 (*0-88001-508-X*) HarpC.

— Foxfire: Confessions of a Girl Gang. LC 94-3897. 336p. 1994. pap. 13.95 (*0-452-27231-9*, W Abrahams Bks) Dutton Plume.

***Oates, Joyce Carol.** George Bellows: American Artist. (Illus.). 69p. 2000. reprint ed. 22.00 (*0-7881-9277-9*) DIANE Pub.

Oates, Joyce Carol. Haunted. 1999. audio 16.95 (*0-453-00955-7*, NAL Bks) NAL.

— Haunted: Tales of the Grotesque. 10.95 (*0-614-32222-7*, Plume) Dutton Plume.

— Haunted: Tales of the Grotesque. 320p. 1995. pap. 13.95 (*0-452-27374-9*, Plume) Dutton Plume.

— Heat: And Other Stories. (Contemporary Fiction Ser.). 416p. 1992. pap. 14.95 (*0-452-26646-7*, W Abrahams Bks) Dutton Plume.

— I Lock My Door Upon Myself. (Fiction on Art Ser.). 112p. 1990. pap. 15.95 (*0-88001-260-9*) HarpC.

— The Life of the Writer, the Life of the Career: Prolegomena to a Personal Ethics. unabridged ed. (Ben Belitt Lectureship Ser.: Vol. 17). (Illus.). 24p. (Orig.). 1995. pap. 5.00 (*0-614-10189-1*) Bennington Coll.

— Man Crazy: A Novel. 288p. 1998. pap. 12.95 (*0-452-27724-8*, Plume) Dutton Plume.

— Man Crazy: A Novel. large type ed. LC 97-41717. 1997. 26.95 (*0-7862-1273-X*) Thorndike Pr.

— Marya: A Life. 320p. 1998. pap. 12.95 (*0-452-28020-6*, Truman Talley) St Martin.

— My Heart Laid Bare. 544p. 1999. pap. 13.95 (*0-452-28006-0*, Plume) Dutton Plume.

— New Heaven, New Earth: The Visionary Experience in Literature. 1978. pap. 2.50 (*0-449-23662-5*, Crest) Fawcett.

— New Heaven, New Earth: The Visionary Experience in Literature. LC 76-371756. 307 p. 1976. write for info. (*0-575-02076-8*) Trafalgar.

— New Plays. LC 97-46802. 284p. 1998. 23.00 (*0-86538-089-9*) Ontario Rev NJ.

***Oates, Joyce Carol.** New Plays. LC 97-46802. 284p. 1998. pap. 13.50 (*0-86538-090-2*) Ontario Rev NJ.

Oates, Joyce Carol. On Boxing. LC 94-17428. (Illus.). 1995. reprint ed. pap. 14.00 (*0-88001-385-0*) HarpC.

— The Perfectionist & Other Plays. 288p. 1998. reprint ed. pap. 15.00 (*0-88001-580-2*) HarpC.

— The Profane Art: Essays & Reviews. 212p. 1985. reprint ed. pap. 9.95 (*0-89255-095-3*) Persea Bks.

— Reading the Fights. (Spectator Ser.). 1990. pap. 9.95 (*0-685-46179-3*) P-H.

— The Rise of Life on Earth. LC 90-48706. 144p. 1991. 16.95 (*0-8112-1171-1*, Pub. by New Directions) Norton.

— The Rise of Life on Earth. LC 92-15118. 144p. 1992. pap. 9.95 (*0-8112-1213-0*, NDP746, Pub. by New Directions) Norton.

***Oates, Joyce Carol.** Solstice. 240p. 2000. reprint ed. pap. 14.95 (*0-86538-100-3*, Pub. by Ontario Rev NJ) Norton.

Oates, Joyce Carol. Son of the Morning. 1979. pap. 2.75 (*0-449-24073-8*, Crest) Fawcett.

***Oates, Joyce Carol.** Tales of H.P. Lovecraft. 352p. 2000. pap. 14.00 (*0-06-095790-5*, Ecco Press) HarperTrade.

Oates, Joyce Carol. Telling Stories: An Anthology for Writers. LC 97-22548. 750p. (C). 1997. pap. 34.75 (*0-393-97176-7*) Norton.

— Tenderness. LC 96-1726. 91p. 1996. pap. 18.95 (*0-86538-085-6*) Ontario Rev NJ.

— Them. 480p. 1984. mass mkt. 6.99 (*0-449-20692-0*, Crest) Fawcett.

***Oates, Joyce Carol.** Them. LC 99-54471. 432p. 2000. 19.95 (*0-679-64025-8*) Random.

Oates, Joyce Carol. Three Plays. LC 80-20210. 157p. 1980. reprint ed. 10.95 (*0-86538-002-3*) Ontario Rev NJ.

— We Were the Mulvaneys. 464p. 1997. pap. 13.95 (*0-452-27720-5*, Plume) Dutton Plume.

— What I Lived For. 624p. 1995. pap. 16.95 (*0-452-27269-6*, Plume) Dutton Plume.

— Where Are You Going, Where Have You Been? LC 94-11284. (Women Writers: Text & Contexts Ser.). 160p. (C). 1995. pap. text 14.00 (*0-8135-2135-1*) Rutgers U Pr.

— Where Are You Going, Where Have You Been? Showalter, Elaine, ed. & intro. by. LC 94-11284. (Women Writers: Text & Contexts Ser.). 160p. (C). 1995. text 30.00 (*0-8135-2134-3*) Rutgers U Pr.

— Where Are You Going, Where Have You Been? Selected Early Stories. LC 92-44899. 522p. 1994. pap. 12.95 (*0-86538-078-3*) Ontario Rev NJ.

— Where Is Here. 1992. 18.95 (*0-88001-283-8*) HarpC.

— Where Is Here. 193p. 1993. pap. 11.00 (*0-88001-338-9*) HarpC.

— Where I've Been & Where I'm Going. LC 98-45234. 400p. 1999. pap. 13.95 (*0-452-28053-2*) NAL.

— Will You Always Love Me? 326p. 1997. pap. 13.95 (*0-452-27413-3*, Plume) Dutton Plume.

— Will You Always Love Me? 28p. 1994. 100.00 (*0-9640454-2-7*) J Cahill Pubng.

— Women Whose Lives Are Food, Men Whose Lives Are Money. Poems. LC 77-17220. (Illus.). 80p. 1978. 15.95 (*0-8071-0391-8*) La State U Pr.

— Wonderland. LC 91-41741. 512p. 1992. reprint ed. pap. 12.95 (*0-86538-075-9*) Ontario Rev NJ.

— You Must Remember This. 448p. 1998. pap. 13.95 (*0-452-28019-2*, Truman Talley) St Martin.

— Zombie. LC 95-8090. 192p. 1996. pap. 10.95 (*0-452-27500-8*, W Abrahams Bks) Dutton Plume.

Oates, Joyce Carol, ed. American Gothic Tales. 560p. 1996. pap. 14.95 (*0-452-27489-3*, W Abrahams Bks) Dutton Plume.

— First Person Singular: Writers on Their Craft. LC 83-21927. 280p. 1983. pap. 9.95 (*0-86538-045-7*) Ontario Rev NJ.

— The Oxford Book of American Short Stories. 784p. 1992. 40.00 (*0-19-507065-8*) OUP.

— The Oxford Book of American Short Stories. 784p. 1994. reprint ed. pap. 18.95 (*0-19-509262-7*) OUP.

***Oates, Joyce Carol & Atwan, Robert, eds.** The Best American Essays of the Century. 544p. 2000. 30.00 (*0-618-04370-5*) HM.

Oates, Joyce Carol & Vachss, Andrew H. Unusual Suspects. Grady, James, ed. 1996. pap. 13.00 (*0-614-97800-9*) Vin Bks.

***Oates, Joyce Carol, et al.** Hover. LC 98-29413. (Illus.). 64p. 1998. 17.50 (*1-891273-00-0*) Artspace Bks.

— Snapshots: 20th Century Mother-Daughter Fiction. Berliner, Janet, ed. 2000. 24.95 (*1-56792-114-0*); pap. 16.95 (*1-56792-172-8*) Godine.

Oates, Joyce Carol, see Smith, Rosamond, pseud.

Oates, Joyce Carol, jt. auth. see Cassill, R. V.

Oates, Joyce Carol, ed. see Dickinson, Emily.

Oates, Joyce Carol, ed. see Lovecraft, H. P.

Oates, Kim. Child Abuse. (Illus.). 320p. 1986. pap. 9.95 (*0-8065-0962-7*, Citadel Pr) Carol Pub Group.

Oates, L. Legal Writing Handbook. 944p. 1993. 33.00 (*0-316-62194-3*, Aspen Law & Bus) Aspen Pub.

Oates, Laurel, et al. The Legal Writing Handbook: Research, Analysis, & Writing. annot. ed. 944p. 1993. write for info. (*0-316-62198-6*, 21986) Aspen Law.

Oates, Laurel C., et al. The Legal Writing Handbook: Research, Analysis & Writing. 2nd ed. LC 97-49350. 1998. pap. text 38.00 (*1-56706-695-X*) Aspen Law.

Oates, LeRoy F. A Date with an Angel. 1998. pap. 7.00 (*1-58235-004-3*) Watermrk Pr.

***Oates, LeRoy F.** My Beloved Angel. 2000. pap. write for info. (*1-58235-329-8*) Watermrk Pr.

Oates, Letty. Decorative Painting. (Illus.). 80p. 1995. write for info. (*1-57215-099-8*) World Pubns.

— Naturally Creative Candles. LC 97-73020. 128p. 1997. pap. 19.95 (*0-8019-9045-9*, NACC) Krause Pubns.

— Step by Step Decoupage. (Illus.). 80p. 1995. write for info. (*1-57215-098-X*) World Pubns.

Oates, Letty. Three Dimensional Decoupage. LC 97-73019. (Illus.). 128p. (Orig.). 1997. pap. 19.95 (*0-8019-9049-1*, THRDE) Krause Pubns.

Oates, Lou. The Complete Book of Ready - to - Finish Furniture. (Illus.). 1984. 21.95 (*0-13-158239-9*, Busn); pap. 12.95 (*0-13-158221-6*, Busn) P-H.

Oates, Marguerite, jt. auth. see Armstrong, Frank H.

Oates, Martha. Death in the School Community: A Handbook for Counselors, Teachers & Administrators. LC 92-21966. 129p. (C). 1993. pap. text 31.95 (*1-55620-099-4*, 72040) Am Coun Assn.

Oates, Mary J. The Catholic Philanthropic Tradition in America. LC 94-13027. (Philanthropic Studies). 252p. 1995. 29.95 (*0-253-34159-0*) Ind U Pr.

— The Role of the Cotton Textile Industry in the Economic Development of the American Southeast: 1900-1940. LC 75-4023. (Dissertations in American Economic History Ser.). (Illus.). 1975. 24.95 (*0-405-07211-2*) Ayer.

Oates, Michael D. & Dubois, Jacques F. Personnages. (FRE.). (C). 1994. text, teacher ed. 46.76 incl. audio (*0-395-72678-6*); pap. text 45.56 incl. audio (*0-395-72677-8*) HM.

Oates, Michael D. & Oukada, Larbi. Entre Amis: An Interactive Approach, 2 vols. (FRE.). (C). 1993. text, teacher ed. 3.96 (*0-395-68256-8*) HM.

— Entre Amis: An Interactive Approach, 2 vols. 2nd ed. (FRE.). 608p. (C). 1993. text 59.56 incl. audio (*0-395-67635-5*) HM.

— Entre Amis: An Interactive Approach, 2 vols. 2nd annot. ed. (FRE.). (C). 1993. text, teacher ed. 60.76 (*0-395-67637-1*) HM.

— Entre Amis: An Interactive Approach. 3rd ed. (FRE.). (C). 1997. pap. text, wbk. ed., lab manual ed. 34.76 (*0-395-87271-5*) HM.

— Entre Amis: An Interactive Approach. 3rd annot. ed. (FRE.). (C). 1997. teacher ed. 61.96 incl. audio (*0-395-88601-5*) HM.

Oates, Phyllis Bennett. The Story of Western Furniture. (Illus.). 256p. 1994. pap. text 22.00 (*1-871569-59-1*, NAB) I R Dee.

— The Story of Western Furniture. 256p. 1999. pap. 24.95 (*1-56131-067-0*, Pub. by I R Dee) Natl Bk Netwk.

Oates, R. Kim. The Spectrum of Child Abuse: Assessment, Treatment, & Prevention. (Basic Principles into Practice Ser.: Vol. 8). 208p. 1996. pap. text 22.95 (*0-87630-807-8*) Brunner-Mazel.

Oates, R. Kim, ed. Understanding & Managing Child Sexual Abuse. (Illus.). 422p. 1990. text 98.00 (*0-7295-0322-4*) Bailliere Tindall.

Oates, Robert. Creating Heaven on Earth: The Mechanics of the impossible. (Illus.). 191p. 1990. pap. 12.50 (*0-685-35778-3*) Heaven On Earth.

Oates, Robert M., jt. auth. see Swanson, Gerald.

Oates, Stephen. The Aftermath of the Fury. Date not set. 16.00 (*0-06-093044-6*) HarpC.

Oates, Stephen B. Abraham Lincoln: The Man Behind the Myths. 240p. 1994. reprint ed. pap. 13.00 (*0-06-092472-1*, Perennial) HarperTrade.

— The Approaching Fury: Voices of the Storm, 1820-1861. 512p. 1998. pap. 15.00 (*0-06-092885-9*, Perennial) HarperTrade.

— Biography As History. LC 90-63742. (Charles Edmondson Historical Lectures). 37p. (Orig.). 1991. pap. text 5.95 (*0-918954-54-1*) Baylor Univ Pr.

— The Confederate Cavalry West of the River. LC 61-10044. (Illus.). 262p. 1992. reprint ed. pap. 14.95 (*0-292-71152-2*) U of Tex Pr.

— The Fires of Jubilee: Nat Turner's Fierce Rebellion. LC 74-1584. 208p. 1990. reprint ed. pap. 13.00 (*0-06-091670-2*, Perennial) HarperTrade.

— Let the Trumpet Sound: The Life of Martin Luther King, Jr. (Illus.). 592p. 1994. reprint ed. pap. 17.00 (*0-06-092473-X*, Perennial) HarperTrade.

— Our Fiery Trial: Abraham Lincoln, John Brown, & the Civil War Era. LC 78-16286. 160p. 1983. pap. 15.95 (*0-87023-397-1*) U of Mass Pr.

— Portrait of America, 6 vols. (C). Date not set. pap., teacher ed., suppl. ed. 31.56 (*0-395-71727-2*) HM.

— Portrait of America, 6 vols., Vol. 2. 6th ed. LC 94-76537. (C). 1994. pap. text 31.56 (*0-395-70888-5*) HM.

— To Purge This Land with Blood: A Biography of John Brown. 2nd ed. LC 84-2635. (Illus.). 448p. 1984. pap. 20.95 (*0-87023-458-7*) U of Mass Pr.

— The Whirlwind of War: Voices of the Storm, 1861-1865. LC 97-51171. 864p. 1998. 35.00 (*0-06-017580-X*) HarpC.

— The Whirlwind of War: Voices of the Storm, 1861-1865. LC 97-51171. 864p. 1999. pap. 18.95 (*0-06-093092-6*) HarpC.

— With Malice Toward None: The Life of Abraham Lincoln. (Illus.). 544p. 1994. reprint ed. pap. 17.00 (*0-06-092471-3*, Perennial) HarperTrade.

— A Woman of Valor: Clara Barton & the Civil War. LC 93-38830. 1994. 27.95 (*0-02-923405-0*) Free Pr.

— A Woman of Valor: Clara Barton & the Civil War. 1995. per. 14.00 (*0-02-874012-2*) Free Pr.

Oates, Stephen B., ed. Biography As High Adventure: Life-Writers Speak on Their Art. LC 85-20847. 160p. (Orig.). 1986. pap. 15.95 (*0-87023-514-1*); lib. bdg. 22.50 (*0-87023-513-3*) U of Mass Pr.

Oates, Stephen B., ed. see Ford, John S.

Oates, Wallace E. The Economics of Environmental Regulation. LC 95-39637. (Economists of the Twentieth Century Ser.). (Illus.). 480p. 1996. 110.00 (*1-85278-743-0*) E Elgar.

***Oates, Wallace E.** Environmental & Public Economics: Essays in Honor of Wallace E. Oates. Panagariya, Arvind et al, eds. LC 98-46623. 368p. 1999. 95.00 (*1-85898-611-7*) E Elgar.

Oates, Wallace E. Fiscal Federalism. (Modern Revivals in Economics Ser.). 272p. 1993. 59.95 (*0-7512-0220-7*, Pub. by Gregg Revivals) Ashgate Pub Co.

— Studies in Fiscal Federalism. (Economists of the Twentieth Century Ser.). 480p. 1991. text 120.00 (*1-85278-520-9*) E Elgar.

Oates, Wallace E., ed. The Economics of Fiscal Federalism & Local Finance. LC 97-43928. (International Library of Critical Writings in Economics). 752p. 1998. 280.00 (*1-85898-355-X*) E Elgar.

— The Economics of the Environment. LC 92-20813. (International Library of Critical Writings in Economics: Vol. 20). 640p. 1992. 230.00 (*1-85278-360-5*) E Elgar.

— The Economics of the Environment. 640p. 1994. pap. 45.00 (*1-85898-002-X*) E Elgar.

— The RFF Reader in Environmental & Resource Management. LC 98-50115. (Illus.). 307p. (C). 1999. pap. text 22.95 (*0-915707-96-9*) Resources Future.

Oates, Wallace E., jt. auth. see Baumol, William J.

Oates, Wayne E. Behind the Masks: Personality Disorders in Religious Behavior. LC 87-8221. 140p. (Orig.). 1987. pap. 14.95 (*0-664-24028-3*) Westminster John Knox.

— The Care of Troublesome People. LC 94-78333. (Church Leader's Core Library). 90p. 1994. pap. 11.25 (*1-56699-133-1*, AL154) Alban Inst.

— The Christian Pastor. 3rd rev. ed. LC 82-4933. 298p. 1982. pap. 17.95 (*0-664-24372-X*) Westminster John Knox.

— Grace Enough: Timeless Words for Trying Times. 56p. (Orig.). 1996. mass mkt. 2.95 (*1-57312-040-5*) Smyth & Helwys.

— Grief, Transition & Loss: A Pastor's Practical Guide. LC 96-49123. (Creative Pastoral Care & Counseling Ser.). 96p. 1997. pap. 15.00 (*0-8006-2864-0*, 1-2864, Fortress Pr) Augsburg Fortress.

— Luck: A Secular Faith. LC 94-19996. 128p. (Orig.). 1995. pap. 13.95 (*0-664-25536-1*) Westminster John Knox.

— Nurturing Silence in a Noisy Heart: How to Find Inner Peace. 128p. 1996. pap. 11.99 (*0-8066-2037-4*, 9-2037) Augsburg Fortress.

— Your Particular Grief. LC 81-3328. 114p. 1981. pap. 14.95 (*0-664-24376-2*) Westminster John Knox.

Oates, Wayne E., ed. see Hewett, John H.

Oates, Whitney. Influence of Simonides of Ceos on Horace. LC 72-122986. (Studies in Comparative Literature: No. 35). 1970. reprint ed. lib. bdg. 75.00 (*0-8383-1119-9*) M S G Haskell Hse.

Oates, Whitney J. Aristotle & the Problem of Value. LC 62-21106. 399p. reprint ed. pap. 123.70 (*0-8357-9493-8*, 201303500083) Bks Demand.

Oates, Whitney J. & O'Neill, Eugene, Jr., eds. Seven Famous Greek Plays. Incl. Agamemnon. Aeschylus. 1955. pap. Alcestis. Euripides. 1955. pap. Antigone. Sophocles. 1955. pap. Aristophanes: Frogs. Aristophanes. 1955. pap. Prometheus Bound. Aeschylus. 1955. pap. 446p. 1955. Set pap. 9.00 (*0-394-70125-9*) Knopf.

Oates, Whitney J., ed. see Euripides.

Oates, Whitney J., ed. see Sophocles.

Oates, William C. The War Between the Union & the Confederacy & Its Lost Opportunities: With a History of the 15th Alabama Regiment & the 48 Battles in Which It Was Engaged. rev. unabridged ed. 808p. 1995. 50.00 (*0-89029-011-3*, Pr of Morningside) Morningside Bkshop.

Oatis, Carol A., jt. auth. see Craik, Rebecca L.

Oatley, Keith & Jenkins, Jennifer M. Understanding Emotions. (Illus.). 512p. (C). 1996. 81.95 (*1-55786-494-2*); pap. 37.95 (*1-55786-495-0*) Blackwell Pubs.

Oatley, Nick. Cities, Economic Competition & Urban Policy. LC 99-164574. 1998. pap. 27.95 (*1-85396-325-9*, Pub. by P Chapman) P H Brookes.

Oatley, Thomas H. Monetary Politics: Exchange Rate Cooperation in the European Community. 240p. (C). 1998. text 47.50 (*0-472-10824-7*, 10824) U of Mich Pr.

Oatman, Eric F. The Jungle (Sinclair) (Barron's Book Notes Ser.). (C). 1984. pap. 2.50 (*0-8120-3424-4*) Barron.

Oatman, Lorenzo D. & Oatman, Olive A. The Captivity of the Oatman Girls among the Apache & Mohave Indians. LC 94-4747. Orig. Title: Life among the Indians: or the Captivity of the Oatman Girls among the Apache & Mohave Indians. (Illus.). 240p. 1994. reprint ed. pap. 7.95 (*0-486-28078-0*) Dover.

Oatman, Mike. Ol' Mikes Philosophy & Foolishness. (Illus.). 160p. (Orig.). 1993. pap. 14.95 (*0-9638429-0-0*) Hearth KS.

Oatman, Miriam E., jt. auth. see Blachly, Frederick F.

Oatman, Olive A., jt. auth. see Oatman, Lorenzo D.

Oatman, Robert L. The Art of Executive Protection. LC 97-68324. (Illus.). 288p. 1997. 27.95 (*1-56167-384-6*) Noble Hse MD.

Oatman, Tamra-Shae. Lone Star Baby: A Consumer Guide for Expectant & New Parents. Van Pilney, Mary, ed. (Orig.). 1988. pap. 8.95 (*0-9620141-0-9*) Oatman-Pilney.

Oba, Sadao. The "Japanese" War: London University's WWII Secret Teaching Programme & the "Experts" Sent to Help Beat Japan. Kaneko, Anne, tr. LC 96-149683. (Japan Library). 224p. (C). 1995. text 42.00 (*1-873410-33-6*, Pub. by Curzon Pr Ltd) UH Pr.

Obaba, Al I. Adam Clayton Powell, Jr. (Great Nubian Quiz Bks.). (Illus.). 43p. (Orig.). (YA). 1989. pap. 3.95 (*0-916157-06-7*) African Islam Miss Pubns.

— Dr. Martin Luther King, Jr. (Great Nubian Quiz Bks.). (Illus.). 43p. (YA). 1989. pap. 5.95 (*0-916157-14-8*) African Islam Miss Pubns.

— Emperor Haile Selassie. (Great Nubian Quiz Bks.). (Illus.). 43p. (Orig.). (YA). 1989. pap. 3.95 (*0-916157-07-5*) African Islam Miss Pubns.

— Malcolm X Great Nubian Quiz. (Great Nubian Quiz Bks.). (Illus.). 43p. (YA). 1988. pap. 5.95 (*0-916157-16-4*) African Islam Miss Pubns.

— Marcus Mosiah Garvey, Jr. Great Nubian Quiz. (Great Nubian Quiz Bks.). (Illus.). 43p. (YA). 1989. pap. 5.95 (*0-916157-15-6*) African Islam Miss Pubns.

— The Papyrus Eber: The First Medical Book in the World. (Illus.). 167p. 1927. pap. text 22.00 (*0-916157-17-2*) African Islam Miss Pubns.

— Sojourner Truth Great Nubian Quiz. (Great Nubian Quiz Bks.). (Illus.). 43p. (YA). 1989. pap. 5.95 (*0-916157-08-3*) African Islam Miss Pubns.

Obaba, Al I., ed. Slave Insurrections "Selected Documents" (Illus.). 176p. 1990. pap. text 17.00 (*0-916157-26-1*) African Islam Miss Pubns.

O

An Asterisk (*) at the beginning of an entry indicates that the title is appearing for the first time.

Obaba, Al I., intro. An Anthology of the Public Utterances. 200p. 1990. pap. text 6.95 (*0-916157-85-7*) African Islam Miss Pubns.

Obaba, Al I., jt. auth. see Abdullah.

Obaba, Al I., ed. see African Islamic Mission Staff.

Obaba, Al I., ed. see Bode, E. A.

Obaba, Al I., ed. see Budge, E. A. Wallis.

Obaba, Al I., ed. see Churchward, Albert.

Obaba, Al I., ed. see Deedat, Ahmed.

Obaba, Al I., ed. see Douglass, Frederick.

Obaba, Al I., ed. see Dudley, Dean.

Obaba, Al I., ed. see Foote, G. W. & Wheeler, J. M.

Obaba, Al I., ed. see Houston, Drusilla D.

Obaba, Al I., ed. see Idowu, E. Bqlaji.

Obaba, Al I., ed. see James, George G.

Obaba, Al I., ed. see Lane-Poole, Stanley.

Obaba, Al I., ed. see Massey, Gerald.

Obaba, Al I., ed. see Morgans, William.

Obaba, Al I., ed. see Mufassir, Sulayman.

Obaba, Al I., ed. see Osei, G. K.

Obaba, Al I., ed. see Owaida, Mohammad T.

Obaba, Al I., ed. see Perry, Rufus L.

Obaba, Al I., ed. see Petrie, W. M.

Obaba, Al I., ed. see Sakr, Ahmad.

Obaba, Al I., ed. see Shorter, Alan W.

Obaba, Al I., ed. see Smith, G. Elliot.

Obaba, Al I., ed. see Volney, C. F.

Obaba, Al I., ed. see Westbrook, Henry S.

Obaba, Al I., ed. see Winchell, Alexander.

Obade, Claire C. Patient Care Decision-Making: A Legal Guide for Providers. annuals rev. ed. LC 91-22470. (Health Law Ser.). 1991. ring bd. 125.00 (*0-87632-819-2*) West Group.

Obadele, Imari A. & Henry, Laurance G. America, the Nation-State: The Politics of the United States from a State-Building Perspective. LC 97-45191. 1998. write for info. (*0-910758-40-9*); pap. write for info. (*0-910758-37-9*) Malcolm Pubns.

***Obadele-Starks, Ernest.** Black Unionism in the Industrial South. LC 99-34233. 2000. 29.95 (*0-89096-912-4*) Tex A&M Univ Pr.

Obagi, Z. E. Obagi Skin Health Restoration & Rejuvenation. (Illus.). 250p. 1998. 135.00 (*0-387-98469-0*) Spr-Verlag.

***Obaidat, Mohammad S., ed.** 1998 Summer Computer Simulation Conference. 696p. 1998. 90.00 (*1-56555-149-4*) Soc Computer Sim.

— 1998 Symposium on the Performance Evaluation of Computer & Telecommunication Systems. 352p. 1998. 50.00 (*1-56555-150-8*) Soc Computer Sim.

***Obaidat, Mohammad S., et al, eds.** 1999 Summer Computer Simulation Conference. 658p. 1999. 180.00 (*1-56555-173-7*) Soc Computer Sim.

Obaidat, Mohammad S. & Illgen, John, eds. Proceedings of the 1997 Summer Computer Simulation Conference Held in Arlington, Virginia July, 1997. 957p. 1998. 180.00 (*1-56555-123-0*, SCSC-97) Soc Computer Sim.

***Obaidat, Mohammad S. & Marsan, Marco Ajmone, eds.** 1999 Symposium on the Performance Evaluation of Computer & Telecommunication Systems. 414p. 1999. pap. 100.00 (*1-56555-174-5*) Soc Computer Sim.

Obal, Philip. What to Look for in Warehouse Management Systems Software. LC 98-96923. 87 p. 1998. 195.00 (*0-9669345-0-4*) Indust Data.

***O'Balance, Edgar.** Sudan Civil War & Terrorism 1956-99. 2000. text 59.95 (*0-312-23360-4*) St Martin.

Obaldia, J., jt. auth. see Obaldia, M.

***Obaldia, M. & Obaldia, J.** Como Coser Libros. (SPA.). 36p. 1999. write for info. (*92-806-3498-4*) U N I C E.

Oballa, Michael C. & Shih, Stuart S., eds. Catalytic Hydroprocessing of Petroleum & Distillates: Proceedings of the AIChE Spring National Meeting, Houston, Texas, 1993. LC 94-12079. (Chemical Industries Ser.: Vol. 58). (Illus.). 480p. 1994. text 190.00 (*0-8247-9255-6*) Dekker.

Oballa, Michael C., jt. ed. see Shis, Stuart S.

O'Ballance, Edgar. Afghan Wars, 1839-1992: What Britain Gave up & the Soviet Union Lost. (Illus.). 260p. 1993. 30.00 (*0-08-040722-6*, Pub. by Brasseys) Brasseys.

— Civil War Lebanon, 1975-92. LC 98-17681. 1998. text 59.95 (*0-312-21593-2*) St Martin.

***O'Ballance, Edgar.** The Congo-Zaire Experience, 1960-98. LC 99-33523. 2000. text 65.00 (*0-312-22795-7*) St Martin.

O'Ballance, Edgar. The Cyanide War: Tamil Insurrection in Sri Lanka 1973-1988. (Illus.). 139p. 1989. 31.95 (*0-08-036695-3*, 3004, Pub. by Brasseys) Brasseys.

— The Gulf War 1980-1987. 240p. 1987. 28.01 (*0-317-66337-2*, Pergamon Pr) Elsevier.

— Islamic Fundamentalist Terrorism, 1979-95: The Iranian Connection. LC 96-12962. 228p. (C). 1996. text 45.00 (*0-8147-6191-7*) NYU Pr.

— Korea, 1950 to 1953. LC 85-14787. 172p. (C). 1985. reprint ed. lib. bdg. 15.00 (*0-89874-885-2*) Krieger.

— No Victor, No Vanquished: The Arab-Israeli War, 1973. LC 76-58756. 384p. 1997. pap. 16.95 (*0-89141-615-3*) Presidio Pr.

— Palestinian Intifada. LC 97-38060. 1998. text 59.95 (*0-312-21172-4*) St Martin.

— Wars in the Caucasus, 1990-1995. LC 96-42273. 255p. 1997. text 45.00 (*0-8147-6192-5*) NYU Pr.

Obama, Barack. Dreams from My Father. 1997. pap. 15.00 (*0-8129-2771-0*, Times Bks) Crown Pub Group.

— Dreams from My Father: A Story of Race & Inheritance. Baker, Deborah, ed. 416p. 1996. reprint ed. pap. 15.00 (*1-56836-162-9*, Kodansha Globe) Kodansha.

O'Banion, John D. Reorienting Rhetoric: The Dialectic of List & Story. 312p. 1991. 40.00 (*0-271-00775-3*) Pa St U Pr.

O'Banion, O. Alpine's. large type ed. (Illus.). 232p. 2000. write for info. (*0-9637174-2-1*) Two O Bks.

— Means to the End. large type ed. 297p. (C). 1996. reprint ed. write for info. (*0-9637174-1-3*) Two O Bks.

— No Longer Alone. large type unabridged ed. 2000. write for info. (*0-9637174-0-5*) Two O Bks.

O'Banion, Terry. Innovation in the Community College. (ACE-Oryx Series on Higher Education). (Illus.). 320p. 1989. 27.95 (*0-02-897291-0*) Oryx Pr.

— A Learning College for the 21st Century. LC 97-8299. (Ace/Oryx Series on Higher Education). 264p. (C). 1997. pap. 27.50 (*1-57356-113-4*) Oryx Pr.

— Teaching & Learning in the Community College. LC 94-224674. (Illus.). 335p. reprint ed. pap. 103.90 (*0-608-08038-1*, 206900300002) Bks Demand.

O'Bannon, Allen. Allen & Mike's Really Cool Backcountry Ski Book: Traveling & Camping Skills for a Winter. (Illus.). 114p. (Orig.). 1996. pap. 12.95 (*1-57540-076-6*) Falcon Pub Inc.

***O'Bannon, Allen & Clelland, Mike.** Allen & Mike's Really Cool Telemark Tips. (Illus.). 112p. 1999. pap. 12.95 (*1-56044-851-2*) Falcon Pub Inc.

***O'Bannon, Barbara K.** Fisheries of the United States, 1997. 174p. 1998. per. 16.00 (*0-16-060919-4*) USGPO.

O'Bannon, Barbara K., ed. Fisheries of the United States, 1996. 1997. per. 16.00 (*0-16-054527-7*) USGPO.

O'Bannon, George W. From Desert & Oasis: Arts of the People of Central Asia. LC 97-44793. (Illus.). 114p. 1998. pap. 30.00 (*0-915977-34-6*) Georgia Museum of Art.

— Oriental Rugs: A Bibliography. LC 94-11116. 757p. 1994. 83.50 (*0-8108-2899-5*) Scarecrow.

***O'Bannon, George W. & Newhall, Amy W.** Tribal & Village Rugs from Arizona Collections. LC 98-74018. (Illus.). 116p. 1998. pap. 50.00 (*0-9653421-1-5*) G W OBannon.

O'Banyon, Constance. El Canto del Ruisenor. Kerrigan, Antonia, tr. (SPA.). 362p. 1998. pap. 6.95 (*84-01-50874-6*) Lectorum Pubns.

— Ecstasy's Promise. 1982. mass mkt. 3.50 (*0-89083-978-6*, Zebra Kensgtn) Kensgtn Pub Corp.

— Enchanted Ecstasy. 496p. 1984. mass mkt. 3.75 (*0-8217-1386-8*, Zebra Kensgtn) Kensgtn Pub Corp.

— Moontide Embrace. 1987. mass mkt. 3.95 (*0-8217-2182-8*, Zebra Kensgtn) Kensgtn Pub Corp.

— Rebel Temptress. (Orig.). 1983. mass mkt. 3.50 (*0-8217-1215-2*, Zebra Kensgtn) Kensgtn Pub Corp.

***O'Banyon, Constance.** San Antonio Rose. 1. 400p. 1999. mass mkt. 5.99 (*0-8439-4563-X*, Pub. by Dorchester Pub Co) CMG.

O'Banyon, Constance. Savage Autumn. 1988. mass mkt. 3.95 (*0-8217-1938-6*, Zebra Kensgtn) Kensgtn Pub Corp.

— Savage Autumn. 1990. pap. 4.50 (*0-8217-3188-2*) NAL.

— Savage Desire. 1983. mass mkt. 3.50 (*0-8217-1120-2*, Zebra Kensgtn) Kensgtn Pub Corp.

— Savage Splendor. 1983. mass mkt. 3.50 (*0-8217-1292-6*, Zebra Kensgtn) Kensgtn Pub Corp.

— Savage Spring. 1988. mass mkt. 3.95 (*0-8217-1715-4*, Zebra Kensgtn) Kensgtn Pub Corp.

— Savage Summer. 448p. 1986. mass mkt. 3.95 (*0-8217-1922-X*, Zebra Kensgtn) Kensgtn Pub Corp.

— Savage Winter. 1988. mass mkt. 3.95 (*0-8217-2372-3*, Zebra Kensgtn) Kensgtn Pub Corp.

— September Moon. 1986. mass mkt. 3.95 (*0-8217-1838-X*, Zebra Kensgtn) Kensgtn Pub Corp.

— Texas Proud. 400p. 1999. mass mkt. 5.99 (*0-8439-4492-7*) Dorchester Pub Co.

***O'Banyon, Constance.** Tykota's Woman. 400p. 2000. pap. 5.99 (*0-8439-4715-2*, Leisure Bks) Dorchester Pub Co.

O'Banyon, Constance. Velvet Chains. 1985. mass mkt. 3.95 (*0-8217-1640-9*, Zebra Kensgtn) Kensgtn Pub Corp.

***O'Banyon, Constance, et al.** Five Gold Rings. 368p. 1999. mass mkt. 5.50 (*0-8439-4612-1*, Leisure Bks) Dorchester Pub Co.

O'Baoill, Manus. Ceolta Gael 2. 80p. pap. 8.95 (*0-85342-738-0*) Dufour.

Obar, Robert A., jt. auth. see Dyer, Betsey D.

Obara, Y., jt. ed. see Sugawara, K.

Obarakpor, Anita M., jt. auth. see Hodgkinson, Harold L.

O'Barr, J. Pink Dust: Comics, 1997: 39th Parallel. LC 98-14186. 1998. 3.50 (*0-87816-585-1*) Kitchen Sink.

***O'Barr, J. & Kramer, Ed, eds.** The Crow: Shattered Lives & Broken Dreams. 384p. 1999. pap. 14.00 (*0-345-41712-7*, Del Rey) Ballantine Pub Grp.

O'Barr, J. & Kramer, Edward E., eds. The Crow Broken Lives & Shattered Dreams. 1998. 200.00 (*1-880418-45-2*) D M Grant.

O'Barr, J., et al. The Crow: Dead Time Collection. Couch, N. C. Christopher, ed. (Illus.). 96p. 1997. pap. 10.95 (*0-87816-547-9*) Kitchen Sink.

O'Barr, James. The Crow. 7th rev. ed. LC 97-124522. (Illus.). 240p. 1996. pap. 15.95 (*0-87816-221-6*) Kitchen Sink.

— Crow: The Author's Edition Hardcover. 1998. 34.95 (*0-87816-634-3*) Kitchen Sink.

O'Barr, James, jt. ed. see Bergin, John.

O'Barr, Jean F. Feminism in Action: Building Institutions & Community Through Women's Studies. LC 93-33313. xiv, 302p. 1994. pap. 19.95 (*0-8078-4439-X*) U of NC Pr.

— Linguistic Evidence: Language, Power & Strategy in the Courtroom. (Illus.). 192p. 1995. reprint ed. pap. text 29.95 (*0-12-523521-6*) Acad Pr.

O'Barr, Jean F., ed. Women & a New Academy: Gender & Cultural Contexts. LC 88-40441. 180p. reprint ed. pap. 55.80 (*0-608-20461-7*, 207171300002) Bks Demand.

O'Barr, Jean F., et al, eds. Ties That Bind: Essays on Mothering & Patriarchy. 312p. 1996. pap. 17.95 (*0-226-61546-4*); lib. bdg. 36.00 (*0-226-61545-6*) U Ch Pr.

O'Barr, Jean F., jt. ed. see Harding, Sandra.

O'Barr, Jean F., jt. ed. see Wyer, Mary.

O'Barr, William M. Culture & the Ad: Exploring Otherness in the World of Advertising. LC 93-44451. (Institutional Structures of Feeling Ser.). (C). 1994. pap. 25.00 (*0-8133-2197-2*, Pub. by Westview) HarpC.

O'Barr, William M. & Jean, F. Languages & Politics. (Contributions to the Sociology of Language Ser.: No. 10). 1977. text 56.95 (*90-279-7761-5*) Mouton.

O'Barr, William M., jt. auth. see Conley, John M.

O'Barry, Richard & Coulbourn, Keith. To Free a Dolphin. 304p. 23.95 (*1-58063-102-9*) Renaissance.

O'Barry, Richard, jt. auth. see Coulbourn, Keith.

Obasanjo, Olusegun. My Command. (African Writers Ser.). (Illus.). 178p. (C). 1981. reprint ed. pap. 9.95 (*0-435-90249-0*, 90249) Heinemann.

Obasanjo, Olusegun, ed. The Challenges of Agricultural Production & Food Security in Africa. 250p. 1992. 65.00 (*0-8448-1724-4*, Crane Russak) Taylor & Francis.

Obasanjo, Olusegun & D'Orville, Hans, eds. Challenges of Leadership in African Government. 200p. 1990. pap. 50.00 (*0-8448-1670-1*, Crane Russak) Taylor & Francis.

— The Leadership Challenge of Economic Reforms in Africa. 112p. 1991. 65.00 (*0-8448-1680-9*, Crane Russak) Taylor & Francis.

Obasanjo, Olusegun, ed. see De'Orville, Hans.

***Obasi, G. O. & Dowdeswell, E.** Climate Change, 1995: IPCC Second Assessment: a Report of the Intergovernmental Panel on Climate Change. (Illus.). 64p. (C). 1998. reprint ed. pap. text 30.00 (*0-7881-3923-1*) DIANE Pub.

Obasi, G. P., jt. auth. see Gringof, I. G.

Obasih, Kem M., et al, eds. Proceedings of the 1995 National Heat Transfer Conference: August 6-9, 1995, Portland, Oregon, Vol. 1. 108p. 1995. 72.00 (*0-7918-1712-1*, H00994) ASME.

Obasih, Kem M., jt. ed. see Eckels, P. W.

***Obata, Chiura.** Topaz Moon: Chiura Obata's Art of the Internment. Hill, Kimi Kodani, ed. LC 99-89212. (Illus.). 147p. 2000. pap. 19.95 (*1-890771-26-0*, Pub. by Heyday Bks) SPD-Small Pr Dist.

Obata, N. White Noise Calculus & Fock Space. (Lecture Notes in Mathematics Ser.: No. 1577). 183p. 1994. 35.95 (*0-387-57985-0*) Spr-Verlag.

Obata, Toshishiro, tr. see Kuniyoshi, Ichiyusai, et al.

Obata, Toshishiro, tr. see Yamamoto, Kansuke.

Obatala, El. Creative Ritual: Combining Yoruba, Santeria & Western Magic Traditions. 2nd ed. LC 96-16319. Orig. Title: Creative Ritual: A Complete Instruction Manual for Creating Magic Rituals (By Thomas Healki). (Illus.). 80p. 1996. reprint ed. pap. 6.95 (*0-87728-898-4*) Weiser.

***Obay, Lamia.** Financial Innovation in the Banking Industry: The Case of Asset Securitization. rev. ed. LC 99-31494. (Financial Sector of the American Economy Ser.). 216p. 1999. 53.00 (*0-8153-3423-0*) Garland.

Obayash, Hiroshi, ed. Death & Afterlife: Perspectives of World Religion. LC 91-3876. (Contributions to the Study of Religion Ser.: No. 33). 240p. 1991. pap. 18.95 (*0-275-94104-3*, B4104, Greenwood Pr) Greenwood.

— Death & Afterlife: Perspectives of World Religion, 33. LC 91-3876. (Contributions to the Study of Religion Ser.: No. 33). 240p. 1991. 55.00 (*0-313-27906-3*, ODE, Greenwood Pr) Greenwood.

Obayashi, Alan W. & Gorgan, Joseph M. Management of Industrial Pollutants by Anaerobic Processes. Patterson, James M., ed. LC 84-23378. (Industrial Waste Management Ser.). (Illus.). 220p. 1984. 119.00 (*0-87371-001-0*, CRC Reprint) Franklin.

Obayashi, Y. Dried BCG Vaccine. (Monographs: No. 28). (ENG & FRE.). 220p. 1955. pap. text 18.00 (*92-4-140028-5*, 1140028) World Health.

Obazee, Philip O. Interest Rate Derivatives: Analysis, Valuation, & Market Applications. 1996. 65.00 (*1-55738-905-5*, Irwn Prfssnl) McGraw-Hill Prof.

Obbagy, William G., jt. auth. see Wood, Edward D., Jr.

Obbard. La Madre: Life & Spirituality. 1996. pap. text 11.95 (*0-8189-9468-1*) Alba.

Obbard, Elizabeth R. Introducing Julian - Woman of Norwich. LC 95-34626. 144p. 1995. pap. 9.95 (*1-56548-047-3*) New City.

— La Madre: The Life & Spirituality of Teresa of Avila. 160p. 1996. pap. 39.95 (*0-85439-468-0*, Pub. by St Paul Pubns) St Mut.

— Poverty: My Riches: A Life of St. Elizabeth of Hungary. 106p. 1997. pap. 16.95 (*1-901157-80-6*) St Austin.

— A Retreat with Therese of Lisieux: Loving Our Way into Holiness. 136p. (Orig.). 1996. pap. 8.95 (*0-86716-242-2*, B2422) St Anthony Mess Pr.

***Obbard, Elizabeth R.** Year with Mary: Prayers & Readings for the Christian Year. 2000. pap. text 12.95 (*1-85311-240-2*) Canterbury Press Norwich.

Obbard, Elizabeth R., ed. see Burrows, Ruth.

O'Bbard, Elizabeth Ruth. The History & Spirituality of Walsingham. (Illus.). 96p. 1996. pap. 8.95 (*1-85311-118-X*, 6347, Pub. by Canterbury Press Norwich) Morehouse Pub.

***O'Bbard, Elizabeth Ruth.** Land of Carmel. 1999. pap. 12.95 (*0-85244-504-0*) Gracewing.

O'Bbard, Elizabeth Ruth. See How I Love You: Meditating on the Way of the Cross with Julian of Norwich. (Illus.). 103p. 1996. pap. 8.95 (*1-85311-141-4*, 857, Pub. by Canterbury Press Norwich) Morehouse Pub.

— A Walshingham Prayer Book: A Meditative Companion & Guide. (Illus.). 128p. 1997. pap. 11.95 (*1-85311-170-8*, 1978, Pub. by Canterbury Press Norwich) Morehouse Pub.

***O'Bbard, Elizabeth Ruth.** A Year with Mary: Prayers & Readings for Marian Feasts & Festivals. 216p. 1999. pap. 14.95 (*0-89622-992-0*) Twenty-Third.

Obbard, John. Early American Furniture a Practical Guide for Collectors. 384p. 1999. pap. text 12.95 (*1-57432-141-2*) Collector Bks.

Obbink, Dirk, ed. Philodemus & Poetry: Poetic Theory & Practice in Lucretius, Philodemus & Horace. 336p. 1995. text 60.00 (*0-19-508815-8*) OUP.

Obbink, Dirk, jt. ed. see Faraone, Christopher A.

Obbink, Dirk, ed. & tr. see Philodemus.

Obbink, Dirk, tr. see Gigante, Marcello.

Obdam, Jack. The Rape of Britannia. 92p. (C). 1989. text 45.00 (*1-872795-80-3*, Pub. by Pentland Pr) St Mut.

Obdidko, V. N., jt. ed. see Stepanov, V. E.

Obdlouk Darovic, Gloria & Franklin, Cory M. Handbook of Hemodynamic Monitoring. Carter, Robin, ed. LC 99-11311. (Illus.). 445p. 1999. pap. text 24.00 (*0-7216-7370-8*, W B Saunders Co) Harcrt Hlth Sci Grp.

Obe, Arnold F. International Air Traffic Control: Management of the World's Airspace. 2nd ed. (Illus.). 275p. 1985. text 47.00 (*0-08-031312-4*, Pergamon Pr) Elsevier.

Obe, Dorothy M. Hilarious Happenings. 93p. (C). 1989. text 45.00 (*0-7855-6971-5*, Pub. by Pentland Pr) St Mut.

— Laughter in Khaki. 138p. (C). 1989. text 50.00 (*0-946270-41-4*, Pub. by Pentland Pr) St Mut.

— Reflections. 189p. (C). 1989. text 50.00 (*0-946270-55-4*, Pub. by Pentland Pr) St Mut.

— Why Forget. 122p. (C). 1989. text 60.00 (*0-946270-54-6*, Pub. by Pentland Pr) St Mut.

Obe, Dorothy M., ed. We Simply Had to Laugh. 85p. (C). 1989. text 39.00 (*1-872795-23-4*, Pub. by Pentland Pr) St Mut.

Obe, G., ed. Advances in Mutagenesis Research, Vol. 2. (Illus.). 384p. 1991. 158.95 (*0-387-52428-2*) Spr-Verlag.

Obe, G., et al, eds. Advances in Mutagenesis Research, Vol. 3. (Illus.). ix, 197p. 1991. 149.00 (*0-387-53359-1*) Spr-Verlag.

— Advances in Mutagenesis Research, Vol. 4. (Illus.). x, 241p. 1993. 202.95 (*0-387-55411-4*) Spr-Verlag.

— Advances in Mutagenesis Research, Vol. 5. (Illus.). 240p. 1994. 219.95 (*0-387-56641-4*) Spr-Verlag.

Obe, G. & Basler, A., eds. Cytogenetics. (Illus.). 415p. 1987. 150.00 (*0-387-18017-6*) Spr-Verlag.

Obe, G. & Natarajan, A. T., eds. Chromosomal Aberrations: Basic & Applied Aspects. (Illus.). xi, 319p. 1990. 158.95 (*0-387-52540-8*) Spr-Verlag.

— Chromosomal Alterations: Origin & Significance. LC 94-8275. 1994. 202.95 (*0-387-57812-9*) Spr-Verlag.

Obe, G., jt. ed. see Sobti, R. C.

***Obe, Julian Evans.** The Forests Handbook. LC 00-21516. 2000. write for info. (*0-632-04823-9*) Blackwell Sci.

Obebe, Bolarinde, et al. Adjustment of Caribbean Immigrants in New York: Educational Dimensions, No. 2. Clarke, Velta, ed. 70p. (Orig.). Date not set. pap. write for info. (*1-878433-02-4*) Caribbean Diaspora Pr.

Obed, Ellen B. A Letter from the Snow. (Illus.). 36p. (J). (gr. 1-4). 1999. pap. 10.00 (*0-9618592-8-8*) Maine Writers.

Obedin, Harry. Peter Penguin & the Polar Sea. LC 88-63171. (Illus.). 32p. (Orig.). (J). (ps-4). 1989. pap. 4.95 (*0-943990-54-8*) Parenting Pr.

Obee, Bruce. The Coastal Birder's Journal. Jones, Elaine, ed. (Illus.). 107p. 1999. reprint ed. pap. text 13.00 (*0-7881-6231-4*) DIANE Pub.

— Guardians of the Whales: The Quest to Study Whales in the Wild. LC 92-15419. (Illus.). 188p. 1992. 34.95 (*0-88240-428-8*, Alaska NW Bks) Gr Arts Ctr Pub.

— The Gulf Islands Explorer: The Outdoor Guide. rev. ed. (Illus.). 208p. 1981. pap. 14.95 (*0-88826-089-X*) Gr Arts Ctr Pub.

— The Pacific Rim Explorer: The Outdoor Guide. (Illus.). 200p. 1994. pap. 14.95 (*0-920620-77-9*) Whitecap Bks.

Obee, Ruth. Es'kia Mphahlele: Themes of Alienation & African Humanism. LC 98-23472. 288p. 1999. pap. text 19.95 (*0-8214-1249-3*) Ohio U Pr.

— Es'kia Mphahlele: Themes of Alientation & African Humanism. LC 98-23472. (Illus.). 243p. 1999. 39.95 (*0-8214-1248-5*) Ohio U Pr.

***Obeidi, Amal.** Political Culture in Libya. 320p. 2000. 80.00 (*0-7007-1229-1*, Pub. by Curzon Pr Ltd) Paul & Co Pubs.

O'Beirne. Reading Nathalie Sarraute: Dialogue & Distance. (Oxford Modern Languages & Literature Monographs). 268p. 1999. text 65.00 (*0-19-815985-4*) OUP.

O'Beirne, H. F. Leaders & Leading Men of the Indian Territory. Goss, Joe R. & Sperry, Phillip A., eds. (Illus.). 326p. 1994. reprint ed. 49.95 (*1-56869-054-1*) Oldbuck Pr.

O'Beirne, Kathleen P. Pass It On! How to Thrive in the Military Lifestyle. LC 91-90191. (Illus.). 528p. (Orig.). 1991. pap. 14.95 (*1-879979-00-4*) Lifescape Enter.

— Pass It On! No. II: Living & Leaving the Military Lifestyle. LC 91-90191. (Illus.). 400p. (Orig.). 1995. pap. 19.95 (*1-879979-01-2*) Lifescape Enter.

O'Beirne, Martin. Family Tree: Ancestral Record. (Illus.). 30p. (Orig.). 1987. pap. 3.95 (*0-948378-01-8*, Pub. by Heraldic Art) Irish Bks Media.

O'Beirne, Patrick. Managing the Euro in Information Systems: Strategies for Successful Changeover. LC 99-28921. (Addison-Wesley Information Technology Ser.). (Illus.). 368p. (C). 1999. pap. 39.95 incl. cd-rom (*0-201-60482-5*) Addison-Wesley.

O'Beirne, T. H., ed. see Schuh, Fred.

O'Beirne, Thomas. Candid-Impartial Narrative of the Transactions of the Fleet Under the Command of Lord Howe. LC 75-77108. (Eyewitness Accounts of the American Revolution Ser.). 1969. reprint ed. 11.95 (*0-405-01170-9*) Ayer.

Obejas, Achy. Memory Mambo. 200p. (Orig.). 1996. pap. 12.95 (*1-57344-017-5*) Cleis Pr.

— We Came All the Way from Cuba So You Could Dress Like This? Stories. LC 94-18194. 160p. (Orig.). 1994. pap. 10.95 (*0-939416-93-X*) Cleis Pr.

Obel, Borge, jt. auth. see Burton, Richard M.

Obel, Borge, jt. ed. see Burton, Richard M.

Obeld, Abu B. El, see El Obeld, Abu B.

O

Obelkevich, James, ed. Religion & the People, 800-1700. LC 78-7847. (Illus.). 351p. reprint ed. pap. 108.90 (*0-8357-3889-2*, 20366210004) Bks Demand.

Obelkevich, James & Catterall, Peter, eds. Understanding Post-War British Society. LC 94-7263. 224p. (C). 1994. pap. 22.99 (*0-415-10940-X*, B4690) Routledge.

Obelkevich, Jim, et al. Disciplines of Faith. 512p. 1987. 59.95 (*0-7102-0750-6*, Routledge Thoemms); pap. 25.00 (*0-7102-0993-2*, Routledge Thoemms) Routledge.

Oben, Freda M. Edith Stein: Scholar-Feminist-Saint. LC 87-24178. 80p. 1988. pap. 5.95 (*0-8189-0523-9*) Alba.

***Oben, Freda M.** The Life & Thought Of St. Edith Stein. LC 00-44179. 2000. write for info. (*0-8189-0846-7*) Alba.

Obenauer, Klaus. Summa Actualitas: Zum Verhaltnis von Einheit und Verschiedenheit in der Dreieinigkeitslehre des Heiligen Bonaventura. (Europaische Hochschulschriften Ser.: Reihe 23, Bd. 559). (GER.). 494p. 1996. 76.95 (*3-631-49031-3*) P Lang Pubng.

Obenaus, W. Handbook of Business English. (ENG & GER.). 380p. 1990. lib. bdg. 95.00 (*0-8288-3887-9*, F107670) Fr & Eur.

Obeng, Eddie. All Change: Project Manager's Secret Handbook. (Financial Times Management Ser.). 256p. 1996. pap. 47.50 (*0-273-62221-8*, Pub. by Pitman Pub) Trans-Atl Phila.

— New Rules For the New World: Cautionary Tales For the New World Manager. 1998. 24.65 (*1-900961-15-6*) Capstone Pub NH.

— Solving Unique Problems: Implementing Strategy Through Projects. LC 95-114792. (Financial Times Management Ser.). 240p. 1996. 25.00 (*0-273-60265-9*) F T P-H.

Obeng, J. Pashington. Asante Catholicism: Religious & Cultural Reproduction among the Akan of Ghana. LC 96-20673. (Studies on Religion in Africa). xvi, 244p. 1996. 97.00 (*90-04-10631-6*) Brill Academic Pubs.

Obeng, Kofi, et al. Modeling Economic Inefficiency Caused by Public Transit Subsidies. LC 96-40535. 216p. 1997. 65.00 (*0-275-95851-5*, Praeger Pubs) Greenwood.

Obenhaus, Victor, ed. Religion & Ethical Issues: Position Guides for Decision Making. LC 91-73417. 262p. (Orig.). 1991. pap. 12.95 (*0-913552-47-X*) Exploration Pr.

Obenhouse, Susan, jt. auth. see Dunne, Patrick M.

Obenski, Kenneth S. & Hill, Paul F. Motorcycle Accident Reconstruction & Litigation. 2nd ed. LC 96-32923. 1133p. 1997. 110.00 (*0-913875-97-X*, 5031-N) Lawyers & Judges.

Obenski, Kenneth S., jt. auth. see Brown, John F.

***Obenzinger, Hilton.** American Palestine: Melville, Twain & the Holy Land Mania. LC 99-20728. 320p. 1999. 55.00 (*0-691-00728-4*, Pub. by Princeton U Pr) Cal Prin Full Svc.

— American Palestine: Melville, Twain & the Holy Land Mania. LC 99-20728. 320p. 1999. pap. 18.95 (*0-691-00973-2*, Pub. by Princeton U Pr) Cal Prin Full Svc.

Obenzinger, Hilton. Cannibal Eliot & the Lost Histories of San Francisco. LC 93-12722. 256p. (Orig.). 1993. pap. 12.95 (*1-56279-047-1*) Mercury Hse Inc.

— New York on Fire. LC 89-10224. (Illus.). 144p. (Orig.). 1989. 24.95 (*0-941104-40-0*); pap. 12.95 (*0-941104-39-7*) Real Comet.

Ober. Business Communication, 2 vols. (C). Date not set. pap., teacher ed., suppl. ed. 11.96 (*0-395-72146-6*) HM.

— Business Communication. (C). 1991. pap. text, teacher ed. 3.16 (*0-395-59235-6*) HM.

— Business Communication, 2 vols. 2nd ed. (C). 1994. pap. text, student ed. 19.96 (*0-395-71165-7*) HM.

— Business Communication Video Guide, 2 vols. (C). Date not set. pap. 11.96 (*0-395-72519-4*) HM.

— Business Communications, 3 vols. (C). Date not set. pap. 11.96 (*0-395-89821-8*) HM.

Ober, jt. auth. see Caller.

Ober, jt. auth. see Stuart.

Ober, C. K., jt. ed. see Weiss, R. A.

Ober, Carol. How Music Came to the World. LC 93-11330. 32p. (J). 1994. 17.00 (*0-395-67523-5*) HM.

Ober, Doris, jt. auth. see Miller, Sukie.

Ober, Doris, jt. ed. see Kirschman, Richard.

Ober, Gary J. Operating Techniques for the Tractor-Loader-Backhoe. (Illus.). 175p. 1983. pap. 24.95 (*0-911785-00-0*) Equip Trning Res.

Ober, J. Fortress Attica: Defense of the Athenian Land Frontier, 404-322 B.C. 1985. pap. 35.00 (*90-04-07243-8*, MNS, 84) Brill Academic Pubs.

Ober, J. Hambleton. Writing: Man's Great Invention. (Illus.). 1965. 19.95 (*0-8392-1139-2*) Astor-Honor.

Ober, Josiah. The Athenian Revolution: Essays on Ancient Greek Democracy & Political Theory. LC 96-19341. 224p. 1997. text 29.95 (*0-691-01095-1*, Pub. by Princeton U Pr) Cal Prin Full Svc.

***Ober, Josiah.** The Athenian Revolution: Essays on Ancient Greek Democracy & Political Theory. 1999. pap. 15.95 (*0-691-00190-1*, Pub. by Princeton U Pr) Cal Prin Full Svc.

Ober, Josiah. Mass & Elite in Democratic Athens: Rhetoric, Ideology, & the Power of the People. 408p. 1989. pap. text 18.95 (*0-691-02864-8*, Pub. by Princeton U Pr) Cal Prin Full Svc.

— Political Dissent in Democratic Athens: Intellectual Critics of Popular Rule. LC 98-7110. (Martin Classical Lectures). 388p. 1998. text 35.00 (*0-691-00122-7*, Pub. by Princeton U Pr) Cal Prin Full Svc.

Ober, Josiah & Hedrick, Charles W., eds. The Birth of Democracy. (Illus.). 179p. 1993. pap. 25.00 (*0-87661-950-2*) Am Sch Athens.

— Demokratia: A Conversation on Democracies, Ancient & Modern. LC 96-33717. 496p. 1996. text 65.00 (*0-691-01109-5*, Pub. by Princeton U Pr); pap. text 24.95 (*0-691-01108-7*, Pub. by Princeton U Pr) Cal Prin Full Svc.

Ober, K. Patrick, ed. Endocrinology of Critical Disease. LC 97-198438. (Contemporary Endocrinology Ser.: Vol. 5). (Illus.). 336p. 1997. 125.00 (*0-89603-422-4*) Humana.

Ober, Kenneth, tr. see Goldschmidt, Meir.

Ober, Kenneth H. Bibliography of Modern Icelandic Literature in Translation: Supplement 1971-1980. LC 89-46232. (Islandica Ser.: No. 47). 325p. 1990. text 49.95 (*0-8014-2475-5*) Cornell U Pr.

Ober, Kenneth H., jt. tr. see Mitchell, P. M.

Ober, Norman, ed. see McQueen-Williams, Morvyth & Apisson, Barbara.

Ober, Richard, jt. auth. see Dobbs, David.

Ober, Scot. Contemporary Business Communication, 2 vols. 2nd ed. 704p. (C). 1994. pap. text 68.76 (*0-395-70745-5*) HM.

— Contemporary Business Communication, 2 vols. 2nd ed. (C). 1995. text, teacher ed. 11.96 incl. trans. (*0-395-71264-5*) HM.

— Gregg College Document Processing for Windows. 8th ed. LC 97-8941. 1997. write for info. (*0-02-803223-3*) Glencoe.

— Gregg College Document Processing for Windows: Lessons 61-120. 8th ed. LC 96-34232. 1996. write for info. (*0-02-803162-8*) Glencoe.

— Gregg College Keyboarding & Document Processing for Windows 95 & Word 7: Take-Home Package. 1998. pap. 49.95 (*0-02-804215-8*) Glencoe.

Ober, Scot, et al. College Keyboarding & Document Processing for Windows, Lessons 1-60. 8th ed. LC 95-48921. 1996. write for info. (*0-02-803126-1*) Glencoe.

— Gregg College Document Processing. 7th ed. LC 92-24928. 1992. write for info. (*0-02-801729-3*) Glencoe.

— Gregg College Document Processing for Microcomputers: Advanced Course. 7th ed. LC 93-16178. (Gregg College Typing Ser.: Series 6). 1993. write for info. (*0-02-801754-4*) Glencoe.

— Gregg College Document Processing for Microcomputers: Intensive Course. 7th ed. LC 92-46513. (Gregg College Typing Ser.). 1993. write for info. (*0-02-801736-6*) Glencoe.

— Gregg College Document Processing for Microcomputers: Intermediate Course. 7th ed. LC 92-30679. 1992. write for info. (*0-02-801753-6*) Glencoe.

— Gregg College Electronic Document Processing: Advanced Course. 7th ed. LC 93-44424. (Gregg College Typing Ser.: Series Six). 1994. write for info. (*0-02-801719-6*) Glencoe.

— Gregg College Keyboarding & Document Processing for Microcomputers, Complete Course. 7th ed. LC 93-25886. (Gregg College Typing Ser.: Series Six). 1993. write for info. (*0-02-801737-4*) Glencoe.

— Gregg College Keyboarding & Electronic Document Processing: Intensive Course. 7th ed. LC 93-44426. (Gregg College Typing Ser.: Series Six). 1994. 32.45 (*0-02-801740-4*) Glencoe.

— Gregg College Typing: Series Six, Kit 1 Basic. 6th ed. 160p. 1988. boxed set 42.50 (*0-07-038393-6*) McGraw.

— Keyboarding: Adapted from Gregg College Keyboarding & Document Processing. 3rd ed. LC 93-8355. 1993. write for info. (*0-02-801747-1*) Glencoe.

Ober, Stuart. Everybody's Guide to Tax Shelters. 1982. pap. 17.95 (*0-8464-1280-2*) Beekman Pubs.

Ober, Stuart. Everything You Wanted to Know About Real Estate Investments. spiral bd. 24.95 (*0-8464-4993-5*) Beekman Pubs.

— How to Evaluate Investment Return. spiral bd. 24.95 (*0-8464-4995-1*) Beekman Pubs.

Ober, Stuart, ed. Tax Shelter Blue Book 1984. 1984. pap. 29.95 (*0-8464-4990-0*) Beekman Pubs.

Ober, Stuart & Richards, Susan. The Joy of Marriage. LC 95-94028. (Illus.). 70p. 1995. 9.95 (*0-8464-4341-4*) Beekman Pubs.

Ober, W. U., ed. Story of the Three Bears. LC 80-28325. 304p. 1981. 50.00 (*0-8201-1362-X*) Schol Facsimiles.

Ober, Warren, jt. auth. see Martin, Walter R.

Ober, Warren U., jt. auth. see Martin, W. R.

Ober, Warren U., ed. see James, Henry.

Ober, William B. Bottoms Up! A Pathologist's Essays on Medicine & the Humanities. 1988. pap. 8.95 (*0-685-44374-4*, Perennial) HarperTrade.

— Bottoms Up! A Pathologist's Essays on Medicine & the Humanities. LC 87-13125. (Illus.). 356p. 1987. 21.95 (*0-8093-1419-3*) S Ill U Pr.

Oberacker, R., jt. auth. see Thummler, F.

Oberai, Amarjit S., ed. Land Settlement Policies & Population Redistribution in Developing Countries: Achievements, Problems & Prospects. LC 87-15837. 409p. 1988. 59.95 (*0-275-92799-7*, C2799, Praeger Pubs) Greenwood.

Oberai, Amarjit S., et al. Determination & Consequences of Internal Migration in India: Studies in Bihar, Kerala & Uttar Pradesh. (Illus.). 168p. 1990. text 19.95 (*0-19-562516-1*) OUP.

Oberai, Amarjit S., jt. auth. see Singh, H. K.

Oberai, M. M., tr. see Fuentes, Albert.

Oberbeil, Klaus. Lose Weight with Apple Vinegar: The Easy Way to the Ideal Body. LC 99-168124.Tr. of Abnehmen mit Apfelessig. 136p. 1998. pap. 12.95 (*1-882330-45-5*) Magni Co.

— 10 Years Younger in 30 Days: 99 Secrets for Perfect Beauty, Health, Mind & Body. 256p. 1999. pap. 16.00 (*3-9802389-1-1*, Pub. by GenPr) BookMasters.

Oberc, Lawrence. Demons. 12p. 1996. pap. 3.00 (*1-57141-027-9*) Runaway Spoon.

Obercht, E., jt. ed. see Favini, A.

Oberdeck, Kathryn J. The Evangelist & the Impresario: Religion, Entertainment & Cultural Politics in America, 1884-1914. LC 98-46628. (New Studies in American Intellectual & Cultural History). 1999. 34.95 (*0-8018-6060-1*) Johns Hopkins.

Oberdieck, Bernard, tr. see Heuck, Sigrid.

Oberdiek, Hans. Tolerance: Between Forbearance & Acceptance. (Philosophy & the Global Context Ser.). 226p. 2000. 57.00 (*0-8476-8785-6*); pap. 23.95 (*0-8476-8788-0*) Rowman.

Oberdiek, Hans, jt. auth. see Tiles, Mary.

Oberdisse, K., ed. Diabetes Mellitus. (Handbuch der Inneren Medigin Ser.: Vol. 7/2). 1977. 392.00 (*0-387-07741-3*) Spr-Verlag.

Oberdorfer. 2 Koreas: A Contemporary History. 496p. 1999. 17.00 (*0-465-08792-2*, Pub. by Basic) HarpC.

Oberdorfer, Bernd. Geselligkeit und Realisierung von Sittlichkeit: Die Theorieentwicklung Friedrich Schleiermachers bis 1799. (Theologische Bibliothek Toepelmann Ser.: No. 69). (GER.). 586p. (C). 1995. lib. bdg. 191.75 (*3-11-014595-2*) De Gruyter.

Oberdorfer, Don. From the Cold War to a New Era: The United States & the Soviet Union, 1983-1991. LC 97-48386. (Illus.). 536p. 1998. pap. text 19.95 (*0-8018-5922-0*) Johns Hopkins.

— Princeton University: The First 250 Years. Miller, J. T., ed. LC 95-20342. (Illus.). 250p. 1995. text 69.50 (*0-691-01122-2*, Pub. by Princeton U Pr) Cal Prin Full Svc.

Oberdorfer, Don, jt. auth. see Palazchenko, Pavel.

Oberdorfer, E. Pflanzensoziologische Studien in Chile. (Illus.). 1960. 48.00 (*3-7682-0011-6*) Lubrecht & Cramer.

Oberer, Walter E., et al. Cases & Materials on Labor Law: Collective Bargaining in a Free Society. 4th ed. (American Casebook Ser.). 866p. (C). 1994. 57.50 (*0-314-03248-7*) West Pub.

— Labor Law: Collective Bargaining in a Free Society. 4th ed. (American Casebook Ser.). 80p. (C). 1995. pap. text, teacher ed. write for info. (*0-314-04826-X*) West Pub.

— Oberer, Hanslowe & Heinsz' Statutory Supplement to Labor Law. 4th ed. (American Casebook Ser.). 866p. (C). 1994. pap. text 22.50 (*0-314-03247-9*) West Pub.

Oberg, Alcestis R., jt. auth. see Sharp.

Oberg, Arthur. Anna's Song. Webber, Joan M. & Blessing, Richard, eds. LC 79-4847. 112p. 1980. 15.00 (*0-295-95681-X*) U of Wash Pr.

***Oberg, Barbara B., ed.** The Papers of Benjamin Franklin, Vol. 35. (Illus.). 832p. 1999. 80.00 (*0-300-07841-2*) Yale U Pr.

Oberg, Barbara B., ed. The Papers of Benjamin Franklin Vol. 32: March 1 Through June 30, 1780. LC 59-12697. (Illus.). 800p. 1997. 80.00 (*0-300-06617-1*) Yale U Pr.

— The Papers of Benjamin Franklin, July 1 Through November 15, 1780 Vol. 33. LC 59-12697. Vol. 33. (Illus.). 672p. 1997. 85.00 (*0-300-07040-3*) Yale U Pr.

Oberg, Barbara B., et al, eds. The Papers of Benjamin Franklin Vol. 34: November 16, 1780, Through April 30, 1781. (Illus.). 720p. 1998. 80.00 (*0-300-07413-1*) Yale U Pr.

Oberg, Barbara B., jt. ed. see Ben-Atar, Doron S.

Oberg, Barbara B., ed. see Franklin, Benjamin.

Oberg, Brent C. & Zapel, Theodore O. Forensics: The Winner's Guide to Speech Contests. LC 95-31868. 192p. (YA). (gr. 9 up). 1995. pap. 14.95 (*1-56608-015-0*, B179) Meriwether Pub.

— Speechcraft: An Introduction to Public Speaking. LC 94-21529. 168p. (YA). (gr. 7 up). 1994. pap. 14.95 (*1-56608-006-1*, B149) Meriwether Pub.

Oberg, Charles N., et al. America's Children: Triumph or Tragedy. LC 96-147980. 94p. 1994. pap. 22.50 (*0-87553-218-7*, 071) Am Pub Health.

Oberg, Charlotte H. A Pagan Prophet, William Morris. LC 77-4730. 199p. reprint ed. pap. 61.70 (*0-8357-3281-9*, 203950400013) Bks Demand.

Oberg, Delroy, compiled by. Daily Readings with a Modern Mystic: Selections from the Writings of Evelyn Underhill. LC 93-60276. 192p. (Orig.). 1993. pap. 9.95 (*0-89622-566-6*) Twenty-Third.

Oberg, Dianne & Steward, Kaye, eds. Connections: School Library Associations & Contact People. 96p. 1994. pap. 15.00 (*1-890861-17-0*) IASL.

Oberg, Eilhart Von, see Von Oberg, Eilhart.

***Oberg, Eric.** Moving Toward Harmony. Thomas, Lesley, ed. (Illus.). 80p. 2000. pap. 14.95 (*0-9678842-0-9*) Far East Pr.

Oberg, Erik. Machinery's Handbook. 1998. pap. 89.95 (*0-8311-2600-0*) Industrial Products Corp.

***Oberg, Erik.** Machinery's Handbook: Toolbox Edition. 25th ed. (Illus.). 1998. 159.95 (*0-8311-2602-7*) Indus Pr.

Oberg, Erik. Machinery's Handbook, Toolbox Edition. 1998. 149.95 (*0-8311-2601-9*) Indus Pr.

Oberg, Erik, et al. Machinery's Handbook. 25th ed. 2545p. 1996. 94.00 (*0-8311-2575-6*) ASM.

Oberg, Erik, et al. Machinery's Handbook. 25th large type ed. 2543p. 1997. 95.00 (*0-8311-2595-0*) Indus Pr.

Oberg, Faye, jt. auth. see Johnson, Dale.

Oberg, Jan, jt. ed. see Nakarada, Radmila.

***Oberg, K.** Role of Somatostatin Analogues i Oncology: European Neuroendocrine Tumour Network (E.N.E.T.), Innsbruck (Austria), February 2000. (Digestion Ser.: 62). 116p. 2000. pap. 34.00 (*3-8055-6931-9*) S Karger.

Oberg, Kalervo. Indian Tribes of Northern Mato Grosso, Brazil. LC 76-44770. (Smithsonian Institution. Institute of Social Anthropology. Publication Ser.: No. 15). reprint ed. 42.50 (*0-404-15958-3*) AMS Pr.

— The Terena & the Caduveo of Southern Mato Grosso, Brazil. LC 76-44771. (Smithsonian Institution. Institute of Social Anthropology. Publication Ser.: No. 9). reprint ed. 42.50 (*0-404-15959-1*) AMS Pr.

Oberg, Larry R., compiled by. Human Services in Postrevolutionary Cuba: An Annotated International Bibliography. LC 83-26527. 433p. 1984. lib. bdg. 65.00 (*0-313-23125-7*, OHS/, Greenwood Pr) Greenwood.

Oberg, Leon. Locomotives of Australia, 1850s-1990s. 3rd ed. (Illus.). 368p. 1997. 42.95 (*0-86417-779-8*, Pub. by Kangaroo Pr) Seven Hills Bk.

Oberg, Michael L. Dominion & Civility: English Imperialism, Native America, & the First American Frontiers, 1585-1685. LC 98-38345. 1999. 42.50 (*0-8014-3564-1*) Cornell U Pr.

Oberg, P. A., jt. ed. see Shepherd, A. P.

Oberg, Pearl, jt. auth. see Stanley, Samuel.

***Oberg, Robert J.** Programming Windows 2000: A Practical Guide for the C/c++ Programmer. 600p. 2000. pap. 49.99 (*0-13-027953-6*, Prentice Hall) P-H.

— Understanding & Programming COM+ A Practical Guide to Windows 2000 DNA. LC 99-56388. (Series on Microsoft Technology). 648p. 2000. pap. text 49.99 (*0-13-023114-2*) P-H.

Oberg, Sture, jt. auth. see Shachar, Arie.

Oberg, Ulf. National Security, Merger & Anti-Trust Policy & International Co-operation in the Defence Industry. 87p. (C). 1998. pap. text 25.00 (*0-7881-4797-8*) DIANE Pub.

Obergfell, Ann M., ed. Law & Ethics in Diagnostic Imaging & Therapeutic Radiology: With Risk Management & Safety Applications. LC 95-10278. (Illus.). 208p. 1995. text 27.00 (*0-7216-5062-7*, W B Saunders Co) Harcrt Hlth Sci Grp.

Oberguggenberger, Michael. Multiplication of Distributions & Applications to Partial Differential Equations. LC 92-4751. (Pitman Research Notes in Mathematics Ser.: No. 259). 330p. 1992. pap. 102.30 (*0-608-05230-2*, 206576700001) Bks Demand.

Oberguggenberger, Michael B. & Rosinger, Elemer E. Solution of Continuous Nonlinear PDEs Through Order Completion. LC 94-19266. (Mathematics Studies: Vol. 181). 448p. 1994. 158.50 (*0-444-82035-3*, North Holland) Elsevier.

Oberhamer, G., ed. Erlosung zu Leben (Jivanmuktih) als Hermeneutisches Problem. (Mededelingen der Koninklijke Nederlandse Akademie van Wetenschappen, Afd. Letterkunde Ser.: No. 55(3)). 14p. pap. 12.50 (*0-444-85749-4*) Elsevier.

Oberhansli-Widmer, Gabrielle. Biblische Figuren in der Rabbinischen Literatur: Gleichnisse und Bilder Zu Adam, Noah und Abraham Im Midrasch Bereschit Rabba. (Judaica et Christiana Serie: Bd. 17). 395p. 1998. 53.95 (*3-906759-66-0*, Pub. by P Lang) P Lang Pubng.

Oberhansly, Dianne Nelson, see Oberttansky, Curtis & Nelson Oberhansly, Dianne.

Oberhau. Professional Selling. 2nd ed. LC 94-70733. (C). 1995. write for info. (*0-03-000639-2*) Harcourt Coll Pubs.

Oberhaus. Professional Selling. 2nd ed. (C). 1997. pap. text 63.50 (*0-15-504405-2*) Harcourt Coll Pubs.

Oberhaus, Dorothy H. Emily Dickinson's Fascicles. (Illus.). 212p. 1995. 45.00 (*0-271-01337-0*) Pa St U Pr.

— Emily Dickinson's Fascicles: Method & Meaning. 272p. 1997. pap. 17.95 (*0-271-01643-4*) Pa St U Pr.

— Skill Building for Professionals. 2nd ed. (C). 1995. pap. text, wbk. ed. 23.50 (*0-03-015859-1*) Harcourt Coll Pubs.

Oberhaus, Mary A. & Ratliffe, Sharon. Video Manual to Accompany Professional Selling. 2nd ed. 64p. (C). 1995. pap. text, wbk. ed. 33.75 (*0-03-010223-5*) Dryden Pr.

Oberhaus, Mary A., et al. Professional Selling: A Relationship Process. 2nd ed. LC 92-75903. 344p. (C). 1995. pap. text, teacher ed. 82.25 incl. trans. (*0-03-010221-9*) Dryden Pr.

— Professional Selling: A Relationship Process, Test bank. 2nd ed. LC 92-75903. 272p. (C). 1995. pap. text, teacher ed. 40.00 (*0-03-010222-7*) Dryden Pr.

Oberheid, K., jt. auth. see Bonnyman, D.

Oberhelman, Harley D. Ernesto Sabato. LC 72-99548. (Twayne's World Authors Ser.). lib. bdg. 20.95 (*0-686-60836-4*) Irvington.

— The Presence of Faulkner in the Writings of Garcia Marquez. (Graduate Studies: No. 22). (Illus.). 43p. 1980. pap. 7.00 (*0-89672-080-2*) Tex Tech Univ Pr.

Oberhelman, Steve M., ed. The Oneirocriticon of Achmet: A Medieval Greek & Arabic Treatise on the Interpretation of Dreams. 320p. 1991. 39.00 (*0-89672-262-7*) Tex Tech Univ Pr.

Oberhelman, Steve M., et al, eds. Epic & Epoch: Essays on the Interpretation & History of a Genre. LC 93-33649. (Studies in Comparative Literature: Vol. 24). 320p. (C). 1994. text 30.00 (*0-89672-331-3*) Tex Tech Univ Pr.

Oberhelman, Steven M. Rhetoric & Homiletics in Fourth-Century Christian Literature: Prose Rhythm, Oratorical Style, & Preaching in the Works of Ambrose, Jerome, & Augustine. 199p. 1991. pap. 19.95 (*1-55540-618-1*) OUP.

Oberhettinger, F. Tables of Bessel Transforms. LC 72-88727. 289p. 1972. 42.95 (*0-387-05997-0*) Spr-Verlag.

— Tables of Mellin Transforms. vii, 275p. 1975. 43.95 (*0-387-06942-9*) Spr-Verlag.

Oberhofer, Ed S. & Vermillion, Robert E. Experimental Physics I. 200p. (C). 1995. spiral bd., lab manual ed. 14.95 (*0-8403-8531-5*) Kendall-Hunt.

Oberhofer, Martin, ed. Advances in Radiation Protection. (C). 1991. text 185.50 (*0-7923-1232-5*) Kluwer Academic.

— Techniques & Management of Personnel Thermoluminescence Dosimetry Services: Based on the Lectures Given During the Eurocourse Techniques & Management of Thermoluminescence Dosimetry Held at the Joint Research Centre, Ispra, Italy, October 19-23, 1992. 446p. (C). 1993. text 241.50 (*0-7923-2436-6*) Kluwer Academic.

An Asterisk (*) at the beginning of an entry indicates that the title is appearing for the first time.

***Oberholser, Harry C.** When Passenger Pigeons Flew in the Killbuck Valley: The Birds of Wayne County, Ohio, 1896. (Illus.). 158p. 1999. pap. 8.95 (*1-888683-96-1*) Wooster Bk.

Oberholser, Warren L. Mind Aerobics. (Illus.). 176p. 1992. pap. 10.00 (*0-963350-0-5*) WarVic Prods.

Oberholtzer, A. H., et al. The Late Fourth Partner: Playscript. rev. ed. LC 97-7171. 64p. (Orig.). 1997. pap. 6.00 (*0-88734-201-9*) Players Pr.

Oberholtzer, Della. Katie & the Neighbors. 1995. pap. 3.50 (*0-87813-559-6*) Christian Light.

— Stories to Grow By. 167p. (J). (gr. 3-6). 1997. pap. 6.95 (*0-87813-566-9*) Christian Light.

Oberholtzer, Ellis P. Jay Cooke, Financier of the Civil War, 2 Vols. LC 68-18222. (Library of Money & Banking History Ser.). 1968. reprint ed. 95.00 (*0-678-00363-7*) Kelley.

— The Morals of the Movie. LC 74-160244. (Moving Pictures Ser.). 251p. 1971. reprint ed. lib. bdg. 28.95 (*0-89198-045-8*) Ozer.

— The Referendum in America. LC 71-119939. (Select Bibliographies Reprint Ser.). 1977. reprint ed. 20.95 (*0-8369-5382-7*) Ayer.

— The Referendum in America. LC 70-153370. (American Constitutional & Legal History Ser). 1971. reprint ed. lib. bdg. 59.50 (*0-306-70149-9*) Da Capo.

— The Referendum in America: A Discussion of Law-Making by Popular Vote. (Political Economy & Public Law Ser.). 225p. 1997. 70.00 (*1-56169-322-7, 14646*) Gaunt.

Oberholtzer, Ellsi P. Jay Cooke, Financier of the Civil War, 2 vols., Set. 1993. reprint ed. lib. bdg. 150.00 (*0-7812-5498-1*) Rprt Serv.

— Philadelphia, a History of the City & Its People, 4 vols. 1993. reprint ed. lib. bdg. 300.00 (*0-7812-5499-X*) Rprt Serv.

Oberholtzer, Ken, jt. auth. see Bertera, Martin.

Oberhuber, Konrad. Drawings Defined. 440p. 1987. 69.50 (*0-89835-274-6*) Abaris Bks.

— Poussin - The Early Years in Rome: The Origins of French Classicism. LC 88-9173. (Illus.). 368p. 1988. 65.00 (*1-55595-002-7*); pap. 24.95 (*1-55595-003-5*) Kimbell Art.

Oberhuber, Konrad, ed. The Illustrated Bartsch Vol. 26, Pt. 1: Marcantonio Raimondi. LC 79-50679. 1978. lib. bdg. 149.00 (*0-89835-026-3*) Abaris Bks.

— The Illustrated Bartsch Vol. 27, Pt. 2: Marcantonio Raimondi. 1978. lib. bdg. 149.00 (*0-89835-027-1*) Abaris Bks.

Oberhuber, Konrad, tr. see Steiner, Rudolf.

Oberhuemer, Pamela & Ulich, Michaela, eds. Working with Young Children in Europe: Provision & Staff Training. LC 97-197495. 256p. 1997. pap. 29.95 (*1-85396-331-3*, Pub. by P Chapman) Taylor & Francis.

Oberhummer, H. Nuclei in the Cosmos. Birman, J. L. et al, eds. (Graduate Texts in Contemporary Physics Ser.). (Illus.). xii, 236p. 1991. 79.95 (*0-387-54198-5*) Spr-Verlag.

Oberi, Amarjit S. Migration, Urbanisation & Development. (Background Paper for Training in Population, Human Resources & Development Planning Ser.: No. 5). vi, 108p. (Orig.). 1990. pap. 13.50 (*92-2-106129-9*) Intl Labour Office.

***Oberkamp, Frances.** Intuition: How to Use It. LC 00-90692. (Illus.). 128p. 2000. pap. 14.95 (*0-9679583-0-X*) Tree of Life CA.

Oberkotter, Mildred, et al, eds. The Possible Dream: Mainstream Experiences of Hearing-Impaired Students. (Centennial Celebration Ser.). 68p. (Orig.). (YA). 1990. pap. text 7.95 (*0-88200-171-X*) Alexander Graham.

Oberland, Kathleen. Show Ring Success: A Rider's Guide to Winning Strategies. LC 93-15115. (Illus.). 192p. 1993. 24.00 (*0-87605-965-5*) Howell Bks.

Oberlander. Project Management for Engineering Construction. 2nd ed. LC 99-53231. 384p. 2000. 76.56 (*0-07-039360-5*) McGraw.

Oberlander, ed. Physical Geography Today. (C). 1998. pap., lab manual ed. write for info. (*0-321-40138-7*) Addison-Wesley.

Oberlander, Clyde G., ed. see Oberlander, June R.

Oberlander, David. Unquestioned Care: Guide for MS Caregivers. 100p. (Orig.). 1999. pap. 8.95 (*0-9654493-4-3*) SunWest MP.

Oberlander, David. Austin's Old 300: With Sketches from the Colony. LC 98-48360. 224p. 1999. 22.95 (*1-57168-291-0*, Eakin Pr) Sunbelt Media.

Oberlander, David H. Sharing the Journey: Personal Stories of MS Caregiving. (Illus.). 200p. (Orig.). 1998. pap. 15.95 (*0-9654493-2-7*) SunWest MP.

***Oberlander, H. Peter & Newbrun, Eva.** Houser: The Life & Work of Catherine Bauer. (Illus.). 356p. 2000. pap. 22.95 (*0-7748-0721-0*, Pub. by UBC Pr) U of Wash Pr.

Oberlander, June R. Measurable Parameters to Profile Child Development from "Slow & Steady, Get Me Ready" The How-to Book That Grows with the Child. Oberlander, Clyde G., ed. 8p. (Orig.). 1993. pap. 3.95 (*0-9622322-3-8*) Bio-Alpha.

— Parametros Mensurables Para Perfilar el Desarrollo Del Nino de "Slow & Steady, Get Me Ready" El Libro de Instrucciones Que Crece Con el Nino. Oberlander, Clyde G., ed. Roig, Jose G., tr. from ENG. (SPA., Illus.). 8p. (Orig.). (J). (ps). 1994. pap. 3.95 (*0-9622322-6-2*) Bio-Alpha.

— Slow & Steady, Get Me Ready: A How-to Book That Grows with the Child. rev. ed. Oberlander, Clyde G., ed. (Illus.). 324p. (Orig.). 1992. pap. 17.95 (*0-9622322-1-1*) Bio Alpha.

— Slow & Steady, Get Me Ready - Despacio y Constantemente, Preparenme: El Libro de Instrucciones que Crece Con Su Nino. Sosa, Juan, ed. Roig, Jose G., tr. from ENG. (SPA., Illus.). 344p. (Orig.). 1994. pap. 17.95 (*0-9622322-4-6*) Bio-Alpha.

Oberlander, Theodore M., ed. Physical Geography Today. (C). 1998. text. write for info. (*0-321-01204-6*); pap. text, student ed. write for info. (*0-321-01205-4*) Addson-Wesley Educ.

Oberlander, Theodore M. & Muller, Robert A. Essentials of Physical Geography Today. 2nd ed. 576p. (C). 1987. 75.31 (*0-07-556615-X*) McGraw.

Oberlander, Theodore M., jt. auth. see Muller, Robert A.

***Oberlander, Todd M.** Why Am I on This Planet? LC 98-90367. 1999. pap. 10.95 (*0-533-12786-6*) Vantage.

***Oberle, Cheryl.** Folk Shawls. LC 99-58836. (Illus.). 144p. 2000. 21.95 (*1-883010-59-4*) Interweave.

Oberle, Ed B. Jacksonville Diary Vol. 1: Behind the Microphone. 296p. 1998. pap. 21.95 (*0-9659897-0-4*) Carobell Co.

Oberle, George H., jt. ed. see Edgley, Betty M.

Oberle, Joseph. Diary of a Mad Househusband: Musings on Life As a Stay-at-Home Dad. LC 96-75064. 144p. 1996. pap. 11.95 (*0-9650741-3-7*) Kimm Pubng.

Oberle, Joseph G. Anchorage. LC 89-26068. (Downtown America Ser.). (Illus.). 60p. (J). (gr. 3 up). 1990. pap. 7.95 (*0-382-24778-7*, Dillon Silver Burdett); lib. bdg. 13.95 (*0-87518-420-0*, Dillon Silver Burdett) Silver Burdett Pr.

Oberle, William F. Calculus & the Computer. (C). 1986. pap. text 50.50 (*0-201-15983-X*) Addison-Wesley.

***Oberleas, Donald, et al.** Minerals: Nutrition & Metabolism. LC 99-93616. 1999. pap. 34.95 (*0-533-13086-7*) Vantage.

Oberleitner, jt. auth. see Poirrier.

Oberleitner, Franz A. Simplicium Leges. Das Ist: Geistliche und Unfehlbare Bauren-Reglen. (GER.). xii, 485p. 1993. reprint ed. write for info. (*3-487-09712-5*) G Olms Pubs.

Oberleitner, J. L., ed. see Speas, W. David.

Oberleitner, John L. Getting PC Cultured: The Young Adult to Senior Citizen (& Everyone in Between) Guide to Personal Computers. (Illus.). 117p. 1995. 24.95 (*1-884889-10-7*) Suarez.

— Stanzi: A Magic Christmas Story. McMahon-Ehalt, Teresa, tr. 33p. (J). 1995. 16.95 (*1-884889-11-5*) Suarez.

Oberlender, Garold. Project Management for Engineers. 448p. (C). 1993. 76.56 (*0-07-048150-4*) McGraw.

Oberlender, Garold D., ed. Earthmoving & Heavy Equipment. (Conference Proceedings Ser.). 201p. 1986. 22.00 (*0-87262-548-6*) Am Soc Civil Eng.

Oberlender, Garold D., jt. auth. see Peurifoy, R. L.

Oberlender, Gary, jt. auth. see Peurifoy, Robert L.

Oberley, Edith T. & Glass, Neal R. Understanding Kidney Transplantation. (Illus.). 160p. (C). 1987. 35.95 (*0-398-05277-8*) C C Thomas.

Oberley, Edith T. & Oberley, Terry D. Understanding Your New Life with Dialysis: A Patient Guide for Physical & Psychological Adjustment. 4th ed. (Illus.). 194p. (C). 1992. pap. text 33.95 (*0-398-05774-5*) C C Thomas.

Oberley, Larry W., ed. Superoxide Dismutase, Vol. I. 168p. 1982. 97.00 (*0-8493-6240-7*, QP603, CRC Reprint) Franklin.

— Superoxide Dismutase, Vol. II. 192p. 1982. 110.00 (*0-8493-6241-5*, CRC Reprint) Franklin.

— Superoxide Dismutase: Pathological States, Vol. III. 280p. 1985. 157.00 (*0-8493-6242-3*, QP603, CRC Reprint) Franklin.

Oberley, Terry D., jt. auth. see Oberley, Edith T.

Oberlin Colloquium in Philosophy Staff. Issues in the Philosophy of Language: Proceedings of the Oberlin Colloquium in Philosophy, 13th, Oberlin College, 1972. MacKay, Alfred F. & Merrill, Daniel D., eds. LC 75-18178. 176p. reprint ed. pap. 54.60 (*0-608-14021-X, 202201800024*) Bks Demand.

— Perception & Personal Identity: Proceedings. Care, Norman S. & Grimm, Robert H., eds. LC 68-9427. 205p. reprint ed. pap. 63.60 (*0-608-30646-0, 200325300021*) Bks Demand.

Oberlin, Loriann H. Working at Home While the Kids Are There Too. LC 97-17757. 192p. 1997. pap. 12.99 (*1-56414-305-8*) Career Pr Inc.

***Oberlin, Loriann Hoff.** Surviving Separation & Divorce: A Woman's Guide to Making it Throught the First Year. LC 99-59250. 288p. 2000. pap. 12.95 (*1-58062-303-4*) Adams Media.

Oberlin, Salley, et al. Quick Course in Windows 3.1: Education/Training Edition. LC 92-60030. (Quick Course Ser.). (Illus.). 133p. (Orig.). 1992. pap. text 14.95 (*1-879399-14-8*) Online Training.

Oberlin, Sarah B. & Ayers, Esther R. A Heritage Money Can't Buy: My Growing up Years as an Old Order Mennonite. LC 97-68938. 1997. mass mkt. 14.95 (*1-889131-19-9*) CasAnanda.

Oberling, Pierre. The Road to Bellapais: The Turkish Cypriot Exodus to Northern Cyprus. (Brooklyn College Studies on Society in Change). 256p. 1982. text 64.50 (*0-88033-000-7*, Pub. by East Eur Monographs) Col U Pr.

Oberlink, jt. auth. see Butler.

Oberly, James W. Sixty Million Acres: American Veterans & the Public Lands Before the Civil War. LC 90-4482. (Illus.). 234p. reprint ed. pap. 72.60 (*0-608-07359-8, 206758700009*) Bks Demand.

Oberly, R. E., et al. General Physics Two Hundred Two. 104p. (C). 1984. pap. text, lab manual ed. 9.95 (*0-89917-442-6*) Tichenor Pub.

Obermaier, Ernst, jt. auth. see Held, Werner.

Obermaier, Hugo. Fossil Man in Spain. LC 70-121293. reprint ed. 49.50 (*0-404-04809-9*) AMS Pr.

— Fossil Man in Spain. LC 69-14012. (Illus.). 495p. 1969. reprint ed. lib. bdg. 75.00 (*0-8371-1504-3*, OBFM, Greenwood Pr) Greenwood.

Obermaier, Otto G. & Morvillo, Robert G., eds. White Collar Crime: Business & Regulatory Offenses. 800p. 1990. ring bd. 110.00 (*0-317-05403-1*, 00610) NY Law Pub.

Oberman, jt. auth. see Rosen.

Oberman, Albert, et al. Principles & Management of Lipid Disorders: A Primary Care Approach. (Illus.). 368p. 1992. 49.00 (*0-683-06623-4*) Lppncott W & W.

Oberman, Bonnie, ed. see Berger, Mary I.

Oberman, Cerise & Kimmage, Dennis, eds. Russian-American Seminar on Critical Thinking & the Library: Papers from the Seminar, Moscow, June 1-5, 1992. (Occasional Papers: No. 200/201). 160p. (Orig.). 1995. pap. 15.00 (*0-614-15032-9*) U of Ill Grad Sch.

Oberman, David. The Science of Humanity. 359p. 1985. 59.00 (*0-7212-0716-2*, Pub. by Regency Pr GBR) St Mut.

Oberman, David, ed. see Bin Idris, Nazmul.

Oberman, David, ed. see Brice, R. Andrew & Koenen, Frank.

Oberman, David, ed. see Crothers, Timothy & Stanger, James.

Oberman, David, ed. see Danks, Brian & Sabol, Jon.

Oberman, David, ed. see Idris, Nazmul Bin.

Oberman, David, ed. see Lane, Patrick T.

Oberman, David, ed. see Lane, Patrick T. & Stanger, James.

Oberman, David, ed. see Stanger, James.

Oberman, David, ed. see Stranger, James.

Oberman, Heiko A. The Dawn of the Reformation: Essays in Late Medieval & Early Reformation Thought. 320p. (C). 1992. reprint ed. pap. 30.00 (*0-8028-0655-4*) Eerdmans.

— The Dawn of the Reformation: The Impact of the Reformation: The Reformation, 3 vols., Set. 1994. pap. 80.00 (*0-8028-0885-9*) Eerdmans.

— Forerunners of the Reformation: The Shape of Late Medieval Thought, Illustrated by Key Documents: Nyhus, Paul L., tr. LC 81-66518. 347p. reprint ed. pap. 107.60 (*0-608-17181-6, 202717500054*) Bks Demand.

— The Impact of the Reformation: Essays. LC 93-42559. 256p. (Orig.). (C). 1994. pap. text 20.00 (*0-8028-0732-1*) Eerdmans.

— Luther. 400p. 1992. pap. 16.95 (*0-385-42278-4*) Doubleday.

— The Reformation: Roots & Ramifications. 288p. (Orig.). 1994. pap. text 30.00 (*0-8028-0825-5*) Eerdmans.

Oberman, Heiko A., ed. see Brady, Thomas.

Oberman, Heiko A., jt. ed. see Dykema, Peter A.

Oberman, Ida, jt. ed. see McLaughlin, Milbrey W.

Oberman, Joseph & Bingham, Robert. Planning & Managing the Economy of the City: Policy Guidelines for the Metropolitan Mayor. LC 72-79544. (Special Studies in U. S. Economic, Social & Political Issues). 1972. 32.50 (*0-275-06160-4*) Irvington.

Oberman, Sheldon. Always Prayer Shawl. LC 93-70874. (Illus.). 32p. (J). (gr. 2 up). 1993. 15.95 (*1-878093-22-3*) Boyds Mills Pr.

Oberman, Sheldon. Always Prayer Shawl. (Picture Puffin Ser.). 1997. 11.19 (*0-606-11034-8*, Pub. by Turtleback) Demco.

Oberman, Sheldon. Always Prayer Shawl. LC 96-33627. (Illus.). 40p. (J). 1997. pap. 5.99 (*0-14-056157-9*) Viking Penguin.

— Always Prayer Shawl. 40p. 1999. pap. 5.99 (*0-14-038214-3*) Viking Penguin.

— By the Hanukkah Light. LC 96-80390. (Illus.). 32p. (J). (gr. 1-4). 1997. 15.95 (*1-56397-658-7*) Boyds Mills Pr.

— The Lion in the Lake (Le Lion dans le Lac) A Bilingual Alphabet (Un Abecedaire Bilingue) (ENG & FRE., Illus.). 56p. (J). (gr. k-3). 1988. text 8.00 (*0-920541-36-4*) Peguis Pubs Ltd.

— This Business with Elijah. 1997. pap. 12.95 (*0-88801-174-1*, Pub. by Turnstone Pr) Genl Dist Srvs.

— The White Stone in the Castle Wall. LC 93-61791. (Illus.). 24p. (J). (gr. k-3). 1995. 14.95 (*0-88776-333-2*) Tundra Bks.

— The White Stone in the Castle Wall. (Illus.). 24p. (gr. 1-4). 1996. pap. 9.95 (*0-88776-379-0*) Tundra Bks.

— The Wisdom Bird. LC 99-63098. (Illus.). 32p. (J). (gr. 1-4). 2000. 15.95 (*1-56397-816-4*) Boyds Mills Pr.

Oberman, Sheldon & Newton, Elaine, eds. Mirror of a People. 256p. 1985. pap. 10.95 (*0-920657-00-1*, Pub. by Coteau) Genl Dist Srvs.

***Oberman, Sheldon & Tookoome, Simon.** A Shaman's Nephew: A Life in the Far North. (Illus.). 56p. (YA). (gr. 4-7). 2000. text 18.95 (*0-7737-3200-4*, Stoddart Kids) Stoddart Publ.

Oberman, Wendy. Family of Strangers. large type ed. (Charnwood Romance Ser.). 576p. 1987. 27.99 (*0-7089-8431-2*, Charnwood) Ulverscroft.

Obermann, C. Esco. The History of Vocational Rehabilitation in America. Phillips, William R. & Rosenberg, Janet, eds. LC 79-6919. (Physically Handicapped in Society Ser.). 1980. reprint ed. lib. bdg. 37.95 (*0-405-13128-3*) Ayer.

Obermann, Julian. New Discoveries at Karatepe. (Connecticut Academy of Arts & Sciences Ser., Trans.: Vol. 38). 1949. pap. 39.50 (*0-685-22903-3*) Elliots Bks.

Obermann, Julian, ed. Nissim Ibn Shahin: The Arabic Original of Ibn Shahin's Book of Comfort. LC 78-63561. (Yale Oriental Series: Researches: No. 17). reprint ed. 72.50 (*0-404-60287-8*) AMS Pr.

Obermann, W. R. Radiology of Carpal Instability: A Practical Approach. LC 95-119769. 200p. 1994. 233.50 (*0-444-82080-9*) Elsevier.

***Obermarck, Philip.** The Celtic Interest Internet Guide. 40p. 1999. pap. 10.00 (*1-883573-37-8*, Lightning Rod) Pride & Imprints.

Obermayer, A., jt. auth. see Herd, E. W.

Obermayer, Heinz. Diccionario Biblico Manual. 3rd ed. (SPA.). 352p. 1987. pap. 14.95 (*0-7859-4887-2*) Fr & Eur.

— Kleines Stuttgarter-Bibellexikon. 3rd ed. (GER.). 344p. 1976. 24.95 (*0-8288-5719-9*, M7507) Fr & Eur.

Obermeier, Bernhardt & Slaby, Wolfgang. Ilias Latina: Concordantia in Iliadem Latinam. 290p. write for info. (*0-318-71962-2*) G Olms Pubs.

Obermeier, Bernhardt & Slaby, Wolfgang, eds. Ilias Latina - Concordantia in Iliadem Latinam. write for info. (*0-318-71152-4*) G Olms Pubs.

Obermeier, Klaus K. Natural Language Processing Technologies in Artificial Intelligence: The Science & Industry Perspective. (Artificial Intelligence Ser.). 1989. text 39.95 (*0-470-21528-3*) P-H.

Obermeier, Otto-Peter & Schuez, Mathias, eds. Risk - Paradise Lost or Gained? A Holistic Approach to the Environment. LC 95-35638. (Illus.). 396p. (C). 1995. text 29.95 (*0-89876-230-8*) Gardner Pr.

Obermen, David, ed. see Lane, Patrick T.

Obermeyer, A. A., et al. Flora of Southern Africa Series, Vol. 5, Pt. 3. (Illus.). 90p. 1992. 23.00 (*1-874907-02-1*, Pub. by Natl Botanical Inst) Balogh.

Obermeyer, Carla M., ed. Family, Gender & Population in the Middle East: Policies in Context. LC 95-960433. 240p. 1995. 35.00 (*977-424-357-9*, Pub. by Am Univ Cairo Pr) Col U Pr.

Obermeyer, Nancy J. Bureaucrats, Clients, & Geography: The Bailly Nuclear Power Plant Battle in Northern Indiana. (Research Papers: No. 216). (Illus.). 140p. 1989. pap. text 14.50 (*0-89065-121-3*) U Ch Pr.

Obermeyer, Nancy J. & Pinto, Jeffrey K. Managing Geographic Information Systems. LC 93-47119. 226p. 1994. lib. bdg. 36.00 (*0-89862-005-8*, 2005) Guilford Pubns.

Obermeyer, Thomas L. Architecture Drawing. 1992. pap. 27.95 (*0-02-800415-9*) Macmillan.

Obermeyer, Vera R. Finding a School in San Francisco: Private Schools. LC 95-81240. (Illus.). xvii, 134p. 1995. pap. text 16.95 (*0-9635882-1-4*) Lrning Assocs.

***Obermeyer, Vera R., et al.** Finding a Preschool for Your Child in San Francisco. (Illus.). 240p. 1999. pap. 19.95 (*0-9648757-2-1*, Pub. by Pince Nez Pr) Sunbelt Pubns.

Obermeyer, Vera R., jt. auth. see Rifkin, Lori.

Obermiller, E. The Doctrine of Prajna-Paramita As Exposed in the Abhisamayalamkara of Maitreya. 153p. 1984. reprint ed. lib. bdg. 22.50 (*0-88181-002-9*) Canon Pubns.

— Nirvana in Tibetan Buddhism. Sobti, Harcharan S., ed. (C). 1987. 11.50 (*81-85132-03-8*) S Asia.

***Obermiller, E.** Prajnaparamitra in Tibetan Buddhism. LC 99-939907. 1998. 21.00 (*81-86230-13-0*, Pub. by Paljor Pubns) S Asia.

Obermiller, E., tr. see Maitreya, Aryasanga.

***Obermiller, Phillip J., et al.** Appalachian Odyssey: Historical Perspectives on the Great Migration. LC 99-54719. 2000. write for info. (*0-275-96851-0*) Greenwood.

Obermiller, Phillip J. & Philliber, William W., eds. Appalachia in an International Context. LC 94-6380. 256p. 1994. 65.00 (*0-275-94835-8*, Praeger Pubs) Greenwood.

Obermiller, Phillip J., jt. ed. see Borman, Kathryn M.

Obermiller, Phillip J., jt. ed. see Philliber, William W.

***Oberneidermaier, Gerhard & Geiss, Marcus.** SAP R/3 Testing with CATT. 400p. 2000. pap. text 49.95 (*0-201-67517-X*) Addison-Wesley.

Oberoi, A. S. Support of the Shaken Sangat: Meetings with Three Masters. Perkins, Russell, ed. LC 84-50911. (Illus.). 256p. (Orig.). 1984. pap. 15.00 (*0-89142-043-6*) Sant Bani Ash.

Oberoi, Harjot. The Construction of Religious Boundaries: Culture, Identity & Diversity in the Sikh Tradition. xxii, 516p. 1994. pap. text 17.95 (*0-226-61593-6*) U Ch Pr.

— The Construction of Religious Boundaries: Culture, Identity & Diversity in the Sikh Tradition. xxii, 516p. 1994. lib. bdg. 49.95 (*0-226-61592-8*) U Ch Pr.

— The Construction of Religious Boundaries: Culture, Identity & Diversity in the Sikh Tradition. LC 98-121332. (Oxford India Paperbacks). (Illus.). 516p. 1997. reprint ed. pap. text 11.95 (*0-19-563780-1*) OUP.

***Oberon Development, Ltd. Staff.** Citation: Bibliographic Software for Legal Research & Writing, Legal Edition. (Illus.). 166p. (C). 1999. pap. 279.00 incl. cd-rom (*0-9677361-2-9*) Oberon.

Oberon, Jake. Snakes As a New Pet. (Illus.). 64p. (Orig.). 1990. pap. 6.95 (*0-86622-623-0*, TU-015) TFH Pubns.

Oberprieler, Ulrich, jt. auth. see Cillie, Burger.

Oberpriller, John, ed. The Development & Regenerative Potential of Cardiac Muscle. xix, 463p. 1991. text 267.00 (*3-7186-0518-X*, Harwood Acad Pubs) Gordon & Breach.

***Oberrecht, Kenn.** California: Scenic Driving Tours along Coastal Highways. (Illus.). 2000. pap. 12.95 (*0-7627-0713-5*) Globe Pequot.

Oberrecht, Kenn. Driving the Pacific Coast: California. 3rd rev. ed. LC 98-15456. (Illus.). 288p. 1998. pap. 12.95 (*0-7627-0136-6*) Globe Pequot.

— Driving the Pacific Coast: Oregon & Washington. 3rd rev. ed. LC 97-30176. (Illus.). 256p. 1998. pap. 12.95 (*0-7627-0137-4*) Globe Pequot.

***Oberrecht, Kenn.** Driving the Pacific Coast - Oregon & Washington: Scenic Driving Tours along Coastal Highways. 4th ed. (Illus.). 256p. 2000. pap. 12.95 (*0-7627-0640-6*) Globe Pequot.

Oberrecht, Kenn. Fish & Shellfish Care & Cookery. (Illus.). 240p. 1997. pap. 19.95 (*0-88317-202-X*) Stoeger Pub Co.

— Home Book of Picture Framing. 2nd ed. LC 97-50142. (Illus.). 272p. 1998. pap. 19.95 (*0-8117-2793-9*) Stackpole.

***Oberrecht, Kenn.** How to Start a Home-Based Crafts Business. 3rd ed. (Home-Based Business Ser.). (Illus.). 288p. 2000. pap. 18.95 (*0-7627-0639-2*) Globe Pequot.

O

Oberrecht, Kenn. How to Start a Home-Based Photography Business. 3rd ed. LC 99-42014. (How to Start a Home-Based Business Ser.). (Illus.). 240p. 2000. pap. text 17.95 (*0-7627-0514-0*) Globe Pequot.

Oberreuter, Ray. A Camera Repairman's Guide to Practical Photography. 178p. 1991. pap. 15.95 (*0-9630169-0-3*) Grassroots.

Oberrheinisches Kardiologen Symposium Staff. Betarezeptoren in der Kardiologie - Probleme aus klinischer Sicht: Proceedings of the Symposium, 1st, Bad Krozingen, October, 1977. Roskamm, H., ed. (Cardiology Ser.: Vol. 63, Suppl. 1). (FRE & GER., Illus.). 1978. 14.00 (*3-8055-2870-1*) S Karger.

O'Berry, Little & Fields Staff. Storytime Around the Curriculum: A Comprehensive Early Childhood Curriculum Presented Through Literature. 1992. pap. 29.95 (*0-933212-03-8*) Partner Pr.

Oberschall, Anthony. Social Movements: Ideologies, Interests & Identities. 402p. 1996. pap. text 29.95 (*1-56000-868-7*) Transaction Pubs.

Oberschelp, Reinhard, ed. Gesamtverzeichnis des Deutschsprachigen Schrifttums, 1911 to 1965, 150 vols., Set. 77000p. 1981. lib. bdg. write for info. (*3-7940-5600-0*) K G Saur Verlag.

Oberschmidt, Randolf. Rubland und die Schleswigholsteinische Frage, 1839-1853. (Illus.). 326p. 1997. 57.95 (*3-631-32129-5*) P Lang Pubng.

Oberschulte, William, ed. Wood-Frame House Construction. 336p. (Orig.). 1992. pap. 25.50 (*0-934041-74-1*) Craftsman.

Obershaw, Richard J. Cry Until You Laugh: A Candid Approach to Grief & Death. 160p. 1996. 10.00 (*1-889279-00-5*) Best Small Pr.

— Cry until You Laugh: A Candid Approach to Grief & Death. 200p. 1996. 18.00 (*0-614-19825-9*) Best Small Pr.

— Cry Until You Laugh: Comforting Guidance for Coping with Grief. LC 97-27942. 192p. 1998. pap. 12.95 (*1-57749-063-0*) Fairview Press.

Oberst, B. B. & Long, J. L. Computers in Private Practice Management. (Illus.). 290p. 1987. 110.00 (*0-387-96502-5*) Spr-Verlag.

Oberst, B. B. & Reid, R. A., eds. Computer Application to Private Office Practices. (Illus.). 145p. 1984. 60.00 (*0-387-90933-8*) Spr-Verlag.

Obert, David L. Philippine Defender: A Fighter Pilot's Diary, 1941-1942. LC 92-71109. 175p. (Orig.). 1992. pap. 12.95 (*0-927562-12-X*) Levite Apache.

Obert, Edward F. Internal Combustion Engines & Air Pollution. 736p. (C). 1997. 105.00 (*0-7002-2183-2*) Addson-Wesley Educ.

Obert, Genevieve. Prince Borghese's Trail: 10,000 Miles over Two Continents, Four Deserts & the Roof of the World in the Peking to Paris Motor Challenge. LC 99-34574. (Illus.). 308p. 1999. 23.95 (*1-57178-085-8*, Pub. by Coun Oak Bks) SPD-Small Pr Dist.

Obert, Jessie C. Community Nutrition. 2nd ed. 496p. (C). 1986. text 70.60 (*0-02-389020-7*, Macmillan Coll) P-H.

Obert, Leonard & Durall, Wilbur I. Rock Mechanics & the Design of Structures in Rock. LC 66-26753. 669p. reprint ed. pap. 200.00 (*0-608-13364-7*, 205576600037) Bks Demand.

Obert, Lois C. Help! Willie's Choking! A Young Child's Introduction to the Heimlich Manuever. Fitting, JanaSue, ed. LC 94-76883. (Illus.). 20p. (J). (ps-3). 1994. teacher ed., spiral bd. 17.95 (*0-923889-49-3*) Inquisitors Pub.

Obert-Westgate, Eleanor. Through the Years. (Orig.). 1996. pap. write for info. (*1-57553-283-2*) Watermrk Pr.

Oberta, Andrew F., ed. Manual on Asbestos Control: Removal, Management, & the Visual Inspection Process. LC 95-25365. (MNL, Manual Ser.: No. 23). (Illus.). 86p. 1995. text 43.00 (*0-8031-2067-2*, MNL23) ASTM.

Oberteuffer, Delbert. Personal Hygiene for College Students. LC 77-177126. (Columbia University. Teachers College. Contributions to Education Ser.: No. 407). (C). reprint ed. 37.50 (*0-404-55407-5*) AMS Pr.

Oberth, Hermann. Primer for Those Who Would Govern. 320p. 1986. pap. 20.00 (*0-914301-06-3*) West-Art.

***Oberthhur, Sebastian & Ott, Hermann.** The Kyoto Protocol: International Climate Policy for the 21st Century. Tarasofsky, R. G., ed. LC 99-45872. (Illus.). 380p. 1999. 59.95 (*3-540-66470-X*) Spr-Verlag.

Oberti, Martha, tr. see Schreuder, Sally A.

Oberto, Martio. Anaphilosophia. Carravetta, Peter & Salamone, Rosa M., trs. from ITA. LC 78-58984. (Illus.). 1984. pap. 17.95 (*0-915570-10-6*) Oolp Pr.

***Obertop, H. & Pedrazzoli, S., eds.** Surgical Treatment of Pancreatic Cancer. (Digestive Surgery Ser.: Vol. 16, No. 4, 1999). (Illus.). 88p. 1999. pap. 34.00 (*3-8055-6937-8*) S Karger.

***Oberttansky, Curtis & Nelson Oberhansly, Dianne.** Half-Lives. 352p. 1999. 24.95 (*1-893448-00-2*) Boaz Pubng.

Oberwager, Jerome. How to Print Posters (UNESCO) (Education Studies & Documents: No. 3). 1969. reprint ed. pap. 25.00 (*0-8115-1327-0*) Periodicals Srv.

Oberweis, Michael. Die Interpolationen im Chronicon Urspergense. (Munchener Beitrage zur Mediavistik und Renaissance-Forschung Ser.: Bd. 40). (GER.). viii, 156p. 1990. 58.00 (*3-615-00170-2*, Pub. by Weidmann) Lubrecht & Cramer.

Oberwinkler, F., jt. ed. see Hertel, H.

Oberwinkler, Franz, jt. auth. see Vanky, Kalman.

Obery, Ingrid, jt. ed. see Moss, Glenn.

Obeyesekere, Gananath. Apotheosis of Captain Cook: European Mythmaking in the Pacific. 344p. 1992. pap. text 17.95 (*0-691-05752-4*, Pub. by Princeton U Pr) Cal Prin Full Svc.

— Cult of Goddess Pattini. (Illus.). 629p. 1987. 65.00 (*0-317-60566-6*, Pub. by Motilal Bnarsidass) S Asia.

— The Cult of the Goddess Pattini. LC 83-5884. (Illus.). 648p. (C). 1984. lib. bdg. 51.00 (*0-226-61602-9*) U Ch Pr.

— Medusa's Hair: An Essay on Personal Symbols & Religious Experiences. LC 80-27372. (Illus.). 232p. 1984. pap. text 11.00 (*0-226-61601-0*) U Ch Pr.

— The Work of Culture: Symbolic Transformation in Psychoanalysis & Anthropology. LC 90-10904. (Lewis Henry Morgan Lectures, 1982). 380p. 1990. pap. text 19.95 (*0-226-61599-5*) U Ch Pr.

— The Work of Culture: Symbolic Transformation in Psychoanalysis & Anthropology. LC 90-10904. (Lewis Henry Morgan Lectures, 1982). 380p. 1990. lib. bdg. 60.00 (*0-226-61598-7*) U Ch Pr.

***Obeyesekere, Ranjini.** Sri Lankan Theater in a Time of Terror: Political Satire in a Permitted Space. LC 98-50748. 1999. write for info. (*0-7619-9302-9*) Sage.

Obeyesekere, Ranjini. Sri Lankan Theater in a Time of Terror: Political Satire in a Permitted Space. LC 98-50748. 280p. 1999. 44.95 (*0-7619-9301-0*) Sage.

Obeyesekere, Ranjini & Fernando, Chitra, eds. An Anthology of Modern Writing from Sri Lanka. LC 81-1140. (Monographs: No. 38). xv, 307p. (C). 1981. 28.00 (*0-8165-0702-3*); pap. 14.00 (*0-8165-0703-1*) Assn Asian Studies.

Obeyeskere, Gananth, jt. auth. see Gombrich, Richard F.

Obholzer, Anton, et al. The Unconscious at Work: Individual & Organizational Stress in the Human Services. 256th ed. LC 93-44323. 256p. (C). 1994. pap. 27.99 (*0-415-10206-5*, B4444) Routledge.

***Obiadi, Boniface.** The Good & the Bad Only in America: The Route from Nigeria to America. Strader, Jennifer, ed. (Illus.). 154p. (YA). 1999. pap. 12.95 (*0-9677864-0-1*) Bons Diversified Invest.

— Nigeria & Her Garbage Dumps: The Environmental Sensitive Nigeria. Fowler, Gary, ed. 69p. 1999. pap. 12.95 (*0-9677864-2-8*) Bons Diversified Invest.

***Obiadi, Boniface N.** Big Bird Little Bird. Strader, Jennifer, ed. (Illus.). 2000. pap. 10.95 (*0-9677864-3-6*) Bons Diversified Invest.

— Why Things Happen: Short Stories about Mankind & His Environment. Strader, Jennifer & Call, Steve, eds. (Illus.). 35p. 1999. pap. 10.95 (*0-9677864-1-X*) Bons Diversified Invest.

Obiakor, Festus. Beyond the Steps. 226p. (C). 1999. pap. text 55.95 (*0-7872-5718-4*, 41571801) Kendall-Hunt.

***Obiakor, Festus.** Beyond the Steps: Multicultural Study Guide. 106p. (C). 1999. per. 24.95 (*0-7872-5717-6*) Kendall-Hunt.

Obiakor, Festus E. Self-Concept of Exceptional Learners: Current Perspectives for Educators. 240p. (C). 1994. per. 41.95 (*0-8403-9545-0*) Kendall-Hunt.

Obiakor, Festus E., et al. Disruption, Disaster, & Death: Helping Students Deal with Crises. LC 96-40939. 109p. 1996. pap. text 26.95 (*0-86586-289-3*, P5190) Coun Exc Child.

Obiakor, Festus E., jt. auth. see Algozzine, Robert.

Obiaya, Joseph O. Mount Zion: The Mystery of God. LC 93-93712. (Illus.). 198p. (C). 1993. lib. bdg. 25.00 (*0-9638850-0-6*) J O Obiaya.

Obichere, Boniface I., ed. Studies in Southern Nigerian History. 278p. 1982. 45.00 (*0-7146-3106-X*, Pub. by F Cass Pubs) Intl Spec Bk.

Obidinski, Eugene & Zand, Helen S. Polish Folkways in America: Community & Family. (Polish Studies: Vol. I). 162p. (Orig.). 1987. pap. text 23.00 (*0-8191-5882-8*); lib. bdg. 44.50 (*0-8191-5881-X*) U Pr of Amer.

Obidinski, Eugene E. Ethnic to Status Group: A Study of Polish Americans in Buffalo. Cordasco, Francesco, ed. LC 80-885. (American Ethnic Groups Ser.). 1981. lib. bdg. 26.95 (*0-405-13446-0*) Ayer.

Obie, Marlene. What Color Is My Collar? 208p. 1985. pap. 2.95 (*0-310-36712-3*, 12491P) Zondervan.

Obiechina, E. N. Onitsha Market Literature. LC 72-76469. 200p. (C). 1972. 17.50 (*0-8419-0122-8*, Africana) Holmes & Meier.

Obiechina, Emmanuel. Locusts. 1976. 2.00 (*0-912678-23-2*, Greenfld Rev Pr) Greenfld Rev Lit.

Obiechina, Emmanuel, ed. Language & Theme: Essays on African Literature. LC 90-34189. 384p. (Orig.). (C). 1990. 26.95 (*0-88258-045-0*); pap. 14.95 (*0-88258-064-7*) Howard U Pr.

Obilade, Akintunde O., jt. ed. see Woodman, Gordon R.

Obilor, John I. The Doctrine of the Resurrection of the Dead & the Igbo Belief in the "Reincarnation" A Systemico-Theological Study. LC 94-195532. (Erfahrung und Theologie Ser.: Vol. 23). 261p. 1994. pap. 45.95 (*3-631-47295-1*) P Lang Pubng.

— The Problem of Language in Religious Education. LC 98-39372. (Beitrage zur Erziehungswissenschaft und Biblischen Bildung Ser.: Vol. 3). 155p. 1998. pap. text 31.95 (*0-8204-3603-8*) P Lang Pubng.

Obilor, John Iheanyichuk. The Problem of Language in Religious Education. 155p. 1998. 31.95 (*3-631-33473-7*) P Lang Pubng.

O'Binna. Foundations of African-American Education. 1998. pap., student ed. 32.81 (*0-07-012211-3*) McGraw.

Obinna, Michael E. Learning & Teaching for Continuous Assessment. LC 97-158430. 88p. 1996. pap. 17.95 (*3-906751-01-5*, Pub. by P Lang) P Lang Pubng.

Obitz, Harry. Golf Magazine's Six Days to Better Golf: The Secrets of Learning the Golf Swing. (Illus.). 192p. 1997. pap. text 10.95 (*0-88486-163-5*, Bristol Park Bks) Arrowood Pr.

Object Management Group Staff, et al. Object Management Architecture Guide. 3rd ed. LC 95-49983. 164p. 1995. pap. 54.99 (*0-471-14193-3*) Wiley.

Object Management Group Staff, jt. auth. see International Enterprise Distributed Object Computing Staff.

Oblad, Alex G., et al, eds. Thermal Hydrocarbon Chemistry: Based on a Symposium Jointly Sponsored by the ACS Divisions of Petroleum Chemistry & Fuel Chemistry at the 175th National Meeting of the American Chemical Society, Anaheim, CA, March 15-16, 1978. LC 79-22817. (Advances in Chemistry Ser.: No. 183). (Illus.). 374p. 1979. reprint ed. pap. 116.00 (*0-608-06752-0*, 206694900009) Bks Demand.

Oblander, Ruth. Sewing Without Pins. LC 76-53269. 1986. 5.95 (*0-933956-01-0*) Sew-Fit.

— Slacks for Perfect Fit: Sew-Fit Method. LC 81-50280. (Illus.). 64p. 1981. pap. 5.95 (*0-933956-07-X*) Sew-Fit.

Oblander, Ruth & Anderson, Joan. Dresses Cut-to-Fit. LC 76-53237. 1976. 5.95 (*0-933956-02-9*) Sew-Fit.

— The Sew-Fit Manual. LC 77-84538. (Illus.). (C). 1978. 29.95 (*0-933956-03-7*) Sew-Fit.

Oblas, Carla. Algebra: Create & Discover. 328p. (C). 1991. pap. text 19.00 (*0-89801-021-7*) NE Univ Pub.

— Problem Solving & Algebra Too. 4th rev. ed. 496p. (C). 1991. pap. text 20.00 (*0-89801-022-5*) NE Univ Pub.

Oblas, Peter B. Perspectives on Race & Culture in Japanese Society: The Mass Media & Ethnicity. LC 94-38356. 236p. 1995. text 89.95 (*0-7734-8986-X*) E Mellen.

Oblensky, S. & Sapountzis, P. Greek Basic Course: Level Three. 210p. 1999. pap. 120.00 incl. audio (*1-58214-024-3*) Mltilingl Bks.

***Oblensky, S., et al.** Greek Basic Course Level Two with 19 Cassettes. 250p. 1999. pap. text 180.00 (*1-58214-023-5*) Mltilingl Bks.

— Greek Basic Course with 17 Cassettes: Foreign Service Greek Level One. (Multilingual Books Intensive Cassette Foreign Language Ser.). 327p. 1999. pap. text 180.00 (*1-58214-022-7*) Mltilingl Bks.

Obler, Loraine & Fein, Deborah, eds. The Exceptional Brain: Neuropsychology of Talent & Special Abilities. LC 86-27136. 522p. 1988. lib. bdg. 55.00 (*0-89862-701-X*) Guilford Pubns.

Obler, Loraine & Gjerlow, Kris. Language & the Brain. (Cambridge Approaches to Linguistics Ser.). (Illus.). 224p. (C). 1998. pap. text 17.95 (*0-521-46641-5*) Cambridge U Pr.

— Language & the Brain. LC 97-47554. (Cambridge Approaches to Linguistics Ser.). (Illus.). 224p. (C). 1999. text 54.95 (*0-521-46095-6*) Cambridge U Pr.

Obler, Loraine K., jt. ed. see Menn, Lise.

Obler, Martin. Moira. LC 92-60567. 304p. 1993. 22.95 (*0-88282-120-2*) New Horizon NJ.

Obler, Martin & Clavin, Thomas. Fatal Analysis: A True Story of Professional Privilege & Serial Murder. LC 96-68934. 288p. 1997. 23.95 (*0-88282-152-0*) New Horizon NJ.

Obligado. Charito's Nest. (J). 1998. 14.00 (*0-671-86747-4*) S&S Bks Yung.

***Obligado, Clara.** Si Un Hombre Vivo Te Hace Iiorar. (SPA.). 1998. 24.95 (*84-08-02506-6*) Planeta Edit.

Obligado, Lilian. Three Little Kittens. 1998. lib. bdg. 7.99 (*0-679-99210-3*, Pub. by Random Bks Yng Read) Random.

— Three Little Kittens. 24p. (J). 1998. 1.99 (*0-679-89210-9*, Pub. by Random Bks Yng Read) Random.

Obligado, Lilli V. Nose to Toes. LC 98-40344. (J). 1999. pap. 3.25 (*0-679-88825-X*, Pub. by Random Bks Yng Read) Random.

Oblinger, Carl. Cornwall: The People & Culture of an Industrial Camelot, 1890-1980. (Illus.). 123p. 1984. pap. text 6.95 (*0-89271-028-4*) Pa Hist & Mus.

— Interviewing the People of Pennsylvania: A Conceptual Guide to Oral History. LC 79-625709. 84p. (Orig.). (C). 1981. pap. 7.95 (*0-911124-94-2*) Pa Hist & Mus.

***Oblinger, Diana G. & Katz, Richard N., eds.** Renewing Administration: Preparing Colleges & Universities for the 21st Century. 375p. (C). 1999. 35.95 (*1-882982-27-4*) Anker Pub.

Oblinger, Diana G. & Rush, Sean C., eds. The Future Compatible Campus: Planning, Designing, & Implementing Information Technology in the Academy. 304p. 1997. 35.95 (*1-882982-19-3*) Anker Pub.

— The Learning Revolution: The Challenge of Information Technology in the Academy. 264p. (C). 1997. text 35.95 (*1-882982-17-7*) Anker Pub.

Oblinger, Diana G., et al. What Business Wants from Higher Education. LC 98-14889. (Series on Higher Education). 200p. 1998. 29.95 (*1-57356-206-8*) Oryx Pr.

***Oblitas, Keith Robert A. & Peter, J. Raymond.** Transferring Irrigation Management to Farmers in Andhra Pradesh, India. LC 99-49102. (Technical Paper Ser.: No. 449). 193p. 1999. pap. 25.00 (*0-8213-4577-X*, 14577) World Bank.

***Oblivion, Brian.** The Hacker's Bible: The Ultimate Guide to Hacking in the Internet Age. (Illus.). 208p. 2000. pap. write for info. (*1-85868-406-4*, Pub. by Carlton Bks Ltd) Natl Bk Netwk.

O'Block, Robert L. Criminal Justice Research Sources. 3rd ed. LC 92-70236. 189p. (C). 1992. pap. text 24.95 (*0-87084-665-5*) Anderson Pub Co.

O'Block, Robert L., et al. Security & Crime Prevention. 2nd ed. 439p. 1991. 44.95 (*0-7506-9007-0*) Buttrwrth-Heinemann.

Obloj, Krysztof, et al. Winning: Continuous Improvement Theory in High Performance Organizations. LC 94-39616. (SUNY Series in International Management). 205p. (C). 1995. text 49.50 (*0-7914-2521-5*); pap. text 16.95 (*0-7914-2522-3*) State U NY Pr.

***Oblong, Angus.** Creepy Susie: And Thirteen Other Tragic Tales for Troubled Children. LC 99-23482. 160p. (J). 1999. 16.95 (*0-345-43301-7*, Ballantine) Ballantine Pub Grp.

Oblozinsky, P & Gandini, A., eds. Nuclear Reaction Data & Nuclear Reactors: Physics, Design & Safety Proceedings of the Workshop ICTP, Trieste, Italy 23 Feb - 27 Mar 1998. LC 99-29343. 560p. 1999. 94.00 (*981-02-3916-5*) World Scientific Pub.

Obm, Shalom Dovbaer Schneersohn. To Know G-D - Ye Yadaata. Touger, Eliyahu, tr. 80p. 1993. pap. 9.00 (*0-8266-0534-6*) Kehot Pubn Soc.

— With Light & with Might. Kaploun, Uri, ed. & tr. by. Touger, Eliyahu, tr. 128p. (Orig.). 1993. pap. 10.00 (*0-8266-0533-8*) Kehot Pubn Soc.

Obm, Yosef Yitchak Schneersohn. Likkutei Dibburim, Vol. 1. Kaploun, Uri, tr. from YID. 360p. 1987. 20.00 (*0-8266-0444-7*) Kehot Pubn Soc.

— Likkutei Dibburim, Vol. 2. Kaploun, Uri, tr. from YID. 328p. 1988. 20.00 (*0-8266-0445-5*) Kehot Pubn Soc.

Obm, Yosef Yitchak Scneersohn. Likkutei Dibburim, Vol. 3. Kaploun, Uri, tr. from YID. 320p. 1990. 20.00 (*0-8266-0446-3*) Kehot Pubn Soc.

Obmascik, Mark. A Consumer's Guide to Water Conservation: Dozens of Ways to Save Water, the Environment, & a Lot of Money. (Illus.). 72p. 1993. mass mkt. 6.75 (*0-89867-726-2*, 10063) Am Water Wks Assn.

Obminsky, Ernest & Bugrov, Andrei. International Economic Security: A Major Factor of Peace. (C). 1988. 14.00 (*0-8364-2394-1*, Pub. by Allied Pubs) S Asia.

Obohuber, Konrad. Raphael: The Paintings. (Illus.). 264p. 1999. 75.00 (*3-7913-2238-9*, Pub. by Prestel) te Neues.

OBOJSKI, BOB. Baseball's Zaniest Moments. LC 99-44615. 96p. 1999. pap. text 6.95 (*0-8069-3767-X*) Sterling.

Obojski, Robert. Baseball's Strangest Moments. LC 87-33319. (Illus.). 128p. 1989. pap. 5.95 (*0-8069-6983-0*) Sterling.

***Obojski, Robert.** Coin Collector's Price Guide. rev. ed. LC 99-462556. (Illus.). 128p. 1999. pap. text 8.95 (*0-8069-6497-9*) Sterling.

Obojski, Robert. A First Stamp Album for Beginners. 1984. pap. 3.95 (*0-486-23843-1*) Dover.

Obojski, Robert, jt. auth. see Hobson, Burton.

Obolensky, D., tr. The Heritage of Russian Verse. LC 75-23893. 544p. reprint ed. pap. 19.95 (*0-253-32736-9*) Ind U Pr.

Obolensky, D., jt. ed. see Auty, R.

***Obolensky, Dimitri.** Bread of Exile: A Russian Family. Willets, Harry, tr. 2000. 30.00 (*1-86046-511-0*, Pub. by Harvill Press) FS&G.

Obolensky, Dimitri. The Byzantine Commonwealth: Eastern Europe, 500-1453. LC 82-16970. (Illus.). 552p. 1983. reprint ed. pap. 19.95 (*0-913836-98-2*) St Vladimirs.

— The Byzantine Inheritance of Eastern Europe. (Collected Studies: No. CS156). (Illus.). 300p. (C). 1982. reprint ed. lib. bdg. 99.95 (*0-86078-102-X*, Pub. by Variorum) Ashgate Pub Co.

— Byzantium & the Slavs. LC 94-25507. 334p. 1994. pap. 18.95 (*0-88141-008-X*) St Vladimirs.

Obolensky, Dmitri. The Bogomils: A Study in Balkan Neo-Manichaeism. LC 77-84712. reprint ed. 39.00 (*0-404-16118-9*) AMS Pr.

Obolensky, George, tr. see Pushkin, Aleksandr, et al.

Obolensky, J. & Auty, B. Introduction to Russian Art & Architecture (Companion to Russian Studies) (C). 1990. pap. 150.00 (*0-7855-4490-9*, Pub. by Collets) St Mut.

Obolensky, Nick. Practical Business Re-Engineering: Tools & Techniques for Achieving Effective Change. LC 95-12523. 346p. 1995. 29.95 (*0-88415-646-X*, 5646) Gulf Pub.

Obolensky, Serge. One Man in His Time. (Illus.). 1958. 20.00 (*0-8392-1080-9*) Astor-Honor.

Obolensky, Serge, et al. Spoken Amharic, Bk. 1. (AMH.). 500p. pap. 190.00 incl. audio (*0-87950-654-7*) Spoken Lang Serv.

Obolensky, Serge, et al. Spoken Amharic, Bk. 1, Units 1-50. (AMH.). 500p. audio 145.00 (*0-87950-652-0*) Spoken Lang Serv.

Obolensky, Serge, et al. Spoken Amharic, Bk. 1, Units 1-50. (AMH.). 500p. 1980. pap. text 45.00 (*0-87950-650-4*) Spoken Lang Serv.

— Spoken Amharic, Bk. 2, Units 51-60. (Spoken Language Ser.). (AMH.). 500p. pap. 110.00 incl. digital audio (*0-87950-655-5*) Spoken Lang Serv.

Obolensky, Serge, et al. Spoken Amharic, Bk. 2, Units 51-60. (Spoken Language Ser.). (AMH.). 500p. audio 65.00 (*0-87950-653-9*) Spoken Lang Serv.

Obolensky, Serge, et al. Spoken Amharic, Book 2, Units Fifty-One to Sixty, Bk. 2, Units 51-60. (Spoken Language Ser.). (AMH.). 500p. 1980. pap. text 45.00 (*0-87950-651-2*); audio 300.00 (*0-87950-656-3*) Spoken Lang Serv.

— Spoken Persian. Panah, Kambiz Y. & Nouri, Fereidoun K., eds. Incl. Book, Units 1-12. LC 73-15155. 401p. 1973. pap. 20.00 (*0-87950-295-9*); LC 73-15155. (Spoken Language Ser.). (C). 1973. (*0-318-55757-6*) Spoken Lang Serv.

Obolensky, Sergie, et al. Amharic Basic Course. (Intensive Cassette Ser.). 501p. 1998. spiral bd. 270.00 incl. audio (*1-58214-006-5*) Mltilingl Bks.

Oboler, Eli M. Defending Intellectual Freedom: The Library & the Censor, 32. LC 79-8585. (Contributions in Librarianship & Information Science Ser.: No. 32). 246p. 1980. 38.50 (*0-313-21472-7*, ODF/, Greenwood Pr) Greenwood.

— Ideas & the University Library: Essays of an Unorthodox Academic Librarian, 20. LC 77-111. (Contributions in Librarianship & Information Science Ser.: No. 20). 203p. 1977. 49.95 (*0-8371-9531-4*, OIS/, Greenwood Pr) Greenwood.

Oboler, Regina S. Women, Power, & Economic Change: The Nandi of Kenya. LC 83-45345. (Illus.). 368p. 1985. 47.50 (*0-8047-1224-7*) Stanford U Pr.

Oboler, Suzanne. Ethnic Labels, Latino Lives: Identity & the Politics of (Re) Presentation. LC 94-22751. 1995. pap. 18.95 (*0-8166-2286-8*) U of Minn Pr.

An Asterisk (*) at the beginning of an entry indicates that the title is appearing for the first time.

Obon de Castro, Concepcion & Rivera Nunez, Diego. A Taxonomic Revision of the Section Sideritis (Genus Sideritis) (Labiatae) LC 96-208276. (Phanerogamarum Monographiae Ser.: Tomus XXI). (Illus.). xii, 640p. 1994. 171.00 (*3-443-78003-2*, Pub. by Gebruder Borntraeger) Balogh.

O'Book, Irene. Maybe My Baby. LC 96-35921. (Illus.). 14p. (J). (ps up). 1998. 5.95 (*0-694-00872-9*) HarpC Child Bks.

***O'Book, Irene.** Scrubbly Bubbly Car Wash. (J). 2001. 15.95 (*0-694-00871-0*) HarpC Child Bks.

Oborn. Pediatrics. Date not set. text. write for info. (*0-323-01199-3*) Mosby Inc.

Oborn, Lynn, jt. auth. see Engler, Nancy.

Oborne, David J. Computers at Work: A Behavioural Approach. LC 84-17335. (Wiley Series in Psychology & Productivity at Work). 436p. reprint ed. pap. 135.20 (*0-7837-3414-X*, 204338100008) Bks Demand.

— Ergonomics & Human Factors, 2 vols., Set. (International Library of Critical Writings in Psychology: No. 7). 1088p. (C). 1995. lib. bdg. 295.00 (*0-8147-6187-9*) NYU Pr.

— Ergonomics & Human Factors, Vol. 1. (C). 1995. lib. bdg. 147.50 (*0-8147-6188-7*) NYU Pr.

— Ergonomics & Human Factors, Vol. 2. (C). 1995. lib. bdg. 147.50 (*0-8147-6189-5*) NYU Pr.

— Ergonomics at Work. LC 81-14642. 331p. reprint ed. pap. 102.70 (*0-608-17554-4*, 203053400069) Bks Demand.

— Ergonomics at Work: Human Factors in Design & Development. 3rd ed. LC 94-28236. 462p. 1995. pap. text 74.50 (*0-471-95235-4*) Wiley.

Oborne, David J. & Gruneberg, Michael M., eds. The Physical Environment at Work. LC 82-23743. (Wiley Series in Psychology & Productivity at Work). 252p. reprint ed. pap. 78.20 (*0-7837-6389-1*, 204610200010) Bks Demand.

Oborne, David J., et al. Person Centered Ergonomics: A Brantonian View of Human Factors. LC 92-29732. 1993. 89.95 (*0-7484-0051-6*) Taylor & Francis.

Oborne, Louise & Builard, Jean. Yes You Can! Help Your Kid Succeed with Math: Even If You think You Can't. Young, Cynthia, ed. LC 97-60736. (Yes You Can! Help Your Kid Ser.: Vol. 1). (Illus.). 64p. 1997. pap. 18.00 (*0-9658044-0-2*, Yes You Can) Bufflehead Pub.

Oborotova, Marina A., jt. ed. see Cross, Sharyl.

***Obosu-Mensah, Kwaku.** Food Production in Urban Areas. LC 99-72607. 248p. 1999. 69.95 (*0-7546-1029-2*) Ashgate Pub Co.

Obosu-Mensah, Kwaku. Ghana's Volta Resettlement Scheme: The Long-Term Consequences of Post-Colonial State Planning. LC 93-42795. 208p. 1996. 69.95 (*1-883255-33-3*, U Pr W Africa); pap. 49.95 (*1-883255-32-5*, U Pr W Africa) Intl Scholars.

O'Boyle, Cornelius. The Art of Medicine: Medical Teaching at the University of Paris, 1250-1400. LC 98-38400. (Education & Society in the Middle Ages & Renaissance Ser.: Vol. 9). (Illus.). 336p. 1998. 106.50 (*90-04-11124-7*) Brill Academic Pubs.

O'Boyle, Edward J. Personalist Economics: Moral Convictions, Economic Realities, & Social Action. LC 98-13615. 1998. 99.95 (*0-7923-8146-7*) Kluwer Academic.

O'Boyle, Edward J., jt. ed. see Davis, John B.

O'Boyle, Edward J., ed. see World Congress of Social Economics Staff.

O'Boyle, Ita. Gertrud Von le Fort: An Introduction to the Prose Work. LC 64-13378. 128p. reprint ed. pap. 39.70 (*0-7837-0459-3*, 204078200018) Bks Demand.

O'Boyle, Jane. Catnip for the Soul. LC 98-56004. (Illus.). 192p. 1999. pap. 9.95 (*0-688-16982-1*, Wm Morrow) Morrow Avon.

***O'Boyle, Jane.** Free Drinks for Ladies with Nuts: Delightfully Mangled English from Around the World. LC 99-45735. 128p. 2000. pap. 10.95 (*0-452-28114-8*, Plume) Dutton Plume.

O'Boyle, Jane. Wrong! The Biggest Missteps & Miscalculations Ever Made by People Who Should Have Known Better. LC 99-27846. 128p. 1999. pap. 11.95 (*0-452-28112-1*, Plume) Dutton Plume.

***O'Boyle, Jane.** Wrong Again! More of the Biggest Mistakes & Miscalculations Ever Made by People Who Should Have Known Better. 2000. pap. 10.00 (*0-452-28201-2*, Plume) Dutton Plume.

O'Boyle, Lily G. Pacific Crossings: A Philippine Cookbook. LC 93-12794. (Illus.). 192p. 1994. 35.00 (*0-944863-25-6*) Acacia Corp.

O'Boyle, Lily G. & Alejandro, Reynaldo. Philippine Hospitality: A Gracious Tradition of the East. Ner, Sonia & Almario, Lyn, eds. 224p. 1988. 55.00 (*0-944863-00-0*) Acacia Corp.

O'Boyle, Michael W., ed. Intelligence, Learning Disability, & Associated Brain Characteristics: A Special Issue of Developmental Neuropsychology. 163p. 1996. pap. 20.00 (*0-8058-9923-5*) L Erlbaum Assocs.

O'Boyle, Monica B., tr. see McIntyre, Sally.

O'Boyle, Thomas F. At Any Cost: Jack Welch, General Electric & the Pursuit of Profit. LC 98-15011. 464p. 1998. 29.95 (*0-679-42132-7*) Knopf.

— At Any Cost: Jack Welch, General Electric & the Pursuit of Profit. 1999. pap. 16.00 (*0-375-70567-8*) Vin Bks.

OBPRA Staff, ed. see New York State of Business Permits Office.

Obradovic, Dragan, jt. auth. see Deco, Gustavo.

Obradovic, Dragon, jt. auth. see Deco, G.

Obradovic, J., jt. ed. see Hein, James R.

Obradovic, Josip & Dunn, William N., eds. Workers' Self-Management & Organizational Power in Yugoslavia. LC 78-16307. 464p. reprint ed. pap. 143.90 (*0-7837-2145-5*, 204243100004) Bks Demand.

Obradovic, Nadezda, jt. ed. see Gorup, Radmilla.

Obradovich, Betty, jt. auth. see Obradovich, John.

Obradovich, John & Obradovich, Betty. 1999 Bahamas & Caribbean Pilot's Guide. 20th rev. ed. (Illus.). 450p. 1998. 44.95 (*0-9660854-1-8*) Pilot Pub.

Obrams, G. I. & Potter, M., eds. Epidemiology & Biology of Multiple Myeloma. (Illus.). xv, 192p. 1991. 48.95 (*0-387-54061-X*) Spr-Verlag.

Obrand, D. I., ed. see Ahn, S. S.

Obrastoff, Sharon, ed. see Blue, Ken.

Obreanu, P. E., jt. ed. see Gould, S. H.

Obrebski, Joseph. The Changing Peasantry of Eastern Europe. (Illus.). 100p. 1976. pap. 21.95 (*0-87073-741-4*) Transaction Pubs.

Obrecht, D., ed. Solid Supported Combinatorial & Parallel Synthesis of Small Molecular-Weight Compound Libraries. LC 98-39458. (Tetrahedron Organic Chemistry Ser.). 400p. 1998. 114.50 (*0-08-043258-1*, Pergamon Pr); pap. 49.50 (*0-08-043257-3*, Pergamon Pr) Elsevier.

Obrecht, Fred. How to Prepare for the CBEST: California Basic Education Skills Test. 4th ed. Mundsack, Alan et al, eds. LC 96-35268. 453p. 1997. pap. 13.95 (*0-8120-9731-9*) Barron.

***Obrecht, Fred.** Minimum Essentials of English. 2nd rev. ed. LC 98-74451. 72p. 1999. ring bd. 6.95 (*0-7641-0745-3*) Barron.

Obrecht, Fred & Ferris, Boak. How to Prepare for the California State University Writing Proficiency Exams: Or the GWAR - Graduation Writing Assessment Requirement. 2nd rev. ed. LC 98-35742. (Illus.). 288p. (YA). 1999. pap. 13.95 (*0-7641-0464-0*) Barron.

Obrecht, G. & Stark, L. W. Presbyopia Research: From Molecular Biology to Visual Adaptation. (Illus.). 318p. (C). 1990. text 85.00 (*0-306-43659-0*, Kluwer Plenum) Kluwer Academic.

Obrecht, J. B. & Dubach, U. C., eds. Medizinische Universitaets Poliklinik Basel, 100 Jahre. (Illus.). 100p. 1975. 26.00 (*3-8055-2280-0*) S Karger.

Obrecht, Jas. Blues Guitar: The Men Who Made the Music. 1990. pap. 19.95 (*0-7935-0074-5*, HL00183632) H Leonard.

Obrecht, Jas, ed. Blues Guitar: The Men Who Made the Music. 2nd ed. (Illus.). 278p. 1993. pap. 22.95 (*0-87930-292-5*) Miller Freeman.

***Obrecht, Jas, ed.** Rollin' & Tumblin' The Postwar Blues Guitarists. (Illus.). 450p. 2000. pap. 19.95 (*0-87930-613-0*) Miller Freeman.

O'Brein, D. P. The Correspondence of Lord Overstone, 3 Vol. 1680p. 1998. 275.00 (*1-85506-624-6*) Thoemmes Pr.

O'Brennen, Junius & Smith, Nopal. The Crystal Icon. (Illus.). vii, 200p. 1981. 50.00 (*0-940578-03-4*) Galahand Pr.

Obreux, Esme. Discipline of the Private House. 2000. mass mkt. 6.95 (*0-352-33459-2*) BLA4.

O'Brian, David Z. How to Avoid Small Business Roadblocks: On the Way to Success. 221p. 1996. pap. 12.95 (*1-881385-04-3*) New Cent Pubns.

— Thirty Reasons Not to Buy or Start a Business. 2nd ed. 201p. 1994. pap. 12.95 (*1-881385-00-0*) New Cent Pubns.

O'Brian, Ellen G. Living the Eternal Way: Spiritual Meaning & Practice for Daily Life. Cawley, Anne, ed. LC 97-75320. (Illus.). 192p. 1997. pap. 22.95 (*0-9660518-0-7*) Ctr for Spirit.

O'Brian, Fitz-James. Ballads of Ireland. (Notable American Authors Ser.). 1999. reprint ed. lib. bdg. 125.00 (*0-7812-4663-6*) Rprt Serv.

— Collected Poems & Stories. (Notable American Authors Ser.). 1999. reprint ed. lib. bdg. 125.00 (*0-7812-4664-4*) Rprt Serv.

— Collected Stories. (Notable American Authors Ser.). 1999. reprint ed. lib. bdg. 125.00 (*0-7812-4666-0*) Rprt Serv.

— A Gentleman from Ireland. (Notable American Authors Ser.). 1999. reprint ed. lib. bdg. 125.00 (*0-7812-4665-2*) Rprt Serv.

O'Brian, John. Degas to Matisse: The Maurice Wertheim Collection. (Illus.). 176p. 1988. pap. 19.95 (*0-916724-65-4*, 4654) Harvard Art Mus.

— Ruthless Hedonism: The American Reception of Matisse. LC 98-22926. (Illus.). 285p. 1999. 45.00 (*0-226-61626-6*) U Ch Pr.

O'Brian, John. Ruthless Hedonism Matisse. 1997. pap. text 15.95 (*0-226-61627-4*) U Ch Pr.

O'Brian, John, ed. see Greenberg, Clement.

O'Brian, L., jt. ed. see Blakeney, A. B.

O'Brian, Patricia, jt. auth. see Bart, Pauline B.

O'Brian, Patrick. Aubrey & Maturin, 18 vols. 1996. 406.50 (*0-393-04117-4*) Norton.

— The Aubrey-Maturin Series, 17 vols. (C). 1995. 382.50 (*0-393-03975-7*) Norton.

— The Aubrey-Maturin Series, 17 vols., Set. (C). 1994. 360.00 (*0-393-03749-5*) Norton.

***O'Brian, Patrick.** Blue at the Mizzen. LC 99-48283. 1999. 30.00 (*0-7862-2046-5*) Mac Lib Ref.

O'Brian, Patrick. Blue at the Mizzen. LC 99-42043. 288p. 1999. 24.00 (*0-393-04844-6*) Norton.

— Blue at the Mizzen. limited ed. 250.00 (*0-393-04874-8*) Norton.

***O'Brian, Patrick.** Blue at the Mizzen. 272p. 2000. reprint ed. pap. 13.95 (*0-393-32107-X*) Norton.

— Caesar: The Life Story of a Panda-Leopard. 100p. 2000. 21.95 (*0-393-04918-3*) Norton.

O'Brian, Patrick. The Commodore. (Aubrey-Maturin Ser.). 288p. 1995. 22.50 (*0-393-03760-6*) Norton.

— The Commodore. (Aubrey-Maturin Ser.). 288p. 1996. pap. 13.95 (*0-393-31459-6*, Norton Paperbks) Norton.

— The Commodore. large type ed. 1995. 24.95 (*1-56895-271-6*, Compass) Wheeler Pub.

— Desolation Island. 325p. 1991. pap. 13.95 (*0-393-30812-X*) Norton.

— Desolation Island. 1994. 24.00 (*0-393-03705-3*) Norton.

O'Brian, Patrick. The Far Side of the World. 1950. 30.00 (*0-7862-1930-0*) Mac Lib Ref.

O'Brian, Patrick. The Far Side of the World. 368p. 1992. pap. 13.95 (*0-393-30862-6*) Norton.

— The Far Side of the World. 1994. 24.00 (*0-393-03710-X*) Norton.

— The Fortune of War. 329p. 1991. pap. 13.95 (*0-393-30813-8*) Norton.

— The Fortune of War. 1994. 24.00 (*0-393-03706-1*) Norton.

— The Golden Ocean. 1994. 24.00 (*0-393-03630-8*) Norton.

— The Golden Ocean. 288p. 1996. pap. 13.95 (*0-393-31537-1*) Norton.

— The Golden Ocean. large type ed. LC 97-13849. (Basic Ser.). 469p. 1997. 26.95 (*0-7862-1147-4*) Thorndike Pr.

— H. M. S. Surprise. 379p. 1991. pap. 13.95 (*0-393-30761-1*) Norton.

— H. M. S. Surprise. 1994. 24.00 (*0-393-03703-7*) Norton.

***O'Brian, Patrick.** H. M. S. Surprise. large type ed. LC 00-23440. (Famous Authors Ser.). 564p. Date not set. 28.95 (*0-7862-1934-3*, MML06400-170754) Thorndike Pr.

O'Brian, Patrick. The Hundred Days. LC 98-35866. 288p. 1998. 24.00 (*0-393-04674-5*) Norton.

— The Hundred Days. 288p. 1999. pap. 13.95 (*0-393-31979-2*) Norton.

— The Hundred Days. large type ed. LC 98-48561. 1950. 30.00 (*0-7862-1749-9*, G K Hall Lrg Type) Mac Lib Ref.

— The Hundred Days. large type ed. LC 98-48561. 1999. 30.00 (*0-7862-1748-0*, G K Hall Lrg Type) Mac Lib Ref.

***O'Brian, Patrick.** Hussein: An Entertainment. 239p. 2000. 23.95 (*0-393-04919-1*) Norton.

O'Brian, Patrick. Industrialization, 4 vols., Set. University of London Staff, ed. LC 97-44965. (Critical Perspectives on the World Economy Ser.). 1544p. (C). 1998. 700.00 (*0-415-12369-0*) Routledge.

— The Ionian Mission. 368p. 1992. pap. 13.95 (*0-393-30821-9*) Norton.

— The Ionian Mission. 1994. 24.00 (*0-393-03708-8*) Norton.

O'Brian, Patrick. The Ionian Mission. large type ed. 1950. 30.00 (*0-7862-1928-9*, G K Hall Lrg Type) Mac Lib Ref.

O'Brian, Patrick. Joseph Banks: A Life. LC 97-24475. ii, 328p. 1997. pap. 15.95 (*0-226-61628-2*) U Ch Pr.

— The Letter of Marque. 1999. 28.95 (*0-7862-1925-4*) Mac Lib Ref.

— The Letter of Marque. 1990. 24.00 (*0-393-02874-7*) Norton.

— The Letter of Marque. 288p. 1992. pap. 13.95 (*0-393-30905-3*) Norton.

— Making College Count: A Real World Look at How to Succeed in & after College. LC 96-94706. (Illus.). 176p. (Orig.). (YA). (gr. 11-12). 1996. pap. 14.95 (*0-9633678-3-8*) Graphic Mngmt.

— Master & Commander. (Aubrey-Maturin Ser.). (Illus.). 411p. 1990. pap. 13.95 (*0-393-30705-0*) Norton.

— Master & Commander. 1994. 24.00 (*0-393-03701-0*) Norton.

— Master & Commander. large type ed. LC 99-26534. 1999. 28.95 (*0-7862-1932-7*) Thorndike Pr.

— The Mauritius Command. 1991. pap. 13.95 (*0-393-30762-X*) Norton.

— The Mauritius Command. 1994. 24.00 (*0-393-03704-5*) Norton.

O'Brian, Patrick. The Mauritius Command. large type ed. 1950. 30.00 (*0-7862-1935-1*) Mac Lib Ref.

O'Brian, Patrick. Men-of-War: Life in Nelson's Navy. 1996. text 23.00 (*0-07-048222-5*) McGraw.

— Men-of-War: Life in Nelson's Navy. LC 95-2297. (Illus.). 96p. 1995. 23.00 (*0-393-03858-0*) Norton.

— The Nutmeg of Consolation. LC 91-3975. 320p. 1991. 24.00 (*0-393-03032-6*) Norton.

— The Nutmeg of Consolation. 320p. 1993. pap. 13.95 (*0-393-30906-1*) Norton.

O'Brian, Patrick. The Nutmeg of Consolation. large type ed. 1950. 30.00 (*0-7862-1938-6*) Mac Lib Ref.

O'Brian, Patrick. Patrick O'Brian: Critical Essays & a Bibliography. 1994. 23.95 (*0-393-03626-X*) Norton.

— Picasso: A Biography. 520p. 1994. pap. 18.95 (*0-393-31107-4*) Norton.

— Post Captain. (Aubrey-Maturin Ser.). 496p. 1990. pap. 13.95 (*0-393-30706-9*) Norton.

— Post Captain. 1994. 24.00 (*0-393-03702-9*) Norton.

***O'Brian, Patrick.** Post Captain. large type ed. LC 00-21929. (Famous Authors Ser.). 689p. 2000. 27.95 (*0-7862-1933-5*, MML06400-17053) Thorndike Pr.

O'Brian, Patrick. The Rendezvous & Other Stories. 240p. 1994. 22.00 (*0-393-03685-5*) Norton.

— The Rendezvous & Other Stories. 256p. 1995. pap. 11.00 (*0-393-31380-8*, Norton Paperbks) Norton.

— The Reverse of the Medal. 288p. 1992. pap. 13.95 (*0-393-30960-6*) Norton.

— The Reverse of the Medal. 1994. 24.00 (*0-393-03711-8*) Norton.

O'Brian, Patrick. The Reverse of the Medal. large type ed. 1950. 30.00 (*0-7862-1931-9*) Mac Lib Ref.

O'Brian, Patrick. The Surgeon's Mate. 384p. 1992. pap. 13.95 (*0-393-30820-0*) Norton.

— The Surgeon's Mate. 1994. 24.00 (*0-393-03707-X*) Norton.

O'Brian, Patrick. The Surgeon's Mate. large type ed. 1950. 30.00 (*0-7862-1936-X*) Mac Lib Ref.

O'Brian, Patrick. Testimonies: A Novel. LC 92-27426. 224p. 1993. 20.95 (*0-393-03483-6*) Norton.

— Testimonies: A Novel. 224p. 1995. pap. 11.95 (*0-393-31316-6*, Norton Paperbks) Norton.

O'Brian, Patrick. The Thirteen-Gun Salute. 1950. 30.00 (*0-7862-1937-8*) Mac Lib Ref.

O'Brian, Patrick. The Thirteen-Gun Salute. LC 91-3455. 1991. 24.00 (*0-393-02974-3*) Norton.

— The Thirteen-Gun Salute. 336p. 1992. pap. 13.95 (*0-393-30907-X*) Norton.

— Treason's Harbour. 334p. 1992. pap. 13.95 (*0-393-30863-4*) Norton.

— Treason's Harbour. 1994. 24.00 (*0-393-03709-6*) Norton.

— The Truelove. 192p. 1992. 24.00 (*0-393-03109-8*) Norton.

— The Truelove. 256p. 1993. pap. 13.95 (*0-393-31016-7*) Norton.

— The Truelove. large type ed. 418p. 1992. reprint ed. lib. bdg. 17.95 (*1-56054-522-4*) Thorndike Pr.

— The Unknown Shore. 1996. text 23.00 (*0-07-048221-7*) McGraw.

— The Unknown Shore. 288p. 1995. 23.00 (*0-393-03859-9*) Norton.

— The Unknown Shore. 316p. 1996. pap. 13.95 (*0-393-31538-X*) Norton.

— The Unknown Shore. large type ed. LC 96-32354. 1996. 24.95 (*1-56895-360-7*, Compass) Wheeler Pub.

— The Wine-Dark Sea. LC 93-1521. 261p. 1993. 24.00 (*0-393-03558-1*) Norton.

— The Wine-Dark Sea. 272p. 1994. pap. 13.95 (*0-393-31244-5*) Norton.

— World of Patrick O'Brian Reading Group Guide. 1998. pap. text. write for info. (*0-393-10165-7*) Norton.

— The Yellow Admiral. 262p. 1996. 24.00 (*0-393-04044-5*) Norton.

— The Yellow Admiral. LC 96-24149. (Illus.). 272p. 1997. pap. 13.95 (*0-393-31704-8*) Norton.

***O'Brian, Patrick.** The Yellow Admiral. 1999. pap. 12.98 (*0-671-04444-3*) PB.

O'Brian, Patrick. The Yellow Admiral. large type ed. LC 97-9697. 1997. 26.95 (*1-56895-430-1*, Compass) Wheeler Pub.

O'Brian, Patrick, jt. ed. see Bruland, Kristine.

O'Brian, Patrick, tr. see Beauvoir, Simone de.

O'Brian, Patrick, tr. see Lacouture, Jean.

O'Brian, Rita C. White Society in Black Africa: The French of Senegal. LC 74-183533. 320p. reprint ed. pap. 99.20 (*0-608-11827-3*, 200687500060) Bks Demand.

O'Brian, Steven. Pancho Villa. (Hispanos Notables Ser.). (SPA., Illus.). 120p. (YA). (gr. 5 up). 1995. pap. 8.95 (*0-7910-3114-4*) Chelsea Hse.

— Ulysses S. Grant. (World Leaders Past & Present Ser.). (Illus.). 120p. (J). (gr. 5 up). 1991. lib. bdg. 19.95 (*1-55546-809-8*) Chelsea Hse.

O'Brian, Thomas A., contrib. by. Human Immunodeficiency Virus Type 1, Reference Material Specifications: Approved Guideline (1991) 1991. 95.00 (*1-56238-134-2*, I/LA13-A) NCCLS.

O'Briant, Don. Backroad Buffets & Country Cafes: A Southern Guide to Meat-&-Threes & Downhome Dining. LC 98-39482. 1998. pap. 13.95 (*0-89587-221-8*) Blair.

— Looking for Tara: The Gone with the Wind Guide to Margaret Mitchell's Atlanta. LC 94-77585. 112p. 1994. pap. 6.95 (*1-56352-172-5*) Longstreet.

***O'Briant, Donald.** Georgia. (Travel Smart Ser.). (Illus.). 240p. 2000. pap. 15.95 (*1-56261-531-9*, Pub. by Avalon Travel) Publishers Group.

O'Briant, Walter H., tr. see Leibniz, Gottfried Wilhelm.

***O'Brien.** Bond Valuation. 2nd ed. (SWC-Finance Ser.). 2002. pap. 22.00 incl. cd-rom (*0-538-87553-4*) Sth-Wstrn College.

O'Brien. Computer Operations Restaurant Management. (Food & Hospitality Ser.). 1991. teacher ed. 10.00 (*0-8273-3684-5*); text 31.95 (*0-8273-3683-7*) Delmar.

O'Brien. Fast Forward in MBA in Business & The Fast Forward MBA in Finance. 576p. pap. 24.95 (*0-471-16763-0*) Wiley.

O'Brien. Introduction to Information Systems. 9th ed. LC 99-31793. 1999. 63.25 (*0-07-229749-2*) McGraw.

— Investments: A Visual Approach. 2nd ed. (FD - Investments Ser.). pap. 68.95 (*0-538-87491-0*) S-W Pub.

— Managers & the Market. 1996. 26.95 (*0-8057-9834-X*, Twyne) Mac Lib Ref.

— Managers & the Market. 1998. per. 15.95 (*0-8057-4502-5*) Macmillan.

— Managing Information Systems Applications. 3rd ed. 1996. text 75.25 (*0-256-23618-6*) McGraw.

— Modern Portfolio Theory: Guide & Exercise. 2nd ed. (FD - Investments Ser.). pap. 27.95 (*0-538-87487-2*) S-W Pub.

— Pollution Prevention & Strategic Environmental Engineering. (C). 1997. text 79.95 (*0-442-02342-1*, VNR) Wiley.

— Refreshed by the Word, Vols. 1-3. 1996. pap. 27.95 (*0-8091-3701-1*) Paulist Pr.

***O'Brien.** Start Now, Succeed Later: Making College Count Career Search a Sucess. (SWC-Business Communication). 64p. 1999. pap. 22.95 (*0-324-01540-2*) Thomson Learn.

O'Brien & Bergstein. Image & Enterprise. Date not set. 50.00 Thames Hudson.

O'Brien & Shipman. Habitats - Forests & Meadows. (Illus.). 48p. (J). (gr. 1-3). 1995. pap., teacher ed. 9.95 (*1-55799-387-4*, 537) Evan-Moor Edu Pubs.

O'Brien - Johnson, Toni. Synge: The Medieval & the Grotesque. (Irish Literary Studies: Vol. # 11). 210p. 1982. 35.00 (*0-86140-104-2*, Pub. by Smyth) Dufour.

O'Brien & Gere Engineers, Inc. Staff. Hazardous Waste Site. (Environmental Engineering Ser.). 1995. pap. 68.95 (*0-442-02023-6*, VNR) Wiley.

O'Brien & Gere Engineers, Inc. Staff. Hazardous Waste Site Remediation: The Engineer's Perspective. Bellandi, Robert, ed. 422p. 1995. pap. 99.00 (*0-471-28693-1*, VNR) Wiley.

O'Brien & Gere Engineers, Inc. Staff. Innovative Engineering Technologies for Hazardous Waste Remediation. Bellandi, Robert, ed. (Environmental Engineering Ser.). 352p. 1994. 99.00 (*0-471-28495-5*, VNR) Wiley.

— Innovative Engineering Technologies for Hazardous Waste Remediation. LC 94-27588. 384p. 1995. text 76.95 (*0-442-01180-6*, VNR) Wiley.

O'Brien, A. Receptor Binding in Drug Research. (Clinical Pharmacology Ser.: Vol. 5). (Illus.). 544p. 1986. text 225.00 (*0-8247-7548-1*) Dekker.

O'Brien, Aileen. The Dine: Orgin Myths of the Navaho Indians. 1988. reprint ed. lib. bdg. 75.00 (*0-7812-0065-2*) Rprt Serv.

O'Brien, Alan. Check-Mate: A Pocket-Size Guide to Everyday Spellings for Dyslexics. 64p. 1993. pap. 9.95 (*1-85302-165-2*) Taylor & Francis.

***O'Brien, Alice R.** Rinks to Arenas: Ten Years of British Ice Hockey. 148p. 1999. pap. 64.00 (*1-897676-89-1*, Pub. by Nottingham Univ Pr) St Mut.

O'Brien, Alison D., jt. auth. see Kaper, James B.

O'Brien, Anita. A Lab Manual for Desktop Publishing: IBM Version for Beginners. 62p. 1992. 24.95 (*1-881950-01-8*) A OBrien.

— A Lab Manual for Desktop Publishing: IBM Version for Intermediates. 62p. 1992. 22.95 (*1-881950-03-4*) A OBrien.

— A Lab Manual for Desktop Publishing: Macintosh Version for Beginners. 62p. 1992. 24.95 (*1-881950-00-X*) A OBrien.

— A Lab Manual for Desktop Publishing: Macintosh Version for Intermediates. 62p. 1992. 22.95 (*1-881950-02-6*) A OBrien.

O'Brien, Anne S. Arco Iris en la Cuidad Bajo la Lluvia. Palacios, Argentina, tr. (Spanish Whole Language Big Bks.).Tr. of Rainy City Rainbow. (SPA., Illus.). 16p. (Orig.). (J). (ps-2). 1993. pap. 14.95 (*1-56784-092-2*) Newbridge Educ.

— The Princess & the Beggar: A Korean Folktale. LC 92-11988. (Illus.). 32p. (J). (gr. k-4). 1993. 14.95 (*0-590-46092-7*) Scholastic Inc.

O'Brien, Anne Sibley, see Burns Knight, Margy & Sibley O'Brien, Anne.

O'Brien, Anthony G. The Ancient Chronology of Thar: The Bhattika, Laukika & Sindh Eras. LC 96-906243. (Oxford University South Asian Studies Ser.). (Illus.). 226p. 1996. text 24.95 (*0-19-563474-8*) OUP.

O'Brien, Anthony P., jt. auth. see O'Driscoll, Ciaran.

O'Brien, Anthony P., jt. ed. see Thornton, Robert J.

O'Brien, Barbara. In Building a Better World. 1997. pap. 56.95 (*1-57553-652-8*) Watermrk Pr.

O'Brien, Bart. Database Decisions: Briefings on the Management of Technology. 288p. (Orig.). 1994. pap. 67.50 (*0-273-60289-6*, Pub. by Pitman Pub) Trans-Atl Phila.

— Information Management Decisions: Briefings & Critical Thinking. 448p. (Orig.). 1994. pap. 59.50 (*0-273-60288-8*, Pub. by Pitman Pub) Trans-Atl Phila.

O'Brien, Bartholomew J. The Cure of ARS: Patron Saint of Parish Priests. LC 87-50942. 133p. 1994. reprint ed. pap. 5.50 (*0-89555-324-4*) TAN Bks Pubs.

— An Introduction to the Promise of Saint Joseph: The Challange of Teenage Chastity. LC 89-60396. 45p. 1989. pap. 2.00 (*0-9618840-8-8*) Queenship Pub.

— Primer of Prayer. Faith Publishing Company Staff, ed. LC 91-71541. 124p. 1991. pap. 4.50 (*0-9625975-8-9*) Queenship Pub.

O'Brien, Bayne P. The Northumberland County, Virginia, 1850 Census. 118p. (Orig.). 1972. reprint ed. pap. 15.00 (*0-89308-307-0*) Southern Hist Pr.

O'Brien, Beatrice. One Track. 1999. pap. text 14.95 (*1-890838-09-8*) Indus Pub.

O'Brien, Bernadette M. & Eggleston, Steven B. Labor & Employment in California Issue 3: A Guide to Employment Laws, Regulations & Practice. 200p. 1999. ring bd. write for info. (*0-327-01416-4*, 8022323) LEXIS Pub.

O'Brien, Bernadette M., jt. auth. see Eggleston, Steven B.

O'Brien, Bernadette M., jt. auth. see O'Brien, David W.

O'Brien, Bernard A., jt. auth. see Mackey, Richard A.

O'Brien, Bernard M. & Morrison, Wayne A. Reconstructive Microsurgery. (Illus.). 540p. 1987. text 300.00 (*0-443-02557-6*) Church.

O'Brien, Betsy. The Seoul Food Guide. 1994. pap. 22.95 (*1-56591-039-7*) Hollym Intl.

— The Seoul Food Guide: A Selection of Restaurants. (Illus.). 280p. 1995. pap. 14.95 (*1-56591-040-0*, Pub. by Hollym Bks) Weatherhill.

O'Brien, Bob R. Our National Parks & the Search for Sustainability. LC 98-9011. 248p. 1999. 40.00 (*0-292-76049-3*); pap. 19.95 (*0-292-76050-7*) U of Tex Pr.

O'Brien, Bonnie B. The Victory of the Lamb. 182p. 1982. pap. 11.50 (*0-311-72280-6*) Casa Bautista.

O'Brien, Brendan. The Long War: The IRA & Sinn Fein, 1985 to Today. 448p. 1995. 19.95 (*0-8156-0319-3*) Syracuse U Pr.

— The Long War: The IRA & Sinn Fein, 1985 to Today. 2nd ed. LC 99-21434. (Irish Studies). 345p. 1999. pap. 19.95 (*0-8156-0597-8*) Syracuse U Pr.

— A Pocket History of the IRA. (Illus.). 144p. 1997. pap. 7.95 (*0-86278-511-1*, Pub. by OBrien Pr) Irish Amer Bk.

***O'Brien, Brendan.** A Pocket History of the IRA. 112p. 2000. pap. 7.95 (*0-86278-642-8*, Pub. by OBrien Pr) IPG Chicago.

O'Brien, Brendan. Speedy Justice: The Tragic Last Voyage of His Majesty's Vessel Speedy. (Publications of the Osgoode Society). (Illus.). 200p. 1992. text 35.00 (*0-8020-2910-8*) U of Toronto Pr.

O'Brien, Bruce R. God's Peace & King's Peace: Laws of Edward the Confessor. LC 98-24540. (Middle Ages Ser.). 296p. 1998. 55.00 (*0-8122-3461-8*) U of Pa Pr.

O'Brien, C., ed. Normal & Impaired Motor Development. (Illus.). 270p. 1994. pap. text 49.50 (*1-56593-148-3*, 0460) Singular Publishing.

O'Brien, C., jt. ed. see Gentili, A.

O'Brien, Caragh M. Mirage. LC 97-94018. 192p. 1997. 18.95 (*0-8034-9256-1*, Avalon Bks) Bouregy.

O'Brien, Carole L. Adult Day Care: A Practical Guide. LC 81-16212. (Nursing-Health Science Ser.). 400p. (C). 1982. 41.25 (*0-8185-0506-0*) Jones & Bartlett.

O'Brien, Carolyn & Hayes, Alan. Normal & Impaired Motor Development: Theory into Practice. LC 94-68790. 256p. 1995. pap. 35.95 (*0-412-47890-0*) Chapman & Hall.

O'Brien, Catherine. Italian Women Poets. 200p. 1996. 39.50 (*0-7165-2603-4*, Pub. by F Cass Pubs); pap. 14.95 (*0-7165-2617-4*, Pub. by F Cass Pubs) Intl Spec Bk.

— Women's Fictional Responses to the First World War. LC 96-131. (Studies in Modern German Literature: No. 82). XI, 204p. (C). 1997. text 44.95 (*0-8204-3141-9*) P Lang Pubng.

O'Brien, Cathy & Phillips, Mark. Trance Formation of America: Trance. 4th rev. unabridged ed. (Illus.). 256p. 1995. pap. 15.00 (*0-9660165-4-8*) Reality Mktg.

O'Brien, Charles, et al, eds. Responding to Child Abuse: Child Protection, Procedures & Practice in Hong Kong. LC 98-107746. 192p. (Orig.). 1997. pap. 34.50 (*962-209-429-5*, Pub. by HK Univ Pr) Coronet Bks.

O'Brien, Charles & Wibmer, Guillermo J. Annotated Checklist of the Weevils of North America, Central America, & the West Indies (Coleoptera: Curculionoidea) (Memoir Ser.: No. 34). 382p. 1982. 45.00 (*1-56665-032-1*) Assoc Pubs FL.

O'Brien, Charles, tr. see Casetti, Francesco.

O'Brien, Charles B. One Thousand One Civil War Trivia. rev. ed. (Illus.). 156p. (Orig.). 1994. pap. text 8.95 (*0-9637602-0-3*) Neirbo Bks.

O'Brien, Charles F. Sir William Dawson: A Life in Science & Religion. LC 71-153381. (American Philosophical Society, Memoirs Ser.: Vol. 84). 217p. reprint ed. pap. 67.30 (*0-608-12107-X*, 202514000042) Bks Demand.

O'Brien, Charles P. & Jaffe, Jerome H., eds. Addictive States. LC 91-31301. (Association for Research in Nervous & Mental Disease Research Publications: Vol. 70). (Illus.). 303p. 1992. reprint ed. pap. 94.00 (*0-608-07194-3*, 206741900009) Bks Demand.

O'Brien, Charles W., jt. auth. see Wibmer, Guillermo J.

***O'Brien, Charmaine.** World Food Deep South. (World Food Ser.). (Illus.). 208p. 2000. pap. 11.95 (*1-86450-110-3*) Lonely Planet.

O'Brien, Chip. Sacramento, CA. (River Journal Ser.: Vol. 4, No. 2). (Illus.). 48p. 1996. pap. 15.95 (*1-57188-051-8*) F Amato Pubns.

O'Brien, Christine. Butterworths Current Law Digest, 1989-1992. 1000p. 1993. boxed set 243.00 (*0-408-71356-9*, NZ, MICHIE) LEXIS Pub.

— My Life Story Vol. 1: From Birth Through Grandparenthood. unabridged ed. (Illus.). 100p. 1997. 29.95 (*1-889972-84-3*) Newpt Media.

O'Brien, Christine & Karunaharan, N. New Zealand Family Law Reports. ring bd. write for info. (*0-409-79037-0*, NZ, MICHIE) LEXIS Pub.

O'Brien, Christine, ed. see Bovo, Mary J.

O'Brien, Christopher. Enter the Valley. LC 99-173821. 1999. mass mkt. 6.99 (*0-312-96835-3*) St Martin.

— Mysterious Valley. 1996. mass mkt. 6.99 (*0-312-95883-8*) St Martin.

***O'Brien, Claire.** Barn Party. (I Am Reading Ser.). (Illus.). 48p. (J). 2000. pap. 3.95 (*0-7534-5120-4*, Kingfisher) LKC.

Obrien, Claire. Sam's Sneaker Search. LC 96-2964. (Illus.). 32p. (J). (ps-2). 1997. mass mkt. 10.95 (*0-689-80169-6*) S&S Bks Yung.

O'Brien, Conan. If They Mated. (Illus.). 160p. (Orig.). (J). 1995. pap. 7.70 (*0-7868-8156-9*, Pub. by Hyperion) Time Warner.

***O'Brien, Conan.** In the Year 2000... LC 99-38811. 1999. pap. 10.95 (*1-57322-771-4*, Riverhd Trade) Berkley Pub.

***O'Brien, Conor.** MCQS in Sports Medicine. 151p. 1999. pap. text 32.50 (*0-7506-2949-5*) Buttrwrth-Heinemann.

O'Brien, Conor C. Ancestral Voices: Religion & Nationalism in Ireland. LC 95-20001. 216p. 1995. pap. 13.95 (*0-226-61652-5*) U Ch Pr.

— The Great Melody: A Thematic Biography of Edmund Burke. lxxvi, 768p. (C). 1993. pap. text 24.95 (*0-226-61651-7*) U Ch Pr.

— The Great Melody: A Thematic Biography of Edmund Burke. LC 92-7302. (Illus.). 768p. 1999. 34.95 (*0-226-61650-9*) U Ch Pr.

— The Long Affair: Thomas Jefferson & the French Revolution, 1785-1800. (Illus.). 360p. 1996. 29.95 (*0-226-61653-3*) U Ch Pr.

— The Long Affair: Thomas Jefferson & the French Revolution, 1785-1800. (Illus.). 368p. 1998. pap. 15.00 (*0-226-61656-8*) U Ch Pr.

— Memoir: My Life & Themes LC 98-233933. 460 p. 1998. write for info. (*1-85371-877-7*) Poolbeg Pr.

***O'Brien, Conor C.** Memoir: My Life & Themes. 2000. 30.00 (*0-8154-1064-6*) Cooper Sq.

O'Brien, Conor C. On the Eve of the Millennium: The Future of Democracy Through an Age of Unreason. LC 95-35636. 1995. 25.00 (*0-02-874098-X*); per. 12.00 (*0-02-874094-7*, M Kessler Bks) Free Pr.

O'Brien, Conor C., et al. The Enduring Edmund Burke: Bicentennial Essays. Crowe, Ian, ed. LC 97-72847. 225p. 1997. 24.95 (*1-882926-16-1*, 242) ISI Books.

— Ireland: A Concise History. 3rd rev. ed. (Illus.). 1985. pap. 16.95 (*0-500-27379-0*, Pub. by Thames Hudson) Norton.

***O'Brien, Conor Cruise.** The French Revolution: A Short History. 144p. 2000. 19.95 (*0-679-64041-X*) Modern Lib NY.

O'Brien, Conor Cruise. God Land: Reflections on Religion & Nationalism. LC 87-32168. (William E. Massey Sr. Lectures in the History of American Civilization). 100p. 1988. text 23.50 (*0-674-35510-5*) HUP.

***O'Brien, Conor Cruise.** God Land: Reflections on Religion & Nationalism. 112p. 1999. 20.95 (*0-7351-0179-5*) Replica Bks.

O'Brien Cousins, Sandra. Exercise, Aging, & Health: Overcoming Barriers to an Active Old Age. LC 97-37825. 250p. 1998. pap. 29.95 (*1-56032-414-7*); boxed set 64.95 (*1-56032-413-9*) Taylor & Francis.

O'Brien Cousins, Sandra & Horne, Tammy. Active Living among Older Adults: Health Benefits & Outcomes. LC 97-38963. 425p. 1998. boxed set 49.95 (*1-56032-585-2*) Taylor & Francis.

O'Brien, Cyril J. Liberation: Marines in the Recapture of Guam. (Illus.). 45p. 1996. reprint ed. pap. text 20.00 (*0-7881-3537-6*) DIANE Pub.

O'Brien, D. Theories of Weight in the Ancient World, Vol. 1. 1981. pap. 62.00 (*90-04-06134-7*, PHA, 37) Brill Academic Pubs.

— Theories of Weight in the Ancient World, Vol. 2. 1984. pap. 66.00 (*90-04-06934-8*, PHA, 41) Brill Academic Pubs.

O'Brien, D. P. J. R. McCulloch: A Study in Classical Economics. (Modern Revivals in Economics Ser.). 452p. 1993. 79.95 (*0-7512-0096-4*, Pub. by Gregg Pub) Ashgate Pub Co.

— Methodology, Money & the Firm: The Collected Essays of D. P. O'Brien, 2 vols., Set. LC 94-3920. (Economists of the Twentieth Century Ser.). 944p. 1994. 200.00 (*1-85278-966-2*) E Elgar.

O'Brien, D. P. Thomas Joplin & Classical Macroeconomics: A Re-Appraisal of Classical Monetary Thought. 304p. 1993. 100.00 (*1-85278-676-0*) E Elgar.

O'Brien, D. P., ed. The Foundations of Business Cycle Theory, 3 vols. LC 97-16995. (Elgar Mini Ser.). 1728p. 1997. 595.00 (*1-85898-422-X*) E Elgar.

***O'Brien, D. P., ed.** The History of Taxation, 8 vols. LC 99-17336. 2800p. 1999. 940.00 (*1-85196-516-5*, Pub. by Pickering & Chatto) Ashgate Pub Co.

O'Brien, D. P. & Creedy, J. Economic Analysis in Historical Perspective. (Modern Revivals in Economics Ser.). 228p. 1992. 61.95 (*0-7512-0088-3*, Pub. by Gregg Revivals) Ashgate Pub Co.

O'Brien, D. P. & Presley, John R., eds. Pioneers of Modern Economics in Britain. LC 79-55496. (Illus.). 292p. 1981. text 53.00 (*0-389-20181-2*, N6622) B&N Imports.

***O'Brien, D. P., et al.** From Classical Economics to the Theory of the Firm: Essays in Honour of D.P. O'Brien. LC 99-16005. 320p. (C). 1999. 95.00 (*1-84064-146-0*) E Elgar.

O'Brien, Dan. Brendan Prairie. 256p. 1997. per. 11.00 (*0-684-80369-0*, Scribner Pap Fic) S&S Trade Pap.

— The Contract Surgeon. LC 99-35243. 288p. 1999. 24.95 (*1-55821-932-3*) Lyons Pr.

***O'Brien, Dan.** Dan O'Brien's Ultimate Workout: The Gold Medal Plan for Reaching Your Peak Performance. LC 97-24500. (Illus.). 256p. (J). 1998. pap. 14.45 (*0-7868-8281-6*, Pub. by Hyperion) Time Warner.

O'Brien, Dan. Eminent Domain. LC 86-30846. (Iowa Short Fiction Award Ser.). 145p. 1987. text 10.00 (*0-87745-170-2*) U of Iowa Pr.

— Equinox: Life, Love, & Birds of Prey. LC 96-41129. (Illus.). 224p. 1997. 22.95 (*1-55821-456-9*) Lyons Pr.

— In the Center of the Nation. 384p. 1992. pap. 10.00 (*0-380-71702-6*, Avon Bks) Morrow Avon.

— The Last Supper Restoration: A Play LC 98-209024. 66p. 1998. write for info. (*0-573-62623-5*) French.

— The Rites of Autumn: A Falconer's Journey Across the American West. LC 96-30496. 1997. pap. 12.95 (*1-55821-457-7*) Lyons Pr.

***O'Brien, Daniel Patrick.** Business Measurements for Safety Performance. 136p. 1999. per. write for info. (*1-56670-408-1*) Lewis Pubs.

O'Brien, Daphne Hamm, ed. see Horne, Meade B.

O'Brien, Darcy. The Hidden Pope. large type ed. LC 98-13687. 575p. 1998. 26.95 (*0-7838-0142-4*, G K Hall Lrg Type) Mac Lib Ref.

— The Hidden Pope: The Untold Story of a Lifelong Friendship That Is Changing the Relationship Between Catholics & Jews. LC 97-48680. 350p. 1998. text 25.00 (*0-87596-478-8*) Rodale Pr Inc.

— Patrick Kavanaugh. (Irish Writers Ser.). 72p. 1975. 8.50 (*0-8387-7884-4*); pap. 1.95 (*0-8387-7985-9*) Bucknell U Pr.

— Power to Hurt. 528p. 1997. mass mkt. 6.50 (*0-06-109600-8*, Harp PBks) HarpC.

— W. R. Rodgers. LC 70-124646. (Irish Writers Ser.). 103p. 1975. pap. 1.95 (*0-8387-7630-2*) Bucknell U Pr.

O'Brien, David. Special Leave to Appeal: The Law & Practice of Special Leave to Appeal to the High Court of Australia. 200p. 1996. pap. 75.00 (*0-455-21421-2*, Pub. by LawBk Co) Gaunt.

***O'Brien, David.** Supreme Court Watch 1999 Pennsylvania. (C). 1999. pap. text 10.50 (*0-393-97546-0*) Norton.

O'Brien, David & Shannon, Thomas A., eds. Catholic Social Thought: The Documentary Heritage. LC 92-3185. 1992. pap. 25.00 (*0-88344-787-8*) Orbis Bks.

O'Brien, David, jt. ed. see Wise, Charles.

O'Brien, David E. Today's Handbook for Solving Bible Difficulties. 496p. 1990. text 19.99 (*0-87123-814-4*) Bethany Hse.

O'Brien, David G., jt. auth. see Moje, Elizabeth B.

O'Brien, David J. From the Heart of the American Church: Catholic Higher Education & American Culture. LC 94-28671. 220p. (Orig.). 1994. pap. 16.00 (*0-88344-985-4*) Orbis Bks.

— Isaac Hecker: An American Catholic. 1992. 25.00 (*0-8091-0397-4*) Paulist Pr.

— Neighborhood Organization & Interest-Group Processes. LC 75-3468. 276p. reprint ed. pap. 85.60 (*0-8357-8966-7*, 203339900085) Bks Demand.

O'Brien, David J. & Fugita, Stephen S. The Japanese American Experience. LC 90-23961. (Minorities in Modern America Ser.: MB-656). (Illus.). 188p. 1991. pap. 10.95 (*0-253-20656-1*, MB-656) Ind U Pr.

***O'Brien, David J., et al.** Household Capital & the Agrarian Problem in Russia. 268p. 1999. text 69.95 (*0-7546-1059-4*, Pub. by Inst Materials) Ashgate Pub Co.

O'Brien, David J., et al. A Research Agenda for Studying Rural Public Service Delivery Alternatives in the North Central Region. 76p. 1994. pap. text 4.00 (*0-936913-09-6*, RRD 167) NCRCRD.

— Services & Quality of Life in Rural Villages in the Former Soviet Union: Data from 1991 & 1993 Surveys. LC 97-41239. 308p. (C). 1997. 47.00 (*0-7618-0954-6*) U Pr of Amer.

O'Brien, David J., jt. auth. see Fugita, Stephen S.

***O'Brien, David M.** Constitutional Law & Politics, Vol. 1. 4th ed. LC 99-27984. 1999. pap. text 48.75 (*0-393-97440-5*) Norton.

— Constitutional Law & Politics, Vol. 2. 4th ed. LC 99-27984. 1999. pap. text 48.75 (*0-393-97441-3*) Norton.

— Governmental Accountability. pap. 34.00 (*0-393-97045-0*) Norton.

O'Brien, David M. Privacy, Law & Public Policy. LC 79-14131. (Praeger Special Studies). 262p. 1979. 67.95 (*0-275-90403-2*, C0403, Praeger Pubs) Greenwood.

— The Public's Right to Know: The Supreme Court & the First Amendment. LC 81-988. 205p. 1981. 55.00 (*0-275-90694-9*, C0694, Praeger Pubs) Greenwood.

— The Right of Privacy: Its Constitutional & Social Dimensions; a Comprehensive Bibliography. (Legal Bibliography Ser.: No. 21). 55p. (Orig.). 1980. pap. 15.00 (*0-935630-04-X*) U of Tex Tarlton Law Lib.

— Storm Center: The Supreme Court in American Politics. 5th ed. LC 99-26041. 1999. (*0-393-97492-8*) Norton.

— What Process Is Due? Courts & Science-Policy Disputes. LC 87-43100. 190p. 1988. text 29.95 (*0-87154-623-X*) Russell Sage.

O'Brien, David M., ed. Judges on Judging: Views from the Bench. LC 96-50991. 384p. (C). 1997. pap. text 26.95 (*1-56643-042-9*, Chatham House Pub) Seven Bridges.

— The Lanahan Readings in Civil Rights & Civil Liberties. 319p. (Orig.). (C). 1999. pap. text 23.75 (*0-9652687-6-4*) Lanahan Pubs.

O'Brien, David M. & Ohkoshi, Yasuo. To Dream of Dreams: Religious Freedom & Constitutional Politics in Postwar Japan. LC 95-45936. (Illus.). 312p. 1996. pap. text 24.00 (*0-8248-1166-6*) UH Pr.

O'Brien, David M., jt. auth. see Craig, Barbara H.

O'Brien, David P., jt. ed. see Braine, Martin.

O'Brien, David W. California Employer-Employee Benefits Handbook: With 1987 Supplement. 6th ed. LC 78-71230. 786p. 1986. pap. text 97.95 (*0-9602204-0-2*) Winterbrook.

— California Workers' Compensation Claims & Benefits, 2 vols. 9th ed. 1100p. 1993. spiral bd. 135.00 (*0-250-47224-4*, MICHIE) LEXIS Pub.

— Misconduct Cases Book. LC 85-51769. 501p. (Orig.). 1985. 49.00 (*0-9602204-1-0*) Winterbrook.

O'Brien, David W. & O'Brien, Bernadette M. California Unemployment & Disability Compensation Programs. 8th ed. 550p. 1994. spiral bd. 129.00 (*1-55943-119-9*, MICHIE) LEXIS Pub.

***O'Brien, David W. & O'Brien, Bernadette M.** California Unemployment & Disability Compensation Programs. 9th ed. 500p. 1999. ring bd. write for info. (*0-327-10138-5*, 8026711) LEXIS Pub.

O'Brien, David W. & O'Brien, Bernadette M. California Workers' Compensation Claims & Benefits. 9th ed. 1100p. 1994. 125.00 (*0-614-10374-6*, MICHIE) LEXIS Pub.

O'Brien, David W., jt. auth. see O'rien, Bernadette M.

O'Brien, Dawn. North Carolina's Historic Restaurants & Their Recipes. 3rd rev. ed. LC 83-2831. (Illus.). 204p. 1990. 14.95 (*0-89587-067-3*) Blair.

— Virginia's Historic Restaurants & Their Recipes. 2nd rev. ed. LC 84-2801. (Illus.). 205p. 1990. 14.95 (*0-89587-068-1*) Blair.

O'Brien, Dawn & Matkov, Rebecca R. Florida's Historic Restaurants & Their Recipes. rev. ed. (Illus.). 224p. 1994. 14.95 (*0-89587-120-3*) Blair.

O'Brien, Dawn & Mulford, Karen S. South Carolina's Historic Restaurants & Their Recipes. rev. ed. (Illus.). 204p. 1992. 15.95 (*0-89587-097-5*) Blair.

O'Brien, Dawn & Schenck, Rebecca. Maryland's Historic Restaurants & Their Recipes. 2nd ed. LC 95-24800. (Historic Restaurant Cookbooks Ser.). (Illus.). 206p. 1996. 15.95 (*0-89587-137-8*) Blair.

O'Brien, Dawn & Spaugh, Jean C. Georgia's Historic Restaurants & Their Recipes. 2nd ed. LC 96-43723. (Historic Restaurant Ser.). (Illus.). 202p. 1997. reprint ed. 16.95 (*0-89587-157-2*) Blair.

O'Brien, Dawn, ed. see Cordeiro, Wayne.

O'Brien, Dean W., ed. Historic Northeast Wisconsin: A Voyageur Guidebook. LC 94-71648. (Illus.). 160p. 1994. pap. 10.00 (*0-9641499-0-7*) Brown County Hist.

O'Brien, Debbee. Character: The Real Thing. Wagner, Karen, ed. 96p. 1998. pap. 8.00 (*0-9666375-0-X*) Leadership Grow.

***O'Brien, Deborah & Fitzgerald, Mairead Ashe.** Celtic Decorative Art: A Living Tradition. (Illus.). 80p. 2000. pap. 16.95 (*0-86278-598-7*, Pub. by OBrien Pr) IPG Chicago.

O'Brien, Deborah, ed. see Levison, Catherine.

An Asterisk (*) at the beginning of an entry indicates that the title is appearing for the first time.

O'Brien, Denis. Empedocles' Cosmic Cycle: A Reconstruction from the Fragments & Secondary Sources. LC 68-10330. 469p. reprint ed. pap. 133.70 (*0-608-10019-6*, 2013218) Bks Demand.

— Theodicee Plotinienne, Theodicee Gnostique. LC 92-9638. (Philosophia Antiqua Ser.: Vol. 57). (FRE.). viii, 118p. 1993. 64.00 (*90-04-09618-3*) Brill Academic Pubs.

O'Brien, Denis, ed. Foundations of Monetary Economics, 6 vols. 1994. 650.00 (*1-85196-190-9*, Pub. by Pickering & Chatto) Ashgate Pub Co.

O'Brien, Denis, jt. auth. see Brown, Judie.

O'Brien, Denis P. & Swann, D. Information Agreements, Competition & Efficiency. LC 72-83156. 248p. 1969. 35.00 (*0-678-07000-8*) Kelley.

O'Brien, Diane R. Ducktrap: Chronicles of a Maine Village. (Illus.). x, 126p. (Orig.). 1994. pap. 20.00 (*0-9650942-0-0*) Schl Hse Mus.

O'Brien, Dianne B. & Overby, James O. Legal Aspects of Sport Entrepreneurships. 468p. (C). 1997. text 46.00 (*1-885693-08-7*) Fit Info Tech.

***O'Brien, Dominic.** Learn to Remember: Practical Techniques & Exercises to Improve Your Memory. (Illus.). 160p. 2000. pap. 14.95 (*0-8118-2715-1*) Chronicle Bks.

O'Brien, Donal B. & Coulon, Christian, eds. Charisma & Brotherhood in African Islam. (Oxford Studies in African Affairs). 232p. 1989. text 59.00 (*0-19-822723-X*) OUP.

***O'Brien, Dora.** From Moscow: Living & Teaching among the Russian in the 1990's. 113p. 2000. pap. 19.95 (*1-900405-07-5*, Pub. by Bramcote Pr) Intl Spec Bk.

O'Brien, Dorothy J., ed. Index to Mariposa Gazette & Miner Commemorative, 1979: Heritage of Law & Press. LC 97-92820. iii, iv, 511p. 1997. pap. 19.10 (*0-9618990-1-8*) Dorothy J OBrien.

O'Brien, Douglas. The Complete Families with Divorce: Books 1,2 & 3 Bks. 1 & 2: What to Know & What to Do to Help Yourself, a Client, or a Friend When "The System" Is Out of Control, Set, Bks. 1 & 2. 610p. (Orig.). 1999. pap. 24.95 (*0-9637496-5-X*) Skid Eighteen Pr.

— Divorce Fear & How to Stop It: Money, Professionals, & Courtroom Games. (Families with Divorce Ser.: Bk. 3). 1998. pap. 14.95 (*0-9637496-3-3*) Skid Eighteen Pr.

— Families with Divorce Bk. 1: Fathers & Mothers in "The System" & the Legal Paper Game, What to Know & What to Do to Help Yourself, a Client, or a Friend When "The System" Is Out of Control. LC 96-92850. (Families with Divorce Ser.: Bk. 2). 272p. (Orig.). 1996. pap. 19.95 (*0-9637496-1-7*) Skid Eighteen Pr.

— The Families with Divorce Workbook. 1999. pap. 18.95 (*0-9637496-4-1*) Skid Eighteen Pr.

— Where Have All the Good Fathers Gone? Bk. 2: Child Support & Custody. LC 96-227336. (Families with Divorce Ser.: Bk. 2). 226p. (Orig.). 1997. pap. 16.95 (*0-9637496-2-5*) Skid Eighteen Pr.

O'Brien, E. Drums. (Learn to Play Ser.). (Illus.). 48p. (J). 1999. 17.95 (*1-58086-202-0*) EDC.

— Reinforced & Prestressed Concrete Design. (C). 1996. pap. 50.95 (*0-582-21883-7*, Pub. by Addison-Wesley) Longman.

O'Brien, E. T. & O'Malley, K. Blood Pressure Measurement. (Handbook of Hypertension Ser.: Vol. 14). 460p. 1991. 285.25 (*0-444-81162-1*) Elsevier.

O'Brien, E. T., et al. ABC of Hypertension. 3rd ed. (Illus.). 79p. 1997. pap. 24.00 (*0-7279-0769-7*, Pub. by BMJ Pub) Login Brothers Bk Co.

— Blood Pressure Measurement. 3rd ed. 27p. 1997. pap. 10.00 (*0-7279-1153-8*, Pub. by BMJ Pub) Login Brothers Bk Co.

O'Brien, Ed & Wilson, Robert. Sinatra 101: The 101 Best Recordings & the Stories Behind Them. LC 96-204851. 192p. 1996. pap. 12.00 (*1-57297-165-7*) Blvd Books.

O'Brien, Edna. Arabian Days. 15.95 (*0-7043-2150-5*, Pub. by Quartet) Charles River Bks.

— The Country Girls. 1963. pap. 1.95 (*0-14-001851-4*) Viking Penguin.

— The Country Girls Trilogy: Second Epilogue. 1987. pap. 15.95 (*0-452-26394-8*, Plume) Dutton Plume.

— The Country Girls Trilogy & Epilogue. 1986. 18.95 (*0-374-13027-2*) FS&G.

— Down by the River. LC 97-37248. 272p. 1998. pap. 12.95 (*0-452-27877-5*, Plume) Dutton Plume.

— Down by the River. LC 96-39251. 256p. 1997. 23.00 (*0-374-14327-7*) FS&G.

— A Fanatic Heart. LC 84-13762. 461p. 1984. text 17.95 (*0-374-15342-6*) FS&G.

— A Fanatic Heart: Selected Stories of Edna O'Brien. LC 85-8935. 480p. 1985. pap. 14.95 (*0-452-26116-3*, Plume) Dutton Plume.

— Girl with Green Eyes. 216p. 1964. pap. 18.99 (*0-14-002108-6*, Penguin Bks) Viking Penguin.

— The High Road. 256p. 1988. 18.95 (*0-374-29273-6*) FS&G.

— House of Splendid Isolation. LC 94-47256. 1995. pap. 12.95 (*0-452-27452-4*, Plume) Dutton Plume.

— House of Splendid Isolation. LC 93-42602. 224p. 1994. text 21.00 (*0-374-17309-5*) FS&G.

— House of Splendid Isolation. large type ed. LC 94-28267. 314p. 1994. lib. bdg. 23.95 (*0-8161-7485-7*, G K Hall Lrg Type) Mac Lib Ref.

***O'Brien, Edna.** James Joyce. LC 99-23214. (Penguin Lives Ser.). 160p. 1999. 19.95 (*0-670-88230-5*) Viking Penguin.

O'Brien, Edna. Lantern Slides. 240p. 1991. reprint ed. pap. 11.95 (*0-452-26628-9*, Plume) Dutton Plume.

***O'Brien, Edna.** Mother Ireland. LC 98-40435. 112p. 1999. pap. 11.95 (*0-452-28050-8*) NAL.

O'Brien, Edna. Nights. 1987. pap. 12.00 (*0-374-52051-8*) FS&G.

— On the Bone. (C). 1990. 35.00 (*0-906887-38-0*, Pub. by Greville Pr) St Mut.

— Time & Tide. LC 92-3962. 325p. 1992. 21.00 (*0-374-27776-1*) FS&G.

***O'Brien, Edna.** Time & Tide. 336p. 1999. pap. 12.95 (*0-452-28051-6*) NAL.

O'Brien, Edna. Virginia: A Play. LC 81-7763. 64p. 1981. 7.95 (*0-15-193762-1*) Harcourt.

***O'Brien, Edna.** Wild Decembers. LC 99-56110. 272p. 2000. 24.00 (*0-618-04567-8*) HM.

O'Brien, Edward J. The Advance of the American Short Story. LC 74-145217. 314p. 1972. reprint ed. 29.00 (*0-403-01134-5*) Scholarly.

— Fifty Best American Short Stories, 1915-1939. (BCL1-PS American Literature Ser.). 868p. 1993. reprint ed. lib. bdg. 119.00 (*0-7812-6936-9*) Rprt Serv.

O'Brien, Edward J., ed. Elizabethan Tales. LC 70-178452. (Short Story Index Reprint Ser.). 1977. reprint ed. 21.95 (*0-8369-4053-9*) Ayer.

O'Brien, Edward J., et al, eds. Memory-Based Text Processing: A Special Issue of "Discourse Processes" 163p. 1998. write for info. (*0-8058-9824-7*) L Erlbaum Assocs.

O'Brien, Edward J., jt. ed. see Lorch, Robert F.

O'Brien, Edward L. Human Rights for All. LC 95-32773. 1994. mass mkt. 27.25 (*0-314-04943-6*) West Pub.

O'Brien, Edward L. & Larkin, Mary C. Democracy for Trade Unions: Civic Education Towards a Democratic Trade Union Culture. Douglas, William A., ed. 80p. (Orig.). 1997. pap. text, teacher ed. write for info. (*1-890922-01-3*) African-Am Labor.

— Democracy for Trade Unions: Civic Education Towards a Democratic Trade Union Culture. Douglas, William A., ed. (Illus.). (Orig.). 1997. pap. text. write for info. (*1-890922-00-5*) African-Am Labor.

— La Democratie: Ouvrage a L'Usage des Syndicats: Education Civique pour un Syndicalisme Democratique. Douglas, William A., ed. Girardeau, Anne, tr. (FRE., Illus.). 140p. (Orig.). 1997. pap. text. write for info. (*1-890922-02-1*) African-Am Labor.

— La Democratie: Ouvrage a L'Usage des Syndicats: Education Civique Pour un Syndicalisme Democratique. Douglas, William A., ed. Girardeau, Anne, tr. (FRE.). (Orig.). 1997. pap. text. write for info. (*1-890922-03-X*) African-Am Labor.

O'Brien, Edward L., et al. Practical Law for Correctional Personnel: A Resource Manual & a Training Curriculum (by the National Street Law Institute) (Illus.). 249p. (C). 1986. reprint ed. pap. text 16.50 (*0-8299-1034-4*) West Pub.

O'Brien-Eggleston, Bernadette M., jt. auth. see Eggleston, Steven B.

O'Brien, Eileen. Hawaiian Host & Hostess. pap. 2.95 (*0-681-02799-1*) Booklines Hawaii.

— Starving to Win: Athletes & Eating Disorders. LC 98-16884. (Teen Health Library of Eating Disorder Prevention). (Illus.). 64p. (YA). (gr. 7-12). 1998. lib. bdg. 17.95 (*0-8239-2764-4*, EDATEA) Rosen Group.

— Story of Music. (Fine Arts Ser.). (Illus.). 32p. (YA). (gr. 5-9). 1998. pap. 6.95 (*0-7460-2423-1*) EDC.

— Story of Music. (Fine Arts Ser.). (Illus.). 32p. (YA). (gr. 5 up). 1998. lib. bdg. 14.95 (*1-58086-014-1*) EDC.

***O'Brien, Eileen.** The Usborne Story of Music. (Illus.). 32p. (J). (gr. 3-5). 2000. 15.00 (*0-7881-9403-8*) DIANE Pub.

***O'Brien, Eileen, ed.** First Book of the Piano with CD. (First Music Ser.). (Illus.). 64p. (J). (gr. 1-4). 2000. pap. 14.95 incl. cd-rom (*0-7460-3713-9*, Pub. by Usbrne Pbng UK) EDC.

O'Brien, Eileen, ed. Learn to Play Drums. (Learn to Play Ser.). (Illus.). 48p. (J). (gr. 4-7). 1999. pap. 9.95 (*0-7460-3044-4*, Usborne) EDC.

O'Brien, Eileen & Miles, John C. First Book of the Piano. rev. ed. (First Music Ser.). (Illus.). 64p. (J). (gr. 4-7). 1998. pap. 10.95 (*0-7460-2985-3*, Usborne) EDC.

— First Book of the Piano. 2nd rev. ed. (First Music Ser.). (Illus.). 64p. (J). (gr. 4-7). 1998. lib. bdg. 18.95 (*1-58086-126-1*, Usborne) EDC.

O'Brien, Eileen & Needham, Kate. Origami. Watt, Fiona, ed. (How to Make Ser.). (Illus.). 32p. (Orig.). (J). (gr. 3-7). 1997. pap. 6.95 (*0-7460-2719-2*, Usborne); lib. bdg. 14.95 (*0-88110-938-X*, Usborne) EDC.

O'Brien, Eileen & Riddel, Diana. Secret Codes. (How to Make Ser.). (Illus.). 32p. (Orig.). (J). (gr. 3-7). 1997. lib. bdg. 14.95 (*0-88110-979-7*, Usborne) EDC.

O'Brien, Eileen & Riddell, Diana. Secret Codes. Miles, Lisa, ed. (How to Make Ser.). (Illus.). 32p. (Orig.). (J). (gr. 3-7). 1997. pap. 6.95 (*0-7460-2329-4*, Usborne) EDC.

O'Brien, Elaine F. Anita of Rancho del Mar. LC 90-19711. (Illus.). 176p. (Orig.). (YA). (gr. 4-8). 1991. pap. 9.95 (*0-931832-79-9*) Fithian Pr.

O'Brien, Elinor. The Land & People of Ireland. rev. ed. LC 76-38335. (Portraits of the Nations Ser.). (Illus.). (J). (gr. 5-9). 1972. lib. bdg. 12.89 (*0-397-31299-7*) HarpC Child Bks.

O'Brien, Elmer, tr. The Essential Plotinus: Representative Treatises from The Enneads. (HPC Classics Ser.). 236p. (C). 1975. pap. text 7.95 (*0-915144-09-3*); lib. bdg. 24.95 (*0-915144-10-7*) Hackett Pub.

O'Brien, Emily, ed. see Piccolomini, Anneas Sylvis.

O'Brien, Eoin. Beckett Country: Samuel Beckett's Ireland. (Illus.). 432p. 1993. reprint ed. 45.00 (*1-55970-229-X*, Pub. by Arcade Pub Inc) Time Warner.

O'Brien, Esse. Art & Artists of Texas. 1993. reprint ed. lib. bdg. 75.00 (*0-7812-5971-1*) Rprt Serv.

O'Brien, Eugene. The Question of Irish Identity in the Writings of William Butler Yeats & James Joyce. LC 98-37620. 300p. 1998. text 89.95 (*0-7734-8237-7*) E Mellen.

O'Brien, Eugene J. & Keogh, Damien L. Bridge Deck Analysis. LC 98-48511. 1998. pap. write for info. (*0-419-22500-5*) Thomson Learn.

O'Brien, F. T. Early Solent Steamers. (C). 1987. 82.00 (*0-85174-417-6*) St Mut.

O'Brien, Felicity. Not Peace but a Sword: John Henry Newman. 188p. (C). 1996. pap. 39.95 (*0-85439-327-7*, Pub. by St Paul Pubns) St Mut.

— Treasure in Heaven Katharine Drexel. 120p. (C). 1990. 45.00 (*0-85439-323-4*, Pub. by St Paul Pubns) St Mut.

O'Brien, Felicity & Gemmell, Suzanne, eds. Piano Lessons: Approaches to "The Piano" 1999. pap. 19.95 (*1-86462-035-8*) Ind U Pr.

O'Brien, Felicity, jt. auth. see Sinclair, Margaret.

O'Brien, Fitz J. Collected Stories. 240p. 1977. 18.95 (*0-8369-4157-8*) Ayer.

O'Brien, Fitz-James. Diamond Lens & Other Stories. LC 70-109502. (Illus.). reprint ed. 26.50 (*0-404-00613-2*) AMS Pr.

— Diamond Lens & Other Stories. LC 76-131791. (Illus.). 1971. reprint ed. 29.00 (*0-403-00678-3*) Scholarly.

— The Poems & Stories of Fitz-James O'Brien. 1972. reprint ed. text 27.95 (*0-8422-8102-9*) Irvington.

O'Brien, Flann. At Swim-Two-Birds. LC 77-368310. 316 p. 1976. write for info. (*0-246-10890-8*) Grfton HrprCllns.

— At Swim-Two-Birds. LC 97-51424. 316p. 1998. reprint ed. pap. 13.95 (*1-56478-181-X*) Dalkey Arch.

— The Best of Myles. LC 98-52436. 400p. 1999. reprint ed. pap. 13.95 (*1-56478-215-8*, Pub. by Dalkey Arch) SPD-Small Pr Dist.

— The Dalkey Archive. LC 92-30923. 224p. 1997. pap. 12.95 (*1-56478-172-0*) Dalkey Arch.

***O'Brien, Flann.** Further Cuttings. LC 00-20973. 189p. 2000. pap. 11.95 (*1-56478-241-7*, Pub. by Dalkey Arch) Chicago Distribution Ctr.

O'Brien, Flann. The Hard Life. 2nd ed. LC 93-21207. 179p. 1996. reprint ed. pap. 11.95 (*1-56478-141-0*) Dalkey Arch.

— The Poor Mouth: A Bad Story about the Hard Life. Power, Patrick C., tr. from GAE. LC 95-26579. (Illus.). 128p. 1996. reprint ed. pap. 10.95 (*1-56478-091-0*) Dalkey Arch.

— The Third Policeman. LC 98-52437. 200p. 1999. reprint ed. pap. 12.95 (*1-56478-214-X*) Dalkey Arch.

O'Brien, Flann & Tracy, Robert. Rhapsody in St. Stephen's Green: The Insect Play. LC 94-233879. 88p. 1994. pap. 12.95 (*1-874675-27-9*) Dufour.

O'Brien, Frances A., jt. auth. see Dyson, Robert G.

O'Brien, Francis P. The High School Failures: A Study of the School Records of Pupils Failing in Academic or Commercial High School Subjects. LC 70-177127. (Columbia University. Teachers College. Contributions to Education Ser.: No. 102). reprint ed. 37.50 (*0-404-55102-5*) AMS Pr.

O'Brien, Frank. Dime Novels. (Illus.). 99p. 1994. reprint ed. pap. 25.00 (*0-87556-183-7*) Saifer.

— Some Smiles & Some Serious Thoughts. Wightman, Kimberly J. & Wightman, Teresa E., eds. 125p. 1999. pap. 10.00 (*1-888911-13-1*) Benson Smythe.

O'Brien, G. & Roebuck, P., eds. Nine Ulster Lives. 178p. 1992. pap. 16.95 (*0-901905-51-8*, Pub. by Ulster Hist Fnd) Irish Bks Media.

O'Brien, Gail W. The Color of the Law: Race, Violence & Justice in the Post-World War II South. LC 98-30827. (John Hope Franklin Series in African American History & Culture). (Illus.). 352p. 1999. 45.00 (*0-8078-2475-5*); pap. 18.95 (*0-8078-4802-6*) U of NC Pr.

***O'Brien, Gary.** A Quest for Happiness. LC 99-96684. 2000. pap. 11.95 (*0-533-13313-0*) Vantage.

O'Brien, Gaynell, jt. auth. see O'Brien, H. V.

O'Brien, Geoffrey. Bardic Deadlines: Reviewing Poetry, 1984-85. LC 98-25510. (Poets on Poetry Ser.). 168p. 1998. text 39.50 (*0-472-09683-4*, 09683) U of Mich Pr.

— A Book of Maps. LC 88-92340. 48p. 1989. pap. 4.00 (*0-87376-061-1*) Red Dust.

***O'Brien, Geoffrey.** The Browser's Ecstacy: A Meditation on Reading. 160p. 2000. text 24.00 (*1-58243-056-X*, Pub. by Counterpt DC) HarpC.

O'Brien, Geoffrey. Hardboiled America: Lurid Paperbacks & the Masters of Noir. expanded ed. LC 96 37486. (Illus.). 216p. 1997. pap. 16.95 (*0-306-80773-4*) Da Capo.

— The Hudson Mystery. 28p. 1995. pap. 4.00 (*0-87376-078-6*) Red Dust.

— The Phantom Empire: Movies in the Mind of the Twentieth Century. (Illus.). 288p. 1995. pap. 12.00 (*0-393-31296-8*, Norton Paperbks) Norton.

— The Times Square Story. LC 98-33977. (Illus.). 96p. 1998. pap. 12.95 (*0-393-31846-X*, Norton Paperbks) Norton.

O'Brien, Geoffrey, ed. Bardic Deadlines: Reviewing Poetry, 1984-85. LC 98-25510. (Poets on Poetry Ser.). 168p. 1998. pap. 14.95 (*0-472-06683-8*, 06683) U of Mich Pr.

O'Brien, Geoffrey, ed. see Library of America Staff.

O'Brien, Geoffrey, tr. see Verge, Roger.

O'Brien, Geofrey. Floating City: Selected Poems, 1978-1996. LC 96-3817. 120p. 1996. 30.50 (*1-883689-39-2*); pap. 10.50 (*1-883689-38-4*) Talisman Hse.

O'Brien, George. Brian Friel. (Twayne's English Authors Ser.: No. 470). 182p. 1989. 23.95 (*0-8057-6980-3*, Twyne) Mac Lib Ref.

— Brian Friel: A Reference Guide. LC 94-30903. (Reference Guide to Literature Ser.). 152p. 1995. 45.00 (*0-8161-7273-0*, G K Hall & Co) Mac Lib Ref.

— Out of Our Minds: "London in the Sixties. Sex, Drugs & Rock 'n' Roll, Politics & Pop" 184p. 1995. pap. 15.95 (*0-85640-541-8*, Pub. by Blackstaff Pr) Dufour.

***O'Brien, George, ed.** Playing the Field: Irish Writers on Sport. 2000. pap. 16.95 (*1-874597-81-2*, Pub. by New Island Books) Dufour.

O'Brien, George, jt. auth. see Dunne, Scban.

O'Brien, George A. An Essay on Medieval Economic Teaching. LC 67-28412. (Reprints of Economic Classics Ser.). viii, 242p. 1967. reprint ed. 39.50 (*0-678-00336-X*) Kelley.

— An Essay on the Economic Effects of the Reformation. LC 68-56556. (Reprints of Economic Classics Ser.). x, 194p. 1970. reprint ed. 35.00 (*0-678-00591-5*) Kelley.

O'Brien, George D. All the Essential Half-Truths about Higher Education. LC 97-14479. 208p. 1997. 19.95 (*0-226-61654-1*) U Ch Pr.

O'Brien, Gerald. This Crazy Mental Health Business. viii, 128p. 1999. pap. 9.00 (*0-944266-25-8*) Maecenas Pr.

O'Brien, Gerard. Anglo-Irish Politics in the Age of Grattan & Pitt. 232p. 1987. 29.95 (*0-7165-2377-9*, Pub. by Irish Acad Pr) Intl Spec Bk.

— Parliament, Politics & People: Essays in Eighteenth Century Irish History. 200p. 1988. 14.95 (*0-7165-2421-X*, I2421, Pub. by Irish Acad Pr) Intl Spec Bk.

— The Politics of Conciliation: The Pursuit of Catholic Emancipation in Ireland, England & Scotland, 1660-1829. 240p. 1997. 45.00 (*0-7165-2535-6*, Pub. by Irish Acad Pr) Intl Spec Bk.

***O'Brien, Gerard, ed.** Derry & Londonderry: History & Society. LC 99-221819. (County History & Society Ser.). (Illus.). 900p. 1998. 79.95 (*0-906602-85-8*, Pub. by Geography Pubns) Irish Bks Media.

O'Brien, Gerard, ed. see Gwynn, Aubrey.

O'Brien, Geri. Secrets of a Successful Mom. 366p. 1995. pap., spiral bd. 6.50 (*1-56245-173-1*) Great Quotations.

O'Brien, Gerry. CBI European Business Handbook 1999 Edition. 1999. pap. text 60.00 (*0-7494-2549-0*) Kogan Page Ltd.

***O'Brien, Gerry.** Cleaning Up. 2000. pap. 9.95 (*0-86140-416-5*, Pub. by Smyth) Dufour.

O'Brien, Gerry & Jolly, Adam, eds. Exporting to Scandinavia. 144p. 1998. pap. 25.00 (*0-7494-2691-8*) Kogan Page Ltd.

O'Brien, Gerry, ed. see Mathews, Peter.

Obrien, Glenn. Rizzi: Plains Myths. 1997. 95.00 (*0-936598-05-0*) J Szoke Edns.

O'Brien, Glenn. Soap Box. 215p. 1998. pap. 27.00 (*90-72191-87-0*, 810551, Pub. by Imschoot) Dist Art Pubs.

***O'Brien, Glenn.** The Style Guy: The Answers to the Questions Men Are Asking on Sex, Manners, Grooming, Fashion, Travel, Women & the Meaning of Life. 256p. 2000. pap. 12.95 (*0-345-42727-0*, Ballantine) Ballantine Pub Grp.

O'Brien, Glenn. The Style Guy Style Book. (Illus.). 1999. pap. write for info. (*0-446-67428-1*) Warner Bks.

O'Brien, Gordon E. Psychology of Work & Unemployment. LC 85-29604. (Wiley Series in Psychology & Productivity at Work). 329p. 1986. pap. 102.00 (*0-7837-8492-9*, 204929900010) Bks Demand.

O'Brien, Greg, ed. A Guide to Nature on Cape Cod & the Islands. expanded rev. ed. (Illus.). 272p. 1995. pap. 13.95 (*0-940160-61-7*) Parnassus Imprints.

— O'Brien's Original Guide to Cape Cod & the Islands. 3rd rev. ed. LC 96-1855. Orig. Title: Insider's Guide to Cape Cod & the Islands. (Illus.). 268p. 1996. pap. 14.95 (*0-940160-66-8*) Parnassus Imprints.

O'Brien, Greg, jt. auth. see Dunford, Fred.

O'Brien, Greg, ed. see Renke, Adria.

O'Brien, Gregory & Yule, William, eds. Behavioral Phenotypes. (Clinics in Developmental Medicine Ser.: No. 138). 224p. 1996. 64.95 (*1-898683-06-9*, Pub. by Mc Keith Pr) Cambridge U Pr.

O'Brien, Gregory, jt. ed. see Gillberg, Christopher.

***O'Brien, Greig, ed.** The Official Kiss Magazine. (Starlog Movie Ser.: No. 2). 1999. pap. 5.99 (*0-934551-93-6*, Pub. by Starlog Grp Inc) Kable News Co Inc.

— Starlog Celebrity Series Presents Shockwave, Vol. 24. 2000. pap. 4.99 (*0-88013-017-2*, Pub. by Starlog Grp Inc) Kable News Co Inc.

O'Brien, H. V. & O'Brien, Gaynell. Painting for Freedom. LC 87-50148. (Illus.). 160p. 1987. 12.95 (*0-9618480-0-6*) Times Pub TX.

O'Brien, Henry. Atlantis in Ireland: Round Towers of Ireland. LC 73-94419. (Illus.). 536p. 1989. reprint ed. pap. 18.95 (*0-89345-245-9*, Steinerbks) Garber Comm.

O'Brien, Horacio H. Estructuras Algebraicas III (Grupos Finitos) OAS General Secretariat, Department of Scientific Research Staff, ed. (Serie de Matematica: No. 14). 138p. (C). 1981. pap. text 2.00 (*0-8270-1298-5*) OAS.

O'Brien, Howard. All Things Considered. (American Autobiography Ser.). 345p. 1995. reprint ed. lib. bdg. 89.00 (*0-7812-8601-8*) Rprt Serv.

Obrien, Ilona. My Baptism Book. 1998. pap. 5.95 (*0-687-08716-3*) Abingdon.

***O'Brien, J.** Flower Garden. (Little Activity Bks.). (J). 2000. pap. 1.00 (*0-486-40983-X*) Dover.

O'Brien, J., et al, eds. The Maillard Reactions in Foods & Medicine. (Special Publication Ser.: Vol. 223). 480p. 1998. 145.00 (*0-85404-733-6*) Spr-Verlag.

O'Brien, J., et al. Religion for a Change, Bk. 2. (C). 1991. text 45.00 (*0-7487-0474-4*, Pub. by S Thornes Pubs) Trans-Atl Phila.

— Religion for a Change, Bk. 3. (C). 1991. text 45.00 (*0-7487-0475-2*, Pub. by S Thornes Pubs) Trans-Atl Phila.

— Religion for a Change Teacher's Book for Books 1 & 2. (C). 1991. text 50.00 (*0-7487-0476-0*, Pub. by S Thornes Pubs) Trans-Atl Phila.

O'Brien, J. E. & Dallman, R. J., eds. Phase Change Heat Transfer, 1993. LC 91-55579. 109p. 1993. pap. 40.00 (*0-7918-1008-9*) ASME.

O'Brien, J. J., jt. auth. see Angel, M. V.

O'Brien, J. J., jt. ed. see Angel, M. V.

O'Brien, J. R. & Verstraete, Marc, eds. Ciclopidine. (Journal: Haemostasis: Vol. 13, Suppl. 1). (Illus.). ii, 54p. 1983. pap. 41.75 (*3-8055-3816-2*) S Karger.

O'Brien, J. S., jt. ed. see Durand, P.

O

O'Brien, Jack. Kiplinger's Complete Job Search Organizer: How to Get a Great Job Fast. 1996. pap. 11.00 (0-614-12599-5) Random.

— Next Step: The Real World: Aggressive Tactics to Get Your Professional Life off to a Fast Start. LC 99-37352. 243p. (C). 1999. pap. 14.95 (0-938721-65-8, Pub. by Kiplinger Bks) Natl Bk Netwk.

— The Return of Silver Chief. (J). 21.95 (0-89190-398-4) Amereon Ltd.

— Silver Chief: Dog of the North. 240p. 1991. reprint ed. lib. bdg. 35.95 (0-89966-823-2) Buccaneer Bks.

— Spike of Swift River. unabridged ed. 200p. 1997. reprint ed. pap. 14.95 (1-57002-043-4) Univ Publng Hse.

***O'Brien, Jacqui.** Train Your Dog: A Weekly Program for a Well-Behaved Dog. LC 98-40604. (Illus.). 128p. 1999. pap. 18.95 (0-7641-0967-7) Barron.

O'Brien, James. Akutagawa & Dazai: Instances of Literary Adaptation. LC 88-70040. (Arizona State University Center for Asian Studies Monograph Ser.: No. 21). 150p. 1988. pap. 10.00 (0-939252-18-X) ASU Ctr Asian.

***O'Brien, James.** CPM in Construction Management. 5th ed. 544p. 1999. 79.95 (0-07-134440-3) McGraw.

O'Brien, James. Music in World Cultures: Understanding Multiculturalism Through the Arts. LC 94-214490. 400p. (C). 1996. pap. text, per. 40.95 (0-8403-9122-6) Kendall-Hunt.

O'Brien, James & Boockholdt, James L. Accounting Systems. 2nd ed. (C). 1994. pap. text 25.95 (0-256-18423-2, Irwn McGrw-H) McGrw-H Hghr Educ.

O'Brien, James, tr. see Dazai, Osamu.

O'Brien, James A. Introduction to Information Systems. 2nd alternate ed. LC 97-36755. 608p. (C). 1997. text 59.50 (0-256-25196-7, Irwn McGrw-H) McGrw-H Hghr Educ.

— Introduction to Information Systems. 8th ed. 544p. (C). 1996. text 68.25 (0-256-20937-5, Irwn McGrw-H) McGrw-H Hghr Educ.

— Introduction to Information Systems: An End User - Enterprise Perspective, Alternate. LC 94-31626. 525p. (C). 1994. text 66.60 (0-256-16221-2, Irwn McGrw-H) McGrw-H Hghr Educ.

***O'Brien, James A.** Introduction to Information Systems: Essentials for the Internetworked E-Business Enterprise. 10th ed. LC 00-33527. 2001. write for info. (0-07-242324-2) McGraw.

O'Brien, James A. Introduction to Information Systems: Select Chapters. 7th ed. (C). 1994. text 43.95 (0-256-18175-6, Irwn McGrw-H) McGrw-H Hghr Educ.

— Liam O'Flaherty. LC 78-126291. (Irish Writers Ser.). 124p. 1975. 8.50 (0-8387-7772-4); pap. 1.95 (0-8387-7773-2) Bucknell U Pr.

— Management Information Systems: A Managerial End-User Perspective. (C). 1990. text 57.95 (0-256-07862-9, Irwn McGrw-H) McGrw-H Hghr Educ.

— Management Information Systems: A Managerial End-User Perspective. 2nd ed. LC 92-17554. 704p. (C). 1992. text 69.95 (0-256-10346-1, Irwn McGrw-H) McGrw-H Hghr Educ.

— Management Information Systems: Managing Information. 3rd ed. 752p. (C). 1995. text 35.50 (0-256-20688-0, Irwn McGrw-H) McGrw-H Hghr Educ.

— Management Information Systems: Managing Information Technology in the Internetworked Enterprise. 4th ed. LC 98-24795. 832p. 1998. 85.00 (0-07-290611-1) McGraw.

— Management Information Systems, International: Managerial End User Perspective. 2nd ed. 728p. (C). 1992. text 35.50 (0-256-10830-7, Irwn McGrw-H) McGrw-H Hghr Educ.

— Management Informations Systems: Managing Information Technology in the Networked Enterprise. 3rd ed. LC 95-38515. (Illus.). 752p. (C). 1998. text 69.95 (0-256-17354-0, Irwn McGrw-H) McGrw-H Hghr Educ.

O'Brien, James A. & Kain, Richard M. George Russell-AE. (Irish Writers Ser.). 93p. 1976. 8.50 (0-8387-1101-4); pap. 1.95 (0-8387-1206-1) Bucknell U Pr.

O'Brien, James A., jt. auth. see Erickson, Fritz J.

O'Brien, James A., jt. auth. see Schultheis, Robert.

***O'Brien, James G., ed.** Self Neglect: Challenges for Helping Professionals. 104p. 1999. 34.95 (0-7890-0975-7) Haworth Pr.

— Self Neglect: Challenges for Helping Professionals. LC 00-21100. 104p. 2000. pap. text 14.95 (0-7890-0993-5) Haworth Pr.

O'Brien, James J. Construction Change Orders: Impact, Avoidance, & Documentation. LC 98-11752. (Illus.). 356p. 1998. text 69.95 (0-07-048234-9) McGraw-Hill Prof.

— Construction Documentation. 3rd ed. LC 95-1088. (Construction Law Library). 368p. 1995. boxed set 150.00 (0-471-11041-8) Wiley.

— CPM in Construction Management. 4th ed. LC 92-24367. 507p. 1992. 85.00 (0-07-047921-6) McGraw.

***O'Brien, James J.** CPM in Construction Management. 5th ed. LC 99-31219. (Illus.). 544p. 1999. 79.95 incl. cd-rom (0-07-048269-1) McGraw.

— Still Deep Water. LC 99-96675. 2000. pap. 9.95 (0-533-13302-5) Vantage.

O'Brien, James J., ed. Advanced Physical Oceanographic Numerical Modelling. 1986. text 267.50 (90-277-2329-X) Kluwer Academic.

— Lawrence D. Miles: Recollections. (Illus.). 124p. 1988. 17.50 (0-9619440-0-5) Value Found.

O'Brien, James J., et al, eds. Standard Handbook of Heavy Construction. 3rd ed. LC 95-45878. (Illus.). 1184p. 1996. 115.00 (0-07-047971-2) McGraw.

O'Brien, James P. The Listening Experience: Elements, Forms, & Styles in Music. 2nd ed. (C). 1995. pap. 35.00 (0-02-872139-X, Schirmer Books) Mac Lib Ref.

— The Listening Experience: Elements, Forms, & Styles in Music. 2nd ed. (C). 1997. teacher ed. write for info. (0-02-872134-9, Schirmer Books) Mac Lib Ref.

O'Brien, James P., jt. auth. see Blaustein, Albert P.

O'Brien, James W. Science Policy, Biotechnology, & American State Government: Recommendations for State Action. (Studies in Technology & Social Change: No. 12). 76p. (Orig.). (C). 1989. pap. 8.00 (0-945271-17-4) ISU-CIKARD.

O'Brien, Janet F., jt. auth. see Garbers, Debbie.

O'Brien, Jean. The Shadow Keeper. LC 97-189691. 50p. 1998. pap. 14.95 (1-897648-79-0, Pub. by Salmon Poetry) Dufour.

O'Brien, Jean M. Dispossession by Degrees: Indian Land & Identity in Natick, Massachusetts, 1650-1790. LC 96-22551. (Studies in North American Indian History: No. 5). (Illus.). 238p. (C). 1997. text 52.95 (0-521-56172-8) Cambridge U Pr.

***O'Brien, Jeff.** Seasons in Upper Turkeyfoot: A Countryman's Journal LC 99-33386. 1999. write for info. (0-9646184-3-5) Lucid Pr.

O'Brien, Jerry, ed. see Stanley, Charles A.

O'Brien, Jim. Dare to Dream: The Steelers of Two Special Seasons. (Illus.). 448p. 1996. 26.95 (1-886348-00-6); pap. 16.95 (1-886348-01-4) J P OBrien.

— Doing It Right: The Steelers of Three Rivers & Four Super Bowls Share Their Secrets for Success. (Pittsburgh Proud Ser.). (Illus.). 536p. (Orig.). 1985. 24.95 (0-916114-09-0) J P OBrien.

— Hometown Heroes: Profiles in Sports & Spirit. O'Brien Zirwas, Sarah, ed. (Pittsburgh Proud Sports Ser.). (Illus.). 416p. (YA). (gr. 4 up). 1999. 26.95 (1-886348-04-9) J P OBrien.

— Keep the Faith: The Steelers of Two Different Eras. O'Brien, Sarah, ed. (Pittsburgh Proud Sports Book Ser.: Vol. 7). (Illus.). 448p. (J). (gr. 4 up). 1997. 26.95 (1-886348-02-2) J P OBrien.

— Maz & the '60 Bucs: When Pittsburgh & Its Pirates Went All the Way. (Pittsburgh Proud Ser.). (Illus.). 512p. 1993. 24.95 (0-916114-12-0) J P OBrien.

— Penguin Profiles: Pittsburgh's Boys of Winter. (Pittsburgh Proud Ser.). (Illus.). 448p. 1994. 24.95 (0-916114-16-3) J P OBrien.

— Remember Roberto: Clemente Recalled by Teammates, Family, Friends & Fans. (Pittsburgh Proud Ser.). (Illus.). 448p. 1994. 24.95 (0-916114-14-7) J P OBrien.

— We Had 'em All the Way: Bob Prince & His Pittsburgh Pirates. O'Brien, Sarah H., ed. (Pittsburgh Proud Sports Book Ser.). (Illus.). 432p. 1998. 26.95 (1-886348-03-0) J P OBrien.

O'Brien, Jim, jt. auth. see Wolfson, Marty.

O'Brien, Joan & Major, Wilfred. In the Beginning: Creation Myths from Ancient Mesopotamia, Israel, & Greece. LC 81-21311. (American Academy of Religion Aids for the Study of Religion Ser.). 211p. (C). 1985. pap. 19.95 (0-89130-559-9, 010311) OUP.

O'Brien, Joan V. The Transformation of Hera: A Study of Ritual, Hero, & the Goddess in the Iliad. LC 92-37157. (Greek Studies: Interdisciplinary Approaches). 240p. (Orig.). (C). 1993. pap. text 26.95 (0-8476-7808-3); lib. bdg. 64.50 (0-8476-7807-5) Rowman.

O'Brien, Joanne & Breuilly, Liz. Religion for a Change: An Integrated Course in Religious & Personal Education, Bk. 2. 80p. (Orig.). (C). 1991. pap. text 42.50 (0-7478-0474-5, Pub. by S Thornes Pubs) Trans-Atl Phila.

O'Brien, Joanne, et al. Religion for a Change: An Integrated Course in Religious & Personal Education. 96p. (Orig.). (C). 1991. pap. 42.50 (0-7478-0475-3, Pub. by S Thornes Pubs) Trans-Atl Phila.

— Religion for a Change: An Integrated Course in Religious & Personal Education, Bk. 1. 96p. (Orig.). (C). 1991. pap. 42.50 (0-7478-0473-7, Pub. by S Thornes Pubs) Trans-Atl Phila.

— Religion for a Change: An Integrated Course in Religious & Personal Education Teacher's Book. (C). 1991. pap. 42.50 (0-7478-0476-1, Pub. by S Thornes Pubs) Trans-Atl Phila.

O'Brien, Joanne, jt. auth. see Kwok Man-Ho.

O'Brien, Joanne, jt. ed. see Palmer, Martin.

O'Brien, Jodi. Social Prisms: Reflections on Everyday Myths & Paradoxes. LC 98-40123. 1999. pap. write for info. (0-8039-9031-6) Pine Forge.

O'Brien, Jodi & Howard, Judith A. Everyday Inequalities: Critical Inquiries. LC 97-47398. 416p. 1998. 59.95 (1-57718-121-2); pap. 26.95 (1-57718-122-0) Blackwell Pubs.

O'Brien, Jodi & Kollock, Peter. The Production of Reality: Essays & Readings on Social Interaction. 2nd ed. LC 96-15615. 608p. (C). 1996. pap. 37.95 (0-7619-8500-X) Pine Forge.

O'Brien, Jodi, et al. The Social Organization of Mental Illness. 2nd ed. (Illus.). 240p. (C). 1996. pap. 19.95 (0-8039-8500-2) Sage.

O'Brien, John. Anacreon Redivivus: A Study of Anacreontic Translation in Mid-Sixteenth-Century France. LC 95-34523. (Recentiores Later Latin Texts & Contexts Ser.). 288p. (C). 1996. text 49.50 (0-472-10617-1, 10617) U of Mich Pr.

— The Assault on Tony's. 224p. 1998. reprint ed. pap. 12.00 (0-8021-3542-0, Grove) Grove-Atltic.

— Break a Leg. 1983. 5.50 (0-87129-489-3, B54) Dramatic Pub.

— Daniel Mannix: Builder of the Australian Church. 1989. pap. 30.00 (1-85390-042-7, Pub. by Veritas Pubns) St Mut.

— Elves, Gnomes & Other Little People Coloring Book. 81st ed. (J). 1980. pap. 2.95 (0-486-24049-5) Dover.

— The Farmer in the Dell. LC 99-60396. (Illus.). 32p. (J). (ps-3). 2000. 14.95 (1-56397-775-3) Boyds Mills Pr.

O'Brien, John. Interviews with Black Writers. LC 72-97488. 274p. 1974. pap. 3.95 (0-87140-085-5) Liveright.

— Investments Vol. I: Modern Portfolio Theory Using CAPM Tutor. (FB-Intro to Finance Ser.). 1995. pap. 34.95 (0-538-84825-1) S-W Pub.

— Investments Vol. III: Bond Valuation Using Bond Tutor, Vol. 3. (FB-Intro to Finance Ser.). 300p. 1996. 55.95 incl. 3.5 hd (0-538-84827-8) S-W Pub.

O'Brien, John. Leaving Las Vegas. 206p. 1991. 19.50 (0-922820-12-0) Watermark Pr.

— Leaving Las Vegas. LC 95-81572. 200p. 1996. reprint ed. pap. 11.00 (0-8021-3445-9, Grove) Grove-Atltic.

— The Man Who Died & Went to Heaven. 32p. (YA). (gr. 10 up). 1980. pap. 3.50 (0-87129-788-4, M47) Dramatic Pub.

— Memory. 1981. pap. 3.50 (0-87129-232-7, M52) Dramatic Pub.

— Mirrors. 1982. 3.50 (0-87129-540-7, M53) Dramatic Pub.

— Mother Hubbard's Christmas. LC 95-83169. (Illus.). 32p. (J). (ps-1). 1996. 14.95 (1-56397-139-9) Boyds Mills Pr.

— Mother Hubbard's Christmas. 32p. (J). (ps-2). 1998. pap. 6.99 (0-440-41450-4) Dell.

O'Brien, John. Mythical Beasts Stickers. (Illus.). (J). 1994. pap. 1.00 (0-486-28282-1) Dover.

Obrien, John. Night Before Christmas Coloring Book. 81st ed. (Illus.). (J). (gr. k-3). 1981. pap. 2.95 (0-486-24169-6) Dover.

O'Brien, John. Please Don't Go Back Where You Came From. 1994. 5.50 (0-87129-434-6, P75) Dramatic Pub.

— Poof! (Illus.). 32p. (J). (ps). 1999. 14.95 (1-56397-815-6) Boyds Mills Pr.

O'Brien, John. Responding to Products Liability Claims. Vol. L1. text 82.00 (0-8205-2405-0) Bender.

O'brien, John. Sam & Spot: A Silly Story. 1995. 11.19 (0-606-09816-X, Pub. by Turtleback) Demco.

O'Brien, John. Softy. 18p. 1991. pap. 3.50 (0-87129-098-7, S94) Dramatic Pub.

— Stripper Lessons. LC 96-44137. 208p. 1997. pap. 12.00 (0-8021-3507-2, Grove) Grove-Atltic.

— Success. 43p. 1984. pap. 3.50 (0-87129-100-2, S70) Dramatic Pub.

***O'Brien, John.** True Lies: 10 Tales for You to Judge. LC 96-7149. 64p. (J). (gr. 3 up). 1998. reprint ed. mass mkt. 4.95 (0-688-16371-8, Wm Morrow) Morrow Avon.

O'Brien, John. The Twelve Days of Christmas. LC 92-73990. (Illus.). 32p. (J). 1993. 14.95 (1-56397-142-9) Boyds Mills Pr.

***O'Brien, John, ed.** Bradford Morrow. (Review of Contemporary Fiction Ser.: Vol. 20.1). (Illus.). 203p. 2000. pap. 8.00 (1-56478-248-4) Dalkey Arch.

O'Brien, John, ed. Curtis White - Milorad Pavic, Vol. 18, No. 2. (Review of Contemporary Fiction Ser.). 224p. 1998. pap. 8.00 (1-56478-191-7) Dalkey Arch.

— Ed Sanders Number. (Review of Contemporary Fiction Ser.: Vol. 19). 256p. 1999. pap. 8.00 (1-56478-220-4) Dalkey Arch.

— Josef Skvorecky/Mario Vargas Llosa. (Review of Contemporary Fiction Ser.: Vol. 17, No. 1). 220p. (Orig.). 1997. pap. 8.00 (1-56478-153-4) Dalkey Arch.

— New French Fiction. (Review of Contemporary Fiction Ser.: Vol. 9, No. 1). 220p. 1989. pap. 8.00 (1-56478-112-7) Dalkey Arch.

— New Latvian Fiction. (Review of Contemporary Fiction Ser.: Vol. 18, No. 1). 256p. 1998. pap. 8.00 (1-56478-178-X) Dalkey Arch.

— Raymond Queneau/Carole Maso. (Review of Contemporary Fiction Ser.). 220p. 1997. pap. 8.00 (1-56478-177-1) Dalkey Arch.

— (Re)Interpretations: Etudes Sur le Seizieme Siecle. (Michigan Romance Studies: Vol. 15). (ENG & FRE., Illus.). 278p. 1995. pap. 15.00 (0-939730-14-6) Mich Romance.

— Richard Powers - Rikki Ducornet, Vol. 18, No. 3. (Review of Contemporary Fiction Ser.). 224p. 1998. pap. 8.00 (1-56478-192-5) Dalkey Arch.

— Samuel Beckett. (Review of Contemporary Fiction Ser.: Vol. 7, No. 2). 220p. 1987. pap. 15.00 (1-56478-108-9) Dalkey Arch.

— Wilson Harris/Alan Burns. (Review of Contemporary Fiction Ser.: Vol. 17, No. 2). 220p. (Orig.). 1997. pap. 8.00 (1-56478-161-5) Dalkey Arch.

O'Brien, John & Srivastava, Sanjay. Investments: A Visual Approach: Bond Valuation & Bond Tutor. LC 95-42295. 1995. write for info. (0-538-84811-1) S-W Pub.

— Modern Portfolio Theory. 1994. write for info. (0-538-84809-X) S-W Pub.

— Option Valuation. LC 94-44758. 1995. write for info. (0-538-84810-3) S-W Pub.

O'Brien, John & Sujono, Monika. Too Many Sisters. LC 91-217610. 108 p. (J). 1991. write for info. (0-340-53575-X, Pub. by Hodder & Stought Ltd) Trafalgar.

O'Brien, John & Travers, Pauric. The Irish Emigrant Experience in Australia. 279p. 1991. pap. 26.00 (1-85371-129-2, Pub. by Poolbeg Pr) Dufour.

O'Brien, John, jt. auth. see Schwartz, Alvin.

O'Brien, John A. The Faith of Millions. rev. ed. LC 74-82119. 438p. 1974. pap. 10.95 (0-87973-830-8) Our Sunday Visitor.

O'Brien, John A. Winning Converts. (Illus.). 258p. 1996. reprint ed. pap. 14.95 (1-888992-00-X) Catholic Answers.

O'Brien, John C. & Goldman, Roger L. Federal Criminal Trial Evidence. LC 89-61440. 726p. 1989. text 15.00 (0-685-45800-8, C1-1184) PLI.

O'Brien, John C., et al. Missouri Evidentiary Foundations. 327p. 1994. 75.00 (1-55834-177-3, 65355-10, MICHIE) LEXIS Pub.

O'Brien, John D., et al, eds. Psychotherapies with Children & Adolescents: Adapting the Psychodynamic Process. 346p. 1992. text 49.50 (0-88048-406-3, 8406) Am Psychiatric.

O'Brien, John E. Refreshed by the Word, Cycle C. 144p. 1994. pap. 10.95 (0-8091-3506-X) Paulist Pr.

— Refreshed by the Word, Cycle A. 160p. 1995. pap. 10.95 (0-8091-3597-3, 1995) Paulist Pr.

— Refreshed by the Word, Cycle B. 160p. 1996. pap. 10.95 (0-8091-3649-X, 3649-X) Paulist Pr.

O'Brien, John J. Defending DWI Cases in Connecticut. 149p. (Orig.). 1992. pap. 50.00 (1-878698-13-3) Atlantic Law.

— Defending DWI Cases in Connecticut. 2nd ed. LC 98-113883. (Illus.). 127p. (Orig.). 1997. pap. 60.00 (1-878698-43-5) Atlantic Law.

Obrien, John J. A Turn of the Verse. 1991. 2.00 (0-9628932-0-X) J Obrien.

O'Brien, John M. Alexander the Great: The Invisible Enemy. (Illus.). 358p. (gr. 13). 1994. pap. 24.99 (0-415-10617-6, B3961) Routledge.

— Medieval Church. (Quality Paperback Ser.: No. 227). 120p. (Orig.). 1968. pap. 11.00 (0-8226-0227-X) Littlefield.

O'Brien, John T., Jr. From Bondage to Citizenship: The Richmond Black Community, 1865-67. LC 90-33971. (Dissertations in Nineteenth-Century American Political & Social History). 528p. 1990. reprint ed. 35.00 (0-8240-0047-1) Garland.

O'Brien, Joseph F. Boss of Bosses: The FBI & Paul Castellano. 384p. 1992. mass mkt. 6.99 (0-440-21229-4) Dell.

O'Brien, Joseph V. William O'Brien & the Course of Irish Politics, 1881-1918. LC 74-22970. (Illus.). 287p. reprint ed. pap. 89.00 (0-608-18292-3, 203154200075) Bks Demand.

O'Brien, Judith. Ashton's Bride. Marrow, Linda, ed. 352p. 1995. mass mkt. 6.50 (0-671-87149-8) PB.

— The Forever Bride. 1999. mass mkt. 6.50 (0-671-00041-1) PB.

— Maiden Voyage. 368p. 1997. per. 5.99 (0-671-50219-0) PB.

— Once upon a Rose. 352p. 1996. mass mkt. 5.99 (0-671-50225-5) S&S Trade.

— Once upon a Rose. large type ed. LC 97-9698. (Large Print Book Ser.). 1997. pap. 22.95 (1-56895-444-1) Wheeler Pub.

Obrien, Judith. One Perfect Knight. 380p. 1998. per. 6.50 (0-671-00040-3) S&S Trade.

O'Brien, Judith. Rhapsody in Time. Marrow, Linda, ed. 304p. (Orig.). 1994. mass mkt. 5.50 (0-671-87148-X) PB.

— To Marry a British Lord. 1997. per. 5.99 (0-671-00039-X) PB.

O'Brien, Judith A. 20 Common Problems in Clinical Laboratory Management. LC 99-13820. (Illus.). 336p. 1999. 45.00 (0-07-048265-9) McGraw-Hill HPD.

***O'Brien, Judith Tate.** Mythic Places. (Chapbook Ser.: Vol. 3). 32p. 2000. 5.00 (0-9659832-3-4) ByLine Pr.

O'Brien, Judy. Once upon a Rose. 1996. pap. 5.99 (0-614-98084-4, Pocket Books) PB.

O'Brien, Julia M. & Horton, Fred L., Jr., eds. The Yahweh-Baal Confrontation & Other Studies in Biblical Literature & Archaeology: Essays in Honour of Emmett Willard Hamrick. LC 95-1377. (Studies in Bible & Early Christianity: Vol. 35). (Illus.). 194p. 1995. text 79.95 (0-7734-2426-1, Mellen Biblical Pr) E Mellen.

O'Brien, Justin. A Meeting of Mystic Paths: Christianity & Yoga. LC 96-14872. 180p. 1996. 16.95 (0-936663-14-6) Yes Intl.

— Walking with a Himalayan Master: An American's Odyssey. LC 98-36530. (Illus.). 425p. 1998. 24.00 (0-936663-19-7) Yes Intl.

— Walking with a Himalayan Master: An American's Odyssey. LC 97-30876. (Illus.). 420p. 1998. pap. 18.00 (0-936663-22-7) Yes Intl.

O'Brien, Justin, ed. see Gide, Andre.

O'Brien, Justin, ed. & intro. see Gide, Andre & Guillaume, Paul.

O'Brien, Justin, tr. see Camus, Albert.

O'Brien, Justin, tr. see Gide, Andre.

O'Brien, Justin, tr. & intro. see Camus, Albert.

O'Brien, Karen. Narratives of Enlightenment: Cosmopolitan History from Voltaire to Gibbon. LC 96-36667. (Studies in Eighteenth-Century English Literature & Thought: Vol. 34). 264p. (C). 1997. text 59.95 (0-521-46533-8) Cambridge U Pr.

— Sacrificing the Forest: Environmental & Social Struggles in Chiapas. LC 97-47343. 210p. (C). 1998. pap. 69.00 (0-8133-6905-3, Pub. by Westview) HarpC.

O'Brien, Karen & White, Robin. A Teacher's Guide to Petroglyph National Monument. 2nd rev. ed. (Illus.). 127p. (gr. k-8). 1997. teacher ed. 12.95 (1-877856-83-5) SW Pks Mnmts.

O'Brien, Karen, jt. auth. see Lieberman, Richard D.

O'Brien, Karen M., jt. auth. see Hill, Clara E.

O'Brien, Kate. Talk of Angels: A Novel. LC 95-17737. 368p. (J). 1997. pap. 12.45 (0-7868-6191-6, Pub. by Hyperion) Time Warner.

O'Brien, Katherine, jt. ed. see Nasr, Seyyed Hossein.

O'Brien, Kathleen. The Daddy Deal. (Presents Ser.: No. 1897). 1997. per. 3.50 (0-373-11897-X, 1-11897-5) Harlequin Bks.

— El Fantasma del Amor (The Phantom of Love) (Deseo Ser.). (SPA.). 1998. per. 3.50 (0-373-33448-6, 1-33448-1) Harlequin Bks.

— A Forgotten Magic. (Presents Ser.). 1994. per. 2.99 (0-373-11642-X, 1-11642-5) Harlequin Bks.

— Herencia de Amor. (Bianca Ser.: No. 170). (SPA.). 1999. per. 3.50 (0-373-33520-2) Harlequin Bks.

O

An Asterisk (*) at the beginning of an entry indicates that the title is appearing for the first time.

— The Husband Contract. (Presents Ser.: No. 116). 1999. mass mkt. 3.75i (*0-373-18716-5*, 1-18716-0) Harlequin Bks.

— Magia Olvidada: A Forgotten Magic. (Bianca Ser.: Vol. 128). (SPA.). 1998. per. 3.50 (*0-373-33478-8*, 1-33478-8) Harlequin Bks.

— Memory Lapse. LC 95-8024. (Temptation Ser.: No. 522). 216p. 1995. per. 3.25 (*0-373-25626-4*, 1-25626-2) Harlequin Bks.

— Michael's Silence. 1994. per. 2.99 (*0-373-11698-5*, 1-11698-7) Harlequin Bks.

— Mistletoe Man. 1996. per. 3.50 (*0-373-11853-8*, 1-11853-8) Harlequin Bks.

— Noche Blanca (White Night) (SPA.). 1997. per. 3.50 (*0-373-33423-0*, 1-33423-4) Harlequin Bks.

— Trial by Seduction. (Presents Ser.). 1998. per. 3.75 (*0-373-11958-5*, 1-11958-5) Harlequin Bks.

— When Dragons Dream. (Presents Plus Ser.). 1993. per. 2.99 (*0-373-11600-4*, 1-11600-3) Harlequin Bks.

O'Brien, Kathleen, jt. auth. see Gamon, David.

O'Brien, Kathleen, ed. see Brock, Jim, et al.

***O'Brien, Keith.** Between Friends. LC 00-130978. 208p. 2000. pap. 13.95 (*0-9679394-4-5*) Global Learn.

O'Brien, Keith. Cut Your Losses: A Smart Retailer's Guide to Loss Prevention. (Business Ser.). 200p. (Orig.). 1996. pap. 17.95 (*1-55180-036-5*) Self-Counsel Pr.

O'Brien, Keith T., jt. auth. see Rao, Natti S.

O'Brien, Kenneth P. & Parsons, Lynn H., eds. The Home-Front War: World War II & American Society, 161. LC 95-3803. (Contributions in American History Ser.: Vol. 161). 224p. 1995. 57.95 (*0-313-29211-6*, Greenwood Pr) Greenwood.

O'Brien, Kevin. But the Gates Were Shut: New Testament Rediscoveries, Vol. II. 540p. 1996. 74.95 (*1-57309-079-4*) Intl Scholars.

— But the Gates Were Shut: New Testament Rediscoveries: Extramural Paradigm Applied to the Jewish Arraignment of Jesus, Vol. II. 540p. 1996. pap. 54.95 (*1-57309-078-6*) Intl Scholars.

— But the Gates Were Shut: Operation of Jerusalem's Perimeter Gates within New Evidence & a New Methodology for Dating & Locating the Last Supper & Identifying the Beloved Disciple in John 13:25 Project, Vol. I. LC 96-39402. 540p. 1996. 74.95 (*1-57309-077-8*) Intl Scholars.

— But the Gates Were Shut Vol. I: Operation of Jerusalem's Perimeter Gates within New Evidence & a New Methodology for Dating & Locating the Last Supper & Identifying the Beloved Disciple in John 13:25. LC 96-39402. 540p. 1996. pap. 54.95 (*1-57309-076-X*) Intl Scholars.

— Only Son. LC 96-77156. 304p. 1997. 21.95 (*1-57566-091-1*, Knsington) Kensgtn Pub Corp.

— Only Son. 352p. 1998. pap. 5.99 (*1-57566-211-6*, Knsington) Kensgtn Pub Corp.

O'Brien, Kevin. The UK Tourism & Leisure Market: Travel Trends & Spending Patterns LC 90-176327. 293 p. 1990. write for info. (*0-85058-328-4*) Economist Intell.

O'Brien, Kevin, jt. auth. see Sullivan, Robert C.

O'Brien, Kevin, tr. see Vertov, Dziga.

O'Brien, Kevin E., ed. My Life in the Irish Brigade: The Civil War Memoirs of Private William McCarter, 116th Pennsylvania Infantry. (Illus.). 288p. 1997. reprint ed. 24.95 (*1-882810-07-4*, 07-4) Savas Pub.

O'Brien, Kevin E., et al. The History of the Irish Brigade: A Collection of Historical Essays. (Illus.). 232p. (C). 1996. pap. 19.95 (*1-887901-03-5*) Sergeant Kirk.

O'Brien, Kevin J. Reform Without Liberalization: China's National People's Congress & the Politics of Institutional Change. (Illus.). 277p. (C). 1990. text 57.95 (*0-521-38086-3*) Cambridge U Pr.

O'Brien, Kimberly. A Competitive Analysis of Electronic Wire & Cable End-Use Markets - Copper vs. Fiber: 1996-2000 Analysis & Forecasts. 70p. 1996. pap. text 2400.00 (*1-878218-70-0*) World Info Tech.

— Electronic Wire & Cable-U. S. Markets & Opportunities: 1996-2000 Analysis & Forecasts. 100p. 1996. pap. text 2700.00 (*1-878218-69-7*) World Info Tech.

— Telecommunications Outside Plant Products, Copper vs. Fiber - U. S. Markets, Customers, & Competitors: 1997-2000 Analysis & Forecasts. 78p. 1997. pap. text 2400.00 (*1-878218-74-3*) World Info Tech.

— U. S. & Canadian Electronic Wire & Cable Manufacturers: 1995 Competitive Analysis. 220p. 1995. pap. text 2900.00 (*1-878218-63-8*) World Info Tech.

— U. S. Distribution Channels for Electronic Wire & Cable: 1995-2000 Analysis & Forecasts. 253p. 1995. pap. text 2700.00 (*1-878218-57-3*) World Info Tech.

— U. S. Electronic Wire & Cable Companies: 1996 Competitive Analysis. 146p. 1996. pap. text 2700.00 (*1-878218-72-7*) World Info Tech.

O'Brien, Kimberly, jt. auth. see McGowan, Kimberly.

O'Brien, Kyran & O'Reilly, Aileen C. Oh Boyz! The New Boyzone Book. (Illus.). 96p. 1997. pap. 12.95 (*0-86278-503-0*, Pub. by OBrien Pr) Irish Amer Bk.

O'Brien, L. Stephen. Traumatic Events & Mental Health. LC 97-22865. (Psychiatry & Medicine Ser.). (Illus.). 312p. (C). 1998. text 100.00 (*0-521-57027-1*); pap. text 44.95 (*0-521-57886-8*) Cambridge U Pr.

O'Brien, Larry & Harris, Frank. Retailing: Shopping, Society & Space. 224p. (C). 1990. pap. 38.95 (*0-8464-1515-1*) Beekman Pubs.

Obrien, Laurie. Guard the Body Save the Soul. 1999. pap. 10.00 (*0-938078-60-7*) Anhinga Pr.

O'Brien, Laurie. Marco Polo at the Millennium. 31p. (Orig.). pap. 8.95 (*0-916092-24-0*) Tex Ctr Writers.

— Our Own Sweet Time. 54p. 1996. pap. 10.00 (*0-944206-04-2*) W FL Lit Fed.

O'Brien, Lawrence J. Bad Medicine: How the American Medical Establishment Is Ruining Our Healthcare System. LC 98-48718. 225p. 1999. 24.95 (*1-57392-260-9*) Prometheus Bks.

O'Brien, Linda. Advance Directives: Making End of Life Decisions. 64p. (C). (gr. 13). 1996. text, pap. text 99.00 incl. VHS (*0-8151-3709-5*, 30522) Mosby Inc.

***O'Brien, Linda.** His Forbidden Touch. 384p. 2000. mass mkt. 5.99 (*0-380-81343-2*, Avon Bks) Morrow Avon.

O'Brien, Linda. Promised to a Stranger. 384p. 1998. mass mkt. 5.99 (*0-380-80206-6*, Avon Bks) Morrow Avon.

O'Brien, Linda, tr. see De Heusch, Luc.

O'Brien, Linda A. Advance Directives - Making End of Life Decisions - Resource Guide & Photo Package. 64p. 1996. write for info. (*0-8151-3628-5*) Mosby Inc.

O'Brien, Lisa. Lights, Camera, Action! Making Movies & TV from the Inside Out. (Illus.). 64p. (YA). (gr. 5 up). 1998. 19.95 (*1-895688-75-2*, Pub. by Greey dePencier); pap. 12.95 (*1-895688-76-0*, Pub. by Greey dePencier) Firefly Bks Ltd.

O'Brien, Liz. Samuel Marx: Furniture & Decoration. (Illus.). 48p. 1996. pap., per. 45.00 (*0-9666205-0-X*) Forty One Liz.

O'Brien, Lynn. Strengthening of Skills: Advanced Teacher's Manual. 206p. 1991. teacher ed. 199.00 (*1-56602-044-1*); student ed. 69.95 (*1-56602-045-X*) Research Better.

— Strengthening of Skills: Basic Teacher's Manual. 3rd ed. 221p. 1991. teacher ed. 199.00 (*1-56602-042-5*); student ed. 69.95 (*1-56602-043-3*) Research Better.

O'Brien, M. Divorce: Facing the Issues. 1993. 64.00 (*1-85594-077-9*) St Mut.

O'Brien, M. C., jt. auth. see Chancey, C. C.

O'Brien, M. J. Archaeology of the Central Salt River Valley: An Overview of the Prehistoric Occupation, Vol. 46. (Missouri Archaeologist Ser.). 1985. pap. 8.00 (*0-943414-66-0*) MO Arch Soc.

O'Brien, M. J., jt. auth. see Majewski, T.

O'Brien, Margaret. Discovering Your Light: Common Journeys of Young Adults. Teutschman, Emilie L., ed. LC 90-66455. 64p. 1991. student ed. 6.95 (*1-878718-09-6*, Resurrection Pr) Catholic Bk Pub.

— My Diary. (American Autobiography Ser.). 117p. 1995. reprint ed. lib. bdg. 69.00 (*0-7812-8602-6*) Rprt Serv.

O'Brien, Margaret, jt. auth. see Brannen, Julia.

O'Brien, Margaret, jt. ed. see Lewis, Charles.

O'Brien, Marie, jt. auth. see Kearns, Kimberly.

O'Brien, Mariellen B., jt. auth. see Chiao, Karen L.

O'Brien, Marion. Inclusive Child Care for Infants & Toddlers: Meeting Special Needs. LC 97-12828. 1997. pap. 34.95 (*1-55766-296-7*) P H Brookes.

O'Brien, Marion, jt. ed. see Horowitz, Frances D.

O'Brien, Mark. Breathing. 2nd rev. ed. 20p. 1997. pap. 4.00 (*1-891420-08-9*) Lemonade Factory.

— The Man in the Iron Lung: Poems by Mark O'Brien. 48p. 1997. pap. 8.00 (*1-891420-03-8*) Lemonade Factory.

— The MBA Answer Book: A Career Guide for the Person Who Means Business. (Illus.). 240p. 1984. 15.50 (*0-13-566779-8*) P-H.

— Sonnets & Strike-Outs: Poems on Love & Baseball. 32p. 1998. 6.00 (*1-891420-09-7*) Lemonade Factory.

O'Brien, Mark & Fernbach, Susan. Love & Baseball: Poems. 36p. 1997. pap. 6.00 (*1-891420-04-6*) Lemonade Factory.

O'Brien, Mark, et al. Five at the Center: Essays on the Disability Experience. 40p. 1999. 6.00 (*1-891420-10-0*) Lemonade Factory.

O'Brien, Mark, jt. auth. see Campbell, Anthony F.

O'Brien, Mark A. The Deuteronomistic History Hypothesis: A Reassessment. (Orbis Biblicus et Orientalis Ser.: Vol. 92). 319p. 1989. text 67.25 (*3-7278-0647-8*, Pub. by Presses Univ Fribourg) Eisenbrauns.

O'Brien, Mark A., jt. auth. see Campbell, Anthony F.

O'Brien, Mark S., ed. Pediatric Neurological Surgery: Sponsored by the Subcommittee on Continuing Education II (Expanded Program), American Association of Neurological Surgeons & Congress of Neurological Surgeons. fac. ed. LC 78-3005. (Seminars in Neurological Surgery Ser.). (Illus.). 216p. pap. 67.00 (*0-7837-7277-7*, 204702900005) Bks Demand.

O'Brien, Martin & Penna, Sue. Theorising Welfare: Enlightenment & Modern Society LC 98-60080. 248 p. 1998. write for info. (*0-8039-8906-7*) Sage.

O'Brien, Martin, et al. Theorizing Modernity: Reflexivity, Enviroment & Identity in Gidden's Social Theory. LC 98-35616. 240p. (C). 1998. pap. 38.00 (*0-582-30743-0*) Longman.

***O'Brien, Mary.** Making Better Environmental Decisions: An Alternative to Risk Assessment. LC 99-56868. (Illus.). 352p. 2000. 55.00 (*0-262-15051-4*) MIT Pr.

— Making Better Environmental Decisions: An Alternative to Risk Assessment. LC 99-56868. (Illus.). 352p. 2000. pap. 22.95 (*0-262-65053-3*) MIT Pr.

O'Brien, Mary & Christie, Clare, eds. Single Women: Affirming Our Spiritual Journey. LC 92-39121. 232p. 1993. 55.00 (*0-89789-321-2*, H321, Bergin & Garvey) Greenwood.

O'Brien, Mary B. Heart of the Trail: The Stories of Eight Covered-Wagon Women. (Illus.). 96p. 1997. pap. 9.95 (*1-56044-562-9*, Two Dot) Falcon Pub Inc.

— Jeannette Rankin: Bright Star in the Big Sky. LC 95-8656. (Illus.). 80p. 1995. pap. 7.95 (*1-56044-360-X*) Falcon Pub Inc.

O'Brien, Mary B., jt. auth. see McCarney-Muldoon, Eileen.

Obrien, Mary Barmeyer. Toward the Setting Sun: Pioneer Girls Traveling the Overland Trails. LC 99-34695. (J). 1999. pap. 8.95 (*1-56044-841-5*, Two Dot) Falcon Pub Inc.

O'Brien, Mary E. The AIDS Challenge: Breaking Through the Boundaries. LC 94-43170. 176p. 1995. 55.00 (*0-86569-247-5*, Auburn Hse) Greenwood.

— Chronic Fatigue Syndrome: Charting Your Course to Recovery. LC 97-199925. (Illus.). 100p. 1997. pap. 14.25 (*0-9646891-9-7*) Anadem Pubng.

— In Sickness & in Health--What Every Man Should Know about the Woman He Loves. LC 90-4408. (Illus.). 208p. (Orig.). 1991. pap. 14.95 (*0-929173-05-8*) Health Press.

— Living with HIV: Experiment in Courage. LC 91-41130. 248p. 1992. 57.95 (*0-86569-040-5*, T040, Auburn Hse); pap. 22.95 (*0-86569-203-3*, R203, Auburn Hse) Greenwood.

— Spirituality in Nursing Practice. LC 98-12662. (Nursing Ser.). 298p. 1999. 31.25 (*0-7637-0644-2*) Jones & Bartlett.

O'Brien, Mary E., jt. ed. see Luteyn, James L.

O'Brien, Mary J. Implementation Plan & Recommendations for Integrated Service Networks (ISNs) & a Regulated All-Payer Option (RAPO) Minnesota Care. 62p. (Orig.). (C). 1994. pap. text 35.00 (*0-7881-1375-5*) DIANE Pub.

***O'Brien, Mary J., ed.** Principles for Maternal & Child Health Services (in Minnesota) 92p. (C). 2000. reprint ed. pap. text 25.00 (*0-7881-8715-5*) DIANE Pub.

O'Brien, Mary K., jt. auth. see Dickey, R. P.

O'Brien, Mary L. Netsuke: A Guide for Collectors. LC 65-11837. (Illus.). 246p. 1965. 45.00 (*0-8048-0423-0*, TR84-1) Tuttle Pubng.

O'Brien, Maryann. Gambler's Desire. 288p. (Orig.). 1995. mass mkt. 5.50 (*0-515-11658-0*, Jove) Berkley Pub.

O'Brien, Matthew J. Chameleon: The March Madness Murders. 300p. 1997. pap. 14.95 (*1-57860-011-1*) Guild Pr IN.

***O'Brien, Matthew J. & Rodriguez, Marty M.** The Complete Idiot's Guide to Online Buying & Selling a House. LC 99-65791. 342p. 2000. pap. 16.99 (*0-7897-2257-7*) Que.

O'Brien, Maureen. Deadly Reflection. 288p. 1995. mass mkt. 11.95 (*0-7472-4374-3*, Pub. by Headline Bk Pub) Trafalgar.

— New Day Journal: A Journey from Grief to Healing. rev. ed. LC 99-76612. 96p. 2000. pap. 9.95 (*0-87946-130-6*, 189) ACTA Pubns.

— Who's Got the Ball? (And Other Nagging Questions about Team Life) A Player's Guide for Work Teams. LC 94-23535. (Management Ser.). 207p. 1995. mass mkt. 21.50 (*0-7879-0057-5*) Jossey-Bass.

***O'Brien, Maureen & Tippins, Sherill.** Watch Me Grow: I'm One: Every Parent's Guide to the Enchanting 12- to 24-Month-Old. 2000. 18.00 (*0-688-16878-7*, HarpRes) HarpInfo.

O'Brien, Maureen, ed. see Bright, Deborah, et al.

O'Brien, Maureen C. A History of the Burke - Bourke Clan. (Illus.). 300p. 1991. 55.00 (*0-9629074-0-5*) Clan Pubns.

— In Support of Liberty: European Paintings at the 1883 Pedestal Fund Art Loan Exhibition. LC 86-60099. (Illus.). 180p. (C). 1986. pap. 20.00 (*0-943526-14-0*) Parrish Art.

O'Brien, Maureen C. & Mandel, Patricia C. The American Painter-Etcher Movement. LC 84-60411. (Illus.). 62p. 1984. pap. 15.00 (*0-943526-11-6*) Parrish Art.

— Nineteenth Century American Etchings in the Collection of the Parrish Art Museum. LC 87-61051. 108p. 1987. pap. 15.00 (*0-943526-16-7*) Parrish Art.

O'Brien, Maureen E., jt. auth. see Bloom, Bernard M.

O'Brien, Maureen M., jt. auth. see Bernard.

O'Brien, Mauryeen. Praying Through Grief: Healing Prayer Services for Those Who Mourn. LC 97-17053. 112p. 1997. pap. 12.95 (*0-87793-629-3*) Ave Maria.

O'Brien, Mayan. Self Enlightenment. 1998. pap. 19.95 (*1-86163-048-4*) Holmes Pub.

O'Brien, Meg. Crashing Down. (Mira Bks.). 408p. 1999. per. 5.99 (*1-55166-516-6*, 1-66516-5, Mira Bks) Harlequin Bks.

— A Dream & Dreamless Sleep. 1996. mass mkt. 5.99 (*0-312-95775-0*) St Martin.

— I'll Love You Till I Die. 1995. mass mkt. 5.99 (*0-312-95586-3*, Pub. by Tor Bks) St Martin.

— The Keeper. LC 92-12247. 288p. 1992. 18.50 (*0-385-42482-5*) Doubleday.

***O'Brien, Meg.** Sacred Trust. 2000. per. 6.50 (*1-55166-586-7*, Mira Bks) Harlequin Bks.

O'Brien, Meg. Take My Breath Away. 1997. mass mkt. 5.99 (*0-312-96158-8*) St Martin.

O'Brien, Meip R., jt. auth. see Breene, Robert G., III.

O'Brien, Michael. Cat Monsters & Head Pots: The Archaeology of Missouri's Pemiscot Bayou. (Illus.). 448p. 1994. text 39.95 (*0-8262-0969-6*) U of Mo Pr.

— A Character of Hugh Legare. LC 85-3207. (Illus.). 371p. 1985. reprint ed. pap. 115.10 (*0-608-07991-X*, 206795600012) Bks Demand.

— Eclipse of the Sun. LC 97-76852. 600p. 1997. 24.95 (*0-89870-687-4*) Ignatius Pr.

— Father Elijah: An Apocalypse. LC 95-79950. 597p. 1996. 24.95 (*0-89870-580-0*) Ignatius Pr.

— Father Elijah: An Apocalypse. 1997. pap. text 14.95 (*0-89870-690-4*) Ignatius Pr.

— The Floor & the Breath. 72p. 1994. pap. 12.00 (*1-886044-03-1*) Cairn Editions.

— Hesburgh: A Biography. LC 98-17978. (Illus.). 346p. 1998. 34.95 (*0-8132-0921-8*) Cath U Pr.

Obrien, Michael. Landscape with Dragons: The Battle for Your Child's Mind. LC 97-76843. 1998. pap. 12.95 (*0-89870-678-5*) Ignatius Pr.

O'Brien, Michael. Mad Boy Chronicles. LC 97-124270. 154p. 1997. pap. text 11.95 (*0-88754-509-2*) Theatre Comm.

— The Mysteries of the Most Holy Rosary. (Illus.). 40p. 1994. spiral bd. 14.95 (*0-9696391-0-4*) Whi4te Horse.

— No Ordinary Joe: The Biography of Joe Paterno. LC 98-19014. 1998. 24.95 (*1-55853-668-X*) Rutledge Hill Pr.

— Phil Hart: The Conscience of the Senate. 250p. 1996. 29.95 (*0-87013-407-8*) Mich St U Pr.

— Plague Journal: A Novel. LC 96-75778. 1999. 19.95 (*0-89870-610-6*) Ignatius Pr.

— Rethinking the South: Essays in Intellectual History. LC 87-32482. 304p. 1988. text 46.00 (*0-8018-3617-4*) Johns Hopkins.

— Rethinking the South: Essays in Intellectual History. LC 92-21424. (Brown Thrasher Bks.). (Illus.). 288p. 1993. reprint ed. pap. 20.00 (*0-8203-1525-7*) U of Ga Pr.

— The Ruin. 32p. 1986. pap. 5.00 (*1-886044-02-3*) Cairn Editions.

***O'Brien, Michael.** Sills: Selected Poems of Michael O'Brien. 112p. 2000. pap. 13.00 (*1-58195-022-5*) Zoland Bks.

O'Brien, Michael. Strangers & Sojourners: A Novel. LC 96-75779. 573p. 1997. 24.95 (*0-89870-609-2*) Ignatius Pr.

— Veil, Hard Rain. 48p. 1986. pap. 5.00 (*1-886044-01-5*) Cairn Editions.

— Vince: A Personal Biography of Vince Lombardi. LC 87-12980. 352p. 1989. pap. 12.95 (*0-688-09204-7*, Quil) HarperTrade.

— We Shall Not Be Moved: The Sit-In at the Jackson Woolworth's. 1999. 26.00 (*0-9647124-5-8*) C River Pr.

O'Brien, Michael, ed. All Clever Men, Who Make Their Way: Critical Discourse in the Old South. LC 92-17539. (Brown Thrasher Bks.). 480p. 1992. reprint ed. pap. 19.95 (*0-8203-1490-0*) U of Ga Pr.

— An Evening When Alone: Four Journals of Single Women in the South, 1827-67. LC 92-39514. (Southern Texts Society Ser.). 512p. (C). 1993. text 45.00 (*0-8139-1440-X*) U Pr of Va.

— An Evening When Alone: Four Journals of Single Women in the South, 1827-67. (Southern Texts Society Ser.). (Illus.). 480p. 1997. reprint ed. pap. text 15.00 (*0-8139-1732-8*) U Pr of Va.

O'Brien, Michael & Moltke-Hansen, David, eds. Intellectual Life in Antebellum Charleston. LC 85-15022. (Illus.). 488p. 1986. text 49.00 (*0-87049-484-8*) U of Tenn Pr.

O'Brien, Michael, jt. auth. see Farber, Joan.

O'Brien, Michael F. & Sibley, Norman. The Photographic Eye: Learning to See with a Camera. rev. ed. LC 93-74644. (Illus.). 228p. (YA). (gr. 9-12). 1995. text 28.60 (*0-87192-283-5*) Davis Mass.

O'Brien, Michael J. Grassland, Forest & Historical Settlement: An Analysis of Dynamics in Northeast Missouri. LC 84-3660. (Studies in North American Archaeology). (Illus.). 367p. reprint ed. pap. 113.80 (*0-7837-6890-7*, 204672000003) Bks Demand.

— A Hidden Phase of American History: Ireland's Part in America's Struggle for Liberty. LC 76-165648. (Select Bibliographies Reprint Ser.). 1977. reprint ed. 42.95 (*0-8369-5957-4*) Ayer.

***O'Brien, Michael J.** A Hidden Phase of American History: Ireland's Part in America's Struggle for Liberty. (Illus.). 632p. 1999. reprint ed. pap. 42.50 (*0-7884-1095-4*, O063) Heritage Bk.

— In Old New York: The Irish Dead in Trinity & St. Paul's Churchyards. 262p. 1997. reprint ed. pap. 26.50 (*0-8063-4709-0*) Clearfield Co.

O'Brien, Michael J. Irish Settlers in America: A Consolidation of Articles from the Journal of the American Irish Historical Society, 2 vols. LC 78-78381. 1282p. 1993. reprint ed. 50.00 (*0-8063-0837-0*) Clearfield Co.

— Paradigms of the Past: The Story of Missouri Archaeology. LC 95-36754. (Illus.). 592p. (C). 1995. pap. text 29.95 (*0-8262-1019-8*) U of Mo Pr.

— Pioneer Irish in New England. 325p. 1998. reprint ed. pap. 27.50 (*0-8063-4790-2*, 9321) Clearfield Co.

— Pioneer Irish in New England. 325p. 1988. reprint ed. pap. 18.00 (*1-55613-106-2*) Heritage Bk.

O'Brien, Michael J., ed. Evolutionary Archaeology: Theory & Application. (Foundations of Archaeological Inquiry). (Illus.). 300p. (Orig.). (C). 1996. text 55.00 (*0-87480-502-3*); pap. text 25.00 (*0-87480-514-7*) U of Utah Pr.

O'Brien, Michael J. & Clarke, J. I. A Hidden Phase of American History. LC 76-165648. (Illus.). 533p. reprint ed. lib. bdg. 20.50 (*0-8290-0493-9*) Irvington.

O'Brien, Michael J. & Lewarch, Dennis E., eds. Plowzone Archeology: Contributions to Theory & Technique. (Vanderbilt University Publications in Anthropology: No. 27). 214p. 1981. pap. 12.15 (*0-935462-18-X*) VUPA.

***O'Brien, Michael J. & Lyman, R. Lee.** Applying Evolutionary Archaeology - A Systematic Approach. LC 99-89696. 470p. 2000. pap. 49.50 (*0-306-46254-0*, Kluwer Plenum) Kluwer Academic.

O'Brien, Michael J. & Lyman, R. Lee. James A. Ford & the Growth of Americanist Archaeology. LC 98-29781. (Illus.). 400p. 1998. 42.50 (*0-8262-1184-4*) U of Mo Pr.

— Measuring the Flow of Time: The Works of James A. Ford, 1935-1941. LC 99-6142. (Classics in Southeastern Archaeology Ser.). (Illus.). 600p. 1999. 39.95 (*0-8173-0991-8*) U of Ala Pr.

***O'Brien, Michael J. & Lyman, R. Lee.** Seriation, Stratigraphy & Index Fossils: The Backbone of Archaeological Dating LC 99-37712. 1999. pap. write for info. (*0-306-46153-6*, Kluwer Plenum) Kluwer Academic.

O'Brien, Michael J. & Shook, Larry. Profit from Experience. 192p. 1998. pap. 10.00 (*0-425-16219-2*) Berkley Pub.

O'Brien, Michael J. & Wood, W. Raymond. The Prehistory of Missouri. LC 97-20654. (Illus.). 488p. 1998. pap. 39.95 (*0-8262-1131-3*) U of Mo Pr.

O

O'Brien, Michael J., et al. Changing Perspectives on the Archaeology of the Central Mississippi River Valley. LC 97-35595. 456p. 1998. pap. text 29.95 (*0-8173-0909-8*) U of Ala Pr.

— A Late Formative Irrigation Settlement below Monte Alban: Survey & Excavation on the Xoxocotlan Piedmont, Oaxaca, Mexico. (Institute of Latin American Studies Special Publication). (Illus.). 254p. 1982. text 27.50 (*0-292-74628-8*) U of Tex Pr.

— Middle & Late Woodland Subsistence & Ceramic Technology in the Central Mississippi River Valley: Selected Studies from the Burkemper Site, Lincoln County, Missouri. (Illinois State Museum Reports of Investigations: Vol. 52). (Orig.). 1996. pap. write for info. (*0-89792-151-8*) Ill St Museum.

O'Brien, Miep R. The Compleat Cricket. (ATS Educational Series Manuals). (Illus.). 15p. 1997. 6.00 (*1-929427-03-4*) American Tarantula.

— Ship It! (ATS Educational Series Manuals). 16p. 1998. 6.00 (*1-929427-02-6*) American Tarantula.

O'Brien, Mike, jt. auth. see Noble, Dennis L.

O'Brien, Mollie M. A Pilgrim Wind. LC 85-60237. 64p. (Orig.). 1985. pap. 5.95 (*0-89390-062-1*) Resource Pubns.

O'Brien, N. R. & Slatt, R. M. Argillaceous Rock Atlas. (Illus.). xv, 141p. 1990. 116.00 (*0-387-97306-0*) Spr-Verlag.

O'Brien-Nabors, Lyn & Gelardi, Robert C., eds. Alternative Sweetners. 2nd ed. (Food Science & Technology Ser.: Vol. 48). (Illus.). 480p. 1991. text 195.00 (*0-8247-8475-8*) Dekker.

O'Brien, Nancy P. Education: A Guide to Reference & Information Sources. 2nd ed. LC 99-44764. (Reference Sources in Social Sciences Ser.). 189p. 2000. 40.00 (*1-56308-626-3*) Libs Unl.

— Test Construction: A Bibliography of Selected Resources. LC 87-25119. 315p. 1988. lib. bdg. 65.00 (*0-313-23435-3*, CTC/, Greenwood Pr) Greenwood.

O'Brien, Niall. Revolution from the Heart. LC DS0686.5.O26. 320p. reprint ed. pap. 99.20 (*0-608-20274-6*, 207153300012) Bks Demand.

O'Brien, Niall, jt. auth. see Gill, Denis.

O'Brien, P. & Jones, A. C. CVD of Compound Semiconductors: Precursor Synthesis, Development & Applications. LC 97-173354. 360p. 1997. 235.00 (*3-527-29294-2*, Wiley-VCH) Wiley.

O'Brien, P., jt. ed. see Treloar, P.

O'Brien, P. J. Will Rogers: Ambassador of Good Will. 1976. 23.95 (*0-8488-1114-3*) Amereon Ltd.

O'Brien, P. K., intro. The Industrial Revolution in Europe, Vol. 1. LC 93-40550. (Industrial Revolutions Ser.: Vols. 4-5). 1994. 124.95 (*0-631-18073-7*) Blackwell Pubs.

— The Industrial Revolution in Europe, Vol. 2. LC 93-40550. (Industrial Revolutions Ser.: Vols. 4-5). 1994. 124.95 (*0-631-18145-8*) Blackwell Pubs.

O'Brien, P. M. The Promoter: His Life & Times. (Illus.). 118p. (YA). (gr. 10-12). 1988. pap. 5.65 (*0-9620540-0-3*) P M OBrien.

O'Brien, P. N., ed. see Jenyon, Malcolm K. & Fitch, Albert A.

O'Brien, P. T. Gospel & Mission in the Writings of Paul: An Exegetical & Theological Analysis. LC 95-16690. 162p. 1995. reprint ed. pap. 9.99 (*0-8010-2052-2*) Baker Bks.

O'Brien, Paddy. Positive Management: Assertiveness for Managers. (People Skills for Professionals Ser.). (Illus.). 170p. 1995. reprint ed. pap. 17.95 (*1-85788-008-0*) Nicholas Brealey.

Obrien, Paddy. Your Life after Birth. 1989. 7.95 (*0-86358-266-4*, Pub. by Pandora) Harper SF.

O'Brien-Palmer, Michelle. Beyond Book Reports. 160p. 1997. pap. text 16.95 (*0-590-76991-X*) Scholastic Inc.

— Book-Write: A Creative Bookmaking Guide for Young Authors. LC 91-68412. (Illus.). 128p. (J). (gr. k-6). 1992. pap. 16.95 (*1-879235-01-3*) MicNik Pubns.

— Great Graphic Organizers for Literature. 160p. 1997. pap. text 16.95 (*0-590-76990-1*) Scholastic Inc.

— Healthy Me: Fun Ways to Develop Good Health & Safety Habits. LC 99-20860. (Illus.). 160p. (J). (gr. k-3). 1999. pap. 12.95 (*1-55652-359-9*) Chicago Review.

— Let's Learn about Story Elements: Character. 64p. 1998. pap. 9.95 (*0-590-10717-8*) Scholastic Inc.

— Let's Learn about Story Elements: Plot. 64p. 1998. pap. 9.95 (*0-590-10716-X*) Scholastic Inc.

— Let's Learn about Story Elements: Setting. 64p. 1998. pap. 9.95 (*0-590-10715-1*) Scholastic Inc.

— Sense-Abilities: Fun Ways to Explore the Senses. LC 98-22983. (Illus.). 128p. (J). (ps-1). 1998. pap. 12.95 (*1-55652-327-0*) Chicago Review.

— Watch Me Grow: Fun Ways to Learn About Cells, Bones, Muscles, Joints. LC 99-20864. (Illus.). 144p. (J). (gr. k-3). 1999. pap. 12.95 (*1-55652-367-X*) Chicago Review.

O'Brien, Pat. The Houseshare. (Black Lace Ser.). 320p. 1996. mass mkt. 5.95 (*0-352-33094-5*, Pub. by Virgin Bks) London Brdge.

O'Brien, Pat A. Outwitting the Hun: My Escape from a German Prison Camp. (American Biography Ser.). 283p. 1991. reprint ed. lib. bdg. 69.00 (*0-7812-8301-9*) Rprt Serv.

O'Brien, Patricia. Colors: Cross-Curriculum Units for Theme Teaching. Mitchell, Judy, ed. (Illus.). 112p. (Orig.). (J). (gr. k-3). 1997. pap., teacher ed. 10.95 (*1-57310-074-9*) Teachng & Lrning Co.

— Good Intentions. 352p. 1998. mass mkt. 5.99 (*1-57566-311-2*) Kensgtn Pub Corp.

— Good Intentions. LC 97-13179. 1997. 22.50 (*0-684-81355-6*) S&S Trade.

— Good Intentions: A Novel. large type ed. LC 98-38048. 357 p. 1998. 25.95 (*1-57490-163-X*, Beeler LP Bks) T T Beeler.

— The Grenfell Obsession: An Anthology. 176p. 1992. 14.35 (*1-895387-08-6*) Creative Bk Pub.

— Ladies Lunch. 1994. 22.00 (*0-671-78906-6*) S&S Trade.

— Ladies Lunch. 1996. mass mkt. 5.99 (*0-312-95789-0*, Pub. by Tor Bks) St Martin.

*__O'Brien, Patricia.__ Making it in the Free World: Women in Transition from Prison. LC 00-36566. (C). 2001. pap. text 18.95 (*0-7914-4862-2*) State U NY Pr.

— Making it in the Free World: Women in Transition from Prison. LC 00-36566. (C). 2001. text 57.50 (*0-7914-4861-4*) State U NY Pr.

O'Brien, Patricia. Seasons: Cross-Curriculum Units for Theme Teaching. Mitchell, Judy, ed. (Illus.). 112p. (Orig.). (J). (gr. k-3). 1997. pap., teacher ed. 10.95 (*1-57310-075-7*) Teachng & Lrning Co.

— Senses: Cross-Curriculum Units for Theme Teaching. Mitchell, Judy, ed. (Illus.). 112p. (Orig.). (J). (gr. k-3). 1997. pap., teacher ed. 10.95 (*1-57310-076-5*) Teachng & Lrning Co.

— The Woman Alone. LC 72-94650. 288p. 1974. write for info. (*0-8129-0344-7*, Times Bks) Crown Pub Group.

*__O'Brien, Patricia & Goodman, Ellen.__ I Know Just What You Mean: The Power of Friendship in Women's Lives. LC 00-24859. (Illus.). 288p. 2000. 25.00 (*0-684-84287-4*) Simon & Schuster.

O'Brien, Patricia, jt. auth. see Goodman, Ellen.

O'Brien, Patricia H., jt. auth. see Bart, Pauline B.

O'Brien, Patricia J. Archeology in Kansas. (Public Education Ser.: No. 9). (Illus.). vii, 144p. (Orig.). 1984. pap. 12.95 (*0-89338-020-2*) U KS Nat Hist Mus.

O'Brien, Patricia J., jt. ed. see Brown, James A.

*__O'Brien, Patrick.__ Encyclopedia of World History. (Illus.). 528p. 2000. 85.00 (*0-8160-4249-7*) Facts on File.

— Extreme Dinosaurs. 2000. pap. text 15.95 (*0-8050-6216-5*) St Martin.

O'Brien, Patrick. Gigantic! LC 98-26038. (Illus.). (J). (gr. k-3). 1999. 15.95 (*0-8050-5738-2*) H Holt & Co.

*__O'Brien, Patrick.__ Hindenberg. LC 99-46687. (Illus.). 40p. (gr. k-3). 2000. text 16.95 (*0-8050-6415-X*) St Martin.

O'Brien, Patrick. The Making of a Knight: How Sir James Earned His Armor. LC 97-36867. (Illus.). 32p. (J). (gr. 1-4). 1998. 15.95 (*0-88106-354-1*) Charlesbridge Pub.

— The Making of a Knight: How Sir James Earned His Armor. LC 97-36867. (Illus.). (J). (ps-3). 1998. pap. 6.95 (*0-88106-355-X*) Charlesbridge Pub.

*__O'Brien, Patrick.__ Megatooth. 2000. pap. text 15.95 (*0-8050-6214-9*) St Martin.

O'Brien, Patrick. Steam, Smoke & Steel: Back in Time with Trains. (Illus.). 32p. (J). (ps-4). 2000. 16.95 (*0-88106-969-8*) Charlesbridge Pub.

O'Brien, Patrick, jt. auth. see Bandon, Alexandra.

O'Brien, Patrick G., compiled by. Herbert Hoover: A Bibliography, 30. LC 92-29467. (Bibliographies of the Presidents of the United States Ser.: No. 30). 416p. 1992. lib. bdg. 75.00 (*0-313-28188-2*, AP30, Greenwood Pr) Greenwood.

O'Brien, Patrick G. & Peak, Kenneth J. Kansas Bootleggers. (Illus.). 135p. (Orig.). 1991. pap. 14.95 (*0-89745-139-2*) Sunflower U Pr.

O'Brien, Patrick K., et al, eds. Atlas of World History: From the Origins of Humanity to the Year 2000. (Illus.). 352p. 1999. 85.00 (*0-19-521567-2*) OUP.

O'Brien, Patrick K. & Quinault, Roland E., eds. The Industrial Revolution & British Society. LC 92-9649. 307p. (C). 1993. pap. text 19.95 (*0-521-43744-X*) Cambridge U Pr.

O'Brien, Paul, jt. auth. see Collard, Clyde.

O'Brien, Paul, jt. ed. see Long, Robert L.

O'Brien, Peggy, ed. Shakespeare Set Free: Teaching Romeo & Juliet, Macbeth, & A Midsummer Night's Dream. 288p. (Orig.). 1993. per. 18.00 (*0-671-76046-7*, WSP) PB.

O'Brien, Peggy & Rosenman, Jane, eds. Teaching Hamlet & Henry IV, Vol. 2, Pt. 1. (Shakespeare Set Free Ser.). 240p. (Orig.). 1994. per. 18.00 (*0-671-76048-3*, WSP) PB.

O'Brien, Peggy, ed. see Boland, Eavan, et al.

O'Brien, Peggy, ed. see Folger Shakespeare Library Staff.

O'Brien, Penny. How to Select the Best Child-Care Option for Your Employees. LC 86-22178. 101p. (Orig.). (C). 1987. pap. 11.95 (*0-930256-15-8*, Vestal Pr) Madison Bks UPA.

O'Brien, Peter. Beyond the Swastika: Liberalism & Nationalism in Post War Germany. 160p. (C). 1996. 75.00 (*0-415-13851-5*); pap. 24.99 (*0-415-13852-3*) Routledge.

O'Brien, Peter & Karmokolias, Yannis. Radical Reform in the Automotive Industry: Policies in Emerging Markets. LC 94-8112. (IFC Discussion Papers: No. 21). 58p. 1994. pap. 22.00 (*0-8213-2806-9*, 12806) World Bank.

O'Brien, Peter T. Colossians, Philemon. (Biblical Commentary Ser.: Vol. 44). 1982. 29.99 (*0-8499-0243-6*) Word Pub.

— The Epistle to the Philippians: A Commentary on the Greek Text. Gasque, W. Ward & Marshall, I. Howard, eds. (New International Greek Testament Commentary Ser.). xl, 560p. 1991. 42.00 (*0-8028-2392-0*) Eerdmans.

*__O'Brien, Peter T.__ Letter to the Ephesians. (Pillar New Testament Commentary Ser.). 608p. 1999. 40.00 (*0-8028-3736-0*) Eerdmans.

O'Brien, Philip. T. E. Lawrence: A Bibliography. (G. K. Hall Reference Ser.). 416p. 1988. lib. bdg. 60.00 (*0-318-32523-3*, Hall Reference) Macmillan.

O'Brien, Phillips P. British & American Naval Power: Politics & Policy, 1900-1936. LC 97-7180. (Praeger Studies in Diplomacy & Strategic Thought). 288p. 1998. 59.95 (*0-275-95898-1*, Praeger Pubs) Greenwood.

O'Brien, Pollyann. Word Families. (Basic Skills Ser.). (Illus.). 32p. (J). (gr. 1). 1997. pap. text 4.95 (*0-88724-405-X*, CD-2105) Carson-Dellos.

O'Brien, R. M. Industrial Behavior Modification. (C). 1982. 70.95 (*0-205-14428-4*, H4428) Allyn.

O'Brien, Rae A., jt. auth. see Rowan, Richard L.

O'Brien, Randall. I Feel Better All over Than I Do Anywhere Else... And Other Stories to Tickle Your Soul. 2nd ed. LC 99-14800. 1999. pap. 10.00 (*1-57312-271-8*) Smyth & Helwys.

O'Brien, Raymond C. & Flannery, Michael T. Long-Term Care: Federal, State & Private Options for the Future. LC 97-1573. 290p. (C). 1997. pap. 24.95 (*0-7890-0261-2*) Haworth Pr.

— Long-Term Care: Federal, State & Private Options for the Future. LC 97-1573. 290p. (C). 1997. 49.95 (*0-7890-0173-X*) Haworth Pr.

O'Brien, Raymond C., jt. auth. see Wadlington, Walter.

O'Brien, Richard. Collecting American-Made Toy Soliders: Identification & Value Guide. 3rd ed. LC 97-170405. (Illus.). 720p. 1996. pap. 32.95 (*0-89689-118-6*, Bks Amrcana) Krause Pubns.

— Collecting Foreign-Made Toy Soldiers: Identification & Value Guide. LC 97-205173. (Illus.). 496p. 1997. pap. 32.95 (*0-89689-122-4*, FMTS) Krause Pubns.

— Global Financial Integration: The End of Geography. 128p. 1992. pap. 14.95 (*0-87609-123-0*) Coun Foreign.

— The Life of Charles Stewart Parnell, 1846-1891, 2 Vols, Set. LC 68-25256. (English Biography Ser.: No. 31). 1969. reprint ed. lib. bdg. 150.00 (*0-8383-0167-3*) M S G Haskell Hse.

— Rocky Horror Picture Show. (Illus.). 72p. 1991. pap. 19.95 (*0-7119-2764-2*, AM86101) Music Sales.

O'Brien, Richard, ed. Finance & the International Economy No. 5: The AMEX Bank Review Prize Essays, 1991. (Illus.). 176p. 1992. pap. 21.00 (*0-19-828766-6*) OUP.

— Finance & the International Economy Vol. 8: The AMEX Bank Review Prize Essays. (Illus.). 168p. 1995. pap. text 19.95 (*0-19-828962-6*) OUP.

O'Brien, Richard, ed. Finance & the International Economy 7: The AMEX Bank Review Prize Essays 1993. (Illus.). 176p. 1994. pap. 18.95 (*0-19-828879-4*) OUP.

O'Brien, Richard & Hewin, Sarah, eds. Finance & the International Economy: The AMEX Bank Review Prize Essays, 1990. (Illus.). 240p. 1991. pap. 21.00 (*0-19-828740-2*) OUP.

O'Brien, Richard & Iverson, Ingrid, eds. Finance & the International Economy 3: The AMEX Bank Review Prize Essays. (Illus.). 208p. 1990. 45.00 (*0-19-829008-X*) OUP.

O'Brien, Richard, jt. ed. see Calverley, John.

O'Brien, Richard C. Dental Radiography: An Introduction for Dental Hygienists & Assistants. 4th ed. (Illus.). 296p. 1982. text 52.00 (*0-7216-6887-9*, W B Saunders Co) Harcrt Hlth Sci Grp.

O'Brien, Richard D. Fats & Oils: Formulating & Processing for Applications. LC 97-61637. 680p. 1997. text 104.95 (*1-56676-363-0*) Technomic.

O'Brien, Richard J. A Descriptive Grammar of Ecclesiastical Latin Based on Modern Structural Analysis. LC 65-25149. (Georgetown University Latin Ser.). 283p. reprint ed. pap. 87.80 (*0-8357-8566-1*, 203493200091) Bks Demand.

— Georgetown University Round Table: Selected Papers on Linguistics, 1961-1965. LC 68-57729. 507p. reprint ed. pap. 157.20 (*0-7837-6348-4*, 204606000010) Bks Demand.

O'Brien, Richard J., ed. see Georgetown University Round Table on Languages & L.

O'Brien, Richard L., ed. see International Leucocyte Culture Conference, 15th:.

O'Brien Riley, Miles. Promises to Keep: People, Places & Parables in Communications from Around the World. (Orig.). 1991. write for info. (*0-9620554-1-7*) Perfect Page Pub.

O'Brien, Rita C., ed. The Political Economy of Underdevelopment: Dependence in Senegal. LC 78-27183. (Sage Series on African Modernization & Development: No. 3). 277p. reprint ed. pap. 85.90 (*0-8357-8502-5*, 203477900091) Bks Demand.

O'Brien, R.L., jt. auth. see Connor, Leonard P.

O'Brien, Robert. This Is San Francisco: A Classic Portrait of the City. LC 94-4578. (Illus.). 372p. 1994. pap. 12.95 (*0-8118-0578-6*) Chronicle Bks.

O'Brien, Robert & Brown, Richard D., eds. The Encyclopedia of New England. LC 82-12097. 623p. 1985. reprint ed. pap. 193.20 (*0-608-02852-5*, 206391600007) Bks Demand.

O'Brien, Robert & Chafetz, Morris. Encyclopedia of Understanding Alcohol & Other Drugs, 2 Vols. (Illus.). 896p. 1998. 195.00 (*0-8160-3970-4*) Facts on File.

O'Brien, Robert & Chafetz, Morris E., eds. The Encyclopedia of Alcoholism. LC HV5017.E5. 398p. 1982. reprint ed. pap. 123.40 (*0-7837-9268-9*, 206000400004) Bks Demand.

*__O'Brien, Robert & Martin, Harold, eds.__ The Encyclopedia of the South (to 1984) (Illus.). 568p. 2000. reprint ed. text 30.00 (*0-7881-6918-1*) DIANE Pub.

O'Brien, Robert & Martin, Harold H., eds. The Encyclopedia of the South. LC 82-12098. (Illus.). 591p. 1985. reprint ed. pap. 183.30 (*0-8357-4237-7*, 203702400007) Bks Demand.

*__O'Brien, Robert, et al.__ Contesting Global Governance: Multilateral Economic Institutions & Global Social Movements. (Cambridge Studies in International Relations Ser.: No. 71). (Illus.). 280p. 2000. 54.95 (*0-521-77315-6*); pap. 19.95 (*0-521-77440-3*) Cambridge U Pr.

O'Brien, Robert, et al. The Encyclopedia of Understanding Alcohol & Other Drugs. LC 98-22491. 1998. write for info. (*0-8160-3971-2*) Facts on File.

O'Brien, Robert C. Mrs. Frisby & the Rats of NIMH. (Rats of NIMH Ser.). (J). (gr. 4-7). 1999. pap. 2.99 (*0-689-82966-3*) Aladdin.

— Mrs. Frisby & the Rats of NIMH. LC 74-134818. (Rats of NIMH Ser.). (Illus.). 240p. (J). (gr. 4-7). 1971. 17.00 (*0-689-20651-8*) Atheneum Yung Read.

*__O'Brien, Robert C.__ Mrs. Frisby & the Rats of NIMH. (Rats of NIMH Ser.). (YA). 1999. 11.95 (*1-56137-532-2*) Novel Units.

— Mrs. Frisby & the Rats of NIMH. (Rats of NIMH Ser.). (J). (gr. 4-7). 1999. 9.95 (*1-56137-273-0*) Novel Units.

O'Brien, Robert C. Mrs. Frisby & the Rats of NIMH. (Rats of NIMH Ser.). (J). (gr. 4-7). 1998. per. 2.65 (*0-689-82171-9*) S&S Childrens.

— Mrs. Frisby & the Rats of NIMH. large type ed. (Rats of NIMH Ser.). (Illus.). (J). (gr. 4-7). 1993. 64.50 (*0-614-09848-3*, L-34129-00) Am Printing Hse.

— Mrs. Frisby & the Rats of NIMH. large type ed. (Rats of NIMH Ser.). (Illus.). (J). (gr. 4-7). 1995. 61.50 (*0-614-09602-2*, L-34828-00) Am Printing Hse.

*__O'Brien, Robert C.__ Mrs. Frisby & the Rats of NIMH. large type ed. (Rats of NIMH Ser.). (Illus.). 300p. (J). (gr. 4-7). 2000. lib. bdg. 29.95 (*1-58118-056-X*, 23470) LRS.

O'Brien, Robert C. Mrs. Frisby & the Rats of NIMH. (Rats of NIMH Ser.). 248p. (J). (gr. 4-7). 1986. reprint ed. mass mkt. 4.50 (*0-689-71068-2*) Aladdin.

O'Brien, Robert C. Mrs. Frisby & the Rats of NIMH. 2nd ed. (Rats of NIMH Ser.). (J). (gr. 4-7). 1986. 9.60 (*0-606-04055-2*, Pub. by Turtleback) Demco.

O'Brien, Robert C. The Secret of NIMH. (Rats of NIMH Ser.). 256p. (J). (gr. 4-7). 1988. pap. 3.99 (*0-590-41708-8*) Scholastic Inc.

— The Secret of NIMH. (Rats of NIMH Ser.). (J). (gr. 4-7). 1971. 9.60 (*0-606-02727-0*, Pub. by Turtleback) Demco.

— Senora Frisby y las Ratas de NIMH. 8th ed. (Rats of NIMH Ser.).Tr. of Mrs. Frisby & the Rats of NIMH. (SPA.). (J). (gr. 4-7). 1985. 11.60 (*0-606-05405-7*, Pub. by Turtleback) Demco.

O'Brien, Robert C. Z for Zachariah. LC 86-23228. (J). 1987. 9.60 (*0-606-03512-5*, Pub. by Turtleback) Demco.

O'Brien, Robert C. Z for Zachariah. LC 86-23228. 256p. (YA). (gr. 7 up). 1987. reprint ed. mass mkt. 4.50 (*0-02-044650-0*) Macmillan.

O'Brien, Robert F. School Songs of America's Colleges & Universities: A Directory. LC 91-11337. 208p. 1991. lib. bdg. 49.95 (*0-313-27890-3*, OSS/, Greenwood Pr) Greenwood.

O'Brien, Robert J., jt. ed. see Dunnette, David A.

O'Brien, Robert M. Crime & Victimization Data. LC 84-29835. (Law & Criminal Justice Ser.: No. 4). 127p. reprint ed. pap. 39.40 (*0-7837-4579-6*, 204410800003) Bks Demand.

O'Brien, Robert W. The Brown Thrush. 1977. text 12.95 (*0-8369-9247-4*, 9101) Ayer.

O'Brien, Robert W. & Daniels, Roger. The College Nisei. LC 78-54829. (Asian Experience in North America Ser.). (Illus.). 1979. reprint ed. lib. bdg. 15.95 (*0-405-11286-6*) Ayer.

O'Brien, Ron. Ron O'Brien's Diving for Gold. LC 91-28668. (Illus.). 200p. 1992. pap. 19.95 (*0-88011-448-7*, POBR0448) Human Kinetics.

O'Brien, Rory, jt. auth. see Theodoulou, Stella Z.

O'Brien, Rory, jt. ed. see Cahn, Matthew A.

*__O'Brien, Rosemary, ed.__ Gertrude Bell: The Arabian Diaries, 1913-1914. (Illus.). 224p. 2000. 29.95 (*0-8156-0672-9*) Syracuse U Pr.

O'Brien, Rourke M. & Thomas, John B. The Quick & Easy Guide to Driveway Detailing. LC 89-85081. (Practice Ring Ser.). (Illus.). 80p. (Orig.). 1993. pap. 9.95 (*0-929758-05-6*) Beeman Jorgensen.

O'Brien, Ruth. Workers' Paradox: The Republican Origins of New Deal Labor Policy, 1886-1935. LC 97-48986. 336p. (C). 1998. pap. 17.95 (*0-8078-4737-2*); lib. bdg. 39.95 (*0-8078-2430-5*) U of NC Pr.

O'Brien, S. A Teacher's Guide to African Narratives. LC 98-9592. 122p. 1998. pap. 21.00 (*0-325-00039-5*) Heinemann.

O'Brien, S. & Cockcroft, James, eds. Political Leaders. (Illus.). 112-128p. (gr. 5). 1996. 139.65 (*0-7910-3528-X*) Chelsea Hse.

O'Brien, Sandy. Thorvo. LC 97-91078. (J). 1998. pap. 8.95 (*0-533-12558-8*) Vantage.

O'Brien, Sarah, ed. see O'Brien, Jim.

O'Brien, Sarah H., ed. see O'Brien, Jim.

*__O'Brien, Seamus.__ Famine & Community in Mullingar Poor Law Union, 1845-1849: Mud Huts & Fat Bullocks. LC 99-29357. (Maynooth Studies in Local History). 64p. 1999. pap. 10.95 (*0-7165-2678-6*, Pub. by Irish Acad Pr) Intl Spec Bk.

*__O'Brien, Sean.__ Best Easy Day Hikes: San Diego. (Illus.). 96p. 1999. pap. 6.95 (*1-56044-864-4*) Falcon Pub Inc.

O'Brien, Sean. The Deregulated Muse: Essays on Contemporary British & Irish Poetry. LC 96-143945. 288p. 1998. 55.00 (*1-85224-281-7*, Pub. by Bloodaxe Bks); pap. 24.95 (*1-85224-282-5*, Pub. by Bloodaxe Bks) Dufour.

— The Frighteners. LC 88-70226. 64p. (Orig.). 1987. pap. 12.95 (*1-85224-013-X*, Pub. by Bloodaxe Bks) Dufour.

— Ghost Train. 62p. (C). 1995. pap. 11.95 (*0-19-283231-X*) OUP.

— The Indoor Park. 64p. 1983. pap. 12.95 (*0-906427-49-5*, Pub. by Bloodaxe Bks) Dufour.

— San Diego Coast. (Twelve Short Hikes Ser.: No. 15). (Illus.). 32p. (Orig.). 1997. pap. 4.95 (*1-57540-080-4*) Falcon Pub Inc.

— San Diego Mountains. (Twelve Short Hikes Ser.: No. 16). (Illus.). 32p. (Orig.). 1997. pap. 4.95 (*1-57540-081-2*) Falcon Pub Inc.

O'Brien, Sean, ed. The Fire Box: Poetry in Britian & Ireland after 1945. 300p. 1998. 27.50 (*0-330-37255-6*, Pub. by Pan); pap. 19.95 (*0-330-36918-0*, Pub. by Pan) Trans-Atl Phila.

O

An Asterisk (*) at the beginning of an entry indicates that the title is appearing for the first time.

O'Brien, Sean Michael. Mountain Partisans: Guerrilla Warfare in the Southern Appalachians, 1861-1865. LC 98-56073. 264p. 1999. 35.00 (0-275-96430-2, C6430, Praeger Pubs) Greenwood.

O'Brien, Seumas. Duty & Other Irish Comedies. LC 77-89724. (One-Act Plays in Reprint Ser.). 1977. reprint ed. 20.00 (0-8486-2029-1) Roth Pub Inc.

O'Brien, Sharon. American Indian Tribal Governments. LC 89-4791. (Illus.). 368p. 1993. pap. 19.95 (0-8061-2564-0) U of Okla Pr.

Obrien, Sharon. Willa Cather: The Emerging Voice. LC 97-172199. (Illus.). 528p. 1996. pap. text 17.95 (0-674-95322-3) HUP.

O'Brien, Sharon, ed. New Essays on Cather's "My Antonia" LC 97-39168. (American Novel Ser.). 144p. (C). 1999. 49.95 (0-521-45275-9); pap. text 14.95 (0-521-45905-2) Cambridge U Pr.

— Write Now: American Literature in the 1980s & 1990s. 296p. 1996. pap. 10.00 (0-8223-6437-9) Duke.

O'Brien, Sharon, ed. see Cather, Willa.

O'Brien, Sharon, ed. & intro. see Cather, Willa.

O'Brien, Shirley. Child Abuse & Neglect: Everyone's Problem. Martin, Lucy P., ed. LC 84-20351. 32p. 1984. 7.50 (0-87173-106-1) ACEI.

— Child Pornography. 208p. 1992. per. 24.95 (0-8403-7845-9) Kendall-Hunt.

O'Brien, Sidney D., jt. auth. see Vaughn, Thad A.

O'Brien, Sinead, jt. auth. see Allan, David G.

O'Brien, Stephen. Genetic Maps. 5th ed. (Illus.). 1156p. 1990. 150.00 (0-87969-338-X) Cold Spring Harbor.

— Using Quickbooks & Quickbooks Pro 6.0. LC 98-84560. 604p. 1998. 29.99 (0-7897-1660-7) Que.

O'Brien, Stephen, ed. Genetic Maps Bk. I: Viruses. (Illus.). 181p. 1990. pap. 17.50 (0-87969-342-8) Cold Spring Harbor.

— Genetic Maps Bk. II: Bacteria, Protozoa & Algae. (Illus.). 134p. 1990. pap. 17.50 (0-87969-343-6) Cold Spring Harbor.

— Genetic Maps Bk. III: Lower Eukaryotes. (Illus.). 201p. 1990. pap. 20.00 (0-87969-344-4) Cold Spring Harbor.

— Genetic Maps Bk. IV: Nonhuman Vertebrates. (Illus.). 175p. 1990. pap. 20.00 (0-87969-345-2) Cold Spring Harbor.

— Genetic Maps Bk. V: Human Maps. (Illus.). 257p. 1990. pap. 20.00 (0-87969-346-0) Cold Spring Harbor.

— Genetic Maps Bk. VI: Plants. (Illus.). 147p. 1990. pap. 20.00 (0-87969-347-9) Cold Spring Harbor.

***O'Brien, Stephen J.** Quickbook 99 Quick Reference, . 192p. 1999. 9.99 (0-7897-2029-9) Que.

— Quicken 2000. (Complete Idiot's Guides (Computers) Ser.). 1999. pap. 16.99 (0-7897-2218-6) Que.

O'Brien, Stephen J. Using Quicken Deluxe 99. LC 98-85289. (Using... Ser.). 1998. pap. 29.99 (0-7897-1723-9) Que.

O'Brien, Stephen J., ed. Genetic Maps: Locus Maps of Complex Genomes, 6 vols., Bk. 1: Viruses. 6th ed. (Illus.). 205p. (C). 1993. pap. text 17.50 (0-87969-415-7) Cold Spring Harbor.

— Genetic Maps: Locus Maps of Complex Genomes, 6 vols., Bk. 2: Bacteria, Algae, & Protozoa. 6th ed. (Illus.). 181p. (C). 1993. pap. text 17.50 (0-87969-416-5) Cold Spring Harbor.

— Genetic Maps: Locus Maps of Complex Genomes, 6 vols., Bk. 3: Lower Eukaryotes. 6th ed. (Illus.). 318p. (C). 1993. pap. text 20.00 (0-87969-417-3) Cold Spring Harbor.

— Genetic Maps: Locus Maps of Complex Genomes, 6 vols., Bk. 4: Nonhuman Vertebrates. 6th ed. (Illus.). 342p. (C). 1993. pap. text 20.00 (0-87969-418-1) Cold Spring Harbor.

— Genetic Maps: Locus Maps of Complex Genomes, 6 vols., Bk. 5: The Human Maps. 6th ed. (Illus.). 310p. (C). 1993. pap. text 20.00 (0-87969-419-X) Cold Spring Harbor.

— Genetic Maps: Locus Maps of Complex Genomes, 6 vols., Bk. 6: Plants. 6th ed. (Illus.). 261p. (C). 1993. pap. text 20.00 (0-87969-420-3) Cold Spring Harbor.

— Genetic Maps: Locus Maps of Complex Genomes, 6 vols., Set. 6th ed. (Illus.). 1620p. (C). 1993. text 120.00 (0-87969-414-9) Cold Spring Harbor.

O'Brien, Stephen K. & Nameroff, Steven. Turbo Pascal 7: The Complete Reference. 864p. 1992. pap. 34.95 (0-07-881793-5) Osborne-McGraw.

O'Brien, Steve. Alexander Hamilton. (World Leaders Past & Present Ser.). (Illus.). 120p. (YA). (gr. 5 up). 1989. lib. bdg. 19.95 (1-55546-810-1) Chelsea Hse.

O'Brien, Steven. Pancho Villa: Mexican Revolutionary. LC 93-37890. (Hispanics of Achievement Ser.). (Illus.). 120p. (YA). (gr. 5 up). 1994. lib. bdg. 19.95 (0-7910-1257-3) Chelsea Hse.

O'Brien, Steven, et al, eds. American Political Leaders: From Colonial Times to the Present. LC 91-30755. 473p. 1991. lib. bdg. 65.00 (0-87436-570-8) ABC-CLIO.

O'Brien, Steven, et al. Antonio Lopez de Santa Anna: Mexican General & Politician. (Hispanics of Achievement Ser.). (Illus.). 120p. (YA). (gr. 5 up). 1993. lib. bdg. 19.95 (0-7910-1245-X) Chelsea Hse.

***O'Brien-Strain, Margaret & Macurdy, Thomas E.** Increasing the Minimum Wage: California's Winners & Losers. LC 00-29347. 2000. write for info. (1-58213-050-7) Pub Policy Inst.

O'Brien-Strain, Margaret, jt. auth. see MaCurdy, Thomas E.

O'Brien, Sue M., compiled by. The Register of Americans of Prominent Descent, Vol. I. LC 81-69243. 545p. 1982. 35.00 (0-686-36318-3) Morten Pub.

O'Brien, Susan K. Complete North Shore Family Guidebook. 1993. pap. 9.95 (0-930100-53-0) H Holt & Co.

O'Brien, Suzanne, tr. see Yoshiaki, Yoshimi.

O'Brien, T., jt. auth. see Dyall-Smith, Delwyn.

O'Brien, T. Kevin, ed. Long-Term Behavior of Composites - STP 813. LC 82-73765. 300p. 1983. 42.00 (0-8031-0252-6, STP813) ASTM.

O'Brien, Terence. The Moonlight War. large type ed. (Non-Fiction Ser.). 1990. 11.50 (0-7089-2176-0) Ulverscroft.

— Out of the Blue: A Pilot with the Chindits. large type ed. (Non-Fiction Ser.). 480p. 1985. 11.50 (0-7089-1392-X) Ulverscroft.

O'Brien, Terence P. The Prehistory of Uganda Protectorate. LC 76-44772. reprint ed. 34.50 (0-404-15874-9) AMS Pr.

O'Brien, Teresa. Man's Work. (GRE.). (J). 1981. 3.99 (0-85953-868-0); 3.99 (0-85953-631-9) Childs Play.

— Memories. LC 90-46155. 5p. (J). 1985. 6.99 (0-85953-319-0) Childs Play.

O'Brien, Teresa, jt. auth. see Beaumont, Mike.

***O'Brien, Teri S.** Pearls for Personal Trainers. (Illus.). 128p. 2000. pap. 16.95 (1-57167-465-9) Coaches Choice.

O'Brien, Teri S. The Personal Trainer's Handbook. LC 96-41431. (Illus.). 192p. (Orig.). 1997. pap. text 25.00 (0-88011-593-9, BOBR0593) Human Kinetics.

O'Brien, Terrence C. The Legend of Tico Bk. 1: The Synthesis of Religions. 80p. 1996. pap. 6.00 (0-9648456-0-1) Tico Enter.

O'Brien, Terry J. Fair Gods & Feathered Serpents: A Search for Ancient America's Bearded White God. (Illus.). 304p. 1997. 22.98 (0-88290-608-9, 1079) Horizon Utah.

O'Brien, Theresa. Animals of the Jungle. (First Flaps First Facts Ser.). (Illus.). (J). (gr. 1-3). 1994. reprint ed. pap. 4.50 (1-884628-06-0, Flyng Frog) Allied Pub MD.

— Animals of the Ocean. (First Flaps First Facts Ser.). (Illus.). (J). (gr. 1-3). 1994. reprint ed. pap. 4.50 (1-884628-08-7, Flyng Frog) Allied Pub MD.

— Little Fish in a Big Pond. (FRE., Illus.). 32p. (J). 1990. pap. 3.99 (0-85953-465-0) Childs Play.

— Little Fish in a Big Pond. LC 90-46519. (Illus.). 32p. (J). (ps-3). 1990. 7.99 (0-85953-390-5); pap. 3.99 (0-85953-391-3) Childs Play.

O'Brien, Thomas C. Odds & Evens. (Young Math Ser.). (Illus.). (J). (gr. 1-4). 1973. pap. 1.45 (0-690-00207-6) HarpC Child Bks.

— Puzzle Tables: Number Problems with Computational Skills. (J). (gr. 4-7). 1995. pap. 8.95 (0-201-48011-5) Addison-Wesley.

— Wollygoggles & Other Creatures: Problems for Developing Thinking Skills. 64p. (J). (gr. 3-12). 1980. pap. text 9.50 (0-914040-85-5) Cuisenaire.

Obrien, Thomas C. Woolygoggles & Other Creatures: Problems for Developing Thinking Skills. (J). (gr. 4-7). 1992. pap. 9.50 (0-201-48018-2) Addison-Wesley.

O'Brien, Thomas C., ed. see International Committee on English in the Liturgy,.

O'Brien, Thomas F. Century of U.S. Capitalism in Latin America. LC 98-33361. (Dialogos Ser.). 1999. pap. text 19.95 (0-8263-1996-3) U of NM Pr.

— Century of U.S. Capitalism in Latin America. LC 98-33361. (Dialogos Ser.). (Illus.). 199p. 1999. 45.00 (0-8263-1995-5) U of NM Pr.

— The Revolutionary Mission: American Business in Latin America, 1900-1945. (Latin American Studies: No. 81). (Illus.). 370p. (C). 1996. text 59.95 (0-521-55015-7) Cambridge U Pr.

***O'Brien, Thomas F.** The Revolutionary Mission: American Enterprise in Latin America, 1900-1945. (Cambridge Latin American Studies: No. 81). (Illus.). 250p. (C). 1999. pap. 19.95 (0-521-66344-X) Cambridge U Pr.

O'Brien, Thomas G., III. Connecticut Corporation Law & Practice. (National Corporation Law Ser.). 886p. 1992. 155.00 (0-13-297623-4) Aspen Law.

— Florida Law of Corporations & Business Organizations. 110.00 (0-13-295007-3) Aspen Law.

— Florida Law of Corporations & Business Organizations. 1992. ring bd. 126.00 (0-13-288226-4) Aspen Law.

O'Brien, Thomas G. & Charlton, Samuel G., eds. Handbook of Human Factors Testing & Evaluation. 376p. 1996. text 69.95 (0-8058-1724-7) L Erlbaum Assocs.

— Handbook of Human Factors Testing & Evaluation. 376p. 1996. pap. 36.00 (0-8058-1725-5) L Erlbaum Assocs.

O'Brien, Thomas J. Global Financial Management. LC 95-9585. 416p. 1995. text 90.95 (0-471-57854-1) Wiley.

O'Brien, Thomas V. The Politics of Race & Schooling: Public Education in Georgia, 1900-1961. LC 99-10348. 256p. 1999. 45.00 (0-7391-0060-2) Lxngtn Bks.

O'Brien, Tim. "?" Question Book. Carle, Cliff, ed. 176p. 1996. pap. 6.99 (0-918259-94-0) CCC Pubns.

***O'Brien, Tim.** The Amusement Park Guide: Coast to Coast Thrills. 3rd ed. LC 99-22424. (Illus.). 288p. 1999. pap. text 14.95 (0-7627-0437-3) Globe Pequot.

O'Brien, Tim. Fun with the Family in Tennessee: Hundreds of Ideas for Day Trips with the Kids. 2nd ed. LC 99-44352. (Illus.). 288p. 2000. pap. text 12.95 (0-7627-0537-X) Globe Pequot.

— Going after Cacciato. LC 99-29275. 352p. 1999. pap. 13.00 (0-7679-0442-7) Broadway BDD.

— Going after Cacciato. 320p. 1979. pap. 11.95 (0-385-28349-0, Delta Trade) Dell.

— Going after Cacciato. LC 77-11723. 1978. 12.09 (0-606-06415-X, Pub. by Turtleback) Demco.

— If I Die in a Combat Zone. LC 99-29406. 224p. 1999. pap. 12.00 (0-7679-0443-5) Broadway BDD.

— If I Die in a Combat Zone. 208p. 1992. mass mkt. 6.99 (0-440-34311-9, LE) Dell.

— In the Lake of the Woods. 303p. 1995. pap. 12.95 (0-14-025094-8, Penguin Bks) Viking Penguin.

***O'Brien, Tim.** Northern Lights. LC 99-28842. 368p. 1999. pap. 13.00 (0-7679-0441-9) Broadway BDD.

O'Brien, Tim. The Nuclear Age. 368p. 1993. mass mkt. 6.99 (0-440-21586-2, LE) Dell.

— The Nuclear Age. 320p. 1996. pap. 13.95 (0-14-025910-4) Viking Penguin.

***O'Brien, Tim.** Tennessee: A Guide to Unique Places. 5th ed. (Off the Beaten Path Ser.). (Illus.). 2000. pap. 12.95 (0-7627-0820-4) Globe Pequot.

O'Brien, Tim. Tennessee: Off the Beaten Path: A Guide to Unique Places. 4th ed. (Off the Beaten Path Ser.). (Illus.). 256p. (Orig.). 1998. pap. 12.95 (0-7627-0279-6) Globe Pequot.

— The Things They Carried. (Contemporary American Fiction Ser.). 288p. (C). 1999. pap. 12.95 (0-14-014773-X) Addson-Wesley Educ.

— The Things They Carried. LC 98-49677. 272p. 1998. pap. 13.00 (0-7679-0289-0) Broadway BDD.

— The Things They Carried. (C). 1997. pap. text. write for info. (0-8013-3149-8) Longman.

— Tomcat in Love. 368p. 1999. pap. 13.00 (0-7679-0204-1) Bantam.

O'Brien, Tim. Tomcat in Love. LC 98-29846. 368p. 1998. 26.00 (0-7679-0202-5) Broadway BDD.

O'Brien, Tim, ed. American Fiction Vol. 7: The Best in Unpublished Short Stories by Emerging Writers. 7th ed. 316p. 1995. pap. 18.95 (0-89823-164-7, Birch Ln Pr) Carol Pub Group.

O'Brien, Tim & Strand, Mark, eds. Ploughshares Winter, 1995-96. 225p. (Orig.). 1995. pap. 8.95 (0-933277-15-6) Ploughshares.

O'Brien, Timothy J. & Gunnell, Margaret. Why Small Christian Communities Work. LC 96-7045. 72p. (Orig.). 1996. pap. 7.95 (0-89390-371-X) Resource Pubns.

O'Brien, Timothy L. Bad Bet: Why the Half-Trillion Dollar Gambling is now the Inside Story of the Glamour, Glitz & Danger of America's Gambling Industry. LC 98-4935. 352p. 1998. 25.00 (0-8129-2807-5, Times Bks) Crown Pub Group.

O'Brien, Timothy M., et al. Microsoft Access 97 Developer's Handbook: Using the New Microsoft Access Object Model & VBA. LC 97-1922. (Solution Developer Ser.). 700p. 1997. pap. 39.99 incl. cd-rom (1-57231-358-7) Microsoft.

O'Brien, Tom, jt. auth. see Cunningham, Vance.

O'Brien, Tony R. Inspirational Poetry by Design. LC 97-90885. 38p. 1998. 10.95 (0-533-12205-8) Vantage.

O'Brien, Vince, ed. Buy Outs. 155p. 1995. 45.00 (1-85564-383-9, Pub. by Euromoney) Am Educ Systs.

O'Brien, Virginia. The Fast Foward MBA in Business. LC 96-28202. 288p. 1996. pap. 12.95 (0-471-14660-9) Wiley.

— Success on Our Own Terms: Tales of Extraordinary, Ordinary Business Women. LC 97-43845. 267p. 1998. 22.95 (0-471-17871-3) Wiley.

O'Brien, W. J., ed. Toolik Lake: Ecology of an Aquatic Ecosystem in Arctic Alaska. LC 92-26746. (Developments in Hydrobiology Ser.: Vol. 78). (C). 1992. text 260.00 (0-7923-1952-4) Kluwer Academic.

O'Brien, W. M., ed. Fenbufen. (Journal: Pharmacology: Vol. 25, Suppl. 1). (Illus.). iv, 96p. 1982. pap. 45.25 (3-8055-3542-2) S Karger.

O'Brien, Walter J. & Marshall, Genevieve E. The American Boiler, Piping & H. V. A. C. Costing Handbook 1997. unabridged ed. (Illus.). xi, 400p. (Orig.). 1996. pap. 95.00 (0-9655162-0-2, 0012596, T-Square Pr) OBrien & Assocs.

O'Brien, Welby Ann. Formerly a Wife: A Survival Guide for Recently Divorced Women. 232p. 1996. pap. 10.99 (0-88965-137-X, Pub. by Horizon Books) Chr Pubns.

O'Brien, William. Bronze Age Copper Mining in Britain & Ireland. (Archaeology Ser.: No. 71). (Illus.). 64p. 1996. pap. 10.50 (0-7478-0321-8, Pub. by Shire Pubns) Parkwest Pubns.

— The Sting of the Scorpion. 1999. pap. text 16.95 (1-56492-276-6) Laredo.

O'Brien, William A. How to Serve Low Mass & Benediction. 2nd ed. 46p. (J). (gr. 2-11). 1997. reprint ed. pap. 3.45 (0-935952-42-X) Angelus Pr.

O'Brien, William F., Jr., jt. auth. see Tuerck, David G.

O'Brien, William H., jt. auth. see Haynes, Stephen N.

O'Brien, William J. Dental Materials: Properties & Selection. 2nd ed. LC 96-48070. 434p. 1997. pap. text 58.00 (0-86715-297-4) Quint Pub Co.

O'Brien, William J., ed. Riding Time Like a River: The Catholic Moral Tradition since Vatican II. LC 93-4394. 192p. 1993. 36.00 (0-87840-542-9) Georgetown U Pr.

— Riding Time Like a River: The Catholic Moral Tradition since Vatican II. LC 93-4394. 126p. 1993. reprint ed. pap. 39.10 (0-608-01817-1, 206246600003) Bks Demand.

— Splendor & Wonder: Jesuit Character, Georgetown Spirit, & Liberal Education. LC 88-24652. 120p. (Orig.). reprint ed. pap. 37.20 (0-7837-6703-X, 204633500011) Bks Demand.

O'Brien, William J., jt. auth. see Craig, Robert G.

O'Brien, William V. The Conduct of a Just & Limited War. LC 81-11883. 495p. 1981. 50.95 (0-275-90693-0, C0693, Praeger Pubs) Greenwood.

O'Brien, Wm. Arctander. Novalis: Signs of Revolution. LC 94-19760. (Post-Contemporary Interventions Ser.). 384p. 1994. text 54.95 (0-8223-1509-2); pap. text 18.95 (0-8223-1519-X) Duke.

O'Brien Zirwas, Sarah, ed. see O'Brien, Jim.

O'Brien'Strain, Margaret, jt. auth. see MaCurdy, Thomas E.

O'Bries, Thomas C. Puzzle Tables. 64p. (J). (gr. 3-8). 1980. pap. text 9.50 (0-914040-83-9) Cuisenaire.

Obrink, K. J. & Flemstrom, G., eds. Gastric Ion Transport. (Illus.). 434p. (Orig.). 1978. pap. text 35.00 (91-22-00254-5) Coronet Bks.

Obrink, Ulla. Hala Sultan Tekke 5: Excavations in Area 22; 1971-1973 & 1975-1978. (Studies in Mediterranean Archaeology: Vol. XLV:5). (Illus.). 144p. (Orig.). 1980. pap. 57.50 (91-85058-91-2) P Astroms.

— Hala Sultan Tekke 6: A Sherd Deposit in Area 22. (Studies in Mediterranean Archaeology: Vol. XLV: 6). (Illus.). 91p. (Orig.). 1979. pap. 37.50 (91-85058-89-0, Pub. by P Astroms) Coronet Bks.

Obrinsky, Mark. Profit Theory & Capitalism. LC 82-40482. (Illus.). 176p. 1983. pap. text 20.95 (0-8122-1147-2) U of Pa Pr.

Obrist, Barbara. Constantine of Pisa: The Book of the Secrets of Alchemy. LC 90-37150. (Collection de Travaux de l'Academie Internationale d'Histoire des Sciences: Vol. 34). (ENG & LAT.). x, 339p. 1990. 119.00 (90-04-09288-9) Brill Academic Pubs.

Obrist, Barbara, jt. ed. see Sider, Sandra.

Obrist, Hans U. & Tortosa, Guy, eds. Unbuilt Roads: 107 Unrealized Projects. 248p. 1998. pap. 39.95 (3-7757-0700-X, 810842, Pub. by Gerd Hatje) Dist Art Pubs.

Obrist, Hans-Ulrich & Altshuler, Bruce. Do It. Grossarth, Ulrike & Marsaldi, Eva, trs. (Illus.). 104p. (C). 1997. pap. 9.95 (0-916365-51-4) Ind Curators.

Obrist, Hans Ulrich & Violette, Robert, eds. The Words of Gilbert & George: Writings, Statements, & Interviews, 1969-1997. (Illus.). 288p. 30.00 (1-900828-00-6, Pub. by Violette) Dist Art Pubs.

Obrist, Hans-Ulrich, ed. see Bourgeois, Louise.

Obrist, Hans Ulrich, ed. see Golub, Leon.

Obrist, Hans-Ulrich, ed. see Richter, Gerhard.

***Obrist, Jurg.** Max & Molly & the Mystery of the Missing Honey. (Illus.). 48p. (J). (gr. 1-4). 2000. 13.95 (0-7358-1266-7, Pub. by North-South Bks NYC) Chronicle Bks.

Obrist, Paul A. Cardiovascular Psychophysiology: A Perspective. LC 80-28582. 246p. 1981. 45.00 (0-306-40599-7, Plenum Trade) Perseus Pubng.

Obrizok, Robert. A Garden of Conifers: Introduction & Selection Guide. LC 93-71498. (Illus.). 120p. 1994. pap. 24.95 (0-913643-08-4) Capabilitys.

O'Brogain, Seamus. The Wolfhound Guide to the Irish Harp. (Illus.). 28p. 1998. pap. 7.95 (0-86327-635-0, Pub. by Wolfhound Press) Irish Amer Bk.

***Obroucheva, Natalie V.** Seed Germination: A Guide to the Early Stages. (Illus.). 158p. 1999. pap. 45.00 (90-5782-040-4, Pub. by Backhuys Pubs) Balogh.

O'Bryan, Aileen. Dine: Origin Myths of the Navaho Indians. (Bureau of American Ethnology Bulletins Ser.). 187p. 1995. lib. bdg. 79.00 (0-7812-4163-4) Rprt Serv.

O'Bryan, Aileen. The Dine: Origin Myths of the Navaho Indians. fac. ed. (Smithsonian Institution, Bureau of American Ethnology, Bulletins Ser.: No. 163). (Illus.). 196p. (C). 1956. reprint ed. pap. text 21.25 (1-55567-761-4) Coyote Press.

O'Bryan, Aileen, tr. Navaho Indian Myths. LC 93-9688. (Illus.). 208p. 1993. reprint ed. pap. 6.95 (0-486-27592-2) Dover.

***O'Bryan, Bonnie.** See It! Say It! Artic Reps! 124 Reproducible Artic Sheets for S, R, L, Blends, SH, CH, F, G, K. (Illus.). 124p. (J). (gr. k-5). 1999. spiral bd., wbk. ed. 26.95 (1-58650-075-9, BK-273) Super Duper.

O'Bryan, Elsie M. Yesterday, As I Pass: A Collection of Poems. LC 97-94780. (Illus.). 64p. 1997. pap. 11.95 (0-9661665-0-7) Bear Paw AK.

O'Bryan, Elsie M., ed. see Backhaus, Phyllis.

O'Bryan, Sharon. Old Fashioned Children's Games: Over 200 Outdoors, Car Trip, Song, Card & Party Activities. (Illus.). 143p. 1998. pap. 23.50 (0-7864-0558-9) McFarland & Co.

O'Bryan, Suzanne. Sauntering. Date not set. pap. 15.95 (0-9621667-2-3) Chengalera Pr.

O'Bryant, David C. Graphics for Engineers: Visualization, Communication, & Design. (Illus.). 620p. (C). 1991. pap. text 41.80 (0-87563-361-7) Stipes.

O'Bryant, David C., jt. auth. see Hartley, T. C.

O'Bryant, Harold S., jt. auth. see Stone, Michael H.

O'Bryant, M. C. Making It As a Sports Official. (Illus.). 90p. (Orig.). 1991. pap. text 12.00 (0-88314-520-0) AAHPERD.

O'Bryant, Michael, ed. Ohio Almanac, 1997-98: An Encyclopedia of Indispensable Information about the Buckeye Universe. rev. ed. (Illus.). 744p. 1997. pap. text 29.95 (1-882203-10-0) Orange Frazer.

O'Bryant-Puentes, Nancy. First Aid for Family Quilts. (Illus.). 34p. (Orig.). 1986. pap. 5.95 (0-9602970-6-5) Leman Pubns.

O'Bryant, Wayne A. The Cleopatra Myth. Sanders, Willease, ed. (Illus.). 29p. 1996. pap. 5.00 (1-891124-50-1) GOD First Prods.

— It Won't Hurt You to Know. Sanders, Willease et al, eds. (Illus.). 54p. 1996. pap. 7.50 (1-891124-51-X) GOD First Prods.

— Teach Me about Christmas. (Illus.). 13p. (J). 1996. pap. 2.50 (1-891124-52-8) GOD First Prods.

— Who Is Ra El? One of the World's Best Kept Secrets - The True Identity of the Africans Brought to America in the Atlantic Slave Trade. Sanders, Willease, ed. (Illus.). 215p. 1997. 19.95 (1-891124-53-6) GOD First Prods.

***O'Bryne, John.** Space. LC 99-39357. (Little Guides Ser.). (Illus.). 320p. 1999. pap. 14.95 (1-875137-60-2) Weldon Owen.

Obrzut, John E. Neuropsychological Foundations of Learning Disabilities: A Handbook of Issues, Methods & Practice. 848p. 1996. pap. text 99.00 (0-12-524039-2) Acad Pr.

Obrzut, John E. & Hynd, George W. Child Neuropsychology, Vol. 1. (Perspectives in Neurolinguistics, Neuropsychology & Psycholinguistics Ser.). 1986. pap. text 55.00 (0-12-524043-0) Acad Pr.

Obsatz, Michael. From Stalemate to Soulmate: A Guide to Mature, Committed & Loving Relationships. LC 97-145457. 112p. 1997. pap. 11.99 (0-8066-2701-8, 9-2701, Augsburg) Augsburg Fortress.

O

An Asterisk (*) at the beginning of an entry indicates that the title is appearing for the first time.

— Raising Nonviolent Children in a Violent World: A Family Handbook. LC 98-38038. 112p. 1998. pap. 11.99 (*0-8066-3700-5*, 9-3700) Augsburg Fortress.

***Obsatz, Micheal.** Healing Our Anger: Seven Ways to Make Peace in a Hostile World. LC 99-53601. 2000. pap. text 12.99 (*0-8066-3890-7*) Augsburg Fortress.

Observer Staff. Chernobyl: The End of the Nuclear Dream. LC 86-22462. 256p. 1986. pap. 4.95 (*0-394-75107-8*) Vin Bks.

— Observer Profiles. Brown, Ivor, ed. LC 78-117330. (Biography Index Reprint Ser.). 1977. reprint ed. 23.95 (*0-8369-8022-0*) Ayer.

Obshey, G., jt. auth. see Tenzin, K. S.

Obshey, O., jt. auth. see Tenzin, K. S.

***Obst, David.** Too Good to Be Forgotten: Changing America in the '60s & '70s. LC 98-8720. 282p. 1998. 24.95 (*0-471-29538-8*) Wiley.

Obst, Lynda. Hello, He Lied: And Other Truths from the Hollywood Trenches. LC 97-25218. (Illus.). 272p. 1997. reprint ed. pap. 14.95 (*0-7679-0041-3*) Broadway BDD.

***Obst, Wesley, et al.** Agribusiness: Financial Management. 326p. 1999. pap. 35.00 (*1-86287-317-8*, Pub. by Federation Pr) Gaunt.

Obstfeld, H., tr. see Aust, W.

Obstfeld, Henri. Spectacle Frame Dispensing. (C). 1998. pap. text 115.00 (*0-7020-1928-3*) Harcourt.

Obstfeld, Lynda R. Hello, He Lied: And Other Truths from the Hollywood Trenches. 246p. 23.95 (*0-614-22237-0*) Little.

Obstfeld, Maurice. EMU, Ready or Not! LC 98-27697. (Essays in International Finance Ser.: No. 209). 36 p. 1998. 10.00 (*0-88165-116-8*) Princeton U Int Finan Econ.

Obstfeld, Maurice & Rogoff, Kenneth. Foundations of International Macroeconomics. (Illus.). 830p. 1996. 65.00 (*0-262-15047-6*) MIT Pr.

Obstfeld, Maurice, jt. auth. see Krugman, Paul R.

Obstfeld, Raymond. The Joker & the Thief. 1994. 9.09 (*0-606-07017-6*, Pub. by Turtleback) Demco.

— Masked Dog. 1986. pap. 3.50 (*0-373-62101-9*) Harlequin Bks.

***Obstfeld, Raymond.** The Novelist's Essential Guide to Crafting Scenes. LC 00-36797. (Novelist's Essential Guide Ser.). 208p. 2000. pap. 14.99 (*0-89879-973-2*, Wrtrs Digest Bks) F & W Pubns Inc.

Obstfeld, Raymond. The Remington Contract. 304p. (Orig.). 1988. spiral bd. 4.50 (*0-373-97095-1*) Harlequin Bks.

***Obstfeld, Raymond & Fitzgerald, Patricia, eds.** Jabberrock: The Ultimate Book of Rock 'n Roll Quotations. (Illus.). 279p. 1999. reprint ed. pap. text 13.00 (*0-7881-6460-0*) DIANE Pub.

Obstfelder, Sigbjorn. A Priest's Diary. McFarlane, James, tr. from NOR. & intro. by. LC 87-63149. (Series B: No. 1). 75p. (Orig.). 1987. pap. 9.95 (*1-870041-01-1*, Pub. by Norvik Pr) Dufour.

Obstler, Mimi. Out of the Earth, into the Fire: A Course in Ceramic Materials for the Studio Potter. Simpson, Robina, ed. LC 95-31026. (Illus.). 1996. 62.00 (*1-57498-001-7*, G021); pap. 52.00 (*1-57498-008-4*, G022) Am Ceramic.

O'Buachalla, Seamas, ed. The Letters of P. H. Pearse. 532p. 1980. 50.00 (*0-901072-87-7*, Pub. by Smyth) Dufour.

Obuchov, V., jt. auth. see Loqinov, V.

Obuchowski, Chester W. Franco-Phonics, Etc. 156p. 1989. pap. 15.00 (*0-8191-7535-8*) U Pr of Amer.

Obudho, Constance E. Black-White Racial Attitudes: An Annotated Bibliography. LC 75-35351. 180p. 1976. lib. bdg. 42.95 (*0-8371-8582-3*, OBW/, Greenwood Pr) Greenwood.

Obudho, Constance E., compiled by. Human Nonverbal Behavior: An Annotated Bibliography. LC 79-7586. 196p. 1979. lib. bdg. 59.95 (*0-313-21094-2*, OBH/, Greenwood Pr) Greenwood.

Obudho, Constance E., ed. Black Marriage & Family Therapy, 72. LC 82-20967. (Contributions in Afro-American & African Studies: No. 72). (Illus.). 269p. 1983. 59.95 (*0-313-22119-7*, OBM/, Greenwood Pr) Greenwood.

Obudho, Robert A., compiled by. Demography, Urbanization, & Spatial Planning in Kenya: A Bibliographical Survey, 7. LC 84-19805. (African Special Bibliographic Ser.: No. 7). 285p. 1985. lib. bdg. 59.95 (*0-313-24420-0*, OBD/, Greenwood Pr) Greenwood.

Obudho, Robert A. & El-Shakhs, Salah S., eds. Development of Urban Systems in Africa. LC 78-19766. 406p. 1979. 65.00 (*0-275-90404-0*, C0404, Praeger Pubs) Greenwood.

Obudho, Robert A. & Mhlanga, Constance C., eds. Slum & Squatter Settlements in Sub-Saharan Africa: Toward a Planning Strategy. LC 87-11705. 440p. 1988. 79.50 (*0-275-92309-6*, C2309, Praeger Pubs) Greenwood.

Obudho, Robert A. & Scott, Jeannine B. Afro-American Demography & Urban Issues: A Bibliography, 8. LC 85-17752. (Bibliographies & Indexes on Afro-American & African Studies Ser.: No. 8). 433p. 1985. lib. bdg. 69.50 (*0-313-24656-4*, OAA/) Greenwood.

Obudho, Robert A. & Waller, P. P. Periodic Markets, Urbanization, & Regional Planning: A Case Study from Western Kenya, 22. LC 75-23867. (Contributions in Afro-American & African Studies: No. 22). (Illus.). 289p. 1976. 55.00 (*0-8371-8375-8*, OPM/) Greenwood.

Obudho, Robert A., jt. ed. see Gooneratne, Wilbert.

Obukhov, Yu N., jt. auth. see Sardanashvily, Gennadi A.

Obukhov, Yu N., jt. ed. see Pronin, P. I.

Oby, Jason. Equity in Operatic Casting As Perceived by African American Male Singers. LC 97-50592. 116p. 1998. text 59.95 (*0-7734-2225-0*) E Mellen.

O'Byrne. Manual of Asthma Management. 1995. pap. text 52.50 (*0-7020-1781-7*, W B Saunders Co) Harcrt Hlth Sci Grp.

***O'Byrne.** Roster of Soldiers & Patriots of the American Revolution Buried in Indiana. 407p. 1999. pap. 34.00 (*0-8063-0266-6*) Clearfield Co.

***O'Byrne, Bill & University of Toronto Staff.** Discovering the Future: Featuring the Career Compass Model. 364p. 1998. 17.95 (*0-7713-0464-1*) Gui3dance Ctr UTP.

O'Byrne, Bob, jt. auth. see Abram, Gary.

O'Byrne, Cathal. From Green Hills of Galilee. LC 71-167464. (Short Story Index Reprint Ser.). 1977. reprint ed. 17.95 (*0-8369-3990-5*) Ayer.

O'Byrne, Denis. Lonely Planet Outback Australia. 2nd ed. (Illus.). 536p. 1998. pap. 21.95 (*0-86442-504-X*) Lonely Planet.

— Lonely Planet South Australia. (Illus.). 336p. 1996. pap. 14.95 (*0-86442-383-7*) Lonely Planet.

***O'Byrne, Denis.** South Australia. 2nd ed. (Illus.). 330p. 1999. pap. 16.95 (*0-86442-716-6*) Lonely Planet.

O'Byrne, Denis & Harcombe, David. Lonely Planet Vanuatu. 3rd ed. 304p. 1999. pap. 15.95 (*0-86442-660-7*) Lonely Planet.

O'Byrne, Denis, jt. auth. see Harcombe, David.

O'Byrne, F. D. Reichenbach's Letters on OD & Magnetism (1852) 119p. 1996. reprint ed. spiral bd. 16.00 (*0-7873-0639-8*) Hlth Research.

O'Byrne, John & Mancini, Rob. Stars & Planets. LC 96-68949. (My First Pocket Guide Ser.). 80p. (J). 1997. write for info. (*0-7922-3450-2*) Natl Geog.

O'Byrne, John, ed. see Burnham, Robert, et al.

O'Byrne, Lorraine. What Is It? A Gallery of Historic Phrases. (Illus.). 48p. 1995. pap. 3.20 (*0-919822-19-3*, Pub. by Boston Mills) Genl Dist Srvs.

O'Byrne, Michael C. History of LaSalle County, 3 vols. in 2, Set. (Illus.). 1148p. 1995. reprint ed. lib. bdg. 109.50 (*0-8328-5003-9*) Higginson Bk Co.

O'Byrne, Paul M., ed. Asthma As an Inflammatory Disease. (Allergic Disease & Therapy Ser.: Vol. 2). (Illus.). 336p. 1990. text 175.00 (*0-8247-8220-8*) Dekker.

O'Byrne, Paul M., jt. ed. see Pauwels, Romain.

O'Byrne-Pelham, Fran, jt. auth. see Balcer, Bernadette.

O'Byrne, Sally, jt. auth. see Thompson, Priscilla M.

O'Byrne, Seamus, ed. Be Reconciled! 113p. 1989. pap. 30.00 (*0-86217-235-7*, Pub. by Veritas Pubns) St Mut.

— Challenge or Crisis? Texts by John Paul II on Religious Life. Romano, Osservatore, tr. from ITA. 312p. (Orig.). 1987. pap. 17.95 (*0-86217-238-1*, Pub. by Veritas Pubns) St Mut.

Oc, Taner, et al. Urban Design: Ornament & Decoration. LC 94-47287. (Illus.). 224p. 1995. 59.95 (*0-7506-0792-0*) Buttrwrth-Heinemann.

Oc, Taner, jt. auth. see Trench, Sylvia.

Oc, Taner, jt. ed. see Trench, Sylvia.

O'C Walshe, M. Buddhism & Christianity: A Positive Approach. 42p. 1987. 2.25 (*955-24-0016-3*, Pub. by Buddhist Pub Soc) Vipassana Res Pubns.

Oca, Elena Montes de, see Montes de Oca, Elena.

Oca, Marco A. Montes De, see Montes De Oca, Marco A.

O'Cadhain, Mairtin. The Road to Brightcity. 112p. 1981. pap. 10.95 (*0-905169-47-6*, Pub. by Poolbeg Pr) Dufour.

O'Cain, Raymond K., jt. auth. see McDavid, Raven I., Jr.

O'Cain, Raymond K., jt. ed. see Davis, Boyd H.

O'Callachan, John. Bit of the Blarney. 1992. pap. 6.95 (*1-882255-00-3*) Hot To Trot.

O'Callaghan, Bryn. History of the Twentieth Century. 1987. pap. text 17.25 (*0-582-33172-2*, 72065) Longman.

O'Callaghan, C. & Stephenson, T. Data Interpretation for Paediatric Examinations. (Illus.). 188p. 1995. pap. write for info. (*0-443-05010-4*) Church.

O'Callaghan, C. A., The MCRP Pt. 1: A System Based Tutorial. (Illus.). 1997. pap. 27.95 (*0-632-04781-X*) Blackwell Sci.

O'Callaghan, Chris, jt. auth. see Stephenson, Terence.

***O'Callaghan, Christopher A. & Brenner, Barry.** The Kidney at a Glance. (At a Glance Ser.). (Illus.). 128p. (C). 2000. pap. 24.95 (*0-632-05206-6*) Blackwell Sci.

O'Callaghan, Conor. The History of Rain. 56p. 1993. pap. 12.95 (*1-85235-116-0*) Dufour.

O'Callaghan, D., jt. ed. see Roche, J. F.

O'Callaghan, E. B. History of New Netherlands, or, New York under the Dutch, 2 vols., Vol. II, 1646-1664. (Illus.). 1101p. 1997. reprint ed. lib. bdg. 105.00 (*0-8328-6090-5*) Higginson Bk Co.

***O'Callaghan, E. B.** Register of New Netherland, 1626-1674. (Illus.). 198p. 1999. pap. 24.50 (*0-8328-9837-6*) Higginson Bk Co.

O'Callaghan, E. B., ed. Names of Persons for Whom Marriage Licenses Were Issued by the Secretary of the Province of New York, Previous to 1784. 480p. 1997. reprint ed. lib. bdg. 49.50 (*0-8328-6089-1*) Higginson Bk Co.

O'Callaghan, Edmund B. Calendar of Historical Manuscripts in the Office of the Secretary of State, Albany, NY. 423p. 1994. reprint ed. lib. bdg. 45.00 (*0-8328-3803-9*) Higginson Bk Co.

— The Documentary History of the State of New York, 4 vols. 4356p. write for info. (*1-886103-00-3*) Fine Books.

— Lists of Inhabitants of Colonial New York. LC 79-52062. 351p. 1999. reprint ed. 25.00 (*0-8063-0847-8*) Genealog Pub.

— The Register of New Netherland, 1626-1674. 198p. 1998. reprint ed. pap. 21.50 (*0-8063-4528-4*, 9294) Clearfield Co.

***O'Callaghan, Edmund Z.** A List of Editions of the Holy Scriptures & Parts Thereof Printed in America Previous to 1860. 415p. 2000. reprint ed. 65.00 (*1-57898-183-2*) Martino Pubng.

O'Callaghan, Gareth. Dare I Die. LC 96-230710. 678p. 1996. pap. 12.95 (*1-85371-635-9*, Pub. by Poolbeg Pr) Dufour.

O'Callaghan, Gary. The Castle Murders. LC 98-96054. 202 p. 1998. write for info. (*0-9662344-0-5*) St Finbarr.

— The Structure & Operation of the World Gold Market. LC 93-22746. (Occasional Papers: No. 105). 60p. 1993. 15.00 (*1-55775-281-8*) Intl Monetary.

O'Callaghan, J. M. Taxation of Estates: The Law in Ireland. 1993. pap. text 91.00 (*1-85475-621-4*, IE, MICHIE) LEXIS Pub.

O'Callaghan, Jane. Algarve. Globetrotter Staff, ed. (Globe Trotter Travel Guides Ser.). (Illus.). 128p. 1996. pap. text 9.95 (*1-85368-436-8*, Pub. by New5 Holland) Globe Pequot.

***O'Callaghan, Jane.** Algarve. 2nd ed. (Globetrotter Travel Guides Ser.). 2001. pap. 10.95 (*1-85974-420-6*) New5 Holland.

O'Callaghan, Jerry. The Red Book: The Hanrahan Case Against Merck, Sharp & Dohme. (Illus.). 228p. (Orig.). 1992. pap. 15.95 (*1-85371-167-5*, Pub. by Poolbeg Pr) Dufour.

O'Callaghan, Jerry A. The Disposition of the Public Domain in Oregon. Bruchey, Stuart, ed. LC 78-53563. (Development of Public Land Law in the U. S. Ser.). 1979. reprint ed. lib. bdg. 15.95 (*0-405-11382-X*) Ayer.

O'Callaghan, Jill. Some Mother's Son. (Orig.). pap. 14.95 (*0-86819-573-1*, Pub. by Currency Pr) Accents Pubns.

***O'Callaghan, John P., ed.** Science, Philosophy & Theology: The Notre Dame Symposium 1997. 432p. 2000. pap. 30.00 (*1-890318-81-7*, Pub. by St Augustines Pr) U Ch Pr.

O'Callaghan, John P. & Hibbs, Thomas S., eds. Recovering Nature: Essays in Natural Philosophy, Ethics & Metaphysics in Honor of Ralph McInerny. LC 99-38120. 272p. 2000. 35.00 (*0-268-01666-6*, Pub. by U of Notre Dame Pr) Chicago Distribution Ctr.

O'Callaghan, Joseph F. Alfonso X & the Cantigas de Santa Maria: A Poetic Biography. LC 98-12852. (Medieval Mediterranean Ser.). 251p. 1998. 99.00 (*90-04-11023-2*) Brill Academic Pubs.

— Alfonso X, the Cortes & Government in Medieval Spain. LC 97-48587. (Variorum Collected Studies Ser.: Vol. 604). 300p. 1998. text 94.95 (*0-86078-692-7*, Pub. by Ashgate Pub) Ashgate Pub Co.

— A History of Medieval Spain. LC 74-7698. 736p. 1983. pap. text 25.00 (*0-8014-9264-5*) Cornell U Pr.

— The Learned King: The Reign of Alfonso X of Castile. LC 93-13417. (Middle Ages Ser.). (Illus.). 408p. (C). 1993. text 51.95 (*0-8122-3226-7*) U of Pa Pr.

O'Callaghan, Joseph F. Heresies of the Early Christian & Medieval Era, 67 titles in 92 vols. (AMS Reprint Ser.). 1965. reprint ed. write for info. (*0-404-16090-5*) AMS Pr.

O'Callaghan, Joseph F., et al. On the Social Origins of Medieval Institutions: Essays in Honor of Joseph F. O'Callaghan. LC 98-35744. (Medieval Mediterranean Ser.). xxiv, 348p. 1998. 128.00 (*90-04-11096-8*) Brill Academic Pubs.

O'Callaghan, Joseph F., tr. see Olin, John C., ed.

O'Callaghan, Julie. Edible Anecdotes. 80p. 1983. pap. 10.95 (*0-85105-414-5*, Pub. by Smyth) Dufour.

— Two Barks. 1997. pap. 15.95 (*1-85224-427-5*, Pub. by Bloodaxe Bks) Dufour.

— What's What. 77p. (Orig.). 1991. pap. 15.95 (*1-85224-161-6*, Pub. by Bloodaxe Bks) Dufour.

O'Callaghan, Margaret. British High Politics & a Nationalist Ireland: Criminality, Land, & the Law Under Forster & Balfour. 220p. 1995. text 65.00 (*0-312-12497-X*) St Martin.

O'Callaghan, Mark A. J. Psycho Surgery. 1983. lib. bdg. 124.00 (*0-942068-06-8*) Kluwer Academic.

O'Callaghan, Mary. The Government Shall Be upon Whose Shoulder? One Family's Chronicle During 40 Years of the Doctrine of Godly Government. Nigh, Kepler, ed. 224p. 1999. pap. 9.99 (*1-884369-99-5*, Serenity Bks) McDougal Pubng.

O'Callaghan, Maxine. Death Is Forever. large type ed. LC 98-46712. 205p. 1999. 19.95 (*0-7862-1729-4*, Five Star MI) Mac Lib Ref.

— Down for the Count: A Delilah West Novel. (WWL Mystery Ser.: No. 294). 1998. per. 4.99 (*0-373-26294-9*, 0-26294-9, Wrldwide Lib) Harlequin Bks.

— Down for the Count: A Delilah West Novel. LC 97-18898. Vol. 60. 240p. 1997. text 20.95 (*0-312-16820-9*) St Martin.

— Down for the Count: A Delilah West Novel. large type ed. LC 97-48566. (Mystery Ser.). 307p. 1998. pap. 24.95 (*0-7838-8404-4*, G K Hall Lrg Type) Mac Lib Ref.

— Only in the Ashes. 320p. 1997. mass mkt. 5.99 (*0-515-12077-4*, Jove) Berkley Pub.

— Shadow of the Child. 336p. 1996. mass mkt. 5.99 (*0-515-11822-2*, Jove) Berkley Pub.

— Trade-Off. (Mystery Ser.). 1996. per. 4.99 (*0-373-26191-8*, 1-26191-6, Wrldwide Lib) Harlequin Bks.

***O'Callaghan, Michelle.** The Shepheard's Nation. (Oxford English Monographs Ser.). 280p. 2000. text 72.00 (*0-19-818638-X*) OUP.

O'Callaghan, Mike, jt. auth. see Hofstede, David.

O'Callaghan, P. O. An Eastern Orthodox Response to Evangelical Claims. 1984. pap. 3.95 (*0-937032-35-2*) Light&Life Pub Co MN.

O'Callaghan, P. W., ed. Energy for Industry. LC 78-41102. (Illus.). 1979. 191.00 (*0-08-022704-X*, Pub. by Pergamon Repr) Franklin.

Ocallaghan, Paul. Energy Management. 464p. 1993. 55.00 (*0-07-707678-8*) McGraw.

O'Callaghan, Paul. Fides Christi: The Justification Debate. 272p. 1997. boxed set 50.00 (*1-85182-316-6*, Pub. by Four Cts Pr) Intl Spec Bk.

O'Callaghan, Paul W. Integrated Environmental Management Handbook. LC 95-52086. 386p. 1996. 115.00 (*0-471-96342-9*) Wiley.

O'Callaghan, Phyllis, ed. A Clashing of Symbols: Method & Meaning in Liberal Studies. LC 87-29950. 164p. reprint ed. pap. 50.90 (*0-608-07021-1*, 206722800009) Bks Demand.

— Values in Conflict: An Interdisciplinary Approach. LC 97-21706. 200p. (C). 1997. 49.00 (*0-7618-0819-1*); pap. 27.50 (*0-7618-0820-5*) U Pr of Amer.

***O'Callaghan, Sean.** To Hell or Barbados: The Ethnic Cleansing of Ireland. 256p. 2000. 29.95 (*0-86322-272-2*, Pub. by Brandon Bk Pubs) Irish Bks Media.

***O'Callaghan, William G.** Putting the Power of Public Engagement to Work for Your Schools & Community. 110p. 1999. ring bd. 49.95 (*0-914607-68-5*, 1748) Master Tchr.

***O'Callaghan, William G., ed.** The Power of Public Engagement: A Beacon of Hope for America's Schools. xiv, 305p. 1999. text 24.95 (*0-914607-67-7*, 1747) Master Tchr.

O'Callahan, Cheryl, jt. auth. see Corwin, Patty.

O'Callahan, D. B. The United States since 1945. 1983. pap. text 9.75 (*0-582-22181-1*, 70893) Longman.

O'Callahan, Jay. The Golden Drum. (YA). (gr. 2 up). 1994. 10.00 incl. audio (*1-877954-04-7*) Artana Prodns.

O'Callahan, Jay. Herman & Marguerite: An Earth Story. LC 94-47561. (Illus.). 36p. (J). (ps-3). 1996. 15.95 (*1-56145-103-7*) Peachtree Pubs.

O'Callahan, Jay. The Herring Shed. (YA). (gr. 9 up). 1983. 10.00 incl. audio (*1-877954-01-2*) Artana Prodns.

— The Island. (J). (gr. 2 up). 1988. 10.00 incl. audio (*1-877954-13-6*) Artana Prodns.

— The Minister of Others Affairs. (J). (gr. 2 up). 1984. 10.00 incl. audio (*1-877954-03-9*) Artana Prodns.

— Mostly Scary. (J). (gr. 2 up). 1987. 10.00 incl. audio (*1-877954-12-8*) Artana Prodns.

O'Callahan, Jay. Orange Cheeks. LC 92-43509. (Illus.). 40p. (J). (ps-3). 1983. 15.95 (*1-56145-073-1*) Peachtree Pubs.

O'Callahan, Jay. Petrukian. (YA). (gr. 2 up). 1994. 10.00 incl. audio (*1-877954-11-X*) Artana Prodns.

— Raspberries. (J). (gr. 2 up). 1983. 10.00 incl. audio (*1-877954-02-0*) Artana Prodns.

— The Silver Stream. (J). (gr. k up). 1990. 10.00 incl. audio (*1-877954-19-5*, A-17-C) Artana Prodns.

— The Strait of Magellan. (YA). (gr. 9 up). 1985. 10.00 incl. audio (*1-877954-06-3*) Artana Prodns.

O'Callahan, Jay. Tulips. LC 96-14701. (Illus.). 28p. (J). (gr. 1-5). 1996. 15.95 (*1-56145-134-7*) Peachtree Pubs.

Ocampo de Gomez, Aurora & Prado Velazquez, Ernesto. Diccionario de Escritores Mexicanos. (SPA.). 69.95 (*0-7859-0713-0*, S-6745) Fr & Eur.

Ocampo, Estela. Diccionario de Terminos Artisticos y Arqueologicos. (SPA.). 240p. 1988. pap. 24.95 (*0-7859-6247-6*, 8476390769) Fr & Eur.

Ocampo, Jose A. & Steiner, Roberto, eds. Foreign Capital in Latin America. 248p. 1994. pap. text 21.50 (*0-940602-77-6*) IADB.

Ocampo, Juan, jt. auth. see Rosenthal, James.

Ocampo, Silvina. La Naranja Maravillosa.Tr. of Marvelous Orange. (Orig.). (J). (gr. 4-7). 1998. pap. text 9.95 (*84-204-3676-3*) Santillana.

Ocamps, Raymond L., Jr., et al. Negotiating & Drafting Software Consulting Agreements. 304p. 1996. ring bd. 119.20 incl. disk (*1-888075-52-X*) Glasser LegalWrks.

***Ocana, Antonio Cortijo.** La Evolucion Generica de la Ficcion Sentimental de los Siglos XV y XVI: Genero Literario y Contexto Social. (Monografias A). (SPA.). 352p. 2000. 75.00 (*1-85566-071-7*, Pub. by Tamesis Bks Ltd) Boydell & Brewer.

O'Canainn, Tomas. A Lifetime of Notes: The Memoirs of Tomas O'Canainn. LC 97-116317. 194p. 1996. pap. 16.95 (*1-898256-18-7*) Dufour.

— Traditional Music in Ireland. (Illus.). 1978. pap. 13.95 (*0-7100-0021-9*, Routledge Thoemms) Routledge.

Ocariz, F., et al. The Mystery of Jesus Christ. LC 95-149485. 123p. 1997. pap. 24.95 (*1-85182-127-9*, Pub. by Four Cts Pr) Intl Spec Bk.

Ocariz, Fernando. God As Father. 53p. 1998. reprint ed. pap. 2.95 (*0-933932-75-8*) Scepter Pubs.

— Opus Dei in the Church. (SPA.). 253p. 1994. pap. 19.95 (*0-933932-79-0*) Scepter Pubs.

O'Carolan, Turlough. Complete Celtic Fingerstyle Guitar Book. Grossman, Stefan et al, trs. 244p. 1995. pap. 22.95 (*0-7866-0100-0*, 95217) Mel Bay.

***O'Carroll, Brendan.** Agnes Browne - The Mammy: MTV. 2000. pap. 10.95 (*0-452-28169-5*, Plume) Dutton Plume.

O'Carroll, Brendan. The Chisellers. 192p. 2000. pap. 11.95 (*0-452-28122-9*, Plume) Dutton Plume.

— The Course: A Play. 128p. 1997. pap. 9.95 (*0-86278-493-X*, Pub. by OBrien Pr) Irish Amer Bk.

***O'Carroll, Brendan.** The Granny. LC 99-89125. 2000. pap. 10.95 (*0-452-28184-9*, Plume) Dutton Plume.

— The Mammy. LC 98-50381. 174p. 1999. pap. 10.95 (*0-452-28103-2*) NAL.

O'Carroll, Brendan. The Mammy. LC 95-123591. 174 p. 1994. write for info. (*0-86278-372-0*) OBrien Pr.

***O'Carroll, Brendan.** The Mammy. large type ed. 225p. 2000. lib. bdg. 26.95 (*1-58547-037-6*) Ctr Point Pubg.

O'Carroll, Ide & Collins, Eoin, eds. Lesbian & Gay Visions of Ireland: Towards the Twenty-First Century. (Lesbian & Gay Studies). 288p. 1996. pap. 21.95 (*0-304-33229-1*) Continuum.

— Lesbian & Gay Visions of Ireland: Towards the Twenty-First Century. (Lesbian & Gay Studies). 288p. 1997. 69.95 (*0-304-33227-5*) Continuum.

O'Carroll, Michael. The Alliance of the Hearts of Jesus & Mary: Hope of the World. LC 97-69221. 112p. 1997. pap. text 4.50 (*1-882972-98-8*, 3631) Queenship Pub.

— Glory of Mary. 32p. 1999. pap. text 2.95 (*1-57918-065-5*) Queen Publ.

— Light from the East. LC 98-65203. 183p. 1998. pap. 9.95 (*1-57918-062-0*, 3632) Queenship Pub.

— Medjugorje: Facts, Documents, Theology. 4th ed. 224p. (Orig.). 1989. pap. 13.95 (*1-85390-073-7*, Pub. by Veritas Pubns) St Mut.

An Asterisk (*) at the beginning of an entry indicates that the title is appearing for the first time.

— Medjugorje Facts Documents Theology. 265p. 1989. 24.00 (*1-85390-141-5*, Pub. by Veritas Pubns) St Mut.

— A Priest in Changing Times: Memories & Opinions of LC 98-145453. 193 p. 1998. write for info. (*1-85607-229-0*) Intl Scholars.

— Verbum Caro: An Encyclopedia on Jesus, the Christ. 216p. (Orig.). 1992. 35.00 (*0-8146-5017-1*, M Glazier) Liturgical Pr.

O'Carroll, Michael, ed. Veni Creator Spiritus: An Encyclopedia of the Holy Spirit. 235p. 1990. 29.95 (*0-8146-5785-0*) Liturgical Pr.

***O'Carroll, Michael, et al.** Contemporary Insights on a Fifth Marian Dogma: Mary Coredemptrix, Mediatrix, Advocate - Theological Foundations III, 2020. Miravalle, Mark I., ed. (Illus.). 2000. pap. 12.50 (*1-57918-125-2*, 2020) Queenship Pub.

O'Casey, Eileen. Cheerio, Titan: The Friendship Between George Bernard Shaw & Eileen & Sean O'Casey. (Illus.). 143p. 1999. reprint ed. text 20.00 (*0-7881-6139-3*) DIANE Pub.

— Sean. LC 78-882085. 318p. 1971. write for info. (*0-333-09442-5*) Macmillan.

O'Casey, Sean. Blasts & Benedictions: Articles & Stories. Ayling, Ronald, ed. LC 75-8487. 314p. 1976. reprint ed. lib. bdg. 45.00 (*0-8371-8158-5*, OCBB, Greenwood Pr) Greenwood.

— Cock-a-Doodle Dandy. LC 90-41574. (Irish Dramatic Texts Ser.). 119p. 1991. 24.95 (*0-8132-0741-X*) Cath U Pr.

— Drums under the Windows. adapted ed. 1961. pap. 5.25 (*0-8222-0336-7*) Dramatists Play.

— I Knock at the Door. adapted ed. 1958. pap. 5.25 (*0-8222-0547-5*) Dramatists Play.

— The Letters of Sean O'Casey. Krause, David, ed. LC 74-11442. 640p. reprint ed. pap. 198.40 (*0-608-20716-0*, 207181400004) Bks Demand.

— The Letters of Sean O'Casey, 1959-1964, Vol. 4. Krause, David, ed. LC 74-11442. (Illus.). 610p. 1992. 49.95 (*0-8132-0678-2*) Cath U Pr.

O'Casey, Sean. Pictures in the Hallway, Vol. 2. LC 72-181386. (His Autobiography Ser.). 240p. 1971. write for info. (*0-330-02717-4*) Pan.

O'Casey, Sean. Purple Dust. 1957. pap. 5.25 (*0-8222-0922-5*) Dramatists Play.

— Sean O'Casey: Plays. 448p. 1998. pap. 16.95 (*0-571-19181-9*) Faber & Faber.

— Sean O'Casey: Plays 2. 448p. 1998. pap. 16.95 (*0-571-19182-7*) Faber & Faber.

— Sean O'Casey, Centenary Essays. Lowery, Robert G. & Krause, David, eds. (Irish Literary Studies: Vol. # 7). 258p. 1980. 54.95 (*0-86140-008-9*, Pub. by Smyth) Dufour.

— Story of the Irish Citizen Army. (C). pap. 8.99 (*0-904526-50-X*, Pub. by Pluto GBR) LPC InBook.

***O'Casey, Sean.** Three Dublin Plays: The Shadow of a Gunman; Juno & the Paycock; The Plough & the Stars. 272p. 2000. pap. 14.00 (*0-571-19552-0*) Faber & Faber.

O'Casey, Sean. Three Plays: Juno & the Paycock; The Shadow of a Gunman & The Plough & the Stars. 218p. 1969. pap. 9.95 (*0-312-80290-0*, Papermac) St Martin.

Ocasio. Chemistry. 1998. pap. text 49.00 (*0-471-32124-9*) Wiley.

Ocasio-Melendez, Marcial E. Capitalism & Development: Tampico, Mexico, 1876-1924. LC 91-43586. (American University Studies: Series IX, Vol. 119). XXXIII, 277p. (C). 1998. text 48.95 (*0-8204-1717-3*) P Lang Pubng.

O'Cathaoir, B. John Blake Dillon, Young Irelander, 1814-66. (Illus.). 208p. 1990. 14.95 (*0-7165-2467-8*, Pub. by Irish Acad Pr) Intl Spec Bk.

***O'Catroux, C. C.** The Dialogues: The Seeker & the Articulate Voice Discusses Life, God, Science, Religion, History, the Meaning of Life & the Search for God & Angels. 88p. 1999. pap. 2.00 (*0-9675578-1-X*) Baavi House.

— The Principles of Business Organization. 89p. 1995. pap. write for info. (*0-9675578-0-1*) Baavi House.

Occamore, David. Essex Potpourri. 1993. pap. 15.00 (*0-86025-271-X*, Pub. by I Henry Pubns) Empire Pub Srvs.

OCCC Montage Staff, ed. see OCCC Press Staff, Students & Friends.

OCCC Press Staff, Students & Friends. Montage, 1990: Anthology of Oregon Coast Community College. OCCC Montage Staff, ed. 56p. (Orig.). 1990. pap. 6.00 (*0-9623452-5-3*) Oregon Coast Cmnty Col.

Occeli & O'Connor, eds. Fluid Cracking Catalysis. LC 97-43570. (Illus.). 368p. 1998. text 145.00 (*0-8247-0079-1*) Dekker.

Occeli, Mario L., ed. Fluid Catalytic Cracking: Role in Modern Refining. LC 88-22151. (Symposium Ser.: No. 375). (Illus.). xii, 356p. 1988. 79.95 (*0-8412-1534-0*) Am Chemical.

Occelli, MArio & Chianelli, Russell. Hydrotreating Technology for Pollution Control: Catalysts, Catalysis, & Processes. LC 96-23962. (Chemical Industries Ser.: Vol. 67). (Illus.). 400p. 1996. text 180.00 (*0-8247-9756-6*) Dekker.

Occelli, Mario L., ed. Fluid Catalytic Cracking: Role in Modern Refining. LC 88-22151. (ACS Symposium Ser.: No. 375). (Illus.). 368p. 1988. reprint ed. pap. 114.10 (*0-608-03279-4*, 206379700007) Bks Demand.

— Fluid Catalytic Cracking Two: Concepts in Catalyst Design. LC 90-23463. (ACS Symposium Ser.: No. 452). (Illus.). 384p. 1991. text 88.00 (*0-8412-1908-7*, Pub. by Am Chemical) OUP.

Occelli, Mario L. & Kessler, Henri, eds. Synthesis of Porous Materials: Zeolites, Clays & Nanostuctures. LC 96-32685. (Chemical Industries Ser.: Vol. 69). (Illus.). 744p. 1996. text 215.00 (*0-8247-9759-0*) Dekker.

Occelli, Mario L. & O'Connor, Paul, eds. Fluid Catalytic Cracking Vol. III: Materials & Processes. LC 94-33553. (Symposium Ser.: No. 571). (Illus.). 370p. 1994. text 110.00 (*0-8412-2996-1*, Pub. by Am Chemical) OUP.

Occelli, Mario L. & Robson, Harry E., eds. Zeolite Synthesis. LC 89-6884. (Symposium Ser.: No. 398). (Illus.). xi, 653p. 1989. 146.95 (*0-8412-1632-0*, Pub. by Am Chemical) OUP.

— Zeolite Synthesis. LC 89-6884. (ACS Symposium Ser.: No. 398). (Illus.). 663p. 1989. reprint ed. pap. 200.00 (*0-608-03146-1*, 206359900007) Bks Demand.

***Occhetti, Dianne R.** Do I Stay or Do I Go? How to Make a Wise Decision about Your Relationship. 2000. pap. 15.95 (*0-9673439-1-7*) InSync Commn.

Occhi, Debra J., jt. ed. see Palmer, Gary B.

Occhiello, Ernesto, jt. ed. see Garbassi, Fabio.

Occhiogrosso, James J. Clipper Developer's Library: Version 5.01. 2nd ed. Leventhal, Lance A., ed. (Lance A. Leventhal Microtrend Ser.). 624p. (Orig.). 1992. pap. 44.95 (*0-915391-69-4*) Slawson Comm.

— Clipper Developer's Library: Version 5.2. 3rd ed. Leventhal, Lance A., ed. LC 93-15438. (Lance A. Leventhal Microtrend Ser.). 624p. (Orig.). 1993. pap. 44.95 (*0-915391-82-1*) Slawson Comm.

Occhiogrosso, Michael G. & Frankel, Martin R. Arbitron Replication II: A Study of the Reliability of Radio Ratings. (Illus.). 148p. (Orig.). 1982. 3.00 (*0-942720-02-4*); pap. 1.50 (*0-942720-03-2*) Fishergate.

***Occhiogrosso, Neill.** Enterprise Development Using COBRA & Java: A4, Version 3.07. Lane, Susan M., ed. (CIW Enterprise Developer Track A4 Ser.). (Illus.). 1999. pap. write for info. (*1-58143-080-9*) Prosoft I-net.

— Enterprise Development Using CORBA & Java: Version 3.07. Lane, Susan M., ed. (CIW Enterprise Developer Track Ser.). (Illus.). 1999. pap. write for info. (*1-58143-044-2*) Prosoft I-net.

Occhiogrosso, Peter. The Joy of Sects: A Spirited Guide to the World's Religious Traditions. (Illus.). 656p. 1997. pap. 21.95 (*0-385-42565-1*, Image Bks) Doubleday.

Occhiogrosso, Peter, jt. auth. see Brodell, James D.

Occhiogrosso, Peter, jt. auth. see Roth, Ron.

Occhionero, Franco. Birth of the Universe & Fundamental Physics: Proceedings of the International Workshop Held in Rome, Italy, 18-21 May 1994, Vol. 455. LC 95-23395. (Lecture Notes in Physics Ser.). 1995. 92.95 (*3-540-60024-8*) Spr-Verlag.

Occhuogrosso, Peter, jt. auth. see Roth, Ron.

Occidental College Staff. Of Excellence & Equity: The 1990 Report of the Occidental College Strategic Planning Steering Committee. (Illus.). 102p. 1991. pap. write for info. (*0-940349-02-7*) Occi Coll ERC.

Occomore, D. Number, Please! History of the London Telephone. 1995. pap. 20.00 (*0-88734-913-7*) Players Pr.

OCCP Health Ser. Staff. Pestline, 2 vols., 1. 1991. text. write for info. (*0-442-00697-7*, VNR) Wiley.

— Pestline, 2 vols., 2. 1991. text. write for info. (*0-442-00698-5*, VNR) Wiley.

Occupational Safety & Health Administration Staff. Hazard Communication Standard Inspection Manual. 4th ed. 180p. 1993. pap. text 79.00 (*0-86587-365-8*) Gov Insts.

— OSHA Field Inspection Reference Manual. 144p. 1995. pap. text 69.00 (*0-86587-426-3*) Gov Insts.

— OSHA Regulated Hazardous Substances: Health, Toxicity, Economic & Technological Data, 2 vols., Set. LC 90-6751. (Illus.). 2294p. 1990. 195.00 (*0-8155-1240-6*) Noyes.

— Process Safety Management Standard Inspection Manual. 2nd ed. 120p. 1994. pap. text 69.00 (*0-86587-427-1*) Gov Insts.

— Standards, Interpretations & Audit Criteria for Performance of Occupational Health Programs. 218p. 1976. 50.00 (*0-932627-15-3*) Am Indus Hygiene.

OCDE Staff. Energy Glossary: Glossaire de l'Energie. (ENG & FRE.). 354p. 1983. pap. 65.00 (*0-7859-4868-6*) Fr & Eur.

— English-French Glossary of the Environment. (ENG & FRE.). 500p. 1995. 250.00 (*0-7859-9275-8*) Fr & Eur.

— Glossaire de l'Agriculture: Anglais-Francais. (ENG & FRE.). 262p. 1982. pap. 49.95 (*0-7859-4908-9*) Fr & Eur.

— Glossaire de l'Economie: Glossary of the Economy: English - French. (ENG & FRE.). 616p. 1992. 195.00 (*0-8288-9195-8*, 9264237453) Fr & Eur.

— Glossaire de l'Energie Nucleaire: Glossary of Nuclear Energy: English - French. (ENG & FRE.). 914p. 1992. 195.00 (*0-8288-9196-6*, 9264237461) Fr & Eur.

Ocean County Historical Society Staff. Along the Toms River. (Images of America Ser.). 128p. 1996. pap. 16.99 (*0-7524-0257-9*) Arcadia Publng.

— Down Shore from Manahawkin to New Gretna. (Images of America Ser.). 1999. pap. 16.99 (*0-7524-0832-1*) Arcadia Publng.

Ocean, Joan. Dolphin Connection: Interdimensional Ways of Living. LC 89-81370. (Illus.). 144p. 1996. reprint ed. pap. 14.95 (*0-9625058-9-7*) Dolphin Connection.

— Dolphins into the Future. 208p. 1997. pap. 16.00 (*0-9625058-8-9*) Dolphin Connection.

Ocean Studies Board, National Research Council Sta. The Ocean's Role in Global Change: Progress of Major Research Programs. 96p. (Orig.). (C). 1994. pap. text 25.00 (*0-309-05043-X*) Natl Acad Pr.

Ocean Studies Board National Research Council Staf. Oceanography & Naval Special Warfare: Opportunities & Challenges. 100p. 1997. pap. text 39.00 (*0-309-05930-5*) Natl Acad Pr.

***Ocean Studies Board Staff & National Research Council Staff.** Oceanography & Mine Warfare. 2000. pap. 26.25 (*0-309-06798-7*) Natl Acad Pr.

***Ocean Studies Board Staff, et al.** Marine Mammals & Low-Frequency Sound: Progress since 1994. 160p. 2000. pap. 35.00 (*0-309-06886-X*) Natl Acad Pr.

Ocean Studies Board Staff, jt. auth. see National Research Council Staff.

Ocean, Suellen. The Acorn Mouse Vol. 1: A Children's Intro to Eating Acorns. large type ed. LC 98-65375. (Illus.). 15p. (J). (gr. k-5). 1999. pap. 3.95 (*0-9651140-4-X*) Ocean Hose.

— Acorns & Eat'em: How-To Vegetarian Cookbook for Acorns. large type ed. (Illus.). 86p. (Orig.). 1993. pap. 11.55 (*0-9651140-0-7*) Ocean Hose.

— Poor Jonny's Cookbook: A Natural Foods Vegetarian Survivalist Cookbook. (Illus.). 130p. 1999. pap. 16.00 (*0-9651140-3-1*) Ocean Hose.

Ocean, Suellen & Hose, Jon. The Common Sense Guide to Good Sex. large type ed. LC 96-92642. (Illus.). 1997. pap. 14.95 (*0-9651140-2-3*) Ocean Hose.

Oceana Publications, Inc. Staff. Constitutions of the U. S. National & State, 7 vols. 2nd ed. 1974. ring bd. 750.00 (*0-379-00186-1*) Oceana.

Oceana Publications, Inc. Staff, ed. Customs Law & Administration: Statutes, 2 vols. 1993. ring bd. 200.00 (*0-379-20872-5*) Oceana.

— Customs Law & Administration: Treaties, 2 binders. LC 97-17874. 1997. ring bd. 200.00 (*0-379-20873-3*) Oceana.

Oceanic Engineering Society (U.S.), jt. auth. see Oceans '98.

Oceanic Society Staff. Field Guide to the Gray Whale. (Sasquatch Field Guide Ser.). (Illus.). 50p. 1989. reprint ed. pap. 6.95 (*0-912365-25-0*) Sasquatch Bks.

Oceanic Society Staff, et al. Field Guide to the Humpback Whale. LC 93-26808. (Sasquatch Field Guide Ser.). (Illus.). 48p. 1993. pap. 5.95 (*0-912365-93-5*) Sasquatch Bks.

Oceano Staff. Diccionario Enciclopedico Exito, 8 vols. (SPA.). 4044p. 1990. write for info. (*0-7859-5044-3*) Fr & Eur.

— Diccionario Enciclopedico Exito, Vol. 1. (SPA.). 456p. 1990. 250.00 (*0-7859-6311-1*, 8477644683) Fr & Eur.

— Diccionario Enciclopedico Exito, Vol. 2. (SPA.). 435p. 1991. 250.00 (*0-7859-6299-9*, 8477640467) Fr & Eur.

— Diccionario Enciclopedico Exito, Vol. 3. 458p. 1991. 250.00 (*0-7859-6300-6*, 8477640475) Fr & Eur.

— Diccionario Enciclopedico Exito, Vol. 4. (SPA.). 468p. 1991. 250.00 (*0-7859-6301-4*, 8477640483) Fr & Eur.

— Diccionario Enciclopedico Exito, Vol. 5. (SPA.). 480p. 1991. 250.00 (*0-7859-6302-2*, 8477640491) Fr & Eur.

— Diccionario Enciclopedico Exito, Vol. 6. (SPA.). 736p. 1990. 250.00 (*0-7859-6496-7*) Fr & Eur.

— Diccionario Enciclopedico Exito, Vol. 8. (SPA.). 508p. 1990. 250.00 (*0-7859-6313-8*, 8477644756) Fr & Eur.

— Diccionario Enciclopedico Oceano, 5 vols., Set. 1990. 695.00 (*0-7859-6303-0*, 8477640998) Fr & Eur.

— Diccionario Enciclopedico Oceano, Vol. 1. (SPA.). 424p. 1990. 150.00 (*0-7859-6304-9*, 8477641005) Fr & Eur.

— Diccionario Enciclopedico Oceano, Vol. 2. (SPA.). 424p. 1990. 150.00 (*0-7859-6305-7*, 8477641013) Fr & Eur.

— Diccionario Enciclopedico Oceano, Vol. 3. (SPA.). 424p. 1990. 150.00 (*0-7859-6495-9*); 150.00 (*0-7859-6306-5*, 8477641021) Fr & Eur.

— Diccionario Enciclopedico Oceano, Vol. 5. (SPA.). 364p. 1990. 150.00 (*0-7859-6307-3*, 8477641048) Fr & Eur.

— Diccionario Espanol-Ingles, Ingles-Espanol, 2 vols., Set. (ENG & SPA.). 1989. 195.00 (*0-7859-6308-1*, 8477644454) Fr & Eur.

— Diccionario Espanol-Ingles, Ingles-Espanol, Vol. 2. (ENG & SPA.). 484p. 1989. 105.00 (*0-7859-6310-3*, 8477644470) Fr & Eur.

— Enciclopedia de la Ciencia y de la Tecnica, 8 vols. 3rd ed. (SPA.). 3191p. 1987. 695.00 (*0-7859-5073-7*) Fr & Eur.

— Enciclopedia de la Ciencia y de la Tecnica: Encyclopedia of Science & Technology, 4 vols. (SPA.). 3063p. 1982. 175.00 (*0-7859-5052-4*) Fr & Eur.

— Enciclopedia General Basica Visual, 5 vols., Set. 1983. 595.00 (*0-8288-2020-1*, S39879) Fr & Eur.

Oceanor Staff. Environmental Conditions in the Barents Sea. 1989. pap. 250.00 (*82-7257-286-9*, Pub. by Oljedirektoratet); pap. 250.00 (*82-7257-285-0*, Pub. by Oljedirektoratet); pap. 250.00 (*82-7257-272-9*, Pub. by Oljedirektoratet) St Mut.

— Environmental Data Collection in the Barents Sea in 1985. 277p. 1988. pap. 250.00 (*82-7257-257-5*, Pub. by Oljedirektoratet) St Mut.

Oceans '98 & Oceanic Engineering Society (U.S.). Oceans '98: Conference Proceedings : 28 September-1 October, 1998, Nice, France, Acropoils Convention Center. LC 98-86363. 1853 p. 1998. write for info. (*0-7803-5048-0*) IEEE Standards.

Ochangco, Armando C. Rationality in Economic Thought: Methodological Ideas on the History of Political Economy. LC 98-23714. (Advances in Economic Methodology Ser.). 352p. 1999. 100.00 (*1-85898-955-8*) E Elgar.

***Ocha'ni Lele.** The Secrets of Afro-Cuban Divination: How to Cast the Diloggun, the Oracle of the Orishas. 304p. 2000. pap. 16.95 (*0-89281-810-7*, Destiny Bks) Inner Tradit.

Ochart, Yvonne. El Fuego de las Cosas. LC 90-36240. (SPA., Illus.). 173p. (Orig.). 1990. pap. 7.50 (*0-8477-3619-9*) U of PR Pr.

Ochawa. Earth Reinforcement, Vol. 1. 1992. 107.00 (*90-5410-094-X*) Ashgate Pub Co.

Ochberg, Frank M. Post-Traumatic Therapy & Victims of Violence. LC 87-26877. (Psychosocial Stress Ser.: No. 11). 384p. 1988. text 47.95 (*0-87630-490-0*) Brunner-Mazel.

Ochberg, Frank M., ed. Victims of Terrorism. LC 82-2572. (Special Studies in National & International Terrorism). 201p. 1982. pap. text 43.00 (*0-89158-463-3*) Westview.

Ochberg, Richard L. Psychobiography & Life Narratives. McAdams, Dan P., ed. LC 88-21922. 325p. 1988. pap. text 27.95 (*0-8223-0892-4*) Duke.

Ochberg, Richard L., jt. ed. see Rosenwald, George C.

***Oches, Norm & Nkomo, Stella.** The Teaching Bridge: A Skills Manual for Part-Time Teachers in Today's Colleges & Universities. (Illus.). 250p. 1999. pap. 29.95 (*0-9672951-0-6*, 50699) Arizona Mission Pr.

***Ochester, Betsy, ed.** Look What You Can Make with Egg Cartons. LC 00-100007. (Illus.). 48p. (J). (ps-7). 2000. pap. 5.95 (*1-56397-906-3*) Boyds Mills Pr.

Ochester, Ed. Changing the Name to Ochester. LC 87-71455. (Poetry Ser.). 1988. pap. 11.95 (*0-88748-069-1*) Carnegie-Mellon.

— Dancing on the Edges of Knives: Poems. LC 73-85458. (Breakthrough Bks.). 64p. 1973. text 18.95 (*0-8262-0153-9*) U of Mo Pr.

— Miracle Mile. LC 83-72900. 1984. pap. 11.95 (*0-915604-89-2*) Carnegie-Mellon.

— Miracle Mile. LC 83-72900. 1984. 20.95 (*0-915604-88-4*) Carnegie-Mellon.

***Ochester, Ed.** Snow White Horses: Selected Poems, 1973-1988. (Poetry Ser.: Vol. 2). (Illus.). 97p. 2000. pap. 14.95 (*0-9669419-1-8*) Autumn Hse Pr.

Ochester, Ed & Oresick, Peter, eds. The Pittsburgh Book of Contemporary American Poetry. LC 92-50846. (Poetry Ser.). (Illus.). 416p. (Orig.). (C). 1993. pap. 15.95 (*0-8229-5506-7*); text 29.95 (*0-8229-3752-2*) U of Pittsburgh Pr.

Ochi, Hironobu, et al, eds. Brain, Heart & Tumor Imaging: Updated PET & MRI: Proceedings of the 2nd International Osaka City University Symposium, Osaka, Japan, 2-4 October 1994. LC 95-25119. (International Congress Ser.: No. 1090). 208p. 1995. 158.75 (*0-444-82155-4*) Elsevier.

Ochi, Michel K. Applied Probability & Stochastic Processes in Engineering & the Physical Sciences. LC 89-34352. (Probability & Mathematical Statistics Ser.). 520p. 1990. 174.95 (*0-471-85742-4*) Wiley.

— Ocean Waves: The Stochastic Approach. LC 97-16355. (Ocean Technology Ser.: No. 6). (Illus.). 332p. (C). 1998. text 110.00 (*0-521-56378-X*) Cambridge U Pr.

Ochi, S., et al. Charge-Coupled Device Technology. (Japanese Technology Reviews Ser.: Vol. 30). 208p. 1997. pap. text 42.00 (*90-5699-001-2*) Gordon & Breach.

Ochiai. Earth Reinforcement, Vol. 2. 1992. 107.00 (*90-5410-095-8*) Ashgate Pub Co.

Ochiai, Derek, jt. auth. see Ochiai, Hidy.

Ochiai, E. I. General Principles of Biochemistry of the Elements. LC 87-20236. (Biochemistry of the Elements Ser.: Vol. 7). (Illus.). 482p. (C). 1987. text 120.00 (*0-306-42647-1*, Kluwer Plenum) Kluwer Academic.

Ochiai, Hidetoshi. Earth Reinforcement: Proceedings of the International Symposium, Fukuoka, Kyushu, Japan, 12-14 November 1996, 2 vols. Yasufuju, N. et al, eds. (Illus.). 1200p. (C). 1996. text 194.00 (*90-5410-833-9*, Pub. by A A Balkema) Ashgate Pub Co.

Ochiai, Hidetoshi, et al, eds. Earth Reinforcement Practice: Proceedings of the International Symposium on Earth Reinforcement Practice Fukuoka, Kyushu, Japan 11-13 November 1992, 2 vols., Set. (Illus.). 1036p. (C). 1992. text 207.00 (*90-5410-093-1*, Pub. by A A Balkema) Ashgate Pub Co.

Ochiai, Hidetoshi, et al. Earth Reinforcement Practice: International Conference on Earth Reinforcement (1996: Fukuoka, Japan), Vol. 1. 855p. 97.00 (*90-5410-834-7*, Pub. by A A Balkema) Ashgate Pub Co.

Ochiai, Hidy. The Essence of Self-Defense. 224p. 1979. pap. 15.95 (*0-8092-7377-2*, 73772) NTC Contemp Pub Co.

— Hidy Ochiai's Complete Book of Self-Defense. (Illus.). 352p. (Orig.). 1991. pap. 18.95 (*0-8092-4055-6*, 405560, Contemporary Bks) NTC Contemp Pub Co.

***Ochiai, Hidy.** Way to Victory: The Annotated Book of Five Rings. LC 00-27016. (Illus.). 248p. 2000. 27.95 (*1-58567-038-3*, Pub. by Overlook Pr) Penguin Putnam.

Ochiai, Hidy & Ochiai, Derek. Hidy Ochiai's Self-Defense for Kids. LC 98-12740. (Illus.). 224p. 1999. pap. 16.95 (*0-8092-2893-9*, 289390, Contemporary Bks) NTC Contemp Pub Co.

Ochiai, K., et al, eds. Endocrine Correlates of Reproduction. (Illus.). xii, 320p. 1984. 97.95 (*0-387-13514-6*) Spr-Verlag.

Ochiai, Kingo, tr. see Mori Ogai, pseud.

Ochiai, R., jt. ed. see Fukushima, K.

Ochiai, Shojiro, ed. Mechanical Properties of Metallic Composites. (Materials Engineering Ser.: Vol. 7). (Illus.). 808p. 1993. text 235.00 (*0-8247-9116-9*) Dekker.

Ochiai, T., jt. auth. see Noguchi, J.

Ochiai Yasufuku. Earth Reinforcement, Vol. 2. 60p. 1997. 97.00 (*90-5410-835-5*) Ashgate Pub Co.

Ochieng, William R. People of the South-Western Highlands: Gusii. (Kenya People Ser.). (Illus.). 34p. (YA). (gr. 6-9). 1991. pap. write for info. (*0-237-49898-7*) EVN1 UK.

Ochildiev, David. David Ochildiev, the Nebushadnezzar's Captives. Malisova, Nataliya, ed. (Illus.). 336p. 1998. pap. 10.00 (*0-9658114-4-1*) Mir Collection.

***Ochiltree, Dianne.** Cats Add Up! LC 97-43659. (Hello Reader! Math Ser.). (Illus.). 48p. (J). (gr. 1-3). 1998. pap. 3.99 (*0-590-12005-0*, Pub. by Scholastic Inc) Penguin Putnam.

***Ochiltree, Dianne & Burns, Marilyn.** Bart's Amazing Charts. LC 99-20216. (Hello Reader! Math Ser.). (Illus.). 32p. (J). (gr. 1-3). 1999. 3.99 (*0-439-09953-6*) Scholastic Inc.

***Ochinko, Walter.** Adults with Severe Disabilities: Federal & State Approaches for Personal Care & Other Services. (Illus.). 87p. (C). 2000. pap. text 20.00 (*0-7881-8809-7*) DIANE Pub.

Ochkin, V. N., jt. ed. see Basov, N. G.

Ochkin, V. N., jt. ed. see Witteman, W. J.

O

***Ochmanek, David A.** NATO's Future: Implications for U. S. Military Capabilities & Posture. LC 99-86504. xiii, 31p. 2000. 7.50 (*0-8330-2809-X*, MR-1162-AF) Rand Corp.

Ochmanek, David A., et al. To Find & Not to Yield: How Advances in Information & Firepower Can Transform Theater Warfare. LC 98-16852. (Illus.). 105p. 1998. pap. 15.00 (*0-8330-2612-7*, MR-958-AF) Rand Corp.

Ochmanek, David A., jt. auth. see Kent, Glen A.

Ochmanek, David A., jt. ed. see Khalilzad, Zalmay M.

Ochnio, Constance M., et al. Cemetery Inscriptions, St. Stanislaus Kostka Cemetery, Dabrowa Bialostocka, Poland. LC 89-61487. (Illus.). 130p. 1989. write for info. (*0-945440-02-2*) Pol Geneal CT.

Ochnio, Constance M., jt. auth. see Shea, Jonathan D.

Ochoa, Anna, jt. auth. see Engle, Shirley H.

Ochoa, Carlos M. The Potatoes of South America: Bolivia. Ugent, Donald, tr. (Illus.). 570p. (C). 1991. text 155.00 (*0-521-38024-3*) Cambridge U Pr.

Ochoa, Emilio, tr. see Olsen, Stephen B., et al.

***Ochoa, Enrique.** Feeding Mexico: The Political Uses of Food Since 1910. LC 99-87310. (Latin American Silhouettes Ser.). 296p. 2000. 55.00 (*0-8420-2812-9*) Scholarly Res Inc.

Ochoa, Esperanza. Siete Del Valle: A Collection of Rio Grande Valley Stories. De La Fuente, Patricia, ed. (Illus.). 209p. 1995. pap. text 15.95 (*0-938738-14-3*) U TX Pan Am Pr.

Ochoa, George. The Fall of Mexico City. (Turning Points in American History Ser.). (Illus.). 64p. (J). (gr. 5 up). 1989. lib. bdg. 14.95 (*0-382-09836-6*) Silver Burdett Pr.

— The Fall of Mexico City. (Turning Points in American History Ser.). (Illus.). 64p. (YA). (gr. 5 up). 1989. pap. 7.95 (*0-382-09853-6*) Silver Burdett Pr.

— The Fall of Quebec & the French & Indian War. (Turning Points in American History Ser.). (Illus.). 64p. (J). (gr. 5 up). 1990. lib. bdg. 14.95 (*0-382-09954-0*) Silver Burdett Pr.

— The Fall of Quebec & the French & Indian War. (Turning Points in American History Ser.). (Illus.). 64p. (YA). (gr. 5 up). 1990. pap. 7.95 (*0-382-09950-8*) Silver Burdett Pr.

***Ochoa, George.** Fitzroy Dearborn Chronology of Ideas. 450p. 1999. lib. bdg. 75.00 (*1-57958-162-5*) Fitzroy Dearborn.

Ochoa, George. The New York Public Library Amazing Hispanic American History: A Book of Answers for Kids. LC 98-23797. (New York Public Library Answer Books for Kids Ser.). (Illus.). 192p. (YA). (gr. 6). 1998. pap. 12.95 (*0-471-19204-X*) Wiley.

***Ochoa, George & Corey, Melinda. Facts about the 20th Century. LC 99-45221. (Facts About Ser.). 625p. 2000. 85.00 (*0-8242-0960-5*) Wilson.**
A comprehensive, alphabetical compilation of important developments that shaped the century, encompassing more than 300 topics, profiles of more than 800 noteworthy figures, plus encompassing on nations & a helpful timeline. To order: H.W.Wilson - 1-800-367-6770 (1-718-588-8400 outside U.S. & Canada); custserv@hwwilson.com, or visit www.hwwilson.com. *Publisher Paid Annotation.*

Ochoa, George & Corey, Melinda. Timeline Book of Ideas. (Timeline Bks.). (Illus.). 416p. 1996. pap. 12.00 (*0-345-38266-8*) Ballantine Pub Grp.

— The Timeline Book of the Arts. (Illus.). 464p. 1995. pap. 12.00 (*0-345-38264-1*) Ballantine Pub Grp.

— The Wilson Chronology of Ideas: A Record of Philosophical, Political, Theological & Social Thought from Ancient Times to the Present. LC 97-17591. 431p. 1998. 160.00 (*0-8242-0935-4*) Wilson.

— The Wilson Chronology of Science & Technology: A Record of Scientific Discovery & Technological Invention from Ancient Times to the Present. LC 97-22060. 440p. 1997. 60.00 (*0-8242-0933-8*) Wilson.

— The Wilson Chronology of the Arts: A Record of Human Creativity from Ancient Times to the Present. LC 97-23541. 476p. 1998. 60.00 (*0-8242-0934-6*) Wilson.

Ochoa, George & Osier, Jeffrey. The Writer's Guide to Creating a Science Fiction Universe. 336p. 1993. 18.95 (*0-89879-536-2*, Wrtrs Digest Bks) F & W Pubns Inc.

Ochoa, George, jt. auth. see Corey, Melinda.

Ochoa, George, ed. see King, Stephen.

Ochoa, Geroge. The Assassination of Julius Caesar. (Turning Points in World History Ser.). (Illus.). 64p. (YA). (gr. 7 up). 1991. pap. 7.95 (*0-382-24136-3*); lib. bdg. 14.95 (*0-382-24130-4*) Silver Burdett Pr.

Ochoa, Holly B., jt. ed. see Palmer, Beverly W.

Ochoa, Jose L., jt. auth. see Rosenbaum, Richard B.

Ochoa, Laurie, jt. auth. see Silverton, Nancy.

Ochoa, Lorenzo. Historia Prehispanica de la Huaxteca. 2nd ed. 182p. 1984. pap. 3.50 (*968-837-076-2*, UN020) UPLAAP.

Ochoa, Orlando A. Growth, Trade, & Endogenous Technology: A Study of OECD Manufacturing. LC 96-4259. 198p. 1996. text 75.00 (*0-312-15845-9*) St Martin.

Ochoa, Salvador Hector, jt. ed. see Tashakkori, Abbas.

Ochojski, Paul M. Monarch Notes on Dickens' Hard Times. (Orig.). (C). 3.95 (*0-671-00823-4*, Arco) Macmillan Gen Ref.

Ocholla-Ayayo, Andrev B. Traditional Ideology & Etics among the Southern Luo. 248p. 1976. write for info. (*91-7106-100-2*, Pub. by Nordic Africa) Transaction Pubs.

Ochorowicz, Julien. Mental Dominance: Classics of Personal Magnetism & Hypnotism. 300p. 1991. reprint ed. 29.98 (*0-941683-04-4*) Instant Improve.

Ochorowicz-Monatowa, Marja. Polish Cookery. Karsavina, Jean, ed. & tr. by. (International Cookbook Ser.). 1968. 15.00 (*0-517-50526-6*, Crown) Crown Pub Group.

Ochosa, Orlino A. & Hilario, Frank A. Pio Del Pilar & Other Heroes. LC 97-946860. xvii, 220 p. 1997. write for info. (*971-10-1009-7*, Pub. by New Day Pub) Cellar.

Ochotta, Emil S. Practical Synthesis of High-Performance Analog Circuits. LC 98-33724. 1998. 120.00 (*0-7923-8237-4*) Kluwer Academic.

Ochowicz, Jim, jt. auth. see Alexander, Don.

Ochroch, Ruth, ed. The Diagnosis & Treatment of Minimal Brain Dysfunction in Children: A Clinical Approach. LC 80-15858. 303p. 1981. 45.95 (*0-87705-503-3*, Kluwer Acad Hman Sci) Kluwer Academic.

Ochs. Introduction to Speech. 2nd ed. (C). 1996. pap. text 28.00 (*0-15-504408-7*) Harcourt.

Ochs & Slobin, Dan I., eds. Variation & Error: A Sociolinguistic Approach to Language Acquisition in Samoa. (Crosslinguistic Study of Language Acquisition Ser.: Vol. 1). 1986. pap. 14.95 (*0-89859-847-8*) L Erlbaum Assocs.

Ochs, Bill. The Clarke Tin Whistle. (Illus.). 80p. (Orig.). (J). (gr. 3 up). 1988. pap. 6.95 (*0-9623456-0-1*); pap. 14.95 incl. audio (*0-9623456-5-2*) Pnnywhstlrs Pr.

— The Clarke Tin Whistle, Incl. Tin Whistle. (Illus.). 80p. (Orig.). (J). (gr. 3 up). 1988. pap. 24.95 incl. audio (*0-9623456-2-8*) Pnnywhstlrs Pr.

Ochs, Carol. The Noah Paradox: Time As Burden, Time As Blessing. LC 90-50969. (C). 1991. text 23.00 (*0-268-01470-1*) U of Notre Dame Pr.

— Song of the Self: Biblical Spirituality & Human Holiness. LC 94-4924. 112p. (Orig.). (C). 1994. pap. 11.00 (*1-56338-096-X*) TPI PA.

— Women & Spirituality. 2nd ed. LC 96-29291. (New Feminist Perspectives Ser.: No. 67). 256p. 1996. 60.50 (*0-8476-8329-X*); pap. 24.95 (*0-8476-8330-3*) Rowman.

Ochs, Carol & Olitzky, Kerry M. Jewish Spiritual Guidance: Finding Our Way to God. LC 97-4877. (Religion in Practice Ser.). 228p. 1997. 22.50 (*0-7879-1059-7*) Jossey-Bass.

Ochs, Carol, et al. Paths of Faithfulness: Personal Essays on Jewish Spirituality. LC 97-5078. 1997. 8.95 (*0-88125-596-3*) Ktav.

Ochs, Carol, ed. see Belford, Fontaine M.

Ochs, Carol P. When I'm Alone. (Illus.). 32p. (J). (ps-3). 1993. lib. bdg. 14.95 (*0-87614-752-X*, Carolrhoda) Lerner Pub.

— When I'm Alone. (Illus.). 32p. (J). (ps-3). 1993. pap. 6.95 (*0-87614-620-5*, Carolrhoda) Lerner Pub.

***Ochs, Cathy & Perry, Marge.** The Secret Weight-Loss Scrolls: 4 Simple Steps to Eating 30-40-30 for Life! Cicero, Christina, ed. (Illus.). 251p. 1999. pap. 29.95 (*0-9674975-0-7*) Redding Weight.

Ochs, Donovan J. Consolatory Rhetoric: Grief, Symbol, & Ritual in the Greco-Roman Era. LC 93-16393. (Studies in Rhetoric & Communication). 144p. (C). 1993. text 29.95 (*0-87249-885-9*) U of SC Pr.

Ochs, Donovan J., et al. A Brief Introduction to Speech. 2nd ed. 240p. (C). 1983. pap. text 18.75 (*0-15-505585-2*) Harcourt Coll Pubs.

Ochs, Ekkehard, et al, eds. Musica Baltica: Interregionale Musikkulturelle Beziehungen im Ostseeraum. (Greifswalder Beitrage zur Musikwissenschaft Ser.: Bd. 4). (GER., Illus.). 322p. 1996. 57.95 (*3-631-30480-3*) P Lang Pubng.

Ochs, Elinor, et al, eds. Interaction & Grammar. (Studies in Interactional Sociolinguistics: No. 13). (Illus.). 480p. (C). 1997. text 74.95 (*0-521-55225-7*) Cambridge U Pr.

Ochs, Elinor, jt. auth. see Capps, Lisa.

Ochs, Elinor, jt. ed. see Jacoby, Sally.

Ochs, Ginger. Recognition & Interpretation of ECG Rhythms. 3rd rev. ed. LC 96-29695. (C). 1997. pap. text 39.95 (*0-8385-4323-5*, A4323-0) Appleton & Lange.

Ochs, Hans D., et al, eds. Genetics of Primary Immunodeficiency Diseases: A Molecular & Genetic Approach. LC 97-46505. (Illus.). 544p. 1998. text 139.50 (*0-19-510486-2*) OUP.

Ochs, Linnea L. & Van Der Reyden, Susan, eds. Secretarial Word Finder. LC 83-8640. 540p. 1983. 19.95 (*0-13-798157-0*, Busn) P-H.

Ochs, Martin. The African Press. 155p. 1987. pap. 17.50 (*977-424-128-2*, Pub. by Am Univ Cairo Pr) Col U Pr.

Ochs, Michael. 1000 Record Covers. (Klotz Ser.). 1996. pap. 29.99 (*3-8228-8595-9*) Taschen Amer.

Ochs, Michael, ed. Music Librarianship in America. 144p. 1991. pap. 22.00 (*0-8108-3521-5*) Scarecrow.

***Ochs, Otto Osip.** Season of the Sacred Fool. LC 00-32445. 72p. 2000. pap. 14.95 (*0-7734-3408-9*) E Mellen.

***Ochs, Paul G.** Tapes. 284p. 2000. pap. 14.95 (*0-595-09687-5*, Writers Club Pr) iUniversecom.

Ochs, Peter. Peirce, Pragmatism, & the Logic of Scripture. 372p. (C). 1998. text 64.95 (*0-521-57041-7*) Cambridge U Pr.

Ochs, Peter, ed. The Return to Scripture in Judaism & Christianity: Essays in Postcritical Scriptural Interpretation. LC 93-24518. (Theological Inquiries Ser.). 384p. (Orig.). 1993. pap. 18.95 (*0-8091-3425-X*) Paulist Pr.

***Ochs, Peter, ed.** Reviewing the Covenant: Eugene Borowitz & the Postmodern Renewal of Jewish Theology. LC 99-37866. (C). 2000. text 59.50 (*0-7914-4533-X*); pap. text 19.95 (*0-7914-4534-8*) State U NY Pr.

***Ochs, Peter, et al.** Reasoning after Revelation: Dialogues in Postmodern Jewish Philosophy. LC 98-20348. (Radical Traditions Ser.). (C). 1998. 28.00 (*0-8133-3506-X*, Pub. by Westview) HarpC.

Ochs, Peter J., 2nd. Maverick Guide to Oman. LC 98-145143. (Illus.). 84p. 1999. pap. 19.95 (*1-56554-241-X*) Pelican.

Ochs, Peter J., 3rd. Maverick Guide to Oman. 2nd ed. (Maverick Guides Ser.). (Illus.). 382p. 1999. pap. 19.95 (*1-56554-687-3*) Pelican.

Ochs, Robyn, ed. Bisexual Resource Guide. 3rd rev. ed. (Illus.). 304p. (Orig.). 1999. pap. 12.95 (*0-9653881-2-3*, Pub. by Bisexual Res) Bookazine Co Inc.

***Ochs, Stephen J.** A Black Patriot & a White Priest: Captain Andre' Cailloux & Claude Paschal Maistre in Civil War New Orleans. LC 99-53403. (Conflicting Worlds Ser.). (Illus.). 328p. 2000. 39.95 (*0-8071-2531-8*) La State U Pr.

Ochs, Stephen J. Desegregating the Altar: The Josephites & the Struggle for Black Priests, 1871-1960. LC 89-48219. (C). 1993. pap. 16.95 (*0-8071-1859-1*) La State U Pr.

Ochs, Steven. Why Everyone Hates You. 96p. 1996. mass mkt. 5.99 (*0-7860-0223-9*, Pinncle Kensgtn) Kensgtn Pub Corp.

Ochs, Vanessa. Words on Fire: One Woman's Journey into the Sacred. 338p. 1992. pap. 12.00 (*0-15-698363-X*, Harvest Bks) Harcourt.

Ochs, Vanessa L. Words on Fire: One Woman's Journey into the Sacred. LC 99-29815. 368p. 1999. 22.00 (*0-8133-6718-2*, Pub. by Westview) HarpC.

Ochse, Orpha C. The History of the Organ in the United States. LC 73-22644. (Illus.). 512p. 1988. pap. 24.95 (*0-253-20495-X*, MB-495) Ind U Pr.

— Organists & Organ Playing in Nineteenth-Century France & Belgium. LC 94-2589. 512p. 1994. 39.95 (*0-253-34161-2*) Ind U Pr.

Ochse, Weston, jt. auth. see Whitman, David.

Ochsenbein, Urs. A New Owner's Guide to Rottweilers: AKC Rank #2. (New Owner's Guide to Ser.). (Illus.). 160p. Date not set. 12.95 (*0-7938-2750-7*, JG-101) TFH Pubns.

Ochsendorf, Falk R. & Fuchs, Jurgen, eds. Oxidative Stress in Male Infertility. 1995. 129.95 (*0-8493-4798-X*, 4798) CRC Pr.

Ochsenius, Claudio & Gruhn, Ruth, eds. Taima-Taima. 138p. 1992. pap. 11.00 (*1-55889-874-3*) Ctr Study First Am.

Ochsenwald, William. Religion, Society & the State in Arabia: The Hijaz under Ottoman Control, 1840-1908. LC 84-7498. (Illus.). 257p. reprint ed. pap. 79.70 (*0-608-09863-9*, 206982800006) Bks Demand.

Ochsenwald, William L. The Hijaz Railroad. LC 80-10505. (Illus.). 187p. reprint ed. pap. 58.00 (*0-8357-3137-5*, 203940000012) Bks Demand.

Ochsenwald, William L., jt. auth. see Fisher, Sydney N.

Ochshorn, Judith & Cole, Ellen, eds. Women's Spirituality, Women's Lives. LC 95-11386. 227p. 1995. 39.95 (*1-56024-722-3*); pap. 19.95 (*1-56023-065-7*, Harrington Park) Haworth Pr.

Ochsman, R. B., jt. ed. see Whitney, P.

Ochsner, et al. Tobacco & Marijuana. 1976. per. 16.00 (*0-88252-048-2*) Paladin Hse.

Ochsner, George H. The Rape of God. Ochsner, Virginia, ed. LC 90-84940. 396p. (Orig.). 1990. pap. 12.95 (*0-945201-16-8*) Gannam-Kubat.

Ochsner, J. Shaping Seattle Architecture: A Historical Guide to the Architects. LC 94-17618. (Illus.). 446p. 1994. 40.00 (*0-295-97365-X*) U of Wash Pr.

— Shaping Seattle Architecture: A Historical Guide to the Architects. LC 94-17618. (Illus.). 446p. 1994. reprint ed. pap. 24.95 (*0-295-97366-8*) U of Wash Pr.

Ochsner, Jeffrey K. H. H. Richardson: Complete Architectural Works. (Illus.). 424p. 1985. pap. text 45.00 (*0-262-65015-0*) MIT Pr.

Ochsner, Othon H., II. Ochsner Guide to the Finest Restaurants & Hotels in the World, 1997-98. 13th rev. ed. Orig. Title: Ochsner Pocket Guide to the Finest Restaurants in the World. (Illus.). 1997. per. 20.00 (*1-881546-03-9*) Ochsner Intl.

— Ochsner Pocket Guide to the Finest Restaurants in the World, 1992-93. 9th ed. (Illus.). 199p. (Orig.). 1992. pap. write for info. (*1-881546-00-4*) Ochsner Intl.

— Ochsner Pocket Guide to the Finest Restaurants in the World, 1993-94. 10th ed. (Illus.). 248p. 1993. pap. 20.00 (*1-881546-01-2*) Ochsner Intl.

— Ochsner Pocket Guide to the Finest Restaurants in the world, 1994-95. 11th ed. (Illus.). 256p. 1994. pap. 20.00 (*1-881546-02-0*) Ochsner Intl.

Ochsner, Robert S. Physical Eloquence & the Biology of Writing. LC 89-38062. (SUNY Series, Literacy, Culture, & Learning). 223p. 1990. pap. text 21.95 (*0-7914-0314-9*) State U NY Pr.

Ochsner, Robert S. Rhythm & Writing. LC 87-50836. vi, 140p. 1989. 35.00 (*0-87875-347-8*) Whitston Pub.

Ochsner, Virginia, ed. see Ochsner, George H.

Ochtrup, Monica. What I Cannot Say/I Will Say. (Minnesota Voices Project Ser.: Vol. 22). 76p. 1984. pap. 3.50 (*0-89823-059-4*) New Rivers Pr.

Ochu, Matthew, et al. Burning Desperation Sticks in the Gateway City. 70p. 1999. pap. 6.00 (*0-7392-0132-8*, PO3052) Morris Pubng.

Ochuizzo, jt. auth. see Ong.

Ochwat, John, jt. auth. see Kaun, David.

***Ociepka, Bob & Ratermann, Dale.** Basketball Playbook 2: More Plays from the Pros. LC 99-88336. (Illus.). 128p. 2000. pap. 14.95 (*0-8092-9870-8*, Contemporary Bks) NTC Contemp Pub Co.

Ociepka, Bob, jt. auth. see Ratermann, Dale.

Ociepka, Bruno, jt. auth. see Gagnon, Patricia J.

OCIME Staff, jt. auth. see ICS Staff.

OCIMF Staff. Anchoring Systems & Procedures for Large Tankers. (C). 1988. 80.00 (*0-900886-73-0*, Pub. by Witherby & Co) St Mut.

— Buoy Mooring Forum SPM Hose Ancillary Equipment Guide. 1975. 45.00 (*0-7855-1762-6*, Pub. by Witherby & Co) St Mut.

— Buoy Mooring Forum SPM Hose System Design Commentary. (C). 1975. 75.00 (*0-7855-3335-4*, Pub. by Witherby & Co) St Mut.

— Design & Construction Specification for Marine Loading Arms. 1986. 310.00 (*0-7855-1764-2*, Pub. by Witherby & Co) St Mut.

— Design & Construction Specification for Marine Loading Arms. (C). 1987. 315.00 (*0-7855-4684-7*, Pub. by Witherby & Co) St Mut.

— Design & Construction Specification for Marine Loading Arms. 1993. 120.00 (*1-85609-071-X*, Pub. by Witherby & Co) St Mut.

— Disabled Tankers: Report of Studies on Drift & Towage. 1981. 450.00 (*0-900886-63-3*, Pub. by Witherby & Co) St Mut.

— Drift Characteristics of Fifty Thousand to Seventy Thousand DWT Tankers. 1982. 180.00 (*0-900886-67-6*) St Mut.

— Drift Characteristics of Fifty Thousand to Seventy Thousand DWT Tankers. (C). 1982. 175.00 (*0-7855-3911-5*, Pub. by Witherby & Co) St Mut.

— Effect on the Operation of Tanker Terminals Following International Tanker Safety & Pollution Prevention Standards. (C). 1981. 24.00 (*0-900886-59-5*, Pub. by Witherby & Co) St Mut.

— Effective Mooring. (C). 1989. 95.00 (*0-948691-88-3*, Pub. by Witherby & Co) St Mut.

— Guide for the Handling, Storage Inspection & Testing of Hoses in the Field. Orig. Title: Buoy Mooring forum Hose Guide. 1993. text 150.00 (*1-85609-070-1*, Pub. by Witherby & Co) St Mut.

— Guide on Marine Terminal Fire Protection & Emergency Evacuation. (C). 1987. 200.00 (*0-948691-28-X*, Pub. by Witherby & Co) St Mut.

— Guide on Terminal Fire Protection & Emergency Evacuation. (C). 1987. 210.00 (*0-948691-30-1*, Pub. by Witherby & Co) St Mut.

— Guidelines & Recommendations for Safe Mooring of Large Ships at Piers & Sea Islands. 1993. 180.00 (*1-85609-041-8*, Pub. by Witherby & Co) St Mut.

— Hawser Guidelines Vol. 1: Guide to Purchasing Hawsers. 1987. 130.00 (*0-948691-31-X*, Pub. by Witherby & Co) St Mut.

— Hawser Guidelines Vol. 2: Procedures for Quality Control & Inspection During Production of Hawsers. (C). 1987. 95.00 (*0-948691-34-4*, Pub. by Witherby & Co) St Mut.

— Hawser Guidelines Vol. 3: Prototype Rope Testing. (C). 1987. 95.00 (*0-948691-35-2*, Pub. by Witherby & Co) St Mut.

— Hawser Test Report. 1982. 250.00 (*0-900886-68-4*, Pub. by Witherby & Co) St Mut.

— Hose Standards. (C). 1988. 100.00 (*0-900886-37-4*, Pub. by Witherby & Co) St Mut.

— Hose Standards. (C). 1990. 195.00 (*0-948691-98-0*, Pub. by Witherby & Co) St Mut.

— Inspection Guidelines for Bulk Oil Carriers. (C). 1989. 110.00 (*0-948691-92-1*, Pub. by Witherby & Co) St Mut.

— Inspection Guidelines for Bulk Oil Carriers. 1993. 55.00 (*1-85609-059-0*, Pub. by Witherby & Co) St Mut.

— Marine & Terminal Operations Survey Guidelines. (C). 1983. 90.00 (*0-900886-86-2*, Pub. by Witherby & Co) St Mut.

— Mooring Equipment Guidelines. 125p. (C). 1992. 195.00 (*1-85609-018-3*, Pub. by Witherby & Co) St Mut.

— Mooring Equipment Guidelines. 1997. pap. 180.00 (*1-85609-088-4*, Pub. by Witherby & Co) St Mut.

— Prediction of Wind & Current Loads on VLCCs. (C). 1977. 400.00 (*0-7855-4682-0*, Pub. by Witherby & Co) St Mut.

— Prediction of Wind & Current Loads on VLCCS. 1993. 240.00 (*1-85609-042-6*, Pub. by Witherby & Co) St Mut.

— Predictions of Wind & Current Loads on VLCC's. 1977. 360.00 (*0-7855-1776-6*, Pub. by Witherby & Co) St Mut.

— Recomendations on Equipment for the Towing of Disabled Tankers. 1981. 150.00 (*0-7855-1783-9*, Pub. by Witherby & Co) St Mut.

— Recommendation for Manifolds Refrigerated Liquefied Natural Gas Carriers, LNG. 1994. 70.00 (*1-85609-066-3*, Pub. by Witherby & Co) St Mut.

— Recommendations for Equipment Employed in the Mooring of Ships at Single Point Moorings. (C). 1988. 80.00 (*0-948691-56-5*, Pub. by Witherby & Co) St Mut.

— Recommendations for Equipment Employed in the Mooring of Ships at Single Point Moorings. (C). 1991. 170.00 (*1-85609-020-5*, Pub. by Witherby & Co) St Mut.

— Recommendations for Manifolds for Refrigerated Liquefied Gas Carriers for Cargoes from 0°C to Minus 104°C. (C). 1988. 80.00 (*0-7855-4681-2*, Pub. by Witherby & Co) St Mut.

— Recommendations for Manifolds for Refrigerated Liquified Gas Carriers for Cargos from 0 C to Minus 104 C. (C). 1987. 90.00 (*0-7855-3916-6*, Pub. by Witherby & Co) St Mut.

— Recommendations for Oil Tanker Manifolds & Associated Equipment. (C). 1991. 115.00 (*1-85609-017-5*, Pub. by Witherby & Co) St Mut.

— Recommendations on Equipment for the Towing of Disabled Tankers. (C). 1981. 160.00 (*0-900886-65-X*, Pub. by Witherby & Co) St Mut.

— Recommendations on Equipment for the Towing of Disabled Tankers. 1997. pap. 200.00 (*1-85609-096-5*, Pub. by Witherby & Co) St Mut.

— Safe Navigation Symposium Papers Washington, D. C. 1978. 198.00 (*0-7855-1784-7*, Pub. by Witherby & Co) St Mut.

— Safety Guide for Terminals Handling Ships Carrying Liquefied Gases in Bulk. (C). 1982. 275.00 (*0-900886-72-2*, Pub. by Witherby & Co) St Mut.

An Asterisk (*) at the beginning of an entry indicates that the title is appearing for the first time.

— Safety Guide for Terminals Handling Ships Carrying Liquefied Gases in Bulk. 1993. 100.00 (1-85609-057-4, Pub. by Witherby & Co) St Mut.
— Safety Inspection Guidelines & Terminal Safety Check List for Gas Carriers. (C). 1979. 95.00 (0-900886-43-9, Pub. by Witherby & Co) St Mut.
— Ship Information Questionnaire for Bulk Oil Carriers. (C). 1989. 85.00 (0-948691-91-3, Pub. by Witherby & Co) St Mut.
— Single Point Mooring Maintenance & Operations Guide. (C). 1985. 200.00 (0-900886-95-1, Pub. by Witherby & Co) St Mut.
— Single Point Mooring Maintenance & Operations Guide. 1993. 80.00 (1-85609-072-8, Pub. by Witherby & Co) St Mut.
— Single Point Morning: Maintenance & Operations Guide. 1985. 162.00 (0-7855-1786-3, Pub. by Witherby & Co) St Mut.
— SPM Hose Ancillary Equipment Guide. (C). 1987. 100.00 (0-948691-54-9, Pub. by Witherby & Co) St Mut.
— SPM Hose System Design Commentary. 1993. 70.00 (1-85609-027-2, Pub. by Witherby & Co) St Mut.
— Standardisation of Manifolds for Refrigerated Liquefied Gas Carriers (LNG) (C). 1979. 55.00 (0-7855-3652-3, Pub. by Witherby & Co) St Mut.
— Standards for Equipment Employed in the Mooring & Ships at Single Point Moorings. 1978. 36.00 (0-7855-1787-1, Pub. by Witherby & Co) St Mut.
— Standards for Oil Tanker Manifolds & Associated Equipment. (C). 1981. 95.00 (0-900886-64-1, Pub. by Witherby & Co) St Mut.
OCIMF Staff, ed. Buoy Mooring Forum Hose Guide. (C). 1974. 75.00 (0-7855-3913-1, Pub. by Witherby & Co) St Mut.
OCIMF Staff & IPIECA Staff. Oil Spills: Their Fate & Impact on the Marine Environment. 1980. 60.00 (0-900886-49-8, Pub. by Witherby & Co) St Mut.
OCIMF Staff & SIGGTO Staff. Prevention of Wind Loads on Large Liquified Gas Carriers. (C). 1985. 600.00 (0-7855-3919-0, Pub. by Witherby & Co) St Mut.
OCIMF Staff & SIGTTO Staff. Inspection Guidelines for Ships Carrying Liquefied Gases in Bulk. (C). 1990. 195.00 (0-948691-96-4, Pub. by Witherby & Co) St Mut.
— Prediction of Wind Loads on Large Liquefied Gas Carriers. (C). 1985. 600.00 (0-900886-97-8, Pub. by Witherby & Co) St Mut.
— Ship Information Questionnaire for Liquefied Gas Carriers. (C). 1990. 125.00 (0-948691-99-9, Pub. by Witherby & Co) St Mut.
OCIMF Staff & SSIGTTO Staff. Predictions of Wind Loads on Large Liquified Gas Carrers. 1987. 540.00 (0-7855-1777-4, Pub. by Witherby & Co) St Mut.
OCIMF Staff, et al. International Safety Guide for Oil Tankers & Terminals (ISGOTT) 4th ed. 1996. pap. 120.00 (1-85609-081-7, Pub. by Witherby & Co) St Mut.
OCIMF Staff, jt. auth. see ICS Staff.
***Ocitti, Jim.** Political Evolution & Democratic Practice in Uganda, 1952-1996. LC 99-53203. (African Studies: Vol. 51). 468p. 2000. 109.95 (0-7734-7860-4) E Mellen.
Ockeghem, Johannes. Johannes Ockeghem: Collected Works, Vol. I. 2nd rev. ed. Plamenac, Dragan, ed. (Studies & Documents). (Illus.). 124p. 1966. pap. 24.00 (1-878528-09-2) Am Musicological.
— Johannes Ockeghem: Collected Works, Vol. II. 2nd rev. ed. Plamenac, Dragan, ed. (Studies & Documents: Vol. 3). (Illus.). 118p. 1966. pap. 24.00 (1-878528-10-6) Am Musicological.
— Johannes Ockeghem: Collected Works, Vol. III. Wexler, Richard & Plamenac, Dragan, eds. (Studies & Documents: Vol. 7). (Illus.). 1992. pap. 85.00 (1-878528-02-5) Am Musicological.
Ockel, Gerhard. Guilt. (C). 1951. pap. 4.00 (0-87574-061-8) Pendle Hill.
Ockelford, Adam. All Join In! 136p. 1996. 70.00 (1-85878-081-0, Pub. by Royal Natl Inst) Am Foun Blind.
Ockelton, Mark. Ockelton: Equity & Trusts. (Butterworths Core Text Ser.). 1997. pap. write for info. (0-406-03313-7, OET, MICHIE) LEXIS Pub.
Ockelton, Mark, jt. auth. see Heydon, J. D.
Ockelton, Mark, ed. see Heydon, J. D.
Ocken, Kathleen Ann Duesel. The ABC's of Crochet: What Every Crocheter Should Know. Royer, Jessica, ed. (Illus.). 60p. 1997. pap. 12.95 (0-9671772-2-7) ICH Inc.
Ocken, Rebecca L. The Relationship Between Site Design & Travel Behavior. LC 95-3538. (CPL Bibliographies Ser.). (Illus.). 31p. 1994. pap. 10.00 (0-86602-312-7, Sage Prdcls Pr) Sage.
Ocken, Stanley. Parametrized Knot Theory. LC 76-3641. (Memoirs Ser.: No. 5/170). 114p. 1976. pap. 22.00 (0-8218-1870-8, MEMO/5/170) Am Math.
Ockenden. Situational Dialogues. Date not set. pap. text. write for info. (0-582-52172-6, Pub. by Addison-Wesley); pap. text. write for info. (0-582-74409-1, Pub. by Addison-Wesley) Longman.
Ockenden, Jonathan & Franklin, Michael. European Agriculture: Making the CAP Fit the Future. (Chatham House Papers). 112p. 1995. 44.95 (1-85567-330-4); pap. 15.95 (1-85567-331-2) Bks Intl VA.
Ockenden, Michael & Jones, Timothy. Around Town. (English As a Second Language Bk.). 1989. 43.09 incl. audio (0-582-79798-5, 75052) Longman.
— Around Town: Situational Conversation Practice. (English As a Second Language Bk.). 1982. pap. text 32.64 (0-582-79772-1, 75026) Longman.
Ockendon, Hilary & Ockendon, John. Viscous Flow. (Texts in Applied Mathematics Ser.: No. 13). (Illus.). 121p. (C). 1995. text 59.95 (0-521-45244-9); pap. text 20.95 (0-521-45881-1) Cambridge U Pr.
Ockendon, Hilary, jt. auth. see Taylor, A. B.
Ockendon, John, et al. Applied Partial Differential Equations. LC 99-34192. (Illus.). 440p. 1999. text 105.00 (0-19-853244-X); pap. text 45.00 (0-19-853243-1) OUP.
Ockendon, John, jt. auth. see Ockendon, Hilary.
Ockene, Ira S. & Ockene, Judith, eds. Prevention of Coronary Heart Disease. LC 92-10336. 1992. 85.00 (0-316-62214-1, Little Brwn Med Div) Lppncott W & W.
Ockene, Judith, jt. ed. see Ockene, Ira S.
Ockenfels, Richard A. Coues White-Tailed Deer (Odocoileus Virginianus Couesi) (Arizona Game & Fish Department Special Reports: No. 18). (Illus.). 106p. (Orig.). 1995. pap. 10.00 (0-917563-26-3) AZ Game & Fish.
Ockenfels, Richard A., et al. Habitat Use & Activity Patterns of Urban-Dwelling Javelina in Prescott, Arizona. (Arizona Game & Fish Department Technical Report: No. 14). (Illus.). 37p. (Orig.). 1994. pap. 5.00 (0-917563-19-0) AZ Game & Fish.
Ockenga, Earl & Rucker, Walt. Money. (Elementary Mathematics Ser.). (Illus.). 16p. (J). (gr. 1). 1990. pap. text 1.25 (1-56281-125-8, M125) Extra Eds.
— Place Value to One Hundred. (Elementary Mathematics Ser.). (Illus.). 16p. (J). (gr. 1). 1990. pap. text 1.25 (1-56281-115-0, M115) Extra Eds.
— Subtracting from Eighteen or Less. (Elementary Mathematics Ser.). (Illus.). 16p. (J). (gr. 1). 1990. pap. text 1.25 (1-56281-135-5, M135) Extra Eds.
— Subtracting from Ten or Less. (Elementary Mathematics Ser.). (Illus.). 16p. (J). (gr. 1). 1990. pap. text 1.25 (1-56281-110-X, M110) Extra Eds.
— Sums Through Eighteen. (Elementary Mathematics Ser.). (Illus.). 16p. (J). (gr. 1). 1990. pap. text 1.25 (1-56281-130-4, M130) Extra Eds.
— Sums Through Ten. (Elementary Mathematics Ser.). (Illus.). 16p. (J). (gr. 1). 1990. pap. text 1.25 (1-56281-105-3, M105) Extra Eds.
— Telling Time. (Elementary Mathematics Ser.). (Illus.). 16p. (J). (gr. 1). 1990. pap. text 1.25 (1-56281-120-7, M120) Extra Eds.
Ockenga, Starr. Earth on Her Hands: The American Woman in Her Garden. LC 98-6323. (Illus.). 256p. 1998. 55.00 (0-517-70561-3) C Potter.
— On Women & Friendship: A Collection of Victorian Keepsakes & Traditions. LC 92-27152. (Illus.). 208p. 1993. 17.50 (1-55670-242-6) Stewart Tabori & Chang.
Ocker, Christopher. Johannes Klenkok: A Friar's Life, c. 1310-1374. LC 93-71200. (Transactions Ser.: Vol. 83, Pt. 5). 115p. 1993. pap. 15.00 (0-87169-835-8, M825-OCC) Am Philos.
Ocker, Christopher, ed. see Sluga, Hans.
Ocker, Jim, et al. Fishing the Mississippi Pools, 15-17. (Mississippi River Ser.). (Illus.). 80p. 1990. pap. 9.95 (0-939314-28-2) Fishing Hot.
— Fishing the Mississippi Pools 18-19. (Mississippi River Ser.). (Illus.). 84p. 1991. pap. 9.95 (0-939314-29-0) Fishing Hot.
***Ockerman, H. W. & Hansen, C. L.** Animal By-Product Processing & Utilization. LC 99-64544. 528p. 1999. text 84.95 (1-56676-777-6) Technomic.
Ockerman, Herbert W. Illustrated Chemistry Laboratory Terminology. 280p. 1991. lib. bdg. 39.95 (0-8493-0152-1, QD51) CRC Pr.
Ockershausen, Jane. The Georgia One-Day Trip Book: A New Way to Explore the State's Romantic Past, Vibrant Present & Olympian Future. LC 93-5351. (Illus.). 415p. 1993. pap. 14.95 (0-939009-71-4, EPM) Howell Pr VA.
— The Maryland One-Day Trip Book. 2nd rev. ed. (Illus.). 288p. 1999. pap. 14.95 (1-57427-089-3, EPM) Howell Pr VA.
— The New Virginia One-Day Trip Book. LC 96-26634. 352p. 1996. 14.95 (1-889324-00-0, EPM) Howell Pr VA.
— The New Washington One-Day Trip Book: One Hundred One Offbeat Excursions in & Around the Nation's Capital. 4th ed. LC 91-46710. 271p. 1992. pap. 9.95 (0-939009-59-5, EPM) Howell Pr VA.
***Ockershausen, Jane.** One-Day Trips Through History. (Illus.). 336p. 2000. pap. 14.95 (1-57427-090-7) Howell Pr VA.
Ockershausen, Jane. The South Carolina One-Day Trip Book: Short Journeys to History, Charm, & Adventure in the Palmetto State. LC 98-5269. 1998. pap. 16.95 (1-889324-08-6, EPM) Howell Pr VA.
Ockert, Carl E. Compassion & Common Sense. LC 79-92791. (Illus.). 172p. (Orig.). 1980. 6.95 (0-9603926-0-2); pap. 4.95 (0-9603926-1-0) MCP Bks.
Ockham, William. A Letter to the Friars Minor & Other Writings. Kilcullen, John & McGrade, Arthur S., eds. (Cambridge Texts in the History of Political Thought Ser.). (Illus.). 433p. (C). 1995. text 64.95 (0-521-35243-6) Cambridge U Pr.
— Opera Politica IV. Offler, H. S., ed. (Auctores Britannici Medii Aevi XIV British Academy). 504p. 1997. text 150.00 (0-19-726127-2) OUP.
— A Short Discourse on Tyrannical Government. Kilcullen, John & McGrade, Arthur S., eds. (Cambridge Texts in the History of Political Thought Ser.). (Illus.). 433p. (C). 1995. pap. text 24.95 (0-521-35804-3) Cambridge U Pr.
Ockham, William. William of Ockham: The Work of Ninety Days (Macintosh) Kilcullen, John & Scott, John, trs. (Past Masters Ser.) (C). write for info. (1-57085-082-8) Intelex.
Ockham, William Of. William of Ockham: Quodlibetal Questions, 2 vols., Set. Freddoso, Alfred J. & Kelley, Francis E., trs. (Yale Library on Medieval Philosophy: No. 1). 336p. 1991. 145.00 (0-300-04832-7) Yale U Pr.
Ockinga. Two Ramesside Tombs at El Mashayakh, No. II. pap. 75.00 (0-85668-566-6, Pub. by Aris & Phillips) David Brown.
Ockinga, ed. Two Ramesside Tombs at El-Mashayikh Vol. 1: The Tomb of Anhurmose the Outer Room. 1988. pap. 75.00 (0-85668-453-8, Pub. by Aris & Phillips) David Brown.
Ockinga, Boyo G. A Tomb from the Reign of Tutankhamun at Awlad Azzaz (Akhmim) (Australian Centre for Egyptology Ser.: Report 10). (Illus.). 144p. 1998. pap. 80.00 (0-85668-801-0) David Brown.
Ockleford, C. D. & Whyte, A., eds. Coated Vesicles. LC 79-17280. 400p. reprint ed. pap. 114.00 (0-608-16943-9, 2027260) Bks Demand.
Ockley, S., jt. auth. see Gibbon, Edward.
Ockley, Simon, tr. see Ibn-Tufail, Abu-Bakr M.
Ockman, Carol. Ingres's Eroticized Bodies: Retracing the Serpentine Line. LC 94-34311. (Publications in the History of Art). 178p. 1995. 47.00 (0-300-05961-2) Yale U Pr.
Ockman, Joan, ed. Architecture Culture 1943-1968: A Documentary Anthology. LC 91-38729. (Readers in Twentieth Century Thought Ser.). (Illus.). 464p. 1993. pap. 35.00 (0-8478-1522-6, Pub. by Rizzoli Intl) St Martin.
Ockman, Sam, jt. auth. see DiBona, Chris.
Ockner, Paula & Pina, Leslie A. Art Deco Aluminum: Kensington. LC 97-21753. 160p. 1997. pap. 29.95 (0-7643-0366-X) Schiffer.
Ockner, Paula, jt. auth. see Pina, Leslie.
Ocko, Jonathan K. Bureaucratic Reform in Provincial China: Ting Jih-ch'ang in Restoration Kiangsu, 1867-1870. (East Asian Monographs: No. 103). 316p. 1983. 32.50 (0-674-08617-1) HUP.
Ocko, Judy Y., ed. The Retail Advertising Manual. (Illus.). 300p. 1987. 89.95 (0-934590-18-4) Visual Refer.
Ocko, Stephanie. Adventure Vacations: A 50-State Guide to Rock Climbing, Horseback Riding, Spelunking, Whitewater Rafting, Snorkeling, Hang Gliding & Ballooning. (Illus.). 352p. 1995. pap. 14.95 (0-8065-1632-1, Citadel Pr) Carol Pub Group.
— Doomsday Denied: A Survivor's Guide to the 21st Century. LC 96-45317. (Millennium 2000 Ser.). (Illus.). 256p. 1997. pap. 14.95 (1-55591-289-3) Fulcrum Pub.
— Water: Almost Enough for Everyone. (Illus.). 144p. (YA). (gr. 5-9). 1995. 16.00 (0-689-31797-2) Atheneum Yung Read.
O'Clair, Charles E., jt. auth. see O'Clair, Rita M.
***O'Clair, Rita M. & Hocker, Katherine M.** Where Is Dinah Diatom? (Illus.). 16p. (J). (ps-4). 2000. pap. write for info. (0-9664245-2-2) Plant Pr AK.
***O'Clair, Rita M. & Lindstrom, Sandra C.** North Pacific Seaweeds. (Illus.). xii, 162p. 2000. pap. 24.95 (0-9664245-1-4) Plant Pr AK.
O'Clair, Rita M. & O'Clair, Charles E. Southeast Alaska's Rock Shores: Animals. LC 98-171724. (Illus.). xii, 564p. 1998. pap. 29.95 (0-9664245-0-6) Plant Pr AK.
O'Clair, Robert, jt. ed. see Ellmann, Richard.
OCLC Online Computer Library Center, Inc. Staff. Diacritics & Special Characters. 2nd ed. LC 98-160383. 1991. write for info. (1-55653-117-6) OCLC Online Comp.
OCLC Staff. Disclit User Guide. 2nd ed. LC 98-229214. viii, 103 p. 1992. write for info. (1-55653-143-5) OCLC Online Comp.
— Epic User Guide. 2nd ed. LC 98-228295. x, 274 p. 1991. write for info. (1-55653-128-1) OCLC Online Comp.
— Firstsearch System Guide. 3rd ed. LC 98-155072. 1993. write for info. (1-55653-193-1) OCLC Online Comp.
— OCLC Authority Control Service Planning Guide. 2nd ed. LC 98-156286. iii, 30p. 1997. write for info. (1-55653-234-2) OCLC Online Comp.
— OCLC Dial TCP/IP Access: A Guide for System Administrators. LC 98-161003. 1997. write for info. (1-55653-237-7) OCLC Online Comp.
OCLC Staff, jt. auth. see Conference of Research Library Directors.
O'Cleary, Helen. Athgreany Stone Circle - The Stones of Time. (Illus.). 203p. (Orig.). 1991. pap. 38.00 (0-9626761-0-1) Al H Morrison.
O'Cleireacain. Political Economy of Western Europe. 1999. text. write for info. (0-312-04776-2) St Martin.
O'Cleireacain, Carol. The Orphaned Capital: Adopting the Right Revenues for the District of Columbia. LC 97-4634. 214p. (Orig.). 1997. pap. 16.95 (0-8157-6425-1) Brookings.
O'Cleireacain, Seamus. Third World Debt & International Public Policy. LC 89-16019. 258p. 1990. 65.00 (0-275-92520-X, C2520, Praeger Pubs) Greenwood.
O'Cleirigh, Nellie & Rowe, Veronica. Limerick Lace: A Social History & a Maker's Manual. LC 95-233670. 92p. 1995. pap. 17.95 (0-86140-368-1, Pub. by Smyth) Dufour.
***O'Cleirigh, Padraig M. & Barrell, Rex A.** An Introduction to Greek Mythology: Story, Symbols & Cultures. LC 00-23078. (Studies in Classics: 12). 288p. 2000. 89.95 (0-7734-7748-9) E Mellen.
O'Cleirigh, Padraig M., tr. see Piux IX.
O'Clery, Conor. Daring Diplomacy: Clinton's Secret Search for Peace in Ireland. 272p. 1997. 22.95 (1-57098-130-2) Roberts Rinehart.
***O'Clery, Conor.** Ireland in Quotes: A History of the 20th Century. 288p. 2000. 24.00 (0-86278-592-8, Pub. by OBrien Pr) IPG Chicago.
O'Clery, Helen. Zodiacal Archetypes in Celtic Myths. Morrison, Al H., ed. (Illus.). 48p. (Orig.). 1993. pap. 11.00 (0-9626761-2-8) Al H Morrison.
O'Clery, Michael, jt. auth. see Dempsey, Eric.
Ocneanu, Adrian. Actions of Discrete Amenable Groups on von Neumann Alegbras. (Lecture Notes in Mathematics Ser.: Vol. 1138). v, 115p. 1985. 49.95 (0-387-15663-1) Spr-Verlag.
O'Collins, Gerald. All Things New: The Promise of Advent, Christmas & the New Year. LC 98-17579. 128p. 1998. pap. 7.95 (0-8091-3824-7) Paulist Pr.
— Christology: A Biblical, Historical & Systematic Study of Jesus Christ. 344p. 1995. pap. text 19.95 (0-19-875502-3) OUP.
***O'Collins, Gerald.** Focus on Jesus: Essays in Christology & Soteriology. 1998. pap. 22.00 (0-85244-360-9) Gra1cewing.
O'Collins, Gerald. Fundamental Theology. LC 80-82809. 288p. (Orig.). 1981. pap. 14.95 (0-8091-2347-9) Paulist Pr.
— Interpreting Jesus. 1983. pap. 14.95 (0-8091-2572-2) Paulist Pr.
— The Resurrection of Jesus Christ. (Pere Marquette Lectures). 1993. 15.00 (0-87462-548-3) Marquette.
— Retrieving Fundamental Theology: The Three Styles of Contemporary Theology. LC 93-28251. 240p. (Orig.). (C). 1993. pap. 14.95 (0-8091-3418-7) Paulist Pr.
— The Tripersonal God: Understanding & Interpreting the Trinity. LC 99-33448. 240p. 1999. pap. 16.95 (0-8091-3887-5) Paulist Pr.
O'Collins, Gerald & Farrugia, Edward G. Concise Dictionary of Theology. LC 91-7187. 272p. 1991. pap. 14.95 (0-8091-3235-4) Paulist Pr.
***O'Collins, Gerald & Farrugia, Edward G.** A Concise Dictionary of Theology. 2nd rev. expanded ed. LC 99-88469. 300p. 2000. pap. 19.95 (0-8091-3929-4) Paulist Pr.
O'Collins, Gerald & Kendall, Daniel. The Bible for Theology: Ten Principles for the Theological Use of Scripture. LC 97-26623. 224p. (Orig.). 1997. pap. 14.95 (0-8091-3743-7, 3743-7) Paulist Pr.
O'Collins, Gerald & Marconi, Gilberto, eds. Luke & Acts. O'Connell, Matthew J., tr. LC 92-35226. 320p. 1993. pap. 10.95 (0-8091-3360-1) Paulist Pr.
O'Collins, Gerald & Venturini, Mary. Believing: Understand the Creed. 182p. 1986. pap. 15.95 (0-00-599292-3, Pub. by T & T Clark) Bks Intl VA.
O'Collins, Gerald S. The Second Journey: Spiritual Awareness & the Midlife Crisis. 105p. 1996. pap. 9.95 (0-85244-321-8, 962, Pub. by Gra1cewing) Morehouse Pub.
O'Con, Robert. Statistical Process Control: A Training Manual & Implementation Guide. Nickel, Amy J., ed. (Illus.). 95p. (C). 1997. pap. 39.00 (1-881113-11-6) Croydon Grp.
O'Con, Robert & Carr, Richard. Advanced Oxyacetlene Flame Cutting. (Series 910). (Orig.). 1985. 7.00 (0-8064-0387-X) Bergwall.
O'Con, Robert, jt. auth. see Carr, Richard.
O'Con, Robert, jt. auth. see Hunter, Richard.
***O'Con, Robert L.** Welding: Management Primer & Employee Training Guide. LC 00-39527. 2000. write for info. (0-8311-3139-X) Indus Pr.
***O'Con, Robert L. & Carr, Richard H.** Metal Fabrication: A Practical Guide. 2nd ed. (Illus.). 334p. (C). 1999. pap. 55.00 (1-881113-12-4) Croydon Grp.
O'Conall, B., jt. ed. see Thimbleby, H.
***O'Conaire, Padraic.** Exile. Mac Eoin, Gearailt, tr. 150p. 2000. pap. 13.95 (1-874700-62-1, Pub. by Clo Iar-Chonnachta) Dufour.
O'Conaire, Padraic O. Finest Stories of Padraic O'Conaire. 210p. 1982. pap. 8.95 (0-905169-54-9, Pub. by Poolbeg Pr) Dufour.
Ocone, D. Complex Fluid Processing. text. write for info. (0-471-49046-6) Wiley.
Ocone, D., jt. ed. see Karatzas, I.
O'Conghaile, Michael, et al. Fourfront: Contemporary Stories Translated from the Irish. LC 98-235780. 148 p. 1998. write for info. (1-902420-01-2) Clo Iar-Chonnachta.
O'Connell. The Car in British Society: Class, Gender, & Motoring, 1896-1939. 208p. 1998. pap. 29.95 (0-7190-5506-7, Pub. by Manchester Univ Pr) St Martin.
— Focus on Advanced English CAE. Date not set. pap. text, student ed. write for info. (0-17-556626-7) Addison-Wesley.
O'Connell. Focus on First Certificate Student Book. 1991. pap. write for info. (0-17-556613-5, Pub. by ITP Nelson) Thomson Learn.
O'Connell. Focus on Proficiency: Full Colour Edition. (Illus.). 1995. pap. text. write for info. (0-17-556981-9) Addison-Wesley.
— Mental Health & Psychiatric Nursing. 1999. pap. text. write for info. (0-7216-6853-4, W B Saunders Co) Harcrt Hlth Sci Grp.
— Speech, Language & Hearing Problems in School. 1996. 42.00 (0-614-22121-8) Aspen Pub.
***O'Connell.** Structural Collapse Rescue. (Fire Science Ser.). (C). 2001. pap. 25.75 (0-7668-0747-9) Delmar.
O'Connell, jt. auth. see Walton.
O'Connell, Agnes N. & Russo, Nancy F., eds. Women in Psychology: A Bio-Bibliographic Sourcebook. LC 89-25787. 456p. 1990. lib. bdg. 75.00 (0-313-26091-5, OWP/, Greenwood Pr) Greenwood.
O'Connell, Agnes N., jt. auth. see Russo, Nancy F.
O'Connell, Ann B., jt. auth. see O'Connell, Brian.
O'Connell, April. Choice & Change. 5th ed. LC 96-18613. 432p. (C). 1996. pap. text 61.00 (0-13-535197-9) P-H.
***O'Connell, April & O'Connell, Vincent.** Choice & Change: Psychological Theory Applied to Personal Growth, Interpersonal Relationships & Living & Working with Others. 6th ed. LC 00-38533. 2001. write for info. (0-13-088413-8) Aspen Law.
O'Connell, Avice M. & Leone, Norma L. Your Child & X-Rays: A Parent's Guide to Radiation, X-Rays & Other Imaging Procedures. LC 87-37854. (Illus.). 104p. (Orig.). 1989. pap. 4.00 (0-936635-05-3) Lion Pr & Vid.
O'Connell, Barry, ed. see Apess, William.

O'Connell, Bill. Foreign Student Education at Two-Year Colleges. 164p. 1994. pap. 19.00 (*0-912207-66-3*) NAFSA Washington.

— On the Map to Your Life. 27p. 1992. pap. 5.00 (*0-933292-20-1*, Dytiscid Pr) Arts End.

— Solution-Focused Therapy: A Casebook. LC 98-61096. (Brief Therapies Ser.). xiii, 160 p. 1998. write for info. (*0-7619-5275-6*) Sage.

O'Connell, Bonnie. The Anti-Warhol Museum Proposals for the Socially Responsible Disposal of Warholia. (Illus.). 1993. pap. 15.00 (*0-932526-48-9*) Nexus Pr.

O'Connell, Brian. America's Voluntary Spirit. 460p. 1983. pap. 14.95 (*0-87954-081-8*) Foundation Ctr.

— America's Voluntary Spirit: A Book of Readings. LC 83-81223. 461p. 1983. 19.95 (*0-87954-079-6*) Foundation Ctr.

— The Board Member's Book: Making a Difference in Voluntary Organizations. 2nd ed. LC 93-26639. 208p. (Orig.). 1993. 24.95 (*0-87954-502-X*) Foundation Ctr.

— Board Overboard: Laughs & Lessons for All but the Perfect Nonprofit. LC 95-33964. (Nonprofit Sector Ser.). 221p. 1995. text 24.00 (*0-7879-0179-2*) Jossey-Bass.

*O'Connell, Brian. B2B.com: Cashing-in on the Business-to-Business E-Commerce Bonanza. 288p. 2000. 24.95 (*1-58062-403-0*) Adams Media.

O'Connell, Brian. Civil Society: The Underpinnings of American Democracy. LC 98-50172. (Civil Society Ser.). 169p. 1999. pap. 14.95 (*0-87451-925-X*); text 35.00 (*0-87451-924-1*) U Pr of New Eng.

— Effective Leadership in Voluntary Organizations. LC 81-69289. 1981. 5.95 (*0-8027-7188-2*) Walker & Co.

— Gen E: Generation Entrepreneur Is Rewriting the Rules of Business - And You Can, Too! LC 99-33490. (Illus.). 300p. 1999. pap. 17.95 (*1-891984-07-1*, Pub. by Entrepreneur) Natl Bk Netwk.

— Our Organization. 1987. pap. 12.95 (*0-8027-1006-9*) Walker & Co.

— People Power: Service, Advocacy, Empowerment : Selected Writings of Brian O'Connell. limited ed. LC 94-23368. 241p. 1994. pap. 24.95 (*0-87954-563-1*) Foundation Ctr.

— Powered by Coalition: The Story of Independent Sector. LC 96-51318. 236p. 1997. 26.95 (*0-7879-0954-8*) Jossey-Bass.

— Voices from the Heart: In Celebration of America's Volunteers. LC 99-163049. 1998. 29.95 (*0-8118-2115-3*); pap. 19.95 (*0-8118-2125-0*) Chronicle Bks.

O'Connell, Brian & O'Connell, Ann B. Volunteers in Action. LC 89-1472. 1989. 24.95 (*0-87954-291-8*); pap. 19.95 (*0-87954-292-6*) Foundation Ctr.

O'Connell, Brian, jt. auth. see Iwaszko, Knute.

O'Connell, C. P., ed. see Spenser, Edmund.

O'Connell, Carol. Judas Child. LC 97-46504. 340p. 1998. 34.99 (*0-399-14380-7*, G P Putnam) Peng Put Young Read.

— Judas Child. 420p. 1999. reprint ed. mass mkt. 6.99 (*0-515-12549-0*, Jove) Berkley Pub.

— Killing Critics. 400p. 1997. mass mkt. 6.99 (*0-515-12086-3*, Jove) Berkley Pub.

— Mallory's Oracle. 329p. 1995. mass mkt. 5.99 (*0-515-11647-5*, Jove) Berkley Pub.

— Mallory's Oracle. large type ed. LC 95-21030. 330p. 1995. lib. bdg. 23.95 (*1-57490-024-2*, Beeler LP Bks) T T Beeler.

— The Man Who Cast Two Shadows. 336p. 1996. mass mkt. 6.99 (*0-515-11890-7*, Jove) Berkley Pub.

— The Man Who Cast Two Shadows. large type ed. 1995. pap. 20.95 (*1-56895-258-9*, Compass) Wheeler Pub.

*O'Connell, Carol. Shell Game. 416p. 2000. mass mkt. 6.99 (*0-425-17603-7*) Berkley Pub.

— Shell Game: Mallory Novel. LC 98-54715. 352p. 1999. 24.95 (*0-399-14495-1*, G P Putnam) Peng Put Young Read.

O'Connell, Carol. Stone Angel. 388p. 1998. mass mkt. 6.99 (*0-515-12298-X*, Jove) Berkley Pub.

— Stone Angel. large type ed. LC 97-32437. 1997. 24.95 (*1-56895-507-3*) Wheeler Pub.

O'Connell, Caroline & Davenport, Megan. The Best Places to Kiss in Southern California: A Romantic Travel Guide. 4th rev. ed. Bulmer, Miriam, ed. (Best Places to Kiss Ser.). 234p. (Orig.). 1997. pap. 13.95 (*1-877988-20-0*) Beginning Pr.

O'Connell, Colette, et al, eds. Directory of Microcomputer Software for Mechanical Engineering Design. LC 85-1540. 431p. reprint ed. pap. 133.70 (*0-7837-4320-3*, 204400600012) Bks Demand.

O'Connell, Colette, jt. auth. see Shupe, Barbara.

O'Connell, Colin, jt. ed. see Elder, Jo-Anne.

O'Connell, Colin B. A Study of Heinrich Ott's Theological Development: His Hermeneutical & Ontological Programme. LC 91-16572. (American University Studies: Theology & Religion: Ser. VII, Vol. 107). XXII, 262p. (C). 1992. text 45.95 (*0-8204-1569-3*) P Lang Pubng.

*O'Connell, Colman, ed. Divine Favor: The Art of Joseph O'Connell. LC 99-37605. (Illus.). 112p. 1999. 39.95 (*0-8146-2573-8*) Liturgical Pr.

O'Connell, Con. Making a Better Confession: A Deeper Examination of Conscience. 1997. pap. text 1.95 (*0-89243-863-0*) Liguori Pubns.

O'Connell, D. C. Critical Essays on Language Use & Psychology. xx, 351p. 1988. 60.95 (*0-387-96703-6*) Spr-Verlag.

O'Connell, Daniel. The Opposition Critics: The Antisymbolist Reaction in the Modern Period. LC 73-80108. (De Proprietatibus Litterarum, Ser. Minor: No. 14). 172p. 1974. pap. text 32.35 (*90-279-3422-3*) Mouton.

O'Connell, Daniel M., ed. see Newman, John Henry.

O'Connell, David. Francois Mauriac Revisited. rev. ed. (Twayne's World Authors Ser.: No. 844). 208p. 1994. 32.00 (*0-8057-4302-2*, Twyne) Mac Lib Ref.

— The Irish Roots of Margaret Mitchell's Gone with the Wind. LC 96-85469. (Illus.). 128p. 1996. 13.95 (*0-9653093-0-4*) Claves Petry.

— Michel de Saint Pierre: A Catholic Novelist at the Crossroads. LC 89-52103. 189p. 1990. lib. bdg. 27.95 (*0-917786-76-9*) Summa Pubns.

O'Connell, David F. Dual Disorders: Essentials for Assessment & Treatment. LC 97-10777. 250p. (C). 1997. pap. 19.95 (*0-7890-0249-3*); pap. 19.95 (*0-7890-0401-1*) Haworth Pr.

— Managing the Dually Diagnosed. 1990. pap. 14.95 (*0-86656-978-2*) Haworth Pr.

O'Connell, David F., ed. Managing the Dually Diagnosed Patient: Current Issues & Clinical Approaches. 265p. 1990. 39.95 (*0-86656-918-9*) Haworth Pr.

O'Connell, Diane, jt. auth. see Braver, Sanford L.

O'Connell, Donald W., ed. Public Sector Labor Relations in Maryland: Issues & Prospects. LC 72-92069. (PSLRCB Publication Ser.: No. 1). (Illus.). (Orig.). 1972. pap. 7.50 (*0-913400-00-9*) Pub Sect Lab Rel.

O'Connell, E. E. Father Browne's Cork: Photographs, 1912-1954. 1996. 39.95 (*0-614-20390-2*) Dufour.

O'Connell, E. Patrick, tr. see De La Touche, Louise M.

O'Connell, Eileen Dubh. Lament for Art O'Leary: A New Translation by Malachi McCormick. McCormick, Malachi, ed. & tr. by. (Illus.). 64p. (C). 1994. pap. 24.00 (*0-943984-64-5*) Stone St Pr.

O'Connell, Eileen M., ed. Rockhurst Review, 1991: A Fine Arts Journal, Vol. IV. 75p. 1991. pap. 5.00 (*1-886761-03-5*) Rockhurst Col.

*O'Connell, Fergus. How to Run Successful High-Tech Project-Based Organizations. LC 99-41776. (Computer Library). 320p. 1999. 59.00 (*1-58053-010-9*) Artech Hse.

O'Connell, Fergus. How to Run Successful Projects. 1994. pap. text 26.25 (*0-685-70921-3*) P-H.

— How to Run Successful Projects. 2nd ed. LC 96-19796. 192p. 1996. pap. 47.00 (*0-13-239856-7*) P-H.

O'Connell, Frances H. Giving & Growing: A Student's Guide for Service Projects. Stamschror, Robert P., ed. 32p. (YA). (gr. 7-12). 1990. teacher ed. 3.95 (*0-88489-225-5*) St Marys.

— Giving & Growing: A Student's Guide for Service Projects. Stamschror, Robert P., ed. (Illus.). 80p. (YA). (gr. 7-12). 1990. text 4.25 (*0-88489-224-7*) St Marys.

O'Connell, Francis A. Plant Closings: Worker Rights, Management Rights, & the Law. (Studies in Social Philosophy & Policy: No. 7). 313p. 1987. 34.95 (*0-912051-07-8*); pap. 21.95 (*0-912051-08-6*) Transaction Pubs.

O'Connell, Gary, jt. auth. see Sachnowsici, Lucia.

O'Connell, Ged, jt. auth. see Hemmert, Amy.

O'Connell, Geoffrey. The Boat Owner's Maintenance Book. 164p. 1989. 17.95 (*0-87201-221-2*) Gulf Pub.

— Southwick: The D-Day Village That Went to War. 1995. 8.95 (*1-85253-299-8*) Cimino Pub Grp.

O'Connell, Helen. Dedicated Lives. (Illus.). 32p. (C). 1993. pap. 7.95 (*0-85598-197-0*, Pub. by Oxfam Pub) Stylus Pub VA.

— Women & Conflict: Gender & Development. (Gender & Development Ser.). (Illus.). 64p. (C). 1993. pap. 12.95 (*0-85598-222-5*, Pub. by Oxfam Pub) Stylus Pub VA.

O'Connell, Helen, ed. Women & the Family. LC 94-2289. (Women & World Development Ser.). (Illus.). 144p. (C). 1994. text 59.95 (*1-85649-105-6*, Pub. by Zed Books); text 22.50 (*1-85649-106-4*, Pub. by Zed Books) St Martin.

O'Connell, J. B., jt. auth. see Fortescue, Adrian.

O'Connell, J. C. A Study of the Special Problems & Needs of American Indians with Handicaps Both on & off the Reservation. 190p. 1987. pap. text. write for info. (*1-888557-12-5*, 100103) No Ariz Univ.

— A Study of the Special Problems & Needs of American Indians with Handicaps Both on & off the Reservation: Appendices. 130p. 1987. pap. text. write for info. (*1-888557-10-9*, 100104) No Ariz Univ.

— A Study of the Special Problems & Needs of American Indians with Handicaps Both on & off the Reservation: Executive Summary. 21p. 1987. pap. text. write for info. (*1-888557-13-3*, 100102) No Ariz Univ.

O'Connell, J. C., jt. auth. see Martin, W. E.

O'Connell, J. Thomas. Mount Zion Field. 101p. 1990. 24.50 (*0-916379-39-6*) Scripta.

O'Connell, J. W. & Korff, Anne, eds. The Book of the Burren. (Illus.). 228p. 1991. 35.95 (*1-873821-05-0*, Pub. by Tir Eolas); pap. 23.95 (*1-873821-00-X*, Pub. by Tir Eolas) Irish Bks Media.

O'Connell, Jack. Box Nine. 336p. 1993. mass mkt. 4.99 (*0-446-40100-5*, Mysterious Paperbk) Warner Bks.

— Derek Jeter: The Yankee Kid. Rains, Rob, ed. (Super Star Ser.). 96p. (J). 1999. pap. 4.95 (*1-58261-043-6*) Sprts Pubng.

— The Skin Palace. 464p. 1996. mass mkt. 5.99 (*0-446-40357-1*) Warner Bks.

— Wireless. 416p. 1993. 19.95 (*0-89296-546-0*) Mysterious Pr.

— Wireless. 416p. 1995. mass mkt. 5.99 (*0-446-40356-3*, Mysterious Paperbk) Warner Bks.

O'Connell, Jack. Word Made Flesh. LC 98-41174. 336p. 1999. 24.00 (*0-06-019209-7*) HarpC.

*O'Connell, Jack. Word Made Flesh. 336p. 2000. pap. 13.00 (*0-06-109722-5*, Perennial) HarperTrade.

O'Connell, James. Meaning of Irish Place Names. 90p. 1979. pap. 5.95 (*0-685-25952-8*, Pub. by Blackstaff Pr) Dufour.

— Meaning of Irish Place Names. 90p. 1986. pap. 5.95 (*0-85640-175-7*) Dufour.

O'Connell, James C., ed. The Pioneer Valley Reader: Prose & Poetry from New England's Heartland. LC 95-8414. (Illus.). 416p. 1995. 27.95 (*0-936399-71-6*) Berkshire Hse.

O'Connell, James F., et al, eds. Perris Reservoir Archeology No. 14: Late Prehistory Demographic Change in Southeastern California. (Publications of the Department of Parks & Recreation: No. 14). (Illus.). 187p. (C). 1974. reprint ed. pap. text 20.00 (*1-55567-465-8*) Coyote Press.

O'Connell, James F., jt. ed. see Madsen, David B.

*O'Connell, Jay. Co-Operative Dreams: A History of the Kaweah Colony. LC 99-64766. (Illus.). 256p. 1999. pap. 17.95 (*0-9673370-0-3*) Raven River Pr.

O'Connell, Jean S. The Dollhouse Caper. LC 75-25501. (Illus.). 96p. (J). (gr. 3-7). 1976. 12.95 (*0-690-01042-7*) HarpC Child Bks.

O'Connell, Jeffrey & Wilson, Wallace H. Car Insurance & Consumer Desires. LC 78-83554. (Illus.). 123p. reprint ed. pap. 38.20 (*0-8357-6047-2*, 203445600090) Bks Demand.

O'Connell, Jeffrey P., jt. auth. see Bell, Peter A.

O'Connell, Jennifer, ed. The Serials Directory No. 5: An International Reference Book. 13th ed. 4119p. 1999. reprint ed. 339.00 (*0-913956-18-X*) EBSCO.

*O'Connell, Jennifer Barrett. Ten Timid Ghosts. LC 99-46427. (Illus.). 32p. (J). (ps-3). 2000. 3.25 (*0-439-15804-4*) Scholastic Inc.

O'Connell, Joanna. Prospero's Daughter: The Prose of Rosario Castellanos. LC 95-3795. (Texas Pan American Ser.). 288p. (Orig.). 1995. 35.00 (*0-292-76041-8*); pap. 17.95 (*0-292-76042-6*) U of Tex Pr.

O'Connell, John. Cartoons for Poolplayers. (Illus.). 55p. 1991. pap. 11.50 (*0-9668821-0-5*) J OConnell.

— Doctor John: Crusading Doctor & Politician. (Illus.). 175p. 1989. pap. 10.95 (*1-85371-025-3*, Pub. by Poolbeg Pr) Dufour.

— Welfare Economic Theory. LC 82-1760. 219p. (C). 1982. 35.00 (*0-86569-087-1*, Auburn Hse); pap. 15.00 (*0-86569-074-X*, Auburn Hse) Greenwood.

O'Connell, John, ed. The Blackwell Encyclopedic Dictionary of International Management. LC 96-27366. (Encyclopedia of Management Ser.). (Illus.). 270p. 1997. 105.95 (*1-55786-924-3*) Blackwell Pubs.

— The Blackwell Encyclopedic Dictionary of International Management. (Blackwell Encyclopedia of Management Ser.). 288p. 1999. reprint ed. pap. 29.95 (*0-631-21081-4*) Blackwell Pubs.

O'Connell, John B., jt. ed. see Engelmeier, Richard S.

O'Connell, John F. Remedies in a Nutshell. 2nd ed. LC 84-19705. (Nutshell Ser.). 320p. (C). 1984. reprint ed. pap. 21.00 (*0-314-85066-X*) West Pub.

O'Connell, John M., jt. auth. see Michaelis, Bill.

O'Connell, Joseph. Twenty Innovative Electronics Projects for Your Home. (Illus.). 256p. 1988. 21.95 (*0-8306-0947-4*); pap. 13.95 (*0-8306-2947-5*) McGraw-Hill Prof.

O'Connell, Joseph J., jt. auth. see Rounds, Stowell.

O'Connell, Joseph T., et al. Sikh History & Religion in the Twentieth Century. (C). 1988. reprint ed. 34.00 (*0-9692907-4-8*, Pub. by Ctre South Asian) S Asia.

O'Connell, Karen, jt. auth. see Chedekel, David.

*O'Connell, Kathleen R. Playing, Learning, Praying: Parish Tools for Gathering Families. LC 99-64812. 64p. 2000. 9.95 (*0-7648-0551-7*) Liguori Pubns.

O'Connell, Katie C. & Chesto, Kathleen O'Connell. Rituals & Icebreakers: Practical Tools for Forming Community. LC 98-75394. 124p. 1999. pap. text 7.95 (*0-7648-0407-3*) Liguori Pubns.

O'Connell, Katie C., et al. Everyday Epiphanies. Weber, Jane, ed. (Anthology of Teachers' Writing Ser.: Vol. 2). 128p. 1997. pap. 9.95 (*0-9666573-1-4*) Plymouth Writers.

— Lessons Learned. Weber, Jane, ed. (Anthology of Teachers' Writing Ser.: Vol. 3). 1998. pap. 9.95 (*0-9666573-2-2*) Plymouth Writers.

— Writers of Passage. (Anthology of Teachers' Writing Ser.: Vol. 1). 146p. 1996. pap. 9.95 (*0-9666573-0-6*) Plymouth Writers.

O'Connell, Kevin. City of Champions: The Story of the 1948 Cleveland Barons, Browns & Indians. 200p. 1997. pap. 20.00 (*0-9659871-0-8*) K T OConnell.

O'Connell, Kevin G., jt. ed. see Dahlberg, Bruce T.

O'Connell, Kevin J., jt. auth. see Levy, David N.

O'Connell, Kevin J., jt. ed. see Wade, Robert G.

O'Connell-Killen, Patricia. Finding Our Voices: Women's Wisdom & Faith. LC 97-37544. 156p. 1997. pap. 14.95 (*0-8245-1610-9*) Crossroad NY.

O'Connell, Lauren M., tr. see Choay, Francoise.

O'Connell, Lenahan & Ryan, James W. Able, Active & Aggressive: History of the O'Connell Family of Massachusetts. (Illus.). 327p. 1994. 35.00 (*0-9641376-0-7*) Elizabeth-James.

O'Connell, Lenahan, jt. auth. see Smith, T. Alexander.

O'Connell, Loraine M., jt. auth. see Smith, Ron F.

O'Connell, M. G. & Bird, Joanna, eds. The Roman Temple at Wanborough. (Surrey Archaeological Collections: Vol. 82, 1994). 235p. 1994. pap. 27.00 incl. mic. form (*0-946897-82-4*, Pub. by Oxbow Bks) David Brown.

O'Connell, M. J., tr. see Calvez, Jean Y.

O'Connell, Margaret. The Magic Cauldron: Witchcraft for Good & Evil. LC 75-26757. (Illus.). 256p. (J). (gr. 9-12). 1975. 38.95 (*0-87599-187-4*) S G Phillips.

O'Connell, Margaret J. Pennington Profile. 2nd ed. (Illus.). 452p. 1986. 25.00 (*0-9617592-1-6*); 50.00 (*0-9617592-0-8*) Pennington Lib.

O'Connell, Marvin R. Blaise Pascal: Reasons of the Heart. LC 97-10578. (Library of Religious Biography). 211p. (Orig.). 1997. pap. 16.00 (*0-8028-0158-7*) Eerdmans.

— Critics on Trial: An Introduction to the Catholic Modernist Crisis. LC 93-41850. 394p. 1994. pap. 24.95 (*0-8132-0800-9*) Cath U Pr.

— John Ireland & the American Catholic Church. (Illus.). xii, 610p. 1988. 34.95 (*0-87351-230-8*) Minn Hist.

— The Oxford Conspirators: A History of the Oxford Movement 1833-45. 478p. (C). 1991. reprint ed. pap. text 38.00 (*0-8191-8074-2*) U Pr of Amer.

O'Connell, Mary. Updike & the Patriachal Dilemma: Masculinity in the Rabbit Novels. LC 94-39038. 288p. (C). 1995. 34.95 (*0-8093-1949-7*) S Ill U Pr.

O'Connell, Mary, jt. auth. see Gardenghi, Monica.

O'Connell, Mathew J., tr. see Horkheimer, Max.

O'Connell, Mattew J., tr. see Gutierrez, Gustavo.

O'Connell, Matthew, tr. see Augustine, Saint.

O'Connell, Matthew, tr. see Cabie, Robert, et al.

O'Connell, Matthew, tr. see Di Sante, Carmine.

O'Connell, Matthew, tr. see Gutierrez, Gustavo.

O'Connell, Matthew, tr. see Martimort, Aime G., et al.

O'Connell, Matthew, tr. see Possidius.

O'Connell, Matthew J., ed. & tr. see Martimort, Aime G., et al.

O'Connell, Matthew J., tr. see Alberigo, Giuseppe, et al, eds.

O'Connell, Matthew J., tr. see Augustine, Saint.

O'Connell, Matthew J., tr. see Back, Siegfried.

O'Connell, Matthew J., tr. see Belo, Fernando.

O'Connell, Matthew J., tr. see Bugnini, Annibale.

O'Connell, Matthew J., tr. see Danneels, Godfried C.

O'Connell, Matthew J., tr. see De Orozco, Alonso.

O'Connell, Matthew J., tr. see Deiss, Lucien.

O'Connell, Matthew J., tr. see Echegaray, Hugo.

O'Connell, Matthew J., tr. see Gonzalez Ruiz, Jose M.

O'Connell, Matthew J., tr. see Martini, Carlo M.

O'Connell, Matthew J., tr. see Mazza, Enrico.

O'Connell, Matthew J., tr. see O'Collins, Gerald & Marconi, Gilberto, eds.

O'Connell, Matthew J., tr. see Pannenberg, Wolfhart.

O'Connell, Matthew J., tr. see Peri, Vittorio.

O'Connell, Matthew J., tr. see Ratzinger, Joseph C.

O'Connell, Matthew J., tr. see Sobrino, Jon.

O'Connell, Matthew J., tr. see Studer, Basil.

O'Connell, Matthew J., tr. see Tamez, Elsa.

O'Connell, Matthew J., tr. see Wa Ilunga, Bakole.

O'Connell, Matthew J., tr. see Zumkeller, Adolar, et al.

O'Connell, Maurice. Daniel O'Connell: The Man & His Politics. 160p. (C). 1990. 29.50 (*0-7165-2446-5*, Pub. by Irish Acad Pr) Intl Spec Bk.

O'Connell, Maurice R. Irish Politics & Social Conflict in the Age of the American Revolution. LC 76-2388. (Illus.). 444p. 1976. reprint ed. lib. bdg. 30.00 (*0-8371-8758-3*, OCIP, Greenwood Pr) Greenwood.

O'Connell, Maurice R., jt. ed. see Nowlan, Kevin B.

O'Connell, Michael. The Idolatrous Eye: Iconoclasm & Theater in Renaissance England. LC 99-22941. (Illus.). 208p. 2000. text 45.00 (*0-19-513205-X*) OUP.

— Mirror & Veil: The Historical Dimension of Spenser's "Faerie Queene" LC 77-1733. 234p. reprint ed. pap. 72.60 (*0-7837-3754-8*, 204357100010) Bks Demand.

O'Connell, Michael, jt. auth. see Huxley, Phil.

O'Connell, Michael A., et al. Working with Sex Offenders: Practical Guidelines for Therapist Selection. 132p. (C). 1990. text 44.00 (*0-8039-3754-7*); pap. text 19.95 (*0-8039-3763-6*) Sage.

O'Connell, Michael A., jt. auth. see Noss, Reed F.

O'Connell, Mike. My Bucket's Got a Hole in It: New Poems by Mike O'Connell. LC 95-95237. (Illus.). 80p. (Orig.). 1995. pap. write for info. (*0-9640408-1-6*) Hugger Mugger.

O'Connell, Mitch. Pwease Wuv Me! More 'Art' of Mitch O'Connell. (Illus.). 84p. 1998. pap. 17.95 (*0-9639762-1-4*) Good Taste.

O'Connell, Nicholas. At the Field's End: Interviews with 22 Pacific Northwest Writers. rev. ed. LC 98-34903. (Illus.). 380p. 1998. pap. 22.95 (*0-295-97723-X*) U of Wash Pr.

— Beyond Risk: Conversation with Climbers. LC 93-22723. (Illus.). 256p. 1993. 19.95 (*0-89886-296-5*) Mountaineers.

— Beyond Risk: Conversations with Climbers. (Illus.). 256p. 1995. pap. text 16.95 (*0-89886-457-7*) Mountaineers.

O'Connell, P. Edna, jt. ed. see Bowles, David S.

O'Connell, P. J. Robert Drew & the Development of Cinema Verite in America. LC 91-39992. 312p. (C). 1992. 36.95 (*0-8093-1779-6*) S Ill U Pr.

O'Connell, Pat. Knight Hawk. 368p. 2000. mass mkt. 5.99 (*0-8439-4253-3*, Leisure Bks) Dorchester Pub Co.

O'Connell, Patricia. The Irish Colleges at Alcala de Henares, 1649-1785. 96p. 1997. boxed set 35.00 (*1-85182-345-X*, Pub. by Four Cts Pr) Intl Spec Bk.

O'Connell, Patrick. Falling in Place. 1997. pap. 7.95 (*0-88801-173-3*, Pub. by Turnstone Pr) Genl Dist Srvs.

— The Inn at Little Washington Cookbook: A Consuming Passion. LC 96-15471. (Illus.). 208p. 1996. 50.00 (*0-679-44736-9*) Random.

— Original Sin in the Light of Modern Science. 128p. 1973. pap. 3.00 (*0-912414-15-4*) Lumen Christi.

— Science of Today & the Problems of Genesis. LC 90-71913. 382p. 1993. pap. 18.50 (*0-89555-438-0*) TAN Bks Pubs.

O'Connell, Patrick, ed. Life & Work of Mother Louise Margaret. LC 86-51579. 230p. 1989. reprint ed. pap. 12.50 (*0-89555-311-2*) TAN Bks Pubs.

O'Connell, Patrick & Carty, Charles M. The Holy Shroud & Four Visions: New Evidence Compared with the Visions of St. Bridget of Sweden, Maria d'Agreda, Anne Catherine Emmerich & Teresa Neumann. (Illus.). 1992. reprint ed. pap. 2.00 (*0-89555-102-0*) TAN Bks Pubs.

O'Connell, Patrick, tr. see Claret de la Touche, Margaret Louise Margaret.

An Asterisk (*) at the beginning of an entry indicates that the title is appearing for the first time.

O'Connell, Patrick, tr. see Croiset, J.
O'Connell, Paul, jt. auth. see Conroy, Larry.
O'Connell, Peggy. Aim for a Job As a Waiter or Waitress. LC 79-15014. (Arco's Career Guidance Ser.). (Illus.). 1980. pap. 4.50 (*0-668-04771-2*, Arco); lib. bdg. 7.95 (*0-668-04767-4*, Arco) Macmillan Gen Ref.
O'Connell, Peter. Greg's Mill. 60p. (C). 1988. text 39.00 (*0-947818-09-X*, Pub. by Old Vicarage) St Mut.
O'Connell, Philip J. & McGinnity, Frances. Working Schemes? Active Labour Market Policy in Ireland. LC 97-73378. 176p. 1997. text 59.95 (*1-85972-624-0*, Pub. by Ashgate Pub) Ashgate Pub Co.
O'Connell, R. J. & Fyfe, W. S., eds. Evolution of the Earth. (Geodynamics Ser.: Vol. 5). 282p. 1981. 25.00 (*0-87590-506-4*) Am Geophysical.
O'Connell, R. T., jt. auth. see Bowerman, B. L.
***O'Connell, Rebecca.** Myrtle of Willendorf. 128p. (YA). (gr. 7 up). 2000. 15.95 (*1-886910-52-9*, Pub. by Front Str) Publishers Group.
O'Connell, Richard. Battle Poems. 1977. pap. 2.50 (*0-686-17592-1*) Atlantis.
— Battle Poems. 1987. pap. 10.00 (*0-318-32928-X*) Atlantis Edns.
— Brazilian Happenings. 1966. pap. 10.00 (*0-685-62617-2*) Atlantis Edns.
— Brazilian Poems. 1928. 35.00 (*0-87556-226-4*) Saifer.
— The Bright Tower. 1997. pap. 15.00 (*3-7052-0058-5*, Pub. by Poetry Salzburg) Intl Spec Bk.
— The Caliban Poems. 1992. pap. 10.00 (*0-685-55467-8*) Atlantis Edns.
— Cries of Flesh & Stone. 1962. pap. 10.00 (*0-685-62608-3*) Atlantis Edns.
— Deaths & Distances. 1965. pap. 10.00 (*0-685-62613-X*) Atlantis Edns.
— Hanging Tough. 1986. pap. 10.00 (*0-317-56161-8*) Atlantis Edns.
— Hudson's Fourth Voyage. 1978. pap. 10.00 (*0-685-87717-5*) Atlantis Edns.
— Lives of the Poets. 1990. pap. 6.00 (*0-685-38406-3*) Atlantis Edns.
— Poems & Epigrams. 1929. pap. 25.00 (*0-87556-227-2*) Saifer.
— Retro Worlds. 1993. pap. 25.00 (*3-7052-0840-3*) Intl Spec Bk.
— RetroWorlds: Selected Poems by Richard O'Connell. 1993. pap. 25.00 (*3-7052-0804-7*, Pub. by Poetry Salzburg) Intl Spec Bk.
— Selected Epigrams. 1990. pap. 10.00 (*0-685-38407-1*) Atlantis Edns.
— Simulations. 1993. pap. 25.00 (*3-7052-0621-4*, Pub. by Poetry Salzburg) Intl Spec Bk.
— Simulations, Selected Translations. 1993. pap. 25.00 (*3-7052-0625-7*, Pub. by Poetry Salzburg) Intl Spec Bk.
— Temple Poems. 1985. pap. 10.00 (*0-317-38870-3*) Atlantis Edns.
— Voyages. 1995. pap. 25.00 (*3-7052-0445-9*, Pub. by Poetry Salzburg) Intl Spec Bk.
O'Connell, Richard, ed. Apollo's Day: Seventeenth Century Songs. 1969. pap. 10.00 (*0-685-62618-0*) Atlantis Edns.
O'Connell, Richard. Thirty Epigrams. 1971. pap. 10.00 (*0-685-62619-9*) Atlantis Edns.
O'Connell, Richard, tr. The Epigrams of Luxorius. 1984. pap. 10.00 (*0-317-17736-2*) Atlantis Edns.
— Irish Monastic Poems. 1984. pap. 10.00 (*0-317-07621-3*) Atlantis Edns.
— Middle English Poems. 1976. pap. 10.00 (*0-685-62624-5*) Atlantis Edns.
— New Epigrams from Martial. 1991. pap. 10.00 (*0-685-55466-X*) Atlantis Edns.
— One Hundred Epigrams: From the Greek Anthology. 1977. pap. 10.00 (*0-685-63924-X*) Atlantis Edns.
O'Connell, Richard, jt. auth. see Bowerman, Bruce L.
O'Connell, Richard, ed. see Martialis, Marcus Valerius Martialis.
O'Connell, Richard L., tr. see Garcia Lorca, Federico.
O'Connell, Richard T., jt. auth. see Bowerman, Bruce L.
O'Connell, Rick M. 365 Easy Italian Recipes Anniversary Edition. 256p. 1996. 12.95 (*0-06-018661-5*) HarpC.
O'Connell, Robert. Imagination & Metaphysics in St. Augustine. LC 85-82595. (Aquinas Lectures). 70p. 1986. 15.00 (*0-87462-227-1*) Marquette.
— Plato & the Human Paradox. LC 96-52170. xviii, 162p. (C). 1997. pap. 15.00 (*0-8232-1758-2*) Fordham.
— Plato & the Human Paradox. 2nd rev. ed. LC 96-52170. xviii, 162p. (C). 1997. 30.00 (*0-8232-1757-4*) Fordham.
— William James on the Courage to Believe. 2nd rev. ed. LC 97-12135. 141p. (C). 1997. pap. 17.00 (*0-8232-1728-0*) Fordham.
— William James on the Courage to Believe. 2nd rev. ed. LC 97-12135. (American Philosophy Ser.: No. 8). x, 223p. (C). 1997. 30.00 (*0-8232-1727-2*) Fordham.
O'Connell, Robert H. Concentricity & Continuity: The Literary Structure of Isaiah. (JSOT Supplement Ser.: No. 188). 272p. 1994. 75.00 (*1-85075-521-3*, Pub. by Sheffield Acad) CUP Services.
O'Connell, Robert H. The Rhetoric of the Book of Judges. LC 95-48238. (Supplements to Vetus Testamentum Ser.: Vol. 63). xxii, 541p. 1995. 175.50 (*90-04-10104-7*) Brill Academic Pubs.
O'Connell, Robert J. Art & the Christian Intelligence in St. Augustine. LC 78-546. 272p. 1978. 37.95 (*0-674-04675-7*) HUP.
— Images of Conversion in St. Augustine's Confessions. xiv, 327p. 1996. 35.00 (*0-8232-1598-9*) Fordham.
— The Origin of the Soul in St. Augustine's Later Works. LC 86-82222. xiii, 363p. (C). 1987. 40.00 (*0-8232-1172-X*) Fordham.
— Saint Augustine's Confessions: The Odyssey of Soul. 2nd ed. LC 69-12731. xvi, 200p. 1989. pap. 19.95 (*0-8232-1265-3*) Fordham.
— Soundings in St. Augustine's Imagination. LC 93-11257. x, 309p. 1993. 40.00 (*0-8232-1347-1*) Fordham.
— Soundings in St. Augustine's Imagination. LC 93-11257. x, 296p. 1995. pap. 19.95 (*0-8232-1348-X*) Fordham.
— St. Augustine's Early Theory of Man, A. D. 386-391. LC 68-21981. 323p. 1969. reprint ed. pap. 100.20 (*0-7837-4173-1*, 205902200012) Bks Demand.
— Teilhard's Vision of the Past: The Making of a Method. LC 82-71279. 205p. 1982. 30.00 (*0-8232-1090-1*) Fordham.
— Teilhard's Vision of the Past: The Making of a Method. LC 82-71279. 205p. 1982. pap. 17.00 (*0-8232-1091-X*) Fordham.
O'Connell, Robert L. Fast Eddie: A Novel in Many Voices. LC 99-11687. 288p. 1999. 24.00 (*0-688-16690-3*, Wm Morrow) Morrow Avon.
— Of Arms & Men: A History of War, Weapons, & Aggression. (Illus.). 384p. 1990. reprint ed. pap. text 16.95 (*0-19-505360-5*) OUP.
— Ride of the Second Horseman: The Birth & Death of War. 305p. 1998. text 27.00 (*0-7881-5619-5*) DIANE Pub.
— Ride of the Second Horseman: The Birth & Death of War. 320p. 1997. pap. 15.95 (*0-19-511920-7*) OUP.
— Sacred Vessels: The Cult of the Battleship & the Rise of the U. S. Navy. LC 92-25712. (Illus.). 432p. (C). 1993. pap. 15.95 (*0-19-508006-8*) OUP.
***O'Connell, Rory.** Legal Theory in the Crucible of Constitutional Justice: A Study of Judges & Political Morality in Canada, Ireland & Italy. LC 00-34253. 2000. write for info. (*0-7546-2097-2*, Pub. by Ashgate Pub) Ashgate Pub Co.
O'Connell-Roussell, Sheila & Nichols, Terri Vorndran. Lectionary-Based Gospel Dramas for Advent, Christmas & Epiphany. (Illus.). 104p. 1997. pap. 23.95 (*0-88489-485-1*) St Marys.
***O'Connell-Roussell, Sheila, et al.** Lectionary-Based Gospel Dramas for Lent & the Easter Triduum. 128p. 1999. spiral bd. 29.95 (*0-88489-627-7*) St Marys.
O'Connell, Sandra E. The Manager As Communicator. (Illus.). 206p. (C). 1986. reprint ed. pap. text 21.50 (*0-8191-5402-4*) U Pr of Amer.
***O'Connell, Sanji.** Theory of Mind. 2000. pap. 12.95 (*0-552-99709-9*, Pub. by Transworld Publishers Ltd) Trafalgar.
O'Connell, Sean. The Car & British Society: Class, Gender, & Motoring, 1896-1939. LC 98-18297. (Studies in Popular Culture). (Illus.). 208p. 1998. text 79.95 (*0-7190-5148-7*, Pub. by Manchester Univ Pr) St Martin.
***O'Connell, Sean.** Cartesian Dreams. (Philosophy-in-Drama Ser.: Vol. 1). 100p. 2000. pap. 8.95 (*0-9686685-0-X*) Phi-Psi Pubs.
O'Connell, Sean, jt. auth. see King-Farlow, John.
***O'Connell, Sean P.** Outspeak: Narrating Identities That Matter. LC 99-86459. (C). 2000. pap. text 18.95 (*0-7914-4738-3*) State U NY Pr.
— Outspeak: Narrating Identities That Matter. LC 99-86459. (C). 2000. text 57.50 (*0-7914-4737-5*) State U NY Pr.
O'Connell, Shannon. That Darn Cat. (Romance Ser.: No. 859). 1992. per. 2.69 (*0-373-08859-0*, 5-08859-6) Silhouette.
O'Connell, Shaun. Imagining Boston: A Literary Landscape. 424p. 1992. pap. 15.00 (*0-8070-5103-9*) Beacon Pr.
— Remarkable, Unspeakable New York: A Literary History. LC 94-36415. 400p. 1997. pap. 14.00 (*0-8070-5003-2*) Beacon Pr.
O'Connell, Sue. Cambridge First Certificate: Listening & Speaking. 1992. teacher ed. 15.95 (*0-521-39696-4*) Cambridge U Pr.
***O'Connell, Sue.** Introduction to Problem Solving: A Resource for the Elementary Grades. LC 99-55425. 2000. pap. text 19.00 (*0-325-00199-5*) Heinemann.
O'Connell, Terry & Wachtel, Ted. Conferencing Handbook: The New Real Justice Training Manual. 128p. 1998. pap. 25.00 (*0-9633887-5-4*) Pipers Pr.
O'Connell, Theodore X., et al. Classic Presentations & Rapid Reviews for USMLE, Step 2. LC 98-66122. 1999. pap. 25.00 (*1-888308-05-2*) J & S Pub VA.
O'Connell, Theodore X., jt. auth. see Huerta, Sergio.
O'Connell, Timothy E. Good People, Tough Choices: Making the Right Decisions Every Day. 128p. 1999. pap. 12.95 (*0-88347-427-1*) T More.
— Let your Spirit Breathe: Living with Joy & Peace. 144p. 1999. pap. 12.95 (*0-88347-439-5*, Pub. by T More) BookWorld.
— Making Disciples: A Handbook of Christian Moral Formation. LC 97-37558. 192p. 1998. pap. 19.95 (*0-8245-1727-X*, Herdr & Herdr) Crossroad NY.
— Principles for a Catholic Morality: Revised Edition. rev. ed. LC 89-45553. 324p. 1990. pap. 18.00 (*0-06-254865-4*) HarpC.
— Tend Your Own Garden: How to Raise Great Kids. LC 98-60970. 112p. 1998. pap. 12.95 (*0-88347-417-4*, 661-028 7417) T More.
O'Connell, Tom. Addicted? A Guide to Understanding Addiction. LC 90-91803. 204p. (Orig.). 1990. pap. text 19.00 (*0-9620318-0-1*) Sanctuary Unltd.
— Danny the Prophet: A Fantastic Adventure. LC 94-92421. 125p. (Orig.). 1996. pap. 12.00 (*0-9620318-4-4*) Sanctuary Unltd.
— Improving Intimacy: Ten Powerful Strategies... A Spiritual Approach. LC 93-92664. 56p. (Orig.). 1993. pap. text 7.00 (*0-9620318-2-8*) Sanctuary Unltd.
— The Monadnock Revelations. A Spiritual Memoir. LC 96-92248. 125p. (Orig.). 1999. pap. 15.00 (*0-9620318-5-2*) Sanctuary Unltd.
— The Odd Duck: A Story for Odd People of All Ages. LC 93-84633. 60p. (Orig.). 1993. pap. 7.00 (*0-9620318-3-6*) Sanctuary Unltd.
O'Connell, Tyne. Sex, Lies & Litigation. 245p. 1998. mass mkt. 12.95 (*0-7472-5613-6*, Pub. by Headline Bk Pub) Trafalgar.
O'Connell, Victoria M., jt. auth. see Kramer, Donald E.
O'Connell, Vincent, jt. auth. see O'Connell, April.
O'Connell, Walter E. Action Therapy & Adlerian Theory: Selected Papers. LC 75-16932. 253p. (Orig.). 1975. pap. text 8.00 (*0-918560-06-3*) Adler Sch Prof Psy.
O'Connell, William. Graphic Communication in Architecture. 148p. 1985. text 23.80 (*0-87563-275-0*) Stipes.
O'Connell, William & Sibson & Company Staff. Reinventing the Sales Team: Building an Effective Sales Organization for Top Line Growth. 240p. 1997. text 34.95 (*0-07-048216-0*) McGraw.
O'Connell, William B. America's Money Trauma: How Washington Blunders Crippled the U. S. Financial System. 176p. (Orig.). 1992. pap. 14.95 (*0-9634395-0-2*) Conversation Pr.
O'Conner, Bridget, et al. Training for Organizations. (KU - Office Procedures Ser.). 358p. (C). 1995. mass mkt. 54.95 (*0-538-71122-1*) S-W Pub.
***O'Conner, Clint.** The Morgan Horse. 272p. 2000. 18.99 (*0-7089-5710-2*) Ulverscroft.
O'Conner, Daniel J. Airplanes & Income Tax. 6th ed. 75p. 1997. pap. 14.00 (*0-9613218-5-7*) Aviation.
O'Conner, David, jt. auth. see Silverman, David P.
O'Conner, Diane V., jt. auth. see Redding, Joan.
O'Conner, Edward. Voice of Prophecy Today. 1999. pap. text 1.95 (*1-57918-063-9*) Queen Publ.
O'Conner, Emmet. Syndicalism in Ireland, 1917-1923. 1988. 39.95 (*0-902561-52-9*, Pub. by Cork Univ) Intl Spec Bk.
***O'Conner, Erin.** Raw Material: Producing Pathology in Victorian Culture. (Illus.). 280p. 2000. lib. bdg. 54.95 (*0-8223-2608-6*) Duke.
O'Conner, Fr. J., tr. see Claudel, Paul.
O'Conner, Frederick. Express Yourself in Written English. 112p. 1994. pap. 13.95 (*0-8442-7692-8*, 76928, Natl Textbk Co) NTC Contemp Pub Co.
O'Conner, Helen K., jt. auth. see Beckham, Sheila.
O'Conner, Jane, jt. auth. see Sweeny, Emma.
***O'Conner, Joey.** I Know You Love Me, But Do You Like Me? How to Become Your Mate's Best Friend. LC 99-24846. 192p. 1999. pap. text 12.99 (*0-8499-3751-5*) Word Pub.
O'Conner, Joseph. Sweet Liberty: Travels in Irish America. 384p. (Orig.). 1997. pap. 17.95 (*0-330-33323-2*, Pub. by Picador) Trans-Atl Phila.
O'Conner, Karen. Essentials of American Government: Continuity & Change. (C). 1998. write for info. (*0-205-28049-8*, Macmillan Coll); write for info. (*0-205-28051-X*, Macmillan Coll) P-H.
O'Conner, Patricia T. Woe Is I: The Grammarphobe's Guide to Better English in Plain English. LC 96-11473. 227p. 1996. 16.95 (*0-399-14196-0*, Grosset-Putnam) Putnam Pub Group.
— Woe Is I: The Grammarphobe's Guide to Better English in Plain English. LC 96-11473. 227p. 1998. reprint ed. pap. 11.00 (*1-57322-625-4*, Riverhead Books) Putnam Pub Group.
O'Conner, Patricia T. Words Fail Me. What Everyone Who Writes Should Know about Writing. LC 99-25610. 240p. (C). 1999. 18.95 (*0-15-100371-8*) Harcourt.
***O'Conner, Patricia T.** Words Fail Me: What Everyone Who Writes Should Know about Writing. 240p. 2000. mass mkt. 12.00 (*0-15-601087-9*) Harcourt.
O'Conner, Richard. Undoing Depression: What Therapy Doesn't Teach You & Medication Can't Give You. 368p. 1999. reprint ed. pap. 12.95 (*0-425-16679-1*) Berkley Pub.
O'Conner, Tom. Eat Like a Horse, Drink Like a Fish: A Bellyfull of Laughter. (Illus.). 272p. 1997. 20.95 (*1-86105-068-2*, Pub. by Robson Bks) Parkwest Pubns.
O'Connor. American Government (C). 2000. pap. text. write for info. (*0-321-06959-5*) Addson-Wesley Educ.
— American Government: Study Guide. 4th ed. 1999. pap. text, student ed. 12.75 (*0-205-29434-0*) S&S Trade.
— Art of Systems Thinking. 1998. pap. 15.00 (*0-7225-3442-6*) Thorsons PA.
O'Connor. Correspondence Theory of Truth. 144p. 1994. 49.95 (*0-7512-0308-4*) Ashgate Pub Co.
O'Connor. Economics: Free Enterprise 1988. 1988. text 65.25 (*0-15-374200-3*); text 75.00 (*0-15-374201-1*) Holt R&W.
— Express Yourself in Written English. 1990. pap., teacher ed. 18.30 (*0-8442-7693-6*) NTC Contemp Pub Co.
— Fitness on Foot Today: Walking, Jogging & Running. (Health Sciences Ser.). 2000. mass mkt. 12.50 (*0-534-36206-0*) Brooks-Cole.
— Flexibility & Fitness Today. (Health Sciences Ser.). 1999. mass mkt. 12.50 (*0-534-36132-3*) Brooks-Cole.
— Life Management Skills. (OX - Home Economic Ser.). 1987. mass mkt., wbk. ed. 19.95 (*0-538-32130-X*) S-W Pub.
— Practical Fire & Arson Investigation. 3p. 1992. lib. bdg. 54.95 (*0-8493-9518-6*) CRC Pr.
— Soccer Today. LC 99-51507. (Health Sciences). 1999. mass mkt. 29.95 (*0-534-36131-5*) Brooks-Cole.
— Speech: Exploring Communication. 3rd ed. 1998. 20.28 (*0-13-827296-4*) P-H.
— Texas Economics: Free Enterprise 1988. 1988. text 75.00 (*0-15-374216-X*); text 65.25 (*0-15-374215-1*) Holt R&W.
— Thinking Through Life. 1998. pap. text 42.00 (*0-02-389042-8*) S&S Childrens.
O'Connor, ed. Constitutional Law. (C). 1998. text 55.75 (*0-673-46356-7*) Addison-Wesley.
O'Connor & Hannan. Laboratory Inspection Manual. LC 93-9055. 408p. 1993. ring bd. 102.00 (*0-8342-0500-9*, S129) Aspen Pub.
O'Connor & Sabato. American Government High School. 3rd ed. 1997. text 64.00 (*0-205-27410-2*) P-H.
O'Connor, jt. auth. see Berman, Daniel M.
O'Connor, jt. auth. see Drewry.
O'Connor, jt. auth. see Gossman.
O'Connor, jt. ed. see Occeli.
O'Connor, Aine, ed. Hollywood Irish in Their Own Words. (Illus.). 144p. 1997. pap. 17.95 (*1-57098-109-4*) Roberts Rinehart.
***O'Connor, Alice.** Poverty Knowledge: Social Science, Social Policy & the Poor in Twentieth-Century U. S. History. LC 00-34682. (Politics & Society in Twentieth-Century America Ser.). 2000. write for info. (*0-691-00917-1*) Princeton U Pr.
O'Connor, Alice, jt. auth. see Gilbert, Jess.
***O'Connor, Allison.** A Message from Heaven: The Life & Crimes of Fr. Sean Fortune. 224p. 2000. 19.95 (*0-86322-270-6*, Pub. by Brandon Bk Pubs) Irish Bks Media.
O'Connor, Ann, ed. Congress A to Z: A Ready Reference Encyclopedia. 2nd ed. LC 93-25926. 560p. (YA). 1993. text 145.00 (*0-87187-826-7*) Congr Quarterly.
O'Connor, Anna T. & Callahan-Young, Sheila. Seven Windows to a Child's World: 100 Ideas for the Multiple Intelligences Classroom - Grades Pre-K - 3. LC 94-78533. xvii, 268 p. 1994. pap. 26.95 (*0-932935-77-X*, NB1261) SkyLght.
O'Connor, Anne Marie, jt. auth. see Williams, Roshumba.
O'Connor, Anthony M. The African City. LC 83-10648. (Illus.). 359p. (C). 1983. 36.00 (*0-8419-0881-8*, Africana) Holmes & Meier.
***O'Connor, B. J. & Giembycz, M. A., eds.** Astha: Epidemiology, Anti-Inflammatory Therapy & Future Trends. (Respiratory Pharmacology & Pharmacotherapy Ser.). 270p. 2000. 195.00 (*3-7643-5858-0*) Birkhauser.
O'Connor, Barbara. Barefoot Dancer: The Story of Isadora Duncan. LC 93-14312. (Trailblazers Ser.). (Illus.). (J). (gr. 4-7). 1994. lib. bdg. 22.60 (*0-87614-807-0*, Carolrhoda) Lerner Pub.
— Beethoven in Paradise. LC 96-17289. 160p. (gr. 5-8). 1997. 15.00 (*0-374-30666-4*) FS&G.
***O'Connor, Barbara.** Beethoven in Paradise. (Illus.). 160p. (YA). (gr. 5-8). 1999. pap. 4.95 (*0-374-40588-3*, Sunburst Bks) FS&G.
— Beethoven in Paradise, Class Set. (YA). 1997. boxed set 97.30 incl. audio (*0-7887-2777-X*, 46097) Recorded Bks.
— Beethoven in Paradise, Homework Set. (YA). (gr. 7). 1997. boxed set 40.20 incl. audio (*0-7887-1845-2*, 40625) Recorded Bks.
O'Connor, Barbara. Katherine Dunham: Pioneer of Black Dance. LC 98-50426. (Trailblazers Biographies Ser.). (Illus.). 112p. (J). (gr. 4-7). 2000. 23.93 (*1-57505-353-5*, Carolrhoda) Lerner Pub.
— Mammolina: A Story about Maria Montessori. LC 92-415. (Creative Minds Ser.). (J). (gr. 3-6). 1993. pap. 2.98 (*0-87614-602-7*, Carolrhoda); lib. bdg. 19.95 (*0-87614-743-0*, Carolrhoda) Lerner Pub.
— Me & Rupert Goody. LC 98-30235. 112p. (YA). (gr. 4-7). 1999. 15.00 (*0-374-34904-5*, Frances Foster) FS&G.
***O'Connor, Barbara.** Moonpie & Ivy. 2001. text. write for info. (*0-374-35059-0*) FS&G.
O'Connor, Barbara. The Soldiers' Voice. The Story of Ernie Pyle. LC 94-44283. (J). 1996. 16.95 (*0-87614-942-5*, Carolrhoda) Lerner Pub.
— The World at His Fingertips: A Story about Louis Braille. LC 96-49950. (Carolrhoda Creative Minds Bks.). (J). 1997. lib. bdg. 14.95 (*1-57505-052-8*, Carolrhoda) Lerner Pub.
O'Connor, Barbara, jt. auth. see Kelly, Mary J.
O'Connor, Barbara H. A Color Atlas & Instruction Manual of Peripheral Blood Morphology. (Illus.). 316p. (C). 1984. pap. text 47.00 (*0-683-06624-2*) Lppncott W & W.
O'Connor, Barney & Scanlon, John A. International Human Rights: A Bibliography, 1970-1975. rev. ed. LC 80-67763. xiii, 172p. 1980. 35.00 (*0-268-01148-6*, 305370) W S Hein.
O'Connor, Basilides A., ed. see Henri D'Arci.
O'Connor, Bill. The Trekking Peaks of Nepal. (Illus.). 224p. 1989. pap. 24.95 (*0-938567-28-4*) Mountaineers.
***O'Connor, Bill.** The Trekking Peaks of Nepal. 224p. 1999. pap. 24.95 (*0-89886-676-6*) Mountaineers.
Oconnor, Bob. Management Training Today. 1989. pap. 19.25 (*0-314-68951-6*) West Pub.
O'Connor, Bob, jt. auth. see Flores, Tom.
O'Connor, Bonnie B. Healing Traditions: Alternative Medicine & the Health Professions. (Studies in Health, Illness, & Caregiving). (Illus.). 288p. (Orig.). (C). 1995. text 39.95 (*0-8122-3184-8*); pap. text 17.95 (*0-8122-1398-X*) U of Pa Pr.
O'Connor, Brendan D., jt. ed. see Keegan, Brendan F.
O'Connor, Brian, ed. The Adorno Reader. LC 99-46075. (Reader Ser.). 352p. 1999. 64.95 (*0-631-21076-8*) Blackwell Pubs.
***O'Connor, Brian, ed.** The Adorno Reader. LC 99-46075. (Reader Ser.). 352p. 2000. pap. 29.95 (*0-631-21077-6*) Blackwell Pubs.
O'Connor, Brian C. Explorations in Indexing & Abstracting: Pointing, Virtue & Power. LC 96-18333. (Library Science Text Ser.). 300p. 1996. lib. bdg. 40.00 (*1-56308-184-9*) Libs Unl.
O'Connor, Brian P., et al. The Role of the Minister in Caring for the Dying Patient & the Bereaved. 18.95 (*0-405-12504-6*) Ayer.
O'Connor, Bridget, jt. auth. see Regan, Elizabeth.
O'Connor, Bridget N., jt. auth. see Regan, Elizabeth A.
O'Connor, C. J. Research Frontiers in Magnetochemistry. LC 93-16991. 424p. 1993. text 109.00 (*981-02-1246-1*) World Scientific Pub.
O'Connor, Carol. Jackie's New Friend. (Illus.). 12p. (J). (ps-1). 1998. pap. 3.75 (*1-880612-71-2*) Seedling Pubns.
— Remember When. unabridged ed. (Illus.). 64p. (Orig.). 1996. pap. 9.95 (*0-9653922-2-8*) Vital Link.

O

An Asterisk (*) at the beginning of an entry indicates that the title is appearing for the first time.

O'Connor, Carol A. The Handbook for Organizational Change: Strategy & Skill for Trainers & Developers. LC 93-21715. (Training Ser.). 1993. write for info. (0-07-707693-1) McGraw.

— The Professional's Guide to Successful Management: The Eight Essentials for Running Your Firm, Practice or Partnership. LC 94-27726. 1994. write for info. (0-07-707999-X) McGraw.

— A Sort of Utopia: Scarsdale, 1891-1981. LC 82-5855. (Illus.). 283p. (C). 1983. text 64.50 (0-87395-659-1); pap. text 21.95 (0-87395-660-5) State U NY Pr.

— Successful Leadership. LC 96-17933. (Barron's Business Success Ser.). 96p. 1997. pap. 6.95 (0-7641-0072-6) Barron.

***O'Connor, Carol M.** Hedgehog Day. 8p. (J). (gr. k-2). 1999. pap. 3.75 (1-880612-93-3) Seedling Pubns.

O'Connor, Carroll. I Think I'm Outta Here: A Memoir of All My Families. 288p. 1998. 24.00 (0-671-01758-6, PB Hardcover) PB.

— I Think I'm Outta Here: A Memoir of All My Families. 288p. 1999. pap. 14.00 (0-671-01759-4) S&S Trade.

— I Think I'm Outta Here: A Memoir of All My Families. 1999. reprint ed. mass mkt. 6.99 (0-671-01760-8) PB.

O'Connor, Catherine. Atormentados (The Tormented Ones) (Bianca Ser.). (SPA.). 1998. per. 3.50 (0-373-33454-0, 1-33454-9) Harlequin Bks.

— Mentiras. (Bianca Ser.: No. 33401).Tr. of Sweet Lies. (SPA.). 1997. per. 3.50 (0-373-33401-X, 1-33401-0) Harlequin Bks.

— On Equal Terms. (Presents Ser.: No. 94). 1998. pap. 3.75 (0-373-18694-0, 1-18694-9) Harlequin Bks.

***O'Connor, Charles.** O'Connor's Classic Movie Guide: The Finest Films Through Seven Decades, 1930-1998. unabridged ed. 306p. 1998. pap. 15.95 (1-893877-03-5) OConnor Hannon.

— O'Connor's Movie Star Treasury Vol. I: 1930-1959. unabridged ed. 272p. 1998. pap. 15.95 (1-893877-01-9) OConnor Hannon.

— O'Connor's Movie Star Treasury Vol. II: 1960-1998. unabridged ed. 274p. 1998. pap. 15.95 (1-893877-02-7) OConnor Hannon.

O'Connor, Charles A., et al. Perspective Drawing & Applications. 2nd ed. LC 97-33980. 96p. (C). 1997. pap. text 39.33 (0-13-633025-8) P-H.

O'Connor, Charles E. Fortuisms. 42p. 1997. pap. 6.95 (0-9661915-0-1) C G Pub.

O'Connor, Charles J. & Litzman, Sidney I., eds. Handbook of Chemical Industry Labeling. LC 83-22108. (Illus.). 487p. 1984. 98.00 (0-8155-0965-0, Noyes Pubns) Noyes.

O'Connor, Claire. Love in Another Room. 254p. 1997. pap. 13.95 (1-86023-019-9, Pub. by Martello Bks) Irish Amer Bk.

O'Connor, Colin. Design of Bridge Superstructures. LC 76-121912. (Illus.). 563p. reprint ed. pap. 174.60 (0-7837-3460-3, 205778600008) Bks Demand.

— Roman Bridges. LC 92-30900. (Illus.). 251p. (C). 1994. text 110.00 (0-521-39326-4) Cambridge U Pr.

***O'Connor, Colin & Shaw, Peter A.** Bridge Loads. LC 00-23894. 2000. write for info. (0-419-24600-2, E & FN Spon) Routledge.

O'Connor, Colleen. They Bury Their Mistakes: How to Survive Your Hospitalization. 100p. (Orig.). 1994. pap. 10.95 (0-9641088-3-6) Valverde Pubns.

O'Connor, Colleen M., jt. ed. see Flemion, Jess.

***O'Connor, Cynthia.** The Pleasing Hours: The Travels of James Caulfeild, 1st Earl of Charlemont, Ireland, 1728-1799. LC 99-196839. (Illus.). 288p. 1999. 35.95 (1-898256-66-7, Pub. by Collins Press) Irish Bks Media.

O'Connor, D. & Fairall, P. A. Criminal Defences. 2nd ed. 1988. 76.00 (0-409-49276-0, AT, MICHIE) LEXIS Pub.

— Criminal Defences. 3rd ed. LC 96-123697. 350p. 1996. write for info. (0-409-30846-3, MICHIE) LEXIS Pub.

O'Connor, D. A. Return to Falling Heath. 370p. mass mkt. 5.99 (1-896329-31-4) Picasso Publ.

O'Connor, D. E., jt. auth. see French, T. W.

O'Connor, D. J. Crime at El Escorial: The 1892 Child Murder, the Press & the Jury. LC 94-41470. (Iberian Studies in History, Literature & Culture). 262p. (C). 1996. text 69.95 (1-883255-89-9); pap. text 54.95 (1-883255-88-0) Intl Scholars.

— An Introduction to the Philosophy of Education. (Modern Revivals in Philosophy Ser.). 156p. 1994. 53.95 (0-7512-0307-6, Pub. by Gregg Revivals) Ashgate Pub Co.

O'Connor, D. J., ed. A Critical History of Western Philosophy. (C). 1985. pap. 18.95 (0-02-923840-4) Free Pr.

O'Connor, D. J., et al, eds. Surface Analysis Methods in Materials Science. (Surface Sciences Ser.: Vol. 23). (Illus.). 480p. 1992. 79.00 (0-387-53611-6) Spr-Verlag.

***O'Connor, D. L.** Representations of the Cuban & Philippine Insurrections on the Spanish Stage 1887-1898. 280p. 2000. pap. 17.00 (0-927534-92-4) Biling Rev-Pr.

O'Connor, D. Thomas, jt. auth. see Burkholder, John.

***O'Connor, Dan.** Clinical Pathology for Athletic Trainers. 250p. (C). 2000. pap. text 32.00 (1-55642-469-8) SLACK Inc.

— The Kauai Golf & Travel Guide. 104p. 2000. pap. 9.95 (0-9667235-0-3) Waterton CA.

— Sugar: A Hawaiian Novel. (Illus.). 320p. 2000. 18.95 (0-9667235-2-X); pap. 12.95 (0-9667235-1-1) Waterton CA.

O'Connor, Dan, jt. auth. see Peterson, Lenka.

O'Connor, Daniel. Gospel, Raj & Swaraj: The Missionary Years of C. F. Andrews, 1904-14. Hollenweger, Walter, ed. (Studies in the Intercultural History of Christianity: Vol. 62). XII, 366p. 1990. pap. 69.00 (3-631-42055-2) P Lang Pubng.

O'Connor, Daniel, tr. see Pieper, Josef.

O'Connor, Daniel D., jt. auth. see Clarke, Duncan L.

O'Connor, Daniel J. Airplanes & Income Tax. 7th rev. ed. Ebersole, Michael J., ed. 64p. 1997. spiral bd. 19.95 (0-9613218-8-1) GCBA.

O'Connor, David. Ancient Egyptian Society. LC 89-85824. (Illus.). 48p. (Orig.). (C). 1990. pap. text 7.95 (0-911239-17-0) Carnegie Mus.

— Ancient Nubia. (Illus.). 224p. (C). 1994. pap. 30.00 (0-924171-28-6) U Museum Pubns.

— God & Inscrutable Evil: In Defense of Theism & Atheism. LC 97-34277. 290p. 1997. 70.50 (0-8476-8763-5); pap. 26.95 (0-8476-8764-3) Rowman.

— The Metaphysics of G. E. Moore. (Philosophical Studies: No. 25). 190p. 1982. text 112.50 (90-277-1352-9, D Reidel) Kluwer Academic.

— A Short History of Ancient Egypt. LC 89-85826. (Illus.). 48p. (Orig.). (C). 1990. pap. text 7.95 (0-911239-16-2) Carnegie Mus.

O'Connor, David, et al, eds. The Future of Asia in the World Economy. 224p. 1998. pap. 38.00 (92-64-16069-8, 41 98 04 1 P, Pub. by Org for Econ) OECD.

O'Connor, David, jt. auth. see Brown, Sarah.

O'Connor, David B. & Cline, Eric H., eds. Amenhotep III: Perspectives on His Reign. LC 97-33738. (Illus.). 448p. (C). 1998. text 59.50 (0-472-10742-9, 10742) U of Mich Pr.

***O'Connor, David E. & Faille, Christopher C.** Basic Economic Principles: A Guide for Students. LC 00-21050. 208p. 2000. 45.00 (0-313-31005-X, GR1005, Greenwood Pr) Greenwood.

O'Connor, Denis. Glue Sniffing & Volatile Substance Abuse: Case Studies of Children & Young Adults. LC 83-16464. 103p. 1983. text 53.95 (0-566-00641-3, Pub. by Avebry) Ashgate Pub Co.

O'Connor, Dennis. Financing the State Water Project. 144p. 1994. pap. write for info. (1-58703-027-6, CRB-94-004) CA St Libry.

— Financing the State Water Project: Options for Change. 70p. 1994. pap. write for info. (1-58703-029-2, CRB-94-005) CA St Libry.

— The Governance of the Metropolitan Water District of Southern California: An Overview of the Issues. 60p. 1998. pap. write for info. (1-58703-092-6, CRB-98-013) CA St Libry.

— Governance of the Metropolitan Water District of Southern California: Options for Change. 45p. 1998. pap. write for info. (1-58703-097-7, CRB-98-018) CA St Libry.

— Is It Time to Talk about Changing the State Water Project's Financing System?, Vol. 3. 5p. 1994. pap. write for info. (1-58703-025-X) CA St Libry.

O'Connor, Dennis & Swenson, Jennifer. Safety & Oversight of Amusement Rides in California. 51p. 1997. pap. write for info. (1-58703-074-8, CRB-97-012) CA St Libry.

O'Connor, Dennis & Swenson, Jennifer. Safety & Oversight of Amusement Rides in California. 51p. (C). 1999. pap. text 20.00 (0-7881-7620-X) DIANE Pub.

O'Connor, Dennis J. & Bueso, Alberto T. Personal Financial Management: A Forecasting & Control Approach. (Illus.). 560p. (C). 1983. text 36.00 (0-13-657940-X) P-H.

O'Connor Di Vito, Nadine. Patterns Across Spoken & Written French: Empirical Research on the Interaction among Forms, Function, & Genres. LC 96-76941. (FRE.). 256p. (C). 1997. pap. text 35.96 (0-669-35173-3) HM Trade Div.

O'Connor, Donal. Job: His Wife, His Friends, & His God. LC 95-226162. 174p. 1997. pap. 49.95 (1-85607-127-8, Pub. by Columba Press) Intl Scholars.

— Job: His Wife, His Friends, & His God. 174p. 1997. 69.95 (1-85607-213-4) Intl Scholars.

O'Connor, Eamonn. Chord Master. 144p. 1997. pap. 19.95 (1-900428-10-5, OS 00112) Music Sales.

O'Connor, Edmund. Education. Yapp, Malcolm, ed. (World History Program Ser.). (Illus.). 32p. (J). (gr. 6-10). 1980. reprint ed. pap. text 5.90 (0-89908-122-3) Greenhaven.

— Roosevelt. Yapp, Malcolm & Killingray, Margaret, eds. (World History Program Ser.). (Illus.). 32p. (YA). (gr. 6-11). 1980. reprint ed. pap. text 5.90 (0-89908-100-2) Greenhaven.

— The Wealth of Japan. Yapp, Malcolm et al, eds. (World History Program Ser.). (Illus.). 32p. (YA). (gr. 6-11). 1980. reprint ed. pap. text 5.90 (0-89908-212-2) Greenhaven.

O'Connor, Edmund, ed. see Doncaster, Islay.

O'Connor, Edmund, ed. see Killingray, David & Killingray, Margaret.

O'Connor, Edmund, ed. see Yapp, Malcolm.

O'Connor, Edward. The Last Hurrah. 437p. Date not set. 28.95 (0-8488-2373-7) Amereon Ltd.

O'Connor, Edward D. The Catholic Vision. LC 91-66667. 480p. 1994. pap. 15.95 (0-87973-736-0, 736) Our Sunday Visitor.

— Marian Apparitions Today - Why So Many? LC 96-67811. (Illus.). 148p. (Orig.). 1996. pap. 7.95 (1-882972-71-6, 3391) Queenship Pub.

O'Connor, Edward F. A Primer on Intellectual property Law & Patent Litigation: Understanding & Defending Your Clients Patents, Trademarks & Copyrights. LC 96-78634. 175p. 1997. pap. 49.95 (1-57073-412-7) Amer Bar Assn.

O'Connor, Edwin. Benjy: A Ferocious Fairy Tale. LC 88-46131. (Pocket Paragon Ser.). (Illus.). 128p. (J). (gr. 4-7). 1996. pap. 11.95 (0-87923-795-3) Godine.

— The Edge of Sadness. 1991. lib. bdg. 21.95 (1-56849-061-5) Buccaneer Bks.

— I Was Dancing. 1966. pap. 5.25 (0-8222-0552-1) Dramatists Play.

***O'Connor, Edwin.** Last Hurrah. 1998. pap. 14.00 (0-316-19092-6, Back Bay) Little.

O'Connor, Edwin. The Last Hurrah. 427p. 1985. reprint ed. pap. 14.95 (0-316-62659-7) Little.

O'Connor, Egan, jt. auth. see Gofman, John W.

O'Connor, Egan, ed. see Gofman, John W.

O'Connor, Elizabeth. Servant Leaders, Servant Structures. (Illus.). 96p. (Orig.). 1991. pap. 7.95 (1-883639-03-4) Servant Ldrship.

O'Connor, Elizabeth R., jt. auth. see Cass, Patricia J.

O'Connor, Ellen. Within Ourselves. 91p. 1982. 7.95 (0-9613897-0-2) Valen Pub.

O'Connor, Ellen M., ed. Myrtilla Miner. LC 79-89384. (Black Heritage Library Collection). 1977. 16.95 (0-8369-8640-7) Ayer.

O'Connor, Ellen M. & Miner, Myrtilla. Myrtilla Miner: A Memoir. LC 73-92235. (American Negro, Ser. 3). 1970. reprint ed. 18.95 (0-405-01933-5) Ayer.

O'Connor, Emily & Fenelon, Mary, compiled by. Business Directory & Buyer's Guide: Orange County, NY. 400p. (Orig.). pap. write for info. (0-945965-02-8) Centers Composition.

***O'Connor, Erin.** Raw Material: Producing Pathology in Victorian Culture. LC 00-30308. (Body, Commodity, Text Ser.). (Illus.). 280p. 2001. pap. 18.95 (0-8223-2616-7) Duke.

O'Connor, Eugene. The Essential Epicurus: Letters, Principal Doctrines, Vatican Sayings, & Fragments. LC 92-42302. (Great Books in Philosophy). 101p. (Orig.). (C). 1993. pap. 5.95 (0-87975-810-4) Prometheus Bks.

O'Connor, Eugene, tr. see Plato.

O'Connor, Evangeline M. Who's Who & What's What in Shakespeare: Over 6,000 Factual & Analytical Entries. 1996. 9.99 (0-517-25923-0) Random Hse Value.

O'Connor, Feargus, et al. The Employer & the Employed, the Chambers' Philosophy Refuted. Thompson, Dorothy, ed. (Chartism, Working-Class Politics in the Industrial Revolution Ser.). 144p. 1987. lib. bdg. 13.00 (0-8240-5592-6) Garland.

O'Connor, Finbarr W., jt. ed. see Klockars, Carl B.

O'Connor, Fionnuala, et al. In Search of a State: Catholics in Northern Ireland. 393p. 1994. pap. 17.95 (0-85640-509-4, Pub. by Blackstaff Pr) Dufour.

O'Connor, Flannery. Les Braves Gens Ne Courent Pas les Rues. (FRE.). 1981. pap. 10.95 (0-7859-4144-4) Fr & Eur.

— Collected Works: Wise Blood; A Good Man Is Hard to Find; The Violent Bear It Away; Everything That Rises Must Converge; Stories, Occasional Prose, & Letters. Fitzgerald, Sally, ed. LC 87-37829. 1281p. 1988. 35.00 (0-940450-37-2, Pub. by Library of America) Penguin Putnam.

— The Complete Stories. LC 72-171492. 555p. 1971. pap. 15.00 (0-374-51536-0) FS&G.

— Everything That Rises Must Converge. 272p. 1965. pap. 13.00 (0-374-50464-4) FS&G.

— A Good Man Is Hard to Find. LC 92-39505. (Women Writers: Text & Contexts Ser.). 1993. pap., pap. text 14.00 (0-8135-1977-2); text 30.00 (0-8135-1976-4) Rutgers U Pr.

— A Good Man Is Hard to Find, & Other Stories. LC 77-3306. 251p. 1977. pap. 12.00 (0-15-636465-4, Harvest Bks) Harcourt.

— A Good Man Is Hard to Find, & Other Stories. 1992. 17.00 (0-15-136504-0) Harcourt.

— The Habit of Being. Fitzgerald, Sally, ed. & intro. by. LC 78-11559. 624p. 1988. pap. 20.00 (0-374-52104-2) FS&G.

— Mystery & Manners: Occasional Prose. Fitzgerald, Robert & Fitzgerald, Sally, eds. LC 69-15409. 256p. 1969. pap. 12.00 (0-374-50804-6) FS&G.

— Three by Flannery O'Connor. 1986. mass mkt. 6.95 (0-451-52514-0, Sig Classics) NAL.

— The Violent Bear It Away. 256p. 1960. pap. 12.00 (0-374-50524-1) FS&G.

— Wise Blood. 232p. 1962. pap. 12.00 (0-374-50584-5) FS&G.

O'Connor, Flannery, jt. auth. see Westarp, Karl-Heinz.

O'Connor, Frances B. Female Face in Patriarchy: Oppression As Culture. LC 98-41217. 1998. pap. 24.95 (0-87013-494-9) Mich St U Pr.

O'Connor, Francine M. ABCs of Christmas. LC 94-76021. (Illus.). 48p. (J). (ps-3). 1994. 14.95 (0-89243-581-X) Liguori Pubns.

— ABCs of Church. LC 96-75982. (Illus.). 32p. (J). (ps-3). 1997. pap. 4.95 (0-7648-0024-8) Liguori Pubns.

— ABCs of the Lessons of Love: Sermon on the Mount for Children. (Illus.). 48p. (J). (gr. 6-8). 1991. pap. 4.95 (0-89243-345-0) Liguori Pubns.

— ABC's of the Mass: For Children. 1998. pap. 9.95 (0-89243-654-9) Liguori Pubns.

— ABCs of the Mass...for Children. (Illus.). 32p. (Orig.). (J). (ps-4). 1988. pap. 4.95 (0-89243-291-8) Liguori Pubns.

***O'Connor, Francine M.** The Commandments: God's Plan for Our Happy Lives. Larkin, Jean, ed. (Active Learning for Catholic Kids Ser.). (Illus.). 28p. (J). (gr. 4-6). 1999. pap. 9.95 (0-937997-56-0) Hi-Time Pflaum.

— First Communion. 1998. pap. text 1.95 (0-7648-0192-9) Liguori Pubns.

O'Connor, Francine M. First Penance. 1998. pap. text 1.95 (0-7648-0194-5, Liguori Triumph) Liguori Pubns.

— Journey of Faith for Children: Leader's Guide. 48p. 1998. pap. 1.95 (0-7648-0160-0) Liguori Pubns.

***O'Connor, Francine M.** Let's Pray: Catholic Prayers & the Mass. Larkin, Jean, ed. (Active Learning for Catholic Kids Ser.). (Illus.). 28p. (J). (gr. 1-3). 1999. pap. 9.95 (0-937997-54-4, 3403) Hi-Time Pflaum.

— My Advent Fun Book: Daily Activities for Children. 32p. 1998. pap. text 1.95 (0-7648-0217-8) Liguori Pubns.

O'Connor, Francine M. My Lenten Fun Book: Daily Activities for Children. 48p. 1998. pap. text 2.95 (0-7648-0218-6) Liguori Pubns.

O'Connor, Francine M. My Lenten Walk with Jesus. (Cycle C Ser.). (Illus.). 32p. (J). (gr. 1-3). 1993. pap., pap. text 2.50 incl. audio (0-89243-421-X); pap., pap. text, teacher ed. 9.95 incl. audio (0-89243-420-1) Liguori Pubns.

— My Lenten Walk with Jesus, Cycle A. (Cycle A Ser.). (Illus.). 32p. (J). (gr. 1-3). 1993. pap. text 2.50 (0-89243-453-8) Liguori Pubns.

— My Lenten Walk with Jesus: Cycle B. (J). (gr. 1-3). 1991. pap., pap. text, teacher ed. 9.95 incl. audio (0-89243-666-2) Liguori Pubns.

— My Lenten Walk with Jesus: Cycle B, Cycle B. 32p. (J). (gr. 1-3). 1991. pap., pap. text 2.50 incl. audio (0-89243-665-4) Liguori Pubns.

— La Primera Comunion. (SPA., Illus.). 32p. 1998. pap. 1.95 (0-7648-0193-7, Libros Liguori) Liguori Pubns.

— La Primera Penitencia. (SPA., Illus.). 1998. pap. 1.95 (0-7648-0195-3, Libros Liguori) Liguori Pubns.

— The Sacraments: Walking with Jesus. Larkin, Jean, ed. (Active Learning for Catholic Kids Ser.). (Illus.). 28p. (J). (gr. 1-3). 1999. pap. 9.95 (0-937997-53-6, 3402) Hi-Time Pflaum.

— The Saints: 21 Models for Good Living. Larkin, Jean, ed. (Active Learning for Catholic Kids Ser.). (Illus.). 28p. (J). (gr. 1-3). 1999. pap. 9.95 (0-937997-52-8, 3401) Hi-Time Pflaum.

O'Connor, Francine M. Wait & Wonder. (Cycle C Ser.). (Illus.). 16p. (J). (gr. 1-3). 1991. pap. text 1.95 (0-89243-419-8) Liguori Pubns.

— Wait & Wonder, Cycle C. (Cycle C Ser.). (Illus.). 16p. (J). (gr. 1-3). 1991. pap. text, teacher ed. 9.95 (0-89243-418-X) Liguori Pubns.

O'Connor, Francine M. Wait & Wonder: Cycle A, Cycle A. (Illus.). 16p. (J). (gr. 1-3). 1992. pap. text 1.95 incl. audio (0-89243-447-3) Liguori Pubns.

— Wait & Wonder: Cycle A, Cycle A. (Illus.). (J). (gr. 1-3). 1992. teacher ed. 9.95 incl. audio (0-89243-448-1) Liguori Pubns.

— Wait & Wonder: Cycle B, Cycle B. 16p. (J). (gr. 1-3). 1993. pap., pap. text 1.95 incl. audio (0-89243-663-8) Liguori Pubns.

— Wait & Wonder: Cycle B, Cycle B. (J). (gr. 1-3). 1993. pap., teacher ed. 9.95 incl. audio (0-89243-664-6) Liguori Pubns.

— We Worship & Pray: The Mass & Traditional Catholic Prayers. Larkin, Jean, ed. (Active Learning for Catholic Kids Ser.). (Illus.). 28p. (J). (gr. 4-6). 1999. pap. 9.95 (0-937997-55-2) Hi-Time Pflaum.

O'Connor, Francine M. You & God: Friends Forever - A Faith Book for Catholic Children. LC 92-75082. (Illus.). 64p. (J). (gr. 1-4). 1993. pap. text 4.95 (0-89243-515-1) Liguori Pubns.

O'Connor, Francine M. & Boswell, Kathryn. ABCs of the Rosary. (Illus.). 32p. (J). (gr. 1-4). 1984. pap. 4.95 (0-89243-221-7) Liguori Pubns.

O'Connor, Francine M., jt. auth. see Boswell, Kathryn.

O'Connor, Francis V., ed. Jackson Pollock: Supplement Number 1 to a Catalogue Raisonne of Paintings, Drawings, & Other Works. 114p. 1995. write for info. (0-9644639-0-3) Pollock-Krasner Found.

O'Connor, Francis V., jt. auth. see Nolan, Leslie.

O'Connor, Frank. Art of the Theatre. LC 74-6483. (Studies in Drama: No. 39). (C). 1974. lib. bdg. 75.00 (0-8383-1909-2) M S G Haskell Hse.

— Big Fellow. LC 97-33373. 224p. 1998. pap. 12.00 (0-312-18050-0) St Martin.

— The Big Fellow. 222p. 1996. reprint ed. pap. 14.95 (0-905169-84-0, Pub. by Poolbeg Pr) Dufour.

— Collected Stories. LC 82-40039. 736p. 1982. pap. 20.00 (0-394-71048-7) Vin Bks.

— Dutch Interior. 296p. 1990. pap. 11.95 (0-85640-432-2, Pub. by Blackstaff Pr) Dufour.

— Guests of the Nation. 199p. 1987. reprint ed. pap. 12.95 (0-905169-89-1, Pub. by Poolbeg Pr) Dufour.

— Kings, Lords & Commons: Irish Poems from the 7th to 17th Century. 188p. 1989. reprint ed. pap. 15.95 (0-926689-00-2) Ford & Bailie Pubs.

— The Midnight Court. LC 74-6477. (English Literature Ser.: No. 33). 1974. lib. bdg. 75.00 (0-8383-1896-7) M S G Haskell Hse.

— Mirror in the Roadway. LC 77-117886. (Select Bibliographies Reprint Ser.). 1977. 24.95 (0-8369-5339-8) Ayer.

— My Father's Son. LC 94-185540. 200 p. 1994. write for info. (0-85640-522-1) Blackstaff Pr.

— My Father's Son. 1999. pap. 17.95 (0-8156-0564-1) Syracuse U Pr.

— An Only Child. (Irish Studies). 290p. 1997. pap. 17.95 (0-8156-0450-5) Syracuse U Pr.

— Saint & Mary Kate. 301p. 1990. reprint ed. pap. 11.95 (0-85640-445-4, Pub. by Blackstaff Pr) Dufour.

— Three Hand Reel: Three One Act Plays Based on Short Stories by Frank O'Connor. adapted ed. 1967. pap. 5.25 (0-8222-1138-6) Dramatists Play.

— Towards an Appreciation of Literature. LC 74-6482. (Studies in Comparative Literature: No. 35). 1974. lib. bdg. 75.00 (0-8383-1907-6) M S G Haskell Hse.

O'Connor, Frank, ed. Classic Irish Short Stories. 352p. 1990. pap. 12.95 (0-19-281918-6) OUP.

— Kings, Lords & Commons. LC 72-75716. (Granger Index Reprint Ser.). 1977. 19.95 (0-8369-6034-3) Ayer.

O'Connor, Frank & Hunt, Hugh. The Invincibles. (Abbey Theatre Ser.). 1980. pap. 2.95 (0-912262-67-2) Proscenium.

— Moses' Rock. Sherry, Ruth, ed. LC 82-23478. (Irish Dramatic Texts Ser.). 110p. 1983. 15.95 (0-8132-0584-0); pap. 7.95 (0-8132-0585-9) Cath U Pr.

O'Connor, Frederick, jt. auth. see Mejia, Elizabeth A.

An Asterisk (*) at the beginning of an entry indicates that the title is appearing for the first time.

O'Connor, Garry. Ralph Richardson: An Actor's Life. expanded rev. ed. (Legends Ser.). (Illus.). 296p. 1999. pap. 16.95 (*1-55783-414-8*) Applause Theatre Bk Pubs.
— Ralph Richardson: An Actor's Life. rev. expanded ed. LC 97-35533. (Illus.). 320p. 1999. 21.95 (*1-55783-300-1*) Applause Theatre Bk Pubs.
— The Secret Woman: A Life of Peggy Ashcroft. LC 97-186459. (Illus.). 352p. 1998. 29.95 (*0-297-81586-5*, Pub. by Weidenfeld & Nicolson) Trafalgar.
— William Shakespeare: A Popular Life. 320p. 2000. 27.95 (*1-55783-401-6*) Applause Theatre Bk Pubs.

O'Connor, Gary. The Secret Woman. large type unabridged ed. 384p. 1998. 26.95 (*0-7531-5050-6*, 150506) ISIS Pub.

***O'Connor, Gemma.** Farewell to the Flesh. 2000. pap. 10.95 (*0-553-50586-6*, Pub. by Transworld Publishers Ltd) Trafalgar.
— Time to Remember. 2000. pap. 10.95 (*0-553-50587-4*, Pub. by Transworld Publishers Ltd) Trafalgar.
— Time to Remember. large type ed. 400p. 2000. write for info. (*0-7505-1512-0*, Pub. by Mgna Lrg Print) Ulverscroft.

O'Connor, Geoffrey. Amazon Journal: Dispatches from a Vanishing Frontier. 384p. 1998. pap. 13.95 (*0-452-27610-1*, Plume) Dutton Plume.

O'Connor, Gerry & Mcnevin, David. Fifty Solos for Irish Tenor Banjo. 80p. pap. 17.95 (*0-7866-1585-0*, 95170WW) Mel Bay.

O'Connor, Greg. The Aikido Student Handbook: A Guide to Philosophy, Spirit, Etiquette & Training Methods of Aikido. LC 93-25763. (Illus.). 108p. 1993. pap. 11.95 (*1-883319-04-8*) Frog Ltd CA.
— The Elements of Aikido. LC 98-37118. (Elements of... Ser.). 128p. 1999. pap. 9.95 (*1-86204-322-1*, Pub. by Element MA) Penguin Putnam.

O'Connor, H., jt. ed. see O'Morain, C. A.

O'Connor, Harold. The Flexibleshaft Machine - Jewelry Techniques. LC 83-70022. (Illus.). 47p. (C). 1983. pap. 12.95 (*0-918820-05-7*) Dunconor Bks.
— The Jeweler's Bench Reference. 11th ed. LC 76-53236. (Illus.). 68p. (C). 1978. student ed. 11.95 (*0-918820-03-0*) Dunconor Bks.

O'Connor, Harvey. The Guggenheims: The Making of an American Dynasty. Bruchey, Stuart & Bruchey, Eleanor, eds. LC 76-5026. (American Business Abroad Ser.). (Illus.). 1976. reprint ed. 45.95 (*0-405-09292-X*) Ayer.

***O'Connor, Helen, et al.** Glucose Revolution Pocket Guide to Sports Nutrition. LC 99-42188. (Illus.). 120p. 2000. mass mkt. 4.95 (*1-56924-676-9*) Marlowe & Co.

O'Connor, Helen K., jt. auth. see Teixeira, Rozalyn K.

O'Connor, Hyla. Cooking on Your Wood Stove. (Illus.). 78p. (Orig.). 1982. pap. 5.95 (*0-9608050-0-1*) Turkey Hill Bks.

O'Connor, Ilett. Calicko, the Tale of the Lickety Cat. (J). (gr. 5-8). 1998. pap. 6.95 (*0-533-12647-9*) Vantage.

O'Connor, J. The Big Game Rifle. (Illus.). 370p. 1994. 37.50 (*1-57157-000-4*) Safari Pr.

O'Connor, J. & Ruddle, H., eds. Business Matters. (C). 1989. 50.00 (*0-946211-87-6*) St Mut.

O'Connor, J., jt. auth. see Galvin, E.

O'Connor, J. D. Better English Pronunciation. 2nd ed. LC 79-41438. (Cambridge English Language Learning Ser.). (Illus.). 159p. 1981. pap. text 15.95 (*0-521-23152-3*) Cambridge U Pr.

O'Connor, J. D. Phonetics. 1992. pap. 19.95 (*0-14-013638-X*, Pub. by Pnguin Bks Ltd) Trafalgar.

O'Connor, J. E. Hydrology, Hydraulics, & Geomorphology of the Bonneville Flood. LC 92-42641. (Special Papers: No. 274). 1993. pap. 13.88 (*0-8137-2274-8*) Geol Soc.

O'Connor, J. F. The Banking Crisis & Recovery under the Roosevelt Administration. LC 73-171696. (FDR & the Era of the New Deal Ser.). 168p. 1971. reprint ed. lib. bdg. 27.50 (*0-306-70366-1*) Da Capo.

O'Connor, J. J. Practical Fire & Arson Investigation. (Practical Aspects of Criminal & Forensic Investigations Ser.). 400p. 1986. 44.95 (*0-444-00874-8*) CRC Pr.

O'Connor, J. Regis. High-Impact Public Speaking for Business & the Professions. 1996. pap. write for info. (*0-8442-3414-1*) NTC Contemp Pub Co.
— High-Impact Public Speaking for Business & the Professions. (Illus.). 192p. 1996. 24.95 (*0-8442-3413-3*, NTC Business Bks) NTC Contemp Pub Co.

***O'Connor, J. Regis.** The Sacred Seal. (New Adventures of Sherlock Holmes Ser.). 1998. 24.00 (*1-55246-110-6*) Battered Silicon.

O'Connor, J. Regis, jt. auth. see Capps, Randall.

O'Connor, Jack. Game in the Desert. 298p. 50.00 (*1-56416-073-4*) Derrydale Pr.

O'Connor, Jack. Jack O'Connor's Gun Book. 1992. 26.00 (*1-879356-11-2*) Wolfe Pub Co.

O'Connor, Jacqueline. Dramatized Dementia: Madness in the Plays of Tennessee Williams. LC 97-20537. 200p. 1997. pap. 15.95 (*0-87972-742-X*) Bowling Green Univ Popular Press.

O'Connor, James. The Father's Son. LC 84-11377. 324p. (C). 1984. pap. 10.95 (*0-8198-2622-7*) Pauline Bks.
— Natural Causes: Essays in Ecological Marxism. LC 97-42398. 350p. 1997. pap. text 19.95 (*1-57230-273-9*); lib. bdg. 39.95 (*1-57230-279-8*, C0273) Guilford Pubns.

***O'Connor, James.** Spirit Walk. large type ed. 180p. 2000. pap. text 7.95 (*0-9652919-0-1*) Golden Chalice.

O'Connor, James. Works of James O'Connor, the Deaf Poet, with a Biography Sketch of the Author. 1972. 59.95 (*0-8490-1330-5*) Gordon Pr.

O'Connor, James T. The Hidden Manna: A Theology of the Eucharist. LC 88-82477. 390p. (Orig.). 1989. 17.95 (*0-89870-288-7*) Ignatius Pr.
— Land of the Living. 1993. pap. 5.95 (*0-89942-174-1*, 174/04) Catholic Bk Pub.

***O'Connor, James V.** Cuss Control: The Complete Book on How to Curb Your Cursing. LC 99-50274. 192p. 2000. pap. 12.95 (*0-609-80546-0*, LAN015000, Three Riv Pr) Crown Pub Group.

O'Connor, Jane. Amy's (Not So) Great Camp-Out: A Brownie Girl Scout Book. LC 92-45881. (Here Comes the Brownies Ser.: No. 4). (Illus.). 64p. (J). (gr. 1-4). 1993. pap. 4.95 (*0-448-40166-5*, G & D) Peng Put Young Read.

O'Connor, Jane. Bad-Luck Penny. LC 95-18326. (Eek! Stories to Make You Shriek Ser.). (J). 1996. 9.15 (*0-606-09054-1*, Pub. by Turtleback) Demco.

O'Connor, Jane. Benny's Big Bubble. LC 95-78718. (All Aboard Reading Picture Readers Ser.). (Illus.). 32p. (Orig.). (J). (ps-1). 1997. pap. 3.95 (*0-448-41303-5*, G & D) Peng Put Young Read.
— Corrie's Secret Pal: A Brownie Girl Scout Book. LC 92-35602. (Here Comes the Brownies Ser.: No. 1). (Illus.). 64p. (J). (gr. 1-4). 1993. pap. 4.95 (*0-448-40160-6*, G & D) Peng Put Young Read.
— Dragon Breath. LC 96-34270. (Eek! Stories to Make You Shriek Ser.). (Illus.). 48p. (J). (gr. 1-3). 1997. pap. 3.95 (*0-448-41558-5*, G & D) Peng Put Young Read.
— Dragon Breath. LC 96-34270. (Eek! Stories to Make You Shriek Ser.). 1997. 9.15 (*0-606-11277-4*, Pub. by Turtleback) Demco.
— Eek! Stories to Make You Shriek. (All Aboard Reading Ser.: Level 2). (Illus.). 48p. (J). (gr. 1-3). 1992. pap. 3.95 (*0-448-40382-X*, G & D) Peng Put Young Read.
— Eek! Stories to Make You Shriek: The Bad-Luck Penny. LC 95-18326. (Eek! Stories to Make You Shriek Ser.). (Illus.). 48p. (J). (gr. 1-3). 1996. pap. 3.95 (*0-448-41254-3*, G & D) Peng Put Young Read.
— Gardening. 2nd ed. LC 99-234457. (Complete Idiot's Guide Ser.). 1998. pap. text 16.95 (*0-02-862767-9*) Macmillan Gen Ref.
— Kate Skates. LC 94-45101. (All Aboard Reading Ser.: Level 1). (Illus.). 32p. (J). (ps-1). 1995. pap. 3.99 (*0-448-40935-6*, G & D) Peng Put Young Read.
— Lulu Goes to Witch School. (I Can Read Bks.). (Illus.). 64p. (J). (gr. 1-3). 1987. 13.00 (*0-06-024628-6*) HarpC Child Bks.
— Lulu Goes to Witch School. LC 87-37. (I Can Read Bks.). (Illus.). 64p. (J). (ps-3). 1990. pap. 3.95 (*0-06-444138-5*, HarpTrophy) HarpC Child Bks.
— Lulu Goes to Witch School. (I Can Read Bks.). (J). (gr. 1-3). 1991. 8.95 (*0-606-04734-4*, Pub. by Turtleback) Demco.
— Make up Your Mind, Marsha! A Brownie Girl Scout Book. LC 92-45880. (Here Comes the Brownies Ser.: No. 3). (Illus.). 64p. (J). (gr. 1-4). 1993. pap. 4.95 (*0-448-40164-9*, G & D) Peng Put Young Read.
— Molly the Brave & Me. (Step into Reading Ser.: A Step 2 Book). (J). (gr. 1-3). 1990. 9.19 (*0-606-12425-X*, Pub. by Turtleback) Demco.

***O'Connor, Jane.** More Flowers. 64p. 1999. pap. text 4.99 (*0-448-41993-9*, G & D) Peng Put Young Read.
— Nina, Nina & the Copycat Ballerina. LC 99-48179. (All Aboard Reading Ser.). (Illus.). 32p. (J). 2000. 13.89 (*0-448-42152-6*, G & D); pap. 3.99 (*0-448-42151-8*, G & D) Peng Put Young Read.

O'Connor, Jane. Nina, Nina Ballerina. LC 92-24465. (All Aboard Reading Ser.: Level 1). (Illus.). 32p. (J). (ps-1). 1993. pap. 3.99 (*0-448-40511-3*, G & D) Peng Put Young Read.
— Nina, Nina Star Ballerina. LC 96-30741. (All Aboard Reading Ser.). (Illus.). 32p. (J). (ps-1). 1997. lib. bdg. 13.89 (*0-448-41611-5*, G & D) Peng Put Young Read.
— Nina, Nina Star Ballerina. LC 96-30741. (All Aboard Reading Ser.: Level 1). (Illus.). 32p. (J). (ps-1). 1997. pap. 3.99 (*0-448-41492-9*, G & D) Peng Put Young Read.
— Sarah's Incredible Idea: A Brownie Girl Scout Book. LC 92-36803. (Here Comes the Brownies Ser.: No. 2). (Illus.). 64p. (J). (ps-3). 1993. pap. 4.95 (*0-448-40162-2*, G & D) Peng Put Young Read.
— Sir Small & the Dragonfly. LC 87-35309. (Step into Reading Ser.: A Step 1 Book). (Illus.). 32p. (J). (ps-3). 1988. pap. 3.99 (*0-394-89625-4*, Pub. by Random Bks Yng Read) Random.

O'Connor, Jane. Sir Small & the Dragonfly. (Step into Reading Ser.: A Step 1 Book). (J). (ps-1). 1988. 9.19 (*0-606-12518-3*, Pub. by Turtleback) Demco.

O'Connor, Jane. Splat! LC 93-34127. (All Aboard Reading Ser.: Level 1). (Illus.). 32p. (J). (ps-1). 1994. pap. 3.95 (*0-448-40219-X*, G & D) Peng Put Young Read.

Oconnor, Jane. Splat! (All Aboard Reading Ser.). (J). 1994. 9.15 (*0-606-06761-2*, Pub. by Turtleback) Demco.

O'Connor, Jane. Super Cluck. (I Can Read Bks.). (J). (gr. 1-3). 1993. 8.95 (*0-606-02917-6*, Pub. by Turtleback) Demco.

O'Connor, Jane. The Teeny Tiny Woman. (Step into Reading Ser.: A Step 1 Book). (J). (ps-1). 1986. 9.19 (*0-606-12533-7*, Pub. by Turtleback) Demco.

O'Connor, Jane. Yours till Niagara Falls, Abby. (J). 1997. 11.05 (*0-606-12128-5*, Pub. by Turtleback) Demco.

O'Connor, Jane & O'Connor, Jim. The Ghost in Tent Nineteen. LC 87-82372. (Stepping Stone Bks). (Illus.). 64p. (J). (gr. 4-7). 1988. pap. 3.99 (*0-394-89800-1*, Pub. by Random Bks Yng Read) Random.

O'Connor, Jane & O'Connor, Robert. Super Cluck. LC 90-32832. (I Can Read Bks.). (Illus.). 64p. (J). (ps-3). 1993. pap. 3.75 (*0-06-444162-8*, HarpTrophy) HarpC Child Bks.

O'Connor, Jane & Sweeney, Emma. Complete Idiot's Guide to Landscaping & Gardening. LC 96-49784. (Illus.). 1996. 16.95 (*0-02-861096-2*) Macmillan Gen Ref.

O'Connor, Jane, et al. Molly the Brave & Me. LC 89-10864: (Step into Reading Ser.: A Step 2 Book). (Illus.). 48p. (J). (ps-3). 1990. pap. 3.99 (*0-394-84175-1*, Pub. by Random Bks Yng Read) Random.

O'Connor, Jerome M. Becoming Human Together: The Pastoral Anthropology of St. Paul, Vol. 2. 242p. 1989. pap. 24.00 (*0-89453-075-5*, Pub. by Veritas Pubns) St Mut.
— Doubleday Bible Commentary: 1 Corinthians. LC 98-15196. 208p. 1998. pap. 11.95 (*0-385-49022-4*) Doubleday.
— Paul the Letter-Writer: His World, His Options, His Skills. LC 94-11566. (Good News Studies: No. 41). 160p. (Orig.). 1995. pap. text 13.95 (*0-8146-5845-8*, M Glazier) Liturgical Pr.

O'Connor, Jerry & Davenport, Mark. Mechanics, Waves & Heat: Physics 1570. (C). 1995. pap. 15.45 (*1-56870-188-8*) RonJon Pub.

O'Connor, Jessie L., et al. Harvey & Jessie: A Couple of Radicals. LC 87-21737. (Illus.). 288p. (C). 1988. 34.95 (*0-87722-519-2*) Temple U Pr.

O'Connor, Jill. Easter Treats: Recipes & Crafts for the Whole Family, a Holiday Celebrations Book. LC 99-10118. (Illus.). 96p. 2000. pap. 14.95 (*0-8118-2384-9*) Chronicle Bks.
— Phyllo: Easy Recipes for Sweet & Savory Treats. LC 96-11107. (Illus.). 96p. 1996. 14.95 (*0-8118-1019-4*) Chronicle Bks.

***O'Connor, Jill.** Simple French Desserts. (Illus.). 144p. 2000. pap. 16.95 (*0-8118-1903-5*) Chronicle Bks.

Oconnor, Jim. Call Me Gretzky! (No Stars Ser.). 1996. 9.09 (*0-606-10896-3*, Pub. by Turtleback) Demco.

***O'Connor, Jim.** Ghost in Tent 19. (Illus.). (J). 1999. pap. 11.10 (*0-8335-2767-3*) Econo-Clad Bks.
— Ghost in Tent 19. (Stepping Stone Bks.). (J). 1988. 9.19 (*0-606-03789-6*, Pub. by Turtleback) Demco.

O'Connor, Jim. Grow up My Child: Christian Maturity. unabridged ed. (Illus.). 148p. (Orig.). 1996. pap. 7.00 (*0-9652919-1-X*) Golden Chalice.
— Jackie Robinson & the Story of All-Black Baseball. LC 88-18466. (Step into Reading Ser.: A Step 4 Book). (Illus.). 48p. (J). (gr. 2-5). 1989. pap. 3.99 (*0-394-82456-3*, Pub. by Random Bks Yng Read) Random.
— Jackie Robinson & the Story of All-Black Baseball. (Step into Reading Ser.: A Step 4 Book). (J). (gr. 2-4). 1989. 9.19 (*0-606-12358-X*, Pub. by Turtleback) Demco.
— Let's Hear It: Shrupps. LC 95-73062. (Illus.). (J). 1996. pap. 3.99 (*0-679-87909-9*) McKay.

Oconnor, Jim. Let's Hear It for the Shrumps! (No Stars Ser.). 1996. 9.09 (*0-606-10897-1*, Pub. by Turtleback) Demco.

O'Connor, Jim. No Girls Allowed, Bk. 1. LC 95-70654. (Illus.). (J). 1996. pap. 3.99 (*0-679-87858-0*) McKay.
— Sticking It Out. 96p. (J). (gr. 2-7). 1996. pap. 3.99 (*0-614-13973-2*, Bullseye Bks) Random Bks Yng Read.
— Sticking It Out. (No Stars Ser.). (J). 1996. 9.09 (*0-606-09695-7*, Pub. by Turtleback) Demco.
— The Story of Roberto Clemente, All-Star Hero. (J). 1996. pap. 3.50 (*0-440-91279-2*) BDD Bks Young Read.

O'Connor, Jim, jt. auth. see O'Connor, Jane.

O'Connor, Jim E. Hydrology, Hydraulics, & Geomorphology of the Bonneville Flood. LC 92-42641. (Geological Society of America, Special Paper: No. 274). (Illus.). 89p. Date not set. reprint ed. pap. 30.00 (*0-608-20644-X*, 207208000003) Bks Demand.

O'Connor, Joan. John Alden Carpenter: A Bio-Bibliography, 54. LC 93-45943. (Bio-Bibliographies in Music Ser.). 256p. 1994. lib. bdg. 65.00 (*0-313-26430-9*, Greenwood Pr) Greenwood.

O'Connor, Joan & Yu, E., eds. Moving Ahead: A Training Manual for Children with Motor Disorders. LC 98-14892. (Illus.). 530p. 1998. pap. 30.00 (*981-3083-27-1*, Pub. by Spr-Verlag) Spr-Verlag.

O'Connor, Joey. Breaking Your Comfort Zones: And 49 Other Extremely Radical Ways to Live for God. LC 95-37517. 224p. (YA). (gr. 6-9). 1996. pap. 8.99 (*0-8007-5584-7*) Revell.
— Excuse Me! I'll Take My Piece of the Planet Now! LC 96-40857. 96p. (YA). (gr. 10). 1997. 9.99 (*0-8010-1132-9*) Baker Bks.

***O'Connor, Joey.** Have Your Wedding Cake & Eat It Too: You Can Be Both Happy & Married. LC 00-36809. 192p. 2000. pap. write for info. (*0-8499-3799-X*) Word Pub.

O'Connor, Joey. Heaven's Not a Crying Place: Teaching Your Child about Funerals, Death, & the Life Beyond. LC 97-37895. 208p. 1997. pap. 11.99 (*0-8007-5643-6*) Revell.
— In His Steps: The Promise. 192p. (YA). (gr. 11). 1998. pap. 8.99 (*0-8007-5678-9*) Revell.

***O'Connor, Joey.** Las Mujeres Siempre Tienen la Razon & los Hombres Nunca Se Equivocan. (SPA.). 1999. pap. 9.99 (*0-88113-551-8*) Caribe Betania.

O'Connor, Joey. Whadd'ya Gonna Do? 25 Secrets for Getting a Life. LC 95-33147. 112p. (J). (gr. 6-9). 1996. 9.99 (*0-8010-1103-5*) Baker Bks.
— Women Are Always Right & Men Are Never Wrong. LC 98-45332. xii, 254 p. 1999. pap. 12.99 (*0-8499-3704-3*) Word Pub.
— You're Grounded for Life: And 49 Other Crazy Things That Parents Say. LC 94-31929. (Illus.). 192p. (Orig.). (YA). (gr. 8-11). 1995. pap. 7.99 (*0-8007-5549-9*) Revell.

O'Connor, Joey, jt. auth. see Schmidt, J. David.

***O'Connor, John.** The 1916 Proclamation. (Illus.) 96p. 1999. pap. 10.95 (*0-937702-19-6*) Irish Bks Media.

O'Connor, John. The Workhouses of Ireland: The Fate of Ireland's Poor. LC 94-117966. (Illus.). 160p. 1997. reprint ed. pap. 15.95 (*0-937702-15-3*) Irish Bks Media.

O'Connor, John, ed. Monitoring Environmental Progress. LC 95-30524. (Environmentally Sustainable Development Occasional Papers: No. 5). 96p. 1995. pap. 22.00 (*0-8213-3365-8*) World Bank.

O'Connor, John & Galvin, Eamonn. Marketing & Information Technology. 320p. 1997. pap. 62.50 (*0-273-62644-2*, Pub. by Pitman Pub) Trans-Atl Phila.

O'Connor, John & Liu, Benjamin. Unseen Warhol. LC 96-19379. (Illus.). 208p. 1996. 50.00 (*0-8478-1967-1*, Pub. by Rizzoli Intl) St Martin.

O'Connor, John, jt. auth. see Lewis, Hilary.

O'Connor, John, jt. auth. see McPhail, David M.

O'Connor, John, jt. ed. see Cohen, Gary.

O'Connor, John, ed. & tr. see Shanghai College of Traditional Chinese Medicine S.

O'Connor, John, tr. see Biver, Paul.

O'Connor, John B. Chapters in the History of Actors & Acting in Ancient Greece. LC 65-21095. (Studies in Drama: No. 39). (C). 1969. reprint ed. lib. bdg. 75.00 (*0-8383-0602-0*) M S G Haskell Hse.

O'Connor, John Cardinal. Covenant of Love: Pastoral Reflections on Marriage. LC 99-17746. 119 p. 1999. pap. 8.95 (*0-7648-0338-7*) Liguori Pubns.
— A Moment of Grace: On the Catechism of the Catholic Church. LC 95-76621. 354p. 1995. pap. 16.95 (*0-89870-554-1*) Ignatius Pr.

O'Connor, John Cardinal, ed. On Being Catholic: Reflections Addressed to Youth. LC 94-30653. 176p. (Orig.). (J). 1994. pap. 8.95 (*0-8189-0718-5*) Alba.

O'Connor, John Cardinal & Koch, Edward Irving. His Eminence & Hizzoner: A Candid Exchange. 352p. 1989. mass mkt. 4.95 (*0-380-70715-2*, Avon Bks) Morrow Avon.

O'Connor, John E. Image As Artifact: The Historical Analysis of Film & Television. LC 88-13854. 356p. (Orig.). 1990. pap. 37.50 (*0-89464-313-4*) Krieger.
— Teaching History with Film & Television. LC 87-72569. (Discussions on Teaching Ser.: No. 2). (Illus.). 86p. 1987. pap. 8.00 (*0-87229-040-9*) Am Hist Assn.
— William Paterson, Lawyer & Statesman, 1745-1806. LC 79-15966. 367p. 1979. reprint ed. pap. 113.80 (*0-7837-5679-8*, 205910700005) Bks Demand.

O'Connor, John E., ed. I Am a Fugitive from a Chain Gang. LC 81-50823. (Warner Bros. Screenplay Ser.). (Illus.). 200p. 1981. pap. 9.95 (*0-299-08754-9*) U of Wis Pr.

O'Connor, John E., jt. ed. see Rollins, Peter C.

O'Connor, John F. The Adobe Book. LC 72-95653. (Illus.). 160p. 1973. pap. 15.95 (*0-941270-19-X*) Ancient City Pr.
— Good Faith in English Law. 200p. 1990. text 71.95 (*1-85521-017-7*, Pub. by Dartmth Pub) Ashgate Pub Co.
— Good Faith in International Law. 144p. 1991. text 71.95 (*1-85521-197-1*, Pub. by Dartmth Pub) Ashgate Pub Co.

O'Connor, John J., jt. auth. see Redsicker, David R.

O'Connor, John P., ed. see Boone, Donald.

O'Connor, John P., Jr., ed. see Brumbaugh, Frank.

O'Connor, John P., Jr., ed. see Davis, Jack I.

O'Connor, John P., ed. see Dove, Tom.

O'Connor, John P., Jr., ed. see Edmunds, Arthur.

O'Connor, John P., Jr., ed. see Edmunds, Artmor.

O'Connor, John P., Jr., ed. see Fleming, John.

O'Connor, John P., ed. see Garrett Mason, Susan.

O'Connor, John P., ed. see Kreisler, Ken.

O'Connor, John P., ed. see Yetman, David S.

O'Connor, John P., Jr., ed. see Zidock, Alex.

O'Connor, John T., jt. auth. see Berman, Daniel M.

O'Connor, John T., jt. auth. see Kessel, Irene.

***O'Connor, John W., Sr. & O'Connor, Kirsten.** Dragons of Hong Kong. 30p. 2000. bds. 10.00 (*1-928776-03-5*, 2500.30) Nitehawk Pubg.
— Wild Flowers of Hong Kong. 30p. 1999. bds. 10.00 (*1-928776-01-9*, 2500.20) Nitehawk Pubg.
— Woodstock II. 30p. 1999. bds. 10.00 (*1-928776-00-0*, 2500.1) Nitehawk Pubg.

***O'Connor, John W., Sr. & O'Connor, Kirsten G.** Angels. 2000. (Illus.). 30p. 2000. 9.95 (*1-928776-02-7*, 2500.10) Nitehawk Pubg.

O'Connor, John William & O'Connor, Kirsten. Gothic in New York City. (Illus.). 30p. Date not set. 10.00 (*1-928776-04-3*, No. 2500.40) Nitehawk Pubg.

***O'Connor, Joseph.** Extraordinary Solutions to Everyday: Simple Strategies That Work. 2000. pap. 8.00 (*0-7225-3933-9*) Thorsons PA.

O'Connor, Joseph. Leading with NLP: Essential Leadership Skills for Influencing & Managing People. (Illus.). 226p. 1999. pap. 16.00 (*0-7225-3767-0*) Thorsons PA.
— Red Roses & Petrol. 1996. pap. 11.95 (*0-413-69990-0*, Methuen Drama) Methn.
— The Salesman. LC 98-51067. (Illus.). 400p. 1999. text 24.00 (*0-312-19998-8*) St Martin.

***O'Connor, Joseph.** The Salesman. 400p. 2000. pap. 14.00 (*0-312-20431-0*, Picador USA) St Martin.

O'Connor, Joseph. The Secret World of the Irish Male. Date not set. pap. 6.99 (*0-7493-2108-3*) Heinemann.
— Sweet Liberty: Travels in Irish America. 384p. 1996. 24.95 (*1-57098-105-1*) Roberts Rinehart.
— Sweet Liberty: Travels in Irish America. 384p. 1997. pap. 15.95 (*1-57098-151-5*) Roberts Rinehart.

***O'Connor, Joseph & Prior, Robin.** NLP & Relationships: Simple Strategies to Make Your Relationships Work. 2000. pap. 16.00 (*0-7225-3868-5*, Pub. by Thorsons PA) HarpC.

O'Connor, Joseph, jt. auth. see McDermott, Ian.

O'Connor, Joseph, tr. see Soltner, Dom L.

O'Connor, Judith. The Planning Committee. 20p. 1997. pap. 12.00 (*0-925299-77-4*) Natl Ctr Nonprofit.

O'Connor, Julia S. Power Resource Theory & the Welfare State: A Critical Approach. LC 98-205029. 368p. 1998. text 60.00 (*0-8020-0809-7*); pap. text 21.95 (*0-8020-7171-6*) U of Toronto Pr.

An Asterisk (*) at the beginning of an entry indicates that the title is appearing for the first time.

al. States, Markets, Families: Gender, al Policy in Australia, Canada, Great United States. LC 98-25258. (Illus.). 320p. text 64.95 (0-521-63092-4); pap. text 24.95 21-63881-X) Cambridge U Pr.

onnor, June. The Quest for Political & Spiritual Liberation: A Study in the Thought of Sri Aurobindo Ghose. LC 75-5249. 153p. (C). 1976. 16.50 (0-8386-1734-4) Fairleigh Dickinson.

O'Connor, June E. The Moral Vision of Dorothy Day: A Feminist Perspective. 200p. 1991. 16.95 (0-8245-1080-1) Crossroad NY.

O'Connor, Justin & Wynne, Derek, eds. From the Margin to the Centre: Cultural Production & Consumption in the Post-Industrial City. (Popular Culture in the City Ser.: No. 13). 288p. 1996. 64.95 (1-85742-332-1, Pub. by Arena); pap. 31.95 (1-85742-333-X, Pub. by Arena) Ashgate Pub Co.

O'Connor, Karen. American Government. 5th ed. 802p. (C). 1999. 70.00 (0-321-07033-X) Addson-Wesley Educ.

— American Government Readings & Cases. LC 94-38283. 608p. 1995. pap. text 37.00 (0-02-388900-4, Macmillan Coll) P-H.

***O'Connor, Karen.** Basket of Blessings: 31 Days to a More Grateful Heart. 192p. 1998. 13.95 (1-57856-011-X) Waterbrook Pr.

O'Connor, Karen. Dan Thuy's New Life in America. (In My Shoes Ser.). (Illus.). 40p. (J). (gr. 4-8). 1992. lib. bdg. 19.93 (0-8225-2555-0, Lerner Publctns) Lerner Pub.

— Essentials of American Government: Continuity & Change. 4th ed. LC 99-45655. 453p. (C). 1999. pap. text 50.00 (0-321-07035-6) Addson-Wesley Educ.

— The Herring Gull. LC 91-40856. (Remarkable Animals Ser.). (Illus.). 60p. (J). (gr. 4 up). 1992. text 13.95 (0-87518-506-1, Dillon Silver Burdett) Silver Burdett Pr.

— Innovative Grandparenting: How Today's Grandparents Build Personal Relationships with Their Grandkids. LC 95-10024. 192p. 1995. pap. 10.99 (0-570-04824-9, 12-3266) Concordia.

— A Kurdish Family. LC 95-33522. (Journey Between Two Worlds Ser.). (J). 1996. lib. bdg. 22.60 (0-8225-3402-9, Lerner Publctns) Lerner Pub.

— The Kurdish Family. (Illus.). 56p. (J). (gr. 3-6). 1996. pap. 8.95 (0-8225-9743-8) Lerner Pub.

— Little-Kids' Olympics. (Illus.). 80p. (J). (ps-3). 1994. pap. 4.99 (0-570-04770-6, 56-1789) Concordia.

— No Neutral Ground? Abortion Politics in an Age of Absolutes. (Dilemmas in American Politics Ser.). 224p. (C). 1996. pap. 19.00 (0-8133-1946-3, Pub. by Westview) HarpC.

— San Diego. (Downtown America Ser.). (Illus.). 60p. (J). (gr. 3 up). 1990. lib. bdg. 13.95 (0-87518-439-1, Dillon Silver Burdett) Silver Burdett Pr.

— Squeeze the Moment: 31 Days to a More Joyful Heart. LC 99-14486. 192p. 1999. 13.95 (1-57856-222-8) Waterbrook Pr.

— Vietnam. LC 98-46344. (Globe-Trotter's Club Ser.). 48p. (J). (gr. 1-5). 1999. 22.60 (1-57505-117-6, Carolrhoda) Lerner Pub.

— Vietnam. LC 98-52660. (Ticket to Ser.). 48p. (J). (gr. 1-5). 1999. lib. bdg. 22.60 (1-57505-142-7, Carolrhoda) Lerner Pub.

O'Connor, Karen & Epstein, Lee. Public Interest Law Groups: Institutional Profiles. LC 88-37382. 278p. 1989. lib. bdg. 75.00 (0-313-24787-0, OPI, Greenwood Pr) Greenwood.

O'Connor, Karen & Sabato. Essentials American Government & Ten Things That Every American Government Student Should Read. 3rd ed. LC 97-26775. 444p. 1997. pap. text 40.00 (0-205-27230-4) P-H.

O'Connor, Karen & Sabato, Larry J. American Government: Continuity & Change. 4th ed. LC 98-25279. 832p. 1998. pap. text 67.00 (0-205-28678-X) Allyn.

***O'Connor, Karen & Sabato, Larry J.** American Government: Continuity & Change. 5th ed. LC 99-45630. (C). 1999. pap. text 65.00 (0-321-07689-3) Longman.

O'Connor, Karen & Sabato, Larry J. American Government: Roots & Reform, Brief Edition. 2nd rev. ed. (C). 1995. pap., teacher ed. write for info. (0-205-19823-6, H9823-9) Allyn.

— American Government: Roots & Reform, Brief Edition, Test Bank. 2nd rev. ed. (C). 1995. pap. write for info. (0-205-19825-2, H9825-4) Allyn.

— American Government Brief: Roots & Reform. 2nd abr. ed. (C). 1995. pap. text 55.00 (0-02-389018-5, Macmillan Coll) P-H.

— American Government 1997. 3rd ed. 1997. pap. text, student ed. 19.00 (0-205-26263-5) Allyn.

— American Government 1997: Continuity & Change. 3rd ed. LC 96-16182. 832p. 1996. pap. text 60.00 (0-205-19811-2) Allyn.

— Essentials of American Government: Continuity & Change. 2nd ed. 1995. pap. text, student ed. 19.00 (0-205-19824-4) Allyn.

O'Connor, Karen, jt. auth. see Mcglen, Nancy E.

O'Connor, Karen, jt. ed. see Griggs, Francis E., Jr.

O'Connor, Katherine. My Sister-Life. 200p. 1989. 32.50 (0-88233-778-5) Ardis Pubs.

O'Connor, Katherine, tr. see Bulgakov, Mikhail Afanasevich.

O'Connor, Katherine T., tr. see Bulgakov, Mikhail Afanasevich.

O'Connor, Kathleen. The Language of Health Care Reform. (Illus.). 48p. (Orig.). 1994. pap. 9.95 (0-9641863-0-6) Understand Busn.

— Robert Musil & the Tradition of the German Novelle. (Studies in Austrian Literature, Culture, & Thought). 192p. 1992. 28.00 (0-929497-45-7) Ariadne CA.

— The Wisdom Literature. (Message of Biblical Spirituality Ser.: Vol. 5). 199p. 1988. pap. 12.95 (0-8146-5571-8) Liturgical Pr.

O'Connor, Kathleen, jt. auth. see Velguth, Gertrude.

***O'Connor, Ken.** The Mindful School: How to Grade for Learning LC 98-61156. xiv, 192p. 1999. write for info. (1-57517-123-6) SkyLght.

***O'Connor, Kevin.** Sweetie: How Haughey Spent the Money. LC 99-490265. 194p. 1999. pap. 19.95 (0-9536302-1-8) Irish Bks Media.

O'Connor, Kevin & Braverman, Lisa M., eds. Play Therapy Theory & Practice: A Comparative Presentation. LC 96-21257. 432p. 1996. 64.50 (0-471-10638-0) Wiley.

O'Connor, Kevin E. & Bucaro, Frank C. When All Else Fails: Finding Solutions to Your Most Persistent Management Problems. 154p. 1992. 19.95 (0-9631170-4-1) Ritmar Pub.

O'Connor, Kevin J. The Play Therapy Primer: In Integration of Theories & Techniques. LC 90-19419. (Series on Personality Processes). 384p. 1991. 74.50 (0-471-52543-X) Wiley.

***O'Connor, Kevin J.** The Play Therapy Primer: In Integration of Theories & Techniques. 2nd ed. LC 99-53399. 384p. 2000. 49.95 (0-471-24873-8) Wiley.

O'Connor, Kevin J. & Ammen, Sue, eds. Play Therapy Treatment Planning & Interventions: The Ecosystemic Model & Workbook. LC 97-25959. (Illus.). 234p. 1997. pap. text 54.95 (0-12-524135-6) Morgan Kaufmann.

O'Connor, Kevin J., jt. auth. see Schaefer, Charles E.

***O'Connor, Kevin M. & Dowding, Charles H.** GeoMeasurements by Pulsing TDR Cables & Probes. LC 98-40834. 424p. 1999. 69.95 (0-8493-0586-1) CRC Pr.

O'Connor, Kirsten, jt. auth. see O'Connor, John W., Sr.

O'Connor, Kirsten, jt. auth. see O'Connor, John William.

O'Connor, Kirsten G., jt. auth. see O'Connor, John W., Sr.

O'Connor, Laura J., jt. ed. see Kratville, William W.

O'Connor, Leo F. The Protestant Sensibility in the American Novel: An Annotated Bibliography. LC 91-38034. 224p. 1991. text 10.00 (0-8240-4605-6, H1082) Garland.

O'Connor, Letitia B. Discover Los Angeles: An Informed Guide to LA's Rich & Varied Cultural Life. LC 97-42692. 176p. 1998. pap. 16.95 (0-89236-479-3, Pub. by J P Getty Trust) OUP.

O'Connor, Letitia Burns & Levy, Dana, eds. America's Spectacular National Parks. (Illus.). 132p. 1999. 75.00 (0-88363-848-7, Pub. by H L Levin) Publishers Group.

***O'Connor, Linda J.** Biology Explorations: Part 1. 208p. (C). 1999. spiral bd. 27.95 (0-7872-6034-7, 41603401) Kendall-Hunt.

O'Connor, Linda J., jt. auth. see Stephenson, Rebecca A.

O'Connor, Lindsey. If Mama Ain't Happy, Ain't Nobody Happy: Making the Choice to Rejoice. 225p. (Orig.). 1996. pap. 9.99 (1-56507-488-2) Harvest Hse.

— Moms Who Have Changed the World: What You Can Learn from Their Stories. LC 98-42735. 191p. 1999. pap. 9.99 (1-56507-655-9) Harvest Hse.

O'Connor, Lisa C. The Newspaper: A Subscription for Success. rev. ed. Drolet, Cindy & Gilles-Brown, C., eds. (Language for Living Ser.). 143p. 1992. spiral bd. 37.00 (0-9609464-8-9, 8004) Imaginart Intl.

O'Connor, Lona. Top Ten Dumb Career Mistakes . . . And How to Avoid Them. LC 98-8344. 192p. 1998. pap. 14.95 (0-8442-6313-3, 63133, VGM Career) NTC Contemp Pub Co.

O'Connor, Louis, jt. ed. see Evans, Roy.

O'Connor, Louise, et al. Drugs: Partnerships for Policy, Prevention & Education. 128p. 1998. 75.00 (0-304-33945-8); pap. 25.95 (0-304-33946-6) Continuum.

O'Connor, Louise S. Cryin' for Daylight: A Ranching Culture in the Texas Coastal Bend. 1991. pap. 24.95 (0-9624821-0-2) Wexford TX.

— Tales from the San'Tone River Bottom: A Cultural History. LC 98-88499. (Texas Coastal Bend Ser.: No. 2). (Illus.). 254p. 1998. 49.95 (0-9624821-1-0) Wexford TX.

O'Connor, Luke J. & Seberry, Jennifer. Cryptographic Significance of the Knapsack Problem: Plus Exercises & Solutions. 186p. (Orig.). (C). 1988. pap. 32.80 (0-89412-150-2) Aegean Park Pr.

O'Connor, M., ed. Writing Successfully in Science. (Illus.). 229p. (Orig.). (C). (gr. 13). 1992. pap. 22.99 (0-412-44630-8, Chap & Hall NY) Chapman & Hall.

O'Connor, M., jt. auth. see Waltke, Bruce K.

O'Connor, M., jt. ed. see Meyers, Carol L.

O'Connor, M. E., et al, eds. Emerging Electromagnetic Medicine. (Illus.). xiii, 307p. 1990. 79.00 (0-387-97224-2) Spr-Verlag.

O'Connor, Maeve. Writing Successfully in Science. 200p. (C). 1992. text 49.95 (0-04-445805-3, A8245); pap. text 14.95 (0-04-445806-1, A8246) Routledge.

O'Connor, Mallory M. Lost Cities of the Ancient Southeast. LC 94-39265. (Illus.). 192p. 1995. 49.95 (0-8130-1350-X) U Press Fla.

O'Connor, Margaret A., ed. & notes see Cather, Willa.

O'Connor, Marion. William Poel & the Elizabethan Stage Society. (Theatre in Focus Ser.). 120p. 1987. pap. write for info. (0-85964-164-3) Chadwyck-Healey.

O'Connor, Marion, jt. ed. see Howard, Jean E.

O'Connor, Mark. Markology. Kiser, Wayne, ed. Carlini, John, tr. 96p. 1997. spiral bd. 16.95 (0-7866-1654-7, 95695) Mel Bay.

— Markology. Carlini, John, tr. 96p. 1997. spiral bd. 31.95 incl. audio compact disk (0-7866-1656-3, 95695CDP) Mel Bay.

O'Connor, Mark & Phillips, Stacy. Mark O'Connor - The Championship Years. 500p. 1991. spiral bd. 17.95 (1-56222-201-5, 94585) Mel Bay.

O'Connor, Martha S., jt. ed. see Lang, Susan M.

O'Connor, Martin. Air Aces of the Austro-Hungarian Empire, 1914-1918. LC 86-8237. (Illus.). 336p. 1994. reprint ed. 49.95 (0-9637110-1-6) Flying Machines.

— The New Zealand European Connection. 172p. (C). 1988. 65.00 (1-86934-018-3, Pub. by Grantham Hse) St Mut.

O'Connor, Martin, ed. Is Capitalism Sustainable? Political Economy & the Politics of Ecology. LC 94-11689. (Democracy & Ecology Ser.). 283p. 1994. pap. text 18.95 (0-89862-594-7, C2594); lib. bdg. 42.00 (0-89862-127-5, C2127) Guilford Pubns.

***O'Connor, Martin & Spash, Clive L., eds.** Valuation & the Environment: Theory, Method & Practice. LC 98-28491. 352p. 1999. 95.00 (1-85898-538-2) E Elgar.

O'Connor, Martin, jt. ed. see Faucheux, Sylvie.

O'Connor, Mary B. Say Yes Quickly: A Cancer Tapestry. LC 97-68939. 91p. (Orig.). 1997. pap. 12.95 (0-9656052-1-3) Pot Shard.

O'Connor, Mary I. Study of the Sources of Han D'Islande & Their Significance in the Literary Development of Victor Hugo. LC 76-115357. (Catholic University Romance Languages Ser.: No. 24). reprint ed. 37.50 (0-404-50324-1) AMS Pr.

O'Connor, Mary L., ed. see Orr, Margaret T.

O'Connor, Marylou & Parker, Elizabeth. Health Promotion: Principles & Practice. 310p. 1996. pap. 29.95 (1-86373-897-5, Pub. by Allen & Unwin Pty) Paul & Co Pubs.

O'Connor, Maura. Flowing to the Sea. Wong, Keola, tr. from HAW. (Illus.). (J). (gr. 4-6). 1994. pap. 14.95 (1-882163-19-2) Moanalua Grdns Fnd.

— The Hummingbird Graveyard. 18p. (Orig.). 1992. pap. 3.00 (0-929730-35-6) Zeitgeist Pr.

— The Romance of Italy & the English Political Imagination. LC 98-21465. 320p. 1998. text 45.00 (0-312-21086-8) St Martin.

O'Connor, Maureen. Equal Rights. LC 96-53582. (What Do We Mean by Human Rights? Ser.). 48p. (J). 1998. 22.00 (0-531-14448-8) Watts.

— Secondary Education. Wragg, C. E., ed. (Education Matters Ser.). 112p. 1990. text 80.00 (0-304-31951-1); pap. text 27.95 (0-304-31956-2) Continuum.

***O'Connor, Michael.** Airfields & Airmen: Ypres. 2000. pap. 16.95 (0-85052-753-8, Pub. by Pen & Sword) Combined Pub.

— Early-Music Degree Programs in North America. 2nd rev. ed. Simmons, Beverly, ed. (EMA Information Resource Ser.). 44p. 2000. pap. 7.50 (1-878206-11-7) Early Music.

O'Connor, Michael. Hebrew Verse Structure. LC 80-68370. xvii, 629p. 1997. text 49.50 (0-931464-02-1) Eisenbrauns.

O'Connor, Michael, et al. O'Connor's Texas Rules Civil Appeals, 1998. (O'Connor's Litigation Ser.). 1024p. (C). 1998. pap. 59.95 (1-884554-20-2) J McClure Pubng.

O'Connor, Michael F. For White Boys Who Have Contemplated Monasteries after Being Dumped on Once Too Often. (Illus.). 1980. write for info. (0-318-51091-X) Blarney Bks.

O'Connor, Michael F. & Yalom, Irvin D. Treating the Psychological Consequences of HIV. LC 96-31519. (Library of Current Clinical Technique). 1996. 28.95 (0-7879-0314-0) Jossey-Bass.

O'Connor, Michael J., jt. auth. see Alessandra, Tony.

O'Connor, Michael J., jt. auth. see Kennedy, Malcolm J.

O'Connor, Michael K., ed. The Mayo Clinic Manual of Nuclear Medicine. LC 96-11649. 592p. 1996. pap. text 89.00 (0-443-07765-7) Church.

O'Connor, Michael P. Pandary. LC 89-11763. 47p. 1990. per. 8.95 (0-934332-50-9) LEpervier Pr.

O'Connor, Michael P. & Erickson, Becky. The MNM Team Building Process for Printers. LC 91-90250. 250p. 1991. pap. 39.95 (0-9629366-7-7) Old Stone Pub.

— The Team Building Book: How to Build Your Staff into a High Performance Team. 250p. (Orig.). 1992. pap. 23.95 (0-9629366-3-4) Old Stone Pub.

O'Connor, Michael P. & Freedman, David N. Backgrounds for the Bible. LC 87-13592. xii, 369p. 1987. text 37.50 (0-931464-30-7) Eisenbrauns.

O'Connor, Micheal G., jt. auth. see Moss, Thomas C.

O'Connor, Michelle, ed. see Bachand, Robert G.

***O'Connor, Michol.** O'Connor's Federal Forms - Civil Trials, 1999. Hughes, D. Bryan et al, eds. (O'Connor's Litigation Ser.). 1032p. 1999. pap. 49.95 (1-884554-28-8) J McClure Pubng.

— O'Connor's Federal Rules - Civil Trials, 2000. Smith, Michael C. & Coleman, Gregory S., eds. (O'Connor's Litigation Ser.). 1068p. 2000. pap. 54.95 (1-884554-36-9) J McClure Pubng.

— O'Connor's Texas Forms - Civil Trials, 2000. Jones McClure Publishing, Inc., Staff, ed. (O'Connor's Litigation Ser.). 1140p. 2000. pap. 54.95 (1-884554-35-0) J McClure Pubng.

— O'Connor's Texas Rules - Civil Appeals, 2000. Amos, Jessie & Guariglia, Diane M., eds. (O'Connor's Litigation Ser.). 2000. pap. 59.95 (1-884554-37-7) J McClure Pubng.

O'Connor, Michol. O'Connor's Texas Rules - Civil Trials, 1991: Civil Trial 1991. Burns, Tracie M., ed. (Texas Lawyer Litigation Ser.). 760p. (Orig.). (C). 1991. pap. 49.95 (1-879590-00-X) Amer Law Media.

***O'Connor, Michol.** O'Connor's Texas Rules - Civil Trials, 2000. Guariglia, Diane M. & Davis, Byron P., eds. (O'Connor's Litigation Ser.). 1018p. 1999. pap. 54.95 (1-884554-34-2) J McClure Pubng.

***O'Connor, Mike, tr.** When I Find You Again, It Will Be in Mountains: Selected Poems of Chia Tao. 160p. 2000. pap. 15.95 (0-86171-172-6) Wisdom MA.

O'Connor, Mike, jt ed. see Pine, Red.

O'Connor, Mike, tr. see Nien, Tung.

O'Connor, N., ed. Recent Soviet Psychology. (C). 1961. 8.00 (0-87140-864-3) Liveright.

O'Connor, Nancy. Letting Go with Love: The Grieving Process. 1994. mass mkt. 4.95 (0-553-85040-7) Bantam.

O'Connor, Nancy. Paterson & Zderad: Humanistic Nursing Theory. (Notes on Nursing Theories Ser.: Vol. 7). (Illus.). 64p. (C). 1992. text 22.95 (0-8039-4798-4) Sage.

— Paterson & Zderad: Humanistic Nursing Theory, No. 7. (Notes on Nursing Theories Ser.: Vol. 7). (Illus.). 64p. (C). 1992. pap. text 9.95 (0-8039-4489-6) Sage.

— Rolling Prairie Cookbook: Over 130 Recipes Celebrating Fresh Produce. LC 99-207445. (Illus.). 219p. 1999. pap. 14.95 (0-9667403-0-0, Pub. by Spring Wheat Nutri) Chelsea Green Pub.

O'Connor, Nancy & O'Connor, Nancy D. Letting Go with Love: The Grieving Process. LC 84-61538. 186p. (C). 1985. 15.95 incl. audio (0-9613714-3-9) La Mariposa.

O'Connor, Nancy D. How to Grow up When You're Grown Up: Achieving Balance in Adulthood. 353p. 1994. 24.95 (0-9613714-6-3); pap. 14.95 (0-9613714-5-5) La Mariposa.

— Letting Go with Love: The Grieving Process. LC 84-61538. 186p. (C). 1985. 24.95 (0-9613714-1-2); pap. 14.95 (0-9613714-0-4) La Mariposa.

O'Connor, Nancy D., jt. auth. see O'Connor, Nancy.

O'Connor, Nancy J., jt. ed. see Bissette, Stephen R.

O'Connor, Nancy L. The Essentials of EXP. LC 88-37867. (Math). 104p. (C). 1989. mass mkt. 28.95 (0-534-10350-2) Brooks-Cole.

O'Connor, Nancy L., jt. auth. see Wenzlik, Virginia C.

O'Connor, Naomi. Wearable Art: Design for the Body. 1997. text 49.95 (90-5703-731-9, Pub. by Craftsman House) Gordon & Breach.

O'Connor, Neal W. The Aviation Awards of Imperial Germany in World War I & the Men Who Earned Them Vol. IV: The Aviation Awards of Wurttemberg, Vol. 1. (Illus.). 288p. (Orig.). (C). 1995. 34.95 (0-9619867-0-0) Fndtn Aviation.

O'Connor, Niobe & Rainger, Amanda. Caminos 3: Pupils Book. 240p. 1998. pap., student ed. 36.00 (0-7487-3898-3) St Mut.

— Caminos 3: Resource & Assessment File. 192p. 1998. pap. 285.00 (0-7487-3890-8) St Mut.

— Caminos 3: Teacher's Book. 176p. 1998. pap., teacher ed. 105.00 (0-7487-3889-4) St Mut.

— Caminos 2: Pupils Book. 176p. 1998. pap., student ed. 36.00 (0-7487-3147-4, Pub. by S Thornes Pubs) Trans-Atl Phila.

— Caminos 2: Resource & Assessment File. 192p. 1998. pap. 320.00 (0-7487-3149-0, Pub. by S Thornes Pubs) Trans-Atl Phila.

— Caminos 2: Teachers Book. 160p. 1998. pap., teacher ed. 120.00 (0-7487-3148-2, Pub. by S Thornes Pubs) Trans-Atl Phila.

O'Connor, Noreen & Joanna, Ryan. Wild Desires & Mistaken Identities: Lesbianism & Psychoanlaysis. 315p. 1998. pap. 17.50 (0-231-10023-X) Col U Pr.

O'Connor, Noreen & Ryan, Joanna. Wild Desires & Mistaken Identities: Lesbianism & Psychoanalysis. LC 93-43814. (Between Men - Between Women Ser.). 1994. 37.50 (0-231-10022-1) Col U Pr.

O'Connor, P., jt. auth. see Healy, G.

O'Connor, P. D. Practical Reliability Eng 3e R. 3rd rev. ed. LC 90-13082. 456p. 1996. pap. 64.95 (0-471-95767-4) Wiley.

— Practical Reliability Engineering. 3rd rev. ed. LC 90-13082. (Quality & Reliability Engineering Ser.). 456p. 1996. 125.00 (0-471-96025-X) Wiley.

O'Connor, P. J. Brendan Behan's 'The Scarperer' (Adaptations Ser.). 1978. 6.95 (0-685-04179-4); pap. 2.95 (0-912262-56-7) Proscenium.

O'Connor, P. J., jt. auth. see Kavanagh, Patrick.

O'Connor, Pat. Friendships Between Women. LC 92-13770. (Series on Personal Relationships). 224p. 1992. pap. text 19.95 (0-89862-981-0) Guilford Pubns.

O'Connor, Patrice M., jt. auth. see Sendor, Virginia F.

O'Connor, Patricia. Hitting the Nail on the Head. Trotter, Candace L., ed. 112p. (Orig.). (YA). (gr. 8 up). 1991. reprint ed. pap. text 9.95 (0-9622684-0-2) Nugget Pub.

— Inner Life of Therese of Lisieux. LC 97-68378. 200p. 1997. pap. text 9.95 (0-87973-932-0) Our Sunday Visitor.

— Therese of Lisieux: A Biography. LC 83-63169. 173p. 1984. pap. 7.95 (0-87973-607-0, 607) Our Sunday Visitor.

***O'Connor, Patricia E.** Speaking of Crime: Narratives of Prisoners. LC 00-27201. (Stages Ser.: Vol. 17). 240p. 2000. pap. text 27.95 (0-8032-8608-2, Bison Books) U of Nebr Pr.

O'Connor, Patricia J. To Love the Good: The Moral Philosophy of Iris Murdoch. LC 92-21786. (American University Studies Series V: Vol. 136). VIII, 297p. (C). 1996. pap. text 32.95 (0-8204-1805-6) P Lang Pubng.

O'Connor, Patricia W. Gregorio & Maria Martinez Sierra. LC 76-45170. (Twayne's World Authors Ser.). 155p. (C). 1977. lib. bdg. 20.95 (0-8057-6252-3) Irvington.

— Plays of the New Democratic Spain (1975-1990) 500p. (Orig.). (C). 1992. pap. text 44.00 (0-8191-8442-X); lib. bdg. 72.50 (0-8191-8441-1) U Pr of Amer.

O'Connor, Patricia W., tr. see Diosdado, Ana.

O'Connor, Patrick. Don't Look Back: A Memoir. 188p. 1996. pap. 12.95 (1-55921-185-7) Moyer Bell.

O'Connor, Patrick D., ed. Reliability Engineering. (Arab School of Science & Technology Ser.). 305p. 1987. 95.00 (0-89116-684-X) Hemisp Pub.

***O'Connor, Patrick J.** Moody's Skidrow Beanery. (Illus.). 1999. pap. 9.00 (1-929731-02-7) Rowfant.

— Tales from a Blackout. (Illus.). 159p. 1997. pap. 9.00 (1-929731-00-0) Rowfant.

— Wichita Blues: Discovery. (Illus.). 119p. 1998. pap. 9.00 (1-929731-01-9) Rowfant.

O'Connor, Patrick J., jt. auth. see Gurrie, Michael.

An Asterisk (*) at the beginning of an entry indicates that the title is appearing for the first time.

O'Connor, Paul. Eskimo Parish. (American Autobiography Ser.). 134p. 1995. reprint ed. lib. bdg. 69.00 (*0-7812-8603-4*) Rprt Serv.
— Grimtooth's Traps Lite. Loomis, Rick, ed. (Illus.). 80p. (Orig.). 1992. pap. 9.95 (*0-940244-87-X*) Flying Buffalo.
— Multiple Sclerosis: The Facts You Need. (Your Personal Health Ser.). 156p. 1999. pap. 14.95 (*1-55209-367-0*) Firefly Bks Ltd.
O'Connor, Paul, ed. Grimtooth's Traps. (Illus.). 1981. 9.95 (*0-940244-75-6*) Flying Buffalo.
— Grimtooth's Traps Ate. (Illus.). 1989. 9.95 (*0-940244-84-5*) Flying Buffalo.
O'Connor, Paul, et al, eds. Deactivation & Testing of Hydrocarbon-Processing Catalysts. LC 96-17665. (ACS Symposium Ser.: No. 634). (Illus.). 464p. 1996. text 130.00 (*0-8412-3411-6*, Pub. by Am Chemical) OUP.
— Grimtooth's Traps Too. (Illus.). 1982. 9.95 (*0-940244-78-0*) Flying Buffalo.
O'Connor, Paul, jt. ed. see Occelli, Mario L.
O'Connor, Peter. Dreams & the Search for Meaning. 264p. 1987. pap. 8.95 (*0-8091-2870-5*) Paulist Pr.
— Electronic Distribution Technology in the Tourism & Hospitality Industries. LC 98-33432. 192p. 1999. text 50.00 (*0-85199-283-8*) OUP.
— Using Computers in Hospitality. 288p. 1998. pap. 28.00 (*0-304-70522-5*) Continuum.
— Using Computers in Hospitality & Tourism. LC 95-10738. (Illus.). 256p. 1995. 90.00 (*0-304-33296-8*); pap. 33.95 (*0-304-33299-2*) Continuum.
O'Connor, Peter D., jt. auth. see Wyne, Marvin D.
O'Connor, Philip, tr. see Mommsen, Hans.
O'Connor, Philip F. Old Morals, Small Continents, Darker Times. LC 70-158043. (Iowa Short Fiction Award Ser.). 198p. 1971. pap. 3.25 (*0-87745-023-4*) U of Iowa Pr.
O'Connor, Philip F., et al. Human Anatomy - Three Fictions; Martin's World by Philip F. O'Connor; A Well of Living Water by Annabel Thomas; Moonless by Jack Matthews. Smith, Larry, ed. (Contemporary Midwest Fiction Ser.). 208p. (Orig.). 1995. pap. 8.95 (*0-933087-27-6*) Bottom Dog Pr.
O'Connor, Raymond. Healthy Home Environment. 1996. pap. 5.50 (*0-425-15443-2*) Berkley Pub.
— Healthy Home Environment Guide. 176p. 1996. mass mkt. 5.50 (*0-425-15128-X*) Berkley Pub.
O'Connor, Raymond G. Diplomacy for Victory: FDR & Unconditional Surrender. LC 70-155986. (Essays in American History Ser.). (Illus.). 143p. (C). 1971. pap. text 11.25 (*0-393-09765-X*) Norton.
O'Connor, Raymond J. The Growth & Development of Birds. LC 84-3724. (Illus.). 325p. 1984. reprint ed. pap. 100.80 (*0-608-07301-6*, 206752900009) Bks Demand.
O'Connor, Richard. Bodyguards: The World of VIP Protection. LC 97-125695. (Illus.). 200p. 1997. 24.95 (*1-85409-322-3*, Pub. by Arms & Armour) Sterling.
— Undoing Depression: What Therapy Doesn't Teach You & Drugs Can't Give You. LC 96-50214. 416p. 1997. 23.95 (*0-316-62643-0*) Little.
O'Connor, Richard A., ed. Tai in Tai Context. (Crossroads Ser.: Ser. 5.1). 122p. 1990. pap. 12.00 (*1-877979-90-2*) SE Asia.
O'Connor, Richard F. How to Market You & Your Book: The Ultimate Insider's Guide to Get Your Book Published with Maximum Sales. LC 96-92785. 192p. (Orig.). 1996. pap. 19.95 (*0-913243-14-0*, Coeur de Lion) O Connor Hse Pubs.
— Ident-a-Kid: The Official Fingerprint Book & Complete Identification Record. rev. ed. LC 97-39388. (Illus.). 56p. 1998. 8.95 (*1-58063-006-5*) Renaissance.
— Personal Meditations. unabridged ed. 1990. pap. 16.95 incl. audio (*1-55927-082-9*) Audio Renaissance.
O'Connor, Richard F., ed. In Remembrance of a Special Cat: A Keepsake Memorial. LC 97-44400. (Illus.). 60p. 1998. 9.95 (*1-58063-004-9*) Renaissance.
— In Remembrance of a Special Dog: A Keepsake Memorial. LC 97-44435. (Illus.). 60p. 1999. 9.95 (*1-58063-005-7*) Renaissance.
O'Connor, Rob, et al. Sports Injuries & Illnesses: Their Prevention & Treatment. (Illus.). 208p. 1998. 40.00 (*1-86126-107-1*, Pub. by Crolwood) Trafalgar.
O'Connor, Robert. Buffalo Soldiers. LC 93-43487. 1994. pap. 13.00 (*0-679-74203-4*) Vin Bks.
O'Connor, Robert, jt. auth. see O'Connor, Jane.
O'Connor, Robert F., ed. Texas Myths: Published for the Texas Committee for the Humanities. LC 85-40743. 264p. 1986. 21.95 (*0-89096-264-2*) Tex A&M Univ Pr.
O'Connor, Robert H., intro. Henry William Bunbury's Tales of the Devil. LC 93-49334. 96p. 1995. 49.95 (*0-7734-9429-4*) E Mellen.
O'Connor, Robert T., ed. Instrumental Analysis of Cotton Cellulose & Modified Cotton Cellulose. LC 72-78243. (Fiber Science Ser.: Vol. 3). 504p. reprint ed. pap. 156.30 (*0-608-16636-7*, 202781100054) Bks Demand.
O'Connor, Rod. Concepts in Chemistry for Environmental Professionals. 1999. 49.95 (*1-56670-349-2*, L1349) Lewis Pubs.
***O'Connor, Rod, et al.** Advanced Problems in Applied Chemistry. LC 99-51333. (Illus.). 320p. 1999. write for info. (*1-56032-883-5*) Taylor & Francis.
O'Connor, Roger, ed. see Fisher, James J.
O'Connor, Rollanda E., et al. Ladders to Literacy: A Kindergarten Activity Book. 272p. (J). (gr. k). 1998. student ed., spiral bd. 44.95 (*1-55766-318-1*, 3181) P H Brookes.
O'Connor, Ronald W. Health Care in Muslim Asia: Development & Disorder in Wartime Afghanistan. LC 94-2655. (Illus.). 312p. (C). 1994. pap. 26.50 (*0-8191-9445-X*); lib. bdg. 62.50 (*0-8191-9444-1*) U Pr of Amer.
O'Connor, Rosanne, ed. see Daniels, Rhonda L.
O'Connor, Rosanne, ed. see Kilpatrick, John A.
O'Connor, S. J., ed. A Calendar of the Cartularies of John Pyel & Adam Fraunceys. (Camden Fifth Ser.: No. 5). 486p. (C). 1995. 54.95 (*0 521 55160 9*) Cambridge U Pr.
O'Connor, Sally. Common Sense Dressage: An Illustrated Guide. LC 90-5375. (Illus.). 178p. 1990. 28.95 (*0-939481-21-9*) Half Halt Pr.
— Practial Eventing. rev. ed. LC 98-44329. (Illus.). 160p. 1998. 28.95 (*0-939481-52-9*) Half Halt Pr.
O'Connor, Sally, ed. The USCTA Book of Eventing: The Official Handbook of the United States Combined Training Association, Inc. 2nd ed. LC 86-51445. (Illus.). 288p. 1987. reprint ed. 18.95 (*0-9617826-0-9*) USCTA.
O'Connor, Sally, jt. auth. see Squires, Gregory D.
O'Connor, Sara & Myers, Sherrill M. Working Space: The Milwaukee Repertory Theater Builds a Home. LC 91-20250. (Illus.). 144p. (Orig.). 1992. pap. 16.95 (*1-55936-033-X*) Theatre Comm.
O'Connor, Seamus, jt. auth. see Bean, J. Ronald.
O'Connor, Sean. Straight Acting: Popular Gay Drama from Wilde to Rattigan. LC 97-13548. 245p. 1997. write for info. (*0-304-32866-9*, Pub. by Cassell); pap. write for info. (*0-304-32864-2*, Pub. by Cassell) Sterling.
O'Connor, Sharon. Afternoon Tea Serenade: Recipes from Famous Tea Rooms, Classical Chamber Music. LC 97-71605. (Sharon O'Connor's Menus & Music Ser.). (Illus.). 224p. 1997. 24.95 incl. audio compact disk (*1-883914-18-3*) Menus & Music.
— Afternoon Tea Serenade: Recipes from Famous Tea Rooms, Classical Chamber Music. LC 97-71605. (Sharon O'Connor's Menus & Music Ser.: Vol. XII). (Illus.). 224p. 1999. pap. 24.95 incl. audio compact disk (*1-883914-30-2*) Menus & Music.
— Bistro: Swinging French Jazz, Favorite Parisian Bistro Recipes. (Sharon O'Connor's Menus & Music Ser.: Vol. XIV). (Illus.). 208p. 1999. pap. 24.95 incl. audio compact disk (*1-883914-28-0*) Menus & Music.
— Dining & the Opera in Manhattan: Recipes form Manhattan Restaurants, Opera Arias. LC 94-78254. (Sharon O'Connor's Menus & Music Ser.). 218p. 1994. 24.95 incl. audio compact disk (*1-883914-04-3*) Menus & Music.
— Dinners for Two: Recipes from Romantic Country Inns, Music by the San Francisco String Quartet. LC 91-90290. (Sharon O'Connor's Menus & Music Ser.). (Illus.). 238p. 1991. 24.95 incl. audio compact disk (*1-883914-07-8*) Menus & Music.
— Holidays: Menu Cookbook, Music by the San Francisco String Quartet. LC 89-92217. (Sharon O'Connor's Menus & Music Ser.). 240p. 1989. 24.95 incl. audio compact disk (*1-883914-05-1*) Menus & Music.
— The Irish Isle: New Irish Cuisine, Traditional Irish Music. LC 96-78371. (Sharon O'Connor's Menus & Music Ser.). (Illus.). 240p. 1996. 24.95 incl. audio compact disk (*1-883914-15-9*) Menus & Music.
— The Irish Isle: New Irish Cuisine, Traditional Irish Music. LC 96-78371. (Sharon O'Connor's Menus & Music Ser.: Vol. XI). (Illus.). 240p. 1999. pap. 24.95 incl. audio compact disk (*1-883914-29-9*) Menus & Music.
***O'Connor, Sharon.** Italian Intermezzo: Recipes by Celebrated Italian Chefs, Romantic Italian Music. (Sharon O'Connor's Menus & Music Ser.). (Illus.). 256p. 2000. pap. 24.95 incl. audio compact disk (*1-883914-22-1*) Menus & Music.
O'Connor, Sharon. Lighthearted Gourmet: Recipes for Lighter, Healthier Dinners, Romantic Solo Piano Music. LC 95-77125. (Sharon O'Connor's Menus & Music Ser.). (Illus.). 240p. 1995. 24.95 incl. audio compact disk (*1-883914-09-4*) Menus & Music.
— Picnics: Picnic Recipes from Summer Music Festivals, Classic Ragtime Music. LC 94-75888. (Sharon O'Connor's Menus & Music Ser.). (Illus.). 248p. 1994. 24.95 incl. audio compact disk (*1-883914-08-6*) Menus & Music.
— Rock & Roll Diner: Popular American Cooking, Classic Rock & Roll Music. LC 96-76188. (Sharon O'Connor's Menus & Music Ser.). (Illus.). 248p. 1996. 24.95 incl. audio compact disk (*1-883914 12 4*) Menus & Music.
— Spa: Favorite Recipes from Celebrated Spas, Soothing Classical Piano Music. LC 98-65843. (Sharon O'Connor's Menus & Music Ser.). (Illus.). 240p. 1998. 24.95 incl. audio compact disk (*1-883914-26-4*) Menus & Music.
O'Connor, Sharon H., jt. auth. see Cohen, Morris L.
O'Connor, Shaun & Chwalek, Kazimierz. MIC - Marians of the Immaculate Conception: Sources of Marian History & Spirituality. Bukowicz, John & Gorski, Thaddeus, eds. 300p. 1988. write for info. (*0-318-62733-7*) Marian Pr.
O'Connor, Sheila. Tokens of Grace: A Novella in Stories. LC 90-5438. (Illus.). 128p. 1990. pap. 9.95 (*0-915943-47-6*) Milkweed Ed.
O'Connor, Sheila, ed. Come Home Before Dark. (Illus.). 149p. (Orig.). 1993. pap. 9.00 (*0-927663-21-X*) COMPAS.
***O'Connor, Shirley Carroll.** Life Is a Circus. LC 99-91850. 103p. 1999. 25.00 (*0-7388-1314-1*); pap. 18.00 (*0-7388-1315-X*) Xlibris Corp.
O'Connor, Sifu R., jt. auth. see Shen-Lang, Zhen.
O'Connor, Simmons O'Shea. Strength Training Today. 2nd ed. LC 99-47559. (Health Sciences). 1999. 29.95 (*0-534-35837-3*) Thomson Learn.
O'Connor, Simon, jt. auth. see Talley, Nicholas J.
O'Connor, Stanley J., jt. auth. see Harrisson, Tom.
***O'Connor, Stephen.** Orphan Trains: The Story of Charles Loring Brace & the Children He Saved & Failed, 1853-1929. (Illus.). 320p. 2001. 26.00 (*0-395-84173-9*) HM.
O'Connor, Stephen. Will My Name Be Shouted Out? 384p. 1997. per. 14.00 (*0-684-83210-0*, Touchstone) S&S Trade Pap.
***O'Connor, Sue & Veth, Peter M., eds.** East of Wallace's Line: Studies of Past & Present Maritime Cultures of the Indo-Pacific Region. (Modern Quaternary Research of Southern Asia Ser.). (Illus.). 200p. (C). 2000. text 76.00 (*90-5809-319-0*, Pub. by A A Balkema) Ashgate Pub Co.
O'Connor, Susan L., jt. auth. see Shaner, Dale L.
O'Connor, T. P., jt. ed. see Nicholson, R. A.
***O'Connor, Teddy.** A New Brain for Igor. LC 00-38711. (Step into Reading Ser.). (Illus.). (J). 2001. pap. write for info. (*0-375-90626-6*) Random Bks Yng Read.
O'Connor, Terrence. 22 Arguments That Win Protests. 29p. 1995. pap. 50.00 (*1-56726-060-8*) Mgmt Concepts.
O'Connor, Terrence M. Winning Negotiations in Federal Contracting. 291p. 1992. 115.00 (*1-56726-004-7*) Mgmt Concepts.
***O'Connor, Terry.** The Archaeology of Animal Bones. (Anthropology Ser.: Vol. 4). (Illus.). 244p. 2000. 34.95 (*0-89096-959-0*) Tex A&M Univ Pr.
O'Connor, Terry, jt. auth. see Evans, John.
O'Connor, Theresa, ed. The Comic Tradition in Irish Women Writers. LC 96-22957. 176p. 1996. 39.95 (*0-8130-1457-3*) U Press Fla.
O'Connor, Therese, jt. auth. see Neuhaus, Thomas.
***O'Connor, Thomas.** Boston A to Z. (Illus.). 384p. 2000. 24.95 (*0-674-00310-1*) HUP.
O'Connor, Thomas. Lotton Art Glass. 1993. 49.95 (*0-915410-45-1*) McGraw.
O'Connor, Thomas A., ed. see De Salazar y Torres, A.
O'Connor, Thomas A., ed. see De Salazar y Torres, Agustin, et al.
***O'Connor, Thomas Austin.** Love in the "Corral" Conjugal Spirituality & Antitheatrical Polemic in Early Modern Spain, 31. (Iberica Ser.: Vol. 31). 395p. (C). 2000. text 64.95 (*0-8204-4493-6*) P Lang Pubng.
O'Connor, Thomas F., ed. Building Sealants: Materials, Properties, & Performance. LC 90-937. (Special Technical Publication (STP) Ser.: STP 1069). (Illus.). 362p. 1990. text 45.00 (*0-8031-1282-3*, STP1069) ASTM.
O'Connor, Thomas H. Bibles, Brahmins, & Bosses: A Short History of Boston. 3rd rev. ed. (Illus.). 271p. (YA). 1991. 12.00 (*0-89073-082-2*, 301) Boston Public Lib.
— Boston Catholics: A History of the Church & Its People. LC 98-18996. (Illus.). 338p. 1998. text 35.00 (*1-55553-359-0*) NE U Pr.
***O'Connor, Thomas H.** Boston Catholics: A History of the Church & Its People. (Illus.). 376p. 2000. pap. text 16.95 (*1-55553-433-3*) NE U Pr.
O'Connor, Thomas H. Boston Irish. 384p. 1997. pap. 14.95 (*0-316-62661-9*) Little.
— The Boston Irish: A Political History. (Illus.). 363p. 1995. text 26.95 (*1-55553-220-9*) NE U Pr.
— Building a New Boston: Politics & Urban Renewal, 1950-1970. 328p. 1993. text 45.00 (*1-55553-161-X*) NE U Pr.
— Building a New Boston: Politics & Urban Renewal, 1950-1970. LC 92-42258. 328p. (C). 1995. pap. text 16.95 (*1-55553-246-2*) NE U Pr.
— Civil War Boston: Home Front & Battlefield. LC 97-15747. (Illus.). 352p. 1997. text 35.00 (*1-55553-318-3*) NE U Pr.
— Civil War Boston: Home Front & Battlefield. 1999. pap. text 16.95 (*1-55553-383-3*) NE U Pr.
— South Boston, My Home Town: The History of an Ethnic Neighborhood. LC 93-43535. 272p. (C). 1994. reprint ed. pap. text 16.95 (*1-55553-188-1*) NE U Pr.
O'Connor, Thomas J. & Robbins, Richard L. The Automated Law Firm: A Complete Guide to Software & Systems. LC 96-47528. 600p. 1996. ring bd. 146.00 (*1-56706-332-2*) Aspen Law.
O'Connor, Thomas P., et al, eds. Physicochemical Processes & Wastes in the Ocean: Oceanic Processes in Marine Pollution, Vol. 2. LC 84-29746. 252p. (C). 1987. lib. bdg. 54.50 (*0-89874-811-9*) Krieger.
O'Connor, Thomas P., jt. ed. see Wolfe, Douglas A.
O'Connor, Thomas S. Clinical Pastoral Supervision & the Theology of Charles Gerkin. (Editions SR Ser.: Vol. 22) 152p. 1998. pap. 24.95 (*0-88920-310-5*) W Laurier U Pr.
O'Connor, Tim. The Feeling of Greatness: The Moe Norman Story. (Illus.). 224p. (Orig.). 1995. pap. 16.95 (*1-57028-086-X*, 8086XH, Mstrs Pr) NTC Contemp Pub Co.
O'Connor, Timothy. Persons & Causes: The Metaphysics of Free Will. LC 99-20501. 160p. 2000. text 35.00 (*0-19-513308-0*) OUP.
O'Connor, Timothy, ed. Agents, Causes, & Events: Essays on Indeterminism & Free Will. 288p. (C). 1995. text 57.00 (*0-19-509156-6*) OUP.
— Agents, Causes & Events: Essays on Indeterminism & Free Will. 288p. 1995. pap. text 24.95 (*0-19-509157-4*) OUP.
O'Connor, Timothy E. The Politics of Soviet Culture: Anatolii Lunacharskii. LC 83-18231. (Studies in the Fine Arts: The Avant-Garde: No. 42). (Illus.). 211p. reprint ed. pap. 65.50 (*0-8357-1468-3*, 207056600001) Bks Demand.
O'Connor, Ulich. Three Noh Plays. (Illus.). 48p. 1997. pap. 4.95 (*0-905473-58-2*, Pub. by Wolfhound Press) Irish Amer Bk.
O'Connor, Ulick. Irish Tales & Sagas. (Illus.). 96p. (Orig.). (J). 1996. pap. 10.95 (*1-57098-106-X*) Roberts Rinehart.
— Irish Tales & Sagas. (Illus.). 96p. (Orig.). 1996. 12.95 (*0-948524-59-6*, Pub. by Town Hse) Roberts Rinehart.
— Irish Troubles. LC 96-45011. 1996. pap. 13.95 (*0-393-31645-9*) Norton.
— Sputnik & Other Poems. (Orig.). pap. 4.95 (*0-8159 6822 1*) Devin.
— Times I've Seen. (Illus.). 1964. 19.95 (*0-8392-1119-8*) Astor-Honor.
O'Connor, Victoria, jt. auth. see Kuebelbeck, Julie.
O'Connor, Vincent D. Nearly Departed: Playscript. 1984. pap. 6.00 (*0-88734-212-4*) Players Pr.
O'Connor, Vincent F. & Hynes, Michael C., eds. Mission Mathematics 5-8: Linking Aerospace & the NCTM Standards. LC 97-42145. (Illus.). 136p. 1997. pap. 22.95 (*0-87353-435-2*) NCTM.
O'Connor, W. F. Folk Tales from Tibet. (Illus.). 176p. (C). 1982. reprint ed. 65.00 (*0-89771-114-9*, Pub. by Ratna Pustak Bhandar) St Mut.
O'Connor, Walter F. Accounting & Taxation. (Barron's Business Library). 320p. 1990. pap. 16.95 (*0-8120-4154-2*) Barron.
— An Inquiry into the Foreign Tax Burdens of U. S. Based Multinational Corporations. Bruchey, Stuart, ed. LC 80-586. (Multinational Corporations Ser.). 1981. lib. bdg. 49.95 (*0-405-13377-4*) Ayer.
O'Connor, William. Sense & Sensibility in Modern Poetry. (BCL1-PS American Literature Ser.). 278p. 1993. reprint ed. lib. bdg. 79.00 (*0-7812-6586-X*) Rprt Serv.
— Three Pillars. (Vampire Ser.). (Illus.). (Orig.). 1997. pap. 18.00 (*1-56504-288-3*, 2809) White Wolf.
O'Connor, William, jt. auth. see Soesbee, Ree.
O'Connor, William E. An Introduction to Airline Economics. 5th ed. LC 94-37883. 256p. 1995. text 45.00 (*0-275-94863-3*, Praeger Pubs) Greenwood.
***O'Connor, William E.** An Introduction to Airline Economics. 6th ed. 264p. 2000. 47.00 (*0-275-96911-8*, C6911, Praeger Pubs) Greenwood.
O'Connor, William J. & Toohey, Phillip S. Regulation Z, Truth-in-Lending: Comprehensive Compliance Manual. rev. ed. 524p. 1991. 254.00 incl. disk (*0-685-62690-3*) Am Bankers.
O'Connor, William J., jt. auth. see American Bankers Association Staff.
O'Connor, William R. Natural Desire for God. (Aquinas Lectures). 1948. 15.00 (*0-87462-113-5*) Marquette.
***O'Connor, William T.** Making Your Bad Back Better with the O'Connor Technique: How You Can Become Your Own Chiropractor. 2nd rev. ed. (Illus.). 402p. 2000. pap. 37.95 (*0-9664991-1-5*, 002) Aegis Genomics.
O'Connor, William V. Ezra Pound. LC 63-62712. (University of Minnesota Pamphlets on American Writers Ser.: No. 26). 48p. (Orig.). reprint ed. pap. 30.00 (*0-7837-2870-0*, 205758500006) Bks Demand.
— Seven Modern American Novelists: An Introduction. LC 64-18175. 308p. reprint ed. pap. 95.50 (*0-608-14129-1*, 205589400039) Bks Demand.
— William Faulkner. LC 59-63269. (University of Minnesota Pamphlets on American Writers Ser.: No. 3). 47p. reprint ed. pap. 30.00 (*0-608-14139-9*, 205592800039) Bks Demand.
O'Connor, William V., ed. see Beach, Joseph W.
O'Connor, William Van, see Van O'Connor, William.
***O'Conohue.** Handbook of Forensic Psychology. 2000. 85.00 (*0-8133-9117-2*, Pub. by Westview) HarpC.
O'Conor, Charles. Letters of Charles O'Conor of Belanagare: A Catholic Voice in Eighteenth-Century Ireland. Ward, Robert E. et al, eds. LC 87-32563. 571p. 1988. reprint ed. pap. 177.10 (*0-7837-9104-6*, 204990600004) Bks Demand.
O'Conor, David, tr. see Speltz, Alexander.
O'Conor, John F., tr. see Sokolov, Nicolai.
O'Conor, Norreys J. Battles & Enchantments Retold from Early Gaelic Literature. LC 71-124247. (Select Bibliographies Reprint Ser.). 1977. reprint ed. 17.95 (*0-8369-5435-1*) Ayer.
O'Conor, William A. Essays in Literature & Ethics. 1977. 17.95 (*0-8369-7234-1*, 8033) Ayer.
OCork, Shannon. Ice Fall. 384p. (Orig.). 1988. pap. 4.50 (*0-373-97084-6*) Harlequin Bks.
Ocork, Shannon. Titanic: A Love Story. rev. ed. (Mira Bks.). 1998. per. 5.50 (*1-55166-506-9*, Mira Bks) Harlequin Bks.
O'Cork, Shannon. Turning Point. 384p. 1988. mass mkt. 4.50 (*0-373-97062-5*) Harlequin Bks.
Ocorr, Dave. Matt & Shawn: Backcourt Duo. LC 98-91433. (Coach's Choice Ser.). 155p. (J). (gr. 4-9). 1998. pap. 8.95 (*0-9660758-2-X*) Perth Pubns.
— Matt & Shawn: Baseball Battery. LC 97-92505. (Coach's Choice Ser.). (J). (gr. 4-9). 1997. pap. 8.95 (*0-9660758-1-1*) Perth Pubns.
— Matt Gray: Frosh Phenom. (Coach's Choice Ser.). 152p. (J). (gr. 4-9). 1997. pap. 8.95 (*0-9660758-0-3*) Perth Pubns.
Ocorr, Karen, jt. auth. see Osgood, Marcy.
O'Corrain, Donncha, jt. ed. see Mac Curtain, Margaret.
O'Coy, Ali. Love's Turbulent Tides. 238p. (Orig.). Date not set. pap. 14.95 (*0-9659023-9-0*) A C Seale.
OCP Publications Staff, ed. see Walsh, Eugene A.
O'Creevey, Mark F. & Nicholson, Nigel. Survey Pack. 50p. 1999. pap. 800.00 (*1-86152-361-0*) Thomson Learn.
O'Crohan, Sean. A Day in Our Life. Enright, Tim, tr. (Illus.). 144p. (Orig.). 1992. 26.95 (*0-19-212603-2*) OUP.
O'Croinin, Breandan, jt. ed. see Grundy, Valerie.
O'Croinin, Connacha, jt. auth. see Dillon, Myles.
O'Croinin, Daibhi, ed. Early Medieval Ireland. LC 94-43307. (History of England Ser.). 384p. (C). 1995. text 55.50 (*0-582-01566-9*, Pub. by Addison-Wesley) Longman.
— Early Medieval Ireland, 400 - 1200. LC 94-43307. (History of England Ser.). 400p. (C). 1995. pap. 39.06 (*0 582 01565-0*) Longman.
O'Croinin, Donncha, jt. auth. see Dillon, Myles.
OCS Marine Staff. Coal-Fired Ships, 3 vols. (C). 1989. text 395.00 (*0-906314-39-9*, Pub. by Lorne & MacLean Marine) St Mut.
— COW - IGS Conference Papers & Proceedings. (C). 1989. text 195.00 (*0-906314-00-3*, Pub. by Lorne & MacLean Marine) St Mut.

O

An Asterisk (*) at the beginning of an entry indicates that the title is appearing for the first time.

— COW - IGS Manual. (C). 1989. text 250.00 (*0-906314-15-1*, Pub. by Lorne & MacLean Marine) St Mut.

— Dry Dock Planning Manual. (C). 1989. text 720.00 (*0-906314-16-X*, Pub. by Lorne & MacLean Marine) St Mut.

— English - Portuguese Marine Engineering Glossary. (C). 1989. text 325.00 (*0-906314-11-9*, Pub. by Lorne & MacLean Marine) St Mut.

— Inert Gas Systems Manual. (C). 1989. text 225.00 (*0-906314-10-0*, Pub. by Lorne & MacLean Marine) St Mut.

— International Manual on Maritime Safety. (C). 1989. text 290.00 (*0-906314-14-3*, Pub. by Lorne & MacLean Marine) St Mut.

— Manual de Controle de Incendio de Buques. (SPA.). (C). 1989. text 195.00 (*0-7855-6968-5*, Pub. by Lorne & MacLean Marine) St Mut.

— Marginal Oilfield Development Manual. (C). 1989. text 350.00 (*0-906314-35-6*, Pub. by Lorne & MacLean Marine) St Mut.

— Operacion y Seguridad en Buques Tanqueros (Tanker Safety Manual) (SPA.). (C). 1989. text 395.00 (*0-906314-04-6*, Pub. by Lorne & MacLean Marine) St Mut.

— S. O. S. (Ship Operational Safety) Manual. (C). 1989. text 425.00 (*0-906314-09-7*, Pub. by Lorne & MacLean Marine) St Mut.

— Ship Squat Manual. (C). 1989. text 290.00 (*0-906314-07-0*, Pub. by Lorne & MacLean Marine) St Mut.

— Shipowners Guide to Yard Repairs. (C). 1989. text 310.00 (*0-906314-29-1*, Pub. by Lorne & MacLean Marine) St Mut.

— Ships Fire-Fighting Manual. (C). 1989. text 195.00 (*0-906314-03-8*, Pub. by Lorne & MacLean Marine) St Mut.

— Steering Gear Systems. (C). 1989. text 150.00 (*0-7855-6969-3*) St Mut.

— Survival Techniques. (C). 1989. text 110.00 (*0-906314-01-1*, Pub. by Lorne & MacLean Marine) St Mut.

OCS Publishing Group Staff. Subsea Production Systems - Can Engineering Reduce Pipeline Costs? 1989. 125.00 (*90-6314-562-4*, Pub. by Lorne & MacLean Marine) St Mut.

Octavio, G., ed. see Dewey, Melvil.

Octogram Publishing Staff. Mac-Graphics Interactive Workshop: A Step-by-Step Visual Guide to Graphics for the Apple Macintosh. 3rd ed. (Illus.). 290p. 1995. pap. 79.95 incl. cd-rom (*0-201-88365-1*) Peachpit Pr.

Octopus, Conran, jt. auth. see Burnett, Sarah.

Octopus, Coran. Sotheby's Art at Auction: The Year in Review, 1995-1996. (Illus.). 256p. 1997. 85.00 (*1-85029-787-8*, Pub. by Conran Octopus) Antique Collect.

Octrue, M. & Guingand, M. Experimental Characterization of Surface Durability of Materials for Worm Gears. (Nineteen Ninety-Two Fall Technical Meeting Ser.: Vol. 92FTM1). (Illus.). 7p. 1992. pap. text 30.00 (*1-55589-581-6*) AGMA.

Octrue, Michel. An Industrial Approach for Load Capacity Calculation of Worm Gears (Verifying & Design) (Nineteen Ninety Fall Technical Meeting Ser.: Vol. 90FTM2). (Illus.). 7p. 1990. pap. text 30.00 (*1-55589-554-9*) AGMA.

— A New Method for Designing Worm-Gear. (Nineteen Eighty-Eight Fall Technical Meeting Ser.: Vol. 88FTM6). (Illus.). 5p. 1988. pap. text 30.00 (*1-55589-511-5*) AGMA.

— Relations Between Wear & Pitting Phenomena in Worm Gears. (Technical Papers: Vol. 97FTM9). (Illus.). 8p. 1997. pap. text 30.00 (*1-55589-703-7*) AGMA.

O'Cuilleanain, Cormac, jt. ed. see Barnes, John.

O'Cuilleanain, Cormac, jt. ed. see Haywood, E.

O'Cuinn, Gerard, ed. Metabolism of Brain Peptides. LC 95-14061. 272p. 1995. boxed set 134.95 (*0-8493-7665-3*, 7665) CRC Pr.

O'Cuinneagain, Mel, et al. Butterworths Ireland Tax Guide, 1993-94. 1993. pap. text 99.00 (*1-85475-626-5*, IE, MICHIE) LEXIS Pub.

Oculi, Okello. Discourse on African Affairs. LC 97-47060. 1997. pap. text 19.95 (*0-86543-557-X*) Africa World.

— Discourses on African Affairs: Directions & Destinies for the 21st Century. LC 97-47060. 136p. 1997. 69.95 (*0-86543-556-1*) Africa World.

O'Curry, Eugene. Lectures on the Manuscript Materials of Ancient Irish History. 750p. 1995. 75.00 (*1-85182-183-X*, Pub. by Four Cts Pr) Intl Spec Bk.

Ocvirk, Otto G., et al. Art Fundamentals: Theory & Practice. 8th ed. LC 96-78734. 352p. (C). 1997. text. write for info. (*0-697-34033-3*, WCB McGr Hill) McGrw-H Hghr Educ.

OCVN Board of Advisors Staff. 1997 Southern California Funding Directory. 3rd rev. ed. 250p. (Orig.). 1996. pap. 29.95 (*0-9655378-0-3*) Orange Cnty Venture.

Oczenski, A. Breathing & Mechanical Support. 1997. 65.00 (*0-632-04859-X*) Blackwell Sci.

Oda & Grice. Japanese Banking, Securities & Anti-Monopoly Law. 200p. 1996. text 100.00 (*0-406-10685-1*, 81279-10, MICHIE) LEXIS Pub.

***Oda, Hiroshi.** Japanese Law. 2nd ed. 496p. 2000. text 115.00 (*0-19-876456-1*) OUP.

Oda, Hiroshi, ed. Japanese Commercial Law in an Era of Internationalization. LC 93-44889. 328p. (C). 1994. lib. bdg. 139.00 (*1-85333-786-2*, Pub. by Graham & Trotman) Kluwer Academic.

— Law & Politics of West-East Technology Transfer. (C). 1991. lib. bdg. 121.50 (*0-7923-0990-1*) Kluwer Academic.

Oda, Hiroshi & Grice, Geoffrey, eds. Japanese Banking, Securities & Anti-Monopoly Law. 170p. 1988. boxed set 85.00 (*0-88063-264-X*, MICHIE) LEXIS Pub.

Oda, Hiroshi, ed. see Rudden, Bernard.

Oda, M. & Iwashita, K. Mechanics of Granular Materials: An Introduction. (Illus.). 383p. (C). 1999. pap. 51.00 (*90-5410-462-7*, Pub. by A A Balkema); text 104.00 (*90-5410-461-9*, Pub. by A A Balkema) Ashgate Pub Co.

Oda, Makoto. The Bomb. Whittaker, D. H., tr. 218p. 1990. 18.95 (*0-87011-981-8*) Kodansha.

— H: A Hiroshima Novel. Whittaker, D. H., tr. from JPN. Orig. Title: The Bomb. 218p. 1995. pap. 10.00 (*4-7700-1947-5*) Kodansha.

Oda, Noritsugu. Danish Chairs. LC 98-8298. (Illus.). 233p. 1999. pap. 29.95 (*0-8118-2257-5*) Chronicle Bks.

Oda, Osamu. Compound Semiconductor Bulk Materials & Characterizations. 250p. 1997. text 59.00 (*981-02-1728-5*) World Scientific Pub.

Oda, Patsy. Heart's Desire. rev. ed. LC 98-60323. 144p. 1998. pap. 9.99 (*1-57921-109-7*, Pub. by WinePress Pub) BookWorld.

Oda, Shigeru. International Control of Sea Resources. rev. ed. (C). 1989. reprint ed. lib. bdg. 101.50 (*90-247-3800-8*) Kluwer Academic.

— International Law of the Resources of the Sea. 144p. 1979. reprint ed. lib. bdg. 41.00 (*90-286-0399-9*) Kluwer Academic.

Oda, Shigeru, et al, eds. The Practice of Japan in International Law, 1961-1970. LC 82-193177. 503p. 1982. reprint ed. pap. 156.00 (*0-608-01257-2*, 206194500001) Bks Demand.

Oda, Stephanie. Hope Lines Journal, No. H40. 1991. 15.95 (*0-8378-2042-1*) Gibson.

Oda, Stephanie C. My Nighttime Book. (Good Little Books for Good Little Children). 12p. (J). (ps). 1986. 3.25 (*0-8378-5091-6*) Gibson.

Oda, Stephanie C., ed. In Sympathy. (Illus.). 1992. 9.50 (*0-8378-2500-8*) Gibson.

Oda, Tadao. Convex Bodies & Algebraic Geometry. (Ergebnisse der Mathematik und Ihrer Grenzgebiete Ser.: Vol. 15, 3 Folge). (Illus.). 280p. 1987. 135.95 (*0-387-17600-4*) Spr-Verlag.

Oda, Takayuki. Periods of Hilbert Modular Surfaces. (Progress in Mathematics Ser.: Vol. 19). 1982. 40.50 (*0-8176-3084-8*) Birkhauser.

Odabasi, Halis & Akyuz, O., eds. Topics in Mathematical Physics: Papers Presented at an International Symposium held July 28-August 2, 1975 at Bogazici University, Istanbul, Turkey. LC 77-84853. (Illus.). 291p. reprint ed. pap. 90.30 (*0-8357-5511-8*, 203512600093) Bks Demand.

Odabasi, Halis, jt. ed. see Brittin, Wesley E.

Odabasi, Halis, ed. see Conference on International Implications of Enviro.

Odada, Eric O., jt. ed. see Johnson, Thomas C.

O'Daffer. Custom Geometry. (C). 1997. pap. text 39.00 (*0-201-33621-9*) Addison-Wesley.

O'Daffer, Phares. Pre-Algebra. (SPA.). 592p. (C). 1992. text 33.33 (*0-201-51868-6*) Addison-Wesley.

— User's Guide for IBM DOS Testgen 3.4 for Math for Elementary School Teachers. (C). 1998. ring bd. write for info. (*0-201-37916-3*) Addison-Wesley.

O'Daffer, Phares G. Geometry: An Investigative Approach to Cooperative Learning. 2nd ed. 110p. (C). 1992. pap. text, lab manual ed. 30.00 (*0-201-21797-X*) Addison-Wesley.

— Mathematics for Elementary School Teachers. Guardino, Karen, ed. 928p. (C). 1997. pap. text. write for info. (*0-201-62099-5*) Addison-Wesley.

Odaga, Adhiambo. Les Filles et L'Ecole en Afrique Subsaharienne: De L'Analyse a L'Action. (World Bank Technical Papers: No. 298).Tr. of Girls & Schools in Sub-Saharan Africa: From Analysis to Action. (FRE.). 130p. 1996. pap. 22.00 (*0-8213-3507-3*, 13507) World Bank.

Odaga, Adhiambo & Heneveld, Ward. Girls & Schools in Sub-Saharan Africa: From Analysis to Action, Vol. 298. LC 95-35063. (World Bank Technical Papers). 124p. 1995. pap. 22.00 (*0-8213-3379-8*) World Bank.

Odagiri, Hiroyuki. Growth Through Competition, Competition Through Growth: Strategic Management & the Economy in Japan. (Illus.). 380p. 1994. reprint ed. pap. text 27.00 (*0-19-828873-5*) OUP.

Odagiri, Hiroyuki & Goto, Akira. Technology & Industrial Development in Japan: Building Capabilities by Learning, Innovation & Public Policy. LC 96-571. (Japan Business & Economics Ser.). (Illus.). 322p. 1996. text 75.00 (*0-19-828802-6*, Clarendon Pr) OUP.

Odagiri, Hiroyuki, jt. ed. see Goto, Akira.

Odahl, C. Early Christian Latin Literature: Readings from the Ancient Texts. (LAT., Illus.). 209p. (C). 1993. pap. text 25.00 (*0-89005-515-7*) Ares.

Odahl, Charles M. Catilinarian Conspiracy. 1972. 16.95 (*0-8084-0032-0*); pap. write for info. (*0-8084-0033-9*) NCUP.

***O'Dair, Sharon.** Class, Critics & Shakespeare: Bottom Lines on the Culture Wars. (Illus.). 200p. (C). 2000. text 44.50 (*0-472-09754-7*, 09754); pap. text 17.95 (*0-472-06754-0*, 06754) U of Mich Pr.

Odaka, Konosuke & Sawai, Minoru, eds. Small Firms, Large Concerns: The Development of Small Business in Comparative Perspective. LC 98-54455. (Illus.). 328p. 1999. text 70.00 (*0-19-829379-8*) OUP.

Odaka, Konosuke, et al. The Automobile Industry in Japan: A Study of Ancillary Firm Development. (Hitotsubashi University Economic Research Ser.: No. 26). 356p. 1988. 85.00 (*4-314-00487-8*) OUP.

Odaka, Kunio. Toward Industrial Democracy: Management & the Workers in Modern Japan. LC 74-82575. (East Asian Monographs: No. 80). 272p. 1975. 18.50 (*0-674-89816-8*) HUP.

O'Daly, Anne, ed. The Encyclopedia of Life Sciences, Set. (J). 1995. 657.07 (*0-7614-0254-3*) Marshall Cavendish.

***O'Daly, Gerard.** Augustine's City of God: A Reader's Guide. LC 98-30960. 336p. 1999. text 85.00 (*0-19-826354-6*) OUP.

O'Daly, Gerard. The Poetry of Boethius. LC 90-2528. xii, 252p. (C). 1991. 59.95 (*0-8078-1989-1*) U of NC Pr.

O'Daly, William, tr. see Neruda, Pablo.

Odam, George. The Sounding Symbol: Music Education in Action. 152p. (Orig.). 1999. pap. 42.50 (*0-7487-2323-4*, Pub. by S Thornes Pubs) Trans-Atl Phila.

***Odam, John.** Start with a Digital Camera: A Guide to Using Digital Photography to Creat High-Quality Graphics. 144p. (C). 1999. pap. text 34.99 (*0-201-35424-1*) Peachpit Pr.

Odam, John, et al. Getting Started with 3D: A Designer's Guide to 3D Graphics & Illustration. LC 99-166993. (Illus.). 176p. (C). 1998. pap. 34.95 (*0-201-69676-2*, Pub. by Peachpit Pr) Addison-Wesley.

Odam, John, jt. auth. see Ashford, Janet.

Odam, Joyce. Nocturnes. 48p. 1995. pap. 6.00 (*0-9648232-1-7*) Frith Pr.

Odamtten, Vincent O. The Art of Ama Ata Aidoo: Polylectics & Reading Against Neocolonialism. LC 93-35009. (Illus.). 216p. (C). 1994. 49.95 (*0-8130-1276-7*); pap. 16.95 (*0-8130-1277-5*) U Press Fla.

Odanaka, T. Dynamic Management Decision & Stochastic Control Processes. 240p. (C). 1990. text 41.00 (*981-02-0092-7*) World Scientific Pub.

O'Daniel, Bill. First Land Buyers in Bossier - Claiborne Parishes, Louisiana: Up to the Civil War. 415p. 1997. pap. 25.00 (*1-57088-048-4*) J&W Ent.

O'Daniel, H. Edward, Jr., text. Kentucky Workers' Compensation Law 1987. 246p. 1988. pap. 41.00 (*0-8322-0219-3*) Banks-Baldwin.

O'Daniel, Michael, jt. auth. see Robertson, Oscar.

O'Daniel, Therman B., ed. James Baldwin: A Critical Evaluation. LC 74-30006. 1981. pap. 12.95 (*0-88258-091-4*) Howard U Pr.

— Jean Toomer: A Critical Evaluation. 576p. 1988. 29.95 (*0-88258-111-2*) Howard U Pr.

Odarty, Bill. A Safari of African Cooking. LC 72-115155. 1971. pap. 12.00 (*0-910296-63-4*) Broadside Pr.

Odate, Gyoju. Japan's Financial Relations with the United States. LC 78-57574. (Columbia University. Studies in the Social Sciences: No. 224). reprint ed. 20.00 (*0-404-51224-0*) AMS Pr.

Odate, Toshio. Japanese Woodworking Tools: Their Tradition, Spirit, & Use. 2nd ed. LC 98-9884. (Illus.). 208p. 1998. reprint ed. pap. 24.95 (*0-941936-46-5*) Linden Pub Fresno.

***Odate, Toshio.** Making Shoji. LC 99-49812. (Illus.). 128p. 2000. pap. 21.95 (*0-941936-47-3*, Pub. by Linden Pub Fresno) IPG Chicago.

O'Day, Alan. Charles Stewart Parnell LC 98-235716. (Historical Association of Ireland / Life & Times Ser.). 85 p. 1998. write for info. (*0-85221-136-8*) Dundalgon Pr.

— The English Face of Irish Nationalism: Parnellite Involvement in British Politics, 1880-86. (Modern Revivals in History Ser.). 224p. 1994. 57.95 (*0-7512-0240-1*, Pub. by Gregg Revivals) Ashgate Pub Co.

— Irish Home Rule, 1867-1921. LC 97-47404. (New Frontiers in History Ser.). 288p. 1998. pap. 27.95 (*0-7190-3776-X*, Pub. by Manchester Univ Pr); text 79.95 (*0-7190-3775-1*, Pub. by Manchester Univ Pr) St Martin.

— The Making of Modern Irish History: Revisionism & the Revisionist Controversy. Boyce, D. George, ed. LC 95-36523. 272p. (C). 1996. 70.00 (*0-415-09819-X*) Routledge.

— Reactions to Irish Nationalism, 1865-1914. 422p. 1987. 55.00 (*0-907628-85-0*) Hambledon Press.

O'Day, Alan, ed. Dimensions of Irish Terrorism. LC 93-38372. (International Library of Terrorism: No. 2). 428p. 1994. 50.00 (*0-8161-7338-9*, G K Hall & Co) Mac Lib Ref.

— Government & Institutions in the Post-1832 United Kingdom. LC 94-38867. (Studies in British History: Vol. 34). 420p. 1995. text 109.95 (*0-7734-8980-0*) E Mellen.

— Political Violence in Northern Ireland: Conflict & Conflict Resolution. LC 96-20681. 264p. 1997. 65.00 (*0-275-95414-5*, Praeger Pubs) Greenwood.

— A Survey of the Irish in England (1872) 174p. 1990. 45.00 (*1-85285-010-8*) Hambledon Press.

— Terrorism's Laboratory: The Case of Northern Ireland. LC 95-3902. 1995. 77.95 (*1-85521-457-1*, Pub. by Dartmth Pub) Ashgate Pub Co.

O'Day, Alan & Alexander, Yonah, eds. Irish Terrorist Trauma. 288p. 1989. 39.95 (*0-685-23482-7*) St Martin.

O'Day, Alan & Stevenson, John, eds. Irish Historical Documents since 1800. 300p. (C). 1992. text 72.50 (*0-389-20971-6*) B&N Imports.

O'Day, Alan, jt. auth. see Alexander, Yonah.

O'Day, Alan, jt. auth. see Boyce, David George.

O'Day, Alan, jt. ed. see Alexander, Yonah.

O'Day, Anita & Eells, George. High Times Hard Times. LC 88-17896. (Illus.). 349p. 1977. reprint ed. pap. 18.00 (*0-87910-118-0*) Limelight Edns.

O'Day, Carol, jt. auth. see Boylston, Eula.

O'Day, Danton. Campus Bound! Are You Ready? (Illus.). 8p. (Orig.). (YA). (gr. 11 up). 1996. pap. 2.50 (*1-884241-69-7*, SPS0021) Energeia Pub.

— Making Quick, Simple & Effective Overheads (for Public Speaking) (Illus.). 8p. (Orig.). 1996. pap. 2.50 (*1-884241-68-9*, SPS0023) Energeia Pub.

O'Day, Danton H. Procrastination: Don't Let It Ruin Your Life. (Illus.). 8p. (Orig.). 1996. pap. 2.50 (*1-884241-70-0*, SPS0022) Energeia Pub.

— Self-Testing Made Easy. (Illus.). 8p. (Orig.). 1997. pap. 2.50 (*0-9626591-4-2*, SPS0340) Energeia Pub.

O'Day, Danton H., ed. Calcium As an Intracellular Messenger in Eucaryotic Microbes. (Illus.). 418p. 1990. 49.00 (*1-55581-023-3*) ASM Pr.

O'Day, Danton H. & Horgen, Paul A., eds. Eucaryotic Microbes As Model Developmental Systems. LC 76-28079. (Microbiology Ser.: No. 2). (Illus.). 456p. reprint ed. pap. 141.40 (*0-8357-6107-X*, 203455800090) Bks Demand.

O'Day, Denis M. Cataract in Adults: Management of Functional Impairment, Clinical Practice Guideline, No. 4. 241p. 1994. per. 9.00 (*0-16-045248-1*) USGPO.

— Management of Cataract in Adults Quick Referene Guide for Clinicians. 4th ed. 15p. 1994. pap. 16.00 (*0-16-045245-7*) USGPO.

O'Day, Flannery C. Bewitched. 400p. 1999. mass mkt. 5.99 (*0-8217-6126-9*) Kensgtn Pub Corp.

O'Day-Flannery, Constance. Anywhere You Are. LC 98-93299. 384p. 1999. mass mkt. 6.50 (*0-380-80169-8*, Avon Bks) Morrow Avon.

***O'Day-Flannery, Constance.** Heaven on Earth. 384p. 2000. mass mkt. 6.50 (*0-380-80805-6*) Morrow Avon.

Oday-Flannery, Constance. Once in a Lifetime. 1994. mass mkt. 5.99 (*0-8217-5918-3*, Zebra Kensgtn) Kensgtn Pub Corp.

O'Day-Flannery, Constance. Seasons. 416p. (Orig.). 1995. mass mkt. 6.50 (*0-446-60107-1*) Warner Bks.

— Second Chances. 400p. 1992. mass mkt. 5.99 (*0-8217-3950-6*, Zebra Kensgtn) Kensgtn Pub Corp.

— Second Chances. 400p. 1998. pap. 5.99 (*0-8217-5917-5*, Zebra Kensgtn) Kensgtn Pub Corp.

— Sunsets. 416p. (Orig.). 1996. mass mkt. 6.50 (*0-446-60307-4*) Warner Bks.

Oday-Flannery, Constance. This Time Forever. 448p. 1998. mass mkt. 5.99 (*0-8217-5964-7*, Zebra Kensgtn) Kensgtn Pub Corp.

— Time for Love. 448p. 1999. mass mkt. 5.99 (*0-8217-6107-2*, Zebra Kensgtn) Kensgtn Pub Corp.

O'Day-Flannery, Constance. Time Kept Promises. 1988. mass mkt. 4.95 (*0-8217-3554-3*, Zebra Kensgtn) Kensgtn Pub Corp.

— Time Kept Promises. (Zebra Bks.). 1998. mass mkt. 5.99 (*0-8217-5963-9*, Zebra Kensgtn) Kensgtn Pub Corp.

— Time Kissed Destiny. 512p. 1998. mass mkt. 5.99 (*0-8217-5962-0*, Zebra Kensgtn) Kensgtn Pub Corp.

— Timeless Passion. 1986. mass mkt. 4.99 (*0-8217-3683-3*, Zebra Kensgtn) Kensgtn Pub Corp.

— Timeswept Lovers. 496p. 1987. mass mkt. 3.95 (*0-8217-2057-0*, Zebra Kensgtn) Kensgtn Pub Corp.

Oday-Flannry. Timeswept Lovers. 1993. pap. 4.99 (*0-8217-4552-2*) NAL.

O'Day, Gabrielle. The Matter of Shiva. 226p. 1991. 24.95 (*0-8191-8202-8*) U Pr of Amer.

O'Day, Gail R. & Long, Thomas G., eds. Listening to the Word: Studies in Honor of Fred B. Craddock. LC 92-38030. 256p. 1993. pap. 16.95 (*0-687-37062-0*) Abingdon.

O'Day, Jennifer A., jt. ed. see Fuhrman, Susan H.

Oday, Kate. The Waite Group's Discovering MS-DOS. 2nd ed. 1991. 19.95 (*0-672-22772-X*, Bobbs) Macmillan.

O'Day, Kate & Tapscott, Linda. The Amazing PhotoDeluxe Book for Macintosh. 244p. 1996. pap. 30.00 (*1-56830-266-5*) Adobe Pr.

— The Amazing PhotoDeluxe Book for Macintosh. 1996. 30.00 (*0-614-14443-4*) Macmillan.

— The Amazing PhotoDeluxe Book for Windows. 264p. 1996. pap. 30.00 (*1-56830-286-X*) Adobe Pr.

— Guerrilla Marketing with Adobe PhotoDeluxe. 275p. 1998. pap. 59.99 incl. cd-rom (*1-56830-486-2*) Adobe Pr.

O'Day, Kate, et al. The Waite Group's Understanding MS-DOS. 2nd ed. (Understanding Ser.). 384p. 1989. 19.95 (*0-672-27298-9*) Sams.

O'Day, Maureen & Steffey, Kevin. Corn Insect Pests: A Diagnostic Guide. (Illus.). 48p. 1999. pap. text 20.00 (*0-7881-7903-9*) DIANE Pub.

O'Day, Rosemary. Longman Companion Tudor. LC 94-9970. (Longman Companions to History Ser.). 336p. (C). 1995. text 62.95 (*0-582-06725-1*, 77010, Pub. by Addison-Wesley) Longman.

O'Day, Rosemary & Englander, David. Mr. Charles Booth's Inquiry: Life & Labour of the People in London Reconsidered. LC 93-356. 256p. 1993. 55.00 (*1-85285-079-5*) Hambledon Press.

O'Day, Rosemary, jt. ed. see Englander, David.

O'Day, Vicki, jt. auth. see Nardi, Bonnie A.

Odback, Asa. Pocket Coach to Parenthood: Good Sports Make Winning Parents. LC 97-71097. 192p. 1997. pap. 13.95 (*0-9657760-8-5*) Light Beams.

Odber de Baubeta, Patricia A. Anticlerical Satire in Medieval Portuguese Literature. LC 92-23339. 356p. 1992. text 99.95 (*0-7734-9607-6*) E Mellen.

Odber de Baubeta, Patricia A., jt. ed. see Coulthard, Malcolm.

Odd, Gilbert, jt. auth. see Sullivan, John L.

Odden. School Finance: Policy Perspectives. 2nd ed. LC 99-15558. 496p. 1999. 53.43 (*0-07-228737-3*) McGraw.

***Odden, Allan & Archibald, Sarah.** How Schools Can Reallocate Resources to Boost Student Achievement. LC 00-8769. 2000. write for info. (*0-7619-7653-1*) Corwin Pr.

Odden, Allan & Busch, Carolyn. Financing Schools for High Performance: Strategies for Improving the Use of Educational Resources. LC 97-44062. 276p. 1998. 31.95 (*0-7879-4060-7*) Jossey-Bass.

Odden, Allan, jt. auth. see Goertz, Margaret E.

Odden, Allan R. Education Policy Implementation. LC 90-43395. (SUNY Series, Educational Leadership). 383p. (C). 1991. text 74.50 (*0-7914-0665-2*); pap. text 24.95 (*0-7914-0666-0*) State U NY Pr.

An Asterisk (*) at the beginning of an entry indicates that the title is appearing for the first time.

Odden, Allan R., ed. Rethinking School Finance: An Agenda for the 1990s. LC 92-11512. (Education-Higher Education Ser.). 384p. 1992. text 38.45 (*1-55542-451-1*) Jossey-Bass.

Odden, Allan R. & Kelley, Carolyn. Paying Teachers for What They Know & Do: New & Smarter Compensation Strategies to Improve Schools. LC 96-25312. (Illus.). 208p. 1996. pap. 24.95 (*0-8039-6459-5*) Corwin Pr.

Odden, Allan R. & Odden, Eleanor R. Educational Leadership for America's Schools. 416p. (C). 1995. 54.69 (*0-07-047489-3*) McGraw.

Odden, Allan R. & Picus, Lawrence O. School Finance: A Policy Perspective. (C). 1991. text 52.74 (*0-07-047486-9*) McGraw.

Odden, Anne Seymour. Child's Medical Record Book. LC 99-90240. 64p. 1999. pap. 12.95 (*0-9670221-1-8*, Pub. by Minot Pubg) ACCESS Pubs Network.

***Odden, Anne Seymour.** Child's Medical Record Book: Your Child's Records in One Convenient Place. 2nd rev. ed. LC 99-90240. 72p. 2000. pap. 12.95 (*0-9670221-3-4*, Pub. by Minot Pubg) ACCESS Pubs Network.

Odden, D., ed. Current Approaches to African Linguistics, Vol. 4. (Publications in African Languages & Linguistics). x, 428p. 1987. pap. 113.85 (*3-11-013103-X*) Mouton.

Odden, David. The Phonology & Morphology of Kimatuumbi. (Phonology of the World's Languages Ser.). 328p. 1996. 80.00 (*0-19-823503-8*) OUP.

Odden, Eleanor R., jt. auth. see Odden, Allan R.

Oddenina, Michael L. Putting Kids First: Walking Away from a Marriage Without Walking over the Kids. LC 96-231499. (Illus.). 151p. 1995. 16.95 (*1-884862-03-9*) Fmly Connect.

Oddenino, Kathy. Bridges of Consciousness. 298p. (Orig.). 1989. pap. 14.95 (*0-923081-01-1*) Joy Pubns MD.

— Healing Ourself: Growing Beyond the True Cause of Disease. (Illus.). 600p. (Orig.). 1994. pap. 24.95 (*0-923081-04-6*) Joy Pubns MD.

— The Journey Home: Our Evolving Consciousness. 525p. 1999. pap. 33.00 (*0-923081-06-2*) Joy Pubns MD.

— The Joy of Health: A Spiritual Concept of Integration & the Practicalities of Living. 300p. (Orig.). 1989. pap. 14.95 (*0-923081-00-3*) Joy Pubns MD.

— Love, Truth & Perception. 288p. (Orig.). (C). 1993. pap. 14.95 (*0-923081-03-8*) Joy Pubns MD.

— Sharing: Self Discovery in Relationships. 354p. (Orig.). 1990. pap. 14.95 (*0-923081-02-X*) Joy Pubns MD.

— A Soul Approach to Depression: Our Normal Transitional Emotions. LC 96-109469. (Illus.). 348p. (Orig.). 1995. pap. 24.95 (*0-923081-05-4*) Joy Pubns MD.

Oddens, B. J. & Vermeulen, A., eds. Androgens in the Aging Male: The Proceedings of a Workshop Organized by the International Health Foundation, Geneva, Switzerland, December 1995. LC 96-29358. (Illus.). 260p. 1996. text 69.00 (*1-85070-763-4*) Prthnon Pub.

Oddey, Alison. Devising Theatre: A Practical & Theoretical Handbook. (Illus.). 272p. (C). 1996. pap. 25.99 (*0-415-04900-8*, A7967) Routledge.

***Oddey, Alison.** Performing Women. LC 99 39867. 299p. 1999. text 39.95 (*0-312-22909-7*) St Martin.

Oddi, Marcia J. Environmental Enforcement Guide: An Overview of Indiana's Environmental Enforcement Process. 152p. 1996. pap., per. 129.00 (*1-883698-13-8*) IN Chamber Comm.

— Indiana Air Permitting Guide: New Source Review & Operating Permits. LC 99-196365. (Illus.). 266p. 1998. pap. write for info. (*1-883698-18-9*) IN Chamber Comm.

Oddi, Marcia J., ed. Indiana Environmental Air Rules, 1992. (Orig.). 1992. pap. 39.95 (*1-880182-03-3*) CEM.

— Indiana Environmental Rules, 1991, Vol. I. 1991. 39.95 (*1-880182-00-9*) CEM.

— Indiana Environmental Rules, 1991, Vol. II. 1991. 39.95 (*1-880182-01-7*) CEM.

— Indiana Environmental Solid & Hazardous Waste Rules, 1992. (Orig.). 1992. pap. 39.95 (*1-880182-05-X*) CEM.

— Indiana Environmental Statutes, 1991. 1991. 39.95 (*1-880182-02-5*) CEM.

— Indiana Environmental Statutes, 1992. (Orig.). 1992. pap. 39.95 (*1-880182-06-8*) CEM.

— Indiana Environmental Water Rules, 1992. (Orig.). 1992. pap. 39.95 (*1-880182-04-1*) CEM.

Oddi, Marsha, ed. Indiana Motor Vehicle Laws 1991 Edition. 624p. 1991. pap. 15.00 (*1-878760-05-X*) Graphics Ltd IN.

Oddie, Bill. Bill Oddie's Birds of Britain & Ireland. 1999. 22.95 (*1-85368-898-3*) Sterling.

***Oddie, Bill.** Bill Oddie's Gripping Yarns: Tales of Birds & Birding. (Illus.). 224p. 2000. pap. 14.95 (*0-7136-5268-3*) A & C Blk.

Oddie, Bill. Bill Oddie's Little Black Bird Book. (Illus.). 150p. 1996. pap. 9.95 (*0-86051-959-7*, Robson-Parkwest) Parkwest Pubns.

— Follow That Bird! Around the World with a Passionate Bird-Watcher. LC 95-73117. (Illus.). 172p. 1996. 21.95 (*0-86051-919-8*, Robson-Parkwest) Parkwest Pubns.

— Follow That Bird! Around the World with a Passionate Bird Watcher. LC 97-69429. (Illus.). 172p. 1997. pap. 11.95 (*1-86105-088-7*, Robson-Parkwest) Parkwest Pubns.

Oddie, Bill & Holden, Peter. Bird in the Nest. LC 97-66442. (Illus.). 146p. 1996. 29.95 (*0-86051-983-X*, Robson-Parkwest) Parkwest Pubns.

— Bird in the Nest. (Illus.). 142p. 1997. pap. 24.95 (*1-86105-039-9*, Robson-Parkwest) Parkwest Pubns.

Oddie, C., et al, eds. Butterworths County Court Precedents & Pleadings. ring bd. 390.00 (*0-406-29211-6*, UK, MICHIE) LEXIS Pub.

Oddie, G. A. Social Protest in India: British Protestant Missionaries & Social Reforms, Eighteen Fifty to Nineteen Hundred. 1979. 17.50 (*0-8364-0195-6*) S Asia.

Oddie, G. A., ed. Religion in South Asia. 204p. 1991. 22.95 (*81-85425-46-9*) Asia Bk Corp.

— Religion in South Asia: Religious Conversion & Revival Movements in South Asia in Medieval & Modern Times. (C). 1991. text 24.00 (*0-945921-18-7*, Pub. by S Asia Pubs) S Asia.

Oddie, Geoffrey. Missionaries, Rebellion & Proto-Nationalism: James Long of Bengal. (SOAS London Studies on South Asia Ser.: Vol. 16). 260p. (C). 1998. text 47.00 (*0-7007-1028-0*, Pub. by Curzon Pr Ltd) UH Pr.

Oddie, Geoffrey A. Popular Religion, Elites & Reform: Hook-Swinging & Its Prohibition in Colonial India. LC 95-910445. (C). 1995. 28.00 (*81-7304-101-6*, Pub. by Manohar) S Asia.

Oddie, Geoffrey A., ed. Religious Conversion Movements in South Asia: Continuities & Change, 1800-1990. (Religion & Society in South Asia Ser.). 280p. (C). 1997. text 48.00 (*0-7007-0472-8*, Pub. by Curzon Pr Ltd) UH Pr.

— Religious Traditions in South Asia: Interaction & Change. LC 97-150922. (Religion & Society in South Asia Ser.). 260p. (C). 1998. text 45.00 (*0-7007-0421-3*, Pub. by Curzon Pr Ltd) UH Pr.

Oddie, Graham. Likeness to Truth. 1986. text 129.50 (*90-277-2238-2*) Kluwer Academic.

Oddie, Graham & Perrett, Roy W., eds. Justice, Ethics, & New Zealand Society. (Illus.). 250p. 1993. pap. text 38.00 (*0-19-558241-1*) OUP.

Oddie, Tasker L. Letters from the Nevada Frontier: Correspondence of Tasker L. Oddie, 1898-1902. Douglass, William A. & Nylen, Robert A., eds. LC 92-54132. (Illus.). 416p. 1992. 45.00 (*0-8061-2448-2*) U of Okla Pr.

Oddie, William. What Will Happen to God? LC 88-81091. 179p. pap. 22.95 incl. audio (*0-89870-211-9*, 108) Ignatius Pr.

Oddo Editorial Staff. Oddo-Matic Teacher Manual. 1977. ring bd. 26.60 (*0-87783-140-8*) Oddo.

Oddo, Eileen, jt. auth. see Patella, Chris.

Oddo, Francine, et al. Coach's Guide to the Memory Jogger Vol. II: The Easy-to-Use, Complete Reference for Working with Improvement & Planning Tools in Teams. 254p. 1995. pap. write for info. (*1-879364-47-6*) GOAL-QPC.

Oddo, Francine, ed. see Brassard, Michael & Ritter, Diane.

Oddo, Francine, ed. see Martin, Paula & Tate, Karen.

Oddo, Francine, ed. see Peach, Robert & Ritter, Diane.

Oddo, Frank. Ford Flathead V8 Builder's Handbook. LC 96-47929. (Illus.). 160p. 1997. pap. 19.95 (*1-55561-119-2*) Fisher Bks.

— Street Rodder's Handbook: How to Build a Street Rod. Sessions, Ron, ed. LC 86-81201. (Illus.). 208p. 1987. pap. 17.95 (*0-89586-369-3*, HP Books) Berkley Pub.

Oddo, Genevieve, ed. see Moore, Silas.

Oddo, Paul C., jt. auth. see Harding, Robert G.

Oddo, Sandra, jt. auth. see Ruchlis, Hy.

Oddo, Victor R., Jr. Kansas City Attractions: The Comprehensive Handbook on How to Enjoy Yourself in the Kansas City's Greater Metropolitan Region. 108p. (Orig.). 1993. pap. 9.95 (*1-883562-00-7*) Natl Pub MO.

— St. Louis Attractions: The Comprehensive Handbook on How to Enjoy Yourself in the Saint Louis Greater Metropolitan Region. LC 95-124109. 108p. (Orig.). 1994. pap. 9.95 (*1-883562-01-5*) Natl Pub MO.

Oddo, Vincent. Playing & Teaching the Strings. 189p. (C). 1979. pap. 20.25 (*0-534-00614-0*) Wadsworth Pub.

— Playing & Teaching the Strings. 2nd ed. LC 94-35620. 189p. 1994. 42.95 (*0-534-22971-9*) Wadsworth Pub.

Oddone, Patrick. Dunkirk, 1940: French Ashes, British Deliverance - The Story of Operation... (Illus.). 128p. pap. 18.99 (*0-7524-2011-9*, Pub. by Tempus Pubng) Arcadia Publng.

Oddou. International Management. (C). 1998. text 47.50 (*0-03-006852-5*, Pub. by Harcourt Coll Pubs) Harcourt.

Oddou, Gary & Mendenhall, Mark, eds. Cases in International Organizational Behavior. LC 98-6189. 256p. (C). 1998. 56.95 (*0-631-21127-6*); pap. 26.95 (*1-55786-735-6*) Blackwell Pubs.

Oddou, Gary, jt. ed. see Mendenhall, Mark.

Odds. Candida & Candidosis. 2nd ed. 448p. 1988. text 126.00 (*0-7020-1265-3*, W B Saunders Co) Harcrt Hlth Sci Grp.

Oddsson, Gisli. Annalium in Islandia Farrago, & De Mirabilibus Islandiae. Hermannsson, Halldor, ed. (Islandica Ser.: Vol. 10). 1917. 25.00 (*0-527-00340-9*) Periodicals Srv.

Oddy, C., et al, eds. Major Financial Institutions of the World, 1999. 865p. 1999. pap. 935.00 (*1-86099-137-8*) Am Educ Systs.

Oddy, Derek J., jt. ed. see Burnett, John.

Oddy, Derek J., jt. ed. see Geissler, Catherine.

Oddy, Dereka J. The Origins & Development of Food Policies in Europe. Burnett, John, ed. 256p. 1994. pap. 25.00 (*0-7185-1694-X*) St Martin.

Oddy, Ian Vaughan. Tempered By Reality. LC 76-360666. 12 p. 1975. write for info. (*0-900182-57-1*) Bow Pubns.

O'Dea & Sykes. Pitman New Era Shorthand Key. anniversary ed. 1992. pap. text. write for info. (*0-273-02901-0*) Addison-Wesley.

O'Dea, Amelia. In a Place of Flame: Prayers for Survivors of Sexual Abuse. LC 96-54808. xi, 114p. 1997. pap. 7.95 (*1-881871-24-X*) Creighton U Pr.

***O'Dea, Jane.** Virtue or Virtuosity? Explorations in the Ethics of Musical Performance, 58. LC 00-24936. (Contributions to the Study of Music & Dance Ser.: Vol. 58). 168p. 2000. 55.00 (*0-313-31568-X*, GM1568, Greenwood Pr) Greenwood.

O'Dea, John. History of the Ancient Order of Hibernians & Ladies' Auxiliary. (C). 1995. text 49.95 (*0-268-01108-7*); pap. text 20.00 (*0-268-01109-5*) U of Notre Dame Pr.

Odea, Mark. Red Bud Women - 4 Dramatic Episodes. LC 76-40391. (One-Act Plays in Reprint Ser.). 1976. 20.00 (*0-8486-2006-2*) Roth Pub Inc.

O'Dea, Michael. Sunfire. LC 98-132056. 62p. 1998. 19.95 (*1-901233-06-5*, Pub. by Dedalus); pap. 12.95 (*1-901233-04-9*, Pub. by Dedalus) Dufour.

***O'Dea, Teresa & Mukherji, Penny.** Understanding Children's Language & Literacy. (Illus.). 256p. 2000. pap. 32.50 (*0-7487-3972-6*, Pub. by S Thornes Pubs) Trans-Atl Phila.

O'Dea, Thomas F. Mormons. LC 57-6984. 1996. pap. text 13.50 (*0-226-61744-0*, P162) U Ch Pr.

— The Mormons. LC 57-6984. 301p. reprint ed. pap. 93.40 (*0-608-09028-X*, 206966300005) Bks Demand.

O'Dea, Thomas F. & Aviad, Janet O. The Sociology of Religion. 2nd ed. 144p. (C). 1983. text 26.00 (*0-13-821066-7*) P-H.

***Odea, Valerie.** Better Business by Phone: A Guide to Effective Telebusiness Management. LC 99-39748. 1999. pap. text 24.95 (*1-55753-155-2*) Purdue U Pr.

Odean, Kathleen. Great Books for Boys. LC 97-45926. 384p. (ps-9). 1998. pap. 12.95 (*0-345-42083-7*) Ballantine Pub Grp.

***Odean, Kathleen.** Great Books for Boys: More Than 600 Books for Boys 2 to 14. 2000. 25.50 (*0-8446-7150-9*) Peter Smith.

Odean, Kathleen. Great Books for Girls. LC 96-44392. 420p. 1997. pap. 12.95 (*0-345-40484-X*) Ballantine Pub Grp.

***Odean, Kathleen.** Great Books for Girls: More Than 600 Books for Girls of All Ages. 2000. 26.00 (*0-8446-7151-7*) Peter Smith.

Oded, Arye. Africa & the Middle East Conflict. LC 87-9576. 244p. 1987. lib. bdg. 40.00 (*1-55587-057-0*) L Rienner.

***Oded, Arye.** Islam & Politics in Kenya. 215p. 2000. lib. bdg. 49.95 (*1-55587-929-2*) L Rienner.

Odedra-Straub, M. & Okut-Uma, Rogers W. Information Technology & Globalisation. 168p. 1995. pap. 16.95 (*0-85092-440-5*, Pub. by Comm Sec) Stylus Pub VA.

***Odefey, Alexander.** Gustav Mahlers Kindertotenlieder: Eine Semantische Analyse. (GER.). 372p. 1999. 56.95 (*3-631-34328-0*) P Lang Pubng.

Odefey, Marvin L., jt. ed. see Culp, Robert D.

Odegaard, Charles, et al. A Comprehensive Introduction to Park Management. 2nd ed. 400p. 1993. 44.95 (*0-915611-58-9*) Sagamore Pub.

Odegaard, Charles E. Dear Doctor: A Personal Letter to a Physician. 172p. (Orig.). 1987. pap. text 3.00 (*0-318-23186-7*) H J Kaiser.

***Odegaard, Charles E.** Pilgrimage Through Universities. LC 99-13655. (Illus.). 244p. 1999. 30.00 (*0-295-97760-4*) U of Wash Pr.

Odegaard, Charles E., et al. Man & Learning in Modern Society. LC 59-15076. (Illus.). 203p. 1959. 20.00 (*0-295-73835-9*) U of Wash Pr.

Odegaard, H., ed. Small Wastewater Treatment Plants. (Water Science & Technology Ser.: No. 22). (Illus.). 374p. 1990. pap. 139.00 (*0-08-040764-1*, Pergamon Pr) Elsevier.

Odegaard, H., ed. see Second International Conference on Design & Operat.

Odegard, Knut. Bee-Buzz, Salmon Leap. Johnston, George, tr. 48p. 1988. pap. 9.95 (*0-921254-01-6*, Pub. by Penumbra Pr) U of Toronto Pr.

Odegard, Peter H. & Helms, E. Allen. American Politics: A Study in Political Dynamics. LC 73-19164. (Politics & People Ser.). 900p. 1974. reprint ed. 69.95 (*0-405-05886-1*) Ayer.

Odeh, R., jt. auth. see Shah, B. K.

Odeh, Robert E. Pocket Book of Statistical Tables. LC 76-28106. (Statistics, Textbooks & Monographs: Vol. 22). 178p. reprint ed. pap. 55.20 (*0-608-08970-2*, 206960500005) Bks Demand.

Odeh, Robert E. & Fox, Martin. Sample Size Choice: Charts for Experiments with Linear Models. LC 75-10347. (Statistics, Textbooks & Monographs: No. 14). 204p. reprint ed. pap. 63.30 (*0-8357-3524-9*, 205230200090) Bks Demand.

Odeh, Robert E. & Owen, D. B. Attribute Sampling Plans, Tables of Tests & Confidence Limits for Proportions. (Statistics: Textbooks & Monographs: Vol. 49). (Illus.). 384p. 1983. text 155.00 (*0-8247-7136-2*) Dekker.

Odeh, Robert E. & Owen, D. B. Parts Per Million Values for Estimating Quality Levels. (Statistics: Textbooks & Monographs: Vol. 87). (Illus.). 360p. 1987. text 167.50 (*0-8247-7950-9*) Dekker.

Odeh, Robert E. & Owen, D. B. Tables for Normal Tolerance Limits, Sampling Plans, & Screening. LC 79-27905. (Statistics, Textbooks & Monographs: No. 32). 332p. reprint ed. pap. 103.00 (*0-7837-7135-5*, 205252900004) Bks Demand.

Odekerken, Peter. A Guide to Lories & Lorikeets, Their Management Care & Breeding. (Illus.). 96p. (Orig.). 1995. pap. 23.95 (*0-9587455-9-5*) Avian Pubns.

Odekon, Mehmet, jt. ed. see Dabir-Alai, Parviz.

Odekon, Mehmet, jt. ed. see Nas, Tevfik F.

Odel, G. C. Annals of New York Stage. 1993. reprint ed. lib. bdg. 90.00 (*0-7812-5282-2*) Rprt Serv.

O'Del, John. Polish Entrepreneurs & American Entrepreneurs: A Comparative Study of Role Motivations. rev. ed. LC 96-30014. (Studies in Entrepreneurship). (Illus.). 104p. 1997. text 37.00 (*0-8153-2850-8*) Garland.

Odel, Kurt G., Society Staff. Computational Logic & Proof Theory: Proceedings, 5th Kurt Godel Colloquium, KGC'97, Vienna, Austria, August 25-29, 1997. Gottlob, G. Colloquim et al, eds. LC 97-30098. (Lecture Notes in Computer Science Ser.: Vol. 1289). viii, 348p. 1997. pap. 61.00 (*3-540-63385-5*) Spr-Verlag.

Odelain, Olivier. Dictionnaire des Noms Propres de la Bible. (FRE.). 536p. 1978. 115.00 (*0-7859-7761-9*, 2204011630) Fr & Eur.

O'Dell. New Rhetoric. pap. text. write for info. (*0-312-24508-4*) St Martin.

Odell, jt. auth. see Kilian, Len.

Odell, Alison. Terra Firma: Land & How We Use It. LC 97-181016. (Illus.). 79p. 1997. write for info. (*0-7622-0276-9*) Creative Pubns.

— Wiggle Your Words: Exploring Poetry with Children. 1990. pap. text 18.95 (*0-201-25121-3*) Addison-Wesley.

O'Dell, Anne M. Ride New York: 35 Horse & Multiple-Use Trails in the Empire State. LC 97-91721. (Illus.). 270p. 1997. pap. 14.95 (*0-9657744-0-6*) Crazy Horse Ranch.

Odell, Bob. Sunsplash! A Spinner Dolphin's Dream. Otake, Ken, tr. (Illus.). 48p. 1998. 15.00 (*0-9672384-0-4*); write for info. (*0-9672384-1-2*) Blue Ocean Inc.

O'Dell, Boyd L. & Sunde, Roger A. Handbook of Nutritionally Essential Minerals. LC 97-55. (Clinical Nutrition in Health & Disease Ser.: Vol. 2). (Illus.). 712p. 1997. text 195.00 (*0-8247-9312-9*) Dekker.

O'Dell, C. R., ed. see International Astronomical Union Staff.

O'Dell, Carla, et al. If Only We Knew What We Know: The Transfer of Internal Knowledge & Best Practice. LC 98-18441. 256p. 1998. 29.50 (*0-684-84474-5*) Free Pr.

— Knowledge Management. Payne, Laurie & Powers, Vicki, eds. (Illus.). 124p. 1996. spiral bd. 495.00 (*1-928593-06-2*) Am Prodtv Qual.

O'Dell, Carla, jt. auth. see Grayson, C. Jackson.

O'Dell, Cary. Women Pioneers in Television: Biographies of Fifteen Industry Leaders. LC 96-46132. (Illus.). 264p. 1997. boxed set 46.50 (*0-7864-0167-2*) McFarland & Co.

Odell, Catherine M. Father Solanus: The Story of Solanus Casey, O. F. M. Cap. rev. ed. LC 87-62387. (Illus.). 240p. 1996. pap. 9.95 (*0-87973-671-2*) Our Sunday Visitor.

O'Dell, Catherine M. Faustina: The Apostle of Divine Mercy. LC 98-65847. 208p. 1998. pap. 9.95 (*0-87973-923-1*) Our Sunday Visitor.

***Odell, Christine.** Intercessions. (Companion to the Revised Common Lectional Ser.). 1998. pap. 17.00 (*0-7162-0517-3*) Epworth Pr.

***Odell, Colin & Le Blanc, Michelle.** Vampire Films. 2000. pap. 5.95 (*1-903047-17-X*, Pub. by Pocket Essentials) Trafalgar.

O'Dell, Dale, photos by. Dale O'Dell - Human Nature. (Illus.). 96p. 1997. pap. 35.00 (*0-9642009-6-1*) Pohlmann Pr.

Odell, Daniel K., jt. auth. see Reynolds, John E., III.

Odell, Daniel K., jt. auth. see Wlodarski, Loran.

O'Dell, De Forest. The History of Journalism Education in the United States. LC 78-177129. (Columbia University. Teachers College. Contributions to Education Ser.: No. 653). reprint ed. 37.50 (*0-404-55653-1*) AMS Pr.

Odell, E. & Rosenthal, H. P., eds. Functional Analysis: Proceedings, the University of Texas at Austin, 1987. (Lecture Notes in Mathematics Ser.: Vol. 1470). viii, 199p. 1991. 40.95 (*0-387-54206-X*) Spr-Verlag.

***Odell, E. W.** Clinical Problem Solving in Dentistry. LC 99-48086. 2000. text. write for info. (*0-443-05631-5*) Church.

Odell, E. W., jt. auth. see Cawson, R. A.

***O'Dell, Earleen Rather.** The Flavour of Home. 2000. pap. 19.95 (*1-57072-102-5*) Overmountain Pr.

Odell, Edward W., jt. auth. see Morgan, P.

Odell, Eric. Robinson Crusoe's Return. Reginald, R. & Menville, Douglas A., eds. LC 75-46298. (Supernatural & Occult Fiction Ser.). 1976. reprint ed. lib. bdg. 17.95 (*0-405-08158-8*) Ayer.

O'Dell, Felicity. CAE Writing Skills. 128p. 1997. pap. text 12.95 (*0-521-46646-6*) Cambridge U Pr.

O'Dell, Felicity A., jt. auth. see McCarthy, Michael.

Odell, G. H. Stone Tools: Theoretical Insights into Human Prehistory. (Interdisciplinary Contributions to Archaeology Ser.). (Illus.). 420p. (C). 1996. 71.00 (*0-306-45198-0*, Plenum Trade) Perseus Pubng.

Odell, George C. Annals of the New York Stage, 15 vols. LC 77-116018. reprint ed. 2175.00 (*0-404-07830-3*) AMS Pr.

— Shakespeare-from Betterton to Irving, 2 vols., Set. LC 63-23277. (Illus.). 1972. reprint ed. 60.95 (*0-405-08824-8*) Ayer.

— Shakespeare-from Betterton to Irving, 2 vols., Vol. 1. LC 63-23277. (Illus.). 1972. reprint ed. 30.95 (*0-405-08825-6*) Ayer.

— Shakespeare-from Betterton to Irving, 2 vols., Vol. 2. LC 63-23277. (Illus.). 1972. reprint ed. 30.95 (*0-405-08826-4*) Ayer.

Odell, George H. Stone Tools & Mobility in the Illinois Valley: From Hunter-Gatherer Camps to Agricultural Villages. LC 96-1824. (Archaeological Ser.: No. 10). (Illus.). xi, 418p. 1996. pap. 49.50 (*1-879621-22-3*); lib. bdg. 78.00 (*1-879621-23-1*) Intl Mono Prehstry.

O'Dell, Gracie. Gracie's Story: Tales of a Sharecropper's Daughter. (Illus.). 120p. (Orig.). 1995. pap. 10.00 (*1-885480-03-2*) Pioneer Pubng.

Odell, J. W., jt. auth. see Cawson, R. A.

Odell, James. An Essay on the Elements, Accents, & Prosody of the English Language. (Anglistica & Americana Ser.: No. 47). vii, 205p. 1969. reprint ed. 44.20 (*0-685-66496-1*, 05102590) G Olms Pubs.

***O'Dell, James Douglas.** The Water Is Never Cold: The Origins of U. S. Naval Combat Demolition. 2000. 24.95 (*1-57488-275-9*) Brasseys.

Odell, James J. Advanced Object-Oriented Analysis & Design Using UML. (SIGS Reference Library: No. 12). 264p. (C). 1998. pap. 34.95 (*0-521-64819-X*) Cambridge U Pr.

Odell, James J., jt. auth. see Martin, James.

O

An Asterisk (*) at the beginning of an entry indicates that the title is appearing for the first time.

O'Dell, James P., ed. see Nee, Watchman.
O'Dell, James R. Crises in Midwifery. LC 88-82207. 33p. (Orig.). 1988. pap. text 5.00 (*0-933856-17-2*) Green Rvr Writers.
— You Will Come Home Again. O'Dell, Mary E., ed. (Orig.). 1997. pap. text 7.50 (*0-9623666-8-4*) Green Rvr Writers.
Odell, Jay S., jt. auth. see Goodway, Martha.
O'Dell, Jennifer. Meditations for Success. Ramsden, Francis, ed. 112p. (Orig.). 1994. pap. 7.95 (*0-9637428-0-9*) Visions Unltd.
***Odell, Jeri.** La Sonadora Escarlata. (SPA.). (J). (gr. 8-12). 1999. mass mkt. 3.99 (*0-7899-0803-4*) Spanish Hse Distributors.
O'Dell, Jerry W., jt. auth. see Karson, Samuel.
Odell, Jim. Delaware & Hudson Color Guide to Freight & Passenger Equipment. LC 97-70599. (Illus.). 128p. 1997. 49.95 (*1-878887-78-5*) Morning NJ.
Odell, John, jt. auth. see Dibble, Anne.
Odell, John, jt. auth. see Lang, David.
Odell, John, jt. auth. see Matzinger-Tchakerian, Margit.
Odell, John P., jt. auth. see Clark, John S.
***Odell, John S.** Negotiating the World Economy. LC 99-55906. (Studies in Political Economy). 288p. 2000. 19.95 (*0-8014-8646-7*) Cornell U Pr.
Odell, John S. & Willett, Thomas D., eds. International Trade Policies: Gains from Exchange Between Economics & Political Science. LC 90-32073. (Studies In International Trade Policy). 298p. (C). 1993. pap. text 27.95 (*0-472-08197-7*, 08197) U of Mich Pr.
Odell, Karen, jt. auth. see Porrazzo, Ed.
O'Dell, Kathy. Contract with the Skin: Masochism, Performance Art & the 1970's. LC 97-45530. 1998. 47.95 (*0-8166-2886-6*); pap. 18.95 (*0-8166-2887-4*) U of Minn Pr.
Odell, Kerry A. Capital Mobilization & Regional Financial Markets: The Pacific Coast States, 1850-1920. rev. ed. LC 92-27793. (Financial Sector of the American Economy Ser.). 240p. 1992. text 20.00 (*0-8153-0959-7*) Garland.
O'Dell, Kimberly. Calhoun County. LC 98-85885. (Images of America Ser.). (Illus.). 128p. 1998. pap. 16.99 (*0-7524-0987-5*) Arcadia Publng.
Odell, Lee, ed. Theory & Practice in the Teaching of Writing: Rethinking the Discipline. LC 92-40547. 352p. (C). 1993. 41.95 (*0-8093-1755-9*); pap. 21.95 (*0-8093-1947-0*) S Ill U Pr.
Odell, Lee & Goswami, Dixie, eds. Writing in Nonacademic Settings. LC 85-27239. (Perspectives in Writing Research Ser.). 553p. 1986. pap. text 28.95 (*0-89862-906-3*) Guilford Pubns.
Odell, Lee, jt. auth. see Cooper, Charles.
O'Dell, Lynne. Our Family Foods: A Journal. (Illus.). 107p. 1996. 19.95 (*0-9651043-0-3*) Kings Mtn.
Odell, Marcia L. Divide & Conquer. Bruchey, Stuart, ed. LC 78-56681. (Management of Public Lands in the United States Ser.). 1979. lib. bdg. 42.95 (*0-405-11347-1*) Ayer.
Odell, Mark & Campbell, Charles E. The Practical Practice of Marriage & Family Therapy: Things My Training Supervisor Never Told Me. LC 97-19857. 276p. (C). 1997. 49.95 (*0-7890-0063-6*); pap. 24.95 (*0-7890-0431-3*) Haworth Pr.
O'Dell, Mary. Poems for the Man Who Weighs Light. LC 98-48975. 72p. 1999. pap. 14.95 (*0-7734-3118-7*, Mellen Poetry Pr) E Mellen.
O'Dell, Mary, ed. see Pile, Virginia.
O'Dell, Mary E. Bridesongs. Xavier Oone' Juaseaux, ed. 43p. (Orig.). 1989. 6.50 (*0-9623666-0-9*) Green Rvr Writers.
O'Dell, Mary E., ed. see Miller, Jim W.
O'Dell, Mary E., ed. see O'Dell, James R.
O'Dell, Mary E., ed. see Palencia, Elaine F.
O'Dell, Mary E., ed. see Pennington, Lee.
Odell, Michael D. Telephony for Network Mechanics. 1986. pap. 26.95 (*0-201-65620-5*) Addison-Wesley.
Odell, Michael E. A Layman's Gold Investment Manual: A Book on Picking & Choosing. Palmquist, Joe, ed. (Illus.). 192p. (Orig.). (C). 1989. pap. 17.95 (*0-924380-00-4*) Veritas Rsch Pub.
***Odell, Michael E.** Marketing Plans for Lemonade Stands: The Micro-Business Owner's How-To Guide to More Sales & Bigger Profits. 112p. 1999. pap. text 24.00 (*0-924380-03-9*) Veritas Rsch Pub.
Odell, Michael E. Silver Investments Volatility & Boredon for the Enduring. Palmquist, Joe, ed. (Illus.). 176p. (C). 1989. pap. text 14.95 (*0-924380-01-2*) Veritas Rsch Pub.
O'Dell, Mike. Telephony for Network Mechanics. (C). 1997. pap. 49.95 (*0-201-85620-4*) Addison-Wesley.
O'Dell, Nancy E. & Cook, Patricia A. Stopping Hyperactivity: A New Solution. LC 97-18860. 208p. 1997. pap. 12.95 (*0-89529-789-2*, Avery) Penguin Putnam.
Odell, P. L. & Newman, T. C. The Generation of Random Variates. 1971. 25.00 (*0-85264-194-X*) Lubrecht & Cramer.
O'Dell, Paula, ed. see Scribner, Ronda.
Odell, Peter R. & Preston, David A. Economies & Societies in Latin America: A Geographical Interpretation. 2nd ed. LC 77-12400. 307p. reprint ed. pap. 95.20 (*0-608-15787-2*, 203102500073) Bks Demand.
Odell, Rice, jt. compiled by see Rodes, Barbara K.
O'Dell, Richard F. Marquette on a Vanishing Frontier. (Illus.). 16p. 1978. pap. 2.50 (*0-938746-09-X*) Marquette Cnty.
— Reaching Out: A History of the Rotary Club of Marquette, Michigan, 1916-1981. Duerfeldt, Pryse H., ed. LC 82-60037. (Illus.). 254p. 1982. 13.00 (*0-9609764-0-X*) Rotary Club.
O'Dell, Roy P., jt. auth. see Jessen, Kenneth C.
O'Dell, Ruth W. Over the Misty Blue Hills: The Story of Cocke County, Tennessee. 436p. 1982. reprint ed. 37.50 (*0-89308-276-7*, TN 53) Southern Hist Pr.
Odell, Sandra J. Mentor Teacher Programs. (What Research Says to the Teacher Ser.). 32p. (Orig.). 1990. pap. 4.95 (*0-614-30866-6*, 1086-8) NEA.
***Odell, Sandra J. & Huling-Austin, Leslie.** Quality Mentoring for Novice Teachers. LC 00-20424. 2000. write for info. (*0-912099-37-2*) Kappa Delta Pi.
Odell, Sandra J., jt. ed. see O'Hair, Mary J.
O'Dell, Scott. Alexandra. 128p. 1987. mass mkt. 4.50 (*0-449-70290-1*) Fawcett.
— Alexandra. (J). 1996. pap. 9.75 (*84-279-3174-3*) Lectorum Pubns.
— Alexandra. 1985. 9.60 (*0-606-00250-2*, Pub. by Turtleback) Demco.
— The Black Pearl. 96p. (YA). (gr. 7 up). 1977. mass mkt. 4.99 (*0-440-90803-5*, LLL BDD) BDD Bks Young Read.
— The Black Pearl. (J). 1995. mass mkt. 4.99 (*0-440-91091-9*) BDD Bks Young Read.
— The Black Pearl. 96p. (J). (gr. 5-9). 1996. pap. 4.99 (*0-440-41146-7*) Dell.
— Black Pearl. (J). 1996. pap. 5.99 (*0-440-91293-8*) BDD Bks Young Read.
— Black Pearl, 001. LC 67-23311. (Illus.). 160p. (J). (gr. 7 up). 1967. 17.00 (*0-395-06961-0*) HM.
— Black Pearl. 1967. 9.60 (*0-606-02045-4*, Pub. by Turtleback) Demco.
— Black Pearl. 1996. 9.70 (*0-606-08698-6*, Pub. by Turtleback) Demco.
— Black Star, Bright Dawn. 103p. (YA). (gr. 7-12). 1990. mass mkt. 4.50 (*0-449-70340-1*, Juniper) Fawcett.
— Black Star, Bright Dawn. LC 87-35351. 144p. (J). (gr. 5-9). 1988. 16.00 (*0-395-47778-6*) HM.
— Black Star, Bright Dawn. 1990. 9.60 (*0-606-01201-X*, Pub. by Turtleback) Demco.
— The Captive, 001. 244p. (J). (gr. 7 up). 1979. 16.00 (*0-395-27811-2*) HM.
— Carlota, 001. LC 77-9468. (Illus.). 176p. (J). (gr. 5-9). 1977. 15.95 (*0-395-25487-6*) HM.
O'Dell, Scott. Carlota. (J). 1977. 9.09 (*0-606-04137-0*, Pub. by Turtleback) Demco.
O'Dell, Scott. Carlotta. 144p. (YA). (gr. k-12). 1989. mass mkt. 4.50 (*0-440-90928-7*, LLL BDD) BDD Bks Young Read.
— Castle in the Sea. 1985. 9.60 (*0-606-01202-8*, Pub. by Turtleback) Demco.
— Estrella Negra, Brillante Amanecer (Black Star, Bright Dawn) 1996. pap. text 9.75 (*84-279-3197-2*) Lectorum Pubns.
— The Hawk That Dare Not Hunt by Day. (Illus.). 182p. (YA). (gr. 7 up). 1986. reprint ed. pap. 6.49 (*0-89084-368-6*, 031062) Bob Jones Univ.
— La Isla de los Deilfines Azules (Island of the Blue Dolphins) (SPA.). (gr. 4-7). 1996. pap. text 7.95 (*84-279-3108-5*) Lectorum Pubns.
***O'Dell, Scott.** La Isla de los Delfines Azules. 15p. 1999. pap. text 7.95 (*84-279-3705-9*) Noguer Edit.
O'Dell, Scott. La Isla de los Delfines Azules. (SPA.). (J). 1960. 16.05 (*0-606-04436-1*, Pub. by Turtleback) Demco.
— Island of the Blue Dolphins. 192p. (J). (gr. 5-8). 1978. mass mkt. 5.99 (*0-440-94000-1*, LLL BDD) BDD Bks Young Read.
— Island of the Blue Dolphins. LC 73-20214. 192p. (J). (gr. 5-8). 1987. pap. 5.99 (*0-440-43988-4*, YB BDD) BDD Bks Young Read.
— Island of the Blue Dolphins. (J). 1995. pap. 5.99 (*0-440-91043-9*) BDD Bks Young Read.
— Island of the Blue Dolphins. (J). write for info. (*0-318-57254-0*) Dell.
— Island of the Blue Dolphins. (J). 1987. write for info. (*0-318-62414-1*) Dell.
— Island of the Blue Dolphins. 192p. (J). 1995. mass mkt. 4.50 (*0-440-80102-8*) Dell.
— Island of the Blue Dolphins. LC 60-5213. 192p. (J). (gr. 5-8). 1960. 16.00 (*0-395-06962-9*) HM.
— Island of the Blue Dolphins. (Illus.). 192p. (YA). (gr. 5 up). 1990. 20.00 (*0-395-53680-4*) HM.
O'Dell, Scott. Island of the Blue Dolphins. 184p. (J). (gr. 3-5). pap. 5.99 (*0-8072-8327-4*) Listening Lib.
O'Dell, Scott. Island of the Blue Dolphins. (J). 1960. 10.60 (*0-606-00877-2*, Pub. by Turtleback) Demco.
— Janey. (YA). (gr. 7-12). 1986. write for info. (*0-318-60130-3*) HM.
— King's Fifth. (Illus.). 272p. (J). (gr. 7-10). 1966. 17.00 (*0-395-06963-7*) HM.
— My Name Is Not Angelica. 144p. (J). (gr. k-6). 1990. pap. 4.99 (*0-440-40379-0*, YB BDD) BDD Bks Young Read.
— My Name Is Not Angelica. 144p. (J). (gr. 5-9). 1989. 18.00 (*0-395-51061-9*) HM.
— My Name Is Not Angelica. (J). 1989. 9.60 (*0-606-04485-X*, Pub. by Turtleback) Demco.
— On Russell. 1999. pap. text 13.95 (*0-534-57616-8*) Thomson Learn.
— La Perla Negra. 7th ed. (Cuatro Vientos Ser.). (SPA.). (J). 1990. 15.05 (*0-606-05404-9*, Pub. by Turtleback) Demco.
— La Perla Negra (The Black Pearl) 7th ed. (Cuatro Vientos). (SPA.). (YA). 1996. pap. 9.75 (*84-279-3112-3*) Lectorum Pubns.
— Representative Photoplays Analyzed. 1972. 44.95 (*0-8490-0947-2*) Gordon Pr.
— The Road to Damietta. 240p. (J). (gr. 7 up). 1987. mass mkt. 4.50 (*0-449-70233-2*, Juniper) Fawcett.
— The Road to Damietta. (J). 1985. 9.60 (*0-606-04403-5*, Pub. by Turtleback) Demco.
— Sarah Bishop, 001. 192p. (J). (gr. 7 up). 1980. 16.00 (*0-395-29185-2*) HM.
— Sarah Bishop. LC 79-28394. (Point Ser.). 230p. (YA). (gr. 7-12). 1988. mass mkt. 4.50 (*0-590-44651-7*, Point) Scholastic Inc.
— Sarah Bishop. (Point Ser.). 1980. 9.60 (*0-606-01175-7*, Pub. by Turtleback) Demco.
— The Serpent Never Sleeps: A Novel of Jamestown & Pocahontas. 192p. (YA). (gr. 8 up). 1989. mass mkt. 4.50 (*0-449-70328-2*, Juniper) Fawcett.
— The Serpent Never Sleeps: A Novel of Jamestown & Pocahontas. (Illus.). 240p. (J). (gr. 5 up). 1987. 17.00 (*0-395-44242-7*) HM.
— The Serpent Never Sleeps: A Novel of Jamestown & Pocahontas. 1989. 9.60 (*0-606-01205-2*, Pub. by Turtleback) Demco.
— Sing down the Moon. 128p. (YA). (gr. 5 up). 1976. mass mkt. 5.50 (*0-440-97975-7*, LLL BDD) BDD Bks Young Read.
— Sing down the Moon. 137p. (YA). (gr. 5-9). 1992. pap. 5.50 (*0-440-40673-0*, YB BDD) BDD Bks Young Read.
— Sing down the Moon. (J). 1991. mass mkt. 4.99 (*0-440-80271-7*) Dell.
— Sing down the Moon, 001. LC 71-98513. 144p. (J). (gr. 4-7). 1970. 17.00 (*0-395-10919-1*) HM.
— Sing down the Moon. (J). 1970. 9.60 (*0-606-00856-X*, Pub. by Turtleback); 9.60 (*0-606-03442-0*, Pub. by Turtleback) Demco.
— Streams to the River, River to the Sea: A Novel of Sacagawea. 163p. (YA). (gr. 7-12). 1988. mass mkt. 4.50 (*0-449-70244-8*, Juniper) Fawcett.
— Streams to the River, River to the Sea: A Novel of Sacagawea. (YA). 1986. 16.00 (*0-395-40430-4*) HM.
— Streams to the River, River to the Sea: A Novel of Sacagawea. LC 86-936. (J). 1986. 9.60 (*0-606-03695-4*, Pub. by Turtleback) Demco.
— Streams to the River, River to the Sea: A Novel of Sacagawea. large type ed. 312p. (YA). (gr. 7 up). 1989. lib. bdg. 14.95 (*0-8161-4811-2*, G K Hall Lrg Type) Mac Lib Ref.
— Thunder Rolling in the Mountains. 144p. (J). 1993. pap. 5.50 (*0-440-40879-2*) Dell.
O'Dell, Scott. Thunder Rolling in the Mountains. 1992. 10.09 (*0-606-06058-8*, Pub. by Turtleback) Demco.
O'Dell, Scott. Zia. (J). 1994. pap. 4.99 (*0-440-91017-X*) BDD Bks Young Read.
— Zia. (J). 1996. pap. 5.99 (*0-440-91115-X*) BDD Bks Young Read.
— Zia. 192p. (J). (gr. 4-7). 1995. pap. 4.99 (*0-440-41001-0*) Dell.
— Zia. 192p. (YA). 1995. mass mkt. 5.50 (*0-440-21956-6*) Dell.
— Zia, 001. LC 75-44156. (Illus.). 224p. (J). (gr. 4-8). 1976. 18.00 (*0-395-24393-9*) HM.
— Zia. (J). 1995. 9.60 (*0-606-01279-6*, Pub. by Turtleback); 9.60 (*0-606-08414-2*, Pub. by Turtleback) Demco.
O'Dell, Scott & Hall, Elizabeth. Thunder Rolling in the Mountains. (Illus.). 144p. (J). (gr. 5-9). 1992. 17.00 (*0-395-59966-0*) HM.
O'Dell, Scott & Hall, Elizabeth. Thunder Rolling in the Mountains, Set. unabridged ed. (J). (gr. 4). 1997. pap. 48.70 incl. audio (*0-7887-2196-8*, 40267) Recorded Bks.
O'Dell, Scott, et al. Newbery Awards, 5 vols., Set. (J). (gr. 4-7). 1990. pap., boxed set 16.75 (*0-440-45963-X*) Dell.
O'Dell, Scott, jt. auth. see Hall, Elizabeth.
Odell-Scott, David W. A Post-Patriarchal Christology. (American Academy of Religion Academy Ser.). 280p. (C). 1991. 29.95 (*1-55540-657-2*, 010178); pap. 19.95 (*1-55540-658-0*, 010178) OUP.
O'Dell, Sean, jt. ed. see Trankina, Len.
O'Dell, Susan M. The Butterfly Customer: Capturing the Loyalty of Today's Elusive Customer. 320p. 1997. 34.95 (*0-471-64197-9*) Wiley.
O'Dell, T. H. Circuits for Electronic Instrumentation. (Illus.). 232p. (C). 1991. text 100.00 (*0-521-40428-2*) Cambridge U Pr.
— Electronic Circuit Design: Art & Practice. 192p. 1988. pap. text 32.95 (*0-521-35858-2*) Cambridge U Pr.
***O'Dell, Tara.** My Gallant Knight. (Zebra Splendor Historical Romances Ser.). 1999. mass mkt. 4.99 (*0-8217-6352-0*, Zebra Kensgtn) Kensgtn Pub Corp.
O'Dell, Tara. Saxon's Daughter. (Zebra Bks.). 384p. 1998. mass mkt. 4.99 (*0-8217-6061-0*, Zebra Kensgtn) Kensgtn Pub Corp.
***O'Dell, Tawni.** Back Roads. LC 00-32531. 2000. write for info. (*0-7862-2762-1*) Thorndike Pr.
— Back Roads: A Novel. LC 99-20649. 338p. 2000. 24.95 (*0-670-89418-4*, Penguin Bks) Viking Penguin.
O'Dell, Tom, et al. Culture Unbound: Americanization & Everyday Life in Sweden. LC 98-202860. (Illus.). 256p. 1997. pap. 49.50 (*91-89116-02-X*, Pub. by Nordic Acad Pr) Coronet Bks.
O'Dell, Tom H. Inventions & Official Secrecy: A History of Secret Patents in the U. K. (Illus.). 160p. 1995. text 45.00 (*0-19-825942-5*) OUP.
Odell, William. What's Special about Being Catholic? Sawyer, Kieran, ed. (Developing Faith Ser.). (Illus.). 128p. 1996. pap. text, teacher ed. 16.95 (*0-87793-567-X*) Ave Maria.
— What's Special about Being Catholic? Sawyer, Kieran, ed. (Developing Faith Ser.). (Illus.). 80p. (YA). (gr. 9-12). 1996. pap. text, student ed. 5.95 (*0-87793-568-8*) Ave Maria.
Odelstad, J. Invariance & Structural Dependence. (Lecture Notes in Economics & Mathematical Systems Ser.: Vol. 380). (Illus.). xii, 245p. 1992. 58.95 (*0-387-55260-X*) Spr-Verlag.
Odem, William O. After the Trenches: The Transformation of U. S. Army Doctrine, 1918-1939. LC 98-30288. (Military History Ser.: Vol. 64). (Illus.). 288p. 1999. 44.95 (*0-89096-838-1*) Tex A&M Univ Pr.
Odem, Mary E. Delinquent Daughters: Protecting & Policing Adolescent Female Sexuality in the United States, 1885-1920. LC 95-13185. (Gender & American Culture Ser.). (Illus.). 288p. (C). 1995. pap. 17.95 (*0-8078-4528-0*); text 49.95 (*0-8078-2215-9*) U of NC Pr.
Odem, Mary E. & Clay-Warner, Jody, eds. Confronting Rape & Sexual Assault. LC 97-16990. (Worlds of Women Ser.: No. 3). 292p. 1997. 55.00 (*0-8420-2598-7*); pap. 18.95 (*0-8420-2599-5*) Scholarly Res Inc.
Odembo, Elkanah & Wright, Keith. Is Health Improving? Information Gathering for Community-Based Health Care. (Illus.). (Orig.). 1996. pap. write for info. (*0-942716-07-8*) World Neigh.
Oden. Path Through Advent for Children. (J). 1994. 1.00 (*0-687-30263-3*) Abingdon.
— Preparing Young Children for Christmas. (J). 1994. pap. 1.00 (*0-687-33915-4*) Abingdon.
Oden, Tinsley, jt. auth. see Kikuchi, N.
Oden, Amy, ed. In Her Words: Women's Writings in the History of Christian Thought. LC 93-23624. 384p. (Orig.). 1994. pap. 19.95 (*0-687-45972-9*) Abingdon.
Oden, Bertil. The Macroeconomic Position of Botswana. (Research Report Ser.: No. 60). 84p. 1981. write for info. (*91-7106-193-2*, Pub. by Nordic Africa) Transaction Pubs.
— Southern African Futures: Critical Factors for Regional Development in Southern Africa. LC 96-231726. (Discussion Papers: Vol. 7). 35p. 1996. pap. text 12.95 (*91-7106-392-7*) Transaction Pubs.
Oden, Bertil, ed. Southern Africa after Apartheid: Regional Integration & External Resources. (Seminar Proceedings Ser.: Vol. 28). 277p. 1993. pap. text 29.95 (*91-7106-332-3*) Transaction Pubs.
Oden, Bertil & Othman, Haroub, eds. Regional Cooperation in Southern Africa: A Post-Apartheid Perspective. (Scandinavian Institute of African Studies). 243p. 1989. 59.00 (*91-7106-298-X*) Coronet Bks.
Oden, Bertil, et al. The South African Tripod: Studies on Economics, Politics & Conflict. (Scandinavian Institute of African Studies). 281p. (Orig.). 1994. pap. 44.50 (*91-7106-341-2*) Coronet Bks.
Oden, Bertil, jt. auth. see Hermele, Kenneth.
Oden, Chester W., Jr., jt. auth. see MacDonald, Scott.
Oden, Fay G. Believe. 48p. (Orig.). 1995. pap., per. 10.00 (*0-9638946-1-7*) Tennedo Pubs.
— Calvin & His Video Camera. 2nd ed. (Illus.). 32p. (J). (gr. 2-4). 1997. reprint ed. spiral bd. 5.00 (*0-9638946-4-1*) Tennedo Pubs.
— Calvin's Curtain Call. 170p. (J). (gr. 4-10). 1999. per. 14.95 (*0-9638946-2-5*) Tennedo Pubs.
— Discover: Discover "Yourself" (Illus.). 107p. 1998. per. 20.00 (*0-9638946-5-X*) Tennedo Pubs.
— I Dream a Journey. large type ed. (Illus.). 63p. (J). (gr. 2-6). 1997. per. 12.00 (*0-9638946-3-3*) Tennedo Pubs.
— Where Is Calvin? (Illus.). 48p. (J). (gr. 2-6). 1994. per. 6.95 (*0-9638946-0-9*) Tennedo Pubs.
Oden, Howard W. Managing Corporate Culture, Innovation, & Entrepreneurship. LC 96-54283. 296p. 1997. 65.00 (*1-56720-047-8*, Quorum Bks) Greenwood.
— Transforming the Organization: A Socio-Technical Approach. LC 99-27827. 360p. 1999. 75.00 (*1-56720-226-8*, Quorum Bks) Greenwood.
Oden, Howard W., et al. Handbook of Material & Capacity Requirements. LC 93-14719. 432p. 1992. 59.50 (*0-07-047909-7*) McGraw.
Oden, J. Tinsley & Becker, E. B. Computational Methods in Nonlinear Mechanics Structures. 1981. pap. 56.00 (*0-08-026153-1*, Pergamon Pr) Elsevier.
Oden, J. Tinsley & Demkowicz, Leszek F. Applied Functional Analysis. LC 95-53832. (Illus.). 672p. 1996. boxed set 99.95 (*0-8493-2551-X*) CRC Pr.
Oden, J. Tinsley, jt. auth. see Ainsworth, Mark.
Oden, J. Tinsley, jt. auth. see Ladeveze, Pierre.
Oden, J. Tinsley, jt. auth. see Rabier, P. J.
Oden, J. Tinsley, ed. see International Conference on Computational Methods.
Oden, Marilyn B. 100 Meditations on Hope. 128p. 1995. 13.00 (*0-8358-0741-X*) Upper Room Bks.
— Through the East Window: Prayers & Promises for Living with Loss. LC 98-16470. 160p. 1998. 15.00 (*0-8358-0852-1*, UR852) Upper Room Bks.
— Wilderness Wanderings: A Lenten Pilgrimage. LC 95-60924. 144p. 1996. pap. text 10.00 (*0-8358-0743-6*) Upper Room Bks.
Oden, Melita H., jt. auth. see Terman, Lewis M.
Oden, Richard L., ed. see Dryden, John & Shadwell, Thomas.
***Oden, Robert A., Jr.** The Bible Without Theology. LC 99-33950. 2000. pap. 14.95 (*0-252-06870-X*) U of Ill Pr.
Oden, Robert A., Jr. Studies in Lucian's De Syria Dea. LC 76-54988. (Harvard Semitic Monographs: No. 15). (Illus.). 189p. reprint ed. pap. 58.60 (*0-7837-5412-4*, 204517600005) Bks Demand.
Oden, Robert A., Jr., jt. auth. see Attridge, Harold W.
Oden, Sherri & Weikart, David P. Introduction: To the Institute for Ideas. LC 94-17644. (Program Guidbook Ser.). 26p. 1994. pap. 8.95 (*0-929816-83-8*, A2000) High-Scope.
Oden, Sherri, et al. Evening Programs: Guidebooks for Institute for Ideas. (Program Guidebook Ser.). 64p. 1994. pap. 10.95 (*0-929816-87-0*, A2003) High-Scope.
***Oden, Sherri, et al.** Into Adulthood: A Study of the Effects of Head Start. LC 99-54686. 2000. write for info. (*1-57379-089-3*) High-Scope.
Oden, Sherri, et al. Work Projects: Program Guidebooks for Institute for Ideas. (Program Guidebook Ser.). 52p. 1994. pap. 10.95 (*0-929816-85-4*, A2002) High-Scope.

O

An Asterisk (*) at the beginning of an entry indicates that the title is appearing for the first time.

— Workshops: Program Guidebooks for Institute for Ideas. (Program Guidebook Ser.). 109p. 1994. pap. 12.95 (*0-929816-84-6*, A2001) High-Scope.

Oden, Thomas C. After Modernity... What? Agenda for Theology. 192p. 1990. 14.95 (*0-310-75390-2*) Zondervan.

— Corrective Love: The Power of Communion Discipline. LC 95-4150. (Scholarship Today Ser.). 224p. 1995. pap. 17.00 (*0-570-04803-6*, 12-3257) Concordia.

— Doctrinal Standards in the Wesleyan Tradition. 256p. 1988. 16.95 (*0-310-75240-X*, 17103) Zondervan.

— First & Second Timothy & Titus. (Interpretation: A Bible Commentary for Teaching & Preaching Ser.). 192p. 1989. 23.00 (*0-8042-3143-5*) Westminster John Knox.

— Life in the Spirit Vol. 3: Systematic Theology, 3 vols. LC 90-55805. 560p. 1994. reprint ed. pap. 26.00 (*0-06-066362-6*, Pub. by Harper SF) HarpC.

— The Living God Vol. 1: Systematic Theology. LC 85-45720. 448p. 1992. reprint ed. pap. 26.00 (*0-06-066363-4*, Pub. by Harper SF) HarpC.

— Pastoral Theology: Essentials of Ministry. LC 82-47753. 384p. (Orig.). 1983. pap. 25.00 (*0-06-066353-7*, RD 415, Pub. by Harper SF) HarpC.

— Requiem a Lament in Three Movements. LC 94-38524. 176p. (Orig.). 1995. 16.95 (*0-687-01160-4*) Abingdon.

— Requiem a Lament in Three Movements. LC 94-38524. 176p. (Orig.). 1995. pap. 11.95 (*0-687-02003-4*) Abingdon.

— The Transforming Power of Grace. 879p. (Orig.). 1993. pap. 16.95 (*0-687-42260-4*) Abingdon.

— The Word of Life Vol. 2: Systematic Theology. LC 88-46011. Vol. 2. 608p. 1992. reprint ed. pap. 26.00 (*0-06-066364-2*, Pub. by Harper SF) HarpC.

Oden, Thomas C., ed. Ancient Christian Commentary on Scripture: Galatians, Ephesians, Phillipians. 400p. 1999. lib. bdg. 40.00 (*1-57958-070-X*) Fitzroy Dearborn.

***Oden, Thomas C., ed.** Colossians, I-II Thessalonians, I-II Timothy. 400p. 1999. 40.00 (*1-57958-134-X*) Fitzroy Dearborn.

— I Corinthians. 348p. 1999. 40.00 (*1-57958-071-8*) Fitzroy Dearborn.

Oden, Thomas C., ed. Parables of Kierkegaard. (Illus.). 212p. (C). 1989. pap. text 10.95 (*0-691-02053-1*, Pub. by Princeton U Pr) Cal Prin Full Svc.

— Phoebe Palmer: Selected Writings. (Sources of American Spirituality Ser.). 384p. 1988. 24.95 (*0-8091-0405-9*) Paulist Pr.

Oden, Thomas C. & Hall, Christopher, eds. Ancient Christian Commentary on Scripture: Mark. 400p. 1998. lib. bdg. 40.00 (*1-57958-036-X*) Fitzroy Dearborn.

Oden, Thomas C. & Longden, Leicester R., eds. The Wesleyan Theological Heritage: Collected Essays of Albert C. Outler. 272p. 1991. pap. 15.99 (*0-310-75471-2*) Zondervan.

Oden, Tom, ed. Albert Outler: Christology. 344p. 1996. 19.95 (*1-885224-08-7*) Bristol Hse.

***Odenbach, Ginny.** The Footprints of Shadows. (Illus.). 24p. 1999. pap. 7.00 (*0-9672078-1-9*) Feathermoon.

Odenbach, Ginny & Osborn, Linda. Feather. Yarnaught, Paula, ed. (Illus.). 88p. (Orig.). (J). (gr. 3-8). 1995. pap. 4.50 (*1-885101-14-7*) Writers Pr ID.

— Feather Resource Guide. Yarnaught, Paula, ed. (Illus.). 28p. (Orig.). 1995. pap., teacher ed. 7.99 (*1-885101-19-8*) Writers Pr ID.

— Sunblade. Kolsen, Wendy S., ed. (Illus.). 54p. (Orig.). (J). (gr. 3-8). 1995. pap. 3.95 (*1-885101-12-0*) Writers Pr ID.

Odenbach, Werner. Biologische Grundlagen der Pflanzenzuechtung (Biological Basis of Plant Propagation) (Illus.). xii, 384p. 1997. 58.00 (*3-8263-3096-X*, Pub. by Blckwell Wissenschafts) Balogh.

Odencrantz, Louise C. Italian Women in Industry: Study of Conditions in New York City. Stein, Leon, ed. LC 77-70523. (Illus.). 1977. reprint ed. lib. bdg. 33.95 (*0-405-10191-0*) Ayer.

Odendaal, Andre, ed. see Forman, Lionel.

Odendaal, H. J. Handbook: A Guide to Effective Spoken & Written Communication. 1993. 96.15 (*0-7021-2667-5*, Pub. by Juta & Co) Gaunt.

Odendaal, P. E., ed. Mine Water Pollution, No. 2. (Water Science & Technology Ser.: Vol. 15). (Illus.). 180p. 1983. pap. 44.00 (*0-08-030423-0*, Pergamon Pr) Elsevier.

Odendahl, Teresa J., ed. America's Wealthy & the Future of Foundations: A Study of Private Philanthropy in America. LC 87-7397. 325p. 1987. 34.95 (*0-87954-197-0*); pap. 24.95 (*0-87954-194-6*) Foundation Ctr.

Odendahl, Teresa J., pref. Conference Proceedings Vol. II: Second Annual Women's Policy Research Conference. LC 91-75395. 325p. (Orig.). (C). 1991. pap. text 30.00 (*1-878428-04-7*) Inst Womens Policy Rsch.

Odendahl, Teresa J., jt. ed. see O'Neill, Michael.

Odenheimer, Micha, tr. see Shapira, Kalonymus K.

Odenheimer, William H. Jerusalem & Its Vicinity: Familiar Lectures on the Sacred Localities Connected with the Week Before the Resurrection. Davis, Moshe, ed. (America & the Holy Land Ser.). (Illus.). 1977. reprint ed. lib. bdg. 23.95 (*0-405-10272-0*) Ayer.

Odens, James A. Lighting the Way to God: Giving People a Context for Understanding the Gospel. LC 99-90126. 110p. 1999. pap. 8.95 (*0-9627088-1-X*) J A Odens.

— Submitting to Christ: Living in Light of His Lordship 214p. (Orig.). 1990. pap. 6.95 (*0-9627088-0-1*) J A Odens.

Odens, Peter R. Ben Hulse: From Mountain Boy to State Senator. LC 84-158219. (Illus.). 56p. 1984. pap. 3.50 (*0-9609484-7-3*) P R Odens.

— The Desert Trackers: Men of the Border Patrol. (Illus.). 70p. (Orig.). 1972. reprint ed. pap., per. 5.00 (*0-9609484-9-X*) P R Odens.

— The Desert's Edge. 5th ed. (Illus.). 102p. 1982. reprint ed. pap. 5.00 (*0-916428-19-2*) P R Odens.

— Dreamers, Adventurers & Storytellers of the American West. (Illus.). 1988. pap. 5.00 (*0-9609484-8-1*) P R Odens.

— Father Garces: The Maverick Priest. (Illus.). 1980. pap. 5.00 (*0-9609484-3-0*) P R Odens.

— Outlaws, Heroes & Jokers of the Old Southwest. (Illus.). 77p. 1975. reprint ed. pap. 5.00 (*0-9609484-6-5*) P R Odens.

— Picacho: Life & Death of a Great Gold Mining Camp. (Illus.). 44p. 1982. reprint ed. lib. bdg. 3.50 (*0-9609484-4-9*) P R Odens.

— Tales from the Southwest Corner. (Illus.). 53p. 1990. pap. 5.00 (*1-878196-00-6*) P R Odens.

Odenstedt, Bengt. On the Origin & Early History of the Runic Script: Typology & Graphic Variation in the Older Futhark. (Acta Academiae Regiae Gustavi Adolphi Ser.: No. 59). 181p. (Orig.). 1990. pap. 48.50 (*91-85352-20-9*) Coronet Bks.

Odenstedt, Bengt & Persson, Gunnar, eds. Instead of Flowers: Papers in Honour of Mats Ryden. (Umea Studies in the Humanities: No. 90). 316p. (Orig.). 1989. pap. 62.50 (*91-7174-416-9*, Pub. by Umea U Bibl) Coronet Bks.

Odent, Michel. Birth Reborn. rev. ed. (Illus.). 123p. 1994. pap. 17.95 (*0-9642036-9-3*) Birth Works.

— Entering the World: The De-Medicalization of Childbirth. Hauch, Christine et al, trs. from FRE. LC 83-6079. (Open Forum Ser.). (Illus.). 154p. 1989. reprint ed. pap. 8.95 (*0-7145-2801-3*) M Boyars Pubs.

— The Nature of Birth & Breastfeeding. LC 91-44076. 160p. 1992. 16.95 (*0-89789-287-9*, H287, Bergin & Garvey) Greenwood.

***Odent, Michel.** The Scientification of Love. 130p. 1999. 25.00 (*1-85343-476-0*, Pub. by Free Assoc Bks) Intl Spec Bk.

Odent, Michel, jt. auth. see Johnson, Jessica.

***Odenthal, Kristen, ed.** Star Rising Magazine, Vol. 3. (Illus.). 160p. 2000. pap. 10.95 (*1-893774-12-0*, Allisone Pr) Star Rising.

***Odenwald.** Astronomy Cafe. 288p. 2000. 8.98 (*1-56731-381-7*, MJF Bks) Fine Comms.

Odenwald, N. Live Oak Splendor. 1992. 35.00 (*0-614-30802-X*, OLIVEO) Claitors.

***Odenwald, Neil G. & Welch, William C.** The Bountiful Flower Garden: Growing & Sharing Cut Flowers in the South. LC 99-55702. (Illus.). 208p. 2000. 32.95 (*0-87833-235-9*) Taylor Pub.

Odenwald, Neil G., et al. Plants for American Landscapes. LC 96-22844. (Illus.). 368p. 1996. 49.95 (*0-8071-2093-6*) La State U Pr.

Odenwald, Neil G., jt. auth. see Turner, James.

Odenwald, Sten F. The Astronomy Cafe: 365 Questions & Answers from Ask the Astronomer. LC 98-2696. (Illus.). 252p. 1998. pap. text 14.95 (*0-7167-3278-5*) St Martin.

— The Astronomy Cafe: 365 Questions & Answers from Ask the Astronomer. LC 98-2696. 1998. 16.75 (*0-7167-3356-0*) W H Freeman.

***Odenwald, Sten F.** The 23rd Cycle: Learning to Live with a Stormy Star. 2001. 27.95 (*0-231-12078-8*) Col U Pr.

Odenwald, Sylvia B. & Matheny, William G. Global Impact: Award Winning Performance Programs from Around the World. LC 96-6441. (Illus.). 224p. 1996. text 35.00 (*0-7863-0958-X*, Irwn Prfssnl) McGraw-Hill Prof.

Odenwaldetal. ID/SEL/USE Sou Plts 3D. 1996. student ed. 37.50 (*0-87511-816-X*, OIDE3S) Claitors.

Odenweller, Arthur L. Predicting the Quality of Teaching: The Predictive Value of Certain Traits for Effectiveness in Teaching. LC 72-177130. (Columbia University. Teachers College. Contributions to Education Ser.: No. 676). reprint ed. 37.50 (*0-404-55676-0*) AMS Pr.

Oder, Phyllis. The Clerihews - One Hundred - of Phyllis Oder. LC 96-92076. (Illus.). 112p. (Orig.). 1996. pap. 11.95 (*0-933243-08-1*) Laurel Pubns New York.

Odera-Straub, Mayuri. Global Information Technology & Socio-Economic Development. 232p. (C). 1996. text 34.95 (*0-9648382-1-4*) Ivy Lcag Pub.

***Oderberg, David S.** Applied Ethics: A Non-Consequentialist Approach. LC 99-45660. 272p. 2000. text 59.95 (*0-631-21904-8*); pap. text 27.95 (*0-631-21905-6*) Blackwell Pubs.

— Moral Theory: A Non-Consequentialist Approach. LC 99-45661. 224p. 2000. text 59.95 (*0-631-21902-1*); pap. text 27.95 (*0-631-21903-X*) Blackwell Pubs.

Oderberg, David S., ed. Form & Matter: Themes in Contemporary Metaphysics. LC 99-19281. (Ratio Ser.: No. 11). 120p. 1999. pap. 11.99 (*0-631-21389-9*) Blackwell Pubs.

***Oderman, Kevin.** How Things Fit Together: Fifteen Essays. (Bakeless Literary Publication Prize for Nonfiction, Bread Loaf Writer's Conference Ser.). (Illus.). 172p. 2000. 26.00 (*1-58465-047-8*) U Pr of New Eng.

***Oderman, Stuart.** Lillian Gish: A Century of Cinema. LC 99-28402. (Illus.). 408p. 1999. boxed set 55.00 (*0-7864-0644-5*) McFarland & Co.

Oderman, Stuart. Roscoe "Fatty" Arbuckle: A Biography of the Silent Film Comedian, 1887-1933. LC 92-56674. (Illus.). 255p. 1994. lib. bdg. 35.00 (*0-89950-872-3*) McFarland & Co.

Odermatt, Jean. Skyscapes. (Illus.). 160p. 1997. 49.95 (*3-931141-61-6*, Pub. by Scalo Pubs) Dist Art Pubs.

Odermatt, Ralph, ed. see Wright, Barbara J.

Oderwald, Richard & Boucher, Britt. Where in the World & What? An Introduction to Global Positioning Systems. 80p. (C). 1996. per. 25.95 (*0-7872-2840-0*, 41284001) Kendall-Hunt.

Odes, S. H., jt. auth. see Madar, Z.

Odescalchi, Edmond P. The Third Crown: A Study in World Government Exercised by the Popes. LC 96-40107. 190p. 1997. text 32.50 (*0-7618-0669-5*) U Pr of Amer.

Odess-Gillett, Jacqueline, ed. see Gifford, Mildred O.

Odesser-Torpey, Marilyn, jt. auth. see Piantanida, Maria.

Odessky, Dick. Fly on the Wall: Recollections of Las Vegas' Good Old, Bad Old Days. (Illus.). 245p. 1999. 21.95 (*0-929712-61-7*) Huntington Pr.

Odetola, Olatunde. Military Regimes & Development: A Comparative Analysis in African Societies. 240p. (C). 1982. pap. text 16.95 (*0-04-301154-3*) Routledge.

Odetola, Theophilus O. Military Politics in Nigeria: Economic Development & Political Stability. LC 76-58232. (Illus.). 180p. 1975. text 34.95 (*0-87855-100-X*) Transaction Pubs.

Odetola, Theophilus O., et al. Man & Society in Africa: An Introduction to Sociology. LC 82-23975. (Illus.). 176p. reprint ed. pap. 54.60 (*0-8357-2967-2*, 203922900011) Bks Demand.

Odets, Clifford. The Big Knife. 1963. pap. 5.25 (*0-8222-0115-1*) Dramatists Play.

— The Country Girl. 1953. pap. 5.25 (*0-8222-0243-3*) Dramatists Play.

— The Flowering Peach. 1973. pap. 5.25 (*0-8222-0411-8*) Dramatists Play.

— Golden Boy. 1948. pap. 5.25 (*0-8222-0456-8*) Dramatists Play.

— Waiting for Lefty. 1989. pap. 3.25 (*0-8222-1215-3*) Dramatists Play.

— Waiting for Lefty: And Other Plays. LC 93-2795. 432p. 1993. pap. 14.00 (*0-8021-3220-0*, Grove) Grove-Atltic.

Odets, Walt. In the Shadow of the Epidemic: Being HIV-Negative in the Age of AIDS. LC 95-1311. (Series Q). 328p. 1995. text 49.95 (*0-8223-1626-9*); pap. text 16.95 (*0-8223-1638-2*) Duke.

Odets, Walt & Shernoff, Michael, eds. The Second Decade of AIDS: A Mental Health Practice Handbook. LC 94-40679. 320p. 1995. pap. 19.95 (*1-886330-01-8*, Pub. by Hatherleigh) Norton.

Odette, Louis L. Intelligent Embedded Systems. 288p. 1990. pap. text 62.95 (*0-201-51753-1*) Addison-Wesley.

Odewahn, Andrew. Oracle Web Applications: PL/SQL Developer's Introduction. Russell, Deborah, ed. (Illus.). 275p. 1999. pap. 29.95 (*1-56592-687-0*) OReilly & Assocs.

Odgaard, Ole. Private Enterprises in Rural China: A Study of Their Impact on Agriculture & Social Stratification. 210p. 1992. 82.95 (*1-85628-405-0*, Pub. by Avebry) Ashgate Pub Co.

Odgaard, Ole, jt. ed. see Bruun, Ole.

Odgaards, A. & Weinans, H. Bone Structure & Remodeling. (Recent Advances in Human Biology Ser.: Vol. 2). 268p. 1995. text 84.00 (*981-02-2190-8*) World Scientific Pub.

Odgen, Annegret S. The Great American Housewife: From Helpmate to Wage Earner, 1776-1986, 61. LC 85-9935. (Contributions in Women's Studies: No. 61). (Illus.). 279p. 1986. 55.00 (*0-313-24752-8*, OGH/, Greenwood Pr) Greenwood.

Odgen, Dunbar H. & Zijlstra, A. Marcel. The Play of Daniel: Critical Essays. LC 96-27276. 1997. pap. 15.00 (*1-879288-77-X*) Medieval Inst.

Odgen, Ellen E. Growing & Using Basil. (Country Wisdom Bulletins: Vol. A-119). 1990. pap. 2.95 (*0-88266-630-4*) Storey Bks.

Odgen, Jack. Ancient Jewellery. 1992. pap. 13.95 (*0-520-08030-0*, Pub. by U CA Pr) Cal Prin Full Svc.

Odgen, Sharon C. Optical Illusions Quilt Designs. LC 93-32469. (Design Library). 48p. 1994. 4.95 (*0-486-27932-4*) Dover.

Odgers, Administrative Office Management. 1997. mass mkt., wbk. ed. 18.00 (*0-314-20707-4*) West Pub.

— All the Sea Between. (Clipper Fiction Ser.). 1991. pap. text. write for info. (*0-582-87537-4*, Pub. by Addison-Wesley) Longman.

— Another Good Friend. (Clipper Fiction Ser.). 1991. pap. text. write for info. (*0-582-87492-0*, Pub. by Addison-Wesley) Longman.

Odgers, Darrel, jt. auth. see Odgers, Sally.

Odgers, Graeme, et al. Utility Regulation: Challenge & Response. (IEA Readings Ser.: No. 42). 137p. 1995. pap. 39.50 (*0-255-36349-4*, Pub. by Inst Economic Affairs) Coronet Bks.

Odgers, J. & Kretschmer, D. Gas Turbine Fuels & Their Influence on Combustion, Vol. 5. LC 85-15633. (Energy & Engineering Science Ser., Abacus Bks.). x, 186p. 1986. text 146.00 (*0-85626-342-7*) Gordon & Breach.

Odgers, Merle M. Latin Parens, Its Meanings & Uses. (Language Dissertations Ser.: No. 3). 1928. pap. 25.00 (*0-527-00749-8*) Periodicals Srv.

Odgers, Pattie. Administrative Office Management. LC 96-37025. 1997. mass mkt. 48.95 (*0-314-09812-7*) West Pub.

Odgers, Peter. Purchasing, Costing & Control. 272p. 1999. pap. 70.00 (*0-7487-0324-1*, Pub. by S Thornes Pubs) Trans-Atl Phila.

Odgers, Sally. Incredible Smell. (Skinny Bks.). 1998. pap. 3.95 (*0-207-19094-1*) HarpC.

— Translations in Celadon. 1999. pap. 7.95 (*0-7322-5908-8*, Pub. by HarpC) Consort Bk Sales.

— Trinity Street. LC 97-221179. 1998. pap. 7.95 (*0-7322-5868-5*) HarpC.

Odgers, Sally & Odgers, Darrel. Tasmania: A Guide. 2nd ed. (Illus.). 240p. 1997. pap. 15.95 (*0-86417-842-5*, Pub. by Kangaroo Pr) Seven Hills Bk.

Odgers, Sally F. Dog Went for a Walk. LC 92-27100. (Illus.). (J). (gr. 3 up). 1993. 2.50 (*0-383-03564-3*) SRA McGraw.

— Mrs. Honey's List. LC 93-6572. (Illus.). (J). 1994. write for info. (*0-383-03703-4*) SRA McGraw.

— Up the Stairs. LC 92-21395. (Voyages Ser.). (Illus.). (J). 1993. 4.25 (*0-383-03601-1*) SRA McGraw.

— Wiz. LC 92-31952. (Voyages Ser.). (Illus.). (J). 1993. 3.75 (*0-383-03608-9*) SRA McGraw.

Odgers, Stephen. Uniform Evidence Law. 353p. 1995. 74.00 (*1-86287-187-6*, Pub. by Federation Pr) Gaunt.

— Uniform Evidence Law. 2nd ed. 372p. 1996. 79.00 (*1-86287-237-6*, Pub. by Federation Pr) Gaunt.

Odgvist, Folke K. Mathematical Theory of Creep & Creep Ruptures. LC 75-306213. (Oxford Mathematical Monographs). (Illus.). 213p. reprint ed. pap. 66.10 (*0-608-30321-6*, 205183400008) Bks Demand.

Odham, Goran, et al, eds. Gas Chromatography-Mass Spectroscopy: Applications in Microbiology. LC 83-16102. 460p. 1984. 120.00 (*0-306-41314-0*, Plenum Trade) Perseus Pubng.

Odhiambo, Atieno, jt. auth. see Ayodo, Awor.

Odhiambo, Christopher, jt. auth. see Musere, Jonathan.

Odhiambo, David N. Diss/Ed Banded Nation. LC 98-88273. 160p. 1999. pap. 13.95 (*1-896095-26-7*) Polstar Bk.

Odhiambo, E. S., jt. auth. see Cohen, David W.

Odhner, Carl T. Michael Servetus, His Life & Teachings. LC 83-45626. reprint ed. 18.50 (*0-404-19844-9*) AMS Pr.

Odhner, Hugo L. The Human Mind: Its Faculties & Degrees a Study of Swedenberg's Psychology. (Illus.). 127p. 1988. reprint ed. 5.50 (*0-915221-66-7*) Swedenborg Sci Assn.

— The Moral Life. 142p. 1985. reprint ed. 3.75 (*0-910557-08-X*) Acad New Church.

— Principles of the New Philosophy. 2nd rev. ed. 36p. 1986. reprint ed. pap. 4.00 (*0-915221-13-6*) Swedenborg Sci Assn.

Odhner, Hugo L., jt. ed. see Pitcairn, Harold F.

Odhner, J. Durban. Alpha & Omega. 63p. (Orig.). 1978. pap. 3.00 (*0-915221-27-6*) Swedenborg Sci Assn.

Odhner, J. Durban, tr. see Swedenborg, Emanuel.

Odhner, John. Light Burden: Easier Ways to Shun Evils. 48p. (Orig.). 1987. pap. 1.00 (*0-910557-16-0*) Acad New Church.

Odhner, John D. Catechism for the New Christian Church Meant by the New Jerusalem in the Revelation: Based on the Teachings of the Seer Emanuel Swedenborg. LC 96-90074. (Illus.). viii, 78p. 1996. pap. write for info. (*0-9650760-0-8*) Newell Pr.

Odhner, John D., ed. see Swedenborg, Emanuel.

Odhner, Matt & Wrox Press Inc., Staff. Professional AppCenter Programming. 800p. Date not set. pap. 49.99 (*1-86100-447-8*) Wrox Pr Inc.

Odhner, Philip N. The Formation of the Church in Man. 184p. 1994. 17.50 (*1-883270-00-6*) Swedenborg Assn.

— The Lord's Prayer. 77p. 1994. 12.50 (*1-883270-01-4*) Swedenborg Assn.

— Reflections on the Book, "The Doctrine of Nova Hierosolyma Concerning the Sacred Scripture" 86p. 1987. 12.50 (*1-883270-07-3*) Swedenborg Assn.

ODI Staff. Making Teams Work: A Guide to Creating & Managing Teams. 142p. 1993. write for info. (*0-9636723-0-4*) ODI.

Odiachi, RoseMarie Rita, jt. auth. see Okut-Uma, Rogers W.

Odiaga, Lola, tr. see Rephann, Richard T.

O'Diam, Eva. Love & Justice. (Covenant Bible Studies). 48p. 1990. pap. 4.95 (*0-87178-543-9*, 8439) Brethren.

Odian. Principles of Polymerization. 3rd ed. 800p. 1994. pap. text 89.95 (*0-471-01005-7*) Wiley.

Odian, jt. auth. see Blei.

Odian, George. Principles of Polymerization. 3rd ed. LC 90-24785. 792p. 1991. 89.95 (*0-471-61020-8*) Wiley.

Odian, George, et al. Schaum's Outline of General, Organic, & Biological Chemistry. 3rd ed. LC 93-37152. 384p. (C). 1994. pap. 14.95 (*0-07-047609-8*) McGraw.

Odian, George G., jt. auth. see Blei, Ira.

O'Diear, James. Season of the Tigers: A Novel of Pre-Pearl Harbor Espionage & Counterespionage. McDonald, Susie & Ball, Terrie, eds. LC 95-958. (Illus.). 319p. (Orig.). 1995. pap. 14.99 (*1-57090-015-9*) Alexander Dist.

Odiear, James. Touching the Clouds: The General Claire Chennault Story. 1998. pap. 19.95 (*1-57090-019-1*) Alexander Dist.

Odier, Antoine. Dictionnaire des Telecommunications. (FRE.). 352p. 1992. pap. 17.95 (*0-7859-7898-4*, 2501016742) Fr & Eur.

Odier, Daniel. Nirvana-Tao: The Secret Meditation Techniques of the Taoist & Buddhist Masters. (Illus.). 208p. (Orig.). 1986. pap. 12.95 (*0-89281-045-9*) Inner Tradit.

— Tantric Quest: An Encounter with Absolute Love. Gladding, Jody, tr. from FRE. LC 97-1786. 192p. 1997. pap. 14.95 (*0-89281-620-1*) Inner Tradit.

Odier, Daniel & Burroughs, William S. The Job: Interview with William Burroughs. LC 72-515422. 192p. 1970. write for info. (*0-224-61811-3*) Jonathan Cape.

Odier, Daniel, jt. auth. see Burroughs, William S.

Odier, Georges. A Revolutionary Approach to Successful Fly Fishing: Swimming Flies. LC 83-51086. (Illus.). 222p. 1984. 19.95 (*0-913276-48-0*) Stone Wall Pr.

Odier, Pierre. The Rock: A History of Alcatraz, the Fort - The Prison. (Illus.). 260p. 1982. 17.00 (*0-9611632-0-8*) Odier CA.

Odievre, Michel, jt. auth. see Alagille, Daniel.

***Odifreddi, P.** Classical Recursion Theory. (Studies in Logic & the Foundations of Mathematics: Vol. 2). 966p. 1999. 147.00 (*0-444-50205-X*, North Holland) Elsevier.

Odifreddi, P. G. Classical Recursion Theory: The Theory Functions & Sets of Natural Numbers. (Studies in Logic & the Foundations of Mathematics. No. 125). 668p. 1989. 176.00 (*0-444-87295-7*, North Holland) Elsevier.

Odifreddi, Piergiorgio, ed. Kreiseliana: About & Around Georg Kreisel. LC 96-38403. 512p. 1996. 60.00 (*1-56881-061-X*) AK Peters.

— Logic & Computer Science. (APIC Studies in Data Processing). 430p. 1990. text 78.00 (*0-12-524220-4*) Acad Pr.

O

Odijk, E., et al, eds. PARLE '89 Vol. II: Parallel Architectures & Languages Europe: Parallel Languages. (Lecture Notes in Computer Science Ser.: Vol. 366). xiii, 442p. 1989. 44.00 (*0-387-51285-3*) Spr-Verlag.

— PARLE '92 Vol. I: Parallel Architectures & Languages Europe: Parallel Architectures. (Lecture Notes in Computer Science Ser.: Vol. 365). xiii, 478p. 1989. 51.00 (*0-387-51284-5*) Spr-Verlag.

Odijk, Michiel A. Railway Timetable Generation. (Illus.). 160p. 1997. pap. 45.00 (*90-407-1611-0*, Pub. by Delft U Pr) Coronet Bks.

Odijk, Pamela. The Ancient World, 12 bks., Set. (Illus.). 48p. (J). (gr. 5-8). 1991. lib. bdg. 179.40 (*0-382-09883-8*) Silver Burdett Pr.

— The Ancient World, 12 bks., Set, 48pg. ea. (Illus.). (J). (gr. 5-8). 1991. pap. 95.40 (*0-382-24258-0*) Silver Burdett Pr.

— The Aztecs. (J). (gr. 5-8). 1990. teacher ed. 4.50 (*0-382-24277-7*) Silver Burdett Pr.

— The Aztecs. (Ancient World Ser.). (Illus.). 48p. (J). (gr. 5-8). 1990. pap. 7.95 (*0-382-24262-9*); lib. bdg. 14.95 (*0-382-09887-0*) Silver Burdett Pr.

— The Chinese. (Ancient World Ser.). (Illus.). 48p. (J). (gr. 5-8). 1991. teacher ed. 4.50 (*0-382-24285-8*); pap. 7.95 (*0-382-24271-8*); lib. bdg. 14.95 (*0-382-09894-3*) Silver Burdett Pr.

— The Egyptians. (Ancient World Ser.). (Illus.). 48p. (J). (gr. 5-8). 1989. teacher ed. 4.50 (*0-382-24276-9*); pap. 7.95 (*0-382-24261-0*); lib. bdg. 14.95 (*0-382-09886-2*) Silver Burdett Pr.

— The Greeks. (Ancient World Ser.). (Illus.). 48p. (J). (gr. 5-8). 1989. teacher ed. 4.50 (*0-382-24274-2*); pap. 7.95 (*0-382-24259-9*) Silver Burdett Pr.

— The Greeks. (Ancient World Ser.). (Illus.). 48p. (J). (gr. 5-8). 1989. lib. bdg. 14.95 (*0-382-09884-6*) Silver Burdett Pr.

— The Incas. (Ancient World Ser.). (Illus.). 48p. (J). (gr. 5-8). 1990. 7.95 (*0-382-24264-5*); teacher ed. 4.50 (*0-382-24279-3*); lib. bdg. 14.95 (*0-382-09889-7*) Silver Burdett Pr.

— The Israelites. (Ancient World Ser.). (Illus.). 48p. (J). (gr. 5-8). 1990. 7.95 (*0-382-24263-7*); teacher ed. 4.50 (*0-382-24278-5*); lib. bdg. 14.95 (*0-382-09888-9*) Silver Burdett Pr.

— The Japanese. (Ancient World Ser.). (Illus.). 48p. (J). (gr. 5-8). 1991. 7.95 (*0-382-24272-6*); teacher ed. 4.50 (*0-382-24286-6*); lib. bdg. 14.95 (*0-382-09898-6*) Silver Burdett Pr.

— The Mayas. (Ancient World Ser.). (Illus.). 48p. (J). (gr. 5-8). 1990. 11.00 (*0-382-24265-3*); teacher ed. 4.50 (*0-382-24280-7*); lib. bdg. 14.95 (*0-382-09890-0*) Silver Burdett Pr.

— The Phoenicians. (Ancient World Ser.). (Illus.). 48p. (J). (gr. 5-8). 1989. 7.95 (*0-382-24266-1*); teacher ed. 4.50 (*0-382-24281-5*); lib. bdg. 14.95 (*0-382-09891-9*) Silver Burdett Pr.

— The Romans. (Ancient World Ser.). (Illus.). 48p. (J). (gr. 5-8). 1989. 7.95 (*0-382-24260-2*); teacher ed. 4.50 (*0-382-24275-0*); lib. bdg. 14.95 (*0-382-09885-4*) Silver Burdett Pr.

— The Sumerians. (Ancient World Ser.). (Illus.). 48p. (J). (gr. 5-8). 1990. 7.95 (*0-382-24268-8*); teacher ed. 4.50 (*0-382-24282-3*); lib. bdg. 14.95 (*0-382-09892-7*) Silver Burdett Pr.

— The Vikings. Easton, Emily, ed. (Ancient World Ser.). (Illus.). 48p. (J). (gr. 5-8). 1990. 7.95 (*0-382-24269-6*); pap., teacher ed. 4.50 (*0-382-24283-1*); lib. bdg. 14.95 (*0-382-09893-5*) Silver Burdett Pr.

Odin, Dexter, jt. auth. see Odin, Paula.

Odin, G. S., ed. Green Marine Clays: Oolitic Ironstone Facies, Verdine Facies, Glaucony Facies & Caledonite - Bearing Rock Facies - A Comparative Study. (Developments in Sedimentology Ser.: No. 45). 446p. 1988. 164.00 (*0-444-87120-9*) Elsevier.

Odin, Gilles S., ed. Numerical Dating in Stratigraphy, Pt. 1. LC 81-14792. (Wiley-Interscience Publications). 658p. reprint ed. pap. 200.00 (*0-7837-3198-1*, 204324500001) Bks Demand.

— Numerical Dating in Stratigraphy, Pt. 2. LC 81-14792. (Wiley-Interscience Publications). 438p. reprint ed. pap. 135.80 (*0-7837-3199-X*, 204324500002) Bks Demand.

***Odin, Jaishree Kak.** To the Other Shore: Lalla's Life & Poetry. 1999. 29.50 (*81-86588-06-X*, Pub. by Vitasta) S Asia.

Odin, Paula & Odin, Dexter. Yachtman's Legal Guide to Co-Ownership. 166p. 1981. 4.95 (*0-8286-0104-6*, 60765) J De Graff.

Odin, Steve. The Social Self in Zen & American Pragmatism. LC 94-33404. (SUNY Series in Constructive Postmodern Thought). 482p. (C). 1996. text 74.50 (*0-7914-2491-X*); pap. text 24.95 (*0-7914-2492-8*) State U NY Pr.

Odingo, Lumumba & Khalifah, H. Khalif. Bumpy Johnson & Lumumba Odingo: Two Uncompromised Black Men in the Slavery Society Called the United States of America. (Illus.). 82p. (Orig.). pap. 7.95 (*1-56411-013-3*) Untd Bros & Sis.

Odio, Elena B., tr. see Delannoy, Luc.

Odio, Elena B., tr. see Zech, Paul.

Odiorne, George S. Green Power: The Corporation & the Urban Crisis. 208p. reprint ed. text 30.50 (*0-8290-0290-1*) Irvington.

— The Human Side of Management. 236p. 1990. 15.95 (*0-669-24826-6*) Lxngtn Bks.

— Management Decisions by Objectives. 1968. 17.95 (*0-13-548529-0*) P-H.

— MBO II: A System of Managerial Leadership. LC 78-72336. 17.95 (*1-56103-977-2*) Ctr Effect Perf.

— Performance Driven Sales Management. 262p. 1991. ring bd. 79.95 (*0-85013-189-8*) Dartnell Corp.

Odiorne, George S., jt. auth. see Rummler.

Odishelidze, Alexander. Dollars Making it...&...Keeping It: The Common Sense Guide to Financial Wellbeing. 208p. 1993. 22.95 (*0-9633405-0-6*) Employ Benefits.

Oditah, Fidelis, ed. The Future for the Global Securities Market--Legal & Regulatory Aspects: Legal & Regulatory Aspects. 311p. 1996. text 75.00 (*0-19-826219-1*, Clarendon Pr) OUP.

Odlaug, Theron O. & Chiasson, Robert B. Laboratory Anatomy of the Fetal Pig. 9th ed. 128p. (C). 1992. spiral bd. write for info. (*0-697-11571-2*, WCB McGr Hill) McGrw-H Hghr Educ.

— Laboratory Anatomy of the Fetal Pig. 9th ed. 136p. (C). 1995. text, lab manual ed. write for info. (*0-697-33297-7*, WCB McGr Hill) McGrw-H Hghr Educ.

— Laboratory Anatomy of the Fetal Pig. 10th ed. 160p. (C). 1994. spiral bd. write for info. (*0-697-15984-1*, WCB McGr Hill) McGrw-H Hghr Educ.

— Laboratory Anatomy of the Fetal Pig. 11th ed. LC 96-61077. 160p. (C). 1996. text 31.25 (*0-697-33324-8*, WCB McGr Hill) McGrw-H Hghr Educ.

Odle, Dean. Grace Abuse: One of the Greatest Hindrances to Genuine Revival. Odle, Susan, ed. Date not set. pap. write for info. (*0-9671221-0-4*) D Odle.

Odle, Joe T. Church Member's Handbook. 1942. pap. 1.50 (*0-8054-9401-4*, 4294-01) Broadman.

Odle, Susan, ed. see Bortolazzo, Paul.

Odle, Susan, ed. see Odle, Dean.

***Odler, Ivan.** Special Inorganic Cements. LC 99-38936. (Civil Engineering Ser.). 1998. pap. 82.50 (*0-419-22790-3*, E & FN Spon) Routledge.

Odlin, Terence. Language Transfer: Cross-Linguistic Influence in Language Learning. (Cambridge Applied Linguistics Ser.). 224p. (C). 1990. pap. text 22.95 (*0-521-37809-5*) Cambridge U Pr.

Odlin, Terence, ed. Perspectives on Pedagogical Grammar. (Applied Linguistics Ser.). (Illus.). 350p. (C). 1994. text 69.95 (*0-521-44530-2*); pap. text 26.95 (*0-521-44990-1*) Cambridge U Pr.

Odlozilik, Otaker. Rembrandt's Polish Nobleman. 32p. 1963. 3.00 (*0-685-25019-9*) Polish Inst Art & Sci.

Odlum, Floyd, jt. auth. see Cochran, Jacqueline.

Odlum, Hortense. A Women's Place. Baxter, Annette K., ed. LC 79-8804. (Signal Lives Ser.). 1980. reprint ed. lib. bdg. 33.95 (*0-405-12850-9*) Ayer.

Odmark, John, ed. Language, Literature & Meaning I: Problems of Literary Theory. (Linguistic & Literary Studies in Eastern Europe: No. 1). x, 467p. 1979. 97.00 (*90-272-1502-2*) J Benjamins Pubng Co.

— Language, Literature & Meaning II: Current Trends in Literary Research. (Linguistic & Literary Studies in Eastern Europe: No. 2). x, 569p. 1980. 124.00 (*90-272-1503-0*, 2) J Benjamins Pubng Co.

Odo, Franklin, et al. Reflections of Internment: The Art of Hawaii's Hiroshi Honda. (Illus.). 33p. (Orig.). 1994. pap. 8.95 (*0-937426-27-X*) Honolu Arts.

***Odo of Deuil.** Journey of Louis VII to the East(De Profectione Ludovici VII in Orientem) rev. ed. 2000. 45.00 (*0-231-12128-8*); pap. text 15.50 (*0-231-12129-6*) Col U Pr.

Odo of Tournai. On Original Sin & A Disputation with the Jew, Leo, Concerning the Advent of Christ, the Son of God: Two Theological Treatises. Resnick, Irven M., tr. from LAT. LC 94-16217. (Middle Ages Ser.). 168p. (Orig.). (C). 1994. text 32.50 (*0-8122-3288-7*) U of Pa Pr.

O'Dochartaigh, Niall. From Civil Rights to Armalites: Derry & the Birth of the Irish Troubles. 240p. 1997. 60.00 (*1-85918-108-2*, Pub. by Cork Univ); pap. 19.95 (*1-85918-109-0*, Pub. by Cork Univ) Stylus Pub VA.

O'Dock, Vincent. Explorations in Microeconomics Test Bank. 136p. (C). 1996. pap. text. write for info. (*1-56226-321-8*) CAT Pub.

Odoevski, I. V. Russian Nights. Koshansky-Olienikov, Olga & Matlaw, Ralph E., trs. LC 96-52851. (European Classics Ser.). 1997. 15.95 (*0-8101-1520-4*) Northwestern U Pr.

***Odoevskii, V.** Odoevskii: Kosmorama. Cockrell, Roger, ed. (Modern Language Ser.). (RUS.). 85p. (C). 1998. pap. text 16.95 (*1-85399-534-7*, Pub. by Brist Class Pr) Focus Pub-R Pullins.

Odoevsky, Vladimir F. The Salamander & Other Gothic Tales. Cornwell, Neil, ed. & tr. by. from RUS. 250p. (Orig.). 1992. pap. 15.95 (*0-8101-1062-8*) Northwestern U Pr.

***O'Doherty, Brian.** Inside the White Cube: The Ideology of the Gallery Space. LC 99-42724. 100p. 1999. pap. 18.95 (*0-520-22040-4*, Pub. by U CA Pr) Cal Prin Full Svc.

O'Doherty, Brian. Joseph Cornell: Dovecotes, Hotels & Other White Spaces. (Illus.). 48p. 1989. pap. write for info. (*1-878283-01-4*) PaceWildenstein.

— William Scharf: Essay. (Illus.). 12p. 1993. pap. 3.00 (*0-685-72255-4*) Michigan Mus.

O'Doherty, Brian, text. John Chamberlain: Recent Sculpture. (Illus.). 460p. 1994. pap. write for info. (*1-878283-47-2*) PaceWildenstein.

O'Doherty, E. F. Helping Disturbed Religious. McNamee, Fintan, ed. (Synthesis Ser.). pap. 1.00 (*0-8199-0234-9*, L38268, Frncscn Herld) Franciscan Pr.

O'Doherty, John K. Half a Hundred Tales of Women: Plus a Collection of Footnotes to History & a Few Miscellaneous Essays. LC 96-92343. (Illus.). v, 207p. (Orig.). 1996. pap. 19.95 (*0-9655669-1-9*, OD-02, Pub. by Watersedge Muse) Bookazine Co Inc.

***O'Doherty, Kathleen.** Woburn. LC 99-69915. (Images of America Ser.). (Illus.). 128p. 2000. pap. 18.99 (*0-7385-0400-9*) Arcadia Publng.

O'Doherty, Malachi. The Trouble with Guns: Republican Strategy & the Provisional IRA. LC 98-173388. 272p. 1998. pap. 22.95 (*0-85640-605-8*, Pub. by Blackstaff Pr) Dufour.

O'Doherty, Mary K. Finklea, Exum, Purcell, Hyman: Their Roots & Branches. large type ed. (Illus.). xii, 190p. 1984. 40.00 (*0-9655669-0-0*, OD-01) Watersedge Muse.

O'Doherty, N. Atlas of the Newborn. 1985. text 124.00 (*0-85200-924-0*) Kluwer Academic.

— Inspecting the Newborn Baby's Eyes. (Atlases of Childhood Ser.). 1986. text 309.00 (*0-85200-857-0*) Kluwer Academic.

— The Neurological Examination of the Newborn. 1986. text 124.00 (*0-85200-877-5*) Kluwer Academic.

O'Doherty, Richard K. Planning, People & Preferences: A Role for Contingent Valuation. 192p. 1996. text 63.95 (*1-85972-176-1*, Pub. by Avebry) Ashgate Pub Co.

Odom. Andrew's Diseases of the Skin. 9th ed. LC 99-58324. 2000. text. write for info. (*0-7216-5832-6*, W B Saunders Co) Harcrt Hlth Sci Grp.

— Nightmare Creatures: The Official Strategy Guide. LC 97-69339. (Secrets of the Game Ser.). 128p. 1997. per. 12.99 (*0-7615-1256-X*) Prima Pub.

Odom, Anne. Russian Enamels: Kievan Rus to Faberge. (Illus.). 208p. 1996. pap. 25.00 (*0-911886-46-X*) Walters Art.

***Odom, Anne.** Russian Imperial Porcelain. LC 99-48115. 1999. write for info. (*0-9654958-6-8*) Hillwood Mus.

Odom, Anne & Arend, Liana P. A Taste for Splendor: Russian Imperial & European Treasures from the Hillwood Museum. LC 97-41835. (Illus.). 340p. 1998. 55.00 (*0-9654958-1-7*) Hillwood Mus.

— A Taste for Splendor: Russian Imperial & European Treasures from the Hillwood Museum. LC 97-41835. (Illus.). 340p. 1999. pap. 39.95 (*0-9654958-2-5*) Hillwood Mus.

Odom, Anne & Johnston, William R. Russian Enamels. (Illus.). 208p. 1996. 45.00 (*0-85667-446-X*, Pub. by P Wilson) Scala Books.

Odom, Anne, et al. A Taste for Splendor: Russian Imperial & European Treasures from the Hillwood Museum. LC 97-41835. (Illus.). 340p. 1998. 55.00 (*0-88397-127-5*) Art Srvc Intl.

***Odom, Anne, et al.** A Taste for Splendor: Russian Imperial & European Treasures from the Hillwood Museum. LC 97-41835. (Illus.). 340p. 1998. pap. 34.95 (*0-88397-128-3*) Art Srvc Intl.

Odom, David. Commissioning Buildings in Hot, Humid Climates: Design & Construction Guidelines. 1999. text 69.00 (*0-13-085911-7*) S&S Trade.

— The End Is Not the Trophy: Reflections on a Life in Coaching. LC 97-77216. 200p. 1998. 19.95 (*0-89089-881-2*) Carolina Acad Pr.

Odom, David, et al. Commissioning Buildings in Hot, Humid Climates: Design & Construction Guidelines. LC 99-25647. 100p. 1999. 69.00 (*0-88173-319-9*) Fairmont Pr.

Odom, E. Dale. An Illustrated History of Denton County, Texas: From Peters Colony to Metroplex. LC 96-92048. (Illus.). 135p. 1996. 24.95 (*0-9651324-0-4*) E D Odom.

Odom, Gene. Lynyrd Skynyrd I'll Never Forget You. 130p. 1983. pap. text 9.95 (*0-9656619-0-3*) A S C Pubng.

Odom, Guy. El Nuevo Conquistador de Mexico: Una Fabula? LC 98-44929. 223p. 1999. 21.95 (*0-8253-0502-0*) Beaufort Bks NY.

Odom, Guy R. America's Man on Horseback: A Fable? LC 97-44904. 186p. 1998. 21.95 (*0-8253-0501-2*) Beaufort Bks NY.

— Mothers, Leadership, & Success. LC 89-23027. 358p. 1990. 22.50 (*0-9624006-0-2*) Polybius Pr.

Odom, J. M., et al, eds. The Sulfate-Reducing Bacteria: Contemporary Perspective. LC 92-2311. (Contemporary Bioscience Ser.). (Illus.). 264p. 1992. 113.00 (*0-387-97865-8*) Spr-Verlag.

Odom, Judy. Blossom, Stalk & Vine. Tickle, Phyllis, ed. 96p. 1990. pap. 8.95 (*0-918518-89-X*) Iris Pr.

Odom, Keith. Only in Louisiana: A Guide for the Adventurous Traveler. 128p. (Orig.). 1994. pap. 6.95 (*0-937552-56-9*) Quail Ridge.

***Odom, Keith C.** Mervin the Purple Three-Toed Schmoo. (Illus.). (J). 1999. pap. text. write for info. (*1-886021-32-5*) J W Wood.

Odom, Mel. Angel Devoid: Face of the Enemy. 240p. 1996. pap. text 19.95 (*0-7615-0424-9*) Prima Pub.

***Odom, Mel.** Barbie: Software for Girls: Official Guide. 1999. pap. 14.99 (*0-7615-2405-3*) Prima Pub.

Odom, Mel. Black Dahlia: The Official Strategy Guide. LC 97-68842. 288p. 1998. per. 19.99 (*0-7615-1213-6*) Prima Pub.

Odom, Mel. Blood: The Official Strategy Guide. LC 96-70604. 224p. 1997. pap., per. 19.99 (*0-7615-0932-1*) Prima Pub.

— By Blood Betrayed, 3. 1999. mass mkt. 5.99 (*0-451-45766-8*, ROC) NAL.

— Draconus: Cult of the Wyrm. (Official Strategy Guides Ser.). 112p. (YA). 2000. pap. 14.99 (*0-7615-2879-2*) Prima Pub.

Odom, Mel. Ecstatica Vol. 2: The Official Strategy Guide. LC 96-72321. 192p. 1997. per. 19.99 (*0-7615-1064-8*) Prima Pub.

— F. R. E. E. Fall. 1996. pap. 5.99 (*0-7869-0493-3*, Pub. by TSR Inc) Random.

— La Femme Nikita, Vol. 2. 2000. mass mkt. 5.99 (*0-06-102012-5*) HarpC.

***Odom, Mel.** Gene Marshall: Girl Star. (Illus.). 192p. 2000. 29.95 (*0-7868-6557-1*, Pub. by Hyperion) Time Warner.

— Glover: Prima's Official Strategy Guide. LC 98-68207. 96p. 1998. pap. 12.99 (*0-7615-1991-2*, Prima Games) Prima Pub.

Odom, Mel. Harvest Moon. (Sabrina, the Teenage Witch Ser.: No. 15). 160p. (YA). (gr. 7-12). 1998. mass mkt. 4.50 (*0-671-02119-2*, Archway) PB.

— Headhunter. (Shadowrun Ser.: No. 27). 1997. mass mkt. 5.99 (*0-451-45614-9*, ROC) NAL.

— I Have No Mouth & I Must Scream: The Official Strategy Guide. 272p. 1995. pap. 19.95 (*0-7615-0359-5*) Prima Pub.

***Odom, Mel.** I'll Zap Manhattan. (Sabrina, the Teenage Witch Ser.: Vol. 18). 176p. (YA). (gr. 7-12). 1999. mass mkt. 4.50 (*0-671-02702-6*, Archway) PB.

Odom, Mel. In Hot Pursuit! (Nickelodeon Ser.). (J). (gr. 3-6). 1998. pap. 3.99 (*0-671-01892-2*, Pocket Books) PB.

— Legacy. (Journey of Allen Strange Ser.: No. 4). (J). (gr. 3-6). 1999. pap. 3.99 (*0-671-02512-0*) PB.

— Leisure Suit Larry: Love for Sail!: The Official Strategy Guide, Vol. 7. LC 96-70479. 240p. 1996. per. 19.99 (*0-7615-0876-7*) Prima Pub.

***Odom, Mel.** Mummy Dearest. (Sabrina, the Teenage Witch Ser.: No. 31). 176p. (YA). (gr. 5 up). 2000. per. 4.50 (*0-671-04068-5*, Archway) PB.

— Redemption. (Angel Ser.: No. 3). 320p. (YA). (gr. 7 up). 2000. per. 5.99 (*0-671-04146-0*, Pocket Pulse) PB.

Odom, Mel. Run Hard, Die Fast, 35. 1999. mass mkt. 5.99 (*0-451-45737-4*, ROC) NAL.

— Sabrina Goes to Rome. (Sabrina, the Teenage Witch Ser.). (YA). (gr. 4-7). 1998. mass mkt. write for info. (*0-671-02772-7*, Archway) PB.

***Odom, Mel.** Sea Devil's Eye: Threat from the Sea, Book III. (Threat from the Sea Ser.: Vol. 3). 352p. 2000. mass mkt. 7.99 (*0-7869-1638-9*) TSR Inc.

— Snow Day. 160p. (J). 2000. per. 4.50 (*0-671-03838-9*, Minstrel Bks) PB.

Odom, Mel. Spacestation Silicon Valley: Prima's Official Strategy Guide. LC 98-67309. 96p. 1998. pap. 12.99 (*0-7615-1806-1*) Prima Pub.

— Under Fallen Stars Bk. II: The Threat from the Sea. (Forgotten Realms Ser.). 1999. pap. 5.99 (*0-7869-1378-9*) TSR Inc.

— Unlock the Secrets of Duke Nukem for the Nintendo 64: The Exclusive Game Guide. LC 97-80911. (Unlock the Secrets of Ser.). 1997. pap. text 12.95 (*1-56893-956-6*) GT Interactive Software.

— Unlock the Secrets of Duke Nukem for the Sony Playstation: The Exclusive Game Guide. (Unlock the Secrets of Ser.). 1997. pap. text 12.95 (*1-56893-957-4*) GT Interactive Software.

— Unlock the Secrets of Oddworld: Official Strategy Guide. (J). pap. 12.95 (*1-56893-960-4*) GT Interactive Software.

***Odom, Mel.** Unnatural Selection. (Buffy the Vampire Slayer Ser.: No. 4). (YA). (gr. 7 up). 1999. pap. 4.99 (*0-671-02630-5*) PB.

Odom, Mel. Young Hercules: TV Tie In. 1999. mass mkt. 3.99 (*0-671-03551-7*) PB.

***Odom, Mel, ed.** Die Hard Trilogy 2: Prima's Official Strategy Guide. LC 99-63033. (Illus.). 96p. 2000. pap. 14.99 (*0-7615-2205-0*) Prima Pub.

Odom, Mel, jt. auth. see Tsr Inc. Staff.

Odom, Robert. Your Companion to Twelve Step Recovery. LC 94-10243. 192p. 1994. pap. 8.95 (*1-56170-098-3*, 161) Hay House.

Odom, Samuel L. & McLean, Mary E., eds. Early Intervention/Early Childhood Special Education: Recommended Practices. LC 95-25823. 460p. 1996. pap. 37.00 (*0-89079-648-3*, 7804) PRO-ED.

Odom, Samuel L., jt. auth. see Favazza, Paddy C.

***Odom, Sara Jo.** How to Keep Insurance Settlements Simple: What Lawyers Don't Want You to Know. Patchen, Robin, ed. (Illus.). 250p. 1999. pap. 16.95 (*0-9674663-0-X*) Pyramis.

***Odom, Sean.** CCNP Switching Exam Prep. (Exam Prep Ser.). (Illus.). 2000. pap. 59.99 (*1-57610-689-6*) Coriolis Grp.

Odom, W. E. Trial after Triumph: East Asia after the Cold War. 151p. (Orig.). (C). 1992. pap. text 12.95 (*1-55813-042-X*) Hudson Instit IN.

Odom, Wendell. CCNA Exam Certification Guide. LC 99-60053. 1999. write for info. (*0-7357-0073-7*) Cisco Press.

— CCNA Exam Certification Guide. 1999. 60.00 (*1-57870-122-8*) Macmillan Tech.

***Odom, Wendell.** Cisco CCNA Exam #640-507: Certification Guide. (Illus.). 2000. pap. 49.95 (*0-7357-0971-8*) Cisco Press.

Odom, William & Schollum, Benno. German for Singers: A Textbook of Diction & Phonetics. 2nd ed. LC 97-20274. 169p. 1997. 28.00 incl. cd-rom (*0-02-864601-0*) Macmillan.

Odom, William E. America's Military Revolution: Strategy & Structure after the Cold War. LC 93-9704. 190p. (C). 1993. lib. bdg. 22.95 (*1-879383-15-2*) Am Univ Pr.

— The Collapse of the Soviet Military. LC 98-17588. (Illus.). 544p. 1998. 37.50 (*0-300-07469-7*) Yale U Pr.

***Odom, William E.** The Collapse of the Soviet Military. LC 98-17588. (Illus.). 544p. 2000. pap. 17.95 (*0-300-08271-1*) Yale U Pr.

Odom, William E. On Internal War: American & Soviet Approaches to Third World Clients & Insurgents. LC 91-18572. 280p. 1991. text 37.95 (*0-8223-1182-8*) Duke.

— The Soviet Volunteers: Modernization & Bureaucracy in a Public Mass Organization. LC 72-6517. 376p. 1973. reprint ed. pap. 116.60 (*0-7837-9406-1*, 206015100004) Bks Demand.

— Unreasonable Sufficiency? Assessing the New Soviet Strategy. (C). 1990. 35.00 (*0-907967-13-2*, Pub. by Inst Euro Def & Strat) St Mut.

Odom, William E. & Dujarric, Robert. Commonwealth or Empire? Russia, Central Asia, & the Transcaucasus. 290p. 1995. text 12.95 (*1-55813-050-0*); pap. text 12.95 (*0-614-16944-5*) Hudson Instit IN.

Odom-Winn, Danni & Dunagan, Dianne E. PreNatally Exposed Kids. Dodson, J. Lynne & Dow, Rosalie, eds. LC 91-77184. (Illus.). 120p. (Orig.). 1991. pap. 14.95 (*0-7925-1867-5*, B302) Ed Activities.

— Teaching the Tough Ones. Dow, Rosalie, ed. (Illus.). 118p. 1991. pap. 14.95 (*0-7925-3213-9*, B305) Ed Activities.

An Asterisk (*) at the beginning of an entry indicates that the title is appearing for the first time.

***Odoms, Mary L.** From the Heart. 40p. 2000. pap. 8.00 (0-8059-4793-0) Dorrance.

Odoms Tennessee Pride Sausage, Inc. Staff. Cooking with Pride: Celebrating Fifty Years. LC 93-70328. 1993. spiral bd. 12.95 (0-87197-366-9) Favorite Recipes.

O'Donahue, William, ed. Sexual Harassment: Theory, Research, & Treatment. 315p. (C). 1996. 73.00 (0-205-16412-9) Allyn.

Odonaill, Eamonn & Nichurraighin, Deirbhile. Irish on Your Own! A Self-Guided Course in the Irish Language. LC 97-43155. 1997. 24.95 (0-8442-2596-7, Passprt Bks) NTC Contemp Pub Co.

O'Donaill, Niall. Focloir Gaeige-Bearla: Irish-English Dictionary. (ENG & IRI.). 533p. 1986. pap. 19.95 (0-8288-1708-1, M6303) Fr & Eur.

O'Donaill, Niall, contrib. by. Irish-English Dictionary (Focloir Gaeilge Bearla) (ENG & IRI.). 1309p. 1992. pap. 47.50 (1-85791-037-0) Colton Bk.

O'Donavan, Maria, jt. auth. see Shanahan, Angie.

Odone, Christina. A Perfect Wife. 217p. 1998. 27.00 (0-7528-1219-X, Pub. by Orion Pubng Grp) Trafalgar.

Odone, Cristina. The Shrine. mass mkt. 13.95 (1-85799-429-9, Pub. by Orion Pubng Grp) Trafalgar.

Odoni, A. R., et al, eds. Flow Control of Congested Networks. (NATO Asi Series F: Vol. 38). x, 355p. 1987. 98.95 (0-387-18398-1) Spr-Verlag.

Odoni, Amedeo R., ed. see Bianco, Lucio.

Odoni, Amedeo R., jt. ed. see Bianco, Lucio.

***Odonkara, Abitimo, tr.** Kit Me Cako Le-He Ki Lok (How to Begin Re-Evaluation Counseling) 16p. 1999. pap. 1.00 (1-58429-063-3) Rational Isl.

Odonkara, Abitimo, tr. see Nickerson, Dan.

O'Donnchada, Diarmuid. The Irish Phrase-Book: An Raleabhar Gaeilge. 96p. 1997. pap. 9.95 (0-85342-752-6, Pub. by Mercier Pr) Irish Amer Bk.

O'Donnel, Kelly. The New '98-'99 Genre Specific Publishers: Reference Book. 1998. pap. 39.95 (1-57532-116-5) Press-Tige Pub.

O'Donnel, Peggy, jt. auth. see Shaevel, Evelyn.

O'Donnell. Automobile Insurance in Ontario. 480p. 1991. boxed set 90.00 (0-409-89361-7, MICHIE) LEXIS Pub.

***O'Donnell.** Bunker. 2000. mass mkt. 18.00 (0-306-80958-3, Pub. by Da Capo) HarpC.

O'Donnell. Directory of the European Medical Device & Biomaterials Industry. LC 96-114298. 1995. pap. 371.00 (1-85617-276-7, Pub. by Elsvr Adv Tech) Elsevier.

— Health Promotion in the Workplace. (Health Services Administration Ser.). 1989. 48.50 (0-8273-4329-9) Delmar.

— Interactive Cases. (C). 1998. pap. text, wbk. ed. 16.75 (0-03-024429-3) Harcourt.

O'Donnell & Benoit. Modern Radio Production. 3rd ed. (Radio/Tv/Film Ser.). 1993. teacher ed. 27.00 (0-534-19081-2) Wadsworth Pub.

O'Donnell & Hausman. Announcing: Broadcast Communications Today. 2nd ed. (Radio/TV/Film Ser.). 1991. mass mkt., teacher ed. write for info. (0-534-14959-6) Wadsworth Pub.

O'Donnell, et al. Advanced WordPerfect 6.0 for DOS. (C). 1994. pap. text 34.00 (0-07-070413-9) McGraw.

— Announcing: Broadcast Communicating Today. 4th ed. LC 99-34591. (Radio/TV/Film Ser.). 1999. pap. 88.95 (0-534-56214-0) Wadsworth Pub.

— Becoming a Reader. 2nd ed. LC 98-8180. 386p. 1998. pap. text 58.00 (0-205-27901-5) Allyn.

O'Donnell, A., jt. auth. see Willet, C. F.

O'Donnell, A. G., jt. ed. see Goodfellow, Michael.

O'Donnell, A. T., jt. auth. see Jackson, P. D.

O'Donnell, Aidan, jt. auth. see Willett, Chris.

O'Donnell, Alejandro, jt. ed. see Bartell, Ernest J.

O'Donnell, Amy & O'Donnell, Charles. Increase Your Child's Learning Potential. (Illus.). 415p. 1992. 39.95 (1-882761-00-6) Spectrum MA.

O'Donnell, Angela M. & King, Alison, eds. Cognitive Perspectives on Peer Learning. LC 98-46511. (Rutgers Invitational Symposium on Education Ser.). 368p. 1999. 79.95 (0-8058-2447-2); pap. 36.00 (0-8058-2448-0) L Erlbaum Assocs.

O'Donnell, Anne, jt. auth. see Kiely, Gabriel.

O'Donnell, Anne M., ed. see Erasmus, Desiderius.

O'Donnell, Anthony G., jt. ed. see Goodfellow, Michael.

ODonnell, Arthur J. American Business in the 20th Century. (20th Century Ser.). 1999. pap. text 9.95 (0-912517-37-9) Bluewood Bks.

O'Donnell, Asta & Lipton, June. Keeping Fit with Asta O'Donnell: An Exercise Program for Problem Backs. (Illus.). 103p. (Orig.). 1983. pap. 12.50 (0-9610564-0-1) J L Prods.

O'Donnell, Barry & Koff, Stephen A., eds. Pediatric Urology. 3rd ed. LC 96-44087. (Illus.). 848p. 1996. text 300.00 (0-7506-1365-3) Buttrwrth-Heinemann.

O'Donnell, Bernard. The Old Bailey & Its Trials. LC 78-2732. (Illus.). 226p. 1978. reprint ed. lib. bdg. 69.50 (0-313-20362-8, ODOB, Greenwood Pr) Greenwood.

O'Donnell, Bob. Personal Computer Secrets. LC 99-27352. 1008p. 1999. pap. 49.99 (0-7645-3133-6) IDG Bks.

O'Donnell, Bob, jt. auth. see Daly, Dan.

O'Donnell, Brennan. The Passion of Meter: A Study of Wordsworth's Metrical Art. LC 94-30735. 340p. 1995. 35.00 (0-87338-510-1) Kent St U Pr.

O'Donnell, C. James. One, Two, Three, You're Hired. 160p. 1992. pap. 9.95 (0-912495-14-6) San Diego Pub Co.

O'Donnell, Cara, ed. see Remakus, Bernard L.

O'Donnell, Carlotta, tr. see Branzinsky, Terri C. & Bowden, Kathi, eds.

O'Donnell, Charles, jt. auth. see O'Donnell, Amy.

O'Donnell, Charles P., ed. see Simon, Yves R.

O'Donnell, Christine. The New Superfund Program: Redefining the Federal-State Partnership. Glass, Karen, ed. 32p. (Orig.). 1988. pap. text 7.50 (1-55877-009-7) Natl Governor.

O'Donnell, Christine & Thompson, Paul. A State Guide to Cleanup & Compliance Issues at Federal Facilities. Feinstein, Gerry & Miller, Mark, eds. 195p. (Orig.). 1991. pap. text 15.00 (1-55877-095-X) Natl Governor.

O'Donnell, Christopher. Commodity Price Stabilization: An Empirical Analysis. 160p. 1993. 66.95 (1-85628-497-2, Pub. by Avebry) Ashgate Pub Co.

— Ecclesia: A Theological Encyclopedia of the Church. LC 96-12532. 520p. (Orig.). 1996. 65.00 (0-8146-5832-6, M Glazier) Liturgical Pr.

O'Donnell, Christopher, jt. auth. see Roberts, Phil.

O'Donnell, Christopher J., jt. auth. see Spiegel, Eugene.

O'Donnell, Chuck. Job Hunter's Workbook: A Complete System for Career Planning & Job Hunting. (Illus.). 200p. 1984. 10.00 (0-9613166-0-8) C O Donnell Pub.

***O'Donnell, Clifford R. & Ferrari, Joseph R.** Employment in Community Psychology: The Diversity of Opportunity. LC 00-28115. 2000. write for info. (0-7890-1036-4) Haworth Pr.

O'Donnell, Clifford R. & Ferrari, Joseph R., eds. Education in Community Psychology: Models for Graduate & Undergraduate Programs. LC 97-759. 107p. 1997. 39.95 (0-7890-0315-5) Haworth Pr.

***O'Donnell, Clifford R. & Ferrari, Joseph R., eds.** Employment in Community Psychology: The Diversity of Opportunity. LC 99-47991. (Journal of Prevention & Intervention in the Community Ser.: Vol. 19, No. 2). 176p. (C). 1999. 39.95 (0-7890-0757-6) Haworth Pr.

O'Donnell, Daniel. Follow Your Dream. LC 93-102723. (Illus.). 160p. 1997. pap. 14.95 (0-86278-319-4, Pub. by OBrien Pr) Irish Amer Bk.

O'Donnell, Derby. Space Bastards. unabridged ed. 242p. 1998. pap. 12.00 (0-9664743-0-9, 980419) Shagnasty Bks.

O'Donnell, Donita. Creating an Environment for Learning Disabilities: A Resource & Planning Guide. 225p. (C). 1994. pap. text 30.00 (1-57337-000-2) WI Dept Pub Instruct.

***O'Donnell, E.** Father Browne's Titanic Album: A Passenger's Photographs & Personal Memoir. LC 98-131994. 120 p. 1998. write for info. (0-86327-598-2, Pub. by Wolfhound Press) Irish Amer Bk.

O'Donnell, E. E. Father Browne's England. LC 97-116153. (Illus.). 128p. 1997. 40.00 (0-86327-490-0, Pub. by Wolfhound Press) Irish Amer Bk.

— Father Browne's Ireland: Remarkable Images of People & Places. LC 89-82287. (Illus.). 112p. 1997. 29.95 (0-86327-200-2, Pub. by Wolfhound Press) Irish Amer Bk.

— Last Days of the Titanic: Photographs & Mementos of the Tragic Maiden Voyage. (Illus.). 120p. 1997. 24.95 (1-57098-201-5) Roberts Rinehart.

O'Donnell, E. E., ed. Images of Aran: Photographs by Father Browne, 1925 & 1938. LC 98-215080. (Illus.). 80p. 1998. pap. 15.95 (0-86327-599-0) Irish Bks Media.

***O'Donnell, Ed.** 1001 Things Everyone Should Know About Irish-American History. 2000. 25.95 (0-7679-0686-1) Broadway BDD.

O'Donnell, Edith. Integrating Computers into the Classroom: The Missing Key. LC 96-14381. 208p. 1996. pap. 19.50 (0-8108-3188-0) Scarecrow.

— Integrating the Internet into the Classroom: The Missing Icon LC 98-42219. 1998. pap. 24.50 (0-8108-3478-2) Scarecrow.

***O'Donnell, Edward J.** Continuing Education for Florida Real Estate Professionals: Necessary & Useful Information for Today's Real Estate Professional, 2000-2001. LC 00-28603. 2000. write for info. (0-7931-3955-4, Real Estate Ed) Dearborn.

O'Donnell, Edward J., jt. auth. see Crawford, Linda L.

O'Donnell, Elizabeth L. Patrick's Day. LC 92-27421. (Illus.). 32p. (YA). (gr. k up). 1994. 15.00 (0-688-07853-2, Wm Morrow) Morrow Avon.

— Winter Visitors. LC 96-38689. (Illus.). 40p. (J). 1997. 16.00 (0-688-13063-1, Wm Morrow) Morrow Avon.

O'Donnell, Elizabeth Lee. I Can't Get My Turtle to Move. LC 88-22046. (Illus.). 32p. (J). (ps-3). 1989. 11.95 (0-688-07323-9, Wm Morrow) Morrow Avon.

O'Donnell, Elliot. The Sorcery Club. Reginald, R. & Menville, Douglas A., eds. LC 75-46295. (Supernatural & Occult Fiction Ser.). (Illus.). 1976. reprint ed. lib. bdg. 29.95 (0-405-08156-1) Ayer.

— Strange Disappearances. 1990. pap. 9.95 (0-8065-1140-0, Citadel Pr) Carol Pub Group.

O'Donnell, Elliot, ed. Trial of Kate Webster, No. 1. (Notable British Trials Ser.). x, 213p. 1995. reprint ed. 68.00 (1-56169-143-7) Gaunt.

O'Donnell, Elliott. Strange Cults & Secret Societies of Modern London. 280p. 1998. reprint ed. pap. 19.95 (0-7661-0285-8) Kessinger Pub.

O'Donnell, Francis & Collins, Claire. Experimental Design & Data Analysis in Agricultural Research. LC 99-10015. 288p. 1999. 124.00 (0-471-96006-3) Wiley.

O'Donnell, Gabriel & Maas, Robin. Spiritual Traditions for the Contemporary Church. 464p. (Orig.). pap. 24.95 (0-687-39233-0) Abingdon.

O'Donnell, Gabriel, et al. The Living Light Vol. 35, No. 2: Special Feature, The Communion of Saints. Marthaler, Berard, ed. 96p. (C). 1999. pap. 8.95 (1-57455-276-7) US Catholic.

O'Donnell, Gayle. Making Grapevine Wreaths. LC 96-1982. (Illus.). 1996. pap. 2.95 (0-88266-445-X, Storey Pub) Storey Bks.

O'Donnell, Gerard, jt. auth. see O'Donnell, Margaret.

O'Donnell, Guillermo. Counterpoints: Selected Essays on Authoritarianism & Democratization. LC 98-48107. 235p. 1999. 40.00 (0-268-00837-X, Pub. by U of Notre Dame Pr); pap. 18.00 (0-268-00838-8, Pub. by U of Notre Dame Pr) Chicago Distribution Ctr.

— Modernization & Bureaucratic-Authoritarianism: Studies in South American Politics. LC 73-620029. (Politics of Modernization Ser.: No. 9). (Illus.). xvi, 226p. 1995. pap. text 15.00 (0-87725-209-2) U of Cal IAS.

O'Donnell, Guillermo, et al, eds. Transitions from Authoritarian Rule: Comparative Perspectives. LC 86-2710. 240p. 1986. pap. text 15.95 (0-8018-3192-X) Johns Hopkins.

— Transitions from Authoritarian Rule: Southern Europe. LC 86-2713. 232p. 1986. pap. text 15.95 (0-8018-3190-3) Johns Hopkins.

O'Donnell, Guillermo & Schmitter, Philippe C., eds. Transitions from Authoritarian Rule: Tentative Conclusions about Uncertain Democracies. LC 86-2714. 96p. 1986. pap. text 10.95 (0-8018-2682-9) Johns Hopkins.

O'Donnell, Guillermo A., jt. auth. see Tokman, Victor E.

O'Donnell, Helen. Common Good: Robert F. Kennedy. LC 98-21128. 352p. 1998. 26.00 (0-688-14861-1, Wm Morrow) Morrow Avon.

O'Donnell, Hugh. Good Times, Bad Times: Soap Operas & Society in Western Europe. LC 97-51601. 1998. 85.00 (0-7185-0045-8); pap. 24.95 (0-7185-0046-6) Bks Intl VA.

O'Donnell, J. D. A Survey of Church History. 1973. pap. 6.95 (0-89265-009-5) Randall Hse.

O'Donnell, J. D. & Hampton, Ralph, Jr. A Survey of the Books of History. 1976. pap. 3.95 (0-89265-032-X) Randall Hse.

— A Survey of the Books of Poetry. 1976. pap. 2.95 (0-89265-033-8) Randall Hse.

O'Donnell, J. D. & Melvin, Billy A. Faith for Today. LC 65-29130. (Sunday School Workers Training Course Ser.: No. 5). 1974. pap. 6.95 (0-89265-000-1) Randall Hse.

O'Donnell, J. D., jt. auth. see Outlaw, W. Stanley.

O'Donnell, J. Reginald, ed. Essays in Honour of Anton Charles Pegis. (Illus.). xx, 187p. 38.29 (0-88844-550-4) Brill Academic Pubs.

O'Donnell, J. T., ed. see Van Rijsbergen, C. J.

O'Donnell, James. Classic Irish Proverbs. 1998. 10.95 (0-8118-1973-6) Chronicle Bks.

***O'Donnell, James.** A Coming of Age: Albania under Enver Hoxha. LC 99-72630. 300p. 1998. 42.00 (0-88033-415-0, 517, Pub. by East Eur Monographs) Col U Pr.

O'Donnell, James. Statistics: Elementary Study Units. 2nd ed. 272p. (C). 1995. pap. text, ring bd. 38.95 (0-7872-0982-1, 41098201) Kendall-Hunt.

O'Donnell, James, jt. ed. see Chavez, Rudolfo C.

O'Donnell, James, jt. ed. see Clark, Christine.

O'Donnell, James, jt. ed. see Okerson, Ann.

O'Donnell, James H. Southern Indians in the American Revolution. LC 76-146662. 185p. reprint ed. pap. 57.40 (0-608-13819-3, 202063000018) Bks Demand.

O'Donnell, James H., jt. ed. see Reichmanis, Elsa.

O'Donnell, James J. Augustine. LC 84-28133. (World Authors Ser.: No. 759). 168p. 1985. 32.00 (0-8057-6609-X, Twyne) Mac Lib Ref.

— Avatars of the Word: From Papyrus to Cyberspace. LC 97-32256. 240p. 1999. text 24.95 (0-674-05545-4) HUP.

***O'Donnell, James J.** Avatars of the Word: From Papyrus to Cyberspace. 2000. pap. 14.95 (0-674-00194-X) HUP.

O'Donnell, James J. Boethius Consolatio Philosophiae. (Latin Commentaries Ser.). 273p. (Orig.). (C). 1984. pap. text 10.00 (0-929524-37-3) Bryn Mawr Commentaries.

— Statistics: Elementary Study Units. 292p. (C). 1995. spiral bd. 31.95 (0-8403-9231-1) Kendall-Hunt.

O'Donnell, James J. & Hall, Bryan D., eds. Penetrance & Variability in Malformation Syndromes. LC 79-5115. (Alan R. Liss Ser.: Vol. 15, No. 5b). 1979. 50.00 (0-685-03295-7) March of Dimes.

O'Donnell, James J. & Reichmanis, Elsa. The Effects of Radiation on High-Technology Polymers. LC 88-39298. (Symposium Ser.: No. 381). (Illus.). xi, 272p. 1988. 54.95 (0-8412-1558-8, Pub. by Am Chemical) OUP.

O'Donnell, James P. Sailing to Byzantium: A Study in the Development of the Later Style & Symbolism in the Poetry of William Butler Yeats. LC 70-120652. (Harvard Honors Theses in English Ser.). 95p. 1971. write for info. (0-374-96141-7) FS&G.

O'Donnell, James T. & Moch, Joseph William. Drug Injury--Liability, Analysis & Prevention. 688p. 2000. text 119.00 (0-913875-09-0, 5090-N) Lawyers & Judges.

O'Donnell, Jane E., jt. auth. see Slater, James A.

O'Donnell, Jeff. Adams County, Nebraska: A Pictorial History. LC 95-31807. 1995. write for info. (0-89865-943-4) Donning Co.

— Amazing Tales of the Old West. Dageforde, Linda J., ed. LC 96-70909. 144p. (Orig.). 1996. pap. 14.95 (1-886225-17-6, 1000) Dageforde Pub.

— Luther North, Frontier Scout. 1995. pap. 13.95 (0-934904-10-3) J & L Lee.

O'Donnell, Jeff & Oliver, Kevin. Starkweather: A Story of Mass Murder on the Great Plains. (Illus.). 208p. (Orig.). 1993. pap. 10.00 (0-934904-31-6) J & L Lee.

O'Donnell, Jeffrey P. Insurance Smart: How to Buy the Right Insurance at the Right Price. LC 90-44826. 236p. 1991. pap. 12.95 (0-471-52711-4) Wiley.

O'Donnell, Jennifer J., jt. auth. see Nordberg, Ken.

O'Donnell, Jennifer J., ed. see Nordberg, Ken.

O'Donnell, Jim. The Day John Met Paul: An Hour-by-Hour Account of How the Beatles Began. LC 99-77840. 164p. 1994. pap. 9.95 (0-9636905-6-6) Hall Fame Bks.

— The Day John Met Paul: An Hour-by-Hour Account of How the Beatles Began. abr. ed. LC 95-564. 176p. 1996. pap. 10.95 incl. audio (0-14-025301-7, Penguin Bks) Viking Penguin.

— Special Edition Using Microsoft Internet Explorer 3. LC 96-68987. 864p. 1996. pap. text 49.99 incl. cd-rom (0-7897-0878-7) Que.

— Wonderful Tonight: Eric Clapton, Les Paul & Queen in Concert. LC 93-78190. 104p. 1993. 9.95 (0-9636905-0-7) Hall Fame Bks.

O'Donnell, Jim & De Freine, Sean. Ireland: The Great Little Answer Book. 152p. 1995. pap. 16.95 (1-898142-06-8, Pub. by Torc) Dufour.

O'Donnell, Jim, jt. auth. see Ladd, Eric.

O'Donnell, Jim, ed. see Geoscience Information Society, Meeting (24th: 198.

O'Donnell, Jim, jt. ed. see Haner, Barbara E.

O'Donnell, Jo Anne, jt. auth. see Cavalline, Jo Jo.

O'Donnell, Joan K., ed. see Dillingham, Rick & Elliott, Melinda.

***O'Donnell, Jodi.** Cowboy Boots & Glass Slippers. (Special Edition Ser.: No. 1284). 1999. per. 4.25 (0-373-24284-0, 1-24284-1) Silhouette.

O'Donnell, Jodi. Daddy Was a Cowboy: (Stetsons & Lace) (Romance Ser.). 1995. per. 2.99 (0-373-19080-8, 1-19080-0) Silhouette.

— Dr. Dad to the Rescue. (Romance Ser.: No. 1385). 1999. per. 3.50 (0-373-19385-8, 1-19385-3) Silhouette.

— The Farmer Takes a Wife. (Romance Ser.). 1994. per. 2.75 (0-373-08992-9, 5-08992-5) Silhouette.

— Of Texas Ladies, Cowboys . . . (Special Edition Ser.). 1996. per. 3.99 (0-373-24045-7, 1-24045-6) Silhouette.

— Real Marriage Material. (Romance Ser.). 1997. per. 3.25 (0-373-19213-4, 1-192137) Silhouette.

— Still Sweet on Him: Premiere. (Romance Ser.). 1993. per. 2.75 (0-373-08969-4, 5-08969-3) Silhouette.

***O'Donnell, Jodi.** When Baby Was Born. (Special Edition Ser.). 2000. mass mkt. 4.50 (0-373-24339-1, 1-24339-3) Silhouette.

O'Donnell, Joe. Birmingham: Magic for the New Millennium. LC 98-44368. (Illus.). 400p. 1998. 45.00 (1-885352-94-8) Community Comm.

O'Donnell, Joe & Reuse, Ruth B. Birmingham: Magic City Renaissance. LC 92-73285. 336p. 1992. 45.00 (0-9630029-3-7) Community Comm.

***O'Donnell, John.** Balthasar. 176p. 2000. pap. 19.95 (0-8264-5080-6) Continuum.

O'Donnell, John. Hans Urs Von Balthasar. Davies, Brian, ed. (Outstanding Christian Thinkers Ser.). 180p. 1992. pap. 12.95 (0-8146-5039-2) Liturgical Pr.

— Mitsubishi Melody. Lester, Genie, ed. 300p. 1997. pap. 14.95 (0-9656874-0-6) Bookmarkers Friend.

O'Donnell, John, jt. auth. see Hall, Cordelia.

O'Donnell, John, jt. ed. see Neese, Harvey.

O'Donnell, John H. The Catholic Hierarchy of the United States, 1790-1922. LC 73-3558. (Catholic University of America. Studies in Romance Languages & Literatures: No. 4). reprint ed. 39.50 (0-404-57754-7) AMS Pr.

***O'Donnell, John J.** A Faith You Can Live With. LC 99-16885. (Come & See Ser.). 302p. 1999. 11.95 (1-58051-065-5) Sheed & Ward WI.

O'Donnell, John L., ed. Adapting Regulation to Shortages, Curtailment & Inflation. LC 77-620033. (MSU Public Utilities Papers: Vol. 1977). 251p. reprint ed. pap. 77.90 (0-608-20508-7, 207176000002) Bks Demand.

O'Donnell, John R. Trumped! Rubenstein, Julie, ed. (Illus.). 392p. 1992. reprint ed. mass mkt. 5.99 (0-671-73818-6) PB.

O'Donnell, Joseph D. & Aycock, Johnnie R. Tuscaloosa: The Tradition, the Spirit, the Vision. Turner, James E. & Hughes, Mary, eds. LC 94-30112. (Illus.). 192p. 1994. pap. 24.95 (1-885352-04-2) Community Comm.

O'Donnell, Joseph F., et al. Oncology for the House Officer. (Illus.). 352p. 1992. 21.95 (0-683-06626-9) Lppncott W & W.

O'Donnell, Joseph M. Hometown Hero: An Action Guide for the Solo Practice. LC 94-48595. 1995. 44.95 (0-87814-435-8) PennWell Bks.

O'Donnell, K. & Pefkaros, S. Trinidad & Tobago Adventure Guide. 2nd rev. ed. (Adventure Guides Ser.). (Illus.). 320p. 1999. pap. 16.95 (1-55650-886-7) Hunter NJ.

O'Donnell, Kate. Defy the Storm. 352p. 1997. mass mkt. 4.99 (0-8217-5573-0, Zebra Kensgtn) Kensgtn Pub Corp.

— An Irish Wind. 320p. 1998. mass mkt. 4.99 (0-8217-5846-2, Zebra Kensgtn) Kensgtn Pub Corp.

O'Donnell, Kathleen M., ed. Handling Residential Real Estate Transactions in Massachusetts. LC 95-78129. 1997. ring bd. 95.00 (0-944490-93-X) Mass CLE.

O'Donnell, Kelly, ed. The Blue Smoke Triology. 120p. (J). (gr. 8). 1998. pap. 9.99 (1-57532-165-3) Press-Tige Pub.

— Confusion on Canary Drive. 90p. 1998. pap. 8.95 (1-57532-156-4) Press-Tige Pub.

— Factory Taunt to Murderous Haunt. (Illus.). (Orig.). 1997. pap. 6.95 (1-57532-037-1) Press-Tige Pub.

— The Microscope. (Illus.). 10p. (Orig.). (J). (gr. 4-7). 1998. pap. text 8.95 (1-57532-153-X) Press-Tige Pub.

— Small Footsteps Vol. 1: Giant Shadows. 300p. 1998. pap. 14.95 (1-57532-166-1) Press-Tige Pub.

O'Donnell, Kelly, ed. see Belkaoui, A. K.

O'Donnell, Kelly, ed. see Elder, Toni.

O'Donnell, Kelly, ed. see Godfrey, M.

O'Donnell, Kelly, ed. see Kimura, Rei.

O'Donnell, Kelly, ed. see Powell, Jack A.

O'Donnell, Kelly S., ed. Missionary Care: Counting the Cost for World Evangelization. LC 92-72009. 560p. (Orig.). (C). 1992. pap. text 13.95 (0-87808-233-6, WCL233-6) William Carey Lib.

O'Donnell, Kevin & Winger, Larry. The Internet for Scientists. 324p. 1997. text 45.00 (90-5702-221-4, Harwood Acad Pubs); pap. text 20.00 (90-5702-222-2, Harwood Acad Pubs) Gordon & Breach.

O'Donnell, L. A. Falling Star. 1980. mass mkt. 1.95 (0-449-24347-8) Ballantine Pub Grp.

O'Donnell, L. A. Irish Voice & Organized Labor in America: A Biographical Study, 49. LC 95-48358. (Contributions in Labor Studies: Vol. 49). 256p. 1997. 59.95 (0-313-29944-7, Greenwood Pr) Greenwood.

O

An Asterisk (*) at the beginning of an entry indicates that the title is appearing for the first time.

O'Donnell, L. A. Wicked Designs. 1981. mass mkt. 2.25 (*0-449-24437-7*) Ballantine Pub Grp.

O'Donnell, Laura. The Lady & the Falconer. 384p. 1998. pap. 4.99 (*0-8217-5953-1*) Kensgtn Pub Corp.

O'Donnell, Laurel. The Angel & the Prince. 448p. 1996. mass mkt. 4.99 (*0-8217-5269-3*, Zebra Kensgtn) Kensgtn Pub Corp.

***O'Donnell, Laurel.** Knight of Honor. (Zebra Splendor Historical Romances Ser.). 1999. mass mkt. 4.99 (*0-8217-6317-2*) Kensgtn Pub Corp.

— Midnight Shadow. (Zebra Historical Romance Ser.). 320p. 2000. mass mkt. 5.99 (*0-8217-6617-1*, Zebra Kensgtn) Kensgtn Pub Corp.

O'Donnell, Lewis B., et al. Announcing: Broadcast Communicating Today. 338p. (C). 1986. pap. 43.95 (*0-534-06582-1*) Wadsworth Pub.

— Announcing: Broadcast Communicating Today. 3rd ed. (C). 1995. pap. 56.50 (*0-534-26088-8*) Wadsworth Pub.

— Modern Radio Production. 258p. (C). 1985. pap. write for info. (*0-534-05064-6*) Wadsworth Pub.

— Modern Radio Production. 2nd ed. 316p. (C). 1989. pap. write for info. (*0-534-11622-1*) Wadsworth Pub.

— Modern Radio Production. 3rd ed. 347p. (C). 1993. mass mkt. 26.75 (*0-534-19080-4*) Wadsworth Pub.

O'Donnell, Liam. The Days of the Servant Boy. LC 97-175715. 160p. 1997. pap. 12.95 (*1-85635-165-3*, Pub. by Mercier Pr) Irish Amer Bk.

O'Donnell, Lillian. The Goddess Affair: A Gwenn Ramadge Mystery. large type ed. LC 97-15911. (Compass Press Large Print Book Ser.). 1997. lib. bdg. 25.95 (*1-56895-461-1*, Compass) Wheeler Pub.

— Lockout: A Norah Mulcahaney Mystery. large type ed. LC 94-25459. (Cloak & Dagger Ser.). 353p. 1994. lib. bdg. 21.95 (*0-7862-0294-7*) Thorndike Pr.

— No Business Being a Cop: A Norah Mulcahaney Mystery. large type ed. LC 92-33704. 346p. 1993. reprint ed. lib. bdg. 17.95 (*1-56054-372-8*) Thorndike Pr.

— The Raggedy Man: A Gwenn Ramadge Mystery. large type ed. LC 95-21831. (Cloak & Dagger Ser.). 381p. 1995. 22.95 (*0-7862-0521-0*) Thorndike Pr.

— Used to Kill. large type ed. LC 93-17005. 321p. 1993. lib. bdg. 21.95 (*1-56054-736-7*) Thorndike Pr.

— Wicked Designs: A Mici Anhalt Mystery. large type ed. LC 92-19379. 341p. 1992. reprint ed. lib. bdg. 17.95 (*1-56054-373-6*) Thorndike Pr.

O'Donnell, M. Developing Health Promotional Programs: HP 620. 102p. (C). 1989. student ed. write for info. (*0-931657-14-8*) Learning Proc Ctr.

O'Donnell, M. C., ed. see Nordberg, Ken.

O'Donnell, M. C., ed. see Nordberg, Ken & O'Donnell, Jennifer J.

O'Donnell, M. R. For I Have Sinned. large type ed. (Charnwood Large Print Ser.). 720p. 1997. 27.99 (*0-7089-8959-4*, Charnwood) Ulverscroft.

— A Woman Scorned. large type ed. (Charnwood Large Print Ser.). 720p. 1996. 27.99 (*0-7089-8919-5*) Ulverscroft.

O'Donnell, Mabel. From Dolphins to Dunes GR1. 1973. pap. text 14.00 (*0-06-516080-0*) HarpC.

O'Donnell, Margaret & O'Donnell, Gerard. Family Values: The Best Gift We Can Give Our Children. (Illus.). 88p. 1993. pap. 6.95 (*1-875570-39-X*) Alba.

***O'Donnell, Marie.** Individual's Filled-In Tax Return Forms: 2000 Edition. 176p. 2000. pap. text 31.00 (*0-8080-0452-2*) CCH INC.

O'Donnell, Mark. Fables for Friends. 1984. pap. 5.25 (*0-8222-0377-4*) Dramatists Play.

— Getting over Homer. 208p. 1997. pap. 11.00 (*0-679-78122-6*); pap. 11.00 (*0-614-27269-6*) Vin Bks.

— Let Nothing You Dismay. LC 98-15883. 224p. 1998. 22.00 (*0-375-40103-2*) Knopf.

— Let Nothing You Dismay. 208p. 1999. 12.00 (*0-375-70096-X*, Vin) Random.

— The Nice & the Nasty. 1987. pap. 5.25 (*0-8222-0815-6*) Dramatists Play.

— Strangers on Earth. 1993. pap. 5.25 (*0-8222-1350-8*) Dramatists Play.

— That's It, Folks! 1983. pap. 5.25 (*0-8222-1128-9*) Dramatists Play.

O'Donnell, Mark, jt. auth. see Irwin, Bill.

O'Donnell, Mark, tr. see Besset, Jean-Marie.

O'Donnell, Mary. HIV/AIDS: Loss, Grief, Challenge, & Hope. LC 95-45406. 200p. 1996. 69.95 (*1-56032-329-9*); pap. 29.95 (*1-56032-330-2*) Taylor & Francis.

— The Light-Makers. 193p. 1992. pap. 14.95 (*1-85371-259-0*, Pub. by Poolbeg Pr) Dufour.

— The Light-Makers. 193p. 1993. 25.00 (*1-85371-177-2*, Pub. by Poolbeg Pr) Dufour.

— Strong Pagans & Other Stories. 258p. 1991. pap. 14.95 (*1-85371-123-3*, Pub. by Poolbeg Pr) Dufour.

— Unlegendary Heroes. LC 98-145439. 96p. 1998. pap. 14.95 (*1-897648-96-0*, Pub. by Salmon Poetry) Dufour.

— Virgin & the Boy. LC 96-227943. 284p. 1997. pap. 14.95 (*1-85371-557-3*, Pub. by Poolbeg Pr) Dufour.

O'Donnell, Mary, ed. see Smith, Joyce.

O'Donnell, Michael. Heart of the Warrior: A Battle Plan for Christian Men. 89p. (Orig.). (C). 1995. pap. 5.99 (*0-89900-706-6*) College Pr Pub.

— How a Man Prepares His Sons for Life. LC 96-10065. (Lifeskills for Men Ser.). 144p. 1996. pap. 7.99 (*1-55661-846-8*) Bethany Hse.

— The Long Walk Home. large type ed. (Adventure Suspense Ser.). 1989. 27.99 (*0-7089-2061-6*) Ulverscroft.

— Marketing Plan: Step-by-Step Workbook. 3rd rev. ed. Gjovig, Bruce, ed. Orig. Title: The Marketing Plan. 160p. 1998. wbk. ed. 29.95 (*0-9626855-5-0*) Ctr for Innov.

— The Marketing Plan - Step-by-Step. 150p. (Orig.). 1991. pap. 49.95 (*0-930204-30-1*) Lord Pub.

— Review for the CLEP General Mathematics Examination. (Illus.). 134p. (C). 1999. pap. 15.95 (*1-56030-120-1*) Comex Systs.

— A Sceptic's Medical Dictionary. 209p. 1997. pap. 27.00 (*0-7279-1204-6*, Pub. by BMJ Pub) Login Brothers Bk Co.

— Writing Business Plans That Get Results. 76p. (Orig.). 1991. pap. 16.95 (*0-8092-4007-6*, 400760, Contemporary Bks) NTC Contemp Pub Co.

O'Donnell, Michael & Morris, Michelle. Heart of the Warrior: A Battle Plan for Fathers to Reclaim Their Families. 1993. pap. 10.95 (*0-89112-233-8*) Abilene Christ U.

O'Donnell, Michael, jt. auth. see Ryan, Leland B.

O'Donnell, Michael, ed. see Ryan, Leland B.

O'Donnell, Michael J. Equational Logic As a Programming Language. (Foundations of Computing Ser.). (Illus.). 250p. 1985. 42.50 (*0-262-15028-X*) MIT Pr.

— Lift up Your Hearts - Year A: Eucharistic Prayers Based on the Revised Common Lectionary. rev. ed. Crouch, Timothy J., ed. 1504p. 1995. spiral bd. 19.95 (*1-878009-23-0*, OSL Pubns) Order St Luke Pubns.

— Lift up Your Hearts - Year B: Eucharistic Prayers Based on the Revised Common Lectionary. rev. ed. Crouch, Timothy J., ed. 148p. 1993. spiral bd. 19.95 (*1-878009-16-8*, OSL Pubns) Order St Luke Pubns.

— Lift up Your Hearts - Year C: Eucharistic Prayers Based on the Revised Common Lectionary. rev. ed. Crouch, Timothy J., ed. 148p. 1994. spiral bd. 19.95 (*1-878009-20-6*, OSL Pubns) Order St Luke Pubns.

O'Donnell, Michael J. & Campbell, J. Duncan. American Military Belt Plates. (Illus.). 614p. 1996. 49.95 (*0-614-29611-0*) North South Trader.

O'Donnell, Michael J., jt. auth. see Sylvia, Stephen W.

O'Donnell, Michael P. & Harris, Jeffrey S. Health Promotion in the Workplace. 2nd ed. LC 93-676. 554p. (C). 1993. pap. 75.95 (*0-8273-4940-8*) Delmar.

***O'Donnell, Michele Longo.** Of Monkeys & Dragons: Freedom from the Tyranny of Disease. 224p. 2000. 21.95 (*0-9676861-0-5*, Pub. by LaVida); pap. 12.95 (*0-9676861-1-3*, Pub. by LaVida) Bk Marketing Plus.

O'Donnell, Mike. The Business Plan: Step-by-Step Workbook. 3rd rev. ed. Gjovig, Bruce, ed. Orig. Title: The Business Plan: A State-of-the-Art Guide. 180p. 1998. wbk. ed. 39.95 (*0-9626855-4-2*) Ctr for Innov.

O'Donnell, Mike & McNeill, Patrick. Age & Generation. LC 85-4792. (Society Now Ser.). 160p. (C). 1985. pap. text 6.50 (*0-422-79360-4*, 9591, Pub. by Tavistock) Routldge.

***O'Donnell, Mike & Sharpe, Sue.** Uncertain Masculinities: Youth, Ethnicity & Class in Contemporary Britain. LC 00-22263. 2000. pap. write for info. (*0-415-15347-6*) Routledge.

O'Donnell, Monica M., ed. Contemporary Theatre, Film & Television, Vol. 1. 554p. 1984. text 155.00 (*0-8103-2064-9*) Gale.

— Contemporary Theatre, Film & Television, Vol. 2. 396p. 1985. text 155.00 (*0-8103-0241-1*) Gale.

— Contemporary Theatre, Film & Television, Vol. 3. 450p. 1986. text 155.00 (*0-8103-2066-5*) Gale.

— Contemporary Theatre, Film, & Television, Vol. 4. 450p. 1987. text 155.00 (*0-8103-2067-3*) Gale.

— Contemporary Theatre, Film & Television, Vol. 5. (Illus.). 450p. 1988. text 155.00 (*0-8103-2068-1*) Gale.

O'Donnell, Nina S. & Galinsky, Ellen. Measuring Progress & Results in Early Childhood System Development. 28p. 1998. pap. 9.00 (*1-888324-12-0*) Families & Work.

O'Donnell, Nina S., ed. see Sazer, Victor.

O'Donnell, Nina Sazer. Early Childhood Action Tips. 19p. pap. 9.00 (*1-888324-27-9*) Families & Work.

— The Seven Lessons of Early Childhood Public Engagement. Date not set. pap. write for info. (*1-888324-29-5*) Families & Work.

O'Donnell, O., jt. auth. see Caffarella, C.

O'Donnell, Owen, ed. Contemporary Theatre, Film, & Television, Vol. 8. LC 84-649371. (Illus.). 500p. 1990. text 155.00 (*0-8103-2071-1*) Gale.

O'Donnell, Owen, ed. see Gale Research Staff.

O'Donnell, Owen, jt. ed. see Hubbard, Linda S.

O'Donnell, P. J., jt. ed. see Castel, B.

O'Donnell, Pat D. Urinary Incontinence. LC 98-132082. (Illus.). 496p. (C). (gr. 13). 1997. text 84.95 (*0-8151-6517-X*, 26546) Mosby Inc.

O'Donnell, Patrick. Echo Chambers: Figuring Voice in Modern Narrative. LC 92-3841. 236p. 1992. text 32.95 (*0-87745-375-6*) U of Iowa Pr.

***O'Donnell, Patrick.** Latent Destinies: Cultural Paranoia & Contemporary U. S. Narrative. LC 00-26812. (New Americanists Ser.). 208p. 2000. pap. 17.95 (*0-8223-2587-X*) Duke.

— Latent Destinies: Cultural Paranoia & Contemporary U. S. Narrative. LC 00-26812. 208p. 2000. lib. bdg. 49.95 (*0-8223-2558-6*) Duke.

O'Donnell, Patrick. Passionate Doubts: Designs of Interpretation in Contemporary American Fiction. LC 85-28865. 213p. 1986. text 27.95 (*0-87745-138-9*) U of Iowa Pr.

O'Donnell, Patrick, ed. New Essays on "The Crying of Lot 49" (American Novel Ser.). 184p. (C). 1992. text 32.95 (*0-521-38163-0*); pap. text 14.95 (*0-521-38833-3*) Cambridge U Pr.

O'Donnell, Patrick & Davis, Robert C., eds. Intertextuality & Contemporary American Fiction. LC 88-46066. 352p. 1989. text 52.00 (*0-8018-3773-1*) Johns Hopkins.

O'Donnell, Patrick, ed. & intro. see Fitzgerald, F. Scott.

O'Donnell, Peadar. The Big Windows. (Classic Irish Fiction Ser.). 212p. 1984. 15.95 (*0-8159-5117-5*) Devin.

O'Donnell, Peggy. Public Library Development Program: Manual for Trainers. LC Z 0670.O366. (Illus.). 154p. reprint ed. pap. 47.80 (*0-7837-5908-8*, 204570600007) Bks Demand.

O'Donnell, Peggy, jt. auth. see Ingram, Anne.

O'Donnell, Peggy, jt. auth. see Phelps, Thomas C.

O'Donnell, Peter. Dead Man's Handle. (Modesty Blaise Adventure Ser.). 1986. 15.95 (*0-89296-245-3*, Pub. by Mysterious Pr); pap. 3.95 (*0-445-40587-2*) Mysterious Pr.

— Dead Man's Handle. (Modesty Blaise Adventure Ser.). 1987. 45.00 (*0-89296-155-4*, Pub. by Mysterious Pr) Little.

— Last Day in Limbo: A Modesty Blaise Novel. 1986. 45.00 (*0-89296-104-X*, Pub. by Mysterious Pr) Little.

— Modesty Blaise: Death in Slow Motion; The Alternative Man; Sweet Caroline. Yronwode, Catherine, ed. (Comic Strip Ser.). (Illus.). 72p. (Orig.). 1986. pap. 5.95 (*0-912277-30-0*) K Pierce Bks.

— Modesty Blaise: The Lady Killer; Garvin's Travels; The Scarlet Maiden. Yronwode, Catherine, ed. & intro. by. (Comic Strip Ser.). (Illus.). 72p. 1984. pap. 5.95 (*0-912277-25-4*) K Pierce Bks.

— Modesty Blaise: The Mind of Mrs. Drake; Uncle Happy. Yronwode, Catherine, ed. (Comic Strip Ser.). (Illus.). 64p. (Orig.). 1981. pap. 5.95 (*0-912277-08-4*) K Pierce Bks.

— Modesty Blaise: The Moon Man; A Few Flowers for the Colonel; The Balloonatic. Yronwode, Catherine, ed. (Comic Strip Ser.). (Illus.). 72p. (Orig.). 1985. pap. 5.95 (*0-912277-28-9*) K Pierce Bks.

— Modesty Blaise: The Return of the Mammoth; Plato's Republic; The Sword of the Bruce. Yronwode, Catherine, ed. (Comic Strip Ser.). (Illus.). 72p. (Orig.). 1986. pap. 5.95 (*0-912277-33-5*) K Pierce Bks.

— The Night of Morningstar. large type ed. 560p. 1996. 27.99 (*0-7089-3543-5*) Ulverscroft.

O'Donnell, Peter. Pieces of Modesty. 1990. mass mkt. write for info. (*0-8125-0732-0*) Tor Bks.

O'Donnell, Peter. Pieces of Modesty. 192p. 1986. reprint ed. 15.45 (*0-89296-172-4*, Pub. by Mysterious Pr) Little.

— The Silver Mistress. LC 84-60559. (Modesty Blaise Ser.). 256p. 1999. reprint ed. 14.45 (*0-89296-101-5*, Pub. by Mysterious Pr) Little.

— A Taste for Death. large type ed. (Large Print Ser.). 528p. 1997. 27.99 (*0-7089-3672-5*) Ulverscroft.

— The Xanadu Talisman. LC 84-60522. 1987. reprint ed. 45.00 (*0-89296-108-2*, Pub. by Mysterious Pr) Little.

— The Xanadu Talisman. LC 84-60522. 1999. reprint ed. 14.95 (*0-89296-107-4*, Pub. by Mysterious Pr) Little.

O'Donnell, Pierce. Dawn's Early Light. Date not set. write for info. (*0-615-11234-X*) Rosebud Pubng.

O'Donnell, Red. Country Gentleman: Biography Chet Atkins. 1976. 21.95 (*0-8488-1115-1*) Amereon Ltd.

***O'Donnell, Riia I.** It Takes a Lot to Make a World. 2000. 9.99 (*1-56245-414-5*) Great Quotations.

O'Donnell, Robert A. Hooked on Philosophy: Thomas Aquinas Made Easy. LC 95-30850. 124p. (Orig.). 1995. pap. 7.95 (*0-8189-0740-1*) Alba.

O'Donnell, Rory, jt. ed. see Nugent, Neill.

O'Donnell-Rosales, John. Hispanic Confederates. LC 99-196355. 90p. 2000. pap. 18.50 (*0-8063-4802-X*) Clearfield Co.

O'Donnell, Rosie, ed. Kids Are Funny 2: More Jokes Sent by Kids to "The Rosie O'Donnell Show" LC PN6371.5.K524 1998. (Illus.). 86p. 1998. 10.00 (*0-446-52540-5*, Pub. by Warner Bks) Little.

O'Donnell, Rosie, intro. Kids Are Punny: Jokes Sent by Kids to the Rosie O'Donnell Show. LC 97-60408. (Illus.). 96p. 1997. 10.00 (*0-446-52323-2*, Pub. by Warner Bks) Little.

***O'Donnell, Rosie, et al.** Bosom Buddies: Lessons & Laughter on Breast Health & Cancer. (Illus.). 336p. 1999. mass mkt. 12.99 (*0-446-67620-9*, Pub. by Warner Bks) Little.

O'Donnell, Ruan. Aftermath: Post-Rebellion Insurgency in Wicklow, 1799-1803. LC 98-43227. (New Directions in Irish History Ser.). (Illus.). 288p. 2000. pap. 24.95 (*0-7165-2638-7*, Pub. by Irish Acad Pr) Intl Spec Bk.

***O'Donnell, Ruan.** Aftermath: Post-Rebellion Insurgency in Wicklow, 1799-1803. LC 98-43227. (New Directions in Irish History Ser.). (Illus.). 288p. 2000. 52.50 (*0-7165-2628-X*, Pub. by Irish Acad Pr) Intl Spec Bk.

O'Donnell, Ruan. The Rebellion in Wicklow, 1798. LC 98-167696. 420p. 1998. 54.50 (*0-7165-2659-X*, Pub. by Irish Acad Pr); pap. 24.95 (*0-7165-2694-8*, Pub. by Irish Acad Pr) Intl Spec Bk.

O'Donnell, Ruan, ed. see Cullen, Luke.

O'Donnell, Ruth, jt. ed. see Mayo, Kathleen.

O'Donnell, S. & Persson, C. G. Directions for New Anti-Asthma Drugs. (Agents & Actions Supplements Ser.: No. 23). 246p. 1988. 97.00 (*0-8176-1957-7*) Birkhauser.

O'Donnell, Sara A., et al. New Choices in Natural Healing for Women: Drug-Free Remedies from the World of Alternative Medicine. LC 97-2481. (Illus.). 544p. 1997. 29.95 (*0-87596-387-0*) Rodale Pr Inc.

O'Donnell, Sara A., jt. auth. see Harrar, Sari.

O'Donnell, Sara Altshul, jt. auth. see Harrar, Sari.

O'Donnell, Sean. Towards Urban Frameworks. (Publications in Architecture & Urban Planning Ser.: Vol. R95-2). 153p. 1995. pap. 15.00 (*0-938744-92-5*) U of Wis Ctr Arch-Urban.

O'Donnell, Terence. An Arrow in the Earth: General Joel Palmer & the Indians of Oregon. (Illus.). 360p. 1991. pap. 14.95 (*0-87595-156-2*) Oregon Hist.

— Cannon Beach: A Place by the Sea. (Illus.). 130p. (Orig.). 1996. pap. 14.95 (*0-87595-260-7*) Oregon Hist.

— Garden of the Brave in War: Recollections of Iran. xvi, 232p. 1988. pap. text 15.95 (*0-226-61764-5*) U Ch Pr.

***O'Donnell, Terence.** Seven Shades of Memory: Stories of Old Iran. LC 99-35117. (Illus.). 150p. 1999. pap. 14.95 (*0-934211-59-0*) Mage Pubs Inc.

O'Donnell, Terence. That Balance So Rare: The Story of Oregon. (Illus.). 152p. (Orig.). 1997. reprint ed. pap. 14.95 (*0-87595-202-X*) Oregon Hist.

O'Donnell, Terence, jt. ed. see Applegate, Shannon.

O'Donnell, Teresa D. & Paiva, Judith L. Independent Writing. 2nd ed. 216p. (J). 1993. mass mkt. 26.95 (*0-8384-4206-4*) Heinle & Heinle.

O'Donnell, Terrence P. DOS 6: A Tutorial Accompany Peter Norton's Introduction to Computers. LC 93-44147. 1994. write for info. (*0-02-801328-X*) Glencoe.

— Lotus 1-2-3, Release 2.4: A Tutorial to Accompany Peter Norton's Introduction to Computers. LC 93-38995. 1994. write for info. (*0-02-801326-3*) Glencoe.

O'Donnell, Theresa, jt. auth. see Morris, Anne.

O'Donnell, Thomas A. Superacids & Acidic Melts As Inorganic Chemical Reaction Media. LC 92-15542. 243p. 1992. 110.00 (*1-56081-035-1*, Wiley-VCH) Wiley.

O'Donnell, Thomas A. Superacids & Acidic Melts As Inorganic Chemical Reaction Media. 243p. 1992. 159.00 (*0-471-18787-9*, Wiley-VCH) Wiley.

O'Donnell, Thomas F., jt. auth. see Jackson, Harry F.

O'Donnell, Thomas F., ed. see Frederic, Harold.

O'Donnell, Thomas F., ed. see Paulding, James K.

O'Donnell, Thomas J. Medicine & Christian Morality. 3rd rev. ed. LC 96-20352. 336p. (Orig.). 1996. pap. 19.95 (*0-8189-0765-7*) Alba.

O'Donnell, Timothy S. World Quality of Life Indicators. (World Facts & Figures Ser.). 1991. lib. bdg. 40.00 (*0-87436-657-7*) ABC-CLIO.

O'Donnell, Timothy T. Heart of the Redeemer. LC 91-76070. (Illus.). 301p. 1992. reprint ed. pap. 14.95 (*0-89870-396-4*) Ignatius Pr.

O'Donnell-Uhlman, Dorothy. Financial Pot O'Goals. unabridged ed. (Success Series: Vol. 1). (C). 1996. pap. 9.95 incl. audio (*0-9666062-0-5*) Uhlman Commns.

— You Are the Healer. (Success Ser.: Vol. 3I). 27p. 2000. pap. 10.95 incl. audio (*0-9666062-2-1*) Uhlman Commns.

O'Donnell-Uhlman, Dorothy. You Are the Star of Your Life. (Success Ser.: Vol. 2). 24p. 1996. pap. 9.95 incl. audio (*0-9666062-1-3*) Uhlman Commns.

O'Donnell, Victoria, jt. auth. see Jowett, Garth.

O'Donnell, W. R. & Todd, Loreto. Variety in Contemporary English. 192p. (Orig.). 1991. pap. 16.95 (*0-04-445737-5*, A8213) Routledge.

O'Donnell, William F. Mother Santa Claus Stories. 1998. lib. bdg. 18.95 (*1-56723-079-2*) Yestermorrow.

— Mother Santa Claus's Stories. (J). 1976. 18.95 (*0-8488-1116-X*) Amereon Ltd.

O'Donnell, William H. A Guide to the Prose Fiction of W. B. Yeats. LC 83-3639. (Studies in Modern Literature: No. 12). 190p. reprint ed. pap. 58.90 (*0-8357-1421-7*, 207056700001) Bks Demand.

O'Donnell, William H., ed. The Collected Works of W. B. Yeats Vol. V: Later Essays, Vol. 5. 296p. 1994. 37.50 (*0-02-632702-3*, Scribners Ref) Mac Lib Ref.

— The Collected Works of W. B. Yeats Vol. 6: Prefaces & Introductions, Vol. 6. 370p. 1990. 35.00 (*0-02-592551-2*) Macmillan.

O'Donnell, William H., ed. see Yeats, William Butler.

O'Donnol, Dion. Listen-No Echo. (Destiny Ser). pap. 5.00 (*0-686-00949-5*) Wagon & Star.

O'Donoghue, B. Black Tides: The Alaska Oil Spill. (Illus.). 40p. 1995. pap. 4.95 (*0-930931-05-X*) Alaska Natural.

***O'Donoghue, Bernard.** Here nor There. 1999. pap. 17.95 (*0-7011-6800-5*, Pub. by Chatto & Windus) Trafalgar.

O'Donoghue, Bernard. Poaching Rights. 32p. 1987. pap. 11.95 (*1-85235-014-8*) Dufour.

ODonoghue, Bernard. Seamus Heaney & the Language of Poetry. 176p. (C). 1995. pap. text 19.95 (*0-13-320763-3*, Pub. by P-H) S&S Trade.

O'Donoghue, Bernard. The Weakness. 80p. 1992. pap. 15.95 (*0-7011-3859-9*, Pub. by Chatto & Windus) Trafalgar.

O'Donoghue, Bernard, ed. Oxford Irish Quotations. LC 98-39813. 336p. 1999. pap. 7.95 (*0-19-860239-1*) OUP.

***O'Donoghue, Brian.** Honest Dogs: A Story of Triumph & Regret from the World's Toughest Sled Dog Race. Brown, Tricia, ed. (Illus.). 320p. 1999. pap. 16.95 (*0-945397-78-X*) Epicenter Pr.

O'Donoghue, Brian P. My Lead Dog Was a Lesbian: An Iditarod Rookie's Tale. (Departures Ser.). Date not set. write for info. (*0-614-10310-X*) Vin Bks.

— My Lead Dog Was a Lesbian: Mushing Across Alaska in the Iditarod - The World's Most Grueling Race. 320p. 1996. pap. 13.00 (*0-679-76411-9*) Vin Bks.

O'Donoghue, David. Hitler's Irish Voices: The Story of German Radio's Wartime Irish Service. LC 98-148113. 236p. 1998. pap. 15.95 (*1-900960-04-4*, Pub. by Beyond the Pale) Irish Bks Media.

O'Donoghue, David J. The Humour of Ireland, Selected. LC 75-28833. (Illus.). reprint ed. 54.00 (*0-404-13823-3*) AMS Pr.

— The Poets of Ireland. 1972. 59.95 (*0-8490-0867-0*) Gordon Pr.

O'Donoghue, David J., ed. see Mangan, James C.

Odonoghue, Declan. Complete Book of Woodworking. LC 98-11761. (Illus.). 232p. 1998. 29.98 (*1-57145-143-9*, Thunder Bay) Advantage Pubs.

O'Donoghue, Florence. No Other Law. 368p. 1986. reprint ed. pap. 13.95 (*0-947962-12-3*, Pub. by Anvil Books Ltd) Irish Bks Media.

***O'Donoghue, Gerad M., et al.** Clinical ENT: An Illustrated Textbook. 2nd ed. LC 99-31868. (Illus.). 257p. 1999. pap. 68.95 (*1-56593-993-X*) Singular Publishing.

O'Donoghue, Gerard, et al. Clinical ENT: An Illustrated Textbook. (Illus.). 240p. 1992. text 49.95 (*0-19-262226-9*) OUP.

O'Donoghue, Gregory. Kicking. 32p. 1975. pap. 6.95 (*0-902996-36-3*) Dufour.

An Asterisk (*) at the beginning of an entry indicates that the title is appearing for the first time.

O'Donoghue, Heather. The Genesis of a Saga Narrative: Verse & Prose in Kormaks Saga. (Oxford English Monographs). 208p. 1991. text 69.00 (*0-19-811783-3*) OUP.

O'Donoghue, Heather, ed. Beowulf: The Fight at Finnsburh. Crossley-Holland, Kevin, tr. from ANG. LC 98-22104. (Oxford World's Classics Ser.). (Illus.). 168p. 1999. pap. 6.95 (*0-19-283320-0*) OUP.

O'Donoghue, Heather, ed. see Woolf, Rosemary.

O'Donoghue, Jo. Brian Moore: A Critical Study. 288p. (C). 1991. text 65.00 (*0-7735-0850-3*, Pub. by McG-Queens Univ Pr) CUP Services.

— Golden Apples. (Illus.). 80p. (J). (gr. 4-7). 1997. pap. 7.95 (*1-85635-122-X*, Pub. by Mercier Pr) Irish Amer Bk.

O'Donoghue, Jo, ed. Taisce Duan: A Treasury of Irish Poems with Translations in English. 270p. (Orig.). 1993. pap. 19.95 (*1-85371-118-7*, Pub. by Poolbeg Pr) Dufour.

O'Donoghue, John L., ed. Neurotoxicity of Industrial & Commercial Chemicals, 2 vols., Vol. 1. LC 84-4261. 232p. 1985. 134.00 (*0-8493-6454-X*, RC347, CRC Reprint) Franklin.

— Neurotoxicity of Industrial & Commercial Chemicals, 2 vols., Vol. 2. LC 84-4261. 224p. 1985. 132.00 (*0-8493-6455-8*, CRC Reprint) Franklin.

O'Donoghue, M. Synthetic, Imitation & Treated Gemstones. LC 97-14620. 224p. 1997. pap. 54.95 (*0-7506-3173-2*) Buttrwrth-Heinemann.

O'Donoghue, Maureen. Jedder's Land. large type ed. (Charnwood Romance Ser.). 592p. 1985. 27.99 (*0-7089-8249-2*) Ulverscroft.

O'Donoghue, Michael. Identifying Man-Made Gems. (Illus.). 221p. 1983. 37.50 (*0-7198-0111-7*, Pub. by NAG Press) Antique Collect.

O'Donoghue, Michael, jt. auth. see Rowland-Entwistle, Theodore.

O'Donoghue, Noel D. Heaven in Ordinarie. 202p. 1979. 14.95 (*0-87243-085-5*) Templegate.

— Heaven in Ordinarie: Prayer As Transcendence. 224p. 1996. pap. 27.95 (*0-567-08510-4*, Pub. by T & T Clark) Bks Intl VA.

— The Mountain Behind the Mountain: Aspects of the Celtic Tradition. 1993. text 37.95 (*0-567-09652-1*, Pub. by T & T Clark) Bks Intl VA.

— Mystics for Our Time. (Orig.). 1997. 39.95 (*0-567-09526-6*, Pub. by T & T Clark) Bks Intl VA.

O'Donoghue, P. E., jt. ed. see Atluri, Satya N.

O'Donoghue, Patrick. Decision-Related Research on the Organization of Service Delivery Systems in Metropolitan Areas: Public Health. LC 79-83820. 1979. write for info. (*0-89138-984-9*) ICPSR.

***O'Donoghue, Tom A.** The Catholic Church & the Secondary School Curriculum in Ireland, 1922-1962. LC 98-37324. (Irish Studies: Vol. 5). 183p. (C). 1999. text 44.95 (*0-8204-4424-3*) P Lang Pubng.

O'Donohoe, Nick. Gnomewrench in the Dwarfworks. 1999. mass mkt. 6.50 (*0-441-00633-7*) Ace Bks.

***O'Donohoe, Nick.** Gnomewrench in the Peopleworks. 2000. mass mkt. 6.50 (*0-441-00760-0*) Ace Bks.

O'Donohoe, Nick. The Healing of Crossroads. 336p. 1996. mass mkt. 5.99 (*0-441-00391-5*) Ace Bks.

— The Magic & the Healing. 352p. (Orig.). 1994. pap. text 4.99 (*0-441-00053-3*) Ace Bks.

— Under the Healing Sun. 352p. (Orig.). 1995. mass mkt. 4.99 (*0-441-00180-7*) Ace Bks.

O'Donohue. Management & Administrative Skills for Mental Health Professionals. 450p. (C). 1999. 39.95 (*0-12-524195-X*) Acad Pr.

O'Donohue, Benedict. File on Sartre. 1996. pap. text. write for info. (*0-413-16530-2*, Methuen Drama) Methn.

O'Donohue, John. Anam Cara: A Book of Celtic Wisdom. LC 97-19212. 256p. 1997. 24.00 (*0-06-018279-2*) HarpC.

— Anam Cara: A Book of Celtic Wisdom. 224p. 1998. pap. 13.00 (*0-06-092943-X*, HarperFlamingo) HarpC.

— Anam Cara: Wisdom from the Celtic World. unabridged ed. 1996. pap. 59.95 incl. audio (*1-56455-376-0*, F039) Sounds True.

***O'Donohue, John.** Conamara Blues. 96p. 2000. 20.00 (*0-06-019644-0*, Pub. by HarperTrade) HarpC.

O'Donohue, John. Echoes of Memory. 1997. pap. 13.95 (*1-897648-30-8*, Pub. by Salmon Poetry) Dufour.

***O'Donohue, John.** Eternal Echoes: Celtic Reflections on Our Yearning to Belong, 304p. 2000. pap. 13.00 (*0-06-095558-9*, Cliff Street) HarperTrade.

O'Donohue, John. Eternal Echoes: Explaining Our Yearning to Belong. LC 98-50256. 304p. 1999. 25.00 (*0-06-018280-6*, Cliff Street) HarperTrade.

***O'Donohue, John.** Eternal Echoes: Exploring Our Yearning to Belong. 273p. 2000. reprint ed. 25.00 (*0-7881-9299-X*) DIANE Pub.

O'Donohue, John, tr. see Renault, Francois.

O'Donohue, W., jt. auth. see Geer, J. H.

O'Donohue, W. T. & Geer, James H., eds. The Sexual Abuse of Children, 2 vols. 424p. 1992. pap. 45.00 (*0-8058-0340-8*); pap. 55.00 (*0-8058-0955-4*) L Erlbaum Assocs.

— The Sexual Abuse of Children. 544p. (C). 1992. 99.95 (*0-8058-0954-6*); 99.95 (*0-8058-0339-4*) L Erlbaum Assocs.

— The Sexual Abuse of Children, 2 vols., Set. 1992. pap. 75.00 (*0-8058-0957-0*); text 165.00 (*0-8058-0956-2*) L Erlbaum Assocs.

O'Donohue, Walter J., Jr., ed. Long Term Oxygen Therapy: Scientific Basis & Clinical Application. LC 94-48767. (Lung Biology in Health & Disease Ser.: Vol. 81). (Illus.). 416p. 1995. text 180.00 (*0-8247-9499-0*) Dekker.

O'Donohue, Walter J., Jr., ed. see Booth, Patricia.

O'Donohue, William. Handbook of Psychological Skills Training: Clinical Techniques & Applications. 640p. 1993. 81.00 (*0-205-15261-9*, Longwood Div) Allyn.

O'Donohue, William. The Philosophy of Psychology. 416p. 1996. 49.50 (*0-7619-5304-3*); pap. 17.99 (*0-7619-5305-1*) Sage.

O'Donohue, William, ed. Learning & Behavior Therapy. LC 97-10769. 568p. (C). 1997. 86.00 (*0-205-18609-2*) Allyn.

O'Donohue, William & Kitchener, Richard, eds. Handbook of Behaviorism. LC 98-85620. (Illus.). 451p. (C). 1998. boxed set 125.00 (*0-12-524190-9*) Acad Pr.

O'Donohue, William & Krasner, Leonard, eds. Theories of Behavior Therapy: Exploring Behavior Change. LC 94-48476. 753p. 1995. text 39.95 (*1-55798-265-1*) Am Psychol.

O'Donohue, William & Krasner, Leonard, eds. Theories of Behavior Therapy: Exploring Behavior Change. 753p. 1995. pap. 29.95 (*1-55798-488-3*) Am Psychol.

O'Donohue, William, jt. ed. see Laws, D. Richard.

O'Donovan-Anderson, Michael. Content & Comportment: On Embodiment & the Epistemic Availability of the World. LC 97-25294. 192p. 1997. 56.00 (*0-8476-8624-8*); pap. 23.95 (*0-8476-8625-6*) Rowman.

O'Donovan-Anderson, Michael, ed. The Incorporated Self: Interdisciplinary Perspectives on Embodiment. 164p. 1996. pap. text 23.95 (*0-8476-8282-X*); lib. bdg. 55.50 (*0-8476-8281-1*) Rowman.

O'Donovan, Daniel, tr. Bernard of Clairvaux: On Grace & Free Choice, in Praise of the New Knighthood. (Cistercian Fathers Ser.: No. CF19A). 1988. pap. 6.00 (*0-87907-070-6*) Cistercian Pubns.

O'Donovan, Daniel J., ed. Nutritional & Acid-Base Aspects of Amino Acid Metabolism: 7th International Ammoniagenesis Workshop, Galway, May 1996. LC 97-23206. (Contributions to Nephrology Ser.: Vol. 121, 1997). (Illus.). x, 172p. 1997. 198.25 (*3-8055-6490-2*) S Karger.

O'Donovan, Dermot. Silas Rat. 112p. 1992. pap. 8.95 (*0-947962-02-6*) Dufour.

O'Donovan, Donal. Little Old Man Cut Short. LC 98-167475. 240p. 1998. pap. 19.95 (*1-900505-90-8*, Pub. by Kestrel Bks) Irish Bks Media.

— The Rock from Which You Were Hewn. (Illus.). 224p. (Orig.). 1989. pap. 12.50 (*0-9623863-0-8*) D ODonovan.

O'Donovan, Edmond. Merv Oasis: Travels & Adventures East of the Caspian During the Years 1879-80-81. LC 71-115570. (Russia Observed Ser., No. 1). 1970. reprint ed. 56.95 (*0-405-03053-3*) Ayer.

O'Donovan, Ita. Organizational Behaviour: A Psychological Approach to Behaviour in the Workplace. (Contemporary Psychology Ser.). 192p. 1996. 75.00 (*0-7484-0358-2*); pap. 24.95 (*0-7484-0359-0*) Taylor & Francis.

O'Donovan, James. McPherson: The Law of Company Liquidation. 3rd ed. lxxxii, 501p. 1987. 110.50 (*0-455-20741-0*, Pub. by LawBk Co) Gaunt.

— McPherson's Law of Company Liquidation. 250p. 1994. pap. 39.00 (*0-455-21232-5*, Pub. by LawBk Co) Gaunt.

O'Donovan, James, jt. auth. see Phillips, John.

O'Donovan, Jeremiah. Irish Immigration in the United States. LC 69-18786. (American Immigration Collection. Series 1). 1969. reprint ed. 18.95 (*0-405-00534-2*) Ayer.

O'Donovan, Joan. Dangerous Worlds. LC 72-75783. (Short Story Index Reprint Ser.). 1977. 17.95 (*0-8369-3008-8*) Ayer.

O'Donovan, Joan E. George Grant & the Twilight of Justice. 208p. 1984. pap. 13.95 (*0-8020-6538-4*) U of Toronto Pr.

O'Donovan, Joan L., jt. ed. see O'Donovan, Oliver.

O'Donovan, John. Antiquities of the Country of Kerry. 1983. pap. 39.95 (*0-946645-01-9*) Dufour.

— Genealogies, Tribes & Customs of Hy-Fiachrach in Ireland: In Gaelic & English. deluxe ed. (Old Ireland Ser.). (ENG & GAE., Illus.). xii, 530p. 1993. reprint ed. lib. bdg. 129.00 (*0-940134-38-1*) Irish Genealog.

— Jonathan, Jack, & GBS: Four Plays about Irish History & Literature. Hogan, Robert T., ed. LC 91-51141. (Illus.). 232p. 1993. 35.00 (*0-87413-452-8*) U Delaware Pr.

— Tribes & Customs of Hy Many Commonly Called O'Kellys Country: In Gaelic & English. deluxe ed. (Old Ireland Ser.). (Illus.). vi, 221p. 1992. reprint ed. lib. bdg. 95.00 (*0-940134-39-X*) Irish Genealog.

O'Donovan, John, ed. Annals of the Four Masters, 7 vols. LC 70-15820. reprint ed. 875.00 (*0-404-04820-X*) AMS Pr.

O'Donovan, K. Sexual Divisions in Law. (Law in Context Ser.). xii, 242p. 1985. 35.00 (*0-297-78664-4*) W S Hein.

O'Donovan, Katherine. Family Law Matters. LC 93-18373. 192p. 1993. pap. 16.95 (*0-7453-0507-5*, Pub. by Pluto GBR) Stylus Pub VA.

— Family Law Matters. LC 93-18373. 192p. (C). 1993. 50.00 (*0-7453-0506-7*, Pub. by Pluto GBR) Stylus Pub VA.

***O'Donovan, Katherine & Rubin, Gerry R., eds.** Human Rights & Legal History: Essays in Honour of Brian Simpson. (Illus.). 300p. 2000. text 65.00 (*0-19-826496-8*) OUP.

O'Donovan, Leo J. A World of Grace: An Introduction to the Themes & Foundations of Karl Rahner's Theology. LC 95-23073. 214p. (C). 1995. pap. 18.95 (*0-87840-596-8*) Georgetown U Pr.

O'Donovan, Leo J., ed. Cooperation Between Theologians & the Ecclesiastical Magisterium: A Report of the Joint Committee of the Canon Law Society of America & the Catholic Theological Society of America. 200p. (Orig.). 1982. pap. 5.00 (*0-943616-12-3*) Canon Law Soc.

O'Donovan, Margaret & Dare, Angela. A Practical Guide to Working with Babies 0-1. 128p. (C). 1994. pap. 32.00 (*0-7478-1743-X*, Pub. by S Thornes Pubs) Trans-Atl Phila.

O'Donovan, Margaret, jt. auth. see Dare, Angela.

O'Donovan, Margeret, jt. auth. see Dare, Angela.

O'Donovan, Mary A. Charters of Sherborne. (Anglo-Saxon Charters Ser.; British Academy: Vol. III). (Illus.). 182p. 1988. 85.00 (*0-19-726051-9*) OUP.

O'Donovan, Michael. The Island Vol. 1: A Photographic Journey of Santa Rosa Island. (Illus.). 104p. 1996. 29.95 (*0-9651034-0-4*) Terra Nova Pub.

— The Road to Stratford. 1988. reprint ed. lib. bdg. 39.00 (*0-7812-0091-1*) Rprt Serv.

— The Road to Stratford. reprint ed. 29.00 (*0-403-04239-9*) Somerset Pub.

***O'Donovan, Molly & Gunning, Brooke.** Towson, Ruxton & Lutherville. (Images of America Ser.). (Illus.). 128p. 1999. pap. 18.99 (*0-7385-0226-X*) Arcadia Publng.

O'Donovan, Oliver. Begotten or Made? Human Procreation & Medical Technique. 94p. 1984. pap. 9.95 (*0-19-826678-2*) OUP.

***O'Donovan, Oliver.** The Desire of the Nations: Rediscovering the Roots of Political Theology. 316p. (C). 1999. pap. 22.95 (*0-521-66516-7*) Cambridge U Pr.

O'Donovan, Oliver. On the Thirty Nine Articles: A Conversation with Tudor Christianity. 160p. 1993. reprint ed. pap. text 16.99 (*0-85364-435-7*) Paternoster Pub.

— The Problem of Self-Love in St. Augustine. LC 80-5397. 229p. reprint ed. pap. 71.00 (*0-8357-8285-9*, 203384600087) Bks Demand.

— Resurrection & Moral Order: An Outline for Evangelical Ethics. rev. ed. 320p. (C). 1994. pap. 23.00 (*0-8028-0692-9*) Eerdmans.

***O'Donovan, Oliver & O'Donovan, Joan L., eds.** From Irenaeus to Grotius: A Sourcebook in Christian Political Thought. 840p. 1999. 70.00 (*0-8028-3876-6*); pap. 45.00 (*0-8028-4209-7*) Eerdmans.

O'Donovan, P. J., jt. ed. see Downes, Ellisa.

O'Donovan, Thomas M. GPSS Simulation Made Simple. LC 79-40520. (Wiley Series in Computing). 139p. 1979. pap. 43.10 (*0-7837-4011-5*, 204384100011) Bks Demand.

— VisiCalc Made Simple. LC 84-3680. 165p. reprint ed. pap. 51.20 (*0-608-17866-7*, 203269600080) Bks Demand.

O'Donovan, Valentine, jt. auth. see Kudsia, Chandra M.

O'Donovan, Wilbur. Biblical Christianity in African Perspective. 2nd ed. xviii, 356p. 1995. reprint ed. pap. 25.00 (*0-85364-711-9*, Pub. by Paternoster Pub) OM Literature.

Odoo, Hans, jt. auth. see Klum, Mattias.

Odor, Harold & Odor, Ruth S. Sharing Your Faith. (Illus.). 16p. (J). (gr. 3-7). 1985. 0.75 (*0-87239-902-8*, 03302) Standard Pub.

Odor, Ruth S. A Child's Book of Manners. Beegle, Shirley, ed. (Happy Day Bks.). (Illus.). 24p. (J). (ps-3). 1994. reprint ed. pap. 1.99 (*0-7847-0252-7*, 04202) Standard Pub.

— A Child's Book of Manners: Preschool Activity. (Activities Bks.). (Illus.). 16p. (J). 1995. pap. 1.69 (*0-7847-0282-9*, 02578) Standard Pub.

***Odor, Ruth S.** Please. LC 99-25377. (Illus.). 32p. (J). 1999. lib. bdg. 18.50 (*1-56766-672-8*) Childs World.

Odor, Ruth S., jt. auth. see Odor, Harold.

***Odor, Ruth Shannon.** Thanks. LC 99-28174. (Thoughts & Feelings Ser.). (Illus.). 32p. (J). 1999. lib. bdg. 18.50 (*1-56766-677-9*) Childs World.

O'Dorisio, T. M., ed. Sandostatin in the Treatment of GEP Endrocine Tumors. 170p. 1989. 50.95 (*0-387-50715-9*) Spr-Verlag.

O'Dorso, Michael, jt. auth. see Cartwright, Madeline.

O'Doughda, Linda, ed. see Norco, Jay E. & Schroder, Thomas.

O'Dougherty, Patrick A. An Existential & Numerical Approach to American History: The American Revolution: A Case Study. LC 96-94077. 151p. (C). 1996. lib. bdg. 10.99 (*0-9626665-0-5*) Irish Catholic.

— Irish Psychology/Irish Psychiatry: Catholic Personalist Intuitionist & Revolution As Therapy--The Tiresias Complex a Critique of Medical Revisionism: Letters Out of Schizophrenia--A Case Study. LC 97-93445. 275p. 1997. lib. bdg. 27.99 (*0-9626665-8-0*) Irish Catholic.

— Life Culture Versus Death Culture & the Death of Literature. LC 95-95349. 50p. (C). 1995. lib. bdg. 10.99 (*0-9626665-3-X*) Irish Catholic.

— Patrick's "Unfinished" An Intellectual History Counterpoint to Franz-Schubert's Symphony No. 8 "Unfinished" unabridged ed. LC 96-94077. 60p. (C). 1996. lib. bdg. 15.99 (*0-9626665-6-4*) Irish Catholic.

— Personalism & Mathematics As Women's Personifestors: Women & the Fior (Which Is Irish for Truth) & the Creation of the Personalist Intuitionist School of Mathematics & Physics. LC 95-79957. 106p. (C). 1995. lib. bdg. 20.99 (*0-9626665-5-6*) Irish Catholic.

— Reinventing Physics: Logic & Physics, a Dialectical Approach to Physics. LC 93-61179. 144p. (C). 1993. lib. bdg. 10.99 (*0-9626665-2-1*) Irish Catholic.

— St. Patrick, the Green Revolution & the Hydrogen Conversion Project: Featuring the International Alliance for Sustainable Agriculture Purple Database. LC 96-94477. (Illus.). 116p. 1996. lib. bdg. 19.99 (*0-9626665-7-2*) Irish Catholic.

— Shaking up Shakespeare: Shakespeare: Dreamwork, Personality & Complexity. LC 97-79439. (Illus.). 169p. (C). 1994. lib. bdg. 19.99 (*0-9626665-4-8*) Irish Catholic.

— Walden III: A Catholic America. LC 96-79986. 92p. (C). 1991. lib. bdg. 10.99 (*0-9626665-1-3*) Irish Catholic.

Odoulov, S. Optical Oscillators with Degenerate Four-Wave Mixing, Dynamic Grating Lasers. (Laser Science & Technology Ser.). 152p. 1991. pap. text 123.00 (*3-7186-4972-1*, Harwood Acad Pubs) Gordon & Breach.

O'Dowd, Anne. Spalpeens & Tatie Hokers: History & Folklore of the Irish Migratory Agricultural Worker in Ireland & Britain. (Illus.). 456p. 1990. 45.00 (*0-7165-2450-3*, Pub. by Irish Acad Pr) Intl Spec Bk.

***O'Dowd, Ben.** In Valiant Company: Diggers in Battle - Korea 1950-51. 212p. 2000. pap. 19.95 (*0-7022-3146-0*, Pub. by Univ Queensland Pr) Intl Spec Bk.

O'Dowd, Desmond. Changing Times: The Story of Religion in 19th Century Celbridge. (Maynooth Studies in Local History). 64p. 1997. pap. 9.95 (*0-7165-2635-2*, Pub. by Irish Acad Pr) Intl Spec Bk.

O'Dowd, Elizabeth & Good, Cynthia. Everyday Bath Book: A Soak for the Soul, 4 vols. (Floating Bath Book Collection). (Illus.). 10p. 1998. pap. 9.95 (*1-56352-456-2*) Longstreet.

— Healthy Bath Book: A Soak for Every Body, 4 vols. (Floating Bath Book Collection). (Illus.). 10p. 1998. pap. 9.95 (*1-56352-457-0*) Longstreet.

— New Mom's Bath Book: A Soak for the Maternal Soul, 4 vols. (Floating Bath Book Collection). (Illus.). 10p. 1998. pap. 9.95 (*1-56352-458-9*) Longstreet.

— The Newlywed Bath Book: A Soak for Two Souls. (Illus.). 10p. 1998. pap. 9.95 (*1-56352-459-7*) Longstreet.

O'Dowd, Elizabeth M. Prepositions & Particles in English: A Discourse-Functional Account. LC 98-18309. 232p. 1998. text 65.00 (*0-19-511102-8*) OUP.

O'Dowd, Elizabeth M., jt. auth. see Mahnke, M. Kathleen.

O'Dowd, Karen. Quick-&-Easy Heart Motif Quilts: Instructions & Full-Size Templates for Applique Projects. (Illus.). 48p. (Orig.). 1986. pap. 4.95 (*0-486-25136-5*) Dover.

O'Dowd, Leonard. The Healing Flame of Love. Otto, Helen T., tr. from RUS. 48p. 1996. pap. write for info. (*0-9639553-5-7*) Verenikia Pr.

O'Dowd, Liam & Thomas, Wilson, eds. Borders, Nations & States: Frontiers of Sovereignty in the New Europe. LC 95-83597. (Perspectives on Europe Ser.). 237p. (C). 1996. 68.95 (*1-85972-158-3*, Pub. by Avebry) Ashgate Pub Co.

***O'Dowd, M.** Calendar of State Papers. 1999. 125.00 (*1-873162-48-0*, Pub. by PRO Pubns) Midpt Trade.

***O'Dowd, M. J. & Philipp, E. E.** The History of Obstetrics & Gynecology. (Illus.). 710p. 2000. pap. 55.00 (*1-85070-040-0*) Prthnon Pub.

O'Dowd, M. J. & Philipp, E. E., eds. The History of Obstetrics & Gynecology. (History of Medicine Ser.). (Illus.). 710p. 1994. 125.00 (*1-85070-224-1*) Prthnon Pub.

O'Dowd, Mary & Wichart, Sabine, eds. Chattel, Servant or Citizen: Women's Status in Church, State & Society. LC 96-100502. 287p. 1996. pap. 25.95 (*0-85389-576-7*, Pub. by Inst Irish Studies) Irish Bks Media.

O'Dowd, Mary, jt. auth. see Valiulis, Maryann Gialanella.

O'Dowd, Mary, jt. ed. see MacCurtain, Margaret.

***O'Dowd, Michael J.** The History of Medications for Women: Materia Medica Woman. (Illus.). 450p. 2000. 85.00 (*1-85070-002-8*) Prthnon Pub.

O'Dowd, Tom & Jewell, David, eds. Men's Health. (Oxford General Practice Ser.: No. 41). (Illus.). 290p. 1998. pap. text 68.00 (*0-19-262581-0*) OUP.

O'Dowda, Brendan. The World of Percy French. LC 97-229300. 192p. 1997. pap. 22.95 (*0-85640-604-X*, Pub. by Blackstaff Pr) Dufour.

— The World of Percy French. 2nd ed. (Illus.). 208p. 1992. pap. 21.00 (*0-85640-482-9*, Pub. by Blackstaff Pr) Dufour.

Odozor, Paulinus I. Richard A. McCormick & the Renewal of Moral Theology. LC 94-15941. (C). 1995. text 34.95 (*0-268-01648-8*) U of Notre Dame Pr.

O'Drago, Alicia S. Radio Dial. LC 88-70857. (Illus.). 133p. (Orig.). 1988. pap. 9.95 (*0-929273-00-1*) AMP Publishing.

O'Drisceoil, Donal. Censorship in Ireland, 1939-1945: Neutrality, Politics & Society. 352p. 1996. 64.95 (*1-85918-073-6*, Pub. by Cork Univ); pap. 26.95 (*1-85918-074-4*, Pub. by Cork Univ) Stylus Pub VA.

***O'Driscoll.** Business Challenges Course Book. 1998. pap., student ed. write for info. (*0-582-22994-4*) Addison-Wesley.

O'Driscoll. Exchange Information Book. 1991. pap. text. write for info. (*0-582-06445-7*, Pub. by Addison-Wesley) Longman.

— Making Contact Book. 1991. pap. text. write for info. (*0-582-06447-3*, Pub. by Addison-Wesley) Longman.

O'Driscoll, jt. auth. see Ellis.

O'Driscoll, Aidan, jt. auth. see Murray, John A.

O'Driscoll, Ciaran. Listening to Different Drummers. 88p. 1993. pap. 11.95 (*1-873790-36-8*) Dufour.

— The Old Women of Magione. LC 98-106067. 72p. 1998. 19.95 (*1-901233-09-X*); pap. 13.95 (*1-901233-08-1*) Dufour.

O'Driscoll, Ciaran & O'Brien, Anthony P. On the Counterscarp: Limerick Writing, 1961-1991. 240p. 1991. pap. 14.95 (*0-948339-85-3*, Pub. by Poolbeg Pr) Dufour.

O'Driscoll, Dennis. Long Story Short. 84p. 1993. pap. 17.95 (*0-85646-256-X*, Pub. by Anvil Press) Dufour.

— Long Story Short. LC 94-132445. Date not set. pap. 11.95 (*1-873790-47-3*) Dufour.

— Quality Time. LC 97-201170. 96p. 1997. pap. 17.95 (*0-85646-290-X*, Pub. by Anvil Press) Dufour.

***O'Driscoll, Dennis.** Weather Permitting. 84p. 2000. pap. 18.95 (*0-85646-315-9*, Pub. by Anvil Press) Dufour.

O'Driscoll, Gerald P., Jr., ed. Adam Smith & Modern Political Economy: Bicentennial Essays on the Wealth of Nations. LC 78-10181. 197p. reprint ed. pap. 61.10 (*0-8357-6757-4*, 203541400095) Bks Demand.

— An Economic Perspective on the Southwest: Defining the Decade: Proceedings of the 1990 Conference on the

O

Southwest Economy Sponsored by the Federal Reserve Bank of Dallas. 176p. (C). 1991. lib. bdg. 73.50 (0-7923-9221-3) Kluwer Academic.

— Free Trade Within North America: Expanding Trade for Prosperity, Proceedings of the 1991 Conference on the Southwest Economy Sponsored by the Federal Reserve Bank of Dallas. LC 92-33253. 1992. lib. bdg. 109.00 (0-7923-9291-4) Kluwer Academic.

O'Driscoll, Gerald P., Jr. & Brown, Stephen P., eds. The Southwest Economy in the 1990s: A Different Decade. 224p. 1990. text 78.00 (0-7923-9092-X) Kluwer Academic.

O'Driscoll, Gerald P., Jr. & Rizzo, Mario J. The Economics of Time & Ignorance. 2nd ed. (Foundations of the Market Economy Ser.). 296p. (C). 1996. pap. 27.99 (0-415-12120-5, C0408) Routledge.

***O'Driscoll, Gerard.** Essential Guide to Digital Set-Top Boxes & Interactive TV. LC 99-54468. (Illus.). 320p. 1999. pap. text 34.99 (0-13-017360-6) P-H.

— Essential Guide to Home Networking Technologies. 300p. 2000. pap. 34.99 (0-13-019846-3, Prentice Hall) P-H.

O'Driscoll, Herbert. Baptism: Saying Yes to Being a Christian. 56p. (Orig.). 1998. pap. 2.95 (0-88028-188-X, 1436) Forward Movement.

— Birth: Holding Your Newborn Child. 40p. 1998. pap. 2.95 (0-88028-193-6, 1441) Forward Movement.

— A Certain Life: Contemporary Meditations on the Way of Christ. 96p. (Orig.). 1984. 5.95 (0-8164-2040-8) Harper SF.

— A Certain Life: Contemporary Meditations on the Way of Christ. large type ed. 192p. (Orig.). 1985. reprint ed. pap. 8.95 (0-8027-2491-4) Walker & Co.

— City Priest, City People. 122p. 1983. pap. 9.95 (0-919891-04-7) Forward Movement.

— Conversations in Time: With Men & Women of the Bible. LC 99-26295. 160p. 1999. pap. 10.95 (1-56101-155-X) Cowley Pubns.

— Crossroads: Times of Decision for People of God. 96p. 1984. 5.95 (0-8164-2432-2) Harper SF.

— Eucharist: The Feast That Never Ends. 56p. (Orig.). 1998. pap. 2.95 (0-88028-192-8, 1440) Forward Movement.

— For All the Saints: Homilies for Saints' & Holy Days. 147p. 1995. pap. 10.95 (1-56101-111-8) Cowley Pubns.

— Grace: For a Time of Sickness. 40p. (Orig.). 1998. pap. 2.95 (0-88028-189-8, 1437) Forward Movement.

— Hope: For a Time of Grieving. 40p. (Orig.). 1998. pap. 2.95 (0-88028-190-1, 1438) Forward Movement.

— The Leap of the Deer: Memories of a Celtic Childhood. LC 93-41744. 154p. 1994. pap. 10.95 (1-56101-086-3) Cowley Pubns.

— Marriage: In the Christian Church. 56p. (Orig.). 1998. pap. 2.95 (0-88028-191-X, 1439) Forward Movement.

— Prayers for the Breaking of Bread: Reflections on the Collects of the Church Year. LC 91-19446. 184p. 1991. pap. 9.95 (1-56101-045-6) Cowley Pubns.

***O'Driscoll, Herbert.** The Road to Donaguile: A Celtic Spiritual Journey. LC 99-49301. 128p. 1999. pap. 9.95 (1-56101-173-8) Cowley Pubns.

O'Driscoll, Kenneth F., jt. ed. see Tsuruta, Teiji.

O'Driscoll, Kenneth F., ed. & frwd. see Sawada, Hideo.

***O'Driscoll, Mervyn.** Irish-German Relations, 1919-1939. 192p. 2000. 55.00 (1-85182-480-4, Pub. by Four Cts Pr) Intl Spec Bk.

O'Driscoll, Robert, ed. The Celtic Consciousness. LC 82-1269. (Illus.). 642p. 1982. 40.00 (0-8076-1041-0) Braziller.

— The Celtic Consciousness. LC 82-1269. (Illus.). 642p. 1985. reprint ed. pap. 29.95 (0-8076-1136-0, Pub. by Braziller) Norton.

O'Driscoll, Robert, ed. see Molloy, M. J.

O'Driscoll, Robert, ed. see Seminar in Irish Studies (2nd: 1968: University of.

O'Driscoll, Sally, tr. see Clement, Catherine.

Oduba, Rebecca E., ed. see Koger, Dorothy P.

O'Duffy, E. Crusade in Spain. 1972. 69.95 (0-87968-972-2) Gordon Pr.

O'Duffy, J. Desmond & Kokmen, Emre, eds. Behcet's Disease: Basic & Clinical Aspects. (Inflammatory Disease & Therapy Ser.: Vol. 8). (Illus.). 696p. 1991. text 265.00 (0-8247-8476-6) Dekker.

***O'Dugan, John.** The Kings of the Race of Eibhear: A Chronological Poem. Daly, John, ed. Kearney, Michael, tr. 88p. 1999. pap. 20.00 (0-9654220-6-2) Gryfons Pubs & Dist.

O'Duigneain, Proinnsios. The Priest & the Protestant Woman: The Trail of Rev. Thomas Maguire, P. P., December 1827. (Maynooth Studies in Local History). 64p. 1997. pap. 9.95 (0-7165-2639-5, Pub. by Irish Acad Pr) Intl Spec Bk.

O'Duignean, Prionnsias. North Leitrim in Famine Times, 1840-1850. (North Leitrim History Ser.). (Illus.). 56p. 1986. pap. 6.95 (1-873437-03-X, Pub. by Drumlin Pubns Ltd) Irish Bks Media.

— North Leitrim in Land League Times, 1880-1884. (North Leitrim History Ser.). (Illus.). 52p. 1992. reprint ed. pap. 6.95 (1-873437-04-8, Pub. by Drumlin Pubns Ltd) Irish Bks Media.

O'Duignean, Prionnsias, ed. see Duibhir, Ciaran O.

O'Duignean, Prionnsios. North Leitrim: The Land War & the Fall of Parnell. (North Leitrim History Ser.). (Illus.). 77p. (Orig.). 1988. pap. 6.95 (1-873437-06-4, Pub. by Drumlin Pubns Ltd) Irish Bks Media.

Odujirin, Adekemi. The Normative Basis of Fault in Criminal Law: History & Theory. LC 98-215019. (History & Theory Ser.). 336p. 1998. text 55.00 (0-8020-4304-6); pap. text 21.95 (0-8020-8132-0) U of Toronto Pr.

Odum. Ecology: Integration Humankind. (C). 1997. text 74.50 (0-03-018292-1) Harcourt Coll Pubs.

— Environment Power & Society. 2nd ed. text 45.00 (0-471-34932-1) Wiley.

— Modeling for All Scales. 448p. (C). 1999. text 79.95 (0-12-524170-4) Acad Pr.

Odum, jt. auth. see Marino.

Odum, Eugene P. Basic Ecology. 613p. (C). 1983. text 87.50 (0-03-058414-0, Pub. by SCP) Harcourt.

— Ecological Vignettes: Ecological Approaches to Dealing with Human Predicaments. 288p. 1998. text 55.00 (90-5702-521-3, ECU46, Harwood Acad Pubs); pap. text 22.00 (90-5702-522-1, ECU18, Harwood Acad Pubs) Gordon & Breach.

— Ecology: A Bridge Between Science & Society. 3rd ed. LC 96-38031. 330p. (C). 1997. pap. text 34.95 (0-87893-630-0) Sinauer Assocs.

***Odum, Eugene P.** Essence of Place. LC 00-29417. 2000. write for info. (0-915977-39-7) Georgia Museum of Art.

Odum, Eugene P., ed. see Brimley, Herbert H.

Odum, H., jt. auth. see Blissett, Marlan.

Odum, Harry. The Vital Singles Ministry. (Effective Church Ser.). 144p. 1992. pap. 3.15 (0-687-43800-4) Abingdon.

Odum, Howard T. Ecological & General Systems: An Introduction to Systems Ecology. rev. ed. LC 93-46846. (Illus.). 664p. (C). 1994. pap. text 49.95 (0-87081-320-X) Univ Pr Colo.

— Environmental Accounting: Energy & Environmental Decision Making. LC 95-11683. 384p. 1995. 110.00 (0-471-11442-1) Wiley.

***Odum, Howard T.** Heavy Metals in the Environment: Using Wetlands for Their Removal. LC 99-89022. 344p. 2000. boxed set 89.95 (1-56670-401-4) Lewis Pubs.

Odum, Howard T. Systems Ecology: An Introduction. LC 82-8650. reprint ed. pap. 178.80 (0-7837-2809-3, 2057663) Bks Demand.

Odum, Howard T., et al. Environment & Society in Florida. LC 97-41621. 480p. 1997. per. 44.95 (1-57444-080-2, SL0802) St Lucie Pr.

Odum, Howard T., jt. auth. see Beyers, Robert J.

Odum, Howard T., ed. see AEC Technical Information Center Staff.

Odum, Howard T., jt. ed. see Carter Ewel, Katherine.

Odum, Howard W. An American Epoch: Southern Portraiture in the National Picture. (BCL1 - United States Local History Ser.). 379p. 1991. reprint ed. lib. bdg. 89.00 (0-7812-6292-5) Rprt Serv.

— American Social Problems. LC 70-128283. (Essay Index Reprint Ser.). 1977. 44.95 (0-8369-1839-8) Ayer.

— Race & Rumors of Race: The American South in the Early Forties. LC 97-14450. 288p. 1997. reprint ed. pap. 14.95 (0-8018-5757-0) Johns Hopkins.

— Social & Mental Traits of the Negro. LC 68-56677. (Columbia University. Studies in the Social Sciences: No. 99). reprint ed. 29.50 (0-404-51099-X) AMS Pr.

Odum, Howard W., ed. Southern Pioneers in Social Interpretation. LC 67-23254. (Essay Index Reprint Ser.). 1977. 19.95 (0-8369-0750-7) Ayer.

Odum, Howard W. & Johnson, Guy B. Negro & His Songs: A Study of Typical Negro Songs in the South. LC 68-55902. 306p. 1969. reprint ed. lib. bdg. 65.00 (0-8371-0596-X, ODS&) Greenwood.

— Negro Workaday Songs. LC 78-89050. 278p. 1970. reprint ed. lib. bdg. 59.50 (0-8371-1938-3, ODW&) Greenwood.

— Negro Workaday Songs. 278p. 1990. reprint ed. lib. bdg. 69.00 (0-7812-9123-2) Rprt Serv.

Odum, Jeffery N. Sterile Product Facility Design & Project Management. (Illus.). 320p. 1996. ring bd. 194.00 (1-57491-020-5) Interpharm.

Odum, Mel. Croc 2: Prima's Official Strategy Guide. (Illus.). 122p. 1999. pap. 12.99 (0-7615-1571-2, Prima Games) Prima Pub.

O'Dunn. Earth. 1995. pap. text. write for info. (0-614-11774-7) P-H.

O'Dunn & Sill. Exploring Geology: Introductory Laboratory Activities. 292p. (C). 1988. pap. text 49.00 (0-13-295668-3) P-H.

O'Dunn, Shannon, jt. auth. see Sill, William D.

Oduyoye, Mercy Amda & Kanyoro, Musimbi R., eds. The Will to Arise: Women, Tradition & the Church in Africa. LC 91-45847. 1992. 18.00 (0-88344-782-7) Orbis Bks.

Oduyoye, Mercy Amda, jt. ed. see Fabella, Virginia.

Odwin, Charles S., et al. Appleton & Lange's Review for the Ultrasonography Examination. 2nd rev. ed. (Illus.). 584p. (C). 1998. pap. text 65.00 (0-8385-9073-X, A9073-6, Apple Lange Med) McGraw.

O'Dwyer. College Physics. (Physics Ser.). 1980. pap., teacher ed. write for info. (0-534-01972-0) Wadsworth Pub.

O'Dwyer, Barry W., tr. from LAT. Stephen of Lexington: Letters from Ireland, 1228-1229. (Cistercian Fathers Ser.: No. 28). Orig. Title: Registrum epistolarum Stephani de Lexinton abbatis de Stannlegia et de Saviagnaco. 1982. 24.95 (0-87907-428-0) Cistercian Pubns.

***O'Dwyer, Bernard.** Modern English Structures. 300p. 2000. pap. 26.95 (1-55111-273-6) Broadview Pr.

— Modern English Structures. 200p. 2000. pap. 17.95 (1-55111-275-2) Broadview Pr.

***O'Dwyer, Caley.** Full Nova. 64p. 2001. pap. 12.95 (0-914061-85-2) Orchises Pr.

O'Dwyer Co. Staff. O'Dwyer's Directory of Public Relations Executives. 2000. 664p. 2000. pap. 120.00 (0-941424-02-2) J R ODwyer.

O'Dwyer, Colm. Car Service Data 1998. 352p. 1997. 24.95 (1-85532-702-3, Pub. by Ospry) Stackpole.

O'Dwyer, Frederick. The Architecture of Deane & Woodward. LC 95-237791. (Illus.). 680p. 1997. 79.95 (0-902561-85-5, Pub. by Cork Univ) Stylus Pub VA.

O'Dwyer, George. Irish Catholic Genesis of Lowell. 80p. 1981. pap. 4.95 (0-942472-02-0) Lowell Museum.

O'Dwyer, J. R., Co., Inc. Staff. O'Dwyer's Directory of Corporate Communications, 1988. (Annual Ser.). 400p. 1999. pap. 130.00 (0-318-32475-X) J R ODwyer.

O'Dwyer, Jack. O'Dwyer's Directory of Public Relations Executives, 2000. 470p. 2000. 175.00 (0-317-62316-8) J R ODwyer.

O'Dwyer, James F. The Art of the Matador. LC 87-72377. (Illus.). 87p. 1988. 19.95 (0-87062-183-1) A H Clark.

O'Dwyer, John J. College Physics. 2nd ed. 808p. (C). 1984. mass mkt. 46.50 (0-534-02950-7) Wadsworth Pub.

O'Dwyer, Michael. Julien Green: A Critical Study. LC 97-101118. 276p. 1997. 45.00 (1-85182-275-5, Pub. by Four Cts Pr) Intl Spec Bk.

O'Dwyer, Peter. Mary: A History of Devotion in Ireland. 331p. 1999. reprint ed. text 25.00 (0-7881-6130-X) DIANE Pub.

— Towards a History of Irish Spirituality. 288p. (Orig.). 1995. pap. 17.95 (1-85607-124-3, Pub. by Columba Press) Whitecap Bks.

O'Dwyer, Tess, tr. see Blest Gana, Alberto.

Ody, Penelope. The Complete Medicinal Herbal. LC 92-53415. (Illus.). 192p. 1993. 29.95 (1-56458-187-X) DK Pub Inc.

***Ody, Penelope.** The Complete Medicinal Herbal. LC 00-25779. (Illus.). 2000. 29.95 (0-7894-6785-2) DK Pub Inc.

— Healing Herbs. LC 98-47382. 1999. 24.95 (1-58017-144-3) Storey Bks.

Ody, Penelope. Herbs for a Healthy Pregnancy. LC 99-33156. 192p. 1999. pap. 14.95 (0-87983-986-4, 39864K, Keats Publng) NTC Contemp Pub Co.

— Herbs for First Aid. LC 97-27554. 96p. 1997. mass mkt. 4.95 (0-87983-825-6, Keats Publng) NTC Contemp Pub Co.

— Herbs for First Aid. LC 99-14253. 128p. 1999. pap. 12.95 (0-87983-981-3, 39813K, Keats Publng) NTC Contemp Pub Co.

— Home Herbal. LC 94-26719. (Illus.). 144p. 1995. 19.95 (1-56458-863-7) DK Pub Inc.

***Ody, Penelope.** Making Time for Me: A Practical Guide to Getting Priorities Right. 1999. pap. 13.95 (1-85626-331-2, Pub. by Cathie Kyle) Trafalgar.

Ody, Penelope. Pocket Medicinal Herbs. LC 96-30991. 96p. 1997. pap. 9.95 (0-7894-1616-6) DK Pub Inc.

Odyniec, M. Solid State Microwave Oscillators. 1987. text. write for info. (0-442-23708-1, VNR) Wiley.

Odyniec, W. & Lewicki, G. Minimal Projections in Banach Spaces: Problems of Existence & Uniqueness & Their Application. (Lecture Notes in Mathematics Ser.: Vol. 1449). (Illus.). viii, 168p. 1990. 35.95 (0-387-53197-1) Spr-Verlag.

Odyssey Group Staff. The ZEV (Zero Emissions Vehicle) Book. (Illus.). 30p. (J). 1995. pap. text 4.00 (1-57074-248-0) Greyden Pr.

***Odyssey Publications Staff.** Autograph Collector Celebrity Autograph Authentication Guide. 1999. pap. text 22.95 (0-9669710-1-9) Odyssey Pubs.

— F. D. N. Y. 2000. 11.95 (962-217-659-3) China Guides.

Odzak, Larry L., ed. see Boylston, Raymond P., Jr.

Odzak, Larry L., ed. see Fortune, Gwen Y.

Odzer, Cleo. Goa Freaks: My Hippie Years in India. (Illus.). 336p. 1996. pap. 17.95 (1-56201-059-X) FoxRock.

— Patpong Sisters: An American Woman's View of the Bangkok Sex World. LC 94-15551. (Illus.). 320p. 1997. pap. 13.45 (1-55970-372-5, Pub. by Arcade Pub Inc) Time Warner.

— Patpong Sisters: Prostitution in Bangkok. LC 94-15551. (Illus.). 320p. 1994. 24.45 (1-55970-281-8, Pub. by Arcade Pub Inc) Time Warner.

— Virtual Spaces: Sex & the Cyber Citizen. LC 97-224016. 192p. 1997. pap. 14.00 (0-425-15986-8) Berkley Pub.

Odzer, Esther. Miss Rogan Poems. (Illus.). 96p. (Orig.). 1984. pap. 4.76 (0-9613572-0-7) E Odzer.

Oe, Emily & Mullen, Sherrie, eds. Kaleidoscope of Play Therapy Stories. LC 95-50408. 136p. 1996. 30.00 (1-56821-786-2) Aronson.

Oe, Kenzaburo. An Echo of Heaven. Mitsutani, Margaret, tr. from JPN. 240p. 1996. 25.00 (4-7700-1986-6) Kodansha.

***Oe, Kenzaburo.** Echo of Heaven. 2000. pap. 14.00 (4-7700-2505-X) Kodansha Intl.

Oe, Kenzaburo. A Healing Family. Shaw, S., ed. Snyder, Stephen, tr. (JPN., Illus.). 160p. 1996. 17.00 (4-7700-2048-1) Kodansha.

Oe, Kenzaburo. Hiroshima Notes. Swain, David L. & Yonezawa, Toshi, trs. (JPN.). 181p. 1995. 22.95 (0-7145-3007-7) M Boyars Pubs.

Oe, Kenzaburo. Hiroshima Notes. Swain, David L. & Yonezawa, Toshi, trs. from JPN. 192p. 1996. reprint ed. pap. 12.00 (0-8021-3464-5, Grove) Grove-Atltic.

— Japan, the Ambiguous & Myself: The Nobel Prize Speech & Other Lectures. (Illus.). 130p. 1995. 15.00 (4-7700-1980-7) Kodansha.

— Nip the Buds, Shoot the Kids: A Novel. Mackintosh, Paul S. & Sugiyama, Maki, trs. from JPN. 189p. 1995. 22.95 (0-7145-2997-4) M Boyars Pubs.

— Nip the Buds, Shoot the Kids: A Novel. Mackintosh, Paul S. & Sugiyama, Maki, trs. from JPN. 192p. 1996. reprint ed. pap. 11.00 (0-8021-3463-7, Grove) Grove-Atltic.

Oe, Kenzaburo. A Personal Matter. Nathan, John, tr. from JPN. LC 68-22007. 176p. 1970. pap. 10.00 (0-8021-5061-6, Grove) Grove-Atltic.

Oe, Kenzaburo. The Pinch Runner Memorandum. Wilson, Michiko N. & Wilson, Michael K., trs. from JPN. LC 93-16114. 265p. (C). (gr. 13). 1994. text 59.95 (1-56324-183-8, East Gate Bk); pap. text 21.95 (1-56324-184-6, East Gate Bk) M E Sharpe.

— A Quiet Life: A Novel. Yanagishita, Kunioki & Wetherall, William, trs. from JPN. 256p. 1998. pap. 12.00 (0-8021-3546-3, Grove) Grove-Atltic.

— Seventeen & J: Two Novels. 204p. 1996. pap. 17.95 (1-56201-091-3) FoxRock.

— Seventeen (The Political Being) & J (The Sexual Being) (Orig.). 1996. pap. 16.95 (1-56201-082-4) Blue Moon Bks.

— The Silent Cry. Shaw, S., ed. 288p. 1994. pap. 11.00 (4-7700-1965-3) Kodansha.

— The Silent Cry. Shaw, S., ed. Bester, John, tr. 284p. 1994. 25.00 (4-7700-0450-8) Kodansha.

— Teach Us to Outgrow Our Madness. Nathan, John, tr. from JPN. LC 76-54582. 288p. 1977. pap. 12.00 (0-8021-5185-X, Grove) Grove-Atltic.

Oe, Kenzaburo, ed. The Crazy Iris & Other Stories of the Atomic Aftermath. Morris, Ivan et al, trs. from JPN. LC 85-71162. 208p. 1985. reprint ed. pap. 11.00 (0-8021-5184-1, Grove) Grove-Atltic.

Oe, Kenzaburo, et al. The Catch & Other War Stories. LC 80-84420. 156p. 1995. pap. 9.00 (0-87011-457-3, L46) Kodansha.

***OECD.** The Appraisal of Investments in Educational Facilities. 236p. 1999. pap. 24.00 (92-64-17036-7, 952000011P, Pub. by Org for Econ) OECD.

— Basic Science & Technology Statistics 1999 Edition. 542p. 2000. pap. 87.00 (92-64-05882-6, 922000013OP, Pub. by Org for Econ) OECD.

— Investing in Education: Analysis of the 1999 World Education Indicators. 192p. 2000. pap. 31.00 (92-64-17183-5, 962000021P, Pub. by Org for Econ) OECD.

— Issues Related to Article 14 of the OECD Model Tax Convention. (Issues in International Taxation Ser.: 7). 48p. 2000. pap. 24.00 (92-64-17643-8, 232000531p, Pub. by Org for Econ) OECD.

OECD (Centre for Co-Operation with the Economies i, contrib. by. Reviews of National Science & Technology Policy: Poland. (ENG & FRE.). 171p. (Orig.). 1996. pap. 30.00 (92-64-14642-3, Pub. by Org for Econ) OECD.

OECD (Int. Energy Agency) Staff. Middle East Oil & Gas. LC 96-175042. (ENG & FRE.). 350p. (Orig.). 1996. pap. 105.00 (92-64-14387-4, Pub. by Org for Econ) OECD.

OECD (International Energy Agency) Staff, contrib. by. Comparing Energy Technologies. (ENG & FRE.). 336p. (Orig.). 1996. pap. 114.00 (92-64-14660-1, Pub. by Org for Econ) OECD.

OECD (Nuclear Energy Agency) Staff. Physics of Plutonium Recycling Vol. IV: Fast Plutonium-Burner Reactors: Beginning of Life. LC 96-123706. (ENG & FRE.). 66p. (Orig.). 1996. pap. 16.00 (92-64-14703-9, Pub. by Org for Econ) OECD.

— Physics of Plutonium Recycling Vol. V: Plutonium Recycling in Fast Reactors. LC 96-123706. (ENG & FRE.). 156p. (Orig.). 1996. pap. 37.00 (92-64-14704-7, Pub. by Org for Econ) OECD.

OECD (Nuclear Energy Agency) Staff, contrib. by. Radioactive Waste Management in Perspective: Nuclear Energy & Information. (ENG & FRE.). 142p. (Orig.). 1996. pap. 63.00 (92-64-14692-X, Pub. by Org for Econ) OECD.

OECD CERI Staff. Decision-Making in 14 OECD Education Systems. LC 96-147464. 136p. (Orig.). 1995. pap. 30.00 (92-64-14421-8, Pub. by Org for Econ) OECD.

— Schools under Scrutiny. LC 96-147461. 156p. (Orig.). 1995. pap. 40.00 (92-64-14567-2, Pub. by Org for Econ) OECD.

OECD Development Centre Staff. Single World, Divided Nations? International Trade & the OECD Labor Markets. LC 96-25252. 146p. 1996. 32.95 (0-8157-5186-9) Brookings.

OECD Int. Energy Agency Staff. Energy Policies of Slovenia, 1996 Survey. 128p. (Orig.). 1996. pap. 46.00 (92-64-14870-1, Pub. by Org for Econ) OECD.

OECD Int Energy Agency Staff & Coal Industry Advisory Board Staff. Factors Affecting the Take-up of Clean Coal Technologies: Overview Report. 68p. (Orig.). 1996. pap. 31.00 (92-64-14872-8, Pub. by Org for Econ) OECD.

OECD International Energy Agency Staff. Energy Policies of South Africa, 1996 Survey. 232p. (Orig.). 1996. pap. 94.00 (92-64-14785-3, Pub. by Org for Econ) OECD.

— Energy Policies of Ukraine, 1996 Survey. 204p. (Orig.). 1996. pap. 86.00 (92-64-14826-4, Pub. by Org for Econ) OECD.

OECD, International Energy Agency Staff. International Energy Technology Collaboration: Benefits & Achievements. (ENG & FRE.). 200p. (Orig.). 1996. pap. 65.00 (92-64-14772-1, Pub. by Org for Econ) OECD.

OECD NEA Staff. Trends in Nuclear Research Institutes. LC 96-185668. 200p. (Orig.). 1996. pap. 68.00 (92-64-14781-0, Pub. by Org for Econ) OECD.

OECD Nuclear Energy Agency. Information Policies of Nuclear Regulatory Organisations: Paris (France) Seminar, 6-8 December 1993, les Politiques d'Information des Organismes de Reglementation Nucleaire: Seminaire de Paris (France), 6-8 Decembre 1993. LC 95-161611. (ENG & FRE.). 223p. 1994. write for info. (92-64-04116-8) Org for Econ.

OECD Nuclear Energy Agency Staff & International Atomic Energy Agency Staff. Uranium, 1995 Resources, Production & Demans. 364p. (Orig.). 1996. pap. 86.00 (92-64-14875-2, Pub. by Org for Econ) OECD.

***OECD Staff.** Action Against Climate Change: The Kyoto Protocol & Beyond. 140p. 1999. pap. 21.00 (92-64-17113-4, 11 1999 03 1 P, Pub. by Org for Econ) OECD.

OECD Staff. Activities of Foreign Affiliates in OECD Countries: Statistical Data, 1985-1994. 272p. 1997. pap. 69.00 (92-64-05522-3, 92-97-06-3, Pub. by Org for Econ) OECD.

An Asterisk (*) at the beginning of an entry indicates that the title is appearing for the first time.

— Adjustment in OECD Agriculture: Reforming Farmland Policies. LC 98-144538. 88p. 1998. pap. 20.00 (*92-64-16027-2*, 51 98 01 1 P, Pub. by Org for Econ) OECD.

— Adult Learning & Technology in OECD Countries. 363p. (Orig.). 1996. pap. 49.00 (*92-64-15320-9*, 96-96-09-1) OECD.

— Advanced Logistics & Road Freight Transport. 184p. (Orig.). 1992. pap. 64.00 (*92-64-13730-0*) OECD.

***OECD Staff.** Agricultural Finance & Credit Infrastructure in Transition Economies: Proceedings of OECD Expert Meeting, Moscow, February 1999. (Proceedings Ser.). 400p. 1999. pap. 87.00 (*92-64-17069-3*, 14 1999 05 1 P, Pub. by Org for Econ) OECD.

OECD Staff. The Agricultural Outlook, 1998-2003. 116p. 1998. pap. 24.00 (*92-64-16028-0*, 51 98 02 1 P, Pub. by Org for Econ) OECD.

— Agricultural Policies in Emerging & Transition Economies: Monitoring & Evaluation 1998. 296p. 1998. pap. 48.00 (*92-64-16074-4*, 1498051P) OECD.

***OECD Staff.** Agricultural Policies in Emerging & Transition Economies, 1999: With Supplement Agriculture at a Glance in Emerging & Transition Economies. 304p. (Orig.). 1999. pap. 78.00 (*92-64-17058-8*, 14 1999 04 1 P, Pub. by Org for Econ) OECD.

— Agricultural Policies in OECD Countries, 1999: Monitoring & Evaluation. 276p. (Orig.). 1999. pap. 67.00 (*92-64-17034-0*, 51-1999-04-1P, Pub. by Org for Econ) OECD.

OECD Staff. Agricultural Policies in Transition Economies: Monitoring & Evaluation, 1997. 240p. 1997. pap. 37.00 (*92-64-15587-2*, 14-97-08-1, Pub. by Org for Econ) OECD.

— Agricultural Policy Reform & the Rural Economy in OECD Countries. LC 98-144334. 316p. 1998. pap. 43.00 (*92-64-16026-4*, 51 98 03 1 P, Pub. by Org for Econ) OECD.

— Agriculture & the Environment: Issues & Policies. 40p. 1998. pap. 8.00 (*92-64-16048-5*, 51 98 07 1 P, Pub. by Org for Econ) OECD.

***OECD Staff.** Agriculture in China & OECD Countries: Past Policies & Future Challenges. (OECD Proceedings Ser.). 332p. 1999. pap. 64.00 (*92-64-17094-4*, 14 1999 07 1 P, Pub. by Org for Econ) OECD.

OECD Staff. Agriculture, Pesticides, & the Environment: Policy Options. LC 98-133487. 72p. 1997. pap. 16.00 (*92-64-15673-9*, 97-97-20-1, Pub. by Org for Econ) OECD.

***OECD Staff.** The Agro-Food Processing Sector in China: Developments & Policy Changes. 336p. 2000. pap. 64.00 (*92-64-17179-7*, 14 200 01 1 P, Pub. by Org for Econ) OECD.

OECD Staff. Aid Activities in Africa,1997-1998. (Creditor Reporting System Ser.). 228p. 1999. pap. 32.00 (*92-64-05847-8*, 43 1999 56 3 P, Pub. by Org for Econ) OECD.

— Aid Activities in Africa, 1997-1998: Creditor Reporting System Gazette Special Edition. 96p. 1998. pap. 20.00 (*92-64-05830-3*, 4398563P) OECD.

***OECD Staff.** Aid Acitivities in Asia, 1997-1998. (Creditor Reporting System Ser.). 172p. (Orig.). 1999. pap. 32.00 (*92-64-05849-4*, 43 1999 58 3 P, Pub. by Org for Econ) OECD.

— Aid Activities in Europe & Oceania, 1997-1998. (Creditor Reporting System Ser.). 84p. (Orig.). 1999. pap. 21.00 (*92-64-05848-6*, 43-1999-57-3 P, Pub. by Org for Econ) OECD.

— Aid Activities in Latin America & the Caribbean, 1997-1998. (Creditor Reporting System Ser.). 172p. (Orig.). 1999. pap. 32.00 (*92-64-05851-6*, 43 1999 60 3 P, Pub. by Org for Econ) OECD.

— Aid Activities in South-East Europe 1990-1998. 116p. 1999. pap. 24.00 (*92-64-05871-0*, 43 1999 61 3 P, Pub. by Org for Econ) OECD.

— The Application of the OECD Model Tax Convention to Partnerships. (Issues in International Taxation Ser.: No. 6). 132p. 1999. pap. 34.00 (*92-64-17077-4*, 23 1999 52 1 P, Pub. by Org for Econ) OECD.

OECD Staff. Applying Market-Based Instruments to Environmental Policies in China & OECD Countries. LC 98-121838. (China in the Global Economy Ser.). 260p. 1998. pap. 45.00 (*92-64-15618-6*, 97-97-17-1, Pub. by Org for Econ) OECD.

***OECD Staff.** Asia & the Global Crisis: The Industrial Dimension. 148p. 1999. pap. 34.00 (*92-64-17099-5*, 92 1999 06 1 P, Pub. by Org for Econ) OECD.

— Assessing the Environmental Effects of Trade Liberalisation Agreements: Methodologies. 364p. 2000. pap. 72.00 (*92-64-17190-8*, 22 2000 01 1 P, Pub. by Org for Econ) OECD.

OECD Staff. Bank Profitability: Financial Statements of Banks, 1997 Edition. 352p. 1997. pap. 78.00 (*92-64-05534-7*, 21-97-07-3, Pub. by Org for Econ) OECD.

— Bank Profitability: Financial Statements of Banks, 1998 Edition. 410p. 1998. pap. 68.00 (*92-64-05816-8*, 21 98 06 3 P, Pub. by European Conference Ministers Transp) OECD.

***OECD Staff.** Bank Profitability: Financial Statements of Banks, 1999 Edition. 352p. 1999. 73.00 (*92-64-05857-5*, 21 1999 04 3 P, Pub. by Org for Econ) OECD.

— The Battle Against Exclusion: Social Assistance in Belgium, the Czech Republic, the Netherlands & Norway. 192p. 1998. pap. 23.00 (*92-64-16192-9*, 8198131P) OECD.

— The Battle Against Exclusion: Social Assistance in Canada & Switzerland. 184p. 1999. pap. 24.00 (*92-64-17108-8*, 81 1999 07 1 P, Pub. by Org for Econ) OECD.

OECD Staff. Behavioural Adaptations to Changes in the Road Transport System. 140p. 1990. pap. 26.00 (*92-64-13389-5*) OECD.

— Best Practice Policies for Small- & Medium-Sized Industries, 1996. 176p. (Orig.). 1997. pap. 49.00 (*92-64-15414-0*, 92-97-01-1, Pub. by Org for Econ) OECD.

— Best Practice Policies for Small & Medium-Sized Enterprises. 210p. 1995. pap. 67.00 (*92-64-14628-8*, Pub. by Org for Econ) OECD.

— Best Practice Policies for Small-& Medium-Sized Enterprises, 1997 Edition. 136p. 1998. pap. 36.00 (*92-64-16012-4*, 92 98 01 1, Pub. by Org for Econ) OECD.

— Bioremediation: The Tokyo '94 Workshop. LC 96-177633. 692p. (Orig.). 1995. pap. 116.00 (*92-64-14634-2*, Pub. by Org for Econ) OECD.

— Biotechnology for Clean Industrial Products & Processes: Towards Industrial Sustainability. 204p. 1998. pap. 53.00 (*92-64-16102-3*, 93 98 03 1 P, Pub. by European Conference Ministers Transp) OECD.

— Biotechnology for Water Use & Conservation: The Mexico '96 Workshop. 732p. 1997. pap. 78.00 (*92-64-15594-5*, 93-97-05-1, Pub. by Org for Econ) OECD.

***OECD Staff.** Boosting Innovation: The Cluster Approach. (OECD Proceedings Ser.). 428p. 1999. pap. 85.00 (*92-64-17080-4*, 92 1999 04 1 P, Pub. by Org for Econ) OECD.

OECD Staff. Budgeting for Results: Perspectives on Public Expenditure Management. 337p. (Orig.). 1995. pap. 73.00 (*92-64-14476-5*, Pub. by Org for Econ) OECD.

***OECD Staff.** Business Incubation: International Case Studies. 180p. 1999. pap. 39.00 (*92-64-17051-0*, 04 1999 03 1 P, Pub. by Org for Econ) OECD.

OECD Staff. Capital Market Development in Transition Economies: Country Experiences & Policies for the Future. LC 99-177185. (OECD Proceedings Ser.). 310p. 1998. pap. 65.00 (*92-64-16119-8*, 1498101P) OECD.

— Caring for Frail Elderly People: New Directions in Care. LC 94-234147. 143p. (Orig.). 1994. pap. 27.00 (*92-64-14160-X*) OECD.

— A Caring World: The New Social Policy Agenda. LC 99-198208. 160p. 1999. pap. 21.00 (*92-64-17007-3*, 81 1999 01 1 P, Pub. by Org for Econ) OECD.

— China in the 21st Century: Long-Term Global Implications. 140p. (Orig.). 1996. pap. 14.00 (*92-64-14924-4*, 03-96-05-1) OECD.

— China's Long March to an Open Economy. 120p. (Orig.). 1994. pap. 19.00 (*92-64-14290-8*) OECD.

— Cities for the 21st Century. LC 96-116333. 204p. (Orig.). 1994. pap. 39.00 (*92-64-14287-8*) OECD.

***OECD Staff.** Classifying Educational Programmes: Manual for ISCED-97 Implementation in OECD Countries--1999 Edition. 116p. 1999. pap. 43.00 (*92-64-17037-5*, 96 1999 04 1 P, Pub. by Org for Econ) OECD.

OECD Staff. Cleaner Production & Waste Minimisation in OECD & Dynamic Non-Member Economies. LC 98-121820. 264p. 1998. pap. 23.00 (*92-64-15686-0*, 97-97-23-1, Pub. by Org for Econ) OECD.

— Climate Change: Policy Initiatives. 184p. (Orig.). 1992. pap. 37.00 (*92-64-13754-8*) OECD.

— Climate Change, Economic Instruments & Income Distribution. LC 96-177630. (ENG & FRE.). 76p. (Orig.). 1996. pap. 19.00 (*92-64-14671-7*, Pub. by Org for Econ) OECD.

— Climate Change Policy Initiatives, 1994 Vol. 1: Update. LC 94-234113. 217p. (Orig.). 1994. pap. 53.00 (*92-64-14142-1*) OECD.

— CO2 Emissions from Transport. LC 98-121296. 212p. 1997. pap. 38.00 (*92-821-1225-X*, 75-97-06-1, Pub. by Org for Econ) OECD.

— Consumer Policy in OECD Countries: 1997 Edition. 152p. 1997. pap. 34.00 (*92-64-15604-6*, 24-97-03-1, Pub. by Org for Econ) OECD.

***OECD Staff.** Consumption Tax Trends, 1999 Edition. 100p. (Orig.). 1999. pap. 33.00 (*92-64-17035-9*, 23 1999 02 1 P, Pub. by Org for Econ) OECD.

OECD Staff. Continuing Professional Education of Highly-Qualified Personnel. LC 96-121952. 105p. (Orig.). 1995. pap. 32.00 (*92-64-14477-3*, Pub. by Org for Econ) OECD.

— Contracting Out Government Services: Best Practice Guidelines & Case Studies. LC 98-144612. (Public Management Occasional Papers: No. 20). 92p. 1998. pap. 12.00 (*92-64-15689-5*, 42-98-70-1, Pub. by Org for Econ) OECD.

— Controlled Foreign Company Legislation in OECD Member Countries. (Studies in Taxation of Foreign Source Income: No. 1). 164p. (Orig.). 1996. pap. 32.00 (*92-64-15337-3*, Pub. by Org for Econ) OECD.

— Coordinating Services for Children & Youth at Risk: A World View. LC 98-220386. 434p. 1998. pap. 47.00 (*92-64-16038-8*, 96 98 01 1 P, Pub. by European Conference Ministers Transp) OECD.

— Corporate Governance, State-Owned Enterprises & Privatisation. LC 98-150620. (Proceedings Ser.). 152p. 1998. pap. 13.00 (*92-64-16075-2*, 21 98 03 1 P, Pub. by Org for Econ) OECD.

— Creativity, Innovation, & Job Creation. LC 97-187951. 264p. (Orig.). 1997. pap. 20.00 (*92-64-15424-8*, 92-97-02-1, Pub. by Org for Econ) OECD.

— Cryptography Policy: The Guidelines & the Issues (The OECD Cryptography Policy Guidelines & the Report on Background & Issues of Cryptography Policy) 40p. 1998. pap. 8.00 (*92-64-16023-X*, 93 98 01 1 P, Pub. by Org for Econ) OECD.

— Decentralising Employment Policy: New Trends & Challenges (The Venice Conference) (OECD Proceedings Ser.). 252p. 1999. 46.00 (*92-64-17055-3*, Pub. by Org for Econ) OECD.

— Development Co-Operation Reviews: Canada, 1998. (Development Cooperation Review Ser.: No. 26). 84p. 1998. pap. 18.00 (*92-64-16098-1*, 43 98 10 1 P, Pub. by European Conference Ministers Transp) OECD.

— Development Co-Operation Reviews No. 27: Spain. 64p. 1998. pap. 18.00 (*92-64-16094-9*, 43 98 09 1 P, Pub. by European Conference Ministers Transp) OECD.

***OECD Staff.** Development Co-operation Reviews No. 33: Denmark 1999. 80p. (Orig.). 1999. pap. 20.00 (*92-64-17070-7*, 43-1999-05-1 P, Pub. by Org for Econ) OECD.

— Development Co-operation Reviews No. 34: Japan 1999. 112p. (Orig.). 1999. pap. 26.00 (*92-64-17085-5*, 43 1999 07 1 P, Pub. by Org for Econ) OECD.

— Development Co-Operation Reviews No. 35: Ireland. 100p. 1999. pap. 22.00 (*92-64-17118-5*, 43 1999 08 1 P, Pub. by Org for Econ) OECD.

OECD Staff. Development Co-operation Reviews Vol. 20: Germany, Vol. 29. (Development Cooperation Reviews Ser.). 72p. 1998. pap. 20.00 (*92-64-16152-X*, 4398151P) OECD.

***OECD Staff.** Development Cooperation Report 1998: Efforts & Policies of the Members of the Development Assistance Committee, 1999 Edition. 254p. 1999. pap. 38.00 (*92-64-17002-2*, 43 1999 02 1 P, Pub. by Org for Econ) OECD.

OECD Staff. Development Cooperation Review: Belgium. (Development Cooperation Review Ser.: No. 23). 48p. 1998. pap. 18.00 (*92-64-16031-0*, 43 98 03 1 P, Pub. by Org for Econ) OECD.

— Development Cooperation Review: France. (Development Cooperation Review Ser.: No. 21). 76p. 1997. pap. 18.00 (*92-64-15517-1*, 43-97-09-1, Pub. by Org for Econ) OECD.

— Development Cooperation Review: Netherlands, 1997, No. 24. 72p. 1998. pap. 18.00 (*92-64-16034-5*, 43 98 04 1 P, Pub. by Org for Econ) OECD.

— Development Cooperation Review: Portugal. (Development Cooperation Review Ser.: No. 22). 52p. 1998. pap. 18.00 (*92-64-15685-2*, 43-97-11-1, Pub. by Org for Econ) OECD.

— Development Cooperation Review, 1996: Switzerland. (Development Cooperation Review Ser.: No. 20). 64p. (Orig.). 1997. pap. 18.00 (*92-64-15458-2*, 43-97-04-1, Pub. by Org for Econ) OECD.

— Development Cooperation Reviews 1998: European Community. (Development Cooperation Reviews Ser.: No. 30). 128p. 1999. pap. 33.00 (*92-64-16965-2*, 43 98 17 1 P) Org for Econ.

— Development Cooperation Reviews Series: United Kingdom, 1997. (Development Cooperation Review Ser.: No. 25). 72p. 1998. pap. 18.00 (*92-64-16070-1*, 43 98 07 1 P, Pub. by Org for Econ) OECD.

***OECD Staff.** Developments in Steelmaking Capacity of Non-OECD Countries, 1999 Edition. 260p. 1999. pap. 62.00 (*92-64-05841-9*, 58 1999 02 3 P, Pub. by Org for Econ) OECD.

OECD Staff. Disabled Youth & Employment. 135p. (Orig.). 1994. pap. 13.00 (*92-64-14152-9*) OECD.

— Disposal of Radioactive Waste: Characterisation of Long-Term Geological Changes for Disposal Sites. 166p. (Orig.). 1996. pap. 40.00 (*92-64-14829-9*, Pub. by Org for Econ) OECD.

— Early Identification of Jobseekers at Risk of Long-Term Unemployment: The Role of Profiling. LC 98-150626. (Proceedings Ser.). 96p. 1998. pap. 16.00 (*92-64-16066-3*, 81 98 04 1 P, Pub. by Org for Econ) OECD.

— Eco-Efficiency. LC 98-144962. 88p. 1998. pap. 13.00 (*92-64-16085-X*, 97 98 07 1 P, Pub. by Org for Econ) OECD.

— Economic Accounts for Agriculture: 1997 Edition. 284p. 1997. pap. 47.00 (*92-64-05529-0*, 51-97-10-3, Pub. by Org for Econ) OECD.

***OECD Staff.** Economic Accounts for Agriculture: 1999 Edition. 340p. 1999. pap. 59.00 (*92-64-05862-1*, 30 1999 04 3 P, Pub. by Org for Econ) OECD.

OECD Staff. Economic Accounts for Agriculture, 1998 Edition. 284p. 1998. pap. 45.00 (*92-64-05767-6*, 30 98 04 3 P, Pub. by European Conference Ministers Transp) OECD.

— Economic Accounts of the European Union, 1996. 1997. 16.00 (*92-828-1881-0*, CA-07-97-466ENC, Pub. by Comm Europ Commun) Bernan Associates.

— Economic Instruments for Environmental Management in Developing Countries. 101p. (Orig.). 1993. pap. 11.00 (*92-64-13952-4*) OECD.

— Education & Employment. LC 95-217922. (FRE.). 110p. (Orig.). 1995. pap. 22.00 (*92-64-04357-8*, Pub. by Org for Econ) OECD.

— Education at a Glance: OECD Indicators 1998 Edition. 416p. 1998. pap. 49.00 (*92-64-16127-9*, 9698041P) OECD.

***OECD Staff.** Education at a Glance: OECD Indicators, 2000 Edition. 384p. 2000. pap. 42.00 (*92-64-17199-1*, 96 2000 04 1 P, Pub. by Org for Econ) OECD.

OECD Staff. Education Policy Analysis: 1998 Edition. 84p. 1998. pap. 20.00 (*92-64-16128-7*, 9698051P) OECD.

***OECD Staff.** Education Policy Analysis: 1999 Edition. 96p. 1999. pap. 20.00 (*92-64-17136-3*, 961999091P, Pub. by Org for Econ) OECD.

OECD Staff. Educational Research & Development: Austria, Germany, Switzerland. (ENG & FRE.). 82p. (Orig.). 1996. pap. 13.00 (*92-64-14554-0*, Pub. by Org for Econ) OECD.

— Educational Research & Development: Trends, Issues & Challenges. LC 96-147459. 180p. (Orig.). 1995. pap. 40.00 (*92-64-14553-2*, Pub. by Org for Econ) OECD.

— Effects of a Worldwide Liberalisation of the Markets for Cereals Oilseeds & Puls. 1997. 35.00 (*92-828-1812-8*, CA-07-97-385ENC, Pub. by Comm Europ Commun) Bernan Associates.

— Electricity Prices, 1990-1997. (E. C. Comprehensive Standing Order English Editions Ser.: Vol. 81450000). 100p. 1997. pap. 20.00 (*92-828-1808-X*, CA-08-97-7113AC, Pub. by Comm Europ Commun) Bernan Associates.

— Electricity Supply Industry: Structure, Ownership & Regulation. 350p. (Orig.). 1994. pap. 113.00 (*92-64-14222-3*) OECD.

— Employment & Growth in the Knowledge-Based Economy. LC 96-181877. 388p. (Orig.). 1996. pap. 60.00 (*92-64-14813-2*, Pub. by Org for Econ) OECD.

— Employment Outlook, June 1998. 224p. 1998. pap. 45.00 (*92-64-16077-9*, 81 98 06 1 P, Pub. by European Conference Ministers Transp) OECD.

***OECD Staff.** EMU: One Year On. (Economic Surveys Ser.). 192p. 2000. pap. 39.00 (*92-64-17639-X*, 11 2000 01 1 P, Pub. by Org for Econ) OECD.

— Energy: The Next Fifty Years. 164p. 1999. pap. 29.00 (*92-64-17016-2*, 03 1999 01 1 P, Pub. by Org for Econ) OECD.

OECD Staff. Energy in Developing Countries: A Sectoral Analysis. 130p. (Orig.). 1994. pap. 42.00 (*92-64-14135-9*) OECD.

— Energy Policies: The Czech & Slovak Federal Republic. 200p. (Orig.). 1992. pap. 46.00 (*92-64-13786-6*) OECD.

— Energy Policies in the Republic of Korea. 123p. (Orig.). 1993. pap. 38.00 (*92-64-13805-6*) OECD.

— Energy Policies of Hungary, 1995 Survey. 214p. (Orig.). 1995. pap. 69.00 (*92-64-14404-8*, Pub. by Org for Econ) OECD.

***OECD Staff.** Energy Policies of IEA Countries: Portugal 2000 Review. (Energy Policies of IEA Countries Ser.). 128p. 2000. pap. 75.00 (*92-64-17680-2*, 612000041P, Pub. by Org for Econ) OECD.

OECD Staff. Energy Policies of IEA Countries (Yr.) Review, 1993. 608p. (Orig.). 1994. pap. 112.00 (*92-64-14199-5*, ECD1995) Bernan Associates.

— Energy Policies of Poland, 1994 Survey. LC 96-117925. 227p. (Orig.). 1995. pap. 65.00 (*92-64-14410-2*, Pub. by Org for Econ) OECD.

— English-French Glossary of the Environment: Glossaire de l'Environnement Anglais-Francais. (ENG & FRE.). 300p. 1981. 35.00 (*0-8288-0940-2*, M14216) Fr & Eur.

***OECD Staff.** Environment in the Transition to a Market Economy: Progress in Central & Eastern Europe & the New Independent States. 248p. 1999. pap. 62.00 (*92-64-17110-X*, 14 1999 08 1 P, Pub. by Org for Econ) OECD.

OECD Staff. The Environment Industry: The Washington Meeting. LC 96-177632. (ENG & FRE.). 286p. (Orig.). 1996. pap. 51.00 (*92-64-14768-3*, Pub. by Org for Econ) OECD.

— Environmental Benefits from Agriculture: Issues & Policies. The Helsinki Seminar. 160p. 1997. pap. 19.00 (*92-64-15416-7*, 51-97-03-1, Pub. by Org for Econ) OECD.

— The Environmental Effects of Agricultural Land Diversion Schemes. LC 97-184948. 96p. (Orig.). 1997. pap. 19.00 (*92-64-15366-7*, 51-97-01-1, Pub. by Org for Econ) OECD.

— The Environmental Effects of Trade. LC 95-160313. (ENG & FRE.). 210p. (Orig.). 1994. pap. 44.00 (*92-64-14094-8*) OECD.

— Environmental Funds in Economies in Transition. (ENG & FRE.). 150p. (Orig.). 1996. pap. 26.00 (*92-64-14653-9*, Pub. by Org for Econ) OECD.

***OECD Staff.** The Environmental Goods & Services Industry: Manual for Data Collection & Analysis. 68p. 1999. pap. 21.00 (*92-64-17109-6*, 70 1999 03 1 P, Pub. by Org for Econ) OECD.

— Environmental Indicators for Agriculture Vol. 2: Issues & Design "The York Workshop" (OECD Proceedings Ser.). 216p. 1999. pap. 40.00 (*92-64-17041-3*, 51 1999 05 1 P, Pub. by Org for Econ) OECD.

OECD Staff. Environmental Learning for the 21st Century. LC 96-147460. 110p. (Orig.). 1995. pap. 31.00 (*92-64-14478-1*, Pub. by Org for Econ) OECD.

— Environmental Performance in OECD Countries: Progress in the 1990s. (ENG & FRE.). 66p. (Orig.). 1996. pap. 19.00 (*92-64-14769-1*, Pub. by Org for Econ) OECD.

— Environmental Performance Review: Belarus. (Environmental Performance Reviews Ser.). 142p. 1997. pap. 35.00 (*92-64-15626-7*, 97-97-18-1, Pub. by Org for Econ) OECD.

— Environmental Performance Reviews: Bulgaria. 165p. (Orig.). 1996. pap. 35.00 (*92-64-14797-7*, Pub. by Org for Econ) OECD.

***OECD Staff.** Environmental Performance Reviews: Czech Republic. (Environmental Performance Reviews Ser.). 204p. (Orig.). 1999. pap. 35.00 (*92-64-17009-X*, 97 1999 02 1 P, Pub. by Org for Econ) OECD.

OECD Staff. Environmental Performance Reviews: Denmark. (OECD Environmental Performance Reviews Ser.). 224p. 1999. pap. 35.00 (*92-64-17008-1*, 97 1999 01 1 P, Pub. by Org for Econ) OECD.

***OECD Staff.** Environmental Performance Reviews: Turkey. 188p. 1999. pap. 35.00 (*92-64-17106-1*, 97 1999 09 1 P, Pub. by Org for Econ) OECD.

OECD Staff. Environmental Policies & Industrial Competitiveness. 180p. (Orig.). 1993. pap. 20.00 (*92-64-03886-8*) OECD.

***OECD Staff.** Environmental Requirements for Industrial Permitting: Vol. 1 - Approaches & Instruments; Vol. 2 - OECD Workshop on the Use of Best Available Technologies & Environmental Quality Objectives, Paris, 9-11 May 1996; Vol. 3 - Regulatory Approaches in OECD Countries. 476p. 1999. pap. 97.00 (*92-64-16193-7*, 97 1999 03 1 P, Pub. by Org for Econ) OECD.

— Environmental Taxes: Recent Developments in China & OECD Countries. (China in the Global Economy Ser.). 328p. 1999. pap. 64.00 (*92-64-17092-8*, 97 1999 07 1 P, Pub. by Org for Econ) OECD.

O

An Asterisk (*) at the beginning of an entry indicates that the title is appearing for the first time.

OECD Staff. Evaluation & the Decision Making Process in Higher Education: French, German, & Spanish Experiences. 204p. (Orig.). 1995. pap. 20.00 (*92-64-14303-3*) OECD.

— Explanatory Report on the Convention on Mutual Administrative Assistance in Tax Matters. (Conventions & Agreements Ser.: No. 127). (ENG & FRE.). 96p. (Orig.). 1989. 21.00 (*92-871-1627-X*, 23-88-10-1, Pub. by Council of Europe) Manhattan Pub Co.

— The Export Credit Arrangement, 1978-1998: Achievements & Challenges. LC 98-150635. 172p. 1998. pap. 15.00 (*92-64-15695-X*, 22 98 53 1 P, Pub. by Org for Econ) OECD.

— The Export Credit Financing Systems in OECD Member & Non-Member Countries. 330p. (Orig.). 1995. pap. 115.00 (*92-64-14559-1*, Pub. by Org for Econ) OECD.

— Export Fruit Boom from the South: A Threat for the North? LC 97-106154. 100p. (Orig.). 1996. pap. 26.00 (*92-64-14898-1*, 51-96-05-1, Pub. by Org for Econ) OECD.

— External Debt Statistics, 1997: The Debt of Developing Countries & CEEC - NIS at End-December, 1995 & End-December, 1996. 34p. 1998. pap. 20.00 (*92-64-15677-1*, 43-97-10-1, Pub. by Org for Econ) OECD.

— External Debt Statistics, 1998 Edition: The Debt of Developing Countries & Countries in Transition at End-1997 & End-1996. 38p. 1998. pap. 34.00 (*92-64-16968-7*, 43 98 16 1 P, Pub. by Org for Econ) OECD.

— External Debt Statistics Supplement 1986/1997: Resource Flows, Debt Stocks & Debt Service, 1998 Edition. 216p. 1998. pap. 39.00 (*92-64-05769-2*, 43 98 11 3 P, Pub. by European Conference Ministers Transp) OECD.

***OECD Staff.** External Debt Statistics Supplement, 1987-1998: Resource Flows, Debt Stocks & Debt Service, 1999 Edition. 212p. (Orig.). 1999. pap. 42.00 (*92-64-05861-3*, 43 1999 06 3 P, Pub. by Org for Econ) OECD.

OECD Staff. Financial Accounts of OECD Countries: Canada, 1981-1996. (Financial Statistics Ser.). 56p. 1998. pap. 15.00 (*92-64-05545-2*, 20-97-33-3, Pub. by Org for Econ) OECD.

***OECD Staff.** Financial Market Trends: October 1999, No. 74. 196p. 1999. pap. 32.00 (*92-64-16165-1*, Pub. by Org for Econ) OECD.

OECD Staff. Financing Higher Education: Current Patterns. 100p. (Orig.). 1990. pap. 21.00 (*92-64-13422-0*) OECD.

***OECD Staff.** Financing Newly Emerging Private Enterprises in Transition Economies. (OECD Proceedings Ser.). 288p. 1999. pap. 61.00 (*92-64-16140-6*, 14 1999 01 1 P, Pub. by Org for Econ) OECD.

OECD Staff. Flows & Stocks of Fixed Capital, 1971-1996 (1997 Edition) 58p. 1998. pap. 23.00 (*92-64-05540-1*, 30-97-06-3-P, Pub. by Org for Econ) OECD.

— Food Safety Evaluation. 180p. (Orig.). 1996. pap. 36.00 (*92-64-14867-1*, Pub. by Org for Econ) OECD.

***OECD Staff.** Foreign Direct Investment & the Environment. (OECD Proceedings Ser.). 140p. 1999. pap. 29.00 (*92-64-17127-4*, 97 1999 12 1 P, Pub. by Org for Econ) OECD.

— Foreign Direct Investment Policy & Promotion in Latin America. 132p. 1999. pap. 34.00 (*92-64-17047-2*, 14 1999 10 1 P, Pub. by Org for Econ) OECD.

OECD Staff. Fostering Entrepreneurship. LC 98-222758. (OECD Jobs Strategy Ser.). 288p. 1998. pap. 29.00 (*92-64-16139-2*, 0498041P) OECD.

***OECD Staff.** Frameworks to Measure Sustainable Development. 168p. 2000. pap. 39.00 (*92-64-17191-6*, 03 2000 01 1 P, Pub. by Org for Econ) OECD.

— From Initial Education to Working Life: Making Transitions Work. 204p. 2000. pap. 37.00 (*92-64-17631-4*, 912000021P, Pub. by Org for Econ) OECD.

OECD Staff. Future Financial Liabilities of Nuclear Activities. LC 96-185667. 98p. (Orig.). 1996. pap. 42.00 (*92-64-14795-0*, Pub. by Org for Econ) OECD.

— Future Global Capital Shortages: Real Threat or Pure Fiction? LC 96-175619. 180p. (Orig.). 1996. pap. 62.00 (*92-64-14644-X*, Pub. by Org for Econ) OECD.

— The Future of Food: Long-Term Prospects for the Agro-Food Sector. LC 98-144643. 200p. 1998. pap. 24.00 (*92-64-15694-1*, 03-98-02-1, Pub. by Org for Econ) OECD.

***OECD Staff.** The Future of the Global Economy: Towards a Long Boom? 200p. 1999. pap. 24.00 (*92-64-17029-4*, 03-1999-02-1 P, Pub. by Org for Econ) OECD.

OECD Staff. Gateways to the Global Market: Consumers & Electronic Commerce. LC 98-184495. (Proceedings Ser.). 133p. 1998. pap. 12.00 (*92-64-16016-7*, 24-98-01-1, Pub. by Org for Econ) OECD.

— Geographical Distribution of Financial Flows to Aid Recipients, 1991-1995. 260p. 1997. pap. 69.00 (*92-64-05256-9*, 43-97-02-3, Pub. by Org for Econ) OECD.

— Geographical Distribution of Financial Flows to Aid Recipients, 1993-1997 (1999 Edition) 320p. 1999. pap. 69.00 (*92-64-05836-2*, 43-1999-01-3) Org for Econ.

***OECD Staff.** Geographical Distribution of Financial Flows to Aid Recipients 1994-1998: (2000 Edition) 324p. 2000. pap. 63.00 (*92-64-05884-2*, 43 2000 01 3 P, Pub. by Org for Econ) OECD.

OECD Staff. Geographical Distribution of Financial Flows to Aid Recipients, 1998 Edition. 272p. 1998. pap. 58.00 (*92-64-05544-4*, 43-98-02-3-P, Pub. by Org for Econ) OECD.

***OECD Staff.** Geological Disposal of Radioactive Waste: Review of Developments in the Last Decade. 108p. 2000. pap. 31.00 (*92-64-17194-0*, 66 1999 17 1 P, Pub. by Org for Econ) OECD.

OECD Staff. The Global Environmental Goods & Services Industry. LC 96-178379. (ENG & FRE.). 55p. (Orig.). 1996. pap. 16.00 (*92-64-14693-8*, Pub. by Org for Econ) OECD.

— The Global Human Genome Programme. 76p. (Orig.). 1995. pap. 21.00 (*92-64-14575-3*, Pub. by Org for Econ) OECD.

— Globalisation & Linkages to 2020: Challenges & Opportunities for OECD Countries: International High-Level Experts Meeting. LC 97-175959. 72p. (Orig.). 1996. pap. 10.00 (*92-64-15351-9*, 03-96-06-1) OECD.

— Globalisation & the Environment: Perspectives from OECD & Dynamic Non-Member Economies. 160p. 1998. pap. 17.00 (*92-64-16083-3*, 97 98 05 1 P, Pub. by Org for Econ) OECD.

***OECD Staff.** Glossary of Insurance Policy Terms. 128p. 1999. pap. 30.00 (*92-64-17083-9*, 14 1999 02 1 P, Pub. by Org for Econ) OECD.

OECD Staff. Governance in Transition: Public Management Reforms in OECD Countries. LC 96-147494. 247p. (Orig.). 1995. pap. 67.00 (*92-64-14486-2*, Pub. by Org for Econ) OECD.

— Guide for Government Officials & Carriers on the Use of the ECMT Multilateral Quota. 57p. (Orig.). 1995. pap. 16.00 (*92-821-0205-X*, Pub. by Org for Econ) OECD.

— Guidelines for the Security of Information Systems. LC 96-181840. 50p. (Orig.). 1996. pap. 17.00 (*92-64-14569-9*, Pub. by Org for Econ) OECD.

— Hazardous Air Pollutants: The London Workshop. LC 96-117532. 342p. (Orig.). 1995. pap. 47.00 (*92-64-14535-4*, Pub. by Org for Econ) OECD.

— Health Quality & Choice. (Health Policy Studies: No. 4). 140p. (Orig.). 1994. pap. 28.00 (*92-64-14213-4*) OECD.

— Historical Statistics, 1960-1995: 1997 Edition. 184p. 1997. pap. 38.00 (*92-64-05531-2*, 30-97-04-3, Pub. by Org for Econ) OECD.

— Household Production in OECD Countries: Data Sources & Measurement Methods. LC 96-121951. 57p. (Orig.). 1995. pap. 12.00 (*92-64-14564-8*, Pub. by Org for Econ) OECD.

— Human Capital Investment: An International Comparison. LC 98-180718. 116p. 1998. pap. 25.00 (*92-64-16067-1*, 96 98 02 1 P, Pub. by Org for Econ) OECD.

— Impacts of National Technology Programmes. 108p. (Orig.). 1995. pap. 42.00 (*92-64-14423-4*, Pub. by Org for Econ) OECD.

— Implementation Strategies for Environmental Taxes. LC 96-175059. (ENG & FRE.). 150p. (Orig.). 1996. pap. 46.00 (*92-64-14686-5*, Pub. by Org for Econ) OECD.

***OECD Staff.** Implementing Domestic Tradable Permits for Environmental Protection. (OECD Proceedings Ser.). 256p. 1999. pap. 69.00 (*92-64-17022-7*, 97 1999 04 1 , Pub. by Org for Econ) OECD.

— Implementing the OECD Jobs Strategy: Assessing Performance & Policy. 192p. 1999. pap. 25.00 (*92-64-17104-5*, 11 1999 02 1 P, Pub. by Org for Econ) OECD.

— Improving Access to Bank Information for Tax Purposes. 120p. 2000. pap. 66.00 (*92-64-17649-7*, 23 2000 03 1 P, Pub. by Org for Econ) OECD.

— Improving the Environment Through Reducing Subsidies: Case Studies. 270p. 2000. pap. 54.00 (*92-64-17093-6*, 97 1999 08 1 P, Pub. by Org for Econ) OECD.

OECD Staff. Improving the Environment Through Reducing Subsidies: Summary & Conclusions: Analysis & Overview of Studies, Pts. I & II. LC 98-180529. 130p. 1998. pap. 30.00 (*92-64-16091-4*, 97 98 09 1 P, Pub. by Org for Econ) OECD.

***OECD Staff.** Indicators of Industrial Activity Supplement: Sources & Methods, Quantitative Indicators. 196p. 1999. pap. 40.00 (*92-64-16191-0*, 37 98 05 1 P, Pub. by Org for Econ) OECD.

OECD Staff. Indicators of Tariff & Non-Tariff Trade Barriers, 1997. LC 98-161994. 78p. 1998. pap. 26.00 (*92-64-15665-8*, 11-97-03-1, Pub. by Org for Econ) OECD.

— Industrial Competitiveness in the Knowledge-Based Economy: The New Role of Governments. LC 98-162001. 256p. 1997. pap. 32.00 (*92-64-15679-8*, 70-97-03-1, Pub. by Org for Econ) OECD.

***OECD Staff.** Industrial Structure Statistics, Vols. 1 & 2. 796p. 2000. pap. 96.00 (*92-64-05887-7*, 30 2000 01 3 P , Pub. by Org for Econ) OECD.

— Industrial Structure Statistics, 1999 Edition, Vols. 1 & 2. 706p. 1999. pap. 101.00 (*92-64-05854-0*, 30 1999 03 3 P, Pub. by Org for Econ) OECD.

OECD Staff. Industrial Structure Statistics, 1994 (1996 Edition) 432p. (Orig.). 1996. pap. 84.00 (*92-64-04835-9*, 70-96-04-3, Pub. by Org for Econ) OECD.

— Industrial Structure Statistics, 1995: 1997 Edition. 450p. 1997. pap. 84.00 (*92-64-05527-4*, 70-97-02-3, Pub. by Org for Econ) OECD.

— Information Technology & the Future of Post-Secondary Education. 140p. (Orig.). 1996. pap. 22.00 (*92-64-14923-6*, 96-96-04-1) OECD.

— Inland Waterway Transport in ECMT Countries to the Year 2000: A New Dimension. 123p. (Orig.). 1990. pap. 24.00 (*92-821-1148-2*) OECD.

— Innovation, Patents & Technological Strategies. (ENG & FRE.). 236p. (Orig.). 1996. pap. 72.00 (*92-64-14661-X*, Pub. by Org for Econ) OECD.

— Institutional Investors in the New Financial Landscape. LC 98-198189. (OECD Proceedings Ser.). 492p. 1998. pap. 57.00 (*92-64-15980-0*, 21 98 02 1 P, Pub. by European Conference Ministers Transp) OECD.

***OECD Staff.** Institutional Investors Statistical Yearbook, 1998. 344p. 1999. pap. 69.00 (*92-64-05855-9*, 21 1999 03 3 P, Pub. by Org for Econ) OECD.

OECD Staff. Insurance Statistics Yearbook, 1989/1996 (1998 Edition) 320p. 1998. pap. 78.00 (*92-64-05763-3*, 21 98 04 3 P, Pub. by European Conference Ministers Transp) OECD.

***OECD Staff.** Insurance Statistics Yearbook 1990/1997 (1999 Edition) 316p. 1999. pap. 83.00 (*92-64-05858-3*, 21 1999 05 3 P, Pub. by Org for Econ) OECD.

OECD Staff. INT Standardisation of Fruit & Vegetables: Kiwifruit. 68p. (Orig.). 1992. pap. 30.00 (*92-64-03697-0*) OECD.

— Integrated Traffic Safety Management in Urban Areas. (Road Transport Research Ser.). 122p. (Orig.). 1990. pap. 25.00 (*92-64-13317-8*) OECD.

— Integrating Services for Children at Risk: Denmark, France, Netherlands, Sweden, United Kingdom (England & Wales) LC 96-181844. 86p. (Orig.). 1996. pap. 17.00 (*92-64-14791-8*, Pub. by Org for Econ) OECD.

***OECD Staff.** Integrating Transport in the City: Reconciling the Economic, Social & Environment Dimensions. 124p. 2000. pap. 22.00 (*92-64-17120-7*, 04 2000 02 1 P, Pub. by Org for Econ) OECD.

OECD Staff. International Direct Investment Statistics Yearbook, 1997. 420p. 1997. pap. 65.00 (*92-64-05535-5*, 21-97-08-3, Pub. by Org for Econ) OECD.

— International Direct Investment Statistics Yearbook, 1998. 440p. 1998. pap. 70.00 (*92-64-05821-4*, 2198073P) OECD.

***OECD Staff.** International Direct Investment Statistics Yearbook, 1999. 452p. 2000. pap. 79.00 (*92-64-05892-3*, 21 2000 01 3 P, Pub. by Org for Econ) OECD.

OECD Staff. International Standardisation of Fruit & Vegetables: Lettuces, Curled-Leaf Endives & Broad-Leaved (Batavian) Endives. (Illus.). 108p. 1996. pap. 20.00 (*92-64-04844-8*, 51-96-04-3, Pub. by Org for Econ) OECD.

— International Standardisation of Fruit & Vegetables: Unshelled Sweet Almonds, Unshelled Hazelnuts. (Illus.). 84p. (Orig.). 1981. pap. text 18.00 (*92-64-02230-9*, 51-81-09-3) OECD.

— International Standardization of Fruit & Vegetables: Aubergines. 55p. (Orig.). 1987. pap. 15.00 (*92-64-02930-3*) OECD.

***OECD Staff.** International Standardization of Fruit & Vegetables: Carrots. (International Standardization of Fruits & Vegetables Ser.). 76p. 2000. pap. 20.00 (*92-64-05890-7*, 512000013P, Pub. by Org for Econ) OECD.

OECD Staff. International Standardization of Fruit & Vegetables: Onions. rev. ed. 50p. 1984. pap. 14.00 (*92-64-02495-6*) OECD.

— International Standardization of Fruit & Vegetables: Witloof Chicories. 84p. (Orig.). 1994. pap. 20.00 (*92-64-04117-6*) OECD.

— International Trade in Professional Services: Assessing Barriers & Encouraging Reform. LC 96-181876. 322p. (Orig.). 1996. pap. 59.00 (*92-64-14873-6*, Pub. by Org for Econ) OECD.

— Internationalisation of Higher Education. LC 96-209135. 140p. (Orig.). 1996. pap. 19.00 (*92-64-15288-1*, 96-96-07-1, Pub. by Org for Econ) OECD.

— Internationalisation of Industrial R&D: Patterns & Trends. LC 99-177203. 108p. 1998. pap. 28.00 (*92-64-16189-9*, 7098041P) OECD.

— Investing in Biological Diversity: The Cairns Conference. LC 97-203232. 408p. 1997. pap. 47.00 (*92-64-15502-3*, 97-97-06-1, Pub. by Org for Econ) OECD.

— Investment Guide for Kazakhstan. LC 98-222759. 164p. 1998. pap. 33.00 (*92-64-16108-2*, 1498081P) OECD.

— Investment Guide for Latvia. LC 98-180896. 235p. 1998. pap. 40.00 (*92-64-16059-0*, 14 98 03 1 P, Pub. by European Conference Ministers Transp) OECD.

— Investment Guide for Lithuania. 164p. 1998. pap. 54.00 (*92-64-16123-6*, 1498121P) OECD.

— Iron & Steel Industry in 1996. 52p. 1998. pap. 20.00 (*92-64-05548-7*, 58-98-01-3-P, Pub. by Org for Econ) OECD.

— Iron & Steel Industry in 1997 (1999 Edition) 52p. 1999. pap. 34.00 (*92-64-05837-0*, 58 1999 01 3 P) Org for Econ.

***OECD Staff.** Iron & Steel Industry in 1998: (2000 Edition) 48p. 2000. pap. 32.00 (*92-64-05883-4*, 58 2000 01 3 P, Pub. by Org for Econ) OECD.

OECD Staff. Issues & Developments in Public Management Survey, 1996-1997. LC 97-199638. 328p. (Orig.). 1997. pap. 69.00 (*92-64-15452-3*, 42-97-01-1, Pub. by Org for Econ) OECD.

— Issues in Education in Asia & the Pacific: An International Perspective. Huges, Philip, ed. LC 94-233543. 196p. (Orig.). 1994. pap. 24.00 (*92-64-14095-6*, 96-94-02-1) OECD.

— Knowledge Bases for Education Policies. LC 96-209136. 170p. (Orig.). 1996. pap. 37.00 (*92-64-14895-7*, 96-96-03-1, Pub. by Org for Econ) OECD.

***OECD Staff.** Knowledge Management in the Learning Society. 260p. 2000. pap. 51.00 (*92-64-17182-7*, 96 2000 01 1 P 1, Pub. by Org for Econ) OECD.

— Labour Force Statistics: 1978/1998, 1999 Edition. 352p. 2000. pap. 72.00 (*92-64-05881-8*, 30 1999 09 3 P, Pub. by Org for Econ) OECD.

OECD Staff. Labour Force Statistics, 1976-1996: 1997 Edition. 592p. 1997. pap. 97.00 (*92-64-05536-3*, 30-97-05-3, Pub. by Org for Econ) OECD.

***OECD Staff.** Labour Force Statistics 1977/1997: 1998 Edition. 588p. 1999. pap. 98.00 (*92-64-05801-X*, 30 98 06 3 P, Pub. by Org for Econ) OECD.

OECD Staff. The Labour Market & Older Workers. LC 96-149704. (Social Policy Studies: No. 17). (ENG & FRE.). 365p. (Orig.). 1996. pap. 64.00 (*92-64-14585-0*, Pub. by Org for Econ) OECD.

— Labour Market & Social Policies in the Slovak Republic. LC 96-231284. 180p. (Orig.). 1996. pap. 40.00 (*92-64-14830-2*, 14-96-10-1, Pub. by Org for Econ) OECD.

— Labour Market Policies in Slovenia. LC 97-224704. 96p. 1997. pap. 19.00 (*92-64-15606-2*, 14-97-09-1, Pub. by Org for Econ) OECD.

***OECD Staff.** Labour Migration & the Recent Financial Crisis in Asia. 248p. 2000. pap. 48.00 (*92-64-17173-8*, 81 2000 01 1 P, Pub. by Org for Econ) OECD.

OECD Staff. Library Association Guidelines for Secondary School Libraries. LC 99-204565. 84p. 1998. 35.00 (*1-85604-278-2*, LAP2782, Pub. by Library Association) Bernan Associates.

— Lifelong Learning for All: Meeting of the Education Committee at Ministerial Level, 16-17 January 1996. LC 96-231285. 230p. (Orig.). 1996. pap. 50.00 (*92-64-14815-9*, Pub. by Org for Econ) OECD.

— Macroeconomic Policies & Structural Reform. 344p. 1996. pap. 42.00 (*92-64-15326-8*, Pub. by Org for Econ) OECD.

— Macrothesaurus for Information Processing in the Field of Economic & Social Development. 5th ed. LC 98-197885. 436p. 1998. pap. 67.00 (*92-64-16025-6*, 40 98 01 1 P, Pub. by European Conference Ministers Transp) OECD.

— Main Economic Indicators: Sources & Definitions. 160p. 1997. pap. 32.00 (*92-64-15602-X*, 31-97-17-1, Pub. by Org for Econ) OECD.

— Main Economic Indicators Sources & Methods: Interest Rates & Share Price Indices. LC 98-157133. 68p. 1998. pap. 18.00 (*92-64-16036-1*, 31-98-14-1, Pub. by Org for Econ) OECD.

— Maintaining Prosperity in an Ageing Society. LC 98-186025. 128p. 1998. pap. 20.00 (*92-64-16093-0*, Pub. by Org for Econ) OECD.

— Making the Curriculum Work. LC 99-176975. 128p. 1998. pap. 20.00 (*92-64-16141-4*, 9698061P) OECD.

— Making Work Pay: Taxation, Benefits, Employment & Unemployment. LC 98-100529. (Jobs Study Ser.). 100p. 1997. pap. 19.00 (*92-64-15666-6*, 21-97-09-1, Pub. by Org for Econ) OECD.

***OECD Staff.** Managing National Innovation Systems. 120p. 1999. pap. 32.00 (*92-64-17038-3*, 92 1999 03 1 P, Pub. by Org for Econ) OECD.

OECD Staff. Managing Structural Deficit Reduction. LC 97-121224. (PUMA Occasional Papers: No. 11). 204p. (Orig.). 1996. pap. 30.00 (*92-64-15294-6*, 42-96-61-1, Pub. by Org for Econ) OECD.

— Managing the Environment with Rapid Industrialisation: Lessons from the East Asian Experience. 218p. (Orig.). 1994. pap. 27.00 (*92-64-14181-2*) OECD.

— Maritime Transport, 1995: (1997 Edition) 180p. (Orig.). 1997. pap. 35.00 (*92-64-15411-6*, 76-97-01-1, Pub. by Org for Econ) OECD.

— Market Access after the Uruguay Round: Investment, Competition & Technology Perspectives. 225p. (Orig.). 1996. pap. 48.00 (*92-64-14823-X*, Pub. by Org for Econ) OECD.

— The Marketing of Traffic Safety. 120p. (Orig.). 1993. pap. 35.00 (*92-64-13903-6*) OECD.

OECD Staff. The Measurement of Scientific & Technical Activities: Proposed Standard Practice for Surveys of Research & Development - Frascati Manual, 1993. 5th ed. 262p. 1994. pap. 71.00 (*92-64-14202-9*) OECD.

— Measuring Student Knowledge & Skills: The PISA 2000 Assessment of Reading, Mathematical & Scientific Literacy. 108p. 2000. pap. 20.00 (*92-64-17646-2*, 96 2000 05 1 P, Pub. by Org for Econ) OECD.

OECD Staff. Measuring What People Know: Human Capital Accounting for the Knowledge Economy. LC 96-181863. 114p. (Orig.). 1996. pap. 29.00 (*92-64-14778-0*, Pub. by Org for Econ) OECD.

— Methods of Privatising Large Enterprises. 208p. (Orig.). 1993. pap. 36.00 (*92-64-03709-8*) OECD.

— Migration & Regional Economic Integration in Asia. LC 98-121824. (Proceedings Ser.). 180p. 1998. pap. 16.00 (*92-64-16039-6*, 81-98-01-1-P, Pub. by Org for Econ) OECD.

— Migration & the Labour Market in Asia: Prospects to the Year 2000. LC 96-175582. (ENG & FRE.). 250p. (Orig.). 1996. pap. 40.00 (*92-64-14775-6*, Pub. by Org for Econ) OECD.

— Model Tax Convention: Four Related Studies. 104p. (Orig.). 1992. pap. 24.00 (*92-64-13801-3*) OECD.

— Model Tax Convention on Income & on Capital June 1998, Condensed Version. 308p. 1998. pap. 35.00 (*92-64-16115-5*, 23 98 51 1 P, Pub. by European Conference Ministers Transp) OECD.

— Multilingual Dictionary of Fish & Fish Products. 1990. pap. 69.95 (*0-8288-7920-6*) Fr & Eur.

— Multilingual Dictionary of Fish & Fish Products. 1990. 180.00 (*0-7855-6946-4*) St Mut.

— Multilingual Dictionary of Fish & Fish Products. 4th ed. 480p. 1995. 59.95 (*0-85238-216-2*) Blackwell Sci.

— National Accounts Vol. I: Main Aggregates, 1960-1995. 166p. (Orig.). 1997. pap. 43.00 (*92-64-05258-5*, 30-97-02-3, Pub. by Org for Econ) OECD.

— National Accounts Vol. I: Main Aggregates, 1960-1996. 180p. 1998. pap. 38.00 (*92-64-05550-9*, 30-98-01-3-P, Pub. by Org for Econ) OECD.

***OECD Staff.** National Accounts Vol. 1: Main Aggregates, 1960-1997 (1999 Edition) 180p. 1999. pap. 53.00 (*92-64-05840-0*, 30 1999 01 3 P, Pub. by Org for Econ) OECD.

OECD Staff. National Accounts Vol. II: Detailed Tables, 1984-1996. 676p. 1998. pap. 142.00 (*92-64-05770-6*, 30 98 05 3 P, Pub. by European Conference Ministers Transp) OECD.

— National Accounts ESA - Detailed Tables by Branch, 1970-1995. (E. C. Non Subscription Comp. Multilingual

An Asterisk (*) at the beginning of an entry indicates that the title is appearing for the first time.

En/Fr Ser.: Vol. 81411000). 173p. 1997. pap. 50.00 (*92-828-1510-2*, CA-08-97-3473AC, Pub. by Comm Europ Commun) Bernan Associates.

*__OECD Staff.__ National Accounts of OECD Countries Vol. 1: Main Aggregates, 1988-1998. 316p. 2000. pap. 71.00 (*92-64-05891-5*, 30 2000 03 3 P, Pub. by Org for Econ) OECD.

— National Climate Policies & the Kyoto Protocol. 88p. 1999. pap. 21.00 (*92-64-17114-2*, 971999101P, Pub. by Org for Econ) OECD.

OECD Staff. National Policies & Agricultural Trade: Finland. 168p. (Orig.). 1989. pap. text 15.00 (*92-64-13240-6*, 51-89-04-1) OECD.

— National Systems for Financing Innovation. 120p. (Orig.). 1995. pap. 40.00 (*92-64-14627-X*, Pub. by Org for Econ) OECD.

— Networks of Enterprises & Local Development. LC 97-135359. 256p. (Orig.). 1997. pap. 43.00 (*92-64-15312-8*, 04-96-09-1, Pub. by Org for Econ) OECD.

— New Directions in Health Care Policies: Improving Cost Control & Effectiveness. LC 96-147497. (Health Care Policy Studies: No. 7). 15p. (Orig.). 1995. pap. 34.00 (*92-64-14545-1*, Pub. by Org for Econ) OECD.

— New Forms of Work Organisation Can Europe Realise Its Potential? Results of a Su. LC 98-125537. 1997. 45.00 (*92-828-1888-8*, SX-09-07-002ENC, Pub. by Comm Europ Commun) Bernan Associates.

— The New Paradigm of Systemic Competitiveness: Toward More Integrated Policies in Latin America. 272p. 1994. pap. 29.00 (*92-64-14259-2*) OECD.

— New Ways of Managing Infrastructure Provision. 200p. (Orig.). 1994. pap. 23.00 (*92-64-14306-8*) OECD.

— The New World Trading System: Readings. 240p. (Orig.). 1994. pap. 29.00 (*92-64-14245-2*) OECD.

*__OECD Staff.__ Development Cooperation Reviews: Norway 1999. 120p. 2000. pap. 22.00 (*92-64-17169-X*, 43 2000 02 1 P, Pub. by Org for Econ) OECD.

OECD Staff. Novel Systems for the Study of Human Disease. LC 98-146020. 400p. 1998. pap. 26.00 (*92-64-16011-6*, 93-98-02-1-P, Pub. by Org for Econ) OECD.

— OECD Agricultural Outlook 1999-2004 (1999 Edition) 152p. 1999. pap. 32.00 (*92-64-16964-4*, Pub. by Org for Econ) OECD.

*__OECD Staff.__ OECD Agricultural Outlook 2000/2005 (2000 Edition) 196p. 2000. pap. 31.00 (*92-64-17641-1*, 51 2000 03 1 P, Pub. by Org for Econ) OECD.

OECD Staff. OECD & ASEAN Economies: The Challenge of Policy Coherence. Fukasaku, K. et al, eds. LC 96-117520. 236p. (Orig.). 1995. pap. 38.00 (*92-64-14482-X*, Pub. by Org for Econ) OECD.

— OECD Benchmark Definition of Foreign Direct Investment. 3rd ed. 58p. (Orig.). 1996. pap. 17.00 (*92-64-15283-0*, 21-96-08-1, Pub. by Org for Econ) OECD.

— OECD Communications Outlook 1999. 256p. 1999. pap. 71.00 (*92-64-17013-8*, 93 1999 02 1 P, Pub. by Org for Econ) OECD.

— OECD Economic Outlook No. 62: December, 1997. 224p. 1997. pap. 35.00 (*92-64-15377-2*, 12-97-62-1, Pub. by Org for Econ) OECD.

— OECD Economic Survey: Switzerland, 1995-1996. 176p. (Orig.). 1996. pap. 26.00 (*92-64-14913-9*, 10-96-26-1, Pub. by Org for Econ) OECD.

*__OECD Staff.__ OECD Economic Survey: Turkey 1999. 184p. 1999. pap. 26.00 (*92-64-16986-5*, Pub. by Org for Econ) OECD.

OECD Staff. OECD Economic Surveys: Australia, 1998. (Economic Surveys Ser.). 188p. 1997. pap. 25.00 (*92-64-15984-3*, 10-98-04-1, Pub. by Org for Econ) OECD.

— OECD Economic Surveys: Australia 1999. (Economic Surveys Ser.). 184p. 1998. pap. 26.00 (*92-64-16971-7*, 10 1999 04 1 P, Pub. by Org for Econ) OECD.

*__OECD Staff.__ OECD Economic Surveys: Australia 2000. 180p. 2000. pap. 30.00 (*92-64-17504-0*, 10 2000 04 1 P, Pub. by Org for Econ) OECD.

OECD Staff. OECD Economic Surveys: Austria, 1997. 208p. (Orig.). 1997. pap. 25.00 (*92-64-15430-2*, 10-97-11-1, Pub. by Org for Econ) OECD.

— OECD Economic Surveys: Austria 1997-1998. (Economic Surveys Ser.). 144p. 1999. pap. 25.00 (*92-64-15989-4*, 10 98 11 1 P, Pub. by Org for Econ) OECD.

*__OECD Staff.__ OECD Economic Surveys: Austria 1999. 148p. (Orig.). 1999. pap. 26.00 (*92-64-16984-9*, 10-1999-11-1P, Pub. by Org for Econ) OECD.

OECD Staff. OECD Economic Surveys: Belgium-Luxembourg, 1997. (Economic Surveys Ser.). 232p. 1997. pap. 25.00 (*92-64-15440-X*, 10-97-29-1, Pub. by Org for Econ) OECD.

— OECD Economic Surveys: Belgium/Luxembourg 1999. (Economic Surveys Ser.). 204p. 1999. pap. 26.00 (*92-64-16970-9*, 10 1999 29 1 P) Org for Econ.

— OECD Economic Surveys: Bulgaria, 1997. 156p. (Orig.). 1997. pap. 25.00 (*92-64-15426-4*, 10-97-35-1, Pub. by Org for Econ) OECD.

— OECD Economic Surveys: Bulgaria 1999. 124p. 1999. pap. 26.00 (*92-64-17052-9*, 10 1999 35 1 P, Pub. by Org for Econ) OECD.

— OECD Economic Surveys: Canada, 1995-1996. 192p. (Orig.). 1996. pap. 26.00 (*92-64-15339-X*, 10-96-01-1, Pub. by Org for Econ) OECD.

— OECD Economic Surveys: Canada, 1997. (Economic Surveys Ser.). 148p. 1997. pap. 23.00 (*92-64-13427-2*, 10-97-01-1, Pub. by Org for Econ) OECD.

— OECD Economic Surveys: Czech Republic, 1998. 156p. 1998. pap. 25.00 (*92-64-15992-4*, 10 98 32 1 P, Pub. by European Conference Ministers Transp) OECD.

*__OECD Staff.__ OECD Economic Surveys: Czech Republic 2000. 232p. 2000. pap. 30.00 (*92-64-17532-6*, 10 2000 32 1 P, Pub. by Org for Econ) OECD.

OECD Staff. OECD Economic Surveys: Denmark 1999. (Economic Surveys Ser.). 164p. 1999. pap. 26.00 (*92-64-16977-6*, 10 1999 13 1 P, Pub. by Org for Econ) OECD.

— OECD Economic Surveys: Finland, 1998. 156p. 1998. pap. 25.00 (*92-64-15996-7*, 10 98 31 1 P, Pub. by European Conference Ministers Transp) OECD.

*__OECD Staff.__ OECD Economic Surveys: Finland 1999. (Economic Surveys Ser.). 148p. (Orig.). 1999. pap. 26.00 (*92-64-16989-X*, 10 1999 31 1 P, Pub. by Org for Econ) OECD.

— OECD Economic Surveys: France 1999. (Economic Surveys Ser.). 188p. 1999. pap. 26.00 (*92-64-16978-4*, 10 1999 14 1 P, Pub. by Org for Econ) OECD.

OECD Staff. OECD Economic Surveys: Germany, 1998. 180p. 1998. pap. 25.00 (*92-64-15993-2*, 10 98 15 1 P, Pub. by European Conference Ministers Transp) OECD.

— OECD Economic Surveys: Greece 1998. (Economic Surveys Ser.). 200p. 1999. pap. 25.00 (*92-64-16002-7*, 10 98 16 1 P) Org for Econ.

— OECD Economic Surveys: Hungary 1999. (Economic Surveys Ser.). 164p. 1999. pap. 26.00 (*92-64-16979-2*, 10 1999 30 1, Pub. by Org for Econ) OECD.

— OECD Economic Surveys: Iceland, 1998. 128p. 1998. pap. 25.00 (*92-64-15991-6*, 10 98 17 1 P, Pub. by Org for Econ) OECD.

*__OECD Staff.__ OECD Economic Surveys: Ireland 1999. 172p. 1999. pap. 26.00 (*92-64-16985-7*, Pub. by Org for Econ) OECD.

OECD Staff. OECD Economic Surveys: Italy, 1997. 176p. (Orig.). 1997. pap. 25.00 (*92-64-15436-1*, 10-97-19-1, Pub. by Org for Econ) OECD.

— OECD Economic Surveys: Italy 1999. (Economic Surveys Ser.). 156p. 1999. pap. 26.00 (*92-64-16969-5*, 10 1999 19 1 P, Pub. by Org for Econ) OECD.

— OECD Economic Surveys: Japan, 1995-1996. 246p. (Orig.). 1997. pap. 26.00 (*92-64-15341-1*, 10-96-03-1, Pub. by Org for Econ) OECD.

— OECD Economic Surveys: Japan, 1997. (Economic Surveys Ser.). 198p. 1997. pap. 25.00 (*92-64-15429-9*, 10-97-03-1, Pub. by Org for Econ) OECD.

— OECD Economic Surveys: Korea 1998. 212p. 1998. pap. 25.00 (*92-64-15997-5*, 1098391P) OECD.

*__OECD Staff.__ OECD Economic Surveys: Korea 1999. (OECD Economic Surveys Ser.). 204p. 1999. pap. 26.00 (*92-64-16991-1*, 10 1999 39 1 P, Pub. by Org for Econ) OECD.

OECD Staff. OECD Economic Surveys: Mexico, 1997. 180p. (Orig.). 1997. pap. 25.00 (*92-64-15412-4*, 92-64-15412-4, Pub. by Org for Econ) OECD.

— OECD Economic Surveys: Mexico, 1998. (Economic Surveys Ser.). 156p. 1998. pap. 25.00 (*92-64-15983-5*, 10-98-40-4-P, Pub. by Org for Econ) OECD.

— OECD Economic Surveys: Mexico 1999. 188p. 1999. pap. 26.00 (*92-64-16981-4*, Pub. by Org for Econ) OECD.

— OECD Economic Surveys: Netherlands, 1998. 180p. 1998. pap. 25.00 (*92-64-15985-1*, 10 98 21 1 P, Pub. by Org for Econ) OECD.

— OECD Economic Surveys: New Zealand, 1998. (Economic Surveys Ser.). 196p. 1998. pap. 25.00 (*92-64-15990-8*, 10 98 05 1 P, Pub. by Org for Econ) OECD.

— OECD Economic Surveys: New Zealand 1999. 152p. 1999. pap. 26.00 (*92-64-16983-0*, 10-1999-05-1-P, Pub. by Org for Econ) OECD.

— OECD Economic Surveys: Norway, 1997. 172p. (Orig.). 1997. pap. 25.00 (*92-64-15437-X*, 10-97-22-1, Pub. by Org for Econ) OECD.

— OECD Economic Surveys: Norway, 1998. 140p. 1998. pap. 25.00 (*92-64-15987-8*, 10 98 22 1 P, Pub. by Org for Econ) OECD.

*__OECD Staff.__ OECD Economic Surveys: Norway 1999. 160p. 1999. pap. 26.00 (*92-64-16980-6*, 10 1999 22 1, Pub. by Org for Econ) OECD.

— OECD Economic Surveys: Norway 2000. 156p. 2000. pap. 30.00 (*92-64-17522-9*, 10 2000 22 1 P, Pub. by Org for Econ) OECD.

OECD Staff. OECD Economic Surveys: Poland, 1996-1997. 188p. (Orig.). 1996. pap. 25.00 (*92-64-15359-4*, 10-97-34-1, Pub. by Org for Econ) OECD.

— OECD Economic Surveys: Poland, 1998. 168p. 1998. pap. 25.00 (*92-64-15995-9*, 10 98 34 1 P, Pub. by European Conference Ministers Transp) OECD.

*__OECD Staff.__ OECD Economic Surveys: Poland 2000. 208p. 2000. pap. 30.00 (*92-64-17534-2*, 10 2000 34 1 P, Pub. by Org for Econ) OECD.

OECD Staff. OECD Economic Surveys: Portugal, 1998. (Economic Surveys Ser.). 128p. 1998. pap. 25.00 (*92-64-15982-7*, 10-98-23-1-P, Pub. by Org for Econ) OECD.

*__OECD Staff.__ OECD Economic Surveys: Portugal 1999. (OECD Economic Surveys Ser.). 162p. 1999. pap. 26.00 (*92-64-16992-X*, 10 1999 23 1 P, Pub. by Org for Econ) OECD.

OECD Staff. OECD Economic Surveys: Romania, 1998. 179p. 1998. pap. 25.00 (*92-64-16006-X*, 10 98 38 1 P, Pub. by Org for Econ) OECD.

— OECD Economic Surveys: Russian Federation, 1997. (Economic Surveys Ser.). 282p. 1997. pap. 25.00 (*92-64-15981-9*, 10-97-37-1, Pub. by Org for Econ) OECD.

*__OECD Staff.__ OECD Economic Surveys: Slovak Republic 1999. 156p. 1999. pap. 26.00 (*92-64-17001-4*, 10 1999 33 1 P, Pub. by Org for Econ) OECD.

OECD Staff. OECD Economic Surveys: Spain, 1998. 208p. 1998. pap. 25.00 (*92-64-15988-6*, 10 98 24 1 P, Pub. by Org for Econ) OECD.

*__OECD Staff.__ OECD Economic Surveys: Spain 2000. 184p. 2000. pap. 30.00 (*92-64-17524-5*, 10 2000 24 1 P, Pub. by Org for Econ) OECD.

OECD Staff. OECD Economic Surveys: Sweden, 1996-1997. 236p. (Orig.). 1997. pap. 25.00 (*92-64-15420-5*, 10-97-25-1, Pub. by Org for Econ) OECD.

— OECD Economic Surveys: Sweden, 1998. 196p. 1998. pap. 25.00 (*92-64-15986-X*, 10 98 25 1 P, Pub. by Org for Econ) OECD.

*__OECD Staff.__ OECD Economic Surveys: Sweden 1999. 186p. (Orig.). 1999. pap. 26.00 (*92-64-16988-1*, 10 99 25 1 P, Pub. by Org for Econ) OECD.

OECD Staff. OECD Economic Surveys: Switzerland, 1997. 172p. 1997. pap. 25.00 (*92-64-15438-8*, 10-97-26-1, Pub. by Org for Econ) OECD.

*__OECD Staff.__ OECD Economic Surveys: Switzerland 1999. 192p. (Orig.). 1999. pap. 26.00 (*92-64-16987-3*, 10 1999 26 1 P, Pub. by Org for Econ) OECD.

— OECD Economic Surveys: The Baltic States. A Regional Economic Assessment 2000. 280p. 2000. pap. 30.00 (*92-64-17541-5*, 10 2000 41 1 P, Pub. by Org for Econ) OECD.

OECD Staff. OECD Economic Surveys: United Kingdom, 1998. 196p. 1998. pap. 25.00 (*92-64-15994-0*, 10 98 28 1 P, Pub. by European Conference Ministers Transp) OECD.

— OECD Economic Surveys: United States, 1997. (Economic Surveys Ser.). 224p. 1997. pap. 25.00 (*92-64-15428-0*, 10-97-02-1, Pub. by Org for Econ) OECD.

— OECD Economic Surveys: United States 1999. 220p. (Orig.). 1999. pap. 26.00 (*92-64-16982-2*, 10-1999-02-1P, Pub. by Org for Econ) OECD.

*__OECD Staff.__ OECD Economic Surveys: United States, 2000. 2000. pap. 30.00 (*92-64-17502-4*, Pub. by Org for Econ) OECD.

OECD Staff. OECD Economics Surveys: Germany, 1997. 184p. 1997. pap. 25.00 (*92-64-15433-7*, 10-97-15-1, Pub. by Org for Econ) OECD.

— OECD Economies at a Glance: Structural Indicators. LC 96-183215. 144p. (Orig.). 1996. pap. 39.00 (*92-64-14805-1*, Pub. by Org for Econ) OECD.

*__OECD Staff.__ OECD Employment Outlook, June 1999. 256p. 1999. pap. 55.00 (*92-64-17063-4*, Pub. by Org for Econ) OECD.

OECD Staff. OECD Environmental Data Compendium, 1997. 292p. 1997. pap. 50.00 (*92-64-05539-8*, 97-97-19-3, Pub. by Org for Econ) OECD.

— OECD Environmental Performance Review: Australia, 1997. (Environmental Performance Reviews Ser.). 212p. 1998. pap. 35.00 (*92-64-16044-2*, 97 98 02 1 P, Pub. by Org for Econ) OECD.

— OECD Environmental Performance Review: Finland. (Environmental Performance Reviews Ser.). 204p. 1997. pap. 35.00 (*92-64-15593-7*, 97-97-16-1, Pub. by Org for Econ) OECD.

— OECD Environmental Performance Review: Mexico, 1997. 220p. 1998. pap. 35.00 (*92-64-16045-0*, 97 98 01 1 P, Pub. by Org for Econ) OECD.

— OECD Environmental Performance Review: Sweden. 150p. (Orig.). 1996. pap. 35.00 (*92-64-15280-6*, 97-96-11-1) OECD.

— OECD Environmental Performance Reviews: Belgium. 228p. 1998. pap. 35.00 (*92-64-16131-7*, 9798101P) OECD.

— OECD Environmental Performance Reviews: France. LC 97-181080. 175p. (Orig.). 1997. pap. 35.00 (*92-64-15443-4*, 97-97-03-1, Pub. by Org for Econ) OECD.

*__OECD Staff.__ OECD Environmental Performance Reviews: Greece. (OECD Environmental Performance Reviews Ser.). 208p. 2000. pap. 32.00 (*92-64-17189-4*, 97 2000 02 1 P, Pub. by Org for Econ) OECD.

OECD Staff. OECD Environmental Performance Reviews: Switzerland. 228p. 1998. pap. 35.00 (*92-64-16132-5*, 9798111P) OECD.

OECD Staff. OECD Guidelines for Testing of Chemicals, 2 vols., Set. 1994. ring bd. 323.00 (*92-64-14018-2*) OECD.

OECD Historical Statistics: 1960/1997 (1999 Edition) 184p. 2000. pap. 40.00 (*92-64-05880-X*, 30 1999 08 3 P, Pub. by Org for Econ) OECD.

OECD Staff. The OECD Input-Output Database. LC 96-147474. (ENG & FRE.). 438p. (Orig.). 1996. pap. 67.00 (*92-64-04612-7*, Pub. by Org for Econ) OECD.

— The OECD International Education Indicators. 118p. (Orig.). 1992. pap. 23.00 (*92-64-13726-2*) OECD.

— The OECD Jobs Strategy: Enhancing the Effectiveness of Active Labour Market Policies. 52p. (Orig.). 1996. pap. 13.00 (*92-64-14908-2*, 81-96-07-1) OECD.

— OECD Jobs Strategy: Technology, Productivity & Job Creation - Best Policy Practices. LC 98-204250. 328p. 1998. pap. 50.00 (*92-64-16096-5*, 92 98 05 1 P, Pub. by European Conference Ministers Transp) OECD.

— The OECD Jobs Study: Evidence & Explanations. 400p. (Orig.). 1994. pap. 60.00 (*92-64-14241-X*) OECD.

*__OECD Staff.__ OECD Principles of Corporate Governance. 48p. 1999. pap. 20.00 (*92-64-17126-6*, 21 1999 06 1 P, Pub. by Org for Econ) OECD.

OECD Staff. OECD Report on Regulatory Reform: Synthesis Report. LC 98-121690. 64p. 1997. pap. 7.00 (*92-64-15556-2*, 42-97-05-1, Pub. by Org for Econ) OECD.

— OECD Report on Regulatory Reform Vols. I & II: Sectoral Studies & Thematic Studies. LC 98-121318. 664p. 1997. pap. 47.00 (*92-64-15519-8*, 42-97-04-1, Pub. by Org for Econ) OECD.

— OECD Review of Agricultural Policies: Slovak Republic. 248p. 1997. pap. 46.00 (*92-64-15568-6*, 14-97-06-1, Pub. by Org for Econ) OECD.

— OECD Reviews of Foreign Direct Investment: Argentina. 68p. 1997. pap. 15.00 (*92-64-15497-3*, 21-97-51-1, Pub. by Org for Econ) OECD.

— OECD Reviews of Foreign Direct Investment: Brazil. 84p. 1998. pap. 20.00 (*92-64-16097-3*, 21 98 51 1 P, Pub. by European Conference Ministers Transp) OECD.

— OECD Reviews of National Policies for Education: Russian Federation. (Reviews of National Policies for Education Ser.). 176p. 1998. pap. 30.00 (*92-64-16058-2*, 91 98 03 1 P, Pub. by Org for Econ) OECD.

*__OECD Staff.__ OECD Science, Technology & Industry Scoreboard 1999: Benchmarking Knowledge-Based Economics. 180p. 1999. pap. 43.00 (*92-64-17107-X*, 92 1999 07 1 P, Pub. by Org for Econ) OECD.

— The OECD STAN Database for Industrial Analysis 1970/1997: 1998 Edition. 376p. 1999. pap. 79.00 (*92-64-05832-X*, 92 1999 01 3 P, Pub. by Org for Econ) OECD.

OECD Staff. OECD Tourism Statistics: Design & Application for Policy. 100p. (Orig.). 1996. pap. 24.00 (*92-64-15327-6*, 78-96-02-1) OECD.

— Open Markets Matter. 176p. 1998. pap. 20.00 (*92-64-16100-7*, 22 98 01 1 P, Pub. by Org for Econ) OECD.

— Overcoming Failure at School. 100p. 1998. pap. 25.00 (*92-64-16151-1*, 9198041P) OECD.

— Participatory Development from Advocacy to Action. Schneider, Hartmut & Libercier, Marie-Helene, eds. 250p. (Orig.). 1995. pap. 50.00 (*92-64-14539-7*, Pub. by Org for Econ) OECD.

— Partnership in the United States: OECD Reviews of Rural Policy. (Reviews of Rural Policy Ser.). 152p. 1997. pap. 25.00 (*92-64-15467-1*, 04-97-02-1, Pub. by Org for Econ) OECD.

— Pathways & Participation in Vocational & Technical Education & Training. LC 98-145090. 396p. 1998. pap. 47.00 (*92-64-15368-3*, 91-98-01-1-P, Pub. by Org for Econ) OECD.

*__OECD Staff.__ Physics & Fuel Performance of Reactor-Based Plutonium Disposition. (OECD Proceedings Ser.). 236p. (Orig.). 1999. pap. 70.00 (*92-64-17050-2*, 66 1999 07 1 P, Pub. by Org for Econ) OECD.

— Policies Towards Full Employment. (Proceedings Ser.). 224p. 2000. pap. 45.00 (*92-64-17661-6*, 03 2000 03 1 P, Pub. by Org for Econ) OECD.

OECD Staff. Policy Evaluation in Innovation & Technology: Towards Best Practices. LC 98-121817. (Proceedings Ser.). 468p. 1998. pap. 27.00 (*92-64-15697-6*, 92-97-10-1, Pub. by Org for Econ) OECD.

— Population & Development Directory of Non-Governmental Organisations in OECD Countries. 360p. (Orig.). 1994. pap. 73.00 (*92-64-04171-0*) OECD.

*__OECD Staff.__ Preparing Youth for the 21st Century: The Transition from Education to the Labour Market: Proceedings of the Washington D. C. Conference, 23-24 February 1999. (OECD Proceedings Ser.). 504p. 1999. pap. 60.00 (*92-64-17076-6*, 91 1999 03 1 P, Pub. by Org for Econ) OECD.

— The Price of Water: Trends in OECD Countries. 176p. 1999. pap. 29.00 (*92-64-17079-0*, 97 1999 06 1, Pub. by Org for Econ) OECD.

— Private Pension Systems & Policy Issues. (Private Pensions Ser.: No. 1). 396p. 2000. pap. 78.00 (*92-64-17634-9*, 21 2000 03 1 P, Pub. by Org for Econ) OECD.

OECD Staff. Private Pensions & Public Policy. 160p. (Orig.). 1992. pap. 35.00 (*92-64-13790-4*) OECD.

— Private Pensions in OECD Countries: The United States. LC 94-183544. 100p. (Orig.). 1993. pap. 22.00 (*92-64-13802-1*) OECD.

*__OECD Staff.__ Privatisation, Competition & Regulation. 216p. 2000. pap. 55.00 (*92-64-17115-0*, 14 2000 02 1 P, Pub. by Org for Econ) OECD.

OECD Staff. Product Liability Rules in OECD Countries. LC 96-161803. 58p. (Orig.). 1995. pap. 18.00 (*92-64-14439-0*, Pub. by Org for Econ) OECD.

— Proposed Guidelines for Collecting & Interpreting Technological Innovation Data: The Oslo Manual. LC 97-180546. (Measurement of Scientific & Technological Activities Ser.). 124p. (Orig.). 1997. pap. 23.00 (*92-64-15464-7*, 92-97-03-1, Pub. by Org for Econ) OECD.

— Public Employment Service: Belgium. LC 97-120045. 140p. 1997. pap. 20.00 (*92-64-15496-5*, 81-97-01-1, Pub. by Org for Econ) OECD.

— The Public Employment Service: Denmark, Finland, Italy. LC 96-181857. 218p. (Orig.). 1996. pap. 50.00 (*92-64-14777-2*, Pub. by Org for Econ) OECD.

— The Public Employment Service: Greece, Ireland, Portugal. LC 99-204589. 264p. 1998. pap. 36.00 (*92-64-16133-3*, 8198091P) OECD.

— The Public Employment Service in Austria, Germany, & Sweden. LC 97-120045. 126p. (Orig.). 1996. pap. 18.00 (*92-64-14930-9*, 81-96-09-1) OECD.

— Public Management: OECD Country Profiles. 470p. (Orig.). 1993. pap. 80.00 (*92-64-13809-9*) OECD.

— Purchasing Power Parities & Real Expenditures EKS Results, 1993 Vol. 1. (ENG & FRE.). 72p. (Orig.). 1995. pap. 29.00 (*92-64-04491-4*, Pub. by Org for Econ) OECD.

*__OECD Staff.__ Purchasing Power Parties & Real Expenditures: 1996 Results (1999 Edition) 168p. 2000. pap. 42.00 (*92-64-05823-0*, 30 1999 06 3 P, Pub. by Org for Econ) OECD.

OECD Staff. Purchasing Power Parities & Real Expenditures Vol. II. GK Results 1993. (ENG & FRE.). 92p. (Orig.). 1996. pap. 32.00 (*92-64-04761-1*, Pub. by Org for Econ) OECD.

— Putting Markets to Work: The Design & Use of Marketable Permits & Obligations. LC 98-144605. (Public Management Occasional Papers: No. 19). 52p. 1998. pap. 7.00 (*92-64-15615-1*, 42-97-69-1, Pub. by Org for Econ) OECD.

***OECD Staff.** Quality & Internationalisation in Higher Education. 272p. 1999. pap. 40.00 (92-64-17049-9, 89 1999 10 1 P, Pub. by Org for Econ) OECD.

OECD Staff. Quality in Teaching. 130p. (Orig.). 1994. pap. 23.00 (92-64-14242-8) OECD.

— Radiation Protection for Emergency Workers the Principles of Ionizing Radiation: Radiation Protection 79. LC 98-196593. 135p. 1997. 45.00 (92-828-1505-6, CR-88-95-929ENC, Pub. by Comm Europ Commun) Bernan Associates.

— Reconciling Trade, Environment, & Development Policies: The Role of Development Cooperation. LC 97-168266. 152p. (Orig.). 1996. pap. 20.00 (92-64-15362-4, 43-96-20-1, Pub. by Org for Econ) OECD.

— Redefining the Place to Learn. (Programme on Educational Building Ser.). 172p. (Orig.). 1995. pap. 37.00 (92-64-14563-X, Pub. by Org for Econ) OECD.

— Redefining the State in Latin America. LC 94-233203. 273p. (Orig.). 1994. pap. 42.00 (92-64-14089-1) OECD.

***OECD Staff.** Reduction of Capital Costs of Nuclear Power Plants. 110p. 2000. pap. 38.00 (92-64-17144-4, 66 2000 03 1 P, Pub. by Org for Econ) OECD.

OECD Staff. Reforming Energy & Transport Subsidies. LC 98-121323. 171p. 1997. pap. 37.00 (92-64-15681-X, 97-97-22-1, Pub. by Org for Econ) OECD.

— A Regional Approach to Industrial Restructuring in the Tomsk Region, Russian Federation. (OECD Proceedings Ser.). 512p. 1998. pap. 65.00 (92-64-16101-5, 14 98 07 1 P, Pub. by European Conference Ministers Transp) OECD.

— Regional Co-Operation & Integration in Asia. Fukasaku, K., ed. 260p. (Orig.). 1995. pap. 48.00 (92-64-14645-8, Pub. by Org for Econ) OECD.

— Regional Integration & Transition Economies: The Case of the Baltic Rim. 212p. (Orig.). 1996. pap. 29.00 (92-64-14929-5, 14-96-11-1, Pub. by Org for Econ) OECD.

— Regionalism & Its Place in the Multilateral Trading System. LC 96-181869. 275p. (Orig.). 1996. pap. 46.00 (92-64-14831-0, Pub. by Org for Econ) OECD.

— Regulatory Reform & International Market Openness. 296p. (Orig.). 1996. pap. 37.00 (92-64-15313-6, 22-96-06-1, Pub. by Org for Econ) OECD.

***OECD Staff.** Regulatory Reform in Korea. (OECD Reviews of Regulatory Reform Ser.). 332p. 2000. 60.00 (92-64-17663-2, 422000021P, Pub. by Org for Econ) OECD.

— Regulatory Reform in Mexico. (OECD Reviews of Regulatory Reform Ser.). 330p. 2000. pap. 69.00 (92-64-17100-2, 42 1999 05 1 P, Pub. by Org for Econ) OECD.

OECD Staff. Regulatory Reform in the Global Economy: Asian & Latin American Perspectives. LC 98-186409. (OECD Proceedings Ser.). 144p. 1998. pap. 20.00 (92-64-16103-1, 22 98 02 1 P, Pub. by European Conference Ministers Transp) OECD.

***OECD Staff.** Regulatory Reform in the Netherlands. (OECD Reviews of Regulatory Reform Ser.). 284p. 1999. pap. 60.00 (92-64-17074-X, P, Pub. by Org for Econ) OECD.

— Regulatory Reform in the United States. (OECD Reviews of Regulatory Reform Ser.). 356p. 1999. pap. 74.00 (92-64-17075-8, 42 1999 03 1 P, Pub. by Org for Econ) OECD.

OECD Staff. Repairing Bridge Substructures. LC 96-123798. (Road Transport Research Ser.). 124p. (Orig.). 1995. pap. 34.00 (92-64-14542-7, Pub. by Org for Econ) OECD.

— Research & Development in Industry: Expenditure & Researchers, Scientists & Engineers, 1975-96. 140p. 1998. pap. 42.00 (92-64-05761-7, 70 98 03 3 P, Pub. by European Conference Ministers Transp) OECD.

***OECD Staff.** Research & Development in Industry, 1976-1997: Expenditure & Researchers, Scientists & Engineers. 156p. (Orig.). 1999. pap. 60.00 (92-64-05845-1, 70 1999 01 3 P, Pub. by Org for Econ) OECD.

OECD Staff. Revenue Statistics, 1965-1996. 280p. 1997. pap. 63.00 (92-64-05521-5, 23-97-03-3, Pub. by Org for Econ) OECD.

— Revenue Statistics, 1965/1997. 272p. 1998. pap. 65.00 (92-64-05766-8, 23 98 06 3 P, Pub. by European Conference Ministers Transp) OECD.

— Review of Agricultural Policies: Hungary. LC 95-105705. 222p. (Orig.). 1994. pap. 49.00 (92-64-14055-7) OECD.

***OECD Staff.** Review of Agricultural Policies: Korea. (National Policies & Agricultural Trade Ser.). 176p. (Orig.). 1999. pap. 30.00 (92-64-17012-X, 51 1999 02 1 P, Pub. by Org for Econ) OECD.

OECD Staff. Review of Agricultural Policies: Latvia. 240p. (Orig.). 1996. pap. 50.00 (92-64-15349-7, 14-96-13-1) OECD.

— Review of Agricultural Policies: Lithuania. 238p. (Orig.). 1996. pap. 50.00 (92-64-15350-0, 14-96-14-1) OECD.

— Review of Agricultural Policies in Mexico. (National Policies & Agricultural Trade Ser.). 252p. 1997. pap. 57.00 (92-64-15486-8, 51-97-09-1, Pub. by Org for Econ) OECD.

***OECD Staff.** Review of Fisheries in OECD Countries: Policies & Summary Statistics: Country Statistics (1999 Edition), 2 vols. 720p. 2000. pap. 129.00 (92-64-17180-0, Pub. by Org for Econ) OECD.

OECD Staff. Review of Fisheries in OECD Countries, 1995 (1997 Edition) 408p. 1998. pap. 89.00 (92-64-15494-9, 53-97-02-1, Pub. by Org for Econ) OECD.

— Reviews of National Policies for Education: Austria. 106p. (Orig.). 1995. pap. 30.00 (92-64-14394-7, Pub. by Org for Econ) OECD.

— Reviews of National Policies for Education: Greece. LC 97-145103. 216p. (Orig.). 1997. pap. 30.00 (92-64-15365-9, 91-97-03-1, Pub. by Org for Econ) OECD.

— Reviews of National Policies for Education: Italy. LC 98-222376. 120p. 1998. pap. 20.00 (92-64-16112-0, 9198061P) OECD.

— Reviews of National Policies for Education: Korea. LC 98-180889. 208p. 1998. pap. 25.00 (92-64-16063-9, 91 98 05 1 P, Pub. by Org for Econ) OECD.

— Reviews of National Policies for Education: Mexico. LC 97-180594. 228p. (Orig.). 1997. pap. 29.00 (92-64-15423-X, 91-97-02-1, Pub. by Org for Econ) OECD.

***OECD Staff.** Reviews of National Policies for Education: Romania. (Reviews of National Policies for Education Ser.). 172p. 2000. pap. 25.00 (92-64-17635-7, 14 2000 05 1 P, Pub. by Org for Econ) OECD.

OECD Staff. Reviews of National Policies for Education Denmark "Educating Youth" LC 96-161351. 126p. (Orig.). 1995. pap. 24.00 (92-64-14475-7, Pub. by Org for Econ) OECD.

— Reviews of National Policies for Education Finland: Higher Education. LC 96-154389. 246p. (Orig.). 1995. pap. 52.00 (92-64-14442-0, Pub. by Org for Econ) OECD.

— Reviews of National Science Policy: United States. Cohen, I. Bernard, ed. LC 79-7979. (Three Centuries of Science in America Ser.). 1980. reprint ed. lib. bdg. 55.95 (0-405-12561-5) Ayer.

— Road Infrastructure Rehabilitation & Safety Strategies in Central & Eastern Europe. (Road Transport Research Ser.). 188p. (Orig.). 1995. pap. 37.00 (92-64-14579-6, Pub. by Org for Econ) OECD.

— Road Maintenance Management Systems in Developing Countries. 208p. (Orig.). 1995. pap. 49.00 (92-64-14300-9) OECD.

— Road Monitoring for Maintenance Management: Road Transport Research, 2 vols., Set. 204p. (Orig.). 1990. pap. 22.95 (92-64-13309-7) OECD.

— Road Safety Principles & Models. (Road Transport Research Ser.). 84p. 1997. pap. 19.00 (92-64-15623-2, 77-97-05-1, Pub. by Org for Econ) OECD.

— Roadside Noise Abatement. LC 96-146987. (Road Transport Research Ser.). 170p. (Orig.). 1995. pap. 50.00 (92-64-14578-8, Pub. by Org for Econ) OECD.

— Route Guidance & In-Car Communications Systems. (Road Transport Research Ser.). 104p. (Orig.). 1988. pap. 16.50 (92-64-23046-7) OECD.

— Safety Strategies for Rural Roads. (Road Transport & Intermodal Research Ser.). 144p. 1999. pap. 42.00 (92-64-17054-5, 77 1999 01 1 P, Pub. by Org for Econ) OECD.

— Saving Biological Diversity: Economic Incentives. 126p. (Orig.). 1996. pap. 39.00 (92-64-14807-8, Pub. by Org for Econ) OECD.

— Schools for Today & Tomorrow: An International Compendium of Exemplary Educational Facilities. (Illus.). 150p. (Orig.). 1996. pap. 30.00 (92-64-15291-1, 95-96-05-1) OECD.

— Science, Technology & Industry Outlook, 1998 Edition. 296p. 1998. pap. 65.00 (92-64-16109-0, 92 98 06 1 P, Pub. by European Conference Ministers Transp) OECD.

— Secondary Education in France. (PEB Papers). 64p. (Orig.). 1995. pap. 18.00 (92-64-14548-6, Pub. by Org for Econ) OECD.

— Securities Markets in OECD Countries: Organisaton & Regulation. LC 96-147496. 104p. (Orig.). 1995. pap. 22.00 (92-64-14632-6, Pub. by Org for Econ) OECD.

— Securitisation: An International Perspective. LC 96-175610. 140p. (Orig.). 1995. pap. 45.00 (92-64-14565-6, Pub. by Org for Econ) OECD.

— Services: Statistics on International Transactions 1970-1994. 444p. (Orig.). 1996. pap. 71.00 (92-64-15333-0, 30-96-14-1, Pub. by Org for Econ) OECD.

— Services: Statistics on Value Added & Employment, 1997 Edition. 327p. 1998. pap. 66.00 (92-64-05760-9, 30 98 03 3 P, Pub. by Org for Econ) OECD.

***OECD Staff.** Services, 1998 Edition: Statistics on International Transactions 1987-1996. (Illus.). 404p. (Orig.). 1999. pap. 70.00 (92-64-05831-1, 30 98 08 3 P, Pub. by Org for Econ) OECD.

OECD Staff. Social & Labour Market Policies in Hungary. LC 96-146711. 190p. (Orig.). 1995. pap. 48.00 (92-64-14525-7, Pub. by Org for Econ) OECD.

***OECD Staff.** The Social Sciences at a Turning Point? LC 99-225140. (OECD Proceedings Ser.). 128p. (Orig.). 1999. pap. 35.00 (92-64-16956-3, 93 1999 05 1 P, Pub. by Org for Econ) OECD.

OECD Staff. Sources of Cadmium in the Environment. 484p. (Orig.). 1996. pap. 67.00 (92-64-15343-8, 97-96-13-1, Pub. by Org for Econ) OECD.

— The Steel Market in 1997 & the Outlook for 1998 & 1999 (1998 Edition) 56p. 1998. pap. 33.00 (92-64-16190-2, 5898021P) OECD.

— The Steel Market in 1996 & the Outlook for 1997 & 1998. LC 98-133329. 46p. 1997. pap. 20.00 (92-64-15613-5, 58-97-02-1, Pub. by Org for Econ) OECD.

— STI Review No. 21: Special Issue on Public Support to Industry. 144p. 1998. pap. 32.00 (92-64-15381-0, 90 97 21 1, Pub. by Org for Econ) OECD.

***OECD Staff.** Strategic Asset Management for Tertiary Institutions. (Programme on Educational Building Ser.). 72p. 1999. pap. 25.00 (92-64-17014-6, 95 1999 01 1 P, Pub. by Org for Econ) OECD.

— Structural Aspects of the East Asian Crisis. LC 99-228375. (OECD Proceedings Ser.). 288p. (Orig.). 1999. pap. 70.00 (92-64-17043-X, 14 1999 03 1 P, Pub. by Org for Econ) OECD.

OECD Staff. Subsidies & Environment: Exploring the Linkages. LC 96-181872. 218p. (Orig.). 1996. pap. 33.00 (92-64-14822-1, Pub. by Org for Econ) OECD.

— Successful Services for Our Children & Families at Risk. 340p. (Orig.). 1996. pap. 43.00 (92-64-15305-5, 96-96-05-1) OECD.

***OECD Staff.** A System of Health Accounts. 208p. 2000. pap. 42.00 (92-64-17655-1, 812000061P, Pub. by Org for Econ) OECD.

OECD Staff. System of National Accounts. 711p. (Orig.). 85.00 (92-1-161352-3) UN.

***OECD Staff.** System of National Accounts, 1993--Glossary. 56p. 2000. pap. 24.00 (92-64-17632-2, 30 2000 02 1 P, Pub. by Org for Econ) OECD.

OECD Staff. Systems for Financing Newly Emerging Private Enterprises in Transition Economies. LC 97-167232. 148p. (Orig.). 1997. pap. 28.00 (92-64-15405-1, 14-97-01-1, Pub. by Org for Econ) OECD.

— The Tax - Benefit Position of Employees, 1995-1996: 1997 Edition. 408p. 1998. pap. 58.00 (92-64-05541-X, 23-98-02-3-P, Pub. by Org for Econ) OECD.

***OECD Staff.** Tax Burdens: Alternative Measures. (Tax Policy Studies: No. 2). 96p. 2000. pap. 24.00 (92-64-17137-1, 23 2000 02 1 P, Pub. by Org for Econ) OECD.

OECD Staff. Tax Expenditures: Recent Experiences. LC 97-114922. 108p. (Orig.). 1996. pap. 39.00 (92-64-14879-5, Pub. by Org for Econ) OECD.

— Tax Sparing: A Reconsideration. 88p. 1998. pap. 22.00 (92-64-16022-1, 23 98 01 1 P, Pub. by Org for Econ) OECD.

***OECD Staff.** Taxation of Cross-Border Portfolio Investment: Mutual Funds & Possible Tax Distortions. LC 99-228533. 176p. (Orig.). 1999. pap. 56.00 (92-64-17045-6, 23 1999 03 1 P, Pub. by Org for Econ) OECD.

OECD Staff. The Taxation of Global Trading of Financial Instruments. LC 98-144987. (Documents Ser.). 72p. 1998. pap. 8.00 (92-64-16057-4, 23 98 03 1 P, Pub. by Org for Econ) OECD.

***OECD Staff.** The Tax/Benefit Position of Employees 1997: 1998 Edition. 384p. 1999. pap. 77.00 (92-64-05833-8, 23 1999 01 3 P, Pub. by Org for Econ) OECD.

— Taxing Powers of State & Local Government. (OECD Tax Policy Studies). 88p. 1999. pap. 24.00 (92-64-17135-5, 23 1999 05 1 P, Pub. by Org for Econ) OECD.

— Taxing Wages 1998/1999: Taxes on Wages & Salaries, Social Security Contributions for Employees & Their Employers, Child Benefits (1999 Edition) 360p. 2000. pap. 72.00 (92-64-05878-8, 23 2000 01 3 P, Pub. by Org for Econ) OECD.

OECD Staff. Technologies for Cleaner Production & Products: Towards Technological Transformation for Sustainable Development. LC 96-175606. 96p. (Orig.). 1995. pap. 30.00 (92-64-14473-0, Pub. by Org for Econ) OECD.

— Technology & Industrial Performance: Technology Diffusion, Productivity, Employment & Skills, International Competitiveness. LC 97-167237. 200p. (Orig.). 1997. pap. 50.00 (92-64-15355-1, 92-96-10-1, Pub. by Org for Econ) OECD.

***OECD Staff.** Tertiary Education & Research in the Russian Federation. (Reviews of National Policies for Education Ser.). 182p. 1999. pap. 38.00 (92-64-17042-1, 91 1999 02 1 P, Pub. by Org for Econ) OECD.

OECD Staff. Tourism Policy & International Tourism in OECD Countries 1993-1994 (1996 Edition) 272p. (Orig.). 1996. pap. 50.00 (92-64-14896-5, 78-96-01-1, Pub. by Org for Econ) OECD.

— Towards a Global Information Society: Global Information Infrastructre--Global Information Society (GII-GIS): Policy Requirements. LC 98-133315. 112p. 1998. pap. 20.00 (92-64-15696-8, 93-97-06-1, Pub. by Org for Econ) OECD.

***OECD Staff.** Towards Lifelong Learning in Hungary. LC 99-228363. (OECD Proceedings Ser.). 92p. (Orig.). 1999. pap. 23.00 (92-64-17023-5, 91 1999 01 1 P, Pub. by Org for Econ) OECD.

OECD Staff. Towards Sustainable Consumption Patterns: A Progress Report on Member Country Initiatives. LC 98-162034. 56p. 1998. pap. 8.00 (92-64-16087-6, 97 98 08 1 P, Pub. by Org for Econ) OECD.

— Towards Sustainable Development: Environmental Indicators. LC 98-183032. 132p. 1998. pap. 26.00 (92-64-16080-9, 97 98 03 1 P, Pub. by Org for Econ) OECD.

— Towards Sustainable Transportation: Proceedings of an OECD Conference Held in Vancouver, Canada, 24-27 March, 1996. LC 98-121121. 192p. 1997. pap. 26.00 (92-64-15573-2, 97-97-11-1, Pub. by Org for Econ) OECD.

***OECD Staff.** Trade & Competition Policies: Exploring the Ways Forward. 68p. 1999. pap. 20.00 (92-64-17122-3, 24 1999 021 P, Pub. by Org for Econ) OECD.

— Trade & Investment & Development: Policy Coherence Matters. 84p. 1999. pap. 21.00 (92-64-17112-6, 22 1999 02 1 P, Pub. by Org for Econ) OECD.

OECD Staff. Trade, Employment, & Labour Standards: A Study of Core Workers' Rights & International Trade. 252p. (Orig.). 1996. pap. 48.00 (92-64-15270-9, 22-96-03-1) OECD.

***OECD Staff.** Trade, Investment & Development: Reaping the Full Benefits of Open Markets. 52p. 1999. pap. 21.00 (92-64-17111-8, 22 1999 01 1 P, Pub. by Org for Econ) OECD.

OECD Staff. Trade Liberalisation Policies in Mexico. 160p. (Orig.). 1996. pap. 24.00 (92-64-15316-0, 22-96-05-1) OECD.

***OECD Staff.** Trade Measures in Multilateral Environmental Agreements. 216p. 1999. pap. 48.00 (92-64-17130-4, 22 1999 05 1 P, Pub. by Org for Econ) OECD.

OECD Staff. Trade Policy & the Transition Process. LC 96-231292. 252p. (Orig.). 1996. pap. 49.00 (92-64-14866-3, Pub. by Org for Econ) OECD.

— Training Truck Drivers. (Road Transport Research Ser.). 98p. (Orig.). 1996. pap. 28.00 (92-64-15275-X, 77-96-02-1) OECD.

— Transfer Pricing & Multinational Enterprises: Three Taxation Issues. 92p. (Orig.). 1984. pap. 20.00 (92-64-12626-0) OECD.

— Transfrontier Movements of Hazardous Wastes, 1992-1993 Statistics. 24p. (Orig.). 1997. pap. 8.00 (92-64-15470-1, 97-97-05-1, Pub. by Org for Econ) OECD.

— The Transition from Work to Retirement. (Social Policy Studies: No. 16). 178p. (Orig.). 1995. pap. 43.00 (92-64-14555-9, Pub. by Org for Econ) OECD.

— Transport Economics: Past Trends & Future Prospects. (ECMT Round Table Ser.: No. 100). (ENG & FRE.). 266p. 1996. pap. 58.00 (92-821-1208-X, Pub. by Org for Econ) OECD.

***OECD Staff.** Trends in International Migration: 1999 Edition. 332p. 1999. pap. 56.00 (92-64-17078-2, Pub. by Org for Econ) OECD.

OECD Staff. 21st Century Technologies: Promises & Perils of a Dynamic Future. LC 98-222756. 176p. 1998. pap. 23.00 (92-64-16052-3, 0398031P) OECD.

— University Research in Transition. LC 98-121910. 108p. 1998. pap. 20.00 (92-64-16030-2, 92-98-02-1-P, Pub. by Org for Econ) OECD.

— Urban Infrastructure: Finance & Management. 92p. (Orig.). 1991. pap. 22.00 (92-64-13584-7) OECD.

***OECD Staff.** Urban Policy in Germany: Towards Urban Sustainable Development. 100p. (Orig.). 1999. pap. 21.00 (92-64-16959-8, 04 1999 01 1 P, Pub. by Org for Econ) OECD.

OECD Staff. Vocational Education & Training for Youth: Towards Coherent Policy & Practice. 180p. (Orig.). 1994. pap. 41.00 (92-64-14285-1) OECD.

***OECD Staff.** Waging the Global War on Poverty: Strategies & Case Studies. 240p. 2000. pap. 38.00 (92-64-17170-3, 41 2000 01 1 P, Pub. by Org for Econ) OECD.

OECD Staff. Women Entrepreneurs in Small & Medium Enterprises. LC 98-162223. (Proceedings Ser.). 280p. 1998. pap. 16.00 (92-64-16040-X, 92 98 03 1 P, Pub. by Org for Econ) OECD.

— Women in the City: Housing, Services, & the Urban Environment. LC 96-121954. 169p. (Orig.). 1995. pap. 37.00 (92-64-14570-2, Pub. by Org for Econ) OECD.

— The World in 2020: Towards a New Global Age. LC 98-121325. 136p. 1997. pap. 17.00 (92-64-15627-5, 03-97-08-1, Pub. by Org for Econ) OECD.

OECD Staff, contrib. by. Integrating Environment & Economy: Progress in the 1990's. LC 96-177016. (ENG & FRE.). 60p. (Orig.). 1996. pap. 19.00 (92-64-14774-8, Pub. by Org for Econ) OECD.

— International Capital Markets Statistics, 1950-1995. LC 96-155006. (ENG & FRE.). 260p. (Orig.). 1996. pap. 65.00 (92-64-04763-8, Pub. by Org for Econ) OECD.

OECD Staff & Bulgarian National Statistical Institute Staff. National Accounts for Bulgaria: Sources, Methods & Estimates. LC 96-181868. 186p. (Orig.). 1996. pap. 52.00 (92-64-14819-1, Pub. by Org for Econ) OECD.

OECD Staff & Centre for Co-Operation with Economies in Transiti. Investment Guide for Bulgaria. 138p. (Orig.). 1996. pap. 26.00 (92-64-14811-6, Pub. by Org for Econ) OECD.

— Investment Guide for Uzbekistan. LC 96-206038. 120p. (Orig.). 1996. pap. 30.00 (92-64-14809-4, Pub. by Org for Econ) OECD.

OECD Staff & IEA Staff. Energy Policies of the Russian Federation: 1995 Survey. 350p. (Orig.). 1995. pap. 123.00 (92-64-14416-1, Pub. by Org for Econ) OECD.

OECD Staff & NEA Staff. Physics of Plutonium Recycling Vol. I: Issues & Perspectives. LC 96-123706. 190p. (Orig.). 1995. pap. 39.00 (92-64-14538-9, Pub. by Org for Econ) OECD.

OECD Staff & Oman, Charles W. Globalisation & Regionalisation: The Challenge for Developing Countries. LC 95-112805. 128p. (Orig.). 1994. pap. 19.00 (92-64-14106-5) OECD.

OECD Staff & Scott, Richard. IEA the First 20 Years Vol. 3: A History of the International Energy Agency: Principal Documents. (ENG & FRE.). 544p. (Orig.). 1996. pap. 84.00 (92-64-14659-8, Pub. by Org for Econ) OECD.

OECD Staff & Taylor, J. Edward. Micro Economy-Wide Models for Migration & Policy Analysis: An Application to Rural Mexico. (ENG & FRE.). 88p. (Orig.). 1996. pap. 18.00 (92-64-14687-3, Pub. by Org for Econ) OECD.

OECD Staff, jt. auth. see Vos St. Smith, H. B.

OECD/IEA Staff. The IEA Natural Gas Security Study. LC 96-175585. 500p. (Orig.). 1995. pap. 154.00 (92-64-14658-X, Pub. by Org for Econ) OECD.

OECD/NEA Staff. The Implementation of Short-Term Countermeasures after a Nuclear Accident: Proceedings of an NEA Workshop Stockholm, Sweden, June 1-3, 1994. (ENG & FRE.). 318p. (Orig.). 1996. pap. 54.00 (92-64-14689-X, Pub. by Org for Econ) OECD.

— Physics of Plutonium Recycling Vol. II: Plutonium Recycling in Pressurized-Water Reactors. LC 96-123706. 176p. (Orig.). 1995. pap. 35.00 (92-64-14590-7, Pub. by Org for Econ) OECD.

— Physics of Plutonium Recycling Vol. III: Void Reactivity Effect in Pressurized-Water Reactors. LC 96-123706. 132p. (Orig.). 1995. pap. 27.00 (92-64-14591-5, Pub. by Org for Econ) OECD.

Oechel, Walter C. Global Change & Arctic Terrestrial Ecosystem. (Ecological Studies: 124). 440p. 1996. 99.95 (0-387-94356-0) Spr-Verlag.

Oechel, Walter C., jt. ed. see Moreno, Jose M.

Oechsle, Robert. Ducky, Ucky & Mucky. (Illus.). 40p. (J). (ps). 1985. pap. 7.95 (*0-9603376-0-1*) Flourtown Pub.

Oechsli, Kelly. Mice at Bat. LC 85-45266. (I Can Read Bks.). (Illus.). 64p. (J). (ps-3). 1986. 11.95 (*0-06-024623-5*) HarpC Child Bks.

— Mice at Bat. LC 85-45266. (I Can Read Bks.). (Illus.). 64p. (J). (ps-3). 1990. pap. 3.95 (*0-06-444139-3*, HarpTrophy) HarpC Child Bks.

Oechsli, Kelly. Mice at Bat (I Can Read Bks.). (J). (ps-3). 1986. 8.95 (*0-606-04476-0*, Pub. by Turtleback) Demco.

Oechsli, Wilhelm. History of Switzerland, Fourteen Ninety-Nine to Nineteen Fourteen. Paul, Eden & Paul, Cedar, trs. from GER. LC 83-45627. reprint ed. 49.50 (*0-404-19845-7*) AMS Pr.

Oechslin, Werner, et al, contrib. by. Mario Botta: Public Buildings, 1990-1998. LC 99-492916. (Illus.). 228p. 1999. 35.00 (*88-8118-321-8*, Pub. by Skira IT) Abbeville Pr.

***Oechsner, Carl.** Ossining. (Images of America Ser.). 128p. 1998. pap. 18.99 (*0-7524-0983-2*) Arcadia Publng.

Oechsner, H., ed. Thin-Film & Depth-Profile Analysis. (Topics in Current Physics Ser.: Vol. 37). (Illus.). 225p. 1984. 69.95 (*0-387-13320-8*) Spr-Verlag.

Oedekerk, Steve. Ace Ventura: When Nature Calls. 1996. pap. 4.99 (*0-590-74151-9*) Scholastic Inc.

Oedkerk, Matthijs, et al. Ultrafast Magnetic Resonance Imaging. 400p. (Orig.). 1997. pap. text 135.00 (*0-632-04179-X*) Blackwell Sci.

Oedkerk, Matthijs, jt. auth. see Heuser, L.

Oedo, Yusuke, ed. Ranka Yearbook, 1991: The Bulletin of the International Go Federation. Power, John, tr. from JPN. (Illus.). 96p. (Orig.). 1991. pap. text 4.00 (*0-685-50760-2*, RY91) Ishi Pr Intl.

OEF International Staff, ed. see Mermel, Anita & Simons, Judy.

Oeffelt, Theo Van, see Koster, Egbert & Van Oeffelt, Theo, eds.

Oeffner, Barbara. CHIEF - Champion of the Everglades: A Biography of Seminole Chief James Billie. LC 95-67410. (Illus.). 256p. 1995. 24.95 (*0-9645266-0-3*) Cape Cod Writers.

Oefinger, Judy F. The Saddlebred - America's Horse of Distinction. Strode, William & Butler, William, eds. (Illus.). 160p. 1991. 45.00 (*0-916509-79-6*) Harmony Hse Pub.

Oeflein, Fred. Oeflein. (C). 1998. pap. text 67.00 (*0-321-04507-6*) Addson-Wesley Educ.

Oegema, Gerbern S. The Anointed & His People: Messianic Expectations from the Maccabees to Bar Kochba. (JSPS Ser.: Vol. 27). 356p. 1998. 85.00 (*1-85075-848-4*, Pub. by Sheffield Acad) CUP Services.

***Oegema, Gerbern S.** Fur Israel und Die Volker: Studien zum Alttestamentlich-Judischen Hintergrund der Paulinischen Theologie. (Novum Testamentum, Supplements Ser.: Vol. 95). (GER., Illus.). Xviii, 310p. 1998. text 109.00 (*90-04-11297-9*) Brill Academic Pubs.

Oegema, Gerbern S. The History of the Shield of David: The Birth of a Symbol. Maier, Johann, ed. (Realms of Judaism Ser.: Vol. 62). (Illus.). 223p. 1996. pap. 44.95 (*3-631-30192-8*) P Lang Pubng.

Oegerle, W., et al, eds. Clusters of Galaxies. (Space Telescope Science Institute Symposium Ser.). (Illus.). 410p. (C). 1990. text 69.95 (*0-521-38462-1*) Cambridge U Pr.

Oeglin, Erhart. Liederbuch von 1512. Eitner, Robert & Maier, Jul J., eds. (Publikation Alterer Praktischer und Theoretischer Musikweke Ser.: Vol. 9). (GER., Illus.). 1966. reprint ed. lib. bdg. 75.00 (*0-8450-1709-8*) Broude.

Oehlbeck, Barbara. The Sabal Palm: A Native Monarch. Bennett, Amy, ed. (Illus.). 100p. 1996. 19.95 (*0-9654019-0-1*) Gulfshore Commun.

Oehlberg, Barbara. Making It Better: Activities for Children in a Stressful World. LC 96-41338. (Illus.). 144p. (Orig.). 1996. pap. 16.95 (*1-884834-26-4*, 3044) Redleaf Pr.

Oehlen, Albert, jt. auth. see Herold, Georg.

Oehler. QED 3.04. (C). 1991. text 40.00 (*0-7167-2253-4*) W H Freeman.

— User's Guide 3.04. (C). 1991. text 20.00 (*0-7167-2254-2*) W H Freeman.

Oehler, C. M. The Great Sioux Uprising. LC 96-36566. (Illus.). 272p. 1997. reprint ed. pap. 14.95 (*0-306-80759-9*) Da Capo.

Oehler, Charles M. Jumping Spiders (Araneae: Salticidae) in the Cincinnati Region of Ohio Including Butler, Clermont, Hamilton, & Warren Counties. (Biological Notes Ser.: No. 13). 1982. pap. text 5.00 (*0-86727-087-X*) Ohio Bio Survey.

***Oehler, Janet.** Nature's Call. (Illus.). 32p. (J). (gr. 4-6). 2000. 18.00 (*0-9671159-0-6*, Pub. by J Oehler) Booksource.

Oehler, Markus. Elia Im Neuen Testament: Untersuchungen zur Bedeutung des Alttestamnetlichen Propheten Im Fruehen Christentum. (Beihefte Zur Zeitschrift Fuer die Neutestamentliche Wissenschaft Ser.: Vol. 88). (GER.). viii, 374p. (C). 1997. lib. bdg. 125.35 (*3-11-015547-8*) De Gruyter.

Oehler, Mike. The Fifty Dollar & up Underground House Book. (Illus.). 1978. pap., per. 13.95 (*0-442-27311-8*) Mole Pub Co.

— One Mexican Sunday. LC 80-82949. (Illus.). 112p. 1981. 8.50 (*0-9604464-1-9*) Mole Pub Co.

Oehler, Paul & Minor, William. Natural Counterpoint. (Illus.). 64p. (Orig.). 1985. pap. 4.95 (*0-9612914-1-9*) Betty's Soup

Oehlers, D. J. & Bradford, M. A. Composite Steel & Concrete Structural Members: Fundamental Behaviour. (Structural & Multidisciplinary Optimization Ser.). 548p. (C). 1995. 148.25 (*0-08-041919-4*, Pergamon Pr) Elsevier.

Oehlers, Deric J., jt. auth. see Bradford, Mark A.

***Oehlert, Gary W.** First Course in Designing Experiments. LC 99-59934. 1999. pap. text. write for info. (*0-7167-3510-5*) W H Freeman.

Oehlert, Mary E., et al. Internship Selection in Professional Psychology: A Comprehensive Guide for Students, Faculty, & Training Directors. LC 97-33695. (Illus.). 172p. 1998. text 42.95 (*0-398-06817-8*); pap. text 27.95 (*0-398-06818-6*) C C Thomas.

Oehlerts, Donald E. Books & Blueprints: Building America's Public Libraries, 69. LC 91-3233. (Contributions in Librarianship & Information Science Ser.: No. 69). 200p. 1991. 52.95 (*0-313-26570-4*, OBB, Greenwood Pr) Greenwood.

Oehling, A. Progress in Allergy & Clinical Immunology Vol. 4: Cancun. LC 97-73937. 436p. 1997. 58.00 (*0-88937-179-2*) Hogrefe & Huber Pubs.

Oehlschlaeger, Fritz, ed. Old Southwest Humor from the St. Louis Reveille, 1844-1850. 304p. 1990. text 34.95 (*0-8262-0741-3*) U of Mo Pr.

Oehlschlaeger, Fritz & Hendrick, George, eds. Toward the Making of Thoreau's Modern Reputation: Selected Correspondence of S. A. Jones, A. W. Hosmer, H. S. Salt, H. G. O. Blake & D. Ricketson. LC 79-12831. (Illus.). 433p. 1980. text 39.95 (*0-252-00725-5*) U of Ill Pr.

Oehlschlaeger, Fritz H., jt. auth. see Graham, Peter W.

Oehme, Chester G., III. Gangs, Groups & Crime: Perceptions & Responses of Community Organizations. LC 97-2318. 326p. 1997. pap. 25.00 (*0-89089-872-3*) Carolina Acad Pr.

Oehme, Frederick W., ed. Toxicity of Heavy Metals in the Environment, Pt. 1. LC 78-14758. (Hazardous & Toxic Substances Ser.: Vol. 2). (Illus.). 528p. 1979. reprint ed. pap. 163.70 (*0-608-06268-5*, 206659700001) Bks Demand.

— Toxicity of Heavy Metals in the Environment, Pt. 2. LC 78-14758. (Hazardous & Toxic Substances Ser.: Vol. 2). (Illus.). 469p. 1979. reprint ed. pap. 145.40 (*0-608-06468-8*, 206659700002) Bks Demand.

Oehme, Wolfgang, jt. auth. see Van Sweden, James.

Oehmich-Russcol, Nancy, jt. auth. see Russcol, Herbert.

Oehmig, H. King. Between the Lines. LC 98-88296. 325p. 1998. 25.00 (*0-7388-0153-4*); pap. 15.00 (*0-7388-0154-2*) Xlibris Corp.

Oehmke, Thomas. International Arbitration. annuals rev. ed. LC 90-60910. (International Business & Law Ser.). 1990. suppl. ed. 145.00 (*0-685-59808-X*) West Group.

Oehmke, Thomas H. Construction Arbitration. LC 88-81923. (Real Property-Zoning Ser.). 1988. 135.00 (*0-685-59798-9*) West Group.

Oehrle, Richard T., et al, eds. Categorial Grammars & Natural Language Structures. (Studies in Linguistics & Philosophy: No. 32). 504p. 1988. pap. text 67.50 (*1-55608-031-X*, D Reidel); lib. bdg. 171.00 (*1-55608-030-1*, D Reidel) Kluwer Academic.

Oehry, Bernhard P., jt. auth. see Molisch, Andreas F.

Oehsen, Barr Von, see Rossman, Allan J. & Von Oehsen, Barr.

Oehsen, H. E. Von, see Gage, Larry S. & Von Oehsen, H. E.

Oehser, Paul H. Sons of Science: The Story of the Smithsonian Institution & Its Leaders. LC 69-10144. (Illus.). 220p. 1969. reprint ed. lib. bdg. 65.00 (*0-8371-0185-9*, OESI, Greenwood Pr) Greenwood.

Oei, Hong L. Genes & Politics: The Recombinant DNA Debate. (Orig.). 1977. pap. 24.95 (*1-57420-050-X*) Chatelaine.

Oei, P. Mushroom Cultivation - with Special Emphasis on Appropriate Techniques for Developing Countries. (Illus.). 284p. 1996. pap. 39.00 (*90-70857-36-7*, Pub. by Tool Bks) Balogh.

Oein, E. Mac, et al, eds. Third International Conference on Minority Languages: Celtic Papers. 1987. 59.00 (*0-905028-64-3*, Pub. by Multilingual Matters) Taylor & Francis.

Oelbermann, Maren, jt. auth. see Milburn, Michael.

***Oelerich, Jeanne.** Chicago Walking Guide: Tourist Information, Maps, Walks, Restaurants, No Hotels! 3rd rev. ed. (Illus.). 16p. 2000. pap. 6.95 (*1-882546-16-4*, Pub. by Just Marvelous) IPG Chicago.

Oelerich, Jeanne. Florence Walking Guide: Where to Go - Where to Eat - What to Do. 2nd rev. ed. (Illus.). 16p. 1998. pap. 6.95 (*1-882546-11-3*) Just Marvelous.

— London Walking Guide: Where to Go - Where to Eat - What to Do. (Illus.). 16p. 1998. pap. 6.95 (*1-882546-10-5*) Just Marvelous.

— Paris Walking Guide: Where to Go, Where to Eat, What to Do. 3rd ed. 1999. pap. text 6.95 (*1-882546-15-6*) Just Marvelous.

— Rome Walking Guide: Where to Go - Where to Eat - What to Do. 2nd rev. ed. (Illus.). 16p. 1998. pap. 6.95 (*1-882546-12-1*) Just Marvelous.

— Venice Walking Guide: Where to Go - Where to Eat - What to Do. 2nd rev. ed. (Illus.). 16p. 1998. pap. 6.95 (*1-882546-13-X*) Just Marvelous.

Oelerich, Marjorie, ed. see Sandell, Elizabeth.

Oelerich, Randall W., jt. auth. see Mannino, Joseph.

Oelert, W., jt. auth. see Hadjimichael, E.

***Oelke, Barbara.** Drawing & Painting Horses. (Illus.). 160p. 2000. 35.00 (*0-8230-1419-3*) Watsn-Guptill.

Oelke, Harry. Die Konfessionsbildung des Sixteen: Jahrunderts in Spiegel Illustrierter Flugblatter. (Arbeiten zur Kirchengeschichte Ser.: Bd. 5). (GER.). x, 477p. (C). 1992. lib. bdg. 136.95 (*3-11-012912-4*) De Gruyter.

***Oelkers, Jurgen & Osterwalder, Fritz.** Die Neue Erziehung: Beitrage zur Internationalitat der Reformpadagogik. (Explorationen. Studien zur Erziehungswissenschaft Ser.). (GER.). 418p. 2000. 56.95 (*3-906764-26-5*, Pub. by P Lang Pubng) P Lang Pubng.

***Oelkers, Jurgen & Rhyn, Heinz.** Dewey & European Education: General Problems & Case Studies. 228p. 2000. pap. 60.00 (*0-7923-6389-2*) Kluwer Academic.

***Oelkers, Kaser.** Sports & Entertainment Marketing. 1999. 38.00 (*0-538-69479-3*) S-W Pub.

Oellerich, Michael, ed. Tobramycin Profile. 39p. 1988. pap. 34.95 (*3-527-27370-0*, Pub. by Wiley) Wiley.

Oellerman, Ortrud R., jt. auth. see Chartrand, Gary.

Oellers-Frahm, K., et al, eds. Dispute Settlement in Public International Law: Texts & Materials. 930p. 1985. 184.95 (*0-387-13190-6*) Spr-Verlag.

Oelman, Timothy, ed. from SPA. Marrano Poets of the Seventeenth Century: An Anthology. (Littman Library of Jewish Civilization). (Illus.). 296p. 1985. 29.95 (*0-19-710047-3*) OUP.

Oelman, Timothy, ed. & tr. see Gomez, Antonio E.

Oelofse, A. N. Suid-Afrikaanse Valutabeheerwetgewing. 190p. 1991. pap. write for info. (*0-7021-2547-4*, Pub. by Juta & Co) Gaunt.

Oelofse, A. N., jt. auth. see Malan, F. R.

Oelrich, Ivan. Conventional Arms Control: The Limits & Their Verification. (Occasional Papers: No. 8). (Illus.). 92p. (C). 1990. pap. text 19.00 (*0-8191-7834-9*); lib. bdg. 38.50 (*0-8191-7833-0*) U Pr of Amer.

Oelrichs Historical Society Staff. In the Shadow of the Butte. 725p. 1984. 30.00 (*0-614-24799-3*) Tesseract SD.

Oelrichs, Ian & Pacific Asia Travel Association Staff. Palau, Belau: Your Future in Tourism: PATA Task Force Study. LC 94-112128. xi, 86 p. 1993. 35.00 (*1-882866-00-2*) Pac Asia Trvl.

Oelschlaeger, Max. Caring for Creation: An Ecumenical Approach to the Environmental Crisis. LC 93-23215. 296p. 1994. 40.00 (*0-300-05817-9*) Yale U Pr.

— Caring for Creation: An Ecumenical Approach to the Environmental Crisis. 1996. pap. 16.00 (*0-300-06645-7*) Yale U Pr.

— The Idea of Wilderness: From Prehistory to the Age of Ecology. LC 90-46016. 488p. (C). 1993. reprint ed. pap. 20.00 (*0-300-05370-3*) Yale U Pr.

Oelschlaeger, Max, ed. After Earth Day: Continuing the Conservation Effort. LC 92-922. (Philosophy & the Environment Ser.: No. 1). 241p. 1992. text 24.50 (*0-929398-44-0*); pap. text 15.95 (*0-929398-40-8*) UNTX Pr.

— The Company of Others: Essays in Celebration of Paul Shepard. LC 95-60390. 296p. (C). 1995. 30.00 (*1-882308-24-7*) Kivaki Pr.

— Postmodern Environmental Ethics. LC 94-32139. 341p. (C). 1995. text 59.50 (*0-7914-2547-9*); pap. text 21.95 (*0-7914-2548-7*) State U NY Pr.

— The Wilderness Condition: Essays on Environment & Civilization. LC 92-52649. 343p. 1992. reprint ed. pap. 17.95 (*1-55963-190-2*) Island Pr.

Oelschlaeger, Max, jt. auth. see Gunter, Pete A.

Oelschlager, H., jt. ed. see Murphy, Gerald P.

Oelschlegel, F. Change of Sight: Classical German Surgery & Pathology As Mirrored in the Fine Arts. (Illus.). 215p. (C). 1994. pap. 29.50 (*0-930329-42-2*) Kabel Pubs.

***Oelschlegel, F.** Wandel Einer Sicht. (GER., Illus.). 1999. 39.50 (*0-930329-38-4*) Kabel Pubs.

Oelsner, G. H. Handbook of Weaves. Dale, Samuel S., ed. 402p. 1952. pap. 10.95 (*0-486-23169-0*) Dover.

Oeltjen, Jody, jt. auth. see Palmer, Elsie.

Oelwein, Patricia L. Teaching Reading to Children with Down Syndrome: A Guide for Parents & Teachers. LC 94-37979. (Topics in Down Syndrome Ser.). (Illus.). 392p. (Orig.). (C). 1995. pap. 16.95 (*0-933149-55-7*) Woodbine House.

Oenen, K. & Diehm, C., eds. Beta-Blockers in the Treatment of Hypertension in the 90s: Experience with Tertatolol. (Journal: Cardiology: Vol. 83, Suppl. 1, 1993). (Illus.). iv, 72p. 1993. pap. 23.50 (*3-8055-5869-4*) S Karger.

Oengus the Culdee. Felire of Oengus the Culdee. Stokes, Whitley, tr. from IRI. 1982. pap. 12.50 (*0-89981-025-X*) Eastern Orthodox.

— Saltair Na Rann. MacCarthy, B., tr. from IRI. 1987. reprint ed. pap. 9.95 (*0-89979-036-4*) British Am Bks.

Oenslager, Donald. The Theatre of Donald Oenslager. LC 77-16026. (Illus.). 194p. reprint ed. pap. 60.20 (*0-608-17823-3*, 203249100079) Bks Demand.

Oergel, Maike. The Return of King Arthur & the Nibelungen: National Myth in Nineteenth-Century English & German Literature. LC 97-50164. (Studies in Literature & the Arts: No. 10). 325p. 1997. 106.00 (*3-11-015084-0*) De Gruyter.

Oeric, O. N., jt. auth. see Oss, O. T.

***Oerke, Andrew H.** Symphony Number One & Selected Poems. LC 99-47305. 92p. 1999. pap. text 19.95 (*0-7734-3119-5*, Mellen Poetry Pr) E Mellen.

Oerke, E. C., et al. Crop Production & Crop Protection. LC 95-116581. 830p. 1994. 188.50 (*0-444-82095-7*) Elsevier.

Oerlemans, J., ed. Glacier Fluctuations & Climatic Change. (C). 1989. text 227.50 (*0-7923-0110-2*) Kluwer Academic.

Oerlemans, J. & Van der Veen, C. J. Ice Sheets & Climates. 1984. text 147.50 (*90-277-1709-5*) Kluwer Academic.

Oerlemans, J., jt. auth. see Van der Veen, C. J.

Oermann, Marilyn H. Professional Nursing Practice. (Orig.). (C). 1996. pap. text 32.95 (*0-8385-8114-5*, A8114-9) Appleton & Lange.

— Professional Nursing Practice: A Conceptual Approach. LC 90-6351. (Illus.). 347p. 1991. reprint ed. pap. 107.60 (*0-608-05811-4*, 205977600007) Bks Demand.

— Trends & Issues in Nursing. 1993. write for info. (*0-397 54919 9*) Lppncott W & W.

Oermann, Marilyn H. & Gaberson, Kathleen B. Evaluating & Testing in Nursing Eduction. LC 97-42741. (Teaching of Nursing Ser.). (Illus.). 336p. 1998. 43.95 (*0-8261-9950-X*) Springer Pub.

Oermann, Marilyn H., jt. auth. see Gaberson, Kathleen B.

Oermann, Marilyn H., jt. auth. see Reilly, Dorothy E.

***Oermann, Robert K.** Century of Country: An Illustrated History of Country Music. LC 99-33596. (Illus.). 320p. 1999. 39.95 (*1-57500-083-0*, Pub. by TV Bks) HarpC.

Oers, Willem T. Van, see Van Oers, Willem T.

Oers, Willem T. Van, see Seestrom, Susan J. & Van Oers, Willem T., eds.

Oertel, Gerhard. Der Pluton von Loch Doon in Suedschottland: Theoretisches Zu Bewegungen in Festen Korpern Bei der Deformation. (Geotektonische Forschungen Ser.: Vol. 11). (GER.). ii, 107p. 1955. pap. 18.00 (*3-510-50902-1*, Pub. by E Schweizerbartsche) Balogh.

— Stress & Deformation: A Handbook on Tensors in Geology. (Illus.). 304p. 1996. text 75.00 (*0-19-509503-0*) OUP.

Oertel, Gunter, ed. Polyurethane Handbook. 2nd ed. LC 93-33469. 688p. (C). 1993. 230.00 (*1-56990-157-0*) Hanser-Gardner.

Oertel, H. & Korner, H., eds. Orbital Transport - Technical, Meteorological & Chemical Aspects: Third Aerospace Symposium Braunschweig 26-28 August, 1991. (Illus.). 492p. 1993. 191.95 (*0-387-56318-0*) Spr-Verlag.

Oertel, H., jt. ed. see Zierep, J.

Oertel, Irmgard, tr. see Schafer, Wilhelm.

Oertel, Patty, ed. The Nonprofit Answer Book: An Executive Director's Guide to Frequently Asked Questions. 272p. 1999. pap. write for info. (*1-892233-01-0*) SCCNM.

Oertel, Wolfgang H., jt. ed. see LeWitt, Peter A.

***Oertelt, Henry.** A Chain of Life: The Story of Henry Oertelt. (Illus.). (YA). (gr. 7-12). 2000. 15.95 (*0-8225-2952-1*, Lerner Publctns) Lerner Pub.

Oerter, A. L. History of Graceham, Frederick County, Maryland. (Illus.). 189p. 1997. reprint ed. lib. bdg. 26.50 (*0-8328-5953-2*) Higginson Bk Co.

Oertling, Sewall J., III. Painting & Calligraphy in the "Wu-tsa-tsu" Conservative Aesthetics in Seventeenth Century China. LC 97-2840. (Michigan Monographs in Chinese Studies: No. 68). 1997. text 50.00 (*0-89264-098-7*) Ctr Chinese Studies.

Oertling, Thomas J. Ships' Bilge Pumps: A History of Their Development, 1500-1900. LC 96-21939. (Studies in Nautical Archaeology: No. 2). (Illus.). 123p. (Orig.). 1996. pap. 17.95 (*0-89096-722-9*) Tex A&M Univ Pr.

Oerton, Sarah. Beyond Hierarchy: Gender, Sexuality & the Social Economy. LC 96-18070. (Gender, Change & Society Ser.). 208p. 1996. 79.95 (*0-7484-0352-3*); pap. 27.95 (*0-7484-0353-1*) Taylor & Francis.

Oertzen, Isabell Von, see Finlayson, C. Max, ed.

Oertzen, Isabell Von, see Finlayson, C. Max & Von Oertzen, Isabell, eds.

Oertzen, W. Von, see Von Oertzen, W., ed.

Oervik, Nils. Europe's Northern Cap & the Soviet Union. LC 73-38763. (Harvard University. Center for International Affairs. Occasional Papers in International Affairs: No. 6). reprint ed. 22.50 (*0-404-54606-4*) AMS Pr.

Oesch, Herbert. Finland Vol. I: The Color & Printing Identification of the 1875 Issues: A New Approach. Aro, Kauko I., tr. from FIN. (Illus.). x, 108p. (C). 1994. pap. text 40.00 (*0-936493-15-1*) Scand Philatelic.

— Finland: The Color & Printing Identification of the 1875 Issues: A New Approach, 2 vols., Set. Aro, Kauko I., tr. from FIN. (Illus.). 672p. (C). 1994. text 85.00 (*0-936493-17-8*) Scand Philatelic.

— Finland: The Color & Printing Identification of the 1875 Issues: A New Approach, Vol. II. Aro, Kauko I., tr. from FIN. (Illus.). iv, 450p. (C). 1994. text 50.00 (*0-936493-16-X*) Scand Philatelic.

Oesch, Josef M. Petucha und Setuma: Untersuchungen Zu Einer Uberlieferten Gliederung Im Hebraeischen Texten des Alten Testaments. (Orbis Biblicus et Orientalis Ser.: Vol. 27). 1979. text 82.50 (*3-7278-0212-X*, Pub. by Ed Univ Fri) Eisenbrauns.

Oesch, Norbert C. The Ten Commandments. LC 96-28876. (Expository Sermon Series). 96p. 1997. 12.99 (*0-570-04878-8*, 12-3301) Concordia.

Oesch, Ronald D., jt. auth. see Parmalee, Paul W.

Oeschger, H., jt. ed. see Eddy, J. A.

Oeser, jt. auth. see Moller, H.

Oeser, Oscar, ed. see Jaensch, Erich.

Oeser, Oscar, tr. see Buhler, Karl.

Oeser, Oscar, tr. see Vossler, Karl.

Oest, O. N., jt. ed. see Bjorner, B.

Oesteicher, Mark. Wild Truth Bible: Lessons 4. pap. 8.99 (*0-310-22366-0*) Zondervan.

Oester, David R., jt. auth. see Gill, Sharon A.

Oesterby, M., ed. Dictionary of the Russian Academy, 7 vols., Set. (RUS.). 1981. reprint ed. 1100.00 (*0-915346-76-1*) A Wofsy Fine Arts.

Oestereich, Bernd. Applying Uml Object Oriented Analys Design. LC 98-55553. (Illus.). 352p. (C). 1999. pap. text 44.95 (*0-201-39826-5*) Addison-Wesley.

Oestereicher, Emil. Thinking, Feeling, & Doing. Hughes, Patrick M., ed. 208p. (Orig.). 1992. pap. 10.00 (*0-9605008-9-8*) Hermes Hse Pr.

***Oesterheld, Christina & Zoller, Claus P., eds.** Of Clowns & Gods, Brahmans & Babus: Humour in South Asian Literature. LC 99-932115. 181p. 1999. 28.50 (*81-7304-260-8*, Pub. by Manohar) St Mut.

Oesterle. Corporation Law: Practitioners Edition. (Hornbook Ser.). Date not set. text. write for info. (*0-314-06607-1*) West Pub.

Oesterle, Dale A. Mergers, Acquisitions, & Reorganizations, the Law Of. (American Casebook Ser.). 1096p. 1991. 68.50 (*0-314-85043-0*) West Pub.

— Mergers, Acquisitions, & Reorganizations, the Law Of. (American Casebook Ser.). 265p. (C). 1992. 20.50 (*0-314-01045-9*) West Pub.

O

Oesterle, J. & Weinstein, A., eds. Analytic Number Theory: Proceedings of a Conference in Honor of Heine Halberstam. (Progress in Mathematics Ser.: Vols. 138 & 139). 885p. 1996. 150.00 (*0-8176-3932-2*) Birkhauser.
— Analytic Number Theory: Proceedings of a Conference in Honor of Heini Halberstam. (Progress in Mathematics Ser.: Vol. 139). xiv, 434p. 1996. 95.00 (*0-8176-3933-0*) Birkhauser.
Oesterle, Jean T., tr. Aristotle - On Interpretation: Commentary by St. Thomas & Cajetan. Incl. Commentary by St. Thomas & Cajetan. 1962. LC 61-17965. (Medieval Philosophical Texts in Translation Ser.). 270p. (C). 15.00 (*0-87462-211-5*) Marquette.
Oesterle, John A. Logic: The Art of Defining & Reasoning. 2nd ed. 1963. pap. text 36.00 (*0-13-539999-8*) P-H.
Oesterle, John A., tr. see Aquinas, Thomas, Saint.
Oesterley, Hermann. Gesta Romanorum. (GER.). viii, 755p. 1980. reprint ed. 188.00 (*3-487-00419-4*, Pub. by Weidmann) Lubrecht & Cramer.
— Wegweiser Durch die Literatur der Urkundensammlungen, 2 vols. vi, 997p. 1969. reprint ed. write for info. (*0-318-71849-9*) G Olms Pubs.
Oesterley, W. O. Wisdom of Egypt & the Old Testament in the Light of the Newly Discovered Teachings of Amen-em-ope. 118p. 1998. reprint ed. pap. 14.95 (*0-7661-0445-1*) Kessinger Pub.
Oesterley, William O. The Jewish Background of the Christian Liturgy. 1925. 16.50 (*0-8446-1329-0*) Peter Smith.
Oesterlin, Pauline J. Hillsborough County, New Hampshire, Court Records 1772-1799. 482p. (Orig.). 1996. pap. 37.00 (*0-7884-0449-0*, O180) Heritage Bk.
— Hopkinton, New Hampshire, Vital Records, Vol. I. 243p. 1998. 32.50 (*0-7884-0953-0*, 0180) Heritage Bk.
— Hopkinton, New Hampshire, Vital Records, Vol. II. 398p. 1998. 38.50 (*0-7884-0974-3*, 0181) Heritage Bk.
— New Hampshire, 1742 Estate List. (Illus.). 432p. 1995. text 31.00 (*0-7884-0129-7*) Heritage Bk.
Oesterling, Joseph E. The ABCs of Prostate Cancer: The Book That Could Save Your Life. LC 96-48316. 1997. pap. text 16.95 (*1-56833-097-9*) Madison Bks UPA.
Oesterling, Joseph E. & Moyad, Mark A. The ABCs of Prostate Cancer: The Book That Could Save Your Life. LC 96-48316. 356p. 1997. write for info. (*1-56833-085-5*) Madison Bks UPA.
Oesterling, Joseph E. & Richie, Jerome. Urologic Oncology. Zorab, Richard, ed. LC 96-41702. 864p. 1997. text 165.00 (*0-7216-6347-8*, W B Saunders Co) Harcrt Hlth Sci Grp.
Oesterling, Joseph E., jt. auth. see Moyad, Mark A.
***Oestermann, Richard.** Born Again. LC 99-30224. 208p. 1999. 16.95 (*965-229-214-1*) Gefen Bks.
Oestermyer, Jeanette M. God, Gardens & Other Wonders: A Collection of Poetry Glorifying God, His Creations, & His Many Wonders. LC 96-60717. 52p. (Orig.). 1996. pap. 6.50 (*1-886467-07-2*) WJM Press.
Oesterreich, Traugott K. Possession: Demoniacal & Other. 400p. 1974. reprint ed. pap. 4.95 (*0-8065-0436-6*, Citadel Pr) Carol Pub Group.
Oesterreicher, Jody, ed. see Goltz, Jay.
Oesterreicher, John M. Walls Are Crumbling. (Illus.). 10.00 (*0-8159-7201-6*) Devin.
Oesterreicher, Michel. Pioneer Family: Life on Florida's 20th-Century Frontier. LC 95-15202. (Illus.). 192p. (Orig.). (C). 1996. pap. 24.95 (*0-8173-0783-4*) U of Ala Pr.
Oesterreicher-Mollwo, Marianne. Dictionnaire des Symboles. (FRE.). 312p. 1992. pap. 59.95 (*0-7859-7903-4*, 2503502458) Fr & Eur.
Oesting, Heather H. Hidden Assets: The Guide to the Best Catalogs. LC 81-90554. 91p. (Orig.). 1982. pap. 6.95 (*0-941552-00-4*) Hidden Assets.
Oestmann, Cord. Lordship & Community: The Lestrange Family & the Village of Hunstanton, Norfolk, in the First Half of the Sixteenth Century. (Illus.). 301p. (C). 1994. 75.00 (*0-85115-351-8*) Boydell & Brewer.
Oestmann, R. English for Military Leaders. (ENG & GER.). 128p. 1987. lib. bdg. 65.00 (*0-8288-3405-9*, F55110) Fr & Eur.
Oestmann, Rainier. English for Military Leaders: German/English/German. 3rd ed. (ENG & GER.). 239p. 1996. 85.00 (*0-320-00529-1*) Fr & Eur.
Oestreich, A. E. How to Measure Angles from Foot Radiographs. (Illus.). 65p. 1989. 36.00 (*0-387-97107-6*) Spr-Verlag.
Oestreich, Alan E., et al. A Centennial History of African Americans in Radiology. unabridged ed. (Illus.). 100p. 1996. 40.00 (*0-9651714-0-X*) Nat Med Assn.
Oestreich, Bernhard. Metaphors & Similes for Yahweh in Hosea 14:2-9(1-8) A Study of Hoseanic Pictorial Language. LC 98-36238. (Friedensauer Schriftenreihe. Reihe A Ser.). 278p. 1998. pap. text 48.95 (*0-8204-3615-1*) P Lang Pubng.
***Oestreich, Bernhard, et al.** Glaube und Zukunftsgestaltung: Festschrift Zum Hundertjahrigen Bestehen der Theologischen Hochschule Friedensau: Aufsatze Zu Theologie, Sozialwissenschaften und Musik. (Illus.). 434p. 1999. 67.95 (*3-631-34547-X*) P Lang Pubng.
Oestreich, Daniel K., jt. auth. see Ryan, Kathleen D.
Oestreich, Nathan. Federal Taxation, 1997 Edition. 10th ed. 408p. (C). 1996. text, student ed. 25.62 (*0-256-17250-1*, Irwn McGrw-H) McGrw-H Hghr Educ.
— Individual Taxation 1997 Edition: Study Guide. 10th ed. 320p. (C). 1996. text 25.62 (*0-256-17027-4*, Irwn McGrw-H) McGrw-H Hghr Educ.
Oestreich, Reed M. Christmas: When & Why. (Illus.). xvi, 182p. 1998. reprint ed. pap. 14.95 (*0-9672115-0-6*) Creek Side Pubg.
Oestreicher. Unmasking the Truth about the Walam Olum. (Illus.). (C). text. write for info. (*0-472-10881-6*) U of Mich Pr.
Oestreicher, Joy & Singer, Richard, eds. Air Fish: An Anthology of Speculative Writing. LC 93-70458. (Illus.). 320p. (Orig.). 1993. pap. 16.95 (*0-9631755-2-1*) Omega Cat Pr.
Oestreicher, Mark. Help! I'm a Junior High Youth Worker! 50 Ways to Survive & Thrive in Ministry to Early Adolescents. LC 96-36848. 64p. 1997. pap. 7.99 (*0-310-21328-2*) Youth Spec.
— Wild Truth Bible Lessons: Pictures of God. LC 99-30185. (Illus.). 96p. 1999. 8.99 (*0-310-22365-2*) HarpC.
— Wild Truth Bible Lessons: 12 Wild Studies for Junior Highers. LC 96-22271. 1996. pap. 12.99 (*0-310-21304-5*) Youth Spec.
— Wild Truth Bible Lessons 2: 12 More Wild Studies for Junior Highers, Based on Wild Bible Characters. LC 97-45509. 1998. pap. 12.99 (*0-310-22024-6*) Zondervan.
— Wild Truth Journal: Fifty Life Lessons from the Scriptures. 112p. 1999. pap. 8.99 (*0-310-22350-4*) HarpC.
— Wild Truth Journal: Fifty Life Lessons from the Scriptures. 112p. 1995. pap. 8.99 (*0-310-20766-5*) Zondervan.
Oestreicher, Richard. Solidarity & Fragmentation: Working People & Class Consciousness in Detroit, 1875-1900. LC 85-1030. (Working Class in American History Ser.). (Illus.). 296p. 1990. pap. text 16.95 (*0-252-06120-9*) U of Ill Pr.
Oeter, D. Herder-Lexikon Medizin. 35.00 (*0-8288-7921-4*, M7446) Fr & Eur.
— Herder-Lexikon Medizin. 2nd ed. (GER.). 240p. pap. 35.00 (*0-686-56479-0*, M-7446) Fr & Eur.
Oeters, Franz. The Metallurgy of Steelmaking. (Illus.). 480p. 1994. 216.00 (*3-514-00465-X*, Pub. by Woodhead Pubng) Am Educ Systs.
Oetgen, Jerome. An American Abbot: Boniface Wimmer, O. S. B., 1809-1887. rev. ed. LC 97-7552. (Illus.). 1997. text 39.95 (*0-8132-0893-9*) Cath U Pr.
***Oetgen, Jerome.** Mission to America: A History of Saint Vincent Archabbey, the First Benedictine Monastery in the United States. LC 99-34694. 2000. 39.95 (*0-8132-0957-9*) Cath U Pr.
***Oetinger, Annis.** Elk for Sale. (Brant Grayson Mystery Ser.: Vol. 2). 224p. 1999. pap. 11.00 (*0-9634757-2-X*) A Oetinger.
Oetinger, Annis. Snow Job. (Illus.). 192p. (Orig.). 1992. pap. 10.95 (*0-9634757-0-3*) A Oetinger.
Oetinger, Annis, et al. Sunriver Lite. unabridged ed. (Illus.). 150p. 1998. pap. 12.00 (*0-9634757-1-1*) A Oetinger.
Oetinger, Friedrich C. Biblisches und Emblematisches Woerterbuch. (GER.). 930p. 1994. 650.00 (*0-7859-8267-1*, 3110049031) Fr & Eur.
— Biblisches und Emblematisches Woerterbuch. (GER.). 880p. 1988. reprint ed. write for info. incl. 3.5 hd (*3-487-02345-8*) G Olms Pubs.
— Biblisches und Emblematisches Worterbuch. 980p. 1998. 300.00 (*3-11-004903-1*) De Gruyter.
Oetjen, Georg-Wilhelm. Freeze-Drying. 260p. 1999. 159.00 (*3-527-29571-2*) Wiley.
***Oetken, Rachel C.** My Home & My Neighborhood: Thematic Unit. Cook, David, ed. 80p. (J). 1999. pap., teacher ed. 9.95 (*1-57690-469-5*, TCM2469) Tchr Create Mat.
Oetker, D. Garnishing Book & Tool Set. 1989. 24.99 (*0-517-69600-2*) Random Hse Value.
Oetliker, O. & Rossi, E. Bern, eds. Nephrologie im Kindesalter III. (Paediatrische Fortbildungskurse fuer die Praxis Ser.: Bd. 45). (GER., Illus.). 1978. 46.25 (*3-8055-2825-6*) S Karger.
Oets, Pim. MS-DOS & PC-DOS: A Practical Guide. 2nd ed. (Computer Science Ser.). (Illus.). 216p. (C). 1988. pap. text 35.00 (*0-333-45440-5*) Scholium Intl.
Oetteking, Bruno. Craniology of the North Pacific Coast. LC 73-3533. (Jessup North Pacific Expedition. Publications: No. 11). reprint ed. 115.00 (*0-404-58111-0*) AMS Pr.
— Skeletal Remains from Santa Barbara, California: I. Craniology. LC 76-43795. (MAI. Indian Notes & Monographs: No. 39). reprint ed. 49.50 (*0-404-15651-7*) AMS Pr.
— The Skeleton from Mesa House. (Illus.). 48p. 1970. reprint ed. pap. 3.50 (*0-916561-61-5*) Southwest Mus.
***Oettel, M., et al, eds.** Estrogens & Antiestrogens I: Physiology & Mechanisms of Action of Estrogens & Antiestrogens. (Handbook of Experimental Pharmacology Ser.: Vol. 135, No. 1). (Illus.). 360p. 1999. 249.00 (*3-540-65016-4*) Spr-Verlag.
— Estrogens & Antiestrogens II: Pharmacology & Clinical Applications of Estrogens & Antiestrogens. (Handbook of Experimental Pharmacology Ser.: Vol. 135, No. 2). (Illus.). 600p. 1999. 399.00 (*3-540-65580-8*) Spr-Verlag.
Oettermann, Stephan. The Panorama: History of a Mass Medium. Schneider, Deborah L., tr. LC 96-30342. 1997. 37.50 (*0-942299-83-3*, Swerve Ed) Zone Bks.
Oettgen, Herbert F., jt. ed. see Mitchell, Malcom S.
Oetting, E. R., jt. auth. see Drake, Lewis E.
***Oetting, Judy.** "M" Is for Missouri's Rocks & Minerals. (Alpha Flight Bks.). (Illus.). 64p. (J). 2000. 17.95 (*1-892920-29-8*) G H B Pubs.
— Missouri Rocks & Minerals: Fun Facts & Games. (Fun Facts & Games Bks.). (Illus.). 64p. (J). 2000. pap. text 5.95 (*1-892920-24-7*) G H B Pubs.
Oetting, Rae. Bobby Bear's Birthday. LC 87-62508. (Bobby Bear Ser.). (Illus.). 32p. (J). (ps-1). 1988. lib. bdg. 11.45 (*0-87783-220-X*) Oddo.
— The Chieftain of Chaucer. LC 73-87806. (Sound Ser.). (Illus.). 32p. (J). (gr. 2-5). 1974. lib. bdg. 9.95 (*0-87783-137-8*) Oddo.
— The Chieftain of Chaucer. deluxe ed. LC 73-87806. (Sound Ser.). (Illus.). 32p. (J). (gr. 2-5). 1974. pap. 3.94 (*0-87783-138-6*) Oddo.
— The Gray Ghosts of Gotham. LC 73-87804. (Sound Ser.). (Illus.). 32p. (J). (gr. 2-5). 1974. lib. bdg. 9.95 (*0-87783-135-1*) Oddo.
— The Gray Ghosts of Gotham. deluxe ed. LC 73-87804. (Sound Ser.). (Illus.). 32p. (J). (gr. 2-5). 1974. pap. 3.94 (*0-87783-136-X*) Oddo.
— Keiki of the Islands. LC 71-108728. (Illus.). 96p. (J). (gr. 3 up). 1970. lib. bdg. 10.95 (*0-87783-018-5*) Oddo.
— Keiki of the Islands. deluxe ed. LC 71-108728. (Illus.). 96p. (J). (gr. 3 up). 1970. pap. 3.94 (*0-87783-096-7*) Oddo.
— Orderly Cricket. LC 68-16395. (Illus.). 32p. (J). (gr. 2-3). 1967. lib. bdg. 9.95 (*0-87783-028-2*) Oddo.
— Prairie Dog Town. LC 68-56829. (Illus.). 48p. (J). (gr. 2-5). 1968. lib. bdg. 10.95 (*0-87783-030-4*) Oddo.
— Prairie Dog Town. deluxe ed. LC 68-56829. (Illus.). 48p. (J). (gr. 2-5). 1968. pap. 3.94 (*0-87783-157-2*) Oddo.
— Quetico Wolf. LC 71-190274. (Illus.). 48p. (J). (gr. 4 up). 1972. lib. bdg. 9.95 (*0-87783-059-2*) Oddo.
— Quetico Wolf. deluxe ed. LC 71-190274. (Illus.). 48p. (J). (gr. 4 up). 1972. pap. 3.94 (*0-87783-103-3*) Oddo.
— Timmy Tiger & the Elephant. LC 73-108730. (Timmy Tiger Ser.). (Illus.). 32p. (J). (ps-2). 1970. lib. bdg. 9.95 (*0-87783-041-X*); audio 7.94 (*0-87783-277-3*) Oddo.
— Timmy Tiger & the Elephant. deluxe ed. LC 73-108730. (Timmy Tiger Ser.). (Illus.). 32p. (J). (ps-2). 1970. pap. 3.94 (*0-87783-111-4*) Oddo.
— Timmy Tiger to the Rescue. LC 70-108733. (Timmy Tiger Ser.). (Illus.). 32p. (J). (ps-4). 1970. lib. bdg. 9.95 (*0-87783-043-6*); audio 7.94 (*0-87783-229-3*) Oddo.
— Timmy Tiger to the Rescue. deluxe ed. LC 70-108733. (Timmy Tiger Ser.). (Illus.). 32p. (J). (ps-4). 1970. pap. 3.94 (*0-87783-112-2*) Oddo.
— Timmy Tiger's New Coat. LC 74-108734. (Timmy Tiger Ser.). (Illus.). 32p. (J). (ps-2). 1970. lib. bdg. 9.95 (*0-87783-044-4*); audio 7.94 (*0-87783-230-7*) Oddo.
— Timmy Tiger's New Coat. deluxe ed. LC 74-108734. (Timmy Tiger Ser.). (Illus.). 32p. (J). (ps-2). 1970. pap. 3.94 (*0-87783-113-0*) Oddo.
— Timmy Tiger's New Friend. LC 77-108732. (Timmy Tiger Ser.). (Illus.). (J). (ps-2). 1970. lib. bdg. 9.95 (*0-87783-042-8*); audio 7.94 (*0-87783-231-5*) Oddo.
— Timmy Tiger's New Friend. deluxe ed. LC 77-108732. (Timmy Tiger Ser.). (Illus.). (J). (ps-2). 1970. pap. 3.94 (*0-87783-114-9*) Oddo.
— When Jesus Was a Lad. LC 68-56816. (Illus.). 32p. (J). (gr. 2-3). 1968. lib. bdg. 9.95 (*0-87783-047-9*) Oddo.
— Wrongway Santa. LC 90-62546. (Illus.). 32p. (J). 1991. lib. bdg. 15.95 (*0-87783-254-4*) Oddo.
Oettingen, Burchard Von, see Von Oettingen, Burchard.
Oettinger, Anthony, jt. auth. see Weinhaus, Carol.
Oettinger, Anthony, ed. see Branscomb, Anne W.
Oettinger, Anthony G. Context for Decisions: Global & Local Information Technology Issues, Vol. I-98-1. unabridged ed. (Illus.). 23p. 1998. pap. text. write for info. (*1-879716-45-3*) Ctr Info Policy.
— Run, Computer, Run: The Mythology of Educational Innovation. LC 71-78522. (Illus.). 323p. reprint ed. pap. 100.20 (*0-7837-5940-1*, 204573900007) Bks Demand.
— Telling Ripe from Hype in Multimedia: The Ecstasy & the Agony. 32p. (Orig.). 1994. pap. text. write for info. (*1-879716-14-3*, I-94-2) Ctr Info Policy.
Oettinger, Anthony G., ed. see Horton, Frank B., et al.
Oettinger, Anthony G., ed. see Tuttle, Jerry O., et al.
Oettinger, Elizabeth N., jt. ed. see Kenny, Dennis E.
Oettinger, Marion, Jr. Discovering the Folk Art of Latin America: Visiones del Pueblo. LC 92-52861. (Illus.). 112p. 1992. 32.50 (*0-525-93435-9*, Dutton Studio) Studio Bks.
— Folk Treasures of Mexico: The Nelson A. Rockefeller Collection. (Illus.). 224p. 1990. 65.00 (*0-8109-1182-5*, Pub. by Abrams) Time Warner.
Oettinger, Marion, Jr., ed. Folk Art of Spain & the Americas: El Alma del Pueblo. LC 97-14719. (Illus.). 200p. 1997. 49.95 (*0-7892-0378-2*) Abbeville Pr.
Oettinger, Marion, ed. see Brandes, Stanley, et al.
Oettli, W., et al, eds. Advances in Optimization: Proceedings of the 6th French-German Colloquium on Optimization, Held at Lambrecht, FRG, June 2-8, 1991. (Lecture Notes in Economics & Mathematical Systems Ser.: Vol. 382). (Illus.). x, 527p. 1992. 93.95 (*0-387-55446-7*) Spr-Verlag.
Oettli, W. & Pallaschke, D., eds. Advances in Optimization: Proceedings of the 6th French-German Colloquium on Optimization, Held at Lambrecht, FRG, June 2-8, 1991. LC 92-5741. (Lecture Notes in Economics & Mathematical Systems Ser.: Vol. 382). 1992. write for info. (*3-540-55446-7*) Spr-Verlag.
Oettmeier, Timothy N., jt. auth. see Pekar, George M.
Oeur, U. Sam & McCullough, Ken, trs. Sacred Vows. LC 97-43267. 150p. 1998. pap. 15.00 (*1-56689-069-1*) Coffee Hse.
***Oevel, W.** Mupad Tutorial: A Version & Platform Independent Introduction. LC 00-41962. 2000. pap. write for info. (*3-540-67546-9*) Spr-Verlag.
Oevering, A. Changing Roles for Local & Regional Government in Environmental Management: Extra Burdens or New Opportunities? xiv, 315p. 1984. lib. bdg. 87.50 (*90-6764-036-0*, Pub. by VSP) Coronet Bks.
Oey, Eric. Java: Garden of the East. (Regional Guides of Indonesia Ser.). (Illus.). 272p. 1992. pap. 15.95 (*0-8442-9903-0*, Passprt Bks) NTC Contemp Pub Co.
— Java: Garden of the East. 2nd ed. (Regional Guides of Indonesia Ser.). (Illus.). 400p. 1994. pap. 17.95 (*0-8442-9947-2*, 99472, Passprt Bks) NTC Contemp Pub Co.
Oey, Eric, ed. Bali. 272p. 1991. pap. 37.50 (*0-945971-32-X*) Periplus.
— Bali. 3rd ed. 312p. 1995. pap. 19.95 (*962-593-028-0*) Periplus.
— Bali: Eiland der Goden. Pessissiron, Sylvia, tr. from ENG. (Indonesie Reisbibliotheek Ser.). (DUT., Illus.). 272p. 1990. 19.95 (*0-945971-17-6*) Periplus.
— Bali: The Emerald Isle. 3rd ed. (Illus.). 296p. (Orig.). 1995. pap. text 19.95 (*0-8442-8996-5*, Passprt Bks) NTC Contemp Pub Co.
— Java. 2nd ed. (DUT.). 416p. 1995. pap. 19.95 (*962-593-013-2*) Periplus.
— Sumatra. 2nd ed. 332p. 1995. pap. 19.95 (*962-593-017-5*) Periplus.
Oey, Eric, ed. see Muller, Kal.
Oey, Thomas G. Everyday Indonesian. (Illus.). 192p. 1994. pap. write for info. (*0-945971-92-3*) Periplus.
— Everyday Indonesian: Phrasebook & Dictionary. 198p. 1992. pap. 11.95 (*0-945971-58-3*) Periplus.
— Indonesissch Fur Reise und Alltag. 200p. 1993. pap. write for info. (*0-945971-85-0*) Periplus.
— Pocket Dictionary: Dutch - Indonesian. (Illus.). 1994. pap. write for info. (*0-945971-94-X*) Periplus.
— Pocket Dictionary: English-Indonesian - Indonesian-English. (IND & ENG.). 72p. (Orig.). 1992. pap. 3.95 (*0-945971-66-4*) Periplus.
Oey, Thomas G. & Hutton, Wendy. Everyday Malay: Phrasebook & Dictionary. 192p. 1994. pap. 14.95 (*0-945971-83-4*) Periplus.
Oey, Thomas G., jt. auth. see Hutton, Wendy.
Oeynhausen, B. Von, see Von Oeynhausen, B.
O'Fahey, R. S., jt. ed. see Hunwick, J. O.
***O'Faircheallaigh, Ciaran, et al.** Public Sector Management in Australia: New Challenges, New Directions. 327p. 2000. 37.95 (*0-7329-4073-7*, Pub. by Macmill Educ) Paul & Co Pubs.
O'Fallon, James M., jt. auth. see Douglas, William O.
O'Faolain, Eileen. Bridge of Feathers. 128p. 1990. pap. 7.95 (*1-85371-049-0*) Dufour.
— Bridge of Feathers. 128p. 1990. pap. 6.95 (*1-85371-053-9*, Pub. by Poolbeg Pr) Dufour.
— Irish Sagas & Folk Tales. 256p. 1986. reprint ed. pap. 11.95 (*0-905169-71-9*, Pub. by Poolbeg Pr) Dufour.
O'Faolain, Nuala. Are You Somebody? The Accidental Memoir of a Dublin Woman. LC 97-29725. 256p. 1998. 21.00 (*0-8050-5663-7*) H Holt & Co.
— Are You Somebody? The Accidental Memoir of a Dublin Woman. 215p. 1999. pap. 11.95 (*0-8050-5664-5*, Owl) H Holt & Co.
— Are You Somebody? The Accidental Memoir of a Dublin Woman. large type ed. LC 98-17244. 1998. 25.95 (*0-7862-1506-2*) Thorndike Pr.
O'Faolain, Sean. And Again? Richardson, Stewart, ed. 290p. 1989. 16.95 (*1-55972-005-4*, Birch Ln Pr) Carol Pub Group.
— The Great O'Neill: A Biography of Hugh O'Neill, Earl of Tyrone, 1550- 284p. 1997. pap. 16.95 (*0-8023-1321-3*) Dufour.
— Irish: A Character Study. 1979. pap. 12.95 (*0-8159-5812-9*) Devin.
— The Man Who Invented Sin. (Illus.). 1974. reprint ed. 12.95 (*0-8159-6212-6*) Devin.
— Nest of Simple Folk. 1990. 17.95 (*1-55972-041-7*, Birch Ln Pr) Carol Pub Group.
— The Short Story. pap. 9.95 (*0-8159-6814-0*) Devin.
— The Short Story. 1989. pap. 19.95 (*0-85342-860-3*) Dufour.
— A Summer in Italy. 12.95 (*0-8159-6831-0*) Devin.
— The Vanishing Hero. LC 71-142686. (Essay Index Reprint Ser.). 1977. 18.95 (*0-8369-2065-1*) Ayer.
— The Vanishing Hero. 1991. reprint ed. lib. bdg. 21.95 (*1-56849-074-7*) Buccaneer Bks.
O'Faolain, Sean, compiled by. Silver Branch. LC 68-58822. (Granger Index Reprint Ser.). 1977. 15.95 (*0-8369-6035-1*) Ayer.
O'Farrell. Small Animal Behavior Problems. (C). 1998. text 55.00 (*0-7020-1789-2*) Bailliere Tindall.
O'Farrell, Brigid & Kornbluh, Joyce L., eds. Rocking the Boat: Women, Unions, & Change, 1915-1975. LC 95-33037. (Illus.). 325p. (C). 1996. text 50.00 (*0-8135-2268-4*); pap. text 17.95 (*0-8135-2269-2*) Rutgers U Pr.
O'Farrell, Brigid, jt. auth. see Friedan, Betty.
O'Farrell, Brigid, ed. see Friedan, Betty.
***O'Farrell, Clare, et al, eds.** Taught Bodies. LC 99-13915. (Eruptions Ser.: No. 5). 224p. 2000. pap. text 29.95 (*0-8204-4297-6*) P Lang Pubng.
O'Farrell, Kathleen. The Fiddler of Kilbroney. 352p. (Orig.). 1994. pap. 15.95 (*0-86322-177-7*, Pub. by Brandon Bk Pubs) Irish Bks Media.
O'Farrell, Larence. Education & the Art of Drama. 69p. (C). 1995. pap. 24.00 (*0-7300-1799-0*, Pub. by Deakin Univ) St Mut.
O'Farrell, M. Brigid, ed. see National Research Council, Panel on Employer Polic.
O'Farrell, Mary A. Telling Complexions: The Nineteenth-Century English Novel & the Blush. LC 96-38211. (Illus.). 192p. 1997. pap. text 16.95 (*0-8223-1895-4*); lib. bdg. 49.95 (*0-8223-1903-9*) Duke.
***O'Farrell, Mary Ann & Vallone, Lynne, eds.** Virtual Gender: Fantasies of Subjectivity & Embodiment. LC 99-6685. 264p. 1999. pap. text 19.95 (*0-472-06708-7*, 06708) U of Mich Pr.
— Virtual Gender: Fantasies of Subjectivity & Embodiment. LC 99-6685. 264p. 2000. text 49.50 (*0-472-09708-3*, 09708) U of Mich Pr.
O'Farrell, Neal. Stepping into Magic: A Handbook for the High Tech Start Up. 362p. 1998. pap. 24.95 (*0-9662435-0-1*) Pylon Bks.
O'Farrell, Padraic. Ancient Irish Legends. LC 95-202363. (Illus.). 96p. (Orig.). 1995. pap. 7.95 (*0-7171-2252-2*, Pub. by Gill & MacMill) Irish Bks Media.
— The Burning of Brinsley MacNamara. (Illus.). 176p. 1990. pap. 11.95 (*0-946640-56-4*, Pub. by Lilliput Pr) Irish Bks Media.

An Asterisk (*) at the beginning of an entry indicates that the title is appearing for the first time.

— Tales for the Telling: True Life Stories of Irish "Scandals" LC 97-102421. 178p. 1996. pap. 13.95 (*1-898256-16-0*, Pub. by Collins Press) Irish Bks Media.

— Who's Who in the Irish War of Independence & the Civil War. 2nd rev. ed. LC 97-162836. Orig. Title: Who's Who in the Irish War of Independence, 1916-1921. 240p. 1997. pap. 19.95 (*1-874675-85-6*, Pub. by Lilliput Pr) Irish Bks Media.

O'Farrell, Padraic, ed. The '98 Reader: An Anthology of Song, Ballads, Prose & Poetry. LC 98-173366. 144p. 1998. pap. 11.95 (*1-901866-03-3*, Pub. by Lilliput Pr) Irish Bks Media.

O'Farrell, Padraig. Irish Fairy Tales. (Illus.). 96p. 1997. pap. 7.95 (*0-7171-2525-4*, Pub. by Gill & MacMill) Irish Bks Media.

O'Farrell, Patrick. The Catholic Church & Community: An Australian History. 3rd rev. ed. 487p. 1988. pap. 19.95 (*0-86840-225-7*, Pub. by New South Wales Univ Pr) Intl Spec Bk.

— The Irish in Australia. (Illus.). 342p. (C). 1989. text 38.00 (*0-268-01164-8*) U of Notre Dame Pr.

***O'Farrell, Patrick.** The Irish in Australia: 1788 to the Present. 3rd ed. 372p. 2000. pap. 24.50 (*0-268-03156-8*, Pub. by U of Notre Dame Pr) Chicago Distribution Ctr.

O'Farrell, Patrick. The Irish in Australia: 1992 Edition. (Illus.). 333p. pap. 29.95 (*0-86840-181-1*, Pub. by New South Wales Univ Pr) Intl Spec Bk.

— Letters from Irish Australia, 1825-1925. 244p. 1990. pap. 24.95 (*0-86840-235-4*, Pub. by New South Wales Univ Pr) Intl Spec Bk.

***O'Farrell, Patrick.** UNSW a Portrait: The University of New South Wales 1948-1998. LC 99-221193. (Illus.). 312p. 1999. 49.95 (*0-86840-417-9*, Pub. by New South Wales Univ Pr) Intl Spec Bk.

O'Farrell, Patrick. Vanished Kingdoms: Irish in Australia & New Zealand. 309p. 1990. 39.95 (*0-86840-148-X*, Pub. by New South Wales Univ Pr) Intl Spec Bk.

O'Farrell, Timothy J., ed. Treating Alcohol Problems: Marital & Family Interventions. LC 93-3061. (Substance Abuse Ser.). 446p. 1993. lib. bdg. 49.00 (*0-89862-195-X*) Guilford Pubns.

O'Farrell, Valerie. Manual of Canine Behaviour. 2nd ed. (Illus.). 132p. 1994. pap. text 51.95 (*0-905214-17-X*, Pub. by BSAVA) Iowa St U Pr.

O'Farrell, Valerie, jt. auth. see Neville, Peter.

Ofcansky, Thomas P. Ethiopia: A Country Study. 448p. 1993. boxed set 31.00 (*0-16-061159-8*) USGPO.

Ofcansky, Thomas P. Paradise Lost: A History of Game Preservation in East Africa. (Illus.). 1997. 22.50 (*0-937058-29-7*) West Va U Pr.

— Uganda: Tarnished Pearl of Africa. LC 95-13468. (Nations of the Modern World: Africa Ser.). 224p. 1995. pap. 69.00 (*0-8133-1059-8*, Pub. by Westview) HarpC.

Ofcansky, Thomas P. & Berry, LaVerle, eds. Ethiopia: A Country Study. 4th ed. LC 92-507. (Area Handbook Ser.: Vol. 550-28). (Illus.). 448p. 1993. boxed set 27.00 (*0-8444-0739-9*) Lib Congress.

Ofcansky, Thomas P. & Maxon, Robert M. Historical Dictionary of Kenya. 2nd ed. LC 98-50070. (African Historical Dictionaries Ser.: No. 77). 808p. 1999. 110.00 (*0-8108-3616-5*) Scarecrow.

Ofcansky, Thomas P. & Yeager, Rodger. Historical Dictionary of Tanzania. 2nd ed. LC 96-35043. (African Historical Dictionaries Ser.). 1997. 69.00 (*0-8108-3244-5*) Scarecrow.

Ofek, Itzhak, jt. ed. see Kahane, Itzhak.

Ofek, Itzhak, ed. see Simon, Melvin I.

Ofenloch, ed. Caecilii Calactini. (GRE.). 1967. reprint ed. 27.95 (*3-519-01120-4*, T1120, Pub. by B G Teubner) U of Mich Pr.

Ofenloch, Jeanne F. Senior Scene: A Compilation. vii, 139p. 1997. pap. 11.95 (*0-9659423-0-9*) Donohue Mkting.

Ofer, Dalia & Weiner, Hannah. Dead-End Journey: The Tragic Story of the Kladovo-Sabec Group. Barber, Anne, tr. from HEB. LC 95-43573. (Studies in the Shoah: Vol. XIV). (Illus.). 254p. (C). 1996. lib. bdg. 42.50 (*0-7618-0199-5*) U Pr of Amer.

Ofer, Dalia & Weitzman, Lenore J., eds. Women in the Holocaust. LC 97-46011. 416p. 1998. 35.00 (*0-300-07354-2*) Yale U Pr.

— Women in the Holocaust. 416p. 1999. pap. 15.95 (*0-300-08080-8*) Yale U Pr.

Ofer, Gur. The Service Sector in Soviet Economic Growth: A Comparative Study. LC 72-87775. (Russian Research Center Studies, No. 71, Economic Studies; No. 141). (Illus.). 216p. 1973. 16.50 (*0-674-80180-6*) HUP.

Ofer, Gur & Vinokur, Aaron. The Soviet Household under the Old Regime: Economic Conditions & Behaviour in the 1970s. (Illus.). 414p. (C). 1992. text 80.00 (*0-521-38398-6*) Cambridge U Pr.

Ofer, Gur, jt. auth. see De Melo, Martha.

Ofer, Gur, jt. ed. see Bosworth, Barry P.

O'Ferrall, Edward M. The Open Forum: Your Gateway to Open & Distance Learning. (Illus.). 352p. 1997. pap. 19.95 (*1-86149-014-3*, Pub. by Edition XII) Baker & Taylor.

— Worldwide Directory of Postgraduate Studies in Arts, Humanities, Economics & Social Sciences. (Edition XII Postgraduate Ser.). (Illus.). 224p. 1998. pap. 14.95 (*1-86149-015-1*, Pub. by Edition XII) Baker & Taylor.

— Worldwide Directory of Postgraduate Studies in Engineering, IT, Computer Science & Mathematics. (Edition XII Postgraduate Ser.). (Illus.). 208p. 1998. pap. 14.95 (*1-86149-017-8*, Pub. by Edition XII) Baker & Taylor.

— Worldwide Directory of Postgraduate Studies in Science. 3rd rev. ed. (Edition XII Postgraduate Ser.). (Illus.). 180p. 1998. pap. 14.95 (*1-86149-016-X*) Baker & Taylor.

O'Ferrall, Edward M., ed. Directory of MBAs. 2nd rev. ed. (Illus.). 720p. 1998. 19.95 (*1-86149-020-8*, Pub. by Edition XII) Baker & Taylor.

O'Ferrall, Fergus. Daniel O'Connell. (Gill's Irish Lives Ser.). (Illus.). 149p. 1998. reprint ed. pap. 13.95 (*0-7171-2689-7*, Pub. by Gill & MacMill) Irish Bks Media.

O'Ferrall, More G., ed. Beef Production from Different Dairy Breeds & Dairy Beef Crosses. 1982. text 207.50 (*90-247-2759-6*) Kluwer Academic.

Off the Curb Publishing Staff, ed. Heart Hiders: Kids Discover How to Memorize God's Word. (Illus.). (J). 1998. pap. 9.95 (*0-9660489-0-3*) Off the Curb Pub.

Offe, Claire & Heinze, Rolf G. Beyond Employment: Time, Work & the Informal Economy. Braley, Alan, tr. (Labor & Social Change Ser.). 248p. 1992. 59.95 (*0-87722-951-1*) Temple U Pr.

Offe, Claus. Contradictions of the Welfare State. Keane, John B., ed. (German Social Thought Ser.). 304p. (Orig.). (C). 1984. pap. text 18.00 (*0-262-65014-2*) MIT Pr.

— Disorganized Capitalism: Contemporary Transformations of Work & Politics. Keane, John B., tr. from GER. (German Social Thought Ser.). 280p. 1985. 30.00 (*0-262-15029-8*); pap. text 17.95 (*0-262-65031-2*) MIT Pr.

— Modernity & the State: East, West. LC 96-3429. (Studies in Contemporary German Social Thought). (Illus.). 288p. 1996. 36.00 (*0-262-15046-8*); pap. text 18.00 (*0-262-65047-9*) MIT Pr.

— Varieties of Transition: East European & East German Experience. LC 96-9046. (Studies in Contemporary German Social Thought). 259p. 1996. 36.00 (*0-262-15048-4*) MIT Pr.

— Varieties of Transition: The East European & East German Experience. LC 96-9046. (Studies in Contemporary German Social Thought). 259p. 1996. pap. text 18.00 (*0-262-65048-7*) MIT Pr.

Offederal, E., jt. ed. see Bjerkholt, Olav.

Offen, H. Scared of a Bear. (Illus.). (J). 1996. pap. text 11.95 (*0-340-65350-7*, Pub. by Hodder & Stought Ltd) Trafalgar.

Offen, H. There Might Be Giants. (Illus.). (J). pap. text 11.95 (*0-340-68149-7*, Pub. by Hodder & Stought Ltd) Trafalgar.

— Watch Out for Witches. (Illus.). (J). 1996. mass mkt. 7.95 (*0-340-66732-X*, Pub. by Hodder & Stought Ltd) Trafalgar.

Offen, Hilda. Bad Day ABC. 32p. (J). pap. 9.96 (*0-14-055653-2*, Pub. by Pnguin Bks Ltd) Trafalgar.

Offen, Hilda. Good Girl, Grace Growler. LC 96-31212. (Illus.). 32p. (J). (ps up). 1996. lib. bdg. 21.27 (*0-8368-1624-2*) Gareth Stevens Inc.

Offen, Hilda. Rita the Rescuer. (Illus.). 32p. (J). pap. 7.95 (*0-14-038598-3*, Pub. by Pnguin Bks Ltd) Trafalgar.

— Roll-Up, Roll-Up It's Rita. (Illus.). 32p. (J). pap. 7.95 (*0-14-038698-X*, Pub. by Pnguin Bks Ltd) Trafalgar.

— SOS for Rita. (Illus.). 32p. (J). 1995. pap. 7.95 (*0-14-037092-7*, Pub. by Pnguin Bks Ltd) Trafalgar.

Offen, Hilda. A Treasury of Bedtime Stories. 160p. (J). (gr. 2 up). 1981. 14.00 (*0-671-44463-8*) S&S Bks Yung.

— A Treasury of Mother Goose. 160p. (J). (ps-3). 1984. pap. 14.00 (*0-671-50118-6*) S&S Bks Yung.

Offen, Kare. European Feminism. 1998. 24.95 (*0-8057-8608-2*, Twyne) Mac Lib Ref.

***Offen, Karen.** European Feminisms, 1700-1950: A Political History. LC 99-44067. 2000. pap. text 19.95 (*0-8047-3420-8*) Stanford U Pr.

Offen, Karen. Paul de Cassagnac & the Authoritarian Tradition in 19th-Century France. rev. ed. LC 91-23151. 416p. 1991. text 45.00 (*0-8153-0479-X*) Garland.

Offen, Karen M., jt. ed. see Bell, Susan G.

Offen, Liz, jt. auth. see Waller, Glenn.

Offen, Neil, jt. auth. see Peithman, Stephen.

Offen, Neil, jt. ed. see Peithman, Stephen.

Offen, Ron. Instead of Gifts. 40p. 1995. pap. 7.95 (*0-944754-26-0*) Pudding Hse Pubns.

Offenbach, J. Tales of Hoffman: Vocal Score. (ENG & FRE.). 332p. 1986. pap. 26.95 (*0-7935-0693-X*, 50338400) H Leonard.

— Tales of Hoffman Libretto: Dialogue Met Version. (ENG & FRE.). 1986. pap. 4.95 (*0-7935-5379-2*, 50340620) H Leonard.

Offenbach, Jacques. Les Contes D'Hoffmann. 1998. pap. 7.95 (*963-8303-18-2*) Konemann.

— Offenbach in America: Notes of a Travelling Musician. LC 74-24172. reprint ed. 37.50 (*0-404-13076-3*) AMS Pr.

— Offenbach's Songs from the Great Operettas. 195p. 1976. pap. 12.95 (*0-486-23341-3*) Dover.

Offenbacker, Beth. Alexandria Virginia: Portrait of a City. (Illus.). 160p. 1998. 34.95 (*1-890291-05-6*) Platinum Pubng.

Offenberg, Adri K. A Choice of Corals. Facets of Fifteenth Century Hebrew Printing. (Illus.). 263p. 1992. 87.50 (*90-6004-421-5*, Pub. by B De Graaf) Coronet Bks.

Offenberg, Adri K., et al, eds. Bibliotheca Rosenthalia: Treasures of Jewish Booklore. LC 95-146605. (C). 1996. 47.50 (*90-5356-088-2*, Pub. by Amsterdam U Pr) U of Mich Pr.

Offenberg, Adri K. & Van Walraven, C. Moed, compiled by. Hebrew Incunabula in Public Collections: A First International Census. 300p. 1990. lib. bdg. 77.50 (*90-6004-404-5*, Pub. by B De Graaf) Coronet Bks.

Offenberger, Niels. Zur Modernen Deutung der Aristotelischen Logik Bd. IV: Niels Offenberger, Zur Vorgeschichte der Mehrwertigen Logik in der Antike. (GER.). viii, 172p. 1990. write for info. (*3-487-09350-2*) G Olms Pubs.

Offenberger, Niels, jt. auth. see Menne, Albert.

Offenberger, Nils & Vigo, Alejandro G. Sudamerikanische Beitrage zur Modernen Deutung der Aristotelischen Logik. (Zur Modernen Deutung der Aristotelischen Logik Ser.: Bd. 7). (GER.). x, 296p. 1997. write for info. (*3-487-10492-X*) G Olms Pubs.

***Offenburger, Andrew.** Over the Hill Twice: A Bio-Narrative of Paul McCorkle. Godwin, Denise M., ed. xi, 176p. 2000. write for info. (*0-9678576-0-0*); pap. write for info. (*0-9678576-1-9*) S & T Pubng.

Offenburger, Chuck. Babe: An Iowa Legend. LC 88-37461. (Illus.). 168p. 1989. reprint ed. pap. 52.10 (*0-608-06856-X*, 206706200009) Bks Demand.

— Iowa Boy: Ten Years of Columns by Chuck Offenburger. LC 87-17269. (Illus.). 250p. (Orig.). 1987. pap. 15.95 (*0-8138-0039-0*) Iowa St U Pr.

Offenburger, Jeffrey & Constant, Nancy. Mind Matters in Selling. unabridged ed. 20p. pap. text 69.50 incl. audio (*0-88432-175-4*, S29600) Audio-Forum.

Offenhauser, Stefan. Reflexion und Freiheit: Zum Verhaltnis von Philosophie und Poesie in Rilkes und Holderlins Spatwerk. (GER.). 240p. 1996. 44.95 (*3-631-30945-7*) P Lang Pubng.

***Offenstadt, Patrick.** Jean Beraud: The Belle Epoque: A Dream of Times Gone By. 1999. 49.99 (*3-8228-6513-3*) Taschen Amer.

***Offentliche Kunstsammlung Basel Staff, et al.** From Schongauer to Holbein: Master Drawings from Basel & Berlin. LC 99-36741. 1999. write for info. (*0-89468-246-6*) Natl Gallery Art.

Offer, Avner. The First World War: An Agrarian Interpretation. (Illus.). 480p. 1991. reprint ed. pap. 25.00 (*0-19-820279-2*) OUP.

— Property & Politics, 1870-1914: Ideology & Urban Development in England. (Modern Revivals in History Ser.). 445p. 1992. 72.95 (*0-7512-0066-2*, Pub. by Gregg Revivals) Ashgate Pub Co.

Offer, Avner, ed. In Pursuit of the Quality of Life. LC 96-31301. (Illus.). 310p. 1997. text 69.00 (*0-19-828002-5*) OUP.

Offer, D., et al. The Teenage World: Adolescents' Self-Image in Ten Countries. LC 88-4127. (Illus.). 288p. (C). 1988. 57.50 (*0-306-42747-8*, Kluwer Plenum) Kluwer Academic.

Offer, Daniel, jt. ed. see Strozier, Charles B.

Offer, John. Herbert Spencer: Critical Assessments. LC 99-20778. 1950p. 2000. write for info. (*0-415-18183-6*) Routledge.

— Social Workers, the Community, & Social Interaction: Intervention & the Sociology of Welfare. 1999. pap. text 29.95 (*1-85302-731-6*) Taylor & Francis.

Offer, John, ed. see Spencer, Herbert.

Offer, Judith S. Gardening Out Loud. (Illus.). 40p. (Orig.). 1997. pap. 11.95 (*0-9649776-1-3*) Plesnt Hill.

Offer, Penny, jt. ed. see Acorn, Sonia.

Offerhaus, J. P., ed. see Verzijl, J. H.

Offerhaus, J. P. S., jt. ed. see Heere, Wybo P.

Offerman, Lynn. The Dress-Up Bears. LC 98-68544. (YA). (ps-2). 1999. pap. 6.95 (*0-7613-1033-9*) Millbrook Pr.

— Little Teddy Bear's Happy Face Sad Face. 12p. (J). (ps-k). 1999. 9.95 (*0-7613-0983-7*, Copper Beech Bks) Millbrook Pr.

***Offerman, Lynn.** Little Teddy Bear's Happy Face Sad Face. 4p. (J). 1998. bds. 12.98 (*1-58048-035-7*) Sandvik Pub.

Offerman, Lynn. My Own Pet. LC 98-68543. (Illus.). 10p. (YA). (ps-k). 1999. pap. 6.95 (*0-7613-1034-7*) Millbrook Pr.

— Where Is It? Hers. (Nuk Bks.). (Illus.). 8p. (J). 1998. 6.95 (*0-7641-7233-6*) Barron.

***Offerman, Susan, ed.** Directory of Grants for Graduate Study & Research Overseas: A Source Book for Students & Scholars from the U. S. A. 10th rev. ed. 305p. 2000. pap. 29.00 (*1-930459-02-5*) Overseas.

— Directory of Grants for Medical Study & Research in the U. S. A. 10th rev. ed. 165p. 2000. pap. 52.00 (*1-930459-01-7*) Overseas.

— Directory of Grants for Study & Research in the U. S. A. A Source Book for Students & Scholars from Other Countries. 14th rev. ed. 285p. 2000. pap. 42.00 (*1-930459-00-9*) Overseas.

Offerman, Theo. Beliefs & Decision Rules in Public Good Games: Theory & Experiments. LC 97-30710. 248p. 1997. 121.00 (*0-7923-9991-9*) Kluwer Academic.

Offerman-Zuckerberg, J. Critical Psychophysical Passages in the Life of a Woman: A Psychodynamic Perspective. LC 88-12615. (Illus.). 310p. (C). 1988. 54.50 (*0-306-42639-0*, Kluwer Plenum) Kluwer Academic.

— Gender in Transition: A New Frontier. (Illus.). 326p. (C). 1989. 59.50 (*0-306-43132-7*, Kluwer Plenum) Kluwer Academic.

— Politics & Psychology: Contemporary Psychodynamic Perspectives. (Illus.). 336p. (C). 1991. 59.50 (*0-306-43864-X*, Plenum Trade) Perseus Pubng.

Offermann, Lynn R. & Gowing, Marilyn K., eds. Organizational Psychology. (Special Issue American Psychologist Ser.: Vol. 45, No. 2). 224p. 1990. pap. 16.00 (*1-55798-092-6*) Am Psychol.

Offers, J. A. Citrus Diseases & Defects Found in the Marketplace. (ENG, FRE, GER & SPA., Illus.). 70p. (Orig.). 1987. pap. 40.00 (*0-614-30365-6*, Pub. by J A Offers) FL Sci Source.

Office de la Langue Francaise Staff. Vocabulary of Banking & Currency. (ENG & FRE.). 39p. 1974. pap. 14.95 (*0-8288-9388-8*) Fr & Eur.

— Vocabulary of Paper Industry Materials: Vocabulaire du Materiel Papetier. (ENG & FRE.). 144p. 1983. 75.00 (*0-8288-4419-4*, M7573) Fr & Eur.

Office des Nations Unies a Geneve. Navigation Interieure (Remplace TERM/15) (FRE.). 205p. 1997. pap. 42.00 (*92-1-000058-7*) UN.

***Office for National Statistics, Social Survey Division Staff, et al.** General Household Survey No. 28: Living in Britain. (Illus.). 344p. 2000. pap. 85.00 (*0-11-621254-3*, HM12543, Pub. by Statnry Office) Balogh.

***Office for National Statistics Staff.** Annual Abstract of Statistics, 2000. 360p. 2000. pap. 90.00 (*0-11-621270-5*, Pub. by Statnry Office) Balogh.

— Birth Statistics. (Series FMI: No. 27). (Illus.). xxxii, 83p. 1998. 60.00 (*0-11-621245-4*, Pub. by Statnry Office) Balogh.

Office for National Statistics Staff. Britain 1999: The Official Yearbook of the United Kingdom. 50th annot. ed. xii, 564p. 1998. 80.00 (*0-11-621037-0*, Pub. by Statnry Office) Balogh.

Office for National Statistics Staff. Cancer Statistics. iv, 72p. Date not set. write for info. (*0-11-621247-0*, Pub. by Statnry Office) Balogh.

— Guide to Official Statistics: 2000 Edition. 200p. 2000. pap. 70.00 (*0-11-621161-X*, HM1161X, Pub. by Statnry Office) Balogh.

— Mortality Statistics: Review of the Registrar General on Deaths by Cause, Sex & Age, in England & Wales, 1998. (Series DH2, 25). (Illus.). xxxii, 250p. 1999. 70.00 (*0-11-621257-8*, Pub. by Statnry Office) Balogh.

Office for National Statistics Staff & Coleman, Michel P. Cancer Survival Trends in England & Wales, 1971-1995: Deprivation & NHS Region. 695p. 1999. 285.00 (*0-11-621031-1*, Pub. by Statnry Office) Balogh.

***Office for National Statistics Staff & HMSO Staff.** Britain, 2000: The Official Yearbook of Great Britain. 576p. 1999. 80.00 (*0-11-621098-2*, HM10982, Pub. by Statnry Office) Balogh.

***Office for Official Publications of the European Communites.** EUR-ASEAN Relations: A Growing Partnership. LC 99-196556. 64p. 1998. write for info. (*92-828-5321-7*, Pub. by Comm Europ Commun) Intl Pubns Serv.

— Panorama of European Business, 1999. 552p. 2000. pap. 65.00 (*92-828-7638-1*, CA25-99-043-EN-C, Pub. by Comm Europ Commun) Balogh.

Office for Official Publications of the European Communites, jt. auth. see European Commission.

Office for Official Publications of the European Communites, jt. auth. see Statistical Office of the European Communities.

Office for Official Publications of the European Communites, jt. auth. see Tacis Technical Dissemination Project Staff.

Office for Official Publications of the European Communities, jt. auth. see Bradbury, Derek.

***Office for Outer Space Affairs United Nations Office at Vienna Staff.** Seminars of the United Nations Programme on Space Applications: Selected Papers on Remote Sensing, Space Science & Information Technology, 1999. 105p. 1999. 30.00 (*92-1-100810-7*) UN.

***Office for Outer Space Affairs, Vienna Staff.** Highlights in Space, 1998: Progress in Space Science, Technology & Applications, International Cooperation & Space Law. 91p. 1999. 25.00 (*92-1-100809-3*) UN.

Office International des Epizooties Staff. Dictionary of Animal Health Terminology in English, French, Spanish, German & Latin. Mack, Roy, ed. (ENG, FRE, GER, LAT & SPA.). 426p. 1992. 250.00 (*0-8288-9215-6*) Fr & Eur.

Office Lighting Committee Staff. Lighting Merchandising Areas: RP-2-85. rev. ed. (Recommended Practices Ser.). (Illus.). 72p. 1986. pap. 18.00 (*0-87995-021-8*, RP-2-85) Illum Eng.

Office Management & Budget Staff. North American Industry Classification System (NAICS) - United States, 1997. 1200p. 1998. pap. 28.50 (*0-934213-57-7*) Natl Tech Info.

***Office of Black Ministries.** But We See Jesus: A Pastoral Letter from the Black Episcopal Bishops to Black Clergy & Laity. LC 99-38454. 48p. 1999. pap. 7.95 (*0-8192-1798-0*, 6077) Morehouse Pub.

Office of Commissioner Federal Judicial Affairs St. Federal Court Reports: Consolidated Index 1989-1992. Rankin, William J., ed. (FRE.). 287p. 1993. 162.50 (*0-660-58036-5*, Pub. by Canadian Govt Pub) Accents Pubns.

Office of Disease Prevention & Health Promotion St, jt. auth. see American Dietetic Association Staff.

Office of Evangelism Ministries, The Episcopal Chu. The Catechumenal Process: Adult Initiation & Formation for Christian Life & Ministry. 304p. 1990. pap. 18.95 (*0-89869-223-7*) Church Pub Inc.

Office of General Assembly Staff, jt. auth. see Presbyterian & Reformed Staff.

***Office of General Counsel Staff & Cosa Member Attorneys Staff.** A School Law Primer, Pt. II. 2000. 300.00 (*0-88364-234-4*, Pub. by Natl Sch Boards) PMDS-AACRAO.

Office of Hawaiian Affairs, contrib. by. Onipa'a: Five Days in the History of the Hawaiian Nation. (Illus.). 208p. 1994. 36.00 (*1-56647-051-X*) Mutual Pub HI.

Office of Home Secretary Staff, ed. see National Academy of Sciences Staff.

Office of International Affairs, National Research. U. S.-Japan Strategic Alliances in the Semiconductor Industry: Technology Transfer, Competition, & Public Policy. 126p. (C). 1992. pap. text 19.00 (*0-309-04779-X*) Natl Acad Pr.

Office of Legal Affairs, Division for Ocean Affair. Conservation & Utilization of the Living Resources of the Exclusive Economic Zone: Conservation & Utilization of the Living Resources of the Exclusive Economic Zone; Legislative History of Articles 61 & 62 of the United Nations Convention on the Law. LC 96-130161. (The Law of the Sea Ser.). 144p. 25.00 (*92-1-133501-9*) UN.

O

***Office of Legal Affairs Staff, ed.** Collection of Essays by Legal Advisers of States: Legal Advisors of International Organizations & Practitioners in the Field of International Law. 523p. 1999. 24.95 (*92-1-033080-3*) UN.

Office of Management & Budget. Guide to Best Practices for Contract Administration. 31p. 1994. pap. 34.99 (*1-56726-059-4*) Mgmt Concepts.

— Guide to Best Practices for Past Performance. 65p. 1995. pap. 34.99 (*1-56726-058-6*) Mgmt Concepts.

Office of Management & Budget Staff. Managing Federal Assistance in the 1980s, 3 vols., Set. 1982. reprint ed. 150.00 (*0-89941-223-8*, 201560) W S Hein.

— North American Industry Classification System (NAICS) - United States, 1997. 1200p. 1998. 32.50 (*0-934213-56-9*) Natl Tech Info.

Office of NAHB General Counsel Staff & C. Flag. Contracts & Liability for Builders & Remodelers. 4th ed. (Illus.). 192p. 1995. pap. 38.50 (*0-86718-417-5*) Home Builder.

***Office of Operations & Technical Assistance Staff.** Decisions of the Federal Labor Relations Authority. 1999. reprint ed. 5112.25 (*1-57588-489-5*) W S Hein.

Office of Personnel Management, Retirement & Insur. Federal Employees Retirement System. 1997. pap. 2.75 (*0-16-048876-1*, 006-000-01429-1) USGPO.

Office of Population Censuses & Surveys Staff. Communicable Disease Statistics. (OPCS Series MB2: No. 22, 1995). 66p. 1997. pap. 45.00 (*0-11-620919-4*, HM09194, Pub. by Statnry Office) Bernan Associates.

— Communicable Disease Statistics (OPCS Series MB2) 1992, No. 19. 66p. 1994. pap. 19.00 (*0-11-691572-2*, HM15722, Pub. by Statnry Office) Bernan Associates.

Office of Research & Policy, Radio Marti Program S. Cuba Annual Report 1985. 400p. 1987. 79.95 (*0-88738-146-4*) Transaction Pubs.

Office of Research & Policy Staff. Cuba Annual Report 1986. 800p. 1989. 79.95 (*0-88738-191-X*) Transaction Pubs.

Office of Research & Policy Staff, et al. Cuba Annual Report, 1987. 800p. 1989. 79.95 (*0-88738-273-8*) Transaction Pubs.

Office of Security Programs University of Illnois. Community Policing for Law Enforcement Managers. Fanning, Paul, ed. LC 95-82387. 169p. 1995. ring bd. write for info. (*0-942715-04-7*) IL Criminal Just.

Office of Solid Waste & Emergency Response, U. S. Composting: Yard & Municipal Solid Waste. 151p. 1995. pap. 64.95 (*1-56676-283-9*, 762839) Technomic.

Office of South Carolina Court Administration Staf. South Carolina Bench Book for Magistrates & Municipal Court Judges. 3rd ed. 1997. ring bd. 100.00 (*0-943856-02-7*, 410) SC Bar CLE.

Office of State-Federal Relations Staff. Summary of the One Hundred First Congress (1989) First Session. (State-Federal Issue Brief Ser.: Vol. 2, No. 11). 10p. 1989. pap. text 6.50 (*1-55516-881-7*, 8500-0211) Natl Conf State Legis.

Office of Technology Assessment Staff. Technologies for Prehistoric & Historic Preservation. LC 87-3304. 210p. 1988. reprint ed. lib. bdg. 27.50 (*0-89464-219-7*) Krieger.

Office of Technology Assessment Staff, compiled by. Wastes in Marine Environments. LC 66-65012. 320p. 1987. 78.95 (*0-89116-793-5*) Hemisp Pub.

Office of Technology Assessment Task Force Staff, ed. Life-Sustaining Technologies & the Elderly. LC 65-20241. 450p. 1988. text 39.95 (*0-397-53024-2*) Lppncott W & W.

Office of the Adj General Staff, compiled by. Record of Officers & Men of New Jersey in the Civil War, 1861-1865, 2 vols., Set. 1996. reprint ed. lib. bdg. 199.00 (*0-8328-5212-0*) Higginson Bk Co.

***Office of the Assistant Chief of Air Intelligence Staff.** German Aircraft & Armament: The U. S. Government's Official Identification Manual. 2000. pap. 26.95 (*1-57488-291-0*) Brasseys.

Office of the Chief of Engineers, U. S. Army Staff, ed. Laws of the United States Relating to the Improvement of Rivers & Harbors from August 11, 1790 to June 29, 1938, 3 vols., Set. LC 73-5434. reprint ed. 125.00 (*0-404-11190-4*) AMS Pr.

Office of the National Environ. Board. The Integrated Management Plan for Ban Don Bay & Phangnga Bay, Thailand. (ICLARM Technical Reports: No. 30). 161p. 1992. per. write for info. (*971-8709-16-9*, Pub. by ICLARM) Intl Spec Bk.

Office of the Secretary of State Staff, compiled by. State of N. J., 3 vols., Set. 1452p. 1996. reprint ed. lib. bdg. 156.00 (*0-8328-5213-9*) Higginson Bk Co.

Office of the Sesquicentennial Fordham University. As I Remember Fordham: Selections from the Sesquicentennial Oral History Project. LC 91-61628. xvi, 208p. 1991. 20.00 (*0-8232-1338-2*) Fordham.

Office of the Special Coordinator for Africa & the. Informal Sector Development in Africa. LC 96-166681. 128p. pap. 10.00 (*92-1-004034-1*, HC800) UN.

Office of the United States Chief of Counsel for P. Nazi Conspiracy & Aggression, Set. LC 96-79659. 1996. reprint ed. 1195.00 (*1-57588-202-7*, 310890) W S Hein.

***Office of Theology & Worship Staff.** Book of Occasional Services. 176p. 1999. pap. 16.95 (*0-664-50098-6*) Geneva Press.

— Book of Occasional Services. deluxe ed. 176p. 1999. lthr. 29.95 (*0-664-50107-9*) Geneva Press.

Office of Transporation Technologies, U. S. Dept.of Energy, contrib. by. Encouraging the Purchase & Use of Electric Motor Vehicles (July, 1995) (Electric Vehicle Information Ser.: Vol. 24). (Illus.). 134p. 1996. pap. 105.00 (*0-89934-287-6*, BT051); lib. bdg. 145.00 (*0-89934-288-4*, BT951) Bus Tech Bks.

Office of Water Resources Research Staff, compiled by. Algae Abstracts: A Guide to the Literature, 3 vols. Incl. Vol. 1. To 1969. 586p. 1973. 95.00 (*0-306-67181-6*, Kluwer Plenum); Vol. 2. 1970 to 1972. 694p. 1973. 95.00 (*0-306-67182-4*, Kluwer Plenum); Vol. 3. 1972 to 1974. 890p. 1976. 95.00 (*0-306-67183-2*, Kluwer Plenum); write for info. (*0-318-53513-0*, Kluwer Plenum) Kluwer Academic.

Office Staff of the Home Secretary. Biographical Memoirs, Vol. 60. 400p. 1991. 70.50 (*0-309-04442-1*) Natl Acad Pr.

Office Stationary Staff. Finance Acts: 1998 Chapter 36. 1998. pap. text 65.00 (*0-10-543698-4*, Pub. by Statnry Office) Bernan Associates.

— Parliamentary Debates, House of Lords No. 583: 10 November-4 December 1997, 1997-98 Edition. (Parliamentary Debates, House of Lords Ser.). 1998. 90.00 (*0-10-780583-9*, Pub. by Statnry Office) Bernan Associates.

***Officer, Charles & Page, Jake.** Earth & You: Tales of the Environment. LC 00-26347. (Illus.). 224p. 2000. write for info. (*0-914339-87-7*, Pub. by P E Randall Pub) U Pr of New Eng.

Officer, Charles B., jt. auth. see Page, Jake.

Officer, James E., ed. see Schuetz-Miller, Mardith, et al.

Officer, Jane. If I Should Die: A Death Row Correspondence. 144p. 1997. pap. 10.95 (*1-873797-22-2*, Pub. by New Clarion) Paul & Co Pubs.

Officer, Lawrence A., ed. International Economics. (C). 1987. lib. bdg. 100.50 (*0-89838-196-7*) Kluwer Academic.

Officer, Lawrence H. Between the Dollar-Sterling Gold Points: Exchange Rates, Parity, & Market Behaviour. (Studies in Monetary & Financial History). 363p. (C). 1996. text 64.95 (*0-521-45462-X*) Cambridge U Pr.

— Econometric Model of Canada under the Fluctuating Exchange Rate. LC 68-14270. (Economic Studies: No. 130). (Illus.). 331p. 1968. 22.50 (*0-674-22500-7*) HUP.

— Purchasing Power Parity & Exchange Rates: Theory, Evidence & Relevance. LC 80-82479. (Contemporary Studies in Economic & Financial Analysis: Vol. 35). 384p. 1982. 78.50 (*0-89232-229-2*) Jai Pr.

Officer, Lawrence H., et al. So You Have to Write an Economics Term Paper. LC 80-80313. x, 149p. (Orig.). 1985. reprint ed. pap. 9.95 (*0-87013-229-6*) Mich St U Pr.

Officer, Robyn. For My Daughter, with Love Mini Edition. LC 98-86357. 1999. 4.95 (*0-8362-7884-4*) Andrews & McMeel.

— For You, Mother Mini Edition. LC 98-86594. 1999. 4.95 (*0-8362-8171-3*) Andrews & McMeel.

***Officer, Robyn.** Language of Love: A Romantic Miscellany, Mini Edition. 2000. 4.95 (*0-7407-0514-8*) Andrews & McMeel.

— A Very Merry Christmas. 80p. 1999. 4.95 (*0-7407-0062-6*) Andrews & McMeel.

Officer, Robyn. Mother Goose's Nursery Rhymes. (Children's Classics Ser.). 32p. (J). (ps-3). 1992. 6.95 (*0-8362-4907-0*) Andrews & McMeel.

Officer X. Ten-Eight: A Cop's Honest Look at Life on the Street. LC 94-68989. 240p. (Orig.). 1994. pap. 14.95 (*0-935878-13-0*) Calibre Pr.

Officers of the U. S. Army Ordinance Dept. Small Arms, 1856: Reports of Experiments with Small Arms for the Military Service. (Illus.). 168p. (C). 1984. reprint ed. 14.95 (*0-939631-01-6*) Thomas Publications.

Official Historians of the Second Bombardment. Defenders of Liberty: Second Bombardment Group. anniversary ed. (Illus.). 488p. Date not set. 54.95 (*1-56311-238-8*) Turner Pub KY.

***Offill, Jenny.** Last Things. 272p. 2000. pap. 11.95 (*0-385-33495-8*, Delta Trade) Dell.

— Last Things. LC 99-10758. 272p. 1999. text 23.00 (*0-374-18405-4*) FS&G.

Offiong, Daniel O. Imperialism & Dependency: Obstacles to African Development. LC 82-15833. 304p. 1982. pap. 12.95 (*0-88258-127-9*) Howard U Pr.

Offit, Avodah K. Night Thoughts: Reflections of a Sex Therapist. rev. ed. LC 94-45758. 256p. 1995. pap. 25.00 (*1-56821-458-8*) Aronson.

— The Sexual Self: How Character Shapes Sexual Experience. 336p. 1995. pap. 25.00 (*1-56821-548-7*) Aronson.

— Virtual Love. LC 93-36227. 1994. 22.00 (*0-671-87436-5*) S&S Trade.

***Offit, Paul A. & Bell, Louis M.** Vaccines: What Every Parent Should Know. 2nd ed. 240p. 1999. 12.95 (*0-02-863861-1*) S&S Trade.

Offit, Paul A., et al. Breaking the Antibiotic Habit: A Parent's Guide to Coughs, Colds, Ear Infections & Sore Throats. LC 98-36478. 186p. 1999. pap. 12.95 (*0-471-31982-1*) Wiley.

Offit, Sidney. He Had it Made. 1999. pap. text 11.95 (*0-931761-63-8*) Beckham Pubns.

— Memoir of Bookie's Son. 176p. 1996. pap. 10.95 (*0-312-14368-0*) St Martin.

Offitt, Kenneth. Clinical Cancer Genetics: Risk Counseling & Management. LC 97-14958. 419p. 1997. 79.95 (*0-471-14655-2*) Wiley.

Offitzer, Karen. Diners. LC 97-36147. 1997. 16.98 (*1-56799-604-3*, MetroBooks) M Friedman Pub Grp Inc.

***Offitzer, Karen.** Great American Emporiums: A Grand History of Department Stores. 80p. 1999. 12.98 (*0-7624-0595-3*) Running Pr.

Offitzer, Karen, compiled by. The Learning Annex Guide to Starting Your Own Import-Export Business. 108p. 1992. pap. 8.95 (*0-8065-1321-7*, Citadel Pr) Carol Pub Group.

Offler, H. S. North of the Tees: Studies in Medieval British History. Doyle, A. I. & Piper, A. J., eds. (Collected Studies: No. CS547). 320p. 1996. 98.95 (*0-86078-599-8*, Pub. by Variorum) Ashgate Pub Co.

Offler, H. S., ed. see Ockham, William.

Offley, Ed, jt. auth. see Owens, William A.

Offner, Arnold A. The Origins of the Second World War: American Foreign Policy & World Politics, 1917-1941. LC 85-23928. 288p. (C). 1986. reprint ed. pap. 19.50 (*0-89464-320-7*); reprint ed. text 23.50 (*0-89874-924-7*) Krieger.

***Offner, Arnold A. & Wilson, Theodore A.** Victory in Europe, 1945: From World War to Cold War. LC 00-39873. (Modern War Studies). 2000. 39.95 (*0-7006-1039-1*) U Pr of KS.

Offner, David. Design Homology: An Introduction to Bionics. 202p. (C). 1995. pap. text 25.00 (*0-9649062-0-1*) D Offner.

Offner, Denny. The Restaurant Phenomenon: An Essential Guide. (Illus.). 114p. 1997. 24.95 (*1-882935-28-4*) Westphalia.

Offner, Hazel. The Fruit of the Spirit. (LifeGuide Bible Studies). 64p. 1987. pap., wbk. ed. 4.99 (*0-8308-1058-7*, 1058) InterVarsity.

— Fruit of the Spirit. rev. ed. (Life Guide Bible Studies Ser.). 57p. 1999. pap. 4.99 (*0-8308-3058-8*, 3058) InterVarsity.

Offner, Herman L. Administrative Procedures for Changing Curriculum Patterns for Selected State Teachers Colleges. LC 76-177131. (Columbia University. Teachers College. Contributions to Education Ser.: No. 898). reprint ed. 37.50 (*0-404-55898-4*) AMS Pr.

Offner, Jerome A. Law & Politics in Aztec Texcoco. LC 82-4368. (Cambridge Latin American Studies: No. 44). (Illus.). 368p. 1984. text 85.00 (*0-521-23475-1*) Cambridge U Pr.

Offner, John L. An Unwanted War: The Diplomacy of the United States & Spain over Cuba, 1895-1898. LC 91-48198. (Illus.). xiv, 306p. (C). 1992. pap. 22.50 (*0-8078-4380-6*) U of NC Pr.

Offner, Paul. Medicaid & the States. LC 98-35591. (Devolution Revolution Ser.). 72p. 1998. pap. 9.95 (*0-87078-426-9*) Century Foundation.

Offner, Richard. Italian Primitives at Yale University. (Illus.). 1927. 100.00 (*0-685-89760-5*) Elliots Bks.

Offner, Richard, et al. A Discerning Eye: Essays on Early Italian Painting. LC 97-13867. 1998. 60.00 (*0-271-01747-3*) Pa St U Pr.

Offner, Richardson R. A Critical & Historical Corpus of Florentine Painting Section IV. 85.00 (*0-685-71750-X*) J J Augustin.

— A Critical & Historical Corpus of Florentine Painting Section IV, IV. 220.00 (*0-685-71749-6*) J J Augustin.

Offner, Rose. The Companion Journal to the Soul. (Illus.). 128p. 1998. pap. 16.95 (*0-89087-872-2*) Celestial Arts.

***Offner, Rose.** Journal to Intimacy: A Couple's Journal for Sustaining Love. 128p. 2000. 19.95 (*0-89087-972-9*) Celestial Arts.

Offner, Rose. Journal to Intimacy: A Couples' Journal for Sustaining Love. (Illus.). 128p. 1998. pap. 19.95 (*0-89087-873-0*) Celestial Arts.

— Journal to the Soul: The Art of Sacred Journal Keeping. (Illus.). 96p. 1996. pap. 19.95 (*0-87905-702-5*) Gibbs Smith Pub.

***Offner, Rose.** Journal to the Soul for Teenagers. 128p. 1999. pap. 16.95 (*0-89087-899-4*) Celestial Arts.

Offner, Rose. Letters from the Soul: Unsent Letters & Stories for Spiritual Growth. (Illus.). 72p. (Orig.). 1997. pap. 19.95 (*0-87905-793-9*) Gibbs Smith Pub.

Offodile, Buchi, compiled by. The Orphan Girl & Other Stories: West African Folk Tales. (Illus.). Date not set. pap. 15.00 (*1-56656-375-5*) Interlink Pub.

***Offor, George.** Memoir of William Tyndale. 1999. pap. 20.00 (*1-58329-010-9*) Lazarus Minist.

Offor, George, ed. see Bunyan, John.

Offord, Carl R. The White Face. LC 73-18596. reprint ed. 32.50 (*0-404-11407-5*) AMS Pr.

Offord, Derek C. Modern Russian: An Advanced Grammar Course. 461p. 1993. pap. 31.95 (*1-85399-361-1*, Pub. by Brist Class Pr) Focus Pub-R Pullins.

— Nineteenth-Century Russia: Opposition to Autocracy. LC 98-55776. 160p. 1999. pap. 12.66 (*0-582-35767-5*) Addison-Wesley.

— The Russian Revolutionary Movement in the 1880s. (Illus.). 232p. 1986. text 59.95 (*0-521-32723-7*) Cambridge U Pr.

— Using Russian: A Guide to Contemporary Usage. LC 97-109160. 437p. (C). 1996. pap. 24.95 (*0-521-45760-2*) Cambridge U Pr.

— Using Russian: A Guide to Contemporary Usage. LC 97-109160. 437p. (C). 1997. text 64.95 (*0-521-45130-2*) Cambridge U Pr.

Offord, Derek C., jt. ed. see Leatherbarrow, William J.

Offord, Kenneth P., jt. auth. see Colligan, Robert C.

***Offord, M. H.** French Words: Past, Present & Future. LC 00-39460. (Modern Languages in Practice Ser.). (FRE & ENG.). 2000. pap. write for info. (*1-85359-496-2*) Taylor & Francis.

Offord, M. H., jt. auth. see Batchelor, R. E.

Offord, M. Y., ed. The Book of the Knight of the Tower Translated by William Caxton. (EETS Supplementary Ser.). 1971. 30.00 (*0-19-722402-4*, Pub. by EETS) Boydell & Brewer.

Offord, Malcolm H., ed. A Reader in French Sociolinguistics. LC 96-3294. (Applications in French Linguistics Ser.: Vol. 1). 213p. 1996. 99.00 (*1-85359-343-5*, Pub. by Multilingual Matters); pap. 34.95 (*1-85359-342-7*, Pub. by Multilingual Matters) Taylor & Francis.

Offord, Malcolm H., jt. auth. see Batchelor, R. E.

Offord, R. M., ed. Jerry McAuley, an Apostle to the Lost. LC 75-124248. (Select Bibliographies Reprint Ser.). (Illus.). 1977. reprint ed. 21.95 (*0-8369-5436-X*) Ayer.

Offord, Robin E. Semisynthetic Proteins. LC 79-40521. (Illus.). 247p. reprint ed. pap. 76.60 (*0-608-17555-2*, 203053500069) Bks Demand.

Offord, Robin E., jt. auth. see Yudkin, Michael.

Offredi, Mariola, ed. Literature, Language & the Media in India. (C). 1992. text 30.00 (*81-85425-75-2*, Pub. by Manohar) S Asia.

Offsey, Sol. Edifice & Other Stories. 56p. 1985. pap. 5.00 (*0-940584-08-5*) Gull Bks.

Offshore Mechanics and Arctic Engineering Division, ASME Staff, contrib. by. International Pipeline Conference, 1998; Proceedings, Vol. 2. LC 98-207925. 1121p. 1998. 220.00 (*0-7918-1580-3*) ASME.

Offshore Mechanics, Arctic Engineering, Deepsea Sy. Proceedings of the First Offshore Mechanics, Arctic Engineering, Deepsea Systems Symposium: Presented at Energy-Sources Technology Conference & Exhibition, New Orleans, Louisiana, March 7-10, 1982, 2 vols., Vol. 1. Chung, Jin S. et al, eds. LC 82-70515. (Illus.). 254p. reprint ed. pap. 78.80 (*0-8357-2838-2*, 203907400001) Bks Demand.

— Proceedings of the First Offshore Mechanics, Arctic Engineering, Deepsea Systems Symposium: Presented at Energy-Sources Technology Conference & Exhibition, New Orleans, Louisiana, March 7-10, 1982, 2 vols., Vol. 2. Chung, Jin S. et al, eds. LC 82-70515. (Illus.). 300p. reprint ed. pap. 93.00 (*0-8357-2839-0*, 203907400002) Bks Demand.

Offut, Andrew J. The Shadow of Sorcery. 240p. (Orig.). 1993. mass mkt. 4.99 (*0-441-76026-0*) Ace Bks.

Offutt, Andrew J. Swords Against Darkness, No. 1. 1990. mass mkt. 3.95 (*0-8217-2972-1*, Zebra Kensgtn) Kensgtn Pub Corp.

Offutt, Andrew J., ed. Swords Against Darkness, No. 5. 1981. mass mkt. 2.50 (*0-89083-839-9*, Zebra Kensgtn) Kensgtn Pub Corp.

Offutt, Charles R., jt. auth. see Offutt, Elizabeth R.

Offutt, Chris. The Good Brother: A Novel. 320p. 1998. per. 12.00 (*0-684-84619-5*) S&S Trade.

— Kentucky Straight. LC 91-5806. 1992. pap. 12.00 (*0-679-73886-X*) Vin Bks.

— Out of the Woods: Stories. LC 98-43041. 192p. 1999. 21.00 (*0-684-82556-2*) S&S Trade.

***Offutt, Chris.** Out of the Woods: Stories. 176p. 2000. per. 11.00 (*0-684-85376-0*) S&S Trade.

Offutt, Chris. The Same River Twice: A Memoir. 192p. 1994. pap. 9.95 (*0-14-023253-2*, Penguin Bks) Viking Penguin.

***Offutt, Chris.** Two-Eleven All Around. deluxe ed. 12p. 1998. pap. 100.00 (*0-9677410-0-9*) Danger Bks.

Offutt, David. A Perishable Good: Selected Poems. Offutt, Janet, ed. LC 98-92400. 53p. 1998. pap. 8.97 (*0-9663605-1-6*) Inflammable Pr.

Offutt, Elizabeth R. Teaching Science in a Multicultural World. 184p. 1996. 14.99 (*0-86653-866-6*, FE3866) Fearon Teacher Aids.

Offutt, Elizabeth R. & Offutt, Charles R. Internet Without Fear! Practical Tips & Activities for the Elementary Classroom. 144p. 1996. teacher ed. 14.99 (*1-56417-853-6*, GA1560) Good Apple.

Offutt, Jane S. Bluegrass Secrets: A Resource Guide for the Home & Garden. (Illus.). 192p. (Orig.). pap. text 12.95 (*1-883554-01-2*) City Secrets.

Offutt, Jane S., jt. auth. see Hodges, Renee.

Offutt, Janet, ed. see Offutt, David.

Offutt, Nelson T. More Than a Cookbook. LC 79-93281. 192p. 1981. pap., spiral bd. 6.95 (*0-89709-019-5*) Liberty Pub.

Offutt, William, jt. auth. see Sween, Jane C.

Offutt, William M. Bethesda: A Social History. rev. ed. (Illus.). 800p. 1995. 50.00 (*0-9643819-3-1*) Innovat Game.

— Bethesda: A Social History. 3rd rev. ed. (Illus.). 800p. 1996. pap. 30.00 (*0-9643819-9-0*) Innovat Game.

Offutt, William M., Jr. Of "Good Laws" & "Good Men" A Law & Society in the Delaware Valley, 1680-1710. 352p. 1995. text 39.95 (*0-252-02152-5*) U of Ill Pr.

Offutt, William M., ed. see Cartwright, William H. & Goeden, Louise E.

***Ofiaja, Nicholas D.** Africa: A Basic Text on Land, People & Culture. LC 99-16605. 1999. write for info. (*0-7734-7924-4*) E Mellen.

Ofiaja, Nicholas D. African Studies: Antiquity to Present. LC 95-25531. 1995. write for info. (*1-881839-43-5*) Educa Vision.

Ofiara, Douglas D & Seneca, Joseph J. Economic Losses From Marine Pollution: A Handbook For Assessment. (Illus.). 203p. 1999. 40.00 (*1-55963-609-2*) Island Pr.

Oficina, Su, tr. see Garcez, Antonio R.

Ofiesh, Mariam Namey. Archbishop Aftimios Ofiesh (1880-1966) A Biography Revealing His Contributions to Orthodoxy & Christendom. Abihider, Aftimios, ed. & illus. by. LC 97-76715. xiv, 274p. 1999. 44.95 (*0-9660908-1-0*) A Abihider.

Ofir, Gaston. El Infernal Negocio de los Secuestros: Arizmendi, S.A.; Escalofriante Red de Complicidades Politicas, Criminales y Policiacas al Descubierto 1999. pap. text 10.98 (*970-661-029-4*) Edamex.

Ofitserov, Dimitri V., jt. auth. see German, Oleg V.

O'Flaherty, Brendan. Making Room: The Economics of Homelessness. (Illus.). 352p. 1996. 44.50 (*0-674-54342-4*) HUP.

— Making Room: The Economics of Homelessness. (Illus.). 368p. 1998. pap. text 17.95 (*0-674-54343-2*) HUP.

— Rational Commitment: A Foundation for Macroeconomics. LC 85-13161. (Duke Press Policy Studies). (Illus.). x, 230p. 1985. text 46.95 (*0-8223-0454-6*) Duke.

O'Flaherty, C. A. Highways: Highway Engineering, Vol. 2. 3rd ed. 704p. (C). 1988. pap. text 75.00 (*0-7131-3596-4*, Pub. by E A) Routldge.

O'Flaherty, C. A., ed. Transport Planning & Traffic Engineering. LC 97-131686. 544p. 69.95 (*0-340-66279-4*, Pub. by E A) Routldge.

O'Flaherty, C. A., jt. auth. see Tough, J. M.

O

An Asterisk (*) at the beginning of an entry indicates that the title is appearing for the first time.

O'Flaherty, Colm A., ed. Transport Planning & Traffic Engineering. LC 97-131686. 560p. 1997. pap. 99.00 (*0-470-23619-1*) Wiley.

***O'Flaherty, Daniel.** General Jo Shelby: Undefeated Rebel. LC 99-89857. (Illus.). 456p. 2000. pap. 18.95 (*0-8078-4878-6*) U of NC Pr.

O'Flaherty, Eamon, tr. see Vovelle, Michel.

O'Flaherty, James, et al, eds. Studies in Nietzsche & the Judaeo-Christian Tradition. LC 84-11963. (University of North Carolina Studies in the Germanic Languages & Literatures: Vol. 103). 405p. reprint ed. pap. 125.60 (*0-608-08618-5*, 206914100003) Bks Demand.

O'Flaherty, James C. The Quarrel of Reason with Itself: Essays on Hamann, Nietzsche, Lessing, & Michaelis. LC 87-70862. (GERM Ser.: Vol. 35). (Illus.). xviii, 260p. 1991. 35.00 (*0-938100-56-4*) Camden Hse.

O'Flaherty, James C., et al, eds. Studies in Nietzsche & the Judaeo-Christian Tradition. LC 84-11963. (Germanic Languages & Literatures Ser.: No. 103). 424p. (C). 1985. lib. bdg. 45.00 (*0-8078-8104-X*) U of NC Pr.

O'Flaherty, James C., tr. & comment see Hamann, Johann G.

O'Flaherty, Jennifer E., jt. auth. see Baum, Victor C.

O'Flaherty, John. Because She Came from Atlanta. 250p. mass mkt. 4.99 (*1-896329-33-0*) Picasso Publ.

— No Place to Sit Down. 2001. pap. 16.95 (*1-57532-230-7*) Press-Tige Pub.

— She Wasn't Fair Game. 2001. pap. 8.95 (*1-57532-225-0*) Press-Tige Pub.

O'Flaherty, Joseph S. An End & a Beginning: The South Coast & Los Angeles 1850-1887. 2nd ed. LC 92-81269. (Illus.). 323p. 1992. 24.95 (*0-914421-05-0*) Hist Soc So CA.

— Those Powerful Years: The South Coast & Los Angeles 1887-1917. 2nd ed. LC 92-81270. (Illus.). 357p. 1992. 29.95 (*0-914421-06-9*) Hist Soc So CA.

O'Flaherty, Joseph T. & Ramwell, Peter W., eds. Platelet-Activating Factor Antagonists: New Developments for Clinical Application. (Advances in Applied Biotechnology Ser.: Vol. 9). (Illus.). 256p. (C). 1990. 55.00 (*0-943255-13-9*) Portfolio Pub.

O'Flaherty, Julie. Intervention in the Early Years: An Evaluation of the High/Scope Curriculum. 160p. 1996. pap. 25.00 (*1-874579-58-X*, Pub. by Natl Childrens Bur) Paul & Co Pubs.

O'Flaherty, Liam. The Assassin. 224p. 1997. pap. 11.95 (*0-86327-368-8*, Pub. by Wolfhound Press) Irish Amer Bk.

— The Black Soul. LC 97-101144. 192p. 1997. pap. 11.95 (*0-86327-478-1*, Pub. by Wolfhound Press) Irish Amer Bk.

— Famine. 448p. 1997. pap. 10.95 (*0-86327-043-3*, Pub. by Wolfhound Press) Irish Amer Bk.

— The Informer. LC 79-26156. 196p. 1980. reprint ed. pap. 10.00 (*0-15-644356-2*, Harvest Bks) Harcourt.

— Insurrection. 224p. 1997. pap. 11.95 (*0-86327-375-0*, Pub. by Wolfhound Press) Irish Amer Bk.

— Joseph Conrad: An Appreciation. LC 72-6945. (Studies in Conrad: No. 8). 1972. reprint ed. lib. bdg. 75.00 (*0-8383-1642-5*) M S G Haskell Hse.

— Mr. Gilhooley. 288p. (Orig.). 1997. pap. 11.95 (*0-86327-289-4*, Pub. by Wolfhound Press); pap. 11.95 (*0-86327-641-5*, Pub. by Wolfhound Press) Irish Amer Bk.

— Mountain Tavern, & Other Stories. LC 73-178453. (Short Story Index Reprint Ser.). 1980. reprint ed. 18.95 (*0-8369-4054-7*) Ayer.

— The Pedlar's Revenge: Short Stories. 224p. 1997. pap. 11.95 (*0-86327-536-2*, Pub. by Wolfhound Press) Irish Amer Bk.

— Return of The Brute. 144p. 1998. pap. 11.95 (*0-86327-628-8*, Pub. by Wolfhound Press) Irish Amer Bk.

— Short Stories: The Pedlar's Revenge. 1991. pap. 10.95 (*0-86327-225-8*) Dufour.

— Skerrett. 224p. 1997. pap. 11.95 (*0-86327-369-6*, Pub. by Wolfhound Press) Irish Amer Bk.

— Spring Sowing. LC 72-10748. (Short Story Index Reprint Ser.). 1977. reprint ed. 21.95 (*0-8369-4221-3*) Ayer.

— Thy Neighbour's Wife. 256p. pap. 11.95 (*0-86327-328-9*, Pub. by Wolfhound Press) Irish Amer Bk.

— A Tourist's Guide to Ireland. LC 99-176612. 96p. 1998. pap. 9.95 (*0-86327-589-3*, Pub. by Wolfhound Press) Irish Amer Bk.

***O'Flaherty, Liam & Kelly, A. A.** The Collected Stories. LC 99-41722. 1999. text 35.00 (*0-312-22905-4*) St Martin.

— The Collected Stories, Vol. 1. LC 99-41722. 396p. 2000. text 35.00 (*0-312-22903-8*) St Martin.

— The Collected Stories, Vol. 2. LC 99-41722. 397p. 2000. text 35.00 (*0-312-22904-6*) St Martin.

O'Flaherty, Louise. The Dreamers. 1984. mass mkt. 3.50 (*0-345-30690-2*) Ballantine Pub Grp.

O'Flaherty, Louise. The Farthest Eden. 1983. mass mkt. 2.50 (*0-345-27400-8*) Ballantine Pub Grp.

— Gospel Swamp. 1980. mass mkt. 1.95 (*0-345-29144-1*) Ballantine Pub Grp.

O'Flaherty, Louise. Poppies in the Wind. 448p. (Orig.). 1981. mass mkt. 2.95 (*0-345-29201-4*) Ballantine Pub Grp.

— This Golden Land. 416p. (Orig.). 1982. mass mkt. 2.95 (*0-345-28346-5*) Ballantine Pub Grp.

O'Flaherty, Michael & Gisvold, Gregory. Post-War Protection of Human Rights in Bosnia & Herzegovina. LC 98-7588. (International Studies in Human Rights). 336p. 1998. 89.00 (*90-411-1020-8*) Kluwer Law Intl.

O'Flaherty, Patrick. The Rock Observed: Studies in the Literature of Newfoundland. LC 80-475278. 254p. reprint ed. pap. 78.80 (*0-608-16639-1*, 202637000049) Bks Demand.

— The Rock Observed: Studies in the Literature of Newfoundland. rev. ed. (Illus.). 304p. 1992. text 40.00 (*0-8020-2807-1*); pap. text 18.95 (*0-8020-7683-1*) U of Toronto Pr.

O'Flaherty, Patrick, jt. ed. see Neary, Peter.

O'Flaherty, Terrence. Masterpiece Theatre: A Celebration of 25 Years of Outstanding Television. LC 95-38710. (Illus.). 256p. (Orig.). 1995. pap. 24.95 (*0-912333-74-X*) BB&T Inc.

O'Flaherty, Wendy D. Dreams, Illusion & Other Realities. LC 83-17944. (Illus.). xvi, 380p. 1986. pap. text 22.95 (*0-226-61855-2*) U Ch Pr.

— Dreams, Illusion & Other Realities. LC 83-17944. (Illus.). xvi, 384p. 1995. 30.00 (*0-226-61854-4*) U Ch Pr.

— Dreams, Illusions & Other Realities. 382p. 1987. 39.95 (*0-318-37018-2*) Asia Bk Corp.

— Dreams, Illusions & Other Realities. (Illus.). 360p. 1987. 24.00 (*81-208-0268-3*, Pub. by Motilal Bnarsidass) S Asia.

— The Origins of Evil in Hindu Mythology. (Hermeneutics: Studies in the History of Religions: No. 6). 1977. pap. 18.95 (*0-520-04098-8*, Pub. by U CA Pr) Cal Prin Full Svc.

— Other People's Myths: The Cave of Echoes. xiv, 226p. 1995. pap. 15.00 (*0-226-61857-9*) U Ch Pr.

— Siva: The Erotic Ascetic. (Illus.). 400p. 1981. reprint ed. pap. 14.95 (*0-19-520250-3*) OUP.

— Tales of Sex & Viloence: Folklore, Sacrifice, & Danger in the Jaiminiya Brahmana. 145p. 1987. 11.50 (*81-208-0267-5*, Pub. by Motilal Bnarsidass) S Asia.

— Tales of Sex & Violence: Folklore, Sacrifice & Danger in the Jaiminiya Brahmana. LC 84-16393. (Illus.). 160p. 1987. 19.95 (*0-226-61852-8*) U Ch Pr.

— Women, Androgynes, & Other Mythical Beasts. LC 79-16128. 408p. 1982. pap. text 22.00 (*0-226-61850-1*) U Ch Pr.

— Women, Androgynes, & Other Mythical Beasts. LC 79-16128. 400p. 1999. lib. bdg. 33.00 (*0-226-61849-8*) U Ch Pr.

O'Flaherty, Wendy D., ed. Textual Sources for the Study of Hinduism. Gold, Daniel H. et al, trs. (Sources for the Textual Study of Religion Ser.). xii, 224p. 1990. pap. text 17.95 (*0-226-61847-1*) U Ch Pr.

O'Flaherty, Wendy D., tr. The Oresteia. LC 88-20492. 262p. 1989. pap. 12.95 (*0-226-00772-3*) U Ch Pr.

O'Flaherty, Wendy D. & Grene, David. The Oresteia. LC 88-20492. 262p. 1997. lib. bdg. 39.00 (*0-226-00771-5*) U Ch Pr.

O'Flaherty, Wendy D., ed. & tr. see Wyatt, Thomas.

O'Flanagan, J. Roderick. Lives of the Lord Chancellors & Keepers of the Great Seal of Ireland, 2 vols. 1971. reprint ed. 65.00 (*0-8377-2500-3*, Rothman) W S Hein.

O'Flanagan, Patrick. Rural Ireland 1600-1900: Modernisation & Change. LC 87-201591. 1987. 35.95 (*0-902561-48-0*) Intl Spec Bk.

O'Flanagan, Patrick & Buttimer, Cornelius, eds. Cork: History & Society. (Illus.). 1000p. 1993. 79.95 (*0-906602-22-X*, Pub. by Geography Pubns) Irish Bks Media.

Oflanagan, R. Dictionary Personnel, Educational Terms: German/English/German. (ENG & GER.). 236p. 1996. 150.00 (*0-320-00126-1*) Fr & Eur.

O'Flanagan, Rory. Dictionary of Personnal & Educational Terms: English, French, German. (ENG, FRE & GER.). 263p. 1991. 125.00 (*0-7859-7111-4*) Fr & Eur.

— Dictionary of Personnel & Educational Terms, German-English/English-German. (ENG & GER.). 263p. 1996. 150.00 (*0-7859-9530-7*) Fr & Eur.

O'Flannabhra, Padraig. Ireland Beyond the Pale: A Photo-Essay. (Illus.). 74p. 1986. 18.95 (*0-85105-448-X*, Pub. by Smyth) Dufour.

O'Flannery, Patsy. Hash & Rehash. 32p. 1994. pap. 4.95 (*1-883849-05-5*) Nine Hund Forty Six Pr.

***O'Flinn, Paul.** How to Study Romantic Poetry. LC 00-42058. 2000. pap. (*0-312-23807-X*) St Martin.

O'Floinn, Raghnall. Irish Shrines & Reliquaries of the Middle Ages. (Treasures of the National Museum of Ireland Ser.). (Illus.). 48p. (Orig.). 1995. pap. 7.95 (*0-946172-40-4*, Pub. by Town Hse) Roberts Rinehart.

O'Flynn, Criostoir. Irish Humorous Poetry. 191p. 1999. pap. 14.95 (*0-7818-0745-X*) Hippocrene Bks.

— There Is An Isle: A Limerick Boyhood. LC 98-148356. 350p. 1998. pap. 15.95 (*1-85635-219-6*, Pub. by Mercier Pr) Irish Amer Bk.

O'Flynn, Criostoir, tr. Blind Raftery. 180p. 1998. pap. 16.95 (*1-900693-07-0*, Pub. by Clo Iar-Chonnachta) Dufour.

O'Flynn, Criostoir, jt. auth. see Raftery, Anthony.

O'Flynn, Joseph P. Nautical Dictionary: Over 3,800 Maritime Terms Defined. (Illus.). 112p. (Orig.). 1992. pap. 11.95 (*0-937360-16-3*) Harbor Hse MI.

O'Flynn, Justine. Guide to Owning a Burmese Cat. LC 99-26001. (Illus.). 64p. (gr. 4-7). 1999. 19.95 (*0-7910-5461-6*) Chelsea Hse.

— Guide to Owning a Burmese Cat. (Illus.). 64p. 1997. pap. 6.95 (*0-7938-2169-X*, RE-402) TFH Pubns.

O'Flynn, Mark. Captain Cook. 143p. (C). 1990. 30.00 (*0-947087-05-2*, Pub. by Pascoe Pub) St Mut.

O'Flynn, Michael F. & Moriarity, Gene M. Linear Systems: Time Domain & Transform Analysis. 512p. 1986. text 99.95 (*0-471-60373-2*) Wiley.

O'Flynn, Silvester. The Good News of Luke's Year: Reflections for Year C. 270p. (Orig.). 1991. pap. 10.95 (*1-85607-038-7*, Pub. by Columba Press) Whitecap Bks.

— The Good News of Mark's Year. 288p. (Orig.). 1990. pap. 10.95 (*1-85607-001-8*, Pub. by Columba Press) Whitecap Bks.

— The Good News of Matthew's Year. 272p. (Orig.). 1989. pap. 10.95 (*0-948183-89-6*, Pub. by Columba Press) Whitecap Bks.

Ofonagoro, W. I. Trade & Imperialism in Southern Nigeria, 1881-1929. LC 78-64521. 263p. 1979. text 23.95 (*0-88357-049-1*) NOK Pubs.

Ofori. Regional Policy & Regional Planning in Ghana. 64.95 (*1-85628-618-5*) Ashgate Pub Co.

Ofori, F., et al. Proceedings of the National Workshop on Soil Fertility Management Action Plan for Ghana: Held at Cape Coast, Ghana, 2nd to 5th, July, 1996. LC 98-28351. 15p. 1998. pap. write for info. (*0-88090-117-9*) Intl Fertilizer.

Ofori, F., jt. auth. see Eden-Green, S. J.

Ofori, George. The Construction Industry: Aspects of Its Economics & Management. 248p. (Orig.). 1990. pap. 39.50 (*9971-69-148-5*, Pub. by Sngapore Univ Pr) Coronet Bks.

— Managing Construction Industry Development: Lessons from Singapore's Experience. 354p. (Orig.). 1993. pap. 47.50 (*9971-69-181-7*, Pub. by Sngapore Univ Pr) Coronet Bks.

Ofori-Yeboah, Kwasi, ed. see Navaratna-Bandara, Abeysinghe M.

Oforiwaa, Yaa, jt. auth. see Addae, Akili.

Ofosu-Amaah, V. National Experience in the Use of Community Health Workers: A Review of Current Issues & Problems. (WHO Offset Publications: No. 71). 49p. 1983. 8.00 (*92-4-170071-8*) World Health.

***Ofosu-Amaah, W. Paatii, et al.** Combating Corruption: A Comparative Review of Selected Legal Aspects of State Practices & Major International Initiatives. LC 99-30183. 124p. 1999. pap. 25.00 (*0-8213-4523-0*, 14523) World Bank.

Ofosu-Appiah, L. H. People in Bondage: African Slavery since the 15th Century. (Illus.). 112p. (YA). (gr. 5 up). 1993. lib. bdg. 17.50 (*0-8225-3150-X*, Runestone Pr) Lerner Pub.

Ofosu-Appiah, L. H., et al. The Encyclopaedia Africana Dictionary of African Biography Vol. 1: Ethiopia-Ghana. Irvine, Keith, ed. LC 76-17954. (Illus.). 1977. 84.00 (*0-917256-01-8*) Ref Pubns.

Ofosu-Appiah, L. H., ed. see Abraham, Arthur, et al.

***Ofrane, Avi & Harte, Lawrence.** Telecom Made Simple; LEC, IXC, PBX & LAN. 1999. pap. text 34.95 (*0-9650658-7-1*) APDG.

O'Frank, Milo. How to Have a Successful Meeting in Half the Time. Rubenstein, Julie, ed. 160p. 1990. reprint ed. pap. 9.00 (*0-671-72601-3*) PB.

Ofrat, Gideon. One Hundred Years of Art in Israel. Kidron, Peretz, tr. LC 97-49058. (Illus.). 400p. 1998. text 50.00 (*0-8133-3377-6*, Pub. by Westview) HarpC.

Ofsanko, Frank J. & Napier, Nancy K., eds. Effective Human Resource Measurement Techniques - A Handbook for Practitioners. 109p. 1990. pap. 15.00 (*0-939900-39-4*, PB18) Soc Human Resc Mgmt.

Ofshe, Lynne & Ofshe, Richard. Utility & Choice in Social Interaction. LC 70-101539. (Illus.). 1970. 39.50 (*0-13-939645-4*) Irvington.

Ofshe, Richard & Watters, Ethan. Making Monsters: False Memories, Psychotherapy, & Sexual Hysteria. 340p. 1998. text 23.00 (*0-7881-5931-3*) DIANE Pub.

— Making Monsters: False Memories, Psychotherapy, & Sexual Hysteria. 340p. 1994. 23.00 (*0-684-19698-0*) S&S Trade.

— Making Monsters: False Memories, Psychotherapy, & Sexual Hysteria. LC 95-49014. 352p. (C). 1996. pap. 15.95 (*0-520-20583-9*, Pub. by U CA Pr) Cal Prin Full Svc.

Ofshe, Richard, jt. auth. see Ofshe, Lynne.

Ofshe, Richard, jt. auth. see Watters, Ethan.

***Ofstad, Kari, et al.** Improving the Exploration Process by Learning from the Past. LC 00-21616. (Norwegian Petroleum Society (NPF) Special Publication Ser.). 2000. write for info. (*0-444-50115-0*) Elsevier.

Ofstedal, Paul. Daily Readings from Spiritual Classics. LC 89-30976. 408p. 1990. kivar 22.99 (*0-8066-2424-8*, 9-2424) Augsburg Fortress.

Ofsthun, N. J., et al, eds. Lymphatic & Non-Lymphatic Fluid Loss from the Peritoneal Cavity. (Journal: Blood Purification: Vol. 10, Nos. 3-4, 1992). (Illus.). 132p. 1993. pap. 88.75 (*3-8055-5769-8*) S Karger.

Oftedal, Sarah. A Window on Eternity: The Life & Poetry of Jane Hess Merchant. LC 82-16276. (Abingdon Classics Ser.). 336p. 1992. pap. 5.95 (*0-687-45602-9*) Abingdon.

Ofuatey-Kodjoe, W. B. The Principle of Self-Determination in International Law. 250p. 1977. text 26.50 (*0-8290-1569-8*) Irvington.

Og, Mandino. Don de la Estrella. (SPA.). 175p. 1997. pap. 15.98 (*968-13-0101-3*, Pub. by Edit Diana) Libros Fronteras.

— Don del Orador. (SPA.). 1997. pap. 15.98 (*968-13-2756-X*, Pub. by Edit Diana) Libros Fronteras.

— Eleccion. (SPA.). 1997. pap. text 15.98 (*968-13-1662-2*) Libros Fronteras.

— Exito Mas Grande Del Mundo. (SPA.). 1997. pap. text 12.98 (*968-13-2007-7*) Libros Fronteras.

— Hacia un Exito Ilimitado. (SPA.). 1997. pap. 17.98 (*968-13-1042-X*, Pub. by Edit Diana) Libros Fronteras.

— Mejor Manera de Vivir. (SPA.). 1997. pap. 16.98 (*968-13-2016-6*, Pub. by Edit Diana) Libros Fronteras.

— Memorandum De Dios. (SPA., Illus.). 63p. 1997. pap. text 13.98 (*968-13-2042-5*) Libros Fronteras.

— Milagro Mas Grande Del Mundo. (SPA.). 1997. pap. text 13.98 (*968-13-2010-7*) Libros Fronteras.

— Misterio Mas Grande del Mundo. (SPA.). 1997. pap. 15.98 (*968-13-3005-6*, Pub. by Edit Diana) Libros Fronteras.

— Operacion Jesucristo y Al Tercer Dia. (SPA.). 1997. pap. text 23.98 (*968-13-0612-0*) Edit Diana.

— Regreso del Trapero. (SPA.). 1997. pap. text 13.98 (*968-13-2269-X*, Pub. by Edit Diana) Libros Fronteras.

— El Secreto Mas Grande del Mundo.Tr. of Greatest Secret in the World. (SPA.). (Orig.). 1997. pap. 16.98 (*968-13-2009-3*, Pub. by Edit Diana) Libros Fronteras.

— Vendedor Mas Grande Parte 2A. (SPA.). 1997. pap. 12.98 (*968-13-1858-7*, Pub. by Edit Diana) Libros Fronteras.

— El Vendedor Mas Grande del Mundo.Tr. of Greatest Salesman in the World. (SPA.). 123p. 1997. pap. 10.98 (*968-13-2008-5*, Pub. by Edit Diana) Libros Fronteras.

***O'Gadhra, Nollaig.** Civil War in Connacht, 1922-1923. 192p. 1999. pap. 17.95 (*1-85635-281-1*) Irish Bks Media.

Ogain, Rionach U. Immortal Dan: Daniel O'Connell in Irish Folk Tradition. LC 95-198894. (Illus.). 260p. (Orig.). 1996. pap. 19.95 (*0-906602-40-8*, Pub. by Geography Pubns) Irish Bks Media.

Ogali, Ogali A. Veronica My Daughter & Other Onitsha Plays & Stories. Sander, Reinhard W. & Ayers, Peter K., eds. LC 80-80886. 376p. (Orig.). 1980. 35.00 (*0-914478-61-3*, Three Contnts); pap. 15.00 (*0-914478-62-1*, Three Contnts) L Rienner.

Ogami, Wolf. Super Taboo. pap. 19.95 (*1-56097-334-X*, Pub. by Fantagraph Bks) Seven Hills Bk.

— Super Taboo Collection, Vol. 2. (Illus.). 128p. 1998. pap. 19.95 (*1-56097-356-0*, Eros Comics) Fantagraph Bks.

Ogan, Beverly J., jt. auth. see Rottier, Jerry.

Ogan, Guy D. Can Anyone Help my Child? Therapies & Treatment for Attention Deficit & Other Learning & Behavioral Disorders in Children, Adolescents, & Adults. rev. ed. 186p. (Orig.). 1991. pap. 9.95 (*0-9631880-1-1*) Faith Pub & Media.

Ogan, Rene, jt. auth. see Rusho, Josie.

Oganessian, Yu T. Heavy Ion Physics: Proceedings of the 6th International School Dubna, Moscow. 1998. 128.00 (*981-02-3531-3*) World Scientific Pub.

Oganessian, Yu T., et al, eds. Heavy Ion Physics: Proceedings of International School Held at Jinr (Dubna, Russia) 10-15 May 1993, 2 vols., Set, Vols. I & II. (Illus.). 1085p. (C). 1995. text 95.00 (*0-614-05122-3*) Hadronic Pr Inc.

Oganesyan, Genrikh A., jt. auth. see Karmanova, Ida G.

Oganesyan, O. V., jt. auth. see Volkov, M. V.

Oganov, Raphael G., jt. ed. see Chazov, Eugene I.

***Ogans, DeBorrah K.** How Do I Love Thee. Ogans, Julian, Sr., ed. & illus. by. 2000. pap. 12.00 (*0-9678486-0-1*) Alpha Seven.

Ogans, Julian, Sr., ed. & illus. see Ogans, DeBorrah K.

O'Gara, Geoffrey. Great Lakes. LC 97-33681. (National Geographic's Driving Guides to America Ser.). 1997. write for info. (*0-7922-3432-4*) Natl Geog.

— The Western Alphabet. LC 83-51556. (Illus.). 64p. (Orig.). 1983. pap. 3.95 (*0-915333-00-7*) Trotevale.

***O'Gara, Geoffrey.** What You See in Clear Water. 2000. 25.00 (*0-679-40415-5*) Knopf.

O'Gara, Gordon C. Theodore Roosevelt & the Rise of the Modern Navy. LC 69-14016. 138p. 1970. reprint ed. lib. bdg. 38.50 (*0-8371-1480-2*, OGTR, Greenwood Pr) Greenwood.

— Theodore Roosevelt & the Rise of the Modern Navy. (History - United States Ser.). 138p. 1993. reprint ed. lib. bdg. 69.00 (*0-7812-4858-2*) Kprt Serv.

Ogara, M. Ecumenical Gift Exchange. 1998. pap. text 14.95 (*0-8146-5893-8*) Liturgical Pr.

O'Gara, Margaret. Triumph in Defeat: Infallibility, Vatican I, & the French Minority Bishops. LC 87-17889. 296p. 1988. 48.95 (*0-8132-0641-3*) Cath U Pr.

O'Gara, W. H. A Black Hills Lady. Meyers, Jean O., ed. (Illus.). (Orig.). 1990. pap. 8.95 (*0-934904-12-X*) J & L Lee.

— In All Its Fury: A History of the Blizzard of January 12, 1888. 3rd ed. Clement, Ora A., ed. (Illus.). 344p. 1988. reprint ed. pap. 9.95 (*0-934904-04-9*) J & L Lee.

O'Gara, William W. Foster's & Nobody Else's: The N. C. Foster Enterprises. (Illus.). 72p. (Orig.). 1988. pap. 8.95 (*0-9622213-0-9*) MCRHSI.

Ogarkov, N. Military Encylopaedic Dictionary. (RUS.). 865p. (C). 1984. 150.00 (*0-7855-6739-9*, Pub. by Collets) St Mut.

Ogasapian, John. Church Organs: A Guide to Selection & Purchase. (Illus.). 144p. (Orig.). 1991. reprint ed. pap. 6.95 (*0-913499-06-4*) Organ Hist Soc.

— English Cathedral Music in New York: Edward Hodges of Trinity Church. (Illus.). x, 244p. 1994. 29.95 (*0-913499-12-9*) Organ Hist Soc.

— Henry Erben: Portrait of a Nineteenth Century Organ Builder. (Illus.). 72p. 1980. pap. 15.00 (*0-913746-13-4*) Organ Lit.

— Organ Building in New York City, 1700 to 1900. LC 78-300889. (Illus.). 1977. pap. text 30.00 (*0-913746-10-X*) Organ Lit.

Ogasawara, Frances. History of the American Lung Association. 172p. 12.50 (*0-915116-19-7*) Am Lung Assn.

Ogasawara, Noboru. Japanese Swords: A Pocket Color Book. 1997. pap. text 9.95 (*0-87040-995-6*) Japan Pubns USA.

Ogasawara, Yuko. Office Ladies & Salaried Men: Power, Gender & Work in Japanese Companies. LC 98-5332. 280p. 1998. pap. text 15.95 (*0-520-21044-1*, Pub. by U CA Pr) Cal Prin Full Svc.

— Office Ladies & Salaried Men: Power, Gender, & Work in Japanese Companies. LC 98-5332. 280p. 1998. 45.00 (*0-520-21043-3*, Pub. by U CA Pr) Cal Prin Full Svc.

Ogata. Modern Control Engineering. 3rd ed. 997p. (C). 1996. 100.00 (*0-13-227307-1*) P-H.

Ogata, Elizabeth, tr. see Ki-Sheok, Chong.

Ogata, Hiromaru, jt. ed. see Okada, Kazuo.

Ogata, Katsuhiko. Discrete-Time Control Systems. 2nd ed. LC 94-19896. 768p. (C). 1994. 105.00 (*0-13-034281-5*) P-H.

— System Dynamics. 3rd ed. LC 97-36383. 758p. (C). 1997. 105.00 (*0-13-675745-6*) P-H.

O

Ogata, S., jt. auth. see Ichimaru, S.

Ogata, Sadako N. Defiance in Manchuria: The Making of Japanese Foreign Policy, 1931-1932. LC 84-543. 259p. (C). 1984. reprint ed. lib. bdg. 41.50 (*0-313-24428-6*, OGDM, Greenwood Pr) Greenwood.

— Normalization with China: A Comparative Study of U. S. & Japanese Processes. (Research Papers & Policy: No. 30). xii, 109p. (Orig.). (C). 1989. pap. 15.00 (*1-55729-013-X*) IEAS.

Ogata, Shijuro, et al. International Financial Integration: The Policy Challenges. (Triangle Papers: No. 37). 36p. (Orig.). 1989. pap. 6.00 (*0-930503-07-4*) Trilateral Comm.

Ogata, Sohaku, tr. The Transmission of the Lamp: Early Masters. rev. ed. LC 89-8125. 475p. 1990. pap. 19.95 (*0-89341-565-0*, Longwood Academic) Hollowbrook.

Ogawa & Katayama, eds. Beautiful Kyoto. (Postcard Book Ser.). (Illus.). 56p. 1994. 8.00 (*4-7700-1674-3*) Kodansha.

Ogawa & Mizuno. Fun & Fancy Sushi, 1. 1998. pap. 13.95 (*4-88996-037-6*, Pub. by Japan JPN) Kodansha.

Ogawa, ed. see Kodansha International Staff.

Ogawa, Akira. Separation of Particles from Air & Gases, Vol. I. 168p. 1984. 97.00 (*0-8493-5787-X*, TH7692, CRC Reprint) Franklin.

— Separation of Particles from Air & Gases, Vol. II. 200p. 1984. 111.00 (*0-8493-5788-8*, CRC Reprint) Franklin.

— Vortex Flow. 336p. 1992. lib. bdg. 239.00 (*0-8493-5782-9*, QA925) CRC Pr.

Ogawa, Brian K. Color of Justice: Culturally Sensitive Treatment of Minority Crime Victims. 2nd ed. LC 98-5359. 216p. (C). 1998. pap. text 31.00 (*0-205-28061-7*) Allyn.

— To Tell the Truth. LC 97-576. (Illus.). (J). 1997. 9.95 (*1-884244-15-7*) Volcano Pr.

— Walking on Eggshells: Practical Counsel for Women in or Leaving a Violent Relationship. LC 89-51441. (Illus.). 68p. (Orig.). 1989. pap. 10.00 (*0-9621260-1-2*) VWAD.

— Walking on Eggshells: Practical Counsel for Women in or Leaving a Violent Relationship. LC 95-52905. 48p. (Orig.). 1996. reprint ed. pap. 8.95 (*1-884244-11-4*) Volcano Pr.

Ogawa, Brian K., et al. To Tell the Truth. LC 88-51256. (Illus.). 40p. (J). (gr. 4-6). 1988. text. write for info. (*0-9621260-0-4*) VWAD.

Ogawa, Dennis M. Jan Ken Po: The World of Hawaii's Japanese Americans. LC 78-9513. (Illus.). 196p. 1978. pap. 9.95 (*0-8248-0398-1*) UH Pr.

Ogawa, Eiji. Modern Production Management: A Japanese Experience. 132p. 1984. 21.70 (*92-833-1071-3*) Productivity Inc.

— Small Business Management Today. LC 95-157981. (Productivity Ser.: No. 25). (Illus.). 119p. 1994. pap. text 7.50 (*92-833-1715-7*, 317157) Productivity Inc.

Ogawa, H., jt. auth. see Nakajima, H.

Ogawa, Hirohide. Enlightenment Through the Art of Basketball. Taniguchi, H. et al, trs. (Illus.). 1979. 13.50 (*0-900891-36-X*); pap. 12.50 (*0-900891-35-1*) Oleander Pr.

Ogawa, Hiromitsu, jt. compiled by see Toda, Teisuke.

Ogawa, Joseph M. & English, Harley. Diseases of Temperate Zone Tree Fruit & Nut Crops. LC 91-65409. (Illus.). 464p. 1991. 65.00 (*0-931876-97-4*, 3345) ANR Pubns CA.

Ogawa, Joshua K. Unlimited Purpose: An Asian Missionary Tells His Story. 1986. pap. 4.95 (*9971-972-46-8*) OMF Bks.

Ogawa, Junjiro. Statistical Theory of the Analysis of Experimental Designs. LC 73-90769. (Statistics, Textbooks & Monographs: Vol. 8). 475p. reprint ed. pap. 147.30 (*0-608-16537-9*, 202733900055) Bks Demand.

Ogawa, Kazuo. Electron Microscopic Cytochemistry in Biomedicine. 816p. 1992. lib. bdg. 297.00 (*0-8493-6012-9*, RB46) CRC Pr.

Ogawa, Kenji. New Intensive Japanese. (ENG & JPN.). 340p. 1997. pap. 32.95 (*4-590-00259-0*, Pub. by Hokuseido Pr) Book East.

Ogawa, Naohiro, et al, eds. Human Resources in Development along the Asia-Pacific Rim. (South-East Asian Social Science Monographs). (Illus.). 442p. 1993. text 65.00 (*0-19-588596-1*) OUP.

Ogawa, Naohiro, jt. auth. see Hodge, Robert W.

Ogawa, Seiva, jt. ed. see Xu, Duanyi.

Ogawa, T., et al, eds. Katachi U Symmetry. (Illus.). 408p. 1996. 129.00 (*4-431-70161-3*) Spr-Verlag.

Ogawa, T. & Kanemitsu, Y. Optical Properties of Low-Dimensional Materials. 400p. 1996. text 99.00 (*981-02-2231-9*) World Scientific Pub.

***Ogawa, Tomoko.** Endgame. (Elementary Go Ser.). (Illus.). (J). 2000. pap. 15.00 (*4-906574-15-7*) KISEIDO.

Ogawa, Tomoko & Davies, James. The Endgame. (Elementary Go Ser.: Vol. 6). 1990. reprint ed. pap. 14.95 (*4-87187-015-4*, G15) Ishi Pr Intl.

Ogawa, Yujiro, jt. ed. see Taira, Asahiko.

Ogbaa, Kalu. Gods, Oracles & Divination: Folkways in Chinua Achebe's Novels. LC 91-72278. 320p. 1992. 49.95 (*0-86543-256-2*); pap. 14.95 (*0-86543-257-0*) Africa World.

— Igbo. LC 94-36608. (Heritage Library of African Peoples). (Illus.). 64p. (YA). (gr. 7-12). 1995. lib. bdg. 16.95 (*0-8239-1977-3*) Rosen Group.

— Understanding Things Fall Apart: A Student Casebook to Issues, Sources & Historical Documents. LC 98-22902. (Greenwood Press Literature in Context Ser.). 256p. 1999. 39.95 (*0-313-30294-4*, Greenwood Pr) Greenwood.

Ogbaa, Kalu, ed. The Gong & the Flute: African Literary Development & Celebration, 173. LC 94-16121. (Contributions in Afro-American & African Studies: No. 173). 224p. 1994. 57.95 (*0-313-29281-7*, Greenwood Pr) Greenwood.

***Ogbankwa-Stevens, Michelle.** All the Right Men. LC 99-91445. 2000. 25.00 (*0-7388-0790-7*); pap. 18.00 (*0-7388-0791-5*) Xlibris Corp.

— All the Right Men. 3rd rev. ed. Blue, Gwendolyn, ed. LC 00-94644. 550p. 2000. 25.00 (*0-9644230-4-9*); pap. 18.00 (*0-9644230-3-0*) Diamond Pubng.

Ogboajah, Frank O., ed. Mass Communication, Culture & Society in West Africa. 335p. 1990. 50.00 (*0-905450-18-3*, Pub. by H Zell Pubs) Seven Hills Bk.

Ogbomo, Onaiwu W. When Men & Women Mattered: A History of Gender Relations among the Owan of Nigeria. LC 97-1501. 232p. 1997. 50.00 (*1-878822-78-0*) Univ Rochester Pr.

Ogbondah, Chris W. Military Regimes & the Press in Nigeria, 1966-1993: Human Rights & National Development. 200p. (Orig.). (C). 1994. pap. text 29.50 (*0-8191-8835-2*) U Pr of Amer.

Ogbondah, Chris W., compiled by. The Press in Nigeria: An Annotated Bibliography, 12. LC 90-3676. (African Special Bibliographic Ser.: No. 12). 144p. 1990. lib. bdg. 47.95 (*0-313-26521-6*, OPN/, Greenwood Pr) Greenwood.

Ogbonnaya, A. On Communitarian Divinity: An African Interpretation of the Trinity. LC 94-12161. 144p. 1995. 29.95 (*1-55778-704-2*) Paragon Hse.

Ogbonnaya, A. Okechukwu. On Communitarian Divinity: An African Interpretation of the Trinity. 144p. 1999. pap. 14.95 (*1-55778-770-0*) Paragon Hse.

***Ogbonnaya, A. Okechukwu & Gates, Denise K.** In Step with the Master. (Discipleship Training Ser.). (Illus.). 64p. 1999. pap., student ed., wbk. ed. 1.25 (*0-940955-55-5*) Urban Ministries.

— In Step with the Master: Leader's Guide. (Discipleship Training Ser.). 126p. 1999. pap., wbk. ed. 7.25 (*0-940955-54-7*) Urban Ministries.

Ogbonnaya, A. Okechukwu, ed. see Trotter, Larry D.

***Ogbonnaya, Okechukwu.** In Step with the Master: Student Book. (Discipleship Training Ser.). (Illus.). 126p. 1999. pap. text 7.95 (*0-940955-53-9*, 6-5110) Urban Ministries.

— Precepts for Living, 1998-1999 Vol. I: The UMI Annual Sunday School Lesson Commentary. (Illus.). 470p. 1998. text 13.50 (*0-940955-46-6*, 11-1998) Urban Ministries.

— Precepts for Living, 1999-2000 Vol. II: The UMI Annual Sunday School Lesson Commentary. 560p. 1999. text 13.50 (*0-940955-57-1*, 11-1999) Urban Ministries.

— Upon This Rock: African Influence in the Christian Church. (Black History Curriculum Ser.). (Illus.). 36p. 1999. pap. text 6.25 (*0-940955-50-4*, 9-9980) Urban Ministries.

Ogbor, Wisdom O. King Zugo's Clan. (Wisdom's Writings Ser.). 175p. (Orig.). 1985. pap. 6.95 (*0-933889-00-3*) Ashiedu Pubns.

— This Young World. (Wisdom's Writings Ser.). 250p. (Orig.). 1985. write for info. (*0-933889-01-1*) Ashiedu Pubns.

***Ogborn, James.** Satire. (Cambridge Contexts in Literature Ser.). 128p. 2000. pap. 13.95 (*0-521-78791-2*) Cambridge U Pr.

Ogborn, Jane, ed. see Tennyson, Alfred Lord, et al.

Ogborn, Jane, ed. see Twain, Mark, pseud.

Ogborn, Jon & Kress, Gunther. Explaining Science in the Classroom. LC 96-13433. 160p. 1996. 92.95 (*0-335-19720-5*) OpUniv Pr.

Ogborn, Jon, et al. Explaining Science in the Classroom. LC 96-13433. 160p. 1996. pap. 27.95 (*0-335-19719-1*) OpUniv Pr.

Ogborn, Jon, jt. ed. see Jennison, Brenda.

Ogborn, Miles. Spaces of Modernity: London's Geographies, 1680-1780. LC 98-13000. (Mappings). 340p. 1998. pap. text 22.95 (*1-57230-365-4*, C0365); lib. bdg. 39.95 (*1-57230-343-3*, C0343) Guilford Pubns.

Ogbourne, C. P., jt. auth. see Jorgensen, R. J.

Ogbourne, C. P., jt. ed. see Armour, J.

Ogbru, Irene O. The Power of Women. 104p. (Orig.). 1993. pap. 10.95 (*1-880365-49-9*) Prof Pr NC.

Ogbu, Ogbonna. African-Igbo Names: How to Choose African Names for Yourself or for Your Loved Ones. Libet, Gayla, ed. 142p. (Orig.). 1995. pap. 8.95 (*1-887848-00-2*) Boug Pubns.

***Ogbu, Osito M. & Mihyo, Paschal.** African Youth on the Information Highway. 130p. 2000. pap. 17.95 (*0-88936-914-3*, Pub. by IDRC Bks) Stylus Pub VA.

***Ogbuene, Chigekwu G.** The Concept of Man in Igbo Myths. LC 99-48010. (European University Ser.: Vol. 597). xii, 292p. (C). 1999. pap. 48.95 (*0-8204-4704-8*) P Lang Pubng.

— The Concept of Man in Myths. (European University Studies: Vol. 597). XII, 292p. 1999. pap. 48.95 (*3-631-35563-7*) P Lang Pubng.

***Ogbuji, Uche.** Linux Database Bible. 650p. 2000. pap. 39.99 (*0-7645-4641-4*) IDG Bks.

Ogburn, Charlton. The Man Who Was Shakespeare: A Summary of the Case Unfolded in "The Mysterious William Shakespeare, the Myth & the Reality" LC 95-21081. 96p. 1995. pap. 5.95 (*0-939009-90-0*) EPM Pubns.

Ogburn, Jacqueline K. The Magic Nesting Doll. LC 98-34397. 2000. lib. bdg. 16.01 (*0-8037-2428-4*, Dial Yng Read) Peng Put Young Read.

— The Magic Nesting Doll. LC 98-34397. (Illus.). 32p. (ps-3). 2000. 16.99 (*0-8037-2414-4*, Dial Yng Read) Peng Put Young Read.

Ogburn, Joyce L., jt. ed. see Rice, Patricia O.

Ogburn, Martha D. Progeny. LC 98-40784. 288p. 1999. pap. 10.99 (*0-8054-1889-X*) Broadman.

Ogburn, William F. Social Characteristics of Cities: A Basis for New Interpretations of the Role of the City in American Life. LC 73-11940. (Metropolitan America Ser.). 80p. 1979. reprint ed. 18.95 (*0-405-05409-2*) Ayer.

Ogburn, William F., ed. American Society in Wartime. LC 72-2380. (FDR & the Era of the New Deal Ser.). 237p. 1972. reprint ed. lib. bdg. 29.50 (*0-306-70484-6*) Da Capo.

— Social Changes During Depression & Recovery. LC 72-2381. (FDR & the Era of the New Deal Ser.). 117p. 1974. reprint ed. lib. bdg. 22.50 (*0-306-70483-8*) Da Capo.

Ogburn, William F. & Bettelheim, Bruno. The Wolf Boy of Agra & Feral Children & Autistic Children. (Reprint Series in Social Sciences). (C). 1993. reprint ed. pap. text 1.90 (*0-8290-2709-2*, S-608) Irvington.

Ogburn, William F. & Goldenweiser, Alexander. The Social Sciences & Their Interrelations. LC 73-14173. (Perspectives in Social Inquiry Ser.). 518p. 1974. reprint ed. 33.95 (*0-405-05516-1*) Ayer.

Ogburn, William F., jt. auth. see Groves, Ernest R.

Ogden. Calculation of Drug Dosages. 6th ed. LC 98-54874. 464p. 1999. pap. text 36.00 (*0-323-00698-1*) Mosby Inc.

— Global Studies of China. 6th ed. 1995. (*1-56134-378-1*, Dshkn McG-Hill) McGrw-H Hghr Educ.

***Ogden, Alan.** Fortresses of Faith: A Pictorial History of the Fortified Saxon Churches of Romania. (Illus.). 144p. 2000. 49.95 (*973-9432-08-5*, Pub. by Ctr Romanian Studies) Intl Spec Bk.

— Romania Revisited: On the Trail of English Travellers, 1602-1941. (Illus.). 239p. 1999. 34.95 (*973-9432-05-0*, Pub. by Ctr Romanian Studies) Intl Spec Bk.

Ogden, Anita & Ogden, Walker. Wooley Meets Horatio: The World's Largest Elephant. (Illus.). 72p. (J). (gr. k-5). 1995. 17.95 (*0-9647159-0-2*) Stage West.

Ogden, Arthur M. The Avenging of the Apostles & Prophets: A Commentary on Revelation. 470p. 19.95 (*0-9646497-1-3*) Ogden Pubns.

— The Development of the New Testament. rev. ed. 100p. reprint ed. pap. text, wbk. ed. 3.95 (*0-9646497-0-5*) Ogden Pubns.

Ogden, August R. The Dies Committee: A Study of the Special House Committee for the Investigation of Un-American Activities, 1938-1944. LC 84-10736. 318p. 1984. reprint ed. lib. bdg. 65.00 (*0-313-24567-3*, OGDC, Greenwood Pr) Greenwood.

— Dies Committee, a Study of the Special House Committee for the Investigation of Un-American Activities, 1938-1944. (History - United States Ser.). 318p. 1993. reprint ed. lib. bdg. 89.00 (*0-7812-4816-7*) Rprt Serv.

Ogden, Betina. Busy Farmyard. (So Tall Board Bks.). 18p. (J). (ps). 1995. bds. 4.95 (*0-448-40945-3*, G & D) Peng Put Young Read.

Ogden, C. K., ed. The Evolutionary Origins of Developmental Psychology: Psyche, 18 vols., Set. 2nd ed. LC 96-163002. 6500p. (C). 1995. 2475.00 (*0-415-12779-3*) Routledge.

Ogden, C. K., tr. see Wittgenstein, Ludwig Josef Johann.

***Ogden, Caroline.** God. (Guides for Beginners - Great Lives Ser.). 2000. pap. 11.95 (*0-340-78080-0*, Pub. by Headway) Trafalgar.

Ogden, Christopher. Legacy: A Biography of Moses & Walter Annenberg. LC 98-51441. 624p. (YA). (gr. 8). 1999. 29.95 (*0-316-63379-8*) Little.

— Life of the Party: The Biography of Pamela Digby Churchill Hayward Harriman. 1998. mass mkt. 6.50 (*0-446-78858-9*) Warner Bks.

— Life of the Party: The Biography of Pamela Digby Churchill Hayward Harriman. (Illus.). 576p. 1995. reprint ed. mass mkt. 6.50 (*0-446-60264-7*, Pub. by Warner Bks) Little.

— Matter of Honor. 1999. 29.95 (*0-316-04491-1*) Little.

Ogden, Clint. Heller from Green Valley. large type ed. 220p. 1992. pap. 18.99 (*1-85389-359-5*) Ulverscroft.

Ogden, Curtis, jt. ed. see Claus, Jeff.

Ogden, D. Kelly & Skinner, Andrew C. New Testament Apostles Testify of Christ: A Guide to Acts Through Revelation. LC 98-35953. 1998. 19.95 (*1-57345-304-8*) Deseret Bk.

Ogden, D. Kelly, jt. auth. see Berrett, LaMar C.

Ogden, Dale. Hoosier Sports Heroes. LC 90-84308. (Hoosier Heritage Ser.). (Illus.). 192p. (YA). 1990. 19.95 (*1-878208-01-2*) Guild Pr IN.

Ogden, Daniel. Greek Bastardy in the Classical & Hellenic Periods. 440p. (C). 1996. text 84.00 (*0-19-815019-9*) OUP.

Ogden, Daniel, ed. Polygamy, Prostitutes & Death: The Hellenistics Dynasties. 1999. 49.50 (*0-7156-2930-1*, Pub. by Classical Pr) David Brown.

Ogden, Daniel M., Jr. & Bone, Hugh A. Washington Politics: Published under the Auspices of the Citizenship Clearing House. LC 80-25647. (Illus.). 77p. 1981. reprint ed. lib. bdg. 35.00 (*0-313-22803-5*, OGWP, Greenwood Pr) Greenwood.

Ogden, David. Dreambirds. (Illus.). 32p. (YA). (ps up). 1997. 16.95 (*0-935699-09-0*) Illum Arts.

— Psalm Songs Psalm Songs. 1998. pap. 23.95 (*0-225-66853-X*) Continuum.

Ogden, David W., jt. auth. see Jacobs, Jerald A.

Ogden, Dayton, jt. auth. see Carey, Dennis C.

Ogden, Donald I. Natural Care of Pets. 65p. 1993. reprint ed. spiral bd. 10.50 (*0-7873-0640-1*) Hlth Research.

Ogden, Dunbar H. & Zijlstra, A. Marcel. The Play of Daniel: Critical Essays. LC 96-27276. 1997. 30.00 (*1-879288-76-1*) Medieval Inst.

Ogden, Eugene C. & Mitchell, Richard S. Identification of Plants with Fleshy Fruits. (Bulletin Ser.: No. 467). (Illus.). 97p. (Orig.). (C). 1990. pap. text 12.95 (*1-55557-188-3*) NYS Museum.

Ogden, Evelyn H. Completing Your Doctoral Dissertation or Master's Thesis: In Two Semesters or Less. 2nd ed. LC 93-60088. 157p. 1997. pap. text 24.95 (*1-56676-035-6*) Scarecrow.

Ogden, Evelyn H. & Germinario, Vito. The At Risk Student: A Practical Guide for Educators. LC 87-51632. 192p. 1994. 29.95 (*0-87762-573-5*) Scarecrow.

— The Nation's Best Schools Vol. 1: Blueprints for Excellence: Elementary & Middle Schools. LC 94-60605. 365p. 1998. 44.95 (*1-56676-148-4*) Scarecrow.

— The Nation's Best Schools Vol. 2: Blueprints for Excellence: Middle & Secondary Schools. LC 94-60605. 445p. 1995. text 44.95 (*1-56676-278-2*) Scarecrow.

Ogden, Frank. The Last Book You'll Ever Read: And Other Lessons from the Future. 224p. 1994. 22.95 (*0-921912-71-4*) MW&R.

Ogden, Frank. Navigating in Cyberspace: A Guide to the Next Millennium. 208p. 1995. text 24.95 (*0-921912-85-4*) MW&R.

Ogden, Fred L., jt. ed. see Nakato, Tatsuaki.

Ogden, Frederic D., ed. see Johnson, Keen.

Ogden, Gary. Biology 2A Syllabus. 72p. 1993. spiral bd. 12.95 (*0-8403-8385-1*) Kendall-Hunt.

Ogden, Gina. Women Who Love Sex. Silvestro, Denise, ed. 288p. 1994. 21.00 (*0-671-86550-1*) PB.

— Women Who Love Sex. Silvestro, Denise, ed. 320p. 1995. mass mkt. 5.99 (*0-671-86551-X*) PB.

— Women Who Love Sex: An Inquiry into the Expanding Spirit of Women's Erotic Experience. rev. ed. LC 99-94005. 224p. 1999. pap. 12.95 (*0-9672705-0-2*) Womanspirit Pr.

Ogden, Graham. Qoheleth. (Readings Ser.). 236p. 1987. 47.50 (*1-85075-071-8*, Pub. by Sheffield Acad) CUP Services.

***Ogden, Graham S.** Handbook on the Song of Songs. LC 98-31386. (Helps for Translators Ser.). 1998. write for info. (*0-8267-0148-5*) Untd Bible Amrcas Svce.

Ogden, Graham S. & Zogbo, Lynell. A Handbook on Ecclesiastes. LC 98-21338. (Helps for Translators Ser.). 1998. write for info. (*0-8267-0121-3*) Untd Bible Soc.

Ogden, Greg. Discipleship Essentials: A Guide to Building Your Life in Christ. LC 98-28070. 223p. 1999. pap. 15.99 (*0-8308-1169-9*, 1169) InterVarsity.

— New Reformation: Returning the Ministry to the People of God. 1990. 14.95 (*0-310-31020-2*) Zondervan.

— The New Reformation: Returning the Ministry to the People of God. 224p. 1991. pap. 12.99 (*0-310-31021-0*) Zondervan.

Ogden, Gregory L., et al. West's California Code Forms with Practice Commentaries, 4 vols. 5th ed. LC 98-36647. 1998. 280.00 (*0-314-23372-5*) West Pub.

Ogden, H. A. Uniforms of the United States Army, 1774-1889. LC 97-46753. (Illus.). 1998. pap. 9.95 (*0-486-40107-3*) Dover.

Ogden, H. V., ed. & tr. see More, Thomas.

Ogden, Hugh. Gift. (Red Hill Ser.). 68p. 1998. pap. 12.95 (*1-879969-08-4*) CRS Outloudbooks.

— Looking for History. (Red Hill Ser.). 64p. 1991. pap. 8.95 (*1-879969-00-9*) CRS Outloudbooks.

— Natural Things: Poems. LC 98-19112. 23p. 1998. pap. 7.00 (*0-916897-35-4*) Andrew Mtn Pr.

— Two Roads & This Spring. (Red Hill Ser.). 88p. (Orig.). 1993. pap. 9.95 (*1-879969-03-3*) CRS Outloudbooks.

***Ogden, James.** Law of Negotiable Instruments. 4th ed. xxii, 846p. 1999. reprint ed. 185.00 (*1-56169-549-1*) Gaunt.

Ogden, James & Scouten, Arthur H., eds. Lear from Study to Stage: Essays in Criticism. LC 96-50339. (Illus.). 304p. 1997. 46.50 (*0-8386-3690-X*) Fairleigh Dickinson.

Ogden, James, ed. see Wycherley, William.

Ogden, James R. The Best Test Preparation for the New TOEFL: Test of English as a Foreign Language. 1998. pap. 19.95 (*0-87891-783-7*) Res & Educ.

— The Best Test Preparation for the TOEFL. 720p. 1998. pap. 34.95 incl. audio (*0-87891-784-5*) Res & Educ.

— Complex Variables Problem Solver. rev. ed. (Illus.). 936p. 1998. pap. 29.95 (*0-87891-604-0*) Res & Educ.

— Developing a Creative & Innovative Integrated Marketing Communications Plan: A Working Model. LC 98-4437. 185p. (C). 1998. pap. text 23.20 (*0-13-778333-7*) P-H.

— Essentials of Advertising. rev. ed. 128p. 1994. pap. text 5.95 (*0-87891-906-6*) Res & Educ.

Ogden, Jane. Health Psychology: A Textbook. LC 95-24922. 192p. 1996. 27.95 (*0-335-19544-X*) OpUniv Pr.

Ogden, Jill E., jt. auth. see Grindley, June N.

Ogden, Joan, ed. see McDermott, Richard E.

Ogden, John, jt. ed. see Davis, Steven.

Ogden, John A. The Medibears Guide to the Doctor's Exam: For Children & Parents. (Illus.). (J). (gr. k-5). 1991. 12.95 (*0-8130-1082-9*) U Press Fla.

— Skeletal Injury in the Child. 2nd ed. 960p. 1989. text 240.00 (*0-7216-2955-5*, W B Saunders Co) Harcrt Hlth Sci Grp.

***Ogden, John A.** Skeletal Injury in the Child. 3rd ed. LC 98-51165. (Illus.). 1200p. 2000. 195.00 (*0-387-98510-7*) Spr-Verlag.

Ogden, John D. Nature Plays for Keeps: Poems. 128p. (Orig.). 1996. pap. 9.50 (*1-56474-166-4*) Fithian Pr.

Ogden, Ken W. Safer Roads: A Guide to Road Safety Engineering. 544p. 1996. 119.95 (*0-291-39829-4*, Pub. by Avebury Technical) Ashgate Pub Co.

— Urban Goods Movement: A Guide to Policy & Planning. 256p. 1991. 101.95 (*1-85742-029-2*, Pub. by Avebry) Ashgate Pub Co.

Ogden, Laura, jt. auth. see Simmons, Glen.

***Ogden, Laurie.** The Chimney Swallows. 1999. pap. 45.00 (*1-85072-219-6*, Pub. by W Sessions) St Mut.

Ogden, Lawrence, jt. auth. see Lounsbury, John F.

Ogden, Margaret, jt. ed. see McVaugh, Michael R.

Ogden, Margaret S., ed. Cyrurgie of Guy de Chauliac Vol. I: Text, Vol. I, Text. (EETS Original Ser.: Vol. 265). 1971. 50.00 (*0-19-722268-4*, Pub. by EETS) Boydell & Brewer.

— Liber de Diversis Medicinis. (EETS, OS Ser.: Vol. 207). 1969. reprint ed. 30.00 (*0-8115-3383-2*) Periodicals Srv.

O

An Asterisk (*) at the beginning of an entry indicates that the title is appearing for the first time.

O

An Asterisk (*) at the beginning of an entry indicates that the title is appearing for the first time.

— The Theology of Plato: Compared with the Principles of Oriental & Grecian Philosophers. xxiii, 205p. 1976. reprint ed. 37.70 (*3-487-05710-7*) G Olms Pubs.

Ogilvie, John F. The Vibrational & Rotational Spectrometry of Diatomic Molecules. LC 98-86160. (Illus.). 432p. (C). 1998. text 120.00 (*0-12-524420-7*) Acad Pr.

Ogilvie, John S. Life & Death of Jay Gould & How He Made His Millions. Bruchey, Stuart, ed. LC 80-1336. (Railroads Ser.). (Illus.). 1981. reprint ed. lib. bdg. 20.95 (*0-405-13809-1*) Ayer.

Ogilvie, John W. Advanced C Structured Programming: Data Structure Design & Implementation in C. LC 90-34645. 432p. 1990. pap. 26.95 (*0-471-51943-X*) Wiley.

Ogilvie, Lloyd J. Acts. (Communicator's Commentary Ser.: Vol. 5). 369p. 22.99 (*0-8499-0158-8*); pap. 14.99 (*0-8499-3321-8*) Word Pub.

— Acts of the Holy Spirit: God's Power for Living. LC 99-19007. 204p. 1999. pap. 12.99 (*0-87788-012-3*, H Shaw Pubs) Waterbrook Pr.

— Asking God Your Hardest Questions. 256p. 1995. pap. 11.99 (*0-87788-059-X*, H Shaw Pubs) Waterbrook Pr.

— Autobiography of God. Fung, Man-chong, tr. from ENG. (CHI.). 1983. pap. write for info. (*0-941598-06-3*) Living Spring Pubns.

— Caer en la Grandeza. Lievano, M. Francisco, tr. from ENG. Orig. Title: Falling into Greatness. (SPA.). 190p. 1985. pap. 6.25 (*0-8297-0702-6*) Vida Pubs.

— Climbing the Rainbow. 224p. 1993. 16.99 (*0-8499-0762-4*) Word Pub.

— Communicator's Commentary: Hosea, Joel, Amos, Obadiah, Jonah. (Mastering the Old & New Testament Ser.: Vol. 20). pap. 14.99 (*0-8499-3558-X*) Word Pub.

— Conversation with God. 1993. pap. 9.99 (*1-56507-048-8*) Harvest Hse.

— Conversation with God: Experience Intimacy with God Through Personal Prayer. 228p: Date not set. 9.99 (*1-56507-930-2*) Harvest Hse.

— Facing the Future Without Fear: Prescriptions for courageous living in the new millennium. LC 99-33769. 196p. 1999. pap. 12.99 (*0-89283-917-1*, Vine Bks) Servant.

***Ogilvie, Lloyd J.** Facing the Future Without Fear: Prescriptions for Courageous Living in the New Millennium. large type ed. LC 00-32053. 297p. 2000. 26.95 (*0-7838-9183-3*, G K Hall Lrg Type) Mac Lib Ref.

Ogilvie, Lloyd J. God's Best for My Life. LC 97-7438. 400p. (Orig.). 1997. 14.99 (*1-56507-699-0*) Harvest Hse.

— The Greatest Counselor in the World: A Fresh, New Look at the Holy Spirit. 208p. 1995. pap. 12.99 (*0-89283-909-0*, Vine Bks) Servant.

— Hosea, Jonah. (Communicator's Commentary Ser.: Vol. 20). 22.99 (*0-8499-0426-9*) Word Pub.

— Lord of the Impossible. LC 84-333. 224p. 1984. pap. 12.95 (*0-687-22710-0*) Abingdon.

— Mayor Consejero del Mundo.Tr. of Greatest Counselor in the World. (SPA.). 1996. pap. 7.99 (*0-8297-0370-5*) Vida Pubs.

***Ogilvie, Lloyd J.** One Quiet Moment: Prayers & Promises for Each New Day. 365p. 2000. 10.99 (*0-7369-0132-9*) Harvest Hse.

Ogilvie, Lloyd J. A Sarca Ainda Arde. Orig. Title: The Bush Is Still Burning. (POR.). 1986. write for info. (*0-8297-1093-0*) Vida Pubs.

— You Are Loved & Forgiven: Paul's letter of hope to the Colossians. rev. ed. LC 86-10186. 192p. 1986. 12.95 (*0-8307-1168-6*, 5111616, Regal Bks) Gospel Lght.

Ogilvie, Lloyd J., ed. The Communicator's Commentary Series: Old Testament. (Communicator's Commentary Ser.: Vol. 7). 22.99 (*0-8499-0412-9*) Word Pub.

— The Communicator's Commentary Series: Old Testament. (Communicator's Commentary Ser.: Vol. 1). 336p. 1982. 22.99 (*0-8499-0154-5*) Word Pub.

Ogilvie, Lloyd J. & Chafin, Kenneth L. New Testament, 1 & 2 Corinthians. (Communicator's Commentary Ser.: Vol. 7). 298p. 1985. 22.99 (*0-8499-0347-5*) Word Pub.

Ogilvie, Lloyd J. & Stuart, Brisco, eds. Mastering the Old Testament. LC 93-39330. (Mastering the Old & New Testament Ser.: Vol. 1). pap. 14.99 (*0-8499-3540-7*) Word Pub.

Ogilvie, Lloyd J. & Wysong, Chuck. The Call to Prayer: Youth Journal. 128p. 1998. spiral bd. 10.99 (*1-56507-936-1*) Harvest Hse.

Ogilvie, Lloyd J., ed. see Marshall, Peter.

Ogilvie, Malcolm A. Photographic Handbook of the Wildfowl of the World. 1999. 49.95 (*1-85368-625-5*) Sterling.

— Wild Geese. LC 77-94181. (Illus.). 1978. 35.00 (*0-931130-00-X*) Harrell Bks.

— Wildfowl of Britain & Europe. 1983. 18.95 (*0-19-217723-0*) OUP.

Ogilvie, Marilyn B. Biographical Dictionary of Women. 1997. text 125.00 (*0-8050-3781-0*) St Martin.

— Women in Science: Antiquity Through Nineteenth Century - A Biographical Dictionary with Annotated Biography. 272p. 1986. 35.00 (*0-262-15031-X*) MIT Pr.

Ogilvie, Marilyn B. & Harvey, Joy D. The Biographical Dictionary of Women in Science, 2 vols. LC 99-17668. 2000. write for info. (*0-415-92040-X*) Routledge.

Ogilvie, Marilyn B. & Meek, Kerry L. Women & Science: An Annotated Bibliography. LC 96-21199. 568p. 1996. text 99.00 (*0-8153-0929-5*, SS859) Garland.

Ogilvie, Marilyn B., jt. ed. see Porter, Roy.

***Ogilvie, Marilyn Bailey & Choquette, Clifford J.** A Dame Full of Vim & Vigor: A Biography of Alice Middleton Boring: Biologist in China. (Women in Science Ser.: Vol. 1). 244p. 1999. text 38.00 (*90-5702-575-2*, Harwood Acad Pubs) Gordon & Breach.

***Ogilvie, Marilyn Bailey & Harvey, Joy Dorothy, eds.** Biographical Dictionary of Women in Science: Pioneering Lives From Ancient Times to Mid-20th Century, 2 vols. Set. LC 99-17668. 1500p. (C). 2000. text 195.00 (*0-415-92038-8*) Routledge.

Ogilvie, Mary G., ed. see Stephen, Caroline.

***Ogilvie, Philip.** Along the Potomac. (Images of America Ser.). (Illus.). 128p. 1999. pap. 18.99 (*0-7385-0352-5*) Arcadia Publng.

Ogilvie, R. M. Romans & Their Gods in the Age of Augustus. (Ancient Culture & Society Ser.). (Illus.). (C). 1970. pap. 12.50 (*0-393-00543-7*) Norton.

Ogilvie, R. M., ed. Ab Urbe Condita, Vol. I, Bks. I-V. 2nd ed. (Oxford Classical Text Ser.). 416p. 1974. text 37.00 (*0-19-814661-2*) OUP.

Ogilvie, R. M. & Winterbottom, M., eds. Agricola, Vol. I: Germania, Agricola. (Loeb Classical Library: No. 35). 1994. 18.95 (*0-674-99039-0*) HUP.

Ogilvie, Robert D. Sleep, Arousal, & Performance. Broughton, Roger J., ed. (Illus.). xvi, 286p. 1991. 109.50 (*0-8176-3518-1*) Birkhauser.

Ogilvie, Robert D., jt. ed. see Harsh, John R.

Ogilvie, Robert M. A Commentary on Livy, Bks. 1-5. (Illus.). 788p. 1965. text 105.00 (*0-19-814432-6*) OUP.

Ogilvie, Sheila A., tr. see Folz, Robert.

Ogilvie, Sheilagh, ed. Germany: A New Social & Economic History 1630-1800, Vol. 2. 448p. 1996. pap. text 24.95 (*0-340-65216-0*, Pub. by E A) OUP.

Ogilvie, Sheilagh C. State Corporatism & Proto-Industry: The Wuttemberg Black Forest, 1580-1797. (Cambridge Studies in Population, Economy & Society in Past Time: No. 33). 539p. (C). 1997. text 80.00 (*0-521-37209-7*) Cambridge U Pr.

Ogilvie, Sheilagh C., ed. Germany - A New Social & Economic History Vol. 2: 1630-1800. 416p. 1996. text 59.95 (*0-340-51395-0*, Pub. by E A) St Martin.

Ogilvie, Sheilagh C. & Cerman, Markus, eds. European Proto-Industrialization. 286p. (C). 1996. text 59.95 (*0-521-49738-8*); pap. text 19.95 (*0-521-49760-4*) Cambridge U Pr.

Ogilvie, T. Francis. Oscillating Pressure Fields on a Free Surface. LC VM0363.O344. (University of Michigan, Dept. of Naval Architecture & Marine Engineering, Report Ser.: No. 30). 64p. reprint ed. pap. 30.00 (*0-608-12982-8*, 202386800034) Bks Demand.

— Wave Resistance: The Low Speed-Limit. LC VM0761.O344. (University of Michigan, Dept. of Naval Architecture & Marine Engineering, Report Ser.). 34p. reprint ed. pap. 30.00 (*0-608-13485-6*, 202262700028) Bks Demand.

Ogilvie-Thompson, S. J., ed. The Index of Middle English Prose Handlist VIII: Manuscripts Containing Middle English Prose in Oxford College Libraries. (Index of Middle English Prose Ser.). 228p. (C). 1991. 75.00 (*0-85991-296-5*) Boydell & Brewer.

***Ogilvie-Thomson, S. J.** The Index of Middle English Prose: Handlist XVI: The Laudian Collection, Bodleian Library, Oxford. 96p. 2000. 55.00 (*0-85991-595-6*) Boydell & Brewer.

Ogilvie-Thomson, Sarah, ed. see Rolle, Richard.

Ogilvie, Timothy H. Large Animal Internal Medicine. LC 97-33109. (The National Veterinary Medical Series for Independent Study). 600p. 1997. write for info. (*0-683-18033-9*) Lppncott W & W.

Ogilvie, William E. Birthright in Land: An Essay on the Right of Property in Land. LC 68-57110. (Reprints of Economic Classics Ser.). xxxii, 436p. 1970. reprint ed. 49.50 (*0-678-00597-4*) Kelley.

— Early Days on the Yukon & the Story of Its Gold Finds, Vol. 15. LC 74-356. (Illus.). 306p. 1974. reprint ed. 24.95 (*0-405-05917-5*) Ayer.

— Pioneer Agricultural Journalists: Brief Biographical Sketches of Some of the Early Editors in the Field of Agricultural Journalism. LC 72-89071. (Rural America Ser.). 1973. reprint ed. 16.00 (*0-8420-1492-6*) Scholarly Res Inc.

Ogilvy, C. Stanley. Excursions in Geometry. (Illus.). 192p. 1990. pap. 6.95 (*0-486-26530-7*) Dover.

— Excursions in Mathematics: Excursions in Mathematics. LC 94-24696. (Illus.). 192p. 1995. pap. text 5.95 (*0-486-28283-X*) Dover.

— Excursions in Number Theory. 168p. 1988. pap. 5.95 (*0-486-25778-9*) Dover.

Ogilvy, Carol & Tinkham, Trudy. Class-Y Christmas Concerts. (Illus.). 112p. (J). (gr. k-7). 1986. student ed. 12.99 (*0-86653-349-4*, GA 795) Good Apple.

— Primary Christmas Concerts. 112p. (J). (gr. k-3). 1989. 12.99 (*0-86653-485-7*, GA1091) Good Apple.

Ogilvy, David. Confessions of an Advertising Man. 172p. 1994. pap. 11.00 (*0-8442-3711-6*, NTC Business Bks) NTC Contemp Pub Co.

— David Ogilvy: An Autobiography. LC 96-45350. (Trailblazers Ser.). 196p. 1997. 24.95 (*0-471-18002-5*) Wiley.

— Ogilvy on Advertising. 1985. pap. 23.00 (*0-394-72903-X*) Vin Bks.

— Old Aeroplanes. 1989. pap. 25.00 (*0-7478-0107-X*, Pub. by Shire Pubns) St Mut.

***Ogilvy, Graham.** Dundee: A Voyage of Discovery. (Illus.). 224p. 1999. 35.00 (*1-84018-218-0*, Pub. by Mainstream Pubng) Trafalgar.

Ogilvy, Graham. The River Tay & Its People. (Illus.). 224p. 1994. 34.95 (*1-85158-406-4*, Pub. by Mainstream Pubng) Trafalgar.

Ogilvy, J. A. Theory of Wave Scattering from Random Rough Surfaces. (Illus.). 292p. 1991. 132.00 (*0-7503-0063-9*) IOP Pub.

Ogilvy, J. D. & Baker, Donald C. Reading "Beowulf" An Introduction to the Poem, Its Background, & Its Style. LC 83-47835. (Illus.). 240p. 1986. reprint ed. pap. 17.95 (*0-8061-2019-3*) U of Okla Pr.

Ogilvy, James, ed. Revisioning Philosophy. LC 91-30803. (SUNY Series in Philosophy). 318p. (C). 1991. pap. text 21.95 (*0-7914-0990-2*) State U NY Pr.

***Ogilvy, James A., et al.** China's Futures: Scenarios for the Impact on Business, the Economy & the World. LC 99-42999. 176p. 2000. 30.00 (*0-7879-5200-1*, Pfffr & Co) Jossey-Bass.

Ogilvy, Susan. Barberesque. 1996. pap. text 24.95 (*0-7935-6623-1*) H Leonard.

— A Classical Terrace: Caves of the Lost Village Carden. 1996. pap. 24.95 incl. 5.25 hd (*0-7935-6447-6*) H Leonard.

— Dance to It! Voyager. 1996. pap. text 24.95 (*0-7935-6604-5*) H Leonard.

— Dream on: Rhythm Matters. 1996. pap. 24.95 (*0-7935-6453-0*) H Leonard.

— Let's Go Baroque Golden Threads Carden. 1996. pap. 24.95 (*0-7935-6465-4*) H Leonard.

— She's the Greatest: Huey's Good News. 1996. pap. 24.95 (*0-7935-6459-X*) H Leonard.

— Silk 'n Clouds: For Ferderick. 1996. pap. text 24.95 (*0-7935-6610-X*) H Leonard.

Ogino, Keizo & Abe, K. Mixed Surfactant Systems. (Surfactant Science Ser.: Vol. 46). (Illus.). 472p. 1992. text 199.00 (*0-8247-8796-X*) Dekker.

Ogino, Yoshisada. Catalysis & Surface Properties of Liquid Metals & Liquid Alloys. (Chemical Industries Ser.: Vol. 29). (Illus.). 224p. 1987. text 165.00 (*0-8247-7699-2*) Dekker.

Ogintz, Eileen. Access Family Travel U. S. A. Date not set. pap. 18.50 (*0-06-277221-X*, Access Trvl) HarpInfo.

— A Kid's Book of Vacation Fun in the Rocky Mountains: Games, Stories, Fun Facts & Much More. LC 95-51756. 128p. (J). 1996. pap. 10.00 (*0-06-258579-7*) Harper SF.

***Ogintz, Eileen, et al.** Kid's Guide to Colonial Williamsburg. LC 99-57277. (Illus.). (J). Date not set. write for info. (*0-87935-204-3*) Colonial Williamsburg.

Oglan, Gerald R. & National Council of Teachers of English Staff. Parents, Learning, & Whole Language Classrooms. LC 97-33187. (Illus.). 96p. 1997. pap. 12.95 (*0-8141-3495-5*) NCTE.

Oglander, John. A Royalist's Notebook: The Commonplace Book of Sir John Oglander. Bamford, Francis, ed. LC 72-174427. (Illus.). 1972. reprint ed. 19.95 (*0-405-08827-2*) Ayer.

Ogle, M. H., et al, eds. Joints in Aluminium - Inalco, 1998: 7th International Conference. 500p. 1999. pap. 315.00 (*1-85573-417-6*) Am Educ Systs.

***Ogle, Amy.** Before Your Pregnancy: Prepare Your Body for a Healthy Pregnancy. (Illus.). ii, 34p. 1999. pap., wbk. ed. 29.95 incl. VHS (*0-9663752-0-3*) Making the Leap.

***Ogle, Arthur.** The Canon Law in Mediaeval England: An Examination of William Lyndwood's "Provinciale," in Reply to the Late Professor F. W. Maitland. fac. ed. LC 99-38827. xv, 220p. 2000. 65.00 (*1-58477-026-0*) Lawbk Exchange.

Ogle, Deborah, tr. see Botermans, Jack.

Ogle, George B. South Korea: Dissent Within the Economic Miracle. LC 90-21221. 192p. (C). 1990. text 22.50 (*1-85649-002-5*, Pub. by Zed Books); text 19.95 (*1-85649-003-3*, Pub. by Zed Books) St Martin.

Ogle, Gini & Noice, Karen. Souvenirs: A Feast of Local Color & Home Cooking. 205p. 1993. 18.95 (*0-9640623-0-5*) Echo Designs.

Ogle, Henry. Ogle - Bertram, Ogle & Bothal: History of the Baronies of Ogle, Bothal & Hepple, & of the Families of Ogle & Bertram Who Held Possession of Those Baronies in Northumberland, to Which Is Added Accounts of Several Branches bearing the Name of Ogle. (Illus.). 496p. 1993. reprint ed. pap. 75.00 (*0-8328-3729-6*); reprint ed. lib. bdg. 85.00 (*0-8328-3728-8*) Higginson Bk Co.

Ogle, John. Colt Memorabilia Price Guide. LC 97-80616. (Illus.), 256p. 1998. pap. 29.95 (*0-87341-514-0*, CCOL) Krause Pubns.

Ogle, Kenneth N., et al. Oculomotor Imbalance in Binocular Vision & Fixation Disparity. LC 67-19139. 384p. reprint ed. pap. 119.10 (*0-608-12683-7*, 205600500043) Bks Demand.

Ogle, Madeline B. From Problems to Profits Vol. 1: The Madson Management System for Pet Grooming Businesses. rev. ed. LC 97-72659. (Illus.). 290p. 1997. pap. 39.95 (*1-878795-25-2*) Madson Group.

Ogle, Marbury B., ed. see Tortarius, Rudolphus.

Ogle, Marc. Abend-94. Wellborn, Montague, ed. (Stories of America along U. S. 60 Ser.: Bk. 2). (Illus.). 240p. 1996. pap. 10.00 (*0-614-28557-7*) Prof Pr NC.

— ABENO-94, 3 vols. LC 97-91784. 230p. 1997. 11.00 (*0-9657841-1-8*) Ogle Develop.

Ogle, Maureen. All the Modern Conveniences: American Household Plumbing, 1840-1890. LC 95-44412. (Johns Hopkins Studies in the History of Technology). (Illus.). 232p. (C). 1996. text 42.00 (*0-8018-5227-7*) Johns Hopkins.

Ogle, Patrick, ed. Facets African-American Video Guide. (Illus.). 230p. 1993. pap. 12.95 (*0-89733-402-7*) Academy Chi Pubs.

Ogle, Robert R., Jr. Crime Scene Investigation & Physical Evidence Manual: Manual of Guidelines - Crime Scene Search & Physical Evidence Collection. 2nd rev. ed. (Illus.). 296p. (C). 1995. ring bd. 69.95 (*0-9661174-0-9*); ring bd. 35.95 (*0-9661174-2-5*) R R Ogle.

Ogle, Robert R. Crime Scene Investigation & Physical Evidence Manual: Manual of Guidelines/Crime Scene Search & Physical Evidence. 2nd ed. (Illus.). 298p. 1998. pap. 43.95 (*0-9661174-4-1*) R R Ogle.

Ogle, Robert R., Jr. O. J. Simpson: Not Guilty by Reason of Insanity: How the LAPD Guaranteed His Acquittal. LC 97-75597. iv, 204p. 1997. pap. 24.95 (*0-9661174-3-3*) R R Ogle.

Ogle, Robert R., Jr. & Fox, Michelle J. Atlas of Human Hair Microscopic Characteristics. LC 98-34752. (Illus.). 96p. 1998. per. 69.95 (*0-8493-8134-7*, 8134) CRC Pr.

Ogle, Thomas P., tr. see Andenaes, Johannes.

Ogle, William, tr. & intro. see Aristotle.

Oglesbee, Rollo B. & Hale, Albert. History of Michigan City. (Illus.). 201p. 1995. reprint ed. lib. bdg. 29.50 (*0-8328-4645-7*) Higginson Bk Co.

Oglesby, jt. auth. see Buckland.

Oglesby, Arthur. Fly Fishing for Salmon & Sea Trout. (Illus.). 320p. 1997. pap. 29.95 (*1-86126-072-5*, Pub. by Cro1wood) Trafalgar.

Oglesby, Carole A., ed. Women & Sport: From Myth to Reality. LC 77-19255. (Illus.). 268p. reprint ed. pap. 83.10 (*0-7837-1492-0*, 205718800023) Bks Demand.

Oglesby, Carole A., et al, eds. Encyclopedia of Women & Sport in America. LC 97-52787. (Illus.). 384p. 1998. boxed set 65.00 (*0-89774-993-6*) Oryx Pr.

Oglesby, Catharine. Modern Primitive Arts of Mexico, Guatemala & the Southwest. LC 75-90670. (Essay Index Reprint Ser.). 1977. 18.95 (*0-8369-1215-2*) Ayer.

Oglesby, Clarkson H. & Hicks, Russell G. Highway Engineering. 4th ed. LC 81-12949. 864p. 1982. text 100.95 (*0-471-02936-X*) Wiley.

Oglesby, Clarkson H., et al. Productivity Improvement in Construction. 1988. pap. text, teacher ed. write for info. (*0-07-047803-1*) McGraw.

— Successful Techniques for Improving Productivity in On-Site Construction. (Illus.). 588p. (C). 1988. 96.88 (*0-07-047802-3*) McGraw.

Oglesby, Dee. Inside Looking Out. 82p. (YA). (gr. 7-12). 1995. pap. 6.95 (*1-57515-053-0*) PPI Pubng.

Oglesby, Dee, told to. Lost Love of a Child. 36p. (YA). (gr. 7-12). 1995. pap. 6.95 (*1-57515-052-2*) PPI Pubng.

Oglesby, E. Hammond. O Lord, Move This Mountain: Racism & Christian Ethics. 128p. 1998. pap. 12.99 (*0-8272-2710-8*) Chalice Pr.

— Ten Principles of Black Self-Esteem: Leffers of Heritage, Lessons of Hope. LC 98-50330. 208p. 1999. pap. 14.95 (*0-8298-1321-7*) Pilgrim OH.

Oglesby, E. W., jt. auth. see Klein, Joe.

Oglesby, Enoch H. God's Divine Arithmetic. Jones, Amos, Jr., ed. LC 84-54498. 150p. (Orig.). 1986. pap. write for info. (*0-910683-06-9*) Townsnd-Pr.

Oglesby, Francis C. An Examination of a Decision Procedure. LC 52-42839. (Memoirs Ser.: No. 1/44). 148p. 1971. reprint ed. pap. 18.00 (*0-8218-1244-0*, MEMO/1/44) Am Math.

Oglesby, K. Thomas. What Black Men Should Do Now: 100 Simple Truths, Ideas & Concepts. LC 98-55907. 160p. 1999. 18.95 (*1-55972-499-4*, Birch Ln Pr) Carol Pub Group.

Oglesby, K. Thomas, jt. ed. see Blalock, Rick.

Oglesby, Lloyd S. The Chemistry of Glitter. (Illus.). 90p. 1989. pap. 19.95 (*0-929931-01-7*) Amer Fireworks.

Oglesby, Mark. Marketing Communications for Solicitors: A Practical Guide to Promoting Your Firm. 247p. 1995. pap. 34.00 (*1-874241-19-8*, Pub. by Cavendish Pubng) Gaunt.

Oglesby, Mira-Lani. Athena Louise Replies. (Morning Chapbook Ser.). 16p. (Orig.). 1989. pap. 15.00 (*0-918273-62-5*) Coffee Hse.

Oglesby, Sabert. Electrostatic Precipitation. LC 77-28984. (Pollution Engineering & Technology Ser.: Vol. 8). (Illus.). 382p. reprint ed. pap. 118.50 (*0-608-08971-0*, 206960600005) Bks Demand.

Oglesby, Stuart R. Prayers for All Occasions. 180p. 1989. reprint ed. pap. 14.95 (*0-8042-2485-4*) Westminster John Knox.

***Oglesby, Virgil.** Watch for the Jaguar. 200p. 2000. 18.95 (*1-58141-014-X*) Rivercross Pub.

Oglesby, William B., Jr. With Wings as Eagles: Toward Personal Christian Maturity. LC 87-51654. 194p. (C). 1987. pap. text 16.00 (*1-55605-036-4*) Wyndham Hall.

Oglesby, William Ellis. Blow Happy, Blow Sad. 247p. mass mkt. 4.99 (*1-55197-321-9*) Picasso Publ.

Oglethorpe, Jean, ed. see Martin, Olive.

***Ogletree, Billy T., et al, eds.** Bridging the Family-Professional Gap: Facilitating Interdisciplinary Services for Children with Disabilities. LC 99-23602. (Illus.). 300p. 1999. pap. 36.95 (*0-398-06989-1*); text 49.95 (*0-398-06988-3*) C C Thomas.

Ogletree, Deakins, Nash, Smoak & Stewart Staff. Americans with Disabilities Act: Public Accommodations & Commercial Facilities. Mook, Jonathan R., ed. LC 96-83131. 1996. 125.00 (*0-8205-2470-0*) Bender.

Ogletree, Frank, et al. Americans with Disabilities Act: Employee Rights & Employee Obligations. Mook, Johnaton R., ed. 1992. 125.00 (*0-8205-1775-5*) Bender.

Ogletree, Madema & Lamb County History Book Committee. Lamb County, Texas. (Illus.). 549p. 1992. 65.00 (*0-88107-195-1*) Curtis Media.

Ogletree, Richard & Fischer, Richard. Top Ten Scientifically Proven Natural Products. 64p. (Orig.). 1997. pap. 11.95 (*0-944351-13-1*) N S D Products.

Ogletree, Roberta J., et al. The Consumer's Guide to School-Based Sexuality Education Curricula. LC 93-46042. 1994. 29.95 (*1-56071-354-2*) ETR Assocs.

***Ogletree, Terry.** Practical Firewalls. 450p. 2000. pap. 34.99 (*0-7897-2416-2*) Que.

Ogley, Adrian. Principles of International Tax: A Multinational Perspective. 1993. 95.00 (*0-9520442-0-X*, Pub. by Interfisc Pub) Intl Info Srvcs Inc.

— Principles of Value Added Tax: A European Perspective. 256p. 1998. 95.00 (*0-9520442-1-8*, Pub. by Interfisc Pub) Intl Info Srvcs Inc.

Ogley, Brian. Exporting: Step by Step to Success. 160p. (C). 1987. 32.00 (*0-7855-2383-9*) St Mut.

O

An Asterisk (*) at the beginning of an entry indicates that the title is appearing for the first time.

Ogley, Roderick C. Internationalizing the Seabed. LC 83-20555. 264p. 1984. text 59.95 (*0-566-00629-4*, Pub. by Dartmth Pub) Ashgate Pub Co.

Ogloff, James R., ed. Law & Psychology: The Broadening of the Discipline. LC 92-71726. 464p. (C). 1992. boxed set 45.00 (*0-89089-475-2*) Carolina Acad Pr.

O'Glove, Thornton. Quality of Earnings: The Investor's Guide to How Much Money a Company Is Really Making. 200p. 1987. 35.00 (*0-02-922630-9*) Free Pr.

Ogne, Steve, jt. auth. see Logan, Robert E.

Ogne, Steven L. & Nebel, Thomas P. Empowering Leaders Through Coaching. (Illus.). 184p. (Orig.). 1996. pap. 85.00 incl. audio (*1-889638-10-2*) ChurchSmart.

Ogne, Steven L., jt. auth. see Logan, Robert E.

Ogniedou, Altan. Phantasmagoria: A Book of Poems. Probstein, Ian E., ed. (Illus.). 80p. 1993. pap. text 6.00 (*0-9635200-0-8*) R E M Pr.

Ogoltsev, V. Common Russian Similes. (Illus.). 174p. (C). 1984. 30.00 (*0-7855-5352-5*, Pub. by Collets) St Mut.

Ogonowska-Coates, Halina. Krystyna's Story. 156p. 1996. pap. 16.95 (*0-908912-87-0*) Paul & Co Pubs.

Ogorkiewicz, R. M., ed. Engineering Properties of Thermoplastics. LC 72-83219. 330p. reprint ed. pap. 102.30 (*0-8357-9885-2*, 205161400097) Bks Demand.

O'Gorman. Late Ruskin. 74.95 (*1-84014-629-X*) Ashgate Pub Co.

O'Gorman, Edmund. St. Francis for Today. 87p. 1991. pap. 7.95 (*0-85244-130-4*, 970, Pub. by Gra1cewing) Morehouse Pub.

O'Gorman, Edmundo. La Invencion de America (The Invention of America) (SPA.). 197p. 1977. pap. 16.99 (*968-16-2371-1*, Pub. by Fondo) Continental Bk.

— The Invention of America. LC 72-6203. 177p. 1972. reprint ed. lib. bdg. 35.00 (*0-8371-6470-2*, OGIA, Greenwood Pr) Greenwood.

O'Gorman, Edward J. Pollution Coverage Issues, 2 vols. LC 98-204276. 1290p. 1998. 198.00 (*1-886813-35-3*) Intl Risk Mgt.

O'Gorman, Eleanor, jt. ed. see Jabri, Vivienne.

***O'Gorman, Ellen.** Irony & Misreading in the "Annals" of Tacitus. LC 99-26462. 208p. (C). 2000. 59.95 (*0-521-66056-4*) Cambridge U Pr.

O'Gorman, F. P. Rationality & Relativity: The Quest for Objective Knowledge. (Avebury Series in Philosophy). 160p. 1989. text 82.95 (*0-566-07035-9*, Pub. by Avebry) Ashgate Pub Co.

O'Gorman, Francis. John Ruskin. 1999. pap. text 9.95 (*0-7509-2142-0*) Sutton Pub Ltd.

O'Gorman, Frank. The Long Eighteenth Century: British Political & Social History, 1688-1832. LC 97-14187. (The Arnold History of Britain Ser.). 432p. 1997. pap. text 24.95 (*0-340-56751-1*) OUP.

O'Gorman, Frank. Voters, Patrons, & Parties: The Unreformed Electorate of Hanoverian England 1734-1832. (Illus.). 464p. 1989. 89.00 (*0-19-820056-0*) OUP.

O'Gorman, Gerald, ed. see Cicero, Marcus Tullius.

O'Gorman, Hubert J. Lawyers & Matrimonial Cases: Study of Informal Pressures in Private Professional Practice. Zuckerman, Harriet & Merton, Robert K., eds. LC 79-3754. (Dissertations on Sociology Ser.). 1980. lib. bdg. 23.95 (*0-405-12986-6*) Ayer.

O'Gorman-Hughes, D. W., jt. auth. see Gupta, J. M.

O'Gorman, J. F., et al. Architecture of Frank Furness. LC 73-77307. (Illus.). 212p. (Orig.). 1987. 52.95 (*0-8122-7957-3*) Phila Mus Art.

O'Gorman, Jack, jt. auth. see Lang, Jovian P.

O'Gorman, James F. ABC of Architecture. LC 97-22616. (Illus.). 144p. (C). (gr. 13). 1997. 26.50 (*0-8122-3423-5*); pap. 14.95 (*0-8122-1631-8*) U of Pa Pr.

— Accomplished in All Departments of Art: Hammatt Billings of Boston, 1818-1874. LC 97-46542. (Studies in Print Culture & the History of the Book). (Illus.). xi, 291p. 1998. 42.50 (*1-55849-148-1*) U of Mass Pr.

— H. H. Richardson: Architectural Forms for an American Society. LC 86-19223. (Illus.). 188p. 1997. pap. text 16.00 (*0-226-62070-0*) U Ch Pr.

— H. H. Richardson: Architectural Forms for an American Society. LC 86-19223. (Illus.). xvi, 188p. (C). 1998. 29.95 (*0-226-62069-7*) U Ch Pr.

Ogorman, James F. Living Architecture: A Biography of H. H. Richardson. LC 97-20534. (Illus.). 176p. 1997. 50.00 (*0-684-83618-1*) Simon & Schuster.

O'Gorman, James F. Three American Architects: Richardson, Sullivan, & Wright, 1865-1915. LC 90-10957. (Illus.). 190p. 1992. pap. 14.95 (*0-226-62072-7*) U Ch Pr.

— Three American Architects: Richardson, Sullivan, & Wright, 1865-1915. LC 90-10957. (Illus.). 192p. 1997. 29.95 (*0-226-62071-9*) U Ch Pr.

O'Gorman, James F., et al. Drawing Toward Building: Philadelphia Architectural Graphics, 1732-1986. (Illus.). 295p. 1986. pap. 19.95 (*0-943836-06-9*) Penn Acad Art.

O'Gorman, Jodie. The Tremaine Site Complex: Oneota Occupation In the La Crosse Locality, Wisconsin. LC 93-38782. 1993. write for info. (*0-87020-273-1*) State Hist Soc Wis.

O'Gorman, Kathleen, ed. Charles Tomlinson: Man & Artist. LC 87-19076. (Illus.). 268p. 1988. text 29.95 (*0-8262-0656-5*) U of Mo Pr.

— On Your Marks: Ready, Set - Learn How to Get a Good Education. (Illus.). 208p. 1994. pap. 9.95 (*0-937247-63-4*) Detroit Pr.

O'Gorman, Lawrence & Kasturi, Rangachar, eds. Document Image Analysis. LC 94-32859. 536p. 1994. 54.00 (*0-8186-6547-5*, BP06547) IEEE Comp Soc.

— Document Image Analysis: An Executive Briefing. LC 97-17283. 107p. 1997. pap. 24.00 (*0-8186-7802-X*, BR07802) IEEE Comp Soc.

O'Gorman, Paschal F., jt. auth. see Boylan, Thomas A.

O'Gorman, Patricia. Dancing Backwards in High Heels: How Women Master the Art of Resilience. LC 94-18598. 208p. (Orig.). 1994. pap. 12.00 (*0-89486-998-1*) Hazelden.

— Patios & Gardens of Mexico. 17p. 1994. reprint ed. 40.00 (*0-8038-0210-2*) Archit CT.

O'Gorman, Patricia W. Tradition of Craftsmanship in Mexican Homes. (Illus.). 272p. 1988. 37.50 (*0-8038-0047-9*) Archit CT.

O'Gorman, Thomas, ed. An Advent Sourcebook. (Seasonal Sourcebook Ser.). 170p. 1988. pap. 15.00 (*0-930467-82-5*, ADVENT) Liturgy Tr Pubns.

O'Gormand, Patricia & Oliver-Diaz, Philip. Twelve Steps to Self Parenting for Adult Children. 1988. pap. 7.95 (*0-932194-68-0*) Health Comm.

Ogorodnikovv, V. A. & Prigarin, S. M. Numerical Modelling of Random Processes & Fields: Algorithms & Applications. 250p. 1996. 155.00 (*90-6764-199-5*, Pub. by VSP) Coronet Bks.

Ogorzaly, Michael A. Waldo Frank, Prophet of Hispanic Regeneration. LC 92-55007. (C). 1994. 36.50 (*0-8387-5233-0*) Bucknell U Pr.

Ogorzaly, Molly C., jt. auth. see Simpson, Beryl B.

***Ogot, B.A.** Africa from the Sixteenth to the Eighteenth Century, Vol. 5. (UNESCO General History of Africa Ser.). 512p. 1999. pap. 24.95 (*0-520-06700-2*, Pub. by U CA Pr) Cal Prin Full Svc.

Ogot, Bethwell A., ed. War & Society in Africa. 276p. 1972. pap. 22.50 (*0-7146-4009-3*, Pub. by F Cass Pubs) Intl Spec Bk.

Ogot, Bethwell A., ed. see UNESCO Staff.

Ogra, Pearay, et al, eds. Mucosal Immunology. 2nd ed. LC 98-36839. (Illus.). 1628p. (C). 1998. boxed set 199.95 (*0-12-524725-7*) Acad Pr.

Ogra, Pearay L., jt. ed. see Bernstein, Joel M.

O'Grada. Irish Economy since Independence. LC 97-12986. 256p. 1997. text 49.95 (*0-7190-4583-5*) St Martin.

O'Grada, Cormac. The Great Irish Famine. (New Studies in Economic & Social History: No. 7). 91p. (C). 1995. text 34.95 (*0-521-55266-4*); pap. text 10.95 (*0-521-55787-9*) Cambridge U Pr.

— Ireland: A New Economic History, 1780-1939. (Illus.). 552p. 1995. pap. text 28.00 (*0-19-820598-8*) OUP.

— Ireland Before & after the Famine: Explorations in Economic History, 1800-1925. 2nd ed. 224p. 1993. text 24.95 (*0-7190-4035-3*, Pub. by Manchester Univ Pr) St Martin.

O'Grada, Cormac, ed. The Economic Development of Ireland since 1870, 2 Vols. (Economic Development of Modern Europe since 1870 Ser.: Vol. 5). 764p. 1994. 295.00 (*1-85278-671-X*) E Elgar.

OGrady. Contemporary Linguistics: Language Introduction. 1996. pap. text 49.50 (*0-312-13795-8*) St Martin.

O'Grady. Lennon & McCartney. (Great Pop Songwriters Ser.). 1998. 45.00 (*0-02-864769-6*) S&S Trade.

O'Grady & Debrovolsky. Contemporary Linguistic Analysis. 1992. pap. text. write for info. (*0-7730-5197-X*) Addison-Wes.

O'Grady, Annie. Past Lifetimes: Keys for Change. (Illus.). 160p. 1997. pap. 12.95 (*1-86351-170-9*, Pub. by Sally Milner) Seven Hills Bk.

***O'Grady, Annmarie.** Everything Irish. LC 99-198473. (Illus.). 80p. (J). (ps-1). 2000. pap. 7.95 (*0-86278-557-X*, Pub. by OBrien Pr) IPG Chicago.

***O'Grady, Carolyn R.** Integrating Service Learning & Multicultural Education in Colleges & Universities. LC 99-87306. 2000. pap. write for info. (*0-8058-3345-5*) L Erlbaum Assocs.

O'Grady, Chris. Love Song to a Long Gone Time: Memoirs of a Moviegoer from Way Back. LC 86-90178. 258p. 1991. 19.95 (*0-9631753-0-0*) C-C OGrady.

***O'Grady, Deidre.** Piave, Boito, Pirandello: From Romantic Realism to Modernism. LC 00-33872. (Studies in Italian Literature). 2000. write for info. (*0-7734-7703-9*) E Mellen.

O'Grady, Dennis E. Taking the Fear Out of Changing. LC 94-28764. 384p. 1994. pap. 14.95 (*1-55850-408-7*) Adams Media.

— Taking the Fear Out of Changing: Guidelines for Getting Through Tough Life Transitions. (Illus.). 480p. (Orig.). 1992. pap. 14.95 (*0-9628476-0-7*) New Insights.

O'Grady, Desmond. Alexandrian Notebook. 32p. 1990. pap. 7.95 (*1-85186-064-9*) Dufour.

— Gododdin. 80p. 1970. 50.00 (*0-85105-310-6*, Pub. by Smyth) Dufour.

— The Golden Odes of Love: An English Verse Rendering. 64p. 1998. pap. 19.50 (*977-424-461-3*, Pub. by Am Univ Cairo Pr) Col U Pr.

— The Headgear of the Tribe: Selected Poems. 98p. 1979. pap. 12.95 (*0-902996-79-7*) Dufour.

— His Skaldcrane's Nest. 52p. 1979. pap. 11.95 (*0-902996-89-4*) Dufour.

— A Limerick Rake: Versions from the Irish. 50p. 1978. pap. 11.95 (*0-902996-68-1*) Dufour.

— The Road Taken: New & Selected Poems, 1956-1996. 487p. 1997. pap. 28.95 (*3-7052-0999-X*, Pub. by Poetry Salzburg) Intl Spec Bk.

— Rome Reshaped: Jubilees, 1300-2000. LC 99-28903. 224p. 1999. 24.50 (*0-8264-1205-X*) Continuum.

— Sing Me Creation. 66p. 1977. pap. 11.95 (*0-902996-56-8*) Dufour.

— Ten Modern Arab Poets. 72p. 1992. pap. 11.95 (*1-873790-04-X*) Dufour.

O'Grady, Desmond. Trawling Tradition: Translations 1954-1994. 606p. write for info. (*3-7052-0920-5*, Pub. by Poetry Salzburg) Intl Spec Bk.

O'Grady, Desmond. The Turned Card: Christianity Before & after the Wall. 2nd ed. LC 96-52196. 200p. 1997. 22.95 (*0-8294-0938-6*) Loyola Pr.

O'Grady, Donald J., jt. ed. see Wester, William C.

O'Grady, Francis, jt. ed. see Lambert, Harold P.

O'Grady, Francis T., ed. Individual Health Insurance. LC 88-6439. 200p. 1988. text 35.00 (*0-938959-00-X*) Soc Actuaries.

O'Grady, G. W. & O'Rourke, K. J. Ryan's Manual of the Law of Income Tax in Australia. 7th ed. xliv, 513p. 1989. 68.00 (*0-455-20906-5*, Pub. by LawBk Co); pap. 42.50 (*0-455-20907-3*, Pub. by LawBk Co) Gaunt.

O'Grady, J. & Rosenthal, M. Obstetrics: Psychological & Psychiatric Syndromes. (Current Topics in Obstetrics & Gynecology Ser.). (Illus.). 383p. (C). (gr. 13). 1991. text 74.95 (*0-412-04601-6*) Chapman & Hall.

O'Grady, J. A., ed. see Paxton, Albert S.

O'Grady, J. P., et al. Vacuum Extraction in Modern Obstetric Practice: Instruments, Operations, Risks & Benefits. LC 94-49184. (Illus.). 154p. 1995. 27.95 (*1-85070-665-4*) Prthnon Pub.

O'Grady, Jennifer. White: Poems by Jennifer O'Grady. LC 99-24501. (First Series Award). 1999. pap. 11.00 (*0-922811-41-5*) Mid-List.

O'Grady, Jim. Dorothy Day: With Love for the Poor. LC 92-84068. (Unsung Americans Ser.). (Illus.). 115p. (J). (gr. 4 up). 1993. pap. 10.95 (*0-9623380-6-0*); lib. bdg. 14.95 (*0-9623380-2-8*) Ward Hill Pr.

O'Grady, Jim, jt. auth. see Polner, Murray.

O'Grady, Joan. Heresy: Heretical Truth or Orthodox Error? A Study of Early Christian Heresies. 164p. 1985. pap. 17.95 (*0-906540-75-5*, Pub. by Element MA) Penguin Putnam.

— Prince of Darkness. 1993. pap. 12.95 (*1-85230-056-6*, Pub. by Element MA) Penguin Putnam.

O'Grady, John. Catholic Charities in the United States: History & Problems. LC 71-137180. (Poverty U. S. A. Historical Record Ser.). 1977. reprint ed. 35.95 (*0-405-03118-1*) Ayer.

Ogrady, John. Early Phase Drug Evaluation in Man. 1990. 115.00 (*0-8493-7708-0*, RM301) CRC Pr.

O'Grady, John. The Life & Works of Sarah Purser. (Illus.). 292p. 1996. boxed set 45.00 (*1-85182-241-0*, Pub. by Four Cts Pr) Intl Spec Bk.

O'Grady, John & Joubert, Pieter H., eds. Handbook of Phase I-II Clinical Drug Trials. LC 96-23811. 576p. 1997. lib. bdg. 159.95 (*0-8493-9230-6*) CRC Pr.

O'Grady, John, jt. ed. see Lewis, Peter J.

O'Grady, John F. According to John: The Witness of the Beloved Disciple. LC 98-47602. 174p. 1999. pap. 12.95 (*0-8091-3852-2*) Paulist Pr.

— Disciples & Leaders: The Origins of Christian Ministry in the New Testament. 1991. pap. 9.95 (*0-8091-3269-9*) Paulist Pr.

— Four Gospels & the Jesus Tradition. 1989. pap. 14.95 (*0-8091-3085-8*) Paulist Pr.

— Models of Jesus Revisited. LC 94-11962. 256p. 1994. pap. 14.95 (*0-8091-3474-8*) Paulist Pr.

— Pillars of Paul's Gospel: Galatians & Romans. LC 91-45556. 192p. 1992. pap. 9.95 (*0-8091-3327-X*) Paulist Pr.

— The Roman Catholic Church: Its Origin & Nature. LC 97-22380. 224p. (Orig.). 1997. pap. 14.95 (*0-8091-3740-2*, 3740 2) Paulist Pr.

O'Grady, John P. Modern Instrumental Delivery. (Illus.). 288p. 1988. 40.00 (*0-683-06632-3*) Lppncott W & W.

— Pilgrims to the Wild: Everett Ruess, Henry David Thoreau, John Muir, Clarence King, Mary Austin. LC 92-29783. 184p. (Orig.). 1993. pap. 16.95 (*0-87480-412-4*) U of Utah Pr.

O'Grady, John P., et al, eds. Operative Obstetrics. LC 95-8734. (Illus.). 512p. 1995. write for info. (*0-683-06633-1*) Lppncott W & W.

O'Grady, John P., et al. Obstetric Syndromes & Conditions. LC 97-33562. (Clinical Handbook Ser.). (Illus.). 408p. 1998. pap. 78.00 (*1-85070-754-5*) Prthnon Pub.

O'Grady, Joseph P. Irish-Americans & Anglo-American Relations, 1880-1888. LC 76-6360. (Irish Americans Ser.). 1976. 29.95 (*0-405-09353-5*) Ayer.

O'Grady, Kathleen, ed. Julia Kristeva: A Bibliography of Primary & Secondary Sources in French & English, 1966-1996. (Bibliographies of Famous Philosophers Ser.). 110p. 1997. 42.00 (*0-912632-68-2*) Philos Document.

O'Grady, Kathleen & Gilroy, Ann L., eds. Bodies, Lives, Voices: Gender in Theology. (Feminist Theology Ser.). 273p. 1998. pap. 24.50 (*1-85075-854-9*, Pub. by Sheffield Acad) CUP Services.

O'Grady, Kathleen & Wansbrough, Paula, eds. Sweet Secrets: Telling Stories of Menstruation. 176p. 1997. pap. 9.95 (*0-929005-33-3*, Pub. by Sec Story Pr) LPC InBook.

O'Grady, Kelly J. Clear the Confederate Way: The Irish in the Army of Northern Virginia. LC 99-63648. (Illus.). 240p. 1999. 24.95 (*1-882810-42-2*) Savas Pub.

O'Grady, Kevin F., et al, eds. Case Management Resource Guide, 4 vols., Set. 4147p. 1999. pap. 225.00 (*1-880874-33-4*) Dorland Hlthcare.

— Case Management Resource Guide Vol. 1: Eastern U. S. 986p. 1998. pap. 60.00 (*1-880874-34-2*) Dorland Hlthcare.

— Case Management Resource Guide Vol. 2: Southern U. S. 1180p. 1998. pap. 60.00 (*1-880874-35-0*) Dorland Hlthcare.

— Case Management Resource Guide Vol. 3: Midwestern U. S. 1123p. 1998. pap. 60.00 (*1-880874-36-9*) Dorland Hlthcare.

— Case Management Resource Guide Vol. 4: Western U. S. 858p. 1998. pap. 60.00 (*1-880874-37-7*) Dorland Hlthcare.

O'Grady, Kieran G., jt. auth. see Morgan, John W.

O'Grady, Lois F., et al, eds. A Practical Approach to Breast Cancer. LC 94-26205. (Illus.). 328p. 1995. pap. text 54.00 (*0-316-63377-1*) Lppncott W & W.

***O'Grady, Michael.** Environmental Statutes Outline: A Guide to Federal Environmental Laws. LC 98-48176. 1998. pap. write for info. (*0-911937-79-X*) Environ Land.

***O'Grady, Michael J., ed.** Environmental Law Deskbook. 6th ed. (Deskbook Ser.). 944p. 2000. pap. 89.95 (*1-58576-006-4*) Environ Law Inst.

***O'Grady, Myles.** Colonfay. LC 99-34810. 254p. 2000. 25.00 (*1-57962-068-X*) Permanent Pr.

O'Grady, Olivia Maria. The Beast of the Apocalypse. unabridged ed. 427p. 1959. reprint ed. 30.00 (*0-945001-66-5*) GSG & Assocs.

O'Grady, Pat B. The Poverty Survival Handbook. LC 86-62681. (Illus.). 72p. (Orig.). 1986. pap. 5.00 (*0-9601846-3-5*) PM Ent.

O'Grady, Patricia. A Recipe for Happy Days. (Illus.). 65p. (Orig.). 1982. pap. 4.25 (*0-9601846-2-7*) PM Ent.

***O'Grady, Patrick.** The Season Starts When? Cycling Cartoons by O'Grady. LC PN6727.O48S43 1999. (Illus.). 160p. 1999. pap. 12.95 (*1-884737-66-8*, Pub. by VeloPress) Publishers Group.

O'Grady, Rohan. Curse of the Montrolfes. 230p. 1983. reprint ed. 22.00 (*0-933256-43-4*) Second Chance.

O'Grady, Ron. Bread & Freedom: Understanding & Acting on Human Rights. LC 81-470289. (Risk Bk.: No. 4). (Illus.). 87p. reprint ed. pap. 30.00 (*0-7837-5996-7*, 204580600008) Bks Demand.

— Tourism in the Third World: Christian Reflections. LC 82-8227. 91p. (Orig.). reprint ed. pap. 30.00 (*0-8357-4076-5*, 203676600005) Bks Demand.

O'Grady, Ron, jt. auth. see Takenaka, Masao.

O'Grady, Scott. Basher Five-Two: The True Story of F-16 Fighter Pilot Captain Scott O'Grady. LC 96-51181. (Illus.). 144p. 1997. 16.95 (*0-385-32300-X*) Doubleday.

— Basher Five-Two: The True Story of F-16 Fighter Pilot Captain Scott O'Grady. 1998. 10.09 (*0-606-13183-3*, Pub. by Turtleback) Demco.

— Return with Honor. 208p. 1996. mass mkt. 6.99 (*0-06-101147-9*, Harp PBks) HarpC.

O'Grady, Scott & Coplon, Jeff. Return with Honor. 224p. 1995. 22.95 (*0-385-48330-9*) Doubleday.

***O'Grady, Scott & Coplon, Jeff.** Return with Honor. (Illus.). 188p. 2000. reprint ed. pap. text 7.00 (*0-7881-6935-1*) DIANE Pub.

O'Grady, Scott & French, Michael. Basher Five-Two: The True Story of F-16 Fighter Pilot Captain Scott O'Grady. (Illus.). 144p. (YA). (gr. 5 up). 1998. reprint ed. pap. 4.99 (*0-440-41313-3*, YB BDD) BDD Bks Young Read.

O'Grady, Standish. Bog of Stars, & Other Stories & Sketches of Elizabethan Ireland. LC 74-125234. (Short Story Index Reprint Ser.). 1977. 16.95 (*0-8369-3601-9*) Ayer.

— Irish Saints from the Silva Gadelica: The Lives of St. Kieran, St. Molasius, St. Magnenn of Kilmainham, St. Cellach of Killala. 1998. pap. text 10.00 (*0-89979-111-5*) British Am Bks.

O'Grady, Standish J. The Flight of the Eagle. LC 79-8428. reprint ed. 44.50 (*0-404-62078-7*) AMS Pr.

***O'Grady, Thomas.** What Really Matters. (The Hugh MacLennan Poetry Ser.). 124p. 2000. pap. 12.95 (*0-7735-1906-8*, Pub. by McG-Queens Univ Pr) CUP Services.

O'Grady, Timothy. I Could Read the Sky. (Illus.). 192p. 1997. 45.00 (*1-86046-386-X*) Harvill Press.

O'Grady, Timothy & Pyke, Steve. I Could Read the Sky. (Illus.). 176p. 1999. pap. 11.00 (*1-86046-508-0*, Pub. by Harvill Press) FS&G.

O'Grady, Timothy, jt. auth. see Griffith, Kenneth.

O'Grady, Tom. In the Room of the Just Born. 72p. (Orig.). 1989. pap. 7.95 (*0-940475-89-8*) Dolphin-Moon.

— James Taylor's Shocked & Amazed! On & off the Midway. Taylor, James & Crawford, Kathleen, eds. (Shocked & Amazed! Ser.). (Illus.). 104p. (Orig.). pap. 12.95 (*0-940475-00-6*) Dolphin-Moon.

— Shaking the Tree: A Book of Works & Days. (Illus.). 197p. (Orig.). 1993. pap. 10.95 (*0-614-05294-7*) Dolphin-Moon.

— Sun, Moon & Stars. LC 96-214709. (Illus.). 64p. (Orig.). 1996. pap. 15.00 (*1-884824-18-8*, Timonier Bks) Tryon Pubng.

O'Grady, Tom, intro. The Hampden-Sydney Poetry Review Anthology (1975-1990) 328p. (Orig.). 1990. pap. 12.95 (*0-940475-91-X*) Dolphin-Moon.

O'Grady, Tom, tr. see Seifert, Jaroslav.

O'Grady, W. E., ed. see Electrocatalysis of Fuel Cell Reactions Workshop S.

***O'Grady, William.** Contemporary Linguistic Analysis. 4th ed. (Illus.). 2000. pap. text. write for info. (*0-201-68481-0*) Addison-Wesley.

O'Grady, William. Contemporary Linguistic Analysis: An Introduction. 4th ed. 2000. pap. text. write for info. (*0-201-47812-9*) Addison-Wesley.

O'Grady, William D. Categories & Case: The Sentence Structure of Korean. LC 90-42137. (Current Issues in Linguistic Theory Ser.: Vol. 71). vii, 294p. 1991. 65.00 (*1-55619-127-8*) J Benjamins Pubng Co.

— Principles of Grammar & Learning. LC 86-11402. 248p. (C). 1987. 33.00 (*0-226-62074-3*) U Ch Pr.

O'Grady, William D., et al. Contemporary Linguistics: An Introduction. LC 96-23860. (Learning about Language Ser.). 1997. pap. write for info. (*0-582-24691-1*, Pub. by Addison-Wesley) Longman.

O'Grady, William D., jt. auth. see Choo, Miho.

O'Grady, William P., jt. auth. see Choo, Miho.

Ogram, Ernest W. The Emerging Pattern of the Multinational Corporation. LC 65-64947. (Georgia State University College of Business Administration Research Monograph Ser.: No. 31). 39p. reprint ed. pap. 30.00 (*0-608-13633-6*, 201905400010) Bks Demand.

Ogrel, Stephen, ed. see Shakespeare, William & Harms, Henry R.

O

Ogren, Goran I. & Bosatta, Ernesto. Theoretical Ecosystem Ecology: Understanding Nutrient Cycles. LC 96-18908. (Illus.). 245p. (C). 1997. text 54.95 (0-521-58022-6) Cambridge U Pr.

Ogren, Kathy J. The Jazz Revolution: Twenties America & the Meaning of Jazz. (Illus.). 240p. 1992. pap. 12.95 (0-19-507479-3) OUP.

Ogren, Robert W. & Jackson, Kenneth M. Defense Procurement Enforcement. LC 84-197577. (Illus.). viii, 796p. 35.00 (0-685-10013-8) Harcourt.

Ogren, Thomas. Happy Hour: Reading Level 3. (Sundown Fiction Collection). 1993. 3.95 (0-88336-218-X) New Readers.

***Ogren, Thomas L.** Allergy-Free Gardening: A Revolutionary Approach to Landscape Planning. (Illus.). 256p. 2000. 32.95 (1-58008-200-9); pap. 19.95 (1-58008-166-5) Ten Speed Pr.

Ogretir, Cemil & Csizmadia, Imre G., eds. Computational Advances in Organic Chemistry: Molecular Structure & Reactivity. (NATO Advanced Science Institutes Series C: Mathematical & Physical Sciences). 432p. 1991. text 218.00 (0-7923-1064-0) Kluwer Academic.

O'Grianna, Seamus. Cith Is Dealan. 130p. 1994. pap. 9.95 (0-85342-448-9, Pub. by Mercier Pr) Irish Amer Bk.

O'Griofa, Mairtin. Book of Irish Weirdness. 496p. 1997. 12.95 (0-8069-9936-5) Sterling.

— A Celtic Christmas: Classic Tales from the Emerald Isle. LC 96-20874. (Illus.). 128p. 1998. 12.95 (0-8069-9586-6) Sterling.

O'Griofa, Mairtin, ed. Irish Tales of the Supernatural. LC 95-26725. (Illus.). 128p. (J). 1996. pap. 6.95 (0-8069-5961-4) Sterling.

Ogrizek, Dore, ed. Winter Book of Switzerland. (Illus.). 383p. 1957. 5.00 (0-686-75372-0) Bookfinger.

***Ogrizek, Michel & Guillery, Jean-Michel.** Communicating in Crisis: A Theoretical & Practical Guide to Crisis Management. Kimball-Brooke, Helen & Brooke, Robert Z., trs. from FRE. LC 99-30182. 110p. 1999. pap. text 14.95 (0-202-30632-1) Aldine de Gruyter.

Ogrizovich, Dorothy M., ed. Sins & Secrets. LC 93-85933. 115p. (Orig.). (C). 1994. pap. 6.95 (0-9639229-0-4) Plautz Enter.

Ogrodnick, Margaret. Instinct & Intimacy: Political Philosophy & Aautobiography in Rousseau. 256p. 1999. text 50.00 (0-8020-0612-4) U of Toronto Pr.

Ogrodnik, Peter J. Fundamental Engineering Mechanics. 256p. (C). 1997. pap. text 44.95 (0-582-29799-0, Pub. by Addison-Wesley) Longman.

Ogrodzki, Jan. Circuit Simulation Methods & Algorithms. 496p. 1994. boxed set 104.95 (0-8493-7894-X, 7894) CRC Pr.

Ogston, Derek. Antifibrinolytic Drugs: Chemistry, Pharmacology, & Clinical Usage. LC 84-13099. (Wiley-Medical Publication). (Illus.). 194p. reprint ed. pap. 60.20 (0-8357-8642-0, 203506600092) Bks Demand.

— The Physiology of Hemostasis. (Illus.). 390p. (C). 1983. 49.95 (0-674-66660-7) HUP.

— Venous Thrombosis: Causation & Prediction. LC 87-8146. (Wiley-Medical Publication). 258p. reprint ed. pap. 80.00 (0-8357-3473-0, 203973500013) Bks Demand.

Ogston, Derek & Bennett, B., eds. Haemostasis: Biochemistry, Physiology, & Pathology. LC 76-44231. 539p. reprint ed. pap. 167.10 (0-608-15421-0, 202927000059) Bks Demand.

Oguchi, Hakuro, ed. see International Symposium on Rarefield Gas Dynamics.

Ogude, James. Ngugi's Novels & African History. LC 99-23065. 1999. write for info. (0-7453-1436-8) LPC InBook.

— Ngugi's Novels & African History: Narrating the Nation. 1999. pap. 19.95 (0-7453-1431-7, Pub. by Pluto GBR) Stylus Pub VA.

Oguhebe, Festus S. The "How to Write" Book. (YA). write for info. (0-9636510-0-5); pap. write for info. (0-9636510-1-3) Hebes Intl.

Ogui, Sensei, jt. auth. see Gove, Mary K.

Oguibe, Olu. Uzo Egonu: An African Artist in the West. 176p. 1995. 32.95 (0-947753-08-7, Pub. by Kala Pr) SPD-Small Pr Dist.

Oguibe, Olu & Enwezor, Okwui. Cross/ing: Time, Space, Movement. (Illus.). 75p. 1998. pap. 20.00 (1-889195-24-3) Smart Art Pr.

Oguibe, Olu & Enwezor, Okwui, eds. Reading the Contemporary: African Art from Theory to the Marketplace. (CUSA Ser.). (Illus.). 348p. 1999. pap. 35.00 (0-262-65051-7) MIT Pr.

O'Guin, C. M. Basic Homiletical Studies. 127p. 1967. pap. 5.95 (1-882449-16-9) Messenger Pub.

Oguin, Michael. Activity Based Costing. 400p. (C). 1991. text 69.95 (0-13-853318-0, Busn) P-H.

Oguinn & Allen, Warren W. Advertising Text. LC 96-46515. (Miscellaneous/Catalogs Ser.). (C). 1997. mass mkt. 60.95 (0-538-86908-9) S-W Pub.

***O'Guinn, et al.** Publicidad. (C). 1999. pap. 87.95 (968-7529-59-8) Thomson Learn.

O'Guinn, Helen Wernle. City Smart: Indianapolis. 2nd ed. (City Smart Ser.). (Illus.). 224p. 1999. pap. 12.95 (1-56261-447-9, City Smart) Avalon Travel.

O'Guinn, Thomas C., et al. Advertising. 2nd ed. LC 99-23028. (Swc-Marketing Ser.). 694p. 1999. pap. 96.95 (0-324-00661-6) Thomson Learn.

Oguinninine, Boris. Essays on Vedic & Indo-european Culture. LC 98-908671. (Mlbd in Linguistics Ser.). viii, 257 p. 1998. pap. 250.00 (81-208-1499-1, Pub. by Motilal Bnarsidass) St Mut.

Ogul, Morris S., jt. auth. see Keefe, William J.

Ogulnick, Karen. Onna Rashiku (Like a Woman) The Diary of a Language Learner in Japan. LC 97-45140. 128p. (C). 1998. text 39.50 (0-7914-3893-7); pap. text 12.95 (0-7914-3894-5) State U NY Pr.

Ogumefu, M. I. Yoruba Legends. LC 78-63217. (Folktale Ser.). 96p. 1985. reprint ed. 27.50 (0-404-16153-7) AMS Pr.

Ogunade, Taiwo. Igbo Wise Sayings, Ibo Proverbs & Greetings. 46p. 1995. lib. bdg. 4.95 (1-881549-06-2) Oluweri Pubns.

— Jeffries, Putting Fire into Whities Ass. 150p. 1995. lib. bdg. 12.50 (1-881549-09-7) Oluweri Pubns.

— Nigerian Musical Styles, Africa's Rhythm of Unity. LC 92-90729. 78p. 1991. lib. bdg. 11.95 (1-881549-01-1) Oluweri Pubns.

— This Side of Harlem, Short Stories about Us. 85p. 1995. lib. bdg. 4.95 (1-881549-08-9) Oluweri Pubns.

Ogunade, Taiyewo. Asose Aworo Onile, a Yoruba Fortune Teller (English) 4p. 1992. 3.50 (1-881549-00-3) Oluweri Pubns.

— Asose Aworo Onile, Oraculo Yoruba. (SPA.). 4p. 1992. 3.50 (1-881549-02-X) Oluweri Pubns.

— Yoruba Religious Worship, Traditional God Worship, Belief & Practice. LC 92-91208. 182p. 1995. lib. bdg. 19.95 (1-881549-03-8) Oluweri Pubns.

Ogunbadejo, Oye. The International Politics of Africa's Strategic Minerals, 88. LC 85-951. (Contributions in Afro-American & African Studies: No. 88). 213p. 1985. 49.95 (0-313-24803-6, OGI/, Greenwood Pr) Greenwood.

Ogundele, Wole. Omuluabi: Ulli Beier, Yoruba Society & Culture. LC 98-37142. 304p. 1998. 79.95 (0-86543-720-3); pap. 21.95 (0-86543-721-1) Africa World.

Ogundijo, Bayo, ed. Yoruba Popular Theatre: Three Plays by the Oyin Adejobi Company. Barter, Karin, tr. LC 94-29997. 1994. 35.00 (0-918456-70-3) African Studies Assn.

Ogundipe, Femi, ed. see Onuzo, Okey.

Ogundipe-Leslie, Molara. Re-Creating Ourselves: African Women & Critical Transformations. LC 93-43967. 250p. 1994. 45.95 (0-86543-411-5); pap. 16.95 (0-86543-412-3) Africa World.

Ogundipe-Leslie, Molara, jt. ed. see Davies, Carole B.

Ogungbesan, Kolawole. The Writings of Peter Abrahams. LC 78-26133. 156p. (C). 1979. 17.50 (0-8419-0480-4, Africana) Holmes & Meier.

***Ogunlana, Stephen O., et al.** Profitable Partnering in Construction Procurement: CIB W 92 (Procurement Systems) CIB TG 23 (Culture in Construction) Joint Symposium. LC 98-53113. (CIB Proceedings Ser.). xii, 735 p. 1999. text. write for info. (0-419-24760-2, E & FN Spon) Routledge.

Ogunnaike, Babatunde A. Instructor's Manual for Process Dynamics, Modeling & Control. 456p. 1997. pap. text. write for info. (0-19-511937-1) OUP.

Ogunnaike, Babatunde A. & Ray, W. Harmon. Process Dynamics, Modeling, & Control. (Topics in Chemical Engineering Ser.). (Illus.). 1296p. (C). 1994. text 92.00 (0-19-509119-1) OUP.

Ogunremi, G. O. The Counting the Camels: The Economics of Transportation in Pre-Industrial Nigeria. LC 79-89989. (Illus.). 1982. 21.50 (0-88357-092-0) NOK Pubs.

Ogunsanwo, Alaba. China's Policy in Africa, Nineteen Fifty-Eight to Nineteen Seventy-One. LC 72-89810. (International Studies). 329p. reprint ed. pap. 93.80 (0-608-13304-3, 2025593) Bks Demand.

Oguntoyinbo, J. S., et al. Nigeria in Maps. Barbour, K. M. et al, eds. 160p. 1982. 49.50 (0-8419-0763-3) Holmes & Meier.

Oguntoyinbo, J. S., jt. auth. see Hayward, D.

Ogunyemi, Chikwenye O. Africa Wo/Man Palava: The Nigerian Novel by Women. (Women in Culture & Society Ser.). 366p. 1996. pap. text 15.95 (0-226-62085-9); lib. bdg. 29.95 (0-226-62084-0) U Ch Pr.

Ogunyemi, Yemi D. The Covenant of the Earth: Yoruba Religious & Philosophical Narratives. 2nd ed. LC 98-71189. Orig. Title: The Covenant of the Earth. (Illus.). 62p. 1998. reprint ed. pap. 10.95 (1-890157-15-5, Pub. by Athelia-Henrietta) BookWorld.

— Introduction to Yoruba Philosophy, Religion & Literature. LC 98-70431. (Illus.). 176p. 1998. pap. 16.95 (1-890157-14-7, Pub. by Athelia-Henrietta) BookWorld.

Ogura, C., et al, eds. Recent Advances in Event-Related Brain Potential Research: Proceedings of the 11th International Conference on Event-Related Potentials (EPIC), Okinawa, Japan, 25-30 June 1995. LC 96-25000. (International Congress Ser.: No. 1099). 1118p. 1996. text 324.25 (0-444-82280-1, Excerpta Medica) Elsevier.

Ogura, F. & Aso, Y. Design of Novel Chalcogen-Containing Organic Metals: Extensively Conjugated Electron Donors & Acceptors with Reduced On-site Coulomb Repulsion, Vol. 11. (Sulfur Reports). 469p. 1992. pap. text 120.00 (3-7186-5295-1) Gordon & Breach.

Ogura, Hideaki. Pharmacological Approach to the Study of the Formation & Resorption Mechanism of Hard Tissues. (Illus.). 192p. 1994. 55.00 (1-56386-021-X, Ishiyaku EuroAmerica) Med Dent Media.

Ogura, Michiko. Verbs in Medieval English: Differences in Verb Choice & Prose. LC 95-4499. (Topics in English Linguistics Ser.: No. 17). xxii, 260p. (C). 1995. lib. bdg. 113.85 (3-11-014426-3) Mouton.

***Ogura, Takekazu.** Agricultural Development in Modern Japan. LC 00-25579. (Japanese Economic History Ser.). 2000. write for info. (0-415-21821-7) Routledge.

Ogura, Takeshi, jt. ed. see Takaku, Fumimaro.

Ogura, Yasuyuki, jt. photos by see Anzai, Shigeo.

Ogura, Yudzuru. Comparative Anatomy of Vegetative Organs of the Pteridophytes. (Handbuch der Pflanzenanatomie Encyclopedia of Plant Anatomy - Traite d' Anatomie Vegetale Ser.: Band VII, Teil 3). (GER., Illus.). viii, 502p. 1972. 135.00 (3-443-14006-8, Pub. by Gebruder Borntraeger) Balogh.

Ogura, Yukiko. Accessories. 80p. 1996. pap. 24.95 (0-9629056-9-0) Quilters Res.

Oguro, Shoichi, et al, eds. Nicholas Love at Waseda: Proceedings of the International Conference, 20-22 July, 1995. LC 97-1851. (Illus.). 305p. 1997. 75.00 (0-85991-500-X, DS Brewer) Boydell & Brewer.

Oguro, Yanao & Takagi, Kunio, eds. Endoscopic Approaches to Cancer Diagnosis & Treatment. (Gann Monographs on Cancer Research: No. 37). 172p. 1990. 125.00 (0-7484-0016-8, Pub. by Tay Francis Ltd) Taylor & Francis.

Oguro, Yanao, jt. ed. see Joffe, S. N.

Ogus, Anthony I. & Barendt, E. M. The Law of Social Security. 3rd ed. 1988. 124.00 (0-406-63372-X, MICHIE); pap. 70.00 (0-406-63370-3, MICHIE) LEXIS Pub.

Ogut, A., jt. ed. see Rohatgi, U. S.

***Ogutcu, Mehmet.** China's Worldwide Quest for Energy Security. 88p. 2000. pap. 100.00 (92-64-17648-9, 61 2000 01 1 P, Pub. by Org for Econ) OECD.

Ogutu, Gilbert E., jt. ed. see Scharlemann, Robert P.

Oguz, Temel, jt. auth. see Ivanov, Leonid I.

Oh. Fitness for the Busy Executive in Only Ten Minutes a Day: A Lifetime Program to Stay in Shape for Your Best Top Level Performance. (Life Management Ser.). Date not set. 25.00 (0-89896-247-1); pap. 20.00 (0-89896-243-9) Larksdale.

Oh & Hassig Pacific Rim Consulting Staff, jt. ed. see Oh, Kongdan.

Oh, Bonnie B., jt. ed. see Stetz, Margaret D.

Oh, Cheol H. Linking Social Science Information to Policy-Making. LC 96-34116. (Political Economy & Public Policy Ser.: Vol. 10). 1996. 78.50 (0-7623-0155-4) Jai Pr.

Oh, Dr. The Happy Marriage Book: How to Turn a Miserable Marriage into a Good Marriage by Using Dr. Oh's Marriage Repair Tool Kit. St. John, Charlotte, ed. (Life Management Ser.). (Illus.). 160p. 1998. pap. 25.00 (0-89896-366-4, Better Life Bks) Larksdale.

***Oh, Ingyu.** Mafioso, Big Business & the Financial Crisis: The State-Business Relations in South Korea & Japan. 218p. 2000. text 65.95 (0-7546-1089-6, Pub. by Ashgate Pub) Ashgate Pub Co.

Oh, J. H., et al. Neural Networks - The Statistical Mechanics Perspective: Proceedings of the CTP - PBSRI Joint Workshop on Thor Physics. (Progress in Neural Processing Ser.: Vol. 1). 300p. 1995. text 76.00 (981-02-2324-2) World Scientific Pub.

Oh, Jae & Seward, James. The Echo Manual. 2nd ed. LC 98-19451. 304p. 1998. text 129.95 (0-7817-1205-X) Lppncott W & W.

Oh, Jae K., et al. The Echo Manual. (Illus.). 336p. 1994. text 94.95 (0-316-63374-7) Lppncott W & W.

Oh, Jai K., ed. see Gold, Joseph.

Oh, John K. Korean Politics: The Quest for Democratization & Economic Development. LC 98-36484. 251p. 1999. 49.95 (0-8014-3447-5); pap. 16.95 (0-8014-8458-8) Cornell U Pr.

Oh, John S., et al, eds. International Financial Management: Problem, Issues, & Experience. LC 81-81655. (Contemporary Studies in Economic & Financial Analysis: Vol. 34). 176p. 1983. 78.50 (0-89232-228-4) Jai Pr.

Oh, Kang-nam, ed. see Chung, David.

Oh, Kara. Men Made Easy: How to Get What You Want from Your Man. Unkefer, Duane & Whitt, Martha, eds. LC 98-96649. 192p. 1999. pap. 15.95 (0-9667875-9-5) Avambre.

***Oh, Kong D.** North Korea Through the Looking Glass. 2000. 39.95 (0-8157-6436-7); pap. write for info. (0-8157-6435-9) Brookings.

***Oh, Kongdan & Oh & Hassig Pacific Rim Consulting Staff, eds.** Korea Briefing, 1997-1999: Challenges & Change at the Turn of the Century. (Asia Society Briefings Ser.). (Illus.). 243p. 2000. text 64.95 (0-7656-0610-0); pap. text 24.95 (0-7656-0611-9, East Gate Bk) M E Sharpe.

Oh, Kongdan, jt. auth. see Fukuyama, Francis.

Oh, Kook S., et al. Practical Gamuts & Differential Diagnosis in Pediatric Radiology. LC 81-19832. 243p. reprint ed. pap. 75.40 (0-8357-7597-6, 205691800096) Bks Demand.

Oh, Lin. Stock Pickers, Pocket Pickers: What Every Widow, Orphan & Prudent Trust Investor Should Know about How to Invest in Wall Street. St. John, Charlotte, ed. LC 93-12370. 160p. (Orig.). 1998. pap. 20.00 (0-89896-201-3, Better Life Bks) Larksdale.

Oh, S. Prevention of Head Injuries in Skiing. (Illus.). viii, 164p. 1985. pap. 42.75 (3-8055-3978-9) S Karger.

Oh, Sae K., ed. PACOMS '96: Proceedings of the 4th Pacific-Asia Offshore Mechanics Symposium, 1996. (Illus.). 325p. 1996. pap. 60.00 (1-880653-27-3) ISOPE.

Oh, Seong-Kyun. Die Materialistisch-Dialektische Fundierung des Epischen Theaters Brechts Als eines Zweidimensionalen Theatralischen Kommunikationssystems. Bollacher, Martin et al, eds. (Bochumer Schriften zur Deutschen Literatur Ser.: Bd. 49). 233p. 1998. pap. 39.95 (3-631-32526-6) P Lang Pubng.

Oh, Shin J. Clinical Electromyography: Nerve Conduction Studies. 2nd ed. LC 92-48896. (Illus.). 720p. 1993. 125.00 (0-683-06644-7) Lppncott W & W.

— Color Atlas of Peripheral Nerve Pathology. (Illus.). 1999. 130.00 (0-8493-1676-6) CRC Pr.

— Principles of Clinical Electromyography: Case Studies. LC 98-10426. 352p. 1998. pap. 50.00 (0-683-18106-8) Lppncott W & W.

Oh, Su Ann. Folk Tales from Iraq. 205p. 1999. reprint ed. pap. text 20.00 (0-7881-6171-7) DIANE Pub.

Oh, Tae-Sok. The Metacultural Theater of Oh Tae-sok: Five Plays from the Korean Avant-Garde. Kim, Ah-jeong & Graves, R. B., trs. from KOR. LC 98-51873. 176p. (C). 1999. 33.00 (0-8248-2099-1); pap. 14.95 (0-8248-2158-0) UH Pr.

Oh, Teik E. Intensive Care Manual. 4th ed. LC 96-38861. 1032p. 1997. pap. text 80.00 (0-7506-2358-6) Buttrwrth-Heinemann.

Oh, Timothy T., jt. ed. see Schmitz, Robert L.

Oh, William, jt. auth. see Tsang, Reginald C.

Oh, Yisok. Microwave Polarimetric Backscattering from Natural Rough Surfaces. fac. ed. LC QC0676.7. (University of Michigan Report: No. RL904). 249p. 1994. pap. 77.20 (0-7837-7699-3, 204745600007) Bks Demand.

Oh, Yong-su. The Good People: Korean Stories. (Writing in Asia Ser.). (Illus.). 162p. (Orig.). (C). 1986. pap. text 10.00 (962-225-171-4, 00271) Heinemann.

Ohadi, M. M. & Conklin, J. C., eds. Advances in Enhanced Heat/Mass Transfer & Energy Efficiency Vol. 320-1: Proceedings of the ASME International Mechanical Engineering Congress & Exposition, 1995, San Francisco, CA. LC 95-81273. (1995 ASME International Mechanical Engineering Congress & Exposition Ser.: HTD-Vol. 320/PID-Vol. 1). 132p. 1995. 56.00 (0-7918-1754-7, H01036) ASME.

Ohaegbulam, F. Ugboaja. A Concise Introduction to American Foreign Policy. LC 98-27377. XIII, 394p. 1999. pap. text 29.95 (0-8204-4182-1, 41821) P Lang Pubng.

Ohaegbulam, Festus U. Nigeria & the U. N. Mission to the Democratic Republic of the Congo: A Case Study of the Formative Stages of Nigeria's Foreign Policy. LC 82-11193. 198p. 1982. reprint ed. pap. 61.40 (0-608-04502-0, 206524700001) Bks Demand.

— Towards an Understanding of the African Experience from Historical & Contemporary Perspectives. 298p. (Orig.). (C). 1990. lib. bdg. 47.00 (0-8191-7940-X) U Pr of Amer.

Ohaeto, Ezenwa. Chinua Achebe: A Biography. LC 97-10961. (Illus.). 1997. 35.00 (0-253-33342-3) Ind U Pr.

O'Hafa, Robert. Insurrection: Holding History. 112p. 1998. pap. 11.95 (1-55936-157-3, Pub. by Theatre Comm) Consort Bk Sales.

O'Hagan. Geraghty's Care for Children. 3rd ed. 1996. pap. text 30.50 (0-7020-1918-6, W B Saunders Co) Harcrt Hlth Sci Grp.

— The School-Marm Tree. LC 78-314425. 256p. 1977. pap. 15.95 (0-88922-129-4, Pub. by Talonbks) Genl Dist Srvs.

O'Hagan, Andrew. The Missing: A Social History of Glasgow & Gloucester. 208p. 1996. 20.00 (1-56584-335-5, Pub. by New Press NY) Norton.

O'Hagan, Andrew. Our Fathers. LC 99-25486. 304p. 1999. 23.00 (0-15-100494-3, Harvest Bks) Harcourt.

***O'Hagan, Andrew.** Our Fathers. 304p. 2000. pap. 13.00 (0-15-601202-2) Harcourt.

O'Hagan, Anthony. Kendall's Advanced Theory of Statistics: Bayesian Inference, Vol. 2B. LC 94-188490. (An Arnold Publication). 304p. 1998. 80.00 (0-340-52922-9, Pub. by E A) OUP.

— Probability: Methods & Measurements. 300p. 1988. text 65.00 (0-412-29530-X) Chapman & Hall.

— Probability: Methods & Measurements. 300p. (gr. 13). 1988. pap. text 49.95 (0-412-29540-7) Chapman & Hall.

O'Hagan, Derek T., ed. Novel Delivery Systems for Oral Vaccines. LC 93-40167. 288p. 1994. lib. bdg. 189.00 (0-8493-4866-8, 4866) CRC Pr.

— Vaccine Adjuvants: Preparation Methods & Research Protocols. (Methods in Molecular Medicine Ser.: Vol. 42). 352p. 2000. 99.50 (0-89603-735-5) Humana.

Ohagan, Howard. Tay John. 274p. 1996. pap. text 7.95 (0-7710-9850-2) McCland & Stewart.

O'Hagan, Howard. Trees Are Lonely Company. 320p. 1993. pap. 16.95 (0-88922-327-0, Pub. by Talonbks) Genl Dist Srvs.

O'Hagan, J., ed. The Economy of Ireland: Policy & Performance of a Small European Country. LC 95-36941. 1995. text 59.95 (0-312-15823-8) St Martin.

O'Hagan, Jacinta, jt. auth. see Fry, Greg.

O'Hagan, James P., ed. Growth & Adjustment in National Agricultures: Four Case Studies & an Overview. LC 77-84411. 200p. 1978. text 42.00 (0-916672-90-5) Rowman.

O'Hagan, John, photos by. Low Virtues: The Value of Human Scale Architecture to Birmingham Urbanism. (Illus.). 28p. 1998. 4.00 (0-943994-23-3) Birmingham Hist Soc.

O'Hagan, John T. High Rise Fire & Life Safety. (Illus.). 1977. 16.00 (0-912212-08-X) Fire Eng.

O'Hagan, John W. The State & the Arts: An Analysis of Key Economic Policy Issues in Europe & the United States. LC 98-6255. 256p. 1998. 85.00 (1-85898-287-1) E Elgar.

O'Hagan, Kieran. Emotional & Psychological Abuse of Children. LC 92-23834. 160p. (C). 1992. 88.00 (0-335-09889-4); pap. 32.50 (0-335-09884-3) U of Toronto Pr.

— Emotional & Psychological Abuse of Children. LC 92-23834. 167p. 1993. pap. text 19.95 (0-8020-7446-4) U of Toronto Pr.

— Working with Child Sexual Abuse: A Post-Cleveland Guide to Effective Principles & Practice. 192p. 1989. pap. 35.95 (0-335-15597-9) OpUniv Pr.

O'Hagan, Kieran, ed. Social Work Competences in Practice. 200p. 1995. pap. 24.95 (1-85302-332-9, Pub. by Jessica Kingsley) Taylor & Francis.

O'Hagan, Kieran & Dillenburger, Karola. The Abuse of Women in Childcare Work. LC 95-3097. 160p. 1995. 113.95 (0-335-19261-0); pap. 31.95 (0-335-19260-2) OpUniv Pr.

O

An Asterisk (*) at the beginning of an entry indicates that the title is appearing for the first time.

***O'Hagan, Maureen & Smith, Maureen.** Early Years: Child Care & Education. 2nd ed. LC 99-32257. 1999. write for info. (*0-7020-2373-6*) W B Saunders.

O'Hagan, Maureen & Smith, Maureen. Special Issues in Child Care: A Comprehensive NVQ-Linked Textbook. (Illus.). 252p. 1993. pap. text 31.00 (*0-7020-1604-7*, Pub. by W B Saunders) Saunders.

O'Hagan, Minako. The Coming Industry of Teletranslation: Overcoming Communication Barriers Through Telecommunication. LC 95-40682. (Topics in Translation Ser.: Vol. 4). 160p. 1996. 59.00 (*1-85359-326-5*, Pub. by Multilingual Matters); pap. 19.95 (*1-85359-325-7*, Pub. by Multilingual Matters) Taylor & Francis.

O'Hagan, Robert E., jt. auth. see Besterfield, Dale H.

O'Hagan, Sheila. The Troubled House. 64p. 1996. pap. 14.95 (*1-897648-16-2*, Pub. by Poolbeg Pr) Dufour.

O'Hagan, Thomas. Essays on Catholic Life. LC 67-22106. (Essay Index Reprint Ser.). 1977. 19.95 (*0-8369-1333-7*) Ayer.

O'Hagan, Tim. Holiday-McKer's Guide to South Africa. LC 95-232832. 210p. 1998. pap. 22.95 (*1-86812-590-4*) Menasha Ridge.

— Wild Places of Southern Africa. LC 97-112865. 352p. pap. 19.95 (*1-86812-667-6*) Menasha Ridge.

O'Hagan, Timothy. Revolution & Enlightenment in Europe. (Enlightenment Rights & Revolution Ser.). 160p. 1991. pap. 37.90 (*0-08-040920-2*, Pub. by Aberdeen U Pr) Macmillan.

O'Hagan, Timothy, ed. Jean-Jacques Rousseau & the Sources of Self. (Series in Philosophy). 144p. 1997. 59.95 (*1-85972-552-X*, Pub. by Avebry) Ashgate Pub Co.

O'Hair. Advancing Competent Communication. pap. text 42.95 (*0-312-17126-9*) St Martin.

O'Hair. ESL Guide for Teaching Public Speaking. 1999. pap. text. write for info. (*0-312-20178-8*) St Martin.

— Foundations of Democratic Educucation. (C). 1999. text 65.50 (*0-03-017348-5*) Harcourt Coll Pubs.

— Public Speaking. Date not set. pap. text. write for info. (*0-312-19219-3*) St Martin.

— Strategic Communication, 3 vols. 3rd ed. LC 97-72528. (C). 1997. pap. text 41.16 (*0-395-85869-0*) HM.

— Strategic Communications, 3 vols. 3rd ed. (C). 1998. 47.96 (*0-395-89766-1*) HM.

O'Hair, ed. The Harpercollins Business Communication Book. (C). 1998. text. write for info. (*0-321-01056-6*) Addson-Wesley Educ.

***O'Hair & O'Rourke.** Web Tutor on Webct to Accompany Business Communication. 2000. pap. 19.00 (*0-324-06483-7*) Sth-Wstrn College.

***O'Hair & Stewart.** Public Speaking: Speech Organizing. 2000. pap. text, wbk. ed. 2.95 (*0-312-25054-1*) St Martin.

— Public Speaking: Choices & Challenges Powerpoint Presentation. pap. text. write for info. (*0-312-20179-6*); pap. text. write for info. (*0-312-20180-X*) St Martin.

***O'Hair, et al.** Speaker's Reference. 2000. pap. text. write for info. (*0-312-25848-8*) St Martin.

O'Hair, Dan. Competent Communication. 1995. pap. text 6.00 (*0-312-04054-7*) St Martin.

— Competent Communication. 2nd ed. LC 95 73212. 1996. pap. 46.95 (*0-312-13857-1*) St Martin.

— Competent Communication 2. 1997. pap. text 10.00 (*0-312-14921-2*) St Martin.

O'Hair, Dan & Kreps, Gary L., eds. Applied Communication Theory & Research. 392p. (C). 1990. pap. 55.00 (*0-8058-0915-5*); text 99.95 (*0-8058-0400-5*) L Erlbaum Assocs.

O'Hair, Dan, et al. Competent Communication. 1995. pap. text, teacher ed. 2.33 (*0-312-04052-0*) St Martin.

— Strategic Communication in Business & the Professions, 2 vols. 2nd ed. 512p. (C). 1994. pap. text 39.16 (*0-395-70889-3*) HM.

— Strategic Communication in Business & the Professions, 2 vols. 2nd ed. (C). 1995. text, teacher ed. 11.96 (*0-395-70890-7*) HM.

O'Hair, Dan, jt. ed. see Kreps, Gary L.

O'Hair, J. Millions Now Dying Will Never Live: A Scriptural Investigation of Russellism As Propagated by the International Bible Students. 22p. 1988. reprint ed. pap. 1.95 (*1-883858-52-6*) Witness CA.

O'Hair, Madalyn. All about Atheists. LC 87-30815. (American Atheist Radio Ser.: Vol. 3). 407p. (Orig.). 1988. pap. 14.00 (*0-910309-44-2*, 5097) Am Atheist.

O'Hair, Madalyn M. Atheist Epic. 2nd ed. LC 89-28711. 302p. 1989. pap. 14.00 (*0-910309-89-2*, 5376) Am Atheist.

— Atheist Heroes & Heroines. LC 91-42408. (American Atheist Radio Ser.: Vol. 4). 370p. (Orig.). 1992. pap. 12.00 (*0-910309-57-4*, 5414) Am Atheist.

— Atheist Magazines: A Sampling, 1927-1970. LC 72-171441. (Atheist Viewpoint Ser.). 554p. 1978. reprint ed. 41.95 (*0-405-03812-7*) Ayer.

— An Atheist Speaks. (American Atheist Radio Ser.: Vol. 2). 322p. (Orig.). 1986. pap. 12.00 (*0-910309-27-2*, 5098) Am Atheist.

— The Atheist World. LC 91-22920. (American Atheist Radio Ser.: Vol. 5). 358p. (Orig.). 1991. pap. 12.00 (*0-910309-69-8*, 5094) Am Atheist.

— Atheists: The Last Minority. LC 90-41448. 24p. (Orig.). 1990. 4.00 (*0-910309-66-3*, 5402) Am Atheist.

— Atheists: Their Dilemma. 11p. (Orig.). 1993. pap. 4.00 (*0-910309-73-6*, 5408) Am Atheist.

— O'Hair on Prayer. 12p. (Orig.). 1980. 1.00 (*0-910309-30-2*) Am Atheist.

— Our Constitution: The Way It Was. rev. ed. 70p. 1988. 6.00 (*0-910309-41-8*, 5400) Am Atheist.

— What on Earth Is an Atheist! LC 71-88701. (Fifty-Two Programs from the American Atheist Radio Ser.). 288p. 1969. pap. 12.00 (*0 911826-00-9*, 5412) Am Atheist.

— What on Earth Is an Atheist! LC 74-161339. (Atheist Viewpoint Ser.). 288p. 1976. reprint ed. 20.95 (*0-405-03802-X*) Ayer.

— Why I Am an Atheist, Including a History of Materialism. 2nd rev. ed. LC 91-26426. 56p. 1991. pap. 9.00 (*0-910309-98-1*, 5416) Am Atheist.

O'Hair, Madalyn M., ed. The Atheist Viewpoint, 25 bks. 1972. 648.00 (*0-405-03791-0*) Ayer.

— The Atheist Viewpoint, 25 bks., Set. 1972. 498.00 (*0-405-03620-5*) Ayer.

O'Hair, Madalyn M., frwd. Women, Food & Sex in History, Set. 1201p. (Orig.). 1989. pap. 40.00 (*0-910309-22-1*, 5427) Am Atheist.

O'Hair, Madalyn M., jt. auth. see Murray, Jon.

O'Hair, Mary J. & Odell, Sandra J., eds. Diversity & Teaching: Teacher Education Yearbook I. 1993. pap. 18.75 (*0-685-74809-X*) Assn Tchr Ed.

— Educating Teachers for Leadership & Change: Teacher Education Yearbook III. (ATE Ser.: Vol. 3). 368p. 1995. 74.95 (*0-8039-6216-9*); pap. 34.95 (*0-8039-6217-7*) Corwin Pr.

O'Hair, Mary J., jt. auth. see McIntyre, D. John.

O'Hair, Michael T., ed. see Engineering Technology Centennial Committee.

O'Hair, Ron. Crosswords about Minnesota. 1997. write for info. (*0-9658660-0-9*) Ohair Crosswds.

O'Hair, Stewart. Public Speaking. LC 97-65197. 1998. pap. text 44.95 (*0-312-13722-2*) St Martin.

— Public Speaking. 1999. pap. text, lab manual ed. 10.00 (*0-312-13721-4*) St Martin.

O'Haire, Daniel, jt. auth. see Connor, Cathy.

O'Haire, Lise, jt. auth. see Evans, Story.

Ohajunwa, Emeka. India-U. S. Security Relations, 1947-1990. (C). 1992. 18.00 (*81-7001-090-X*, Pub. by Chanakya) S Asia.

Ohala, Catherine, ed. see Palika, Liz.

Ohala, Catherine, ed. see Parkin, Jacqueline.

Ohalla, N. S., ed. Methods in Studying Cardiac Membranes, Vol. I. 320p. 1984. 181.00 (*0-8493-5995-3*, QP114, CRC Reprint) Franklin.

O'Hallaron, David R. Language, Compilers & Run-Time Systems for Scalable Computers: Selected Papers From The 4th International Workshop, Lcr '98, Pittsburgh, Pa, U. S. A., May 1998. LC 98-45572. 151. 1998. pap. 67.00 (*3-540-65172-1*) Spr-Verlag.

O'Hallaron, David R., jt. auth. see Gross, Thomas.

O'Hallaron, David R., jt. auth. see O'Hallaron, Richard D.

***O'Hallaron, Richard D. & O'Hallaron, David R.** The Mission Primer: Four Steps to an Effective Mission Statement. LC 99-91651. 136p. 2000. per. 19.00 (*0-9676635-0-4*) Mission Inc.

O'Hallmurain, Gearoid. The Pocket History of Irish Traditional Music. (Pocket History Ser.). 144p. 1998. pap. 7.95 (*0-86278-555-3*, Pub. by OBrien Pr) Irish Amer Bk.

O'Halloran. Welfare of the Child. pap. 33.95 (*1-85742-291-0*) Ashgate Pub Co.

O'Halloran, Bethany J. View from Another Dimension: An Angel Speaks. rev. ed. Adams, T. Dean & Rico, Daniel T., eds. LC 97-71221. (Illus.). 192p. 1997. pap. 14.95 (*0-9655288-1-2*) Interdimensional Pubns.

O'Halloran, D., et al, eds. Geological & Landscape Conservation: Proceedings of the Malvern International Conference, 1993. (Illus.). 544p. 1994. 117.00 (*1-897799-09-8*, 232, Pub. by Geol Soc Pub Hse) AAPG.

O'Halloran, James. Signs of Hope: Developing Small Christian Communities. LC 90-46180. 176p. reprint ed. pap. 54.60 (*0-608-20216-9*, 207147500012) Bks Demand.

— Small Christian Communities: A Pastoral Companion. rev. ed. LC 96-10160. Orig. Title: Signs of Hope. 187p. (Orig.). 1996. pap. 13.00 (*1-57075-077-7*) Orbis Bks.

— When the Acacia Bird Sings LC 99-191310. 109p. 1999. write for info. (*1-85607-254-1*) Intl Scholars.

O'Halloran, Jamie, ed. see Arroyo, Robert, Jr. & Wynne, Robert.

O'Halloran, Jamie, ed. see Brown, Derrick, et al.

O'Halloran, Jamie, ed. see Gardner, Howard.

O'Halloran, Jamie, ed. see Saenz, Alicia Vogl.

O'Halloran, Jamie, ed. see Wesley, Jan.

***O'Halloran, Jim.** Arson About. LC 99-224286. (Illus.). 1998. write for info. (*0-7541-0599-7*, Pub. by Minerva Pr) Unity Dist.

O'Halloran, Kerry. Adoption in the Two Jurisdictions of Ireland: A Comparative Study. 256p. 1994. 65.95 (*1-85628-904-4*, Pub. by Avebry) Ashgate Pub Co.

***O'Halloran, Kerry.** The Welfare of the Child. LC 99-76362. 327p. 1999. text 78.95 (*1-85742-290-2*, Pub. by Arena) Ashgate Pub Co.

O'Halloran, M. Sean. Focus on Eating Disorders. LC 93-37136. (Teenage Perspectives Ser.). 297p. 1993. lib. bdg. 39.50 (*0-87436-692-5*) ABC-CLIO.

O'Halloran, Maura S. Pure Heart, Enlightened Mind: The Zen Journal & Letters of Maura "Shoshin" O'Halloran. LC 95-22765. (Illus.). 320p. 1995. pap. 14.00 (*1-57322-503-7*, Riverhd Trade) Berkley Pub.

— Pure Heart, Enlightened Mind: The Zen Journal & Letters of Maura Soshin O'Halloran. (Illus.). 192p. (Orig.). 1994. pap. 18.00 (*0-8048-1977-7*) Tuttle Pubng.

O'Halloran, Sharyn. Politics, Process & American Trade Policy. 216p. 1994. text 47.50 (*0-472-10516-7*, 10516) U of Mich Pr.

O'Halloran, Sharyn, jt. auth. see Epstein, David.

O'Halloran, Susan & Delattre, Susan. The Woman Who Lost Her Heart: A Tale of Reawakening. rev. ed. LC 92-8661. 148p. (Orig.). 1997. pap. 12.95 (*1-880913-27-5*) Innisfree Pr.

O'Halloran, Susan, jt. auth. see Delattre, Susan.

O'Halloran, Terence P. Mountains Out of Molehills. 250p. (C). 1993. 110.00 (*1-85609-048-5*, Pub. by Witherby & Co) St Mut.

— You Sign. 100p. 1992. 75.00 (*1-85609-038-8*, Pub. by Witherby & Co) St Mut.

***O'Halpin, Eunan.** Defending Ireland: The Irish State & Its Enemies since 1922. LC DA964.A2O39 1999. 398p. 1999. 42.00 (*0-19-820426-4*) OUP.

Ohama, ed. Disposal & Recycling of Organic & Polymeric Construction Materials: Proceedings of the International Rilem Workshop. LC 96-142040. (Rilem Proceedings Ser.). (Illus.). 324p. (C). 1995. 140.00 (*0-419-20550-0*, E & FN Spon) Routledge.

Ohama, Gary. Determining Your First Step to Success. 48p. 1988. pap. 2.95 (*0-88144-119-8*) Christian Pub.

Ohama, Yoshihiko. Handbook of Polymer-Modified Mortars & Concrete: Properties & Process Technology. LC 94-15235. (Illus.). 236p. 1995. 139.00 (*0-8155-1358-5*) Noyes.

O'Hamaguchi & Clifton, Talbot. Fortune Telling by Japanese Swords: "From Old Japanese MSS." (Illus.). 44p. 1995. pap. 7.95 (*0-910704-95-3*) Hawley.

***Ohana, Chris.** Crossing Borders: Connecting Knowledge in a University-School Partnership. 2000. pap. text. write for info. (*0-325-00297-5*) Heinemann.

Ohana, David, jt. ed. see Wistrich, Robert.

O'Handley, Robert C. Modern Magnetic Materials: Principles & Applications. LC 99-21372. 740p. 1999. 125.00 (*0-471-15566-7*) Wiley.

***Ohanesian.** Macaroni Math. 27p. (J). 2000. pap. 7.95 (*0-07-134826-3*) McGraw.

O'Hanesian, Diane. Science: Seeds & Plants. (Illus.). 32p. (J). (gr. 2-3). 1997. pap., wbk. ed. 2.25 (*0-88743-293-X*, 02161) Sch Zone Pub Co.

O'hanesian, Jordan. Splish Splash Fun-in-the-Tub: Bathtime Science ActivitiesfFor Kids. LC 98-27310. (Illus.). 27p. (J). (ps-3). 1998. pap. 12.95 (*0-07-079061-2*) McGraw.

Ohanian. The Principles of Physics. 1995. pap. text, teacher ed., suppl. ed. write for info. (*0-393-96586-4*) Norton.

— The Principles of Physics: Answer Pamphlet. (C). 1994. pap. text 6.00 (*0-393-96394-2*) Norton.

Ohanian, C. M. The Vegetarian Traveler's Guide to North America. iv, 76p. 1993. pap. 8.95 (*1-883138-00-0*) Cold Sprng.

Ohanian, Edward J. What Price Mink? (Illus.). 240p. (Orig.). 1983. pap. 9.95 (*0-317-13105-2*) Ohanian.

O'Hanian, Hans. Physics. 2nd ed. (C). 1990. text 70.00 (*0-393-96038-2*) Norton.

— The Principles of Physics: Student Solution Manual. (C). Date not set. student ed. write for info. (*0-393-96781-6*) Norton.

Ohanian, Hans C. Modern Physics. 2nd ed. LC 94-38687. 576p. (C). 1995. 66.00 (*0-13-124439-6*) P-H.

Ohanian, Hans C. One Volume Edition, Regular with Study Guide. pap. 62.00 (*0-393-96037-4*) Norton.

Ohanian, Hans C. Physics, 2. 2nd ed. (C). 1989. 97.25 (*0-393-95750-0*) Norton.

— Physics, Vol. 1. 2nd ed. (C). 1989. 47.00 (*0-393-95748-9*) Norton.

— Physics, Vol. 2. 2nd ed. (C). 1989. 65,50 (*0-393-95786-1*) Norton.

— Physics, Vols. I & II. (C). 1989. student ed. write for info. incl. trans. (*0-393-95763-2*) Norton.

— Physics, Vols. I & II. (C). 1990. pap. text, teacher ed., student ed. write for info. (*0-393-95754-3*) Norton.

— Physics, Vols. I & II. 2nd ed. (C). 1989. 87.00 (*0-393-95746-2*) Norton.

— Physics: Answers to Problems, Vols. I & II. 2nd ed. (Orig.). (C). 1990. pap. text, student ed. 6.25 (*0-393-95756-X*) Norton.

Ohanian, Hans C. Physics ANS Supplement Problems. pap. text 0.00 (*0-393-95684-9*) Norton.

Ohanian, Hans C. The Principles of Physics. (C). 1994. pap. text 97.25 (*0-393-95773-X*) Norton.

— The Principles of Physics. (C). 1994. pap. text. write for info. (*0-393-96336-5*) Norton.

— The Principles of Physics: Study Guide. (C). 1994. pap. text 27.25 (*0-393-95780-2*) Norton.

— Principles of Quantum Mechanics. 384p. (C). 1989. text 66.00 (*0-13-712795-2*) P-H.

Ohanian, Hans C. & Rufkin, Reno. Gravitation & Spacetime. 2nd ed. LC 93-34408. (Illus.). 500p. (C). 1994. text 63.25 (*0-393-96501-5*) Norton.

Ohanian, Hans C., et al. Physics, Vols. I & II. 2nd ed. (C). 1989. pap., student ed. 32.00 (*0-393-95752-7*) Norton.

Ohanian, Lee E. The Macroeconomic Effects of War Finance in the United States: Taxes, Inflation & Deficit Finance. rev. ed. LC 98-39521. (Financial Sector of the American Economy Ser.). (Illus.). 144p. 1998. 42.00 (*0-8153-3040-5*) Garland.

Ohanian, Nancy K. The American Pulp & Paper Industry, 1900-1940: Mill Survival, Firm Structure, & Industry Relocation, Vol. 140. LC 92-18362. (Contributions in Economics & Economic History Ser.: No. 140). 240p. 1993. 55.00 (*0-313-27366-9*, KPJ, Greenwood Pr) Greenwood.

Ohanian, Susan. All about Bears. LC 93-28988. (Illus.). (J). 1994. 4.25 (*0-383-03735-2*) SRA McGraw.

— Ask Ms. Class. 232p. (C). 1995. pap. text 17.00 (*1-57110-025-3*) Stenhse Pubs.

— From Pumpkin Time to Valentines: Sneaking Language Arts Strategies into Holiday Celebrations. xi, 131p. 1994. pap. text 17.50 (*1-56308-171-7*) Teacher Ideas Pr.

O'Hanian, Susan. Garbage Pizzas, Patchwork Quilts & Math Magic: Stories about Teachers Who Love to Teach. 256p. 1994. pap. 12.95 (*0-7167-2584-3*) W H Freeman.

Ohanian, Susan. Math As a Way of Knowing. LC 96-45740. (Strategies for Teaching & Learning Ser.). 96p. (C). 1996. reprint ed. pap. text 15.00 (*1-57110-051-2*) Stenhse Pubs.

— Math at a Glance: A Month-by-Month Celebration of the Numbers Around Us. LC 94-46723. 115p. 1995. pap. 13.95 (*0-435-08364-3*, 08364) Heinemann.

— 145 Wonderful Writing Prompts: From Favorite Literature. 1998. pap. text 10.95 (*0-590-01973-2*) Scholastic Inc.

— One Size Fits Few: The Folly of Educational Standards. LC 98-54482. 154p. 1999. pap. text 16.00 (*0-325-00158-8*, E00158) Heinemann.

— Standards, Plain English, & the Ugly Duckling: Lessons about What Teachers Really Do. LC 98-68068. 75p. 1998. pap. 12.00 (*0-87367-809-5*) Phi Delta Kappa.

— Who's in Charge? A Teacher Speaks Her Mind. LC 94-5586. 249p. 1994. pap. 19.95 (*0-86709-339-0*, 0339, Pub. by Boynton Cook Pubs) Heinemann.

— Wolves. LC 93-28973. (Voyages Ser.). (Illus.). (J). 1994. 4.25 (*0-383-03742-5*) SRA McGraw.

Ohanian, Susan & Burns, Marilyn. Division, Grades 3-4. (Math by All Means Ser.). 212p. 1995. pap. text. write for info. (*0-941355-06-3*) Math Solns Pubns.

Ohanian, Thomas A. Digital Nonlinear Editing: Editing Film & Video on the Desktop. 2nd ed. LC 97-46778. 384p. 1998. 49.95 (*0-240-80225-X*, Focal) Buttrwrth-Heinemann.

Ohanian, Thomas A. & Phillips, Michael E. Digital Filmmaking: The Changing Art & Craft of Making Motion Pictures. (Illus.). 298p. 1996. pap. 49.95 (*0-240-80219-5*, Focal) Buttrwrth-Heinemann.

***Ohanian, Thomas A. & Phillips, Michael E.** Digital Filmmaking: The Changing Art & Craft of Making Motion Pictures. 2nd ed. (Illus.). 368p. 2000. pap. 49.95 (*0-240-80427-9*, Focal) Buttrwrth-Heinemann.

O'Hanlan, Katherine A., jt. auth. see Perry, Susan.

O'Hanley, David S. Serpentinites: Recorders of Tectonic & Petrological History. (Oxford Monographs on Geology & Geophysics: No. 34). (Illus.). 296p. 1996. text 100.00 (*0-19-508254-0*) OUP.

O'Hanlon. Experimental Psychopharmacology. text. write for info. (*0-471-49045-8*) Wiley.

O'Hanlon. A Guide to Possibility Land: Fifty-One Methods for Doing Brief, Respectful Thearpy. LC 98-31885. (Illus.). 86p. 1999. pap. 13.00 (*0-393-70297-9*) Norton.

O'Hanlon, Alvin M. Reflections, Sharing Thoughts: One-on-One. LC 86-61409. 1986. 17.50 (*0-9616898-0-3*) Phoenix Pr FL.

***O'Hanlon, Ann & O'Hanlon, Dick.** Seeing/Perception: Looking at the World Through an Artist's Eye. (Illus.). 96p. 2001. pap. 22.00 (*0-9657015-4-9*) Arctos Pr.

***O'Hanlon, Ardal.** Knick Knack Paddy Whack: A Novel. LC 99-40754. 244p. 2000. 23.00 (*0-8050-6330-7*) H Holt & Co.

O'Hanlon, Ardal. The Talk of the Town. abr. ed. pap. text 16.95 incl. audio (*1-85998-974-8*) Trafalgar.

O'Hanlon, Bill. Do One Thing Different: And Other Uncommonly Sensible Solutions to Life's Persistent Problems. LC 99-21578. (Illus.). 224p. 1999. 22.00 (*0-688-16499-4*, Wm Morrow) Morrow Avon.

***O'Hanlon, Bill.** Do One Thing Different: And Other Uncommonly Simple Solutions to Life's Persistent Problems. 224p. 2000. pap. 13.00 (*0-688-17794-8*, Quil) HarperTrade.

O'Hanlon, Bill & Hudson, Pat. Love Is A Verb: How to Stop Analyzing Your Relationship, Start Making It Great! 160p. 1995. 19.95 (*0-393-03734-7*) Norton.

— Stop Blaming, Start Loving: A Solution-Oriented Approach to Improving Your Relationship. 192p. 1996. pap. 11.00 (*0-393-31461-8*, Norton Paperbks) Norton.

O'Hanlon, Bill & Wilk, James. Shifting Contexts: The Generation of Effective Psychotherapy. LC 86-26986. 289p. 1987. lib. bdg. 38.00 (*0-89862-677-3*) Guilford Pubns.

***O'Hanlon, Bill, et al.** Even from a Broken Web: Brief, Respectful Solution-Oriented Therapy for Sexual Abuse & Trauma. LC 97-35488. 208p. 1998. 47.50 (*0-471-19403-4*) Wiley.

O'Hanlon, Bill, jt. auth. see Rowan, Tim.

***O'Hanlon, Brenda.** Overcoming Sleep Disorders: A Natural Approach. LC 00-30709. 2000. pap. 10.95 (*1-58091-014-9*) Crossing Pr.

O'Hanlon, Brenda. Pocket Guide to Stress Reduction. LC 99-36916. (Crossing Press Pocket Ser.). Orig. Title: Stress - The Common Sense Approach. 112p. 1999. pap. 6.95 (*1-58091-011-4*) Crossing Pr.

O'Hanlon, Carol. The Knockout Punch: Facets & Ways of Coping with a Sudden Death. 32p. 1999. pap. 7.00 (*0-8059-4551-2*) Dorrance.

O'Hanlon, Christine. Special Education Integration in Europe. 192p. 1993. pap. 32.00 (*1-85346-236-5*, Pub. by David Fulton) Taylor & Francis.

O'Hanlon, Christine, ed. Inclusive Education in Europe. LC 96-127645. 160p. 1995. pap. 29.95 (*1-85346-405-8*, Pub. by David Fulton) Taylor & Francis.

— Professional Development Through Action Research in Educational Settings. LC 96-12656. 224p. 1996. 79.95 (*0-7507-0507-8*, Falmer Pr); pap. 29.95 (*0-7507-0508-6*, Falmer Pr) Taylor & Francis.

O'Hanlon, Daniel P., tr. from LAT. Macer's Virtue of Herbs. Orig. Title: Macer Floridus De Viribus Herbarum. 125p. (C). 10.00 (*0-89744-243-1*) Auromere.

O'Hanlon, Dick, jt. auth. see O'Hanlon, Ann.

O'Hanlon, Gerard F. The Immutability of God in the Theology of Hans Urs von Balthasar. 243p. (C). 1990. text 69.95 (*0-521-36649-6*) Cambridge U Pr.

O'Hanlon, John F. A User's Guide to Vacuum Technology. 2nd ed. LC 88-27327. 512p. 1989. 94.50 (*0-471-81242-0*) Wiley.

O'Hanlon, Joseph. Beginning the Bible. 120p. 1994. pap. 35.00 (*0-85439-496-6*, Pub. by St Paul Pubns) St Mut.

— The Dance of the Merrymakers. 255p. (C). 1990. 39.00 (*0-85439-331-5*, Pub. by St Paul Pubns) St Mut.

O

— Mark My Words: A Commentary on the Gospel of Mark. 316p. 1996. pap. 19.95 (*0-85439-472-9*, Pub. by St Paul Pubns) St Mut.

O'Hanlon, Katherine, jt. auth. see Perry, Susan.

***O'Hanlon, Lynne.** CD-Rom for Introduction to Computer Programming Logic. (C). 2000. audio compact disk 24.95 (*0-7872-7249-3*) Kendall-Hunt.

O'Hanlon, Lynne. Introduction to Computer Programming Logic. 2nd ed. 550p. (C). 1997. spiral bd. 58.95 (*0-7872-3308-0*, 41330801) Kendall-Hunt.

***O'Hanlon, Michael.** The Colorado Sangre de Cristo: A Complete Trail Guide. 3rd rev. ed. Thomason, Bob, tr. (Illus.). 80p. 1999. pap. 12.95 (*0-9671829-0-5*) Hungry Gulch.

O'Hanlon, Michael. Defense Planning for the Late 1990s: Beyond the Desert Stom Framework. LC 95-22189. 150p. (C). 1995. pap. 16.95 (*0-8157-6449-9*) Brookings.

— How to Be a Cheap Hawk: The 1999 & 2000 Defense Budgets. LC 98-8940. 178p. 1998. pap. 16.95 (*0-8157-6443-X*) Brookings.

— Stopping Civil Conflict with Force: Military Criteria for Humanitarian Interventions. LC 97-21239. (Occasional Papers). 86p. 1996. pap. 12.95 (*0-8157-6447-2*) Brookings.

O'Hanlon, Michael. Technological Change & the Future of Warfare. LC 99-50470. (Illus.). 197p. 2000. 42.95 (*0-8157-6440-5*) Brookings.

***O'Hanlon, Michael.** Technological Change & the Future of Warfare. LC 99-50470. (Illus.). 197p. 2000. pap. 18.95 (*0-8157-6439-1*) Brookings.

O'Hanlon, Michael & Graham, Carol. A Half Penny on the Federal Dollar: The Future of Development Aid. LC 97-4697. 102p. (Orig.). 1997. pap. text 14.95 (*0-8157-6445-6*) Brookings.

O'Hanlon, Michael, jt. ed. see Hirsch, Eric.

O'Hanlon, Michael E. The Art of War in the Age of Peace: U. S. Military Posture for the Post-Cold War World. LC 91-47086. 176p. 1992. 47.95 (*0-275-94259-7*, C4259, Praeger Pubs) Greenwood.

O'Hanlon, Michael E., et al. Enhancing U.S. Security Through Foreign Aid. (Illus.). 90p. (Orig.). (YA). (gr. 12 up). 1994. pap. text 30.00 (*0-7881-0831-X*) DIANE Pub.

O'Hanlon, Michael E., jt. auth. see Daalder, Ivo H.

O'Hanlon, P. J., jt. ed. see Bentley, P. H.

O'Hanlon, Ray. The New Irish Americans. LC 97-52317. (Illus.). 256p. 1998. pap. text 15.95 (*1-57098-212-0*) Roberts Rinehart.

O'Hanlon, Redmond. In Trouble Again. LC 89-40563. (Vintage Departures Ser.). 288p. 1990. pap. 13.00 (*0-679-72714-0*) Vin Bks.

— Into the Heart of Borneo. LC 87-40084. (Vintage Departures Ser.). 204p. 1987. pap. 12.00 (*0-394-75540-5*) Vin Bks.

— No Mercy: A Journey to the Heart of the Congo. LC 96-36677. (Illus.). 462p. 1997. 29.95 (*0-679-40655-7*) Knopf.

— No Mercy: A Journey to the Heart of the Congo. 480p. 1998. pap. 14.00 (*0-679-73732-4*) Vin Bks.

O'Hanlon, Rosalind. A Comparison Between Women & Men: Tarabai Shinde & the Critique of Gender Relations in Colonial India. 154p. 1994. text 16.95 (*0-19-563266-4*) OUP.

O'Hanlon, Tim. Accessing Federal Adoption Subsidies after Legalization. LC 95-143985. (Orig.). 1995. pap. text 14.95 (*0-87868-569-3*) Child Welfare.

O'Hanlon, Tim, jt. auth. see Laws, Rita.

O'Hanlon, Tom. The Company You Keep: 150 Years with New York Life. Robbins, Ceila D., ed. (Illus.). 240p. 1995. write for info. (*0-944641-14-8*) Greenwich Pub Group.

O'Hanlon, W. M. Walks among the Poor of Belfast. 1971. reprint ed. 22.00 (*0-8464-0961-5*) Beekman Pubs.

O'Hanlon, William H. Taproots: Underlying Principles of Milton Erickson's Therapy & Hypnosis. (Professional Bks.). 1987. 22.95 (*0-393-70031-3*) Norton.

O'Hanlon, William H. & Martin, Michael. Solution-Oriented Hypnosis: An Ericksonian Approach. LC 92-16410. 180p. (C). 1992. 25.00 (*0-393-70149-2*) Norton.

O'Hanlon, William H. & Weiner-Davis, Michele. In Search of Solutions: Creating a Context for Change. 1988. 25.00 (*0-393-70061-5*) Norton.

O'Hanlon, William H., jt. auth. see Bertolino, Bob.

O'Hanlon, William H., jt. auth. see Cade, Brian.

O'Hanlon, William H., jt. auth. see Hudson, Patricia O.

***O'Hanlon, William Hudson.** Evolving Possibilities: Selected Works of Bill O'Hanlon. LC 99-28379. 1999. pap. text 29.95 (*0-87630-980-5*) Brunner-Mazel.

***Ohanna, Karin.** Star Crossed: A Novel. LC 98-90898. 1999. pap. 12.95 (*0-533-12976-1*) Vantage.

Ohanneson, Joan. Scarlet Music: A Life of Hildegard Von Bingen. LC 96-47125. (Crossroad Fiction Program Ser.). 228p. 1997. pap. 14.95 (*0-8245-1646-X*) Crossroad NY.

Ohannessian, Sirarpi, et al, eds. Language Surveys in Developing Nations: Papers & Reports on Sociolinguistic Surveys. LC 75-7584. 234p. reprint ed. pap. 72.60 (*0-8357-3369-6*, 203961000013) Bks Demand.

Ohannessian, Sirarpi & Kashoki, Mubanga E., eds. Language in Zambia. LC 78-325190. (Ford Foundation Language Surveys Ser.). 472p. 1978. reprint ed. pap. 146.40 (*0-8357-3022-0*, 205710900010) Bks Demand.

Ohaodha, M. & Robinson, Lennox. Pictures at the Abbey: The Collection of the Irish National Theatre. (Illus.). 64p. 1983. 21.00 (*0-85105-418-8*, Pub. by Smyth); pap. 11.95 (*0-85105-399-8*, Pub. by Smyth) Dufour.

O'Hara & Gardner, eds. Write to One Million: Turn Your Dreams into Dollars. (Illus.). 162p. (Orig.). 1990. pap. 15.00 (*0-9625725-0-0*) Cat Tale Pr.

O'Hara, jt. auth. see Matherly, Donna M.

O'Hara, Aidan. I'll Live 'til I Die: The Story of Delia Murphy. LC 97-189522. (Illus.). 208p. 1997. pap. 19.95 (*1-873437-17-X*, Pub. by Drumlin Pubns Ltd) Irish Bks Media.

O'Hara, Arnold. As Burns Said . . . (C). 1988. 60.00 (*0-907526-30-6*, Pub. by Alloway Pub) St Mut.

O'Hara, Bruce. Put Work in Its Place: How to Redesign Your Job to Fit Your Life. 2nd rev. ed. (Illus.). 298p. 1994. pap. 12.00 (*0-921586-40-X*, Pub. by New Star Bks) Genl Dist Srvs.

O'Hara, Bruce. Working Harder Isn't Working: How We Can Save the Environment, the Economy & Our Sanity by Working Less & Enjoying Life More. (Illus.). 310p. 1993. pap. 12.95 (*0-921586-33-7*, Pub. by New Star Bks) Genl Dist Srvs.

O'Hara, Carol. From Concept Through Creation: Carol O'Haras Guide to the Lucrative Publishing Business. 3rd rev. ed. 20p. 1997. ring bd. 20.00 (*0-9625725-2-7*) Cat Tale Pr.

O'Hara, Carol, tr. see Phillipps, Marilyn.

***O'Hara, Catherine L.** The Perfect Setting: Menus & Memories from Cincinnati's Taft Museum. 144p. 1999. 21.95 (*0-915577-30-5*) Taft Museum.

O'Hara, Catherine L. Tarleton Blackwell: The Greatest Show of Hogs. (Illus.). 44p. (Orig.). 1993. pap. 12.00 (*0-915577-25-9*) Taft Museum.

O'Hara, Catherine L. & Meyer, Ruth K. Tyrone Geter: Images of Africa & Recent Works. (Illus.). 20p. (Orig.). 1989. pap. 5.00 (*0-915577-18-6*) Taft Museum.

O'Hara, Charles E. & O'Hara, Gregory L. Fundamentals of Criminal Investigation. 6th ed. LC 93-26172. (Illus.). 1010p. (C). 1994. text 49.95 (*0-398-05889-X*) C C Thomas.

O'Hara, Charles E., jt. auth. see O'Hara, Gregory L.

O'Hara, Christopher B. The Bloody Mary: A Connoisseur's Guide to the World's Most Complex Cocktail. LC 98-31906. (Illus.). 112p. 1999. 18.95 (*1-55821-786-X*) Lyons Pr.

***O'Hara, Christopher B.** Ribs: A Connoisseur's Guide to Barbecuing & Grilling. 128p. 2000. 18.95 (*1-58574-171-X*) Lyons Pr.

O'Hara, Craig. Philosophy of Punk: More Than Noise. (Illus.). 148p. (Orig.). 1995. pap. 10.00 (*1-873176-43-0*) AK Pr Dist.

— Philosophy of Punk: More Than Noise. (Orig.). 1999. pap. text 12.00 (*1-873176-16-3*) AK Pr Dist.

O'Hara, Cynthia O. The Harried Housewife's Cookbook: (Easy, Quick & Delicious Recipes for the Busy Household!) LC 96-90605. (Illus.). 180p. (Orig.). 1997. spiral bd. 14.95 (*0-9654385-0-3*) Upstate Pubng.

O'Hara, Daniel, ed. Why Nietzsche Now? LC 84-48455. 453p. reprint ed. pap. 140.50 (*0-608-09355-6*, 205410100002) Bks Demand.

O'Hara, Daniel T. Lionel Trilling: The Work of Liberation. LC 87-37178. 332p. (Orig.). (C). 1988. pap. text 19.95 (*0-299-11314-0*) U of Wis Pr.

— Radical Parody: American Culture & Critical Agency after Foucault. 264p. 1992. text 57.50 (*0-231-07692-4*) Col U Pr.

O'Hara, Daniel T., ed. Why Nietzsche Now?? LC 84-48455. (Illus.). 460p. 1985. 31.50 (*0-253-36530-9*) Ind U Pr.

O'Hara, Daniel T. & Singer, Alan, eds. Thinking Through Art: Aesthetic Agency & Global Modernity, Vol. 25, No. 1. 250p. 1998. pap. 12.00 (*0-8223-6453-0*) Duke.

O'Hara, Delta. Cabaret Noir. 1995. pap. 3.00 (*0-929730-56-9*) Zeitgeist Pr.

***O'Hara, Dennis Patrick & St. John, Donald P.** Merton & Ecology: A Double Issue. (Teilhard Studies Ser.: Vol. 37). 1999. pap. 3.50 (*0-89012-080-3*) Am Teilhard.

O'Hara-Devereaux, Mary, et al, eds. Eldercare: A Practical Guide to Clinical Geriatrics. (Illus.). 368p. 1981. text 54.00 (*0-8089-1285-2*, 793190, Grune & Strat) Harcrt Hlth Sci Grp.

O'Hara-Devereaux, Mary & Johansen, Robert. Globalwork: Bridging Distance, Culture & Time. LC 94-4431. (Business-Management Ser.). (Illus.). 471p. 1994. mass mkt. 30.00 (*1-55542-602-6*) Jossey-Bass.

***O'Hara, Diana.** Courtship & Constraint: Rethinking the Making of Marriage in Tudor England. LC 99-43121. (Politics, Culture & Society in Early Modern Britain Ser.). 2000. 79.95 (*0-7190-5074-X*, Pub. by Manchester Univ Pr) St Martin.

O'Hara, Edgar, jt. ed. see Ramos-Garcia, Luis A.

O'Hara, Edwin V. The Church & the Country Community. 1978. 17.95 (*0-405-10846-X*, 11849) Ayer.

O'Hara, Eileen. Silent Wisdom, Hidden Light. 1997. pap. 7.95 (*0-85305-425-8*, 6361, Pub. by Arthur James) Morehouse Pub.

O'Hara, Elizabeth, et al. The Hiring Fair. 176p. (J). (gr. 5-9). 1994. pap. 8.95 (*1-85371-275-2*, Pub. by Poolbeg Pr) Dufour.

O'Hara, F., tr. see Leger, E., et al.

O'Hara, Frank. Amorous Nightmares of Delay: Selected Plays. LC 96-38486. (PAJ Bks.). 230p. 1997. reprint ed. pap. text 14.95 (*0-8018-5529-2*) Johns Hopkins.

— Art Chronicles: 1954-1966. LC 74-77526. 1990. pap. 14.95 (*0-8076-0756-8*) Braziller.

— Biotherm. limited ed. (Illus.). 1990. 2750.00 (*0-910457-21-2*) Arion Pr.

— The Collected Poems of Frank O'Hara. Donald, Allen, ed. LC 94-24660. 1995. pap. 19.95 (*0-520-20166-3*, Pub. by U CA Pr) Cal Prin Full Svc.

— Invitation to the Theater. LC 76-109299. 211p. 1971. reprint ed. lib. bdg. 59.50 (*0-8371-3842-6*, OHIT, Greenwood Pr) Greenwood.

— Lunch Poems. LC 64-8689. (Pocket Poets Ser.: No. 19). 1964. pap. 7.95 (*0-87286-035-3*) City Lights.

— Meditations in an Emergency. 64p. 1996. reprint ed. pap. 10.00 (*0-8021-3452-1*, Grove) Grove-Atltic.

— Poems Retrieved. 2nd rev. ed. Allen, Donald, ed. LC 77-554. 272p. 1996. pap. 13.95 (*0-912516-19-4*) Grey Fox.

— Standing Still & Walking in New York. Allen, Donald, ed. LC 74-75455. 192p. 1975. reprint ed. pap. 6.95 (*0-912516-12-7*) Grey Fox.

— Today in American Drama. LC 69-14018. (Illus.). 277p. 1969. reprint ed. lib. bdg. 35.00 (*0-8371-0600-1*, OHAD, Greenwood Pr) Greenwood.

— Today in American Drama. (BCL1-PS American Literature Ser.). 277p. 1993. reprint ed. lib. bdg. 79.00 (*0-7812-6588-6*) Rprt Serv.

***O'Hara, Frank.** What's with Modern Art? 33p. 1999. pap. 5.00 (*0-9671035-0-9*, Pub. by Mike & Dale) SPD-Small Pr Dist.

O'Hara, Frederic J. A Guide to Publications of the Executive Branch. LC 78-66368. 1979. 39.50 (*0-87650-072-6*); pap. 24.50 (*0-87650-088-2*) Pierian.

O'Hara, Frederic J., ed. Informing the Nation: A Handbook of Government Information for Librarians. LC 90-34263. 584p. 1990. lib. bdg. 75.00 (*0-313-27267-0*, OHG, Greenwood Pr) Greenwood.

***O'Hara, Frederick M., Jr.** Handbook of United States Economic & Financial Indicators, 20. rev. ed. LC 99-54281. (Bibliographies & Indexes in Economics & Economic History Ser.: Vol. 20). 408p. 2000. lib. bdg. 89.50 (*0-313-27450-9*, Greenwood Pr) Greenwood.

O'Hara, Frederick M., Jr., ed. see Hirst, Eric, et al.

O'Hara, G. I Walked Today Where Jesus Walked. 12p. 1986. pap. 1.25 (*0-7935-5512-4*, 50299840) H Leonard.

O'Hara, Gregory, jt. auth. see Hamel, William.

O'Hara, Gregory L. & O'Hara, Charles E. A Review Guide for the Fundamentals of Criminal Investigation. 6th ed. LC 98-17048. 260p. 1998. pap. text 26.95 (*0-398-06880-1*) C C Thomas.

O'Hara, Gregory L., jt. auth. see O'Hara, Charles E.

O'Hara, Gwydion. The Magic of Aromatherapy: The Use of Scent for Healing Body, Mind, & Spirit. LC 97-32117. (Illus.). 320p. 1999. pap. 14.95 (*1-56718-348-4*) Llewellyn Pubns.

— Moon Lore: Myths & Folklore from Around the World. LC 95-51456. (Illus.). 216p. 1999. pap. 9.95 (*1-56718-342-5*) Llewellyn Pubns.

— Pagan Ways: Finding Your Spirituality in Nature. LC 97-22994. (Illus.). 208p. (Orig.). 1999. pap. 7.95 (*1-56718-341-7*) Llewellyn Pubns.

— Sun Lore: Myths & Folklore from Around the World. LC 97-17276. (Illus.). 224p. 1999. pap. 9.95 (*1-56718-343-3*) Llewellyn Pubns.

Ohara, H. Ikebana of Japan. 1996. pap. 10.95 (*4-07-973139-6*) Shufu No.

O'Hara, J. Integrated System Validation: Methodology & Review Criteria. 122p. 1997. per. 15.00 (*0-16-062802-4*) USGPO.

O'Hara, J. D. Samuel Beckett's Hidden Drives: Structural Uses of Depth Psychology. LC 97-16090. (CrossCurrents). 432p. 1997. 49.95 (*0-8130-1527-8*) U Press Fla.

O'Hara, J. G. & Pricha, W. Hertz & the Maxwellians. (History of Technology Ser.: No. 8). 168p. 1987. 42.00 (*0-86341-101-0*, HT008) INSPEC Inc.

***O'Hara, J. M.** Advanced Information Systems Design: Technical Basis & Human Factors Review. 156p. 2000. per. 16.00 (*0-16-059206-2*) USGPO.

— Computer-Based Procedure Systems: Technical Basis & Human Factors Review. 153p. 2000. per. 16.00 (*0-16-059207-0*) USGPO.

O'Hara, J. T. The Gift of Happiness Belongs to Those Who Unwrap It: And Other Tidbits for Living the Good Life by One Smart Cookie. LC 98-5939. (Illus.). 144p. 1998. pap. 7.95 (*0-8362-6770-2*) Andrews & McMeel.

O'Hara, James. John Cheever: A Study of the Short Fiction. (Twayne's Studies in Short Fiction: No. 9). 168p. 1989. 29.00 (*0-8057-8310-5*) Macmillan.

— True Names: Vergil & the Alexandrian Tradition of Etymological Wordplay. LC 96-4240. 344p. (C). 1996. text 47.50 (*0-472-10660-0*, 10660) U of Mich Pr.

O'Hara, Jean & Sperlinger, Anthea. Adults with Learning Disabilities: A Practical Approach for Health Professionals. LC 97-17410. 256p. 1997. pap. 36.50 (*0-471-97664-4*) Wiley.

O'Hara, Jean & Sperlinger, Anthea. Adults with Learning Disabilities: A Practical Approach for Health Professionals. LC 97-17410. 256p. 1997. 82.50 (*0-471-97665-2*) Wiley.

O'Hara, Jean, jt. auth. see Rebert, Jo.

O'Hara, Jim & Walle, Grace. Collage: A Resource Book for Christian Youth Groups. 86p. (Orig.). 1976. pap. 4.00 (*0-9608124-5-8*) Marianist Com Ctr.

O'Hara, Joe, jt. auth. see McCormack, Vincent.

O'Hara, John. Appointment in Samarra. 364p. 1994. 14.50 (*0-679-60110-4*) Modern Lib NY.

— Appointment in Samarra. LC 82-40029. 256p. 1982. pap. 10.00 (*0-394-71192-0*) Random.

— Appointment in Samarra. large type ed. LC 98-37020. 1998. 24.95 (*0-7838-0376-1*, G K Hall Lrg Type) Mac Lib Ref.

— Appointment in Samarra. 1993. reprint ed. lib. bdg. 89.00 (*0-7812-5481-7*) Rprt Serv.

— The Big Laugh: A Novel. LC 97-17230. 320p. 1997. pap. 15.00 (*0-88001-575-6*) HarpC.

— Butterfield Eight. 1976. 23.95 (*0-8488-1441-X*) Amereon Ltd.

— Forty-Nine Stories. 28.95 (*0-89190-393-3*) Amereon Ltd.

***O'Hara, John.** From the Terrace. 2nd ed. 897p. 1999. pap. text 16.95 (*0-7867-0682-1*) Carroll & Graf.

O'Hara, John. Gibbsville, PA. Bruccoli, Matthew J., ed. 864p. 1994. pap. 17.95 (*0-7867-0082-3*) Carroll & Graf.

— Hellbox. large type ed. LC 98-54308. 228p. 1999. 24.95 (*1-56000-480-0*) Transaction Pubns.

— A Mug's Game: A History of Gaming & Betting in Australia. 288p. 27.95 (*0-86840-298-2*, Pub. by New South Wales Univ Pr); pap. 27.95 (*0-614-13107-3*, Pub. by New South Wales Univ Pr) Intl Spec Bk.

O'Hara, John. North Frederick. 416p. 27.95 (*0-8488-2492-X*) Amereon Ltd.

O'Hara, John. The Novellas of John O'Hara. large type ed. 608p. 1995. 19.00 (*0-679-60167-8*) Random.

— A Rage to Live. LC 97-2092. 1997. 22.00 (*0-679-60266-6*) Modern Lib NY.

— A Rage to Live. 542p. 1986. reprint ed. mass mkt. 4.95 (*0-88184-216-8*) Carroll & Graf.

— The Second Ewings: A Facsimile of the Manuscript. 1977. boxed set 60.00 (*0-89723-012-4*) Bruccoli.

— Sermons & Soda Water. 336p. 1986. pap. 4.95 (*0-88184-271-0*) Carroll & Graf.

— Ten North Frederick. 408p. 1985. mass mkt. 4.50 (*0-88184-173-0*) Carroll & Graf.

— We'll Have Fun. 1996. 1.99 (*0-679-77100-X*) Modern Lib NY.

O'Hara, John, jt. auth. see Levin, Laura Victoria.

***O'Hara, Jonathan Patrick.** How It Was: A Vietnam Story. 125p. 2000. pap. 12.95 (*1-55571-516-8*, Hellgate Pr) PSI Resch.

O'Hara, Kathryn J. & Iudicello, Suzanne. A Citizen's Guide to Plastic in the Ocean: More Than a Litter Problem. (Illus.). 140p. (Orig.). 1988. pap. write for info. (*0-9615294-2-3*) Ctr Env Educ.

***O'Hara-Kelly, Katie.** What Are You Looking At? (Illus.). 32p. (J). (gr. k-3). 2000. 6.95 (*1-878441-11-6*) Sequoia Nat Hist Assn.

Ohara, Ken. One. 496p. 1997. 29.99 (*3-8228-7866-9*, Pub. by Benedikt Taschen) Bks Nippan.

O'Hara, Kevin, jt. auth. see Walters, Annette.

O'Hara, Kieron, ed. see DGE Acquisition Workshop Staff.

O'Hara, Kirk B., jt. auth. see Backer, Thomas E.

***O'Hara, Kristen.** Sex As Nature Intended It: The Most Important Thing You Need to Know about Making Love. (Illus.). 348p. 2000. pap. 19.95 (*0-9700442-0-8*) Turning Point Pub.

O'Hara, Larry. Turning up the Heat: MI5 after the Cold War. 96p. (Orig.). 1994. pap. 10.95 (*0-948984-29-5*, Pub. by Phoenix Pr) AK Pr Dist.

Ohara, Leander L. Jurisprudence & Organ Procurements: Index of Authors & Subjects. 180p. 1993. 47.50 (*1-55914-938-8*); pap. 44.50 (*1-55914-939-6*) ABBE Pubs Assn.

O'Hara, Leo. An Emerging Profession: Philadelphia Doctors, 1860-1900. (Medical Care in the United States Ser.: Vol. 10). 270p. 1989. text 25.00 (*0-8240-8339-3*) Garland.

O'Hara, M. W. & Alloy, L. B. Postpartum Depression: Causes & Consequences. (Series in Psychopathology). 256p. 1994. 90.00 (*0-387-94261-0*) Spr-Verlag.

Ohara, Maricarmen. Amiguitos. (SPA., Illus.). 144p. (J). (gr. k-3). 23.00 (*0-944356-22-2*) Alegria Hispana Pubns.

— Capullitos. (SPA., Illus.). 70p. (J). (gr. k-3). 15.00 (*0-944356-03-6*) Alegria Hispana Pubns.

— La Odisea de Penelope. (SPA.). 112p. 1997. 23.00 (*0-944356-16-8*) Alegria Hispana Pubns.

— Tesoro de Lenguaje Popular. (SPA.). 96p. 1997. 23.00 (*0-944356-15-X*) Alegria Hispana Pubns.

— Tesoro de Poesia Juvenil. (SPA.). 144p. 20.00 (*0-944356-09-5*) Alegria Hispana Pubns.

***O'Hara, Marie, et al.** NAFSA's Guide to International Student Recruitment. LC 00-30541. 2000. pap. write for info. (*0-912207-84-1*) NAFSA Washington.

O'Hara, Mark. The Composer's Dream. 32p. 1995. pap. 5.50 (*0-9647127-2-5*) Coreopsis Bks.

O'Hara, Martin. EMC at Component & PCB Level. (Illus.). 208p. 1998. pap. text 44.95 (*0-7506-3355-7*, Newnes) Buttrwrth-Heinemann.

O'Hara, Mary. The Catch Colt. 1964. pap. 6.00 (*0-8222-0190-9*) Dramatists Play.

— My Friend Flicka. (J). 1988. 10.85 (*0-606-02855-2*, Pub. by Turtleback) Demco.

— My Friend Flicka. (Illus.). 320p. (YA). 1999. reprint ed. 37.95 (*1-56849-725-3*) Buccaneer Bks.

— My Friend Flicka. LC 87-45654. 304p. (YA). (gr. 4-7). 1988. reprint ed. mass mkt. 6.00 (*0-06-080902-7*, P-902, Perennial) HarperTrade.

— My Friend Flicka. rev. ed. LC 73-6611. (Illus.). 272p. (J). (gr. 7-9). 1973. 15.95 (*0-397-00981-X*, Lippnctt) Lppncott W & W.

— Thunderhead. (J). 1971. 12.60 (*0-606-02864-1*, Pub. by Turtleback) Demco.

— Thunderhead. LC 87-45653. 384p. (YA). (gr. 4-7). 1988. reprint ed. mass mkt. 7.50 (*0-06-080903-5*, P-903, Perennial) HarperTrade.

O'Hara, Mary L. The Logic of Human Personality: An Onto-logical Account. LC 99-10400. 1999. write for info. (*1-57392-671-X*, Humanity Bks) Prometheus Bks.

— The Logic of Human Personality: An Ontological Account. LC 96-39586. 176p. (C). 1997. text 45.00 (*0-391-04022-7*) Humanities.

O'Hara, Mary L., tr. see Marias, Julian.

O'Hara, Maureen. Market Microstructure Theory. LC 94-28078. (Illus.). 300p. (C). 1994. text 55.95 (*1-55786-443-8*) Blackwell Pubs.

— Market Microstructure Theory. LC 94-28078. (Illus.). 300p. (C). 1997. pap. text 36.95 (*0-631-20761-9*) Blackwell Pubs.

O'Hara, Megan. Blue Earth. (Living History Ser.). (J). (gr. 2-7). 1999. 84.00 (*0-516-29731-7*) Childrens.

***O'Hara, Megan.** Charles A. Lindbergh: The Boyhood Diary of the Famous Aviator. (Diaries, Letters & Memoirs Ser.). 32p. (J). (gr. 2-7). 2000. lib. bdg. 22.60 (*0-7368-0600-8*, Blue Earth Bks) Capstone Pr.

O'Hara, Megan. Frontier Fort: Fort Life on the Upper Mississippi, 1826. (Illus.). (J). (gr. 2-3). 1998. 21.00 (*1-56065-724-3*, Blue Earth Bks) Capstone Pr.

O

— Frontier Fort: Fort Life on the Upper Mississippi, 1826. LC 97-31877. (Living History Ser.). 32p. 1998. lib. bdg. 21.00 (*1-56065-725-1*, Blue Earth Bks) Capstone Pr.

— General Store: A Country Store in 1902. LC 97-31876. (Living History Ser.). (J). 1998. lib. bdg. 21.00 (*1-56065-723-5*, Blue Earth Bks) Capstone Pr.

— Lighthouse: Living in a Great Lakes Lighthouse, 1910 to 1940. 32p. (J). 1998. 21.00 (*0-516-21252-4*) Childrens.

— Living History, 4 Vols. 1999. 84.00 (*1-56065-823-1*) Capstone Pr.

— Pioneer Farm: Living on a Farm in the 1880s. LC 97-31874. (Living History Ser.). (Illus.). 32p. (J). (gr. 2-3). 1998. lib. bdg. 21.00 (*1-56065-726-X*, Blue Earth Bks) Capstone Pr.

***O'Hara, Megan.** Wanda Gag: The Girlhood Diary of a Young Adult. (Diaries, Letters & Memoirs Ser.). 32p. (J). (gr. 2-7). 2000. lib. bdg. 22.60 (*0-7368-0598-2*, Blue Earth Bks) Capstone Pr.

— A Whaling Captain's Daughter: The Diary of Laura Jernegan, 1868-1871. (Diaries, Letters & Memoirs Ser.). 32p. (J). (gr. 2-7). 1999. 21.00 (*0-516-21851-4*, Bridgestone Bks) Capstone Pr.

***O'Hara, Megan, ed.** A Colonial Quaker Girl: The Diary of Sally Wister, 1777-1778. (Diaries, Letters & Memoirs Ser.). (Illus.). 32p. (J). (gr. 2-7). 1999. 21.00 (*0-516-21852-2*) Childrens.

O'Hara, Megan, ed. A Colonial Quaker Girl: The Diary of Sally Wister, 1777-1778. (Diaries, Letters & Memoirs Ser.). 32p. (J). (gr. 2-7). 2000. lib. bdg. 22.60 (*0-7368-0349-1*, Blue Earth Bks) Capstone Pr.

O'Hara, Megan, ed. see Jernegan, Laura.

O'Hara, Michael, et al, eds. Psychological Aspects of Women's Reproductive Health. LC 94-36163. 368p. 1995. 43.95 (*0-8261-8660-2*) Springer Pub.

O'Hara, Monica, jt. auth. see Keeton, Joe.

O'Hara, Myochi Nancy, jt. auth. see Farrey, Seppo Ed.

O'Hara, Nancy. Find a Quiet Corner: A Simple Guide to Self-Peace. 128p. (Orig.). 1995. mass mkt. 9.99 (*0-446-67111-8*, Pub. by Warner Bks) Little.

O'Hara, Nancy. Just Listen: A Guide to Finding Your Own True Voice. 288p. 1998. reprint ed. pap. 13.00 (*0-7679-0023-5*) Broadway BDD.

O'Hara, P. Pain Management for Health Professionals. (Illus.). 192p. (Orig.). 1996. pap. 39.95 (*1-56593-436-9*, 1105) Singular Publishing.

O'Hara, Pat, photos by. Nature's Holy Realm: Verses for Living in the Natural World. LC 96-84599. (Illus.). 128p. 1997. 19.95 (*1-55971-598-7*, NorthWord Pr) Creat Pub Intl.

O'Hara, Pat, jt. auth. see Smithson, Michael.

O'Hara, Patricia. Partners in Production? Women, Farm & Family in Ireland. LC 97-38373. 192p. 1998. 55.00 (*1-57181-939-8*); pap. 16.50 (*1-57181-969-X*) Berghahn Bks.

O'Hara, Patrick. SBA Microloan & Specialty Handbook. LC 95-53995. 212p. 1996. 49.95 (*0-471-13915-7*); pap. 19.95 (*0-471-13914-9*) Wiley.

O'Hara, Patrick D. SBA Loan: A Step-by-Step Guide. 3rd ed. LC 97-27647. 352p. 1998. pap. 19.95 (*0-471-23347-1*) Wiley.

— The Total Business Plan: How to Write, Rewrite & Revise. 2nd ed. LC 94-17935. 320p. 1994. pap. 49.95 incl. disk (*0-471-07829-8*) Wiley.

O'Hara, Peg, compiled by. Corporate Governance Today & Tomorrow: The Thoughts of Seven Leading Players. 96p. (Orig.). 1992. pap. 25.00 (*1-879775-00-X*) IRRC Inc DC.

O'Hara, Peg, ed. see Baker, Amy J.

O'Hara, Peg, ed. see Light, Sharon.

O'Hara, Phillip A. Encyclopedia of Political Economy. LC 97-48471. 1998. write for info. (*0-415-18718-4*) Routledge.

O'Hara, Phillip A., ed. Encyclopedia of Political Economy, Vols. 1 & 2 LC 97-48471. (Illus.). 1208p. (C). 1998. 265.00 (*0-415-15426-X*, D6570) Routledge.

***O'Hara, Phillip Anthony.** Encyclopedia of Political Economy, 2 vols. LC 00-42491. 2001. pap. write for info. (*0-415-24187-1*) Routledge.

O'Hara, R. A. Guide to Highway Law for Architects, Engineers, Surveyors & Contractors. (Illus.). 144p. (C). 1991. 90.00 (*0-419-17330-7*, E & FN Spon) Routledge.

Ohara, Rei, photos by. Manatee. LC 98-12678. (Illus.). 96p. 1998. 14.95 (*0-8118-1920-5*) Chronicle Bks.

O'Hara, Robert. Insurrection: Holding History. Date not set. pap. 5.95 (*0-8222-1771-6*) Dramatists Play.

O'Hara, Robert. Introducing Microsoft Windows CE: Your Guide to the New Version of Microsoft Windows for Your Handheld PC, 6 vols. 2nd ed. LC 97-833. 256p. 1997. pap. text 16.99 (*1-57231-515-6*) Microsoft.

O'Hara, Robert C. Language & Meaning. 224p. (C). 1993. per. 31.95 (*0-8403-8600-1*) Kendall-Hunt.

O'Hara, Sabine, jt. auth. see Gowdy, John.

O'Hara, Scott. Autopornography: A Life in the Lust Lane. LC 96-41442. 210p. (C). 1997. pap. 14.95 (*1-56023-898-4*, Harrington Park) Haworth Pr.

— Autopornography: A Memoir of Life in the Lust Lane. LC 96-41442. 210p. (C). 1997. 29.95 (*0-7890-0144-6*) Haworth Pr.

— Do-It-Yourself Piston Polishing. (Orig.). 1996. mass mkt. 6.50 (*1-56333-489-5*, Badboy) Masquerade.

— Rarely Pure & Never Simple: Selected Essays of Scott O'Hara. LC 98-28104. xiii, 217 p. 1999. 39.95 (*0-7890-0573-5*) Haworth Pr.

— Rarely Pure & Never Simple: Selected Essays of Scott O'Hara. 1999. pap. text 19.95 (*1-56023-939-5*, Harrington Park) Haworth Pr.

O'Hara, Scott R. Operation Air Traffic Controller: Secrets of Air Traffic Controller Exam. 290p. (Orig.). 1991. pap. 14.95 (*0-9629713-0-8*) Intercntl News.

O'Hara, Shannon. Reunion. 24p. 1999. pap. 6.00 (*0-8059-4416-8*) Dorrance.

O'Hara, Sharon. Pearls from the Moon: Rays from the Sun. 176p. 1995. 17.95 (*0-9646460-0-5*) Growing Place.

O'Hara, Shelley. The Complete Idiot's Guide to Buying & Selling a Home. 384p. 1994. 16.95 (*1-56761-510-4*, Alpha Ref) Macmillan Gen Ref.

— Complete Idiot's Guide to Buying & Selling a Home. 2nd ed. LC 97-73172. (Illus.). 352p. 1997. 17.95 (*0-02-861959-5*) Macmillan Gen Ref.

— Easy Excel 5 for Windows. 2nd ed. (Illus.). 246p. 1994. 19.95 (*1-56529-540-4*) Que.

— Easy OS-2. (Illus.). 192p. 1993. 16.95 (*1-56529-145-X*) Que.

***O'Hara, Shelley.** Easy Windows Millennium. (Illus.). 300p. 2000. pap. 19.99 (*0-7897-2406-5*) Que.

— Easy Windows 2000 Professional. LC 99-63897. 240p. 2000. pap. 19.99 (*0-7897-2187-2*) Que.

O'Hara, Shelley. Easy Windows 95. 3rd ed. LC 98-85581. (Easy Ser.). 1998. pap. 19.99 (*0-7897-1738-7*) Que.

— Easy Windows 98. LC QA76.76.O63O349 1998. 272p. 1998. pap. 19.99 (*0-7897-1484-1*) Que.

***O'Hara, Shelley.** Easy Windows 98. 2nd ed. 260p. 1999. 19.99 (*0-7897-2134-1*) Que.

O'Hara, Shelley. Easy Word for Windows. 2nd ed. 272p. (Orig.). 1993. 19.95 (*1-56529-444-0*) Que.

— Easy WordPerfect for Windows Version 6. (Easy Ser.). (Illus.). 278p. (Orig.). 1993. 19.95 (*1-56529-230-8*) Que.

— Easy WordPerfect 6. 256p. (Orig.). 1993. pap. 16.95 (*0-685-70409-2*) Que.

— Easy Works for Windows. (Easy Ser.). (Illus.). 246p. 1992. 19.95 (*1-56529-063-1*) Que.

— Excel 97. (Lazy Way Ser.). 304p. 1999. pap. text 12.95 (*0-02-863016-5*) Macmillan.

***O'Hara, Shelley.** Master Microsoft Word 2000 Visually. LC 99-26495. 704p. 2000. pap. 39.99 (*0-7645-6046-8*) IDG Bks.

O'Hara, Shelley. PC's Cheat Sheet. LC 98-87210. 334p. 1999. 14.99 (*0-7897-1874-X*) Que.

***O'Hara, Shelley.** Sams Teach Yourself Act! 2000 in 10 Minutes. LC 99-64532. (Illus.). 192p. 1999. pap. 12.99 (*0-672-31772-9*) Sams.

— Select: Internet Explorer 4.0 Brief (Projects 1-4) 128p. (C). 1998. pap. text 19.00 (*0-201-35207-9*, Prentice Hall) P-H.

— Select Internet Explorer 5.0. 400p. (C). 1999. pap. text. write for info. (*0-201-45904-3*) Addison-Wesley.

O'Hara, Shelley. Teach Yourself PCs in 10 Minutes. LC 98-84599. (Teach Yourself Ser.). 1998. pap. 12.99 (*0-672-31322-7*) Sams.

— 10 Minute Guide to ACT! for Windows. (Illus.). 166p. 1994. 10.99 (*1-56761-539-2*, Alpha Ref) Macmillan Gen Ref.

— 10 Minute Guide to Approach for Windows 95. (Illus.). (Orig.). Date not set. pap. 12.99 (*0-614-10396-7*) Que.

O'Hara, Shelley. Transition to Windows 95 for Windows 3.X Users. 1995. pap. text 27.99 (*1-57576-251-X*) Que Educ & Trng.

O'Hara, Shelley. Windows 98. LC 98-87537. 319p. 1998. pap. text 14.99 (*0-7897-1901-0*) Que.

O'Hara, Shelley & Warner, Nancy. Easy Microsoft Excel 2000. (Easy ... / Que Ser.). (Illus.). 216p. 1999. pap. 19.99 (*0-7897-1867-7*) Que.

O'Hara, Shelley, jt. auth. see Alpha Development Group Staff.

Ohara, Shelly. Discover Windows 95. LC 96-80456. 448p. 1997. pap. 19.99 (*0-7645-3078-X*) IDG Bks.

O'Hara, Shelly. Ten Minute Guide to PC Computing. LC 97-69188. (10 Minute Guide Ser.). 160p. 1997. pap. text 14.99 (*0-7897-1483-3*) Que.

O'Hara, Susan P. & Graves, Gregory. Saving California's Coast: Army Engineers at Oceanside & Humboldt Bay. (Western Lands & Waters Ser.: No. 16). (Illus.). 278p. 1991. 38.50 (*0-87062-201-3*) A H Clark.

O'Hara, Suzanne. Studying @ University & College. 128p. 1998. pap. 9.95 (*0-7494-2273-4*, Kogan Pg Educ) Stylus Pub VA.

Ohara, Tetsuo, ed. see Konishi, Shiro.

***O'Hara, Thomas.** Marine Corps Air Station El Toro. (Images of America Ser.). (Illus.). 128p. 1999. pap. 18.99 (*0-7385-0186-7*) Arcadia Publng.

O'Hara, Thomas & Janke, Kenneth S., Sr. Starting & Running a Profitable Investment Club. LC 99-215159. 304p. (J). 1998. pap. 15.00 (*0-8129-3008-8*, Times Bks) Crown Pub Group.

O'Hara, Thomas E. & McLane, Helen J. Taking Control of Your Financial Future: Making Smart Investment Decisions With Stocks & Mutual Funds. LC 94-25001. 272p. 1994. text 25.00 (*0-7863-0139-2*, Irwn Prfssnl) McGraw-Hill Prof.

O'Hara, Valerie. Five Weeks to Healing Stress: The Wellness Option. rev. ed. LC 96-67943. Orig. Title: The Fitness Option. (Illus.). 216p. 1996. pap. 17.95 (*1-57224-055-5*) New Harbinger.

— Wellness at Work: Building Resilience to Job Stress. LC 95-69482. (Illus.). 238p. (Orig.). 1995. pap. 17.95 (*1-57224-030-X*) New Harbinger.

***O'Hara, Valerie.** Wellness 9-5 - Managing Stress at Work. 256p. 1999. 9.98 (*1-56731-298-5*, MJF Bks) Fine Comms.

O'Hara, Walter J. Mariner's Gyro-Navigation Manual for Masters, Mates, Marine Engineers. LC 51-7444. (Illus.). 192p. reprint ed. pap. 59.60 (*0-608-30806-4*, 201130500076) Bks Demand.

O'Hara, William T. & Hill, John T., Jr. The Student, the College, the Law. LC 72-87116. 234p. 1972. reprint ed. pap. 72.60 (*0-608-02105-9*, 202604900048) Bks Demand.

O'Hare. Artificial Recharge. 1986. 238.00 (*0-87371-050-9*, TD404, CRC Reprint) Franklin.

Ohare & Funk. Modern Writers. 5th ed. LC 99-25711. 688p. 1999. 34.00 (*0-205-29899-0*, Longwood Div) Allyn.

***Ohare & Funk.** Modern Writers. 5th ed. LC 99-25711. 655p. 1999. pap. text 22.00 (*0-205-29900-8*, Longwood Div) Allyn.

O'Hare & Krizan, A. C. Business Communication. LC 99-86565. (Business Communication Ser.). 2000. pap. 52.50 (*0-324-01415-5*) Sth-Wstrn College.

— Writer's Guide - Business Communication. (SWC-Business Communication Ser.). 2000. pap. 16.95 (*0-324-01425-2*) Sth-Wstrn College.

O'Hare, Carol. Cycling the San Francisco Bay Area: Thirty Rides to Historic Sites & Scenic Places. LC 93-83823. (Illus.). 272p. 1996. pap. 12.95 (*0-933201-57-5*) MBI Pubg.

O'Hare, Carol, ed. see Stevens, Doris.

O'Hare, Carol, ed. see Willard, Frances E.

O'Hare, D., jt. auth. see Bruce, D. W.

***O'Hare, David, ed.** Human Performance in General Aviation. LC 99-45177. 344p. 1999. text 78.95 (*0-291-39852-9*, Pub. by Ashgate Pub) Ashgate Pub Co.

O'Hare, David & Roscoe, Stanley N. Flightdeck Performance: The Human Factor. LC 89-19904. (Illus.). 308p. 1990. pap. 24.95 (*0-8138-0173-7*) Iowa St U Pr.

O'Hare, Frank. Sentence Combining: Improving Student Writing Without Formal Grammar Instruction. LC 72-95432. (NCTE Research Reports: No. 15). 121p. 1973. reprint ed. pap. 37.60 (*0-608-00858-3*, 206164900010) Bks Demand.

***O'Hare, Frank & Funk, Robert.** The Modern Writer's Handbook. 5th ed. LC 99-25711. 704p. 1999. write for info. (*0-205-30923-2*) Allyn.

O'Hare, Frank & Memering, W. Dean. The Writer's Work: A Guide to Effective Composition. 3rd ed. 592p. (C). 1989. 47.00 (*0-13-969635-0*) P-H.

O'Hare, G. & Sweeney. CFIG Atmospheric System. 1986. pap. text. write for info. (*0-05-003742-0*) Addison-Wesley.

O'Hare, G., jt. auth. see Tivy, Joy.

O'Hare, G., jt. ed. see Kirn, Stefan.

O'Hare, G. M. & Jennings, N. R., eds. Foundations of Distributed Artificial Intelligence. LC 95-238. (Sixth-Generation Computer Technologies Ser.). 592p. 1996. 105.00 (*0-471-00675-0*) Wiley.

***O'Hare, Jeff.** The Big Book of Puzzle Fun: Over 500 Puzzles, Quizzes & Brain Teasers. (Illus.). 144p. (YA). (gr. 2 up). 2000. pap. 8.95 (*1-56397-879-2*) Boyds Mills Pr.

O'Hare, Jeff. Bogus Beasts: In Search of Imaginary Animals. (Illus.). 32p. (J). (gr. 2). 1999. pap. 7.95 (*1-56397-812-1*) Boyds Mills Pr.

— Giant Book of Mazes. LC 96-80394. (Illus.). 72p. (J). (gr. 2-7). 1997. pap., student ed. 7.95 (*1-56397-675-7*) Boyds Mills Pr.

— Hanukkah, Happy Hanukkah: Crafts, Recipes, Games, Puzzles, Songs, & More for the Joyous Celebration of the Festival of Lights. LC 93-73302. (Illus.). 32p. (J). (ps-5). 1994. pap. 4.95 (*1-56397-369-3*) Boyds Mills Pr.

— Searchin' Safari: Looking for Camouflaged Creatures. LC 91-72974. (Illus.). 32p. (J). (gr. 2-7). 1999. pap. 7.95 (*1-56397-817-2*) Boyds Mills Pr.

— Secret Codes & Hidden Messages. LC 96-86534. (Illus.). 48p. (J). (gr. 3-7). 1997. pap. 4.95 (*1-56397-652-8*) Boyds Mills Pr.

***O'Hare, Jeff, ed.** Hanukkah: Festival of Lights. LC 99-69851. (Illus.). 64p. (J). (gr. k-7). 2000. pap. 7.95 (*1-56397-907-1*) Boyds Mills Pr.

— Puzzlemania Superchallenge, Bk. 1. (Illus.). 48p. (YA). (gr. 5 up). 1999. pap. 6.95 (*1-56397-789-3*) Boyds Mills Pr.

O'Hare, Jeff, ed. Puzzlemania Superchallenge, Bk. 2. (Illus.). 48p. (YA). (gr. 5 up). 1999. pap. 6.95 (*1-56397-790-7*) Boyds Mills Pr.

— Puzzlemania Superchallenge, Bk. 3. (Illus.). 48p. (YA). (gr. 5 up). 1999. pap. 6.95 (*1-56397-791-5*) Boyds Mills Pr.

O'Hare, Jeff, ed. see Highlights Staff.

O'Hare, Julianna. Heroes. 450p. 1994. pap. 14.95 (*0-9640345-9-X*) Bk Factory.

O'Hare, Kate R. Kate Richards O'Hare: Selected Writings & Speeches. fac. ed. Foner, Philip S. & Miller, Sally M., eds. LC 81-15667. 371p. 1982. reprint ed. pap. 115.10 (*0-7837-7732-9*, 204748800007) Bks Demand.

O'Hare, Laura, jt. auth. see Stanko, Ronald T.

O'Hare, Mark. Citizen Dog: The First Collection. (Illus.). 128p. 1998. pap. 9.95 (*0-8362-5186-5*) Andrews & McMeel.

***O'Hare, Mark.** D Is for Dog. (Citizen Dog Ser.). (Illus.). (J). 2000. pap. 9.95 (*0-7407-0457-5*) Andrews & McMeel.

O'Hare, Mark. Dog's Best Friend: More Citizen Dog Reflections. LC 98-88674. 1999. pap. text 9.95 (*0-8362-6751-6*) Andrews & McMeel.

O'Hare, Martin, jt. ed. see Drysdale, Peter.

***O'Hare, Mick, ed.** The Last Word: Questions & Answers from the Popular Column on Everyday Science. LC 99-204863. (Illus.). 238p. 1999. pap. 12.95 (*0-19-286199-9*) OUP.

O'Hare, O. Introduction to Documentary Credits. (C). 1989. 90.00 (*0-85297-264-4*, Pub. by Chartered Bank) St Mut.

O'Hare, P. A., jt. auth. see Marsh, K. N.

O'Hare, P. A. G., jt. auth. see Leonidov, Vladimir.

O'Hare, Padraic. The Enduring Covenant: The Education of Christians & the End of Antisemitism. LC 96-42304. 192p. (Orig.). 1997. pap. 17.00 (*1-56338-186-9*) TPI PA.

— Way of Faithfulness: Contemplation & Formation in the Church. LC 93-22668. 192p. 1993. pap. 13.50 (*1-56338-066-8*) TPI PA.

O'Hare, Patricia & Terry, Margret. Discharge Planning: Assuring the Continuity of Care. 196p. 1987. 72.00 (*0-87189-895-0*, 89895) Aspen Pub.

O'Hare, Patrick F. The Facts about Luther. LC 87-50945. 378p. 1992. reprint ed. pap. 16.50 (*0-89555-322-8*) TAN Bks Pubs.

O'Hare, S., jt. ed. see Pentreath, V.

O'Hare, Sheila & Atterwill, Christopher K., eds. In Vitro Toxicity Testing Protocols. LC 95-3384. (Methods in Molecular Biology Ser.: Vol. 43). (Illus.). 346p. 1995. spiral bd. 89.50 (*0-89603-282-5*) Humana.

***O'Hare, Thomas P.** Individual Medical Expense Insurance. 200p. 2000. 30.00 (*1-57996-025-1*, Pub. by Amer College) Maple-Vail Bk.

***O'Hare, W. H.** The Ubiquitous Rapture: A Christmasy Quantum Ghost Story. LC 99-93697. 155p. 2000. 16.95 (*0-533-13109-X*) Vantage.

O'Harper, Marilynn. Twelfth Night Notes. (Cliffs Notes Ser.). 64p. 1960. pap. 4.95 (*0-8220-0094-6*, Cliff) IDG Bks.

O'Harra, Brooke, jt. auth. see Eide, Kristbjorg.

O'Harra, Marjorie L. Southern Oregon: Short Trips into History. (Illus.). 200p. 1985. pap. 11.95 (*0-943388-06-6*) South Oregon.

O'Harrow, Stephen D., jt. auth. see Ton, Kim T.

O'Harrow, Stephen D., ed. see Thompson, Laurence C.

O'Hart, John. Irish & Anglo Irish Landed Gentry. O'Laughlin, Michael C., ed. (Collected Works of O'Hart). (Illus.). 900p. 1998. reprint ed. 65.00 (*0-940134-10-1*) Irish Genealog.

***O'Hart, John.** The Irish & Anglo-Irish Landed Gentry: When Cromwell Came to Ireland; or a Supplement ot Irish Pedigrees. 774p. 2000. reprint ed. pap. 59.95 (*0-8063-4951-4*, Pub. by Clearfield Co) ACCESS Pubs Network.

O'Hart, John. Irish Pedigrees: The Origin & the Stem of the Irish Nation, 2 vols. LC 76-12097. 1896p. 1999. reprint ed. 150.00 (*0-8063-0737-4*) Genealog Pub.

— Irish Pedigrees: The Origins & Stem of the Irish Nation. O'Laughlin, Michael C., ed. (Collected Works of O'Hart: Vol. 1). (Illus.). 950p. 1998. reprint ed. 95.00 (*0-940134-26-8*) Irish Genealog.

Ohashi. Vibration & Oscillation of Hydraulic Machinery. 1991. 97.95 (*1-85628-185-X*) Ashgate Pub Co.

Ohashi, Y., jt. ed. see Kinoshita, S.

Ohashi, Haruzo. Japanese Courtyard Gardens. 106p. 1997. 29.00 (*0-87040-993-X*) Japan Pubns USA.

— The Japanese Garden: Islands of Serenity. (Illus.). 100p. 1997. bds. 29.00 (*0-87040-989-1*) Japan Pubns USA.

— Japanese Gardens of the Modern Era. (Illus.). 104p. 2000. pap. 32.00 (*4-88996-055-4*) Japan Pubn Trad.

Ohashi, Haruzo. Japanese Gardens of the Modern Era. LC 87-45213. (Illus.). 100p. 1987. 34.00 (*0-87040-743-0*) Japan Pubns USA.

Ohashi, Isao & Tachibanaki, Toshiaki. Internal Labour Markets, Incentives & Employment. LC 97-38225. 276p. 1998. text 75.00 (*0-312-21193-7*) St Martin.

Ohashi, Kenzaburo, ed. Melville & Melville Studies in Japan, 103. LC 92-36613. (Contributions in American Studies: No. 103). 272p. 1993. 67.95 (*0-313-28622-1*, OMS, Greenwood Pr) Greenwood.

Ohashi, Pamela, jt. ed. see Bleuthmann, Horst.

Ohashi, Tadahiko, jt. ed. see Klass, Donald L.

***Ohashi, Tomio, photos by.** Kisho Kurokawa: Kuala Lumpur International Airport. (Opus Ser.: Vol. 24). (Illus.). 48p. 1999. 42.00 (*3-930698-24-2*, Pub. by Edition A Menges) Natl Bk Netwk.

Ohashi, Watari & Monte, Tom. Reading the Body: Ohashi's Book of Oriental Diagnosis. 156p. (Orig.). 1991. pap. 19.95 (*0-14-019362-6*, Arkana) Viking Penguin.

Ohashi, Wataru. The Ohashi Bodywork Book: Beyond Shiatsu with the Ohashiatsu Method. DeAngelis, Paul, ed. (Illus.). 208p. 1996. pap. 24.00 (*1-56836-096-7*) Kodansha.

Ohashi, Wataru, jt. auth. see Masunaga, Shizuto.

O'Haver, M. E. Solving Cipher Secrets: A Collection of Weekly Articles & Problems Concerning Codes & Ciphers That Appeared in "Flynn's Weekly" 162p. 1983. pap. 30.80 (*0-89412-057-3*, C-37) Aegean Park Pr.

Ohay, Nicole. California Wine Country Guide. 2nd ed. LC 97-76017. 216p. 1998. pap. text 12.95 (*1-883323-77-0*) Open Rd Pub.

O'Hay, Rochelle, ed. see Francen, Mike.

O'Hay, Rochelle, ed. see Francer, Mike.

Ohayon, Roger. Structural Acoustics & Vibration: Mechanical Models, Variational Formulations & Discretization. LC 97-43103. (Illus.). 436p. 1997. text 69.95 (*0-12-524945-4*) Morgan Kaufmann.

Ohayon, Roger, jt. auth. see Morand, Henri J.

***Ohba, Hideaki.** The Himalayan Plants. 590p. 1999. 225.00 (*0-86008-527-9*, Pub. by U of Tokyo) Col U Pr.

Ohba, Hideaki & Malla, Samal B., eds. The Himalayan Plants, Vol. 1. 1988. 225.00 (*0-86008-427-2*, Pub. by U of Tokyo) Col U Pr.

Ohba, Hideaki & Malla, Sarah B. The Himalayan Plants, Vol. 2. (Illus.). 360p. 1991. text 200.00 (*0-86008-459-0*, Pub. by U of Tokyo) Col U Pr.

Ohba, K., jt. ed. see Gerbsch, R. A.

Ohba, Y., ed. Intelligent Sensor Technology. LC 92-18809. (Series in Measurement Science & Technology). 184p. 1993. 210.00 (*0-471-93423-2*) Wiley.

Ohba, Yoko, jt. auth. see Tsuyuki, Hiroshi.

Ohdomari, I., ed. see First International Symposium Staff.

***Ohe, Tadasu.** Tadasu Ohe Plantec Architects: Protocols of Architecture. (Illus.). 2000. pap. text 25.00 (*88-7838-066-0*) L'Arca IT.

O'Healy, Aine, tr. see De Marinis, Marco.

O'Healy, Anne-Marie. Cesare Pavese. (Twayne World Authors Ser.: No. 785). 192p. (C). 1988. 26.95 (*0-8057-8242-7*, 398, Twayne) Mac Lib Ref.

O'Hear, Ann. Power Relations in Nigeria: Ilorin Slaves & Their Successors. LC 97-20263. (Rochester Studies in African History & the Diaspora: Vol. 1). (Illus.). 352p. 1997. 65.00 (*1-878822-86-1*) Univ Rochester Pr.

O

O'Hear, Ann, ed. see Carnegie, David W.

***O'Hear, Anthony.** After Progress: Finding the Old Way Forward. 270p. 2000. 27.50 (*1-58234-040-4*) Bloomsbury Pubg.

— Beyond Evolution: Human Nature & the Limits of Evolutionary Explanation. 230p. 1999. pap. 18.95 (*0-19-825004-5*) OUP.

— Cambridge Philosophers. LC 00-8719. 160p. 2000. pap. text 18.00 (*1-890318-09-4*, Pub. by St Augustines Pr) U Ch Pr.

— Current Issues in Philosophy of Mind. LC 99-162555. 1998. write for info. (*0-521-63927-1*) Cambridge U Pr.

O'Hear, Anthony. Education, Society & Human Nature: An Introduction to the Philosophy of Education. 192p. (C). 1981. pap. 13.95 (*0-7100-0748-5*, Routledge Thoemms) Routledge.

— The Element of Fire: Science, Art & the Human World. LC 88-306. 190p. reprint ed. pap. 58.90 (*0-608-20367-X*, 207162000002) Bks Demand.

— Experience, Explanation & Faith: An Introduction to the Philosophy of Religion. LC 83-15957. 266p. (Orig.). 1984. pap. 13.95 (*0-7100-9768-9*, Routledge Thoemms) Routledge.

***O'Hear, Anthony.** German Philosophy since Kant. LC 99-35520. 1999. write for info. (*0-521-66782-8*) Cambridge U Pr.

O'Hear, Anthony. An Introduction to the Philosophy of Science. 250p. (C). 1989. pap. text 18.95 (*0-19-824813-X*) OUP.

O'Hear, Anthony, ed. Karl Popper: Philosophy & Problems. (Royal Institute of Philosophy Supplements Ser.: No. 39). 308p. (C). 1996. pap. text 22.95 (*0-521-55815-8*) Cambridge U Pr.

***O'Hear, Anthony, ed.** Philosophy, the Good, the True & the Beautiful. 320p. 2000. pap. text 24.95 (*0-521-78511-1*) Cambridge U Pr.

O'Hear, Anthony, ed. Verstehen & Humane Understanding. (Royal Institute of Philosophy Supplements Ser.: Vol. 41). (Illus.). 318p. (C). 1997. pap. text 22.95 (*0-521-58742-5*) Cambridge U Pr.

O'Hear, Michael D. Empty Beds. (Lewiston Poetry Ser.: Vol. 12). (Illus.). 64p. 1989. lib. bdg. 24.95 (*0-88946-893-1*) E Mellen.

O'Hear, Philip & White, John, eds. Assessing the National Curriculum. 128p. 1993. pap. 27.00 (*1-85396-232-5*, Pub. by P Chapman) Taylor & Francis.

Ohearn. Hercules the Harbor Tug. 1995. 6.95 (*0-08-810688-8*, Pub. by Aberdeen U Pr) Macmillan.

O'Hearn, Bill. From the Heart of a Child & Other Lessons to Live By. LC 91-72584. 144p. (Orig.). 1991. pap. 11.95 (*0-9626161-0-9*) Entheos Pub.

— The Heart of the Matter. LC 95-83105. 1996. pap. 12.00 (*0-9626161-2-5*) Entheos Pub.

— Life More Abundant: An Owner's Manual. LC 99-42617. 108p. 2000. pap. 12.00 (*1-58151-045-4*, Pub. by BookPartners) Midpt Trade.

— Live Only Love. Bacon, Thorn, ed. 140p. (Orig.). 1998. pap. 12.95 (*0-9626161-3-3*) Entheos Pub.

O'Hearn, Claudine C. Monkey in the Middle: Writers on Growing up Biracial & Bicultural. LC 97-49597. 224p. 1998. pap. 13.00 (*0-375-70011-0*) Random.

O'Hearn, Denis. Inside the Celtic Tiger: The Irish Economy & the Asian Model. LC 98-24903. (Contemporary Irish Studies). 224p. 1998. 59.95 (*0-7453-1288-8*, Pub. by Pluto GBR) Stylus Pub VA.

— Inside the Celtic Tiger: The Irish Economy & the Asian Model. LC 98-24903. (Contemporary Irish Studies). 224p. 1998. pap. 22.50 (*0-7453-1283-7*, Pub. by Pluto GBR) Stylus Pub VA.

O'Hearn, Denis, ed. see Munck, Ronaldo.

O'Hearn, Frank, tr. see Dent, Robert L.

O'Hearn, Michael. Hercules the Harbor Tug. LC 93-27191. (Illus.). 32p. (J). (ps-4). 1995. pap. 6.95 (*0-88106-888-8*) Charlesbridge Pub.

— Look at the Night. LC 95-61438. (Illus.). 48p. 1996. pap. 9.95 (*1-883650-24-0*) Windswept Hse.

O'Hearn, P. Algol-like Languages, 2 vols. 650p. 1997. write for info. (*3-7643-3936-5*) Birkhauser.

— Algol-like Languages, 2 vols., Vol. 1. 294p. 1997. write for info. (*3-7643-3880-6*) Birkhauser.

— Algol-like Languages, 2 vols., Vol. 2. 356p. 1997. write for info. (*3-7643-3937-3*) Birkhauser.

O'Hearn, Peter W. & Tennent, R. D. Algol-Like Languages, 2 vols. LC 96-46972. (Progress in Theoretical Computer Science Ser.). 600p. 1996. 99.00 (*0-8176-3936-5*) Birkhauser.

— Algol-Like Languages. LC 96-46972. (Progress in Theoretical Computer Science Ser.: Vol. 2). 280p. 1996. 69.50 (*0-8176-3937-3*) Birkhauser.

— Algol-Like Languages, Vol. I. (Progress in Theoretical Computer Science Ser.). 270p. 1996. 49.50 (*0-8176-3880-6*) Birkhauser.

O'Heffernan, Mahon. Who Will Buy a Poem? Seventeenth Century. McCormick, Malachi, ed. & tr. by. (Miniatures Ser.). 24p. 1991. 7.00 (*0-943984-41-6*); 7.00 (*0-685-65461-3*) Stone St Pr.

O'Heffernan, Patrick. Mass Media & American Foreign Policy: Insider Perspectives on Global Journalism & the Foreign Policy Process. 288p. 1991. pap. 39.50 (*0-89391-729-X*); text 73.25 (*0-89391-728-1*) Ablx Pub.

O'Hegarty, Patrick Sarsfield. Victory of Sinn Fein: How it Won & How it Used it. LC 98-229567. 1999. pap. text 21.00 (*1-900621-17-7*, Pub. by Univ Coll Dublin Pr) Dufour.

Oheh, Robert & Fox, M. Sample Size Choice: Charts for Experiments with Linear Models. 2nd ed. (Statistics: Textbooks & Monographs: Vol. 122). (Illus.). 216p. 1991. text 95.00 (*0-8247-8600-9*) Dekker.

O'Hehir, Brendan. Harmony from Discords: A Life of Sir John Denham. LC 68-27162. 308p. reprint ed. pap. 95.50 (*0-608-18293-1*, 203154300075) Bks Demand.

O'Hehir, Brendan & Dillon, John M. A Classical Lexicon for Finnegans Wake: A Glossary of the Greek & Latin in the Major Works of Joyce, Including Finnegans Wake, the Poems, Dubliners, Stephen Hero, a Portrait of the Artist as a Young Man, Exiles, & Ulysses. LC 77-372235. 675p. reprint ed. pap. 200.00 (*0-7837-4691-1*, 204443800003) Bks Demand.

O'Hehir, Diana. Spells for Not Dying Again: Poems. LC 96-32793. 80p. 1997. 26.00 (*0-910055-30-0*); pap. 14.00 (*0-910055-31-9*) East Wash Univ.

— Summoned: Poems. LC 76-16011. (Breakthrough Bks.). 64p. 1976. text 18.95 (*0-8262-0204-7*) U of Mo Pr.

O'Heigeartaigh, M., et al, eds. Combinatorial Optimization: Annotated Bibliographies. LC 84-5081. 212p. reprint ed. pap. 65.80 (*0-7837-6391-3*, 204610400010) Bks Demand.

O'Heithir, Breandan. Lead Us into Temptation. 142p. 1991. pap. 10.95 (*1-85371-120-9*) Dufour.

***O'Heithir, Breandan.** A Pocket History of Ireland. 2nd ed. 112p. 2000. pap. 7.95 (*0-86278-633-9*, Pub. by OBrien Pr) IPG Chicago.

***Oheneba-Sakyi, Yaw.** Female Autonomy, Family Decision Making & Demographic Behavior in Africa. LC 99-34530. (Studies in African Economic & Social Development: Vol. 12). 244p. 1999. text 89.95 (*0-7734-7981-3*) E Mellen.

Oheneba-Sakyi, Yaw, ed. Family Planning & Reproductive Health Services in Ghana: An Annotated Bibliography, 18. LC 94-10358. (African Special Bibliographic Ser.: No. 18). 176p. 1994. lib. bdg. 59.95 (*0-313-28900-X*, Greenwood Pr) Greenwood.

O'Henry. The Misty Treasury. (J). 1997. 11.95 (*0-689-82046-1*) S&S Bks Yung.

— The Stories of O'Henry. (Scribner Classic Ser.). (J). 2000. 25.00 (*0-689-82000-3*) Atheneum Yung Read.

O'Henry & Glennon, William. The Last Leaf. 56p. 1996. pap. 3.50 (*0-87129-691-8*, L84) Dramatic Pub.

Oher, James M., ed. The Employee Assistance Handbook. LC 98-31699. 554p. 1999. 75.00 (*0-471-24252-7*) Wiley.

Oher, James M., et al. The Employee Assistance Treatment Planner. LC 98-23046. 176p. 1998. pap. 39.95 (*0-471-24709-X*); pap. text 175.00 incl. disk (*0-471-24730-8*) Wiley.

O'Hern, T. J., ed. Cavitation & Gas-Liquid Flow in Fluid Machinery & Devices. LC 94-71579. (Fluid Engineering Division Conference Ser.: Vol. 190). 343p. 1994. pap. text 55.00 (*0-7918-1373-8*) ASME.

O'Hern, William J., jt. auth. see Smith, Richard.

O'Heron, Edward J. Your Life Story: Self-Discovery & Beyond. 181p. 1993. pap. 8.95 (*0-86716-177-9*) St Anthony Mess Pr.

Oherova, Jana. Business & Legal Dictionary, Czech-English. (CZE & ENG.). 1996. 150.00 (*0-7859-9710-5*) Fr & Eur.

O'Herron, Paul. An Alembic of Philosophy. LC 95-105307. 192p. (C). 1994. pap. 15.00 (*0-9641821-0-6*) Okapi Press.

O'Herron, Thomas F., ed. Terms of Trade: The Language of International Trade Policy, Law, & Diplomacy. 2nd rev. ed. LC 97-74868. 230p. 1999. pap. 14.95 (*0-9624861-0-8*, Pub. by IAS Pub) Direct Mail.

***Ohgushi, H., et al, eds.** Bioceramics 12: Proceedings of the 12th International Conference on Ceramics in Medicine. 600p. 1999. 138.00 (*981-02-4099-6*) World Scientific Pub.

Oh'hne, Sage. Our Journey Home Vol. 1: A Guide for Conscious Ascension. (Illus.). 184p. (Orig.). 1996. pap. 16.95 (*0-9643360-0-6*) New Earth WI.

— Our Journey Home Vol. 2: A Guide for Conscious Ascension. (Illus.). 360p. (Orig.). 1996. pap. 16.95 (*0-9643360-7-3*) New Earth WI.

***Ohi, Debbie Ridpath.** The Writer's Online Marketplace: How & Where to Get Published Online. 240p. 2000. pap. 17.99 (*1-58297-016-5*, Wrtrs Digest Bks) F & W Pubns Inc.

O'Hickey, S., jt. ed. see Frank, R. M.

Ohigashi, H. Food Factors for Cancer Prevention. LC 97-16526. xvi, 684p. 1997. text. write for info. (*4-431-70196-6*) Spr-Verlag.

***Ohigginhs, Michael.** Beating the Dow. rev. ed. 2000. pap. 15.00 (*0-06-662052-X*) HarpC.

O'Higgins. Anthony Collins: The Man & His Works. (International Archives of the History of Ideas Ser.: No. 35). 277p. 1970. lib. bdg. 99.50 (*90-247-5007-5*, Pub. by M Nijhoff) Kluwer Academic.

O'Higgins, Harvey J. From the Life: Imaginary Portraits of Some Distinguished Americans. LC 75-130069. (Short Story Index Reprint Ser.). 1977. 20.95 (*0-8369-3650-7*) Ayer.

— Silent Sam, & Other Stories of Our Day. 1977. 23.95 (*0-8369-4251-5*, 6061) Ayer.

— The Smoke Eaters: The Story of a Fire Crew. 1977. 21.95 (*0-8369-4249-3*, 6059) Ayer.

— Some Distinguished Americans: Imaginary Portraits. LC 78-144166. (Short Story Index Reprint Ser.). 1977. reprint ed. 23.95 (*0-8369-3781-3*) Ayer.

O'Higgins, James. Determinism & Freewill. (International Archives of the History of Ideas Ser.: No. 18). 131p. 1976. pap. text 78.50 (*90-247-1776-0*) Kluwer Academic.

— Yves de Vallone: The Making of an Espirit-Fort. 1982. lib. bdg. 112.50 (*90-247-2520-8*) Kluwer Academic.

O'Higgins, Kathleen. Disruption, Displacement, Discontinuity: Children in Care & Their Families in Ireland. 240p. 1996. 72.95 (*1-85972-235-0*, Pub. by Avebry) Ashgate Pub Co.

Ohiggins, Maria J. De, see De Ohiggins, Maria J.

O'Higgins, Michael & Downes, John. Beating the Dow: A High Return, Low-Risk Method for Investing in the Dow Jones Industrial Stocks with As Little As 5,000 Dollars. LC 89-46551. 304p. 1992. reprint ed. pap. 14.00 (*0-06-098404-X*, Perennial) HarperTrade.

O'Higgins, Michael & Downes, John. Beating the Dow: O'Higgins,&Michael B. abr. ed. 1990. audio 12.00 (*1-55994-285-1*, CPN 1870) HarperAudio.

***O'Higgins, Michael B.** Beating The Dow Revised Edition: A High-Return, Low-Risk Method for Investing in the Dow Jones Industrial Stockswith as Little as $5,000. rev. ed. 320p. 2000. pap. 15.00 (*0-06-662047-3*) HarpC.

O'Higgins, Michael B. Beating the Dow with Bonds. 2000. pap. 15.00 (*0-88730-883-X*, HarpBusn) HarpInfo.

***O'Higgins, Michael B.** Beating the Dow with Bonds: A High-Return, Low-Risk Strategy for Outperforming the Pros Even When Stocks Go South. 1999. audio 18.00 (*0-694-52089-6*) HarperAudio.

O'Higgins, Michael B. & McCarthy, John. Beating the Dow with T-Bills, T-Bonds, & Stocks: A High-Return, Low-Risk Method for Outperforming the Pros 95of the Time - Regarding of Market Conditions. LC 98-31065. 288p. 1999. 24.00 (*0-88730-947-X*, HarpBusn) HarpInfo.

***O'Higgins, Niall.** Youth Unemployment & Employment Policy in Global Perspective. 200p. 2000. pap. 18.95 (*92-2-111384-1*, Pub. by ILO) ILO Pubns Ctr.

O'Higgins, Nuala, jt. auth. see O'Higgins, Paul.

***O'Higgins, Paul & Cohn, Martin.** Vertebrate Ontogeny & Evolution. (Illus.). 238p. 1999. 74.95 (*0-12-524965-9*) Morgan Kaufmann.

O'Higgins, Paul & O'Higgins, Nuala. Christianity Without Religion. 2nd rev. ed. 1997. pap. 6.95 (*0-944795-00-5*) Recon Outreach.

— The Feasts of the Lord: And the Fullness of Redemption. 48p. 1997. mass mkt. 3.95 (*0-944795-03-X*) Recon Outreach.

— Fresh Bread: Manna for Kingdom Living Today. 2nd ed. (Orig.). 1987. pap. 6.95 (*0-944795-02-1*) Recon Outreach.

— In Israel Today with Yeshua. 3rd ed. 1987. reprint ed. pap. 6.95 (*0-944795-01-3*) Recon Outreach.

— New Testament Believers & the Law. pap. 3.95 (*0-944795-04-8*) Recon Outreach.

— Women in the Church. mass mkt. 3.95 (*0-944795-06-4*) Recon Outreach.

O'Higgins, Paul, jt. auth. see Hepple, B. A.

O'Higgins, Paul, ed. see Elias, Patrick & Ewing, K. D.

O'Higgins, Paul, ed. see Fredman, Sandra & Morris, Gillian S.

O'Higgins, Paul, ed. see Hepple, B.

O'Higgins, Paul, ed. see Szyszczak, Erika M.

O'Higgins, R., jt. ed. see McEldowney, J.

***Ohio Adjutant General's Dept.** Roster of Ohio Soldiers in the War of 1812. 157p. 1999. 18.50 (*0-8063-0267-4*) Clearfield Co.

Ohio Archaeological Council, jt. auth. see Pacheco, Paul J.

Ohio Coal Development Office Staff, contrib. by. Dry Scrubbing Technologies for Flue Gas Desulfurization. LC 98-42064. 12p. 1998. 190.00 (*0-7923-8346-X*) Kluwer Academic.

Ohio, Denise. Blue. LC 93-29091. 192p. 1993. pap. 12.00 (*0-929701-30-5*) McPherson & Co.

— The Finer Grain. 224p. 1988. pap. 8.95 (*0-941483-11-8*) Naiad Pr.

Ohio Department of Education Staff. Becoming a Better Problem Solver, Bk. 1. 1997. text 9.50 (*0-86651-083-4*) Seymour Pubns.

— A Resource for Problem Solving, Bk. 2. 1997. pap. text 9.50 (*0-86651-084-2*) Seymour Pubns.

Ohio Environmental Protection Agency Staff, contrib. by. Ohio EPA Laws & Regulations, 3 vols. 4090p. 1993. 185.00 (*1-58360-091-4*) Anderson Pub Co.

Ohio Genealogical Society Staff. Ohio Source Records from "The Ohio Genealogical Quarterly" 666p. 1993. reprint ed. 29.95 (*0-8063-1137-1*, 4308) Genealog Pub.

Ohio Historical Society Staff. Union Bibliography of Ohio Printed State Documents, 1803-1970. 750p. 1973. 20.00 (*0-318-03190-6*) Ohio Hist Soc.

Ohio Historical Society Staff & Kitchen, Judith L. Old Building Owner's Manual. 86p. 1983. spiral bd. 9.95 (*0-87758-016-2*) Ohio Hist Soc.

Ohio Judicial Conference, Jury Instruction Committ. Ohio Jury Instructions, 4 vols., Set. 1997. pap. 220.00 (*0-87084-675-2*) Anderson Pub Co.

Ohio Math Project, Inc. Staff. Introduction to Algebra & Statistics. Anthony, Edward F., ed. (Illus.). 456p. (YA). (gr. 8-10). 1993. teacher ed. 68.00 (*1-880251-11-6*); text 37.30 (*1-880251-10-8*) EFA & Assocs.

— Mathematics Across the Curriculum. Anthony, Edward F., ed. (Illus.). 575p. (YA). (gr. 8-10). 1992. text 37.80 (*1-880251-06-X*) EFA & Assocs.

— Mathematics Across the Curriculum. Anthony, Edward F., ed. (Illus.). 575p. (YA). (gr. 8-10). 1992. teacher ed. 70.00 (*1-880251-08-6*) EFA & Assocs.

Ohio Otterbein College Staff, ed. see Humesky, Assya & Shamraj, Ruth.

Ohio Recorders' Association Staff. Ohio County Recorder Laws, 1998. LC 98-228821. 557 p. 1998. write for info. (*0-8322-0737-3*) Banks-Baldwin.

Ohio, State Bar Association, Administrative Law Committee. Ohio Purchasing Laws & Rules. LC 98-152104. iv, 36 p. 1997. 0.00 (*0-8322-0640-7*) Banks-Baldwin.

Ohio State Grange Staff. The Ohio State Grange Cookbook. LC 92-20292. 1992. spiral bd. write for info. (*0-87197-339-1*) Favorite Recipes.

Ohio State Medical Association Staff, et al. Sports Medicine Roles & Responsibilities for High School Team Physicians & Athletic Trainers. LC 96-70418. 72p. (Orig.). 1997. pap. 9.95 (*0-944183-20-4*) PRC Pub.

Ohio State University, Department of Home Economic. Home Economics Education: A Review & Synthesis of the Research. 5th ed. 55p. 1986. 7.00 (*0-317-01422-6*, IN 313) Ctr Educ Trng Employ.

Ohio State University, Department of Linguistics S. Language Files: Materials for an Introduction to Language & Linguistics. 6th ed. 477p. (C). 1994. pap. text 37.50 (*0-8142-0645-X*) Ohio St U Pr.

Ohio State University Staff. Laboratory Manual for Geological Sciences 100. 148p. (C). 1995. per. 14.95 (*0-8403-9457-8*) Kendall-Hunt.

***Ohio State University Staff.** Retrieving the American Past: A Customized U.S. History Reader, Revised Edition. 1999. pap. text. write for info. (*0-13-025774-5*) P-H.

Ohio State University Staff, et al. Language Files: Materials for an Introduction to Language & Linguistics. 7th ed. LC 97-51188. 523p. 1998. pap. text 37.50 (*0-8142-5003-3*) Ohio St U Pr.

Ohio State University Staff, jt. auth. see Hawthorne, Nathaniel.

Ohio University Staff. The University Experience. 302p. (C). 1997. per. 25.95 (*0-7872-3794-9*) Kendall-Hunt.

— The University Experience. 5th ed. 302p. (C). 1998. per. 33.95 (*0-7872-4993-9*, 41499301) Kendall-Hunt.

Ohio Veterinary Medical Association Staff. A Century of Caring. Flournoy & Gibbs, Inc. Staff, ed. (Illus.). 132p. 1984. 30.00 (*0-9613273-0-8*) Ohio Vet.

Ohiorhenuan, John F. Capital & the State in Nigeria, 122. LC 88-7710. (Contributions in Afro-American & African Studies). 280p. 1989. 65.00 (*0-313-26460-0*, OCN, Greenwood Pr) Greenwood.

Ohiorhenuan, John F. & Wunker, Stephen M. Capacity Building Requirements for Global Environmental Protection. LC 95-203532. (Working Papers: No. 12). 36p. (Orig.). (C). 1995. pap. 6.95 (*1-884122-13-2*) Global Environ.

Ohira, Goro, ed. see Niyama, Eisuke.

Ohira, Nine-Dan S. Appreciating Famous Games. Fairbairn, John, tr. from JPN. 1977. 13.95 (*4-87187-025-1*, G25) Ishi Pr Intl.

Ohishi, Hiroshi. Photometric Determination of Traces of Metals: Individual Metals Magnesium, Vol. 1, Pt. 2B, Individual Metals Magnesium to Zik. 4th ed. 848p. 1989. 425.00 (*0-471-84694-5*) Wiley.

Ohishi, Yasutake, ed. see Shimizu, Makoto, et al.

Ohiwerei, Godwin O., ed. The Developing Strategies for Excellence in Urban Education. LC 96-21873. (Illus.). 247p. (C). 1996. lib. bdg. 95.00 (*1-56072-356-4*) Nova Sci Pubs.

Ohkawa, Kazushi, et al, eds. Patterns of Japanese Economic Development: A Quantitative Appraisal. LC 78-23317. (Economic Growth Center, Yale University, & the Council on East Asian Studies, Yale University Publication Ser.). (Illus.). 428p. reprint ed. pap. 132.70 (*0-8357-8261-1*, 203384700087) Bks Demand.

Ohkawa, Kazushi & Kohama, Hirohisa. Lectures on Economic Development: Japan's Experience & Its Relevance. 380p. 1989. 57.50 (*0-86008-438-8*, Pub. by U of Tokyo) Col U Pr.

Ohkawa, Kazushi & Rosovsky, Henry. Japanese Economic Growth: Trend Acceleration in the Twentieth Century. LC 72-97203. (Studies of Economic Growth in Industrialized Countries). 352p. 1973. 45.00 (*0-8047-0833-9*) Stanford U Pr.

Ohkawa, Kazushi, et al. Growth Mechanism of Developing Economies: Investment, Productivity, & Employment. LC 92-33578. 524p. 1992. pap. 24.95 (*1-55815-193-1*) ICS Pr.

Ohkawa, Kazushi, ed. see International Conference on Economic Growth Staff.

Ohkawa, Y., et al, eds. Proceedings of the 16th International Conference on Offshore Mechanics & Arctic Engineering, Yokohama, Japan, April 13-17, 1997 Vol. VI: Ocean Space Utilization. 16th ed. 304p. 1997. 120.00 (*0-7918-1804-7*, H01085) ASME Pr.

Ohki-Close, Emiko, jt. auth. see Close, Paul.

Ohki, S., ed. Cell & Model Membrane Interactions. (Illus.). 304p. (C). 1992. text 114.00 (*0-306-44097-0*, Kluwer Plenum) Kluwer Academic.

Ohkoshi, Yasuo, jt. auth. see O'Brien, David M.

Ohkusu, M., ed. Advances in Marine Hydrodynamics. 384p. 1996. 121.00 (*1-85312-287-4*) Computational Mech MA.

Ohkusu, M., ed. Advances in Marine Hydrodynamics. LC 95-67471. (Advances in Fluid Mechanics Ser.: Vol. 5). 384p. 1996. 170.00 (*1-56252-211-6*, 2874) Computational Mech MA.

Ohl, Dana A., jt. auth. see Lechtenberg, Richard.

Ohl, John K. Hugh S. Johnson & the New Deal. (Illus.). 374p. 1985. 35.00 (*0-87580-110-2*) N Ill U Pr.

— Supplying the Troops: General Somervell & American Logistics in WW II. LC 93-39869. (Illus.). 325p. 1994. lib. bdg. 35.00 (*0-87580-185-4*) N Ill U Pr.

***Ohl, John Kennedy.** Minuteman: The Military Career of General Robert S. Beightler. 280p. (YA). 2000. 59.95 (*1-55587-923-3*) L Rienner.

Ohl, S. S., et al. Guide to Modern Meals. 4th ed. 640p. 1985. text, student ed. 30.12 (*0-07-047513-X*) McGraw.

Ohlander, Ben, jt. auth. see Drake, David.

Ohlander, Ben, jt. auth. see Forstchen, William R.

Ohlander, Stephen. Dramatic Suspense in Euripides' & Seneca's "Medea" (American University Studies: Classical Languages & Literature: Ser. XVII, Vol. 6). 342p. (C). 1989. text 49.50 (*0-8204-0873-5*) P Lang Pubng.

Ohlander, U. Studies on Co-Ordinate Expressions in Middle English. (Lund Studies in English: Vol. 5). 1974. reprint ed. pap. 30.00 (*0-8115-0548-0*) Periodicals Srv.

Ohlbach, Hans J., ed. GWAI-92 - Advances in Artificial Intelligence: Proceedings of the 16th German Conference on Artificial Intelligence, Bonn Germany, August 31-September 3, 1992. LC 93-15233. (Lecture Notes in Computer Science Ser.: Vol. 671). 1993. 61.95 (*0-387-56667-8*) Spr-Verlag.

Ohlbach, Hans J., jt. auth. see Gabbay, Dov M.

An Asterisk (*) at the beginning of an entry indicates that the title is appearing for the first time.

An Asterisk (*) at the beginning of an entry indicates that the title is appearing for the first time.

(Arbeiten Zur Kirchengeschichte Ser.: ...R.). 620p. (C). 1997. lib. bdg. 220.00 (...89-8) De Gruyter.

...man. Foreign Language Grammatical Glossary. ...d. Ohme, Jean, ed. (Illus.). 80p. 1989. pap. 6.00 (...-936047-07-0) CA Educ Plan.

— Learn How to Learn Study Skills. rev. ed. Ohme, Jean, ed. (Illus.). 256p. 1989. pap. 12.00 (*0-936047-00-3*) CA Educ Plan.

— Motivation & Concentration. rev. ed. Ohme, Jean, ed. (Illus.). 48p. 1989. pap. 5.00 (*0-936047-01-1*) CA Educ Plan.

— Organization & Time Management. rev. ed. Ohme, Jean, ed. (Illus.). 48p. 1989. pap. 5.00 (*0-936047-03-8*) CA Educ Plan.

— Parent Guide to Study Skills. rev. ed. Ohme, Jean, ed. (Illus.). 48p. 1989. pap. 5.00 (*0-936047-06-2*) CA Educ Plan.

— Teacher Guide to "Learn How to Learn" Study Skills. rev. ed. Ohme, Jean, ed. (Illus.). 24p. 1989. pap. 5.00 (*0-936047-02-X*) CA Educ Plan.

— Test Taking. rev. ed. Ohme, Jean, ed. (Illus.). 54p. 1989. pap. 5.00 (*0-936047-05-4*) CA Educ Plan.

Ohme, Herman & Ohme, Jean. Notetaking & Report Writing. rev. ed. (Illus.). 56p. 1989. pap. 5.00 (*0-936047-11-9*) CA Educ Plan.

Ohme, Jean, jt. auth. see Ohme, Herman.

Ohme, Jean, ed. see Ohme, Herman.

Ohmi, Ayano, jt. auth. see Hamanaka, Sheila.

Ohmi, T. Ultra-Clean Technology Handbook Vol. 1: Ultra-Pure Water. (Illus.). 944p. 1993. text 255.00 (*0-8247-8753-6*) Dekker.

Ohmori, Koichiro. Over the Himalaya. (Illus.). 108p. 1994. 29.95 (*0-938567-37-3*) Mountaineers.

Ohmori, Shingo, et al. Mobile Satellite Communications. LC 97-41708. 1997. 99.00 (*0-89006-843-7*) Artech Hse.

***Ohmsha.** Dictionary Science & Engineering. (ENG & JPN.). 1998. 795.00 (*0-320-02288-9*); 795.00 (*0-320-02289-7*) Fr & Eur.

Ohnaka, I. & Stefanescu, D. M., eds. Solidification Science & Processing. (Illus.). 307p. 1995. 20.00 (*0-87339-338-4*, 3384) Minerals Metals.

Ohnami, Masateru, ed. Fracture & Society. LC 92-53265. 420p. (gr. 12). 1992. 105.00 (*90-5199-092-8*, Pub. by IOS Pr) IOS Press.

Ohnemus, Sylvia. An Ethnology of the Admiralty Islanders. (Illus.). 432p. 1998. text 99.00 (*0-8248-2084-3*) UH Pr.

Ohnesorg, Aenne. Inselionische Marmordaecher. Deutsches Archaeologisches Institut Staff, ed. (Denkmaeler Antiker Architektur Ser.: No. 18, 2). (GER., Illus.). xvi, 160p. (C). 1993. lib. bdg. 186.15 (*3-11-013718-6*) De Gruyter.

Ohnesorg, Stephanie, jt. auth. see Moser, Beverly.

Ohngren, Bo, jt. ed. see Ohman, Arne.

***Ohnishi, M., ed.** Glycoenzymes. (Illus.). x, 264p. 2000. 231.50 (*3-8055-7076-7*) S Karger.

Ohnishi, S. Tsuyoshi. Malignant Hyperthermia Membrane-Linked Diseases, Vol. III. 352p. 1993. lib. bdg. 160.00 (*0-8493-8093-6*, RD82) CRC Pr.

— Membrane Associated Abnormalities - Sickle Cell Diseases - Membrane Linked Diseases, Vol. II. 304p. 1993. lib. bdg. 115.00 (*0-8493-8092-8*, RC641) CRC Pr.

Ohnishi, S. Tsuyoshi & Ohnishi, Tomoko, eds. Central Nervous System Trauma Research Techniques, Vol. 4. (Membrane-Linked Diseases Ser.). 592p. 1995. boxed set 199.95 (*0-8493-8094-4*, 8094) CRC Pr.

Ohnishi, Tomoko, jt. ed. see Ohnishi, S. Tsuyoshi.

Ohno, A. Solidification. (Illus.). 130p. 1987. 65.95 (*0-387-18233-0*) Spr-Verlag.

Ohno, A., jt. auth. see Oae, S.

Ohno, Izumi, jt. auth. see Ohno, Kenichi.

Ohno, Izumi, ed. see Symposium on Electroless Deposition of Metals & Al.

Ohno, John. Comprehensive Medical Thesaurus with Concise Etymological Analysis. 304p. 1999. pap. 29.95 (*1-58244-012-3*) Rutledge Bks.

Ohno, Kenichi & Ohno, Izumi. Japanese Views on Economic Development: Diverse Paths to the Market. LC 97-29027. 320p. (C). 1998. 90.00 (*0-415-15639-4*) Routledge.

Ohno, M., et al, eds. Seaweed Cultivation & Marine Ranching. (World Biodiversity Database Ser.). 1997. 71.95 incl. cd-rom (*3-540-14549-4*) Spr-Verlag.

Ohno, M., jt. ed. see Lukacs, Gabor.

Ohno, Shigeaki. Uveitis Today: Proceedings of the Fourth International Symposium on Uveitis, Held in Yokohama, Japan, 10-14 October, 1997. LC 98-18044. 333p. 1998. write for info. (*0-444-82983-0*) Elsevier.

Ohno, Shigeaki, ed. see Forrester, John V., et al.

Ohno, Shuho. Modern Senryu in English. (Illus.). 256p. (C). 1988. 18.50 (*0-9620359-0-4*) Hokubei Intl.

Ohno, T. & Yamamoto, R., eds. Multilayers No. IMAM-10: Materials Research Society International Symposium Proceedings. 619p. 1989. text 17.50 (*1-55899-039-9*, IMAM-10) Materials Res.

Ohno, Taiichi. El Sistema de Produccion Toyota: Mas Alla de la Produccion de Toyota. (SPA., Illus.). 172p. (Orig.). 1991. pap. 40.00 (*84-87022-52-9*) Productivity Inc.

— Toyota Production System: Beyond Large-Scale Production. LC 87-43172. (Illus.). 162p. 1988. 45.00 (*0-915299-14-3*) Productivity Inc.

Ohno, Y., ed. Distributed Environments: Software Paradigms & Workstations. (Illus.). xi, 322p. 1991. 122.95 (*0-387-70075-7*) Spr-Verlag.

Ohno, Yutaka, jt. auth. see Matsumoto, Yoshihio.

Ohnstad, Arik T., ed. see Ditchey, Karen M. & Novak, Pamela K.

Ohnstad, Bob. Scissors & Comb Haircutting: A Cut-by-Cut Guide for Home Haircutters. LC 84-90072. (Illus.). 186p. 1985. pap. 18.95 (*0-916819-01-9*, Pub. by You Can Pub) IPG Chicago.

Ohnuki, Masako, tr. see Asada, Toshi, ed.

Ohnuki-Tierney, Emiko. Culture Through Time: Anthropological Approaches. LC 90-36662. 344p. 1991. 47.50 (*0-8047-1792-3*); pap. 15.95 (*0-8047-1791-5*) Stanford U Pr.

— Illness & Culture in Contemporary Japan: An Anthropological View. LC 83-14415. 250p. 1984. pap. text 19.95 (*0-521-27786-8*) Cambridge U Pr.

— Illness & Healing among the Sakhalin Ainu: A Symbolic Interpretation. LC 80-24268. 261p. reprint ed. pap. 74.40 (*0-608-15760-0*, 2031701) Bks Demand.

Ohnuki, Y. Unitary Representations of the Poincare Group & Relativistic Wave Equations. 228p. (C). 1988. text 54.00 (*9971-5-0250-X*) World Scientific Pub.

Ohnuki, Y. & Kamefuchi, S. Quantum Field Theory & Parastatistics. (Illus.). 489p. 1982. 120.00 (*0-387-11643-5*) Spr-Verlag.

Ohnuma, Toshiro. Radiation Phenomena in Plasmas. 326p. 1994. text 74.00 (*981-02-1840-0*) World Scientific Pub.

Ohnysty, James. Aids to Ethics & Professional Conduct for Student Radiologic Technologists. 2nd ed. 176p. 1979. pap., spiral bd. 29.95 (*0-398-01419-1*) C C Thomas.

Ohogain. Celtic Warrios. 1999. text 24.95 (*0-312-20509-0*) St Martin.

O'Hogain, Daithi. The Sacred Isle: Pre-Christian Religions in Ireland. LC 99-17518. 256p. 1999. 45.00 (*0-85115-747-5*) Boydell & Brewer.

Oholo Biological Conference Staff. Skin: Drug Application & Evaluation of Environmental Hazards, Proceedings of the Oholo Biological Conference, 22nd, Ma'alot, March 1977. Mali, J. W. et al, eds. (Current Problems in Dermatology Ser.: Vol. 7). (Illus.). 1977. 86.25 (*3-8055-2797-7*) S Karger.

O'Hooper, David. The Peace Tree: A Modern Christmas Fable. (Illus.). 32p. (J). (gr. k-8). 1994. 12.50 (*0-9640684-3-5*) Pixie Dust.

O'Hora, Jill & Varga, Anna, eds. The Ties That No Longer Bind: Russians & Americans Talk to Each Other. LC 96-85036. (West & the Wider World: Vol. 10). (Illus.). 250p. (Orig.). 1996. pap. 21.95 (*0-940121-37-9*, P305) Cross Cultural Pubns. Here the editors present vivid pictures of life in Russia & America. Some dialogues take place in Russia--in tiny apartments or sunny dachas--while other meetings are held in Los Angeles. Participants of both nationalities begin by trying to lay to rest the cliches that each group attributes to the culture of the other. The photographs that accompany this text are by turns dramatic, insightful, touching & revealing. Some pictures are paired to show parallel views of life, while other pairs show vivid contrasts. Remarkably open & honest conversations sparkle with real life, real concerns & real humanity.
Publisher Paid Annotation.

Ohotin, Nicholas A., tr. see Soloveichik, Svetlana A.

Ohovwore, Nizza. Things Fall Apart. LC 97-91322. 49p. 2000. pap. 8.95 (*0-533-12633-9*) Vantage.

Ohr, Karlfriedrich. Die Basilika In Pompeji: Unter Mitarbeit von Jurgen J. Rasch. (Denkmaeler Antiker Architektur Ser.: Vol. 17). (GER., Illus.). x, 87p. (C). 1991. lib. bdg. 152.35 (*3-11-012283-9*) De Gruyter.

Ohr, R., jt. ed. see Lang, F. P.

Ohr, Tim. Florida's Fabulous Natural Places. Williams, Winston, ed. (Florida's Fabulous Nature Ser.). (Illus.). 160p. 1998. pap. 15.95 (*0-911977-19-8*) Wrld Tampa.

***Ohr, Tim.** Florida's Fabulous Natural Places. Williams, Winston, ed. LC 98-90875. (Illus.). 160p. 1999. 24.95 (*0-911977-20-1*) Wrld Tampa.

— Florida's Illustrated Canoe & Kayak Adventures. (Illus.). 108p. 2000. pap. 15.95 (*1-884942-23-7*) Carmichael Pubns.

— Florida's Illustrated Trails: Hiking, Bicycling, Equestrian Trails. (Illus.). 128p. 2000. pap. 15.95 (*1-884942-24-5*) Carmichael Pubns.

Ohr, Tim, ed. see Carmichael, Pele & Hill, Leonard.

Ohr, Tim, ed. see Lamar, William.

Ohr, Tim, ed. see Oxley, Richard.

Ohr, Tim, ed. see Whitaker, John, Jr. & Reeves, Randall R.

***Ohrbach, Barbara.** Assorted Barbara Ohrbach. 2000. 25.00 (*5-550-02743-7*) Nairi.

Ohrbach, Barbara M. Antiques at Home. 1989. 30.00 (*0-517-56986-8*) C Potter.

— Food for the Soul: Delicious Thoughts to Nourish Mind & Heart. LC 97-6208. 64p. 1996. pap. 8.00 (*0-517-88770-3*) C Potter.

— If You Think You Can . . . You Can! (Illus.). 64p. 1998. pap. 8.00 (*0-609-80317-4*) C Potter.

— Merry Christmas: Festive Stories, Songs, Poems, Recipes, & Gift Ideas for the Holidays. (Illus.). 64p. 1992. 12.00 (*0-517-58626-6*) C Potter.

— The Scented Room: Cherchez's Book of Dried Flowers, Fragrance, & Potpourri. (Illus.). 1986. 20.00 (*0-517-56081-X*) C Potter.

— Tabletops: Easy, Practical, Beautiful Ways to Decorate. LC 97-219769. 1997. 24.00 (*0-517-70332-7*) Random Hse Value.

— A Token of Friendship: A Collection of Sentiments, Thoughts, Gift Ideas, & Recipes for Special Friends. deluxe ed. (Illus.). 64p. 1987. 10.00 (*0-517-56657-5*) C Potter.

Ohrbach, Barbara Milo. All Things are Possible: Pass the Word. LC 94-37344. 64p. (J). 1995. pap. 8.00 (*0-517-88426-7*) C Potter.

— Roses from the Scented Room. LC 99-32988. (Illus.). 144p. 2000. 25.00 (*0-609-60107-5*) C Potter.

***Ohrbach, Barbara Milo.** A Token of Love: A Little Book of Romance. LC 99-89064. (Illus.). 64p. 2000. 12.00 (*0-609-60501-1*) C Potter.

Ohrbach, Karl-Heinz. The Parat Dictionary of Ecology: English-German, German-English. (ENG & GER.). 330p. 1991. 175.00 (*0-7859-6955-1*) Fr & Eur.

Ohrback, B. Scented Room. 12.95 (*1-56305-897-9*) Workman Pub.

Ohren, Margaret, ed. Taking Time Out: Managing Employment Breaks. 160p. (C). 1991. pap. text 65.00 (*0-85292-460-7*, Pub. by IPM Hse) St Mut.

***Ohren, Peter.** Catch of the Day. 2001. 25.00 (*1-929871-00-7*) Van Neste.

Ohrenstein, Roman A. & Gordon, Barry. Economic Analysis in Talmudic Literature: Rabbinic Thought in the Light of Modern Economics. LC 91-41392. (Studia Post-Biblica Ser.: No. 40). (Illus.). xviii, 152p. 1992. 56.50 (*90-04-09540-3*) Brill Academic Pubs.

Ohri, Vishwa C. On the Origins of the Pahari Painting. (C). 1991. 25.00 (*81-85182-53-1*, Pub. by Motilal Bnarsidass) S Asia.

Ohri, Vishwa C., ed. History & Culture of the Chamba State. (C). 1988. 110.00 (*81-85016-25-9*, Pub. by Bks & Bks) S Asia.

Ohriner, Evan K., et al, eds. Iridium. (Illus.). 440p. pap. 68.00 (*0-87339-461-5*) Minerals Metals.

Ohring, G. & Bolle, H. J., eds. Space Observations for Climate Studies: Proceedings of Symposium 4 of the COSPAR Twenty-Fifth Plenary Meeting Held in Graz Austria, 25 June-7 July 1984. (Illus.). 404p. 1985. pap. 54.00 (*0-08-033195-5*, Pub. by PPL) Elsevier.

Ohring, Milton. Engineering Materials for Science. 1995. pap. text, student ed. 10.00 (*0-12-524998-5*) Acad Pr.

— Engineering Materials Science. (Illus.). 827p. 1995. text 74.00 (*0-12-524995-0*) Acad Pr.

— The Materials Science of Thin Films. (Illus.). 704p. 1991 text 93.00 (*0-12-524990-X*) Acad Pr.

— Reliability & Failure of Electronic Materials & Devices. LC 98-16084. (Illus.). 692p. 1998. boxed set 95.... (*0-12-524985-3*) Acad Pr.

Ohrlander, Gunnar. ...Story: A Child's Struggle, a Family's Victory Against All Odds. LC 91-53080. 1991. 18.95 (*0-88282-041-9*) New Horizon NJ.

Ohrloff, C., jt. ed. see Wegener, A.

Ohrn, Deborah G., ed. Her Story. 1999. pap. 6.99 (*0-14-038074-4*) Viking Penguin.

Ohrn, Deborah G. & Ashby, Ruth, eds. Herstory: Women Who Changed the World. LC 94-61492. (Illus.). 304p. (YA). (gr. 7-12). 1995. 24.99 (*0-670-85434-4*, Viking) Viking Penguin.

***Ohrn, Yngve N.** Elements of Molecular Symmetry. LC 99-39819. 375p. 2000. text 69.95 (*0-471-36323-5*, Wiley-Interscience) Wiley.

Ohrnberger, D. Bamboos of the World: A Preliminary Study of the Names & Distribution of the Herbaceous & Woody Bamboos (Bambusoideae Nees V. Esenb) 1112p. (C). 1990. 160.00 (*0-7855-6877-8*, Pub. by Intl Bk Distr) St Mut.

— The Bamboos of the World: Annotated Nomenclature & Literature of the Species & the Higher & Lower Taxa. LC 98-32276. 596p. 1999. 210.50 (*0-444-50020-0*) Elsevier.

O'hrs, Herman R. & Lenhart, Volker. Progressive Education Across the Continents: A Handbook. LC 95-23815. (Heidelberger Studien zur Erziehungswissenschaft Ser.: Bd. 44). 446p. 1995. 69.95 (*0-8204-2914-7*, 68705) P Lang Pubng.

Ohrstrom, Peter & Hasle, Per F. Temporal Logic: From Ancient Ideas to Artificial Intelligence. LC 95-22191. (Studies in Linguistics & Philosophy: Vol. 57). 424p. (C). 1995. lib. bdg. 99.00 (*0-7923-3586-4*, Pub. by Kluwer Academic) Kluwer Academic.

***Ohrt, Robert & Koch, Uwe.** Raymond Pettibon: The Books, 1978-1998. (Illus.). 992p. 2000. pap. 50.00 (*1-891024-18-3*, A20301) Dist Art Pubs.

Ohrt, Wallace. Defiant Peacemaker: Nicholas Trist in the Mexican War. LC 97-35669. (Elma Dill Russell Spencer Series in the West & Southwest: No. 17). (Illus.). 224p. 1997. 29.95 (*0-89096-778-4*) Tex A&M Univ Pr.

Ohry, Abraham, jt. auth. see Kossoy, Edward.

Ohsako, Toshio. Violence at School: Global Issues & Interventions. LC 98-144066. 1998. 25.00 (*92-3-185004-0*, U5004, Pub. by UNESCO) Bernan Associates.

***Ohsako, Toshio, ed.** Violence at School: Global Issues & Intervention. 127p. 1999. reprint ed. pap. text 30.00 (*0-7881-8178-5*) DIANE Pub.

Ohsawa, George. The Art of Peace: A New Translation of the Book of Judo. Rothman, Sandy, ed. Gleason, William, tr. from FRE. LC 90-82077. 152p. 1990. pap. 7.95 (*0-918860-50-4*) G Ohsawa.

— Gandhi: The Eternal Youth. Burns, Kenneth G., tr. from JPN. & intro. by. LC 86-80512. (FRE.). 142p. (Orig.). 1986. pap. 6.95 (*0-918860-45-8*) G Ohsawa.

— Macrobiotic Guidebook for Living: And Other Essays. rev. ed. 130p. 1985. pap. 7.95 (*0-918860-41-5*) G Ohsawa.

— Macrobiotics: An Invitation to Health & Happiness. 77p. 1984. reprint ed. pap. 5.95 (*0-918860-02-4*) G Ohsawa.

— Order of the Universe: The Spiralic Concept of Man. Poggi, Jim, ed. (Illus.). 103p. 1986. pap. 7.95 (*0-918860-46-6*) G Ohsawa.

— Philosophy of Oriental Medicine: Key to Your Personal Judging Ability. Aihara, Herman & Rothman, Sandy, eds. LC 91-76486. 153p. 1991. pap. 7.95 (*0-918860-52-0*) G Ohsawa.

— Zen Macrobiotics: The Art of Rejuvenation & Longevity. unabridged ed. Ferre, Carl, ed. LC 95-69712. 208p. 1995. pap. 9.95 (*0-918860-54-7*) G Ohsawa.

Ohsawa, George, Macrobiotic Foundation Staff. The First Macrobiotic Cookbook: Formerly Zen Cookery. rev. ed. Ruggles, Laurel, ed. (Illus.). 134p. 1985. 9.95 (*0-918860-42-3*) G Ohsawa.

Ohsawa, Georges & De Langre, Jacques. But I Love Fruits. (Illus.). 1993. pap. 3.50 (*0-916508-32-3*) Happiness Pr.

Ohsawa, T., jt. ed. see Noguchi, J.

Ohse, D. Handbook of Thermodynamic & Transport Properties of Alkali Metals. 1991. 187.00 (*0-632-01447-4*) CRC Pr.

Ohshima, Hiroyuki & Furusawa, Kunio. Electrical Phenomena at Interfaces. 2nd ed. LC 98-29986. (Surfactant Science Ser.). (Illus.). 664p. 1998. text 235.00 (*0-8247-9039-1*) Dekker.

Ohshima, T., jt. ed. see Kato, Shinzi.

Ohshima, Tsutomu. Notes on Training. LC 99-158941. 252 p. 1998. 40.00 (*0-937663-32-8*) Idyll Arbor.

— Notes on Training. 252p. 1998. 40.00 (*1-882883-36-5*, Pine Winds Pr) Idyll Arbor.

Ohshima, Tsutomu, tr. see Funakoshi, Gichin.

Ohshiro, Toshio. Laser Treatment for Naevi. 292p. 1995. 315.00 (*0-471-95243-5*) Wiley.

— The Role of the Laser in Dermatology: An Atlas. LC 96-30947. 294p. 1997. 442.00 (*0-471-96630-4*) W...

Ohshiro, Toshio & Calderhead, R. G., eds. P...00002) Laser Therapy: Selected Papers from ... ILTA Congress. LC 91-24452. (I... ...e Industry: A reprint ed. pap. 76.30 (*0-60...* ...ate & Market Structures. Bks Demand.

Ohsono, Tomokaz... ...0.00 (*0-304-33395-6*) Continuum.

Graphical ed. Frequency Control of Semiconductor (Illus.). LC 95-24632. (Microwave & Optical Oh... Engineering Ser.). 256p. 1996. 98.95 (*0-471-01341-2*, Wiley-Interscience) Wiley.

Ohsuga, S., ed. Virtual Reality & Multimedia. LC 97-75041. (Frontiers in Artificial Intelligence Applications Ser.: Vol. 42). 500p. Date not set. 99.00 (*90-5199-356-0*) IOS Press.

Ohsuga, S., et al, eds. Algorithmic Learning Theory: First International Workshop on Algorithmic Learning Theory (ALT '90), Tokyo, Japan, 8-10 October 1990. xi, 441p. 1991. 79.00 (*0-387-19661-7*) Spr-Verlag.

— Information Modelling & Knowledge Bases III. LC 91-77697. (Frontiers in Artificial Intelligence & Applications Ser.: Vol. 13). 712p. (gr. 12). 1992. 135.00 (*90-5199-073-1*, Pub. by IOS Pr) IOS Press.

***Ohta, Amy Snyder.** Second Language Acquisition in the Classroom: Learning Japanese. (A Volume in the Second Language Acquisition Research Series). 272p. 2001. write for info. (*0-8058-3800-7*); pap. write for info. (*0-8058-3801-5*) L Erlbaum Assocs.

Ohta, Hiroshi. Spatial Price Theory of Imperfect Competition. LC 87-22333. (Economics Ser.: No. 8). (Illus.). 254p. 1988. lib. bdg. 39.95 (*0-89096-372-X*) Tex A&M Univ Pr.

Ohta, Kaoru. Advances in Cryptology-Asiacrypt '98 International Conference on the Theory & Applications of Cryptology & Information Security, Beijing, China, October, 1998, Vol. 151. (Lecture Notes in Computer Science Ser.). 1998. pap. 67.00 (*3-540-65109-8*) Spr-Verlag.

— Japanese Grammar & Usage: A Companion to Modern Japanese, A Basic Reader. (JPN.). 416p. (C). 1991. pap. text 39.95 (*0-88710-163-1*) Yale Far Eastern Pubns.

Ohta, M. & Remand, B. Tours Symposium on Nuclear Physics. 364p. 1992. text 102.00 (*981-02-0892-8*) World Scientific Pub.

Ohta, Masahiro. Japanese Guide to the Grand Canyon. LC 82-82562. (Illus.). 26p. 1982. pap. 6.95 (*0-938216-18-X*) GCA.

Ohta, Naohisa. Packet Video: Modeling & Signal Processing. LC 93-38080. 207p. 1994. 79.00 (*0-89006-519-5*) Artech Hse.

Ohta, Naohisa, ed. Digital Compression Technologies & Systems for Video Communications. (Europto Ser.: Vol. 2952). 710p. 1996. 118.00 (*0-8194-2356-4*) SPIE.

Ohta, Naohisa, et al. Super-High Definition Images: Beyond HDTV. LC 94-49709. 154p. 1995. text 77.00 (*0-89006-674-4*) Artech Hse.

Ohta, T. Evolution & Variation of Multigene Families. (Lecture Notes in Biomathematics Ser.: Vol. 37). 131p. 1980. 34.95 (*0-387-09998-0*) Spr-Verlag.

Ohta, T., ed. Solar-Hydrogen Energy System: An Authoritative Review of Water-Splitting Systems by Solar Beam & Solar Heat; Hydrogen Production, Storage & Utilization. LC 79-40694. (Illus.). 1979. 119.00 (*0-08-022713-9*, Pub. by Pergamon Repr) Franklin.

Ohta, T. & Aoki, K., eds. Population Genetics & Molecular Evolution. 400p. 1986. 94.00 (*0-387-15584-8*) Spr-Verlag.

Ohta, T., jt. ed. see Cheng, K. E.

Ohta, Tokio. Energy Technology: Sources, Systems, & Frontier Conversion. LC 94-11525. 244p. 1994. text. write for info. (*0-08-042132-6*, Pergamon Pr) Elsevier.

Ohta, Y., ed. Color Vision Deficiencies. LC 90-5233. (Illus.). 267p. 1990. lib. bdg. 71.50 (*90-6299-063-0*, Pub. by Kugler) Kugler Pubns.

Ohta, Y. & Tamura, H., eds. Mixed Reality - Merging Real & Virtual Worlds: International Symposium on Mixed Reality, Yokohama, March 9-11, 1999. 400p. 1999. 75.00 (*3-540-65623-5*) Spr-Verlag.

Ohta, Yuichi. Knowledge-Based Interpretation of Outdoor Natural Color Scenes. (Research Notes in Artificial Intelligence Ser.). 1998. pap. text 30.95 (*0-273-08673-1*) Morgan Kaufmann.

An Asterisk (*) at the beginning of an entry indicates that the title is appearing for the first time.

***Ohta, Yukie, tr. from JPN.** A Rainbow in the Desert: An Anthology of Early Twentieth Century Japanese Children's Literature. 188p. 2000. pap. text 19.95 (*0-7656-0556-2*, East Gate Bk) M E Sharpe.

— A Rainbow in the Desert: An Anthology of Early 20th Century Japanese Children's Literature. (Illus.). 188p. 2000. 49.95 (*0-7656-0555-4*, East Gate Bk) M E Sharpe.

Ohtaishi, N. & Sheng, H. L., eds. Deer of China: Biology & Management: Proceedings of the International Symposium on Deer of China, Held in Shanghai, China, 21-23 November 1992. LC 93-33240. (Developments in Animal & Veterinary Science Ser.: Vol. 26). 432p. 1993. 211.25 (*0-444-81540-6*) Elsevier.

Ohtaka, Kassie, tr. see Bergen, Marty.

Ohtake, Noriko. Creative Sources for the Music of Toru Takemitsu. LC 92-28294. 118p. 1993. 61.95 (*0-85967-954-3*, Pub. by Scolar Pr) Ashgate Pub Co.

Ohtake, Shinro. Atlanta, 1945 + 50. (Illus.). 32p. 1996. 90.00 (*0-932526-55-1*) Nexus Pr.

Ohtaki, H., ed. Crystallization Processes. LC 97-21772. (Wiley Series in Solution Chemistry: Vol. 3). 220p. 1997. 165.00 (*0-471-97396-3*) Wiley.

Ohtaki, H. & Yamatera, H., eds. Structure & Dynamics of Solutions. LC 92-16273. (Studies in Physical & Theoretical Chemistry: Vol. 79). 344p. 1992. 228.50 (*0-444-89651-1*) Elsevier.

Ohtani, Kiyotaka, jt. ed. see Loughlin, Thomas R.

Ohtani, Nobuoki, et al. Japanese Product Design & Development. LC 96-43275. (Design Council Ser.). 190p. 1997. text 65.95 (*0-566-07718-3*, Pub. by Gower) Ashgate Pub Co.

***Ohtani, Shin-ichi, et al, eds.** Magnetospheric Current Systems. (Geophysical Monograph Ser.: Vol. 118). 2000. write for info. (*0-87590-976-0*) Am Geophysical.

Ohtsu, M., ed. Near-Field Nano/Atom Optics & Technology. LC 98-21851. (Illus.). xiv, 306p. 1998. 74.95 (*4-431-70228-8*) Spr-Verlag.

Ohtsu, M. & Hori, H. Near-Field Nano-Optics: From Basic Principles to Nano-Fabrication & Nano-Photonics. LC 99-14419. (Lasers, Photonics, & Electro-Optics Ser.). (Illus.). 390p. (C). 1999. write for info. (*0-306-45897-7*, Plenum Trade) Perseus Pubng.

Ohtsu, Motoichi. Coherent Quantum Optics & Technology. LC 92-38956. (Advances in Optoelectronics Ser.: Vol. 5). 250p. (C). 1993. text 183.00 (*0-7923-2079-4*) Kluwer Academic.

Ohtsuka, Ryutaro. Oriomo Papuans: Ecology of Sago-Eaters in Lowland Papua. (Illus.). 197p. 1983. 30.00 (*0-86008-327-6*, Pub. by U of Tokyo) Col U Pr.

Ohtsuka, Ryutaro & Suzuki, Tsuguyoshi, eds. Population Ecology of Human Survival. 300p. 1990. text 52.50 (*0-86008-456-6*, Pub. by U of Tokyo) Col U Pr.

Ohtsuki, H. Y., ed. Recent Theoretical (Computational) Developments in Atomic Collisions in Solids: Proceedings of a Conference, Strasbourg, France, July 14-16, 1981. 162p. 1983. 46.00 (*9971-950-33-2*) World Scientific Pub.

Ohtsuki, Y. H., ed. Science of Ball Lightning (Fire Ball) 352p. (C). 1989. text 98.00 (*9971-5-0723-4*) World Scientific Pub.

O'Huigin, Sean. The Ghost Horse of the Mounties. LC 87-46287. (Illus.). 72p. (J). (gr. 4-6). 1991. 14.95 (*0-87923-721-X*) Godine.

— Scary Poems for Rotten Kids. (J). 1988. 10.15 (*0-606-04314-4*, Pub. by Turtleback) Demco.

O'Hussey, Bonaventura & Winzet, Ninian. Dan Do Rinne. LC 79-370435. (English Recusant Literature, 1558-1640 Ser.). 281p. 1978. write for info. (*0-85967-507-6*) Scolar Pr.

Ohya, H., et al. Polymide Membranes: Applications, Fabrications, & Properties. 328p. 1996. text 78.00 (*90-5699-024-1*, ECU100) Gordon & Breach.

Ohya, Masanori & Petz, Denes. Quantum Entropy & Its Use. LC 92-29580. (Texts & Monographs in Physics). 1993. 107.95 (*0-387-54881-5*) Spr-Verlag.

Ohya-Nishiguchi, H. & Packer, Lester, eds. Bioradicals Detected by ESR Spectroscopy. (Molecular & Cell Biology Updates Ser.). 337p. 1995. 139.00 (*3-7643-5077-6*) Birkhauser.

Ohye, Chihiro, et al, eds. Asian Society for Stereotactic, Functional & Computer-Assisted Neurosurgery: 2nd Congress, Nagano Prefecture, November 1996 - Invited Papers & Abstracts. (Stereotactic & Functional Neurosurgery Ser.: Vol. 70, Nos. 2-4). (Illus.). viii, 150p. 1998. pap. 99.25 (*3-8055-6797-9*) S Karger.

Ohye, Chihiro, ed. see Annual Meeting of the Japanese Society for Stereot.

Ohye, Chihiro, ed. see International Basal Ganglia Society Staff.

Ohzu, Hitoshi, ed. see International Conference on Optics within Life Sci.

Oi, Jean C. Rural China Takes Off: The Institutional Foundations of Economic Reform. LC 98-26762. 259p. 1999. 35.00 (*0-520-20006-3*, Pub. by U CA Pr); pap. 17.95 (*0-520-21727-6*, Pub. by U CA Pr) Cal Prin Full Svc.

— State & Peasant in Contemporary China: The Political Economy of Village Government. (Illus.). 308p. 1991. reprint ed. pap. 16.95 (*0-520-07637-0*, Pub. by U CA Pr) Cal Prin Full Svc.

Oi, Jean C. & Walder, Andrew G. Property Rights & Economic Reform in China LC 99-11806. 1999. 22.95 (*0-8047-3788-6*) Stanford U Pr.

***Oi, Jean C. & Walder, Andrew G., eds.** Property Rights & Economic Reform in China. LC 99-11806. 354p. 1999. 60.00 (*0-8047-3456-9*) Stanford U Pr.

Oickle, Alvin E., ed. see Oickle, Matthew S.

Oickle, Matthew S. Raw Courage New Growth: A Dying Man's Struggle with Cancer: From the Poetry Notebooks of Matthew Scott Oickle. Oickle, Alvin E., ed. LC 98-96959. 64p. (Orig.). 1999. pap. 6.00 (*0-9664556-1-4*, LSP) L Slater Pubg.

Oida, Marshall, jt. auth. see Yoshi.

Oida, Yoshi. An Actor Adrift. 188p. 1995. pap. 19.95 (*0-413-65840-6*, A0741, Methuen Drama) Methn.

Oieroset, Marit, jt. ed. see Hultqvist, Bengt.

Oifer, Jessica. Jungle Animals. (Hidden Pictures Coloring Bks.). 48p. (J). pap. 3.95 (*1-56565-246-0*, 02460W, Pub. by Lowell Hse Juvenile) NTC Contemp Pub Co.

Oikawa, Mona, et al, eds. Out Rage: Dykes & Bis Resist Homophobia. 286p. pap. 12.95 (*0-88961-188-2*, Pub. by Womens Pr) LPC InBook.

— Resist! Essays Against a Homophobic Culture. 242p. pap. 13.95 (*0-88961-197-1*, Pub. by Womens Pr) LPC InBook.

Oikawa, Mona, jt. auth. see Kobayashi.

Oikkonen, J. & Vaananen, J., eds. Logic Colloquium, 1990: ASL Summer Meeting in Helsinki. (Lecture Notes in Logic Ser.: Vol. 2). (Illus.). vii, 305p. 1994. 62.95 (*0-387-57094-2*) Spr-Verlag.

Oikonomides, Al. N. Abbreviations in Greek: Inscriptions, Papyri, Manuscripts & Early Printed Books. 214p. (Orig.). 1986. 25.00 (*0-89005-049-X*) Ares.

Oikonomides, Al N., ed. Supplementum Inscriptionum Atticarum V. 1984. 45.00 (*0-89005-531-9*) Ares.

— Supplementum Inscriptionum Atticarum IV. 1980. 45.00 (*0-89005-377-4*) Ares.

— Supplementum Inscriptionum Atticarum I. 1976. 45.00 (*0-89005-126-7*) Ares.

Oikonomides, Al. N., ed. Supplementum Inscriptionum Atticarum III. 1979. 45.00 (*0-89005-275-1*) Ares.

Oikonomides, Al N., ed. Supplementum Inscriptionum Atticarum II. 1978. 45.00 (*0-89005-249-2*) Ares.

Oikonomides, Al N., ed. see Hanno the Carthaginian.

Oikonomides, Nicolas. Byzantine Lead Seals. (Byzantine Collection Publications: No. 7). (Illus.). 28p. (Orig.). 1985. pap. 6.00 (*0-88402-144-0*) Dumbarton Oaks.

— Byzantium from the Ninth Century to the Fourth Crusade: Studies, Texts, Monuments. (Collected Studies: Vol. CS369). 207p. 1992. 117.95 (*0-86078-321-9*, Pub. by Variorum) Ashgate Pub Co.

— A Collection of Dated Byzantine Lead Seals. LC 86-6191. (Illus.). 176p. (Orig.). 1986. pap. text 15.00 (*0-88402-150-5*, OIDLP) Dumbarton Oaks.

Oikonomides, Nicolas, ed. Studies in Byzantine Sigillography, No. 2. LC 90-33600. (Illus.). 328p. 1990. pap. 45.00 (*0-88402-188-2*, OBS2P, Dumbarton Rsch Lib) Dumbarton Oaks.

— Studies in Byzantine Sigillography, No. 3. (Illus.). 244p. 1993. pap. 25.00 (*0-88402-218-8*) Dumbarton Oaks.

Oikonomides, Nicolas, jt. auth. see Nesbitt, John.

Oikonomides, Nicolas, jt. ed. see Nesbitt, John.

Oil & Colour Chemists' Association of Australia St. Surface Coatings: Paints & Their Applications, Vol. 2. 2nd ed. 480p. 1985. 85.00 (*0-412-26710-1*, NO. 9245) Chapman & Hall.

***Oil & Gas Direcorate Department of Trade & Industry Staff.** The Energy Report - The Brown Book, Vol. 2 2000. 140p. 2000. pap. 90.00 (*0-11-515499-X*, Pub. by Statnry Office) Balogh.

Oil & Gas Journal Staff. OGJ International Energy Statistics Sourcebook. 8th ed. 736p. 1996. 295.00 (*0-685-71331-8*, E1283) PennWell Bks.

Oil & Gas Journal Staff, ed. International Petroleum Encyclopedia, 1990. 400p. 1990. 55.00 (*0-87814-358-0*) PennWell Bks.

Oilfield Publications, Inc. Staff. Field Development Concepts of the World: Incorporating Offshore Production Concepts. (Illus.). 250p. 1997. pap. 111.00 (*1-870945-78-6*) Oilfield Publns.

— Gulf of Mexico Field Development Guide, 1998-1999: Offshore Texas, Louisiana, Mississippi, Alabama. (Illus.). 900p. 1997. pap. 416.00 (*1-870945-92-1*) Oilfield Publns.

— World Offshore Field Development Guide Vol. 3: North & South America. 2nd ed. (Illus.). 385p. 1997. pap. 332.00 (*1-870945-80-8*) Oilfield Publns.

Oilfield Publications, Inc. Staff, ed. Anchor Handling Tugs & Supply Vessels of the World, 1997-1998: The Nobile Denton Towing Vessel Register. (Illus.). 325p. 1997. pap. 280.00 (*1-870945-98-0*) Oilfield Publns.

— Mobile Drilling Units of the World, 1997-1998. (Illus.). 910p. 1997. pap. 383.00 (*1-870945-97-2*) Oilfield Publns.

Oilfield Publications Limited Staff. Construction Vessels of the World, 1998-1999. 4th ed. (Illus.). 456p. 1998. pap. 416.00 (*1-870945-18-2*, P1757) Oilfield Publns.

— European Continental Shelf Guide 1996/97. (Illus.). 500p. 1996. pap. 495.00 (*1-870945-82-4*) Oilfield Publns.

— Guidelines for Marine Operations. 185p. 1997. pap. 281.00 (*1-870945-95-6*) Oilfield Publns.

— Handbook for ROV Pilot/Technicians. 350p. 1997. pap. 162.00 (*1-870945-85-9*) Oilfield Publns.

— An Introduction to Offshore Maintenance. (Illus.). 256p. (C). 1992. pap. 140.00 (*1-870945-21-2*) Oilfield Publns.

— Introduction to Oil & Gas Joint Ventures. 162p. 1997. pap. 162.00 (*1-870945-96-4*) Oilfield Publns.

— Mobile Production Systems of the World. (Vessels of the World Ser.). (Illus.). 400p. (C). 1994. pap. 355.00 (*1-870945-66-2*) Oilfield Publns.

— The North Sea Atlas. (Illus.). 48p. 1994. pap. 145.00 (*1-870945-64-6*) Oilfield Publns.

— North Sea Facts. 2nd ed. (Illus.). 400p. 1993. pap. 125.00 (*1-870945-45-X*) Oilfield Publns.

— The North Sea Field Development Guide, 1997-1998 Vols. 1 & 2: Northern North Sea & Southern North Sea. 6th ed. (Illus.). 1400p. 1997. pap. 502.00 (*1-870945-88-3*) Oilfield Publns.

— The North Sea Subsea Atlas. (Illus.). 104p. (C). 1992. pap. 89.95 (*1-870945-34-4*) Oilfield Publns.

— The Offshore Field Development Atlas of North West Europe: 1998 Edition. 2nd ed. (Illus.). 48p. 1997. pap. 162.00 (*1-870945-84-0*) Oilfield Publns.

— Offshore Production Concepts. 2nd ed. (Illus.). 200p. 1993. pap. 155.00 (*1-870945-46-8*, P7496) Oilfield Publns.

— Platform Abandonment & Decommissioning: History & Techniques, Vol. 1. (Illus.). 200p. 1995. pap. 295.00 (*1-870945-74-3*) Oilfield Publns.

— Remotely Operated Vehicles of the World. (Vessels of the World Ser.). (Illus.). 400p. 1994. pap. 213.00 (*1-870945-59-X*) Oilfield Publns.

— Russia & the CIS Oil & Gas Industry Guide. 2nd ed. 550p. (C). 1997. pap. 1105.00 (*1-870945-31-X*) Oilfield Publns.

— Russia & the Commonwealth of Independent States Oil & Gas Industry Report. 2nd ed. (Illus.). 550p. 1994. pap. 1850.00 (*1-870945-58-1*) Oilfield Publns.

— Single Point Moorings of the World. 4th ed. (Illus.). 300p. 1994. pap. 285.00 (*1-870945-83-2*) Oilfield Publns.

— Standby Vessels of the World. (Vessels of the World Ser.). (Illus.). 300p. (C). 1992. pap. 195.00 (*1-870945-24-7*) Oilfield Publns.

— Survey Vessels of the World. (Vessels of the World Ser.). (Illus.). 240p. 1995. pap. 285.00 (*1-870945-72-7*) Oilfield Publns.

— The World Offshore Field Development Guide, 3. (World Offshore Field Development Guide Ser.). (Illus.). 1885p. 1995. pap. 695.00 (*1-870945-60-3*) Oilfield Publns.

— The World Offshore Field Development Guide Vol. 1: Africa, Mediterranean, & Middle East. (Illus.). 750p. 1995. pap. 350.00 (*1-870945-69-7*) Oilfield Publns.

— The World Offshore Field Development Guide Vol. 2: Asia, Indian Sub-Continent. 2nd ed. (World Offshore Field Development Guide Ser.). (Illus.). 385p. 1995. pap. 350.00 (*1-870945-70-0*) Oilfield Publns.

— World Oil & Gas Atlas, 1995-96 Edition. (Illus.). 36p. 1995. pap. 79.00 (*1-870945-73-5*) Oilfield Publns.

Oilfield Publishing Staff. Mobile Productions Systems of the World, 1997-1998. (Illus.). 400p. 1997. pap. 383.00 (*1-870945-93-X*) Oilfield Publns.

Oinas, Felix J. Basic Course in Estonian. 3rd rev. ed. LC 66-63527. (Uralic & Altaic Ser.: Vol. 54). (EST.). 393p. 1968. reprint ed. 39.00 (*0-87750-018-5*) Res Inst Inner Asian Studies.

Oinas, Felix J. Estonian, Basic. unabridged ed. 393p. 1993. text 295.00 incl. audio (*0-88432-460-5*, AFET10) Audio-Forum.

Oinas, Felix J. Estonian General Reader. 2nd rev. ed. LC 73-64410. (Uralic & Altaic Ser.: Vol. 34). 1972. write for info. (*0-87750-007-X*) Curzon Pr Ltd.

— Studies in Finnic Folklore. LC 84-80930. (Uralic & Altaic Ser.: Vol. 147). 219p. (Orig.). (C). 1985. pap. 30.00 (*0-933070-15-2*) Res Inst Inner Asian Studies.

Oinas, Felix J., ed. Heroic Epic & Saga: An Introduction to the World's Great Folk Epics. LC 77-9637. 383p. reprint ed. pap. 118.80 (*0-8357-3948-1*, 205704300004) Bks Demand.

Oinas, Felix J. & Soudakoff, Stephen. The Study of Russian Folklore. (Indian Univ. Folklore Ser.: No. 25). 341p. 1975. text 73.85 (*90-279-3147-X*) Mouton.

Oinas, Paivi, jt. ed. see Malecki, Edward J.

Oinckle, Alvin F. Jonathan Walker, the Man with the Branded Hand: An [SIC] Historical Biography. LC 98-90402. xi, 264p. 1998. 12.00 (*0-9664556-0-6*) L Slater Pubg.

Oines, Charles. Voidstriker. Lidbert, Paul A., ed. (Illus.). (YA). 1994. 8.95 (*1-929332-02-5*, CFE0050) Crunchy Frog.

***Oingman, Vera.** Aunt Vera's Bedtime Stories. 128p. (J). (gr. 1-6). 1999. 5.00 (*0-7392-0325-8*) Morris Pubng.

Oinstein. Israel Yearbook on Human Rights, 1995, Vol. 25. 1996. text 185.00 (*90-411-0258-2*) Kluwer Law Intl.

Oinstrin. May The Best Man Lose. 1999. text. write for info. (*0-312-00224-6*) St Martin.

Oiringel, I. M., jt. auth. see Tstovich, V. N.

Oirschot, J. T. Van, see Van Oirschot, J. T., ed.

Oirsouw, Robert R. Van, see Van Oirsouw, Robert R.

Oishi, Emily & Thompson, Sue. Before It's Too Late. 57p. (Orig.). 1996. pap., spiral bd., wbk. ed. 14.95 (*0-9657016-0-3*) Before Its Too Late.

Oishi, Sabine, jt. auth. see Simons, Jeanne.

Oishi, Sabine M., jt. auth. see Frey, James H.

Oishi, Shinsaburo, jt. auth. see Nakane, Chie.

Oisteanu, Valery. Do Not Defuse. 1980. pap. 2.50 (*0-9601870-2-2*) Pass.

— Pasport to Eternal Life. 68p. 1990. pap. 8.00 (*0-685-46237-4*) Pass.

— Passport to Eternal Life: Poetry, 1980-1990. Sheinman, Allen J., ed. (Illus.). 72p. (Orig.). 1990. pap. text 8.00 (*0-685-45645-5*) Pass.

Oistenau, Valery. Underground Shadows. 1977. pap. 1.50 (*0-9601870-0-6*) Pass.

Oister, Lisa, ed. see Fowler, Raymond E.

Oiticica, Helio. Helio Oiticica. 280p. 1992. pap. 45.00 (*90-73362-18-0*, Pub. by Witte De With CFCA) Dist Art Pubs.

Oiticica, Helio, et al. Cahier 2: Mutti-Vati Kultur. (Cahiers Ser.). 210p. 1995. pap. 29.95 (*90-73362-28-8*) Dist Art Pubs.

***Oittinen, Ritta.** Translating for Children. (Children's Literature & Culture Ser.: 11). 275p. 2000. 60.00 (*0-8153-3335-8*) Garland.

Oiwa, Keibo, jt. auth. see Suzuki, David.

Oiwa, Keibo, jt. auth. see Suzuki, David T.

Oizumi, Akio. A Bibliography of Writings on Chaucer's English. 112p. 1995. write for info. (*3-487-10007-X*) G Olms Pubs.

— Towards a Comprehensive Concordance to the Works of Geoffrey Chaucer. (GER.). 22p. 1995. write for info. (*3-487-09976-4*) G Olms Pubs.

Oizumi, Akio, ed. A Rhyme Concordance to the Poetical Works of Geoffrey Chaucer. (Supplement Ser.: Vol. XI). 1994. write for info. (*3-487-09821-0*) G Olms Pubs.

— A Rhyme Concordance to the Poetical Works of Geoffrey Chaucer. (Supplement Ser.: Vol. XII). 1994. write for info. (*3-487-09822-9*) G Olms Pubs.

Oizumi, Akio, jt. ed. see Fisiak, Jacek.

Oizumi, Akio, ed. A Complete Concordance to the Works of Geoffrey Chaucer, 10 vols., Set. (Alpha-Omega Series C. English Authors: Vol. 1). 9510p. 1992. 2587.00 incl. 3.5 hd (*3-487-09412-6*) G Olms Pubs.

Oja. Student Writing in Philosophy: A Companion to Cover & Garns (Custom Publication) (C). 1990. pap. 8.44 (*0-07-013274-7*) McGraw.

Oja, et al. E-Course Microsoft Office 95. 512p. (C). 1997. pap., mass mkt. 52.95 incl. cd-rom (*0-7600-5372-3*) Course Tech.

— E-Course Microsoft Office 97. 512p. (C). 1997. pap., mass mkt. 38.50 incl. cd-rom (*0-7600-5360-X*) Course Tech.

Oja, jt. auth. see Carey.

Oja, jt. auth. see Parson.

Oja, jt. auth. see Parsons.

Oja, Carol J. Colin McPhee: Composer in Two Worlds. LC 89-600387. (Studies of American Musicians). (Illus.). 376p. 1990. text 42.00 (*0-87474-732-5*) Smithsonian.

***Oja, Carol J.** Making Music Modern: New York in the 1920s. LC 99-52604. 512p. 2000. 45.00 (*0-19-505849-6*) OUP.

Oja, Carol J., ed. American Music Recordings: A Discography of 20th-Century U. S. Composers. LC 82-83008. 368p. (Orig.). 1982. pap. 60.00 (*0-914678-19-1*) Inst Am Music.

— Stravinsky in Modern Music. LC 82-1473. (Music Reprint Ser.). 1982. reprint ed. 39.50 (*0-306-76108-4*) Da Capo.

Oja, Dan. E-Course Microsoft PowerPoint 97: E-Course Microsoft PowerPoint 7. 96p. (C). 1997. teacher ed. 18.50 (*0-7600-5369-3*) Course Tech.

— E-Course Microsoft PowerPoint 7. 96p. (C). 1997. pap., mass mkt. 21.95 incl. cd-rom (*0-7600-5395-2*) Course Tech.

— E-Course Microsoft PowerPoint 97. 10th ed. 96p. (C). 1997. pap., mass mkt. 21.95 incl. cd-rom (*0-7600-5368-5*) Course Tech.

— E-Course Netscape Navigator. 10th ed. 144p. (C). 1997. pap., mass mkt. 21.95 incl. cd-rom (*0-7600-5370-7*) Course Tech.

***Oja, Dan & Parsons, June.** Computer Concepts: Illustrated Brief. 3rd ed. (C). 2000. pap. 12.95 (*0-619-01739-2*) Course Tech.

— Microsoft Windows 95 New Perspectives. (C). 1997. spiral bd. 36.00 (*0-7600-7264-7*) Thomson Learn.

Oja, Dan & Parsons, June J. E-Course Microsoft Excel 97: E-Course Microsoft Excel 7. 144p. (C). 1997. teacher ed. 18.50 (*0-7600-5365-0*) Course Tech.

— E-Course Microsoft Excel 97. 144p. (C). 1997. pap., mass mkt. 19.75 incl. cd-rom (*0-7600-5364-2*) Course Tech.

Oja, Dan & Zeanchock, John. E-Course Microsoft Word 97. 144p. (C). 1997. teacher ed. 18.50 (*0-7600-5363-4*) Course Tech.

— E-Course Microsoft Word 97. 10th ed. 144p. (C). 1997. pap., mass mkt. 19.75 incl. cd-rom (*0-7600-5362-6*) Course Tech.

Oja, Dan, et al. E-Course Microsoft Access 97. 10th ed. 144p. (C). 1997. pap., mass mkt. 26.95 incl. cd-rom (*0-7600-5366-9*) Course Tech.

— E-Course Microsoft Windows 95: E-Course Microsoft Windows NT Workstation 4.0. 96p. (C). 1997. teacher ed. 18.50 (*0-7600-5359-6*); teacher ed. 18.50 (*0-7600-5402-9*) Course Tech.

— E-Course Microsoft Windows NT Workstation 4.0. 10th ed. 96p. (C). 1997. pap., mass mkt. 21.95 incl. cd-rom (*0-7600-5401-0*) Course Tech.

— E-Course Microsoft Windows 95. 10th ed. 96p. (C). 1997. pap., mass mkt. 21.95 incl. cd-rom (*0-7600-5358-8*) Course Tech.

Oja, Dan, jt. auth. see Parsons, June.

Oja, Dan, jt. auth. see Parsons, June J.

Oja, Dan, jt. auth. see Parsons, June Jamrich.

***Oja, Erkki & Kaski, Samuel.** Kohonen Maps LC 99-35682. 1999. write for info. (*0-444-50270-X*) Elsevier.

Oja, V., jt. auth. see Laisk, A.

Ojaide, Tanure. The Blood of Peace & Other Poems. (African Writers Ser.). 128p. (Orig.). (C). 1991. pap. 8.95 (*0-435-91193-7*, 91193) Heinemann.

— Children of Iroko. 1973. per. 3.00 (*0-912678-09-7*, Greenfld Rev Pr) Greenfld Rev Lit.

— The Eagle's Vision. LC 87-46316. 104p. (Orig.). 1987. pap., per. 8.00 (*0-916418-66-9*) Lotus.

— Great Boys: An African Childhood. LC 97-13297. 209p. 1997. write for info. (*0-86543-574-X*) Africa World.

— Invoking the Warrior Spirit: New & Selected Poems. LC 98-41398. 246p. 1998. 59.95 (*0-86543-710-6*); pap. 18.95 (*0-86543-711-4*) Africa World.

— Labyrinths of the Delta. 1986. 9.95 (*0-912678-67-4*, Greenfld Rev Pr) Greenfld Rev Lit.

— Poetic Imagination in Black Africa: Essays on African Poetry. LC 96-16122. 168p. (Orig.). 1996. pap. 20.00 (*0-89089-855-3*) Carolina Acad Pr.

***Ojaide, Tanure & Sallah, Tijan M., eds.** The New African Poetry. LC 99-29889. (Three Continents Ser.). 234p. 2000. 49.95 (*0-89410-879-4*, Three Contnts) L Rienner.

— The New African Poetry: An Anthology. 233p. 2000. pap. 17.95 (*0-89410-891-3*, Three Contnts) L Rienner.

Ojakangas, Beatrice. The Great Scandinavian Baking Book. LC 99-29064. (Illus.). 328p. 1999. pap. 18.95 (*0-8166-3496-3*, Pub. by U of Minn Pr) Chicago Distribution Ctr.

***Ojakangas, Beatrice.** Light & Easy Baking. (Illus.). 240p. 2000. 9.99 (*0-517-20962-4*) Random Hse Value.

Ojakangas, Beatrice. Whole Grain Breads by Hand Or Machine. LC 98-16927. 416p. 1998. 27.50 (*0-02-861847-5*) Macmillan.

O

Ojakangas, Beatrice A. Best of Honey Recipes. 108p. 1992. 5.95 (*0-934860-68-8*) Adventure Pubns.
— The Best of Pancake & Waffle Recipes. 108p. (Orig.). 1992. pap. 5.95 (*0-934860-59-9*) Adventure Pubns.
— The Best of the Liberated Cook. 96p. 1991. pap. 9.95 (*0-9609408-0-4*) Adventure Pubns.
— The Best of Wild Rice Recipes. 108p. 1989. pap. 5.95 (*0-934860-56-4*) Adventure Pubns.
— The Best of Wild Rice Recipes-Giftpack. 1989. pap. 13.95 (*0-934860-58-0*) Adventure Pubns.
— The Book of Heartland Cooking. (Illus.). 120p. 1992. pap. 11.95 (*1-55788-073-5*, HP Books) Berkley Pub.
— Finnish Cook Book. (International Cookbook Ser.). 1964. 14.00 (*0-517-50111-2*, Crown) Crown Pub Group.
— Light Muffins: 60 Recipes for Sweet & Savory Low-Fat Muffins & Spreads. LC 94-42664. 96p. 1995. 12.00 (*0-517-70066-2*) C Potter.
— Pot Pies: Forty Savory Suppers. LC 92-16447. 112p. 1993. 14.00 (*0-517-58573-1*) C Potter.
Ojakangas, Beatrice A., ed. Fantastically Finnish: Recipes & Traditions. LC 85-61029. (Illus.). 88p. 1985. pap. 8.95 (*0-941016-22-6*) Penfield.
Ojakangas, R. W., et al, eds. Middle Proterozoic to Cambrian Rifting, Central North America. LC 96-48160. (Special Papers: No. 312). 1997. pap. 100.00 (*0-8137-2312-4*) Geol Soc.
Ojakangas, Richard W., ed. see International Conference on Basement Tectonics Sta.
Ojala, Jeanne A. Auguste de Colbert: Aristocratic Survival in an Era of Upheaval, 1793-1809. LC 79-4872. 213p. reprint ed. pap. 66.10 (*0-8357-5883-4*, 202716900054) Bks Demand.
Ojala, Jeanne A. & Ojala, William T. Madame de Sevigne: A Seventeenth-Century Life. LC 89-37007. (Women's Ser.). 234p. 1990. 19.50 (*0-85496-169-0*) Berg Pubs.
Ojala, William T., jt. auth. see Ojala, Jeanne A.
Ojalvo, Morris. Thin-Walled Bars with Open Profiles. Straw, Richard, ed. LC 90-60103. (Illus.). 208p. (C). 1990. lib. bdg. 27.50 (*0-9627025-0-1*) Olive Press.
Ojanen, Hanna. The Plurality of Truth: A Critique of Research on the State & European Integration. LC 98-24497. 377p. 1998. text 72.95 (*1-84014-402-5*, JA86.O46, Pub. by Ashgate Pub) Ashgate Pub Co.
Ojanpera, Tero. Wideband CDMA for Third Generation Mobile Communications: Wireless Communications Engineering. Prasad, Ramjee, ed. LC 98-33857. 320p. 1998. 99.00 (*0-89006-735-X*) Artech Hse.
Ojea, Patricia & Quigley, Barbara. Women's Studies, 1999-2000. (Annual Ser.). (Illus.). 240p. 1998. pap. text 12.25 (*0-07-303197-6*, Dshkn McG-Hill) McGrw-H Hghr Educ.
Ojeda, Almerindo E. Linguistic Individuals. LC 92-5935. (Center for the Study of Language & Information-Lecture Notes Ser.: No. 31). 200p. (C). 1993. 54.95 (*0-937073-85-7*); pap. 18.95 (*0-937073-84-9*) CSLI.
Ojeda, Almerindo E., jt. ed. see Huck, Geoffrey J.
Ojeda, Almerindo E., jt. ed. see Kreiman, Jody.
Ojeda-Castaneda, Jorge & Gomez-Reino, Carlos. Selected Papers on Zone Plates. LC 96-9781. (SPIE Milestone Ser.). 1996. 100.00 (*0-8194-2302-5*, MS128) SPIE.
Ojeda, Enriave. Jorge Carrera Andrade: Introduccion a Su Vida. 1972. 16.95 (*0-88303-003-9*); pap. 12.95 (*0-685-73209-6*) E Torres & Sons.
Ojeda, Felix. Programa para Todo el Pueblo. (SPA.). 1966. pap. 0.25 (*0-87898-013-X*) New Outlook.
Ojeda, Felix, ed. Vito Marcantonio y Puerto Rico. 156p. 1978. pap. 6.95 (*0-940238-40-3*) Ediciones Huracan.
Ojeda, Linda. Her Healthy Heart: A Woman's Guide to Preventing & Reversing Heart Disease Naturally. LC 98-35412. 352p. 1998. pap. 14.95 (*0-89793-225-0*) Hunter Hse.
— Her Healthy Heart: A Woman's Guide to Preventing & Reversing Heart Disease Naturally. LC 98-35412. (Illus.). 352p. 1998. 24.95 (*0-89793-226-9*) Hunter Hse.
— Menopause Without Medicine. 3rd ed. LC 95-2607. (Illus.). 352p. 1995. 23.95 (*0-89793-178-5*); pap. 14.95 (*0-89793-177-7*) Hunter Hse.
***Ojeda, Linda.** Menopause Without Medicine. 4th rev. ed. (Illus.). 352p. 2000. 25.95 (*0-89793-282-X*, Pub. by Hunter Hse) Publishers Group.
— Menopause Without Medicine. 4th rev. ed. LC 00-38884. (Illus.). 352p. 2000. pap. 15.95 (*0-89793-281-1*, Pub. by Hunter Hse) Publishers Group.
Ojeda, Linda. Safe Dieting for Teens. LC 92-26432. 120p. (Orig.). (YA). (gr. 7-12). 1992. pap. 9.95 (*0-89793-113-0*) Hunter Hse.
Ojeda, Linda, jt. auth. see Liew, Lana.
Ojeda, Osacr R. The New American House: Innovations in Residential Design & Construction. (Illus.). 264p. 1995. pap. 55.00 (*0-8230-3163-2*) Watsn-Guptill.
Ojeda, Oscar. Moore, Ruble & Yudell: Houses & Housing. 1994. pap. 29.99 (*1-56496-279-2*) Rockport Pubs.
Ojeda, Oscar R. Alberto Rebecchi. (Art & Architecture Ser.). (Illus.). 132p. 1999. pap. 24.99 (*1-56496-449-3*) Rockport Pubs.
— Alfredo De Vido Architects. (Ten Houses Ser.). (Illus.). 108p. 1998. pap. 19.99 (*1-56496-409-4*) Rockport Pubs.
— Campo Baeza. (Contemporary World Architects Ser.: Vol. 4). (Illus.). 132p. 1996. pap. 19.99 (*1-56496-340-3*) Rockport Pubs.
— Central Office of Architecture. (Contemporary World Architects Ser.). (Illus.). 132p. 1998. pap. 19.99 (*1-56496-407-8*) Rockport Pubs.
— Contemporary World Architects: James Cutler Architects. (Contemporary World Architects Ser.: Vol. 5). (Illus.). 132p. 1996. pap. 19.99 (*1-56496-341-1*) Rockport Pubs.
— Enrique Brown. (Ten Houses Ser.). (Illus.). 108p. (Orig.). 1997. pap. 19.99 (*1-56496-391-8*) Rockport Pubs.
— Gwathmey Siegel Associates. (Ten Houses Ser.). 108p. 1995. pap. 19.99 (*1-56496-216-4*) Rockport Pubs.
— Henri Ciriani. (Illus.). 132p. 1997. pap. text 19.99 (*1-56496-234-2*) Rockport Pubs.
— Jorge Peralta Urquiza. (Art & Architecture Ser.). (Illus.). 132p. 1999. pap. 24.99 (*1-56496-490-6*) Rockport Pubs.
— Kuwabara Payne McKenna Blumberg. (Contemporary World Architects Ser.). (Illus.). 132p. 1997. pap. 19.99 (*1-56496-408-6*) Rockport Pubs.
— Lacroze-Miguens-Prati. (Ten Houses Ser.). (Illus.). 108p. 1996. pap. 19.99 (*1-56496-326-8*) Rockport Pubs.
— Lake/Flato Architects. (Illus.). 132p. 1995. pap. 19.99 (*1-56496-233-4*) Rockport Pubs.
***Ojeda, Oscar R.** Office D. A. (Contemporary World Architects Ser.). (Illus.). 132p. 1999. pap. 25.00 (*1-56496-546-5*) Rockport Pubs.
Ojeda, Oscar R. Peter Forbes Architects & Associates. (Ten Houses Ser.). 1995. 19.99 (*1-56496-183-4*) Rockport Pubs.
— Peter L. Gluck & Partners. (Ten Houses Ser.). (Illus.). 108p. 1997. pap. 19.99 (*1-56496-314-4*) Rockport Pubs.
— Phoenix Central Library: Bruder/DWL Architects. (Single Building Ser.). (Illus.). 120p. 1999. pap. 19.99 (*1-56496-525-2*) Rockport Pubs.
— Robert Marino. (Contemporary World Architects Ser.). (Illus.). 132p. 1999. pap. 19.99 (*1-56496-452-3*) Rockport Pubs.
— Souto Moura. (Ten Houses Ser.). (Illus.). 108p. (Orig.). 1997. pap. 19.99 (*1-56496-394-2*) Rockport Pubs.
— Ten Houses: Christian De Groote. (Ten Houses Ser.). (Illus.). 108p. 1999. pap. 19.99 (*1-56496-492-2*) Rockport Pubs.
— Type/Variant House: Vincent James. (Single Building Ser.). (Illus.). 132p. 1999. pap. 25.00 (*1-56496-523-6*) Rockport Pubs.
— Whanki Museum: Kyu Sung Woo. (Single Building Ser.). (Illus.). 120p. 1998. pap. 19.99 (*1-56496-524-4*) Rockport Pubs.
Ojeda, Oscar R., ed. Adrian Luchini. (Contemporary World Architects Ser.). (Illus.). 132p. 1999. pap. 19.99 (*1-56496-503-1*) Rockport Pubs.
— Lorcan O'Herlihy. (Contemporary World Architects Ser.). (Illus.). 132p. 1999. pap. 19.99 (*1-56496-504-X*) Rockport Pubs.
— Miller/Hull Partnership. (Ten Houses Ser.). (Illus.). 108p. 1999. pap. 25.00 (*1-56496-450-7*) Rockport Pubs.
— The New American House 2: Innovations in Residential Design & Construction: 30 Case Studies. 2nd ed. (Illus.). 264p. 1997. 55.00 (*0-8230-3164-0*) Watsn-Guptill.
— Pasanella Klein Stolzman & Berg. (Contemporary World Architects Ser.). (Illus.). 132p. 1999. pap. 19.99 (*1-56496-505-8*) Rockport Pubs.
— Richter et Dahl Rocha. (Contemporary World Architects Ser.). (Illus.). 132p. 1999. pap. 19.99 (*1-56496-451-5*) Rockport Pubs.
— Wheeler Kearns Architects. (Ten Houses Ser.). (Illus.). 124p. 1999. pap. 19.99 (*1-56496-493-0*) Rockport Pubs.
Ojeda, Oscar R. & Guerra, Lucas H. Hyper-Realistic: Computer-Generated Architectural Renderings. 192p. write for info. incl. cd-rom (*1-56496-281-4*) Rockport Pubs.
— Moore Ruble Yudell: Campus & Community. (Illus.). 192p. 1997. 39.99 (*1-56496-230-X*) Rockport Pubs.
Ojeda, Oscar R., ed. see Fuksas, Massimiliano.
Ojeda, Oscar R., ed. see Kagan, Michel.
Ojeda, Oscar Riera. Burnett Studio Residence. (Single Building Ser.). (Illus.). 120p. 2000. pap. 25.00 (*1-56496-522-8*) Rockport Pubs.
***Ojeda, Oscar Riera.** Contemporary World Architects: Jose Paolo Dos Santos. 2000. pap. 25.00 (*1-56496-573-2*) Rockport Pubs.
Ojeda, Oscar Riera. Greenway Plaza Apartment. (Single Building Ser.). (Illus.). 120p. 2000. pap. 25.00 (*1-56496-520-1*) Rockport Pubs.
***Ojeda, Oscar Riera.** Hyper-Realistic: Computer Generated Architectural Rendering, 2000. pap. text 25.00 (*1-56496-686-0*) Rockport Pubs.
Ojeda, Oscar Riera. Ledge House: Bohlin Cywinski Jackson. (Single Building Ser.). 1999. pap. text 19.99 (*1-56496-521-X*) Rockport Pubs.
***Ojeda, Oscar Riera.** National Airport Terminal. (Single Building Ser.). (Illus.). 120p. 2000. pap. 25.00 (*1-56496-545-7*) Rockport Pubs.
Ojeda, Oscar Riera. Ten Houses: Ace Architects. (Ten Houses Ser.). (Illus.). 108p. 1999. pap. text 19.99 (*1-56496-491-4*) Rockport Pubs.
***Ojeda, Oscar Riera.** Wheeler Kearn's Architects. (Ten Houses Ser.). 1999. pap. 25.00 (*1-56496-538-4*) Rockport Pubs.
***Ojeda, Oscar Riera, compiled by.** Olson Sundberg Kundig Allen Architects: Architecture, Art & Craft. (Illus.). 256p. 2000. 65.00 (*1-58093-078-6*, Pub. by Monacelli Pr) Penguin Putnam.
Ojeda, Raquel, ed. see Schwartz, Robert M.
Ojeda Reyes, Felix. Peregrinos de la Libertad. (SPA., Illus.). 272p. 1992. pap. 29.95 (*0-8477-5664-5*) U of PR Pr.
Ojeda, Sergio R., jt. ed. see Griffin, James E.
Ojeda, Sergio R., jt. ed. see Griffin, James.
Ojedo, Oscar R. & Guerra, Lucas H. Hyper-Realistic: Computer-Generated Architectural Renderings. 192p. 1996. 39.99 (*1-56496-184-2*) Rockport Pubs.
Ojemann, George A., jt. auth. see Calvin, William H.
Ojemann, Robert G., et al. Surgical Management of Neurovascular Disease. 3rd ed. LC 94-40513. (Illus.). 624p. 1995. 175.00 (*0-683-06629-3*) Lppncott W & W.
Ojendal, Joakim. Regionalization in East Asia-Pacific? An Elusive Process. 57p. (Orig.). (C). 1999. pap. text 20.00 (*0-7881-7403-7*) DIANE Pub.
— Regionalization in East Asia-Pacific? An Elusive Process. (World Development Studies: No. 11). 57p. (Orig.). 1997. pap. 12.00 (*952-9520-49-2*) UN.
Ojetti, Ugo. As They Seemed to Me. Furst, H., tr. LC 68-54364. (Essay Index Reprint Ser.). 1977. 20.95 (*0-8369-0751-5*) Ayer.
Ojha, Brahm S & Singh, Jasbir. Resource Planning Atlas. (C). 1993. text 50.00 (*81-85135-73-8*) S Asia.
Ojha, D. C. Computer Application in Library & Information Science. 1995. pap. 160.00 (*81-7233-123-1*, Pub. by Scientific Pubs) St Mut.
Ojha, D. C., jt. ed. see Sharma, C. D.
Ojha, Divakar & Kumar, Ashok. Panchakrma Therapy in Ayurveda. 219p. 1979. pap. 18.95 (*0-89744-057-9*) Auromere.
Ojha, E. Raj. Agricultural Terracing Development Perspectives. 1997. pap. 66.00 (*0-7855-7359-3*, Pub. by Ratna Pustak Bhandar) St Mut.
Ojha, G. K. Predictive Astrology of the Hindus. (Illus.). 347p. 1990. 19.95 (*0-318-36380-1*) Asia Bk Corp.
Ojha, Pandit G., et al. Aspects in Vedic Astrology. 180p. 1993. pap. 13.95 (*1-878423-15-0*) Morson Pub.
Ojha, Purana C. Asvattha in Every Day Life as Related in Puranas. (C). 1991. 30.00 (*81-85067-64-3*, Pub. by Sundeep Prak) S Asia.
Ojha, S. K. Flight Performance of the Aircraft. LC 95-4456. (Education Ser.). 500p. (C). 1995. text 84.95 (*1-56347-113-2*, 13-2) AIAA.
Oji, Hiroi. Samurai Crusader: Sunrise over Shanghai. (Illus.). 240p. 1997. pap. text 16.95 (*1-56931-236-2*, Viz Comics) Viz Commns Inc.
— Samurai Crusader: The Kumomaru Chronicles. (Illus.). 224p. 1996. pap. text 15.95 (*1-56931-130-7*) Viz Commns Inc.
— Way of the Dragon. (Samurai Crusader Ser.). (Illus.). 232p. 1997. pap. text 15.95 (*1-56931-164-1*, Viz Comics) Viz Commns Inc.
Ojiambo, Joseph B., ed. see Tallman, Julie I.
***Ojima, Iwao.** Catalytic Asymmetric Synthesis. 2nd ed. 550p. 2000. 89.95 (*0-471-29805-0*) Wiley.
Ojima, Iwao, ed. Catalytic Asymmetric Synthesis. LC 93-19389. (Illus.). xviii, 476p. 1993. 110.00 (*1-56081-532-9*, Wiley-VCH) Wiley.
Ojima, Iwao, ed. Catalytic Asymmetric Synthesis. 496p. 1995. pap. 84.95 (*0-471-18625-2*, Wiley-VCH) Wiley.
Ojima, Iwao, ed. Catalytic Asymmetric Synthesis. (Illus.). xviii, 476p. 1995. pap. 59.95 (*1-56081-911-1*, Wiley-VCH) Wiley.
Ojima, Iwao, et al, eds. Biomedical Frontiers of Fluorine Chemistry, Vol. 639. LC 96-24784. (ACS Symposium Ser.: No. 639). (Illus.). 368p. 1996. text 105.00 (*0-8412-3442-6*, Pub. by Am Chemical) OUP.
Ojima, Iwao & Nakanishi, N. Covariant Operator Formalism of Gauge Theories & Quantum Gravity. 452p. 1990. text 85.00 (*9971-5-0238-0*); pap. text 39.00 (*9971-5-0239-9*) World Scientific Pub.
Ojinmah, Umelo. Witi Ihimaera: A Changing Vision. 158p. 1996. pap. 24.95 (*0-908569-57-2*, Pub. by Univ Otago Pr) Intl Spec Bk.
Ojior, Omoh J. Africa & Africans in the Diaspora: An Evaluation of the Impact They Have on Each Other. unabridged ed. 200p. (Orig.). 1996. pap. 12.00 (*1-56411-139-3*, 4BBG0143) Untd Bros & Sis.
***Ojo-Ade, Femi.** Death of a Myth: Critical Essays on Nigeria. LC 99-30086. 1999. write for info. (*0-86543-790-4*) Africa World.
Ojo-Ade, Femi. Rene Maran: The Black Frenchman: A Biocritical Study. LC 81-51663. (Illus.). 277p. 1984. 18.00 (*1-57889-052-7*); pap. 12.00 (*1-57889-051-9*) Passeggiata.
***Ojo-Ade, Femi.** Saro Wiwa: A Bio-Critical Study. 300p. 1999. pap. 22.50 (*0-9663837-1-0*, ALP.FOA) Africana Leg Pr.
Ojo-Ade, Femi, ed. Of Dreams Deferred, Dead or Alive: African Perspectives on African-American Writers, 180. LC 95-45960. (Contributions in Afro-American & African Studies: Vol. 180). 208p. 1996. 59.95 (*0-313-26475-9*, Greenwood Pr) Greenwood.
Ojo, Bamidele A. Human Rights & the New World Order: Questions of Universality, Acceptability & Human Diversity. LC 97-209605. 245p. (C). 1997. lib. bdg. 75.00 (*1-56072-438-2*) Nova Sci Pubs.
Ojo, Bamidele A., ed. Contemporary African Politics: A Comparative Study of Political Transition to Democratic Legitimacy. LC 98-32387. 176p. 1999. 47.00 (*0-7618-1327-6*); pap. 27.50 (*0-7618-1328-4*) U Pr of Amer.
Ojo-Igbinoba, M. E. The Practice of Conservation of Library Materials in Sub-Saharan Africa. 61p. 1993. 7.00 (*0-941934-65-9*) Indiana Africa.
Ojo, Olatunde J., et al. African International Relations. LC 85-794. 192p. 1985. reprint ed. pap. 59.60 (*0-608-03609-9*, 206443200009) Bks Demand.
Ojo, Olatunde J., jt. ed. see Koehn, Peter H.
Ojo, Onukada A. In the Eyes of Time. (Illus.). 224p. 1997. pap. write for info. (*1-57579-074-2*) Pine Hill Pr.
Ojofeitimi, jt. auth. see Oke, O. L.
Ojugo. Practical Food & Beverage Cost Control. LC 98-25767. (Food & Hospitality Ser.). 432p. (C). 1998. text 57.95 (*0-7668-0038-5*) Delmar.
Ok, Tae H., et al, eds. Change & Challenge on the Korean Peninsula: Developments, Trends, & Issues. (Asian Studies Report). 81p. (C). 1996. pap. text 10.95 (*0-89206-342-4*) CSIS.
OK-9, jt. auth. see Tamiran, David.
Oka. Deformation & Progressive Failure in Geomechanics (IS-NAGDYA'97) LC 97-224403. 952p. 1997. text 225.00 (*0-08-042838-X*) Elsevier.
Oka, Christine K., jt. auth. see LaGuardia, Cheryl.
Oka, Hisao, et al, eds. Chemical Analysis for Antibiotics Used in Agriculture. LC 95-232303. 452p. 1995. pap. 95.00 (*0-935584-57-9*) AOAC Intl.
Oka, Isaburo. Hiroshige: Japan's Great Landscape Artist. 1997. pap. text 25.00 (*4-7700-2121-6*) FS&G.
— Hiroshige: Japan's Great Landscape Artist. Carpenter, Juliet W., tr. 96p. 1992. 32.00 (*4-7700-1658-1*) Kodansha.
Oka, K. Collected Papers. 245p. 1984. 169.00 (*0-387-13240-6*) Spr-Verlag.
Oka, Melvin S. & Rupp, Randall G., eds. Cell Biology & Biotechnology: Novel Approaches to Increased Cellular Productivity. LC 92-37369. 176p. 1993. 99.00 (*0-387-97951-4*) Spr-Verlag.
Oka, Sheoten. Cardiovascular Hemorheology. LC 80-41338. 220p. reprint ed. pap. 62.70 (*0-608-15761-9*, 2031702) Bks Demand.
Oka, Takashi. Prying Open the Door: Foreign Workers in Japan. LC 94-20944. (Contemporary Issue Papers: Vol. 2). 83p. (C). 1994. pap. 8.95 (*0-87003-053-1*) Carnegie Endow.
Oka, Takeshi, tr. see Tomonaga.
Oka, Yasu, et al, eds. Clinical Transesophageal Echocardiography: A Problem-Oriented Approach. LC 95-35651. (Illus.). 382p. 1995. text 156.00. (*0-397-51426-3*) Lppncott W & W.
Oka, Yasu & Goldiner, Paul L. Transesophageal Echocardiography. LC 91-42380. (Illus.). 364p. 1992. reprint ed. pap. 112.90 (*0-608-05818-1*, 205978300007) Bks Demand.
Okabayashi, Hidekazu, et al, eds. Stress Induced Phenomena in Metallization: Fourth International Workshop. LC 97-77868. (AIP Conference Proceedings Ser.: Vol. 418). (Illus.). ix, 519 p. 1998. 135.00 (*1-56396-682-4*) Am Inst Physics.
Okabayashi, S. Visual Optics of Head-Up Displays (HUDs) in Automotive Applications. 140p. 1996. pap. text 36.00 (*2-88449-033-7*) Gordon & Breach.
Okabe, Hideo. Photochemistry of Small Molecules. LC 78-6704. (Illus.). 447p. reprint ed. pap. 138.60 (*0-608-17420-3*, 205645500067) Bks Demand.
Okabe, Michiko. Spatial Tessallation. 2nd ed. LC 99-13149. 1999. text 120.00 (*0-471-98635-6*) Wiley.
Okabe, Mitsuaki. The Structure of the Japanese Economy: Changes in the Domestic & International Character. LC 94-17219. (Studies in the Modern Japanese Economy). 1994. text 59.95 (*0-312-12219-5*) St Martin.
Okabe, Mitsuaki, jt. ed. see Suzuki, Yoshio.
Okabe, S. & Takeuchi, K., eds. International Conference on Ulcer Research, 8th Meeting, Kyoto-Japan, November 1994: Abstracts. (Journal: Digestion: Vol. 55, Supplement 2, 1994). (Illus.). ii, 62p. 1994. pap. 28.00 (*3-8055-6069-9*) S Karger.
Okada. Western Writers in Japan. LC 98-39735. 224p. 1999. text 59.95 (*0-312-21670-X*) St Martin.
Okada, Amina & Joshi, M. C. Taj Mahal. (Illus.). 240p. 1993. 75.00 (*1-55859-617-8*) Abbeville Pr.
Okada, Barbara T. Symbol & Substance in Japanese Lacquer: Lacquer Boxes from the Collection of Elaine Ehrenkranz. (Illus.). 192p. 1995. 60.00 (*0-8348-0316-X*) Weatherhill.
Okada, Barbara T. & Okada, Nancy T. Do's & Don'ts for the Japanese Businessman Abroad. 130p. 1973. pap. text 4.75 (*0-88345-208-1*, 18133) Prentice ESL.
Okada, Florence, tr. see Kikuchi, Shigeo.
Okada, H. Richard. Figures of Resistance: Language, Poetry, & Narrating in The Tale of the Genji & Other Mid-Heian Texts. LC 91-13312. (Post-Contemporary Interventions Ser.). 400p. 1992. text 59.95 (*0-8223-1185-2*); pap. text 23.95 (*0-8223-1192-5*) Duke.
***Okada, H. Richard & Mateer, Niall J.** Cretaceous Environments of Asia. LC 00-23203. (Developments in Palaeontology & Stratigraphy Ser.). 264p. 2000. 154.50 (*0-444-50276-9*) Elsevier.
Okada, Jo, jt. auth. see Shiraichi, Masami.
Okada, John. No-No Boy. LC 79-55834. 176p. 1980. reprint ed. pap. 14.95 (*0-295-95525-2*) U of Wash Pr.
Okada, K., et al. Mullite & Mullite Ceramics. LC 93-36459. 266p. 1994. 265.00 (*0-471-94249-9*) Wiley.
Okada, Kazuo & Ogata, Hiromaru, eds. Shock, from Molecular & Cellular Level to Whole Body: Proceedings of the Third International Shock Congress, Shock '95, Hamamatsu, Japan, 21-23 October 1995. LC 96-5881. (International Congress Ser.: No. 1102). 410p. 1996. 194.50 (*0-444-82285-2*) Elsevier.
Okada, M., jt. auth. see Suzuki, M.
Okada, Miyo. Language of Courtesy: Honorific Speech of Japanese. 97p. 1954. 8.95 (*0-88710-041-4*) Yale Far Eastern Pubns.
Okada, Mokichi. Health & the New Civilization. LC 91-60112. 96p. (Orig.). 1991. pap. 3.75 (*0-9629183-0-X*) Johrei Fellow.
Okada, Nancy T., jt. auth. see Okada, Barbara T.
Okada, Shintaro, et al. Biochemical Basis of Inherited Human Disease. 1973. 32.50 (*0-8422-7087-6*) Irvington.
Okada, T. S. Transdifferentiation: Flexibility in Cell Differentiation. (Illus.). 248p. 1991. 105.00 (*0-19-854281-X*) OUP.
***Okada, Y., ed.** Japan's Industrial Technology Development: The Role of Cooperative Learning & Institutions. (Illus.). x, 202p. 1999. pap. 74.95 (*4-431-70265-2*) Spr-Verlag.
Okada, Y., ed. The Role of Adenosine in the Nervous System: Proceedings of an International Symposium on Adenosine in the Nervous System, Kobe, Japan, 13-16 July 1996. LC 97-38557. (International Congress Ser.: No. 1140). 288p. 1997. 185.75 (*0-444-82643-2*) Elsevier.
Okada, Yasue. Public Lands & Pioneer Farmers, Gage County, Nebraska, 1850-1900. Bruchey, Stuart, ed. LC 78-56687. (Management of Public Lands in the U. S. Ser.). (Illus.). 1979. reprint ed. lib. bdg. 18.95 (*0-405-11348-X*) Ayer.
Okada Yasunobu Tion. Cell Volume Regulation: The Molecular Mechanism & Volume Sening Machinery: Proceedings of the 23rd Taniguchi Foundation

An Asterisk (*) at the beginning of an entry indicates that the title is appearing for the first time.

Biophysics Symposium Held in Okazaki, Japan, 17-21 November, 1997. LC 98-8800. (International Congress Ser.). 214p. 1998. 155.00 (*0-444-82951-2*) Elsevier.

Okada, Yoshitaka, jt. auth. see Kojima, Sakura.

Okafor, Dubem. Dance of Death: Nigerian History & Christopher Okigbo's Poetry. LC 97-15056. 232p. 1997. pap. text 21.95 (*0-86543-555-3*) Africa World.

— The Dance of Death: Nigerian History & Christopher Okigbo's Poetry. LC 97-15056. 232p. 1997. 79.95 (*0-86543-554-5*) Africa Wrld Bks.

***Okafor, Dubem, ed.** Meditations on African Literature, 201. LC 99-462059. (Contributions in Afro-American & African Studies: Vol. 201). 296p. 2000. 59.00 (*0-313-29866-1*, GM9866, Greenwood Pr) Greenwood.

***Okafor, Obiora Chinedu.** Re-Defining Legitimate Statehood: International Law & State Fragmentation in Africa. LC 00-21886. (Developments in International Law Ser.: Vol. 36). 2000. 77.00 (*90-411-1353-3*) Kluwer Law Intl.

Okagaki, Alan & Benson, Jim. County Energy Plan Guidebook. 2nd ed. (Illus.). 200p. (Orig.). (C). 1979. pap. text 10.00 (*0-937786-01-2*) Inst Ecological.

Okagaki, Lynn & Sternberg, Robert J., eds. Directors of Development: Influences on the Development of Children's Thinking. 304p. 1991. pap. 34.50 (*0-8058-0628-8*); text 59.95 (*0-8058-0627-X*) L Erlbaum Assocs.

Okagaki, Lynn, jt. ed. see Luster, Tom.

Okai, Matthew. Social Valuation in Agricultural Policy Analysis: Its Significance for Sub-Saharan Africa. LC 99-72333. 446p. 1999. text 83.95 (*1-84014-885-3*, Pub. by Ashgate Pub) Ashgate Pub Co.

Okaichi, T., et al, eds. Red Tides: Biology, Environmental Science, & Toxicology. 489p. 1988. 97.50 (*0-444-01343-1*) P-H.

O'Kain, David & Carmack, Joyce, contrib. by. Proceedings of the Flywheel Energy Storage Workshop (October, 1995) (Flywheel Energy Information Ser.: No. II). 475p. 1996. lib. bdg. 205.00 (*0-89934-328-7*, BT966) Bus Tech Bks.

***O'Kain, Dennis, photos by.** The Most Beautiful Villages & Towns of the South. LC 99-96559. (Most Beautiful Villages of... Ser.). (Illus.). 208p. 2000. 40.00 (*0-500-01999-1*, Pub. by Thames Hudson) Norton.

Okaiye, Anthony. Story of an Abused Priest. LC 95-70228. 76p. (Orig.). (C). 1995. pap. text 14.95 (*1-882792-16-5*) Proctor Pubns.

Okakura, Kakuzo. Book of Tea. Bleiler, Everett F., ed. 94p. 1964. pap. 3.95 (*0-486-20070-1*) Dover.

— The Book of Tea. 144p. 1991. reprint ed. pap. 10.00 (*4-7700-1542-9*) Kodansha.

Okakura, Y. The Japanese Spirit. 1972. lib. bdg. 250.00 (*0-87968-549-2*) Krishna Pr.

Okal, ed. Rubigalli Pannonii, Pauli. (LAT.). 1980. 22.95 (*3-322-00860-6*, T1924, Pub. by B G Teubner) U of Mich Pr.

Okal, Emile A., ed. Advances in Volcanic Seismology. 248p. 1988. reprint ed. 48.50 (*0-8176-1927-5*) Birkhauser.

— Aspects of Pacific Seismicity. 200p. 1991. reprint ed. 27.50 (*0-8176-2589-5*) Birkhauser.

Okali, Christine. Cocoa & Kinship in Ghana: The Matrilineal Akan of Ghana. 200p. 1983. pap. 25.00 (*0-7103-0041-7*) Routledge.

Okali, Christine, et al. Farmer Participatory Research: Rhetoric & Reality. 156p. 1994. pap. 19.50 (*1-85339-252-9*, Pub. by Intermed Tech) Stylus Pub VA.

Okali, Christine, jt. auth. see Sumberg, James E.

Okamoto, Ariel R. Guide to the Parks: Golden Gate National Recreation Area. (Illus.). 96p. (Orig.). 1995. pap. 9.95 (*0-9625206-0-8*) Gldn Gate Natl Parks Assoc.

Okamoto, Garret T. Smart Antenna Systems & Wireless Lans, Vol. 474. LC 98-44078. (The Kluwer International Series in Engineering & Computer Science). 19p. 1998. 98.00 (*0-7923-8335-4*) Kluwer Academic.

Okamoto, H., jt. ed. see Tanner, L. E.

Okamoto, Hiroaki, ed. Phase Diagrams of Binary Iron Alloys. LC 93-70331. (Monograph Series on Alloy Phase Diagrams). (Illus.). 472p. 1993. 326.00 (*0-87170-469-2*, 57733G) ASM.

Okamoto, Hiroaki & White, C. E., eds. Phase Diagrams of Indium Alloys & Their Engineering Applications. (Monograph Series on Alloy Phase Diagrams: No. 8). (Illus.). 338p. 1991. text 297.00 (*0-87170-438-2*, 57727G) ASM.

Okamoto, Hiroaki, et al. Handbook of Ternary Alloy Phase Diagrams, 10 vols., Set. Incl. Handbook of Ternary Alloy Phase Diagrams Vol. 1: Ac-Gd. LC 94-41540. 1994. Not sold separately (*0-87170-526-5*); LC 94-41540. (Illus.). 15000p. 1995. 6825.00 (*0-87170-525-7*, 57706G) ASM.

Okamoto, Hiroshi, ed. Molecular Biology of the Islets of Langerhans. (Illus.). 362p. (C). 1990. text 105.00 (*0-521-36204-0*) Cambridge U Pr.

Okamoto, Kanoko. The House Spirit: And Other Stories. LC 94-48092. 160p. (Orig.). 1995. pap. 10.95 (*0-88496-392-6*) Capra Pr.

***Okamoto, Katsunari.** Fundamentals of Optical Waveguides. 2000. 95.00 (*0-12-525095-9*) Acad Pr.

Okamoto, Lorina R. & Westmore, Gerald J. Ice Hockey FANFOLD. 2p. 1996. 2.95 (*0-9628248-2-8*) L R Okamoto.

Okamoto, Lorina R., jt. auth. see Huff, Helen E.

Okamoto, M., jt. ed. see Tajima, T.

Okamoto, Naomi. Japanese Ink Painting: The Art of Sumi-e. LC 94-40844 Tr. of Japanische Tuschmalerei fur Einsteiger. (ENG & GER., Illus.). 96p. (Orig.). 1995. 19.95 (*0-8069-0832-7*) Sterling.

— Japanese Ink Painting: The Art of Sumi-e.Tr. of Japanische Tuschmalerei fur Einsteiger. (Illus.). 96p. (Orig.). 1996. pap. 14.95 (*0-8069-0833-5*) Sterling.

Okamoto, Osamu. Sam Okamoto's Incredible Vegetables. LC 94-8520. (Illus.). 336p. 1993. 25.00 (*1-56554-025-5*) Pelican.

Okamoto, Rai Y. & Williams, Frank E. Urban Design Manhattan. (Illus.). 130p. (C). 1969. text 10.00 (*0-318-19021-4*) Regional Plan Assn.

Okamoto, Shumpei. Impressions of the Front: Woodcuts of the Sino-Japanese War, 1894-95. LC 83-4096. (Illus.). 56p. (Orig.). 1983. pap. 7.50 (*0-87633-049-9*) Phila Mus Art.

— The Japanese Oligarchy & the Russo-Japanese War. LC 74-114259. 372p. reprint ed. pap. 115.40 (*0-8357-3728-4*, 203645000003) Bks Demand.

Okamoto, Shumpei, tr. see Yoshitake, Oka.

Okamoto, Shunzo. Introduction to Earthquake Engineering. 2nd ed. 629p. 1984. reprint ed. 122.50 (*0-86008-361-6*, Pub. by U of Tokyo) Col U Pr.

Okamoto, Shunzo, et al, eds. Static & Dynamic Behavior of Kurobe Dam: Record of Measurements & Observations on a High Arch Dam. LC 88-206004. 437p. 1988. reprint ed. pap. 135.50 (*0-608-01259-9*, 206194700001) Bks Demand.

Okamoto, Tatsuaki, ed. see Qing, Sihan.

Okamoto, Yukari, jt. auth. see Case, Robbie.

Okamura, Arthur, jt. auth. see Kowit, Steve.

Okamura, Hajime, jt. ed. see Meyer, Christian.

Okamura, Jonathan Y. Imagining the Filipino American Diaspora: Transnational Relations, Identities, & Communities. LC 98-28383. (Asian Americans). 155p. 1998. 43.00 (*0-8153-3183-5*) Garland.

Okamura, Kichiemon, jt. auth. see Muraoka, Kageo.

Okamura, Sandanori. History of Electron Tubes. LC 93-80285. 230p. (gr. 12). 1994. 79.00 (*90-5199-145-2*) IOS Press.

Okamura, Sandanori, ed. Recent Trends in Radiation Polymer Chemistry. (Advances in Polymer Science Ser.: Vol. 105). (Illus.). 166p. 1993. 119.95 (*0-387-55812-8*) Spr-Verlag.

Okamura, William H., jt. ed. see Dawson, Marcia I.

***Okana.** Znaki: Slavic Charms. (Illus.). 16p. 1999. pap. 25.00 (*0-9678050-3-1*) Okanas Web.

Okandan, Ender, ed. Geothermal Reservoir Engineering. (C). 1988. text 191.00 (*90-247-3751-6*) Kluwer Academic.

— Heavy Crude Oil Recovery. 1984. text 185.50 (*90-247-2951-3*) Kluwer Academic.

O'Kane & Kranis. Radiology on Call: A Survival Handbook. (Illus.). 320p. (C). (gr. 13). 1999. pap. text 39.00 (*0-8151-4487-3*, 29953) Mosby Inc.

O'Kane, Bernard. Studies in Persian Art & Architecture. (Illus.). 334p. 1996. 39.00 (*977-424-370-6*, Pub. by Am Univ Cairo Pr) Col U Pr.

— Timurid Architecture in Khurasan. LC 85-43494. (Islamic Art & Architecture Ser.: Vol. 3). (Illus.). 520p. 1987. lib. bdg. 55.00 (*0-939214-35-0*) Mazda Pubs.

O'Kane, Francoise. Scared Chaos. LC 95-838293. (Studies in Jungian Psychology). 144p. 1995. pap. 16.00 (*0-919123-65-1*, Pub. by Inner City Bks) BookWorld.

O'Kane, Hugh P. & O'Kane, Monica. The Nolan Family Tree. (Illus.). 253p. 1983. 25.00 (*0-9609198-2-1*) Diction Bks.

O'Kane, J. Philip, ed. Advances in Theoretical Hydrology: A Tribute to Jim Dooge. LC 92-35090. (European Geophysical Society Series in Hydrological Sciences: Vol. 1). 254p. 1992. 182.25 (*0-444-89831-X*) Elsevier.

O'Kane, James M. The Crooked Ladder: Gangsters, Ethnicity, & the American Dream. 185p. (C). 1992. 39.95 (*1-56000-021-X*) Transaction Pubs.

O'Kane, John, tr. see Bozorg Alavi.

O'Kane, John, tr. see Radtke, Bernd, ed.

O'Kane, John, jt. tr. see Radtke, Bernd.

O'Kane, John, tr. see Vilhjalmsson, Thor.

Okane, Judith Coupe. Communication before Speech: Development & Assessment. 2nd ed. 1998. pap. text 32.95 (*1-85346-486-4*) David Fulton.

O'Kane, Leslie. The Cold, Hard Fax: A Molly Masters Mystery. 1998. mass mkt. 5.99 (*0-449-00158-X*, GM) Fawcett.

— Death & Faxes. 1997. per. 4.99 (*0-373-26248-5*, 1-26248-4, Wrldwide Lib) Harlequin Bks.

— Death & Faxes. LC 95-40802. 240p. 1996. 19.95 (*0-312-13960-8*) St Martin.

***O'Kane, Leslie.** The Fax of Life. large type ed. LC 99-54811. (Mystery Ser.). 390p. 2000. 26.95 (*0-7862-2328-6*) Thorndike Pr.

O'Kane, Leslie. The Fax of Life, 1. 1999. mass mkt. 5.99 (*0-449-00160-1*) Fawcett.

— Just the Fax, Ma'am. 1997. per. 4.99 (*0-373-26254-X*, 1-26254-2, Wrldwide Lib) Harlequin Bks.

— Play Dead. LC 98-96043. 261p. 1998. mass mkt. 5.99 (*0-449-00159-8*, GM) Fawcett.

***O'Kane, Leslie.** Play Dead. large type ed. LC 99-56053. 377p. 2000. 27.95 (*0-7862-2329-4*) Thorndike Pr.

— Ruff Way to Go. 2000. mass mkt. 6.50 (*0-449-00161-X*) Fawcett.

— The School Board Murder. 240p. 2000. mass mkt. 6.50 (*0-449-00567-4*, GM) Fawcett.

O'Kane, Monica, jt. auth. see O'Kane, Hugh P.

O'Kane, Patrick. Rapid Access Guide to Internal Medicine: Companion to Kelley's Textbook of Internal Medicine. 3rd ed. LC 96-15026. 416p. 1996. pap. text 24.95 (*0-397-51255-4*) Lppncott W & W.

O'Kane, Richard H. Clear the Bridge! The War Patrols of the U. S. S. Tang. LC 88-27104. (Illus.). 480p. 1997. pap. 19.95 (*0-89141-573-4*) Presidio Pr.

— Wahoo: The Patrols of America's Most Famous WWII Submarine. LC 87-6925. 376p. 1996. pap. 18.95 (*0-89141-572-6*) Presidio Pr.

O'Kane, Rosemary H. Likelihood of Coups. 160p. 1987. text 72.95 (*0-566-05006-4*) Ashgate Pub Co.

— Revolution: Critical Concepts in Political Science, Set, Vol. 4. LC 99-13576. 1999. text. write for info. (*0-415-20132-2*) Routledge.

— Terror, Force & States: The Path from Modernity. LC 95-34568. 224p. 1996. 90.00 (*1-85278-694-9*) E Elgar.

***Okane, Sean.** Church of Chains. 1999. pap. text 9.99 (*1-897809-60-3*) Silver Moon.

Okane, Trish. Guatemala: A Guide to the People, Politics & Culture. LC 98-27653. (In Focus Guides Ser.). (Illus.). 94p. 1999. pap. text 12.95 (*1-56656-242-2*) Interlink Pub.

O'Kane, Walter C. Sun in the Sky. LC 50-7404. (Civilization of the American Indian Ser.: No. 30). (Illus.). 274p. reprint ed. 85.00 (*0-8357-9742-2*, 201624500002) Bks Demand.

***O'Kane, William & Kerr, Eoin.** Irish Gravestone Inscriptions: A Guide to Sources in Ulster. 57p. 1999. pap. 7.95 (*0-8063-1616-0*) Genealog Pub.

Okano, Isai. Vital Judo: Grappling Techniques. pap. 14.95 (*0-685-70712-1*) Wehman.

Okano, Isai, jt. auth. see Sato, T.

Okano, K. School to Work Transition in Japan. 1992. pap. 44.95 (*1-85359-162-9*, Pub. by Multilingual Matters) Taylor & Francis.

Okano, Kaori. School to Work Transition in Japan: An Ethnographic Study. LC 92-20817. (Language & Education Library: No. 3). 1992. 99.00 (*1-85359-163-7*, Pub. by Multilingual Matters) Taylor & Francis.

Okano, Kaori & Oprandy, Robert. Education in Contemporary Japan: Inequality & Diversity. LC 98-43666. (Contemporary Japanese Society Ser.). (Illus.). 272p. (C). 1999. pap. 19.95 (*0-521-62686-2*) Cambridge U Pr.

Okano, T., et al, eds. Advanced Biomaterials in Biomedical Engineering & Drug Delivery Systems. (Illus.). xxii, 378p. 1996. 130.00 (*4-431-70163-X*) Spr-Verlag.

Okano, Teruo, ed. Biorelated Polymers & Gels: Controlled Release & Applications in Biomedical Engineering. LC 97-50406. (Polymers, Interfaces, & Biomaterials Ser.). (Illus.). 257p. 1998. text 95.00 (*0-12-525090-8*) Acad Pr.

Okano, Teruo, jt. auth. see Ikada, Yoshito.

Okantah, Mwatabu S. Afreeka Brass. (Cleveland Poets Ser.: No. 35). 28p. (Orig.). 1983. pap. 3.50 (*0-914946-41-2*) Cleveland St Univ Poetry Ctr.

— Collage. LC 83-82776. 68p. 1984. pap., per. 5.00 (*0-916418-56-1*) Lotus.

Okaori, Kaori & Tsuchiya, Motonori. Education in Contemporary Japan: Inequality & Diversity. LC 98-43666. (Contemporary Japanese Society Ser.). (Illus.). 272p. (C). 1999. text 64.95 (*0-521-62252-2*) Cambridge U Pr.

Okas, John. Freewayfarers' Book of the Dead. LC 94-31751. 268p. 1995. 24.00 (*1-877946-60-5*) Permanent Pr.

— Routes. LC 93-27528. 225p. 1994. 22.00 (*1-877946-43-5*) Permanent Pr.

Okasaki, Chris. Purely Functional Data Structures. LC 98-15367. 232p. (C). 1998. text 39.95 (*0-521-63124-6*) Cambridge U Pr.

***Okasaki, Chris.** Purely Functional Data Structures. 230p. (C). 1999. pap. 24.95 (*0-521-66350-4*) Cambridge U Pr.

Okasaki-Ward, Lola. Management, Education & Training in Japan: Background & Practice. LC 93-22622. 640p. (C). 1993. lib. bdg. 208.00 (*1-85333-781-1*, Pub. by Graham & Trotman) Kluwer Academic.

O'Kash, Alex. Beyond the Law: A Tale of Two Cities - Superior-Duluth. 130p. (Orig.). 1996. pap. 9.95 (*0-9653027-3-3*) Paper Moon Pub.

— Stop in the Name of the Law. 1994. pap. 9.95 (*1-886028-00-1*) Savage Pr.

***Okasha, Ahmed, et al, eds.** Ethics, Culture & Psychiatry: International Perspectives. LC 99-40828. 288p. 2000. pap. 29.95 (*0-88048-999-5*) Am Psychiatric.

Okasha, Elisabeth. Corpus of Early Christian Inscribed Stones. LC 93-9951. (Studies in the Early History of Britain). 256p. 1993. 95.00 (*0-7185-1475-0*) St Martin.

***Okasha, Elisabeth & Forsyth, Katherine S.** Early Christian Inscriptions of Munster: A Corpus of the Inscribed Stones (Excluding Ogham) 320p. 2000. 85.00 (*1-85918-170-8*, Pub. by Cork Univ) Stylus Pub VA.

Okasha, Sarwat. Encyclopaedic Dictionary of Cultural Terms: English-French-Arabic. (ARA, ENG & FRE.). 580p. 1990. 48.00 (*0-86685-500-9*, LDL5009, Pub. by Librairie du Liban) Intl Bk Ctr.

Okawa, Essei. The Adventures of the One Inch Boy. Ooka, Diane T., tr. from JPN. (Japanese Fairy Tale Ser.: No. 4). (Illus.). 32p. (J). (gr. k-6). 1985. 12.95 (*0-89346-258-6*) Heian Intl.

— The Fisherman & the Grateful Turtle. Ooka, Diane T., tr. from JPN. (Japanese Fairy Tale Ser.: No. 3). (Illus.). 32p. (J). (gr. k-6). 1985. 12.95 (*0-89346-257-8*) Heian Intl.

Okawa, M., jt. auth. see Meier-Evert, K.

Okawa, Naomi. Edo Architecture: Katsura & Nikko. Woodhull, Alan & Miyamoto, Akito, trs. from JPN. LC 74-23786. (Heibonsha Survey of Japanese Art Ser.: Vol. 20). (Illus.). 164p. 1975. 20.00 (*0-8348-1027-1*) Weatherhill.

***Okawa, Ryuho.** The Essence of Buddha: The Path to Enlightenment. 160p. 2000. pap. 16.95 (*1-86204-836-3*) Element MA.

— The Golden Laws: The Buddhist Path to a Spiritual Dawn. (Illus.). 2000. pap. 16.95 (*1-86204-731-6*, Pub. by Element MA) Penguin Putnam.

Okawa, Ryuho. Law of the Sun: The Spiritual Laws & History Governing Past, Present & Future. 1996. pap. 11.95 (*1-85230-807-9*, Pub. by Element MA) Penguin Putnam.

— Laws of Eternity: A Time of New Hope for the World. 128p. 1998. pap. 9.95 (*1-86204-292-6*, Pub. by Element MA) Penguin Putnam.

— The Laws of the Sun. Date not set. write for info. (*0-614-17667-0*) Penguin Putnam.

Okawara, M., et al. Organic Colorants: A Handbook of Data of Selected Dyes for Electro-Optical Applications. (Physical Sciences Data Ser.: No. 35). 504p. 1989. 404.50 (*0-444-98884-X*) Elsevier.

Okawara, Nobuo, jt. auth. see Katzenstein, Peter J.

Okayama, Kotaro. Zur Grundlegung Christlicher Ethik Theologische Konzeptionen der Gegenwart im Lichte des Analogie-Problems. (Theologische Bibliothek Toepelmann Ser.: Vol. 30). (C). 1977. 75.40 (*3-11-005812-X*) De Gruyter.

Okazaki, Chieko N. Aloha! LC 94-45860. 256p. 1995. 14.95 (*0-87579-979-5*) Deseret Bk.

— Cat's Cradle. 1993. 14.95 (*0-88494-904-4*) Bookcraft Inc.

— Disciples. LC 98-27282. 1998. 17.95 (*1-57345-413-3*) Deseret Bk.

— Lighten Up! Finding Real Joy in Real Life. LC 92-40396. 232p. 1993. 12.95 (*0-87579-668-0*) Deseret Bk.

— Sanctuary. LC 97-3488. vii, 211p. 1997. 15.95 (*1-57345-154-1*) Deseret Bk.

— Shared Motherhood. 1994. pap. 1.95 (*0-88494-932-X*) Bookcraft Inc.

Okazaki, Chieko N., et al. Corporate Governance In Japan:towards New Thinking 2000. pap. text 19.99 (*1-86152-481-1*) Thomson Learn.

Okazaki, Haruo. Fundamentals of Neuropathology. 2nd ed. LC 89-2048. (Illus.). 328p. 1989. 79.00 (*0-89640-156-1*) Igaku-Shoin.

Okazaki, Renji, jt. auth. see Inagaki, Yoshio.

Okazaki, Teruyuki. The Textbook of Modern Karate. 1997. pap. 32.95 (*4-7700-2141-0*, Pub. by Kodansha Int) OUP.

Okazaki, Tetsuji, jt. ed. see Okuno-Fujiwara, Masahiro.

Okazawa-Rey, Margo, jt. auth. see Kirk, Gwyn.

Oke, Barbara & Oke, Deborah. The Oke Family Cookbook: Favorite Recipes of Janette's Family. LC 94-37627. (Illus.). 224p. 1994. pap. 9.99 (*1-55661-529-9*) Bethany Hse.

Oke, Deborah, jt. auth. see Oke, Barbara.

***Oke, Janette.** Beyond the Gathering Storm. 256p. 2000. 15.99 (*0-7642-2401-8*); pap. 10.99 (*0-7642-2400-X*) Bethany Hse.

— Beyond the Gathering Storm. large type ed. 368p. 2000. pap. 15.99 (*0-7642-2403-4*) Bethany Hse.

Oke, Janette. The Bluebird & the Sparrow. LC 95-16974. (The Women of the West Ser.: Vol. 10). 256p. 1995. pap. 8.99 (*1-55661-612-0*) Bethany Hse.

— The Bluebird & the Sparrow. large type ed. 336p. (J). 1995. pap. 12.99 (*1-55661-613-9*) Bethany Hse.

— The Bluebird & the Sparrow. large type ed. LC 95-30933. 305p. 1995. 22.95 (*0-7838-1479-8*, G K Hall Lrg Type) Mac Lib Ref.

— A Bride for Donnigan. (Women of the West Ser.). 224p. 1993. pap. 8.99 (*1-55661-327-X*) Bethany Hse.

— A Bride for Donnigan. (Women of the West Ser.). 288p. 1999. pap. text 5.99 (*0-7642-2244-9*) Bethany Hse.

— A Bride for Donnigan. large type ed. (Women of the West Ser.). 24p. 1993. pap. 10.99 (*1-55661-328-8*) Bethany Hse.

— The Calling of Emily Evans. LC 89-78543. 224p. 1990. pap. 8.99 (*1-55661-118-8*) Bethany Hse.

— The Calling of Emily Evans. LC 98-13843. (Women of the West Ser.: Bk. 1). 288p. 1998. mass mkt. 5.99 (*0-7642-2098-5*, 202098) Bethany Hse.

***Oke, Janette.** The Calling of Emily Evans. LC 00-33755. 2000. write for info. (*0-7862-2701-X*) Thorndike Pr.

Oke, Janette. The Calling of Emily Evans. large type ed. 224p. 1990. pap. 10.99 (*1-55661-121-8*) Bethany Hse.

— Canadian West Gifset, 4 bks., Set. boxed set 35.99 (*0-87123-972-8*) Bethany Hse.

Oke, Janette. Canadian West Saga 4-in-1. 656p. 1995. 12.99 (*0-88486-112-0*, Inspirational Pr) Arrowood Pr.

Oke, Janette. Celebrating the Inner Beauty of Woman. LC 97-45437. 1p. 1998. text 14.99 (*0-7642-2041-1*) Bethany Hse.

***Oke, Janette.** A Cote of Many Colors. (Oke Children's Classics Ser.). (Illus.). 128p. (Orig.). (J). (gr. 3 up). 1998. pap. 5.99 (*0-934998-27-2*) Bethany Hse.

— Drums of Change. (Women of the West Ser.). 288p. 2000. mass mkt. 5.99 (*0-7642-2383-6*) Bethany Hse.

Oke, Janette. The Drums of Change: The Story of Running Fawn. (The Women of the West Ser.: Vol. 12). 24p. 1996. pap. 8.99 (*1-55661-812-3*) Bethany Hse.

— The Drums of Change: The Story of Running Fawn. large type ed. 352p. 1996. pap. 12.99 (*1-55661-817-4*) Bethany Hse.

***Oke, Janette.** Ducktails. (Oke Children's Classics Ser.). (Illus.). 131p. (J). (gr. 3 up). 1998. pap. 4.99 (*0-934998-20-5*) Bethany Hse.

Oke, Janette. The Father of Love. 28p. 1989. text 11.99 (*1-55661-064-5*) Bethany Hse.

— A Gown of Spanish Lace. LC 95-467. (Women of the West Ser.). 256p. 1995. text 14.99 (*1-55661-690-2*) Bethany Hse.

— A Gown of Spanish Lace. LC 95-467. (Women of the West Ser.: Vol. 11). 256p. 1995. pap. 8.99 (*1-55661-683-X*) Bethany Hse.

— A Gown of Spanish Lace. 288p. 1997. mass mkt. 5.99 (*0-7642-2017-9*) Bethany Hse.

— A Gown of Spanish Lace. large type ed. LC 97-214. (Women of the West Ser.). 368p. 1995. pap. 12.99 (*1-55661-684-8*) Bethany Hse.

— A Gown of Spanish Lace. large type ed. 367p. 1996. 22.95 (*0-7838-1595-6*, G K Hall Lrg Type) Mac Lib Ref.

— Heart of the Wilderness. 24p. 1993. pap. 8.99 (*1-55661-362-8*) Bethany Hse.

— Heart of the Wilderness. 288p. 1997. mass mkt. 5.99 (*0-7642-2016-0*) Bethany Hse.

— Heart of the Wilderness. large type ed. 248p. 1993. pap. 10.99 (*1-55661-363-6*) Bethany Hse.

— Hey, Teacher! (Illus.). 94p. 1981. pap. 4.99 (*0-934998-06-X*) Evangel Indiana.

O

***Oke, Janette.** The Impatient Turtle. Peterson, Pete, ed. (Oke Children's Classics Ser.). (Illus.). 110p. (Orig.). (J). (gr. 3 up). 1998. pap. 5.99 (*0-934998-24-8*) Bethany Hse.

— Impatient Turtle. (Janette Oke's Animal Friends Ser.). (Illus.). (J). 2000. pap. 5.99 (*0-7642-2407-7*) Bethany Hse.

— Janette Oke Engagement Diary, 2000 Ed. 1999. 12.99 (*0-7642-2984-2*) Bethany Hse.

Oke, Janette. Janette Oke's Reflections on the Christmas Story. LC 94-39586. (Illus.). 112p. 1994. text 10.99 (*1-55661-528-0*) Bethany Hse.

— Julia's Last Hope. 28p. 1990. pap. 8.99 (*1-55661-153-6*) Bethany Hse.

***Oke, Janette.** Julia's Last Hope. LC 90-42091. (Women of the West Ser.). 288p. 2000. mass mkt. 5.99 (*0-7642-2384-4*) Bethany Hse.

— Like Gold Refined. LC 00-8127. (Prairie Legacy Ser.: Vol. 4). 256p. 2000. 15.99 (*0-7642-2162-0*); pap. 10.99 (*0-7642-2161-2*) Bethany Hse.

— Like Gold Refined. large type ed. (Prairie Legacy Ser.: Vol. 4). 384p. 2000. 15.99 (*0-7642-2163-9*) Bethany Hse.

Oke, Janette. Love Comes Softly. LC 79-16421. (Love Comes Softly Ser.: Vol. 1). 192p. 1979. pap. 8.99 (*0-87123-342-8*) Bethany Hse.

Oke, Janette. Love Comes Softly. 1979. 14.09 (*0-606-03052-2*, Pub. by Turtleback) Demco.

Oke, Janette. Love Comes Softly, 4 vols., Vol. 5-8. 1993. boxed set 35.99 (*1-55661-778-X*) Bethany Hse.

— Love Comes Softly: Gift Set, 4 vols., Vol. 1-4. (Orig.). 1993. pap. text 35.99 (*1-55661-777-1*) Bethany Hse.

— Love Finds a Home. large type ed. (Love Comes Softly Ser.: Vol. 8). 224p. 1989. pap. 8.99 (*1-55661-086-6*) Bethany Hse.

— Love Takes Wing. LC 88-19276. (Love Comes Softly Ser.: Vol. 7). 224p. (Orig.). 1988. pap. 8.99 (*1-55661-035-1*) Bethany Hse.

— Love Takes Wing. large type ed. LC 94-43842. 322p. (Orig.). 1995. 22.95 (*0-7838-1206-X*, G K Hall Lrg Type) Mac Lib Ref.

— Love's Abiding Joy. LC 83-15503. (Love Comes Softly Ser.: Vol. 4). 224p. (Orig.). 1983. pap. 8.99 (*0-87123-401-7*) Bethany Hse.

— Love's Enduring Promise. LC 80-22993. (Love Comes Softly Ser.: Vol. 2). 208p. 1980. pap. 8.99 (*0-87123-345-2*) Bethany Hse.

— Love's Enduring Promise. large type ed. LC 80-22993. (Love Comes Softly Ser.: Vol. 2). 28p. 1985. pap. 10.99 (*0-87123-829-2*) Bethany Hse.

— Love's Long Journey. large type ed. LC 82-9469. (Love Comes Softly Ser.: Vol. 3). 28p. 1982. pap. 8.99 (*0-87123-315-0*) Bethany Hse.

— Love's Unending Legacy. LC 84-18412. (Love Comes Softly Ser: Vol. 5). 224p. 1984. pap. 8.99 (*0-87123-616-8*) Bethany Hse.

— Love's Unfolding Dream. large type ed. LC 87-15780. (Love Comes Softly Ser.: Vol. 6). 224p. (J). (gr. 4 up). 1987. pap. 8.99 (*0-87123-979-5*) Bethany Hse.

— Love's Unfolding Dream. large type ed. LC 84-18412. 224p. 1987. pap. 10.99 (*0-87123-980-9*) Bethany Hse.

— Making Memories. LC 99-6737. 32p. 1999. 14.99 (*0-7642-2190-6*) Bethany Hse.

— The Matchmakers. LC 97-33830. 144p. 1997. pap. 12.99 (*0-7642-2020-9*); text 12.99 (*0-7642-2002-0*) Bethany Hse.

***Oke, Janette.** Maury Had a Little Lamb. (Oke Children's Classics Ser.). (Illus.). 144p. (Orig.). (J). (gr. 3 up). 1998. pap. 5.99 (*0-934998-34-5*) Bethany Hse.

Oke, Janette. The Measure of a Heart. (Women of the West Ser.: No. 6). 224p. 1992. pap. 8.99 (*1-55661-296-6*) Bethany Hse.

— The Measure of a Heart. LC 98-13840. (Women of the West Ser.: Bk. 6). 288p. 1998. mass mkt. 5.99 (*0-7642-2100-0*, 202100) Bethany Hse.

— The Measure of a Heart. large type ed. (Women of the West Ser.: No. 6). 224p. 1992. pap. 10.99 (*1-55661-297-4*) Bethany Hse.

— The Measure of a Heart. large type ed. LC 93-36155. 293p. 1994. 19.95 (*0-8161-5850-9*, G K Hall Lrg Type) Mac Lib Ref.

— Nana's Gift: Some Things in This World Are Very Expensive, but Others Are Priceless. LC 96-25352. 144p. 1996. text 12.99 (*1-55661-898-0*) Bethany Hse.

— Nana's Gift: Some Things in This World Are Very Expensive, but Others Are Priceless. large type ed. LC 96-45045. (Inspirational Ser.). 1997. lib. bdg. 23.95 (*0-7838-2019-4*, G K Hall Lrg Type) Mac Lib Ref.

***Oke, Janette.** New Kid in Town. (Oke Children's Classics Ser.). (Illus.). 136p. (Orig.). (J). (gr. 3 up). 1998. pap. 5.99 (*0-934998-16-7*) Bethany Hse.

Oke, Janette. Once Upon a Summer. LC 81-10183. 28p. 1981. pap. 8.99 (*0-87123-413-0*) Bethany Hse.

Oke, Janette. Once Upon a Summer. 1981. 14.09 (*0-606-03051-4*, Pub. by Turtleback) Demco.

Oke, Janette. Once Upon a Summer. large type ed. LC 81-10183. 28p. 1987. pap. 10.99 (*0-87123-981-7*) Bethany Hse.

— Once Upon a Summer, Vol. 1. LC 99-21866. 1999. 23.95 (*0-7862-1970-X*) Thorndike Pr.

Oke, Janette. Pordy's Prickly Problem, Vol. 11. Pettifor, Grace, ed. LC 96-738. (Illus.). 100p. (J). (gr. 3 up). 1993. pap. 5.99 (*0-934998-50-7*) Bethany Hse.

— Prairie Dog Town. (Illus.). 140p. (J). (gr. 3 up). 1998. pap. 5.99 (*0-934998-31-0*) Bethany Hse.

— Prairie Legacy: Tender Years; Searching Heart; Quiet Strength; Like Gold Refined, Vols. 1-4. 2000. pap., boxed set 43.99 (*0-7642-8650-1*) Bethany Hse.

— The Prodigal Cat. (Oke Children's Classics Ser.). (Illus.). 160p. (Orig.). (J). (gr. 3 up). 1998. pap. 5.99 (*0-934998-19-1*) Bethany Hse.

— Prodigal Cat. (Janette Oke's Animal Friends Ser.). (Illus.). (J). 2000. pap. 5.99 (*0-7642-2406-9*) Bethany Hse.

— Quiet Places, Warm Thoughts. 112p. 1998. pap. 6.99 (*0-934998-15-9*) Bethany Hse.

— A Quiet Strength. LC 99-6539. No. 3. 256p. 1999. 15.99 (*0-7642-2157-4*) Bethany Hse.

— Quiet Strength, 3. LC 99-6539. (Prairie Legacy Ser.). 1999. 15.99 (*0-7642-2158-2*) Bethany Hse.

— Quiet Strength, No. 3. LC 99-6539. (Prairie Legacy Ser.). 256p. 1999. pap. text 10.99 (*0-7642-2156-6*) Bethany Hse.

— A Quiet Strength: A Prairie Legacy. large type ed. LC 99-46977. (G. K. Hall Inspirational Ser.). 1999. 27.95 (*0-7838-8813-9*, G K Hall Lrg Type) Mac Lib Ref.

Oke, Janette. The Red Geranium. LC 95-481. 8p. 1995. text 10.99 (*1-55661-662-7*) Bethany Hse.

— Roses for Mama. 224p. (Orig.). 1991. pap. 8.99 (*1-55661-185-4*) Bethany Hse.

— Roses for Mama. (Women of the West Ser.). 288p. (Orig.). 1999. pap. text 5.99 (*0-7642-2243-0*) Bethany Hse.

***Oke, Janette.** A Searching Heart. LC 98-217080. (Prairie Legacy Ser.: Bk. 2). 272p. 1998. 15.99 (*0-7642-2140-X*) Bethany Hse.

— A Searching Heart. Vol. 2. 256p. 1998. pap. 10.99 (*0-7642-2139-6*) Bethany Hse.

— A Searching Heart. large type ed. 352p. 1998. pap. 15.99 (*0-7642-2142-6*) Bethany Hse.

— A Searching Heart. large type ed. LC 98-44163. 312p. 1999. write for info. (*0-7540-3614-6*) Chivers N Amer.

Oke, Janette. A Searching Heart. large type ed. LC 98-44163. Date not set. 26.95 (*0-7838-0404-0*) Mac Lib Ref.

— Seasons of the Heart, 4 vols. in 1. 576p. 1993. 12.99 (*0-88486-088-4*) Arrowood Pr.

— Seasons of the Heart, Vols. 1-4. (Seasons of the Heart Ser.). 1989. pap., boxed set 35.99 (*1-55661-756-9*, 252756) Bethany Hse.

— Spring's Gentle Promise. LC 89-22. (Seasons of the Heart Ser.). 224p. 1989. pap. 8.99 (*1-55661-059-9*) Bethany Hse.

— Spring's Gentle Promise. large type ed. LC 89-22. (Seasons of the Heart Ser.: Vol. 4). 224p. 1989. pap. 10.99 (*1-55661-074-2*) Bethany Hse.

***Oke, Janette.** Spring's Gentle Promise. large type ed. LC 99-58237. (Christian Fiction Ser.). 2000. 26.95 (*0-7862-2377-4*) Thorndike Pr.

— Spunky's Camping Adventure. 32p. (J). 1998. text 9.99 (*0-7642-2145-0*) Bethany Hse.

Oke, Janette. Spunky's Circus Adventure. (Spunky Ser.). 32p. (J). 1999. text 9.99 (*0-7642-2194-9*) Bethany Hse.

***Oke, Janette.** Spunky's Diary. (Oke Children's Classics Ser.). (Illus.). 100p. (J). (gr. 3 up). 1998. pap. 5.99 (*0-934998-11-6*) Bethany Hse.

— Spunky's Diary. (Janette Oke's Animal Friends Ser.). (Illus.). (J). 2000. pap. 5.99 (*0-7642-2405-0*) Bethany Hse.

Oke, Janette. Spunky's First Christmas. LC 97-33882. 33p. (J). 1997. text 9.99 (*0-7642-2052-7*) Bethany Hse.

— The Tender Years. LC 97-21037. (Prairie Legacy Ser.: No. 1). 384p. 1997. pap. 15.99 (*1-55661-953-7*); text 15.99 (*1-55661-952-9*) Bethany Hse.

— The Tender Years. (Prairie Legacy Ser.: Bk. 1). 270p. 1997. pap. 10.99 (*1-55661-951-0*, 211951) Bethany Hse.

— The Tender Years. large type ed. LC 97-32572. (Inspirational Ser.: Vol. 1). 319p. 1998. 25.95 (*0-7838-8374-9*, G K Hall & Co) Mac Lib Ref.

— They Called Her Mrs. Doc. (Women of the West Ser.: Vol. 5). 224p. 1992. pap. 8.99 (*1-55661-246-X*) Bethany Hse.

— They Called Her Mrs. Doc. (Women of the West Ser.). 288p. 1999. pap. text 5.99 (*0-7642-2245-7*) Bethany Hse.

***Oke, Janette.** This Little Pig. Pettifor, Grace, ed. (Illus.). 145p. (Orig.). (J). (gr. 3 up). 1998. pap. 5.99 (*0-934998-43-4*) Bethany Hse.

Oke, Janette. Too Long a Stranger. (Women of the West Ser.: Bk. 9). 34p. 1994. pap. 9.99 (*1-55661-456-X*) Bethany Hse.

***Oke, Janette.** Too Long a Stranger. LC 94-7586. (Women of the West Ser.). 288p. 2000. mass mkt. 5.99 (*0-7642-2385-2*) Bethany Hse.

Oke, Janette. Too Long a Stranger. large type ed. (Women of the West Ser.: Bk. 9). 384p. 1994. pap. 13.99 (*1-55661-457-8*) Bethany Hse.

***Oke, Janette.** Trouble in a Fur Coat. (Oke Children's Classics Ser.). (Illus.). 152p. (Orig.). (J). (gr. 3 up). 1998. pap. 5.99 (*0-934998-38-8*) Bethany Hse.

Oke, Janette. When Breaks the Dawn. LC 86-3405. (Canadian West Ser.). 224p. (Orig.). 1986. pap. 8.99 (*0-87123-882-9*) Bethany Hse.

— When Breaks the Dawn. large type ed. LC 86-3405. (Canadian West Ser.: Vol. 3). 224p. (Orig.). 1986. pap. 10.99 (*0-87123-895-0*) Bethany Hse.

— When Calls the Heart. LC 82-24451. (Canadian West Ser.: Vol. 1). (Illus.). 224p. 1983. pap. 8.99 (*0-87123-611-7*) Bethany Hse.

— When Comes the Spring. LC 85-11261. (Canadian West Ser.: Vol. 2). 256p. 1985. pap. 8.99 (*0-87123-795-4*) Bethany Hse.

— When Comes the Spring. large type ed. LC 85-11261. (Canadian West Ser.: Vol. 2). 256p. 1985. pap. 10.99 (*0-87123-884-5*) Bethany Hse.

— When Hope Springs New. LC 86-13664. (Canadian West Ser.). 224p. 1986. pap. 8.99 (*0-87123-657-5*) Bethany Hse.

— The Winds of Autumn. LC 86-34299. (Seasons of Heart Ser.: No. 2). 224p. 1987. pap. 8.99 (*0-87123-946-9*) Bethany Hse.

— The Winds of Autumn. large type ed. (Seasons of Heart Ser.: No. 2). 28p. 1987. pap. 10.99 (*0-87123-982-5*) Bethany Hse.

— The Winds of Autumn. large type ed. LC 99-16094. 1999. pap. 23.95 (*0-7862-2054-6*) Mac Lib Ref.

— Winter Is Not Forever. large type ed. LC 88-2882. (Seasons of Heart Ser.: No. 3). 224p. 1988. pap. 8.99 (*1-55661-002-5*) Bethany Hse.

***Oke, Janette.** Winter Is Not Forever. large type ed. LC 99-36545. 1999. 24.95 (*0-7862-2145-3*) Mac Lib Ref.

Oke, Janette. A Woman Named Damaris. (Women of the West Ser.: No. 4). 224p. (Orig.). 1991. pap. 8.99 (*1-55661-225-7*) Bethany Hse.

— A Woman Named Damaris. 288p. (Orig.). 1997. mass mkt. 5.99 (*0-7642-2018-7*) Bethany Hse.

— A Woman Named Damaris. large type ed. (Women of the West Ser.: No. 4). 224p. (Orig.). 1991. pap. 10.99 (*1-55661-226-5*) Bethany Hse.

***Oke, Janette.** Women of the West I. 2000. boxed set 17.99 (*0-7642-8496-7*) Bethany Hse.

Oke, Janette. Women of the West II, Vols. 5-8. (Women of the West Ser.). 1993. pap., boxed set 35.99 (*1-55661-773-9*, 252773) Bethany Hse.

— Women of the West III: Too Long a Stranger, The Bluebird & the Sparrow, 4 vols. 1996. pap. text, boxed set 36.99 (*0-7642-8025-2*) Bethany Hse.

— Women of the West I: Calling of Emily Evans, Julia's Last Hope, Roses for Mama, Woman Named Damaris. 1991. boxed set 35.99 (*1-55661-761-5*) Bethany Hse.

***Oke, Janette.** Women of the West II: Drums of Change; Julia's Last Hope; Too Long a Stranger, 3 bks. 2000. mass mkt., boxed set 17.99 (*0-7642-8648-X*) Bethany Hse.

Oke, Janette & Bunn, T. Davis. Another Homecoming. LC 97-4669. 256p. 1997. pap. 9.99 (*1-55661-934-0*) Bethany Hse.

— Another Homecoming. large type ed. LC 97-4669. 384p. 1997. pap. 12.99 (*1-55661-979-0*) Bethany Hse.

— Another Homecoming. large type ed. LC 97-31794. 1997. 25.95 (*0-7838-8332-3*, G K Hall & Co) Mac Lib Ref.

— The Meeting Place. LC 99-6376. 256p. 1999. 15.99 (*0-7642-2177-9*); pap. 10.99 (*0-7642-2176-0*) Bethany Hse.

***Oke, Janette & Bunn, T. Davis.** The Meeting Place. LC 99-6376. 1999. audio 14.99 (*0-7642-2179-5*) Bethany Hse.

Oke, Janette & Bunn, T. Davis. The Meeting Place. LC 99-23487. 1999. 26.95 (*0-7838-8658-6*) Thorndike Pr.

— The Meeting Place. large type ed. LC 99-6376. 432p. 1999. pap. 15.99 (*0-7642-2178-7*) Bethany Hse.

— Return to Harmony. large type ed. LC 97-13182. (Inspirational Ser.). 273p. 1997. lib. bdg. 24.95 (*0-7838-8220-3*, G K Hall Lrg Type) Mac Lib Ref.

— Return to Harmony: A Novel. 224p. 1996. pap. 9.99 (*1-55661-878-6*) Bethany Hse.

— Return to Harmony: A Novel. large type ed. 288p. 1996. pap. 12.99 (*1-55661-902-2*) Bethany Hse.

***Oke, Janette & Bunn, T. Davis.** The Sacred Shore. 256p. 1999. pap. 10.99 (*0-7642-2247-3*) Bethany Hse.

— The Sacred Shore. LC 99-6839. 256p. 2000. 15.99 (*0-7642-2249-X*) Bethany Hse.

— The Sacred Shore. large type ed. 356p. 1999. pap. 15.99 (*0-7642-2248-1*) Bethany Hse.

— The Sacred Shore. large type ed. LC 00-39601. 394p. 2000. 27.95 (*0-7838-9090-7*, G K Hall & Co) Mac Lib Ref.

Oke, Janette & Bunn, T. Davis. Tomorrow's Dream. 224p. 1998. pap. 9.99 (*0-7642-2054-3*); text 15.99 (*0-7642-2055-1*) Bethany Hse.

— Tomorrow's Dream. large type ed. 256p. 1998. pap. 12.99 (*0-7642-2056-X*) Bethany Hse.

Oke, Norman R. Search the Scriptures, New Testament Vol. 2: Mark. 1953. pap. 1.99 (*0-8341-0012-6*) Nazarene.

— Search the Scriptures, New Testament Vol. 9: Galatians. 1962. pap. 1.99 (*0-8341-0019-3*) Beacon Hill.

— What a Price! 76p. 1987. pap. 5.99 (*0-8341-1210-8*) Nazarene.

Oke, O. L. & Ojofeitimi. Nutrition for Nurses. 1985. pap. text. write for info. (*0-582-77705-4*, Pub. by Addison-Wesley) Longman.

Oke, Oluremilekun A. Psychosomatics, Bk. 1. LC 92-96858. 200p. 1996. 15.00 (*0-533-10441-6*) Vantage.

Oke, T. R. Boundary Layer Climates. 2nd ed. 450p. (C). 1988. pap. 35.00 (*0-415-04319-0*) Routledge.

— Boundary Layer Climates. 2nd ed. (Illus.). 416p. 1988. pap. text 35.00 (*0-416-04432-8*, A1485); lib. bdg. 99.00 (*0-416-04422-0*, A1481) Routledge.

Oke, Tayo. Radicalism, Political Power & Foreign Policy in Nigeria. LC 99-20550. (African Studies: Vol. 49). 247p. 1999. pap. text 89.95 (*0-7734-8034-X*) E Mellen.

O'Keafe, Cynthia, jt. auth. see Crawley, Amy.

Okeay, T. The Story of Venice. (Mediaeval Towns Ser.: Vol. 31). 1974. reprint ed. 65.00 (*0-8115-0873-0*) Periodicals Srv.

O'Keef, Richard D. How to Make More Money Babysitting: What Works, What Doesn't, & Why. LC 91-92960. (Illus.). 136p. (Orig.). (YA). (gr. 6-10). 1992. pap. 8.95 (*0-9630531-3-2*) Diamond Bks UT.

O'Keefe. Bridging the Gap. LC 99-43022. 292p. 1999. pap. text 30.80 (*0-13-079774-X*) P-H.

O'Keefe. CPR: MS Excel 97 Advanced. (Illustrated Ser.). (C). 1997. pap. 20.95 (*0-7600-5821-0*) Course Tech.

— CPR: MS Excel 97 Intermediate. (Illustrated Ser.). (C). 1997. pap. 20.95 (*0-7600-5820-2*) Course Tech.

— Crse Gde: Ill Ms Excel 2000 Advanced. (Illustrated Ser.). (C). 1999. pap. text 21.95 (*0-7600-6391-5*) Course Tech.

— Crse Gde: Ill Ms Excel 2000 Intermediate. (Illustrated Ser.). (C). 1999. pap. text 21.95 (*0-7600-6390-7*) Course Tech.

— MS Excel 2000: Illustrated 2nd Course. (C). 1999. pap. 21.95 (*0-7600-6063-0*) Thomson Learn.

O'Keefe. The Path Less Taken. 1996. 6.95 (*0-7667-0386-X*) Gibson.

O'Keefe & Reding. CPR: MS Excel 97 Basic. (Illustrated Ser.). (C). 1997. pap. 20.95 (*0-7600-5819-9*) Course Tech.

O'Keefe, et al. The ECG Criteria & ACLS Handbook. (Illus.). 202p. (C). 1998. pap. text 12.95 (*1-890114-03-0*) Physicians Pr.

O'Keefe, jt. auth. see Reding.

O'Keefe, Betty & Macdonald, Ian. The Final Voyage of the Princess Sophia: Did They All Have to Die? LC 98-910806. (Illus.). 192p. 1998. pap. 16.95 (*0-938665-61-8*) Fine Edge Prods.

— The Final Voyage of the Princess Sophia: Did They All Have to Die? LC 99-202996. 1998. pap. 16.95 (*1-895811-64-3*) Heritage Hse.

O'Keefe, Betty, jt. auth. see Macdonald, Ian.

O'Keefe, Bob, jt. auth. see McEachern, Tim.

O'Keefe Bolick, Nancy. Mail Call! The History of the U. S. Mail Service. LC 94-49. (First Bks.). (Illus.). 64p. (J). (gr. 4-6). 1994. lib. bdg. 22.00 (*0-531-20170-8*) Watts.

O'Keefe, Brendan. Medicine at War. (Official History of Australia's Involvement in Southeast Asian Conflicts Ser.: Vol. III). (Illus.). 536p. 1994. 59.95 (*1-86373-301-9*, Pub. by Allen & Unwin Pty) Paul & Co Pubs.

— Simeon Pearce's Randwick: Dream & Reality. (Illus.). 75p. pap. 9.95 (*0-86840-305-9*, Pub. by New South Wales Univ Pr) Intl Spec Bk.

O'Keefe, Chap. The Gunman & the Actress. large type ed. (Linford Western Large Print Ser.). 256p. 1997. pap. 16.99 (*0-7089-5049-3*) Ulverscroft.

— Gunsmoke Night. large type ed. (Linford Western Library). 256p. 1996. pap. 16.99 (*0-7089-7815-0*, Linford) Ulverscroft.

O'Keefe, Charles. Void & Voice: Questioning Narrative Conventions in Andre Gide's Major First-Person Narratives. LC 95-21311. (University of North Carolina Studies in the Romance Languages & Literature Sero: Vol. 251). 425p. (C). 1996. pap. text 34.95 (*0-8078-9255-6*) U of NC Pr.

O'Keefe, Christine. How to Successfully Flirt, Date & Mate. 103p. 1990. wbk. ed. 89.95 incl. audio (*0-9667974-0-X*) C OKeefe.

***O'Keefe, Claudia, ed.** Father: Famous Writers Celebrate the Bond Between Father & Child. 2000. 12.00 (*0-671-04217-3*, PB Hardcover) PB.

— Father: Famous Writers Celebrate the Bond Between Father & Child. 368p. 2000. reprint ed. per. 13.95 (*0-671-00791-2*) PB.

O'Keefe, Claudia, ed. Forever Sisters: Famous Writers Celebrate the Power of Sisterhood with Short Stories, Essays & Memoirs. LC 98-43729. 320p. 1999. 23.00 (*0-671-00792-0*) PB.

***O'Keefe, Claudia, ed.** Forever Sisters: Famous Writers Celebrate the Power of Sisterhoood with Short Stories, Essays & Me. 320p. 2000. reprint ed. per. 13.95 (*0-671-04216-5*) PB.

O'Keefe, Claudia, ed. Ghosttide. (Illus.). 1992. pap. write for info. (*0-944494-22-6*) Lifeboat Bks.

— Mother: Twenty Famous Writers Celebrate Mother with a Treasury of Short Stories, Essays, Poems. 256p. 1996. pap. 12.00 (*0-671-52998-6*, PB Trade Paper) PB.

O'Keefe, Claudia, ed. see Clark, Mary Higgins, et al.

O'Keefe, Constance, jt. auth. see Kanno, Eiji.

O'Keefe, Cynthia A. Exploring the Real World: Middle School Edition. 200p. (Orig.). (J). Date not set. pap. 85.00 (*0-913956-89-9*) EBSCO.

— Exploring the Real World: Primary School Edition. 200p. (Orig.). (J). (gr. 4-6). Date not set. pap. 65.00 (*0-913956-88-0*) EBSCO.

— Exploring the Real World: Secondary Edition. 366p. (Orig.). (YA). (gr. 7-12). Date not set. pap. 283.00 (*0-913956-87-2*) EBSCO.

***O'Keefe, Deborah.** Good Girl Messages: How Young Women Were Misled by Their Favorite Books. LC 99-88181. 216p. 2000. 26.95 (*0-8264-1236-X*) Continuum.

O'Keefe, Dennis & Stoll, Patricia. Issues in School Attendance & Truancy. 1995. pap. 54.50 (*0-273-61686-2*, Pub. by F T P-H) Trans-Atl Phila.

O'Keefe, Donald H. Mountain of the Lion: The Great Revival in Sierra Leone, West Africa. LC 96-20617. 172p. (Orig.). 1996. pap. 8.99 (*1-56722-192-0*) Word Aflame.

O'Keefe, Donna. Linn's Philatelic Gems, No. 4. (Illus.). 167p. 1989. pap. 9.95 (*0-940403-12-9*) Linns Stamp News.

— Philatelic Gems, No. 2. (Illus.). 168p. 1985. reprint ed. pap. 9.95 (*0-940403-03-X*) Linns Stamp News.

— Philatelic Gems, No. 3. (Illus.). 168p. 1987. pap. 9.95 (*0-940403-02-1*) Linns Stamp News.

— Philatelic Gems, No. 3. (Illus.). 168p. 1987. reprint ed. pap. 9.95 (*0-940403-04-8*) Linns Stamp News.

— Philatelic Gems, No. 4. (Illus.). 168p. 1989. 30.00 (*0-940403-17-X*) Linns Stamp News.

— Philatelic Gems, No. 5. (Illus.). 168p. 1991. 30.00 (*0-940403-45-5*); pap. 9.95 (*0-940403-44-7*) Linns Stamp News.

— Philatelic Gems, Set. 1989. pap. 55.00 (*0-940403-16-1*) Linns Stamp News.

O'Keefe, Donna, ed. Linn's Stamp Identifier. LC 93-2693. 144p. (Orig.). 1993. pap. 9.95 (*0-940403-52-8*) Linns Stamp News.

O'Keefe, Edward & Berger, Donna. Instructor's Guide to Self-Management for College Students. (Orig.). 1995. pap. text 6.95 (*0-9637801-1-5*) Partridge Hill.

O'Keefe, Edward & Berger, Donna S. Self-Management for College Students: The ABC Approach. 1999. 2nd ed. LC 93-85780. 1999. pap. 24.95 (*0-9637801-3-1*) Partridge Hill.

***O'Keefe, Eric.** West Texas & the Big Bend. LC 99-29206. 1999. pap. text 15.95 (*0-89123-037-8*, 3037) Gulf Pub.

O

An Asterisk (*) at the beginning of an entry indicates that the title is appearing for the first time.

O'Keefe, Eric. Who Rules America: The People vs. The Political Class. LC 98-96756. 1998. pap. 12.95 (*0-9667559-0-1*) Citizen Govt Found.

O'Keefe, Frank. School Stinks. 132p. (YA). (gr. 7-11). 1991. pap. 4.95 (*0-7736-7294-X*) Stoddart Publ.

O'Keefe, Garrett J., et al. Taking a Bite Out of Crime: The Impact of a National Prevention Campaign. LC 96-25179. 176p. 1996. pap. 19.95 (*0-8039-5989-3*) Sage.

O'Keefe, Gavin, ed. see Blake, William.

O'keefe, Georgia. One Hundred Flowered Postcards. 1990. pap. write for info. (*0-316-88849-4*) Little.

O'Keefe, Georgia. One Hundred Flowers: Address Book. 1990. pap. write for info. (*0-316-88850-8*) Little.

O'Keefe, J. A. & Farrand, W. L. Introduction to New Zealand Law. 4th ed. 650p. 1986. pap. 63.00 (*0-409-65537-6*, NZ, MICHIE) LEXIS Pub.

O'Keefe, J. G., ed. The Day of Judgement. 1997. pap. 1.50 (*0-89979-094-1*) British Am Bks.

O'Keefe, J. G., ed. On the Observance of Sunday. (IRI.). 1996. pap. 1.50 (*0-89979-083-6*) British Am Bks.

O'Keefe, Jack. Reading to Writing: Form & Meaning. 352p. (C). 1990. pap. text 35.50 (*0-15-575784-9*, Pub. by Harcourt Coll Pubs) Harcourt.

O'Keefe, Jackie. Handlettering for Decorative Artists. LC 98-13041. (Illus.). 128p. 1998. pap. 22.99 (*0-89134-825-5*, North Lght Bks) F & W Pubns Inc.

O'Keefe, James H., et al. The Complete Guide to ECGs: A Comprehensive Study Guide to Improve ECG Interpretation Skills. (Illus.). 607p. (C). 1997. pap. text 49.95 (*1-890114-00-6*) Physicians Pr.

O'Keefe, Janet, jt. ed. see Bruyere, Susanne M.

O'Keefe, Jared. Pendulums. (Illus.). 128p. 1999. pap. 6.95 (*965-494-090-6*) Astrolog Pub.

OKeefe, JoAnna. Come to the Garden: An Invitation to Serenity. Mitchell, Julie, ed. (Illus.). 1992. 6.95 (*0-8378-2502-4*) Gibson.

O'Keefe, JoAnna. The Path Less Taken. (Illus.). 1996. 6.95 (*0-614-20841-6*) Gibson.

O'Keefe, John. Shimmer & Other Texts. LC 89-20312. 72p. (Orig.). 1989. pap. 6.95 (*1-55936-002-X*) Theatre Comm.

— What Color Is Your Swimming Pool? The Guide to Trouble-Free Pool Maintenance. Clarkson, Sarah M., ed. LC 85-61479. (Illus.). 120p. 1987. pap. 12.95 (*0-88266-408-5*, Storey Pub) Storey Bks.

O'Keefe, John & Shield, William. John O'Keefe & William Shield: The Poor Soldier (1783) Brasmer, William & Osborne, William, eds. (Recent Researches in American Music Ser.: No. RRAM6). (Illus.). 82, xiiip. 1978. pap. 35.00 (*0-89579-103-X*) A-R Eds.

O'Keefe, John J., jt. auth. see Allsopp, Michael E.

O'Keefe, John M. What Color Is Your Swimming Pool? The Guide to Trouble-Free Pool Maintenance. 2nd ed. LC 97-51750. (Illus.). 128p. 1998. pap. 12.95 (*1-58017-036-6*) Storey Bks.

O'Keefe, Joseph, jt. ed. see Haney, Regina.

O'Keefe, Joseph, ed. see O'Keeffe, Bernadette.

O'Keefe, Katherine O. Old English Shorter Poems: Basic Readings. LC 94-10194. (Basic Readings on Anglo-Saxon England Ser.: Vol. 3). 456p. 1994. text 77.00 (*0-8153-0097-2*, H1432) Garland.

O'Keefe, Katherine O., jt. ed. see Freese, Delores.

O'Keefe, Laura K., ed. Records of the National Council of Women of the United States, Inc., 1988-ca. 1970: A Guide to the Microfiche Edition. 41p. 1988. pap. 15.00 (*0-8357-0799-7*) Univ Microfilms.

O'Keefe, Lawrence P. Technology Assessment for State & Local Government: A Guide to Decision Making. LC 82-71314. 222p. reprint ed. pap. 68.90 (*0-608-12702-7*, 202352000033) Bks Demand.

O'Keefe, M. & Hyde, B. G. Symmetry & Structures of Crystals. 600p. 1997. text 97.00 (*981-02-1701-3*) World Scientific Pub.

O'Keefe, M. Timothy. Hiking Florida. LC 96-46307. (Illus.). 272p. 1997. pap. 14.95 (*1-56044-467-3*) Falcon Pub Inc.

***O'Keefe, M. Timothy.** Hiking Florida. (Illus.). 262p. 1999. pap. 14.95 (*1-56044-876-8*) Falcon Pub Inc.

O'Keefe, M. Timothy. Manatees - Our Vanishing Mermaids. LC 93-79803. (Illus.). 128p. (Orig.). 1993. pap. text 8.95 (*0-936513-43-8*) Larsens Outdoor.

— Sea Turtles: The Watchers Guide. LC 95-75545. (Illus.). 128p. (Orig.). 1993. pap. text 8.95 (*0-936513-47-0*) Larsens Outdoor.

— Seasonal Guide to the Natural Year: Florida with Georgia & Alabama Coasts. (Seasonal Guides to the Natural Year Ser.). (Illus.). 360p. (Orig.). 1996. pap. 16.95 (*1-55591-269-9*) Fulcrum Pub.

O'Keefe, M. Timothy, jt. auth. see Larsen, Larry.

O'Keefe, Mark. Becoming Good, Becoming Holy: On the Relationship of Christian Ethics & Spirituality. LC 95-16977. 192p. (Orig.). (C). 1995. pap. 11.95 (*0-8091-3593-0*) Paulist Pr.

O'Keefe, Mark, et al. The Living Light Vol. 31, No. 4: Summer 1995. Marthaler, Berard L., ed. 93p. (Orig.). 1995. pap. 8.95 (*1-55586-060-5*) US Catholic.

O'Keefe, Martin, ed. see De Aldama, Antonio M.

O'Keefe, Martin D. Known from the Things That Are: Fundamental Theory of the Moral Life. LC 87-16496. 348p. 1987. pap. 15.00 (*0-685-31935-0*) Ctr Thomistic.

— Known from the Things That Are: Fundamental Theory of the Moral Life. LC 87-16496. 348p. (C). 1987. pap. text 15.00 (*0-268-01228-8*) U of Notre Dame Pr.

O'Keefe, Martin D., tr. from LAT. A Guide for Delegates to a Province Congregation. LC 98-72984. (Series I: Vol. 18). Orig. Title: Manuale Congregationis Provinciae. vi, 44p. 1998. pap. 3.00 (*1-880810-34-4*) Inst Jesuit.

— Oremus: Speaking with God in the Words of the Roman Rite. LC 93-61062. (Series V: No. 2). (LAT.). viii, 390p. 1993. pap. 32.95 (*1-880810-28-X*) Inst Jesuit.

O'Keefe, Martin D., tr. see McCarthy, John L., ed.

O'Keefe, Mary E. Nursing Practice & the Law: Avoiding Malpractice & Other Legal Risks. (Illus.). 432p. 2000. 29.95 (*0-8036-0602-8*) Davis Co.

O'Keefe, Michael, ed. see Minerals, Metals & Materials Society Staff.

O'Keefe, Michael F., et al. Essentials of Emergency Care: A Refresher for the Practicing EMT-B. Dickinson, Edward T., ed. LC 95-19433. 496p. 1995. pap. text 44.00 (*0-8359-4963-X*) P-H.

O'Keefe, Michael F., ed. see Limmer.

O'Keefe, Nicolett, ed. see Higgins, Patrick W.

O'Keefe, Patrick J., jt. ed. see Harvey, Archer St. Clair.

O'Keefe, Peggy, ed. see Crane, Dick.

O'Keefe, Phil. Energy & Development in Southern Africa: SADCC Country Studies, Pt. II. Munslow, Barry, ed. (Energy, Environment & Development in Africa Ser.: No. 4). 227p. 1984. write for info. (*91-7106-231-9*, Pub. by Nordic Africa) Transaction Pubs.

O'Keefe, Phil, et al, eds. Energy & Development in Kenya: Opportunities & Constraints. (Energy, Environment & Development in Africa Ser.: No. 1). 190p. 1984. write for info. (*91-7106-225-4*, Pub. by Nordic Africa) Transaction Pubs.

O'Keefe, Phil & Munslow, Barry, eds. Energy & Development in Southern Africa: SADCC Country Studies, Pt. I. (Energy, Environment & Development in Africa Ser.: No. 3). 193p. 1984. write for info. (*91-7106-229-7*, Pub. by Nordic Africa) Transaction Pubs.

O'Keefe, Phil & Wisner, Ben, eds. Landuse & Development. LC 78-308975. (African Environment: Special Reports: Vol. 5). 242p. reprint ed. pap. 75.10 (*0-8357-3023-9*, 205711000010) Bks Demand.

O'Keefe, Phil, jt. auth. see Middleton, Neil.

O'Keefe, Philip & Van Gelder, Barry. The New Forester. 128p. (Orig.). 1995. pap. 19.50 (*1-85339-232-4*, Pub. by Intermed Tech) Stylus Pub VA.

O'Keefe, Philip, jt. auth. see Middleton, Neil.

O'Keefe, Richard A. The Craft of Prolog. (Logic Programming Ser.). 410p. 1990. 55.00 (*0-262-15039-5*) MIT Pr.

O'Keefe, Richard R. Mythic Archetypes in Ralph Waldo Emerson: A Blakean Reading. LC 95-1707. 232p. 1995. text 35.00 (*0-87338-518-7*) Kent St U Pr.

O'Keefe, Roger. Trusted Faces Violating Private Places: Teaching Your Children How to Protect Themselves from Sexual Assault. LC 95-18155. (Illus.). 150p. (Orig.). 1995. pap. 14.95 (*0-942963-56-3*) Distinctive Pub.

O'Keefe, Rose A. Cooking on the Coast: From Cajun-Creole to Caviar. 1994. pap. 14.95 (*0-9641501-0-7*) R A OKeefe.

O'Keefe, Ruth A. Starter One Hundred One, Bk. 8. AEVAC, Inc. Staff, ed. (Structured Beginning Reading Program Ser.). 96p. student ed. 3.50 (*0-913356-14-X*) AEVAC.

O'Keefe, S. T. Revision of the Nearctic Genus Lophioderus Casey: (Coleoptera: Scydmaenidae) (Thomas Say Publications in Entomology). (Illus.). 97p. 1996. pap. 35.00 (*0-938522-56-6*, ESATSP7) Entomol Soc.

***O'Keefe, Sarah.** Framemaker 5.5.6 for Dummies. (For Dummies Ser.). 384p. 1999. pap. 24.99 incl. cd-rom (*0-7645-0637-4*) IDG Bks.

O'Keefe, Sarah, jt. auth. see Prendergast, Alexia.

O'Keefe, Sean, jt. auth. see Susman, Gerald I.

O'Keefe, Steve. Publicity on the Internet: Creating Successful PublicityCampaigns on the internet & the Commercial online Services. LC 96-32539. (Illus.). 416p. 1996. pap. 29.95 (*0-471-16175-6*) Wiley.

O'Keefe, Susan H. Countdown to Christmas: Advent Thoughts, Prayers, & Activities. LC 95-16257. (Illus.). 96p. (Orig.). (J). (gr. 4-8). 1995. pap. 7.95 (*0-8091-6628-3*) Paulist Pr.

— One Hungry Monster: A Counting Book in Rhyme. (Illus.). 32p. (J). (ps-3). 1989. 12.95 (*0-316-63385-2*, Joy St Bks) Little.

— One Hungry Monster: A Counting Book in Rhyme. (Illus.). 32p. (J). (gr. k-3). 1992. pap. 5.95 (*0-316-63388-7*, Joy St Bks) Little.

— One Hungry Monster: A Counting Book in Rhyme. (J). 1989. 11.15 (*0-606-01417-9*, Pub. by Turtleback) Demco.

O'Keefe, Susan H., ed. see Stroman, J. & Wilson, K.

O'Keefe, Susan Heyboer. Master the ACT: 2000 Edition. 2000th ed. LC 99-61614. (Arco ACT). (Illus.). 693p. 1999. pap. 13.95 (*0-02-863238-9*, Arc) IDG Bks.

Okeefe, Susan Heyboer. Angel Prayers: Prayers for All Children. LC 98-88220. (Illus.). 32p. (J). (ps-1). 1999. 15.95 (*1-56397-683-8*) Boyds Mills Pr.

— Good Night, God Bless. LC 98-42724. 32p. (J). (gr. k-2). 1999. 15.95 (*0-8050-6008-1*) H Holt & Co.

Okeefe, Susan Heyboer, jt. auth. see Malanga, Tara.

***O'Keefe, Tallig.** Medieval Ireland. (Illus.). 1999. 32.50 (*0-7524-1464-X*, Pub. by Tempus Pubng) Arcadia Publng.

O'Keefe, Tara. Microsoft Excel 97. 1997. pap. text 24.99 (*0-7600-5609-9*) Course Tech.

— Microsoft Excel 7 for Windows 95 - Illustrated Plus, Incl. instr. resource kit, test mgr., Web pg. (Illustrated Ser.). (Illus.). 384p. 1996. text, mass mkt. 38.95 incl. 3.5 ld (*0-7600-3742-6*) Course Tech.

O'Keefe, Tara, jt. auth. see Reding, Elizabeth E.

O'Keefe, Tara Lynn, jt. auth. see Reding, Elizabeth Eisner.

O'Keefe, Theodore J., ed. Journal of Historical Review Vol. 7, Nos. 1-4: 1987 Index. 544p. 1988. 40.00 (*0-939484-48-X*, 1007, Inst Hist Rev) Legion Survival.

— Journal of Historical Review Vol. 8, Nos. 1-4: 1988 Index. 522p. 1989. 40.00 (*0-939484-34-X*, 1008, Inst Hist Rev) Legion Survival.

— Journal of Historical Review Vol. 9, Nos. 1-4: 1989 Index. 545p. 1990. 40.00 (*0-939484-41-2*, 1009, Inst Hist Rev) Legion Survival.

— Journal of Historical Review Vol. 10, Nos. 1-4: 1990 Index. 519p. 1991. 40.00 (*0-939484-42-0*, 1010, Inst Hist Rev) Legion Survival.

— Journal of Historical Review Vol. 11, Nos. 1-4: 1991 Index. 544p. 1992. 40.00 (*0-939484-43-9*, 1011, Inst Hist Rev) Legion Survival.

O'Keefe, Thomas A. Latin American Trade Agreements. 500p. 1997. ring bd. 185.00 (*1-57105-027-2*) Transnatl Pubs.

O'Keefe, Tim. Great Adventures in Florida. (Illus.). 192p. (Orig.). 1995. pap. 14.95 (*0-89732-183-9*) Menasha Ridge.

— Spicy Camp Cookbook. LC 96-48481. (Illus.). 128p. (Orig.). 1996. pap. 12.95 (*0-89732-188-X*) Menasha Ridge.

***O'Keefe, Timothy.** Florida. (Rails-to-Trails Ser.). (Illus.). 256p. 2000. pap. 14.95 (*0-7627-0712-7*) Globe Pequot.

O'Keefe, Timothy, jt. auth. see Mills, Heidi.

O'Keefe, Timothy, jt. auth. see Simos, Michele.

O'Keefe, Timothy J., ed. Columbus, Confrontation, Christianity: The European-American Encounter Revisited. LC 94-66842. (Illus.). 256p. (Orig.). 1994. pap. 19.95 (*0-9636059-1-7*) Forbes Mill.

O'Keefe, Timothy J., jt. auth. see Walsh, James P.

O'Keefe, Tom. The Art of Ray Swanson: Celebrating People & Lifestyles. Westheimer, Mary et al, eds. LC 92-82070. (Illus.). 208p. 1994. 45.00 (*0-9638565-0-2*) Old Paint.

***O'Keefe, Virginia.** Developing Critical Thinking: The Speaking/listening Connection. LC 99-30811. 100p. 1999. text 14.50 (*0-86709-491-5*, Pub. by Boynton Cook Pubs) Heinemann.

O'Keefe, Virginia. Speaking to Think/Thinking to Speak: The Importance of Talk in the Learning Process. LC 94-45175. 183p. 1995. pap. text 25.00 (*0-86709-358-7*, 0358, Pub. by Boynton Cook Pubs) Heinemann.

O'Keefe-Young, Mary, jt. auth. see Weidt, Maryann N.

O'Keeffe, B. Emer, jt. ed. see Harris, Ruth-Ann.

O'Keeffe, Bernadette. The Contemporary Catholic School: Context, Identity, & Diversity. McLaughlin, Terence H. & O'Keefe, Joseph, eds. LC 96-12660. 320p. 1996. 79.95 (*0-7507-0471-3*, Falmer Pr); pap. 27.95 (*0-7507-0472-1*, Falmer Pr) Taylor & Francis.

O'Keeffe, D. J. Truancy in English Secondary Schools: A Report Prepared for the DFE. 134p. 1994. pap. 19.00 (*0-11-270870-6*, HM08706, Pub. by Statnry Office) Bernan Associates.

O'Keeffe, Daniel, 2nd. One Heartbeat from Heaven: O'Keeffe Hunting Camp, 1914-1965. Cashion, Gerald, ed. (Illus.). 85p. 1997. pap. 11.95 (*0-9654280-1-X*) Sunset Ent.

O'Keeffe, David, et al, eds. Butterworths Expert Guide to the European Union. 296p. 1996. pap. write for info. (*0-406-04839-8*, BEGE, MICHIE) LEXIS Pub.

***O'Keeffe, David, et al.** Judicial Review in European Union Law: Essays in Honour of Lord Slynn. LC 00-39124. 2000. write for info. (*90-411-1372-X*) Kluwer Law Intl.

O'Keeffe, David, jt. ed. see Hervey, Tamara K.

O'Keeffe, David, jt. ed. see Twomey, Patrick.

***O'Keeffe, Dennis.** Political Correctness & Public Finance. 114p. 1999. 22.50 (*0-255-36478-4*, Pub. by Inst Economic Affairs) Coronet Bks.

O'Keeffe, Georgia. Essential Emergency Care. 1995. pap., teacher ed., suppl. ed. 44.00 (*0-8359-4975-3*) P-H.

— Georgia O'Keeffe. (Illus.). 224p. 1995. 29.98 (*1-884822-29-0*) Blck Dog & Leventhal.

— Georgia O'Keeffe: One Hundred Flowers. Callaway, Nicholas, ed. LC 87-45235. (Illus.). 160p. 1987. 100.00 (*0-394-56218-6*) Knopf.

— Georgia O'Keeffe: One Hundred Flowers. 1990. pap. 12.95 (*0-679-73323-X*) Knopf.

— Poppy, 1927. (Fine Art Jigsaw Puzzles Ser.). 1989. 9.95 (*0-934967-49-0*) Battle Rd Pr.

— Reading to Writing. (C). 1991. pap. text, teacher ed. 3.75 (*0-15-575785-7*) Harcourt Coll Pubs.

— Some Memories of Drawings. LC 74-14986. 1974. 250.00 (*0-686-17542-5*, Archway) PB.

O'Keeffe, Georgia, et al. Georgia O'Keeffe: One Hundred Flowers. (Illus.). 1995. 49.99 (*0-614-15409-X*) Random Hse Value.

O'Keeffe, John. Business Beyond the Box: Applying Your Mind for Breakthrough Results. (Illus.). 244p. 1999. pap. 16.00 (*1-85788-213-X*) Nicholas Brealey.

— Recollections of the Life of John O'Keeffe, 2 vols. LC 70-89711. 1972. 48.95 (*0-405-08828-0*) Ayer.

— Wild Oats. 96p. (Orig.). 1996. pap. 12.95 (*1-85459-229-7*, Pub. by N Hern Bks) Theatre Comm.

O'Keeffe, Katherine O., ed. Reading Old English Texts. LC 96-47374. 244p. (C). 1997. text 64.95 (*0-521-46575-3*); pap. text 19.95 (*0-521-46970-8*) Cambridge U Pr.

O'Keeffe, Katherine O., jt. ed. see Keefer, Sarah L.

O'Keeffe, Katherine O'Brien, jt. ed. see Ezell, Margaret J. M.

O'Keeffe, Linda. Shoes: A Celebration of Pumps, Sandals, Slippers & More. LC 96-20755. (Illus.). 512p. 1996. pap. 11.95 (*0-7611-0114-4*, 10114) Workman Pub.

***O'Keeffe, Michael, ed.** Residue Analysis in Food: Principles & Applications. 324p. 1999. text 95.00 (*90-5702-441-1*, Harwood Acad Pubs) Gordon & Breach.

O'Keeffe, Michael & Hyde, B. G. Crystal Structures No. I: I. Patterns & Symmetry. (Mineralogical Society of America Monograph Ser.). (Illus.). 453p. (C). 1996. 36.00 (*0-939950-40-5*) Mineralogical Soc.

O'Keeffe, Michael, jt. ed. see Twite, Garry.

O'Keeffe, Pat. Kick Boxing: A Framework for Success. (Illus.). 1998. pap. 19.95 (*1-873475-23-3*, Pub. by Summers) Howell Pr VA.

— Kick Boxing: A Framework for Success. 2nd rev. ed. 160p. 1999. pap. 19.95 (*1-84024-093-8*, Pub. by Summers) Seven Hills Bk.

O'Keeffe, Peter & Simington, Tom. Irish Stone Bridges: History & Heritage. (Illus.). 352p. 1991. 42.50 (*0-7165-2465-1*, Pub. by Irish Acad Pr) Intl Spec Bk.

Okehie-Offoha, Marcellina U. & Sadiku, Matthew N. Diversity & Culture in Multiethnic Nigeria. Date not set. pap. 18.95 (*0-86543-283-X*) Africa World.

Okehie-Offoha, Marcellina U. & Sadiku, Matthew N., eds. Ethnic & Cultural Diversity in Nigeria. 1995. 59.95 (*0-86543-282-1*) Africa World.

Okeke, Chika. Fante. Bond, George, ed. LC 95-20128. (Heritage Library of African Peoples). (Illus.). 64p. (YA). (gr. 7-12). 1997. lib. bdg. 16.95 (*0-8239-1981-1*) Rosen Group.

— Kongo. LC 96-7892. (Heritage Library of African Peoples). (Illus.). 64p. (YA). (gr. 7-12). 1997. lib. bdg. 16.95 (*0-8239-2001-1*) Rosen Group.

Okeke-Ibezim, Felicia. O. J. Simpson: The Trial of the Century. LC 97-94874. (Illus.). 124p. 1997. pap. 9.95 (*0-9661598-0-2*) Ekwike Bks & Pub.

Okell, John. Burmese: A Course in Four Volumes, 4 vols. (Illus.). 1994. pap. text 179.95 incl. audio (*1-877979-49-X*) SE Asia.

— Burmese: An Introduction to the Literary Style. (Southeast Asian Language Text Ser.). 1994. pap. 23.00 incl. audio (*1-877979-44-9*) SE Asia.

— Burmese: An Introduction to the Script. (Southeast Asian Language Text Ser.). 1994. pap. 51.00 incl. audio (*1-877979-43-0*) SE Asia.

— Burmese: An Introduction to the Spoken Language, Bk. 1. (Southeast Asian Language Text Ser.). 1994. pap. 56.00 incl. audio (*1-877979-41-4*) SE Asia.

— Burmese: An Introduction to the Spoken Language, Bk. 2. (Southeast Asian Language Text Ser.). 1994. pap. 62.00 incl. audio (*1-877979-42-2*) SE Asia.

O'Kelley, Charles R., Jr. & Thompson, Robert B. Corporations & Other Business Associations: Cases & Materials. 2nd ed. LC 95-81928. 1282p. 1996. teacher ed. write for info. (*0-316-63816-1*, 38161) Aspen Law.

O'Kelley, Charles R. & Thompson, Robert B. Corporations & Other Business Associations: Cases & Materials. 3rd ed. LC 98-55064. 1999. boxed set 58.00 (*0-7355-0211-0*) Panel Pubs.

— Corporations & Other Business Associations: Selected Statutes, Rules, & Forms: 1997 Edition. 850p. 1997. write for info. (*1-56706-571-6*, 65716) Panel Pubs.

***O'Kelley, Charles R. & Thompson, Robert B.** Corporations & Other Business Associations: Selected Statutes, Rules, & Forms: 1999-2000 Supplement. 912p. 1999. pap. text, suppl. ed. 26.95 (*0-7355-0030-4*, 00304, Aspen Law & Bus) Aspen Pub.

O'Kelley, Hallie H. Screen Printing for Quilters. 1995. pap. 17.95 (*1-881320-44-8*, Black Belt) Black Belt Communs.

O'Kelley, Joyce. Love Letters to God. 1989. 7.95 (*0-86544-053-0*) Salv Army Suppl South.

Okello, James. Mcheshi Goes to the Market: Mcheshi Aenda Sokoni. 1991. 13.15 (*0-606-08819-9*, Pub. by Turtleback) Demco.

O'Kelly, Bernard & Jarrott, Catherine A., eds. John Colet's Commentary on First Corinthians: A New Edition of the Latin Text, With Translation, Annotations & Introduction. LC 82-12403. (Medieval & Renaissance Texts & Studies: Vol. 21). (Illus.). 352p. 1985. 30.00 (*0-86698-056-3*, MR21) MRTS.

O'Kelly, Charlotte G. Women & Men in Society: Cross-Cultural Perspectives on Gender Stratification. (Sociology - Introductory Level Ser.). 1980. pap. 9.75 (*0-534-25794-1*) Wadsworth Pub.

O'Kelly, Donal. Catalpa. (Nick Hern Bks.). 96p. 1997. pap. 14.95 (*1-85459-357-9*, Pub. by N Hern Bks) Theatre Comm.

O'Kelly, Kevin. Richland Street. LC 96-61466. 283p. (Orig.). 1997. reprint ed. pap. 18.95 (*0-9653864-5-7*) Wacahoota Pr.

O'Kelly, M. E., jt. auth. see Fotheringham, A. S.

O'Kelly, Michael J. Early Ireland: An Introduction to Irish Prehistory. 392p. 1989. pap. text 37.95 (*0-521-33687-2*) Cambridge U Pr.

— Here Kitty, Kitty: Here Kiddy, Kiddy. (Illus.). 565p. (C). 1989. 29.95 (*0-685-26324-X*); text 24.95 (*0-685-26325-8*); pap. text 9.95 (*0-685-26326-6*) M J OKelly.

— Newgrange: Archaeology, Art & Legend. LC 81-86413. (New Aspects of Antiquity Ser.). (Illus.). 240p. 1995. pap. 22.50 (*0-500-27371-5*, Pub. by Thames Hudson) Norton.

O'Kelly, Seumas. The Lady of Deer Park. LC 96-60146. 320p. (Orig.). 2000. pap. 14.95 (*1-885983-14-X*) Turtle Point Pr.

— Waysiders: Stories of Connacht. LC 73-150480. (Short Story Index Reprint Ser.). 1977. reprint ed. 19.95 (*0-8369-3821-6*) Ayer.

Okely, Judith. Anthropological Practice: Fieldwork & the Ethnographic Method. 352p. (C). 1999. 65.00 (*0-415-11361-X*) Routledge.

— Own or Other Culture. LC 95-25985. 256p. (C). 1996. 90.00 (*0-415-11512-4*); pap. 25.99 (*0-415-11513-2*) Routledge.

— The Traveller-Gypsies. LC 82-9478. (Illus.). 272p. 1983. pap. text 24.95 (*0-521-28870-3*) Cambridge U Pr.

Okely, Judith & Callaway, Helen, eds. Anthropology & Autobiography. LC 91-32485. (ASA Monographs Ser.: No. 29). (Illus.). 272p. (C). (gr. 13). 1992. pap. 25.99 (*0-415-05189-4*, A5912) Routledge.

Okema, Michael. Political Culture of Tanzania. LC 95-30882. 172p. 1996. 79.95 (*0-7734-8921-5*) E Mellen.

Oken, Alan. Alan Oken's Complete Astrology. 2nd rev. ed. LC 87-47885. (Illus.). 640p. 1988. pap. 17.95 (*0-553-34537-0*) Bantam.

***Oken, Alan.** The Hidden Rulers of the Horoscope: The Inner Structure of the Natal Chart. 200p. 2000. pap. 18.95 (*0-89594-998-9*, Pub. by Crossing Pr) Publishers Group.

Oken, Alan. Houses of the Horoscope: An Introduction. LC 98-55281. 128p. 1999. pap. 14.95 (*0-89594-932-6*) Crossing Pr.

— Pocket Guide to Astrology. (Crossing Press Pocket Ser.). (Illus.). 128p. 1996. pap. 6.95 (*0-89594-820-6*) Crossing Pr.

— Pocket Guide to Numerology. (Crossing Press Pocket Ser.). 96p. (Orig.). 1996. pap. 6.95 (*0-89594-826-5*) Crossing Pr.

— Pocket Guide to Tarot. (Crossing Press Pocket Ser.). (Illus.). 176p. (Orig.). 1996. pap. 6.95 (*0-89594-822-2*) Crossing Pr.

— Soul-Centered Astrology: A Key to Your Expanding Self. (Illus.). 450p. 1996. pap. 18.95 (*0-89594-811-7*) Crossing Pr.

Oken, Carole & Asch, Beth J. Encouraging Recruiter Achievement: A Recent History of Military Recruiter Incentive Programs. LC 97-37885. (Illus.). 111p. 1997. pap. 9.00 (*0-8330-2552-X*, MR-845-OSD/A) Rand Corp.

Oken, Lorenz. Lehrbuch der Naturphilosophie. (GER.). 1997. reprint ed. 128.00 (*3-487-09453-3*) G Olms Pubs.

Okenfuss, Max J. The Rise & Fall of Latin Humanism in Early-Modern Russia: Pagan Authors, Ukrainians, & the Resiliency of Muscovy. LC 95-15028. (Studies in Intellectual History: Vol. 64). (Illus.). 312p. 1995. 99.50 (*90-04-10331-7*) Brill Academic Pubs.

Okenfuss, Max J., tr. & intro. see Tolstoi, Peter.

Okenimkpe, Michael, jt. auth. see Cook, David.

O'Kennedy, R. & Thornes, R. D., eds. Coumarins: Biology, Applications & Mode of Action. LC 96-31627. 358p. 1997. 175.00 (*0-471-96997-4*) Wiley.

Okeragori, Abel. Totems of the Kisii. 1995. 14.95 (*9966-884-74-2*) Nocturnal Sun.

Okere, Theophilus, ed. Identity & Change: Nigerian Philosophical Studies I. LC 94-40762. (Cultural Heritage & Contemporary Change, Ser. II, Africa: Vol. 3). 1995. pap. 17.50 (*1-56518-072-0*) Coun Res Values.

Okereke, Okoro. Agrarian Development Programmes of African Countries: A Reappraisal of Problems of Policy. (Research Report Ser.: No. 28). 20p. 1975. write for info. (*91-7106-086-3*, Pub. by Nordic Africa) Transaction Pubs.

Okerlund, Twila. Stepping Toward Control: A Book for People Who Live with Diabetes. Allen, Susan D. & Holloran, Colleen A., eds. (Illus.). 64p. pap. text 3.75 (*0-916999-15-7*) HERC Inc.

***Okerlund, William C.** For Love or Nothing: Lessons to Illuminate the Path to Love. 144p. (C). 2000. pap. 11.95 (*0-9678713-0-1*, Pub. by Guidepost) BookMasters.

O'Kerry, Janeen. Mistress of the Waters. (Love Spell Ser.). 320p. 1999. mass mkt. 4.99 (*0-505-52309-4*, Love Spell) Dorchester Pub Co.

— Queen of the Sun. 320p. 1998. mass mkt. 4.99 (*0-505-52269-1*, Love Spell) Dorchester Pub Co.

Okerson, Ann, ed. Filling the Pipeline & Paying the Piper: Proceedings of the Fourth Symposium. LC 96-173703. 260p. 1995. 20.00 (*0-918006-25-2*) ARL.

— Visions & Opportunities in Electronic Publishing: Proceedings of the 2nd Symposium. 175p. 1993. pap. 20.00 (*0-918006-61-9*) ARL.

Okerson, Ann & O'Donnell, James, eds. Scholarly Journals at the Crossroads: A Subversive Proposal for Electronic Publishing. 250p. 1995. pap. 20.00 (*0-918006-26-0*) ARL.

Okerson, Anne, ed. Gateways, Gatekeepers & Roles in the Information Omniverse: Proceedings of the Third Symposium. 176p. 1994. pap. 20.00 (*0-918006-73-2*) ARL.

Okerstrom, Dennis & Morgan, Sarah J. Peace & War: Readings for Writers. 512p. (C). 1992. pap. 37.00 (*0-205-13603-6*, H3603-1) Allyn.

Okerstrom, Dennis, jt. auth. see Morgan, Sarah J.

Okeshia, Alma. Darker Than a Thousand Midnights. 35p. 1998. pap. 9.95 (*1-892896-37-0*) Buy Books.

Okeson, Jeffrey P. Bell's Orofacial Pains. 5th ed. LC 95-1313. (Illus.). 400p. 1995. text 68.00 (*0-86715-293-1*) Quint Pub Co.

— Management of Temporomandibular Disorders & Occlusion. 4th ed. LC 97-35663. (Illus.). 656p. (C). (gr. 13). 1997. text 71.00 (*0-8151-6939-6*, 27162) Mosby Inc.

Okeson, Jeffrey P., ed. see American Academy of Orofacial Pain Staff.

Okey, Robin. Eastern Europe, 1740-1985: Feudalism to Communism. 2nd ed. LC 86-11319. (Illus.). 264p. (C). 1987. pap. 18.95 (*0-8166-1561-6*) U of Minn Pr.

Okey, Robin. The Habsburg Monarchy: From Enlightenment to Eclipse. text 35.00 (*0-312-23375-2*) St Martin.

Okey, T. The Story of Paris. (Mediaeval Towns Ser.: Vol. 15). 1974. reprint ed. 65.00 (*0-8115-0857-9*) Periodicals Srv.

Okeze, Ignatius. Hope for Your Marriage. 110p. 1997. pap. 10.95 (*0-9662098-0-X*) Light of Life.

Okhee Kim, tr. see ChiWhan Yoo.

Okhi, S., et al, eds. Molecular Mechanisms of Membrane Fusion. LC 87-29163. (Illus.). 598p. 1988. 125.00 (*0-306-42773-7*, Plenum Trade) Perseus Pubng.

Okholm, Dennis L. The Gospel in Black & White: Theological Resources for Racial Reconciliation. LC 96-29817. 196p. (Orig.). 1997. pap. 15.99 (*0-8308-1887-1*, 1887) InterVarsity.

Okholm, Dennis L., jt. ed. see Phillips, Timothy R.

Okhravi, Narciss. Manual of Primary Eye Care. LC 97-144804. (Illus.). 192p. 1997. text 45.00 (*0-7506-2221-0*) Buttrwrth-Heinemann.

***Okhravi, Narciss.** Manual of Primary Eye Care. 176p. 1999. reprint ed. 35.00 (*0-7506-4467-2*) Buttrwrth-Heinemann.

Okhubo, Hitoshi, tr. see Fukuda, Tadashi.

Oki, Michinori. Applications of Dynamic NMR Spectroscopy to Organic Chemistry. LC 84-20844. (Methods in Stereochemical Analysis Ser.: Vol. 4). 423p. 1985. lib. bdg. 140.00 (*0-89573-120-7*, Wiley-VCH) Wiley.

Oki, Michinori & Ito, Sho. The Chemistry of Rotational Isomers. LC 92-37400. (Reactivity & Structure Ser.: Vol. 30). 1993. 159.95 (*0-387-56193-5*) Spr-Verlag.

Oki, Morihiro, photos by. India: Fairs & Festivals. (Illus.). 160p. 1989. 29.95 (*0-87040-823-2*) Japan Pubns USA.

Okidegbe, Nwanze. Agriculture Sector Programs: Sourcebook. LC 98-30553. (Technical Paper Ser.: No. 418F). 87p. 1998. pap. 22.00 (*0-8213-4323-8*, 14323) World Bank.

— Agriculture Sector Programs: Sourcebook. (Technical Paper Ser.: No. 418F). (FRE.). 100p. 1999. pap. 22.00 (*0-8213-4453-6*, 14453) World Bank.

— Fostering Sustainable Development: The Sector Investment Program. LC 97-15318. (Discussion Paper Ser.: No. 363). 36p. 1997. pap. 22.00 (*0-8213-3941-9*, 13941) World Bank.

Okie, Laird. Augustan Historical Writing: Histories of England in the English Enlightenment. 248p. (C). 1991. lib. bdg. 48.00 (*0-8191-8050-5*) U Pr of Amer.

Okie, Susan, jt. auth. see Ride, Sally.

O'Kieffe, Charley. Western Story: The Recollections of Charley O'Kieffe, 1884-1898. LC 60-5381. (Pioneer Heritage Ser.: No. 2). 239p. 1974. reprint ed. pap. 74.10 (*0-608-01396-X*, 206215900002) Bks Demand.

Okigbo, Pius N. Africa & the Common Market. LC 67-18007. 199p. reprint ed. pap. 61.70 (*0-8357-5223-2*, 201671800004) Bks Demand.

— National Development Planning in Nigeria, 1900-1992. 229p. (C). 1989. text 40.00 (*0-435-08039-3*, 08039) Heinemann.

— Nigerian Public Finance. LC 65-15473. (Northwestern University African Studies Ser.: No. 15). 259p. reprint ed. pap. 80.30 (*0-608-13053-2*, 201485500096) Bks Demand.

— Nigeria's Financial System. LC 82-158952. 300p. reprint ed. pap. 93.00 (*0-8357-2969-9*, 203923100011) Bks Demand.

Okihiro, Gary Y. Cane Fires: The Anti-Japanese Movement in Hawaii, 1865-1945. (Asian American History & Culture Ser.). 1991. pap. 22.95 (*0-87722-945-7*) Temple U Pr.

— Margins & Mainstreams: Asians in American History & Culture. LC 93-44382. 222p. (C). 1994. 25.00 (*0-295-97338-2*); pap. 13.95 (*0-295-97339-0*) U of Wash Pr.

***Okihiro, Gary Y.** A Social History of the Bakwena & Peoples of the Kalahari of Southern Africa, 19th Century. LC 99-57090. (African Studies: Vol. 52). (Illus.). 220p. 2000. text 89.95 (*0-7734-7839-6*) E Mellen.

Okihiro, Gary Y. Stories Lives: Japanese American Students & World War II. LC 98-51100. (Scott & Laurie Oki Series in Asian American Studies). 1999. write for info. (*0-295-97764-7*) U of Wash Pr.

***Okihiro, Gary Y.** Stories Lives: Japanese American Students & World War II. LC 98-51100. (Scott & Laurie Oki Series in Asian American Studies). (Illus.). 208p. 1999. 17.50 (*0-295-97796-5*) U of Wash Pr.

Okihiro, Gary Y. Teaching Asian American History. Painter, Nell I. & Rios-Bustamante, Antonio, eds. LC 97-73462. (Teaching Diversity Ser.). 57p. 1997. pap. 8.00 (*0-87229-077-8*) Am Hist Assn.

— Whispered Silences: Japanese Americans & World War II. LC 95-21895. (Samuel & Althea Stroum Bks.). (Illus.). 256p. 1996. pap. 29.95 (*0-295-97498-2*); text 60.00 (*0-295-97497-4*) U of Wash Pr.

Okihiro, Gary Y., ed. In Resistance: Studies in African, Caribbean, & Afro-American History. LC 85-28874. 240p. 1986. reprint ed. pap. 74.40 (*0-7837-9205-0*, 204995500004) Bks Demand.

Okihiro, Norman. Mounties, Moose, & Moonshine: The Patterns & Context of Outport Crime. LC 97-139115. (Illus.). 224p. 1997. text 45.00 (*0-8020-0891-7*); pap. text 19.95 (*0-8020-7874-5*) U of Toronto Pr.

Okihiro, Norman, jt. auth. see Waller, Irvin.

Okiji, A. & Kawakami, N., eds. Correlation Effects in Low-Dimensional Electron Systems: Proceedings of the 16th Taniguchi Symposium, Kashkojima, Japan, October 25-29, 1993. LC 94-8947. (Springer Series in Solid-State Sciences: Vol. 118). 1994. 86.95 (*0-387-57878-1*) Spr-Verlag.

Okiji, A., ed. see Kasai, H.

Okiko, Miyake & Biesel, Diane, eds. Proceedings of the Fourth Pacific Rim Conference on Children's Literature: Children's Rights in the Multimedia Age, August 24-28, 1993, Kyoto, Japan. LC 97-10055. 240p. 1996. 68.00 (*0-8108-3206-2*) Scarecrow.

***Okilo, Melford.** The Law of Balance. 26p. 1999. pap. text 5.00 (*1-879605-61-9*) U Sci & Philos.

— The Law of Giving. 15p. 1999. pap. 5.00 (*1-879605-63-5*) U Sci & Philos.

Okilo, Melford. The Law of Life. 250p. 1991. text 5.00 (*1-879605-03-1*) U Sci & Philos.

***Okilo, Melford.** The Law of Love. 48p. 1999. pap. 5.00 (*1-879605-62-7*) U Sci & Philos.

Okilo, Melford. Love Creates Balance. 1991. 3.00 (*1-879605-04-X*) U Sci & Philos.

***Okilo, Melford.** Man's New Cycle. 45p. 1999. pap. 5.00 (*1-879605-65-1*) U Sci & Philos.

— Man's Secret Power. 19p. 1999. pap. 5.00 (*1-879605-64-3*) U Sci & Philos.

Okimoto, Daniel I. Between MITI & the Market: Japanese Industrial Policy for High Technology. LC 88-39837. (ISIS Studies in International Policy). 288p. 1989. pap. 14.95 (*0-8047-1812-1*) Stanford U Pr.

— The Japan-America Security Alliance: Prospects for the 21st Century. 60p. 1998. pap. 7.50 (*0-9653935-4-2*) Asia-Pacific Res.

Okimoto, Daniel I., et al, eds. Competitive Edge: The Semiconductor Industry in the U. S. & Japan. LC 83-40107. (ISIS Studies in International Policy). xviii, 275p. 1984. 39.50 (*0-8047-1225-5*) Stanford U Pr.

Okimoto, Daniel I. & Rohlen, Thomas P., eds. Inside the Japanese System: Readings on Contemporary Society & Political Economy. LC 87-18820. xiv, 286p. 1988. pap. 15.95 (*0-8047-1423-1*) Stanford U Pr.

Okimoto, Daniel I., et al. The Semiconductor Competition & National Security. (Special Report of the Northeast Asia-United States Forum on International Policy, Stanford University Ser.). 87p. (Orig.). 1987. pap. 12.00 (*0-935371-16-8*) CFISAC.

Okimoto, Daniel I., et al. A United States Policy for the Changing Realities of East Asia: Toward a New Consensus. unabridged ed. xii, 64p. (Orig.). 1996. pap. 10.00 (*0-9653935-0-X*, 96-04) Asia-Pacific Res.

Okimoto, Daniel I., jt. ed. see Inoguchi, Takashi.

Okimoto, Jean D. Blumpoe Grumpoe Meets Arnold C, Vol. 1. (J). (ps-3). 1990. 13.95 (*0-316-63811-0*, Joy St Bks) Little.

— Blumpoe the Grumpoe Meets Arnold the Cat. 2nd ed. (Illus.). 28p. (J). (gr. k-5). 1997. reprint ed. 15.00 (*0-9661149-0-6*, 1) TigerHorse.

— The Eclipse of Moonbeam Dawson. LC 97-19533. 192p. (J). (gr. 7-10). 1997. text 17.95 (*0-312-86244-X*) St Martin.

— The Eclipse of Moonbeam Dawson. (J). 1997. 18.95 (*0-614-29310-3*) Tor Bks.

— Jason's Women. LC 85-28655. 210p. (YA). (gr. 7 up). 1986. 14.95 (*0-316-63809-9*, 638099, Joy St Bks) Little.

— No Dear, Not Here: The Marbled Murrelets' Quest for a Nest in the Pacific Northwest. (Illus.). 32p. (J). (ps-2). 1995. 14.95 (*1-57061-019-3*) Sasquatch Bks.

— A Place for Grace. (Illus.). 32p. (J). (ps up). 1996. reprint ed. pap. 7.95 (*1-57061-069-X*) Sasquatch Bks.

— Take a Chance, Gramps! (J). (gr. 3-7). 1996. mass mkt. 3.99 (*0-8125-4323-8*, Pub. by Tor Bks) St Martin.

— Take a Chance, Gramps! (J). 1996. 9.09 (*0-606-12531-0*, Pub. by Turtleback) Demco.

— Talent Night. LC 93-34591. 176p. (YA). (gr. 7-9). 1995. 14.95 (*0-590-47809-5*) Scholastic Inc.

Okimoto, Jean Davies. Eclipse of Moonbeam Dawson. (YA). (gr. 10 up). 1998. pap. 4.99 (*0-8125-6172-4*, Pub. by Tor Bks) St Martin.

***Okimoto, Jean Davies.** To JayKae: Life Stinx. LC 99-38398. 192p. (YA). (gr. 9 up). 1999. 18.95 (*0-312-86732-8*, Pub. by Tor Bks) St Martin.

Okin, Louis, jt. ed. see Burstein, Stanley M.

Okin, Milton, ed. From the Heart Easy Piano. 64p. (YA). pap. text 9.95 (*0-89524-885-9*) Cherry Lane.

Okin, Susan M. Justice, Gender & the Family. LC 89-42519. 224p. 1991. pap. 15.00 (*0-465-03703-8*, Pub. by Basic) HarpC.

— Women in Western Political Thought. LC 79-84004. 384p. 1979. pap. text 18.95 (*0-691-02191-0*, Pub. by Princeton U Pr) Cal Prin Full Svc.

Okin, Susan M. & Mansbridge, Jane, eds. Feminism, 2 vols. (Schools of Thought in Politics Ser.: Vol. 6). 896p. 1994. 295.00 (*1-85278-565-9*) E Elgar.

Okin, Susan M., et al. Is Multiculturalism Bad for Women? LC 99-21303. 146p. 1999. 12.95 (*0-691-00432-3*, Pub. by Princeton U Pr) Cal Prin Full Svc.

***Okin, Susan Moller.** Is Multiculturalism Bad for Women? LC 99-21303. 146p. 1999. 29.95 (*0-691-00431-5*, Pub. by Princeton U Pr) Cal Prin Full Svc.

Okin, Susan Moller, ed. & intro. see Mill, John Stuart.

Okita, Dwight. Crossing with the Light. 60p. 1992. pap. 6.95 (*0-9624287-9-5*) Tia Chucha Pr.

Okita, K., ed. HCV & Related Liver Diseases. (Illus.). 132p. 1999. 79.00 (*4-431-70235-0*) Spr-Verlag.

***Okita, K., ed.** Progress in Hepatocellular Carcinoma Treatment. LC 99-48955. xii, 112p. 2000. 79.00 (*4-431-70257-1*) Spr-Verlag.

Okita, Saburo. The Developing Economics of Japan. 284p. 1980. 37.50 (*0-86008-271-7*, Pub. by U of Tokyo) Col U Pr.

— Japan in the World Economy of the 1980s. 270p. 1989. text 37.50 (*0-86008-451-5*, Pub. by U of Tokyo) Col U Pr.

— Postwar Reconstruction of the Japanese Economy. 200p. 1992. text 44.50 (*0-86008-478-7*, Pub. by U of Tokyo) Col U Pr.

Okkema, Kathleen. Cognition & Perception in the Stroke Patient: A Guide to Functional Outcomes in Occupational Therapy. LC 92-48191. (Rehabilitation Institute of Chicago Publication Ser.). 220p. 1993. 64.00 (*0-8342-0362-6*, 20362) Aspen Pub.

Okken, Albert A. & Koch, Jochim J., eds. Thermoregulation of Sick & Low Birth Weight Neonates: Temperature Control, Temperature Monitoring, Thermal Environment. (Illus.). 256p. 1995. 104.00 (*3-540-60169-4*) Spr-Verlag.

Okken, P. A., et al, eds. Climate & Energy: The Feasibility of Controlling CO2 Emissions. (C). 1989. text 160.00 (*0-7923-0519-1*) Kluwer Academic.

Okker, Patricia. Our Sister Editors: Sarah J. Hale & the Tradition of Nineteenth-Century American Women Editors. LC 94-15269. (Illus.). 280p. 1995. 40.00 (*0-8203-1686-5*) U of Ga Pr.

Okkonen, Marc. Federal League. 64p. 1989. pap. 12.00 (*0-910137-37-4*) Soc Am Baseball Res.

— Minor League Baseball Towns of Michigan: Adrian to Ypsilanti. (Illus.). 186p. 1997. pap. 16.95 (*1-882376-43-9*) Thunder Bay Pr.

— USS Silversides SS236: An Illustrated Record of Silversides' War Patrol Period, Dec. 1941-Aug. 1945. (Illus.). 48p. 1998. pap. 14.95 (*0-9665487-9-5*) T Carlson.

Okladnikov, Aleksei P. Ancient Population of Siberia & Its Cultures. Maurin, Vladimir M., tr. LC 76-38729. (Harvard University. Peabody Museum of Archaeology & Ethnology. Antiquities of the New World Ser.: Vol. 1, No. 1). reprint ed. 47.50 (*0-404-52641-1*) AMS Pr.

Okladnikov, Alekseui P. Yakutia Before Its Incorporation into the Russian State. LC 71-102976. (Arctic Institute of North America-Anthropology of the North; Translation from Russian Sources Ser.: No. 8). (Illus.). 541p. reprint ed. pap. 167.80 (*0-7837-1171-9*, 204170000022) Bks Demand.

Oklahoma City Community College - Division of Science & Math Staff. Human Anatomy & Physiology (Bio 1314) Laboratory Manual. 1996. text 7.13 (*1-56870-252-3*) RonJon Pub.

Oklahoma City Document Management Team Staff. City of Oklahoma City Final Report, Alfred P. Murrah Federal Building Bombing, April 19, 1995. LC 96-85340. (Illus.). 350p. 1996. pap. text 17.50 (*0-87939-130-8*, 35942) IFSTA.

Oklahoma City Orchestra Staff. Applause. 1995. pap. text 17.95 (*0-9643907-0-1*) OK City Orchestra.

Oklahoma, D. K. The Light in the Mill. 80p. (YA). (gr. 10 up). 1989. pap. 5.50 (*0-87129-900-3*, L64) Dramatic Pub.

Oklahoma Department of Libraries Staff. Directory of Oklahoma: State Almanac. 43rd ed. Vesely, Marilyn & Lester, Patricia, eds. (Illus.). 792p. 1991. pap. 12.00 (*1-880438-00-3*) OK Dept Lib.

Oklahoma Department of Libraries Staff, et al, eds. Oklahoma Almanac. 44th ed. 792p. 1993. pap. 12.00 (*1-880438-01-1*) OK Dept Lib.

Oklahoma Department of Wildlife Conservation Staff. Oklahoma Watchable Wildlife Viewing Guide, 2 vols. 84p. 1993. pap. 7.95 (*0-614-06141-5*) Falcon Pub Inc.

Oklahoma Dept. of Vo-Tech Education Staff. Peak: Practical Exercises in Applying Knowledge - PeakMath. 2nd rev. ed. (Illus.). 300p. (YA). (gr. 9-12). 1995. ring bd. 195.00 (*1-892312-06-9*) Coin Eductnl.

— Peak: Practical Exercises in Applying Knowledge - PeakScience. 2nd rev. ed. (Illus.). 300p. (YA). (gr. 9-12). 1995. ring bd. 195.00 (*1-892312-16-6*) Coin Eductnl.

Oklahoma Future Homemakers of America Staff. Discover Oklahoma Cookin' LC 93-72517. 1993. write for info. (*0-87197-388-X*) Favorite Recipes.

— Oklahoma Recipe Roundup. LC 92-20293. 1992. pap. write for info. (*0-87197-340-5*) Favorite Recipes.

Oklahoma State Staff. Making Connections: Arts & Sciences 1111. 126p. (C). 1997. per. 10.95 (*0-7872-4187-3*, 41418701) Kendall-Hunt.

Oklahoma State University Staff. Geography 1114. 172p. (C). 1999. spiral bd., lab manual ed. 20.95 (*0-7872-5688-9*, 41568802) Kendall-Hunt.

Oklahoma West Publishing Company Staff. Wildlife Laws of Oklahoma: Oklahoma Statutes: Title 29, Game & Fish, & Title 22, Double Section Symbol 1111 Through 1113 As Amended Through Laws of the 1984 Regular Session of the Legislature. 1984. write for info. (*0-318-59005-0*) West Pub.

Okland, J. Lakes & Snails. Environment & Gastropoda in 1500 Norwegian Lakes, Ponds & Rivers: Environment & Gastropoda in 1500 Norwegian Lakes, Ponds & Rivers. (Illus.). 516p. 1990. 120.00 (*90-73348-02-1*, Pub. by Backhuys Pubs) Balogh.

Oklobdzija, Vojin G. High-Performance System Design: Circuits & Logic. LC 98-32107. 560p. 1999. 89.95 (*0-7803-4716-1*) Inst Electrical.

Okninski, A. Catastrophe Theory. (Comprehensive Chemical Kinetics Ser.: Vol. 33). 286p. 1992. 228.50 (*0-444-98742-8*) Elsevier.

Okninski, Jan. Semigroups of Matrices. (Series in Algebra: Vol. 6). 320p. 1998. 54.00 (*981-02-3445-7*) World Scientific Pub.

Okninski, Jan, ed. Semigroup Algebras. (Pure & Applied Mathematics Ser.: Vol. 138). (Illus.). 376p. 1990. text 155.00 (*0-8247-8356-5*) Dekker.

Oknuki-Tierney, Emiko. Rice As Self: Japanese Identities Through Time. 198p. 1993. pap. text 14.95 (*0-691-02110-4*, Pub. by Princeton U Pr) Cal Prin Full Svc.

Oko, R. J., jt. auth. see Barth, A. D.

Okoampa-Ahoofe, Kwame, Jr. Dorkordicky Ponkorhythms. LC 97-60862. 70p. (Orig.). 1997. pap. 7.95 (*0-938999-09-5*) Turn of River.

***Okoampa-Ahoofe, Kwame, Jr.** Obaasima. 104p. 2000. pap. 8.95 (*0-938999-13-3*) Yuganta Pr.

Okochi, Akio & Inoue, Tadakatsu, eds. Overseas Business Activities: The International Conference on Business History, 9. 296p. 1984. 42.50 (*0-86008-325-X*, Pub. by U of Tokyo) Col U Pr.

Okochi, Akio & Yasuoka, Shigeaki, eds. Family Business in the Era of Industrial Growth. (International Conferences on Business History Ser.: No. 10). 318p. 1984. 42.50 (*0-86008-346-2*, Pub. by U of Tokyo) Col U Pr.

Okochi, Akio & Yonekawa, Shin-ichi, eds. The Textile Industry & Its Business Climate, No. 8. 299p. 1982. 42.50 (*0-86008-298-9*, Pub. by U of Tokyo) Col U Pr.

Okoko, K. A. Socialism & Self-Reliance in Tanzania. 200p. 1985. 65.00 (*0-7103-0269-X*) Routledge.

Okokon, Susan. Black Londoners, 1880-1990. LC 99-187581. 1998. pap. 12.95 (*0-7509-1548-X*, Pub. by Sutton Pub Ltd) Intl Pubs Mktg.

Okolicsanyi, L., ed. see Familial Disorders of Hepatic Bilirubin Metabolism.

An Asterisk (*) at the beginning of an entry indicates that the title is appearing for the first time.

Okolie, Charles C. International Law Perspectives of the Developing Countries. LC 74-81841. 1978. 24.95 (*0-88357-011-4*); pap. 9.95 (*0-88357-042-4*) NOK Pubs.

Okolo, Eucharia Nnadi, ed. Health Research & Design. 272p. 1990. lib. bdg. 159.00 (*0-8493-4627-4*, R850) CRC Pr.

Okolo, Julius E. & Shaw, Timothy M., eds. The Political Economy of Foreign Policy in ECOWAS. LC 93-29482. (International Political Economy Ser.). 1994. text 65.00 (*0-312-10646-7*) St Martin.

Okolov, Vladislav, jt. auth. see Samarin, Viktor.

Okome, Mojubaolu O. A Sapped Democracy: The Political Economy of the Structural Adjustment Program & the Political Transition in Nigeria, 1983-1993. LC 97-32886. 344p. (C). 1997. text 62.00 (*0-7618-0984-8*); pap. text 36.50 (*0-7618-0985-6*) U Pr of Amer.

***Okome, Onookome.** Ogun's Children: The Literature & Politics of Wole Soyinka since the Nobel Prize LC 99-22539. 1999. write for info. (*0-86543-667-3*) Africa World.

Okon, Phyllis. Winds of Destiny. 176p. 1999. pap. 13.00 (*0-8059-4559-8*) Dorrance.

Okon, Yaacov, ed. Azospirillum - Plant Associations. LC 93-26203. 192p. 1993. lib. bdg. 179.00 (*0-8493-4925-7*, QR82) CRC Pr.

Okonek, Christian, et al. Vector Bundles on Complex Projective Spaces. (Progress in Mathematics Ser.: No. 3). 396p. 1980. 49.00 (*0-8176-3000-7*) Birkhauser.

Okonjo, I. M. British Administration in Nigeria, 1900-1950: A Nigerian View. LC 73-84372. (Library of African Affairs). 390p. 1974. text 21.50 (*0-88357-002-5*) NOK Pubs.

***Okonkwo.** Decolonization Agonistics in Postcolonial Fiction. LC 98-53052. 236p. 1999. text 49.95 (*0-312-22068-5*) St Martin.

Okonkwo, Rina. Protest Movements in Lagos, 1908-1930. LC 94-33462. (African Studies: Vol. 37). 134p. 1995. text 69.95 (*0-7734-9049-3*) E Mellen.

Okonomie & Okologie Team e. V. Staff, ed. Arbeit und Umwelt: Gegensatz Oder Partnerschaft. (Illus.). VII, 324p. 1998. pap. 51.95 (*3-631-31858-8*) P Lang Pubng.

Okonowicz, Ed. Crying in the Kitchen. (Spirits Between the Bays Ser.: Vol. VI). (Illus.). 112p. 1998. pap. 9.95 (*0-9643244-8-2*) Myst & Lace.

— Disappearing Delmarva: Portraits of the Peninsula People. (Illus.). 208p. 1997. 38.00 (*1-890690-00-7*) Myst & Lace.

— Fired! (Del Marva Murder Mystery Ser.). (Illus.). 320p. 1998. pap. 9.95 (*1-890690-01-5*) Myst & Lace.

— Halloween House No. 2: DelMarva Murder Mystery. (Illus.). 320p. 1999. pap. 9.95 (*1-890690-03-1*, Pub. by Myst & Lace) Wash Bk Distrib.

***Okonowicz, Ed.** Horror in the Hallway. (Spirits Between the Boys Ser.: Vol. VIII). (Illus.). 112p. (Orig.). 1999. pap. 9.95 (*1-890690-04-X*, Pub. by Myst & Lace) Koen Bk Distributors.

Okonowicz, Ed. In the Vestibule, Vol. IV. (Spirits Between the Bays Ser.). (Illus.). 112p. (Orig.). 1996. pap. 9.95 (*0-9643244-6-6*) Myst & Lace.

— Opening the Door, Vol. 2. (Spirits Between the Bays Ser.). (Illus.). 96p. (Orig.). 1995. pap. 8.95 (*0-9643244-3-1*) Myst & Lace.

***Okonowicz, Ed.** Phantom in the Bedchamber. (Spirits Between the Bays Ser.: Vol. 9). (Illus.). 112p. 2000. pap. 9.95 (*1-890690-05-8*) Myst & Lace.

Okonowicz, Ed. Possessed Possessions: Haunted Antiques, Furniture & Collectibles. 112p. (Orig.). 1996. pap. 9.95 (*0-9643244-5-8*) Myst & Lace.

— Possessed Posessions 2: More Haunted Antiques, Furniture & Collectibles. 112p. 1998. pap. 9.95 (*1-890690-02-3*) Myst & Lace.

— Presence in the Parlor, Vol. 5. (Spirits Between the Bays Ser.). (Illus.). (Orig.). 1997. pap. 9.95 (*0-9643244-7-4*) Myst & Lace.

— Pulling Back the Curtain, Vol. I. (Spirits Between the Bays Ser.). (Illus.). 64p. (Orig.). 1994. pap. 8.95 (*0-9643244-0-7*) Myst & Lace.

— Stairway over the Brandywine: A Love Story. 24p. (Orig.). 1995. pap. 5.00 (*0-9643244-2-3*) Myst & Lace.

***Okonowicz, Ed.** Up the Back Stairway. (Spirits Between the Bays Ser.: Vol. VII). (Illus.). 112p. 1999. pap. text 9.95 (*0-9643244-9-0*) Myst & Lace.

Okonowicz, Ed. Welcome Inn, Vol. 3. (Spirits Between the Bays Ser.). (Illus.). 96p. (Orig.). 1995. pap. 8.95 (*0-9643244-4-X*) Myst & Lace.

O'Konski, Chester T., ed. Molecular Electro-Optics, Pt. 1. LC 75-43047. (Electro-Optics Ser.: Vol. 1). 544p. 1976. reprint ed. pap. 168.70 (*0-608-03579-3*, 206440200001) Bks Demand.

— Molecular Electro-Optics, Pt. 2. LC 75-43047. (Electro-Optics Ser.: Vol. 1). 351p. 1976. reprint ed. pap. 108.90 (*0-608-03580-7*, 206440200002) Bks Demand.

Okonski, Walter. Wartime Poland, 1939-1945: A Select Annotated Bibliography of Books in English, 45. LC 96-33027. (Bibliographies & Indexes in World History Ser.). 128p. 1997. lib. bdg. 65.00 (*0-313-30004-6*) Greenwood.

Okonta, Ike. Nietzsche: The Politics of Power. LC 91-31790. (American University Studies: Philosophy: Ser. V, Vol. 132). 192p. (C). 1992. text 38.95 (*0-8204-1727-0*) P Lang Pubng.

— Where Vultures Feast: 40 Years of Shell in the Niger Delta. 1998. 65.00 (*0-7453-1332-9*) LPC InBook.

Okonta, Ike & Douglas, Oronto. Where Vultures Feast: Forty Years of Shell in the Niger Delta. 1999. pap. 24.95 (*0-7453-1327-5*) Stylus Pub VA.

Okoro, Ephraim, ed. see Wuzor, Geoffrey O.

Okoro, Mariagorretti. The Orphan Child. (Orig.). (J). (gr. 2-6). 1997. pap. 6.95 (*0-533-12111-6*) Vantage.

Okorocha, Cyril C., jt. auth. see Kew, Richard.

Okoroche, Cyril C. Meaning of Religious Conversion: The Case of the Igbo of Nigeria. (Avebury Series in Philosophy). 354p. 1987. text 101.95 (*0-566-05030-7*, Pub. by Avebury) Ashgate Pub Co.

***Okoronta, E. Ogemdi.** In the Land of the Broken Clock. 75p. 1999. write for info. (*1-85863-559-4*, Pub. by Minerva Pr) Unity Dist.

Okos, Martin R., jt. ed. see Barbosa-Canovas, Gustavo V.

Okoshi, Takanori. Planar Circuits. (Electrophysics Ser.: Vol. 18). (Illus.). 220p. 1985. 86.95 (*0-387-13853-6*) Spr-Verlag.

Okoshi, Takanori & Kikuchi, K. Coherent Optical Fiber Communications. (C). 1988. text 260.00 (*90-277-2677-9*) Kluwer Academic.

Okoshi, Takanori & Sueta, T. Ultra-Fast, Ultra-Parallel Optoelectronics. LC 95-9102. 620p. 1996. 185.00 (*0-471-95665-1*) Wiley.

Okosky, Kristen. New Baby's Nativity. (First Bible Collection). (Illus.). 8p. (J). (gr. k-3). 1999. 10.99 (*1-57584-329-3*, Pub. by Rdrs Digest) Random.

***Okosun.** First Year Orientation. 1999. pap. text 23.00 (*0-536-02543-6*) Pearson Custom.

Okosun, T. Y. Ambivalence, Belief? In Search of Social Well-Being. (Orig.). 1996. pap. write for info. (*0-9637979-4-8*) T Y Okosun.

***Okosun, T. Y.** Honduras: Once upon a Memory. 110p. 2000. pap. write for info. (*0-9637979-6-4*) T Y Okosun.

Okosun, T. Y. How Much Longer? Racism, Broken Children, African Americans & Anti-Human Churches. LC 93-73406. 155p. 1993. pap. 9.00 (*0-9637979-0-5*) T Y Okosun.

— My University Life: The First Steps. 1998. pap. write for info. (*0-9637979-5-6*) T Y Okosun.

— Violence, Values & Inner-City Children. (Orig.). 1994. pap. 8.00 (*0-9637979-2-1*) T Y Okosun.

Okot, Kotber B., jt. ed. see Watson, J. A.

***Okowa, Phoebe.** State Responsibility for Transboundary Air Pollution. (Oxford Monographs in International Law). 400p. 2000. text 115.00 (*0-19-826097-0*) OUP.

Okoye, John I. Speech in Ben Sira with Special Reference to 5, 9-6, 1. (European University Studies: Series 23, Vol. 535). xix, 208p. 1995. pap. 44.95 (*3-631-48923-4*) P Lang Pubng.

***Okoye-Johnson, Ogo.** Oma the Faithful Daughter. 32p. (J). (gr. k-8). 1999. 15.00 (*0-9670024-9-4*) Noon Prodns.

Okoye, Mokwugo. African Responses. 420p. 1987. 40.00 (*0-7223-0018-2*, Pub. by A H S Ltd) St Mut.

— The Beard of Prometheus. 220p. 1985. 35.00 (*0-7855-0781-7*, Pub. by A H S Ltd) St Mut.

— The Beard of Prometheus. 220p. 1987. 50.00 (*0-7223-9988-X*, Pub. by A H S Ltd) St Mut.

Okpako, David T. Principles of Pharmacology: A Tropical Approach. (Illus.). 590p. (C). 1991. text 170.00 (*0-521-34095-0*) Cambridge U Pr.

Okpaku, Joseph, Sr. Nigeria: Hundred Questions & Answers. 100p. 1992. 19.95 (*0-89388-226-7*); pap. 9.95 (*0-89388-227-5*) Okpaku Communications.

Okpaku, Joseph. Superfight No. II: The Story Behind the Fights Between Muhammad Ali & Joe Frazier. LC 74-74429. 1974. 20.00 (*0-89388-165-1*) Okpaku Communications.

— Verdict: The Exclusive Picture Story of the Trial of the Chicago 8. LC 79-129568. (Illus.). 160p. 1970. 30.00 (*0-89388-008-6*); pap. 20.00 (*0-89388-009-4*) Okpaku Communications.

Okpaku, Joseph, ed. Nigeria - Dilemma of Nationhood: An African Analysis of the Biafran Conflict. LC 73-83162. 426p. 1974. reprint ed. pap. 15.95 (*0-89388-088-4*) Okpaku Communications.

Okpaku, Joseph, Sr., ed. Nigeria & the Organisation of African Unity: In Search of an African Reality. LC 91-67250. 446p. 1991. 50.00 (*0-685-59746-6*) Okpaku Communications.

— Nigeria at the United Nation: Partnership for a Better World. LC 91-67251. 742p. 60.00 (*0-89388-211-9*) Okpaku Communications.

Okpaku, Joseph, ed. Nigeria, Dilemma of Nationhood: An African Analysis of the Biafran Conflict, 12. LC 78-111266. (Contributions in Afro-American & African Studies: No. 12). 426p. (C). 1970. 47.95 (*0-8371-4668-2*, OKN/, Greenwood Pr) Greenwood.

Okpaku, Joseph O., ed. New African Literature & the Arts, Vol. 3. LC 76-109903. 224p. 1973. 29.95 (*0-685-29060-3*); pap. 14.95 (*0-89388-083-3*) Okpaku Communications.

Okpaku, Samuel O. Mental Health in Africa & the Americas Today. 507p. (C). 1993. pap. text 49.95 (*0-916085-01-5*) Chrisolith Bks.

— Sex, Orgasm & Depression: Their Inner Relationship in a Changing Society. LC 83-63524. 160p. (Orig.). 1984. 12.95 (*0-916085-00-7*) Chrisolith Bks.

Okpaku, Samuel O., ed. Clinical Methods in Transcultural Psychiatry. 496p. 1998. text 67.00 (*0-88048-710-0*, 8710) Am Psychiatric.

Okpala, Chukwudi. The Visible Man. 124p. 1995. pap. 10.95 (*1-885392-25-7*) Allied Publishers.

Okpalaonwuka, James-Michael. Morality & Politics in Nigeria: Moral Integration in Nigerian Politics As a Way Out. (European University Studies: Ser. 23). xii, 306p. 1997. 57.95 (*3-631-31532-5*) P Lang Pubng.

— Morality & Politics in Nigeria: Moral Integration in Nigerian Politics As a Way Out. (European University Studies, Seris 23: No. 599). XII, 306p. 1997. 57.95 (*0-8204-3268-7*) P Lang Pubng.

Okpara, Mzee L. Life Sentences: Freeing Black Relationships. 85p. 1993. pap. 8.00 (*0-88378-146-8*) Third World.

Okpewho. Law Victims. 1995. pap. text. write for info. (*0-582-26502-9*, Pub. by Addison-Wesley) Longman.

Okpewho, Isadore. The Victims. (Longman African Writers Ser.). (C). 1995. pap. text 10.66 (*0-582-26520-7*) Addison-Wesley.

Okpewho, Isidore. African Oral Literature: Backgrounds, Character, & Continuity. LC 91-25671. (Illus.). 408p. 1992. text 45.00 (*0-253-34167-1*); pap. text 19.95 (*0-253-20710-X*, MB-710) Ind U Pr.

— The Epic in Africa. 312p. 1991. pap. text 20.50 (*0-231-04401-1*) Col U Pr.

— Once upon a Kingdom: Myth, Hegemony, & Identity. LC 98-19792. (Illus.). 288p. 1998. 39.95 (*0-253-33396-2*) Ind U Pr.

— Once upon a Kingdom: Myth, Hegemony & Identity. LC 98-19792. (Illus.). 288p. 1998. pap. 19.95 (*0-253-21189-1*) Ind U Pr.

Okpewho, Isidore, ed. The Heritage of African Poetry. (Illus.). 256p. (C). 1985. pap. text 27.50 (*0-582-72704-9*, 74743) Longman.

***Okpewho, Isidore, et al, eds.** The African Diaspora: African Origins & New World Identities. 566p. 1998. 59.95 (*0-253-33425-X*) Ind U Pr.

Okpi, Kalu. The Jasmine Candle. (Heartbeats Ser.). 112p. (YA). (gr. 7 up). 1994. pap. 5.95 (*0-7910-2932-8*) Chelsea Hse.

— Love Changes Everything. (Heartbeats Ser.). 112p. (YA). (gr. 7 up). 1994. pap. 4.99 (*0-7910-2934-4*) Chelsea Hse.

***Okpodu, Camellia Moses.** Investigating Plant Physiology Laboratory Manual. (Illus.). 176p. (C). 2000. pap. text 19.95 (*0-89582-516-3*) Morton Pub.

***Okposin, Samuel B.** The Extent of Singapore's Investments Abroad. LC 98-74637. 226p. 1999. text 65.95 (*0-7546-1010-1*, Pub. by Ashgate Pub) Ashgate Pub Co.

Okrand, Marc. The Klingon Dictionary. Stern, Dave, ed. 192p. 1992. per. 12.00 (*0-671-74559-X*) PB.

— Klingon for the Galactic Traveler. 224p. 1997. per. 12.00 (*0-671-00995-8*, PB Trade Paper) PB.

— The Klingon Way: A Warrior's Guide. 224p. 1996. per. 12.00 (*0-671-53755-5*, PB Trade Paper) PB.

Okrand, Mark & Lovine, Barry. Power Klingon, 1. abr. ed. (Star Trek Original Ser.). 1993. audio 12.00 (*0-671-87975-8*, Pimsleur) S&S Trade.

Okrant, Mark J. Judson's Island. (Illus.). 131p. (Orig.). (C). 1995. pap. text 13.95 (*0-9646061-1-9*) Wayfarer Pr.

Okrend, Elise & Okrend, Philip. Blintzes for Blitzen. (Illus.). 32p. (Orig.). (J). (ps up). 1996. pap. text 8.95 (*0-9651475-0-9*) MixedBlessing.

Okrend, Philip, jt. auth. see Okrend, Elise.

O'Krent. Legal Terminology/Legal Dict/ Thesaurus Package. (Paralegal Law Library). (C). 1995. 52.00 (*0-8273-7295-7*, VNR) Wiley.

Okrent, Cathy J. Civil Litigation for the Paralegal: New York. 2nd ed. 128p. (C). 1996. pap., suppl. ed. 16.95 (*0-8273-7574-3*) Delmar.

— Civil Litigation for the Paralegal New York State Student Pocket Part. 1992. pap., student ed. 10.50 (*0-8273-5294-8*) Delmar.

— Legal Terminology. 96p. 1995. pap. text 15.50 (*0-8273-6522-5*) Delmar.

— Legal Terminology with Flashcards. LC 94-38109. 384p. (C). 1994. mass mkt. 46.95 (*0-8273-6521-7*) Delmar.

Okrent, Cathy J., jt. auth. see Buckley.

Okrent, Cathy J., jt. auth. see Buckley, William R.

Okrent, Daniel. The Baseball Book. pap. write for info. (*0-318-61607-6*, Penguin Bks) Viking Penguin.

— Nine Innings: The Anatomy of a Baseball Game. 288p. 1994. pap. 12.00 (*0-395-71040-5*) HM.

***Okrent, Daniel.** The Ultimate Baseball Book: The Classic Illustrated History of the World's Greatest Game. LC 99-86020. (Illus.). 432p. 2000. pap. 29.95 (*0-618-05668-8*) HM.

Okrent, Daniel & Lewine, Harris, eds. The Ultimate Baseball Book. rev. ed. (Illus.). 384p. 1991. pap. 30.00 (*0-395-59697-1*) HM.

Okrent, Daniel & Wulf, Steve. Baseball Anecdotes. 368p. (C). 1989. 19.95 (*0-19-504396-0*) OUP.

Okrent, Daniel & Wulf, Steve. Baseball Anecdotes RI. LC 89-45793. 368p. 1993. reprint ed. pap. 15.00 (*0-06-273206-4*, Harper Ref) HarpC.

Okrent, David. Nuclear Reactor Safety: On the History of the Regulatory Process. LC 80-53958. 389p. 1981. reprint ed. pap. 120.60 (*0-608-01888-0*, 206254000003) Bks Demand.

Okrent, Mark. Heidegger's Pragmatism: Understanding, Being, & the Critique of Metaphysics. LC 87-26014. 320p. 1988. text 42.50 (*0-8014-2094-6*) Cornell U Pr.

Okrent, Rebecca Lazear. A Food Lover's Guide To New York. 1999. write for info. (*0-316-63005-5*) Little.

O'Krent, Ted. Thoughts for Living Wisely. 132p. Date not set. pap. write for info. (*0-9649275-0-0*) Heirloom TX.

Okroi, Loren J. Galbraith, Harrington, Heilbroner: Economics & Dissent in an Age of Optimism. LC 87-35416. 290p. reprint ed. pap. 89.90 (*0-608-06295-2*, 206665700008) Bks Demand.

Okruhlik, Kathleen & Brown, James R., eds. The Natural Philosophy of Leibniz. 352p. 1985. text 160.00 (*90-277-2145-9*, D Reidel) Kluwer Academic.

Okruhlik, Kathleen, jt. ed. see Harvey, Elizabeth D.

Oks, Eugene & Pirideola, Michael S., eds. Atomic Processes in Plasmas: Eleventh APS Topical Conference. LC 98-86803. (AIP Conference Proceedings Ser.: Vol. 443). (Illus.). xi, 381 p. 1998. 105.00 (*1-56396-802-9*) Am Inst Physics.

Oks, Eugene A. Plasma Spectroscopy: The Influence of Microwave & Laser Fields. LC 94-35448. (Series on Atoms & Plasmas: Vol. 9). 1995. 83.95 (*0-387-54100-4*) Spr-Verlag.

— Spectral Line Shapes. 12th ICSLS. (AIP Conference Proceedings Ser.: No. 328). (Illus.). 448p. (C). 1995. text 140.00 (*1-56396-326-4*, AIP Pr) Spr-Verlag.

Oksas, Richard M., jt. auth. see Pallasch, Thomas J.

Oksche, A., et al, eds. The Subcommissural Organ: An Ependymal Brain Gland. LC 93-9609. 1993. 174.00 (*0-387-56336-9*) Spr-Verlag.

Oksche, A. & Vollrath, L., eds. Teeth. (Handbook of Microscopic Anatomy Ser.: Vol. V/6). (Illus.). 605p. 1988. 464.00 (*0-387-19331-6*) Spr-Verlag.

Oksefjell, Signe, jt. ed. see Johansson, Stip.

Oksenberg, Jorge R., et al. Polymerase Chain Reaction & the Analysis of the T Cell Receptor Repertoire. (Medical Intelligence Unit Ser.). 125p. 1992. 99.00 (*1-879702-47-9*) Landes Bioscience.

Oksenberg, Michael & Economy, Elizabeth, eds. China Joins the World: Progress & Prospects. LC 99-19186. (Illus.). 360p. 1997. pap. 22.95 (*0-87609-225-3*) Coun Foreign.

Oksenberg, Micheal, jt. auth. see Jacobson, Harold K.

Oksenberg, Michel. Beijing Spring, 1989: Confrontation & Conflict: The Basic Documents. Lambert, marc et al, eds. LC 90-8077. 448p. (C). (gr. 13). 1990. pap. text 35.95 (*0-87332-684-9*, East Gate Bk) M E Sharpe.

Oksenberg, Michel, et al, eds. Beijing Spring, 1989: Confrontation & Conflict: The Basic Documents. LC 90-8077. 448p. (C). (gr. 13). 1990. text 81.95 (*0-87332-683-0*, East Gate Bk) M E Sharpe.

Oksenberg, Michel & Economy, Elizabeth. China's Accession to the Implementation of International Environmental Accords, 1978-95. vi, 46p. 1998. pap. 7.50 (*0-9653935-6-9*) Asia-Pacific Res.

— Shaping U. S.-China Relations: A Long-Term Strategy. (Council on Foreign Relations Study Group Reports). 1998. pap. 5.00 (*0-87609-228-8*) Coun Foreign.

Oksenberg, Michel & Henderson, Gail, eds. Research Guide to People's Daily Editorials, 1949-1975. LC 82-4408. 212p. 1982. pap. text 20.00 (*0-89264-949-6*) Ctr Chinese Studies.

Oksendal, B. Stochastic Differential Equations: An Introduction with Applications. 5th rev. ed. LC 98-4563. (Universitext Ser.). (Illus.). xviii, 324p. 1998. pap. 34.95 (*3-540-63720-6*) Spr-Verlag.

Oksendal, Bernt K. Stochastic Differential Equations. (Universitext Ser.). xiii, 205p. 1985. pap. 29.00 (*0-387-15292-X*) Spr-Verlag.

— Stochastic Differential Equations. 2nd ed. (Universitext Ser.). 208p. 1989. pap. 29.95 (*0-387-51740-5*) Spr-Verlag.

— Stochastic Differential Equations: An Introduction with Applications. 3rd ed. (Universitext Ser.). xiii, 224p. (C). 1993. pap. text 32.00 (*0-387-53335-4*) Spr-Verlag.

— Stochastic Differential Equations: An Introduction with Applications. 4th ed. 1995. pap. text 36.00 (*0-387-60243-7*) Spr-Verlag.

Oksendal, Bernt K. & Lund, D., eds. Stochastic Models & Option Values: Applications to Resources, Environment & Investment Problems. (Contributions to Economic Analysis Ser.: No. 200). 302p. 1991. 131.50 (*0-444-88630-3*, North Holland) Elsevier.

Oksendal, Bernt K., et al. Stochastic Analysis & Related Topics V: The Silivri Workshop, 1994. LC 95-49835. (Progress in Probability Ser.: No. 38). 294p. 1995. 82.00 (*0-8176-3887-3*); write for info. (*3-7643-3887-3*) Birkhauser.

Oksford, Mike. Rationality in an Uncertain World: Essays on the Cognitive Science of Human Reasoning. 336p. 1998. 54.95 (*0-86377-534-9*) Taylor & Francis.

Okshansky, Robert B. Landslide Hazard in the United States: Case Studies in Planning & Policy Development. LC 90-43660. (Environment: Problems & Solutions Ser.). 240p. 1990. text 15.00 (*0-8240-0472-8*) Garland.

Oksner, William, jt. auth. see Green, Bruce M.

Oktavec. Answered Prayers: Miracles & Milagros along the Border. (Illus.). 239p. 1995. pap. 22.50 (*0-8165-1581-6*) U of Ariz Pr.

Oktavec, Eileen, photos by. Great Walks of Acadia National Park & Mount Desert Island. LC 94-75232. (Great Walks Ser.: No. 1). (Illus.). 176p. (Orig.). 1994. pap. 8.95 (*1-879741-00-8*) Great Walks.

— Great Walks of Big Bend National Park. (Great Walks Ser.: No. 3). (Illus.). 44p. (Orig.). 1991. pap. 3.95 (*1-879741-03-2*) Great Walks.

— Great Walks of Sequoia & Kings Canyon National Parks. LC 93-77483. (Great Walks Ser.: No. 6). (Illus.). 208p. (Orig.). 1994. pap. 8.95 (*1-879741-06-7*) Great Walks.

— Great Walks of Southern Arizona. (Great Walks Ser.: No. 2). (Illus.). 46p. (Orig.). 1990. pap. 3.95 (*1-879741-02-4*) Great Walks.

— Great Walks of the Great Smokies. (Great Walks Ser.: No. 4). (Illus.). 120p. (Orig.). 1992. pap. 5.95 (*1-879741-04-0*) Great Walks.

— Great Walks of Yosemite National Park. (Great Walks Ser.: No. 5). (Illus.). 192p. (Orig.). 1993. pap. 8.95 (*1-879741-05-9*) Great Walks.

Oktay, Julianne S. & Walter, Carolyn, eds. Breast Cancer in the Life Course: Women's Experiences. (Social Work Ser.: Vol. 20). 232p. 1991. 28.95 (*0-8261-7110-9*) Springer Pub.

Oktay, Julianne S., jt. ed. see Palley, Howard A.

Oktemgil, Mehmet, jt. auth. see Cheeseright, Paul.

Oktenberg, Adrian. The Bosnia Elegies: Poems. LC 96-25030. 64p. (Orig.). 1997. pap. 10.95 (*0-9638183-5-X*) Paris Pr MA.

Oku, Hachiro. Plant Pathogenesis & Disease Resistance. 208p. 1993. lib. bdg. 99.95 (*0-87371-727-9*, L727) Lewis Pubs.

Oku, Milton. Dave Matthews Band: Under the Table & Dreaming. 88p. (YA). 1995. pap. 19.95 (*0-89524-987-1*, Pub. by Cherry Lane) H Leonard.

Oku, Milton, ed. Dave Matthews Band: Under the Table & Dreaming - Piano/Vocal. 103p. 17.95 (*0-89524-995-2*, Pub. by Cherry Lane) H Leonard.

— Roxette for Easy Piano. 48p. (YA). pap. text 9.95 (*0-89524-889-1*, 02505509) Cherry Lane.

O

An Asterisk (*) at the beginning of an entry indicates that the title is appearing for the first time.

Okubayashi, Koji, et al. Organisation for Japanese Technology: The Japanese Style of Management in the New Generation. (Series on Technology Management). 230p. 1999. 38.00 (*1-86094-142-7*, Pub. by Imperial College) World Scientific Pub.

Okubo, Akira. Oceanic Mixing. LC 73-133442. 151p. 1970. 19.00 (*0-403-04523-1*) Scholarly.

Okubo, Derek. Governance & Diversity: Findings from Los Angeles. 1994. 8.00 (*0-916450-48-1*) Nat Civic League.

— Governance & Diversity: Oakland CA. 1995. 8.00 (*0-916450-53-8*) Nat Civic League.

Okubo, Mine. Citizen, 13660. LC 82-20221. (Illus.). 226p. (Orig.). 1983. pap. 14.95 (*0-295-95989-4*) U of Wash Pr.

Okubo, Susumo. Introduction to Octonion & Other Non-Associative Algebras in Physics. (Montroll Memorial Lecture Series in Mathematical Physics: Vol. 2). (Illus.). 148p. (C). 1995. text 54.95 (*0-521-47215-6*) Cambridge U Pr.

Okubo, T. Differential Geometry. (Pure & Applied Mathematics Ser.: Vol. 112). 816p. 1987. text 225.00 (*0-8247-7700-X*) Dekker.

Okubo, Toshiteru, jt. ed. see Reich, Michael R.

Okubo, Yukimi, jt. auth. see Goris, Richard C.

Okuda. Liver Cancer. 1997. text 150.00 (*0-443-05481-9*, W B Saunders Co) Harcrt Hlth Sci Grp.

***Okuda, Akinori.** Raising Genius: Midori & Her Mother. 168p. 2000. pap. 14.95 (*1-56931-444-6*, Pub. by Viz Commns Inc) Publishers Group.

Okuda, Denise & Okuda, Michael. The Star Trek Encyclopedia. rev. ed. 1999. 60.00 (*0-671-03475-8*) PB.

Okuda, Denise, et al. The Star Trek Encyclopedia. rev. ed. 752p. 1999. per. 27.95 (*0-671-53609-5*, Star Trek) PB.

Okuda, Denise, jt. auth. see Okuda, Michael.

Okuda, Haruyuki, et al, eds. Diffuse Infrared Radiation & the IRTS: Proceedings of a Symposium Held at the Institute of Space & Astronautical Science, Sagamihara, Kanagawa, Japan, November 11-14, 1996. (ASP Conference Series Proceedings: Vol. 124). 495p. 1997. 34.00 (*1-886733-44-9*) Astron Soc Pacific.

Okuda, Hitoshi. Magical Girl Pretty Sammy: No Need for Tenchi. (Illus.). 184p. 1998. pap. 15.95 (*1-56931-288-5*, Cadence Bks) Viz Commns Inc.

— No Need for Tenchi! (Illus.). 184p. 1997. pap. text 15.95 (*1-56931-180-3*, Viz Comics) Viz Commns Inc.

***Okuda, Hitoshi.** No Need for Tenchi: Dream a Little Scheme. (No Need for Tenchi Ser.). (Illus.). 176p. 1999. pap. text 15.95 (*1-56931-429-2*, Pub. by Viz Commns Inc) Publishers Group.

Okuda, Hitoshi. No Need for Tenchi: Sword Play. (Illus.). 176p. 1998. pap. text 15.95 (*1-56931-254-0*, Viz Comics) Viz Commns Inc.

***Okuda, Hitoshi.** No Need for Tenchi! Unreal Genius. (Illus.). 176p. 1999. pap. text 15.95 (*1-56931-365-2*) Viz Commns Inc.

Okuda, Hitoshi. No Need for Tenchi: Samurai Space Opera. 1998. pap. text 15.95 (*1-56931-339-3*) Viz Commns Inc.

***Okuda, Hitoshi.** Tenchi in Love. (No Need for Tenchi Ser.). (Illus.). (J). 2000. pap. 15.95 (*1-56931-470-5*, Viz Comics) Viz Commns Inc.

Okuda, K., ed. International Congress on Clinical Enzymology, Osaka, 7th, September 1988, Abstracts. (Journal: Enzymology: Vol. 40, Suppl. 1, 1988). ii, 66p. 1988. pap. 21.00 (*3-8055-4915-6*) S Karger.

Okuda, K., jt. auth. see Takayasu, K.

Okuda, Kunio & Benhamou, J. P., eds. Portal Hypertension: Clinical & Physiological Aspects. (Illus.). 592p. 1991. 336.00 (*0-387-70054-4*) Spr-Verlag.

Okuda, Kunio & Ishak, Kamal G. Neoplasms of the Liver. (Illus.). 500p. 1987. 391.00 (*0-387-70020-X*) Spr-Verlag.

Okuda, Kunio, ed. see International Symposium on Idiopathic Portal Hyper.

Okuda, Michael. Star Trek Chronology. LC 97-120510. (Star Trek Ser.). 352p. 1996. per. 25.00 (*0-671-53610-9*, Star Trek) PB.

Okuda, Michael, ed. The Star Trek Encyclopedia. (Illus.). 400p. 1994. 30.00 (*0-671-88684-3*); per. 22.00 (*0-671-86905-1*) PB.

Okuda, Michael & Okuda, Denise. Star Trek: Chronology. 1996. pap. 25.00 (*0-614-20458-5*) PB.

— Star Trek Chronology: The History of the Future. Stern, Dave, ed. (Orig.). 1993. pap. 14.00 (*0-671-79611-9*) PB.

— The Star Trek Encyclopedia. expanded rev. ed. (Illus.). 640p. 1997. 50.00 (*0-671-53607-9*, PB Hardcover) PB.

Okuda, Michael, et al. Star Trek Sticker Book. (Illus.). 32p. 1999. per. 20.00 (*0-671-01472-2*, Star Trek) PB.

Okuda, Michael, jt. auth. see Okuda, Denise.

Okuda, Michael, jt. auth. see Sternbach, Rick.

Okuda, Minoru. Progress in Allergy & Clinical Immunology: Kyoto, Vol. 2. Miyamoto, Terumasa, ed. LC 92-53196. (Illus.). 747p. 1992. text 50.00 (*0-88937-087-7*) Hogrefe & Huber Pubs.

Okuda, Setsuo, et al, eds. The Physical Processes of Lake Biwa, Japan. LC 95-1870. (Coastal & Estuarine Studies: Vol. 48). 216p. 1995. 45.00 (*0-87590-262-6*) Am Geophysical.

***Okuda, Ted.** The Monogram Checklist: The Films of Monogram Pictures Corporation, 1931-1952. LC 86-43089. (Illus.). 399p. 1999. per. 25.00 (*0-7864-0750-6*, McFarland Cls) McFarland & Co.

Okuda, Ted. The Monogram Checklist: The Films of Monogram Pictures Corporation, 1931-1958. LC 86-43089. (Illus.). 399p. 1987. lib. bdg. 29.95 (*0-89950-286-5*) McFarland & Co.

Okuda, Ted & Watz, Edward. The Columbia Comedy Shorts: Two-Reel Hollywood Film Comedies, 1933-1958. LC 84-43241. (Illus.). 272p. 1998. per. 25.00 (*0-7864-0577-5*, McFarland Cls) McFarland & Co.

Okuda, Ted, jt. auth. see Neibaur, James L.

Okuda, Yoko, tr. see Zenji, Torei E.

O

Okudaira, Hideo. Narrative Picture Scrolls. Rosenfield, John, ed. Ten Grotenhuis, Elizabeth, tr. from JPN. LC 73-9619. (Arts of Japan Ser.: Vol. 5). (Illus.). 152p. 1973. 15.00 (*0-8348-2710-7*) Weatherhill.

Okudzhava, Bulat. Songs: Bulat Okudzhava, Vol. II. Frumkin, Vladimir, ed. Wolfson, Tanya et al, trs. (ENG & RUS.). 117p. 1986. pap. text 11.95 (*0-87501-022-9*) Ardis Pubs.

Okuguchi, K. & Szidarovsky, F. The Theory of Oligopoly with Multi-Product Firms. 2nd enl. rev. ed. LC 99-30478. (Illus.). viii, 268p. 1999. 89.95 (*3-540-65779-7*) Spr-Verlag.

Okuguchi, K. & Szidarovszky. The Theory of Oligopoly with Multi-Product Firms. (Lecture Notes in Economics & Mathematical Systems Ser.: Vol. 342). v, 167p. 1990. 29.90 (*0-387-52567-X*) Spr-Verlag.

Okuizumi, Hiraku. The Stones Cry Out. Westerhoven, James, tr. from JPN. LC 98-14434. 160p. 1999. 20.00 (*0-15-100365-3*) Harcourt.

Okujava, V. M. Mechanisms of Cortical Inhibition. 147p. (C). 1997. lib. bdg. 95.00 (*1-56072-375-0*) Nova Sci Pubs.

Okulam, Frodo. The Julian Mystique: Her Life & Teachings. LC 97-60964. 88p. 1998. pap. 7.95 (*0-89622-743-X*) Twenty-Third.

Okulicz, Karen. Try! A Survival Guide to Unemployment. 70p. 1995. pap. 10.00 (*0-9644260-0-5*) K-Slaw.

Okum, Stacy & Town & Country Staff. Town & Country Weddings. 1924. write for info. (*0-688-16257-6*, Hearst) Hearst Commns.

Okuma, Augustine Ichiro. Awakening to Prayer. Hiraki, Theresa Kazue & Yamato, Albert Masaru, trs. from JPN. LC 93-33061. (Illus.). 98p. 1994. pap. 8.95 (*0-935216-22-7*) ICS Pubns.

Okuma, Thomas M. Angola in Ferment: The Background & Prospects of Angolan Nationalism. LC 73-17929. (Illus.). 137p. 1974. reprint ed. lib. bdg. 55.00 (*0-8371-7272-1*, OKAF, Greenwood Pr) Greenwood.

O'Kuma, Tom, et al, eds. Ranking Task Exercises in Physics. LC 99-32915. 217p. 1999. pap. text 23.20 incl. audio compact disk (*0-13-022355-7*) P-H.

Okumiya, Masatake, et al. Zero: The Air War in the Pacific in World War II, from the Japanese Viewpoint. LC 79-20670. 1979. reprint ed. 25.00 (*0-89201-082-7*) Zenger Pub.

Okumiya, Masatake, jt. auth. see Fuchida, Mitsuo.

Okumu, Washington. Lumumba's Congo. 1962. 12.95 (*0-8392-1062-0*) Astor-Honor.

***Okumura, Hiroshi.** Corporate Capitalism in Japan. LC 99-53113. 2000. 65.00 (*0-312-23083-4*) St Martin.

Okumura, Nobuyoshi, tr. see Shimomura, Kojin.

***Okumura, Shohaku & Warner, Jisho, eds.** Nothing Is Hidden: Essays on Zen Master Dogen's Instructions for the Cook. 2000. pap. 14.95 (*0-8348-0478-6*) Weatherhill.

Okumura, Shohaku, jt. tr. see Leighton, Taigen D.

Okumura, Shohaku, tr. see Uchiyama, Kosho.

***Okun.** Effective Helping: Interviewing & Counseling Techniques. 6th ed. (C). 2001. text 31.25 (*0-534-51384-0*) Wadsworth Pub.

Okun, Arthur M. Economics for Policymaking: Selected Essays by Arthur M. Okun. Pechman, Joseph A., ed. (Illus.). 679p. 1983. 55.00 (*0-262-15025-5*) MIT Pr.

— Equality & Efficiency: The Big Tradeoff. LC 75-5162. 124p. 1975. pap. 10.95 (*0-8157-6475-8*) Brookings.

— The Political Economy of Prosperity. LC 76-108835. 122p. 1970. 19.95 (*0-8157-6478-2*) Brookings.

— Prices & Quantities: A Macroeconomic Analysis. LC 80-70076. 367p. 1981. pap. 18.95 (*0-8157-6479-0*) Brookings.

Okun, Arthur M. & Perry, George L., eds. Brookings Papers on Economic Activity: No. 1-1978. LC 74-129564. 238p. reprint ed. pap. 73.80 (*0-8357-7442-2*, 202539400043) Bks Demand.

— Brookings Papers on Economic Activity: No. 2-1979. LC 74-129564. 226p. reprint ed. pap. 70.10 (*0-8357-7444-9*, 202539600043) Bks Demand.

— Brookings Papers on Economic Activity: No. 3-1978. LC 74-129564. 370p. reprint ed. pap. 114.70 (*0-8357-7443-0*, 202539500043) Bks Demand.

— Curing Chronic Inflation. LC 78-11859. 311p. reprint ed. pap. 96.50 (*0-608-12456-7*, 202539300043) Bks Demand.

Okun, Barbara F. Effective Helping: Interviewing & Counseling Techniques. 3rd ed. LC 86-6128. (Counseling-Psychology Ser.). 293p. (C). 1986. pap. 22.25 (*0-534-06588-0*) Brooks-Cole.

— Effective Helping: Interviewing & Counseling Techniques. 4th ed. 283p. (C). 1992. pap. 23.25 (*0-534-14544-2*) Brooks-Cole.

Okun, Barbara F. Effective Helping: Interviewing & Counseling Techniques. 5th ed. LC 96-25606. (Counseling Ser.). 272p. (C). 1996. pap. 43.95 (*0-534-34173-X*) Brooks-Cole.

Okun, Barbara F. Understanding Diverse Families: What Practitioners Need to Know. LC 96-35441. 376p. 1996. lib. bdg. 37.95 (*1-57230-056-6*, 0056) Guilford Pubns.

— Understanding Diverse Families: What Practitioners Need to Know. 376p. 1998. pap. text 23.00 (*1-57230-417-0*) Guilford Pubns.

Okun, Barbara F., et al. Understanding Diversity: A Learning-As-Practice Primer. LC 98-22621. 1998. pap. 34.95 (*0-534-34810-6*) Brooks-Cole.

Okun, Barbara F., jt. ed. see Kantor, David.

Okun, Daniel A. Regionalization of Water Management: A Revolution in England & Wales. (Illus.). 377p. 1977. 74.00 (*0-85334-738-7*) Elsevier.

Okun, Daniel A. & Ponghis, G. Community Wastewater Collection & Disposal. 1975. pap. text 37.80 (*92-4-156045-2*, 1150026) World Health.

Okun, Daniel A., jt. auth. see Fair, Gordon M.

Okun, James D. & Goodmere, Evangilita. Erasing Scars: Herpes & Healing. Roberts, Ed et al, eds. LC 96-92867. (Illus.). 180p. (YA). 1997. pap. 15.95 (*0-9649093-0-8*) Jane Pubns.

Okun, L. B. Leptons & Quarks. (North-Holland Personal Library: Vol. 2). xiv, 362p. 1987. reprint ed. pap. 68.00 (*0-444-86924-7*, North Holland) Elsevier.

— Particle Physics: The Quest for Substance of Substance. (Contemporary Concepts in Physics Ser.: Vol. 2). xiv, 224p. 1985. text 132.00 (*3-7186-0228-8*); pap. text 36.00 (*3-7186-0229-6*) Gordon & Breach.

— A Primer in Particle Physics, Alpha, Beta, Gamma...Z. xii, 114p. 1987. text 52.00 (*3-7186-0374-8*); pap. text 24.00 (*3-7186-0405-1*) Gordon & Breach.

— The Relations of Particles: Lecture Notes in Physics, Vol. 42. 168p. 1991. text 48.00 (*981-02-0453-1*); pap. text 23.00 (*981-02-0454-X*) World Scientific Pub.

Okun, Lewis. Woman Abuse: Facts Replacing Myths. LC 84-26912. 298p. (C). 1985. text 64.50 (*0-88706-077-3*); pap. text 21.95 (*0-88706-079-X*) State U NY Pr.

Okun, Milton. Just the Right Mix: Piano/Vocal/Guitar. 141p. (YA). pap. text 14.95 (*0-89524-977-4*) Cherry Lane.

Okun, Milton, ed. Ain't Broadway Grand - A Brand New 1948 Musical. pap. 14.95 (*0-89524-747-X*) Cherry Lane.

— All My Life - Karla Bonoff (Piano - Vocal) (Illus.). 64p. (Orig.). (YA). pap. 14.95 (*0-89524-707-0*) Cherry Lane.

— Andrea Marcovicci: New Words. 157p. Date not set. pap. 22.95 (*0-89524-984-7*) Cherry Lane.

— The Authentic Guitar Style of Harry Chapin. (Illus.). 55p. (Orig.). 1990. pap. text 14.95 (*0-89524-384-9*, Pub. by Cherry Lane) H Leonard.

— Barbra Streisand: The Concert. 288p. 1995. pap. 22.95 (*0-614-03545-7*) Cherry Lane.

— Barbra Streisand - A Collection: Greatest Hits...& More. 1989. pap. 17.95 (*0-89524-504-3*, Pub. by Cherry Lane) H Leonard.

— Barbra Streisand - Till I Loved You (Piano - Vocal) (Illus.). 56p. (Orig.). 1990. pap. text 14.95 (*0-89524-421-7*) Cherry Lane.

— Best of Boston P-V-G. 80p. (YA). 1995. pap. 17.95 (*0-89524-920-0*, Pub. by Cherry Lane) H Leonard.

— The Best of Contemporary Folk. (Illus.). 120p. (Orig.). (YA). 1995. pap. 17.95 (*0-89524-861-1*) Cherry Lane.

— The Best of Huey Lewis & the News: Piano - Vocal. (Illus.). 158p. (Orig.). 1990. pap. text 17.95 (*0-89524-341-5*) Cherry Lane.

— Best of John Denver for Easy Guitar. 64p. (YA). 1995. pap. text 9.95 (*0-89524-913-8*, Pub. by Cherry Lane) H Leonard.

— Best of John Denver for Easy Piano. 63p. 1995. pap. text 9.95 (*0-89524-910-3*, Pub. by Cherry Lane) H Leonard.

— Best of Lenny Kravitz. 1994. pap. text 12.95 (*0-89524-829-8*, Pub. by Cherry Lane) H Leonard.

— The Best of Roxette. 1994. pap. text 12.95 (*0-89524-827-1*, Pub. by Cherry Lane) H Leonard.

— Best of Steve Wariner. pap. 14.95 (*0-89524-672-4*) Cherry Lane.

— Bonnie Raitt - Longing in Their Hearts (Piano-Vocal-Guitar) 71p. (Orig.). (YA). 1994. pap. 16.95 (*0-89524-844-1*, 02502139, Pub. by Cherry Lane) H Leonard.

— Bonnie Raitt - Luck of the Draw. 1990. pap. 14.95 (*0-89524-646-5*, Pub. by Cherry Lane) H Leonard.

— Bonnie Raitt - Nick of Time. 1991. pap. 14.95 (*0-89524-440-3*, Pub. by Cherry Lane) H Leonard.

Okun, Milton, ed. The Bottom Line 20th Anniversary Songbook. (Illus.). 149p. (Orig.). (YA). 1994. pap. 19.95 (*0-89524-852-2*, Pub. by Cherry Lane) H Leonard.

Okun, Milton, ed. Broadway Today. 1994. per. 14.95 (*0-89524-814-X*) Cherry Lane.

— Bruce Hornsby & the Range - A Night on the Town. pap. 14.95 (*0-89524-580-9*) Cherry Lane.

— Bruce Hornsby & the Range - Five of the Best. pap. 9.95 (*0-89524-539-6*) Cherry Lane.

— The Cherry Lane Gospel Songbook. pap. 17.95 (*0-89524-703-8*, Pub. by Cherry Lane) H Leonard.

— Christine Lavin Songbook. pap. 17.95 (*0-89524-712-7*, Pub. by Cherry Lane) H Leonard.

Okun, Milton, ed. Christmas Carols for Piano Duet. 63p. (YA). pap. 14.95 (*0-89524-948-0*, 02505651); pap. 17.95 (*0-89524-949-9*, 02505652, Pub. by Cherry Lane) H Leonard.

Okun, Milton, ed. Classic Country Encore. pap. 14.95 (*0-89524-755-0*) Cherry Lane.

— Classic Country Round-Up. 144p. 1995. pap. 14.95 (*0-89524-981-2*) Cherry Lane.

— Classic Love Songs: Piano - Vocal. rev. ed. (Illus.). 128p. (Orig.). 1990. pap. text 12.95 (*0-89524-377-6*) Cherry Lane.

— Cliff Eberhardt Songbook. 56p. (YA). Date not set. pap. 15.95 (*0-89524-957-X*) Cherry Lane.

— Concrete Blonde- Bloodletting. pap. 12.95 (*0-89524-624-4*) Cherry Lane.

— Contemporary Christian Today. pap. 14.95 (*0-89524-793-3*) Cherry Lane.

— Contemporary Folk - Five of the Best. pap. 7.95 (*0-89524-637-6*) Cherry Lane.

— Country Chartbusters - Five of the Best. pap. 6.95 (*0-89524-641-4*) Cherry Lane.

— Country Ladies. (Illus.). 128p. (Orig.). 1995. pap. 12.95 (*0-89524-819-0*, HL02502129) Cherry Lane.

— Deck the Halls: Fifty Beloved Traditional & Contemporary Christmas Favorites. 143p. (Orig.). (YA). 1994. pap. 12.95 (*0-89524-858-1*, Pub. by Cherry Lane) H Leonard.

— Dick Clark's American Bandstand Gold Vol. 2: 1965-1975. 142p. (Orig.). (YA). 1994. pap. 16.95 (*0-89524-815-8*, 02502123) Cherry Lane.

— Eric Andersen Selected Songs (Piano - Vocal) (Illus.). 96p. (Orig.). (YA). 1993. pap. text 17.95 (*0-89524-733-X*) Cherry Lane.

— Erroll Garner for Easy Piano. (Illus.). 31p. (YA). pap. text 10.95 (*0-89524-860-3*, 02505504, Pub. by Cherry Lane) H Leonard.

— Follow That Road: Martha's Vineyard II Songbook. 92p. (Orig.). (YA). pap. 22.95 (*0-89524-875-1*, 02506919) Cherry Lane.

— From a Distance & Thirty-Three More Easy Listening Classics. 1994. pap. 14.95 (*0-89524-813-1*) Cherry Lane.

— From a Distance & Twenty-Four Other Easy Listening Favorites for Easy Piano. 119p. (Orig.). (YA). pap. 12.95 (*0-89524-871-9*, 02505508) Cherry Lane.

Okun, Milton, ed. From the Heart - 30 Love Songs. 117p. (Orig.). (YA). pap. 14.95 (*0-89524-864-6*, 02502146) Cherry Lane.

Okun, Milton, ed. Grand Hotel - The Musical. pap. 10.95 (*0-89524-603-1*, Pub. by Cherry Lane) H Leonard.

— Great Rock Ballads. 104p. (YA). pap. 15.95 (*0-89524-936-7*, 02502173) Cherry Lane.

— Great Songs of the Eighties. pap. 16.95 (*0-89524-792-5*, Pub. by Cherry Lane) H Leonard.

— Great TV Themes - Five of the Best. pap. 5.95 (*0-89524-636-8*) Cherry Lane.

— Guns n' Roses - Appetite for Destruction: Piano - Vocal. (Illus.). 112p. (Orig.). 1990. pap. text 19.95 (*0-89524-417-9*) Cherry Lane.

— Guns n' Roses for Easy Piano. 1994. pap. text 9.95 (*0-89524-808-5*) Cherry Lane.

— Hal Ketchum - Past the Point of Rescue. pap. 14.95 (*0-89524-719-4*) Cherry Lane.

— Hal Ketchum - Sure Love. 1994. pap. text 14.95 (*0-89524-739-9*) Cherry Lane.

— Harry Chapin Tribute: Piano - Vocal. (Illus.). 103p. (Orig.). 1990. pap. text 17.95 (*0-89524-418-7*, Pub. by Cherry Lane) H Leonard.

— Heavy Metal Bass Lines: Play-it-Like-It-Is Bass, Vol. 2. pap. 14.95 (*0-89524-444-6*) Cherry Lane.

— Heavy Metal Guitar, Vol. 1. (Illus.). 127p. (Orig.). 1990. pap. text 14.95 (*0-89524-221-4*) Cherry Lane.

— Highlights from Jekyll & Hyde: Piano - Vocal - Guitar. (Illus.). 64p. (Orig.). 1990. pap. text 12.95 (*0-89524-531-0*) Cherry Lane.

— Indian Runner - Soundtrack. pap. 12.95 (*0-89524-648-1*) Cherry Lane.

— John Berry: Standing on the Edge. 64p. 1995. pap. 15.95 (*0-89524-967-7*) Cherry Lane.

— John Denver: A Legacy of Song. (Illus.). 156p. (YA). 1996. pap. 24.95 (*0-89524-926-X*, 02502151, Pub. by Cherry Lane) H Leonard.

— John Denver - Aerie. pap. 10.95 (*0-89524-004-1*) Cherry Lane.

— John Denver - Authentic Guitar Style: Acoustic Guitar Transcriptions. pap. text 14.95 (*0-89524-376-8*, Pub. by Cherry Lane) H Leonard.

— John Denver - Five of the Best. pap. 6.95 (*0-89524-638-4*) Cherry Lane.

— John Denver - Flower That Shattered the Stone. pap. 12.95 (*0-89524-615-5*) Cherry Lane.

— John Denver - Greatest Hits Vol. 3: Piano - Vocal. (Illus.). 67p. (Orig.). 1990. pap. text 14.95 (*0-89524-294-X*) Cherry Lane.

— John Denver - It's about Time: Piano - Vocal. (Illus.). 72p. (Orig.). 1990. pap. text 12.95 (*0-89524-196-X*) Cherry Lane.

— John Denver - JD. pap. 10.95 (*0-89524-051-3*) Cherry Lane.

— John Denver - Rocky Mountain High: Piano - Vocal. (Illus.). 79p. (Orig.). 1990. pap. text 10.95 (*0-89524-118-8*) Cherry Lane.

— John Denver - Spirit. pap. 10.95 (*0-89524-005-X*) Cherry Lane.

— John Denver's Greatest Hits, Vols. 1-3. 152p. (YA). 1995. pap. 17.95 (*0-89524-914-6*, Pub. by Cherry Lane) H Leonard.

— John Hiatt Songbook (Piano - Vocal) (Illus.). 64p. (Orig.). 1990. pap. text 14.95 (*0-89524-479-9*) Cherry Lane.

— John Tesh - Victory: Solo Piano. 80p. (YA). Date not set. pap. 15.95 (*1-57560-020-X*) Cherry Lane.

— Johnny Cash - A Man & His Music. 1994. pap. 16.95 (*0-89524-778-X*) Cherry Lane.

— Just for Kids. 32p. (YA). pap. 7.95 (*0-89524-950-2*, 02505506) Cherry Lane.

— Just for Kids Not! Classics. 32p. (YA). 1995. pap. 7.95 (*0-89524-985-5*, Pub. by Cherry Lane) H Leonard.

— Kenny Rogers: Gideon. 1980. 6.95 (*0-89898-011-9*) Almo Pubns.

— Lenny Kravitz - Are You Gonna Go My Way. 1994. pap. 14.95 (*0-89524-776-3*) Cherry Lane.

— Lenny Kravitz - Mama Said. pap. 14.95 (*0-89524-634-1*) Cherry Lane.

— The Leslie Bricusse Christmas Songbook. 94p. (YA). Date not set. pap. 17.95 (*1-57560-025-0*, Pub. by Cherry Lane) H Leonard.

— Leslie Bricusse Theatre Book. 224p. (YA). pap., per. 24.95 (*0-89524-882-4*, 02502148) Cherry Lane.

— Linda Ronstadt - Cry Like a Rainstorm, Howl Like the Wind: Piano - Vocal. (Illus.). 52p. (Orig.). 1990. pap. text 14.95 (*0-89524-501-9*) Cherry Lane.

— Lionel Richie - Can't Slow Down. pap. 9.95 (*0-89524-194-3*) Cherry Lane.

— Lionel Richie - Complete: Piano - Vocal. (Illus.). 264p. (Orig.). 1990. pap. text 24.95 (*0-89524-370-9*) Cherry Lane.

— Lionel Richie - Dancing on the Ceiling: Piano - Vocal. (Illus.). 61p. (Orig.). 1990. pap. text 9.95 (*0-89524-324-5*) Cherry Lane.

— Lionel Richie - Love Ballads. pap. 12.95 (*0-89524-355-5*) Cherry Lane.

An Asterisk (*) at the beginning of an entry indicates that the title is appearing for the first time.

— Lionel Richie Greatest Hits: Ez Piano. (Illus.). 72p. (Orig.). 1990. pap. text 10.95 (*0-89524-292-3*) Cherry Lane.

— The Love Ballads of Lionel Richie (Piano - Vocal) (Illus.). 95p. (Orig.). 1990. pap. text 14.95 (*0-89524-343-1*) Cherry Lane.

— Love Is . . . 25 Songs of Love. 128p. (YA). 1995. pap. 14.95 (*0-89524-978-2*) Cherry Lane.

— Lucinda Williams - Sweet Old World. pap. 14.95 (*0-89524-744-5*) Cherry Lane.

— Magic of Music - Children's Song: Piano - Vocal. (Illus.). 80p. (Orig.). (J). 1988. pap. text 9.95 (*0-89524-372-5*) Cherry Lane.

— Magic of Music - Christmas Songs: Piano - Vocal. (Illus.). 56p. (Orig.). 1988. pap. text 9.95 (*0-89524-457-8*) Cherry Lane.

— Magic of Music - Holiday Songs: Piano - Vocal. (Illus.). 63p. (Orig.). 1990. pap. text 7.95 (*0-89524-380-6*) Cherry Lane.

— Mary Chapin Carpenter: Stones in the Road. (Illus.). 92p. (Orig.). (YA). 1995. pap. 17.95 (*0-89524-901-4*, Pub. by Cherry Lane) H Leonard.

— Maury Yeston - December Songs. pap. 16.95 (*0-89524-679-1*) Cherry Lane.

— Modern County P/U/G: 22 Contemporary Country Hits. 112p. (YA). Date not set. pap. 14.95 (*1-57560-006-4*) Cherry Lane.

— Modern Rock - Piano/Vocal/Guitar. 93p. Date not set. pap. 15.95 (*1-57560-009-9*) Cherry Lane.

— Music of Bruce Hornsby. (Easy Piano Ser.). pap. 9.95 (*0-89524-339-3*) Cherry Lane.

— The Music of John Denver Made Easy for Guitar. (Easy Guitar Ser.). pap. 9.95 (*0-89524-018-1*) Cherry Lane.

— The Music of Richard Marx (Easy Piano) (Illus.). 56p. (Orig.). 1990. pap. text 10.95 (*0-89524-478-0*) Cherry Lane.

— Nine. pap. 17.95 (*0-89524-820-4*) Cherry Lane.

— Of Love & Hope - Selections from "Beauty & the Beast" pap. 12.95 (*0-89524-484-5*) Cherry Lane.

— On the Back Porch with Barry & Holly Tashian. 32p. (YA). 1995. pap. 12.95 (*0-89524-974-X*) Cherry Lane.

— Ozzy Ozbourne Songbook: Guitar - Vocal. (Illus.). 175p. (Orig.). 1990. pap. text 24.95 (*0-89524-237-0*, Pub. by Cherry Lane) H Leonard.

— Patty Loveless: Only What I Feel. 57p. (Orig.). (YA). pap. 14.95 (*0-89524-898-0*, Pub. by Cherry Lane) H Leonard.

— Patty Loveless: When Fallen Angels Fly. 70p. (Orig.). (YA). pap. 14.95 (*0-89524-897-2*, 02502161) Cherry Lane.

— Phantom - The American Musical Sensation. pap. 12.95 (*0-89524-727-5*, Pub. by Cherry Lane) H Leonard.

— Pixies - Bossanova. pap. 12.95 (*0-89524-608-2*) Cherry Lane.

— Pop Songs for the Wedding. 1994. pap. 14.95 (*0-89524-822-0*) Cherry Lane.

— Queens of Pop. 104p. 1995. pap. 12.95 (*0-89524-976-6*) Cherry Lane.

— Richard Marx - Five of the Best. pap. 6.95 (*0-89524-538-8*) Cherry Lane.

— Richard Marx - Repeat Offender. pap. 14.95 (*0-89524-441-1*) Cherry Lane.

— Richard Marx - Rush Street. pap. 14.95 (*0-89524-692-9*) Cherry Lane.

— Richard Marx (Piano - Vocal) (Illus.). 63p. (Orig.). 1990. pap. text 14.95 (*0-89524-346-6*) Cherry Lane.

— Ricky Lee Jones - Flying Cowboys: Piano - Vocal. (Illus.). 67p. (Orig.). 1990. pap. text 14.95 (*0-89524-505-1*) Cherry Lane.

— Roberta Flack - Oasis. pap. 12.95 (*0-89524-428-4*) Cherry Lane.

— Roxette - Five of the Best. pap. 6.95 (*0-89524-540-X*) Cherry Lane.

— Roxette - Joyride. pap. 14.95 (*0-89524-673-2*) Cherry Lane.

— Roxette - Look Sharp. pap. 14.95 (*0-89524-473-X*) Cherry Lane.

— Roxette - Tourism. pap. 16.95 (*0-89524-729-1*, Pub. by Cherry Lane) H Leonard.

— Sawyer Brown: This Thing Called Wantin' & Havin' It All. 64p. (YA). 1995. pap. 15.95 (*0-89524-992-8*) Cherry Lane.

— Sawyer Brown Greatest Hits P-V-G, 1990-1995. 64p. (YA). 1995. pap. 15.95 (*0-89524-935-9*) Cherry Lane.

— Scrooge - The Musical. pap. 14.95 (*0-89524-726-7*) Cherry Lane.

— Scrooge Revised Vocal Selections. 88p. (YA). 1995. pap. 19.95 (*0-89524-988-X*, Pub. by Cherry Lane) H Leonard.

— Searchin' for Love. 128p. (YA). 1995. pap. 14.95 (*0-89524-979-0*) Cherry Lane.

— Shawn Colvin - Cover Girl. 32p. (Orig.). (YA). pap. text 12.95 (*0-89524-867-0*, 02506918) Cherry Lane.

— Shawn Colvin - Steady On: Piano - Vocal. (Illus.). 55p. (Orig.). 1990. pap. text 14.95 (*0-89524-516-7*) Cherry Lane.

— Sherlock Holmes. pap. 19.95 (*0-89524-745-3*) Cherry Lane.

— Skid. pap. 14.95 (*0-89524-667-8*) Cherry Lane.

— Skid: Drum. pap. 16.95 (*0-89524-601-5*) Cherry Lane.

— Skid: Easy Guitar. pap. 9.95 (*0-89524-656-2*) Cherry Lane.

— Skid: Play-It-Like-It-Is-Bass. pap. 14.95 (*0-89524-579-5*) Cherry Lane.

— Statler Brothers Anthology. pap. 14.95 (*0-89524-044-0*) Cherry Lane.

— Suzanne Vega - Days of Open Hand. pap. 14.95 (*0-89524-545-0*) Cherry Lane.

— Suzanne Vega - Solitude Standing. pap. 12.95 (*0-89524-345-8*) Cherry Lane.

— Today's Country Hits. 1994. pap. 12.95 (*0-89524-789-5*) Cherry Lane.

— Today's Country Hits: Easy Piano. pap. 14.95 (*0-89524-801-8*) Cherry Lane.

— Tom Chapin: Zag Zig. (Illus.). 45p. (Orig.). (YA). pap. 15.95 (*0-89524-905-7*, Pub. by Cherry Lane) H Leonard.

— Tom Paxton - Authentic Guitar Style: Guitar Transcriptions. pap. 14.95 (*0-89524-448-9*, Pub. by Cherry Lane) H Leonard.

— Tom Paxton - Politics: Guitar/Vocal Arrangements. pap. 9.95 (*0-89524-435-7*, Pub. by Cherry Lane) H Leonard.

— Tom Paxton - Wearing the Time. 63p. (YA). 1994. pap. 14.95 (*0-89524-881-6*, 02502157, Pub. by Cherry Lane) H Leonard.

— Twin Peaks. pap. 12.95 (*0-89524-613-9*) Cherry Lane.

— Van Halen - 5150. pap. 14.95 (*0-89524-460-8*) Cherry Lane.

Okun, Milton & Fox, Dan, eds. Donald Fagen: The Nightfly. (Illus.). 64p. 1983. pap. 14.95 (*0-89524-176-5*) Cherry Lane.

— John Denver: Some Days Are Diamonds. (Illus.). 71p. 1981. pap. 10.95 (*0-89524-143-9*, 9016) Cherry Lane.

— John Denver Anthology: Easy Guitar. (Illus.). 255p. 1981. pap. 17.95 (*0-89524-142-0*, 9091) Cherry Lane.

— Kenny Rogers Greatest Hits: Easy Piano. 48p. 1980. pap. 9.95 (*0-89524-105-6*) Cherry Lane.

— Lionel Richie. (Illus.). 64p. 1982. pap. 9.95 (*0-89524-175-7*) Cherry Lane.

Okun, Milton, ed. see Alger, Pat.

Okun, Milton, ed. see Blonde, Concrete.

Okun, Milton, ed. see Bricusse, Leslie.

Okun, Milton, ed. see Burgie, Irving.

Okun, Milton, ed. see Chapin, Harry.

Okun, Milton, ed. see Denver, John.

Okun, Milton, ed. see Eder, Linda.

Okun, Milton, ed. see Gold, Julie, et al.

Okun, Milton, ed. see Guns N' Roses.

Okun, Milton, ed. see Koller, Fred.

Okun, Milton, ed. see McBroom, Amanda.

Okun, Milton, ed. see Overstreet, Paul.

Okun, Milton, jt. ed. see Phillips, Mark.

Okun, Milton, ed. see Wheeler, Cheryl, et al.

Okun, Milton R., et al. Gross & Microscopic Pathology of the Skin, 2 vols., Set. 2nd ed. LC 87-71751. (Illus.). 1988. 375.00 (*0-9618536-0-3*) Derma Found Pr.

Okun, Mitchell. Fair Play in the Marketplace: The First Battle for Pure Food & Drugs. LC 85-25921. 1986. 32.00 (*0-87580-115-3*) N Ill U Pr.

***Okun, Stacey.** Town & Country Elegant Weddings. LC 00-39612. (Illus.). 2001. write for info. (*1-58816-000-9*, Hearst) Hearst Commns.

Okun, Tema & Wood, Peter, eds. Through the Hoop. (Southern Exposure Ser.). (Illus.). 128p. (Orig.). (C). 1979. pap. 4.00 (*0-943810-07-8*) Inst Southern Studies.

Okunade, Albert A., jt. auth. see Willis, William J.

Okunev, Yuri. Phase & Phase-Difference Modulation in Digital Communications. LC 97-21324. (Signal Processing Technology Ser.). 392p. 1997. 109.00 (*0-89006-937-9*) Artech Hse.

O'Kunewick, James P. & Meredith, Ruby F., eds. Graft vs. Leukemia in Man & Animal Models. 288p. 1981. 157.00 (*0-8493-5745-4*, RC643) CRC Pr.

Okuno-Fujiwara, Masahiro & Okazaki, Tetsuji, eds. The Japanese Economic System & Its Historical Origins. Herbert, susan, tr. (Japan Business & Economics Ser.). (Illus.). 304p. 1999. text 78.00 (*0-19-828901-4*) OUP.

Okuno, Hirishi G., jt. ed. see Rosenthal, David F.

Okuno, Hiroshi G., jt. ed. see Rosenthal, David F.

Okunor, Shiame. Politics, Misunderstandings, Misconceptions: The History of Colonial Universities. LC 90-22144. (American University Studies: Education: Ser. XIV, Vol. 26). 196p. (C). 1991. text 34.95 (*0-8204-1176-0*) P Lang Pubng.

Okuntseff, Nik. Programming MS Exchange Server. (Illus.). 318p. 1999. pap. 39.95 incl. cd-rom (*0-87930-567-3*, Pub. by C M P Books) Publishers Group.

— Windows NT Security: Programming Easy-to-Use Security Options. (Illus.). 277p. (Orig.). 1997. pap. 39.95 incl. disk (*0-87930-473-1*) C M P Books.

***Okupa, Effa.** International Bibliography of African Customary Law. 280p. 1999. pap. text 59.95 (*3-8258-4009-3*, Pub. by CE24) Transaction Pubs.

Okur, Nilgun A. Contemporary African American Theater: Afrocentricity in the Works of Larry Neal, Amiri Baraka, & Charles Fuller. LC 97-16545. (Studies in African American History & Culture). 236p. 1997. text 50.00 (*0-8153-2872-9*) Garland.

Okura, Nagatsune. Seiyu Roku: Oil Manufacturing in Japan in 1836. Ariga, Eiko, tr. LC 74-6761. (Illus.). 79p. 1974. 25.00 (*0-917526-01-5*) Olearius Edns.

Okure, Teresa. Johannine Approach to Mission: A Contextual Study of John 4: 1-42. 370p. 1987. lib. bdg. 63.50 (*3-16-145049-3*, Pub. by JCB Mohr) Coronet Bks.

***Okut-Uma, Rogers W.** Information Technology & Globalization. 150p. 1998. pap. 16.95 (*0-85092-517-7*, Pub. by Comm Sec) Stylus Pub VA.

***Okut-Uma, Rogers W. & Odiachi, RoseMarie Rita.** Biodiversity & Gender for Sustainable Development. 201p. 2000. pap. 45.00 (*0-85092-558-4*, Pub. by Comm Sec) Stylus Pub VA.

Okut-Uma, Rogers W., jt. auth. see Caffrey, Larry.

Okut-Uma, Rogers W., jt. auth. see Nagarajan, V.

Okut-Uma, Rogers W., jt. auth. see Odedra-Straub, M.

Okutoro, Lydia. Quiet Storm. LC 98-30346. 128p. (J). (gr. 7-12). 1999. lib. bdg. 17.49 (*0-7868-2403-4*, Pub. by Hyprn Child) Little.

— Quiet Storm. (J). 2005. pap. write for info. (*0-7868-1320-2*) Hyprn Child.

— Quiet Storm: Voices of Young Black Poets. LC 98-30346. 128p. (J). (gr. 7-12). 1999. 16.99 (*0-7868-0461-0*, Pub. by Hyprn Child) Time Warner.

Okuturo. Quiet Storm. LC 97-39832. (J). 1998. 16.00 (*0-689-81039-3*) S&S Childrens.

Okuyama, Shinichi & Mishina, Hitoshi. Evolution of Cancer. 1990. text 67.50 (*0-86008-460-4*, Pub. by U of Tokyo) Col U Pr.

Okuyama, Y. Absolute Summability of Fourier Series & Orthogonal Series. (Lecture Notes in Mathematics Ser.: Vol. 1067). vi, 118p. 1984. 29.95 (*0-387-13355-0*) Spr-Verlag.

***Okwu, Julian C. R.** As I Am: Young African American Women in a Critical Age. LC 98-29557. (Illus.). 160p. 1999. pap. 22.95 (*0-8118-2073-4*) Chronicle Bks.

Okwu, Julian C. R. Face Forward: Young African American Men in a Critical Age. LC 96-42319. 1997. 35.00 (*0-8118-1631-1*) Chronicle Bks.

— Face Forward: Young African American Men in a Critical Age. LC 96-42319. 1999. pap. 19.95 (*0-8118-1215-4*) Chronicle Bks.

***Okwudili, Jacqueline.** How to Use Microsoft Access 2000. (How to Use ... (Que) Series). 1999. pap. text 24.99 (*0-672-31491-6*) Sams.

Okwumabua, Theresa M., jt. ed. see Morgan, Sam B.

Okyayuz-Baklouti, I., jt. ed. see Stefanovich, V.

Ola Abdel Hammid Soliman. Diccionario Espanol-Frances-Arabe. (ARA, FRE & SPA.). 787p. 1991. 45.00 (*0-86685-465-7*, LDL4657, Pub. by Librairie du Liban) Intl Bk Ctr.

Ola, R. O. Public Administration in Nigeria. 220p. 1984. pap. 24.50 (*0-7103-0044-1*) Routledge.

Ola, S. Tropical Soils of Nigeria in Engineering Practice. 336p. (C). 1983. text 181.00 (*90-6191-264-4*, Pub. by A A Balkema) Ashgate Pub Co.

Ola, Virginia U. The Life & Works of Bessie Head. LC 94-20128. 108p. 1994. text 59.95 (*0-7734-9018-3*) E Mellen.

Olabisi, Olagoke. Handbook of Thermoplastics. LC 97-58. (Plastics Engineering Ser.: Vol. 41). (Illus.). 1080p. 1997. text 250.00 (*0-8247-9797-3*) Dekker.

Oladele, Folasade. Awakening Students Talents: A Teacher's Guide to Developing Skills in Reading, Thinking, & Writing. Aromolaran, Adebisi T., ed. & intro. by. 122p. (C). 1998. teacher ed. 15.95 (*0-9635862-4-6*) Meroe Pub.

Oladipo, Caleb O. The Development of the Doctrine of the Holy Spirit in the Yoruba (African) Indigenous Christian Movement. LC 94-35601. (American University Studies VII: Vol. 185). XIII, 192p. (C). 1997. pap. 25.95 (*0-8204-2708-X*) P Lang Pubng.

Olafemi, Michael A. Black Assasin: Rage. LC 95-92344. (Illus.). 65p. 1995. pap. text 6.95 (*1-887778-00-4*) Free Mind Free Spirit.

Olafson, Frederick A. The Dialectic of Action: A Philosophical Interpretation of History & the Humanities. LC 79-10316. 303p. reprint ed. pap. 94.00 (*0-608-18215-X*, 205661900078) Bks Demand.

— Heidegger & the Ground of Ethics: A Study of "Mitsein" LC 98-16539. (Modern European Philosophy Ser.). 128p. (C). 1998. text 49.95 (*0-521-63094-0*); pap. text 17.95 (*0-521-63879-8*) Cambridge U Pr.

— Principles & Persons: An Ethical Interpretation of Existentialism. LC 67-16038. 276p. reprint ed. pap. 85.60 (*0-7837-6426-X*, 204642400012) Bks Demand.

— What Is a Human Being? A Heideggerian View. (Modern European Philosophy Ser.). 272p. (C). 1995. text 64.95 (*0-521-47395-0*); pap. text 21.95 (*0-521-47937-1*) Cambridge U Pr.

Olafson, Peter. Thunderscape: The World of Aden. 272p. 1995. pap. text 19.95 (*0-7615-0312-9*) Prima Pub.

Olafsson, Bjorn G. Small States in the Global System: Analysis & Illustrations from the Case of Iceland. LC 97-76951. (Illus.). 164p. 1998. text 55.95 (*1-84014-129-8*, Pub. by Ashgate Pub) Ashgate Pub Co.

Olafsson, Gestur, jt. auth. see Hilgert, Joachim.

***Olafsson, Olaf.** The Journey Home. 272p. 2000. 24.00 (*0-375-42061-4*) Knopf.

Olafsson, R., jt. auth. see Pau, L. F.

Olagoke, D. Olu. The Incorruptible Judge. (Evans Africa Plays Ser.). 48p. 1991. pap. write for info. (*0-237-49522-8*) EVN1 UK.

Olaguer, Eduardo P., Jr. Born from Above: A Commentary on John's Gospel. LC 98-72598. 87p. 1998. pap. 7.50 (*0-9646439-3-6*) Ambasdr Bks.

Olah. The Many Facets of Chemistry: Reflections & Changes. 300p. 24.95 (*0-471-15743-0*) Wiley.

— Superacids in Organic Synthesis. 250p. 1998. 1.00 (*0-12-525435-0*) Acad Pr.

***Olah, Brian.** Impromptu Startup!! 580p. 2000. pap. 42.00 (*0-13-019115-9*) P-H.

Ola'h, G. M. A New Way to Grow Edible Mushrooms: White Pleurotus. (Illus.). xii, 92p. 1981. pap. text 15.00 (*2-7637-6963-2*) Lubrecht & Cramer.

Olah, George A., ed. Cage Hydrocarbons. LC 89-29217. 432p. 1990. 150.00 (*0-471-62292-3*) Wiley.

Olah, George A., et al, eds. Electron Deficient Boron & Carbon Clusters. LC 90-41326. 379p. 1991. 120.00 (*0-471 52795-5*) Wiley.

Olah, George A. & Malhotra, Ripudaman. Nitration: Methods & Mechanisms. (Organic Nitro Chemistry Ser.). 330p. 1989. 120.00 (*0-471-18695-3*, Wiley-VCH) Wiley.

Olah, George A. & Molnar, Arpad. Hydrocarbon Chemistry. LC 94-31442. 656p. 1995. 89.95 (*0-471-11359-X*) Wiley.

Olah, George A. & Squire, David R., eds. Chemistry of Energetic Materials. (Illus.). 212p. (C). 1991. text 93.00 (*0-12-525440-7*) Acad Pr.

Olah, George A., et al. Nitration: Methods & Mechanisms. LC 89-16582. (Organic Nitro Chemistry Ser.). 330p. 1989. 75.00 (*0-89573-144-4*, Wiley-VCH) Wiley.

— Onium Ions. LC 97-43337. 528p. 1998. 110.00 (*0-471-14877-6*, Wiley-Interscience) Wiley.

— Synthetic Fluorine Chemistry. LC 91-25155. 416p. 1992. 165.00 (*0-471-54370-5*) Wiley.

Olah, J. Fish, Pathogens & Environment in European Polyculture: Proceedings of an International Seminar, Szarvas, Hungary, June 23-27, 1981. 264p. (C). 1984. 85.00 (*963-05-3614-5*, Pub. by Akade Kiado) St Mut.

Olah, Suzann M. My Phone Book. 18p. (J). (ps-2). 1991. pap. 3.50 (*0-9630985-0-0*) RJB Enter.

Olaisen, Bjonar, et al, eds. Progress in Forensic Genetics 7. 580p. 1998. 244.00 (*0-444-82965-2*, Excerpta Medica) Elsevier.

Olaitan, Samson O. & Agusiobo, Obiora N. Introduction to the Teaching of Home Economics. LC 80-40288. (Education in Africa Ser.). 341p. reprint ed. pap. 105.80 (*0-8357-6941-0*, 203900000009) Bks Demand.

Olaizola, Jose L. The Thirteenth Summer. Ouriou, Susan, tr. 288p. 1993. pap. 12.95 (*0-88995-094-6*, Pub. by Red Deer) Genl Dist Srvs.

Olajide, D., jt. ed. see Ndegwa, David.

Olajide, Michael, Jr. & Berger, Phil. Aerobox: A High Performance Fitness Program. 192p. (Orig.). 1995. mass mkt. 12.99 (*0-446-67116-9*, Pub. by Warner Bks) Little.

Olajos, Eugene, jt. auth. see Salem, Harry.

Olakanpo, Toyin. Beautiful, First Daughter. 224p. 1999. pap. write for info. (*0-9673126-7-1*) T K D Bks.

***Olakanpo, Toyin.** Poetry for the Spirit: Poem Meditations. 60p. 1999. pap. 10.00 (*0-9673126-6-3*) T K D Bks.

Olakanpo, Toyin. You & Him: A Stroll with God. iv, 370p. 1999. pap. 15.00 (*0-9673126-5-5*) T K D Bks.

Olaleye, Isaac. Bitter Bananas. LC 93-73306. (Illus.). 32p. (J). (ps-3). 1994. 14.95 (*1-56397-039-2*) Boyds Mills Pr.

Olaleye, Isaac. Bitter Bananas. LC 93-73306. (J). 1996. 11.19 (*0-606-09080-0*, Pub. by Turtleback) Demco.

Olaleye, Isaac. Distant Talking Drum: Poems from Nigeria. LC 94-60260. (Illus.). 32p. (J). (gr. 3-6). 1995. 15.95 (*1-56397-095-3*, Wordsong) Boyds Mills Pr.

— In the Rainfield: Who Is the Greatest? LC 97-39861. (Illus.). 32p. (J). (ps-4). 2000. 16.95 (*0-590-48363-3*, Blue Sky Press) Scholastic Inc.

— Lake of the Big Snake: An African Rain Forest Adventure. LC 95-80780. (Illus.). 32p. (J). (ps-3). 1998. 15.95 (*1-56397-096-1*) Boyds Mills Pr.

***Olaleye, Isaac & Demarest, Chris L.** Bikes for Rent! LC 99-58403. (J). 2000. lib. bdg. write for info. (*0-531-33290-X*) Orchard Bks Watts.

Olalquiaga, Celeste. The Artificial Kingdom: A Treasury of the Kitsch Experience. LC 98-14530. (Illus.). 336p. 1998. 30.00 (*0-679-43393-7*) Pantheon.

— Megalopolis: Contemporary Cultural Sensibilities. LC 91-12383. (Illus.). 136p. (C). 1992. pap. 13.95 (*0-8166-1999-9*) U of Minn Pr.

***Olam, Joseph.** Another Gender: Exposing the Theft of God-Given Authority. 128p. 2000. pap. 12.95 (*1-57921-253-0*, 924-173, Pub. by WinePress Pub) BookWorld.

***Oland, C. B.** Marble Hill Annealing Demonstration Evaluation. 164p. 1998. per. 38.00 (*0-16-062902-0*) USGPO.

— Repair Practices for Nuclear Power Plant Containment Metallic Pressure Boundaries. 127p. 1998. per. 10.00 (*0-16-062921-7*) USGPO.

***Oland, C. B., et al.** Marble Hill Annealing Demonstration Evaluation. LC 98-174523. xvii, 117p. 1998. write for info. (*0-16-049502-4*) USGPO.

Oland, Dwight D. North Apennines: United States Army Campaigns of World War 2. 31p. 1996. pap. 1.75 (*0-16-061321-3*) USGPO.

Olander, Donald R. Fundamental Aspects of Nuclear Reactor Fuel Elements, 2 vols., Vol. 1. LC 76-6485. (ERDA Technical Information Center Ser.). 625p. 1976. pap. 23.50 (*0-87079-031-5*, TID-26711-P1); fiche 9.00 (*0-685-01475-4*, TID-26711-P2) DOE.

— Fundamental Aspects of Nuclear Reactor Fuel Elements, 2 vols., Vol. 2. LC 76-6485. (ERDA Technical Information Center Ser.). 565p. 1976. pap. 22.00 (*0-685-01474-6*, TID-26711-P2); fiche 9.00 (*0-87079-467-1*, TID-26711-P2) DOE.

Olander, Folke, ed. European Consumer Policy after Maastricht. LC 94-7632. 344p. (C). 1994. lib. bdg. 153.00 (*0-7923-2770-5*) Kluwer Academic.

Olander, Folke, jt. ed. see Grunert, Klaus G.

Olander, Joseph D., et al, eds. School & Society Through Science Fiction. LC 81-40587. (Illus.). 404p. 1982. reprint ed. pap. text 31.00 (*0-8191-1997-0*) U Pr of Amer.

Olander, Tom, jt. auth. see Vantassel, Stephen.

Olander, William, et al, contrib. by. Fake: A Meditation on Authenticity. LC 87-42689. (Illus.). 50p. (Orig.). 1987. pap. 8.00 (*0-915557-58-4*) New Mus Contemp Art.

Olander, William & Debavpatnaik, P. Contemporary Afro-American Photography. LC 83-72603. (Illus.). 32p. 1983. pap. 3.00 (*0-942946-03-0*) Ober Coll Allen.

Olander, William & Grundberg, Andy. Drawings: After Photography. LC 89-82028. (Illus.). 48p. 1984. pap. 18.00 (*0-916365-12-3*) Ind Curators.

Olaniyan, R. Omotayo. Foreign Aid, Self-Reliance & Economic Development in West Africa. LC 96-10425. 224p. 1996. 62.95 (*0-275-95501-X*, Praeger Pubs) Greenwood.

Olaniyan, Tejumola. Scars of Conquest - Masks of Resistance: The Invention of Cultural Identities in African, African-American, & Caribbean Drama. 208p. 1995. text 55.00 (*0-19-509405-0*) OUP.

Olano, Pamela J., jt. auth. see McNaron, Toni A.

O

An Asterisk (*) at the beginning of an entry indicates that the title is appearing for the first time.

Olanow, Charles W. & Youdim, Moussa B. Neurodegeneration & Neuroprotection in Parkinson's Disease. (Neuroscience Perspectives Ser.). (Illus.). 224p. 1996. text 65.00 (0-12-525445-8) Acad Pr.
Olanrewaju, S. A., jt. ed. see Falola, Toyin.
Olaoye, Elain H. Passions of the Soul. 65p. 1998. pap. text. write for info. (1-880764-14-8) Northwind NJ.
***Olap, Train.** Olap Services Fundamentals. LC 99-86771. 1999. pap. text 39.99 (0-7356-0904-7) Microsoft.
Olarewaju, jt. auth. see Cottell.
***Olariu, S. & Wu, J., eds.** 12th International Conference on Parallel & Distributed Computing Systems: PDCS 99 Proceedings August 18-20, 1999, Ft. Lauderdale, FL. 572p. (C). 1999. write for info. (1-880843-29-3) Int Soc Comp App.
Olariu, Stephan, jt. auth. see Tanimoto, Steven L.
Olarsch, I. Gerald. Electrolytes: Your Body's Strongest Health Link! 44p. 1998. pap. 4.95 (0-9640539-8-5, 139) Natures Pubng.
Olarte, Efrain Gonzales de, see Gonzales de Olarte, Efrain, ed.
Olaru, Victor, tr. see Chufu, Gabriel.
Olasiji, Thompson, jt. auth. see Henderson, George.
***Olasky, Marvin.** The American Leadership Tradition: The Inevitable Impact of a Leader's Faith on a Nation's Destiny. Orig. Title: The American Leadership Tradition: Moral Vision from Washington to Clinton. 320p. 2000. reprint ed. pap. 15.99 (1-58134-176-8) Crossway Bks.
— Compassionate Conservatism: What It Is, What It Does, & How It Can Transform America. 240p. 2000. 24.00 (0-7432-0131-0) Free Pr.
Olasky, Marvin. God, Sex & Statesmanship: The Morals & Politics of Great American Leaders. LC 98-43422. (Illus.). 320p. 1999. 24.50 (0-684-83449-9) Free Pr.
Olasky, Marvin N. Abortion Rites: A Social History of Abortion in America. LC 92-12118. 320p. 1992. pap. 19.99 (0-89107-687-5) Crossway Bks.
— Abortion Rites: A Social History of Abortion in America. LC 95-24312. 336p. 1995. reprint ed. pap. 14.95 (0-89526-723-3) Regnery Pub.
— Central Ideas in the Development of American Journalism: A Narrative History. 208p. 1990. text 36.00 (0-8058-0893-0) L Erlbaum Assocs.
— Corporate Public Relations: A New Historical Perspective. 192p. 1987. pap. 36.00 (0-8058-0052-2) L Erlbaum Assocs.
— Fighting for Liberty & Virtue. 316p. 1996. 24.95 (0-89526-712-8) Regnery Pub.
— The Press & Abortion, 1838-1988. (Communication Ser.). 208p. (C). 1988. pap. text 27.50 (0-8058-0485-4) L Erlbaum Assocs.
— Prodigal Press: The Anti-Christian Bias of the American News Media. LC 87-72951. (Turning Point Christian Worldview Ser.). 256p. 1988. pap. 14.99 (0-89107-476-7) Crossway Bks.
— Renewing American Compassion. 208p. 1996. 20.50 (0-684-83000-0) Free Pr.
— Renewing American Compassion: How Compassion for the Needy Can Turn Ordinary Citizens into Heroes. LC 97-7707. 208p. 1997. pap. 12.95 (0-89526-414-5) Regnery Pub.
— Telling the Truth: How to Revitalize Christian Journalism. LC 95-42467. 320p. 1996. pap. 20.00 (0-89107-885-1) Crossway Bks.
— The Tragedy of American Compassion. 299p. 1995. pap. 14.95 (0-89526-725-X) Regnery Pub.
Olasky, Marvin N. & Olasky, Susan. More Than Kindness: A Compassionate Approach to Crisis Childbearing. LC 90-80625. 224p. 1990. pap. 14.99 (0-89107-584-4) Crossway Bks.
Olasky, Marvin N., et al. Whirled Views: Tracking Today's Culture Storms. LC 96-51913. 243p. 1997. pap. 12.99 (0-89107-938-6) Crossway Bks.
Olasky, Susan. Annie Henry & the Birth of Liberty. LC 94-45739. (Adventures of the American Revolution Ser.: Vol. 2). 128p. (J). (gr. 4-6). 1995. pap. 5.99 (0-89107-842-8) Crossway Bks.
— Annie Henry & the Mysterious Stranger. LC 96-29070. (Adventures of the American Revolution Ser.: Vol. 3). 144p. (J). (gr. 3-7). 1996. pap. 5.99 (0-89107-907-6) Crossway Bks.
— Annie Henry & the Redcoats. LC 96-33031. (Adventures of the American Revolution Ser.: Vol. 4). 128p. (J). (gr. 3-7). 1996. pap. 5.99 (0-89107-908-4) Crossway Bks.
— Annie Henry & the Secret Mission. LC 94-38671. (Adventures of the American Revolution Ser.: Vol. 1). 128p. (J). (gr. 3-7). 1995. pap. 5.99 (0-89107-830-4) Crossway Bks.
Olasky, Susan, jt. auth. see Olasky, Marvin N.
Olatunde, Njideka N. Reflexology Today - A Family Affair: A Self-Help Guide for Family Wellness. (Illus.). 116p. 1999. pap. write for info. (0-7392-0171-9, PO3132) Morris Pubng.
Olatunji, Sunday. Faith That Produces Miracles. 30p. (Orig.). 1997. pap. write for info. (0-9622241-5-4) Olatunji Bks.
— Free Money Grants & How to Get It. 32p. 1997. pap. write for info. (0-9622241-6-2) Olatunji Bks.
— Free Money in America & How to Get It. 200p. (Orig.). (C). 1989. pap. text. write for info. (0-318-64799-0) Olatunji Bks.
— How to Get a Government Job. 36p. (Orig.). 1997. pap. write for info. (0-9622241-4-6) Olatunji Bks.
— How to Inspect & Buy a Used Car. 40p. (Orig.). 1997. pap. write for info. (0-9622241-0-3) Olatunji Bks.
Olatunji, Sunday O. Bad Credit - No Credit You Can Get a Mortgage & Buy a House. 36p. (Orig.). 1997. pap. write for info. (0-9622241-3-8) Olatunji Bks.
— Free Money Grants in America & How to Get It. 50p. 1997. pap. write for info. (0-9622241-7-0) Olatunji Bks.
O'Laughlin, Jay, jt. auth. see Cubbage, Frederick W.
O'Laughlin, M. Families of County Dublin, Ireland: Including Old Irish & Settlers from the Earliest Times to the 20th Century. (Families of Ireland Ser.: Vol. 7). (Illus.). 256p. 1999. 34.00 (0-940134-30-6) Irish Genealog.
O'Laughlin, Michael, ed. see Keating, Geoffrey.
O'Laughlin, Michael C. Beginner's Guide to Irish Genealogy. (Common Sense Guide Ser.). (Illus.). 50p. 1988. pap. 15.00 (0-940134-03-9) Irish Genealog.
— The Book of Irish Families: Great & Small. 2nd anniversary ed. (Annals of Irish Family History Ser.: Vol. 1). (Illus.). 360p. 1997. 34.95 (0-940134-15-2) Irish Genealog.
— The Complete Book of Irish Family Names: The Master I.G.G. Index. 311p. 1987. 24.00 (0-940134-41-1) Irish Genealog.
***O'Laughlin, Michael C.** Families of County Clare, Ireland: Including Old Irish & Settler Families from the Earliest Times to the 20th Century. 2nd rev. enl. ed. (Families of Ireland Ser.: Vol. 3). (Illus.). 172p. 2000. 34.00 (0-940134-98-5) Irish Genealog.
O'Laughlin, Michael C. Families of County Cork, Ireland: Irish Family Surnames with Locations & Origins. (Irish Families Ser.: Vol. 4). (Illus.). 219p. 1999. 34.00 (0-940134-35-7) Irish Genealog.
***O'Laughlin, Michael C.** Families of County Donegal, Ireland: Including Old Irish & Settlers from the Earliest Times to the 20th Century. (Families of Ireland Ser.: Vol. 8). (Illus.). 168p. 2000. 34.00 (0-940134-75-6) Irish Genealog.
O'Laughlin, Michael C. Families of County Galway, Ireland: Irish Family Surnames with Locations & Origins. (Families of Ireland Ser.: Vol. 6). 207p. 1999. 34.00 (0-940134-00-4) Irish Genealog.
— Families of County Kerry, Ireland: Irish Family Surnames with Locations & Origins. (Irish Families Ser.: Vol. 2). (Illus.). 244p. 1999. 34.00 (0-940134-36-5) Irish Genealog.
— Families of County Limerick, Ireland: Irish Family Surnames with Locations & Origins. (Families of Ireland Ser.: Vol. 5). (Illus.). 184p. 1999. 34.00 (0-940134-31-4) Irish Genealog.
— The Flaherty Book. (Irish Family Histories Ser.). (ENG & GAE., Illus.). 40p. 1983. 15.00 (0-940134-22-5) Irish Genealog.
— Irish Settlers on the American Frontier, Vol. 1: Gateway West. Donahue, P. J., ed. (Irish West of the Mississippi Ser.). (Illus.). 250p. 1983. lib. bdg. 34.00 (0-940134-25-X) Irish Genealog.
— The Kelly Book. (Irish Family Histories Ser.). (Illus.). 50p. 1981. 15.00 (0-940134-19-5) Irish Genealog.
— Master Book of Irish Placenames: Master Atlas & Book of Irish Placenames. (Illus.). 270p. 1994. 19.95 (0-940134-33-0) Irish Genealog.
— Master Book of Irish Surnames: Locations, Origins & Ethnicity. (Illus.). 304p. 1993. 23.95 (0-940134-32-2) Irish Genealog.
— The Murphy Book. (Irish Family Histories Ser.). (Illus.). 1981. 15.00 (0-940134-20-9) Irish Genealog.
— The O'Donaghue Book. (Irish Family Histories Ser.). 50p. 1981. 15.00 (0-940134-16-0) Irish Genealog.
— The O'Laughlin Book. (Irish Family Histories Ser.). 50p. 1981. 15.00 (0-940134-17-9) Irish Genealog.
— The O'Reilly Book. (Irish Family Histories Ser.). (Illus.). 50p. 1981. 15.00 (0-940134-21-7) Irish Genealog.
— The O'Sullivan Book. (Irish Family Histories Ser.). (Illus.). 50p. 1981. 15.00 (0-940134-18-7) Irish Genealog.
O'Laughlin, Michael C., ed. see O'Hart, John.
O'Laughlin, Robert J., jt. auth. see Bukowski, Richard W.
***Olausen, Judy.** Mother. 96p. 2000. pap. 15.95 (0-14-029084-2, Viking); pap. 15.95 (0-14-026362-4) Viking Penguin.
Olaussen, Maria. Forceful Creation in Harsh Terrain: Place & Identity in Three Novels by Bessie Head. LC 97-25383. (European University Studies, Series 14: Vol. 325). 337p. 1997. pap. 57.95 (3-631-31421-3) P Lang Pubng.
— Forceful Creation in Harsh Terrain: Place & Identity in Three Novels by Bessie Head. LC 97-25383. (European University Studies, Series 14: Vol. 325). 337p. 1997. pap. 57.95 (0-8204-3254-7) P Lang Pubng.
Olausson, Eric & Cato, Ingemar, eds. Chemistry & Biogeochemistry of Estuaries. LC 79-41211. (Illus.). 462p. reprint ed. pap. 143.30 (0-608-17590-0, 203043400069) Bks Demand.
Olave, Baden-Powell, jt. auth. see Hillcourt, William.
O'Laverty, H. Mother of God & Her Glorious Feasts. LC 87-50580. (Illus.). 200p. 1987. pap. 10.00 (0-89555-317-1) TAN Bks Pubs.
Olawsky, Lynn A. Colors of Australia. LC 96-45651. (Colors of the World Ser.). (Illus.). 24p. (J). (gr. 2-5). 1997. 14.21 (0-87614-884-4, Lerner Publctns) Lerner Pub.
— Colors of Australia. LC 96-45651. (Colors of the World Ser.). (Illus.). 24p. (J). (gr. 2-5). 1997. pap. text 5.95 (1-57505-213-X, Carolrhoda) Lerner Pub.
— Colors of Mexico. LC 96-42523. (Colors of the World Ser.). (Illus.). 24p. (J). 1997. lib. bdg. 19.93 (0-87614-886-0, Carolrhoda) Lerner Pub.
— Colors of Mexico. (Colors of the World Ser.). (Illus.). 24p. (J). (gr. k-3). 1997. pap. text 5.95 (1-57505-216-4, Carolrhoda) Lerner Pub.
Olayiwola, Peter O. Petroleum & Structural Change in a Developing Country: The Case of Nigeria. LC 86-21216. 225p. 1986. 59.95 (0-275-92115-8, C2115, Praeger Pubs) Greenwood.
Olazaga. Sorpresasa with List Cass. 2nd ed. (C). 1996. student ed. 38.50 (0-03-018839-3) Harcourt.
Olazagasti-Segovia, Elena. Sorpresas. 2nd ed. 240p. (C). 1996. pap. text 37.00 (0-03-017524-0) Holt R&W.
Olazagasti-Segovia, Elena, tr. see Ortiz Cofer, Judith.
Olbe, L., ed. Proton Pump Inhibitors: Milestones in Drug Therapy. 250p. 1999. 138.00 (3-7643-5897-1) Birkhauser.
***Olbe, Lars.** Proton Pump Inhibitors. LC 98-49154. (Milestones in Drug Therapy Ser.). 1999. write for info. (0-8176-5897-1) Birkhauser.
Olberg, Gabriele Von, see Von Olberg, Gabriele.
Olbermann, Keith & Patrick, Dan. The Big Show. 1997. 23.00 (0-614-28167-9) PB.
— The Big Show: A Tribute to ESPN's SportsCenter. 256p. 1984. per. 1.50 (0-671-00919-2, 857835) PB.
Olbertz, Hella. Verbal Periphrases in a Functional Grammar of Spanish. LC 98-4782. (Functional Grammar Ser.: No. 22). (SPA.). 585p. 1998. 155.00 (3-11-015402-1) De Gruyter.
Olbertz, Hella, et al, eds. The Structure of the Lexicon in Functional Grammar, Vol. 16. LC 98-18695. (Studies in Language Companion Ser.: Vol. 43). xii, 312p. 1998. 69.00 (1-55619-929-5) J Benjamins Pubng Co.
Olbey, J., ed. see Olney, Richard.
Olbinski, Rafal. Rafal Olbinski "Posters" LC 96-69653. (Illus.). 76p. (Orig.). 1996. pap. 28.95 (1-878768-00-X) Nahan Editions.
Olbinsky, Carol. Federal Income Taxes of Decedents & Estates. 18th ed. 160p. 1997. pap. text 37.50 (0-8080-0228-7, 0545100) CCH INC.
***Olbracht, Ivan.** Nikola the Outlaw. 2001. pap. 18.95 (0-8101-1827-0) Northwestern U Pr.
Olbracht, Ivan. The Sorrowful Eyes of Hannah Karajich. Lewitova, Iris U., tr. from CZE. LC 99-41491. (Central European Classics Series). 200p. 1999. pap. 16.95 (963-9116-47-5) Ctrl Europ Univ.
Olbrechts-Tyteca, L., jt. auth. see Perelman, Chaim.
Olbrich, Dieter & Plassmann, Reinhard, eds. Psychosomatische Rehabilitation und Sozialmedizin. (Illus.). 210p. 1997. pap. 37.95 (3-631-31866-9) P Lang Pubng.
Olbrich, Emil. Development of Sentiment on Negro Suffrage to 1860. Fish, Carl R., ed. LC 72-154085. (Black Heritage Library Collection). 1977. 17.95 (0-8369-8796-9) Ayer.
Olbrich, Freny. Desouza in Stardust. large type ed. (Mystery Ser.). 384p. 1983. 27.99 (0-7089-0951-5) Ulverscroft.
— Desouza Pays the Price. large type ed. (Mystery Ser.). 352p. 1982. 27.99 (0-7089-0844-6) Ulverscroft.
Olbrich, Joseph M. Ideen von Olbrich. (GER., Illus.). 196p. boxed set 75.00 (3-925369-15-5, Pub. by Arnoldsche Art Pubs) Antique Collect.
Olbrich, Martin, jt. auth. see Bunke, Ulrich.
Olbricht, Thomas H. Clinical Dermatology. 432p. 1992. spiral bd. 34.95 (0-316-09425-0) Lppncott W & W.
— Hearing God's Voice: My Life with Scripture in the Churches of Christ. LC 96-83724. 447p. (Orig.). 1996. pap. 19.95 (0-89112-018-1) Abilene Christ U.
Olbricht, Thomas H., jt. ed. see Porter, Stanley E.
Olby, Robert C. The Origins of Mendelism. LC 84-2491. (Illus.). xviii, 328p. 1996. pap. text 18.00 (0-226-62592-3) U Ch Pr.
— The Path to the Double Helix: The Discovery of DNA. (Illus.). xxvi, 526p. 1994. reprint ed. pap. 13.95 (0-486-68117-3) Dover.
Olby, Robert C., jt. ed. see Cantor, G. N.
Olcen, Mehmet A. Vetluga Memoir: A Turkish Prisoner of War in Russia, 1916-1918. Leiser, Gary, ed. & tr. by. from TUR. LC 94-48881. (Illus.). 264p. 1995. 49.95 (0-8130-1353-4) U Press Fla.
***Olcese, James.** Melatonin after Four Decades: An Assessment of Its Potential LC 99-31757. (Advances in Experimental Medicine & Biology Ser.). 1999. write for info. (0-306-46134-X, Kluwer Plenum) Kluwer Academic.
Olcheski, Bill. One Hundred Trivia Quizzes for Stamp Collectors. 130p. 1982. pap. 4.95 (0-933580-09-6) Am Philatelic Society.
Olcott, Anthony. Murder at the Red October. (Academy First Mystery Ser.). 320p. 1990. reprint ed. pap. 5.95 (0-89733-327-6) Academy Chi Pubs.
— Rough Beast: A Novel by the Author of Murder at the Red October. 320p. 1992. text 20.00 (0-684-19406-6) S&S Trade.
Olcott, Anthony, tr. see Markish, Shimon.
Olcott, Anthony, tr. see Moscovit, Andrei, pseud.
Olcott, Charles, compiled by. Two Lectures on the Subjects of Slavery & Abolition. LC 71-164391. (Black Heritage Library Collection). 1977. reprint ed. 17.95 (0-8369-8850-7) Ayer.
Olcott, Charles S. Life of William McKinley, 2 vols., Set. LC 79-128946. (American Statesmen Ser.: Nos. 38, 39). reprint ed. 90.00 (0-404-50893-6) AMS Pr.
Olcott, Edward S. 20th Century Summit. (Illus.). iv, 82p. 1998. pap. 15.00 (0-9666996-0-2) City of Summit.
Olcott, Frances J. Good Stories for Anniversaries. LC 89-43342. (Tower Bks.). (Illus.). 264p. 1990. reprint ed. lib. bdg. 48.00 (1-55888-876-4) Omnigraphics Inc.
Olcott, Frances J., compiled by. Story-Telling Poems. LC 77-128155. (Granger Index Reprint Ser.). xvi, 384p. 1977. 21.95 (0-8369-6182-X) Ayer.
Olcott, Henry S. Buddhist Catechism. 120p. 1998. reprint ed. pap. 16.95 (0-7661-0430-3) Kessinger Pub.
— The Golden Rules of Buddhism Compiled from the Bana Books. 50p. 1992. reprint ed. pap. 3.00 (1-56459-256-1) Kessinger Pub.
— Old Diary Leaves. 1974. 9.50 (0-8356-7106-2) Theos Pub Hse.
— Old Diary Leaves, II. 1973. 9.50 (0-8356-7123-2) Theos Pub Hse.
— Old Diary Leaves, III. 1973. 9.50 (0-8356-7480-0) Theos Pub Hse.
— Old Diary Leaves, IV. 1973. 9.50 (0-8356-7484-3) Theos Pub Hse.
— Old Diary Leaves, V. 1973. 9.50 (0-8356-7487-8) Theos Pub Hse.
— Old Diary Leaves, VI. 1973. 9.50 (0-8356-7491-6) Theos Pub Hse.
— People from the Other World. 492p. 1996. reprint ed. spiral bd. 31.00 (0-7873-0641-X) Hlth Research.
— People from the Other World. 492p. 1996. reprint ed. pap. 29.95 (1-56459-829-2) Kessinger Pub.
— Theosophy: Religion & Occult Theosophy. 384p. 1993. reprint ed. pap. 24.95 (1-56459-390-8) Kessinger Pub.
Olcott, Henry S., ed. see D'Assier, Adolphe.
Olcott, Lynn, jt. auth. see O'Lill, Ruth.
Olcott, Martha B. Central Asia's New States: Independence, Foreign Policy, & Regional Security. LC 95-30153. 1995. pap. text 19.95 (1-878379-51-8) US Inst Peace.
***Olcott, Martha B.** Getting It Wrong: Regional Cooperation & the Commonwealth of Independent States. 2000. pap. 19.95 (0-87003-171-6) Carnegie Endow.
Olcott, Martha B. The Kazakhs. 2nd ed. (Publication Ser.: No. 427). (Illus.). 388p. (C). 1995. 38.95 (0-8179-9351-7); pap. 20.95 (0-8179-9352-5) Hoover Inst Pr.
Olcott, Martha B., et al, eds. The Soviet Multinational State: Readings & Documents. LC 88-36747. (USSR in Transition: Readings & Documents Ser.). 616p. (C). (gr. 13). 1990. text 88.95 (0-87332-389-0) M E Sharpe.
Olcott, Martha B., jt. ed. see Aslund, Anders.
Olcott, Martha B., ed. & intro. see Poliakov, Sergei P.
Olcott, Martha B., ed. & intro. see Poliakov, Sergie P.
Olcott, Nick, tr. see Lehmann, Rudolf.
Olcott, William A. Make a Note of It: Wit & Wisdom from Fund Raisers for Fund Raisers. LC 97-51685. 138p. 1998. 24.95 (1-56625-102-8) Bonus Books.
Olcott, William R. Maintaining the Profession: A Fieldbook for Clinical Supervisors. 238p. 1996. 19.95 (1-889346-00-4) Rainmaker Pr.
Olcott, William T. Star Lore of All Ages. 452p. 1996. reprint ed. spiral bd. 38.00 (0-7873-1096-4) Hlth Research.
— Star Lore of All Ages: A Collection of Myths, Legends, & Facts Concerning the Constellations of the Northern Hemisphere (1911) 475p. 1996. reprint ed. pap. 29.95 (1-56459-770-9) Kessinger Pub.
Olczak, Anatole. The Bourne Shell Quick Reference Guide. 2nd ed. 44p. (Orig.). 1998. pap. text 7.95 (0-935739-22-X) ASP.
— C Reference Card. (Orig.). 1985. pap. 2.95 (0-935739-01-7) ASP.
— JavaScript Quick Reference Guide. 65p. 1998. pap. 7.95 (0-935739-28-9) ASP.
— Korn Shell Quick Reference Guide. 2nd ed. 1998. pap. 7.95 (0-935739-21-1) ASP.
— KornShell User & Programming Manual. rev. ed. LC 97-14395. 424p. (C). 1997. pap. text 44.95 (0-201-17688-2) Addison-Wesley.
— UNIX Quick Reference Guide. 5th ed. 161p. 1996. pap. text 9.95 (0-935739-25-4) ASP.
— VI Reference Card. 4th ed. (Orig.). 1996. pap. 2.95 (0-935739-19-X) ASP.
Olczak, Anatole, jt. auth. see Waechter, Parker.
Olczak, Paul V., jt. auth. see Grosch, James W.
Old, Alan R. De, see Sheets, Everett & De Old, Alan R.
Old California Preservation Society Staff, ed. California Historic Sites. (Illus.). 1986. pap. 4.95 (0-913290-69-6) Camaro Pub.
— Historic Restaurants of California. (Illus.). 1986. pap. 4.95 (0-913290-60-2) Camaro Pub.
Old Campbell County Historical Society Staff. Campbell County, Georgia Superior Court Deeds & Mortgages Grantee/Grantor Index 1829-1931. Redmond, LaGroon, ed. LC 94-60683. 528p. (C). 1994. text. write for info. (1-883793-04-1) Wolfe Pubng.
Old Farmer's Almanac Almanac Editorial Staff, ed. see Halvorson, Christine, et al.
Old Farmers' Almanac Editors, jt. auth. see White, Martha.
Old Farmers Almanac Editors, ed. see Bannister, Polly.
Old Farmer's Almanac Editors, ed. see Van Hasinga, Cynthia.
Old Farmer's Almanac Staff. Old Farmer's Almanac. 1997. pap. 4.95 (0-375-75037-1) Villard Books.
Old Farmers Almanac Staff. Old Farmers Almanac, '99. 1998. write for info. (0-676-57785-7) Villard Books.
Old, Hughes O. Guides to the Reformed Tradition: Worship. LC 83-19616. 194p. 1984. pap. 17.95 (0-8042-3252-0) Westminster John Knox.
— Leading in Prayer: A Workbook for Worship. 381p. (Orig.). 1995. pap. 20.00 (0-8028-0821-2) Eerdmans.
— The Reading & Preaching of the Scriptures in the Worship of the Christian Church: The Biblical Period. LC 97-30624. 346p. (Orig.). 1997. pap. 35.00 (0-8028-4356-5) Eerdmans.
— The Reading & Preaching of the Scriptures in the Worship of the Christian Church Vol. 2: The Ancient Church. LC 97-30624. 480p. 1998. pap. 42.00 (0-8028-4357-3) Eerdmans.
— The Reading & Preaching of the Scriptures in the Worship of the Christian Church Vol. 3: The Medieval Church. 3rd ed. 640p. 1999. pap. 45.00 (0-8028-4619-X) Eerdmans.

O

An Asterisk (*) at the beginning of an entry indicates that the title is appearing for the first time.

age of 92. What is the secret - what are these successful older people doing right? To find the secrets of longevity & good health, he went to the experts - those that have aged successfully, & simply asked the, "To what do you owe your health & longevity?" The secrets they have revealed to their Family Doctor will intrigue everyone, regardless of age. The book consists of fascinating anecdotes & lively examples from Dr. Old's medical practice as his older patients reveal their pragmatic, workable, personal secrets of successful aging. There is incredible value in older "Vintage People." Chapters include such topics as: "Chronologically Gifted," "Use it or Lose It," & "Spirituality." Old presents chapters dealing with personal triumph over tragedy & also includes statistics to back him up. The bottom line, however, is that attitude makes a big difference, & that is something we all have control over.
Publisher Paid Annotation.

Old, John & Shafto, Tony. Introduction to Business Economics: Workbook. 208p. 1998. pap., wbk. ed. 39.00 (*0-7487-1359-X*) St Mut.

Old Nordenski, Erland. The Cultural History of the South American Indians. Lindberg, Christer, ed. & intro. by. LC 96-20345. (Studies in Cultural History: Vol. 4). 223p. 1996. 82.50 (*0-404-64254-3*) AMS Pr.

Old Northwest Genealogical Quarterly Staff. Ohio Cemetery Records Extracted from the "Old Northwest" Genealogical Quarterly. LC 84-80083. 495p. 1989. reprint ed. 30.00 (*0-8063-1071-5*) Genealog Pub.

Old, O., jt. auth. see Shafto, S.

***Old, Scofield Readers Staff .** The New Scofield Reader's Study Bible. 1760p. 1998. pap. 39.99 (*0-19-528145-4*) OUP.

— Old Scofield Study Bible. 1616p. 1998. 54.99 (*0-19-527433-4*) OUP.

***Old, Scofield Readers Staff .** Old Scofield Reader Edition Study Bible. 1616p. 1998. 44.99 (*0-19-527415-6*) OUP.

Old Scofield Readers Staff. Old Scofield Readers Edition Study Bible. 1616p. 1998. 75.00 (*0-19-527446-6*) OUP.

***Old Scofield Readers Staff.** Old Scofield Study Bible. 1616p. 1998. 86.99 (*0-19-527439-3*) OUP.

Old Scofield Staff. King James Old Scofield Study Bible Black Genuine Leather Wide Margin. 1616p. 1997. 96.99 (*0-19-527323-0*) OUP.

***Old Scofield Staff.** KJV 269RRL Old Scofield Readers Edition Study Bible. 1616p. 1998. 81.00 (*0-19-527447-4*) OUP.

— Old Scofield Readers Study Bible. 1616p. 1998. 44.99 (*0-19-527419-9*) OUP.

— Old Scofield Readers Study Bible: 274RRL. 1616p. 1998. 54.99 (*0-19-527437-7*) OUP.

Old Scofield Staff, ed. Bible: New Scofield Ed. 1824p. 1998. 49.99 (*0-19-527725-2*) OUP.

— Bible: New Scofield Ed. 1824p. 1999. bond lthr. 79.99 (*0-19-527727-9*) OUP.

— Bible: New Scofield Ed. 1824p. 1999. bond lthr. 86.99 (*0-19-527728-7*); bond lthr. 86.99 (*0-19-527730-9*) OUP.

— Bible: New Scofield Edition. 1824p. 1999. 56.99 (*0-19-527726-0*) OUP.

— Bible: Old Scofield Ed. 1616p. 1998. lthr. 100.00 (*0-19-527410-5*) OUP.

— Bible: Old Scofield Ed. 1616p. 1998. lthr. 107.00 (*0-19-527411-3*); lthr. 100.00 (*0-19-527412-1*) OUP.

— Bible: Old Scofield Edition. 1616p. 1998. lthr. 107.00 (*0-19-527413-X*) OUP.

Old Settlers' Union Committee. History & Reminiscences: From the Records of Old Settlers' Union of Princeville & Vicinity, 4 vols. (Illus.). 567p. 1997. reprint ed. lib. bdg. 49.00 (*0-8328-5783-1*) Higginson Bk Co.

Old Slave Mart Museum & Library Staff. Catalog of the Old Slave Mart Museum & Library. 1978. 175.00 (*0-8161-0073-X*, G K Hall & Co) Mac Lib Ref.

Old Time Publications Staff, ed. see Goss, Carrie F.

Old Vicarage Publications Staff. Antiqvarivm Forense. (C). 1982. pap. text 40.00 (*0-7855-3131-9*, Pub. by Old Vicarage) St Mut.

— Athens. (C). 1982. pap. text 50.00 (*0-9508635-5-6*, Pub. by Old Vicarage) St Mut.

— Cave of Tiberius. 66p. (C). 1982. pap. text 60.00 (*0-7855-3134-3*, Pub. by Old Vicarage) St Mut.

— Corinth-Mycenae-Nauplion-Tiryns-Epidauros. 50p. (C). 1982. pap. text 50.00 (*0-9508635-7-2*, Pub. by Old Vicarage) St Mut.

— Crete. (C). 1982. pap. text 40.00 (*0-9508635-4-8*, Pub. by Old Vicarage) St Mut.

— Delphi. 96p. (C). 1982. pap. text 40.00 (*0-947818-01-4*, Pub. by Old Vicarage) St Mut.

— M Sixty-Three - Motorway Through a Town. 80p. (C). 1982. pap. text 39.00 (*0-9508635-0-5*, Pub. by Old Vicarage) St Mut.

— Paestum. (C). 1982. pap. text 60.00 (*0-7855-3135-1*, Pub. by Old Vicarage) St Mut.

— The Palatine. 94p. (C). 1982. pap. text 34.00 (*0-7855-3132-7*, Pub. by Old Vicarage) St Mut.

— Phlegraean Fields. 168p. (C). 1982. pap. text 45.00 (*0-7855-3130-0*, Pub. by Old Vicarage) St Mut.

— Piazza Armerina Imperial Villa. 92p. (C). 1982. pap. text 65.00 (*0-7855-3133-5*, Pub. by Old Vicarage) St Mut.

— The Quincentenary Year of Stockport Grammar School. 128p. (C). 1988. pap. text 39.00 (*0-947818-10-3*, Pub. by Old Vicarage) St Mut.

— The Roman Forum. 104p. (C). 1982. pap. text 34.00 (*0-7855-5991-4*, Pub. by Old Vicarage) St Mut.

— Rome & Environs. 240p. (C). 1982. pap. text 45.00 (*0-7855-3136-X*, Pub. by Old Vicarage) St Mut.

— Tivoli Hadrian's Villa & Villa D'Este. 70p. (C). 1982. pap. text 65.00 (*0-7855-3129-7*, Pub. by Old Vicarage) St Mut.

Old, W. Gorn. The Yoga of Yama. 64p. 1996. reprint ed. spiral bd. 12.00 (*0-7873-1169-3*) Hlth Research.

Old, Wendie. Stacy Had a Little Sister: A Concept Book. Grant, Christy, ed. (Illus.). 32p. (J). (ps-3). 1994. lib. bdg. 14.95 (*0-8075-7598-4*) A Whitman.

Old, Wendie C. Duke Ellington: Giant of Jazz. LC 96-3279. (African-American Biographies Ser.). (Illus.). 128p. (YA). (gr. 6 up). 1996. lib. bdg. 20.95 (*0-89490-691-7*) Enslow Pubs.

— George Washington. LC 96-43571. (United States Presidents Ser.). (Illus.). 128p. (YA). (gr. 5 up). 1997. lib. bdg. 20.95 (*0-89490-832-4*) Enslow Pubs.

— James Monroe. LC 97-43699. (United States Presidents Ser.). 128p. (YA). (gr. 5 up). 1998. lib. bdg. 20.95 (*0-89490-941-X*) Enslow Pubs.

— Louis Armstrong: King of Jazz. LC 97-35860. (African-American Biographies Ser.). (Illus.). 128p. (YA). (gr. 6 up). 1998. lib. bdg. 20.95 (*0-89490-997-5*) Enslow Pubs.

— Marian Wright Edelman: Fighting for Children's Rights. LC 95-7508. (People to Know Ser.). (Illus.). 128p. (YA). (gr. 6 up). 1995. lib. bdg. 20.95 (*0-89490-623-2*) Enslow Pubs.

— Thomas Jefferson. LC 97-7273. (United States Presidents Ser.). (Illus.). 112p. (YA). (gr. 5 up). 1997. lib. bdg. 20.95 (*0-89490-837-5*) Enslow Pubs.

***Old, Wendie C.** The Wright Brothers: Inventors of the Airplane. LC 99-39585. (Historical American Biographies Ser.). (Illus.). 128p. (gr. 6 up). 2000. lib. bdg. 20.95 (*0-7660-1095-3*) Enslow Pubs.

Old Woodbury Historical Society Staff, compiled by. Homes of Old Woodbury. (Illus.). 262p. 1995. reprint ed. lib. bdg. 35.00 (*0-8328-4992-8*) Higginson Bk Co.

Old World Farmer's Almanac Staff, jt. auth. see Schultz, Christine.

Old World Wisconsin Staff. Taste of Tradition: Old World Wisconsin Cooking. Larson, Carolyn, ed. & pref. by. (Illus.). 208p. (Orig.). 1988. 12.50 (*0-9620365-0-1*) Friends Old World WI.

Oldach, Mark. Creativity for Graphic Designers. (Illus.). 144p. 1995. 29.99 (*0-89134-583-3*, North Lght Bks) F & W Pubns Inc.

***Oldach, Mark.** Creativity for Graphic Designers. (Illus.). 144p. 2000. pap. 19.99 (*1-58180-055-X*, North Lght Bks) F & W Pubns Inc.

Oldacre, Ellen, jt. auth. see Bruce, Debra F.

***Oldak, Emily.** Comedy for Real Life: A Guide to Helping Kids Survive in an Imperfect World. Peterson, Nicholas, ed. (Illus.). 126p. 1999. pap. 19.95 (*0-9676828-0-0*) Comedy Presc.

***Oldaker, Wilfred H.** Aristophanes' Scenes from The Birds. (Classical Reprints Ser.). (GRE.). 76p. (C). 1999. reprint ed. pap. text 16.95 (*1-58510-006-4*) Focus Pub-R Pullins.

Oldakowski, Ray, et al, eds. Growth, Technology, Planning, & Geographic Education in Central Florida: Images & Encounters. LC 98-161522. (Illus.). 144p. 1998. pap. 12.00 (*1-884136-11-7*) NCFGE.

Oldal, E., jt. auth. see Redl, E.

***Oldale, Peter.** Practical Picture Restoration. (Illus.). 160p. 2000. pap. 35.00 (*1-86126-239-6*, Pub. by Crolwood) Trafalgar.

Oldani, Barbara A. Golf Colorado: Complete Guide to Public Golf Courses. (Colorado Recreation Guides Ser.). 180p. (Orig.). 1995. pap. 7.95 (*1-887430-00-8*) Global Inc.

Oldani, Robert W., jt. auth. see Emerson, Caryl.

Oldberg, Ingmar, jt. ed. see Bergstrand, Bengt-Goran.

Oldcorn, Anthony, tr. see Bonfil, Robert.

Oldcorn, Anthony, tr. see Goldoni, Carlo.

Oldcorn, Roger & Parker, David. Strategic Investment Decision: Evaluating Opportunities in Dynamic Markets. (Financial Times Management Ser.). (Illus.). 256p. 1996. 39.95 (*0-273-61779-6*) F T P-H.

Olde, Peter & Marriott, Neil. The Grevillea Book, 3 vols., Vols. 1-3, Set. (Illus.). 768p. 1995. 149.85 (*0-88192-308-7*) Timber.

Oldehoeft, Rodney R., jt. ed. see Matsuoka, Satoshi.

Oldeman, R. A. Forests: Elements of Silvology. (Illus.). 640p. 1990. 227.95 (*0-387-51883-5*) Spr-Verlag.

Olden, Anthony. Libraries in Africa: Pioneers, Policies, Problems. 190p. 1995. 39.50 (*0-8108-3093-0*) Scarecrow.

Olden, Anthony & Wise, Michael, eds. Information & Libraries in the Developing World, No. 3: Arab States. 272p. 1994. 90.00 (*1-85604-085-2*, LAP0852, Pub. by Library Association) Bernan Associates.

Olden, Anthony, jt. ed. see Wise, Michael.

Olden, Diana J. & Smith, Vicki. Pendleton Pennywise Presents the Money Book - Just for You: A Budget Book for Children. 44p. (J). (gr. 3-5). 1991. spiral bd. 11.95 (*0-9630463-0-6*) S & D.

***Olden, Kenneth, ed.** Niehs Report on Health Effects from Exposure to Power-Line Frequency Electric & Magnetic Fields. 67p. (C). 1999. pap. text 20.00 (*0-7881-8373-7*) DIANE Pub.

Olden, Kenneth, ed. NTP Workshop on Validation & Regulatory Acceptance of Alternative Toxicological Test Methods: Final Report. (Illus.). 41p. (C). 1997. pap. text 30.00 (*0-7881-4233-X*) DIANE Pub.

Olden, Kevin W., ed. Handbook of Functional Gastrointestinal Disorders, No. 4. (Medical Psychiatry Ser.: Vol. 4). (Illus.). 436p. 1996. text 150.00 (*0-8247-9409-5*) Dekker.

Olden, Marc. Fear's Justice. 352p. 1999. mass mkt. 6.50 (*0-671-00379-8*) PB.

— The Ghost. 400p. 2000. per. 6.99 (*0-671-00418-2*, Pocket Star Bks) PB.

***Olden, Marc.** The Ghost: A Novel, 1. LC 99-21761. 320p. 1999. 23.50 (*0-684-83467-7*) Simon & Schuster.

Olden, Marc. Kisaeng. 416p. 1992. reprint ed. mass mkt. 5.99 (*0-8217-3897-6*, Zebra Kensgtn) Kensgtn Pub Corp.

Olden, Roger. Victims. LC 95-68400. 204p. 1995. lib. bdg. 50.00 (*0-923687-35-1*) Celo Valley Bks.

Oldenberg, Hermann. Dipavamsa. 232p. 1986. reprint ed. 20.00 (*0-8364-1747-X*, Pub. by Manohar) S Asia.

— The Dipavamsa: An Ancient Buddhist Historical Record. (C). 1982. 17.00 (*0-8364-2831-5*, Pub. by Asian Educ Servs) S Asia.

— The Doctrine of the Upanisads & the Early Buddhism. (C). 1991. 26.00 (*81-208-0830-4*, Pub. by Motilal Bnarsidass) S Asia.

— The Religion of the Veda. Shrotri, Shridhar B., tr. (C). 1988. 42.50 (*81-208-0392-2*, Pub. by Motilal Bnarsidass) S Asia.

Oldenberg, Hermann, ed. The Dipavamsa: An Ancient Buddhist Historical Record. LC 78-72428. (ENG & PLI.). reprint ed. 27.00 (*0-404-17289-X*) AMS Pr.

Oldenberg, Hermann, jt. auth. see Muller, F. Max.

Oldenberg, Otto & Rasmussen, Norman C. Modern Physics for Engineers. (Illus.). 489p. (C). 1992. reprint ed. text 81.00 (*1-878907-47-6*) TechBooks.

***Oldenbourg, Lennart.** Business Dictionary. (ENG & SWE.). 404p. 1998. 195.00 (*0-320-02205-6*) Fr & Eur.

Oldenbourg, Lennart. Engelsk-Svensk Affarsordbok: English-Swedish Business Dictionary. (ENG & SWE.). 376p. 1994. 195.00 (*0-7859-8582-4*, 9127570576) Fr & Eur.

Oldenbourg, Rudolf C. & Sartorius, Hans. The Dynamics of Automatic Controls. Mason, H. L., ed. LC 49-2386. 276p. reprint ed. pap. 85.60 (*0-608-30564-2*, 205194500015) Bks Demand.

Oldenbourg, Zoe. Argile et Cendres, Tome I. 1979. pap. 15.95 (*0-7859-4126-6*) Fr & Eur.

— Les Brules. (FRE.). 1975. pap. 13.95 (*0-7859-4043-X*, 2070366855) Fr & Eur.

— Les Cites Charnelles. (FRE.). 1983. pap. 20.95 (*0-7859-4189-4*) Fr & Eur.

— The Cornerstone. 496p. 1998. pap. 14.95 (*0-7867-0524-8*) Carroll & Graf.

— Destiny of Fire. 384p. 1998. pap. 13.95 (*0-7867-0577-9*) Carroll & Graf.

— La Joie des Pauvres, Tome I. (FRE.). 1981. pap. 13.95 (*0-7859-4153-3*) Fr & Eur.

— La Joie des Pauvres, Tome II. (FRE.). 1981. pap. 13.95 (*0-7859-4154-1*) Fr & Eur.

— La Joie-Souffrance, Tome I. (FRE.). 1985. pap. 20.95 (*0-7859-4226-2*) Fr & Eur.

— La Joie-Souffrance, Tome II. (FRE.). 1985. pap. 20.95 (*0-7859-4227-0*) Fr & Eur.

— La Pierre Angulaire. (FRE.). 1972. pap. 17.95 (*0-7859-3986-5*) Fr & Eur.

— Reveilles de la Vie. (FRE.). 1974. pap. 11.95 (*0-7859-4035-9*) Fr & Eur.

— Visages d'un Autoportrait. (FRE.). 409p. 1988. pap. 17.95 (*0-7859-4284-X*, 2070379167) Fr & Eur.

— The World Is Not Enough. Trask, Willard R., tr. LC 97-17488. 512p. 1998. mass mkt. 13.95 (*0-7867-0489-6*) Carroll & Graf.

Oldenburg, Ann & Oldenburg, Don. Washington, D. C. & Baltimore Dog Lover's Companion: The Inside Scoop on Where to Take Your Dog. (Illus.). 450p. 1998. pap. text 17.95 (*1-57354-041-2*) Avalon Travel.

Oldenburg, Brian, ed. Health, Work, & the Workplace: A Special Issue of the International Journal of Behavioral Medicine. 88p. 1999. pap. 20.00 (*0-8058-9797-6*) L Erlbaum Assocs.

Oldenburg, Claes & Van Bruggen, Coosje. Large-Scale Projects: Claes Oldenburg Coosje van Bruggen. LC 94-76579. (Illus.). 584p. 1994. 95.00 (*1-885254-04-0*, Pub. by Monacelli Pr) Penguin Putnam.

Oldenburg, Don, jt. auth. see Oldenburg, Ann.

Oldenburg, Douglas W., jt. auth. see Whittall, Kenneth P.

Oldenburg, Henry. The Correspondence of Henry Oldenburg, 1641-1662, Vol. 1. Hall, A. Rupert & Hall, Marie B., eds. & trs. by. LC 65-11201. (Illus.). 547p. 1965. reprint ed. pap. 169.60 (*0-608-07467-5*, 206769400001) Bks Demand.

— The Correspondence of Henry Oldenburg, 1663-1665, Vol. 2. Hall, A. Rupert & Hall, Marie B., eds. LC 65-11201. (Illus.). 706p. 1965. reprint ed. pap. 200.00 (*0-608-07468-3*, 206769400002) Bks Demand.

— The Correspondence of Henry Oldenburg, 1667-1668, Vol. 4. Hall, A. Rupert & Hall, Marie B., eds. LC 65-11201. (Illus.). 629p. 1965. reprint ed. pap. 195.00 (*0-608-07469-1*, 206769400004) Bks Demand.

— The Correspondence of Henry Oldenburg, 1668-1669, Vol. 5. Hall, A. Rupert & Hall, Marie B., eds. LC 65-11201. (Illus.). 632p. 1965. reprint ed. pap. 196.00 (*0-608-07470-5*, 206769400005) Bks Demand.

— The Correspondence of Henry Oldenburg, 1669-1670, Vol. 6. Hall, A. Rupert & Hall, Marie B., eds. LC 65-11201. (Illus.). 690p. 1965. reprint ed. pap. 200.00 (*0-608-07471-3*, 206769400006) Bks Demand.

— The Correspondence of Henry Oldenburg, 1672-1673, Vol. 9. Hall, A. Rupert & Hall, Marie B., eds. LC 65-11201. (Illus.). 738p. 1965. reprint ed. pap. 200.00 (*0-608-07472-1*, 206769400009) Bks Demand.

Oldenburg, Kirsten U., jt. auth. see Hirschhorn, Joel S.

Oldenburg, L. Business Dictionary. (ENG & FIN.). 393p. 1997. 175.00 (*0-320-02424-5*) Fr & Eur.

Oldenburg, Philip. Big City Government in India: Councilor, Administrator, & Citizen in Delhi. (Monographs: No. 31). xiii, 400p. 1976. pap. 18.00 (*0-614-97994-3*) Assn Asian Studies.

Oldenburg, Philip, ed. India Briefing: Staying the Course. (Asia Society Briefings Ser.). 252p. (C). 1995. pap. 30.95 (*1-56324-610-4*, East Gate Bk) M E Sharpe.

— India Briefing: Staying the Course. (Asia Society Briefings Ser.). 252p. (gr. 13). 1995. 75.95 (*1-56324-609-0*, East Gate Bk) M E Sharpe.

Oldenburg, Philip, jt. ed. see Bouton, Marshall M.

***Oldenburg, Ray.** The Great Good Place: Cafes, Coffee Shops, Bookstores, Bars, Hair Salons & Other Hangouts at the Heart of a Community. 3rd ed. LC 99-29168. (Illus.). 368p. 1999. pap. 15.95 (*1-56924-681-5*) Marlowe & Co.

Oldenburg, Ray. The Great Good Place: Cafes, Coffee Shops, Community Centers, Beauty Parlors, General Stores, Bars, Hangouts, & How They Get You Through the Day. 338p. 1994. pap. 14.95 (*1-56924-907-5*) Marlowe & Co.

— The Great Good Place: Cafes, Coffee Shops, Community Centers, Beauty Parlors, General Stores, Bars, Hangouts, & How They Get You Through the Day. 2nd ed. 1997. pap. 14.95 (*1-56924-778-1*) Marlowe & Co.

***Oldenburg, Ray, ed.** Celebrating the Third Place: Inspiring Stories about the "Great Good Places" at the Heart of Our Communities. (Illus.). 2000. pap. 14.95 (*1-56924-612-2*) Marlowe & Co.

Oldenburg, Rick. Conducting the Phonothon. (Illus.). 44p. 1991. pap. 8.00 (*1-55833-109-3*) Natl Cath Educ.

Oldenburg, Veena T. The Making of Colonial Lucknow, 1856-1877. LC 83-16008. 314p. 1984. reprint ed. pap. 97.40 (*0-7837-9407-X*, 206015200004) Bks Demand.

— Say It in Hindi. (Say It Ser.). 192p. (Orig.). 1981. pap. 4.95 (*0-486-23959-4*) Dover.

Oldendorf, Donna, ed. see Commire, Anne.

Oldendorf, Walter P., jt. ed. see Rud, Anthony G., Jr.

Oldendorf, William H., Jr. Basic of Magnetic Resonance Imaging. (Topics in Neurology Ser.). (C). 1988. text 133.00 (*0-89838-964-X*) Kluwer Academic.

— MRI Primer. 240p. 1991. text 53.50 (*0-88167-769-8*) Lppncott W & W.

Oldendorf, William H. The Quest for an Image of Brain: Computerized Tomography in the Perspective of Past & Future Imaging Methods. LC 79-62971. 167p. 1980. reprint ed. pap. 51.80 (*0-608-00420-0*, 206113500007) Bks Demand.

Oldenquist, Andrew. The Non-Suicidal Society. LC 85-45804. 276p. 1986. pap. 85.60 (*0-608-05038-5*, 205969900004) Bks Demand.

Oldenquist, Andrew G. The Non-Suicidal Society. LC 85-45804. (Illus.). 280p. (C). 1986. 10.95 (*0-253-34107-8*) Ind U Pr.

Oldenquist, Andrew G., ed. Can Democracy Be Taught? LC 96-68281. 150p. 1996. pap. 14.50 (*0-87367-489-8*) Phi Delta Kappa.

Oldenquist, Andrew G. & Rosner, Menachem, eds. Alienation, Community, & Work, 96. LC 91-6282. (Contributions in Sociology Ser.: No. 96). 224p. 1991. 55.00 (*0-313-27541-6*, OAL, Greenwood Pr) Greenwood.

Oldenquist, Andrew G., jt. ed. see Garner, Richard T.

Oldenski, Thomas. Liberation Theology & Critical Pedagogy in Today's Catholic Schools: Social Justice in Action. LC 96-51085. (Critical Education Practice Ser.: Vol. 11). (Illus.). 264p. 1997. text 44.00 (*0-8153-2379-4*); pap. text 22.95 (*0-8153-2375-1*) Garland.

Oldenverg, Herman. Buddha: His Life, His Doctrine, His Order. (C). 1992. 27.00 (*81-7062-177-1*, Pub. by Lancer India) S Asia.

Oldenziel, Ruth. Making Technology Masculine: Men, Women & Modern Machines in America, 1870-1945. LC 99-496066. 1999. pap. 24.95 (*90-5356-381-4*, Pub. by Amsterdam U Pr) U of Mich Pr.

Older, Anne, et al. In & Around Albany, Schenectady & Troy. 3rd ed. (Illus.). 368p. 1992. pap. 14.95 (*1-881324-00-1*) Wash Park.

Older, Cora M. Love Stories of Old California. LC 94-43777. 320p. 1995. pap. 15.95 (*1-55709-400-4*) Applewood.

— Love Stories of Old California. LC 75-167165. (Short Story Index Reprint Ser.). 1977. reprint ed. 26.95 (*0-8369-3991-3*) Ayer.

Older, Effin. Birthday Party. LC 99-186742. (You're Invited to Mary-Kate & Ashley's Ser.). (Illus.). 48p. (J). (gr. 2-4). 1998. 12.95 (*0-590-22593-6*) Scholastic Inc.

— Ice Dreams. (Silver Blades Figure Eight Ser.: No. 1). 80p. (J). (gr. 1-4). 1996. pap. 3.50 (*0-553-48491-5*) Bantam.

***Older, Effin.** My Two Grandmothers. LC 99-6092. (Illus.). 32p. (J). (ps-3). 2000. 16.00 (*0-15-200785-7*, Harcourt Child Bks) Harcourt.

Older, Effin. Randi Goes for the Gold! (Silver Blades Figure Eights Ser.: No. 2). (Illus.). 96p. (J). (gr. 1-4). 1998. pap. 3.99 (*0-553-48522-9*, Skylark BDD) BDD Bks Young Read.

— Randi's Pet Surprise. (Silver Blades Figure Eights Ser.: No. 8). (Illus.). 96p. (Orig.). (J). (gr. 1-4). 1997. pap. 3.50 (*0-553-48514-8*) BDD Bks Young Read.

— Snowboarding. LC 99-17541. (Illus.). 112p. 1999. pap. 14.95 (*0-8117-2931-1*) Stackpole.

Older, Fremont. My Own Story. rev. ed. (BCL1 - United States Local History Ser.). 340p. 1991. reprint ed. lib. bdg. 89.00 (*0-7812-6343-3*) Rprt Serv.

— William Randolph Hearst, American. LC 72-7195. (Select Bibliographies Reprint Ser.). 1977. reprint ed. 42.95 (*0-8369-6951-0*) Ayer.

Older, Jay J. Eyelid Tumors: Clinical Diagnosis & Surgical Treatment. LC 85-43152. (Illus.). 128p. 1987. reprint ed. pap. 39.70 (*0-608-05872-6*, 205983900007) Bks Demand.

Older, John, ed. Bone Implant Grafting. LC 92-2327. xviii, 226p. 1992. 247.00 (*0-387-19720-6*) Spr-Verlag.

— Bone Implant Grafting. LC 92-2327. xviii, 226p. 1992. write for info. (*3-540-19720-6*) Spr-Verlag.

O

An Asterisk (*) at the beginning of an entry indicates that the title is appearing for the first time.

Older, Jules. Anita! The Woman Behind the Body Shop. LC 97-41906. (Illus.). (YA). (gr. 3 up). 1998. 13.95 (0-88106-979-5) Charlesbridge Pub.
***Older, Jules.** Backroad & Offroad Biking. LC 00-25640. (Illus.). 2000. pap. 19.95 (0-8117-3150-2) Stackpole.
Older, Jules. Cow. LC 96-947. (Illus.). (J). 1997. pap. 6.95 (0-88106-956-6) Charlesbridge Pub.
— Cow. LC 96-947. (Illus.). 32p. (J). (ps-4). 1997. 15.95 (0-88106-957-4) Charlesbridge Pub.
— Cross-Country Skiing for Everyone. LC 98-12789. (Illus.). 192p. 1998. 16.95 (0-8117-2708-4) Stackpole.
— Ski Vermont: A Complete Guide to the Best Vermont Skiing. LC 91-16650. (Illus.). 141p. reprint ed. pap. 43.80 (0-608-08584-7, 206910700002) Bks Demand.
***Older, Jules.** Telling Time: How to Tell Time on Digital & Analog Clocks! LC 99-18764. (Illus.). 32p. (J). (ps-2). 2000. 16.95 (0-88106-396-7); pap. 6.95 (0-88106-397-5) Charlesbridge Pub.
Older, Julia. Endometriosis. (Illus.). 221p. 1985. pap. 10.95 (0-684-18505-9, Scribners Ref) Mac Lib Ref.
***Older, Julia.** Hermaphroditus in America. LC 00-36271. 2000. write for info. (0-9627162-9-4) Appledore Bks.
Older, Julia. Higher Latitudes. LC 95-79509. 61p. (Orig.). 1995. pap. 8.00 (0-9627162-3-5) Appledore Bks.
— The Island Queen: Celia Thaxter of the Isles of Shoals. LC 94-70760. 206p. (Orig.). 1998. reprint ed. pap. 12.00 (0-9627162-2-7) Appledore Bks.
— A Little Wild: Poems & Woodcuts. (Illus.). 40p. 1987. 28.00 (0-930126-19-X) Typographeum.
— Oonts & Others. 72p. 1982. 17.50 (0-87775-150-1); pap. 9.95 (0-87775-151-X) Unicorn Pr.
Older, Julia & Sherman, Steve. Nature Walks in Southern New Hampshire. (Nature Walks Guides Ser.). (Illus.). 256p. 1994. pap. 10.95 (1-878239-35-X) AMC Books.
— Nature Walks in the New Hampshire Lakes Region. LC 97-6637. (Nature Walks Guide Ser.). (Illus.). 336p. (Orig.). 1997. pap. 12.95 (1-878239-59-7) AMC Books.
Older, Julia, ed. see Thaxter, Celia.
Older, Julia, ed. & tr. see Vian, Boris.
Older, Ricki, jt. auth. see Reynolds, Dona.
Older, Robert A., jt. auth. see Resnick, Martin I.
Olderman, Raymond M. Beyond the Waste Land: A Study of the American Novel in the Nineteen-Sixties. LC 73-182210. 269p. reprint ed. pap. 83.40 (0-8357-8042-2, 203384800087) Bks Demand.
— 10 Minute Guide to Business Communication. (10 Minute Guides). 144p. 1997. pap. 10.95 (0-02-861600-6) Macmillan.
Olderog, E. R., jt. ed. see Steffen, Bernhard.
Olderog, Ernst R. Nets, Terms & Formulas: Three Views of Concurrent Processes & Their Relationship. (Tracts in Theoretical Computer Science Ser.: No. 23). 277p. (C). 1991. text 59.95 (0-521-40044-9) Cambridge U Pr.
Olderog, Ernst R., ed. Programming Concepts, Methods & Calculi: Proceedings of the IFIP TC2/WG2.1/WG2.2/WG2.3 Working Conference on Programming Concepts, Methods, & Calculi (PROCOMET '94), San Miniato, Italy, 6-10 June 1994. LC 94-36660. (IFIP Transactions & Computer Science & Technology Ser.). 602p. 1994. 178.50 (0-444-82020-5) Elsevier.
Olderog, Ernst R. & Apt, K. R. Verification of Sequential & Concurrent Programs. 2nd ed. LC 96-29771. (Graduate Texts in Computer Science Ser.). 424p. 1997. 39.95 (0-387-94896-1) Spr-Verlag.
Olderog, F. R., jt. auth. see Apt, K. R.
Olderr, Steven. Mystery Index: Subjects, Settings, & Sleuths of 10,000 Mystery Novels. LC 87-1294. 448p. 1987. text 20.00 (0-8389-0461-0) ALA.
— Olderr's Fiction Subject Headings: A Supplement & Guide to the LC Thesaurus. LC 91-8679. 160p. (C). 1991. pap. text 35.00 (0-8389-0562-5) ALA.
— Reverse Symbolism Dictionary: Symbols Listed by Subject. LC 90-53517. 191p. 1992. lib. bdg. 35.00 (0-89950-561-9) McFarland & Co.
Olderr, Steven, compiled by. Symbolism: A Comprehensive Dictionary. LC 85-42833. 159p. 1986. lib. bdg. 32.00 (0-89950-187-7) McFarland & Co.
Olderr, Steven, ed. Olderr's Fiction Index, 1987. 87th ed. 350p. 1988. 65.00 (0-912289-85-6) St James Pr.
— Olderr's Fiction Index, 1988. 88th ed. 1989. 65.00 (1-55862-028-1) St James Pr.
— Olderr's Fiction Index, 1989. 89th ed. 450p. 1990. 65.00 (1-55862-057-5) St James Pr.
— Olderr's Fiction Index, 1990. 90th ed. 557p. 1991. 65.00 (1-55862-090-7, 200143) St James Pr.
— Olderr's Young Adult Fiction Index, 1990. 90th ed. 310p. 1991. 65.00 (1-55862-091-5, 200144) St James Pr.
— Olderr's Young Adult Fiction Index, 1988. 88th ed. 1989. 65.00 (1-55862-020-6) St James Pr.
— Olderr's Young Adult Fiction Index, 1989. 89th ed. 250p. 1990. 65.00 (1-55862-058-3) St James Pr.
Oldershaw, Callie. Oceans. LC 91-45079. (Our Planet Ser.). (Illus.). 32p. (J). (gr. 4-6). 1993. pap. 4.95 (0-8167-2754-6) Troll Communs.
— Oceans. LC 91-45079. (Our Planet Ser.). (Illus.). 32p. (J). (gr. 4-6). 1997. lib. bdg. 17.25 (0-8167-2753-8) Troll Communs.
***Oldershaw, Cally.** Deserts & Wastelands. LC 99-45544. (Closer Look at Ser.). 32p. (J). (gr. 4-6). 2000. lib. bdg. 21.90 (0-7613-1152-1, Copper Beech Bks) Millbrook Pr.
Oldertz, Carl & Tidefelt, Eva, eds. Compensation for Personal Injury in Sweden & 17 Other Countries. 408p. 1988. 109.00 (91-7598-197-1) Coronet Bks.
Oldfather, C. H., tr. see Von Pufendorf, Samuel.
Oldfather, Penny, et al. Learning Through Children's Eyes: Social Constructivism & the Desire to Learn. LC 99-12929. (Division 15 Ser.: Vol. 12). 120p. 1999. pap. text 17.95 (1-55798-587-1, 431619A) Am Psychol.
Oldfather, W. A., tr. see Von Pufendorf, Samuel.
Oldfather, William A. A Bibliography of Epictetus. 177p. 1952. 20.00 (0-685-02325-7) Holmes.
— Contributions Toward a Bibliography of Epictetus: A Supplement. Harman, Marion, ed. LC 28-2296. 197p. reprint ed. pap. 61.10 (0-608-11104-X, 202087000020) Bks Demand.
Oldfather, William A., et al. Index Verborum Ciceronis Epistularum. 583p. 1965. reprint ed. write for info. (0-318-72059-0) G Olms Pubs.
— Index Verborum Quae in Senecae Fabulis Necnon in Octavia Praetexta Reperiuntur. 272p. 1964. reprint ed. write for info. (0-318-72060-4) G Olms Pubs.
— Index Verborum Quae in Senecae Fabulis Necnon in Octavia Praetexta Reperiuntur. (University of Illinois Studies in Language & Literature: Vol. IV, 2-4). 272p. 1983. reprint ed. write for info. (3-487-00658-8) G Olms Pubs.
Oldfather, William A., et al. Index Verborum Ciceronis Epistularum. 583p. 1988. reprint ed. write for info. (3-487-00880-7) G Olms Pubs.
Oldfield, Audrey. Woman Suffrage in Australia: A Gift or a Struggle? (Studies in Australian History). (Illus.). 277p. (C). 1993. text 69.95 (0-521-40380-4); pap. text 22.95 (0-521-43611-7) Cambridge U Pr.
Oldfield, Barney & Moriarty, John J. Amphibians & Reptiles Native to Minnesota. LC 93-45018. (C). 1994. 29.95 (0-8166-2384-8) U of Minn Pr.
Oldfield, Duane M. The Right & the Righteous: The Christian Right Confronts the Republican Party. (Religious Forces in the Modern Political World). 294p. (C). 1996. 27.95 (0-8476-8190-4) Rowman.
Oldfield, Elizabeth. Amor en Peligro: Looking after Dad. (Bianca Ser.: Vol. 461).Tr. of Love at Risk. (SPA.). 1998. per. 3.50 (0-373-33461-3, 1-33461-4) Harlequin Bks.
— Backlash. large type ed. (Magna Large Print Ser.). 1994. 27.99 (0-7505-0667-9, Pub. by Mgna Lrg Print) Ulverscroft.
— The Bedroom Incident: Do Not Disturb. 1998. per. 3.75 (0-373-11994-1, 1-11994-0) Harlequin Bks.
— Beloved Stranger. large type ed. (Magna Romance Ser.). 1992. 17.95 (0-7505-0401-3, Pub. by Mgna Lrg Print) Ulverscroft.
— Bodycheck. large type ed. 264p. 1993. 27.99 (0-7505-0555-9, Pub. by Mgna Lrg Print) Ulverscroft.
— Close Proximity. large type ed. (Magna Large Print Ser.). 1994. 27.99 (0-7505-0739-X, Pub. by Mgna Lrg Print) Ulverscroft.
— Dark Victory. large type ed. 1995. lib. bdg. 18.95 (0-263-13940-9) Thorndike Pr.
— Dark Victory (Dangerous Liaisons) LC 96-700. 189p. 1996. per. 3.50 (0-373-11800-7, 1-11800-9) Harlequin Bks.
— Designed to Annoy. (Presents Ser.). 1994. per. 2.99 (0-373-11636-5, 1-11636-7) Harlequin Bks.
— Ennemis et Complices. (Azur Ser.). 1999. mass mkt. 3.50 (0-373-34771-5, 1-34771-5) Harlequin Bks.
— Fast & Loose. (Presents Ser.). 1996. per. 3.50 (0-373-11831-7, 1-11831-4) Harlequin Bks.
— La Fausse Declaration. (Azur Ser.: Bk. 740). 1999. mass mkt. 3.50 (0-373-34740-5, 1-34740-0) Harlequin Bks.
— Fighting Lady. large type ed. 305p. 1993. 27.99 (0-7505-0474-9) Ulverscroft.
— Final Surrender. LC 95-6879. (Presents Ser.). 188p. 1995. per. 3.25 (0-373-11747-7, 1-11747-2) Harlequin Bks.
— His Sleeping Partner. large type ed. (Mills & Boon Large Print Ser.). 288p. 1997. 23.99 (0-263-14972-2) Ulverscroft.
— Imperfect Stranger. 1999. pap. 3.75 (0-373-18701-7, 1-18701-2, Harlequin) Harlequin Bks.
— Imperfect Stranger. large type ed. 288p. 1995. 23.99 (0-263-14292-2, Pub. by Mills & Boon) Ulverscroft.
— Living Dangerously. large type ed. 255p. 1992. 11.50 (0-7505-0317-3, Pub. by Mgna Lrg Print) Ulverscroft.
— Looking after Dad. (From Here to Paternity Ser.). 1997. per. 3.50 (0-373-11879-1, 1-11879-3) Harlequin Bks.
— Looking after Dad. large type ed. (Mills & Boon Large Print Ser.). 288p. 1997. 23.99 (0-263-15170-0, Pub. by Mills & Boon) Ulverscroft.
— Love's Prisoner (Presents Plus) LC 96-551. 189p. 1995. mass mkt. 3.25 (0-373-11773-6) Harlequin Bks.
— Relaciones Intimas (Intimate Relations), Vol. 420. (Harlequin Bianca Ser.). (SPA.). 1997. per. 3.50 (0-373-33420-6, 1-33420-0) Harlequin Bks.
***Oldfield, Elizabeth.** Reluctant Father. 1999. mass mkt. 3.50 (0-373-18712-2) Harlequin Bks.
Oldfield, Elizabeth. Solution: Seduction! large type ed. (Mills & Boon Large Print Ser.). 288p. 1997. 23.99 (0-263-15299-5, Pub. by Mills & Boon) Ulverscroft.
— Sudden Fire. large type ed. (Harlequin Ser.). 1994. lib. bdg. 19.95 (0-263-13778-3) Thorndike Pr.
Oldfield, George S., Jr. Implications of Regulation on Bank Expansion: A Simulation Analysis. Altman, Edward I. & Walter, Ingo I., eds. LC 76-10399. (Contemporary Studies in Economic & Financial Analysis: Vol. 10). 140p. 1978. 78.50 (0-89232-015-X) Jai Pr.
Oldfield, Harry, jt. auth. see Coghill, Roger.
Oldfield, J. Abandoned, Bk. 2. (Illus.). (J). 1997. mass mkt. 7.95 (0-340-68170-5, Pub. by Hodder & Stought Ltd) Trafalgar.
— Blind Alley, Bk. 7. (Illus.). (J). mass mkt. 8.95 (0-340-70873-5, Pub. by Hodder & Stought Ltd) Trafalgar.
— X-Mas Special. (Illus.). (J). 1997. mass mkt. 7.95 (0-340-70399-7, Pub. by Hodder & Stought Ltd) Trafalgar.
— Crash. (Illus.). (J). mass mkt. 7.95 (0-340-70869-7, Pub. by Hodder & Stought Ltd) Trafalgar.
— Grievous Bodily Injury, Bk. 9. (Illus.). (J). mass mkt. 7.95 (0-340-70875-1, Pub. by Hodder & Stought Ltd) Trafalgar.
— Homeless. (Home Farm Twins Ser.: No. 3). (Illus.). (J). 1996. mass mkt. 7.95 (0-340-66129-1, Pub. by Hodder & Stought Ltd) Trafalgar.
— Intensive Care. (Illus.). (J). 1997. mass mkt. 7.95 (0-340-68169-1, Pub. by Hodder & Stought Ltd) Trafalgar.
— Killer on the Loose, Bk. 3. (J). 1997. mass mkt. 7.95 (0-340-68171-3, Pub. by Hodder & Stought Ltd) Trafalgar.
— Living Proof, Bk. 8. (Illus.). (J). mass mkt. 7.95 (0-340-70874-3, Pub. by Hodder & Stought Ltd) Trafalgar.
— Quarantine, Bk. 4. (J). 1998. mass mkt. 7.95 (0-340-68172-1, Pub. by Hodder & Stought Ltd) Trafalgar.
— Running Wild, Bk. 10. (Illus.). (J). mass mkt. 8.95 (0-340-70876-X, Pub. by Hodder & Stought Ltd) Trafalgar.
— Sinbad Runaway. (Home Farm Twins Ser.: No. 2). (Illus.). (J). 1996. mass mkt. 7.95 (0-340-66128-3) Hodder & Stought Ltd.
— Skin & Bone, Vol. 5. (J). mass mkt. 7.95 (0-340-70878-6, Pub. by Hodder & Stought Ltd) Trafalgar.
— Skye Champion, Bk. 13. (Illus.). (J). mass mkt. 7.95 (0-340-69985-X, Pub. by Hodder & Stought Ltd) Trafalgar.
— Snip/Snap Trauant. (Home Farm Twins Ser.: No. 6). (Illus.). (J). 1996. mass mkt. 7.95 (0-340-66132-1, Pub. by Hodder & Stought Ltd) Trafalgar.
— Socks Survivor. (Home Farm Twins Ser.: Vol. 8). (J). 1997. mass mkt. 7.95 (0-340-68991-9, Pub. by Hodder & Stought Ltd) Trafalgar.
— Sophie Showoff, Bk. 15. (J). mass mkt. 7.95 (0-340-69987-6, Pub. by Hodder & Stought Ltd) Trafalgar.
— Sorrel Substitute, Bk. 12. (Illus.). (J). mass mkt. 7.95 (0-340-69984-1, Pub. by Hodder & Stought Ltd) Trafalgar.
— Speckled Stray. (Home Farm Twins Ser.: No. 1). (Illus.). (J). 1996. mass mkt. 7.95 (0-340-66127-5, Pub. by Hodder & Stought Ltd) Trafalgar.
— Spike the Tramp. (Home Farm Twins Ser.: No. 5). (Illus.). (J). 1996. mass mkt. 7.95 (0-340-66131-3, Pub. by Hodder & Stought Ltd) Trafalgar.
— Stanley Troublemaker. (J). mass mkt. 8.95 (0-340-72675-X, Pub. by Hodder & Stought Ltd) Trafalgar.
— Stevie Rebel. (Home Farm Twins Ser.: Vol. 9). (Illus.). (J). mass mkt. 7.95 (0-340-68992-7, Pub. by Hodder & Stought Ltd) Trafalgar.
— Sugar & Spice, Bk. 14. (Illus.). (J). mass mkt. 7.95 (0-340-69986-8, Pub. by Hodder & Stought Ltd) Trafalgar.
— Sultan Patient, Vol. 2. (Illus.). (J). mass mkt. 7.95 (0-340-69983-3, Pub. by Hodder & Stought Ltd) Trafalgar.
— Sunny Hero. (Home Farm Twins Ser.: No. 7). (J). mass mkt. 7.95 (0-340-68990-0, Pub. by Hodder & Stought Ltd) Trafalgar.
— Susie Orphan. (Home Farm Twins Ser.: No. 4). (Illus.). (J). 1996. mass mkt. 7.95 (0-340-66130-5, Pub. by Hodder & Stought Ltd) Trafalgar.
Oldfield, J. E., jt. auth. see Kains, M. G.
Oldfield, J. R. Alexander Crummell (Eighteen Nineteen to Eighteen Ninety-Eight) & the Creation of an African-American Church in Liberia. LC 90-31353. (Studies in the History of Missions: Vol. 6). 180p. 1990. lib. bdg. 79.95 (0-88946-074-4) E Mellen.
— Popular Politics & British Anti-Slavery: The Mobilisation of Public Opinion Against the Slave Trade, 1787-1807. LC 98-29907. (Studies in Slave & Post-Slave Societies & Cultures). (Illus.). 216p. 1998. pap. 26.50 (0-7146-4462-5, Pub. by F Cass Pubs) Intl Spec Bk.
Oldfield, J. R., ed. Civilization & Black Progress: Selected Writings of Alexander Crummell on the South. (Southern Texts Society Ser.). 320p. (C). 1995. text 38.50 (0-8139-1602-X) U Pr of Va.
Oldfield, Jenny. After Hours. large type ed. LC 97-52108. (Romance Ser.). 1998. 24.95 (0-7862-1397-3) Thorndike Pr.
— All Fall Down. LC 98-11022. 551 p. 1998. write for info. (0-7540-2120-3) Mac Lib Ref.
— All Fall Down. large type ed. LC 98-11022. 1998. 24.95 (0-7862-1393-0) Thorndike Pr.
— Deadline. 192p. 1996. 22.00 (0-7278-5157-8) Severn Hse.
— Paradise Court large type ed. LC 97-12886. 603 p. 1997. write for info. (0-7540-2011-8, Galaxy Child Lrg Print) Chivers N Amer.
Oldfield, Jim, Jr. Your Family Tree: Using Your PC. LC 97-132903. (Illus.). 220p. (Orig.). 1997. pap. 25.95 incl. cd-rom (1-55755-310-6) Abacus MI.
Oldfield, John V. & Dorf, Richard C. Field-Programmable Gate Arrays: Reconfigurable Logic for Rapid Prototyping & Implementation of Digital Systems. 360p. 1995. 87.95 (0-471-55665-3) Wiley.
Oldfield, Josiah. Eat Nature's Food & Live Long. 84p. 1996. reprint ed. spiral bd. 10.00 (0-7873-0642-8) Hlth Research.
Oldfield, Margaret J. Costumes & Customs of Many Lands. (Illus.). (J). (gr. k-3). 1970. reprint ed. pap. 2.95 (0-934876-19-3) Creative Storytime.
— Fat Cat & Ebenezer Geezer: The Teeny Tiny Mouse. 2nd ed. (Illus.). (J). (gr. k-2). 1974. pap. 3.00 (0-934876-13-4) Creative Storytime.
— Finger Puppets & Finger Plays. (Illus.). (J). (ps-3). 1979. reprint ed. pap. 3.00 (0-934876-18-5) Creative Storytime.
— Lots More Tell & Draw Stories. (Illus.). (J). (ps-3). 1973. pap. 6.95 (0-934876-03-7) Creative Storytime.
— Lots More Tell & Draw Stories. (Illus.). (J). (ps-3). 1973. lib. bdg. 11.95 (0-934876-07-X) Creative Storytime.
— More Tell & Draw Stories. (Illus.). (J). (ps-3). 1969. pap. 6.95 (0-934876-02-9); lib. bdg. 11.95 (0-934876-06-1) Creative Storytime.
— Tell & Draw Paper Bag Puppet Book. 2nd ed. (Illus.). (J). (gr. k-2). 1978. pap. 6.95 (0-934876-16-9) Creative Storytime.
— Tell & Draw Paper Cut-Outs. (Illus.). (Orig.). (J). (gr. k-2). 1988. pap. 4.00 (0-934876-23-1, 23) Creative Storytime.
Oldfield, Mary. Please Communicate. 1956. pap. 5.25 (0-8222-0900-4) Dramatists Play.
Oldfield, Maurice. Tolley's Understanding Occupational Pension Schemes. 5th ed. Orig. Title: Tolley's Understanding Pension Schemes. 150p. (C). 1994. 60.00 (1-85190-878-1, Pub. by Tolley Pubng) St Mut.
— Understanding Occupational Pension Schemes. 5th ed. 170p. 1994. pap. 100.00 (0-85459-878-2, Pub. by Tolley Pubng) St Mut.
— Understanding Pension Schemes. 4th ed. 182p. 1992. 45.00 (1-85190-168-X, Pub. by Tolley Pubng) St Mut.
Oldfield, Maurice, ed. Tolley's Understanding Occupational Pension Schemes. 5th ed. Orig. Title: Tolley's Understanding Pension Schemes. 150p. 1994. 60.00 (0-7855-2693-5, Pub. by Tolley Pubng) St Mut.
Oldfield, Nina. Adequacy of Foster Care Allowances. LC 97-71458. (Studies in Cash & Care). (Illus.). 224p. 1997. text 69.95 (1-85972-427-2, Pub. by Ashgate Pub) Ashgate Pub Co.
Oldfield, Pamela. After the Storm. large type ed. 605p. 1995. 27.99 (0-7505-0621-0) Ulverscroft.
— The Bright Dawning. 416p. 1999. 26.00 (0-7278-2294-2, Pub. by Severn Hse) Chivers N Amer.
— The Gilded Land. 432p. 1998. 25.00 (0-7278-5286-8) Severn Hse.
— Golden Tally. large type ed. (Magna Large Print Ser.). 515p. 1997. 27.99 (0-7505-1177-X, Pub. by Mgna Lrg Print) Ulverscroft.
— Lady of the Night. LC 99-18843. 1999. 24.95 (0-7862-1892-4) Mac Lib Ref.
***Oldfield, Pamela.** Lady of the Night. large type ed. LC 99-18843. 444p. 1999. write for info. (0-7540-2231-5, Black Dagger) Chivers N Amer.
Oldfield, Pamela. Lowering Skies. 400p. 1998. 25.00 (0-7278-2205-5) Severn Hse.
— The Rich Earth. large type ed. (Magna Large Print Ser.). 1994. 27.99 (0-7505-0619-9, Pub. by Mgna Lrg Print) Ulverscroft.
— Somebody's Lover. large type ed. (Ulverscroft Large Print Ser.). 640p. 1998. 29.99 (0-7089-3881-7) Ulverscroft.
— String of Blue Beads. large type ed. LC 94-45926. 509p. 1995. reprint ed. lib. bdg. 21.95 (0-7838-1240-X, G K Hall Lrg Type) Mac Lib Ref.
— This Ravished Land. large type ed. 595p. 1995. 27.99 (0-7505-0620-2) Ulverscroft.
— White Water. large type ed. 550p. 1995. 11.50 (0-7505-0622-9) Ulverscroft.
Oldfield, R. A., jt. auth. see Laird, MacGregor.
Oldfield, Ronald Jowett, jt. auth. see Rost, F. W. D.
Oldfield, Sara. Rain Forests. LC 95-39685. (Endangered People & Places Ser.). (J). 1996. lib. bdg. 22.60 (0-8225-2778-2, Lerner Publctns) Lerner Pub.
***Oldfield, Sybil.** Alternative to Militarism, 1900-1989: Women Against the Iron Fist. LC 00-32451. 256p. 2000. 89.95 (0-7734-7765-9) E Mellen.
Oldfield, Sybil. Collective Biography of Women in England, 1550-1900: A Select Annotated Bibliography. LC 97-38287. 1999. 85.00 (0-7201-2321-6) Continuum.
***Oldfield, Sybil.** Women Humanitarians: Docrs of the Word: A Biographical Dictionary of British Women Active Between, 1900-1950. LC 00-34573. (Illus.). 2001. write for info. (0-8264-4962-X) Continuum.
Oldfield, Sybil & Purvis, June, eds. This Working Day World: A Social, Political, & Cultural History of Women's Lives, 1914-1945. LC 93-41225. (Gender & society Series: Feminist Perspectives on the Past & Present). 224p. 1994. 75.00 (0-7484-0107-5, Pub. by Tay Francis Ltd); pap. 27.50 (0-7484-0108-3, Pub. by Tay Francis Ltd) Taylor & Francis.
Oldfield, Wendy, jt. auth. see Davies, Kay.
Oldford-Matchim, Joan. Help Your Child Become a Reader: A Guide for Reading Conversations, Activities & Games. (Illus.). 120p. (Orig.). 1995. pap. text 13.50 (1-887176-01-2) Globl Age Pub.
Oldford, R. W., jt. ed. see Cheeseman, P.
Oldgate, Karl. Karate. rev. ed. (Play the Game Ser.). (Illus.). 80p. (YA). (gr. 10-12). 1993. pap. 8.95 (0-7137-2410-2, Pub. by Blandford Pr) Sterling.
— Play the Game: Karate. (Illus.). 80p. 1998. pap. 10.95 (0-7063-7714-1, Pub. by WrLock) Sterling.
Oldhafer, K. J., et al, eds. Isolated Liver Perfusion in Hepatic Tumors. LC 97-36940. (Recent Results in Cancer Research Ser.: Vol. 147). (Illus.). 175p. 1998. 109.00 (3-540-63336-7) Spr-Verlag.
Oldhafer, K. J., et al. Isolated Liver Perfusion in Hepatic Tumors, Vol. 147. LC 97-36940. (Recent Results in Cancer Research Ser.). 1997. write for info. (0-354-06336-7) Spr-Verlag.
Oldham, Brian. Dream Killers. 635p. mass mkt. 4.99 (1-896329-71-3) Picasso Publ.
Oldham, C. E., jt. ed. see Temple, R. C.
Oldham, Charles, jt. ed. see Yehling, Robert.
Oldham, Edward U., tr. see Basov, N. G., ed.
Oldham, Elizabeth, ed. see Miller, Richard F. & Mooney, Robert F.
Oldham, Eric. British Railways Steam in Retrospect: The Post-War Era. (Illus.). 124p. 1998. pap. 39.95 (0-7509-1768-7, Pub. by Sutton Pub Ltd) Intl Pubs Mktg.
Oldham, G. The Future of Research: SHRE Leverhulme IV. 220p. 1982. pap. 28.00 (0-900868-86-4) Taylor & Francis.

An Asterisk (*) at the beginning of an entry indicates that the title is appearing for the first time.

Oldham, Gabriella. First Cut: Conversations with Film Editors. LC 91-47713. 1992. 45.00 (*0-520-07586-2*, Pub. by U CA Pr) Cal Prin Full Svc.

— First Cut: Conversations with Film Editors. LC 91-47713. 417p. 1995. pap. 17.95 (*0-520-07588-9*, Pub. by U CA Pr) Cal Prin Full Svc.

— Keaton's Silent Shorts: Beyond the Laughter. LC 95-13970. (Illus.). 398p. (C). 1996. 39.95 (*0-8093-1951-9*); pap. 24.95 (*0-8093-1952-7*) S Ill U Pr.

— Old-Fashioned All-Occasion Postcards. 1990. pap. text 4.95 (*0-486-26265-0*) Dover.

Oldham, George E. Dictionary of Business & Finance Terms. 1993. pap. 9.95 (*1-882912-01-2*) Sunrise TN.

***Oldham, J. Thomas.** Child Support: The Next Frontier. 248p. (C). 2000. text 44.50 (*0-472-11057-8*, 11057) U of Mich Pr.

Oldham, J. Thomas. Texas Marital Property Rights. 2nd ed. 588p. (Orig.). 1992. pap. 55.00 (*0-916081-30-3*) J Marshall Pub Co.

Oldham, Jack, jt. auth. see Goldstein, Bernard.

Oldham, James. The Mansfield Manuscripts & the Growth of English Law in the Eighteenth Century, 2 vols., Set. LC 91-46199. (Studies in Legal History). (C). 1992. 250.00 (*0-8078-2052-0*) U of NC Pr.

Oldham, James B. Blind Panels of English Binders. (History of Bookbinding & Design Ser.). (Illus.). 144p. 1990. reprint ed. text 40.00 (*0-8240-4048-1*) Garland.

— English Blind-stamped Bindings. LC 52-9808. (Sanders Lectures: 1949). 212p. reprint ed. pap. 60.50 (*0-608-13036-2*, 2024507) Bks Demand.

— English Blind-Stamped Bindings, Vol. 18. (History of Bookbinding & Design Ser.). (Illus.). 142p. 1990. text 40.00 (*0-8240-4047-3*) Garland.

— Shrewsbury School Library Bindings, Vol. 17. (History of Bookbinding & Design Ser.). (Illus.). 296p. 1990. reprint ed. text 70.00 (*0-8240-4046-5*) Garland.

Oldham, John. Selected Poems. Robinson, Ken, ed. 88p. 1980. pap. 10.95 (*0-906427-12-6*, Pub. by Bloodaxe Bks) Dufour.

— Works of Mr. John Oldham. LC 79-26304. 720p. 1980. reprint ed. 90.00 (*0-8201-1337-9*) Schol Facsimiles.

Oldham, John, jt. auth. see Oldham, Ray.

Oldham, John M. Personality Disorders: New Perspectives on Diagnostic Validity. LC 89-18135. (Progress in Psychiatry Ser.). 217p. 1991. reprint ed. pap. 67.30 (*0-608-06667-2*, 206686400009) Bks Demand.

Oldham, John M., et al, eds. American Psychiatric Press Review of Psychiatry, Vol. 12. 872p. 1993. text 15.00 (*0-88048-439-X*, 8439) Am Psychiatric.

— Impulsivity & Compulsivity. 306p. 1996. text 42.00 (*0-88048-676-7*, 8676) Am Psychiatric.

Oldham, John M. & Bone, Stanley, eds. Paranoia: New Psychoanalytic Perspectives. 166p. 1994. 27.50 (*0-8236-3985-1*) Intl Univs Pr.

Oldham, John M. & Liebert, Robert S. The Middle Years: New Psychoanalytic Perspectives. 304p. (C). 1990. 37.50 (*0-300-04418-6*) Yale U Pr.

Oldham, John M. & Liebert, Robert S., eds. The Middle Years: New Psychoanalytic Perspectives. LC 89-8939. (Illus.). 311p. 1989. reprint ed. pap. 96.50 (*0-608-07841-7*, 205401700010) Bks Demand.

Oldham, John M. & Morris, Lois B. The New Personality Self-Portrait: Why You Think, Work, Love & Act the Way You Do. rev. ed. LC 95-12233. Orig. Title: The Personality Self-Portrait. 464p. 1995. pap. 14.95 (*0-553-37393-5*) Bantam.

Oldham, John M. & Riba, Michelle B., eds. American Psychiatric Press Review of Psychiatry, Vol. 13. 804p. 1994. 15.00 (*0-88048-440-3*, 8440) Am Psychiatric.

— American Psychiatric Press Review of Psychiatry, Vol. 14. 960p. 1995. text 59.95 (*0-88048-441-1*, 8441) Am Psychiatric.

Oldham, John M. & Russakoff, L. Mark. Dynamic Therapy in Brief Hospitalization. LC 87-12629. 235p. 1987. 40.00 (*0-87668-965-9*) Aronson.

Oldham, John R., ed. China's Legal Development. LC 85-18321. 327p. 1986. reprint ed. pap. 101.40 (*0-7837-9984-5*, 206071100006) Bks Demand.

Oldham, Joseph H. Christianity & the Race Problem. LC 73-75534. 280p. 1969. reprint ed. lib. bdg. 59.50 (*0-8371-1112-9*, OLC&) Greenwood.

Oldham, June. Found. LC 96-12992. 208p. (J). (gr. 5-9). 1996. 16.95 (*0-531-09543-6*); lib. bdg. 17.99 (*0-531-08893-6*) Orchard Bks Watts.

Oldham, K. G., jt. ed. see Evans, E. A.

Oldham, K. M. Accounting Systems & Practice in Europe. 3rd ed. 335p. 1987. text 84.95 (*0-566-02612-0*, Pub. by Gower) Ashgate Pub Co.

Oldham, Keith B. & Myland, Jan C. Fundamentals of Electrochemical Science. (Illus.). 496p. 1993. text 59.00 (*0-12-525545-4*) Acad Pr.

Oldham, Keith B., jt. auth. see Spanier, Jerome.

Oldham, Keith T. Surgery of Infants & Children: Scientific Principles & Practice. LC 96-43070. 1,888p. 1996. text 263.00 (*0-397-51417-4*) Lppncott W & W.

Oldham, Kenneth. Steam in Wartime Britain. LC 92-45036. 1993. 26.95 (*0-7509-0325-2*, Pub. by Sutton Pub Ltd) Intl Pubs Mktg.

Oldham, Larry, jt. auth. see Koplen, Barry.

Oldham, Lea Leever. Creating Brochures That Get Results. (Illus.). 68p. 1998. pap. 7.95 (*0-942923-07-3*) NETWIC.

— The Lindsay Letters, 1828-1838. LC 98-92948. 83p. 1998. per. 10.00 (*1-55856-279-6*, 185) Closson Pr.

— Newsletters with Impact. 72p. 1998. pap. text 7.95 (*0-942923-09-X*) NETWIC.

— Non-Credit Instruction: A Guide for Continuing & Adult Education Programs. Greive, Donald, ed. 34p. (Orig.). (C). 1995. pap. text 5.95 (*0-940017-20-2*) Info Tec OH.

— Self Publishing: 101. 72p. (Orig.). 1997. pap. 6.95 (*0-942923-04-9*) NETWIC.

— Selling What You Make. 72p. (Orig.). 1997. pap. 5.95 (*0-942923-03-0*) NETWIC.

Oldham, Lea Leever, jt. auth. see Allen, Nancy.

Oldham, Linda, jt. auth. see Lee, Nancy.

Oldham, Mary. Alwena's Garden. (YA). (gr. 6-12). 1998. pap. 17.95 (*0-8464-4604-9*) Beekman Pubs.

— Something's Burning. 183p. (YA). (gr. 6). 1995. pap. 14.95 (*0-8464-4815-7*) Beekman Pubs.

Oldham-Merrill, Jan & Reed-Scott, Jutta. Preservation Planning Program: An Assisted Self-Study Manual for Libraries. 3rd rev. ed. 138p. 1993. pap. 45.00 (*0-918006-69-4*) ARL.

Oldham, Mika. Blackstone's Statutes on Family Law: International Student Edition. 6th ed. 518p. 1998. pap., student ed. 30.00 (*1-85431-664-8*, Pub. by Blackstone Pr) Gaunt.

— Blackstone's Statutes on Family Law, 1996-97. 5th ed. 474p. 1996. pap. 30.00 (*1-85431-562-5*, Pub. by Blackstone Pr) Gaunt.

***Oldham, Mika, ed.** Blackstone's Statutes on Family Law 1999-2000. 8th ed. 500p. 1999. pap. 26.50 (*1-85431-929-9*, 18423, Pub. by Blackstone Pr) Gaunt.

Oldham, Neild B. Studying Smart: Thinking & Study Skills for School & the Workplace. 260p. 1993. teacher ed. 8.00 (*1-56118-529-9*); pap. text 16.95 (*1-56118-528-0*) Paradigm MN.

Oldham, Neild B., jt. auth. see Fruehling, Rosemary T.

***Oldham, Nile.** NIST Multifunction Calibration System. 28p. 1998. pap. 3.00 (*0-16-060871-6*) USGPO.

Oldham, Peter. Hindenburg Line: Arras. (Illus.). 1998. pap. 16.95 (*0-85052-568-3*, Pub. by Leo Cooper) Combined Pub.

— Messines Ridge: Ypres. (Illus.). 1998. pap. 16.95 (*0-85052-624-8*, Pub. by Leo Cooper) Combined Pub.

— Pill Boxes on the Western Front: A Guide to the Design, Construction & Use of Concrete Pill Boxes, 1914-1918. (Illus.). 208p. 1995. 31.95 (*0-85052-418-0*, Pub. by Leo Cooper) Trans-Atl Phila.

Oldham, Ray & Oldham, John. Western Heritage Pt. I: A Study of the Colonial Architecture of Perth, Western Australia. LC 79-670392. 1987. 15.00 (*0-85564-134-7*, Pub. by Univ of West Aust Pr) Intl Spec Bk.

— Western Heritage Pt. II: George Temple-Poole: Architect of the Golden Years 1885-1897. 1997. lthr. 35.00 (*0-85564-173-8*) Intl Spec Bk.

Oldham, Richard. Poetry, Vol. 1. 32p. 1997. pap. 6.30 (*0-9655710-7-6*) With Heart Bks.

— Poetry, Vol. 2. unabridged ed. 30p. 1997. pap. 6.30 (*0-9655710-8-4*) With Heart Bks.

Oldham, Richard L. End to End. unabridged ed. 25p. 1997. pap. 6.30 (*0-9655710-9-2*) With Heart Bks.

— Lessons of the Grandfather, Vol. 1. unabridged ed. 35p. 1997. pap. 6.30 (*0-9655710-4-1*) With Heart Bks.

— Lessons of the Grandfather, Vol. 2. unabridged ed. 35p. 1997. pap. 6.30 (*0-9655710-5-X*) With Heart Bks.

— Lessons of the Grandfather, Vol. 3. 3rd ed. 1997. pap. 6.30 (*0-9655710-6-8*) With Heart Bks.

Oldham, Robert K. The Cure. LC 90-92322. 343p. (Orig.). 1991. pap. write for info. (*0-9628850-0-2*) Media Amer.

Oldham, Robert K., ed. Principles of Cancer Biotherapy. LC 86-42899. 512p. 1987. reprint ed. pap. 158.80 (*0-608-00356-5*, 206107300007) Bks Demand.

— Principles of Cancer Biotherapy. 2nd rev. ed. 696p. 1991. text 185.00 (*0-8247-8504-5*) Dekker.

— Principles of Cancer Biotherapy. 3rd ed. LC 97-2588. 892p. 1997. lib. bdg. 380.00 (*0-7923-3507-4*) Kluwer Academic.

Oldham, Thomas J. Divorce, Separation & the Distribution of Property. 400p. 1987. ring bd. 65.00 (*0-318-23153-0*, 00604) Law Journal.

— Divorce, Separation & the Distribution of Property. ring bd. 98.00 (*0-318-23686-9*) NY Law Pub.

Oldham, Timothy R., ed. Ionizing Radiation Effects in MOS Oxides. 130p. 1998. 28.00 (*981-02-3326-4*) World Scientific Pub.

***Oldham, Todd & Art Guys Group Staff.** Suits: The Clothes Make the Man. LC 00-20004. (Illus.). 128p. 2000. 34.95 (*0-8109-4198-8*, Pub. by Abrams) Time Warner.

Oldham, Todd & Aucoin, Kevyn. Todd Oldham Without Boundries. 1997. pap. 27.50 (*0-7893-0044-3*); text 45.00 (*0-7893-0043-5*) St Martin.

Oldham, Tom, jt. auth. see Alderman, Richard.

Oldham, William G., jt. auth. see Schwarz, Stephen E.

Oldham, William G., jt. auth. see Schwarz, Steven E.

Olding, L. B., ed. Reproductive Immunology. (Current Topics in Microbiology & Immunology Ser.: Vol. 222). (Illus.). 320p. 1997. 154.95 (*3-540-61888-0*) Spr-Verlag.

Olding, Simon. London: Exploring Museums. xiii, 110p. 1986. 16.00 (*0-11-290465-3*, Pub. by Statnry Office) Balogh.

Olding, Simon. Martyn Brewster. LC 97-66328. (Illus.). 96p. 1997. text 39.95 (*1-85928-414-0*, Pub. by Ashgate Pub) Ashgate Pub Co.

— Martyn Brewster. limited ed. LC 97-66328. (Illus.). 96p. 1997. text 209.95 (*1-85928-415-9*, Pub. by Ashgate Pub) Ashgate Pub Co.

Oldis, Daniel. Albert. LC 85-91094. 1986. 12.95 (*0-87212-196-8*) Libra.

Oldknow, Adrian J. Microcomputers in Geometry. LC 86-27874. (Mathematics & Its Applications Ser.). 21p. 1987. text 78.95 (*0-470-20805-8*) P-H.

— Microcomputers in Geometry. LC 86-27874. (Mathematics & Its Applications Ser.). 21p. 1987. pap. text 31.95 (*0-470-20814-7*) P-H.

Oldknow, Adrian J. & Smith, D. V. Learning Mathematics with Micros. LC 83-12642. (Mathematics & Its Applications Ser.). 268p. 1983. text 64.95 (*0-470-27488-3*); pap. text 31.95 (*0-470-27487-5*) P-H.

Oldknow, Antony. Consolation for Beggars. 48p. 1998. pap. text 5.00 (*1-881604-37-3*) Scopcraeft.

— Cow-in-a-Green-Field Charm. 2nd ed. Orig. Title: More Sonnets by Oldknow. 23p. 1998. reprint ed. pap. text 5.00 (*1-881604-34-9*) Scopcraeft.

— Lost Allegory. 35p. 1998. reprint ed. pap. text 5.00 (*1-881604-36-5*) Scopcraeft.

— Precision Writing. 188p. 1998. pap. text 18.00 (*1-881604-26-8*) Scopcraeft.

— Scene Without Act: Fourteen Sonnets. 2nd rev. ed. 23p. 1998. reprint ed. pap. text 5.00 (*1-881604-40-3*) Scopcraeft.

— Sheets for LInguistic Study. 35p. (C). 1997. pap. text 12.00 (*1-881604-30-6*) Scopcraeft.

— Ten Small Songs. 15p. 1998. reprint ed. pap. text 5.00 (*1-881604-35-7*) Scopcraeft.

— Wanderers: Selected Poems & Translations. 80p. 1994. 8.00 (*1-881604-19-5*) Scopcraeft.

Oldknow, Antony, ed. Four Short Novels: Carmilla, the Strange Case of Dr. Jekyll & Mr. Hyde, the Sign of the Four, & the Snows of Kilimanjaro. 295p. 1998. pap. text 18.00 (*1-881604-32-2*) Scopcraeft.

— Roots of Science Fiction. 217p. (C). 1997. pap. text 20.00 (*1-881604-24-1*) Scopcraeft.

— Selected Arthurian Texts. 306p. (C). 1997. pap. text 18.00 (*1-881604-23-3*) Scopcraeft.

— Selected Texts for Intertextual Bible Study. 112p. (C). 1997. pap. text 15.00 (*1-881604-28-4*) Scopcraeft.

— A Short Anthology of Modern World Literature. 182p. (C). 1998. pap. text 15.00 (*1-881604-31-4*) Scopcraeft.

Oldknow, Antony, jt. auth. see Hendershot, Cynthia.

Oldknow, Antony, jt. ed. see Hendershot, Cyndy.

Oldknow, Antony, jt. ed. see Hendershot, Cynthia.

Oldknow, Antony, tr. see Jammes, Francis.

Oldknow, Tina. Pilchuck: A Glass School. LC 96-16615. (Illus.). 296p. 1996. 60.00 (*0-295-97559-8*) U of Wash Pr.

— Richard Marquis Objects. LC 98-117805. (Illus.). 144p. 1998. 35.00 (*0-295-97687-X*) U of Wash Pr.

***Oldman, Alf & Tomkins, Cyril.** Cost Management & Its Interplay with Business Strategy & Context. LC 98-45771. 346p. 1999. text 74.95 (*1-84014-579-X*, Pub. by Ashgate Pub) Ashgate Pub Co.

Oldman, C., et al. The Effects of Benefit on Housing Decisions. (DSS Research Report Ser.). 1994. 35.00 (*0-11-762157-9*, Pub. by Statnry Office) Bernan Associates.

— Housing Benefit & Service Charges. (DSS Research Report Ser.). 1996. write for info. (*0-11-762399-7*, Pub. by Statnry Office) Bernan Associates.

***Oldman, Mark & Vault.com Staff.** The Vault.com Guide to Schmoozing. rev. ed. (Illus.). 2000. pap. 15.00 (*1-58131-117-6*) Vaultcom.

Oldman, Oliver, jt. ed. see Bird, Richard M.

Oldman, Oliver S. State & Local Finance. Date not set. text 22.00 (*0-88277-396-8*) West Pub.

— State & Local Taxation, Vols. 1 & 2. 3rd rev. ed. Pomp, Richard D., ed. LC 98-227182. 1152p. (Orig.). (C). 1998. pap. text 59.00 (*0-9653722-0-0*) R D Pomp.

Oldman, Oliver S. & Popkin, William D. The Deduction for Business Expenses & Losses. LC 71-172245. (Tax Technique Handbook Ser.). (Illus.). 112p. (Orig.). 1973. pap. 5.00 (*0-915506-14-9*) Harvard Law Intl Tax.

Oldman, Oliver S., et al. Financing Urban Development in Mexico City: A Case Study of Property Tax, Land Use, Housing, & Urban Planning. Herrman, Lawrence M. & Lee, Lawrence D., trs. LC 67-20878. 374p. reprint ed. pap. 116.00 (*0-7837-2307-5*, 205739500004) Bks Demand.

Oldmeadow, K. Fritjof Schuon & the Meaning of Tradition. 1996. pap. 24.95 (*0-614-21219-7*, 321) Kazi Pubns.

***Oldmeadow, Kenneth.** Traditionalism: Religion in the Light of the Perennial Philosophy. 224p. 2000. 37.50 (*955-9028-04-9*, Pub. by Sri Lanka Inst) Paul & Co Pubs.

Oldmixon, John W. The Arts of Logick & Rhetorick: Interpreted & Explain'd by ... Bouhours. (Anglistica & Americana Ser.: No. 163). xxxii, 418p. 1976. reprint ed. 76.70 (*3-487-05926-0*) G Olms Pubs.

Oldpath, Obadiah. (Lynn) Lin: Or Notable People & Notable Things in the Early History of Lynn, the Third Plantation of Massachusetts Colony (History & Reminiscences) (Illus.). 500p. 1998. reprint ed. lib. bdg. 52.00 (*0-8328-7120-6*) Higginson Bk Co.

***Oldridge, Darren.** Devil in Early Modern England. (Illus.). 224p. 2000. 34.95 (*0-7509-2092-0*) Sutton Publng.

Oldridge, Darren. Religion & Society in Early Stuart England. LC 97-38533. 172p. 1998. 61.95 (*1-85928-312-8*, BX93342.O53, Pub. by Ashgate Pub) Ashgate Pub Co.

Oldridge, Les. Basic Benchwork. (Workshop Practice Ser.: No. 18). (Illus.). 128p. (Orig.). 1988. pap. 18.50 (*0-85242-920-7*, Pub. by Nexus Special Interests) Trans-Atl Phila.

Oldridge, N. B., et al, eds. Cardiac Rehabilitation & Clinical Exercise Programs: Theory & Practice. (Illus.). 300p. 1988. pap. 34.95 (*0-317-59354-4*) Mouvement Pubns.

Oldridge, S. G., et al. Wild Mushroom & Toadstool Poisoning. 23p. 1989. pap. 10.00 (*0-947643-18-4*, Pub. by Royal Botnic Grdns) Balogh.

Oldring, Peter K. & Hayward, G. Resins for Surface Coatings. (C). 1989. 305.00 (*0-7855-4923-4*, Pub. by Fuel Metallurgical Jrnl); 900.00 (*0-86108-200-1*, Pub. by Fuel Metallurgical Jrnl) St Mut.

Oldrizzi, L., ed. The Progressive Nature of Renal Diseases: Myths & Facts. (Contributions to Nephrology Ser.: Vol. 75). (Illus.). viii, 218p. 1989. 29.75 (*3-8055-5021-9*) S Karger.

Oldroyd, David R. The Highlands Controversy: Constructing Geological Knowledge Through Fieldwork in Nineteenth-Century. LC 89-20610. (Science & Its Conceptual Foundations Ser.). (Illus.). 456p. 1990. pap. text 36.00 (*0-226-62635-0*) U Ch Pr.

— The Highlands Controversy: Constructing Geological Knowledge Through Fieldwork in Nineteenth-Century Britain. LC 89-20610. (Science & Its Conceptual Foundations Ser.). (Illus.). 448p. 1990. lib. bdg. 78.00 (*0-226-62634-2*) U Ch Pr.

— Thinking about the Earth: A History of Ideas in Geology. LC 95-48234. (Illus.). 448p. (C). 1996. 48.95 (*0-674-88382-9*) HUP.

Oldroyd, David R. & Langham, Ian G., eds. The Wider Domain of Evolutionary Thought. (Australasian Studies in History & Philosophy of Science: 2). 336p. 1983. lib. bdg. 176.50 (*90-277-1477-0*, D Reidel) Kluwer Academic.

Oldroyd, David R., et al. Educational Management Today: A Concise Dictionary & Guide. LC 96-209134. (One-Off Ser.). 136p. 1996. (*1-85396-328-3*); pap. (*1-85396-326-7*) Corwin Pr.

Oldroyd, George. The Technique & Spirit of Fugue: An Historical Study. LC 85-27089. 228p. 1986. reprint ed. lib. bdg. 59.75 (*0-313-25052-9*, OLTS, Greenwood Pr) Greenwood.

Oldroyd, Ida S. The Marine Shells of the West Coast of North America, 4 vols., Set. (Illus.). 1530p. 1927. 149.50 (*0-8047-0987-4*) Stanford U Pr.

Oldroyd, Margaret. Staff Development in Academic Libraries: Present Practice & Future Challenges. 192p. 1996. 60.00 (*1-85604-174-3*, LAP1743, Pub. by Library Association) Bernan Associates.

Oldroyd, Michael, jt. auth. see Hatton, Angela.

Oldroyd, Stephen & Stoffers, Kenneth. Hypodermics. 48p. 1980. lthr. 45.00 (*0-88014-022-4*) Mosaic Pr OH.

Oldroyo. Sales & Marketing Environment. 286p. pap. text. write for info. (*0-7506-4036-7*) Buttrwrth-Heinemann.

***Olds, Anita Rui.** Child Care Design Guide. 2000. 69.95 (*0-07-047449-4*) McGraw.

Olds, Arthur F. It's No Bull! The True Story of the Taming of Northeast Pinellas County. 300p. 1992. pap. 18.50 (*0-9632576-3-3*) Boot Ranch Pub.

Olds, Carl D. Continued Fractions. LC 61-12185. (New Mathematical Library: No. 9). 162p. 1963. pap. text 8.00 (*0-88385-609-3*, NML-09) Math Assn.

Olds, Clifton C., jt. auth. see Hall, Donald.

Olds, Edward C., jt. auth. see Freeman, Leon L.

Olds, Elizabeth F. Women of the Four Winds. 1999. pap. 15.00 (*0-395-95784-2*) HM.

Olds-Ellingson, Alice. The Devil Won't Let Me In. 70p. (Orig.). 1990. pap. 6.95 (*0-916397-11-4*) Manic D Pr.

Olds, Gloria M. Stepping Stones. LC 97-90809. 1998. 13.95 (*0-533-12482-4*) Vantage.

Olds, Henry F. The Computer As an Educational Tool. LC 86-3132. (Computers in the Schools Ser.: Vol. 3, No. 1). 99p. 1986. text 29.95 (*0-86656-559-0*) Haworth Pr.

Olds, Hugh W., Jr. Public Opinion in Kyrgyzstan: 1996. (Illus.). iv, 116p. 1997. pap. text 13.00 (*1-879720-21-3*) Intl Fndt Elect.

Olds, Jacqueline, et al. Overcoming Loneliness in Everyday Life. 256p. 1996. 19.95 (*1-55972-343-2*, Birch Ln Pr) Carol Pub Group.

Olds, Jacqueline, jt. auth. see Schwartz, Richard S.

Olds, Jennifer. Rodeo & the Mimosa Tree. LC 91-74038. 80p. 1991. pap. 9.95 (*0-9627501-4-X*) Event Horizon.

Olds, Kris. Globalisation & the Asia-Pacific: Contested Territories. LC 98-31539. (Warwick Studies in Globalization Ser.). 1999. 100.00 (*0-415-19919-0*); pap. 32.99 (*0-415-19920-4*) Routledge.

***Olds, Kris.** Globalization & Urban Change: Capital, Culture, & Pacific Rim Mega-Projects. (Oxford Geographical & Environmental Studies). (Illus.). 280p. 2000. text 65.00 (*0-19-823361-2*) OUP.

Olds, Kris, jt. auth. see Yeung, Henry W.

Olds, Linda E. Metaphors of Interrelatedness: Toward a Systems Theory of Psychology. LC 91-18490. (SUNY Series, Alternatives in Psychology). 217p. (C). 1992. text 49.50 (*0-7914-1011-0*); pap. text 18.95 (*0-7914-1012-9*) State U NY Pr.

Olds, Margaret, ed. see Creber, Ann & King, Elisabeth.

Olds, Marshall C. Analysis of the Interchurch World Movement Report on the Steel Strike. LC 70-172223. (Right Wing Individualist Tradition in America Ser.). 1972. reprint ed. 35.95 (*0-405-00432-X*) Ayer.

— Analysis of the Interchurch World Movement Report on the Steel Strike. LC 73-139199. (Civil Liberties in American History Ser.). 1971. reprint ed. lib. bdg. 65.00 (*0-306-70082-4*) Da Capo.

— Desire Seeking Expression: Mallarme's Prose pour des Esseintes. LC 82-82431. (French Forum Monographs: No. 42). 129p. (Orig.). 1983. pap. 10.95 (*0-917058-41-0*) French Forum.

Olds, Marshall C., ed. see Rogers, Peter S.

Olds, Patrick C. The Barbie Doll Years. 3rd ed. LC 99-215371. 336p. 1999. pap. text 18.95 (*1-57432-100-5*) Collector Bks.

***Olds, Patrick C.** Barbie Doll Years: A Comprehensive Listing & Value Guide of Dolls & Accessories. 4th ed. (Illus.). 320p. 2000. pap. 19.95 (*1-57432-185-4*) Collector Bks.

Olds, Robert. Helldiver Squadron: The Story of Carrier Bombing Squadron 17 with Task Force 58. LC 79-16872. 1980. reprint ed. 23.95 (*0-89201-054-1*) Zenger Pub.

Olds, S., tr. see Szymborska, Wislawa.

***Olds, Sally.** Maternal Newborn Nursing. 6th ed. (C). 2000. pap. text, student ed., wbk. ed. 25.31 (*0-8053-8074-4*) Benjamin-Cummings.

Olds, Sally B. Clinical Handbook for Maternal Newborn Nursing. (C). 1992. pap. text 25.31 (*0-8053-5588-X*) Addison-Wesley.

— Maternal Newborn Nursing. 4th ed. Cleary, Patti, ed. 1328p. (C). 1992. pap. text 18.75 (*0-8053-5581-2*) Addison-Wesley.

O

An Asterisk (*) at the beginning of an entry indicates that the title is appearing for the first time.

— Maternal Newborn Nursing: Clinical Handbook. 6th ed. (C). 2000. pap. text 25.31 (*0-8053-8076-0*) Benjamin-Cummings.
— Trans Matnl Newborn Nrsg. 4th ed. Cleary, Patti, ed. 1328p. (C). 1994. pap. text 211.73 (*0-8053-5583-9*) Addison-Wesley.
Olds, Sally B., et al. Maternal Newborn Nursing. 5th ed. LC 95-38372. 1142p. (C). 1995. 84.00 (*0-8053-5612-6*) Addison-Wesley.
— Maternal-Newborn Nursing Care: A Family-Centered Approach. 2nd ed. 1168p. 1984. write for info. (*0-201-12797-0*, Health Sci) Addison-Wesley.
— Maternal-Newborn Nursing Care: A Workbook. 2nd ed. 1984. pap. write for info. (*0-201-12799-7*) Addison-Wesley.
Olds, Sally W. A Child's World: Infancy Through Adolescence. 7th ed. (C). 1995. pap., student ed. 23.75 (*0-07-048769-3*) McGraw.
— Human Development. 7th ed. LC 97-73170. 768p. (C). 1997. 70.63 (*0-07-048772-3*) McGraw.
Olds, Sally W., jt. auth. see Eiger, Marvin S.
Olds, Sally W., jt. auth. see Papalia, Diane E.
Olds, Sally W., jt. auth. see Simon, Sidney B.
Olds, Sally Wenkos, see Eiger, Marvin S. & Wenkos Olds, Sally.
***Olds, Sharon.** Blood, Tin & Straw. LC 99-15602. 112p. 1999. pap. 15.00 (*0-375-70735-2*) Knopf.
— Blood, Tin, Straw. LC 99-15602. 112p. 1999. 24.00 (*0-375-40742-1*) Knopf.
Olds, Sharon. The Dead & the Living. LC 83-47780. (Poetry Ser.: No. 12). 96p. 1984. pap. 15.00 (*0-394-71563-2*) Knopf.
— The Father. 1992. pap. 14.00 (*0-679-74002-3*) Knopf.
— The Gold Cell. 1987. pap. 15.00 (*0-394-74770-4*) Knopf.
— Satan Says. LC 79-24300. (Poetry Ser.). 72p. 1980. pap. 10.95 (*0-8229-5314-5*) U of Pittsburgh Pr.
— The Wellspring: Poems. LC 95-15835. 112p. 1996. pap. 14.00 (*0-679-76560-3*) Knopf.
Olds, Sharon, et al. The Maverick Poets: An Anthology. (Illus.). 146p. (Orig.). 1988. 18.50 (*0-9610454-3-4*); pap. 12.00 (*0-9610454-2-6*) Gorilla Pr.
Olds, Tim, jt. ed. see Norton, Kevin.
Olds, Timothy & Norton, Kevin. Pre-Exercise Health Screening Guide. LC 99-24274. 85p. 1999. pap. write for info. (*0-7360-0210-3*) Human Kinetics.
Oldsey, Bernard. Hemingway's Hidden Craft: The Writing of "A Farewell to Arms" LC 79-743. (Illus.). 1979. 30.00 (*0-271-00213-1*) Pa St U Pr.
Oldsey, Bernard, ed. British Novelists, 1930-1959, 2 vols. (Dictionary of Literary Biography Ser.: Vol. 15). (Illus.). 376p. 1983. text 296.00 (*0-8103-0938-6*) Gale.
Oldsey, Bernard, ed. British Novelists, 1930-1959, 2 vols., Set. (Dictionary of Literary Biography Ser.: Vol. 15). 713p. 1983. pap. 280.00 (*0-8103-1637-4*, 006392-M99348) Gale.
Oldsfield, Wendy, jt. auth. see Davis, Kay.
Oldson, William O. The Historical & Nationalistic Thought of Nicolae Iorga. (East European Monographs: No. 5). 135p. 1974. text 60.00 (*0-231-03747-3*, Pub. by East Eur Monographs) Col U Pr.
— A Providential Anti-Semitism: Nationalism & Polity in Nineteenth-Century Romania. LC 90-56109. (Memoirs Ser.: Vol. 193). (Illus.). 177p. (Orig.). (C). 1991. pap. 20.00 (*0-87169-193-0*, M193-OLW) Am Philos.
Oldstone, M. B. & Notkins, A. L., eds. Concepts in Viral Pathogenesis III. 415p. 1989. 109.00 (*0-387-96974-8*, 2692) Spr-Verlag.
Oldstone, Michael B. Current Topics in Microbiology & Immunology, Vol. 161 Vol. 161: Picornaviruses. 228p. 1990. 108.00 (*0-387-52429-0*) Spr-Verlag.
— Viruses, Plagues & History. LC 97-9545. (Illus.). 224p. 1998. 25.00 (*0-19-511723-9*) OUP.
Oldstone, Michael B., ed. Animal Virus Pathogenesis: A Practical Approach. (Practical Approach Ser.). (Illus.). 192p. 1990. pap. 45.00 (*0-19-963101-8*) OUP.
— Molecular Mimicry. (Current Topics in Microbiology & Immunology Ser.: Vol. 145). (Illus.). 145p. 1989. 84.00 (*0-387-50929-1*) Spr-Verlag.
Oldstone, Michael B., et al, eds. Current Topics in Microbiology & Immunology V0l. 180: Pathogenesis of Shigellosis. (Illus.). 160p. 1992. 140.00 (*0-387-55058-5*) Spr-Verlag.
— Current Topics in Microbiology & Immunology Vol. 158: Viral Expression Vectors. (Illus.). 192p. 1992. 134.00 (*0-387-52431-2*) Spr-Verlag.
— Current Topics in Microbiology & Immunology Vol. 163: Poxviruses. 256p. 1990. 96.00 (*0-387-52430-4*) Spr-Verlag.
— Current Topics in Microbiology & Immunology Vol. 164: Human Diabetes: Genetics, Environmental & Autoimmune Etiology. (Illus.). 216p. 1990. 120.00 (*0-387-52652-8*) Spr-Verlag.
— Current Topics in Microbiology & Immunology Vol. 165: Neuronal Growth Factors. (Illus.). 192p. 1991. 88.00 (*0-387-52654-4*) Spr-Verlag.
— Current Topics in Microbiology & Immunology Vol. 166: Mechanisms in B-Cell Neoplasia 1990: Workshop at the National Cancer Institute, National Institutes of Health, Bethesda, MD, U.S.A., March 28-30, 1990. (Illus.). xix, 380p. 1990. 129.00 (*0-387-52886-5*) Spr-Verlag.
— Current Topics in Microbiology & Immunology Vol. 172: Transmissible Spongiform Encephalopathies, Scrapie, BSE & Related Human Disorders. (Illus.). ix, 288p. 1991. 123.00 (*0-387-53883-6*) Spr-Verlag.
— Current Topics in Microbiology & Immunology Vol. 174: Superantigens. (Illus.). 160p. 1991. 114.00 (*0-387-54205-1*) Spr-Verlag.
— Current Topics in Microbiology & Immunology Vol. 175: ADP-Ribosylating Toxins. (Illus.). 160p. 1992. 126.00 (*0-387-54598-0*) Spr-Verlag.
— Current Topics in Microbiology & Immunology Vol. 177: Hematopoietic Stem Cells: Animal Models & Human Transplantation. (Illus.). 256p. 1992. 125.00 (*0-387-54531-X*) Spr-Verlag.
— Current Topics in Microbiology & Immunology Vol. 178: Membrane Defenses Against Attack by Complement & Perforins. (Illus.). 192p. 1992. 144.00 (*0-387-54653-7*) Spr-Verlag.
— Current Topics in Microbiology & Immunology Vol. 183: Neutralization of Animal Viruses. (Illus.). 160p. 1993. 131.95 (*0-387-56030-0*) Spr-Verlag.
— Current Topics in Microbiology & Immunology Vol. 206: Transgenic Models of Human Viral & Immunological Disease, No. 206. (Illus.). 350p. 1995. 163.95 (*3-540-59341-1*) Spr-Verlag.
— Hepadnaviruses: Molecular Biololgy & Pathogenesis. (Current Topics in Microbiology & Immunology Ser.: Vol. 168). (Illus.). ix, 206p. 1991. 138.00 (*0-387-53060-6*) Spr-Verlag.
— Mechanisms in B-Cell Neoplasia, 1992: Workshop at the National Cancer Institute, National Institutes of Health, Bethesda, MD, U. S. A., April 21-23, 1992. (Current Topics in Microbiology & Immunology Ser.: Vol. 182). (Illus.). 528p. 1992. 188.95 (*0-387-55658-3*) Spr-Verlag.
Oldstone, Michael B. & Haase, A. T., eds. In Situ Hybridization. (Current Topics in Microbiology & Immunology Ser.: Vol. 143). (Illus.). 80p. 1989. 88.95 (*0-387-50761-2*) Spr-Verlag.
Oldstone, Michael B. & Koprowski, Hilary, eds. Retroviruses Infections of the Nervous System. (Current Topics in Microbiology & Immunology Ser.: Vol. 160). (Illus.). 176p. 1990. 105.00 (*0-387-51939-4*) Spr-Verlag.
Oldstone, Michael B. & Notkins, A. L., eds. Concepts in Viral Pathogenesis. (Illus.). 390p. 1984. 79.00 (*0-387-90982-6*) Spr-Verlag.
— Concepts in Viral Pathogenesis II. (Illus.). 450p. 1986. 103.95 (*0-387-96322-7*) Spr-Verlag.
Oldstone, Michael B. & Vitkovic, L., eds. HIV & Dementia: Proceedings of the NIMH-Sponsored Conference "Pathogenesis of HIV Infection of the Brain: Impact on Function & Behavior", No. 202. (Current Topics in Microbiology & Immunology Ser.: Vol. 202). (Illus.). 336p. 1995. 167.95 (*3-540-59117-6*) Spr-Verlag.
Oldstone, Michael B., jt. auth. see McConnell, I.
Oldstone, Michael B., jt. ed. see Koprowski, Hilary.
***Oldstone, Michael B. A.** Viruses, Plagues & History. (Illus.). 240p. 2000. pap. 14.95 (*0-19-513422-2*) OUP.
***Oldstone-Moore, Christopher.** Hugh Price Hughes: Founder of a New Methodism, Conscience of a New Nonconformity. (Illus.). 393p. 1999. 49.95 (*0-7083-1468-6*, Pub. by U Wales Pr) Paul & Co Pubs.
Oldt, Franklin T., ed. History of Dubuque County, Iowa. (Illus.). 943p. 1993. reprint ed. lib. bdg. 92.50 (*0-8328-2950-1*) Higginson Bk Co.
Oldt, Linda. Mad Money: How to Preserve, Protect & Multiply Your Personal Injury Lawsuit Settlement. Oldt, Thomas R., ed. LC 94-96293. 160p. (Orig.). 1994. pap. 24.95 (*0-9642858-0-7*) Invest Informat.
Oldt, Thomas R., ed. see Oldt, Linda.
***Olea, R. A.** Geostatistics for Engineers & Earth Scientists LC 99-24689. 1999. write for info. (*0-7923-8523-3*) Kluwer Academic.
Olea, Ricardo A., ed. Geostatistical Glossary & Multilingual Dictionary. (International Association for Mathematical Geology: Studies in Mathematical Geology: No. 3). (Illus.). 192p. 1991. text 50.00 (*0-19-506689-8*) OUP.
***O'Lear, Joseph K.** A Devotional Note Book No. 1: John & Paul. 172p. 2000. 19.95 (*0-9701268-0-8*) J K OLear.
O'Leary. Advanced Office 2000. 784p. 1999. spiral bd. 54.69 (*0-07-237879-4*) McGraw.
— Computer Essentials. 1997. text 24.00 (*0-07-012567-8*); text 34.25 (*0-07-561040-X*) McGraw.
— Computing Essentials: Annual Edition, 1990. 12th ed. 2000. pap. text 34.00 (*0-07-236168-9*) McGraw.
***O'Leary.** Ise Computer Essential 2000-2001. 2000. write for info. (*0-07-116610-6*, McGraw-H College) McGraw-H Hghr Educ.
O'Leary. Lotus 1-2-3 Tutorial Guide. (C). 1992. text, student ed. 32.00 incl. 3.5 hd (*0-201-60585-6*) Addison-Wesley.
— Microcomputer Custom Bdr. 93-94. 1993. 6.56 (*0-07-911544-6*) McGraw.
— Microsoft Access 2.0 Windows. 1995. 22.50 (*0-07-049070-8*) McGraw.
— Microsoft Excel 5.0 Windows. 232p. 1995. pap. 27.50 (*0-07-049076-7*) McGraw.
— Microsoft Office Professional for Windows 95 with Powerpoint. (C). 1996. pap. text 43.00 (*0-07-049112-7*) McGraw.
— Microsoft Office with Windows 3.1, Word 6.0, Excel 5.0, Access 2.0, Itegration, & Powerpoint. (C). 1995. pap. text 43.00 (*0-07-049102-X*) McGraw.
— Microsoft Office with Windows 3.1, Word 6.0, Excel 5.0, Access 2.0, & Integration. (C). 1995. pap. text 37.00 (*0-07-049101-1*) McGraw.
— Microsoft Powerpoint 97. 1999. pap., student ed. 27.50 (*0-07-231669-1*) McGraw.
— MS Windows 98. LC 98-33571. 144p. 1998. pap. 27.50 (*0-07-092041-9*) McGraw.
O'Leary. Nationalism. 129.95 (*1-85521-387-7*) Ashgate Pub Co.
O'Leary. Netscape Communicator. 216p. 1998. pap. 27.50 (*0-07-012579-1*) McGraw.
— Production Line to Frontline. 1998. 19.95 (*1-85532-703-1*, 847845Q, Pub. by Ospry) Stackpole.
— Shaping Chinese Foreign Policy. (Australian National University Press Ser.). 1996. write for info. (*0-08-033000-2*, Pergamon Pr) Elsevier.
— Tutorial Guide to Lotus 1-2-3 Release 2.2: 3.5 Tutorial Guide. 1992. 32.00 incl. 3.5 hd (*0-201-60584-8*) Addison-Wesley.
***O'Leary.** Website Microsoft Office 2000. 1999. write for info. (*0-07-236858-6*, McGrw-H College) McGrw-H Hghr Educ.
O'Leary, jt. auth. see Wilson.
O'Leary, jt. tr. see De Lacey.
O'Leary, A. P. Jane's Electro-Optic Systems, 1997-98: The Complete Source for Military Laser, Thermal Imaging & Image Intensifying Systems. 3rd ed. 1997. 320.00 (*0-7106-1545-0*) Janes Info Group.
O'Leary, Alice. Pigs on the Links: Hidden Hazards for the Woman. LC 94-77832. (Illus.). 88p. (Orig.). 1994. pap. 11.95 (*0-936485-09-4*) Lkng Glass Pubns.
O'Leary, Alice M., jt. auth. see Randall, Robert C.
O'Leary, Ann. Julia's Song. LC 97-52749. 224p. (Orig.). 1998. pap. 11.95 (*1-56280-197-X*) Naiad Pr.
— Letting Go. LC 97-10006. 256p. (Orig.). 1997. pap. 11.95 (*1-56280-183-X*) Naiad Pr.
— The Other Woman. LC 98-31633. 208p. 1999. pap. 11.95 (*1-56280-234-8*) Naiad Pr.
O'Leary, Ann & Jemmott, Loretta S., eds. Women & AIDS: Coping & Care. LC 96-3254. (AIDS Prevention & Mental Health Ser.). (Illus.). 263p. 1996. 54.00 (*0-306-45258-8*, Kluwer Plenum) Kluwer Academic.
— Women at Risk: Issues in the Primary Prevention of AIDS. (AIDS Prevention & Mental Health Ser.). (Illus.). 292p. (C). 1995. text 59.00 (*0-306-45041-0*, Kluwer Plenum) Kluwer Academic.
O'Leary, Ann S. The Adirondack Style. 1998. 37.50 (*0-609-60127-X*) C Potter.
— The Adirondack Style. LC 98-9172. 1998. pap. write for info. (*0-609-80235-6*) C Potter.
— The Adirondack Style. (Illus.). 180p. 1998. 37.50 (*0-609-60361-2*) Random Hse Value.
***O'Leary, Arthur.** Guide to Successful Construction: Effective Contract Administration. 3rd rev. ed. 1999. pap. 60.00 (*1-55701-313-6*) BNI Pubns.
O'Leary, Barrie. A Field Guide to Australian Opals. (Illus.). 159p. 1984. 36.50 (*0-7270-0387-9*, Pub. by NAG Press) Antique Collect.
O'Leary, Bradley S. Are You a Republican or a Democrat? 1998. pap. 5.95 (*1-887161-22-8*) Boru Pubng.
— Bed & Champagne: Top Romantic Hideaways. Weeks, Stephen, ed. LC 96-45471. (Illus.). 250p. 1996. pap. 13.95 (*1-887161-08-2*) Boru Pubng.
— Bed & Champagne: World's Top Romantic Hideaways. 1998. pap. 14.95 (*1-887161-24-4*) Boru Pubng.
— Dining by Candlelight: America's 200 Most Romantic Restaurants. Weeks, Stephen, ed. LC 96-45472. (Illus.). 250p. 1996. pap. 13.95 (*1-887161-10-4*) Boru Pubng.
— Dining by Candlelight: World's Most Romantic Restaurants. 1998. pap. 14.95 (*1-887161-23-6*) Boru Pubng.
— Top 200 Reasons Not to Vote for Bill Clinton. LC 96-85055. 128p. 1996. pap. 5.95 (*1-887161-11-2*) Boru Pubng.
O'Leary, Bradley S. & Hallow, Ralph Z. Presidential Follies: Those Who Would Be President & Those Who Should Think Again! Weems, Ann O., ed. 250p. 1995. text 19.95 (*1-887161-00-7*, Boru Bks); pap. text 7.95 (*1-887161-07-4*, Boru Bks) Boru Pubng.
O'Leary, Bradley S. & Kamber, Victor. Are You Conservative or a Liberal? Weeks, Stephen, ed. LC 96-85050. 170p. (Orig.). 1996. pap. 5.95 (*1-887161-09-0*) Boru Pubng.
Oleary, Brendan. The Politics of Antagonism: Understanding Northern Ireland. (Conflict & Change in Britain - A New Audit Ser.). (C). 1996. pap. 22.50 (*0-485-80110-8*) Humanities.
O'Leary, Brendan, jt. auth. see McGarry, John.
O'Leary, Brendan, jt. ed. see McGarry, John.
O'Leary, Brian. Exploring Inner & Outer Space: A Scientist's Perspective on Personal & Planetary Transformation. (Illus.). 240p. (Orig.). 1989. pap. 14.95 (*1-55643-068-X*) North Atlantic.
— Miracle in the Void: Free Energy, UFO's & Other Scientific Revelations. 262p. 1997. pap. 9.95 (*0-9647826-0-X*) Kamapua a Pr.
— The Second Coming of Science: An Intimate Report on the New Science. LC 92-29954. 220p. (Orig.). 1993. pap. 12.95 (*1-55643-152-X*) North Atlantic.
O'Leary, Brian, ed. Space Industrialization, Vol. I. 176p. 1982. 105.00 (*0-8493-5890-6*, TL797, CRC Reprint) Franklin.
— Space Industrialization, Vol. II. 240p. 1982. 136.00 (*0-8493-5891-4*, CRC Reprint) Franklin.
O'Leary, Cecilia E. To Die For: The Paradox of American Patriotism. LC 98-25235. 336p. 1998. text 29.95 (*0-691-01686-0*, Pub. by Princeton U Pr) Cal Prin Full Svc.
***O'Leary, Cecilia E.** To Die For: The Paradox of American Patriotism. (Illus.). 336p. 2000. pap. 17.95 (*0-691-07052-0*) Princeton U Pr.
O'Leary, Christopher J. & Wandner, Stephen A. Unemployment Insurance in the United States: Analysis of Policy Issues. LC 97-40086. 762p. (C). 1997. text 50.00 (*0-88099-174-7*); pap. text 33.00 (*0-88099-173-9*) W E Upjohn.
O'Leary, D. E. & Watkins, Paul R. Expert Systems in Finance. (Studies in Management Science & Systems: Vol. 19). 268p. 1992. 106.50 (*0-444-88860-8*, North Holland) Elsevier.
O'Leary, D. L. How Greek Science Passed to the Arabs. 196p. 1979. pap. 20.00 (*0-89005-282-4*) Ares.
O'Leary, Dale. The Gender Agenda: Redefining Equality. LC 96-60583. 224p. (Orig.). 1997. pap. 11.99 (*1-56384-122-3*, Vital Issue Pr) Huntington Hse.
O'Leary, Dan, jt. ed. see Vasarhelyi, Miklos A.
O'Leary, Daniel & Preece, Alun, eds. Verification & Validation of Knowledge-Based Systems: Papers from the AAAI Workshop. (Technical Reports: Vol. WS-98-11). (Illus.). 51p. 1998. spiral bd. 25.00 (*1-57735-064-2*) AAAI Pr.
O'Leary, Daniel, jt. ed. see Staab, Steffen.
***O'Leary, Daniel E.** Enterprise Resource Planning Systems: Systems, Life Cycles, Electronic Commerce & Risk. (Illus.). 240p. (C). 2000. text Price not set. (*0-521-79152-9*) Cambridge U Pr.
O'Leary, Daniel E. Journeys over Water: The Paintings of Stephen Etnier. Ransom, Susan L., ed. LC 98-65386. (Illus.). 64p. 1998. pap. 14.95 (*0-916857-13-1*) Port Mus Art.
O'Leary, Daniel E. & Gamble, Rose, eds. Using AI in Electronic Commerce, Virtual Organizations, & Enterprise Knowledge Management to Reengineer the Corporation. (Technical Reports: No. WS-97-02). 66p. 1997. spiral bd. 25.00 (*1-57735-029-4*) AAAI Pr.
O'Leary, Daniel E. & Watkins, Paul R. Expert Systems & Artificial Intelligence in Internal Auditing. (Rutgers Series in Accounting Research). 194p. (C). 1995. text 49.95 (*1-55876-086-5*) Wiener Pubs Inc.
***O'Leary, Daniel E., et al.** N. C. Wyeth: Precious Time. Ransom, Susan L., ed. (Illus.). 40p. 2000. pap. write for info. (*0-916857-21-2*) Port Mus Art.
O'Leary, Daniel J. Passion for the Possible: A Spirituality of Hope for a New Millennium LC 98-215634. 294p. 1998. write for info. (*1-85607-235-5*) Intl Scholars.
O'Leary, De Lacy. Coptic Hymns-Fragments from the Wadi n Narrun, Pt. 1, Translation. 1973. pap. 3.95 (*0-89979-008-9*) British Am Bks.
O'Leary, De Lacy E. Arabia Before Muhammad. LC 74-180373. (Illus.). reprint ed. 39.50 (*0-404-56313-9*) AMS Pr.
— Arabic Thought & Its Place in History. rev. ed. LC 80-1917. 1981. reprint ed. 35.00 (*0-404-18982-2*) AMS Pr.
— Islam at the Cross Roads: A Brief Survey of the Present Position & Problems of the World of Islam. LC 80-1916. 1981. reprint ed. 26.50 (*0-404-18983-0*) AMS Pr.
***O'Leary, Donal.** Vocationalism & Social Catholicism in Twentieth-Century Ireland. LC 99-59621. (Social Sciences Research Centre Ser.). (Illus.). 288p. 2000. 57.50 (*0-7165-2667-0*) Intl Spec Bk.
O'Leary, Donal & Sallnow, Teresa. Religious Education & Young Adults. (C). 1988. 60.00 (*0-85439-229-7*, Pub. by St Paul Pubns) St Mut.
O'Leary, E. Counseling Older Adults. 224p. 1995. 45.00 (*1-56593-281-1*, 0605) Singular Publishing.
O'Leary, Eleanor. Gestalt Therapy: Theory, Practice & Research. LC 92-17085. 148p. 1992. 44.75 (*1-56593-036-3*, 0284) Singular Publishing.
O'Leary, Elizabeth L. At Beck & Call: The Representation of Domestic Servants in Nineteenth-Century American Painting. (Illus.). 344p. 1996. pap. text 34.95 (*1-56098-606-9*) Smithsonian.
O'Leary, Fred. Corkscrews: 1000 Patented Ways to Open a Bottle. LC 95-53671. (Schiffer Book for Collectors Ser.). (Illus.). 340p. (YA). (gr. 10-13). 1996. write for info. (*0-7643-0018-0*) Schiffer.
O'Leary, Greg, ed. Adjusting to Capitalism: Chinese Workers & the State. LC 97-33545. (Socialism & Social Movements Ser.). 200p. (C). (gr. 13). 1997. text 66.95 (*0-7656-0039-0*, East Gate Bk) M E Sharpe.
O'Leary-Hawthorne, John, jt. auth. see Cover, J. A.
O'Leary-Hawthorne, John, jt. auth. see Lance, Mark N.
O'Leary, J. Patrick & Capote, Lea R., eds. The Physiologic Basis of Surgery. 2nd ed. LC 96-4702. (Illus.). 752p. 1996. write for info. (*0-683-06616-1*) Lppncott W & W.
O'Leary, James, ed. see Katchmer, George A.
O'Leary, James, ed. see Seabourne, Tom.
O'Leary, James, Jr., ed. see Yang, Jwing-Ming.
O'Leary, James, ed. see Zhang, Hong-Chao.
O'Leary, James A. Shoulder Dystocia & Birth Injury: Prevention & Treatment. (Illus.). 200p. 1992. text 42.00 (*0-07-105393-X*) McGraw-Hill HPD.
O'Leary, James C., ed. The Poems of Tai Chi Chuan: Selected Readings from the Masters. Jwing-Ming, Yang, tr. LC 98-61694. (Tai Chi Treasures Ser.). 128p. 1999. pap. 12.95 (*1-886969-71-X*, B035\71X) YMAA Pubn.
O'Leary, James C., ed. see Chuckrow, Robert.
O'Leary, James C., ed. see Jwing-Ming, Yang.
O'Leary, James C., ed. see Yang, Jwing-Ming.
O'Leary, James J. Stagnation or Healthy Growth? The Economic Challenge to the United States in the Nineties. 162p. (C). 1992. lib. bdg. 42.50 (*0-8191-8839-5*) U Pr of Amer.
O'Leary, James L. & Goldring, Sidney. Science & Epilepsy: Neuroscience Gains in Epilepsy Research. LC 75-21860. 303p. 1976. text 62.00 (*0-89004-072-9*) Lppncott W & W.
O'Leary, Jenifer. Write Your Own Curriculum: A Complete Guide to Planning, Organizing & Documenting Homeschool Curriculums, Family. LC 93-60801. (Illus.). 130p. (Orig.). 1994. 29.95 (*1-883947-23-5*) Whole Life.
— Write Your Own Curriculum: A Complete Guide to Planning, Organizing & Documenting Homeschool Curriculums, High School. LC 93-60801. (Illus.). 130p. (Orig.). 1994. student ed. 29.95 (*1-883947-22-7*) Whole Life.
O'Leary, Joan, et al. Winning Strategies for Nursing Managers. (Illus.). 165p. 1986. text 16.95 (*0-397-54541-X*, Lippncott) Lppncott W & W.
O'Leary, Joann & Task Force of Parents. A Fragile Beginning: Parenting Your Early Baby. (SPA.). (Orig.). 1997. pap. 2.85 (*1-891633-01-5*) Abbott NW Hosp.

O

An Asterisk (*) at the beginning of an entry indicates that the title is appearing for the first time.

O

Olefsky, Jerrold M. & Sherwin, Robert S., eds. Diabetes Mellitus: Management & Complications. (Contemporary Issues in Endocrinology & Metabolism Ser.: Vol. 1). (Illus.). 399p. 1985. text 50.00 (0-443-08379-7) Church.

— Diabetes Mellitus: Management & Complications. fac. ed. LC 84-29258. (Contemporary Issues in Endocrinology & Metabolism Ser.). (Illus.). 413p. 1985. reprint ed. pap. 128.10 (0-7837-7899-6, 204765500008) Bks Demand.

Olefsky, Jerrold M., jt. ed. see Manolagas, Stavros C.

Olefsky, Jerrold M., jt. ed. see Steinberg, Daniel.

Oleinick, Peter N. Parallel Algorithms on a Multiprocessor. Stone, Harold S., ed. LC 82-4954. (Computer Science: Systems Programming Ser.: No. 4). 124p. 1982. reprint ed. pap. 38.50 (0-8357-1327-X, 207007900063) Bks Demand.

Oleinik, O. A. I. G. Petrowsky: Selected Works., 2 vols., Vol. 2. (Classics of Soviet Mathematics Ser.). 992p. 1996. text 192.00 (2-88124-980-9) Gordon & Breach.

— I. G. Petrowsky - Selected Works Pt. 1: Systems of Partial Differential Equations; Algebraic Geometry, Vol. 1. (Classics of Soviet Mathematics Ser). 528p. 1995. text 198.00 (2-88124-978-7) Gordon & Breach.

— I. G. Petrowsky - Selected Works Pt. 2: Differential Equations; Probability Theory, Vol. 2. (Classics of Soviet Mathematics Ser.). 464p. 1996. text 108.00 (2-88124-979-5) Gordon & Breach.

— Second Order Equations with Nonnegative Characteristic Form. Fife, Paul C., tr. LC 73-16453. 267p. 1973. reprint ed. pap. 82.80 (0-608-05462-3, 206593100006) Bks Demand.

***Oleinik, O. A. & Samokhin, V. N.** Mathematical Models in Boundary Layer Theory. LC 99-25191. 528p. 1999. boxed set 74.95 (1-58488-015-5, Chap & Hall CRC) CRC Pr.

— Mathematical Models in Boundary Layer Theory. 528p. 1999. 74.95 (0-8493-0840-2) CRC Pr.

Oleinik, O. A., et al. Mathematical Problems in Elasticity & Homogenization. LC 92-15390. (Studies in Mathematics & Its Applications: Vol. 26). 412p. 1992. 169.50 (0-444-88441-6, North Holland) Elsevier.

Oleinik, Olga. Some Asymptotic Problems in the Theory of Partial Differential Equations. (Lezioni Lincee Lectures). 213p. (C). 1996. text 59.95 (0-521-48083-3) Cambridge U Pr.

— Some Asymptotic Problems in the Theory of Partial Differential Equations. (Lezioni Lincee Lectures). 213p. (C). 1996. pap. text 22.95 (0-521-48537-1) Cambridge U Pr.

Olejar, Thomas, jt. auth. see Drate, Spencer.

Olejarczyk, Matt, jt. auth. see Zito, Matt.

Olejniczak, Anne, jt. auth. see Olejniczak, Denise.

Olejniczak, Denise & Olejniczak, Anne. Best Junior Handler: A Guide to Showing Successfully in Junior Showmanship. Luther, Luana, ed. LC 95-71341. 1997. pap. 16.95 (0-944875-45-9) Doral Pub.

Olejniczak, Verena. Wirkungsstrukturen in Ausgewahlten Texten T. S. Eliots und Virginia Woolfs. (Anglistische und Amerikanistische Texte und Studien Ser.: No. 3). 386p. 1987. write for info. (3-487-07885-6) G Olms Pubs.

Olejnik, Renee M. & Masters, Marie, eds. Rules for Inboard, Inboard Endurance & Unlimited Racing, 1989. 98p. 1990. 10.00 (0-318-41009-5) Am Power Boat.

— Rules for Offshore Racing, 1989. 62p. 1990. 10.00 (0-318-41010-9) Am Power Boat.

— Rules for Stock Outboard, PRO Outboard, Modified Outboard, & Outboard Performance Craft, 1989. 86p. 1990. 5.00 (0-318-41011-7) Am Power Boat.

Olek, Jan, jt. auth. see Hansen, Robert.

***Olekamma, Innocent Uhuegbu.** The Healing of Blind Bartimaeus (Mk 10,46-52) in the Markan Context: Two Ways of Asking. LC 99-49225. (European University Studies: Vol. 672). 316p. (C). 1999. pap. 48.95 (0-8204-4341-7) P Lang Pubng.

— The Healing of Blind Bartimaeus (MK 10,46-52) in the Markan Context: Two Ways of Asking. (European University Studies: Vol. 672). 316p. 1999. pap. 48.95 (3-631-34798-7) P Lang Pubng.

Oleksa, Michael J, Orthodox Alaska: A Theology of Mission. LC 92-37026. 1993. pap. 11.95 (0-88141-092-6) St Vladimirs.

Oleksiw, Andrew. A Guide to Analyzing Foreign Banks. Burke, Sarah A., ed. LC 88-23611. 64p. (Orig.). 1988. pap. text 37.00 (0-936742-57-7, 34041) Robt Morris Assocs.

Oleksiw, Barbara, ed. see Rubino, Lisa.

Oleksiw, Susan P. Double Take. (Chief Joe Silva Ser.). 256p. 1994. text 20.00 (0-684-19656-5, Scribners Ref) Mac Lib Ref.

— Family Album. LC 94-19679. (Chief Joe Silva Ser.). 1995. 20.00 (0-684-19731-6) S&S Trade.

— Murder in Mellingham. 288p. 1993. 20.00 (0-684-19528-3, Scribners Ref) Mac Lib Ref.

— Readers Guide to Classic British Mysteries. 1989. pap. 19.45 (0-89296-968-7, Pub. by Mysterious Pr) Little.

— A Reader's Guide to the Classic British Mystery. 300p. 1988. 50.00 (0-8161-8787-8, Hall Reference) Macmillan.

Oleksowicz, Ruth J., jt. auth. see Blair, Jane.

Oleksy. Elonic Troubleshooting. 2nd ed. 1990. 35.34 (0-02-676390-7) McGraw.

Oleksy, Elzbieta. Plight in Common: Hawthorne & Percy. LC 92-4487. (American University Studies: American Literature: Ser. XXIV, Vol. 34). VI, 244p. (C). 1993. text 35.95 (0-8204-1848-X) P Lang Pubng.

Oleksy, Elzbieta, ed. American Cultures: Assimilation & Multiculturalism. 166p. 1996. 69.95 (1-57309-013-1); pap. 49.95 (1-57309-012-3) Intl Scholars.

Oleksy, Elzbieta, jt. ed. see Lawson, Lewis A.

Oleksy, Walter. Business & Industry. LC 95-20415. (Information Revolution Ser.). (Illus.). 128p. (J). 1996. 19.95 (0-8160-3075-8) Facts on File.

***Oleksy, Walter.** Christopher Reeve. LC 99-29830. (People in the News Ser.). (Illus.). 144p. (YA). (gr. 6-9). 2000. lib. bdg. 23.70 (1-56006-534-6) Lucent Bks.

Oleksy, Walter. Entertainment. LC 95-22110. (The Information Revolution Ser.). (Illus.). 128p. (YA). (gr. 5-12). 1996. 19.95 (0-8160-3077-4) Facts on File.

— Experiments with Heat. LC 85-30860. (New True Books Ser.). (Illus.). 48p. (J). (ps-3). 1986. lib. bdg. 21.00 (0-516-01277-0) Childrens.

— Hispanic-American Scientists. LC 98-6558. (American Profiles Ser.). (Illus.). 160p. 1998. 19.95 (0-8160-3704-3) Facts on File.

— Military Leaders of World War II. LC 93-33641. (American Profiles Ser.). (Illus.). 160p. (J). (gr. 5-12). 1994. 19.95 (0-8160-3008-1) Facts on File.

— Science & Medicine. (Information Revolution Ser.). (Illus.). 128p. (YA). (gr. 5-12). 1995. 19.95 (0-8160-3076-6) Facts on File.

Oleksy, Walter, jt. auth. see Emerson, Larry.

Oleksy, Walter, jt. auth. see Kozlowski, Joseph G.

***Oleksy, Walter G.** Barefoot Waterskiing. LC 99-47922. (Extreme Sports Ser.). 48p. (YA). (gr. 5 up). 2000. lib. bdg. 21.26 (0-7368-0480-3) Capstone Pr.

— Choosing a Career as a Firefighter. LC 99-59417. (World of Work Ser.). (Illus.). (J). 2000. lib. bdg. write for info. (0-8239-3245-1) Rosen Group.

— The Circulatory System. LC 00-9417. (Insider's Guide to the Body Ser.). (Illus.). 2000. lib. bdg. write for info. (0-8239-3336-9) Rosen Group.

Oleksy, Walter G. Information Revolution, 4 Vols. 1995. 71.80 (0-8160-3836-8) Facts on File.

***Oleksy, Walter G.** James Dean. LC 00-9236. (Illus.). (J). 2001. write for info. (1-56006-698-9) Lucent Bks.

— The Nervous System. LC 00-9381. (Insider's Guide to the Body Ser.). (Illus.). 2000. lib. bdg. write for info. (0-8239-3341-5) Rosen Group.

— The Philippines. LC 99-13701. (Enchantment of the World Ser.). 2000. 32.00 (0-516-21010-6) Childrens.

— Princess Diana. LC 99-53455. 144p. (YA). (gr. 4-12). 2000. 18.96 (1-56006-579-6) Lucent Bks.

Oleksy, Wieslaw & Swan, Oscar E. W Labiryncie (Labyrinth of Life) An Advanced Polish Course. (Illus.). xiv, 378p. (Orig.). (C). 1993. pap. text 22.95 (0-89357-242-X) Slavica.

Oleksyn, J., jt. ed. see Innes, J. L.

Olem. Applying Ethics. 6th ed. LC 98-13955. 1998. 56.95 (0-534-55175-0) Wadsworth Pub.

Olem, H., ed. Diffuse Pollution. (Water Science & Technology Ser.: Vol. 28). 738p. 1993. pap. 346.50 (0-08-042345-0) Elsevier.

Olem, Harvey. Liming Acidic Surface Waters. (Illus.). 384p. 1990. lib. bdg. 99.95 (0-87371-243-9, L243) Lewis Pubs.

Olem, Harvey, jt. auth. see Novotny, Vladimir.

Olema, A. History of Evangelical Christianity in Russia. 8.99 (1-56632-082-8) Revival Lit.

Oleman, ed. see Gomez, Antonio-Enriquez.

***Olemskoi, A.** Theory of Structure Transformations in Non-Equilibrium Condensed Matter. LC 99-43599. (Illus.). 285p. 1999. 89.00 (1-56072-732-2) Nova Sci Pubs.

Olemskoi, Al, jt. ed. see Katsnel'son, A. A.

***Olemskoi, Alexander.** Fractals in Condensed Matter Physics. (Physics Reviews Ser.). 150p. 1999. pap. text 75.00 (3-7186-5937-9, Harwood Acad Pubs) Gordon & Breach.

Olen. Persons & Their World. 1983. teacher ed. 16.00 (0-07-554386-9) McGraw.

***Olen & Barry.** Applying Ethics. 6th ed. (Philosophy Ser.). (C). 2001. text 40.75 (0-534-56153-5) Wadsworth Pub.

Olen, Dale R. Accepting Yourself: Liking Yourself All of the Time. (Illus.). 212p. (Orig.). 1992. pap. 5.95 (1-56583-005-9) JODA.

— Being Intimate: Achieving Union with Others Without Losing Yourself. (Illus.). 212p. (Orig.). 1992. pap. 5.95 (1-56583-008-3) JODA.

— Communicating: Speaking & Listening to End Misunderstanding & Promote Friendship. (Illus.). 212p. (Orig.). 1992. pap. 5.95 (1-56583-007-5) JODA.

— Defeating Depression: Lifting Yourself from Sadness into Joy. (Illus.). 212p. (Orig.). 1992. pap. 5.95 (1-56583-011-3) JODA.

— Managing Stress: Learning to Pace Your Chase Through Life. 212p. (Orig.). 1992. pap. 5.95 (1-56583-003-2) JODA.

— Overcoming Fear: Reaching for Your Dreams & Knowing Peace of Mind. (Illus.). 212p. (Orig.). 1992. pap. 5.95 (1-56583-010-5) JODA.

— Parenting for the First Time. 195p. 1994. pap. 8.95 (1-56583-015-6) JODA.

— Reducing Anger: Harnessing Passion & Fury to Work for You - Not Against Others. (Illus.). 212p. (Orig.). 1992. pap. text 5.95 (1-56583-009-1) JODA.

— Resolving Conflict: Learning How You Both Can Win & Keep Your Relationship. (Illus.). 212p. (Orig.). 1992. pap. text 5.95 (1-56583-012-1) JODA.

— Self-Esteem for Children: A Parent's Gift That Lasts Forever. (Life Skills Parenting Ser.). (Illus.). 195p. (Orig.). 1996. pap. 9.95 (1-56583-016-4) JODA.

— The Thoughtful Art of Discipline: Teaching Responsibility When Your Child Misbehaves. (Life Skills Parenting Ser.). (Illus.). 195p. (Orig.). 1994. pap. 8.95 (1-56583-014-8) JODA.

Olen, Dale R. Meeting Life Head On: Moving into Life with Courage - Not Backing Away in Fear. 212p. (Orig.). 1992. pap. 5.95 (1-56583-006-7) JODA.

— Thinking Reasonably: Reaching Emotional Peace Through Mental Toughness. 212p. (Orig.). 1992. pap. 5.95 (1-56583-004-0) JODA.

Olen, Jeffrey. Moral Freedom. LC 88-15916. 149p. (C). 1988. 27.95 (0-87722-578-8) Temple U Pr.

— Persons & Their World: An Introduction to Philosophy. 608p. (C). 1983. text 41.74 (0-07-554311-7) McGraw.

Olen, Jeffrey & Barry, Vincent E. Applying Ethics: A Text with Readings. 3rd ed. 471p. (C). 1988. pap. write for info. (0-534-10152-6) Wadsworth Pub.

— Applying Ethics: A Text with Readings. 4th ed. 470p. (C). 1991. mass mkt. 29.75 (0-534-16470-6) Wadsworth Pub.

— Applying Ethics: A Text with Readings. 5th ed. LC 95-11852. 499p. 1995. pap. 36.25 (0-534-26316-X) Wadsworth Pub.

Olen, Stephanie, jt. auth. see Giangrande, Patricia.

Olenchak, F. Richard. Digging Through Archaeology: A Triad in Inquiry & Discovery. Smith, Linda, ed. (Triad Prototype Ser.). 40p. 1989. pap. 5.00 (0-936386-49-5) Creative Learning.

— They Say My Kid's Gifted - Now What? Ideas for Parents for Understanding & Working with Schools. 98p. (Orig.). 1998. pap. 19.95 (1-882664-44-2) Prufrock Pr.

Olender, Maurice. The Languages of Paradise: Race, Religion, & Philology in the Nineteenth Century. Goldhammer, Arthur, tr. from FRE. 208p. (C). 1992. 36.50 (0-674-51052-6) HUP.

Olendorf. Notable Twentieth-Century Scientists Supplement. LC 98-14016. 617p. 1998. 90.00 (0-7876-2766-6) Gale.

Olendorf, Bill. Paris Sketchbook: An American Retrospective of a Beautiful City. (Sketchbook Ser.). (Illus.). 144p. 1990. 40.00 (0-923078-02-9) Olendorf Graph.

Olendorf, Donna. Contemporary Authors, Vol. 144. 500p. 1994. text 150.00 (0-8103-5692-9) Gale.

— Something about the Author, Vol. 63. 275p. 1991. text 108.00 (0-8103-2273-0) Gale.

— Something about the Author, Vol. 64. 275p. 1991. text 108.00 (0-8103-2274-9) Gale.

Olendorf, Donna, ed. Something about the Author, Vol. 65. 275p. 1991. text 108.00 (0-8103-2275-7) Gale.

— Something about the Author, Vol. 66. 275p. 1991. text 108.00 (0-8103-2276-5) Gale.

Olendorf, Donna, et al. The Gale Encyclopedia of Medicine. LC 98-37918. 1998. write for info. (0-7876-1869-1); write for info. (0-7876-1870-5); write for info. (0-7876-1871-3); write for info. (0-7876-1872-1); write for info. (0-7876-1873-X) Gale.

Olendorf, Donna, ed. see Commire, Anne.

Olendorf, Donna, jt. ed. see McMurray, Emily J.

Olendzenski, Lorraine, jt. ed. see Margulis, Lynn.

Olenick, Arnold J. Managing to Have Profits: The Secrets Japan Learned but the U. S. Forgot. (Illus.). xii, 210p. 1992. reprint ed. 14.95 (1-880561-00-X) CashFlow Bks.

Olenick, Arnold J. & Olenick, Phil, eds. Making the Non-Profit Organization Work: A Legal & Accounting Guide for Administrators. LC 83-12885. 416p. 1983. 49.95 (0-87624-354-5, Inst Busn Plan) P-H.

Olenick, Arnold J. & Olenick, Philip R. Nonprofit Organization Operating Manual: Planning for Survival & Growth. LC 91-12292. 484p. (Orig.). 1991. pap. text 29.95 (0-87954-293-4) Foundation Ctr.

Olenick, Phil, jt. ed. see Olenick, Arnold J.

Olenick, Philip R., jt. auth. see Olenick, Arnold J.

Olenick, Rhoda & Prarie, Arleen. The Developing Child. rev. ed. 117p. 1996. student ed. 18.50 (1-55740-186-1) Magna Systems.

Olenick, Rhoda & Gonzalez-Mena, Janet, contrib. by. Early Childhood Training. 50p. (Orig.). 1995. pap. text, wbk. ed. 18.50 (1-55740-269-8) Magna Systems.

Olenick, Susan. Real Estate License Examination Review Program for the ASI Exam, The. 62p. (C). 1990. pap. text 63.00 (0-13-291733-5) P-H.

Olenjnik. Biology & Industry. (UK - Science Ser.). 1989. pap. 88.95 (0-17-448210-8) S-W Pub.

Oler, J. W. & Jordan, D. P. GRPHX: A High-Level System of Graphics Rountines Version 1.6. (Illus.). (C). 1989. pap. 9.95 (0-89672-195-7) Tex Tech Univ Pr.

Olere, David. Witness: Images of Auschwitz. LC 98-25406. 1998. 36.00 (0-941037-69-X, WstWind) D & F Scott.

Olerich, Henry. Cityless & Countryless World: An Outline of Practical Cooperative Individualism. LC 73-154455. (Utopian Literature Ser.). 1976. reprint ed. 35.95 (0-405-03537-3) Ayer.

Olerud, Lesley A., jt. auth. see Morse, Jerome G.

***Oles, Carole.** Sympathetic Systems. LC 99-47312. 1999. write for info. (0-89924-105-0) Lynx Hse.

— Sympathetic Systems: Poems. LC 99-47312. 70p. 2000. 12.95 (0-89924-104-2) Lynx Hse.

Oles, Carole S. The Deed: Poems by Carole Simmons Oles. LC 91-3931. 72p. 1991. pap. 7.95 (0-8071-1702-1); text 15.95 (0-8071-1701-3) La State U Pr.

— Night Watches: Inventions on the Life of Maria Mitchell. LC 85-70621. 72p. 1985. 6.95 (0-914086-56-1); pap. 9.95 (0-914086-57-X) Alice James Bks.

Oles, James. South of the Border: Mexico in the American Imagination, 1914-1947. LC 92-41507. (Illus.). 354p. 1993. pap. 34.95 (1-56098-295-0); text 75.00 (1-56098-294-2) Smithsonian.

Oles, James, tr. see Debroise, Olivier.

Oles, Judy. Keys to Business Math: 10 Key Electronic Calculator & Computer Numeric Keypad. (Illus.). 55p. 1998. pap. text, teacher ed., wbk. ed. write for info. (0-9666558-0-X) Plateau Pub Co.

Oles, Judy H. Keys to Business Math: 10 Key Electronic Calculator & Computer Numeric Keypad. (Illus.). 200p. 1998. pap. text, wbk. ed. write for info. (0-9666558-1-8) Plateau Pub Co.

***Olesen, Henning Salling & Jensen, Jens Hojgaard, eds.** Project Studies: A Late Modern University Reform? 305p. 1999. 34.00 (87-16-13482-6, Pub. by Copenhagen Busn Schl) Bks Intl VA.

Olesen, Asta. Afghan Craftsmen: The Cultures of Three Itinerant Communities. LC 94-60295. (Carlsberg Nomad Ser.). (Illus.). 320p. 1994. 50.00 (0-500-01612-7, Pub. by Thames Hudson) Norton.

— Islam & Politics in Afghanistan. LC 95-115079. 350p. (C). 1995. text 75.00 (0-7007-0299-7, Pub. by Curzon Pr Ltd) Paul & Co Pubs.

— Islam & Politics in Afghanistan. LC 95-115079. (Scandinavian Institute of Asian Studies: No. 67). 350p. (C). 1995. pap. 35.00 (0-7007-0296-2, Pub. by Curzon Pr Ltd) Paul & Co Pubs.

Olesen, David. North of Reliance: A Personal Story of Living Beyond the Wilderness. LC 94-12981. (Illus.). 176p. 1994. pap. 12.95 (1-55971-433-6, NorthWord Pr) Creat Pub Intl.

Olesen, Jens. Snail. LC 86-10084. (Stopwatch Ser.). (Illus.). 25p. (J). (gr. k-4). 1986. pap. 3.95 (0-382-24019-7); lib. bdg. 9.95 (0-382-09289-9, Silver Pr NJ) Silver Burdett Pr.

Olesen, Jes. Migraine & Other Headaches: The Vascular Mechanisms. (Frontiers in Headache Research Ser.: Vol. 1). 368p. 1991. text 99.50 (0-88167-795-7) Lppncott W & W.

Olesen, Jes, et al, eds. The Headaches. LC 93-19517. 928p. 1993. text 182.00 (0-7817-0069-8) Lppncott W & W.

Olesen, Jes & Bousser, Marie-Germaine. Genetics of Headache Disorders, Vol. 8. 294p. text 110.00 (0-7817-2648-4) Lppncott W & W.

Olesen, Jes & Edvinsson, Lars, eds. Headache Pathogenesis: Monoamines, Neuropeptides, Purines, & Nitric Oxide. LC 97-8666. 352p. 1997. text 100.00 (0-7817-1208-4) Lppncott W & W.

***Olesen, Jes & Goadsby, Peter J., eds.** Cluster Headache & Related Conditions. LC 99-44816. (Frontiers in Headache Research Ser.). (Illus.). 320p. 2000. text 79.50 (0-19-263073-3) OUP.

Olesen, Jes & Saxena, Pramod R., eds. Five-Hydroxytryptamine Mechanisms in Primary Headaches. LC 92-17140. (Frontiers in Headache Research Ser.: Vol. 2). 384p. 1992. text 105.00 (0-88167-927-5) Lppncott W & W.

Olesen, Jes & Schoenen, Jean, eds. Tension-Type Headache: Classification, Mechanisms, & Treatment. LC 93-19572. (Frontiers in Headache Research Ser.: Vol. 3). 320p. 1993. text 105.00 (0-7817-0070-1) Lppncott W & W.

Olesen, Jes, et al. The Headaches. 2nd ed. LC 99-21427. 950p. 1999. text. write for info. (0-7817-1597-0) Lppncott W & W.

Olesen, Sigrid. Summer Is from Winter Until Winter. (Illus.). 80p. (C). 1980. 4.95 (0-936748-02-8); pap. 3.50 (0-685-01610-2) Fade In.

Olesen, Virginia L. & Whittaker, Elvi W. The Silent Dialogue: A Study in the Social Psychology of Professional Socialization. LC 68-21320. (Jossey-Bass Behavioral Science Ser.). 328p. reprint ed. pap. 101.70 (0-608-14929-2, 202567800045) Bks Demand.

Olesen, Virginia L. & Woods, Nancy F., eds. Culture, Society & Menstruation. LC 66-55252. 186p. 1986. 65.00 (0-89116-557-6) Hemisp Pub.

Olesen, Virginia L., jt. auth. see Clarke, Adele.

Olesen, Virginia L., jt. ed. see Clarke, Adele E.

Olesha, IUrii Karlovich. Envy. Berczynski, Thomas, tr. from RUS. (Orig.). 1979. pap. 12.95 (0-88233-091-8) Ardis Pubs.

— No Day Without a Line: From Notebooks by Yury Olesha. Rosengrant, Judson, tr. from RUS. LC 98-17688. (Studies in Russian Literature & Theory). 272p. 1998. pap. text 19.95 (0-8101-1382-1) Northwestern U Pr.

Oleske, Denise M., ed. Epidemiology & the Delivery of Health Care Services: Methods & Applications. LC 95-9426. (Illus.). 252p. (C). 1995. text 54.00 (0-306-44968-4, Kluwer Plenum) Kluwer Academic.

Olesker, Michael. Michael Olesker's Baltimore: If You Live Here, You're Home. 176p. 1995. 22.95 (0-8018-5203-X) Johns Hopkins.

Olesker, Michael, jt. auth. see Bretholz, Leo.

***Oleski, Joseph.** The Poppy Field. LC 98-90934. 1999. pap. 12.95 (0-533-12992-3) Vantage.

Olesko. Osiris, Vol. 5. 1991. lib. bdg. 39.00 (0-934235-12-0) U Ch Pr.

— Osiris, Vol. 5. 1993. pap. text 25.00 (0-934235-13-9) U Ch Pr.

Olesko, Kathryn M. Physics As a Calling: Discipline & Practice in the Konigsberg Seminar for Physics. LC 90-55717. (History of Science Ser.). (Illus.). 496p. 1991. text 52.50 (0-8014-2248-5) Cornell U Pr.

Olesky, J. & Rutkowski, George B. Microprocessor & Digital Computer Technology. 1981. text 54.00 (0-13-581116-3) P-H.

Olesky, Rio. Astrology & Consciousness: The Wheel of Light. LC 95-74973. (Illus.). 384p. (Orig.). 1995. pap. 16.95 (1-56184-123-4) New Falcon Pubns.

***Olesky, Walter.** Choosing a Career in Agriculture. LC 00-9603. (World of Work Ser.). (Illus.). 2000. lib. bdg. write for info. (0-8239-3332-6) Rosen Group.

Oleson, Alexandra & Brown, Sanborn C., eds. The Pursuit of Knowledge in the Early American Republic: American Scientific & Learned Societies from Colonial Times to the Civil War. LC 75-36941. 400p. reprint ed. pap. 124.00 (0-8357-8294-8, 203411700088) Bks Demand.

Oleson, Alexandra & Voss, John, eds. The Organization of Knowledge in Modern America, 1860-1920. LC 78-20521. 503p. reprint ed. pap. 156.00 (0-608-15187-4, 202737500055) Bks Demand.

An Asterisk (*) at the beginning of an entry indicates that the title is appearing for the first time.

Oleson, Emery. How to Create/Market/Operate a Mini Storage Complex. rev. ed. LC 93-92654. (Illus.). 84p. 1993. vinyl bd. write for info. (*0-9636920-0-3*) Ole & Co.

Oleson, John D. Pathways to Agility: Mass Customization in Action. LC 97-31608. (Illus.). 263p. 1998. 39.95 (*0-471-19175-2*) Wiley.

Oleson, John D., ed. Technology Vision 2020: The U. S. Chemical Industry. 91p. (C). 1998. pap. text 25.00 (*0-7881-7177-1*) DIANE Pub.

Oleson, John P. Greek & Roman Mechanical Water-Lifting Devices: The History of Technology. (Phoenix Supplementary Volumes Ser.: Vol. 16). (Illus.). 624p. 1984. text 95.00 (*0-8020-5597-4*) U of Toronto Pr.

— Greek Numismatic Art: Coins of the Arthur Stone Dewing Collection. (Illus.). 152p. 1975. pap. 4.95 (*0-916724-02-6*) Harvard Art Mus.

Oleson, Karen. Develop a Powerful Speaking Voice. (Speakease Ser.). 8p. 1991. 11.95 incl. audio (*1-886789-01-0*, 0506-74) VoiceTech WA.

Oleson, Karen. I'm Not Crazy, I'm Vocalizing. rev. ed. (Vocalizing Ser.). (Illus.). 8p. (J). 1991. 15.95 incl. audio (*1-886789-06-1*, 1214-41); 19.95 incl. audio compact disk (*1-886789-07-X*, 1214-41) VoiceTech WA.

Oleson, Karen. You Can Teach Yourself to Sing. 72p. 1997. pap. 9.95 (*0-7866-0278-3*, 95294) Mel Bay.

Oleson, Karen. You Can Teach Yourself to Sing. 72p. 1998. pap. 18.95 incl. audio (*0-7866-1257-6*, 95294P) Mel Bay.

— You Can Teach Yourself to Sing. 72p. 1998. pap. 24.95 incl. audio compact disk (*0-7866-2539-2*, 95294CDP) Mel Bay.

Oleson, Keith. Food Safety: Opportunities to Redirect Federal Resources & Funds Can Enhance Effectiveness. (Illus.). 48p. (C). 1999. text 20.00 (*0-7881-7932-2*) DIANE Pub.

Oleson, Keith W. Food-Related Services: Opportunities Exist to Recover Costs by Charging Beneficiaries. 64p. (C). 1999. reprint ed. text 20.00 (*0-7881-7931-4*) DIANE Pub.

— Water Quality: A Catalog of Related Federal Programs. 64p. 1998. pap. text 20.00 (*0-7881-7219-0*) DIANE Pub.

Oleson, Keith W. & Richards, Dennis. Food Safety: Federal Efforts to Ensure the Safety of Imported Foods Are Inconsistent & Unreliable. (Illus.). 64p. 1998. pap. text 20.00 (*0-7881-7380-4*) DIANE Pub.

Oleson, Sue. Asteroid Survival Manual. (Illus.). xii, 105p. 2000. spiral bd. 17.97 (*1-891829-04-1*) Peaceful Angel.

— Inner-Biography: Write Your Life Story from a Feeling Level. (Illus.). xii, 110p. 2000. spiral bd., wbk. ed. 17.97 (*1-891829-01-7*) Peaceful Angel.

— El Nino Survival Cookbook: Cooking Without Conveniences. (Illus.). xii, 89p. 2000. spiral bd. 17.95 (*1-891829-00-9*) Peaceful Angel.

— Renaissance Womyn: Women of the New Millennium. (Illus.). 130p. 2000. spiral bd., wbk. ed. 17.97 (*1-891829-02-5*) Peaceful Angel.

Oleson, Terry. Auriculotherapy Manual: Chinese & Western Systems of Ear Acupuncture. 2nd ed. LC 96-77437. (Illus.). ill, 244 p. 1996. pap. 42.00 (*0-9629415-5-7*) Hlth Care Altern.

— International Handbook of Ear Reflex Points. (Illus.). 239p. 1995. pap. 39.00 (*0-9629415-3-0*) Hlth Care Altern.

Oleson, Trygovi J. The Witenagemot in the Reign of Edward the Confessor: A Study in the Constitutional History of Eleventh-Century England. LC 80-2217. 1981. reprint ed. 32.50 (*0-404-18769-2*) AMS Pr.

Oleson, W. B., jt. auth. see Stevens, John L.

Oleszczuk, Thomas. Political Justice in the Soviet Union: Dissent & Repression in Lithuania, 1969-1987. (East European Monographs: No. 247). 221p. 1988. text 59.50 (*0-88033-144-5*, Pub. by East Eur Monographs) Col U Pr.

Oleszczuk, Thomas A., jt. auth. see Smith, Theresa C.

***Oleszczuk, Tom.** Gazing into the Pond. (Illus.). 40p. 1999. pap. 5.00 (*1-893043-02-9*) Petit Pois.

— Time off for Good Behavior. 2000. pap. 5.00 (*1-893043-03-7*) Petit Pois.

Oleszczuk, Tom, jt. auth. see Ivy, Evie.

***Oleszek, W. & Marston, A.** Saponins in Food, Feedstuffs & Medicinal Plants. LC 00-30658. (Proceedings of the Phytochemical Society Ser.). 2000. write for info. (*0-7923-6023-0*) Kluwer Academic.

***Oleszek, Walter J.** Congressional Procedures & Policy Process. 5th ed. 2000. 44.95 (*1-56802-492-4*) CQ Pr.

— Congressional Procedures & Policy Process. 5th ed. (Illus.). 2000. pap. 28.95 (*1-56802-448-7*) CQ Pr.

Oleszek, Walter J. Congressional Procedures & the Policy Process. 4th ed. LC 95-31596. 373p. (YA). (gr. 11). 1995. pap. text 26.95 (*0-87187-703-1*) Congr Quarterly.

— Congressional Procedures & the Policy Process. 4th ed. LC 95-31596. 373p. (C). 1995. text 42.95 (*0-87187-704-X*) Congr Quarterly.

Oleszek, Walter J., jt. auth. see Davidson, Roger H.

Oleszewski, Wes. Ghost Ships, Gales & Forgotten Tales: True Adventures on the Great Lakes. 2nd ed. LC 95-79791. (Illus.). 1995. pap. 13.95 (*0-932212-83-2*) Avery Color.

— Great Lakes Lighthouses, American & Canadian: A Comprehensive Directory - Guide to Great Lakes Lighthouses. (Illus.). 202p. 1998. pap. 16.95 (*0-932212-98-0*) Avery Color.

— Ice Water Museum: Forgotten Great Lakes Shipwrecks. (Illus.). 192p. 1993. 13.95 (*0-932212-78-6*) Avery Color.

***Oleszewski, Wes.** Keepers of Valor: Lighthouses, Lake Boats & Lifesavers. (Illus.). 320p. 2000. pap. 16.95 (*1-892384-04-3*) Avery Color.

Oleszewski, Wes. Lighthouse Adventures: Heroes, Haunts & Havoc on the Great Lakes. LC 99-72160. 224p. 1999. pap. 16.95 (*1-892384-01-9*) Avery Color.

— Mysteries & Histories of the Great Lakes: Shipwrecks of the Great Lakes. LC 97-70282. (Illus.). 312p. 1997. pap. 13.95 (*0-932212-92-1*) Avery Color.

— Sounds of Disaster: Great Lakes Shipwrecks. 2nd ed. LC 92-75915. (Illus.). 144p. 1993. pap. 12.95 (*0-932212-76-X*) Avery Color.

Oleszowksi, Wes. Stormy Seas: Triumphs & Tragedies of Great Lakes Ships. 3rd ed. LC 90-86206. 1991. pap. 12.95 (*0-932212-67-0*) Avery Color.

Olev, Kulno. Maritime Dictionary English-Estonian-Russian. (ENG, EST & RUS.). 560p. 1981. 35.00 (*0-8288-0430-3*, M 15461) Fr & Eur.

O'Levenson, Jordan, ed. Irish in Memorium Poetry: The Book of Tears. LC 82-90968. (Orig.). 1983. pap. 15.95 (*0-914442-10-4*) Levenson Pr.

Olevianus, Caspar. A Firm Foundation: An Aid to Interpreting the Heidelberg Cathechism. Bierma, Lyle D., ed. & tr. by. from GER. LC 95-12360. (Texts & Studies in Reformation & Post-Reformation Thought). 134p. 1995. pap. 17.99 (*0-8010-2022-0*) Baker Bks.

Olevitch, Barbara A. Using Cognitive Approaches with the Seriously Mentally Ill: Dialogue Across the Barrier. LC 95-6348. 184p. 1995. 59.95 (*0-275-95244-4*, Praeger Pubs) Greenwood.

Olevnik, Peter P. American Higher Education: A Guide to Reference Sources, 12. LC 93-25015. (Bibliographies & Indexes in Education Ser.: No. 12). 232p. 1993. lib. bdg. 59.95 (*0-313-27749-4*, OHU/, Greenwood Pr) Greenwood.

Olewiler, David B. Solar Device Design Vol. 1: Sustainable Development. Wilde, David, ed. (Illus.). 95p. 1997. 35.00 (*1-882204-20-4*) Wilde Pub.

***Olexiewicz, Charlene.** Super More Origami Crafts. (50 Nifty Ser.). (Illus.). 80p. (J). (gr. 3-7). 2000. pap. 6.95 (*0-7373-0481-2*, 04812W, Pub. by Lowell Hse Juvenile) NTC Contemp Pub Co.

Olexiewicz, Charlene, jt. auth. see Fister, Nancy.

Olexson, Dennis W., jt. auth. see Bellamy, James E. C.

Olexy, Ronald T., et al. Cantus - An Aquitanian Antiphoner: Toledo, Biblioteca Capitular, 44.2. (Wissenschaftliche Abhandlungen-Musicological Studies: Vol. 55, Pt. 1). 185p. 1992. 80.00 (*0-931902-71-1*) Inst Mediaeval Mus.

Oley, Norman. Germanville: A Struggle for Power in the Early Pennsylvania Coal Region. Goldbeck, Christine M., ed. LC 97-90102. 260p. (Orig.). 1997. mass mkt. 13.95 (*0-9657050-0-5*) Valhalla Bks.

Oleynik, Igor S. Russian Regional Investment & Business Guide: Stategic Information & Data for Corporate Executives on Russia. 1996. pap. 59.00 (*0-9646241-1-7*) Intl Business Pubns.

Oleynik, Igor S., ed. Russian Business White & Yellow Pages: 25,000 Business Contacts in Russia & Worldwide. (Illus.). 1200p. (Orig.). (C). 1996. pap. 99.00 (*0-9646241-0-9*) Intl Business Pubns.

Oleynik, Igor S. & Musin, Oleg. Russian Regional Explorer: Geography, Government, Economy, Ecology. (Illus.). 500p. (C). 1996. 120.00 rom, audio compact disk 149.00 (*0-9646241-9-2*) Intl Business Pubns.

Oleynik, Igor S., ed. see Russian Info & Business Center, U. S. A. Staff.

Oleynik, Igor S., ed. see Russian Information & Business Center, Inc. Staff.

Oleynikol, Nikolai. Fronichiskie Stikhi: Fronical Verses. 2nd ed. Poliak, Gregory, ed. (RUS., Illus.). 96p. (Orig.). pap. 8.00 (*0-940294-04-4*) Silver Age Pub.

Olf. Biochemistry. 1994. pap. text 36.00 (*0-443-05272-7*, W B Saunders Co) Harcrt Hlth Sci Grp.

— Contemporary Social Policy. 1995. pap. text 31.00 (*0-443-05360-X*, W B Saunders Co) Harcrt Hlth Sci Grp.

— Descriptive Statistics. 1995. pap. text 30.00 (*0-443-05341-3*, W B Saunders Co) Harcrt Hlth Sci Grp.

— Experimental Research. 1994. pap. text 50.00 (*0-443-05270-0*, W B Saunders Co) Harcrt Hlth Sci Grp.

— Genetics. 1994. pap. text 36.00 (*0-443-05273-5*, W B Saunders Co) Harcrt Hlth Sci Grp.

— Legal Aspects of Health Care. 1995. pap. text 53.00 (*0-443-05359-6*, W B Saunders Co) Harcrt Hlth Sci Grp.

— People in Organisations. LC 96-52855. 1997. 47.95 (*0-631-20181-5*) Blackwell Pubs.

— Psychology. 1994. pap. text 34.00 (*0-443-05274-3*, W B Saunders Co) Harcrt Hlth Sci Grp.

Olf, Lillian. Their Name Is Pius. LC 74-107729. (Essay Index Reprint Ser.). 1977. 30.95 (*0-8369-1768-5*) Ayer.

Olfe, Julie T., ed. see Andrews, Lawrence F.

Olfenbuttel, Robert F., jt. ed. see Hinchee, Robert E.

Olff, M., et al, eds. Quantification of Human Defense Mechanisms. (Recent Research in Psychology Ser.). (Illus.). vi, 327p. 1991. 70.95 (*0-387-53821-6*) Spr-Verlag.

Olfman, Lorne, ed. Organizational Memory Systems: A Special Double Issue of the Journal of Organizational Computing & Electronic Commerce. 136p. 1999. pap. 34.50 (*0-8058-9796-8*) L Erlbaum Assocs.

Olford, A. Stephen. A Graca de Dar. Orig. Title: The Grace of Giving. (POR.). 128p. 1986. pap. 3.95 (*0-8297-1602-5*) Vida Pubs.

Olford, David L., jt. auth. see Olford, Stephen F.

***Olford, Stephen.** Time for Truth. 1999. 16.99 (*0-89957-846-2*) AMG Pubs.

Olford, Stephen F. Answers to Personal Problems Sermon Outlines. 64p. (Orig.). 1998. pap. 4.99 (*0-8010-9056-3*) Baker Bks.

— Bible Character Sermon Outlines: David, Elisha, Samson, Caleb, Isaiah, the Blind Man & Lazarus. 64p. (Orig.). 1998. pap. 4.99 (*0-8010-9055-5*) Baker Bks.

— The Christian Message for Contemporary Life: The Gospel's Power to Change Lives. LC 99-18856. 112p. 1999. pap. 7.99 (*0-8254-3361-4*) Kregel.

— Expository Preaching Outlines, Vol. 1. 3rd ed. 1998. reprint ed. ring bd. 69.95 (*1-879028-03-4*) Encounter Minist.

— Expository Preaching Outlines, Vol. 2. 3rd ed. 1981. reprint ed. ring bd. 69.95 (*1-879028-04-2*) Encounter Minist.

— Expository Preaching Outlines, Vol. 3. 3rd ed. 1982. reprint ed. ring bd. 69.95 (*1-879028-05-0*) Encounter Minist.

— Expository Preaching Outlines, Vol. 5. 3rd ed. 1985. reprint ed. ring bd. 69.95 (*1-879028-07-7*) Encounter Minist.

— Expository Preaching Outlines, Vol. 6. 3rd ed. 1987. reprint ed. ring bd. 69.95 (*1-879028-08-5*) Encounter Minist.

— Expository Preaching Outlines, Vol. 7. 3rd ed. 1989. reprint ed. ring bd. 69.95 (*1-879028-09-3*) Encounter Minist.

— The Grace of Giving. 1986. mass mkt. 3.75 (*0-8297-1263-1*) Vida Pubs.

— The Grace of Giving: Biblical Expositions. 2nd rev. ed. 119p. 1990. pap. 6.95 (*1-879028-00-X*) Encounter Minist.

— Inviting People to Christ: Evangelistic Expository Messages. LC 99-176672. (Stephen Olford Biblical Preaching Library). 128p. 1998. pap. 10.99 (*0-8010-9062-8*) Baker Bks.

— Manna in the Morning. 6th ed. 13p. 1962. 0.50 (*1-879028-01-8*) Encounter Minist.

— Not I, but Christ. LC 96-39643. 192p. 1997. reprint ed. pap. 12.99 (*0-89107-943-2*) Crossway Bks.

— Proclaiming the Good News: Evangelistic Expository Messages. (Stephen Olford Biblical Preaching Library). 128p. 1998. pap. 10.99 (*0-8010-9061-X*) Baker Bks.

— The Secret of Soul Winning. LC 94-167798. 126p. (Orig.). 1994. pap. 8.99 (*1-56043-800-2*, Treasure Hse) Destiny Image.

— Sermon Outlines on the Cross. 64p. 1997. pap. 5.99 (*0-8010-9045-8*) Baker Bks.

— Special-Day Sermon Outlines. 64p. 1997. pap. 5.99 (*0-8010-9046-6*) Baker Bks.

— The Tabernacle: Camping with God. LC 78-173686. 187p. 1971. 16.99 (*0-87213-675-2*) Loizeaux.

— The Way of Holiness. LC 97-29012. 160p. 1998. 14.99 (*0-89107-977-7*) Crossway Bks.

Olford, Stephen F. & Barclay, Ian. Expository Preaching Outlines, Vol. 4. 3rd ed. 1983. reprint ed. ring bd. 69.95 (*1-879028-06-9*) Encounter Minist.

Olford, Stephen F. & Olford, David L. Anointed Expository Preaching. LC 97-31305. 304p. 1998. text 24.99 (*0-8054-6085-3*) Broadman.

***Olgac, Nejat, ed.** ASME Dynamic Systems & Control Division. (DSC Ser.: Vol. 67). 959p. 1999. 240.00 (*0-7918-1634-6*) ASME Pr.

Olgiati, Charlie, jt. auth. see Gross, Jim.

Olgiati, Vittorio, jt. auth. see Podgorecki, Adam.

Ol'gin, Olgert, jt. auth. see Krivitch, Mikhail.

Olgivie-Gordon, Maria M., tr. see Von Zittel, K. A.

Olgyay, Aladar. Solar Control & Shading Devices. LC 57-5455. (Illus.). 208p. reprint ed. pap. 64.50 (*0-8357-3703-9*, 203642800003) Bks Demand.

Olgyay, Nora. Safety Symbols Art: Camera-Ready Disk Art for Designers. 213p. 1995. pap. 59.95 (*0-471-29029-7*, VNR) Wiley.

Olhausen, Pam, jt. auth. see Russo, Ron.

Olhoff, Neils, jt. ed. see Eschenauer, H. A.

Olhoff, Niels & Rozvany, George I., eds. Structural & Multidisciplinary Optimization: Proceedings of the First World Congress of Multidisciplinary Optimization, Goslar, Germany, Held May 28-June 2, 1995. 960p. 1996. 188.50 (*0-08-042267-5*, Pergamon Pr) Elsevier.

Olhovych, Orest, ed. An Interview with Political Prisoners in a Soviet Perm Camp. 2nd ed. Drozd, Taras, tr. from UKR. (Documents of Ukrainian Samvydav Ser.: No. 2). 1978. 1.00 (*0-686-58232-2*) Smoloskyp.

Olhovych, Orest, jt. ed. see Harasowska, Marta.

Oli, G. C., jt. ed. see Devoto, G.

Oli, Krishna Prasad. Environmental Study of Napal's Begnas & Rupa Lakes. 1996. pap. 37.00 (*0-7855-7389-5*, Pub. by Ratna Pustak Bhandar) St Mut.

— Phewal Lake Conservation Action Plan. 1997. pap. 22.00 (*0-7855-7472-7*, Pub. by Ratna Pustak Bhandar) St Mut.

***Olia, Masoud, et al.** How to Prepare for the Fundamentals of Engineering: FE/FEIT Exam. LC 99-45283. 450p. 1999. pap. 18.95 (*0-7641-0651-1*) Barron.

Olian, Joanne. Everyday Fashions of the Forties As Pictured in Sears Catalogs. (Illus.). 128p. 1991. pap. 12.95 (*0-486-26918-3*) Dover.

Olian, JoAnne, ed. Authentic French Fashions of the Twenties. 144p. 1990. pap. 9.95 (*0-486-26187-5*) Dover.

Olian, Joanne, ed. 80 Godey's Full-Color Fashion Plates. (Illus.). 96p. 1998. pap. 12.95 (*0-486-40222-3*) Dover.

— Everyday Fashions of the Sixties As Pictured in Sears Catalogs. LC 99-37107. (Illus.). 96p. 1998. pap. 10.95 (*0-486-40120-0*) Dover.

Olian, JoAnne, ed. Everyday Fashions, 1910-1920, as Pictured in Sears Catalogs. (Illus.). 144p. 1995. pap. 12.95 (*0-486-28628-2*) Dover.

— Full-Color Victorian Fashions, 1870-1893. LC 99-14122. (Illus.). 64p. 1999. pap. text 16.95 (*0-486-40484-6*) Dover.

Olian, Joanne, ed. Victorian & Edwardian Fashions from "La Mode Illustree" LC 98-29316. (Illus.). 256p. (Orig.). 1997. reprint ed. pap. text 16.95 (*0-486-29711-X*) Dover.

Olian, JoAnne, ed. Wedding Fashions, 1860-1912: Three Hundred Eighty Designs from "La Mode Illustree" (Illus.). 96p. 1994. reprint ed. pap. text 9.95 (*0-486-27882-4*) Dover.

Olian, JoAnne, intro. Children's Fashions, 1860-1912: One Thousand Sixty-Five Costume Designs from "La Mode Illustree" (Illus.). 128p. 1993. pap. 10.95 (*0-486-27615-5*) Dover.

Olian, JoAnne, tr. see Leniston, Florence, ed.

***Olick, Hilda.** Kaviam Iqvaryallra (When the Fox Went Berry Picking) large type ed. (ESK., Illus.). 8p. (J). (gr. k-3). 1999. pap. text 14.50 (*1-58084-057-4*) Lower Kuskokwim.

— Kavviar Paunerssuyallrim (When the Fox Went Berry Picking) large type ed. (ESK., Illus.). 8p. (J). (gr. k-3). 1999. pap. text 14.50 (*1-58084-114-7*) Lower Kuskokwim.

— Kayuqtuq Aullaqsrugiaman (When the Fox Went Berry Picking) large type ed. (ESK., Illus.). 8p. (J). (gr. k-3). 1999. pap. text 14.50 (*1-58084-119-8*) Lower Kuskokwim.

— Kayuqturuuq Ahiariarnirman (When the Fox Went Berry Picking) large type ed. (ESK., Illus.). 8p. (J). (gr. k-3). 1999. pap. text 14.50 (*1-58084-142-2*) Lower Kuskokwim.

Olick, Hilda. Pisukti Asianik Pukugiarami (When the Fox Went Berry Picking) large type ed. (ESK., Illus.). 8p. (J). (gr. k-3). 1999. pap. text 14.50 (*1-58084-128-7*) Lower Kuskokwim.

***Olick, Hilda.** Tiriganniaq Kablatariahuni Ahiariaqtuqhani (When the Fox Went Berry Picking) large type ed. (ESK., Illus.). 8p. (J). (gr. k-3). 1999. pap. text 14.50 (*1-58084-135-X*) Lower Kuskokwim.

Olick, Hilda. When the Fox Went Berry Picking. large type ed. (Illus.). 8p. (J). (gr. k-3). 1999. pap. text 14.50 (*1-58084-056-6*) Lower Kuskokwim.

Olick, Hilda & Nicori, Helen. Nasaurluq Nunalinqigtelleq. large type ed. (ESK., Illus.). 8p. (J). (gr. k-3). 1997. pap. text 6.00 (*1-58084-009-4*) Lower Kuskokwim.

— Wavigcuk Watqapik-llu. large type ed. (ESK., Illus.). 8p. (J). (gr. k-3). 1998. pap. text 6.00 (*1-58084-019-1*) Lower Kuskokwim.

Olidort, Baila. Just Like Mommy. LC 92-20591. (Illus.). 1992. 8.00 (*0-8266-0359-9*, Merkos LInyonei Chinuch) Kehot Pubn Soc.

— Quarters & Dimes & Nickels & Pennies. LC 98-20559. (Illus.). 24p. (J). 1993. reprint ed. 12.00 (*0-8266-0358-0*, Merkos LInyonei Chinuch) Kehot Pubn Soc.

Olidort, Baila, ed. Feeding among the Lilies: Exploring the Inner Dimension of Torah & Soul. 272p. (Orig.). 1999. pap. 18.00 (*0-8266-1305-5*, Wellsprings) Kehot Pubn Soc.

Oliemans, R. V., ed. Computational Fluid Dynamics for the Petrochemical Process Industry. 242p. (C). 1991. text 175.00 (*0-7923-1360-7*) Kluwer Academic.

Olien, Charles R. & Smith, Myrtle N. Analysis & Improvement of Plant Cold Hardiness. 224p. 1981. 130.00 (*0-8493-5397-1*, SB781, CRC Reprint) Franklin.

Olien, Diana D., jt. auth. see Olien, Roger M.

Olien, Rebecca. Splish Splash Science: Learning about Water with Easy Fun-Filled Activities. 64p. (J). 1999. pap. 10.95 (*0-590-11595-2*) Scholastic Inc.

— Walk This Way! Classroom Hikes to Learning. LC 98-17810. (Beeline Ser.). 1998. pap. 9.95 (*0-325-00022-0*) Heinemann.

Olien, Roger M. From Token to Triumph: The Texas Republicans since 1920. LC 81-13589. (Illus.). 320p. 1982. 15.00 (*0-87074-180-2*) SMU Press.

***Olien, Roger M.** Oil & Ideology: The Cultural Creation of the American Petroleum Industry. LC 99-29765. (Luther Hartwell Hodges Series on Business, Society & the State). 416p. 2000. lib. bdg. 49.95 (*0-8078-2523-9*) U of NC Pr.

Olien, Roger M. & Olien, Diana D. Easy Money: Oil Promoters & Investers in the Jazz Age. LC 90-50017. 230p. 1990. pap. 71.30 (*0-608-05208-6*, 206574500001) Bks Demand.

***Olien, Roger M. & Olien, Diana D.** Oil & Ideology: The Cultural Creation of the American Petroleum Industry. LC 99-29765. (Luther Hartwell Hodges Series on Business, Society & the State). 416p. 2000. pap. 18.95 (*0-8078-4835-2*) U of NC Pr.

Olien, Roger M. & Olien, Diana D. Oil Booms: Social Change in Five Texas Towns. LC 81-11686. (Illus.). 238p. reprint ed. pap. 73.80 (*0-7837-4668-7*, 204439500002) Bks Demand.

Oliensis, Adam. Ring of Men. 1995. pap. 3.25 (*0-8222-1468-7*) Dramatists Play.

Oliensis, Ellen. Horace & the Rhetoric of Authority. LC 97-33353. 254p. (C). 1998. text 59.95 (*0-521-57315-7*) Cambridge U Pr.

Olifant, Patty & Harrier, Kathy. FTCE Technology. (C). 1998. per. 10.00 (*1-58197-088-9*) XAM.

Oliff, Douglas, ed. The Ultimate Book of Mastiff Breeds. LC 99-461700. (Illus.). 200p. 1999. 34.95 (*1-58245-080-3*) Howell Bks.

Oliff, Douglas B. Mastiff & Bullmastiff Handbook. (Illus.). 230p. 1988. 25.95 (*0-85115-485-9*) Howell Bks.

Oliga, J. C. Power, Ideology, & Control. (Contemporary Systems Thinking Ser.). (Illus.). 344p. (C). 1996. 69.50 (*0-306-45160-3*, Plenum Trade) Perseus Pubng.

Oliger, Joseph, jt. ed. see Golub, Gene H.

Oligney, Ronald, jt. auth. see Economides, Michael J.

Oligny, Paul J., tr. see Lekeux, Martial.

Oliker, Ishai, ed. see American Society of Mechanical Engineers Staff.

Oliker, Stacey J. Best Friends & Marriage: Exchange among Women. 1989. 30.00 (*0-520-06392-9*, Pub. by U CA Pr) Cal Prin Full Svc.

Oliker, Vladimir & Treibergs, Andrejs, eds. Geometry & Nonlinear Partial Differential Equations. LC 92-4421. (Contemporary Mathematics Ser.: Vol. 127). 154p. 1992. pap. 36.00 (*0-8218-5135-7*, CONM/127) Am Math.

O'Lill, Ruth & Olcott, Lynn. Songs to Sisters: A Celebration of Being Women. LC 98-20397. 169p. 1999. 9.95 (*0-9659214-1-7*) J Dunn.

O

An Asterisk (*) at the beginning of an entry indicates that the title is appearing for the first time.

Olim, Jason, et al. The CDnow Story: Rags to Riches on the Internet. LC 98-86474. (Illus.). 256p. 1998. pap. 19.95 (0-9661032-6-2) Top Floor Pub.

Olimpio, Sal. Taxpayer, Dragonslayer: The Consumer's Guide to Solving IRS Problems. Donovan, Jim, ed. 280p. 1995. pap. 17.95 (1-880925-06-0) Equitable Media.

Olin, Bernie R., et al. Patient Drug Facts. (C). 59.95 (0-03-268636-6) Lppncott W & W.

Olin, Caroline & Dutton, Bertha P. Southwest Indians Bk. 1: (Navajo, Pima, Apache), Bk. 1. (Illus.). (J). (gr. 5). 1978. pap. 4.95 (0-88388-049-0) Bellerophon Bks.

Olin, George. House in the Sun: A Natural History of the Sonoran Desert. 2nd ed. LC 93-86936. 230p. 1994. pap. 12.95 (1-877856-39-8) SW Pks Mnmts.

— Mammals of the Southwest Desert. rev. ed. Houk, Rose et al, eds. LC 81-86094. (Illus.). 100p. 1982. pap. 5.95 (0-911408-60-6) SW Pks Mnmts.

***Olin, George.** Up Close: A Lifetime of Observing & Photographing Desert Animals. LC 99-50880. (Illus.). 240p. 2000. pap. 19.95 (0-8165-2004-6) U of Ariz Pr.

— Up Close: A Lifetime of Observing & Photographing Desert Animals. LC 99-50880. (Illus.). 240p. 2000. 45.00 (0-8165-2003-8) U of Ariz Pr.

Olin, Harold. Construction: Principles, Materials & Methods. 6th ed. (Building Construction Ser.). 262p. 1995. pap. 29.95 (0-471-29020-3, VNR) Wiley.

Olin, Harold. Construction Im. 6th ed. 1995. text. write for info. (0-471-28575-7) Wiley.

Olin, Harold B. Construction: Principle Matters & Methods. 6th ed. 1994. text 66.95 (0-442-00605-5, VNR) Wiley.

— Construction Principles: Materials & Methods. 6th ed. (Architecture Ser.). 1995. text 86.95 (0-442-02263-8, VNR) Wiley.

— Construction Principles & Material. 6th ed. (Building Construction Ser.). 1995. teacher ed. write for info. (0-442-01575-5, VNR) Wiley.

Olin, Harold B., et al. Construction Methods: Principles, Materials, & Textbook & Student Workbook. 6th ed. 1434p. 1995. 94.95 (0-471-28762-8) Wiley.

— Construction Principles, Materials, & Methods: Principles, Materials & Methods. 6th ed. (Building Construction Ser.). 1172p. 1994. 79.00 (0-471-28416-5, VNR) Wiley.

Olin, Harold B., jt. auth. see Schmidt, John.

Olin, Jacqueline S., jt. ed. see Fitzhugh, William W.

Olin, Jason T. & Keatinge, Carolyn. Rapid Psychological Assessment. LC 97-45506. 336p. 1998. 59.95 (0-471-18181-1) Wiley.

Olin, Jeni. A Valentine to Frank O'Hara. 32p. 1999. pap. 6.95 (0-9658877-4-X) Smokeproof Pr.

Olin, John C. Catholic Reform from Cardinal Ximenes to the Council of Trent, 1495-1563: An Essay with Illustrative Documents & a Brief Study of St. Ignatius Loyola. LC 90-80702. (Illus.). xiii, 152p. 1990. 35.00 (0-8232-1280-7) Fordham.

— Catholic Reform from Cardinal Ximenes to the Council of Trent, 1495-1563: An Essay with Illustrative Documents & a Brief Study of St. Ignatius Loyola. LC 90-80702. (Illus.). xiii, 152p. 1990. pap. 17.50 (0-8232-1281-5) Fordham.

— Erasmus, Utopia & the Jesuits: Essays on the Outreach of Humanism. (Illus.). xi, 125p. 1994. text 25.00 (0-8232-1600-4); pap. text 15.95 (0-8232-1601-2) Fordham.

— Six Essays on Erasmus: And a Translation of Erasmus' Letter to Carondelet, 1523. LC 76-18467. (Illus.). xi, 125p. 1979. pap. 17.50 (0-8232-1024-3) Fordham.

Olin, John C., compiled by. The Catholic Reformation: Savonarola to St. Ignatius Loyola. LC 92-29865. xxiv, 218p. (C). 1993. reprint ed. pap. 17.00 (0-8232-1478-8) Fordham.

Olin, John C., ed. The Autobiography of St. Ignatius of Loyola: With Related Documents. O'Callaghan, Joseph F., tr. from LAT. LC 92-32959. vii, 113p. 1993. pap. 15.00 (0-8232-1480-X) Fordham.

— Christian Humanism & the Reformation: Selected Writings of Erasmus, with His Life by Beatus Rhenanus & a Biographical Sketch by the Editor. 3rd ed. LC 65-10218. (Illus.). x, 202p. 1980. pap. 17.00 (0-8232-1192-4) Fordham.

— Interpreting Thomas More's Utopia. LC 89-80149. (Illus.). xiii, 98p. 1989. 27.50 (0-8232-1233-5) Fordham.

— A Reformation Debate. 129p. 1999. 30.00 (0-8232-1990-9, Pub. by Fordham); pap. 17.50 (0-8232-1991-7, Pub. by Fordham) BookMasters.

Olin, John C., et al, eds. Luther, Erasmus & the Reformation: A Catholic-Protestant Reappraisal. LC 68-8749. 160p. reprint ed. pap. 45.60 (0-7837-0460-7, 2040783) Bks Demand.

— Luther, Erasmus & the Reformation: A Catholic-Protestant Reappraisal. LC 82-15500. 150p. 1982. reprint ed. lib. bdg. 55.00 (0-313-23652-6, OLLE, Greenwood Pr) Greenwood.

Olin, John C., ed. & tr. see Erasmus, Desiderius.

***Olin, Laurie.** Across the Open Field: Essays Drawn from English Landscapes. LC 99-15965. 1999. 42.50 (0-8122-3531-2) U of Pa Pr.

Olin, Laurie. Transforming the Common-Place: Selections from Laurie Olin's Sketchbooks. LC 96-76087. (Illus.). 72p. (Orig.). 1997. 24.95 (1-878271-88-1) Princeton Arch.

Olin, Margaret. Forms of Representation in Alois Riegl's Theory of Art. (Illus.). 272p. 1992. text 48.50 (0-271-00777-X) Pa St U Pr.

***Olin, Meike.** The Standard Guide to Workers Compensation. 4th ed. 192p. 1998. pap. 68.50 (0-923240-25-X) Stndrd Publishing.

Olin Metals Research Laboratory Staff. Corrosion Testing of Welded Copper-Nickel Clad Steel. 49p. 1977. 7.35 (0-317-34504-4, 227) Intl Copper.

— Forming Limit Analysis for Enchanced Fabrication. (INCRA Monographs). 137p. 1983. 30.00 (0-943642-09-4) Intl Copper.

Olin, Oscar E., et al, eds. Centennial History of Akron, Ohio, 1825-1925. (Illus.). 666p. 1997. reprint ed. lib. bdg. 68.50 (0-8328-7150-8) Higginson Bk Co.

Olin, Phillip S. Treasure, the Business & Technology. (Illus.). 188p. (Orig.). 1991. pap. 19.95 (1-880502-00-3) Omicron Grp.

Olin, R. F., jt. auth. see Conway, J. B.

Olin, Spencer C. California's Prodigal Sons: Hiram Johnson & the Progressives, 1911-1917. LC 68-11968. 267p. reprint ed. pap. 82.80 (0-8357-7975-0, 203130900074) Bks Demand.

Olin, Spencer C., jt. auth. see Chan, Sucheng.

Olin, Spencer C., jt. auth. see Nelson, Keith L.

Olin, Stephen. Travels in Egypt, Arabia Petraea & the Holy Land, 2 vols. Davis, Moshe, ed. LC 77-70727. (America & the Holy Land Ser.). 1977. lib. bdg. 81.95 (0-405-10273-9) Ayer.

Olin, Warren G. 300 Years of Joseph Olin & His Descendants, Vol. 1. Powell, A. Joyce Olin, ed. LC 96-68406. (Illus.). 700p. 1996. write for info. (0-9651495-0-1) Type-O-Graphics.

Olinde, Kacoo, jt. ed. see Olinde, Ralph.

Olinde, Ralph & Olinde, Kacoo, eds. Ralph & Kacoo, a Taste of Louisiana. 2nd ed. (Illus.). 348p. 1988. reprint ed. 13.95 (0-9613196-0-7) Cajun Bayou.

Olinder, Bjorn & Pohl, Ingrid. San Giovenale Vol. II, Fasc. 4: The Semi-Subterranean Building in Area B. (Acta Instituti Romani Regni Sueciae, Series in 4 Degrees: Vol. XXVI:II,4). (Illus.). 120p. 1981. pap. 65.00 (91-7042-079-3, Pub. by P Astroms) Coronet Bks.

Oline, Larry. When the Foundations Crumble. LC 98-84445. (Illus.). 128p. 1998. pap. 8.95 (1-883928-31-1) Longwood.

Oliner & Gay. Race, Ethnicity & Gender: A Global Perspective. 406p. (C). 1997. pap. text 50.95 (0-7872-3678-0, 41367801) Kendall-Hunt.

Oliner, Arthur A., ed. see Phased Array Antenna Symposium (1970: Polytechnic.

Oliner, Marion M. Cultivating Freud's Garden in France. LC 87-31908. 332p. 1988. 60.00 (0-87668-995-0) Aronson.

Oliner, Pearl M. & Oliner, Samuel P. Toward a Caring Society: Ideas into Action. LC 95-3339. 256p. 1995. 65.00 (0-275-95198-7, Praeger Pubs) Greenwood.

Oliner, Pearl M. & Smolenska, M. Zuzanna. Embracing the Other: Philosophical, Psychological, & Historical Perspectives on Altruism. 450p. (C). 1995. pap. text 20.00 (0-8147-6190-9) NYU Pr.

***Oliner, Samuel P.** Narrow Escapes: Childhood Memories of the Holocaust & Their Legacy. 2nd rev. ed. 238p. 2000. pap. 14.95 (1-55778-792-1) Paragon Hse.

Oliner, Samuel P. Restless Memories: Recollections of the Holocaust Years. 2nd rev. ed. LC 85-82084. 215p. (Orig.). 1986. pap. 9.95 (0-943376-28-9) Magnes Mus.

— Toward a Caring Society. 1994. 22.95 (0-02-923835-8) S&S Trade.

Oliner, Samuel P., et al, eds. Embracing the Other: Philosophical, Psychological, & Historical Perspectives on Altruism. 450p. (C). 1992. text 55.00 (0-8147-6175-5) NYU Pr.

Oliner, Samuel P. & Lee, Kathleen M. Who Shall Live? The Wilhelm Bachner Story. LC 96-24750. 277p. 1996. 25.00 (0-89733-437-X) Academy Chi Pubs.

Oliner, Samuel P., jt. auth. see Oliner, Pearl M.

Olinescu, Radu, et al. The Body's Battle Against Pollution. LC 97-38186. 226p. 1997. lib. bdg. 65.00 (1-56072-503-6) Nova Sci Pubs.

Olinger, Christine W., jt. auth. see Grant, Elliot.

Olinger, Paula. Images of Transformation in Traditional Hispanic Poetry. 185p. 1985. 16.50 (0-936388-21-8) Juan de la Cuesta.

Olinick, Michael. Intro Math Modl Soc Life. LC 77-77758. (Illus.). 1978. text 38.36 (0-201-05448-5) Addison-Wesley.

***Olinick, Michael.** Introduction to Math Modeling. 2nd ed. 1999. 49.95 (0-12-525570-5) Morgan Kaufmann.

Olinick, Michael, et al. Calculus. 6th ed. (Mathematics Ser.: Vol. 1). 1994. mass mkt., student ed. 26.75 (0-534-93626-1) PWS Pubs.

Olinick, Michael, jt. auth. see Swokowski.

Olinick, Stanley L. The Psychotherapeutic Instrument. LC 80-620. 216p. 1980. 40.00 (0-87668-403-7) Aronson.

Olinka, Sharon. A Face Not My Own. 67p. (Orig.). 1995. pap. 8.95 (0-931122-82-1) West End.

Olins. Corporate Identity. 224p. 1990. 50.00 (0-07-103301-7) McGraw.

Olins, Wally. Corporate Identity: Making Business Strategy Visible Through Design. 224p. (C). 1992. pap. 27.95 (0-87584-368-9) Harvard Busn.

— Corporate Identity: Making Business Strategy Visible Through Design. 224p. 1992. reprint ed. 50.00 (0-87584-250-X) Harvard Busn.

— The New Wolff Olins Guide to Identity: How to Create & Sustain Change Through Managing Identity. 110p. 1996. pap. 33.95 (0-566-07737-X, Pub. by Gower) Ashgate Pub Co.

Olins, Wally, ed. International Corporate Identity, Vol. 1. (Illus.). 192p. 1996. 55.00 (1-85669-067-9, Pub. by Law King Ltd) Trafalgar.

Olinser, Chauncey G., Jr., jt. ed. see Kuhn, James W.

Olinsky, Frank. Buddha Book: A Meeting of Images. LC 97-2165. 96p. 1997. 19.95 (0-8118-1777-6) Chronicle Bks.

Olinto, Angela, et al. Eighteenth Texas Symposium on Relativistic Astrophysics & Cosmology: "Texas in Chicago," December 15-20, 1996. LC 98-16902. 1998. 118.00 (981-02-3487-2) World Scientific Pub.

Olinzock, Anthony A. Microcomputer Activities for the Office. 2nd ed. (KM - Office Procedures Ser.). 1988. mass mkt. 10.50 (0-538-60021-7) S-W Pub.

— Microcomputer Simulations in Business. (KM - Office Procedures Ser.). 1986. pap. 13.95 (0-538-13620-0) S-W Pub.

— Office Procedures: Learning & Instructions. (KU - Office Procedures Ser.). 1983. mass mkt. 23.25 (0-538-24140-3) S-W Pub.

Olinzock, Anthony A. & Lazarony. Advanced Applications for Reinforcement. 1997. pap. 32.95 (0-538-71945-1) Thomson Learn.

— MS Office for Windows 95 & 3.1 & Mac. (Computer Applications Ser.). 1996. pap. 32.95 (0-538-71484-0) Sth-Wstrn College.

Olinzock, Anthony A. & Santos. Wall Street Office Systems. (KM - Office Procedures Ser.). 1989. mass mkt. 10.25 (0-538-11324-3) S-W Pub.

— Wall Street Office Systems, Integrated. (KM - Office Procedures Ser.). 1990. mass mkt., wbk. ed. 6.00 (0-538-11337-5) S-W Pub.

— Wall Street Office Systems, Integrated. (KM - Office Procedures Ser.). 1991. mass mkt., wbk. ed. 6.00 (0-538-11339-1) S-W Pub.

— Wall Street Office Systems, Integrated. (KM - Office Procedures Ser.). 1992. mass mkt., wbk. ed. 6.00 (0-538-11338-3) S-W Pub.

***Olinzock, Anthony A., et al.** Integrated Business Projects. 1999. pap. 20.00 (0-538-72152-9) Thomson Learn.

Oliphant, B. J. Death Served up Cold. (Orig.). 1994. mass mkt. 4.99 (0-449-14896-3, GM) Fawcett.

— Here's to the Newly Dead. 1997. mass mkt. 5.99 (0-449-14992-7, GM) Fawcett.

Oliphant, Betty. Miss O: My Life in Dance. LC 97-100358. (Illus.). 288p. 1996. 22.95 (0-88801-210-1, Pub. by Turnstone Pr) Genl Dist Srvs.

Oliphant, Dale. Oliphants of the Civil War (1861-1865) (Illus.). 120p. 1998. 30.00 (0-8059-4273-4) Dorrance.

Oliphant, Dave. Civilization & Barbarism: A Guide to the Teaching of Latin American Literature. (Latin American Curriculum Units for Junior & Community Colleges Ser.). v, 94p. (Orig.). (C). 1979. pap. text 4.95 (0-86728-002-6) U TX Inst Lat Am Stud.

***Oliphant, Dave.** Memories of Texas Towns & Cities. (Illus.). 286p. 2000. 25.00 (0-924047-18-6); pap. 12.00 (0-924047-19-4) Host Pubns.

Oliphant, Dave. On a High Horse: Views Mostly of Latin American & Texan Poetry. 1983. pap. 9.95 (0-933384-11-4) Prickly Pear.

— Texan Jazz. (Illus.). 480p. (C). 1996. pap. 24.95 (0-292-76045-0); text 50.00 (0-292-76044-2) U of Tex Pr.

Oliphant, Dave, ed. The Bebop Revolution in Words & Music. (Illus.). 227p. 1994. pap. 20.00 (0-87959-131-5) U of Tex H Ransom Ctr.

— The Company They Kept: Alfred A. & Blanche W. Knopf, Publishers: An Exhibition Catalog. LC 97-188718. (Illus.). 276p. 1995. pap. 25.00 (0-87959-135-8) U of Tex H Ransom Ctr.

— Conservation & Preservation of Humanities Research Collections. (Illus.). 166p. 1989. pap. 17.95 (0-87959-109-9) U of Tex H Ransom Ctr.

— Hopkins Lives: An Exhibition & Catalogue. (Illus.). 187p. 1989. 25.00 (0-87959-115-3); pap. 17.95 (0-87959-110-2) U of Tex H Ransom Ctr.

— Perspectives on Australia. (Illus.). 204p. 1988. pap. 18.95 (0-87959-108-0) U of Tex H Ransom Ctr.

***Oliphant, Dave, ed.** Roundup: An Anthology of Texas Poets from 1973 until 1998. (Illus.). 228p. 1999. pap. 15.00 (0-933384-23-8) Prickly Pear.

Oliphant, Dave, ed. The State & Fate of Publishing: A "Flair" Symposium. (Illus.). 1995. pap. 15.00 (0-87959-134-X) U of Tex H Ransom Ctr.

Oliphant, Dave, ed. Gendered Territory: Photographs of Women by Julia Margaret Cameron. (Illus.). 1996. pap. 15.00 (0-87959-136-6) U of Tex H Ransom Ctr.

Oliphant, Dave, et al, eds. New Poetry from a New Spain: The Generation of 1970: A Bilingual Anthology. Sulllivan, Constance et al, trs. from SPA. (Poiesis Ser.: No. 8). (Illus.). 400p. (C). 1993. 15.95 (0-934840-15-6) Studia Hispanica.

Oliphant, Dave, intro. Nahuatl to Rayuela: The Latin American Collection at Texas. (Illus.). 160p. 1992. 15.00 (0-87959-128-5) U of Tex H Ransom Ctr.

— Rossetti to Sexton: Six Women Poets at Texas. (Illus.). 237p. (Orig.). (C). 1992. pap. 20.00 (0-87959-127-7) U of Tex H Ransom Ctr.

***Oliphant, Dave, tr.** Figures of Speech: Poems by Enrique Lihn. (ENG & SPA.). ix, 188p. 2000. pap. 12.00 (0-924047-17-8) Host Pubns.

Oliphant, Dave & Carver, Larry, eds. New Directions in Textual Studies. (Illus.). 185p. 1990. pap. 20.00 (0-87959-111-0) U of Tex H Ransom Ctr.

Oliphant, Dave & Dagel, Gena, eds. Lawrence, Jarry, Zukofsky: A Triptych. (Manuscript Collections at the Harry Ransom Humanities Research Center). (Illus.). 1986. pap. 20.00 (0-87959-106-4) U of Tex H Ransom Ctr.

Oliphant, Dave & Zigal, Thomas, eds. Joyce at Texas. (Illus.). 172p. 1983. pap. 20.00 (0-87959-099-8) U of Tex H Ransom Ctr.

— Perspectives on Music. (Illus.). 235p. 1984. pap. 16.95 (0-87959-102-1) U of Tex H Ransom Ctr.

— WCW & Others. (Illus.). 128p. 1984. pap. 16.95 (0-87959-103-X) U of Tex H Ransom Ctr.

Oliphant, Dave, ed. see Barney, William.

Oliphant, Dave, ed. see Behlen, Charles.

Oliphant, Dave, jt. ed. see Henderson, Cathy.

Oliphant, Dave, ed. see Murphey, Joseph C.

Oliphant, Dave, tr. see Ramos-Garcia, Luis A., ed.

Oliphant, David & Slobody, Lawrence B., eds. The Golden Years: A 12-Step Anti-Aging Plan for a Healthier, Longer, & Happier Life. LC 95-44322. 192p. 1996. 19.95 (0-89789-474-X, Bergin & Garvey) Greenwood.

Oliphant, David, ed. see Lynn, Sandra.

Oliphant, Ernest H. The Plays of Beaumont & Fletcher. LC 73-126657. reprint ed. 37.50 (0-404-04814-5) AMS Pr.

— The Plays of Beaumont & Fletcher: An Attempt to Determine Their Respective Shares & the Shares of Others. (BCL1-PR English Literature Ser.). 553p. 1992. reprint ed. lib. bdg. 99.00 (0-7812-7236-X) Rprt Serv.

— The Plays of Beaumont & Fletcher: An Attempt to Determine Their Respective Shares & the Shares of Others. 1971. reprint ed. 10.00 (0-403-01138-8) Scholarly.

Oliphant, Grant. Webwalkers. LC 96-29213. 1997. 24.00 (0-517-70408-0) Crown Pub Group.

Oliphant, Herman & Hope, Theodore S. A Study of Day Calendars. 1979. 15.95 (0-405-10618-1) Ayer.

Oliphant, J. Orin, ed. see Jackson, William E.

Oliphant, James. Victorian Novelists. LC 02-26320. reprint ed. 29.50 (0-404-04816-1) AMS Pr.

***Oliphant, John.** Peace & War on the Anglo-Cherokee Frontier, 1756-63. 272p. 2000. 39.95 (0-8071-2637-3) La State U Pr.

Oliphant, Ken, jt. auth. see Lunney, Mark.

Oliphant, Laurence. Elgin's Mission to China & Japan, 2 vols. (Oxford in Asia Historical Reprints Ser.). 1970. 22.25 (0-19-641004-5) OUP.

— Journey to Katmandu, Capital of Nepaul, with the Camp of Jung Bahadoor Including a Sketch of the Nepaulese Ambassador at Home. (C). 1994. reprint ed. 18.00 (81-206-0941-7, Pub. by Asian Educ Servs) S Asia.

— Russian Shores of the Black Sea: In the Autumn of 1852 with a Voyage Down the Volga, & a Tour Through the Country of the Don Cossacks. LC 75-115571. (Russia Observed, Series I). 1970. reprint ed. 19.95 (0-405-03054-1) Ayer.

Oliphant, Lawrence. Russian Shores of the Black Sea. (Cloth Bound Pocket Ser.). 1998. 7.95 (3-8290-0894-5, 520654) Konemann.

Oliphant, M. Jerusalem, the Holy City. 600p. 1985. 365.00 (1-85077-083-2) St Mut.

Oliphant, Margaret. Miss Marjoribanks. LC 99-461808. 1999. pap. 12.95 (0-14-043630-8, PuffinBks) Peng Put Young Read.

Oliphant, Margaret & Gray, Margaret K. Selected Short Stories of the Supernatural. LC 86-147476. (Association for Literary Studies). 256 p. 1985. write for info. (0-7073-0478-4) Scottish Acdmc.

Oliphant, Margaret O. Annals of a Publishing House: William Blackwood & His Son, Their Magazine & Friends, 3 vols. LC 70-148282. reprint ed. 205.00 (0-404-07730-7) AMS Pr.

— The Autobiography of Mrs. Oliphant. xxiv, 162p. 1994. pap. 9.95 (0-226-62651-2) U Ch Pr.

— Beleaguered City. LC 79-98862. 267p. 1970. reprint ed. lib. bdg. 55.00 (0-8371-3137-5, OLBC, Greenwood Pr) Greenwood.

— A Beleaguered City. (BCL1-PR English Literature Ser.). 267p. 1992. reprint ed. lib. bdg. 79.00 (0-7812-7610-1) Rprt Serv.

— The Earliest Civilizations. (Illustrated History of the World Ser.). (Illus.). 80p. (J). (gr. 2-6). 1993. 19.95 (0-8160-2785-4) Facts on File.

— The Greatest Heiress in England, 3 vols., 2 bks., Set. LC 79-8184. reprint ed. 84.50 (0-404-62082-5) AMS Pr.

— Literary History of England in the End of the Eighteenth & Beginning of the Nineteenth Century, 3 vols. LC 76-121021. reprint ed. 45.00 (0-404-04830-7) AMS Pr.

— Makers of Venice: Doges, Conquerors, Painters & Men of Letters. LC 77-173089. (Illus.). reprint ed. 39.50 (0-404-04815-3) AMS Pr.

— Memoir of the Life of Laurence Oliphant & of Alice Oliphant, His Wife. LC 75-36915. (Occult Ser.). 1976. reprint ed. 35.95 (0-405-07970-2) Ayer.

— The Minister's Wife, 3 vols., 2 bks., Set. LC 79-8185. reprint ed. 84.50 (0-404-62098-1) AMS Pr.

— Stories of the Seen & the Unseen. LC 72-113682. (Short Story Index Reprint Ser.). 1977. 36.95 (0-8369-3411-3) Ayer.

— Stories of the Seen & the Unseen. 316p. 1971. reprint ed. spiral bd. 19.00 (0-7873-0643-6) Hlth Research.

Oliphant, Pat. Are We There Yet? An Oliphant Collection, 1 vol. 160p. 1999. pap. 12.95 (0-7407-0211-4) Andrews & McMeel.

— But Seriously, Folks! (Illus.). 160p. (Orig.). 1983. pap. 6.95 (0-8362-1199-5) Andrews & McMeel.

— Fashions for the New World Order. (Illus.). 160p. (Orig.). 1991. pap. 9.95 (0-8362-1879-5) Andrews & McMeel.

***Oliphant, Pat.** Now We're Going to Have to Spray for Politicians. 160p. 2000. pap. 12.95 (0-7407-0614-4) Andrews & McMeel.

Oliphant, Pat. So That's Where They Came From! An Oliphant Collection. LC 97-51785. (Illus.). 160p. (Orig.). 1997. pap. 10.95 (0-8362-3687-4) Andrews & McMeel.

Oliphant, Pat & Katz, Harry. Oliphant's Anthem: Pat Oliphant at the Library of Congress. Day, Sara, ed. LC 97-51785. (Illus.). 130p. 1998. pap. 24.95 (0-8362-5898-3) Andrews & McMeel.

Oliphant, Patrick. Ban This Book! LC 82-72414. (Illus.). 160p. 1982. pap. 6.95 (0-8362-1251-7) Andrews & McMeel.

— Between Rock & a Hard Place. (Illus.). 160p. (Orig.). 1986. pap. 8.95 (0-8362-2084-6) Andrews & McMeel.

— Just Say No! More Cartoons by Pat Oliphant. (Illus.). 160p. (Orig.). 1992. pap. 9.95 (0-8362-1700-4) Andrews & McMeel.

— Make My Day. (Illus.). 160p. 1992. pap. 8.95 (0-8362-2072-2) Andrews & McMeel.

O

An Asterisk (*) at the beginning of an entry indicates that the title is appearing for the first time.

— Nothing Basically Wrong. (Illus.). 160p. (Orig.). 1988. pap. 8.95 (*0-8362-1833-7*) Andrews & McMeel.
— Off to the Revolution. (Illus.). 160p. 1995. pap. 9.95 (*0-8362-0429-8*) Andrews & McMeel.
— Oliphant: The New World Order in Drawing & Sculpture, 1983-1993. LC 94-2147. (Illus.). 96p. 1994. pap. 12.95 (*0-8362-1755-1*) Andrews & McMeel.
— Oliphant's Presidents: Twenty-Five Years of Caricature. (Illus.). 96p. (Orig.). 1990. pap. 12.95 (*0-8362-1813-2*) Andrews & McMeel.
— Reaffirm the Status Quo! (Illus.). 160p. (Orig.). 1996. pap. 10.95 (*0-8362-2135-4*) Andrews & McMeel.
— Up to There in Alligators. (Illus.). 160p. (Orig.). 1987. pap. 8.95 (*0-8362-2095-1*) Andrews & McMeel.
— Waiting for the Other Shoe to Drop. LC 94-77996. (Illus.). 160p. 1994. pap. 9.95 (*0-8362-1765-9*) Andrews & McMeel.
— What Those People Need Is a Puppy! More Cartoons by Pat Oliphant. (Illus.). 160p. (Orig.). 1989. pap. 8.95 (*0-8362-1857-4*) Andrews & McMeel.
— Why Do I Feel Uneasy? (Illus.). 160p. (Orig.). 1993. pap. 9.95 (*0-8362-1719-5*) Andrews & McMeel.
— The Year of Living Perilously. (Illus.). 160p. 1992. pap. 6.95 (*0-8362-2056-0*) Andrews & McMeel.
Oliphant, Robert, ed. see Younger, Irving.
Oliphant, Susan, ed. see Frederickson, Jeanette A. & Holton, Court C.
Oliphant, Zan. Programming Netscape Plug-Ins. LC 96-67543. 448p. 1996. 39.99 (*1-57521-098-3*) Sams.
Olis, Colleen, jt. auth. see Gerstl, Lorraine.
Olishey, O., jt. auth. see Tenzin, T.
Olishifski, Julian B., ed. see National Safety Council Staff.
Olislagers, Robert P. Fields of Flying in the Southwest: A History of Airports. Parks, Lori, ed. LC 97-143902. (Illus.). 250p. 1997. 39.95 (*1-886483-04-3*) Heritge Media.
Olito, Michael. Atli's Tale. 193p. pap. 14.95 (*0-88801-204-7*, Pub. by Turnstone Pr) Genl Dist Srvs.
Olito, Michael & Smith, Doug. The Best Possible Face: L. B. Foote's Winnipeg. 1997. pap. 10.95 (*0-88801-097-4*, Pub. by Turnstone Pr) Genl Dist Srvs.
Olitsky, Matis, jt. auth. see Mlotek, Joseph.
Olitt, Arnold, jt. auth. see Gladden, Scott C.
Olitzki, A. Enteric Fevers: Causing Organisims & Host's Reactions. Grumbach, A., ed. (Bibliotheca Microbiologica Ser.: Vol. 10). 1971. pap. 126.25 (*3-8055-1237-6*) S Karger.
— Immunological Methods in Brucellosis Research: Procedures, Pt. 2. (Bibliotheca Microbiologica Ser.: Vol 9) 1970. pap. 92.25 (*3-8055-0149-8*) S Karger.
***Olitzky, Kerry.** From Your Father's House: Reflections for Modern Jewish Men. LC 98-54863. 160p. 1999. pap. 9.95 (*0-8276-0666-4*) JPS Phila.
Olitzky, Kerry M. The American Synagogue: A Historical Dictionary & Sourcebook. LC 95-49681. 432p. 1996. lib. bdg. 105.00 (*0-313-28856-9*, Greenwood Pr) Greenwood.
— Eight Nights, Eight Lights. (Illus.). 64p. (Orig.). (C). 1994. pap. 8.95 (*1-881283-09-7*) Alef Design.
— Grief in Our Seasons: A Mourner's Kaddish Companion. LC 97-35986. 448p. 1998. pap. 15.95 (*1-879045-55-9*) Jewish Lights.
***Olitzky, Kerry M.** Jewish Paths toward Healing & Wholeness: A Personal Guide to Dealing with Suffering. 192p. 2000. pap. 15.95 (*1-58023-068-7*) Jewish Lights.
Olitzky, Kerry M. The Jewish Wedding Ceremony. LC 96-16437. 1996. 2.00 (*0-88125-557-2*) Ktav.
— One Hundred Blessings Every Day: Daily Twelve Step Recovery Affirmations, Exercises for Personal Growth & Renewal Reflecting Seasons of the Jewish Year. LC 93-9090. 432p. (Orig.). 1993. pap. 14.95 (*1-879045-30-3*) Jewish Lights.
— Recovery from Codependence: A Jewish Twelve Steps Guide to Healing Your Soul. LC 93-20051. (Illus.). 160p. (Orig.). 1993. 21.95 (*1-879045-27-3*); pap. 13.95 (*1-879045-32-X*) Jewish Lights.
Olitzky, Kerry M., ed. In Celebration: An American Jewish Perspective on the Bicentennial of the United States Constitution. LC 88-27867. 142p. (Orig.). (C). 1989. pap. text 19.50 (*0-8191-7222-7*); lib. bdg. 41.00 (*0-8191-7221-9*) U Pr of Amer.
— Interfaith Ministry to the Aged: A Survey of Models, A Special Issue of Journal of Aging & Judaism. 58p. 1988. pap. 14.95 (*0-89885-432-6*, Kluwer Acad Hman Sci) Kluwer Academic.
Olitzky, Kerry M., et al, eds. Reform Judaism in America: A Biographical Dictionary & Sourcebook. LC 92-25794. (Jewish Denominations in America Ser.). 384p. 1993. lib. bdg. 85.00 (*0-313-24628-9*, SUJ, Greenwood Pr) Greenwood.
***Olitzky, Kerry M. & Forman, Lori.** Restful Reflections: Nighttime Inspiration to Calm the Soul, Dased on Jewish Wisdom. 2000. pap. 15.95 (*1-58023-091-1*) Jewish Lights.
Olitzky, Kerry M. & Forman, Lori. Sacred Intentions: Daily Inspiration to Strengthen the Spirit, Based on Jewish Wisdom. LC 99-36862. 448p. 1999. pap. 15.95 (*1-58023-061-X*) Jewish Lights.
Olitzky, Kerry M. & Isaacs, Ronald H. A Glossary of Jewish Life. LC 91-12399. 264p. 1992. 40.00 (*0-87668-547-5*) Aronson.
— A Glossary of Jewish Life. LC 91-12399. (Illus.). 264p. 1997. pap. 30.00 (*1-56821-965-2*) Aronson.
— The How-to-Handbook for Jewish Living. LC 93-14594. 1993. pap. 12.95 (*0-88125-290-5*) Ktav.
***Olitzky, Kerry M. & Isaacs, Ronald H.** I Believe: The Thirteen Principles of Faith: A Confirmation Textbook. LC 99-29439. 1999. 12.95 (*0-88125-627-7*) Ktav.
Olitzky, Kerry M. & Isaacs, Ronald H. Rediscovering Judaism: Bar & Bat Mitzvah for Adults. LC 97-24081. xviii, 397p. 1997. 25.00 (*0-88125-566-1*) Ktav.
— Sacred Celebrations: A Jewish Holiday Handbook. LC 94-1391. 1994. 19.95 (*0-88125-484-3*); pap. 12.95 (*0-88125-496-7*) Ktav.
— The Second How-to Handbook for Jewish Living. LC 95-46769. 216p. 1996. 24.95 (*0-88125-534-3*); pap. 13.95 (*0-88125-550-5*) Ktav.
— The Second How-To Handbook for Jewish Living. LC 95-46769. 216p. 1996. 24.95 (*0-88125-539-4*) Ktav.
Olitzky, Kerry M. & Isaacs, Ronald H., eds. Critical Documents of Jewish History: A Sourcebook. LC 94-44933. 392p. 1995. 40.00 (*1-56821-392-1*) Aronson.
***Olitzky, Kerry M. & Kravitz, Leonard S., eds.** Shemonah Perakim: A Treatise on the Soul. 160p. 2000. pap. 12.95 (*0-8074-0704-6*, 160508) UAHC.
***Olitzky, Kerry M. & Raphael, Marc Lee.** An Encyclopedia of American Synagogue Ritual. LC 99-54418. 184p. 2000. lib. bdg. 75.00 (*0-313-30814-4*, Greenwood Pr) Greenwood.
Olitzky, Kerry M. & Z., Aaron. Renewed Each Day Vol. 2: Daily Twelve Step Recovery Meditations Based on the Bible. LC 92-8517. Vol. 2. (Illus.). 280p. 1992. pap. 14.95 (*1-879045-13-3*) Jewish Lights.
Olitzky, Kerry M., et al. Renewed Each Day Vol. 1: Daily Twelve Step Recovery Meditations Based on the Bible. LC 92-8517. Vol. 1. (Illus.). 224p. 1992. pap. 14.95 (*1-879045-12-5*) Jewish Lights.
— Twelve Jewish Steps to Recovery: A Personal Guide to Turning from Alcoholism & Other Addictions--Drugs, Food, Gambling, Sex... LC 91-25346. (Illus.). 144p. 1992. pap. 13.95 (*1-879045-09-5*) Jewish Lights.
— When Your Jewish Child Asks Why: Answers for Tough Questions. LC 92-37176. 1992. 19.95 (*0-88125-452-5*); pap. 12.95 (*0-88125-451-7*) Ktav.
Olitzky, Kerry M., jt. auth. see Kasakove, David P.
Olitzky, Kerry M., jt. auth. see Kushner, Lawrence S.
Olitzky, Kerry M., jt. auth. see Ochs, Carol.
Olitzky, Kerry M., jt. auth. see Patz, Naomi.
Olitzky, Kerry M., jt. ed. see Isaacs, Ronald H.
Olitzky, Kerry M., jt. ed. see Kravitz, Leonard S.
Olitzky, Kerry M., jt. ed. see Kravitz, Leonard.
Oliu, Walter E. Writing That Works. 6th ed. LC 97-65193. 662p. 1997. pap. text 50.95 (*0-312-15391-0*) St Martin.
— Writing That Works. 6th ed. 1998. pap. text 5.00 (*0-312-15390-2*) St Martin.
Oliu, Walter E., et al. Writing that Works. 5th ed. 1995. pap. text, teacher ed. 35.00 (*0-312-10378-6*) St Martin.
— Writing That Works. 7th ed. 2000. pap. text. write for info. (*0-312-25629-9*) St Martin.
Oliva. Supervision Today. 5th ed. 656p. 1997. 74.95 (*0-471-36488-6*) Wiley.
***Oliva, Achille Bonito.** Pignatelli. 2000. pap. 29.95 (*88-8158-252-X*) Charta.
— Viaggiatori Senza Bagaglio: Travelers Without Baggage. (ITA & ENG.). 2000. pap. 35.00 (*88-8158-224-4*) Charta.
Oliva, Bonita M., jt. auth. see Oliva, Leo E.
Oliva, Cesar, ed. see Del Valle-Inclan, Ramon.
Oliva, Jorge E. Snake & Wings. 40p. (J). (gr. 1-6). 1990. pap. 5.00 (*0-9629756-0-5*) Wings Bks.
Oliva, Juan, contrib. by. A Portolan Atlas of the Mediterranean Sea & Western European Waters, with a World Map. LC 87-675334. 12p. 1987. 15.95 (*0-8444-0572-8*) Lib Congress.
Oliva, Judy L. David Hare: Theatricalizing Politics. LC 89-27751. (Theatre & Dramatic Studies: No. 66). 216p. (C). reprint ed. 67.00 (*0-8357-2048-9*, 207074700004) Bks Demand.
— New Theatre Vistas: Modern Movements in International Theatre. King, Kimball, ed. LC 95-30422. (Studies in Modern Drama: Vol. 7). 234p. 1995. text 46.00 (*0-8153-1670-4*, H1840) Garland.
Oliva, Lawrence. Partners, Not Competitors: The Age of Teamwork & Technology. LC 90-82962. 256p. (C). 1992. pap. text 32.95 (*1-878289-09-8*) Idea Group Pub.
***Oliva, Leo E.** Fort Dodge. LC 98-86546. (Kansas Forts Ser.). x, 115 p. 1998. write for info. (*0-87726-049-4*) Kansas St Hist.
Oliva, Leo E. Fort Hays, Frontier Army Post, 1865 1889. LC 80-82227. (Illus.). 66p. 1980. pap. 3.50 (*0-87726-020-6*) Kansas St Hist.
— Fort Larned on the Santa Fe Trail. LC 82-80495. (Illus.). 84p. 1982. pap. 3.50 (*0-87726-024-9*) Kansas St Hist.
— Fort Scott on the Indian Frontier. LC 84-81183. (Illus.). 78p. 1984. pap. 3.50 (*0-87726-027-3*) Kansas St Hist.
***Oliva, Leo E.** Fort Wallace: Sentinel on the Smoky Hill Trail. LC 97-81105. (Kansas Forts Ser.). xi, 132 p. 1998. write for info. (*0-87726-048-6*) Kansas St Hist.
Oliva, Leo E. Woodston: The Story of a Kansas Country Town. (Illus.). viii, 237p. (Orig.). 1985. pap. 15.00 (*0-685-66152-0*) Western Bks.
Oliva, Leo E., ed. Adventure on the Santa Fe Trail. LC 88-50922. (Illus.). 127p. 1988. pap. 7.95 (*0-87726-033-8*) Kansas St Hist.
Oliva, Leo E. & Oliva, Bonita M. Santa Fe Trail Trivia. 2nd ed. iv, 56p. (Orig.). 1987. pap. 1.95 (*0-685-66153-9*) Western Bks.
— Santa Fe Trail Trivia. 3rd ed. viii, 68p. (Orig.). 1989. pap. 2.95 (*0-938463-04-7*) Western Bks.
Oliva, Marilyn. The Convent & the Community in Late Medieval England: Female Monasteries in the Diocese of Norwich, 1350-1540. LC 97-28874. (Studies Hist Med Religion: Vol. 12). 288p. 1998. 90.00 (*0-85115-576-6*, Boydell Pr) Boydell & Brewer.
Oliva, Max. Free to Pray, Free to Love. 1994. pap. 39.00 (*1-85390-275-6*, Pub. by Veritas Pubns) St Mut.
— The Masculine Spirit: Resources for Reflective Living. LC 97-20164. 160p. 1997. pap. 8.95 (*0-87793-630-7*) Ave Maria.
— Praying the Beatitudes: A Retreat on the Sermon on the Mount. 126p. 1989. pap. 30.00 (*1-85390-039-7*, Pub. by Veritas Pubns) St Mut.
Oliva, Peter F. Developing Curriculum. 4th ed. LC 96-9233. 608p. (C). 1997. 87.00 (*0-673-52455-8*) Addson-Wesley Educ.
Oliva, Peter F. & Pawlas, George E. Supervision for Today's Schools. 5th ed. LC 96-6458. (C). 1997. text 61.88 (*0-8013-1650-2*) Longman.
***Oliva, Peter F. & Pawlas, George E.** Supervision for Today's Schools. 6th ed. 672p. (C). 2001. write for info. (*0-471-36435-5*) Wiley.
Oliva, Peter R. Developing the Curriculum. (C). 1982. text 24.95 (*0-316-64995-3*) Little.
Oliva-Rasbich, Jean. Viva la Mediterranean: A Cultural Feast from Healthmark. LC 95-151189. 1994. 21.95 (*0-9624784-2-3*) HealthMark.
Oliva, S. & Buxton, A. Catalan-English Dictionary. (CAT & SPA.). 842p. 1989. 50.00 (*84-85194-39-X*) IBD Ltd.
— English Catalan Dictionary: Bilingual General Dictionary. 2nd rev. ed. (CAT & ENG.). 1107p. 1989. 69.95 (*0-685-52395-0*, S39887) Fr & Eur.
Olivares, Cecilia, tr. see Hildton, Nette.
Olivares, Julian. Cuentos Hispanos de los Estados Unidos. (SPA.). 1993. 20.10 (*0-606-01319-9*, Pub. by Turtleback) Demco.
— Tomas Rivera Complete Works. 447p. 1995. 38.95 (*1-55885-153-4*) Arte Publico.
Olivares, Julian, ed. Cuentos Hispanos de los Estados Unidos. 2nd ed. (SPA.). 228p. 1998. pap. 16.95 (*1-55885-260-3*) Arte Publico.
— Decade II: A Twentieth Anniversary Anthology. LC 92-35458. 256p. (Orig.). 1993. pap. 12.00 (*1-55885-062-7*) Arte Publico.
Olivares, Julian, ed. see Rivera, Tomas.
Olivares, Rafael A. NTC's Dictionary of Latin American Spanish. (ENG & SPA.). 384p. 1999. pap. 17.95 (*0-8442-7964-1*, 79641) NTC Contemp Pub Co.
— Using the Newspaper to Teach ESL Learners. LC 93-988. 104p. 1993. pap. 11.95 (*0-87207-237-1*) Intl Reading.
Olivarez, Anna, ed. Uncle Nacho's Hat Read-Along. (ENG & SPA.). (YA). (gr. 1 up). 1990. 25.95 incl. audio (*0-89239-061-1*) Childrens Book Pr.
Olivarez, Anna, ed. The Adventures of Connie & Diego/Las a Venturasde Connie y Diego. (Tales of the Americas Ser.). (ENG & SPA.). (YA). (gr. 1 up). 9.95 incl. audio (*0-89239-051-4*) Childrens Book Pr.
Olivarez, Anna, ed. see Anchondo, Mary.
Olivarez, Anna, ed. see Roehmer, Harriet.
Olivarez, Lori J. Reflections of You. LC 97-91172. 1998. pap. 10.95 (*0-533-12588-X*) Vantage.
Olivari, Mariolina. Giovanni Bellini. Brierley, Anthony, tr. from ITA. (Library of Great Masters). (Illus.). 80p. (Orig.). 1990. pap. 14.99 (*1-878351-09-5*) Riverside NY.
— Giovanni Bellini. (Grandes Maestros del Arte Ser.). (SPA., Illus.). 80p. (Orig.). 1993. pap. 12.99 (*1-878351-32-X*) Riverside NY.
Olivart, Jose-Maria A. Diccionari de Noms de Persona. 6th ed. (CAT.). 368p. 1991. 39.95 (*0-7859-5877-0*, 8429715738) Fr & Eur.
Olivas, Michael A. The Law & Higher Education: Cases & Materials on Colleges in Court. 1056p. 1993. suppl. ed. 14.95 (*0-89089-009-9*) Carolina Acad Pr.
— The Law & Higher Education: Cases & Materials on Colleges in Court. 2nd ed. LC 96-47275. 1176p. 1997. boxed set 80.00 (*0-89089-866-9*) Carolina Acad Pr.
Olivas, Michael A., ed. Latino College Students. LC 86-5697. (Bilingual Education Ser.). 384p. reprint ed. pap. 119.10 (*0-608-08642-8*, 206916500003) Bks Demand.
***Olivastri, Valentina, ed.** Sicily. (World Bibliographical Ser.: Vol. 213). 220p. 1999. lib. bdg. 63.00 (*1-85109-291-9*) ABC-CLIO.
Olive. Diagnostic Imaging in Gynecology. 1998. text. write for info. (*0-7216-5890-3*, W B Saunders Co) Harcrt Hlth Sci Grp.
Olive, A., et al, eds. Advanced Information Systems Engineering: 9th International Conference, CAISE/97, Barcelona, Catalonia, Spain, June 16-20, 1997, Proceedings. LC 97-14854. (Lecture Notes in Computer Science Ser.: No. 1250). xi, 451p. 1997. pap. 76.00 (*3-540-63107-0*) Spr-Verlag.
Olive, Barbara. Time to Say Goodbye: Your Guide to Empowerment During Life-Threatening Illness, Aging & Life's Final Passages. LC 98-67916. (Illus.). 192p. 1998. pap. 14.95 (*0-9667269-0-1*) Lemieux Intl Ltd.
Olive, D. & West, P., eds. Duality & Supersymmetric Theories. LC 99-18753. (Publications of the Newton Institute: No. 13). (Illus.). 450p. (C). 1999. text 69.95 (*0-521-64158-6*) Cambridge U Pr.
Olive, D., jt. ed. see Goddard, P.
Olive, David. Business Babble: A Cynic's Dictionary of Corporate Jargon. LC 91-9209. (Illus.). 192p. 1991. 14.95 (*0-471-54789-1*) Wiley.
— More Political Babble: The Dumbest Things Politicians Ever Said. LC 95-37784. 244p. 1996. 16.95 (*0-471-13548-8*) Wiley.
Olive, David L., et al. Novak's Gynecology Self-Assessment & Review: Study Guide for Novak's Gynecology. LC 97-50305. 369p. 1997. 32.00 (*0-683-00589-8*) Lppncott W & W.
Olive, David L., jt. ed. see Blackwell, Richard E.
Olive, Diane. Think Before You Eat: Smarter Food Choices for You & Your Family. 224p. 1996. pap. text 16.95 (*1-888824-01-8*) Bridgeport Bks.
Olive, G., et al, eds. International Colloquium of Developmental Pharmacology, 4th, Paris, May 1983. (Journal: Developmental Pharmacology & Therapeutics: Vol. 7, Suppl. 1). (Illus.). viii, 224p. 1984. pap. 61.00 (*3-8055-3997-5*) S Karger.
Olive, J. Fred. The Educational Technology Profession: A Bibliographic Overview of a Profession in Search of Itself; a Selected Bibliography. LC 94-27747. (Educational Technology Selected Bibliography Ser.: Vol. 12). 1995. pap. 24.95 (*0-87778-277-6*) Educ Tech Pubns.
Olive, J. P., et al. Acoustics of American English Speech: A Dynamic Approach. LC 92-44839. 408p. 1995. 59.95 (*0-387-97984-0*) Spr-Verlag.
Olive, Jenny. Maths - A Students' Survival Guide: A Self-Help Workbook for Science & Engineering Students. LC 97-28653. (Illus.). 584p. (C). 1998. text, student ed., wbk. ed. 74.95 (*0-521-57306-8*); pap. text, student ed., wbk. ed. 29.95 (*0-521-57586-9*) Cambridge U Pr.
Olive, John. Killers. 1990. pap. 5.25 (*0-8222-0612-9*) Dramatists Play.
— Minnesota Moon. 48p. (Orig.). 1990. 5.95 (*0-317-91359-X*) Playsmith.
— Standing on My Knees. 1983. pap. 5.25 (*0-8222-1071-1*) Dramatists Play.
Olive, John H. & Smith, Kenneth R. Benthic Macroinvertebrates as Indexes of Water Quality in the Scioto River Basin, Ohio. 1975. pap. text 10.00 (*0-86727-077-2*) Ohio Bio Survey.
Olive, Martin, et al, eds. Forging the Valley. 144p. 1997. 24.50 (*1-85075-647-3*, Pub. by Sheffield Acad) CUP Services.
Olive, Martin-Maria. Praxedes: Wife, Mother, Widow, & Lay Dominican. LC 87-50548. 203p. 1992. pap. 12.00 (*0-89555-309-0*) TAN Bks Pubs.
Olive Natural Heritage Society Staff, jt. auth. see Bierhorst, John.
Olive, Noel, ed. Karijini Mirlimirli: Aboriginal Histories from the Pilbara. 256p. 1997. pap. 19.95 (*1-86368-204-X*, Pub. by Fremantle Arts) Intl Spec Bk.
***Olive, Phyllis Carol.** The Lost Lands of the Book of Mormon. LC 94-98119. (Illus.). 348p. 2000. pap. write for info. (*0-9678223-0-0*) P C Olive.
Olive, S., ed. see Shutov, F. A.
Olive, Terence A., jt. ed. see Fenner, William R.
Olive, Teresa. Kind Samaritan: Luke 10:25-37. LC 97-156346. (Arch Bks.). 24p. 1995. pap. 1.99 (*0-570-07502-5*, 59-1475) Concordia.
— Life after TV: Slaying the One-Eyed Monster. (Contemporary Christian Living Ser.). 51p. (Orig.). 1992. pap. 1.99 (*0-87509-470-8*) Chr Pubns.
— Three Men in the Fiery Furnace: Daniel 3:1-30. (Arch Bks.). (Illus.). 24p. (J). (ps-3). 1994. pap. 1.99 (*0-570-09043-1*, 59-1466) Concordia.
Olive, William J., jt. ed. see Kirby, Thomas A.
Oliveira, AnaBela, jt. auth. see Gordon, Timothy E.
***Oliveira, Arantes E., et al, eds.** Computational Methods in Engineering & Science. 1450p. 1999. 266.50 (*0-08-043570-X*) Elsevier.
Oliveira, Armando, ed. Hypermedia Courseware: Structures of Communication & Intelligent Help. LC 92-35693. x, 241p. 1992. 84.00 (*0-387-55810-1*) Spr-Verlag.
Oliveira, Claire De, see De Oliveira, Claire.
Oliveira, David. Storytelling. 12p. (Orig.). 1993. pap. 5.00 (*0-9638843-0-1*) Mille Grazie.
Oliveira, David B. Immunological Aspects of Renal Disease. (Reviews in Clinical Immunology Ser.: No. 2). 239p. (C). 1992. text 74.95 (*0-521-40174-7*) Cambridge U Pr.
Oliveira, Emanuelle, tr. see De Jesus, Carolina M.
Oliveira, Evandro De, see Sekhar, Laligam N. & De Oliveira, Evandro.
Oliveira, F., jt. ed. see Ferraz, A.
Oliveira, F. A. De, see De Araujo, C. B. & De Oliveira, F. A.
Oliveira, Fernanda A. R. & Oliveira, Jorge C. Processing Foods: Quality Optimization & Process Assessment. LC 98-46086. (Food Engineering & Manufacturing Ser.). 1999. 99.95 (*0-8493-7905-9*) CRC Pr.
Oliveira, Fernanda A. R., jt. ed. see Singh, R. Paul.
***Oliveira, Jacquelyn Frances.** The Case for Life Beyond Death. Roerden, Chris, ed. 240p. 1999. write for info. (*0-9674041-0-X*) Laughton Pubs.
Oliveira, Joanyr F. De, see De Oliveira, Joanyr F.
Oliveira, Jocy De, see De Oliveira, Jocy.
Oliveira, Jorge C., jt. auth. see Oliveira, Fernanda A. R.
Oliveira, Jose A. De, see De Oliveira, Jose A.
Oliveira, Joseph G. De, see De Oliveira, Joseph G.
Oliveira, Jura. Living Portuguese: Conversational Manual. rev. ed. (Complete Living Language Course Ser.). (ENG & POR.). 1993. pap. 6.00 (*0-517-59035-2*) Liv Lang.
— Living Portuguese: Dictionary. (Complete Living Language Course Ser.). (ENG & POR.). 1993. pap. 5.00 (*0-517-59036-0*) Liv Lang.
Oliveira, Karla, jt. auth. see Gardener, Christopher.
Oliveira Lima, Manuel De, see De Oliveira Lima, Manuel.
Oliveira, Marcelo F., jt. auth. see Branemark, Per-Ingvar.
Oliveira, Marques A. A History of Portugal, Vol. 1. 1972. text 67.00 (*0-231-03159-9*) Col U Pr.
Oliveira, Marta K. & Valsiner, Jane. Literacy in Human Development. LC 97-35105. 1998. 73.25 (*1-56750-366-7*); pap. 39.50 (*1-56750-367-5*) Ablx Pub.
Oliveira, Miguel D. De, see De Oliveira, Miguel D., ed.
Oliveira, Nicholas De, see De Oliveira, Nicholas.
Oliveira, Nicolas De, see De Oliveira, Nicolas.
Oliveira, Nuno. Reflections on Equestrian Art. 130p. 1990. 22.95 (*0-85131-461-9*, Pub. by J A Allen) Trafalgar.
Oliveira, Plinio C. de, see De Oliveira, Plinio C.
Oliveira, Plinio Correa de, see Correa de Oliveira, Plinio.
Oliveira Setubal, Paulo De, see De Oliveira Setubal, Paulo.
Oliveira-Smith, Pamela J. De, see De Oliveira-Smith, Pamela J.
Oliveira, Solange R. De, see McGuirk, Bernard & De Oliveira, Solange R., eds.

O

Oliveira, Tony & Hedman, Ray. Blood of Heroes: The Superhero-and the Villain-Roleplaying Game. Hedman, June, ed. (Illus.). 350p. 1998. pap. 25.00 (*0-9665280-0-X*, PUL1158.2500) Pulsar Games.

Oliveira, Tony, jt. auth. see Marquart, Josh.

Olivella, J. & Brebbia, Carlos A., eds. Maritime Engineering & Ports II. (Water Studies). 350p. 2000. 173.00 (*1-85312-829-5*, 8295, Pub. by WIT Pr) Computational Mech MA.

Olivella, Manuel Z. Chambacu: Black Slum. Tittler, Jonathan, tr. from SPA. LC 89-12406. (Discoveries Ser.). 128p. 1989. pap. 12.95 (*0-935480-39-0*) Lat Am Lit Rev Pr.

Olivelle, Patrick. The Asrama System: The History & Hermeneutics of a Religious Institution. LC 92-38998. 288p. (C). 1993. text 65.00 (*0-19-508327-X*) OUP.

— The Dharmasutras: The Law Codes of Ancient India. (Oxford World's Classics Ser.). 480p. 1999. pap. 12.95 (*0-19-283882-2*) OUP.

— Rule & Regulations of Brahmanical Asceticism. LC 94-36124. (SUNY Series in Religious Studies). 458p. (C). 1994. pap. text 18.95 (*0-7914-2284-4*) State U NY Pr.

— Rule & Regulations of Brahmanical Asceticism. LC 94-36124. (SUNY Series in Religious Studies). 458p. (C). 1994. text 57.50 (*0-7914-2283-6*) State U NY Pr.

— The Samnyasa Upanisads: Hindu Scriptures on Asceticism & Renunciation. 336p. (C). 1992. pap. text 25.95 (*0-19-507045-3*) OUP.

— Upanisads. (Oxford World's Classics Ser.). (Illus.). 506p. 1998. pap. 6.95 (*0-19-283576-9*) OUP.

Olivelle, Patrick, ed. The Early Upanisads: Annotated Text & Translation. LC 98-17677. (South Asia Research Ser.). (Illus.). 704p. 1998. text 65.00 (*0-19-512435-9*) OUP.

— Pancatantra: The Book of India's Folk Wisdom. LC 97-2843. (The World's Classics Ser.). 256p. 1998. pap. 11.95 (*0-19-283299-9*) OUP.

Oliven, Ruben. Tradition Matters: Modern Gaucho Identity in Brazil. Tesser, Carmen C., tr. (Illus.). 160p. 1996. pap. 18.50 (*0-231-10425-1*) Col U Pr.

Oliver. Back in Line. LC 99-182125. 120p. 1998. pap. text 22.50 (*0-7506-2872-3*) Buttrwrth-Heinemann.

***Oliver.** The Leaf & the Cloud. 64p. 2000. 22.00 (*0-306-80993-1*) Da Capo.

— Lotus Domino 5 Programming Bible. (Bible Ser.). 600p. 2000. 39.99 (*0-7645-4724-0*) IDG Bks.

Oliver. Lotus Web Development Exam 190-281: Accelerated Lotus Study Guide. LC 98-55405. (Accelerated Ser.). 1999. pap., student ed. 29.99 (*0-07-134533-7*) McGraw.

***Oliver.** Making Racial Inequality. 2000. 25.00 (*0-465-05200-2*, Pub. by Basic); pap. 18.00 (*0-465-05201-0*, Pub. by Basic) HarpC.

— Mars: Back Care. 1996. 3.5 hd 205.00 (*0-7506-2672-0*) Buttrwrth-Heinemann.

Oliver. Modern Electronic Communication. 6th ed. 1998. pap. text, lab manual ed. 34.00 (*0-13-860917-9*) P-H.

— The Politics of Disablement. 1997. text 21.95 (*0-333-43293-2*, Pub. by Macmillan) St Martin.

Oliver, et al. Spanish for Law Enforcement. 5th ed. 284p. (C). 1996. pap. text 33.16 (*0-669-35461-9*) HM Trade Div.

Oliver, jt. auth. see Jarvis, Ana C.

Oliver, jt. auth. see Wright.

O

***Oliver, Dawn.** The Public/Private Divide. 256p. 1999. pap. 39.95 (*0-406-98303-8*, Pub. by Buttrwrth Co Ltd) Northwestern U Pr.

Oliver, Dawn, jt. ed. see Jowell, Jeffrey.

Oliver, Dennis J. Inside Out Northern California: Camping, Biking, Loding & Surfing. 2nd ed. (Inside Out Ser.). 688p. 1999. pap. 21.95 (*1-57061-166-1*) Sasquatch Bks.

Oliver, Katie T. Try God, You'll Like Him. (Uplook Ser.). 1975. pap. 0.99 (*0-8163-0178-6*, 20340-6) Pacific Pr Pub Assn.

***Oliver, Willie.** Overland Through Southern Africa. 1998. pap. text 29.95 (*1-86872-105-1*) Struik Pubs.

Oliver, Willie & Oliver, Sandra. Hiking Trails of Southern Africa. LC 95-227467. 400p. 1998. pap. 18.95 (*1-86812-514-9*) Menasha Ridge.

— Visitors' Guide to Namibia. LC 96-145284. 254p. 1998. pap. 17.95 (*1-86812-427-4*) Menasha Ridge.

Oliver, A. Richard. Charles Nodier, Pilot of Romanticism. LC 64-8670. (Illus.). 1964. 39.95 (*0-8156-2073-X*) Syracuse U Pr.

Oliver, Akilah. The She Said Dialogues: Flesh Memory. 85p. 1999. pap. 10.95 (*0-9658877-5-8*, Pub. by Smokeproof Pr) SPD-Small Pr Dist.

Oliver, Alan. Watercolor: Planning & Painting. LC 98-53455. (Illus.). 128p. 1998. 24.95 (*0-8069-2059-9*, Pub. by D & C Pub) Sterling.

Oliver, Alan C. Dampness in Buildings. 2nd ed. LC 96-20739. 240p. 1996. pap. text 44.95 (*0-632-04085-8*) Blackwell Sci.

Oliver, Alex, jt. ed. see Mellor, D. H.

Oliver, Alex W., jt. auth. see Schultz, Roger E.

Oliver, Alisa B., ed. see Kivi, Judy.

Oliver, Alisa B., ed. see Kyser, Eric.

Oliver, Alisa B., ed. see Swinnerton, Dick.

Oliver, Alisa B., ed. see Vantornhout, Kris.

Oliver, Andrew. The Portraits of John Marshall. LC 76-13648. (Illus.). 233p. reprint ed. pap. 72.30 (*0-7837-4355-6*, 204406500012) Bks Demand.

— Portraits of John Quincy Adams & His Wife. LC 70-128349. (Adams Papers: No. 4, Adams Family Portraits). (Illus.). 335p. 1970. 46.50 (*0-674-69152-0*) HUP.

Oliver, Andrew, ed. Journal of Samuel Curwen, Loyalist, 2 vols., Set. LC 72-180150. (Illus.). 1972. 49.95 (*0-88389-096-8*, PEMP184, Essx Institute) Peabody Essex Mus.

Oliver, Andrew & Tolles, Bryant F., Jr. Windows on the Past: Portraits at the Essex Institute. LC 80-70017. (E.I. Museum Booklet Ser.). (Illus.). 64p. (Orig.). 1981. pap. 5.95 (*0-88389-079-8*, PEMP195, Essx Institute) Peabody Essex Mus.

Oliver, Andrew, et al. Portraits in the Massachusetts Historical Society. LC 88-2936. (Illus.). 163p. 1988. 50.00 (*0-934909-26-1*, Pub. by Mass Hist Soc) NE U Pr.

Oliver, Andrew, Jr., jt. auth. see Davinson, Patricia.

Oliver, Andrew, ed. see Curwen, Samuel.

Oliver, Annette. Italian Greyhounds Today. (Illus.). 160p. 1993. pap. 25.95 (*0-87605-191-3*) Howell Bks.

Oliver, Anthony M. Hawaii: Facts & Reference. 1995. pap. text 18.00 (*0-614-05582-2*) Blackwell Sci.

— Hawaii Fact & Reference Book: Recent & Historical Facts & Events in the Fiftieth State. 300p. 1995. pap. 12.95 (*1-56647-061-7*) Mutual Pub HI.

Oliver, Barry D. SDA Organizational Structure: Past, Present, & Future. (Andrews University Seminary Doctoral Dissertation Ser.: Vol. 15). 488p. (Orig.). 1989. pap. 19.99 (*0-943872-97-9*) Andrews Univ Pr.

Oliver, Benjamin L. Law Summary: A Collection of Legal Tracts on Subjects of General Application in Business. 2nd enl. ed. 391p. 1995. reprint ed. 52.50 (*0-8377-2450-3*, Rothman) W S Hein.

— The Rights of an American Citizen. LC 76-119940. (Select Bibliographies Reprint Ser.). 1977. reprint ed. 25.95 (*0-8369-5383-5*) Ayer.

Oliver, Bernard J., Jr. Marriage & You. 1964. 14.95 (*0-8084-0211-0*); pap. 16.95 (*0-8084-0212-9*) NCUP.

— Sexual Deviation in American Society: A Social-Psychological Study of Sexual Nonconformity. 1967. pap. 18.95 (*0-8084-0277-3*) NCUP.

Oliver, Bernard M., ed. see Cyclops Design Team Staff.

Oliver, Beverly. Nightmare in Dallas: The "Babushka Lady" LC 94-66617. 304p. 1994. 19.95 (*0-914984-60-8*) Starburst.

— Shelbyville: A Pictorial History. (Indiana Pictorial History Ser.). (Illus.). 1996. write for info. (*0-943963-53-2*) G Bradley.

Oliver, Bill. Women & Children First: Stories. LC 97-44887. (First Series). 192p. (Orig.). 1998. pap. 14.00 (*0-922811-35-0*) Mid-List.

Oliver, Bill, jt. auth. see Lyons, Bonnie.

Oliver, Bobbie. Peacemongers: Conscientious Objectors to Military Service in Australia, 1811-1845. 1997. pap. 19.95 (*1-86368-184-1*, Pub. by Fremantle Arts) Intl Spec Bk.

— War & Peace in Western Australia: The Social & Political Impact of the Great War 1914-1926. LC 96-133986. 314p. 1995. pap. 24.95 (*1-875560-57-2*, Pub. by Univ of West Aust Pr) Intl Spec Bk.

Oliver Brachfeld, F. Inferiority Feelings in the Individual & the Group. Gabain, Marjorie, tr. from FRE. LC 70-169849. 301p. 1973. reprint ed. lib. bdg. 65.00 (*0-8371-6245-9*, OLIF, Greenwood Pr) Greenwood.

Oliver, Brett. Creating Cool Intelligent Agents for Windows. LC 96-76258. 288p. 1996. pap. 29.99 (*1-56884-823-4*) IDG Bks.

— Extending Clipper 5: Includes Version 5.01. 1992. pap. write for info. (*0-201-56783-0*) Addison-Wesley.

Oliver, Brian, jt. auth. see Wotton, Peter.

Oliver, Bruce, jt. auth. see Berjeron-Oliver, Sherry.

***Oliver, Caroline.** The Policy Governance Fieldbook: Practical Lessons, Tips & Tools from the Experiences of Real-World. LC 99-6258. 256p. 1999. pap. text 29.95 (*0-7879-4366-5*) Jossey-Bass.

Oliver, Caroline. Western Women in Colonial Africa, 12. LC 81-24194. (Contributions in Comparative Colonial Studies: No. 12). 201p. 1982. 52.95 (*0-313-23388-8*, OWA/, Greenwood Pr) Greenwood.

Oliver, Carolyn C. & McCormick, Ellen R. A Good Teacher. (Illus.). 112p. 1992. pap. 9.95 (*0-9629972-6-9*) Meredith VA.

Oliver, Carrie, jt. auth. see Oliver, Gary.

Oliver, Celia. Enduring Grace: Quilts from the Shelburne Museum Collection. Jonsson, Lee, ed. LC 96-44403. (Illus.). 112p. (Orig.). 1997. pap. 24.95 (*1-57120-022-3*, 10146) C & T Pub.

Oliver, Chad. Another World. 1993. reprint ed. lib. bdg. 18.95 (*0-89968-356-8*, Lghtyr Pr) Buccaneer Bks.

— Shadows in the Sun. 1993. reprint ed. lib. bdg. 18.95 (*0-89968-357-6*, Lghtyr Pr) Buccaneer Bks.

Oliver, Chadwick & Larson, Bruce C. Forest Stand Dynamics. 520p. 1996. pap. 48.95 (*0-471-13833-9*) Wiley.

Oliver, Charles. Ernest Hemingway A to Z: The Essential Reference to His Life & Work. LC 98-30042. (Literary A to Z Ser.). (Illus.). 452p. (YA). 1999. 50.00 (*0-8160-3467-2*) Facts on File.

— How to Take Standardized Tests. 215p. (Orig.). (gr. 10-12). 1981. pap. text 5.50 (*0-89285-155-4*) ELS Educ Servs.

— How to Take Standardized Tests. 215p. (Orig.). (YA). (gr. 10-12). 1981. audio 16.95 (*0-89285-157-0*) ELS Educ Servs.

Oliver, Charles, ed. see Van Hook, Beverly.

Oliver, Charles M. Ernest Hemingway A to Z: The Essential Reference to His Life & Work. 464p. 1999. pap. 17.95 (*0-8160-3934-8*) Facts on File.

Oliver, Charles M., ed. A Moving Picture Feast: A Filmgoer's Hemingway. LC 88-32292. 202p. 1989. 55.00 (*0-275-93146-3*, C3146, Praeger Pubs) Greenwood.

***Oliver, Charly.** Winter Trails of the Front Range. (Illus.). 56p. 1999. pap. 7.95 (*1-892540-04-5*) Sharp End.

Oliver, Chris J. & Quegan, Shaun. Understanding Synthetic Aperture Radar Images. LC 97-41709. (Remote Sensing Library). 464p. 1998. 115.00 (*0-89006-850-X*) Artech Hse.

Oliver, Chuck. On the Throne with the King. 224p. 1998. pap. 5.99 (*0-7860-0543-2*, Pinncle Kensgtn) Kensgtn Pub Corp.

— On the Throne with the King: The Ultimate Elvis Bathroom Book. 300p. 1999. pap. 14.95 (*1-891847-06-6*, Pub. by Dowling Pr) Midpt Trade.

***Oliver, Clare.** Animals Helping with Special Needs. (Animals That Help Us Ser.). (Illus.). (J). 2000. pap. 6.95 (*0-531-15404-1*) Watts.

— Animals in Dangerous Places. (Animals That Help Us Ser.). (Illus.). 2000. 20.00 (*0-531-14566-2*) Watts.

— Animals in Dangerous Places. (Animals That Help Us Ser.). (Illus.). (J). 2000. pap. 6.95 (*0-531-15408-4*) Watts.

— Animals on the Move. (Animals That Help Us Ser.). (Illus.). 2000. 20.00 (*0-531-14562-X*) Watts.

— Animals on the Move. (Animals That Help Us Ser.). (Illus.). (J). 2000. pap. 6.95 (*0-531-15405-X*) Watts.

Oliver, Clare. Mountains Gush Lava & Ash: And Other Amazing Facts about Volcanoes. LC 98-18033. (I Didn't Know That... Ser.). (Illus.). 32p. (J). (gr. 1-3). 1998. 8.95 (*0-7613-0739-7*, Copper Beech Bks); lib. bdg. 20.90 (*0-7613-0820-2*, Copper Beech Bks) Millbrook Pr.

— Natural Disasters. (Totally Amazing Ser.). 32p. 1999. pap. 5.99 (*0-307-20165-1*) Gldn Bks Pub Co.

— Quakes Split The Ground Open: And Other Amazing Facts about Earthquakes. LC 98-54110. (I Didn't Know That... Ser.). (Illus.). 32p. (J). 1999. 8.95 (*0-7613-0795-8*, Copper Beech Bks) Millbrook Pr.

***Oliver, Clare.** Quakes Split the Ground Open: And Other Amazing Facts about Earthquakes. LC 98-54110. (I Didn't Know That... Ser.). (Illus.). 32p. (J). 1999. lib. bdg. 21.90 (*0-7613-0912-8*, Copper Beech Bks) Millbrook Pr.

Oliver, Clare. Some Boats Have Wings: And Other Amazing Facts about Ships & Submarines. LC 98-6803. (I Didn't Know That... Ser.). (Illus.). 32p. (J). (gr. 1-3). 1998. 8.95 (*0-7613-0736-2*, Copper Beech Bks); lib. bdg. 20.90 (*0-7613-0817-2*, Copper Beech Bks) Millbrook Pr.

***Oliver, Clare & Sherman, Jane.** Blue Plane: Match the Shape. (Match-the-Shape Ser.). (Illus.). 6p. (J). 2000. bds. 7.95 (*0-8118-2749-6*) Chronicle Bks.

— Silver Train: Match the Shape. (Match-the-Shape Ser.). (Illus.). 6p. (J). 2000. bds. 7.95 (*0-8118-2761-5*) Chronicle Bks.

Oliver, Clifford. Operations Manual for Machine Tool Technology. LC 82-13489. 272p. (C). 1982. pap. text 29.95 (*0-471-04744-9*) P-H.

Oliver, Constance, ed. Cell Biology of Trauma. LC 94-30688. 384p. 1995. boxed set 149.95 (*0-8493-2453-X*) CRC Pr.

Oliver, Cora H. Hazen. Genealogy of Samuel & Elizabeth (Dewitt) Hazen & Their Descendants. 142p. 1997. reprint ed. pap. 22.00 (*0-8328-9068-5*); reprint ed. lib. bdg. 32.00 (*0-8328-9067-7*) Higginson Bk Co.

Oliver, Cordelia. Joan Eardley, RSA. (Illus.). 120p. 1993. 34.95 (*1-85158-166-9*, Pub. by Mainstream Pubng) Trafalgar.

Oliver, Covey T., et al. The International Legal System, Cases & Materials. 4th ed. (University Casebook Ser.). 1771p. 1995. text 52.95 (*1-56662-135-6*) Foundation Pr.

Oliver, D., jt. ed. see Higgins, E.

Oliver, D. L. Studies in the Anthropology of Bougainville, Solomon Islands. (HU PMP Ser.). 1974. reprint ed. 30.00 (*0-527-01274-2*) Periodicals Srv.

***Oliver, Dana J.** Drum Grooves Presents: Groovin' to the Music. (Illus.). 72p. 2000. pap. 29.95 incl. cd-rom (*0-9679362-0-9*) Drum Grooves.

Oliver, Daniel T. Animal Rights: The Inhumane Crusade. 2nd ed. Huberty, Robert, ed. LC 99-14055. (Studies in Organization Trends: Vol. 13). 260p. 1999. pap. 14.95 (*0-936783-23-0*) Merril Pr.

Oliver, David. Flying Boats & Amphibians since 1945. LC 87-61279. (Illus.). 144p. 1996. reprint ed. 29.95 (*0-87021-898-0*) Naval Inst Pr.

— The Shaggy Steed of Physics: Mathematical Beauty in the Physical World. LC 93-33015. (Illus.). 298p. 1994. 48.95 (*0-387-94163-0*) Spr-Verlag.

— Wings over Water: Waterbirds of the Atlantic. 1999. 17.99 (*0-7858-1043-9*) Bk Sales Inc.

***Oliver, David, et al, eds.** Palliative Care in Amyotrophic Lateral Sclerosis: Motor Neurone Disease. (Illus.). 240p. 2001. text 79.50 (*0-19-263166-7*) OUP.

Oliver, David, jt. auth. see Ryan, Mike.

Oliver, David, jt. ed. see Feskens, Theo.

Oliver, David B., ed. New Directions in Religion & Aging. 205p. 1987. 39.95 (*0-86656-553-1*) Haworth Pr.

Oliver, David B. & Tureman, Sally, eds. The Human Factor in Nursing Home Care. LC 87-36625. (Activities, Adaptation & Aging Ser.: Vol. 10, Nos. 3 & 4). (Illus.). 202p. 1988. pap. text 14.95 (*0-86656-732-1*) Haworth Pr.

— The Human Factor in Nursing Home Care. LC 87-36625. (Activities, Adaptation & Aging Ser.: Vol. 10, Nos. 3 & 4). (Illus.). 202p. 1988. text 39.95 (*0-86656-715-1*) Haworth Pr.

Oliver, David J. & Snelgrove, John H. Butterworths Estate Planning for U. K. Individuals Residing & Investing Abroad. 1996. ring bd. write for info. (*0-406-06324-9*, BEPU, MICHIE) LEXIS Pub.

Oliver, David M. Gifts We Bring to Honor the King: Sermon & Worship Resources for Advent Christmas. LC 97-15983. 1997. pap. 10.25 (*0-7880-1124-3*) CSS OH.

Oliver, David W., et al. Engineering Complex Systems: With Models & Objects. LC 97-4055. (Illus.). 297p. 1997. 60.00 (*0-07-048188-1*) McGraw.

Oliver, Dawn H. Government in the United Kingdom: The Search for Accountability, Effectiveness & Citizenship. 224p. 1991. pap. 41.95 (*0-335-15639-8*) OpUniv Pr.

Oliver, Dawn H. & Drewry, Gavin. Public Service Reforms Issues of Accountability & Public Law: Towards Efficiency & Empowerment. LC 96-529. (Constitutional Reform Ser.). 192p. (C). 1996. text 99.00 (*1-85567-391-6*) Bks Intl VA.

Oliver, Dawn H. & Freeman, M. D., eds. Current Legal Problems Vol. 47, Pt. 2: Collected Papers. 386p. 1995. text 55.00 (*0-19-826000-8*) OUP.

Oliver, Deborah, jt. auth. see Oliver, Marina.

Oliver-Diaz, Philip, jt. auth. see O'Gormand, Patricia.

Oliver, Dick. Teach Yourself HTML 4 in 24 Hours. 2nd ed. LC 97-68549. 440p. 1997. 19.99 (*1-57521-366-4*) Sams.

Oliver, Dick. Teach Yourself HTML 4 in 24 Hours. 4th ed. (Teach Yourself Ser.). 512p. 1999. 19.99 (*0-672-31724-9*) Sams.

— Teach Yourself HTML in 24 Hours. LC 96-71214. 416p. 1997. 19.99 (*1-57521-235-8*) Sams.

— Teach Yourself Microsoft FrontPage 2000 in 24 Hours. LC 98-87801. (Teach Yourself Ser.). 1999. pap. 19.99 (*0-672-31500-9*) Sams.

— Web Page Wizardry. LC 96-67210. 448p. 1996. pap. text 39.99 incl. cd-rom (*1-57521-092-4*) Sams.

Oliver, Donald. Auditioning for the Musical Theater. 160p. 1995. pap. 11.95 (*1-880399-58-X*) Smith & Kraus.

Oliver, Donald & Butler, Dan. The Case of the Dead Flamingo Dancer. LC 97-212142. 113 p. 1997. write for info. (*0-573-69620-9*) S French Trade.

Oliver, Donald W. & Gershman, Kathleen W., eds. Education, Modernity, & Fractured Meaning: Toward a Process Theory of Teaching & Learning. LC 88-20990. (SUNY Series, the Philosophy of Education). 261p. (C). 1989. pap. text 22.95 (*0-88706-942-8*) State U NY Pr.

Oliver, Douglas. Kind: Collected Poems. (Illus.). 192p. (Orig.). 1987. 24.00 (*0-907954-04-9*) SPD-Small Pr Dist.

— Kind: Collected Poems. (Agneau 2 Paperbook Ser.: No. 3). (Illus.). 192p. (Orig.). 1987. pap. 12.00 (*0-907954-05-7*) SPD-Small Pr Dist.

***Oliver, Douglas.** A Salvo for Africa. 2000. pap. 18.95 (*1-85224-475-5*, Pub. by Bloodaxe Bks) Dufour.

Oliver, Douglas. Selected Poems. 120p. 1996. 30.50 (*1-883689-35-X*); pap. 10.50 (*1-883689-34-1*) Talisman Hse.

Oliver, Douglas, et al. Penniless Politics: A Satirical Poem. 77p. 1995. pap. 16.95 (*1-85224-269-8*, Pub. by Bloodaxe Bks) Dufour.

Oliver, Douglas L. Black Islanders: A Personal Perspective of Bougainville, 1937-1991. LC 91-57969. (Illus.). 348p. (C). 1991. pap. text 18.00 (*0-947062-82-3*) UH Pr.

— Native Cultures of the Pacific Islands. LC 88-20625. (Illus.). 184p. (C). 1989. pap. text 15.00 (*0-8248-1182-8*) UH Pr.

— Oceania: The Native Cultures of Australia & the Pacific Islands, 2 vols. LC 88-29551. (Illus.). 1264p. 1988. text 95.00 (*0-8248-1019-8*) UH Pr.

— The Pacific Islands. 3rd ed. LC 88-38668. (Illus.). 336p. (C). 1989. pap. text 18.00 (*0-8248-1233-6*) UH Pr.

— Two Tahitian Villages: A Study in Comparison. (Illus.). 572p. 1983. text 25.00 (*0-939154-22-6*) Inst Polynesian.

Oliver, E. Eugene. Greece. (Pelham Guides Ser.). 23p. (Orig.). (C). 1996. 22.00 (*0-929851-95-1*) Am Assn Coll Registrars.

— Greece; A Study of the Educational System of Greece & a Guide to the Academic Placement of Students in Educational Institutions of the United States. LC 81-20595. (World Education Ser.). (Illus.). 134p. reprint ed. pap. 41.60 (*0-8357-3115-4*, 203937200012) Bks Demand.

— Saudi Arabia. (Pelham Guides Ser.). 70p. (Orig.). (C). 1996. 22.00 (*0-929851-85-4*) Am Assn Coll Registrars.

— Saudi Arabia: A Study of the Educational System of Saudi Arabia & a Guide to the Academic Placement of Students in Educational Institutions of the United States. LC 87-1204. (World Education Ser.). 132p. 1987. reprint ed. pap. 41.00 (*0-8357-8660-9*, 203510800092) Bks Demand.

***Oliver, Eileen C.** Afro-Brazilian Religions: A Selective, Annotated Bibliography: 1900-1997 LC 99-205774. xxiv, 197p. 1998. write for info. (*0-917617-57-6*) SALALM.

Oliver, Eileenn I., jt. ed. see Hollins, Etta R.

Oliver, Elisa B., ed. see Gregory, Sharon.

Oliver, Elizabeth M. Black Mother Goose Book. 2nd ed. LC 81-83427. (Illus.). 48p. 1981. pap. 7.95 (*0-912444-12-6*) DARE Bks.

— Black Mother Goose Book. 2nd ed. LC 81-83427. (Illus.). 48p. (J). (gr. k-3). 1994. reprint ed. 12.95 (*0-912444-35-5*) DARE Bks.

Oliver, Elma, jt. auth. see Schwartz, Anna J.

Oliver, Eric. The Human Factor at Work: A Guide to Self-Reliance & Consumer Protection for the Mind. Beacon, Ursula, ed. (Orig.). 1993. pap. 14.95 (*0-9636980-0-1*) Metasystems.

Oliver, Eric & Wilson, John. Security Manual. 6th ed. (Illus.). 250p. (Orig.). 1994. pap. 15.95 (*0-566-07443-5*, Pub. by Gower) Ashgate Pub Co.

Oliver, Evelyn D., jt. auth. see Lewis, James R.

Oliver, F. W., ed. The Natural History of Plants, 2 vols., Set. (C). 1988. text 800.00 (*0-7855-3156-4*, Pub. by Scientific) St Mut.

Oliver, Fitch E., ed. see Pynchon, William.

Oliver, Frederick S. Endless Adventure, Set, 3 vols. LC 78-123762. reprint ed. 165.00 (*0-404-04840-4*) AMS Pr.

Oliver, G. Marketing Today. 425p. (C). 1988. 100.00 (*0-7855-3782-1*, Pub. by Inst Pur & Supply) St Mut.

— Marketing Today. 425p. (C). 1990. 200.00 (*0-7855-5656-7*, Pub. by Inst Pur & Supply) St Mut.

— La Masculinidad Ante las Encrucijadas. (Hombres de Integridad Ser.).Tr. of Masculinity at the Crossroads. (SPA.). 53p. 1995. 2.99 (*1-56063-574-6*, 495677) Editorial Unilit.

An Asterisk (*) at the beginning of an entry indicates that the title is appearing for the first time.

Oliver, G., ed. Marketing Today. 425p. (C). 1989. 173.00 (*0-7855-4626-X*, Pub. by Inst Pur & Supply) St Mut.

Oliver, Garret H., jt. auth. see Harper, Timothy.

Oliver, Gary. Buford Bears, Bad News Blues. 32p. (J). 1995. 7.99 (*1-56476-461-3*, 6-3461) Chariot Victor.

— Casino Poker Without Fear. (Orig.). 1996. pap. 8.95 (*0-9635909-2-8*) Poker Tips Pr.

— How to Get It Right After You've Gotten It Wrong. LC 98-142366. 208p. 1998. pap. 10.99 (*1-56476-719-1*, Victor Bks) Chariot Victor.

— Low Limit Seven-Card Stud. 28p. (Orig.). 1991. pap. 6.95 (*0-9635909-1-X*) Poker Tips Pr.

— Poker Humor. 100p. 1993. pap. 5.95 (*0-9635909-0-1*) Poker Tips Pr.

— Ric & Rac's Woodland Adventures. (J). 1995. write for info. (*7-900882-26-X*, Chariot Bks) Chariot Victor.

***Oliver, Gary & Oliver, Carrie.** Raising Sons & Loving It! 2000. pap. 12.99 (*0-310-22801-8*) Zondervan.

Oliver, Gary, jt. auth. see Wright, Norman.

Oliver, Gary D. Enigma at Tumacacori Arizona. 112p. 1992. pap. 9.95 (*0-9633813-0-X*) G D Oliver.

Oliver, Gary J. How to Get It Right After You've Gotten It Wrong. LC 96-110983. 176p. 1995. 15.99 (*1-56476-486-9*, 6-3486, Victor Bks) Chariot Victor.

Oliver, Gary J. & Wright, Norman. Good Women Get Angry: A Woman's Guide to Handling Her Anger, Depression, Anxiety & Stress. LC 95-23763. (Illus.). 320p. 1995. pap. 12.99 (*0-89283-935-X*, Vine Bks) Servant.

— When Anger Hits Home: Taking Care of Your Anger Without Taking It Out on Your Family. 18.99 (*0-8024-9237-1*, 322) Moody.

Oliver, Gary J., et al. Promoting Change Through Brief Therapy in Christian Counseling. LC 97-25133. (AACC Counseling Library Ser.). 1997. 24.99 (*0-8423-5059-4*) Tyndale Hse.

Oliver, Gary J., jt. auth. see Lee, Ron.

Oliver, Gary J., jt. auth. see Wright, Norman.

Oliver, Gary J., ed. see Osterhaus, James P.

Oliver, Gene David. Life & the Art of Change: A Journey to Consciousness, Awareness & Personal Growth. LC 98-53163. 137p. 1999. 12.95 (*0-9668441-7-3*) LifeChange Pr.

Oliver, George. Origin of the Royal Arch: English Royal Arch Degree (1867) 242p. 1999. reprint ed. pap. 17.95 (*0-7661-0814-7*) Kessinger Pub.

— Revelations of a Square Exhibiting a Graphic Display of the Savings & Doings or Eminent Free & Accepted Masons, from the Revival in 1717 by Dr. Desauguliers, to the Reunion in 1813 by Their R.H. The Duke of Kent & Sussex. 330p. 1995. reprint ed. pap. 24.95 (*1-56459-477-7*) Kessinger Pub.

— Widdershins. Reginald, R. & Manville, Douglas, eds. LC 75-46297. (Supernatural & Occult Fiction Ser.). 1976. reprint ed. lib. bdg. 25.95 (*0-405-08157-X*) Ayer.

Oliver, George R. The Antiquities of Freemasonry Comprising Illustrations of the Five Grand Periods of Masonry from the Creation of the World to the Dedication of King Solomon's Temple. 250p. 1993. reprint ed. pap. 16.95 (*1-56459-398-3*) Kessinger Pub.

— The History of Initiation in Twelve Lectures Comprising a Detailed Account of the Rites & Ceremonies, Doctrines & Discipline of All the Secret & Mysterious Institutions of the Ancient World. 236p. 1993. reprint ed. pap. 17.00 (*1-56459-301-0*) Kessinger Pub.

— The Pythagorean Triangle: The Science of Numbers. 260p. 1993. reprint ed. pap. 17.95 (*1-56459-372-X*) Kessinger Pub.

— Signs & Symbols Illustrated & Explained in a Course of Twelve Lectures on Freemasonry. 210p. 1993. reprint ed. pap. 17.00 (*1-56459-302-9*) Kessinger Pub.

Oliver, Gordon. Marketing Today. 4th ed. 550p. 1995. pap. 63.00 (*0-13-203001-2*) P-H.

Oliver, H. J., ed. see Shakespeare, William.

Oliver, Harold H. A Relational Metaphysics. (Studies in Philosophy & Religion: No. 4). 242p. 1981. lib. bdg. 153.00 (*90-247-2457-0*, Pub. by M Nijhoff) Kluwer Academic.

Oliver, Harold H., tr. see Buri, Fritz.

Oliver, Harry R., III. Business Persons' Guide to Taxation in the 90's: Starting & Running Your Business. 212p. 1990. 19.95 (*0-9622569-1-9*) El Dorado Pr.

Oliver, Heddy, ed. see Jones, Mark.

Oliver, Henry M. Economic Opinion & Policy in Ceylon. LC 57-13023. (Commonwealth Studies Center: No. 6). 160p. reprint ed. 49.60 (*0-8357-9103-3*, 201792000010) Bks Demand.

Oliver, Hermia. Flaubert & an English Governess: The Quest for Juliet Herbert. (Illus.). 1980. 45.00 (*0-19-815764-9*) OUP.

Oliver, Howard R. & Oliver, Sylvia A., eds. The Role of Water & the Hydrological Cycle in Global Change. (NATO ASI Ser.: Ser. I, Vol. 31). (Illus.). 480p. 1995. 244.95 (*3-540-59429-9*) Spr-Verlag.

Oliver, Hugh, ed. see Quarter, Jack.

Oliver, I. Madsin, ed. Algebraic Topology, Aarhus 1982: Proceedings of a Conference Held in Aarhus, August 1-7, 1982. (Lecture Notes in Mathematics Ser.: Vol. 1051). (FRE & GER.). x, 665p. 1984. 62.95 (*0-387-12902-2*) Spr-Verlag.

Oliver, Ian. Programming Classics PHA: Implementing the World's Best Algorithms. LC 93-32080. 500p. 1994. text 60.00 (*0-13-100413-1*) Prntice Hall Bks.

Oliver, J. A. Green Heads & Black Bass: 60 Years of Hunting & Fishing in South Louisiana. (Illus.). 200p. 1999. pap. 14.95 (*0-9671048-0-7*, 1) Sorrel Pubg.

Oliver, J. David & Rogers, Ian T., eds. Permanent Establishment As a Basis for Tax - A Case Study. 208p. 1991. pap. text 75.00 (*1-56423-003-1*) Ntl Ctr Tax Ed.

Oliver, J. E. Shocks & Rocks: Seismology in the Plate Tectonics Revolution: The Story of Earthquakes & the Great Earth Science Revolution of the 1960s. LC 96-2723. (History of Geophysics Ser.: Vol. 6). 1996. 28.00 (*0-87590-280-4*) Am Geophysical.

Oliver, J. M., jt. auth. see Webster, G. H.

Oliver, J. P. Quality of Life & Mental Health Services. LC 96-44152. (Illus.). 256p. (C). 1997. pap. 27.99 (*0-415-16151-7*) Routledge.

Oliver, Jack. The Incomplete Guide to the Art of Discovery. (Illus.). 232p. 1991. text 55.50 (*0-231-07620-7*) Col U Pr.

— The Lifetime Financial Plan: The Seven Ages of Financial Health. 288p. 1998. pap. 57.50 (*0-273-63052-0*, Pub. by Pitman Pub) Trans-Atl Phila.

Oliver, James, tr. see Kersten, Felix.

Oliver, James E. Educational Interest Inventory (Package of 25 Answer Sheets, Profile & Interpretation Guides) 9p. (Orig.). (YA). (gr. 12). 1989. pap., student ed. 35.00 (*0-933510-84-5*, Wintergreen-Orchard) Riverside Pub Co.

— Educational Interest Inventory (Reusable Test Booklet) 12p. (Orig.). (YA). (gr. 12). 1989. pap., student ed. 3.00 (*0-933510-83-7*, Wintergreen-Orchard) Riverside Pub Co.

Oliver, James E., des. Career Guidance Inventory. enl. rev. ed. 1989. pap. 3.00 (*0-933510-85-3*, Wintergreen-Orchard) Riverside Pub Co.

— Career Guidance Inventory (Package of 25 Answer Sheets, Profile & Interpretation Guide) enl. rev. ed. 1989. pap. 35.00 (*0-933510-86-1*, Wintergreen-Orchard) Riverside Pub Co.

— Educational Interest Inventory & Career Guidance Inventory, Set. enl. rev. ed. 1989. pap., teacher ed. 16.00 (*0-685-53405-7*, Wintergreen-Orchard) Riverside Pub Co.

Oliver, James H. The Civic Tradition & Roman Athens. LC 82-16180. 182p. reprint ed. pap. 56.50 (*0-7837-0338-4*, 204065700018) Bks Demand.

— Demokratia, the Gods, & the Free World. Vlastos, Gregory, ed. LC 78-19378. (Morals & Law in Ancient Greece Ser.). (ENG, GRE & LAT., Illus.). 1979. reprint ed. lib. bdg. 18.95 (*0-405-11564-4*) Ayer.

— Greek Constitutions of Early Roman Emperors from Inscriptions & Papyri. LC 86-72884. (American Philosophical Society, Memoirs Ser.: No. 178). (Illus.). 670p. 1989. reprint ed. pap. 200.00 (*0-7837-6704-8*, 204633700011) Bks Demand.

— Marcus Aurelius: Aspects of Civic & Cultural Policy in the East. LC 72-22588. (Hesperia Supplement Ser.: No. 13). (Illus.). xv, 160p. 1970. pap. 15.00 (*0-87661-513-2*) Am Sch Athens.

Oliver, James K., jt. auth. see Nathan, James A.

Oliver, James S., et al, eds. Early Hominid Behavioural Ecology: New Looks at Old Questions. (Illus.). 328p. 1994. pap. text 39.95 (*0-12-525660-4*) Acad Pr.

***Oliver, Jamie.** The Naked Chef. LC 99-54555. 256p. 2000. 34.95 (*0-7868-6617-9*, Pub. by Hyperion) Time Warner.

Oliver, Jane. Blue Heaven Bends over All: A Novel of the Life of Sir Walter Scott. 384p. (Orig.). 1993. pap. 14.95 (*0-85640-450-0*, Pub. by Blackstaff Pr) Dufour.

***Oliver, Jane.** Morning for Mr. Prothero. LC 99-80172. 320p. 2000. write for info. (*1-893766-18-7*) Aeon Pub Co.

Oliver, Jane S., jt. auth. see Kami, Karen R.

Oliver, Jean. Back Care: An Illustrated Guide. (Illus.). 192p. 1994. pap. text 42.00 (*0-7506-0191-4*) Buttrwrth-Heinemann.

***Oliver, Jean.** Back Care: An Illustrated Guide. 2nd ed. (Illus.). 224p. 2000. pap. text 45.00 (*0-7506-4689-6*) Buttrwrth-Heinemann.

Oliver, Jean & Middleditch, Alison. Functional Anatomy of the Spine. (Illus.). 304p. 1991. text 52.50 (*0-7506-0052-7*) Buttrwrth-Heinemann.

— Functional Anatomy of the Spine. 2nd ed. (Illus.). 224p. 1997. pap. 50.00 (*0-7506-2717-4*) Buttrwrth-Heinemann.

Oliver, Jeanne. Frommer's Memorable Walks in Paris. 3rd ed. 168p. 1998. 12.95 (*0-02-862247-2*, Pub. by Macmillan) S&S Trade.

— Frommer's Memorable Walks in Paris. 3rd ed. 1998. 12.95 (*0-02-862263-4*) Macmillan.

— Frommer's Paris from $70 a Day 98. 288p. 1997. 14.95 (*0-02-861869-6*) Macmillan.

***Oliver, Jeanne.** Lonely Planet Crete. Lonely Planet Publications Staff, ed. (Travel Guides Ser.). (Illus.). 256p. 2000. pap. text 15.95 (*1-86450-074-3*) Lonely Planet.

— Lonely Planet Crete: Crete Condensed. Lonely Planet Publications Staff, ed. (Travel Guides Ser.). (Illus.). 128p. 2000. pap. text 9.95 (*1-86450-042-5*) Lonely Planet.

Oliver, Jeanne. Lonely Planet Croatia. 288p. 1999. pap. 16.95 (*0-86442-646-1*) Lonely Planet.

Oliver, Jim. Closing Distance: A Novel. LC 02-9648. 288p. 1997. reprint ed. pap. 9.95 (*1-55583-376-4*) Alyson Pubns.

— Experiencing God's Promises in Colombian Trenches. unabridged ed. 191p. 1998. 10.00 (*0-9667639-0-4*) J Oliver.

— Wings in the Snow. LC 98-7837. 288p. 1998. pap. 12.95 (*1-55583-462-0*, Alyson Bks) Alyson Pubns.

Oliver, Jim, jt. auth. see Freeman, Holly.

Oliver, Joan Duncan. Contemplative Living. LC 99-39248 (Omega Institute Mind, Body & Spirit Bks.). 240p. 2000. pap. 12.95 (*0-440-50869-X*, Dell Trade Pbks) Dell.

Oliver, John, ed. see Hill, Elizabeth C.

Oliver, John E., et al. Perspectives on Applied Physical Geography. 2nd ed. LC 97-73137. 196p. 1997. per. 52.95 (*0-7872-2516-9*, 41251601) Kendall-Hunt.

Oliver, John E., jt. auth. see Hidore, John J.

Oliver, John L., Jr. Emanuel County, GA. LC 98-88251. (Images of America Ser.). (Illus.). 128p. 1998. pap. 18.99 (*0-7524-1381-3*) Arcadia Publng.

— Hartsville & Trousdale County, Tennessee. (Images of America Ser.). (Illus.). 128p. 1996. pap. 16.99 (*0-7524-0533-0*) Arcadia Publng.

Oliver, John W. History of American Technology. LC 56-6269. 686p. reprint ed. pap. 200.00 (*0-608-11391-3*, 201252100081) Bks Demand.

Oliver, John W. & Roberts, Arthur O., eds. J. Walter Malone: The Autobiography of an Evangelical Quaker. LC 93-2204. (Illus.). 122p. (Orig.). (C). 1993. lib. bdg. 49.50 (*0-8191-9207-4*) U Pr of Amer.

Oliver, Joseph R. Eleven Twenty Handbook. 600p. 1988. 49.95 (*0-13-635129-8*, Busn) P-H.

— Preparing the Consolidated Return, 1992. 360p. 1992. 54.95 (*0-7811-0004-6*, Maxwell Macmillan) Macmillan.

— Preparing the 1120 Return, 1992. 580p. 1992. 54.95 (*0-7811-0002-X*, Maxwell Macmillan) Macmillan.

— Preparing the 1120 Return, 1993. rev. ed. LC 88-60292. (Professional Tax Advisor's Guide Ser.). (Illus.). 1992. pap. text 56.00 (*0-7811-0060-7*) Res Inst Am.

Oliver, Jr., John E. Handbook of Veterinary Neurology. 3rd ed. LC 96-38603. (Illus.). x, 453p. (C). 1997. pap. text 55.00 (*0-7216-7140-3*) Harcourt.

Oliver, Julia M., ed. see McCoy, Henry D., II.

Oliver, June. Polysymetrics: The Art of Making Geometric Patterns. 40p. 1982. pap. 3.95 (*0-685-05678-3*) P-H.

— Polysymetrics: The Art of Making Geometric Patterns. (Illus.). 32p. (J). (gr. 5-9). 1986. pap. 7.95 (*0-906212-09-X*, Pub. by Tarquin Pubns) Parkwest Pubns.

Oliver, Katherine M., jt. auth. see Fletcher, Robert.

***Oliver, Kathleen.** Swollen Tongues. 1999. pap. 14.95 (*0-88754-572-6*) Theatre Comm.

Oliver, Kelly. Family Values: Subjects Between Nature & Culture. LC 97-183209. 208p. (C). 1997. 65.00 (*0-415-91365-9*); pap. 17.99 (*0-415-91366-7*) Routledge.

— Reading Kristeva: Unraveling the Double-Bind. LC 92-9543. 240p. (C). 1993. pap. 15.95 (*0-253-20761-4*, MB-761) Ind U Pr.

***Oliver, Kelly.** Subjectivity Without Subjects: From Abject Fathers to Desiring Mothers. LC 98-35602. 192p. 1998. pap. 18.95 (*0-8476-9253-1*, Pub. by Rowman) Natl Bk Netwk.

Oliver, Kelly. Womanizing Nietzsche: Philosophy's Relation to "the Feminine" 256p. (C). 1994. pap. 20.99 (*0-415-90682-2*, A9545) Routledge.

— Womanizing Nietzsche: Philosophy's Relation to "the Feminine" 224p. (C). (gr. 13). 1994. 70.00 (*0-415-90681-4*, A9541) Routledge.

Oliver, Kelly, ed. Ethics, Politics, & Difference in Julia Kristeva's Writings: A Collection of Essays. LC 92-47482. 288p. (C). 1993. pap. 18.99 (*0-415-90704-7*, A9783) Routledge.

***Oliver, Kelly, ed.** French Feminism Reader. LC 99-86127. 352p. 2000. 65.00 (*0-8476-9766 5*) Rowman.

— French Feminism Reader. LC 99-86127. 352p. 2000. pap. 21.95 (*0-8476-9767-3*) Rowman.

Oliver, Kelly & Kristeva, Julia. The Portable Kristeva. LC 96-34403. 464p. (C). 1997. pap. 18.50 (*0-231-10505-3*) Col U Pr.

Oliver, Kelly & Pearsall, Marilyn, eds. Feminist Interpretations of Friedrich Nietzsche. LC 97-33640. (Re-Reading the Canon Ser.: No. 10). 352p. 1998. 55.00 (*0-271-01763-5*); pap. 19.95 (*0-271-01764-3*) Pa St U Pr.

Oliver, Kelly, jt. auth. see Kristeva, Julia.

Oliver, Kelly, jt. ed. see Deutscher, Penelope.

Oliver, Kelly, jt. ed. see Hendricks, Christina.

***Oliver, Kelly H.** Witnessing: Beyond Recognition. LC 00-9646. 2001. write for info. (*0-8166-3628-1*) U of Minn Pr.

Oliver, Kenneth. The Way English Works: How to Understand It & Use It. 288p. (Orig.). 1994. pap. 19.95 (*1-56883-036-X*) Colonial Pr AL.

Oliver, Kenneth G. Basic Industrial Electricity: A Training & Maintenance Manual. (Illus.). 384p. (C). 1990. pap. text 34.95 (*0-8311-3006-7*) Indus Pr.

— Industrial Boiler Management: An Operator's Guide. (Illus.). 412p. 1989. 32.95 (*0-8311-3018-0*) Indus Pr.

— Under the Southern Cross: A Petty Officer's Chronicle of the U.S.S. Octans, Banana Boat Become World War II Supply Ship for the Southern Pacific Fleet. LC 94-31153. (Illus.). 312p. 1995. pap. 29.95 (*0-89950-999-1*) McFarland & Co.

Oliver, Kevin, jt. auth. see O'Donnell, Jeff.

***Oliver, Kitty.** Race & Change in Hollywood, Florida. (Voices of America Ser.). (Illus.). 128p. 2000. pap. 18.99 (*0-7385-0569-2*) Arcadia Publng.

Oliver, Lawrence J. Brander Matthews, Theodore Roosevelt & the Politics of American Literature, 1880-1920. LC 91-24627. 272p. (C). 1992. text 31.00 (*0-87049-738-3*) U of Tenn Pr.

Oliver, Lawrence J., ed. The Letters of Theodore Roosevelt & Brander Matthews. LC 94-18766. (Illus.). 272p. (C). 1995. text 28.00 (*0-87049-894-0*) U of Tenn Pr.

Oliver, Lawrence J., jt. ed. see Price, Kenneth M.

Oliver, Leonard P. Study Circles: Coming Together for Personal Growth & Social Change. LC 87-12874. (Illus.). 165p. (Orig.). 1987. pap. 9.95 (*0-932020-47-X*) Seven Locks Pr.

***Oliver-Leonhardt, Gayle.** Execume: It's More Than a Resume, It's a Reflection of You. Fox, Erica, ed. 280p. 1999. pap., wbk. ed. 29.95 incl. cd-rom (*0-9672358-0-4*) Empower-U.

Oliver, Lewis. Estiyut Omayat: Creek Writing. (Illus.). 17p. 1985. pap. 2.00 (*0-940392-16-X*) Indian U Pr OK.

***Oliver, Lianabel.** The Cost Management Toolbox: The Manager's Guide to Controlling Costs & Boosting Profits. LC 99-36915. 320p. 1999. pap. 28.95 (*0-8144-7053-X*) AMACOM.

Oliver, Libbey, jt. auth. see Theobold, Mary M.

Oliver, Libbey Hodges. Colonial Williamsburg Decorates for Christmas: Step-by-Step Illustrated Instructions for Christmas Decorations That You Can Make for Your Home. LC 81-10103. (Illus.). 80p. 1981. 15.95 (*0-87935-056-3*); pap. 10.95 (*0-87935-058-X*) Colonial Williamsburg.

***Oliver, Libbey Hodges.** Flowers Are Almost Forever: The Care & Handling of Cut Flowers. LC 99-16969. (Illus.). 1999. pap. 12.00 (*1-883911-35-4*) Brandylane.

***Oliver, Libbey Hodges, et al.** Williamsburg Christmas. LC 98-53974. (Illus.). 128p. 1999. 24.95 (*0-8109-4551-7*, Pub. by Abrams) Time Warner.

Oliver, Lilian H. Some Boone Descendants & Kindred of the St. Charles District. LC 84-70107. 442p. 1984. pap. 47.00 (*0-939052-02-4*) Dean Pubns.

***Oliver, Lin.** Beezy's Big Boy. large type ed. (Illus.). 32p. (J). 2000. pap. 14.99 incl. audio (*1-890647-61-6*) Lrning Curve.

— Beezy's Big Boy. large type ed. (Illus.). 32p. (J). (gr. k-4). 2000. 14.95 (*1-890647-60-8*) Lrning Curve.

Oliver, Lin. Daylight Limited. 1999. pap. 14.95 (*1-56799-866-6*, Friedman-Fairfax) M Friedman Pub Grp Inc.

***Oliver, Lin.** The Daylight Limited. LC 98-85455. (Great Railway Adventures Ser.). 1998. write for info. (*1-890647-53-5*) Lrning Curve.

— Journey of the Jupiter. large type ed. (Illus.). 32p. (J). 2000. pap. 14.99 incl. audio (*1-890647-59-4*) Lrning Curve.

— Journey of the Jupiter. large type ed. (Great Railway Adventures Ser.). (Illus.). 32p. (J). (gr. k-4). 2000. 14.95 (*1-890647-58-6*) Lrning Curve.

Oliver, Lin. The Mighty Mogul. LC 99-28601. (Great Railway Adventures Ser.: Vol. 2;1). (Illus.). 32p. (J). (gr. k-4). 1999. 14.95 (*1-890647-56-X*); pap. 9.99 incl. audio (*1-890647-57-8*) Lrning Curve.

— The President Express. 1999. 14.95 (*1-56799-867-4*) M Friedman Pub Grp Inc.

***Oliver, Lin.** The President Express LC 98-85456. (Great Railway Adventures Ser.). 1998. write for info. (*1-890647-54-3*) Lrning Curve.

Oliver, Lin. Torpedo Run. 1999. 14.95 (*1-56799-868-2*) M Friedman Pub Grp Inc.

***Oliver, Lin.** The Torpedo Run LC 98-85457. (Great Railway Adventures Ser.). 1998. write for info. (*1-890647-55-1*) Lrning Curve.

Oliver, Lin, jt. auth. see Mooser, Stephen.

Oliver, Lloyd F. Houses of Strother Descendants of William Strother I King George County, Virginia, Vol. I: William Storther II (CA. 1653-1726) & His Descendants. LC 93-84938. (Orig.). 1993. pap. write for info. (*0-9637624-0-0*) W Strother Soc.

Oliver, Louis. Horned Snake. Barken, Stanley H., ed. (Cross-Cultural Review Chapbook Ser.: No. 15). 16p. 1981. 15.00 (*0-89304-839-9*, CCC142); pap. 5.00 (*0-89304-814-3*) Cross-Cultrl NY.

Oliver, Louis L. Caught in a Willow Net. LC 83-80757. (American Indian Poetry Ser.). 88p. 1983. 5.00 (*0-912678-57-7*, Greenfld Rev Pr) Greenfld Rev Lit.

— Chasers of the Sun: Creek Indian Thoughts, Poems & Stories. 105p. 1990. 9.95 (*0-912678-70-4*) Greenfld Rev Lit.

Oliver, Lucy. The Meditator's Guidebook: Pathways to Greater Awareness & Creativity. 160p. (Orig.). 1991. pap. 9.95 (*0-89281-360-1*) Inner Tradit.

Oliver, M. Agent Arthur's Desert Challenge. (Puzzle Adventures Ser.). (Illus.). 48p. (J). (gr. 3-8). 1994. pap. 5.95 (*0-7460-1406-6*, Usborne) EDC.

— Agent Arthur's Desert Challenge. (Puzzle Adventures Ser.). (Illus.). 48p. (J). (gr. 3-8). 1999. lib. bdg. 13.95 (*0-88110-696-8*, Usborne) EDC.

— Agent Arthur's Jungle Journey. (Puzzle Adventures Ser.). (Illus.). 48p. (J). (gr. 3-8). 1989. pap. 5.95 (*0-7460-0141-X*) EDC.

— The Intergalactic Bus Trip. (Puzzle Adventures Ser.). (Illus.). 48p. (J). (gr. 3-8). 1988. pap. 5.95 (*0-7460-0151-7*); lib. bdg. 13.95 (*0-88110-301-2*) EDC.

— Search for the Sunken City. (Puzzle Adventures Ser.). (Illus.). 48p. (J). (gr. 3-8). 1989. pap. 5.95 (*0-7460-0304-8*) EDC.

— Search for the Sunken City. (Puzzle Adventures Ser.). (Illus.). 48p. (J). (gr. 3-8). 1999. lib. bdg. 13.95 (*0-88110-409-4*) EDC.

Oliver, M., jt. auth. see Fischel, Emma.

Oliver, M. A., jt. auth. see Webster, R.

Oliver, M. C. & Marshall, E. A. Company Law. 485p. (C). 1987. 100.00 (*0-7855-5676-1*, Pub. by Inst Pur & Supply) St Mut.

Oliver, M. F., et al. Intensive Coronary Care. 1974. pap. text 10.80 (*92-4-154046-X*, 1150082) World Health.

Oliver, M. R., jt. auth. see Reid, G. S.

Oliver, M. S., et al. Coated Metal Roofing & Cladding. 178p. 1997. 92.00 (*0-7277-2620-X*, 2620, Pub. by T Telford) RCH.

Oliver, Marcelo. Rapid Review: Anatomy Reference Guide. Liskar, Nancy, ed. (Illus.). 77p. (YA). (gr. 9 up). 1996. pap. 32.95 (*0-9603730-9-8*) Anatomical Chart.

Oliver, Marcelo V. Expressions of Love. 99p. (Orig.). 1996. pap. 9.95 (*0-9650640-0-X*) P D Mayo.

Oliver, Margo. Margo Oliver's Cookbook for Seniors: Nutritious Recipes for One- Two- or More. (Retirement Ser.). (Illus.). 272p. 1989. pap. 9.95 (*0-88908-695-8*) Self-Counsel Pr.

Oliver, Maria-Antaonia & McNerney, Kathleen. Blue Roses for A Dead-- Lady. LC 98-60097. 121 p. 1998. write for info. (*1-889431-30-3*) Univ Pr South.

O

...bbie.

..., Pam.

...of the Air Ministries, Inc.

...Mainstay Church Resources Staff.

... Alcatraz Prison in American History. LC ...n American History Ser.). 128p. (YA). (gr. 5 ...). lib. bdg. 20.95 (*0-89490-990-8*) Enslow Pubs.

...arilyn T. Drugs: Should They Be Legalized? LC ...-12265. (Issues in Focus Ser.). (Illus.). 128p. (YA). (gr. 6 up). 1996. lib. bdg. 20.95 (*0-89490-738-7*) Enslow Pubs.

— Gangs: Trouble in the Streets. LC 94-34619. (Issues in Focus Ser.). (Illus.). 128p. (YA). (gr. 6 up). 1995. lib. bdg. 20.95 (*0-89490-492-2*) Enslow Pubs.

— Gay & Lesbian Rights: A Struggle. LC 98-21258. (Issues in Focus Ser.). (Illus.). 128p. (YA). (gr. 6 up). 1998. lib. bdg. 20.95 (*0-89490-958-4*) Enslow Pubs.

— Natural Crafts: Seventy-Two Easy Projects. (Illus.). 245p. 1994. pap. 16.95 (*0-8117-2564-2*) Stackpole.

— Prisons: Today's Debate. LC 96-40137. (Issues in Focus Ser.). 128p. (YA). (gr. 6 up). 1997. lib. bdg. 20.95 (*0-89490-906-1*) Enslow Pubs.

Oliver, Marina. The Baron's Bride. large type ed. (Linford Romance Library). 1991. pap. 16.99 (*0-7089-7107-5*, Linford) Ulverscroft.

— Campaign for a Bride. large type ed. 320p. 1994. 11.50 (*0-7089-3117-0*) Ulverscroft.

— Cavalier Courtship. large type ed. (Romance Ser.). 1991. 27.99 (*0-7089-2466-2*) Ulverscroft.

— The Cobweb Cage. large type ed. 653p. 1995. 27.99 (*0-7505-0729-2*, Pub. by Mgna Lrg Print) Ulverscroft.

— Gavotte. large type ed. 184p. 1990. 20.95 (*0-7451-1093-2*, G K Hall Lrg Type) Mac Lib Ref.

— Highland Destiny. large type ed. (Historical Romance Ser.). 1991. 27.99 (*0-7089-2411-5*) Ulverscroft.

— Highwayman's Hazard. large type ed. (Dales Large Print Ser.). 231p. 1998. pap. 19.99 (*1-85389-803-1*, Dales) Ulverscroft.

— Lord Hugo's Bride. large type ed. (Linford Romance Library). 1991. pap. 16.99 (*0-7089-7101-6*, Linford) Ulverscroft.

— Lord Hugo's Wedding. large type ed. (Linford Romance Library). 320p. 1993. pap. 16.99 (*0-7089-7459-7*, Linford) Ulverscroft.

— Masquerade for the King. large type ed. (Historical Romance Ser.). 272p. 1992. 27.99 (*0-7089-2679-7*) Ulverscroft.

— Player's Wench. large type ed. (Dales Large Print Ser.). 1994. pap. 18.99 (*1-85389-511-3*, Pub. by Mgna Lrg Print) Ulverscroft.

— Runaway Hill. large type ed. (Historical Romance Ser.). 288p. 1992. 11.50 (*0-7089-2592-8*) Ulverscroft.

— Strife Beyond Tamar. large type ed. (Dales Large Print Ser.). 1995. pap. 18.99 (*1-85389-573-3*, Dales) Ulverscroft.

— Veiled Destiny. 224p. 25.00 (*0-7278-5246-9*) Severn Hse.

— Veiled Destiny. large type ed. (Magna Large Print Ser.). 320p. 1998. 29.99 (*0-7505-1252-0*, Pub. by Mgna Lrg Print) Ulverscroft.

***Oliver, Marina.** Write & Sell Your Novel: The Fiction Writer's Guide to Writing for Publication. 2nd ed. (Creative Writing Ser.). (Illus.). 144p. 2000. pap. 19.95 (*1-85703-575-5*, Pub. by How To Bks) Midpt Trade.

Oliver, Marina. Writing & Selling a Novel: How to Craft Your Fiction for Publication. (Successful Writing Ser.). 144p. 1996. pap. 19.95 (*1-85703-406-6*, Pub. by How To Bks) Trans-Atl Phila.

— Writing Historical Fiction: How to Create Authentic Historical Fiction & Get It Published. 144p. 2000. pap. 19.95 (*1-85703-294-2*, Pub. by How To Bks) Midpt Trade.

— Writing Romantic Fiction: How to Make a Success of Your Creative Work. (Successful Writing Ser.). 128p. 1997. pap. 19.95 (*1-85703-466-X*, Pub. by How To Bks) Trans-Atl Phila.

— Writing Romantic Fiction: How to Make a Success of Your Creative Work. 160p. 2000. pap. 14.95 (*1-85703-147-4*, Pub. by How To Bks) Midpt Trade.

Oliver, Marina & Oliver, Deborah. Starting to Write: How to Create Written Work for Publication & Profit. (Successful Writing Ser.). 128p. 1996. pap. 19.95 (*1-85703-401-5*, Pub. by How To Bks) Trans-Atl Phila.

Oliver, Mark A., jt. auth. see Talbot, Steven R.

Oliver, Mark E. Modern Communications. 3rd ed. (Illus.). 176p. (C). 1988. student ed. 21.00 (*0-317-64538-2*) P-H.

Oliver, Martin. Agent Arthur's Jungle Journey. (Usborne Puzzle Adventures Ser.). (Illus.). 48p. (J). (gr. 4-7). 1989. lib. bdg. 13.95 (*0-88110-334-9*) EDC.

Oliver, Martin. What's Wrong? The Fletcher Family's Picnic Puzzle. (Illus.). 32p. (YA). (gr. 1-3). 1999. pap. 6.95 (*0-7641-0905-7*) Barron.

Oliver-Martin, Felix. L' Organisation Corporative de la France d'Ancien Regime. xiii, 565p. reprint ed. write for info. (*0-318-71385-3*) G Olms Pubs.

Oliver, Marvin. Individualized Reading: A Whole Language Approach. 64p. (C). 1998. pap. text 12.95 (*0-935435-03-4*) High Impact Pr.

— Visual Imagery Response Scale: Manual of Directions. 22p. (C). 1998. pap. text 13.95 (*0-935435-12-3*) High Impact Pr.

Oliver, Marvin E. Word Identification for Teachers. rev. ed. Gibson, Victoria L., ed. LC 86-82262. 80p. (C). 1992. pap. text 9.95 (*0-935435-00-X*) High Impact Pr.

— Writing Student Papers. LC 94-77264. (Illus.). (Orig.). 1994. pap. 7.95 (*0-935435-10-7*) High Impact Pr.

Oliver, Mary. American Primitive. 88p. 1983. pap. 13.95 (*0-316-65004-8*) Little.

— American Primitive. 1998. mass mkt. 12.95 (*0-316-19145-0*, Back Bay) Little.

— Blue Pastures. LC 95-16881. 136p. 1995. 22.00 (*0-15-100190-1*); pap. 14.00 (*0-15-600215-9*) Harcourt.

— Dream Work. LC 86-7656. 96p. 1986. pap. 10.95 (*0-87113-069-6*, Atlntc Mnthly) Grove-Atltic.

— House of Light. LC 89-46059. 96p. 1992. pap. 13.00 (*0-8070-6811-X*) Beacon Pr.

— New & Selected Poems. LC 92-7767. 272p. 1993. 28.50 (*0-8070-6818-7*) Beacon Pr.

— New & Selected Poems. LC 92-7767. 255p. 1993. pap. 16.00 (*0-8070-6819-5*) Beacon Pr.

— A Poetry Handbook. LC 93-49676. 132p. 1994. pap. 12.00 (*0-15-672400-6*, Harvest Bks) Harcourt.

— Rules for the Dance. LC 98-2625. 224p. 1998. pap. 13.00 (*0-395-85086-X*, Mariner Bks) HM.

— Twelve Moons. LC 79-10428. 77p. 1979. pap. 12.95 (*0-316-65000-5*) Little.

***Oliver, Mary.** Twelve Moons. 1998. mass mkt. 12.95 (*0-316-19148-5*, Back Bay) Little.

Oliver, Mary. West Wind. LC 97-2986. 96p. 1997. 21.00 (*0-395-85082-7*) HM.

— West Wind. 64p. 1998. pap. 14.00 (*0-395-85085-1*) HM.

— West Wind. 1996. pap. 11.95 (*0-15-600213-2*) Harcourt.

— West Wind. 1996. 19.95 (*0-15-100159-6*) Harcourt.

— White Pine: Poems & Prose Poems. LC 94-20112. 80p. 1994. 19.95 (*0-15-100131-6*); pap. 13.00 (*0-15-600120-9*) Harcourt.

— Winter Hours: Prose, Prose Poems, & Poems. LC 99-19141. 109p. 1999. 22.00 (*0-395-85084-3*) HM.

***Oliver, Mary.** Winter Hours: Prose, Prose Poems & Poems. 144p. 2000. pap. 14.00 (*0-395-85087-8*, Mariner Bks) HM.

Oliver, Mary A. Conjugal Spirituality: The Primacy of Mutual Love in Christian Tradition. 176p. (Orig.). (C). 1994. pap. 12.95 (*1-55612-312-4*) Sheed & Ward WI.

Oliver, Mary M. & Surovell, Edward, eds. Story of an Ordinary Woman: The Extraordinary Life of Florence Cushman Milner. (Illus.). 135p. 1989. 10.00 (*0-9614344-3-0*) Historical Soc MI.

Oliver, Melvin L. Black Wealth White Wealth: A New Perspective on Racial Inquality. (Illus.). 256p. 1996. pap. 18.99 (*0-415-91847-2*) Routledge.

Oliver, Melvin L. & Shapiro, Thomas M. Black Wealth/White Wealth: A New Perspective on Racial Inequality. LC 95-17000. 256p. (C). 1995. 35.00 (*0-415-91375-6*) Routledge.

Oliver, Merle J., jt. auth. see Fay, Jessica B.

Oliver, Michael. Alden Nowlan & His Works. 58p. (C). 1990. pap. 9.95 (*1-55022-067-5*, Pub. by ECW) Genl Dist Srvs.

— Benjamin Britten. (20th Century Composers Ser.). (Illus.). 240p. (Orig.). 1996. pap. 19.95 (*0-7148-3277-4*, Pub. by Phaidon Press) Phaidon Pr.

— Disability Politics. LC 96-208111. 240p. (C). 1996. 75.00 (*0-415-07998-5*); pap. 22.99 (*0-415-07999-3*) Routledge.

— Igor Stravinsky. (20th Century Composers Ser.). (Illus.). 240p. 1995. pap. 19.95 (*0-7148-3158-1*, Pub. by Phaidon Press) Phaidon Pr.

— Lotus 49. (Illus.). 256p. 1999. 49.95 (*1-901295-51-6*, 129154AE, Pub. by Vloce Pub) Motorbooks Intl.

— The Politics of Disablement: A Sociological Approach. LC 90-8133. 168p. 1990. text 29.95 (*0-312-04658-8*) St Martin.

— Understanding Disability: From Theory to Practice. 1995. pap. 19.95 (*0-312-15803-3*); text 49.95 (*0-312-15794-0*) St Martin.

Oliver, Michael, ed. Social Work: Disabled People & Disabling Environments. 160p. 1991. 49.50 (*1-85302-042-7*) Taylor & Francis.

— Social Work: Disabled People & Disabling Environments. 208p. 1992. pap. 19.95 (*1-85302-178-4*) Taylor & Francis.

***Oliver, Michael & Partridge, Richard.** Napoleonic Army Handbook: The British Army & Her Allies. (Illus.). 80p. 2000. 75.00 (*0-09-477630-X*, Pub. by Constable & Co) Trafalgar.

Oliver, Michael, ed. see Workshop on Strategies for Screening for Risk of C.

Oliver, Michael J. Hegel's Revenge. LC 83-8834. 1987. pap. 13.95 (*0-87949-236-8*) Ashley Bks.

— Whatever Happened to Monetarism? Economic Policy Making & Social Learning in the United Kingdom since 1979. LC 97-14589. (Modern Social & Economic History Ser.: Vol. 2). (Illus.). 204p. 1997. text 78.95 (*1-85928-433-7*, Pub. by Scolar Pr) Ashgate Pub Co.

Oliver, Michael J., jt. auth. see Aldcroft, Derek H.

Oliver, Michael R. DSF Plan. 54p. (Orig.). 1995. pap. 17.99 (*0-9645047-0-7*) DSF Plan.

Oliver, Mona A., ed. see Savage, Gary.

Oliver, N. T. Lee's Priceless Recipes. (Classic Reprint Ser.). 370p. 1995. reprint ed. pap. 5.95 (*0-921335-17-2*, Pub. by LVTL) Veritas Tools.

Oliver, Nancy. Autumn. (American Homestead Cookbook Ser.). 128p. 1999. mass mkt. 5.00 (*1-885507-20-8*) Fundco Printers.

— Southwestern Sampler: Live Health-Low Fat. 128p. 1998. mass mkt. 5.00 (*1-885507-11-9*) Fundco Printers.

— Summer. (American Homestead Cookbook Ser.: Vol. 3). 128p. 1999. mass mkt. 5.00 (*1-885507-19-4*) Fundco Printers.

***Oliver, Nancy, ed.** American Homestead. 4 vols., Set. 128p. 1999. mass mkt., boxed set 20.00 (*1-885507-21-6*) Fundco Printers.

Oliver, Nancy, ed. Cookin in the U. S. A. Vol. 2: Live Healthy - Low Fat. 128p. 1998. mass mkt. 5.00 (*1-885507-07-0*) Fundco Printers.

— Down Home Cooking Vol. 3: Live Healthy - Low Fat. 128p. 1998. mass mkt. 5.00 (*1-885507-08-9*) Fundco Printers.

— Holiday Favorites Vol. 4: Live Healthy - Low Fat. 128p. 1998. mass mkt. 5.00 (*1-885507-09-7*) Fundco Printers.

— Holiday Favorites: Down Home Cooking: Cookin in the U. S. A.: Southwestern. (Live Healthy . . . Live Better Ser.). 1998. mass mkt. 20.00 (*1-885507-10-0*) Fundco Printers.

***Oliver, Nancy, ed.** Spring. (American Homestead Cookbook Ser.: Vol. 2). 128p. 1999. mass mkt. 5.00 (*1-885507-18-6*) Fundco Printers.

Oliver, Nancy, ed. Twas the Meal Before Christmas. 144p. 1998. mass mkt. 5.00 (*1-885507-06-2*) Fundco Printers.

***Oliver, Nancy, ed.** Winter. (American Homestead Cookbook Ser.: Vol. 1). 128p. 1999. mass mkt. 5.00 (*1-885507-17-8*) Fundco Printers.

Oliver, Naomi. Passion. 24p. 1999. pap. 7.00 (*0-8059-4659-4*) Dorrance.

Oliver, Narelle. The Best Beak in Boonaroo Bay. LC 95-8075. (Illus.). 32p. (J). (ps-3). 1995. 8.00 (*1-55591-227-3*) Fulcrum Pub.

— The Hunt. (Illus.). 32p. (J). (gr. 2-5). 1998. pap. 6.95 (*1-887734-43-0*) Star Brght Bks.

Oliver, O., jt. auth. see Allwright, A. D.

Oliver, Owen L. Colorado Real Estate Transactions. LC 85-80619. (Practice Systems Library Manual). 1985. 120.00 (*0-318-18298-X*); 67.50 (*0-317-03274-7*) West Group.

Oliver, P. Black Music in Britain. 208p. 1990. 123.00 (*0-335-15298-8*); pap. 34.95 (*0-335-15297-X*) OpUniv Pr.

Oliver, P. M. Donne's Religious Writing. LC 96-33543. (Medieval & Renaissance Library). (C). 1997. 65.00 (*0-582-25018-8*) Longman.

— Donne's Religious Writing: A Discourse of Feigned Devotion. LC 96-33543. (Medieval & Renaissance Library). 304p. (C). 1997. pap. 33.53 (*0-582-25017-X*) Longman.

Oliver, Pam D., ed. Subject Bibliographies of Government Publications: A Compilation of Books, Reports, & Pamphlets Available from the U. S. Government Printing Office at the Time of Their Publication. 932p. 1989. 85.00 (*1-55888-813-6*) Omnigraphics Inc.

Oliver, Pamela, jt. auth. see Marwell, Gerald.

Oliver, Patricia. Lady in Gray, 1 vol. (Signet Regency Romance Ser.). 221p. 1999. mass mkt. 4.99 (*0-451-19500-0*) NAL.

***Oliver, Patricia.** Lady Jane's Nemesis. (Regency Romance Ser.). 2000. mass mkt. 4.99 (*0-451-20069-1*, Sig) NAL.

— Scandalous Secrets. (Signet Regency Romance Ser.). 224p. 1999. mass mkt. 4.99 (*0-451-19886-7*, Sig) NAL.

Oliver, Patricia. An Unsuitable Match. 1999. mass mkt. 5.50 (*0-451-18801-2*, Sig) NAL.

Oliver, Paul. Blues off the Record: Thirty Years of Blues Commentary. (Quality Paperbacks Ser.). (Illus.). 132p. 1988. reprint ed. pap. 13.95 (*0-306-80321-6*) Da Capo.

— Conversation with the Blues. 2nd ed. LC 96-47887. (Illus.). 224p. (C). 1997. 54.95 (*0-521-59181-3*) Cambridge U Pr.

— Conversation with the Blues. 3rd ed. LC 96-47887. (Illus.). 175p. 1997. pap. write for info. (*0-521-59826-5*) Cambridge U Pr.

— Dwellings: The House across the World. (Illus.). 256p. 1987. 40.00 (*0-292-71554-4*) U of Tex Pr.

— Gospel Blues. rev. ed. 1997. pap. 16.95 (*0-393-30357-8*) Norton.

— How to Study. (Teach Yourself Ser.). 192p. 1998. pap. 9.95 (*0-8442-0232-0*, 02320, Teach Yrslf) NTC Contemp Pub Co.

— Research: For Business Marketing & Education. (Teach Yourself Ser.). (Illus.). 192p. 1998. pap. 9.95 (*0-8442-0015-8*, 00158, Teach Yrslf) NTC Contemp Pub Co.

— Screening the Blues: Aspects of the Blues Tradition. (Quality Paperbacks Ser.). (Illus.). 302p. 1989. reprint ed. pap. 13.95 (*0-306-80344-5*) Da Capo.

— The Story of the Blues. rev. ed. LC 98-12192. (Illus.). 288p. 1998. text 50.00 (*1-55553-355-8*); pap. text 16.95 (*1-55553-354-X*) NE U Pr.

Oliver, Paul, compiled by. Early Blues Songbook. (Illus.). 192p. 1982. pap. 21.95 (*0-86001-942-X*, AM29083) Music Sales.

Oliver, Paul, ed. Encyclopedia of Vernacular Architecture of the World, 3 vols. LC 97-6060. (Illus.). 2450p. (C). 1998. text 995.00 (*0-521-56422-0*) Cambridge U Pr.

— Lifelong & Continuing Education: What Is a Learning Society? LC 99-71887. (Monitoring Change in Education Ser.). 240p. 1999. text 65.95 (*1-84014-905-1*, Pub. by Ashgate Pub) Ashgate Pub Co.

— The Management of Educational Change: A Case Study Approach. (Monitoring Change in Education Ser.). 250p. 1996. text 64.95 (*1-85742-379-8*, Pub. by Arena) Ashgate Pub Co.

— Shelter, Sign & Symbol. LC 77-77089. (Illus.). 1977. 40.00 (*0-87951-068-4*, Pub. by Overlook Pr) Penguin Putnam.

— Shelter, Sign & Symbol. LC 77-77089. (Illus.). 1980. pap. 16.95 (*0-87951-112-5*, Pub. by Overlook Pr) Penguin Putnam.

Oliver, Paul, et al. Dunroamin' The Suburban Semi & Its Enemies. (Illus.). 224p. 1995. pap. 22.95 (*0-7126-6029-1*, Pub. by Pimlico) Trafalgar.

Oliver, Paul, jt. auth. see Cowley, John.

Oliver, Pearl M. & Oliver, Samuel P. Toward a Caring Society: Ideas into Action. LC 95-3339. 256p. 1995. pap. 19.95 (*0-275-95453-6*, Praeger Pubs) Greenwood.

Oliver, Peter. Bicycling: A Complete Guide. LC 95-5526. (Trailside Series Guide). (Illus.). 192p. 1995. pap. 17.95 (*0-393-31337-9*) Norton.

— G. Howard Ferguson: Ontario Tory. (Ontario Historical Studies). 1977. text 27.50 (*0-8020-3346-6*) U of Toronto Pr.

— Insider's Guide to the Best Skiing in New England. rev. ed. (Illus.). 192p. 1994. pap. 12.95 (*0-89732-154-5*) Menasha Ridge.

— Peter Oliver's "Origin & Progress of the American Rebellion" A Tory View. Adair, Douglass & Schutz, John A., eds. xxiv, 176p. 1961. pap. 10.95 (*0-8047-0601-8*) Stanford U Pr.

— A Poem Sacred to the Memory of the Honorable Josiah Willard. (Notable American Authors Ser.). 1999. reprint ed. lib. bdg. 125.00 (*0-7812-4668-7*) Rprt Serv.

— The Puritan Commonwealth. LC 75-31127. reprint ed. 41.50 (*0-404-13606-0*) AMS Pr.

— Saints of Chaos. LC 67-23255. (Essay Index Reprint Ser.). 1977. 19.95 (*0-8369-0752-3*) Ayer.

— Scripture Lexicon. (Notable American Authors Ser.). 1999. reprint ed. lib. bdg. 125.00 (*0-7812-4669-5*) Rprt Serv.

— A Speech... After Death of Isaac Lothrop. (Notable American Authors Ser.). 1999. reprint ed. lib. bdg. 125.00 (*0-7812-4667-9*) Rprt Serv.

— Terror to Evil-Doers: Prisons & Punishments in Nineteenth-Century Ontario. LC 97-93258. (Illus.). 575p. 1997. text. write for info. (*0-8020-4345-3*) U of Toronto Pr.

***Oliver, Peter, et al, eds.** Faith in Law: Essays in Legal Theory. 256p. 1999. 40.00 (*1-901362-95-7*, Pub. by Hart Pub) Intl Spec Bk.

Oliver, Peter N. "Terror to Evil-Doers" Prisons & Punishment in Nineteenth-Century Ontario. (Illus.). 632p. 1998. pap. text 45.00 (*0-8020-8166-5*) U of Toronto Pr.

Oliver, Philip D. & Peel, Fred W., Jr. Readings & Materials on Tax Policy. LC 96-213627. (University Casebook Ser.). 803p. 1996. text. write for info. (*1-56662-427-4*) Foundation Pr.

— Teachers' Manual to Accompany Readings & Materials on Tax Policy. (University Casebook Ser.). 1996. pap. text, teacher ed. write for info. (*1-56662-435-5*) Foundation Pr.

Oliver, Philip M. The Oliver System--Using the Factor Ranking-Benchmark-Guidechart Evaluation Plan, 2 vols. LC 84-90567. (Illus.). 267p. 1984. 90.00 (*0-9617464-2-4*) P M Oliver.

— The Oliver System--Using the Factor Ranking-Benchmark-Guidechart Evaluation Plan, 2 vols., Set. LC 84-90567. (Illus.). 267p. 1984. 90.00 (*0-9617464-0-8*) P M Oliver.

Oliver, R. & Taylor, L. Logarithmic Descriptions of Whitehead Groups & Class Groups for P-Groups. LC 88-22226. (Memoirs Ser.: No. 76/392). 97p. 1988. pap. 16.00 (*0-8218-2455-4*, MEMO/76/392) Am Math.

Oliver, R. A., jt. ed. see Fage, J. D.

Oliver, R. D. Bottum (& Longbottom) Family Album: An Historical & Biographical Genealogy of the Descendants of Daniel (-1732) & Elizabeth (Lamb) Longbottom of Norwich, Ct. (Illus.). 341p. 1995. reprint ed. pap. 52.00 (*0-8328-4746-1*); reprint ed. lib. bdg. 62.00 (*0-8328-4745-3*) Higginson Bk Co.

Oliver, R. M. & Smith, J. Q., eds. Influence Diagrams, Belief Nets & Decision Analysis. LC 89-38933. 500p. 1990. 270.00 (*0-471-92381-8*) Wiley.

Oliver, R. T. & Coptcoat, M. J., eds. Bladder Cancer. LC 97-78239. (Cancer Surveys Ser.). (Illus.). 170p. (C). 1998. text 93.00 (*0-87969-529-3*) Cold Spring Harbor.

Oliver, R. W., ed. HPLC of Macromolecules: A Practical Approach. 2nd ed. LC 97-42708. (Practical Approach Ser.: Vol. 190). (Illus.). 224p. 1998. pap. text 45.00 (*0-19-963570-6*) OUP.

Oliver, R. W. & Allwright, A. D. Terms & Conditions of Contract. 125p. 1989. 65.00 (*0-7855-1098-2*, Pub. by Inst Pur & Supply) St Mut.

Oliver, R. W., jt. auth. see Allwright, A. D.

Oliver, Raylynn. Contraceptive Use in Ghana: The Role of Service Availability, Quality & Price, 111. LC 94-31691. (LSMS Working Papers). 60p. 1995. pap. 22.00 (*0-8213-3020-9*, 13020) World Bank.

— Model Living Standards Measurement Study Survey Questionnaire for the Countries of the Former Soviet Union. LC 97-19577. (Living Standards Measurement Survey Working Paper Ser.: No. 130). 144p. 1997. pap. 22.00 (*0-8213-3934-6*, 13934) World Bank.

Oliver, Reggie. Imaginary Lines: A Comedy. LC 88-173613. ii, 58p. 1987. write for info. (*0-573-11241-X*) S French Trade.

Oliver, Regina M., jt. auth. see Meehan, Bridget M.

Oliver-Rehorn, Marcy. The Adoption Directory: Connecting You to the Perfect Professionals for a Successful Adoption. Keefer, Carol, ed. LC 97-95361. (Illus.). 136p. 1998. pap. 12.95 (*0-9660786-3-2*) Cherub Pub.

— The Adoption Planner: An Adoption Consultation with Marcy Oliver-Rehorn. 34p. 1999. 19.95 (*0-9660786-4-0*) Cherub Pub.

Oliver, Revilo P. Mrcchakatika the Little Clay Cart: A Drama in Ten Acts. LC 74-14116. 1975. lib. bdg. 59.50 (*0-8371-7789-8*, SULC, Greenwood Pr) Greenwood.

Oliver, Rice D. Lone Woman of Ghalas-Hat. (Illus.). 32p. (J). (gr. 4-8). 1993. pap. 6.00 (*0-936778-51-2*); lib. bdg. 13.00 (*0-936778-52-0*) Calif Weekly.

***Oliver, Rice D.** Student Atlas of California. 5th ed. LC 91-71717. 67p. 1999. pap. 12.00 (*0-936778-07-5*) Calif Weekly.

Oliver, Rice D. Student Atlas of California. 5th rev. ed. LC 91-71717. (Illus.). 66p. 1999. lib. bdg., teacher ed. 15.00 (*0-936778-09-1*) Calif Weekly.

— Student Atlas of California. 5th rev. ed. LC 91-71717. (Illus.). 66p. (J). (gr. 4-12). 1999. pap. 13.00 (*0-936778-08-3*) Calif Weekly.

***Oliver, Richard & Leipold, Craig.** Hockey Tonk: The Amazing Story of the Nashville Predators. 2000. 22.99 (*0-7852-6841-3*) Nelson.

Oliver, Richard, jt. auth. see Cotton, Bob.

Oliver, Richard G., jt. auth. see Jones, Malcolm L.

Oliver, Richard G., jt. ed. see Jones, Malcolm L.

An Asterisk (*) at the beginning of an entry indicates that the title is appearing for the first time.

Oliver, Richard L. Satisfaction: A Behavioral Perspective on the Consumer. LC 96-17899. 448p. (C). 1996. 79.06 (*0-07-048025-7*) McGraw.
Oliver, Richard L., jt. ed. see Rust, Roland T.
Oliver, Richard P. & Schweizer, Michael, eds. Molecular Fungal Biology. LC 99-10041. (Illus.). 320p. (C). 1999. text 80.00 (*0-521-56116-7*); pap. text 34.95 (*0-521-56784-X*) Cambridge U Pr.
Oliver, Richard R., jt. auth. see Kain, Roger J.
Oliver, Richard W. The Coming Biotech Age: The Business of Bio-Materials. LC 99-53282. 266p. 1999. 24.95 (*0-07-135020-9*) McGraw.
— The Shape of Things to Come: 7 Imperatives for Winning in the New World of Business. LC 98-8119. 256p. 1998. 24.95 (*0-07-048263-2*) McGraw.
Oliver, Robert. El Arqueopterix. (Biblioteca de Dinosaurios).Tr. of Archaeopteryx. 24p. (J). Date not set. lib. bdg. 13.95 (*0-86593-224-7*) Rourke Corp.
— Career Unrest: A Source of Creativity. 1981. text 20.00 (*0-685-09088-4*) CU Ctr Career Res.
— Cave Bear. (Ice-Age Monsters Ser.). 24p. (J). lib. bdg. 18.60 (*0-86592-844-4*) Rourke Enter.
— Dinosaur Library, 3 bks., Set I. (Illus.). 312p. (J). 1984. lib. bdg. 55.80 (*0-86592-200-4*) Rourke Enter.
— Dinosaur Library, 6 bks., Set III. (Illus.). 144p. (J). 1986. lib. bdg. write for info. (*0-86592-214-4*) Rourke Enter.
— Glyptodon. (Ice-Age Monsters Ser.). 24p. (J). 1986. lib. bdg. 13.95 (*0-86592-843-6*) Rourke Enter.
— El Iguanodon. (Biblioteca de Dinosaurios). 24p. (J). Date not set. lib. bdg. 13.95 (*0-86593-226-3*) Rourke Corp.
— Megaceros. (Ice-Age Monsters Ser.). 24p. (J). 1986. lib. bdg. 18.60 (*0-86592-846-0*) Rourke Enter.
— Woolly Rhinoceros. (Ice-Age Monsters Ser.). 24p. (J). 1986. lib. bdg. 18.60 (*0-86592-848-7*) Rourke Enter.
Oliver, Robert & Endersby, Colin. Teaching & Assessing Nurses: A Handbook for Preceptors. (Illus.). 166p. 1995. pap. text 29.50 (*0-7020-1720-5*, Pub. by W B Saunders) Saunders.
Oliver, Robert & Langrish, Bob. A Photographic Guide to Conformation. 250p. 1990. 68.00 (*0-85131-522-4*, Pub. by J A Allen) Trafalgar.
Oliver, Robert, jt. auth. see Stafford, Christine.
Oliver, Robert A. & Johnson, Dewayne J. Beginning Swimming. (Illus.). 52p. (C). 1982. pap. text 9.95 (*0-89641-282-2*) American Pr.
Oliver, Robert A., jt. auth. see Johnson, Dewayne J.
Oliver, Robert M. & Marshall, Kneale T. Decision Analysis & Forecasting. 1995. pap. text, student ed. write for info. (*0-07-048028-1*) McGraw.
Oliver, Robert M., jt. auth. see Marshall, Kneale T.
Oliver, Robert T. Communication & Culture in Ancient India & China. LC 75-151717. 326p. 1971. reprint ed. pap. 101.10 (*0-608-06987-6*, 206719500009) Bks Demand.
— Four Who Spoke Out. LC 75-101831. (Biography Index Reprint Ser.). 1977. 21.95 (*0-8369-8005-0*) Ayer.
— History of Public Speaking in America. LC 78-13428. 566p. 1978. reprint ed. lib. bdg. 47.50 (*0-313-21152-3*, OLPS, Greenwood Pr) Greenwood.
— A History of the Korean People in Modern Times: 1800 to the Present. LC 92-50486. (C). 1993. 49.50 (*0-87413-477-3*) U Delaware Pr.
— The Influence of Rhetoric in the Shaping of Great Britain: From the Roman Invasion to the Early Nineteenth Century. LC 85-40519. 320p. 1986. 50.00 (*0-87413-289-4*) U Delaware Pr.
— Leadership in Asia: Persuasive Communication in the Making of Nations, 1850-1950. 1989. 47.50 (*0-87413-353-X*) U Delaware Pr.
— Public Speaking in the Reshaping of Great Britain. LC 86-40355. (Illus.). 248p. 1987. 40.00 (*0-87413-315-7*) U Delaware Pr.
Oliver, Robert W. George Woods & the World Bank. LC 94-8738. 228p. 1994. lib. bdg. 32.00 (*1-55587-503-3*) L Rienner.
Oliver, Rocky, jt. auth. see Kreisle, Bill.
Oliver, Roderick T., et al, eds. Preventing Prostate Cancer: Screening Versus Chemoprevention Pros & Cons Based on New Views of Its Biology, Early Events & Clinical Behaviour. LC 95-175636. (Cancer Surveys Ser.: Vol. 23). (Illus.). 351p. reprint ed. pap. 108.90 (*0-608-09129-4*, 206976100006) Bks Demand.
Oliver, Roger W., ed. Ingmar Bergman: An Artist's Journey. LC 94-46211. (Illus.). 192p. 1995. pap. 17.45 (*1-55970-295-8*, Pub. by Arcade Pub Inc) Time Warner.
***Oliver, Roland.** African Experience: From Olduvai Gorge to the 21st Century. 2nd ed. 351p. 2000. pap. 24.00 (*0-8133-9042-7*) Westview.
Oliver, Roland Anthony. African Experience. LC 91-57950. (Illus.). 304p. 1992. pap. 28.00 (*0-06-430218-0*, Perennial) HarperTrade.
Oliver, Roland Anthony. In the Realms of Gold: Pioneering in African History. LC 97-7217. (Illus.). 425p. 1997. 59.95 (*0-299-15650-8*); pap. 24.95 (*0-299-15654-0*) U of Wis Pr.
Oliver, Roland Anthony & Atmore, Anthony. Africa since 1800. LC 93-9779. (Illus.). 320p. (C). 1994. text 59.95 (*0-521-41946-8*) Cambridge U Pr.
— Africa since 1800. 4th ed. LC 93-9779. (Illus.). 320p. (C). 1994. pap. text 20.95 (*0-521-42970-6*) Cambridge U Pr.
Oliver, Ronald, jt. auth. see Hoover, John.
Oliver, Rose & Bock, Frances. Coping with Alzheimer's: A Caregiver's Emotional Survival Guide. 1989. pap. 10.00 (*0-87980-424-6*) Wilshire.
Oliver, Ruby L. My Unusual Journey to Success: Based on a True Story. LC 96-92997. 160p. 12.95 (*0-9655770-9-0*) Oliver Prods.
Oliver, S. G., jt. auth. see Tuite, M. F.
Oliver, S. Pasfield. Pendennis & St. Mawes: An Historical Sketch of Two Cornish Castles. (C). 1989. 70.00 (*0-907566-90-1*, Pub. by Dyllansow Truran) St Mut.
Oliver, Sally, ed. see Broili, June.
Oliver, Samuel L. What the Dying Teach Us: Lessons on Living. LC 97-43515. (Illus.). 128p. 1998. 29.95 (*0-7890-0475-5*, Haworth Pastrl); pap. 14.95 (*0-7890-0476-3*, Haworth Pastrl) Haworth Pr.
Oliver, Samuel P., jt. auth. see Oliver, Pearl M.
Oliver, Sandra, jt. auth. see Oliver, Willie.
Oliver, Sandra L. Saltwater Foodways: New Englanders & Their Food, at Sea & Ashore, in the Nineteenth Century. (Illus.). xiii, 442p. 1995. 39.95 (*0-913372-72-2*) Mystic Seaport.
Oliver-Smith, Anthony. Angry Earth: Disaster in Anthropological Perspective. LC 98-49959. 1999. text. write for info. (*0-415-91986-X*) Routledge.
***Oliver-Smith, Anthony.** Angry Earth: Disaster in Anthropological Perspective. LC 98-49959. 1999. pap. 27.99 (*0-415-91987-8*) Routledge.
Oliver-Smith, Anthony. Involuntary Migration & Resettlement: The Problems & Responses of Dislocated People. Hansen, Art, ed. (Special Studies). (Illus.). 1982. text 43.50 (*0-89158-976-7*) Westview.
Oliver, Stefan. Illuminated Letters: Paint Your Own. 1999. pap. text 12.99 (*0-7858-1064-1*) Bk Sales Inc.
Oliver, Stephanie S. Seven Soulful Sisters. 1999. 22.95 (*0-385-48767-3*) Doubleday.
Oliver, Stephanie Stokes. Daily Cornbread: 365 Secrets for a Healthy Mind, Body & Soul. LC 99-24396. 384p. 1999. 22.95 (*0-385-48769-X*) Doubleday.
Oliver, Stephen, photos by. My First Look at Numbers. LC 89-63088. (Illus.). 24p. (J). (ps). 1990. 9.00 (*0-679-80533-8*, Pub. by Random Bks Yng Read) Random.
Oliver, Steve. Clueless in Seattle. (Illus.). 137p. (Orig.). 1995. pap. 10.95 (*0-9644138-6-8*) OffByOne.
***Oliver, Steve.** Lotus Domino 5 Programming Bible. (Illus.). 2000. pap. text 39.99 (*0-7645-4722-4*) IDG Bks.
Oliver, Steve. Moody Forever. LC 98-21446. 272p. 1998. text 22.95 (*0-312-19301-7*) St Martin.
— Moody Forever. 272p. 1999. pap. 5.99 (*0-312-96923-6*, St Martins Paperbacks) St Martin.
— Moody Gets the Blues. (Illus.). 256p. 1996. 21.95 (*0-9644138-7-6*) OffByOne.
— Moody Gets the Blues, Vol. 1. 1998. 5.99 (*0-312-96502-8*, Pub. by Tor Bks) St Martin.
Oliver, Steve & Wood, Pete. Lotus Domino Web Site Development. LC 98-24387. 615p. 1998. pap. 44.99 incl. cd-rom (*0-07-913755-5*) McGraw.
Oliver, Sylvia A., jt. ed. see Oliver, Howard R.
***Oliver, Taye.** Folk Art Angels Coloring Book. (Museo Mundo Activity Bks.). 24p. 1999. pap. 4.99 (*0-9677409-0-8*) MNMF.
— Folk Art Toys & Figurines Coloring Book. (Museo Mundo Activity Bks.). 24p. (J). (gr. k-7). 1999. pap. 4.99 (*0-9677409-1-6*) MNMF.
Oliver, Terri Hume, ed. see Du Bois, W. E. B.
Oliver, Tess. Red, Red Rose. 3rd ed. LC 96-72079. 192p. 2000. pap. 21.33 (*0-671-57014-5*) S&S Trade.
Oliver, Theodore J. Classic Period Settlement in the Uplands of Tonto Basin: Report on the Uplands Complex, Roosevelt Platform Mound Study. LC 97-24380. (Anthropological Field Studies: No. 34). 1998. write for info. (*1-886067-05-8*) ASU Office Cultural Res.
Oliver, Theodore J., et al. Salado Residential Settlements on Tonto Creek: Roosevelt Platform Mound Study: Report on the Cline Mesa Sites, Cline Terrace Complex, Pts. I & II. LC 97-37106. (Anthropological Field Studies: No. 38). 1997. write for info. (*1-886067-09-0*) ASU Office Cultural Res.
Oliver, Thomas W., 4th. A Narrative History of Cotton in Alabama: A Tour of the Old Alabama Town Cotton Gin. (Illus.). 96p. (Orig.). 1992. pap. 8.00 (*0-7012-5775-X*) Landmarks Found.
Oliver, Thomas W. The United Nations in Bangladesh. LC 77-85554. 253p. 1978. reprint ed. pap. 78.50 (*0-7837-9408-8*, 206015300004) Bks Demand.
Oliver, Tony. Touring Bikes: A Practical Guide. (Illus.). 176p. 1991. 39.95 (*1-85223-339-7*, Pub. by Cro1wood) Trafalgar.
Oliver, Valerie B. Fashion & Costume in American Popular Culture: A Bibliographical Guide. LC 96-161. (American Popular Culture Ser.). 296p. 1996. lib. bdg. 69.50 (*0-313-29412-7*, Greenwood Pr) Greenwood.
Oliver, Vickie. Kalyn's Life Adventures: Not Even in a Book. 32p. (J). (gr. 4-10). 1991. 4.95 (*1-877610-07-0*) Sea Island.
Oliver, Virginia H. Apocalypse of Green: A Study of Emily Dickinson's Eschatology. (American University Studies: American Literature: Ser. XXIV, Vol. 4). IX, 252p. 1989. text 38.00 (*0-8204-0887-5*) P Lang Pubng.
Oliver, W. C., et al, eds. Thin Films - Stresses & Mechanical Properties II Vol. 188: Symposium Proceedings. 365p. 1990. text 17.50 (*1-55899-077-1*) Materials Res.
Oliver, W. R. Genus Coprosma. (BMB Ser.: No. 132). 1969. reprint ed. 35.00 (*0-527-02238-1*) Periodicals Srv.
Oliver, Wade W. Stalkers of Pestilence: The Story of Man's Ideas of Infection. LC 77-119210. 1930. 21.95 (*0-8434-0092-7*, Pub. by McGrath NH) Ayer.
Oliver, Wendy, ed. Focus on Dance, Twelve: Dance in Higher Education. (Illus.). 128p. (Orig.). (C). 1992. pap. text 24.00 (*0-88314-521-9*) AAHPERD.
***Oliver, Wesley B.** Country Doctor. LC 98-68268. 160p. 1999. pap. 13.95 (*1-57197-149-1*) Pentland Pr.
Oliver, Willard M. Community Oriented Policing: A Systemic Approach to Policing. LC 97-23651. 444p. 1997. 70.00 (*0-13-524869-8*) P-H.
Oliver, William. The Violent Social World of Black Men. LC 98-7266. (Psychology Ser.). 208p. 1998. reprint ed. pap. 22.95 (*0-7879-4305-3*) Jossey-Bass.
Oliver, William, ed. Pigs, Peccaries & Hippos: An Action Plan for the Suiformes. (C). 1995. pap. text 27.00 (*2-8317-0057-4*, Pub. by IUCN) Island Pr.
Oliver, William, jt. auth. see Cross, Henry.
Oliver, William I., tr. see de Vega, Lope.
***Oliver, William J.** Primitive Peoples Without Salt: A Perspective for Industrialized Societies LC 97-92346. 290 p. 1998. write for info. (*0-9658325-0-3*) W J Oliver.
Oliver, William W. Why We Should Abolish the Income Tax: A Guide to the Principal Proposals. LC 95-71215. 150p. (Orig.). 1996. pap. 15.95 (*0-940121-33-6*, P303) Cross Cultural Pubns.
Olivera, Bernardo. How Far to Follow? The Martyrs of Atlas. Roberts, Augustine, tr. from FRE. LC 97-4714. 100p. (Orig.). 1997. pap. 14.95 (*1-879007-24-X*) St Bedes Pubns.
***Olivera, George.** Virtue in Diverse Traditions: An Introduction. LC 98-915553. 1998. write for info. (*81-7086-215-9*) Asian Trad Corp.
Olivera, Nuno. Junge Pferde - Junge Reiter. (Documenta Hippologica Ser.: Bd. 2). (Illus.). 120p. 1997. 32.00 (*3-487-08356-6*) G Olms Pubs.
— Klassische Grundsatze der Kunst, Pferde Auszubilden. (Schriften Ser.: Bd. 1). (Illus.). 172p. 1996. write for info. (*3-487-08355-8*) G Olms Pubs.
Olivera, Otto. Bibliografia de la Literatura Dominicana (1960-1982) LC 83-51004. (SPA.). 86p. 1984. pap. 18.00 (*0-89295-027-7*) Society Sp & Sp-Am.
— La Literatura en Periodicos & Revistas de Puerto Rico: Siglo XIX. LC 85-1143. (Comunicacion Ser.: No. 74). (SPA.). 410p. 1987. pap. 10.00 (*0-8477-0074-7*) U of PR Pr.
— La Literatura en Publicaciones Periodicas de Guatemala: Siglo XIX, Vol. 5. 273p. 1974. pap. 7.00 (*0-912788-04-6*) Tulane Romance Lang.
— Viajeros en Cuba, (1800-1850) LC 97-80546. (Coleccion Cuba y Sus Jueces Ser.). (Illus.). 291p. 1998. pap. 19.95 (*0-89729-860-8*) Ediciones.
Olivera, Ruth R. & Crete, Liliane. Life in Mexico under Santa Ana, 1822-1855. LC 90-50693. (Illus.). 280p. 1991. 28.95 (*0-8061-2320-6*) U of Okla Pr.
Oliveras, Elizabeth, jt. auth. see McIntosh, Noel.
Oliveras, Elizabeth, ed. see Blumenthal, Paul D. & McIntosh, Noel.
Oliveras, Elizabeth, ed. see McIntosh, Noel & Blumenthal, Paul.
Oliveras, Elizabeth, ed. see McIntosh, Noel & Blumenthal, Paul D.
Oliveras, Elizabeth, jt. ed. see McIntosh, Noel.
Oliveres, Raphael. NTC's Dictionary of Latin American Spanish. LC 97-22112. (SPA., Illus.). 384p. Date not set. 19.95 (*0-8442-7963-3*, 79633) NTC Contemp Pub Co.
Oliveri. Shakespeare Without Fear. (C). 1999. pap. 32.50 (*0-15-508038-5*) Harcourt Coll Pubs.
Oliveri, Ernest J. Latin American Debt & the Politics of International Finance. LC 91-30394. 256p. 1992. 55.00 (*0-275-94123-X*, C4123, Praeger Pubs) Greenwood.
Oliveri, Gianluigi, jt. ed. see McGuinness, Brian.
Oliveri-Lopez, Angel M. Key to an Enigma: British Sources Disprove British Claims to the Falkland/Malvinas Islands. LC 94-31531. 160p. 1994. lib. bdg. 30.00 (*1-55587-521-1*) L Rienner.
Oliveri, Mario. The Representatives: The Real Nature & Function of Papal Legates. LC 81-108272. 192p. (Orig.). (C). 1981. reprint ed. pap. 4.95 (*0-905715-20-9*) Wanderer Pr.
Oliveria, Paulo M. De, see De Oliveria, Paulo M.
Oliveria, Plinio Correa De, see Lee, Hannah S.
Oliverio. The Office: Procedures & Technology. (KM - Office Procedures Ser.). 1987. mass mkt. 36.50 (*0-538-11353-7*) S-W Pub.
— Office: Procedures & Technology. (KM - Office Procedures Ser.). 1991. mass mkt. 34.25 (*0-538-61747-0*) S-W Pub.
— Office: Procedures & Technology. 2nd ed. (KM - Office Procedures Ser.). 1992. 3.00 (*0-538-60902-8*); mass mkt., wbk. ed. 16.25 (*0-538-60901-X*) S-W Pub.
— Office Procedures & Technology, Tests 1-15. (KM - Office Procedures Ser.). 1987. 3.00 (*0-538-11355-3*) S-W Pub.
— Secretarial Office Procedures Supplement. 10th ed. (KM - Office Procedures Ser.). 1982. pap., wbk. ed. 18.95 (*0-538-11341-3*) S-W Pub.
Oliverio & White. The Office: Procedure & Technology. 3rd ed. (KF - Office Education Ser.). 1998. pap., teacher ed. 71.95 (*0-538-66739-7*); pap., teacher ed. 16.95 (*0-538-66740-0*) S-W Pub.
— The Office: Procedures & Technology. 3rd ed. (KF - Office Education Ser.). 1997. pap. 15.50 (*0-538-66737-0*) S-W Pub.
Oliverio, Annamarie. The State of Terror. LC 97-17274. (SUNY Series in Deviance & Social Control). 192p. (C). 1998. text 59.50 (*0-7914-3707-8*); pap. text 19.95 (*0-7914-3708-6*) State U NY Pr.
Oliverio, Mary E. The Office: Procedures & Technology. 2nd ed. (KM - Office Procedures Ser.). 1992. mass mkt. 34.25 (*0-538-60900-1*) S-W Pub.
Oliverio, Mary E., jt. auth. see Newman, Bernard H.
Oliverios. S&M Theory: Theory & Practices. 1999. text. write for info. (*0-312-09378-0*) St Martin.
Olivero, Federico. Edgar Allan Poe. LC 79-144666. (ITA.). reprint ed. 42.50 (*0-404-04818-8*) AMS Pr.
Olivero, Michael J. Honor, Violence, & Upward Mobility: A Case Study of Chicago Gangs During the 1970s & 1980s. (Illus.). 186p. (Orig.). (C). 1991. pap. text 12.95 (*0-938738-10-0*) U TX Pan Am Pr.
Olivero, Raymond. Robert Kushner: Paintings. (Illus.). 15p. 1989. pap. 1.00 (*0-939324-41-5*) Wichita Art Mus.
Oliveroff, Andre. Flight of the Swan: A Memory of Anna Pavlova. LC 79-17902. (Series in Dance). 1979. reprint ed. 29.50 (*0-306-79580-9*) Da Capo.
Oliveros, Chuck. The Pterodactyl in the Wilderness. 56p. (Orig.). 1983. pap. 3.00 (*0-911757-00-7*) Dead Angel.
Oliveros, Gumersindo, jt. auth. see Dillon, K. Burke.
Oliveros, Pauline & Cohen, Becky. Initiation Dream. (Illus.). 50p. (Orig.). 1981. pap. 10.00 (*0-937122-07-6*) Astro Artz Eighteenth St.
Oliverson, Ray & McKenna, Ted. Glossary of Maintenance & Reliability Terms. LC 97-17097. 1997. pap. 30.00 (*0-88415-360-6*, 5360) Gulf Pub.
Oliverus. The Capture of Damietta. Gavigan, John J., tr. LC 78-63353. (Crusades & Military Orders Ser.: Second Series). reprint ed. 34.50 (*0-404-17026-9*) AMS Pr.
Oliveto, G. & Brebbia, C. A., eds. Earthquake Resistant Engineering Structures II: Proceedings of the 2nd International Conference. (Advances in Earthquake Engineering Ser.: Vol. 4). 823p. 1999. 395.00 (*1-85312-689-6*, Pub. by WIT Pr) Computational Mech MA.
Olivetti. English-Spanish Dictionary of Computer Science. 11th ed. (ENG & SPA.). 270p. 1992. pap. 25.25 (*84-283-1230-3*, Pub. by Paraninfo) IBD Ltd.
— Olivetti English-Spanish Computer Dictionary (Diccionario de Informatica Olivetti Ingles-Espanol) 10th ed. (ENG & SPA.). 271p. 1991. pap. 39.95 (*0-7859-4873-2*) Fr & Eur.
Olivetti Staff. Diccionario de Informatica Ingles-Espanol. (ENG & SPA.). 272p. 1989. pap. 39.95 (*0-685-53860-5*, S50364) Fr & Eur.
Olivey, Captain. Sea Stories. (C). 1989. text 59.00 (*1-85821-031-3*, Pub. by Pentland Pr) St Mut.
Olivi, Jan. The Complete Book of Cat Care. 1994. 14.98 (*0-7858-0133-2*) Bk Sales Inc.
— The Complete Book of Dog Care. 1994. 14.98 (*0-7858-0132-4*) Bk Sales Inc.
Olivi, Terry, jt. ed. see Petofi, Janos S.
Olivia. Erotic Astrology: About Him for Her. LC 96-97080. 1997. pap. 12.95 (*0-345-40978-7*) Ballantine Pub Grp.
— Olivia. LC 75-12342. (Homosexuality Ser.). 1975. reprint ed. 22.55 (*0-405-07382-8*) Ayer.
Olivie, Jean-Luc, tr. Dale Chihuly: Objects de Verre. (ENG & FRE., Illus.). 40p. 1986. pap. 15.00 (*1-57684-026-3*) Portland Pr.
Oliviennes, F., ed. see Hamamah, S. & Mieusset, R.
Olivier, A., et al, eds. American Society for Stereotactic & Functional Neurosurgery, Montreal, Quebec, June 1987: Journal: Applied Neurophysiology, Vol. 50, Nos. 1-6, 1987. xii, 512p. 1988. pap. 205.25 (*3-8055-4756-0*) S Karger.
Olivier, B., et al, eds. Animal Models in Psychopharmacology. (Advances in Pharmacological Sciences Ser.). 476p. 1991. 132.50 (*0-8176-2503-8*) Birkhauser.
— Ethopharmacology of Agonistic Behaviour in Animals & Humans. (Topics in the Neurosciences Ser.). (C). 1987. text 176.50 (*0-89838-972-0*) Kluwer Academic.
Olivier, Berend, et al, eds. Serotonin Receptors & Their Ligands, Vol. 27. LC 97-24994. (Pharmacochemistry Library). 380p. 1997. 297.00 (*0-444-82041-8*) Elsevier.
Olivier, Bernard V. The Implementation of China's Nationality Policy in the Northeastern Provinces. LC 93-539. 340p. 1993. text 99.95 (*0-7734-2228-5*) E Mellen.
***Olivier, Burgundy Luticia.** I Love Spinach. LC 00-190390. (Illus.). 275p. 2000. 19.95 (*0-9677273-0-8*) Green Toque.
Olivier, Cadot, et al, eds. European Casebook on Industrial & Trade Policy. LC 95-34219. (European Casebook Series on Management). 1995. 44.95 (*0-13-353574-6*) P-H.
Olivier, Carolyn & Bowler, Rosemary. Learning to Learn. LC 96-18548. 288p. 1996. per. 12.00 (*0-684-80990-7*) S&S Trade.
Olivier, Cas. How to Educate & Train: Outcomes Based. LC 98-188147. xiii, 73 p. 1998. write for info. (*0-627-02355-X*) J L Van Schaik.
Olivier, Christine. Jocasta's Children. 192p. 1989. 39.95 (*0-415-01434-4*); pap. 13.95 (*0-415-01435-2*) Routledge.
Olivier, D. Luther's Faith: The Cause of the Gospel in the Church. LC 12-2961. 240p. 1982. pap. 17.00 (*0-570-03868-5*, 12-2961) Concordia.
Olivier, David, et al. Negawatt Power Pt. 3b: Demand-Side Electricity Resources in Western Europe. (Energy Policy in the Greenhouse Ser.: Vol. 2). 150p. (Orig.). 1996. pap. 35.00 (*1-883774-04-7*) IPSEP.
Olivier, Julien, jt. auth. see Parent, Michael.
Olivier, Laurence. Death of King George. abr. ed. LC 56-322. 1977. audio 14.00 (*0-694-50000-3*, SWC 1003, Caedmon) HarperAudio.
Olivier-Martin, R., jt. ed. see Pichot, P.
Olivier, N. J., Jr., et al. Indigenous Law. (Lawsa Student Text Ser.). 288p. 1995. student ed. write for info. (*0-409-04600-0*, MICHIE) LEXIS Pub.
Olivier, N. J., et al. Law of Property Students' Handbook. 2nd ed. 337p. 1993. pap. 30.00 (*0-7021-2937-2*, Pub. by Juta & Co) Gaunt.
— Sakereg Studentehandboek. 2nd ed. 355p. 1993. pap. write for info. (*0-7021-2938-0*, Pub. by Juta & Co) Gaunt.
— Statutere Sakereg. 700p. 1988. ring bd. write for info. (*0-7021-1994-6*, Pub. by Juta & Co) Gaunt.
Olivier, N. J., jt. auth. see Delport, H. J.
Olivier, P. A. & Van Den Berg, G. P. Praktiese Boedelbeplanning. 307p. 1991. pap. write for info. (*0-7021-2623-3*, Pub. by Juta & Co) Gaunt.
Olivier, Patrick, ed. Cognitive & Computational Models of Spatial Representation: Papers from the 1996 Spring Symposium. (Technical Reports). (Illus.). 109p. 1996. spiral bd. 25.00 (*1-57735-005-7*) AAAI Pr.
Olivier, Patrick & Gapp, Klaus-Peter, eds. Representation & Processing of Spatial Expressions. LC 97-4129. 250p. 1997. text. write for info. (*0-8058-2285-2*) L Erlbaum Assocs.

O

An Asterisk (*) at the beginning of an entry indicates that the title is appearing for the first time.

***Olivier, Paul A.** The Universe Is One: Towards a Theory of Knowledge & Life. LC 99-30492. 248p. 1999. 45.00 (*0-7618-1437-X*) U Pr of Amer.

Olivier, Rejean. Dictionnaire Biographique des Createurs de la Region de Joli. (FRE.). 1975. write for info. (*0-7859-8255-8*, 2-920249-28-2) Fr & Eur.

Olivier, Richard. Melting the Stone: A Journey Around My Father. 232p. 1995. pap. 18.50 (*0-88214-370-0*) Spring Pubns.

Olivier, Robert L. Tidoon. LC 70-18934. 104p. 1972. pap. 12.95 (*1-56554-642-3*) Pelican.

***Olivier, Suzannah.** Stress Protection Plan: Everyday Ways to Beat Stress & Enjoy Life. 2000. pap. 19.95 (*1-85585-743-X*, Pub. by Collins & Br) Sterling.

Olivier, Sydney H. The Anatomy of African Misery. LC 74-38017. (Black Heritage Library Collection). 1977. reprint ed. 21.95 (*0-8369-8984-8*) Ayer.

Olivier, William P. Videodiscs in Vocational Educational. 35p. 1985. 4.75 (*0-317-01301-7*, IN299) Ctr Educ Trng Employ.

Oliviera. Engineering Geology 7th Intl, Vol. 2. 1994. 110.00 (*90-5410-505-4*) Ashgate Pub Co.

— Engineering Geology 7th Intl, Vol. 3. 1994. 110.00 (*90-5410-506-2*) Ashgate Pub Co.

— Engineering Geology 7th Intl, Vol. 4. 1994. 110.00 (*90-5410-507-0*) Ashgate Pub Co.

— Engineering Geology 7th Intl, Vol. 5. 1994. 110.00 (*90-5410-508-9*) Ashgate Pub Co.

— Engineering Geology 7th Intl, Vol. 6. 1994. 110.00 (*90-5410-509-7*) Ashgate Pub Co.

Oliviera, Gerry. Engineering Geology 7th Intl, Vol. 1. 1994. 110.00 (*90-5410-504-6*) Ashgate Pub Co.

Oliviera, Jose A. De, see De Oliviera, Jose A.

Oliviera, R., et al, eds. 7th International Congress International Association of Engineering Geology, Lisbon, Portugal, 5-9 September 1994, 6 vols. (Illus.). 5240p. (C). 1994. text 539.00 (*90-5410-503-8*, Pub. by A A Balkema) Ashgate Pub Co.

Oliviere, David. Good Practices in Palliative Care: A Psychosocial Perspective. Hargreaves, Rosalind & Monroe, Barbara, eds. LC 98-12751. 210p. 1998. pap. 42.95 (*1-85742-396-8*, R726.8.O45, Pub. by Ashgate Pub) Ashgate Pub Co.

Oliviere, David, et al. Good Practices in Palliative Care (H) A Psychosocial Perspective. LC 98-12751. 210p. 1998. text 59.95 (*1-85742-395-X*, R726.8.O45, Pub. by Ashgate Pub) Ashgate Pub Co.

Olivieri, A., jt. auth. see Arangio-Ruis, V.

Olivieri, D., ed. Interstitial Lung Disease & Bronchial Hyperreactivity: Selected Papers from the Meeting of the Italian Chapter of ACCP, Parma, May 1987, Journal: Respiration, Vol. 54, Supplement 1. iv, 122p. 1988. pap. 39.25 (*3-8055-4891-5*) S Karger.

Olivieri, D. & Bianco, S., eds. Airway Obstruction & Inflammation: Present Status & Perspectives. (Progress in Respiratory Research Ser.: Vol. 24). (Illus.). viii, 288p. 1990. 242.75 (*3-8055-5006-5*) S Karger.

Olivieri, D. & Nadel, Jay A., eds. Chronic Bronchitis in the 90's Vol. 58, Supp. 1: Journal: Respiration. (Illus.). vi, 58p. 1991. pap. 28.00 (*3-8055-5452-4*) S Karger.

Olivieri, D., et al. Asthma Treatment: A Multidisciplinary Approach. (NATO ASI Ser.: Vol. 299). (Illus.). 306p. (C). 1992. text 105.00 (*0-306-44215-9*, Kluwer Plenum) Kluwer Academic.

Olivieri, Francesca. Muppet Babies Noisy Book. (Little Nugget Bks.). (Illus.). 18p. (J). 1998. bds. 3.49 (*0-307-13052-5*, 13052, Goldn Books) Gldn Bks Pub Co.

Olivieri, Joseph. How to Design Heating-Cooling Comfort Systems. 4th ed. LC 85-31387. 316p. 1987. 12.95 (*0-912524-36-7*) Busn News.

Olivieri, Matilde Vilarino De, see Vilarino De Olivieri, Matilde.

Olivieri, Rafael C. Ritual. (Aqui y Ahora Ser.). 1997. pap. 6.95 (*0-8477-0322-3*) U of PR Pr.

Oliviero, Jamie. The Day Sun Was Stolen. LC 94-19374. (Illus.). 32p. (J). (ps-3). 1995. 14.95 (*0-7868-0031-3*, Pub. by Hyprn Child); lib. bdg. 14.89 (*0-7868-2026-8*, Pub. by Hyprn Child) Little.

— The Day Sun Was Stolen. large type ed. (Illus.). 40p. (J). (ps-3). 1995. write for info. (*1-895340-08-X*) Hyperion Pr.

— The Fish Skin. large type ed. (Illus.). 40p. (J). (ps-2). 1993. write for info. (*0-920534-94-5*) Hyperion Pr.

— Som See & the Magic Elephant. large type ed. (Illus.). 32p. (J). (gr. k-4). 1994. write for info. (*1-895340-04-7*) Hyperion Pr.

— Som See & the Magic Elephant. large type ed. LC 94-1164. (Illus.). 32p. (J). (ps-3). 1995. 14.95 (*0-7868-0025-9*, Pub. by Hyprn Child) Little.

Oliviero, Jeffrey. Motion Picture Players' Credits: Worldwide Performers of 1967 Through 1980 with Filmographies of Their Entire Careers, 1905-1983. LC 89-13644. 1023p. 1991. lib. bdg. 145.00 (*0-89950-315-2*) McFarland & Co.

Olivio, Christiane. Creating a Democratic Civil Society in Eastern Germany. text. write for info. (*0-312-23401-5*) St Martin.

Olivio, P. D., et al. Basic Blueprint Reading & Sketching. 7th ed. LC 98-44492. 240p. (C). 1998. 50.95 (*0-7668-0841-6*) Delmar.

***Olivo.** Basic Blueprint Reading & Sketching: Instructor's Guide. 7th ed. 192p. 1999. teacher ed. 30.95 (*0-7668-1111-5*) Delmar.

Olivo, C. Thomas. Advanced Machine Technology. (C). 1982. mass mkt. 39.95 (*0-534-01040-7*); mass mkt., student ed. 14.00 (*0-534-01041-5*) Wadsworth Pub.

— Advanced Machine Technology. (C). 1982. teacher ed. 6.60 (*0-534-01042-3*) Wadsworth Pub.

— Advanced Machine Tool Technology & Manufacturing Processes. Putnam, H. G., ed. LC 89-64000. (Illus.). 608p. (C). 1991. student ed. 9.95 (*0-938561-05-7*) C T Olivo.

— Advanced Machine Tool Technology & Manufacturing Processes. 3rd ed. Putnam, H. G., ed. LC 89-64000. (Illus.). 608p. (C). 1991. teacher ed. 15.95 (*0-938561-06-5*) C T Olivo.

— Advanced Machine Tool Technology & Manufacturing Processes. 3rd ed. Putnam, H. G., ed. LC 89-64000. (Illus.). 608p. (C). 1990. text 45.25 (*0-938561-04-9*) Thomson Learn.

— Basic Machine Technology. 1980. 21.95 (*0-672-97171-2*, Bobbs) Macmillan.

— Basic Technical Mathematics Simplified: Instructor's Guide. 6th ed. 1992. pap. 16.00 (*0-8273-4642-5*) Delmar.

— Basic Vocational Technical Mathematics: Fundamentals Edition. 5th ed. Olivo, Thomas P., ed. 448p. (C). 1983. pap. 34.95 (*0-8273-2225-9*); text 39.95 (*0-8273-2226-7*) Delmar.

— Basic Vocational Technical Mathematics: Fundamentals Edition. 5th ed. Olivo, Thomas P., ed. 448p. (C). 1985. teacher ed. 15.00 (*0-8273-2228-3*) Delmar.

— Fundamentals of Machine Tool Technology & Manufacturing Processes. Putnam, H. G., ed. LC 89-64001. (Illus.). 544p. (C). 1991. teacher ed. 9.95 (*0-938561-01-4*) C T Olivo.

— Fundamentals of Machine Tool Technology & Manufacturing Processes. 3rd ed. Putnam, H. G., ed. LC 89-64001. (Illus.). 544p. (C). 1991. teacher ed. 15.95 (*0-938561-02-2*); text 34.95 (*0-938561-00-6*) C T Olivo.

— Machine Tool Technology & Manufacturing Processes. Putnam, H. G., ed. LC 86-18216. (Illus.). 640p. 1987. teacher ed. 15.95 (*0-938561-10-3*); student ed. 8.95 (*0-938561-09-X*) C T Olivo.

— Machine Tool Technology & Manufacturing Processes. Putnam, H. G., ed. LC 86-18216. (Illus.). 640p. 1986. pap. 42.75 (*0-938561-08-1*) Thomson Learn.

— Principles of Refrigeration. 3rd ed. (Heating, Ventilation & Air Conditioning Ser.). 1990. pap., teacher ed. 14.95 (*0-8273-3559-8*) Delmar.

Olivo, C. Thomas & Cubbler, Telecommunications: Concpets & Applications. (DF - Computer Applications Ser.). 1990. mass mkt. 20.95 (*0-538-60360-7*) S-W Pub.

Olivo, C. Thomas & Marsh, R. W. Principles of Refrigeration. 3rd ed. LC 76-14089. 1990. mass mkt. 46.50 (*0-8273-3557-1*) Delmar.

Olivo, C. Thomas & Olivo, T. Fundamentals of Applied Physics. 3rd ed. LC 83-71503. 440p. (C). 1984. pap. 82.95 (*0-8273-2159-7*) Delmar.

Olivo, C. Thomas & Olivo, Thomas P. Basic Blueprint Reading & Sketching. 6th ed. 1993. trans. 103.95 (*0-8273-5924-1*) Delmar.

— Basic Technical Mathematics. 6th ed. 694p. 1992. text 42.50 (*0-8273-4666-2*) Delmar.

— Basic Technical Mathematics Fundamentals. 6th ed. 384p. (C). 1992. mass mkt. 40.95 (*0-8273-4958-0*) Delmar.

— Basic Vocational Technical Mathematics: Fundamentals Edition. 5th ed. LC 84-23257. 352p. (C). 1985. pap. 24.95 (*0-8273-2227-5*) Delmar.

— Industrial Drawings Supplement for Basic Blueprint Reading & Sketching. 6th ed. 1993. 27.00 (*0-8273-5923-3*) Delmar.

— Teacher's Resource Guide to Accompany Basic Blueprint Reading & Sketching. 6th ed. 154p. 1993. teacher ed. 24.50 (*0-8273-5921-7*) Delmar.

Olivo, C. Thomas & Rotner, Shelley. Close, Closer, Closet. LC 96-15837. (Illus.). 40p. (J). (ps-2). 1997. 13.00 (*0-689-80762-7*) S&S Bks Yung.

Olivo, C. Thomas, jt. auth. see Olivo, T.

Olivo, C. Thomas, jt. auth. see Olivo, Thomas P.

Olivo, Richard, jt. auth. see Rotner, Shelley.

Olivo Staff. Fundamentals of Machine Tool Technology. 3rd ed. (MACHINE TRADES). 1994. pap. 42.75 (*0-938561-13-8*) Thomson Learn.

Olivo, T. & Olivo, C. Thomas. Fundamentals of Applied Physics. 3rd ed. LC 83-71503. 440p. (C). 1984. teacher ed. 21.00 (*0-8273-2160-0*); student ed. 23.00 (*0-8273-2161-9*) Delmar.

Olivo, T., jt. auth. see Olivo, C. Thomas.

Olivo, Thomas P. Blueprint Reading & Technical Sketching for Industry: Instructor's Guide. 2nd ed. 1992. 14.95 (*0-8273-5078-3*) Delmar.

Olivo, Thomas P. & Olivo, C. Thomas. Basic Vocational Technical Math. 6th ed. (C). 1992. mass mkt. 35.00 (*0-8273-4641-7*) Delmar.

— Blueprint Reading & Technical Sketching for Industry. LC 83-26174. 464p. (C). 1985. teacher ed. 13.95 (*0-8273-2206-2*) Delmar.

Olivo, Thomas P., jt. auth. see C. Thomas Olivo & Associates Staff.

Olivo, Thomas P., jt. auth. see Olivo, C. Thomas.

Olivo, Thomas P., ed. see Olivo, C. Thomas.

Olivova, Vera. The Doomed Democracy: Czechoslovakia in a Disrupted Europe, 1914-38. Theiner, George, tr. from CZE. LC 78-189266. 294p. reprint ed. pap. 91.20 (*0-7837-1018-6*, 204132900020) Bks Demand.

Olk, R. Joseph & Lee, Carol M. Diabetic Retinopathy: Practical Management. LC 92-48876. 224p. 1993. text 103.00 (*0-397-51167-1*) Lppncott W & W.

Olken, Charles E., et al. The Connoisseurs' Handbook of California Wines. 3rd ed. LC 84-47864. (Illus.). 256p. 1984. pap. 6.95 (*0-685-08624-0*) Knopf.

Olken, Charles E., jt. auth. see Roby, Norman S.

Olken, Hyman. The High-Tech Industry Manual: Conversion of U. S. Industry to High Technology Through Technology Transfer. 144p. 1986. pap. 20.00 (*0-934818-02-9*) Olken Pubns.

— Memory: The Physiological Mechanism of Memory in the Human Center. (Illus.). 87p. 1990. 12.00 (*0-685-47603-0*) Olken Pubns.

— Opening the Door to the Brain: Granular Cell Neuron Masses. (Illus.). 30p. (Orig.). pap. 12.00 (*0-934818-05-3*) Olken Pubns.

— The Technical Communicator's Handbook of Technology Transfer. 144p. 1980. pap. 12.50 (*0-934818-01-0*) Olken Pubns.

— Technology Transfer: How to Make It Work, a Management Handbook. 92p. 1972. pap. 7.00 (*0-934818-00-2*) Olken Pubns.

Olken, Ilene T. & Mazzola, Claudio. Racconti Del Novecento: Realta Regionali. 320p. (C). 1990. pap. text 31.60 (*0-13-750001-7*) P-H.

Olker, J. Florida Attorney's - Secretary's Handbook, 1993. 1992. 59.00 (*1-880919-02-8*) Namar Comms.

— Florida Attorney's - Secretary's Handbook, 1994. 1993. 59.00 (*1-880919-05-2*) Namar Comms.

— Illinois Attorney's - Secretary's Handbook: 1992 Edition. 650p. 1991. ring bd. 63.00 (*1-880919-00-1*) Namar Comms.

— Illinois Attorney's - Secretary's Handbook, 1993. 1993. 63.00 (*1-880919-03-6*) Namar Comms.

— Illinois Attorney's - Secretary's Handbook, 1994. 1994. 63.00 (*1-880919-06-0*) Namar Comms.

— Wisconsin Attorney's - Secretary's Handbook, 1993-94. 1993. 59.00 (*1-880919-04-4*) Namar Comms.

— Wisconsin Attorney's - Secretary's Handbook, 1994-95. 1994. 59.00 (*1-880919-07-9*) Namar Comms.

Olkes, Cheryl, jt. auth. see Stoller, Paul.

Olkhovsky, Andrey. Music under the Soviets: The Agony of an Art, No. 11--11. LC 74-20341. (Studies of the Research Program of the U. S. S. R.: No. 11). 427p. 1975. reprint ed. lib. bdg. 72.50 (*0-8371-7856-8*, OLMS, Greenwood Pr) Greenwood.

Olkhovsky, Yuri. Vladimir Stasov & Russian National Culture. LC 83-3528. (Russian Music Studies: No. 6). (Illus.). 207p. reprint ed. pap. 64.20 (*0-8357-1412-8*, 207051500097) Bks Demand.

Olkier, Stacey, jt. auth. see Cancian, Francesca M.

Olkin, Ingram. Classification & Dissimilarity Analysis. LC 94-35226. (Lecture Notes in Statistics Ser.: Vol. 93). 238p. 1994. 52.95 (*0-387-94400-1*) Spr-Verlag.

— Indirect Estimators in U. S. Federal Programs. LC 95-42186. (Lecture Notes in Statistics Ser.: Vol. 108). 208p. 1995. 54.95 (*0-387-94616-0*) Spr-Verlag.

Olkin, Ingram & Zeger, Scott L. Applications of Computer Aided Time Series Modeling. LC 96-38868. (Lecture Notes in Statistics Ser.: Vol. 119). 352p. 1996. pap. 43.95 (*0-387-94751-5*) Spr-Verlag.

Olkin, Ingram, et al. Bilinear Forms & Zonal Polynomials. LC 95-22682. (Lecture Notes in Statistics Ser.: Vol. 102). x, 378p. 1995. 48.95 (*0-387-94522-9*) Spr-Verlag.

Olkin, Ingram, jt. auth. see Hedges, Larry V.

Olkin, Ingram, jt. auth. see Marshall, Albert.

Olkin, Ingram, ed. see Berger, M. A. & Fienberg, Stephen E.

Olkin, Ingram, ed. see Finkelstein, Michael O. & Levin, B.

Olkin, Ingram, ed. see Jobson, J. D.

Olkin, Ingram, ed. see Karr, Alan F.

Olkin, Ingram, ed. see Mueller, Ralph O.

Olkin, Ingram, ed. see Srivastava, M. & Sen, Amartya K.

Olkin, Ingram, ed. see Whittle, P.

***Olkin, Rhoda.** What Psychotherapists Should Know about Disability. LC 99-33774. 360p. 1999. lib. bdg. 36.00 (*1-57230-227-5*, CO227) Guilford Pubns.

Olkin, Sylvia K. Positive Parenting Fitness: A Total Approach to Caring for the Physical & Emotional Needs of Your New Family. LC 91-28933. (Illus.). 344p. (Orig.). pap. 14.95 (*0-89529-481-8*, Avery) Penguin Putnam.

— Positive Pregnancy Fitness: A Guide to a More Comfortable Pregnancy & Easier Birth Through Exercise & Relaxation. LC 87-18844. (Illus.). 272p. pap. 12.95 (*0-89529-373-0*, Avery) Penguin Putnam.

Olkin, Sylvia K. Relax & Enjoy Your Baby. (Illus.). 12p. 1996. 16.95 incl. audio (*1-55961-346-7*, BP7506, Pub. by Relaxtn Co) Publishers Group.

Olko, Robert S., jt. ed. see Friedman, Steven J.

Olkowski, Dorothea. Gilles Deleuze & the Ruin of Representation. LC 98-38667. 250p. 1999. 48.00 (*0-520-21691-1*, Pub. by U CA Pr); pap. 18.95 (*0-520-21693-8*, Pub. by U CA Pr) Cal Prin Full Svc.

***Olkowski, Dorothea.** Resistance, Flight, Creation: Feminist Enactments of French Philosophy. LC 99-59369. 2000. pap. write for info. (*0-8014-8645-9*) Cornell U Pr.

Olkowski, Dorothea & Morley, James, eds. Merleau-Ponty, Interiority & Exteriority, Psychic Life & the World. LC 98-49628. 288p. (C). 1999. text 65.50 (*0-7914-4277-2*); pap. text 21.95 (*0-7914-4278-0*) State U NY Pr.

Olkowski, Dorothea, jt. ed. see Boundas, Constantin V.

Olkowski, Dorothea, jt. ed. see Hass, Lawrence.

Olkowski, Mary. From the Garden of My Soul. unabridged ed. LC 98-96834. (Illus.). 50p. 1998. pap. 12.99 (*0-9668781-0-8*) Limpid Butterfly.

***Olkowski, Mary.** Life's a Cinch with Just One Inch. unabridged ed. LC 99-95296. (Illus.). 100p. (YA). (gr. 4 up). 1999. 19.95 (*0-9668781-2-4*, 1003-1004); pap. 14.95 (*0-9668781-3-2*, 1003-1004) Limpid Butterfly.

Olkowski, Mary. The Mysteries of the Limpid Butterfly. LC 99-94342. (Illus.). 300p. 1999. pap. 14.99 (*0-9668781-1-6*, 1002) Limpid Butterfly.

Olkowski, Thomas T. & Parker, Lynn. Moving with Children: A Parent's Guide to Moving with Children. LC 93-19123. (Illus.). 196p. (Orig.). 1993. pap. 12.95 (*1-880197-08-1*) Gylantic Pub.

Olkowski, William, et al. Common-Sense Pest Control. (Illus.). 736p. (C). 1991. 39.95 (*0-942391-63-2*, 070110) Taunton.

— The Gardener's Guide to Common-Sense Pest Control. LC 95-51204. (Illus.). 300p. 1996. pap. 19.95 (*1-56158-149-6*, 070276) Taunton.

Olla, B. L., jt. auth. see Burger, J.

Olla, Bori L., jt. auth. see Winn, Howard E.

***Olla, Debbie.** R & R for Teens: Retreats & Days of Reflection. Cannizzo, Karen, ed. (Youth Ministry Resource Library). 96p. 2000. pap. 19.95 (*0-937997-78-1*, 3213) Hi-Time Pflaum.

Ollagnier, J. Moulin. Ergodic Theory & Statistical Mechanics. (Lecture Notes in Mathematics Ser.: Vol. 1115). vi, 147p. 1985. 34.95 (*0-387-15192-3*) Spr-Verlag.

Ollapally, Deepa M. Confronting Conflict: Domestic Factors & U. S. Policymaking in the Third World, 324. LC 92-45073. (Contributions in Political Science Ser.: No. 324). 232p. 1993. 62.95 (*0-313-28824-0*, GM8824, Greenwood Pr) Greenwood.

Ollard, Eric A. Installation & Maintenance in Electroplating Shops. (C). 1988. 160.00 (*0-85218-021-7*, Pub. by Fuel Metallurgical Jrnl) St Mut.

***Ollard, Richard.** Character Sketches: Pepys & his Circle. (Illus.). 64p. 2000. 11.95 (*1-85514-281-3*, Pub. by Natl Port Gall) Antique Collect.

Ollason, Robert J. Penguin Parade. LC 94-6433. (Illus.). 40p. (J). (gr. 4-6). 1994. lib. bdg. 19.95 (*0-8225-1491-5*, Lerner Publctns) Lerner Pub.

Ollawa, Patrick E. Participatory Democracy in Zambia. 520p. 1985. 60.00 (*0-7855-0784-1*, Pub. by A H S Ltd); pap. 60.00 (*0-7855-0785-X*, Pub. by A H S Ltd) St Mut.

— Participatory Democracy in Zambia. 520p. (C). 1990. 60.00 (*0-7855-6535-3*, Pub. by A H S Ltd); pap. 50.00 (*0-7223-1214-8*, Pub. by A H S Ltd) St Mut.

Olle, Annette & Lyneham, Paul, eds. Andrew Olle: A Tribute. 200p. 1996. pap. 14.95 (*0-86840-367-9*, Pub. by New South Wales Univ Pr) Intl Spec Bk.

Olle, James G. A Guide to Sources of Information in Libraries. LC 84-4066. 178p. 1984. text 54.95 (*0-566-03477-8*, Pub. by Gower) Ashgate Pub Co.

Olle, T. William. The CODASYL Approach to Data Base Management. LC 77-12375. 307p. reprint ed. pap. 95.20 (*0-608-18447-0*, 203266300080) Bks Demand.

— Information Systems Methodologies: A Framework for Understanding. (Illus.). 190p. (C). 1988. pap. text 34.50 (*0-201-41610-7*) Addison-Wesley.

Olle, T. William, jt. ed. see Verrijn-Stuart, A. A.

Ollefen, William Van, see Ross, Steven & Van Ollefen, William.

Ollenberger, Ben C., et al, eds. The Flowering of Old Testament Theology: A Reader in Twentieth-Century Old Testament Theology, 1930-1990. LC 91-24963. (Sources for Biblical & Theological Study Ser.: Bk. 1). xii, 547p. 1991. text 37.95 (*0-931464-62-5*) Eisenbrauns.

Ollenberger, Jane C. & Moore, Helen A. Sociology of Women. 2nd ed. LC 97-24490. 251p. (C). 1997. pap. text 35.20 (*0-13-671637-7*) P-H.

***Ollenborger, Mindy.** TAC, 1969-1999, One Vision, One Company LC 99-35016. 1999. write for info. (*1-57864-080-6*) Donning Co.

Ollenburger, Ben C. Zion, the City of the Great King: A Theological Symbol of the Jerusalem Cult. (JSOT Supplement Ser.: No. 41). 271p. 1987. pap. 24.50 (*1-85075-014-9*, Pub. by Sheffield Acad) CUP Services.

Ollenburger, Ben C., ed. So Wide a Sea: Essays on Biblical & Systematic Theology. (Text-Reader Ser.: No. 4). 145p. (Orig.). 1991. pap. text 10.00 (*0-936273-18-6*) Inst Mennonite.

Ollenburger, Ben C., jt. auth. see Kraftchick, Steven J.

Ollenburger, Jane C., jt. auth. see Grana, Sheryl J.

Ollendick, Thomas H., et al, eds. Handbook of Child Psychopathology. 3rd ed. LC 97-40923. 694p. 1997. 97.50 (*0-306-45321-5*, Kluwer Plenum) Kluwer Academic.

— International Handbook of Phobic & Anxiety Disorders in Children & Adolescents. (Illus.). 510p. (C). 1994. 85.00 (*0-306-44759-2*, Plenum Trade) Perseus Pubng.

Ollendick, Thomas H. & Cerny, Jerome A. Clinical Behavior Therapy with Children. LC 81-17891. (Applied Clinical Psychology Ser.). (Illus.). 364p. (C). 1981. text 71.00 (*0-306-40774-4*, Kluwer Plenum) Kluwer Academic.

Ollendick, Thomas H. & Hersen, Michael, eds. Handbook of Child & Adoloscent Assessment. LC 90-49071. Vol. 167. 564p. (C). 1992. 89.00 (*0-205-14592-2*, Longwood Div) Allyn.

Ollendick, Thomas H. & Hersen, Michael, eds. Handbook of Child Psychopathology. 2nd ed. (Illus.). 570p. 1989. 85.00 (*0-306-42975-6*, Plenum Trade) Perseus Pubng.

Ollendick, Thomas H. & Prinz, Ronald J., eds. Advances in Clinical Child Psychology. (Clinical Child Psychology Ser.: Vol. 20). (Illus.). 330p. (C). 1998. 85.00 (*0-306-45667-2*, Plenum Trade) Perseus Pubng.

Ollendick, Thomas H. & Prinz, Ronald J., eds. Advances in Clinical Child Psychology, Vol. 15. (Illus.). 360p. (C). 1993. 85.00 (*0-306-44273-6*, Plenum Trade) Perseus Pubng.

Ollendick, Thomas H. & Prinz, Ronald J., eds. Advances in Clinical Child Psychology, Vol. 16. (Illus.). 332p. (C). 1993. 85.00 (*0-306-44552-2*, Plenum Trade) Perseus Pubng.

— Advances in Clinical Child Psychology, Vol. 17. LC 77-643411. (Illus.). 422p. (C). 1994. 85.00 (*0-306-44799-1*, Kluwer Plenum) Kluwer Academic.

— Advances in Clinical Child Psychology, Vol. 18. (Illus.). 388p. (C). 1996. 85.00 (*0-306-45143-3*, Plenum Trade) Perseus Pubng.

— Advances in Clinical Child Psychology, Vol. 19. 388p. 1997. 85.00 (*0-306-45447-5*, Kluwer Plenum) Kluwer Academic.

Ollendick, Thomas H., jt. ed. see Russ, Sandra Walker.

Ollendick, Thomas K., jt. ed. see Silverman, Wendy K.

An Asterisk (*) at the beginning of an entry indicates that the title is appearing for the first time.

Oller, John. Jean Arthur: The Actress Nobody Knew. LC 99-11144. (Illus.). 358p. 1999. reprint ed. pap. 18.95 (*0-87910-278-0*) Limelight Edns.

***Oller, Bobby.** Comedies Useful: Southern Theatre History, 1775-1812. LC 97-78002. 1998. pap. 21.95 (*0-9636489-2-6*) Celest Pr.

Oller, D. Kimbrough. The Emergence of the Speech Capacity. LC 99-52021. 450p. 1999. write for info. (*0-8058-2628-9*) L Erlbaum Assocs.

— The Emergence of the Speech Capacity. LC 99-52021. 450p. 1999. pap. write for info. (*0-8058-2629-7*) L Erlbaum Assocs.

Oller, John W., Jr. Coding Information in Natural Languages. LC 74-182465. (Janua Linguarum, Ser. Minor: No. 123). (Illus.). 120p. (Orig.). 1971. pap. text 15.40 (*3-10-800282-1*) Mouton.

— Language & Bilingualism: More Tests of Tests. LC 90-55874. 192p. 1991. 32.50 (*0-8387-5210-1*) Bucknell U Pr.

Oller, John W. Language Tests at School: A Pragmatic Approach. LC 79-322102. (Applied Linguistics & Language Studies). 512p. 1979. reprint ed. pap. 158.80 (*0-608-03619-6*, 206444500009) Bks Demand.

***Oller, John W. & Giardetti, J. Roland.** Images That Work: Creating Successful Messages in Marketing & High Stakes Communication. LC 99-13622. 256p. 1999. 59.95 (*1-56720-184-9*) Greenwood.

Oller, John W. & Jonz, Jon. Cloze & Coherence. LC 94-11856. 1994. 45.00 (*0-8387-5303-5*) Bucknell U Pr.

Ollerenshaw, Chris & Ritchie, Ron. Primary Science: Making it Work. (Primary Curriculum Ser.). 192p. 1993. pap. 32.00 (*1-85346-199-7*, Pub. by David Fulton) Taylor & Francis.

— Primary Science - Making It Work. 2nd ed. LC 97-196074. (Primary Curriculum Ser.). 240p. 1997. pap. 32.00 (*1-85346-439-2*, Pub. by David Fulton) Taylor & Francis.

Ollero, A., ed. Intelligent Components for Vehicles: Proceedings of the IFAC Workshop, Seville, Spain, 23-24 March 1998. LC 98-44152. 436p. 1998. pap. 99.50 (*0-08-043232-8*) Elsevier.

Ollero, A. & Camacho, E. F., eds. Intelligent Components & Instruments for Control Applications: Selected Papers from the IFAC Symposium, Malaga, Spain, 20-22 May, 1992. LC 92-44354. (IFAC Symposia Ser.). 554p. 1993. 206.25 (*0-08-041899-6*, Pergamon Pr) Elsevier.

Olleros, Angel Rodriguez. Canto a la Raza: Composicion Sangvinea De Estudiantes De la Universidad De Puerto Rico. 94p. 1974. 2.00 (*0-8477-2314-3*) U of PR Pr.

Olleson, jt. auth. see Kassler.

Olleson, Philip, ed. see Wesley, Samuel.

Olley, John W. Righteousness in the Septuagint of Isaiah: A Contextual Study. LC 78-3425. (Society of Biblical Literature. Septuagint & Cognate Studies: No. 8). 201p. reprint ed. pap. 62.40 (*0-7837-5438-8*, 204520300005) Bks Demand.

O'Lley, Michelle. Adonis: Masterpieces of Erotic Male Photography. 224p. 1999. pap. 27.50 (*1-56025-220-0*, Thunders Mouth) Avalon NY.

***O'Lley, Michelle.** Venus: Masterpieces of Modern Erotic Photography. (Illus.). 2000. pap. 27.50 (*1-56025-272-3*, Thunders Mouth) Avalon NY.

Olley, Peter M., jt. ed. see Coceani, Flavio.

Ollgaard, B. Flora of Ecuador: Lycopodiaceae. (Opera Botanica Series B). 155p. 1988. pap. 54.00 (*1-878762-07-9*, Pub. by Coun Nordic Pubs) Balogh.

Ollgaard, Benjamin & Molau, Ulf, eds. Current Scandinavian Botanical Research in Ecuador. (Reports from the Botanical Institute, University of Aarhus: No. 15). (Illus.). 86p. (C). 1986. pap. 12.95 (*87-87600-19-6*, Pub. by Aarhus Univ Pr) David Brown.

Ollgaard, Benjamin, ed. see Lawesson, J. E., et al.

Ollie. Suzann Says, Vol. I. (Illus.). 48p. (Orig.). 1992. pap. 5.95 (*0-9624100-6-3*) Bell Buckle.

***Ollie, Michelle, ed.** Aribert Munzner: Teacher, Colleague, Artist. (Emeritus Faculty Ser.). (Illus.). 64p. 2000. write for info. (*0-9611672-2-X*) Minneapolis Coll Art.

Ollier, Brigitte. Doisneau - Paris. (Illus.). 688p. (Orig.). 1996. pap. 55.00 (*3-927258-34-2*) Gingko Press.

Ollier, C. D. Ancient Landforms. 240p. 1992. text 59.00 (*1-85293-074-8*) St Martin.

Ollier, Claude. Disconnection. Di Bernardi, Dominic, tr. from FRE. LC 89-35215. 130p. 1989. 19.95 (*0-916583-47-3*) Dalkey Arch.

— Law & Order. Molinaro, Ursule, tr. from FRE. LC 76-133248. (French Ser.). Orig. Title: Le Maintien De L'ordre. 126p. 1971. 4.95 (*0-87376-015-8*) Red Dust.

***Ollier, Claude.** The Mise-en-Scene. Di Bernardi, Dominic, tr. from FRE. & afterword by by. LC 87-73069. 256p. 2000. pap. 12.50 (*1-56478-232-8*, Pub. by Dalkey Arch) Chicago Distribution Ctr.

Ollier, Cliff & Pain, Colin. Regolith, Soils & Landforms. 326p. 1996. 165.00 (*0-471-96121-3*) Wiley.

Ollier, Francois. La Mirage Spartiate Pt. 1: Etude sur l'Idealisation de Sparte dans l'Antiquite Greque de ' Origine Jusqu'aux Cyniques, 2 vols. LC 72-7903. (Greek History Ser.). (FRE.). 1979. reprint ed. 53.95 (*0-405-04799-1*) Ayer.

Ollier, Kate, jt. auth. see Hobday, Angela.

Ollier, Susan, jt. auth. see Davies, Robert J.

Olliff, ed. Auburn World Atlas (C). 1996. text 20.63 (*0-673-67616-1*) Addison-Wesley.

Ollila, Dale G., jt. auth. see Renes, Robert M.

Ollila, Lloyd O., ed. The Kindergarten Child & Reading. LC 77-4318. 88p. (Orig.). reprint ed. pap. 30.00 (*0-8357-8198-4*, 203408300087) Bks Demand.

Olling, G. J., et al. Machining Impossible Shapes: IFIP TC5 WG5.3 International Conference on Sculptured Surfaces (SSM98), November 5-11, 1998 Chrysler Technology Center, Michigan / LC 99-30260. (International Federation for Information Processing Ser.). 1999. write for info. (*0-412-84680-2*) Chapman & Hall.

Olling, Gustav, jt. ed. see Wozny, Michael J.

Ollinger, Michael. Organizational Form & Business Strategy in the U. S. Petroleum Industry. LC 92-41876. 166p. (C). 1993. lib. bdg. 39.50 (*0-8191-8990-1*) U Pr of Amer.

Olliphant, Jo A. Total Physical Fun: Strategies & Activities for Teaching & Learning Language Through Cooperative Play. (Illus.). 168p. 1997. reprint ed. pap. text 24.95 (*1-879725-00-2*) Sahmarsh Pub.

Ollis, David F. & Al-Ekabi, Hussain, eds. Photocatalytical Purification & Treatment of Water & Air: Proceedings of the First International Conference on TiO2 Photocatalytical Purification & Treatment of Water & Air, London, Ontario, Canada, 8-13 November, 1992. LC 93-20734. (Trace Metals in the Environment Ser.: Vol. 3). 836p. 1993. 307.00 (*0-444-89855-7*) Elsevier.

Ollis, David F., jt. auth. see Bailey, James.

Ollis, W. D., jt. ed. see Barton, Derek H.

Ollison, Larry. God's Plan for Handling Stress. 64p. 1997. pap. 4.95 (*0-9653202-0-0*) L Ollison.

— Is Faith Really Important? 64p. 1997. pap. 4.95 (*0-9653202-1-9*) L Ollison.

Ollivant, Alfred. Bob, Son of Battle. 24.95 (*0-8488-0137-7*) Amereon Ltd.

— Bob, Son of Battle. Hinkle, Don, ed. LC 87-15477. (Illus.). 48p. (J). (gr. 3-6). 1997. pap. 5.95 (*0-8167-1212-3*) Troll Communs.

Olliver, Jane, ed. A Treasury of Animal Stories. LC 92-53110. (Treasury of Stories Ser.). (Illus.). 160p. (J). (ps-4). 1992. pap. 7.95 (*1-85697-831-1*) LKC.

— A Treasury of Giant & Monster Stories. LC 92-53112. (Treasury of Stories Ser.). (Illus.). 160p. (J). (ps-4). 1992. pap. 6.95 (*1-85697-832-X*) LKC.

— A Treasury of Spooky Stories. LC 92-53111. (Treasury of Stories Ser.). (Illus.). 160p. (J). (ps-4). 1992. pap. 6.95 (*1-85697-830-3*) LKC.

Ollivier, Ann J., tr. see Kilham, Christopher S.

Ollivier, Emile. The Franco-Prussian War & Its Hidden Causes. Ives, George B., tr. LC 71-140369. (Select Bibliographies Reprint Ser.). 1977. reprint ed. 31.95 (*0-8369-5612-5*) Ayer.

Ollivier, Eric. L' Orphelin de Mer, Ou, Les Memoires de Monsieur Non. (FRE.). 1984. pap. 10.95 (*0-7859-4200-9*) Fr & Eur.

Ollivier, Jacqueline. Grammaire Francaise. 2nd ed. (FRE.). 480p. (C). 1993. pap. text 7.00 (*0-15-501032-8*, Pub. by Harcourt Coll Pubs) Harcourt.

— Grammaire Francaise 2E. 2nd ed. (FRE.). 486p. (C). 1993. pap. text 50.00 (*0-15-500661-4*) Harcourt Coll Pubs.

Ollivier, Jacqueline, et al. Appel: Initiation Au Francais D'Jourd'Hui. 2nd ed. 557p. (C). 1988. pap. text, teacher ed. 17.50 (*0-15-502929-0*) Harcourt Coll Pubs.

— KIT: APPEL 2E:LM/WKBK + CASSET. 2nd ed. 557p. (C). 1988. pap. text, student ed. 40.50 (*0-15-502928-2*) Harcourt Coll Pubs.

Ollivier, John J. Fun with Nursery Rhymes: Or What Was the Real Ending of Humpty Dumpty? (Illus.). 72p. (Orig.). 1990. pap. text 9.95 (*0-9626821-0-1*) J Ollivier.

— Tick Tock Clock. (Wisdom Series for Children). (Illus.). 13p. (Orig.). (J). (gr. k-1). 1996. pap. 5.49 (*1-888995-00-9*) MI GALS.

Ollivier, Larry. The Voice of All Things, Singing. 90p. (Orig.). 1997. pap. 12.00 (*0-944920-27-6*) Bellowing Ark Pr.

Ollivier, Louis, jt. ed. see Straszewska, Sophie.

***Ollman, Arthur.** The Model Wife. LC 99-17301. (Illus.). 212p. 1999. 65.00 (*0-8212-2170-1*, Pub. by Bulfinch Pr) Little.

Ollman, Arthur, jt. auth. see Goldberg, Vicki.

Ollman, B. Alienation. 2nd ed. LC 76-4234. (Studies in the History & Theory of Politics). 339p. 1977. pap. text 26.95 (*0-521-29083-X*) Cambridge U Pr.

***Ollman, Bertell.** How to Take an Exam... & Win the World. 2000. 48.99 (*1-55164-171-2*) Black Rose.

— How to Take an Exam... & Win the World. (Illus.). 260p. 2000. pap. 19.99 (*1-55164-170-4*) Black Rose.

Ollman, Bertell. Market Socialism: Debate among Socialists. LC 97-18313. 192p. (C). 1998. 70.00 (*0-415-91966-5*) Routledge.

— Social & Sexual Revolution. 228p. write for info. (*0-919618-85-5*); pap. write for info. (*0-919618-84-7*) Black Rose.

— Social & Sexual Revolution: Essays on Marx & Reich. LC 78-71204. 228p. 1979. 20.00 (*0-89608-081-1*) South End Pr.

Ollman, Bertell, ed. Market Socialism: Debate among Socialists. LC 97-18313. 192p. (C). 1997. pap. 20.99 (*0-415-91967-3*) Routledge.

Ollman, Bertell & Birnbaum, Jonathan, eds. U. S. Constitution: Two Hundred Years of Anti-Federalist, Abolitionist, Feminist, Muckraking, Progressive, & Especially Socialist Criticism. 416p. (C). 1990. text 55.00 (*0-8147-6169-0*); pap. text 18.50 (*0-8147-6170-4*) NYU Pr.

Ollman, Bertell & Vernoff, Edward, eds. The Left Academy: Marxist Scholarship on American Campuses, Vol. 2. LC 81-12365. 290p. (Orig.). (C). 1984. 59.95 (*0-275-91237-X*, C12372, Praeger Pubs) Greenwood.

The Left Academy: Marxist Scholarship on American Campuses, Vol. 3. LC 86-9321. 322p. (Orig.). 1986. 59.95 (*0-275-92116-6*, C21163, Praeger Pubs) Greenwood.

— The Left Academy: Marxist Scholarship on American Campuses, Vol. 3. LC 86-9321. 322p. (Orig.). 1986. pap. 19.95 (*0-275-92117-4*, B21173, Praeger Pubs) Greenwood.

Ollman, John, ed. Ceramic Sculptures: Eugene Von Bruenchenhein. LC 98-70092. (Illus.). 54p. 1998. pap. 15.00 (*0-9621506-5-7*) Fleisher Ollman Gallery.

Ollman, John E., ed. Joseph Yoakum: Animistic Landscapes. (Illus.). 56p. (Orig.). 1989. pap. 15.00 (*0-9621506-1-4*) Fleisher Ollman Gallery.

— Miracles: The Sculptures of William Edmondson. LC 94-73210. (Illus.). 60p. Date not set. pap. 15.00 (*0-9621506-3-0*) Fleisher Ollman Gallery.

Ollman, John E., ed. see Fitzpatrick, Tony.

Ollmane, John, ed. A Silent Voice: Drawings & Constructions of James Castle. LC 98-70091. (Illus.). 54p. 1998. pap. 15.00 (*0-9621506-4-9*) Fleisher Ollman Gallery.

Ollosson, Marc. Real Ales for the Home Brewer. (Illus.). 176p. (Orig.). 1997. pap. 20.00 (*1-85486-151-4*) Nexus Special Interests.

***Ollsin, Don.** Pathways to Healing: A Guide to Herbs, Ayurveda, Dreambody & Shamanism. (Illus.). 208p. 1999. pap. 14.95 (*1-58394-011-1*) Frog Ltd CA.

Ollson, Thomas. Swedish Lotto Systems: Guaranteed & Tested Strategies. (LOMAP Ser.: Vol. 4). (Illus.). 80p. 1986. pap. 9.95 (*0-936918-08-X*) Intergalactic NJ.

Ollswang, Jeffrey E., jt. auth. see Ambrose, James E.

Olm, Carroll J. Fairhaven: God's Mighty Oak. LC 97-92827. (Illus.). 180p. 1997. write for info. (*1-57579-098-X*) Pine Hill Pr.

***Olm, Carroll J.** Fairhaven Vol. II: God's Mighty Oak: The Development of the Fairhaven Ministry. LC 97-92827. (Illus.). 232p. 1999. 24.95 (*1-57579-180-3*) Pine Hill Pr.

Olm-Stoelting, Paul. A Quiet Witness. 268p. 1998. pap. write for info. (*1-57502-718-6*, PO2018) Morris Pubng.

Olman, John M. The Squire: The Legendary Golfing Life of Gene Sarazen. LC 87-5714. (Illus.). 176p. 1987. 29.95 (*0-942117-00-X*) Market St Pr.

— The Squire: The Legendary Golfing Life of Gene Sarazen. deluxe limited ed. LC 87-5714. (Illus.). 176p. 1987. lthr. 140.00 (*0-942117-01-8*) Market St Pr.

Olman, John M. & Olman, Morton W. Golf Antiques: And Other Treasures of the Game. abr. rev. ed. LC 93-78337. (Illus.). 312p. 1997. pap. 19.95 (*0-942117-16-6*) Market St Pr.

— Olmans' Guide to Golf Antiques: And Other Treasures of the Game. (Illus.). 280p. 1992. 24.95 (*0-942117-02-6*) Market St Pr.

— St. Andrews & Golf. LC 93-78338. (Illus.). 208p. (Orig.). 1995. 55.00 (*0-942117-20-4*) Market St Pr.

Olman, Morton W., jt. auth. see Olman, John M.

Olmedo, Andres Soria, see Garcia Lorca, Federico & Soria Olmedo, Andres.

Olmedo, Esteban L. & Walker, Verna R., eds. Hispanics in the United States: Abstracts of the Psychological & Behavioral Literature, 1980-1989. LC 90-1218. (PsycINFO Bibliographies in Psychology Ser.: No. 8). 307p. 1990. pap. 19.95 (*1-55798-103-5*) Am Psychol.

Olmedo, Francisco Lopez-Casero, see Lopez-Casero Olmedo, Francisco.

Olmedo, Teofilo E., tr. see Synowiec, Bertie Ryan.

Olmert, Michael. The Smithsonian Book of Books. LC 91-39590. (Illus.). 320p. 1992. 49.95 (*0-89599-030-X*) Smithsonian Bks.

Olmert, Michael, et al. Official Guide to Colonial Williamsburg. LC 98-17476. 176p. 1998. pap. 6.95 (*0-87935-184-5*) Colonial Williamsburg.

Olmesdahl, et al. Marvel Super Heroes Adventure Games. 1998. 24.95 (*0-7869-1227-8*, Pub. by TSR Inc) Random.

Olmesdahl, Bill. A Guide to Marvel Earth. 1998. 15.95 (*0-7869-1230-8*, Pub. by TSR Inc) Random.

***Olmesdahl, Bill.** Scalders, Vol. 1. 1998. 6.95 (*0-7869-0687-1*, Pub. by TSR Inc) Random.

Olmi, M. The Dryinidae & Embolemidae (Hymenoptera: Chrysidoidea) of Fennoscandia & Denmark. (Fauna Entomologica Scandinavica Ser.: 30). 98p. 1994. lib. bdg. 54.00 (*90-04-10224-8*) Brill Academic Pubs.

— Revision of the Dryinidae (Hymenoptera), 2 vols. (Memoir Ser.: No. 37). (Illus.). 1938p. 1984. 130.00 (*1-56665-035-6*) Assoc Pubs FL.

***Olmo, E. & Redi, C. A., eds.** Chromosomes Today, Vol. 13. (Illus.). 350p. 2000. 139.00 (*3-7643-5799-1*) Birkhauser.

Olmo, Ettore. A. Reptilia. (Animal Cytogenetics Ser.: Vol. 4: Chordata 3). (Illus.). 100p. 1986. pap. text 54.60 (*0-685-59739-3*) Lubrecht & Cramer.

— Animal Cytogenetics Vol. 4, Chordata 3A: Reptilia. John, Bernard et al, eds. (Publications in Zoology). (Illus.). iv, 100p. 1986. 51.00 (*3-443-26012-8*) Balogh.

— Animal Cytogenetics, Vol. 4: Chordata, Pt. 3: Reptilia. (Illus.). 104p. 1986. text 62.50 (*0-685-55889-4*) Lubrecht & Cramer.

— Cytogenetics of Amphibians & Reptiles. (Advances in Life Sciences Ser.). 280p. 1990. 76.50 (*0-8176-2358-2*) Birkhauser.

Olmo, Ettore, ed. International Chromosome Conference: 13th Conference, Ancona, September 1998, No.2, Vol.81. (Cytogenetics & Cell Genetics Ser.: Vol. 81, No. 2 (1998)). 78p. 1998. pap. 51.50 (*3-8055-6759-6*) S Karger.

Olmo, Lauro. Camisa English Spoken - S. Garcia. 3rd ed. 234p. 1986. pap. 9.95 (*0-7859-5184-9*) Fr & Eur.

Olmo, Lauro, jt. auth. see Enciso, Pilar.

Olmo Lete, Gregorio Del, see Del Olmo Lete, Gregorio.

Olmos, Dan, jt. auth. see Hay, Louise L.

Olmos, Dan, ed. see Dean, Amy E.

Olmos, Dan, ed. see Fox, Arnold & Fox, Barry.

Olmos, Dan, ed. see Hay, Louise L.

Olmos, Dan, ed. see Hay, Louise L. & Tomchin, Linda C.

Olmos, Dan, ed. see Peterson, Wilferd A.

Olmos, Dan, ed. see Scolastico, Ron.

Olmos, Dan, ed. see Shultz, J. Kennedy.

Olmos, Edward J., et al. Latins Anonymous: Plays. LC 96-26649. 103p. 1996. pap. 11.95 (*1-55885-172-0*, Pub. by Arte Publico) Empire Pub Srvs.

Olmos, Edward James. Americanos: Latino Life in the United States. Monterrey, Manuel, ed. LC 98-51930. (Illus.). 176p. 1999. pap. 25.00 (*0-316-64909-0*) Little.

— Americanos: Latino Life in the United States (La Vida Latina en los Estados Unidos) LC 98-51930. 176p. (gr. 8). 1999. 40.00 (*0-316-64914-7*) Little.

Olmos, Jaime & Sharon, Ariel, eds. Simulators, Vol. 11. 559p. 1994. 120.00 (*1-56555-071-4*, SS-26-3) Soc Computer Sim.

Olmos, Margarite Fernandez. Rudolfo A. Anaya: A Critical Companion. LC 99-17843. (Critical Companions to Popular Contemporary Writers Ser.). 176p. 1999. 29.95 (*0-313-30641-9*) Greenwood.

Olmos, Margarite Fernandez & Paravisini-Gebert, Lizabeth, eds. Remaking & Lost Harmony: Stories from the Hispanic Caribbean. (Dispatches Ser.: Vol. 3). 250p. (Orig.). 1995. pap. 17.00 (*1-877727-36-9*) White Pine.

Olmos, Margarite Fernandez, jt. ed. see Augenbraum, Harold Fernandez.

Olmos, Vicente-Juan B. A Catalogue of Two Hundred Type-I UFO Events in Spain & Portugal. (Illus.). 91p. (C). 1976. pap. 6.00 (*0-929343-50-6*) J A Hynek Ctr UFO.

Olmstead. Math Matters. (Academic Math Ser.: Bk. 3). 1994. text 221.95 (*0-538-61131-6*) S-W Pub.

— Math Matters. (MA - Academic Math Ser.: Bk. 2). 1995. teacher ed. 191.95 (*0-538-63955-5*) S-W Pub.

— Math Matters, Bk. 3. (MA - Academic Math Ser.). (C). 1997. mass mkt. 52.95 (*0-538-68111-X*) S-W Pub.

— Math Matters: Alternate Assessment. (Academic Math Ser.: Bk. 3). 1994. text 72.95 (*0-538-63389-1*) S-W Pub.

— Math Matters: An Integrated Approach, Vol. 1. (Academic Math Ser.). 1994. mass mkt. 29.95 (*0-538-63968-7*) S-W Pub.

— Math Matters: An Integrated Approach, Vol. 2. (Academic Math Ser.). 1995. text 29.95 (*0-538-63969-5*) S-W Pub.

— Math Matters Bk. 2: Copyright Update. (Academic Math Ser.). 1995. text 59.95 (*0-538-63954-7*) S-W Pub.

— Trail of Hearts Blood Wherever. LC 98-6698. 408p. 1998. pap. 14.00 (*0-8050-5843-5*, Owl) H Holt & Co.

Olmstead & Lynch. Math Matters: An Integrated Approach. (MA - Academic Math Ser.: Bk. 3). 1994. mass mkt., wbk. ed. 12.95 (*0-538-61125-1*) S-W Pub.

Olmstead, jt. auth. see Lynch.

Olmstead, Adrienne. My Nature Journal: A Personal Nature Guide for Young People. unabridged ed. Olmstead, Donald, ed. & des. by. (ACE., Illus.). 176p. (gr. 3-8). 2000. 17.95 (*0-9672459-1-5*) Pajaro.

Olmstead, Albert T. History of Assyria. LC 23-17167. (Midway Reprint Ser.). 727p. reprint ed. pap. 200.00 (*0-608-12115-0*, 202406100035) Bks Demand.

***Olmstead, Andrea.** Juilliard: A History. LC 98-58043. (Music in American Life Ser.). 400p. 1999. 37.50 (*0-252-02487-7*) U of Ill Pr.

Olmstead, Arthur T. History of the Persian Empire. LC 48-7317. (Illus.). 661p. 1959. pap. 24.00 (*0-226-62777-2*, P36) U Ch Pr.

Olmstead, Cresencia & Olmstead, Dale. Mission Santa Ines: The Hidden Gem. LC 95-661321. (Illus.). 25p. (Orig.). 1995. pap. 8.95 (*0-9646858-0-9*) Old Mission Santa Ines.

Olmstead, Dale, jt. auth. see Olmstead, Cresencia.

Olmstead, Donald, ed. & des. see Olmstead, Adrienne.

Olmstead, Earl P. Blackcoats among the Delaware: David Zeisberger on the Ohio Frontier. LC 90-47576. (Illus.). 296p. 1991. pap. 17.50 (*0-87338-434-2*) Kent St U Pr.

Olmstead, Earl P. & Zeisberger, David. David Zeisberger: A Life among the Indians. LC 96-3083. (Illus.). 488p. 1997. 39.00 (*0-87338-568-3*) Kent St U Pr.

Olmstead, Ellen, jt. ed. see Kutenplon, Deborah.

Olmstead, Frederick L. The Yosemite Valley & the Mariposa Big Trees: A Preliminary Report, 1865. LC 93-22909. (Illus.). 1995. 85.00 (*0-939666-68-5*); pap. 6.95 (*0-939666-69-3*) Yosemite Assn.

Olmstead, Gene. Problem Solving with the TI-83. 160p. (YA). (gr. 9-12). 1997. spiral bd. 27.00 (*1-886018-11-1*) Venture Pubng.

Olmstead, Jean E. Itinerant Teaching: Tricks of the Trade for Teachers of Blind & Visually Impaired Students. LC 91-8392. 136p. 1991. pap. 27.95 (*0-89128-190-8*) Am Foun Blind.

***Olmstead, Joseph A.** Executive Leadership: Building World-Class Organization. LC 99-88701. 514p. 2000. pap. 24.95 (*0-87719-369-X*, Cashman Dud) Gulf Pub.

Olmstead, Judith. Woman Between Two Worlds: Portrait of an Ethiopian Rural Leader. LC 96-10068. 280p. 1997. text 39.95 (*0-252-02283-1*); pap. text 19.95 (*0-252-06587-5*) U of Ill Pr.

Olmstead, Lois. Breast Cancer & Me: One Woman's Story of Victory over a Deadly Disease. LC 97-157229. 1996. pap. 10.99 (*0-87509-686-7*) Chr Pubns.

Olmstead, Marty. Hidden Georgia. (Hidden Travel Ser.). (Illus.). 350p. 1999. pap. 16.95 (*1-56975-180-3*) Ulysses Pr.

— Hidden Tennessee. 2nd rev. ed. (Hidden Travel Ser.). (Illus.). 352p. 1999. pap. 15.95 (*1-56975-172-2*) Ulysses Pr.

Olmstead, Marvin L. Small Animal Orthopedics. (Illus.). 592p. (C). (gr. 13). 1995. text 80.00 (*0-8016-5874-8*, 05874) Mosby Inc.

Olmstead, P. & Weikart, David P. How Nations Serve Young Children: Profiles of Care & Education in 14 Countries. LC 89-35026. 438p. (C). 1989. pap. text 29.95 (*0-929816-07-2*, R1029) High-Scope.

Olmstead, P. & Weikart, David P., eds. Families Speak: Early Childhood Care & Education in 11 Countries. LC 94-26948. 390p. 1994. 29.95 (*0-929816-89-7*, R1038) High-Scope.

Olmstead, Phyllis M., ed. & illus. see Champagne, David W.

An Asterisk (*) at the beginning of an entry indicates that the title is appearing for the first time.

O

Olmstead, Robert. America by Land. LC 97-1751. 1997. pap. 12.00 (*0-8050-5119-8*) H Holt & Co.
— Elements of the Writing Craft. LC 96-50165. 272p. 1997. 19.99 (*1-884910-29-7*, Story Press) F & W Pubns Inc.
— River Dogs. LC 97-1749. 1997. pap. 12.00 (*0-8050-5120-1*) H Holt & Co.
— Stay Here with Me. large type ed. (Niagara Large Print Ser.). 332p. 1997. 29.50 (*0-7089-5872-9*) Ulverscroft.
— Stay Here with Me: A Memoir. 1997. pap. text 12.00 (*0-8050-5358-1*, Owl) H Holt & Co.
— A Trail of Heart's Blood Wherever We Go. 416p. 1992. reprint ed. pap. 11.00 (*0-380-71548-1*, Avon Bks) Morrow Avon.
Olmstead. Chemistry. 1994. student ed. (*0-8151-6408-4*); lab manual ed. write for info. (*0-8151-6409-2*) Mosby Inc.
— Chemistry. annot. ed. 1994. teacher ed. 14.06 (*0-8151-6519-6*) Mosby Inc.
— Chemistry: Molecular Science. 1994. 29.37 (*0-697-40329-7*, WCB McGr Hill) McGrw-H Hghr Educ.
Olmsted & Williams. General Chemistry Lab Manual. (C). 1994. text 37.50 (*0-8016-5072-0*) Mosby Inc.
Olmsted, Barney & Smith, Suzanne. Creating a Flexible Workplace: How to Select & Manage Alternative Work Options. 2nd ed. LC 94-28096. 384p. 1994. 59.95 (*0-8144-0214-3*) AMACOM.
— The Job Sharing Handbook. 116p. 1996. pap. 15.00 (*0-14-046544-8*) New Ways Work.
***Olmsted, Charles L. & Ybarra, Edward C.** Juan Coy: Texas Outlaw & Lawman. LC 99-28428. 2000. 19.95 (*1-57168-324-0*, Eakin Pr) Sunbelt Media.
Olmsted, Cheryl. Alphabet Cooking Cards. (J). (gr. k-1). 1990. pap. 12.99 (*0-8224-0454-0*) Fearon Teacher Aids.
Olmsted, D. L. Out of the Mouth of Babes: Earliest Stages in Language Learning. LC 70-17001. (Janua Linguarum, Ser. Minor: No. 117). (Illus.). 260p. (Orig.). 1971. pap. text 44.65 (*90-279-1892-9*) Mouton.
Olmsted, Denison. Memoir of Eli Whitney, Esq. LC 72-5065. (Technology & Society Ser.). 90p. 1977. reprint ed. 19.95 (*0-405-04716-9*) Ayer.
Olmsted, Frederick L. Civilizing American Cities: Writings on City Landscapes. Sutton, S. B., ed. LC 96-47983. (Illus.). 318p. 1997. pap. 14.95 (*0-306-80765-3*) Da Capo.
— A Consideration of the Justifying Value of a Public Park. (Notable American Authors Ser.). 1999. reprint ed. lib. bdg. 125.00 (*0-7812-4676-8*) Rprt Serv.
— The Cotton Kingdom. Powell, Lawrence et al, eds. (Modern Library College Editions). 624p. (C). 1983. pap. 8.44 (*0-07-554413-X*) McGraw.
— The Cotton Kingdom. (Notable American Authors Ser.). 1999. reprint ed. lib. bdg. 125.00 (*0-7812-4674-1*) Rprt Serv.
— The Cotton Kingdom: A Traveller's Observations on Cotton & Slavery in the American Slave States. unabridged ed. Schlesinger, Arthur Meier, Jr., ed. LC 96-24350. 708p. 1996. reprint ed. pap. 18.95 (*0-306-80723-8*) Da Capo.
— Frederick Law Olmsted, Professional Papers. (Notable American Authors Ser.). 1999. reprint ed. lib. bdg. 125.00 (*0-7812-4677-6*) Rprt Serv.
— A Journey in the Black Country. (Notable American Authors Ser.). 1999. reprint ed. lib. bdg. 125,00 (*0-7812-4673-3*) Rprt Serv.
— A Journey in the Seaboard Slave States. (Notable American Authors Ser.). 1999. reprint ed. lib. bdg. 125.00 (*0-7812-4671-7*) Rprt Serv.
— Journey in the Seaboard Slave States, with Remarks on Their Economy. LC 68-55903. (Illus.). 723p. 1969. reprint ed. lib. bdg. 35.00 (*0-8371-0601-X*, OLJ&) Greenwood.
— Journey Through Texas. 1993. reprint ed. lib. bdg. 75.00 (*0-7812-5891-X*) Rprt Serv.
— A Journey Through Texas: or A Saddle-Trip on the Southwestern Frontier. (American Biography Ser.). 516p. 1991. reprint ed. lib. bdg. 99.00 (*0-7812-8302-7*) Rprt Serv.
Olmsted, Frederick L., Jr. Public Parks & the Enlargement of Towns. LC 76-112564. (Rise of Urban America Ser.). 1973. reprint ed. 15.95 (*0-405-02469-X*) Ayer.
Olmsted, Frederick L. Public Parks & the Enlargement of Towns. (Notable American Authors Ser.). 1999. reprint ed. lib. bdg. 125.00 (*0-7812-4675-X*) Rprt Serv.
— Slavery & the South, 1852-1857. Beveridge, Charles E. & McLaughlin, Charles C., eds. LC 80-8881. (Papers of Frederick Law Olmsted: Vol. 2). 527p. 1981. reprint ed. pap. 163.40 (*0-608-03669-2*, 206449500009) Bks Demand.
— Walks & Talks of an American Farmer in England. (Notable American Authors Ser.). 1999. reprint ed. lib. bdg. 125.00 (*0-7812-4670-9*) Rprt Serv.
Olmsted, Frederick L., Jr. & Kimball, Theodora. Frederick Law Olmsted, Landscape Architect: 1822-1903, 2 vols., 1 bk. LC 68-57756. (Illus.). 1972. reprint ed. 38.95 (*0-405-08829-9*) Ayer.
Olmsted, Gerald W. A Rambler's Guide to the Trails of Mt. Tamalpais & the Marin Headlands: Complete Guide to Hiking, Biking, Horse Trails. 8th rev. ed. (Illus.). 1998. pap. 6.95 (*0-941969-05-3*) Olmsted Bros Map.
— A Rambler's Guide to the Trails of the East Bay Hills: Central Section Including Redwood, Chabot, Las Trampas, Sibley & Joaquin Miller Parks & Lands of East Bay MUD. (Illus.). 1987. 6.95 (*0-941969-00-2*) Olmsted Bros Map.
Olmsted, Helen E., ed. Homicide Host Presents. 300p. 1996. 25.00 (*1-885173-14-8*) Write Way.
Olmsted, Henry K. & Ward, George K. Olmsted Family in America. LC 93-79946. (Illus.). 550p. 1994. reprint ed. 60.00 (*1-55787-046-2*) Hrt of the Lakes.
Olmsted, J. M. Francois Magendie. Cohen, I. Bernard, ed. LC 80-2139. (Illus.). 1981. reprint ed. lib. bdg. 30.95 (*0-405-13894-6*) Ayer.
Olmsted, J. M., jt. auth. see Gelbaum, Bernard R.
Olmsted, James F., jt. auth. see Whitney, Philip R.
Olmsted, Jane, jt. ed. see Oakes, Elizabeth.
***Olmsted, John & Williams, Gregory.** Chemistry: A Molecular Science. 3rd ed. (Illus.). (C). 2000. text 83.75 (*0-7637-0896-8*) JB Pubns.
Olmsted, John A., jt. auth. see Tikkanen, Wayne.
Olmsted, John M. Second Course in Calculus. LC 68-14041. (Century Mathematics Ser.). (Illus.). 336p. (C). 1968. 39.50 (*0-89197-395-8*) Irvington.
Olmsted, Kathryn S. Challenging the Secret Government: The Post-Watergate Investigations of the CIA & FBI. LC 95-23354. (Illus.). 272p. 1996. lib. bdg. 45.00 (*0-8078-2254-X*) U of NC Pr.
— Challenging the Secret Government: The Post-Watergate Investigations of the CIA & FBI. LC 95-23354. (Illus.). 272p. (C). 1996. pap. 18.95 (*0-8078-4562-0*) U of NC Pr.
Olmsted, Larry. A Trailside Guide: Snowshoeing. LC 97-22846. 192p. 1998. pap. 17.95 (*0-393-31720-X*) Norton.
Olmsted, Merle C. The 357th over Europe: The 357th Fighter Group in World War II. 164p. 1997. reprint ed. pap. 24.95 (*0-933424-73-6*) Specialty Pr.
Olmsted, Nancy. The Ferry Building: Witness to a Century of Change, 1898-1998. LC 98-40386. (Illus.). 240p. 1998. pap. 30.00 (*1-890771-12-0*) Heyday Bks.
Olmsted, Nancy, ed. see Olmsted, Roger.
Olmsted, Patricia P., et al. Parent Education: The Contributions of Ira J. Gordon. Sunderlin, Sylvia, ed. LC 80-12211. (Illus.). 64p. (Orig.). 1980. 4.75 (*0-87173-094-4*) ACEI.
Olmsted, Patricia P., jt. ed. see Weikart, David P.
Olmsted, Robert. The Shotgun. 16p. 1991. pap. 1.50 (*0-89754-077-8*) Dan River Pr.
Olmsted, Robert, ed. see Diamond, Olivia.
Olmsted, Robert W. Wild Strawberries at 3000 Feet. LC 86-60424. 64p. (Orig.). 1986. pap. 6.95 (*0-89002-244-5*) Am Hist Pr.
— Wild Strawberries at 3000 Feet. LC 86-60424. 64p. (Orig.). 1986. 19.95 (*0-89002-245-3*) Northwoods Pr.
Olmsted, Roger. Scow Schooners of San Francisco Bay. Olmsted, Nancy, ed. (Local History Studies: Vol. 33). 112p. 1988. pap. 14.95 (*0-935089-12-8*) CA History Ctr.
Olmsted, Sterling. Motions of Love: Woolman As Mystic & Activist. LC 93-85961. (Orig.). 1993. pap. 4.00 (*0-87574-312-9*) Pendle Hill.
Olmsted, Sterling & Hellex, Mike, eds. John Woolman: A Nonviolence & Social Change Source Book. 150p. (Orig.). (C). 1997. pap. text. write for info. (*0-9658866-0-3*) WC Peace Res Ctr.
Olmsted, Wendy, jt. auth. see Jost, Walter.
Olmsted, Wendy, jt. ed. see Jost, Walter.
Olmypic Scientific Congress (1984: Eugene, OR) Sta. Sport & Disabled Athletes. Sherrill, Claudine, ed. LC 85-18112. (1984 Olympic Scientific Congress Proceedings Ser.: No. 9). (Illus.). 315p. reprint ed. pap. 97.70 (*0-608-07049-1*, 206725500009) Bks Demand.
Oln, Ross R., jt. auth. see Henson, Burt.
Olness, Karen. Parenting Happy Healthy Children. 1981. pap. 8.95 (*0-9602790-4-0*) Hlth Frontiers.
— Practical Pediatrics in Less-Developed Countries. 1980. pap. 9.95 (*0-9602790-2-4*) Hlth Frontiers.
— Raising Happy Healthy Children. 1981. pap. 3.95 (*0-9602790-5-9*) Hlth Frontiers.
Olness, Karen & Kohen, Daniel P. Hypnosis & Hypnotherapy with Children. 3rd ed. LC 95-26800. (Illus.). 457p. 1996. lib. bdg. 50.00 (*1-57230-054-X*, 0054) Guilford Pubns.
Olney, Clarke, ed. see Norton, Caroline Sheridan.
Olney, Claude W. The Bucks Start Here: How to Turn Your Hidden Assets into Money. LC 53-86047. (Illus.). 236p. 1991. pap. 8.00 (*0-9617886-4-X*) Olney Seminars.
— Where There's a Will There's an A: How to Get Better Grades in College. (Illus.). 32p. 1986. 44.95 (*0-9617886-0-7*) Olney Seminars.
Olney, Dick & Moore, Roslyn. Walking in Beauty: A Collection of the Psychological Insights & Spiritual Wisdom of Dick Olney. 120p. (Orig.). 1996. pap. 14.95 (*0-9646999-0-7*) DO Publng.
Olney, J. Modern Geography As of 1828. (Illus.). 200p. 1994. pap. 25.00 (*0-87556-789-4*) Saifer.
***Olney, James.** Memory & Narrative: The Weave of Life-Writing. LC 98-17135. (Illus.). 496p. 1999. 35.00 (*0-226-62816-7*) U Ch Pr.
Olney, James. Metaphors of Self: The Meaning of Autobiography. LC 71-173758. 358p. reprint ed. pap. 111.00 (*0-7837-1412-2*, 204176600023) Bks Demand.
Olney, James, ed. Afro-American Writing Today: An Anniversary Issue of the Southern Review. LC 88-39021. (Illus.). 328p. 1989. text 45.00 (*0-8071-1482-0*) La State U Pr.
— T. S. Eliot: Essays from the Southern Review. (Illus.). 368p. 1988. text 90.00 (*0-19-818575-8*) OUP.
Olney, Judith. The Farm Market Cookbook. 296p. Date not set. 25.00 (*0-88365-865-8*) Galahad Bks.
— The Joy of Chocolate. 208p. 1989. pap. 14.95 (*0-8120-4279-4*) Barron.
Olney, Kathryn. Girl Geeks: Making Sure That Girls Are Not Left Behind in the Technological Revolution. 256p. 2000. 24.00 (*0-465-02650-8*, Pub. by Basic) HarpC.
Olney, Marguerite, jt. ed. see Flanders, Helen H.
Olney, Martha L. Buy Now, Pay Later: Advertising, Credit, & Consumer Durables in the 1920s. LC 90-49565. 444p. reprint ed. pap. 137.70 (*0-608-06012-7*, 206634000008) Bks Demand.
Olney, Pat, jt. auth. see Olney, Ross R.
Olney, Richard. Reflexions. Olbey, J., ed. (Illus.). 400p. 1998. 34.95 (*1-883283-20-5*) Brick Tower.
— Richard Olney's French Wine & Food: A Wine Lover's Cookbook. LC 97-24713. (Illus.). 128p. 1997. write for info. (*1-56656-226-0*) Interlink Inc.
— Simple French Food. (Illus.). 448p. 1992. reprint ed. pap. 15.95 (*0-02-010060-4*) Macmillan.
— Ten Vineyard Lunches. LC 88-21936. (Ten Menus Ser.). (Illus.). 128p. 1988. 19.95 (*0-940793-23-7*) Interlink Pub.
Olney, Ross R. & Olney, Pat. Easy to Make Magic. (gr. 1-3). 1981. pap. 3.95 (*0-13-222570-0*) P-H.
Olney, Ross Robert. The Farm Combine. LC 84-5288. (Inventions That Changed Our Lives Ser.). (Illus.). 64p. (J). (gr. 4 up). 1984. lib. bdg. 10.85 (*0-8027-6568-8*) Walker & Co.
— Internal Combustion Engine. LC 81-48604. (Illus.). 48p. (J). (gr. 3-5). 1982. 11.95 (*0-397-32009-4*); lib. bdg. 11.89 (*0-397-32010-8*) HarpC Child Bks.
Olney, Ross Robert. Lyn St. James: Driven to Be First. LC 96-16239. (Achievers Ser.). (J). 1997. lib. bdg. 19.93 (*0-8225-2890-8*, Lerner Publctns) Lerner Pub.
Olney, Ross Robert. Lyn St. James: Driven to Be First. LC 96-16239. (Achievers Ser.). (Illus.). 64p. (J). 1997. pap. 5.95 (*0-8225-9749-7*, Lerner Publctns) Lerner Pub.
Olney, Ross Robert, jt. auth. see Sorrentino, Amedeo J.
Olney, Shauna L. Unions in a Changing World: Problems & Prospects in Selected Industrialized Countries. LC 97-162274. xii, 99p. 1996. pap. 18.00 (*92-2-109504-5*) Intl Labour Office.
Olney Street Group Staff. The Olney Street Anthology. LC 88-92293. 120p. (Orig.). 1988. pap. 5.00 (*0-9621084-0-5*) Olney St Pr.
O'Loan, Kathryn, jt. ed. see Filho, Walter L.
Oloff, Lawrence M., ed. Musculoskeletal Disorders of the Lower Extremities. LC 93-7250. 1994. text 142.00 (*0-7216-3716-7*, W B Saunders Co) Harcrt Hlth Sci Grp.
Olofson, Jack. Best of Colorado Four Wheel Drive Roads. 68p. 1998. pap. 12.95 (*0-930657-40-3*) Outdr Bks & Maps.
***Olofson, Jack.** Colorado's Guide to Hunting. 112p. 1999. pap. 14.95 (*0-930657-42-X*) Outdr Bks & Maps.
Olofson, Jack O. Best of Rocky Mountain National Park Hiking Trails. 48p. 1998. pap. 9.95 (*0-930657-39-X*) Outdr Bks & Maps.
Olofson, Margareta S. Acquarossa: The Head Antefixes & Relief Plaque; a Reconstruction of a Terracotta Decoration & Its Architectural Setting. (Acta Instituti Romani Regni Sueciae Ser.: Series 4, XXXVIII:V, 1). (Illus.). 160p. (Orig.). 1984. pap. 72.50 (*91-7042-097-1*, Pub. by P Astroms) Coronet Bks.
Olofsson, Anna, jt. ed. see Englis, Basil.
Olofsson, Staffan. God Is My Rock: A Study of Translation Technique & Theological Exegesis in the Septuagint. (Coniectanea Biblica. Old Testament Ser.: No. 31). 208p. (Orig.). 1990. pap. 46.50 (*91-22-01394-6*) Coronet Bks.
— The LXX Version: A Guide to the Translation Technique of the Septuagint. (Coniectanea Biblica. Old Testament Ser.: No. 30). 105p. (Orig.). 1990. pap. 36.50 (*91-22-01392-X*) Coronet Bks.
Olofsson, Tommy. Elemental Poems. Pearson, Jean, tr. 136p. 1991. pap. 7.00 (*1-877727-09-1*) White Pine.
Olomalaiye, P. Improvng Constrctn Prodc. (C). 1997. 143.95 (*0-582-09603-0*) Addison-Wesley.
Oloman, Colin. Electrochemical Processing for the Pulp & Paper Industry. (Illus.). xxv, 244p. (Orig.). 1996. 95.00 (*0-9517307-2-X*) Electrosyn Co.
O'Longaigh, David, ed. We Irish in Oregon: A Historical Account of the Irish in Oregon from the Pioneer Times to the Present Day. LC 99-490571. (Illus.). 105p. 1998. pap. 12.95 (*0-9661518-1-X*, Pub. by Celtic Chronicles) All-Ireland Cultural.
***Olonisakin, Funmi.** Reinventing Peacekeeping in Africa: Conceptual & Legal Issues in ECOMOG Operations. LC 99-89237. 272p. 2000. 71.55 (*90-411-1321-5*) Kluwer Law Intl.
Oloniyo, N. Living by Faith. 204p. 1993. pap. 5.95 (*0-88172-201-4*) Believers Bkshelf.
O'Looney, John. Beyond Maps: GIS & Decision Making in Local Government. LC 98-105647. (Special Reports). 152p. 1997. pap. text 48.00 (*0-87326-156-9*) Intl City-Cnty Mgt.
— Economic Development & Environmental Control: Balancing Business & Community in Age of NIMBYS & LULUS. LC 94-45283. 360p. 1995. 75.00 (*0-89930-940-2*, Quorum Bks) Greenwood.
***O'Looney, John.** Local Government On-Line: Putting the Internet to Work. LC 00-21451. 2000. write for info. (*0-87326-170-4*) Intl City-Cnty Mgt.
O'Looney, John. Redesigning the Work of Human Services. LC 95-24915. 344p. 1996. 72.95 (*0-89930-941-0*, Quorum Bks) Greenwood.
***O'Looney, John A.** Beyond Maps: GIS & Decision Making in Local Government. 315p. 2000. pap. 39.95 (*1-879102-79-X*, Pub. by ESR Inst) IPG Chicago.
O'Looney, John A. Emergency 911 Services: A Guide for Georgia Local Governments. LC 97-27934. 25p. 1997. pap. 8.95 (*0-89854-188-3*) U of GA Inst Govt.
— Outsourcing State & Local Government Services: Decision-Making Strategies & Management Methods. LC 98-18502. 256p. 1998. 59.95 (*1-56720-169-5*, Quorum Bks) Greenwood.
Olorenshaw, R. Teach Yourself French, Further. (Teach Yourself Ser.). 1992. 15.95 (*0-8288-8328-9*); 45.00 incl. audio (*0-8288-8329-7*) Fr & Eur.
— Teach Yourself Further French, 2 cass., Set. (FRE.). 240p. 1994. pap. 19.95 incl. audio (*0-8442-3884-8*, Teach Yrslf) NTC Contemp Pub Co.
Olorode, Omotoye. Taxonomy of West African Flowering Plants. (Illus.). 176p. 1984. text 25.95 (*0-582-64429-1*) Longman.
***Olotu, Oluyemisi.** Vision: A Plain Ole Love Story. LC 99-91775. vi, 311p. 2000. pap. 10.00 (*0-9676973-0-1*) Iwe Yemi Pr.
O'Loughlin, Edward T., ed. Hearst & His Enemies. LC 76-125710. (American Journalists Ser.). 1974. reprint ed. 16.95 (*0-405-01691-3*) Ayer.
O'Loughlin, John, ed. Dictionary of Geopolitics. LC 93-25072. 304p. 1993. lib. bdg. 79.50 (*0-313-26313-2*, ODG/, Greenwood Pr) Greenwood.
O'Loughlin, John & Friedrichs, Juergen, eds. Social Polarization in Post-Industrial Metropolises. (Illus.). xiv, 335p. (C). 1996. lib. bdg. 49.95 (*3-11-013728-3*, 111/96) De Gruyter.
O'Loughlin, John & Van der Wusten, Herman. The New Political Geography of Eastern Europe. LC 92-36085. 320p. 1993. 130.00 (*0-471-94812-8*) Wiley.
***O'Loughlin, Luanne, et al.** Online Auctions: The Internet Guide for Bargain Hunters & Collectors. 291p. 2000. pap. 14.95 (*0-07-135303-8*) McGraw.
O'Loughlin, Miceal. Another Nation: New & Selected Poems. 105p. (Orig.). 1996. pap. 13.95 (*1-874597-03-0*, Pub. by New Island Books) Irish Bks Media.
O'Loughlin, Michale, tr. see Achterberg, Gerrit.
O'Loughlin, Raphael. Basilian Leaders from Texas. Whitebird, J., ed. (Texas-Church History Ser.). (Illus.). 112p. (Orig.). 1992. pap. 20.00 (*0-930324-17-X*) Wings Pr.
O'Loughlin, Sean, jt. auth. see Muir, Kenneth.
O'Loughlin, Thomas. Cardinal Newman: Seeker of Truth. 1989. pap. 22.00 (*1-85390-096-6*, Pub. by Veritas Pubns) St Mut.
***O'Loughlin, Thomas.** Celtic Theology: Humanity, World & God in Early Irish Writings. 224p. 2000. 74.95 (*0-8264-4870-4*); pap. 28.95 (*0-8264-4871-2*) Continuum.
— Journeys on the Edges: The Celtic Tradition. 144p. 2000. pap. 14.00 (*1-57075-337-7*) Orbis Bks.
O'Loughlin, Thomas. St. Patrick: The Man & His Works. 1999. pap. text 9.95 (*0-281-05211-5*) Society Prom Christ Know.
Olovsson, Paul, jt. ed. see Klevmarken, Anders.
Olowofoyeku, Abimbola. Suing Judges: A Study of Judicial Immunity. 258p. 1994. text 65.00 (*0-19-825793-7*) OUP.
Olowomeye, Richard. The Management of Solid Waste in Nigerian Cities. LC 90-27893. (Environment: Problems & Solutions Ser.). 224p. 1991. text 20.00 (*0-8240-9274-0*) Garland.
Olowu, Dele, jt. ed. see Wunsch, James S.
Oloyede, Olajide. Coping under Recession: Workers in a Nigerian Factory. (Studia Sociologica Upsaliensia: No. 34). 177p. (Orig.). 1991. pap. 42.00 (*91-554-2801-0*) Coronet Bks.
Olphen, H. Van, see Van Olphen, H., ed.
Olpin, Robert S., et al, eds. Artists of Utah. LC 99-17190. (Illus.). 320p. 1999. 50.00 (*0-87905-905-2*) Gibbs Smith Pub.
Olpin, Robert S., ed. see Harwood, James T.
Olrik, Alex, intro. A Book of Danish Ballads. 337p. 1977. 18.95 (*0-8369-6036-X*) Ayer.
Olrik, Axel. Principles for Oral Narrative Research. Wolf, Kirsten & Jensen, Jody, trs. LC 88-46034. (Folklore Studies in Translation). 240p. 1992. text 31.95 (*0-253-34175-2*) Ind U Pr.
Olroyd, D. R. Darwinian Impacts: An Introduction to the Darwinian Revolution. 416p. 1980. pap. 16.99 (*0-335-09001-X*) OpUniv Pr.
Olsa, Aaron C., tr. see Hutchinson, Hanna.
Olsberg, Diana. Ageing & Money: Australia's Retirement Revolution. LC 97-148512. 224p. 1997. pap. 24.95 (*1-86448-047-5*, Pub. by Allen & Unwin Pty) Paul & Co Pubs.
Olsby, Gary. Basic Bible Studies for Children: Grades 1-6. 100p. 1999. pap. 9.99 (*0-89900-853-4*) College Pr Pub.
— A Heart for God. (Studies in the Life of King David). 109p. 1996. pap. 14.99 (*0-89900-735-X*, T96-735-X) College Pr Pub.
Olscamp, Paul J. An Introduction to Philosophy. LC 77-144104. 523p. reprint ed. pap. 162.20 (*0-608-10045-5*, 201252200081) Bks Demand.
— The Moral Philosophy of George Berkeley. (International Archives of the History of Ideas Ser.: No. 33). 251p. 1970. lib. bdg. 88.00 (*90-247-0303-4*) Kluwer Academic.
Olscamp, Paul J., jt. ed. see Lennon, Thomas M.
Olschewski, Andreas, jt. auth. see Groth, Wolfgang.
Olschki, Leo. Choix de Livres Anciens Rares et Curieux, Vols. 1-13. (Illus.). 1966p. 1998. pap. 450.00 (*1-57898-084-4*) Martino Pubng.
Olsder, G. J., jt. auth. see Basar, T.
Olsder, Geert J., ed. New Trends in Dynamic Games & Appications, Vol. 3. LC 95-33319. (Annals of the International Society of Dynamic Games Ser.). 482p. 1995. 104.00 (*0-8176-3812-1*) Birkhauser.
Olsen. Being Healthy: Grade 6. 1990. student ed. 34.25 (*0-15-368770-3*) Harcourt Schl Pubs.
— Being Healthy 90: Grade 4. 1991. student ed. 31.95 (*0-15-368768-1*) Harcourt Schl Pubs.
— Being Healthy 90: Grade 5. 1990. 33.00 (*0-15-368769-X*) Harcourt Schl Pubs.
— Being Healthy 90: Grade 7. 1990. 36.00 (*0-15-368771-1*) Harcourt Schl Pubs.
— Being Healthy 90: Grade 8. 1990. student ed. 36.00 (*0-15-368772-X*) Harcourt Schl Pubs.
— Criminal Tax Procedure. LC 95-77096. 1995. 125.00 (*0-316-65045-5*, Aspen Law & Bus) Aspen Pub.
— Handbook of Avian Medicine. (Illus.). 512p. (C). (gr. 13). 1999. pap. text 49.95 (*0-8151-8466-2*, 28825) Mosby Inc.
— Hasand to Grave, Vol. 1. 352p. Date not set. 6.99 (*0-312-96699-7*, Pub. by Tor Bks) St Martin.

An Asterisk (*) at the beginning of an entry indicates that the title is appearing for the first time.

— Silver Unicorn: A Telecommunications Simulation. (KM - Office Procedures Ser.). 1992. mass mkt. 15.50 (*0-538-61066-2*) S-W Pub.
— Societal Dynamics. (C). 1994. pap. text 41.20 (*0-13-157397-7*) P-H.
Olsen, ed. Tectonic, Depositional, & Paleoecological History of Early Mesozoic Rift Basins, Eastern North America, No. T351. (IGC Field Trip Guidebooks Ser.). 184p. 1989. 35.00 (*0-87590-658-3*) Am Geophysical.
Olsen, et al. Immunology & Immunopathology of Domestic Animals. 2nd ed. LC 95-106545. (Illus.). 208p. (C). (gr. 13). 1994. text 81.95 (*0-8016-6398-9*, 06398) Mosby Inc.
Olsen, Afton S. Afternoon in the Garden. 81p. 1996. write for info. (*0-9629616-2-0*) Magden Assocs.
Olsen, Afton S., jt. auth. see McFarland, Minnie B.
Olsen, Alan R. & Sidebottom, Thomas H. Fundamentals of Microanalytical Entomology: A Practical Guide to Detecting & Identifying Filth in Foods. 320p. 1995. boxed set 129.95 (*0-8493-8925-9*, 8925) CRC Pr.
Olsen, Alexandra Hennessey. Between Ernest & Game: The Literary Artistry of the Confessio Amantis. LC 89-133292. (American University Studies: English Language & Literature: Ser. IV, Vol. 110). IX, 130p. 1990. text 31.50 (*0-8204-1141-8*) P Lang Pubng.
Olsen, Alexandra Hennessey, ed. Poems & Prose from the Old English. Raffel, Burton, tr. from ANG. LC 97-22556. 273p. 1998. 32.50 (*0-300-06994-4*) Yale U Pr.
Olsen, Alexandra Hennessey, jt. auth. see Raffel, Burton.
Olsen, Alexandra Hennessey, jt. ed. see Damico, Helen.
Olsen, Alexandra Hennessey, tr. see Boccaccio, Giovanni.
Olsen, Alfa B., jt. auth. see Efron, Marshall.
Olsen, Alfred O. & Clark, Franklin. On Line Criminal Activity: An Investigative Primer for Law. (Practical Aspects Of Criminal & Forensic Investigation Ser.). 1998. 69.95 (*0-8493-8161-4*) CRC Pr.
Olsen, Allison, tr. see Tonnessen, Tor I.
Olsen, Anders, et al. Systems Engineering Using SDL-92. LC 94-31557. 480p. 1994. 167.50 (*0-444-89872-7*, North Holland) Elsevier.
Olsen, Andrea. BodyStories: A Guide to Experiential Anatomy. 2nd rev. ed. (Illus.). 176p. 1998. pap. 26.95 (*1-58177-023-5*) Barrytown Ltd.
Olsen, Arthur M., et al, eds. The Call to Care: Dimensions & Dilemmas of Caring. LC 98-74834. (Illus.). 496p. 1999. pap. 29.95 (*0-944287-22-0*) Ex Machina.
Olsen, Ashley, jt. auth. see Olsen, Mary-Kate.
***Olsen, Austin.** Apache Ambush. 2000. mass mkt. 5.99 (*0-7860-1148-3*, Pinncle Kensgtn) Kensgtn Pub Corp.
Olsen, Bent O., jt. auth. see Larsen, Ivind.
Olsen, Bernard A. Upon the Tented Field. LC 93-80311. (Illus.). 336p. 1993. 34.95 (*0-9638729-0-7*) Historic Proj.
Olsen, Birger M., jt. auth. see Mann, Nicholas E.
***Olsen, Birgit A.** The Noun in Biblical Armenian: Origin & Word Formation: with Special Emphasis on the Indo-European Heritage. LC 99-11550. (Trends in Linguistics Ser.). xiiv, 1100p. 1999. 125.35 (*3-11-016483-3*) De Gruyter.
Olsen, Bjorn R. & Nimni, Marcel E. Molecular Biology, Vol. 4. LC 87-20946. (Collagen Ser.: Vol. IV). 208p. 1988. 110.00 (*0-8493-4604-5*, QP552) Franklin.
Olsen, Brad. Hawaii. 252p. 1998. pap. text 13.95 (*1-55650-809-3*) Hunter NJ.
— Northern California. (Extreme Adventure Guide). 252p. 1998. pap. text 13.95 (*1-55650-808-5*) Hunter NJ.
***Olsen, Brad.** Sacred Places: 101 Spiritual Sites Around the World. Cambron, Beverly, ed. LC 98-92920. (Illus.). 288p. 1999. pap. 16.95 (*1-888729-02-3*, 420-3) Cnsrtm Cllctive Cnscnss.
Olsen, Brad. World Stompers: A Guide to Travel Manifesto. 3rd rev. ed. LC 96-86305. (Illus.). 280p. 1997. pap. 16.95 (*1-888729-01-5*) Cnsrtm Cllctive Cnscnss.
— World Stompers: A Guide to Travel Manifesto. 4th rev. ed. Nardini, Jerry & Cambron, Beverly, eds. LC 96-86305. (Illus.). 284p. 1998. pap. 17.95 (*1-888729-04-X*, 420-1) Cnsrtm Cllctive Cnscnss.
Olsen, Brad, jt. auth. see Northam, Bruce.
Olsen, Bruce, tr. see Cho Chikun Nine-Dan.
Olsen, Bruce L., jt. auth. see Garrison, Marc S.
Olsen, Byron D. Great Northern Railway 1945-1970 Photo Archive, Vol. 2. LC 97-75285. (Photo Archive Ser.: Vol. 2). (Illus.). 128p. 1998. pap. 29.95 (*1-882256-79-4*) Iconografix.
Olsen, Byron D., ed. Great Northern Railway 1945-1970 Photo Archive. LC 96-76224. (Photo Archive Ser.). (Illus.). 128p. 1996. pap. 29.95 (*1-882256-56-5*) Iconografix.
***Olsen, Byron D. & Lyons, Dan.** Station Wagons. LC 99-86227. (Illus.). 128p. 2000. pap. 19.95 (*0-7603-0632-X*, 129823AE, Pub. by MBI Pubg) Motorbooks Intl.
Olsen, Carol. Left-Over Louie. (Illus.). 169p. (Orig.). (J). 1993. 29.95 (*1-883078-75-X*) Gig Harbor Pr.
— Left-Over Louie. 2nd ed. (Illus.). 168p. (Orig.). (J). (gr. 2 up). 1993. pap. 11.95 (*1-883078-76-8*) Gig Harbor Pr.
— Slime: Slugs Have Feelings Too. (Left-over Louie Ser.: 1). (Illus.). 26p. (Orig.). (J). (gr. 6). 1994. pap. 6.95 (*1-883078-80-6*) Gig Harbor Pr.
Olsen, Catherine. Index Theory in Von Neumann Algebras. LC 83-22519. (Memoirs Ser.: No. 47/294). 71p. 1984. pap. 15.00 (*0-8218-2295-0*, MEMO/47/294) Am Math.
Olsen, Charles M. Transforming Church Boards: Into Communities of Spiritual Leaders. LC 95-75680. 208p. 1995. pap. 15.25 (*1-56699-148-X*, AL158) Alban Inst.
Olsen, Charles M., jt. auth. see Morris, Danney E.
Olsen, Charles M., jt. auth. see Morris, Danny E.
Olsen, Christina. The Art of Tarot. LC 95-15102. (Tiny Folios Ser.). (Illus.). 320p. 1996. pap. 11.95 (*0-7892-0016-3*) Abbeville Pr.
***Olsen, Christopher J.** The Political Culture of Secession Mississippi, 1830-1860. LC 99-49213. (Illus.). 320p. 2000. text. write for info. (*0-19-513147-9*) OUP.
Olsen, Claudia, jt. auth. see Allred, Jacki.
Olsen, Cynthia B. El Aceite de Arbol de Te Australiano Manual de Primeros Auxilios: 101 Maneras de Usar el Aceite de Arbol de Te. (Illus.). 47p. 1998. pap. 3.50 (*0-9628882-3-0*) Kali Pr.
— Australian Tea Tree Oil Guide: First Aid Kit in a Bottle: With Photographs & Updated Resource Guide. LC 98-35973. 1998. pap. 8.50 (*1-890941-01-8*) Kali Pr.
Olsen, Cynthia B., et al. Australian Tea Tree Oil Handbook: 101 Plus Ways to Use Tea Tree Oil. 96p. 1999. per. 6.95 (*1-890941-02-6*) Kali Pr.
— Essiac: A Native Herbal Cancer Remedy. 2nd ed. LC 98-35978. (Illus.). 1998. pap. 12.50 (*1-890941-00-X*) Kali Pr.
Olsen, D. H. & Straub, B. E. Delaware Bay Fishing Guide: New Jersey Edition. 128p. (Orig.). 1991. pap. 9.95 (*0-9629749-1-9*) Vayu Pr.
Olsen, Dale A. Music of the Warao of Venezuela: Song People of the Rain Forest. LC 95-46549. (Illus.). 432p. (C). 1996. lib. bdg. 49.95 incl. cd-rom (*0-8130-1390-9*) U Press Fla.
— Musics Many Cultures. 280p. (C). 1996. pap. text 23.95 (*0-7872-1245-8*) Kendall-Hunt.
***Olsen, Dale A. & Sheehy, Daniel E., eds.** The Garland Handbook of Latin American Music. (Reference Library of Humanities). (Illus.). 464p. 2000. pap. 39.95 (*0-8153-3833-3*) Garland.
Olsen, Dale A. & Sheehy, Daniel E., eds. South America, Mexico, Central America, & the Caribbean. LC 97-9671. (Encyclopedia of World Music Ser.: Vol. 2). (Illus.). 1082p. 1998. 165.00 (*0-8240-4947-0*, H1193) Garland.
Olsen, Dale A., et al. Sounds of the World: Music of Latin America (Teacher's Guide) (Sounds of the World Ser.). (Illus.). 5p. 1987. pap., teacher ed. write for info. incl. audio (*1-56545-053-1*, 3032) MENC.
Olsen, Dan, jt. ed. see Gluver, Henrik.
Olsen, Dan R., Jr. Developing User Interfaces. LC 97-45231. 414p. (Orig.). 1998. pap. 49.95 (*1-55860-418-9*) Morgan Kaufmann.
— User Interface Management Systems: Models & Algorithms. LC 91-41076. (Morgan Kaufmann Series in Computers Graphics & Geometric Modeling). 231p. 1992. text 54.95 (*1-55860-220-8*, QA76.9) Morgan Kaufmann.
***Olsen, Darren S. & Potyondy, John P., eds.** Wildland Hydrology. 536p. 1999. pap. 80.00 (*1-882132-47-5*, TPS-99-3) Am Water Resources.
Olsen, Dave, ed. The Greatest Country Music. rev. ed. (New Home Library Ser.). 112p. (Orig.). 1995. reprint ed. pap. text 12.95 (*0-89724-630-6*, THL2009B) Wrner Bros.
***Olsen, Dave, et al.** Starbucks Passion for Coffee: A Starbucks Coffee Cookbook. (Illus.). 96p. 2000. reprint ed. 15.00 (*0-7881-9311-2*) DIANE Pub.
Olsen, Dave C., ed. The Book of Golden Big Band Favorites. 112p. (YA). 1994. pap. 13.95 (*0-7692-0256-X*) Wrner Bros.
***Olsen, David.** Lazy Daisy. LC 00-29558. (Illus.). 32p. (J). (ps-5). 2000. 15.95 (*1-57102-162-0*, Ideals Child) Hambleton-Hill.
Olsen, David. Socio-Economic Survey of Recreational Boating & Fishing in the U. S. Virgin Islands. (Illus.). 80p. 1979. 12.00 (*0-318-14618-5*) Isl Resources.
— Words You Should Know. 260p. 1991. pap. 7.95 (*1-55850-018-9*) Adams Media.
Olsen, David C. Integrative Family Therapy. LC 92-44125. (Creative Pastoral Care & Counseling Ser.). 96p. 1993. pap. 15.00 (*0-8006-2638-9*, 1-2638, Fortress Pr) Augsburg Fortress.
Olsen, David C., ed. Atkins - Knopfler: Neck & Neck. 132p. 1991. pap. text 16.95 (*0-89898-635-4*, P0906GTX) Wrner Bros.
— The Greatest Songs of 1890 1920. 112p. (Orig.). (YA). 1990. pap. text 12.95 (*0-89898-599-4*, THL1001B) Wrner Bros.
— The Greatest Songs of 1940-1960. 112p. (Orig.). (YA). 1990. pap. text 12.95 (*0-89898-601-X*, THL1003B) Wrner Bros.
— Life of the Christmas Party. rev. ed. 160p. (Orig.). (YA). 1996. pap. text 19.95 (*0-89898-645-1*, TMF0182C) Wrner Bros.
— The World's Best Piano. 280p. (Orig.). (YA). 1991. pap. text 19.95 (*0-89898-598-6*, TMF0227) Wrner Bros.
Olsen, David C., jt. auth. see Grosch, William N.
Olsen, David R. Reclaiming Reality: Healing the Scars of Addiction. LC 96-92387. 90p. 1996. pap. write for info. (*0-7880-0692-4*, Fairway Pr) CSS OH.
Olsen, Debbie & Peterson, Chris. I Love the Internet, but I Want My Privacy, Too! Simple Steps Anyone Can Take to Enjoy the Net Without Worry. LC 98-22383. 226p. 1998. per. 19.95 (*0-7615-1436-8*) Prima Pub.
Olsen, Del. Made in God's Image. 128p. (Orig.). 1985. pap. 3.70 (*0-310-46381-5*, 18382P) Zondervan.
Olsen, Dietmar. Das Kaufrechtliche Sachmangelgewahrleistungsrecht des Code Civil in der Rechtsprechung Deutscher Gerichte im 19. Jahrhundert: Ein Beitrag zur Ablosung der Partikularrechte durch das BGB. (Rechtshistorische Reihe: Bd. 159). (GER.). 198p. 1996. pap. 42.95 (*3-631-30884-1*) P Lang Pubng.
Olsen, Donald. The Complete Idiot's Travel Guide to London. (Complete Idiot's Travel Guide Ser.). (Illus.). 354p. 1999. pap. 15.95 (*0-02-862899-3*) Macmillan Gen Ref.
Olsen, Donald J. The City As a Work of Art: London, Paris, Vienna. LC 85-24639. 360p. 1986. 65.00 (*0-300-02870-9*) Yale U Pr.
— The City As a Work of Art: London, Paris, Vienna. LC 85-24639. 360p. (C). 1988. reprint ed. pap. 25.00 (*0-300-04212-4*) Yale U Pr.
— Town Planning in London: The Eighteenth & Nineteenth Centuries. LC 82-50440. (Illus.). 246p. 1982. pap. 23.00 (*0-300-02915-2*, Y-443) Yale U Pr.
Olsen, Douglas, et al, eds. Textbook of Videoscopic Surgery. 1996. text 220.00 (*3-7186-5495-4*, Harwood Acad Pubs) Gordon & Breach.
— Textbook of Videoscopic Surgery. 384p. 1997. text 98.00 (*90-5702-230-3*, Harwood Acad Pubs) Gordon & Breach.
Olsen, E. A. Adrift on a Raft. LC 68-16397. (Oceanography Ser.). (Illus.). 48p. (J). (gr. 3 up). 1970. lib. bdg. 10.95 (*0-87783-000-2*); audio 10.60 (*0-87783-176-9*) Oddo.
— Adrift on a Raft. deluxe ed. LC 68-16397. (Oceanography Ser.). (Illus.). 48p. (J). (gr. 3 up). 1970. pap. 3.94 (*0-87783-078-9*) Oddo.
— Killer in the Trap. LC 68-16399. (Oceanography Ser.). (Illus.). 48p. (J). (gr. 3 up). 1970. lib. bdg. 10.95 (*0-87783-019-3*); audio 10.60 (*0-87783-190-4*) Oddo.
— Killer in the Trap. deluxe ed. LC 68-16399. (Oceanography Ser.). (Illus.). 48p. (J). (gr. 3 up). 1970. pap. 3.94 (*0-87783-097-5*) Oddo.
— Lobster King. LC 68-16400. (Oceanography Ser.). (Illus.). 48p. (J). (gr. 3 up). 1970. lib. bdg. 10.95 (*0-87783-024-X*); audio 10.60 (*0-87783-192-0*) Oddo.
— Lobster King. deluxe ed. LC 68-16400. (Oceanography Ser.). (Illus.). 48p. (J). (gr. 3 up). 1970. pap. 3.94 (*0-87783-099-1*) Oddo.
— Mystery at Salvage Rock. LC 68-16401. (Oceanography Ser.). (Illus.). 48p. (J). (gr. 3 up). 1970. lib. bdg. 10.95 (*0-87783-027-4*); audio 10.60 (*0-87783-195-5*) Oddo.
— Mystery at Salvage Rock. deluxe ed. LC 68-16401. (Oceanography Ser.). (Illus.). 48p. (J). (gr. 3 up). 1970. pap. 3.94 (*0-87783-101-7*) Oddo.
Olsen, E. G. Atlas of Cardiovascular Pathology. 1987. text 268.50 (*0-85200-866-X*) Kluwer Academic.
Olsen, E. G., jt. ed. see Goodwin, J. F.
Olsen-Ecker, Bradley H. Lady of the Water. (Illus.). 36p. 1985. pap. 6.95 (*0-9671658-1-4*) B Olsen-Ecker.
— The Y2K Computer Problem Will Cause Havoc & Worldwide Panic: Civilization as We Know It Will Cease to Exist & a Wave of Fear Will Cover the Earth, Unless You Read This Book. large type ed. (Illus.). 24p. 1999. pap. 8.95 (*0-9671658-0-6*) B Olsen-Ecker.
Olsen, Eddie, jt. auth. see Patterson, Jerry L.
Olsen, Edward A. U. S. - Japan Strategic Reciprocity: A Neo-Internationalist View. (Publication Ser.: No. 307). xiii, 194p. 1985. 9.98 (*0-8179-8071-7*); pap. 4.38 (*0-8179-8072-5*) Hoover Inst Pr.
Olsen, Edward A., jt. ed. see Kwak, Tae-Hwan.
Olsen, Elise A., ed. Disorders of Hair Growth: Diagnosis & Treatment. (Illus.). 448p. 1993. text 125.00 (*0-07-047934-8*) McGraw-Hill HPD.
Olsen, Ellyn. God's Blueprint for Mankind: As Revealed in the Feasts of the Lord. LC 83-72382. (Illus.). 96p. 1983. pap. 3.95 (*0-913961-00-0*) Bless Israel.
Olsen, Eric. Encyclopedia of Record Producers. LC 99-32191. 1998. pap. text 24.95 (*0-8230-7607-5*) Watsn-Guptill.
— On the Right Track: A Spectator's Guide to the Olympic Running Events. xiv, 225 p. 1984. pap. write for info. (*0-672-52807-X*) Macmillan.
— This Business of Networking in the Music Industry. (Illus.). 320p. 1999. 21.95 (*0-8230-7710-1*) Watsn-Guptill.
Olsen, Eric, jt. auth. see Paffenbarger, Ralph S.
Olsen, Erica S., ed. see Delo, David M.
Olsen, Frances E. Feminist Legal Theory, Set. (C). 1995. pap. text 59.00 (*0-8147-6184-4*) NYU Pr.
Olsen, Frances E., ed. Feminist Legal Theory, 2 vols. Incl. Vol. 1. Feminist Legal Theory., 2 vols. LC 94-30376. (C). 1995. lib. bdg. 125.00 (*0-8147-6179-8*); Vol. 2. Feminist Legal Theory., 2 vols. LC 94-30376. (C). 1995. lib. bdg. 125.00 (*0-8147-6180-1*); LC 94-30376. (International Library of Essays in Law & Legal Theory, Schools: Vol. 15). (C). 1995. Set lib. bdg. 250.00 (*0-8147-6177-1*) NYU Pr.
— Feminist Legal Theory Vol. I: Foundations & Outlooks. 574p. (C). 1995. pap. text 32.50 (*0-8147-6185-2*) NYU Pr.
— Feminist Legal Theory Vol. II: Positioning Feminist Theory Within the Law. 593p. (C). 1995. pap. text 32.50 (*0-8147-6186-0*) NYU Pr.
Olsen, Fred. Indian Creek. LC 74-5959. (Illus.). 100p. 1975. pap. 9.95 (*0-8061-1208-5*) U of Okla Pr.
Olsen, Fred A., ed. Technology: A Reign of Benevolence & Destruction. LC 73-16385. 1974. 32.50 (*0-8422-5130-8*) Irvington.
***Olsen, Frederick.** Kiln Book: Materials, Specifications & Construction. 3rd rev. ed. LC 00-101578. (Illus.). 320p. 2000. 44.95 (*0-87341-910-3*, KILN3) Krause Pubns.
Olsen, Frederick I., et al. Frederick Layton & His World, 1888. Tilendis, Robert M., ed. LC 87-61767. (Illus.). 283p. (Orig.). 1988. pap. 19.95 (*0-944110-23-1*) Milwauk Art Mus.
Olsen, Frederick L. The Kiln Book. 2nd ed. LC 81-71090. 291p. 1983. 40.00 (*0-8019-7071-7*) Krause Pubns.
***Olsen, G.** Delta Natural Blondes. 1998. mass mkt. 6.95 (*0-7472-5681-0*, Pub. by Headline Bk Pub) Trafalgar.
Olsen, G. James. Why Angels Have Wings. LC 99-176833. 96p. (Orig.). 1997. pap. 7.50 (*1-57353-114-6*, Eschaton Bks) Eschaton Prods.
Olsen, Gary. Getting Started in Multimedia Design. LC 96-35944. (Illus.). 144p. 1997. pap. 29.99 (*0-89134-716-X*, North Lght Bks) F & W Pubns Inc.
— MasterPath: The Divine Science of Light & Sound. (Illus.). 230p. 1999. pap. 20.00 (*1-885949-01-4*) MasterPath.
Olsen, George D., jt. ed. see Konkol, Richard J.
Olsen, George H. The Beginner's Handbook of Electronics. 1980. 17.95 (*0-13-074211-2*) P-H.
Olsen, Gerald W., intro. Religion & Revolution in Early-Industrial England: The Halevy Thesis & Its Critics. LC 89-36361. 252p. (Orig.). (C). 1990. pap. text 26.50 (*0-8191-7555-2*); lib. bdg. 44.50 (*0-8191-7554-4*) U Pr of Amer.
Olsen-Gisel, H. Developments in Stamens of Viola Odorata. (Dissertationes Botanicae Ser.: Vol. 70). (Illus.). 192p. 1983. pap. text 64.00 (*3-7682-1362-5*) Lubrecht & Cramer.
Olsen, Glenda P. Birds of Prey. (Nature Books Ser.). (Illus.). 32p. (J). (gr. 2-6). 1994. lib. bdg. 22.79 (*1-56766-059-2*) Childs World.
Olsen, Glenn, jt. auth. see Fuller, Mary Lou.
Olsen, Greg. Expressions of Faith. (Illus.). 80p. 1999. 20.00 (*0-8010-1186-8*) Baker Bks.
Olsen, Gregg. Mockingbird: A Mother, a Child, a Murder. 336p. 1995. mass mkt. 5.99 (*0-446-60095-4*, Pub. by Warner Bks) Little.
— Starvation Heights: The True Story of an American Doctor & the Murder of a British Heiress. 440p. (Orig.). 1997. mass mkt. 6.50 (*0-446-60341-4*, Pub. by Warner Bks) Little.
Olsen, Gregg M. If Loving You is Wrong. 1999. mass mkt. 6.50 (*0-312-97012-9*, St Martins Paperbacks) St Martin.
— The Struggle for Economic Democracy in Sweden. 159p. 1992. 82.95 (*1-85628-298-8*, Pub. by Avebry) Ashgate Pub Co.
Olsen, H. N., et al. Temperature Measurements in Seeded Air & Nitrogen Plasmas. LC 79-131016. 133p. 1970. 19.00 (*0-403-04524-X*) Scholarly.
Olsen, Hans C. The Work of Boards of Education. LC 77-177134. (Columbia University. Teachers College. Contributions to Education Ser.: No. 213). reprint ed. 37.50 (*0-404-55213-7*) AMS Pr.
Olsen, Harry, ed. see Riekes, Linda & Ackerly, Sally M.
***Olsen, Henrik Palmer & Toddington, Stuart.** Law in Its Own Right. (Legal Theory Today Ser.). 124p. 1999. 35.00 (*1-84113-034-6*, Pub. by Hart Pub); 14.95 (*1-84113-028-1*, Pub. by Hart Pub) Intl Spec Bk.
Olsen, Howard J. Wounded Warriors Chosen Lives: Healing for Vietnam Veterans. 244p. 1997. pap. 12.95 (*0-9637741-2-3*) Clear Stream.
Olsen, Inger, jt. auth. see Isaacson, Lanae.
Olsen, J., jt. ed. see Nilsen, B.
Olsen, J. W., jt. auth. see Mansfield, Ron.
Olsen, Jack. Charmer: A Ladies' Man & His Victims. 384p. 1995. mass mkt. 6.50 (*0-380-71601-1*, Avon Bks) Morrow Avon.
— Climb up to Hell. LC 98-33794. 240p. 1998. pap. 12.95 (*0-312-19450-1*) St Martin.
***Olsen, Jack.** The Climb Up To Hell. 256 + 8pp p. 2000. 6.99 (*0-312-97506-6*) St Martin.
Olsen, Jack. Hastened to the Grave: The Gypsy Murder Investigation. LC 98-10239. 288p. 1998. text 24.95 (*0-312-18362-3*) St Martin.
***Olsen, Jack.** Last Man Standing: The Tragedy & Triumph of Geronimo Pratt. LC 00-29436. 384p. 2000. 26.95 (*0-385-49367-3*) Doubleday.
Olsen, Jack. Night of the Grizzlies. LC 96-3072. 224p. 1996. reprint ed. pap. 14.95 (*0-943972-48-5*) Homestead WY.
— Salt of the Earth: One Family's Journey Through the Violent American Landscape. 1997. mass mkt. 6.99 (*0-312-95998-2*) St Martin.
Olsen, James S., et al. U. S. in the 20th Century: America since 1945, 2 vols., Vol. 2. 426p. 1995. pap. text 32.95 (*0-312-08437-4*) St Martin.
Olsen, Jan. Electronic Journal Literature: Implications for Scholars. LC 93-6314. 100p. 1994. 25.00 (*0-88736-925-1*) Mecklermedia.
Olsen, Jan Z. Cursive Handwriting. 2nd rev. ed. (Illus.). 80p. (J). (gr. 3). 1996. pap. text 4.75 (*1-891627-04-X*) Handwriting.
— Cursive Teacher's Guide. 4th ed. (Illus.). 52p. 1998. pap. text, teacher ed. 4.75 (*1-891627-06-6*) Handwriting.
— My Printing Book. 4th rev. ed. (Illus.). 72p. (J). (gr. 1). 1997. pap. text, teacher ed. 4.75 (*1-891627-01-5*) Handwriting.
— Printing Power. 3rd rev. ed. (Illus.). 64p. (J). (gr. 2). 1997. pap. text 4.75 (*1-891627-02-3*) Handwriting.
— Printing Teacher's Guide. 2nd ed. (Illus.). 48p. 1997. pap. text, teacher ed. 4.75 (*1-891627-03-1*) Handwriting.
***Olsen, Jan Z.** Cursive Success. 80p. (YA). (gr. 4 up). 1999. pap. text 4.75 (*1-891627-11-2*) Handwriting.
Olsen, Janice Z. Draw & Write Notebook. (Illus.). 32p. (J). (gr. 1-2). 1998. pap. text, student ed., wbk. ed. 1.50 (*1-891627-09-0*) Handwriting.
— Handwriting Without Tears. 7th rev. ed. (Illus.). 81p. (J). 1998. pap. text 6.50 (*1-891627-07-4*) Handwriting.
— Letters & Numbers for Me. (Illus.). 72p. (J). (gr. k-1). 1999. pap. text, wbk. ed. 4.75 (*1-891627-10-4*) Handwriting.
— Writing Notebook. 32p. (J). (gr. 3-4). 1998. pap., student ed., wbk. ed. 1.50 (*1-891627-08-2*) Handwriting.
Olsen, Jean, tr. see Paludan, Lis.
Olsen, Jennifer & Princen, Thomas. Hazardous Waste Trade, North & South: The Case of Italy & Koko, Nigeria. (Pew Case Studies in International Affairs). 50p. (C). 1994. pap. text 3.50 (*1-56927-161-5*, GU Schl Foreign) Geo U Inst Dplmcy.
***Olsen, Jerry & Cooper, Paul.** Dealing with Disruptive Students in the Classroom. 176p. 2000. pap. 22.50 (*0-7494-3132-6*, Kogan Pg Educ) Stylus Pub VA.
Olsen, Johan P. Organized Democracy: Political Institutions in a Welfare State - The Case of Norway. 246p. 1985. pap. 32.00 (*82-00-06442-5*) Scandnvan Univ Pr.
Olsen, Johan P. & Peters, B. Guy, eds. Lessons from Experience: Experiential Learning in Administrative Reforms in Eight Democracies. 339p. (C). 1996. pap. text 41.00 (*82-00-22565-8*) Scandnvan Univ Pr.
Olsen, Johan P., jt. auth. see March, James G.
Olsen, Johan P., jt. auth. see Marsh, James G.

O

An Asterisk (*) at the beginning of an entry indicates that the title is appearing for the first time.

jt. auth. see Brunsson, Nils.

B., jt. auth. see Eadie, Douglas C.

ohn W. Vertebrate Faunal Remains from rasshopper Pueblo, Arizona. LC 90-6183. (Anthropological Papers Ser.: No. 83). (Illus.). xvi, 200p. (Orig.). 1990. pap. 15.00 (*0-915703-21-1*) U Mich Mus Anthro.

Olsen, John W. & Rukang, Wu, eds. Palaeoanthropology & Palaeolithic Archaeology in the People's Republic of China. 1985. text 55.00 (*0-12-601720-4*) Acad Pr.

***Olsen, Jonathan.** Nature & Nationalism: Right-wing Ecology & The Politics of Identity in Contemporary Germany. LC 99-17474. 1999. text 45.00 (*0-312-22071-5*) St Martin.

Olsen, Jorgen L. Electron Transport in Metals. LC 61-17893. (Interscience Tracts on Physics & Astronomy Ser.: No. 12). 129p. reprint ed. pap. 40.00 (*0-608-30475-1*, 201196200080) Bks Demand.

Olsen, Jorn. Searching for Causes of Work-Related Diseases: An Introduction to Epidemiology at the Work Site. 100p. 1991. pap. 19.95 (*0-19-261819-9*) OUP.

Olsen, Judy E., ed. Communication-Starters & Other Activities for the ESL Classroom. (Illus.). 129p. (C). 1990. pap., teacher ed. 19.00 (*0-13-155656-8*) Alemany Pr.

Olsen, Judy W. Look Again Pictures: For Language Development & Lifeskills. rev. ed. (Illus.). xx, 112p. 1998. pap. text 19.95 (*1-882483-70-7*) Alta Bk Ctr.

Olsen, June L. Fundamentals of Nursing. LC 90-9636. (Nursetest: A Review Ser.). 336p. (Orig.). 1991. pap. 21.95 (*0-87434-302-X*) Springhouse Corp.

— Medical Dosage Calculations. 4th ed. 1987. pap. text 14.36 (*0-201-19185-7*) Addison-Wesley.

— Medical Dosage Calculations. 5th ed. 246p. (C). 1991. pap. text 25.95 (*0-8053-5603-7*) Addison-Wesley.

— Medical Dosage Calculations. 7th ed. LC 99-34128. (Illus.). 358p. (C). 1999. pap. text 36.40 incl. cd-rom (*0-8053-9162-2*) Addison-Wesley.

Olsen, June L. & Murray, Eugenia B. Dosage Calculations. LC 91-4828. (Nursetest Ser.). (Illus.). 304p. 1991. pap. 21.95 (*0-87434-301-1*) Springhouse Corp.

Olsen, K. H. Continental Rifts: Evolution, Structure, Tectonics. (Developments in Geotectonics Ser.: Vol. 25). 490p. 1995. pap. 99.50 (*0-444-89567-1*) Elsevier.

— Continental Rifts: Evolution, Structure, Tectonics. 490p. 1995. 231.50 (*0-444-89566-3*) Elsevier.

Olsen, Karen & Tebbutt, John. The Impact of the FCC's Open Networks Architecture on NS/NP Telecomunications Security. (Illus.). 34p. (C). 1996. reprint ed. pap. text 25.00 (*0-7881-3509-0*) DIANE Pub.

Olsen, Karen, jt. auth. see Pearson, Sue.

Olsen, Karen D. The California Mentor Teacher Role: Owner's Manual. 1998. pap. text 21.95 (*0-9624475-7-9*) Bks Educators.

***Olsen, Karen D.** Making Bodybrain-Compatible Education a Reality: Coaching for the ITI Model. 214p. 1999. spiral bd. 24.95 (*0-9624475-8-7*) Bks Educators.

Olsen, Karen D. Science Continuum of Concepts: For Grades K-6. 55p. 1995. pap., teacher ed. 7.95 (*0-9630547-3-2*) Bks Educators.

— Synergy: Transforming America's High Schools Through Integrated Thematic Instruction. (Illus.). 278p. (Orig.). 1995. pap. 27.50 (*1-878631-25-X*, Pub. by S Kovalik) Bks Educators.

Olsen, Karen D. & Kovalik, Susan. ITI Schoolwide Rubric: Planning & Assessing Schoolwide Implementation of Brain-Compatible Education. 56p. 1997. pap. text 6.50 (*1-878631-38-1*) S Kovalik.

***Olsen, Karen D. & Kovalik, Susan J.** ITI Classroom Stages of Implementation: Assessing Implementation of Bodybrain-Compatible Learning. rev. ed. 17p. 1999. pap. text 6.50 (*1-878631-53-5*, Pub. by S Kovalik) Bks Educators.

Olsen, Karen D., jt. auth. see Kovalik, Susan J.

Olsen, Karen D., jt. auth. see Ross, Ann.

Olsen, Karen D., ed. see Hart, Leslie A.

Olsen, Karen D., ed. see Pearson, Sue.

Olsen, Ken, et al. Cross-Country Skiing Yellowstone Country. LC 92-85241. (Illus.). 164p. (Orig.). 1992. pap. 10.95 (*1-56044-191-7*) Falcon Pub Inc.

Olsen, Ken, jt. auth. see Baker, Vernon J.

Olsen, Kenneth R., tr. see Ingarden, Roman.

Olsen, Kim. I Missed My Molly Morrow Certificate by a Stitch. Isackson, Darla, ed. (Illus.). Date not set. pap. 5.95 (*0-9664447-0-1*) Stellar Pubg.

Olsen, Kirstin. Chronology of Women's History. LC 93-50542. 528p. 1994. 39.95 (*0-313-28803-8*) Greenwood.

— Daily Life in 18th-Century England. LC 98-44593. (Daily Life Through History Ser.). 416p. 1999. 45.00 (*0-313-29933-1*) Greenwood.

Olsen, Kirstin. Remember the Ladies: A Woman's Book of Days. LC 93-16868. 1993. 14.95 (*0-8061-2558-6*) U of Okla Pr.

***Olsen, Kirstin.** Understanding Lord of the Flies: A Student Casebook to Issues, Sources & Historical Documents. LC 99-89787. (The Greenwood Press 'Literature in Context' Ser.). (Illus.). 232p. 2000. 39.95 (*0-313-30723-7*, GR0723, Greenwood Pr) Greenwood.

Olsen, Klaus M. Skuas & Jaegers. LC 97-60338. (Illus.). 156p. 1997. 35.00 (*0-300-07269-4*) Yale U Pr.

Olsen, Klaus M. & Larsson, Hans. Terns of Europe & North America. LC 94-39312. 176p. 1995. text 42.50 (*0-691-04387-6*, Pub. by Princeton U Pr) Cal Prin Full Svc.

Olsen, Lance. Burnt. Memmott, David, ed. (Wordcraft Speculative Writers Ser.). 172p. (Orig.). 1996. pap. 11.95 (*1-877655-20-1*) Wordcraft Oregon.

— Elipse of Uncertainty: An Introduction to Postmodern Fantasy, 26. LC 86-22789. (Contributions to Postmodern Fantasy Ser.: No. 26). 145p. 1987. 49.95 (*0-313-25511-3*, OEU, Greenwood Pr) Greenwood.

— Lolita: A Janus Text. LC 94-24562. (Twayne's Masterwork Studies: Vol. 153). 1995. pap. 18.00 (*0-8057-8593-0*, Twyne) Mac Lib Ref.

— Lolita: A Janus Text. LC 94-24562. (Twayne's Masterwork Studies: Vol. 153). 1995. 29.00 (*0-8057-8355-5*, Twyne) Mac Lib Ref.

***Olsen, Lance.** Sewing Shut My Eyes. 115p. 2000. pap. 11.95 (*1-57366-083-3*) Fiction Coll.

Olsen, Lance. Time Famine. 328p. (Orig.). 1996. pap. 12.95 (*1-882633-15-6*) Permeable.

— Tonguing the Zeitgeist. LC 94-232725. 192p. (Orig.). 1994. pap. 11.95 (*1-882633-04-0*) Permeable.

Olsen, Lance, ed. Surfing Tomorrow: Essays on the Future of American Fiction. 105p. 1995. pap. 9.95 (*1-884754-22-8*) Potpourri Pubns.

Olsen, Lance, jt. auth. see Worley, Jeff.

Olsen, Lance, jt. ed. see Amerika, Mark.

Olsen, Larry D. Outdoor Survival Skills. 1990. pap. 5.99 (*0-671-72298-0*) S&S Trade.

— Outdoor Survival Skills. rev. ed. (Illus.). 1988. pap. 9.95 (*0-9620429-0-0*) Salmon Falls Pub.

— Outdoor Survival Skills. 6th rev. ed. LC 97-20442. (Illus.). 272p. 1997. pap. 14.95 (*1-55652-323-8*) Chicago Review.

Olsen, Larry K. & Monismith, Samuel W. Introduction to Health & Disease. 3rd ed. 192p. (C). 1996. per. 29.95 (*0-7872-1897-9*, 41189701) Kendall-Hunt.

Olsen, Larry K., et al. Health Today. 656p. (C). 1986. teacher ed. write for info. (*0-318-59089-1*) Macmillan.

Olsen, Larry K., jt. ed. see Mahoney, Beverly S.

Olsen, Lauri. Big Sky Dreams. LC 97-93464. 192p. 1997. lib. bdg. 18.95 (*0-8034-9233-2*, Avalon Bks) Bouregy.

— Cold Moon Honor. LC 97-97111. 192p. 1998. 18.95 (*0-8034-9272-3*, Avalon Bks) Bouregy.

Olsen, Laurie. Made in America. 1997. 25.00 (*1-56584-400-9*, Pub. by New Press NY) Norton.

— Made in America: Immigrant Students in Our Public Schools. 288p. 1998. pap. 14.95 (*1-56584-471-8*, Pub. by New Press NY) Norton.

Olsen, Laurie & Chen, Marcia T. Crossing the Schoolhouse Border: Immigrant Students & the California Public Schools. 128p. 1988. pap. 16.00 (*1-887039-00-7*) Calif Tomorrow.

Olsen, Laurie & Mullen, Nina A. Embracing Diversity: Teachers' Voices from California's Classrooms. 115p. 1990. pap. 20.00 (*1-887039-03-1*) Calif Tomorrow.

Olsen, Laurie & Raffel, Lisa, eds. California Perspectives Vol. 4: An Anthology from California Tomorrow Special Issue: Community Canons. 110p. 1994. pap. 17.00 (*1-887039-11-2*) Calif Tomorrow.

Olsen, Laurie, et al. The Unfinished Journey: Restructuring Schools in a Diverse Society. 362p. 1994. pap. 27.00 (*1-887039-09-0*) Calif Tomorrow.

Olsen, Leslie A. Technical Writing & Professional Communication. 2nd ed. 768p. (C). 1991. pap. 71.88 (*0-07-047823-6*) McGraw.

Olsen, Leslie A., ed. & intro. see Skinner, Ernest M. & Skinner, Richmond H.

Olsen, Lester P. Cybernetics - Come of Age. (Illus.). 173p. (Orig.). (C). 1992. write for info. (*0-9632625-0-5*) Winchester NE.

***Olsen, Lise Arends.** La Femme et l'Enfant dans les Union Illegitimes a Rome. (Publications Universitaires Europeennes: Vol. 2714). (Illus.). xiv, 249p. 1999. 40.95 (*3-906763-49-8*, Pub. by P Lang) P Lang Pubng.

Olsen, Lois C. Contentment Is Great Gain. (Illus.). 250p. (Orig.). 1996. pap. 11.00 (*0-9654488-0-0*) Leone Pr.

Olsen, M., ed. Financial Management. 50p. 1984. pap. 23.00 (*0-08-031290-X*, Pergamon Pr) Elsevier.

Olsen, Madeleine. Hieroglyphics. (Illus.). (J). (gr. 3-7). 1997. pap. 7.95 (*0-8167-4402-5*) Troll Communs.

Olsen, Madeline. Native American Sign Language. LC 98-106314. (Illus.). 32p. (J). (gr. 3-7). 1998. pap. 4.95 (*0-8167-4509-9*) Troll Communs.

Olsen, Mahlon E. History of the Origin & Progress of Seventh-Day Adventists. LC 76-134375. reprint ed. 67.50 (*0-404-08423-0*) AMS Pr.

***Olsen, Mancur.** Power & Prosperity: Outgrowing Communist & Capitalist Dictatorships. LC 99-52774. 272p. 1999. 41.00 (*0-465-05195-2*, Pub. by Basic) HarpC.

Olsen, Margaret. The Platinum & Palladium Buyer's Guide. Matthews, Alison, ed. LC 97-60830. (Illus.). 272p. (Orig.). 1998. pap. 24.95 (*0-9630498-2-8*, 97-60830) Westminster CO.

Olsen, Margaret A. & Matthews, Alison F. The Gold Book: A Guide to Commonly Traded Gold Bullion Coins & Bars. (Illus.). (Orig.). 1992. pap. 19.95 (*0-9630498-4-4*) Westminster CO.

Olsen, Mari B. A Semantic & Pragmatic Model of Lexical & Grammatical Aspect. Horn, Laurence, ed. LC 97-17027. (Outstanding Dissertations in Linguistics Ser.). 340p. 1997. text 74.00 (*0-8153-2849-4*) Garland.

Olsen, Mark. The Actor with a Thousand Faces. LC 97-28473. (Illus.). 192p. 1999. pap. 18.95 (*1-55783-306-0*) Applause Theatre Bk Pubs.

— The Golden Buddha Changing Masks: Essays on the Spiritual Dimension of Acting. LC 89-1409. (Illus.). 210p. (Orig.). 1990. pap. 15.95 (*0-89556-058-5*) Gateways Bks & Tapes.

— Refuge. 180p. (Orig.). 1996. pap. 9.95 (*0-9639465-2-8*) Sardis Pr.

Olsen, Mark & Avital, Samuel. The Conception Mandala: Creative Techniques for Inviting a Child into Your Life. (Illus.). 96p. (Orig.). 1992. pap. 8.95 (*0-89281-356-3*) Inner Tradit.

Olsen, Marvin E. & Micklin, Michael, eds. Handbook of Applied Sociology: Frontiers of Contemporary Research. LC 81-5891. 616p. 1981. 89.50 (*0-275-90695-7*, C0695, Praeger Pubs) Greenwood.

***Olsen, Mary-Kate & Olsen, Ashley.** The Case of the Flying Phantom. (New Adventures of Mary-Kate & Ashley Ser.: Vol. 18). (Illus.). 96p. (J). (gr. 1-5). 2000. mass mkt. 4.25 (*0-06-106591-9*) HarpC Child Bks.

— The Cool Club. (Two of a Kind Ser.: No. 12). 112p. (J). (gr. 3-7). 2000. mass mkt. 4.25 (*0-06-106582-X*, HarpEntertain) Morrow Avon.

— How to Flunk Your First Date. (Two of a Kind Ser.: No. 2). (Illus.). 112p. (J). (gr. 3-7). 1999. mass mkt. 3.99 (*0-06-106572-2*) HarpC.

— Mary-Kate & Ashley. (Illus.). 32p. (ps-3). 1999. 13.95 (*0-06-107566-3*, HarpCollins) HarperTrade.

— Mary-Kate & Ashley Our Story: Mary-Kate & Ashley Olsen's Official Biography. 96p. (gr. 3-7). 2000. mass mkt. 4.99 (*0-06-107569-8*) HarpC.

— Mary-Kate & Ashley Switching Goals. 128p. (J). (gr. 3-7). 2000. 4.99 (*0-06-107603-1*, HarpEntertain) Morrow Avon.

— Mary-Kate & Ashley's Passport to Paris Scrapbook. (Illus.). 48p. (gr. 3-7). 2000. mass mkt. 7.95 (*0-06-107570-1*, HarpEntertain) Morrow Avon.

— P. S. Wish You Were Here. (Two of a Kind Ser.: no. 11). 112p. (J). (gr. 3-7). 2000. mass mkt. 4.25 (*0-06-106581-1*) HarpC.

— Passport to Paris. 2000. mass mkt. 7.95 (*0-694-01043-X*) HarpC.

Olsen, Mary L. More Creative Connections: Literature & the Reading Program, Grades 4-6. (Illus.). xvii, 319p. 1993. pap. text 25.00 (*1-56308-027-3*) Teacher Ideas Pr.

Olsen, Mary M. & Harris, Kenneth R. Color Vision Deficiency & Color Blindness. 62p. (Orig.). 1988. pap. 8.50 (*0-9615332-2-6*) Fern Ridge Pr.

Olsen, Maryann & Berrey, Henry. A Pictorial Guide to Yosemite.Tr. of Bildfuhrer fur Yosemite. (Illus.). 22p. 1981. pap. 2.95 (*0-939666-37-5*) Yosemite Assn.

— A Pictorial Guide to Yosemite. Stock, Edith, tr. from GER.Tr. of Bildfuhrer fur Yosemite. (Illus.). 22p. 1981. pap. 2.95 (*0-939666-35-9*) Yosemite Assn.

Olsen, Maryann, et al. Guia Ilustrada de Yosemite.Tr. of Pictorial Guide to Yosemite. (Illus.). 22p. 1987. pap. 2.95 (*0-939666-48-0*) Yosemite Assn.

— Guide Illustre de Yosemite. Billot, Michel & Tech-Tran, Agnew, trs. from FRE. Orig. Title: Pictorial Guide to Yosemite. (FRE., Illus.). 22p. (Orig.). 1979. pap. 2.95 (*0-939666-36-7*) Yosemite Assn.

Olsen, Michael D. Strategic Management in the Hospitality Industry. 392p. 1992. text 49.95 (*0-442-00246-7*, VNR) Wiley.

***Olsen, Michael D., et al.** Strategic Management in the Hospitality Industry. 2nd ed. LC 98-22037. 400p. 1998. 54.95 (*0-471-29239-7*, VNR) Wiley.

Olsen, Michael D., jt. ed. see Teare, Richard.

***Olsen, Neil.** Albania. 80p. 2000. pap. 9.95 (*0-85598-432-5*, Pub. by Oxfam Pub) Stylus Pub VA.

Olsen, Nils A. Journal of a Tamed Bureaucrat: Nils A. Olsen & the BAE. Lowitt, Richard, ed. LC 79-20342. 253p. 1980. reprint ed. pap. 78.50 (*0-608-00183-X*, 206096500006) Bks Demand.

Olsen, O. Wilford. Animal Parasites: Their Life Cycles & Ecology. 564p. 1986. reprint ed. pap. text 19.95 (*0-486-65126-6*) Dover.

Olsen, O. Wilford, jt. auth. see Meyer, Marvin C.

Olsen, Ole, jt. auth. see Speiks, Mike.

Olsen, Otto H. Carpetbagger's Crusade: The Life of Albion Winegar Tourgee. LC 65-13522. (Illus.). 413p. reprint ed. pap. 128.10 (*0-608-17898-5*, 202790000057) Bks Demand.

Olsen, Paul T. Comprehensive Psychotherapy, Vol. 3. 183p. 1984. pap. 109.00 (*0-677-16369-X*) Gordon & Breach.

Olsen, Paul T., ed. Comprehensive Psychotherapy, Vol. 1. viii, 176p. 1980. pap. 75.00 (*0-685-37404-1*) Gordon & Breach.

— Comprehensive Psychotherapy, Vol. 2. vi, 122p. 1981. pap. 90.00 (*0-685-01948-9*) Gordon & Breach.

— Emotional Flooding: An Official Publication of the National Institute for the Psychotherapies. LC 74-12620. (New Directions in Psychotherapy Ser.: Vol. I). 270p. 1976. 35.95 (*0-87705-239-5*, Kluwer Acad Hman Sci) Kluwer Academic.

Olsen, Paul T. & Cornet, Bruce. Early to Middle Carnian (Triassic) Flora & Fauna of the Richmond & Taylorsville Basins. 92p. 1990. 22.00 (*0-9625801-1-2*) VA Mus Natl Hist.

Olsen, Paul T. & Murrell, Sandra. Mathematics for the Health Sciences. (Developmental & Precalculus Math Ser.). (Illus.). 432p. 1981. pap. text. write for info. (*0-201-04647-4*) Addison-Wesley.

Olsen, Paul T., jt. ed. see Grayson, Henry.

Olsen, Penny. Australian Birds of Prey: The Biology & Ecology of Raptors. LC 95-40813. (Illus.). 240p. (C). 1996. 49.95 (*0-8018-5357-5*) Johns Hopkins.

Olsen, Penny, jt. ed. see Newton, Ian.

Olsen, Phyllis J., jt. auth. see Coombs, Gary B.

Olsen, R. W., jt. ed. see Lunt, George G.

***Olsen, Rachel.** Wedding Wishes. 2000. 4.99 (*1-56245-407-2*) Great Quotations.

Olsen, Ray, ed. see Red Herring Staff.

Olsen, Rex N., ed. see Freije, Matthew R.

Olsen, Richard G., ed. Feline Leukemia. LC 80-24314. 184p. 1981. 107.00 (*0-8493-6070-6*, SF986, CRC Reprint) Franklin.

Olsen, Richard G., et al, eds. Comparative Pathobiology of Viral Diseases. 232p. 1985. 130.00 (*0-8493-5945-7*, SF780, CRC Reprint) Franklin.

— Comparative Pathobiology of Viral Diseases. 232p. 1985. 134.00 (*0-8493-5946-5*, SF780, CRC Reprint) Franklin.

Olsen, Richard P. Practical Dreamer. 1990. pap. 8.95 (*0-687-60906-2*) Abingdon.

Olsen, Richard W., jt. auth. see Martin, David L.

Olsen, Robert, jt. ed. see Rothkrug, Paul.

Olsen, Robert D., Sr. Scott's Fingerprint Mechanics. (Illus.). 480p. 1978. 77.95 (*0-398-03730-2*); pap. 54.95 (*0-398-06308-7*) C C Thomas.

Olsen, Roberta J. Fire & Ice: A History of Comets in Art. LC 85-7295. (Illus.). 134p. 1985. 24.95 (*0-8027-0855-2*); pap. 14.95 (*0-8027-7283-8*) Walker & Co.

Olsen, Rodney D. Dancing in Chains: The Youth of William Dean Howells. (American Social Experience Ser.). (Illus.). 320p. (C). 1991. text 52.50 (*0-8147-6172-0*) NYU Pr.

— Dancing in Chains: The Youth of William Dean Howells. (American Social Experience Ser.). 288p. (C). 1992. pap. text 19.00 (*0-8147-6178-X*) NYU Pr.

Olsen, Rolf, jt. ed. see Wing, J. K.

Olsen, S., jt. auth. see Johansen, P.

Olsen, S., jt. ed. see Johansen, P.

Olsen, Sandi. The Upside-Down Christmas. (Illus.). 32p. 1996. pap. 6.95 (*0-89036-634-9*) Liahona Pub Trust.

Olsen, Sandra L., ed. Horses Through Time. (Illus.). 221p. 1996. 35.00 (*1-57098-060-8*) Roberts Rinehart.

Olsen, Sandra L. & Solecki, Ralph S. Ancient Peoples & Landscapes. Johnson, Eileen, ed. (Illus.). 368p. (Orig.). (C). 1995. pap. 34.95 (*0-9640188-1-0*) Mus TX Tech.

Olsen, Sharon J., jt. auth. see Stromborg, Marilyn F.

Olsen, Solveig, ed. Computer-Aided Instruction in the Humanities. LC 85-13740. (Technology & the Humanities Ser.: No. 2). 294p. 1985. pap. 91.20 (*0-608-05589-1*, 206604900006) Bks Demand.

Olsen, Sondra S. Traps. LC 91-19062. (Iowa Short Fiction Award Ser.). 159p. 1991. 11.50 (*0-87745-346-2*) U of Iowa Pr.

Olsen, Stanley J. Fish, Amphibian & Reptile Remains from Archaeological Sites Pt. I: Southeastern & Southwestern United States; Appendix: The Osteology of the Wild Turkey. LC 68-56643. (Papers of the Peabody Museum of Archaeology & Ethnology: Vol. 56, No. 2). (Illus.). 137p. (C). 1996. reprint ed. pap. 35.00 (*0-87365-163-4*, P56-2) Peabody Harvard.

— Mammal Remains from Archaeological Sites Pt. 1: Southeastern & Southwestern United States. LC 85-176642. (Papers of the Peabody Museum of Archaeology & Ethnology: Vol. 56, No. 1). (Illus.). 176p. (C). 1996. reprint ed. pap. 35.00 (*0-87365-162-6*, P56-1) Peabody Harvard.

— Osteology for the Archaeologist: The American Mastodon & the Woolly Mammoth; North American Birds: Skulls & Mandibles & Postcranial Skeletons. rev. ed. LC 79-65654. (Peabody Museum Papers: Vol. 56, Nos. 3, 4, & 5). (Illus.). 196p. 1979. pap. 35.00 (*0-87365-197-9*) Peabody Harvard.

— An Osteology of Some Maya Mammals. LC 81-85463. (Peabody Museum Papers: No. 73). (Illus.). 92p. 1982. pap. 18.00 (*0-87365-199-5*) Peabody Harvard.

Olsen, Stanley J. & Wheeler, Richard P. Bones from Awatovi: Northeastern Arizona: The Faunal Analysis; Bone & Antler Artifacts. LC 78-67471. (Peabody Museum Papers: Vol. 70, 1 & 2). (Illus.). 74p. 1978. pap. 15.00 (*0-87365-195-2*) Peabody Harvard.

Olsen, Steen. Tumors of the Kidney & Urinary Tract. (Illus.). 291p. 1985. text 142.00 (*0-7216-1588-0*, W B Saunders Co) Harcrt Hlth Sci Grp.

Olsen, Stein H., jt. auth. see Lamarque, Peter.

Olsen, Stephen, et al. Atacames Special Area Management Plan: Atacames-Sua Muisne. 68p. 1994. write for info. (*1-885454-01-5*) Coastal Res.

Olsen, Stephen, et al. Survey of Current Purposes & Methods for Evaluating Coastal Management Projects & Programs Funded by International Donors. (Coastal Management Report Ser.: Vol. 2200). 1997. pap. write for info. (*1-885454-20-1*) Coastal Res.

***Olsen, Stephen B.** Coastal Management: What Are We Learning from U. S. & International Experience? (Coastal Management Report Ser.: Vol. 2218). 14p. 1999. pap. write for info. (*1-885454-26-0*) Coastal Res.

— Educating for Governance of Coastal Ecosystems: The Dimension of the Challenge. (Coastal Management Report Ser.: Vol. 2219). 13p. 1999. pap. write for info. (*1-885454-27-9*) Coastal Res.

— Increasing the Efficiency of Integrated Coastal Management. (Coastal Management Report Ser.: Vol. 2220). (Illus.). 1999. pap. write for info. (*1-885454-28-7*) Coastal Res.

***Olsen, Stephen B. & Kerr, Meg.** Building Constituencies for Coastal Management: A Handbook for the Planning Phase. 153p. 1999. pap. write for info. (*1-885454-17-1*) Coastal Res.

***Olsen, Stephen B. & Ngoile, Magnus.** Final Evaluation Global Environment Facility: Belize - Sustainable Development & Management of Biologically Diverse Coastal Resources. (Coastal Management Report Ser.: Vol. 2207). 40p. 1998. pap. write for info. (*1-885454-07-4*) Coastal Res.

Olsen, Stephen B. & Tobey, James A. Final Evaluation Global Environment Facility: Patagonian Coastal Zone Management Plan. (Coastal Management Report Ser.: Vol. 2208). 46p. 1997. pap. write for info. (*1-885454-08-2*) Coastal Res.

***Olsen, Stephen B., et al.** Final Evaluation Global Environment Facility Dominican Republic - Conservation & Management in the Coastal Zone of the Dominican Republic. (Coastal Management Ser.: Vol. 2215). 52p. 1999. write for info. (*1-885454-18-X*) Coastal Res.

— Final Evaluation Global Environmental Facility: Protecting Biodiversity & Sustainable Development of

the Sabana-Camaguey Project. (Coastal Management Report Ser.: Vol. 2201). 1997. pap. write for info. (*1-885454-21-X*) Coastal Res.
— A Framework for a Common Methodology. (Coastal Management Report Ser.: Vol. 2221). (Illus.). 18p. 2000. pap. write for info. (*1-885454-29-5*) Coastal Res.
— Una Guia para Evaluar el Progreso en el Manejo Costero (A Manual for Assessing Progress in Coastal Management) Ochoa, Emilio, tr. (Coastal Management Report Ser.: Vol. 2211). (SPA.). 1999. pap. write for info. (*1-885454-12-0*) Coastal Res.
— A Manual for Assessing Progress in Coastal Management. (Coastal Management Report Ser.: Vol. 2211). (Illus.). 1999. pap. write for info. (*1-885454-11-2*) Coastal Res.
Olsen, Stephen B., jt. auth. see Johnston, Robert J.
***Olsen, Susan U.** Just Not Quite Right. LC 99-90395. (Illus.). 32p. (YA). (gr. 6-9). 2000. 20.00 (*0-9672018-0-2*) Mind Set Pr.
Olsen, T. V. Blood Rage. 192p. 1999. mass mkt. 3.99 (*0-8439-4500-1*) Dorchester Pub Co.
***Olsen, T. V.** Canyon of the Gun. large type ed. LC 99-39439. 2000. 30.00 (*0-7838-8733-7*, G K Hall Lrg Type) Mac Lib Ref.
Olsen, T. V. Deadly Pursuit. 240p. 1998. mass mkt. 4.50 (*0-8439-4463-3*, Leisure Bks) Dorchester Pub Co.
— Deadly Pursuit. large type ed. 1996. 20.00 (*0-7838-1403-8*) Thorndike Pr.
— Deadly Pursuit. large type ed. 294p. 1996. pap. 17.95 (*0-7862-0717-5*) Thorndike Pr.
— Deadly Pursuit: A Western Story. LC 95-20010. (Five-Star Western Ser.). 200p. 1995. 16.95 (*0-7862-0507-5*) Thorndike Pr.
— Eye of the Wolf. 192p. 1998. reprint ed. mass mkt. 3.99 (*0-8439-4390-4*, Leisure Bks) Dorchester Pub Co.
***Olsen, T. V.** Haven of the Hunted. large type ed. LC 99-29285. 1999. pap. 19.95 (*0-7838-8649-7*, G K Hall & Co) Mac Lib Ref.
Olsen, T. V. Keno. 176p. 1998. reprint ed. mass mkt. 3.99 (*0-8439-4347-5*, Leisure Bks) Dorchester Pub Co.
— The Lost Colony. LC 99-35658. (Westerns Ser.). 250p. 1999. 19.95 (*0-7862-1582-8*) Five Star.
— The Lost Colony. large type ed. 275p. 2000. 30.00 (*0-7862-1588-7*) Thorndike Pr.
***Olsen, T. V.** Rattlesnake. 208p. 1999. pap. 4.50 (*0-8439-4620-2*, Leisure Bks) Dorchester Pub Co.
Olsen, T. V. Savage Sierra. large type ed. LC 97-50194. 242p. 1998. pap. 21.95 (*0-7838-8420-6*, G K Hall Lrg Type) Mac Lib Ref.
— Starbuck's Brand. 192p. 1997. reprint ed. mass mkt. 3.99 (*0-8439-4326-2*, Leisure Bks) Dorchester Pub Co.
— Track the Man Down. 208p. 1998. reprint ed. mass mkt. 4.50 (*0-8439-4369-6*, Leisure Bks) Dorchester Pub Co.
Olsen, Terry. My Father My Hero: Becoming Your Child's Best Friend. LC 95-200756. 191p. (Orig.). 1995. pap. 9.95 (*1-883893-13-5*) WinePress Pub.
Olsen, Theodore V. Arrow in the Sun. 272p. 1996. reprint ed. pap. text, mass mkt. 4.55 (*0-8439-3948-6*) Dorchester Pub Co.
— Blood of the Breed. large type ed. 1985. 15.95 (*0-7089-1262-1*) Ulverscroft.
— Blood of the Breed. 192p. 1997. reprint ed. mass mkt. 3.99 (*0-8439-4158-8*) Dorchester Pub Co.
— Bonner's Stallion. 256p. 1997. reprint ed. mass mkt. 4.50 (*0-8439-4276-2*, Leisure Bks) Dorchester Pub Co.
— Break the Young Land. 224p. 1988. pap. 2.75 (*0-380-75290-5*, Avon Bks) Morrow Avon.
— Break the Young Land. 224p. 1997. reprint ed. mass mkt. 4.50 (*0-8439-4226-6*) Dorchester Pub Co.
— Eye of the Wolf. large type ed. LC 98-10487. 256p. 1998. pap. 18.95 (*0-7838-8457-5*, G K Hall & Co) Mac Lib Ref.
— The Golden Chance. large type ed. LC 93-27028. 220p. 1993. lib. bdg. 18.95 (*0-8161-5861-4*, G K Hall Lrg Type) Mac Lib Ref.
— Gunswift. large type ed. (Linford Western Library). 1991. pap. 16.99 (*0-7089-6967-4*) Ulverscroft.
— A Killer Is Waiting, 1. (Love Spell Ser.). 208p. 1999. mass mkt. 4.50 (*0-8439-4549-4*) Dorchester Pub Co.
Olsen, Theodore V. Lazlo's Strike. 192p. 1996. reprint ed. mass mkt. 3.99 (*0-8439-4114-6*) Dorchester Pub Co.
Olsen, Theodore V. Lonesome Gun. large type ed. (Linford Western Large Print Ser.). 1993. pap. 16.99 (*0-7089-7367-1*, Linford) Ulverscroft.
— A Man Called Brazos. large type ed. (Linford Western Library). 1991. pap. 16.99 (*0-7089-7015-X*, Linford) Ulverscroft.
— The Man from Nowhere. large type ed. (Linford Western Library). 1990. pap. 16.99 (*0-7089-6946-1*, Linford) Ulverscroft.
— Run to the Mountain/Day of the Buzzard, 2 bks. in 1. 368p. 1996. reprint ed. mass mkt. 4.99 (*0-8439-4059-X*, Leisure Bks) Dorchester Pub Co.
— The Stalking Moon. 256p. 1997. reprint ed. mass mkt. 4.50 (*0-8439-4180-4*) Dorchester Pub Co.
— Starbuck's Brand. large type ed. LC 92-19929. (Nightingale Ser.). 311p. 1992. pap. 14.95 (*0-8161-5594-1*, G K Hall Lrg Type) Mac Lib Ref.
— There Was a Season. 448p. 1994. reprint ed. pap. text, mass mkt. 4.99 (*0-8439-3652-5*) Dorchester Pub Co.
— Treasures of the Sun: A South-Western Story. LC 98-28226. 1998. 18.95 (*0-7862-0995-X*) Thorndike Pr.
***Olsen, Theodore V.** Treasures of the Sun: A South-Western Story. large type ed. LC 99-41470. (Thorndike Western Ser.). 1999. 30.00 (*0-7862-1034-6*) Thorndike Pr.
Olsen, Theodore V. Under the Gun. large type ed. LC 94-1037. 223p. 1994. lib. bdg. 19.95 (*0-8161-5862-2*, G K Hall Lrg Type) Mac Lib Ref.
— Westward They Rode. 224p. 1996. reprint ed. mass mkt. 4.50 (*0-8439-4021-2*) Dorchester Pub Co.
Olsen, Tillie. Tell Me a Riddle. LC 94-231378. 128p. 1971. pap. 12.95 (*0-385-29010-1*, Delta Trade) Dell.
— Tell Me a Riddle. 1984. 24.50 (*0-8446-6090-6*) Peter Smith.
— Tell Me a Riddle. Rosenfelt, Deborah S., ed. (Women Writers: Text & Contexts Ser.). 200p. (C). 1995. text 38.00 (*0-8135-2136-X*); pap. text 14.00 (*0-8135-2137-8*) Rutgers U Pr.
— Yonnondio. 160p. 1989. pap. 13.95 (*0-385-29179-5*, Delta Trade) Dell.
— Yonnondio. 1984. 24.50 (*0-8446-6089-2*) Peter Smith.
Olsen, Tillie, ed. Mother to Daughter, Daughter to Mother: A Daybook & Reader. LC 84-21038. 312p. 1984. 19.95 (*1-55861-008-1*, Pub. by Feminist Pr); pap. 10.95 (*0-935312-37-4*) Feminist Pr.
Olsen, Tillie, ed. see Davis, Rebecca H.
***Olsen, Tim, ed.** The Big Red Book of American Lutherie, 1985-1987, Vol. 1. (Illus.). 521p. 2000. 40.00 (*0-9626447-2-2*) Guild Amer Luthiers.
Olsen, Tim & Burton, Cyndy. Lutherie Tools: Making Hand & Power Tools for String Instrument Building. (Guild of American Luthiers Resource Bk.: No. 1). 122p. 1990. 25.00 (*0-9626447-0-6*) Guild Amer Luthiers.
— Lutherie Woods & Steel String Guitars: A Guide to Tonewoods with a Compilaition of Repair & Construction Techniques. (Guild of American Luthiers Resource Bk.: No. 2). 154p. 1998. 25.00 (*0-9626447-1-4*) Guild Amer Luthiers.
Olsen, Tina, jt. auth. see Catts, Hugh.
Olsen, T.V. Lone Hand: Frontier Stories. large type ed. LC 96-53929. 262p. 1997. 17.95 (*0-7862-0738-8*) Thorndike Pr.
— Lone Hand: Frontier Stories. large type ed. LC 98-5429. 1998. 19.95 (*0-7862-0761-2*) Thorndike Pr.
Olsen, V. Norskov. Christian Faith & Religious Freedom. LC 96-60631. 112p. 1996. per. 8.95 (*1-57258-118-2*) Teach Servs.
— The New Relatedness for Man & Woman in Christ: A Mirror of the Divine. LC 93-13440. 1993. pap. 9.95 (*1-881127-01-X*) LLU Ctr Christ Bio.
— The New Testament Logia on Divorce. vi, 161p. 1994. pap. 36.50 (*3-16-131441-7*, Pub. by JCB Mohr) Coronet Bks.
— Papal Supremacy & American Democracy. LC 87-83037. 190p. (Orig.). 1988. pap. 10.95 (*0-944450-01-6*) La Sierra U Pr.
Olsen, Victoria C., jt. ed. see Boufis, Christina.
Olsen, Viggo. Daktar: Diplomat in Bangladesh. LC 95-21032. 352p. 1996. pap. 14.99 (*0-8254-3368-1*) Kregel.
Olsen, W. H., jt. auth. see Riddell, Francis A.
Olsen, W. Scott. Meeting the Neighbors: Sketches of Life on the Northern Prairie. LC 93-12827. 1993. pap. 9.95 (*0-87839-080-4*) North Star.
Olsen, W. Scott, ed. Best of Writers at Work, 1995. 217p. 1995. pap. 12.95 (*1-877603-30-9*) Pecan Grove.
Olsen, W. Scott & Cairns, Scott, eds. The Sacred Place: Witnessing the Holy in the Physical World. 360p. 1996. 49.95 (*0-87480-523-6*); pap. 19.95 (*0-87480-524-4*) U of Utah Pr.
Olsen, W. Scott, et al. When We Say We're Home: A Quartet of Place & Memory. LC 98-54376. 344p. 1999. pap. 19.95 (*0-87480-592-9*) U of Utah Pr.
***Olsen, W. Scott, et al.** When We Say We're Home: A Quartet of Place & Memory. LC 98-54376. 344p. 1999. 45.00 (*0-87480-591-0*) U of Utah Pr.
Olsen, Wallace C. Agricultural Economics & Rural Sociology: The Contemporary Core Literature. LC 95-20394. 304p. 1991. text 57.50 (*0-8014-2677-4*) Cornell U Pr.
Olsen, Wallace C., ed. The Literature of Animal Science & Health. 400p. 1993. text 79.95 (*0-8014-2886-6*) Cornell U Pr.
— The Literature of Crop Science. (Literature of the Agricultural Sciences Ser.). (Illus.). 544p. 1995. text 79.95 (*0-8014-3138-7*) Cornell U Pr.
Olsen, Wallace C., jt. ed. see Brogdon, Jennie L.
Olsen, Wallace C., jt. ed. see Hall, Carl W.
Olsen, Warren & Rinden, David. Explanation of Luther's Small Catechism. 128p. (J). (gr. 7-8). 1988. text 7.95 (*0-943167-12-4*) Faith & Fellowship Pr.
Olsen, Warren & Rinden, David, eds. Explanation of Luther's Small Catechism. 2nd ed. 128p. (J). (gr. 7-8). 1992. text 7.95 (*0-943167-20-5*) Faith & Fellowship Pr.
Olsen, Warren, jt. auth. see Larson, Luther.
Olsen, Wendy K. Rural Indian Social Relations: A Study of Southern Andhra Pradesh. LC 96-902145. (Illus.). 368p. (C). 1996. text 35.00 (*0-19-563641-4*) OUP.
Olsen, William. The Hand of God & a Few Bright Flowers. Poems. LC 87-24507. (National Poetry Ser.). 80p. 1988. pap. 9.95 (*0-252-06001-6*) U of Ill Pr.
— Vision of a Storm Cloud. LC 96-1876. (Illus.). 136p. 1996. pap. 13.95 (*0-8101-5044-1*); text 29.95 (*0-8101-5043-3*) Northwestern U Pr.
Olsen, William H. Archaeological Investigations at Sutter's Fort State Historical Monument. (Publications of the Department of Parks & Recreation: No. 1). (Illus.). 83p. (C). 1961. reprint ed. pap. text 9.38 (*1-55567-453-4*) Coyote Press.
Olsen, William H. & Payen, Louis A. Archeology of the Grayson Site, Merced County, California. (Publications of the Department of Parks & Recreation: No. 12). (Illus.). 148p. (C). 1969. reprint ed. pap. text 16.25 (*1-55567-463-1*) Coyote Press.
— Archeology of the Little Panocke Reservoir, Fresno County, California. (Publications of the Department of Parks & Recreation: No. 11). (Illus.). 170p. (C). 1968. reprint ed. pap. text 18.13 (*1-55567-462-3*) Coyote Press.
Olsen, William H. & Wilson, Norman. The Salvage Archaeology of the Bear Creek Site (SJo-112) A Terminal Central California Early Horizon Site. fac. ed. (Sacramento Anthropological Society, Sacramento State College Ser.: No. 1). (Illus.). 61p. 1964. reprint ed. pap. text 7.19 (*1-55567-557-3*) Coyote Press.
Olsenius, Christine, jt. auth. see Olsenius, Richard.
Olsenius, Richard. Distant Shores: Music & Photographs from Lake Superior & Lake Michigan. 112p. 1990. pap. 19.95 incl. audio (*0-9609064-4-4*); pap. 14.95 (*0-9609064-5-2*); audio 9.95 (*0-9609064-6-0*) Bluestem Prod.
— Distant Shores: Music & Photographs from Lake Superior & Lake Michigan. 112p. 1993. pap. 24.95 incl. cd-rom (*0-9609064-8-7*) Bluestem Prod.
Olsenius, Richard & Olsenius, Christine. Arctic Odyssey: Music, Images & CD-Rom from the Northwest Passage. LC 98-96817. (Illus.). 72p. (YA). 1998. 22.95 (*0-9609064-9-5*) Bluestem Prod.
Olsgaard, John N., ed. Principles & Applications of Information Science for Library Professionals. LC 88-36876. 152p. reprint ed. pap. 47.20 (*0-7837-5922-3*, 204572100007) Bks Demand.
Olshaker, Bennett. The Child As a Work of Art. 1985. reprint ed. pap. 6.95 (*0-9617697-0-X*) Marko Bks.
Olshaker, Mark, jt. auth. see Douglas, John.
Olshaker, Mark, jt. auth. see Douglas, John E.
Olshaker, Mark, jt. auth. see Peters, C. J.
Olshan, A. F., jt. ed. see Mattison, D. R.
Olshan, Al. My Life, My Way. 300p. (Orig.). 1992. pap. write for info. (*0-9632134-0-7*) Al Olshan.
Olshan, Joseph. Nightswimmer. 320p. 1996. reprint ed. mass mkt. 6.99 (*0-425-15190-5*) Berkley Pub.
— Vanitas. LC 98-15551. 288p. 1998. 23.00 (*0-684-83396-4*) S&S Trade.
Olshan, Marc A., jt. ed. see Kraybill, Donald B.
Olshan, Neal H. Golden Handcuffs: How Women Can Break Free of Financial Dependence in Their Intimate Relationships. 208p. 1993. 17.95 (*1-55972-202-9*, Birch Ln Pr) Carol Pub Group.
***Olshan, Neal H.** Golden Handcuffs: How Women Can Break Free of Financial Dependence in Their Intimate Relationships. 149p. 1999. reprint ed. text 18.00 (*0-7881-6820-7*) DIANE Pub.
Olshanetsky, M. A., jt. ed. see Morozov, A. Yu.
Olshanksy, Robert B. Reducing Earthquake Hazards in the Central U. S. Seismic Building Codes. (Illus.). 85p. (C). 1999. reprint ed. text 25.00 (*0-7881-7736-2*) DIANE Pub.
Olshanski, G. I., ed. Kirillov's Seminar on Representation Theory. Sossinsky, A. B., tr. LC 91-640741. (Mathematical Society Translations Ser.: Series 2, Vol. 181). 271p. 1997. text 99.00 (*0-8218-0669-6*) Am Math.
Ol'shanskii, A. Yu. Geometry of Defining Relations in Groups. 544p. (C). 1991. text 332.00 (*0-7923-1394-1*) Kluwer Academic.
***Olshansky.** Integrated Women's Health Care. 2000. pap. 35.00 (*0-8342-1219-6*) Aspen Pub.
Olshansky, Brian, jt. ed. see Grubb, Blair P.
***Olshansky, Robert B.** Promoting the Adoption & Enforcement of Seismic Building Codes: A Guidebook for State Earthquake & Mitigation Managers. (Illus.). 205p. (C). 1999. pap. text 35.00 (*0-7881-7632-3*) DIANE Pub.
Olshansky, Robert B. Reducing Earthquake Hazards in the Central U. S. Seismic Safety of Existing Buildings. 71p. (C). 1999. reprint ed. pap. text 20.00 (*0-7881-7738-9*) DIANE Pub.
Olshansky, S. Jay & Carnes, Bruce A. The Quest for Immortality: Science at the Frontiers of Aging. 176p. 2001. text 25.95 (*0-393-04836-5*) Norton.
Olshausen, Hans-Gustav. VDI-Lexikon Bauingenieurwesen. (GER.). 649p. 1991. 250.00 (*0-7859-8287-6*, 3184008975) Fr & Eur.
Olshausen, Rainer von, see Peschke, Egon & von Olshausen, Rainer.
Olshavsky, Richard W., ed. see Attitude Research Conference Staff.
Olshefski, Jacqueline, jt. auth. see Olshefski, Tom.
Olshefski, Tom & Olshefski, Jacqueline. PIZZAstrology: How to Interpret Your Sauce Sign for Fun & Prophet! (Illus.). iv, 108p. 1998. pap. 14.95 (*0-9666873-0-2*) Life Enhancing Pubns.
Olshen, Barry N. & Feldman, Yael, eds. Approaches to Teaching the Hebrew Bible As Literature in Translation. LC 89-32332. (Approaches to Teaching World Literature Ser.: No. 25). x, 156p. 1989. pap. 18.00 (*0-87352-524-8*, AP25P); lib. bdg. 37.50 (*0-87352-523-X*, AP25C) Modern Lang.
Olsher, David. Words in Motion. LC 95-13830. 76p. 1996. pap. text, teacher ed. 8.95 (*0-19-434459-2*) OUP.
— Words in Motion: An Interactive Approach to Writing Student Books. (Illus.). 128p. 1995. pap. text 12.95 (*0-19-434452-5*) OUP.
Olshevky, V. & Ponomarev, A. Revolutionary Guide to OOP Using C++ LC 94-78388. 600p. 1994. pap. 39.95 incl. disk (*1-874416-18-4*) Wrox Pr Inc.
***Olshevski, Jody.** Stress Reduction for Caregivers. LC 98-55754. 1999. pap. text 24.95 (*0-87630-941-4*) Brunner-Mazel.
Olshevskii, Viktor V. Statistical Methods in Sonar. Middleton, David, ed. LC 78-18196. (Studies in Soviet Science). 262p. 1978. reprint ed. pap. 81.30 (*0-608-05413-5*, 206588200006) Bks Demand.
Olshevsky, Moshe, et al. The Manual of Natural Therapy. 384p. 1990. pap. 14.95 (*0-8065-1202-4*, Citadel Pr) Carol Pub Group.
— The Manual of Natural Therapy: A Practical Guide to Alternative Medicine. (Illus.). 386p. 1999. reprint ed. 39.95 (*0-7351-0088-8*) Replica Bks.
— The Manual of Natural Therapy: A Succint Catalog of Complementary Treatments. LC 88-24410. (Illus.). 384p. reprint ed. pap. 119.10 (*0-7837-6694-7*, 204631100011) Bks Demand.
Olshewsky, Thomas M., jt. ed. see Colapietro, Vincent M.
Olshtain, Elite, et al. The Junior Files No. 1: English for Today & Tomorrow. rev. ed. (Illus.). ix, 246p. (YA). (gr. 6-12). 1993. pap. text 16.95 (*1-882483-04-9*) Alta Bk Ctr.
— The Junior Files No. 2: English for Tomorrow. (Illus.). 288p. (YA). (gr. 6-12). 1993. pap. text 16.50 (*1-882483-08-1*) Alta Bk Ctr.
— The Junior Files, File 1: English for Today & Tomorrow. rev. ed. Berman, Aaron & Chapman, Charles, eds. (Illus.). 270p. (J). (gr. 6-10). 1991. pap. write for info. (*1-878598-02-3*) Alta Bk Co Pubs.
— The Junior Files Teacher's Guide No. 1: English for Today & Tomorrow. (Junior Files Ser.). (Illus.). 88p. 1996. teacher ed. 11.50 (*1-882483-07-3*) Alta Bk Ctr.
— The Junior Files Teacher's Guide No. 2: English for Tomorrow. (Junior Files Ser.). (Illus.). 104p. (YA). (gr. 6-12). 1996. teacher ed. 11.50 (*1-882483-11-1*) Alta Bk Ctr.
Olshtain, Elite, jt. auth. see Celce-Murcia, Marianne.
Olshtain, Elite, jt. auth. see Dubin, Fraida.
Olski, Jennifer, ed. see Mills, Laurel.
Olsnes, S., jt. auth. see Potter, M.
Olson. American Odessey, 2. 2000. 73.00 (*0-07-048226-8*) McGraw.
— American Odyssey. 2001. 73.00 (*0-07-048223-3*) McGraw.
— American Odyssey, 1. 2001. 73.00 (*0-07-048225-X*) McGraw.
— Confessions of Black Widow, Vol. 1. 288p. 1998. 6.50 (*0-312-96503-6*, Pub. by Tor Bks) St Martin.
***Olson.** Functional Human Anatomy. 5th ed. 1999. pap. text, lab manual ed. 22.00 (*0-536-02786-2*) Pearson Custom.
Olson. The Gender Reader. 2nd ed. LC 99-26099. 498p. (C). 1999. pap. text 36.00 (*0-205-28530-9*, Macmillan Coll) P-H.
***Olson.** Healing the Dying. 2nd ed. (C). 2001. pap. 18.50 (*0-7668-2572-8*) Delmar.
Olson. A History of Breast Cancer. 1997. 25.00 (*0-02-923836-6*); 25.00 (*0-684-82806-5*) Free Pr.
— Introduction to Fire Protection. 120p. (C). 1997. pap., student ed. 19.95 (*0-8273-8229-4*) Delmar.
— Job Wars. 1996. 24.95 (*0-02-874035-1*) Free Pr.
— My Lai Massacre. LC 97-74967. 222p. 1998. pap. text 11.95 (*0-312-14227-7*) St Martin.
***Olson.** Power & Prosperity. 2000. pap. 18.00 (*0-465-05196-0*, Pub. by Basic) HarpC.
Olson. Reading Critically: The Harper Collins Concise Handbook. (C). 1997. pap. text 14.66 (*0-06-502024-3*) Addson-Wesley Educ.
— Real World Fitness. LC 98-37293. 192p. 1998. pap. 19.95 (*1-58238-026-0*, Whitman Coin) St Martin.
— U S in the Twentieth Century. 1995. pap. text 34.20 (*0-312-13796-6*) St Martin.
Olson & Courtney. Decision Support Models & Expert Systems. LC 97-68556. 1997. 74.95 (*0-87393-663-9*) Dame Pubns.
Olson & Hanratty. Key Factor to Motivation. LC 81-66054. 64p. 1981. 9.00 (*0-86690-008-X*, O1359-014) Am Fed Astrologers.
— Your Motive Factor. 24p. 1981. 8.00 (*0-86690-218-X*, O1361-014) Am Fed Astrologers.
Olson, jt. auth. see Lee.
Olson, jt. auth. see Lockerbie.
Olson, Charles E. Cost Considerations for Efficient Electricity Supply. LC 70-629562. (MSU Public Utilities Studies: Vol. 1970). (Illus.). 111p. reprint ed. pap. 34.50 (*0-608-20509-5*, 207176100002) Bks Demand.
Olson, Adolf. A Centenary History As Related to the Baptist General Conference of America. Ganstad, Edwin S., ed. LC 79-52602. (Baptist Tradition Ser.). (Illus.). 1980. reprint ed. lib. bdg. 61.95 (*0-405-12467-8*) Ayer.
Olson, Alan M. Hegel & the Spirit: Philosophy as Pneumatology. 176p. 1992. text 37.50 (*0-691-07411-9*, Pub. by Princeton U Pr) Cal Prin Full Svc.
Olson, Alan M., et al, eds. Video Icons & Values. LC 89-49240. (SUNY Series in Speech Communication). 189p. 1990. pap. text 21.95 (*0-7914-0412-9*) State U NY Pr.
— Video Icons & Values. LC 89-49240. (SUNY Series in Speech Communication). 189p. 1991. text 64.50 (*0-7914-0411-0*) State U NY Pr.
Olson, Alan M. & Rouner, Leroy S., eds. Transcendence & the Sacred. LC 81-50456. (Boston University Studies in Philosophy & Religion: Vol. 2). 256p. (C). 1981. text 34.50 (*0-268-01841-3*) U of Notre Dame Pr.
— Transcendence & the Sacred. LC 81-50456. (Boston University Studies in Philosophy & Religion: Vol. 2). (C). 1994. reprint ed. pap. text 13.00 (*0-268-01888-X*) U of Notre Dame Pr.
Olson, Alan P., jt. auth. see Ambler, J. Richard.
Olson, Alger James, jt. auth. see Barnett, Cheryl Kay.
Olson, Alison G. Making the Empire Work: London & American Interest Groups, 1690-1790. 272p. 1992. 51.95 (*0-674-54318-1*) HUP.
Olson, Alton T. Mathematics Through Paper Folding. LC 75-16115. (Illus.). 60p. 1975. pap. 8.95 (*0-87353-076-4*) NCTM.
Olson, Ann S., ed. see Tampa Museum of Art Staff.
Olson, Ardis L., ed. see Singer, George H., et al.
Olson, Arielle N. & Schwartz, Howard. Ask the Bones: Scary Stories from around the World. LC 98-19108. (Illus.). 160p. (J). (gr. 3-7). 1999. 15.99 (*0-670-87581-3*) Viking Penguin.
Olson, Arnold T. The Significance of Silence. LC 80-70698. (Heritage Ser.: Vol. 2). 208p. 1981. 8.95 (*7-100-07628-5*) Free Church Pubns.
— Stumbling Toward Maturity. LC 81-66943. (Heritage Ser.: Vol. 3). 208p. 1981. 8.95 (*0-911802-50-9*) Free Church Pubns.

O

An Asterisk (*) at the beginning of an entry indicates that the title is appearing for the first time.

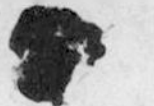

Olson, Arnold T., ed. The Search for Identity. LC 80-66030. (Heritage Ser.: Vol. 1). 160p. 1980. 8.95 (*0-911802-46-0*); pap. 6.95 (*7-100-07621-8*) Free Church Pubns.

Olson, Audrey L. St. Louis Germans, 1850-1920: The Nature of an Immigrant Community & Its Relation to the Assimilation Process. Cordasco, Francesco, ed. LC 80-886. (American Ethnic Groups Ser.). 1981. lib. bdg. 42.95 (*0-405-13447-9*) Ayer.

Olson, B. G. Interior Alaska: Including Fairbanks & Denali Park. (Umbrella Guides Ser.). (Illus.). 160p. (Orig.). 1995. pap. 12.95 (*0-945397-39-9*, Umbrella Bks) Epicenter Pr.

Olson, B. G., jt. auth. see Stockley, Tom.

Olson, B. G., ed. see Nelson, Sharlene P. & Nelson, Ted.

Olson, Barbara. Hell to Pay: The Unfolding Story of Hillary Rodham Clinton. LC 99-47548. 380p. 1999. 27.95 (*0-89526-274-6*, Pub. by Regnery Pub) Natl Bk Netwk.

Olson, Barbara, et al. Experimenting for Breakthrough Improvement. (Illus.). 367p. (C). 1994. ring bd. 69.95 (*1-882307-02-X*) Res Engineering.

Olson, Barbara K. Authorial Divinity in the Twentieth Century: Omniscient Narration in Woolf, Hemingway, & Others. LC 96-27062. 152p. 1997. 29.50 (*0-8387-5316-7*) Bucknell U Pr.

Olson, Beverly & Lazzara, Judy. Country Flower Drying. LC 87-26705. (Illus.). 132p. 1988. pap. 9.95 (*0-8069-6746-3*) Sterling.

Olson, Bill & Linkert, Lo. Beat the Links: A Simplified Instructional Guide for the Weekend Golfer. (Illus.). 96p. 1997. reprint ed. pap. text 5.00 (*0-7881-5129-0*) DIANE Pub.

Olson, Bob. Memories with a Christmas Attitude. LC 96-61542. 96p. 1996. pap. 9.00 (*1-883893-76-3*, Pub. by WinePress Pub) BookWorld.

Olson, Bob & Olson, Melissa. Win the Battle: The 3-Step Lifesaving Conquering Depression & Behavior Disorder. LC 98-74420. 156p. 1999. 17.95 (*1-886284-31-8*, Pub. by Chandler Hse) Natl Bk Netwk.

Olson, Bonnie F., ed. see Foell, Lillian A.

***Olson, Brad.** To Those Who Dream. 55p. 1999. pap. 5.00 (*0-7392-0365-7*, PO3567) Morris Pubng.

Olson, Brent. Lay of the Land. (Illus.). 188p. 1998. pap. 11.95 (*0-934904-36-7*, 36-7) J & L Lee.

Olson, Bruce. Bruchko. LC 73-81494. 208p. (Orig.). 1973. pap. 12.99 (*0-88419-133-8*) Creation House.

Olson, Bruce H., jt. auth. see Marple, Elliot.

Olson-Buchanan, Julie B., jt. ed. see Drasgow, Fritz.

Olson, C. Gordon. What in the World is God Doing? The Essentials of Global Missions. 3rd ed. (Illus.). 320p. 1994. pap. text 11.95 (*0-9624850-2-0*) Global Gospel Pubs.

— What in the World Is God Doing? The Essentials of Global Missions. 4th ed. (Illus.). 368p. (Orig.). (C). 1998. pap. text 12.00 (*0-9624850-3-9*) Global Gospel Pubs.

Olson, C. L. & Schumacher, U. Collective Ion Acceleration. (Tracts in Modern Physics Ser.: Vol. 84). (Illus.). 1979. 46.00 (*0-387-09066-5*) Spr-Verlag.

Olson, Carl. The Indian Renouncer & Postmodern Poison: A Cross-Cultural Encounter. LC 95-40652. (New Perspectives in Philosophical Scholarship Series: Texts & Issues: Vol. 7). XVI, 367p. (C). 1997. text 58.95 (*0-8204-3022-6*) P Lang Pubng.

— The Mysterious Play of Kali: An Interpretive Study of Ramakrishna. 140p. 1990. 29.95 (*1-55540-339-5*, 01 00 56); pap. 19.95 (*1-55540-340-9*) OUP.

***Olson, Carl.** Zen & the Art of Postmodern Philosophy: Two Paths of Liberation from the Representational Mode of Thinking. LC 99-58390. (C). 2000. pap. text 21.95 (*0-7914-4654-9*) State U NY Pr.

— Zen & the Art of Postmodern Philosophy: Two Paths of Liberation from the Representational Mode of Thinking. LC 99-58390. (C). 2000. text 65.50 (*0-7914-4653-0*) State U NY Pr.

Olson, Carl A. & Werner, Floyd G. Insects of the Southwest: How to Identify Helpful Harmful. LC 94-29991. (Illus.). 192p. (Orig.). 1994. pap. 12.95 (*1-55561-060-9*) Fisher Bks.

Olson, Carl R., jt. ed. see Hanson, Stephen J.

Olson, Carol B. Practical Ideas for Teaching Writing As a Process. (Illus.). 224p. (C). 1996. reprint ed. pap. text 30.00 (*0-7881-2718-7*) DIANE Pub.

— Practical Ideas for Teaching Writing As a Process, Elementary & Middle Grade Levels. (Illus.). 320p. 1996. pap. 18.00 (*0-8011-1221-4*) Calif Education.

Olson, Carol T. The Life of Illness: One Woman's Journey. LC 91-33457. (SUNY Series, The Body in Culture, History, & Religion). 203p. (C). 1992. text 18.50 (*0-7914-1199-0*) State U NY Pr.

Olson, Charles. Call Me Ishmael. (BCL1-PS American Literature Ser.). 119p. 1993. reprint ed. lib. bdg. 69.00 (*0-7812-6991-1*) Rprt Serv.

— Collected Poems of Charles Olson: Excluding the Maximus Poems. 1997. pap. text 42.50 (*0-520-21231-2*, Pub. by U CA Pr) Cal Prin Full Svc.

— The Maximus Poems. Butterick, George F., ed. LC 79-65759. 664p. 1995. pap. 37.50 (*0-520-05595-0*, Pub. by U CA Pr) Cal Prin Full Svc.

— Maximus to Gloucester: The Letters & Poems of Charles Olson to the Editor of the Gloucester Daily Times, 1962-1969. Anastas, Peter, ed. (Illus.). 161p. (Orig.). 1992. pap. 15.00 (*0-938459-07-4*) Ten Pound Isl Bk.

Olson, Charles. A Nation of Nothing but Poetry: Supplementary Poems. LC 88-36879. 226p. (Orig.). (C). 1989. pap. 12.50 (*0-87685-750-0*) Black Sparrow.

Olson, Charles. The Post Office. LC 74-75456. (Illus.). 66p. 1975. pap. 4.95 (*0-912516-14-3*) Grey Fox.

— Selected Poems. Creeley, Robert, ed. LC 92-23838. 1993. 35.00 (*0-520-07528-5*, Pub. by U CA Pr) Cal Prin Full Svc.

— Selected Poems. 1997. pap. text 15.95 (*0-520-21232-0*, Pub. by U CA Pr) Cal Prin Full Svc.

— Selected Writings. Creeley, Robert, ed. LC 66-27613. (Orig.). 1967. pap. 12.95 (*0-8112-0128-7*, NDP231, Pub. by New Directions) Norton.

— The Special View of History. Charters, Ann, ed. 128p. 2000. pap. 14.95 (*1-886449-67-8*, P9678, Pub. by Barrytown Ltd) Consort Bk Sales.

Olson, Charles & Boldereff, Frances. Charles Olson & Frances Boldereff: A Modern Correspondence. Maud, Ralph & Thesen, Sharon, eds. LC 98-41954. (Illus.). 564p. 1999. pap. 24.95 (*0-8195-6364-1*, Pub. by U Pr of New Eng); text 60.00 (*0-8195-6363-3*, Wesleyan Univ Pr) U Pr of New Eng.

Olson, Charles & Creeley, Robert. Charles Olson & Robert Creeley: The Complete Correspondence, Vol. 1. Butterick, George F., ed. LC 80-12222. (Illus.). 184p. (Orig.). 1980. 20.00 (*0-87685-400-5*) Black Sparrow.

— Charles Olson & Robert Creeley: The Complete Correspondence, Vol. 1. Butterick, George F., ed. LC 80-12222. (Illus.). 184p. (Orig.). 1980. pap. 12.50 (*0-87685-399-8*) Black Sparrow.

— Charles Olson & Robert Creeley: The Complete Correspondence, Vol. 2. Butterick, George F., ed. LC 80-12222. (Illus.). 184p. (Orig.). 1980. pap. 12.50 (*0-87685-440-4*) Black Sparrow.

— Charles Olson & Robert Creeley: The Complete Correspondence, Vol. 3. Butterick, George F., ed. LC 80-12222. (Illus.). 175p. (Orig.). (C). 1981. 20.00 (*0-87685-483-8*); pap. 12.50 (*0-87685-482-X*) Black Sparrow.

— Charles Olson & Robert Creeley: The Complete Correspondence, Vol. 3, signed ed. deluxe ed. Butterick, George F., ed. LC 80-12222. (Illus.). 175p. (Orig.). (C). 1981. 30.00 (*0-87685-484-6*) Black Sparrow.

— Charles Olson & Robert Creeley: The Complete Correspondence, Vol. 4. Butterick, George F., ed. LC 80-12222. (Illus.). 158p. (Orig.). (C). 1982. pap. 12.50 (*0-87685-485-4*) Black Sparrow.

— Charles Olson & Robert Creeley: The Complete Correspondence, Vol. 6. LC 80-12222. (Illus.). 247p. (Orig.). 1985. 20.00 (*0-87685-586-9*) Black Sparrow.

— Charles Olson & Robert Creeley: The Complete Correspondence, Vol. 6. LC 80-12222. (Illus.). 247p. (Orig.). 1985. pap. 15.00 (*0-87685-585-0*) Black Sparrow.

— Charles Olson & Robert Creeley: The Complete Correspondence, Vol. 7. Butterick, George F., ed. LC 80-12222. (Illus.). 286p. (Orig.). 1987. pap. 15.00 (*0-87685-689-X*) Black Sparrow.

— Charles Olson & Robert Creeley: The Complete Correspondence, Vol. 7, signed ed. deluxe ed. Butterick, George F., ed. LC 80-12222. (Illus.). 286p. (Orig.). 1987. 30.00 (*0-87685-691-1*) Black Sparrow.

— Charles Olson & Robert Creeley: The Complete Correspondence, Vol. 8. LC 80-12222. (Illus.). 284p. (Orig.). (C). 1987. pap. 15.00 (*0-87685-704-7*) Black Sparrow.

— Charles Olson & Robert Creeley: The Complete Correspondence, Vol. 8, signed ed. deluxe ed. LC 80-12222. (Illus.). 284p. (Orig.). (C). 1987. 30.00 (*0-87685-706-3*) Black Sparrow.

— Charles Olson & Robert Creeley: The Complete Correspondence, Vol. 9. Blevins, Richard W., ed. LC 80-12222. (Illus.). 346p. (Orig.). (C). 1990. 25.00 (*0-87685-782-9*) Black Sparrow.

— Charles Olson & Robert Creeley: The Complete Correspondence, Vol. 9. Blevins, Richard W., ed. LC 80-12222. Vol. 9. (Illus.). 346p. (Orig.). (C). 1990. pap. 15.00 (*0-87685-781-0*) Black Sparrow.

— Charles Olson & Robert Creeley: The Complete Correspondence, Vol. 9, signed ed. deluxe ed. Blevins, Richard W., ed. LC 80-12222. (Illus.). 346p. (Orig.). (C). 1990. 35.00 (*0-87685-783-7*) Black Sparrow.

— Charles Olson & Robert Creeley Vol. 10: The Complete Correspondence, Vol. 10. Blevins, Richard W., ed. LC 80-12222. (Illus.). 325p. (Orig.). (C). 1996. 27.50 (*1-57423-005-0*); pap. 17.50 (*1-57423-004-2*) Black Sparrow.

— Charles Olson & Robert Creeley Vol. 10: The Complete Correspondence, Vol. 10. limited ed. Blevins, Richard W., ed. LC 80-12222. (Illus.). 325p. (Orig.). (C). 1996. 35.00 (*1-57423-006-9*) Black Sparrow.

Olson, Charles & Den Boer, James. Olson-Den Boer: A Letter. 1977. pap. 6.00 (*0-87922-051-1*) Christophers Bks.

***Olson, Charles & Maud, Ralph.** Selected Letters of Charles Olson. LC 99-48424. (Illus.). 464p. 2000. 60.00 (*0-520-20580-4*, Pub. by U CA Pr) Cal Prin Full Svc.

Olson, Charles, et al. Charles Olson & Robert Creeley: The Complete Correspondence, Vol. 5. Butterick, George F., ed. LC 80-12222. (Illus.). 222p. (Orig.). (C). 1983. 20.00 (*0-87685-561-3*) Black Sparrow.

— Charles Olson & Robert Creeley: The Complete Correspondence, Vol. 5. Butterick, George F., ed. LC 80-12222. (Illus.). 222p. (Orig.). (C). 1983. pap. 12.50 (*0-87685-560-5*) Black Sparrow.

— Collected Prose. LC 97-5390. 382p. 1997. 50.00 (*0-520-20319-4*, Pub. by U CA Pr); pap. 22.50 (*0-520-20873-0*, Pub. by U CA Pr) Cal Prin Full Svc.

Olson, Charles J., jt. auth. see Olson, William H.

Olson, Charles L., et al. Consumer & Business Arithmetic. LC 79-57434. 1981. teacher ed. 5.96 (*0-02-831240-6*); student ed. 9.32 (*0-02-831230-9*); text 22.64 (*0-02-831220-1*) Glencoe.

Olson, Charles R. A Teaching Guide to Writing English. LC 98-90209. 1999. pap. 12.95 (*0-533-12736-X*) Vantage.

Olson, Chester L. Essentials of Statistics: Data. 1987. text, teacher ed. 14.38 (*0-697-06945-1*, WCB McGr Hill) McGrw-H Hghr Educ.

Olson, Christine A. Libraries Through the Seasons Vol. 3, Pt. 2: Spring. (Olson's Library Clip Art). (Illus.). 16p. (Orig.). 1995. pap. text 33.00 (*1-56984-009-1*) C Olson & Assocs.

Olson, Christine A., ed. Americans with Disabilities Act Vol. 2: (ADA) Images & Symbols. (Olson's Library Clip Art Ser.). (Illus.). 9p. (Orig.). 1993. pap. text 23.75 (*1-56984-005-9*) C Olson & Assocs.

— Libraries Through the Seasons Vol. 3: Winter, Spring, Summer & Fall. (Olson's Library Clip Art). (Illus.). 64p. (Orig.). 1995. pap. text 112.00 (*1-56984-020-2*) C Olson & Assocs.

— Libraries Through the Seasons Vol. 3, Pt. 1: Winter. (Olson's Library Clip Art). (Illus.). 16p. (Orig.). 1995. pap. text 33.00 (*1-56984-008-3*) C Olson & Assocs.

— Libraries Through the Seasons Vol. 3, Pt. 3: Summer. (Olson's Library Clip Art). (Illus.). 16p. (Orig.). 1995. pap. text 33.00 (*1-56984-010-5*) C Olson & Assocs.

— Libraries Through the Seasons Vol. 3, Pt. 4: Fall. (Olson's Library Clip Art). (Illus.). 16p. (Orig.). 1995. pap. text 33.00 (*1-56984-011-3*) C Olson & Assocs.

— Olson's Book of Library Clip Art Vol. 1: 204 Original Library Graphics for All Types of Libraries. (Olson's Library Clip Art Ser.). (Illus.). 30p. (Orig.). 1992. pap. text 45.00 (*0-9632754-0-2*) C Olson & Assocs.

Olson, Clair C., ed. see Rickert, Edith.

Olson, Clifford G., jt. auth. see Lynch, David W.

Olson, Colleen M. Domestic Relations Law for Paralegals. LC 93-72661. 270p. (C). 1993. pap. 28.95 (*0-87084-681-7*) Anderson Pub Co.

Olson, Craig R., jt. auth. see Breaza, Michael.

Olson, D. Decision Aids for Selection Problems, Vol. VII. Glynn, P., ed. LC 95-34191. (Series in Operations Research). (Illus.). 293p. 1995. 59.95 (*0-387-94560-1*) Spr-Verlag.

Olson, D. H., ed. & intro. see Wandrei, Howard.

Olson, D. L., et al, eds. Welding: Theory & Practice. (Materials Processing Theory & Practice Ser.: No. 8). 390p. 1990. 216.75 (*0-444-87427-5*, North Holland) Elsevier.

Olson, D. L. & North, T. H., eds. Ferrous Alloy Weldments. 422p. 1992. text 183.00 (*0-87849-544-4*, Pub. by Trans T Pub) Enfield Pubs NH.

Olson, Dale P. Modern Civil Practice in West Virginia. 8th ed. 697p. 1984. 55.00 (*0-614-05907-0*, MICHIE) LEXIS Pub.

Olson, Dale W. Knowing Your Intuitive Mind. 3rd ed. Johnson, David et al, eds. (Illus.). 196p. 1990. per. 14.95 (*1-879246-00-7*) Crystalline Pubns.

— The Pendulum Bridge to Infinite Knowing: Beginning Through Advanced Instruction. rev. ed. Goins, Kalani, ed. Orig. Title: Advanced Pendulum Instruction & Application. (Illus.). 224p. (Orig.). 1997. per. 14.95 (*1-879246-08-2*) Crystalline Pubns.

— Pendulum Charts: Knowing Your Intuitive Mind. (Illus.). 25p. 1989. spiral bd. 14.95 (*1-879246-02-3*) Crystalline Pubns.

Olson, Dana. Prince Madoc: Founder of Clark County Indiana. (Illus.). 128p. 1987. pap. 10.00 (*0-9677903-0-1*) Olson Enter.

Olson, Daniel M., ed. see Nordenskiold, Gustaf E.

Olson, Daniel V. A., jt. auth. see Swatos, William H.

Olson, David, jt. auth. see Olson, Linda.

Olson, David A. The Cost of Select Recreation & Leisure Activities, 1993. 78p. 1994. pap. text 25.00 (*0-614-06283-7*) U CO Busn Res Div.

Olson, David C., jt. ed. see Cuellar, Carol.

Olson, David H. Family Perspectives in Child & Youth Services. LC 88-32006. (Child & Youth Services Ser.: Vol. 11, No. 1). (Illus.). 211p. 1989. text 49.95 (*0-86656-850-6*) Haworth Pr.

Olson, David H., et al, eds. Circumplex Model: Systemic Assessment & Treatment of Families. LC 88-30151. (Journal of Psychotherapy & the Family: Vol. 4, Nos. 1 & 2). (Illus.). 296p. 1989. text 49.95 (*0-86656-776-3*) Haworth Pr.

— Circumplex Model: Systemic Assessment & Treatment of Families. 283p. 1989. pap. 17.95 (*0-86656-955-3*) Haworth Pr.

Olson, David H. & DeFrain, John D. Marriage & the Family: Diversity & Strengths. 3rd ed. LC 99-22761. xxviii, 692p. 1999. text 63.95 (*0-7674-1209-5*, 12095) Mayfield Pub.

Olson, David H. & Hanson, Meredith K., eds. 2001: Preparing Families for the Future: NCFR Presidential Report. (Illus.). 40p. (Orig.). (C). 1990. pap. text 13.00 (*0-916174-26-3*) Natl Coun Family.

***Olson, David H., et al.** Building Relationships: Developing Skills for Life. (Illus.). 258p. (YA). (gr. 6 up). 1999. pap. 14.95 (*0-9671983-0-5*) Life Innov.

— Building Relationships: Teacher's Manual. 128p. 1999. pap., teacher ed. write for info. (*0-9671983-1-3*) Life Innov.

Olson, David H., et al. Families: What Makes Them Work. 316p. (C). 1989. 42.00 (*0-8039-2011-3*); pap. text 22.50 (*0-8039-2854-8*) Sage.

— Families, What Makes Them Work. LC 89-24231. 315p. 1989. reprint ed. pap. 97.70 (*0-608-01529-6*, 2059573) Bks Demand.

***Olson, David H., et al.** Marriage & the Family Study Guide: Diversity & Strength. 3rd ed. iv, 220p. (C). 1999. pap. text 19.95 (*0-7674-1211-7*, 1211-7) Mayfield Pub.

Olson, David H., jt. ed. see Miller, Brent C.

Olson, David J., jt. auth. see Lipsky, Michael.

Olson, David J., jt. ed. see Gardiner, John A.

Olson, David L., et al, eds. Handbook Vol. 6: Welding, Brazing & Soldering. rev. ed. LC 90-115. (Illus.). 1299p. 1993. 186.00 (*0-87170-382-3*, 6480) ASM.

Olson, David L., jt. auth. see Evans, James R.

Olson, David L., ed. see Daly, Lawrence W.

***Olson, David Louis.** Introduction to Information Systems Project Management. LC 00-27782. 2001. pap. write for info. (*0-07-229498-1*, McGrw-H College) McGrw-H Hghr Educ.

Olson, David M. Democratic Legislative Institutions: A Comparative View. LC 94-18913. (Comparative Politics Ser.). (Illus.). 200p. (gr. 13). 1994. text 74.95 (*1-56324-314-8*) M E Sharpe.

Olson, David M. Democratic Legislative Institutions: A Comparative View. LC 94-18913. (Comparative Politics Ser.). (Illus.). 200p. (gr. 13). 1994. pap. text 32.95 (*1-56324-315-6*) M E Sharpe.

Olson, David M. & Franks, C. E. S., eds. Representation & Policy Formation in Federal Systems: Canada & the United States. LC 93-19575. 325p. 1993. pap. 24.95 (*0-87772-340-0*) UCB IGS.

Olson, David M. & Mezey, Michael L., eds. Legislatures in the Policy Process: The Dilemmas of Economic Policy. (Advances in Political Science Ser.). (Illus.). 237p. (C). 1991. text 65.00 (*0-521-38103-7*) Cambridge U Pr.

Olson, David M. & Norton, Philip, eds. The New Parliaments of Central & Eastern Europe. 264p. (C). 1996. 52.50 (*0-7146-4715-2*, Pub. by F Cass Pubs); pap. 24.50 (*0-7146-4261-4*, Pub. by F Cass Pubs) Intl Spec Bk.

Olson, David R. Cognitive Development: The Child's Acquisition of Diagonality. 240p. 1996. pap. 29.95 (*0-8058-2302-6*) L Erlbaum Assocs.

— The World on Paper: The Conceptual & Cognitive Implications of Writing & Reading. (Illus.). 338p. 1996. pap. text 22.95 (*0-521-57558-3*) Cambridge U Pr.

Olson, David R., ed. Media & Symbols: The Forms of Expression, Communication, & Education. LC 06-16938. (National Society for the Study of Education Publication Ser.: No. 73, Pt. 1). 560p. 1974. 10.00 (*0-226-60114-5*) U Ch Pr.

Olson, David R. & Bialystok, Ellen. Spatial Cognition: The Structure & Development of Mental Representations of Spatial Relations. 296p. 1983. text 69.95 (*0-89859-252-6*) L Erlbaum Assocs.

Olson, David R. & Torrance, Nancy. The Handbook of Education & Human Development: A Student's Guide to the Information & Communication Technologies. LC 98-28704. 272p. 1999. pap. 34.95 (*1-85554-823-2*) Blackwell Pubs.

— The Handbook of Education & Human Development: New Models of Learning, Teaching & Schooling. 816p. 1998. pap. 34.95 (*0-631-21186-1*) Blackwell Pubs.

Olson, David R. & Torrance, Nancy, eds. Literacy & Orality. (Illus.). 300p. (C). 1991. text 69.95 (*0-521-39217-9*); pap. text 23.95 (*0-521-39850-9*) Cambridge U Pr.

— Modes of Thought: Explorations in Culture & Cognition. LC 97-591. (Illus.). 313p. (C). 1996. text 59.95 (*0-521-49610-1*); pap. text 21.95 (*0-521-56644-4*) Cambridge U Pr.

Olson, David R., jt. ed. see Van Holthoon, Frits.

Olson, David V. Badges & Distinctive Branch Insignia of the U. S. Army Quartermaster Corps, 1775-1995: U. S. Army Quartermaster Corps Branch Insignia, 1775-1995. (Illus.). 60p. (Orig.). 1994. pap. 15.00 (*0-929757-16-5*) D V Olson RQM.

— Badges & Distinctive Insignia of the Kingdom of Saudi Arabia Vol. 1: Saudi Arabian Army Insignia. (Illus.). 192p. 1981. pap. 5.00 (*0-9609690-0-4*) D V Olson RQM.

Olson, Dean. Industrial Arts for the General Shop. 4th ed. 1973. text 24.28 (*0-13-459131-3*) P-H.

Olson, Dean, jt. auth. see Carey, Omer.

Olson, Dennis L. Cougars: Solitary Spirits. LC 96-13258. (Wildlife Ser.). (Illus.). 144p. (Orig.). 1996. pap. 14.95 (*1-55971-574-X*, NorthWord Pr) Creat Pub Intl.

— Shared Spirits: Wildlife & Native Americans. 176p. 1999. pap. text 19.95 (*1-55971-676-2*) NorthSound Music.

— Special Gifts. LC 98-49215. (Illus.). 1999. pap. text 12.95 (*1-55971-679-7*, NorthWord Pr) Creat Pub Intl.

— Way of the Whitetail: Magic & Mystery. LC 94-20648. (Illus.). 160p. 1994. 35.00 (*1-55971-427-1*, NorthWord Pr) Creat Pub Intl.

— Wisdom Warrior & Other Animal Legends. LC 99-21047. (Illus.). 64p. 1999. 9.95 (*1-55971-709-2*, NorthWord Pr) Creat Pub Intl.

Olson, Dennis T. Deuteronomy & the Death of Moses: A Theological Reading. LC 94-12729. (Overtures to Bibical Theology Ser.). 208p. 1994. pap. 19.00 (*0-8006-2639-7*, 1-2639, Fortress Pr) Augsburg Fortress.

— Numbers. (Interpretation Ser.). 208p. 1996. 24.95 (*0-8042-3104-4*) Westminster John Knox.

Olson, Don. Movie. 1990. pap. 8.95 (*0-8216-2008-8*, Univ Books) Carol Pub Group.

***Olson, Donald.** London for Dummies. (For Dummies Ser.). 384p. 2000. pap. 15.99 (*0-7645-6194-4*) IDG Bks.

— Queer Corners. 1999. pap. text 15.95 (*0-9623683-6-9*) BridgeCity Bks.

Olson, E. Van. Retiree Nonpension Benefits: Management Guidelines. (Current Issues Ser.: No. 2). 32p. 1993. reprint ed. 5.50 (*0-89215-137-4*) U Cal LA Indus Rel.

Olson, Edna M., jt. auth. see Sperandio, Richard G.

Olson, Edward C. & Christoffersen, Ralph E., eds. Computer-Assisted Drug Design. LC 79-21038. (ACS Symposium Ser.: Vol. 112). 631p. 1979. reprint ed. pap. 195.70 (*0-608-03052-X*, 206350500007) Bks Demand.

Olson, Edward C., jt. auth. see Jones, Laurence.

Olson, Edward C., jt. ed. see Christoffersen, Ralph E.

Olson, Elder. Aristotle's Poetics & English Literature: A Collection of Critical Essays. LC 65-24430. (Gemini Bks: Patterns of Literary Criticism). 264p. reprint ed. pap. 81.90 (*0-8357-5734-X*, 202673700051) Bks Demand.

— Collected Poems. LC 63-22589. 1993. pap. 3.95 (*0-226-62914-7*, PP8) U Ch Pr.

An Asterisk (*) at the beginning of an entry indicates that the title is appearing for the first time.

— Last Poems. LC 84-136. 72p. (C). 1996. pap. 8.95 (*0-226-62898-1*) U Ch Pr.

— Olson's Penny Arcade. LC 75-5080. 1993. reprint ed. pap. 2.95 (*0-226-62894-9*, PP16) U Ch Pr.

— On Value in the Arts & Other Essays. LC 75-9057. 380p. 1992. lib. bdg. 24.00 (*0-226-62895-7*) U Ch Pr.

— Plays & Poems, 1948-58. LC 58-11951. (Midway Reprint Ser.). 179p. reprint ed. pap. 55.50 (*0-608-09029-8*, 206966400005) Bks Demand.

— Plays & Poems, 1948-58. LC 58-11951. (Midway Reprint Ser.). x, 170p. 1993. reprint ed. pap. text 5.95 (*0-226-62896-5*) U Ch Pr.

— Poetry of Dylan Thomas. LC 54-9580. 1993. pap. 1.75 (*0-226-62917-1*, P72) U Ch Pr.

Olson, Eleanor. Wayne Estes: A Hero's Legacy. (Illus.). (YA). (gr. 7-12). 1991. pap. text 6.00 (*0-9628317-0-0*) E Olson.

Olson, Eleonora & Olson, Ethel. Yust for Fun. (Illus.). 60p. 1979. reprint ed. pap. 2.50 (*0-9602914-1-5*) Eggs Pr.

Olson, Elizabeth, ed. Dollars for College: The Quick Guide to Financial Aid for Education. LC 95-1364. (Dollars for College Ser.). 79p. 1997. pap. 6.95 (*0-89434-196-0*) Ferguson.

— Dollars for College Disabled: The Quick Guide to Financial Aid for the Disabled. 1997. pap. 6.95 (*0-89434-181-2*, GP186) Ferguson.

Olson, Elizabeth, jt. auth. see Simpson, Alan.

Olson, Elizabeth A., ed. Big Opportunities for Women: The Directory of Women's Organizations. LC 96-50328. 450p. (Orig.). 1996. pap. 39.95 (*0-89434-183-9*, F646) Ferguson.

Olson, Elizabeth A., jt. auth. see Young, Rosalie F.

Olson, Elizabeth A., jt. ed. see Young, Rosalie F.

Olson, Ellen, et al, eds. Controversies in Ethics in Long-Term Care. LC 94-23161. 176p. 1994. 34.95 (*0-8261-8600-9*) Springer Pub.

Olson, Eric. So Close & Yet So Far: Mexico's Mid-Term Elections & the Struggle for Democracy. Washington Office on Latin America, ed. 44p. (C). 1997. pap. text. write for info. (*0-929513-38-X*) WOLA.

Olson, Eric T. The Human Animal: Personal Identity Without Psychology. LC 96-7018. (Philosophy of Mind Ser.). 200p. 1997. 45.00 (*0-19-510506-0*) OUP.

— The Human Animal: Personal Identity Without Psychology. 200p. 1999. pap. 14.95 (*0-19-513423-0*) OUP.

Olson, Ernest. How to Hang Loose in an Uptight World: Discovering Leisure in Everyday Life. 16.95 (*0-933025-71-8*) Angel Dawn.

— Personal Development & Discovery Through Leisure. 300p. (C). 1999. per. 32.95 (*0-7872-6296-X*, 41629602) Kendall-Hunt.

Olson, Ernest W. & Lawson, Evald B. Augustana Book Concern & Christine Nilsson's Visit to Brockton, Mass. in November, 1870. (Augustana Historical Society Publications: Vol. 3). 96p. 1933. pap. 3.00 (*0-910184-03-8*) Augustana.

Olson, Ernst W., et al. History of the Swedes of Illinois, 2 vols., Set. Scott, Franklyn D., ed. LC 78-15844. (Scandinavians in America Ser.). (Illus.). 1979. reprint ed. lib. bdg. 101.95 (*0-405-11656-X*) Ayer.

Olson, Esther E. Let's Make Up. 1945. pap. 3.25 (*0-8222-0653-6*) Dramatists Play.

Olson, Ethel, jt. auth. see Olson, Eleonora.

Olson, Eugene E., jt. auth. see Tobin, Michael C.

Olson, Everett C. Morphological Integration. LC 99-24323. 1999. pap. text 19.00 (*0-226-62905-8*) U Ch Pr.

— The Other Side of the Medal: A Paleobiologist Reflects on the Art & Serendipity of Science. LC 90-5612. (Illus.). xiv, 182p. 1990. 19.95 (*0-939923-13-0*) M & W Pub Co.

Olson, Everett C., jt. ed. see Czerkas, Sylvia J.

Olson, F. W., et al, eds. Symposium on Small Hydropower & Fisheries. LC 85 72260. 497p. 1985. text 29.00 (*0-913235-37-7*, 530.11C) Am Fisheries Soc.

Olson, Frederick I., jt. auth. see Anderson, Harry H.

Olson, G. B., ed. see Cohen, Morris.

Olson, G. Elaine. Blest Be the Tie. LC 95-70333. 278p. (Orig.). 1995. pap. 8.95 (*0-9645085-3-2*) Prtnrshp Bk Servs.

Olson, G. Keith. Counseling Teenagers: The Complete Christian Guide to Understanding & Helping Adolescents. 528p. 1984. pap. 21.99 (*0-931529-67-0*) Group Pub.

Olson, Gary & Moran, Thomas, eds. Experimental Comparisons of Usability Evaluations Methods: A Special Issue of Human-Computer Interactions. 113p. 1998. pap. write for info. (*0-8058-9813-1*) L Erlbaum Assocs.

Olson, Gary A., ed. Philosophy, Rhetoric, Literary Criticism: Inter-Views. LC 93-38349. 264p. (C). 1994. 26.95 (*0-8093-1908-X*) S Ill U Pr.

Olson, Gary A., et al, eds. Advanced Placement English: Theory, Politics & Pedagogy. LC 89-31480. 205p. (Orig.). (C). 1989. pap. text 24.00 (*0-86709-246-7*, 0246, Pub. by Boynton Cook Pubs) Heinemann.

Olson, Gary A. & Dobrin, Sidney I., eds. Composition Theory for the Postmodern Classroom. LC 94-8605. 360p. (C). 1994. text 64.50 (*0-7914-2305-0*); pap. text 21.95 (*0-7914-2306-9*) State U NY Pr.

Olson, Gary A. & Drew, Julie, eds. Landmark Essays on Advanced Composition. (Landmark Essays Ser.: Vol. 10). 250p. (Orig.). 1996. pap. 19.95 (*1-880393-25-5*, Hermagoras) L Erlbaum Assocs.

Olson, Gary A. & Gale, Irene, eds. Interviews: Cross-Disciplinary Perspectives on Rhetoric & Literacy. LC 91-17653. 200p. 1991. 21.95 (*0-8093-1737-0*) S Ill U Pr.

Olson, Gary A. & Hirsh, Elizabeth, eds. Women Writing Culture. LC 95-34122. (SUNY Series, Interruptions). 204p. (C). 1995. text 59.50 (*0-7914-2963-6*); pap. text 16.95 (*0-7914-2964-4*) State U NY Pr.

Olson, Gary A. & Taylor, Todd W., eds. Publishing in Rhetoric & Composition. LC 96-36302. 247p. (C). 1997. text 59.50 (*0-7914-3395-1*); pap. text 19.95 (*0-7914-3396-X*) State U NY Pr.

Olson, Gary A. & Worsham, Lynn, eds. Race, Rhetoric, & the Postcolonial. LC 98-34971. 259p. (C). 1998. pap. text 18.95 (*0-7914-4174-1*) State U NY Pr.

— Race, Rhetoric, & the Postcolonial. LC 98-34971. 259p. (C). 1999. text 57.50 (*0-7914-4173-3*) State U NY Pr.

Olson, Gary M., et al, eds. Coordination Theory & Collaboration Technology. (Volume in the Computers, Cognition, & Work Ser.). 350p. 1999. write for info. (*0-8058-3403-6*) L Erlbaum Assocs.

Olson, Gene. Skunk River Anthology. (Illus.). 166p. 1992. pap. 9.95 (*1-878488-59-7*) Quixote Pr IA.

Olson, Georgine N., ed. Fiction Acquisition/Fiction Management: Education & Training. LC 97-49336. 120p. 1998. 29.95 (*0-7890-0391-0*) Haworth Pr.

Olson, Georgine N. & Allen, Barbara, eds. Cooperative Collection Management: The Conspectus Approach. LC 94-20036. 107p. 1994. 32.95 (*1-55570-200-7*) Neal-Schuman.

Olson, Gerald W. Soils & the Environment: A Guide to Their Applications. 191p. 1982. pap. 19.95 (*0-412-23760-1*, 6587) Chapman & Hall.

Olson, Glending, ed. see Chaucer, Geoffrey.

***Olson, Gordon C.** Holiness & Sin. (Illus.). 55p. 1999. reprint ed. pap. 1.00 (*0-9664597-3-3*) Rev Theol Prom.

Olson, Gordon C. The Kindness of God Our Saviour. (Illus.). 126p. 1993. pap. text 2.50 (*0-9664597-1-7*) Rev Theol Prom.

***Olson, Gordon C.** The Moral Government of God. (Illus.). 48p. 1999. reprint ed. pap. 1.00 (*0-9664597-2-5*) Rev Theol Prom.

Olson, Gordon C. The Truth Shall Make You Free. large type ed. (Illus.). 240p. 1998. reprint ed. pap. text 4.00 (*0-9664597-0-9*) Rev Theol Prom.

Olson, Gordon L. A City Renewed: A History of Grand Rapids, Michigan since World War II. (Illus.). 184p. 1996. 29.95 (*0-9617708-6-4*) GRMI Hist Comm.

— The Grand Rapids Furniture Record, 1900-1930: Printed Index to the Microfilm Edition. LC 97-30882. 1997. 50.00 (*0-88354-179-3*) N Ross.

— A Grand Rapids Sampler. LC 92-72735. (Illus.). 240p. (C). 1992. 29.95 (*0-9617708-3-X*) GRMI Hist Comm.

Olson, Grant, ed. Crossroads: General Issue. (Interdisciplinary Journal of Southeast Asian Studies: Vol. 4.2). 114p. 1989. pap. 12.00 (*1-877979-89-9*) SE Asia.

— Crossroads: General Issue. (Interdisciplinary Journal of Southeast Asian Studies: Vol. 5.2). 162p. 1990. pap. 12.00 (*1-877979-91-0*) SE Asia.

— Crossroads: General Issue. (Interdisciplinary Journal of Southeast Asian Studies: Vol. 6.2). 142p. 1991. pap. 12.00 (*1-877979-93-7*) SE Asia.

— Crossroads: General Issue. (Interdisciplinary Journal of Southeast Asian Studies: Vol. 7.1). 139p. 1992. pap 12.00 (*1-877979-94-5*) SE Asia.

— Crossroads: General Issue. (Interdisciplinary Journal of Southeast Asian Studies: Vol. 8.1). 178p. 1993. pap. 12.00 (*1-877979-96-1*) SE Asia.

— Modern Southeast Asian Literature in Translation: A Resource for Teaching. LC 98-127912. 116p. 1997. pap. text 12.95 (*1-881044-14-9*) ASU Prog SE Asian.

Olson, Grant A., tr. see Payutto, Phra P.

Olson, Greg. Aikido: A Beginner's Text. 124p. (C). 1996. pap. text 31.95 (*0-7872-2830-3*) Kendall-Hunt.

Olson, Gregory A. Mansfield & Vietnam: A Study in Rhetorical Adaptation. 1995. 39.95 (*0-87013-386-1*) Mich St U Pr.

Olson, Greta J., ed. see Comes, Juan Baptista.

Olson, Gretchen. Joyride. LC 97-70580. 200p. (YA). (gr. 7-12). 1999. pap. 8.95 (*1-56397-758-3*) Boyds Mills Pr.

Olson, Gust, tr. see Tumonov, Alla.

Olson, H. W. The Earthworms of Ohio. (Bulletin Ser.: No. 17). 1928. pap. text 2.00 (*0-86727-016-0*) Ohio Bio Survey.

Olson, Harry A. 8 Keys to Becoming Wildly Successful & Happy, 1. 1998. pap. text 16.95 (*1-885640-40-4*) Intl Netwrk.

— Power Strategies of Jesus Christ: Principles of Leadership from the Greatest Motivator of All Time. LC 98-47544. 192p. 1999. 5.99 (*0-517-20334-0*) Random Hse Value.

— Power Strategies of Jesus Christ: Principles of Leadership from the Greatest Motivator of All Time. LC 91-11891. 192p. 1991. reprint ed. pap. 9.95 (*0-89243-505-4*, Liguori Triumph) Liguori Pubns.

Olson, Harry F. Music, Physics, & Engineering. enl. rev. ed. (Illus.). 460p. 1966. pap. 10.95 (*0-486-21769-8*) Dover.

Olson, Helen, ed. Please Listen . . . LC 94-69790. 153p. 1994. pap. text 5.95 (*1-882972-52-X*, 3155) Queenship Pub.

Olson, Helen, jt. auth. see Olson, Virgil J.

Olson Higgins, Susan. There's a Giggle in My Pocket. 2nd rev. ed. Orig. Title: What Do You Do With a Poem or Two?. (Illus.). 100p. (J). (ps-6). 1992. pap. write for info. (*0-939973-43-X*, 0013) Pumpkin Pr Pub Hse.

Olson, Hilary C., jt. ed. see Graham, Stephan A.

***Olson, Ivan.** The Arts & Critical Thinking in American Education. LC 98 30497. (Critical Perspectives on Culture & Society Ser.). 1999. write for info. (*0-313-30844-6*, Greenwood Pr) Greenwood.

Olson, Ivan. The Arts & Critical Thinking in American Education. LC 98-30497. 160p. 1999. 59.95 (*0-89789-694-7*, Bergin & Garvey) Greenwood.

Olson, Iver. Baptism & Spiritual Life. rev. ed. 86p. 1984. reprint ed. pap. 4.50 (*1-58572-011-9*) Ambasdor Pubns.

Olson, J. M., et al, eds. Green Photosynthetic Bacteria. LC 88-12419. (Illus.). 338p. 1988. 85.00 (*0-306-42920-9*, Plenum Trade) Perseus Pubng.

Olson, Jack. Deaf Communities: A Worldwide Perspective. (Illus.). 96p. (Orig.). 1995. pap. text 9.95 (*1-884362-01-X*) Butte Pubns.

Olson, Jack, jt. auth. see Bragg, Bernard.

Olson, Jack, jt. auth. see Price, Wilson.

Olson, James. Clinical Pharmacology Made Ridiculously Simple. (Illus.). 162p. (C). 1998. pap. text 19.95 (*0-940780-17-8*) MedMaster.

Olson, James, jt. auth. see Roberts, Randy.

Olson, James A., et al. Modern Nutrition in Health & Disease, 2 vols., 1. 8th ed. (Illus.). 2200p. 1993. lib. bdg. 67.50 (*0-8121-1751-4*) Lppncott W & W.

— Modern Nutrition in Health & Disease, 2 vols., 2. 8th ed. (Illus.). 3036p. 1993. lib. bdg. 67.50 (*0-8121-1752-2*) Lppncott W & W.

— Modern Nutrition in Health & Disease, 2 vols., Set. 8th ed. (Illus.). 2200p. 1993. lib. bdg. 99.50 (*0-8121-1485-X*) Lppncott W & W.

Olson, James C. Serving the University of Missouri: A Memoir of Campus & System Administration. (Illus.). 232p. 1993. text 34.95 (*0-8262-0924-6*) U of Mo Pr.

Olson, James C. & Naugle, Ronald C. History of Nebraska. 3rd ed. LC 96-27320. (Illus.). xii, 506p. 1997. pap. 25.00 (*0-8032-8605-8*, Bison Books); text 45.00 (*0-8032-3559-3*) U of Nebr Pr.

Olson, James C. & Olson, Vera B. The University of Missouri: An Illustrated History. LC 88-1158. (Illus.). 312p. 1988. 29.95 (*0-8262-0678-6*) U of Mo Pr.

Olson, James D. Minnesota Residential Real Estate. 1994. ring bd., suppl. ed. 45.00 (*0-318-68686-4*, MICHIE) LEXIS Pub.

— Minnesota Residential Real Estate, Issue 16. 210p. 1999. ring bd. write for info. (*0-327-01083-5*, 8185026) LEXIS Pub.

***Olson, James D.** Minnesota Residential Real Estate, Issue 17. Davidson, Neil, ed. 150p. 1999. ring bd. write for info. (*0-327-01698-1*, 8185027) LEXIS Pub.

Olson, James D. Minnesota Residential Real Estate, 2 vols., Set. 980p. 1994. spiral bd. 179.00 (*0-88063-862-1*, 81846-10, MICHIE) LEXIS Pub.

Olson, James E., et al, eds. Historical Dictionary of the British Empire. LC 94-871. 1328p. 1996. lib. bdg. 195.00 (*0-313-27917-9*) Greenwood.

Olson, James M., et al, eds. Relative Deprivation & Social Comparison: The Ontario Symposium, Vol. 4. (Ontario Symposia on Personality Ser.). 272p. (C). 1986. text 49.95 (*0-89859-704-8*) L Erlbaum Assocs.

Olson, James M. & Zanna, Mark P., eds. Self-Inference Processes: The Ontario Symposium, Vol. 6. 336p. (C). 1990. text 69.95 (*0-8058-0551-6*) L Erlbaum Assocs.

Olson, James M., jt. auth. see Maio, Gregory R.

Olson, James M., jt. ed. see Roese, Neal J.

Olson, James M., jt. ed. see Zanna, Mark P.

Olson, James N., jt. auth. see Roberts, Randy.

Olson, James S. Dark Mirror. LC 97-74967. 1998. text 35.00 (*0-312-17767-4*) St Martin.

— Dictionary of United States Economic History. LC 91-32193. 680p. 1992. lib. bdg. 99.50 (*0-313-26532-1*, OEH/, Greenwood Pr) Greenwood.

— The Ethnic Dimension in American History. 3rd rev. ed. 384p. (C). 1999. pap. text 19.50 (*1-881089-87-8*) Brandywine Press.

— An Ethnohistorical Dictionary of China. LC 97-27110. 448p. 1998. lib. bdg. 89.50 (*0-313-28853-4*, Greenwood Pr) Greenwood.

— The Historical Dictionary of the 1960s. LC 97-2231. 560p. 1999. lib. bdg. 95.00 (*0-313-29271-X*, Greenwood Pr) Greenwood.

— Historical Dictionary of the Nineteen Twenties: From World War I to the New Deal, 1919-1933. LC 87-29987. 420p. 1988. lib. bdg. 69.50 (*0-313-25683-7*, OHD/, Greenwood Pr) Greenwood.

— The History of Cancer: An Annotated Bibliography, 3. LC 89-2174. (Bibliographies & Indexes in Medical Studies: No. 3). 434p. 1989. lib. bdg. 99.50 (*0-313-25889-9*, OHY/, Greenwood Pr) Greenwood.

— The Indians of Latin America: An Ethnohistorical Dictionary. LC 90-47503. 528p. 1991. lib. bdg. 85.00 (*0-313-26387-6*, OIL/, Greenwood Pr) Greenwood.

— The Peoples of Africa. LC 95-36433. 696p. 1996. lib. bdg. 110.00 (*0-313-27918-7*, Greenwood Pr) Greenwood.

— Slave Life in America: A Historiography & Selected Bibliography. 128p. (Orig.). (C). 1983. lib. bdg. 47.50 (*0-8191-3285-3*) U Pr of Amer.

— The Vietnam War: Handbook of the Literature & Research. LC 92-25626. 536p. 1993. lib. bdg. 85.00 (*0-313-27422-3*, OVA, Greenwood Pr) Greenwood.

Olson, James S., ed. Dictionary of the Vietnam War. LC 87-12023. 593p. 1988. lib. bdg. 79.50 (*0-313-24943-1*, OVW/, Greenwood Pr) Greenwood.

— Historical Dictionary of the New Deal: From Inauguration to Preparation for War. LC 84-19792. 611p. 1985. lib. bdg. 79.50 (*0-313-23873-1*, ODN/, Greenwood Pr) Greenwood.

— The Historical Dictionary of the 1970s. LC 98-46818. 424p. 1999. lib. bdg. 89.50 (*0-313-30543-9*) Greenwood.

Olson, James S., et al, eds. Encyclopedia of American Indian Civil Rights. LC 96-35352. 448p. 1997. 65.00 (*0-313-29338-4*, Greenwood Pr) Greenwood.

— Historical Dictionary of European Imperialism. LC 90-38413. 804p. 1991. lib. bdg. 115.00 (*0-313-26257-8*, OIM, Greenwood Pr) Greenwood.

— Historical Dictionary of the British Empire: A-J, Vol. 1. LC 94-871. 632p. 1996. lib. bdg. 195.00 (*0-313-29366-X*, Greenwood Pr) Greenwood.

— Historical Dictionary of the British Empire: K-Z, Vol. 2. LC 94-871. 656p. 1996. lib. bdg. 195.00 (*0-313-29367-8*, Greenwood Pr) Greenwood.

— Historical Dictionary of the Spanish Empire, 1402-1975. LC 91-8250. 720p. 1991. lib. bdg. 105.00 (*0-313-26413-9*, OSR, Greenwood Pr) Greenwood.

Olson, James S. & Olson, Judith E. The Cuban Americans: From Trauma to Triumph. LC 94-34365. (Immigrant Heritage of America Ser.). 1995. 33.00 (*0-8057-8430-6*, Twyne); pap. 20.00 (*0-8057-8439-X*, Twyne) Mac Lib Ref.

Olson, James S. & Roberts, Randy. Where the Domino Fell: America & Vietnam, 1945 to 1990. (Illus.). 321p. 1997. reprint ed. text 20.00 (*0-7881-5138-X*) DIANE Pub.

— Where the Domino Fell: America & Vietnam, 1945-1990. (Illus.). 321p. 1998. pap. text 14.00 (*0-7881-5575-X*) DIANE Pub.

— Where the Domino Fell: America & Vietnam, 1945-1995. 3rd ed. 326p. (C). 1999. pap. text 19.50 (*1-881089-79-7*) Brandywine Press.

Olson, James S. & Wilson, Raymond. Native Americans in the Twentieth Century. (Illus.). 248p. 1986. text 29.95 (*0-252-01286-0*); pap. text 14.95 (*0-252-01285-2*) U of Ill Pr.

Olson, James S., et al. An Ethnohistorical Dictionary of the Russian & Soviet Empires. LC 93-18149. 848p. 1994. lib. bdg. 145.00 (*0-313-27497-5*, OEA/, Greenwood Pr) Greenwood.

— U. S. in the 20th Century: America, 1900-1945, 2 vols., Vol. 1. 333p. 1995. pap. text 32.95 (*0-312-10104-X*) St Martin.

Olson, James S., jt. auth. see Roberts, Randy.

Olson, James S., ed. see Riordon, William L.

***Olson, James Stuart.** Historical Dictionary of the 1950's. LC 99-49694. 360p. 2000. lib. bdg. 79.95 (*0-313-30619-2*) Greenwood.

Olson, Janet L. Envisioning Writing: Toward an Integration of Drawing & Writing. LC 92-7322. 176p. (C). 1992. pap. text 23.00 (*0-435-08700-2*, 08700) Heinemann.

Olson, Janet S. Your Total Communications Image. Scanlon, Kelly, ed. LC 96-71252. (Self-Study Sourcebook Ser.). (Illus.). 177p. 1997. pap. 15.95 (*1-57294-075-1*, 13-0025) SkillPath Pubns.

Olson, Jean L., jt. auth. see Jennette, J. Charles.

Olson, Jeannette R., et al. Public School Restructuring: A Selected Bibliography. LC 95-23157. (Educational Technology Selected Bibliography Ser.). 50p. 1996. pap. 24.95 (*0-87778-291-1*) Educ Tech Pubns.

Olson, Jeannine E. Calvin & Social Welfare: Deacons & the Bourse Francaise. LC 86-43234. (Illus.). 344p. 1989. 60.00 (*0-941664-85-6*) Susquehanna U Pr.

Olson, Jeff. The Agile Manager's Guide to Cutting Costs. LC 97-90826. (Agile Manager Ser.). (Illus.). 96p. 1997. pap. 9.95 (*0-9659193-3-1*) Velocity Busn.

— The Agile Manager's Guide to Getting Organized. (Agile Manager Ser.). (Illus.). 96p. 1997. pap. 9.95 (*0-9659193-0-7*) Velocity Busn.

— The Agile Manager's Guide to Giving Great Presentations. LC 97-90829. (Agile Manager Ser.). (Illus.). 96p. 1997. pap. 9.95 (*0-9659193-1-5*) Velocity Busn.

Olson, Jenni, ed. The Ultimate Guide to Lesbian & Gay Film & Video. LC 95-72972. (Illus.). 350p. (Orig.). 1996. pap. 25.00 (*1-85242-339-0*) Serpents Tail.

Olson, Jerome A., jt. auth. see Gamkhar, Shama.

Olson, Jerry, jt. auth. see Whitman, John.

Olson, Jerry C. David D. Clarke: Narrative of a Surveyor & Engineer in the Pacific Northwest 1864-1920. (Illus.). 224p. 1996. 39.95 (*0-9642883-3-8*) J C Olson.

Olson, Jerry C. & Sentis, Keith, eds. Advertising & Consumer Psychology, Vol. 3. LC 86-12219. 302p. 1986. 55.00 (*0-275-92154-9*, C21543, Praeger Pubs) Greenwood.

Olson, Jerry C., jt. auth. see Peter, J. Paul.

Olson, Jerry C., jt. ed. see Reynolds, Thomas J.

Olson, Jim. Environmental Law: A Citizens Guide in the 1980's. 344p. 1981. pap. 21.95 (*0-943806-01-1*) Neahtawanta Pr.

— The Reindeer & the Easter Bunny. Van Vleck, Jane & Olson, Sally, eds. (Illus.). 18p. (Orig.). (J). (gr. 1-4). 1981. pap. 6.95 (*0-943806-00-3*) Neahtawanta Pr.

Olson, Jim & Kozar, Elaine. Half Headed People. (Green Legend Ser.). (Illus.). 80p. (Orig.). pap. 7.95 (*0-943806-04-6*) Neahtawanta Pr.

Olson, Jim, jt. auth. see Olson, Lori.

***Olson, John.** Echo Regime. 94p. 2000. pap. 9.00 (*0-9675144-3-6*, Black Sq) Neko Buildings.

Olson, John. Eggs & Mirrors. (Illus.). 28p. 1999. 28.00 (*1-890654-17-5*); pap. 8.00 (*1-890654-16-7*) Wood Work.

— Too Proud to Beg: Self-Empowerment for Today's Dog. LC 96-85788. (Illus.). 96p. (Orig.). 1997. pap. 10.95 (*0-8362-2772-7*) Andrews & McMeel.

— Understanding Teaching: Beyond Expertise. (Developing Teachers & Teaching Ser.). 160p. 1991. 123.00 (*0-335-09289-6*); pap. 35.95 (*0-335-09288-8*) OpUniv Pr.

Olson, John E. Anywhere - Anytime. (Illus.). 238p. 1991. 13.50 (*0-9644432-2-8*) J E Olson.

— The Guerrilla & the Hostage. LC 95-152641. (Illus.). 256p. (Orig.). 1994. pap. 13.50 (*0-9644432-0-1*) J E Olson.

— Twenty-First Virginia Cavalry. (Virginia Regimental Histories Ser.). (Illus.). 91p. 1989. 19.95 (*0-930919-81-5*) H E Howard.

Olson, John F. & Goldstein, Arnold A. The Inclusion of Students with Disabilities & Limited English Proficient Students in Large-scale Assessments: A Summary of Recent Progress. LC 97-215363. 117p. 1997. pap. write for info. (*0-16-049132-0*) USGPO.

Olson, John F., jt. auth. see Johnston, Joseph J.

Olson, John F., jt. ed. see Goodman, Amy L.

Olson, John M., et al. Wisconsin Corporations. 2nd ed. LC 96-137930. 700p. 1995. text. write for info. (*0-7620-0035-X*) West Group.

O

Olson, John R. Collecting the Mercedes-Benz SL, 1954-1993. 235p. 1993. 19.95 (0-9635394-0-X); pap. 17.95 (0-9635394-1-8) SL Mkt Letter.

— Facility & Equipment Management for Sport Directors. LC 96-28490. (Sport Director Ser.). (Illus.). 168p. (Orig.). 1996. pap. text 22.00 (0-87322-940-1, POLS0940) Human Kinetics.

— Make Money Owning Your Car (And Enjoy Every Minute) rev. ed. (Illus.). 184p. 1976. 9.95 (0-686-09315-1) Electronic Flea.

***Olson, John R.** The Mercedes-Benz SL Experience: Five Decades of the Mercedes-Benz SL. 3rd rev. ed. Orig. Title: Collecting the Mercedes-Benz SL, 1954-1993. (Illus.). 330p. 2000. 49.95 (0-9635394-2-6) SL Mkt Letter.

Olson, John R., jt. auth. see Schniederjans, Marc J.

Olson, Jon, ed. Minnesota Business Almanac: Minnesota's Guide to Business, 1996-1997. (Illus.). 740p. (Orig.). 1996. pap. write for info. (0-9641908-7-7) MSP Communs.

Olson, Joseph E. Federal Taxation of Intellectual Property Transfers. 400p. ring bd. 70.00 (0-318-21432-6, 00597) NY Law Pub.

— Federal Taxation of Intellectual Property Transfers. 500p. 1986. ring bd. 85.00 (0-317-05389-2, 00597) NY Law Pub.

Olson, Joubert W. Craps: There are No Secrets to This Game! LC 93-93744. (Illus.). 160p. 1993. pap. 19.95 (1-883067-24-3) South Shore.

Olson, Joy, jt. auth. see Isacson, Adam.

Olson, Judith. Writing Skills Success in 20 Minutes a Day. LC 98-17969. 1998. pap. 16.00 (1-57685-128-1) LrningExprss.

Olson, Judith E., jt. auth. see Olson, James S.

Olson, Judith F. Grammar Essentials. Gish, Jim, ed. LC 97-4361. (Basics Made Easy Ser.). 192p. (Orig.). 1997. pap. 13.95 (1-57685-062-5) LrningExprss.

***Olson, Judith F.** Grammar Essentials: Learn to Express Yourself Clearly & Correctly. 2nd ed. (Illus.). 208p. 2000. pap. text 14.95 (1-57685-306-3) LrningExprss.

Olson, Judith F. Writing Skills for College Students. LC 97-43620. (Learning Express Basic Skills for College Students Ser.). 214p. (C). 1997. pap. text 20.40 (0-13-080256-5) P-H.

Olson, Judy. Teaching Children & Adolescents with Special Needs. 3rd ed. LC 99-18770. (Illus.). 427p. (C). 1999. pap. text 60.00 (0-13-099949-0) P-H.

Olson, Judy, jt. auth. see Platt, Jennifer.

Olson, Karen, jt. ed. see Brown, Cheryl L.

Olson, Karla, ed. see Eskes, David.

Olson, Kathleen. Something to Talk About: A Reproducible Conversion Resource for Teachers & Tutors. (Illus.). 110p. (C). pap. text 24.95 (0-472-08760-6) U of Mich Pr.

***Olson, Kathy.** ExCet Computer Science Sample Test. (ExCet Teacher Certification Ser.). (C). 1999. per. 10.00 (1-58197-121-4) XAM.

Olson, Kathy, ed. see Romig, Dennis A.

Olson, Kaye. Surgery & Recovery: How to Reduce Anxiety & Promote Healthy Healing. LC 97-67641. 224p. 1997. pap. 12.95 (1-890394-03-3) Rhodes & Easton.

Olson, Keith G. The Art of Steve Hanks: Poised Between Heartbeats. LC 94-75613. (Illus.). 128p. 1994. 74.95 (0-9618978-2-1) Hadley Hse Pub.

— The Art of Steve Hanks: Poised Between Heartbeats. deluxe limited ed. LC 94-75613. (Illus.). 128p. 1994. lthr. 200.00 (0-9618978-3-X) Hadley Hse Pub.

— The Art of Terry Redlin: Master of Memories. LC 97-71557. (Illus.). 124p. 1997. 75.00 (0-9618978-4-8) Hadley Hse Pub.

— The ART of Terry Redlin: Opening Windows to the Wild. 6th ed. LC 87-81872. (Illus.). 132p. 1987. 75.00 (0-9618978-0-5) Hadley Hse Pub.

Olson, Keith R., jt. auth. see Park, Mary J.

Olson, Keith W. Biography of a Progressive: Franklin K. Lane, 1864-1920, 78. LC 78-57766. (Contributions in American History Ser.: No. 78). 233p. 1979. 62.95 (0-313-20613-9, OBP/, Greenwood Pr) Greenwood.

Olson, Ken, jt. auth. see Baker, Vernon J.

Olson, Kenneth B. One Doctor Learns to Be a Patient. Wills, Susan E., ed. LC 93-83044. (Illus.). 320p. 1993. 29.00 (1-883122-00-7) Pearce Pub.

Olson, Kenneth E. Music & Musket: Bands & Bandsmen of the American Civil War, 1. LC 79-6195. (Contributions to the Study of Music & Dance Ser.: No. 1). (Illus.). 299p. 1981. 65.00 (0-313-22112-X, OMM/, Greenwood Pr) Greenwood.

Olson, Kenneth R. An Essay on Facts. LC 86-72171. (Center for the Study of Language & Information-Lecture Notes Ser.: No. 6). 160p. 1987. 49.95 (0-937073-07-5); pap. text 12.95 (0-937073-08-3) CSLI.

Olson, Kent. Legal Information: How to Find It, How to Use It. 344p. 1998. pap. 39.50 (0-89774-963-4); boxed set 59.95 (0-89774-961-8) Oryx Pr.

Olson, Kent C. & Berring, Robert C. Practical Approaches to Legal Research. LC 88-6800. (Legal Reference Services Quarterly Ser.: Supp. No. 1). 143p. 1988. text 39.95 (0-86656-253-2); pap. text 19.95 (0-86656-853-0) Haworth Pr.

Olson, Kent C., jt. auth. see Cohen, Morris L.

Olson, Kent R. Poisoning & Drug Overdose. 2nd ed. (Illus.). 592p. (C). 1994. pap. text 32.95 (0-8385-1108-2, A1108-8) Appleton & Lange.

— Poisoning & Drug Overdose: A Lange Clinical Manual. 4th ed. 1998. pap. text 36.95 (0-8385-8172-2) Appleton & Lange.

— Poisoning & Drug Overdose: Clinical Manual. 3rd ed. (Illus.). 569p. 1999. spiral bd. 36.95 (0-8385-0260-1, Apple Lange Med) McGraw.

Olson, Kent W., et al. State Policy & Economic Development in Oklahoma: A Report to Oklahoma 2000, Inc., 1996. unabridged ed. (Illus.). 69p. (Orig.). 1996. mass mkt. write for info. (1-890100-01-3) OK Two-Thousand.

Olson, Kerry, jt. auth. see Means, Barbara.

Olson-Kilcup, Susan, ed. see Kilcup, Dan.

***Olson, Kirby.** Comedy after Postmodernism: Rereading Comedy from Edward Lear to Charles Willeford. 2001. 29.95 (0-89672-440-9) Tex Tech Univ Pr.

***Olson, Kris Ellingboe.** Crabby Abby. Wise, Noreen, ed. (Book-a-Day Collection). (Illus.). 32p. (YA). (ps up). 2000. pap. 5.95 (1-58584-375-X) Huckleberry CT.

Olson, L. Rowlf's Very Own First Piano Book. 24p. 1987. pap. 5.95 (0-7935-2431-8, 00240835) H Leonard.

Olson, L., et al, eds. Applied Mechanics Division: Book of Abstracts: Proceedings ASME International Mechanical Engineering Congress & Exposition, 1998 Anaheim, CA. LC 99-182515. (AMD Ser.: Vol. 229). 211p. 1998. 120.00 (0-7918-1585-4) ASME.

Olson, L. & Saigal, S., eds. Computational Methods for Solution of Inverse Problems in Mechanics: Proceedings ASME International Mechanical Engineering Congress & Exposition 1998, Anaheim, CA. LC 98-74425. (AMD Ser.: Vol. 228). 107p. 1998. 80.00 (0-7918-1584-6) ASME.

Olson, Lance. Circus of the Mind in Motion: Postmodernism & the Comic Vision. LC 89-39857. 172p. (C). 1990. text 34.95 (0-8143-2132-1) Wayne St U Pr.

Olson, Laura K., ed. The Graying of the World: Who Will Care for the Frail Elderly? LC 92-1661. (Illus.). 320p. 1994. lib. bdg. 69.95 (1-56024-363-5) Haworth Pr.

Olson, Laura K., jt. ed. see Browne, William P.

***Olson, Laura R.** Filled with Spirit & Power: Protestant Clergy in Politics. LC 99-41450. (C). 2000. pap. text 18.95 (0-7914-4590-9) State U NY Pr.

— Filled with Spirit & Power: Protestant Clergy in Politics. LC 99-41450. (C). 2000. text 57.50 (0-7914-4589-5) State U NY Pr.

Olson, Laura R. & Jelen, Ted G., compiled by. The Religious Dimension of Political Behavior: A Critical Analysis & Annotated Bibliography, 47. LC 98-28016. (Bibliographies & Indexes in Religious Studies: Vol. 47). 168p. 1998. lib. bdg. 65.00 (0-313-28484-9, Greenwood Pr) Greenwood.

Olson, Lawrence. The Ambivalent Moderns: Portraits in Japanese Cultural Identity. 200p. (C). 1992. text 66.00 (0-8476-7738-9); pap. text 22.95 (0-8476-7739-7) Rowman.

Olson, Lawrence A. Japan in Postwar Asia. LC 79-101674. 302p. reprint ed. pap. 93.70 (0-608-30367-4, 200295400016) Bks Demand.

Olson, Lawrence O. When You Lose Touch. (Stepping Stones Ser.). 32p. (Orig.). 1992. pap. 1.95 (0-8100-0455-0, 12N2002) Northwest Pub.

***Olson, Leanne.** A Cruel Paradise: Journals of an International Relief Worker. 192p. 2000. pap. 15.99 (1-895837-82-0) Insomniac.

***Olson, Leonard T.** Masters Track & Field: A History. (Illus.). 320p. 2000. 65.00 (0-7864-0889-8) McFarland & Co.

Olson, Linda & Olson, David. Listening Prayer: My Sheep Hear My Voice. unabridged ed. 189p. 1997. 16.95 (1-893498-01-8); pap. 12.95 (1-893498-00-X) Listen Prayer.

Olson, Linda A. New Psalms for New Moms: A Keepsake Journal. LC 98-53387. (Illus.). 1999. 15.00 (0-8170-1298-2) Judson.

Olson, Linda L. & Bywater, Tim. Guide to Exploring Grand Teton National Park. rev. ed. LC 90-61339. (Illus.). 160p. (Orig.). 1995. pap. 10.95 (0-9621511-1-4) RNM Pr.

Olson, Lloyd C., ed. Virus Infections: Modern Concepts & Status. LC 82-5097. (Microbiology Ser.: No. 6). 303p. 1982. reprint ed. pap. 94.00 (0-608-01308-0, 206205300001) Bks Demand.

Olson, Lori & Olson, Jim. Norsk Hostfest: Heritage Comes Alive. (Illus.). (Orig.). 1995. pap. 8.00 (1-56037-078-5) Am Wrld Geog.

Olson, Lynette. Early Monasteries in Cornwall. (Studies in Celtic History: No. XI). (Illus.). 160p. 1989. 75.00 (0-85115-478-6) Boydell & Brewer.

Olson, Lynn. School-to-Work Revolution: How Employers & Educators Are Joining Forces to Prepare Tomorrow's Workers. LC 98-86619. 352p. 1998. reprint ed. pap. text 14.00 (0-7382-0029-8) Perseus Pubng.

— Sculpting with Cement: Direct Modeling in a Permanent Medium. rev. ed. LC 81-708. (Illus.). 109p. (Orig.). (C). 1997. reprint ed. pap. 30.00 (0-9605678-0-1) Steelstone.

Olson, Lynn F. Essential Keyboard Repertoire, Bk. 1. 1993. pap. 14.95 (0-88284-857-7) Alfred Pub.

— Exploring More Piano Literature. (Illus.). 1980. pap. 7.50 (0-8258-0057-9, 0-5082) Fischer Inc NY.

— Exploring Piano Literature. (Illus.). 48p. 1978. pap. 7.95 (0-8258-0056-0, 0-5041) Fischer Inc NY.

Olson, Lynn F., jt. auth. see Hilley, Martha.

Olson, Lynn F., jt. auth. see Reilly, Mary L.

Olson, Lynn Freeman. A Happy Secret. 4p. 1986. pap. 2.50 (0-7390-0532-4, 2372) Alfred Pub.

— Italian Festival. 4p. 1985. pap. 1.95 (0-7390-0840-4, 2511) Alfred Pub.

Olson, Lynn Freeman, ed. Debussy/Le Petit Negre. 4p. 1985. pap. 2.50 (0-7390-0672-X, 2547) Alfred Pub.

— Essential Keyboard Repertoire, Bk. 2. 144p. 1997. pap. 14.95 (0-7390-0619-3, 16777) Alfred Pub.

— Essential Keyboard Repertoire Vol. 2: Baroque to Modern. 144p. 1994. pap. 25.90 incl. audio compact disk (0-7390-0618-5, 503C) Alfred Pub.

— Villa-Lobos - O Polichinelo (Punch) (Alfred Masterwork Edition Ser.). 8p. 1987. pap. 2.95 (0-7390-0774-2, 885) Alfred Pub.

Olson, Lynn Freeman & Hilley, Martha, eds. Essential Keyboard Repertoire Vol. 3: 16 Early/Late Intermediate Sonatinas in Their Original Form. 152p. 1988. pap. 14.95 (0-7390-0547-2, 505) Alfred Pub.

— Essential Keyboard Repertoire Vol. 3: 16 Early/Late Intermediate Sonatinas in Their Original Form. 1997. pap. 23.90 incl. audio compact disk (0-7390-0548-0, 16776) Alfred Pub.

Olson, Lynn Freeman, jt. auth. see Reilly, Mary Louise.

Olson, Lynn T. The Soul of Sound. (Illus.). 160p. (Orig.). 1996. pap. 29.95 (0-9653367-0-0) Nutshell High Fidlty.

***Olson, Lynne.** Freedom's Daughters. 2001. 27.50 (0-684-85012-5) Scribner.

Olson, Lynne, jt. auth. see Cloud, Stanley.

Olson, M. Genevieve. From Ax & Plow to Here & Now. (Illus.). 188p. (Orig.). 1991. pap. 13.50 (0-9629033-1-0) Farmstead MN.

Olson, M. H., ed. Technological Support for Work Group Collaboration. (John Seely Brown Ser.). 208p. 1988. 29.95 (0-8058-0304-1) L Erlbaum Assocs.

Olson, Mancur, Jr. The Logic of Collective Action: Public Goods & the Theory of Groups. (Economic Studies: Vol. No. 124). 186p. (C). 1965. pap. 15.50 (0-674-53751-3) HUP.

— The Logic of Collective Action: Public Goods & the Theory of Groups. rev. ed. LC 65-19826. (Economic Studies: No. 24). 1965. pap. 6.95 (0-674-03751-0) HUP.

Olson, Mancur. The Rise & Decline of Nations: Economic Growth, Stagflation, & Social Rigidities. LC 82-40163. 287p. 1984. reprint ed. pap. 16.00 (0-300-03079-7, Y-487) Yale U Pr.

Olson, Mancur & Kahkohnen, Satu, eds. A Not-So-dismal Science: A Broader View of Economies & Societies. LC 98-33705. (Illus.). 286p. 2000. pap. text 19.95 (0-19-829490-5) OUP.

— A Not-So-Dismal Science: A Broader View of Economies & Societies. LC 98-33705. (Illus.). 286p. 2000. text 65.00 (0-19-829369-0) OUP.

Olson, Mancur, Jr. & Landsberg, Hans H., eds. The No-Growth Society. 259p. (C). 1974. 11.25 (0-393-01111-9) Norton.

Olson, Mancur L., Jr. Economics of Wartime Shortages: A History of British Food Supplies in the Napoleonic War & in World War I & World War II. LC 63-17328. 160p. reprint ed. 49.60 (0-8357-9104-1, 201791700010) Bks Demand.

Olson, Mar J., ed. see Evseeff, David D.

Olson, Marcy. Tae Kwon Do. LC 98-33676. (World of Sports Ser.). (Illus.). 32p. (YA). (gr. 4 up). 2000. lib. bdg. 22.60 (1-887068-55-4) Smart Apple.

Olson, Margaret J. Aloysious Alligator. 2nd ed. (Illus.). (J). (gr. k-2). 1964. pap. 3.00 (0-934876-14-2) Creative Storytime.

— Tell & Draw Animal Cut-Outs. 3rd ed. (J). (gr. k-2). 1963. pap. 4.00 (0-934876-15-0) Creative Storytime.

— Tell & Draw Stories. (Illus.). (J). (ps-3). 1963. pap. 6.95 (0-934876-01-0); lib. bdg. 11.95 (0-934876-05-3) Creative Storytime.

Olson, Margot A. & Forrest, Mary L. Shared Meaning: An Introduction to Speech Communication. 3rd ed. 312p. (C). 1996. per. 34.59 (0-8403-9290-7) Kendall-Hunt.

— Shared Meaning: An Introduction to Speech Communication. 5th ed. 376p. (C). 1999. per. 42.95 (0-7872-5664-1, 41566401) Kendall-Hunt.

Olson, Marian. Facing the Wind. 108p. 1990. write for info. (0-9625862-1-8) Raven Pr CA.

***Olson, Marianne.** Over the Waves. LC 99-64152. (Illus.). iv, 147p. (YA). (gr. 4 up). 1999. pap. 9.95 (0-9673497-0-2) Rafter Five Pr.

Olson, Marianne E. Crossroads... A Journey of Commitment. (Illus.). 250p. 1999. pap. 14.95 (0-9662512-1-0) Planning Innovat.

— The Standard: "Because We've Always Done It That Way Here!" LC 97-76166. (Illus.). 334p. 1998. text 29.95 (0-9662512-0-2) Planning Innovat.

***Olson, Marie.** Notes on the Psalms by Marie Olson. Dick, Louise, ed. 500p. (Orig.). 1999. pap. 19.95 (0-935899-09-X) LeTourneau Pr.

— Tlingit Coloring Book. (ENG.). 24p. (J). pap. 6.00 (1-57833-051-3) Todd Commns.

Olson, Marie M. & Reisbick, Anna M., eds. Norka: A German Village in Russia. 2nd rev. ed. 49p. 1986. 6.00 (0-914222-22-8) Am Hist Soc Ger.

Olson, Marilyn. Newsschool: Using the Newspaper to Teach Math, Science & Health. 1997. pap. text 11.85 (0-86651-261-6) Seymour Pubns.

— Newsschool: Using the Newspaper to Teach Social Studies. 1997. pap. text 11.85 (0-86651-262-4) Seymour Pubns.

Olson, Marilynn S. Ellen Raskin. (Twayne's United States Authors Ser.: No. 579). 152p. 1991. 21.95 (0-8057-7627-3) Macmillan.

Olson, Mark. Innerer Klang. (Illus.). 28p. 1981. 25.00 (0-939622-20-3); pap. 5.00 (0-939622-19-X) Four Zoas Night Ltd.

— The Woodcutter. (Chickadee Ser.: No. 4). 1992. pap. 7.00 (1-55780-117-7) Juniper Pr ME.

Olson, Mark, jt. ed. see Bridwell-Bowles, Lillian.

Olson, Mark, ed. see Ganguli, Aparna B. & Henry, Richard.

Olson, Mark, ed. see Henderson, Zenna.

Olson, Mark, ed. see Homstad, Torild & Thorson, Helga.

Olson, Mark, ed. see Kassner, Linda A. & Collins, Terence.

Olson, Mark, ed. see Miller, Hildy & Ashcroft, Mary E.

Olson, Mark, ed. see Nereson, Sally.

Olson, Mark, ed. see Olson, Wilma R.

Olson, Mark, ed. see Schmitz, James.

Olson, Mark D. Go Public - Thirty Days: The Comprehensive Course on Regulation D. (Illus.). (C). 1989. 225.00 (0-685-24733-3) C Counsel Inc.

Olson, Mark J. Irenaeus, the Valentinian Gnostics, & the Kingdom of God (A.H. Book V) LC 92-29432. (Biblical Press Ser.: Vol. 4). 164p. 1992. text 79.95 (0-7734-2352-4) E Mellen.

***Olson, Mark L. & Lewis, Anthony R., eds.** The Essential Hal Clement: Trio for Slide Rule & Typewriter, Vol. 1. 524p. 1999. 25.00 (1-886778-06-X, NESFA Pr) New Eng SF Assoc.

Olson, Mark L., ed. see Clement, Hal.

Olson, Mark L., ed. see White, James.

Olson, Marla, ed. see Roberts, Lisa M.

Olson, Mary. An Alligator Ate My Brother. LC 98-89692. (Illus.). 32p. (J). (gr. k-3). 2000. 15.95 (1-56397-803-2) Boyds Mills Pr.

***Olson, Mary E.** Feminism, Community & Communication. LC 00-40748. 2000. write for info. (0-7890-1152-2) Haworth Pr.

Olson, Mary V. Nice Try, Tooth Fairy. LC 98-22749. Orig. Title: Dear Tooth Fairy. (Illus.). 32p. (J). (ps-3). 2000. per. 15.00 (0-689-82422-X) S&S Bks Yung.

Olson, Mary W., ed. Opening the Door to Classroom Research. LC 89-28255. 166p. 1990. reprint ed. pap. 51.50 (0-608-00503-7, 206132300008) Bks Demand.

Olson, Mary W. & Miller, Samuel D. Reading & Language Arts Programs: A Guide to Evaluation. (Essential Tools for Educators Ser.). 120p. 1993. pap. 24.95 (0-8039-6042-5) Corwin Pr.

Olson, Matthew H., jt. auth. see Hergenhahn, B. R.

Olson, Mel, jt. auth. see Henderson, Frank.

Olson, Melfried. Mathematics Activities for Elementary Teachers. 168p. (C). 1996. pap. text, spiral bd. 20.95 (0-8403-9930-8) Kendall-Hunt.

Olson, Melissa, jt. auth. see Olson, Bob.

Olson, Melodie. Healing the Dying. LC 95-45489. (Nurse as Healer Ser.). (Illus.). 272p. 1996. mass mkt. 21.95 (0-8273-6603-5) Delmar.

Olson, Melvin, jt. auth. see Krause, Andreas.

Olson, Meredith B. Page's Pencilsharpener. LC 97-94520. (Illus.). 64p. (J). (gr. 3-4). 1998. 11.95 (0-9657061-7-6) Glenhaven.

— Willis's Windowslats. LC 98-92486. (Illus.). 64p. (J). (gr. 3-4). 1999. 15.95 (0-9657061-6-8) Glenhaven.

Olson, Michael. MetroFarm: The Guide to Growing for Big Profit on a Small Parcel of Land. (Illus.). 576p. 1995. pap. 29.95 (0-9637876-0-8) T S Bks.

Olson, Milton C. & Haber, F. Barry. Business Mathematics. 1981. student ed. write for info. (0-672-97328-6); pap. write for info. (0-672-97327-8) Macmillan.

***Olson, Miriam M., ed.** Crafts in A Flash: Quick, Quicker & Quickest Projects. LC 98-147770. 160 p. 1998. 24.95 (0-86573-195-0) Creat Pub Intl.

Olson, Miriam M., ed. Women's Health & Social Work: Feminist Perspectives. LC 94-3951. (Social Work in Health Care Ser.: Vol. 19, Nos. 3-4). 175p. 1994. 39.95 (1-56024-683-9) Haworth Pr.

Olson, Myrle, jt. auth. see Metcalfe, Kathy.

Olson, Myrna, jt. auth. see Chalmers, Lynne.

Olson, Myrna R. Longing to Die - Fighting to Live: An Incest Survivor's Story. LC 97-65412. 111p. 1997. pap. 10.00 (0-9620254-1-0) Nathan Star Pr.

— Women's Journeys Through Crisis. LC 88-60778. (Illus.). (Orig.). 1988. pap. 12.00 (0-9620254-0-2) Nathan Star Pr.

Olson, Myrna R. & Mangold, Sally S. Guidelines & Games for Teaching Efficient Braille Reading. LC 81-14906. (Illus.). 116p. 1981. pap. 24.95 (0-89128-105-3) Am Foun Blind.

Olson, Nancy. Garvarni's Carnival Lithographs. (Illus.). 1979. pap. 1.00 (0-89467-009-3) Yale Art Gallery.

— MicroStation 95 Fundamentals. 600p. 1996. pap. text 39.99 (1-56205-607-7) New Riders Pub.

Olson, Nancy B. Audiovisual Material Glossary. (Library, Information, & Computer Science Ser.: No. 7). (Illus.). 56p. (Orig.). 1988. pap. text 8.50 (1-55653-026-9) OCLC Online Comp.

— Cataloging Motion Pictures & Videorecordings. (Minnesota AACR Two Trainers Ser.: No. 1). (Illus.). 159p. 1991. pap. 30.00 (0-936996-38-2) Soldier Creek.

— Cataloging of Audiovisual Materials & Other Special Materials: A Manual Based on AACR2. 4th rev. ed. LC 98-5787. (Illus.). 350p. 1997. pap. 75.00 (0-933474-53-9) Media Mktg Group.

— 1996 Update to Cataloging Motion Pictures & Videorecordings. (Minnesota AACR Two Trainers Ser.). 24p. 1996. 4.00 (0-936996-71-4) Soldier Creek.

— 1996 Update to Cataloging Computer Files. (Minnesota AACR Two Trainers Ser.). 26p. 1996. 4.00 (0-936996-72-2) Soldier Creek.

***Olson, Nancy B., compiled by.** Cataloging Service Bulletin Index: Index to Bulletins 1-82 (Summer 1978-Fall 1998) annuals 90p. 1999. 40.00 (0-936996-79-X) Soldier Creek.

***Olson, Nancy Kruger.** We Flew with Our Own Wings: A Family Odyssey. Elvehjem, Joyce, tr. (Illus.). 170p. 2000. write for info. (0-9659896-9-0) Asgard MN.

Olson, Norman. I Can Read About Trucks & Cars. LC 72-96957. (Illus.). (J). (gr. 2-4). 1973. pap. 2.95 (0-89375-055-7) Troll Communs.

Olson, O. Charles. Diagnosis & Management of Diabetes Mellitus: A Clinical Manual for Medical Students, Residents, & Primary Care Physicians. LC 80-27025. (Illus.). 308p. reprint ed. pap. 95.50 (0-8357-7652-2, 205697800096) Bks Demand.

— Prevention of Football Injuries: Protecting the Health of the Student Athlete. LC 70-157472. 136p. reprint ed. 42.20 (0-8357-9413-X, 201456900094) Bks Demand.

Olson, O. N. A. J. Lindstrom. LC 58-2906. (Augustana Historical Society Publications: Vol. 16). 47p. 1957. pap. 3.00 (0-910184-16-X) Augustana.

O

An Asterisk (*) at the beginning of an entry indicates that the title is appearing for the first time.

Olson, Oscar N. Olof Christian Telemak Andren, Ambassador of Good Will. LC 55-2674. (Augustana Historical Society Publications: Vol. 14). 103p. 1954. pap. 3.00 (*0-910184-14-3*) Augustana.
— Sward & Johnston, Biographical Sketches of Augustana Leaders. LC 56-5870. (Augustana Historical Society Publications: No. 15). 80p. 1955. pap. 3.00 (*0-910184-15-1*) Augustana.
Olson, Pamela, jt. auth. see Marx, Pamela.
Olson, Patricia S. And Suddenly They're Gone: What Parents Need to Know about the Empty Nest. LC 92-61770. 237p. (Orig.). 1993. pap. 14.00 (*0-9634523-0-4*) Tiffany Pr CO.
Olson, Paul A. The Journey to Wisdom: Self-Education in Patristic & Medieval Literature. LC 95-3042. xx, 299p. 1995. text 50.00 (*0-8032-3562-3*) U of Nebr Pr.
Olson, Paul A., ed. The Struggle for the Land: Indigenous Insight & Industrial Empire in the Semiarid World. LC 89-22422. (Illus.). x, 317p. 1990. text 50.00 (*0-8032-3555-0*) U of Nebr Pr.
Olson, Paul L. Forensic Aspects of Driver Perception & Response. LC 96-6158. (Illus.). 213p. 1996. 75.00 (*0-913875-22-8*, 5228-N) Lawyers & Judges.
Olson, Paul R. Circle of Paradox: Time & Essence in the Poetry of Juan Ramon Jimenez. LC 67-21581. 248p. reprint ed. pap. 76.90 (*0-608-13739-1*, 202073000018) Bks Demand.
Olson, Paul W. Beyond the Blue Ridge. (Illus.). (Orig.). 1990. pap. write for info. (*1-879077-50-7*) Olson Pub Co.
Olson, Peggy M. Hiking the Inner Gorge: Life's Little Lessons As Taught by the Grand Canyon. 80p. 1995. pap. text, spiral bd. 9.95 (*1-887414-01-0*) PMO Pubns.
— In the Garden: Nature's Way to Understanding. 28p. 1995. pap. text 7.95 (*1-887414-00-2*) PMO Pubns.
— Now You Can . . . 42p. 1995. pap. text, spiral bd. 7.95 (*1-887414-02-9*) PMO Pubns.
Olson, Phillip. The Discipline of Freedom: A Kantian View of the Role of Moral Precepts in Zen Practice. LC 91-26526. (SUNY Series in Buddhist Studies). 217p. (C). 1993. text 64.50 (*0-7914-1115-X*); pap. text 21.95 (*0-7914-1116-8*) State U NY Pr.
Olson, Pierce. Landmarks of the Rocky Mountain Fur Trade: Two One-Day Self-Guided Tours from Jackson, Wyoming. LC 97-43163. (Center Bks.: Vol. 3). (Illus.). 132p. 1997. pap. 11.95 (*1-886402-02-7*) Jackson Hole Hist.
Olson, Priscilla, ed. An Ornament to His Profession. (NESFA's Choice Ser.). 537p. 1998. 25.00 (*1-886778-09-4*) New Eng SF Assoc.
Olson, Priscilla, ed. see Henderson, Zenna.
Olson, R., et al. Exploring the Role of Diversity in Sustainable Agriculture. LC 96-176089. 249p. 1995. 24.00 (*0-89118-128-8*) Am Soc Agron.
Olson, R. A. & Frey, K. J. Nutritional Quality of Cereal Grains: Genetic & Agronomic Improvement. (Agronomy Monograph Ser.: No. 28). 512p. 1987. 37.50 (*0-89118-092-3*) Am Soc Agron.
Olson, R. E., jt. auth. see Pascale, J.
Olson, R. L., ed. see Gifford, Edward W.
***Olson, R. Paul.** The Reconciled Life. 2000. pap. 19.95 (*1-56563-608-2*) Hendrickson MA.
Olson, R. Paul. The Reconciled Life: A Critical Theory of Counseling. LC 97-11084. 280p. 1997. 62.95 (*0-275-95630-X*, Praeger Pubs) Greenwood.
Olson, Rachel. 'Twas the Night Before: A Picture-Story of the Nativity. Wray, Rhonda, ed. LC 93-26740. (Illus.). 24p. (Orig.). (J). (gr. k-3). 1993. 14.95 (*0-916260-85-2*, B143) Meriwether Pub.
Olson, Randy. Spring Wildflowers. (Illus.). 156p. 1993. pap. 9.95 (*1-55109-050-3*) Nimbus Publ.
Olson, Randy, jt. photos by see Salaverry, Philip.
Olson, Randy M. Views of the Present . . . Visions of the Past. Kremer, William N., ed. (Illus.). 225p. (Orig.). 1984. pap. text 22.50 (*0-318-03518-9*) Gazette Print.
Olson, Raymond E. & Paul, Anthony M., eds. Contemporary Philosophy in Scandinavia. LC 70-148242. 520p. reprint ed. pap. 161.20 (*0-608-15871-2*, 203074700070) Bks Demand.
Olson, Reginald D. Toward a Social Technology of Peace: A Sociology of Conflict Resolution. LC 96-212894. 340p. (Orig.). 1996. pap. text 35.95 (*0-9653403-0-9*) R Olson.
Olson, Richard. The Emergence of the Social Sciences, 1642-1792. (Studies in Intellectual & Cultural History). 260p. 1993. pap. 14.95 (*0-8057-8632-5*); text 26.95 (*0-8057-8607-4*) Macmillan.
— Emergence of the Social Sciences, 1642-1792. 1992. pap. 13.95 (*0-8057-8617-1*, Twyne) Mac Lib Ref.
— Science Deified & Science Defied: The Historical Significance of Science in Western Culture: From the Early Modern Age Through the Early Romantic Era ca.1640-ca.1820, Vol. 2. (Illus.). 445p. 1995. pap. 18.95 (*0-520-20167-1*, Pub. by U CA Pr) Cal Prin Full Svc.
Olson, Richard & Lyson, Thomas A., eds. Under the Blade: The Conversion of Agricultural Landscapes. LC 98-42069. 352p. 1998. 65.00 (*0-8133-3596-5*, Pub. by Westview) HarpC.
***Olson, Richard & Lyson, Thomas A., eds.** Under the Blade: The Conversion of Agricultural Landscapes. LC 98-42069. 352p. 2000. 35.00 (*0-8133-3597-3*, Pub. by Westview) HarpC.
Olson, Richard & Smith, Roger. Biographical Encyclopedia of Scientists, 5 vols. LC 97-23877. (Illus.). 1460p. (YA). (gr. 6 up). 1997. 514.21 (*0-7614-7064-6*) Marshall Cavendish.
Olson, Richard K., jt. ed. see Poincelot, Raymond P.
Olson, Richard L. Gulf War Air Power Survey: Logistics & Support, Vol. 3. 786p. 1994. per. 47.00 (*0-16-042911-0*) USGPO.
Olson, Richard P. A Different Kind of Man: Changing Male Roles in Today's World. LC 97-52186. 1998. pap. 15.00 (*0-8170-1263-X*) Judson.
— Midlife Journeys: A Traveler's Guide. LC 96-30146. 312p. (Orig.). 1996. pap. 16.95 (*0-8298-1142-7*) Pilgrim OH.
— Privileged Conversations: Dramatic Stories for Christmas. LC 95-51168. 136p. (Orig.). 1996. pap. 10.95 (*0-8298-1078-1*) Pilgrim OH.
Olson, Richard P. & Froyd, Helen E. Discoveries: Expanding Your Child's Vocational Horizons. LC 95-16997. (Illus.). 224p. (Orig.). 1995. pap. 14.95 (*0-8298-1106-0*) Pilgrim OH.
Olson, Richard P. & Leonard, Joe H., Jr. A New Day for Family Ministry. LC 95-83895. 170p. 1996. pap. 15.75 (*1-56699-166-8*, AL170) Alban Inst.
Olson, Richard P. & Pia-Terry, Carole D. Help for Remarried Couples & Families. LC 84-813. (Judson Family Life Ser.). 159p. 1984. reprint ed. pap. 49.30 (*0-608-00219-4*, 206101300006) Bks Demand.
Olson, Richard S. The Politics of Earthquake Prediction. LC 88-22101. 199p. 1989. reprint ed. pap. 61.70 (*0-608-06481-5*, 206677800009) Bks Demand.
***Olson, Richard Stuart, et al.** Some Buildings Just Can't Dance: Politics, Life Safety & Disaster. LC 99-51719. (Contemporary Studies in Applied Behavioral Science). 188p. 1999. write for info. (*0-7623-0528-2*) Jai Pr.
Olson, Robert. Art Direction for Film & Video. (Illus.). 160p. 1993. pap. 29.95 (*0-240-80189-X*, Focal) Buttrwrth-Heinemann.
— Art Direction for Film & Video. 2nd rev. ed. LC 98-25752. 144p. 1998. pap. 24.95 (*0-240-80338-8*, Focal) Buttrwrth-Heinemann.
Olson, Robert, ed. Islamic & Middle Eastern Societies. 293p. (Orig.). 1987. pap. 9.95 (*0-915597-46-2*) Amana Bks.
— The Kurdish Nationalist Movement & Its Impact on Turkey in the 1990's. 224p. 1996. pap. text 18.00 (*0-8131-0896-9*) U Pr of Ky.
Olson, Robert, tr. see Hodgson, Thomas C.
Olson, Robert A. & Thiel, Charles C., Jr., eds. Earthquake Damage Mitigation for Computer Systems: Workshop Proceedings, July 12, 1983. 128p. 1983. pap. 12.00 (*0-685-14421-6*) Earthquake Eng.
Olson, Robert C. Motto, Context, Essay: The Classical Background of Samuel Johnson's "Rambler" & "Adventurer" Essays. 398p. (Orig.). 1985. pap. text 32.00 (*0-8191-4236-0*) U Pr of Amer.
Olson, Robert E., ed. Annual Review of Nutrition, Vol. 7. (Illus.). 1987. text 43.00 (*0-8243-2807-8*) Annual Reviews.
— Annual Review of Nutrition, Vol. 13. (Illus.). 1993. text 45.00 (*0-8243-2813-2*) Annual Reviews.
— Perspectives in Biological Chemistry. LC 78-103834. (Illus.). 298p. reprint ed. pap. 92.40 (*0-7837-0960-9*, 204126500019) Bks Demand.
Olson, Robert E., et al, eds. Annual Review of Nutrition, Vol. 5. (Illus.). (C). 1985. text 43.00 (*0-8243-2805-1*) Annual Reviews.
— Annual Review of Nutrition, Vol. 6. (Illus.). 1986. text 43.00 (*0-8243-2806-X*) Annual Reviews.
— Annual Review of Nutrition, Vol. 8. (Illus.). 1988. text 43.00 (*0-8243-2808-6*) Annual Reviews.
— Annual Review of Nutrition, Vol. 9. 1989. text 43.00 (*0-8243-2809-4*) Annual Reviews.
— Annual Review of Nutrition, Vol. 10. 1990. text 43.00 (*0-8243-2810-8*) Annual Reviews.
— Annual Review of Nutrition, Vol. 11. 1991. text 43.00 (*0-8243-2811-6*) Annual Reviews.
— Annual Review of Nutrition, Vol. 12. 1992. text 45.00 (*0-8243-2812-4*) Annual Reviews.
— Annual Review of Nutrition, Vol. 14. (Illus.). 1994. text 48.00 (*0-8243-2814-0*) Annual Reviews.
Olson, Robert G. An Introduction to Existentialism. 221p. (Orig.). 1962. pap. text 6.95 (*0-486-20055-8*) Dover.
Olson, Robert K., jt. auth. see Wadman, Robert C.
Olson, Robert L., jt. auth. see Bonnett, Thomas W.
Olson, Robert L., jt. ed. see Bezold, Clement.
Olson, Robert M., III, jt. ed. see Merrell, Ronald C.
Olson, Robert W. The Kurdish Question & Turkish-Iranian Relations: From World War I to 1998. LC 98-9898. (Kurdish Studies Ser.: Vol. 1). 115p. 1998. text 19.95 (*1-56859-067-9*) Mazda Pubs.
— Stepping Out Within: The Ennegram & Essence. (Illus.). 276p. (Orig.). 1993. pap. 14.95 (*0-9634860-0-4*) Awakened Pr.
Olson, Roberta A. The Florentine Tondo. (Illus.). 400p. 2000. text 145.00 (*0-19-817425-X*) OUP.
Olson, Roberta A., et al, eds. The Sourcebook of Pediatric Psychology. 608p. (C). 1994. 89.00 (*0-205-15182-5*, Longwood Div) Allyn.
Olson, Roberta A., jt. ed. see Seibert, Jeffrey M.
Olson, Roberta J. Italian Renaissance Sculpture. LC 91-65310. (World of Art Ser.). (Illus.). 216p. (Orig.). 1992. pap. 14.95 (*0-500-20253-2*, Pub. by Thames Hudson) Norton.
— Ottocento: Romanticism & Revolution in 19th-Century Italian Painting. LC 92-30898. (Illus.). 296p. 1992. 67.95 (*0-917418-94-8*) Am Fed Arts.
— Ottocento: Romanticism & Revolution in 19th-Century Italian Painting. LC 92-30898. (Illus.). 296p. (C). 1993. text 69.95 (*0-8122-3207-0*, Pub. by Centro Di) U of Pa Pr.
Olson, Roberta J. & Pasachoff, Jay M. Fire in the Sky: Comets & Meteors, the Decisive Centuries, in Art & Science. LC 97-46513. (Illus.). 384p. (C). 1998. text 74.95 (*0-521-63060-6*) Cambridge U Pr.
***Olson, Roberta J. & Pasachoff, Jay M.** Fire in the Sky: Comets & Meteors, the Decisive Centuries, in Art & Science. (Illus.). 410p. 1999. pap. 29.95 (*0-521-66359-8*) Cambridge U Pr.
Olson, Roberta K., jt. ed. see Vance, Connie.
Olson, Roger E. The Story of Christian Theology: Twenty Centuries of Tradition & Reform. LC 99-18734. 656p. 1999. 34.99 (*0-8308-1505-8*, 1505) InterVarsity.
Olson, Roger E., jt. auth. see Grenz, Stanley J.
Olson, Ron. Half Life. LC 84-70678. (Orig.). 1984. pap. 3.95 (*0-916027-01-5*) Bannack Pub Co.
— Three for the Bobcat. LC 84-70024. 187p. (Orig.). 1984. pap. 2.95 (*0-916027-00-7*) Bannack Pub Co.
***Olson, Ron A.** American Zen. 2000. 7.95 (*0-533-13257-6*) Vantage.
Olson, Ronald. Chumash Prehistory. fac. ed. (University of California Publications in American Archaeology & Ethnology: No. 28). (Illus.). 25p. 1930. reprint ed. pap. text 2.81 (*1-55567-854-8*) Coyote Press.
Olson, Ronald, jt. auth. see Voight, Randall L.
Olson, Ronald L. Clan & Moiety in Native America. fac. ed. (University of California Publications in American Archaeology & Ethnology: Vol. 33: 4). 80p. (C). 1933. reprint ed. pap. text 9.06 (*1-55567-291-4*) Coyote Press.
— Notes on the Bella Bella Kwakiutl. fac. ed. Heizer, R. F. et al, eds. (University of California Publications: No. 14:5). 33p. (C). 1955. reprint ed. pap. 3.75 (*1-55567-138-1*) Coyote Press.
— Social Life of the Owikeno. fac. ed. Heizer, R. F. et al, eds. (University of California Publications: No. 14:3). (Illus.). 54p. (C). 1954. reprint ed. pap. 6.56 (*1-55567-136-5*) Coyote Press.
— The Social Organization of the Haisla of British Columbia. fac. ed. Kroeber, A. L. & Lowie, Robert H., eds. (University of California Publications: No. 2:5). 37p. (C). 1940. reprint ed. pap. 4.06 (*1-55567-124-1*) Coyote Press.
Olson, Ronald L. & Treganza, Adam E. The Topanga Culture First Season's Excavation of the Tank Site, 1947. fac. ed. (University of California Publications: No. 12:4). 56p. (C). 1950. reprint ed. pap. 6.88 (*1-55567-129-2*) Coyote Press.
Olson, Ronald L., et al. An Archaeological Survey of the Yuki Area. fac. ed. (University of California Publications: No. 12:3). (Illus.). 20p. (C). 1950. reprint ed. pap. 2.50 (*1-55567-128-4*) Coyote Press.
Olson, Ronald L., ed. see Cook, S. F.
Olson, Ronald L., ed. see Garth, Thomas R.
Olson, Ronald L., ed. see Heizer, R. F.
Olson, Ronald L., ed. see Heizer, Robert F.
Olson, Ronald L., ed. see Kroeber, A. L.
Olson, Ronald L., ed. see Kroeber, A. L. & Harner, Michael.
Olson, Ronald L., ed. see Lowie, Robert H.
Olson, Ronald L., ed. see Merghan, Clement W.
***Olson, Russell L.** The Independent Fiduciary: Investing for Pension Funds & Endowment Funds. LC 99-22802. (Frontiers in Finance Ser.). 336p. 1999. 69.95 (*0-471-35387-6*) Wiley.
***Olson, Ruth.** Jesus Loves You This I Know. 1998. pap. 10.00 (*0-9656749-7-5*) ACW Press.
Olson, S. Dean, ed. see Kale, W. Wilford.
Olson, S. Douglas. Aristophanes' "Plutus" (Greek Commentaries Ser.). 101p. (Orig.). (C). 1989. pap. text 7.00 (*0-929524-63-2*) Bryn Mawr Commentaries.
— Blood & Iron: Story & Storytelling in Homer's Odyssey. LC 94-45655. (Mnemosyne, Bibliotheca Classica Batava Ser.: Vol. 148). 1995. 89.00 (*90-04-10251-5*) Brill Academic Pubs.
***Olson, S. Douglas.** Euripides' Cyclops. (Greek Commentaries Ser.). 76p. 1999. pap. 6.00 (*0-929524-91-8*) Bryn Mawr Commentaries.
***Olson, S. Douglas & Sens, Alexander.** Matro of Pitane & the Tradition of Epic Parody in the Fourth Century BCE: Text, Translation & Commentary. LC 99-50172. (American Philological Association American Classical Studies). 174p. 1999. 34.95 (*0-7885-0614-5*, 400444); pap. 19.95 (*0-7885-0615-3*, 400444) OUP.
Olson, S. Douglas, ed. see Archestratos of Gela Staff.
Olson, S. Douglas, ed. see Aristophanes.
Olson, S. L. & James, H. F. Descriptions of Thirty-Two Species of Birds from the Hawaiian Islands: Part I: Non-Passerines; Part II: Passerines. (Ornithological Monographs: Vols. 45-46). (Illus.). 176p. 1991. 25.00 (*0-935868-54-2*) Am Ornithologists.
Olson, Sally, ed. see Olson, Jim.
***Olson, Sandra.** Rebirth. 236p. 2000. pap. 19.95 (*0-938041-77-0*) Arc Pr AR.
Olson, Sandra, ed. Career Counseling of Older Adults: Pioneers & Prophets - A Special Issue of Journal of Career Development. 69p. 1987. pap. 14.95 (*0-89885-347-8*, Kluwer Acad Hman Sci) Kluwer Academic.
Olson, Sandra S. Dental Radiology Laboratory Manual. LC 94-8369. (Illus.). 256p. 1994. pap. text, lab manual ed. 28.00 (*0-7216-6455-5*, W B Saunders Co) Harcrt Hlth Sci Grp.
Olson, Sarah E. Becoming One: A Story of Triumph Over Multiple Personality Disorder. LC 96-61720. 288p. (Orig.). 1997. pap. 16.95 (*0-9623879-8-3*) Trilogy Bks.
Olson, Scott R. Hollywood Planet: American Competitive Advantage & the Transparent Apparatus of Global Media. LC 98-55063. (LEA's Communication Ser.). 232p. 1999. pap. 24.50 (*0-8058-3230-0*) L Erlbaum Assocs.
— Hollywood Planet: Global Media & the Competitive Advantage of Narrative Transparency. LC 98-55063. (Communication Ser.). 232p. 1999. 45.00 (*0-8058-3229-7*) L Erlbaum Assocs.
Olson, Scott S., jt. auth. see Montgomery, Nancy L.
***Olson, Shannon.** Welcome to My Planet: Where English Is Sometimes Spoken. LC 00-24549. 243p. 2000. 22.95 (*0-670-89208-4*, Viking) Viking Penguin.
Olson, Sharon. Into the Light: For Women Experiencing the Transformative Nature of Grief. (Illus.). 64p. 1993. 24.45 (*0-9638984-0-X*) Seasons.
Olson, Sharon L., ed. see Battery, Lee, et al.
Olson, Sheldon R. Issues in the Sociology of Criminal Justice. LC 74-31261. (Studies in Sociology). 58p. 1975. pap. text 2.50 (*0-672-61348-4*, Bobbs) Macmillan.
Olson, Sherry H. Baltimore: The Building of an American City. expanded ed. LC 97-10692. (Illus.). 432p. 1997. pap. 24.95 (*0-8018-5640-X*) Johns Hopkins.
— Baltimore: The Building of an American City. LC 79-21950. (Illus.). 446p. reprint ed. pap. 138.30 (*0-8357-4334-9*, 203713400007) Bks Demand.
***Olson, Sherry H.** Breakfast at the Wayside. 96p. 2000. pap. 12.00 (*0-9678022-0-2*, BP0001) Boyer Pub.
Olson, Sherry H. Depletion Myth: A History of Railroad Use of Timber. LC 70-148940. (Illus.). 246p. 1971. 29.00 (*0-674-19820-4*) HUP.
Olson, Sheryl L., jt. auth. see Thorpe, Geoffrey L.
Olson, Sidney. Young Henry Ford: A Picture History of the First Forty Years. (Illus.). 204p. 1997. reprint ed. 29.95 (*0-8143-1224-1*) Wayne St U Pr.
Olson, Sigurd F. Listening Point. LC 97-22180. (Fesler-Lampert Minnesota Heritage Book Ser.). 1997. write for info. (*0-8166-2996-X*) U of Minn Pr.
— The Lonely Land. LC 97-22181. (The Fesler-Lampert Minnesota Heritage Book Ser.). 1997. write for info. (*0-8166-2997-8*) U of Minn Pr.
— Of Time & Place. LC 98-21096. (Fesler-Lampert Minnesota Heritage Book Ser.). 192p. 1998. pap. 14.95 (*0-8166-2995-1*) U of Minn Pr.
— Open Horizons. LC 98-21095. (Fesler-Lampert Minnesota Heritage Book Ser.). 256p. 1998. pap. 14.95 (*0-8166-3037-2*) U of Minn Pr.
— Reflections from the North Country. (Illus.). 1976. 27.50 (*0-394-40265-0*) Knopf.
— Reflections from the North Country. LC 98-21094. (Fesler-Lampert Minnesota Heritage Book Ser.). 192p. 1998. pap. 14.95 (*0-8166-2993-5*) U of Minn Pr.
— Runes of the North. LC 97-22170. (Fesler-Lampert Minnesota Heritage Book Ser.). 1997. write for info. (*0-8166-2994-3*) U of Minn Pr.
— The Singing Wilderness. (Illus.). 1956. 25.00 (*0-394-44560-0*) Knopf.
— The Singing Wilderness. LC 97-13328. (Fesler-Lampert Minnesota Heritage Book Ser.). 1997. write for info. (*0-8166-2992-7*) U of Minn Pr.
— Songs of the North. 288p. 1987. pap. 11.95 (*0-14-025218-5*, Penguin Bks) Viking Penguin.
Olson, Steiner, jt. auth. see Ferno.
Olson, Steve. Biotechnology: An Industry Comes of Age. LC 85-28442. (Illus.). 128p. (Orig.). reprint ed. pap. 39.70 (*0-8357-4214-8*, 203699600003) Bks Demand.
— The Last Valkyrie. Kirsch, J. Allen, ed. 224p. (Orig.). 1997. pap. 12.95 (*1-878569-49-X*) Badger Bks Inc.
— Shaping the Future: Biology & Human Values. 132p. 1989. 17.95 (*0-309-03947-9*) Natl Acad Pr.
***Olson, Steve & Loucks-Horsley, Susan.** Inquiry & the National Science Education Standards: A Guide for Teaching & Learning. 224p. 2000. pap. 21.95 (*0-309-06476-7*) Natl Acad Pr.
Olson, Steve, et al. Alcohol in America: Taking Action to Prevent Abuse. LC 85-13667. (Illus.). 125p. 1985. pap. 14.95 (*0-309-03449-3*) Natl Acad Pr.
Olson, Steven. The Prairie in Nineteenth-Century American Poetry. LC 93-32550. (Illus.). 224p. 1995. pap. 15.95 (*0-8061-2640-X*) U of Okla Pr.
Olson, Stuart. The Little Book of Qi-Gong: The Easiest, Most Effective Seated Qi-Gong Exercises for Better Meditation. 88p. 1998. pap. 12.95 (*1-889633-15-1*) Jade Forest.
Olson, Stuart A. Eight Brocades Seated Ch'I-Kung. Gross, Patrick D., ed. LC 96-78391. 232p. 1997. otabind 24.95 (*1-889633-00-3*) Jade Forest.
— Tai Chi: Sensing Hands. LC 98-68620. (Illus.). 153p. 1999. pap. text 19.95 (*1-892515-15-6*) Multi-Media Commns.
— T'ai Chi Changes: T'ai Chi According to the Book of Changes. 180p. Date not set. otabind 1.95 (*1-889633-02-X*) Jade Forest.
— Tai Chi Thirteen Sword: A Sword Master's Manual. LC 98-68619. (Illus.). 259p. 1999. pap. text 19.95 (*1-892515-14-8*) Multi-Media Commns.
Olson, Susan M. Clients & Lawyers: Securing the Rights of Disabled Persons, 28. LC 83-11724. (Contributions in Legal Studies: No. 28). (Illus.). 236p. 1984. 62.95 (*0-313-24105-8*, OCL/, Greenwood Pr) Greenwood.
Olson-Sutton, Judith, jt. auth. see Satterwhite, Marilyn.
Olson-Sutton, Judith, jt. auth. see Satterwhite, Marilyn L.
Olson, Syble, ed. see DuBos, Denise.
Olson, Tamara, jt. auth. see Squibb, Ronald.
Olson, Ted. Blue Ridge Folklife. LC 97-27218. (Folklife in the South Ser.). (Illus.). 256p. 1997. pap. 18.00 (*1-57806-023-0*) U Pr of Miss.
— Blue Ridge Folklife. LC 97-27218. (Folklife in the South Ser.). (Illus.). 256p. 1998. 45.00 (*1-57806-022-2*) U Pr of Miss.
— Ranch on the Laramie. LC 72-8985. x, 240p. 1973. write for info. (*0-316-65052-8*) Little.
Olson, Theodore. Millennialism, Utopianism, & Progress. 1981. text 45.00 (*0-8020-5506-0*) U of Toronto Pr.
***Olson, Theodore B.** Constitutional Challenges to Punitive Damages after BMW V. Gore. LC 98-161287. 1998. write for info. (*0-937299-68-5*) Natl Legal Ctr Pub Interest.
***Olson, Theresa.** His Holiness Maharishi Mahesh Yogi a Living Saint for the New: Stories of His First Visit to the U. S. A. As Told by Helena Olson. 2nd ed. (Illus.). 250p. 2000. pap. 16.95 (*1-929297-02-5*, Pub. by Samhita Prodns) ACCESS Pubs Network.
— Maharishi Mahesh Yogi: A Living Saint for the New Millennium. 1999. pap. text. write for info. (*1-57582-040-4*) Samhita Enterprises.
Olson, Toby. Changing Appearance. 1975. pap. 15.00 (*0-87924-021-0*) Membrane Pr.

O

— Home. 1976. pap. 5.00 (0-87924-035-0) Membrane Pr.

*Olson, Toby. Human Nature. LC PS3565.L84H86 2000. 2000. pap. 14.95 (0-8112-1440-0, Pub. by New Directions) Norton.

Olson, Toby. Seaview. LC 88-22359. 288p. 1982. 9.95 (0-8112-0828-1, Pub. by New Directions) Norton.

— Unfinished Building. LC 93-15299. 96p. (Orig.). 1993. pap. 11.95 (1-56689-009-8) Coffee Hse.

*Olson, Toby. Utah, Vol. 49. (Illus.). 2000. pap. 12.95 (1-892295-35-0) Green Integer.

Olson, Toby. We Are the Fire: A Selection of Poems. LC 84-4772. 128p. 1984. 14.95 (0-8112-0913-X, Pub. by New Directions); pap. 7.50 (0-8112-0914-8, NDP580, Pub. by New Directions) Norton.

*Olson, Toby. Write Letter to Billy. 368p. 2000. pap. 15.95 (1-56689-103-5, Pub. by Coffee Hse) Consort Bk Sales.

Olson, Toby, jt. ed. see Siegel, Muffy E.

Olson, Todd. PDR Atlas of Anatomy. LC 98-171711. (Illus.). 500p. 1997. text 54.95 (1-56363-279-9) Med Econ.

Olson, Todd R. A. D. A. M. Student Atlas of Anatomy: Keepsake. (Illus.). (C). 1998. write for info. (0-683-30179-9) Lppncott W & W.

— A. D. A. M.'s Student Atlas: Animated Dissection of Anatomy for Medicine. LC 95-11593. (Illus.). 544p. 1996. pap. text 39.95 (0-683-00042-X) Lppncott W & W.

Olson, Vera B., jt. auth. see Olson, James C.

Olson, Virgil J. & Olson, Helen. Capitol Reef: The Story Behind the Scenery. Sommer, Sigrid, tr. (GER., Illus.). 48p. (Orig.). 1994. pap. 8.95 (0-88714-778-X) KC Pubns.

— Capitol Reef: The Story Behind the Scenery. rev. ed. LC 90-60036. (Illus.). 48p. (Orig.). 1990. pap. 7.95 (0-88714-043-2) KC Pubns.

Olson, W. K., et al, eds. Structure & Expression: DNA Bending & Curvature, Vol. 3. (Structure & Expression Ser.). (Illus.). 280p. 1988. lib. bdg. 100.00 (0-940030-23-3) Adenine Pr.

— Structure & Expression: From Proteins to Ribosomes; DNA & Its Drug Complexes; DNA Bending & Curvature, 3 vols., Set. (Illus.). 1988. lib. bdg. 300.00 (0-940030-24-1) Adenine Pr.

Olson, W. Scott. Acts of Illumination: Opening Conversation for the Writing Classroom. (Illus.). 47p. (Orig.). (C). 1996. pap. text 7.50 (0-945632-16-9) St Marys Univ Pr.

Olson, W. T., jt. ed. see Hawthorne, William R.

Olson, Waldemar. Methods of Teaching Elementary School Mathematics. LC 68-56887. 281p. reprint ed. pap. 87.20 (0-608-30448-4, 200347400030) Bks Demand.

Olson, Wallace M. History of Fort Durham. (ENG.). 77p. 1994. pap. text 13.00 (1-57833-050-5) Todd Commns.

Olson, Wallace M. The Tlingit: An Introduction to Their Culture & History. 3rd ed. LC E99.T6047 1997. (Illus.). 111p. 1997. pap. 12.50 (0-9659009-0-8) Heritage Research.

Olson, Wallace M., anno. Alaska Travel Journal of Archibald Menzies, 1793-1794. LC 93-1334. xvi, 247p. (C). 1993. pap. 17.50 (0-912006-70-6) U of Alaska Pr.

Olson, Walter. Job Lock: How Employment Laws Are Paralyzing the American Workplace. 1997. 25.00 (0-614-27991-7) Free Pr LA.

Olson, Walter K. Getting Away with It. 240p. 1999. text 23.95 (0-525-94278-5) NAL.

Olson, Waltler K. The Excuse Factory. LC 97-7114. 336p. 1997. 24.50 (0-684-82732-8) Free Pr.

Olson, Warren E., jt. auth. see Hertzke, Eugene R.

Olson, Wayne, ed. Automated Microbiological Identification & Quantitation: Technologies for the 2000's. (Illus.). 397p. 1996. 197.00 (0-935184-82-1) Interpharm.

Olson, Wayne & Groves, M., eds. Aseptic Pharmaceutical Manufacturing: Technology for the 1990s. 430p. 1987. 79.50 (0-935184-06-6) Interpharm.

Olson, Wayne, jt. auth. see Lassanyi, Mary E.

Olson, Wayne, ed. see Schwartz, Frederick J.

Olson, Wayne K. Agriculture & the Gatt: A Retrospective Bibliography, 1948-1980. 55p. (C). 1998. reprint ed. pap. text 20.00 (0-7881-7446-0) DIANE Pub.

Olson, Wayne P., ed. Separations Technology: Pharmaceutical & Biotechnology Applications. 505p. 1995. 179.00 (0-935184-72-4) Interpharm.

Olson, Wayne P., jt. ed. see Nordhauser, Fred M.

Olson, Willard C. The Measurement of Nervous Habits in Normal Children, Vol. 3. LC 73-9228. 97p. 1970. reprint ed. lib. bdg. 45.00 (0-8371-6991-7, CWOH, Greenwood Pr) Greenwood.

Olson, William C. Congressional Power in International Relations. (C). 2000. pap. 65.00 (0-8133-1060-1); pap. text 19.95 (0-8133-1061-X) Westview.

Olson, William C. & Groom, A. J. R. International Relations Then & Now: Origins & Trends in Interpretation. LC 92-22900. 1992. write for info. (0-415-09080-6) Routledge.

Olson, William H. Island Haiku. 36p. (Orig.). 1997. pap. 5.50 (1-890352-02-0) Jackson Harbor.

— Island Verse: Poems Relating to Washington Island. 61p. (Orig.). 1995. pap. 3.99 (0-9640210-2-1) Jackson Harbor.

— Island Verse: Poems Relating to Washington Island. (Illus.). 61p. (Orig.). 1995. 13.99 (0-9640210-4-8) Jackson Harbor.

*Olson, William H. The Islanders. 172p. 1999. pap. 10.95 (1-890352-09-8) Jackson Harbor.

Olson, William H. North of Death's Door. LC 92-3505. (Illus.). vi, 66p. 1992. 10.00 (0-940473-25-9) Wm Caxton.

Olson, William H. & Olson, Charles J. Cyclist's Guide to Washington Island. LC 97-71788. (Illus.). 49p. (Orig.). 1997. spiral bd. 4.95 (1-890352-00-4) Jackson Harbor.

— Washington Island Guidebook. LC 94-179864. 52p. 1994. pap. 4.98 (0-9640210-0-5) Jackson Harbor.

— Washington Island Guidebook. (Illus.). 56p. 1995. 14.99 (0-9640210-6-4) Jackson Harbor.

Olson, William H., et al. Handbook of Symptom Oriented Neurology. 2nd ed. (Illus.). 632p. (C). (gr. 13). 1993. pap. text 37.95 (0-8016-7779-3, 07779) Mosby Inc.

Olson, William H., jt. auth. see Burns, Robert.

Olson, William H., jt. auth. see Lindquist, William J.

Olson, William J. Anglo-Iranian Relations During the First World War. 305p. 1986. 49.50 (0-7146-3178-7, Pub. by F Cass Pubs) Intl Spec Bk.

Olson, William J., ed. Small Wars. LC 94-68309. (Annals of the American Academy of Political & Social Science Ser.: Vol. 541). 1995. 28.00 (0-8039-7124-9); pap. 18.00 (0-8039-7125-7) Am Acad Pol Soc Sci.

Olson, Wilma R. Olancha Remembered. unabridged ed. Olson, Mark, ed. LC 97-92709. (Illus.). 180p. 1997. pap. 7.95 (0-9659709-3-0) W R Olson.

Olssen, Erik. Building the New World: Work, Politics & Society in Caversham 1880s-1920s. (Illus.). 300p. 1995. pap. 29.95 (1-86940-106-9, Pub. by Auckland Univ) Paul & Co Pubs.

— The Red Feds: Revolutionary Industrial Unionism & the New Zealand Federation of Labor 1908-1914. 312p. 1988. 59.00 (0-19-558122-9) OUP.

*Olssen, Mark. Michel Foucault: Materialism & Education. LC 98-49933. (Critical Studies in Education & Culture). 216p. 1999. 59.95 (0-89789-587-8, Bergin & Garvey) Greenwood.

Olsson, jt. auth. see Barger, Vernon.

Olsson, A. A. Papers on Neogene Mollusks No. 19: Special Publication. 163p. 1993. 16.00 (0-87710-428-X) Paleo Res.

Olsson, Anders. The Swedish Wage Negotiation System. 220p. 1990. text 66.95 (1-85521-203-X, Pub. by Dartmth Pub) Ashgate Pub Co.

Olsson, Anders G., jt. ed. see Carlson, Lars A.

Olsson, Axel A. Neogene Mollusks from Northwestern Ecuador No. 4: Special Publication. (Illus.). 258p. 1964. 12.00 (0-87710-367-4) Paleo Res.

Olsson, Birger, jt. ed. see Hartman, Lars.

Olsson, Birgur. Structure & Meaning in the Fourth Gospel: A Text-Linguistic Analysis of John. (New Testament Ser.: No. 6). 328p. 1974. pap. 53.00 (91-40-03344-9, Pub. by LiberUtbildning) Coronet Bks.

Olsson, David E. Management by Objectives. LC 67-21207. (Illus.). xiv, 112p. 1968. 15.95 (0-87015-168-1) Pacific Bks.

Olsson, David L., et al. Opportunities in Chemical Engineering. (Opportunities In . . . Ser.). (Illus.). 160p. pap. 12.95 (0-8442-6588-8, 297ICHEME, VGM Career) NTC Contemp Pub Co.

Olsson, David L., jt. auth. see Raphael, Harold J.

Olsson, Gunnar. Lines of Power - Limits of Language. (Illus.). 144p. (C). 1991. 24.95 (0-8166-1949-2) U of Minn Pr.

Olsson, Gunnar, jt. ed. see Gale, Stephen.

Olsson, Gustaf. Selected Papers on Reticles & Their Applications. LC 99-10802. (Milestone Ser.). 668p. 1999. 110.00 (0-8194-3225-3) SPIE.

Olsson, Hagar. The Woodcarver & Death (Trasnidaren Och d Oden) Schoolfield, George C., tr. from SWE. LC 65-24187. (Nordic Translation Ser.). 176p. reprint ed. pap. 54.60 (0-608-20464-1, 207171600002) Bks Demand.

Olsson, Jennifer. Cast Again: Tales of a Fly-Fishing Guide. (Illus.). 160p. 1996. 19.95 (1-55821-442-9, 14429) Lyons Pr.

— Cast Again: Tales of a Fly-Fishing Guide. 160p. 1997. reprint ed. pap. 12.95 (1-55821-580-8) Lyons Pr.

Olsson, Karl A. By One Spirit. (Illus.). 1962. pap. 12.95 (0-910452-10-5) Covenant.

— A Family of Faith. 157p. 1975. pap. 5.45 (0-910452-24-5) Covenant.

Olsson, Kurt. John Gower & the Structures of Conversion: A Reading of the Confessio Amantis. (Publications of John Gower Society: Vol. 4). 283p. (C). 1992. 75.00 (0-85991-314-7) Boydell & Brewer.

Olsson, Lars. On the Threshold of the People's Home of Sweden. LC 97-14995. 176p. (Orig.). 1997. pap. 19.95 (1-57703-002-8) CMS.

Olsson, Nils-Olof. Stockholm: Seen by Five Centuries of Artists. Austin, Paul Britten, tr. from SWE. LC 98-135030. (Illus.). 212p. 1997. 87.50 (91-7031-075-0) Coronet Bks.

Olsson, Nils W. Swedish Passenger Arrivals in New York, 1820-1850. LC 67-21056. 392p. 1967. 5.00 (0-318-03677-0) Swedish-Am.

Olsson, Nils W., ed. A Pioneer in Northwest America, 1841-1858, 2 vols. LC 60-11209. 1960. 16.00 (0-318-03680-0) Swedish-Am.

*Olsson, Nils William, ed. Swedish Voters in Chicago 1888: Based Upon the Voter Registrations of 1888. LC 99-76487. (Studies in Swedish American Genealogy: Vol. 5). (Illus.). 320p. 1999. 42.50 (0-9616105-3-0) SAG Pubns.

Olsson, O. Roentgen Diagnosis of the Urogenital System. LC 73-14486. (Encyclopedia of Medical Radiology Ser.: Vol. 13, Pt. 1). (Illus.). 690p. 1974. 300.00 (0-387-06514-8) Spr-Verlag.

Olsson, Rolf, jt. ed. see Tygstrup, Niels.

*Olsson, S. Bertil, et al, eds. Dispersion of Ventricular Repolarization: State of the Art. (Illus.). 300p. 2000. write for info. (0-87993-458-1) Futura Pub.

Olsson-Seffer, Pehr. Genesis & Development of Sand Formations on Marine Coast & the Sand Strand Flora of Marine Coasts. LC 11-22544. (Augustana College Library Publications: No. 7). 183p. 1910. pap. 1.00 (0-910182-04-3) Augustana Coll.

*Olsson, Shoren, et al. In Ned's Head. LC 99-86169. (J). 2000. write for info. (0-689-83870-0) Atheneum Yung Read.

Olsson, Sten E. The Radiological Diagnosis in Canine & Feline Emergencies: An Atlas of Thoracic & Abdominal Changes. LC 71-146031. 223p. reprint ed. pap. 69.20 (0-608-10273-3, 205657200074) Bks Demand.

Olsson, Suzann, ed. The Gender Factor: Women in New Zealand Organizations. (Orig.). 1992. pap. 35.00 (0-86469-167-X) Intl Spec Bk.

Olsson, Sven E., ed. Social Policy & Welfare State in Sweden. 2nd ed. (Lund Studies in Social Welfare: No. 3). 348p. (Orig.). 1992. pap. 63.00 (91-7924-053-4) Coronet Bks.

Olsson, Tord, et al, eds. Alevi Identity: Cultural, Religious & Social Perspectives. 188p. 1998. 65.00 (0-7007-1087-6, Pub. by Curzon Pr Ltd); pap. 29.95 (0-7007-1088-4, Pub. by Curzon Pr Ltd) Paul & Co Pubs.

Olsson, Torsten, jt. auth. see Hansson, Elisabeth.

Olsson, Y., jt. ed. see Sharma, H. S.

*Olstad, Geneva Roth. Main Street, North Dakota Vol. 1: In Vintage Postcards. (Postcard History Ser.). (Illus.). 128p. 2000. pap. 18.99 (0-7385-0726-1) Arcadia Publng.

— Main Street, North Dakota Vol. 2: In Vintage Postcards. (Postcard History Ser.). (Illus.). 128p. 2000. pap. 18.99 (0-7385-0760-1) Arcadia Publng.

Olstad, Kathy G. Housetraining 101: For Dogs of All Ages. Grant, Diane K., ed. (Illus.). 52p. 1996. pap. text 10.00 (0-9659671-0-7) Box R Pubns.

Olstedt, Christine E., ed. see Karstedt, Mark J.

Olstein, Judi. Sensational Desserts. 93p. 1994. write for info. (1-57215-001-7) World Pubns.

Olstein, Judi, jt. auth. see Buff, Sheila.

Olsten, Haley, jt. auth. see Bradley, Don.

Olster, David M. The Politics of Usurpation in the Seventh Century: Rhetoric & Revolution in Byzantium. vii, 209p. 1993. pap. 80.00 (90-256-1010-2, Pub. by AM Hakkert) BookLink Distributors.

— Roman Defeat, Christian Response, & the Literary Construction of the Jew. LC 93-42841. (Middle Ages Ser.). 224p. (C). 1994. text 33.95 (0-8122-3152-X) U of Pa Pr.

Olster, Fredi, et al, eds. Discovering Shakespeare: Romeo & Juliet: a Workbook for Students. LC 96-15959. 144p. (Orig.). (J). 1996. pap. 19.95 (1-57525-044-6) Smith & Kraus.

Olster, Fredi & Hamilton, Rick. Discovering Shakespeare: A Midsummer's Night Dream: A Workbook for Students. LC 96-15955. (Young Actors Ser.). 112p. (J). 1996. pap., student ed. 19.95 (1-57525-042-X) Smith & Kraus.

— Discovering Shakespeare: MacBeth. (Young Actors Ser.). 144p. (YA). (gr. 7-12). 1999. wbk. ed. 19.95 (1-57525-149-3) Smith & Kraus.

— Discovering Shakespeare: Much Ado about Nothing: A Workbook for Students & Teachers. LC 98-7822. (Young Actors Ser.). 160p. (YA). (gr. 7 up). 1998. pap. text, wbk. ed. 19.95 (1-57525-143-4) Smith & Kraus.

— Discovering Shakespeare: The Taming of the Shrew: A Workbook for Students. (Young Actors Ser.). 168p. (J). 1996. pap., wbk. ed. 19.95 (1-57525-046-2) Smith & Kraus.

Olster, Stacey. Reminiscence & Re-Creation in Contemporary American Fiction. 232p. (C). 1989. text 64.95 (0-521-36383-7) Cambridge U Pr.

Olsthoom, Xander & European Commission. Economic Evaluation of Air Quality Targets for Sulphur Dioxide, Nitrogen Dioxide, Fine & Suspended Particulate Matter & Lead: Final Report. LC 98-196591. 1998. 30.00 (92-828-3063-2, Pub. by Comm Europ Commun) Bernan Associates.

Olswang, Lesley B., et al. Assessing Prelinguistic & Linguistic Behaviors in Developmentally Young Children. 164p. 1987. ring bd. 50.00 (0-295-96560-6) U of Wash Pr.

Olswang, Steven G. & Lee, Barbara A. Faculty Freedoms & Institutional Accountability: Interactions & Conflicts. Fife, Jonathan D., ed. LC 84-73305. (ASHE-ERIC Higher Education Reports: No. 84-5). 92p. (Orig.). 1985. pap. 24.00 (0-913317-14-4) GWU Grad Schl E&HD.

Olswanger, Anna. Sweet Potato Pudding. LC 99-72737. (Illus.). 60p. 1999. pap. text 6.95 (1-58521-008-0) Bks Black Chldn.

Olswanger, Anna, ed. The Memphis Music of Berl Olswanger. 82p. (Orig.). 1985. pap. 14.95 (0-9614598-3-2) Anna Olswanger.

Olszak, W., ed. Thin Shell Theory: New Trends & Applications. (CISM Courses & Lectures: Vol. 240). (Illus.). 301p. 1981. 50.95 (0-387-81602-X) Spr-Verlag.

Olszer, Krystyna, ed. Treasury of Love Poems by Adam Mickiewicz (Bilingual) LC 98-36272. 128p. 1998. 11.95 (0-7818-0652-6) Hippocrene Bks.

Olszer, Krystyna M., ed. Informator Dla Nowoprzybytych Z Polski: Guide for Newcomers from Poland. 84p. 1983. 4.00 (0-940962-48-9) Polish Inst Art & Sci.

Olszer, Krystyna M. & Olszer, Ryszard. Polish Handy Extra Dictionary. (POL.). 125p. (Orig.). 1996. pap. 11.95 (0-7818-0504-X) Hippocrene Bks.

Olszer, Ryszard, jt. auth. see Olszer, Krystyna M.

Olszewska, E. S., jt. tr. see Turville-Petre, Gabriel.

Olszewski, Bruce J. & Schiavo, Frank R. Readings in Environmental Studies. 416p. (C). 1992. pap. text 27.95 (0-8403-7324-4) Kendall-Hunt.

Olszewski, Deborah I. & Dibble, Harold L., eds. The Paleolithic Prehistory of the Zagros-Taurus. LC 93-12382. (University Museum Monographs: Vol. 83/V). xiii, 237p. (C). 1983. 50.00 (0-924171-24-3) U Museum Pubns.

Olszewski, Edward J., jt. ed. see Dunbar, Burton L.

Olszewski-Kubilius, Paula & Vantassel-Baska, Joyce, eds. Patterns of Influence on Gifted Learners: The Home, the Self, & the School. LC 88-29486. (Education & Psychology of the Gifted Ser.). 261p. 1989. reprint ed. pap. 81.00 (0-608-03016-3, 206346600006) Bks Demand.

Olszewski, Lema J., ed. see Ward, Fred & Ward, Betty.

Olszewski, Mike, jt. auth. see Sweed, Ron.

Olszewski, Waldemar L. Handbook of Microsurgery, Vol. 1. LC 83-15087. 1984. lib. bdg. 182.00 (0-8493-3920-0, CRC Reprint) Franklin.

— Handbook of Microsurgery, Vol. 2. LC 82-15087. 1984. lib. bdg. 182.00 (0-8493-3921-9, CRC Reprint) Franklin.

— In Vivo Migration of Immune Cells. 280p. 1987. 156.00 (0-8493-5076-X, CRC Reprint) Franklin.

— Lymph Stasis: Pathophysiology, Diagnosis, & Treatment. (Illus.). 592p. 1991. lib. bdg. 259.00 (0-8493-6499-X, RC646) CRC Pr.

— Peripheral Lymph: Formation & Immune Function. 176p. 1985. 105.00 (0-8493-6137-0, QP115, CRC Reprint) Franklin.

Olszewski, Waldemar L., ed. see European Society for Surgical Research Staff.

Olszewsky, J. & Baxter, D. Cytoarchitecture of the Human Brain Stem. 2nd ed. (Illus.). 200p. 1981. 242.75 (3-8055-2210-X) S Karger.

Olszowka, Albert J., et al. Blood Gases: Hemoglobin, Base Excess & Maldistribution; Nomograms for Normal & Abnormal Bloods, Effects of Maldistribution. LC 72-12923. 179p. reprint ed. pap. 55.50 (0-8357-7327-2, 205543900022) Bks Demand.

Olszowy-Schlanger, Judith. Karaite Marriage Contracts from the Cairo Geniza: Legal Traditions & Community Life in Medieval Egypt & Palestine. LC 97-40007. (Etudes sur le Judaisme Medieval Ser.: No. 20). (Illus.). 570p. 1997. 185.00 (90-04-10886-6) Brill Academic Pubs.

Olthoff, James K., ed. Gaseous Electronics Conference Radio-Frequency Reference Cell. (Illus.). 175p. (Orig.). (C). 1996. pap. text 50.00 (0-7881-2708-X) DIANE Pub.

Olthoff, James K., jt. ed. see Christophorou, Loucas G.

Olthoff, Walter, et al, eds. ECOOP '95 - Object-Oriented Programming: 9th European Conference, Aarhus, Denmark, August 7-11, 1995, Proceedings, Vol. XI. LC 95-35671. (Lecture Notes in Computer Science Ser.: Vol. 952). 471p. 1995. 75.00 (3-540-60160-0) Spr-Verlag.

Olthuis, James H. Knowing Other-Wise: Philosophy at the Threshold of Spirituality. LC 97-7412. (Perspectives in Continental Philosophy Ser.: Vol. 4). viii, 268p. 1997. 35.00 (0-8232-1780-9); pap. 19.00 (0-8232-1781-7) Fordham.

Olthuis, James H., ed. see Canadian Corporation for Studies in Religion Staff.

*Oltion, Jerry. Abandon in Place. 2000. text 24.95 (0-312-87264-X) Tor Bks.

Oltion, Jerry. Mudd in Your Eye. (Star Trek Ser.). 1997. per. 5.99 (0-671-00260-0, Star Trek) PB.

— Twilight's End. (Star Trek Ser.: Vol. 77). 1996. mass mkt. 5.99 (0-671-53873-X, Pocket Books) PB.

*Oltion, Jerry & Oltion, Kathy. The Flaming Arrow. (Star Trek Ser.: Vol. 4). 320p. 2000. per. 6.50 (0-671-78562-1, Star Trek) PB.

Oltion, Jerry & Pike, Christopher. Where Sea Meets Sky. (Star Trek: The Captain's Table Ser.: No. 6). 267p. 1998. mass mkt. 6.50 (0-671-02400-0) PB.

Oltion, Kathy, jt. auth. see Oltion, Jerry.

Oltjenbruns, Kevin A., jt. auth. see Cook, Alicia S.

Oltman, Deborah O. Statistics for Business & Economics. (Business Statistics Ser.). 1991. pap., student ed. 26.95 (0-534-14433-0) Wadsworth Pub.

Oltman, Debra O. & Lackritz, James R. Statistics for Business & Economics. LC 90-2148. 984p. (C). 1991. text 80.95 (0-534-14430-6) Wadsworth Pub.

Oltmanns. Abnormal Psychology. 2nd ed. 1997. pap. text, student ed. 20.00 (0-13-750258-3, Pub. by P-H) S&S Trade.

Oltmanns, Michael J. European Company Structures: A Guide to Establishing a Business Entity in a European Country. LC 98-180444. (Ernst & Young Legal Ser.). xi, 266p. 1998. 95.00 (90-411-0746-0) Kluwer Law Intl.

Oltmanns, Thomas F. & Emery, Robert E. Abnormal Psychology. LC 94-35274. 704p. 1994. text 88.00 (0-13-007295-8) P-H.

— Abnormal Psychology. 2nd ed. LC 97-14478. 761p. 1997. 85.33 (0-13-728197-8) P-H.

Oltmanns, Thomas F. & Maher, Brendan A., eds. Delusional Beliefs. LC 87-25328. (Personality Processes Ser.). 352p. 1988. 125.00 (0-471-83635-4) Wiley.

Oltmanns, Thomas F., et al. Case Studies in Abnormal Psychology. 4th ed. 416p. 1995. pap. 46.95 (0-471-00581-9) Wiley.

— Case Studies in Abnormal Psychology. 5th ed. LC 98-35239. 416p. 1998. pap. 37.95 (0-471-25216-6) Wiley.

Olton, David S. & Kesner, R., eds. Neurobiology of Comparative Cognition. (Roitblat Bever Olton Ser.). 488p. (C). 1990. pap. 45.00 (0-8058-0639-3); text 99.95 (0-8058-0133-2) L Erlbaum Assocs.

Olton, Roy, jt. auth. see Plano, J. P.

Olton, Roy, jt. auth. see Plano, Jack C.

Oltrogge, Keith. Massey Tractor Data Book. LC 99-43587. (Tractor Data Bks.). (Illus.). 160p. 1999. pap. text 11.95 (0-7603-0599-4, 128922AP, Pub. by MBI Pubg) Motorbooks Intl.

Olu, Easmon C. Bisi & the Golden Disc. LC 89-77347. (Illus.). 32p. (J). 1990. 13.95 (0-940793-56-3, Crocodile Bks) Interlink Pub.

Oluer-Zimmerman, Joelle, jt. auth. see LesPes, Claudine.

Olufs, Dick, jt. auth. see Schuman, David.

An Asterisk (*) at the beginning of an entry indicates that the title is appearing for the first time.

Olufs, Dick W., 3rd. The Making of Telecommunication Policy. LC 98-7499. (Explorations in Public Policy Ser.). 214p. 1998. 49.95 (*1-55587-707-9*) L Rienner.

Olufs, Dick W., III, jt. auth. see Schuman, David F.

Olugbala, Wanda. If Glory Wore a Hat She Would Wear Feathers. 128p. (Orig.). 1997. pap. 15.00 (*0-9657107-2-6*) Olugbalas Way.

— Mountaintop Blues. pap. 6.00 (*0-9657107-0-X*) Olugbalas Way.

— My Grandmother's Posture. pap. 6.00 (*0-9657107-1-8*) Olugbalas Way.

Olugbile, Femi. Lonely Men. LC 88-139532. (Drumbeat Novel Ser.). 183 p. 1987. write for info. (*0-582-98500-5*) Longman.

Oluikpe, B. O. Swazi. LC 96-32821. (Heritage Library of African Peoples: Set 4). (Illus.). 64p. (J). (gr. 7-12). 1997. lib. bdg. 16.95 (*0-8239-2012-7*, D2012-7) Rosen Group.

Olujic, Grozdana. Rose of Mother-of-Pearl. Kessler, Jascha, tr. LC 83-18254. (CRO & SER., Illus.). 19p. (Orig.). (J). (gr. 4 up). 1983. pap. 12.00 (*0-915124-90-4*) Coffee Hse.

Olukoshi, Adebayo O. The Elusive Prince of Denmark: Structural Adjustment & the Crisis of Governance in Africa LC 98-233911. 59 p. 1998. write for info. (*91-7106-428-1*) Nordic Africa.

— Politics of Structural Adjustment in Nigeria. 144p. (C). 1993. text 50.00 (*0-435-08072-5*, 08072) Heinemann.

Olukoshi, Adebayo O., ed. The Politics of Opposition in Contemporary Africa. LC 98-215444. 230p. 1998. pap. 26.95 (*91-7106-419-2*) Transaction Pubs.

Olukoshi, Adebayo O. & Laakso, Liisa, eds. Challenges to the Nation-State in Africa. LC 97-160893. 213p. (Orig.). 1996. pap. 52.50 (*91-7106-381-1*, Pub. by Nordisk Afrikainstitutet) Coronet Bks.

Olukoshi, Adebayo O. & Wohlgemuth, Lennart, eds. A Road to Development: Africa in the 21st Century. (Papers Presented at the Nordic Africa Institute). 84p. 1995. pap. 29.50 (*91-7106-360-9*) Coronet Bks.

Olukoshi, Adebayo O., jt. auth. see Gibbon, Peter.

Olukunmi, Egbelade, jt. auth. see Weaver, LLoyd.

Oluleye, Ibiyinka, jt. auth. see Oluleye, Kunmi.

Oluleye, Kunmi & Oluleye, Ibiyinka. The Cure of Chronic Hepatitis B: One Family's Experience. LC 96-94867. (Illus.). 192p. (Orig.). 1997. pr. 19.95 (*0-9654801-9-4*) Irok Solutions.

***Olum, Adhiambo.** Twins a Step Behind. (Illus.). 44p. (J). (gr. 1-8). 1999. pap. 7.95 (*1-881524-56-6*) Milligan Bks.

Olum, Paul. Invariants for Effective Homotopy Classification & Extension of Mappings. LC 52-42839. (Memoirs Ser.: No. 1/37). 69p. 1989. reprint ed. pap. 22.00 (*0-8218-1237-8*, MEMO/1/37) Am Math.

— Invariants for Effective Homotopy Classification & Extension of Mappings. LC QA0003.A57. (Memoirs of the American Mathematical Society Ser.: No. 37). 75p. reprint ed. pap. 30.00 (*0-7837-7000-6*, 204681300004) Bks Demand.

***Oluonye, Mary N.** Madagascar. LC 99-38138. (Ticket to Ser.). (Illus.). 48p. (J). (gr. k-2). 2000. lib. bdg. 22.60 (*1-57505-145-1*, Carolrhoda) Lerner Pub.

Oluonye, Mary N. Madagascar. LC 98-54225. (Globe-Trotters Club Ser.). (Illus.). 48p. (J). (gr. 3-5). 2000. lib. bdg. 22.60 (*1-57505-120-6*, Carolrhoda) Lerner Pub.

— Nigeria. LC 97-16567. (Globe-Trotters Club Ser.). 1998. 22.60 (*1-57505-113-3*, Carolrhoda) Lerner Pub.

— South Africa. LC 98-54223. (Ticket to Ser.). 48p. (J). (gr. k-2). 1999. lib. bdg. 22.60 (*1-57505-141-9*, Carolrhoda) Lerner Pub.

***Oluonye, Mary N.** South Africa. LC 98-28175. (Globe-Trotters Club Ser.). 48p. (J). (gr. 3-5). 1999. lib. bdg. 22.60 (*1-57505-116-8*, Carolrhoda) Lerner Pub.

Oluonye, Mary N. A Ticket to Nigeria. LC 97-51174. (Ticket to . . . Ser.). (J). 1998. lib. bdg. 19.93 (*1-57505-138-9*, Carolrhoda) Lerner Pub.

Olupona, Jacob, et al, eds. The Study of Religions in Africa: Past, Present & Prospects. (Religions of Africa Ser.: No. 1). 366p. 1996. pap. 59.50 (*0-9525772-2-4*, Pub. by Almqvist Wiksell) Coronet Bks.

Olupona, Jacob K. Kingship, Religion & Rituals in a Nigerian Community: A Phenomenological Study of Ondo Yoruba Festivals. (Stockholm Studies in Comparative Religion: No. 28). (Illus.). 195p. (Orig.). 1991. pap. 47.50 (*91-22-01382-2*) Coronet Bks.

Olupona, Jacob K., intro. African Traditional Religion in Contemporary Society. LC 89-77137. 212p. 1991. pap. 12.95 (*0-89226-079-3*) Paragon Hse.

Olupona, Jacob K. & Nyang, Sulayman S., eds. Religious Plurality in Africa: Essays in Honor of John S. Mbiti. LC 93-7392. (Religion & Society Ser.: No. 32). xxi, 455p. (C). 1993. lib. bdg. 175.40 (*3-11-012220-0*) Mouton.

— Religious Plurality in Africa: Essays in Honor of John S. Mbiti. (Religion & Society Ser.: No. 32). xxi, 445p. (C). 1995. pap. text 36.95 (*3-11-014789-0*) Mouton.

Olusegun, Ayobumi. "Secrets" That Little Girls Hide: The Journey of Ayobumi Olusegun. Matlock-Abdullah, Arriama, ed. 364p. (Orig.). 1997. pap. 18.95 (*0-9660907-3-X*) Univ Breath.

Olusegun Wallace, R. S., et al, eds. Research in Accounting in Emerging Economies, Vol. 1.Tr. of Research in Third World Accounting. 290p. 1991. 78.50 (*1-55938-134-5*) Jai Pr.

— Research in Accounting in Emerging Economies, Vol. 2.Tr. of Research in Third World Accounting. 397p. 1993. 78.50 (*1-55938-419-0*) Jai Pr.

— Research in Accounting in Emerging Economies, Vol. 3.Tr. of Research in Third World Accounting. 1996. 78.50 (*1-55938-697-5*) Jai Pr.

— Research in Accounting in Emerging Economies, Vol. 4.Tr. of Research in Third World Accounting. Date not set. 78.50 (*1-55938-995-8*) Jai Pr.

Olve. Performance Drivers. 362p. 1999. 43.95 (*0-471-98623-2*) Wiley.

Olver. Microwave & Optical Transmission S. O. L. 86p. 1992. pap. text 2.00 (*0-471-93767-3*) Wiley.

Olver, A. D., et al. Microwave Horns & Feeds. 512p. 1994. 99.95 (*0-7803-1115-9*, PC4689) Inst Electrical.

Olver, A. David, et al, eds. The Handbook of Antenna Design, Vols. 1 & 2. (Electromagnetic Waves Ser.: No. 15). 1696p. 1986. pap. 165.00 (*0-86341-052-9*, EW015Z) INSPEC Inc.

Olver, A. David, jt. auth. see Clarricoats, P. J.

Olver, Frank W. Asymptotics & Special Functions. 2nd rev. ed. LC 97-377. (Illus.). 592p. (C). 1997. text 69.00 (*1-56881-069-5*) AK Peters.

Olver, Graham. A French-English Dictionary of Legal & Commercial Terms. (ENG & FRE.). xi, 170p. 1988. reprint ed. lib. bdg. 35.00 (*0-8377-2515-1*, Rothman) W S Hein.

***Olver, Jane.** Color Atlas of Lacrimal Surgery. (Illus.). 176p. 2000. 130.00 (*0-7506-4486-9*) Buttrwrth-Heinemann.

***Olver, P. J.** Applications of Lie Groups to Differential Equations. 2nd ed. (Illus.). 513p. 2000. 39.95 (*0-387-95000-1*) Spr-Verlag.

Olver, Peter J. Applications of Lie Groups to Differential Equations. (Graduate Texts in Mathematics Ser.: Vol. 107). (Illus.). 495p. 1986. 54.00 (*0-387-96250-6*) Spr-Verlag.

— Applications of Lie Groups to Differential Equations. 2nd ed. LC 92-44573. (Illus.). 513p. 1994. 64.95 (*0-387-94007-3*) Spr-Verlag.

— Classical Invariant Theory. LC 98-33722. (London Mathematical Society Student Texts Ser.: Vol. 44). (Illus.). 259p. (C). 1999. 57.95 (*0-521-55243-5*); pap. 21.95 (*0-521-55821-2*) Cambridge U Pr.

— Equivalence, Invariants, & Symmetry. (Illus.). 541p. (C). 1995. text 49.95 (*0-521-47811-1*) Cambridge U Pr.

Olver, Peter J., ed. Solitons in Physics, Mathematics, & Nonlinear Optics. (IMA Volumes in Mathematics & Its Applications Ser.: Vol. 25). (Illus.). xiii, 215p. 1990. 42.95 (*0-387-97309-5*) Spr-Verlag.

Olver, Peter J., jt. ed. see Kamran, Niky.

Olver, Rob & Olver, Stuart. Dawn till Dusk in the Stirling & Porongurup Ranges. 192p. 1998. 49.95 (*1-876268-10-7*, Pub. by Univ of West Aust Pr); pap. 34.95 (*1-876268-09-3*, Pub. by Univ of West Aust Pr) Intl Spec Bk.

Olver, Stuart, jt. auth. see Olver, Rob.

Olweiler, David B. Cowboy Boots in Africa. pap. write for info. (*1-882204-21-2*) Wilde Pub.

Olwell, David H., jt. auth. see Hawkins, Douglas M.

Olwell, Robert. Masters, Slaves, & Subjects: The Culture of Power in the South Carolina Low Country, 1740-1790. LC 97-53061. (Illus.). 296p. 1998. text 49.95 (*0-8014-3488-2*) Cornell U Pr.

— Masters, Slaves & Subjects: The Culture of Power in the South Carolina Low Country, 1740-1790. LC 97-53061. (Illus.). 296p. 1998. pap. 17.95 (*0-8014-8491-X*) Cornell U Pr.

Olweny, Ch. L., et al, eds. Kaposi's Sarcoma. (Antibiotics & Chemotherapy Ser.: Vol. 29). (Illus.). xii, 104p. 1981. 77.50 (*3-8055-2076-X*) S Karger.

Olwer, James S. Grandpa's Very Short Stories... For Every Month of the Year. 108p. 1997. pap. 9.95 (*1-57502-635-X*, PO1797) Morris Pubng.

Olweus, Dan. Bullying at School: What We Know & What We Can Do. (Understanding Children's Worlds Ser.). (Illus.). 136p. 1993. pap. 22.95 (*0-631-19241-7*) Blackwell Pubs.

Olwig, Karen F. Cultural Adaptation & Resistance on St. John: Three Centuries of Afro-Caribbean Life. LC 85-13414. (Illus.). 240p. (Orig.). 1985. pap. 24.95 (*0-8130-0818-2*) U Press Fla.

Olwig, Karen F. Global Culture, Island Identity: Continuity & Change in the Afro-Caribbean Community. LC 92-35262. (Studies in Anthropology & History: No. 8). 256p. 1993. text 72.00 (*3-7186-5329-X*) Gordon & Breach.

Olwig, Karen F. Global Culture, Island Identity: Continuity & Change in the Afro-Caribbean Community of Nevis. (Studies in Anthropology & History). 256p. 1996. pap. text 12.00 (*3-7186-0624-0*, Harwood Acad Pubs) Gordon & Breach.

Olwig, Karen F. & Hastrup, Kirsten, eds. Siting Culture: The Anthropological Object on the Move. 328p. (C). 1996. 85.00 (*0-415-15001-9*) Routledge.

— Siting Culture: The Anthropological Object on the Move. (Illus.). 328p. (C). 1996. pap. 25.99 (*0-415-15002-7*) Routledge.

Olwig, Kenneth R. Nature's Ideological Landscape. (London Research Series in Geography: No. 5). (Illus.). 144p. 1984. text 60.00 (*0-04-710002-8*) Routledge.

Olwyler, Kelle, jt. auth. see Fletcher, Jerry L.

***Olya, Cherentsova.** Gorod V Tekhase. LC 99-35225. (RUS., Illus.). 168p. 1999. pap. 10.00 (*1-55779-121-X*) Hermitage Pubs.

Olyamast. Control Volatile Organic Compound Emiss. (Environmental Engineering Ser.). (C). 1999. text 69.95 (*0-442-02605-6*, VNR) Wiley.

Olyan, Saul M. A Thousand Thousands Served Him: Exegesis & the Naming of Angels in Ancient Judaism. (Texte und Studien zum Antiken Judentum: No. 36). 148p. 1993. 97.50 (*3-16-146063-4*, Pub. by JCB Mohr) Coronet Bks.

Olyan, Saul M. & Nussbaum, Martha C., eds. Sexual Orientation & Human Rights in American Religious Discourse. 288p. 1998. 29.95 (*0-19-511942-8*) OUP.

Olyan, Saul M., jt. ed. see Anderson, Gary A.

Olyanova, Nadya. Handwriting Tells. 1976. pap. 7.00 (*0-87980-046-1*) Wilshire.

— Psychology of Handwriting. (Illus.). 395p. 1978. pap. 10.00 (*0-87980-128-X*) Wilshire.

Olyff, Clotilde. 1 2 3. LC 94-1238. (Illus.). 22p. (J). (ps-3). 1994. 13.95 (*0-395-70736-6*, Pub. by Ticknor & Fields) HM.

Olympia, Daniel, et al. Homework Teams: Homework Management Strategies for the Classroom. (Homework Partners Ser.). (Illus.). 76p. 1993. pap. text, teacher ed. 16.50 (*0-944584-50-0*, 44TEAM) Sopris.

— Sanity Savers for Parents: Tips for Tackling Homework. (Homework Partners Ser.). (Illus.). 66p. 1996. pap. 16.50 (*1-57035-002-7*, 44SAN) Sopris.

Olympia, Peter L. Developing Foxpro Applications. 2nd ed. 496p. (C). 1991. pap. text 26.95 (*0-201-56786-5*) Addison-Wesley.

Olympic Co-Ordination Authority Staff. Homebush Bay Ecological Studies 1993-1994, 2 vols., Vols. 1 & 2. LC 96-207960. (Illus.). 414p. (Orig.). 1996. pap. 44.95 (*0-643-05858-3*, Pub. by CSIRO) Accents Pubns.

Olympic Mountain Rescue Staff. Climber's Guide to the Olympic Mountains. 3rd ed. LC 88-17636. (Illus.). 260p. (Orig.). 1988. pap. 14.95 (*0-89886-154-3*) Mountaineers.

Olympic Scientific Congress (1984, Eugene, OR) Staff. The Dancer as Athlete. Shell, Caroline G., ed. LC 85-18119. (Olympic Scientific Conference Proceedings 1984 Ser.: Vol. 8). (Illus.). 255p. reprint ed. pap. 79.10 (*0-608-20833-7*, 207193200003) Bks Demand.

— Sport & Human Genetics. Malina, Robert M. & Bouchard, Claude, eds. LC 85-18116. (Olympic Scientific Conference Proceedings 1984 Ser.: Vol. 4). 200p. reprint ed. pap. 62.00 (*0-608-20827-2*, 207192600003) Bks Demand.

Olympic Scientific Congress (1984: Eugene, OR) Sta. The Dancer As Athlete. Shell, Caroline G., ed. LC 85-18119. (Nineteen Eighty-Four Olympic Scientific Congress Proceedings Ser.: No. 8). (Illus.). 255p. reprint ed. pap. 79.10 (*0-608-07051-3*, 206725700009) Bks Demand.

— Perspectives in Kinanthropometry. Day, James A., ed. LC 85-18118. (Nineteen Eighty-Four Olympic Scientific Congress Proceedings Ser.: No. 1). (Illus.). 300p. 1986. reprint ed. pap. 93.00 (*0-608-06447-5*, 206728300009) Bks Demand.

— Sport & Aging. McPherson, Barry D., ed. LC 85-18124. (Nineteen Eighty-Four Olympic Scientific Congress Proceedings Ser.: No. 5). (Illus.). 296p. reprint ed. pap. 91.80 (*0-608-06456-4*, 206729400009) Bks Demand.

— Sport & Elite Performers. Landers, Daniel M., ed. LC 85-18115. (1984 Olympic Scientific Congress Proceedings Ser.: No. 3). (Illus.). 212p. reprint ed. pap. 65.80 (*0-608-06451-3*, 206728900009) Bks Demand.

— Sport & Human Genetics. Malina, Robert M. & Bouchard, Claude, eds. LC 85-18116. (Nineteen Eighty-Four Olympic Scientific Congress Proceedings Ser.: No. 4). (Illus.). 200p. reprint ed. pap. 62.00 (*0-608-06458-0*, 206729600009) Bks Demand.

— Sport & Politics. Redmond, Gerald, ed. LC 85-18114. (Nineteen Eighty-Four Olympic Scientific Congress Proceedings Ser.: No. 7). 236p. reprint ed. pap. 73.20 (*0-608-07039-4*, 206724600009) Bks Demand.

— Sport for Children & Youths. Weiss, Maureen R. & Gould, Daniel, eds. LC 85-18111. (Nineteen Eighty-Four Olympic Scientific Congress Proceedings Ser.: No. 10). (Illus.). 302p. reprint ed. pap. 93.70 (*0-608-07044-0*, 206725100009) Bks Demand.

— Sport, Health, & Nutrition. Katch, Frank I., ed. LC 85-18117. (Nineteen Eighty-Four Olympic Scientific Congress Proceedings Ser.: No. 2). (Illus.). 242p. reprint ed. pap. 75.10 (*0-608-07081-5*, 206731000009) Bks Demand.

— Sport Pedagogy. Pieron, Maurice & Graham, George, eds. LC 85-18113. (1984 Olympic Scientific Congress Proceedings Ser.: No. 6). (Illus.). 220p. reprint ed. pap. 68.20 (*0-608-07042-4*, 206724900009) Bks Demand.

Olympiodorus. Olympiodorus: Commentary on Platos "Gorgias" Tarrant, Harold et al, trs. LC 98-16149. (Philosophia Antiqua Ser.: No. 78). (ENG & GRE.). 336p. 1998. 118.00 (*90-04-10972-2*) Brill Academic Pubs.

Olyniec, James H., ed. Transition in the Nuclear Industry: Proceedings of a Symposium Sponsored by the Construction & Energy Division. 237p. 1985. 5.00 (*0-87262-443-9*) Am Soc Civil Eng.

Olynyk, Frank. Stars & Bars: A Tribute to the American Fighter Ace 1920-1973. (Illus.). 698p. 1995. 69.95 (*1-898697-17-5*, Pub. by Grub St) Seven Hills Bk.

Olynyk, M., tr. see Zinkewych, Osyp & Hula, Volodymyr.

Olyott, Stuart, tr. see Calvin, John.

Olyott, Stuart J. Alive in Christ. 1994. pap. 10.99 (*0-85234-315-9*, Pub. by Evangelical Pr) P & R Pubng.

— Gospel As It Really Is (Romans) (Welwyn Commentary Ser.). 1979. pap. 10.99 (*0-85234-124-5*, Pub. by Evangelical Pr) P & R Pubng.

— A Life Worth Living: Ecclesiastes & Song of Solomon. (Welwyn Commentary Ser.). 1983. pap. 8.99 (*0-85234-173-3*, Pub. by Evangelical Pr) P & R Pubng.

— The Three Are One. 1979. pap. 3.99 (*0-85234-138-5*, Pub. by Evangelical Pr) P & R Pubng.

— You Might Have Asked. 1983. pap. 8.99 (*0-85234-175-X*, Pub. by Evangelical Pr) P & R Pubng.

Olyslager, Frank. Electromagnetic Waveguides & Transmission Lines. LC 99-10126. (Oxford Engineering Science Ser.: Vol. 51). (Illus.). 238p. 1999. text 110.00 (*0-19-856450-3*) OUP.

Olzak, Susan. The Dynamics of Ethnic Competition & Conflict. 288p. (C). 1992. 45.00 (*0-8047-2028-2*) Stanford U Pr.

— Dynamics of Ethnic Competition & Conflict. xvi, 271p. 1994. pap. 14.95 (*0-8047-2337-0*) Stanford U Pr.

Olzendam, Roderic M. & Keith, Gordon. It Came to Pass in the San Juan Islands. LC 78-73807. (Illus.). 152p. 1978. 7.95 (*0-8323-0318-6*) Binford Mort.

Olzog, Gunther, jt. auth. see Vinz, Curt.

OM Association, Inc. Staff. Creativity Around Us. 1995. vdisk 64.95 (*0-7872-0972-4*) Kendall-Hunt.

Om, Brita G., jt. auth. see Manning, Mick.

Om, Hari. Beyond the Kashmir Valley. LC 98-917049. 218p. 1998. write for info. (*81-241-0558-8*) Har-Anand Pubns.

Om, R. Hari. Muslims of Jammu & Kashmir. 160p. 1986. 150.00 (*0-7855-1822-3*, Pub. by Archives Pubs) St Mut.

— Muslims of Jammu & Kashmir: A Study in the Spread of Education & Consciousness, 1857-1925. 156p. 1986. 12.00 (*0-685-58187-X*, Pub. by Archives Pubs) Nataraj Bks.

Om-ra-zeti, Khafra. World Economic Collapse: The Last Decade & the Global Depression. LC 93-78028. (Illus.). 278p. (Orig.). 1995. pap. 18.95 (*0-9635645-0-1*) KMT Pubns.

OM Staff. Global Action: Personal Discipleship Manual for the World Christian. Briggs, Richard, ed. 247p. 1997. reprint ed. pap. 16.99 (*1-85078-277-6*, Pub. by O M Pubng) OM Literature.

— Logos, Doulos & Logos II. 1995. 4.99 (*1-85985-035-9*) O M Lit.

Omaar, Rakiya, jt. ed. see Brittain, Victoria.

Omachonu, Vincent K. Health Care Quality Management. LC 98-31216. 1998. 49.95 (*0-89806-187-3*, OMACH) Eng Mgmt Pr.

Omachonu, Vincent K., et al. Principles of Total Quality. 2nd ed. (Illus.). 400p. 1997. lib. bdg. 49.95 (*1-57444-094-2*) St Lucie Pr.

Omae, I. Applications of Organometallic Compounds. 526p. 1998. 215.00 (*0-471-97604-0*) Wiley.

Omae, Kinjiro & Tachibana, Yuzuru. The Book of Sushi. LC 81-80658. 128p. 1988. pap. 19.95 (*0-87011-866-8*) Kodansha.

Omaggio, Alice C. Teaching Language In Context. (Teaching Methods). 479p. (J). 1986. mass mkt. 25.00 (*0-8384-1372-2*) Heinle & Heinle.

Omaggio, Alice C., ed. Proficiency, Curriculum, Articulation: The Ties That Bind. (Reports of the Northeast Conference on the Teaching of Foreign Languages). 220p. 1985. pap. 10.95 (*0-915432-85-4*) NE Conf Teach Foreign.

Omaggio, Alice C., et al. Kaleidoscope: Grammaire en Contexte. 3rd ed. LC 92-25063. 384p. (C). 1992. pap. 59.38 (*0-07-047319-6*) McGraw.

Omaggio, Hadley A., et al. Kaleidoscope: Grammaire en Contexte. 3rd ed. (C). 1993. pap., wbk. ed. 28.13 (*0-07-047320-X*) McGraw.

***Omaha World-Herald Staff.** Omaha, Times Remembered. Gerber, Kristine, ed. (Illus.). 176p. 1999. 39.95 (*0-9674995-0-X*) Kids Prodns.

O'Mahoney, Bernard. So This Is Ecstasy? (Illus.). 192p. 1997. pap. 17.95 (*1-85158-896-5*, Pub. by Mainstream Pubng) Trafalgar.

***O'Mahoney, Bernard & McGovern, Mick.** A Soldier of the Queen. (Illus.). 256p. 2000. 29.95 (*0-86322-262-5*, Pub. by Brandon Bk Pubs) Irish Bks Media.

O'Mahoney, Dan. Four Letter Word: Selecting Writings, 1993-1995. 80p. (Orig.). 1996. pap. 6.95 (*1-873176-29-5*) AK Pr Dist.

O'Mahoney, M. J., jt. ed. see Spirit, D. M.

O'Mahoney, Patrick D. The Fantasy of Human Rights. 192p. 1978. pap. 6.50 (*0-85597-256-4*) Attic Pr.

Omahony. Crime Community & Locale. 56.95 (*1-84014-555-2*) Ashgate Pub Co.

O'Mahony, Charles. Blue Battlefields. Frisque, Tom, ed. (Illus.). 153p. 1994. 39.95 (*0-9623080-6-4*) Aviation Usk.

O'Mahony, Christopher, ed. from FRE. St. Therese of Lisieux: By Those Who Knew Her. 287p. (Orig.). 1975. pap. 14.95 (*0-901810-84-3*, Pub. by Veritas Pubns) St Mut.

O'Mahony, David, jt. auth. see Fanning, Connell.

O'Mahony, Denis & Martin, Una. Practical Therapeutics for Older Patients. LC 98-36751. 284p. 1999. pap. 50.00 (*0-471-98594-5*) Wiley.

O'Mahony, Donal, et al. Electronic Payment Systems. LC 97-9405. (Computing Ser.). 232p. 1997. 69.00 (*0-89006-925-5*) Artech Hse.

O'Mahony, Felicity, ed. Book of Kells: Proceedings of a Conference at Trinity College, Dublin, 1994. LC 94-38638. (Illus.). 640p. 1994. 139.95 (*0-85967-967-5*, Pub. by Scolar Pr) Ashgate Pub Co.

O'Mahony, Gerald. Abba! Father! (C). 1988. 39.00 (*0-85439-194-0*, Pub. by St Paul Pubns) St Mut.

— The Cup That I Drink. (C). 1988. 39.00 (*0-85439-240-8*, Pub. by St Paul Pubns) St Mut.

— Living & Believing, 4 bks. (C). 1988. write for info. (*0-7855-2582-3*, Pub. by St Paul Pubns) St Mut.

— Living & Believing, 4 bks., Bk. 1. (C). 1988. 60.00 (*0-85439-163-0*, Pub. by St Paul Pubns) St Mut.

— Living & Believing, 4 bks., Bk. 2. (C). 1988. 50.00 (*0-85439-174-6*, Pub. by St Paul Pubns) St Mut.

— Living & Believing, 4 bks., Bk. 3. (C). 1988. 50.00 (*0-85439-175-4*, Pub. by St Paul Pubns) St Mut.

— Living & Believing, 4 bks., Bk. 4. (C). 1988. 50.00 (*0-85439-176-2*, Pub. by St Paul Pubns) St Mut.

O'Mahony, Gerald & Lucey, James V., eds. Understanding Psychiatric Treatment: Therapy for Serious Mental Disorder in Adults. LC 97-43723. 172p. 1998. pap. 49.50 (*0-471-97570-2*) Wiley.

O'Mahony, Kieran. The Dictionary of Geographical Literacy: The Complete Geography Reference. (Illus.). 380p. (Orig.). (C). 1993. pap. 19.95 (*0-944638-08-2*) EduCare Pr.

— Geographical Literacy: What Every American Needs to Know about Geography. (Illus.). (Orig.). 1992. pap. 14.95 (*0-944638-06-6*) EduCare Pr.

— Geography & Education. 250p. (C). 1988. text 24.95 (*0-944638-00-7*) EduCare Pr.

O'Mahony, Kieran, ed. see Buchanan, Courtney, et al.

O'Mahony, Kieran, ed. see Jacobson, Sheldon A.

O

An Asterisk (*) at the beginning of an entry indicates that the title is appearing for the first time.

O'Mahony, Kieran, ed. see King, Patrick.

O'Mahony, Kieran, ed. see Lee, Grace.

O'Mahony, Kieran, ed. see Zehr, Ellen.

O'Mahony, Laim, jt. auth. see Seaver, Matt.

O'Mahony, Marie, jt. auth. see Braddock, Sarah E.

O'Mahony, Mary, jt. auth. see Oulton, Nicholas.

O'Mahony, Michael. Sensory Evaluation of Food: Statistical Methods & Procedure. (Food Science & Technology Ser.: Vol. 16). (Illus.). 512p. 1986. text 175.00 (*0-8247-7337-3*) Dekker.

O'Mahony, Patrick J. Nature, Risk & Responsibility: Discourses of Biotechnology LC 98-37245. 1999. 80.00 (*0-415-92290-9*); pap. 24.99 (*0-415-92291-7*) Routledge.

***O'Mahony, Paul.** Prison Policy in Ireland. 72p. 2000. pap. 8.95 (*1-85918-243-7*, Pub. by Cork Univ) Stylus Pub VA.

O'Mahony, T. P. Lynch Years. 125p. 1986. pap. 10.95 (*0-85105-449-8*, Pub. by Smyth) Dufour.

O'Maitiu, Seamas & O'Reilly, Barry. Ballyknockan: A Wicklow Stonecutters' Village. LC 97-213048. (Illus.). 109p. 1997. pap. 19.95 (*0-9528453-5-0*, Pub. by Woodfield Pr) Irish Bks Media.

O'Maitiu, Seamas, jt. auth. see James, Dermot.

O'Maitiu, Seamus. The Humours of Donnybrook: Dublin's Famous Fair & Its Suppression. 64p. 1995. pap. 9.95 (*0-7165-2569-0*, Pub. by Irish Acad Pr) Intl Spec Bk.

Omaji, Paul, jt. auth. see Beresford, Quentin.

***Omakoko, Augustin O.** L'enseignement de l/'Histoire en Republique Democratique du Congo (Ex-Zaire) xv, 339p. 1999. 47.95 (*3-906762-42-4*) P Lang Pubng.

Omalia, Michael. Beginner's Guide to Window Cleaning. Bradley, Austin, ed. & illus. by. (Orig.). 1992. pap. 9.95 (*0-9633996-9-1*) Ready Bks.

O'Malley. Integrated Direct Marketing. LC 99-187893. (ITBP Acquisitions Ser.). 1998. pap. 23.99 (*1-86152-402-1*) Thomson Learn.

O'Malley, jt. auth. see Daley, Jr., Henry O.

O'Malley, Bert W., et al, eds. Hormones & Signalling, Vol. 1. (Illus.). 364p. 1997. text 69.95 (*0-12-312411-5*) Morgan Kaufmann.

O'Malley, Bert W., jt. auth. see Means, Anthony R.

O'Malley, Bert W., ed. see Argenteuil Symposium Staff.

O'Malley, Brendan. Celtic Blessings & Prayers: Making All Things Sacred. LC 98-75050. 176p. 1999. pap. 12.95 (*0-89622-957-2*) Twenty-Third.

***O'Malley, Brendan.** Cyprus Conspiracy. 268p. 2000. text 29.95 (*1-86064-439-2*, Pub. by I B T) St Martin.

— God at Every Gate: Prayers & Blessing for Pilgrims. 192p. 2000. 13.95 (*0-8192-1846-4*, 6291) Morehouse Pub.

O'Malley, Brendan. God at Every Gate: Prayers & Blessings for Pilgrims. 160p. 2000. pap. 13.95 (*1-85311-162-7*, 1981, Pub. by Canterbury Press Norwich) Morehouse Pub.

O'Malley, Brendan, ed. A Welsh Pilgrim's Manual. 147p. (C). 1989. pap. 20.00 (*0-86383-583-X*, Pub. by Gomer Pr) St Mut.

— A Welsh Pilgrim's Manual. 2nd ed. 147p. 1997. reprint ed. pap. 14.95 (*0-8464-4642-1*) Beekman Pubs.

O'Malley, Brian. The Secret of the Mountains. 40p. (J). (gr. 1-6). 1993. 14.95 (*0-9634446-0-3*) Spirit of Advent.

O'Malley, C., ed. see O'Malley, Ernie.

O'Malley, C. D., jt. auth. see Clarke, Edwin.

O'Malley, Charles T. Low Bridges & High Water: On the New York State Barge Canal. (Illus.). 284p. 1991. pap. 19.95 (*0-925168-38-6*) North Country.

O'Malley, Claire, ed. Computer Supported Collaborative Learning. LC 94-40220. (NATO ASI F Computer & Systems Sciences Ser.: Vol. 128). x, 305p. 1994. 79.95 (*0-387-57740-8*) Spr-Verlag.

— Computer Supported Collaborative Learning. LC 94-40220. (NATO ASI F Computer & Systems Sciences Ser.: Vol. 128). x, 305p. 1995. write for info. (*3-540-57740-8*) Spr-Verlag.

O'Malley, Colleen, jt. auth. see Wincek, Jean.

O'Malley, Cormac, jt. auth. see English, Richard.

O'Malley, Ernie. On Another Man's Wound. 343p. 1979. reprint ed. pap. 17.95 (*0-947962-31-X*, Pub. by Anvil Books Ltd) Irish Bks Media.

— On Another Man's Wound: A Personal History of Ireland's War of Independence. 336p. 1999. reprint ed. pap. 14.95 (*1-57098-277-5*) Roberts Rinehart.

— Prisoners: The Civil War Letters of Ernie O'Malley. English, R. & O'Malley, C., eds. 164p. 1991. pap. 15.95 (*1-85371-140-3*, Pub. by Poolbeg Pr) Dufour.

— The Singing Flame. 2nd ed. 312p. 1992. reprint ed. pap. 15.95 (*0-947962-32-8*, Pub. by Anvil Books Ltd) Irish Bks Media.

O'Malley, Ilene V. The Myth of the Revolution: Hero Cults & the Institutionalization of the Mexican State, 1920-1940, 1. LC 85-30488. (Contributions to the Study of World History Ser.: No. 1). 211p. 1986. 49.95 (*0-313-25184-3*, OMR/, Greenwood Pr) Greenwood.

O'Malley, J. J., et al, eds. Hegel & the History of Philosophy. 248p. 1975. pap. text 106.00 (*90-247-1712-4*) Kluwer Academic.

O'Malley, J. J. & Green, Bill. The Glen - 50 Years of Road Racing Excellence. LC 99-173454. (Illus.). 224p. 1998. 39.95 (*0-943860-14-8*) UMI Pubns.

O'Malley, J. Michael & Chamot, Anna U. Learning Strategies in Second Language Acquisition. (Cambridge Applied Linguistics Ser.). (Illus.). 272p. (C). 1990. pap. text 22.95 (*0-521-35837-X*) Cambridge U Pr.

O'Malley, J. Michael, jt. auth. see Chamot, Anna U.

O'Malley, J. Steven. Early German-American Evangelicalism: Pietist Sources on Discipleship & Sanctification, 7 Vols., Vol. 7. LC 94-21622. (Pietist & Wesleyan Studies: No. 7). (Illus.). 362p. 1995. 65.50 (*0-8108-2873-1*) Scarecrow.

O'Malley, Jan. The Politics of Community Action. 180p. (C). 1988. 60.00 (*0-85124-184-0*); pap. 45.00 (*0-85124-183-2*) St Mut.

O'Malley, Jeanne, jt. auth. see Thompson, Terry.

O'Malley, Jeannette, jt. ed. see Kirst, Lynn.

***O'Malley, John.** Introduction to PSpice for Windows. (Illus.). 200p. 2000. pap. 32.00 (*0-13-915661-5*) P-H.

O'Malley, John. Schaum's Outline of Basic Circuit Analysis. 2nd ed. LC 90-26615. (Schaum's Outline Ser.). 484p. (C). 1992. pap. 15.95 (*0-07-047824-4*) McGraw.

O'Malley, John F. Managed Care Referral: Development & Management Strategies - How to Develop a Systematic Plan for Building Your Referral Business in Today's Healthcare Environment. LC 96-3675. 288p. 1996. text 45.00 (*0-7863-0878-8*, Irwn Prfssnl) McGraw-Hill Prof.

— Ultimate Patient Satisfaction: Designing & Implementing an Effective Patient Satisfaction Program. LC 97-26913. 1997. 55.00 (*0-7863-1219-X*, Irwn Prfssnl) McGraw-Hill Prof.

O'Malley, John W. The First Jesuits. 480p. (C). 1993. 43.50 (*0-674-30312-1*) HUP.

— The First Jesuits. (Illus.). 480p. 1995. pap. 16.95 (*0-674-30313-X*, OMAFIX) HUP.

— Religious Culture in the Sixteenth Century: Preaching, Rhetoric, Spirituality, & Reform. (Collected Studies: No. CS 404). 294p. 1993. 104.95 (*0-86078-369-3*, Pub. by Variorum) Ashgate Pub Co.

Omalley, John W. Spiritualia & Pastoralia. (Collected Works of Erasmus: Vol. 69). 660p. 1998. text 125.00 (*0-8020-4309-7*) U of Toronto Pr.

***O'Malley, John W.** Trent & All That: Renaming Catholicism in the Early Modern Era. LC 99-41584. (Illus.). 240p. 2000. 24.95 (*0-674-00087-0*) HUP.

O'Malley, John W., ed. Catholicism in Early Modern History: A Guide to Research. (Reformation Guides to Research Ser.: Vol. II). 346p. 1988. 29.50 (*0-910345-02-3*) Center Reform.

— Humanity & Divinity in Renaissance & Reformation: Essays In Honor of Charles Trinkaus. LC 93-14242. (Studies in the History of Christian Thought: Vol. 51). x, 328p. 1993. 126.50 (*90-04-09804-6*) Brill Academic Pubs.

O'Malley, John W., et al, eds. The Jesuits: Cultures, Sciences, & the Arts, 1540-1773. (Illus.). 872p. 1999. text 80.00 (*0-8020-4287-2*) U of Toronto Pr.

O'Malley, John W., ed. see Erasmus, Desiderius.

O'Malley, John W., ed. see Martin, Francis X.

O'Malley, Joseph, ed. see Marx, Karl.

O'Malley, Julie. Magistrates Court. 2nd ed. (Cavendish Practice Notes Ser.). 1996. pap. 32.00 (*1-85941-301-3*, Pub. by Cavendish Pubng) Gaunt.

O'Malley, K., jt. auth. see O'Brien, E. T.

O'Malley, Kathleen, jt. auth. see Crispin, A. C.

O'Malley, Kathleen, ed. see Thompson, Victoria.

***O'Malley, Kevin.** Bud. LC 99-52869. (Illus.). 32p. (J). (gr. k-3). 2000. 15.95 (*0-8027-8718-5*); lib. bdg. 16.85 (*0-8027-8719-3*) Walker & Co.

O'Malley, Kevin. Camptown Races. 32p. 1996. pap. 8.95 (*1-56189-399-4*) Amer Educ Pub.

— Leo Cockroach... Toy Tester. LC 98-27989. (Illus.). 32p. (J). (ps-2). 1999. 15.95 (*0-8027-8689-8*); lib. bdg. 16.85 (*0-8027-8690-1*) Walker & Co.

— My Lucky Hat. LC 98-43057. (Illus.). 32p. (J). (gr. 5-9). 1999. 15.95 (*1-57255-710-9*) Mondo Pubng.

O'Malley, Kevin. O'Malley Picture Book. (Illus.). 14.89 (*0-06-027627-4*) HarpC Child Bks.

O'Malley, Kevin. Roller Coaster. LC 94-79123. (Illus.). 24p. (J). (ps up). 1995. 16.00 (*0-688-13971-X*); lib. bdg. 15.93 (*0-688-13972-8*) Lothrop.

— Velcome. LC 96-51577. (Illus.). 32p. (J). (gr. k-3). 1999. lib. bdg. 16.95 (*0-8027-8629-4*) Walker & Co.

***O'Malley, Kevin.** Velcome. (Illus.). 32p. (J). (gr. k-3). 1999. reprint ed. pap. 6.95 (*0-8027-7568-3*) Walker & Co.

O'Malley, Kevin. Who Killed Cock Robin? LC 92-40340. (Illus.). 32p. (J). (gr. k-3). 1993. lib. bdg. 14.93 (*0-688-12431-3*) Lothrop.

O'Malley, Kevin. There Was a Crooked Man. (J). (ps). 1995. 9.95 (*0-671-89477-3*) Litle Simon.

O'Malley, Kevin, et al. Velcome. LC 96-51577. (Illus.). 32p. (J). (gr. k-3). 1999. 15.95 (*0-8027-8628-6*) Walker & Co.

O'Malley, Lewis S. Hinduism: The Religion of the Masses. 1986. 175.00 (*0-7855-1965-3*, Pub. by Scientific) St Mut.

***O'Malley, Lurana Donnels, compiled by.** Two Comedies by Catherine the Great, Empress of Russia: Oh, These Times & the Siberian Shaman. 116p. 1998. pap. text 24.00 (*90-5755-023-7*, Harwood Acad Pubs) Gordon & Breach.

***O'Malley, Lurana Donnels, ed.** Two Comedies by Catherine the Great, Empress of Russia: Oh, These Times & the Siberian Shaman. 116p. 1998. text 46.00 (*90-5755-022-9*, Harwood Acad Pubs) Gordon & Breach.

O'Malley, Lurana Donnels, jt. auth. see Donnels, Johnny.

O'Malley, M. Hinduism: The Religion of the Masses. (C). 1985. text 100.00 (*81-85046-21-2*, Pub. by Scientific Pubs) St Mut.

O'Malley, Martin, jt. auth. see Pungente, John J.

O'Malley, Martin J. The Lun Yu of Kung Fu. LC 75-19749. 20p. 1975. pap. 1.00 (*0-9606610-0-X*) M J O'Malley.

— The Tao of Mao Tse-Tung. 1977. pap. 1.00 (*0-9606610-1-8*) M J O'Malley.

O'Malley, Michael. Creating Commitment: How to Attract & Retain Talented Employees by Building Relationships That Last. 259p. 2000. text 29.95 (*0-471-35897-5*) Wiley.

O'Malley, Michael, Jr. The Family Business: How to Work with Your Family & Still Enjoy Sunday Dinner. (Illus.). 128p. (Orig.). pap. 8.95 (*0-9639548-0-6*) Family Busn.

O'Malley, Michael. Keeping Watch: A History of American Time. LC 95-40809. (Illus.). 384p. 1996. pap. text 17.95 (*1-56098-672-7*) Smithsonian.

O'Malley, Michael F. Are You Paid What You're Worth. LC 97-47523. 272p. 1998. pap. 15.95 (*0-7679-0131-2*) Broadway BDD.

— Ferry Travel Adventures in Washington, British Columbia & Alaska. LC 95-72701. 292p. 1996. pap. 24.95 (*1-887187-06-5*) RSH Media.

O'Malley, Michael J. Authentic Assessment for English Learners. LC 96-162949. 288p. 1996. pap. text 35.28 (*0-201-59151-0*) Addison-Wesley.

O'Malley, Mike. Diverting Devotion: A Play. LC 98-232329. 98 p. 1997. write for info. (*0-573-66034-4*) French.

O'Malley, Nancy. Sailing South. LC 94-68046. 1994. 17.95 (*1-877978-68-X*, FLF Pr) FL Lit Foundation.

O'Malley, Padraig. Biting at the Grave: The Irish Hunger Strikes & the Politics of Despair. LC 89-43076. 344p. 1991. pap. 19.00 (*0-8070-0209-7*) Beacon Pr.

— Shades of Difference. 1999. 29.95 (*0-670-85233-3*) Viking Penguin.

— The Uncivil Wars: Ireland Today. 3rd ed. 560p. 1997. pap. 19.00 (*0-8070-0223-2*) Beacon Pr.

O'Malley, Padraig, ed. AIDS: A Special Issue of the "New England Journal of Public Policy" 526p. 1988. pap. 21.95 (*0-87023-657-1*) U of Mass Pr.

— Homelessness: New England & Beyond: A Special Issue of the "New England Journal of Public Policy" 816p. 1992. pap. 29.95 (*0-87023-825-6*) U of Mass Pr.

O'Malley, Pam, jt. ed. see Boyd-Barrett, Oliver.

O'Malley, Pat, ed. Crime & the Risk Society. LC 98-12101. (International Library of Criminology, Criminal Justice, & Penology). 490p. 1998. text 162.95 (*1-84014-027-5*, Pub. by Ashgate Pub) Ashgate Pub Co.

O'Malley, Pat & Sutton, Adam, eds. Crime Prevention in Australia: Issues in Policy & Research. 295p. 1997. pap. 39.00 (*1-86287-230-9*, Pub. by Federation Pr) Gaunt.

O'Malley, Patricia Trainor. Bradford: The End of an Era. LC 97-112640. (Images of America Ser.). 1996. pap. 16.99 (*0-7524-0426-1*) Arcadia Publng.

***O'Malley, Patricia Trainor.** Bradford College: Massachusetts. LC 00-101192. (College History Ser.). (Illus.). 128p. 2000. pap. 19.99 (*0-7385-0409-2*) Arcadia Publng.

O'Malley, Patricia Trainor. Haverhill: From Town to City. (Images of America Ser.). 1999. pap. 16.99 (*0-7524-0840-2*) Arcadia Publng.

***O'Malley, Patricia Trainor.** Haverhill's Immigrants at the Turn of the Century. (Images of America Ser.). 128p. 1999. pap. 18.99 (*0-7524-1363-5*) Arcadia Publng.

O'Malley, Patricia Trainor. The Irish in Haverhill. (Images of America Ser.). 128p. 1998. pap. 16.99 (*0-7524-0877-1*) Arcadia Publng.

***O'Malley, Patricia Trainor.** The Irish in Haverhill, Vol. 2. (Images of America Ser.). 1999. pap. 18.99 (*0-7524-1359-7*) Arcadia Publng.

O'Malley, R. E., Jr. Singular Perturbation Methods for Ordinary Differential Equations. John, F. et al, eds. (Applied Mathematical Sciences Ser.: Vol. 89). (Illus.). 248p. 1991. 59.95 (*0-387-97556-X*) Spr-Verlag.

O'Malley, Robert E., Jr. Thinking about Ordinary Differential Equations. (Texts in Applied Mathematics Ser.: No. 18). (Illus.). 257p. (C). 1997. text 69.95 (*0-521-55314-8*) Cambridge U Pr.

— Thinking about Ordinary Differential Equations. (Texts in Applied Mathematics Ser.: No. 18). (Illus.). 257p. (C). 1997. pap. text 24.95 (*0-521-55742-9*) Cambridge U Pr.

O'Malley, Robert E., Jr., ed. Asymptotic Methods & Singular Perturbations: New York, April 1976. LC 76-27872. (SIAM-AMS Proceedings Ser.: Vol. 10). 154p. 1976. text 42.00 (*0-8218-1330-7*, SIAMS/10) Am Math.

— ICIAM 91: Proceedings of the Second International Conference on Industrial & Applied Mathematics. LC 92-16500. (Proceedings in Applied Mathematics Ser.: No. 61). xvii, 391p. 1992. text 81.50 (*0-89871-302-1*) Soc Indus-Appl Math.

O'Malley, Robert E., Jr., jt. auth. see Cronin, Jane.

O'Malley, Sarah, jt. auth. see Eimer, Robert.

O'Malley, Sarah A. We Were There: A Way of the Cross. LC 97-147128. (Illus.). 40p. (Orig.). 1996. pap. 1.95 (*0-8146-2355-7*, Liturg Pr Bks) Liturgical Pr.

O'Malley, Sarah A. & Eimer, Robert D. Journey of Decision: A Way of the Cross. 32p. 1991. pap. 2.95 (*0-8146-2016-7*) Liturgical Pr.

O'Malley, Sarah A., jt. auth. see Eimer, Robert D.

O'Malley, Suzanne, jt. auth. see Greenburg, Dan.

O'Malley, T. J. Artillery: Guns & Rocket Systems. LC 94-13570. (Military Manuals Ser.). 160p. 1994. 19.95 (*1-85367-188-6*, 5404) Stackpole.

— Fighting Vehicles: Armoured Personnel Carriers & Infantry Fighting Vehicles. LC 95-15140. (Military Manuals Ser.). (Illus.). 144p. 1995. 19.95 (*1-85367-211-4*, Pub. by Greenhill Bks) Stackpole.

— Military Transport: Trucks & Transporters. LC 94-41840. (Greenhill Military Manuals Ser.: Vol. 3). (Illus.). 160p. 1995. 19.95 (*1-85367-202-5*, Pub. by Greenhill Bks) Stackpole.

O'Malley, Terry, jt. auth. see Fulmer, Terry.

O'Malley, Therese & Trieb, Marc, eds. Regional Garden Design in the United States. LC 93-23720. (Colloquium on the History of Landscape Architecture Ser.: No. 15). 1995. 50.00 (*0-88402-223-4*) Dumbarton Oaks.

O'Malley, Therese, jt. ed. see Wolschke-Bulmahn, Joachim.

O'Malley, Thomas. The Easter Yegg. 22p. (J). (gr. k-5). 1997. mass mkt. 7.00 (*1-58193-162-X*) Brown Bag Prods.

— Once upon a Christmas. 19p. (J). (gr. k-5). 1997. mass mkt. 7.00 (*1-58193-168-9*) Brown Bag Prods.

O'Malley, Thomas & White, Jane D. The Christmas Caper. 18p. (J). (gr. k-5). 1997. mass mkt. 7.00 (*1-58193-160-3*) Brown Bag Prods.

O'Malley, Timothy. Artificial Intelligence Project for Commodore. 1991. 19.95 (*0-8306-6420-3*) McGraw-Hill Prof.

O'Malley, Tom. Closedown? The BBC & Government Broadcasting Policy 1979-92. LC 94-18521. 256p. (C). 1994. 54.95 (*0-7453-0570-9*, Pub. by Pluto GBR) Stylus Pub VA.

— Journey Backward. LC 98-145652. 96p. 1998. pap. 14.95 (*1-897648-14-6*, Pub. by Salmon Poetry) Dufour.

***O'Malley, Tom.** Regulating the Press. 2000. pap. 22.50 (*0-7453-1197-0*) Pluto GBR.

O'Malley, Tom, jt. auth. see Bromley, Michael.

O'Malley, Tom, jt. ed. see Harris, Michael.

***O'Malley, Vincent J.** Ordinary Suffering of Extraordinary Saints. LC 99-75034. 272p. 2000. pap. 12.95 (*0-87973-893-6*) Our Sunday Visitor.

O'Malley, Vincent J., ed. Saintly Companions. LC 95-3115. 353p. (Orig.). 1995. pap. 9.95 (*0-8189-0693-6*) Alba.

O'Malley, William. Converting the Baptized: A Survival Manual for Parents, Teachers, & Pastors. 263p. (Orig.). 1991. pap. 9.40 (*1-55924-490-9*, 22038) Res Christian Liv.

— Young People And . . . You Know What: Eroding the New Paganism. (Spirit Life Ser.). 40p. 1993. pap. 3.95 (*1-878718-13-4*, Resurrection Pr) Catholic Bk Pub.

O'Malley, William D., jt. auth. see Howe, Robert D.

O'Malley, William J. Daily Prayers for Busy People. (Illus.). 192p. 1990. spiral bd. 10.95 (*0-88489-248-4*) St Marys.

— Daily Prayers for Busy People. Koch, Carl, ed. LC 91-815555. (Illus.). 192p. 1990. pap. 8.95 (*0-88489-242-5*) St Marys.

— The Fifth Week. 2nd rev. ed. LC 96-41077. 256p. 1996. pap. 5.95 (*0-8294-0928-9*, Jesuit Way) Loyola Pr.

***O'Malley, William J.** God: The Oldest Question. LC 00-25507. 2000. pap. 12.95 (*0-8294-1515-7*) Loyola Pr.

O'Malley, William J. Heart to Heart: Guiding Your Kids Toward Courage, Character & Values. 256p. 1999. pap. 16.95 (*1-886284-51-2*, Pub. by Chandler Hse) Natl Bk Netwk.

— Matthew, Mark, Luke, & You: Unraveling the Gospel. 264p. (Orig.). 1996. pap. 13.95 (*0-88347-286-4*, 7286) Res Christian Liv.

— Meeting the Living God. 3rd rev. ed. LC 98-5532. 336p. (YA). (gr. 9-12). 1998. pap. 14.95 (*0-8091-9576-3*, 9576-3) Paulist Pr.

— More Daily Prayers for Busy People. 192p. 1999. spiral bd. 10.95 (*0-88489-634-X*); per. 8.95 (*0-88489-618-8*) St Marys.

— The Pursuit of Happiness: Evolving a Soul. LC 98-122580. 320p. (C). 1998. 18.95 (*0-88347-333-X*) T More.

— Redemptive Suffering: Understanding Suffering, Living with It, Growing Through It. LC 97-15540. 144p. 1997. pap. 11.95 (*0-8245-1680-X*) Crossroad NY.

— Soul of a Christian Man: A Scriptural look at Spirituality. LC 99-70054. 128p. 1999. pap. 12.95 (*0-88347-431-X*, Pub. by T More) BookWorld.

— Why Not? Daring to Live the Challenge of Christ. LC 86-14059. 169p. (Orig.). 1986. pap. 6.95 (*0-8189-0504-2*) Alba.

O'Malley, William T., compiled by. Anglo-Irish Literature: A Bibliography of Dissertations, 1873-1989. 26. LC 89-78163. (Bibliographies & Indexes in World Literature Ser.: No. 26). 312p. 1990. lib. bdg. 79.50 (*0-313-27303-0*, ODL/, Greenwood Pr) Greenwood.

Omalu, Mirian Kene, see Kene Omalu, Mirian.

Oman, Anne. 25 Bicycle Tours in & Around Washington, D. C. From the Capitol Steps to Country Roads. 2nd ed. LC 98-13692. (25 Bicycle Tours Ser.). (Illus.). 176p. 1998. pap. 14.95 (*0-88150-422-X*, Pub. by Countryman) Norton.

Oman, Anne H. 25 Bicycle Tours in Maryland: From the Allegheny Mountains to the Atlantic Ocean. LC 93-45462. (25 Bicycle Tours Ser.). (Illus.). 200p. (Orig.). 1994. pap. 14.00 (*0-88150-287-1*, Pub. by Countryman) Norton.

Oman, Carola. Nelson. (Illus.). 816p. 1996. 46.95 (*1-55750-618-3*) Naval Inst Pr.

Oman, Charles. History of the Art of War in the 16th Century. LC 99-39574. (Illus.). 400p. 1999. pap. 29.95 (*1-85367-384-6*, Pub. by Greenhill Bks) Stackpole.

— History of the Peninsular War, Vol. 5. 59.95 (*1-85367-225-4*, Pub. by Greenhill Bks) Stackpole.

Oman, Charles. A History of the Peninsular War Vol. 6: September 1, 1812-August 5, 1813. 832p. 59.95 (*1-85367-226-2*, Pub. by Greenhill Bks) Stackpole.

— A History of the Peninsular War Vol. 7: August 1813-April 14, 1814. 59.95 (*1-85367-227-0*, Pub. by Greenhill Bks) Stackpole.

Oman, Charles P., et al, eds. Investing in Asia. LC 97-163243. (Development Centre Seminar Ser.). 252p. (Orig.). 1997. pap. 45.00 (*92-64-15408-6*, 41-97-01-1, Pub. by Org for Econ) OECD.

Oman, Charles P. & Wignaraja, Ganeshan. The Postwar Evolution of Development Thinking. LC 91-27768. 288p. 1991. pap. 19.95 (*0-312-07185-X*) St Martin.

Oman, Charles W. The Art of War in the Middle Ages: A.D. 378-1515. rev. ed. Beeler, John H., ed. (Illus.). 194p. 1960. pap. text 10.95 (*0-8014-9062-6*) Cornell U Pr.

Oman, Charles W. Great Revolt of 1381. LC 69-14020. 219p. 1969. reprint ed. lib. bdg. 35.00 (*0-8371-1860-3*, OMGR, Greenwood Pr) Greenwood.

Oman, Charles W. Great Revolt of 1381. LC 68-25257. (British History Ser.: No. 30). 1969. reprint ed. lib. bdg. 75.00 (*0-8383-0224-6*) M S G Haskell Hse.

— The Great Revolt of 1381. 232p. 35.00 (*1-85367-045-6*, 5515) Stackpole.

O

— History of England. LC 71-39469. (Select Bibliographies Reprint Ser.). 1977. reprint ed. 37.95 (*0-8369-9920-7*) Ayer.
— History of England from the Accession of Richard Second to the Death of Richard Third. LC 71-5632. (Political History of England Ser.: No. 4). reprint ed. 45.00 (*0-404-50774-3*) AMS Pr.
— A History of the Art of War in the Middle Ages. LC 98-4145. (Illus.). 608p. 1998. pap. 29.95 (*1-85367-331-5*, Pub. by Greenhill Bks); pap. 29.95 (*1-85367-332-3*, Pub. by Greenhill Bks) Stackpole.
— A History of the Art of War in the Sixteenth Century. 810p. 1989. 50.00 (*0-947898-69-7*, 5454) Stackpole.
— A History of the Art of War in the Sixteenth Century. LC 75-41204. reprint ed. 67.50 (*0-404-14579-5*) AMS Pr.
— History of the Peninsular War, 7 vols., Set. Incl. Vol. 1. From the Treaty of Fontainebleau to the Battle of Corunna, 1807-1809. LC 77-93687. (*0-404-16961-9*); Vol. 2. From the Battle of Corunna to the End of the Talavera, Jan.-Sept., 1809. LC 77-93687. 49.50 (*0-404-16962-7*); Vol. 3. Ocana, Cadiz, Bussaco, Torres Vedras, Sept.-Dec., 1810. LC 77-93687. 49.50 (*0-404-16963-5*); Vol. 4. Massena's Retreat, Fuentes de Onoro, Albuera, Tarragona, Dec. 1810-Dec. 1811. LC 77-93687. 49.50 (*0-404-16964-3*); Vol. 5. Valencia, Ciudad Rodrigo, Badajos, Salamanca, Madrid, Oct. 1811-Aug. 31, 1812. LC 77-93687. 49.50 (*0-404-16965-1*); Vol. 6. Siege of Burgos, the Retreat from Burgos the Campaign of Vittoria, the Battles of the Pyrennes, Sept. 1, 1812-Aug. 5, 1813. LC 77-93687. 49.50 (*0-404-16966-X*); Vol. 7. Capture of St. Sebastian, Wellington's Invasion of France, Battles of Nivelle, the Nive Orthez & Toulouse, Aug. 1813-Apr. 1814. LC 77-93687. (*0-404-16967-8*); LC 77-93687. (Illus.). 345.00 (*0-404-16960-0*) AMS Pr.
— A History of the Peninsular War Vol. 3: September 1809-December 1810. (Illus.). 624p. 1996. 59.95 (*1-85367-223-8*, Pub. by Greenhill Bks) Stackpole.
— A History of the Peninsular War Vol. 4: December 1810-December 1811. (Illus.). 736p. 1996. 59.95 (*1-85367-224-6*, Pub. by Greenhill Bks) Stackpole.
— A History of the Peninsular War, January to September 1809 Vol. 2: From the Battle of Corunna to the End of the Talavera Campaign. (Illus.). 720p. 1995. 59.95 (*1-85367-215-7*, Pub. by Greenhill Bks) Stackpole.
— A History of the Peninsular War, 1807-1809 Vol. 1: From the Treaty of Fontainebleau to the Battle of Corunna. (Illus.). 704p. 1995. 59.95 (*1-85367-214-9*, Pub. by Greenhill Bks) Stackpole.
— Seven Roman Statesmen of the Later Republic. LC 75-156699. (Essay Index Reprint Ser.). 1977. reprint ed. 30.95 (*0-8369-2288-3*) Ayer.
— The Sixteenth Century. LC 75-25517. 247p. 1976. reprint ed. lib. bdg. 65.00 (*0-8371-8118-6*, OMSIC, Greenwood Pr) Greenwood.
— Warwick the Kingmaker. LC 79-137383. (Select Bibliographies Reprint Ser.). 1977. reprint ed. 18.95 (*0-8369-5584-6*) Ayer.
— Wellington's Army, 1809-1814. 440p. 1986. 40.00 (*0-947898-41-7*) Stackpole.

Oman, Charles W., jt. auth. see OECD Staff.

Oman, Daniel, jt. auth. see Oman, Robert.

Oman, Frydman R. & Phelps, E. Individual Forecasting & Aggregate Outcomes: "Rational Expectations Examined" (Illus.). 256p. 1987. pap. text 25.95 (*0-521-31095-4*) Cambridge U Pr.

Oman, John C. The Brahmans, Theists & Muslims of India. LC 76-179231. (Illus.). reprint ed. 49.50 (*0-404-54858-X*) AMS Pr.
— Cults, Customs, & Superstitions of India: Being a Revised & Enlarged Edition of Indian Life, Religious & Social. LC 70-179232. (Illus.). reprint ed. 59.50 (*0-404-54859-8*) AMS Pr.
— Great Indian Epics: The Stories of the Ramayana & the Mahabharata with Notes Appendices & Illustrations. (C) 1995. reprint ed. 17.50 (*81-206-0994-8*, Pub. by Asian Educ Servs) S Asia.
— The Mystics, Ascetics & Saints of India: A Study of Sadhmaism with an Account of the Yogis, Sanyasis, Bairagis, & other Strange Hindu Sectarians. 308p. 1984. text 38.50 (*0-89563-650-6*) Coronet Bks.

Oman, John C. & Schleiermacher, Friedrich Daniel Ernst. On Religion: Speeches to Its Cultured Despisers. 312p. 1994. pap. 18.95 (*0-664-25556-6*) Westminster John Knox.

Oman, John W. The Natural & the Supernatural. LC 79-39696. (Select Bibliographies Reprint Ser.). 1977. reprint ed. 22.95 (*0-8369-9941-X*) Ayer.

Oman, Lela K. The Epic of Qayaq: The Longest Story Ever Told by My People. Tyler, Priscilla & Brooks, Maree, eds. (Illus.). 144p. 1996. pap. 22.50 (*0-295-97531-8*) U of Wash Pr.

Oman, Maggie, ed. Prayers for Healing: 365 Blessings, Poems & Meditations from Around the World. LC 97-19158. 294p. 1997. 14.95 (*1-57324-089-3*) Conari Press.

***Oman, Maggie, ed.** Prayers for Healing: 365 Blessings, Poems & Meditations from Around the World. 2000. reprint ed. pap. 13.95 (*1-57324-522-4*) Conari Press.

Oman, Mark. Golf Astrology: Your Pars Are in the Stars!: Your Astrological Guide to Better Golf. LC 94-96668. (Illus.). 168p. (Orig.). 1995. pap. 9.95 (*0-917346-06-8*) Golfaholics Anon.
— The Nine Commandments of Golf . . . According to the Pro Upstairs. LC 88-81603. (Illus.). 112p. (Orig.). 1988. pap. 8.95 (*0-917346-07-6*) Golfaholics Anon.
— The Sensuous Golfer. LC 76-19347. (Illus.). 1976. pap. 7.95 (*0-917346-01-7*) Golfaholics Anon.

Oman, Mark & Gevertz, Hal. World's Greatest Golf Excuses: All the Good Reasons for Playing So Bad in the 1990's. LC 89-81851. (Illus.). 112p. (Orig.). 1990. pap. 9.95 (*0-917346-03-3*) Golfaholics Anon.

Oman, Mary, jt. auth. see Favazza, Armando R.

Oman, P. W., et al. Leafhoppers (Cicadellidae) A Bibliography, Generic Check-List & Index to the World Literature, 1956-1985. 384p. 1990. text 120.00 (*0-85198-690-0*) OUP.

Oman, Paul. Pursuing the Ten Million Dollar Dream, 3 vols., Set. 1991. pap. text 30.00 (*1-879317-05-2*) Success Info Mktg.
— Pursuing the Ten Million Dollar Dream: A Field Guide for All Entrepreneurs. (Illus.). 156p. (Orig.). 1990. pap. 21.95 (*1-879317-00-1*) Success Info Mktg.
— Pursuing the Ten Million Dollar Dream No. 1: The Lifestyle. 114p. (Orig.). 1991. pap. text 10.00 (*1-879317-02-8*) Success Info Mktg.

Oman, Paul, ed. Pursuing the Ten Million Dollar Dream No. 2: Tips & Tricks. 119p. (Orig.). 1991. pap. text 10.00 (*1-879317-03-6*) Success Info Mktg.
— Pursuing the Ten Million Dollar Dream No. 3: How to - How Come. 118p. 1991. pap. text 10.00 (*1-879317-04-4*) Success Info Mktg.

Oman, Paul W. & Pfleeger, Shari L., eds. Applying Software Metrics. LC 96-29059. 344p. 1996. pap. 50.00 (*0-8186-7645-0*) IEEE Standards.

Oman, Ray C., et al. Management Analysis in Public Organizations: History, Concepts, & Techniques. LC 91-25533. 224p. 1992. 59.95 (*0-89930-403-6*, OMA, Quorum Bks) Greenwood.

Oman, Robert & Oman, Daniel. Calculus for the Utterly Confused. LC 98-25802. (Illus.). 208p. 1998. pap. 15.95 (*0-07-048261-6*) McGraw.
— Physics for the Utterly Confused. LC 98-25808. (Illus.). 208p. 1998. pap. 15.95 (*0-07-048262-4*) McGraw.

Oman, Robert M. The Easy Way to Higher Grades. 40p. (C). 1978. pap. 2.95 (*0-931660-01-7*) R Oman Pub.
— Graphing Algebraic Functions. (C). 1979. pap. 2.95 (*0-931660-02-5*) R Oman Pub.

Oman, Robert M., et al. How to Solve Physics Problems & Make the Grade: Including Hundreds of Solved Problems. LC 96-32639. (Illus.). 352p. (C). 1996. pap. 15.95 (*0-07-048166-0*) McGraw.

Omand, Donald. The Borders Book. LC 98-131302. (Illus.). 230p. 1998. pap. 33.95 (*1-874744-73-4*, Pub. by Birlinn Ltd) Dufour.
— Perthshire Book. 1. LC 99-219555. 1999. 33.95 (*1-874744-84-X*) Dufour.

O'Manique, John & Lerner, Michael. World Leadership & International Development. 138p. 1986. mass mkt. 20.00 (*0-86346-011-9*, Tycooly Pub) Weidner & Sons.

Omans, Glen A. Passion in Poe: The Development of a Critical Term. 1986. pap. 2.95 (*0-910556-22-9*) Enoch Pratt.

Omanson, Roger L. & Ellington, John. A Handbook on Paul's Second Letter to the Corinthians. LC 93-4494. (UBS Handbook Ser.). viii, 272p. 1994. pap. 14.99 (*0-8267 0162-0*, 105034) Untd Bible Soc.

Omanson, Roger L. & Noss, Philip A. A Handbook on the Book of Esther. LC 96-37687. (UBS Handbook Ser.). x, 379p. 1997. pap. 13.99 (*0-8267-0116-7*, 105918) Untd Bible Soc.

O'Maolalaigh, Roibeard, jt. auth. see MacAonghuis, Iain.

Omar, Adisa M. '60 to '80: Songs for the Black Struggle. Alston, Robert, ed. (Illus.). 42p. 1998. reprint ed. pap. 9.95 (*0-939366-00-2*) AKU Pr.

Omar, Ariffin. Bangsa Melayu: Malay Concepts of Democracy & Community, 1945-1950. LC 92-40292. (South-East Asian Historical Monographs). (Illus.). 276p. (C). 1993. text 55.00 (*0-19-588613-5*) OUP.

Omar, B. K. Human Radiological Anatomy. (C). 1989. 60.00 (*0-89771-358-3*, Pub. by Current Dist) St Mut.
— Normal Radiographic Anatomy. 1983. 90.00 (*0-7855-0795-7*, Pub. by Current Dist) St Mut.

Omar, H. A. The Great Warriors. 1984. pap. 30.00 (*0-7212-0631-X*, Pub. by Regency Pr GBR) St Mut.
— The Human Perfection. 96p. (C). 1988. 40.00 (*0-7212-0701-4*, Pub. by Regency Pr GBR) St Mut.
— The Paragon of Human Perfection. 85p. 1984. 25.00 (*0-7212-0566-6*, Pub. by Regency Pr GBR) St Mut.

Omar, Imtiaz. Rights, Emergencies & Judicial Review. LC 96-14431. 412p. 1996. 150.00 (*90-411-0229-9*) Kluwer Law Intl.

Omar, Ishak H. Market Power, Vertical Linkages, & Government Policy: The Fish Industry in Peninsular Malaysia. (South-East Asian Social Science Monographs). (Illus.). 204p. 1995. text 49.95 (*967-65-3056-5*) OUP.

Omar, Ka. Wolof Phonology & Morphology. LC 93-30604. 160p. (Orig.). (C). 1993. pap. text 29.50 (*0-8191-9288-0*) U Pr of Amer.

Omar, M. Ali. Elementary Solid State Physics. 688p. 1993. 95.00 (*0-201-60733-6*) Addison-Wesley.

Omar, Margaret K. The Acquisition of Egyptian Arabic As a Native Language. 1973. pap. text 67.70 (*90-279-2468-6*) Mouton.
— Saudi Arabic Basic Course: Urban Hajazi Dialect. rev. ed. 288p. (Orig.). 1994. pap. 14.95 (*0-7818-0257-1*) Hippocrene Bks.

Omar, Maryaret K. Saudi Arabic Intensive Course. (Intensive Cassette Ser.). 287p. 1998. spiral bd. 180.00 incl. audio (*1-58214-004-9*) Mltilingl Bks.

Omar, Najwa, tr. see Al-Salihi, Joan.

***Omar, Ogenyi.** Retail Marketing. 320p. (Orig.). 2000. pap. 57.50 (*0-273-63859-9*) F T P H.

Omar, Rdean. Death on Your Doorstep: One Hundred One Weapons in the Average Home. (Illus.). 75p. 1992. pap. 7.95 (*0-939427-85-0*) Alpha Pubns OH.

Omar, Saleh B. Ibn-Al-Haytham's Optics: A Study of the Origins of Experimental Science. LC 76-42611. (Studies in Islamic Philosophy & Science). (Illus.). 1977. 30.00 (*0-88297-015-1*) Bibliotheca.

Omar, Samira A., et al, eds. Range Management in Arid Zones: Proceedings of the Second International Conference on Range Management in the Arabian Gulf. LC 93-37668. (Illus.). 325p. 1996. 212.50 (*0-7103-0472-2*, Pub. by Kegan Paul Intl) Col U Pr.

Omar, Samira A. S., et al, eds. Sustainable Development in Arid Zones Vols. 1 & 2: Assessment & Monitoring of Desert Ecosystems, Management & Improvement of Desert Resources. (Illus.). 772p. (C). 1998. text 151.00 (*90-5410-452-X*) Ashgate Pub Co.

Omar, Sharifah M. Myths & the Malay Ruling Class. 144p. 1993. pap. 12.50 (*981-210-025-3*, Pub. by Times Academic) Intl Spec Bk.

***Omar, Sharrieff.** Questions of Love. 72p. 1999. 8.00 (*1-56411-226-8*) Untd Bros & Sis.

Omar, Sharrieff. The Second Civil War in the U.S.A. America Erupts in Turmoil. 65p. (Orig.). 1997. pap. 7.00 (*1-56411-165-2*) Untd Bros & Sis.

Omar, Sydney. My World of Astrology. 1976. pap. 10.00 (*0-87980-103-4*) Wilshire.
— Thought Dial. 1975. pap. 7.00 (*0-87980-164-6*) Wilshire.

O'Mara, Anna. Deserts. (Read-&-Discover Bks.). (Illus.). 24p. (J). (gr. k-3). 1996. 14.00 (*0-516-20125-5*) Childrens.
— Mountains. (Read-&-Discover Bks.). (Illus.). 24p. (J). (gr. k-3). 1996. 14.00 (*0-516-20127-1*) Childrens.
— Oceans. (Read-&-Discover Bks.). (Illus.). 24p. (J). (gr. k-3). 1996. lib. bdg. 14.00 (*0-516-20126-3*) Childrens.
— Rain Forests. (Read-&-Discover Bks.). (Illus.). 24p. (J). (gr. k-3). 1996. 14.00 (*0-516-20128-X*) Childrens.
— Read-&-Discover Science Series, 4 bks. Incl. Deserts. LC 95-43240. (Illus.). 24p. (J). (gr. 2-3). 1996. lib. bdg. 13.75 (*1-56065-338-8*, Bridgestone Bks); Mountains. LC 95-47650. (Illus.). 24p. (J). (gr. 2-3). 1996. lib. bdg. 13.75 (*1-56065-337-X*, Bridgestone Bks); Oceans. LC 95-47653. (Illus.). 24p. (J). (gr. 2-3). 1996. lib. bdg. 13.75 (*1-56065-339-6*, Bridgestone Bks); Rain Forests. (Illus.). 24p. (J). (gr. 2-3). 1996. lib. bdg. 13.75 (*1-56065-336-1*, Bridgestone Bks); 55.00 (*1-56065-630-1*, Bridgestone Bks) Capstone Pr.

O'Mara, B., ed. see Electrochemical Society Staff.

O'Mara, Bill. The Godspell Solution: An Extraordinary Dialog with God. LC 99-57380. 145p. 1999. per. 11.95 (*1-893183-20-3*) Granite Pub.

O'Mara, Carmel. Good Morning. 2001. write for info. (*0-15-202135-3*) Harcourt.
— Good Morning, Good Night. (J). (ps-k). 1997. bds. 5.95 (*0-614-28822-3*, Red Wagon Bks) Harcourt.
— Good Night. 2001. write for info. (*0-15-202136-1*) Harcourt.

Omara, Ed L. Classic Erotic Tales. 256p. 1994. 8.98 (*0-7858-0198-7*) Bk Sales Inc.

Omara, George. Mastering AutoCAD14: Premium Edition. LC 98-85873. (Mastering Ser.). (Illus.). 1440p. 1998. 59.99 (*0-7821-2338-4*) Sybex.

O'Mara, Gillian, jt. compiled by see Erickson, Rica.

O'Mara, Julie. Diversity Activities & Training Designs. LC 94-65469. (Illus.). 400p. 1994. ring bd. 159.00 (*0-88390-436-5*, Pfiffr & Co) Jossey-Bass.

O'Mara, Julie, jt. auth. see Jamieson, David.

O'Mara, Karen, jt. auth. see Goldberg, Jack.

O'Mara, Kate. When She Was Bad. large type ed. (Black Satin Romance Ser.). 464p. 1996. 27.99 (*1-86110-022-1*) Ulverscroft.

O'Mara, Lesley. Best Dog Stories. (Illus.). 256p. 1991. reprint ed. 8.99 (*0-517-06498-7*) Random Hse Value.
— Best Horse Stories. (Illus.). 256p. 1992. reprint ed. 8.99 (*0-517-07251-3*) Random Hse Value.
— Classic Animal Stories. (Illus.). 32p. (J). (gr. k-3). 18.95 (*0-316-18929-4*) Little.

***O'Mara, Lesley.** Great Cat Tales. 256p. 2000. pap. 12.95 (*0-7867-0765-8*, Pub. by Carroll & Graf) Publishers Group.

Omara, Lesley. Great Cat Tales. 1991. 7.98 (*1-55521-757-5*) Bk Sales Inc.

O'Mara, Lesley, ed. Best Cat Stories. (Illus.). 256p. 1992. reprint ed. 8.99 (*0-517 07391-9*) Random Hse Value.

O'Mara, Leslie. Best-Loved Cat Stories. LC 97-33388. 275p. 1998. 19.95 (*0-7621-0050-8*, Pub. by RD Assn) Penguin Putnam.
— Greatest Cat Stories. 1995. 8.98 (*0-7858-0462-5*) Bk Sales Inc.
— Which Way to the Vomitorium: Vernacular Latin for All Occasions. Williams, Rose, tr. 128p. 1999. text 11.95 (*0-312-24276-X*) St Martin.

***O'Mara, Martha A.** Strategy & Place: Corporate Real Estate & Facilities Management. LC 99-22122. (Illus.). 368p. 1999. 34.50 (*0-684-83489-8*) Free Pr.

O'Mara, Michael. Bath Time with Foam Duck. (Illus.). (J). (ps up). 1997. pap. 8.95 (*1-85479-317-9*) Trans-Atl Phila.
— Bath Time with Foam Whale: A Waterproof Plastic Book. (Illus.). (J). (ps up). 1997. pap. 8.95 (*1-85479-309-8*) Trans-Atl Phila.
— Ireland. LC 96-48923. (Illus.). 160p. 1996. text 29.95 (*0-312-14209-9*) St Martin.
— Tales of Old Ireland. 1994. 8.98 (*0-7858-0087-5*) Bk Sales Inc.

***O'Mara, Michael, ed. Facts about the World's Nations. LC 98-51148. 1065p. 1999. 65.00 (*0-8242-0955-9*) Wilson.**

New in the acclaimed Fact Series, this is a comprehensive, data-filled sourcebook on the world's nations & the majority of their territories around the globe. Students, travelers, business people, & general readers will appreciate complete coverage of each nation's (or territory's) history; constitution & government; international relations; economy, industry & commerce; geography; climate; cities & towns; population; religion; language; communications; education & welfare.The volume also provides basic maps for most countries. The historical accounts take readers from a country's first inhabitants through centuries of power struggles & from modern governmental transitions to current events.They provide a detailed snapshot of even the smallest countries, such as Tuvalu in the South Pacific & San Marino, the tiny principality in the middle of Italy. In addition, there are chapters on such supranational entities as the Commonwealth of the Independent States & the European Union - even the Vatican has its own chapter. As a helpful way of providing access to even more information, a handy web site section at the end of each entry provides Internet addresses for as many nations as possible. Hundreds of web sites are listed, including official government, embassy, & United Nations permanent mission home pages - themselves loaded with many links. To Order: H.W. Wilson -- 1-800-367-6770 (1-718-588-8400 outside U.S. and Canada), or visit www.hwwilson.com." *Publisher Paid Annotation.*

O'Mara, Michael, ed. Tales of Old Ireland. 247p. 1994. 42.50 (*1-85479-981-9*, Pub. by Pan) Trans-Atl Phila.

O'Mara, Michael, et al. Adobe Web Design & Publishing Unleashed. LC 96-71506. 1075p. 1997. 49.99 (*1-57521-252-8*) Sams.

O'Mara, Patrick F. Egyptian Hieroglyphics: An Easy Introduction for History & Art Students. 2nd ed. (Illus.). 55p. (Orig.). (C). 1976. pap. text 18.00 (*0-686-30248-6*) Paulette Pub.
— The Palermo Stone & the Archaic Kings of Egypt. (Studies in the Structural Archaeology of Ancient Egypt: Vol. I). (Illus.). xvi, 208p. (Orig.). 1979. pap. 22.00 (*0-686-30249-4*) Paulette Pub.
— Some Indirect Sothic & Lunar Dates from the Late Middle Kingdom in Egypt. x, 69p. (Orig.). 1997. pap. 16.00 (*0-614-32422-X*) Paulette Pub.

O'Mara, Peggy. Way Back Home. 1993. pap. 10.95 (*0-914257-09-9*) Mothering Magazine.

O'Mara, Peggy, ed. Vaccination! The Issues of Our Times. 1997. pap. 14.95 (*0-914257-17-X*) Mothering Magazine.

O'Mara, Peggy & McConnell, Jane L. Natural Family Living: The Mothering Magazine Guide to Parenting. LC 99-89667. (Illus.). 384p. 2000. per. 17.95 (*0-671-02744-1*, PB Trade Paper) PB.

O'Mara, Philip. The Franciscan Leader. (Pathways Ser.). 103p. 1997. pap. text 8.00 (*1-57659-126-3*) Franciscan Inst.

O'Mara, Shane M., jt. ed. see Lynch, Marina A.

O'Mara, V. M., jt. ed. see Pickering, O. S.

O'Mara, W. Paul & Casazza, John A. Office Development Handbook. LC 82-50078. (Community Builders Handbook Ser.). (Illus.). 272p. 1982. 64.95 (*0-87420-607-3*, OD1) Urban Land.

O'Mara, W. Paul, et al. Developing Power Centers. LC 96-60515. 153p. 1996. pap. text 59.95 (*0-87420-785-1*, P12) Urban Land.
— Rental Housing. LC 84-51908. 167p. reprint ed. pap. 51.80 (*0-7837-1008-9*, 204131800020) Bks Demand.

O'Mara, W. Paul, jt. auth. see Beyard, Michael D.

O'Mara, William C., et al, eds. Handbook of Semiconductor Silicon Technology. LC 89-77067. (Illus.). 795p. 1990. 145.00 (*0-8155-1237-6*) Noyes.

Omarbetade, T. Prisma Modern Swedish-English Dictionary. (ENG & SWE.). 394p. 1980. 24.95 (*0-8288-1678-6*, M9450) Fr & Eur.

Omari, C. K. Socio-Cultural Factors in Modern Family Planning Methods in Tanzania. LC 88-9352. (Studies in African Health & Medicine: Vol. 3). 250p. 1989. lib. bdg. 89.95 (*0-88946-189-9*) E Mellen

Omari, C. K., jt. auth. see Creighton, Colin.

Omari, C. K., jt. ed. see Creighton, Colin.

O'Marie, Carol Anne. Death of an Angel: A Sister Mary Helen Mystery. LC 96-48770. 256p. 1996. 21.95 (*0-312-15107-1*, Thomas Dunne) St Martin.
— Death of an Angel: A Sister Mary Helen Mystery. large type ed. LC 97-9213. 1997. pap. 22.95 (*1-56895-442-5*) Wheeler Pub.
— Death of an Angel: A Sister Mary Helen Mystery. 3rd ed. (Sister Mary Helen Mystery Ser.). 304p. 1997. mass mkt. 5.99 (*0-312-96396-3*, St Martins Paperbacks) St Martin.
— Death Takes Up a Collection: A Sister Mary Helen Mystery. LC 98-21148. 224p. 1998. text 21.95 (*0-312-19256-8*) St Martin.
— Death Takes Up a Collection: A Sister Mary Helen Mystery. 256p. 1999. mass mkt. 5.99 (*0-312-97193-1*, St Martins Paperbacks) St Martin.
— Death Takes Up a Collection: A Sister Mary Helen Mystery. large type ed. Date not set. 30.00 (*0-7862-1663-8*) Thorndike Pr.

***O'Marie, Carol Anne.** Requiem at the Refuge: A Sister Mary Helen Mystery. 288p. 2000. text 23.95 (*0-312-20906-1*) St Martin.

Omark, Donald R., jt. ed. see Chance, Michael R.

Omarr, Sydney. Answer in the Sky, Almost: Confessions of an Astrologer. 208p. (Orig.). 1995. pap. 11.95 (*1-57174-028-7*) Hampton Roads Pub Co.
— Aquarius, 1987. 1987. pap. 2.95 (*0-317-47657-2*, Sig) NAL.
— Astrological Guide for You in 2000, 1 vol. 352p. 1999. mass mkt. 6.99 (*0-451-19354-7*) NAL.

An Asterisk (*) at the beginning of an entry indicates that the title is appearing for the first time.

O

— Astrology: Off the Top. 128p. 1975. 10.50 (*0-86690-135-3*, O1362-014) Am Fed Astrologers.

— Sydney Omarr Presenta la Astrologia en el Sexo y el Amor: Descubra el Amor Con la Ayuda de las Estrellas! (SPA.). 264p. 1999. pap. 9.95 (*1-56718-502-9*, K-502-9) Llewellyn Pubns.

***Omarr, Sydney.** Sydney Omarr y Sus Revelaciones Astrologicas. 2000. pap. 9.95 (*1-56718-501-0*, Llewellyn Esp) Llewellyn Pubns.

— Sydney Omarr's Astrological Guide for You in 2001. 2000. mass mkt. 6.99 (*0-451-19369-5*, Sig) NAL.

Omarr, Sydney. Sydney Omarr's Astrological Guide to Love & Romance. LC 98-33307. 368p. 1999. 12.95 (*1-56718-505-3*, K505) Llewellyn Pubns.

— Sydney Omarr's Astrological Revelations about You. 288p. 1998. pap. 12.95 (*1-56718-504-5*, K504) Llewellyn Pubns.

***Omarr, Sydney.** Sydney Omarr's Day-by-Day Astrological Guide for Aquarius 2001. 304p. 2000. mass mkt. 5.99 (*0-451-20067-5*, Sig) NAL.

— Sydney Omarr's Day-by-Day Astrological Guide for Aries 2001. 304p. 2000. mass mkt. 5.99 (*0-451-20057-8*, Sig) NAL.

— Sydney Omarr's Day-by-Day Astrological Guide for Cancer 2001. 304p. 2000. mass mkt. 5.99 (*0-451-20061-6*, Sig) NAL.

— Sydney Omarr's Day-by-Day Astrological Guide for Capricorn 2001. 304p. 2000. mass mkt. 5.99 (*0-451-20068-3*, Sig) NAL.

— Sydney Omarr's Day-by-Day Astrological Guide for Gemini 2001. 304p. 2000. mass mkt. 5.99 (*0-451-20060-8*, Sig) NAL.

— Sydney Omarr's Day-by-Day Astrological Guide for Leo 2001. 304p. 2000. mass mkt. 5.99 (*0-451-20062-4*, Sig) NAL.

— Sydney Omarr's Day-by-Day Astrological Guide for Libra 2001. 304p. 2000. mass mkt. 5.99 (*0-451-20064-0*, Sig) NAL.

— Sydney Omarr's Day-by-Day Astrological Guide for Pisces 2001. 304p. 2000. mass mkt. 5.99 (*0-451-20059-4*, Sig) NAL.

— Sydney Omarr's Day-by-Day Astrological Guide for Sagittarius 2001. 304p. 2000. mass mkt. 5.99 (*0-451-20066-7*, Sig) NAL.

— Sydney Omarr's Day-by-Day Astrological Guide for Scorpio 2001. 304p. 2000. mass mkt. 5.99 (*0-451-20065-9*, Sig) NAL.

— Sydney Omarr's Day-by-Day Astrological Guide for Taurus 2001. 304p. 2000. mass mkt. 5.99 (*0-451-20058-6*, Sig) NAL.

Omarr, Sydney. Sydney Omarr's Day-By-Day Astrological Guide for the New Millennium: Capricorn. 1999. mass mkt. 5.99 (*0-451-19356-3*) NAL.

— Sydney Omarr's Day-By-Day Astrological Guide for the New Millennium: Aquarius. 1999. mass mkt. 5.99 (*0-451-19352-0*) NAL.

— Sydney Omarr's Day-By-Day Astrological Guide for the New Millennum: Aries. 1999. mass mkt. 5.99 (*0-451-19353-9*) NAL.

— Sydney Omarr's Day-By-Day Astrological Guide for the New Millennum: Cancer. 1999. mass mkt. 5.99 (*0-451-19355-5*) NAL.

— Sydney Omarr's Day-By-Day Astrological Guide for the New Millennum: Gemini. 1999. mass mkt. 5.99 (*0-451-19357-1*) NAL.

— Sydney Omarr's Day-By-Day Astrological Guide for the New Millennum: Leo. 1999. mass mkt. 5.99 (*0-451-19359-8*) NAL.

— Sydney Omarr's Day-By-Day Astrological Guide for the New Millennum: Libra. 1999. mass mkt. 5.99 (*0-451-19360-1*) NAL.

— Sydney Omarr's Day-By-Day Astrological Guide for the New Millennum: Pisces. 1999. mass mkt. 5.99 (*0-451-19362-8*) NAL.

— Sydney Omarr's Day-By-Day Astrological Guide for the New Millennum: Sagittarius. 1999. mass mkt. 5.99 (*0-451-19363-6*) NAL.

— Sydney Omarr's Day-By-Day Astrological Guide for the New Millennum: Scorpio. 1999. mass mkt. 5.99 (*0-451-19364-4*) NAL.

— Sydney Omarr's Day-By-Day Astrological Guide for the New Millennum: Taurus. 1999. mass mkt. 5.99 (*0-451-19365-2*) NAL.

— Sydney Omarr's Day-By-Day Astrological Guide for the New Millennum: Virgo. 1999. mass mkt. 5.99 (*0-451-19366-0*) NAL.

***Omarr, Sydney.** Sydney Omarr's Day-by-Day Astrological Guide for Virgo 2001. 304p. 2000. mass mkt. 5.99 (*0-451-20063-2*, Sig) NAL.

Omarr, Sydney. Sydney Omarr's New Millennium Guide. 1999. mass mkt. 6.99 (*0-451-19829-8*, Sig) NAL.

Omarr, Sydney & Roy, Mike. Sydney Omarr's Cooking with Astrology. 2nd ed. LC 98-39313. 392p. 1999. 17.95 (*1-56718-506-1*, K506) Llewellyn Pubns.

Omartian, S. Llaves de la Salud Emocional. (Actualidades Ser.).Tr. of Keys to Emotional Health. (SPA.). 1986. 2.29 (*1-56063-161-9*, 498123); pap. write for info. (*0-614-27073-1*) Editorial Unilit.

Omartian, Stormie. Better Body Management. LC 93-23876. 1993. 10.95 (*0-917143-25-6*) Sparrow TN.

***Omartian, Stormie.** Child of Promise: When Love Came down at Christmas. gif. ed. (Illus.). 112p. 2000. 24.99 (*0-7369-0250-3*) Harvest Hse.

— Finding Peace for Your Heart. rev. ed. LC 98-44532. 288p. 1999. pap. 12.99 (*0-7852-7038-8*) Nelson.

Omartian, Stormie. Greater Health God's Way. 208p. 1984. pap. 5.95 (*0-917143-00-0*) Sparrow TN.

— Greater Health God's Way: Seven Steps to Inner & Outer Beauty. 276p. 1999. pap. 9.99 (*0-7369-0061-6*) Harvest Hse.

— Just Enough Light for the Step I'm On: Following God in Simple Faith. LC 98-42889. 179p. 1999. pap. 9.99 (*0-7369-0012-8*) Harvest Hse.

***Omartian, Stormie.** Love Binds Us Together. (Moment Meditation Ser.). 64p. 2000. pap. 7.99 (*0-7369-0193-0*) Harvest Hse.

Omartian, Stormie. The Power of a Praying Kid. 80p. Date not set. pap. 7.99 (*0-7369-0122-1*) Harvest Hse.

— The Power of a Praying Parent. LC 95-8627. 213p. 1995. pap. 9.99 (*1-56507-354-1*) Harvest Hse.

***Omartian, Stormie.** The Power of a Praying Parent Prayer & Study Guide. 144p. 2000. pap., student ed. 6.99 (*0-7369-0343-7*) Harvest Hse.

Omartian, Stormie. The Power of a Praying Wife. LC 97-7436. 203p. 1997. pap. 9.99 (*1-56507-572-2*) Harvest Hse.

Omartian, Stormie. The Power of a Praying Wife, Set. audio 16.99 (*0-7369-0054-3*) Harvest Hse.

— The Power of a Praying Wife Prayer & Study Guide. 144p. 2000. pap. 6.99 (*0-7369-0317-8*) Harvest Hse.

— The Power of a Praying Woman Prayer Journal. 208p. 1999. 11.99 (*0-7369-0130-2*) Harvest Hse.

— Prayers of the Heart. (Moment Meditations Ser.). 64p. 1999. pap. 7.99 (*0-7369-0207-4*) Harvest Hse.

Omartian, Stormie. Stormie. 192p. (Orig.). 1997. reprint ed. pap. 8.99 (*1-56507-832-2*) Harvest Hse.

— That's What Love Is For. LC 98-4071. 48p. 1998. 12.99 (*1-56507-914-0*) Harvest Hse.

Omartian, Stormie, et al. Can I Afford Time for Friendships? Answers to Questions Women Ask about Friends. LC 94-27810. 192p. 1994. pap. 8.99 (*1-55661-517-5*) Bethany Hse.

O'Mary, Barbara. This Woman: Poetry of Love & Change. LC 72-95283. (Illus.). 64p. (Orig.). 1973. pap. 3.25 (*0-87810-024-5*) Times Change.

Omarzu, Julia, jt. auth. see Harvey, John H.

Omas, Anders Hjort af, see Hjort af Omas, Anders, ed.

Omasa, K., et al, eds. Climate Change & Plants in East Asia. (Illus.). 206p. 1996. 117.00 (*4-431-70176-1*) Spr-Verlag.

Omata, Masao, ed. see International Symposium on Idiopathic Portal Hyper.

O'Mathuna, Diarmuid. Mechanics, Boundary Layers & Function Spaces. 240p. 1989. 68.50 (*0-8176-3464-9*) Birkhauser.

O'Mathuna, Sean P. William Bathe, S. J., 1564-1614: A Pioneer in Linguistics. LC 86-11791. (Studies in the History of Language Sciences: Vol. 37). (Illus.). iv, 211p. 1986. 55.00 (*90-272-4520-7*) J Benjamins Pubng Co.

Omatu, Sigeru & Seinfeld, John H. Distributed Parameter Systems: Theory & Applications. (Oxford Mathematical Monographs). (Illus.). 448p. 1989. 110.00 (*0-19-853295-4*) OUP.

Omatu, Sigeru, et al. Neuro-Control & Its Applications. LC 95-20218. (Advances in Industrial Control Ser.). 272p. 1996. 59.00 (*3-540-19965-9*) Spr-Verlag.

Omax, Paul & Cadenhead, Roger. Laura Lemay's Web Workshop: ActiveX & VBScript. LC 96-70390. 450p. 1996. 39.99 (*1-57521-207-2*) Sams.

Omaye, Stanley T., jt. ed. see Bidlak, Wayne R.

Ombelet, W., et al, eds. Modern Art in the 2000s: Andrology in the Nineties. LC 98-10330. (Studies in Profertility Ser.: Vol. 8). (Illus.). 238p. 1998. 58.00 (*1-85070-043-5*) Prthnon Pub.

Ombregt. A System of Orthopaedic Medicine. 1995. text 136.50 (*0-7020-1595-4*, W B Saunders Co) Harcrt Hlth Sci Grp.

Omchery, Deepti B., jt. ed. see Omchery, Leela.

Omchery, Leela. Studies in Indian Music & Applied Arts. 1990. 180.00 (*0-317-99586-3*, Pub. by Sundeep Prak) S Asia.

Omchery, Leela & Omchery, Deepti B., eds. Immortals of Indian Music. LC 98-903067. (Illus.). 240p. 1998. 26.00 (*81-212-0456-9*, Pub. by Gyan Publishing Hse) Nataraj Bks.

Omdahl, Becky. Cognitive Appraisal, Emotion, & Empathy. 274p. 1995. text 59.95 (*0-8058-1479-5*) L Erlbaum Assocs.

***Omdorf, Eleanor & Moore, Jo Ellen.** Poetry Patterns. Evans, Marilyn, ed. (Illus.). 96p. 1999. pap., teacher ed. 10.95 (*1-55799-733-0*, 733) Evan-Moor Edu Pubs.

Omdra 6 Staff. Dreamrise. 2nd ed. 1977. pap. 2.95 (*0-930472-00-4*) G Stempien.

— Elltradonnic City. 1979. pap. 3.95 (*0-930472-02-0*) G Stempien.

O'Meally, Robert G. History & Memory in African American Culture. Fabre, Genevieve E., ed. (Illus.). 336p. 1994. text 60.00 (*0-19-508396-2*) OUP.

***O'Meally, Robert G.** Lady Day: The Many Faces of Billie Holiday. (Illus.). 208p. 2000. pap. text 20.00 (*0-306-80959-1*) Da Capo.

O'Meally, Robert G., ed. The Jazz Cadence of American Culture. LC 98-14768. (Illus.). 576p. 1998. pap. 22.50 (*0-231-10449-9*); lib. bdg. 49.50 (*0-231-10448-0*) Col U Pr.

O'Meally, Robert G., ed. see Adams, Edward C.

O'Meally, Robert G., jt. ed. see Fabre, Genevieve E.

O'Mealy, Joseph H., et al. Language, Linguistics, & Leadership: Essays in Honor of Carol M. K. Eastman. LC 98-40514. (Literary Studies--East & West). 1998. 28.00 (*0-8248-1971-3*) UH Pr.

O'Mear, Anthony. Experience, Explanation & Faith: A Study in the Philosophy of Religion. (Modern Revivals in Philosophy Ser.). 285p. 1992. 58.95 (*0-7512-0052-2*, Pub. by Gregg Pub) Ashgate Pub Co.

O'Meara, ed. Pselli, Michaelis Vol. II: Philosophica Minora. (GRE.). 1989. 75.00 (*3-322-00462-7*, T1661, Pub. by B G Teubner) U of Mich Pr.

O'Meara, Barry E. Napoleon in Exile, 2 vols. LC 74-106520. reprint ed. 57.50 (*0-404-00610-8*) AMS Pr.

***O'Meara-Brown Publications Inc. Staff.** Lakeland Boating Ports 'O Call Vol. II: Lake Huron Cruise Guide. 2nd rev. ed. (Illus.). 1999. spiral bd. 44.95 (*1-890839-06-X*) OMeara-Brown Pubns.

O'Meara, Carra F. Monarchy & Consent: The Coronation Book of Charles V of France. (Illus.). 350p. 1999. text 95.00 (*1-872501-10-9*) Gordon & Breach.

O'Meara, D. Structures Hierarchiques dans la Pensee de Plotin: Etude historique et interpretative. (FRE.). 1975. pap. 35.00 (*90-04-04372-1*, PHA, 27) Brill Academic Pubs.

O'Meara, Dan. Forty Lost Years: The Apartheid State & the Politics of the National Party 1948-1994. LC 96-18303. (African Studies). (Illus.). 618p. (Orig.). (C). 1997. pap. text 29.95 (*0-8214-1173-X*) Ohio U Pr.

— Volkskapitalisme: Class, Capital & Ideology in the Development of Afrikaner Nationalism, 1934-1948. LC 82-9504. (African Studies: No. 34). (Illus.). 304p. 1983. text 85.00 (*0-521-24285-1*) Cambridge U Pr.

O'Meara, Daniel P. Protecting the Growing Number of Older Workers: The Age Discrimination in Employment Act. LC 88-80365. (Labor Relations & Public Policy Ser.: No. 33). 384p. 1989. pap. 30.00 (*0-89546-069-6*) U PA Ctr Hum Res.

***O'Meara, David.** Storm Still. (Harbinger Poetry Ser.). 72p. 1999. pap. 12.95 (*0-88629-360-X*) McG-Queens Univ Pr.

O'Meara, David & Murray, Ted. Tennis Unlimited. LC 96-51750. (Winning Edge of Sports Ser.). (Illus.). 64p. (Orig.). 1997. pap. 9.95 (*1-57034-059-5*) Globe Pequot.

***O'Meara, Doc.** Colt's Single Action Army Revolver. LC 99-67652. (Illus.). 160p. 2000. 34.95 (*0-87341-794-1*) Krause Pubns.

O'Meara, Dominic. The Structure of Being & the Search for Good: Essays on Ancient & Early Medieval Platonism. LC 98-35486. (Variorum Collected Studies: No. CS629). 320p. (C). 1998. text 91.95 (*0-86078-765-6*, B517.O44, Pub. by Variorum) Ashgate Pub Co.

O'Meara, Dominic J. Plotinus: An Introduction to the Enneads. (Illus.). 154p. 1995. pap. text 17.95 (*0-19-875147-8*) OUP.

— Pythagoras Revived: Mathematics & Philosophy in Late Antiquity. 264p. 1991. reprint ed. pap. text 29.95 (*0-19-823913-0*) OUP.

O'Meara, Dominic J., ed. Neoplatonism & Christian Thought. LC 81-5272. (Studies in Neoplatonism: Ancient & Modern: Vol. 3). 297p. 1981. text 21.50 (*0-87395-492-0*) State U NY Pr.

— Studies in Aristotle. LC 81-4381. (Studies in Philosophy & the History of Philosophy: No. 9). 321p. reprint ed. pap. 99.60 (*0-7837-1000-3*, 204130700020) Bks Demand.

O'Meara, Donna D., jt. auth. see O'Meara, Stephen J.

O'Meara, J. J., jt. auth. see De'Angeli, Daniel.

O'Meara, Jan. Alaska Backyard Wines. (Illus.). 64p. (Orig.). 1988. pap. 7.95 (*0-9621543-5-0*) Wizard Works.

— Alaska Dictionary & Pronunciation Guide. (Illus.). (Orig.). 1995. reprint ed. pap. 11.95 (*0-9621543-6-9*) Wizard Works.

— Bed & Breakfast Alaska Style! 5th rev. ed. (Illus.). 224p. (Orig.). 1997. pap. 16.95 (*0-9621543-9-3*) Wizard Works.

— Kids' Guide to Common Alaska Critters. (Illus.). 32p. (Orig.). (J). (gr. k-7). 1995. pap. text 7.95 (*0-9621543-3-4*) Wizard Works.

O'Meara, Jan, ed. Bed & Breakfast, Alaska Style! 6th rev. ed. (Illus.). 192p. 1999. pap. 16.95 (*1-890692-01-8*) Wizard Works.

— Flights of Fancy: Alaska Birds in Verse. (Illus.). 64p. (Orig.). 1994. pap. 7.95 (*0-9621543-4-2*) Wizard Works.

O'Meara, Jan, ed. see Niebergall, Jane.

***O'Meara, John.** Defending Her Son. (Prose Ser.: No. 51). 190p. 2000. pap. 15.00 (*1-55071-105-9*, , Pub. by Guernica Editions) Paul & Co Pubs.

O'Meara, John. Delaware-English/English-Delaware Dictionary. LC 96-147437. (DEL.). 650p. 1996. text 75.00 (*0-8020-0670-1*) U of Toronto Pr.

— Delaware Reference Grammar. 168p. 1998. text 30.00 (*0-8020-4386-0*) U of Toronto Pr.

— Othello's Sacrifice: Essays on Shakespeare & Romantic Tradition. LC 95-81892. 128p. Date not set. pap. 10.00 (*1-55071-040-0*) Guernica Editions.

— Otherworldly Hamlet: Four Essays. 112p. 1991. pap. 10.00 (*0-920717-50-0*) SPD-Small Pr Dist.

— The Singing-Masters. 1996. 23.95 (*0-946640-68-8*, Pub. by Lilliput Pr) Irish Bks Media.

— Studies in Augustine & Eriugena. Halton, Thomas P., ed. LC 92-7188. 362p. 1993. text 59.95 (*0-8132-0768-1*) Cath U Pr.

O'Meara, John, tr. see Gerarld of Wales.

O'Meara, John J. Eriugena. (Illus.). 248p. 1988. text 69.00 (*0-19-826674-X*) OUP.

— Studies in St. Augustine. 200p. 1996. 65.00 (*1-85182-272-0*, Pub. by Four Cts Pr) Intl Spec Bk.

***O'Meara, John J.** The Young Augustine. 2nd rev. ed. LC 99-49350. (C). 2001. pap. 14.95 (*0-8189-0833-5*) Alba.

O'Meara, John J., tr. The Voyage of St. Brendan. 1981. pap. 9.95 (*0-85105-384-X*, Pub. by Smyth) Dufour.

O'Meara, John J., tr. see Cambrensis, Giraldus.

O'Meara, Lynn, ed. see MacCubbin, Tom.

O'Meara, Mark L. Here I Am: Finding Oneself Through Healing & Letting Go. 208p. (Orig.). 1998. pap. 12.95 (*0-9680459-1-X*, Pub. by Soul Care Pub) New Leaf Dist.

O'Meara, Megan. The Shamrock Diary. 240p. 1998. pap. 10.95 (*0-9665175-1-2*) Magnolia Mansions.

***O'Meara, Molly.** Building Cities for People & the Planet. Peterson, Jane A., ed. LC 99-71314. (Paper Ser.: Vol. 147). 80p. 1999. pap. 5.00 (*1-878071-49-1*) Worldwatch Inst.

O'Meara, O. Timothy. Lectures on Linear Groups. LC 74-8773. (CBMS Regional Conference Series in Mathematics: No. 22). 87p. 1974. reprint ed. pap. 19.00 (*0-8218-1672-1*, CBMS/22) Am Math.

— Symplectic Groups. LC 78-19101. (Mathematical Surveys & Monographs). 122p. 1978. reprint ed. pap. 49.00 (*0-8218-1516-4*, SURV/16) Am Math.

O'Meara, O. Timothy, jt. auth. see Hahn, Alexander J.

O'Meara, Patrick. K. F. Ryleev: A Political Biography of the Decembrist Poet. LC 83-24658. 381p. 1984. reprint ed. pap. 118.20 (*0-7837-9405-3*, 206015000004) Bks Demand.

***O'Meara, Patrick, et al.** Changing Perspectives on International Education. LC 00-38876. 2000. write for info. (*0-253-33816-6*) Ind U Pr.

— Globalization & the Challenges of a New Century: A Reader. Newman, Roxanna Ma, ed. LC 99-37634. 576p. 2000. pap. 19.95 (*0-253-21355-X*); lib. bdg. 49.95 (*0-253-33658-9*) Ind U Pr.

O'Meara, Patrick, jt. ed. see Carter, Gwendolen M.

O'Meara, Patrick, jt. ed. see Carter, Gwendolyn M.

O'Meara, Patrick, jt. ed. see Martin, Phyllis M.

O'Meara, Stephen J. Deep-Sky Companions: The Messier Objects: A New Look at the Most Famous Deep-Sky Wonders in the Heavens. LC 96-51773. (Illus.). 240p. (C). 1999. 34.95 (*0-521-55332-6*) Cambridge U Pr.

O'Meara, Stephen J. & O'Meara, Donna D. Volcanoes: Passion & Fury. LC 93-47387. (Illus.). 96p. (J). 1994. pap. 16.95 (*0-933346-70-0*) Sky Pub.

O'Meara, Stephen J., jt. auth. see Houston, Walter S.

***O'Meara, T. O.** Introduction to Quadratic Forms. LC 99-58347. (Classics in Mathematics). (Illus.). xiv, 344p. 2000. pap. 39.95 (*3-540-66564-1*) Spr-Verlag.

O'Meara, Thomas F. The Pattern of Our Days: Liturgies & Resources For Worship. 2nd ed. Galloway, Kathy, ed. LC 98-56177. 224p. 1999. pap. 13.95 (*0-8091-3860-3*) Paulist Pr.

— Theology of Ministry. 2nd rev. ed. LC 99-13339. 320p. 1999. pap. 21.95 (*0-8091-3856-5*) Paulist Pr.

— Thomas Aquinas Theologian. LC 96-26438. 368p. 1997. text 36.00 (*0-268-01898-7*); pap. text 16.95 (*0-268-04201-2*) U of Notre Dame Pr.

O'Meara, Tim. Samoan Planters. 200p. (C). 1990. pap. text 23.50 (*0-03-022847-6*) Harcourt Coll Pubs.

O'Meara, Walter. Guns at the Forks. LC 79-4000. (Illus.). 280p. 1979. pap. 15.95 (*0-8229-5309-9*) U of Pittsburgh Pr.

— Lakeland Boating Ports O' Call Lake Erie & Lk. St. Claire: Includes the Detroit & St. Claire Rivers. 2nd rev. ed. Hess, Randall W., ed. (Lakeland Boating Ports O'Call Ser.). (Illus.). 304p. 1998. spiral bd. 44.95 (*1-890839-05-1*) OMeara-Brown Pubns.

— We Made It Through the Winter. (Illus.). xi, 128p. 1987. pap. 7.95 (*0-87351-212-X*) Minn Hist.

***Omega, Ryan.** Anime Trivia Quizbook Episode 1: From Easy to Otaku Obscure. Vol. 1. (Illus.). 176p. 2000. pap. 14.95 (*1-880656-44-2*) Stone Bridge Pr.

— Torments from the Top 20. (Anime Trivia Quizbks.: Vol. 2). (Illus.). 176p. 2000. pap. 14.95 (*1-880656-55-8*) Stone Bridge Pr.

O'Meilia, Matt. Garth Brooks: The Road Out of Santa Fe. LC 96-42095. 220p. 1997. 19.95 (*0-8061-2907-7*) U of Okla Pr.

Omelchenko, William, ed. see Doroshenko, Dmytro.

O'Melia, Charles R., ed. Environmental Engineering. LC 90-881. 940p. 1990. pap. text 85.00 (*0-87262-768-3*) Am Soc Civil Eng.

O'Melia, Charles R., jt. auth. see Becker, William C.

O'Melia, Michael, jt. auth. see Miley, Karla K.

O'Melia, Micheal, jt. auth. see Miley, Karla K.

***Omelianuk, Scott & Allen, Ted.** Esquire'sThings a Man Should Know about Marriage: A Groom's Guide to the Wedding & Beyond. LC 99-48056. 1999. pap. 10.95 (*1-57322-777-3*, Riverhd Trade) Berkley Pub.

Omelianuk, Scott & Allen, Ted. Things a Man Should Know about Style. LC 99-25788. 144p. 1999. pap. 10.95 (*1-57322-763-3*) Berkley Pub.

O'Melveny, Henry W. William G. Kerckhoff: Utility Empire Builder. 2nd ed. Orig. Title: William G. Kerckhoff, a Memorial. (Illus.). 76p. 1998. reprint ed. pap. 15.00 (*0-9669508-0-1*) Upland Public.

O'Melveny, Regina. Blue Wolves. Rogers, Bertha, ed. (Poetry Book Award Ser.: Vol. 2). 64p. (Orig.). 1998. mass mkt. 12.00 (*0-9646844-7-0*) Bright Hill.

Omenana Collective Research Group Staff. Maatics: African Ethical Foundations. (Laying the Foundations into the Heart Ser.). 60p. (Orig.). 1985. pap. 5.95 (*0-943324-21-1*) Omenana.

Omenana Collective Research Group Staff, ed. see Ntalaja, Nzongola.

Omenana Collective Research Group Staff, ed. see Nwafor, Azinna.

Omenana Research Group Staff. Buna-Kima or Theologia Africana, Vol. I. 200p. (Orig.). 1982. pap. 9.95 (*0-943324-03-3*) Omenana.

— Corporate Class Ethics & Apartheid. 120p. (Orig.). 1982. pap. 3.95 (*0-943324-04-1*) Omenana.

Omenetto, P., jt. ed. see Boissonnas, J.

Omenka, Nicholas I. The School in the Service of Evangelization: The Catholic Educational Impact in Eastern Nigeria 1886-1950. LC 88-37555. (Studies on Religion in Africa - Supplements to the Journal of Religion in Africa: Vol. 6). xv, 317p. 1989. 101.50 (*90-04-08632-3*) Brill Academic Pubs.

Omenn, Gilbert S., ed. Annual Review of Pubic Health, Vol. 16. 1995. text 52.00 (*0-8243-2716-0*) Annual Reviews.

— Environmental Biotechnology: Reducing Risks from Environmental Chemicals Through Biotechnology. LC 88-17886. (Basic Life Sciences Ser.: Vol. 45). (Illus.). 520p. 1988. 125.00 (*0-306-42984-5*, Plenum Trade) Perseus Pubng.

An Asterisk (*) at the beginning of an entry indicates that the title is appearing for the first time.

Omenn, Gilbert S., et al, eds. Annual Review of Public Health, Vol. 12. 1991. text 45.00 (*0-8243-2712-8*) Annual Reviews.
— Annual Review of Public Health, Vol. 13. 1992. text 49.00 (*0-8243-2713-6*) Annual Reviews.
— Annual Review of Public Health, Vol. 14. (Illus.). 1993. text 49.00 (*0-8243-2714-4*) Annual Reviews.
— Annual Review of Public Health, Vol. 15. (Illus.). 1994. text 52.00 (*0-8243-2715-2*) Annual Reviews.
— Annual Review of Public Health, Vol. 17. (Illus.). 1996. text 57.00 (*0-8243-2717-9*) Annual Reviews.

Omenn, Gilbert S. & Gelboin, Harry V., eds. Genetic Variability in Responses to Chemical Exposure. LC 84-4947. (Banbury Report: No. 16). 433p. reprint ed. pap. 134.30 (*0-7837-2011-4*, 204228500002) Bks Demand.

Omenn, Gilbert S. & Hollaender, Alexander, eds. Genetic Control of Environmental Pollutants. LC 82-26942. (Basic Life Sciences Ser.: Vol. 28). 418p. 1984. 95.00 (*0-306-41624-7*, Plenum Trade) Perseus Pubng.

Omenn, Gilbert S. & Teich, Albert H., eds. Biotechnology & the Environment: Research Needs. LC 86-18181. (Illus.). 169p. 1987. 36.00 (*0-8155-1105-1*) Noyes.

Omenn, Gilbert S., jt. auth. see Lave, Lester B.

Omer, Amatul Rahma, tr. see Nooruddin, Allamah.

Omer-Cooper, J. D. The Zulu Aftermath. Date not set. pap. text. write for info. (*0-582-64531-X*, Pub. by Addison-Wesley) Longman.

Omer-Cooper, John D. History of Southern Africa. 2nd ed. LC 93-40500. 322p. (Orig.). 1994. pap. 22.50 (*0-435-08095-4*, 08095) Heinemann.

Omer, Devorah. Once There Was a Hassid. (Illus.). 28p. (J). (gr. 4 up). 1987. 9.95 (*0-915361-73-6*) Lambda Pubs.

Omer, Elhaj B. Danagla Traders of Northern Sudan. (Sudan Studies: No. 10). 105p. 1985. 25.00 (*0-685-14919-6*) Evergreen Dist.

Omer, Haim. Critical Interventions in Psychotherapy. 192p. 1994. 23.00 (*0-393-70182-4*) Norton.
— Parental Presence: Reclaiming a Leadership Role in Bringing up Our Children. LC 99-34352. 160p. 2000. pap. 19.95 (*1-891944-39-8*) Zeig Tucker.

Omer, Haim & Alon, Nahi. Constructing Therapeutic Narratives. LC 96-13384. 280p. 1997. 50.00 (*1-56821-856-7*) Aronson.

Omer, Jason. History of Southern Africa. 2nd ed. LC 93-40500. 1997. pap. text 22.50 (*0-85255-715-9*) J Currey.

Omer-Man, Jonathan, jt. ed. see Wiener, Shohama H.

***Omer, Mordechai.** Enzo Cucchi. 2000. pap. 29.95 (*88-8158-270-8*) Charta.

Omer, Mordechai. J. M. W. Turner & the Romantic Vision of the Holy Land & the Bible. Grinnell, Jennifer, ed. LC 96-77722. (Illus.). 149p. (Orig.). 1996. pap. text 19.95 (*0-9640153-5-8*) McMullen Mus Art.

O'Mera, Jan, ed. see Fry, Bill.

Omerod, A. Textile Project Management. 1992. 360.00 (*1-870812-38-7*, Pub. by Textile Inst) St Mut.

Omerod, A. & Sondhelm, W. S. Weaving: Technology & Operations. 1995. 90.00 (*1-870812-76-X*, Pub. by Textile Inst) St Mut.

Omerod, Jan. Miss Mouse Takes Off. (J). Date not set. 14.95 (*0-688-17870-7*, Wm Morrow) Morrow Avon.

O'Merry, Rory. Doctor Smog's Used Car Lemon Check: The Used Car Buying Guide for Smart People. 96p. (Orig.). 1995. reprint ed. pap. 12.95 (*0-9625048-4-X*) Dr Smogs Clean Air.

Omery, Anna & Kasper, Christine E. In Search of Nursing Science. 328p. 1995. text 54.00 (*0-8039-5093-4*); pap. text 25.00 (*0-8039-5094-2*) Sage.

Ometrics & Beman, Jude. First Steps Beyond. 1976. 13.95 (*0-89190-964-8*, Rivercity Pr) Amereon Ltd.

Omi, Michael & Winant, Howard A. Racial Formation in the United States: 1960-1990. 2nd ed. LC 93-336254. 224p. (C). 1994. pap. 17.99 (*0-415-90864-7*) Routledge.
— Racial Formation in the United States from the 1960's to the 1980's. 224p. 1986. pap. 13.95 (*0-7102-0970-3*, 09703, Routledge Thoemms) Routledge.

OMI Staff, et al. O Blessed Night: Theological Underpinnings for Recovery from Addiction. LC 90-19635. 205p. (Orig.). 1991. pap. 9.95 (*0-8189-0587-5*) Alba.

Omichi, Toshikatsu. Drought Conciliation & Water Rights: Japanese Experience. (Illus.). 104p. (C). 1999. pap. text 25.00 (*0-7881-4369-7*) DIANE Pub.

Omid, Homa. Islam & the Post-Revolutionary State in Iran. 288p. 1994. text 69.95 (*0-312-10737-4*) St Martin.

Omidian, Patricia A. Aging & Family in an Afghan Refugee Community: Transitions & Transformations. rev. ed. LC 95-47462. (Studies on the Elderly in America). 227p. 1996. text 20.00 (*0-8153-2279-8*) Garland.

Omidvar, Omid & Dayhoff, Judith, eds. Neural Networks & Pattern Recognition. LC 97-25466. (Illus.). 351p. 1997. text 49.95 (*0-12-526420-8*) Acad Pr.

Omidvar, Omid M. & Van Der Smagt, Patric, eds. Neural Systems for Robotics. LC 96-29555. (Illus.). 346p. 1997. text 49.95 (*0-12-526280-9*) Morgan Kaufmann.

Omidvar, Omid M., jt. ed. see Elliott, David.

***Omidyar, Cambyse Guy.** Mobile & Wireless Communications Networks: Proceedings of the IFIP - TC6/European Union Networking 2000 International Workshop, MWCN 2000, Paris, France, May 2000. LC 00-33819. (Lecture Notes in Computer Science). 2000. pap. write for info. (*3-540-67543-4*) Spr-Verlag.

Omikron. Letters from Paulos: A Leader in Wisdom to HUS Pupils 10 Korinthos, 1920. 304p. 1998. reprint ed. pap. 24.95 (*0-7661-0610-1*) Kessinger Pub.

Omilian, Susan M. Sex-Based Employment Discrimination. 1990. 130.00 (*0-685-46258-7*) West Group.
— What Every Employer Should Be Doing about Sexual Harassment. rev. ed. LC 98-202626. 128p. 1986. per. 29.95 (*1-55645-443-0*, 443) Busn Legal Reports.

Ominsky, Harris. Real Estate Practice: New Perspectives. 480p. (Orig.). 1996. pap. 29.00 (*1-57804-000-0*, PBI Pr) PA Bar Inst.

Omishi, Ray, jt. auth. see Akahori, Satoru.

Omisky, Dave. Football Made Simple: A Spectator's Guide. 2nd ed. 129p. 1998. pap. 9.95 (*1-884309-08-9*) First Base Spts.

Omissi, David E., jt. auth. see Killingray, David.

Omiya, James K., jt. auth. see Gutierrez, Jorge A.

Omiya, Shiro. The Hidden Roots of Aikido: Aiki Jujutsu Daitoryu. 1999. 30.00 (*4-7700-2327-8*, Pub. by Kodansha Intl) Kodansha.

Omizo, Naomi, jt. auth. see Peterson, Hiromi.

Omland, Omar K. The Third Mile: A Biblical View of Codependency. 105p. (Orig.). 1992. pap. 8.95 (*0-943167-11-6*) Faith & Fellowship Pr.

Omlin, Christian W. Knowledge Acquisition & Representation in Recurrent Neural Networks: Progress in Neural Processes. 1998. 45.00 (*981-02-3607-7*) World Scientific Pub.

Omlor, Georg. Isolated Hyperthermic Limb Perfusion. Vaupel, Peter & Alexander, Cristof, eds. LC 95-17288. (Medical Intelligence Unit Ser.). 120p. 1995. 69.00 (*1-57059-178-4*) Landes Bioscience.

Omlor, J. Dennis. Efficiency Analysis of File Organization & Information. Stone, Harold S., ed. LC 81-11693. (Computer Science: Distributed Database Systems Ser.: No. 10). 124p. 1981. reprint ed. pap. 38.50 (*0-8357-1226-5*, 207016100064) Bks Demand.

Omlor, Patrick. Has the Church the Right? (Illus.). 1997. pap. 2.50 (*1-929968-01-9*) Catholic Research Inst.
— Insights into Heresy. 1997. pap. 2.00 (*1-929968-06-X*) Catholic Research Inst.
— Questioning the Validity of Masses Using the New All-English Canon. 1997. pap. 5.00 (*1-929968-05-1*) Catholic Research Inst.
— The Robber Church: An Interdum Reprint. 1997. pap. 4.00 (*1-929968-04-3*) Catholic Research Inst.
— The Ventriloquists. 1997. pap. 2.00 (*1-929968-02-7*) Catholic Research Inst.

Ommagio-Hadley, Alice. Teaching Language in Context. 2nd ed. 532p. (C). 1993. mass mkt. 37.95 (*0-8384-4067-3*) Heinle & Heinle.
— Teaching Language in Context. 2nd ed. (C). 1993. mass mkt., student ed. 19.95 (*0-8384-4068-1*) Heinle & Heinle.

Ommanney, Francis D. The Shoals of Capricorn. LC 74-15555. (Illus.). 322p. 1975. reprint ed. lib. bdg. 65.00 (*0-8371-7823-1*, OMSC, Greenwood Pr) Greenwood.

Ommanney, K. A. & Schanker, Harry H. The Stage & the School. 5th ed. 1982. text 29.76 (*0-07-047671-3*) McGraw.

***Ommeln, Miriam.** Die Verkorperung von Friedrich Nietzsches Asthetik Ist der Surrealismus. (Europaische Hochschulschriften, Reihe 20). V, 295p. 1999. 51.95 (*3-631-35100-3*) P Lang Pubng.

Ommen, G. J. Van, see Van Ommen, G. J., ed.

Ommen, Thomas B. The Hermeneutic of Dogma. LC 75-29493. (American Academy of Religion. Dissertation Ser.: No. 11). 262p. reprint ed. pap. 81.30 (*0-7837-5468-X*, 204523300005) Bks Demand.

Ommer, Rosemary E. From Outpost to Outport: A Structural Analysis of the Jersey-Gasp[00e9] Cod Fishery, 1767-1886. 264p. (C). 1990. text 65.00 (*0-7735-0730-2*, Pub. by McG-Queens Univ Pr) CUP Services.

Ommer, Rosemary E., jt. ed. see Newell, Diane.

Ommer, Uwe. Asian Ladies. 2000. 29.99 (*3-8228-7181-8*) Taschen Amer.

***Ommer, Uwe.** 1000 Families. 2000. 39.99 (*3-8228-6213-4*) Taschen Amer.

Ommerborn, Wolfgang. Die Einheit der Welt: Die Qi-Theorie des Neo-Konfuzianers Zhang Zai (1020-1077) LC 96-6460. (Bochumer Studien zur Philosophie Ser.: Vol. 23). iv, 349p. 1996. lib. bdg. 85.00 (*90-6032-344-0*) J Benjamins Pubng Co.

Ommeren, Hans Von, see Von Ommeren, Hans, photos by.

Ommundsenand, Wenche & Rowley, Hazel. From a Distance. LC 97-161211. 1996. pap. 70.00 (*0-949823-56-2*, Pub. by Deakin Univ) St Mut.

Omnaes, Roland. Quantum Philosophy: Understanding & Interpreting Contemporary Science. LC 98-42445. 1999. text 29.95 (*0-691-02787-0*, Pub. by Princeton U Pr) Cal Prin Full Svc.

Omnes, Roland. The Interpretation of Quantum Mechanics. LC 93-47445. (Physics Ser.). 568p. (C). 1994. text 95.00 (*0-691-03336-6*, Pub. by Princeton U Pr); pap. text 39.50 (*0-691-03669-1*, Pub. by Princeton U Pr) Cal Prin Full Svc.
— Understanding Quantum Mechanics. LC 98-42442. 1999. 35.00 (*0-691-00435-8*, Pub. by Princeton U Pr) Cal Prin Full Svc.

***Omnibus Press Staff.** Classical Good CD Guide: 2000 Edition. 1999. pap. text 27.95 (*1-902274-06-7*) Gramophone.

Omnibus Press Staff. The Story of Live Spice: The Fab Five on Tour. Dimery, Robert, ed. (Illus.). 32p. (YA). 1998. pap. 9.95 (*0-7119-6940-X*, OP48084) Omnibus NY.

Omnigraphics Inc Staff. Stately Homes in America. 2000. 58.00 (*0-7808-0160-1*) Omnigraphics Inc.

Omnik, Tukummiq C. & Lowenstein, Tom, trs. The Things That Were Said of Them: Shaman Stories & Oral Histories of the Tikigaq People. 285p. 1992. 40.00 (*0-520-06569-7*, Pub. by U CA Pr) Cal Prin Full Svc.

Omo-Osagie, Solomon I., II. Native Voices. 108p. 1995. pap. 6.50 (*0-9647217-0-8*) S I Omo-Osagie.

Omohundro Institute of Early American History & Cu, jt. auth. see Morgan, Philip D.

Omohundro, John T. Careers in Anthropology. LC 97-37783. viii, 119p. 1997. pap. text 13.95 (*0-7674-0263-4*, 20263) Mayfield Pub.

Omohundro, John T. & Goodman, Kathleen. Mystery Fossil 1: A Physical Anthropology Laboratory Exercise for the Macintosh. (Mystery Fossil Ser.). (C). 1993. pap. text 24.95 incl. disk (*1-55934-264-1*, 1264) Mayfield Pub.
— Mystery Fossil 2: A Physical Anthropology Laboratory Exercise for the Macintosh. (Mystery Fossil Ser.). (C). 1993. pap. text 24.95 incl. disk (*1-55934-275-7*, 1275) Mayfield Pub.

Omohundro, Malvern H. Omohundro Genealogical Record: The Omohundro & Allied Families in America . . . From the First Omohundro in Westmoreland County, Va., 1670 . . . To 1950. (Illus.). 1287p. 1998. reprint ed. pap. 159.00 (*0-8328-9483-4*); reprint ed. lib. bdg. 169.00 (*0-8328-9482-6*) Higginson Bk Co.

Omohundro, S. M. Geometric Perturbation Theory in Physics. 584p. 1986. text 77.00 (*9971-5-0136-8*) World Scientific Pub.

***Omoigui, Sota.** Sota Omoigui's Anesthesia Drugs Handbook. 3rd ed. LC 99-24987. 628p. 1999. pap. 39.95 (*0-632-04421-7*) Blackwell Sci.
— Sota Omoigui's Pain Drugs Handbook. 2nd ed. LC 98-40987. (Illus.). 1999. pap. 39.95 (*0-632-04419-5*) Blackwell Sci.

Omoigui, Sota. Universal Drug Infusion Ruler. (Illus.). 4p. 1995. spiral bd. 29.00 (*0-9650767-0-9*) St-of-the-Art Tech.

Omoike, Isaac I. Euthanasia, Right or Wrong? (Or Tell-Tale Signs of Murders) LC 94-90564. 169p. (Orig.). (C). 1995. pap. text 19.95 (*0-9632236-3-1*) I Omoike Bks.
— Genocide: The Ultimate Threat of the Next Milleniums. LC 91-70487. 228p. (Orig.). 1991. pap. text 16.99 (*0-9632236-0-7*) I Omoike Bks.
— Insider America. LC 91-90721. 106p. (Orig.). 1993. pap. 11.00 (*0-9632236-8-2*) I Omoike Bks.
— The Murder of a Princess? An Investigational Analysis of the Death of Princess Diana. LC 98-91270. (Illus.). 109p. 1998. pap. 13.99 (*0-9632236-4-X*) I Omoike Bks.

***Omoike, Isaac I.** A Tribute to John F. Kennedy, Jr. LC 00-102047. 2000. pap. text 19.95 (*0-9632236-5-8*) I Omoike Bks.

Omolade, Barbara. It's a Family Affair: The Real Lives of Black Single Mother. (Freedom Organizing Pamphlet Ser.). 16p. (Orig.). 1986. pap. 3.95 (*0-913175-10-2*) Kitchen Table.
— The Rising Song of African American Women. LC 94-4752. 288p. (C). (gr. 13). 1994. 75.00 (*0-415-90760-8*) Routledge.
— The Rising Song of African American Women. 288p. (C). (gr. 13). 1994. pap. 19.99 (*0-415-90761-6*, Pub. by Tavistock) Routledge.

Omond, James. Orkney Eighty Years Ago: With Special Attention to Evie. LC 77-87683. reprint ed. 27.50 (*0-404-16479-X*) AMS Pr.

Omond, Thomas S. The Romantic Triumph. LC 74-38364. (Select Bibliographies Reprint Ser.). 1977. reprint ed. 25.95 (*0-8369-6781-X*) Ayer.

Omonde, Lois G., jt. auth. see Mattallano, Jane.

Omondi, Amos R. The Microarchitecture of Pipelined & Superscalar Computers. LC 99-13874. 1999. write for info. (*0-7923-8463-6*) Kluwer Academic.

Omont, Henri A. Facsimiles De Manuscrits Grecs Des XVe et XVIe Siecles. 65p. 1974. reprint ed. write for info. (*3-487-05259-8*) G Olms Pubs.

O'Moore, R. R., et al. Medical Informatics Europe, 1990 Vol. 40: Proceedings Glasgow, Scotland, August 20-23, 1990. Rienhoff, O. & Lindberg, D. A., eds. (Lecture Notes Ser.). xxv, 820p. 1990. 146.00 (*0-387-52936-5*) Spr-Verlag.

O'Morain, C. A. & O'Connor, H., eds. Helicobacter Pylori: Implications & Practice. LC 94-66536. 1994. pap. 25.00 (*0-926592-14-9*) Normed Verlag.

O'Morain, C. A., jt. ed. see Moran, A. P.

O'Morain, Calm A. Ulcerative Colitis. 208p. 1991. lib. bdg. 129.00 (*0-8493-5498-6*, RC862) CRC Pr.

O'More, Peggy. Dinah Mason, Reporter. large type ed. (Linford Mystery Library). 272p. 1996. pap. 16.99 (*0-7089-7909-2*) Ulverscroft.
— I'll Never Love Again. large type ed. (Linford Romance Library). 368p. 1996. pap. 16.99 (*0-7089-7838-X*, Linford) Ulverscroft.
— Love's Inner Beauty. large type ed. (Linford Romance Library). 1991. pap. 16.99 (*0-7089-6984-4*, Linford) Ulverscroft.
— Marta. large type ed. 1994. 27.99 (*0-7089-3205-3*) Ulverscroft.
— Mary Contrary. large type ed. 212p. 1994. pap. 18.99 (*1-85389-437-0*, Dales) Ulverscroft.
— No Place for Love. large type ed. (Linford Romance Library). 320p. 1993. pap. 16.99 (*0-7089-7410-4*, Linford) Ulverscroft.
— Pixie. large type ed. (Linford Romance Library). 256p. 1995. pap. 16.99 (*0-7089-7664-6*, Linford) Ulverscroft.
— Stand-By Nurse. large type ed. (Linford Romance Library). 1995. pap. 16.99 (*0-7089-7682-4*, Linford) Ulverscroft.
— Vacation with Love. large type ed. (Linford Romance Library). 1990. pap. 16.99 (*0-7089-6917-8*) Ulverscroft.

O'More, Peggy, jt. auth. see Covert, Alice L.

Omori, Annie S. & Kochi, Doi, trs. Diaries of Court Ladies of Old Japan. LC 72-111775. reprint ed. 29.50 (*0-404-04819-6*) AMS Pr.

Omori, Frances, et al. Strength Through Cooperation: Military Force in the Asian-Pacific Region. LC 97-31822. 1997. write for info. (*1-57906-005-6*) Natl Defense.

Omori, Hideki, tr. from JPN. Infinite-Dimensional Lie Groups. LC 96-38349. (Translations Of Mathematical Monographs: Vol. 158). 415p. 1996. text 99.00 (*0-8218-4575-6*, MMONO/158) Am Math.

Omori, Makoto & Tsutomu, Ikeda. Methods in Marine Zooplankton Ecology. LC 91-24425. 348p. (C). 1992. reprint ed. lib. bdg. 59.95 (*0-89464-653-2*) Krieger.

Omori, Rotaishi S. Zen & Budo. Wong, Brenda, ed. Tanouye, Tenshin, tr. from JPN. (Illus.). 23p. (Orig.). 1989. pap. 5.00 (*1-877982-02-4*) Daihonzan Chozen-ji.

Omori, T., jt. ed. see Yoshibara, K.

O'Morrow, Gerald & Reynolds, Ron. Study Guide for National Certification in Therapeutic Recreation. LC 90-71335. 89p. 1990. 11.95 (*0-910251-38-X*) Venture Pub PA.

O'Morrow, Gerald S. & Carter, Marcia J. Effective Management in Therapeutic Recreation Service. LC 96-61938. 412p. 1997. text 39.95 (*0-910251-87-8*, ETR91) Venture Pub PA.

O'Morrow, Gerald S. & Reynolds, Ronald P. Therapeutic Recreation. 3rd ed. 352p. 1988. text 84.00 (*0-13-914896-5*) P-H.

O'Morrow, Gerald S., jt. auth. see Reynolds, Ronald P.

Omotani, Les M. Konnichi Wa, Japan. (JPN., Illus.). 128p. (YA). (gr. 7-12). 1995. pap. 15.95 (*0-8442-8497-1*, 84971, Natl Textbk Co) NTC Contemp Pub Co.

Omoto, Keiichi, jt. ed. see Tobias, Philip V.

Omoto, Sadayoshi, intro. Early Michigan Paintings. (Illus.). 130p. (Orig.). 1976. pap. 6.50 (*1-879147-02-5*) Kresge Art Mus.

Omoto, Sadayoshi & Van Liere, Eldon N. The Michigan Experience. (Illus.). 176p. (Orig.). 1986. pap. 8.00 (*1-879147-08-4*) Kresge Art Mus.

Omotoso, Kole. Achebe or Soyinka? A Re-Interpretation & a Study in Contrasts. (New Perspectives on African Literature Ser.: No. 3). 188p. 1995. lib. bdg. 75.00 (*0-905450-38-8*, Pub. by H Zell Pubs) Seven Hills Bk.

Omoyajowo, J. A. Cherubim & Seraphim: The History of an African Independent Church. LC 78-64624. 256p. (Orig.). 1982. 21.50 (*0-88357-068-8*); pap. 8.95 (*0-88357-069-6*) NOK Pubs.

Omran, Abdel R. Egypt: Population Problems & Prospects. 448p. 1973. pap. 6.50 (*0-89055-106-5*) Carolina Pop Ctr.

Omran, Abdel R., ed. Liberalization of Abortion Laws: Implications. LC 75-42005. 305p. 1976. pap. 5.00 (*0-89055-115-4*) Carolina Pop Ctr.

Omran, Elsayed M., tr. & intro. see El-Zein, Samih A.

Omraseu, Khafra K. & Jenkins, Timothy L. Black Futurists in the Information Age: Vision of a 21st Century Technological Renaissance. LC 96-79952. 284p. 1997. pap. 19.95 (*0-9635645-6-0*) KMT Pubns.

Omrcanin, Ivo. Anglo-American Croatian Rapprochement. 650p. 1989. 25.00 (*0-9613814-6-9*) Ivor Pr.
— Boljsevici Kolju Sami Sebe. (CRO.). 72p. 1995. pap. 7.00 (*0-614-06282-9*) Ivor Pr.
— Croatia Rediviva. (CRO.). 72p. 1995. pap. 10.00 (*0-614-06281-0*) Ivor Pr.
— Diplomatische und Politische Geschichte Kroatiens. rev. ed. 416p. 1990. 25.00 (*1-878716-03-4*) Ivor Pr.
— Diplomatska i Politicka Povijest Hrvatske, 4 vols., Set. (CRO.). 298p. 1992. pap. 25.00 (*1-878716-06-9*) Ivor Pr.
— Hrvatska Backa. (CRO.). 104p. (Orig.). 1995. pap. 10.00 (*1-878716-19-0*) Ivor Pr.
— Hrvatska 1944. 500p. 1990. pap. 25.00 (*1-878716-01-8*) Ivor Pr.
— Hrvatska, 1945. (CRO.). 400p. (Orig.). 1992. pap. 25.00 (*1-878716-05-0*) Ivor Pr.
— Hrvatski Boljsevici (su) Srpski Drek. (CRO.). 104p. 1993. pap. 10.00 (*1-878716-10-7*) Ivor Pr.
— Hrvatski Srijem. (CRO.). 160p. (Orig.). 1944. pap. 10.00 (*1-878716-18-2*) Ivor Pr.
— Hrvatsko Kraljevstvo Slavnikovica. (CRO., Illus.). 104p. (Orig.). 1994. pap. 10.00 (*1-878716-16-6*) Ivor Pr.
— Hrvatsko Kraljevstvo Slavnikovica (The Slavnik Kingdom of Croatia) (CRO.). 104p. 1994. pap. 10.00 (*1-878716-14-X*) Ivor Pr.
— Ime Pobjede Krscanstvo Hrvata: Name Victories Christianity of Croatians. (CRO.). 24p. 1993. pap. 2.00 (*1-878716-12-3*) Ivor Pr.
— L' Influence du Droit Canonique sur le Droit Coutumier Croate. (FRE.). 100p. 1990. 5.00 (*1-878716-00-X*) Ivor Pr.
— Mi i Drugi u Sedmom Stoljecu: Us & Others in the Seventh Century. (CRO., Illus.). 160p. 1993. pap. 10.00 (*1-878716-13-1*) Ivor Pr.
— Mit Bogova u Predpovijesti Hrvatske. (CRO.). 158p. (Orig.). 1993. pap. 10.00 (*1-878716-09-3*) Ivor Pr.
— Ratna Povijest Hrvatske (Military History of Croatia), 4 vols. (CRO.). 1993. pap. 5.00 (*1-878716-08-5*) Ivor Pr.
— 7 Ne Ofanziva - 7 Non Offensives. (CRO.). 72p. (Orig.). 1996. pap. 10.00 (*0-614-15880-X*) Ivor Pr.
— Sjeca Svecenika U Hrvatskoj.Tr. of Slaughter of Priests in Croatia. (CRO.). 72p. (Orig.). 1995. pap. 7.00 (*0-614-10151-4*) Ivor Pr.
— Spasio Sam Ustastvo. (CRO.). 104p. 1994. pap. 10.00 (*1-878716-17-4*) Ivor Pr.
— Ubijaj Boljsevicke Lazi i Zlocine (Kill Bolshevik Lies & Crimes) (CRO.). 104p. 1993. pap. 10.00 (*1-878716-11-5*) Ivor Pr.
— Velika Hrvatska. (CRO.). 104p. 1994. pap. 10.00 (*1-878716-15-8*) Ivor Pr.
— Vlasi U Hrvatskoj Nisu Raci.Tr. of Vlahs in Croatia Are Not Serbians. (CRO.). 72p. (Orig.). 1995. pap. 7.00 (*0-614-10152-2*) Ivor Pr.

Omrcanin, Margaret S. Goodbye - Zbogom Srbijo. (CRO.). 126p. 1991. write for info. (*1-878716-04-2*) Ivor Pr.
— Margaret Thatcher's Doctrine on Recognition of Croatia. 82p. (Orig.). 1992. pap. 5.00 (*1-878716-07-7*) Ivor Pr.
— Los Von Serbien: Kroatien und das Skandinavische Modell. 2nd ed. Rullman, Hans P., tr. (GER.). 100p. 1990. pap. 7.00 (*1-878716-02-6*) Ivor Pr.

Omstead, Daniel R., ed. Computer Control of Fermentation Processes. 320p. 1989. lib. bdg. 239.00 (*0-8493-5496-X*, TP156) CRC Pr.

O

An Asterisk (*) at the beginning of an entry indicates that the title is appearing for the first time.

***Omsted, Robert P.** Remembering Santa Fe. (Illus.). 128p. 1999. 39.95 (*0-934228-18-3*) McMillan Pubns.

Omta, S. W. Critical Success Factors in Biomedical Research & Pharmaceutical Innovation: The Joint Impact of Management Control & Contingencies on Performance & Effectiveness in Research Laboratories in Medical. . . LC 95-17479. 294p. 1995. text 129.00 (*0-7923-3563-5*) Kluwer Academic.

Omtvedt, Tamara, jt. ed. see Harris, Tara.

***O'Muilleoir, Mairtin.** Belfast's Dome of Delight: City Hall Politics 1981-2000. 226p. 2000. pap. 16.95 (*1-900960-08-7*, Pub. by Beyond the Pale) Irish Bks Media.

O'Muircheartaigh, Colm A. & Payne, Clive, eds. The Analysis of Survey Data, 2 vols., 1. LC 76-951. (Illus.). 289p. 1977. reprint ed. pap. 89.60 (*0-8357-8798-2*, 203362000001) Bks Demand.

— The Analysis of Survey Data, 2 vols., 2. LC 76-951. (Illus.). 271p. 1977. reprint ed. pap. 84.10 (*0-8357-8799-0*, 203362000002) Bks Demand.

O'Muirithe, Diarmaid. A Word in Your Ear. 134p. 1997. pap. 15.00 (*1-85182-339-5*, Pub. by Four Cts Pr) Intl Spec Bk.

O'Muirithe, Diarmuid, ed. Wexford Carols. (Illus.). 96p. 1982. pap. 14.95 (*0-85105-376-9*, Pub. by Smyth) Dufour.

O'Muirthile, Liam. Dialann Bothair. 60p. 1992. pap. 12.95 (*1-85235-098-9*) Dufour.

O'Mulgreavey, Seamus. Bonkie the Great Bank Blagger. 264p. (C). 1990. 39.00 (*1-86305-003-5*, Pub. by Pascoe Pub) St Mut.

Omura, George. Mastering AutoCAD 14. LC 97-67593. (Illus.). 1312p. 1997. pap. text 49.99 incl. cd-rom (*0-7821-2109-8*) Sybex.

Omura, George. Mastering AutoCAD LT for Windows 95. LC 96-69282. 896p. 1996. pap. text 34.99 incl. cd-rom (*0-7821-1855-0*) Sybex.

Omura, George. Mastering AutoCAD 3D. LC 96-67845. (Illus.). 1104p. (Orig.). 1996. pap. 49.99 incl. cd-rom (*0-7821-1850-X*) Sybex.

Omura, George. Mastering AutoCAD 2000. LC 99-61306. (Mastering Ser.). 1504p. 1999. pap. 49.99 (*0-7821-2501-8*) Sybex.

— Mastering AutoCAD 2000: Premium Edition. 3rd ed. (Mastering Ser.). 1664p. 1999. 59.99 (*0-7821-2499-2*) Sybex.

— Mastering AutoCAD 2000 for Mechanical Engineers. 3rd ed. (Mastering Ser.). 1376p. 1999. pap. 54.99 (*0-7821-2500-X*) Sybex.

***Omura, George.** Mastering 3D Studio Viz 3.0. 656p. 2000. pap. text 39.99 (*0-7821-2775-4*) Sybex.

Omura, George & Callori, B. Robert. AutoCAD 14 Instant Reference. LC 97-67761. 368p. 1997. pap. text 19.99 (*0-7821-2129-2*) Sybex.

***Omura, George & Callori, B. Robert.** AutoCAD 2000 Instant Reference. LC 99-61304. (Instant Reference Ser.). (Illus.). 608p. 1999. pap. 19.99 (*0-7821-2497-6*) Sybex.

Omura, George, jt. auth. see Keith, Stephen.

Omura, Satoshi, ed. The Search for Bioactive Compounds from Microorganisms. (Contemporary Bioscience Ser.). (Illus.). 376p. 1992. 102.00 (*0-387-97755-4*) Spr-Verlag.

Omura, Tsuneo, jt. ed. see Tagashira, Yusaku.

Omura, Yoshiaki. Acupuncture Medicine: Its Historical & Clinical Background. (Illus.). 288p. 1996. pap. 42.50 (*1-882345-09-6*) Cognizant Comm.

***O'Murchu, Diarmuid.** Our World in Transition: Making Sense of a Changing World. 160p. 2000. pap. 16.95 (*0-8245-1862-4*, Pub. by Crossroad NY) Natl Bk Netwk.

O'Murchu, Diarmuid. Poverty, Celibacy & Obedience: A Radical Option for Life. LC 98-41199. (Orig.). 1999. pap. 14.95 (*0-8245-1473-4*) Crossroad NY.

— Quantum Theology. LC 96-49656. 1997. pap. text 19.95 (*0-8245-1630-3*) Crossroad NY.

— Reclaiming Spirituality. LC 97-67572. 196p. 1998. pap. 15.95 (*0-8245-1723-7*, Crsrd) Crossroad NY.

— Reframing Religious Life: An Expanded Vision for the Future. 159p. 1994. pap. 35.00 (*0-85439-499-0*, Pub. by St Paul Pubns) St Mut.

***O'Murchu, Diarmuid.** Religion in Exile: A Spiritual Homecoming. 208p. 2000. pap. 15.95 (*0-8245-1841-1*, Pub. by Crossroad NY) Natl Bk Netwk.

Omvedt, Gail. Dalits & the Democratic Revolution: Dr. Ambedkar & the Dalit Movement in Colonial India. LC 93-11778. 348p. (C). 1994. text 44.95 (*0-8039-9139-8*) Sage.

— Reinventing Revolution: New Social Movements & the Socialist Tradition in India. LC 92-46911. (Socialism & Social Movements Ser.). 384p. (C). (gr. 13). 1993. text 81.95 (*0-87332-784-5*, East Gate Bk) M E Sharpe.

Omvedt, Gail. Reinventing Revolution: New Social Movements & the Socialist Tradition in India. LC 92-46911. (Socialism & Social Movements Ser.). 384p. (C). (gr. 13). 1993. pap. text 35.95 (*0-87332-785-3*, East Gate Bk) M E Sharpe.

Omvedt, Gail. Violence Against Women: New Movements & New Theories in India. 42p. 1990. pap. 6.95 (*81-85107-28-9*) Women Ink.

— We Will Smash This Prison! Indian Women in Struggle. 189p. 1979. 19.95 (*0-318-37315-7*) Asia Bk Corp.

Omvedt, Gail, tr. see Moon, Vasant.

On, Danny & Sumner, David, photos by. Along the Trail: A Photographic Essay of Glacier National Park & the Northern Rockies. LC 79-53223. (Illus.). 128p. 1980. 20.00 (*0-913504-53-X*); pap. 12.95 (*0-913504-54-8*) Lowell Pr.

On, Danny, jt. auth. see Shaw, Richard J.

On Demand Data, Inc. Staff. The Corporate Tree: Directory of Corporate Linkage in the U. S. 1231p. (Orig.). 1989. 369.00 (*0-9625174-1-0*) On Demand Data.

— The Corporate Tree: Directory of Corporate Linkage in the U. S. Ward-Wuller, Patti, ed. 1180p. (Orig.). 1990. pap. 369.00 (*0-9625174-0-2*) On Demand Data.

On Wheels Staff. Arizona & New Mexico on Wheels. 208p. 1995. 13.95 (*0-02-860144-0*) Macmillan.

Onacewicz, Wlodzimierz. Empires by Conquest, 2 vols., Set. (Illus.). (C). 1986. 29.95 (*0-915979-04-7*) NOVA Pubns.

Onaga, Christine, jt. auth. see Niesen, Karen L.

Onaga, Christine Y., jt. auth. see Niesen, Karen L.

Onah, Godfrey I. Self-Transcendence & Human History in Wolfhart Pannenberg. LC 99-15085. 256p. 1999. pap. 29.50 (*0-7618-1416-7*) U Pr of Amer.

Onaitis, Susan. Negotiate Like the Big Guys: How Small & Mid-Size Companies Can Balance the Power in Dealing with Corporate Giants. 334p. 1998. pap. 29.95 (*1-56343-167-X*) Silver Lake.

***OnalBroy, M.** Requirements Targeting Software & Systems Engineering: International Workshop RTSE '97, Bernried, Germany, October 12-14, 1997: Proceedings, Vol.152. LC 98-32083. (Lecture Notes in Computer Science Ser.). 1998. 59.00 (*3-540-65309-0*) Spr-Verlag.

O'Nan, Michael & Enderton, Herbert B. Linear Algebra. 3rd ed. 461p. (C). 1989. pap. text 20.75 (*0-15-551009-6*) SCP.

***O'Nan, Stewart.** The Circus Fire: A True Story. LC 99-42051. (Illus.). 320p. 2000. 24.95 (*0-385-49684-2*) Doubleday.

O'Nan, Stewart. The Names of the Dead. 416p. 1997. pap. 11.95 (*0-14-026309-8*) Viking Penguin.

— A Prayer for the Dying: A Novel. LC 98-39613. 195p. 1999. 22.00 (*0-8050-6147-9*) H Holt & Co.

***O'Nan, Stewart.** A Prayer for the Dying: A Novel. LC 99-85964. 208p. 2000. pap. 13.00 (*0-312-25501-2*, Picador USA) St Martin.

— A Prayer for the Dying: A Novel. large type ed. LC 99-86694. 2000. 25.95 (*1-56895-841-2*) Wheeler Pub.

O'Nan, Stewart. Snow Angels: A Novel. 320p. 1995. pap. 10.95 (*0-14-025096-4*, Penguin Bks) Viking Penguin.

— Transmission. 2nd ed. LC 87-30635. (Illus.). 26p. 1987. pap. text 2.00 (*0-943123-04-6*) Arjuna Lib Pr.

— The Vietnam Reader: The Definitive Collection of American Fiction & Nonfiction on the War. LC 98-15575. (Illus.). 736p. 1998. pap. 15.95 (*0-385-49118-2*) Doubleday.

— A World Away: A Novel. LC 97-36727. 338p. 1998. 23.00 (*0-8050-5774-9*) H Holt & Co.

— A World Away: A Novel. 352p. 1999. pap. 13.00 (*0-8050-5775-7*, Pub. by H Holt & Co) VHPS.

O'Nan, Stewart, jt. auth. see Gardner, John.

O'Nan, Stewart, ed. see Gardner, John.

Onaro, Esther. Jacobs & Jenkins Family Roots. (Illus.). 100p. (Orig.). 1996. pap. write for info. (*0-9644473-3-9*) Adept Pubng.

***Onarres, Sheryl Ann & Shelton, Kathleen I.** The Walker & Cane Heist. St. James, Charlotte, ed. LC 99-75842. 180p. 1999. pap. 12.99 (*1-929316-02-X*) Moon At Mid Day Pr.

Onasch, Konrad & Schnieper, Annemarie. Icons: The Fascination & the Reality. (Illus.). 302p. 1997. 99.00 (*1-878351-53-2*) Riverside NY.

Onassis, Jacqueline Kennedy. A Look at Relapse. 10p. 1974. pap. 1.65 (*0-89486-007-0*, 1380B) Hazelden.

Onassis, Jacqueline Kennedy, ed. In the Russian Style. LC 97-75626. (Illus.). 144p. 1998. reprint ed. 14.98 (*1-56731-256-X*, MJF Bks) Fine Comms.

O'Nate, E. Computational Methods in Engineering. text. write for info. (*0-471-49047-4*) Wiley.

O'Nate, E., et al, eds. The Finite Element Method in the Nineteen Ninety's: A Book Dedicated to O.C. Zienkiewicz. (Illus.). 650p. 1992. 206.95 (*0-387-54930-7*) Spr-Verlag.

O'Nate, E., jt. ed. see Chenot, Jean-Loup.

O'Nate, E., jt. ed. see Kratzig, W. B.

Onazi, jt. auth. see Youdeouwei.

Onbargi, Salim. Born Again with Dr. Dahesh. (Illus.). 226p. 1993. 18.00 (*0-935359-39-7*) Daheshist.

Once Upon a Planet, Inc. Staff. Let's Hug! (Illus.). 32p. 1994. 2.50 (*0-88009-071-5*) Once Upon A Planet.

Onchulenko, Gene & Gillham, Skip. The Ships of the Paterson Fleet. (Great Lakes Marine History Ser.). (Illus.). 144p. 1996. pap. 19.95 (*0-9697606-4-7*, Pub. by RivT) Partners Pubs Grp.

Oncina, Jose, jt. ed. see Carrasco, R. C.

Oncken, O. Basement Tectonics No. 11: Proceedings of the Eleventh International Conference on Basement Tectonics, Held in Potsdam, Germany, July 1994. Janssen, C., ed. LC 95-42181. (Proceedings of the International Conferences on Basement Tectonics Ser.: Vol. 5). 200p. (C). 1996. text 110.50 (*0-7923-3797-2*) Kluwer Academic.

Oncken, William, III. Monkey Business: Are You Controlling Events or Are Events Controlling You? 192p. 1999. 22.95 (*1-890009-24-5*) Exec Excell.

Oncology Nursing Soc. (ONS) Staff. Core Curriculum for Oncology Nursing. 3rd ed. Itano, Joanne et al, eds. LC 97-14399. (Illus.). 784p. 1997. pap. text 45.00 (*0-7216-7156-X*, W B Saunders Co) Harcrt Hlth Sci Grp.

Oncology Nursing Society Staff. Guidelines for Oncology Nursing Practice. 2nd ed. (Illus.). 476p. 1991. pap. text 58.00 (*0-7216-3419-2*, W B Saunders Co) Harcrt Hlth Sci Grp.

Oncology Nursing Society Staff, jt. auth. see American Nurses Association Staff.

Oncu, Ayse, jt. ed. see Weyland, Petra.

Onda, John R. Visual Basic Developer's Toolkit. 2nd ed. Engelmann, Eric, ed. (Developer's Toolkit Ser.). 320p. 1997. pap. 39.95 (*1-889671-26-6*) Advice Pr.

Onda, John R. & Engelmann, Eric. Access Developer's Toolkit. 2nd ed. 300p. (YA). (gr. 9 up). 1997. 39.95 incl. cd-rom (*1-889671-05-3*) Advice Pr.

***Ondaatje, Christopher.** Journey to the Source of the Nile. (Illus.). 384p. 1999. pap. 25.00 (*1-55209-371-9*) Firefly Bks Ltd.

Ondaatje, Elizabeth H. Policy Options for Army Involvement in Youth Development. LC 93-21331. 1993. pap. 15.00 (*0-8330-1460-9*, MR-352-A) Rand Corp.

Ondaatje, Kim. Toronto, My City: A Photographic Memoir. (Illus.). 144p. 1993. 25.00 (*1-55082-062-1*, Pub. by Quarry Pr) LPC InBook.

***Ondaatje, Michael.** Anil's Ghost. LC 99-59208. 320p. 2000. 25.00 (*0-375-41053-8*, Evrymans Lib Childs) Knopf.

— Anil's Ghost. large type ed. LC 00-42351. 2000. write for info. (*0-7862-2791-5*) Thorndike Pr.

Ondaatje, Michael. The Cinnamon Peeler: Selected Poems. LC 97-111363. 1997. pap. 14.00 (*0-679-77913-2*) Vin Bks.

— The Collected Works of Billy the Kid. LC 95-46415. 1996. pap. 10.00 (*0-679-76786-X*) Vin Bks.

— Coming Through Slaughter. 1996. pap. 10.00 (*0-679-76785-1*) Vin Bks.

— Elimination Dance - La Danse Eliminatoire. Tostevin, Lola Lemire, tr. (FRE & ENG.). 56p. 1991. pap. 10.00 (*0-919626-55-6*, Pub. by Brick Bks) Genl Dist Srvs.

— Elimination Dance - La Danse Eliminatoire. large type ed. Tostevin, Lola L., tr. 56p. 1995. pap. 10.00 (*0-919626-79-3*, Pub. by Brick Bks) Genl Dist Srvs.

— The English Patient. 1996. reprint ed. pap. 12.00 (*0-676-51420-0*) Vin Bks.

— The English Patient: A Novel. LC 92-53089. 1992. 25.00 (*0-679-41678-1*) Knopf.

— The English Patient: A Novel. LC 93-10492. 302p. 1993. pap. 12.00 (*0-679-74520-3*) Vin Bks.

***Ondaatje, Michael.** Handwriting: Poems. LC 98-41731. 78p. 1999. 22.00 (*0-375-40559-3*) Knopf.

Ondaatje, Michael. Handwriting: Poems. LC 98-41731. 1999. pap. write for info. (*0-375-70535-X*) Random.

***Ondaatje, Michael.** Handwriting: Poems. 2000. pap. 11.00 (*0-375-70541-4*) Vin Bks.

Ondaatje, Michael. In the Skin of a Lion: A Novel. LC 97-111370. 1997. pap. 12.00 (*0-679-77266-9*) McKay.

***Ondaatje, Michael.** Lost Classics. 2000. write for info. (*0-676-97299-3*, Pub. by Knopf) Random House.

Ondaatje, Michael. Paciente Ingles. 1998. pap. 6.95 (*84-01-46329-7*) Lectorum Pubns.

— Running in the Family. LC 93-10494. 1993. pap. 11.00 (*0-679-74669-2*) Vin Bks.

Ondaatje, Michael & Minghella, Anthony. The English Patient: A Screenplay. LC 96-42250. (Illus.). 208p. (J). 1996. pap. 10.45 (*0-7868-8245-X*, Pub. by Hyperion) Time Warner.

Ondaatje, Michael, ed. see Nichol, B. P.

Ondar, O., ed. Correspondence Between A. A. Markov & A. A. Chuprov on the Theory of Probability & Mathematical Statistics. 192p. 1981. 105.95 (*0-387-90585-5*) Spr-Verlag.

Ondeck, Deborah A., jt. auth. see Gingerich, Barbara S.

Ondemir, Ali R. Judeo-Christianity from the Perspective of Morality & Other Sciences. (Orig.). 1995. pap. 30.00 (*0-9645912-0-0*) A R Ondemir.

Onderdonk, A., jt. auth. see Onderdonk, E.

Onderdonk, E. & Onderdonk, A. Genealogy of the Onderdonk Family in America. (Illus.). 374p. 1989. reprint ed. pap. 56.00 (*0-8328-0923-3*); reprint ed. lib. bdg. 64.00 (*0-8328-0922-5*) Higginson Bk Co.

Onderdonk, Francis S., Jr. The Ferro-Concrete Style: Reinforced Concrete in Modern Architecture. LC 98-9649. (Illus.). 1998. 55.00 (*0-940512-09-2*) Hennessey.

Onderdonk, Francis S. 1144 Paths to Happiness: The Emerging Science. LC 95-61410. 1997. 24.95 (*0-533-11622-8*) Vantage.

Onderdonk, Henry, Jr. Queens Documents & Letters Intended to Illustrate Revolutionary Incidents of Queens County, with Connecting Narratives, Explanatory Notes & Additions. 70p. 1997. reprint ed. pap. 14.00 (*0-8328-6206-1*) Higginson Bk Co.

Onderdonk, Henry, Jr., ed. Queens County Documents & Letters Intended to the Revolutionary Incidents of Queens County, with Connecting Narratives, Explanatory Notes & Additions. (Illus.). 264p. 1997. reprint ed. lib. bdg. 34.50 (*0-8328-6207-X*) Higginson Bk Co.

— Revolutionary Incidents of Suffolk & Kings Counties, with an Account of the Battle of Long Island & the British Prisons & Prison-ships at New York. (Illus.). 268p. 1997. reprint ed. lib. bdg. 35.00 (*0-8328-6254-1*) Higginson Bk Co.

Onderwater, Hans. Gentlemen in Blue: The History of No. 600 "City of London" Squadron. (Illus.). 512p. 1998. 49.95 (*0-85052-575-6*, Pub. by Leo Cooper) Trans-Atl Phila.

Ondich, Gregory. Pollution Prevention Research Program (EPA) 67p. (Orig.). 1996. reprint ed. pap. text 25.00 (*0-7881-2957-0*) DIANE Pub.

Ondik, H. M. & McMurdie, H. F., eds. Phase Diagrams for Zirconium & Zirconia Systems. (Illus.). 750p. 1998. 150.00 (*1-57498-055-6*, PhZr) Am Ceramic.

Ondori, contrib. by. Huck Embroidery. (Illus.). 116p. 1997. pap. 18.00 (*0-916896-89-7*, LE36) Lacis Pubns.

Ondori Publishing Company Staff. American Patchwork Quilt Designs. (Illus.). 78p. (Orig.). 1987. pap. 13.95 (*0-87040-744-9*) Japan Pubns USA.

— Attractive Cross Stitch Designs. LC 81-80834. (Illus.). 104p. (Orig.). 1981. pap. 15.95 (*0-87040-501-2*) Japan Pubns USA.

— Basic Knit Sweaters: Step-by-Step. (Illus.). 64p. 1985. pap. 15.00 (*0-87040-654-X*) Japan Pubns USA.

— Basic Patchwork with Patterns. (Illus.). 72p. (Orig.). 1990. pap. 13.95 (*0-87040-818-6*) Japan Pubns USA.

— Classic Quilting of Sashiko. 1990. pap. 19.00 (*0-87040-854-2*) Japan Pubns USA.

— Creative Embroidery Designs. (Illus.). 1979. pap. 16.00 (*0-87040-452-0*) Japan Pubns USA.

— Crochet Lace with Complete Diagrams. (Ondori Needlecraft Ser.). (Illus.). 1979. pap. 14.95 (*0-87040-415-6*) Japan Pubns USA.

— Cross Stitch: Three Hundred Motifs. LC 81-84804. (Illus.). 100p. 1982. pap. 16.00 (*0-87040-506-3*) Japan Pubns USA.

— Cross Stitch Designs. (Ondori Handicrafts Ser.). (Illus.). 96p. 1980. pap. 13.95 (*0-87040-366-4*) Japan Pubns USA.

— Cross Stitch for Your Home. (Illus.). 134p. (Orig.). 1986. pap. 14.95 (*0-87040-734-1*) Japan Pubns USA.

— Danish Cross-Stitch. (Illus.). 112p. 1985. pap. 14.95 (*0-87040-627-2*) Japan Pubns USA.

— Easy Cross-Stitch. (Illus.). 124p. (Orig.). 1984. pap. 15.95 (*0-87040-604-3*) Japan Pubns USA.

— Easy Embroidery. rev. ed. (Illus.). 96p. (Orig.). 1984. pap. 13.95 (*0-87040-608-6*) Japan Pubns USA.

— Elegant Cross-Stitch Embroidery. (Illus.). 100p. (Orig.). 1983. pap. 15.95 (*0-87040-538-1*) Japan Pubns USA.

— An Embroidery Sampler. (Illus.). 102p. 1988. pap. 15.00 (*0-87040-758-9*) Japan Pubns USA.

— Fine Patchwork & Quilting. (Illus.). 80p. 1983. pap. 11.95 (*0-87040-557-8*) Japan Pubns USA.

— Full Color Illustrated Basic Knit. (Illus.). 40p. (Orig.). 1987. pap. 9.95 (*0-87040-745-7*) Japan Pubns USA.

— Glass Bead Artistry: Over 200 Playful Designs. (Illus.). 48p. (Orig.). 1992. pap. 15.00 (*0-87040-890-9*) Japan Pubns USA.

— Gorgeous Crochet Laces for Interior Decoration. LC 80-81039. 1980. pap. 17.00 (*0-87040-487-3*) Japan Pubns USA.

— Handcraft for Baby: Cotton Wares up to Two Years Old. (Illus.). 96p. (Orig.). 1993. pap. 14.95 (*0-87040-606-X*) Japan Pubns USA.

— Home Embroidery. (Illus.). 64p. (Orig.). 1993. pap. 15.95 (*0-87040-927-1*) Japan Pubns USA.

— Living with Cross-Stitch. (Illus.). 96p. (Orig.). 1988. pap. 11.95 (*0-87040-760-0*) Japan Pubns USA.

— Lovely Embroidery Patterns. LC 79-66301. (Illus.). 1980. pap. 13.95 (*0-87040-465-2*) Japan Pubns USA.

— Modern Patchwork. LC 81-84806. (Illus.). 108p. 1982. 12.95 (*0-87040-507-1*) Japan Pubns USA.

— My Lace. (Illus.). 94p. 1987. pap. 11.95 (*0-87040-736-8*) Japan Pubns USA.

— New Embroidery for Beginners. (Illus.). 48p. 1986. pap. 11.95 (*0-87040-702-3*) Japan Pubns USA.

— A New Look for Needlework, Embroidery & Cross Stitch. (Illus.). 112p. (Orig.). 1983. pap. 13.95 (*0-87040-568-3*) Japan Pubns USA.

— Patchwork & Quilting Book. LC 81-80836. (Illus.). 104p. (Orig.). 1981. pap. 16.00 (*0-87040-498-9*) Japan Pubns USA.

— Patchwork Made Perfect. 1990. pap. 15.95 (*0-87040-855-0*) Japan Pubns USA.

— Playful Patchwork: Great Gift Ideas for Children. (Illus.). 84p. 1993. pap. 18.00 (*0-87040-913-1*) Kodansha.

— Quilting & Applique All Around the House. (Illus.). 120p. 1986. 15.95 (*0-87040-703-1*) Japan Pubns USA.

— Simple Embroidery Designs. (Illus.). 103p. (Orig.). 1985. pap. 10.95 (*0-87040-647-7*) Japan Pubns USA.

— Simple Patchwork. (Illus.). 64p. (Orig.). 1993. pap. 15.95 (*0-87040-928-X*) Japan Pubns USA.

— Simple Tiny Cross-Stitch. (Illus.). 72p. (Orig.). 1990. pap. 12.95 (*0-87040-864-X*) Japan Pubns USA.

— Small Embroidery Gifts. (Illus.). 124p. (Orig.). 1989. pap. 13.95 (*0-87040-819-4*) Japan Pubns USA.

— Tole Painting Made Easy. (Illus.). 96p. (Orig.). 1996. pap. 17.00 (*0-87040-985-9*) Kodansha.

Ondori Publishing Company Staff & Onoue, Masano. The World of Cross Stitch. (Illus.). 100p. (Orig.). 1983. pap. 15.00 (*0-87040-558-6*) Japan Pubns USA.

***Ondori Staff.** Art of Antique Beading. (Illus.). 88p. 2000. pap. 19.00 (*4-88996-062-7*) Japan Pubn Trad.

Ondori Staff. Fun & Fancy Cross-Stitch. (Illus.). 120p. 1988. pap. 17.00 (*0-87040-754-6*) Japan Pubns USA.

Ondra, Nancy J. Easy Plant Propagation: Filling Your Garden with Plants from Seeds, Cuttings, Divisions, & Layers. LC 97-39672. (Taylor's Weekend Gardening Guides Ser.). (Illus.). 128p. 1998. pap. 12.95 (*0-395-86295-7*) HM.

***Ondra, Nancy J.** Landscaping with Herbs: Beautify Your Yard & Garden with Easy-Care Herbs. LC 99-50813. (Essential Herbal Handbooks Ser.). (Illus.). 160p. 2000. pap. 14.95 (*0-87596-858-9*, Pub. by Rodale Pr Inc) St Martin.

Ondra, Nancy J. Taylor's Weekend Gardening Guide to Soil & Composting. LC 97-46590. (Taylor's Weekend Gardening Guides Ser.). (Illus.). 128p. 1998. pap. 12.95 (*0-395-86294-9*, Mariner Bks) HM.

Ondra, Winona H. Lonesome & Coping. unabridged ed. LC 96-95210. (Illus.). 320p. (Orig.). 1997. pap. 20.00 (*0-9655858-0-8*) Boyden Pub.

Ondrackova, Jana. The Physiological Activity of the Speech Organs: An Analysis of the Speech-Organs During the Phonation of Sung, Spoken, & Whispered Czech Vowels on the Basis of X-Ray Methods. Short, D., tr. from DUT. LC 72-94494. (Illus.). 105p. 1973. text 46.15 (*90-279-2374-4*) Mouton.

Ondrejack, Larry. Always There for You: Incidents That Bring God to Mind. 87p. 1994. pap. 3.95 (*0-88172-213-8*) Believers Bkshelf.

Ondreka, Arthur J. Portable Calibrator for Across-the-Road Radar Systems. 37p. 1998. pap. 3.50 (*0-16-056690-8*) USGPO.

Ondrey, Patrick, jt. auth. see Avanzini, John F.

Ondrich, Jan & Wasylenko, Michael. Foreign Direct Investment in the United States: Issues, Magnitudes & Location Choice of New Manufacturing Plants, 1978 to 1987. LC 93-32159. 160p. 1993. pap. 14.00 (*0-88099-139-9*); text 33.00 (*0-88099-140-2*) W E Upjohn.

Ondryas, I. S. & Fransson, T. H., eds. 1900 ASME COGEN-TURBO: International Symposium on Gas Turbines in Cogeneration, Repowering, & Peak-Load Power Generation, 4th, Held in New Orleans, Louisiana, August 27-29, 1990. LC 90-195623. (IGTI Ser.: Vol. 5). 264p. 1990. reprint ed. pap. 81.90 (*0-7837-1448-3*, 205242300017) Bks Demand.

One Hundred & Third Ohio Volunteer Infantry Member. Personal Reminiscences & Experiences. 444p. 1984. reprint ed. 25.00 (*0-9613625-0-2*) OH Volunteer.

***One Year Chronological Staff.** One Year Chronological Bible. 2000. 24.99 (*0-8423-3530-7*); pap. 19.99 (*0-8423-3531-5*) Tyndale Hse.

O'Neal, Adella D. Splashings of Peace. 1997. pap. write for info. (*1-57553-551-3*) Watermrk Pr.

O'Neal, Agnes. Borne on Eagles Wings. 100p. 1999. pap. write for info. (*1-57579-149-8*) Pine Hill Pr.

O'Neal, Alexandra, jt. auth. see Quick, Jennifer.

O'Neal, Bill. The American Association: A Baseball History, 1902-1991. LC 91-24176. 410p. 1992. pap. 21.95 (*0-89015-812-6*) Sunbelt Media.

— The Arizona Rangers. Eakin, Edwin M., ed. (Illus.). 232p. 1988. pap. 15.95 (*0-89015-610-7*) Sunbelt Media.

— Best of the West. LC 97-67523. (Illus.). 312p. 1997. write for info. (*0-7853-2428-3*) Pubns Intl Ltd.

***O'Neal, Bill.** The Bloody Legacy of Pink Higgins: Half a Century of Violence in Texas. LC 99-17586. 1999. pap. 18.95 (*1-57168-304-6*, Eakin Pr) Sunbelt Media.

O'Neal, Bill. Encyclopedia of Western Gunfighters. LC 78-21380. (Illus.). 1980. 34.95 (*0-8061-1508-4*) U of Okla Pr.

— Encyclopedia of Western Gunfighters. LC 78-21380. (Illus.). 400p. 1991. pap. 19.95 (*0-8061-2335-4*) U of Okla Pr.

— Fighting Men of the Indian Wars: A Biographical Encyclopedia of the Mountain Men, Soldiers, Cowboys, & Pioneers Who Took up Arms During America's Westward Expansion. LC 91-36114. (Illus.). 272p. 1992. 26.95 (*0-935269-07-X*) Western Pubns.

***O'Neal, Bill.** Great Gunfighters of the Wild West: Twenty Courageous Westerners Who Struggled with Right & Wrong, Good & Evil, Law & Order. LC 99-51316. 1999. write for info. (*1-57168-374-7*) Sunbelt Media.

O'Neal, Bill. Historic Ranches of the Old West. LC 97-15250. (Illus.). 376p. 1997. 28.95 (*1-57168-167-1*, Eakin Pr) Sunbelt Media.

— The International League: A Baseball History, 1884-1991. 450p. 1992. pap. 21.95 (*0-89015-856-8*) Sunbelt Media.

— Pacific Coast League, 1903-1988. Roberts, Melissa, ed. (Illus.). 356p. 1990. 21.95 (*0-89015-776-6*) Sunbelt Media.

O'Neal, Bill. Panola College: The First Half Century. 200p. 1997. 16.95 (*1-57168-211-2*) Sunbelt Media.

O'Neal, Bill. The Southern League: Baseball in Dixie, 1885-1994. LC 93-47554. 292p. 1994. pap. 21.95 (*0-89015-952-1*) Sunbelt Media.

— Tex Ritter: America's Most Beloved Cowboy. LC 98-28565. (Illus.). 168p. (Orig.). 1998. pap. 21.95 (*1-57168-249-X*, Eakin Pr) Sunbelt Media.

— The Texas League: A Century of Baseball. Roberts, Melissa, ed. (Illus.). 408p. 1987. pap. 21.95 (*0 89015-609-3*) Sunbelt Media.

O'Neal, Bill, ed. see Vanbuskirk, Robert.

O'Neal, Charles. Developing a Winning Just-in-time Marketing Strategy: The Industrial Marketer's Guide. 1990. text 31.67 (*0-13-205303-9*) P-H.

— Three Wishes for Jamie. 1976. 22.95 (*0-8488-0184-9*) Amereon Ltd.

— Three Wishes for Jamie. large type ed. LC 93-42059. 368p. 1994. lib. bdg. 17.95 (*0-7862-0140-1*) Thorndike Pr.

— Three Wishes for Jamie. LC 79-66116. 256p. 1980. reprint ed. 22.00 (*0-933256-08-6*); reprint ed. pap. text 16.00 (*0-933256-09-4*) Second Chance.

O'Neal, Christopher. Frankenstein: The Monster Play. 52p. 1980. pap. 4.00 (*0-88680-056-0*) I E Clark.

O'Neal, D. L. Las Navidades Van Asomando en Libro de Cuentas.Tr. of Christmas Pop-Up Counting Book. (SPA.). (J). 1994. 6.49 (*1-56063-768-4*, 490325) Editorial Unilit.

O'Neal, D. L., et al, eds. 1995 ASME International Mechanical Engineering Congress & Exposition Vol. 34: Heat Pump & Refrigeration Systems Design, Analysis & Applications - 1995. 240p. 88.00 (*0-614-97062-8*, H01001) ASME.

— Thermodynamics & the Design, Analysis, & Improvement of Energy Systems, 1995 Vol. 35: Proceedings of the ASME International Mechanical Engineering Congress & Exposition, 1995, San Francisco, CA. LC 97-155101. (1995 ASME International Mechanical Engineering Congress & Exposition Ser.: AES-Vol. 35). 460p. 1995. 110.00 (*0-7918-1764-4*, H01045) ASME.

O'Neal, Daisy E. Man in the Kitchen Texas Style! 150p. (Orig.). 1990. pap. 9.95 (*0-9626482-0-5*) Star-Daze Prodns.

O'Neal, David. Choosing to Kill: A Novel of Crime, Justice & Conscience. (Dying Game Trilogy Ser.). 268p. 1999. mass mkt. 5.99 (*0-9660851-2-4*) Pac Coast Pr.

— The Pact with Bruno. 248p. 1998. pap. 6.50 (*0-9660851-1-6*) Pac Coast Pr.

— What Goes Around. 240p. 1998. per. 5.99 (*0-9660851-0-8*) Pac Coast Pr.

O'Neal, David, ed. Meister Eckhart, from Whom God Hid Nothing: Sermons, Writings, & Sayings. LC 95-22647. (Illus.). 160p. (Orig.). 1996. pap. 13.95 (*1-57062-139-X*, Pub. by Shambhala Pubns) Random.

O'Neal, David, ed. see Hort, Barbara E.

***O'Neal, Debbie & Satchell, Jonathan.** The Big Bedtime Book of Bible Stories & Prayers. 64p. 1999. pap. 22.00 (*1-85608-356-X*, Pub. by Hunt GBR) St Mut.

O'Neal, Debbie T. The Advent Wreath: A Light in the Darkness. 16p. 1989. pap. 1.99 (*0-8066-2375-6*, 10-23756) Augsburg Fortress.

— Before & after Christmas: Activities & Ideas for Advent & Epiphany. LC 91-9988. (Illus.). 64p. 1991. pap. 10.99 (*0-8066-2534-1*, 9-2534) Augsburg Fortress.

— Before & after Easter: Activities & Ideas for Lent to Pentecost. LC 92-32415. (Illus.). 64p. 1993. pap. 10.99 (*0-8066-2604-6*, 9-2604) Augsburg Fortress.

— The Big Bedtime Book of Bible Stories & Prayers. 64p. (J). (gr. k-3). 1995. 9.95 (*0-687-00126-9*) Abingdon.

— I Can Pray with Jesus: The Lord's Prayer for Children. LC 97-71855. (Illus.). 32p. (J). (ps-k). 1997. pap. 6.99 (*0-8066-3328-X*, 9-3328, Augsburg) Augsburg Fortress.

— More Than Glue & Glitter: Classroom Guide for Volunteer Teachers. LC 91-47157. 96p. 1992. pap. 11.99 (*0-8066-2561-9*, 9-2561) Augsburg Fortress.

— Now I Lay Me down to Sleep: Action Prayers, Poems, & Songs for Bedtime. LC 94-71213. (Illus.). 32p. (J). (ps-k). 1994. pap. 6.99 (*0-8066-2602-X*, 9-2602, Augsburg) Augsburg Fortress.

— 101 Things to Do for Christmas. LC 94-46532. (Illus.). 64p. (J). (gr. 1). 1995. pap. 10.99 (*0-8066-2792-1*, 9-2792) Augsburg Fortress.

— Thank You for This Food: Action Prayers, Songs, & Blessings for Mealtime. LC 94-78747. (Illus.). 32p. (J). (ps). 1994. pap. 6.99 (*0-8066-2603-8*, 9-2603, Augsburg) Augsburg Fortress.

***O'Neal, Debbie Trafton.** Family Hand-Me-Down Book: Creating & Celebrating Family Traditions. LC 99-58204. (Illus.). 96p. 2000. pap. 12.99 (*0-8066-4035-9*) Augsburg Fortress.

O'Neal, Debbie Trafton. Family Time: 101 Great Ideas for Sunday Afternoons. LC 93-5065. 144p. (Orig.). 1994. pap. 1.88 (*0-687-38507-5*) Dimen for Liv.

— Family Fun: 105 Easy Ways to Make the Most of Busy Days. 160p. (Orig.). 1995. pap. 1.88 (*0-687-01023-3*) Dimen for Liv.

***O'Neal, Debbie Trafton.** Thank You for This Day: Action Prayers, Songs & Blessings for Every Day. LC 00-26644. (Illus.). (J). 2000. write for info. (*0-8066-4069-3*, Augsburg) Augsburg Fortress.

O'Neal, Don, jt. auth. see Thomas, Howard.

O'Neal, F. Hodge, ed. Corporate Practice Commentator, 1966-1990, 25 vols. write for info. (*0-318-61075-2*) West Group.

— Corporate Practice Commentator, 1966-1990, 25 vols. annuals LC 68-3938. 135.00 (*0-685-14553-0*) West Group.

— Corporate Practice Commentator, 1966-1990, 25 vols., Set. LC 68-3938. 515.00 (*0-685-14552-2*) West Group.

O'Neal, F. Hodge & Thompson, Robert B. O'Neal Close Corporations: Law & Practice, 2 vols., No. 12. 1990. 200.00 (*0-685-33314-0*); write for info. (*0-318-66850-5*); write for info. (*0-318-66851-3*) West Group.

— O'Neal's Oppression of Minority Shareholders, 2 vols. 3rd ed. LC 85-7867. 1990. 230.00 (*0-318-42412-6*); write for info. (*0-318-65004-5*) West Group.

O'Neal, F. Hodge, jt. auth. see Hazen, Thomas L.

O'Neal, Glenn. Make the Bible Live. pap. 3.50 (*0-88469-020-2*) BMH Bks.

O'Neal, James. Workers in American History. 32nd ed. LC 78 156437. (American Labor Ser., No. 2). 1977. reprint ed. 19.95 (*0-405-02935-7*) Ayer.

O'Neal, Janet. The Complete Idiot's Guide to Seduction. LC 98-88313. (Complete Idiot's Guides Ser.). (Illus.). 352p. 1998. pap. 16.95 (*0-02-862738-5*) Macmillan Gen Ref.

— Cracking the Love Code. 240p. 1999. reprint ed. pap. 12.00 (*0-7679-0168-1*) Broadway BDD.

O'Neal, Jim. Confessions of a Mass Murderer. 117p. (Orig.). 1993. pap. text 10.95 (*1-883457-02-5*) J ONeal Publng.

— Dumferling Castle & Other Plays. 235p. 1993. pap. 11.95 (*1-883457-03-3*) J ONeal Publng.

— Poems Especially for You. 24p. 1993. pap. 9.95 (*1-883457-32-7*) J ONeal Publng.

— Professor Rubin. 118p. (Orig.). 1993. pap. text 10.95 (*1-883457-00-9*) J ONeal Publng.

— The Wretch. 318p. (Orig.). 1993. pap. text 12.95 (*1-883457-01-7*) J ONeal Publng.

O'Neal, John C. The Authority of Experience: Sensationist Theory in the French Enlightenment. LC 95-18091. (Literature & Philosophy Ser.). 272p. 1996. 48.50 (*0-271-01515-2*) Pa St U Pr.

O'Neal, Jon T. The Bloodborne Pathogens Standard: A Pragmatic Approach. 336p. 1996. text 60.95 (*0-442-01779-0*, VNR) Wiley.

O'Neal, Katherine. Bride of Danger. 352p. 1997. mass mkt. 5.99 (*0-553-57379-9*) Bantam.

***O'Neal, Katherine.** My One & Only. 352p. 2000. mass mkt. 5.99 (*0-553-58121-X*) Bantam.

O'Neal, Katherine. Written in the Stars. 352p. 1998. mass mkt. 5.99 (*0-553-57380-2*) Bantam.

O'Neal, Kathleen M. Redemption of Light. (Powers of Light Ser.: Bk. 3). 1991. mass mkt. 4.99 (*0-88677-470-5*, Pub. by DAW Bks) Penguin Putnam.

***O'Neal, Kelly, et al, photos by.** U. S. Sailing Is... (Illus.). 10p. 1999. write for info. (*1-882502-76-0*) US Sail Assn.

O'Neal, L. Thomas. Maya in Sankara: Measuring the Immeasurable. 1980. 16.00 (*0-8364-0611-7*) S Asia.

O'Neal, LuLu M. My Life 'N' Doins. Spears-Stewart, Reta, ed. 1998. pap. 10.00 (*1-892477-06-8*) Barnabs Pub.

O'Neal, Lyman & Weinland, Linda. Ecosystems of Southwest Florida: Laboratory Manual. 232p. (C). 1996. spiral bd. 38.95 (*0-7872-3258-0*, 41325801) Kendall-Hunt.

O'Neal, Malinda K., jt. auth. see Franklin, Gordon T.

O'Neal, Michael. The Assassination of Abraham Lincoln: Opposing Viewpoints. LC 91-13682. (Great Mysteries Ser.). (Illus.). 96p. (J). (gr. 5-8). 1991. lib. bdg. 22.45 (*0-89908-092-8*) Greenhaven.

— President Truman & the Atomic Bomb. LC 90-35611. (Great Mysteries Ser.). (Illus.). 112p. (J). (gr. 5-8). 1990. lib. bdg. 22.45 (*0-89908-079-0*) Greenhaven.

— Pyramids: Opposing Viewpoints. (Opposing Viewpoints Juniors Ser.). (Illus.). 96p. (J). (gr. 5-12). 1995. lib. bdg. 22.45 (*1-56510-216-9*, 2169) Greenhaven.

O'Neal, Michael J. The Atomic Bomb. 39.00 (*1-56696-102-5*) Jackdaw.

***O'Neal, Nanette.** To Love's Hell & Back. LC 99-91948. 2000. 25.00 (*0-7388-1438-5*); pap. 18.00 (*0-7388-1439-3*) Xlibris Corp.

O'Neal, Patrick H., jt. ed. see McElligott, Mary E.

O'Neal, Reagan, pseud. The Fallon Blood. 1996. mass mkt. 6.99 (*0-8125-4397-1*, Pub. by Forge NYC) St Martin.

— The Fallon Pride. LC 96-8303. 384p. 1996. 24.95 (*0-312-86231-8*) Forge NYC.

— The Fallon Pride. 1997. mass mkt. 6.99 (*0-8125-6760-9*, Pub. by Forge NYC) St Martin.

O'Neal, S. D., ed. see Stryde, E. T.

O'Neal, Sean. Elvis Inc. The Fall & Rise of the Presley Empire. 256p. 1997. per. 14.00 (*0-7615-1127-X*) Prima Pub.

— Elvis, Inc. The Rise & Fall of the Presley Empire. LC 96-1427. (Illus.). 256p. 1996. boxed set 23.95 (*0-7615-0398-6*) Prima Pub.

— My Boy Elvis: The Colonel Tom Parker Story. LC 98-3056. 1998. write for info. (*1-56980-127-4*) Barricade Bks.

O'Neal, Sean, jt. auth. see Tunzi, Joseph A.

O'Neal, Shaquille. Shaq & the Beanstalk: And Other Very Tall Tales. LC 98-52007. (Illus.). 80p. (J). (gr. 1-4). 1999. 15.95 (*0-590-91823-0*, Pub. by Scholastic Inc) Penguin Putnam.

O'Neal, Ted. Garden Therapy. LC 98-74886. (Elf-Help Books Ser.). (Illus.). 88p. 1999. pap. 4.95 (*0-87029-325-7*, 20116) Abbey.

***O'Neal, Terry.** Motion Sickness. Burrise, Andrea, ed. 103p. 2000. pap. 7.95 (*0-9679446-0-0*) Motion Pubns.

O'Neal, Virginia. Beecher. large type ed. LC 93-34590. 346p. 1993. lib. bdg. 17.95 (*0-7862-0078-2*) Thorndike Pr.

O'Neal, William B. Jefferson's Fine Arts Library: His Selections for the University of Virginia Together with His Own Architectural Books at Monticello. LC 75-33229. (Illus.). 409p. 1976. 40.00 (*0-8139-0282-7*) U Pr of Va.

O'Neal, William B. & Weeks, Christopher. The Work of William Lawrence Bottomley in Richmond. LC 84-20800. (Illus.). 286p. 1985. reprint ed. pap. 88.70 (*0-7837-9230-1*, 204998100004) Bks Demand.

O'Neal, William J., ed. see Lazzarelli, Ludovico.

O'Neal, Zibby. Grandma Moses. (J). 1987. pap. 4.99 (*0-14-032220-5*, PuffinBks) Peng Put Young Read.

— Grandma Moses: Painter of Rural America. (Women of Our Time Ser.). (Illus.). (J). (gr. 2-6). reprint ed. pap. 3.50 (*0-317-62289-7*, PuffinBks) Peng Put Young Read.

O'Neal, Zibby. Grandma Moses, Painter of Rural America. (Women of Our Time Ser.). (J). 1986. 10.19 (*0-606-03586-9*, Pub. by Turtleback) Demco.

Oneal, Zibby. The Language of Goldfish. Brodie, D., ed. (J). 1990. pap. 4.99 (*0-14-034540-X*, PuffinBks) Peng Put Young Read.

O'Neal, Zibby. Language of Goldfish: A Novel. (J). 1990. 10.09 (*0-606-04728-X*, Pub. by Turtleback) Demco.

— A Long Way to Go: A Story of Women's Right to Vote. (Once Upon America Ser.). (Illus.). 64p. (J). (gr. 2-6). 1992. pap. 4.99 (*0-14-032950-1*, PuffinBks) Peng Put Young Read.

O'Neal, Zibby. A Long Way to Go: A Story of Women's Right to Vote. (Once upon America Ser.). (J). 1992. 10.19 (*0-606-01718-6*, Pub. by Turtleback) Demco.

O'Neal, Zibby. Maude & Walter. LC 84-48357. (Illus.). 32p. (J). (ps-2). 1985. 11.95 (*0-397-32150-3*) HarpC Child Bks.

Oneal, Zibby. Turtle & Snail. LC 78-14826. (Lippincott-I-Like-to-Read Bks.). (Illus.). (J). (gr. k-2). 1979. 11.95 (*0-397-31829-4*) HarpC Child Bks.

O'Neale, K., jt. ed. see Bennett, S. W.

O'Neale, Lila M. Yurok-Karok Basket Weavers. LC 95-36643. (Classics in California Anthropology Ser.). 1995. write for info. (*0-936127-06-6*); pap. write for info. (*0-936127-04-X*) P A Hearst Mus.

— Yurok-Karok Basket Weavers. fac. ed. (University of California Publications in American Archaeology & Ethnology: Vol. 32: 1). (Illus.). 244p. (C). 1932. reprint ed. pap. text 25.63 (*1-55567-287-6*) Coyote Press.

O'Neale, Sondra. Jupiter Hammon & the Biblical Beginnings of African-American Literature. LC 91-38904. (American Theological Library Association Monograph: No. 28). 303p. 1993. 46.00 (*0-8108-2479-5*) Scarecrow.

O'Neall, John B. Biographical Sketches of the Bench & Bar of South Carolina, 2 vols., Set. Incl. Vol. 1. LC 75-1159. 470p. 1975. 22.50 (*0-87152-198-9*); Vol. 2. LC 75-1159. 620p. 1975. 22.50 (*0-87152-199-7*); LC 75-1159. 1975. reprint ed. 45.00 (*0-87152-300-0*) Reprint.

O'Neall, John B. & Chapman, John A. The Annals of Newberry, South Carolina, Historical Biographical & Anecodotal: Also Religious Medical & Literary, 2 vols., Set. iii, 890p. 1993. reprint ed. pap. text 51.00 (*1-55613-772-9*) Heritage Bk.

O'Neall, John B., jt. auth. see Chapman, John A.

Oneda, Susana, ed. Hadron Spectroscopy - 1985, (International Conference, University of Maryland. LC 85-72537. (AIP Conference Proceedings Ser.: No. 132). 504p. 1985. lib. bdg. 49.75 (*0-88318-331-5*) Am Inst Physics.

Oneda, Susana & Koide, Y. Asymptotic Symmetry & Its Implication in Elementary Particle Physics. 300p. 1991. text 61.00 (*981-02-0498-1*) World Scientific Pub.

Oneda, Susana & Peaslee, David C. Hadron 91: Proceedings of the International Conference, University of Maryland, College Park, U. S. A., 12-16 August 1991. 500p. 1992. text 135.00 (*981-02-1003-5*) World Scientific Pub.

O'Neeall, Parris, et al. Caribbean Family Planning Guide: A Self Instruction Manual for Health Professionals. 432p. 1990. 25.00 (*0-916683-24-9*) Intl Plan Parent.

Onega, Susana. Metafiction & Myth in the Novels of Peter Ackroyd. LC 98-52962. (Studies in English & American Literature, Linguistics, & Culture). (Illus.). 190p. 1999. 50.00 (*1-57113-006-3*) Camden Hse.

Onega, Susana, ed. Peter Ackroyd. pap. 22.50 (*0-7463-0839-6*, Pub. by Northcote House) Trans-Atl Phila.

Onega, Susana & Landa, Jose A. Narratology. (Critical Readers Ser.). 336p. (C). 1996. pap. 31.20 (*0-582-25543-0*); text 63.00 (*0-582-25542-2*) Longman.

Oneglia, Mario F. Contemporary Conducting Techniques. LC 79-66924. (Illus.). (Orig.). 1979. spiral bd. 20.00 (*0-9603470-0-3*) Tritone Music.

Oneida Community Staff. Annual Report: 1848-1851, 3 vols., bk.1. LC 78-72358. (Free Love in America Ser.). reprint ed. 42.50 (*0-404-60982-1*) AMS Pr.

— Bible Communism: A Compilation from the Annual Reports & Other Publications of the Oneida Association & Its Branches. LC 72-2978. reprint ed. 27.50 (*0-404-10742-7*) AMS Pr.

— Hand-book of the Oneida Community, with a Sketch of Its Founder, & an Outline of Its Constitution & Doctrines, 3 vols. in 1. Incl. Hand-Book of the Oneida Community, Containing a Brief Sketch of Its Present Condition, Internal Economy & Leading Principles. LC 72-2977. Mutual Criticism. LC 72-2977. LC 72-2977. reprint ed. 47.50 (*0-404-10741-9*) AMS Pr.

Oneida County Historical Society Staff. Focus on the Fifties: Utica & Vicinity, 1950-1962. (Illus.). 1995. 29.95 (*0-925168-43-2*) North Country.

O'Neil. Advanced Engineering Math. 3rd ed. (Mathematics Ser.). 1991. mass mkt., student ed. 24.25 (*0-534-13585-4*) PWS Pubns.

— Advanced Engineering Mathematics. 4th ed. 1994. teacher ed. 27.25 (*0-534-94322-5*) Brooks-Cole.

— Ans-sol Advanced Engineering Mathematics. (Math). 1983. student ed. 15.00 (*0-534-01880-7*) Brooks-Cole.

— Ans/sol Advanced Engineering Math. 2nd ed. (Math). 1986. student ed. 17.50 (*0-534-06793-X*) Brooks-Cole.

O'Neil & Rowe. Pediatric Surgery. 5th ed. LC 97-51987. (Illus.). 2176p. (C). (gr. 13). 1998. text 295.00 (*0-8151-6518-8*, 26544) Mosby Inc.

O'Neil, jt. auth. see Keyser.

O'Neil & Company Staff. Going Green. (Illus.). 64p. (Orig.). 1995. pap. text. write for info. (*0-9641863-2-2*) Understand Busn.

O'Neil, A. W. & Palmer, Paul C. A Checklist of the Birds of Brooks County, Texas. 6p. (Orig.). 1988. pap. 0.50 (*0-9611604-4-6*) C Del Grullo.

O'Neil, Alex & Statham, Daphne, eds. Shaping Futures: Rights, Welfare & Personal Social Services. 1998. pap. 43.00 (*1-899942-29-7*, Pub. by Natl Inst Soc Work) St Mut.

O'Neil, Amanda. The Complete Book of the Dog. 19.98 (*1-55521-492-4*) Bk Sales Inc.

— Complete Encyclopedia of Needlework & Sewing Techniques. (Illus.). 336p. 19.99 (*1-57215-229-X*, JG229X) World Pubns.

Oneil, Amanda. Spiders Spin Webs: And Other Questions about Insects. (I Wonder Why Ser.). (J). (gr. 1-4). 1998. pap. 7.95 (*1-85697-665-3*) LKC.

O'Neil, Amanda & Hillyard, Paul. I Wonder Why Spiders Spin Webs: And Other Questions about Creepy Crawlies. LC 94-45121. (I Wonder Why Ser.). (Illus.). (J). (gr. k-4). 1995. 11.95 (*1-85697-581-9*, Kingfisher) LKC.

O'Neil, Anelle T., ed. see Piggott, Mattie G., et al.

O'Neil, Barbara. Saving on a Shoestring: How to Cut Expenses, Reduce Debt, Stash More Cash. 352p. 1996. reprint ed. mass mkt. 6.99 (*0-425-15344-4*) Berkley Pub.

O'Neil, Barbara T. & Foreman, George C. The Prairie Print Makers. 2nd ed. Ellington, Howard W., ed. (Illus.). 60p. 1984. reprint ed. pap. 10.00 (*0-9614307-0-2*) Gallery Ellington.

***O'Neil, Bill.** Fairest of Them All. 368p. 1999. mass mkt. 5.50 (*0-8439-4513-3*, Leisure Bks) Dorchester Pub Co.

O'Neil, Bill. A Field Guide for the Sight-Impaired Reader: A Comprehensive Resource for Students, Teachers & Librarians. LC 99-21788. 280p. 1999. 49.95 (*0-313-30969-8*) Greenwood.

O'Neil, Bill, jt. auth. see Turner, Michael.

O'Neil, Bill, tr. see Solomos, Dionysios.

O'Neil, Brian. Acting as a Business: Strategies for Success. LC 93-9183. 116p. 1993. pap. 13.95 (*0-435-08623-5*, 08623) Heinemann.

— Acting as a Business: Strategies for Success. 2nd ed. LC 98-43832. 116p. 1999. pap. 15.95 (*0-325-00123-5*) Heinemann.

— Actors Take Action: A Career Guide for the Competitive Actor. LC 96-14546. 112p. 1996. pap. 13.95 (*0-435-07012-6*) Heinemann.

O'Neil, Bryan H. Castles & Cannon. LC 74-30843. (Illus.). 121p. 1975. reprint ed. lib. bdg. 35.00 (*0-8371-7933-5*, ONCC, Greenwood Pr) Greenwood.

O'Neil, Buck. I Was Right on Time. 256p. 1997. per. 12.00 (*0-684-83247-X*) S&S Trade Pap.

***O'Neil, Carol.** Rose of Sharon. 1999. pap. write for info. (*1-58235-224-0*) Watermrk Pr.

***O'Neil, Catherine.** Fine & Dandy. Wise, Noreen, ed. (Lemonade Collection). (YA). (gr. 4 up). 2000. pap. 6.95 (*1-58584-250-8*) Huckleberry CT.

O'Neil, Charles. Military Adventures of Charles O'Neil. 1997. 29.95 (*1-885119-45-3*) Sarpedon.

O'Neil, Charles. Military Adventures of Charles O'Neil. 272p. 1997. 80.00 (*1-873376-74-X*, Pub. by Spellmnt Pubs) St Mut.

O'Neil, Charles J. Imprudence in Saint Thomas Aquinas. LC 55-9017. (Aquinas Lectures). 1955. 15.00 (*0-87462-120-8*) Marquette.

O'Neil, Colleen, ed. see O'Neil, Leslie S.

O'Neil, Daniel X. Boilerplate: Being a List of Eight Ways in Which the Dead at Waco Were a Lot Like the Rest of Us. 32p. 1994. pap. 5.00 (*0-9646137-1-9*) Juggernaut.

— Bricks: A New Book of Poems by Daniel X. O'Neil. 53p. 1992. pap. 10.00 (*0-9646137-0-0*) Juggernaut.

— Memo to All Employees: Poetry by Daniel X. O'Neil. (Illus.). 48p. 1995. 12.00 (*0-9646137-2-7*) Juggernaut.

O'Neil, Dennis. Azrael/Ash. (Illus.). 48p. 1997. pap. 4.95 (*1-56389-292-8*) DC Comics.

— Batman: Birth of the Demon. Goodwin, Archie, ed. (Illus.). 112p. 1993. pap. 12.95 (*1-56389-081-X*) DC Comics.

— Batman: Forever Movie Adaptation. Peterson, ed. (Illus.). 64p. 1995. pap. 5.95 (*1-56389-199-9*) DC Comics.

***O'Neil, Dennis.** Batman: Shaman. Kahan, Bob, ed. (Illus.). 136p. 1998. pap. 12.95 (*1-56389-083-6*, Pub. by DC Comics) Time Warner.

— Batman: Sword of Azrael. Kahan, Bob, ed. (Illus.). 112p. 1993. pap. 9.95 (*1-56389-100-X*, Pub. by DC Comics) Time Warner.

O'Neil, Dennis. Batman: Tales of the Demon. Levitz, Paul et al, eds. LC 92-112766. (Illus.). 208p. 1998. mass mkt. 17.95 (*0-930289-94-3*, Pub. by Warner Bks) Little.

O'Neil, Dennis. Batman: Venom. Kahan, Bob, ed. (Illus.). 136p. 1993. pap. 9.95 (*1-56389-101-8*, Pub. by DC Comics) Time Warner.

O'Neil, Dennis. Batman - Green Arrow: The Poison Tomorrow. Goodwin, Archie, ed. (Illus.). 64p. 1992. pap. 5.95 (*0-930289-15-3*) DC Comics.

— Batman - Punisher: Lake of Fire. Goodwin, A., ed. (Illus.). 48p. 1994. pap. 4.95 (*1-56389-161-1*) DC Comics.

— Batman & Robin Movie Adaptation. LC 97-221835. (Illus.). 64p. (Orig.). 1997. pap. 5.95 (*1-56389-306-1*) DC Comics.

***O'Neil, Dennis.** Batman in the Seventies. (Illus.). 192p. 2000. pap. 19.95 (*1-56389-565-X*, Pub. by DC Comics) Time Warner.

O'Neil, Dennis & Grant, Alan. Nightwing: Ties that Bind. Land, Greg & Giordano, Dick, eds. LC 98-100054. (Illus.). 144p. 1997. pap. text 12.95 (*1-56389-328-2*, Pub. by DC Comics) Time Warner.

O'Neil, Dennis, et al. Batman: Shaman. 136p. 1993. mass mkt. 12.99 (*0-446-39522-6*, Pub. by Warner Bks) Little.

— Batman: The Movies. LC 97-191432. (Illus.). 280p. 1997. pap. text 19.95 (*1-56389-326-6*, Pub. by DC Comics) Time Warner.

O'Neil, Dennis, ed. see Abnett, Dan & Lanning, Andy.

O'Neil, Dennis, ed. see Augustyn, Brian.

O'Neil, Dennis, ed. see Barr, Mike W.

O'Neil, Dennis, ed. see Barretto.

O'Neil, Dennis, ed. see Byrne, John.

O'Neil, Dennis, ed. see Chaykin, Howard.

O'Neil, Dennis, ed. see Chaykin, Howard & Moore, J. F.

O'Neil, Dennis, ed. see Dixon, C. & Grant, A.

O'Neil, Dennis, ed. see Moench, D.

O'Neil, Dennis, ed. see Moench, Doug.

O'Neil, Dennis, ed. see Moench, D., et al.

O'Neil, Dennis, ed. see Moore, Alan.

O'Neil, Dennis, ed. see Newell, Mindy.

O'Neil, Dennis, ed. see Niven, Larry & Byrne, John.

O'Neil, Dennis, ed. see Ostrander, John.

O'Neil, Dennis, ed. see Starlin, Jim.

O'Neil, Dennis, ed. see Wagner, John & Grant, Alan.

O'Neil, Dennis, ed. see Wagner, M.

O'Neil, Dennis, ed. see Wagner & Grant Staff.

O'Neil, Dennis V. Trail Tools: Yosemite Valley: Trail Maps, Trail Profiles, Mileage Charts, & Destination Charts for Hikers & Backpackers. LC 96-92038. (Illus.). 112p. (Orig.). 1996. pap. 12.95 (*0-931285-05-4*) ONeill Soft.

O'Neil, Di & Scott, Dorothy. Beyond Child Rescue: Developing Family Centered Practice at St. Luke's. 160p. 1997. pap. 24.95 (*1-86448-164-1*, Pub. by Allen & Unwin Pty) Paul & Co Pubs.

O'Neil, Dominic, jt. auth. see McKibbin, Elizabeth.

O'Neil, Doris C. Life: The Sixties. (Illus.). 1989. 35.00 (*0-8212-1752-6*) Little.

O'Neil, Doris C., ed. see Eisenstaedt, Alfred.

O'Neil, Edward H. & Coffman, Janet. Seven Strategies for the Future of Nursing. LC 97-45454. 288p. 1998. 36.95 (*0-7879-4028-3*) Jossey-Bass.

O'Neil, Elizabeth, jt. auth. see O'Neil, Patrick.

O'Neil, Elizabeth M., ed. see Williams, William Carlos.

O'Neil, Floyd A., ed. see Lyman, Stanley D.

O'Neil, Floyd A., jt. ed. see Milner, Clyde A., II.

O'Neil, Frank. The Mammoth Book of Oddities. LC 96-38173. 512p. 1996. pap. 8.95 (*0-7867-0375-X*) Carroll & Graf.

O'Neil, George & O'Neil, Gisela. Human Life. pap. 28.00 (*0-929979-01-X*, 1531) Merc Pr NY.

O'Neil, Gerard. The High Frontier: Human Colonies in Space. (Illus.). 326p. 1989. pap. 9.95 (*0-9622379-0-6*) SSIP.

O'Neil, Ginger R., ed. see Manasevit, Leigh, et al.

O'Neil, Ginger R., ed. see Schwahn, Chuck J. & Spady, William G.

O'Neil, Ginger R., ed. see Spady, William G.

O'Neil, Gisela, jt. auth. see O'Neil, George.

O'Neil, Gisela, ed. see Steiner, Rudolf.

O'Neil, Gladys, jt. ed. see Helfrich, G. W.

O'Neil, Harold F., Jr., ed. Workforce Readiness: Competencies & Assessment. LC 97-13791. 375p. 1997. 89.95 (*0-8058-2149-X*) L Erlbaum Assocs.

— Workforce Readiness: Competencies & Assessment. LC 97-13791. 375p. 1997. pap. 45.00 (*0-8058-2150-3*) L Erlbaum Assocs.

O'Neil, Harold F., jt. ed. see Baker, Eva L.

O'Neil, Harold F., jt. ed. see Drillings, Michael.

O'Neil, Isabel. The Art of the Painted Finish for Furniture & Decoration. LC 70-151928. (Illus.). 1980. reprint ed. pap. 19.95 (*0-688-06070-6*, Quil) HarperTrade.

O'Neil, J. J. The Prodigal Genius: The Life & Mind of Nikola Tesla. (Nikola Tesla Ser.). 1986. lib. bdg. 79.95 (*0-8490-3839-1*) Gordon Pr.

O'Neil, Jackie. Guide to Owning a Miniature Pinscher. (Illus.). 64p. 1997. pap. 6.95 (*0-7938-1891-5*, RE-340) TFH Pubns.

— Guide to Owning an Irish Setter. (Illus.). 64p. 1997. pap. 6.95 (*0-7938-1888-5*, RE-338) TFH Pubns.

O'Neil, Jacqueline. All about Agility: A Concise Guide to the Agility Scene. LC 97-38166. (Illus.). 180p. 1998. 22.95 (*0-87605-412-2*) Howell Bks.

***O'Neil, Jacqueline.** Chihuahuas for Dummies. (Illus.). 288p. 2000. pap. 15.99 (*0-7645-5284-8*) IDG Bks.

O'Neil, Jacqueline. Guide to Owning a Boston Terrier. (Guide to Owning Ser.). 64p. 1998. pap. text 6.95 (*0-7938-1885-0*, RE335) TFH Pubns.

— Guide to Owning an English Springer Spaniel. (Guide to Owning Ser.). 64p. 1998. pap. text 6.95 (*0-7938-1886-9*, RE336) TFH Pubns.

— A New Owner's Guide to Miniature Pinschers: AKC Rank #18. (New Owner's Guide to Ser.). (Illus.). 160p. 1997. 12.95 (*0-7938-2768-X*, JG-119) TFH Pubns.

***O'Neil, Jacqueline F.** All about Agility. rev. unabridged ed. 192p. 1999. pap. text 12.95 (*1-58245-123-0*) Howell Bks.

O'Neil, James. Qwik-Sane: Topological Puzzle. 1970. 3.00 (*0-911624-10-4*) Wffn Proof.

O'Neil, James, jt. auth. see Griffith, Barbara S.

O'Neil, James L. The Origins & Development of Ancient Greek Democracy. (Greek Studies: Interdisciplinary Approaches). 195p. 1995. pap. 23.95 (*0-8476-7957-8*); lib. bdg. 60.50 (*0-8476-7956-X*) Rowman.

O'Neil, James M., jt. ed. see Conyne, Robert K.

O'Neil, James M., jt. ed. see Harway, Michele.

O'Neil, Jean. Asegurando el Futuro/Securing the Future. Kirby, Judy, ed. (SPA.). 40p. (Orig.). 1998. pap. write for info. (*0-934513-70-8*) Natl Crime DC.

— Barter, Bargain, & Borrow. 8p. 1987. pap. 3.95 (*0-934513-40-6*, R4B) Natl Crime DC.

— Finding Federal Funds (And Other Resources) to Prevent Crime. Kirby, Judy, ed. 44p. 1997. pap. 12.95 (*0-934513-15-5*, R12A) Natl Crime DC.

— Helping Communities Mobilize Against Crime, Drugs, & Other Problems. 28p. 1992. pap. 5.95 (*0-934513-20-1*, M32A) Natl Crime DC.

— Ink & Airtime: Working Effectively with the Media. 124p. 1987. pap. 14.95 (*0-934513-41-4*, M5B) Natl Crime DC.

***O'Neil, Jean.** Lessons from Indian Country: McGruff & Scruff's Drug & Violence Prevention Story & Activity Book & Leaders Guide. Kirby, Judy, ed. (Illus.). 21p. (Orig.). (J). 1998. pap. Price not set. (*0-934513-75-9*) Natl Crime DC.

— Making It Happen. Kirby, Judy, ed. 12p. 1999. pap. 5.95 (*0-934513-90-2*) Natl Crime DC.

O'Neil, Jean. Planning Is a Verb. 84p. 1988. pap. 14.95 (*0-934513-44-9*, M10B) Natl Crime DC.

— Reaching Out: School-Based Community Service Programs. 109p. (Orig.). 1991. pap. 14.95 (*0-934513-81-3*) Natl Crime DC.

— Securing the Future for Safer Youth & Communities. Kirby, Judy, ed. LC 98-233043. 20p. 1998. pap. write for info. (*0-934513-69-4*, M52) Natl Crime DC.

— Uniting Communities Through Crime Prevention. 2nd ed. Kirby, Judy, ed. (Special Focus Ser.). 80p. (Orig.). 1994. reprint ed. pap. 14.95 (*0-934513-07-4*, M35) Natl Crime DC.

***O'Neil, Jean.** Youth Action Packets. Kirby, Judy, ed. (Illus.). 40p. (YA). 1998. pap. 17.95 (*0-934513-76-7*) Natl Crime DC.

O'Neil, Jean, ed. Achieving Success in Drug Prevention: Community-Law Enforcement Partnerships. 12p. 1991. pap. 5.95 (*0-934513-17-1*, R9B) Natl Crime DC.

— Being Healthy & Safe with McGruff & Scruff: Activity Book for Preschool, Head Start, & Other Child Care Programs. (Illus.). 72p. 1995. pap. 24.95 (*0-934513-26-0*, K25) Natl Crime DC.

— Bringing Up a Drug-Free Generation: How Communities Can Support Parents. 31p. (Orig.). 1992. pap. 5.95 (*0-934513-79-1*) Natl Crime DC.

— Building & Crossing Bridges: Refugees & Law Enforcement Working Together. 60p. 1994. pap. 14.95 (*0-934513-18-X*, M36) Natl Crime DC.

O'Neil, Jean, ed. Challenges & Opportunities in Drug Prevention: A Demand Reduction Resource Guide for Law Enforcement Officers. 219p. (Orig.). 1990. pap. 24.95 (*0-934513-82-1*) Natl Crime DC.

O'Neil, Jean, ed. Changing Our Course: Youth As Resources Program Guide. 146p. 1992. 24.95 (*0-934513-32-5*, M25) Natl Crime DC.

— Changing Perspectives: Youth As Resources. 88p. 1990. pap. 14.95 (*0-934513-33-3*, M16B) Natl Crime DC.

— Cops Helping Kids: Teaching Preschoolers Violence Prevention & Safety. (Illus.). 64p. 1995. pap. 19.95 (*0-934513-27-9*, K30) Natl Crime DC.

O'Neil, Jean, ed. Given the Opportunity: How Three Communities Engaged Teens as Reources in Drug Abuse Prevention. 56p. (Orig.). 1992. pap. 11.95 (*0-934513-80-5*) Natl Crime DC.

O'Neil, Jean, ed. Helping Kids Handle Conflict: A Guide for Those Teaching Children. (Illus.). 104p. 1995. pap. 24.95 (*0-934513-28-7*) Natl Crime DC.

— How Communities Can Bring up Youth Free from Fear & Violence. 70p. 1995. pap. 11.95 (*0-934513-21-X*, M45) Natl Crime DC.

— Let's Drive Con Artists Out of Business. 24p. 1992. pap. 7.95 (*0-934513-42-2*, R11A) Natl Crime DC.

— El Libro de McGruff - McGruff's Activity Book. (SPA., Illus.). 96p. 1993. pap. 22.95 (*0-934513-50-3*, K9) Natl Crime DC.

— Maintaining Neighborhood Watch. 4p. 1986. pap. 3.95 (*0-934513-23-6*, R1A) Natl Crime DC.

— McGruff's Drug Abuse Prevention Kit. 1989. 44.95 (*0-934513-83-X*) Natl Crime DC.

— McGruff's Elementary Drug Prevention Activity Book. (Illus.). 64p. 1992. pap. 19.95 (*0-934513-29-5*, K8) Natl Crime DC.

— Organizing for Small Business Crime Prevention. 12p. 1988. pap. 5.95 (*0-934513-43-0*, M13B) Natl Crime DC.

— Partner with the Media to Build Safer Communities. 72p. 1995. pap. 19.95 (*0-934513-59-7*, K20) Natl Crime DC.

— Preventing Violence: Program Ideas & Examples. 80p. 1992. pap. 11.95 (*0-934513-45-7*, M21A) Natl Crime DC.

— Put a Stop to Auto Theft. 12p. 1991. pap. 7.95 (*0-934513-46-5*, R10A) Natl Crime DC.

— Selling Crime Prevention. 4p. 1987. pap. 3.95 (*0-934513-47-3*, R3B) Natl Crime DC.

— Spanish & English Masters for Crime Prevention. (ENG & SPA.). 16p. 1995. pap. 9.95 (*0-934513-52-X*) Natl Crime DC.

— Success of Community Crime Prevention. 8p. 1987. pap. 3.95 (*0-934513-48-1*, R5B) Natl Crime DC.

— Taking the Offensive to Prevent Crime: How Seven Cities Did It. 116p. 1994. pap. 14.95 (*0-934513-24-4*, M34) Natl Crime DC.

— Teen Power: Don't Fight Drugs Without It. 106p. (Orig.). pap. 14.95 (*0-934513-77-5*) Natl Crime DC.

— Teens, Crime, & the Community Implementation Guide. 2nd rev. ed. 177p. 1997. 39.95 (*0-934513-37-6*, M26A) Natl Crime DC.

— Tools to Involve Parents in Gang Prevention. 50p. 1992. pap. 24.95 (*0-934513-38-4*, M31) Natl Crime DC.

— When a Child Reports a Crime: Encouraging Children to Report Crime & Responding Appropriately When They Do. 84p. 1992. pap. 14.95 (*0-934513-31-7*, M27) Natl Crime DC.

— Working with Older Americans. 12p. 1990. pap. 5.95 (*0-934513-39-2*, R8B) Natl Crime DC.

O'Neil, Jean & Modglin, Terrence. Charting Success: A Workbook for Developing Crime Prevention & Other Community Service Projects. 3rd rev. ed. Kirby, Judy, ed. (Illus.). 48p. (Orig.). (YA). 1995. pap., wbk. ed. 7.95 (*0-934513-06-6*, M11B) Natl Crime DC.

O'Neil, Jean, jt. auth. see Brosler, Lauren.

O'Neil, Jean, jt. auth. see Kelly, Theresa.

O'Neil, Jean, jt. auth. see Zahm, Diane.

O'Neil, Jean, ed. see Carlson, Andrea.

O'Neil, Jean, ed. see Donovan, Erin.

O'Neil, Jean, ed. see Marvin, Mary J.

O'Neil, Jean, ed. see Marvin, Mary Jo.

O'Neil, Joe. Teach Yourself Java 1.2. LC 99-161885. 1998. pap. text 29.99 (*0-07-882570-9*) Osborne-McGraw.

O'Neil, Joe, jt. auth. see Schildt, Herbert.

O'Neil, John. Leadership Aikido: 6 Business Practices that Can Turn Your Life Around. LC 97-13489. 1997. 25.00 (*0-517-70575-3*) Random.

— Leadership Aikido: 6 Business Practices That Can Turn Your Life Around. 256p. 1999. pap. 14.00 (*0-609-80221-6*) Harmony Bks.

— Plato's Cave: Desire, Power, & the Specular Functions of the Media. 224p. 1991. pap. 39.50 (*1-56750-080-3*) Ablx Pub.

— Plato's Cave: Desire, Power, & the Specular Functions of the the Media. 224p. 1991. text 73.25 (*0-89391-722-2*) Ablx Pub.

O'Neil, John & Willis, Scott. ASCD Update Compilation, 2 vols. 1998. pap. 32.95 (*0-87120-312-X*, 198198) ASCD.

O'Neil, John & Willis, Scott, eds. Revitalizing the Disciplines: The Best of ASCD's Curriculum Update. LC 98-15117. 286p. 1998. pap. 20.95 (*0-87120-309-X*, 198051) ASCD.

O'Neil, John, et al. Transforming Classroom Practice: The Best of ASCD's Update Newsletters. LC 98-3546. (Illus.). 283p. 1998. pap. 20.95 (*0-87120-310-3*, 198052) ASCD.

O'Neil, Joseph. Visual InterDev 6 from the Ground Up. LC 98-87439. 608p. 1998. pap. 34.99 (*0-07-882509-1*) Osborne-McGraw.

O'Neil, Joseph & Schildt, Herbert. Java Beans Programming from the Ground Up. LC 98-176410. 487p. 1998. pap. text 34.99 (*0-07-882477-X*) McGraw.

O'Neil, Karen E. Health & Medicine Projects for Young Scientists. LC 92-42745. (Projects for Young Scientists Ser.). (Illus.). 128p. (YA). (gr. 9-12). 1993. lib. bdg. 24.00 (*0-531-11050-8*) Watts.

O'Neil, Katherine, jt. auth. see Mahan, Sue.

O'Neil, Kevin R. American Buddhist Directory. 2nd ed. 116p. (Orig.). 1985. pap. 20.00 (*0-685-11198-9*) Crises Res Pr.

— The American Buddhist Directory, 1982. 96p. 1982. pap. 7.00 (*0-86627-003-5*) Crises Res Pr.

— Awakening of Faith in Mahayana. (Orig.). 1984. pap. 14.95 (*0-685-09623-8*) Crises Res Pr.

— Basic Buddhism. 41p. (Orig.). 1981. pap. 5.00 (*0-86627-006-X*) Crises Res Pr.

— The Diamond Sutra. 1978. pap. 5.00 (*0-86627-004-3*) Crises Res Pr.

— How to Protect Your Family from Terrorists. 106p. 1979. pap. 15.00 (*0-86627-007-8*) Crises Res Pr.

— An Introduction to Nichiren Shoshu Buddhism. 111p. 1980. pap. 5.00 (*0-86627-002-7*) Crises Res Pr.

— Realm of Totality. 49p. (Orig.). 1984. pap. 6.00 (*0-86627-011-6*) Crises Res Pr.

— What to Tell Your Children about Cults. 52p. (Orig.). 1982. pap. 9.95 (*0-86627-001-9*) Crises Res Pr.

O'Neil, Kevin R., ed. American Buddhist Newsletter, 1981-1982, Vol. I. 136p. (Orig.). 1982. pap. 35.00 (*0-86627-000-0*) Crises Res Pr.

— The Sutra Spoken by Vimilakirti. pap. 6.00 (*0-86627-009-4*) Crises Res Pr.

O'Neil, Kimberly, jt. auth. see Mock, John.

O'Neil, L. Peat. Travel Writing: A Guide to Research, Writing & Selling. LC 95-34121. 256p. 1996. 18.99 (*0-89879-671-7*, Wrtrs Digest Bks) F & W Pubns Inc.

***O'Neil, L. Peat.** Travel Writing: A Guide to Research, Writing & Selling. (Illus.). 256p. 2000. pap. 14.99 (*1-58297-000-9*, Wrtrs Digest Bks) F & W Pubns Inc.

O'Neil, Laura. The Case of the Ballet Bandit. (New Adventures of Mary-Kate & Ashley Ser.). (Illus.). 87p. (J). (gr. 2-4). 1998. pap. 3.99 (*0-590-29542-X*) Scholastic Inc.

— The Case of the Hotel Who-Done-It. (Adventures of Mary-Kate & Ashley Ser.). 88p. (J). (gr. 2-4). 1997. pap. 3.99 (*0-590-88013-6*) Scholastic Inc.

— Hello Birthday, Goodbye Friend. (Full House Stephanie Ser.: Vol. 30). 144p. (J). (gr. 4-7). 1999. pap. 3.99 (*0-671-02160-5*) PB.

— Major League Trouble. (Full House Michelle Ser.). 96p. (J). (gr. 4-7). 1996. per. 3.99 (*0-671-53575-7*, PB Trade Paper) PB.

— Second Noah. (J). (gr. 4-7). 1996. pap. text 3.99 (*0-590-93710-3*) Scholastic Inc.

O'Neil, Laura, jt. auth. see Weyn, Suzanne.

O'Neil, Leo E. The Living Fire: Selected Poetry of Leo E. O'Neil, 1973-1997. Gamachi, Ray, ed. (Illus.). 240p. 1998. pap. 14.95 (*0-9646061-2-7*) Wayfarer Pr.

O'Neil, Leslie S. My Nanny: From a Small Country Town, to the Entertainment Capital of the World. Moreau, Michael & O'Neil, Colleen, eds. LC 97-94475. 368p. 1998. pap. 16.95 (*0-9660519-0-4*) Crown Pt Publ.

O'Neil, Luke A., jt. ed. see Murphy, Michael P.

O'Neil, M. E. & Chorlton, Frank. Viscous & Compressible Fluid Dynamics. 1989. text 79.95 (*0-470-21263-2*) P-H.

O'Neil, Marnie H., jt. ed. see Carter, David.

O'Neil, Martin F., jt. auth. see Blonchek, Robert M.

O'Neil, Mike S. Power to Choose: Twelve Steps to Wholeness. 209p. (Orig.). 1991. pap. 19.95 (*0-9633454-0-0*) Sonlight Pub.

O'Neil, Mike S., jt. auth. see Newbold, Charles E.

O'Neil, Mike S., jt. ed. see Nightingale, Peggy.

O'Neil, P. Fundamental Concepts of Topology. xvi, 320p. 1972. text 306.00 (*0-677-03420-2*) Gordon & Breach.

— Traveller's Guide to Cape Breton. 1999. pap. text 12.95 (*1-896792-00-6*) So7lus.

O'Neil, Pat. Explore Cape Breton: A Field Guide to Adventure. (Illus.). 176p. 1994. pap. 10.95 (*1-55109-085-6*) Nimbus Publ.

— What Now? 60p. (Orig.). 1989. pap. text 7.95 (*0-9627243-0-0*) Pat Pubns.

— What Now?! (This Book Is User Friendly) 61p. 1991. 7.95 (*0-9627243-1-9*) Pat Pubns.

O'Neil, Patrick. Revolution from Within: The Hungarian Socialist Workers' Party & the Collapse of Communism. LC 97-35438. (Studies of Communism in Transition). 288p. 1998. 85.00 (*1-85898-766-0*) E Elgar.

O'Neil, Patrick & O'Neil, Elizabeth. Database: Principles, Programming, Performance. 2nd ed. Gray, Jim, ed. LC 99-89041. (Data Management Systems Ser.). 1000p. (C). 2000. 74.95 (*1-55860-438-3*, Pub. by Morgan Kaufmann) Harcourt.

***O'Neil, Patrick & O'Neil, Elizabeth.** Database--Principles, Programming & Performance. 2nd ed. LC 99-89041. 2000. pap. write for info. (*1-55860-580-0*) Morgan Kaufmann.

O'Neil, Patrick B. The Cosmology of John Ross. LC 94-61226. 136p. (Orig.). 1995. pap. 10.00 (*1-884570-14-3*) Research Triangle.

O'Neil, Patrick E. Database: Principles, Programming & Performance. LC 94-26710. 874p. 1994. text 74.95 (*1-55860-219-4*) Morgan Kaufmann.

O'Neil, Patrick H., ed. Communicating Democracy: The Media & Political Translations. LC 97-39364. 226p. 1998. lib. bdg. 55.00 (*1-55587-669-2*) L Rienner.

— Post-Communism & the Media in Eastern Europe. LC 96-39923. 152p. (Orig.). (C). 1997. 37.50 (*0-7146-4765-9*, Pub. by F Cass Pubs); pap. 19.50 (*0-7146-4311-4*, Pub. by F Cass Pubs) Intl Spec Bk.

O'Neil, Peggy Sailer, jt. auth. see Kusler, Ruth Weil.

O'Neil, Peter. Health Crisis 2000. 1983. pap. text 25.00 (*92-890-1009-6*) World Health.

O'Neil, Peter V. Advanced Engineering Mathematics. (Math). 1232p. (C). 1983. mass mkt. 43.00 (*0-534-01136-5*) PWS Pubs.

— Advanced Engineering Mathematics. 2nd ed. (Math). 1122p. (C). 1986. mass mkt. 58.00 (*0-534-06792-1*) PWS Pubs.

An Asterisk (*) at the beginning of an entry indicates that the title is appearing for the first time.

O

O'Neill, Eugene. The Last Will & Testament of an Extremely Distinguished Dog. (Illus.). 48p. 1999. 18.00 (*0-9633560-5-4*) Durand Pr.

***O'Neill, Eugene.** The Last Will & Testament of an Extremely Distinguished Dog. LC 99-36351. (Illus.). 48p. 1999. 15.00 (*0-8050-6170-3*) H Holt & Co.

O'Neill, Eugene. The Later Plays. Bogard, Travis, ed. 409p. (C). 1967. pap. 8.44 (*0-07-553664-1*) McGraw.

— Long Day's Journey into Night. 19.95 (*0-89190-370-4*) Amereon Ltd.

— Long Day's Journey into Night. 176p. 1950. 20.00 (*0-300-04600-6*) Yale U Pr.

O'Neill, Eugene. Long Day's Journey into Night. LC 89-50523. 176p. 1989. pap. 10.00 (*0-300-04601-4*) Yale U Pr.

O'Neill, Eugene. The Long Voyage Home: 7 Plays of the Sea. 21.95 (*0-89190-369-0*) Amereon Ltd.

— The Long Voyage Home & Other Plays. unabridged ed. (Thrift Editions Ser.). (Illus.). 80p. 1995. reprint ed. pap. text 1.00 (*0-486-28755-6*) Dover.

— Love & Admiration & Respect: The O'Neill-Commins Correspondence. Commins, Dorothy, ed. LC 86-6195. xxi, 248p. 1986. text 41.00 (*0-8223-0668-9*) Duke.

— A Moon for the Misbegotten. LC 74-5218. 115p. 1974. pap. 8.00 (*0-394-71236-6*) Vin Bks.

— More Stately Mansions. abr. ed. Gallup, Donald, ed. (Illus.). (Orig.). 1964. pap. 11.00 (*0-300-00177-0*, Y101) Yale U Pr.

— O'Neill: 3 Plays. 320p. 1998. mass mkt. 4.95 (*0-451-52667-8*, Penguin Classics) Viking Penguin.

— Selected Letters of Eugene O'Neill. Bogard, Travis & Bryer, Jackson R., eds. (Illus.). 602p. (C). 1988. 55.00 (*0-300-04374-0*) Yale U Pr.

— Selected Letters of Eugene O'Neill. Bryer, Jackson R. & Bogard, Travis, eds. LC 94-28978. (Illus.). 614p. 1994. reprint ed. pap. 18.95 (*0-87910-181-4*) Limelight Edns.

— Six Plays. 1976. 24.95 (*0-8488-0600-X*) Amereon Ltd.

— Ten "Lost" Plays. 320p. 1995. pap. text 8.95 (*0-486-28367-4*) Dover.

— The Theatre We Worked For: The Letters of Eugene O'Neill to Kenneth Macgowan. Bryer, Jackson R. & Alvarez, Ruth M., eds. LC 81-299. (Illus.). 292p. (C). 1982. 45.00 (*0-300-02583-1*) Yale U Pr.

— Three Plays. 384p. 1995. pap. 12.00 (*0-679-76396-1*) Random.

— A Touch of the Poet. 1994. pap. 5.25 (*0-8222-1393-1*) Dramatists Play.

— The Unknown O'Neill: Unpublished & Unfamiliar Writings of Eugene O'Neill. Bogard, Travis, ed. & comment by. LC 87-24637. 352p. (C). 1988. 55.00 (*0-300-03985-9*) Yale U Pr.

O'Neill, Eugene, ed. Seven Famous Greek Plays. (C). 1950. pap. text. write for info. (*0-07-553629-3*) McGraw.

O'Neill, Eugene, jt. auth. see Center for Learning Network Staff.

O'Neill, Eugene, Jr., ed. see Euripides.

O'Neill, Eugene, Jr., jt. ed. see Oates, Whitney J.

O'Neill, Eugene, Jr., ed. see Sophocles.

O'Neill, Eugene S., ed. The Psychiatric Emergency: Its Recognition & Management. LC 85-21986. (Emergency Health Services Review Ser.: Vol. 3, No. 1). 128p. 1986. text 4.95 (*0-86656-518-3*) Haworth Pr.

O'Neill, Francis. Irish Minstrels & Musicians: The Story of Irish Music. (Illus.). 497p. 1987. reprint ed. pap. 30.00 (*0-85342-801-8*) Dufour.

— O'Neill's Irish Music: Arranged for Piano or Violin. 192p. 1987. pap. 21.00 (*0-85342-800-X*) Dufour.

O'Neill, Francis, ed. O'Neill's Music of Ireland: Intermediate Level. 368p. 1996. spiral bd. 29.95 (*0-7866-2498-1*, 96322) Mel Bay.

O'Neill, Frank Q., jt. ed. see Greene, Harlan.

O'Neill, Gerard, jt. auth. see Lehr, Dick.

O'Neill, Gerard K. The Technology Edge: Opportunities for America in World Competition. 299p. 1983. pap. 9.95 (*0-671-44766-1*) SSIP.

O'Neill, Gilda. A Night Out with the Girls: Women Having a Good Time. 212p. 1997. pap. 15.95 (*0-7043-4353-3*, Pub. by Womens Press) Trafalgar.

— Pull No More Bines: Hop Picking-Memories of a Vanished Way of Life. pap. 17.95 (*0-7043-4229-4*, Pub. by Womens Press) Trafalgar.

— Pull No More Bines: Memoirs of a Vanished Way of Life. large type ed. (Reminiscence Ser.). 22.95 (*1-85695-079-4*, Pub. by ISIS Lrg Prnt) Transaction Pubs.

O'Neill, H., jt. ed. see Dearden, J.

O'Neill, Harold F. Effects of Stress on State Anxiety & Performance in Computer-Assisted Learning. LC 79-136729. 1970. 25.00 (*0-403-04525-8*) Scholarly.

O'Neill, Helen. Managing Anger. 1999. pap. 36.95 (*1-86156-107-5*) Whurr Pub.

O'Neill, Helen, ed. Third World Debt: How Sustainable Are Current Strategies & Solutions? 1990. text 42.50 (*0-7146-3409-3*, Pub. by F Cass Pubs) Intl Spec Bk.

O'Neill, Hlly A. Afghanistan. LC 95-15772. (OIES Country Guide Ser.). 1995. 22.00 (*0-929851-39-0*) Am Assn Coll Registrars.

O'Neill, Holly A. Sudan. LC 95-22478. (Oles Country Guide Ser.). 1996. 22.00 (*0-929851-60-9*) Am Assn Coll Registrars.

— Zambia. LC 95-22477. (Oles Country Guide Series Report from the AACRAO-AID Project). 1996. 22.00 (*0-929851-64-1*) Am Assn Coll Registrars.

O'Neill, Hugh. The Complete Spindle Turner: Spindle Turning for Furniture & Decoration. (Illus.). 160p. 1998. pap. 29.95 (*1-86126-059-8*, Pub. by Cro1wood) Trafalgar.

— Creating Opportunity: Strategies for Reducing Poverty Through Economic Development. LC 85-5931. 207p. 1985. 16.95 (*0-934842-41-8*) CSPA.

— A Man Called Daddy. LC 95-26787. 223p. 1996. 12.95 (*1-55853-393-1*) Rutledge Hill Pr.

— Police Officer. 12th ed. (Illus.). 480p. 1994. pap. 14.00 (*0-671-89231-2*) P-H.

***O'Neill, Hugh.** Upholstery: A Manual of Techniques. (Illus.). 208p. 2000. pap. 35.00 (*1-86126-140-3*, Pub. by Cro1wood) Trafalgar.

O'Neill, Hugh. Woodturning: A Guide to Advanced Techniques. (Illus.). 192p. 1998. pap. 24.95 (*1-85223-994-8*, Pub. by Cro1wood) Trafalgar.

— Woodturning: A Manual of Techniques. (Illus.). 192p. 1993. pap. 29.95 (*1-85223-723-6*, Pub. by Cro1wood) Trafalgar.

O'Neill, Hugh & Hammer, Hy. Police Officer. 13th ed. 1996. 13.95 (*0-02-861188-8*) Macmillan.

O'Neill, Hugh, et al. Police Officer. 13th ed. 480p. 1996. pap. 13.95 (*0-02-861518-2*, Arco) Macmillan Gen Ref.

— Where the Jobs Are: How Labor Market Conditions in the New York Area Will Affect the Employment Prospects of Public Assistance Recipients. 83p. (Orig.). 1997. mass mkt. 12.00 (*0-88156-201-7*) Comm Serv Soc NY.

O'Neill, I. K., et al, eds. Environmental Carcinogens: Methods of Analysis & Exposure Measurement, Vol. 9-Passive Smoking. (IARC Scientific Publications: No. 81). (Illus.). 383p. 1988. 80.00 (*92-832-1181-2*) OUP.

— Relevance to Human Cancer of N-Nitroso Compounds, Tobacco Smoke & Mycotoxins. (IARC Scientific Publications: No. 105). (Illus.). 642p. 1991. pap. 150.00 (*92-832-2105-2*) OUP.

O'Neill, I. K., jt. ed. see Fishbein, L.

O'Neill, I. K., ed. see International Agency for Research on Cancer Staff.

O'Neill, J. Leaving Home. 1997. mass mkt. 13.95 (*0-340-69496-3*, Pub. by Hodder & Stought Ltd) Trafalgar.

O'Neill, J. O'Neill's One Thousand One Collection. 1986. pap. 20.95 (*0-7866-1603-2*, 95188WW) Mel Bay.

O'Neill, J. C. The Bible's Authority: A Portrait Gallery of Thinkers from Lessing to Bultmann. 312p. 1991. pap. 29.95 (*0-567-29189-8*, Pub. by T & T Clark) Bks Intl VA.

— Who Did Jesus Think He Was? (Biblical Interpretation Ser.: Vol. 11). 238p. 1995. 90.00 (*90-04-10429-1*) Brill Academic Pubs.

O'Neill, J. P. The Great New England Sea Serpent: An Account of Unknown Creatures Sighted by Many Respectable Persons Between 1638 & the Present Day. LC 99-29121. 288p. 1999. pap. 15.95 (*0-89272-461-7*) Down East.

O'Neill, Jack. Stress Busters: Twenty-One Thoughts for Your Emotional Wellness. LC 93-70088. 160p. 1993. pap. 9.95 (*1-883000-00-9*) Derrymore West.

O'Neill, Jaime. We're History! The 20th Century Survivor's Final Exam. LC 98-6512. 384p. 1998. mass mkt. 14.00 (*0-684-82922-3*, Fireside) S&S Trade Pap.

***O'Neill, Jaime.** What Do You Know? 2000. 8.99 (*0-517-16259-8*) Random Hse Value.

O'Neill, James. Sci-Fi on Tape: A Comprehensive Guide to Science Fiction & Fantasy Films on Video. LC 96-52599. (Illus.). 272p. 1997. 16.95 (*0-8230-7659-8*, Billboard Bks) Watsn-Guptill.

— Terror on Tape: A Complete Guide to over 2,000 Horror Movies on Video. LC 94-25496. (Illus.). 400p. 1994. pap. 16.95 (*0-8230-7612-1*, Billboard Bks) Watsn-Guptill.

O'Neill, James, Jr., et al. Upon This Rock: A New History of the Trenton Diocese. (Illus.). 593p. 1993. 39.00 (*0-9638128-0-7*) Diocese of Trenton.

O'Neill, James A., Jr., jt. ed. see Dean, Richard H.

O'Neill, James E. & Krauskopf, Robert, eds. World War II: An Account of Its Documents. LC 74-34112. (National Archives Conference Ser.: Vol. 8). (Illus.). 1976. 24.50 (*0-88258-053-1*) Howard U Pr.

O'Neill, James L. & Cushing, Michael A. The Impact of Shift Work on Police Officers. LC 91-66816. 75p. (Orig.). 1991. pap. 16.50 (*1-878734-26-1*) Police Exec Res.

O'Neill, James M. Making Colonial Furniture: Instructions & Diagrams for 24 Projects. LC 97-137. (Illus.). 142p. 1997. reprint ed. pap. text 9.95 (*0-486-29666-0*) Dover.

O'Neill, Jan, jt. auth. see Conzemius, Anne.

O'Neill, Jane. World of the Brontes: The Lives, Times & Works of Charlotte, Emily & Anne Bronte. 144p. 1999. 24.95 (*1-85868-341-6*, Pub. by Carlton Bks Ltd) Natl Bk Netwk.

Oneill, Jasmin Lee. Through the Eyes of Aliens: A Book about Autistic People. LC 98-11662. 1998. pap. text 18.95 (*1-85302-710-3*) Taylor & Francis.

***O'Neill, Jean.** Lewis & Clark in the Bitterroot. 216p. 1998. 19.95 (*0-912299-76-2*); pap. 14.95 (*0-912299-71-1*) Stoneydale Pr Pub.

O'Neill, Jennifer. Surviving Myself. LC 99-10051. 256p. 1999. 25.00 (*0-688-15992-3*, Wm Morrow) Morrow Avon.

O'Neill, Joan. Bread & Sugar. 254p. 1993. pap. 10.95 (*1-85371-313-9*, Pub. by Poolbeg Pr) Dufour.

O'Neill, John. The Communicative Body: Studies in Communicative Philosophy, Politics & Sociology. (Studies in Phenomenology & Existential Philosophy). 264p. 1989. pap. 19.95 (*0-8101-0802-X*) Northwestern U Pr.

— Ecology, Policy, & Politics: Human Well-Being & the Natural World. LC 93-16367. (Environmental Philosophies Ser.). 240p. (C). 1993. pap. 22.99 (*0-415-07300-6*, B2478) Routledge.

— Five Bodies: The Human Shape of Modern Society. LC 84-22947. (Illus.). 184p. 1985. pap. text 13.95 (*0-8014-9455-9*) Cornell U Pr.

— For Marx Against Althusser & Other Essays. LC 82-17353. (Current Continental Research Ser.). (Illus.). 192p. (Orig.). 1983. pap. text 19.50 (*0-8191-2816-3*) U Pr of Amer.

— The Jazz Method for Clarinet. (Illus.). 112p. (YA). 1993. pap. text 19.95 (*0-946535-21-3*, Pub. by Schott & Co) Eur-Am Music.

— The Jazz Method for Flute. (Illus.). 104p. (YA). 1994. pap. 19.95 (*0-946535-24-8*, Pub. by Schott & Co) Eur-Am Music.

— The Jazz Method for Saxophone. (Illus.). 108p. (YA). 1992. pap. 19.95 (*0-946535-20-5*, Pub. by Schott & Co) Eur-Am Music.

— Love in Alaska. 96p. 1994. pap. text 11.95 (*0-88982-135-6*, Pub. by Oolichan Bks) Genl Dist Srvs.

— The Missing Child in Liberal Theory: Towards a Covenant Theory of Family, Community Welfare & the Civic State. 136p. 1994. text 40.00 (*0-8020-0627-2*); pap. text 14.95 (*0-8020-7586-X*) U of Toronto Pr.

— Perception, Expression, & History: The Social Phenomenology of Maurice Merleau-Ponty. (Studies in Phenomenology & Existential Philosophy). 101p. 1970. 39.95 (*0-8101-0299-4*) Northwestern U Pr.

— The Poverty of Postmodernism. LC 94-7260. (Social Futures Ser.). 240p. (Orig.). (C). 1994. pap. 24.99 (*0-415-11687-2*, B4746) Routledge.

O'Neill, John, ed. Freud & the Passions. LC 97-16894. (Literature & Philosophy Ser.). (Illus.). 236p. 1996. 45.00 (*0-271-01529-2*); pap. 19.95 (*0-271-01530-6*) Pa St U Pr.

— Hegel's Dialectic of Desire & Recognition: Texts & Commentary. LC 95-5523. (SUNY Series in the Philosophy of the Social Sciences). 331p. (C). 1996. text 59.50 (*0-7914-2713-7*); pap. text 19.95 (*0-7914-2714-5*) State U NY Pr.

— On Critical Theory. 270p. (C). 1989. reprint ed. pap. text 25.00 (*0-8191-7514-5*) U Pr of Amer.

O'Neill, John & O'Neill, Pat. Concerned Intervention: When Your Loved One Won't Quit Alcohol or Drugs. LC 92-61813. 208p. (Orig.). 1992. pap. 13.95 (*1-879237-36-9*) New Harbinger.

O'Neill, John & Waterman, Steve. The Jazz Method for Trumpet. (Illus.). 120p. (YA). 1995. pap. 19.95 (*0-946535-25-6*, Pub. by Schott & Co) Eur-Am Music.

O'Neill, John, jt. auth. see Fanning, Patrick.

O'Neill, John, jt. auth. see Hayward, Tim.

O'Neill, John, ed. see De Villena, Enrique.

O'Neill, John, tr. see Merleau-Ponty, Maurice.

O'Neill, John, tr. & intro. see Merleau-Ponty, Maurice.

O'Neill, John J. Management of Industrial Construction Projects. 285p. 1990. 49.95 (*0-89397-357-2*) Nichols Pub.

— Prodigal Genius: The Life of Nikola Tesla. 326p. reprint ed. 12.00 (*0-913022-40-3*) Angriff Pr.

O'Neill, John J. Prodigal Genius: The Life of Nikola Tesla. unabridged ed. 326p. 1978. reprint ed. 25.00 (*0-945001-22-3*) GSG & Assocs.

— Prodigal Genius: The Life of Nikola Tesla. unabridged ed. 326p. 1978. reprint ed. pap. 15.00 (*0-945001-21-5*) GSG & Assocs.

O'Neill, John J. Tesla - Prodigal Genius: The Life of Nikola Tesla. (Illus.). 330p. 1998. reprint ed. pap. 15.95 (*0-914732-33-1*) Bro Life Inc.

O'Neill, John J., jt. auth. see Colladay, Morrison.

O'Neill, John P. Barnett Newman: Selected Writings & Interviews. 1992. pap. 17.95 (*0-520-07817-9*, Pub. by U CA Pr) Cal Prin Full Svc.

— Great Texas Birds. Winckler, Suzanne, ed. LC 98-47137. 128p. 1999. 34.95 (*0-292-76053-1*) U of Tex Pr.

— Just for Today, Lord. 192p. (Orig.). 1993. pap. 10.00 (*0-9637937-0-5*) DEO Bks.

— Metropolitan Cats. LC 81-9590. (Illus.). 112p. 1981. 16.95 (*0-87099-276-7*) Metro Mus Art.

O'Neill, John R. The Paradox of Success: When Winning at Work Means Losing at Life: A Book of Renewal for Leaders. 272p. 1994. pap. 13.95 (*0-87477-772-0*, Tarcher Putnam) Putnam Pub Group.

O'Neill, John T., jt. auth. see Fanning, Patrick.

***O'Neill, Joseph.** The Black Shore. Lynch, M. Kelly, ed. LC 99-45135. (Illus.). 264p. 2000. 42.50 (*0-8387-5431-7*) Bucknell U Pr.

O'Neill, Joseph. Land under England. LC 80-14273. 312p. 1981. reprint ed. 22.50 (*0-87951-117-6*, Pub. by Overlook Pr) Penguin Putnam.

— This Is the Life. 224p. 1991. 18.95 (*0-374-27590-4*) FS&G.

O'Neill, Joseph E., ed. Fifty Years of Thought: Representative Selections. LC 30-22096. 630p. reprint ed. pap. 195.30 (*0-7837-5585-6*, 204537700005) Bks Demand.

O'Neill, Judith, ed. Critics on Blake. LC 75-142198. (Readings in Literary Criticism Ser.: No. 7). 1970. pap. 19.95 (*0-87024-189-3*) U of Miami Pr.

— Critics on Charlotte & Emily Bronte. LC 68-54477. (Readings in Literary Criticism Ser.: No. 2). 1979. pap. 19.95 (*0-87024-098-6*) U of Miami Pr.

— Critics on Jane Austen. LC 69-15928. (Readings in Literary Criticism Ser.: No. 5). 1970. pap. 19.95 (*0-87024-117-6*) U of Miami Pr.

— Critics on Marlowe. LC 69-15927. (Readings in Literary Criticism Ser.: No. 4). 1970. pap. 19.95 (*0-87024-121-4*) U of Miami Pr.

— Critics on Pope. LC 68-54478. (Readings in Literary Criticism Ser.: No. 3). (C). 1968. 19.95 (*0-87024-099-4*) U of Miami Pr.

O'Neill, Julia K. & Warda, Mark. How to Start a Business in Massachusetts. 2nd ed. LC 99-44317. (Legal Survival Guides Ser.). 208p. 1999. pap. 16.95 (*1-57248-106-4*, Sphinx Pubng) Sourcebks.

O'Neill, June. Work & Welfare in Massachusetts: An Evaluation of the ET Program. (Pioneer Paper Ser.: No. 3). 114p. (Orig.). 1990. pap. 10.00 (*0-929930-03-7*) Pioneer Inst.

O'Neill, June E., ed. The Economic & Budget Outlook: An Update (1998) (Illus.). 87p. (C). 1999. reprint ed. pap. text 25.00 (*0-7881-7711-7*) DIANE Pub.

O'Neill, June E. & O'Neill, Dave M. The Employment & Distributional Effects of Mandated Benefits. (Studies in Health Reform). 35p. (Orig.). 1994. pap. 9.95 (*0-8447-7021-3*, AEI Pr) Am Enterprise.

O'Neill, June E., jt. auth. see O'Neill, Dave M.

O'Neill, Karen, ed. see Leary, Edward J.

***O'Neill, Kate.** Waste Trading among Rich Nations: Building a New Theory of Environmental Regulation. LC 99-88564. (American & Comparative Environmental Policy Ser.). (Illus.). 310p. 2000. 60.00 (*0-262-15050-6*); pap. 22.00 (*0-262-65052-5*) MIT Pr.

O'Neill, Kathleen, jt. auth. see Laskin, David.

O'Neill, Kelly. Emerging Markets for Family Farms: Opportunities to Prosper Through Social & Environmental Responsibility. (Illus.). 61p. 1998. pap. text 20.00 (*0-7881-7035-X*) DIANE Pub.

O'Neill Ketchum, Mary. Aloha in Chinatown. (Illus.). 32p. (J). (gr. k-4). 1995. 12.95 (*0-89610-286-6*, 24032) Island Heritage.

O'Neill, Kevin. Family & Farm in Pre-Famine Ireland: The Parish of Killashandra. LC 84-40154. 247p. reprint ed. pap. 76.60 (*0-608-20462-5*, 207171400002) Bks Demand.

O'Neill, Kevin, jt. auth. see Mills, Pat.

O'Neill, Kevin, ed. see Albright, David, et al.

O'Neill, Kevin, tr. see Finkielkraut, Alain.

O'Neill, Kevin M., jt. auth. see Evans, Howard E.

***O'Neill, Kim.** Discover Your Spiritual Destiny: Unlock the Secrets of Your Soul to Build a Better Life. LC 98-94825. 256p. 1999. mass mkt. 5.99 (*0-380-80306-2*, Avon Bks) Morrow Avon.

O'Neill, Kim. H T Talk with Angels. 224p. 1995. mass mkt. 5.99 (*0-380-78194-8*, Avon Bks) Morrow Avon.

O'Neill, Kitty. Snack Attack: How to Stick to a Diet, Eat Lots of Snacks, & Still Lose Weight. LC 94-60670. 100p. (Orig.). 1994. pap. 12.95 (*0-9641463-4-7*) Ctr for Design.

O'Neill, L. J., jt. ed. see Oakely, I. T.

Oneill, Laurie. Wounded Knee: The Death of a Dream. (Spotlight on American History Ser.). 1993. 11.15 (*0-606-06894-5*, Pub. by Turtleback) Demco.

O'Neill, Laurie A. The Boston Tea Party. LC 95-26442. (Spotlight on American History Ser.). (Illus.). 64p. (J). (gr. 4-6). 1996. lib. bdg. 21.90 (*0-7613-0006-6*) Millbrook Pr.

— Little Rock: The Desegregation of Central High. LC 93-29057. (Spotlight on American History Ser.). (Illus.). 64p. (J). (gr. 4-6). 1994. lib. bdg. 21.90 (*1-56294-354-5*) Millbrook Pr.

— Wounded Knee: Death of a Dream. LC 92-12998. (Spotlight on American History Ser.). (Illus.). 64p. (J). (gr. 4-6). 1993. pap. 5.95 (*1-56294-748-6*); lib. bdg. 21.90 (*1-56294-253-0*) Millbrook Pr.

O'Neill, Linda. History, Memory, & Ethnic Identification: Rediscovering Community in Bishop Hill, Illinois. LC 96-21680. 100p. (Orig.). 1996. pap. text 15.95 (*1-879528-19-3*) Ed Studies Pr.

O'Neill, Lois D., ed. The Women's Book of World Records & Achievements. (Quality Paperbacks Ser.). (Illus.). xiii, 800p. 1983. reprint ed. pap. 14.95 (*0-306-80206-6*) Da Capo.

O'Neill, Luke, ed. Interleukin Protocols. (Methods in Molecular Medicine Ser.). 350p. 2000. 99.50 (*0-89603-738-X*) Humana.

O'Neill, Luke A., jt. ed. see Murphy, Michael P.

***O'Neill, Maggie.** Prostitution & Feminism. 2001. 59.95 (*0-7456-1204-0*, Pub. by Polity Pr); pap. 24.95 (*0-7456-1921-5*, Pub. by Polity Pr) Blackwell Pubs.

O'Neill, Margaret. No Longer a Stranger. large type ed. 288p. 1995. 23.99 (*0-263-14332-5*, Pub. by Mills & Boon) Ulverscroft.

***O'Neill, Margaret.** A Practice Wife. large type ed. 1999. 25.99 (*0-263-15992-2*, Pub. by Mills & Boon) Ulverscroft.

***O'Neill, Marie.** Grace Gifford Plunkett & Irish Freedom: Tragic Bride of 1916. LC 99-36022. (Women in Irish History Ser.). 136p. 2000. pap. 18.50 (*0-7165-2713-8*, Pub. by Irish Acad Pr) Intl Spec Bk.

— Grace Gifford Plunkett & Irish Freedom: Tragic Bride of 1916. LC 99-36022. (Women in Irish History Ser.). (Illus.). 136p. 2000. 35.00 (*0-7165-2666-2*, Pub. by Irish Acad Pr) Intl Spec Bk.

O'Neill, Marnie H., jt. ed. see Carter, David S.G.

O'Neill, Marnie H., jt. ed. see Carter, David.

O'Neill, Martha, jt. auth. see Snyder, Thomas F.

O'Neill, Martha, ed. see Chamberlain, Valerie M., et al.

O'Neill, Martha, ed. see Shand, Dorothy E., et al.

O'Neill, Martha, ed. see Snyder, Thomas F.

O'Neill, Martha, ed. see Tsumura, Ted K. & Jones, Lorraine H.

O'Neill, Mary. Air Scare. LC 89-49626. (SOS Planet Earth Ser.). (Illus.). 32p. (J). (gr. 3-6). 1996. pap. 5.95 (*0-8167-2083-5*) Troll Communs.

— Hailstones & Halibut Bones: Adventures in Color. (Illus.). 64p. (J). 1989. 15.95 (*0-385-24484-3*) Doubleday.

— Hailstones & Halibut Bones: Adventures in Color. 64p. (J). 1990. pap. 8.95 (*0-385-41078-6*) Doubleday.

— Hailstones & Halibut Bones: Adventures in Color. (J). 1961. 13.15 (*0-606-04393-4*, Pub. by Turtleback) Demco.

— Power Failure. LC 90-11148. (SOS Planet Earth Ser.). (Illus.). 32p. (J). (gr. 3-6). 1997. pap. 4.95 (*0-8167-2289-7*) Troll Communs.

— Water Squeeze. LC 89-77456. (SOS Planet Earth Ser.). (Illus.). 32p. (J). (gr. 3-6). 1997. pap. 5.95 (*0-8167-2081-9*) Troll Communs.

— What Is Orange? (Illus.). (J). (gr. k-2). 1993. pap. 8.95 incl. audio (*0-7608-0500-8*); pap. 4.95 (*0-88741-933-X*) Sundance Pub.

— What Is Orange?, Big bk. (Illus.). (J). (gr. k-2). 1993. pap. 17.95 (*0-88741-932-1*) Sundance Pub.

O'Neill, Mary, jt. ed. see Correard, Marie-Helene.

O'Neill, Mary, jt. ed. see Correard, Marie H.

O'Neill, Mary, tr. see Harnoncourt, Nikolaus.

O'Neill, Mary A. Religion Literacy Indicator. 1996. 9.95 (*1-55612-110-5*, SS1110) Sheed & Ward WI.

O'Neill, Mary B. Pearls of Faith. 1997. pap. write for info. (*1-57553-546-7*) Watermrk Pr.

***O'Neill, Mary Beth.** Executive Coaching with Backbone & Heart: A Systems Approach to Engaging Leaders with Their Challenges. LC 99-6928. (Business & Management Ser.). 272p. 2000. 30.00 (*0-7879-5016-5*, Pfffr & Co) Jossey-Bass.

O'Neill, Mary L. The Sound of Day: The Sound of Night. LC 98-24041. (Illus.). (J). 1999. write for info. (*0-7894-2567-X*) DK Pub Inc.

O'Neill, Matthew. The Seasons at Walden Inn: Signature Recipes from an Elegant Country Inn. 150p. 1999. 21.95 (*1-57860-004-9*) Guild Pr IN.

O'Neill, Maura. Women Speaking, Women Listening: Women in Interreligious Dialogue. LC 90-35123. (Faith Meets Faith Ser.). 143p. reprint ed. pap. 44.40 (*0-608-20246-0*, 207150500012) Bks Demand.

O'Neill-McGivern, Diane, jt. auth. see Mezey, Mathy D.

O'Neill, Michael. Green Parties & Political Change in Contemporary Europe: New Politics, Old Predicaments. LC 97-25958. 544p. 1997. 91.95 (*1-85521-786-4*, Pub. by Ashgate Pub); pap. 36.95 (*1-85521-790-2*, Pub. by Ashgate Pub) Ashgate Pub Co.

— The Human Mind's Imaginings: Conflict & Achievement in Shelley's Poetry. (Illus.). 232p. 1989. 70.00 (*0-19-811748-5*) OUP.

O'Neill, Michael. Keats: Bicentenary Readings. 208p. 1997. lib. bdg. 60.00 (*0-7486-0899-0*, Pub. by Edinburgh U Pr) Col U Pr.

O'Neill, Michael. Romanticism & the Self-Conscious Poem. LC 97-2025. 352p. 1997. text 75.00 (*0-19-812285-3*) OUP.

O'Neill, Michael, ed. Literature of the Romantic Period: A Bibliographical Guide. 418p. 1998. text 79.00 (*0-19-871120-4*) OUP.

— Literature of the Romantic Period: A Bibliographical Guide. 418p. 1998. pap. text 24.95 (*0-19-871121-2*) OUP.

— Politics of European Integration. 360p. (C). 1996. pap. 24.99 (*0-415-11298-2*) Routledge.

O'Neill, Michael, intro. Shelly. (Longman Critical Readers Ser.). (C). 1994. text 83.75 (*0-582-08668-X*) Longman.

O'Neill, Michael & Fletcher, Kathleen, eds. Nonprofit Management Education: U. S. & World Perspectives. LC 98-14904. 176p. 1998. 55.00 (*0-275-96115-X*, Praeger Pubs) Greenwood.

O'Neill, Michael & Odendahl, Teresa J., eds. Women & Power in the Nonprofit Sector. LC 93-47558. (Nonprofit Sector-Public Administration Ser.). 353p. 1994. text 36.95 (*1-55542-650-6*) Jossey-Bass.

O'Neill, Michael & Young, Dennis R., eds. Educating Managers of Nonprofit Organizations. LC 87-25869. 190p. 1988. 49.95 (*0-275-92609-5*, C2609, Praeger Pubs) Greenwood.

O'Neill, Michael, jt. auth. see Gallegos, Herman.

O'Neill, Michael, jt. ed. see Austin, Dennis.

O'Neill, Michael, ed. see Shelley, Percy Bysshe.

O'Neill, Michael E. & Chorlton, Frank. Ideal & Incompressible Fluid Dynamics. LC 85-30194. (Mathematics & Its Applications Ser.). 412p. 1986. text 99.95 (*0-470-20273-4*) P-H.

O'Neill, Michael E., jt. auth. see More, Harry W., Jr.

O'Neill, Michael E., jt. auth. see More, Harry W.

O'Neill, Michael J. Ergonomic Design for Organizational Effectiveness. LC 97-47028. 432p. 1998. boxed set 64.95 (*1-56670-252-6*) CRC Pr.

— Terrorist Spectaculars: Should TV Coverage Be Curbed? - A Twentieth Century Fund Paper. 109p. (Orig.). (C). 1986. pap. text 7.50 (*0-87078-202-9*) Century Foundation.

O'Neill, Michael T. A. P. Richardson: The Ethics of a Humanist, Original Anthology, Brief, Richard P., ed. LC 80-1461. (Dimensions of Accounting Theory & Practice Ser.). 1980. lib. bdg. 31.95 (*0-405-13483-5*) Ayer.

O'Neill, Michael W. & Dobry, Ricardo, eds. Dynamic Response of Pile Foundations: Analytical Aspects. LC 80-69151. 118p. 1980. pap. 13.00 (*0-87262-257-6*) Am Soc Civil Eng.

O'Neill, Michelle L. Creative Childbirth: The Leclaire Method of Easy Birthing Through Hypnosis & Rational-Intuitive Thought. LC 92-81691. (Illus.). 105p. (Orig.). 1993. pap. 11.95 (*0-9633087-3-4*) Papyrus Pr.

O'Neill, Mochael, ed. Politics of European Integration. 360p. (C). 1996. 90.00 (*0-415-11297-4*) Routledge.

O'Neill, Molly. A Feast of Irish Cooking. 96p. 1986. pap. 8.95 (*0-85105-450-1*, Pub. by Smyth) Dufour.

— New York Cookbook. LC 92-50280. (Illus.). 512p. 1992. pap. 17.95 (*0-89480-698-X*, 1698) Workman Pub.

— The Pleasure of Your Company. 1996. 26.95 (*0-614-19404-0*) Viking Penguin.

O'Neill, Nancy G., jt. auth. see Klingner, Donald E.

O'Neill, Nick & Handley, Robin. Retreat from Injustice: Human Rights in Australian Law. 544p. 1994. pap. 59.00 (*1-86287-121-3*, Pub. by Federation Pr) Gaunt.

***O'Neill, Onora.** Bounds of Justice. LC 99-56414. 226p. (C). 2000. write for info. (*0-521-44232-X*); pap. write for info. (*0-521-44744-5*) Cambridge U Pr.

O'Neill, Onora. Constructions of Reason: Explorations of Kant's Practical Philosophy. 261p. (C). 1990. text 69.95 (*0-521-38121-5*); pap. text 23.95 (*0-521-38816-3*) Cambridge U Pr.

— Towards Justice & Virtue: A Constructive Account of Practical Reasoning. 240p. (C). 1996. pap. text 18.95 (*0-521-48559-2*) Cambridge U Pr.

O'Neill, P., et al, eds. Microdosimetry: An Interdisciplinary Approach. 450p. 1997. 180.00 (*0-85404-737-9*) Am Chemical.

O'Neill, P., jt. ed. see Fielden, E. M.

O'Neill, P. G. Japanese Kana Workbook. 128p. 1973. pap. 10.00 (*0-87011-039-X*) Kodansha.

— Japanese Kana Workbook. LC 94-48166. 128p. 1995. pap. 9.95 (*0-8348-0337-2*) Weatherhill.

O'Neill, P. G., ed. Tradition & Modern Japan. 320p. (C). 1996. text 37.00 (*0-904404-36-6*, Pub. by Curzon Pr Ltd) UH Pr.

O'Neill, Paige J. Tips & Tales of the Tennis Court. LC 97-166864. (Illus.). 180p. (Orig.). 1995. pap. 9.95 (*0-9649392-0-7*) P ONeill.

***O'Neill, Pat.** From the Bottom Up: The Story of the Irish in Kansas City. LC 99-91486. (Illus.). 256p. 1999. pap. 25.95 (*0-9676375-0-3*) Seat-O-The-Pants.

O'Neill, Pat, jt. auth. see O'Neill, John.

O'Neill, Patricia, ed. Core Curriculum for Noenatal Intensive Care Nursing. 2nd ed. LC 99-25873. (Illus.). 735p. 1998. write for info. (*0-7216-7489-5*, W B Saunders Co) Harcrt Hlth Sci Grp.

O'Neill, Patrick. Acts of Narrative: Textual Strategies in Modern German Fiction. LC 97-102588. (Theory/Culture Ser.). 205p. 1996. text 45.00 (*0-8020-0982-4*) U of Toronto Pr.

— Alfred Doeblin's Babylonische Wanderung: A Study. (Canadian Studies in German Language & Literature: Vol. 13). 142p. 1974. 34.00 (*3-261-01014-2*) P Lang Pubng.

— The Comedy of Entropy: Humour, Narrative & Reading. 320p. 1990. text 50.00 (*0-8020-2737-7*) U of Toronto Pr.

— Fictions of Discourse: Reading Narrative Theory. (Theory/Culture Ser.). 190p. 1994. pap. text 16.95 (*0-8020-7948-2*) U of Toronto Pr.

— Fictions of Discourse: Reading Narrative Theory. (Theory/Culture Ser.). 190p. 1994. text 35.00 (*0-8020-0468-7*) U of Toronto Pr.

— Gunter Grass: A Bibliography, 1955-1975. LC 76-17278. 116p. reprint ed. pap. 36.00 (*0-608-12874-0*, 202365700033) Bks Demand.

— Gunter Grass Revisited. LC 98-33278. 1999. 32.00 (*0-8057-4571-8*, Twayne) Mac Lib Ref.

— Negotiating Consent in Psychotherapy. LC 98-25349. (Qualitative Studies in Psychology Ser.). 200p. 1998. text 55.00 (*0-8147-6194-1*); pap. text 18.50 (*0-8147-6195-X*) NYU Pr.

O'Neill, Patrick I. & Trickett, Edison J. Community Consultation. LC 82-48062. (Jossey-Bass Social & Behavioral Science Ser.). 307p. reprint ed. pap. 95.20 (*0-8357-4914-2*, 203784400009) Bks Demand.

O'Neill, Paul. Selling Services: Marketing for the Consulting Professional. 80p. 1999. pap. 14.95 (*1-55571-461-7*, SSRVP, Oasis Pr) PSI Resch.

O'Neill, Peter. Environmental Chemistry. (Illus.). 176p. (C). 1985. text 60.00 (*0-04-551085-7*); pap. text 19.95 (*0-04-551086-5*) Routledge.

***O'Neill, Peter.** Wolves Howling in the Land: A Tale of Chechnya. 350p. 2000. 24.95 (*1-885003-58-7*, Pub. by R D Reed Pubs) Midpt Trade.

O'Neill, Philip. Wilkie Collins: Women, Property & Propriety. 1988. 50.00 (*0-389-20771-3*) Rowman.

O'Neill, Philomena. Cat Story. LC 97-10045. 24p. 1999. 7.99 (*0-679-88537-4*, Pub. by Random Bks Yng Read) Random.

O'Neill, Pierre-George. Too Good to Be True: The Perils & Pitfalls of Work-at-Home Programs. 128p. (Orig.). 1990. pap. 12.95 (*0-9693942-0-9*, Pub. by Factfinder) Quality Bks IL.

O'Neill, R. Fourth Dimension. Date not set. pap. text, student ed. write for info. (*0-582-03182-6*, Pub. by Addison-Wesley); pap. text, student ed. write for info. (*0-582-91720-4*, Pub. by Addison-Wesley) Longman.

O'Neill, R., et al. T/M Amer Third Dimension. (Illus.). 1993. pap. text, teacher ed. 18.95 (*0-8013-0852-6*) Longman.

O'Neill, R. V., jt. ed. see Innis, G. S.

O'Neill, Reginald F. Theories of Knowledge: With a New Preface. 242p. 1980. reprint ed. text 32.50 (*0-8290-0227-8*); reprint ed. pap. text 18.95 (*0-8290-0386-X*) Irvington.

O'Neill, Reginald F., ed. Readings in Epistemology. LC 61-18427. 1979. reprint ed. pap. text 17.95 (*0-89197-604-3*) Irvington.

O'Neill, Richard. Suicide Squads. (Classic Conflicts Ser.). 1999. pap. text 16.95 (*1-84065-082-6*) Salamander.

O'Neill, Robert. The Cavalry Battles of Aldie, Middleburg & Upperville: Small but Important Riots, June 10 - 27, 1863. (Virginia Civil War Battles & Leaders Ser.). 1994. 19.95 (*1-56190-052-4*) H E Howard.

— Functional Analysis of Problem Behavior. (Special Education Ser.). 85p. 1993. pap. 25.95 (*0-534-21654-4*) Wadsworth Pub.

O'Neill, Robert, et al. AKL Beg Workbook. (English As a Second Language Bk.). 1981. pap. text, student ed. 8.95 (*0-582-79899-X*, 75132) Longman.

— American Kernel Lessons: Advanced Student Book. (Illus.). 142p. (Orig.). 1981. student ed. 8.95 incl. audio (*0-582-79764-0*, 75018) Longman.

— American Kernel Lessons: Advanced Student Book, No. 2. (Illus.). 142p. (Orig.). 1981. audio. write for info. (*0-582-79766-7*, 75020) Longman.

— American Kernel Lessons: Beginning Level, No. 2. (English As a Second Language Bk.). 1981. audio 69.95 (*0-582-79800-0*, 75054) Longman.

O'Neill, Robert, Jr., et al. American Kernel Lessons: Intermediate Level. (English As a Second Language Bk.). (Illus.). 1978. teacher ed. 8.95 (*0-582-79708-X*, 74975) Longman.

O'Neill, Robert, et al. American Kernel Lessons Beginning Tapescript for Lab Drills. (English As a Second Language Bk.). 1981. student ed. 8.95 incl. audio (*0-582-78342-9*, 74909) Longman.

O'Neill, Robert, Jr., et al. American Kernel Lessons Intermediate Tapescript for Lab Drills. (English As a Second Language Bk.). (Illus.). 1978. audio 8.95 (*0-582-79709-8*, 74976) Longman.

O'Neill, Robert, et al. Functional Analysis of Problem Behavior: A Practical Assessment Guide. Repp, Alan C. & Singh, Nirbhay N., eds. 85p. (C). 1990. pap. text 21.95 (*0-9625233-2-1*) Sycamore Pub.

O'Neill, Robert, jt. auth. see Brunelle, Wallace.

O'Neill, Robert, jt. auth. see LaPorte, Penny.

***O'Neill, Robert J. & Donahoe, Carol Cheney.** Focus on Luke: A Study Guide for Groups & Individuals. rev. ed. (Focus Bible Study Ser.: Vol. 3). 176p. 2000. pap. 11.95 (*1-889108-67-7*) Liv Good News.

O'Neill, Robert John, jt. ed. see Baylis, John.

O'Neill, Robert K. Archives, Museums, & Ancestoral Heritage Centres. LC 97-163682. 176p. 1997. pap. 14.00 (*0-901905-79-8*, Pub. by Ulster Hist Fnd) Irish Bks Media.

O'Neill, Robert K., compiled by. English-Language Dictionaries, Sixteen Hundred Four - Nineteen Hundred: The Catalog of the Warren N. & Suzanne B. Cordell Collection, 1. LC 87-35947. (Bibliographies & Indexes in Library & Information Science: No. 1). 509p. 1988. lib. bdg. 145.00 (*0-313-25522-9*, OEL/) Greenwood.

O'Neill, Robert K., ed. Management of Library & Archival Security: From the Outside Looking In. LC 98-4912. (Journal of Library Science). 120p. 1998. 29.95 (*0-7890-0519-0*) Haworth Pr.

O'Neill, Robert V. A Hierarchical Concept of Ecosystems. LC 86-9423. (Monographs in Population Biology: No. 23). (Illus.). 262p. reprint ed. pap. 81.30 (*0-608-20160-X*, 205444100011) Bks Demand.

O'Neill, Robin. The Weekend Chef: A New Approach to Everyday Cooking. (Illus.). 160p. 1999. pap. 12.95 (*1-55867-223-0*) Bristol Pub Ent CA.

— Wish You Were Here: France. 224p. (YA). 1996. mass mkt. 4.50 (*0-425-14944-7*) Berkley Pub.

— Wish You Were Here: Ireland. 224p. (YA). 1996. mass mkt. 4.50 (*0-425-15416-5*) Berkley Pub.

— Wish You Were Here: New Orleans. (YA). 1996. mass mkt. 4.50 (*0-425-14984-6*) Berkley Pub.

O'Neill, Roger A., jt. ed. see Khan, Shaheer H.

O'Neill, Rosary H. The Actor's Checklist. 256p. (C). 1992. pap. text 20.00 (*0-03-073142-9*, Pub. by Harcourt Coll Pubs) Harcourt.

O'Neill, Rowan. The Making of a Seaman. 3rd ed. (Illus.). 164p. 1982. pap. 2.95 (*0-933704-45-3*) Dawn Pr.

— The Making of a Seaman. 4th ed. (Illus.). 164p. 1988. pap. 5.95 (*0-933704-53-4*) Dawn Pr.

O'Neill, Scott L., et al, eds. Influential Passengers: Inherited Microorganisms & Arthropod Reproduction. LC 97-18603. (Illus.). 226p. 1998. text 95.00 (*0-19-857786-9*); pap. text 45.00 (*0-19-850173-0*) OUP.

O'Neill, Sean P., jt. ed. see Golla, Victor.

O'Neill, Shane. Impartiality in Context: Grounding Justice in a Pluralist World. LC 96-34723. (SUNY Series in Social & Political Thought). 288p. (C). 1997. text 57.50 (*0-7914-3387-0*); pap. text 18.95 (*0-7914-3388-9*) State U NY Pr.

O'Neill, Sharon G. Lurning: 147 Inspiring Thoughts for Learning on the Job. LC 93-1277. 93p. 1993. pap. 7.95 (*0-89815-536-3*) Ten Speed Pr.

O'Neill, Stephan D., jt. ed. see Bilby, Joseph G.

O'Neill, Susan, jt. auth. see Nobles, Robin.

O'Neill, Suzanne B. & Sparkman, Catherine G. From Law School to Law Practice: The New Associate's Guide. LC 89-80281. 286p. 1989. text 83.00 (*0-8318-0593-5*, B593) Am Law Inst.

— From Law School to Law Practice: The New Associate's Guide. 2nd ed. LC 98-87077. xix, 298 p. 1998. 65.00 (*0-8318-0765-2*) Am Law Inst.

O'Neill, Teresa. The Homeless: Distinguishing Between Fact & Opinion. LC 90-45283. (Opposing Viewpoints Juniors Ser.). (Illus.). 36p. (J). (gr. 3-6). 1990. lib. bdg. 16.20 (*0-89908-605-5*) Greenhaven.

O'Neill, Teresa, ed. Immigration: Opposing Viewpoints. LC 92-21794. (American History Ser.). 312p. (YA). 1992. pap. 16.20 (*1-56510-006-9*); lib. bdg. 26.20 (*1-56510-007-7*) Greenhaven.

O'Neill, Terry. Constantine's Circus. 61p. (YA). (gr. 8-10). 1995. pap. 14.95 (*0-9649322-0-2*) Tom Tyger.

***O'Neill, Terry.** Gun Control. LC 99-48707. (Opposing Viewpoints Digests Ser.). (Illus.). 144p. (YA). (gr. 6-10). 2000. pap. text 14.95 (*1-56510-878-7*); lib. bdg. 23.70 (*1-56510-879-5*) Greenhaven.

— Readings on "To Kill a Mockingbird" (Literary Companion Ser.). 224p. (YA). (gr. 9-11). 2000. pap. 17.45 (*1-56510-575-3*) Greenhaven.

— Readings on "To Kill a Mockingbird" (Literary Companion Ser.). 127p. (YA). (gr. 9-12). 2000. lib. bdg. 27.45 (*1-56510-576-1*) Greenhaven.

O'Neill, Terry. Zoos: Identifying Propaganda Techniques. LC 90-3247. (Opposing Viewpoints Juniors Ser.). (Illus.). 36p. (J). (gr. 3-6). 1990. pap. text 16.20 (*0-89908-600-4*) Greenhaven.

O'Neill, Terry, ed. All Quiet on the Western Front. LC 98-33585. (Literary Companion Ser.). 128p. (YA). (gr. 9-12). 1998. pap. 17.45 (*1-56510-824-8*); lib. bdg. 27.45 (*1-56510-825-6*) Greenhaven.

— Animal Farm. (Literary Companion Ser.). 144p. (YA). (gr. 7 up). 1997. pap. 13.96 (*1-56510-650-4*); lib. bdg. 20.96 (*1-56510-651-2*) Greenhaven.

— Biomedical Ethics: Opposing Viewpoints. LC 93-7260. 312p. 1994. pap. 16.20 (*1-56510-061-1*); lib. bdg. 26.20 (*1-56510-062-X*) Greenhaven.

O'Neill, Terry, ed. Out of Time & Place: Amazing Accounts That Challenge Our View of Human History. LC 98-33309. (Illus.). 272p. 1999. 9.95 (*1-56718-261-5*) Llewellyn Pubns.

O'Neill, Terry, ed. see Behr, Ashley F.

O'Neill, Thomas. Lakes, Peaks, & Prairies: Discovering the United States-Canadian Border. Crump, Donald J., ed. LC 84-22775. (Special Publications Series 19: No. 3). (Illus.). 200p. 1984. 12.95 (*0-87044-478-6*); lib. bdg. 12.95 (*0-87044-483-2*) Natl Geog.

O'Neill, Thomas J., jt. auth. see Gentry, Donald W.

O'Neill, Thomas P., jt. auth. see Longford, Frank P.

O'Neill, Tim. Airy Plumeflights: A Beginner's Guide to Celtic Script & Design. LC 95-101894. (Illus.). 48p. (Orig.). 1994. pap. 11.95 (*1-874675-35-X*, Pub. by Lilliput Pr) Irish Bks Media.

O'Neill, Timothy. Irish Hand: Scribes & Their Manuscripts from the Earliest Times. (Illus.). 128p. 1984. 40.00 (*0-85105-411-0*, Pub. by Smyth) Dufour.

— Merchants & Mariners in Medieval Ireland. LC 87-180747. 164p. 1987. write for info. (*0-7165-2399-X*) Intl Spec Bk.

— Merchants & Mariners in Medieval Ireland. (Illus.). 164p. 1987. 25.00 (*0-7165-2398-1*, Pub. by Irish Acad Pr) Intl Spec Bk.

O'Neill, Timothy J. Bakke & the Politics of Equality: Friends & Foes in the Classroom of Litigation. LC 83-26122. 344p. 1985. reprint ed. pap. 106.70 (*0-608-02296-9*, 206293700004) Bks Demand.

O'Neill, Timothy P., jt. auth. see Nolan, William.

O'Neill, Tip & Hymel, Gary. All Politics Is Local: And Other Rules of the Game. 1995. pap. 7.95 (*1-55850-470-2*) Adams Media.

O'Neill, Tom, ed. The Shared Horizon. 216p. 1989. 39.50 (*0-7165-2414-7*, Pub. by Irish Acad Pr) Intl Spec Bk.

O'Neill, Vincent, ed. see Kelly, Joseph M.

O'Neill, Vincent J., Jr. O'Neill's California Confessions Law: A Comprehensive Outline, Including Detailed Summaries of All Relevant State & Federal Decisions & Statutes. 1993. ring bd. 124.95 (*1-883952-09-3*) Hse of Steno.

O'Neill, W. Charles. Atlas of Renal Ultrasonography. (Illus.). 255p. Date not set. text. write for info. (*0-7216-8913-2*, W B Saunders Co) Harcrt Hlth Sci Grp.

O'Neill, William. The Ethics of Our Climate: Hermeneutics & Ethical Theory. 160p. 1994. 40.00 (*0-87840-565-8*) Georgetown U Pr.

***O'Neill, William.** 24 Essential Lessons for Investment Success: Learn the Most Important Investment Techniques form the Founder of Investor's Business Daily. (Illus.). 176p. 1999. pap. 10.95 (*0-07-135754-8*) McGraw.

O'Neill, William, ed. see Doggett, Martha.

O'Neill, William G., ed. see Ross, James D.

O'Neill, William J., Jr., ed. Family - The First Imperative: A Symposium in Search of Root Causes of Family Strength & Family Disintegration. LC 95-71661. 344p. 1995. pap. 12.00 (*0-9649220-0-2*) ONeill Fnd.

O'Neill, William J., Jr., ed, see Campbell, John H.

O'Neill, William L. American High: The Years of Confidence, 1945-1960. 336p. 1989. pap. 14.95 (*0-02-923679-7*) Free Pr.

— A Better World: Stalinism & the American Intellectuals. 464p. 1989. pap. 24.95 (*0-88738-631-8*) Transaction Pubs.

— Coming Apart: An Informal History of America in the 1960's. LC 79-152098. (Illus.). 480p. 1974. reprint ed. write for info. (*0-8129-0190-8*, Times Bks); reprint ed. pap. 16.00 (*0-8129-6223-0*, Times Bks) Crown Pub Group.

— A Democracy at War: America's Fight at Home & Abroad in World War II. (Illus.). 512p. (C). 1995. pap. 17.95 (*0-674-19737-2*) HUP.

— Divorce in the Progressive Era. LC 67-24507. 309p. reprint ed. pap. 95.80 (*0-608-10707-7*, 202202500024) Bks Demand.

— Feminism in America: A History. 2nd rev. ed. 408p. 1994. pap. 24.95 (*0-88738-761-6*) Transaction Pubs.

— The Great Schism: Stalinism & the American Intellectuals. (Illus.). 447p. 17.95 (*0-686-43340-8*) S&S Trade.

— The Last Romantic: A Life of Max Eastman. 350p. (C). 1990. pap. 24.95 (*0-88738-859-0*) Transaction Pubs.

— Women at Work. LC 72-182506. 384p. 1972. pap. 4.95 (*0-8129-6237-0*, Times Bks) Crown Pub Group.

— World War II: A Student Companion. LC D743.7.O49 1999. (Student Companions to American History Ser.). (Illus.). 384p. (YA). (gr. 7 up). 1999. text 40.00 (*0-19-510800-0*) OUP.

O'Neill, William L., ed. Echoes of Revolt: The Masses 1911-1917. (Illus.). 304p. 1989. reprint ed. pap. text 18.95 (*0-929587-15-4*, Elephant Paperbacks) I R Dee.

O'Neill, Ynez V. Speech & Speech Disorders in Western Thought Before 1600, 3. LC 79-7361. (Contributions in Medical History Ser.: No. 3). 246p. 1980. 55.00 (*0-313-21058-6*, OSD, Greenwood Pr) Greenwood.

O'Neill, Theresa Deleane. Disciplined Hearts: History, Identity & Depression in an American Indian Community. LC 95-35126. (Illus.). 265p. (C). 1996. 40.00 (*0-520-20229-5*, Pub. by U CA Pr) Cal Prin Full Svc.

— Disciplined Hearts: History, Identity & Depression in an American Indian Community. (Illus.). 265p. 1998. pap. 18.95 (*0-520-21446-3*, Pub. by U CA Pr) Cal Prin Full Svc.

Onen, H. Dictionnaire de la Medecine du Sommeil. (FRE.). 1998. 59.95 (*0-320-00245-4*) Fr & Eur.

Onenko, S. N. Nanaisk-Russian Dictionary. (RUS.). 1980. 24.95 (*0-8288-1627-1*, F47740) Fr & Eur.

O'Neoill. Third Dimension. Date not set. pap. text, teacher ed. write for info. (*0-582-01720-3*, Pub. by Addison-Wesley) Longman.

O

***Oness, C. Mikal.** Water Becomes Bone. 2000. pap. 12.00 (*0-932826-89-X*) WMU Poetry & Prose.

***Oness, Elizabeth.** Articles of Faith. (Iowa Short Fiction Award Ser.). 152p. 2000. pap. 14.95 (*0-87745-726-3*) U of Iowa Pr.

Onet, Ionel. ABC de Esperanto. (RUM.). 15p. 1994. pap. 1.00 (*1-882251-08-3*) Eldonejo Bero.

***Onet, Ionel.** Documente Esperanto, No. 3. Vlad, Sasha, ed. & tr. by. from ENG.Tr. of Esperanto documents. (RUM.). 44p. 1999. mass mkt. 4.25 (*1-882251-17-2*) Eldonejo Bero.

Onet, Ionel. Primii Pasi in Esperanto. (RUM.). 68p. 1993. pap. text 5.00 (*1-882251-03-2*) Eldonejo Bero.

— Usono Nigre-Blanke. (ESP., Illus.). 110p. 1998. pap. 8.30 (*1-882251-26-1*) Eldonejo Bero.

Onet, Ionel, ed. & intro. see Sylva, Carmen.

Onet, Ionel, tr. see Brancusi, Constantin.

Onet, Ionel, tr. see Naum, Gellu.

Onet, Ionel, tr. & intro. see Canache, George, et al.

Onetti, Juan Carlos. Brief Life. (Extraordinary Classics Ser.). 300p. 1994. pap. 15.99 (*1-85242-301-3*) Serpents Tail.

— Cuando Ya No Importe (When It Matters No More) 218p. 1995. pap. 14.95 (*0-679-76094-6*) Vin Bks.

***Onetti, Juan Carlos.** Cuentos Completos, Onetti. LC 94-202133. (SPA.). 1998. pap. 21.95 (*84-204-8117-3*) Santillana.

Onetti, Juan Carlos. Let the Wind Speak. Lane, Helen, tr. from SPA. (Extraordinary Classics Ser.). (SPA.). 288p. (Orig.). (C). 1997. pap. 15.99 (*1-85242-196-7*) Serpents Tail.

— Shipyard. (Extraordinary Classics Ser.). 192p. 1993. pap. 14.99 (*1-85242-191-6*) Serpents Tail.

***Oneworld Publications Staff.** Wisdom of the Quran. 2000. 15.95 (*1-85168-224-4*, Pub. by Onewrld Pubns) Penguin Putnam.

***Oney, Walter.** Programming the Microsoft Windows Driver Model. LC 99-33878. (C). (gr. 8). 1999. pap. 49.99 (*0-7356-0588-2*) Microsoft.

Ong. The Practice of Health Services Research. 174p. 1993. pap. 54.25 (*1-56593-214-5*, 0567) Singular Publishing.

Ong & Ochuizzo. Crosscurrents Activity, Bk. 2. 1996. pap. text. write for info. (*0-582-07621-8*, Pub. by Addison-Wesley) Longman.

Ong, A. S. & Packer, Lester, eds. Lipid-Soluble Antioxidants: Biochemistry & Clinical Applications. LC 92-49649. (Molecular & Cell Biology Updates Ser.). xii, 640p. 1992. 165.00 (*0-8176-2667-0*, Pub. by Birkhauser) Princeton Arch.

Ong, A. S., jt. auth. see Niki, E.

Ong, Aihwa. Flexible Citizenship: The Cultural Logics of Transnationality. LC 98-33678. 1998. pap. 17.95 (*0-8223-2269-2*); lib. bdg. 49.95 (*0-8223-2250-1*) Duke.

— Spirits of Resistance & Capitalist Discipline: Factory Women in Malaysia. LC 86-22980. (SUNY Series in the Anthropology of Work). 268p. (C). 1987. text 59.50 (*0-88706-380-2*); pap. text 19.95 (*0-88706-381-0*) State U NY Pr.

Ong, Aihwa, ed. Ungrounded Empires: The Cultural Politics of Modern Chinese Transnationalism. 352p. (C). 1996. 80.00 (*0-415-91542-2*); pap. 23.99 (*0-415-91543-0*) Routledge.

Ong, Aihwa & Peletz, Michael G., eds. Bewitching Women, Pious Men: Gender & Body Politics in Southeast Asia. LC 94-22740. (Illus.). 314p. 1995. 50.00 (*0-520-08860-3*, Pub. by U CA Pr); pap. 17.95 (*0-520-08861-1*, Pub. by U CA Pr) Cal Prin Full Svc.

Ong, Andy, jt. auth. see Douglas, Peter.

Ong, Augustine S., jt. ed. see Packer, Lester.

Ong, Bie N. Rapid Appraisal & Health Policy. (Illus.). 152p. (Orig.). 1996. pap. 49.95 (*1-56593-736-8*, 1432) Singular Publishing.

Ong, Chee-Mun. Dynamic Simulations of Electric Machinery. LC 97-20313. 688p. (C). 1997. 94.00 (*0-13-723785-5*) P-H.

Ong, Chin K. & Huxley, P. A., eds. Tree-Crop Interactions: A Physiological Approach. LC 97-117527. 408p. 1996. pap. text 50.00 (*0-85198-987-X*) OUP.

Ong, Colin. Cross-Border Litigation within ASEAN: The Prospect for Harmonization of Civil & Commercial Litigation. LC 97-8399. 828p. 1997. 232.00 (*90-411-0396-1*) Kluwer Academic.

***Ong, Cristina.** Colors: The Little Engine That Could, 1 vol. (Illus.). 24p. (ps). 1999. bds. 1.99 (*0-448-41971-8*) Putnam Pub Group.

Ong, Cristina. Little Engine That Could. (Wee Sing Ser.). (Illus.). 12p. (J). 1998. mass mkt. 9.99 incl. audio (*0-8431-7837-X*) Putnam Pub Group.

***Ong, Cristina.** Little Engine That Could Helps Out, 1 vol. 32p. (ps-1). 1999. pap. text 3.99 (*0-448-41973-4*) Putnam Pub Group.

— Numbers: The Little That Could, 1 vol. (Illus.). 24p. (ps). 1999. bds. 1.99 (*0-448-41972-6*) Putnam Pub Group.

Ong, Cristina. Tub Time: With the Little Engine That Could, 1, 10p. (ps). 1999. pap. text 4.99 (*0-448-42052-X*) Putnam Pub Group.

Ong, Cristina. The Little Engine That Could Let's Sing ABC. 24p. (J). (ps). 1993. 12.95 (*0-448-40509-1*, Plat & Munk) Peng Put Young Read.

— The Little Engine That Could Pudgy Word Book. (Pudgy Board Bks.). 18p. (J). (ps up). 1988. bds. 3.99 (*0-448-19054-0*, Plat & Munk) Peng Put Young Read.

— The Little Engine That Could Rides Again. (Sticker Stories Ser.). 16p. (J). (ps-1). 1996. pap. text 4.99 (*0-448-41145-8*, G & D) Peng Put Young Read.

Ong, Editha & Ciuffreda, Kenneth J. Accommodation Nearwork & Myopia. LC 96-51078. (Illus.). (C). 1997. lib. bdg. 21.00 (*0-943599-88-1*) OEPF.

Ong, Helen. Amal & the Letter from the King. (Illus.). (J). 1995. 16.95 (*1-85430-290-6*) Magi Pubns.

Ong, Helen, jt. auth. see Gajadin, Chitra.

Ong Jin Hui, et al, eds. Understanding Singapore Society. LC 97-945801. 608p. 1997. pap. 29.00 (*981-210-052-0*, Pub. by Times Academic) Intl Spec Bk.

Ong, L. S., jt. auth. see Cheung, J. S.

Ong, Lina, ed. Burma Studies Issue. (Crossroads Ser.: Ser. 4.1). 151p. 1988. pap. 12.00 (*1-877979-88-0*) SE Asia.

Ong, Paul, ed. The Impact of Affirmative Action: Policies & Consequences in California. LC 99-6108. 224p. 1999. pap. 23.95 (*0-7619-9056-9*) AltaMira Pr.

***Ong, Paul, ed.** The Impact of Affirmative Action: Policies & Consequences in California. LC 99-6108. 224p. 1999. 62.00 (*0-7619-9055-0*) AltaMira Pr.

Ong, Paul & Hee, Suzanne. Losses in the Los Angeles Civil Unrest, April 29-May 1, 1992: Lists of the Damaged Properties & Korean Merchants & the L. A. Riot - Rebellion. 138p. 1993. pap. 6.95 (*1-883191-00-9*) U CA Ctr Pac Rim.

***Ong, Paul M., ed.** The State of Asian Pacific America: Transforming Race Relations. 507p. 2000. pap. 20.00 (*0-934052-33-6*) UCLA Asian Am Studies Ctr.

Ong, S. H. A Strategy for a Metaphorical Reading of the Epistle of James. 194p. (Orig.). (C). 1995. pap. text 26.00 (*0-7618-0150-2*); lib. bdg. 51.00 (*0-7618-0149-9*) U Pr of Amer.

Ong, Walter J. American Catholic Crossroads: Religious-Secular Encounters in the Modern World. LC 80-29660. 160p. 1981. reprint ed. lib. bdg. 55.00 (*0-313-22467-6*, 0NAM, Greenwood Pr) Greenwood.

— Hopkins, the Self & God. 194p. 1986. text 32.50 (*0-8020-5688-1*) U of Toronto Pr.

— Hopkins, the self & God. 194p. 1986. pap. text 17.95 (*0-8020-7413-8*) U of Toronto Pr.

— Orality & Literacy: The Technologizing of the World. 212p. 1982. pap. 18.99 (*0-415-02796-9*, NO. 6526) Routledge.

— Ramus, Method, & the Decay of Dialogue: From the Art of Discourse to the Art of Reason. 432p. 1983. pap. 16.50 (*0-674-74802-6*) HUP.

Ong, Walter J., ed. see Ramus, Petrus.

Onge, Ronald, et al. Interaction Text/Audio CD Package. 5th ed. 409p. pap. 52.95 (*0-8384-1018-9*, Pub. by Heinle & Heinle) Thomson Learn.

***Ongile, Grace Atieno.** Gender & Agricultural Supply Responses to Structural Adjustment Programs. LC 99-212250. 186p. 1999. pap. 16.95 (*91-7106-440-0*) Almqvist Wiksell.

***Ongman, Gudrun Geibel.** The Sleep Ponies. LC 00-90088. (Illus.). 32p. (J). 2000. 16.95 (*0-9677204-0-0*) Mindcastle Bks.

Ongong'a, Jude J. & Gray, Kenneth R., eds. Bottlenecks to National Identity: Ethnic Co-Operation Towards Nation Building. 142p. 1989. pap. text 9.95 (*9966-835-24-5*) Prof World Peace.

OnGuard Inc. Staff. Fire Attack: Strategy & Tactics of Initial Company Response. 120p. 1987. pap. text 13.95 (*1-56916-001-5*); teacher ed., ring bd. 35.95 (*1-56916-002-3*) OnGuard.

— Hazardous Materials Emergency Response Handbook. 1995. pap. 69.95 (*0-614-03568-6*, VNR) Wiley.

OnGUARD Inc. Staff. Hazardous Materials Handbook for Emergency Responders. Varela, Joe, ed. (Industrial Health & Safety Ser.). 552p. 1995. 99.95 (*0-471-28713-X*, VNR) Wiley.

OnGuard Inc. Staff. Making a Difference: The Fire Officer's Role. 232p. 1988. pap. text, student ed. 14.95 (*1-56916-110-0*); teacher ed., ring bd. 35.95 (*1-56916-111-9*) OnGuard.

— Recruiting, Training & Maintaining Volunteer Firefighters: The Volunteer Firefighter: A Breed Apart Resource Manual. 264p. 1993. student ed., ring bd. 16.95 (*1-56916-057-0*) OnGuard.

— Silent War: Infection Control for Emergency Responders. (Student Textbook Ser.). 232p. 1992. pap. text, student ed. 13.95 (*1-56916-403-7*); teacher ed., ring bd. 35.95 (*1-56916-402-9*) OnGuard.

— Silent War: Infection Control for Law Enforcement. Peterson, Susan, ed. (Illus.). 144p. 1996. pap. text 7.95 (*1-56916-710-9*, 40SWP) OnGuard.

— Silent War: Infection Control for Law Enforcement: Post-Incident Procedures. (Illus.). 116p. 1993. teacher ed., ring bd. 30.95 (*1-56916-709-5*) OnGuard.

— Silent War: Infection Control for Law Enforcement: Reducing Your Risk. (Illus.). 59p. 1993. teacher ed., ring bd. 30.95 (*1-56916-706-0*) OnGuard.

— Silent War: Infection Control for Law Enforcement: Understanding Contagious Diseases. (Illus.). 53p. 1993. teacher ed., ring bd. 30.95 (*1-56916-703-6*) OnGuard.

OnGuard Inc. Staff & Bruegman, Randy R. Surviving the Hazardous Materials Incident, Pt. 1. 3rd ed. Varela, Joe R. & Peterson, Susan, eds. 304p. 1996. pap. text, student ed. 13.95 (*1-56916-200-X*, 20HAZ P1) OnGuard.

— Surviving the Hazardous Materials Incident, Pt. 2. 2nd ed. Varela, Joe R. & Peterson, Susan, eds. 288p. 1995. pap. text 13.95 (*1-56916-213-1*) OnGuard.

OnGUARD Staff. Hazardous Materials Emergency Response Handbook. Varela, Joe, ed. (Industrial Health & Safety Ser.). 544p. 1995. text 76.95 (*0-442-02104-6*, VNR) Wiley.

Ongwamuhana, Kibuta. The Taxation of Income from Foreign Investments: A Tax Study of Developing Countries. 156p. 1991. pap. 40.00 (*90-6544-542-0*) Kluwer Law Intl.

Onheiber, Marissa & Swanson, Vern G. Historic Treasures: Utopian Spirit Russian Impressionism, 1930-1980s. (Illus.). 95p. 1998. pap. 20.00 (*0-9617882-7-5*) FFCA Pub.

***Oni-Eseleh, Ohiro D.** In Pursuit of Dreams: The Truth about Immigration. LC 99-67378. 190p. 1999. pap. 14.95 (*1-893162-04-4*) Erica Hse.

— Thy Will Not Mine: Accepting the Will of God. 2000. pap. 7.99 (*0-615-11303-6*) Choice Pub.

Oni, Lola, et al. Care & Management of People with Sickle Cell & Thalassaemia. (Illus.). 288p. 2000. pap. text 55.00 (*0-7506-3000-0*) Buttrwrth-Heinemann.

Oni, Olusola O. Who Should Run the Health Service? Realignment & Reconstruction. LC 96-33577. 1996. write for info. (*1-85775-169-8*, Radcliffe Med Pr) Scovill Paterson.

Oni, Sauda. What Kwanzaa Means to Me. (Illus.). 36p. (J). (gr. k-3). 1992. pap. 3.95 (*0-912444-38-X*) DARE Bks.

Onians, Dick. Essential Woodcarving Techniques. LC 97-198856. (Illus.). 192p. 1997. pap. text 17.95 (*1-86108-042-5*, Pub. by Guild Master) Sterling.

Onians, John. Bearers of Meaning: The Classical Orders in Antiquity, the Middle Ages, & the Renaissance. (Illus.). 400p. (Orig.). 1989. pap. text 35.00 (*0-691-00219-3*, Pub. by Princeton U Pr) Cal Prin Full Svc.

— Classical Art & the Cultures of Greece & Rome. LC 98-43738. (Illus.). 306p. 1999. 50.00 (*0-300-07533-2*) Yale U Pr.

Onians, John. Sight & Insight: Essays on Art & Culture in Honor of E. H. Gombrich at 85. LC 94-192568. (Illus.). 420p. (C). 1994. text 59.95 (*0-7148-2971-4*, Pub. by Phaidon Press) Phaidon Pr.

Onians, Richard B. The Origins of European Thought About the Body, the Mind, the Soul, the World, Time, & Fate. LC 72-9298. (Philosophy of Plato & Aristotle Ser.). 1980. reprint ed. 43.95 (*0-405-04853-X*) Ayer.

— The Origins of European Thought about the Body, the Mind, the Soul, the World, Time, & Fate: New Interpretations of Greek, Roman, & Kindred Evidence, Also of Some Basic Jewish & Christian Beliefs. 2nd ed. (Illus.). 608p. 1988. pap. text 32.95 (*0-521-34794-7*) Cambridge U Pr.

Onicescu, O. Invariantive Mechanics. (International Centre for Mechanical Sciences Ser.: No. 218). 1976. 27.95 (*0-387-81349-7*) Spr-Verlag.

O'Niel, Charles J., ed. An Etienne Gilson Tribute. LC 59-8092. 355p. reprint ed. pap. 110.10 (*0-608-10156-7*, 201201500081) Bks Demand.

O'Niell, John, ed. Modes of Individualism & Collectivism. (Modern Revivals in Philosophy Ser.). 368p. 1993. 72.95 (*0-7512-0050-6*, Pub. by Gregg Pub) Ashgate Pub Co.

O'Niell, Terry, jt. ed. see Swisher, Karin L.

Onieva, Antonio. Diccionario Multiple. 4th ed. (SPA.). 1987. write for info. (*0-7859-3678-5*, 8428304009) Fr & Eur.

— Lengua Espanola. 299p. 1969. 9.95 (*0-8288-7480-8*) Fr & Eur.

Onieva Morales, Juan L. Curso de Comunicacion Activa: Desarrollo de las Destrezas Basicas del Espanol. 9th ed. (SPA.). 312p. (C). 1991. reprint ed. pap. text 14.95 (*1-56328-009-4*) Edit Plaza Mayor.

Onieva-Morales, Juan L. Intercomunicacion, Supplement No. 1: Curso Basico para el Aprendizaje Activo del Espanol. 13th ed. (Textbook Ser.). (SPA.). 260p. (Orig.). (C). 1991. reprint ed. pap. text 14.95 (*1-56328-001-9*) Edit Plaza Mayor.

— Intercomunicacion, Supplement No. 2: Curso Basico para el Aprendizaje Activo del Espanol. 10th ed. (Textbook Ser.). (SPA.). 216p. (Orig.). (C). 1991. reprint ed. pap. text 14.95 (*1-56328-002-7*) Edit Plaza Mayor.

— Introduccion a los Generos Literarios a Traves del Comentario de Textos. 3rd ed. (SPA.). 372p. (C). 1993. pap. text 14.95 (*1-56328-036-1*) Edit Plaza Mayor.

Onik, Gary M., et al, eds. Percutaneous Prostate Cryoablation. LC 94-34029. (Illus.). 172p. 1994. text 75.00 (*0-942219-66-X*) Quality Med Pub.

Onik, Gary M., ed. see Morris, D. L., et al.

Onion, Cathy, jt. auth. see Taylor, Gordy.

Onion, Daniel K. The Little Black Book of Primary Care: Pearls & References. 2nd ed. 600p. (C). 1995. pap. write for info. (*0-393-71024-6*) Norton.

— The Little Black Book of Primary Care: Pearls & References. 3rd ed. LC 98-17781. 700p. 1996. spiral bd. 34.95 (*0-86542-489-6*) Blackwell Sci.

— The Little Black Book of Primary Care: Pearls & References. 3rd ed. LC 98-17781. (Little Black Book Ser.). (Illus.). 923p. 1998. pap. 39.95 (*0-632-04345-8*) Blackwell Sci.

Onion, Susan. Beverly Cleary. (Favorite Authors Ser.). (Illus.). 1994. 11.95 (*1-55734-457-4*) Tchr Create Mat.

— Big Wave. 1998. pap. 7.95 (*1-55734-616-X*) Tchr Create Mat.

— The Cricket in Times Square: A Literature Unit. (Literature Units Ser.). (Illus.). 48p. (Orig.). 1993. pap., student ed. 7.95 (*1-55734-419-1*) Tchr Create Mat.

Onion, Susan, et al. Survival. (Interdisciplinary Units Ser.). 1995. pap. text 14.95 (*1-55734-604-6*) Tchr Create Mat.

Onion Writers Staff, jt. auth. see Dikkers, Scott.

Onions, A. H., jt. ed. see Smith, D.

Onions, Charles T. A Shakespeare Glossary. 3rd enl. rev. ed. Eagleson, Robert D., ed. 342p. 1986. pap. text 17.95 (*0-19-812521-6*) OUP.

Onions, Charles T., et al, eds. Oxford Dictionary of English Etymology. 1,042p. 1966. 65.00 (*0-19-861112-9*) OUP.

Onions, H. S., jt. auth. see Smith, D.

Onions, Oliver. A Case in Camera. 320p. 1980. reprint ed. lib. bdg. 19.95 (*0-89968-205-7*, Lghtyr Pr) Buccaneer Bks.

— Widdershins. 1993. reprint ed. lib. bdg. 18.95 (*0-89968-438-6*, Lghtyr Pr) Buccaneer Bks.

Onipko, Alexander I., tr. see Ostapenko, N. I., et al.

Onischchik, A. L. & Vinberg, Ernst B., eds. Lie Groups & Lie Algebra Three: Structure of Lie Groups & Lie Algebras. LC 93-33446. (Encyclopedia of Mathematical Sciences Ser.: Vol. 41). 1994. write for info. (*0-387-54683-9*) Spr-Verlag.

Onischenko, George T., tr. see Blinkov, Samuil Mikha'ilovich & Smirnov, N. A.

***Onish, Liane.** The Alphabet Eurps & the 4 Seasons. (Eurps Concept Bks.). (Illus.). (J). 1999. 7.95 (*1-892522-08-X*) Eurpsville USA.

— The Alphabet Eurps Build Eurpsville. (Eurps Concept Bks.). (Illus.). (J). 1999. 7.95 (*1-892522-05-5*) Eurpsville USA.

— Alphabet Eurps Meet Bipple. (Eurps Concept Bks.). (Illus.). (J). 1999. 7.95 (*1-892522-03-9*) Eurpsville USA.

— The Alphabet Eurps on the Farm. (Illus.). (J). 1999. 7.95 (*1-892522-07-1*) Eurpsville USA.

— The Alphabet Eurps Ride a Rainbow. (Eurps Concept Bks.). (Illus.). (J). 1999. 7.95 (*1-892522-06-3*) Eurpsville USA.

— The Alphabet Eurps Visit School. (Eurps Concept Bks.). (Illus.). 32p. (J). 1999. 7.95 (*1-892522-04-7*) Eurpsville USA.

Onish, Liane. Doug's Word Book. LC PE1449.O56 1999. (Doug Ser.). 48p. (J). 1999. 9.99 (*0-7364-0021-4*, Pub. by Mouse Works) Time Warner.

***Onish, Liane.** Kindergarten: Math Readiness. (Jumpstart Ser.). (Illus.). 32p. 2000. pap. text 3.99 (*0-439-16419-2*) Scholastic Inc.

— Kindergarten: Reading Readiness. (Illus.). 2000. pap. text 3.99 (*0-439-16420-6*) Scholastic Inc.

— Lowercase Letters. (Jumpstart Workbooks Ser.). (Illus.). (J). (ps-k). 2000. pap. text 3.99 (*0-439-16418-4*) Scholastic Inc.

Onish, Liane. Mickey Mouse's Bedtime Stories Picture Book. (Illus.). (J). 1999. 12.99 (*0-7364-0030-3*, Pub. by Mouse Works) Time Warner.

***Onish, Liane B.** Fairy Tale Theater: The Story of Rapunzel. (Little Golden Bks.). (Illus.). 24p. (J). 1998. 2.29 (*0-307-98290-4*, 98290, Goldn Books) Gldn Bks Pub Co.

Onishchik, A. I. & Vinberg, E. B., eds. Lie Groups & Lie Algebras No. II: Discrete Subgroups of Lie Groups, Cohomologies of Lie Groups & Lie Algebras. (Encyclopedia of Mathematical Sciences Ser.: Vol. 21). 230p. 2000. 95.00 (*3-540-50585-7*) Spr-Verlag.

Onishchik, A. L. Foundations of Lie Theory & Lie Transformation Groups. LC 98-193499. 235p. 1997. pap. text 54.50 (*3-540-61222-X*) Spr-Verlag.

Onishchik, A. L., ed. Lie Groups & Lie Algebras I. LC 92-21600. (Encyclopedia of Mathematical Sciences Ser.: Vol. 20). 1993. 118.95 (*0-387-18697-2*) Spr-Verlag.

Onishchik, A. L. & Vinberg, Ernst B. Lie Groups & Algebraic Groups Springer-Verlag. (Illus.). 352p. 1990. 86.95 (*0-387-50614-4*) Spr-Verlag.

Onishchik, A. L. & Vinberg, Ernst B., eds. Lie Groups & Lie Algebras II: Discrete Subgroups of Lie Groups, Cohomologies of Lie Groups & Lie Algebras. 250p. 1996. write for info. (*0-387-50585-7*) Spr-Verlag.

Onishenko, Gary, jt. auth. see Roberts, Edmund B.

Onishi, Hiroshi. On a Riverboat Journey: A Handscroll by Ito Jakuchu, with Poems by Daiten. LC 89-62484. (Illus.). 180p. 1990. boxed set 45.00 (*0-8076-1229-4*) Braziller.

— Photometric Determination of Traces of Metals, Vol. 1 Set. 4th ed. 1733p. 1989. 599.00 (*0-471-52748-3*) Wiley.

— Photometric Determination of Traces of Metals: Individual Metals, Aluminum to Lithium, Vol. 1, Pt. 2A, Individual Metals, Aluminum to Lit. 4th ed. 885p. 1986. 375.00 (*0-471-86139-1*) Wiley.

Onishi, Hiroshi, jt. auth. see Sandell, Ernest B.

Onishi, K., jt. auth. see Ninomiya, H.

Onishi, Yoshinori. Feminine Multiplicity. (C). 1997. 22.00 (*81-7030-513-6*, Pub. by Sri Satguru Pubns) S Asia.

Onissi, T. R. Elsevier's Dictionary of the Cement Industry. (ENG, FRE, GER, JPN & SPA.). 520p. 1987. 350.00 (*0-8288-9285-7*, M1535) Fr & Eur.

— Elsevier's Dictionary of the Cement Industry: In English, French, German, Spanish, & Japanese. 532p. 1987. 282.75 (*0-444-42629-9*) Elsevier.

Onizuka, Richard, jt. auth. see Glodava, Mila.

Onken, Lisa S. Beyond the Therapeutic Alliance: Keeping the Drug-Dependent Individual in Treatment. 259p. 1997. pap. text 18.00 (*0-16-049092-8*) USGPO.

Onken, Lisa S., et al, eds. Behavioral Treatments for Drug Abuse & Dependence. (Illus.). 329p. (C). 1995. pap. text 35.00 (*0-7881-1871-4*) DIANE Pub.

— Integrating Behavioral Therapies with Medications in the Treatment of Drug Dependence. (Illus.). 190p. (Orig.). (C). 1995. pap. text 30.00 (*0-7881-2466-8*) DIANE Pub.

— Treatment of Drug Dependent Individuals with Comorbid Mental Disorders. (Illus.). 170p. (C). 1998. pap. text 35.00 (*0-7881-2782-9*) DIANE Pub.

Onken, Lisa Simon. Treatment of Drug Dependent Individuals with Comorbid Mental Disorders. 174p. 1997. per. 10.00 (*0-16-061517-8*) USGPO.

Onken, U., jt. auth. see Gmehling, J.

Onkenhout, Debra F., tr. see Van Maarsen, Jacqueline.

Onkvisit, Sak & Shaw, John J. International Marketing: Analysis & Strategy. 2nd ed. LC 92-83811. 960p. (C). 1992. text 82.00 (*0-02-389343-5*, Macmillan Coll) P-H.

— International Marketing: Analysis & Strategy. 3rd ed. LC 96-46485. (Illus.). 750p. (C). 1996. 94.00 (*0-13-272451-0*, Prentice Hall) P-H.

— Product Life Cycles & Product Management. LC 88-26509. 172p. 1989. 55.00 (*0-89930-319-6*, OKV, Quorum Bks) Greenwood.

Onley, Elaine H. Crying on Sunday: Surviving Forced Termination in Ministry. LC 94-14018. 80p. 1994. pap. 7.00 (*1-880837-47-1*) Smyth & Helwys.

***Onley, Glen.** Beyond Contentment: A Contemporary Novel. 256p. 2000. 24.95 (*0-86534-311-X*) Sunstone Pr.

Onley, Joy. Memories of Frederick - Over on the Other Side. (Illus.). 175p. (Orig.). 1995. pap. 15.95 (*0-9650433-0-4*) J Onley.

***Onley, Toni.** Toni Onley's British Columbia: A Tribute. (Illus.). 64p. 2000. 19.95 (*1-55192-236-3*) Raincoast Bk.

O

An Asterisk (*) at the beginning of an entry indicates that the title is appearing for the first time.

Online Computer Library Center, Inc. Staff. U. S. Newspaper Program: National Union List. 3rd ed. 1989. fiche 275.00 (*0-685-25894-7*) OCLC Online Comp.

Online Press Inc. Staff. Quick Course Access 97 Workbook Instructor's Resource Packet. (Quick Course Ser.). (Illus.). 1997. pap. text 11.95 (*1-879399-84-9*) Online Training.

— Quick Course Excel 97 Workbook Instructor's Resource Packet. (Quick Course Ser.). (Illus.). 1997. pap. text 11.95 (*1-879399-85-7*) Online Training.

***Online Press, Inc., Staff.** Quick Course in Microsoft Access 97. 192p. 2000. pap. 9.99 (*0-7356-1072-X*) Microsoft Pr.

— Quick Course in Microsoft Access 2000. 2000. pap. 9.99 (*0-7356-1082-7*) Microsoft.

— Quick Course in Microsoft Excel 2000. (Quick Course Ser.). (Illus.). 2000. pap. 9.99 (*0-7356-1081-9*) Microsoft.

— Quick Course In Microsoft Excel 97. 2000. pap. 9.99 (*0-7356-1073-8*) Microsoft Pr.

— Quick Course in Microsoft FrontPage 2000. (Quick Course Ser.). (Illus.). 2000. pap. 9.99 (*0-7356-1086-X*) Microsoft.

Online Press, Inc., Staff. Quick Course in Microsoft Internet Explorer 4. LC 97-31807. 1997. 14.99 (*1-57231-804-X*) Microsoft.

***Online Press, Inc., Staff.** Quick Course in Microsoft Internet Explorer 5. (Quick Course Ser.). (Illus.). 2000. pap. 9.99 (*0-7356-1087-8*) Microsoft.

— Quick Course in Microsoft Office 97. (Quick Course Ser.). (Illus.). 2000. pap. 9.99 (*0-7356-1076-2*) Microsoft.

— Quick Course in Microsoft Office 2000. (Quick Course Ser.). (Illus.). 2000. pap. 9.99 (*0-7356-1083-5*) Microsoft.

— Quick Course in Microsoft Outlook 2000. (Quick Course Ser.). (Illus.). 2000. pap. 9.99 (*0-7356-1089-4*) Microsoft.

— Quick Course in Microsoft Outlook 98. 192p. 2000. pap. 9.99 (*0-7356-1080-0*) Microsoft Pr.

— Quick Course in Microsoft PowerPoint 2000. (Quick Course Ser.). (Illus.). 2000. pap. 9.99 (*0-7356-1084-3*) Microsoft.

— Quick Course in Microsoft PowerPoint 97. (Quick Course Ser.). (Illus.). 2000. pap. 9.99 (*0-7356-1074-6*) Microsoft.

— Quick Course in Microsoft Publisher 2000. (Quick Course Ser.). (Illus.). 2000. pap. 9.99 (*0-7356-1088-6*) Microsoft.

— Quick Course in Microsoft Windows 95. (Quick Course Ser.). (Illus.). 2000. pap. 9.99 (*0-7356-1077-0*) Microsoft.

— Quick Course in Microsoft Windows NT 4 Workstation. (Quick Course Ser.). (Illus.). 2000. pap. 9.99 (*0-7356-1079-7*) Microsoft.

Online Press Inc. Staff. Quick Course In Microsoft Windows 2000 (C). (gr. 8). 1999. pap. 16.99 (*1-57231-845-7*) Little.

***Online Press, Inc., Staff.** Quick Course in Microsoft Windows 98. (Quick Course Ser.). (Illus.). 2000. pap. 9.99 (*0-7356-1078-9*) Microsoft.

Online Press Inc. Staff. Quick Course in Microsoft Word 2000. 60p. 11.95 (*1-58278-011-0*) Online Training.

***Online Press, Inc., Staff.** Quick Course in Microsoft Word 2000. (Quick Course Ser.). (Illus.). 2000. pap. 9.99 (*0-7356-1085-1*) Microsoft.

— Quick Course in Microsoft Word 97. (Quick Course Ser.). (Illus.). 2000. pap. 9.99 (*0-7356-1075-4*) Microsoft.

Online Press Inc. Staff. Quick Course in PowerPoint 97. (Quick Course Ser.). (Illus.). 60p. 1997. pap. text, wbk. ed. 11.95 (*1-879399-79-2*) Online Training.

Online Press Inc. Staff. Quick Course in Windows 2000. 224p. 15.95 (*1-58278-000-5*); wbk. ed. 12.75 (*1-58278-009-9*) Online Training.

Online Press Inc. Staff. Quick Course Office 97 Workbook Instructor's Resource Packet. (Quick Course Ser.). (Illus.). 1997. pap. text 14.95 (*1-879399-83-0*) Online Training.

— Quick Course PowerPoint 97 Workbook Instructor's Resource Packet. (Quick Course Ser.). (Illus.). 1997. pap. text 11.95 (*1-879399-86-5*) Online Training.

— Quick Course Word 97 Workbook Instructor's Resource Packet. (Quick Course Ser.). (Illus.). 1997. pap. text 11.95 (*1-879399-87-3*) Online Training.

— Workbook for Quick Course in Access 97. (Quick Course Ser.). (Illus.). 60p. (Orig.). 1997. pap. text, wbk. ed. 11.95 (*1-879399-78-4*) Online Training.

— Workbook for Quick Course in Excel 97. (Quick Course Ser.). (Illus.). 60p. 1997. pap. text, wbk. ed. 11.95 (*1-879399-77-6*) Online Training.

— Workbook for Quick Course in Microsoft Office for Windows 95 & Windows NT. 108p. 1996. pap. text 14.95 (*1-879399-65-2*) Online Training.

— Workbook for Quick Course in Office 97: Education/Training Edition. (Quick Course Ser.). (Illus.). 123p. 1997. pap. text, wbk. ed. 14.95 (*1-879399-74-1*) Online Training.

— Workbook for Quick Course in Word 97. (Quick Course Ser.). (Illus.). 60p. 1997. pap. text, wbk. ed. 11.95 (*1-879399-76-8*) Online Training.

Online Press Inc. Staff, contrib. by. Quick Course Windows 98 Workbook Instructor's Resource Packet. (Quick Course). (Illus.). 1998. pap. text 12.95 (*1-879399-89-X*) Online Training.

***Online Press Staff.** Workbook for Quick Course in Microsoft Excel 2000. (Quick Course Ser.). (Illus.). 60p. 1999. pap. text 11.95 (*1-58278-012-9*) Online Training.

Online Press Staff. Workbook for Quick Course in Microsoft Office 2000: Education/Training Edition. (Quick Course Ser.). 144p. 1999. pap. text 14.95 (*1-58278-010-2*) Online Training.

***Online Trading Academy Staff.** Electronic Trading Guide for NASDAQ Level 2. 3rd rev. ed. Jimenez, Jorge et al, eds. (Illus.). 107p. 2000. ring bd. 29.95 (*0-9668115-0-X*) Online Trading.

Onlinecomputer Library Center, Inc. Staff. USNP National Unionfest, 1989. 3rd ed. 2000p. 1989. 275.00 incl. fiche (*1-55653-074-9*) OCLC Online Comp.

Onlonez, Maria. English for Progress (Ingles para Progresar), Vol. 1. 3rd ed. Smith, Darvel D. et al, eds. LC 87-71460. (ENG & SPA., Illus.). 304p. 1987. pap. text 15.95 (*0-942885-02-3*) Casa Blanca Pr.

Onn, Gerald, tr. see Von Rauch, Georg.

***Onnepalu, Tonu.** Border State. LC 99-462232. 120p. 2000. 49.95 (*0-8101-1779-7*) Northwestern U Pr.

Onnerfors, ed. Taciti, P. Corneli Tom. II, Fascicule 2: De Origine et Situ Germanorum. (Annales Ser.). (LAT.). 1983. pap. 21.95 (*3-519-01838-1*, T1838, Pub. by B G Teubner) U of Mich Pr.

— Vegetii, P. Flavii. (LAT.). 1995. 79.50 (*3-519-01872-1*, T1872, Pub. by B G Teubner) U of Mich Pr.

Onnerfors, Alf. Kleine Schriften Zur Lateinischen Sprache und Literatur der Antike und des Mittelalters. Maaz, W. et al, eds. (Spolia Berolinensia Ser.: Bd. 10). (Illus.). 272p. 1998. 88.00 (*3-615-00186-9*, Pub. by Weidmann) Lubrecht & Cramer.

Onnerfors, Alf, et al, eds. Bibliotheca Graeca et Latina Suppletoria, Bd. II: Physica Plinii Bambergensis. 174p. 1976. write for info. (*0-318-70725-X*) G Olms Pubs.

Onnerfors, Alf, ed. see Plinius Secundus, C.

Onnes, Keike K. Through Measurement to Knowledge: The Selected Papers of Heike Kamerlingh Onnes, 1853-1926. Gavroglu, Kostas & Goudaroulis, Yorgos, eds. 688p. (C). 1990. lib. bdg. 253.00 (*0-7923-0825-5*, Pub. by Kluwer Academic) Kluwer Academic.

Onnias, Arturo. The Language of Total Quality. 1993. 24.95 (*0-614-30073-8*) Juran Inst.

Ono, Hideichi. Japanese Grammar. (ENG & JPN.). 368p. 1997. pap. 32.95 (*4-590-00399-6*, Pub. by Hokuseido Pr) Book East.

— A Practical Guide to Japanese-English Onomatopoeia & Mimesis. 408p. 1997. boxed set 42.95 (*4-590-00722-3*, Pub. by Hokuseido Pr) Book East.

Ono, Hiroko, tr. see Kamimura, Ikuro.

Ono, Ichiro, photos by. Divine Excess: Mexican Ultra-Baroque. LC 96-17874. (Illus.). 96p. 1996. 14.95 (*0-8118-1483-1*) Chronicle Bks.

Ono, K., et al, eds. Lumbar Fusion & Stabilization. LC 92-46674. 1993. 174.00 (*0-387-70116-8*) Spr-Verlag.

Ono, K., et al. Introduction to Color & Composition. (Easy Start Guide Ser.). (Illus.). 112p. 1992. 37.95 (*4-7661-0629-6*, Pub. by Graphic-Sha) Bks Nippan.

Ono, K., jt. ed. see Uchida, A.

Ono, K. A., jt. auth. see Trillmich, F.

Ono, Ken I. & Sugiyama, Tomoo. Visual Feedback Photography: Making Your 5S Implementation Click. LC 96-45256. (Shopfloor Ser.). 1996. teacher ed., ring bd. 150.00 (*1-56327-090-0*) Productivity Inc.

***Ono, Kinji, ed.** Digital Convergence for Creative Divergence: Proceedings of the International Conference on Computer Communication 1999. (Illus.). 1200p. 1999. pap. 250.00 (*1-891365-05-3*) ICCC Pr.

Ono, Koichi. Little Panda Bear. (Shaggies Ser.). (Illus.). 12p. (J). (ps-2). 1982. 4.95 (*0-671-42549-8*) Litle Simon.

Ono, Michio. Atlas of the Cerebral Sulci. (Illus.). 232p. 1990. text 189.00 (*0-86577-362-9*) Thieme Med Pubs.

Ono, Mikio, jt. ed. see Stuessy, Tod F.

Ono, Nobuko, ed. The Consumer Movement. Saito, Fujiko, tr. (JPN., Illus.). 336p. 1996. pap. write for info. (*4-8265-0215-X*) Family Econ Trust.

Ono, R. Dana. Business of Biotechnology: From the Bench to the Street. 392p. 1991. text 79.95 (*0-7506-9119-0*) Buttrwrth-Heinemann.

Ono, Sokyo. Shinto: The Kami Way. (Illus.). 144p. 1994. pap. 8.95 (*0-8048-1960-2*) Tuttle Pubng.

Ono, T. An Introduction to Algebraic Number Theory. LC 90-30155. (University Series in Mathematics). (Illus.). 234p. (C). 1990. text 55.00 (*0-306-43436-9*, Kluwer Plenum) Kluwer Academic.

— Variations on a Theme of Euler: Quadratic Forms, Elliptic Curves, & Hopf Maps. (University Series in Mathematics). (Illus.). 360p. (C). 1994. text 89.50 (*0-306-44789-4*, Kluwer Plenum) Kluwer Academic.

Ono, Taketoshi. Perception, Memory & Emotion: Frontiers in Neuroscience. LC 96-2868. (Pergamon Studies in Neuroscience: Vol. 13). 632p. 1996. 196.50 (*0-08-042735-9*, Pergamon Pr) Elsevier.

Ono, Taketoshi, et al, eds. Brain Mechanisms of Perception & Memory: From Neuron to Behavior. LC 92-49789. (Illus.). 722p. 1993. text 125.00 (*0-19-507770-9*) OUP.

Ono, Taketoshi, jt. ed. see Nakajima, Teruo.

***Ono, Tom.** Might & Magic VII: For Blood & Honor - Prima's Official Strategy Guide. LC 99-70045. 240p. 1999. pap. 19.99 (*0-7615-2069-4*) Prima Pub.

***Ono, Toshihiro.** Pokemon: Electric Pikachu Boogaloo. (Illus.). 168p. 2000. pap. 12.95 (*1-56931-436-5*, Pub. by Viz Commns Inc) Publishers Group.

— Pokemon: Pikachu Shocks Back. (Illus.). 160p. 1999. pap. 12.95 (*1-56931-411-X*, Viz Comics) Viz Commns Inc.

Ono, Toshihiro. Pokemon: The Electric Tale of Pikachu! (Illus.). 160p. (J). (gr. 4-7). 1999. pap. 12.95 (*1-56931-378-4*, Pub. by Viz Commns Inc) Publishers Group.

***Ono, Toshihiro.** Surf's up, Pikachu! (Pokemon Ser.). (Illus.). (J). 2000. pap. 12.95 (*1-56931-494-2*, Viz Comics) Viz Commns Inc.

Ono, Y. Somatoform Disorders: A Worldwide Perspective. LC 99-14495. (Keio University Symposia for Life Science & Medicine Ser.). xx, 288p. 1999. write for info. (*4-431-70248-2*) Spr-Verlag.

***Ono, Yoko.** Grapefruit: A Book of Instructions & Drawings by Yoko Ono. (Illus.). 320p. 2000. write for info. (*0-7432-0110-8*) Simon & Schuster.

Ono, Yoko. Instruction Paintings. LC 95-16907. (Illus.). 64p. 1995. boxed set 19.95 (*0-8348-0348-8*) Weatherhill.

***Ono, Yoko.** Instruction Paintings. (Illus.). 63p. 1999. reprint ed. pap. text 20.00 (*0-7881-6800-2*) DIANE Pub.

Ono, Yoshimasa A., jt. ed. see Fujikawa, K.

Ono, Yoshiyasu. Money, Interest, & Stagnation: Dynamic Theory & a Monetary Economy. (Illus.). 216p. 1994. text 49.95 (*0-19-828837-9*) OUP.

Onoapoi, A. M. Mirror Mimes Mankind's Mind. LC 96-94708. 56p. (Orig.). 1996. pap. 12.05 (*0-9654513-1-3*) Think Pen.

— Themes They Try to Tame. unabridged ed. LC 96-94707. 56p. (Orig.). 1996. pap. 12.95 (*0-9654513-0-5*); lib. bdg. 18.95 (*0-614-24606-7*) Think Pen.

Onoda, George, jt. ed. see Jillarenkatesa, Ajit.

Onoda, George Y., Jr. & Hench, Larry L., eds. Ceramic Processing before Firing. 512p. 1978. 297.50 (*0-471-65410-8*, Wiley-Interscience) Wiley.

***Onoda, Hiroo.** No Surrender: My Thirty-Year War. LC 99-23484. 1999. pap. 15.95 (*1-55750-663-9*) Naval Inst Pr.

***Onoda, T.** Lanchester Theory: Science to Win the Competition, Vol. 1. 1999. pap. text 55.00 (*1-57321-015-3*) Lanchester Pr.

Onodaga Historical Association Staff. Syracuse. (Images of America Ser.). 1997. pap. 16.99 (*0-7524-0551-9*) Arcadia Publng.

Onodera, Ryoji, et al, eds. Rumen Microbes & Digestive Physiology in Ruminants: Satellite Symposium of the 8th Animal Science Congress, Kyoto October 1996. LC 98-117971. (Illus.). x, 260p. 1997. text 222.75 (*3-8055-6588-7*) S Karger.

Onodera, T. & Kawai, S. A Formal Model of Visualization in Computer Graphics Systems. (Lecture Notes in Computer Science Ser.: Vol. 421). x, 100p. 1990. 24.50 (*0-387-52395-2*) Spr-Verlag.

Onoe, Morio, et al, eds. Real-Time Medical Image Processing. LC 80-23779. (Illus.). 268p. 1980. reprint ed. pap. 83.10 (*0-608-05449-6*, 206591800006) Bks Demand.

Onofrey, Bruce. Clinical Optometric Pharmacology & Therapeutics: Clinical Text, Annual New. (Illus.). 170p. 1992. ring bd. 115.00 (*0-397-52133-2*) Lppncott W & W.

Onofrey, Bruce E., et al. Ocular Therapeutics Handbook: A Clinical Manual. LC 97-25437. 400p. 1997. spiral bd. 49.95 (*0-397-51392-5*) Lppncott W & W.

Onofri, M. & Tesei, A., eds. Fluid Dynamical Aspects of Combusion Theory. LC 89-13183. (Pitman Research Notes in Mathematics Ser.: No. 223). 380p. 1991. pap. 117.80 (*0-608-05234-5*, 206577100001) Bks Demand.

***Onofri, Silvano, et al.** Italians in the History of Mycology: Proceedings of a Symposium Held in the Archivo Centrale Dello Stato, Rome, 4-5 October 1955. (Illus.). 163p. 1999. pap. 35.00 (*0-930845-09-9*) Mycotaxon Ltd.

Onoh, J. Money & Banking in Africa. 1982. pap. text. write for info. (*0-582-64336-8*, Pub. by Addison-Wesley) Longman.

Onoh, J. K. Money & Banking in Africa. LC 82-15266. 224p. reprint ed. pap. 69.50 (*0-8357-2968-0*, 203923000011) Bks Demand.

Onokerhoraye, A. G. Social Services in Nigeria: An Introduction. LC 82-17156. 354p. 1983. pap. 18.50 (*0-7103-0042-5*) Routledge.

O'Nolan, Niall, ed. see O'Nuallain, Ciaran.

Onolehmemhen, Durrenda & Gessesse, Kebede. The Black Jews of Ethiopia: The Last Exodus. LC 97-46025. (ATLA Monographs: No. 45). (Illus.). 152p. 1998. 39.50 (*0-8108-3414-6*) Scarecrow.

Onon, Temujin, tr. see Shirendev, Bazaryn.

Onon, Urgunge. The History & the Life of Chinggis Khan: The Secret History of the Mongols. LC 90-2136. xix, 183p. 1990. 71.50 (*90-04-09236-6*) Brill Academic Pubs.

Onon, Urgunge, ed. Mongollan Heroes of the Twentieth Century. LC 76-23980. (Asian Studies: No. 1). (Illus.). 1976. lib. bdg. 32.50 (*0-404-15402-6*) AMS Pr.

Onon, Urgunge, jt. auth. see Humphrey, Caroline.

Onorato, Mary, jt. ed. see Evans, Denise.

Onorato, Michael P. Forgotten Heroes: Japan's Imprisonment of American Civilians in the Phillipines, 1942-1945. LC 89-13402. (Oral History Ser.). 344p. 1989. 79.50 (*0-313-28084-3*, OFH/, Greenwood Pr) Greenwood.

Onorato, Michael P., ed. Another Time, Another World: Coney Island Memories. 1988. 25.00 (*0-930046-09-9*) CSUF Oral Hist.

***Onorato, Michael P., ed.** Another Time, Another World: Coney Island Memories. 2nd rev. ed. (Illus.). 2000. pap. write for info. (*0-930046-14-5*) CSUF Oral Hist.

Onorato, Michael P., ed. Steeplechase Park: Sales & Closure, 1965-1966 - Diary & Papers of James J. Onorato. LC 98-65799. (Illus.). 100p. 1998. 35.00 (*0-9620979-6-9*) Pac Rim Bks.

Onorato, Michael P., jt. ed. see Cariaga-Barden, Regina.

Onorato, Richard J. The Character of the Poet: Wordsworth in the Prelude. LC 74-131126. 447p. 1971. reprint ed. pap. 138.60 (*0-7837-9409-6*, 206015400004) Bks Demand.

Onorato, Ronald J. Douglas Huebler. LC 88-81414. 52p. 1988. pap. text 14.00 (*0-934418-30-6*) Mus Contemp Art.

— Maria Nordman: Trabajos en la Ciudad de Ondas. LC 85-80104. (Illus.). 20p. 1985. 5.00 (*0-934418-23-3*) Mus Contemp Art.

— Wendy Edwards: Paintings & Drawings. (Illus.). 16p. (Orig.). 1989. pap. 5.00 (*0-933519-18-4*) D W Bell Gallery.

Onorato, Ronald J., et al. Satellite Intelligence: Boston-San Diego New Art Exchange. LC 90-61071. (Illus.). 36p. (Orig.). 1990. pap. 10.00 (*0-934418-35-7*) Mus Contemp Art.

Onorato, Ronald J., jt. auth. see Davies, Hugh M.

***Onorato, William T., et al.** World Bank Group Assistance for Coal Sector Development & Reform in Member Countries. LC 98-5910. (Technical Paper Ser.: No. 405). 42p. 1998. pap. 22.00 (*0-8213-4203-7*, 14203) World Bank.

Onore, Cynthia S., jt. auth. see Lester, Nancy B.

Onori, S. & Tabet, E., eds. Physics in Environmental & Biomedical Research: Rome, Italy, November 26-29, 1985. 608p. 1986. text 144.00 (*9971-5-0110-4*) World Scientific Pub.

Onosko, Tim. Funland U. S. A. 1978. 15.95 (*0-405-11151-7*) Ayer.

Onoue, Masano, jt. auth. see Ondori Publishing Company Staff.

Onoura, Lesley I., jt. ed. see Haubold, Hans J.

***Onouye, Barry S.** Statics & Strength of Materials for Construction & Architecture. LC 98-21972. 548p. (C). 1998. 93.00 (*0-13-639246-6*) P-H.

***Onqueme, Tess.** Why the Elephants Has No Butt. LC 00-100872. 168p. 2000. pap. write for info. (*0-9663837-2-9*) Africana Leg Pr.

***ONS (Oncology Nursing Society) Staff.** Study Guide for the Core Curriculum for Oncology Nursing. 3rd ed. Eoyang, Thomas, ed. 215p. 1999. pap. text. write for info. (*0-7216-7157-8*, W B Saunders Co) Harcrt Hlth Sci Grp.

Onsager, Lars. The Collected Works of Lars Onsager. 1088p. 1996. lib. bdg. 39.00 (*981-02-2718-3*) World Scientific Pub.

Onsager, Richard C. Arizona Limited Liability Company Forms & Practice Manual, Vol. 2. LC 96-3980. 828p. 1996. ring bd. 239.90 (*1-57400-013-6*) Data Trace Pubng.

Onshage, A. C. Mercury Cadmium Telluride Imagers: A Patent-Oriented Survey. (Handbook of Sensors & Actuators Ser.: No. 5). 456p. 1997. 215.75 (*0-444-82790-0*) Elsevier.

***Onslow, Barbara.** Women of the Press in Nineteenth-Century Britain. LC 00-33333. 2000. write for info. (*0-312-23602-6*) St Martin.

Onslow-Ford, Gordon. Creation. (Illus.). 123p. 1978. text 35.00 (*0-9612760-0-2*) Bishop Pine.

Onslow, Mark. Behavioral Management of Stuttering. (Illus.). 232p. (C). 1995. reprint ed. pap. 45.00 (*1-56593-633-7*, 1312) Thomson Learn.

Onslow, Mark & Packman, Ann, eds. The Handbook of Early Stuttering. LC 98-55683. 300p. 1999. pap. 39.95 (*1-56593-970-0*, 1920) Thomson Learn.

Onslow, Sue. Backbench Debate Within the Conservative Party & Its Influence on Foreign Policy, 1948-57. LC 96-28389. 256p. 1997. text 65.00 (*0-312-16471-8*) St Martin.

Onsrud, Harlan J., ed. Proceedings of the Conference on Law & Information Policy for Spatial Databases. LC 97-156416. (Illus.). 331p. (C). 1995. pap. text 35.00 (*0-9648267-0-4*) U ME Nat Ctr Geog.

Onsrud, Harlan J. & Cook, David W., eds. Geographic & Land Information Systems for Practicing Surveyors. 219p. 1990. pap. 45.00 (*0-614-06118-0*, L293) Am Congrs Survey.

Onsrud, Harlan J. & Rushton, Gerard, eds. Sharing Geographic Information. LC 94-19192. (Illus.). 528p. (C). 1995. 44.95 (*0-88285-152-7*) Ctr Urban Pol Res.

Onsrud, Harlan J., jt. ed. see Masser, Ian.

Onstad, Diane. Whole Foods Companion: A Guide for Adventurous Cooks, Curious Shoppers, & Lovers of Natural Foods. LC 96-33441. (Illus.). 400p. 1996. pap. 29.00 (*0-930031-83-0*) Chelsea Green Pub.

— Whole Foods Companion: A Guide for Adventurous Cooks, Curious Shoppers, & Lovers of Natural Foods. 1996. 55.00 (*0-930031-89-X*) Chelsea Green Pub.

Onstad, Esther. Courage for Today, A Hope for Tomorrow: A Study of the Revelation. expanded rev. ed. LC 75-2829. 160p. 1993. pap. 13.99 (*0-8066-2651-8*, 9-2651) Augsburg Fortress.

Onstad, Preston E., ed. see Hilleary, William M.

O'nstein, Allan. Institutionalized Learning in America. 248p. 1990. 39.95 (*0-88738-331-9*) Transaction Pubs.

Onstine, Burton W. Oregon Votes, 1858-1972. LC 73-88980. 395p. 1973. pap. 9.95 (*0-87595-043-4*) Oregon Hist.

Onstot, T. G. Pioneers of Menard & Mason Counties . . . Including Personal Reminiscences of Abraham Lincoln & Peter Cartwright. (Illus.). 400p. 1997. reprint ed. lib. bdg. 45.00 (*0-8328-5770-X*) Higginson Bk Co.

Onstott, T. G. Pioneers of Menard & Mason Counties, Illinois. 404p. 1987. reprint ed. pap. 19.95 (*1-877869-08-2*) Mason Cnty Hist Proj.

Ontario, jt. auth. see Canadian Wildlife Service Staff.

Ontario Science Center Staff. Science Express. 1991. 14.38 (*0-201-57773-9*) Addison-Wesley.

— Science Express. 1991. pap. 8.95 (*0-201-57725-9*) Addison-Wesley.

— Scienceworks: Sixty-Five Experiments That Introduce the Fun & Wonder of Science. (Illus.). (J). (gr. 2-7). 1986. pap. 11.95 (*0-201-16780-8*) Addison-Wesley.

Ontario Science Center Staff, jt. auth. see Gold, Carol.

Ontario Science Centre Staff. The Jumbo Book of Science. (Illus.). 192p. (J). 1994. pap. 12.00 (*1-55074-197-7*) Kids Can Pr.

— Plants. unabridged ed. (Starting with Science Ser.). 32p. (J). (gr. k-4). 2000. pap. 6.95 (*1-55074-395-3*, Pub. by Kids Can Pr) Genl Dist Srvs.

— Science Express. (Illus.). 96p. (J). 1991. pap. text 9.95 (*1-55074-017-2*) Kids Can Pr.

An Asterisk (*) at the beginning of an entry indicates that the title is appearing for the first time.

— Science Express. (Illus.). 96p. (J). 1995. text 19.95 (*1-55074-015-6*) Kids Can Pr.

— Solids, Liquids & Gases. (Starting with Science Ser.). 32p. (J). (gr. k-4). 2000. pap. 6.95 (*1-55074-401-1*, Pub. by Kids Can Pr) Genl Dist Srvs.

Ontario Science Centre Staff. Sportsworks: More Than Fifty Fun Games & Activities That Explore the Science of Sports. 1989. pap. 9.95 (*0-201-15296-7*) Addison-Wesley.

Ontario Symposium on Personality & Social Psycholo. Consistency in Social Behavior. Zanna, Mark P. et al, eds. LC 82-11489. (Ontario Symposium Ser.: No. 2). (Illus.). 328p. 1982. reprint ed. pap. 101.70 (*0-7837-9050-3*, 20498010003) Bks Demand.

Ontiveros, Erlinda. San Ramon Chapel Pioneers & Their California Heritage. LC 90-7934. 572p. 1990. 50.00 (*0-933380-06-2*) Olive Pr Pubns.

Ontiveros, Suzanne R. Global Terrorism: A Historical Bibliography. (ABC-CLIO Research Guides: No. 16). 168p. 1986. lib. bdg. 19.80 (*0-87436-453-1*) ABC-CLIO.

Ontiveros, Suzanne R. & Kinnell, Susan K. American Maritime History: A Bibliography. (ABC-CLIO Research Guides: No.17). 260p. 1986. lib. bdg. 49.50 (*0-87436-471-X*) ABC-CLIO.

Ontko, Andrew G. Thunder over the Ochoco, Vol. I, Pts. 1 & 2. LC 93-18698. (Illus.). 400p. (Orig.). 1993. pap. 16.95 (*0-89288-232-8*) Maverick.

Ontko, Andrew G. Trails to the Ochoco Valley. (Illus.). 1992. 12.95 (*1-930405-05-7*) Crook County Hist.

Ontko, Gale. Thunder over the Ochoco: Distant Thunder, Vol. II. 400p. 1994. pap. 16.95 (*0-89288-248-4*) Maverick.

— Thunder over the Ochoco Vol. 3: Lightning Strikes! (Illus.). 560p. 1998. pap. 19.95 (*0-89288-265-4*) Maverick.

— Thunder over the Ochoco Vol. IV: Rain of Tears. (Illus.). 464p. 1998. pap. 19.95 (*0-89288-275-1*) Maverick.

***Ontko, Gale.** Thunder over the Ochoco Vol. 5: And the Juniper Trees Bore Fruit. LC 93-18698. (Illus.). 480p. 1999. pap. 19.95 (*0-89288-276-X*) Maverick.

Ontza, J. Diccionarios del Saber Moderno: La Politica en Su Entorno Historico Actual. (SPA.). 671p. 1980. 45.00 (*0-8288-2269-7*, S35606) Fr & Eur.

O'Nuallain, Ciaran. The Early Years of Brian O'Nolan, Flann O'Brien, Myles na gCopaleen. 2nd rev. ed. O'Nolan, Niall, ed. LC 99-165866. 128p. 1998. pap. 13.95 (*1-901866-18-1*, Pub. by Lilliput Pr) Irish Bks Media.

***O'Nuallain, Sean.** Being Human: The Search for Order. 192p. 2000. 34.95 (*1-84150-025-9*, Pub. by Intellect) Intl Spec Bk.

O'Nuallain, Sean, et al, eds. Two Sciences of Mind: Readings in Cognitive Science & Consciousness. LC 96-52164. (Advances in Consciousness Research Ser.: Vol. 9). xii, 490p. 1997. pap. 79.00 (*1-55619-189-8*) J Benjamins Pubng Co.

Onuf, Nicholas G. The Republican Legacy in International Thought. LC 97-11810. (Studies in International Relations: Vol. 59). 302p. (C). 1998. text 64.95 (*0-521-58444-2*); pap. text 24.95 (*0-521-58599-6*) Cambridge U Pr.

Onuf, Nicholas G., jt. auth. see Onuf, Peter S.

Onuf, Peter, ed. Thomas Jefferson: An Anthology. 268p. 1999. pap. 19.50 (*1-881089-57-6*) Brandywine Press.

***Onuf, Peter S.** Jefferson's Empire: The Language of American Nationhood. LC 99-39129. (Jeffersonian America Ser.). 250p. 2000. 27.95 (*0-8139-1930-4*) U Pr of Va.

Onuf, Peter S. Statehood & Union: A History of the Northwest Ordinance. LC 86-43046. (Midwestern History & Culture Ser.). 218p. reprint ed. pap. 67.60 (*0-608-09356-4*, 205410200002) Bks Demand.

Onuf, Peter S., ed. America & the World: Diplomacy, Politics, & War. LC 91-15487. (New American Nation, 1775-1820 Ser.: Vol. 9). 472p. 1991. text 10.00 (*0-8153-0444-7*) Garland.

— American Culture, 1776-1815. LC 91-15465. (New American Nation, 1775-1820 Ser.: Vol. 12). 508p. 1991. text 10.00 (*0-8153-0447-1*) Garland.

— American Society, 1776-1815. LC 91-13745. (New American Nation, 1775-1820 Ser.: Vol. 11). 550p. 1991. text 10.00 (*0-8153-0446-3*) Garland.

— Congress & the Confederation. LC 91-13165. (New American Nation, 1775-1820 Ser.: Vol. 4). 460p. 1991. text 10.00 (*0-8153-0439-0*) Garland.

— Establishing the New Regime: The Washington Administration. LC 91-3515. (New American Nation, 1775-1820 Ser.: Vol. 7). 476p. 1991. text 10.00 (*0-8153-0442-0*) Garland.

— The Federal Constitution. LC 91-13164. (New American Nation, 1775-1820 Ser.: Vol. 5). 626p. 1991. text 10.00 (*0-8153-0440-4*) Garland.

— Federalists & Republicans. LC 91-15475. (New American Nation, 1775-1820 Ser.: Vol. 8). 400p. 1991. text 10.00 (*0-8153-0443-9*) Garland.

— Jeffersonian Legacies. 528p. (C). 1993. pap. text 19.50 (*0-8139-1463-9*) U Pr of Va.

Onuf, Peter S., intro. Ratifying, Amending, & Interpreting the Constitution. LC 91-3502. (New American Nation, 1775-1820 Ser.: Vol. 6). 536p. 1991. text 10.00 (*0-8153-0441-2*) Garland.

— State & Local Politics in the New Nation. LC 91-15466. (New American Nation, 1775-1820 Ser.: Vol. 10). 600p. 1991. text 10.00 (*0-8153-0445-5*) Garland.

Onuf, Peter S. & Onuf, Nicholas G. Federal Union, Modern World: The Law of Nations in an Age of Revolutions, 1776-1814. 250p. 1994. text 29.95 (*0-945612-34-6*) Madison Hse.

Onuf, Peter S., jt. auth. see Cayton, Andrew R.

Onuf, Peter S., jt. auth. see Lewis, Jan.

Onuf, Peter S., jt. auth. see Matson, Cathy D.

Onuf, Peter S., ed. see Dulany, Daniel.

Onuf, Peter S., jt. ed. see Lewis, Jan E.

Onuh, Charles O. Christianity & the Igbo Rites of Passage: The Prospects of Inculturation. LC 92-15800. (European University Studies: Theology, 0721-3409: Ser. 23, Vol. 462). XVIII, 263p. 1992. 50.00 (*3-631-44974-7*) P Lang Pubng.

Onuki, A. & Kawasaki, K., eds. Dynamics & Patterns in Complex Fluids: New Aspects of the Physics-Chemistry Interface: Proceedings of the 4th Nishinomiya-Yukawa Memorial Symposium Nishinomiya City, Japan, October 26-27, 1989. (Proceedings in Physics Ser.: Vol. 52). (Illus.). x, 223p. 1990. 68.00 (*0-387-53051-7*) Spr-Verlag.

Onuki, Takashi. Gnosis und Stoa: Eine Untersuchung Zum Apokryphon des Johannes. (Novum Testamentum et Orbis Antiquus Ser.: Vol. 9). 198p. 1989. text 43.50 (*3-7278-0606-0*, Pub. by Presses Univ Fribourg) Eisenbrauns.

Onuma, Hideharu, et al. Kyudo: The Essence & Practice of Japanese Archery. LC 92-30473. (Illus.). 176p. 1993. 32.00 (*4-7700-1734-0*) Kodansha.

Onuma, Tadayoshi, tr. see Yoshioka, Minoru & Iijima, Koichi.

Onuma, Yasuaki & Crawford, James, eds. A Normative Approach to War: Peace, War, & Justice in Hugo Grotius. LC 92-2466. 440p. 1993. text 85.00 (*0-19-825709-0*, Clarendon Pr) OUP.

Onuoha, Everest C., jt. auth. see Alden, Richard.

Onursal, Bekir & Gautam, Surhid P. Contaminacion Atmosferica por Vehiculos Automotores: Experiencias Recogidas en Siete Centros Urbanos de America Latina. (Technical Paper Ser.: No. 373). (SPA.). 332p. 1997. pap. 40.00 (*0-8213-4017-4*, 14017) World Bank.

— Vehicular Air Pollution: Experiences from Seven Latin American Urban Centers. LC 97-18346. (Technical Paper Ser.: No. 373). 332p. 1997. pap. 40.00 (*0-8213-4016-6*, 14016) World Bank.

Onuska, Francis I. & Karasek, Francis W. Open Tubular Column Gas Chromatography in Environmental Sciences. LC 84-4806. 294p. 1984. 79.50 (*0-306-41589-5*, Plenum Trade) Perseus Pubng.

Onuzo, Okey. The Convert & the Counsellor. Ogundipe, Femi, ed. 120p. (Orig.). (C). 1990. pap. 5.00 (*978-30915-0-6*) Life Link.

— The Convert & the Counsellor: Following up New Christians. 2nd ed. Ndego, Anne, ed. 122p. 1993. pap. text 6.99 (*1-880608-00-6*) Life Link.

— Dimensions of Faith. Ogundipe, Femi, ed. 168p. (Orig.). 1992. pap. text 17.50 (*1-880608-01-4*) Life Link.

— Minspi. 385p. 1998. pap. 7.00 (*1-880608-08-1*, LL-BK-06) Life Link.

— You May Kiss the Bride: Choice, Engagement, Courtship, Marriage, Divorce, Remarriage, Polygamy...& the Christian. Ndego, Anne, ed. 209p. (Orig.). 1992. pap. text 8.50 (*1-880608-02-2*) Life Link.

Onvural, R. O. & Nilsson, A. Local Area Network Interconnection. LC 93-6370. (Illus.). 368p. (C). 1993. 110.00 (*0-306-44630-8*, Plenum Trade) Perseus Pubng.

Onvural, R. O., jt. auth. see Viniotis, Y.

Onvural, Raid O. & Cherukuri, Rao. Signaling in ATM Networks. LC 97-30791. 420p. 1997. 87.00 (*0-89006-871-2*) Artech Hse.

Onvural, Raif O. Asynchronous Transfer Mode Networks: Performance Issues. 2nd ed. LC 95-33936. 535p. 1995. 95.00 (*0-89006-804-6*) Artech Hse.

Onvural, Raif O., ed. Political Science Abstracts, 1992: Annual Supplement. (Illus.). 2086p. (C). 1993. 750.00 (*0-306-69042-X*, Plenum Trade) Perseus Pubng.

Onvural, Raif O. & Marin, Gerald. Asynchronous Transfer Mode Networking: Standards. (C). 2000. 43.00 (*0-13-567967-2*, Macmillan Coll) P-H.

Onwonga, Billy M. Coming to America. LC 96-92011. 133p. (Orig.). 1996. pap. text 9.95 (*1-57579-012-2*) Pine Hill Pr.

OnWord Press Development Team Staff & Hicks, Cliff. Five Steps to SunSoft Solaris 2. 208p. (C). 1993. pap. 29.95 (*0-934605-80-7*) Thomson Learn.

Onword Press Development Team Staff & Hicks, Clint. SunSoft Solaris 2.0 Quick Reference. 224p. (C). 1993. pap. 21.95 (*0-934605-76-9*) Thomson Learn.

Onword Press Development Team Staff & Kimery, Sam. SunSoft Solaris 2.0 User's Guide. 336p. (C). 1993. pap. 29.95 (*0-934605-74-2*) Thomson Learn.

Onword Press Development Team Staff & Rice, Jim. Five Steps To Hp-Ux. LC 92-61886. 144p. (C). 1993. pap. 28.95 (*0-934605-24-6*, 5092) Thomson Learn.

Onword Press Development Team Staff, et al. Inside Pro-Jr. LC 95-1000. (Illus.). 688p. (C). 1995. pap. 56.95 (*1-56690-082-4*) Thomson Learn.

OnWord Press Development Team Staff, jt. auth. see Sahaj, Ranjit.

Onwuanibe, Richard C. A Critique of Revolutionary Humanism: Frantz Fanon. 168p. 1983. 15.50 (*0-87527-296-7*) Green.

Onwubiko. Computer Aided Design. (West Engineering Ser.). 1989. text 65.95 (*0-534-93835-3*) PWS Pubs.

***Onwubiko, Chinyere.** Engineering Design Optimization. LC 99-32305. 312p. (C). 1999. 100.00 (*0-201-47673-8*, Prentice Hall) P-H.

Onwudiwe. Globalization of Terrorism. 61.95 (*0-7546-1095-0*) Ashgate Pub Co.

Onwueme, I. C. The Tropical Tuber Crops: Yam, Cassava, Sweet Potato, Cocoyams. LC 77-20932. 248p. reprint ed. 76.90 (*0-8357-9996-4*, 205182300008) Bks Demand.

Onwueme, Osonye T. The Missing Face. LC 96-95387. (Musical Drama for the Voices of Color Ser.). 76p. (Orig.). (YA). (gr. 5 up). 1997. pap. 10.00 (*1-57579-053-X*, 1) Pine Hill Pr.

— Tell It to Women: An Epic Drama for Women. LC 97-450. (African American Life Ser.). 176p. (Orig.). 1997. pap. text 18.95 (*0-8143-2649-8*) Wayne St U Pr.

Onwueme, Tess. Three Plays: "The Broken Calabash," "Parables for a Season," & "The Reign of Wazobia" LC 92-47582. (African American Life Ser.). 174p. 1993. text 29.95 (*0-8143-2444-4*); pap. text 17.95 (*0-8143-2445-2*) Wayne St U Pr.

Onwukike, Uche F. Democracy in Nigeria: Its Anthropological & Social Requirements. (European University Studies, Series 23: Vol. 608). 359p. 1997. pap. 57.95 (*3-631-32143-0*) P Lang Pubng.

— Democracy in Nigeria: Its Anthropological & Social Requirements. LC 97-29499. (European University Studies, Seris 23: Vol. 608). 359p. 1997. pap. 57.95 (*0-8204-3503-1*) P Lang Pubng.

Onwumechili, C. Agodi. The Equatorial Electrojet. 648p. 1997. text 101.00 (*90-5699-069-1*) Gordon & Breach.

Onwumechili, Chuka. African Democratization & Military Coups. LC 98-18068. 136p. 1998. 49.95 (*0-275-96325-X*, Praeger Pubs) Greenwood.

Onwyneme, Osonye T. Riot in Heaven. (Musical Drama for the Voices of Color Ser.). 136p. (Orig.). (YA). (gr. 5 up). 1997. pap. 10.00 (*1-57579-054-8*, 2) Pine Hill Pr.

***Onyeani, Chika A.** Capitalist Nigger: The Spider-Web Doctrine. 208p. 2000. 24.95 (*0-9678460-0-5*) Timbuktu.

Onyeberechi, Sydney E. Critical Essays: Achebe, Baldwin, Cullen, Ngugi & Tutuola. LC 99-33351. 98p. (C). 1999. pap. text 9.95 (*1-890279-79-X*) Rising Star MD.

Onyefulu, Ifeoma. A Is for Africa. LC 92-39964. (Illus.). 32p. (J). (ps-3). 1993. 15.99 (*0-525-65147-0*, Dutton Child) Peng Put Young Read.

— A Is for Africa. 1997. 10.19 (*0-606-11015-1*, Pub. by Turtleback) Demco.

— Chidi Only Likes Blue: An African Book of Colours. LC 97-218846. (Illus.). 32p. (J). 1997. 14.99 (*0-525-65243-4*) NAL.

***Onyefulu, Ifeoma.** Ebele's Favourite: A Book of African Games. (Illus.). 32p. (J). (gr. k-3). 1999. 18.99 (*0-7112-1279-1*) F Lincoln.

Onyefulu, Ifeoma. Emeka's Gift. 24p. (J). (ps-3). 1999. pap. 5.99 (*0-14-056500-0*, PuffinBks) Peng Put Young Read.

— Grandfather's Work: A Traditional Healer in Nigeria. LC 97-35815. (Illus.). 32p. (J). (gr. 2-4). 1998. lib. bdg. 19.90 (*0-7613-0412-6*) Millbrook Pr.

— Ogbo: Sharing Life in an African Village. LC 95-8882. (Illus.). 32p. (J). (gr. 2-6). 1996. 15.00 (*0-15-200498-X*, Gulliver Bks) Harcourt.

Onyemelukwe, Clement C. Economic Underdevelopment: An Inside View. LC 75-302086. (Illus.). 127p. reprint ed. pap. 39.40 (*0-8357-6101-0*, 203449700090) Bks Demand.

***Onyemelukwe, Clement C.** The Science of Economic Development. (Illus.). 384p. 2000. 74.95 (*0-7656-0604-6*) M E Sharpe.

Onyenorah, Edith. The Gorgeous Black Prince. 1987. 40.00 (*0-7223-2173-2*, Pub. by A H S Ltd) St Mut.

Onyett. Case Management in Mental Health. 280p. 1992. pap. 44.95 (*1-56593-018-5*, 0261) Thomson Learn.

Onyett, Gail, jt. auth. see Onyett, Lloyd C.

Onyett, Lloyd C. & Onyett, Gail. Essentials of Lotus 1-2-3 Release 2.2. (Illus.). 272p. (C). 1991. pap. text 17.95 (*1-878748-69-6*); disk 44.95 (*1-878748-67-X*); disk 44.95 (*1-878748-68-8*) Course Tech.

— Essentials of Lotus 1-2-3 Release 2.3. (Illus.). 384p. (C). 1992. teacher ed. write for info. (*0-318-69235-X*); pap. text 19.95 (*1-878748-91-2*); disk 49.95 (*1-878748-89-0*); disk 49.95 (*1-878748-90-4*) Course Tech.

Onyette, Lloyd. Excel 97 Smartstart Plus. 1997. 39.99 (*1-57576-881-X*) Que Educ & Trng.

Onyszkiewicz, Janusz, jt. auth. see Marek, Wiktor.

***Onyx, Jenny, et al, eds.** Revisioning Aging: Empowerment of Older Women. LC 98-26794. (Eruptions Ser.: Vol. 4). (Illus.). 259p. (C). 1999. pap. text 29.95 (*0-8204-4131-7*) P Lang Pubng.

Onyx Staff. Cost of Honor/Desperate Viscount/Duke's Double/Incurable Matchmaker/Indigo Moon/Julia's Spirit. 1997. mass mkt. 72.84 (*0-451-93462-8*) NAL.

Oo, N. K. The Book of Aquarius Vol. 11: An Enchiridion. 80p. 1998. 12.95 (*1-56313-891-3*) BrownTrout Pubs Inc.

— The Book of Aries Vol. 3: An Enchiridion. 80p. 1998. 12.95 (*1-56313-883-2*) BrownTrout Pubs Inc.

— The Book of Cancer Vol. 6: An Enchiridion. 80p. 1998. 12.95 (*1-56313-886-7*) BrownTrout Pubs Inc.

— The Book of Capricorn Vol. 10: An Enchiridion. 80p. 1998. 12.95 (*1-56313-890-5*) BrownTrout Pubs Inc.

— The Book of Gemini Vol. 5: An Enchiridion. 80p. 1998. 12.95 (*1-56313-885-9*) BrownTrout Pubs Inc.

— The Book of Leo, (Enchiridions Ser.: Vol. 1 of 12). 96p. 1995. 14.95 (*1-56313-461-6*) BrownTrout Pubs Inc.

— The Book of Libra Vol. 8: An Enchiridion. 80p. 1998. 12.95 (*1-56313-888-3*) BrownTrout Pubs Inc.

— The Book of Pisces Vol. 12: An Enchiridion. 80p. 1998. 12.95 (*1-56313-892-1*) BrownTrout Pubs Inc.

— The Book of Sagittarius Vol. 9: An Enchiridion. 80p. 1998. 12.95 (*1-56313-889-1*) BrownTrout Pubs Inc.

— The Book of Scorpio, Vol. 2. (Enchiridions Ser.: Vol. 2 of 12). 80p. 1995. 14.95 (*1-56313-639-2*) BrownTrout Pubs Inc.

— The Book of Taurus Vol. 4: An Enchiridion. 80p. 1998. 12.95 (*1-56313-884-0*) BrownTrout Pubs Inc.

— The Book of Virgo Vol. 7: An Enchiridion. 80p. 1998. 12.95 (*1-56313-887-5*) BrownTrout Pubs Inc.

Oodan, A. P., et al. Quality of Service in Telecommunications. (Telecommunications Ser.: No. 39). 400p. 1998. 95.00 (*0-85296-919-8*, TE039) INSPEC Inc.

Oody, T. Eugene. The Bible Goes to Kruka Town. (Illus.). 74p. (Orig.). 1994. pap. 5.00 (*0-9640888-0-0*) T E Oody.

Ooi, B. C. Efficient Query Processing in Geographic Information Systems. (Lecture Notes in Computer Science Ser.: Vol. 471). viii, 208p. 1990. 29.00 (*0-387-53474-1*) Spr-Verlag.

Ooi, B. C., jt. auth. see Lu, H. J.

Ooi, B. C., jt. ed. see Abel, D.

Ooi, Beng Chin, jt. auth. see Tan, Kian-Lee.

Ooi, James M. Coding for Channels with Feedback. LC 98-23720. (Engineering & Computer Science Ser.). 1998. 97.50 (*0-7923-8207-2*) Kluwer Academic.

Ooi, Jin-Bee. Peninsular Malaysia. LC 75-42166. (Geographies for Advances Study Ser.). 453p. reprint ed. pap. 140.50 (*0-608-17116-6*, 202771000056) Bks Demand.

Ooi, Keat. Rising Sun over Borneo: The Japanese Period in Sarawak, 1941-1945. LC 98-38442. 140p. 1999. text 55.00 (*0-312-21714-5*) St Martin.

Ooi, Vincent. Computer Corpus Lexicography. LC 98-170036. 224p. 1998. 68.00 (*0-7486-0996-2*, Pub. by Edinburgh U Pr); pap. 25.00 (*0-7486-0815-X*, Pub. by Edinburgh U Pr) Col U Pr.

***Ooi, Vincent, ed.** Evolving Identities: The English in Singapore & Malaysia. 136p. 2000. pap. 25.00 (*981-210-156-X*, Pub. by Times Academic) Intl Spec Bk.

Ooij Van. Corrosion Control of Metals by Organic Coatings. 1995. 99.95 (*0-8493-8958-5*) CRC Pr.

Ooijen, Els Van, see Van Ooijen, Els.

Ooka, Diane T., ed. see Ger, Lily.

Ooka, Diane T., tr. see Kawahata, Aliyoshi.

Ooka, Diane T., tr. see Masui, Mitsuko.

Ooka, Diane T., tr. see Okawa, Essei.

Ooka, Diane T., tr. see Watanabe, Yuichi.

Ooka, Diane T., tr. see Yazaki, Setsuo.

Ooka, Makoto. Beneath the Restless Turning of the Planets: Selected Poems, 1972-1989. Fitzsimmons, Thomas, ed. Beichman, Janine, tr. from JPN. LC 95-41648. (Asian Poetry in Translation Ser.: No. 17). (Illus.). 178p. (C). 1996. text 30.00 (*0-942668-45-6*) Katydid Bks.

— Poetry & Poetics of Ancient Japan. Fitzsimmons, Thomas, tr. from JPN. LC 97-19908. (Reflections Ser.: No. 6). (Illus.). 144p. 1997. 30.00 (*0-942668-51-0*); pap. text 19.95 (*0-942668-52-9*) Katydid Bks.

— A String Around Autumn: Selected Poems, 1952-1980. Fitzsimmons, Thomas, ed. & tr. by. from JPN. LC 82-80672. (Asian Poetry in Translation Ser.: No. 3). 94p. 1982. text 20.00 (*0-942668-13-8*) Katydid Bks.

Ooka, Makoto, et al. What the Kite Thinks: A Linked Poem. 88p. 1994. pap. text 11.00 (*0-8248-1599-8*) U HI Summer Sess.

Ooka, Shohei. Fires on the Plain. Morris, Ivan, tr. from JPN Tr. of Nobi. 254p. 1957. pap. 12.95 (*0-8048-1379-5*) Tuttle Pubng.

— Fires on the Plain. Morris, Ivan, tr. from JPN. LC 78-16916.Tr. of Nobi. 246p. 1978. reprint ed. lib. bdg. 38.50 (*0-313-20567-1*, OOFP, Greenwood Pr) Greenwood.

Oomah, B. D., jt. ed. see Mazza, G.

***Oomen, Anne-Marie, ed.** Looking over My Shoulder: Reflections on the 20th Century. LC 00-100916. (Illus.). 104p. 2000. pap. 15.00 (*0-9679632-0-6*) Nrthwst MI Col.

Oomen, Francine. My Friends. (Peephole Board Bks). (Illus.). 6p. (J). 1995. 2.25 (*0-689-80260-9*, Mac Bks Young Read) S&S Childrens.

Oomen, Francine, jt. auth. see Stam, Dagmar.

Oomens, C. W., jt. ed. see Sol, H.

Oomi, G., et al. Transport & Thermal Properties of T-Electron Systems. (Illus.). 322p. (C). 1993. text 110.00 (*0-306-44531-X*, Kluwer Plenum) Kluwer Academic.

Oommachan, M. & Srivatava, J. L. The Flora of Jabalpur. 1996. pap. 215.00 (*81-7233-110-X*, Pub. by Scientific Pubs) St Mut.

Oommen, George. Paths of Dalit Liberation in Kerala: Interaction with Christianity & Communism, 1854-1966. (Religion & Society in South Asia Ser.). 240p. (C). 1998. text 45.00 (*0-7007-0423-X*, Pub. by Curzon Pr Ltd) UH Pr.

Oommen, M. A. Economics of Indian Cinema. (C). 1991. 17.50 (*81-204-0575-7*, Pub. by Oxford IBH) S Asia.

— Issues in Teaching of Economics in Indian Universities. (C). 1987. 18.50 (*81-204-0203-0*, Pub. by Oxford IBH) S Asia.

Oommen, M. A., jt. ed. see Ramachandran, P.

Oommen, T. K. Alien Concepts & South Asian Reality: Responses & Reformulations. 220p. 1995. 29.95 (*0-8039-9204-1*) Sage.

— Citizenship, Nationality & Ethnicity: Reconsiling Competing Identities. LC 96-35367. 272p. 1997. pap. 28.95 (*0-7456-1620-8*, Pub. by Polity Pr); text 60.95 (*0-7456-1619-4*, Pub. by Polity Pr) Blackwell Pubs.

— From Mobilization to Institutionalization: The Dynamics of Agrarian Movement in Twentieth Century Kerala. 1985. 27.50 (*0-8364-1407-1*, Pub. by Popular Prakashan) S Asia.

— Protest & Change: Studies in Social Movements. 304p. (C). 1990. text 32.50 (*0-8039-9652-7*) Sage.

— State & Society in India: Studies in Nation Building. 210p. (C). 1990. text 26.00 (*0-8039-9656-X*) Sage.

Oommen, T. K., ed. Citizenship & National Identity: From Colonialism to Globalism. LC 96-45160. 284p. (C). 1997. 36.00 (*0-8039-9358-7*, 93587) Sage.

— Sociological Literature South Asia, 1992: 1992, Vol. 1. (C). 1993. 62.00 (*81-900333-0-1*, Pub. by Deep & Deep Pubns) S Asia.

***Oommen, T. K. & Mabry, Hunter P.** The Christian Clergy in India. LC 00-22299. 2000. write for info. (*0-7619-9418-1*) Sage.

Oommen, T. K. & Mukherji, P. N., eds. Indian Sociology: Reflections & Introspections. (C). 1986. 28.00 (*0-86132-133-2*, Pub. by Popular Prakashan) S Asia.

Oommen, T. K. & Venugogal, C. N. Sociology for Law Students. (C). 1993. 32.50 (*81-7012-375-5*, Pub. by Eastern Book) St Mut.

Oommen, T. K. & Venugopal, C. N. Sociology. (C). 1988. 80.00 (*0-7855-3519-5*) St Mut.

An Asterisk (*) at the beginning of an entry indicates that the title is appearing for the first time.

Oommen, T. R. & Mukhopadhyay, S., eds. Sociological Literature, South Asia, 1993. xvii, 354p. 1997. 45.00 (*81-86562-24-9*, Pub. by Manak Pubns Pvt Ltd) Nataraj Bks.

Ooms, Emily G. Women & Millenarian Protest in Meiji, Japan: Deguchi Nao & Omotokyo. (Cornell East Asia Ser.: No. 61). 163p. (C). 1993. pap. 11.90 (*0-939657-61-9*) Cornell East Asia Pgm.

Ooms, Herman. Tokugawa Ideology: Early Constructs, 1570-1680. LC 97-51687. (Michigan Monograph Series in Japanese Studies: No. 18). 348p. 1998. pap. 18.95 (*0-939512-85-8*) U MI Japan.

— Tokugawa Village Practice: Class, Status, Power, Law. LC 95-41444. (Philip E. Lilienthal Bk.). (Illus.). 424p. (C). 1996. 48.00 (*0-520-20209-0*, Pub. by U CA Pr) Cal Prin Full Svc.

Ooms, L. A. & Degryse, A. D., eds. Physiological & Pharmacological Aspects of the Reticulo-rumen. (Current Topics in Veterinary Medicine & Animal Science Ser.). (C). 1987. text 218.00 (*0-89838-878-3*) Kluwer Academic.

Ooms, Marius. Empirical Vector Autoregressive Modeling. LC 93-46882. (Lecture Notes in Economics & Mathematical Systems Ser.: Vol. 407). (Illus.). xiv, 380p. 1994. pap. 64.00 (*0-387-57707-6*) Spr-Verlag.

Ooms, Theodora, jt. auth. see Whitehead, Barbara Dafoe.

Ooms, Theodora, jt. ed. see Snyder, Wendy.

Ooms, Theodora J., jt. ed. see Lerman, Robert I.

Oomura, Y., ed. Emotions. (Illus.). xiv, 446p. 1986. 233.25 (*3-8055-4405-7*) S Karger.

***Oon, Helen.** Malaysia. 2nd ed. (Globetrotter Travel Guides Ser.). (Illus.). 128p. 2000. pap. 10.95 (*1-85974-435-4*) New5 Holland.

— Singapore. 2nd ed. (Globetrotter Travel Guides Ser.). (Illus.). 128p. 2000. pap. 10.95 (*1-85974-368-4*) New5 Holland.

Oon, Helen. Travel Guide Malaysia. 2nd ed. (Globetrotter Travel Guide Ser.). 1998. pap. 10.95 (*1-85368-894-0*) Globe Pequot.

***Oord, Thomas J.** Generation Xers Talk about the Church LC 99-38543. 160p. 1999. 19.99 (*0-8341-1815-7*) Nazarene.

Oorde, Willem V. Lexikon Aetherianum. viii, 219p. 1963. reprint ed. write for info. (*0-318-72061-2*) G Olms Pubs.

Oorde, Willem Van, see Van Oorde, Willem.

Oordt, Kari van, tr. see Steiner, Rudolf.

Oorschot, D. E. Realizing Rights. 400p. 1995. 82.95 (*1-85972-071-4*) Ashgate Pub Co.

Oorschot, D. E. & Jones, D. G. Axonal Regeneration in the Mammalian Central Nervous System. (Advances in Anatomy, Embryology & Cell Biology Ser.: Vol. 119). (Illus.). 128p. 1990. 58.00 (*0-387-51757-X*) Spr-Verlag.

Oorschot, Paul C. Van, see Vanstone, Scott A. & Van Oorschot, Paul C.

Oorschot, Paul C. Van, see Kranakis, Evangelos & Van Oorschot, Paul C.

Oort, A. J. P. Nutritional Requirements of Lactarius Species, & Cultural Characters in Relation to Taxonomy. (Verhandelingen der Koninklijke Nederlandse Akademie van Wetenschappen, Afd. Natuurkunde Ser.: No. 76). 96p. 1981. pap. text 47.00 (*0-444-85533-5*) Elsevier.

Oort, Frans. Moduli of Supersingular Abelian Varieties. Li, Ke-Zheng, ed. LC 97-48780. (Lecture Notes in Mathematics Ser.: Vol. 1680). v, 116p. 1998. pap. 27.00 (*3-540-63923-3*) Spr-Verlag.

Oort, H. A. Van, see Van Oort, H. A.

Oort, J., jt. auth. see Baak, J. P.

Oort, Johannes Van, see Van Oort, Johannes.

Oort, Johannes Van, see Van Den Broek, R. & Van Oort, Johannes.

Oort, Marianne S., jt. auth. see Kolff, Dirk H.

Oosawa, Fumio. Polyelectrolytes. LC 70-134786. (Illus.). 167p. reprint ed. pap. 51.80 (*0-608-30542-1*, 205501000007) Bks Demand.

Oosawa, Fumio, et al, eds. Transmembrane Signaling & Sensation. (Taniguchi Symposia on Brain Sciences Ser.: No. 7). 278p. 1984. lib. bdg. 112.00 (*90-6764-041-7*, Pub. by VSP) Coronet Bks.

Oost, Stewart I. Roman Policy in Epirus & Acarnania in the Age of the Roman Conquest of Greece. LC 75-7333. (Roman History Ser.). 1975. reprint ed. 12.95 (*0-405-07050-0*) Ayer.

Oost, W. A., jt. ed. see Komen, G. J.

Oostdam, Ron, jt. auth. see Rijlaarsdam, Gert.

Oosten, Jarich G., jt. ed. see Claessen, Henri J.

Oostendorp, Cora. The Bryophytes of the Palaeozoic & the Mesozoic. Gradstein, S. R., ed. (Bryophytorum Bibliotheca: Vol. 34). (GER., Illus.). 216p. 1987. pap. 71.00 (*3-443-62006-X*, Pub. by Gebruder Borntraeger) Balogh.

Oostendorp, Herre Van, see Goldman, Susan R. & Van Oostendorp, Herre, eds.

Oostendorp, Herre Van, see Van Oostendorp, Herre, ed.

Oostendorp, Herre Van, see De Mul, Sjaak & Van Oostendorp, Herre, eds.

Oosterbaan, Amanda. Freddy the Fire Truck. LC 94-94353. (Illus.). 32p. (Orig.). (J). (ps-2). 1994. pap. 8.95 (*0-9643138-9-8*); text 166.95 (*0-9643138-8-X*) Chldrns Pubng.

Oosterbroek, Pjotr. The Families of Diptera of the Malay Archipelago. LC 98-38381. (Fauna Malesiana Handbks.: Vol. 1). xii, 228p. 1998. 112.00 (*90-04-11053-4*) Brill Academic Pubs.

Oosterhaven, Jan, jt. auth. see Folmer, Hendrik.

Oosterhof, Albert. Developing & Using Classroom Assessments. 2nd ed. LC 98-7089. 245p. (gr. 1). 1998. pap. text 37.67 (*0-13-080130-5*, Pub. by P-H) S&S Trade.

Oosterhof, Albert C. Classroom Applications of Educational Measurement. 2nd ed. 544p. (C). 1994. 91.00 (*0-02-389350-8*, Macmillan Coll) P-H.

— Developing & Using Classroom Assessments. 250p. (C). 1996. pap. text 33.00 (*0-13-373747-0*, Merrill Pub Co) Macmillan.

Oosterhoff, O. H., tr. & intro. see Van Bruggen, J.

***Oosterhouse, Jim.** F.A.I.T.H. Unfolded. 2000. pap. 0.75 (*1-56212-555-9*, 150930) CRC Pubns.

Oosterhouse, Kenneth, et al. Born of a Glorious Thunder: Real Life Accounts of Foreign Christian Work. Kortenhoeven, Helen, tr. 304p. (Orig.). 1986. pap. 6.95 (*0-318-22002-4*) West Indies Pub.

Oosterhuis, D. M., jt. ed. see Miley, W. N.

Oosterhuis, Frans, et al. Product Policy in Europe: New Environmental Perspectives. LC 96-16837. (Environment & Policy Ser.). 320p. (C). 1996. text 166.00 (*0-7923-4078-7*, D Reidel) Kluwer Academic.

Oosterhuis, Hans J., jt. ed. see De Baets, Marc H.

***Oosterhuis, Harry.** Krafft-Ebing's Stepchildren of Nature: Psychiatry & the Making of Sexuality. LC 00-23399. (Series on Sexuality, History & Society). 1999. 30.00 (*0-226-63059-5*) U Ch Pr.

Oosterhuis, Harry, ed. Homosexuality & Male Bonding in Pre-Nazi Germany - The Youth Movement, the Gay Movement & Male Bonding Before Hitler's Rise: Original Transcripts from "Der Eigene", the First Gay Journal in the World. LC 91-27666. (Journal of Homosexuality). 297p. 1992. lib. bdg. 8.95 (*1-56024-164-0*) Haworth Pr.

— Homosexuality & Male Bonding in the Pre-Nazi Germany - The Youth Movement, the Gay Movement & Male Bonding Before Hitler's Rise: Original Transcripts from "Der Eigene", the First Gay Journal in the World. LC 91-27388. (Journal of Homosexuality Ser.). 297p. 1992. lib. bdg. 19.95 (*1-56023-008-8*, Harrington Park) Haworth Pr.

Oosterhuis, Huub. The Children of the Poor Man. Kaan, Fred, tr. LC 84-240947. (Risk Bk.: No. 7). (Illus.). 60p. reprint ed. pap. 30.00 (*0-7837-5998-3*, 204580800008) Bks Demand.

— Your Word Is Near: Contemporary Christian Prayers. Smith, N. David, tr. LC 68-20848. 164p. reprint ed. pap. 50.90 (*0-8357-4631-3*, 203756000008) Bks Demand.

Oosterhuis, J. W., et al, eds. Pathobiology of Human Germ Cell Neoplasia. (Recent Results in Cancer Research Ser.: Vol. 123). (Illus.). 192p. 1991. 106.00 (*0-387-53928-X*) Spr-Verlag.

Oosterhuis, Jendo A., ed. Ophthalmic Tumours. (Monographs in Ophthalmology). 1985. text 233.50 (*90-6193-528-8*) Kluwer Academic.

Oosterling, Henk. Denken Unterwegs: Philosophie im Kratefeld Sozialen und Politischen Engagements. Festschrift fur Heinz Kimmerle Zu Seinem 60. Geburstag. De Jong, Frans, ed. (Schriften Zur Philosophie der Differenz Ser.: No. 4). xxiv, 436p. 1990. 83.00 (*90-6032-317-3*, Pub. by B R Gruner) Humanities.

Oosterman, Margaret A., et al, eds. Earth Science Investigations. (Illus.). 238p. (Orig.). 1990. pap. 43.75 (*0-922152-07-1*) Am Geol.

Oosterom, A. T. Van, see Van Dam, Raymond & Van Oosterom, A. T., eds.

Oosterom, A. T. Van, see Van Oosterom, A. T.

Oosterveen, Karla, tr. see Mitterauer, Michael & Sieder, Reinhard.

Oosterveld-Egas, jt. auth. see Raparaz, M. C.

Oosterveld, Marinus W. Practical Design of Ships & Mobile Units: Proceedings Of The 7th International Symposium on Practical Design of Ships & Mobile Units, The Netherlands, September, 1998. LC 98-37581. 1998. write for info. (*0-444-82918-0*) Elsevier.

Oosterveld, Wilhelmus J., ed. Meniere's Disease: A Comprehensive Appraisal. LC 83-5962. (Wiley-Medical Publication). 145p. reprint ed. pap. 45.00 (*0-8357-7878-9*, 203629600002) Bks Demand.

— Otoneurology. LC 84-3717. (Wiley-Medical Publication). (Illus.). 284p. reprint ed. pap. 88.10 (*0-8357-7929-7*, 205232900002) Bks Demand.

Oosterwegel, Annerieke & Oppenheimer, Louis. The Self-System: Developmental Changes Between & Within Self-Concepts. 208p. 1993. text 39.95 (*0-8058-1216-4*) L Erlbaum Assocs.

Oosterwegel, Annerieke & Wicklund, Robert A., eds. The Self in European & North American Culture: Development & Processes: Proceedings of the NATO Advanced Research Workshop, Chersonnisos, Crete, Greece, January 10-14, 1994. LC 95-34233. (NATO Advanced Science Institutes Ser.: Series D, Vol. 84). 408p. (C). 1995. lib. bdg. 209.50 (*0-7923-3672-0*) Kluwer Academic.

Oosterzee, Penny Van, see Van Oosterzee, Penny.

Oosthoek, Hans & Vroeijenstijn, T. Higher Education & New Technology: Proceedings 5th Congress European Association Research & Development-High Education April 22-25, 1987. LC 89-4029. 558p. 1989. 253.00 (*0-08-037261-9*, Pub. by Pergamon Repr) Franklin.

Oosthout, Henri. Modes of Knowledge & the Transcendental: An Introduction to Plotinus Ennead 5.3 (49) with a Commentary & Translation. LC 91-23974. (Bochumer Studien zur Philosophie Ser.: Vol. 17). vii, 200p. 1991. 65.00 (*90-6032-319-X*, Pub. by B R Gruner) Humanities.

Oosthuizen, G. C., et al, eds. Afro-Christian Religion & Healing in Southern Africa. LC 88-8894. (African Studies: Vol. 8). 450p. 1990. lib. bdg. 109.95 (*0-88946-282-8*) E Mellen.

Oosthuizen, G. C., jt. ed. see Hexham, Irving.

Oosthuizen, Gerhardus C. The Healer-Prophet in Afro-Christian Churches. LC 92-15125. (Studies in Christian Mission: Vol. 3). (Illus.). xxviii, 202p. 1992. 78.00 (*90-04-09468-7*) Brill Academic Pubs.

Oosthuizen, Gerhardus C. & Becken, H. J., eds. Afro-Christianity at the Grassroots: Its Dynamics & Strategies. LC 94-26023. (Studies of Religion in Africa: 9). 1994. 94.00 (*90-04-10035-0*) Brill Academic Pubs.

Oosthuizen, Gerhardus C. & Hexham, Irving. The Story of Isaiah Shembe: History & Traditions Centered on Ekuphakameni & Mount Nhlangakazi, 2 vols. LC 96-48564. (Sacred History & Traditions of the Amanazaretha Ser.). 1997. write for info. (*0-7734-8773-5*) E Mellen.

Oosthuizen, Gerhardus C. & Hexham, Irving, eds. Afro-Christian Religion at the Grassroots in Southern Africa. LC 91-10173. (African Studies: Vol. 19). 440p. 1991. lib. bdg. 109.95 (*0-88946-226-7*) E Mellen.

— Empirical Studies of African Independent- Indigenous Churches. LC 92-22083. 356p. 1992. text 99.95 (*0-7734-9588-6*) E Mellen.

Oosthuizen, Gerhardus C., et al. Religion, Intergroup Relations, & Social Change in South Africa, 24. LC 88-15430. (Contributions in Ethnic Studies: No. 24). 249p. 1988. 55.00 (*0-313-26360-4*, HSG/, Greenwood Pr) Greenwood.

Oosthuizen, Gerhardus C., jt. ed. see Hexham, Irving.

Oosthuizen, P. H., et al, eds. National Heat Transfer Conference: Fundamentals of Convection, Turbulent Heat Transfer, & Mixed Convection Heat Transfer Proceedings, National Heat Transfer Conference (32nd, 1997, Baltimore, Maryland) LC 97-74082. (HTD Ser.: Vol. 346). 195p. 1997. pap. 90.00 (*0-7918-1813-6*) ASME.

Oosthuizen, P. H. & Carscallen, William E. Compressible Fluid Flow. LC 96-9908. (Illus.). xx, 548p. 1996. write for info. (*0-07-048198-9*) McGraw.

— Compressible Fluid Flow. LC 96-9908. 576p. (C). 1997. 102.81 (*0-07-048197-0*) McGraw.

Oosthuizen, P. H. & Kroeger, P. G., eds. Fundamentals of Phase Change, Sublimation & Solidification: Proceedings: International Mechanical Engineering Congress & Exposition (1994: Chicago, IL) LC 94-78968. (HTD Ser.: Vol. 286). 61p. 1995. pap. 40.00 (*0-7918-1395-9*, G00890) ASME Pr.

Oosthuizen, P. H. & Naylor, David. An Introduction to Convective Heat Transfer Analysis. LC 98-5484. 624p. 1998. 98.75 (*0-07-048201-2*) McGraw.

Oosthuizen, P. H., jt. ed. see Ebadian, M. A.

Oosthuizen, Susan. Cambridgeshire from the Air. (Illus.). 128p. 1996. 35.95 (*0-7509-1064-X*, Pub. by Sutton Pub Ltd) Intl Pubs Mktg.

Oostinde, Gert. Fifty Years Later: Antislavery, Capitalism & Modernity in the Dutch Orbit. 269p. (Orig.). (C). 1996. pap. 22.50 (*0-8229-5587-3*); text 45.00 (*0-8229-3929-0*) U of Pittsburgh Pr.

Oosting, Katrina A. Maenad: Mary's Song. LC 97-68875. 208p. 1998. 13.95 (*1-887750-73-8*) Rutledge Bks.

Oosting, Richard. Toward a New Durable & Environmentally Compliant Adhesive Bonding Process for Aluminum Alloys. (Illus.). 273p. (Orig.). 1995. pap. 67.50 (*90-407-1170-4*, Pub. by Delft U Pr) Coronet Bks.

Oostra, B. A., ed. Trinucleotide Diseases & Instability. LC 97-51981. (Results & Problems in Cell Differentiation Ser.: Vol. 21). (Illus.). 170p. 1998. 109.00 (*3-540-63993-4*) Spr-Verlag.

***Oostveen, Job.** Strongly Stabilizable Distributed Parameter Systems. (Frontiers in Applied Mathematics Ser.: No. 20). (Illus.). 150p. 2000. 56.00 (*0-89871-455-9*, FR0020) Soc Indus-Appl Math.

Oothoudt, Michael, jt. ed. see Lillberg, John.

Oots, Kent L. A Political Organization Approach to Transnational Terrorism, 141. LC 85-17030. (Contributions to Political Science Ser.: No. 141). (Illus.). 188p. 1986. 49.95 (*0-313-25105-3*, OPO/, Greenwood Pr) Greenwood.

***OOverstreet & Rock, ed.** Catamaran & Cabana Checkbook. 2nd ed. 46p. 1999. pap. text 8.00 (*0-536-02631-9*) P-H.

— Catamarans & Cabanas. 2nd ed. 144p. 1999. pap. text 13.00 (*0-536-02632-7*) P-H.

Op De Beeck, Bart, jt. auth. see Callewaert, Winand M.

Op Den Kamp, J. A., ed. Biological Membranes: Structure, Biogenesis & Dynamics. LC 94-2915. (NATO ASI Series H: Cell Biology: Vol. 82). (Illus.). 366p. 1994. 154.00 (*0-387-57731-9*) Spr-Verlag.

Op den Kamp, J. A., ed. Dynamics of Membrane Assembly. (NATO ASI Series H: Cell Biology: Vol. 63). (Illus.). 393p. 1992. 238.95 (*0-387-53149-1*) Spr-Verlag.

Op Den Kamp, J. A., ed. Membrane Biogenesis. (NATO ASI Series H: Vol. 16). (Illus.). viii, 477p. 1988. 206.95 (*0-387-18566-6*) Spr-Verlag.

Op den Velde, W., jt. ed. see De Loos, W. S.

Opachak, Mark, ed. Industrial Fluids: Controls, Concerns & Costs. LC 82-60442. (Manufacturing Update Ser.). 276p. reprint ed. pap. 85.60 (*0-608-15927-1*, 203089700071) Bks Demand.

Opalek, Kazimierz & Wolenski, Jan. Kazimierz Opalek: Selected Papers in Legal Philosophy. LC 99-22862. (Law & Philosophy Library). 1999. write for info. (*0-7923-5732-9*) Kluwer Academic.

Opalewski, Dave & Robertson, Joel. Crises Response Planning: A Procedure Manual for Schools. LC 97-72328. 180p. 1998. pap. 49.00 (*0-9655436-3-3*) Balance Grp.

Opalski, Magdalena & Bartal, Israel. Poles & Jews: A Failed Brotherhood. LC 92-53865. (Tauber Institute Ser.: Vol. 13). 205p. 1992. pap. 17.95 (*0-87451-602-1*) U Pr of New Eng.

Oparenko, Christina, retold by. Ukrainian Folk-Tales. (Oxford Myths & Legends Ser.). (Illus.). 160p. (J). (gr. 7 up). 1996. pap. 12.95 (*0-19-274168-3*) OUP.

Oparil, Suzanne & Weber, Michael A. Hypertension: A Companion to Brenner & Rector's the Kidney. Zorab, Richard, ed. LC 98-47451. (Illus.). 757p. 1999. text 95.00 (*0-7216-7764-9*, W B Saunders Co) Harcrt Hlth Sci Grp.

Oparil, Suzanne, jt. auth. see Snider, Arthur J.

Oparka, K. J., jt. ed. see Harris, N.

Opatoshu, Joseph. A Day in Regensburg: Short Stories. Sloan, Jacob, tr. LC 68-15788. 252p. reprint ed. pap. 78.20 (*0-608-17262-6*, 202921300059) Bks Demand.

Opatowski, Michel, jt. auth. see Duncan, Andrew.

Opatrny, Josef. Historical Pre-Conditions of the Origin of the Cuban Nation. LC 92-32972. 264p. 1993. text 89.95 (*0-7734-2304-4*) E Mellen.

— U. S. Expansionism & Cuban Annexationism in the 1850s. LC 93-15343. 324p. 1993. text 99.95 (*0-7734-2308-7*) E Mellen.

Opatz, Joseph P., ed. Health Promotion Evaluation: Measuring the Organizational Impact. (Illus.). (Orig.). 1987. pap. 22.95 (*0-940981-00-9*) Natl Wellness Inst.

Opatz, Joseph P., ed. see Association for Worksite Health Promotion Staff.

Opatz, Patricia G. Sincerely Yours: Letters from the Heart. LC 96-19518. 176p. (Orig.). 1996. pap. 11.95 (*0-8146-2422-7*, Liturg Pr Bks) Liturgical Pr.

OPCS Staff. Mortality Statistics - Injuries & Poisoning. (OPCS Series DH4: No. 19). 50p. 1997. pap. 60.00 (*0-11-691698-2*, HM16982, Pub. by Statnry Office) Bernan Associates.

OPD Working Group. Operationalized Psychodynamic Diagnostics (OPD) 250p. 2000. 29.50 (*0-88937-188-1*) Hogrefe & Huber Pubs.

Opdahl, Keith. Novels of Saul Bellow: An Introduction. LC 67-16197. 1967. 30.00 (*0-271-73118-4*) Pa St U Pr.

***Opdahl, Lise.** LY or Zero Suffix? A Study in Variation of Dual-Form Adverbs in Present-Day English Volume 1: Overview & Volume 2: Adverbial Profiles. LC 99-86060. 862p. 2000. pap. 89.95 (*0-8204-4399-9*) P Lang Pubng.

Opden Kamp, Jos A., ed. Molecular Dynamics of Biomembranes. LC 96-1972. (NATO ASI Series H: Cell Biology: No. 96). 404p. 1996. 197.00 (*3-540-60764-1*) Spr-Verlag.

Opdycke, John B. Harper's English Grammar. 288p. 1983. reprint ed. mass mkt. 4.99 (*0-446-31184-7*, Pub. by Warner Bks) Little.

Opdycke, Leonard E. French Aeroplanes Before the Great War. LC 98-87946. (Illus.). 288p. 1999. 59.95 (*0-7643-0752-5*) Schiffer.

***Opdycke, Sandra.** No One Was Turned Away. (Illus.). 240p. 2000. pap. 18.95 (*0-19-514059-1*) OUP.

Opdycke, Sandra. No One Was Turned Away: The Role of Public Hospitals in New York City Since 1900. LC 98-3753. (Illus.). 264p. 1999. 29.95 (*0-19-511950-9*) OUP.

***Opdycke, Sandra.** The Routledge Historical Atlas of Women in America. LC 99-53346. (Historical Atlas of American History Ser.). 144p. 2000. pap. 17.95 (*0-415-92138-4*); text 60.00 (*0-415-92132-5*) Routledge.

Opdyke, C. W. Opdyke: Genealogy, Containing the Opdyck-Opdycke-Updike American Descendants of the Wesel & Holland Families. 499p. 1991. reprint ed. pap. 77.50 (*0-8328-1825-9*); reprint ed. lib. bdg. 87.50 (*0-8328-1824-0*) Higginson Bk Co.

Opdyke, D. L., ed. Monographs on Fragrance Raw Materials. (Illus.). 1979. 323.00 (*0-08-023775-4*, Pub. by Pergamon Repr) Franklin.

Opdyke, George. A Treatise on Political Economy. LC 68-56559. (Reprints of Economic Classics Ser.). xxxiv, 339p. 1973. reprint ed. 49.50 (*0-678-00802-7*) Kelley.

Opdyke, Irene Gut. In My Hands: Memories of a Holocaust Rescuer. LC 98-54095. (Illus.). 240p. (J). (gr. 5-9). 1999. 18.00 (*0-679-89181-1*, Pub. by Knopf Bks Yng Read) Random.

Opdyke, Irene Gut & Armstrong, Jennifer. In My Hands: Memories of a Holocaust Rescuer. LC 98-54095. (Illus.). 240p. (YA). (gr. 5-9). 1998. lib. bdg. 19.99 (*0-679-99181-6*, Pub. by Knopf Bks Yng Read) Random.

Opdyke, N. D. & Channell, J. G. Magneticstratigraphy. LC 96-5925. (International Geophysics Ser.: Vol. 64). (Illus.). 349p. 1996. text 99.00 (*0-12-527470-X*) Acad Pr.

Opdyke, Steven. The Printed Elvis: The Complete Guide to Books about the King, 75. LC 99-11132. (Music Reference Collection: Vol. 75). 352p. 1999. lib. bdg. 49.95 (*0-313-30815-2*) Greenwood.

— Willie Nelson Sings America. LC 99-160749. (Illus.). 528p. (Orig.). 1998. pap. 24.95 (*1-57168-265-1*, Eakin Pr) Sunbelt Media.

O'Pecko, Michael T. & Hofstetter, Eleanore O. The Twentieth-Century German Novel: A Bibliography of English Language Criticism, 1945-1986. LC 89-10872. 816p. 1989. 68.50 (*0-8108-2262-8*) Scarecrow.

Opeka, Kay. Keep Them Thinking: A Handbook of Model Lessons, Level 1. 2nd ed. LC 91-61813. (Illus.). 80p. (Orig.). 1991. pap. text 9.95 (*0-932935-34-6*) SkyLght.

Opeka, Kay, jt. auth. see Fogarty, Robin.

Opeke, Lawrence K. Tropical Tree Crops. LC 81-11501. 330p. reprint ed. pap. 102.30 (*0-608-18064-5*, 202789500057) Bks Demand.

Opel, Adolf, ed. Against the Grain: New Anthology of Contemporary Austrian Prose. (Studies in Austrian Literature, Culture, & Thought). 330p. (Orig.). 1997. pap. 25.00 (*1-57241-031-0*) Ariadne CA.

— Relationships: An Anthology of Contemporary Austrian Prose. (Studies in Austrian Literature, Culture, & Thought. Translation Ser.). 362p. 1991. pap. 25.00 (*0-929497-05-8*) Ariadne CA.

Opel, Heinz Von, see Von Opel, Heinz.

Opelima, Ecniv. God Unveiled & Demystified: The Master Key Revealed for Happiness, Love, Wisdom & Power. LC 93-74912. (Illus.). 192p. (Orig.). 1994. pap. 19.95 (*1-884767-00-1*) Celestial Lodge.

Opella, Stanley J., jt. ed. see Lu, P.

Opella, Stanley J., jt. ed. see Markley, John L.

O

***Opello, Walter C., Jr. & Rosow, Stephen J.** The Nation - State & Global Order: A Historical Introduction to Contemporary Politics. LC 98-28937. 290p. 1999. lib. bdg. 55.00 (*1-55587-811-3*) L Rienner.

Opello, Walter C., Jr. & Rosow, Stephen J. The Nation-State & Global Order: A Historical Introduction to Contemporary Politics. LC 98-28937. 290p. 1999. pap. 19.95 (*1-55587-832-6*) L Rienner.

Open City Staff. Backlash Retrospective, Part 2, Vol. 14. 1999. pap. text 7.50 (*1-888984-07-4*) Baffler.

Open Group Staff. Data Storage Management: A Systems Approach. 196p. (C). 1997. pap. 50.00 (*0-13-890187-2*) P-H.

— Event Management Services. 256p. (C). 1997. pap. 50.00 (*0-13-890203-8*) P-H.

Open House Staff. Photos on CD: The Ultimate Search Tool for Finding Just the Right Photo on CD-ROM. 1995. pap. 49.95 incl. cd-rom (*1-56609-173-X*) Peachpit Pr.

Open Learning Foundation Staff. Business Functions: An Active Learning Approach. LC 98-8588. 608p. 1998. pap. 68.95 (*0-631-20177-7*) Blackwell Pubs.

— Business Skills: An Active Learning Approach. LC 97-45213. 608p. 1998. pap. 68.95 (*0-631-20801-1*) Blackwell Pubs.

— Caring for Older People in a Mixed Economy. 146p. 1996. pap. write for info. (*0-443-05734-6*) Church.

— Inferential Statistics in Nursing & Healthcare. 143p. 1998. pap. write for info. (*0-443-05740-0*) Church.

— Learning Disability & the Social Context of Caring. 142p. 1997. pap. write for info. (*0-443-05735-4*) Church.

— Lifespan Development in a Mixed Economy of Care. 112p. 1996. pap. write for info. (*0-443-05736-2*) Church.

— Psychological Aspects of Caring in a Mixed Economy. 130p. 1996. pap. write for info. (*0-443-05733-8*) Church.

— Qualitative Research Methodology in Nursing & Health Care. 120p. 1997. pap. write for info. (*0-443-05738-9*) Church.

— Research Methodology in Nursing & Health Care. 144p. 1996. pap. write for info. (*0-443-05737-0*) Church.

— The Social Context of Caring in a Mixed Economy. 144p. 1996. pap. write for info. (*0-443-05732-X*) Church.

***Open Linguistics Forum Staff.** The Minimalist Parameter: Selected Papers from the Open Linguistics Forum, Ottawa, 21-23 March, 1997. Alexandrova, Galina M. & Arnaudova, Olga, eds. LC 99-88575. (Current Issues in Linguistic Theory Ser.: Vol. 192). viii, 374p. 2000. 79.00 (*1-55619-970-8*) J Benjamins Pubng Co.

Open Media Research Institute Staff. The OMRI Annual Survey of Eastern Europe & the Former Soviet Republic: 1995: Buidling Democracy. LC 96-19263. (Illus.). 344p. (C). (gr. 13). 1996. text 94.95 (*1-56324-924-3*) M E Sharpe.

Open Media Research Institute Staff, Prague. The OMRI Annual Survey of Eastern Europe & the Former Soviet: 1996: Forging Ahead, Falling Behind. (Illus.). 344p. (C). (gr. 13). 1997. text 94.95 (*1-56324-925-1*) M E Sharpe.

Open Media Research Institute Staff, Prague, et al. The Russian Parliamentary Elections of 1995: The Battle for the Duma. LC 96-29822. (Omri Bks.). 220p. (C). (gr. 13). 1997. text 74.95 (*0-7656-0084-6*) M E Sharpe.

Open Path Staff. Namgyal Rinpoche: Unfolding Through Art. Wongmo, Karma C., ed. (Illus.). 157p. (Orig.). (C). 1982. text 75.00 (*0-9602722-2-4*); pap. text 25.00 (*0-685-07078-6*) Open Path.

Open School in Soweto Staff. Two Dogs & Freedom: Black Children of South Africa Speak Out. 56p. (J). 1987. pap. 4.95 (*0-8050-0637-0*) FoxRock.

Open Software Foundation Staff. Application Development Reference, Vol. 2. 2nd ed. 848p. 1995. pap. 62.00 (*0-13-241464-3*, Macmillan Coll) P-H.

— Applications Environment Specification Distributed Computing. 960p. (C). 1994. pap. 45.00 (*0-13-043688-7*) P-H.

— Introduction to OSF DCE. 272p. 1995. pap. 47.00 (*0-13-185810-6*) P-H.

— OSF - Motif Programmer's Guide Release 1.2. 650p. 1992. pap. 65.00 (*0-13-643107-0*) P-H.

— OSF - Motif Programmer's Reference Release 1.2. 1260p. 1992. pap. 86.00 (*0-13-643115-1*) P-H.

— OSF - Motif Style Guide Release 1.2. 400p. 1992. pap. 46.00 (*0-13-643123-2*) P-H.

— OSF - Motif User's Guide Release 1.2. 176p. 1992. pap. 31.60 (*0-13-643131-3*) P-H.

Open Software Foundation Staff. Osf Dce Administration Guide Core Components. 800p. 1995. pap. 60.00 (*0-13-185844-0*, Prentice Hall) P-H.

Open Software Foundation Staff. OSF DCE Application Development Guide, Vol. 2. 912p. 1995. pap. 65.00 (*0-13-185885-8*) P-H.

— OSF DCE Application Development Guide, Vol. 3. 640p. 1995. pap. 64.00 (*0-13-185893-9*) P-H.

— OSF DCE Application Development Guide 1.1, Vol. 1. 416p. 1995. pap. 57.00 (*0-13-185877-7*) P-H.

— OSF DCE Application Development Reference. 880p. 1995. pap. 65.00 (*0-13-185869-6*) P-H.

— OSF DCE Command Reference. 740p. 1996. pap. 62.00 (*0-13-185851-3*) P-H.

— OSF DCE DFS Adm. Guide & Reference 1.1. 1056p. 1996. pap. 72.00 (*0-13-185828-9*) P-H.

— OSF Dce. Gds. Admin. Guide & Reference. 704p. 1995. pap. 46.60 (*0-13-185901-3*) P-H.

— OSF DCE User's Guide & Reference. 208p. 1998. pap. 28.60 (*0-13-643842-3*) P-H.

Open System Foundation Staff. Guidebook of Open System Foundation Distributed Computing Environment. (C). 1993. pap. text. write for info. (*0-201-59466-8*) Addison-Wesley.

***Open University Course Team Staff.** Bordo: Get Ready for Spanish. 160p. (C). (gr. 13). 1999. pap. 49.99 incl. audio (*0-415-19901-8*) Routledge.

Open University Course Team Staff, ed. Ocean Chemistry & Deep-Sea Sediments, Vol. 5. (Illus.). 128p. 1989. pap. text 39.95 (*0-08-036373-3*, Pergamon Press) Buttrwrth-Heinemann.

Open University Program Staff. Ocean Basins: Structure. 2nd ed. 1998. pap. text 37.95 (*0-7506-3983-0*) Buttrwrth-Heinemann.

Open University Program Staff. Ocean Circulation. 1989. pap. text 39.95 (*0-7506-3716-1*) Buttrwrth-Heinemann.

***Open University Staff.** Bordo: Get Ready for Spanish. LC 99-204333. 221p. 1998. pap. text. write for info. (*0-415-19899-2*) Routledge.

Open University Staff, jt. auth. see Ferguson, John.

Open University Team Staff. Case Studies in Oceanography. (Open University Oceanography Ser.). 1991. pap. text 16.40 (*0-08-036935-9*, Pergamon Pr) Elsevier.

— Ocean Basins. (Open University Oceanography Ser.). 1988. pap. text 11.75 (*0-08-036930-8*, Pergamon Pr) Elsevier.

— Ocean Chemistry. (Open University Oceanography Ser.). 1989. pap. text 11.70 (*0-08-036934-0*, Pergamon Pr) Elsevier.

— Ocean Circulation. (Open University Oceanography Ser.). 1989. pap. text 11.70 (*0-08-036932-4*, Pergamon Pr) Elsevier.

— Seawater. (Open University Oceanography Ser.). 1989. pap. text 11.75 (*0-08-036931-6*, Pergamon Pr) Elsevier.

— Seawater: Its Composition, Properties & Behavior. 2nd ed. (Illus.). 166p. 1995. pap. text 34.95 (*0-7506-3715-3*, Pergamon Press) Buttrwrth-Heinemann.

— Waves & Tides. (Open University Oceanography Ser.). 1989. pap. text 11.75 (*0-08-036933-2*, Pergamon Pr) Elsevier.

— Waves, Tides & Shallow-Water Processes. 187p. 2000. pap. text 37.95 (*0-7506-2827-8*) Buttrwrth-Heinemann.

Open University Team Staff, ed. Ocean Basins: Their Structure & Evolution. (Open University Oceonography Ser.). (Illus.). 120p. (C). 1988. pap. text 34.95 (*0-08-036365-2*, Pergamon Press) Buttrwrth-Heinemann.

***Open University Team Staff, ed.** Waves, Tides & Shallow Water Processes. 2nd ed. 228p. 2000. pap. 37.95 (*0-7506-4281-5*) Buttrwrth-Heinemann.

Open University Team Staff & Englander, David. Understanding Comparative History: Britain & America, 1760-1970. LC 96-36470. 352p. 1997. 47.00 (*0-300-06977-4*); pap. 20.00 (*0-300-06978-2*) Yale U Pr.

Open University Team Staff, et al. Families, Education & Social Differences. LC 96-33064. (Exploring Educational Issues Ser.). (Illus.). 256p. (C). 1997. pap. 20.99 (*0-415-15540-1*) Routledge.

— The Welsh & Their Country: Selected Readings in the Social Sciences. 365p. (C). 1986. pap. 30.00 (*0-86383-245-8*, Pub. by Gomer Pr) St Mut.

***Open Universitty Tea Staff.** Electronic Materials. 2nd ed. LC TK7871.E438 1998. (Materials in Action Ser.). 423p. 1999. pap. text 49.95 (*0-7506-4387-0*, Newnes) Buttrwrth-Heinemann.

Openbare Leeszaal van Curapcao Staff & University of Western Ontario Philosophy Colloquim, 4th. A Short-title Catalog of Sixteenth, Seventeenth, & Eighteenth Century Books in the Openbare Leeszaal Van Curapcao (Netherlands Antilles) LC 84-172259. (Whstc Library Catalog.). 47p. 1983. write for info. (*0-7714-0409-3*) UWO2.

Opengart, Bea. Erotica. 47p. 1995. pap. 12.00 (*0-937669-54-7*) Owl Creek Pr.

***Opengl Architecture Review Board, Architecture Review Board.** Opengl Programming Guide: The Official Guide to Learning Opengl, Version 1.2. 3rd ed. LC 99-31356. 784p. 1999. pap. text 49.95 (*0-201-60458-2*) Addison-Wesley.

OpenGL Architecture Review Staff. OpenGL Reference Manual: The Official Reference Document for OpenGL, Release 1. 400p. (C). 1992. pap. text 34.95 (*0-201-63276-4*) Addison-Wesley.

OpenGL Architecture Review Staff & Kempf, Renate. The Reference Manual: The Official Reference Document to OpenGL Release 1.1. 2nd ed. LC 96-37076. 512p. (C). 1997. pap. text 41.95 (*0-201-46140-4*) Addison-Wesley.

OpenGL Architecture Review Staff, et al. The OpenGL Programming Guide: The Official Guide to Learning OpenGL, Release 1. LC 93-3162. 560p. (C). 1993. pap. text 34.95 (*0-201-63274-8*) Addison-Wesley.

OpenInventor Architecture Group Staff. Open Inventor C++ Reference Manual: The Official Reference Document for Open Inventor, Release 2. LC 94-8378. 336p. (C). 1994. pap. 33.95 (*0-201-62493-1*) Addison-Wesley.

Openo, Woodward D. The Sarah Mildred Long Bridge: The History of the Maine-New Hampshire Interstate Bridge. (Portsmouth Marine Society Ser.: No. 13). (Illus.). 130p. 1989. 30.00 (*0-915819-12-0*) Portsmouth Marine Soc.

— Tugboats on the Piscataqua: A Brief History of Towing on One of America's Toughest Rivers. (Illus.). 184p. 1992. 25.00 (*0-915819-17-1*) Portsmouth Marine Soc.

Openshaw, jt. auth. see Eaton.

Openshaw, Christine, jt. auth. see Openshaw, Stan.

Openshaw, Eli C., et al. Might, Mind & Strength: Autobiography of Eli Carlos Openshaw. Lund, Mark W., ed. (Illus.). 442p. 1997. 30.00 (*0-9660894-0-5*, 9701) Eli Pr.

Openshaw, Florence. Advanced Hairdressing Science. LC 81-25729. (Illus.). 239p. reprint ed. pap. 74.10 (*0-608-08061-6*, 206902600002) Bks Demand.

Openshaw, Gene, jt. auth. see Steves, Rick.

Openshaw, Jennifer, ed. see UCLA Students.

Openshaw, K. Cost & Financial Accounting in Forestry. 1980. reprint ed. text 94.00 (*0-08-021456-8*, CRC Reprint) Franklin.

Openshaw, Leona Holdworth, jt. auth. see Lovejoy, Ann.

Openshaw, Stan. Nuclear Power: Siting & Safety. (Illus.). 337p. 1986. text 45.00 (*0-7102-0183-4*, Routledge Thoemms) Routledge.

***Openshaw, Stan & Abrahart, Robert J.** Geocomputation. LC 99-29605. 1999. 150.00 (*0-7484-0900-9*) Taylor & Francis.

Openshaw, Stan & Openshaw, Christine. Artificial Intelligence in Geography. LC 96-45100. 348p. 1997. 120.00 (*0-471-96991-5*) Wiley.

Openshaw, Stan & Turton, Ian. High Performance Computing & Art of Parallel Programming: An Introduction for Geographers, Social Scientists, & Engineers. LC 99-18439. 1999. text. write for info. (*0-415-15692-0*) Routledge.

Openshaw, Stanley, ed. Census Users' Handbook. 460p. 1995. pap. text 49.95 (*0-470-23481-4*) Halsted Pr.

Opera Guild Staff. Intermission. (Illus.). 222p. 1992. 15.95 (*0-9637382-0-8*) Sprngfld Reg.

Opera Society of Fort Lauderdale Staff. Libretto: Opera Society Menu Cookbook. Camp, Melanie & Gamble, Marion, eds. 192p. 1987. 17.95 (*0-9618686-0-0*) Opera Soc Ft Lauderdale.

Operation Explore Staff. Experiential Learning. 112p. 1995. pap., per. 15.99 (*0-7872-1600-3*) Kendall-Hunt.

Operation Smile International Staff. A Smile Is the Beginning: Operation Smile International the First Ten Years. 196p. 1993. 50.00 (*0-9635271-0-X*) Oper Smile Intl.

Operations Evaluation Department Staff, World Bank. New Lessons from Old Projects: The Workings of Rural Development in Northeast Brazil. LC 93-14543. (Operations Evaluation Studies). 126p. 1993. pap. 22.00 (*0-8213-2512-4*, 12512) World Bank.

Operkola, Pauline N. Stamps & Philately Honors in Science & Medicine: Index of Modern Authors & Subjects with Guide for Rapid Research. LC 90-56321. 170p. 1991. 47.50 (*1-55914-436-X*); pap. 44.50 (*1-55914-437-8*) ABBE Pubs Assn.

***Opeskin, Brian & Wheeler, Fiona, eds.** The Australian Federal Judicial System. 550p. 2000. 79.95 (*0-522-84889-3*, Pub. by Melbourne Univ Pr) Paul & Co Pubs.

Opfell, Olga S. The Lady Laureates: Women Who Have Won the Nobel Prize. 2nd ed. LC 85-19670. 334p. 1986. 36.00 (*0-8108-1851-5*) Scarecrow.

— Queens, Empresses, Grand Duchesses & Regents: Women Rulers of Europe, A.D. 1328-1989. LC 88-43484. (Illus.). 296p. 1989. lib. bdg. 39.95 (*0-89950-385-3*) McFarland & Co.

— Special Visions: Profiles of Fifteen Women Artists from the Renaissance to the Present Day. LC 90-53603. (Illus.). 231p. 1991. lib. bdg. 37.50 (*0-89950-603-8*) McFarland & Co.

— Women Prime Ministers & Presidents. LC 92-56675. (Illus.). 237p. (YA). (gr. 9-12). 1993. lib. bdg. 38.50 (*0-89950-790-5*) McFarland & Co.

Opfermann, Ulrich F. Dass Sie den Zigeuner-Habit Ablegen. 2nd ed. Hohmann, Joachim S., ed. (Studien Zur Tsiganologie und Folkloristik Ser.: Vol. 17). 263p. 1997. pap. 51.95 (*3-631-31635-6*) P Lang Pubng.

Ophee, Matanya. Luigi Boccherini's Guitar Quintets - New Evidence. LC 82-181560. (Studies in Guitar History Ser.). (Illus.). 88p. (Orig.). 1981. pap. 7.00 (*0-936186-06-2*) Edit Orphee.

Ophee, Matanya, intro. Dictionary of Guitarists: A Biographical-Bibliographical-Historical-Critical Dictionary of Guitars (Related Instruments), Guitarists (Teachers-Composers-Performers-Luthiers-Amateurs), Guitar-Makers (Luthiers), Dances & Songs - Terminology. LC 86-80463. (SPA.). 488p. 1988. reprint ed. 135.00 (*0-936186-18-6*) Edit Orphee.

Ophee, Matanya, ed. see Chaine, Jacques.

Ophee, Matanya, ed. see Johnson, John.

Ophee, Matanya, ed. see Pujol, Emilio.

O'Phelan, Cesar A., jt. ed. see Barkin, Jamie S.

Ophiel. Art & Practice of Astral Projection. LC 92-18477. 124p. (Orig.). 1974. pap. 9.95 (*0-87728-246-3*) Weiser.

— The Art & Practice of Creative Visualization. rev. ed. LC 96-51424. Orig. Title: The Art & Practice of Getting Material Things Through Creative Visualizations. (Illus.). 112p. (Orig.). 1997. pap. 9.95 (*1-57863-001-0*) Weiser.

Ophir, Adi. Plato's Republic & the Space of Discourse. 300p. (C). 1990. text 64.00 (*0-389-20930-9*) Rowman.

Ophir, Jacqueline. A Perfect Mistress. (Illus.). 144p. 39.95 (*1-899861-14-9*, Pub. by AKS Bks) Xclusiv Distrib.

Ophthalmic Microsurgery Study Group Staff. Surgery of the Iris & the Ciliary Body: Proceedings of the Ophthalmic Microsurgery Study Group, 4th, Lund, Sweden, July 4-7, 1972. Palm, E. & Mackensen, G., eds. (Advances in Ophthalmology Ser.: Vol. 30). 300p. 1975. 172.25 (*3-8055-1844-7*) S Karger.

Ophthalmic Microsurgery Study Group Symposium Staf. Microsurgery of Cataract, Vitreous & Astigmatism: Proceedings of the Ophthalmic Microsurgery Study Group Symposium, 5th, London, June 1974. Kersley, J. & Pierse, D., eds. (Advances in Ophthalmology Ser.: Vol.33). 400p. 1976. 155.75 (*3-8055-2323-8*) S Karger.

Ophthalmology Annual Staff. Ophthalmology Annual, 1988. Reinecke, Robert D., ed. LC 85-646190. (Illus.). 256p. 1988. pap. 79.40 (*0-7837-8356-6*, 204914600010) Bks Demand.

Ophuijsen, J. M. van, et al. Linguistics into Interpretation: Speeches of War in Herodotus VII 5 & 8-18. LC 99-23081. (Mnemosyne, Bibliotheca Classica Batava: Supplementum Ser.). 368p. 1999. 126.50 (*90-04-11455-6*) Brill Academic Pubs.

Ophuijsen, J. M. Van, see Van Ophuijsen, J. M.

Ophuijsen, J. M. Van, see Sicking, C. M. & Van Ophuijsen, J. M.

Ophuijsen, Johannes M. Van, see Van Ophuijsen, Johannes M., ed.

Ophuls, Marcel. Hotel Terminus: The Life & Times of Klaus Barbie. 1993. 18.95 (*0-671-68703-4*) S&S Trade.

Ophuls, William. Requiem for Modern Politics: The Tragedy of the Enlightenment & the Challenge of the New Millennium. 336p. 1998. pap. text 28.00 (*0-8133-3516-7*, Pub. by Westview) HarpC.

Opi, Sergio B. U. S./E. U. Merger Control: How Should the U. S. Experience Influence the Enforcement of Council Regulation 4064/89 on the Control of Concentrations Between Undertakings. (Leuven Law Ser.: Vol. 8). 75p. 1997. pap. 37.50 (*90-6186-820-3*, Pub. by Leuven Univ) Coronet Bks.

Opic, B. & Kufner, A. Hardy-Type Inequalities. LC 89-14502. (Pitman Research Notes in Mathematics Ser.: Vol. 219). 351p. 1990. reprint ed. pap. 108.90 (*0-608-03598-X*, 206442100009) Bks Demand.

Opic, P., jt. auth. see Seret, B.

Opie. Nature's Nation. 27p. (C). 1998. pap. text 37.00 (*0-15-500219-8*, Pub. by Harcourt Coll Pubs) Harcourt.

Opie, A., jt. auth. see Brown, G.

Opie, Amelia. Adeline Mowbray. King, Shelley & Pierce, John, eds. (Oxford World's Classics Ser.). 304p. 2000. pap. 12.95 (*0-19-283330-8*) OUP.

— Adeline Mowbray 1805. LC 94-44529. (Revolution & Romanticism, 1789-1834 Ser.). 1995. 85.00 (*1-85477-188-4*) Continuum.

Opie, Amelia A. Memorials of the Life of Amelia Opie. LC 79-37711. reprint ed. 67.50 (*0-404-56774-6*) AMS Pr.

— The Works of Mrs. Amelia Opie, 3 vols., Set. LC 70-37706. (Women of Letters Ser.). reprint ed. 270.00 (*0-404-56796-7*) AMS Pr.

***Opie, Anne.** Thinking Teams / Thinking Clients: Knowledge-Based Team Work. 256p. 2000. text 49.50 (*0-231-11684-5*); pap. text 21.50 (*0-231-11685-3*) Col U Pr.

Opie, Anne, et al. There's Nobody There: Community Care of Confused Older People. (Studies in Health, Illness, & Caregiving). 232p. (Orig.). (C). 1992. pap. text 19.95 (*0-8122-1419-6*) U of Pa Pr.

Opie, Brenda. Masterminds - Pre-Algebra: Reproducible Skill Builders & Higher Order Thinking Activities Based on NCTM Standards. (Illus.). 96p. (Orig.). (J). (gr. 4-7). 1995. pap. text 10.95 (*0-86530-338-X*, IP 200-6) Incentive Pubns.

Opie, Brenda & McAvinn, Douglas. Effective Language Arts Techniques for Middle Grades (4-8) An Integrated Approach. (Illus.). 84p. (Orig.). (J). (gr. 4-8). 1989. pap. text 7.95 (*0-685-26803-9*) Masterminds Pubns.

***Opie, Brenda & McAvinn, Douglas.** Masterminds Skills Boosters for the Reluctant Math Student: Reproducible Skill Builders & Higher Order Thinking Activities Based on NCTM Standards. (Masterminds Riddle Math Ser.). (Illus.). 96p. (J). (gr. 4-8). 2000. pap. text 10.95 (*0-86530-448-3*, IP 200-7) Incentive Pubns.

Opie, Brenda & McKenzie, Douglas. Effective Language Arts Techniques for Middle Grades: An Integrated Approach. (Illus.). 96p. (Orig.). (J). (gr. 4-8). 1995. pap. text 10.95 (*0-86530-306-1*, 201-0) Incentive Pubns.

Opie, Brenda, et al. Masterminds Addition, Subtraction, Place Value, & Other Numeration Systems: Reproducible Skill Builders & Higher Order Thinking Activities Based on NCTM Standards. (Illus.). 96p. (Orig.). (J). (gr. 3-7). 1995. pap. text 10.95 (*0-86530-303-7*, 200-3) Incentive Pubns.

— Masterminds Decimals, Percentages, Metric System, & Consumer Math: Reproducible Skill Builders & Higher Order Thinking Activities Based on NCTM Standards. (Illus.). 96p. (Orig.). (J). (gr. 4-8). 1995. pap. text 10.95 (*0-86530-301-0*, 200-1) Incentive Pubns.

— Masterminds Fractions, Ratio, Probability, & Standard Measurement: Reproducible Skill Builders & Higher Order Thinking Activities Based on NCTM Standards. (Illus.). 96p. (Orig.). (J). (gr. 3-7). 1995. pap. text 10.95 (*0-86530-302-9*, 200-2) Incentive Pubns.

— Masterminds Geometry & Graphing: Reproducible Skill Builders & Higher Order Thinking Activities Based on NCTM Standards. (Illus.). 96p. (Orig.). (J). (gr. 4-8). 1995. pap. text 10.95 (*0-86530-305-3*, 200-5) Incentive Pubns.

— Masterminds Multiplication & Division: Reproducible Skill Builders & Higher Order Thinking Activities Based on NCTM Standards. (Illus.). 96p. (Orig.). (J). (gr. 4-7). 1995. pap. text 10.95 (*0-86530-304-5*, 200-4) Incentive Pubns.

Opie, Christine A., jt. auth. see Miller, Robert H.

***Opie, Iona.** Here Comes Mother Goose. LC 99-14256. (Illus.). 108p. (J). 1999. 21.99 (*0-7636-0683-9*) Candlewick Pr.

— My Mother Goose Library, 2 vols. (Illus.). 108p. (J). 2000. boxed set 40.00 (*0-7636-1177-8*) Candlewick Pr.

Opie, Iona. The People in the Playground. LC 92-12172. (Illus.). 256p. 1993. 25.00 (*0-19-811265-3*) OUP.

Opie, Iona, ed. Humpty Dumpty & Other Rhymes. LC 97-65083. (My Very First Mother Goose Board Bks.). (Illus.). 16p. (J). (ps). 1997. bds. 6.99 (*0-7636-0353-8*) Candlewick Pr.

— Little Boy Blue & Other Rhymes. LC 97-65085. (My Very First Mother Goose Board Bks.). (Illus.). 16p. (J). (ps). 1997. bds. 6.99 (*0-7636-0354-6*) Candlewick Pr.

— My Very First Mother Goose. LC 96-4904. (Illus.). 108p. (J). (ps-k). 1996. 19.99 (*1-56402-620-5*) Candlewick Pr.

— Pussycat, Pussycat & Other Rhymes. LC 97-65082. (My Very First Mother Goose Board Bks.). (Illus.). 16p. (J). (ps). 1997. bds. 6.99 (*0-7636-0355-4*) Candlewick Pr.

— Wee Willie Winkie & Other Rhymes. LC 97-65084. (My Very First Mother Goose Board Bks.). (Illus.). 16p. (J). (ps). 1997. 6.99 (*0-7636-0356-2*) Candlewick Pr.

Opie, Iona & Opie, Peter. Children's Games with Things. (Illus.). 366p. 1998. 35.00 (*0-19-215963-1*) OUP.

— The Classic Fairy Tales. (Illus.). 256p. 1980. pap. text 15.95 (*0-19-520219-8*) OUP.

— The Lore & Language of Schoolchildren. (Illus.). 448p. 1987. pap. 10.95 (0-19-282059-1) OUP.

Opie, Iona & Opie, Peter, compiled by. The Opie Collection of Children's Literature: A Guide to the Microfiche Collection, Unit 1. v, 79p. 1992. pap. 20.00 (0-8357-2151-5) Univ Microfilms.

— The Opie Collection of Children's Literature: A Guide to the Microfiche Collection, Unit 2. v, 65p. 1992. pap. 20.00 (0-8357-2152-3) Univ Microfilms.

Opie, Iona & Opie, Peter, eds. I Saw Esau: A Schoolchild's Pocket Book. LC 91-71845. (Illus.). 160p. (J). (ps up). 1992. 19.95 (1-56402-046-0) Candlewick Pr.

— The Oxford Book of Children's Verse. (Illus.). 440p. (J). 1995. reprint ed. pap. 15.95 (0-19-282349-3) OUP.

— The Oxford Dictionary of Nursery Rhymes. 2nd ed. (Illus.). 588p. (J). 1998. 49.95 (0-19-860088-7) OUP.

Opie, Iona, et al. The Treasures of Childhood: Books, Toys & Games from the Opie Collection. (Illus.). 192p. 1995. pap. 29.95 (1-85793-624-8, Pub. by Pavilion Bks Ltd) Trafalgar.

***Opie, Iona A.** I Saw Esau: The Schoolchild's Pocket Book. (Illus.). 160p. (J). 2000. pap. 9.99 (0-7636-1199-9) Candlewick Pr.

Opie, James. Collecting Toy Soldiers. (Pincushion Press Collectibles Ser.). 144p. pap. 19.95 (1-872727-76-X) Pincushion Pr.

— The Great Book of Britains: 100 Years of Britains Toy Soldiers 1893-1993. limited ed. (Illus.). 640p. 1996. 125.00 (1-872727-32-8, Pub. by New Cavendish) Pincushion Pr.

— The Great Book of Britains: 100 Years of Britains Toy Soldiers 1893-1993. limited ed. 1996. 250.00 (1-872727-42-5) Pincushion Pr.

— Opie's Pocket Price Guide to Britains Hollowcast Toy Soldiers. 128p. 12.95 (1-872727-82-4, Pub. by New Cavendish) Pincushion Pr.

— Toy Soldiers. 1989. pap. 25.00 (0-85263-632-6, Pub. by Shire Pubns) St Mut.

— Tribal Rugs. 1997. 95.00 (1-85669-025-3, Pub. by L King Pubng) Bks Nippan.

— Tribal Rugs: A Complete Guide to Nomadic & Village Carpets, Vol. 1. (Illus.). 328p. (gr. 8). 1998. 75.00 (0-8212-2547-2) Little.

— Tribal Rugs: Nomadic & Village Weavers from the Near East & Central Asia. Gill, Spencer & Collins, Sophie, eds. LC 92-72906. (Illus.). 328p. 1992. 95.00 (0-9633689-0-7) Tolstoy Pr.

Opie, Jamesnce. Collector's Guide to Twentieth Century Toys. 1990. 12.98 (1-55521-544-0) Bk Sales Inc.

Opie, Jennifer. Scandinavia: Ceramics & Glass in the Twentieth Century. (Illus.). 183p. 1997. pap. 29.50 (1-85177-071-2, Pub. by V&A Ent) Antique Collect.

Opie, John. The Law of the Land: Two Hundred Years of American Farmland Policy. LC 94-28389. (Illus.). xxii, 231p. 1987. reprint ed. pap. text 17.95 (0-8032-8607-4, Bison Books) U of Nebr Pr.

— Ogallala: Water for a Dry Land. LC 92-26718. (Our Sustainable Future Ser.: Vol. 1). (Illus.). xxi, 412p. 1993. text 50.00 (0-8032-3557-7) U of Nebr Pr.

— Ogallala: Water for a Dry Land. 2nd ed. LC 99-42161. (Our Sustainable Future Ser.). (Illus.). 536p. 2000. pap. text 25.00 (0-8032-8614-7) U of Nebr Pr.

Opie, John N. A Rebel Cavalryman: With Lee, Stuart & Jackson. 2nd ed. (Illus.). 336p. 1975. reprint ed. 32.50 (0-89029-012-1) Morningside Bkshop.

Opie, Lionel H. Angiotensin Converting Enzyme Inhibitors. 2nd ed. 309p. 1994. pap. 79.95 (0-471-11195-3) Wiley.

— Clinical Use of Calcium Antagonist Drugs. (C). 1989. text 145.00 (0-7923-0155-2) Kluwer Academic.

— Drugs for the Heart. 4th rev. ed. 1997. pap. text 35.00 (0-7216-7525-5, W B Saunders Co) Harcrt Hlth Sci Grp.

— The Heart: Physiology & Metabolism. 2nd ed. (Illus.). 528p. 1991. 89.50 (0-88167-751-5) Lppncott W & W.

— The Heart: Physiology, from Cell to Circulation. 3rd ed. LC 97-41380. 560p. 1998. text 68.00 (0-7817-1560-1) Lppncott W & W.

Opie, Lionel H., ed. Myocardial Protection by Calcium Antagonists. 195p. 1994. pap. 79.95 (0-471-07669-4) Wiley.

— Stunning, Hibernation, & Calcium in Myocardial Ischemia & Reperfusion. LC 92-17257. (C). 1992. pap. text 132.50 (0-7923-1793-9) Kluwer Academic.

Opie, Lionel H., et al, eds. Metabolic & Molecular Aspects of Cardiomyopathy. LC 92-173761. (Cardiomyopathy Update Ser.: No. 4). 259p. 1991. reprint ed. pap. 80.30 (0-608-01544-X, 206195100001) Bks Demand.

Opie, Lionel H. & Messerli, Franz H. Combination Drug Therapy for Hypertension. 190p. 1997. pap. text 52.00 (1-881063-05-4) Lppncott W & W.

Opie, Lionel H. & Sabino, F., eds. Heart Failure Today. (Journal: Cardiology: Vol. 75, Suppl. 1, 1988). (Illus.). iv, 160p. 1988. pap. 48.75 (3-8055-4929-6) S Karger.

Opie, Lionel H., jt. auth. see Ferrari, Roberto.

Opie, Lionel H., ed. see International Society & Federation of Cardiology S.

Opie, Mary-Jane. Eyewitness Art: Sculpture. LC 93-2593. 1994. 16.95 (1-56458-613-8) DK Pub Inc.

Opie, Peter, jt. auth. see Opie, Iona.

Opie, Peter, jt. compiled by see Opie, Iona.

Opie, Peter, jt. ed. see Opie, Iona.

Opie, Redvers, tr. see Schumpeter, Joseph Alois.

Opie, Robert. Advertising Tins: A Collector's Guide. LC 99-495088. (Miller's Collector's Guides Ser.). (Illus.). 64p. 1999. pap. 11.95 (1-84000-067-8) Antique Collect.

— 1950s Scrapbook. 1998. 24.95 (1-872727-63-8, Pub. by New Cavendish) Pincushion Pr.

— 1930s Scrapbook. 1997. 24.95 (1-872727-33-6, Pub. by White Mouse) Abbeville Pr.

— Remember When: A Nostalgic Trip Through the 20th Century. 1999. 35.00 (1-84000-129-1) Millers Pubns.

***Opie, Robert.** Sweet Memories. (Illus.). 128p. 1999. pap. 16.95 (1-86205-309-X, Pub. by Pavilion Bks Ltd) Trafalgar.

— Victorian Scrapbook. (Illus.). 62p. 2000. 24.95 (1-872727-73-5) New Cavendish.

Opie, Robert. Wartime Scrapbook: From Blitz to Victory, 1939-1945. (Illus.). 64p. 1995. 17.95 (1-872727-08-5) Pincushion Pr.

Opie, William. Shenandoah Spector. 120p. (Orig.). (YA). 1989. pap. write for info. (0-318-65487-3) Opie Pub.

Opiela, Kenneth S. & Stammer, Robert E., eds. Microcomputer Applications in Transportation III. LC 90-716. 1320p. 1990. pap. text 105.00 (0-87262-757-8) Am Soc Civil Eng.

Opies, Redvers, tr. see Schumpeter, Joseph Alois.

Opila, R. L., et al, eds. Polymer/Inorganic Interfaces. (Symposium Proceedings Ser.: Vol. 304). 235p. 1993. text 30.00 (1-55899-200-6) Materials Res.

Opinion Research Corporation Staff. Implementation & Enforcement Codes of Ethics in Corporations & Associations. (Opinion Research Corporation Studies: No. 65334). 256p. 1980. 17.50 (0-916152-05-7) Ethics Res Ctr.

Opinion Research Serv. Staff. American Public Opinion Index, 1997. LC 83-64638. 1998. 195.00 (0-913577-67-7) ORS Pubg.

Opio, Aba J. Casting Shadows. 24p. 1991. 3.00 (1-877610-04-6) Sea Island.

Opitz, Bruce K., ed. Geographic Information Systems in Government, 2 vols., Set. 968p. 1986. 94.00 (0-937194-20-4) A Deepak Pub.

Opitz, Edmund A. Religion: Foundation of the Free Society. LC 95-83491. 270p. 1996. reprint ed. pap. 14.95 (0-910614-92-X) Foun Econ Ed.

— Religion & Capitalism: Allies, Not Enemies. 2nd ed. 322p. 1992. reprint ed. pap. 19.95 (0-910614-81-4) Foun Econ Ed.

Opitz, Edmund A., ed. Leviathan at War. (Freeman Classics Ser.). 195p. 1995. pap. 9.95 (1-57246-009-1) Foun Econ Ed.

Opitz, Edmund A. & Hallberg, Charles. The Libertarian Theology of Freedom. LC 99-72105. 160p. 1999. 19.95 (0-87319-046-7) Hallberg Pub Corp.

Opitz, Glenn B. Chinese & Other Far Eastern Art. (Illus.). 400p. 1988. reprint ed. 65.00 (0-938290-09-6) Apollo.

— Stable & Barn Fixtures. 182p. 1987. reprint ed. 65.00 (0-938290-07-X) Apollo.

Opitz, Glenn B., ed. Dictionary of American Sculptors: Eighteenth Century to the Present. (Illus.). 656p. 1984. 65.00 (0-938290-03-7) Dealers Choice.

Opitz, Glenn B., jt. auth. see Fielding, Mantle.

Opitz, Helmut & Schmid, F. Enciclopedia Pediatrica, 12 vols., Set. (SPA.). 13429p. 1974. 1495.00 (0-8288-6036-X, S50558) Fr & Eur.

— Enciclopedia Pediatrica Vol. 1, Pt. 1: Historia De. 960p. 1973. 275.00 (0-7859-6113-5, 8471121352) Fr & Eur.

— Enciclopedia Pediatrica Vol. 1, Pt. 2: Fisio-Patologia del Recien. 570p. 1974. 275.00 (0-7859-6115-1, 8471121433) Fr & Eur.

— Enciclopedia Pediatrica Vol. 2, Pt. 2: Terapeutica Pediatrica. 806p. 1971. 275.00 (0-7859-6117-8, 8471121875) Fr & Eur.

— Enciclopedia Pediatrica Vol. 3: Immunologia. Pediatria Social. 1366p. 1969. 295.00 (0-7859-6118-6, 8471121883) Fr & Eur.

— Enciclopedia Pediatrica Vol. 4: Metabolismo, Nutricion, Digestion. 1376p. 1967. 295.00 (0-7859-6119-4, 8471121891) Fr & Eur.

— Enciclopedia Pediatrica Vol. 5: Enfermedades Infecciosas. 1398p. 1967. 295.00 (0-7859-6120-8, 8471121905) Fr & Eur.

— Enciclopedia Pediatrica Vol. 6: Enfermedades de los Tejidos De. 1353p. 1970. 295.00 (0-7859-6121-6, 8471121913) Fr & Eur.

— Enciclopedia Pediatrica Vol. 7: Enfermedades del Aparato Respirato. 1450p. 1968. 295.00 (0-7859-6122-4, 8471121921) Fr & Eur.

— Enciclopedia Pediatrica Vol. 8, Pt. 1: Neurologia, Psicologia. 1136p. 1971. 275.00 (0-7859-6481-9) Fr & Eur.

— Enciclopedia Pediatrica Vol. 8, Pt. 2: Tumores en la Infancia. 840p. 1974. 275.00 (0-7859-6114-3, 8471121417) Fr & Eur.

— Enciclopedia Pediatrica Vol. 9: Ojos, Nariz, Dientes, Piel. 997p. 1972. 295.00 (0-7859-6112-7, 8471121174) Fr & Eur.

Opitz, Joachim L., jt. ed. see Martin, Gordon M.

Opitz, John M. & Paul, Natalie W. Blastogenesis: Normal & Abnormal, No. 29. 424p. 1993. 325.00 (0-471-59789-9) Wiley.

Opitz, Marion. Gozzoli. (Masters of Italian Art Ser.). (Illus.). 140p. 1998. 19.95 (3-8290-0250-5, 520530) Konemann.

— Monumentale Hollendarstellungen Im Trecento in der Toskana. (Europaische Hochschulschriften Ser.: Reihe 28, Vol. 320320). (Illus.). 273p. 1998. pap. 51.95 (3-631-32997-0) P Lang Pubng.

Opitz, May, et al, eds. Showing Our Colors: Afro-German Women Speak Out. Adams, Anne V., tr. from GER. LC 91-17061. (Illus.). 272p. (C). 1991. pap. 18.95 (0-87023-760-8); lib. bdg. 40.00 (0-87023-759-4) U of Mass Pr.

Opitz, Michael F. Flexible Grouping in Reading: Practical Ways to Help All Students Become Better Readers. 96p. 1998. pap. text 12.95 (0-590-96390-2) Scholastic Inc.

— Getting the Most from Predictable Books: Strategies & Activities for Teaching with More Than 75 Favorite Children's Books. LC 96-108604. 112p. 1996. pap. text 14.95 (0-590-27049-4) Scholastic Inc.

— Learning Centers: Getting Them Started, Keeping Them Going. LC 94-218729. 96p. 1994. pap. 12.95 (0-590-49554-2) Scholastic Inc.

***Opitz, Michael F.** Rhymes & Reasons: Literature & Language Play. 128p. 2000. pap. text 15.00 (0-325-00246-0) Heinemann.

Opitz, Michael F. & International Reading Association Staff. Literacy Instruction for Culturally & Linguistically Diverse Students: A Collection of Articles & Commentaries. LC 98-27561. 1998. 29.95 (0-87207-194-4) Intl Reading.

Opitz, Michael F. & Rasinski, Tim. Goodbye Round Robin: 25 Effective Oral Reading Strategies. LC 98-37936. 1998. pap. text 12.00 (0-325-00098-0) Heinemann.

Opitz, Otto, ed. Conceptual & Numerical Analysis of Data. (Illus.). 560p. 1989. 110.95 (0-387-51641-7, 3488) Spr-Verlag.

Opitz, Otto, et al, eds. Information & Classification: Concepts, Methods, & Applications: Proceedings of the 16th Annual Conference of the "Gesellschaft Fur Klassifikation E. V." University of Dortmund, April 1-3, 1992. LC 93-5237. (Studies in Classification, Data Analysis, & Knowledge Organization). (Illus.). xii, 517p. 1993. 119.95 (0-387-56736-4) Spr-Verlag.

— Ordinal & Symbolic Data Analysis: Proceedings of the International Conference on Ordinal & Symbolic Data Analysis--Osda '95, Paris, June 20-23, 1995. LC 96-23140. (Studies in Classification, Data Analysis, & Knowledge Organization). 372p. 1996. 99.50 (3-540-61081-2) Spr-Verlag.

Opitz, Otto, jt. ed. see Klar, Rudiger.

Opitz, S. Quantitative Models of Trophic Interactions in Caribbean Coral Reefs. (ICLARM Technical Reports: No. 43). 350p. 1996. pap. 27.00 (971-8709-60-6, Pub. by ICLARM) Intl Spec Bk.

Opland, Greg. Phoenix Rock II. 2nd rev. ed. (Illus.). 272p. 1996. pap. 25.00 (1-57540-023-5) Falcon Pub Inc.

Opland, Jeff. Anglo-Saxon Oral Poetry: A Study of the Traditions. LC 79-24202. 301p. 1980. reprint ed. pap. 93.40 (0-8357-3754-3, 203648000003) Bks Demand.

Oplatka, Matthias. Dictionary of Soil Bioengineering, English, French, German & Italian. (ENG, FRE, GER & ITA.). 256p. 1995. 75.00 (0-7859-9883-7) Fr & Eur.

Opler, Lewis A. & Bialkowski, Carol. Prozac & Other Psychiatric Drugs: Everything You Need to Know. LC 96-222142. 1996. per. 6.99 (0-671-51070-3) PB.

Opler, Morris E. An Apache Life-Way: The Economic, Social & Religious Institutions of the Chiricahua Indians. LC 96-24886. (Illus.). xxi, 530p. 1996. pap. 22.50 (0-8032-8610-4, Bison Books) U of Nebr Pr.

— Apache Odyssey: A Journey Between Two Worlds. Spindler, Louise S. & Spindler, George D., eds. LC 82-23355. (Case Studies in Cultural Anthropology). (Illus.). 320p. 1983. reprint ed. pap. text 19.95 (0-8290-1267-2) Irvington.

— Childhood & Youth in Jicarilla Apache Society. LC 76-43797. reprint ed. 37.50 (0-404-15653-3) AMS Pr.

— Childhood & Youth in Jicarilla Apache Society. (Frederick Webb Hodge Publications: No. 5). (Illus.). xii, 170p. 1964. reprint ed. pap. 5.00 (0-916561-13-5) Southwest Mus.

— Dirty Boy: A Jicarilla Tale of Raid & War. LC 39-14218. (American Anthropological Association Memoirs Ser.). 1938. 25.00 (0-527-00551-7) Periodicals Srv.

— Myths & Tales of the Jicarilla Apache Indians. LC 94-27548. (Sources of American Indian Oral Literature Ser.). xxxviii, 407p. 1994. reprint ed. pap. 14.95 (0-8032-8603-1, Bison Books) U of Nebr Pr.

— Myths & Tales of the Jicarilla Apache Indians. unabridged ed. 406p. 1994. pap. text 9.95 (0-486-28324-0) Dover.

Opler, Morris E., compiled by. Myths & Tales of the Chiricahua Apache Indians. LC 94-12396. (Sources of American Indian Oral Literature Ser.). xxvi, 115p. 1994. pap. 6.95 (0-8032-8602-3, Bison Books) U of Nebr Pr.

Opler, Morris E., jt. auth. see Hoijer, Harry.

Opler, Paul A. Butterflies: Flashguides. (Illus.). 24p. 1997. pap. 7.95 (0-395-82996-8) HM.

— Butterflies East & West: A Book to Color. (Illus.). 96p. (Orig.). (J). (gr. 1-6). 1993. pap. 8.95 (1-879373-45-9) Roberts Rinehart.

— Western Butterflies. 2nd ed. LC 98-43204. (Peterson Field Guides Ser.). 1999. 32.00 (0-395-79152-9) HM.

***Opler, Paul A.** Western Butterflies. 2nd ed. (Peterson Field Guides Ser.). 1999. pap. 24.00 (0-395-79151-0) HM.

Opler, Paul A. & Krizek, George O. Butterflies East of the Great Plains: An Illustrated Natural History. LC 83-6197. (Illus.). 312p. 1984. 49.50 (0-8018-2938-0) Johns Hopkins.

Opler, Paul A., jt. auth. see Strawn, Susan.

Oplinger, Carl S. & Halma, J. Robert. The Poconos: An Illustrated Natural History Guide. (Illus.). 280p. (C). 1988. pap. 14.95 (0-8135-1294-8) Rutgers U Pr.

Oplinger, Carl S., jt. auth. see Halma, Robert.

Oplinger, Jon. The Politics of Demonology: The European Witchcraze & the Mass Production of Deviance. LC 89-43149. 312p. 1990. 44.50 (0-945636-11-3) Susquehanna U Pr.

— Quang Tri Cadence: Memoir of a Rifle Platoon Leader in the Mountains of Vietnam. LC 92-56676. (Illus.). 220p. 1993. pap. 17.95 (0-89950-873-1) McFarland & Co.

Opoczky, L., jt. auth. see Juhasz, Z. A.

Opoku, Kofi A., et al. Healing for God's World: Remedies from Three Continents. (Orig.). 1991. pap. 10.95 (0-377-00229-1) Friendship Pr.

Opolka, H., jt. auth. see Scharlau, Winfried.

Opolot, James S. An Introduction to Private Security: A Comparative Introduction to an International Phenomena. LC 98-56508. 336p. 1998. 54.95 (1-57292-138-2); pap. 32.95 (1-57292-137-4) Austin & Winfield.

***Oppedisano, Jeannette M.** Historical Encyclopedia of American Women Entrepreneurs: 1776 to the Present. LC 99-88204. 2000. lib. bdg. write for info. (0-313-30647-8, Greenwood Pr) Greenwood.

Oppedisano, Joe. Joe Oppedisano. 72p. 1999. pap. 19.95 (88-8158-211-2, Pub. by Charta) Dist Art Pubs.

Oppedisano-Reich, Marie, jt. auth. see Cohen, Lily.

***Oppel, Andrew J. & Albert, Thomas Milton.** Essential Guide to Databases. 300p. (C). 2000. pap. 34.99 (0-13-017368-1) P-H.

Oppel, Ed. Fish & Seafood Cooking. 1994. 12.98 (0-7858-0195-2) Bk Sales Inc.

Oppel, F. Limericks, Limericks, Limericks, Limericks. 1992. 7.98 (1-55521-783-4) Bk Sales Inc.

— Tales of Alaska & the Yukon. 1992. 8.98 (1-55521-119-4) Bk Sales Inc.

— Tales of the Great Lakes. 480p. 1992. 8.98 (1-55521-120-8) Bk Sales Inc.

— Tales of the West. 480p. 1992. 7.98 (0-89009-796-8) Bk Sales Inc.

— True Tales of the West. 1994. 8.98 (0-89009-874-3) Bk Sales Inc.

— Winning System. 1993. 12.98 (1-55521-966-7) Bk Sales Inc.

Oppel, Frances N. Mask & Tragedy: Yeats & Nietzsche, 1902-10. LC 86-24652. 267p. reprint ed. pap. 82.80 (0-7837-4366-1, 204407600012) Bks Demand.

Oppel, Frank. Tales of Old Florida. 480p. 1988. 9.98 (1-55521-225-5) Bk Sales Inc.

— Tales of the New England Coast. (Illus.). 480p. 1997. 9.98 (0-89009-873-5) Bk Sales Inc.

***Oppel, Kenneth.** Emma's Emu. (First Flight Chapter Bk.). (Illus.). 64p. (YA). (gr. 3 up). 1999. pap. 3.95 (1-55041-524-7) Fitzhenry & W Ltd.

Oppel, Kenneth. Follow That Star. unabridged ed. (Illus.). 32p. (J). (gr. k-2). 1994. 12.95 (1-55074-134-9, Pub. by Kids Can Pr) Genl Dist Srvs.

— Silverwing. LC 97-10977. 192p. (J). (gr. 3-7). 1997. per. 16.00 (0-689-81529-8) S&S Childrens.

— Silverwing. LC 97-10977. 224p. (J). (gr. 3-7). 1999. per. 4.99 (0-689-82558-7, 076714004993) S&S Childrens.

***Oppel, Kenneth.** Sunwing. LC 99-25322. (Illus.). 266p. (J). (gr. 4-8). 2000. per. 16.00 (0-689-82674-5) S&S Childrens.

Oppel, Kenneth & LaFave, Kim. Follow That Star. (FRE., Illus.). 32p. (J). pap. 7.99 (0-590-16022-2) Scholastic Inc.

Oppelt, Norman T. Earth, Water & Fire: The Prehistoric Pottery of Mesa Verde. rev. ed. LC 91-75686. (Illus.). 91p. (YA). 1998. reprint ed. pap. 14.95 (0-9662845-0-X) Oppelt Pubns.

— Southwestern Pottery: An Annotated Bibliography & List of Types & Wares. LC 88-6424. (Illus.). 333p. 1988. 47.50 (0-8108-2119-2) Scarecrow.

— The Tribally Controlled Indian College. 1990. pap. 20.00 (0-912586-67-2) Dine College Pr.

Oppen, George. Collected Poems. LC 75-6965. 1976. pap. 11.95 (0-8112-0615-7, NDP418, Pub. by New Directions) Norton.

— This in Which. LC 65-15674. (ND Paperbook Ser.: No. 201). 89p. (Orig.). 1965. reprint ed. pap. 30.00 (0-608-05911-0, 206624600008) Bks Demand.

Oppen, Mary. Meaning a Life. LC 78-6223. (Illus.). 214p. 1990. reprint ed. 25.00 (0-87685-375-0); reprint ed. pap. 12.50 (0-87685-374-2) Black Sparrow.

Oppen, William A. The Riel Rebellions: A Cartographic History (Le Recit Cartographique des Affaires Riel) LC 80-453679. (Illus.). 119p. reprint ed. pap. 36.90 (0-8357-4000-5, 203670100005) Bks Demand.

Oppeneer, P. M., jt. auth. see Kubler, J.

Oppenheim. Listening to American Jews. 1987. 16.95 (1-55774-004-6) Lambda Pubs.

— The Maritime History of Devon. 202p. 1968. text 35.00 (0-900771-00-3, Pub. by Univ Exeter Pr) Northwestern U Pr.

— Rob-Pat Act, 1. 1971. 47.00 (0-316-65090-0) Little.

— Rob-Pat Act, 2. 1971. 47.00 (0-316-65091-9) Little.

— Rob-Pat Act, 3. 1971. 47.00 (0-316-65092-7) Little.

— Rob-Pat Act, 4. 1971. 47.00 (0-316-65093-5) Little.

— Science Is Fun. 32p. 1996. teacher ed. 12.50 (0-8273-7337-6) Delmar.

***Oppenheim.** The Storybook Prince. 2000. pap. write for info. (0-15-202691-6) Harcourt.

Oppenheim, et al. Discrete Time Signal Proc., 1. 2nd ed. LC 98-50398. (Illus.). 950p. 1998. 105.00 (0-13-754920-2) P-H.

Oppenheim, A. Leo. Ancient Mesopotamia: Portrait of a Dead Civilization. 2nd rev. ed. LC 64-19847. (Illus.). 496p. 1977. pap. text 19.00 (0-226-63187-7) U Ch Pr.

Oppenheim, A. Leo, ed. The Assyrian Dictionary of the Oriental Institute of the University of Chicago, Vol. 5, G. LC 56-58292. (AKK & ENG.). 1956. lib. bdg. 45.00 (0-918986-11-7) Orient Inst.

— The Assyrian Dictionary of the Oriental Institute of the University of Chicago, Vol. 6, H. LC 56-58292. (AKK & ENG.). 1956. lib. bdg. 50.00 (0-918986-12-5) Orient Inst.

Oppenheim, A. Leo, et al, eds. The Assyrian Dictionary of the Oriental Institute of the University of Chicago, Vol. 2, B. LC 56-58292. (AKK.). 1966. lib. bdg. 40.00 (0-918986-08-7) Orient Inst.

— The Assyrian Dictionary of the Oriental Institute of the University of Chicago, Vol. 8, K. LC 56-58292. 1971. lib. bdg. 80.00 (0-918986-14-1) Orient Inst.

Oppenheim, A. Leo & Reiner, Erica, eds. The Assyrian Dictionary of the Oriental Institute of the University of Chicago, Vol. 1, A, Pt. 1. LC 56-58292. (AKK.). 1964. lib. bdg. 55.00 (0-918986-06-0) Orient Inst.

— The Assyrian Dictionary of the Oriental Institute of the University of Chicago, Vol. 3, D. (AKK.). 1989. reprint ed. lib. bdg. 35.00 (0-918986-09-5) Orient Inst.

— The Assyrian Dictionary of the Oriental Institute of the University of Chicago, Vol. 9, L. (AKK.). 1978. reprint ed. lib. bdg. 40.00 (0-918986-15-X) Orient Inst.

O

— The Assyrian Dictionary of the Oriental Institute of the University of Chicago, Vol. 10, M, Pts. 1 & 2. LC 56-58292. (AKK.). 1991. reprint ed. lib. bdg. 130.00 (0-918986-16-8) Orient Inst.
— The Assyrian Dictionary of the Oriental Institute of the University of Chicago, Vol. 16, S. LC 56-58292. (AKK.). 1989. reprint ed. lib. bdg. 40.00 (0-918986-18-4) Orient Inst.
— The Assyrian Dictionary of the Oriental Institute of the University of Chicago, Vol. 21, Z. LC 56-58292. 1961. lib. bdg. 45.00 (0-918986-19-2) Orient Inst.
Oppenheim, A. Leo, et al. Glass & Glassmaking in Ancient Mesopotamia. LC 75-131303. (Illus.). 296p. 1988. 60.00 (0-87290-058-4) Corning.
Oppenheim, A. N. The Chosen People: The Story of the '222 Transport' from Bergen-Belsen to Palestine. 200p. 1996. pap. 19.50 (0-85303-330-7, Pub. by M Vallentine & Co); text 39.50 (0-85303-323-4, Pub. by M Vallentine & Co) Intl Spec Bk.
— Questionnaire Design, Interviewing, & Attitude Measurement. LC 92-15306. 310p. 1993. pap. text 29.95 (1-85567-044-5) Bks Intl VA.
— Questionnaire Design, Interviewing, & Attitude Measurement. LC 92-15306. 1992. text 59.00 (1-85567-043-7) St Martin.
Oppenheim, Alan V. & Schafer, Ronald W. Digital Signal Processing. LC 74-17280. (Illus.). 608p. 1975. 105.00 (0-13-214635-5) P-H.
Oppenheim, Alan V., et al. Signals & Systems. 2nd ed. 957p. (C). 1996. 100.00 (0-13-814757-4) P-H.
Oppenheim, Carol. Science Is Fun: For Families & Classroom Groups. (Early Childhood Education Ser.). 416p. (Orig.). (C). 1995. mass mkt. 29.95 (0-8273-7336-8) Delmar.
Oppenheim, Carolyn T., ed. Listening to American Jews. 210p. 1988. pap. 13.95 (1-55774-002-X) Lambda Pubs.
Oppenheim, D. E., jt. auth. see Freud, Sigmund.
Oppenheim, E. P. The Light Beyond. 319p. Date not set. 24.95 (0-8488-2376-1) Amereon Ltd.
Oppenheim, E. Phillips. Advice Limited. LC 74-134972. (Short Story Index Reprint Ser.). 1977. 20.95 (0-8369-3703-1) Ayer.
— Ask Miss Mott. LC 79-128745. (Short Story Index Reprint Ser.). 1977. 19.95 (0-8369-3636-1) Ayer.
— The Ex-Detective. LC 77-150481. (Short Story Index Reprint Ser.). 1977. reprint ed. 19.95 (0-8369-3822-4) Ayer.
— The Golden Beast. reprint ed. lib. bdg. 23.95 (0-89190-411-5, Rivercity Pr) Amereon Ltd.
— The Great Impersonation. (Illus.). 1976. reprint ed. lib. bdg. 21.95 (0-89190-412-3, Rivercity Pr) Amereon Ltd.
— The Great Impersonation. 1990. reprint ed. lib. bdg. 19.95 (0-89968-542-0) Buccaneer Bks.
— The Kingdom of the Blind. LC 97-22026. (Classics in Espionage Ser.). 1997. write for info. (0-7146-4806-X, Pub. by F Cass Pubs) Intl Spec Bk.
— Murder at the Monte Carlo. reprint ed. lib. bdg. 24.95 (0-89190-413-1, Rivercity Pr) Amereon Ltd.
— The Oppenheim Secret Service Omnibus, 2 vols., Vol. 1. (Spies & Intrigues Ser.: No. 1). 525p. 1984. pap. 8.95 (0-918172-13-6) Leetes Isl.
— The Oppenheim Secret Service Omnibus, 2 vols., Vol. 2. (Spies & Intrigues Ser.: No. 1). 440p. 1984. pap. 8.95 (0-918172-14-4) Leetes Isl.
— Pawns Count. 24.95 (0-8488-0304-3) Amereon Ltd.
— Seven Conundrums. LC 78-134973. (Short Story Index Reprint Ser.). (Illus.). 1977. 20.95 (0-8369-3704-X) Ayer.
— The Spy Paramount. reprint ed. lib. bdg. 23.95 (0-89190-414-X, Rivercity Pr) Amereon Ltd.
— Treasure House of Martin Hews. reprint ed. lib. bdg. 26.95 (0-89190-415-8, Rivercity Pr) Amereon Ltd.
— The Vanished Messenger. reprint ed. lib. bdg. 25.95 (0-89190-416-6, Rivercity Pr) Amereon Ltd.
Oppenheim, Edward P. The Kingdom of the Blind. LC 97-22026. (Classics in Espionage Ser.). 1997. pap. write for info. (0-7146-4358-0, Pub. by F Cass Pubs) Intl Spec Bk.
Oppenheim, Elliott B. Before & After: Spoliation of Evidence in Medical Negligence Litigation. 5th ed. 200p. 1996. 180.00 (1-930263-03-1) Terra Firma NM.
— Emtala: Y2K: Its First Decade - A Retrospective Analysis. 5th ed. 85p. 1996. 100.00 (1-930263-00-7) Terra Firma NM.
— The Law of Evidence & the Medical Record: A Trial Lawyer's Guide. 5th ed. 120p. 1997. 125.00 (1-930263-01-5) Terra Firma NM.
Oppenheim, Elliott B. The Medical Record As Evidence. LC 98-84349. xxxi, 968 p. 1998. 110.00 (1-55834-889-1) LEXIS Pub.
***Oppenheim, Elliott B.** The Medical Record As Evidence, 1999 Supplement: Pocketpart. 50p. 1999. suppl. ed. write for info. (0-327-01701-5, 6606210) LEXIS Pub.
— Obstetric Litigation: A Trial Lawyer's Guide. 300p. 1999. 300.00 (1-930263-02-3) Terra Firma NM.
— Scientific Evidence in Personal Injury Litigation. 250p. 2000. 250.00 (1-930263-04-X) Terra Firma NM.
Oppenheim, Eve, contrib. by. Electronic Trading Systems: Which, Why, Where. 182p. 1996. 2750.00 (1-56965-074-8, G-183) BCC.
Oppenheim, Felix E. Political Concepts: A Reconstruction. LC 80-23846. 240p. 1996. pap. text 7.00 (0-226-63185-0) U Ch Pr.
— Political Concepts, a Reconstruction. LC 80-23846. 237p. reprint ed. pap. 73.50 (0-608-09490-0, 205429100005) Bks Demand.
Oppenheim, Frank M. Royce's Mature Ethics. LC 92-53531. (C). 1993. text 42.50 (0-268-01642-9) U of Notre Dame Pr.
— Royce's Voyage Down Under: A Journey of the Mind. LC 79-4007. 136p. reprint ed. pap. 42.20 (0-7837-5786-7, 204545200006) Bks Demand.
Oppenheim, Frank M., ed. The Reasoning Heart: Toward a North American Theology. LC 86-4655. 159p. (Orig.). reprint ed. pap. 49.30 (0-7837-6336-0, 204604800010) Bks Demand.
Oppenheim, Frank M. & Swift, Helen C. Behind the Bits: Managing the Media Maze. 236p. 1998. pap. 25.50 (0-7618-1170-2) U Pr of Amer.
Oppenheim, Gary S., jt. auth. see Richards, Regina.
Oppenheim, I., jt. ed. see Tokuyama, M.
Oppenheim, Irwin, jt. ed. see Tokuyama, Michio.
Oppenheim, Israel. The Struggle of Jewish Youth for Productivization. 240p. 1989. text 55.50 (0-88033-170-4, Pub. by East Eur Monographs) Col U Pr.
***Oppenheim, J. & Van der Wolf, W., eds.** The International Tribunal for the Former Yugoslavia: Facts, Cases & Documents, Vol. 1. 1999. 120.00 (90-5644-017-9, Pub. by Global Law Assn) Gaunt.
Oppenheim, James. The Nine-Tenths. LC 68-57543. (Muckrakers Ser.). 1979. reprint ed. lib. bdg. 29.00 (0-8398-1453-4) Irvington.
— Pay Envelopes: Tales of the Mill, the Mine & the City Street, Vol. 1. LC 72-3288. (Short Story Index Reprint Ser.). (Illus.). 1977. reprint ed. 18.95 (0-8369-4158-6) Ayer.
Oppenheim, Janet. The Other World: Spiritualism & Psychical Research in England, 1850-1914. (Illus.). 504p. 1985. text 80.00 (0-521-26505-3) Cambridge U Pr.
— The Other World: Spiritualism & Psychical Research in England, 1850-1914. (Illus.). 518p. 1988. pap. text 21.95 (0-521-34767-X) Cambridge U Pr.
Oppenheim, Joanne. Black Hawk, Frontier Warrior. 1979. 8.70 (0-606-01478-0, Pub. by Turtleback) Demco.
— Have You Seen Birds? (J). 1986. 10.19 (0-606-03805-1, Pub. by Turtleback) Demco.
Oppenheim, Joanne. Osceola, Seminole Warrior. (J). 1979. 8.70 (0-606-01695-3, Pub. by Turtleback) Demco.
— Painting with Air: A Blopens Craft Package. (Illus.). 32p. (J). (gr. 2-5). 1999. per. 17.95 (0-689-82528-5) Litle Simon.
Oppenheim, Joanne. Rooter Remembers. 1999. pap. 3.99 (0-14-054091-1) NAL.
***Oppenheim, Joanne & Zimmerman, Jerry.** Bug Riddles. LC 99-39190. (Illus.). (J). Date not set. pap. write for info. (0-439-08749-X) Scholastic Inc.

***Oppenheim, Joanne, et al. Oppenheim Toy Portfolio 2001: The Best Toys, Books, Videos, Music & Software for Kids. annuals 378p. 2000. 12.00 (0-9664823-6-0) Oppenheim Toy.**
More than 150,000 sold, this annual book has been featured on Oprah, NBC's Today Show & CNN. The experts from the Oppenheim Toy Portfolio, the nationally recognized consumer organization, help guide parents to find the best designed & most educational toys, books, recordings, videos & software for children from infancy to age ten. With reviews of more than 1,000 expert & kid-tested new & classic products, the book also contains features on products for kids with special needs, multicultural toys, books & videos plus the 2001 Platinum Award Lists. The guide is recommended by Family Circle, USA Today, Baby Talk & Working Mother Magazine. For information contact: Oppenheim Toy Portfolio, Inc., 40 East 9th Street, Suite 14M, New York, NY 10003; Phone: 212-598-0502; Fax: 212-598-9709; website: www.toyportfolio.com; e-mail: stephanie@toyportfolio.com. ***Publisher Paid Annotation.***

Oppenheim, Joanne F. The Best Toys, Books, Videos & Software for Kids - 1997: Oppenheim Toy Portfolio. (Illus.). 320p. 1996. pap., per. 13.00 (0-7615-0705-1) Prima Pub.
Oppenheim, Joanne F. Black Hawk, Frontier Warrior. LC 78-18049. (Illus.). 48p. (J). (gr. 4-6). 1979. pap. 3.50 (0-89375-147-2) Troll Communs.
— Do You Like Cats? LC 92-14113. (Bank Street Ready-to-Read Ser.). (Illus.). 32p. (J). 1993. pap. 4.50 (0-553-37107-X, Litl Rooster) BDD Bks Young Read.
— Eency Weency Spider. 32p. (J). (ps-3). 1991. pap. 4.50 (0-553-35304-7) Bantam.
— Gift for Noche Buena. 1999. 14.99 (0-525-45202-8) NAL.
— Have You Seen Birds? (Illus.). (J). (ps-2). 1988. pap. 2.95 (0-590-40890-9) Scholastic Inc.
— Have You Seen Bugs? LC 96-46140. (Illus.). 32p. (J). (gr. k-3). 1997. 15.95 (0-590-05963-7) Scholastic Inc.
— Have You Seen the Birds? (Illus.). 32p. (J). (ps-3). 1988. pap. 4.99 (0-590-27030-3) Scholastic Inc.
Oppenheim, Joanne F. Kids & Play. 1984. pap. write for info. (0-345-30517-5) Ballantine Pub Grp.
Oppenheim, Joanne F. Money. LC 94-12740. (United Nations Bookshelf Ser.). (J). 1994. text 14.95 (0-689-31910-X) Atheneum Yung Read.
— The Not Now! Said the Cow-Bank Street. 32p. (J). (ps-3). 1981. pap. 4.50 (0-553-34691-1) Bantam.
— Oppenheim Toy Portfolio: Baby & Toddler Play Book. (Oppenheim Toy Portfolio Ser.). 1999. pap. 5.95 (0-9664823-3-6) Oppenheim Toy.
— Osceola, Seminole Warrior. LC 78-60116. (Illus.). 48p. (J). (gr. 4-6). 1979. pap. 3.50 (0-89375-148-0) Troll Communs.
— Sequoyah, Cherokee Hero. LC 78-60117. (Illus.). 48p. (J). (gr. 4-6). 1979. pap. 3.50 (0-89375-149-9); lib. bdg. 15.85 (0-89375-159-6) Troll Communs.
— Wake Up, Baby. (Bank Street Ready-to-Read Ser.). (J). (ps-3). 1990. pap. 3.50 (0-685-46039-8, Litl Rooster); lib. bdg. 9.99 (0-685-54065-0, Litl Rooster) BDD Bks Young Read.
Oppenheim, Joanne F. & Oppenheim, Stephanie. The Best Toys, Books & Videos for Kids: 1996 Edition. (Illus.). 320p. 1995. pap. 13.00 (0-06-273379-6, Perennial) HarperTrade.
Oppenheim, Joanne F., et al. Oppenheim Toy Portfolio: 2000 Edition: The Best Toys, Books, Video, Music & Software for Kids. 7th rev. ed. (Oppenheim Toy Portfolio Ser.). (Illus.), 342p. 1999. pap. 12.00 (0-9664823-2-8) Oppenheim Toy.
Oppenheim, Joost J., et al, eds. Clinical Applications of Cytokines: Role in Pathogenesis, Diagnosis, & Therapy. LC 92-49062. (Illus.). 400p. 1993. text 150.00 (0-19-507129-8) OUP.
***Oppenheim, Joost J., et al, eds.** Cytokine Encyclopedia, 2 Vols. Set. (Illus.). 1800p. 2000. 495.00 (0-12-252670-8) Acad Pr.
***Oppenheim, Joost J. & Feldmann, Marc, eds.** Cytokine Reference: A Compendium of Cytokines & Other Mediators of Host Defense. 1950p. 2000. 695.00 (0-12-252673-2) Acad Pr.
Oppenheim, Joost J. & Shevach, Ethan M., eds. Immunophysiology: The Role of Cells & Cytokines in Immunity & Inflammation. (Illus.). 448p. 1991. reprint ed. pap. text 59.95 (0-19-507064-X) OUP.
Oppenheim, Klara & Power, Jenny. Hungarian Business Law. 2nd ed. LC 98-39195. 1998. 78.00 (90-411-1088-7) Kluwer Law Intl.
***Oppenheim, L., ed.** The Collected Papers of John Westlake on Public International Law. xxix, 705p. 2000. 185.00 (1-56169-595-5) Gaunt.
Oppenheim, Leo. The Interpretation of Dreams in the Ancient Near East. LC 78-72754. (Ancient Mesopotamian Texts & Studies). reprint ed. 40.00 (0-404-18198-8) AMS Pr.
Oppenheim, Lois. Directing Beckett. LC 94-13121. (Illus.). 336p. 1994. text 49.50 (0-472-10535-3, 10535) U of Mich Pr.
— Intentionality & Intersubjectivity: A Phenomenological Study of Butor's La Modification. LC 79-53399. (French Forum Monographs: No. 16). 187p. (Orig.). 1980. pap. 12.95 (0-917058-15-1) French Forum.
***Oppenheim, Lois.** The Painted Word: Samuel Beckett's Dialogue with Art. LC 99-50634. (Theater Ser.). (Illus.). 248p. 2000. text 49.50 (0-472-11117-5, 11117) U of Mich Pr.
Oppenheim, Lois. Politics in Chile: Democracy, Authoritarianism, & the Search for Development. 2nd ed. LC 98-20755. 320p. 1998. text 65.00 (0-8133-3565-5, Pub. by Westview) HarpC.
Oppenheim, Lois, ed. Directing Beckett. 336p. (C). 1997. pap. text 19.95 (0-472-08436-4, 08436) U of Mich Pr.
— Improvisations on Butor: Transformation of Writing, by Michel Butor. Miller, Elinor S., tr. (Crosscurrents Ser.). 224p. (C). 1996. lib. bdg. 34.95 (0-8130-1378-X) U Press Fla.
— Samuel Beckett & the Arts: Music, Visual Arts, & Non-Print Media. LC 98-46328. (Border Crossings Ser.: Vol. 2). 416p. 1998. 75.00 (0-8153-2527-4, H2036) Garland.
Oppenheim, Lois & Buning, Marius, eds. Beckett on & On... LC 95-20868. 264p. 1996. 39.50 (0-8386-3623-3) Fairleigh Dickinson.
Oppenheim, Lois, ed. & anno. see Smith, Nigel J.
Oppenheim, Lois H. Politics in Chile: Democracy, Authoritarianism, & the Search for Development. 2nd ed. LC 98-20755. 320p. (C). 1998. pap. text 28.00 (0-8133-3415-2, Pub. by Westview) HarpC.
— Women & Politics in Chile. (C). 1996. pap. text 33.50 (0-8133-8121-5) Westview.
Oppenheim, M., ed. see Helps, Arthur.
Oppenheim, Max F. Von, see Von Oppenheim, Max F.
Oppenheim, Meret. Meret Oppenheim: Beyond the Teacup. 1996. pap. 29.95 (0-614-25261-X) Dist Art Pubs.
Oppenheim, Meret. Beyond the Teacup. LC 95-81295. 176p. 1996. 49.95 (0-916365-45-X, 620141) Ind Curators.
Oppenheim, Michael. Mutual Upholding: Fashioning Jewish Philosophy Through Letters. LC 91-36045. (Revisioning Philosophy Ser.: Vol. 9). 186p. (C). 1992. text 36.95 (0-8204-1685-1) P Lang Pubng.
— Speaking/Writing of God: Jewish Philosophical Reflections on the Life with Others. LC 96-41186. (SUNY Series in Jewish Philosophy). 201p. (C). 1997. text 59.50 (0-7914-3457-5); pap. text 19.95 (0-7914-3458-3) State U NY Pr.
— What Does Revelation Mean for the Modern Jew? LC 85-18929. (Symposium Ser.: Vol. 17). 152p. 1985. lib. bdg. 79.95 (0-88946-708-0) E Mellen.
Oppenheim, Mike. The Man's Health Book. LC 94-4872. 370p. (C). 1994. pap. text 16.95 (0-13-880550-4) P-H.
— One Hundred Drugs That Work: A Guide to Prescription & Non-Prescription Drugs. 348p. 1994. 22.95 (1-56565-115-4) Lowell Hse.
Oppenheim, Peter K. International Banking. 400p. 1991. 51.00 (0-89982-369-6, 050290) Am Bankers.
— The Language of International Finance in English: Money & Banking. (English for Careers Ser). (Illus.). (YA). (gr. 10 up). 1976. pap. text 4.25 (0-88345-272-3, 18504) Prentice ESL.
Oppenheim, Phillip. Japan Without Blinders: Coming to Terms with Japan's Economic Success. 448p. 1992. 24.95 (4-7700-1682-4) Kodansha.
Oppenheim, Robert. 101 Salon Promotions. LC 98-4064. (Milady - Cosmetology). 256p. 1999. pap. text 31.95 (1-56253-358-4) Thomson Learn.
— Urban Travel Demand Modeling: From Individual Choices to General Equilibrium. 480p. 1995. 99.00 (0-471-55723-4) Wiley.
Oppenheim, Rosalind C. Effective Teaching Methods for Autistic Children. 124p. 1977. 30.95 (0-398-02858-3); pap. 20.95 (0-398-06309-5) C C Thomas.
Oppenheim, Samuel. Early History of the Jews in New York. 96p. 1993. reprint ed. lib. bdg. 69.00 (0-7812-5313-6) Rprt Serv.
Oppenheim, Shulamith. The Hundredth Name. LC 94-72255. (Illus.). 32p. (J). (ps-3). 1997. pap. 7.95 (1-56397-694-3) Boyds Mills Pr.
Oppenheim, Shulamith L. Appleblossom. Yolen, Jane, ed. LC 89-24575. (Illus.). 40p. (J). (gr. 1-7). 1991. 14.95 (0-15-203750-0, Harcourt Child Bks) Harcourt.
— Fireflies for Nathan. LC 93-29568. (Illus.). (J). 1994. 16.00 (0-688-12147-0, Wm Morrow) Morrow Avon.
— The Hundredth Name. 32p. (J). 1996. 14.95 (0-614-21008-9, 1501) Kazi Pubns.
— I Love You, Bunny Rabbit. (Illus.). 32p. (J). 1997. pap. 4.99 (0-440-41172-6, Yearling) BDD Bks Young Read.
— I Love You, Bunny Rabbit. LC 94-70683. (Illus.). 32p. (J). (ps-2). 1995. 14.95 (1-56397-322-7) Boyds Mills Pr.
— Iblis: An Islamic Tale. LC 92-15060. (Illus.). 32p. (J). (ps-3). 1994. 15.95 (0-15-238016-7) Harcourt.
— The Lily Cupboard. 2nd ed. LC 90-38592. (Charlotte Zolotow Bk.). (Illus.). 32p. (J). (ps-3). 1995. pap. 5.95 (0-06-443393-5, HarpTrophy) HarpC Child Bks.
— The Selchie's Seed. LC 96-2279. (Illus.). 96p. (J). 1996. pap. 7.00 (0-15-201412-8) Harcourt.
— Waiting for Noah. LC 89-35561. (Charlotte Zolotow Bk.). (Illus.). 32p. (J). (ps-2). 1990. 12.95 (0-06-024633-2) HarpC Child Bks.
— What Is the Moon Full Of? LC 96-80399. (Illus.). 32p. (J). (ps-3). 1997. 14.95 (1-56397-479-7) Boyds Mills Pr.
— Yanni Rubbish. LC 98-71791. (Illus.). 32p. (J). (ps-4). 1999. 15.95 (1-56397-668-4) Boyds Mills Pr.
Oppenheim, Shulamith Levey. Fireflies for Nathan. LC 96-6239. 1996. 10.19 (0-606-09278-1, Pub. by Turtleback) Demco.
— Lily Cupboard. (J). 1992. 11.40 (0-606-07789-8) Turtleback.
***Oppenheim, Shulamith Levey.** What Is the Full Moon Full Of? (Illus.). 32p. (J). 2000. 6.99 (0-440-41640-X) Dell Yearling.
Oppenheim, Stephanie, jt. auth. see Oppenheim, Joanne F.
Oppenheim, Vicki. The Money Project. 1992. pap. text, teacher ed. 29.95 (1-882247-00-0) Dansi Pr.
— The Money Project. (YA). (gr. 9-12). 1992. pap. text, student ed., wbk. ed. 10.95 (1-882247-01-9) Dansi Pr.
— The Money Project II. 1995. pap. text, teacher ed. 31.95 (1-882247-02-7) Dansi Pr.
— The Money Project II. (YA). (gr. 9-12). 1995. pap. text, student ed., wbk. ed. 10.95 (1-882247-03-5) Dansi Pr.
Oppenheim, Vicki A. & Sierra, Luis F. Building Blocks: Community-Based Strategies to Counteract Housing Disinvestment & Abandonment in New York City. 236p. (Orig.). 1994. pap. 15.00 (0-88156-158-4) Comm Serv Soc NY.
Oppenheim, Yvonne, tr. see Heidenreich, Manfred.
Oppenheimer. Survey of Electronics. (C). 1990. pap. text, teacher ed. 38.25 (0-03-020843-2) Harcourt Coll Pubs.
Oppenheimer, Andres. Bordering on Chaos: Mexico's Roller-Coaster Journey to Prosperity. LC 99-198298. (Illus.). 416p. 1998. pap. 15.00 (0-316-65025-0) Little.
Oppenheimer, Andrew, ed. European Community Law & National Law: Cases on Their Relationship. 1029p. (C). 1995. text 200.00 (0-521-47296-2) Cambridge U Pr.
Oppenheimer, Betty. The Candlemaker's Companion. Balmuth, Deborah, ed. LC 97-13119. (Illus.). 176p. 1997. pap. 18.95 (0-88266-994-X, Storey Pub) Storey Bks.
— Gifts for Herb Lovers. Balmuth, Deborah, ed. LC 97-13882. (Illus.). 128p. 1997. pap. 14.95 (0-88266-983-4, Storey Pub) Storey Bks.
***Oppenheimer, Betty.** Making Hand-Dipped Candles. LC 99-14635. 1999. pap. 3.95 (1-58017-205-9) Storey Bks.
Oppenheimer, Betty. Sewing Packs, Pouches, Seats & Sacks: 30 Easy Projects. LC 98-13402. (Illus.). 147p. 1998. pap. 19.95 (1-58017-049-8) Storey Bks.
Oppenheimer, Bruce I., jt. auth. see Dodd, Lawrence C.
Oppenheimer, Bruce I., jt. auth. see Lee, Frances E.
Oppenheimer, Catherine, jt. auth. see Jacoby, Robin.
***Oppenheimer, Christine Crawford.** Long-Distance Genealogy. (Illus.). 208p. 2000. pap. 18.99 (1-55870-535-X, Betrwy Bks) F & W Pubns Inc.
Oppenheimer, David, et al. System Security: A Management Perspective. Geer, Dan, ed. & frwd. by. (Orig.). 1997. pap. text 7.50 (1-880446-85-5) USENIX Assn.
Oppenheimer, David B. Rowe vs. Pacific Quad, Inc. 3rd ed. 150p. 1993. pap. 22.95 (1-55681-376-7) Natl Inst Trial Ad.
Oppenheimer, Deborah, jt. auth. see Harris, Mark Jonathan.
Oppenheimer, Ernest J. Balancing the Federal Budget: The Cure for U. S. Wealth Dissipation. LC 90-62918. 181p. 1991. 20.00 (0-9603982-6-0) Pen & Podium.
— Budget Therapy. LC 96-92237. 190p. 1996. 30.00 (0-9603982-9-5) Pen & Podium.
— Gasoline Tax Advantages. 90p. (Orig.). 1987. pap. 10.00 (0-9603982-5-2) Pen & Podium.
— Natural Gas, the Best Energy Choice. LC 89-63205. 188p. 1990. 30.00 (0-9603982-7-9) Pen & Podium.
— A Realistic Approach to U. S. Energy Independence. (Orig.). 1980. pap. 5.00 (0-9603982-0-1) Pen & Podium.
— Solving the U. S. Energy Problem. 50p. (Orig.). 1984. pap. 5.00 (0-9603982-4-4) Pen & Podium.
Oppenheimer, Evelyn. A Book Lover in Texas. LC 94-49021. 181p. 1995. 16.95 (0-929398-89-0) UNTX Pr.
— Gilbert Onderdonk: The Nurseryman of Mission Valley, Pioneer Horticulturist. LC 90-28231. (Illus.). 159p. 1991. pap. 12.95 (0-929398-23-8) UNTX Pr.

O

An Asterisk (*) at the beginning of an entry indicates that the title is appearing for the first time.

— Heroes of Texas. (Illus.). 1964. 24.95 (0-87244-001-X) Texian.

— Oral Book Reviewing to Stimulate Reading: A Practical Guide in Technique for Lecture & Broadcast. LC 80-20006. 168p. 1980. 21.00 (0-8108-1352-1) Scarecrow.

Oppenheimer, Evelyn, ed. see Tolbert, Frank.

Oppenheimer, Francis J. Ezekiel to Einstein: Israel's Gifts to Science & Invention. LC 70-167398. (Essay Index Reprint Ser.). 1977. reprint ed. 12.95 (0-8369-2438-X) Ayer.

Oppenheimer, Franz. Selected Writings. 1973. 300.00 (0-8490-1022-5) Gordon Pr.

— The State. Gitterman, John M., tr. from GER. 122p. 1975. pap. 12.99 (0-919618-59-6, Pub. by Black Rose) Consort Bk Sales.

— The State. 1984. lib. bdg. 250.00 (0-87700-647-4) Revisionist Pr.

— The State. Gitterman, John M., tr. from GER. lvi, 148p. 1997. reprint ed. 22.95 (0-930073-22-3); reprint ed. pap. 12.95 (0-930073-23-1) Fox & Wilkes.

— The State: Its History & Development Viewed Sociologically. LC 98-27093. 312p. 1998. pap. 24.95 (1-56000-965-9) Transaction Pubs.

— State: Its History & Development Viewed Sociologically. Gitterman, John M., tr. LC 73-172224. (Right Wing Individualist Tradition in America Ser.). 1978. reprint ed. 25.95 (0-405-00433-8) Ayer.

Oppenheimer, George, jt. auth. see Kober, Arthur.

Oppenheimer, Gerald M., jt. auth. see Bayer, Ronald.

Oppenheimer, Gregg, jt. auth. see Oppenheimer, Jess.

Oppenheimer, Heinrich. Rationale of Punishment: With Intro. & Index Added. LC 72-172579. (Criminology, Law Enforcement, & Social Problems Ser.: No. 167). 1975. 24.00 (0-87585-167-3) Patterson Smith.

Oppenheimer, Helen. Helping Children Find God: A Book for Parents, Teachers & Clergy. LC 95-20804. 176p. 1995. reprint ed. pap. 12.95 (0-8192-1650-X) Morehouse Pub.

***Oppenheimer, J. A.** Evaluation of Cryptosporidium Inactivation in Natural Waters. LC 00-42070. 2000. write for info. (1-58321-027-X) Am Water Wks Assn.

Oppenheimer, James. Poems. 1972. 69.95 (0-8490-0847-6) Gordon Pr.

Oppenheimer, Jane M. Autobiography of Dr. Karl Ernst von Baer. LC 86-1924. 1986. 25.00 (0-88135-079-6) Watson Pub Intl.

Oppenheimer, Jane M., tr. & intro. see Groeben, Christiane, ed.

Oppenheimer, Jerry. Martha Stewart - Just Desserts: The Unauthorized Biography. 496p. 1998. mass mkt. 6.99 (0-380-73164-9, Avon Bks) Morrow Avon.

— The Other Mrs. Kennedy. 4th ed. 752+16p. 1995. mass mkt. 7.99 (0-312-95600-2) St Martin.

— State of a Union. 2000. pap. 6.99 (0-06-109843-4) HarpC.

— State of a Union: Inside the Complex Marriage of Bill & Hillary Clinton. (Illus.). 320p. 2000. 25.00 (0-06-019392-1) HarpC.

Oppenheimer, Jess & Oppenheimer, Gregg. Laughs, Luck... & Lucy: How I Came to Create the Most Popular Sitcom of All Time (with Lucy Audio CD) LC 96-20756. (Television Ser.). (Illus.). 312p. 1996. 39.95 incl. audio compact disk (0-8156-0406-8, OPLL) Syracuse U Pr.

— Laughs, Luck...& Lucy: How I Came to Create the Most Popular Sitcom of All Time (with I Love Lucy's Lost Scenes Audio CD) (Illus.). 312p. 1999. pap. 19.95 incl. audio compact disk (0-8156-0584-6) Syracuse U Pr.

Oppenheimer, Joachim. Take Your Brother by the Hand. LC 91-71463. (Illus.). 186p. (Orig.). 1991. pap. 17.95 (0-9629401-0-0) J Oppenheimer.

Oppenheimer, Joan. Gardine vs. Hanover. LC 81-43390. 160p. (J). (gr. 5-7). 1982. 11.95 (0-690-04190-X) HarpC Child Bks.

Oppenheimer, Joan L. Trouble at the Gabourys' 1987. 16.95 (0-8027-0981-8) Walker & Co.

Oppenheimer, Joe A., jt. auth. see Frohlich, Norman.

Oppenheimer, Joel. Collected Later Poems of Joel Oppenheimer. Bertholf, Robert J., ed. (Illus.). 500p. (Orig.). (C). 1996. 24.95 (0-922668-15-9); pap. 14.95 (0-922668-16-7) SUNYB Poetry Rare Bks.

— Drawing from Life: A Selection of Joel Oppenheimer's Writings from "The Village Voice" Bertholf, Robert & Landrey, David, eds. LC 96-43470. 382p. 1997. 24.95 (1-55921-197-0, Asphodel Pr) Moyer Bell.

— The Ghost Lover. 16p. 1993. pap. 3.00 (0-9632962-0-5) A Mann Kaye.

— The Ghost Lover. limited ed. 16p. 1993. 10.00 (0-9632962-1-3) A Mann Kaye.

— Names & Local Habitations: Selected Poems. 1990. 30.00 (0-912330-66-X) Jargon Soc.

— New Spaces: Poems, 1975-1983. LC 85-9060. 151p. (Orig.). 1985. pap. 8.50 (0-87685-640-7) Black Sparrow.

— Pan's Eyes. LC 74-77760. (Haystack Bks.). 64p. 1974. pap. 3.50 (0-685-46899-2) Mulch Pr.

— Why Not? 46p. 1987. 7.00 (0-934834-32-6) White Pine.

— The Woman Poems. LC 74-17641. 128p. 1975. 7.95 (0-672-52025-7, Bobbs); pap. 4.95 (0-672-52026-5, Bobbs) Macmillan.

Oppenheimer, Josh & Reckitt, Helena, eds. Acting on AIDS, Vol. 1. LC 96-69725. 256p. (Orig.). 1997. pap. 19.99 (1-85242-553-9) Serpents Tail.

***Oppenheimer, L.** The Future of International Law. LC 99-47539. 2000. write for info. (1-57588-592-1) W S Hein.

Oppenheimer, L., ed. The Self-Concept: European Perspectives on Its Development, Aspects, & Applications. (Recent Research in Psychology Ser.). (Illus.). viii, 160p. 1990. 42.95 (0-387-52371-5) Spr-Verlag.

Oppenheimer, L. & Valsiner, Jaan, eds. The Origins of Action: Interdisciplinary & International Perspectives. (Illus.). xv, 265p. 1991. 79.95 (0-387-97510-1) Spr-Verlag.

Oppenheimer, Lillian & Epstein, Natalie. Decorative Napkin Folding for Beginners. (Illus.). 48p. 1980. pap. 2.95 (0-486-23797-4) Dover.

— More Decorative Napkin Folding. (Cookery, Wine, Nutrition Ser.). 48p. 1984. pap. 2.95 (0-486-24673-6) Dover.

Oppenheimer, Lillian, jt. auth. see Lewis, Shari.

***Oppenheimer, Lisa.** Hidden Disneyland & Beyond. (Hidden Travel Ser.). (Illus.). 290p. 2000. pap. 13.95 (1-56975-209-5, Pub. by Ulysses Pr) Publishers Group.

Oppenheimer, Lisa, jt. auth. see Ritz, Stacy.

***Oppenheimer, Lorna.** Lorna Oppenheimer's Trade Secrets: Home Decorating Kit. Weber, Beth, ed. (Illus.). 67p. 1999. 49.95 (1-893635-01-5) Trade Sec.

Oppenheimer, Louis, jt. auth. see Oosterwegel, Annerieke.

Oppenheimer, M., jt. auth. see Donley, Thomas.

***Oppenheimer, Martin.** The State in Modern Society. LC 99-87115. 230p. 2000. 44.95 (1-57392-822-4, Humanity Bks) Prometheus Bks.

Oppenheimer, Martin. White Collar Politics. 288p. 1985. 26.00 (0-85345-659-3, Pub. by Monthly Rev); pap. 12.00 (0-85345-660-7, Pub. by Monthly Rev) NYU Pr.

Oppenheimer, Martin, ed. The American Military. LC 73-78698. (Society Bks.). 180p. (C). 1971. reprint ed. 32.95 (0-87855-056-9); reprint ed. pap. text 19.95 (0-87855-549-8) Transaction Pubs.

Oppenheimer, Martin, et al, eds. Radical Sociologists & the Movement: Experiences, Lessons, & Legacies. 256p. 1991. 32.95 (0-87722-745-4) Temple U Pr.

Oppenheimer, Mary, jt. auth. see Fitch, Robert B.

***Oppenheimer, Max, Jr.** An Innocent Yank at Home Abroad: Footnotes to History, 1922-1945. (Illus.). 270p. 1999. pap. 22.95 (0-89745-230-5) Sunflower U Pr.

Oppenheimer, Max, Jr. & Calderon de la Barca, Pedro. Pedro Balderon de la Barca's "The Fake Astrologer" A Critical Spanish Text & English Translation. LC 93-12701. (Iberica Ser.: Vol. 9). 258p. (C). 1994. text 48.95 (0-8204-2166-9) P Lang Pubng.

Oppenheimer, Max, Jr., tr. see De Molina, Tirso.

Oppenheimer, Nathaniel, jt. auth. see Friedman, Donald.

Oppenheimer, Norman J., et al, eds. Nuclear Magnetic Resonance Pt. B: Structure & Mechanism. (Methods in Enzymology Ser.: Vol. 177). 550p. 1989. text 125.00 (0-12-182078-5) Acad Pr.

***Oppenheimer, Pamela.** Wine Wallet Wizard: A Portable Consultant for Matching Foods with Wines. 3rd rev. ed. 1p. 1999. 2.50 (0-9673154-1-7) Cosper Corp.

***Oppenheimer, Paul.** Blood Memoir: The First Three Days of Creation. 1999. pap. text 14.95 (1-56886-067-6, Pub. by Marsilio Pubs) Consort Bk Sales.

Oppenheimer, Paul. Evil & the Demonic: A New Theory of Monstrous Behavior. LC 96-22374. (Illus.). 256p. (C). 1999. text 45.00 (0-8147-6193-3) NYU Pr.

— Evil & the Demonic: A Theory of Monstrous Behavior. 1999. pap. 18.95 (0-8147-6196-8) NYU Pr.

Oppenheimer, Paul J., tr. Till Eulenspiegel: His Adventures. (World's Classics Ser.). (Illus.). 248p. 1995. pap. 9.95 (0-19-282343-4) OUP.

Oppenheimer, Peter. Mirror by the Road: A Transforming Journey of Spirituality in Everyday Life. (Illus.). 208p. (Orig.). 1988. pap. 12.95 (0-945925-03-4) Inner Wealth Pr.

Oppenheimer, Priscilla. Top-Down Network Design. LC 98-84274. 1998. 55.00 (1-57870-069-8) Cisco Press.

Oppenheimer, Richard, ed. see Schuyler, Arlene A.

Oppenheimer, Robert. Robert Oppenheimer: Letters & Recollections. Smith, Alice K. & Weiner, Charles, eds. LC 80-10106. (Harvard Paperbacks Ser.). (Illus.). 387p. 1980. text 37.50 (0-674-77605-4) HUP.

— Robert Oppenheimer: Letters & Recollections. Smith, Alice K. & Weiner, Charles, eds. LC 80-10106. (Harvard Paperbacks Ser.). 387p. 1981. pap. text 12.50 (0-674-77606-2) HUP.

Oppenheimer, Stephen. Eden in the East: The Drowned Continent of Southeast Asia. (Illus.). 560p. 1999. 35.00 (0-297-81816-3, Pub. by Weidenfeld & Nicolson) Trafalgar.

***Oppenheimer, Stephen.** Eden in the East: The Drowned Continent of Southeast Asia. (Illus.). 560p. 2000. reprint ed. pap. 17.95 (0-7538-0679-7, Pub. by Phoenix Hse) Trafalgar.

Oppenheimer, Valerie K. The Female Labor Force in the United States, Vol. 5. LC 76-4536. (Population Monograph: No. 5). (Illus.). 197p. 1976. reprint ed. lib. bdg. 25.00 (0-8371-8829-6, OPFL, Greenwood Pr) Greenwood.

Oppenheimer, William. El Dorado: Lament for the Gold Double Eagle. LC 94-77949. 152p. 1994. 23.00 (0-913559-25-3); pap. 14.00 (0-913559-24-5) Birch Brook Pr.

Oppenlander, Ella Ann & Dickens, Charles. Dickens' "All the Year Round" Descriptive Index & Contributor List. LC 82-50403. viii, 752p. 1984. 55.00 (0-87875-252-8) Whitston Pub.

Oppenlander, Karl H., ed. Business Cycle Indicators. 304p. 1997. text 78.95 (1-85972-436-1, Pub. by Avebry) Ashgate Pub Co.

Oppenlander, Karl H. & Poser, Gunter. Business Cycle Analysis by Means of Economic Surveys, Pt. II: Papers Presented at the 20th CIRET Conference Proceedings, Budapest 1991. 480p. 1993. 91.95 (1-85628-429-8, Pub. by Avebry) Ashgate Pub Co.

— Business Cycle Analysis by Means of Economic Surveys, Pt. 1: Papers Presented at the 20th CIRET Conference Proceedings, Budapest 1991. 453p. 1992. 109.95 (1-85628-260-0, Pub. by Avebry) Ashgate Pub Co.

— Business Cycle Surveys: Forecasting Issues & Methodological Aspects: Selected Papers Presented at the 22nd CIRET Conference, Singapore 1995. LC 96-85548. (CIRET Ser.). 456p. 1996. text 106.95 (1-85972-267-9, Pub. by Avebry) Ashgate Pub Co.

— Business Cycle Surveys with Special Reference to the Pacific Basin Economies: Papers Presented at the 19th CIRET Conference Proceedings, OSaka, 1989. (CIRET Conference Proceedings Ser.). 761p. 1990. text 142.95 (1-85628-123-X, Pub. by Avebry) Ashgate Pub Co.

Oppenlander, Karl H. & Poser, Gunter, eds. The Explanatory Powers of Business Cycle Surveys: Papers Presented at the 21st Ciret Conference Proceedings, Stellenbosch, 1993. 736p. 1994. 142.95 (1-85628-575-8, Pub. by Avebry) Ashgate Pub Co.

— Social Structural Change - Consequences for Business Cycle Surveys: Selected Papers Presented at the 23rd CIRET Conference, Helsinki. LC 98-72622. (CIRET Conference Proceedings Ser.). 512p. 1998. text 97.95 (1-84014-536-6, Pub. by Avebry) Ashgate Pub Co.

Oppenlander, Meredith & Coulton, Mia. Math Set "B" Includes "In the Hen House," "The Bird Feeder," "How to Make Snack Mix," "How Much Does This Hold?", 4 vols. (Illus.). (J). (gr. k-2). Date not set. pap. 19.25 (1-57874-071-1) Kaeden Corp.

Oppenneer, Betsy. Breads from Betsy's Kitchen. Oppenneer, Mark E., ed. LC 98-92808. (Illus.). 192p. 1998. 17.95 (0-9627665-4-2) Breadworks.

— Perfect Bread: Fun with Creative Shapes. 1992. 29.95 incl. VHS (0-9627665-3-4) Breadworks.

— Perfect Bread: How to Conquer Bread Baking. 1991. 29.95 incl. VHS (0-9627665-1-8) Breadworks.

Oppenneer, Mark E., ed. see Oppenneer, Betsy.

Oppenoorth, Harry, jt. auth. see Hilhorstand, Thea.

Opper & Mott. A Study Guide to Planet Earth. 92p. 1997. ring bd. 9.56 (0-88725-244-3) Hunter Textbks.

Opper, Jacob. Science & the Arts: A Study in Relationships from 1600-1900. LC 70-178042. 226p. 1973. 32.50 (0-8386-1054-4) Fairleigh Dickinson.

Opper, L. Hong Kong's Young Children: Their Early Development & Learning. 304p. (Orig.). 1996. pap. 42.50 (962-209-414-7, Pub. by HK Univ Pr) Coronet Bks.

Opper, S. Carl. A Study Guide for Planet Earth: A Telecourse. 80p. (C). 1992. spiral bd. 7.60 (1-880847-01-9) DEWMAR Hse.

Opper, Susan, et al. The Impact on Study Abroad Programmes on Students & Graduates, Vol. 2. (Higher Education Policy Ser.: No. 11). 250p. 1990. 49.95 (1-85302-523-2) Taylor & Francis.

Opper, Sylvia. Hong Kong's Young Children: Their Preschools & Families. LC LB1140.25.H8. 231p. (Orig.). 1992. reprint ed. pap. 71.70 (0-608-01391-9, 206215200002) Bks Demand.

Opper, Sylvia, jt. auth. see Ginsburg, Herbert P.

Opper, Sylvia, jt. auth. see Ginsbury, Herbert.

Opperheimer-Dekker, A., jt. ed. see Van Mierop, L. H.

Opperman, Pam L. & Wedge, Connie S. Organizing A Home Filing System. (Illus.). 28p. 1998. pap. 9.95 (0-9669466-3-4) Hope River.

Opperman, Cathleen S. & Cassandra, Kathleen A. Contemporary Pediatric Nursing. LC 97-42370. (Illus.). 576p. (C). (gr. 13). 1998. teacher ed. write for info. (0-8151-2897-5, 30096) Mosby Inc.

— Study Guide T-A Contemporary Pediatric Nursing. (Illus.). 224p. 1998. student ed. write for info. (0-8151-2898-3) Mosby Inc.

Opperman, George W., jt. auth. see Spahr, Sidney L.

Opperman, Hal N. Jean-Baptiste Oudry Sixteen Eighty-Six to Seventeen Fifty-Five. LC 82-84544. 226p. (C). 1983. pap. 24.95 (0-295-96015-9) U of Wash Pr.

— Jean-Baptiste Oudry, 1686 to 1755. 250p. 1983. pap. 24.95 (0-912804-12-2) Kimbell Art.

Opperman, Henry V. & Butcher, Tina G., eds. Specifications, Tolerances, & Other Technical Requirements for Weighing & Measuring Devices. (Illus.). 300p. (Orig.). (C). 1995. pap. text 50.00 (0-7881-2464-1) DIANE Pub.

***Opperman, Joachim.** Dinosaurs (Dinosaurier) (Start Me Up Ser.: Vol. 2). (Illus.). 48p. (J). (gr. 4-7). 1998. pap. 12.95 (1-58185-001-8, Tessloff Publishing) Quadrillion Media.

Opperman, Joseph. Winter Dreams, Summer Balms. (Illus.). 160p. 1995. pap. 15.95 (1-879418-98-3) Audenreed Pr.

Opperman, K., jt. ed. see Kroner, W.

Opperman, Mark. The Art of Veterinary Practice Management. LC 98-61301. (Illus.). 240p. 1999. 34.95 (0-935078-74-6) Veterinary Med.

Opperman, Martin, ed. Sex Tourism & Prostitution: Aspects of Leisure, Recreation & Work. LC 98-4404. (Tourism Dynamics Ser.). (Illus.). 300p. (C). 1998. pap. 30.00 (1-882345-15-0); text 38.00 (1-882345-14-2) Cognizant Comm.

Opperman, Martin, jt. auth. see Chon, Sun.

Opperman, Pam L., jt. auth. see Wedge, Connie S.

Oppermann, et al. Accounting Standards. LC 99-215269. 872p. 1998. pap. 105.00 (0-7021-4363-4, Pub. by Juta & Co) Intl Spec Bk.

Oppermann, Alfred. Dictionary of Dataprocessing. 2nd ed. (ENG & GER.). 1973. pap. 55.00 (0-8288-6244-3, M-7116) Fr & Eur.

— Dictionary of Electronics, Vol. 1. (ENG & GER.). 1987p. 195.00 (0-8288-0294-7, M 15118) Fr & Eur.

— Dictionary of Electronics, Vol. 2. (ENG & GER.). 800p. 1987. 225.00 (0-8288-0293-9, M8702) Fr & Eur.

— Dictionary of Modern Technology: English-German, 2 vols., Vol. 1. 2nd ed. (ENG & GER.). 1935p. 1990. 375.00 (0-8288-0631-4, M6982) Fr & Eur.

— Dictionary of Modern Technology: English-German, 2 vols., Vol. 2. (ENG & GER.). 2044p. 1987. 375.00 (0-8288-0632-2) Fr & Eur.

— Woerterbuch der Modernen Technik. (ENG & GER.). 350.00 (0-685-01777-X, M-6982) Fr & Eur.

— Woerterbuch Kybernetik: Dictionary of Cybernetics. (ENG & GER.). 1969. pap. 22.50 (3-7940-3258-6, M-6915) Fr & Eur.

***Oppermann, Charles J.** Programming Active Directory Services. 400p. 2000. 49.99 (0-7356-1037-1) Microsoft.

Oppermann, Friedrich W. Dissertations Botanicae, Band 298. (ENG & GER., Illus.). 214p. 1998. 59.00 (3-443-64210-1, Pub. by Gebruder Borntraeger) Balogh.

Oppermann, Helga. Das Engelsmuster - Zur Theorie und Geschichte, Analyse und Interpretation eines Kulturellen Deutungsmusters Des Weiblichen. (Anglistische und Amerikanistische Texte und Studien Ser.: No. 2). xvi, 518p. 1986. write for info. (3-487-07747-7) G Olms Pubs.

Oppermann, Martin, ed. Geography & Tourism Marketing. LC 97-26368. 186p. 1997. pap. 19.95 (0-7890-0336-8) Haworth Pr.

— Geography & Tourism Marketing. LC 97-26368. 186p. 1997. 39.95 (0-7890-0335-X) Haworth Pr.

— Pacific Rim Tourism. LC 97-34916. (A CAB International Publication). 288p. 1998. text 65.00 (0-85199-221-8) OUP.

Oppermann, Reinhard, ed. Adaptive User Support: Ergonomic Design of Manually & Automatically Adaptable Software. (Computers, Cognition, & Work Ser.). 272p. 1994. text 49.95 (0-8058-1655-0) L Erlbaum Assocs.

Oppersdorff, Mathias, photos by. People of the Road: The Irish Travellers. LC 97-20568. (Illus.). 96p. 1997. 39.95 (0-8156-0476-9) Syracuse U Pr.

Oppersdorff, Tony. Coastal Labrador: A Northern Odyssey. (Illus.). 96p. 1991. 24.95 (0-921054-84-X) Nimbus Publ.

Oppert, Gustav. On the Original Inhabitants of Bharatavarsa or India. Bolle, Kees W., ed. (Mythology Ser.). 1978. reprint ed. lib. bdg. 60.95 (0-405-10557-6) Ayer.

Oppewal, Donald, ed. Voices from the Past: Reformed Educators. LC 97-3169. 352p. 1997. pap. 37.50 (0-7618-0767-5) U Pr of Amer.

Oppian. Poems. (Loeb Classical Library: No. 219). 15.50 (0-674-99241-5) HUP.

Oppianus. Index in Halieutica Oppiani Cilicis et in Cynegetica Poetae Apameensis. James, A. W., ed. 132p. 1970. write for info. (0-318-70990-2) G Olms Pubs.

Oppitz, Joseph. Alphonsus Liguori - The Redeeming Love of Christ: Selected Spiritual Writings. 136p. 1996. pap. text 9.95 (1-56548-045-7) New City.

Oppliger, Jurg. Get That Job! LC 96-40123. 1997. 8.95 (1-56853-035-8, Signal Hill) New Readers.

***Oppliger, Peter.** Green Tea: The Delicious Everyday Health Drink. 1998. pap. 19.95 (0-85207-321-6) C W Daniel.

Oppliger, Rolf. Authentication Systems for Secure Networks. LC 95-53773. 186p. 1996. write for info. (0-89006-510-1) Artech Hse.

— Internet & Intranet Security. LC 97-42908. 376p. 1997. 79.00 (0-89006-829-1) Artech Hse.

***Oppliger, Rolf.** Security Technologies for the World Wide Web. LC 99-45835. (Computer Library). (Illus.). 419p. 1999. 69.00 (1-58053-045-1) Artech Hse.

Opplt, J. J., jt. ed. see Lewis, L. A.

Oppman, R. Scott, jt. ed. see von Meyer, Nancy R.

Oppo, G. L., ed. Quantum Dynamics of Simple Systems: Proceedings of the Scottish Universities Summer School in Physics, 1994, Stirling, Scotland. 44th ed. 373p. 1996. pap. 53.00 (0-7503-0490-1) IOP Pub.

Oppo, G. L., et al. Quantum Dynamics of Simple Systems: Proceedings of the 44th Scottish Universities Summer School in Physics, University of Stirling, 15-26 August, 1994. (Scottish Universities Summer School in Physics, a NATO Advanced Study Institute Ser.: Vol. 44). (Illus.). 300p. 1996. 180.00 (0-7503-0351-4) IOP Pub.

Oppold, Robert S. Iowa Bankruptcy, 1984-1992. 420p. 1992. ring bd. 105.00 (0-86678-370-9, MICHIE) LEXIS Pub.

Oppong, Christine, ed. Female & Male in West Africa. 280p. (C). 1983. pap. text 47.95 (0-04-301158-6) Routledge.

— Sex Roles, Population & Development in West Africa. LC 87-27386. 242p. (C). 1988. 40.00 (0-435-08022-9, 08022) Heinemann.

Oppong, Christine & Abu, Katharine. Seven Roles of Women: Impact of Education, Migration & Employment on Ghanian Mothers. (Women, Work & Development Ser.: No. 13). xi, 127p. (Orig.). (C). 1987. pap. 18.00 (92-2-105858-1) Intl Labour Office.

Oppong, Christine, jt. auth. see Adepoju, Aderanti.

Oppy, Graham. Ontological Arguments & Belief in God. LC 95-6458. 396p. (C). 1996. text 74.95 (0-521-48120-1) Cambridge U Pr.

Oprandy, Robert, jt. auth. see Burge, Richard.

Oprandy, Robert, jt. auth. see Gebhard, Jerry G.

Oprandy, Robert, jt. auth. see Okano, Kaori.

O'Pray, Michael. British Avant-Garde Film. LC 97-115519. 1997. 34.95 (1-86020-004-4, Pub. by U of Luton Pr) Bks Intl VA.

— Derek Jarman: Dreams of England. (Distributed for the British Film Institute Ser.). (Illus.). 184p. 1996. 29.95 (0-85170-590-1, Pub. by British Film Inst) Ind U Pr.

O'Pray, Michael, ed. Andy Warhol: The Film Factory. (Illus.). 196p. 1990. 13.50 (0-85170-250-3, Pub. by British Film Inst); pap. 19.95 (0-85170-243-0, Pub. by British Film Inst) Ind U Pr.

Oprea, A. G., jt. auth. see Cuculescu, I.

Oprea, C. & Dan, F. Macromolecular Mechanochemistry, 2 vols. Incl. Polymer Mechanochemistry. 380p. 1999. 149.00 (1-898326-72-X); Polymers with Chemomechanical Function. 360p. 2000. 146.00 (1-898326-73-8); 1999. 146.00 (1-898326-76-2) CISP.

Oprea, John. Differential Geometry & Its Applications. LC 96-9009. 387p. (C). 1996. 90.67 (0-13-340738-1) P-H.

O

An Asterisk (*) at the beginning of an entry indicates that the title is appearing for the first time.

***Oprea, John.** The Mathematics of Soap Films: Explorations with Maple. LC 00-41614. (Student Mathematical Library: Vol. 10). (Illus.). 277p. (J). 2000. pap. 29.00 (*0-8218-2118-0*) Am Math.

Oprea, John & Tralle, Aleksy. Symplectic Manifolds with No Kahler Structure, Vol. 166. LC 97-20491. (Lecture Notes in Mathematics Ser.). viii, 207p. 1997. pap. text. write for info. (*3-540-63105-4*) Spr-Verlag.

Opremack, E. Mitchel. Uveitis: A Clinical Manual for Ocular Inflammation. LC 94-13826. (Illus.). 278p. 1994. 149.00 (*0-387-94247-5*) Spr-Verlag.

Oprendek, Donald V., jt. auth. see Davis, Patricia A.

O'Prey, Kevin P. The Arms Export Challenge: Cooperative Approaches to Export Management & Defense Conversion. 56p. (C). 1995. pap. 9.95 (*0-8157-6499-5*) Brookings.

— A Farewell to Arms? Russia's Struggle with Defense Conversion. 143p. (C). 1995. pap. 9.95 (*0-87078-375-0*) Century Foundation.

***O'Prey, Paul, ed.** Collected Writings on Poetry. 1999. (*1-85754-172-3*, Pub. by Carcanet Pr) Paul & Co Pubs.

O'Prey, Philip, tr. see Tubiana, Joseph.

Opromolla, Diltor V., jt. ed. see Hastings, Robert C.

Opsahl, Benjamin, ed. see Kabana, Joni.

Opsal, Knut. Business Strategy & Ethnic Identity. (Bergen Studies in Social Anthropology: No. 44). 127p. (Orig.). 1989. pap. text 13.95 (*0-936508-73-6*) Barber Pr.

Opsal, Philip M. Lineman's Quick Reference on Wood Safety. LC 95-51663. 1996. 39.95 (*0-87814-474-9*) PennWell Bks.

Opschoor, A. Conformations of Polyethylene & Polypropylene. x, 68p. 1966. text 141.00 (*0-677-61220-6*) Gordon & Breach.

Opschoor, J. B., ed. Persistent Pollutants. (Economy & Environment Ser.). (C). 1991. lib. bdg. 171.00 (*0-7923-1168-X*) Kluwer Academic.

Opschoor, J. B., et al, eds. Environmental Economics & Development. LC 99-14856. (Environmental Analysis & Economics Policy Ser.). 619p. 1999. 235.00 (*1-85898-740-7*) E Elgar.

Opschoor, J. B. & Turner, R. K., eds. Economic Incentives & Environmental Policies: Principles & Practice. LC 93-41913. 312p. (C). 1994. lib. bdg. 178.50 (*0-7923-2601-6*) Kluwer Academic.

Opsomer, Carmelia. Opsomer, Carmelia: Index de la Pharmacopee Latine du Ler Au Xe Siecle, 2 vols., Set. (Alpha-Omega, Reihe A Ser.: Bd. CV). (GER.). lxxxviii, 824p. 1989. write for info. (*3-487-09190-9*) G Olms Pubs.

Opstal, Machteld Van, see Van Eeckhoutte, Willy & Van Opstal, Machteld, eds.

Optic, Oliver. Bear & Forbear: Getting Along. unabridged ed. (Lakeshore Ser.: Vol. 6). (Illus.). 312p. 1998. reprint ed. 15.00 (*1-889128-55-4*) Mantle Ministries.

— Duty Bound: The Lightning Express. unabridged ed. (Lakeshore Ser.: Vol. 2). (Illus.). 312p. 1998. reprint ed. 15.00 (*1-889128-51-1*) Mantle Ministries.

— Fighting for the Right. LC 99-61016. (Blue & the Gray Ser.). (Illus.). 376p. (YA). (gr. 4 up). 2000. reprint ed. pap. 14.95 (*1-890623-12-1*) Lost Classics.

— Forgive & Forget: The Young Captain. unabridged ed. (Lakeshore Ser.: Vol. 3). (Illus.). 288p. (J). 1998. reprint ed. 15.00 (*1-889128-52-X*) Mantle Ministries.

— Heaping Coals: The War of the Students. unabridged ed. (Lakeshore Ser.: Vol. 4). (Illus.). 288p. 1998. reprint ed. 15.00 (*1-889128-53-8*) Mantle Ministries.

— Hope & Have: Fanny Grant among the Indians. LC 96-79125. (Illus.). xi, 264p. (J). (gr. 3-7). 1997. reprint ed. pap. 14.95 (*0-9652735-6-3*) Lost Classics.

— On the Blockade. LC 98-88130. (Blue & the Gray Ser.). (Illus.). 354p. (YA). (gr. 4 up). 1999. reprint ed. pap. 14.95 (*1-890623-10-5*) Lost Classics.

— Stand by the Union. (Blue & the Gray Ser.). (Illus.). 360p. (YA). (gr. 4 up). 2000. reprint ed. pap. 14.95 (*1-890623-11-3*) Lost Classics.

— Taken by the Enemy. LC 98-84649. (Blue & the Gray Ser.). (Illus.). 351p. (YA). (gr. 4 up). 1998. reprint ed. pap. 14.95 (*1-890623-03-2*) Lost Classics.

— Through by Daylight: The Young Engineer. unabridged ed. (Lakeshore Ser.: Vol. 1). (Illus.). 312p. 1998. reprint ed. 15.00 (*1-889128-50-3*) Mantle Ministries.

— Tried & True: The Young Peacemakers. unabridged ed. (Lakeshore Ser.: Vol. 5). (Illus.). 304p. 1998. reprint ed. 15.00 (*1-889128-54-6*) Mantle Ministries.

— A Victorious Union. LC 99-61015. (Blue & the Gray Ser.). (Illus.). 360p. (YA). (gr. 4 up). 2000. reprint ed. pap. 14.95 (*1-890623-13-X*) Lost Classics.

— Within the Enemy's Lines. LC 98-86833. (Blue & the Gray Ser.). (Illus.). 352p. (YA). (gr. 4 up). 1998. reprint ed. pap. 14.95 (*1-890623-09-1*) Lost Classics.

***Optical Image Staff.** The Great Jelly World Fair. (Jelly Flap Bks.). 16p. (J). 2000. pap. 4.99 (*1-57584-689-6*, Pub. by Rdrs Digest) S&S Trade.

— Jelly Bath Fun. (Soft Bath Book Ser.). 3p. (J). (ps). 2000. 6.99 (*1-57584-690-X*, Pub. by Rdrs Digest) S&S Trade.

— Where Is Pepper? (Jelly Flap Bks.). 16p. (J). (ps-k). 2000. pap. 4.99 (*1-57584-688-8*, Pub. by Rdrs Digest) S&S Trade.

***Optical Society of America Staff.** Fiber Optics. (Handbook of Optics Ser.: Vol. 4). (Illus.). 900p. 2000. 125.00 (*0-07-136456-0*) McGraw.

Optical Society of America Staff. Handbook of Optics, 2 vols., Vol. 1. 2nd ed. 2600p. 1994. 199.00 (*0-07-911807-0*) McGraw.

— Handbook of Optics, Vol. 2. 2nd ed. Vol. 1. (Illus.). 1664p. 1994. 125.00 (*0-07-047740-X*) McGraw.

— Handbook of Optics, Vol. 3. 2nd ed. (Illus.). 1568p. 1994. 125.00 (*0-07-047974-7*) McGraw.

— The Handbook of Optics on CD-ROM. 2nd ed. (Illus.). 3500p. 1996. 149.50 incl. cd-rom (*0-07-852993-X*) McGraw.

— Nonlinear Guided Waves & Their Applications: Technical Digest : Collocated with the Workshop on Novel Solitons & Nonlinear Periodic Structures, Integrated Photonics Research, April 1-3, 1998, Victoria Conference Centre, Victoria, British Columbia, Canada. LC 98-84329. xxxvii, 300 p. 1998. write for info. (*1-55752-537-4*) Optical Soc.

Optical Society of America Staff, compiled by. Applications of High-Field & Short Wavelength Sources. LC 97-65496. (Nineteen Ninety-Seven Technical Digest Ser.: Vol. 7). (Illus.). 294p. 1997. pap. 75.00 (*1-55752-489-0*) Optical Soc.

— Conference on Lasers & Electro-Optics. LC 97-65506. (Nineteen Ninety-Seven Technical Digest Ser.: Vol. 11). 662p. (Orig.). 1997. pap. 92.00 (*1-55752-499-8*) Optical Soc.

— Fourier Transform Spectroscopy. LC 96-72427. (Nineteen Ninety-Seven Technical Digest Ser.: Vol. 3). (Illus.). 250p. 1997. pap. 66.00 (*1-55752-475-0*) Optical Soc.

— Lasers in Dermatology: Bio-Optics & Treatment of Human Skin. LC 97-68772. (Nineteen Ninety-Seven Technical Digest Ser.: Vol. 15). (Illus.). 72p. 1997. pap. 75.00 (*1-55752-513-7*) Optical Soc.

— Nonastronimical Adaptive Optics. LC 97-68221. (Nineteen Ninety-Seven Technical Digest Ser.: Vol. 13). (Illus.). 69p. 1997. pap. 75.00 (*1-55752-507-2*) Optical Soc.

— Optics in Computing. LC 97-65498. (Nineteen Ninety-Seven Technical Digest Ser.: Vol. 8). (Illus.). 298p. 1997. pap. 75.00 (*1-55752-491-2*) Optical Soc.

— Organic Thin Films for Photonics Applications. LC 97-68770. (Nineteen Ninety-Seven Technical Digest Ser.: Vol. 14). (Illus.). 269p. 1997. pap. 74.00 (*1-55752-511-0*) Optical Soc.

— Quantum Optoelectronics. LC 97-65500. (Nineteen Ninety-Seven Technical Digest Ser.: Vol. 9). (Illus.). 152p. 1997. pap. 75.00 (*1-55752-493-9*) Optical Soc.

Optical Society of America Staff & American Academy of Optometry. Vision Science & Its Applications: February 6-9, 1998 : Eldorado Hotel, Santa Fe, New Mexico. LC 97-81326. (1998 Technical Digest Series). 236 p. 1998. write for info. (*1-55752-521-8*) Optical Soc.

***Optical Society of America Staff & Laser Institute of America Staff.** Laser Applications to Chemical & Environmental Analysis: March 9-11, 1998, Sheraton World Resort Orlando, Orlando, Florida. LC 97-81333. xiii, 214 p. 1998. write for info. (*1-55752-533-1*) Optical Soc.

Optical Society of America Staff & Lasers & Electro-Optics Society (IEEE) Staff. Nonlinear Optics '98: Materials, Fundamentals & Applications Topical Meeting, 10-14 August 1998, Princeville Hotel, Princeville, Kauai, Hawaii. LC 98-85597. 468 p. 1998. pap. write for info. (*0-7803-4952-0*) IEEE Standards.

Optical Society of America Staff, et al. Solid State Lasers, Materials & Applications: Sino-American Topical Meeting & Tabletop Exhibit, July 8-11 1997, Nankai University, Tianjin, PRC. LC 97-68177. xi, 168 p. 1997. write for info. (*1-55752-508-0*) Optical Soc.

Optical Spectrometric Measurements of High Tempera. Optical Spectrometric Measurements of High Temperatures. Dickerman, Philip J., ed. LC 61-5607. 397p. reprint ed. pap. 123.10 (*0-608-30369-0*, 200513900050) Bks Demand.

Opticians Association of America Staff. Professional Dispensing for Opticianry. 2nd ed. 1996. text 80.00 (*0-7506-9889-6*) Buttrwrth-Heinemann.

Options, Inc. Staff & Robbins, Wendy H. The Job Seeker's Guide to the Delaware Valley: A Source Book Linking People to Jobs. LC 92-40246. (Illus.). 162p. (Orig.). 1993. pap. 11.95 (*0-940159-22-8*) Camino Bks.

Options Institute Staff. Options: Essential Concepts & Trading Strategies. 2nd ed. 430p. 1994. text 55.00 (*0-7863-0272-0*, Irwn Prfssnl) McGraw-Hill Prof.

***Options Institute Staff.** Options: Essential Concepts & Trading Strategies. 3rd ed. LC 99-18006. (Illus.). 441p. 1999. 55.00 (*0-07-134169-2*) McGraw.

Opton, Gene. Williams-Sonoma Mandoline Cookbook. LC 97-39477. (Williams-Sonoma Cookware Ser.). (Illus.). 95p. 1998. reprint ed. pap. 12.95 (*1-887451-13-7*) Wldon Owen Ref.

***Opton, Gene & Hughes, Nancie.** Honey: A Connoisseur's Guide with Recipes. LC 99-54700. (Illus.). 144p. 2000. pap. 14.95 (*1-58008-177-0*) Ten Speed Pr.

Opubor, A., jt. ed. see Nwuneli, O.

Opus Communication Staff, jt. auth. see Greeley, Hugh P.

Opuszynski, Karol & Shireman, Jerome V. Herbivorous Fish: Culture & Use For Weed Management. LC 94-13708. 234p. 1994. lib. bdg. 179.00 (*0-8493-4988-5*) CRC Pr.

Oputa, C. A., jt. auth. see Oputa, Justice C.

Oputa, Justice C. & Oputa, C. A. Conduct at the Bar & the Unwritten Law of the Legal Profession. LC 81-85780. xiv, 69p. 1982. reprint ed. 35.00 (*0-912004-20-7*) Gaunt.

— Modern Bar Advocacy. LC 81-85779. xix, 224p. 1982. reprint ed. 60.00 (*0-912004-19-3*) Gaunt.

***Opyr, Linda.** Earth Time: Poems. Axelrod, David B., ed. & pref. by. 72p. 2000. pap. 12.00 (*0-925062-21-9*, Pub. by Writers Ink Pr) LIPS.

Opyr, Linda. Small Sightings. 1996. pap. 5.00 (*1-878173-46-4*) Birnham Wood.

Opyr, Linda E. No Moon: New Poems. 72p. 1998. pap. 12.00 (*0-925062-16-2*) Writers Ink Pr.

Opyt, Barbara, jt. auth. see Dale, Robert.

***O'Quinn, Donnie.** Digital Prepress Guide. 800p. 2000. 49.99 (*0-7897-2102-3*) Que.

O'Quinn, Donnie. Photoshop in a Nutshell. 2nd ed. Mott, Troy S., ed. (In a Nutshell Ser.). (Illus.). 656p. 1999. pap. 24.95 (*1-56592-565-3*) OReilly & Assocs.

— Quark XPress in a Nutshell. (Illus.). 546p. 1998. pap. 24.95 (*1-56592-399-5*) OReilly & Assocs.

O'Quinn, Garland, Jr. & Hickman, E. Jessica. Teaching Developmental Gymnastics: Skills to Take Through Life. (Illus.). 224p. 1990. 39.95 (*0-292-78101-6*); pap. 24.95 (*0-292-78104-0*) U of Tex Pr.

O'Quinn, Nancy K. What the Doctors & Nurses Don't Tell You: A Nurse's Battle with Breast Cancer: A Journal. LC 97-90977. 78p. 1998. pap. 8.95 (*0-533-12531-6*) Vantage.

Oquli, Ramon & Melendez, Carlos. Escritos de Jose Cecilio del Valle: Una Seleccion. OAS General Secretariat, Department of Cultural Affairs Staff, tr. from SPA. (SPA.). 255p. (C). 1982. pap. text 20.00 (*0-8270-1271-3*) OAS.

Or, Amir, tr. see Bogot, Howard I.

Or, Dani, jt. auth. see Dasberg, S.

Or, Eidan. Meditation: The Journey to Your Inner World. (Astrolog Complete Guide Ser.). (Illus.). 128p. 1998. mass mkt. 6.95 (*965-494-008-6*, Pub. by Astrolog Pub) Assoc Pubs Grp.

Or, Galia B., jt. auth. see Ahronson, Meir.

***Orabone, Laura A.** Elena & the Coin: Exploring Tucson's Presidio Heritage. (Illus.). 1999. pap. write for info. (*1-886398-40-2*) Desert Archaeol.

Oracle. Earth Magick. unabridged ed. LC 92-12569. (Modern Witchcraft Ser.). (Illus.). 240p. 1999. pap. 9.95 incl. audio (*0-87542-591-7*, L-591) Llewellyn Pubns.

Oraevsky, Anatolii N. Gaussian Beams & Optical Resonators. (Proceedings of the Lebedev Physics Institute Ser.: Vol. 222). 107p. 1998. 125.00 (*1-56072-249-5*) Nova Sci Pubs.

Orage, A. R. On Love & Psychological Exercises, 2 vols. in 1. LC 97-43968. 200p. 1998. reprint ed. pap. 14.95 (*1-57863-100-9*) Weiser.

Orage, Alfred R. Nietzsche in Outline & Aphorism. 1974. 250.00 (*0-8490-0733-X*) Gordon Pr.

— Political & Economic Writings. 1973. 250.00 (*0-8490-0872-7*) Gordon Pr.

— Political & Economic Writings from the New English Weekly, 1932-1934. LC 67-28762. (Essay Index Reprint Ser.). 1977. 19.95 (*0-8369-0753-1*) Ayer.

— Readers & Writers. LC 72-99714. (Essay Index Reprint Ser.). 1977. 19.95 (*0-8369-1367-1*) Ayer.

— Selected Essays & Critical Writings. Read, Herbert E. & Saurat, Denis, eds. LC 67-30225. (Essay Index Reprint Ser.). 1977. 19.95 (*0-8369-0754-X*) Ayer.

Orah-Keeton, Monica. I Died on the Titanic. 1998. pap. text 12.95 (*0-907768-86-5*) Countyvise.

O'Rahilly. Irish Dialects: Past & Present. 1988. reprint ed. 40.00 (*0-901282-55-3*) Colton Bk.

O'Rahilly, Egan. The Poems of Egan O'Rahilly: To Which Are Added Miscellaneous Pieces Illustrating Their Subjects & Language. Dinneen, Patrick S., ed. LC 75-28837. reprint ed. 30.00 (*0-404-13826-8*) AMS Pr.

O'Rahilly, Ronan & Muller, Fabiola. Developmental Stages in Human Embryos. LC 87-70669. (Illus.). 320p. 1987. 52.00 (*0-87279-666-3*, 637) Carnegie Inst.

— The Embryonic Human Brain: An Atlas of Developmental Stages. (Illus.). 352p. 1994. 219.95 (*0-471-58845-8*, Wiley-Interscience) Wiley.

— The Embryonic Human Brain: An Atlas of Developmental Stages. 2nd ed. LC 98-42193. 464p. 1999. 199.95 (*0-471-25450-9*) Wiley.

— Human Embryology & Teratology. 2nd ed. LC 95-48297. (Illus.). 480p. 1996. 279.95 (*0-471-13351-5*) Wiley.

O'Rahilly, Thomas F. Danfhocail: Irish Epigrams in Verse. LC 75-28834. reprint ed. 29.50 (*0-404-13824-1*) AMS Pr.

O'Rahilly, Thomas F. Danta Gradha. 148p. 1925. pap. 12.95 (*0-902561-09-X*, Pub. by Cork Univ) Stylus Pub VA.

O'Raifeartaigh, Lochlainn. The Dawning of Gauge Theory. LC 96-43337. (Princeton Series in Physics). 272p. 1997. text 69.50 (*0-691-02978-4*, Pub. by Princeton U Pr); pap. text 29.95 (*0-691-02977-6*, Pub. by Princeton U Pr) Cal Prin Full Svc.

Orakwue, Stella. Pitch Invaders: The Modern Black Football Revolution. (Illus.). 256p. 1998. pap. 22.95 (*0-575-06118-9*, Pub. by V Gollancz) Trafalgar.

Oral History Association Staff. Oral History Evaluation Guidelines. (Pamphlet Ser.: Vol. 3). (Orig.). 1992. pap. text 5.00 (*0-614-32271-5*) Oral Hist.

Oral, O., ed. see Sahin, I.

Oram, Alison. Women Teachers. 320p. 1996. text 74.95 (*0-7190-2759-4*) St Martin.

— Women Teachers & Feminist Politics, 1900-1939. LC 95-36983. 1996. 79.95 (*0-7190-2959-7*, Pub. by Manchester Univ Pr) St Martin.

Oram, Allan E., jt. auth. see Gellinas, Ulric J., Jr.

Oram, Andrew, jt. auth. see Talbott, Steve.

Oram, Andy, jt. auth. see Loukides, Mike.

Oram, Andy, ed. see Alhir, Sinan Si.

Oram, Andy, ed. see Barr, Michael, et al.

Oram, Andy, ed. see Friedl, Jeffrey E. F.

Oram, Andy, ed. see Glickstein, Bob.

Oram, Andy, ed. see Gundavaram, Shishir.

Oram, Andy, ed. see Jameson, Kevin.

Oram, Andy, ed. see Kelly, Peter, et al.

Oram, Andy, ed. see Kirch, Olaf.

Oram, Andy, ed. see Kirch, Olaf & Dawson, Terry.

Oram, Andy, ed. see Loudon, Kyle.

Oram, Andy, ed. see Nichols, Bradford, et al.

Oram, Andy, ed. see Oualline, Steve.

Oram, Andy, ed. see Raines, Paul & Tranter, Jeff.

Oram, Andy, ed. see Rubini, Alessandro.

Oram, Andy, ed. see Schwartz, Ed.

Oram, Andy, ed. see Schwartz, Randal L.

Oram, Andy, ed. see Schwartz, Randal L., et al.

Oram, Andy, ed. see Scott, Charlie, et al.

Oram, Andy, ed. see Shirley, John, et al.

Oram, Andy, ed. see Siever, Ellen & O'Reilly & Associates Staff.

Oram, Andy, ed. see Sydow, Dan P.

Oram, Andy, ed. see Thai, Thuan L.

Oram, Andy, ed. see Tranter, Jeff.

Oram, Andy, ed. see Welsh, Matthew, et al.

Oram, Andy, ed. see Welsh, Matt & Kaufman, Lar.

Oram, Andy, ed. see Yarger, Randy J., et al.

Oram, Barbara, jt. auth. see Maclean, Heather.

Oram, Elizabeth, jt. auth. see Baker, Robin.

Oram, Helen, jt. auth. see Oram, Tom.

Oram, Hiawyn. Angry Arthur. LC 96-61813. (Illus.). 32p. (J). (ps-3). 1997. pap. text 4.95 (*0-374-40386-4*) FS&G.

— Angry Arthur. (J). 1997. 11.15 (*0-606-13125-6*, Pub. by Turtleback) Demco.

— Badger's Bad Mood. LC 97-20651. (Illus.). 32p. (J). (ps-3). 1998. 15.95 (*0-590-18920-4*) Scholastic Inc.

— Badger's Bring Something Party. LC 94-77456. (Illus.). 32p. (J). (ps up). 1995. 15.00 (*0-688-14082-3*) Lothrop.

— Fernando Furioso (Angry Arthur) (SPA., Illus.). 32p. (J). (ps-1). pap. 6.95 (*980-257-061-3*, Pub. by Ediciones Ekare) Kane-Miller Bk.

***Oram, Hiawyn.** Gerda the Goose. (Illus.). 32p. (J). 2000. pap. 6.95 (*0-7641-1484-0*) Barron.

Oram, Hiawyn. The Good Time Boys. unabridged ed. (Curtain Up! Ser.: Vol. 8). (Illus.). 48p. (J). (gr. 2-6). 1998. pap. 16.95 (*0-7136-4627-6*, Pub. by A & C Blk) Midpt Trade.

— In the Attic. LC 84-15570. (Illus.). 32p. (J). (ps-2). 1995. 13.95 (*0-8050-0779-2*, Bks Young Read); pap. 4.95 (*0-8050-0780-6*, Bks Young Read) H Holt & Co.

— Just Dog. LC 98-17238. 32p. (J). (ps-2). 1998. 13.95 (*0-8118-2247-8*) Chronicle Bks.

***Oram, Hiawyn.** Kiss It Better. (Illus.). 32p. (J). (ps-1). 2000. 12.99 (*0-525-46386-0*, Dutton Child) Peng Put Young Read.

Oram, Hiawyn. Ned & the Joybaloo. LC 88-46178. (Illus.). 28p. (J). (ps up). 1989. 11.95 (*0-374-35501-0*) FS&G.

— Ned & the Joybaloo. 26p. (ps-3). 1990. pap. 3.95 (*0-374-45492-2*) FS&G.

— Not-So-Grizzly Bear Stories. LC 98-17388. (Illus.). 96p. (J). (ps-2). 1998. 16.95 (*1-888444-41-X*) Little Tiger.

***Oram, Hiawyn.** Princess Chamomile Gets Her Way. (Illus.). 32p. (J). (ps-4). 1999. 15.99 (*0-525-46148-5*, Dutton Child) Peng Put Young Read.

— Princess Chamomile's Garden. LC 99-87242. (Illus.). 32p. (J). (ps-4). 2000. 16.95 (*0-525-46387-9*, Dutton Child) Peng Put Young Read.

— The Wrong Overcoat. LC 99-44222. (Picture Bks.). (Illus.). 32p. (J). (ps-3). 2000. 15.95 (*1-57505-453-1*, Carolrhoda) Lerner Pub.

***Oram, Hiawyn & Brown, Ken.** Little Giant & Jabber-Jabber. (Illus.). 32p. (J). 1998. 19.95 (*0-86264-798-3*, Pub. by Random) Trafalgar.

Oram, Hiawyn & Kitamura, Satoshi. Alex Quiere un Dinosaurio (A Boy Wants a Dinosaur) (SPA., Illus.). 28p. (J). (gr. 1-3). 1993. pap. 14.95 (*968-16-4114-0*, Pub. by Fondo) Continental Bk.

— En el Desvan (In the Attic) Dominguez, Catalina, tr. (SPA., Illus.). 28p. (J). (gr. 1-3). 1993. pap. 14.95 (*968-16-4112-4*, Pub. by Fondo) Continental Bk.

***Oram, Hiawyn & Langley, Jonathan.** Where Are You Hiding, Little Lamb? (Illus.). 16p. (J). (ps-1). 1999. 10.95 (*0-7641-5196-7*) Barron.

Oram, Hugh. All about Ireland: Facts & Figures. (Pocket Guide Ser.). (Illus.). 72p. (Orig.). 1990. pap. 7.95 (*0-86281-231-3*, Pub. by Appletree Pr) Irish Bks Media.

Oram, Michael & Wellins, Richard S. Re-Engineering's Missing Ingredient: The Human Factor. 256p. 1995. pap. 54.00 (*0-85292-621-9*, Pub. by IPM Hse) St Mut.

Oram, Peter A. & De Haan, Cornelis. Technologies for Rainfed Agriculture in Mediterranean Climates: A Review of World Bank Experiences. LC 95-37034. (World Bank Technical Papers: No. 300). 192p. 1996. pap. 22.00 (*0-8213-3433-6*) World Bank.

Oram, R. B. Cargo Handling in a Modern Port. 1964. pap. 88.00 (*0-08-011305-2*, Pub. by Pergamon Repr) Franklin.

Oram, R. B., jt. auth. see Course, A. G.

Oram, R. N., ed. Register of Australian Herbage Plant Cultivars. 3rd ed. 300p. 1990. pap. 75.00 (*0-643-05054-X*, Pub. by CSIRO) Accents Pubns.

Oram, Richard. Angus & the Mearns: A Historical Guide. (Illus.). 268p. pap. 15.95 (*1-874744-47-5*, Pub. by Birlinn Ltd) Dufour.

— Moray & Badenoch: A Historical Guide. (Illus.). 190p. pap. 15.95 (*1-874744-46-7*, Pub. by Birlinn Ltd) Dufour.

— Scotland's Kings & Queens: Royalty & the Realm. (Discovering Historic Scotland Ser.). (Illus.). 108p. 1997. pap. 26.00 (*0-11-495783-5*, Pub. by Statnry Office) Balogh.

— Scottish Prehistory. LC 97-122630. (Illus.). 256p. pap. 17.95 (*1-874744-69-6*, Pub. by Birlinn Ltd) Dufour.

Oram, Tom & Oram, Helen. Book Sales in America: Your Guide to Used Book Bargains, 1997 Edition. (Orig.). 1997. pap. 19.95 (*0-9640950-1-7*) Baysys Pubng.

Oram, William A., ed. see Spenser, Edmund.

Oram, William Allan. Edmund Spenser. LC 96-44377. 1997. 35.00 (*0-8057-8622-8*) Mac Lib Ref.

Oramas, Nelson. Drug Enforcement in Minority Communities: Minneapolis Police Department. LC 94-61300. (Case Studies in Police Decision-Making: Vol. 2). 28p. (Orig.). 1994. pap. 6.50 (*1-878734-36-9*) Police Exec Res.

Orams, Mark. Marine Tourism: Development, Impacts & Management. LC 98-18191. 1998. write for info. (*0-415-19572-1*); pap. 14.95 (*0-415-13938-4*) Routledge.

Oran, Daniel. Dictionary of the Law. 3rd ed. (C). 1999. pap. text 39.95 (*0-7668-1742-3*) Delmar.

— Law Dictionary for Non-Lawyers. 2nd ed. 337p. 1984. pap. text 13.75 (*0-314-85283-2*) West Pub.

— Law Dictionary for Non-Lawyers. 3rd ed. 303p. 1991. pap. 15.50 (*0-314-87532-8*) West Pub.

An Asterisk (*) at the beginning of an entry indicates that the title is appearing for the first time.

O

An Asterisk (*) at the beginning of an entry indicates that the title is appearing for the first time.

Orbell, John, et al. From Cape to Cape: This History of Lyle Shipping. (Illus.). 1978. 30.00 (0-8464-0433-8) Beekman Pubs.

Orbell, Margaret R. A Concise Encyclopedia of Maori Myth & Legend. LC 98-229002. 232 p. 1998. pap. 19.95 (0-908812-56-6, Pub. by Canterbury Univ) Accents Pubns.

— The Illustrated Encyclopedia of Maori Myth & Legend. (Illus.). 276p. (C). 1995. 69.95 (0-908812-45-0, Pub. by Canterbury Univ) Accents Pubns.

— The Illustrated Encyclopedia of Maori Myth & Legend. (Illus.). 276p. 1996. pap. 39.95 (0-908812-47-7, Pub. by Canterbury Univ) Accents Pubns.

— Illustrated Encyclopedia of Maori Myth & Legend. (Illus.). 310p. 1997. pap. 34.95 (0-86840-416-0, Pub. by New South Wales Univ Pr) Intl Spec Bk.

Orbell, Margaret R., jt. ed. see Finnegan, Ruth H.

Orben, Robert. Joke-Teller's Handbook: or 1,999 Belly Laughs. 1976. reprint ed. pap. 10.00 (0-87980-323-1) Wilshire.

***Orben, Robert.** Speaker's Handbook of Humor. 2000. pap. 14.95 (0-87779-629-7) Merriam-Webster Inc.

Orben, Robert. Twenty-Five Hundred Jokes to Start 'Em Laughing. 1987. 10.00 (0-87980-387-8) Wilshire.

— Two Thousand Four Hundred Jokes to Brighten Your Speeches. 1989. pap. 10.00 (0-87980-425-4) Wilshire.

— Two Thousand New Laughs for Speakers. 1980. pap. 7.00 (0-87980-382-7) Wilshire.

— Two Thousand One Hundred Laughs for All Occasions. LC 82-45448. 240p. 1986. pap. 9.95 (0-385-23488-0) Doubleday.

— Two Thousand Sure Fire Jokes for Speakers & Writers. LC 86-24240. 240p. 1986. pap. 9.95 (0-385-23465-1) Doubleday.

Orberg, Hans H. Lingua Latina: Colloqvia Personarvm. 96p. 1994. pap. 7.00 (87-88073-75-0, Pub. by Mus Tusculanum) Paul & Co Pubs.

— Lingua Latina: Exercitia Latina. 154p. 1994. pap. 9.00 (87-88073-77-7, Pub. by Mus Tusculanum) Paul & Co Pubs.

— Lingua Latina: Grammatica Latina. 38p. 1994. pap. 6.00 (87-88073-07-6, Pub. by Mus Tusculanum) Paul & Co Pubs.

— Lingua Latina Pt. 1: Familia Romana. 328p. 1994. pap. 34.00 (87-7289-139-4, Pub. by Mus Tusculanum) Paul & Co Pubs.

— Lingua Latina Pt. II: Roma Aeterna. 424p. 1994. pap. 55.00 (87-7289-107-6, Pub. by Mus Tusculanum) Paul & Co Pubs.

Orbey, Hasan & Sandler, Stanley I. Modeling Vapor-Liquid Equilibria: Cubic Equations of State & Their Mixing Rules. LC 97-43340. (Series in Chemical Engineering). (Illus.). 250p. (C). 1998. text 80.00 (0-521-62027-9) Cambridge U Pr.

Orbi, Joseph. Peter's Choice. 1998. text 24.00 (0-9661619-0-4) Rom Pub.

Orbigny, A. D'. Foraminiferes Fossiles du Bassin Tertiaire de Vienne. 1963. reprint ed. 25.00 (0-934454-39-6) Lubrecht & Cramer.

— Memoire sur les Foraminiferes de la Craie Blanche du Bassin de Paris. 1964. reprint ed. pap. 5.00 (0-934454-63-9) Lubrecht & Cramer.

Orbis Direct Staff. How to Quit: The National Wellness Stop Smoking Campaign. 59.95 (0-9640449-0-0) Orbis Direct.

Orbis Staff. Woerterbuch der Synonyme. (GER.). 352p. 1993. 29.95 (0-7859-8437-2, 3572006309) Fr & Eur.

Orbison, Roy. The Definitive Roy Orbison Collection. 176p. 1997. otabind 19.95 (0-7935-6258-9) H Leonard.

Orbitz, Harry. Six Days to Better Golf. 1995. 7.98 (0-88365-896-8) Galahad Bks.

***Orborne, Rick.** I Want to Know about the Church. LC 98-17209. (Illus.). 32p. (J). 1998. 9.99 (0-310-22094-7) Zondervan.

Orbuch, Terri L., ed. Close Relationship Loss: Theoretical Approaches. (Illus.). xvi, 233p. 1992. 123.00 (0-387-97727-9) Spr-Verlag.

Orbuch, Terri L., jt. auth. see Cohen, Bruce J.

Orca Staff. Strategies for Studying: A Handbook of Study Skills. 160p. 1996. pap. 12.95 (1-55143-063-0) Orca Bk Pubs.

Orchanian, Robert, ed. see Buono, Anthony & Nemerson, Roy.

Orchanian, Robert, ed. see Pettigrew, David.

Orchard. Synopsis of Four Gospels. (Studies of the New Testament & Its World). 1994. 43.95 (0-567-09331-X, Pub. by T & T Clark) Bks Intl VA.

Orchard, jt. auth. see Horn.

Orchard, Andy. Cassell Dictionary of Norse Myth & Legend. 1999. pap. text 19.95 (0-304-35134-2) Continuum.

— The Poetic Art of Aldhelm. (Cambridge Studies in Anglo-Saxon England: No. 8). (Illus.). 328p. (C). 1994. text 85.00 (0-521-45090-X) Cambridge U Pr.

— Pride & Prodigies: Studies in the Monsters of the Beowulf-Manuscript. 360p. (C). 1995. 75.00 (0-85991-456-9, DS Brewer) Boydell & Brewer.

Orchard, Anthony A. Flora of Australia Vol. 55: Lichens: Lecanorales 2, Parmeliaceae. (Illus.). 360p. 1994. pap. 49.95 (0-643-05674-2, Pub. by CSIRO) Accents Pubns.

***Orchard, Bernard, ed.** Josephus' Jewish War & its Slavonic Version: A Synoptic Comparison. LC 99-30230. (Arbeiten zur Geschichte des Antiken Judentums und des Urchristentums Ser.). (Illus.). 1999. 212.00 (90-04-11438-6) Brill Academic Pubs.

Orchard, Bernard & Riley, Harold. The Order of the Synoptics: Why Three Synoptic Gospels? LC 87-5593. 384p. 1987. 38.95 (0-86554-222-8, MUP H-199) Mercer Univ Pr.

Orchard, Bernard, tr. see Vanhoye, Albert.

***Orchard, David M., et al.** Figuratively Speaking in the Computer Age: Techniques for Preparing & Delivering Presentations. (Special Publication Ser.). (Illus.). xi, 101p. 2000. spiral bd. 49.00 (0-89181-822-7, 601) AAPG.

Orchard, E. W., et al. Business Economics: An Active Learning Approach. LC 97-27442. 696p. 1997. pap. 64.95 (0-631-20179-3) Blackwell Pubs.

Orchard, G. A., ed. Neural Computing Research & Applications: Proceedings of the Second Irish Neural Networks Conference, Queen's University, Belfast, Northern Ireland, 25-26 June, 1992. 336p. 1993. 159.00 (0-7503-0259-3) IOP Pub.

Orchard, G. Edward, jt. auth. see Peyerle, Hans G.

Orchard, G. Edward, ed. & tr. see Bussow, Conrad.

Orchard, Harry F. Charles Lanman: Landscapes & Nature Studies. (Illus.). 28p. 1983. pap. 4.00 (0-9613046-0-X) Morris Mus.

Orchard, Harry F., et al. Julian Rockmore: The American Scene . . . Then & Now. (Illus.). 40p. 1984. pap. 4.00 (0-9613046-1-8) Morris Mus.

***Orchard, Helen C.** Courting Betrayal: Jesus as Victim in the Gospel of John. LC 98-171018. (JSNT Supplement Ser.: No. 161). 293p. 1998. 85.00 (1-85075-892-1, Pub. by Sheffield Acad); pap. 24.50 (1-85075-884-0, Pub. by Sheffield Acad) CUP Services.

Orchard, Hugh. Old Orchard Farm. Sharp, Paul, ed. LC 87-34488. (Iowa Heritage Collection). (Illus.). 252p. 1988. reprint ed. pap. 9.95 (0-8138-0084-6) Iowa St U Pr.

Orchard, J. E., jt. ed. see Clarke, P. A.

Orchard, Janet, jt. auth. see Perry, Garry P.

Orchard, Jeff. Gold, Gold? in New Hampshire. 2nd ed. (Illus.). 74p. 1995. pap. text 8.95 (0-9645890-0-1) Cider Pr NH.

***Orchard, John E.** Japan's Economic Position. LC 00-25580. (Japanese Economic History Ser.). 2000. write for info. (0-415-21822-5) Routledge.

Orchard, Lauren W. Letters from Prison. (Spiritual Discovery Ser.). 128p. 1997. pap., teacher ed. 9.95 (0-88243-221-4, 02-0221); pap., student ed. 4.95 (0-88243-121-8) Gospel Pub.

Orchard, Lionel & Dare, Robert. Market Morals & Public Policy. 240p. 1989. pap. 41.00 (1-86287-624-X, Pub. by Federation Pr) Gaunt.

***Orchard, Paul.** Mangoes Restaurant Key West, Cool Recipes for Turned-On Cooks: Anthology of a Restaurant. Culver-Aversa, Amy, ed. (Illus.). 46p. 1998. pap. 20.00 (0-9673660-0-3) P A G Key West.

Orchard, Thomas N. Astronomy of Milton's Paradise Lost. LC 68-4178. (Studies in Milton: No. 22). (Illus.). 1969. reprint ed. lib. bdg. 75.00 (0-8383-0672-1) M S G Haskell Hse.

Orchard, Vance. Just Rambling Around Blue Mountain Country. 184p. 1981. 15.95 (0-936546-03-4); pap. 10.95 (0-936546-04-2) Pioneer Pr Bks.

— Life on the Dry Side: A Nostalgic Journey down the Backroads of the Inland Northwest. 192p. 1984. 15.95 (0-936546-09-3) Pioneer Pr Bks.

Orchard, W. G. A Dictionary of Cornish Mining Terms. (C). 1989. pap. 35.00 (1-85022-053-0, Pub. by Dyllansow Truran) St Mut.

Orchard, W. R. & Sherratt, A. F., eds. Combined Heat & Power: Whole City Heating, Planning Tomorrow's Energy Economy. LC 80-41444. 248p. reprint ed. pap. 76.90 (0-608-13100-8, 202521400043) Bks Demand.

Orchard, William C. The Technique of Porcupine Quill Decoration among the Indians of North America. Smith, Monte, ed. (Illus.). 88p. 1982. reprint ed. per. 9.95 (0-943604-00-1, BOO/01) Eagles View.

Orchard, William C., et al. Indian Notes. (Museum of the American Indian, Heye Foundation - Quarterly Ser.: No. 3:2). (Illus.). 92p. (C). 1926. pap. text 10.31 (1-55567-754-1) Coyote Press.

Orchid Society of South East Asia Staff, ed. Orchid Growing in the Tropics. (Illus.). 208p. 1994. 32.95 (981-204-108-7) Timber.

Orcutt, Ada M. Tillamook: Land of Many Waters. 296p. 1997. pap. write for info. (0-9661150-0-7) Tillamook County.

Orcutt, Ben A. Science & Inquiry in Social Work Practice. 256p. 1990. text 50.00 (0-231-07040-3) Col U Pr.

Orcutt, Ben A., et al, eds. Social Work & Thanatology. LC 79-22448. 300p. 1980. lib. bdg. 27.95 (0-405-12621-2) Ayer.

***Orcutt, Christopher.** Nick Chase's Great Escape. LC 99-91079. 1999. 25.00 (0-7388-0602-1); pap. 18.00 (0-7388-0603-X) Xlibris Corp.

***Orcutt, David M. & Nilsen, Erik T.** The Physiology of Plants under Stress: Soil & Biotic Factors. 550p. 2000. text 125.00 (0-471-17008-9) Wiley.

Orcutt, David M., jt. auth. see Nilsen, Erik T.

Orcutt, Georgia. Soups, Chowders & Stews. Taylor, Sandra, ed. LC 80-53728. (Flavor of New England Ser.). 144p. 1981. pap. 10.95 (0-911658-17-3, 80-150-9) Yankee Bks.

Orcutt, Georgia & Taylor, Sandra, eds. Flavor of New England: Breads, Rolls & Pastries. LC 81-50147. (Illus.). 144p. 1981. pap. 9.95 (0-911658-28-9, 80-151-1) Yankee Bks.

Orcutt, Jane. The Fugitive Heart. LC 99-217190. (Heart's True Desire Ser.: Vol. 1). 352p. 1998. pap. 7.95 (1-57856-022-5) Waterbrook Pr.

— The Hidden Heart. LC 00-502482. (Heart's True Desire Ser.: Bk. 2). 336p. 1998. pap. 7.95 (1-57856-053-5) Waterbrook Pr.

***Orcutt, Jane.** The Living Stone. 352p. 2000. pap. 10.95 (1-57856-292-9) Waterbrook Pr.

Orcutt, Jane, et al. Porch Swings & Picket Fences: Love in a Small Town. LC 99-22466. 352p. 1999. pap. 10.95 (1-57856-226-0) Waterbrook Pr.

Orcutt, John. Betty & Pansy's Severe Queer Review of San Francisco. 2nd ed. (Illus.). 1992. pap. text 8.95 (0-9633048-0-1) Bedpan Prods.

Orcutt, Samuel. History of the Old Town of Derby, Connecticut, 1642-1880, Vols. 1 & 2. LC 98-168901. (Illus.). 844p. 1998. reprint ed. pap. 57.00 (0-7884-0907-7, 0618) Heritage Bk.

— A History of the Old Town of Stratford & the City of Bridgeport, Connecticut, Pt. I. (Illus.). 692p. 1988. reprint ed. lib. bdg. 70.00 (0-8328-0014-7, CT0014) Higginson Bk Co.

— A History of the Old Town of Stratford & the City of Bridgeport, Connecticut, Pt. II. (Illus.). 700p. 1988. reprint ed. lib. bdg. 70.00 (0-8328-0015-5, CT0015) Higginson Bk Co.

— History of the Town of Wolcott, Connecticut, from 1731 to 1874. 608p. 1992. reprint ed. lib. bdg. 60.00 (0-8328-2270-1) Higginson Bk Co.

— History of the Towns of New Milford & Bridgewater, 1703-1882. 909p. 1992. reprint ed. lib. bdg. 90.00 (0-8328-2265-5) Higginson Bk Co.

— History of Torrington, Connecticut: From Its First Settlement in 1737 with Biographies & Genealogies. (Illus.). 817p. 1988. reprint ed. lib. bdg. 85.00 (0-8328-0016-3, CT0024) Higginson Bk Co.

— Indians of the Housatonic & Naugatuck Valleys, Connecticut. (Illus.). 220p. 1997. reprint ed. lib. bdg. 32.50 (0-8328-5618-5) Higginson Bk Co.

Orcutt, Samuel & Beardsley, A. History of the Old Town of Derby, Connecticut, 1642-1880: With Biographies & Genealogies. (Illus.). 843p. 1988. reprint ed. lib. bdg. 87.00 (0-8328-0001-5, CT0002) Higginson Bk Co.

Orcutt, Ted L. Magicians of the Soul: Exploring the World of Paranormal & Mystical Experience. LC 95-94237. 264p. 1995. 35.00 (0-9623434-4-7) Global Village.

— No Beggars Just Balloons: A Practical Approach to Self-Transformation. 248p. 1989. 19.95 (0-9623434-2-0) Global Village.

Orcutt, Ted L. & Prell, Jan R. Integrative Paradigms of Psychotherapy. LC 93-24551. 272p. (C). 1993. 68.00 (0-205-14823-9, Longwood Div) Allyn.

Orcutt, William D. Celebrities off Parade. LC 79-93369. (Essay Index Reprint Ser.). 1977. 23.95 (0-8369-1424-4) Ayer.

— In Quest of the Perfect Book. LC 74-121495. (Essay Index Reprint Ser.). 1977. 28.95 (0-8369-1769-3) Ayer.

— Magic of the Book. LC 79-107730. (Essay Index Reprint Ser.). 1977. 36.95 (0-8369-2009-0) Ayer.

— Mary Baker Eddy & Her Books. (Twentieth-Century Biographers Ser.). (Illus.). 224p. 1992. 14.95 (0-87510-274-3) Writings of Mary Baker.

— The Stradivari Memorial. LC 76-58561. (Music Reprint Ser.). 1977. reprint ed. lib. bdg. 21.50 (0-306-70865-5) Da Capo.

***Orczy, Baroness.** The First Sir Percy. 320p. 2000. reprint ed. 37.95 (1-56849-734-2) Buccaneer Bks.

— I Will Repay. 192p. 2000. reprint ed. 29.95 (1-56849-732-6) Buccaneer Bks.

— The Scarlet Pimpernel. 288p. 2000. mass mkt. 4.95 (0-451-52762-3, Sig) NAL.

— Sir Percy Hits Back. 320p. 2000. reprint ed. 37.95 (1-56849-733-4) Buccaneer Bks.

Orczy, Emmuska. Adventures of the Scarlet Pimpernel. 321p. 1983. reprint ed. lib. bdg. 35.95 (0-89966-459-8) Buccaneer Bks.

— Eldorado. lib. bdg. 22.95 (0-8488-2010-X) Amereon Ltd.

— Eldorado. 435p. 1980. reprint ed. lib. bdg. 35.95 (0-89968-195-6, Lghtyr Pr) Buccaneer Bks.

— The Elusive Pimpernel. 419p. 1984. lib. bdg. 35.95 (0-89966-488-1) Buccaneer Bks.

Orczy, Emmuska. Elusive Pimpernel. 288p. 23.95 (0-8488-2521-7) Amereon Ltd.

Orczy, Emmuska. Emperor's Candlesticks. 1976. lib. bdg. 13.75 (0-89968-075-5, Lghtyr Pr) Buccaneer Bks.

— Lady Molly of Scotland Yard. LC 75-32771. (Literature of Mystery & Detection Ser.). 1976. reprint ed. 25.95 (0-405-07890-0) Ayer.

— The Laughing Cavalier. 1976. lib. bdg. 18.50 (0-89968-076-3, Lghtyr Pr) Buccaneer Bks.

— The League of the Scarlet Pimpernel. 282p. Date not set. 23.95 (0-8488-2377-X) Amereon Ltd.

— The League of the Scarlet Pimpernel. 238p. 1981. reprint ed. lib. bdg. 35.95 (0-89966-286-2) Buccaneer Bks.

— Lord Tony's Wife. (J). 1986. reprint ed. lib. bdg. 37.95 (0-89966-553-5) Buccaneer Bks.

***Orczy, Emmuska.** The Old Man in the Corner. 1998. lib. bdg. 16.95 (1-56723-080-6) Yestermorrow.

Orczy, Emmuska. The Old Man in the Corner. 340p. 1980. reprint ed. lib. bdg. 15.95 (0-89968-196-4, Lghtyr Pr) Buccaneer Bks.

Orczy, Emmuska. Pimpernel & Rosemary. 312p. 24.95 (0-8488-2543-8) Amereon Ltd.

Orczy, Emmuska. Pimpernel & Rosemary. 1996. 37.95 (0-89966-462-8) Buccaneer Bks.

— The Scarlet Pimpernel. (Illustrated Classics Collection 4). 64p. 1994. pap. 4.95 (0-7854-0755-3, 40518) Am Guidance.

— The Scarlet Pimpernel. 20.95 (0-8488-0601-8) Amereon Ltd.

— The Scarlet Pimpernel. (Bantam Classics Ser.). 264p. 1992. mass mkt. 4.95 (0-553-21402-0, Bantam Classics) Bantam.

***Orczy, Emmuska.** The Scarlet Pimpernel. 1999. 14.95 (0-375-40658-1) Everymns Lib.

Orczy, Emmuska. The Scarlet Pimpernel. (Signet Classics Ser.). 248p. (J). 1974. mass mkt. 4.95 (0-451-52315-6, Sig Classics) NAL.

— The Scarlet Pimpernel. Farr, Naunerle C., ed. (Now Age Illustrated IV Ser.). (Illus.). (J). (gr. 4-12). 1978. student ed. 1.25 (0-88301-345-2); pap. text 2.95 (0-88301-321-5) Pendulum Pr.

— The Scarlet Pimpernel. 1985. 11.95 (0-396-08690-X, G P Putnam) Peng Put Young Read.

— The Scarlet Pimpernel. LC 98-10741. 1998. pap. 12.95 (0-89526-365-3, Gateway Editions) Regnery Pub.

— The Scarlet Pimpernel. 1974. 10.05 (0-606-00955-8, Pub. by Turtleback) Demco.

— The Scarlet Pimpernel. 256p. 1984. reprint ed. lib. bdg. 21.95 (0-89966-508-X) Buccaneer Bks.

— The Scarlet Pimpernel Readalong. (Illustrated Classics Collection 4). 64p. 1994. pap. 14.95 incl. audio (0-7854-0771-5, 40520) Am Guidance.

Orczy, Emmuska. Triumph of the Scarlet Pimpernel. 320p. 24.95 (0-8488-2557-8) Amereon Ltd.

Orczy, Emmuska. The Triumph of the Scarlet Pimpernel. 321p. 1983. reprint ed. lib. bdg. 35.95 (0-89966-460-1) Buccaneer Bks.

— The Way of the Scarlet Pimpernel. 24.95 (0-8488-1442-8) Amereon Ltd.

— The Way of the Scarlet Pimpernel. 318p. 1983. reprint ed. lib. bdg. 37.95 (0-89966-461-X) Buccaneer Bks.

Orczy, Emmuska, jt. auth. see Center for Learning Network Staff.

Ord, Alan J. Songs for Bass Voice: An Annotated Guide to Works for Bass Voice. 228p. 1994. 34.50 (0-8108-2897-9) Scarecrow.

Ord, Alison, et al, eds. Localization of Deformation in Rocks & Metals. LC 92-22431. (PAGEOPH Reprint from Pure & Applied Geophysics Ser.: Vol. 137). v, 150p. 1992. 58.00 (3-7643-2772-3, Pub. by Birkhauser); 20.50 (0-8176-2772-3, Pub. by Birkhauser) Princeton Arch.

Ord, David R. & Coote, Robert B. Is the Bible True? Understanding the Bible Today. LC 93-37570. 100p. (Orig.). 1994. pap. 12.00 (0-88344-948-X) Orbis Bks.

Ord, Hubert W. Chaucer & the Rival Poet in Shakespeare's Sonnets, a New Theory. LC 71-173810. reprint ed. 21.50 (0-404-07829-X) AMS Pr.

Ord-Hume, Arthur W. The Musical Box. LC 94-37334. (Illus.). 336p. 1995. 79.95 (0-88740-764-1) Schiffer.

— Pianola: The History of the Self-Playing Piano. (Illus.). 360p. 1984. 70.00 (0-04-789009-6) Routledge.

— Restoring Pianolas & Other Self Playing Pianos. (Illus.). 160p. 1983. 45.00 (0-04-789008-8) Routledge.

Ord, Irene. Bolero. large type ed. (Linford Romance Library). 288p. 1993. pap. 16.99 (0-7089-7320-5, Linford) Ulverscroft.

— Desert Doctor. large type ed. (Linford Romance Library). 304p. 1996. pap. 16.99 (0-7089-7921-1) Ulverscroft.

— The Doctor Takes a Bride. large type ed. (Dales Large Print Ser.). 230p. 1997. pap. 18.99 (1-85389-727-2) Ulverscroft.

— Flower of the Desert. large type ed. (Linford Romance Library). 1990. pap. 16.99 (0-7089-6826-0) Ulverscroft.

— The Fragrance of Love. large type ed. (Romance Ser.). 304p. 1988. 27.99 (0-7089-1853-0) Ulverscroft.

— The Hawk & the Angel. large type ed. (Linford Romance Library). 304p. 1988. pap. 16.99 (0-7089-6583-0, Linford) Ulverscroft.

— Island Interlude. large type ed. 160p. 1992. 15.95 (0-7451-1568-3, G K Hall Lrg Type) Mac Lib Ref.

— Not the Marrying Kind. large type ed. (Linford Romance Library). 1991. pap. 16.99 (0-7089-7119-9, Linford) Ulverscroft.

— Passion in Paradise. large type ed. (Linford Romance Library). 272p. 1989. pap. 16.99 (0-7089-6705-1; Linford) Ulverscroft.

— Stand-In for Love. large type ed. (Linford Romance Library). 1989. pap. 16.99 (0-7089-6787-6) Ulverscroft.

***Ord, Irene.** Strange Enchantment. large type ed. 320p. 1999. pap. 18.99 (0-7089-5488-X, Linford) Ulverscroft.

Ord, J. Keith. Families of Frequency Distributions. (Griffin's Statistical Monographs: No. 30). 231p. 1972. 27.50 (0-85264-137-0) Lubrecht & Cramer.

Ord, J. Keith, jt. auth. see Stuart, Alan.

Ord, J. Keith, jt. ed. see Cormack, R. M.

Ord, M. J., et al, eds. The Use of Computers & Statistics in Toxicology, Vol. 10. 102p. 1985. 32.00 (0-85066-977-4) Taylor & Francis.

Ord, Margaret G. & Stocken, Lloyd A. Foundations of Modern Biochemistry: A Multi-Volume Treatise, Vol. 4. 1998. 128.50 (0-7623-0351-4) Jai Pr.

Ord, Margery G. & Stocken, Lloyd A., eds. Foundations of Modern Biochemistry Vol. 1: Early Adventures in Biochemistry. LC 95-17048. 219p. 1995. 128.50 (1-55938-960-5) Jai Pr.

— Foundations of Modern Biochemistry Vol. 2: Quantum Leaps in Biochemistry. 257p. 1996. 128.50 (0-7623-0077-9) Jai Pr.

— Foundations of Modern Biochemistry Vol. 3: More Milestones in Biochemistry. 346p. 1997. 128.50 (0-7623-0078-7) Jai Pr.

***Ord, Robert A. & Blanchaert, Remy H.** Oral Cancer. LC 99-40839. 244p. 1999. write for info. (0-86715-357-1) Quint Pub Co.

Ord-Smith, R. J. & Stephenson, J. Computer Simulation of Continuous Systems. LC 74-12957. (Cambridge Computer Science Texts Ser.: No. 3). 333p. reprint ed. pap. 95.00 (0-608-15762-7, 2031703) Bks Demand.

Ordahl. Current Topics in Developmental Biology, Vol. 41. Pedersen, Roger A. & Schatten, Gerald P., eds. (Illus.). 197p. (C). 1998. boxed set. write for info. (0-12-153141-4) Acad Pr.

***Ordahl, Charles P.** Somitogenesis, Pt. II. (Current Topics in Developmental Biology Ser.: Vol. 48). (Illus.). 416p. 1999. 99.95 (0-12-153148-1) Acad Pr.

Ordan, Dena, tr. see David, Abraham, ed.

Ordaz, Amado N. Poemas. 7th ed. 1983. pap. 9.95 (0-7859-5191-1) Fr & Eur.

Ordaz, Luis, jt. auth. see Neglia, Herminio G.

Orde. The Eclipse of Great Britain. LC 96-7160. 272p. 1996. text 59.95 (0-312-16140-9) St Martin.

An Asterisk (*) at the beginning of an entry indicates that the title is appearing for the first time.

— Eclipse of Great Britain. LC 96-7160. 272p. 1996. pap. 19.95 (*0-312-16141-7*) St Martin.

Orde, A. J. A Little Neighborhood Murder. large type ed. (Linford Mystery Library). 448p. 1992. pap. 16.99 (*0-7089-7163-6*, Linford) Ulverscroft.

Orde-Browne, Granville S. The African Labourer. LC 33-28584. 248p. reprint ed. pap. 76.90 (*0-8357-3024-7*, 205711100010) Bks Demand.

Orde, H. L., tr. see Ewing, J. H., et al, eds.

Orde, Julian. Conjurors. (C). 1990. 35.00 (*0-906887-25-9*, Pub. by Greville Pr) St Mut.

Orde, L. Eagles. 1989. pap. 4.50 (*0-8217-2746-X*) NAL.

— Heritage. 1982. pap. 3.95 (*0-8217-2397-9*) NAL.

Orde, Lewis. Dreams of Gold. 532p. 1993. 20.00 (*0-8217-4015-6*, Zebra Kensgtn) Kensgtn Pub Corp.

Orde, Lewis. Dreams of Gold. 576p. 1993. mass mkt. 4.99 (*0-8217-4395-3*, Zebra Kensgtn) Kensgtn Pub Corp.

— Eagles. 1984. mass mkt. 3.95 (*0-8217-1500-3*, Zebra Kensgtn) Kensgtn Pub Corp.

— Heritage. 1982. mass mkt. 3.75 (*0-8217-1100-8*, Zebra Kensgtn) Kensgtn Pub Corp.

— The Lion's Way. 1987. mass mkt. 4.50 (*0-8217-2087-2*, Zebra Kensgtn) Kensgtn Pub Corp.

— Munich Ten. 1983. mass mkt. 3.95 (*0-8217-1300-0*, Zebra Kensgtn) Kensgtn Pub Corp.

— The Proprietor's Daughter. 1988. 18.95 (*0-316-67340-4*) Little.

— The Tiger's Heart. 720p. 1987. mass mkt. 4.50 (*0-8217-2086-4*, Zebra Kensgtn) Kensgtn Pub Corp.

***Ordelheide, Dieter & KPMG Worldwide Staff.** Transnational Accounting, 3 vols. 2nd ed. 3200p. 2000. 650.00 (*1-56159-246-3*) Groves Dictionaries.

Ordelheide, Dieter & Pfaff, Dieter. Germany. LC 93-36088. (European Financial Reporting Ser.). (Illus.). 256p. (C). (gr. 13). 1993. pap. 114.95 (*0-415-06775-8*, B0276) Thomson Learn.

Ordeman, John T. The Aquatints, Drypoints & Etchings of the Derrydale Press. 2nd ed. 64p. 1995. pap. text 35.00 (*1-881755-06-1*) Sunrise OH.

Orden, Al Van, see Van Orden, Al.

***Orden, David, et al.** Policy Reform in American Agriculture: Analysis & Prognosis. LC 98-55710. (Illus.). 248p. 1999. 38.00 (*0-226-63264-4*) U Ch Pr.

Orden, M. D. Van, see Van Orden, M. D.

Orden, Phyllis J. Van, see Van Orden, Phyllis J.

Order-Disorder Transformations in Alloys Internati. Proceedings of the Order-Disorder Transformations in Alloys International Symposium, Tubinger, Germany, September 1973. Warlimont, H., ed. (Reine Uno Angewandte Metallkunde in Einzel-Darstellungen Ser.: Vol. 24). (Illus.). viii, 556p. 1974. 94.95 (*0-387-06766-3*) Spr-Verlag.

Order of Americans of Armorial Ancestry Staff. The Order of Americans of Armorial Ancestry Lineage of Members. LC 97-215271. 690 p. 45.00 (*0-8063-4719-8*) Clearfield Co.

Order of Buddhist Contemplatives Monks Staff & Jiyu-Kennett, P. T. Serene Reflection Meditation. 6th rev. ed. LC 96-67050. Orig. Title: Zen Meditation. (Illus.). 102p. (Orig.). 1996. pap. 6.00 (*0-930066-16-2*, B301) Shasta Abbey.

Order of Mercy, Mt. St. Joseph Seminary Staff, tr. A Year with the Saints. 2nd ed. LC 88-50638. (Illus.). 364p. 1988. reprint ed. pap. 16.50 (*0-89555-339-2*) TAN Bks Pubs.

Order of the Secret Chief of the Rosicrucian Order. The Book of the Goetia: The Lesser Key of Solomon the King. 82p. 1976. reprint ed. pap. 15.00 (*0-7873-0644-4*) Hlth Research.

Order, S. E. & Donaldson, S. S. Radiation Therapy of Benign Diseases: A Clinical Guide. 2nd rev. ed. LC 97-30099. (Medical Radiology Ser.). 250p. 1997. 129.00 (*3-540-58865-5*) Spr-Verlag.

Order, S. E. & Donaldson, S. Radiation Therapy of Benign Diseases. (Medical Radiology, Diagnostic Imaging & Radiation Oncology Ser.). viii, 213p. 1991. 104.00 (*0-387-50901-1*) Spr-Verlag.

Order Sons of Italy in America Staff. Cucina Classica: Maintaining a Tradition. 1995. 15.00 (*0-9647376-0-4*) Order Sons Italy.

Ordericus Vitalis Staff. Ecclesiastical History of England & Normandy, 4 Vols, Set. Forrester, T., tr. LC 68-57872. (Bohn's Antiquarian Library). reprint ed. 185.00 (*0-404-50040-4*) AMS Pr.

Ordermatt, Rick, jt. auth. see Cozza, Carm.

Ordeshook, Peter C. Game Theory & Political Theory: An Introduction. (Illus.). 527p. 1986. pap. text 30.95 (*0-521-31593-X*) Cambridge U Pr.

***Ordeshook, Peter C.** Lessons for Citizens of a New Democracy. LC 97-38257. (Shaftesbury Papers: Vol. 10). 144p. (C). 1998. pap. 15.00 (*1-85898-545-5*) E Elgar.

Ordeshook, Peter C. A Political Theory Primer. (Illus.). 272p. (C). 1992. pap. 20.99 (*0-415-90241-X*, A4116) Routledge.

Ordeshook, Peter C., ed. Models of Strategic Choice in Politics. 392p. 1989. text 57.50 (*0-472-10122-6*, 10122) U of Mich Pr.

Ordeshook, Peter C. & Shepsle, Kenneth A. Political Equilibrium. (Studies in Public Choice). 1982. lib. bdg. 111.00 (*0-89838-073-1*) Kluwer Academic.

Ordeshook, Peter C., et al. The Balance of Power: Stability & Instability in International Systems. (Illus.). 367p. (C). 1989. text 80.00 (*0-521-37471-5*) Cambridge U Pr.

Ordesky, Maxine. Complete Home Organizer: A Guide to Functional Storage Space for All the Rooms in Your Home. LC 92-36125. 192p. 1993. pap. 22.00 (*0-8021-3340-1*, Grove) Grove-Atltic.

Ordet, Stephen M. & Grand, Leonard S. Dynamics of Clinical Rehabilitative Exercise: Dynamics of Clinical Rehabilitative Exercise. (Illus.). 304p. 1991. 55.00 (*0-683-06654-4*) Lppncott W & W.

Ordidge, Paul D. Simple Case Books for Small Businesses. 96p. (Orig.). 1990. pap. 14.95 (*0-8464-1379-5*) Beekman Pubs.

Ordin, Robert L. Contesting Confirmation: A Creditor's Perspective. 524p. 1993. 110.00 (*0-13-296955-6*) Aspen Law.

— Contesting Confirmation: A Creditor's Perspective. LC 93-7740. 1993. 150.00 (*0-13-359183-2*) Prntice Hall Bks.

— Contesting Confirmation: A Creditor's Perspective. 2nd ed. 708p. ring bd. 165.00 (*1-56706-155-9*, 61560) Panel Pubs.

Ordin, Robert L., jt. auth. see Henry, Sally M.

Ordinary Differential Equations Symposium Staff. Proceedings of the Ordinary Differential Equations Symposium, Minneapolis, May 1972. Harris, W. A., Jr. & Sibuya, Y., eds. LC 72-97022. (Lecture Notes in Mathematics Ser.: Vol. 312). (Illus.). 204p. 1973. 37.95 (*0-387-06146-0*) Spr-Verlag.

Ordine, Bill. Fatal Match. LC 98-222967. 368p. 1998. mass mkt. 6.99 (*0-380-79105-6*, Avon Bks) Morrow Avon.

Ordine, Nuccio. Giordano Bruno & the Philosophy of the Ass. LC 95-39256. (Illus.). 271p. 1996. 40.00 (*0-300-05852-7*) Yale U Pr.

Ordiz, Javier, ed. see Fuentes, Carlos.

Ordman, Kathryn A. & Ralli, Mary P. What People Say. 5th ed. LC 76-6143. 1976. pap. text 11.95 (*0-88200-073-X*, B0990) Alexander Graham.

Ordnance Survey Pathfinder Guild Staff. Brecon Beacons & Glamorgan Walks. (Pathfinder Guides Ser.). (Illus.). 80p. (Orig.). 1994. pap. 14.95 (*0-7117-0671-9*) Seven Hills Bk.

— Cairngorms Walks. 1996. pap. text 16.95 (*0-7117-0852-5*, Pub. by JARR UK) Seven Hills Bk.

— Skye & North West Highlands Walks. 1996. pap. text 16.95 (*0-7117-0850-9*, Pub. by JARR UK) Seven Hills Bk.

— South Devon & Dartmoor Walks. 1996. pap. text 16.95 (*0-7117-0851-7*, Pub. by JARR UK) Seven Hills Bk.

Ordnance Survey Staff. South Pennines Walks. (Ordnance Survey Pathfinder Guides Ser.). (Illus.). 80p. 1996. pap. 16.95 (*0-7117-0849-5*, Pub. by JARR UK) Seven Hills Bk.

***Ordodnez, Margaret T. & Costume Society of America Staff.** Your Vintage Keepsake: A CSA Guide to Costume Storage & Display. LC 00-28031. (Illus.). 32p. 2000. pap. 5.00 (*0-9676445-0-X*) Costume Soc of Amer.

Ordog, Gary, ed. Management of Gunshot Wounds. 477p. (C). 1992. pap. text 120.00 (*0-8385-5713-9*, A5713-1, Apple Lange Med) McGraw.

Ordon, Edmund, ed. Ten Contemporary Polish Stories. LC 74-2842. 252p. 1974. reprint ed. lib. bdg. 47.50 (*0-8371-7436-8*, ORPS, Greenwood Pr) Greenwood.

Ordonez, C., jt. auth. see Starfield, B.

Ordonez, Elizabeth J. Voices of Their Own: Contemporary Spanish Narrative by Women. LC 90-55690. 256p. 1991. 42.50 (*0-8387-5203-9*) Bucknell U Pr.

Ordonez, Hernan, jt. auth. see Cadavid, Gilberto.

Ordonez-Hernandez, Maria. English for Progress. Smith, Daniel D. et al, eds. LC 87-71460. (Illus.). 304p. (Orig.). 1987. pap. write for info. (*0-942995-02-3*) Casa Blanca Pr.

Ordonez, Jose A. The Education of a Schoolmaster: My Years at St. Paul's School. LC 98-73061. (Illus.). 248p. 1998. 32.00 (*0-9665051-0-7*) Francis Pr.

Ordonez, Juan Pablo. No Human Being Is Disposable: Social Cleansing, Human Rights & Sexual Orientation. 78p. 1995. pap. 12.00 (*1-884955-01-0*) Intl Gay & Lesbian.

Ordonez, Margaret T., jt. auth. see Welters, Linda.

Ordonez, Maria A., jt. auth. see Pico, Fernando.

Ordonez, Robert L. When I Was a Boy: One Year in Vietnam. Ziegler, Lenda, ed. LC 96-96065. (Illus.). 320p. (Orig.). 1997. pap. 13.95 (*0-9656070-0-3*) CIMA Pub.

Ordonez y Montalvo, Jose A., ed. The Pictorial History of St. Paul's School. 242p. 1991. 155.00 (*0-9630522-0-9*) St Pauls Sch.

Ordorica, Ray, ed. Handguns '99. 11th ed. LC 88-72115. (Illus.). 352p. 1998. pap. 22.95 (*0-87349-205-6*, H99) Krause Pubns.

Ordovas, Jose M. Lipoprotein Protocols. LC 98-228469. (Methods in Molecular Biology Ser.: Vol. 110). (Illus.). 304p. 1998. 79.50 (*0-89603-420-8*) Humana.

Ordovensky, Pat. College Planning for Dummies. (For Dummies Ser.). 368p. 1995. pap. 16.99 (*1-56884-382-8*) IDG Bks.

— College Planning for Dummies. 3rd ed. (For Dummies Ser.). 356p. 1999. pap. 19.99 (*0-7645-5164-7*, Dummies Trade Pr) IDG Bks.

— U. S. A. Today Financial Aid for College: A Quick Guide to Everything You Need to Know, with the New 1996 Forms! rev. ed. LC 95-26614. 160p. 1995. pap. 8.95 (*1-56079-568-9*) Petersons.

— U. S. A. Today Getting into College: A Quick Guide to Everything You Need to Know. LC 95-12443. 160p. (Orig.). 1995. pap. 8.95 (*1-56079-463-1*) Petersons.

Ordovensky, Pat, jt. auth. see Carris, Joan D.

Ordovensky, Pat, jt. auth. see Marx, Gary.

Ordover, Abraham P. Flinders v. Mismo: Tort - Arson. 5th rev. ed. 140p. 1992. pap. 22.95 (*1-55681-299-X*) Natl Inst Trial Ad.

— Fordyce vs. Harris & Felson. 5th rev. ed. 138p. 1992. pap. 22.95 (*1-55681-301-5*) Natl Inst Trial Ad.

Ordover, Eileen L. & Boundy, Kathleen B. Educational Rights of Children with Disabilities. 120p. 1991. pap. 12.50 (*0-912585-06-4*) Ctr Law & Ed.

Ordover, Janusz A., jt. ed. see Baumol, William J.

Ordover, John, ed. Warchild. (Star Trek: Deep Space Nine Ser.: No. 7). 288p. 1994. mass mkt. 5.50 (*0-671-88116-7*) PB.

Ordover, John, ed. see Archer, Nathan.

Ordover, John, ed. see Graf, L. A.

Ordover, John, ed. see Hambly, Barbara.

Ordover, John, ed. see Hugh, Dafydd ab.

Ordover, John, ed. see Johnson, Kij.

Ordover, John, ed. see Schofield, Sandy.

Ordover, John, ed. see Scott, Melissa.

Ordover, John, ed. see Weinstein, Howard.

Ordover, John J., et al. Strange New Worlds, No. I. Smith, Dean Wesley, ed. (Star Trek Ser.). 496p. 2000. reprint ed. per. 6.50 (*0-671-01447-1*, Star Trek) PB.

***Ordover, John J., et al.** Strange New Worlds Two. Smith, Dean Wesley et al, eds. (Star Trek Ser.: Vol. 2). (Illus.). 448p. 2000. per. 6.50 (*0-671-02693-3*, Star Trek) PB.

Ordronaux, John. Hints on the Preservation of Health in Armies: Bound with: Manual of Instructions for Military Surgeons. (American Civil War Medical Ser.: No. 1). 238p. 1990. reprint ed. 45.00 (*0-930405-34-X*) Norman SF.

— Jurisprudence in Medicine in Relation to the Law. LC 73-5158. (Mental Illness & Social Policy; the American Experience Ser.). 1973. reprint ed. 26.95 (*0-405-05239-1*) Ayer.

Ordway, Frederick I., 3rd, ed. History of Rocketry & Astronautics. LC 57-43769. (AAS History Ser.: Vol. 9). (Illus.). 330p. 1989. 50.00 (*0-87703-309-9*, Am Astronaut Soc); pap. 35.00 (*0-87703-310-2*, Am Astronaut Soc) Univelt Inc.

Ordway, Frederick I., III & Sharpe, Mitchell R. The Rocket Team. (Illus.). 496p. 1982. reprint ed. pap. text 12.95 (*0-262-65013-4*) MIT Pr.

Ordway, Frederick I., III, et al. Blueprint for Space: Science Fiction to Science Fact. LC 91-3160. (Illus.). 224p. (C). 1992. pap. 24.95 (*1-56098-073-7*) Smithsonian.

Ordway, Frederick I., III, jt. auth. see Stuhlinger, Ernst.

Ordway, Greg. Are You What God Is Looking For? 220p. 1999. pap. 11.95 (*0-9672849-0-2*) Good News Pubs.

Ordway, Jerry. The Power of Shazam! Carlin, Mike, ed. LC 94-158497. (Illus.). 96p. 1995. mass mkt. 7.50 (*1-56389-153-0*, Pub. by DC Comics) Time Warner.

Ordway, Nicholas O. Real Estate Math Made Easy: A Step-by-Step Instructional Approach. 2nd ed. (C). 1985. pap. text 31.60 (*0-8359-6485-X*) P-H.

Ordway, Nicholas O., jt. auth. see Tosh, Dennis S., Jr.

Ordys, A. W., et al. Modelling & Simulation of Power Generation Plants. LC 94-27489. (Advances in Industrial Control Ser.). 1994. 75.95 (*0-387-19907-1*) Spr-Verlag.

Ore, H. T., et al. Rogers Ridge (4-SBr-5250) A Fossil Spring Site of the Lake Mojave & Pinto Periods - Phase 2 Test Excavations & Site Evaluation - Appendices. fac. ed. (Fort Irwin Archaeology Project, Research Reports: No. 18: Appendices). 60p. 1985. reprint ed. pap. text 7.19 (*1-55567-544-1*) Coyote Press.

Ore, Oystein. Graphs & Their Uses. rev. ed. (New Mathematical Library: No. 34). 160p. 1990. pap. text 20.50 (*0-88385-635-2*, NML-34) Math Assn.

— Invitation to Number Theory. LC 67 20607. (New Mathematical Library: No. 20). 129p. 1967. pap. text 18.75 (*0-88385-620-4*, NML-20) Math Assn.

— Niels Hendrik Abel, Mathematician Extraordinary. LC 73-14693. (Illus.). viii, 277p. 1974. reprint ed. text 19.95 (*0-8284-0274-4*) Chelsea Pub.

— Number Theory & Its History. (Illus.). 380p. 1988. reprint ed. pap. text 10.95 (*0-486-65620-9*) Dover.

— Theory of Graphs. LC 61-15687. (Colloquium Publications: Vol. 38). 270p. 1962. reprint ed. pap. 24.00 (*0-8218-1038-3*, COLL/38) Am Math.

Ore, Rebecca. Alien Bootlegger & Other Stories. 1993. mass mkt. 3.99 (*0-8125-1278-2*, Pub. by Tor Bks) St Martin.

— Alien Bootlegger & Other Stories. 1995. pap. 14.95 (*0-312-89030-3*) Tor Bks.

— Becoming Alien. (Illus.). 320p. 1989. pap. 3.95 (*0-8125-0313-9*) Tor Bks.

— Gaia's Toys. 1997. pap. text 9.99 (*0-8125-3908-7*, Pub. by Tor Bks) St Martin.

— Human to Human. 1990. pap. 3.95 (*0 8125-0045-8*) Tor Bks.

— Illegal Rebirth of Billy the Kid. 1991. pap. 3.95 (*0-8125-0672-3*, Pub. by Tor Bks) St Martin.

***Ore, Rebecca.** Outlaw School. 320p. 2000. pap. 13.50 (*0-380-79250-8*, Avon Bks) Morrow Avon.

Ore, Rebecca. Slow Funeral. 320p. 1995. 4.99 (*0-8125-1604-4*, Pub. by Tor Bks) St Martin.

***Ore, Tracy E.** The Social Construction of Difference & Inequality: Race, Class, Gender & Sexuality. LC 99-42782. xvi, 619p. 2000. 33.95 (*0-7674-1167-6*, 1167-6) Mayfield Pub.

Oread Literary Club Staff, compiled by. History of the Town of Johnson, Vt., 1784-1907. (Illus.). 83p. 1996. reprint ed. pap. 15.00 (*0-8328-5179-5*); reprint ed. lib. bdg. 25.00 (*0-8328-5178-7*) Higginson Bk Co.

O'Rear, C. E. & Llewellyn, G. C., eds. Biodeterioration Research: General Biodeterioration, Degradation, Mycotoxins, Biotoxins, & Wood Decay, Vol. 2. (Illus.). 720p. 1989. 135.00 (*0-306-43229-3*, Plenum Trade) Perseus Pubng.

O'Rear, C. E., jt. ed. see Llewellyn, G. C.

***O'Rear, Charles.** Chardonnay: Photographs from Around the World. LC 98-37641. (Illus.). 144p. 1999. 19.98 (*0-7651-1028-8*) Smithmark.

***O'Rear, Charles & Creedman, Michael.** Cabernet: A Photographic Journey from Vine to Wine. LC 98-16436. (Illus.). 144p. 1998. 19.98 (*0-7651-0791-0*) Smithmark.

Orear, Elizabeth, jt. auth. see Orear, Gordon.

Orear, Gordon & Orear, Elizabeth. Sarkis. LC 94-43015. (Illus.). 170p. 1995. 29.95 (*0 8143-2517-3*, Great Lks Bks) Wayne St U Pr.

Orear, Leslie F., ed. On the Job in Illinois, Then & Now. (Illus.). 1976. 8.00 (*0-916884-04-X*); pap. 7.50 (*0-916884-02-3*) Ill Labor Hist Soc.

O'Rear, Sybil J. Charles Goodnight: Pioneer Cowman. LC 89-48652. (Illus.). 80p. (J). (gr. 6-7). 1990. 12.95 (*0-89015-741-3*) Sunbelt Media.

— Jesse Chisholm: Trailblazer & a Peacemaker. LC 96-24039. (Illus.). 112p. (J). (gr. 4-6). 1997. 12.95 (*1-57168-110-8*, Eakin Pr) Sunbelt Media.

Orebaugh, Walter W. & Jose, Carol. The Consul. 2nd rev. ed. LC 94-70993. (Illus.). 336p. 1994. pap. 9.95 (*1-878398-08-3*) Blue Note Pubns.

— Guerrilla in Striped Pants: A U. S. Diplomat Joins the Italian Resistance. LC 91-32212. 264p. 1992. 55.00 (*0-275-94149-3*, C4149, Praeger Pubs) Greenwood.

Orecchia, Ferruccio & Chiantini, Luca, eds. Zero-Dimensional Schemes: Proceedings of the International Conference held in Ravello, Italy, June 8-13, 1992. LC 94-20654. vii, 339p. (C). 1994. lib. bdg. 112.95 (*3-11-013934-0*) De Gruyter.

Oredson, Olivia, jt. auth. see Kushi, Michio.

***O'Ree, Willie.** Story of Willie O'Ree. (Illus.). (J). 2000. 13.89 (*1-58184-085-3*) Somerville Hse.

***O'Ree, Willie & McKinley, Michael.** Story of Willie O'Ree. (NHL Coolest Books on Earth Ser.). 96p. (J). (gr. 3-7). 2000. pap. 4.99 (*1-58184-071-3*) Somerville Hse.

Orefice, Gabriella, et al. Atlas of Florence. (Illus.). 384p. 1994. 185.00 (*1-56886-006-4*) Marsilio Pubs.

Orefjaerd, Curth. Bhagavan Sri Sathya Sai Baba, My Divine Teacher. (C). 1995. 14.00 (*81-208-1269-7*, Pub. by Motilal Bnarsidass) S Asia.

Orefudo, Antonio, jt. auth. see Gonzalez Vela, Helena.

O'Regan. Understanding Company Accounts. pap. text. write for info. (*0-471-48923-9*) Wiley.

O'Regan, Brigitte. Self & Existence: J. M. R. Lenz's Subjective Point of View. LC 95-45534. (Studies in Modern German Literature: No. 73). XVI, 145p. (C). 1997. text 39.95 (*0-8204-2524-9*) P Lang Pubng.

O'Regan, Catherine, jt. auth. see Murray, Christina.

O'Regan, Cyril. The Heterodox Hegel. LC 93-36365. (SUNY Series in Hegelian Studies). 517p. (C). 1994. text 74.50 (*0-7914-2005-1*); pap. text 24.95 (*0-7914-2006-X*) State U NY Pr.

O'Regan, Daphne. Rhetoric, Comedy & the Violence of Language in Aristophanes' Clouds. 224p. 1992. text 70.00 (*0-19-507017-8*) OUP.

O'Regan, Donal. Theory of Singular Boundary Value Problems. 168p. 1994. text 48.00 (*981-02-1760-9*) World Scientific Pub.

O'Regan, Donal & Meehan, Maria. Existence Theory for Nonlinear Integral & Integrodifferential Equations. LC 98-21020. (Mathematics & Its Applications Ser.). 228p. 1998. 102.00 (*0-7923-5089-8*) Kluwer Academic.

O'Regan, Donal, jt. ed. see Agarwal, Ravi P.

O'Regan, G., et al, eds. 1st Irish Workshop on Formal Methods: Proceedings of the 1st Irish Workshop on Formal Methods, Dublin, 3-4 July, 1997. (Electronic Workshops in Computing Ser.). vi, 10p. 1997. pap. 44.95 (*3-540-76196-9*) Spr-Verlag.

O'Regan, John. From Empire to Commonwealth: Reflections on a Career in Britain's Overseas Service. (Studies in Imperialism). 192p. 1994. text 45.00 (*1-85043-777-7*) I B T.

O'Regan, Marie B., jt. auth. see Detty, Michael R.

O'Regan, Pauline. There Is Hope for a Tree. 200p. 1996. pap. 19.95 (*1-86940-132-8*, Pub. by Auckland Univ) Paul & Co Pubs.

***O'Regan, Philip.** Archbishop William King (1650-1729) & the Constitution in Church & State. 256p. 2000. 55.00 (*1-85182-464-2*, Pub. by Four Cts Pr) Intl Spec Bk.

O'Regan, R. G., et al. Arterial Chemoreceptors: Cell to System, 360. (Advances in Experimental Medicine & Biology Ser.). (Illus.). 416p. (C). 1994. text 115.00 (*0-306-44824-6*, Kluwer Plenum) Kluwer Academic.

O'Regan, R. S. New Essays on the Australian Criminal Codes. xxii, 125p. 1988. pap. 39.00 (*0-455-20797-6*, Pub. by LawBk Co) Gaunt.

O'Regan, Tom. Australian National Cinema. LC 96-1055. (National Cinemas Ser.). (Illus.). 416p. (C). 1996. 80.00 (*0-415-05730-2*); pap. 24.99 (*0-415-05731-0*) Routledge.

O'Regan, Tom, jt. ed. see Moran, Albert.

***O'Regan, Valerie R.** Gender Matters: Female Policymakers' Influence in the Industrialized Nations. LC 99-55879. 168p. 2000. 49.95 (*0-275-96884-7*, Praeger Pubs) Greenwood.

***Oregon.** Oregon Insurance Laws. LC 98-66068. 1999. write for info. (*0-89246-496-8*) NILS Pub.

Oregon Biodiversity Project Staff. Oregon's Living Landscape: Strategies & Opportunities to Conserve Biodiversity. LC 98-15394. (Illus.). 220p. 1998. pap. 29.95 (*0-926549-01-4*) Defend Wildlife.

Oregon Business Professionals. The Gold Book: Starting & Mining Success in Business. Smith, R. G., ed. (Illus.). 160p. (Orig.). 1988. pap. 7.95 (*0-944312-01-2*) Minds Ink Pub.

Oregon Department of Transportation Staff. U. S. Highway 26 Widening Agreement Through the Villages of Oregon's Mount Hood Westside. (Illus.). 76p. 1995. 13.00 (*0-89904-503-0*, Cascade Geog Soc) Crumb Elbow Pub.

Oregon Dietitians Staff. Tastefully Oregon. LC 96-179261. (Illus.). 292p. (Orig.). 1997. 15.95 (*0-9650697-0-2*) Oregon Dietetic.

Oregon Historical Society Staff. One Average Day: Oregon Project Dayshoot Photographs - 15 July 1983. (Illus.). 152p. (Orig.). 1984. 21.95 (*0-87595-132-5*); pap. 14.95 (*0-87595-133-3*) Oregon Hist.

Oregon. Insurance Division & National Insurance Law Service. Oregon Regulations: Containing Insurance Division Regulations. LC 97-67933. (Illus.). 1997. write for info. (*0-89246-475-5*) NILS Pub.

Oregon Nikkei Endowment Staff. Touching the Stones. 112p. 34.95 (*0-9644806-0-3*); pap. 19.95 (*0-9644806-1-1*) OR Nikkei Endow.

O

Oregon Secretary of State Staff. Oregon Blue Book, 1997-1998. (Illus.). 480p. (Orig.). 1997. pap. 14.00 (*0-924540-02-8*) Oregon Secy.

Oregon State University Staff. Writing Philosophy Papers. 112p. (C). 1997. student ed., spiral bd. 12.95 (*0-7872-4271-3*, 41427101) Kendall-Hunt.

Oregon Writers Colony Staff. In Our Own Voices Vol. 5: Anthology of the Oregon Writers Colony, 1993-1997. Bolton, Elizabeth, ed. (Illus.). 100p. 1997. 10.50 (*1-891535-00-5*) Oregon Writers.

***Oregonian Staff, compiled by.** The Oregon Story, 1850-2000. 2000. 29.95 (*1-55868-543-X*) Gr Arts Ctr Pub.

Oreibi, Misbah, et al. Contribution of Islamic Thought to Modern Economics: Proceedings of the Economics Seminar Held Jointly by Al Azhar University & the International Institute of Islamic Thought, Cairo, 1409-1988. LC 97-41875. (Islamization of Knowledge 17 Ser.). 1997. write for info. (*1-56564-262-7*) IIIT VA.

Oreier, John C., ed. The Alliance for Progress: Problems & Perspectives. LC 62-18508. 166p. reprint ed. pap. 51.50 (*0-8357-5319-0*, 202076500018) Bks Demand.

O'Reilley, Mary. The Peaceable Classroom. LC 93-17781. 160p. 1993. pap. text 21.50 (*0-86709-328-5*, 0328, Pub. by Boynton Cook Pubs) Heinemann.

O'Reilley, Mary R. Radical Presence: Teaching As Contemplative Practice. LC 97-44855. 1998. pap. 14.00 (*0-86709-427-3*, Pub. by Boynton Cook Pubs) Heinemann.

— Radical Presence: Teaching As Contemplative Practice. LC 97-44855. 1998. write for info. (*0-86709-449-4*) Boynton Cook Pubs.

***O'Reilley, Mary Rose.** The Barn at the End of the World: The Apprenticeship of a Quaker, Buddhist Shepherd. LC 99-16274. 316p. 2000. 22.95 (*1-57131-237-4*) Milkweed Ed.

O'Reilly. Another World. 1992. pap. text. write for info. (*0-582-06418-X*, Pub. by Addison-Wesley) Longman.

— Environmental & Workplace Safety Binder. (C). 1996. 74.95 (*0-442-02366-9*, VNR) Wiley.

— Whole Internete Guide/Catalog: Academy Education. (Multimedia). 1995. pap. 25.95 (*0-534-50674-7*) Brooks-Cole.

O'Reilly, et al. Diagnostic Techniques in Urology. (Illus.). 640p. 1990. text 240.00 (*0-7216-3116-9*, W B Saunders Co) Harcrt Hlth Sci Grp.

O'Reilly, jt. auth. see Empey.

***O'Reilly & Associates, Inc. Staff.** Java Enterprise CD Bookshelf. Walsh, Linda, ed. (Illus.). 622p. 2000. pap. 89.95 incl. cd-rom (*1-56592-850-4*) OReilly & Assocs.

— Oracle PL/SQL CD Bookshelf. Walsh, Linda, ed. (Illus.). 272p. 2000. pap. 89.95 incl. cd-rom (*1-56592-849-0*) OReilly & Assocs.

— Web Board Host Master. Peck, Susan, ed. (Illus.). 300p. 2000. pap. 699.00 incl. cd-rom (*1-56592-745-1*) OReilly & Assocs.

O'Reilly & Associates Staff. Assorted O'Reilly Annoyances. 1997. pap. 26.20 (*1-56592-476-2*) OReilly & Assocs.

— The Perl CD Bookshelf. Walsh, Linda, ed. (Illus.). 1999. pap. 59.95 incl. cd-rom (*1-56592-462-2*) OReilly & Assocs.

***O'Reilly & Associates Staff.** The UNIX CD Bookshelf. 2nd ed. Walsh, Linda, ed. (Illus.). 624p. 2000. pap. 69.95 (*1-56592-815-6*) OReilly & Assocs.

O'Reilly & Associates Staff. Website 1.1. 2nd ed. (Illus.). 500p. (Orig.). 1996. pap. 249.00 (*1-56592-173-9*) Thomson Learn.

***O'Reilly & Associates Staff, ed.** The Networking CD Bookshelf. (Illus.). 456p. 1998. pap. 79.95 incl. cd-rom (*1-56592-523-8*) OReilly & Assocs.

O'Reilly & Associates Staff & Cutler, Ellie. SCO UNIX in a Nutshell. Mui, Peter, ed. LC 94-173420. (Illus.). 590p. 1994. pap. 24.95 (*1-56592-037-6*) Thomson Learn.

O'Reilly & Associates Staff & Mitchell, Carolyn B. The Harvard Conference on the Internet & Society. 1997. pap. text 27.95 (*0-674-45931-8*) HUP.

— Internet & Society. 1997. pap. text 32.95 incl. cd-rom (*0-674-45932-6*) HUP.

***O'Reilly & Associates Staff, et al.** UNIX in a Nutshell: System V Edition. 3rd ed. Loukides, Mike, ed. (Illus.). 624p. 1999. pap. 24.95 (*1-56592-427-4*) OReilly & Assocs.

O'Reilly & Associates Staff, jt. auth. see Siever, Ellen.

O'Reilly & Associates Staff, ed. see Gilly, Daniel.

O'Reilly, A. J. The Martyrs of the Coliseum with Historical Records of the Great Amphitheater of Ancient Rome. LC 82-50595. 450p. 1994. reprint ed. pap. 18.50 (*0-89555-192-6*) TAN Bks Pubs.

O'Reilly, Aileen C., jt. auth. see O'Brien, Kyran.

O'Reilly, Aleia N. & St. Germain. Rainbow Warriors Awake! An Invitation to Remember. 240p. 1995. pap. 15.95 (*0-9642096-0-8*) Little Hummingbird.

***O'Reilly, Andrea & Abbey, Sharon, eds.** Mothers & Daughters: Connection, Empowerment & Transformation. LC 99-45590. 336p. 2000. pap. 25.95 (*0-8476-9487-9*); text 65.00 (*0-8476-9486-0*) Rowman.

O'Reilly, Andrea, jt. ed. see Abbey, Sharon M.

O'Reilly, Anne. Intro to Human Development: 141. 224p. (C). 1995. pap. 18.95 (*0-7872-1311-X*) Kendall-Hunt.

— Introduction to Human Development: Psychology 141. 2nd ed. 170p. (C). 1997. spiral bd. 22.00 (*0-7872-4330-2*) Kendall-Hunt.

O'Reilly, Barbi L., ed. Manhattan Dance School Directory. LC 78-10411. (Dance Program Ser.: Vol. 13). 191p. reprint ed. pap. 59.30 (*0-608-16660-X*, 202781500054) Bks Demand.

O'Reilly, Barry, jt. auth. see O'Maitiu, Seamas.

***O'Reilly, Bill.** The O'Reilly Factor: The Good, the Bad, & the Completely Ridiculous in American Life. 224p. 2000. 23.00 (*0-7679-0528-8*) Broadway BDD.

O'Reilly, Bill. Those Who Trespass: A Novel of Murder & Television. 332p. (Orig.). 1998. pap. 24.00 (*0-9631246-8-4*) Bancroft MD.

***O'Reilly, Bill.** Those Who Trespass: A Novel of Murder & Television. 382p. (Orig.). 1999. reprint ed. mass mkt. 6.99 (*0-451-40882-9*, Onyx) NAL.

O'Reilly, Camille. The Irish Language in Northern Ireland: The Politics of Culture & Identity. LC 98-19152. 256p. 1999. text 65.00 (*0-312-21790-0*) St Martin.

***O'Reilly, Charles A., III & Pfeffer, Jeffrey.** Hidden Value: How Great Companies Achieve Extraordinary Results from Ordinary People. LC 00-25016. 2000. 27.50 (*0-87584-898-2*) Harvard Busn.

O'Reilly, Charles A., jt. auth. see Tushman, Michael L.

O'Reilly, Ciaron. Bomber Grounded, Runway Closed: Prison Letters & Court Notes of a Gulf War Resister. Sprong, Michael, ed. 175p. (Orig.). 1994. pap. 9.95 (*0-9636224-2-0*) Rose Hill Bks.

***O'Reilly, Dave, et al.** Developing the Capable Practitioner: Professional Capability Through Higher Education. LC 99-234364. (Illus.). 224p. 1999. pap. 32.50 (*0-7494-2876-7*, Kogan Pg Educ) Stylus Pub VA.

O'Reilly, David, et al. Baculovirus Expression Vectors: A Laboratory Manual. LC 93-43895. (Illus.). 364p. (C). 1993. spiral bd., lab manual ed. 65.00 (*0-19-509131-0*) OUP.

O'Reilly, Diane. Retard. LC 88-83478. 200p. 1989. 18.95 (*0-944435-05-X*) Glenbridge Pub.

O'Reilly, Donal. The Supermarket Shopper's Guide to Fat Free Foods. 108p. (Orig.). 1995. pap. 3.95 (*0-9643726-6-5*) Onomy Hse.

O'Reilly, E. Heroic Spain. 1976. lib. bdg. 59.95 (*0-8490-1948-6*) Gordon Pr.

O'Reilly, Edmund B. Sobering Tales: Narratives of Alcoholism & Recovery. LC 96-20323. 264p. (C). 1997. 50.00 (*1-55849-064-7*); pap. 17.95 (*1-55849-065-5*) U of Mass Pr.

O'Reilly, Edward. Brown Pelican at the Pond. LC 78-58689. (Illus.). (J). (gr. k-4). 1979. 7.95 (*0-931644-01-1*) Manzanita Pr.

***O'Reilly, Emily.** Veronica Guerin: The Life & Death of a Crime Reporter. 190p. 1998. pap. 13.95 (*0-09-976151-3*, Pub. by Random) Trafalgar.

O'Reilly, Emma-Louise. Perfect Country Rooms. (Illus.). 144p. 1996. 35.00 (*0-7892-0121-6*) Abbeville Pr.

O'Reilly, Evelyn M. Decoding the Cultural Stereotypes about Aging: New Perspectives on Aging Talk & Aging Issues. rev. ed. Bruchey, Stuart, ed. LC 97-33172. (Studies on the Elderly in America). 136p. 1997. text 43.00 (*0-8153-3023-5*) Garland.

O'Reilly, F. D. & McDonald, P. I. Thailand's Agriculture. 98p. 1983. write for info. (*963-05-3360-X*, Pub. by Akade Kiado) St Mut.

O'Reilly, Frank A. The Fredericksburg Campaign "Stonewall" Jackson at Fredericksburg: The Battle of Prospect Hill. (Virginia Civil War Battles & Leaders Ser.). (Illus.). 243p. 1993. 19.95 (*1-56190-050-8*) H E Howard.

O'Reilly, Gerald, ed. Planning for Field Safety. LC 89-83681. 197p. (Orig.). 1992. pap. text 18.75 (*0-913312-93-2*) Am Geol.

O'Reilly, Gretchen, jt. auth. see Reading, Lee.

O'Reilly, Helen. New Owner's Guide to Sugar Gliders. 160p. 1998. 12.95 (*0-7938-2825-2*, JG-200) TFH Pubns.

O'Reilly, Henry. Settlement in the West. 468p. 1993. reprint ed. lib. bdg. 99.00 (*0-7812-5193-1*) Rprt Serv.

O'Reilly, J. Multivariable Control for Industrial Applications. (Control Engineering Ser.: No. 32). 466p. 1987. 99.00 (*0-86341-117-7*, CE032) INSPEC Inc.

O'Reilly, J. J. Principios de Telecomunicaciones. 2nd ed. (SPA.). 192p. (C). 1994. pap. text 12.66 (*0-201-62563-6*) Addison-Wesley.

O'Reilly, Jacqueline. Banking on Flexibility: A Comparison of Flexible Employment Strategies in the Retail Banking Sector in Britain & France. 310p. 1994. 77.95 (*1-85628-549-9*, Pub. by Avebry) Ashgate Pub Co.

O'Reilly, Jacqueline & Fagan, Colette, eds. Part Time Prospects: International Comparison of Part Time Work in Europe, North America & the Pacific Rim. LC 98-166828. 272p. (C). 1998. pap. 29.99 (*0-415-15670-X*) Routledge.

— Part Time Prospects: International Comparison of Part Time Work in Europe, North America & the Pacific Rim. LC 98-166828. (Illus.). 304p. (C). 1998. 90.00 (*0-415-15669-6*) Routledge.

O'Reilly, James, et al, eds. Danger! True Stories of Trouble & Survival. LC 99-18518. (Travelers' Tales Ser.). 336p. 1999. pap. 17.95 (*1-885211-32-5*) Trvlers Tale.

— The Gift of Travel: The Best of Travelers' Tales. (Travelers' Tales Ser.). 240p. 1998. pap. 14.95 (*1-885211-25-2*, 25-2) Trvlers Tale.

***O'Reilly, James, et al, eds.** Grand Canyon: True Stories of Life Below the Rim. LC 99-26917. (Travelers' Tales Ser.). 320p. 1999. pap. 17.95 (*1-885211-34-1*) Trvlers Tale.

O'Reilly, James, et al, eds. Paris. (Travelers' Tales Guides Ser.). 417p. 1997. pap. 17.95 (*1-885211-10-4*) Trvlers Tale.

— Testosterone Planet: True Stories from a Man's World. LC 99-35884. (Travelers' Tales Ser.). 384p. 1999. pap. 17.95 (*1-885211-43-0*, 43-0, Pub. by Trvlers Tale) OReilly & Assocs.

— Traveler's Tales France. (Illus.). 517p. 1995. pap. 17.95 (*1-885211-02-3*) Thomson Learn.

— Traveler's Tales Hong Kong. (Travelers' Tales Guides Ser.). (Illus.). 439p. 1996. pap. 17.95 (*1-885211-03-1*) Thomson Learn.

***O'Reilly, James, et al, eds.** Travelers Tales Ireland: True Stories of Life on the Emerald Isle. LC 99-86872. (Travelers' Tales Guides Ser.). 368p. 2000. pap. 17.95 (*1-885211-46-5*, 46-5, Pub. by Trvlers Tale) Publishers Group.

O'Reilly, James, et al, eds. Travelers Tales San Francisco. (Computer Science). 491p. 1996. pap. 17.95 (*1-885211-08-2*) Thomson Learn.

***O'Reilly, James, et al, eds.** The Ultimate Journey: Inspiring Stories of Living & Dying. LC 99-42251. 336p. 2000. pap. 17.95 (*1-885211-38-4*, 38-4, Pub. by Trvlers Tale) Publishers Group.

O'Reilly, James & Habegger, Larry, eds. Traveler's Tales India. (Travelers' Tales Guides Ser.). (Illus.). 435p. 1995. pap. 17.95 (*1-885211-01-5*) Thomson Learn.

— Travelers' Tales of Mexico. (Travelers' Tales Guides Ser.). (Illus.). 463p. 1994. pap. 17.95 (*1-885211-00-7*) Thomson Learn.

— Travelers' Tales Thailand. (Illus.). 405p. 1993. pap. 15.95 (*1-56592-900-4*) Thomson Learn.

— Traveler's Tales Thailand. rev. ed. (Travelers' Tales Guides Ser.). (Illus.). 483p. 1993. pap. 17.95 (*1-885211-05-8*) Thomson Learn.

***O'Reilly, James & O'Reilly, Sean, eds.** Pilgrimage: Adventures of the Spirit. (Illus.). 344p. 2000. pap. 16.95 (*1-885211-56-2*) Trvlers Tale.

O'Reilly, James T. Administrative Rule Making: 1996 Supplement. Davis, Russ, ed. 226p. 1996. pap. text, suppl. ed. write for info. (*0-7620-0062-7*) West Group.

— American Environmental Liability Risks. (International Environmental Law & Policy Ser.). 256p. (C). 1995. lib. bdg. 103.50 (*1-85966-093-2*, Pub. by Graham & Trotman) Kluwer Academic.

— Federal Information Disclosure: Procedures, Forms & the Law, 2 vols. LC 77-21381. 1344p. 1977. 200.00 (*0-07-047825-2*) Shepards.

— Federal Information Disclosure: Procedures, Forms & the Law (New Material) 2nd ed. Davis, Russ, ed. 308p. 1996. text. write for info. (*0-7620-0071-6*) West Group.

— Federal Information Disclosure: Procedures, Forms & the Law (1996 Supplement) 2nd ed. Davis, Russ, ed. 308p. 1996. text, suppl. ed. write for info. (*0-7620-0072-4*) West Group.

— Ohio Public Employee Collective Bargaining Law. 2nd ed. (Anderson's Ohio Practice Manual Ser.). 439p. 1992. pap. 50.00 (*0-87084-668-X*) Anderson Pub Co.

***O'Reilly, James T.** Product Warnings, Defects & Hazards. 2nd ed. LC 98-47268. 1999. ring bd. 164.00 (*0-7355-0299-4*) Aspen Law.

O'Reilly, James T. Toxic Torts Practice Guide. 2nd ed. LC 92-39224. 1158p. 1993. text 105.00 (*0-07-172430-3*) Shepards.

O'Reilly, James T. & Aronson, Jodi C. Unions' Rights to Company Information. rev. ed. LC 85-82257. (Labor Relations & Public Policy Ser.: Vol. 21). 312p. 1987. pap. 37.50 (*0-89546-060-2*) U PA Ctr Hum Res.

O'Reilly, James T. & Cody, Nancy C. Ohio Products Liability Manual. (Ohio Practice Manual Ser.). 299p. (Orig.). 1992. pap. 40.00 (*0-87084-670-1*) Anderson Pub Co.

O'Reilly, James T. & Simon, Gale P. Unions' Rights to Company Information. LC 80-53300. (Labor Relations & Public Policy Ser.: No. 21). 292p. reprint ed. pap. 90.60 (*0-608-14862-8*, 202591300047) Bks Demand.

O'Reilly, James T., et al. Environmental & Workplace Safety: A Guide for University, Hospital, & School Managers. (Industrial Health & Safety Ser.). 352p. 1996. 89.95 (*0-471-28723-7*, VNR) Wiley.

O'Reilly, James T., et al. Federal Regulation of the Chemical Industry. LC 80-11488. (Regulatory Manual Ser.). 1184p. 1980. text 95.00 (*0-07-047728-0*) Shepards.

— Keeping Buildings Healthy: How to Monitor & Prevent Indoor Environmental Problems. LC 98-3365. 361p. 1998. 87.95 (*0-471-29228-1*, VNR) Wiley.

— RCRA & Superfund: A Practice Guide with Forms. 2nd ed. LC 93-40258. 1994. 99.00 (*0-07-172535-0*) McGraw.

— Sick or Healthy Building? (Occupational Health & Safety Ser.). (Illus.). 400p. 1998. 69.95 (*0-442-02507-6*, VNR) Wiley.

— University Hospitals & School Managers Guide to Environment: A Guide for University, Hospital, & School Managers. LC 95-38757. (Industrial Health & Safety Ser.). 368p. 1996. text 78.95 (*0-442-02123-2*, VNR) Wiley.

O'Reilly, Jane. Quick Escapes from Minneapolis - St. Paul: 25 Weekend Getaways from the Twin Cities. LC 97-47753. (Quick Escapes Ser.). (Illus.). 256p. 1998. pap. 14.95 (*0-7627-0199-4*) Globe Pequot.

***O'Reilly, Jane H.** Quick Escapes - Minneapolis/St. Paul: 25 Weekend Getaways in & Around the Twin Cities. 2nd ed. (Quick Escapes Ser.). (Illus.). 320p. 2000. pap. 15.95 (*0-7627-0637-6*) Globe Pequot.

O'Reilly, Jean J., jt. auth. see Pritsker, A. Alan B.

O'Reilly, John, ed. Observers for Linear Systems. (Mathematics in Science & Engineering Ser.). 1983. text 116.00 (*0-12-527780-6*) Acad Pr.

O'Reilly, John & Kinyon, John. Yamaha Band Student, B-Flat Clarinet, Bk. 3. (Yamaha Band Student Ser.). 32p. 1991. pap. 5.95 (*0-7390-0674-6*, 5216) Alfred Pub.

— Yamaha Band Student, Bb-Flat Trumpet/Cornet, Bk. 3. (Yamaha Band Student Ser.). 32p. 1991. pap. 5.95 (*0-7390-0673-8*, 5223) Alfred Pub.

O'Reilly, John & Williams, Mark. Accent on Achievement, Bk. 1. 1997. audio compact disk 14.95 (*0-7390-0483-2*, 17144) Alfred Pub.

— Accent on Achievement, B-Flat Bass Clarinet, Bk. 1. (Accent on Achievement Ser.). 48p. 1997. pap. 6.95 (*0-7390-0484-0*, 17086) Alfred Pub.

— Accent on Achievement, B-Flat Bass Clarinet, Bk. 2. (Accent on Achievement Ser.). 48p. 1998. pap. 6.95 (*0-7390-0460-3*, 18260) Alfred Pub.

— Accent on Achievement, B-Flat Bass Clarinet, Bk. 3. (Accent on Achievement Ser.). 40p. 1999. pap. 6.95 (*0-7390-0627-4*, 18058) Alfred Pub.

— Accent on Achievement. B-Flat Clarinet, Bk. 1. (Accent on Achievement Ser.). 48p. 1997. pap. 6.95 (*0-7390-0485-9*, 17084) Alfred Pub.

— Accent on Achievement, B-Flat Clarinet, Bk. 2. (Accent on Achievement Ser.). 48p. 1998. pap. 6.95 (*0-7390-0461-1*, 18258) Alfred Pub.

— Accent on Achievement, B-Flat Clarinet, Bk. 3. (Accent on Achievement Ser.). 40p. 1999. pap. 6.95 (*0-7390-0625-8*, 18056) Alfred Pub.

— Accent on Achievement, B-Flat Tenor Saxophone, Bk. 1. (Accent on Achievement Ser.). 48p. 1997. pap. 6.95 (*0-7390-0486-7*, 17088) Alfred Pub.

— Accent on Achievement, B-Flat Tenor Saxophone, Bk. 2. (Accent on Achievement Ser.). 48p. 1998. pap. 6.95 (*0-7390-0462-X*, 18262) Alfred Pub.

— Accent on Achievement, B-Flat Tenor Saxophone, Bk. 3. (Accent on Achievement Ser.). 40p. 1999. pap. 6.95 (*0-7390-0629-0*, 18060) Alfred Pub.

— Accent on Achievement, B-Flat Trumpet, Bk. 1. (Accent on Achievement Ser.). 48p. 1997. pap. 6.95 (*0-7390-0487-5*, 17090) Alfred Pub.

— Accent on Achievement, B-Flat Trumpet, Bk. 2. (Accent on Achievement Ser.). 48p. 1998. pap. 6.95 (*0-7390-0463-8*, 18264) Alfred Pub.

— Accent on Achievement, B-Flat Trumpet/Cornet, Bk. 3. (Accent on Achievement Ser.). 40p. 1999. pap. 6.95 (*0-7390-0631-2*, 18062) Alfred Pub.

— Accent on Achievement, Baritone B. C., Bk. 1. (Accent on Achievement Ser.). 48p. 1997. pap. 6.95 (*0-7390-0488-3*, 17093) Alfred Pub.

— Accent on Achievement, Baritone B. C., Bk. 2. (Accent on Achievement Ser.). 48p. 1998. pap. 6.95 (*0-7390-0464-6*, 18267) Alfred Pub.

— Accent on Achievement, Baritone B. C., Bk. 3. (Accent on Achievement Ser.). 40p. 1999. pap. 6.95 (*0-7390-0634-7*, 18065) Alfred Pub.

— Accent on Achievement, Baritone T. C., Bk. 1. (Accent on Achievement Ser.). 48p. 1997. pap. 6.95 (*0-7390-0489-1*, 17094) Alfred Pub.

— Accent on Achievement, Baritone T. C., Bk. 2. (Accent on Achievement Ser.). 48p. 1998. pap. 6.95 (*0-7390-0465-4*, 18268) Alfred Pub.

— Accent on Achievement, Baritone T. C., Bk. 3. (Accent on Achievement Ser.). 40p. 1999. pap. 6.95 (*0-7390-0635-5*, 18066) Alfred Pub.

— Accent on Achievement, Bassoon, Bk. 1. (Accent on Achievement Ser.). 48p. 1997. pap. 6.95 (*0-7390-0490-5*, 17083) Alfred Pub.

— Accent on Achievement, Bassoon, Bk. 2. (Accent on Achievement Ser.). 48p. 1998. pap. 6.95 (*0-7390-0466-2*, 18257) Alfred Pub.

— Accent on Achievement, Bassoon, Bk. 3. (Accent on Achievement Ser.). 40p. 1999. pap. 6.95 (*0-7390-0624-X*, 18055) Alfred Pub.

— Accent on Achievement, Combined Percussion, Bk. 1. (Accent on Achievement Ser.). 92p. 1997. pap. 9.95 (*0-7390-0491-3*, 17099) Alfred Pub.

— Accent on Achievement, Combined Percussion, Bk. 2. (Accent on Achievement Ser.). 92p. 1998. pap. 9.95 (*0-7390-0467-0*, 18273) Alfred Pub.

— Accent on Achievement, Combined Percussion, Bk. 3. (Accent on Achievement Ser.). 80p. 1999. pap. 9.95 (*0-7390-0709-2*, 18071) Alfred Pub.

— Accent on Achievement, Conductor's Score, Bk. 1. (Accent on Achievement Ser.). 388p. 1997. pap. 49.95 (*0-7390-0492-1*, 17101) Alfred Pub.

— Accent on Achievement, Conductor's Score, Bk. 2. (Accent on Achievement Ser.). 400p. 1998. pap. 49.95 (*0-7390-0468-9*, 18275) Alfred Pub.

— Accent on Achievement, Conductor's Score, Bk. 3. (Accent on Achievement Ser.). 354p. 1999. pap. 49.95 (*0-7390-0641-X*, 18072) Alfred Pub.

— Accent on Achievement, E-Flat Alto Clarinet, Bk. 2. (Accent on Achievement Ser.). 48p. 1998. pap. 6.95 (*0-7390-0469-7*, 18259) Alfred Pub.

— Accent on Achievement, E-Flat Alto Clarinet, Bk. 3. (Accent on Achievement Ser.). 40p. 1999. pap. 6.95 (*0-7390-0626-6*, 18057) Alfred Pub.

— Accent on Achievement, E-Flat Alto Saxophone, Bk. 1. (Accent on Achievement Ser.). 48p. 1997. pap. 6.95 (*0-7390-0508-1*, 17087) Alfred Pub.

— Accent on Achievement, E-Flat Alto Saxophone, Bk. 2. (Accent on Achievement Ser.). 48p. 1998. pap. 6.95 (*0-7390-0470-0*, 18261) Alfred Pub.

— Accent on Achievement, E-Flat Alto Saxophone, Bk. 3. (Accent on Achievement Ser.). 40p. 1999. pap. 6.95 (*0-7390-0628-2*, 18059) Alfred Pub.

— Accent on Achievement, E-Flat Baritone Saxophone, Bk. 1. (Accent on Achievement Ser.). 48p. 1997. pap. 6.95 (*0-7390-0509-X*, 17089) Alfred Pub.

— Accent on Achievement, E-Flat Baritone Saxophone, Bk. 2. (Accent on Achievement Ser.). 48p. 1998. pap. 6.95 (*0-7390-0471-9*, 18263) Alfred Pub.

— Accent on Achievement, E-Flat Baritone Saxophone, Bk. 3. (Accent on Achievement Ser.). 40p. 1999. pap. 6.95 (*0-7390-0630-4*, 18061) Alfred Pub.

— Accent on Achievement, E-Flat Clarinet, Bk. 1. (Accent on Achievement Ser.). 48p. 1997. pap. 6.95 (*0-7390-0507-3*, 17085) Alfred Pub.

— Accent on Achievement, Electric Bass, Bk. 1. (Accent on Achievement Ser.). 48p. 1997. pap. 6.95 (*0-7390-0510-3*, 17096) Alfred Pub.

— Accent on Achievement, Electric Bass, Bk. 2. (Accent on Achievement Ser.). 48p. 1998. pap. 6.95 (*0-7390-0472-7*, 18270) Alfred Pub.

— Accent on Achievement, Electric Bass, Bk. 3. (Accent on Achievement Ser.). 40p. 1999. pap. 6.95 (*0-7390-0637-1*, 18068) Alfred Pub.

— Accent on Achievement, Flute, Bk. 1. (Accent on Achievement Ser.). 48p. 1997. pap. 6.95 (*0-7390-0511-1*, 17081) Alfred Pub.

O

An Asterisk (*) at the beginning of an entry indicates that the title is appearing for the first time.

— Accent on Achievement, Flute, Bk. 2. (Accent on Achievement Ser.). 48p. 1998. pap. 6.95 (*0-7390-0473-5*, 18255) Alfred Pub.
— Accent on Achievement, Flute, Bk. 3. (Accent on Achievement Ser.). 40p. 1999. pap. 6.95 (*0-7390-0622-3*, 18053) Alfred Pub.
— Accent on Achievement, Horn in F, Bk. 1. (Accent on Achievement Ser.). 64p. 1997. pap. 6.95 (*0-7390-0512-X*, 17091) Alfred Pub.
— Accent on Achievement, Horn in F, Bk. 2. (Accent on Achievement Ser.). 48p. 1998. pap. 6.95 (*0-7390-0474-3*, 18265) Alfred Pub.
— Accent on Achievement, Horn in F, Bk. 3. (Accent on Achievement Ser.). 40p. 1999. pap. 6.95 (*0-7390-0632-0*, 18063) Alfred Pub.
— Accent on Achievement, Mallet Percussion, Bk. 1. (Accent on Achievement Ser.). 48p. 1997. pap. 6.95 (*0-7390-0513-8*, 17098) Alfred Pub.
— Accent on Achievement, Mallet Percussion, Bk. 3. (Accent on Achievement Ser.). 40p. 1999. pap. 6.95 (*0-7390-0639-8*, 18070) Alfred Pub.
— Accent on Achievement, Mallet Percussion & Timpani, Bk. 2. (Accent on Achievement Ser.). 48p. 1998. pap. 6.95 (*0-7390-0475-1*, 18272) Alfred Pub.
— Accent on Achievement, Oboe, Bk. 1. (Accent on Achievement Ser.). 56p. 1997. pap. 6.95 (*0-7390-0514-6*, 17082) Alfred Pub.
— Accent on Achievement, Oboe, Bk. 2. (Accent on Achievement Ser.). 48p. 1998. pap. 6.95 (*0-7390-0476-X*, 18256) Alfred Pub.
— Accent on Achievement, Oboe, Bk. 3. (Accent on Achievement Ser.). 40p. 1999. pap. 6.95 (*0-7390-0623-1*, 18054) Alfred Pub.
— Accent on Achievement, Percussion, Bk. 1. (Accent on Achievement Ser.). 48p. 1997. pap. 6.95 (*0-7390-0515-4*, 17097) Alfred Pub.
— Accent on Achievement, Percussion, Bk. 2. (Accent on Achievement Ser.). 48p. 1998. pap. 6.95 (*0-7390-0477-8*, 18271) Alfred Pub.
— Accent on Achievement, Percussion, Bk. 3. (Accent on Achievement Ser.). 40p. 1999. pap. 6.95 (*0-7390-0638-X*, 18069) Alfred Pub.
— Accent on Achievement, Piano Accompaniment, Bk. 1. (Accent on Achievement Ser.). 68p. 1997. pap. 9.95 (*0-7390-0516-2*, 17100) Alfred Pub.
— Accent on Achievement, Piano Accompaniment, Bk. 2. (Accent on Achievement Ser.). 48p. 1998. pap. 9.95 (*0-7390-0478-6*, 18274) Alfred Pub.
— Accent on Achievement, Teacher's Resource Kit, Bk. 1. (Accent on Achievement Ser.). 1997. pap. 29.95 (*0-7390-0517-0*) Alfred Pub.
— Accent on Achievement, Teacher's Resource Kit, Bk. 2. (Accent on Achievement Ser.). 86p. 1998. teacher ed. 29.95 (*0-7390-0479-4*, 18276) Alfred Pub.
— Accent on Achievement, Trombone, Bk. 1. (Accent on Achievement Ser.). 48p. 1997. pap. 6.95 (*0-7390-0518-9*, 17092) Alfred Pub.
— Accent on Achievement, Trombone, Bk. 2. (Accent on Achievement Ser.). 48p. 1998. pap. 6.95 (*0-7390-0480-8*, 18266) Alfred Pub.
— Accent on Achievement, Trombone, Bk. 3. (Accent on Achievement Ser.). 40p. 1999. pap. 6.95 (*0-7390-0633-9*, 18064) Alfred Pub.
— Accent on Achievement, Tuba, Bk. 1. (Accent on Achievement Ser.). 48p. 1997. pap. 6.95 (*0-7390-0519-7*, 17095) Alfred Pub.
— Accent on Achievement, Tuba, Bk. 2. (Accent on Achievement Ser.). 48p. 1998. pap. 6.95 (*0-7390-0481-6*, 18269) Alfred Pub.
— Accent on Achievement, Tuba, Bk. 3. (Accent on Achievement Ser.). 40p. 1999. pap. 6.95 (*0-7390-0636-3*, 18067) Alfred Pub.

O'Reilly, John, jt. auth. see Bach, Steve.

O'Reilly, John, jt. auth. see Feldstein, Sandy.

O'Reilly, John, jt. auth. see Feldstein, Saul.

O'Reilly, John, jt. auth. see Kinyon, John.

O'Reilly, John, ed. see DeCesare, Ruth.

O'Reilly, John B., compiled by. The Poetry & Song of Old Ireland. (Illus.). 852p. 1985. 35.00 (*0-940134-43-8*) Irish Genealog.

O'Reilly, John B., jt. auth. see Evans, A. G.

O'Reilly, John L. The Smoldering Wick: Never Too Late for New Life. (Illus.). 144p. (Orig.). 1990. write for info. (*0-9625748-0-5*); write for info. (*0-9625748-1-3*); write for info. (*0-9625748-9-9*); teacher ed. write for info. (*0-9625748-6-4*); student ed. write for info. (*0-9625748-7-2*); student ed. write for info. (*0-9625748-8-0*); pap. 12.00 (*0-9625748-4-8*); text. write for info. (*0-9625748-3-X*); pap. text. write for info. (*0-9625748-5-6*); lib. bdg. write for info. (*0-9625748-2-1*) J L OReilly.

***O'Reilly, Karen.** The British on the Costa del Sol: Transnational Identities & Local Communities. LC 00-21537. 2000. pap. write for info. (*1-84142-047-6*, Pub. by UCL Pr Ltd) Taylor & Francis.

O'Reilly, Kellie W., ed. Managing the Rapids: Stories from the Forefront of the Learning Organization. LC 95-69858. (Illus.). 124p. 1995. pap. 17.95 (*1-883823-08-0*, OL004) Pegasus Comm.

O'Reilly, Kellie W., ed. see Seagal, Sandra & Horne, David.

O'Reilly, Kenneth. Nixon's Piano: Presidents & the Politics of Race from Washington to Clinton. 512p. 1995. 27.00 (*0-02-923685-1*) Free Pr.

O'Reilly, Kevin. Critical Thinking in United States History Book 1: Colonies to Constitution. 2nd ed. (Critical Thinking in United States History Ser.). Orig. Title: Critical Thinking in American History, Vol 1. 148p. (YA). 1990. pap., teacher ed. 16.95 (*0-89455-414-X*) Crit Think Bks.
— Critical Thinking in United States History Book 1: Colonies to Constitution. 2nd rev. ed. (Critical Thinking in United States History Ser.). Orig. Title: Critical Thinking in American History, Vol 1. (Illus.). 130p. (YA). (gr. 6 up). 1990. pap. 22.95 (*0-89455-413-1*) Crit Think Bks.
— Critical Thinking in United States History Book 2: New Republic to Civil War. 2nd ed. (Critical Thinking in United States History Ser.). Orig. Title: Critical Thinking in American History, Vol 2. 142p. (YA). 1993. pap., teacher ed. 16.95 (*0-89455-416-6*) Crit Think Bks.
— Critical Thinking in United States History Book 2: New Republic to Civil War. 2nd rev. ed. (Critical Thinking in United States History Ser.). Orig. Title: Critical Thinking in American History, Vol 2. (Illus.). 193p. (YA). (gr. 6 up). 1993. pap. 22.95 (*0-89455-415-8*) Crit Think Bks.
— Critical Thinking in United States History Book 3: Reconstruction to Progressivism. 2nd ed. (Critical Thinking in United States History Ser.). Orig. Title: Critical Thinking in American History, Vol 3. 148p. (YA). 1991. pap., teacher ed. 16.95 (*0-89455-418-2*) Crit Think Bks.
— Critical Thinking in United States History Book 3: Reconstruction to Progressivism. 2nd rev. ed. (Critical Thinking in United States History Ser.). Orig. Title: Critical Thinking in American History, Vol 3. (Illus.). 197p. (YA). (gr. 6 up). 1991. pap. 22.95 (*0-89455-417-4*) Crit Think Bks.
— Critical Thinking in United States History Book 4: Spanish-American War to Vietnam War. 2nd ed. (Critical Thinking in United States History Ser.). Orig. Title: Critical Thinking in American History, Vol 4. 150p. (YA). 1991. pap., teacher ed. 16.95 (*0-89455-420-4*) Crit Think Bks.
— Critical Thinking in United States History Book 4: Spanish-American War to Vietnam War. 2nd rev. ed. (Critical Thinking in United States History Ser.). Orig. Title: Critical Thinking in American History, Vol 4. (Illus.). 170p. (YA). (gr. 6 up). 1991. pap. 22.95 (*0-89455-419-0*) Crit Think Bks.

O'Reilly, M. P., ed. Cyclic Loading of Soils. 1991. mass mkt. 139.95 (*0-442-30410-2*, VNR) Wiley.

O'Reilly, Marjorie I., jt. auth. see O'Reilly, Robert C.

O'Reilly, Mark F., jt. auth. see Leslie, Julian.

O'Reilly, Martin. The Challenge of Being a Religious in Africa Today. LC 97-981282. (Publications Spearhead). xiii, 241p. 1996. write for info. (*9966-836-20-9*) Gaba Pubns.

O'Reilly, Maureen. Current Concepts in Pediatrics. (Newsletter Ser.: No. 2). 4p. (Orig.). 1994. write for info. (*0-944036-99-6*) Medicine Grp USA.
— Current Concepts in Pediatrics, Vol. 1, No. 1. 4p. (Orig.). 1994. write for info. (*0-944036-97-X*) Medicine Grp USA.

O'Reilly, Maureen, ed. The Challenges in Studying the Socioeconomic Dimensions in Cancer Therapy. 88p. (Orig.). 1995. write for info. (*1-57130-013-9*) Medicine Grp USA.
— The Challenges in Studying the Socioeconomic Dimensions in Cancer Therapy: Proceedings of a Symposium held in Cologne, Germany. (Illus.). 124p. (Orig.). 1995. write for info. (*1-57130-016-3*) Medicine Grp USA.

O'Reilly, Meg, jt. auth. see Morgan, Chris.

O'Reilly, Michael. Civil Engineering Construction Contracts. LC 96-232698. 418p. 1996. 67.00 (*0-7277-2530-0*) Am Soc Civil Eng.
— Costs in Arbitration Proceedings. 92p. 1995. text 55.00 (*1-85044-979-1*) LLP.

O'Reilly, Michael P. Principles of Construction Law. xxiii, 300p. (C). 1993. 71.95 (*0-582-21585-4*, 15740) Gaunt.

O'Reilly, Montagu. Who Has Been Tampering with These Pianos? 1988. pap. 10.00 (*0-947757-18-X*, Pub. by Atlas Pr) Serpents Tail.

O'Reilly, Pat. Harnessing the Unicorn: How to Create Opportunity & Manage Risk. LC 98-5371. 200p. 1998. 56.95 (*0-566-07974-7*, Pub. by Gower) Ashgate Pub Co.
— Matching the Hatch: Stillwater, River & Stream. (Illus.). 224p. 1998. 24.95 (*1-85310-822-7*) Swan Hill Pr.
— The Skills Development Handbook for Busy Managers. LC 92-45730. 1993. write for info. (*0-07-707682-6*) McGraw.

O'Reilly, Pat & Hoskin, Derek. An Introduction to Fly Tying. (Illus.). 112p. 1993. 29.95 (*1-85223-647-7*, Pub. by Crolwood) Trafalgar.

O'Reilly, Patrick W. Computer Aided Engineering Electronics. 1986. pap. 30.95 (*0-442-31747-6*) Thomson Learn.

***O'Reilly, Patrick W., photos by.** I Wanna Learn to Serge: 50+ Serger Projects. vii, 82p. 1999. pap. 16.95 (*0-9700204-0-6*) Sew-Biz.

O'Reilly, Peter. Loughs of Ireland: An Angler's Guide. 3rd ed. (Fly Fishing International Ser.). (Illus.). 335p. 1999. 34.95 (*0-8117-1025-4*) Stackpole.
— Rivers of Ireland: An Angler's Guide. 4th ed. (Illus.). 335p. 1999. 34.95 (*0-8117-1433-0*) Stackpole.
— Trout & Salmon Flies of Ireland. (Fly Fishing International Ser.). (Illus.). 176p. 1996. 34.95 (*0-8117-1610-4*) Stackpole.
— Trout & Salmon Rivers of Ireland: An Angler's Guide. (Fly Fishing International Ser.). (Illus.). 336p. 1995. 24.95 (*0-8117-1758-5*) Stackpole.

O'Reilly, Priscilla. Preservation Guide No. 3: Paintings. LC 84-106237. (Illus.). ii, 14p. 1986. pap. 3.95 (*0-917860-22-5*) Historic New Orleans.

O'Reilly, Priscilla & Lord, Allyn, eds. Basic Condition Reporting: A Handbook. 2nd expanded rev. ed. LC 88-62138. 56p. 1988. pap. 9.45 (*0-9621348-0-5*) SERA LA.
— Basic Condition Reporting: A Handbook. 2nd rev. ed. LC 88-62138. 1988. pap. 7.95 (*0-685-44324-8*) SERA LA.

***O'Reilly, Randall C. & Munakata, Yuko.** Computational Explorations in Cognitive Neuroscience: Understanding the Mind by Stimulating the Brain. LC 99-86066. (Illus.). 512p. 2000. pap. 50.00 (*0-262-65054-1*, Bradford Bks) MIT Pr.

O'Reilly, Robert C. & Green, Edward T. School Law for the 1990s: A Handbook. LC 91-27237. 312p. 1992. 49.95 (*0-313-27817-2*, OSL/, Greenwood Pr) Greenwood.
— School Law for the Practitioner, 6. LC 82-11982. (Contributions to the Study of Education Ser.: No. 6). (Illus.). 314p. 1983. 36.95 (*0-313-23639-9*, ORS/, Greenwood Pr) Greenwood.

O'Reilly, Robert C. & O'Reilly, Marjorie I. Librarians & Labor Relations: Employment under Union Contracts, 35. LC 80-1049. (Contributions in Librarianship & Information Science Ser.: No. 35). 191p. 1981. 52.95 (*0-313-22485-4*, OLL/) Greenwood.

O'Reilly, Sean. Irish Churches & Monasteries. LC 97-216413. 128p. 1997. pap. 15.95 (*1-898256-14-4*, Pub. by Collins Press) Irish Bks Media.
— Irish Houses & Gardens: From the Archives of Country Life. (Illus.). 1998. 60.00 (*1-85410-580-9*, Pub. by Aurum Pr) London Brdge.

O'Reilly, Sean, et al, eds. The Road Within: True Stories of Transformation & the Soul. (Travelers' Tales Guides Ser.). 459p. 1997. pap. 17.95 (*1-885211-19-8*, 19-8) Trvlers Tale.

O'Reilly, Sean, jt. ed. see Habegger, Larry.

O'Reilly, Sean, jt. ed. see O'Reilly, James.

O'Reilly, Susan. Arts & Crafts. 1998. 59.92 (*0-8172-4598-7*) Raintree Steck-V.

O'Reilly, Susan M. On Track: The Railway Mail Service in Canada. (Illus.). 152p. 1993. pap. 14.95 (*0-660-14005-5*, Pub. by CN Mus Civilization) U of Wash Pr.

O'Reilly, Susie. Knitting & Crochet. (Arts & Crafts Ser.). (Illus.). 32p. (J). (gr. 1-6). 1994. lib. bdg. 21.40 (*1-56847-221-8*) Raintree Steck-V.
— Needlecraft. (Arts & Crafts Ser.). (Illus.). 32p. (J). 1994. lib. bdg. 21.40 (*1-56847-220-X*) Raintree Steck-V.
— Papermaking. LC 93-24397. (Arts & Crafts Ser.). (Illus.). 32p. (J). (gr. 1-6). 1994. lib. bdg. 21.40 (*1-56847-069-X*) Raintree Steck-V.
— Stencils & Screens. LC 93-28349. (Arts & Crafts Ser.). (Illus.). 32p. (J). (gr. 1-6). 1994. lib. bdg. 21.40 (*1-56847-068-1*) Raintree Steck-V.

O'Reilly, Terence, jt. auth. see Stopp, Elisabeth.

O'Reilly, Tim & Mott, Troy. Windows 98 in a Nutshell. (Illus.). 600p. 1999. pap. 24.95 (*1-56592-486-X*) OReilly & Assocs.
— Windows 95 in a Nutshell. (Nutshell Ser.). (Illus.). 528p. (Orig.). 1998. pap. 24.95 (*1-56592-316-2*) OReilly & Assocs.

O'Reilly, Tim & Todino, Grace. Managing UUCP & USENET. 10th ed. (Computer Science). 368p. 1992. pap. 27.95 (*0-937175-93-5*) Thomson Learn.

O'Reilly, Tim, jt. auth. see Nye, Adrian.

O'Reilly, Tim, jt. auth. see Quercia, Valerie.

O'Reilly, Tim, ed. see Costales, Bryan, et al.

O'Reilly, Tim, ed. see Flanagan, David.

O'Reilly, Tim, ed. see Internet Multicasting Services Staff.

O'Reilly, Tim, ed. see Levine, John R. & Nelson, Russell.

O'Reilly, Tim, ed. see Libes, Don.

O'Reilly, Tim, ed. see Moncur, Michael.

O'Reilly, Tim, ed. see Mui, Linda & Pearce, Eric.

O'Reilly, Tim, ed. see Mui, Linda & Quercia, Valerie.

O'Reilly, Tim, ed. see Nuberg, Matt.

O'Reilly, Tim, ed. see Peek, Jerry.

O'Reilly, Tim, ed. see Pogue, David.

O'Reilly, Tim, ed. see Raymond, Eric S.

O'Reilly, Tim, ed. see Todino, Grace, et al.

O'Reilly, Tom, ed. see Costales, Bryan & Allman, Eric.

O'Reilly, Victor. The Devil's Footprint. 448p. 1998. mass mkt. 7.50 (*0-425-16186-2*) Berkley Pub.
— Games of the Hangman. 512p. 1992. mass mkt. 7.50 (*0-425-13456-3*) Berkley Pub.
— Rules of the Hunt. 512p. 1995. mass mkt. 6.99 (*0-425-15097-6*) Berkley Pub.

O'Reilly, Vincent M., et al. Montgomery's Auditing. 2nd ed. 1344p. 1998. 175.00 (*0-471-14063-5*) Wiley.
— Montgomery's Auditing Continuing Professional Education. 694p. 1999. 85.00 (*0-471-34605-5*) Wiley.

O'Reilly, W., ed. Magnetism, Planetary Rotation, & Convention in the Solar System: Retrospect & Prospect, Vol. 7. (Geophysical Surveys Ser.: Nos. 1, 2 & 3). 1985. text 171.50 (*90-277-2050-9*) Kluwer Academic.

***O'Reilly, Wenda B.** The Renaissance Art Book: Discover Thirty Glorious Masterpieces by Leonardo da Vinci, Michelangelo, Raphael, Fra Angelico, Botticelli. (Illus.). 80p. 2000. pap. (*1-889613-03-7*) Birdcage Bks.
— The Renaissance Art Game: Discover Thirty Glorious Masterpieces in a Delightful Game for All Ages. (Illus.). 80p. 2000. pap. (*1-889613-02-9*) Birdcage Bks.

O'Reilly, Wenda Brewster, ed. see Hahnemann, Samuel.

O'Reirdan, Terry, jt. auth. see Roffey, Sue.

Orejas, Fernando & Diaz, J. TAPSOFT '89, Vol. 1. (Lecture Notes in Computer Science Ser.: Vol. 351). x, 383p. 1989. 45.00 (*0-387-50939-9*) Spr-Verlag.
— TAPSOFT '89, Vol. 2. x, 389p. 1989. 45.00 (*0-387-50940-2*) Spr-Verlag.

Orejas, Fernando, jt. ed. see Ehrig, Hartmut.

Orejudo, Antonio. Las Epistolas Familiares de Antonio de Guevara en el Contexto Epistolar del Renacimiento. (SPA.). xv, 204p. 1994. 25.00 (*1-56954-026-8*) Hispanic Seminary.

Orel. Charles Darwin: Interviews & Recollections. LC 99-18934. 176p. 1999. text 55.00 (*0-312-22100-2*) St Martin.

Orel, Harold. Critical Essays on Sir Arthur Conan Doyle. (Critical Essays on British Literature Ser.). 250p. 1992. 49.00 (*0-8161-8865-3*, Hall Reference) Macmillan.
— A Kipling Chronology. (Chronologies-Reference Ser.). 1990. 40.00 (*0-8161-9090-9*, Hall Reference) Macmillan.
— Popular Fiction in England, 1914-1918. LC 91-36651. 256p. 1992. 29.95 (*0-8131-1789-5*) U Pr of Ky.
— Thomas Hardy's Epic-Drama: A Study of the Dynasts. LC 69-14022. 122p. 1969. reprint ed. lib. bdg. 49.50 (*0-8371-0602-8*, ORTD, Greenwood Pr) Greenwood.

Orel, Harold, ed. The Brontes: Interviews & Recollections. LC 96-60149. 230p. 1997. text 24.95 (*0-87745-537-6*) U of Iowa Pr.
— Critical Essays on Rudyard Kipling. (Critical Essays on British Literature Ser.). 248p. 1989. 48.00 (*0-8161-8767-3*, G K Hall & Co) Mac Lib Ref.
— Gilbert & Sullivan: Interviews & Recollections. LC 93-60769. 232p. 1994. reprint ed. pap. 15.95 (*0-87745-476-0*) U of Iowa Pr.
— Sir Arthur Conan Doyle: Interviews & Recollections. LC 90-44945. 296p. 1991. text 45.00 (*0-312-05374-6*) St Martin.
— Victorian Short Stories 2: The Trials of Love. 287p. 1991. pap. 8.95 (*0-460-87007-6*, Everyman's Classic Lib) Tuttle Pubng.
— World of Victorian Humor. LC 61-8018. (Goldentree Books in English Literature). (Illus.). (Orig.). 1961. pap. text 15.95 (*0-89197-474-1*) Irvington.

Orel, Sara E., ed. Death & Taxes in the Ancient Near East. LC 92-4673. (Illus.). 256p. 1992. lib. bdg. 89.95 (*0-7734-9512-6*) E Mellen.

Orel, Vladimir E. Albanian Etymological Dictionary. LC 98-13217. 670p. 1998. 186.50 (*90-04-11024-0*) Brill Academic Pubs.

***Orel, Vladimir E.** A Concise Historical Grammar of the Albanian Language: Reconstruction of Proto-Albanian. LC 99-53799. 352p. 2000. 138.00 (*90-04-11647-8*) Brill Academic Pubs.

Orel, Vladimir E. The Language of Phrygians: Description & Analysis. LC 97-44326. 504p. 1997. 75.00 (*0-88206-089-9*) Caravan Bks.

Orel, Vladimir E. & Stolbova, Olga V. Hamito-Semitic Etymological Dictionary: Materials for Reconstruction. LC 94-32911. (Handbuch der Orientalistik, Erste Abteilung, Nahe und Mittlere Osten Ser.). 652p. 1994. 250.50 (*90-04-10051-2*) Brill Academic Pubs.

Orelheide, Dieter, ed. see KPMG Peat Marwick Staff.

Orell, Svante R. & Philips, Jeanette. The Thyroid: Fine-Needle Biopsy & Cytological Diagnosis of Thyroid Lesions. LC 96-53276. (Monographs in Clinical Cytology Ser.: Vol. 14, 1997). (Illus.). x, 206p. 1997. 97.50 (*3-8055-6383-3*) S Karger.

Orell, Svente R., et al. Manual & Atlas of Fine Needle Aspiration Cytology. 2nd ed. (Illus.). 341p. 1992. text 240.00 (*0-443-04239-X*) Church.

Orellana, Juan & Friedman, Alan H. Clinico-Pathological Atlas of Congenital Fundus Disorders. LC 92-49529. 1993. 199.00 (*0-387-97936-0*) Spr-Verlag.

Orellana, Juan, et al. Color Atlas of Ocular Manifestations of AIDS: Diagnosis & Management. LC 94-33155. 120p. 1995. 98.50 (*0-89640-273-8*) Igaku-Shoin.

Orellana, Marina. International Glossary for Translators, Spanish-English, English-Spanish. 3rd ed. (ENG & SPA.). 648p. 1993. pap. 95.00 (*0-8288-9422-1*) Fr & Eur.

Orellana, Sandra L. Ethnohistory of the Pacific Coast. LC 94-77124. (Illus.). 176p. (Orig.). 1995. pap. 22.00 (*0-911437-33-9*) Labyrinthos.
— The Tzutujil Mayas: Continuity & Change, 1250-1630. LC 83-47837. (Civilization of the American Indian Ser.: Vol. 162). (Illus.). 320p. 1984. 42.95 (*0-8061-1739-7*) U of Okla Pr.

Orellano, Perez. Y Cristo Me Liberto - And Jesus Set Me Free. (SPA.). 1991. write for info. (*1-56063-121-X*) Editorial Unilit.

Orelli, J. C. & Baiter, J. G. Onomasticon Tullianum, 3 vols. 1965. reprint ed. write for info. (*0-318-72062-0*) G Olms Pubs.

Orelove, Frank P., jt. auth. see Garner, Howard Glenn.

Orelove, Fred P. & Garner, Howard, eds. Teamwork: Parents & Professionals Speak for Themselves. LC 98-23708. 220p. 1998. pap. 16.95 (*0-87868-602-9*, 602-9) Child Welfare.

Orelove, Fred P. & Sobsey, Dick, eds. Educating Children with Multiple Disabilities: A Transdisciplinary Approach. 3rd ed. LC 96-7912. 480p. (Orig.). 1996. pap. text 38.00 (*1-55766-246-0*, 2460) P H Brookes.

Orelove, Fred P., jt. auth. see Power-deFur, Lissa A.

Orem, David S. The Wonderful White Lion. 160p. (J). (gr. 4-6). 1998. pap. 9.95 (*0-9665466-0-1*) Tidewatch Pubs.

Orem, Donna, jt. compiled by see Burnett, Jefferson G.

Orem, Dorothea E. Nursing: Concepts of Practice. 5th ed. LC 94-47916. (Illus.). 448p. (C). (gr. 13). 1995. pap. text 39.00 (*0-8151-6552-8*, 24728) Mosby Inc.

Orem, Howard & Snyder, Suzen. Country Land & Its Uses, Vol. 1. LC 74-22154. (Illus.). 310p. 1975. pap. 9.95 (*0-87961-030-1*) Naturegraph.

Orem, Reginald C., jt. auth. see Amos, William E.

Orem, Sara & Demarest, Larry. Living Simply: Timeless Thoughts for a Balanced Life. LC 94-23548. (Illus.). 200p. (Orig.). 1994. pap. 9.95 (*1-55874-321-9*, 3219) Health Comm.

Orem, Sue D. & Brue, Deborah F., eds. Practical Programming in Continuing Professional Education: Examples for Understanding & Improving Practice. 1991. 13.95 (*0-88379-050-5*) A A A C E.

***Orem, William.** Zombi, You My Love. LC 98-66969. 225p. 1999. pap. 12.00 (*0-9644348-2-2*) La Questa Pr.

O

Oremland, Jerome, ed. Protecting the Emotional Development of the Ill Child: The Essence of the Child Life Profession. LC 99-17720. 275p. 1999. 45.00 (*1-887841-20-2*, 64385, Psychosocial) Intl Univs Pr.

Oremland, Jerome D. Interpretation & Interaction: Psychoanalysis or Psychotherapy? 192p. 1991. text 29.95 (*0-88163-127-2*) Analytic Pr.

— The Origins & Psychodynamics of Creativity: A Psychoanalytic Perspective. LC 96-43194. 224p. 1997. 32.50 (*0-8236-3905-3*, 03905) Intl Univs Pr.

Oremland, Ronald S., ed. The Biogeochemistry of Global Change: Radiatively Active Trace Gases. LC 93-19052. 1993. write for info. (*0-04-120304-6*) Routledge.

Oremling, Ferdinand J., Jr., jt. ed. see Anson, R. W.

Oren, Aharon. Microbiology & Biogeochemistry of Hypersaline Environments. LC 98-18052. (Microbiology of Extreme & Unusual Environments Ser.). 384p. 1998. boxed set 159.95 (*0-8493-8363-3*) CRC Pr.

Oren, Aras. Please, No Police: A Novella. Sipahigil, Teoman, tr. from TUR. LC 92-75236. (Modern Middle Eastern Literature in Translation Ser.). 174p. 1992. pap. 8.95 (*0-292-76038-8*, Pub. by Ctr Mid East Stud) U of Tex Pr.

Oren, Birta, ed. Proceedings, 1995 Summer Computer Simulation Conference: Summer Computer Simulation Proceedings. (Illus.). 900p. 1995. 180.00 (*1-56555-081-1*, SCSC-95) Soc Computer Sim.

Oren, Dan A. Joining the Club: A History of Jews & Yale. LC 85-14252. (Yale Scene, University Ser.: No. 4). 448p. 1986. 55.00 (*0-300-03330-3*) Yale U Pr.

— Joining the Club: A History of Jews & Yale. 448p. (C). 1988. reprint ed. pap. 25.00 (*0-300-04384-8*) Yale U Pr.

Oren, Dan A., et al. How to Beat Jet Lag: A Practical Guide for Air Travelers. LC 93-17190. (Illus.). 144p. 1995. pap. 14.95 (*0-8050-2687-8*) H Holt & Co.

Oren, Eliezer D. The Hyksos: New Historical & Archaeological Perspectives. LC 96-51278. (University Museum Monographs: Vol. 96, Series 8). (Illus.). xxvi, 433p. 1997. 50.00 (*0-924171-46-4*) U Museum Pubns.

Oren, Israel. Taberna Pauperum: The Development of a New Background to the Nativity of Christ in the Fourteenth & Fifteenth Centuries in the North. LC 93-31501. (Hermeneutics of Art Ser.: Vol. 3). 1994. write for info. (*0-8204-2073-5*) P Lang Pubng.

Oren, John W., jt. auth. see Brown, Ronald.

Oren, Michael B. The Origins of the Second Arab-Israel War: Egypt, Israel & the Great Powers, 1952-56. 199p. 1993. 49.50 (*0-7146-3430-1*, Pub. by F Cass Pubs) Intl Spec Bk.

Oren, Nissan. Bulgarian Communism: The Road to Power 1934-1944. LC 84-25247. 290p. (C). 1985. reprint ed. lib. bdg. 75.00 (*0-313-24741-2*, 0RBC, Greenwood Pr) Greenwood.

— Prudence in Victory: The Dynamics of Post-War Settlements. 16p. (Orig.). 1977. pap. text 11.00 (*0-8191-5830-5*) U Pr of Amer.

— Revolution Administered: Agrarianism & Communism in Bulgaria. LC 72-8831. (Integration & Community Building in Eastern Europe Ser.: EE8). 224p. reprint ed. pap. 69.50 (*0-608-14606-4*, 202310800032) Bks Demand.

Oren, Nurit. Ancient Stories Living Today: Retrieved from the Riches of the Cache. (Illus.). 120p. (Orig.). 1995. pap. 12.95 (*0-919842-23-2*, NYOB1) Sun-Scape Ent.

Oren, Shmuel S. & Smith, Stephen A., eds. Service Opportunities for Electric Utilities: Creating Differentiated Products. LC 92-44559. (Topics in Regulatory Economics & Policy Ser.). 352p. (C). 1993. lib. bdg. 120.00 (*0-7923-9319-8*) Kluwer Academic.

Oren, Tuncer I., ed. Advances in Artificial Intelligence in Software Engineering, Vol. 1. 332p. 1990. 90.25 (*0-89232-854-1*) Jai Pr.

Oren, Tuncer I. & Klir, George J., eds. Computer Aided Systems Theory: Proceedings of the CAST International Workshop, 4th, Ottawa, Ontario, Canada, Held May 16-20, 1994. LC 96-27897. (Lecture Notes in Computer Science Ser.). 439p. 1996. pap. 68.00 (*3-540-61478-8*) Spr-Verlag.

***Orend, Brian.** War & International Justice: A Kantian Perspective. LC 99-931118. 248p. 2000. 44.95 (*0-88920-337-7*) Wilfrid Laurier.

Orendi, Diana, jt. ed. see Feldman, Linda E.

Orenhorn, Douglas, ed. Money for Visual Artists: A Comprehensive Arts Resource Guide. 2nd ed. LC 91-13168. 317p. (Orig.). 1993. pap. 14.95 (*0-915400-91-X*, ACA Bks) Am for the Arts.

***Orenstein.** Little Red Riding Hood Uncloaked. 2000. 25.00 (*0-465-04125-6*, Pub. by Basic) HarpC.

***Orenstein, Alex & Kotatko, Peter.** Knowledge, Language & Logic: Questions for Quine. LC 99-45976. (Boston Studies in the Philosophy of Science). 448p. 1999. pap. write for info. (*0-7923-5986-0*) Kluwer Academic.

Orenstein, Alex & Stern, Raphael. Developments in Semantics. LC 83-83299. (Language, Logic & Linguistics Ser.). 402p. (C). 1984. 65.00 (*0-930586-34-4*) Haven Pubns.

Orenstein, Alex & Stern, Raphael, eds. Developments in Semantics. LC 83-83299. (Language, Logic & Linguistics Ser.). 402p. (C). 1984. pap. text 29.00 (*0-930586-13-1*) Haven Pubns.

Orenstein, Arbie. Ravel: Man & Musician. (Illus.). 352p. 1991. pap. 9.95 (*0-486-26633-8*) Dover.

Orenstein, Aviel, ed. Mishnah Berurah Vol. 2B: Covering Chapters 157-201 of the Shulchan Aruch Orach Chaim. (HEB.). 570p. 1988. 22.95 (*0-87306-445-3*) Feldheim.

— Mishnah Berurah Vol. 2B: Covering Chapters 157-201 of the Shulchan Aruch Orach Chaim. large type ed. (HEB.). 570p. 1988. 28.95 (*0-87306-444-5*) Feldheim.

Orenstein, Aviel, tr. Mishnah Berurah Vol. 1A: Laws of Daily Conduct. 1993. 20.95 (*0-87306-604-9*) Feldheim.

— Mishnah Berurah Vol. 1A: Laws of Daily Conduct. large type ed. 1993. 25.95 (*0-87306-603-0*) Feldheim.

— Mishnah Berurah Vol. 1B: Laws of Tefillin. 1993. 20.95 (*0-87306-623-5*) Feldheim.

— Mishnah Berurah Vol. 1B: Laws of Tefillin. large type ed. 1993. 25.95 (*0-87306-624-3*) Feldheim.

— Mishnah Berurah Vol. 1C: Laws of Daily Prayer. 1991. 22.95 (*0-87306-552-2*) Feldheim.

— Mishnah Berurah Vol. 1C: Laws of Daily Prayer. large type ed. 1991. 27.95 (*0-87306-551-4*) Feldheim.

— Mishnah Berurah Vol. 1D: Laws of Daily Prayer. 1991. 20.95 (*0-87306-554-9*) Feldheim.

— Mishnah Berurah Vol. 1D: Laws of Daily Prayer. large type ed. 1991. 25.95 (*0-87306-553-0*) Feldheim.

Orenstein, Aviel, tr. see Chaim-Chofet.

Orenstein, Aviel, tr. see Ha-Cohen, Yisroel Meir.

Orenstein, Aviel, tr. see Yisroel Meir Ha-Cohen.

Orenstein, Claudia. Festive Revolutions: The Politics of Popular Theater & the San Francisco Mime Troupe. LC 98-28413. (Illus.). 176p. 1999. 45.00 (*1-57806-063-X*); pap. 18.00 (*1-57806-079-6*) U Pr of Miss.

Orenstein, David M. Cystic Fibrosis: A Guide for Patient & Family. 2nd ed. LC 96-27001. 368p. 1996. pap. text 25.95 (*0-397-51653-3*) Lppncott W & W.

— Social Questions. Date not set. pap. text, teacher ed. write for info. (*0-314-77939-6*) West Pub.

Orenstein, David M., et al. Cystic Fibrosis: Medical Care. LC 99-55489. 384p. 2000. pap. text 46.00 (*0-7817-1798-1*) Lppncott W & W.

Orenstein, David Michael, jt. auth. see Ashley, David.

Orenstein, Debra, ed. Lifecycles Vol. 1: Jewish Women on Life Passages & Personal Milestones. LC 94-14799. 480p. 1994. 24.95 (*1-879045-14-1*) Jewish Lights.

— Lifecycles Vol. 1: Jewish Women on Life Passages & Personal Milestones. 480p. 1998. pap. 19.95 (*1-58023-018-0*) Jewish Lights.

— Lifecycles Vol. 3: Jewish Women on Holy Days & Communal Celebrations. LC 94-14799. (Lifecycles Ser.: Vol. 3). 300p. 24.95 (*1-879045-18-4*) Jewish Lights.

Orenstein, Debra & Litman, Jane R., eds. Lifecycles Vol. 2: Jewish Women on Biblical Themes in Contemporary Life. LC 94-14799. 464p. 1997. 24.95 (*1-879045-15-X*) Jewish Lights.

— Lifecycles Vol. 2: Jewish Women on Biblical Themes in Contemporary Life. Vol. 2. 464p. 1998. pap. 19.95 (*1-58023-019-9*) Jewish Lights.

Orenstein, Denise G. When the Wind Blows Hard. LC 84-46027. (Illus.). (J). 1982. 11.95 (*0-201-10740-6*) HarpC Child Bks.

Orenstein, Frank. A Vintage Year for Dying. (WWL Mystery Ser.). 1996. per. 4.99 (*0-373-26196-9*, 1-26196-5, Wrldwide Lib) Harlequin Bks.

Orenstein, Gloria F. The Reflowering of the Goddess. (Athene Ser.). 256p. (C). 1990. text 47.50 (*0-8077-6243-1*); pap. text 17.95 (*0-8077-6242-3*) Tchrs Coll.

— The Reflowering of the Goddess: Contemporary Journeys & Cycles of Empowerment. (Athene Ser.). (Illus.). 250p. 1990. text 47.50 (*0-08-035179-4*, 2707, Pub. by PPI); pap. text 17.95 (*0-08-035178-6*, Pub. by PPI) Elsevier.

Orenstein, Gloria F., jt. auth. see Diamond, Irene.

Orenstein, Harold. Entertainment Law & Business Issue 13: Guide to Law & Business Practice of Entertainment Industry. 100p. 1999. ring bd. write for info. (*0-327-01082-7*, 8040515) LEXIS Pub.

Orenstein, Harold & Sinacore-Guinn, David. Entertainment Law & Business, 1989-1993: A Guide to the Law & Business Practices of the Entertainment Industry. 1991. ring bd. 180.00 (*0-88063-163-5*, 80401-10, MICHIE); suppl. ed. 55.00 (*1-56257-152-4*, MICHIE) LEXIS Pub.

Orenstein, Harold S. Soviet Documents on the Use of War Experiences Vol. 3: Military Operations, 1941-1942. LC 91-11452. 224p. 1993. 45.00 (*0-7146-3402-6*, Pub. by F Cass Pubs) Intl Spec Bk.

Orenstein, Harold S., tr. Soviet Documents on the Use of War Experience Vol. 1: The Initial Period of War 1941. 83p. 1991. text 37.50 (*0-7146-3392-5*, Pub. by F Cass Pubs) Intl Spec Bk.

— Soviet Documents on the Use of War Experience Vol. 2: The Winter Campaign, 1941-1942. 255p. 1991. text 45.00 (*0-7146-3393-3*, Pub. by F Cass Pubs) Intl Spec Bk.

Orenstein, Harold S., jt. ed. see Glantz, David M.

Orenstein, Harold S., tr. see Glantz, David M.

Orenstein, Henry. Abram: The Life of an Israeli Patriot. (Illus.). 224p. 1999. 21.95 (*0-8253-0503-9*) Beaufort Bks NY.

— Gaon: Conflict & Cohesion in an Indian Village. LC 65-12991. (Illus.). 349p. reprint ed. pap. 108.20 (*0-8357-4397-7*, 205706700007) Bks Demand.

— I Shall Live. 1997. pap. 14.95 (*0-8253-0500-4*) Beaufort Bks NY.

— I Shall Live: Surviving Against All Odds, 1939-1945. 1987. 16.95 (*0-8253-0441-5*) Beaufort Bks NY.

Orenstein, Herta. Die Refrainformen Im Chansonnier de L'Arsenal. (Wissenschaftliche Abhandlungen-Musicological Studies: Vol. 19). (GER.). 120p. 1972. lib. bdg. 54.00 (*0-912024-89-5*) Inst Mediaeval Mus.

Orenstein, Jack A. & Vassiliou, Marius S. Object-Oriented Approach to Spatial Data Processing. (C). 2001. 39.00 (*0-13-119876-9*, Macmillan Coll) P-H.

Orenstein, Jeffrey R., jt. auth. see Fowler, Robert B.

***Orenstein, Julian.** 365 Tips for Baby's First Year. LC 00-38569. 400p. 2000. pap. 7.95 (*1-58062-296-8*) Adams Media.

Orenstein, Julian. 365 Ways to Calm Your Crying Baby. LC 98-17607. 416p. 1998. pap. 7.95 (*1-58062-011-6*) Adams Media.

Orenstein, Mel. MACRS Depreciation Handbook. 160p. 1995. pap. text 39.50 (*0-7811-0106-9*) Res Inst Am.

***Orenstein, Myrna, ed.** Smart but Stuck: What Every Therapist Needs to Know about Learning Disabilities. LC 99-16077. 216p. (C). 1999. pap. text 24.95 (*0-7890-0888-5*) Haworth Pr.

— Smart But Stuck: What Every Therapist Needs to Know about Learning Disabilities & Imprisoned Intelligence. LC 99-16077. 242p. (C). 1999. lib. bdg. 34.95 (*0-7890-0853-X*) Haworth Pr.

Orenstein, Neil, ed. see Anderson, Nina, et al.

***Orenstein, Peggy.** Flux: Women on Sex, Work, Love, Kids & Life in a Half-Changed World. LC 00-27626. 304p. 2000. 25.00 (*0-385-49886-1*) Doubleday.

Orenstein, Peggy. SchoolGirls: Young Women, Self-Esteem & the Confidence Gap. 368p. 1995. reprint ed. pap. 14.95 (*0-385-42576-7*, Anchor NY) Doubleday.

Orenstein, Ronald. Songbirds. LC 97-9668. 1997. 35.00 (*0-87156-947-7*, Pub. by Sierra) Random.

Orenstein, Ruth, ed. Full Text Sources Online. 558p. 1998. pap. text 118.00 (*1-879258-20-X*) BiblioData.

— Fulltext Sources Online. rev. ed. 1998. pap. 118.00 (*1-879258-21-8*) BiblioData.

Orenstein, Vik. Creative Techniques for Photographing Children. 144p. 1993. pap. 26.99 (*0-89879-543-5*, 10358, Wrtrs Digest Bks) F & W Pubns Inc.

Orenstein, Walter. Etched in Stone: A Study of Biblical Personalities. 177p. 1989. 13.95 (*0-932351-24-7*) B P Marketing.

— Letters to My Daughter: A Father Writes about Torah & the Jewish Woman. LC 94-45801. 280p. 1995. 30.00 (*1-56821-387-5*) Aronson.

Orenstein, Walter & Frankel, Hertz. The Passover Haggadah. 197p. 1962. 3.50 (*0-88482-364-4*) Hebrew Pub.

Orenstein, Walter A., jt. auth. see Plotkin, Stanley A.

Orenstein, Walter R. The Transformation of a Skeptic: A Jewish Perspective. LC 99-20640. 240p. 2001. 30.00 (*0-7657-6100-9*) Aronson.

Orent, Sander. Stress & the Heart: Storm in a Bottle. LC 87-7540. 256p. 1989. text 24.95 (*0-89876-139-5*) Gardner Pr.

Orent, Tom. Extreme Customer Service. 220p. 1998. pap. 32.00 (*0-9651544-3-2*) Gems Pubng.

— Freedom from Chronic Pain: MPD Facial & Headache Relief Secrets Revealed. Berman, Lynn, ed. (Illus.). 48p. (Orig.). 1996. pap. 16.77 (*0-9651544-0-8*) Gems Pubng.

Orentlicher, Diane, et al. The Twentieth Century Fund Century Foundation Task Force Report on Apprehending Indicted War Criminals. LC 98-5924. 354p. 1998. write for info. (*0-87078-421-8*) Century Foundation.

Orentsein, David M. & Stern, Robert C., eds. Treatment of Hospitalized Cystic Fibrosis Patient. LC 97-31070. (Lung Biology in Health & Disease Ser.). (Illus.). 472p. 1997. text 180.00 (*0-8247-9500-8*) Dekker.

***Oreopoulos, D. G.** Nephrology & Geriatrics Integrated. LC 00-21825. 2000. write for info. (*0-7923-6181-4*) Kluwer Academic.

Oreopoulos, Dimitrious G., ed. Geriatric Nephrology. (Developments in Nephrology Ser.). 1986. text 232.00 (*0-89838-781-7*) Kluwer Academic.

Oreopoulos, Dimitrious G., et al, eds. Nephrology & Urology in the Aged Patient. LC 92-48668. 1993. text 392.50 (*0-7923-2019-0*) Kluwer Academic.

Orero, Pilar, ed. see Pontiero, Giovanni.

Oreshkin, A. V., tr. see Klevezal, Galina A.

Oreshkin, V. A., jt. auth. see Davydov, O. D.

Oresick, Peter. Definitions. LC 90-12346. 72p. (C). 1990. 18.95 (*0-931122-59-7*); pap. 8.95 (*0-931122-58-9*) West End.

Oresick, Peter & Coles, Nicholas, eds. Working Classics: Poems on Industrial Life. 304p. 1990. 17.95 (*0-252-06133-0*); text 34.95 (*0-252-01730-7*) U of Ill Pr.

Oresick, Peter, jt. auth. see Romano, Frank J.

Oresick, Peter, jt. ed. see Coles, Nicholas.

Oresick, Peter, ed. see Dobler, Patricia.

Oresick, Peter, ed. see Ignatow, David.

Oresick, Peter, jt. ed. see Ochester, Ed.

Oreskes, Irwin, jt. auth. see Spiera, Harry.

Oreskes, Naomi. The Rejection of Continental Drift: Theory & Method in American Earth Science. LC 98-4161. (Illus.). 432p. 1999. pap. 29.95 (*0-19-511733-6*) OUP.

***Oreskes, Naomi.** The Rejection of Continental Drift: Theory & Method in American Earth Science. LC 98-4161. (Illus.). 432p. 1999. text 60.00 (*0-19-511732-8*) OUP.

Oresko, Robert, ed. The Works in Architecture of Robert & James Adam. (Academy Architecture Ser.). (Illus.). 184p. 1982. pap. 19.95 (*0-312-88954-2*) St Martin.

Oresko, Robert, et al, eds. Royal & Republican Sovereignty in Early Modern Europe: Essays in Memory of Ragnhild Hatton. 692p. 1997. text 95.00 (*0-521-41910-7*) Cambridge U Pr.

Oresman, Janice C. New Vistas: Contemporary American Landscapes. (Illus.). 55p. (Orig.). 1984. pap. 4.75 (*0-943651-20-4*) Hudson Riv.

— Twentieth Century American Watercolor. (Illus.). 56p. 1983. 15.00 (*0-934483-03-5*) Gal Assn NY.

Oresme, Nicole. De Proportionibus Proportionum & Ad Pauca Respicientes. Grant, Edward, ed. & tr. by. LC 65-20640. (Publications in Medieval Science). 488p. reprint ed. pap. 151.30 (*0-608-20430-7*, 207168300002) Bks Demand.

— Le Livre du Ciel et du Monde. Menut, Albert D., ed. & tr. by. Denomy, Alexander J., ed. LC 67-11061. (University of Wisconsin Publications in Medieval Science). (ENG & FRE., Illus.). 792p. 1968. reprint ed. pap. 200.00 (*0-7837-9787-7*, 206051600005) Bks Demand.

— Nicole Oresme & the Kinematics of Circular Motion: Tractatus de Commensurabilitate Vel Incommensurabilitate Motuum Celi. Grant, Edward, ed. & tr. by. LC 79-133238. (Publications in Medieval Science). (Illus.). 438p. reprint ed. pap. 135.80 (*0-608-20431-5*, 207168400002) Bks Demand.

— Nicole Oresme & the Marvels. Hansen, Bert, ed. pap. text 59.43 (*0-88844-068-5*) Brill Academic Pubs.

— Nicole Oresme & the Medieval Geometry of Qualities & Motions: A Treatise on the Uniformity & Difformity of Intensities Known As Tractatus de Configurationibus Qualitatum et Motuum. Clagett, Marshall, ed. LC 68-14031. (University of Wisconsin Publications in Medieval Science). (Illus.). 736p. reprint ed. pap. 200.00 (*0-7837-5901-0*, 204569200007) Bks Demand.

Orevkov, P. & Sanin, M. A., eds. Problems in the Constructive Trend in Mathematics, IV, Vol. 93. 329p. 1967. 69.00 (*0-8218-1893-7*, STEKLO/93C) Am Math.

Orevkov, V. P. Complexity of Proofs & Their Transformations in Axiomatic Theories. Louvish, David, ed. Bochman, Alexander, tr. from RUS. LC 93-11139.Tr. of Slozhnost Dokazatelstviikh Preobrazovanii Aksiomatizirovannykh Teoriiakh. (ENG.). 153p. 1993. text 86.00 (*0-8218-4576-4*, MMONO/128) Am Math.

Orevkov, V. P., ed. Logical & Logico-Mathematical Calculi, 2: Proceedings. LC 74-8854. 183p. 1974. pap. 66.00 (*0-8218-3021-X*, STEKLO/121) Am Math.

Orevkov, V. p. & Sanin, Nikolai A., eds. Problems in the Constructive Trend in Mathematics, Pt. VI. LC 75-11951. (Proceedings of the Steklov Institute of Mathematics Ser.: No. 129). 272p. 1976. pap. 135.00 (*0-8218-3029-5*, STEKLO/129) Am Math.

Orevkov, V. P. & Sanin, Nikolai A., eds. Problems in the Constructive Trend in Mathematics Pt. V: Proceedings. (Proceedings of the Steklov Institute of Mathematics Ser.: No. 113). 287p. 1972. pap. 66.00 (*0-8218-3013-9*, STEKLO/113) Am Math.

Orevkov, V. P., ed. see Steklov Institute of Mathematics, Academy of Scien.

Orey, Cal. Epilepsy. LC 98-39298. (Essential Guide to Natural Pet Care Ser.: Vol. 4). (Illus.). 64p. (Orig.). 1999. pap. 6.95 (*1-889540-34-X*) Bowtie Press.

***Orey, Cal.** Healing Powers of Vinegar: A Complete Guide to Nature's Most Remarkable Remedy. (Illus.). 2000. pap. 12.00 (*1-57566-609-X*) Kensgtn Pub Corp.

Orey, Carl. Cancer. LC 98-43387. (Essential Guide to Natural Pet Care Ser.: Vol. 2). (Illus.). 64p. (Orig.). 1999. pap. 6.95 (*1-889540-35-8*) Bowtie Press.

Orey, Maureen. Successfully Staffing in a Diverse Workplace: A Practical Guide to Building an Effective & Diverse Staff. LC 95-83809. (Workplace Diversity Ser.). (Illus.). 120p. 1995. pap. 12.95 (*1-883553-67-9*) R Chang Assocs.

***Orey, Michael.** Assuming the Risk: The Mavericks, the Lawyers & the Whistle-Blowers Who Beat Big Tobacco. LC 99-20616. (Illus.). 400p. (gr. 8). 1999. 24.95 (*0-316-66489-8*) Little.

Oreyegui, P. Buenaventura De, see Aberlaitz & De Oreyegui, P. Buenaventura.

Orfalea. The Lost Battalion. 1996. 24.95 (*0-02-923455-7*) Free Pr.

Orfalea, Gregory. The Capital of Solitude. LC 87-81729. (Ithaca House Ser.). 84p. 1988. pap. 9.95 (*0-87886-129-7*, Greenfld Rev Pr) Greenfld Rev Lit.

— The Lost Battalion. LC 96-43681. 448p. 1997. 27.00 (*0-684-82804-9*) Free Pr.

— U. S. - Arab Relations: The Literary Dimension, No. 2. 44p. (Orig.). 1984. pap. 4.00 (*0-916729-01-X*) Natl Coun Arab.

Orfalea, Gregory & Elmusa, Sharif, eds. Grape Leaves: A Century of Arab-American Poetry. 330p. 2000. pap. 17.95 (*1-56656-338-0*) Interlink Pub.

Orfalea, Gregory & Elmusa, Sharif S., eds. Grape Leaves: A Century of Arab American Poetry. LC 88-19041. (Illus.). 330p. reprint ed. pap. 102.30 (*0-7837-5537-6*, 204531000005) Bks Demand.

Orfali, J. Sebastian, jt. auth. see Potter, Beverly A.

Orfali, Jacob G. An Armenian from Jerusalem. (Illus.). 154p. 1987. pap. 9.95 (*0-914171-09-7*) Ronin Pub.

— Everywhere You Go People Are the Same. (Illus.). 176p. (Orig.). 1995. pap. 14.95 (*0-914171-75-5*) Ronin Pub.

Orfali, Robert & Harkey, Dan. Client/Server Programming with Enterprise JavaBeans. 512p. 2000. pap. 49.99 incl. cd-rom (*0-471-18931-6*) Wiley.

***Orfali, Robert & Harkey, Dan.** Client/Server Programming with Java & CORBA. 2nd ed. LC 98-10456. 1072p. 1998. pap. 54.99 (*0-471-24578-X*) Wiley.

Orfali, Robert & Harkey, Daniel. Client/Server Survival Guide with OS/2. 1008p. 1995. pap. 39.95 (*0-471-13118-0*) Wiley.

Orfali, Robert, et al. The Essential Distributed Objects Survival Guide. LC 96-216401. 640p. 1995. pap. 39.99 (*0-471-12993-3*) Wiley.

— Instant Corba. LC 97-7518. 336p. 1997. pap. 29.99 (*0-471-18333-4*) Wiley.

— Object Web Survival Guide. 672p. 1998. pap. 39.99 (*0-471-24546-1*) Wiley.

Orfali, Sebastian J., ed. Computer Comics. (Illus.). 96p. (Orig.). 1984. pap. 5.95 (*0-914171-03-8*) Ronin Pub.

Orfali, Sebastian J., jt. auth. see Potter, Beverly A.

Orfali, Sebastian J., ed. see Leary, Timothy.

Orfali, Sebastian J., ed. see Stafford, Peter.

Orfali, Stephanie. A Jewish Girl Finds New Roots. (Illus.). 96p. (Orig.). 1996. pap. 14.95 (*0-914171-91-7*) Ronin Pub.

— A Jewish Girl in the Weimar Republic. (Illus.). 192p. 1987. pap. 9.95 (*0-914171-10-0*) Ronin Pub.

Orfall, Robert, et al. Client/Server Survival Guide. 3rd ed. LC 99-19494. 800p. 1999. pap. 39.99 (*0-471-31615-6*) Wiley.

Orfanidis, Sophocles J. Introduction to Signal Processing. LC 95-10970. 798p. 1995. 105.00 (*0-13-209172-0*) P-H.

An Asterisk (*) at the beginning of an entry indicates that the title is appearing for the first time.

— Optimal Signal Processing. 1985. 34.95 (*0-02-949860-0*) Free Pr.

Orfanos, C. E., ed. Recent Developments in Clinical Research. (Current Problems in Dermatology Ser.: Vol. 13). (Illus.). viii, 192p. 1984. 142.75 (*3-8055-3928-2*) S Karger.

Orfanos, C. E. & Happle, R., eds. Hair & Hair Diseases. (Illus.). 1070p. 1990. 318.00 (*0-387-50960-7*) Spr-Verlag.

Orfanos, C. E. & Schuppli, R., eds. Oral Retinoids in Dermatology Workshop Held on the 15th International Congress of Dermatology, Mexico City, October 1977. 1978. pap. 22.75 (*3-8055-2950-3*) S Karger.

Orfanos, Spyros D., et al, eds. Education & Greek Americans: Process & Prospects. 216p. 1987. pap. text 11.00 (*0-918618-36-3*) Pella Pub.

Orfeo, Christine V. My First Book about Mary. LC 96-20218. (Illus.). 80p. (Orig.). (J). (ps-2). 1996. pap. 9.95 (*0-8198-4789-5*) Pauline Bks.

Orfer-Lucius, Gudrun K., jt. auth. see Lobo, Crispino.

Orfeuil, Maurice. Electric Process Heating: Technologies, Equipment, Applications. LC 86-3531. 832p. 1987. 95.00 (*0-935470-26-3*) Battelle.

Orff, Carl. The Schulwerk, Vol. 3. Murray, Margaret, tr. from GER. (Carl Orff Documentation Ser.). 1978. pap. 25.00 (*0-930448-06-5*, STAP065) Eur-Am Music.

Orfield, Gary. Dismantling Desegregation. 1997. pap. 17.95 (*1-56584-401-7*, Pub. by New Press NY) Norton.

Orfield, Gary, et al, eds. Chilling Admissions: The Affirmative Action Crisis & the Search for Alternatives. LC 98-71079. (Illus.). 140p. 1998. pap. 16.95 (*1-891792-00-8*) HEPG.

Orfield, Gary & Ashkinaze, Carole. The Closing Door: Conservative Policy & Black Opportunity. LC 90-48542. (Illus.). 274p. 1991. 27.00 (*0-226-63272-5*) U Ch Pr.

— The Closing Door: Conservative Policy & Black Opportunity. LC 90-48542. (Illus.). xx, 280p. 1993. pap. 11.95 (*0-226-63273-3*) U Ch Pr.

***Orfield, Gary & Debray, Elizabeth H.** Hard Work for Good Schools. LC 99-89654. 2000. pap. 12.95 (*0-87078-445-5*) Century Foundation.

Orfield, Gary & Lebowitz, Holly. Religion & Civil Rights: New Visions for A More Diverse Society. LC 99-18241. 1999. write for info. (*0-87078-433-1*) Century Foundation.

Orfield, Gary & Monfort, Franklin. Status of School Desegregation: The Next Generation. 39p. (Orig.). 1992. pap. 10.00 (*0-88364-174-7*, 05-132) Natl Sch Boards.

Orfield, Gary, et al. The Growth of Segregation in American Schools: Changing Patterns of Separation & Poverty since 1968. 34p. (Orig.). 1993. pap. 15.00 (*0-88364-179-8*, 05-133) Natl Sch Boards.

— Status of School Desegregation, 1968-1986: Segregation, Integration, & Public Policy: National, State, & Metropolitan Trends in Public Schools. 31p. (Orig.). 1989. pap. text 10.00 (*0-88364-171-2*, 05-104) Natl Sch Boards.

Orfield, Lester B. Amending of the Federal Constitution. LC 74-146151. (American Constitutional & Legal History Ser). (Illus.). 1971. reprint ed. lib. bdg. 29.50 (*0-306-70094-8*) Da Capo.

— The Amending of the Federal Constitution. LC 42-36735. (Michigan Legal Publications). xxvii, 242p. 1984. reprint ed. lib. bdg. 38.50 (*0-89941-324-2*, 303160) W S Hein.

Orfield, Myron W. Metropolitics: A Regional Agenda for Community & Stability. LC 96-45202. (Illus.). 224p. 1998. pap. 18.95 (*0-8157-6639-4*); text 42.95 (*0-8157-6640-8*) Brookings.

Orford, Ellen. Understanding Your 11 Year Old. Osborne, Elsie, ed. (Understanding Your Child Ser.: Vol. 12). 96p. 1997. pap. 8.95 (*1-894020-11-1*) Warwick Publ.

Orford, Jim. Community Psychology: Theory & Practice. LC 91-30651. 302p. 1992. pap. 79.95 (*0-471-93810-6*) Wiley.

Orford, Jim. Excessive Appetites. pap. 39.95 (*0-471-98231-8*) Wiley.

Orford, Jim. Excessive Appetites: A Psychological View of Addictions. LC 84-22066. 378p. 1995. pap. 95.00 (*0-471-93613-8*) Wiley.

Orford, Jim, ed. Treating the Disorder, Treating the Family. LC 87-3159. 310p. 1987. reprint ed. pap. 96.10 (*0-608-03672-2*, 206449800009) Bks Demand.

Orford, Jim & Edwards, Griffith. Alcoholism: A Comparison of Treatment & Advice, with a Study of the Influence of Marriage. (Maudsley Monographs: No. 26). (Illus.). 1978. text 24.95 (*0-19-712148-9*) OUP.

Orford, Jim, jt. auth. see Otto, Shirley.

Orford, Jim, jt. auth. see Velleman, Richard.

Orford, Margaret. The King's Daughter. large type ed. (Linford Romance Library). 1991. pap. 16.99 (*0-7089-7108-3*) Ulverscroft.

Orford, Scott. Valuing the Built Environment: GIS & House Price Analysis. 232p. 1999. text 69.95 (*0-7546-1012-8*, Pub. by Ashgate Pub) Ashgate Pub Co.

Orga, Ates. Beethoven. (Illustrated Lives of the Great Composers Ser.). (Illus.). 176p. 1996. 17.95 (*0-7119-0251-8*, OP 42373) Omnibus NY.

— Chopin. (Illustrated Lives of the Great Composers Ser.). (Illus.). 144p. 1996. 17.95 (*0-7119-0247-X*, OP 42332) Omnibus NY.

Organ, Barbara E. Judaism for Gentiles. LC 96-15396. vii, 207 p. 1996. pap. 14.95 (*0-941037-41-X*, BIBAL Press) D & F Scott.

***Organ, Claude H., Jr., ed.** The Best of Archives of Surgery. 250p. 1999. 50.00 (*1-57947-059-9*) AMA.

Organ, Claude H., Jr. & Smith, R. Stephen. Gasless Laparoscopy with Conventional Instruments: The Next Phase in Minimally Invasive Surgery. LC 93-26738. (Illus.). 153p. 1993. 98.00 (*0-930405-61-7*) Norman SF.

Organ, Claude H., Jr., jt. auth. see Henderson, Vernon J.

Organ, Claude H., jt. ed. see Tsoi, Edmund K.

***Organ Committee of St. Christopher's by-the-River.** The Hradetzky Organ of St. Christopher's by-the-River: The Story of the Hradetzky Organ of the Parish of St. Christopher's by-the-River, Gates Mills, Ohio. (Illus.). 24p. 1998. pap. write for info. (*0-9617637-3-6*) CL Stock Images.

Organ, Dennis M. Tennyson's Dramas: A Critical Study. (Graduate Studies: No. 17). 125p. 1979. pap. 7.00 (*0-89672-066-7*) Tex Tech Univ Pr.

Organ, Dennis W. & Bateman, Thomas S. CPS Organizational Behavior, Select Chapters. 4th ed. 432p. (C). 1996. text 28.00 (*0-256-21540-5*, Irwn McGrw-H) McGrw-H Hghr Educ.

Organ, L. W., ed. see Toronto University, Dept. of Physiology Staff.

Organ, Richard. Avro Arrow. LC 97-181269. (Illus.). 176p. 1995. reprint ed. pap. 19.95 (*1-55046-047-1*, Pub. by Boston Mills) Genl Dist Srvs.

Organ, Sue. Salt Dough Models. (Illus.). 48p. (YA). 1993. pap. 12.95 (*0-85532-756-1*, 756-1, Pub. by Srch Pr) A Schwartz & Co.

Organ, Troy W. The Hindu Quest for the Perfection of Man. 450p. 1994. 36.50 (*81-215-0642-5*, Pub. by M Manoharial) Coronet Bks.

— Index to Aristotle. LC 66-19085. 181p. 1966. reprint ed. 75.00 (*0-87752-079-8*) Gordian.

— The One: East & West. 464p. (Orig.). (C). 1991. lib. bdg. 52.00 (*0-8191-7877-2*) U Pr of Amer.

— Philosophy & the Self: East & West. LC 86-62506. 240p. 1987. 42.50 (*0-941664-80-5*) Susquehanna U Pr.

— Philosophy for the Left Hand. (Revisioning Philosophy Ser.: Vol. 3). 398p. (C). 1991. text 54.95 (*0-8204-1308-9*) P Lang Pubng.

— The Self in Its Worlds: East & West. LC 87-42799. 256p. 1988. 36.50 (*0-941664-88-0*) Susquehanna U Pr.

***Organ, Troy Wilson.** The Hindu Quest for the Perfection of Man. 450p. 1998. pap. 35.00 (*1-57910-141-0*) Wipf & Stock.

Organessian, Yu T. & Kalpakchieva, R. EPS XV Nuclear Physics Divisional Conference: Low Energy Nuclear Dynamics (LEND '95) 500p. 1995. text 118.00 (*981-02-2392-7*) World Scientific Pub.

***Organic Gardening Editors.** Gardener to Gardener Almanac & Pest Control Primer: A Month-by-Month Guide & Journal for Planning, Planting. Bradley, Fern, ed. (Illus.). 256p. 2000. pap. 27.70 (*0-87596-862-7*) Rodale Pr Inc.

***Organic Gardening Magazine Staff.** Organic Gardening in Basic Lawns. LC 99-50442. (Illus.). 112p. 2000. pap. 14.95 (*0-87596-837-6*) Rodale Pr Inc.

— Organic Gardening with Roses. LC 99-50445. (Illus.). 112p. 2000. pap. text 14.95 (*0-87596-839-2*) Rodale Pr Inc.

— Organic Gardening with Soil. LC 99-50443. (Illus.). 2000. pap. 14.95 (*0-87596-838-4*) Rodale Pr Inc.

— Organic Gardening with Vegetables. LC 99-50444. (Illus.). 112p. 2000. pap. text 14.95 (*0-87596-840-6*) Rodale Pr Inc.

Organic Gardening Magazine Staff, jt. ed. see Bucks, Christine.

Organic Gardening Staff, jt. auth. see Long, Cheryl.

Organic Reaction Mechanisms Staff. Organic Reaction Mechanisms, 1987: An Annual Survey Covering the Literature Dated December, 1986 to November 1987. Knipe, A. C. & Watts, W. E., eds. LC 66-23143. 666p. reprint ed. pap. 200.00 (*0-608-20227-4*, 207148600012) Bks Demand.

Organic Reaction Mechanisms Staff. Organic Reaction Mechanisms, 1988: An Annual Survey Covering the Literature Dated December, 1987 to November 1988. Knipe, A. C. & Watts, W. E., eds. LC 66-23143. (Illus.). 754p. reprint ed. pap. 200.00 (*0-608-20226-6*, 207148500012) Bks Demand.

Organic Reaction Mechanisms Staff. Organic Reaction Mechanisms, 1989: An Annual Survey Covering the Literature Dated December, 1988 to November 1989. Knipe, A. C. & Watts, W. E., eds. LC 66-23143. (Illus.). 721p. reprint ed. pap. 200.00 (*0-608-20225-8*, 207148400012) Bks Demand.

Organic Reaction Mechanisms Staff. Organic Reaction Mechanisms, 1990: An Annual Survey Covering the Literature Dated December, 1989 to November 1990. Knipe, A. C. & Watts, W. E., eds. LC 66-23143. (Illus.). 664p. reprint ed. pap. 200.00 (*0-608-20229-0*, 207148800012) Bks Demand.

— Organic Reaction Mechanisms, 1991: An Annual Survey Covering the Literature Dated December, 1990 & November 1991. Knipe, A. C. & Watts, W. E., eds. LC 66-23143. (Illus.). 626p. reprint ed. pap. 194.10 (*0-608-20228-2*, 207148700012) Bks Demand.

Organic Reactions Catalysis Society Staff, jt. auth. see Herkes, Frank E.

Organic Trade Association Staff, compiled by. The Organic Pages: Organic Trade Association's 1998 North American Resource Directory. 270p. 1998. spiral bd. 44.95 (*1-881427-99-4*) OTA Press.

Organick, Avrum B. Blessings. iii, 250p. 1999. pap. 13.50 (*0-9671068-0-X*) Red Lake Pr.

***Organick, Avrum B.** Blessings. 2nd ed. 270p. 2000. 22.95 (*0-9671068-2-6*) Red Lake Pr.

— Blessings. 2nd rev. ed. 270p. 2000. pap. 14.50 (*0-9671068-1-8*) Red Lake Pr.

Organick, Elliot I., jt. auth. see Meissner, Loren P.

Organisation for Economic Co-operation & Development Staff. Benefit Systems & Work Incentives 1998. LC 98-196455. (FRE.). 59 p. 1998. write for info. (*92-64-26073-0*) Org for Econ.

— Harmful Tax Competition: An Emerging Global Issue. LC 98-180118. 80 p. 1998. write for info. (*92-64-16090-6*) Org for Econ.

— Immigrants, Integration & Cities: Exploring the Links. LC 98-180150. (OECD Proceedings Ser.). 194 p. 1998. write for info. (*92-64-16068-X*) Org for Econ.

— The Role of the Competition Agency in Regulatory Reform: Proceedings of a Workshop by the OECD & the Fair Trade Commission of Japan. LC 98-178212. (Proceedings Ser.). 92 p. 1997. pap. write for info. (*92-64-15692-5*) Org for Econ.

Organisation for Economic Co-operation & Development Staff, jt. auth. see Blondal, Jon.

Organisation for Economic Co-operation & Development Staff, jt. auth. see Maddison, Angus.

Organisation for Economic Co-operation and Development Staff. Economic Globalization & the Environment. LC 98-143792. 92p. 1997. pap. 12.00 (*92-64-15514-7*, 97-97-08-1, Pub. by Org for Econ) OECD.

Organization for Economic Co-operation & Development & Inter-Organization Programme for the Sound Management of Chemicals. Fertilizers as a Source of Cadmium. LC 97-120634. (OECD Proceedings Ser.). 252p. 1996. write for info. (*92-64-15342-X*) Org for Econ.

Organization for Economic Co-operation and Development Staff. Domestic Finance. LC 98-145315. (Sources & Methods Ser.). 81p. 1998. write for info. (*92-64-16035-3*) European Conference Ministers Transp.

Organization for Economic Cooperation & Developmen. Adult Illiteracy & Economic Performance. 88p. (Orig.). 1992. pap. 24.00 (*92-64-13597-9*) OECD.

— Enterprising Women: Local Initiatives for Job Creation. 100p. (Orig.). 1991. pap. 20.00 (*92-64-13436-0*) OECD.

— Restoring Financial Flows to Latin America. Iglesias, Enrique V. & Emmerij, Louis, eds. 251p. 1991. pap. 18.50 (*92-64-13476-X*, Pub. by European Conference Ministers Transp) OECD.

Organization for Obstetric, Gynecologic & Neonatal. Core Curriculum for Maternal-Newborn Nursing. Mattson, Susan & Smith, Judy E., eds. (Illus.). 816p. 1992. pap. text 63.00 (*0-7216-3122-3*, W B Saunders Co) Harcrt Hlth Sci Grp.

— Core Curriculum for Neonatal Intensive Care Nursing. Beachy, Patricia O. & Deacon, Jane, eds. (Illus.). 746p. 1992. pap. text 64.00 (*0-7216-3121-5*, W B Saunders Co) Harcrt Hlth Sci Grp.

Organization of American Historians Staff, et al. Historians & Archivists: Educating the Next Generation. (Illus.). 59p. (C). 1993. 5.00 (*1-884141-00-5*) Org Am Historians.

Organization of American States - Bogota Staff. American Treaty of Peaceful Settlement: Pact of Bogota. rev. ed. (Treaty Ser.: No. 17). (ENG, FRE, POR & SPA.). 1978. pap. 1.00 (*0-8270-0355-2*) OAS.

Organization of American States Editors. Index to Latin American Periodical Literature, 1929-1960, 8 Vols, Set. 1970. 620.00 (*0-8161-0501-4*, G K Hall & Co) Mac Lib Ref.

— Index to Latin American Periodical Literature, 1966-1970. 1980. 255.00 (*0-8161-0314-3*, G K Hall & Co) Mac Lib Ref.

Organization of American States General Secretaria. Biogeografia de America Latina. 2nd ed. (Serie de Biologia: No. 13). (SPA., Illus.). 122p. (C). 1980. pap. 3.50 (*0-8270-1233-0*) OAS.

Organization of American States General Secretaria, ed. see Piscoya, Francisco M.

Organization of American States Staff. Charter of the Organization of American States, Bogota, 1948. (Treaty Ser.: No. 1). (ENG, FRE, POR & SPA.). 1948. pap. 1.00 (*0-8270-0245-9*) OAS.

***Organization of American States Staff.** House of the Americas. LC 99-38869. (ENG, POR, SPA & FRE.). 1999. write for info. (*0-8270-4033-4*) OAS.

Organization of American States Staff. Sectoral Study of Transnational Enterprises in Latin America: The Banana Industry. 1978. reprint ed. pap. text 5.00 (*0 685-03624-3*); reprint ed. write for info. (*0-8270-3310-9*) OAS.

Organization of American States Staff, tr. see Black, Donald E.

Organization of Peace Commission & Holcombe, Arthur N. Strengthening the United Nations. LC 74-7536. 276p. 1976. reprint ed. lib. bdg. 69.50 (*0-8371-7579-8*, HOUN, Greenwood Pr) Greenwood.

Organization of the Petroleum Exporting Countries. Selected Documents of the International Petroleum Industry: 1966-1978 (with Pre-1966 Reports), 15 bks., Set. 1983. reprint ed. 485.00 (*0-89941-291-2*, 201610) W S Hein.

Organizations for Professional Women Staff, jt. auth. see American Psychological Association, Women & Health.

Organizers Against Deportation & Refugees in Oakda. On Loving Neighbors & Aliens. (Common Ground Ser.: Vol. II). (Illus.). 24p. (Orig.). 1986. pap. 5.00 (*1-884478-01-8*) Common Grnd.

Organos, Minnie, jt. ed. see Northwest U Staff.

Organski, A. F. The Thirty-Six Billion Dollar Bargain. 315p. 1991. pap. text 20.00 (*0-231-07197-3*) Col U Pr.

Organski, A. F. & Kugler, Jacek. The War Ledger. LC 79-23366. (Illus.). 304p. 1981. pap. text 14.50 (*0-226-63280-6*) U Ch Pr.

— The War Ledger. LC 79-23366. (Illus.). 1992. lib. bdg. 25.00 (*0-226-63279-2*) U Ch Pr.

Organski, A. F., et al. Births, Deaths & Taxes: The Demographic & Political Transitions. LC 83-17989. 174p. (C). 1998. lib. bdg. 24.00 (*0-226 63281-4*) U Ch Pr.

Orgel, D. Show-&-Tell Frog. (LVL Ser.: No. 2). (Illus.). 32p. (J). 1992. pap. 4.50 (*0-553-35147-8*) Bantam.

***Orgel, Doris.** Ariadne, Awake! (Illus.). 74p. (gr. 6-11). 1999. reprint ed. text 16.00 (*0-7881-6477-5*) DIANE Pub.

Orgel, Doris. Button Soup. LC 93-14087. (Bank Street Ready-to-Read Ser.). (Illus.). 32p. (J). 1994. pap. 4.50 (*0-553-37341-2*) Bantam.

— The Devil in Vienna. (J). 1988. pap. 5.99 (*0-14-032500-X*, PuffinBks) Peng Put Young Read.

— The Devil in Vienna. (J). 1995. 19.50 (*0-8446-6797-8*) Peter Smith.

Orgel, Doris. The Devil in Vienna. (J). 1978. 11.09 (*0-606-03565-6*, Pub. by Turtleback) Demco.

Orgel, Doris. Don't Call Me Slob-O. LC 95-4822. (West Side Kids Ser.: No. 2). (Illus.). 80p. (J). (gr. 2-5). 1996. lib. bdg. 13.89 (*0-7868-2086-1*, Pub. by Hyprn Child) Little.

— Don't Call Me Slob-O. LC 95-4822. (West Side Kids Ser.). 1996. 9.05 (*0-606-10038-5*, Pub. by Turtleback) Demco.

— Friends to the Rescue. LC 95-33605. (West Side Kids Ser.: No. 3). (Illus.). 80p. (J). (gr. 2-5). 1996. pap. 3.95 (*0-7868-1045-9*, Pub. by Hyprn Ppbks) Little.

— Friends to the Rescue. LC 95-33605. (West Side Kids Ser.). 1996. 9.15 (*0-606-10359-7*, Pub. by Turtleback) Demco.

***Orgel, Doris.** The Lion & the Mouse: And Other Aesop's Fables. (Illus.). 40p. (J). (ps-3). 2000. 16.95 (*0-7894-2665-X*) DK Pub Inc.

Orgel, Doris. Pegasus. unabridged ed. (Stories to Remember Ser.). (J). (gr. 1-5). 1993. pap. 8.98 incl. audio (*1-879496-13-5*) Lightyear Entrtnmnt.

— The Princess & the God. 128p. (YA). (gr. 9 up). 1997. mass mkt. 4.50 (*0-440-22691-0*) BDD Bks Young Read.

— The Princess & the God. LC 95-33527. 128p. (YA). (gr. 6 up). 1996. lib. bdg. 16.99 (*0-531-08866-9*) Orchard Bks Watts.

— The Princess & the God. 1997. 9.60 (*0-606-13723-8*, Pub. by Turtleback) Demco.

— Sarah's Room. LC 63-13675. (Illus.). (J). (gr. k-3). 1963. 11.95 (*0-06-024605-7*); lib. bdg. 14.89 (*0-06-024606-5*) HarpC Child Bks.

— Sarah's Room. LC 63-13675. (Trophy Picture Bk.). (Illus.). 48p. (J). (ps-3). 1991. pap. 4.95 (*0-06-443238-6*, HarpTrophy) HarpC Child Bks.

Orgel, Doris. Two Crows Counting. (J). 1995. mass mkt. 4.99 (*0-553-54204-4*) BDD Bks Young Read.

Orgel, Doris. Two Crows Counting. (J). 1995. 19.95 (*0-553-53119-0*) BDD Bks Young Read.

— Two Crows Counting. LC 94-32240. (Ready-to-Read Ser.). (Illus.). 32p. (J). (ps-1). 1995. pap. 4.50 (*0-553-37573-3*) BDD Bks Young Read.

— We Goddesses: Athena, Aphrodite, Hera. LC 98-41155. (Illus.). 144p. (YA). (gr. 5-9). 1999. 22.95 (*0-7894-2586-6*) DK Pub Inc.

Orgel, Doris & Schecter, Ellen. The Flower of Sheba. LC 92-33477. (Bank Street Ready-to-Read Ser.). (Illus.). 32p. (J). 1994. pap. 4.50 (*0-553-37235-1*, Litl Rooster) BDD Bks Young Read.

Orgel, Doris, et al. Don't Call Me Slob-O. LC 95-4822. (West Side Kids Ser.: No. 2). (Illus.). 80p. (J). (ps-3). 1996. pap. 3.95 (*0-7868-1044-0*, Pub. by Hyprn Ppbks) Little.

Orgel, Irene. Odd Tales of Irene Orgel. LC 67-14531. 116p. 1966. 30.00 (*0-87130-015-X*) Eakins.

***Orgel, Joseph R.** Building an Enriched Vocabulary. 594p. 1999. pap., teacher ed. 22.50 (*0-87105-502-3*) Sadlier-Oxford.

— Building an Enriched Vocabulary. rev. ed. 498p. (YA). (gr. 9-12). 1999. text 24.90 (*0-87105-501-5*) Sadlier-Oxford.

— Building an Enriched Vocabulary: Supplementary Exercise & Testing Program. 92p. (YA). (gr. 9-12). 1999. pap. 7.95 (*0-87105-503-1*) Sadlier-Oxford.

Orgel, Joseph R. Families, Families: Big Book, Theme 2. large type ed. (Worlds of Poetry Ser.). (Illus.). 16p. (J). (gr. k-3). 1998. pap. text 28.95 (*0-8215-0510-6*) Sadlier.

Orgel, Shelly & Fine, Bernard D., eds. Clinical Psychoanalysis. LC 79-51910. (Downstate Psychoanalytic Institute Twenty-Fifth Anniversary Ser.: Vol. III). 360p. 1979. 60.00 (*0 87668-368-5*) Aronson.

Orgel, Stephen. The Illusion of Power: Political Theater in the English Renaissance. 95p. 1991. reprint ed. pap. 14.95 (*0-520-02741-8*, Pub. by U CA Pr) Cal Prin Full Svc.

— Impersonations: The Performance of Gender in Shakespeare's England. (Illus.). 195p. 1996. pap. text 17.95 (*0-521-56842-0*) Cambridge U Pr.

***Orgel, Stephen.** King Lear: The Quarto & the Folio Texts. (Pelican Shakespeare Ser.). 270p. 2000. pap. 4.95 (*0-14-071490-1*) Viking Penguin.

Orgel, Stephen. Shakespeare's Poems. LC 99-49783. (Scholarly Literature Ser.). 1999. write for info. (*0-8153-2964-4*) Garland.

Orgel, Stephen, ed. Shakespeare & Gender. LC 99-48820. (Scholarly Literature Ser.). 1999. write for info. (*0-8153-2962-8*) Garland.

— Shakespeare & the Arts. LC 99-48822. (Scholarly Literature Ser.). 1999. write for info. (*0-8153-2961-X*) Garland.

— Shakespeare & the Editorial Tradition. LC 99-49782. (Scholarly Literature Ser.). 1999. write for info. (*0-8153-2965-2*) Garland.

— Studies on Industrial Productivity, Set. LC 94-484. 192p. 1993. 783.00 (*0-8153-1529-5*) Garland.

Orgel, Stephen, ed. William Shakespeare: The Scholarly Literature. Date not set. 80.00 (*0-8153-2970-9*) Garland.

Orgel, Stephen, ed. William Shakespeare: The Scholarly Literature. LC 99-54097. 1999. write for info. (*0-8153-2968-7*) Garland.

— William Shakespeare: The Scholarly Literature. LC 99-48821. 1999. write for info. (*0-8153-2963-6*) Garland.

O

An Asterisk (*) at the beginning of an entry indicates that the title is appearing for the first time.

— William Shakespeare Vol. 6: The Scholarly Literature. LC 99-50173. 1999. 80.00 (*0-8153-2966-0*) Garland.

— William Shakespeare Vol. 7: The Scholarly Literature. LC 99-50161. 1999. 80.00 (*0-8153-2967-9*) Garland.

— William Shakespeare Vol. 9: The Scholarly Literature. LC 99-50160. 1999. 80.00 (*0-8153-2969-5*) Garland.

***Orgel, Stephen & Keilen, Sean, eds.** Shakespeare: The Critical Complex, 10 vols. 1999. 800.00 (*0-8153-2960-1*) Garland.

Orgel, Stephen, ed. see Jonson, Ben.

Orgel, Stephen, jt. ed. see Lytle, Guy F.

Orgel, Stephen, ed. see Milton, John.

Orgel, Stephen, ed. see Shakespeare, William.

Orgel, Stephen, ed. see Wharton, Edith.

Orgel, Stephen, ed. & intro. see Trollope, Anthony.

***Orgeldinger, Sybille.** Standardisierung Und Purismus Bei Joachim Heinrich Campe. ix, 481p. 1999. 158.70 (*3-11-016312-8*) De Gruyter.

Orgelfinger, Gail, ed. The Hystorye of Olyuer of Castylle. LC 88-7223. (Medieval Texts Ser.: Vol. 14). 291p. 1988. text 20.00 (*0-8240-8500-0*, 746) Garland.

Orgell, Doris. Bunny & Grandma. (Illus.). (J). 1999. pap. write for info. (*0-14-054293-0*) NAL.

Orgera. Here Comes the Bride. (Illus.). (YA). 1996. 9.99 (*0-590-60799-5*) Scholastic Inc.

Orgill. A Canaries Rockers & Red Hot Mamas: A Century of American Popular Girl Singers. LC 99-54374. (J). (gr. 7). 2001. per. 18.00 (*0-689-81991-9*) S&S Childrens.

Orgill, Andrew. The 1990-91 Gulf War: Crisis, Conflict, Aftermath: An Annotated Bibliography. LC 94-28447. 224p. 1995. 110.00 (*0-7201-2174-4*) Continuum.

Orgill, Roxanne. If I Only Had a Horn: Young Louis Armstrong. LC 96-15380. (Illus.). 32p. (J). (ps-3). 1997. 16.00 (*0-395-75919-6*) HM.

Orgogozo, J. M. & Dyken, M., eds. Advances in Stroke Prevention: Sanofi-Winthrop Symposium, Second European Stroke Conference, Lausanne, June 1992. (Journal: Cerebrovascular Diseases Ser.: Vol. 3, Suppl. 1, 1993). (Illus.). iv, 44p. 1993. pap. 21.00 (*3-8055-5787-6*) S Karger.

Orgogozo, J. M. & Lenzi, G. L., eds. Assessment of Stroke Outcome: Round Table. (Journal: Cerebrovascular Diseases Ser.: Vol. 4, Suppl. 2, 1994). (Illus.). iv, 30p. 1994. pap. 15.00 (*3-8055-6064-8*) S Karger.

Orgogozo, J. M. & Warlow, Charles P., eds. Advances in Stroke Prevention: New Outlooks. (Journal Ser.: Vol. 6, Suppl. 1, 1996). (Illus.). iv, 40p. 1995. pap., suppl. ed. 21.75 (*3-8055-6278-0*) S Karger.

Orgun, M. A. & Ashcroft, E. A. Intensional Programming - Based on the Papers at ISLIP 95. 308p. 1996. text 98.00 (*981-02-2400-1*) World Scientific Pub.

Orh, Kenneth Orh, jt. auth. see Winkelman, Robert.

Orhelein, Ann, ed. see Perez, Ramon.

Orhon, Derin & Artan, Nazik. Modelling of Activated Sludge Systems. (Illus.). 585p. 1994. 116.95 (*1-56676-101-8*) Technomic.

Ori, Amos, ed. see International Research Workshop on Internal Struct.

Ori, Kan, jt. auth. see Benjamin, Roger.

Oria, Tomas G. Martí y el Krausismo. LC 86-63038. (SPA.). 176p. 1987. pap. 30.00 (*0-89295-047-1*) Society Sp & Sp-Am.

O'Riagain, Padraig. Language Policy & Social Reproduction: Ireland 1893-1993. LC 96-39193. (Oxford Studies in Language Contact). (Illus.). 312p. 1997. text 80.00 (*0-19-823518-6*, Clarendon Pr) OUP.

Oriani, G., et al, eds. Handbook on Hyperbaric Medicine. 900p. 1996. 198.00 (*3-540-75016-9*) Spr-Verlag.

Oriani, G. & Wattel, F., eds. Proceedings of the 12th International Congress on Hyperbaric Medicine. LC 97-73095. (Illus.). 320p. 1998. 64.00 (*0-941332-63-2*, D938) Best Pub Co.

Orianne, Andre, tr. see Levinas, Emmanuel.

Orians, Gordon H. Blackbirds of Americas. LC 85-40352. (Illus.). 164p. 1985. pap. 35.00 (*0-295-96253-4*) U of Wash Pr.

— Some Adaptations of Marsh-Nesting Blackbirds. LC 79-84005. (Monographs in Population Biology: Vol. 14). (Illus.). 308p. reprint ed. pap. 95.50 (*0-608-06470-X*, 206676700009) Bks Demand.

Orians, Gordon H., et al, eds. Biodiversity & Ecosystem Processes in Tropical Forests. LC 96-1606. (Ecological Studies: Vol. 122). 232p. 1996. 79.95 (*3-540-59275-X*) Spr-Verlag.

— The Preservation & Valuation of Biological Resources. LC 90-12118. 304p. 1990. 40.00 (*0-295-97004-9*) U of Wash Pr.

Orians, Gordon H., jt. auth. see Beletsky, Les D.

Orians, Thomas, jt. ed. see Leopold, Kathleen.

***Oriard, Lewis L.** The Effects of Vibrations & Environmental forces: A Guide for the Investigation of Structures. LC 99-76570. (Illus.). 296p. 1999. text 49.00 (*1-892396-10-6*) Intl Soc Explosives.

Oriard, Michael. Reading Football: How the Popular Press Created an American Spectacle. LC 92-42840. (Cultural Studies of the United States). 352p. 1998. pap. 18.95 (*0-8078-4751-8*) U of NC Pr.

— Sporting with the Gods: The Rhetoric of Play & Game in American Literature. (Cambridge Studies in Latin American LIterature & Culture: No. 45). (Illus.). 608p. (C). 1991. text 74.95 (*0-521-39113-X*) Cambridge U Pr.

Oribe, E., jt. auth. see Appenzeller, O.

Oribe, Emilio, jt. auth. see Appenzeller, Otto.

Oribe, Jose. The Fine Guitar. 96p. 1985. 19.95 (*0-9615906-1-0*) Vel-or Co.

— Jose Oribe: The Fine Guitar. (Illus.). 96p. 1996. pap. 19.95 (*0-7866-1367-X*, MB95629) Mel Bay.

Oribello, William A. Candle Burning with the Psalms. 100p. 10.00 (*0-938294-58-X*) Inner Light.

— Godspells: Written Spells, Spoken Spells & Spell Enhancers. 70p. 15.00 (*0-938294-49-0*) Inner Light.

— The Sacred Magic. 96p. (Orig.). 15.00 (*0-938294-26-1*) Inner Light.

— The Sealed Magical Book of Moses. (Illus.). 96p. 15.00 (*0-938294-68-7*) Inner Light.

Oribello, William A. & Hamilton, William, III. Using Candle Burning to Contact Your Guardian Angel. 96p. 15.00 (*0-938294-75-X*) Inner Light.

Orichowski, Rose M., jt. auth. see Johnson, Rachel P.

Oriedo, Ollie O., jt. ed. see Gibson, Stephanie.

Oriel, Charles. Writing & Inscription in Golden Age Drama. LC 92-26368. (Studies in Romance Literatures: Vol. 1). 200p. 1992. reprint ed. pap. 21.95 (*1-55753-074-2*) Purdue U Pr.

Oriel Incorporated Staff. Guiding Successful Projects. 1997. 14.95 (*1-884731-14-7*) Oriel Inc.

Oriel, J. D. The Scars of Venus: A History of Venereology. LC 93-34554. (Illus.). 248p. 1994. 98.00 (*3-540-19844-X*) Spr-Verlag.

— The Scars of Venus: A History of Venereology. LC 93-34554. vii, 248p. 1994. 98.00 (*0-387-19844-X*) Spr-Verlag.

O'Rielly, Lily & Murphy, Deanna. Teacher's Manual to Accompany Arithmetic for Adults: An Alternative Approach. 218p. (C). pap. text. write for info. (*0-7872-6585-3*) Kendall-Hunt.

O'Rielly, Terence. From Ignatius to John of the Cross. (Collected Studies: Vol. CS484). 300p. 1995. 98.95 (*0-86078-459-2*, Pub. by Variorum) Ashgate Pub Co.

O'rien, Bernadette M. & O'Brien, David W. California Unemployment & Disability Compensation Programs, No. 1. 8th ed. 1993. suppl. ed. 35.00 (*0-685-74366-7*, MICHIE) LEXIS Pub.

Orient, Grand. The Book of Destiny & the Art of Reading Therein. 277p. 1986. spiral bd. 24.50 (*0-7873-0647-9*) Hlth Research.

— A Handbook of Cartomancy: Fortune-Telling & Occult Divination. 114p. 1996. reprint ed. spiral bd. 12.50 (*0-7873-0645-2*) Hlth Research.

— A Manual of Cartomancy, Fortune-Telling & Occult Divination. 278p. 1996. reprint ed. spiral bd. 18.00 (*0-7873-0646-0*) Hlth Research.

— The Occult Science of Jewels: The Symbolism of Precious Stones. Holmes, J. D., ed. 1995. pap. 6.95 (*1-55818-316-7*, Sure Fire) Holmes Pub.

Orient, Grand & Holmes, J. D., eds. Divination by Flowers: Being in Accordance with the Hermetic Doctrine Concerning Solar & Lunar Influences. 1995. reprint ed. pap. 6.95 (*1-55818-315-9*, Sure Fire) Holmes Pub.

Orient, Jane M. & Wright, Linda J. Sutton's Law. unabridged ed. LC 97-72143. 299p. 1997. 21.95 (*0-9641077-1-6*) Hacienda Pub.

Oriental Division of the New York Public Library S, jt. auth. see LC Marc Tapes Staff.

Oriental Institute Staff. The 1905-1907 Breasted Expeditions to Egypt & the Sudan: A Photographic Study, 2 vols., Vol. 1. LC 76-22621. (Illus.). 21p. 1976. lib. bdg. 15.00 incl. fiche (*0-226-69471-2*) U Ch Pr.

Oriental Institute Staff. The 1905-1907 Breasted Expeditions to Egypt & the Sudan: A Photographic Study, 2 vols., Vol. 2. LC 76-22621. (Illus.). 24p. 1976. lib. bdg. 15.00 incl. fiche (*0-226-69472-0*) U Ch Pr.

— The 1919-1920 Breasted Expedition to the Near East. LC 77-2731. 36p. 1978. lib. bdg. 20.50 incl. fiche (*0-226-69473-9*) U Ch Pr.

— Persepolis & Ancient Iran. LC 76-7942. 57p. 1976. lib. bdg. 66.00 incl. fiche (*0-226-69493-3*) U Ch Pr.

— Studies in Honor of John A. Wilson. LC 76-81081. 124p. 1969. pap. text 11.00 (*0-226-62408-0*, SAOC35) U Ch Pr.

Oriental Institute Staff & Nasgowitz, David. Ptolemais Cyrenaica. LC 80-26769. (Illus.). 84p. 1981. lib. bdg. 60.00 incl. fiche (*0-226-69474-7*) U Ch Pr.

Orier, Anthony L. Life Between Seedtime & Harvest. LC 98-91103. 200p. 1999. pap. 12.95 (*1-889448-52-4*) NBN Publishers Group.

Orieux, Jean. L' Aigle de Fer. (FRE.). 1985. pap. 17.95 (*0-7859-4234-3*) Fr & Eur.

Oriev, Uri. The Island on Bird Street. 176p. (J). (gr. 4-7). 1992. pap. 5.95 (*0-395-61623-9*) HM.

***Origami, Ball.** Kusudama. (Illus.). 76p. 2000. pap. text 14.00 (*4-88996-049-X*) Japan Pubn Trad.

Origen. Commentary on the Gospel of John, Bks. 1-10. Heine, Ronald E., tr. LC 88-20406. (Fathers of the Church Ser.: Vol. 80). 344p. 1989. 36.95 (*0-8132-0080-6*) Cath U Pr.

— Commentary on the Gospel of John, Bks. 13-32. Heine, Ronald E., tr. from GRE. LC 88-20406. (Fathers of the Church Ser.: Vol. 89). 436p. 1993. 36.95 (*0-8132-0089-X*) Cath U Pr.

— Homilies on Genesis & Exodus. Heine, Ronald E., tr. LC 82-4124. (Fathers of the Church Ser.: Vol. 71). 435p. (C). 1982. 31.95 (*0-8132-0071-7*) Cath U Pr.

— Homilies on Leviticus. Barkley, Gary W., tr. LC 89-78173. (Fathers of the Church Ser.: Vol. 83). 294p. 1990. 33.95 (*0-8132-0083-0*) Cath U Pr.

— Homilies on Luke. Lienhard, Joseph T., tr. from GRE. LC 95-39207. (Fathers of the Church Ser.: Vol. 94). 246p. 1996. 31.95 (*0-8132-0094-6*) Cath U Pr.

— On First Principles: Being Koetschau's Text of the De Principiis. Butterworth, G. W., tr. 1990. 27.00 (*0-8446-2685-6*) Peter Smith.

— The Philocalia of Origen. LC 80-2359. reprint ed. 39.50 (*0-404-18911-3*) AMS Pr.

Origen, et al. The Pilgrim Road. Roberts, Alexnder et al, trs. from GRE. 192p. (Orig.). 1991. pap. 7.95 (*0-924722-04-5*) Scroll Pub.

Origenes. Hexaplorum Quae Supersunt, 2 vols., Set. ci, 1918p. 1964. reprint ed. write for info. (*0-318-70992-9*) G Olms Pubs.

Origer, Thomas M. Temporal Control in the Southern North Coast Ranges of California: The Application of Obsidian Hydration Analyses. fac. ed. (Northern California Anthropological Group). (Illus.). 180p. (C). 1987. reprint ed. pap. text 19.38 (*1-55567-812-2*) Coyote Press.

Origin Special Staff. 688 (I) Hunter/Killer: The Official Strategy Guide. LC 96-71781. 192p. 1997. per. 19.99 (*0-7615-1036-2*) Prima Pub.

Origin Staff. F-15: Prima's Official Strategy Guide. LC 97-76318. 320p. 1998. per. 19.99 (*0-7615-1516-X*) Prima Pub.

Origin Systems Inc. Staff. Official Guide to Janes Advanced Tactical Fighters. 1996. pap. text 19.95 (*0-7845-0739-2*) Elect Arts.

— Origins Official Guide to Wing Commander IV. 1996. pap. text 19.95 (*0-929373-37-5*) Elect Arts.

Original Publications, tr. from SPA. Helping Yourself With Selected Prayers. 1984. pap. 4.95 (*0-942272-01-3*) Original Pubns.

Origo, Iris. Images & Shadows: Part of a Life. LC 99-23132. (Nonpareil Ser.). (Illus.). 588p. 1999. pap. 15.95 (*1-56792-103-5*, Non Pareil Bk) Godine.

***Origo, Iris.** The Last Attachment: The Story of Byron & Teresa Guiccioli. 320p. 2000. pap. 16.95 (*1-885586-50-7*, Pub. by Turtle Point Pr) Dist Art Pubs.

Origo, Iris. Leopardi: A Study in Solitude. 396p. (Orig.). 1999. pap. 16.95 (*1-885983-44-1*, Helen Mx) Turtle Point Pr.

***Origo, Iris.** A Need to Testify. 320p. 2000. pap. 16.95 (*1-885586-51-5*, Pub. by Turtle Point Pr) Dist Art Pubs.

Origo, Iris. War in Val d'Orcia: An Italian War Diary, 1943-1944. LC 82-49344. (Nonpareil Bks.: Vol. 13). 256p. 1984. pap. 14.95 (*0-87923-476-8*) Godine.

Orihel, Thomas C., jt. auth. see Ash, Lawrence R.

Orihuela, Maria L. Calle Ocho. LC 97-80335. (Coleccion Caniqui). (SPA.). 152p. 1998. pap. 12.00 (*0-89729-855-1*, 855-1) Ediciones.

Oriji, John N. Ngwa History: A Study of Social & Economic Changes in Igbo Mini-States in Time Perspective. 2nd ed. LC 98-141338. XII, 195p. 1998. pap. 24.95 (*0-8204-4042-6*) P Lang Pubng.

— Traditions of Igbo Origin: A Study of Pre-Colonial Population Movements in Africa. 2nd rev. ed. LC 93-43268. (Am. Univ. Studies, XI: Vol. 48). XII, 234p. (C). 1994. pap. text 24.95 (*0-8204-2481-1*) P Lang Pubng.

O'Riley, Carolyn A. Go Within Feel the Love. (Illus.). 60p. 1997. spiral bd. 10.00 (*1-891870-00-9*, 00100) Archangels Pen.

— Grandma Are You Old. (Illus.). 30p. (J). (ps-2). 1998. spiral bd. 15.00 incl. audio (*1-891870-05-X*, 00600) Archangels Pen.

— How High Is Heaven. (Illus.). 24p. (J). (ps-2). 1998. spiral bd. 15.00 incl. audio (*1-891870-07-6*, 00800) Archangels Pen.

— If I Were a Kangaroo Would You Love Me Too? (Illus.). 26p. (J). (ps-2). 1998. spiral bd. 15.00 incl. audio (*1-891870-03-3*, 00400) Archangels Pen.

— Look Inside. (Illus.). 30p. (J). (ps-2). 1998. spiral bd. 10.00 (*1-891870-01-7*, 00200) Archangels Pen.

— Pink, Yellow, Black & Green What Do All the Differences Mean? (Illus.). 36p. (J). (ps-2). 1998. spiral bd. 15.00 incl. audio (*1-891870-04-1*, 00500) Archangels Pen.

— What Is a Gift. (Illus.). 26p. (J). (ps-2). 1998. spiral bd. 15.00 incl. audio (*1-891870-06-8*, 00700) Archangels Pen.

— Where Is God. (Illus.). 22p. (J). (ps-2). 1998. spiral bd. 15.00 incl. audio (*1-891870-08-4*, 00900) Archangels Pen.

— You Are One of a Kind. (Illus.). 18p. (J). (ps-2). 1998. spiral bd. 15.00 incl. audio (*1-891870-02-5*, 00300) Archangels Pen.

***O'Riley, Carolyn Ann.** The Journey Within. (Archangel Michael Speaks Ser.: Bk. I). 100p. 2000. spiral bd. 15.00 (*1-891870-10-6*) Archangels Pen.

O'Riley, Jade. 56 Days in the History of Love. LC 99-18940. 64p. 1999. pap. text 14.95 (*0-7734-3103-9*) E Mellen.

O'Riley, Ronald P. Electrical Grounding. 2nd ed. (Electrical Trades Ser.). 1990. pap. 23.95 (*0-8273-3853-8*); pap., teacher ed. 13.95 (*0-8273-3854-6*) Delmar.

— Electrical Grounding. 4th ed. (Electrical Trades Ser.). 1996. teacher ed. 15.95 (*0-8273-6658-2*, VNR) Wiley.

— Electrical Grounding: Bringing Grounding Back to Earth. 4th ed. LC 95-13272. 304p. 1995. mass mkt. 25.75 (*0-8273-6657-4*) Delmar.

— Illustrated Changes in NEC. 2nd ed. LC 95-7607. (Illus.). 368p. 1995. mass mkt. 27.75 (*0-8273-6773-2*) Delmar.

— Illustrated Changes in the National Electrical Code, 1993. LC 92-17310. 1993. pap. 34.95 (*0-8273-5304-9*) Delmar.

— Illustrated Changes in the 1993 National Electrical Code: Instructor's Guide. 1993. teacher ed. 13.50 (*0-8273-5616-1*); trans. 249.95 (*0-8273-5615-3*) Delmar.

— Illustrated Changes in the 1996 NEC. 2nd ed. (Electrical Trades Ser.). (Illus.). 1996. teacher ed. 13.50 (*0-8273-6774-0*) Delmar.

— Illustrated Changes in the 1999 National Electrical Code. 3rd ed. LC 98-17860. (Illus.). 304p. (C). 1998. text 31.95 (*0-7668-0763-0*) Delmar.

Orilia, Francesco, et al. Thought, Language & Ontology: Essays in Memory of Hector-Neri Castaneda. LC 98-28935. (Philosophical Studies). 1998. 135.00 (*0-7923-5197-5*) Kluwer Academic.

Orimalade, Adeyinka. Petroleum Refining in Africa: Origin, Growth & Prospects. (C). 1989. 22.00 (*81-7023-211-2*, Pub. by Allied Pubs) S Asia.

Orimo, H., ed. Fifth Symposium by the Nine Winners of the Grants from Sandoz Foundation for Gerontological Research: Annual Meeting of the Japan Gerontological Society, Sapporo, Japan, September 1993, No. 40. (Journal: Gerontology: Supplement 2, 1994). (Illus.). iv, 72p. 1994. pap. 33.25 (*3-8055-6044-3*) S Karger.

— The First Symposium by the Six Winners of the Grants from Sandoz Foundation for Gerontological Research: Annual Meeting of the Japan Gerontological Society, Nagoya, Japan, November 1989 - Journal: Gerontology, Vol. 36, Suppl. 1, 1990. (Illus.). vi, 50p. 1990. pap. 24.50 (*3-8055-5240-8*) S Karger.

— Fourth Symposium by the Five Winners of the Grants from Sandoz Foundation for Gerontological Research, Annual Meeting of the Japan Gerontological Society, Kanazawa, Japan, November 1992. (Journal: Gerontology: Vol. 39, Suppl. 1, 1993). (Illus.). vi, 38p. 1993. pap. 14.00 (*3-8055-5823-6*) S Karger.

— The Second Symposium by the Eight Winners of the Grants from Sandoz Foundation for Gerontological Research: Annual Meeting of the Japan Gerontological Society, Kochi-Japan, November 1990 - Journal: Gerontology, Vol. 37, Suppl. 1, 1991. (Illus.). iv, 64p. 1991. pap. 21.00 (*3-8055-5473-7*) S Karger.

— The 7th Symposium by the 8 Winners of the Grants from Sandoz Foundation for Gerontological Research: Annual Meeting of the Japan Gerontological Society Osaka, October 20, 1995. (Journal: Gerontology: Vol. 42, Suppl. 11, 1996). (Illus.). iv, 78p. 1996. pap. 25.25 (*3-8055-6334-5*) S Karger.

— The Sixth Symposium by the 5 Winners of the Grants from Sandoz Foundation for Gerontological Research: Annual Meeting of the Japan Gerontological Society, Tokyo, Japan, September 1994. (Journal: Gerontology: Vol. 41, Suppl. 1, 1995). (Illus.). iv, 34p. 1995. pap. 21.75 (*3-8055-6235-7*) S Karger.

— Third Symposium by the Seven Winners of the Grants from Sandoz Foundation for Gerontological Research, Annual Meeting of the Japan Gerontological Society, Yokohama, November 1991. (Journal: Gerontology: Vol. 38, Suppl. 1, 1992). (Illus.). vi, 50p. 1992. pap. 17.50 (*3-8055-5661-6*) S Karger.

Orimo, Hajime, ed. The Eighth Symposium by the 6 Winners of the Grants from Sandoz Foundation for Gerontological Research, Makuhari, June 1996. (Journal: Vol. 43, Suppl. 1, 1997). (Illus.). iv, 54p. 1997. pap. 21.75 (*3-8055-6489-9*) S Karger.

Oring, Elliott. Humor & the Individual. LC 84-70061. (Orig.). 1984. pap. 8.95 (*0-914563-02-5*) CA Folklore Soc.

— Israeli Humor: The Content & Structure of the Chizbat of the Palmah. LC 80-25483. (SUNY Series in Modern Jewish Literature & Culture). 295p. (C). 1981. text 21.50 (*0-87395-512-9*) State U NY Pr.

— Jokes & Their Relations. LC 91-35254. 184p. 1992. text 25.00 (*0-8131-1774-7*) U Pr of Ky.

— The Jokes of Sigmund Freud: A Study in Humor & Jewish Identity. LC 96-37012. 168p. 1997. pap. 25.00 (*0-7657-5976-4*) Aronson.

Oring, Elliott, ed. Folk Groups & Folklore Genres: A Reader. 394p. 1989. pap. text 19.95 (*0-87421-140-9*) Utah St U Pr.

— Folk Groups & Folklore Genres: An Introduction. (Illus.). 272p. 1986. pap. text 19.95 (*0-87421-128-X*) Utah St U Pr.

Oring, Stuart A. A Beginner's Guide to Pictures. (Illus.). 33p. (Orig.). 1997. pap. 9.00 (*0-9630896-1-7*) ISIS Visual.

— Understanding Pictures: A Teacher's Planning Guide. 29p. (Orig.). 1996. pap. 7.00 (*0-9630896-2-5*) ISIS Visual.

–Understanding Pictures: Theories, Exercises, & Procedures. enl. rev. ed. LC 91-75593. (Illus.). 233p. 1992. reprint ed. spiral bd. 38.00 (*0-9630896-0-9*) ISIS Visual.

If you are interested in the visual image -- whether you are an art historian or a teacher of photography or art -- you will want to add this book to your library. It is a comprehensive look at pictures & how to approach them in order to understand them better. Combining traditional & revolutionary approaches, the book describes in detail how to use both your conscious & unconscious mind in order to obtain as much in insight about pictures as possible. It gives well proven procedures for looking at pictures in both an active & a passive manner. But, most importantly, it will show you how to determine if your emotional response to a picture is on track or not through logical-rational analysis. And, just so that you don't overlook anything important when you look at a picture, the book will show you how checklists can help you to organize the experience in an effective & organized way. Book Ordering Information: Copies of the book UNDERSTANDING PICTURES can be ordered from: Stuart A. Oring, c/o Isis Visual Communications, 2570 Redbud Lane, Owings, MD 20736. The price of the book is $38.00 plus $4.00 shipping & handling. Maryland residents must add an additional 5 percent sales tax on all orders. Also available from Isis Visual Communications are: A TEACHER'S PLANNING GUIDE that describes how to effectively present the material in the book UNDERSTANDING PICTURES

An Asterisk (*) at the beginning of an entry indicates that the title is appearing for the first time.

in the classroom. The Guide shows the instructor how to put together effective classroom sessions & suggest student learning assignments. $9.00. A BEGINNER'S GUIDE TO PICTURES that is packed with useful information in easy-to-understand language. It also provides a worksheet for helping the reader to look at pictures in an organized way. "The Guide" can be used effectively as a student "handout" in the classroom. $12.00. *Publisher Paid Annotation.*

Oringel, Sandy & Silverman, Helene. Math Activities with Dominoes. 80p. (J). (gr. k-3). 1997. pap. text 9.95 (*0-938587-97-8*) Cuisenaire.

— Math Activities with Dominoes. 80p. (J). (gr. 3-8). 1997. pap. text 9.95 (*1-57452-027-X*) Cuisenaire.

Orio, Miguel. The Feather Chest: Te Waka Huia. LC 97-179558. 797p. 1997. 32.00 (*1-85756-259-3*, Pub. by Janus Pubng) Paul & Co Pubs.

Oriol, William E. Aging in All Nations: A Special Report on the United Nations World Assembly on Aging. Incl. Aging in North America. 1982. 200p. 1982. Set pap. 14.00 (*0-910883-00-9*, 4166) Natl Coun Aging.

Oriol, William E., compiled by. Federal Public Policy on Aging since 1960: An Annotated Bibliography, Vol. 5. LC 87-8343. (Bibliographies & Indexes in Gerontology Ser.: No. 5). 141p. 1987. lib. bdg. 59.95 (*0-313-25286-6*, OPP/, Greenwood Pr) Greenwood.

Oriol, Yves, ed. see Siebert, Jerome B.

Orioli, Giuseppe, ed. see Lawrence, D. H.

Oriolo, Leonardo. How to Say It: English-Amharic-Italian. LC 98-22103. 1997. pap. 14.95 (*1-56902-076-0*) Red Sea Pr.

— How to Say It in English-Amharic-Italian. LC 98-22103. (AMH & ITA.). 1998. 49.95 (*1-56902-078-7*) Red Sea Pr.

Oriolo, Leonardo, ed. Tigrinya Phrase Book. LC 98-981241. 64p. 1998. pap. 4.95 (*1-56902-083-3*) Red Sea Pr.

Oriolo, Leonardo, et al. How to Say It: English-Tigrinya-Italian. LC 97-2021. (ENG, ITA & TIR.). 1997. pap. 14.95 (*1-56902-054-X*) Red Sea Pr.

— How to Say It in English, Tigrinya, Italian. LC 97-2021. (ENG, ITA & TIR.). 1997. write for info. (*1-56902-055-8*); write for info. (*1-56902-056-6*) Red Sea Pr.

Orion. Pronouncing American English. 2nd ed. (College ESL Ser.). (J). 1998. mass mkt., suppl. ed. 6.00 (*0-8384-6334-7*) Heinle & Heinle.

Orion Agency, Inc. Staff. Obtaining Your Private Investigator's License. 64p. (Orig.). 1986. pap. 10.00 (*0-87364-390-9*) Paladin Pr.

***Orion Center for the Study of the Dead Sea Scrolls, et al.** The Damascus Document: A Centennial of Discovery: Proceedings of the 3rd International Symposium of the Orion Center for the Study of the Dead Sea Scrolls & Associated Literature, 4-8 February, 1998. LC 99-51404. (Studies on the Texts of the Desert of Judah). 1999. write for info. (*90-04-11462-9*) Brill Academic Pubs.

Orion Center for the Study of the Dead Sea Scrolls, et al. Pseudepigraphic Perspectives: The Apogrypha & Pseudepigrapha in Light of the Dead Sea Scrolls: Proceedings of the International Symposium of the Orion Center for the Study of the Dead Sea Scrolls & Associated Literature, 12-14 January, 1997. LC 98-34509. (Studies on the Texts of the Desert of Judah). 1998. 94.50 (*90-04-11164-6*) Brill Academic Pubs.

Orion, Doreen. I Know You Really Love Me. 384p. 1998. mass mkt. 6.50 (*0-440-22599-X*) Doubleday.

***Orion, Doreen.** I Know You Really Love Me: A Psychiatrist's Journal of Erotomania, Stalking, & Obsessive Love. 312p. 1999. reprint ed. text 24.00 (*0-7881-6484-8*) DIANE Pub.

Orion, Doreen R. I Know You Really Love Me: A Psychiatrist's Journal of Erotomania, Stalking & Obsessive Love. LC 97-14348. 288p. 1997. 23.95 (*0-02-861665-0*) Macmillan.

Orion, Gertrude. Pronouncing American English: Sounds, Stress, & Intonation. 321p. (J). 1987. pap., teacher ed. 11.95 (*0-8384-2696-4*, Newbury) Heinle & Heinle.

Orion, Getrude F. Pronouncing American English. 2nd ed. LC 96-51549. (College ESL Ser.). (J). 1997. pap. 32.95 (*0-8384-6332-0*) Heinle & Heinle.

Orion, Janice, tr. see Calame, Claude.

***Orion, Jonathan.** Poems of Love. 35p. 1999. (*1-891232-09-6*, Closet Bks) R Crane Pub.

Orion, Loretta. Never Again the Burning Times: Paganism Revived. (Illus.). 322p. (C). 1995. pap. text 13.95 (*0-88133-835-4*) Waveland Pr.

***Orion, Rae.** Astrology for Dummies. (For Dummies Ser.). 408p. 1999. pap. 19.99 (*0-7645-5217-1*) IDG Bks.

Orion Research Corporation Staff, compiled by. Computer Blue Book - Quarterly - Winter. rev. ed. 1999. lib. bdg. 129.00 (*0-932089-18-6*) Orion Res.

Orion Research Corporation Staff, ed. Vintage Guitar Blue Book - Quarterly - Winter. rev. ed. 732p. 1999. lib. bdg. 54.00 (*0-932089-50-X*) Orion Res.

O'Riordain, John J. Irish Catholic Spirituality: Celtic & Roman. LC 98-215604. 155 p. 1998. write for info. (*1-85607-243-6*) Intl Scholars.

— The Music of What Happens: Celtic Spirituality: A View from the Inside. 120p. 1996. pap. 9.95 (*0-88489-514-9*) St Marys.

***O'Riordan.** Environment Science for Enviromental Management. 2nd ed. 544p. 1999. pap. 46.95 (*0-582-35633-4*) Longman.

O'Riordan, Brian, jt. auth. see Meyer, Bruce.

O'Riordan, Jane. Rhone Appetit: Food to Serve with American Rhone Varietals. LC 98-60471. (Wine-Friendly Food Ser.). (Illus.). 112p. 1998. pap. text 17.95 (*0-9642901-3-8*) Toyon Hill Pr.

***O'Riordan, Linda.** The Art of Sufi Healing. 180p. 2000. pap. 12.95 (*0-910735-63-8*, Pub. by MTO Printing & Pubn Ctr) ACCESS Pubs Network.

O'Riordan, Ruth M. Aspects of Littorinid Biology, 133. LC 98-45179. 1999. 156.00 (*0-7923-5461-3*) Kluwer Academic.

O'Riordan, Tim & Cameron, James, eds. Interpreting the Precautionary Principle. (Environmental Law Ser.). 300p. 1994. 115.00 (*1-874698-45-7*, Pub. by Cameron May) Gaunt.

O'Riordan, Tim & Jager, Jill, eds. Politics of Climate Change: A European Perspective. LC 95-42459. (Global Environmental Change Ser.). (Illus.). 416p. (C). 1996. 85.00 (*0-415-12573-1*); pap. 27.99 (*0-415-12574-X*) Routledge.

O'Riordan, Tim & Voisey, Heather, eds. The Politics of Sustainable Development: A European Perspective. 288p. 1997. write for info. (*1-85383-469-6*, Pub. by Escan Pubns) Island Pr.

O'Riordan, Timothy, ed. Progress in Resource Management & Environmental Planning, 4 vols., Vol. 1. LC 80-646092. 335p. reprint ed. pap. 103.90 (*0-8357-4623-2*, 203755500001) Bks Demand.

— Progress in Resource Management & Environmental Planning, 4 vols., Vol. 2. LC 80-646092. 256p. reprint ed. pap. 79.40 (*0-8357-4624-0*, 203755500002) Bks Demand.

— Progress in Resource Management & Environmental Planning, 4 vols., Vol. 3. LC 80-646092. 340p. reprint ed. pap. 105.40 (*0-8357-4625-9*, 203755500003) Bks Demand.

— Progress in Resource Management & Environmental Planning, 4 vols., Vol. 4. LC 80-646092. 322p. reprint ed. pap. 99.90 (*0-8357-4626-7*, 203755500004) Bks Demand.

O'Riordan, Timothy & Sewell, W. R., eds. Project Appraisal & Policy Review. LC 80-40847. (Wiley Series on Studies in Environmental Management & Resource Development). (Illus.). 316p. reprint ed. pap. 98.00 (*0-8357-4622-4*, 203755400008) Bks Demand.

O'Riordan, Timothy & Voisey, Heather, eds. Sustainable Development in Western Europe: Coming to Terms with Agenda 21. LC 97-17430. 177p. 1997. 52.50 (*0-7146-4830-2*, Pub. by F Cass Pubs); pap. 19.50 (*0-7146-4376-9*, Pub. by F Cass Pubs) Intl Spec Bk.

O'Riordan, Timothy, jt. auth. see Cameron, James.

O'Riordan, Timothy, jt. ed. see Watson, J. Wreford.

O'Riorden. Points of Contention. 1996. pap. 22.19 (*0-07-048192-X*) McGraw.

Orishimo, Isao. Urbanization & Environmental Quality. (Studies in Applied Regional Science). 192p. 1982. lib. bdg. 111.00 (*0-89838-080-4*) Kluwer Academic.

Orissa University of Agriculture & Technology Staff, jt. auth. see Seminar on Current & Emerging Trends in Aquaculture & Its Impact on Rural Development Staff.

Oristaglio, Michael L. & Spies, Brian R., eds. Three-Dimensional Electromagnetics. LC 98-30016. (Geophysical Developments Ser.: Vol. 7). (Illus.). 724p. 1999. 152.00 (*1-56080-079-8*) Soc Expl Geophys.

Orivel, Francois, ed. see Schriewer, Jurgen.

Orizet, Jean. Anthologie de la Poesie Francaise. (FRE.). Date not set. 150.00 (*0-7859-9307-X*) Fr & Eur.

— Tiers of Survival: Selected Poems. DeWees, Aletha, tr. from FRE. Orig. Title: Niveaux de Survie. 120p. (Orig.). 1984. pap. 8.00 (*0-939378-03-5*) Mundus Artium.

***Orji, Cyril U.** Lamentation: An Immigrant's Dilemma. LC 99-93173. 300p. 1999. pap. write for info. (*0-9670657-0-4*) C U Orji.

Orkand, Robert, jt. auth. see Bogot, Howard.

Orkeny, Elte A., jt. auth. see Csepeli, Gyorgy.

Orkeny, Istvan. The Flower Show-The Toth Family. Heim, Michael & Gyorgyey, Clara, trs. LC 81-22373. 160p. 1982. 8.95 (*0-8112-0836-2*, Pub. by New Directions) Norton.

***Orkeny, Istvan.** One Minute Stories. 128p. 1999. pap. 21.00 (*963-13-4783-4*, Pub. by Corvina Bks) St Mut.

Orkeny, Istvan. Unuminutaj Noveloj. Ertl, Istvan, ed. & intro. by. Kamaco, Georgo, intro. (ESP.). 120p. 1995. pap. 7.95 (*1-882251-06-7*) Eldonejo Bero.

Orkin. What Are the Odds? Chance & Probability. LC 99-51731. 208p. 1999. pap. text 14.95 (*0-7167-3560-1*, Sci Am Lib) W H Freeman.

Orkin, Mark. Canajan, Eh? 3rd rev. ed. LC 97-931962. (Illus.). 144p. 1997. pap. 15.95 (*0-7737-5906-9*) Stoddart Publ.

Orkin, Mark, ed. Sanctions Against Apartheid. (C). 1996. text 48.50 (*0-8133-7927-X*) Westview.

Orkin, Mark M., jt. auth. see Bickerstaff, Isaac.

Orkin, Martin. Drama & the South African State. Dollimore, Jonathan & Sinfield, Alan, eds. LC 90-6556. (Cultural Politics Ser.). 192p. 1991. text 79.95 (*0-7190-2576-1*, Pub. by Manchester Univ Pr) St Martin.

Orkin, Martin, jt. ed. see Loomba, Ania.

Orkin, Michael. Can You Win? (C). 1991. pap. text 12.95 (*0-7167-2155-4*) W H Freeman.

Orkin, Milton & Maibach, Howard I. Cutaneous Infestations & Insect Bites. LC 84-22977. (Dermatology Ser.: Vol. 4). (Illus.). 368p. 1985. text 175.00 (*0-8247-7273-3*) Dekker.

Orkin, Milton, et al. Dermatology. (Illus.). 696p. (C). 1992. pap. text 43.95 (*0-8385-1288-7*, A1288-8, Apple Lange Med) McGraw.

Orkin, Stuart H., jt. auth. see Nathan, David G.

Orkow, Ben. The First Actress. 1976. pap. 5.25 (*0-8222-0401-0*) Dramatists Play.

Orlach, Manfred G. Englishes Around the World Vol. 1: General Studies: British Isles, North America: Studies in Honor of Manfred Gorlach. Schneider, Edgar W., ed. LC 97-15215. (Varieties of English Around the World General Ser.: Vol. G18). vi, 329p. 1997. lib. bdg. 79.00 (*1-55619-449-8*) J Benjamins Pubng Co.

— Englishes Around the World Vol. 2: Caribbean, Africa, Asia, Australasia: Studies in Honor of Manfred Gorlach. Schneider, Edgar W., ed. LC 97-15215. (Varieties of English Around the World General Ser.: Vol. G19). viii, 358p. 1997. lib. bdg. 85.00 (*1-55619-716-0*) J Benjamins Pubng Co.

Orlady, Harry W. & Orlady, Linda M. Human Factors in Multi-Crew Flight Operations. LC 99-26346. (Illus.). 628p. 1999. text 99.95 (*0-291-39838-3*, Pub. by Avebury Technical); pap. text 48.95 (*0-291-39839-1*, Pub. by Avebury Technical) Ashgate Pub Co.

Orlady, Harry W., ed. see Hawkins, Frank H.

Orlady, Linda M., jt. auth. see Orlady, Harry W.

Orlan. Orlan: This Is My Body . . . This Is My Software . . . (ENG & FRE., Illus.). 80p. 1996. pap. 39.95 incl. cd-rom (*0-9521773-6-6*, Pub. by Art Bks Intl) Partners Pubs Grp.

Orlan, Pierre M. A Bord de l'Etoile Matutine. (FRE.). 1983. pap. 10.95 (*0-7859-4188-6*) Fr & Eur.

— Le Bal du Pont du Nord Suivi d'Entre Deux Jours. (FRE.). 1984. pap. 11.95 (*0-7859-4208-4*) Fr & Eur.

— La Cavaliere Elsa. (FRE.). 1980. pap. 10.95 (*0-7859-4136-3*) Fr & Eur.

— Mademoiselle Bambu, Filles et Ports d'Europe-Pere Barbancon. (FRE.). 1982. pap. 10.95 (*0-7859-4163-0*) Fr & Eur.

— La Venus Internationale suivi de Dinah Miami. (FRE.). 1981. pap. 11.95 (*0-7859-4160-6*) Fr & Eur.

Orlan, Pierre Mac, see Mac Orlan, Pierre.

Orland, Henri, jt. auth. see Negele, John W.

Orland, Leonard, ed. Corporate & White Collar Crime: An Anthology. LC 95-11892. 438p. 1995. pap. 34.95 (*0-87084-870-4*) Anderson Pub Co.

Orland, Martin E., ed. Promises to Keep: Creating High Standards for American Students: Report to the National Education Goals Panel. 69p. 1998. pap. text 20.00 (*0-7881-4181-3*) DIANE Pub.

Orland, Ted. Scenes of Wonder & Curiosity: The Photographs & Writings of Ted Orland. LC 88-45333. (Illus.). 128p. 1988. 35.00 (*0-87923-768-6*) Godine.

Orland, Ted, jt. auth. see Bayles, David.

Orland, Ted, jt. auth. see Mazza, Cris.

Orland, Ted N. Man & Yosemite: A Photographer's View of the Early Years. (Illus.). 96p. (Orig.). 1985. 19.95 (*0-9614547-0-9*); pap. 10.95 (*0-9614547-1-7*) Image Continuum.

Orlande, Helcio R., jt. auth. see Ozisik, M. Necati.

Orlandello, John. O'Neill on Film. LC 80-70627. 192p. 1982. 32.50 (*0-8386-2291-7*) Fairleigh Dickinson.

***Orlandersmith, Dael.** Beauty's Daughter, Monster, The Gimmick: Three Plays by Dael Orlandersmith. 2000. pap. 12.00 (*0-375-70871 5*) Vin Bks.

Orlandi, Camillo, et al, eds. Recent Advances in Prenatal Diagnosis: Proceedings of the First International Symposium on Recent Advances in Prenatal Diagnosis, Bologna, September 15-16, 1980. LC 81-198305. (Illus.). 344p. reprint ed. pap. 106.70 (*0-608-15576-4*, 202963800062) Bks Demand.

Orlandi, M. Quelques Mots sur l'Acier, Lexique des Utilsateurs. (FRE.). 1998. 39.95 (*0-320-00154-7*) Fr & Eur.

Orlandi, Mario A., ed. Cultural Competence for Evaluators: A Guide for Alcohol & Other Drug Abuse Prevention Practitioners Working with Ethnic - Racial Communities. (Illus.). 299p. (C). 1998. pap. text 45.00 (*0-7881-4751-X*) DIANE Pub.

Orlandi, Pellegrino A. Abcedario Pittorico. fac. ed. (Documents of Art & Architectural History Ser.: Vol. 6). (ITA., Illus.). 447p. 1981. lib. bdg. 50.00 (*0-89371-106-3*) Broude Intl Edns.

Orlandini, Alberto. El Estes (Stress) Que Es y Como Evitarlo (What Is It & How to Avoid It) (SPA.). 165p 1996. pap. 15.99 (*950-557-217-4*, Pub. by Fondo) Continental Bk.

***Orlandini, Ervin.** Pesticide Removal by Combined Ozonation & Granular Activated Carbon Filtration. (IHE Dissertation Ser.: Vol. 16). (Illus.). 182p. (C). 1999. pap. text 40.00 (*90-5410-414-7*, Pub. by A A Balkema) Ashgate Pub Co.

Orlandini, G. E. & Orlandini, S. Zeechi, eds. The Tenth European Anatomical Congress Firenze, September 17-21, 1995, Abstracts: With the Participation of the American Association of Anatomists. (Journal: Acta Anatomica: Vol. 152, No. 4, 1995). iv, 130p. 1995. pap. 100.00 (*3-8055-6233-0*) S Karger.

Orlandini, John B. Ancient Native Americans of the Wyoming Valley: 10,000 Years of Prehistory. 190p. (Orig.). 1996. pap. 15.95 (*1-57502-128-5*) Morris Pubng.

Orlandini, S. Zeechi, jt. ed. see Orlandini, G. E.

Orlando. Thinking Critically about Reading, Writing, & Study Skills. (C). 1996. pap. text. write for info. (*0-15-501030-1*); pap. text, teacher ed. write for info. (*0-15-501637-7*) Harcourt Coll Pubs.

— Unto Him Vol. 1: Biblical Ballads of People & Events in God's Word. (Illus.). vii, 51p. (Orig.). 1997. pap. 6.95 (*0-9658387-0-6*) desktop.

Orlando & Levy. Tools for Teachers: A Guide to Understanding & Using Instructional Techniques. 300p. (C). 1998. spiral bd. 26.25 (*0-7872-4288-8*) Kendall-Hunt.

Orlando, jt. auth. see Banks.

Orlando, Anne S. The Wasted: A Play in Four Acts. (Illus.). 40p. 1999. pap. 7.00 (*0-8059-4714-0*) Dorrance.

Orlando, Bob. Indonesian Fighting Fundamentals: The Brutal Arts of the Archipelago. (Illus.). 200p. 1996. pap. 40.00 (*0-87364-892-7*) Paladin Pr.

— Martial Arts America: A Western Approach to Eastern Arts. LC 97-38087. (Illus.). 200p. 1998. pap. 14.95 (*1-883319-67-6*) Frog Ltd CA.

Orlando, Edward A. Delayed Disaster: One Life to Live & Give. LC 96-96429. (Illus.). x, 168p. (Orig.). 1996. pap. 20.00 (*0-9653007-0-6*) Englan Pub.

Orlando, Francesco. Toward a Freudian Theory of Literature: With an Analysis of Racine's Phedre. Lee, Charmaine, tr. LC 78-7577. 224p. reprint ed. pap. 69.50 (*0-8357-6622-5*, 203526700094) Bks Demand.

Orlando, Frank & Orlando, Regina. How to Own a New Home & Save Thousands: The Modular Home Manual. (Illus.). 113p. (Orig.). 1993. pap. 29.95 (*0-9642015-0-X*) Proven Methods.

Orlando, Henri, jt. auth. see Negele, John W.

Orlando, Janet Cucinell, see Wilkinson, Roy.

Orlando, Joseph. The San Francisco Waterfront Cookbook. (Illus.). 144p. 1991. reprint ed. pap. 9.95 (*0-89087-652-5*) Celestial Arts.

Orlando, Joseph A. Cogeneration Planner's Handbook. 1991. 74.00 (*0-88173-111-0*) Fairmont Pr.

— Cogeneration Planner's Handbook. 1992. 79.00 (*0-87814-674-1*) PennWell Bks.

Orlando, Lou. The Ultimate Phillies Trivia Quiz. 80p. (Orig.). 1994. write for info. (*0-9641936-0-4*) Rockford Assocs.

— Ultimate Phillies Trivia Quiz, 1997 Update. (Illus.). 80p. (Orig.). 1997. pap. write for info. (*0-614-30168-8*) Rockford Assocs.

Orlando, M. The Sleeping Palace. (Orig.). 1997. mass mkt. 6.95 (*1-56333-582-4*) Masquerade.

Orlando, Regina, jt. auth. see Orlando, Frank.

Orlando, Roy C. Esophagus & Pharynx, Vol. 5. LC 96-18669. (Gastroenterology & Hepatology Ser.). 1997. text 105.00 (*0-443-07855-6*) Church.

Orlando, S., jt. auth. see Meyer, A.

Orlando, Terry P. & Delin, Kevin A. Foundations of Applied Superconductivity. (Electrical Engineering Ser.). (Illus.). 544p. (C). 1991. 105.00 (*0-201-18323-4*) Addison-Wesley.

***Orlando, Valerie.** Nomadic Voices of Exile: Feminine Identity in Francophone Literature of the Maghreb. LC 98-32063. 256p. 1999. 36.95 (*0-8214-1262-0*) Ohio U Pr.

Orlans, F. Barbara. Animal Care from Protozoa to Small Mammals. 1977. text 22.00 (*0-201-05484-1*) Addison-Wesley.

— In the Name of Science: Issues in Responsible Animal Experimentation. LC 92-39344. (Illus.). 312p. 1993. text 39.95 (*0-19-507043-7*) OUP.

— In the Name of Science: Issues in Responsible Animal Experimentation. (Illus.). 312p. 1996. reprint ed. pap. text 21.95 (*0-19-510871-X*) OUP.

Orlans, F. Barbara, ed. Field Research Guidelines: Impact on Animal Care & Use Committees. (Illus.). 23p. (Orig.). 1988. pap. text 10.00 (*0-9620700-0-9*) Scientists Ctr.

Orlans, F. Barbara, et al, eds. The Human Use of Animals: Case Studies in Ethical Choice. (Illus.). 352p. 1998. pap. 29.50 (*0-19-511908-8*) OUP.

— The Human Use of Animals: Case Studies in Ethical Choice. (Illus.). 352p. (C). 1998. 59.50 (*0-19-511907-X*) OUP.

Orlans, Harold. Contracting for Atoms. LC 80-58. (Illus.). xvii, 242p. 1980. reprint ed. lib. bdg. 75.00 (*0-313-22287-8*, ORCA, Greenwood Pr) Greenwood.

Orlans, Harold, ed. Adjustment to Adult Hearing Loss. (Illus.). 217p. (C). 1991. reprint ed. pap. 32.95 (*1-879105-47-0*, A056) Thomson Learn.

Orlans, Harold, ed. see Lawrence, T. E.

Orlans, Michael, jt. auth. see Levy, Terry M.

Orlean. Passion. Date not set. pap. write for info. (*0-449-22423-6*) Fawcett.

Orlean, Rene, jt. auth. see Cooke, Barclay.

***Orlean, Susan.** The Orchid Thief. 304p. 2000. pap. 14.00 (*0-449 00371-X*) Ballantine Pub Grp.

Orlean, Susan. The Orchid Thief: A True Story of Beauty & Obsession. LC 98-16829. 284p. 1998. 25.00 (*0-679-44739-3*) Random.

— Saturday Night. 1990. 19.95 (*0-317-99650-9*) Knopf.

— Saturday Night. LC 97-49228. 287p. 1997. reprint ed. lib. bdg. 29.95 (*0-7351-0009-8*) Replica Bks.

Orleans, C. Tracy & Slade, John, eds. Nicotine Addiction: Principles & Management. LC 92-29443. (Illus.). 456p. 1993. text 69.50 (*0-19-506441-0*) OUP.

Orleans, Charlotte-Elisabeth. A Woman's Life in the Court of the Sun King: Letters of Liselotte von der Pfalz, Elisabeth Charlotte, Duchesse d'Orleans, 1652-1722. Forster, Elborg, tr. & intro. by. LC 84-5718. 349p. reprint ed. pap. 108.20 (*0-7837-3391-7*, 204334900008) Bks Demand.

Orleans, Henri P. Around Tonkin & Siam. Pitman, C. B., tr. LC 77-87071. (Illus.). reprint ed. 37.50 (*0-404-16847-7*) AMS Pr.

Orleans, Jacob S. A Study of the Nature of Difficulty. LC 74-177136. (Columbia University. Teachers College. Contributions to Education Ser.: No. 206). reprint ed. 37.50 (*0-404-55206-4*) AMS Pr.

Orleans, Jacob S., jt. auth. see Jacobson, Edmund.

Orleans, Leo A., ed. Chinese Approaches to Family Planning. LC 79-64372. 232p. (gr. 13). 1979. text 66.95 (*0-87332-139-1*) M E Sharpe.

Orleans, Peter & Ellis, William R., eds. Race, Change & Urban Society. LC 70-127992. (Urban Affairs Annual Reviews Ser.: Vol. 5). 640p. reprint ed. pap. 198.40 (*0-608-30980-X*, 202193900026) Bks Demand.

Orlebeke, Charles J. Federal Aid to Chicago. LC 82-74097. 80p. 1983. pap. 8.95 (*0-8157-6649-1*) Brookings.

— New Life at Ground Zero: New York, Home Ownership,

O

An Asterisk (*) at the beginning of an entry indicates that the title is appearing for the first time.

& the Future of American Cities. LC 97-27654. (Illus.). 300p. 1997. 42.95 (*0-914341-52-9*, Rockefeller Inst Pr); pap. 18.95 (*0-914341-51-0*, Rockefeller Inst Pr) Nelson Rockefeller Inst Govt.

Orleck, Annelise. Common Sense & a Little Fire: Women & Working-Class Politics in the United States, 1900-1965. LC 94-24544. (Gender & American Culture Ser.). (Illus.). 410p. 1995. pap. 17.95 (*0-8078-4511-6*); text 49.95 (*0-8078-2199-3*) U of NC Pr.

— The Soviet Jewish Americans. LC 98-22917. (New Americans Ser.). 232p. 1999. 39.95 (*0-313-30074-7*, Greenwood Pr) Greenwood.

Orledge, R. Charles Koechlin (Eighteen Sixty-Seven to Nineteen Fifty) His Life & Works. (Contemporary Music Studies: Vol. 1). xxvi, 458p. 1989. text 83.00 (*3-7186-4898-9*) Gordon & Breach.

Orledge, Robert. Charles Koechlin, 1867-1950: His Life & Works. (Contemporary Music Studies). xxvi, 458p. 1989. pap. text 122.00 (*3-7186-0609-7*, Harwood Acad Pubs) Gordon & Breach.

— Satie Remembered. (Illus.). 272p. 1995. 29.95 (*1-57467-000-X*, Amadeus Pr); pap. 19.95 (*1-57467-001-8*, Amadeus Pr) Timber.

Orleman, Jane. Telling Secrets: An Artist's Journey Through Childhood Trauma. LC 97-51413. (Illus.). 115p. 1998. pap. 15.95 (*0-87868-729-7*, 7297) Child Welfare.

Orlemann, Clinton & Stevenson, Hollis. Cincinnati: Paintings & Sketches. (Illus.). 116p. 1987. reprint ed. 19.95 (*0-9618069-1-5*) C Orlemann.

***Orlemann, Eric.** Building Giant Earthmovers. (Illus.). 128p. 2000. pap. 17.95 (*0-7603-0640-0*, 129793AP, Pub. by MBI Pubg) Motorbooks Intl.

Orlemann, Eric. Caterpillar. LC 98-3913. (Enthusiast Color Ser.). (Illus.). 96p. 1998. pap. 13.95 (*0-7603-0529-3*) Motorbooks Intl.

***Orlemann, Eric.** Caterpillar Chronicle: History of the Greatest Earthmovers. LC 00-25722. (Illus.). 168p. 2000. pap. 29.95 (*0-7603-0667-2*, 129790AP, Pub. by MBI Pubg) Motorbooks Intl.

Orlemann, Eric. Super Duty Earthmovers. LC 98-32302. (Illus.). 128p. 1999. pap. 21.95 (*0-7603-0645-1*, 128066AP) MBI Pubg.

Orlemann, Eric C. Euclid & Terex Earth Moving Machines. LC 97-15493. (Illus.). 160p. 1997. pap. 26.95 (*0-7603-0293-6*) MBI Pubg.

Orlen, Steve. The Bridge of Sighs: Poems. LC 92-8418. (Miami University Press Poetry Ser.). 60p. (C). 1992. 15.95 (*1-881163-00-8*); pap. 9.95 (*1-881163-01-6*) Miami Univ Pr.

— Kisses. LC 97-7287. (Miami University Press Poetry Ser.). 73p. 1997. 19.95 (*1-881163-20-2*); pap. 11.95 (*1-881163-21-0*) Miami Univ Pr.

Orlens, Willehalm Von, see Deutschen Akademie der Wissenschaften Staff & Von Orlens, Willehalm.

Orlet-Schoen, Julie. Jackie Jack the Brave Little Boy. (Illus.). 56p. 1998. 12.95 (*0-9663076-0-7*); pap. 6.95 (*0-9663076-1-5*) Woodland Studios.

Orletsky, David, jt. auth. see Stillion, John.

Orlev, Uri. La Abuela Tejedora (Granny Knitts) (SPA., Illus.). (YA). 1997. pap. 6.99 (*968-16-5442-0*, Pub. by Fondo) Continental Bk.

— Hairy Tuesday. LC 98-50375. (YA). (gr. 6-10). 1999. 15.95 (*1-57255-651-X*) Mondo Pubng.

— The Island on Bird Street, 001. Halkin, Hillel, tr. from HEB. 176p. (J). (gr. 5 up). 1984. 16.00 (*0-395-33887-5*, 5-92515) HM.

— Island on Bird Street. 1984. 11.05 (*0-606-00521-8*, Pub. by Turtleback) Demco.

— The Lady with the Hat. Halkin, Hillel, tr. 192p. (YA). (gr. 7). 1995. 14.95 (*0-395-69957-6*) HM.

— The Lady with the Hat. 1997. 10.09 (*0-606-13562-6*, Pub. by Turtleback) Demco.

***Orlev, Uri.** A Lion for Michael. (Illus.). 32p. (J). (gr. k-4). 2000. 15.95 (*1-58653-172-7*) Mondo Pubng.

Orlev, Uri. Lydia, Queen of Palestine. 1995. 9.09 (*0-606-07817-7*, Pub. by Turtleback) Demco.

— The Man from the Other Side. Halkin, Hillel, tr. LC 90-47898. 144p. (J). (gr. 5 up). 1991. 16.00 (*0-395-53808-4*) HM.

— The Man from the Other Side. Halkin, Hillel, tr. LC 94-30189. (Illus.). 192p. (J). (gr. 1-8). 1995. pap. 4.99 (*0-14-037088-9*, PuffinBks) Peng Put Young Read.

— The Man from the Other Side. 1995. 9.09 (*0-606-07834-7*, Pub. by Turtleback) Demco.

Orley, J. & Kuyken, W., eds. Quality of Life Assessment - International Perspectives: Proceedings of the Joint Meeting Organized by the World Health Organization & the Foundation IPSEN in Paris, July 2-3,1993. LC 94-26934. 1994. 96.95 (*0-387-58205-3*) Spr-Verlag.

Orliac, Catherine & Orliac, Michel. Easter Island: Mystery of the Stone Giants. Bahn, Paul G., tr. (Discoveries Ser.). (Illus.). 144p. 1995. pap. 12.95 (*0-8109-2834-5*, Pub. by Abrams) Time Warner.

Orliac, Michel, jt. auth. see Orliac, Catherine.

Orlic, David & Kanz, Lothar, eds. Hematopoietic Stem Cells: Biology & Transplantation. LC 99-26840. 375p. 1999. text 120.00 (*1-57331-188-X*) NY Acad Sci.

Orlich, Donald C. Designing Successful Grant Proposals. LC 96-9962. 130p. (Orig.). 1996. pap. 20.95 (*0-87120-264-6*, 196022) ASCD.

Orlich, Donald C., et al. Hematopoietic Stem Cells: Biology & Transplantation LC 99-26840. (Annals of the New York Academy of Science Ser.). 1999. write for info. (*1-57331-189-8*) NY Acad Sci.

Orlich, Donald C., et al. Teaching Strategies: A Guide to Better Instruction. 4th ed. (C). 1994. text, teacher ed. 2.66 (*0-669-34961-5*) HM Trade Div.

Orlich, Donald C., et al. Teaching Strategies: A Guide to Better Instruction. 4th ed. 400p. (C). 1994. pap. text 52.36 (*0-669-34960-7*) HM Trade Div.

Orlick, Terry. Coaches Training Manual to Psyching for Sport. LC 85-31837. (Illus.). 103p. (Orig.). 1986. reprint ed. pap. 32.00 (*0-608-07108-0*, 206733500009) Bks Demand.

— Cooperative Sports & Game Book. 144p. 1996. pap. text, per. 15.00 (*0-7872-1928-2*) Kendall-Hunt.

— The Cooperative Sports & Games Book: Challenge Without Competition. LC 77-88771. 1978. pap. 21.00 (*0-394-73494-7*) Pantheon.

— Embracing Your Potential. LC 97-45746. (Illus.). 208p. 1998. pap. 15.95 (*0-88011-831-8*, PORL0831) Human Kinetics.

***Orlick, Terry.** In Pursuit of Excellence: How to Win in Sport & Life Through Mental Training. 3rd rev. ed. LC 00-24335. (Illus.). 242p. 2000. pap. 15.95 (*0-7360-3186-3*) Human Kinetics.

Orlick, Terry. The Second Cooperative Sports & Game Book. 288p. 1996. pap. text, per. 17.00 (*0-7872-1929-0*) Kendall-Hunt.

— The Second Cooperative Sports & Games Book: Over 200 Brand-New Noncompetitive Games for Kids & Adults Both. 255p. 1982. pap. 17.00 (*0-394-74813-1*) NASCO.

Orlick, Terry & Botterill, Carl. Every Kid Can Win. LC 74-19385. 202p. 1975. pap. text 20.95 (*0-88229-471-7*) Burnham Inc.

Orlicz, W. Linear Functional Analysis. Lee Peng Yee, tr. from CHI. (Series in Real Analysis: Vol. 4). 220p. 1992. text 48.00 (*981-02-0853-7*) World Scientific Pub.

Orlie, Melissa A. Living Ethically, Acting Politically. LC 97-14935. 248p. 1997. pap. 16.95 (*0-8014-8472-3*); text 39.95 (*0-8014-3355-X*) Cornell U Pr.

Orlik, Deborah K. The California Ethics Supplement. Kaiser, Janet, ed. 136p. (Orig.). (C). 1995. pap. text 5.95 (*0-9633276-5-8*) Marlen Hill Pub.

— How to Teach. (Orig.). 1996. pap. text 10.95 (*0-9633276-7-4*) Marlen Hill Pub.

Orlik, Deborah K., ed. Ethics for the Legal Assistant. 3rd rev. ed. (Illus.). 360p. (C). 1994. pap. text 20.95 (*0-9633276-2-3*) Marlen Hill Pub.

Orlik, Deborah K., jt. auth. see Kligerman, Susan D.

Orlik, P. P. Introduction to Arrangements. LC 89-14893. (CBMS Regional Conference Series in Mathematics: No. 72). 110p. 1989. pap. 16.00 (*0-8218-0723-4*, CBMS/72) Am Math.

Orlik, P. P. & Terao, H. Arrangements of Hyperplanes. Berger, M. et al, eds. (Grundlehren der Mathematischen Wissenschaften Ser.: Vol. 300). (Illus.). xvii, 325p. 1992. 103.95 (*0-387-55259-6*) Spr-Verlag.

Orlik, Peter, ed. Singularities: Proceedings of Symposia in Pure Mathematics, Pt. 1. LC 83-2529. (Proceedings of Symposia in Pure Mathematics Ser.: Vol. 40). 676p. 1983. text 80.00 (*0-8218-1450-8*, PSPUM/40.1) Am Math.

— Singularities: Proceedings of Symposia in Pure Mathematics, Pt. 2. LC 83-2529. (Proceedings of Symposia in Pure Mathematics Ser.: Vol. 40). 680p. 1983. text 80.00 (*0-8218-1466-4*, PSPUM/40.2) Am Math.

— Singularities: Proceedings of Symposia in Pure Mathematics, Set. LC 83-2529. (Proceedings of Symposia in Pure Mathematics Ser.: Vol. 40). 1356p. 1983. text 138.00 (*0-8218-1443-5*, PSPUM/40) Am Math.

Orlik, Peter B. Broadcast Cable Copywriting. 6th ed. LC 97-9115. 492p. 1997. pap. text 56.00 (*0-205-27143-X*) Allyn.

— Broadcast Cable Copywriting. 6th ed. 128p. (C). 1997. pap. text, teacher ed. write for info. (*0-205-27395-5*, T7395-1) Allyn.

— The Electronic Media: An Introduction to the Profession. 2nd ed. LC 96-45422. (Illus.). 684p. 1997. 52.95 (*0-8138-2438-9*) Iowa St U Pr.

— Electronic Media Criticism: Applied Perspectives. LC 93-43678. (Illus.). 352p. 1994. pap. 42.95 (*0-240-80162-8*, Focal) Buttrwrth-Heinemann.

***Orlik, Peter B.** Electronic Media Criticism: Applied Perspectives. 352p. 1999. pap. 49.95 (*0-8058-3667-5*) L Erlbaum Assocs.

— Electronic Media Criticism: Applied Perspectives. 2nd ed. (A Volume in LEA's Communication Series). 376p. 2000. pap. write for info. (*0-8058-3641-1*) L Erlbaum Assocs.

Orlikoff, James. Quality from the Top. 1990. 39.95 (*0-944496-15-6*) Precept Pr.

Orlikoff, James E. Trustee Guide to Boardroom Basics in Health Care. 1998. pap. text 15.00 (*1-55648-221-3*) AHPI.

— Trustee Guide to Strategic Planning & Information in Health Care. 1998. pap. text 15.95 (*1-55648-223-X*) AHPI.

Orlikoff, James E. & Fifer, William R. Malpractice Prevention & Liability Control for Hospitals. LC 85-4063. vii, 146p. 1981. 24.75 (*0-939450-62-3*) AHPI.

Orlikoff, James E. & Totten, Mary K. The Board's Role in Quality Care: A Practical Guide for Hospital Trustees. LC 90-14512. 157p. (Orig.). 1991. pap. 32.95 (*1-55648-061-X*, 196126) AHPI.

— The Future of Health Care Governance: Redesigning Boards for a New Era. LC 96-852. 1996. pap. 35.00 (*1-55648-160-8*, 196112) AHPI.

Orlikoff, James E., et al. The Trustee Handbook for Health Care Governance. LC 97-31677. 1998. 55.00 (*1-55648-220-5*) AHPI.

Orlikoff, James E., jt. auth. see Pointer, Dennis D.

Orlikoff, James E., jt. auth. see Totten, Mary K.

Orlikoff, Robert F. & Baken, Ronald J. Clinical Speech & Voice Measurement: Laboratory Exercises. LC 93-14930. (Illus.). 488p. (Orig.). (C). 1993. pap. text 55.00 (*1-879105-91-8*, 0354) Thomson Learn.

— Clinical Speech & Voice Measurement Laboratory Exercises: Instructor's Manual. (Illus.). 150p. (Orig.). (C). 1993. pap. text 24.95 (*1-56593-215-3*, 0576) Singular Publishing.

Orlikoff, Robert F., jt. auth. see Baken, R. J.

Orlin, Eric M. Temples, Religion & Politics in the Roman Republic. (Mnemosyne, Supplements Ser.: Vol. 164). (ENG & GRE.). 184p. 1996. 71.00 (*90-04-10708-8*) Brill Academic Pubs.

Orlin, Lena C. Elizabethan Households: An Anthology. (Illus.). 176p. (C). 1995. pap. 24.95 (*0-295-97464-8*) U of Wash Pr.

— Private Matters & Public Culture in Post-Reformation England. (Illus.). 328p. 1994. text 45.00 (*0-8014-2858-0*) Cornell U Pr.

***Orlin, Lena Cowen.** Material London, C. A. 1600. LC 99-54378. (New Cultural Studies). 2000. pap. 26.50 (*0-8122-1721-7*) U of Pa Pr.

Orlin, Louis L. Assyrian Colonies in Cappadocia. (Orig.). 1970. pap. text 67.70 (*3-10-800110-8*) Mouton.

Orlin, Louis L., ed. Janus: Essays in Ancient & Modern Studies. LC 75-18943. 255p. 1975. pap. 10.00 (*0-89824-424-2*) Trillium Pr.

Orling, Merry, tr. see Menotti, Giulia.

Orlinsky, Harry M. Ancient Israel. 2nd ed. (Development of Western Civilization Ser.). (Illus.). 164p. 1960. pap. text 8.95 (*0-8014-9849-X*) Cornell U Pr.

— International Organization for Masoretic Studies, 1972 & 1973 Proceedings & Papers. LC 74-16568. (Society of Biblical Literature, Masoretic Studies). 175p. reprint ed. 54.30 (*0-8357-9573-X*, 201753500007) Bks Demand.

— Israel Exploration Journal Reader, 2 vols., Set. (Library of Biblical Studies). 1982. 99.50 (*0-87068-267-9*) Ktav.

Orlman, Mark. The Teacher's Book of Wit: Quips, Quotes & Anecdotes to Make Learning More Fun. LC 95-61631. 96p. (Orig.). 1996. pap. 9.95 (*0-9634699-7-5*) Wise Owl Bks & Mus.

Orloci, L., jt. auth. see De Patta Pillar.

Orloci, Laszlo. Conapack: Program for Canonical Analysis of Classification Tables. (Ecological Computations Ser.: Vol. 4). 126p. 1991. pap. 30.00 (*90-5103-063-0*, Pub. by SPB Acad Pub) Balogh.

— Ecological Programs for Instructional Computing on the Macintosh. (Ecological Computations Ser.: Vol. 2). x, 131p. 1991. pap. 35.00 (*90-5103-060-6*, Pub. by SPB Acad Pub) Balogh.

— Entropy & Information. (Ecological Computations Ser.: Vol. 3). xiv, 72p. 1991. pap. 30.00 (*90-5103-062-2*, Pub. by SPB Acad Pub) Balogh.

— Multivariate Analysis in Vegetation Research. 1978. text 155.50 (*90-6193-567-9*) Kluwer Academic.

Orloci, Laszlo, et al, eds. Multivariate Methods in Ecological Work. (Statistical Ecology Ser.: Vol. 7). 580p. 1980. 50.00 (*0-89974-004-9*) Intl Co-Op.

Orloci, Laszlo & Wildi, O. Numerical Exploration of Community Patterns. (Ecological Computations Ser.: No. 1). (Illus.). 124p. 1990. 32.00 (*90-5103-037-1*, Pub. by SPB Acad Pub) Balogh.

Orloci, Laszlo, jt. ed. see Feoli, E.

Orlock, Carol. The End of Aging: How Medical Science is Changing Our Concept of Old Age. LC 95-19242. 240p. 1995. 19.95 (*1-55972-319-X*, Birch Ln Pr) Carol Pub Group.

— Inner Time: The Science of Body Clocks & What Makes Us Tick. 208p. 1993. 18.95 (*1-55972-194-4*, Birch Ln Pr) Carol Pub Group.

— Know Your Body Clock. 204p. 1995. pap. 9.95 (*0-8065-1703-4*, Citadel Pr) Carol Pub Group.

***Orloff, Alvin.** I Married an Earthling: A Novel. LC 00-8961. 240p. 2000. pap. 13.95 (*0-916397-64-5*) Manic D Pr.

Orloff, Alvin, jt. auth. see Lake, Bambi.

Orloff, Ann S. The Politics of Pensions: A Comparative Analysis of Britain, Canada, & the United States, 1880-1940. LC 92-50256. (Illus.). 398p. (Orig.). (C). 1993. pap. 19.95 (*0-299-13224-2*); lib. bdg. 60.00 (*0-299-13220-X*) U of Wis Pr.

Orloff, Chet, jt. auth. see Gleason, Norma C.

Orloff, Erica & Baker, JoAnn. The Big Sleep: True Tales & Twisted Trivia about Death. Morrell, Pam, tr. LC 98-61119. (True Tales & Twisted Trivia Ser.: Vol. 1). 192p. 1998. pap. 12.95 (*1-885843-09-7*) Saturn Press.

Orloff, Erica, ed. see Baker, JoAnn.

Orloff, Erica, ed. see Buchbinder, Ligaya H.

Orloff, Erica, ed. see Lampert, Lawrence D.

Orloff, Erica, ed. see Levinson, Kathy.

Orloff, Erica, ed. see Pedder, Nancy Shank.

Orloff, Jack & Berliner, Robert W., eds. Handbook of Physiology: Section 8, Renal Physiology. (American Physiological Society Book). (Illus.). 1090p. 1988. text 130.00 (*0-19-520683-5*) OUP.

Orloff, Jon, ed. Handbook of High Resolution Charged Particle Optics. LC 96-49553. 528p. 1997. boxed set 149.95 (*0-8493-2513-7*) CRC Pr.

Orloff, Judith. Dr. Judith Orloff's Guide to Intuitive Healing: Five Steps to Physical, Emotional & Sexual Wellness. LC 99-42499. 320p. 2000. 24.00 (*0-8129-3097-5*, Times Bks) Crown Pub Group.

***Orloff, Judith.** The Life Awareness Manual: A Simple Recipe for Living Life. rev. ed. 144p. 2000. 19.95 (*0-8129-3270-6*, Times Bks) Crown Pub Group.

Orloff, Judith. Second Sight. 1997. mass mkt. write for info. (*0-446-60422-4*) Warner Bks.

Orloff, M. Judith. Second Sight. 384p. 1997. mass mkt. 14.95 (*0-446-67335-8*, Pub. by Warner Bks) Little.

Orloff, Nicolas, tr. Horologion: A Primer for Elementary Village Schools. Incl. Ferial Menaion, or the Book of Services for the Twelve Great Festivals & the New Year's Day, 4 vols. Ferial Menaion, or the Book of Services for the Twelve Great Festivals & the New Year's Day., 4 vols. 30.00 (*0-404-04850-1*); General Menaion, or the Book of Services Common to the Festivals of Our Lord Jesus Christ, of the Holy Virgin, & of the Different Orders of Saints. Octoechos: or The Book of the Eight Tones. Bk. 1. Ferial Menaion, or the Book of Services for the Twelve Great Festivals & the New Year's Day., 4 vols. 30.00 (*0-404-04851-X*); Bk. 2. Ferial Menaion, or the Book of Services for the Twelve Great Festivals & the New Year's Day., 4 vols. 30.00 (*0-404-04852-8*); Bk. 3. Ferial Menaion, or the Book of Services for the Twelve Great Festivals & the New Year's Day., 4 vols. 30.00 (*0-404-04853-6*); Bk. 4. Ferial Menaion, or the Book of Services for the Twelve Great Festivals & the New Year's Day., 4 vols. 30.00 (*0-404-04854-4*); reprint ed. write for info. (*0-318-50613-0*) AMS Pr.

Orloff, Steve, ed. Intermountain Alfalfa Production. LC 94-61790. 144p. 1997. pap. 18.00 (*1-879906-24-4*, 3366) ANR Pubns CA.

Orloff, Tracey M. & Tymann, Barbara. Rural Health: An Evolving System of Accessible Services. 293p. 1996. pap. 33.00 (*1-55877-250-2*) Natl Governor.

Orloff, Tracy M., et al. Medicaid Cost-Based Reimbursement for State & Local Health Department Clinic Services. Glass, Karen, ed. 97p. (Orig.). 1993. pap. text 15.00 (*1-55877-222-7*) Natl Governor.

Orlofsky, Myron, jt. auth. see Orlofsky, Patsy.

Orlofsky, Patsy & Orlofsky, Myron. Quilts in America. (Illus.). 368p. 1992. 65.00 (*1-55859-334-9*) Abbeville Pr.

Orlosky, Donald E. Society, Schools & Teacher Preparation. LC 88-80932. 1988. pap. 6.25 (*0-89333-050-7*) Assn Tchr Ed.

Orlosky, Donald E., et al. Educational Administration Today. 368p. (C). 1990. text 57.00 (*0-675-20110-1*, Merrill Coll) P-H.

Orlov, D. S. Humic Substance of Soils & General Theory of Humification. Kothekar, V. S., tr. from RUS. (Russian Translation Ser.: No. 111). (Illus.). 323p. (C). 1995. text 123.00 (*90-6191-955-X*, Pub. by A A Balkema) Ashgate Pub Co.

— Humus Acids of Soils. Kothekar, V. S., tr. from RUS. 388p. (C). 1985. text 110.00 (*90-6191-453-1*, Pub. by A A Balkema) Ashgate Pub Co.

— Soil Chemistry. Kothekar, V. S., ed. (Russian Translation Ser.: No. 92). (RUS., Illus.). 402p. (C). 1992. text 123.00 (*90-6191-915-0*, Pub. by A A Balkema) Ashgate Pub Co.

Orlov, Darlene, et al. What Every Manager Needs to Know about Sexual Harassment. LC 98-28708. 240p. 1999. 24.95 (*0-8144-0492-8*) AMACOM.

Orlov, Georgi. Black Knights' Tango. 1998. pap. text 19.95 (*0-7134-8349-0*, Pub. by B T B) Branford.

Orlov, Henry, ed. Vblizi Vestnikov: Near the Messengers - Vblizi Vestnikov Russian. LC 88-91215. (RUS., Illus.). 325p. (Orig.). 1988. pap. 15.00 (*0-929647-00-9*) H A Frager & Co.

Orlov, Henry, tr. see Perelman, N.

Orlov, Paul A. An American Tragedy: Perils of the Self Seeking "Success" LC 97-6139. (Illus.). 248p. 1998. 41.50 (*0-8387-5350-7*) Bucknell U Pr.

Orlov, S. B., ed. English-Russian Dictionary of Networks & Network Technologies. 301p. (C). 1997. pap. 24.00 (*0-8285-5505-2*) Firebird NY.

Orlov, Vladimir N. Letters from Russia. (Illus.). 48p. (Orig.). 1993. 5.95 (*1-878116-19-3*) JVC Bks.

— Russian-English-German-French Mathematics Dictionary. 300p. (C). 1987. 90.00 (*0-7855-5057-7*, Pub. by Collets) St Mut.

Orlov, Vladimir N. & Bulatova, N. S. Population Radiation Cytogenetics of Animals, Vol. 3. iv, 62p. 1989. text 59.00 (*3-7186-4882-2*) Gordon & Breach.

Orlov, Y. I., jt. auth. see Kravtsov, Y. A.

Orlov, Yu I., jt. auth. see Kravtsov, Yurii A.

Orlova, Aleksandra A. Musorgsky's Days & Works: A Biography in Documents. Guenther, Roy J., ed. & tr. by. LC 82-4826. (Russian Music Studies: No. 4). 719p. reprint ed. pap. 200.00 (*0-8357-1324-5*, 207043600089) Bks Demand.

Orlove, Ben. In My Father's Study. LC 94-37406. (Singular Lives: The Iowa Series in North American Autobiography). (Illus.). 344p. 1995. pap. 16.95 (*0-87745-491-4*); text 39.95 (*0-87745-490-6*) U of Iowa Pr.

Orlove, Benjamin S., ed. The Allure of the Foreign: Imported Goods in Postcolonial Latin America. LC 96-45899. 240p. (C). 1997. text 44.50 (*0-472-10664-3*, 10664) U of Mich Pr.

Orlove, Benjamin S. & Custred, Glynn, eds. Land & Power in Latin America: Agrarian Economics & Social Process in the Andes. LC 79-26598. 258p. 1980. 39.50 (*0-8419-0476-6*) Holmes & Meier.

Orlovski, Sergei A. Calculus of Properties, Fuzzy Sets, & Decisions. LC 94-2015. 1994. 75.00 (*0-89864-066-0*) Allerton Pr.

Orlovski, Sergei A., jt. ed. see Kacprzyk, Janusz.

Orlovsky, Archimandrite D. New Confessors of Russia Vol. I: Nizhny-Novgorod Province. LC 98-86309. (Illus.). 430p. 1998. pap. 19.00 (*1-887904-34-4*) St Herman Pr.

Orlovsky, Daniel T. The Limits of Reform: The Ministry of Internal Affairs in Imperial Russia, 1802-1881. LC 80-18868. (Russian Research Center Studies: No. 81). 311p. 1981. reprint ed. pap. 96.50 (*0-7837-4708-X*, 205906000002) Bks Demand.

Orlovsky, Daniel T., ed. Beyond Soviet Studies. 400p. (Orig.). 1995. pap. text 24.95 (*0-943875-69-2*) Johns Hopkins.

— Social & Economic History of Prerevolutionary Russia. LC 91-44282. (Articles on Russian & Soviet History, 1500-1991 Ser.: Vol. 4). 696p. 1992. text 35.00 (*0-8153-0561-3*) Garland.

Orlovsky, Grigori, et al. Neuronal Control of Locomotion: From Mollusc to Man. LC 99-15701. (Illus.). 336p. 1999. text 59.50 (*0-19-852405-6*) OUP.

An Asterisk (*) at the beginning of an entry indicates that the title is appearing for the first time.

O

An Asterisk (*) at the beginning of an entry indicates that the title is appearing for the first time.

Ormond, J. Will & Rose, Lucy A. Preaching Eyes for Listening Ears: Sermons & Commentary for Preachers & Students of Preaching. LC 98-48038. 184p. 1999. pap. 15.95 (*0-7880-1320-3*) CSS OH.

Ormond, Mark. Craig Rubadoux: Works on Paper, 1962-1984. LC 85-80749. (Illus.). 48p. (Orig.). 1985. pap. 10.00 (*0-916758-20-6*) Ringling Mus Art.

— Joel Shapiro. LC 86-82010. (Illus.). 38p. 1986. pap. 10.00 (*0-916758-22-2*) Ringling Mus Art.

— Robert Rauschenberg: Works from the Salvage Ser. LC 85-60057. (Illus.). 20p. 1985. pap. 3.00 (*0-916758-17-6*) Ringling Mus Art.

Ormond, Mark, ed. see Conforti, Michael, et al.

Ormond, Richard. John Singer Sargent: The Early Portraits, Vol. 1. LC 97-27380. (The Complete Paintings Ser.: Vol. 1). 278p. 1997. 60.00 (*0-300-07245-7*) Yale U Pr.

Ormond, Richard, et al. Frederic, Lord Leighton: Eminent Victorian Artist. (Illus.). 256p. 1996. 49.50 (*0-8109-3578-3*, Pub. by Abrams) Time Warner.

Ormond, Richard, jt. auth. see Kemp, Peter.

Ormond, Richard, jt. ed. see Kilmurray, Elaine.

Ormond, Riette & Ormond, George. Unique Program for Staying Healthy, Young, & Trim. 44p. (Orig.). 1982. pap. 6.95 (*0-9620518-0-2*) Ormond Assocs.

Ormond, Riette S., jt. auth. see Ormond, George.

Ormond, Roger. A Dip into Murder. large type ed. 304p. 1994. pap. 16.99 (*0-7089-7570-4*) Ulverscroft.

Ormond, Rupert F., et al, eds. Marine Biodiversity: Patterns & Processes. LC 96-9334. (Illus.). 472p. (C). 1998. text 80.00 (*0-521-55222-2*) Cambridge U Pr.

Ormond, Rupert F., jt. auth. see Bemert, Gunnar.

Ormond, Suzanne. Recipes from an Old New Orleans Kitchen, 1. LC 88-12478. 100p. 1999. pap. 7.95 (*1-56554-673-3*) Pelican.

Ormond, Suzanne, et al. Favorite New Orleans Recipes. LC 78-18841. 100p. 1979. spiral bd. 6.95 (*0-88289-198-7*) Pelican.

Ormonde, Jimmy. Tap Dancing at a Glance. LC 96-85686. (Illus.). 96p. (Orig.). 1996. reprint ed. pap. 9.95 (*1-55709-435-7*) Applewood.

Ormondroyd, Albert, III. Crazy Al's Cook Book & Party Book. LC 83-51789. (Illus.). 136p. 1984. pap. 8.95 (*0-915949-10-5*) Whitinsville Bk.

Ormondroyd, Edward. Broderick. LC 77-83752. (Illus.). (J). (gr. k-3). 1969. lib. bdg. 4.77 (*0-686-86580-4*) HM.

***Ormondroyd, Edward.** David & the Phoenix. LC 00-104408. (Illus.). iii, 173p. (YA). 2000. write for info. (*1-930900-00-7*) Purple Hse Pr.

Ormondroyd, Edward. Theodore's Rival. LC 76-156876. (Illus.). 40p. (J). (ps-3). 1971. lib. bdg. 4.59 (*0-87466-001-7*) HM.

Ormont, Louis. The Group Therapy Experience: From Theory to Practice. 5th ed. 256p. 1991. text 24.95 (*0-312-07036-5*) St Martin.

Ormos, Maria. From Padua to the Trianon, 1918-1920. 409p. 1990. pap. 75.00 (*963-05-5328-7*, Pub. by Akade Kiado) St Mut.

— From Padua to Trianon, 1918-1920. 1991. text 62.00 (*0-88033-195-X*, Pub. by East Eur Monographs) Col U Pr.

Ormrod. Human Learning. 3rd ed. LC 98-21670. 557p. 1998. 71.00 (*0-13-875684-8*) P-H.

Ormrod, David & North, Michael, eds. Art Markets in Europe, 1400-1800. LC 98-18916. 288p. 1998. text 83.95 (*1-84014-630-3*, N8600.A737, Pub. by Ashgate Pub) Ashgate Pub Co.

Ormrod, Jeanne E. Using Your Head: An Owner's Manual. LC 89-30780. (Illus.). 224p. 1989. 24.95 (*0-87778-216-4*) Educ Tech Pubns.

Ormrod, Jeanne Ellis. Educational Psychology: Developing Learners. 3rd ed. LC 99-29741. 773p. 1999. pap. text 69.00 (*0-13-013648-4*) S&S Trade.

Ormrod, John & Francis, Dennis, eds. Molecular & Cell Biology of the Plant Cell Cycle: Proceedings of a Meeting Held at Lancaster University, 9-10 April 1992. LC 92-36385. 236p. (C). 1993. text 169.50 (*0-7923-1767-X*) Kluwer Academic.

Ormrod, John, tr. see Schacherl, Lillian.

Ormrod, Sarah J., ed. Cambridge Contributions. LC 98-21478. 250p. (C). 1999. 59.95 (*0-521-59243-7*); pap. 22.95 (*0-521-59738-2*) Cambridge U Pr.

Ormrod, Susan, jt. auth. see Cockburn, Cynthia.

Ormrod, W. M. Political Life in Medieval England, 1300-1450. LC 95-8258. (British History in Perspective Ser.). 1995. text 45.00 (*0-312-12722-7*) St Martin.

***Ormrod, W. M.** Reign of Edward III. (Illus.). 224p. 1999. 34.99 (*0-7524-1773-8*, Pub. by Tempus Pubng) Arcadia Publng.

Ormrod, W. M., jt. auth. see Musson, Anthony.

Ormsbee, Helen. Backstage with Actors. LC 70-84522. (Illus.). 1972. 29.95 (*0-405-08830-2*) Ayer.

— Backstage with Actors, from the Time of Skakespeare to the Present Day. (Illus.). 343p. 1977. 23.95 (*0-8369-1934-3*) Ayer.

Ormsby, Alison. The Prairie. LC 97-39444. (Ecosystems of North America Ser.). (Illus.). (YA). (gr. 6 up). 1998. lib. bdg. 27.07 (*0-7614-0897-5*, Benchmark NY) Marshall Cavendish.

Ormsby, Charles C., Jr. & Salafia, Philip M., Jr. 9-1-1 Liability: A Call for Answers. LC 97-75907. (Illus.). 208p. 1998. 69.95 (*0-9661395-0-X*) PowerPhone.

Ormsby, Eric L. Bavarian Shrine & Other Poems. 62p. (C). 1990. pap. text 12.00 (*1-55022-107-8*, Pub. by ECW) Genl Dist Srvs.

— Coastlines. 48p. (C). 1992. pap. 12.00 (*1-55022-176-0*, Pub. by ECW) Genl Dist Srvs.

— For a Modest God: New & Selected Poems. LC 96-35472. 160p. 1997. 20.00 (*0-8021-1607-8*, Grove) Grove-Atltic.

— Theodicy in Islamic Thought: The Dispute over al-Ghazali's "Best of All Possible Worlds" LC 84-3396. 326p. 1984. reprint ed. pap. 101.10 (*0-608-06471-8*, 206676800009) Bks Demand.

Ormsby, Eric L., ed. Moses Maimonides & His Time. LC 88-18910. (Studies in Philosophy & the History of Philosophy: No. 19). 188p. 1989. reprint ed. pap. 58.30 (*0-7837-9105-4*, 204990700004) Bks Demand.

Ormsby, Frank. The Ghost Train. 54p. 1997. pap. 12.95 (*1-85235-172-1*) Dufour.

— A Northern Spring. 54p. 1986. pap. 12.95 (*0-904011-92-5*) Dufour.

— Poets from the North of Ireland. 312p. 1990. pap. 22.00 (*0-85640-444-6*, Pub. by Blackstaff Pr) Dufour.

— A Store of Candles. 58p. 1986. pap. 12.95 (*0-904011-98-4*) Dufour.

Ormsby, Frank, ed. The Collected Poems of John Hewitt. 708p. 1991. 50.00 (*0-85640-459-4*, Pub. by Blackstaff Pr) Dufour.

— The Collected Poems of John Hewitt. 708p. 1993. pap. 35.00 (*0-85640-494-2*, Pub. by Blackstaff Pr) Dufour.

— Northern Windows: An Anthology of Ulster Autobiography. 256p. 1987. 22.00 (*0-85640-375-X*, Pub. by Blackstaff Pr) Dufour.

Ormsby, Gregory & Cook, Wendy, eds. The Big Green Book: Northwest Music Industry Directory & Guide, 1993. 5th ed. (Illus.). 214p. 1993. pap. 19.95 (*0-9632474-5-X*) NW Intl Enter.

Ormsby, John R., Jr., jt. auth. see Johnson, James A.

Ormsby, Lawrence, illus. see Clark, Tim W.

Ormsby-Lennon, Hugh, jt. ed. see Roberts, Marie.

Ormsby, Margaret, ed. A Pioneer Gentlewoman in British Columbia: The Recollections of Susan Allison. (Pioneers of British Columbia Ser.). (Illus.). 196p. 1976. pap. 15.95 (*0-7748-0392-4*) U of Wash Pr.

Ormsby, Michael. Preparing Students for CLAS (California Learning Assessment Systems) Reading & Writing-Elementary. 213p. 1994. pap. text 18.95 (*0-9643281-0-0*) Catalysts for Lrning.

Ormsby, R. H. The Angels of Autumn. LC 96-92121. 432p. (Orig.). 1996. pap. 6.50 (*0-9651362-5-6*) Chessie Pub.

Ormsby, Ralph. A Man of Vision, Francis H. McLean, 1869-1945. LC 75-99972. 158p. reprint ed. pap. 49.00 (*0-608-18325-3*, 203160100075) Bks Demand.

Ormsby, Waterman L. The Butterfield Overland Mail. Wright, Lyle H. & Bynum, Josephine M., eds. LC 91-22092. (Illus.). 194p. 1998. reprint ed. pap. 12.95 (*0-87328-095-4*, Pub. by Huntington Lib) A Schwartz & Co.

***Ormsten, Franklin D.** A Primer on Securities Arbitration Law for Investors, Brokers & Attorneys. LC 99-93322. 115p. 1999. pap. 49.99 (*0-9673982-0-7*) Cadrey Pubg.

Ormulum. The Ormulum, with the Notes & Glossary of Dr. Robert Meadows White, 2 vols. Holt, Robert, ed. LC 72-178548. reprint ed. 85.00 (*0-404-56654-5*) AMS Pr.

***Orna, Elizabeth.** Practical Information Policies. 2nd ed. LC 98-40510. 200p. 1999. 87.95 (*0-566-07693-4*, Pub. by Gower) Ashgate Pub Co.

Orna, Elizabeth. Practical Information Policies: How to Manage Information Flow in Organizations. 263p. 1991. text 76.95 (*0-566-03632-0*, Pub. by Gower) Ashgate Pub Co.

Orna, Elizabeth & Pettitt, Charles. Information Handling in Museums. fac. ed. LC 81-140240. 198p. 1980. reprint ed. pap. 61.40 (*0-7837-8201-2*, 204795900008) Bks Demand.

Orna, Elizabeth & Stevens, Graham. Managing Information for Research. LC 95-13767. 160p. 1995. pap. 27.95 (*0-335-19397-8*) OpUniv Pr.

Orna, Mary V., ed. Archaeological Chemistry: Organic, Inorganic, & Biochemical Analysis. LC 96-4812. (ACS Symposium Ser.: No. 625). (Illus.). 472p. 1996. text 115.00 (*0-8412-3395-0*, Pub. by Am Chemical) OUP.

Orna, Mary V., et al, eds. Sourcebook Vol. 1: Hard Copy Version. (Illus.). (Orig.). (C). 1994. pap. text. write for info. (*0-9637747-2-7*) Chemsource.

— Sourcebook Vol. 2: Hard Copy Version. (Illus.). (Orig.). (C). 1994. pap. text. write for info. (*0-9637747-3-5*) Chemsource.

— Sourcebook Vol. 3: Hard Copy Version. (Illus.). (Orig.). (C). 1994. pap. text. write for info. (*0-9637747-4-3*) Chemsource.

— Sourcebook Vol. 4: Hard Copy Version. (Illus.). (Orig.). (C). 1994. pap. text. write for info. (*0-9637747-5-1*) Chemsource.

— Sourcebook Vols. 1-4: Hardcopy Version Overall Bound Volumes, 4 Vols., Set. (Illus.). 2100p. (Orig.). (C). 1994. pap. text 70.00 (*0-9637747-1-9*) Chemsource.

Orna, Mary V. & Goodstein, Madeline. Chemistry & Artists' Colors. (Illus.). 426p. (C). 1993. pap. text 22.00 (*0-9637747-0-0*) Chemsource.

Orna, Mary V. & James, M. Lynn, eds. Guidebook to Pre-Service Use of Chemsource. 95p. (Orig.). (C). 1994. pap. text 15.00 (*0-9637747-7-8*) Chemsource.

Orna, Mary V., jt. ed. see Stock, John T.

Orna, Wlizabeth & Pettitt, Charles. Information Management in Museums. 2nd ed. LC 97-17222. 290p. 1998. text 87.95 (*0-566-07776-0*, Pub. by Gower) Ashgate Pub Co.

Ornas, Anders H. & Dahl, Gudrun. Responsible Man: The Atmaan Beja of Northeastern Sudan. (Stockholm Studies in Social Anthropology). 195p. (Orig.). 1991. pap. 47.50 (*91-7146-905-2*) Coronet Bks.

Ornato, Joseph P., ed. Cardiovascular Emergencies. LC 86-17130. (Clinics in Emergency Medicine Ser.: No. 9). (Illus.). 272p. reprint ed. pap. 84.40 (*0-7837-6250-X*, 204596200010) Bks Demand.

Ornato, Joseph P. & Gonzalez, Edgar R., eds. Drug Therapy in Emergency Medicine. (Illus.). 607p. 1990. text 78.00 (*0-443-08599-4*) Church.

Ornatowski, Cezar, jt. ed. see Staples, Katherine.

Ornauer, H., ed. Images of the World in the Year Two Thousand: A Comparative Ten-Nation Study. (Publications of the European Coordination Centre for Research & Documentation). 719p. 1976. text 103.10 (*90-279-7551-5*) Mouton.

***Orndorf, Brenda.** Whisperings. 1999. pap. write for info. (*1-58235-251-8*) Watermrk Pr.

***Orndorf, Brenda M.** Whisperings. 94p. 2000. 17.95 (*0-7541-1329-9*, Pub. by Minerva Pr) Unity Dist.

***Orndorff, Beverly.** Magical Acts, Hypercubes & Pie: Meanderings Through Science, Medicine & Mathematics. Witschey, Walter R. T., ed. 180p. 1999. write for info. (*0-9674451-0-8*) Science Mus VA.

Orndorff, Christopher N. & Syal, Ashin. Investing Local Government Funds: A Guide for Municipal Finance Professionals, Board Members & Investment Managers. LC 96-40003. 240p. 1997. 55.00 (*0-7863-0816-8*, Irwn Prfssnl) McGraw-Hill Prof.

Orndorff, John C. Prince Michael & the Dragon (A True Story) LC 99-65997. (Illus.). vi, 87p. (J). (gr. 5-8). 1998. pap. 5.95 (*1-893213-00-5*) Amulet.

Orndorff, Kata, ed. Bi Lives: Bisexual Women Reveal Their Stories. 1999. pap. 14.95 (*1-884365-09-4*) See Sharp Pr.

Orndorff, Mary. Messages of Despair, Messages of Hope: A Guide to the Recovery from Eating Disorders. 70p. 1990. 8.95 (*0-9636536-0-1*) Garkakee.

***Orndorff, Richard L., et al.** Geology Underfoot in Central Nevada. (Geology Underfoot Ser.). (Illus.). 272p. 2000. pap. 16.00 (*0-87842-418-0*) Mountain Pr.

Ornduff, Donald R. The First Forty-Nine. LC 81-84498. (Illus.). 280p. 1981. 12.95 (*0-913504-73-4*) Lowell Pr.

Ornduff, Robert. Introduction to California Plant Life. (California Natural History Guides Ser.: No. 35). (Illus.). 1974. pap. 13.95 (*0-520-02735-3*, Pub. by U CA Pr) Cal Prin Full Svc.

Orne, Martin T. On the Social Psychology of the Psychological Experiment: With Particular Reference to Demand Characteristics & Their Implications. (Irvington Reprint Series in Psychology). (C). 1991. reprint ed. pap. text 1.30 (*0-8290-2624-X*, Y-678) Irvington.

Ornea, Liviu, jt. auth. see Dragomir, Sorin.

***Ornea, Z.** The Romanian Extreme Right: The 1930's. 480p. 1999. 58.00 (*0-88033-430-4*, 532, Pub. by East Eur Monographs) Col U Pr.

Ornelas, ed. see Singer, Dan.

Ornelas, Bernada, ed. see Stowe, Gayle.

Ornelas, Kriemhild Conee, jt. ed. see Kiple, Kenneth F.

Ornelas, Michael. Between the Conquests: Readings in Early Chicano History. 2nd ed. 290p. (C). 1998. per. 31.25 (*0-7872-4764-2*, 41476402) Kendall-Hunt.

— Beyond 1848: Readings. 2nd ed. LC 99-193687. 318p. (C). 1999. per. 39.95 (*0-7872-5691-9*, 41569101) Kendall-Hunt.

Ornelas, Michael R. Between the Conquests: Readings in Early Chicano History. 288p. (C). 1996. pap. text, per. 22.95 (*0-7872-2368-9*) Kendall-Hunt.

Ornelas-Struve, Carole M. & Coulter, Fredrick L. Memphis, 1800-1900, 3 vols., set. Hassell, Joan, ed. LC 81-17920. (Illus.). 384p. 1982. pap., boxed set 24.95 (0-941684-03-2) Powers Pub.

A must for scholars & American history buffs, Memphis: 1800 - 1900 is an historical work that captures the indomitable spirit of a freewheeling century. This richly illustrated set of books traces the turbulent birth & growth of Memphis: its roots--its philosophes--its politics--its triumphs & its tragedies. From raw frontier, to the tragic Civil War years, to renewal, Memphis emerges with exciting courage & dignity. Full of information & insight, the city comes alive with an easy fluency of style & delightful glimpses of everyday life. To order your 3-volume set of Memphis: 1800 - 1900, please send a check or money order for $21.95 (plus applicable shipping & handling*) to: Powers Publishing, P O Box 172345, Memphis TN 38187-2345 *Shipping & Handling US=$2.75, Canada=$3.25, International=$4.50. Note: Bookstores, libraries & schools receive a 30 discount & purchase orders accepted. www.powerspublishing.com, e-mail: info@powerspublishing.com *Publisher Paid Annotation.*

— Memphis, 1800-1900, 3 Bks. in slipcase, Vol. I: Years of Challenge, 1800-1860. Hassell, Joan, ed. LC 81-17920. (Illus.). 384p. 1982. pap. 9.95 (*0-941684-00-8*) Powers Pub.

— Memphis, 1800-1900, 3 Bks. in slipcase, Vol. II: Years of Crisis, 1860-1870. Hassell, Joan, ed. LC 81-17920. (Illus.). 384p. 1982. pap. 9.95 (*0-941684-01-6*) Powers Pub.

— Memphis, 1800-1900, 3 Bks. in slipcase, Vol. III: Years of Courage, 1870-1900. Hassell, Joan, ed. LC 81-17920. (Illus.). 384p. 1982. pap. 9.95 (*0-941684-02-4*) Powers Pub.

Orner, Christian K., jt. ed. see Chapin, F. Stuart, III.

Orner, Eric. Ethan Green: Exposed. 144p. 1999. pap. 10.95 (*0-312-20040-4*) St Martin.

— Ethan Green Chronicles: His Still Unfabulous Life & Times. LC 96-9458. (Illus.). 128p. 1997. pap. 10.95 (*0-312-14742-2*) St Martin.

— The Mostly Unfabulous Social Life of Ethan Green. (Illus.). 128p. 1992. pap. 8.95 (*0-312-07635-5*) St Martin.

— The Seven Deadly Sins of Love: The Still Unfabulous Social Life of Ethan Green. 128p. 1994. pap. 8.95 (*0-312-10539-8*) St Martin.

Ornest, Noemi, ed. see Bonnick, Bertrand.

Ornig, Joseph. My Last Chance to Be a Boy: Theodore Roosevelt's South American Expedition of 1913-1914. (Illus.). 320p. 1994. 29.95 (*0-8117-1098-X*) Stackpole.

Ornig, Joseph R. My Last Chance to Be a Boy: Theodore Roosevelt's South American Expedition of 1913-1914. LC 97-51138. (Illus.). 320p. 1998. pap. 16.95 (*0-8071-2271-8*) La State U Pr.

Ornish, Dean. Dr. Dean Ornish's Program for Reversing Heart Disease Without Drugs Or Surgery. LC 91-91878. (Illus.). 631p. 1992. pap. 15.00 (*0-345-37353-7*) Ballantine Pub Grp.

— Dr. Dean Ornish's Program for Reversing Heart Disease: The Only System Scientifically Proven to Reverse Heart Disease Without Drugs or Surgery. LC 95-94897. 638p. 1996. mass mkt. 6.99 (*0-8041-1038-7*) Ivy Books.

— Eat More, Weigh Less: Dr. Dean Ornish's Life Choice Program for Losing Weight Safely While Eating Abundantly. Brown, Shirley, ed. 480p. 1997. mass mkt. 6.99 (*0-06-109627-X*, Pub. by Harper SF) HarpC.

— Eat More Weigh Less: Dr. Dean Ornish's Life Choice Program for Losing Weight Safely While Eating Abundantly. LC 92-53326. 448p. 1994. pap. 15.00 (*0-06-092545-0*, Perennial) HarperTrade.

Ornish, Dean. Eat More, Weigh Less: Ornish,&Dean. abr. ed. 1993. audio 12.00 (*1-55994-715-2*, CPN 1959) HarperAudio.

— Everyday Cooking WIth Dr. Dean Ornish: Ornish,&Dean. abr. ed. 1996. audio 12.00 (*0-694-51627-9*, CPN 10066) HarperAudio.

Ornish, Dean. Love & Survival: The Scientific Basis for the Healing Power of Intimacy. 320p. 1999. pap. 14.00 (*0-06-093020-9*) HarpC.

***Ornish, Dean.** Love & Survival: The Scientific Basis for the Healing Power of Intimacy. abr. ed. 1998. audio 18.00 (*0-694-51875-1*, CPN2685) HarperAudio.

Ornish, Dean. Love & Survival: The Scientific Basis for the Healing Power of Intimacy. large type ed. LC 98-26645. 450p. 1998. 26.95 (*0-7862-1550-X*) Thorndike Pr.

— Stress, Diet, & Your Heart. 398p. 1984. mass mkt. 6.99 (*0-451-17113-6*, ROC) NAL.

Ornish, Dean, et al. Everyday Cooking with Dean Ornish: 150 Easy, Low-Fat, High-Flavor Recipes. LC 95-47392. 368p. 1997. pap. 16.00 (*0-06-092811-5*, Perennial) HarperTrade.

Ornish, Natalie. Pioneer Jewish Texans: Their Impact on Texas & American History for 400 Years, 1590-1990. (Illus.). 336p. 1989. 39.95 (*0-9620755-0-7*) TX Heritage Pr.

Ornish, Natalie & Ehrenberg, Herman. Ehrenberg: Goliad Survivor, Old West Explorer. LC 97-23996. (Illus.). 424p. 1997. 29.95 (*0-9620755-1-5*) TX Heritage Pr.

Ornitz, Barbara E. Oil Crisis in Our Oceans: Coral: Roadkill on the Petrohighway. LC 97-107751. (Illus.). 320p. (Orig.). 1996. pap. 30.00 (*0-9638385-1-2*) Tageh Pr.

Ornitz, Hilda, jt. auth. see Knapp, Terence.

Ornitz, Laurel, ed. see Allen, Sam.

Ornitz, Samuel. Alrightniks Row: The Making of a Professional Jew, Haunch, Paunch & Jowl. LC 85-40730. (Masterworks of Modern Jewish Writing Ser.). 323p. 1986. reprint ed. 18.95 (*0-910129-49-5*); reprint ed. pap. 9.95 (*0-910129-46-0*) Wiener Pubs Inc.

Ornoy, Asher, ed. Animal Models of Human Related Calcium Metabolic Disorders. LC 95-18262. 256p. 1995. boxed set 174.95 (*0-8493-6024-2*, 6024) CRC Pr.

***Ornsby, Tim & Alvi, Jonell.** Extending ArcView GIS: With Network Analyst, Spatial Analyst, & 3D Analyst. 1999. pap. 49.95 incl. cd-rom (*1-879102-05-6*) ESR Inst.

Ornstein. Campaign Finance: An Illustrated Guide. LC 98-129309. (Illus.). 1997. pap. 9.95 (*0-8447-7108-2*) Am Enterprise.

— Found Educ Tsts, 6 vols. (C). 1996. pap., teacher ed. 11.96 (*0-395-77105-6*) HM.

— Foundations of Education, 5 vols. (C). 1992. text 66.36 (*0-395-63782-1*) HM.

— Life of the Mind. 2001. write for info. (*0-15-100423-4*) Harcourt.

— Strategies for Effective Teaching. 2nd ed. 1995. teacher ed. 12.18 (*0-697-25093-8*, WCB McGr Hill) McGrw-H Hghr Educ.

***Ornstein & Waxman.** Secondary & Middle School Methods. 1998. pap. text 40.00 (*0-205-26376-3*) P-H.

Ornstein, Allan C. Strategies for Effective Teaching. 2nd ed. 512p. (C). 1994. text. write for info. (*0-697-24415-6*) Brown & Benchmark.

— Strategies for Effective Teaching. 3rd ed. LC 99-34637. 576p. 1999. pap. 45.93 (*0-697-29885-X*) McGraw.

Ornstein, Allan C. Teaching: Theory into Practice. LC 94-27202. 400p. 1994. pap. text 66.00 (*0-205-15778-5*) Allyn.

Ornstein, Allan C. Teaching: Theory into Practice. (C). 1994. pap., teacher ed. write for info. (*0-205-16606-7*, H6606-1) Allyn.

— Teaching in a New Era. 1976. pap. text 6.80 (*0-87563-110-X*) Stipes.

Ornstein, Allan C. & Behar-Horenstein, Linda S. Contemporary Issues in Curriculum. 2nd ed. LC 97-48490. 456p. 1998. pap. text 73.00 (*0-205-28323-3*) Allyn.

Ornstein, Allan C. & Behar, Unda S., eds. Our Evolving Curriculum Pt. I: A Special Issue of the Peabody Journal of Education, Vol. 69, No. 3, 1996. 1996. reprint ed. pap. 20.00 (*0-8058-9897-2*) L Erlbaum Assocs.

Ornstein, Allan C. & Hunkins, Francis P. Curriculum. 3rd ed. LC 97-24347. 416p. 1997. 79.00 (*0-205-27702-0*) P-H.

O

An Asterisk (*) at the beginning of an entry indicates that the title is appearing for the first time.

Ornstein, Allan C., et al. Foundations of Education. 6 vols. 6th ed. 640p. (C). 1996. text 66.36 (*0-395-77104-8*) HM.
— An Introduction to the Foundations of Education. 4th ed. 1988. teacher ed. write for info. (*0-318-63327-2*); trans. write for info. (*0-318-63328-0*) HM.
Ornstein, Allan C., jt. auth. see Lunenburg, Frederick C.
Ornstein, Beverly J., jt. auth. see Schatz, Howard.
Ornstein, Donald, et al. Equivalence of Measure Preserving Transformations. LC 82-4005. (Memoirs Ser.: No. 37/262). 120p. 1985. reprint ed. pap. 17.00 (*0-8218-2262-4*, MEMO/37/262) Am Math.
Ornstein, Donald S., et al. Equivalence of Measure Preserving Transformations. LC 82-4005. (American Mathematical Society Ser.: No. 262). 132p. reprint ed. pap. 41.00 (*0-608-09216-9*, 205272000005) Bks Demand.
Ornstein-Galicia, Jacob L. Jewish Farmer in America: The Unknown Chronicle. LC 92-44246. (Illus.). 264p. 1993. text 89.95 (*0-7734-9229-1*) E Mellen.
Ornstein-Galicia, Jacob L., ed. Form & Function in Chicano English. LC 87-3379. 256p. (C). 1988. reprint ed. lib. bdg. 29.50 (*0-89464-233-2*) Krieger.
***Ornstein, H. L.** Evaluation of Air-operated Valves at United States Light-water Reactors. 32p. 2000. pap. 3.50 (*0-16-059120-1*) USGPO.
Ornstein, J. H. The Mind & the Brain: A Multi-Aspect Interpretation. 183p. 1972. pap. text 99.50 (*90-247-1339-0*) Kluwer Academic.
Ornstein, Jacob, ed. Three Essays on Linguistic Diversity in the Spanish-Speaking World: The U. S. Southwest & the River Plate Area. (Janua Linguarum, Ser Practica: No. 174). (Illus.). (Orig.). 1976. pap. text 24.65 (*90-279-3167-4*) Mouton.
Ornstein, Jacob, jt. ed. see Gilbert, Glenn G.
Ornstein, Jacob, jt. ed. see Mackey, William F.
Ornstein, Judy, ed. see Peskoff, Joel.
Ornstein, Martha. The Role of Scientific Societies in the Seventeenth Century. LC 74-26282. (History, Philosophy & Sociology of Science Ser.). 1980. reprint ed. 25.95 (*0-405-06609-0*) Ayer.
Ornstein, Michael D., jt. auth. see Stevenson, H. Michael.
Ornstein, Norman J. Lessons & Legacies: Farewell Addresses from the Senate. Gutmann, Henning, ed. LC 96-46021. 240p. (Orig.). 1996. pap. 12.00 (*0-201-69579-0*) Addison-Wesley.
— The Permanent Democratic Congress. (Essay Ser.: No. 3). 31p. (C). 1991. pap. text 3.00 (*1-878802-02-X*) J M Ashbrook Ctr Pub Affairs.
Ornstein, Norman J. & Lambert, Richard D., eds. Changing Congress: The Committee System. LC 73-89780. (Annals Ser.: No. 411). 1974. pap. 18.00 (*0-87761-177-6*) Am Acad Pol Soc Sci.
***Ornstein, Norman J. & Mann, Thomas E., eds.** The Permanent Campaign & Its Future. 250p. 2000. 39.95 (*0-8447-4133-7*, Pub. by Am Enterprise); pap. 16.95 (*0-8447-4134-5*, Pub. by Am Enterprise) Pub Resources Inc.
Ornstein, Norman J., et al. Vital Statistics on Congress, 1997-1998. LC 87-659232. 292p. (C). 1997. text 30.57 (*1-56802-298-0*); pap. text 23.97 (*1-56802-299-9*) Congr Quarterly.
***Ornstein, Norman J., et al.** Vital Statistics on Congress, 1999-2000. 10th ed. 300p. 1999. 39.95 (*0-8447-4115-9*, Pub. by Am Enterprise) Pub Resources Inc.
— Vital Statistics on Congress,1999-2000. 10th ed. 300p. 1999. pap. 16.95 (*0-8447-4116-7*, Pub. by Am Enterprise) Pub Resources Inc.
Ornstein, Norman J., jt. auth. see Mann, Thomas E.
Ornstein, Norman J., ed. see Mann, Thomas E.
Ornstein, Norman J., jt. ed. see Mann, Thomas E.
Ornstein, Pamela O. Granny Poo's Restaurant Review. 60p. (Orig.). 1994. 19.95 (*0-944105-02-5*) Candico Prods.
Ornstein, Paul H., ed. The Search for the Self: Selected Writings of Heinz Kohut, Vol. 3. 400p. 1991. 62.50 (*0-8236-6017-6*) Intl Univs Pr.
— The Search for the Self: Selected Writings of Heinz Kohut, Vol. 4. 500p. 1991. 67.50 (*0-8236-6018-4*) Intl Univs Pr.
— The Search for the Self: Selected Writings of Heinz Kohut 1950-1978, 4 vols., 1. LC 77-90229. 1978. 75.00 (*0-8236-6015-X*) Intl Univs Pr.
— The Search for the Self: Selected Writings of Heinz Kohut 1950-1978, 4 vols., 2. LC 77-90229. 1978. 67.50 (*0-8236-6016-8*) Intl Univs Pr.
Ornstein, Richard. Flatten Your Tummy: Lose the Jelly from the Belly. (Illus.). 36p. 1997. pap. 10.95 (*0-8038-9388-4*) Hastings.
Ornstein, Rick L. Biomacromolecules: From 3-D Structure to Applications. LC 96-27519. 368p. 1997. pap. 57.50 (*1-57477-019-5*) Battelle.
Ornstein, Robert. A Kingdom for a Stage: The Achievement of Shakespeare's History Plays. LC 88-70855. 231p. (C). 1988. reprint ed. 24.75 (*0-9620257-0-4*) Arden Pr OH.
— Right Mind. LC 97-21659. 200p. 1997. 22.00 (*0-15-100324-6*) Harcourt.
— The Right Mind. 224p. (C). 1998. 12.00 (*0-15-600627-8*, Harvest Bks) Harcourt.
Ornstein, Robert & Sobel, David. The Healing Brain: Breakthrough Discoveries about How the Brain Keeps Us Healthy. LC 98-52480. 301p. 1999. reprint ed. pap. 16.00 (*1-883536-17-0*) ISHK.
Ornstein, Robert & Swencionis, Charles, eds. The Healing Brain: A Scientific Reader. LC 89-16968. 262p. 1991. reprint ed. pap. text 24.00 (*0-89862-463-0*) Guilford Pubns.
Ornstein, Robert, jt. auth. see Sobel, David S.
Ornstein, Robert E. The Evolution of Consciousness: The Origins of the Way We Think. (Illus.). 320p. 1992. pap. 14.00 (*0-671-79224-5*, Touchstone) S&S Trade Pap.
— Healthy Pleasures. 1989. 16.95 (*0-201-12669-9*) Addison-Wesley.
— Healthy Pleasures. 1990. pap. 11.00 (*0-201-52385-X*) Addison-Wesley.
— The Mind Field: A Personal Essay. 3rd ed. LC 95-81219. 144p. 1996. reprint ed. pap. 15.00 (*1-883536-00-6*, Malor Bks) ISHK.
— The Moral Vision of Jacobean Tragedy. LC 74-25893. 299p. 1975. reprint ed. lib. bdg. 45.00 (*0-8371-7864-9*, ORJT, Greenwood Pr) Greenwood.
— Physiological Studies of Consciousness. 20p. 1973. pap. 6.00 (*0-904674-00-2*, Pub. by Octagon Pr) ISHK.
— Shakespeare's Comedies: From Roman Farce to Romantic Mystery. (Illus.). 272p. 1994. pap. 17.95 (*0-87413-541-9*) U Delaware Pr.
Ornstein, Robert E. & Sobel, David S. The Healing Brain: Breakthrough Medical Discoveries about How the Brain Manages Health. 304p. 1988. pap. 12.00 (*0-671-66236-8*, Touchstone) S&S Trade Pap.
Ornstein, Robert E. & Thompson, Richard F. The Amazing Brain. (Illus.). 224p. 1991. pap. 15.95 (*0-395-58572-4*) HM.
Ornstein, Robert E., jt. auth. see Burke, James.
Ornstein, Yevrah. Forging the New Fathers: Why Contemporary Fatherhood Must Change. unabridged ed. LC 96-94686. 244p. (Orig.). (C). 1997. pap. 12.95 (*0-9629211-6-5*) Harmonia.
— From the Hearts of Men. LC 91-72316. 352p. 1991. pap. 16.95 (*0-9629211-5-7*) Harmonia.
Ornston, L. Nicholas. Annual Review of Microbiology, Vol. 49. LC 49-432. 1995. text 48.00 (*0-8243-1149-3*) Annual Reviews.
Ornston, L. Nicholas, ed. Annual Review of Microbiology, Vol. 50. LC 49-432. 1996. text 53.00 (*0-8243-1150-7*) Annual Reviews.
— Annual Review of Microbiology, Vol. 51. LC 49-432. 1997. text 60.00 (*0-8243-1151-5*) Annual Reviews.
— Annual Review of Microbiology, Vol. 52. LC 49-432. 847p. 1998. text 60.00 (*0-8243-1152-3*) Annual Reviews.
***Ornston, L. Nicholas, ed.** Annual Review of Microbiology, Vol. 53. 706p. 1999. 120.00 (*0-8243-1153-1*) Annual Reviews.
Ornston, L. Nicholas, et al, eds. Annual Review of Microbiology, Vol. 37. LC 49-432. (Illus.). 1983. text 41.00 (*0-8243-1137-X*) Annual Reviews.
— Annual Review of Microbiology, Vol. 38. LC 49-432. (Illus.). 1984. text 41.00 (*0-8243-1138-8*) Annual Reviews.
— Annual Review of Microbiology, Vol. 39. LC 49-432. (Illus.). (C). 1985. text 41.00 (*0-8243-1139-6*) Annual Reviews.
— Annual Review of Microbiology, Vol. 40. LC 49-432. (Illus.). 1986. text 41.00 (*0-8243-1140-X*) Annual Reviews.
— Annual Review of Microbiology, Vol. 41. LC 49-432. (Illus.). 1987. text 41.00 (*0-8243-1141-8*) Annual Reviews.
— Annual Review of Microbiology, Vol. 42. LC 49-432. (Illus.). 1988. text 41.00 (*0-8243-1142-6*) Annual Reviews.
— Annual Review of Microbiology, Vol. 43. LC 49-432. 1989. text 41.00 (*0-8243-1143-4*) Annual Reviews.
— Annual Review of Microbiology, Vol. 44. LC 49-432. 1990. text 41.00 (*0-8243-1144-2*) Annual Reviews.
— Annual Review of Microbiology, Vol. 45. LC 49-432. 1991. text 41.00 (*0-8243-1145-0*) Annual Reviews.
— Annual Review of Microbiology, Vol. 46. LC 49-432. 1992. text 45.00 (*0-8243-1146-9*) Annual Reviews.
— Annual Review of Microbiology, Vol. 47. LC 49-432. (Illus.). 1993. text 45.00 (*0-8243-1147-7*) Annual Reviews.
— Annual Review of Microbiology, Vol. 48. LC 49-432. (Illus.). 1994. text 48.00 (*0-8243-1148-5*) Annual Reviews.
Ornum, William E. Van, see Van Ornum, William E.
Oro, J., ed. Life Sciences & Space Research XXIII (1) Exobiology Science & Primitive Solar System Bodies: Proceedings of Workshop XXII of the COSPAR 27th Plenary Meeting Held is Espoo, Finland, 18-29 July, 1988. (Advances in Space Research Ser.: Vol. 9). 125p. 1989. pap. 79.00 (*0-08-037381-X*, Pergamon Pr) Elsevier.
Oro, J., et al, eds. Life Sciences & Space Research XXIV (3) Planetary Biology & Origins of Life: Proceedings of the Topical Meeting of the COSPAR Interdisciplinary Scientific Commission F (Meetings F7, F1, F8 & F9) of the COSPAR 28th Plenary Meeting Held in The Hague, The Netherlands, 25 June-6 July, 1990. (Advances in Space Research Ser.: Vol. 12). 288p. 1992. pap. 165.00 (*0-08-041845-7*, Pergamon Pr) Elsevier.
Oro, J., ed. see International Conference on the Origin of Life Sta, et al.
Oro, Julius E. Nyang, see Nyang Oro, Julius E.
***O'Roark, Ann M.** The Quest for Executive Effectiveness: Turning Vision Inside-Out: Charismatic-Participatory Leadership. 352p. 2000. pap. 19.95 (*1-57733-058-7*) B Dolphin Pub.
O'Roark, Ann M. & Exner, John E., Jr., eds. History & Directory: Society for Personality Assessment Fiftieth Anniversary. 192p. 1989. pap. 39.95 (*0-8058-0569-9*) L Erlbaum Assocs.
Orobitg, Christine. L' Humeur Noire: Melancolie, Ecriture et Pensee en Espagne aux XVIeme et XVIIeme Siecles. 236p. 1996. 69.95 (*1-57309-073-5*); pap. 49.95 (*1-57309-072-7*) Intl Scholars.
Orodenker, Richard. The Writers Game: Nonfiction Baseball Prose. 1996. pap. 32.00 (*0-8057-3998-X*, Hall Reference) Macmillan.
Orodenker, Richard, ed. The Phillies Reader. LC 96-26884. 256p. 1996. 24.95 (*1-56639-503-8*) Temple U Pr.
Orodenker, Sylvia Z. Family Caregiving in a Changing Society: The Effects of Employment on Caregiver Stress. LC 91-29925. (Studies on the Elderly in America). 160p. 1991. text 25.00 (*0-8153-0521-4*) Garland.
Orofino, James F., ed. Structural Materials. LC 89-6764. 592p. 1989. pap. text 7.00 (*0-87262-699-7*, 699) Am Soc Civil Eng.
Orol, Brian. Real Life Guide to Personal Finance after College: How to Survive on a Starting Salary. Foster, Kerry, ed. (Real Life Guide Ser.). 335p. 1998. pap. 16.95 (*1-890586-01-3*) Pipeline Pr.
Oropallo, Kathy, jt. auth. see Radencich, Marguerite C.
Oropesa, Jose D. Cosmologia: El Humanismo Cristiano. LC 90-82885. 140p. (Orig.). 1990. pap. 9.95 (*0-89729-573-0*) Ediciones.
— Historiologia Cubana, 4 vols., II. LC 74-81336. (Coleccion Cuba y sus Jueces). (SPA.). (Orig.). 1993. pap. 25.00 (*0-685-74171-0*) Ediciones.
— Historiologia Cubana, 4 vols., III. LC 74-81336. (Coleccion Cuba y sus Jueces). (SPA.). (Orig.). 1993. pap. 25.00 (*84-399-2582-4*) Ediciones.
— Historiologia Cubana, 4 vols., Vol. I: Desde la Era Mesozoica Hasta 1898. LC 74-81336. (Coleccion Cuba y sus Jueces). (SPA.). 430p. (Orig.). 1993. pap. 25.00 (*0-89729-490-4*) Ediciones.
— Historiologia Cubana, 4 vols., Vol. IV: Desde 1959 Hasta 1980. LC 74-81336. (Coleccion Cuba y sus Jueces). (SPA.). 682p. (Orig.). 1993. pap. 39.00 (*0-89729-623-0*) Ediciones.
Oropeza, B. J. 99 Answers to Questions about Angels, Demons & Spiritual Warfare. LC 97-14368. 216p. 1997. pap. 10.99 (*0-8308-1968-1*, 1968) InterVarsity.
— 99 Reasons Why No One Knows When Christ Will Return. LC 94-3576. 180p. (Orig.). 1994. pap. 10.99 (*0-8308-1636-4*, 1636, Saltshaker Bk) InterVarsity.
***Oropeza, B. J.** Paul & Apostasy: Eschatology, Perseverance & Falling Away in the Corinthian Congregation. (Wissenshaftliche Untersuchungen zum Neuen Testament Ser.: Vol. 2). 320p. 2000. pap. 110.00 (*3-16-147307-8*, Pub. by JCB Mohr) Coronet Bks.
Oropeza, C., et al, eds. Lethal Yellowing: Research & Practical Aspects, Vol. 5. LC 95-37539. (Developments in Plant Pathology Ser.). 268p. (C). 1995. text 121.50 (*0-7923-3723-9*) Kluwer Academic.
Oropeza, Luis J. Tutelary Pluralism: A Critical Approach to Venezuelan Democracy. (Harvard Studies in International Affairs: No. 46). 144p. 1984. reprint ed. pap. text 18.00 (*0-8191-4120-8*) U Pr of Amer.
***O'Rorke, Torena.** Always Another Dawn. LC 99-65312. 224p. 2000. pap. 11.95 (*1-56315-262-2*, Pub. by SterlingHse) Natl Bk Netwk.
Oros, John G., ed. see Masson, Dubos J.
Orosius, Paulus. Historiarum Adversum Paganos Libri Septem. (GER.). xxxix, 819p. 1967. reprint ed. write for info. (*3-318-70524-9*) G Olms Pubs.
— King Alfred's Orosius, Pt. 1. Sweet, H., ed. (EETS, OS Ser.: No. 79). 1969. 50.00 (*0-527-00079-5*) Periodicals Srv.
— Seven Books of History Against the Pagans. Deferrari, Ray J., tr. LC 64-8670. (Fathers of the Church Ser.: Vol. 50). 415p. 1964. 24.95 (*0-8132-0050-4*) Cath U Pr.
Orosz, Carmen. From the Ganges to the Indus: Religions, Shrines & Traveling. LC 93-72947. 1994. pap. 11.95 (*0-8158-0496-2*) Chris Mass.
Orosz, Charles. Avian Surgical Anatomy. 1992. text 99.00 (*0-7216-3654-3*, W B Saunders Co) Harcrt Hlth Sci Grp.
— Transplant Vascular Sclerosis. LC 95-31248. (Medical Intelligence Unit Ser.). 222p. 1996. 99.00 (*1-57059-287-X*) Landes Bioscience.
***Orosz, Istvan.** Istvan Orosz: Etchings & Posters. Torok, Andras & Lord, Roberta, eds. (Illus.). 90p. 2000. pap. 40.00 (*0-9678409-1-0*) GrafikArchive.
Orosz, Joel J. Curators & Culture: The Museum Movement in America, 1740-1870. LC 89-33865. (History of American Science & Technology Ser.). 318p. reprint ed. pap. 98.60 (*0-608-03807-5*, 206465800009) Bks Demand.
— The Curious Case of the Coin Collectors Kline. Bowers, Q. David, ed. (Bowers & Merena Galleries' Little Editions Ser.). (Illus.). 24p. 1997. pap. 5.95 (*0-943161-73-8*) Bowers & Merena.
— The Eagle That Is Forgotten: Pierre Eugene Du Simitiere, Founding Father of American Numismatics. (Illus.). 76p. 1988. 19.95 (*0-943161-16-9*); pap. 9.95 (*0-943161-08-8*) Bowers & Merena.
***Orosz, Joel J.** The Insider's Guide to Grantmaking: How Foundations Find, Fund & Manage Effective Programs. LC 00-8263. (Nonprofit & Public Management Ser.). 2000. 32.95 (*0-7879-5238-9*) Jossey-Bass.
Orosz, Joel J., ed. see Fugate, Sandy.
Orosz, Kathryn S. Miami: Oasis. (Illus.). 80p. 1995. 28.00 (*0-9644807-0-0*) Orosz FL.
Orosz, Nicholas, jt. ed. see McCorquodale, Robert.
Oroszi, Dave, jt. auth. see Reynolds, Kirk.
Orou, Franz-Martin. Der Schutz des Industrial Design im Deutschsprachigen Raum: Ein Rechtsvergleich Zwischen Osterreich, Deutschland und der Schweiz unter Berucksichtigung Internationaler Abkommen und der Europaischen Rechtssetzung. (Europaische Hochschulschriften: Reihe 2: Bd. 2138). (GER., Illus.). 268p. 1997. 51.95 (*3-631-31221-0*) P Lang Pubng.
O'Rouke, T. D., ed. Guidelines for Tunnel Lining Design. 94p. 1984. 17.00 (*0-87262-402-1*) Am Soc Civil Eng.
Orourke. Beginning Your Career Search. 64p. (C). 1997. pap. text 8.00 (*0-13-790312-X*, Macmillan Coll) P-H.
O'Rourke, jt. auth. see O'Hair.
O'Rourke, jt. auth. see Rose.
O'Rourke, A. Desmond. The World Apple Market. LC 93-7919. (Illus.). 238p. 1994. lib. bdg. 59.95 (*1-56022-041-4*) Haworth Pr.
O'Rourke, A. Desmond, ed. Understanding the Japanese Food & Agrimarket: A Multifaceted Opportunity. LC 92-20076. (Illus.). 212p. 1994. lib. bdg. 89.95 (*1-56022-029-5*) Haworth Jrnl Co-Edits.
O'Rourke, Betty. Island of the Gods. large type ed. (Linford Mystery Library). 240p. 1996. pap. 16.99 (*0-7089-7870-3*, Linford) Ulverscroft.
— Mists of Remembrance. large type ed. (Linford Romance Library). 256p. 1992. pap. 16.99 (*0-7089-7135-0*, Linford) Ulverscroft.
— Nightingale Summer. large type ed. (Ulverscroft Large Print Ser.). 400p. 1997. 27.99 (*0-7089-3794-2*) Ulverscroft.
***O'Rourke, Betty.** Penhaligon's Rock. 352p. 2000. 31.99 (*0-7089-4208-3*) Ulverscroft.
O'Rourke Boyle, Marjorie. Loyola's Acts: The Rhetoric of the Self. LC 97-2132. (New Historicism Ser.: Vol. 36). (Illus.). 277p. 1997. 48.00 (*0-520-20937-0*, Pub. by U CA Pr) Cal Prin Full Svc.
O'Rourke, Brian. Pale Rainbow: Gaelic Folksongs with English Translations. 96p. 1989. 25.00 (*0-7165-2425-2*, Pub. by Irish Acad Pr) Intl Spec Bk.
O'Rourke, Carol J. Sea Critters Vol. 1: The Case of the Stolen Pearl. (Illus.). 14p. (J). (gr. k-4). 1998. pap. 2.95 (*0-9665692-0-2*) Sea Critters.
— Sea Critters Vol. 2: The Splangywangba Adventure. (Illus.). 14p. (J). (gr. k-4). 1998. pap. 2.95 (*0-9665692-1-0*) Sea Critters.
O'Rourke, Charles M., jt. auth. see Punderson, James M., 4th.
O'Rourke, Colleen M. & Colarusso, Ron. Special Education for Teachers. 2nd ed. 442p. (C). 1999. per. 48.95 (*0-7872-5673-0*, 41567301) Kendall-Hunt.
O'Rourke, David K. Demons by Definition: Social Idealism, Religious Nationalism, & the Demonizing of Dissent. LC 98-2642. (Berkeley Insights in Linguistics & Semiotics Ser.: Vol. 35). 147p. (C). 1998. text 38.95 (*0-8204-3928-2*) P Lang Pubng.
O'Rourke, Donny. The Waistband & Other Poems. 88p. 1998. pap. 10.95 (*0-7486-6232-4*, Pub. by Polygon) Subterranean Co.
O'Rourke, Donny, ed. Dream State: The New Scottish Poets. LC 94-143675. 278p. 1993. 19.95 (*0-7486-6169-7*, Pub. by Polygon) Subterranean Co.
O'Rourke, Dori. I Found the Golf God: Ten Secrets for Golfing Success. 99p. 1991. pap. 9.95 (*0-9628854-0-1*) On Target Life.
— The Mystery of Feeling Great: Discover the World's Greatest Secret. 191p. (Orig.). 1996. pap. 14.95 (*0-9628854-1-X*) On Target Life.
O'Rourke, Edward J. Jesus, the Divine Teacher: Five New Decades of the Rosary. 32p. 1994. pap. 1.95 (*0-89243-680-8*) Liguori Pubns.
O'Rourke, Edward W. Roots of Human Rights. (Synthesis Ser.). 117p. 1981. pap. 1.00 (*0-8199-0373-6*, Frncscn Herld) Franciscan Pr.
O'Rourke, Everett V. The Highest School in California: A Story of Bodie, California. (Illus.). 32p. (Orig.). (J). (gr. 1-4). 1978. 4.00 (*0-9621369-0-5*) E ORourke.
— Sounds & Images of the Fabulous Fifties: History of the Tahoe Truckee Unified School District: 1949-1956. (Illus.). (Orig.). 1990. pap. text 10.00 (*0-9621369-1-3*) E ORourke.
***O'Rourke, Felicity.** Irish Facts. LC 99-43267. 2000. 5.99 (*0-517-20805-9*) Random Hse Value.
O'Rourke, Fran. Pseudo-Dionysius & the Metaphysics of Aquinas. LC 92-13959. (Studien und Texte zur Geistesgeschichte des Mittelalters Ser.: Vol. 32). xvi, 300p. 1992. 104.50 (*90-04-09466-0*) Brill Academic Pubs.
O'Rourke, Fran, ed. At the Heart of the Real: Philosophical Essays in Honour of Archbishop Desmond Connell. 420p. 1992. 45.00 (*0-7165-2464-3*, Pub. by Irish Acad Pr) Intl Spec Bk.
O'Rourke, Frank. Ambuscade. 1980. mass mkt. 1.75 (*0-451-09490-5*, Sig) NAL.
— Ambuscade. 144p. 1988. pap. 2.75 (*0-671-63604-7*) PB.
— Burton & Stanley. LC 96-67486. (Illus.). 64p. (J). (gr. 4-7). 1996. pap. 4.95 (*0-374-40989-7*) FS&G.
— Burton & Stanley. (Illus.). 64p. (J). (gr. 4-7). 1993. 15.95 (*0-87923-824-0*) Godine.
— Burton & Stanley. 1996. 10.15 (*0-606-11176-X*, Pub. by Turtleback) Demco.
— Ellen & the Barber: Three Love Stories of the Thirties. LC 98-18715. 208p. 1998. text 20.95 (*0-312-19263-0*) St Martin.
O'Rourke, G. G. & Wooldridge, E. T. Night Fighters over Korea. LC 98-16424. 1998. 34.95 (*1-55750-653-1*) Naval Inst Pr.
O'Rourke, Hugh S. Stories of the Greatest Holy Leaf. 44p. (J). (gr. 1-6). 1997. 15.95 (*1-870989-77-5*) Bahai.
O'Rourke, J. Computer Technology & the Disabled. 1992. text. write for info. (*0-442-00507-5*, VNR) Wiley.
O'Rourke, J. Barry. How to Photograph Women - Beautifully. (Illus.). 144p. 1986. pap. 22.50 (*0-8174-4004-6*, Amphoto) Watsn-Guptill.
***O'Rourke, Jack.** A Giant in My Life. 2000. pap. 8.95 (*0-533-13560-5*) Vantage.
O'Rourke, James. Keats's Odes & Contemporary Criticism. LC 98-6635. (Illus.). 256p. 1998. 39.95 (*0-8130-1590-1*) U Press Fla.
O'Rourke, James J. The Problem of Freedom in Marxist Thought: An Analysis of the Treatment of Human Freedom by Marx, Engels, Lenin & Contemporary Soviet Philosophy. LC 73-86095. (Sovietica Ser.: No. 32). 240p. 1974. lib. bdg. 126.50 (*90-277-0383-3*) Kluwer Academic.
O'Rourke, James J., jt. auth. see Blakeley, Thomas J.

O

An Asterisk (*) at the beginning of an entry indicates that the title is appearing for the first time.

O'Rourke, Joseph. Art Gallery Theorems & Algorithms. (International Series of Monographs on Computer Science: No. 3). (Illus.). 304p. 1987. text 60.00 (0-19-503965-3) OUP.

— Computational Geometry in C. 2nd expanded rev. ed. LC 98-15363. (Illus.). 424p. (C). 1998. 74.95 (0-521-64010-5); pap. 74.95 (0-521-64976-5) Cambridge U Pr.

O'Rourke, Joseph, jt. auth. see Dale, Edgar.

O'Rourke, Joseph, jt. ed. see Goodman, Jacob E.

O'Rourke, Joseph P. Toward a Science of Vocabulary Development. LC 73-87530. (Janua Linguarum, Ser.: No. 183). (Illus.). 1974. pap. text 44.65 (90-279-2663-8) Mouton.

O'Rourke, K. J., jt. auth. see O'Grady, G. W.

O'Rourke, Kathleen & Worzbyt, John C. Support Groups for Children. 425p. 1996. pap. 39.95 (1-56032-395-7) Hemisp Pub.

O'Rourke, Kelly. The Mad House. (Halloween Ser.). 1998. mass mkt. 4.50 (1-57297-342-0) Blvd Books.

— The Old Myers Place. (Halloween Ser.: No. 2). 1997. mass mkt. 4.50 (1-57297-341-2) Blvd Books.

***O'Rourke, Kevin, ed.** Looking for the Cow: Modern Korean Poems. 168p. 2000. pap. 14.95 (1-901233-51-0, Pub. by Dedalus) Dufour.

O'Rourke, Kevin D. Development of Church Teaching on Prolonging Life. 20p. 1988. pap. 3.00 (0-87125-152-3, 217) Cath Health.

***O'Rourke, Kevin D., ed.** A Primer for Health Care Ethics. 2nd ed. LC 00-25273. 240p. 2000. pap. text 21.95 (0-87840-802-9) Georgetown U Pr.

O'Rourke, Kevin D. & Boyle, Philip. Medical Ethics: Sources of Catholic Teaching. 3rd rev. ed. LC 98-44647. 442p. (Orig.). 1999. pap. 37.50 (0-87840-722-7) Georgetown U Pr.

O'Rourke, Kevin D. & Boyle, Philip, eds. Medical Ethics: Sources of Catholic Teaching. 2nd ed. LC 93-4895. 368p. (Orig.). 1993. pap. text 35.00 (0-87840-540-2) Georgetown U Pr.

O'Rourke, Kevin D., jt. auth. see Ashley, Benedict.

O'Rourke, Kevin D., jt. auth. see Ashley, Benedict M.

O'Rourke, Kevin D., jt. auth. see So Chong-Ju.

O'Rourke, Kevin D., jt. auth. see Yi, Kry-bo.

O'Rourke, Kevin D., tr. see Ch'on Sang Pyong.

O'Rourke, Kevin H. & Williamson, Jeffrey G. Globalization & History: The Evolution of a Nineteenth-Century Atlantic Economy. LC 99-17963. (Illus.). 400p. 1999. 40.00 (0-262-15049-2) MIT Pr.

O'Rourke, Lorenzo, ed. see Taine, Hippolyte A.

O'Rourke, Lorenzo, tr. see Hugo, Victor.

O'Rourke, Mary-Jo & Shrestha, Bimal. Nepali: Language Survival Kit. 3rd ed. (Illus.). 228p. 1996. pap. 5.95 (0-86442-345-4) Lonely Planet.

O'Rourke, Mary K. No Sparrow Shall Fall: Leaving the Convent after Forty-Five Years Under Vows. (Illus.). 192p. 1988. 17.95 (0-941974-10-3) Baranski Pub Co.

O'Rourke, Maureen. Hydrotherapy & Heliotherapy: Natural Healing with Water, Herbs, & Sunlight. 88p. (C). 1995. pap. text 14.95 (0-9649356-0-0) Educ Hands.

O'Rourke, Michael. Meteor's Tale. Smith, Sally, ed. 160p. 1999. 20.00 (1-891437-01-1) Victorian Essence.

— Principles of Three-Dimensional Computer Animation: Modeling, Rendering, & Animating with 3D Graphics. rev. ed. LC 98-4553. (Illus.). 256p. 1998. 55.00 (0-393-73024-7) Norton.

— The Scream Factory. (Halloween Ser.: No. 1). 160p. (J). (gr. 5-11). 1997. mass mkt. 4.50 (1-57297-298-X) Blvd Books.

O'Rourke, Michael, et al, eds. Arterial Vasodilation, Mechanisms & Therapy. LC 92-49292. (Illus.). 231p. 1993. text 89.50 (0-8121-1671-2) Lppncott W & W.

***O'Rourke, Michael, et al, eds.** Truth & Meaning. 304p. (C). 2000. pap. 26.95 (1-889119-55-5) Seven Bridges.

O'Rourke, Michael & Liu, Xuejie. Response of Buried Pipelines Subject to Earthquake Effects. (Monograph Ser.: Vol. 3). (Illus.). 260p. 1999. pap. 25.00 (0-9656682-3-1) Multidisciplinary Ctr.

O'Rourke, Michael F., jt. auth. see Nichols, Wilmer W.

O'Rourke, Michael G., ed. see Emmett, Anthony J.

O'Rourke, Michael J., ed. Lifeline Earthquake Engineering: Proceedings of the Fourth U. S. Conference; San Francisco, California, August 10-12, 1995. (Monograph Ser.: No. 6). 824p. 1995. 78.00 (0-7844-0101-2) Am Soc Civil Eng.

O'Rourke, Mike D. & Marich, Stephen, intros. International Heavy Haul Railway Conference, Fourth, 1989: Railways in Action. (Illus.). 682p. 1989. 115.25 (0-85825-469-7, Pub. by Inst Engrs Aust-EA Bks) Accents Pubns.

O'Rourke, Nancy. Punctuation. 1997. pap., wbk. ed. 2.25 (1-56293-916-5, McClanahan Book) Learn Horizon.

O'Rourke, P. J. Age & Guile Beat Youth, Innocence & a Bad Haircut: Twenty-Five Years of P. J. O'Rourke. LC 95-16430. 368p. 1996. reprint ed. pap. 12.00 (0-87113-653-8, Atlntc Mnthly) Grove-Atltic.

— All the Trouble in the World: The Lighter Side of Overpopulation, Famine, Ecological Disaster, Ethnic Hatred, Plague, & Poverty. LC 94-21547. 368p. 1995. pap. 12.00 (0-87113-611-2, Atlntc Mnthly) Grove-Atltic.

— The Bachelor Home Companion: A Practical Guide to Keeping House Like a Pig. 176p. 1997. pap. 11.00 (0-87113-686-4, Atlntc Mnthly) Grove-Atltic.

— Eat the Rich: A Treatise on Economics. LC 98-27100. 272p. 1998. pap. 24.00 (0-87113-719-4, Atlntc Mnthly) Grove-Atltic.

***O'Rourke, P. J.** Eat the Rich: A Treatise on Economics. 272p. 1999. pap. 13.00 (0-87113-760-7, Atlntc Mnthly) Grove-Atltic.

O'Rourke, P. J. The Enemies List: Flushing Out Liberals in the Age of Clinton. LC 96-4887. 176p. 1996. pap. 11.00 (0-87113-632-5, Atlntc Mnthly) Grove-Atltic.

— Give War a Chance: Eyewitness Accounts of Mankind's Struggle Against Tyranny, Injustice, & Alcohol-Free Beer. LC 92-50591. 1993. pap. 13.00 (0-679-74201-8) Vin Bks.

— Holidays in Hell. 1989. pap. 13.00 (0-679-72422-2) Vin Bks.

— Holidays in Hell. 1992. pap. 12.00 (0-394-23898-2) Vin Bks.

***O'Rourke, P. J.** Holidays in Hell: In Which Our Intrepid Reporter Travels to the World's Worst Places & Asks "What's Funny about This" 272p. 2000. reprint ed. pap. 12.00 (0-8021-3701-6, Pub. by Grove-Atltic) Publishers Group.

O'Rourke, P. J. Modern Manners: An Etiquette Book for Rude People. LC 88-31834. 300p. 1990. pap. 12.00 (0-87113-375-X, Atlntc Mnthly) Grove-Atltic.

— Parliament of Whores: A Lone Humorist Attempts to Explain the Entire U. S. Government. 1992. pap. 12.00 (0-679-73789-8) Vin Bks.

— Public Enemies: PJ's Irreverent Hit List of Institutions, Individuals, Assorted Morons. 1995. pap. 8.95 (0-9629072-1-9) Amer Spectator.

— Republican Party Reptile. LC 86-26504. 240p. 1995. pap. 12.00 (0-87113-622-8, Atlntc Mnthly) Grove-Atltic.

Orourke, Page E. Dollhouse Family. (Sticker Stories Ser.). 16p. 1998. pap. text 4.99 (0-448-41831-2, G & D) Peng Put Young Read.

O'Rourke, Patricia, jt. auth. see Godley, Lee N.

O'Rourke, Paul F., jt. auth. see Polakoff, Phillip L.

O'Rourke, Raymond J. European Food Law. LC 99-486995. 200p. 1998. pap. 78.20 (1-902558-00-6, Pub. by Palladian Law) Gaunt.

***O'Rourke, Raymond J.** European Food Law with 1999 Update. 276p. 1999. pap. write for info. (1-902558-33-2, Pub. by Palladian Law) Gaunt.

— Food Safety & Product Liability. 200p. 2000. pap. 92.00 (1-902558-22-7, Pub. by Palladian Law) Gaunt.

O'Rourke, Rebecca. Reflecting on the Well of Loneliness: Stephen Gordon, a Lesbian's Heroine? (Heroines? Ser.). 96p. 1989. pap. 9.95 (0-415-01841-2) Routledge.

O'Rourke, Robert. The AHA Cardiac Consult. 700p. 59.95 (0-683-30748-7) Lppncott W & W.

O'Rourke, Robert A. Hurst's The Heart. 8th ed. 1995. pap. text 45.00 (0-07-048157-1) McGraw.

O'Rourke, Robert A., ed. Hurst's the Heart: Update 1. 8th ed. Orig. Title: The Heart. (Illus.). 192p. 1995. text, suppl. ed. 45.00 (0-07-048207-1) McGraw-Hill HPD.

***O'Rourke, Shane.** Warriors & Peasants. LC 99-40595. (St. Antony's Ser.). 2000. text 65.00 (0-312-22774-4) St Martin.

O'Rourke, T. D. & Hobelman, A. G., eds. Excavation & Support for the Urban Infrastructure: Papers Presented for Sessions Sponsored by the Geotechnical Engineering Division of the American Society of Civil Engineers in Conjunction with the ASCE International Convention & Exposition, September 14 & 15, 1992 in New York, New York. LC 92-27782. (Geotechnical Special Publications: No. 33). 272p. 1992. 28.00 (0-87262-906-6) Am Soc Civil Eng.

O'Rourke, Terrence J. A Basic Course in Manual Communication. (Illus.). 1973. 11.95 (0-913072-01-X) Natl Assn Deaf.

— A Basic Vocabulary: American Sign Language for Parents & Children. 1978. pap. 8.95 (0-932666-00-0) T J Pubs.

O'Rourke, Terrence J., et al. A Basic Course in American Sign Language. (Illus.). 280p. 1980. spiral bd. 26.95 (0-932666-24-8, 7544S) T J Pubs.

— A Basic Course in American Sign Language. (Illus.). 288p. 1994. spiral bd. 29.95 (0-932666-42-6, 013S) T J Pubs.

— A Basic Course in American Sign Language. 2nd ed. (Illus.). 288p. 1994. text 36.95 (0-932666-43-4, 013H) T J Pubs.

O'Rourke, Thomas, jt. auth. see Collins, Denis.

O'Rourke, Thomas D., ed. The Loma Prieta, California, Earthquake of October 17, 1989 - Marina District. (Illus.). 215p. (Orig.). (C). 1993. pap. text 45.00 (0-7881-0175-7) DIANE Pub.

O'Rourke, Thomas J., jt. auth. see Shaw, G. Jerry.

O'Rourke, Thomas P. The Franciscan Missions in Texas (1690-1793) LC 73-3559. (Catholic University of America. Studies in Romance Languages & Literatures: No. 5). reprint ed. 27.50 (0-404-57755-5) AMS Pr.

O'Rourke, Timothy. The Impact of Reapportionment. LC 78-62883. 325p. 1979. 39.95 (0-87855-290-1) Transaction Pubs.

O'Rourke, Vernon A. The Juristic Status of Egypt & the Sudan, Series LIII, No. 1--1. LC 75-138619. 184p. 1973. reprint ed. lib. bdg. 55.00 (0-8371-5731-5, ORJS, Greenwood Pr) Greenwood.

O'Rourke, William. Campaign America '96: The View from the Couch with a New, Updated Epilogue: "From Monica to Milosevic, 1998-1999" 2nd ed. LC 99-462322. 528p. 2000. reprint ed. pap. 20.00 (0-268-02251-8, Pub. by U of Notre Dame Pr) Chicago Distribution Ctr.

— Signs of the Literary Times: Essays, Reviews, Profiles 1970-1992. LC 92-43027. (SUNY Series, The Margins of Literature). 250p. (C). 1993. pap. text 19.95 (0-7914-1682-8) State U NY Pr.

— Signs of the Literary Times: Essays, Reviews, Profiles 1970-1992. LC 92-43027. (SUNY Series, The Margins of Literature). 250p. (C). 1993. text 59.50 (0-7914-1681-X) State U NY Pr.

***O'Rourke, William, et al.** The Notre Dame Review Vol. 9: Soft Millennium. 176p. 2000. pap. 8.00 (1-892492-08-3) Notre Dame Rev.

— The Notre Dame Review Vol. 10: Body & Soul. 176p. 2000. pap. 8.00 (1-892492-09-1) Notre Dame Rev.

O'Rourke, William & Matthias, John, eds. The Notre Dame Review Vol. 7: Work. (Illus.). 1998. pap. 8.00 (1-892492-06-7) Notre Dame Rev.

— The Notre Dame Review Vol. 8: Place-Displacement. (Illus.). 1999. pap. 8.00 (1-892492-07-5) Notre Dame Rev.

***Orovetskii, Yu. P.** Mantle Plumes. (Illus.). 250p. 1999. text 95.00 (90-5410-792-8, Pub. by A A Balkema) Ashgate Pub Co.

Orow, Michael. Captive in Russia. LC 98-65634. 224p. 1998. pap. 14.95 (1-57197-113-0) Pentland Pr.

***Orowe, Marc.** Howie the Rookie. 64p. 1999. pap. 14.95 (1-85459-422-2, Pub. by Theatre Comm) Consort Bk Sales.

Oroyan, Susanna. Anatomy of a Doll: The Fabric Sculptors Handbook. Lanzarotti, Sally & Kuhn, Barbara K., eds. LC 96-37077. (Illus.). 144p. (Orig.). 1997. pap. 25.95 (1-57120-024-X, 10148) C & T Pub.

***Oroyan, Susanna.** Designing the Doll: From Concept to Construction. Rymer, Cyndy & MacFarland, Sara, eds. LC 98-30312. (Illus.). 160p. 1999. pap. 27.95 (1-57120-060-6, 10186) C & T Pub.

Oroyan, Susanna. Fantastic Figures: Ideas & Techniques Using the New Clays. LC 94-4645. (Illus.). 128p. 1995. pap. 21.95 (0-914881-00-0, 10099) C & T Pub.

Orozco. Educational Leadership. 2000. pap. text 11.97 (0-395-97214-0) HM.

Orozco, Alonso De, see De Orozco, Alonso.

Orozco, C. R. Spanish-English, English-Spanish Commercial Dictionary. (ENG & SPA.). 208p. 1969. pap. 35.25 (0-08-006380-2, Pergamon Pr) Elsevier.

Orozco, Carlos R. Spanish-English/English-Spanish Commercial Dictionary. (ENG & SPA.). 200p. 1996. pap. 49.95 (0-7859-9641-9) Fr & Eur.

Orozco, David J., ed. see Imatani, Wendy J.

Orozco, David J., ed. & intro. see Twain, Mark, pseud, et al.

Orozco, E. C. Republican Protestantism in Aztalan. LC 80-82906. 261p. 1980. pap. 24.00 (0-9606102-2-7) Petereins Pr.

Orozco, Enrique. The Chicano Labyrinth of Solitude: A Study in the Making of the Chicano Mind & Character. 160p. (C). 1996. pap. text, per. 35.95 (0-7872-1966-5) Kendall-Hunt.

Orozco, Fernando. Conquista de Mexico. (J). 1997. pap. text 9.98 (968-38-0289-3) Panorama Edit.

Orozco, Fernando. Fechas Historicas de Mexico. 1997. pap. text 9.98 (968-38-0295-8) Panorama Edit.

Orozco, Fernando. Grandes Personajes de Mexico. 1997. pap. text 10.50 (968-38-0317-2) Panorama Edit.

***Orozco, Gabriel, et al.** Gabriel Orozco: Photogravity: Texts from Gabriel Orozco's Notebooks, 1992-99. LC 99-48794. 184p. 2000. 35.00 (0-87633-128-2, Pub. by Phila Mus Art) Dist Art Pubs.

Orozco, Jose-Luis. Diez Deditos & Other Play Rhymes & Action Songs From Latin America. (SPA., Illus.). 48p. (J). (ps up). 1997. 18.99 (0-525-45736-4, Dutton Child) Peng Put Young Read.

Orozco, Jose-Luis, tr. De Colores & Other Latin-American Folk Songs for Children. (Illus.). 56p. (J). 1994. 17.99 (0-525-45260-5, Dutton Child) Peng Put Young Read.

***Orozco, Olga.** Relampagos de lo Invisible. 312p. 1998. pap. 9.99 (950-557-240-9) Fondo CA.

***Orozco, R., et al.** Atlas of Internal Fixation: Fractures of Long Bones. (Illus.). 370p. 2000. 199.00 (3-540-65621-9) Spr-Verlag.

Orozco, Ruben G. La Historia Puertorriquena de Rodriguez Julia. 1997. pap. 12.95 (0-8477-0285-5) U of PR Pr.

Orozco, Samuel, jt. auth. see Street, Richard S.

Orpen, Adela E. The Chronicles of the Sid, or, the Life & Travels of Adelia Gates. LC 72-5585. (Black Heritage Library Collection). 1977. reprint ed. 41.95 (0-8369-9145-1) Ayer.

Orpen, Valerie, tr. see Alera, Don B.

Orphanides, Andreas G. Bronze Age Anthropomorphic Figurines in the Cesnola Collection at the Metropolitan Museum of Art. (Studies in Mediterranean Archaeology & Literature: No. 20). (Illus.). 80p. (Orig.). 1983. pap. 29.50 (91-86098-09-8, Pub. by P Astroms) Coronet Bks.

Orphanides, Andreas G., jt. ed. see Wallace, Paul W.

Orphee, Elvira. El Angels Last Conquest. (Orig.). 1985. pap. 4.95 (0-345-31821-8, Ballantine) Ballantine Pub Grp.

Orpheus. Hymni. Quant, Wilhelm, ed. 93p. 1973. write for info. (3-296-14800-0) G Olms Pubs.

Orpin, Colin G., jt. ed. see Mountfort, Douglas O.

Orput, Fran, ed. see Bordenave, Eileen.

Orr. Designing Library Buildings. (C). 1977. text 16.00 (0-233-96230-1) Westview.

— Geology of the Pacific Northwest. (C). Date not set. pap. text. write for info. (0-03-007444-4) Harcourt Coll Pubs.

— J. G. Ballard. 1997. 22.95 (0-8057-4511-4, Twyne) Mac Lib Ref.

***Orr.** Mouth Madness. (C). 1999. pap. text 42.00 (0-12-785028-7) Acad Pr.

Orr. Mouth Madness. 1998. 42.00 (0-7616-4850-X, W B Saunders Co) Harcrt Hlth Sci Grp.

— Oregon Fossils. 390p. 1998. per. 40.95 (0-7872-5454-1) Kendall-Hunt.

***Orr & Gamble.** Arabella. (Illus.). 32p. (ps-1). 2000. pap. 7.00 (0-207-19904-3) CARP.

Orr & Schutte. Language of Science. 1992. 52.95 (0-409-11165-1) Buttrwrth-Heinemann.

Orr, Trevor L. & Farrell, Eric R. Geotechnical Design to Eurocode 7. LC 98-51614. 175p. 1999. 119.00 (1-85233-038-4, Pub. by Spr-Verlag) Spr-Verlag.

Orr & Reno P. A. Staff. New Hampshire Environmental Practice: Regulation & Compliance. Platt, Thomas C. & Johnston, Cordell A., eds. LC 92-14890. 680p. 1994. ring bd. 95.00 (1-56257-190-7, 83350-10, MICHIE) LEXIS Pub.

— New Hampshire Environmental Practice: Regulation & Compliance. Platt, Thomas C. & Johnston, Cordell A., eds. LC 92-14890. 1993. ring bd., suppl. ed. 50.00 (0-685-74438-8, MICHIE) LEXIS Pub.

Orr, A., ed. see Livio, Mario, et al.

Orr, Akiva. Israel: Politics, Myths & Identity Crises. LC 94-2269. (Middle Eastern Ser.). 180p. (C). 1994. 49.95 (0-7453-0766-3, Pub. by Pluto GBR); pap. 16.95 (0-7453-0767-1, Pub. by Pluto GBR) Stylus Pub VA.

Orr, Alberta L. Issues in Aging & Vision: A Curriculum. LC 98-6543. 264p. (Orig.). 1998. 27.95 (0-89128-947-X) Am Foun Blind.

Orr, Alberta L., ed. Vision & Aging: Crossroads for Service Delivery. LC 92-5088. 392p. 1992. pap. 47.95 (0-89128-216-5) Am Foun Blind.

Orr, Alexandra L. Life & Letters of Robert Browning. (BCL1-PR English Literature Ser.). 431p. 1992. reprint ed. lib. bdg. 99.00 (0-7812-7465-6) Rprt Serv.

Orr, Alice. Dear Santa. (Intrigue Ser.: No. 494). 1998. per. 3.99 (0-373-22494-X, 1-22494-8) Harlequin Bks.

— Heat of Passion. (Intrigue Ser.). 1998. per. 3.99 (0-373-22464-8, 1-22464-1) Harlequin Bks.

Orr, Alice H. Camp Fear. (Intrigue Ser.). 1994. per. 2.99 (0-373-22266-1, 1-22266-0) Harlequin Bks.

— Cold Summer. (Intrigue Ser.). 1993. per. 2.89 (0-373-22216-5, 1-22216-5) Harlequin Bks.

— Key West Heat. LC 95-13555. (Intrigue Ser.: 324). 248p. 1995. per. 3.50 (0-373-22324-2, 1-22324-7) Harlequin Bks.

— Manhattan Heat. (Intrigue Ser.). 1996. per. 3.75 (0-373-22369-2, 1-22369-2) Harlequin Bks.

— Protect Me, Love. 1996. per. 3.75 (0-373-22398-6, 1-22398-1) Harlequin Bks.

Orr, Anne. Anne Orr's Afghans to Crochet & Knit. (Illus.). 32p. 1987. reprint ed. pap. 3.50 (0-486-25440-2) Dover.

— Anne Orr's Charted Designs. (Needlework Ser.). (Illus.). 40p. 1979. pap. 3.95 (0-486-23704-4) Dover.

— Anne Orr's Classic Tatting Patterns. 60th ed. LC 85-4523. (Illus.). 32p. 1985. reprint ed. pap. 3.95 (0-486-24897-6) Dover.

— Crochet Designs of Anne Orr. LC 77-92502. (Needlework Ser.). (Illus.). 48p. 1978. pap. 3.50 (0-486-23621-8) Dover.

— Crocheting with Anne Orr. (Illus.). 48p. (Orig.). 1988. pap. 3.50 (0-486-25672-3) Dover.

— Favorite Charted Designs. 40p. (Orig.). 1983. pap. 3.50 (0-486-24484-9) Dover.

— Quilting with Anne Orr. 32p. 1990. pap. 3.50 (0-486-26325-8) Dover.

— Tatting with Anne Orr. (Illus.). 32p. (J). 1989. pap. 3.50 (0-486-25982-X) Dover.

Orr, Bartholomew. Learning to Read & Make Mechanical Drawings. 6th ed. 112p. 1988. text 12.72 (0-02-676350-8) Glencoe.

Orr, Ben, jt. ed. see Orr, Eliza C.

Orr, Bernadette M. Americas: Telecourse Faculty Guide. 184p. 1993. pap. text (0-19-507796-2) OUP.

Orr, Bill. The Global Economy in the Nineties: A User's Guide. (Illus.). 330p. (C). 1992. text 75.00 (0-8147-6176-3) NYU Pr.

— The Global Economy in the 1990s: A User's Guide. (Illus.). 320p. (C). 1993. pap. text 25.00 (0-8147-6181-X) NYU Pr.

— HarperCollins College Outline College Algebra. LC 91-55381. (Outline Ser.). (Illus.). 448p. (C). 1992. pap. 17.00 (0-06-467140-2, Harper Ref) HarpC.

Orr, Bob & Orr, Helen. The Gossip. unabridged ed. Landes, William-Alan, ed. LC 97-39067. 55p. 1998. pap. 5.00 (0-88734-752-5) Players Pr.

Orr, Bob, jt. auth. see Orr, Helen.

Orr, Bud. Anthology of Mandolin Music. 224p. 1983. spiral bd. 24.95 (1-56222-009-8, 93952) Mel Bay.

— Deluxe Country Mandolin Method. 96p. 1981. spiral bd. 11.95 (0-87166-962-5, 93719) Mel Bay.

— Learn to Play Bluegrass Mandolin. 48p. 1980. pap. 7.95 (0-87166-683-9, 93720) Mel Bay.

Orr, C. E. Food for Lambs. 168p. pap. 4.00 (0-686-29109-3) Faith Pub Hse.

— Heavenly Life for Earthly Living. 60p. pap. 1.50 (0-686-29111-5) Faith Pub Hse.

— Helps to Holy Living. 64p. pap. 1.50 (0-686-29112-3); pap. 1.00 (0-686-29113-1) Faith Pub Hse.

— The Hidden Life. 112p. pap. 2.00 (0-686-29149-2) Faith Pub Hse.

— How to Live a Holy Life. 112p. pap. 2.00 (0-686-29120-4) Faith Pub Hse.

— Odors from Golden Vials. 78p. pap. 2.00 (0-686-29131-X) Faith Pub Hse.

Orr, C. W. The Making of Northern Nigeria. 320p. 1986. 250.00 (1-85077-138-3, Pub. by Darf Pubs Ltd) St Mut.

Orr-Cahall, Christina. Addison Mizner, Architect of Dreams & Realities, 1872-1933. 64p. 1977. 16.95 (0-614-32158-1) Norton Gal Art.

Orr-Cahall, Christina & Tucker, Paul H. Claude Monet: An Impression. 24p. 1993. 12.95 (0-943411-22-X) Norton Gal Art.

Orr-Cahall, Christina, et al. Norton Museum of Art: The American Collection. (Illus.). 293p. 1995. pap. 35.00 (0-943411-29-7) Norton Gal Art.

Orr, Carol A., jt. auth. see Banks, Susan V.

Orr, Casey. Portraits of Anarchists. (Illus.). (Orig.). 1997. pap. 24.95 incl. audio compact disk (1-873176-37-6) AK Pr Dist.

Orr, Charles A. History of the Pequot War: The Contemporary Accounts of Mason, Underhill, Vincent & Gardener. LC 76-43799. 1980. reprint ed. 37.50 (0-404-15655-X) AMS Pr.

— Stalin's Slave Camps. LC 74-22754. (Labor Movement in Fiction & Non-Fiction Ser.). reprint ed. 27.50 (0-404-58507-8) AMS Pr.

Orr, Chris, et al. A First Poetry Book. 128p. (J). (gr. 2-3). 1987. pap. 8.95 (0-19-918112-8) OUP.

An Asterisk (*) at the beginning of an entry indicates that the title is appearing for the first time.

Orr, Clarice C. The Joy of Grandma's Cooking. Dageforde, Linda J., ed. LC 99-40213. (Illus.). 220p. 1999. pap. 16.95 (*1-886225-45-1*) Dageforde Pub.

— The Joy of Grandparenting: Grandparents Make a Difference. LC 95-67533. (Illus.). 224p. (Orig.). 1995. pap. 10.00 (*1-886225-00-1*) Dageforde Pub.

Orr, Clarissa C., ed. Wollstonecraft's Daughters? Womanhood in England & France, 1780-1920. (Illus.). 256p. 1996. text 79.95 (*0-7190-4241-0*, Pub. by Manchester Univ Pr) St Martin.

— Women in the Victorian Art World. (Illus.). 256p. 1995. text 24.95 (*0-7190-4123-6*, Pub. by Manchester Univ Pr) St Martin.

Orr, Clive, ed. see Matteson, Michael J.

Orr, Clyde, ed. Filtration: Principles & Practices, Pt. 1. LC 75-18059. (Chemical Processing & Engineering Ser.: No. 10). (Illus.). 544p. reprint ed. pap. 168.70 (*0-8357-6113-4*, 203455900001) Bks Demand.

— Filtration: Principles & Practices, Pt. 2. LC 75-18059. (Chemical Processing & Engineering Ser.: No. 10). 419p. pap. 129.90 (*0-7837-0036-9*, 203455900002) Bks Demand.

Orr, Clyde, jt. auth. see Webb, Paul A.

Orr, D., ed. see Orr European Geophysical Symposium Staff.

Orr, Dan & Clendenen, Bill. Pocket Guide to First Aid for Scuba Diving. (Illus.). 28p. 1998. pap. text 12.95 (*1-886127-17-4*) Troutbeck Pub.

Orr, David. Italian Renaissance Drama in England Before 1625. LC 77-17260. (University of North Carolina Studies in Comparative Literature: No. 49). 151p. reprint ed. 46.90 (*0-8357-9704-X*, 201723000006) Bks Demand.

Orr, David B. Fundamentals of Applied Statistics & Surveys. LC 94-11048. (Illus.). 352p. (Orig.). 1995. ring bd. 54.95 (*0-412-98821-6*, Chap & Hall CRC) CRC Pr.

Orr, David B., ed. New Directions in Employability: Reducing Barriers to Full Employment. LC 73-6094. (Special Studies in U. S. Economic, Social & Political Issues). 1973. 42.50 (*0-275-28838-2*) Irvington.

Orr, David W. Earth in Mind: On Education, Environment, & the Human Prospect. LC 94-17546. 224p. 1994. 35.00 (*1-55963-294-1*); pap. 18.95 (*1-55963-295-X*) Island Pr.

— Ecological Literacy: Education & the Transition to a Postmodern World. LC 90-28767. (SUNY Series in Constructive Postmodern Thought). 210p. (C). 1991. pap. text 18.95 (*0-7914-0874-4*) State U NY Pr.

Orr, David W. & Soroos, Marvin S., eds. The Global Predicament: Ecological Perspectives on World Order. LC 78-10207. 414p. reprint ed. pap. 128.40 (*0-8357-4404-3*, 203722400008) Bks Demand.

Orr, David W., jt. ed. see Eagan, David J.

Orr, Dorothy B., jt. auth. see Orr, Robert T.

***Orr, Douglas M., Jr. & Stuart, Alfred W., eds.** The North Carolina Atlas: Portrait for a New Century. LC 99-17353. (Illus.). 480p. 2000. 45.00 (*0-8078-2507-7*) U of NC Pr.

Orr, Ed. Enigmas: After de Chirico. 1986. pap. 5.00 (*0-941240-06-1*) Ommation Pr.

Orr, Edward W. Performance Enhancement in Coatings. LC 98-30429. 2p. 1998. 98.00 (*1-56990-263-1*) Hanser-Gardner.

Orr, Elaine N. Subject to Negotiation: Reading Feminist Criticism & American Women's Fictions. LC 96-44391. 204p. 1997. text 32.50 (*0-8139-1715-8*) U Pr of Va.

Orr, Eleanor. Twice As Less. LC 98-115953. 256p. 1997. pap. 12.95 (*0-393-31741-2*) Norton.

Orr, Eliza C. & Orr, Ben, eds. Qanemcikarluni Tekitnarqelartuq: One Must Arrive with a Story to Tell: Traditional Narratives by the Elders of Tununak, Alaska. LC 95-2303. (ESK.). xxx, 377p. 1995. pap. 19.00 (*1-55500-052-5*) Alaska Native.

Orr, Eliza C., et al. Ellangellemni: When I Became Aware. LC 97-2509. (ENG & ESK.). 1997. pap. 26.00 (*1-55500-061-4*) Alaska Native.

Orr, Elizabeth L. Geology of Oregon. 260p. (C). 1996. pap. 33.95 (*0-8403-8058-5*) Kendall-Hunt.

Orr, Elizabeth L., jt. auth. see Orr, William.

Orr, Emma R. Principles of Druidry: The Only Introduction You'll Ever Need. (Illus.). 160p. 1999. pap. 11.00 (*0-7225-3674-7*) Thorsons PA.

***Orr, Emma Restall.** Spirits of the Sacred Grove: The World of a Druid Priestess. LC 99-205432. 272p. 1998. pap. 16.00 (*0-7225-3596-1*, Pub. by Thorsons MD) Natl Bk Netwk.

Orr European Geophysical Symposium Staff. Geomagnetic Pulsations: Proceedings of the Orr European Geophysical Symposium, Budapest, August 1980. Orr, D., ed. 100p. 1983. pap. 30.00 (*0-08-026508-1*, Pergamon Pr) Elsevier.

***Orr-Ewing, Malcolm.** Asia Pacific Business Travel Guide 1999. (Illus.). 328p. 1999. pap. 19.95 (*1-871985-30-7*) Priory Pubns.

Orr, F. William & Singh, Gurmit. Bone Metastasis. (Medical Intelligence Unit Ser.). 225p. 1995. 89.95 (*1-57059-319-1*) Landes Bioscience.

Orr, F. William, et al. Microcirculation in Cancer Metastasis. LC 96-6236. (Illus.). 304p. 1991. lib. bdg. 202.00 (*0-8493-6154-0*, RC269) CRC Pr.

Orr, Fred. How to Pass Exams. 2nd ed. Orig. Title: Test Taking Power. (Illus.). 160p. 1998. pap. 7.95 (*1-86448-482-9*) IPG Chicago.

— How to Succeed at Part-Time Study. 1988. pap. 12.95 (*0-04-305007-7*, Pub. by Allen & Unwin Pty) Paul & Co Pubs.

— Study Skills for Successful Students. 1992. pap. 10.95 (*1-86373-118-0*, Pub. by Allen & Unwin Pty) Paul & Co Pubs.

Orr, Genevieve B., jt. ed. see Muller, Klaus-Robert.

Orr, Gilbert MacWilliams, Jr., jt. ed. see Orr, Lois Harlan.

Orr, Gregory. Burning the Empty Nests. LC 96-83416. (Classic Contemporaries Ser.). 80p. 1997. reprint ed. pap. 12.95 (*0-88748-250-3*) Carnegie-Mellon.

— City of Salt. LC 94-42339. (Poetry Ser.). 80p. 1995. pap. 10.95 (*0-8229-5557-1*); text 24.95 (*0-8229-3876-6*) U of Pittsburgh Pr.

***Orr, Gregory.** Orpheus & Eurydice: A Lyric Sequence. 80p. 2001. pap. 12.00 (*1-55659-151-9*) Copper Canyon.

Orr, Gregory. Richer Entanglements: Essays & Notes on Poetry & Poems. LC 93-10796. (Poets on Poetry Ser.). 192p. (C). 1993. pap. 13.95 (*0-472-06525-4*, 06525) U of Mich Pr.

— Stanley Kunitz: An Introduction to the Poetry. LC 84-23213. (Columbia Introductions to Twentieth Century American Poetry Ser.). 296p. 1985. text 44.00 (*0-231-05234-0*) Col U Pr.

Orr, Gregory & Voight, Ellen B., eds. Poets Teaching Poets: Self & the World. LC 96-4234. 288p. (C). 1996. text 47.50 (*0-472-09621-4*, 09621) U of Mich Pr.

Orr, Gregory & Voigt, Ellen B., eds. Poets Teaching Poets: Self & the World. LC 96-4234. 288p. 1996. pap. 17.95 (*0-472-06621-8*, 06621) U of Mich Pr.

Orr, Gregory, tr. see Volkova, Bronislava, et al.

Orr, H. Winnett. On the Contributions of Hugh Owen Thomas of Liverpool, Sir Robert Jones of Liverpool & London, John Ridlon, M. D. of New York & Chicago to Modern Orthopedic Surgery. Phillips, William R. & Rosenberg, Janet, eds. LC 79-6920. (Physically Handicapped in Society Ser.). 1980. reprint ed. lib. bdg. 26.95 (*0-405-13129-1*) Ayer.

Orr, Helen & Orr, Bob. The Europeans. unabridged ed. Landes, William-Alan, ed. LC 98-15804. 55p. 1998. pap. 6.00 (*0-88734-773-8*) Players Pr.

Orr, Helen, jt. auth. see Orr, Bob.

Orr, J. B., et al. What Science Stands For. LC 72-134157. (Essay Index Reprint Ser.). 1977. 17.95 (*0-8369-1938-6*) Ayer.

Orr, J. Edwin. An Apprenticeship of Faith. rev. ed. Roberts, Richard O., ed. xvi, 144p. 1993. mass mkt. 6.95 (*0-940033-49-6*) R O Roberts.

— Campus Aflame: A History of Evangelical Awakenings in Collegiate Communities. Roberts, Richard O., ed. LC 93-78598. 286p. 1994. pap. 14.95 (*0-940033-48-8*) R O Roberts.

— The Event of the Century: The 1857-1858 Awakening. Roberts, Richard O., ed. xviii, 384p. 1989. 27.50 (*0-940033-39-9*) R O Roberts.

— My All His All. Roberts, Richard O., ed. xiv, 170p. 1989. 14.95 (*0-940033-40-2*) R O Roberts.

Orr, J. M. Libraries As Communication Systems, 17. LC 76-8739. (Contributions in Librarianship & Information Science Ser.: No. 17). 221p. 1977. 55.00 (*0-8371-8936-5*, ORL, Greenwood Pr) Greenwood.

Orr, Jack. Black Athlete: His Story in American History. (J). (gr. 6 up). 1969. lib. bdg. 15.95 (*0-87460-104-5*) Lion Bks.

Orr, James. The Christian View of God & the World. LC 89-2580. 512p. 1989. pap. 18.99 (*0-8254-3370-3*, Kregel Class) Kregel.

— God's Image in Man: And Its Defacement in Light of Modern Denials. 332p. 1997. pap. 25.00 (*1-57910-043-0*) Wipf & Stock.

— A Guide to Putting Yourself in the Movies. 246p. 1987. per. 9.95 (*0-943629-01-2*) Swan Pub.

— The Resurrection of Jesus. 292p. 1997. pap. 22.00 (*1-57910-042-2*) Wipf & Stock.

Orr, James, ed. International Standard Bible Encyclopedia, 4 vols., Set. 3200p. 1994. 179.95 (*1-56563-026-2*) Hendrickson MA.

Orr, James E. An Apprenticeship of Faith. LC 89-82774. Orig. Title: Can God. xvi, 144p. (Orig.). 1993. pap. 6.95 (*0-926474-04-9*) Intl Awakening Pr.

— Campus Aflame: A History of Evangelical Awakenings in Collegiate Communities. rev. ed. LC 93-78598. 286p. 1994. pap. text 14.95 (*0-926474-07-3*) Intl Awakening Pr.

— The Event of the Century. 300p. 1989. lib. bdg. 27.50 (*0-926474-01-4*) Intl Awakening Pr.

— My All, His All. rev. ed. 215p. 1989. reprint ed. lib. bdg. 14.95 (*0-926474-02-2*) Intl Awakening Pr.

Orr, James M. & D'Amico, Francesca. Summer Bridge Activities - Middle School Vol. 8: Sixth-Seventh Grade. VanLeeuwen, Michele, ed. (Illus.). 176p. (J). (gr. 6-7). 1998. mass mkt. 12.95 (*1-887923-09-8*) Rainbow UT.

Orr, James M., et al. Summer Bridge Activities - Middle School Vol. 9: Seventh-Eighth Grade. VanLeeuwen, Michele, ed. (Illus.). (Orig.). (J). (gr. 7-8). 1998. mass mkt. 12.95 (*1-887923-10-1*) Rainbow UT.

Orr, James R., et al. A Guide To...Putting Yourself in the Movies. Billac, Pete, ed. LC 87-91245. 246p. (gr. 12 up). 1987. pap. 9.95 (*0-943629-26-8*) Swan Pub.

Orr, James W., Jr., et al. Complications in Gynecologic Surgery: Prevention, Recognition & Management. Sims, J. Marion, ed. LC 93-41475. (Illus.). 360p. 1994. text 88.00 (*0-397-51269-4*, Lippnctt) Lppncott W & W.

Orr, James W., jt. auth. see Shingleton, Hugh M.

Orr, Jean, jt. auth. see Luker, Karen A.

Orr, Jessie F. Dare to Believe You Live after Death. 347p. (C). 1988. 40.00 (*0-7212-0747-2*, Pub. by Regency Pr GBR) St Mut.

Orr, Joe B. The Boatguy Company Boat Log Book. 124p. 1998. pap. 13.95 (*0-9667138-0-X*) Boatguy Co.

Orr, John. Cinema & Modernity. (Illus.). 232p. 1993. pap. text 26.95 (*0-7456-1186-9*) Blackwell Pubs.

***Orr, John.** Contemporary Cinema. 224p. 1998. 26.00 (*0-7486-0836-2*, Pub. by Edinburgh U Pr) Col U Pr.

Orr, John & Klaic, Dragan, eds. Terrorism & Modern Drama. 1991. text 68.00 (*0-7486-0173-2*, Pub. by Edinburgh U Pr) Col U Pr.

— Terrorism & Modern Drama. 288p. 1992. pap. 25.00 (*0-7486-0195-3*, Pub. by Edinburgh U Pr) Col U Pr.

Orr, John, jt. auth. see Bartholomew, Roy A.

Orr, John, jt. ed. see Nicholson, Colin.

Orr, John, tr. see Jordan, Jorgu.

Orr, John L. Triangular Algebras & Ideals of Nest Algebras. LC 95-382. (Memoirs of the American Mathematical Society Ser.: No. 562). 49p. 1995. pap. 28.00 (*0-8218-0405-7*, MEMO/117/562) Am Math.

Orr, John W., Jr. Reflections from the Shrine: An Anecdotal History of HIghtstown & East Windsor. Martin, David G., ed. (Illus.). 424p. 1998. 40.00 (*0-944413-49-8*, 138) Longstreet Hse.

***Orr, John W., Jr.** Set up Running: The Life of a Pennsylvania Railroad Engineman. LC 00-28818. 2000. write for info. (*0-271-02056-3*) Pa St U Pr.

Orr, Julian E. Talking about Machines: An Ethnography of a Modern Job. LC 96-23924. (IRL Press Book/Collection on Technology & Work). 192p. 1996. text 32.50 (*0-8014-3297-9*) Cornell U Pr.

— Talking about Machines: An Ethnography of a Modern Job. (IRL Press Book/Collection on Technology & Work). 192p. 1996. pap. text 13.95 (*0-8014-8390-5*) Cornell U Pr.

Orr, Julian E., jt. ed. see Barley, Stephen R.

Orr, Julie. Finders Keepers. Hoffman, Joan, ed. (Jump Ahead Bk.). (Illus.). 32p. (J). (ps-3). 1994. student ed. 2.25 (*0-88743-111-9*, 02081) Sch Zone Pub Co.

Orr, Katherine S. The Coral Reef Coloring Book. LC 90-101277. (NaturEncyclopedia Ser.). (Illus.). 48p. (J). (gr. 4-7). 1988. pap. 6.95 (*0-88045-090-8*) Stemmer Hse.

— The Hawaiian Coral Reef Coloring Book. 5th ed. (NaturEncyclopedia Ser.). (Illus.). 48p. (J). (gr. 1-6). 1992. pap. 5.95 (*0-88045-122-X*, Intl Design) Stemmer Hse.

— My Grandpa & the Sea. LC 89-23876. (Illus.). 32p. (J). (gr. k-4). 1990. lib. bdg. 19.95 (*0-87614-409-1*, Carolrhoda) Lerner Pub.

— My Grandpa & the Sea. (Illus.). 32p. (J). (gr. k-4). 1991. pap. 5.95 (*0-87614-525-X*, Carolrhoda) Lerner Pub.

— Story of a Dolphin. (Illus.). 32p. (J). (gr. k-4). pap. 6.95 (*0-87614-951-4*, Carolrhoda) Lerner Pub.

— Story of a Dolphin. LC 92-28656. (Illus.). 32p. (J). (gr. k-4). 1993. lib. bdg. 14.95 (*0-87614-777-5*, Carolrhoda) Lerner Pub.

— Wondrous World of the Mangrove Swamps. (Illus.). 32p. 1989. pap. 3.95 (*0-9613236-2-0*) Florida Flair Bks.

Orr, Katherine S. & Berg, Carl J., Jr. The Queen Conch. (Illus.). 32p. 1987. pap. 2.95 (*0-89317-038-0*) Windward Pub.

Orr, Katherine S., jt. auth. see Weiss, Jaqueline S.

Orr, Kathy. A Christmas Garland. 40p. (J). 1991. lib. bdg. 8.95 (*0-8378-2069-3*) Gibson.

— Dearly Beloved Wedding Album. 64p. 1994. 20.00 (*0-8378-2243-2*) Gibson.

— Dearly Beloved Wedding Guest Book. 48p. 1994. 13.00 (*0-614-04419-7*) Gibson.

— Dearly Beloved Wedding Organizer. 1994. 20.00 (*0-8378-2245-9*) Gibson.

Orr, Ken. The One Minute Methodology. LC 84-61222. 66p. 1990. pap. 12.95 (*0-932633-17-X*) Dorset Hse Pub Co.

Orr, Ken, jt. auth. see Higgins, Dave.

Orr, Kenneth G. Field Notes on the Burmese Standard of Living. LC 77-87019. reprint ed. 35.00 (*0-404-16848-5*) AMS Pr.

Orr, Kenneth G., et al. The Zimmerman Site: A Report of Excavations at the Grand Village of Kaskaskia, LaSalle County, Illinois. Brown, James A., ed. (Reports of Investigations: No. 9). (Illus.). 86p. 1974. pap. 2.10 (*0-89792-021-X*) Ill St Museum.

Orr, Kenneth T. Structured Systems Development. LC 77-88593. (Illus.). 192p. (Orig.). 1986. pap. 19.95 (*0-917072-06-5*, Yourdon) P-H.

Orr, Kevin. Overcoming by the Blood: Of the Lamb & by the Word of Your Testimony. 50p. (Orig.). 1996. pap. write for info. (*1-57502-149-8*) Morris Pubng.

Orr, Kim. Seafare: A Collection of Favorite Recipes of Those Who Serve in the United States Navy. 150p. 1998. spiral bd. 16.00 (*0-9657312-0-0*) SFN Inc.

Orr, Kimbel, ed. see Gephardt, Dennis & Bullard, Lacy.

Orr, Larry, et al. Does Training for the Disadvantaged Work? Evidence from the National JTPA Study. 375p. 1996. pap. text 36.50 (*0-87766-647-4*); lib. bdg. 73.00 (*0-87766-646-6*) Urban Inst.

Orr, Larry L. Social Experiments: Evaluating Public Programs with Experimental Methods. LC 98-25337. 217p. 1998. 69.95 (*0-7619-1294-0*); pap. 29.95 (*0-7619-1295-9*) Sage.

Orr, Leonard. About Your Femininity. 1994. 5.00 (*0-945793-22-7*) Inspir Univ.

— Breaking the Death Habit: The Story of Bhartriji, Immortal Yogi of 2000 Years. LC 97-39685. (Illus.). 120p. 1998. pap. 14.95 (*1-883319-68-4*) Frog Ltd CA.

Orr, Leonard. A Catalogue Checklist of English Prose Fiction: 1750-1800. LC 79-64848. x, 204p. 1979. 39.00 (*0-87875-171-8*) Whitston Pub.

— Existentialism & Phenomenology: A Guide for Research. LC 77-93782. xiv, 197p. 1978. 35.00 (*0-87875-141-6*) Whitston Pub.

Orr, Leonard. Fire. 1997. 20.00 (*0-945793-21-9*) Inspir Univ.

— Healing Power of Birth & Rebirth. 1994. 20.00 (*0-945793-19-7*) Inspir Univ.

— Personal Energy Management. 1996. 20.00 (*0-945793-20-0*) Inspir Univ.

Orr, Leonard. Semiotic & Structuralist Analyses of Fiction: An Introduction & a Bibliographic Survey. LC 86-50685. vi, 224p. 1987. 48.00 (*0-87875-331-1*) Whitston Pub.

Orr, Leonard, ed. De-Structing the Novel: Essays in Applied Post-Modern Hermeneutics. LC 81-52811. xii, 263p. (C). 1982. 45.00 (*0-87875-223-4*) Whitston Pub.

Orr, Leonard & Billy, Ted, eds. A Joseph Conrad Companion. LC 98-46819. 360p. 1999. lib. bdg. 85.00 (*0-313-29289-2*) Greenwood.

Orr, Leonard D. Babaji, the Angel of the Lord. 1995. 20.00 (*0-945793-18-9*) Inspir Univ.

— Bhartriji - Immortal Yogi of Two Thousand Years. 1990. 22.00 (*0-945793-05-7*) Inspir Univ.

— Breath Awareness: Breath Awareness for Public Schools, Medical Profession. (YA). (gr. 7 up). 1988. pap. 20.00 (*0-945793-02-2*) Inspir Univ.

— The Common Sense of Physical Immortality. 1992. pap. write for info. (*0-318-23459-9*) L Orr.

— Common Sense of Physical Immortality. rev. ed. 1992. pap. 20.00 (*0-945793-00-6*) Inspir Univ.

— Critical Essays on Coleridge. (Critical Essays on British Literature Ser.). 208p. 1994. 48.00 (*0-8161-8867-X*, Twyne) Mac Lib Ref.

— The Death Urge. 1995. 20.00 (*0-945793-15-4*) Inspir Univ.

— A Dictionary of Critical Theory. LC 90-22816. 488p. 1991. lib. bdg. 85.00 (*0-313-23527-9*, ODC, Greenwood Pr) Greenwood.

— The Energy of Success. 1990. 20.00 (*0-945793-12-X*) Inspir Univ.

— Government Without Taxes. 1991. 20.00 (*0-945793-14-6*) Inspir Univ.

— How to Be Successful in the Self Improvement Business. 1990. 20.00 (*0-945793-07-3*) Inspir Univ.

— How to Make Democracy Work. 1990. 22.00 (*0-945793-06-5*) Inspir Univ.

— How to Make Democracy Work. 1990. pap. write for info. (*0-318-23461-0*) L Orr.

— The Money Seminar. 1990. 20.00 (*0-945793-11-1*) Inspir Univ.

— The Money System. 1990. 20.00 (*0-945793-13-8*) Inspir Univ.

— Physical Immortality. (YA). (gr. 7 up). 1988. pap. 11.00 (*0-945793-01-4*) Inspir Univ.

— Physical Immortality for Christians. (YA). (gr. 7 up). 1986. 22.00 (*0-945793-03-0*) Inspir Univ.

— Problems & Poetics of the Nonaristotelian Novel. LC 89-46139. 176p. 1991. 32.50 (*0-8387-5182-2*) Bucknell U Pr.

— Prosperity Consciousness Consultation. 1990. 20.00 (*0-945793-10-3*) Inspir Univ.

— The Science of Everlasting Life. 1988. pap. write for info. (*0-318-62542-3*) L Orr.

— Secrets of Youthing. 1994. 22.00 (*0-945793-16-2*) Inspir Univ.

— The Story of Rebirthing. 1990. 5.00 (*0-945793-08-1*) Inspir Univ.

— Turning Senility Misery into Victory. 1990. 10.00 (*0-945793-17-0*) Inspir Univ.

Orr, Leonard D., compiled by. Research in Critical Theory since 1985: A Classified Bibliography, 21. LC 89-16863. (Bibliographies & Indexes in World Literature Ser.: No. 21). 480p. 1989. lib. bdg. 89.50 (*0-313-26388-4*, ORC/, Greenwood Pr) Greenwood.

Orr, Leonard D., ed. Yeats & Postmodernism. (Irish Studies). 192p. 1990. text 39.95 (*0-8156-2506-5*) Syracuse U Pr.

Orr, Leonard D., et al, eds. Critical Theory, Cultural Politics, & Latin American Narrative. LC 92-53744. (C). 1993. text 34.50 (*0-268-00795-0*) U of Notre Dame Pr.

Orr, Leonard D. & Ray, Sondra. Rebirthing in the New Age. LC 76-53337. 240p. 1983. pap. write for info. (*0-89087-134-5*) Celestial Arts.

Orr, Leonard H., ed. see Herman, Stewart W., et al.

Orr, Leslie C. Donors, Devotees & the Daughters of God: Temple Women in Medieval Tamilnadu. LC 98-7533. (South Asia Research Ser.). (Illus.). 318p. 2000. text 45.00 (*0-19-509962-1*) OUP.

Orr, Linda. Headless History: Nineteenth-Century French Historiography of the Revolution. LC 89-22140. (Illus.). 216p. 1990. text 35.00 (*0-8014-2379-1*) Cornell U Pr.

— Jules Michelet: Nature, History, & Language. LC 76-13662. 256p. 1976. text 37.50 (*0-8014-0976-4*) Cornell U Pr.

Orr, Lisa, et al, eds. Working Class Studies. (Womens Studies Quarterly Ser.: Vol. 98, Nos. 1 & 2). 256p. 1998. pap. 18.00 (*1-55861-191-6*) Feminist Pr.

***Orr, Lois Harlan & Orr, Gilbert MacWilliams, Jr., eds.** Maury County Remembered: The Gilbert MacWilliams Orr Family Collection. (Tennessee Heritage Library Bicentennial Collection). (Illus.). 192p. 1999. 32.95 (*1-57736-164-4*, Hillsboro Pr) Providence Hse.

Orr, Lynn F., et al. Monet: Late Paintings of Giverny from the Musee Marmottan. (Illus.). 88p. 1995. pap. 14.95 (*0-8109-2610-5*, Pub. by Abrams) Time Warner.

Orr, Margaret T. Evaluating School to Work Transition. (Education Reform & School-to-Work Transition Ser.). 36p. 1995. pap. text, teacher ed. 12.00 (*0-614-24520-6*) Natl Inst Work.

— What to Do about Youth Dropouts? A Summary of Solutions. O'Connor, Mary L., ed. 32p. (Orig.). 1987. pap. 5.00 (*0-943567-00-9*) SEEDCO.

Orr, Marion. Black Social Capital: The Politics of School Reform in Baltimore, 1986-1998. LC 99-22219. (Studies in Government & Public Policy). 256p. 1999. pap. 17.95 (*0-7006-0982-2*) U Pr of KS.

***Orr, Marion.** Black Social Capital: The Politics of School Reform in Baltimore, 1986-1998. LC 99-22219. (Studies in Government & Public Policy). 256p. 1999. 35.00 (*0-7006-0981-4*) U Pr of KS.

Orr, Marjorie. Illustrated Guide to the Zodiac. LC 98-47759. 1999. 21.95 (*0-8069-2417-9*) Sterling.

Orr, Marsha E., jt. ed. see Hennessy, Kathryn A.

Orr, Mary. Claude Simon: The Intertextual Dimension. 224p. 1993. 60.00 (*0-85261-372-5*, Pub. by Univ of Glasgow) St Mut.

O

*Orr, Mary. Flaubert: Writing the Masculine. LC 99-48440. 256p. 2000. write for info. (0-19-815969-2) OUP.

Orr, Mary. Grass Widows. 1976. pap. 5.25 (0-8222-0477-0) Dramatists Play.

— Madame Bovary: Representations of the Masculine. (Romanticism & after in France/Le Romantisme et apres en France Ser.: Vol. 3). 229p. 1999. pap. text 37.95 (0-8204-4247-X) P Lang Pubng.

*Orr, Mary. Madame Bovary -- Representations of the Masculine. Raitt, Allan W., ed. (Romanticism & after in France Ser.). 229p. 1999. pap. 37.95 (3-906762-90-4, Pub. by P Lang) P Lang Pubng.

Orr, Mary. Roommates. 1989. pap. 3.25 (0-8222-0964-0) Dramatists Play.

— The Wisdom of Eve. rev. ed. 1994. pap. 5.25 (0-8222-1429-6) Dramatists Play.

— Women Must Weep & Women Must Work. 1963. pap. 5.25 (0-8222-1273-0) Dramatists Play.

— Women Still Weep: A Sequel to Women Must Weep. 1980. pap. 5.25 (0-8222-1275-7) Dramatists Play.

Orr, Mary & Denham, Reginald. Be Your Age: Manuscript Edition. 1953. pap. 13.00 (0-8222-1301-X) Dramatists Play.

— Dead Giveaway. 1982. pap. 5.25 (0-8222-0283-2) Dramatists Play.

— Minor Murder: Manuscript Edition. 1967. pap. 13.00 (0-8222-0760-5) Dramatists Play.

Orr, Mary, jt. ed. see Williams, Tony.

Orr, N. Lee. Church Music Handbook: For Pastors & Musicians. 1991. pap. 11.95 (0-687-07853-9) Abingdon.

— Church Music Handbook: For Pastors & Musicians. 1995. pap. text 12.95 (0-687-01624-X) Abingdon.

Orr, N. Lee & Bertrand, Lynn W., eds. The Collected Works of John Hill Hewitt. LC 94-76. (Nineteenth-Century American Musical Theater Ser.: No. 6). 328p. 1994. reprint ed. text 121.00 (0-8153-1370-5) Garland.

*Orr, N. Lee & Hardin, W. Dan. Choral Music in Nineteenth-Century America: A Guide to the Sources. LC 99-31630. 152p. 1999. 25.00 (0-8108-3664-5) Scarecrow.

Orr, Nancy, jt. auth. see McKean, Kay S.

Orr, Oliver H., Jr. Saving American Birds: T. Gilbert Pearson & the Founding of the Audubon Movement. (Illus.). 272p. 1992. 39.95 (0-8130-1129-9) U Press Fla.

Orr, P. C., jt. auth. see Gifford, Edward W.

*Orr, Patrick J. Exceptionally Preserved Conchostracans & Other Crustaceans from the Upper Carboniferous of Ireland, 62. (Special Papers in Palaeontology Ser.). (Illus.). 2000. pap. text 70.00 (0-901702-68-4) The Palaeontological Assn.

Orr, Phil C. Archaeology of Mescalitan Island & Customs of the Canalina. (Santa Barbara Museum of Natural History Occasional Papers). (Illus.). 68p. (C). 1943. pap. text 8.13 (1-55567-735-5) Coyote Press.

— Archaeology of Mescalitan Island & Customs of the Canalino. (Santa Barbara Museum of Natural History Occasional Papers: No. 5). (Illus.). 84p. (C). 1943. pap. 9.69 (1-55567-645-6) Coyote Press.

— Excavations in Moaning Cave. (Illus.). 22p. (C). 1952. pap. text 2.81 (1-55567-726-6) Coyote Press.

— Radiocarbon Dates from Santa Rosa Island, I. (Illus.). 13p. (C). 1956. pap. text 1.88 (1-55567-727-4) Coyote Press.

— Radiocarbon Dates from Santa Rosa Island, II. (Illus.). 13p. (C). 1960. pap. text 1.88 (1-55567-728-2) Coyote Press.

Orr, Philip. The Road to the Somme: Men of the Ulster Division Tell Their Story. LC 87-18228. (Illus.). 248p. 1992. pap. 29.00 (0-85640-390-3, Pub. by Blackstaff Pr) Dufour.

Orr, Priscilla. Jugglers & Tides: Poems. LC 96-79972. 92p. 1997. 21.95 (1-889262-02-1) Hannacroix.

Orr, Richard. O&CB Streetcars of Omaha & Council Bluffs. (Illus.). viii, 348p. 1996. 59.95 (0-9653505-0-9) R Orr.

— Richard Orr's Nature Cross-Sections. (Illus.). (J). 22.99 (0-590-24633-X) Scholastic Inc.

Orr, Robert. Religion in China. 144p. (Orig.). 1980. 4.95 (0-318-16788-3) US-China Peoples Friendship.

*Orr, Robert D. Death of an Insurance Salesman? The Sale of Insurance & Financial Services in the Internet Age. LC 00-133111. 256p. 2000. pap. 19.95 (1-58597-037-9) Leathers Pub.

Orr, Robert M., Jr. The Emergence of Japan's Foreign Aid Power. 178p. (C). 1992. pap. 17.50 (0-231-07047-0) Col U Pr.

Orr, Robert T. Mammals of Lake Tahoe. (Illus.). 127p. 1949. 7.50 (0-940228-07-6) Calif Acad Sci.

Orr, Robert T. & Moffitt, James. Birds of the Lake Tahoe Region. (Illus.). 150p. 1971. 8.00 (0-940228-08-4) Calif Acad Sci.

Orr, Robert T. & Orr, Dorothy B. Mushrooms of Western North America. LC 77-93468. (California Natural History Guides Ser.: No.42). (Illus.). 1979. 45.00 (0-520-03656-5, Pub. by U CA Pr); pap. 13.95 (0-520-03660-3, Pub. by U CA Pr) Cal Prin Full Svc.

Orr, Robert T., et al. Marine Mammals of California. LC 78-165233. (California Natural History Guides Ser.: No. 29). 92p. 1972. pap. 12.95 (0-520-06515-8, Pub. by U CA Pr) Cal Prin Full Svc.

Orr, Robin A., et al. Introduction to Consumer-Based Nutrition. LC 89-84650. (Illus.). 160p. 1989. reprint ed. pap. 49.60 (0-608-06873-X, 206708100009) Bks Demand.

Orr, Ruth, ed. see Savitch, Cary.

Orr, Ryan. Adolescent Boys & Dealing with Sex. (Illus.). 60p. 1998. wbk. ed. 14.95 (0-9641861-2-8) Redhawk Pubng.

— The Ranch. 1982. 204p. (YA). (gr. 6 up). Date not set. pap. 18.95 (0-9641861-4-4) Redhawk Pubng.

Orr, S. Kiiluuq. (ESK.). 17p. (J). 1975. pap. 2.00 (0-933769-70-9) Alaska Native.

Orr, Salile & S. I. Artists Staff. Barbie: Mile 1. LC 98-86205. (Barbie Ser.). (Illus.). 32p. 1998. pap. 3.99 (0-307-26106-9, Goldn Books) Gldn Bks Pub Co.

Orr, Sandra. Huron: Grand Bend to Southampton. Hudson, Noel, ed. (Illus.). 160p. 1993. 35.00 (1-55046-059-5, Pub. by Boston Mills) Genl Dist Srvs.

Orr, Susan. Jerusalem & Athens: Reason & Revelation in the Works of Leo Strauss. 260p. 1995. pap. text 23.95 (0-8476-8011-8); lib. bdg. 59.00 (0-8476-8010-X) Rowman.

Orr, Tracy. No Right Way. 1995. pap. 12.95 (1-85727-087-8) LPC InBook.

Orr, Verlena. Woman Who Hears Voices: Poems. 28p. 1998. 3.00 (0-9653194-7-4) Future Tense.

Orr, Wendy. Aa-Choo! (Illus.). 32p. (J). (ps-3). 1992. pap. 4.95 (1-55037-208-4, Pub. by Annick); lib. bdg. 14.95 (1-55037-209-2, Pub. by Annick) Firefly Bks Ltd.

— Arabella. 1998. 16.00 (0-207-19164-6) HarpC.

*Orr, Wendy. Ark in the Park. LC 99-33342. (Illus.). 64p. (J). 2000. 15.95 (0-8050-6221-1) H Holt & Co.

Orr, Wendy. Bully Biscuit Gang. (Skinny Bks.). 1998. pap. 3.95 (0-207-19095-X) HarpC.

— A Light in Space. (Illus.). 124p. (J). (gr. 4-6). 1994. lib. bdg. 14.95 (1-55037-368-4, Pub. by Annick) Firefly Bks Ltd.

— A Light in Space. (Illus.). 124p. (J). (gr. 5-7). 1994. pap. 5.95 (1-55037-975-5, Pub. by Annick) Firefly Bks Ltd.

*Orr, Wendy. Nim's Island. 2001. mass mkt. 16.99 (0-375-91123-5, Pub. by Random Bks Yng Read); mass mkt. 14.95 (0-375-81123-0, Pub. by Random Bks Yng Read) Random.

Orr, Wendy. Peeling the Onion. 166p. (YA). (gr. 7-12). 1999. mass mkt. 4.50 (0-440-22773-9, LLL BDD) BDD Bks Young Read.

— Peeling the Onion. LC 96-42353. 176p. (J). (gr. 7-12). 1997. 16.95 (0-8234-1289-X) Holiday.

— Pegasus & Ooloo-Moo-Loo. (Illus.). 32p. (J). 1993. pap. 4.95 (1-55037-279-3, Pub. by Annick); lib. bdg. 14.95 (1-55037-278-5, Pub. by Annick) Firefly Bks Ltd.

— A Train to the City. (Illus.). 32p. 1993. pap. 4.95 (1-55037-283-1, Pub. by Annick); lib. bdg. 14.95 (1-55037-282-3, Pub. by Annick) Firefly Bks Ltd.

— The Wedding. (Illus.). 32p. 1993. pap. 4.95 (1-55037-281-5, Pub. by Annick); lib. bdg. 14.95 (1-55037-280-7, Pub. by Annick) Firefly Bks Ltd.

Orr, William & Guy, William. Living Hope: A Study of the New Testament Theme of Birth from Above. LC 88-34841. 208p. (Orig.). 1989. pap. 10.95 (0-86534-132-X) Sunstone Pr.

Orr, William & Orr, Elizabeth L. Geology of the Pacific Northwest. 406p. (C). 1995. pap. 54.69 (0-07-048018-4) McGraw.

— Rivers of the West: A Guide to the Geology & History. LC 85-61228. (Illus.). 342p. (Orig.). 1985. 14.95 (0-9606502-1-0) W&E Orr.

*Orr, William, et al. Geology of Oregon. 5th ed. 268p. (C). 1999. per. 41.95 (0-7872-6608-6) Kendall-Hunt.

Orr, William C., jt. ed. see Champion, Malcolm C.

Orr, William C., jt. ed. see Pressman, Mark R.

Orr, William D. Conversational Computers. LC 68-30916. 261p. reprint ed. pap. 81.00 (0-608-30462-X, 201195400080) Bks Demand.

— First Gentleman's Cookbook. Holloway-Eiche, Pamela, ed. (Illus.). 360p. (Orig.). 1989. pap. 12.50 (0-9622297-7-6) Gov Mansion Restor.

Orr, William F. Corinthians I. LC 75-42441. (Anchor Bible Ser.: Vol. 32). 416p. 1976. 34.00 (0-385-02853-9) Doubleday.

Orr, William I. All about VHF Amateur Radio. 1991. pap. 11.95 (0-933616-10-4) Radio Pubns.

— All about VHF Amateur Radio. (Illus.). 172p. pap. 13.95 (0-8230-8705-0, RAC Bks) Watsn-Guptill.

— The W6SAI HF Antenna Handbook. LC 96-84315. (Illus.). 172p. (Orig.). 1996. pap. 19.95 (0-943016-15-0) CQ Commns Inc.

Orr, William I. & Cowan, S. D. Simple Low-Cost Wire Antennas for Radio Amateurs. 2nd ed. LC 76-190590. (Illus.). 192p. 1972. 11.95 (0-933616-02-3) Radio Pubns.

Orr, William I. & Cowan, Stuart. The Truth about CB Antennas. (Illus.). 240p. 1990. pap. 13.95 (0-8230-8708-5, RAC Bks) Watsn-Guptill.

Orr, William I. & Cowan, Stuart D. All about Cubical Quad Antennas. 3rd ed. LC 82-80282. (Illus.). 112p. 1982. 9.95 (0-933616-03-1) Radio Pubns.

— All About Vertical Antennas. LC 86-61499. (Illus.). 192p. 1986. 10.95 (0-933616-09-0) Radio Pubns.

— All about Vertical Antennas. (Illus.). 192p. pap. 13.95 (0-8230-8710-7, RAC Bks) Watsn-Guptill.

— Beam Antenna Handbook. LC 83-61824. (Illus.). 271p. 1983. 11.95 (0-933616-04-X) Radio Pubns.

Orr, William I. & Cowan, Stuart D. Beam Antenna Handbook. (Illus.). 112p. pap. 13.95 (0-8230-8704-2, RAC Bks) Watsn-Guptill.

Orr, William I. & Cowan, Stuart D. Better Shortwave Reception. 5th ed. LC 57-14916. (Illus.). 160p. 1957. 9.95 (0-933616-05-8) Radio Pubns.

— The Radio Amateur Antenna Handbook. LC 78-53340. (Illus.). 191p. 1978. 11.95 (0-933616-07-4) Radio Pubns.

— The Radio Amateur Antenna Handbook. (Illus.). 192p. 1991. pap. 13.95 (0-8230-8706-9, RAC Bks) Watsn-Guptill.

— Simple, Low-Cost Wire Antennas for Radio Amateurs. (Illus.). 192p. 1990. pap. 13.95 (0-8230-8707-7, RAC Bks) Watsn-Guptill.

— The Truth about CB Antennas. 2nd ed. LC 70-164932. (Illus.). 240p. 1971. 11.95 (0-933616-08-2) Radio Pubns.

Orr, William I., jt. auth. see Cowan, Stuart D.

Orr, William I., ed. see Nelson, William.

Orr, William J. Radio Handbook. 23rd ed. 672p. 1987. pap. text 52.95 (0-7506-9947-7) Buttrwrth-Heinemann.

Orr, William J., Jr., ed. see Zeh, Frederick.

Orr, William W. The Anguish of Earth's Tribulation. (Prophecy Ser.). 48p. reprint ed. pap. 3.50 (0-944412-01-7) Glad Tid.

— Believer's First Bible Course. (Basic Bible Ser.). 48p. reprint ed. pap. 3.50 (0-944412-00-9) Glad Tid.

— What Is Heaven Like? (Bible Answers Ser.). 48p. reprint ed. pap. 3.50 (0-944412-02-5) Glad Tid.

Orr, Willie. Discovering Argyll, Mull & Iona. (Discovering Ser.). 224p. (C). 1996. pap. 26.85 (0-85976-269-6, Pub. by J Donald) St Mut.

Orr, Wilson L. & White, Curt M., eds. Geochemistry of Sulfur in Fossil Fuels. LC 90-239. (ACS Symposium Ser.: No. 429). (Illus.). 693p. 1990. text 120.00 (0-8412-1804-8, Pub. by Am Chemical) OUP.

Orrell & Elston. Microsoft Works 2.0. 1992. pap. text. write for info. (0-273-03833-8) Addison-Wesley.

Orrell, John, jt. auth. see Gurr, Andrew.

*Orrell, Robert. Blowout. LC 99-53396. (Illus.). 192p. 2000. pap. 14.95 (1-57409-109-3) Sheridan.

Orren, Gary R., ed. Blurring the Lines: Candidates & Journalists in American Elections. 320p. 1992. 24.95 (0-02-923476-X) Free Pr.

Orren, Gary R., jt. auth. see Verba, Sidney.

Orren, Gary R., jt. ed. see Mann, Thomas E.

Orren, Karen. Belated Feudalism: Labor, the Law & Liberal Development in the United States. 250p. (C). 1992. text 59.95 (0-521-41039-8); pap. text 18.95 (0-521-42254-X) Cambridge U Pr.

— Corporate Power & Social Change: The Politics of the Life Insurance Industry. LC 73-8118. (Illus.). 224p. reprint ed. pap. 69.50 (0-608-14756-7, 202586200046) Bks Demand.

Orren, Karen & Skowronek, Stephen. American Political Development. 2000. pap. write for info. (0-393-97397-2) Norton.

— Studies in American Political Development: An Annual, Vol. 3. Vol. 3. 352p. (C). 1989. pap. 18.00 (0-300-04487-9); text 38.00 (0-300-04486-0) Yale U Pr.

Orrey, Leslie. The Foundations of Harmony & Composition: Music Book Index. 137p. 1993. reprint ed. lib. bdg. 69.00 (0-7812-9662-5) Rprt Serv.

— Opera: A Concise History. LC 86-51512. (World of Art Ser.). (Illus.). 252p. 1987. pap. 14.95 (0-500-20217-6, Pub. by Thames Hudson) Norton.

Orrick, Bentley & Crumpacker, Harry L. The Tampa Tribune: A Century of Florida Journalism. LC 97-45368. 1998. write for info. (1-879852-57-8) Univ Tampa.

Orrick, James. Matthew Arnold & Goethe. LC 70-179267. (Studies in Comparative Literature: No. 35). 1972. reprint ed. lib. bdg. 75.00 (0-8383-1368-X) M S G Haskell Hse.

Orridge, Dia. A Girl Called Judith. large type ed. (Linford Romance Library). 224p. 1988. pap. 16.99 (0-7089-6587-3, Linford) Ulverscroft.

— Through the Ivory Gate. large type ed. (Romance Ser.). 1989. 27.99 (0-7089-2062-4) Ulverscroft.

Orridge, Martin. Another 75 Ways to Liven Up Your Training A Second Collection of Energizing Activities. LC 98-45607. 1999. write for info. (0-566-08152-0) Ashgate Pub Co.

— How to Deliver Training. LC 97-31502. 160p. 1998. pap. 61.95 (0-566-07913-5, Pub. by Gower) Ashgate Pub Co.

— 75 Ways to Liven up Your Training. LC 96-8092. (Illus.). 250p. 1996. 59.95 (0-566-07774-4, Pub. by Gower) Ashgate Pub Co.

Orrieux, Claude & Pantel, Pauline S. A History of Greece. LC 98-56267.Tr. of Histoire Greque. (Illus.). 528p. (C). 1999. text 69.95 (0-631-20308-7) Blackwell Pubs.

*Orrieux, Claude & Pantel, Pauline S. A History of Greece. LC 98-56267.Tr. of Histoire Greque. (Illus.). 528p. (C). 1999. pap. text 34.95 (0-631-20309-5) Blackwell Pubs.

Orrill, Robert. Education & Democracy: Re-Imagining Liberal Learning in America. 1997. 29.95 (0-87447-588-0) College Bd.

Orrill, Robert. Education & Democracy: Re-Imagining Liberal Learning in America. 1998. pap. 22.95 (0-87447-589-9) College Bd.

Orrin, Geoffrey R. Medieval Churches in the Vale of Glamorgan. 550p. (C). 1989. 175.00 (0-905928-80-6, Pub. by D Brown & Sons Ltd) St Mut.

— Medieval Churches in the Vale of Glamorgan. deluxe limited ed. 550p. (C). 1989. 350.00 (0-905928-92-X, Pub. by D Brown & Sons Ltd) St Mut.

Orringer, Oscar, ed. Residual Stress in Rails, 2 vols. (Engineering Application of Fracture Mechanics Ser.). 492p. (C). 1992. text 340.50 (0-7923-1651-7) Kluwer Academic.

Orringer, Oscar, jt ed. see Tong, Pin.

Orringer, Stephanie L. Pedro Salinas' Theater of Self-Authentication. LC 94-28221. (AUS II: Vol. 199). 137p. (C). 1995. text 39.95 (0-8204-1994-X) P Lang Pubng.

Orriols, Antoni L. Diccionari de la Ciencia i la Tecnologia Nuclears. (CAT.). 316p. 1979. pap. 29.95 (0-7859-5876-2, 8429714766) Fr & Eur.

Orrios, Angel G., ed. & tr. see Garcia Lorca, Federico.

*Orris, J. Burdeane. Excel 2000 Essentials Advanced with CD-ROM. 240p. (C). 1999. pap. text 18.67 incl. audio compact disk (1-58076-303-0, Prentice Hall) P-H.

Orrison, Estrella H. Eckert Record: Story of Georg Bernhardt Eckert & His Descendants, 1793-1957. (Illus.). 124p. 1997. reprint ed. pap. 19.50 (0-8328-8436-7); reprint ed. lib. bdg. 29.50 (0-8328-8435-9) Higginson Bk Co.

Orrison, Katherine. Written in Stone: Making Cecil B. DeMille's Epic, The Ten Commandments. LC 98-51596. (Illus.). 206p. (Orig.). 1998. pap. 33.00 (1-879511-24-X, Vestal Pr) Madison Bks UPA.

Orrison, Katherine, jt. auth. see Wilcoxon, Henry.

Orrison, William W. Atlas of Brain Function. LC 94-45686. 176p. 1995. pap. 49.00 (0-86577-528-1) Thieme Med Pubs.

— Introduction to Neuroimaging. (Illus.). 384p. 1988. 88.00 (0-316-66492-8, Little Brwn Med Div) Lppncott W & W.

— Neuroimaging, 5 Vols. LC 97-39761. 1999. text. write for info. (0-7216-6799-6, W B Saunders Co) Harcrt Hlth Sci Grp.

Orrison, William W., et al. Functional Brain Imaging. (Illus.). 496p. (C). (gr. 13). 1994. text 98.00 (0-8151-6509-9, 24274) Mosby Inc.

Orriss, Mike. Delphi Fat FAQs. (Illus.). 560p. 1998. pap., pap. text 39.95 incl. cd-rom (0-07-913263-4) McGraw.

Orriss, N., tr. see Babin, Claude, ed.

Orrit, L., tr. see Lalanne, J. R., et al.

Orrmont, Arthur & Rosenstiel, Leonie. Literary Agents of North America. 5th rev. ed. (Orig.). 1993. pap. 33.00 (0-911085-12-2) Author Aid.

Orrmont, Arthur & Rosenstiel, Leonie, eds. Literary Agents of North America. 3rd ed. 200p. (Orig.). 1988. pap. 19.95 (0-911085-04-1) Author Aid.

Orru, Marco, et al. The Economic Organization of East Asian Capitalism. 426p. 1996. 58.00 (0-7619-0479-4) Sage.

Orrye, B. Dictionnaire Noms Famille Pays Creusois. (FRE.). 1998. 59.95 (0-320-00204-7) Fr & Eur.

Orsag, Ann, jt. auth. see Fishman, Joel.

*Orsatti, A., et al. Abelian Groups, Module Theory & Topology: Proceedings in Honor of Adalberto Orsatti's 60th Birthday. LC 98-29983. (Lecture Notes in Pure & Applied Mathematics Ser.). (Illus.). 472p. 1998. pap. text 165.00 (0-8247-1937-9) Dekker.

Orsay, Jonathan. Examkrackers MCAT Biology. Hsu, Linda, ed. (Illus.). 254p. 1999. pap. 38.95 (1-893858-00-6) OSO Pubg.

— Examkrackers MCAT Chemistry. (Illus.). 184p. 1999. pap. 32.95 (1-893858-03-0) OSO Pubg.

— Examkrackers MCAT Organic Chemistry. (Illus.). 124p. 1999. pap. 21.95 (1-893858-02-2) OSO Pubg.

— Examkrackers MCAT Physics. (Illus.). 230p. 1999. pap. 34.95 (1-893858-01-4) OSO Pubg.

*Orsay, Jonathan. Examkrackers 1001 Questions in MCAT Physics. Calvin, Scott, ed. (Illus.). 160p. (C). 2000. pap. 29.95 (1-893858-04-9) OSO Pubg.

Orsborn, Carol. Art of Resilience: One Hundred Paths to Wisdom & Strength in an Uncertain World. LC 97-200927. 1997. pap. 15.00 (0-609-80061-2) Harmony Bks.

— How Would Confucius Ask for a Raise? 336p. 1995. reprint ed. pap. 11.00 (0-380-72250-X, Avon Bks) Morrow Avon.

*Orsborn, Carol. How Would Confucius Ask for a Raise? 100 Enlightened Solutions for Business Problems. 331p. 2000. reprint ed. 23.00 (0-7881-9324-4) DIANE Pub.

— Inner Excellence at Work: The Path to Meaning, Spirit & Success. LC 99-29738. 150p. 1999. pap. 14.95 (0-8144-7041-6) AMACOM.

Orsborn, Carol M. Return from Exile: One Woman's Journey Back to Judaism. LC 84-28048. 220p. 1998. 19.95 (0-8264-1102-9) Continuum.

Orsburn, Douglas K. Spares Management: An Introduction. (Illus.). 250p. 1991. 49.95 (0-8306-7626-0, 3626) TAB Bks.

— Spares Management Handbook. 496p. 1991. 49.95 (0-07-157637-1) McGraw.

Orsburn, Jack, et al. The New Self-Directed Work Teams: Mastering the Challenge. 2nd ed. LC 99-30690. (Illus.). 416p. 1999. 45.00 (0-07-043414-X) McGraw.

Orsburn, Jack D., et al. Self-Directed Work Teams: The New American Challenge. 353p. 1990. 40.00 (1-55623-341-8, Irwn Prfssnl) McGraw-Hill Prof.

Orsden, Donald B. The Holy Bible - the Final Testament: What Is the Significance of 666? (Illus.). 48p. (Orig.). (C). 1992. pap. 9.99 (1-881373-00-2) Orsden Pr.

Orselli, Paul, ed. The Cheapbook: A Compendium of Inexpensive Exhibit Ideas. (Orig.). 1996. pap. 11.95 (0-944040-42-X) AST Ctrs.

Orsen, Susan M., ed. & photos by see Coghill, Elstan.

Orsenna, Erik. History of the World in 9 Guitars. LC 99-31625. 112p. 1999. 12.95 (1-56649-046-4) Welcome Rain.

Orser, C. E., Jr. A Historical Archaeology of the Modern World. LC 95-26380. (Contributions to Global Historical Archaeology Ser.). (Illus.). 264p. (C). 1996. 41.00 (0-306-45173-5) Plenum.

Orser, Charles E., Jr., ed. Images of the Recent Past: Readings in Historical Archaeology. LC 96-10102. (Illus.). 480p. 1996. 69.00 (0-7619-9141-7); pap. 26.95 (0-7619-9142-5) AltaMira Pr.

Orser, Charles E., Jr., et al. Historical Archaeology. LC 94-18994. 291p. (C). 1997. pap. text 38.60 (0-673-99094-X) Addson-Wesley Educ.

Orser, Stanton. Dancing with the Wind. LC 96-38811. (Illus.). 32p. (J). (gr. k-3). 1997. lib. bdg. 14.95 (0-87358-639-5, Rising Moon Bks) Northland AZ.

Orser, W. Edward. Blockbusting in Baltimore: The Edmondson Village Story. (Illus.). 256p. (C). 1994. pap. text 21.00 (0-8131-0935-3) U Pr of Ky.

Orshalick, David, jt. auth. see Dale, Nell.

Orshalick, David W., jt. auth. see Dale, Nell B.

Orshan, G., ed. Plant Pheno. Morphological Studies in Mediterranean Type Ecosystems. (Geobotany Ser.). (C). 1988. text 354.00 (90-6193-656-X) Kluwer Academic.

Orshan, G., jt. auth. see Danin, A.

O

An Asterisk (*) at the beginning of an entry indicates that the title is appearing for the first time.

Orsher. An Atlas of Diseases of the Ear in Dog & Cat. 1994. write for info. (*0-397-51199-X*) Lppncott W & W.

Orsi-Battaglini, Andrea & Karpen, Ulrich, eds. Scientific Research in the Federal Republic of Germany: Essays on the Constitutional, Administrative & Financial Problems. 279p. 1990. 53.00 (*3-7890-1913-5*, Pub. by Nomos Verlags) Intl Bk Import.

Orsi, Giuseppe, et al. Arbeit - Arbeitslosigkeit. (Rechtsphilosophische Hefte Ser.: Bd. 5). (GER.). 160p. 1996. 34.95 (*3-631-30440-4*) P Lang Pubng.

Orsi, Jan, jt. auth. see Strikes, Thunder.

Orsi, Maria. The Red Lion: The Elixir of Eternal Life. 364p. 1987. pap. 8.95 (*0-9632370-0-4*) Comput Composit.

Orsi, Michael P., et al. Touching the Truth: A Summary & Commentary on the Splendor of Truth. 64p. (Orig.). 1995. pap. 2.25 (*0-8198-7379-9*) Pauline Bks.

Orsi, Pietro. Cavour & the Making of Modern Italy. LC 73-14461. (Heroes of the Nations Ser.). reprint ed. 30.00 (*0-404-58279-6*) AMS Pr.

Orsi, Richard J., et al, eds. Yosemite & Sequoia: A Century of California National Parks. LC 92-42370. 1993. pap. 17.95 (*0-520-08161-7*, Pub. by U CA Pr) Cal Prin Full Svc.

Orsi, Richard J., jt. auth. see Gutierrez, Ramona.

Orsi, Richard J., jt. ed. see Starr, Kevin.

Orsi, Robert A. The Madonna of 115th Street: Faith & Community in Italian Harlem, 1880-1950. LC 85-10799. 366p. (C). 1988. reprint ed. pap. 17.00 (*0-300-04264-7*) Yale U Pr.

— Thank You, St. Jude: Women's Devotion to the Patron Saint of Hopeless Causes. LC 95-26017. (Illus.). 336p. 1996. 35.00 (*0-300-06476-4*); pap. 18.00 (*0-300-07659-2*) Yale U Pr.

Orsi, Robert A., ed. Gods of the City: Religion & the American Urban Landscape. LC 98-48338. (Religion in North America Ser.). (Illus.). 581p. 1999. pap. 19.95 (*0-253-21276-6*) Ind U Pr.

***Orsi, Robert A., ed.** Gods of the City: Religion & the American Urban Landscape. LC 98-48338. (Religion in North America Ser.). (Illus.). 581p. 1999. text 39.95 (*0-253-33499-3*) Ind U Pr.

Orsini, Ann. Can I Go Home Now? 237p. (Orig.). 1994. pap. 14.95 (*0-9642267-0-7*) Phoenix Sparks.

Orsini, D. L., et al. The Neuropsychology Casebook. (Illus.). 300p. 1988. 92.95 (*0-387-96681-1*) Spr-Verlag.

***Orsini, Jacqueline.** Mary: Images of the Holy Mother. LC 00-22361. (Illus.). 2000. 19.95 (*0-8118-2850-6*) Chronicle Bks.

Orsini, James A. & Divers, Thomas J. Manual of Equine Emergencies: Treatment & Procedures. 6th ed. Donley, Stephanie, ed. LC 97-35784. (Illus.). 592p. (C). 1998. text 55.00 (*0-7216-2425-1*, W B Saunders Co) Harcrt Hlth Sci Grp.

***Orsini, Joseph.** Italian Family Cooking: Unlocking a Treasury of Recipes & Stories. LC 99-56353. (Illus.). 167p. 2000. text 27.50 (*0-312-24225-5*) St Martin.

Orsini, Joseph E. Father Orsini's Italian Kitchen. (Illus.). 288p. 1993. pap. 12.95 (*0-312-09524-4*) St Martin.

Orsini, Joseph L., jt. ed. see Kassarjian, Harold H.

Orsini, Larry, et al. World Accounting Series, 3 vols. 1987. ring bd. 590.00 (*0-8205-1835-2*) Bender.

Orsino, Joseph. Storage Battery Manufacturing Manual. 3rd ed. 1985. 35.00 (*0-685-12355-3*) IBMA Pubns.

Orska, Krystyna. Illustrated Poems for Children. (Illus.). (J). 1985. 12.95 (*0-02-689410-6*) Macmillan.

Orski, C. Kenneth, et al. TDM Beyond the Crossroads. 14p. 1999. pap. text 15.00 (*0-935403-30-2*, IR-096) Inst Trans Eng.

Orskov, E. R. Protein Nutrition in Ruminants. 2nd ed. (Illus.). 175p. 1992. text 62.00 (*0-12-528481-0*) Acad Pr.

Orsman, H. W., ed. The Dictionary of New Zealand English: A Dictionary of New Zealandisms on Historical Principles. 982p. 1998. text 175.00 (*0-19-558347-7*) OUP.

Orso, Ethelyn G. The Macha of Chira, Costa Rica: Confessions of an Anthropologist. (Illus.). 170p. (Orig.). (C). 1991. pap. 13.95 (*0-9630475-0-7*) Lakeview LA.

— Modern Greek Humor: A Collection of Jokes & Ribald Tales. LC 78-24845. 288p. reprint ed. pap. 89.30 (*0-608-13206-3*, 205604900044) Bks Demand.

— St. Joseph Altar Traditions of South Louisiana. LC 90-82375. (Louisiana Life Ser.: No. 4). 57p. 1990. pap. 5.00 (*0-940984-59-8*) Univ LA Lafayette.

Orso, Mary E. The Crab Lover's Book: Recipes & More. LC 94-44277. 256p. 1995. pap. 16.95 (*0-87805-796-X*) U Pr of Miss.

Orso, Steven N. Philip IV & the Decoration of the Alcazar of Madrid. LC 85-19442. (Illus.). 330p. 1986. reprint ed. pap. 102.30 (*0-608-07163-3*, 206738800009) Bks Demand.

— Velazquez, "Los Borrachos," & Painting at the Court of Philip Fourth. LC 93-493. (Illus.). 224p. (C). 1994. text 80.00 (*0-521-44452-7*) Cambridge U Pr.

Orsolini, Keith R. The Non-Intimidating Computer Book: The Absolute Bare Bones, Nuts & Bolts Couldn't Be Simpler, Guide to Understanding & Using Personal Computers. (Illus.). 84p. (Orig.). (C). 1989. pap. text. write for info. (*0-318-65725-2*) KRO Enterprises.

Orsrofisan, Fremir. Moruontodun & Other Plays. LC 85-840264. 138 p. 1982. write for info. (*0-582-78575-8*) Longman.

Orsted, Bent & Schlichtkrull, Henrik. Algebraic & Analytic Methods in Representation Theory. LC 96-22985. (Perspectives in Mathematics Ser.: Vol. 17). (Illus.). 343p. 1996. text 59.95 (*0-12-625440-0*) Acad Pr.

Orsted, Hans C., et al. Selected Scientific Works of Hans Christian Orsted. LC 97-6179. 664p. 1998. text 89.50 (*0-691-04334-5*, Pub. by Princeton U Pr) Cal Prin Full Svc.

***Orsted, Peter, et al, eds.** Africa Proconsularis, Regional Studies in the Segermes Valley Vol. III: Historical Conclusions. (Illus.). 384p. 2000. 59.95 (*87-7288-828-8*, Pub. by Aarhus Univ Pr) David Brown.

Orstein, Norman J., jt. auth. see Mann, Thomas E.

Orster, Eckart, jt. auth. see Henrich, Dieter.

Orstrom. Dynamics & Use of Sardinella Resources from Upwelling off Ghana & Ivory Coast (Dynamique et Usage des Ressources en Sardinelles de l'Upwelling Cotier de Ghana et de la Cote-D'Ivoire) Bard, F. X. & Koranteg, K. A., eds. 440p. 1993. pap. 30.00 (*2-7099-1258-9*, Pub. by LInstitut Francais) Balogh.

— La Vegetation de L'Afrique (The Vegetation of Africa)Tr. of Vegetation of Africa. (FRE.). 384p. 1986. pap. 50.00 (*2-7099-0832-8*, Pub. by LInstitut Francais) Balogh.

Orsucci, Franco. The Complex Matters of the Mind. LC 98-2516. (Studies of Nonlinear Phenomena in Life Sciences: Vol. 6). 300p. 1998. 64.00 (*981-02-3339-6*) World Scientific Pub.

Orsulak. Methods in Clinical Toxicology. 420p. 1999. 73.95 (*0-8493-7883-4*) CRC Pr.

Orsund-Gassiot, Cindy A. & Lindsey, Sharon, eds. Handbook of Medical Staff Management. (Health Care Administration Ser.). 336p. 1990. 85.00 (*0-8342-0177-1*) Aspen Pub.

Orsuto, Donna L., jt. ed. see Billy, Dennis J.

Orsy, Ladislas M. From Vision to Legislation. From The Council to a Code of Laws. LC 85-60746. (Pere Marquette Lectures). 50p. 1985. 15.00 (*0-87462-540-8*) Marquette.

— The Lord of Confusion. 1969. 10.00 (*0-87193-064-1*) Dimension Bks.

— Theology & Canon Law: New Horizons for Legislation & Interpretation. 200p. (Orig.). 1992. pap. text 19.95 (*0-8146-5011-2*) Liturgical Pr.

***Orszag, M.** Quantum Optics. LC 99-33296. (Illus.). 400p. 1999. 79.95 (*3-540-65008-3*) Spr-Verlag.

Orszag, S. A., jt. auth. see Bender, Carl M.

Orszag, S. A., jt. auth. see Mendez, Raul H.

Orszag, S. A., ed. see Amini, S., et al.

Orszag, S. A., ed. see Bruch, E.

Orszag, S. A., ed. see Camp, C. V. & Gipson, G. Steven.

Orszag, S. A., ed. see Deconinck, J., et al.

Orszag, S. A., ed. see Hayami, K.

Orszag, Steven A., jt. auth. see Gottlieb, David.

Orszagh, L., et al, eds. Hungarian-English Classical Comprehensive Dictionary. (ENG & HUN.). 2000p. 1998. 225.00 (*963-05-7515-9*, Pub. by Akade Kiado) Intl Spec Bk.

Orszagh, L. & Magay, T. English-Hungarian Classical Comprehensive Dictionary. (ENG & HUN.). 2000p. 1998. 225.00 (*963-05-7514-0*, Pub. by Akade Kiado) St Mut.

Orszagh, L., ed. see Futasz, D. & Kovecses, Z.

Orszagh, Laszlo. Comprehensive Hungarian-English Dictionary. 9th ed. 1991. 87.00 (*0-7859-8943-9*) Fr & Eur.

— English-Hungarian: Little. 17th ed. (ENG & HUN.). 608p. 1994. 18.00 (*963-05-6942-6*) IBD Ltd.

— English-Hungarian Comprehensive Dictionary. 1995. 995.00 (*963-05-6963-9*, Pub. by Akade Kiado) St Mut.

— English-Hungarian Comprehensive Dictionary. 11th ed. (ENG & HUN.). 2319p. 1992. 100.00 (*0-7859-8856-4*) Fr & Eur.

— English-Hungarian Comprehensive Dictionary, Vol. 2, N-Z. (ENG & HUN.). 1992. Not sold separately (*0-614-32197-2*) Fr & Eur.

— English-Hungarian Concise Dictionary. 12th rev. ed. (ENG & HUN.). 1052p. 1986. 59.95 (*0-8288-0511-3*, M8553) Fr & Eur.

— English-Hungarian Dictionary. (ENG & HUN.). 791p. 42.50 (*0-87557-043-7*) Saphrograph.

— English-Hungarian Pocket Dictionary. 608p. (C). 1992. 21.00 (*963-05-6358-4*, Pub. by Akade Kiado) St Mut.

— English-Hungarian Pocket Dictionary. 14th ed. (ENG & HUN.). 608p. 1984. pap. 19.95 (*0-8288-0512-1*, M8771) Fr & Eur.

— English to Hungarian Classical Comprehensive Dictionary. rev. ed. (ENG & HUN.). 2000p. 1998. 150.00 (*0-320-00000-1*) Fr & Eur.

— Hungarian-English Comprehensive Dictionary, 2 vols., Set. 8th rev. ed. (ENG & HUN.). 2319p. 1985. 150.00 (*0-8288-0513-X*, M8552) Fr & Eur.

— Hungarian-English Comprehensive Dictionary Vol. 1: A-K; Vol. 2: L-ZS, 2 vols., Set. 2159p. (C). 1992. 145.00 (*963-05-6254-5*, Pub. by Akade Kiado) St Mut.

— Hungarian-English Concise Dictionary. (ENG & HUN.). 1996. 38.00 (*0-7859-9685-0*) Fr & Eur.

— Hungarian-English Concise Dictionary. 10th ed. (ENG & HUN.). 1179p. 1985. 39.95 (*0-8288-0514-8*, M 8554) Fr & Eur.

— Hungarian-English Dictionary, Magyar Angol Szotar, 2 vols. (ENG & HUN.). 49.50 (*0-87557-042-9*) Saphrograph.

— Hungarian-English Pocket Dictionary. 464p. (C). 1992. 21.00 (*963-05-6359-2*, Pub. by Akade Kiado) St Mut.

— Hungarian-English Pocket Dictionary. 14th ed. (ENG & HUN.). 464p. 1984. 17.95 (*0-8288-0515-6*, M3168) Fr & Eur.

— Hungarian to English Classical Comprehensive Dictionary. rev. ed. (ENG & HUN.). 2000p. 1998. 150.00 (*0-320-00001-X*) Fr & Eur.

Orszagh, Laszlo, jt. auth. see Magay, Tamas.

Orszagh, Laszlo, jt. ed. see Magay, Tamas.

Orszagh, Laszlo, jt. ed. see Maqay, T.

Orszagh, V. A Concise English-Hungarian Dictionary. (ENG & HUN.). 1091p. 1981. 110.00 (*0-569-00407-1*) St Mut.

— A Concise Hungarian-English Dictionary. (ENG & HUN.). 1180p. 1987. 95.00 (*0-569-00343-1*, Pub. by Collets) St Mut.

— English-Hungarian Dictionary, 2 vols. (ENG & HUN.). 2336p. 1988. 190.00 (*0-569-00359-8*, Pub. by Collets) St Mut.

— Hungarian-English Dictionary, 2 vols. (ENG & HUN.). 2160p. 1988. 190.00 (*0-569-00409-8*, Pub. by Collets) St Mut.

***Orszula, Ed.** Just Steel: A Justin Steel Mystery/Thriller. 228p. 2000. pap. 12.95 (*0-9701596-0-9*) Chris Mystery.

Orszula, Edward. One More Time. Chris Mystery Publishing Staff, ed. 240p. 1999. pap. 12.95 (*0-7392-0298-7*, PO3418) Morris Pubng.

Orszulik, S. T., ed. Environmental Technology in the Oil Industry. (Illus.). 352p. 1996. pap. write for info. (*0-7514-0347-4*) Kluwer Academic.

Orszulik, S. T., jt. auth. see Mortier, R. M.

Orszulik, S. T., jt. ed. see Mortier, K. M.

Ort, Daniel. Is This the End of Little Rico? LC 98-12917. 72p. 1998. pap. 12.95 (*0-914061-73-9*) Orchises Pr.

— My Mother Always Called Me by My Brother's Name. 128p. (Orig.). 1994. pap. 14.95 (*0-914061-45-3*) Orchises Pr.

— Ort Bran. LC 90-34158. 128p. (Orig.). 1990. pap. 14.95 (*0-914061-15-1*); boxed set 20.00 (*0-914061-18-6*) Orchises Pr.

Ort, Donald, ed. Oxygenic Photosynthesis: The Light Reactions. (Advances in Photosynthesis Ser.). 696p. (C). 1996. pap. text 147.00 (*0-7923-3684-4*) Kluwer Academic.

Ort, Donald, ed. see Yocum, Charles F.

Ort, Harry H. Structured Data Processing Design. LC 84-14506. 224p. 1985. pap. text 17.56 (*0-201-05425-6*) Addison-Wesley.

Ort, Kathleen, ed. see Caldwell, D. W.

Ort, Kathleen, ed. see Clarke, Herbert.

Ort, Kathleen, ed. see Constantz, George.

Ort, Kathleen, ed. see Gray, Mary T.

Ort, Kathleen, ed. see Horn, Elizabeth L.

Ort, Kathleen, ed. see Ippisch, Hanneke.

Ort, Kathleen, ed. see Norton, O. Richard.

Ort, Kathleen, ed. see Rutter, Michael.

Ort, Kathleen, ed. see Taylor, Ronald J.

Ort, Kathleen, ed. see Taylor, Ronald J. & Douglas, George.

Ort, Kathleen, ed. see Wassink, Jan L.

Ort, Myron. Preserving Perishables with Vacuum Packing. 130p. (Orig.). 1981. pap. text. write for info. (*0-941446-00-X*) Tethys Pr.

Orta, G. D. Colloquies on the Simples & Drug of India. (C). 1988. 115.00 (*0-7855-2293-X*, Pub. by Scientific) St Mut.

— Colloquies on the Simples & Drugs of India. 509p. (C). 1985. text 300.00 (*0-89771-616-7*, Pub. by Intl Bk Distr) St Mut.

— Colloquies on the Simples & Drugs of India. 509p. (C). 1979. reprint ed. 300.00 (*0-7855-3127-0*, Pub. by Intl Bk Distr) St Mut.

Orta, John. Computer Applications in Nutrition & Dietetics: An Annotated Bibliography. LC 87-30450. 256p. 1988. text 15.00 (*0-8240-6621-9*) Garland.

Ortado, Judy. Didn't You Know? (Illus.). 23p. (J). (ps-4). 1995. 19.50 (*1-57529-007-3*) Kabel Pubs.

— A Koala Carrying a Polka-Dot Bowl. (Illus.). 24p. (J). (gr. 1-4). 1997. 29.50 (*1-57529-054-5*) Kabel Pubs.

— A Koala Carrying a Polka-Dot Bowl. large type unabridged ed. (Illus.). 24p. (J). (ps-5). 1997. 24.50 (*1-57529-055-3*) Kabel Pubs.

***Ortakovski, Vladimir.** Minorities in the Balkans. LC 00-23470. 300p. 2000. 95.00 (*1-57105-129-5*) Transnatl Pubs.

Ortalda, Robert A., Jr. How to Live Within Your Means & Still Finance Your Dreams. 384p. 1990. pap. 11.00 (*0-671-69607-6*, Fireside) S&S Trade Pap.

Ortaldo, John R., jt. ed. see Chambers, William H.

Ortaldo, John R., jt. ed. see Ransom, Janet H.

Ortalli, Ida, jt. auth. see International Conference on the Applications of the Mhossbauer Effect Staff.

***Ortberg.** Groups. (Pursuing Spiritual Transformation Ser.). 2000. pap. 10.99 (*0-310-22076-9*) Zondervan.

***Ortberg & Poling.** Fully Devoted. (Pursuing Spiritual Transformation Ser.). 2000. pap. 7.99 (*0-310-22073-4*) Zondervan.

— Gifts. (Pursuing Spiritual Transformation Ser.). 2000. pap. 10.99 (*0-310-22077-7*) Zondervan.

— Giving. (Pursuing Spiritual Transformation Ser.). 2000. pap. 7.99 (*0-310-22078-5*) Zondervan.

— Grace. (Pursuing Spiritual Transformation Ser.). 2000. pap. 7.99 (*0-310-22074-2*) Zondervan.

— Growth. (Pursuing Spiritual Transformation Ser.). 2000. pap. 7.99 (*0-310-22075-0*) Zondervan.

Ortberg, John. Christianity Illustrated. Date not set. 16.99 (*0-310-22863-8*) HarpC.

— In the Life You've Always Wanted. 240p. 1998. pap. 12.99 (*0-310-22699-6*) Zondervan.

Ortberg, John. An Inside Look at the Willow Creek Worship Service: Building a New Community. 29.99 incl. VHS (*0-310-22357-1*) Zondervan.

Ortberg, John. The Life You've Always Wanted: Spiritual Disciplines for Ordinary People. LC 97-29959. 208p. 1997. 15.99 (*0-310-21214-6*) Zondervan.

— Love Beyond Reason: Moving God's Love from Your Head to Your Heart. LC 98-26062. 208p. 1998. 16.99 (*0-310-21215-4*) Zondervan.

Ortberg, John, Jr., jt. auth. see Tan, Siang-Yang.

ORTE Architekturnetzwerk Niederosterreich Staff. Architecture in Lower Austria 1986-1997. (Illus.). 224p. 1997. 40.00 (*3-7643-5746-0*, Pub. by Birkhauser) Princeton Arch.

Ortega, jt. auth. see Benford.

Ortega, A. & Mulay, S. P., eds. Proceedings of the 1995 National Heat Transfer Conference: August 6-9, 1995, Portland, Oregon, Vol. 1. 164p. 1995. 88.00 (*0-7918-1702-4*, H00984) ASME.

Ortega, Adolfo. Calo Arbis: Semiotic Aspects of a Chicano Language Variety. LC 90-25441. (American University Studies: Linguistics: Ser. XIII, Vol. 21). XXXI, 264p. (C). 1991. text 45.95 (*0-8204-1542-1*) P Lang Pubng.

Ortega-Alcalde, D., jt. ed. see Candell-Riera, J.

Ortega, Antonia L. Moonlit: Short Stories by Antonio Lupez Ortega. Budoff, Nathon, tr. from SPA. LC 98-33715.Tr. of Lunar. 208p. (Orig.). 1998. pap. 15.95 (*1-57129-057-5*, Lumen Eds) Brookline Bks.

Ortega, Bob. In Sam We Trust: The Untold Story of Sam Walton & How Wal-Mart Is Devouring America. LC 98-21598. (Illus.). 384p. 1998. 25.95 (*0-8129-6377-6*, Times Bks) Crown Pub Group.

— In Sam We Trust: The Untold Story of Sam Walton & How Wal-Mart Is Devouring America. large type ed. 2000. pap. 16.00 (*0-8129-3297-8*) Random Hse Lrg Prnt.

Ortega, Catherine P. Cowbirds & Other Brood Parasites. LC 98-8911. (Illus.). 380p. 1998. 65.00 (*0-8165-1527-1*) U of Ariz Pr.

Ortega Cavero, David. Diccionario Portugues-Espanol, Espanol-Portugues, 2 vols., Set. (POR & SPA.). 1856p. 1975. 175.00 (*0-8288-5832-2*, S12405) Fr & Eur.

Ortega, Cesar. Costos: The Cost of Building in Mexico. (SPA.). (Orig.). 1996. pap. 450.00 (*968-6735-04-6*, COSTOS) R S Means.

Ortega, Claudia. Religious Clip Art Book. (Illus.). 32p. (Orig.). 1989. pap. 24.95 (*1-55612-311-6*) Sheed & Ward WI.

Ortega, Cristina. Los Ojos del Tejedor: Through the Eyes of the Weaver. LC 96-11137. (Illus.). 64p. (YA). 1997. pap. 14.95 (*0-940666-81-2*) Clear Light.

Ortega, Daniel & Sheehan, Daniel. Assault on Nicaragua: The Untold Story of the U. S. 'Secret War' Holt, Rod, ed. 115p. (Orig.). 1987. pap. write for info. (*0-929405-00-5*) Walnut Pub.

Ortega, Emilio, tr. see Jones, Allan F.

Ortega, Hector. The Comic Trial of Joseph K. Text & Context. Flores, Manuel, ed. (Illus.). 136p. 1997. pap. 22.50 (*1-879691-40-X*) SDSU Press.

Ortega, Hernan & Vari, Richard P. Annotated Checklist of the Freshwater Fishes of Peru. LC 86-600237. (Smithsonian Contributions to Zoology Ser.: No. 437). 29p. reprint ed. pap. 30.00 (*0-8357-5612-2*, 202955400061) Bks Demand.

Ortega, Idsa A., jt. ed. see Ortiz, Angel R.

Ortega, Idsa E. Alegria, see Alegria Ortega, Idsa E.

Ortega, J., jt. intro. see Fuentes, Carlos.

Ortega, J. M. Introduction to Parallel & Vector Solution of Linear Systems. LC 88-721. (Frontiers of Computer Science Ser.). (Illus.). 318p. (C). 1988. 75.00 (*0-306-42862-8*, Plenum Trade) Perseus Pubng.

— Matrix Theory: A Second Course. LC 86-30312. (University Series in Mathematics). (Illus.). 274p. (C). 1987. text 49.50 (*0-306-42433-9*, Kluwer Plenum) Kluwer Academic.

Ortega, James M. Numerical Analysis: A Second Course. LC 89-48562. (Classics in Applied Mathematics Ser.: No. 3). xiii, 201p. 1990. pap. 34.50 (*0-89871-250-5*) Soc Indus-Appl Math.

Ortega, James M. & Grimshaw, Andrew S. An Introduction to C++ & Numerical Methods. LC 97-36115. (Illus.). 288p. 1998. pap. text 36.95 (*0-19-511767-0*) OUP.

***Ortega, James M. & Rheinboldt, W. C.** Iterative Solution of Nonlinear Equations in Several Variables. (Classics in Applied Mathematics: No. 30). (Illus.). 580p. 2000. reprint ed. pap. 58.00 (*0-89871-461-3*, CL0030) Soc Indus-Appl Math.

Ortega, James M. & Voigt, Robert G. Solution of Partial Differential Equations on Vector & Parallel Computers. LC 85-61387. (Miscellaneous Bks.: No. 13). iii, 96p. 1985. pap. 22.00 (*0-89871-055-3*) Soc Indus-Appl Math.

Ortega, James M., jt. auth. see Golub, Gene H.

Ortega, Josbe, jt. auth. see Hayes, Joe.

Ortega, Jose. Alienacion y Agnesion en Juan Goytisolo en Senas de Identidad y Reivindicacion Del Conde Don Julian. 1973. 10.50 (*0-88303-012-8*); pap. 7.50 (*0-685-73216-9*) E Torres & Sons.

Ortega, Jose & Gassett, Jose O. Meditations on Hunting. LC 95-61397. (Illus.). 1995. 60.00 (*1-885106-18-1*) Wild Adven Pr.

Ortega, Jose R. Estudio Ceramografico y Petrografico del Area de San Cristobal de las Casas, Chiapas. 160p. 1990. pap. 7.00 (*968-6487-19-0*, IN024) UPLAAP.

***Ortega, Joshua.** Frequencies. LC 99-90380. 394p. 1999. pap. 19.99 (*0-9671120-4-4*) Omega Point.

Ortega, Julio. Ayacucho, Goodbye & Moscow's Gold: Two Novellas on Peruvian Politics & Violence. Miller, Yvette E., ed. Grossman, Edith & Kelly, Alita, trs. from SPA. LC 94-3634. (Discoveries Ser.). (SPA.). 104p. 1994. pap. 13.95 (*0-935480-66-8*) Lat Am Lit Rev Pr.

— Poetics of Change: The New Spanish-American Narrative. Greaser, Galen D., tr. (Texas Pan American Ser.). 200p. (C). 1984. reprint ed. pap. 10.95 (*0-292-76508-8*); reprint ed. text 20.00 (*0-292-76488-X*) U of Tex Pr.

— Reapropiaciones: Cultura y Nueva Escritura en Puerto Rico. 264p. 1991. pap. 10.50 (*0-8477-3620-2*) U of PR Pr.

Ortega, Julio, ed. La Cervantiada. 1994. 12.95 (*0-8477-0182-4*) U of PR Pr.

Ortega, Julio, ed. see Arguedas, Jose Maria.

Ortega, Koryne. Proud Ones: Poems by Koryne Ortega. (Illus.). 46p. (Orig.). 1988. pap. 5.00 (*0-943557-00-3*) Esoterica Pr.

Ortega, Leda, ed. see Finkel, Raphael A.

O

Ortega, Leda, ed. see Savitch, Walter J. & Main, Michael G.
Ortega, Leda, ed. see Wolfe, Michael.
Ortega, Mary, tr. see Telesis Corp. Staff.
Ortega, Pedro R. Christmas in Old Santa Fe: Stories. LC 73-90581. (Illus.). 107p. 1982. pap. 8.95 (*0-913270-25-3*) Sunstone Pr.
Ortega, Pedro R., tr. see Dressman, John.
Ortega, Rafael C. Anthology of Mexican American Literature. LC 94-61116. 203p. (C). 1995. pap. 24.00 (*0-9643219-0-4*) Tara Pubng.
Ortega, Roberto. For Humanity: Teachings of Life & Truth. 325p. (Orig.). 1992. pap. write for info. (*0-9631824-0-4*) Three Eras.
Ortega, Romeo. Passivity-Based Control of Euler-Lagrange Systems. LC 98-23128. 1998. 89.95 (*1-85233-016-3*) Spr-Verlag.
Ortega, Romeo, et al, eds. Advances in Adaptive Control. LC 91-16922. (Illus.). 424p. (C). 1991. text 89.95 (*0-87942-278-5*, PC0272-5) Inst Electrical.
***Ortega, Rosario Guarino.** Los Comentarios Al Ibis de Ovidio: El Largo Recorrido de Una Exegesis. 503p. 1999. 79.95 (*3-631-34051-6*) P Lang Pubng.
Ortega, Spottorno J. Relatos en Espiral. (Nueva Austral Ser.: Vol. 143). (SPA.). 1991. pap. text 24.95 (*84-239-1943-9*) Elliots Bks.
Ortega-Velez, Ruth. La Mujer en la Obra de Enrique Laguerre. LC 89-5382. 114p. (Orig.). 1990. pap. text 8.95 (*0-8477-3636-9*) U of PR Pr.
Ortega, Violeta & Velasco, Marina. Espanol Activo, Vol. 1. (Illus.). 112p. (YA). (gr. 5-8). 1996. pap. 14.73 (*1-928882-12-9*) CCLS Pubg Hse.
— Espanol Activo, Vol. 2. (Illus.). 112p. (YA). (gr. 5-8). 1996. pap. 16.03 (*1-928882-13-7*) CCLS Pubg Hse.
— Espanol Activo, Vol. 3. (Illus.). 112p. (YA). (gr. 5-8). 1996. pap. 16.03 (*1-928882-14-5*) CCLS Pubg Hse.
— Espanol Activo, 4 vols., Vol. 4. (Illus.). 112p. (YA). (gr. 5-8). 1996. pap. 16.03 (*1-928882-15-3*) CCLS Pubg Hse.
Ortega y Gasset, Jose. The Dehumanization of Art: And Other Essays on Art, Culture, & Literature. LC 68-8963. (Princeton Paperbacks Ser.: Vol. 128). 210p. 1968. reprint ed. pap. 65.10 (*0-7837-9281-6*, 206002000004) Bks Demand.
— La Deshumanizacion del Arte. (Nueva Austral Ser.: Vol. 13). (SPA.). 1991. pap. text 24.95 (*84-239-1813-0*) Elliots Bks.
— History As a System & Other Essays Toward a Philosophy of History. LC 81-13359. 269p. 1981. reprint ed. lib. bdg. 59.75 (*0-313-23112-5*, ORHS, Greenwood Pr) Greenwood.
— Mission of the University. 120p. (C). 1991. pap. text 24.95 (*1-56000-560-2*) Transaction Pubs.
***Ortega y Gasset, Jose.** The Origin of Philosophy. LC 99-56002. 2000. pap. 10.00 (*0-252-06896-3*) U of Ill Pr.
Ortega y Gasset, Jose. The Revolt of the Masses. LC 93-29295. 192p. 1994. pap. 10.95 (*0-393-31095-7*) Norton.
— El Tema de Nuestro Tiempo. (Nueva Austral Ser.: Vol. 28). (SPA.). 1991. pap. text 24.95 (*84-239-1828-9*) Elliots Bks.
Ortego, Hasa. Christmas Eve on the Big Bayou. 1974. 3.95 (*0-87511-091-6*) Claitors.
Ortego, Pedro R., tr. see LaFarge, Oliver.
Orten & McCracken. Small Animals Thoracic Surgery. (Illus.). 350p. 1994. 79.00 (*0-683-06670-6*) Lppncott W & W.
Ortenberg, Veronica. The English Church & the Continent in the Tenth & Eleventh Centuries: Cultural, Spiritual, & Artistic Exchanges. (Illus.). 352p. 1992. 85.00 (*0-19-820159-1*) OUP.
Ortenburger, Leigh N. & Jackson, Reynold G. A Climber's Guide to the Teton Range. 3rd ed. (Illus.). 544p. 1996. 35.00 (*0-89886-480-1*) Mountaineers.
Ortenburger, Rick. Black Forest Clocks. LC 90-63797. (Illus.). 300p. 1991. 79.95 (*0-88740-300-X*) Schiffer.
— Vienna Regulator Clocks. LC 89-64090. (Illus.). 180p. 1990. 39.95 (*0-88740-224-0*) Schiffer.
Ortese, Anna M. The Iguana. Martin, Henry, tr. from ITA. LC 87-20258.Tr. of L'Iguana. 208p. 1988. 14.95 (*0-914232-87-8*); pap. 9.00 (*0-914232-95-9*) McPherson & Co.
— The Lament of the Linnet. Creagh, Patrick, tr. from ITA. LC 98-159990. 325p. 1999. 24.00 (*1-86046-206-5*, Pub. by Harvill Press) FS&G.
— A Music Behind the Wall Vol. 1: Selected Stories. Martin, Henry, tr. & intro. by. 160p. 1994. 20.00 (*0-929701-39-9*) McPherson & Co.
***Ortese, Anna M.** A Music Behind the Wall Vol. 2: Selected Stories. Martin, Henry, tr. 224p. 1998. 22.00 (*0-929701-56-9*) McPherson & Co.
Orteu, Henri, jt. auth. see Norman, Jill.
Ortez, Sandra. Walk Across the Lawn. 1999. pap. write for info. (*1-58235-039-6*) Watermrk Pr.
Orth, D. L. Calculus in a New Key. (Illus.). (Orig.). 1976. pap. text 15.00 (*0-917326-05-9*) APL Pr.
Orth, Donald, ed. Place Names of America. (International Library of Names). 400p. (C). text. write for info. (*0-8290-1210-9*) Irvington.
Orth, Donald J. Dictionary of Alaska Place Names. 210.00 (*0-944780-02-4*) Todd Commns.
Orth, Donald S. Handbook of Cosmetic Microbiology. (Cosmetic Science & Technology Ser.: Vol. 12). (Illus.). 608p. 1993. text 250.00 (*0-8247-9012-X*) Dekker.
Orth, Donald S., jt. ed. see Kabara, Jon J.
Orth, Ghita. The Music of What Happens. LC 82-10280. (Eileen W. Barnes Award Ser.). (Illus.). 70p. (Orig.). 1982. pap. 5.50 (*0-938158-01-5*) Saturday Pr.
Orth-Gomer, Kristina, et al, eds. Women, Stress, & Heart Disease. LC 97-44966. 400p. 1996. 69.95 (*0-8058-2124-4*) L Erlbaum Assocs.
Orth-Gomer, Kristina & Schneiderman, Neil, eds. Behavioral Medicine Approaches to Cardiovascular Disease Prevention. LC 95-2986. 336p. 1995. text 69.95 (*0-8058-1820-0*) L Erlbaum Assocs.
Orth, Jane, ed. see Maddox, Kathleen B.
Orth, Jennifer, jt. auth. see Downs, Deeann.
Orth, John M. Solving Your Financial Puzzle: Making Ends Meet Plus More. LC 96-92828. (Illus.). xvi, 373p. (Orig.). 1996. pap. 24.95 (*0-9655379-0-0*, Pub. by Fin Sol Ltd) Johnson Bks.
Orth, John V. Combination & Conspiracy: A Legal History of Trade Unionism, 1721-1906. 224p. 1991. text 85.00 (*0-19-825299-4*) OUP.
— The North Carolina State Constitution: A Reference Guide, 16. LC 92-42676. (Reference Guides to the State Constitutions of the United States Ser.: No. 16). 216p. 1993. lib. bdg. 75.00 (*0-313-27570-X*, ONC, Greenwood Pr) Greenwood.
— The North Carolina State Constitution: With History & Commentary. LC 95-14496. (Reference Guides to the State Constitutions of the United States Ser.: No. 16). 212p. (C). 1995. text 24.95 (*0-8078-4551-5*) U of NC Pr.
Orth, Joy. Island: Our Alaskan Dream & Reality. LC 87-1308. (Illus.). 125p. (Orig.). 1987. pap. 9.95 (*0-88240-321-4*, Alaska NW Bks) Gr Arts Ctr Pub.
***Orth, Maureen.** Vulgar Favors. 560p. 2000. mass mkt. 7.50 (*0-440-22585-X*) Dell.
Orth, Maureen. Vulgar Favors: Andrew Cunanan, Gianni Versace & the Largest Failed Manhunt in U.S. History. LC 98-54318. 464p. 1999. 24.95 (*0-385-33286-6*) Delacorte.
Orth, Ralph H., ed. see Emerson, Ralph Waldo.
Orth, Robert E., jt. auth. see Fisher, T. W.
Orth, Samuel P. Centralization of Administration in Ohio. LC 68-56679. (Columbia University Studies in the Social Sciences Ser.: No. 43). reprint ed. 27.50 (*0-404-51043-4*) AMS Pr.
— Five American Politicians: Study in Evolution of American Politics. LC 73-19165. 448p. 1974. reprint ed. 34.95 (*0-405-05887-X*) Ayer.
Orth, Samuel P., ed. Readings on the Relation of Government to Property & Industry. LC 73-2527. (Big Business; Economic Power in a Free Society Ser.). 1973. reprint ed. 44.95 (*0-405-05106-9*) Ayer.
Orthner, Dennis K., jt. ed. see Bowen, Gary L.
Orthner, Donald P. Wellsprings of Life: Understanding Proverbs. (Illus.). xii, 228p. (Orig.). (YA). (gr. 9 up). 1989. pap. 7.95 (*0-317-93833-9*) Adon Bks.
Orthner, Jerry. Angels: Friends in High Places: Who They Are & What They Do. LC 97-191589. 274p. 1997. pap. 12.99 (*0-88965-138-8*, Pub. by Horizon Books) Chr Pubns.
Ortho Books-How to Staff, jt. auth. see Beckstrom, Robert J.
Ortho Books-Reference Staff. The Ortho Problem Solver. 4th rev. ed. Smith, Michael D., ed. LC 94-65696. (Illus.). 960p. 1994. 225.00 (*0-89721-268-1*, UPC 06021, Ortho Bks) Meredith Bks.
Ortho Books-Reference Staff, jt. auth. see Smith, Michael.
Ortho Books Staff. All about Growing Fruits, Berries & Nuts. Ferguson, Barbara, ed. LC 87-70194. (Illus.). 112p. (Orig.). 1987. pap. 9.95 (*0-89721-096-4*, Ortho Bks) Meredith Bks.
— Gardening in Containers. Burke, Ken R., ed. LC 83-61314. (Illus.). 96p. (Orig.). 1983. pap. 9.95 (*0-89721-020-4*, Ortho Bks) Meredith Bks.
— Gardening in Containers. rev. ed. 96p. 1997. pap. 9.95 (*0-89721-282-7*) Meredith Bks.
— How to Install Ceramic Tile. LC 87-72099. (Illus.). 96p. (Orig.). 1989. pap. 9.95 (*0-89721-142-1*) Meredith Bks.
— 1997 Garden Planner Mid-Atlantic Edition. 1996. pap. text 10.95 (*0-89721-308-4*, Ortho Bks) Meredith Bks.
— 1997 Garden Planner Midwest Edition. 1996. pap. text 10.95 (*0-89721-309-2*, Ortho Bks) Meredith Bks.
— 1997 Garden Planner Northwest Edition. 1996. pap. text 10.95 (*0-89721-306-8*, Ortho Bks) Meredith Bks.
— 1997 Garden Planner Southwest Edition. 1996. pap. text 10.95 (*0-89721-307-6*, Ortho Bks) Meredith Bks.
— 1997 Garden Planner South Edition. 1996. pap. text 10.95 (*0-89721-311-4*, Ortho Bks) Meredith Bks.
— Ortho Garden Planner 95-MID-NE. 1995. pap. 10.95 (*0-89721-262-2*, Ortho Bks) Meredith Bks.
— Ortho Garden Planner 96-SE. 1995. pap. 10.95 (*0-89721-278-9*, Ortho Bks) Meredith Bks.
— Ortho Garden Planner 96-West. 1995. pap. 10.95 (*0-89721-277-0*, Ortho Bks) Meredith Bks.
— Ortho's Guide to Creative Home Landscaping. rev. ed. 336p. 1991. pap. 24.95 (*0-89721-279-7*) Meredith Bks.
— Ortho's Guide to Enjoying Birds. (Illus.). 352p. 1991. pap. 24.95 (*0-89721-280-0*) Meredith Bks.
— Ortho's Vegetable Gardening. Date not set. write for info. (*0-89721-324-6*, Ortho Bks) Meredith Bks.
— Projects for Woodworkers. (Illus.). 96p. 1995. pap. 9.95 (*0-89721-258-4*) Meredith Bks.
Ortho Books Staff, ed. How to Design & Build Decks & Patios. LC 79-52994. (Illus.). 112p. 1980. pap. 9.95 (*0-917102-78-9*, Ortho Bks) Meredith Bks.
— The World of Cactus & Succulents. LC 77-89689. (Illus.). 96p. 1977. pap. 9.95 (*0-917102-59-2*) Meredith Bks.
Ortho Books Staff & Fox, Jill. How to Install Ceramic Tile. (Illus.). 96p. (Orig.). Date not set. 14.95 (*0-89721-362-9*, Ortho Bks) Meredith Bks.
Ortho Books Staff & Hildebrand, Ron. Wood Projects for the Home. LC 80-66343. (Illus.). 96p. (Orig.). 1981. pap. 9.95 (*0-917102-85-1*) Meredith Bks.
Ortho Books Staff & Kellum, Jo. All about Landscaping. LC 98-66918. (Ortho's All about Ser.). (Illus.). 96p. 1998. pap. 11.95 (*0-89721-434-X*, Ortho Bks) Meredith Bks.
Ortho Books Staff & Williams, T. Jeff. Basic Carpentry Techniques. LC 80-85220. (Illus.). 112p. 1982. pap. 9.95 (*0-917102-95-9*, Ortho Bks) Meredith Bks.
Ortho Staff. Ortho's All about Sprinklers & Drip Systems. LC 97-75856. (Illus.). 96p. 1998. pap. 11.95 (*0-89721-413-7*, Ortho Bks) Meredith Bks.
— Ortho's Deck Plans. LC 97-75854. (Illus.). 96p. 1996. pap. 11.95 (*0-89721-411-0*, Ortho Bks) Meredith Bks.
***Orthodox America Staff.** St. Jonah of Manchuria. 1999. pap. 0.50 (*0-89981-224-4*) Eastern Orthodox.
Orthodox Christian Educational Society Staff, ed. see Agapius, et al.
Orthodox Christian Educational Society Staff, ed. see DeBallester, Archimandrite P.
Orthodox Christian Educational Society Staff, ed. see Holy Synod of the Ecumenical Patriarchate Staff & Anthimus.
Orthodox Christian Educational Society Staff, ed. see Livadeas, Themistocles & Charitos, Minas.
Orthodox Christian Educational Society Staff, ed. see Makrakis, Apostolos.
Orthodox Christian Educational Society Staff, ed. see Philaretos, S. D.
Orthodox Christian Educational Society Staff, ed. see Philaretos, Sotirios D.
Orthodox Christian Educational Society Staff, ed. see Photiou, Paul.
Orthodox Christian Educational Society Staff, ed. see Vassilakos, Aristarchus.
Orthodox Church in America Staff & Arhipov, Sergei. The Epistles of the Holy Apostles: Epistle Readings, Prokimena, Alleluia Verses, & Antiphons for the Entire Liturgical Year. LC 96-44477. 1996. write for info. (*1-878997-49-1*) St Tikhons Pr.
Orthodox Eastern Church Staff. Akathist to Great Martyr George. 1993. pap. 0.50 (*0-89981-142-6*) Eastern Orthodox.
— Liturgies of Saints Mark, James, Clement, Chrysostom, & the Church of Malabar. LC 76-83374. reprint ed. 42.00 (*0-404-04658-4*) AMS Pr.
— Liturgies of Saints Mark, James, Clement, Chrysostom, Basil. LC 79-80721. 1969. reprint ed. 42.00 (*0-404-04657-6*) AMS Pr.
— Offices of the Oriental Church. LC 73-79805. reprint ed. 34.50 (*0-404-00874-7*) AMS Pr.
— Prayer for the Dead. 1991. pap. 1.50 (*0-89981-045-4*) Eastern Orthodox.
— Prayers for the Sick. 1993. pap. 1.00 (*0-89981-114-0*) Eastern Orthodox.
— Service to a Fool for Christ Sake. 1976. pap. 0.75 (*0-89981-093-4*) Eastern Orthodox.
— Suffering of the Forty Holy Martyrs in Sebaste in Armenia. 1990. pap. 1.00 (*0-89981-122-1*) Eastern Orthodox.
— Synod of 1672: Acts & Decrees of the Jerusalem Synod Held Under Dositheus, Containing the Confession Published Name of Cyril Lukaris. Robertson, J. N., tr. LC 78-81769. 1969. reprint ed. 41.50 (*0-404-03567-1*) AMS Pr.
Orthodox Eastern Church-Synod of Jerusalem Staff. Acts & Decrees of the Synod of Jerusalem, 1672. 1978. pap. 1.95 (*0-89981-001-2*) Eastern Orthodox.
Orthodox Woodriver District Baptist Association Staff. Treasured Talents in God's Time. large type unabridged ed. Fisher, Suzanne, ed. (WeWrite Kids! Ser.: Vol. 42). (Illus.). 39p. (YA). (gr. 4-12). 1999. pap. 3.95 (*1-57635-024-X*) WeWrite.
Orthos Books Staff, ed. see Lammers, Susan.
Orthwein, Jayne, jt. auth. see Morris, Richard.
Orthwein, William C. Clutches & Brakes: Design & Selection. (Mechanical Engineering Ser.: Vol. 50). (Illus.). 368p. 1986. text 155.00 (*0-8247-7393-4*) Dekker.
Ortigao, J. A. Soil Mechanics in the Light of Critical State Theories: An Introduction. (Illus.). 160p. (C). 1995. pap. 41.00 (*90-5410-195-4*, Pub. by A A Balkema); text 82.00 (*90-5410-194-6*, Pub. by A A Balkema) Ashgate Pub Co.
Ortigoza, Brenda. How Institutions Voted on Social Policy Shareholder Resolutions in the 1993 Proxy Season. Mathiasen, Carolyn, ed. (Illus.). 137p. (Orig.). 1993. pap. text 35.00 (*1-879775-13-1*) IRRC Inc DC.
***Ortigoza-Guerrero, Lauro & Aghvami, A. Hamid.** Resource Allocation in Hierarchical Cellular Systems. LC 99-45831. (Mobile Communications Library). 208p. 1999. 85.00 (*1-58053-066-4*) Artech Hse.
Ortin, Felix De Latassa y, see De Latassa y Ortin, Felix.
Ortin, Lavinia, ed. Media Courses U. K., 1996. 1995. pap. 14.95 (*0-85170-521-9*, Pub. by British Film Inst) Ind U Pr.
***Ortins, Ana Patuleia.** Portuguese Homestyle Cooking. (Illus.). 2000. 25.00 (*1-56656-373-9*) Interlink Pub.
Ortiz. After Before Lightin St. LC 94-5761. (Sun Tracks Ser.: Vol. 28). 127p. (Orig.). 1994. pap. 17.95 (*0-8165-1448-8*) U of Ariz Pr.
Ortiz, Adalberto. El Animal Herido: Antologia Poetica. (B. E. Ser.: No. 24). (SPA.). 1959. 25.00 (*0-8115-2975-4*) Periodicals Srv.
— Juyungo. Tittler, Jonathan & Hill, Susan, trs. from SPA. LC 81-51674. x, 226p. (Orig.). 1982. reprint ed. pap. 13.95 (*0-89410-091-2*, Three Contnts) L Rienner.
— Juyungo: Historia de un Negro, una Isla y Otros Negros. (B. E. Ser.: No. 23). (SPA.). 1943. 30.00 (*0-8115-2974-6*) Periodicals Srv.
Ortiz, Alejandro & Zierer, Ernesto. Set Theory & Linguistics. (Janua Linguarum, Ser. Minor: No. 70). (Orig.). 1968. pap. text 12.70 (*90-279-0597-5*) Mouton.
Ortiz, Alfonso. Tewa World: Space, Time, Being, & Becoming in a Pueblo Society. LC 72-94079. 216p. 1972. pap. text 11.00 (*0-226-63307-1*, P447) U Ch Pr.
Ortiz, Alfonso, ed. Southwest. LC 77-17162. (Handbook of North American Indians Ser.: Vol. 9). (Illus.). 702p. 1980. 49.00 (*0-87474-189-0*, ORV9) Smithsonian.
— Southwest, Vol. 10. LC 77-17162. (Handbook of North American Indians Ser.). (Illus.). 868p. 1983. 52.00 (*0-87474-190-4*) Smithsonian.
Ortiz, Alfonso, jt. auth. see Sturtevant, William C.
Ortiz, Alfonso, jt. ed. see DeMallie, Raymond J.
Ortiz, Alfonso, jt. ed. see Erdoes, Richard.
Ortiz, Alfonzo, jt. auth. see Sturtevant, William C.
***Ortiz, Alicia Dujovne.** Eva Peron. 1998. 9.95 (*950-511-205-X*) Santillana.
Ortiz, Alicia Dujovne. Eva Peron: A Biography. Fields, Shawn, tr. (Illus.). 336p. 1997. pap. 14.95 (*0-312-16827-6*) St Martin.
Ortiz, Altagracia. Eighteenth Century Reforms in the Caribbean: Miguel De Muesas, Governor of Puerto Rico, 1769-76. LC 79-56408. (Illus.). 256p. 1983. 35.00 (*0-8386-3008-1*) Fairleigh Dickinson.
Ortiz, Altagracia, ed. Puerto Rican Women & Work: Bridges in Transnational Labor. LC 95-43822. (Puerto Rican Studies). 272p. (C). 1996. pap. 22.95 (*1-56639-451-1*) Temple U Pr.
— Puerto Rican Women & Work: Bridges in Transnational Labor. LC 95-43822. (Puerto Rican Studies). 272p. (C). 1996. 69.95 (*1-56639-450-3*) Temple U Pr.
Ortiz, Angel R. & Ortega, Idsa A., eds. Puerto Rico en la Economia Politica del Caribe. LC 90-80515. 204p. 1990. pap. 12.50 (*0-929157-06-0*) Ediciones Huracan.
— Puerto Rico en las Relaciones Internacionales del Caribe. LC 90-80514. 197p. 1990. pap. 12.50 (*0-929157-05-2*) Ediciones Huracan.
Ortiz, Antonio D., et al. Velazquez. 1989. 45.00 (*0-87099-554-5*); pap. 19.95 (*0-87099-555-3*) Metro Mus Art.
Ortiz-Aponte, Sally & Cabezas, Juan A. Las Mujeres De Clarin: Espermentos y Camafeos. 200p. (C). 1971. pap. 3.00 (*0-8477-3141-3*) U of PR Pr.
Ortiz, Beverly. It Will Live Forever: Traditional Yosemite Acorn Preparation. 2nd ed. LC 91-76689. (Illus.). 160p. (Orig.). 1996. reprint ed. pap. 12.95 (*0-930588-45-2*) Heyday Bks.
Ortiz-Blanco, Luis. European Community Competition Procedure. Frame, Iain, tr. LC 95-49266. (Illus.). 700p. (C). 1996. text 225.00 (*0-19-825967-0*, Clarendon Pr) OUP.
Ortiz-Blanco, Luis & Van Houtte, Ben. EC Competition Law in the Transport Sector. LC 96-29006. 336p. 1997. text 145.00 (*0-19-826089-X*) OUP.
Ortiz Blasco, M. Tauromaquia A-Z: Diccionario Enciclopedico de la Historia, la Tecnica, del Arte, 2 vols. (SPA.). 1614p. 1993. 425.00 (*0-7859-9235-9*) Fr & Eur.
— Tauromaquia A-Z: Diccionario Enciclopedico de la Historia la Tecnica y la Cultura Del Arte Del Toreo, 2 vols., Set. (SPA., Illus.). 1614p. 1993. 450.00 (*84-239-5888-4*) Elliots Bks.
Ortiz, Bobbye, tr. see Debray, Regis.
Ortiz-Buonafina, Marta. Profitable Export Marketing: A Strategy for U. S. Business. LC 92-15752. 1992. pap. 29.50 (*0-8191-8733-X*) U Pr of Amer.
Ortiz, C., jt. ed. see Poker, D. B.
Ortiz-Carboneres, Salvador, ed. Spanish History: Selected Texts from the Fall of Granada in 1492 to Modern Times. LC 89-31905. 221p. 1989. 19.50 (*0-85496-095-3*) Berg Pubs.
Ortiz-Carboneres, Salvador, jt. auth. see Leigh, Heather.
Ortiz, Carlos Buitrago, see Buitrago Ortiz, Carlos.
Ortiz Cofer, Judith. Bailando en Silencio: Escenas de una Ninez Puertorriquena. Olazagasti-Segovia, Elena, tr.Tr. of Silent Dancing: A Partial Remembrance of a Puerto Rican Childhood. 160p. (J). (gr. 6). 1997. pap. 12.95 (*1-55885-205-0*) Arte Publico.
Ortiz-Cofer, Judith. Una Isla Como Tu (An Island Like You) (SPA.). (YA). 1997. pap. 6.99 (*968-16-5441-2*, Pub. by Fondo) Continental Bk.
Ortiz Cofer, Judith. An Island Like You: Stories of the Barrio. LC 94-32496. 176p. (YA). (gr. 7 up). 1995. 15.95 (*0-531-06897-8*); lib. bdg. 16.99 (*0-531-08747-6*) Orchard Bks Watts.
Ortiz Cofer, Judith. An Island Like You: Stories of the Barrio. 1996. 10.09 (*0-606-10740-1*, Pub. by Turtleback) Demco.
— Woman in Front of the Sun: On Becoming a Writer. LC 00-36882. 2000. pap. write for info. (*0-8203-2261-X*) U of Ga Pr.
Ortiz, Darlene. Public Speaking Made Easy. (Four-H Ser.). (Illus.). 12p. (J). (gr. 6-8). 1991. pap. 2.25 (*1-57753-210-4*, 105M-1-4) Corn Coop Ext.
Ortiz, Darwin. Casino Gambling for the Clueless: A Beginner's Guide to Playing & Winning. (Illus.). 272p. 1998. pap. 16.95 (*0-8184-0609-7*, L Stuart) Carol Pub Group.
— Darwin Ortiz on Casino Gambling: The Complete Guide to Playing & Winning. (Illus.). 1990. reprint ed. pap. 8.95 (*0-8184-0525-2*, Citadel Pr) Carol Pub Group.
— Gambling Scams: How They Work - How to Detect Them - How to Protect Yourself. (Illus.). 262p. 1990. reprint ed. pap. 12.95 (*0-8184-0529-5*, Citadel Pr) Carol Pub Group.
Ortiz, Darwin & Dunlap, Leslie. Darwin Ortiz on Casino Gambling: The Complete Guide to Playing & Winning. (Illus.). 288p. 1999. reprint ed. 34.95 (*0-7351-0098-5*) Replica Bks.
***Ortiz, David.** Paper Liberals: Press & Politics in Restoration Spain, 73. LC 99-55208. (Contributions to the Study of World History Ser.: Vol. 73). 2000. write for info. (*0-313-31216-8*, Greenwood Pr) Greenwood.
Ortiz, David & Chesler, Phyllis. La Memoria Extraviada. LC 94-21995. 131p. 1995. pap. text. write for info. (*1-56758-038-6*) Edit Cultl.

O

An Asterisk (*) at the beginning of an entry indicates that the title is appearing for the first time.

O

An Asterisk (*) at the beginning of an entry indicates that the title is appearing for the first time.

Ortolani, Benito. The Japanese Theatre: From Shamanistic Ritual to Contemporary Pluralism. 424p. 1995. pap. text 24.95 (*0-691-04333-7*, Pub. by Princeton U Pr) Cal Prin Full Svc.

— Luigi Pirandello: Lettere a Marta Abba. 1700p. 1996. text 75.00 (*88-04-39379-3*, Pub. by Mondadori & Il) Princeton U Pr.

***Ortolani, Benito, ed.** International Bibliography of Theatre, 1997. 750p. 1999. lib. bdg. 285.00 (*0-945419-08-2*) Theatre Rsch Data Ctr.

Ortolani, Benito, ed. International Bibliography of Theatre, 1996. 741p. 1998. lib. bdg. 280.00 (*0-945419-07-4*) Theatre Rsch Data Ctr.

Ortolani, Benito, et al, eds. International Bibliography of Theatre, 1982. 186p. 1985. lib. bdg. 70.00 (*0-89062-207-8*) Theatre Rsch Data Ctr.

— International Bibliography of Theatre, 1983. 388p. 1986. lib. bdg. 90.00 (*0-89062-219-1*) Theatre Rsch Data Ctr.

— International Bibliography of Theatre, 1984. 852p. 1987. lib. bdg. 120.00 (*0-89062-225-6*) Theatre Rsch Data Ctr.

— International Bibliography of Theatre, 1985. 1211p. 1989. lib. bdg. 145.00 (*0-945419-00-7*) Theatre Rsch Data Ctr.

— International Bibliography of Theatre, 1986. 706p. 1991. lib. bdg. 145.00 (*0-945419-01-5*) Theatre Rsch Data Ctr.

— International Bibliography of Theatre, 1987. 704p. 1992. lib. bdg. 175.00 (*0-945419-02-3*) Theatre Rsch Data Ctr.

— International Bibliography of Theatre, 1988-89. 951p. 1993. lib. bdg. 270.00 (*0-945419-03-1*) Theatre Rsch Data Ctr.

— International Bibliography of Theatre, 1990-91. 1023p. 1994. lib. bdg. 270.00 (*0-945419-04-X*) Theatre Rsch Data Ctr.

— International Bibliography of Theatre, 1992-93. 1035p. 1995. lib. bdg. 270.00 (*0-945419-05-8*) Theatre Rsch Data Ctr.

— International Bibliography of Theatre, 1994-95. 1180p. 1997. lib. bdg. 280.00 (*0-945419-06-6*) Theatre Rsch Data Ctr.

Ortolani, Benito, et al. Japanese Theatre in the World. Leiter, Samuel, ed. LC 97-73947. (Illus.). 1997. pap. write for info. (*0-913304-44-1*) Japan Soc.

Ortolani, Benito, ed. & tr. see Pirandello, Luigi.

Ortolani, C., jt. ed. see Wuethrich, B.

Ortolani, S. & Schnack, D. D. The Magnetohydrodynamics of Plasma Relaxation. 200p. 1993. text 61.00 (*981-02-0860-X*) World Scientific Pub.

Ortolano, Leonard. Environmental Planning & Decision Making. LC 83-19820. 448p. (C). 1984. text 102.95 (*0-471-87071-4*) Wiley.

— Environmental Regulation & Impact Assessment. LC 96-26400. 620p. 1997. text 106.95 (*0-471-31004-2*) Wiley.

Ortolano, Leonard, jt. auth. see Ma, Xiaoying.

Ortolano, Leonard, jt. auth. see Sinkule, Barbara J.

Ortoleva, Peter J. Geochemical Self-Organization. (Oxford Monographs on Geology & Geophysics: No. 23). (Illus.). 432p. 1994. text 115.00 (*0-19-504476-2*) OUP.

Ortoleva, Peter J., ed. Basin Compartments & Seals. (AAPG Memoir Ser.: No. 61). (Illus.). xxxi, 477p. 1994. 149.00 (*0-89181-340-3*, 589) AAPG.

Ortoleva, Peter J., jt. ed. see Meshri, Indu D.

***Ortolja-Baird, Ljiljana, ed.** Animals in Art. (National Gallery Ser.). (Illus.). 2000. pap. 14.95 (*0-8230-0339-6*) Watsn-Guptill.

— Flowers in Art. (National Gallery Ser.). (Illus.). 144p. 2000. pap. 14.95 (*0-8230-0340-X*) Watsn-Guptill.

Ortoll, Servando, jt. ed. see Arrom, Silvia M.

***Ortolon, Julie.** Drive Me Wild. 400p. 2000. mass mkt. 5.99 (*0-440-23618-5*, Dell Trade Pbks) Dell.

Orton, Andrew. Functional Appliances: Atlas of Clinical Prescription & Laboratory Construction. (Illus.). 373p. 1990. text 72.00 (*1-85097-012-2*) Quint Pub Co.

— The Way We Build Now. (Illus.). 530p. 1988. pap. 80.95 (*0-7476-0011-2*) Chapman & Hall.

— The Way We Build Now: Form, Scale & Technique. (Illus.). 544p. (Orig.). 1991. pap. text 99.95 (*0-419-15780-8*, E & FN Spon) Routledge.

Orton, Ann W. Eternally Yours. 1994. pap. 1.95 (*0-88494-946-X*) Bookcraft Inc.

Orton, Anthony. Learning Mathematics. 2nd ed. 192p. 1992. text 100.00 (*0-304-32553-8*); pap. text 35.95 (*0-304-32555-4*) Continuum.

— Pattern in the Teaching & Learning of Mathematics. LC 80-5342. 224p. 1999. 75.00 (*0-304-70051-7*); pap. 27.95 (*0-304-70052-5*) Continuum.

Orton, Anthony & Frobisher, Leonard. Insights into Teaching Mathematics. (Introduction to Education Ser.). (Illus.). 288p. 1996. 99.50 (*0-304-33218-6*); pap. 35.00 (*0-304-33220-8*) Continuum.

Orton, Chad M. More Faith Than Fear: The Los Angeles Stake Story. 1987. 12.95 (*0-88494-646-0*) Bookcraft Inc.

Orton, Charles W. & Marsh, Diann. The Colorful Coast: An Illustrated History of Newport Beach & Harbor. Parks, Lori, ed. LC 97-71125. (Illus.). 200p. 1997. 39.95 (*1-886483-12-4*) Heritge Media.

Orton, Christine. Sharing Your Home. (C). 1989. 30.00 (*0-86242-060-1*, Pub. by Age Concern Eng) St Mut.

***Orton, Clive.** Sampling in Archaeology. (Manuals in Archaeology Ser.). (Illus.). 250p. (C). 2000. text 74.95 (*0-521-56226-0*); pap. text 27.95 (*0-521-56666-5*) Cambridge U Pr.

Orton, Clive, et al. Pottery in Archaeology. LC 92-25814. (Manuals in Archaeology Ser.). (Illus.). 287p. (C). 1993. pap. text 23.95 (*0-521-44597-3*) Cambridge U Pr.

Orton, Colin G., ed. Progress in Medical Radiation Physics, Vol. 1. 402p. 1982. 95.00 (*0-306-40713-2*, Plenum Trade) Perseus Pubng.

— Progress in Medical Radiation Physics, Vol. 2. 248p. 1985. 95.00 (*0-306-41789-8*, Plenum Trade) Perseus Pubng.

— Radiation Dosimetry: Physical & Biological Aspects. (Illus.). 340p. (C). 1986. text 107.00 (*0-306-42056-2*, Kluwer Plenum) Kluwer Academic.

***Orton, D. E.** Poetry in the Hebrew Bible, Selected Studies from Vetus Testamentum. (Readers in Biblical Studies). 2000. 35.00 (*90-04-11161-1*) Brill Academic Pubs.

Orton, David, ed. Online Searching in Science & Technology: An Introductory Guide to Equipment, Databases & Search Techniques. 3rd ed. (Information in Focus Ser.). 128p. 1995. pap. 49.95 (*0-7123-0802-4*, Pub. by SRIS) L Erlbaum Assocs.

***Orton, David E.** Composition of Mark's Gospel: Selected Studies from Novum Testamentum. (Punto Saggi Ser.). 1999. pap. text 35.00 (*90-04-11340-1*) Brill Academic Pubs.

— Prophecy in the Hebrew Bible: Selected Studies from Vetus Testamentum. LC 99-51406. (Brill's Readers in Biblical Studies). 1999. write for info. (*90-04-11160-3*) Brill Academic Pubs.

— Synoptic Problem & Questions. 1999. pap. text 35.00 (*90-04-11342-8*) Brill Academic Pubs.

— The Understanding Scribe: Matthew & the Apocalyptic Ideal. (JSNT Supplement Ser.: No. 25). 280p. 1989. 80.00 (*1-85075-181-1*, Pub. by Sheffield Acad) CUP Services.

Orton, David E., compiled by. The Composition of John's Gospel: Selected Studies from Novum Testamentum. LC 99-174428. viii, 278p. 1998. pap. 35.00 (*90-04-11158-1*) Brill Academic Pubs.

Orton, David E., tr. see Raisanen, Heikki.

Orton, Diane & Malouf, Renee. Homemaking Blueprints. LC 95-79195. 1995. pap. 8.95 (*1-57008-187-5*) Bookcraft Inc.

Orton, Diane B. & Malouf, Renee B. More Homemaking Blueprints. LC 97-74881. 1997. pap. 9.95 (*1-57008-333-9*) Bookcraft Inc.

Orton, Donald A. & Green, Thomas L. Coincide: The Orton System of Pest Management. 189p. (Orig.). (C). pap. text 20.95 (*1-887619-03-8*) Plantsmans Pubns.

Orton, Ed. A. & Wain, Geoffrey. Issues in Teaching Mathematics. (Education Ser.). (Illus.). 256p. 1994. pap. 35.00 (*0-304-32680-1*) Continuum.

Orton, Fred. Avant-Gardes & Partisans Reviewed: A Social History of Art. LC 97-129794. (Illus.). 380p. 1997. text 27.95 (*0-7190-4399-9*, Pub. by Manchester Univ Pr) St Martin.

— Figuring Jasper Johns. LC 94-12431. (Essays in Art & Culture Ser.). (Illus.). 208p. 1994. text 46.95 (*0-674-30117-X*, ORTFIG) HUP.

— Figuring Jasper Johns. (Essays in Art & Culture Ser.). (Illus.). 208p. 1996. pap. 23.50 (*0-674-30118-8*) HUP.

Orton, Fred & Pollock, Griselda. Avant-Gardes & Partisans Reviewed: A Social History of Art. LC 97-129794. (Illus.). 380p. 1997. text 59.95 (*0-7190-4398-0*) St Martin.

Orton, Geraldine L. Strategies for Counseling with Children & Their Parents. 1996. mass mkt., wbk. ed. 16.50 (*0-534-34566-2*) Brooks-Cole.

— Strategies for Counseling with Children & Their Parents. LC 96-41264. (Counseling Ser.). 390p. (C). 1996. mass mkt. 74.95 (*0-534-23280-9*) Brooks-Cole.

Orton, H. E. Insulated Conductors. (Electrical Engineering & Electronics Ser.). Date not set. write for info. (*0-8247-9934-8*) Dekker.

Orton, Harold & Halliday, Wilfrid J., eds. Survey of English Dialects: Introduction & Basic Materials, 13 vols., Set. LC 97-51151. 17p. (C). (gr. 13). 1993. 1360.00 (*0-415-18178-X*) Routledge.

Orton, Harold & Sanderson, Stewart F., eds. The Linguistic Atlas of England. (Illus.). 488p. (C). 1998. 195.00 (*0-415-15129-5*) Routledge.

Orton, Helen F. The Gold-Laced Coat. rev. ed. (Illus.). 226p. (J). (gr. 4-8). 1988. reprint ed. pap. 5.95 (*0-941967-07-7*) Old Fort Niagara Assn.

— Mystery in the Old Cave. (Illus.). (J). (gr. 4-6). 1950. 11.95 (*0-397-30173-1*) HarpC Child Bks.

— Mystery of the Lost Letter. LC 46-7568. (Illus.). (J). (gr. 4-6). 1946. 11.95 (*0-397-31598-8*, Lippnctt) Lppncott W & W.

— The Treasure in the Little Trunk. (Illus.). 208p. (J). (gr. 4). 1989. reprint ed. pap. text 5.95 (*1-878233-00-9*) Niagara Cnty Hist Soc.

Orton, J. Robert, Jr. Benevolence & Blasphemy: Memoirs of a Contemporary Art Collector. LC 95-60520. 288p. (Orig.). 1995. pap. 13.95 (*1-885983-05-0*) Turtle Point Pr.

Orton, J. W. Electron Paramagnetic Resonance. 240p. (C). 1969. 155.00 (*0-677-61900-6*) Gordon & Breach.

Orton, J. W. & Blood, Peter. The Electrical Characterisation of Semiconductors: Measurement of Minority Carrier Properties. (Techniques of Physics Ser.: Vol. 13). 291p. 1990. text 103.00 (*0-12-528625-2*) Acad Pr.

Orton, Job. Discourses to the Aged. Stein, Leon, ed. LC 79-8697. (Growing Old Ser.). 1980. reprint ed. lib. bdg. 33.95 (*0-405-12795-2*) Ayer.

Orton, Joe. Between Us Girls: A Novel. 224p. 1999. pap. 12.00 (*0-8021-3644-3*) Grove-Atltic.

— Complete Plays of Orton: Entertaining Mr. Sloane; Loot; What the Butler Saw; & Four Shorter Plays. LC 90-3069. 448p. 1990. pap. 14.00 (*0-8021-3215-4*) Grove-Atltic.

***Orton, Joe.** Head to Toe: A Novel & up Against It: A Screenplay for the Beatles. LC 97-39767. 275p. 1998. reprint ed. pap. 14.95 (*0-306-80836-6*) Da Capo.

— The Visitors & Fred & Madge. LC 99-30227. 192p. 1999. pap. 13.00 (*0-8021-3628-1*, Grove) Grove-Atltic.

Orton, Joe & Lahr, John, eds. The Orton Diaries: Including the Correspondence of Edna Welthorpe & Others. LC 96-18361. (Illus.). 332p. 1996. pap. 14.95 (*0-306-80733-5*) Da Capo.

Orton, Kay. Entree to Malta & Gozo. 1992. pap. 20.00 (*1-870948-61-0*, Pub. by Quiller Pr) St Mut.

Orton, Ken, jt. auth. see Windham, Laurie.

Orton, Larry J. & Jackson, Scott S., contrib. by. Utah Publicity Source Book. 17th rev. ed. 468p. 1998. lib. bdg. 135.00 (*1-884689-09-4*); ring bd. 135.00 (*1-884689-08-6*) Orton Grp.

Orton, Larry J., tr. see Jackson, Scott S., ed.

***Orton, Lavinia.** Media Courses U. K, 2000 Edition. 1999. pap. 24.95 (*0-85170-740-8*) British Film Inst.

Orton, Lavinia, ed. Media Courses U. K., 1998. 230p. 1998. 15.95 (*0-85170-649-5*, Pub. by British Film Inst) Ind U Pr.

— Media Courses U. K., 1997. (Distributed for the British Film Institute Ser.). 230p. 1996. pap. 14.95 (*0-85170-587-1*, Pub. by British Film Inst) Ind U Pr.

— Media Courses UK, 1999. (Distributed for the British Film Institute Ser.). 288p. Date not set. pap. 15.95 (*0-85170-683-5*, Pub. by British Film Inst) Ind U Pr.

Orton, Lawrence D. Polish Detroit & the Kolasinski Affair. LC 80-25290. 230p. reprint ed. pap. 71.30 (*0-608-10595-3*, 207121600009) Bks Demand.

— The Prague Slav Congress of 1848. (East European Monographs: No. 46). 187p. 1978. text 60.00 (*0-914710-39-7*, Pub. by East Eur Monographs) Col U Pr.

Orton, Louis. Hypnotism Made Practical. 1976. pap. 5.00 (*0-87980-079-8*) Wilshire.

Orton, Michelle D., jt. auth. see Lamet, Jerome S.

Orton-Montanari, Ellen. One Hundred One Ways to Build Enrollment in Your Early Childhood Program. 135p. 1992. pap. text 12.95 (*1-882149-39-4*) CPG Pub.

Orton, P. D., et al. British Fungus Flora No. 6: Pluteaceae, Pluteus & Volvariella. (British Fungus Flora (Agarics & Boleti) Ser.: Pt. 4). (Illus.). ii, 100p. 1986. pap. 20.00 (*0-9504270-4-7*, Pub. by Royal Botanic Edinburgh) Balogh.

***Orton, Peter & Hill, Claire, eds.** The General Practice Management Handbook: A Volume in The Management Of Health Care. (Illus.). 270p. 1998. pap. write for info. (*0-7020-2204-7*) W B Saunders.

Orton, Peter Z. LSAT Preparation Guide: Law School Admission Test. (Cliffs Test Preparation Ser.). 336p. (Orig.). (C). 1993. pap. text 9.95 (*0-8220-2066-1*, Cliff) IDG Bks.

Orton, Peter Z., jt. auth. see Bobrow, Jerry.

Orton, Peter Z., jt. auth. see Covino, William A.

Orton, Peter Z., jt. auth. see Rimal, Rajiv N.

Orton, Peter Z., jt. auth. see Voelker, David H.

***Orton, Ray.** Moving People: From Street to Platform, 100 Years Underground. Gale, John & Lipley, Grey, trs. (Illus.). 77p. 1999. 49.95 (*1-886536-25-2*) Elevator Wrld.

Orton, Richard H., compiled by. Records of California Men in the War of the Rebellion, 1861 to 1867. (Illus.). 887p. 1997. reprint ed. lib. bdg. 89.00 (*0-8328-7048-X*) Higginson Bk Co.

Orton, Stephen A. Pan the Man: Kids vs. Drugs in 2 Acts. 36p. (YA). (gr. 7-12). 1991. pap. 3.50 (*0-88680-355-1*) I E Clark.

Orton, T. J., jt. ed. see Tanksley, S. D.

Orton, Terry C., jt. ed. see Tucker, Mary J.

Orton, Thomas. The Lost Glass Plates of Wilfred Eng: A Novel. LC 99-34803. 256p. 1999. text 24.00 (*1-58243-023-3*, Pub. by Counterpt DC) HarpC.

***Orton, Thomas.** The Lost Glass Plates of Wilfred Eng: A Novel. 2001. reprint ed. pap. 13.00 (*1-58243-125-6*) Counterpt DC.

Orton, Vrest. The American Cider Book. 136p. 1995. pap. text 9.00 (*0-86547-484-2*) N Point Pr.

— Calvin Coolidge's Unique Vermont Inauguration. LC 81-66760. 96p. 1981. pap. 4.50 (*0-914960-31-8*) Academy Bks.

— Dreiserana. 1999. lib. bdg. 17.95 (*1-56723-159-4*) Yestermorrow.

— Dreiserana: A Book about His Books. LC 72-6287. (American Literature Ser.: No. 49). 84p. (C). 1972. reprint ed. lib. bdg. 75.00 (*0-8383-1629-8*) M S G Haskell Hse.

***Orton, Vrest.** The Forgotten Art of Building a Good Fireplace. LC 00-35075. (Illus.). 64p. (Orig.). 2000. pap. 12.50 (*0-911469-17-6*) A C Hood.

Orton, Vrest. The Forgotten Art of Building a Good Fireplace. LC 70-9285. (Forgotten Arts Ser.). (Illus.). 64p. (Orig.). 1969. pap. 6.95 (*0-911658-53-X*, 80-250-8) Yankee Bks.

***Orton, Vrest.** The Forgotten Art of Building a Good Fireplace: The Story of Sir Benjamin Thompson, Count Rumford, an American Genius. (Illus.). 62p. 2000. reprint ed. pap. text 9.00 (*0-7881-6488-0*) DIANE Pub.

***Orton, Vrest.** Vermont Afternoons with Robert Frost. LC 00-35102. (Illus.). 64p. 2000. pap. 10.00 (*0-911469-18-4*) A C Hood.

Orton, Vrest. Vermont Afternoons with Robert Frost. LC 70-134029. 64p. 1981. pap. 4.50 (*0-914960-34-2*) Academy Bks.

***Ortonne, Jean-Paul & Marks, Ronald.** Photodamaged Skin: Clinical Signs, Causes & Management. 149p. 1999. 89.95 (*1-85317-345-2*, Pub. by Martin Dunitz) Mosby Inc.

Ortony, Andrew, ed. Metaphor & Thought. 2nd ed. LC 92-37625. (Illus.). 694p. (C). 1993. pap. text 32.95 (*0-521-40561-0*) Cambridge U Pr.

— Metaphor & Thought. 2nd ed. LC 92-37625. (Illus.). 694p. (C). 1994. text 80.00 (*0-521-40547-5*) Cambridge U Pr.

Ortony, Andrew, et al, eds. Communication from an Artificial Intelligence Perspective: Theoretical & Applied Issues. LC 92-31538. xi, 260p. 1992. write for info. (*3-540-55881-0*); 82.95 (*0-387-55881-0*) Spr-Verlag.

Orts, J. C., et al. Breve Diccionario Espanol-Ruso: Ruso-Espanol de Terminos Cientificos & Tecnicos. deluxe ed. (RUS & SPA.). 438p. 1960. 35.00 (*0-8288-6832-8*, S-31835) Fr & Eur.

Orts, Neil E. Watch & Pray: Meditations in Dramatic Form for the Season of Lent. LC 95-25340. 1996. pap. 8.25 (*0-7880-0390-9*) CSS OH.

Orttung, Robert W. From Leningrad to St. Petersburg: Democratization in a Russian City. LC 94-40057. 320p. 1995. text 55.00 (*0-312-12080-X*) St Martin.

Ortuando, J. M. Nautical Dictionary, Spanish-English/ English-Spanish. (ENG & SPA.). 1996. 50.00 (*0-7859-9689-3*) Fr & Eur.

Ortuno. Senales de Identidad. (SPA.). 1998. 33.00 (*0-07-428932-2*) McGraw.

Ortuondo, J. M. Malagon, see Malagon Ortuondo, J. M.

Ortuzar, Adolfo. Chile of Today: Its Commerce Production & Resources. 1976. lib. bdg. 69.95 (*0-8490-1605-3*) Gordon Pr.

Ortwein, Terrence. Shel's Sister. 1994. 3.50 (*0-87129-476-1*, S32) Dramatic Pub.

Ortwerth, John & Nicks, Mel J. P. E. Curriculum Guide. (Illus.). 160p. 1984. student ed. 12.99 (*0-86653-262-5*, GA 599) Good Apple.

Ortz, Nick. Poetry for the Soul: A Poetic Review of 12 Best Sellers. 208p. 1998. pap. 14.95 (*1-892896-09-5*) Buy Books.

Ortzen, Len, tr. see Ousmane, Sembene.

Ortzen, Tony. When Dead Kings Speak. 144p. (C). 1988. pap. 40.00 (*0-7212-0785-5*, Pub. by Regency Pr GBR) St Mut.

O'Ruanaidh, Joseph J. & Fitzgerald, William J. Numerical Bayesian Methods Applied to Signal Processing. LC 95-44635. 1996. write for info. (*0-614-09506-9*) Spr-Verlag.

O'Ruanaidh, Joseph J., jt. auth. see Fitzgerald, W. J.

Orucu, Esin, et al, eds. Studies in Legal Systems: Mixed & Mixing. LC 95-51331. 1996. 101.50 (*90-411-0906-4*) Kluwer Law Intl.

***Orui, Makoto.** L'Amour: French Glamour Girls: Retro Nudes of the 1950s & 60s. (Illus.). 144p. 2000. pap. 24.95 (*4-7661-1133-8*) Graphic-Sha.

Oruka, J. Odera, ed. Philosophy, Humanity & Ecology Vol. 1: Philosophy of Nature & Environmental Ethics. 367p. (Orig.). (C). 1996. pap. text 55.00 (*0-7881-2676-8*) DIANE Pub.

Orullion, Peter, ed. see Hixson, Jon, et al.

***Orum.** Introduction to Political Sociology. 4th ed. 320p. 2000. pap. 37.33 (*0-13-927153-8*, Prentice Hall) P-H.

Orum, ed. Sociology. (C). 1998. text. write for info. (*0-321-01368-9*); pap. text, student ed. write for info. (*0-321-01369-7*) Addson-Wesley Educ.

Orum, Anthony, et al. Changing Societies: Essential Sociology for Our Times. LC 98-44548. 500p. 1999. pap. 24.95 (*0-8476-9329-5*) Rowman.

***O'Rush, Claire.** The Enchanted Garden: Discovering & Enhancing the Magical Healing Properties in Your Garden. LC 00-23843. 110p. 2000. 9.99 (*0-517-16242-3*) Gramrcy Bks.

***Orvaschel, et al.** Handbook of Conceptualization & Treatment of Child Psychopathology. 1999. text 174.01 (*0-08-043362-6*, Pergamon Pr) Elsevier.

Orvell, Miles. After the Machine: Visual Arts & the Erasing of Cultural Boundaries. LC 95-15919. (Illus.). 240p. 1995. pap. 16.95 (*0-87805-755-2*); text 40.00 (*0-87805-754-4*) U Pr of Miss.

— Flannery O'Connor: An Introduction. LC 91-26494. 1991. pap. 17.00 (*0-87805-542-8*) U Pr of Miss.

— The Real Thing: Imitation & Authenticity in American Culture, 1880-1940. LC 88-20886. (Cultural Studies of the United States). (Illus.). xxvi, 382p. (C). 1989. pap. 19.95 (*0-8078-4246-X*) U of NC Pr.

Orvik, Nils. Decline of Neutrality, 1914-1941. 310p. 1971. 30.00 (*0-7146-2696-1*, Pub. by F Cass Pubs) Intl Spec Bk.

Orvik, Tore U., jt. auth. see Satzinger, John W.

Orville-Thomas, W. J. & Redshaw, Mavis, eds. Internal Rotation in Molecules. LC 73-2791. (Wiley Monographs in Chemical Physics). (Illus.). 624p. reprint ed. pap. 193.50 (*0-608-17589-7*, 203043200069) Bks Demand.

Orville-Thomas, W. J., jt. auth. see Gribov, L. A.

Orville-Thomas, W. J., jt. auth. see Maksic, Z. B.

Orville-Thomas, W. J., jt. ed. see Jones, Hamlyn G.

Orvin, George H. Understanding the Adolescent. 224p. 1995. 22.95 (*0-88048-651-1*, 8651) Am Psychiatric.

Orvis, Bill. VBScript Web Page Interactivity. LC 96-68057. 504p. 1996. per. 40.00 incl. cd-rom (*0-7615-0684-5*) Prima Pub.

Orvis, Bruce R., et al. Ensuring Personnel Readiness in the Army Reserve Components. LC 95-47570. 122p. 1996. pap. text 15.00 (*0-8330-2342-X*, MR-659-A) Rand Corp.

— Military Recruiting Outlook: Recent Trends in Enlistment Propensity & Conversion of Potential Enlisted Supply. LC 96-48738. xvii, 68p. 1997. pap. 15.00 (*0-8330-2461-2*, MR-677-A/OSO) Rand Corp.

Orvis, Bruce R., jt. auth. see Asch, Beth J.

***Orvis, James.** Weight Training Workouts That Work: The Portable Handbook That Shows You Exactly What to Do at Every Workout. (Illus.). 150p. 2000. pap. 14.95 (*0-9675188-2-2*) Ideal Pubg.

***Orvis Shooting School Staff.** The Orvis Shooting School Method of Wingshooting: An Orvis Guide. (Orvis Guides Ser.). (Illus.). 128p. 2000. 16.95 (*1-57223-314-1*) Willow Creek Pr.

Orvis, Stephen. The Agrarian Question in Kenya. LC 96-17923. 223p. 1997. 49.95 (*0-8130-1498-0*) U Press Fla.

Orvis, William J. Excel for Scientists & Engineers. 2nd ed. LC 95-71900. 576p. 1995. pap. text 39.99 incl. disk (*0-7821-1761-9*) Sybex.

O

Orwant, Jon. Perl 5 Interactive Course: Certified Edition. LC 97-11857. 884p. 1997. 49.99 (*1-57169-113-8*) Macmillan Gen Ref.

Orwant, Jon & Kobes, Randy. Perl Developer's Toolkit. 2nd ed. 320p. (gr. 9 up). 1998. pap. 39.95 incl. audio compact disk (*1-889671-17-7*) Advice Pr.

Orwant, Jon, et al. Mastering Algorithms with Perl. (Illus.). 684p. 1999. pap. 34.95 (*1-56592-398-7*) OReilly & Assocs.

Orwell, George. Animal Farm. 1989. pap. text. write for info. (*0-582-02173-1*, Pub. by Addison-Wesley) Longman.

— Animal Farm. 1991. pap. text. write for info. (*0-582-06010-9*, Pub. by Addison-Wesley) Longman.

— Animal Farm. Bloom, Harold, ed. LC 98-15483. (Modern Critical Interpretations Ser.). 176p. (YA). 1999. 34.95 (*0-7910-4774-1*) Chelsea Hse.

— Animal Farm. 1999. mass mkt. write for info. (*0-451-52536-1*, Sig Classics) NAL.

***Orwell, George.** Animal Farm. large type ed. LC 98-39553. (Isis Large Print Bks.). 1998. pap. write for info. (*1-56000-520-3*) Transaction Pubs.

Orwell, George. Animal Farm. 50th anniversary ed. 1996. mass mkt. 5.95 (*0-451-52634-1*, Sig Classics) NAL.

— Animal Farm: A Fairy Story. 17.95 (*0-8488-0120-2*) Amereon Ltd.

— Animal Farm: A Fairy Story. LC 92-54299. 1993. 15.00 (*0-679-42039-8*) Everymns Lib.

— Animal Farm: A Fairy Story. 132p. 1990. 18.00 (*0-15-107255-8*) Harcourt.

— Animal Farm: A Fairy Story. 1946. 11.05 (*0-606-00102-6*, Pub. by Turtleback) Demco.

— Animal Farm: A Fairy Story. 1982. reprint ed. lib. bdg. 27.95 (*0-89966-369-9*) Buccaneer Bks.

— Animal Farm: A Fairy Story. 50th anniversary ed. (Illus.). 192p. 1996. 30.00 (*0-15-100217-7*) Harcourt.

— Animal Farm: 50th Anniversary Edition. anniversary ed. 1996. pap. 9.95 (*0-452-27750-7*, Plume) Dutton Plume.

— Animal Farm - Musical. 85p. 1986. pap. 5.95 (*0-87129-695-0*, A06) Dramatic Pub.

— Burmese Days. 23.95 (*0-8488-0602-6*) Amereon Ltd.

— Burmese Days. LC 34-35694. 288p. 1950. 8.95 (*0-15-114975-5*) Harcourt.

— Burmese Days: A Novel. LC 73-12947. 288p. 1974. reprint ed. pap. 12.00 (*0-15-614850-1*, Harvest Bks) Harcourt.

— A Clergyman's Daughter. LC 60-10943. 320p. 1950. reprint ed. pap. 15.00 (*0-15-618065-0*, Harvest Bks) Harcourt.

— Collected Essays, Journalism & Letters Vol. 1: An Age Like This, 1920-1940. Orwell, Sonia & Angus, Ian, eds. LC 68-12591. 574p. 1968. reprint ed. 17.95 (*0-15-118546 8*) Harcourt.

— Collected Essays, Journalism & Letters Vol. 2: My Country Right or Left, 1940-1943. Orwell, Sonia & Angus, Ian, eds. LC 68-12591. 477p. 1968. reprint ed. 15.95 (*0-15-118547-6*) Harcourt.

— Collected Essays, Journalism & Letters Vol. 3: As I Please, 1943-1945. Orwell, Sonia & Angus, Ian, eds. LC 68-12591. 1968. reprint ed. 15.95 (*0-15-118548-4*) Harcourt.

— The Collected Essays, Journalism, & Letters of George Orwell, 4 vols. Angus, Ian, ed. Incl. Vol. II. My Country Right or Left, 1940-1943. 477p. 1971. pap. 6.95 (*0-15-618621-7*, Harvest Bks); Vol. III. As I Please: 1943-1945. 435p. 1971. pap. 6.95 (*0-15-618622-5*, Harvest Bks); Vol. IV. In Front of Your Nose: 1945-1950. 576p. 1971. pap. 17.95 (*0-15-618623-3*, Harvest Bks); 1971. Set pap. 29.95 (*0-15-618624-1*, Harvest Bks) Harcourt.

***Orwell, George.** The Collected Essays, Journalism & Letters of George Orwell Vol. 1: An Age Like This, 1920-1940. Orwell, Sonia & Angus, Ian, eds. (Nonpareil Ser.: Vol. 86). 600p. 2000. reprint ed. pap. 17.95 (*1-56792-133-7*) Godine.

— The Collected Essays, Journalism & Letters of George Orwell Vol. 2: My Country Right or Left, 1940-1943. Orwell, Sonia & Angus, Ian, eds. (Nonpareil Ser.: Vol. 87). 496p. 2000. reprint ed. pap. 17.95 (*1-56792-134-5*) Godine.

— The Collected Essays, Journalism & Letters of George Orwell Vol. 3: As I Please, 1943-1945. Orwell, Sonia & Angus, Ian, eds. (Nonpareil Ser.: Vol. 88). 496p. 2000. reprint ed. pap. 17.95 (*1-56792-135-3*) Godine.

— The Collected Essays, Journalism & Letters of George Orwell Vol. 4: In Front of Your Nose, 1945-1950. Orwell, Sonia & Angus, Ian, eds. (Nonpareil Ser.: Vol. 89). 496p. 2000. reprint ed. pap. 17.95 (*1-56792-136-1*) Godine.

Orwell, George. A Collection of Essays. LC 54-7594. 324p. (C). 1970. reprint ed. pap. 12.00 (*0-15-618600-4*, Harvest Bks) Harcourt.

— Coming up for Air. LC 50-5002. 292p. (C). 1969. reprint ed. pap. 12.00 (*0-15-619625-5*, HPL44, Harvest Bks) Harcourt.

— Dickens, Dali & Others. 1998. lib. bdg. 20.95 (*1-56723-081-4*) Yestermorrow.

— Down & Out in Paris & London. LC 65-67354. 228p. (C). 1972. reprint ed. pap. 12.00 (*0-15 626224-X*, Harvest Bks) Harcourt.

— The English People. LC 74-7022. (British History Ser.: No. 30). 1974. lib. bdg. 75.00 (*0-8383-1897-5*) M S G Haskell Hse.

— La Ferme des Animaux. (FRE.). 1984. pap. 8.95 (*0-7859-4198-3*) Fr & Eur.

— Homage to Catalonia. LC 52-6442. 264p. (C). 1969. reprint ed. pap. 12.00 (*0-15-642117-8*, Harvest Bks) Harcourt.

— Keep the Aspidistra Flying. 22.95 (*0-8488-0603-4*) Amereon Ltd.

— Keep the Aspidistra Flying. LC 56-5326. 264p. (C). 1969. reprint ed. pap. 12.00 (*0-15-646899-9*, Harvest Bks) Harcourt.

— The Lion & the Unicorn: Socialism & the English Genius. LC 75-41205. reprint ed. 22.50 (*0-404-14691-0*) AMS Pr.

— Monarch Quick & Easy Notes: "Nineteen Eighty-Four" by George Orwell. write for info. (*0-318-58794-7*) S&S Trade.

— 1984. 1991. pap. text. write for info. (*0-582-06018-4*, Pub. by Addison-Wesley) Longman.

— 1984. 1998. pap. 5.95 (*0-451-52493-4*) Addson-Wesley Educ.

— 1984. 1963. 5.60 (*0-87129-542-3*, N15) Dramatic Pub.

***Orwell, George.** 1984. 1999. pap. 13.35 (*0-88103-036-8*) Econo-Clad Bks.

Orwell, George. 1984. LC 92-52906. 384p. 1992. 17.00 (*0-679-41739-7*) Everymns Lib.

— 1984. LC 83-18442. 320p. 1983. 12.95 (*0-15-166038-7*) Harcourt.

— 1984. write for info. (*0-614-22114-5*, Sig Classics) NAL.

Orwell, George. 1984. 294p. 1989. pap. 12.95 (*0-452-26293-3*) NAL.

Orwell, George. 1984. (Signet Classics). 1949. 11.05 (*0-606-00199-9*, Pub. by Turtleback) Demco.

— 1984. 1982. reprint ed. 29.95 (*0-89966-368-0*) Buccaneer Bks.

— 1984: The Facsimile of the extant manuscript. fac. ed. LC 81-3848. 416p. 1984. 75.00 (*0-15-166034-4*) Harcourt.

— 1984: The Fascimile of the Extant Manuscript. deluxe limited ed. Davison, Peter, ed. 406p. 1984. boxed set 525.00 (*0-87730-015-1*); lthr. 275.00 (*0-87730-012-7*) M & S Pr.

— Orwell: The Lost Writings. West, W. J., ed. 352p. 1988. mass mkt. 5.95 (*0-380-70118-9*, Avon Bks) Morrow Avon.

— The Orwell Reader: Fiction, Essays, & Reportage. LC 61-1439. 480p. 1961. pap. 15.00 (*0-15-670176-6*, Harvest Bks) Harcourt.

— Orwell's 1984: Text, Sources, Criticism. 2nd ed. Howe, Irving & Levin, David, eds. (Harbrace Sourcebooks Ser.). 450p. (C). 1982. pap. text 32.50 (*0-15-565811-5*, Pub. by Harcourt Coll Pubs) Harcourt.

— Rebelion en la Granja. (SPA.). pap. 14.95 (*84-233-0922-3*, Pub. by Destino) Continental Bk.

— The Road to Wigan Pier. LC 58-10888. 264p. (C). 1972. reprint ed. pap. 12.00 (*0-15-676750-3*, Harvest Bks) Harcourt.

— Shooting an Elephant & other essays. LC 50-10343. 200p. 1950. 12.95 (*0-15-182043-0*) Harcourt.

Orwell, George & Angus, Ian, eds. The Collected Essays, Journalism, & Letters of George Orwell, 4 vols. 1969. 67.80 (*0-15-118545-X*) Harcourt.

***Orwell, George & MacGregor, Lona.** Animal Farm. LC 98-73081. (Literature Made Easy Ser.). (Illus.). 96p. (YA). 1999. pap. 4.95 (*0-7641-0819-0*) Barron.

Orwell, Sonia, ed. see Orwell, George.

Orwen, Gifford P. Upgrade Your Italian: A Review Grammar. 1983. pap. 15.00 (*0-913298-12-3*) S F Vanni.

Orwicz, Michael R., ed. Art Criticism & Its Institutions in Nineteenth-Century France. LC 93-46023. 1994. text 24.95 (*0-7190-3860-X*, Pub. by Manchester Univ Pr) St Martin.

Orwig, Gary W., jt. auth. see Barron, Ann E.

Orwig, Sara. Amor Arriesgado: A Baby for Mommy. (Deseo Ser.: Vol. 120).Tr. of Risky Love. (SPA.). 1998. per. 3.50 (*0-373-35250-6*, 1-35250-9) Harlequin Bks.

***Orwig, Sara.** Amor Verdadero. (Harlequin Deseo Ser.: Vol. 158).Tr. of True Love. (SPA.). 156p. 1999. per. 3.50 (*0-373-35288-3*, 1-35288-9) Harlequin Bks.

Orwig, Sara. Babes in Arms. 1997. per. 3.50 (*0-373-76094-9*, 1-76094-1) Silhouette.

— A Baby for Mommy. (Desire Ser.). 1997. per. 3.50 (*0-373-76060-4*, 1-76060-2) Silhouette.

— The Bride's Choice. (Desire Ser.). 1996. per. 3.50 (*0-373-76019-1*, 1-76019-8) Silhouette.

— Comanche Dancer. 384p. 1998. pap. 4.99 (*0-8217-5951-5*) Kensgtn Pub Corp.

— Comanche Passion, 1. 384p. 1999. mass mkt. 4.99 (*0-8217-6286-9*) Kensgtn Pub Corp.

— The Consummate Cowboy. (Desire Ser.). 1998. per. 3.75 (*0-373-76164-3*, 1-76164-2) Silhouette.

— The Cowboy's Seductive Proposal. 1998. per. 3.75 (*0-373-76192-9*, 1-76192-3, Mira Bks) Harlequin Bks.

— Esposos y Amantes. (SPA.). 1997. per. 3.50 (*0-373-35189-5*, 1-35189-9) Harlequin Bks.

— Falcon's Lair. (Desire Ser.). 1995. per. 3.25 (*0-373-05938-8*, 1-05938-5) Silhouette.

— Family Fortunes. 352p. (Orig.). 1989. mass mkt. 4.50 (*0-446-35410-4*, Pub. by Warner Bks) Little.

— Favors of the Rich. 1991. mass mkt. 4.95 (*0-446-35632-8*, Pub. by Warner Bks) Little.

***Orwig, Sara.** Galahad in Blue Jeans: Way Out West. (Intimate Moments Ser.). 1999. mass mkt. 4.25 (*0-373-07971-0*) Silhouette.

Orwig, Sara. Her Torrid Temporary Marriage. (Desire Ser.: No. 1125). 1998. per. 3.75 (*0-373-76125-2*, 1-76125-3) Silhouette.

— Hide in Plain Sight. 1995. per. 3.75 (*0-373-07679-7*, 1 07679-3) Silhouette.

***Orwig, Sara.** Lazos de Conveniencia. (Deseo Ser.: No. 182).Tr. of Bonds of Convenience. (SPA.). 1999. per. 3.50 (*0-373-35312-X*, 1-35312-7) Harlequin Bks.

Orwig, Sara. Lightning Season. 320p. 1993. mass mkt. 3.99 (*0-8217-4052-0*, Zebra Kensgtn) Kensgtn Pub Corp.

— The Mad, the Bad & the Dangerous. (Superromance Ser.). 1993. mass mkt. 3.50 (*0-373-70563-8*, 1-70563-1) Harlequin Bks.

— Sweeter Than Sin. 368p. (Orig.). 1992. mass mkt. 4.99 (*0-446-36084-8*, Pub. by Warner Bks) Little.

— Texas Passion. 432p. 1994. mass mkt. 4.50 (*0-8217-4746-0*, Zebra Kensgtn) Kensgtn Pub Corp.

— Troublante Ennemie. (FRE.). 1998. mass mkt. 3.50 (*0-373-37478-X*, 1-37478-4) Harlequin Bks.

— Una Vida Nueva: Babes in Arms. (Deseo Ser.: Vol. 114).Tr. of New Life. (SPA.). 1998. per. 3.50 (*0-373-35244-1*, 1-35244-2) Harlequin Bks.

— Warrior Moon. 384p. 1995. mass mkt. 4.99 (*0-8217-5041-0*, Zebra Kensgtn) Kensgtn Pub Corp.

Orwin, Clifford. The Humanity of Thucydides. LC 94-3111. 256p. 1994. text 45.00 (*0-691-03449-4*, Pub. by Princeton U Pr) Cal Prin Full Svc.

— Humanity of Thucydides. 249p. 1994. pap. text 17.95 (*0-691-01726-3*, Pub. by Princeton U Pr) Cal Prin Full Svc.

Orwin, Clifford & Tarcov, Nathan, eds. The Legacy of Rousseau. LC 96-8908. 296p. 1997. pap. text 17.95 (*0-226-63856-1*) U Ch Pr.

— The Legacy of Rousseau. LC 96-8908. 296p. 1998. lib. bdg. 45.00 (*0-226-63855-3*) U Ch Pr.

Orwin, Donna T. Tolstoy's Art & Thought, 1847-1880. LC 92-37860. 296p. (C). 1993. text 42.50 (*0-691-06991-3*, Pub. by Princeton U Pr) Cal Prin Full Svc.

Orwin, Donna T., ed. see Feuer, Katherine B.

Orwin, Joanna, jt. auth. see Cormack, Syd.

Orwin, Martin. Colloquial Somali: A Complete Language Course. LC 95-3131. (Colloquials Ser.). (SOM.). 304p. (gr. 13). 1995. pap. 27.99 (*0-415-10009-7*, B4032) Routledge.

— Colloquial Somali: A Complete Language Course. (Colloquials Ser.). 304p. (C). (gr. 13). 1995. audio 29.99 (*0-415-10010-0*, B4036) Routledge.

— Colloquial Somali: A Complete Language Course. (Colloquials Ser.). (SOM.). 304p. (gr. 13). 1995. pap. 55.00 incl. audio (*0-415-10011-9*, B4040) Routledge.

Orwoll, Bruce & Orwoll, Eric S. Osteoporosis in Men: The Effects of Gender on Skeletal Health. LC 98-83125. (Illus.). 582p. 1999. 99.95 (*0-12-528640-6*) Acad Pr.

Orwoll, Eric S., jt. auth. see Orwoll, Bruce.

***Orwoll, Mark.** Sams Teach Yourself E-Travel Today: Planning Vacations, Finding Bargains & Booking Reservations. (Teach Yourself Today Ser.). (Illus.). 1999. pap. 17.99 (*0-672-31822-9*) Sams.

Ory, John C. & Ryan, Katherine E. Testing & Grading: Tips for Classroom Practice. (Survival Skills for Scholars Ser.: Vol. 4). (Illus.). 128p. (C). 1993. text 37.00 (*0-8039-4973-1*); pap. text 16.50 (*0-8039-4974-X*) Sage.

Ory, John C., jt. auth. see Braskamp, Larry A.

Ory, Marcia G. Aging & Health Care: Social Science & Policy Perspectives. 284p. 1993. pap. 95.00 (*1-56593-576-4*, 0684) Singular Publishing.

Ory, Marcia G., et al, eds. Aging, Health, & Behavior. LC 91-18529. (Illus.). 392p. 1992. pap. 121.60 (*0-608-05062-8*, 206561700005) Bks Demand.

— Aging, Health, & Behavior. 400p. (C). 1991. 58.00 (*0-8039-4342-3*); pap. 26.00 (*0-8039-4343-1*) Sage.

Ory, Marcia G. & Bond, Kathleen, eds. Aging & Health Care: Social Science & Policy Perspectives. (Contemporary Issues in Health, Medicine, & Social Policy Ser.). 320p. 1989. 49.95 (*0-415-01716-5*); pap. 19.95 (*0-415-01717-3*) Routledge.

Ory, Marcia G. & DeFriese, Gordon H., eds. Self-Care in Later Life: Research, Program & Policy Issues. LC 97-43506. (Illus.). 296p. 1998. 48.95 (*0-8261-1186-6*) Springer Pub.

Ory, Marcia G. & Duncker, Alfred P., eds. In-Home Care for Older People: Health & Supportive Services. 224p. (C). 1991. text 42.00 (*0-8039-4413-6*); pap. text 18.95 (*0-8039-4414-4*) Sage.

— In-Home Care for Older People: Health & Supportive Services. LC 91-30887. 224p. 1992. reprint ed. pap. 69.50 (*0-608-03374-X*, 205963800008) Bks Demand.

Ory, Marcia G. & Warner, Huber R., eds. Gender, Health & Longevity: Multidisciplinary Perspectives. LC 90-35541. 208p. 1990. 39.95 (*0-8261-7140-0*) Springer Pub.

Ory, Robert L. Antinutrients & Natural Toxicants in Foods. 378p. 1981. 74.00 (*0-917678-15-X*) Food & Nut Pr.

— Grandma Called It Roughage: Fiber Facts & Fallacies. LC 91-24259. (Illus.). 170p. 1991. text 26.00 (*0-8412-1749-1*, Pub. by Am Chemical); pap. text 15.95 (*0-8412-1764-5*, Pub. by Am Chemical) OUP.

Ory, Robert L., ed. Plant Proteins: Applications, Biological Effects, & Chemistry. LC 86-10848. (ACS Symposium Ser.: No. 312). (Illus.). 296p. 1986. text 75.00 (*0-8412-0976-6*, Pub. by Am Chemical) OUP.

Ory, Robert L. & Rittig, Falk R. Bioregulators: Chemistry & Uses. LC 84-10987. (ACS Symposium Ser.: No. 257). 296p. 1984. 49.95 (*0-8412-0853-0*) Am Chemical.

Ory, Robert L. & Rittig, Falk R., eds. Bioregulators, Chemistry & Uses. LC 84-10987. (ACS Symposium Ser.: No. 257). (Illus.). 293p. 1984. reprint ed. pap. 90.90 (*0-608-03138-0*, 206359100007) Bks Demand.

Ory, Robert L. & St. Angelo, Allen J., eds. Enzymes in Food & Beverage Processing. LC 77-6645. (ACS Symposium Ser.: No. 47). 1977. 38.95 (*0-8412-0375-X*) Am Chemical.

— Enzymes in Food & Beverage Processing. LC 77-6645. (ACS Symposium Ser.: Vol. 47). 335p. 1977. reprint ed. pap. 103.90 (*0-608-03838-5*, 206428500008) Bks Demand.

Ory, Steven J., jt. auth. see Leach, Richard E.

Oryan, Baba T. The Rubaiyat of Baba Tahir Oryan of Hamadan. Nakosteen, Mehdi K., tr. from PEO. & intro. by. (PER., Illus.). 60p. (C). 1988. text 25.00 (*0-936347-42-2*) IBEX.

O'Ryan, S., jt. auth. see Foreman, C.

***Oryu, S., et al, eds.** Few-Body Problems in Physics '99: Proceedings of the 1st Asian-Pacific Conference, Tokyo, Japan, August 23-28, 1999. (Illus.). 550p. 2000. 124.00 (*3-211-83503-2*) Spr-Verlag.

Oryu, S. & Sawada, T., eds. Few-Body Approaches to Nuclear Reactions: Proceedings of the International Workshop on Few-Body Approaches to Nuclear Reactions in Tandem & Cyclotron Energy Regions, Tokyo, Japan, August 22-24, 1986. 308p. 1987. text 97.00 (*9971-5-0218-6*) World Scientific Pub.

Oryx Press Staff. The Hutchinson Guide to the World. 3rd ed. (Illus.). 666p. 1998. boxed set 69.50 (*1-57356-220-3*) Oryx Pr.

***Oryx Press Staff.** Operating Grants for Nonprofit Organizations. 296p. 2000. pap. 29.95 (*1-57356-396-X*) Oryx Pr.

Oryx Press Staff, ed. Directory of Biomedical & Health Care Grants 2000. 14th ed. 904p. 1999. pap. 84.50 (*1-57356-191-6*) Oryx Pr.

— Directory of Child Day Care Centers, 4 vols. Incl. South. 440p. 1986. pap. 26.95 (*0-89774-330-X*); Vol. 1. Northeast. 440p. 1986. 26.95 (*0-89774-256-7*); Vol. 2. North Central. 464p. 1986. 26.95 (*0-89774-328-8*); Vol. 3. West. 528p. 1986. 26.95 (*0-89774-329-6*); Set pap. 250.00 (*0-685-12389-8*) Oryx Pr.

***Oryx Press Staff, ed.** Directory of Grants in the Humanities 2000-2001. 14th ed. 888p. 2000. pap. 84.50 (*1-57356-270-X*) Oryx Pr.

Oryx Press Staff, ed. Directory of Research Grants 2000. 25th ed. 1264p. 1999. pap. 135.00 (*1-57356-189-4*) Oryx Pr.

***Oryx Press Staff, ed.** Funding Sources for Community & Economic Development 1999: A Guide to Current Sources for Local Programs & Projects. 600p. 1999. pap. 64.95 (*1-57356-197-5*) Oryx Pr.

— Funding Sources for Community & Economic Development, 2000: A Guide to Current Sources for Local Programs & Projects. 6th ed. 704p. 2000. pap. text 64.95 (*1-57356-268-8*) Oryx Pr.

***Orza, Vincent F.** When I Want Your Opinion I'll Tell It to You, 1vol. 1999. pap. text 6.95 (*0-9675617-0-1*) Great Thoughts.

***Orzak, Carol.** Grandpa & the Boys. (Illus.). 24p. (J). 2000. write for info. (*0-9679747-0-4*) Details.

Orzalesi, N., jt. ed. see Bonomi, L.

Orzech, Charles D. Politics & Transcendent Wisdom: The Scripture for Humane Kings in the Creation of Chinese Buddhism. LC 96-52407. (Hermeneutics Ser.: No. 8). 424p. 1998. 55.00 (*0-271-01715-5*) Pa St U Pr.

Orzech, Morris. Plane Algebraic Curves. (Pure & Applied Mathematics Ser.: Vol. 61). (Illus.). 240p. 1981. text 135.00 (*0-8247-1159-9*) Dekker.

Orzechowski, Peter, jt. auth. see Slater, William.

Orzechowski, Tom, ed. see McFarlane, Todd.

Orzechowski, Tom, ed. see McFarlane, Todd, et al.

Orzechowski, Z., jt. ed. see Bayvel, L. P.

Orzeck, Art Z. Emily Dickinson & Audience. LC 96-18592. 288p. (C). 1996. text 52.50 (*0-472-10325-3*, 10325) U of Mich Pr.

— Psychology in a Physical World: Forty Years of Just Thinking About Science. 108p. (Orig.). (C). 1995. pap. text 18.50 (*0-8191-9799-8*) U Pr of Amer.

Orzeck, Art Z., jt. auth. see Hendrickson, Al.

Orzel, Susan, jt. auth. see Biggs, Hayes.

Orzessek, Michael, jt. auth. see Sommer, Peter.

Orzeszkowa, Eliza. The Forsaken. Konigsberger, Edward, tr. from POL. 248p. (C). 1980. 65.00 (*0-9508203-0-X*, Pub. by Delamare) St Mut.

O's. The World's Best Irish Jokes. 96p. 1998. pap. 6.95 (*0-00-638409-9*, Pub. by HarpC) Trafalgar.

Os, Henk Van, see Van Os, Henk.

Os, Jaap Van, see Gosman, Martin & Van Os, Jaap, eds.

Os, M. Van, see Van Os, M., ed.

O's, Mr. & MacGregor, Cynthia. O'Brien & Fitzgerald Walk into a Bar . . . The Worlds Best Irish Jokes. LC 95-4827. (Illus.). 1995. pap. 7.95 (*0-8065-1663-1*, Citadel Pr) Carol Pub Group.

Os, N. M. Van, see Van Os, N. M.

Os-Saltaneh, Taj. Khaterat-e Taj Os-Saltaneh: The Memoirs of Taj Os-Saltaneh. Sadounian, Cyrus, ed. (PER.). 136p. (C). 1991. reprint ed. pap. 15.00 (*0-936347-22-8*) IBEX.

Os, Van, ed. Nonionic Surfactants: Organic Chemistry. LC 97-43114. (Surfactant Science Ser.). (Illus.). 312p. 1997. text 145.00 (*0-8247-9997-6*) Dekker.

Os, W. A. Van, see Hafez, E. S. & Van Os, W. A., eds.

Osa. The Collected Optics Papers of Lord Rayleigh. LC 94-68292. 1300p. reprint ed. 150.00 (*1-55752-367-3*) Optical Soc.

Osa, Nancy, ed. see Roberts, Suzanne.

Osa, Osayimwense. African Children's & Youth Literature. LC 94-44450. (Twayne's World Authors Ser.: Vol. 853). 1995. 32.00 (*0-8057-4524-6*, Twyne) Mac Lib Ref.

Osa, Osayimwense, ed. The All White World of Children's Books & African American Children's Literature. 1995. pap. 14.95 (*0-86543-477-8*) Africa World.

— The All White World of Children's Books & African American Children's Literature. 1996. 45.95 (*0-86543-476-X*) Africa World.

OSA Standards Committee. ISO 10110: Optics & Optical Instruments - Preparation of Drawings for Optical Elements & Systems: a User's Guide. Kimmel, Ronald K. & Parks, Robert E., eds. LC 93-85841. 1993. pap. 50.00 (*1-55752-271-5*) Optical Soc.

Osa, Tetsuo, ed. New Challenges in Organic Electrochemistry. 384p. 1998. text 59.00 (*90-5699-146-9*, ECU75) Gordon & Breach.

Osa, Tetsuo, jt. ed. see Atwood, Jerry L.

Osabu-Kle, Daniel T. Introduction to Polimetrics. 1997. 29.95 (*1-55111-161-6*) Broadview.

***Osada, H., ed.** Bioprobes: Biochemical Tools for Investigating Cell Function. LC 99-49857. viii, 319p. 1999. 149.00 (*4-431-70247-4*) Spr-Verlag.

Osada, Takashi. The Five S's: Five Keys to a Total Quality Environment. 224p. 1991. text 32.95 (*92-833-1115-9*, 311159); pap. text 27.50 (*92-833-1116-7*, 311167) Productivity Inc.

Osada, Takashi, jt. auth. see Takahasi, Yoshikazu.

Osada, Y., jt. auth. see Biederman, H.

***Osada, Yoshihito.** Gels Handbook. 3 vols. 1500p. 2000. 1200.00 (*0-12-394690-5*) Acad Pr.

***Osada, Yoshihito & De Rossi, Danilo E., eds.** Polymer Sensors & Actuators: With Contributions by Various Experts. LC 99-16715. (Macromolecular Systems - Materials Approach Ser.). (Illus.). 430p. 1999. 159.00 (*3-540-65487-9*) Spr-Verlag.

Osada, Yoshihito & Nakagawa, Hidemi, eds. Membrane Science & Technology. (Illus.). 488p. 1992. text 215.00 (*0-8247-8694-7*) Dekker.

Osadchy, Mykhaylo, ed. Kafedra, Issue 7. LC 89-80449. 224p. 1989. 10.00 (*0-914834-61-4*) Smoloskyp.

— Kafedra, Issue 8. LC 89-80449. 264p. 1989. 12.50 (*0-914834-62-2*) Smoloskyp.

Osadebay, Dennis C., jt. auth. see Dei-Anang, Michael F.

Osafsky, Joy D. & Fenichel, Emily. Islands of Safety: Assessing & Treating Young Victims of Violence. LC 96-60719. 40p. (Orig.). 1996. pap. 6.00 (*0-943657-37-7*) ZERO TO THREE.

Osaghae, Eghosa E. The Crippled Giant: Nigeria since Independence. LC 97-32892. (C). 1998. pap. 18.95 (*0-253-21197-2*); text 39.95 (*0-253-33410-1*) Ind U Pr.

— Structural Adjustment & Ethnicity in Nigeria. LC 96-219355. (Scandinavian Institute of African Studies: No. 98). 66p. (Orig.). 1995. pap. 20.00 (*91-7106-373-0*) Coronet Bks.

***Osagie, Lyunolu F.** Amistad Revolt: Memory, Slavery & the Politics of Identity in the United Stated & Sierra. LC 99-87625. 2000. 35.00 (*0-8203-2224-5*) U of Ga Pr.

Osaigbovo, Rebecca F. Chosen Vessels: Women of Color, Keys to Change. LC 92-85567. (Illus.). 216p. (Orig.). 1993. pap. 9.95 (*1-880560-57-7*) DaBaR Srvs.

— Movin' on Up: A Woman's Guide Beyond Religion to Spirit Living. 1997. 17.95 (*1-880560-55-0*) DaBaR Srvs.

— Moving on Up: A Woman's Guide to Spirit Living. 1996. pap. text 9.95 (*1-880560-54-2*) DaBaR Srvs.

***Osaka, T., et al, eds.** Electrochemical Technology Applications in Electronics III. 434p. 2000. 84.00 (*1-56677-257-5*, PV 99-34) Electrochem Soc.

Osaka, T., et al, eds. Electrochemical Technology, Innovation & New Technologies. xii, 440p. 1996. text 72.00 (*90-5699-002-0*) Gordon & Breach.

***Osaka, Tetsuya & Datta, Madhav, eds.** Energy Storage Systems in Electronics. Vol. 1. 512p. 1999. text 145.00 (*90-5699-176-0*) Gordon & Breach.

Osaki, Norio. Madhubani Paintings: Indian Native. (Arts Collection Ser.: Vol. 120). (Illus.). 256p. 1998. pap. 14.95 (*4-7636-1620-X*, Pub. by Kyoto Shoin) Bks Nippan.

Osaki, Shunji. Applied Stochastic System Modeling. (Illus.). 280p. 1992. 94.95 (*0-387-54927-7*) Spr-Verlag.

— Stochastic System Reliability Modeling. (Series in Modern Applied Mathematics: Vol. 5). 300p. 1985. text 44.00 (*9971-978-56-3*) World Scientific Pub.

Osaki, Shunji & Cao, J., eds. Reliability Theory & Applications: Proceedings of China-Japan Symposium. 448p. (C). 1987. text 100.00 (*9971-5-0347-6*) World Scientific Pub.

Osaki, Shunji & Murth, D. N. Stochastic Models in Engineering, Technology & Management: Proceeding of the 1st Australia-Japan Workshop. 500p. 1993. text 121.00 (*981-02-1452-9*) World Scientific Pub.

Osaki, Shunji & Nishio, T. Reliability Evaluation of Some Fault-Tolerant Computer Architectures. (Lecture Notes in Computer Science Ser.: Vol. 97). 129p. 1980. 21.00 (*0-387-10274-4*) Spr-Verlag.

Osaki, Shunji, jt. auth. see Mine, Hisashi.

Osaki, Yuji, et al, eds. Progress of Seismology of the Sun & Stars: Proceedings of the Oji International Seminar Held at Hakone, Japan, December 11-14, 1989. (Lecture Notes in Physics Ser.: Vol. 367). xiii, 467p. 1990. 59.00 (*0-387-53091-6*) Spr-Verlag.

Osakwe, Christopher. Co-Venturing in the Soviet Union. 1994. 25.00 (*0-02-923465-4*) S&S Trade.

— Joint Ventures with the Soviet Republics: Law & Practice. 400p. 1993. ring bd. 125.00 (*0-88063-374-3*, MICHIE); ring bd., suppl. ed. 55.00 (*0-318-67229-4*, MICHIE) LEXIS Pub.

— Soviet Business Law: Institutions, Principles & Processes. 1992. ring bd., suppl. ed. 90.00 (*1-56257-194-X*, MICHIE) LEXIS Pub.

Osakwe, Christopher, ed. see Glendon, Mary Ann.

Osalcik, J. Adsorption. (Physical Chemistry Ser.). 206p. 1983. text 94.00 (*0-470-27218-X*) P-H.

Osama, Abdul R. The Dilemma of Development in the Arabian Peninsula. 208p. 1986. 59.50 (*0-7099-4240-0*, Pub. by C Helm) Routldge.

Osamu Sato. Art of Computer Designing. (Illus.). 128p. 1993. pap. 36.95 (*4-7661-0736-5*, Pub. by Graphic-Sha) Bks Nippan.

Osamu, Yoshida, tr. see Numata Center for Buddhist Translation & Research.

Osamura, K. & Hirabayashi, I., eds. Advances in Superconductivity X: Proceedings of the 10th International Symposium on Superconductivity, 2 vols. 1500p. 1997. 298.00 (*4-431-70219-9*) Spr-Verlag.

Osamura, Yoshihiro. Composite Superconductors. (Applied Physics Ser.: Vol. 3). (Illus.). 440p. 1993. text 215.00 (*0-8247-9117-7*) Dekker.

Osancova, K., tr. see Parizkova, Jana.

Osanka, Frank, jt. auth. see Johann, Sara L.

Osanka, Frank M., jt. auth. see Linedecker, Clifford L.

Osaragi, Jiro. The Journey. Morris, Ivan, tr. from JPN.Tr. of Tahiji. 350p. 1960. pap. 12.95 (*0-8048-1377-9*) Tuttle Pubng.

***Osaragi, Jiro.** The Journey. Morris, Ivan, tr.Tr. of Tahiji. 352p. 2000. pap. 12.95 (*0-8048-3255-2*) Tuttle Pubng.

***Osato, T., et al.** Epstein-Barr Virus & Human Cancer. LC 98-164993. (Gann Monograph on Cancer Research Ser.). viii, 190 p. 1998. write for info. (*4-7622-1874-X*) Jap Sci Soc Pr.

Osato, Toyoro, et al, eds. Epstein-Barr Virus & Human Cancer. (Gann Monograph on Cancer Research Ser.: No. 45, 1998). (Illus.). viii, 190p. 1998. 243.50 (*3-8055-6663-8*) S Karger.

Osawa, E. & Yonemitsu, O., eds. Carbocylic Cage Compounds: Chemistry & Applications. (Methods in Stereochemical Analysis Ser.). 409p. 1992. 145.00 (*0-471-18742-9*, Wiley-VCH) Wiley.

Osawa, Eiji & Yonemitsu, Osamu. Carbocyclic Cage Compounds: Chemistry & Applications. (Methods in Stereochemical Analysis Ser.). (Illus.). 409p. 1992. text 95.00 (*0-89573-728-0*, Wiley-VCH) Wiley.

Osawa, Syozo. Evolution of the Genetic Code. (Illus.). 220p. 1995. text 115.00 (*0-19-854781-1*) OUP.

Osawa, Syozo & Honjo, T., eds. Evolution of Life: Fossils, Molecules, & Culture. xiii, 460p. 1991. 199.95 (*0-387-70064-1*) Spr-Verlag.

Osawa, T. & Bonavida, B., eds. Tumor Necrosis Factor: Structure Function Relationship & Clinical Application. (Illus.). x, 292p. 1992. 242.75 (*3-8055-5458-3*) S Karger.

Osawa, Yasu, jt. auth. see Schatz, Dennis.

Osband, Gillian. Castles. LC 91-60082. (Illus.). 16p. (J). 1991. 18.95 (*0-531-05949-9*) Orchard Bks Watts.

Osband, Gillian, ed. The National Trust Family Handbook. (Illus.). 204p. 1993. pap. 8.95 (*0-7078-0171-0*, Pub. by Natl Trust) Trafalgar.

***Osband, Linda.** Victorian Gothic House Style: An Architectural & Interior Design Source Book. (Illus.). 2000. 27.95 (*0-7153-0969-2*, Pub. by D & C Pub) Sterling.

Osband, Linda. Victorian House Style. (Illus.). 192p. 1992. 39.95 (*0-7153-9841-5*, Pub. by D & C Pub) Sterling.

***Osbeck, Kenneth W.** Amazing Grace: Gift Edition. (Illus.). 64p. 1999. 15.99 (*0-8254-3433-5*) Kregel.

Osbeck, Kenneth W. Amazing Grace: 366 Inspiring Hymn Stories for Daily Devotions. LC 90-37888. 400p. 1990. pap. 14.99 (*0-8254-3425-4*) Kregel.

— Devotional Warm-Ups for Church Choirs. LC 85-17222. 96p. 1985. pap. 5.99 (*0-8254-3421-1*) Kregel.

— 52 Bible Characters Dramatized. 192p. 1996. pap. 10.99 (*0-8254-3429-7*) Kregel.

— 52 Hymn Stories Dramatized. LC 91-39320. 176p. 1992. pap. 10.99 (*0-8254-3428-9*) Kregel.

***Osbeck, Kenneth W.** Hallelujah! What a Savior. 128p. 2000. pap. 8.99 (*0-8254-3432-7*) Kregel.

Osbeck, Kenneth W. Himnos Dramatizados. (SPA.). 176p. 1996. pap. 7.99 (*0-8254-1543-8*, Edit Portavoz) Kregel.

***Osbeck, Kenneth W.** Joy to the World! The Stories Behind Your Favorite Christmas Carols. LC 99-16479. 112p. 1999. pap. 8.99 (*0-8254-3431-9*) Kregel.

Osbeck, Kenneth W. The Ministry of Music. LC 61-14865. 192p. 1975. pap. 11.99 (*0-8254-3410-6*) Kregel.

— My Music Workbook. 144p. 1982. pap. 8.99 (*0-8254-3415-7*) Kregel.

— 101 Hymn Stories. LC 81-17165. 288p. (C). 1982. pap. 12.99 (*0-8254-3416-5*) Kregel.

— 101 More Hymn Stories. LC 84-27847. 328p. (C). 1985. pap. 12.99 (*0-8254-3420-3*) Kregel.

— Pocket Guide for the Church Choir Member. 48p. 1969. pap. 2.50 (*0-8254-3408-4*) Kregel.

***Osbeck, Kenneth W.** 25 Most Treasured Gospel Hymn Stories. LC 98-45851. 112p. 1999. pap. text 7.99 (*0-8254-3430-0*) Kregel.

Osberg, Lars, ed. Economic Inequality & Poverty: International Perspectives. LC 90-31795. 272p. (gr. 13). 1991. text 74.95 (*0-87332-528-1*) M E Sharpe.

Osberg, Lars, ed. Economic Inequality & Poverty: International Perspectives. LC 90-31795. 272p. (gr. 13). 1991. pap. text 36.95 (*0-87332-540-0*) M E Sharpe.

Osberg, Lars & Caledon Institute of Social Policy Staff. The Equity, Efficiency, & Symbolism of National Standards in an Era of Provincialism. LC 96-231521. 10 p. 1996. write for info. (*1-895796-46-6*) CISP.

Osberg, Lars & Fortin, Pierre, eds. Unnecessary Debts. LC 96-156230. 200p. 24.95 (*1-55028-497-5*, Pub. by J Lorimer); pap. 19.95 (*1-55028-496-7*, Pub. by J Lorimer) Formac Dist Ltd.

Osberg, Lars, et al. Vanishing Jobs: The Labour Market In The 1990s. LC 96-112533. 223p. 29.95 (*1-55028-483-5*, Pub. by J Lorimer); pap. 19.95 (*1-55028-482-7*, Pub. by J Lorimer) Formac Dist Ltd.

Osberg, Lars, jt. ed. see MacLean, Brian K.

***Osberg, Len.** Coronado the Crown City: Life on the Island, Places to Go & How to Get There. 136p. 1999. spiral bd. 11.95 (*0-9676029-0-4*) L Osber Pubg Co.

Osberg, Richard H. Sir Gawain & the Green Knight. LC 89-13304. (American University Studies: English Language & Literature: Ser. IV, Vol. 112). XXII, 274p. 1989. text 45.95 (*0-8204-1160-4*) P Lang Pubng.

Osberg, Richard H., ed. The Poems of Laurence Minot, 1333-1352. LC 96-6482. (Middle English Texts Ser.). (Illus.). 1996. pap. 12.00 (*1-879288-67-2*) Medieval Inst.

Osberger, Madeleine, jt. auth. see Wilson, Randy J.

Osbey, Brenda M. All Saints: New & Selected Poems. 128p. 1997. pap. 15.95 (*0-8071-2198-3*); text 22.95 (*0-8071-2197-5*) La State U Pr.

— Desperate Circumstances, Dangerous Woman. 96p. (Orig.). 1991. pap. 9.95 (*0-934257-57-4*) Story Line.

Osborn. Public Speaking, 3 vols. 3rd ed. LC 93-78696. (C). 1993. pap. text 39.96 (*0-395-67578-2*) HM.

***Osborn.** Public Speaking. 5th ed. 1999. pap. text, teacher ed. 8.97 (*0-395-96048-7*) HM.

Osborn. Public Speaking: Testbank, 4 vols. (C). 1996. pap., teacher ed. 11.96 (*0-395-80884-7*) HM.

— Public Speaking Transcripts, 2 vols. 2nd ed. (C). 1991. 25.96 (*0-395-57299-1*) HM.

— Public Speaking Video Guide, 3 vols. (C). 1993. pap. 9.96 (*0-395-67580-4*) HM.

***Osborn.** Statistical Applications for Health Information Management. 2000. pap. 55.00 (*0-8342-1243-9*) Aspen Pub.

Osborn. Understanding Communications. (C). Date not set. pap. write for info. (*0-395-67561-8*) HM.

— Understanding Communications. (C). 1998. pap. text 32.97 (*0-395-63206-4*) HM.

Osborn, Noel D. & Hatton, Howard. A Handbook on Exodus. LC 98-35644. (Handbook Ser.). (Illus.). 946p. 1999. pap. write for info. (*0-8267-0101-9*, 105920, Pub. by Untd Bible Soc) Am Bible.

Osborn, Albert S. Mind of the Juror As Judge of the Facts: or The Layman's View of the Law. xv, 239p. 1982. reprint ed. 40.00 (*0-8377-0926-1*, Rothman) W S Hein.

— Problem of Proof: Especially As Exemplified in Disputed Documents Trials. LC 75-20212. 564p. 1975. reprint ed. text 57.95 (*0-88229-300-1*) Burnham Inc.

***Osborn, Albert S.** Problem of Proof: Especially As Exemplified in Disputed Documents Trials. xxi, 526p. 1999. reprint ed. 165.00 (*1-56169-477-0*) Gaunt.

Osborn, Albert S. Questioned Document Problems: The Discovery & Proof of the Facts. LC 84-14716. (Criminology, Law Enforcement, & Social Problems Ser.: No. 172). (Illus.). 570p. 1991. 45.00 (*0-87585-172-X*) Patterson Smith.

***Osborn, Albert S.** Questioned Documents. xxiv, 501p. 1999. reprint ed. 158.00 (*1-56169-476-2*) Gaunt.

Osborn, Albert S. Questioned Documents. 2nd ed. LC 74-78841. (Illus.). 1072p. 1974. reprint ed. text 57.95 (*0-88229-190-4*) Burnham Inc.

— Questioned Documents. 2nd rev. ed. LC 73-9875. (Criminology, Law Enforcement, & Social Problems Ser.: No. 207). (Illus.). 760p. 1973. lib. bdg. 27.50 (*0-87585-207-6*) Patterson Smith.

***Osborn, Alex F.** Let Us Honor the Creator & Other Poems. 2000. write for info. (*1-58235-490-1*) Watermrk Pr.

Osborn, Anne G. Atlas of Diagnostic Neuroradiology. (Illus.). 960p. (C). (gr. 13). 1993. text 250.00 (*0-8016-7486-7*, 04008) Mosby Inc.

— Cerebral Angiography. 2nd ed. LC 98-39295. 462p. 1998. text 135.00 (*0-397-58404-0*) Lppncott W & W.

— An Introduction to Cerebral Angiography. (Illus.). 436p. 1980. text 92.00 (*0-06-141829-3*, 14-18292) Lppncott W & W.

— 1998 Year Book Of Diagnostic Radiology. (Illus.). 640p. (C). (gr. 13). 1998. text 79.00 (*0-8151-9616-4*, 24953) Mosby Inc.

Osborn, Anne G. & Tong, Karen A. Handbook of Neuroradiology: Brain & Skull. 2nd ed. LC 95-25936. (Illus.). 736p. (C). (gr. 13). 1995. pap. text 46.95 (*0-8151-6593-5*, 25690) Mosby Inc.

Osborn, Anne G., ed. see Year Book of Neuroradiology Staff.

Osborn, Averil. Taking Part in Community Care Planning: The Involvement of User Groups, Career Groups & Voluntary Groups. (C). 1991. 60.00 (*0-946505-84-5*, Pub. by Age Concern Eng) St Mut.

Osborn, Caroline. Mortgage Fraud. 314p. 1995. pap. 60.00 (*1-85811-025-4*, Pub. by CLT Prof) Gaunt.

Osborn, Carolyn. Warriors & Maidens. LC 90-49280. 188p. (C). 1991. 19.95 (*0-87565-084-8*) Tex Christian.

***Osborn, Caryn.** I Touched the Ocean. 1999. pap. write for info. (*1-58235-358-1*) Watermrk Pr.

Osborn, Chase. The Soo-Scenes in & about Sault Ste. Marie, Michigan in 1887. (Illus.). 46p. 1983. pap. 8.00 (*0-912382-30-9*) Black Letter.

Osborn, Claudia L. Over My Head: A Doctor's Account of Head Injury from the Inside Looking Out. LC 97-40542. 256p. 1998. 21.95 (*0-8362-5419-8*) Andrews & McMeel.

— Over My Head: A Doctor's Account of Head Injury from the Inside Looking Out. LC 97-67529. iv, 240p. 1997. pap. 18.95 (*0-9658750-0-8*) Peripatetic Pub.

***Osborn, Claudia L.** Over My Head: A Doctor's Own Story of Head Injury from the Inside Looking Out. 2000. pap. 12.95 (*0-7407-0598-9*) Andrews & McMeel.

Osborn, Cynthia J., jt. auth. see Davis, Thomas E.

Osborn, D. Keith. Early Childhood Education in Historical Perspective. 3rd rev. ed. LC 90-23294. 224p. (C). 1991. pap. 24.95 (*0-918772-22-2*) Daye Pr.

Osborn, D. Keith & Osborn, Janie D. Discipline & Classroom Management. 3rd ed. (Illus.). 224p. 1989. lib. bdg. 17.95 (*0-918772-18-4*) Daye Pr.

Osborn, D. Keith, jt. auth. see Osborn, Janie D.

Osborn, Daisy. 5 Choices for Women Who Win. 2nd ed. (RUS., Illus.). (Orig.). 1995. reprint ed. mass mkt. write for info. (*1-890863-05-X*) Wrld Wide Print.

— New Life for Women. 2nd ed. (RUS., Illus.). (Orig.). 1995. reprint ed. mass mkt. write for info. (*1-890863-07-6*) Wrld Wide Print.

— Women & Self-Esteem. 2nd ed. (RUS., Illus.). (Orig.). 1995. mass mkt. write for info. (*1-890863-13-0*) Wrld Wide Print.

— The Women Believer. 2nd ed. (RUS.). (Orig.). 1995. mass mkt. write for info. (*1-890863-12-2*) Wrld Wide Print.

— Women Without Limits. 2nd ed. (RUS., Illus.). (Orig.). 1995. mass mkt. write for info. (*1-890863-14-9*) Wrld Wide Print.

Osborn, Daisy, jt. auth. see Osborn, T. L.

Osborn, Dale J. The Mammals of Ancient Egypt. (Natural History of Egypt Ser.). 224p. 1998. pap. 75.00 (*0-85668-510-0*, Pub. by Aris & Phillips) David Brown.

— The Mammals of Ancient Egypt. (Natural History of Egypt Ser.). (Illus.). 224p. 1998. 95.00 (*0-85668-522-4*, Pub. by Aris & Phillips) David Brown.

Osborn, Dale J. & Helmy, Ibrahim. The Contemporary Land Mammals of Egypt: Including Sinai. LC 79-51549. (Field Museum of Natural History, Publication 1309, Anthropological Ser.: No. 5). 601p. reprint ed. pap. 186.40 (*0-608-03790-7*, 206464900009) Bks Demand.

Osborn, David. Murder in the Napa Valley. 224p. 1995. mass mkt. 4.99 (*0-8217-4844-0*, Zebra Kensgtn) Kensgtn Pub Corp.

— Murder in the Napa Valley: A Margaret Barlow Mystery. 224p. 1993. 19.00 (*0-671-70487-7*) S&S Trade.

— Murder on the Chesapeake: A Margaret Barlow Mystery. 304p. 1993. mass mkt. 3.99 (*0-8217-4165-9*, Zebra Kensgtn) Kensgtn Pub Corp.

***Osborn, David A.** Squirrel Dog Basics: A Guide to Hunting Squirrels with Dogs. LC 99-90379. (Illus.). ix, 157p. 1999. pap. 18.50 (*0-9671700-0-1*) Treetop Pubns.

Osborn, Diana, jt. auth. see Osborn, Lawrence.

Osborn, Diane, selected by. The Joseph Campbell Companion: Reflections on the Art of Living. LC 90-56391. (Illus.). 320p. 1992. 27.00 (*0-06-016718-1*) HarperTrade.

Osborn, Diane K., ed. A Joseph Campbell Companion. LC 90-56391. 320p. 1995. pap. 14.00 (*0-06-092617-1*, Perennial) HarperTrade.

Osborn, Donald E., ed. Selected Papers on Solar Radiation & Solar Thermal Systems. LC 92-19411. (Milestone Ser.: Vol. 54). 1992. pap. 45.00 (*0-8194-0984-7*) SPIE.

— Selected Papers on Solar Radiation & Solar Thermal Systems. LC 92-19411. (Milestone Ser.: Vol. MS 54/HC). 1992. 55.00 (*0-8194-0983-9*) SPIE.

Osborn, Donald L. Joseph Brunner of Rothenstein, Schifferstadt, & Frederick. LC 91-60136. (Illus.). xiv, 586p. 1991. 150.00 (*0-9629126-1-1*) D L Osborn.

— Knowing the Bruners: Ancestry & Descendants of Samuel Bruner & His Wife, Catharine Briggs. LC 68-20641. (Illus.). xiv, 240p. 1968. 100.00 (*0-9629126-0-3*) D L Osborn.

Osborn, Donald W. & Dwyer, David J. A Fulfulde (Masina)-English-French Lexicon: A Root Based Compilation Drawn from Extant Sources Followed by English-Fulfulde & French-Fulfulde Listings. LC 92-35325. 1993. 69.95 (*0-87013-326-8*) Mich St U Pr.

***Osborn, Dorisanne.** Sasha Dolls: Throughout the Years. (Illus.). 56p. 1999. 35.00 (*0-912823-86-0*, BT-182, Pub. by Gold Horse); pap. 29.00 (*0-912823-85-2*, BT-182S, Pub. by Gold Horse) Dollmasters.

Osborn, Duffield. Secret of the Crater. 1979. reprint ed. 8.50 (*0-686-65259-2*) Bookfinger.

Osborn, Edward B. Literature & Life: Things Seen, Heard & Read. LC 68-16963. (Essay Index Reprint Ser.). 1977. reprint ed. 17.95 (*0-8369-0755-8*) Ayer.

Osborn, Edward B., jt. auth. see McManus, Judith A.

Osborn, Elane. The Cop & Calamity Jane. 1999. per. 4.25 (*0-373-07923-0*, 1-07923-5) Silhouette.

— Honeymoon with a Handsome Stranger. 1996. per. 3.99 (*0-373-07748-3*, 1-07748-6) Silhouette.

— Shelter in His Arms. (Intimate Moments Ser.). 1995. per. 3.75 (*0-373-07642-8*, 1-07642-1) Silhouette.

Osborn, Elizabeth, jt. auth. see Sakheim, George A.

Osborn, Eric. Tertullian, First Theologian of the West. 308p. (C). 1997. text 64.95 (*0-521-59035-3*) Cambridge U Pr.

Osborn, Eric F. Ethical Patterns in Early Christian Thought. LC 75-10040. 262p. reprint ed. pap. 74.70 (*0-608-16509-3*, 2026351) Bks Demand.

Osborn, Fairfield, ed. Our Crowded Planet: Essays on the Pressures of Population. LC 82-21145. 240p. 1983. reprint ed. lib. bdg. 65.00 (*0-313-22639-3*, OSOC, Greenwood Pr) Greenwood.

Osborn, Garth, jt. auth. see Ohmans, Patricia.

Osborn, George. The R. L. Stevenson Trail Through the Cevennes. (C). 1989. pap. text 55.00 (*0-9515838-0-8*, Pub. by GTBS Pubns) St Mut.

Osborn, George C. John James Tigert: American Educator. LC 74-6314. (Illus.). 560p. reprint ed. pap. 173.60 (*0-7837-4947-3*, 204461300004) Bks Demand.

— Woodrow Wilson: The Early Years. LC 68-13451. 367p. 1968. pap. 113.80 (*0-7837-8507-0*, 204931500011) Bks Demand.

Osborn, Guy, jt. auth. see Greenfield, Steve.

Osborn, H. Cicadellidae of Hawaii. (BMB Ser.: No. 134). 1972. reprint ed. pap. 25.00 (*0-527-02240-3*) Periodicals Srv.

Osborn, H. Low-Dimensional Topology & Quantum Field Theory. (NATO ASI Ser.: Vol. 315). (Illus.). 332p. (C). 1993. text 110.00 (*0-306-44578-6*, Kluwer Plenum) Kluwer Academic.

Osborn, H. S. How to Prospect for Gold, Silver Gems. (Illus.). 200p. 1998. reprint ed. pap. 14.95 (*1-57002-086-8*) Univ Publng Hse.

Osborn, Hazel. Room for Loving, Room for Learning: Finding the Space You Need in Your Family Child Care Home. LC 94-2503. 109p. 1994. pap. 11.95 (*0-934140-98-7*, 1090) Redleaf Pr.

Osborn, Hazel, jt. auth. see Rothschild, Michael.

***Osborn, Helen M. I. & Khan, Tariq H.** Oligosaccharides: Their Synthesis & Biological Role. (Illus.). 208p. 2000. text 65.00 (*0-19-850265-6*); pap. text 34.95 (*0-19-850260-5*) OUP.

Osborn, Henry F. Cope: Master Naturalist: Life & Letters of Edward Drinker Cope, with a Bibliography of His Writings. LC 77-81135. (Biologists & Their World Ser.). (Illus.). 1978. reprint ed. lib. bdg. 65.95 (*0-405-10735-8*) Ayer.

— The Elephants & Mastodons Arrive in America. fac. ed. (Shorey Historical Ser.). (Illus.). 23p. 1925. reprint ed. pap. 10.00 (*0-8466-6021-0*, U-21) Shoreys Bkstore.

An Asterisk (*) at the beginning of an entry indicates that the title is appearing for the first time.

— From the Greeks to Darwin. LC 74-26283. (History, Philosophy & Sociology of Science Ser.). 1975. reprint ed. 34.95 (0-405-06610-4) Ayer.
— Men of the Old Stone Age, Their Environment, Life & Art. LC 78-72705. (Illus.). reprint ed. 47.00 (0-404-18276-3) AMS Pr.
— The Origin & Evolution of Life: On the Theory of Action, Reaction & Interaction of Energy. Gould, Stephen Jay, ed. LC 79-8340. (History of Paleontology Ser.). (Illus.). 1980. reprint ed. lib. bdg. 36.95 (0-405-12728-6) Ayer.
Osborn, Henry F., ed. Naturalist in the Bahamas: October 12, 1861 - June 25, 1891. LC 10-13587. 1910. 24.50 (0-404-04794-7) AMS Pr.
Osborn, Henry F., et al. Major Papers on Early Primates, Compiled from the Publications of the American Museum of Natural History, 1982-1948. LC 78-72712. 1980. 55.50 (0-404-18282-8) AMS Pr.
Osborn, Henry F., jt. auth. see Department of the Interior, U. S. Geological Surve.
Osborn, Herbert. Bibliography of Ohio Zoology. (Bulletin Ser.: No. 23). 1930. pap. text 2.00 (0-86727-022-5) Ohio Bio Survey.
— The Fulgoridae of Ohio. (Bulletin Ser.: No. 35). 1938. pap. text 4.00 (0-86727-034-9) Ohio Bio Survey.
— The Leafhoppers of Ohio. (Bulletin Ser.: No. 14). 1928. pap. text 2.00 (0-86727-013-6) Ohio Bio Survey.
— The Membracidae of Ohio. (Bulletin Ser.: No. 37). 1940. pap. text 3.00 (0-86727-036-5) Ohio Bio Survey.
Osborn, Herbert, et al. Recent Insect Invasions in Ohio. 1948. pap. text 3.00 (0-86727-039-X) Ohio Bio Survey.
Osborn, Ian. Tormenting Thoughts & Secret Rituals: The Hidden Epidemic of Obsessive-Compulsive Disorder. 1999. pap. 12.95 (0-440-50847-9) Dell.
— Tormenting Thoughts & Secret Rituals: The Hidden Epidemic of Obsessive-Compulsive Disorder. LC 97-31226. 320p. 1998. 25.00 (0-679-44222-7) Pantheon.
Osborn, J., jt. ed. see Benkart, G.
Osborn, J. A., ed. see Conference on Magnetism & Magnetic Materials Staff.
Osborn, J. M., jt. ed. see Benkart, G.
Osborn, Jack L. Personal Information: Privacy at the Workplace. LC 78-18223. (AMA Management Briefing Ser.). 52p. reprint ed. pap. 30.00 (0-608-30703-3, 205039100078) Bks Demand.
Osborn, James. Area, Development Policy, & the Middle City in Malaysia. LC 73-92650. (University of Chicago, Department of Geography, Research Paper Ser.: No. 153). 304p. 1974. reprint ed. pap. 94.30 (0-608-02281-0, 206292200004) Bks Demand.
— Neo-Philobiblon: Ruminations on Manuscript Collecting. LC 72-619565. (Bibliographical Monograph: No. 7). (Illus.). 1973. 10.00 (0-87959-049-1) U of Tex H Ransom Ctr.
Osborn, James M. Young Philip Sidney, 1572 to 1577. LC 77-151584. (Elizabethan Club Ser.: No. 5). 591p. reprint ed. pap. 183.30 (0-608-14025-2, 202202600024) Bks Demand.
Osborn, James M., jt. auth. see Neale, John.
Osborn, Janie D. & Osborn, D. Keith. Cognition in Early Childhood. LC 83-71727. (Illus.). 237p. (C). 1983. pap. text 9.95 (0-918772-12-5) Daye Pr.
Osborn, Janie D., jt. auth. see Osborn, D. Keith.
Osborn, Jean & Lehr, Fran, eds. Literacy for All: Issues in Teaching & Learning. LC 98-6175. 353p. 1998. pap. text 25.00 (1-57230-349-2, C0349); lib. bdg. 45.00 (1-57230-348-4, C0348) Guilford Pubns.
Osborn, Jean, jt. ed. see Lehr, Fran.
Osborn, Jen, jt. ed. see Harris, Tara.
Osborn, John J., Jr., jt. auth. see Neuwirth, Donald.
Osborn, John J., Jr., jt. auth. see Robinette, Joseph.
Osborn, John M., ed. see McCoy, Betsy.
Osborn, June E., pref. AIDS Health Services at the Crossroads: Lessons for Community Care. LC 91-67786. 136p. (Orig.). 1991. pap. write for info. (0-942054-04-0) R W Johnson Found.
Osborn, Karen. Beyond the River. 2001. write for info. (0-688-15899-4, Wm Morrow) Morrow Avon.
— Patchwork. 324p. 1992. pap. 8.95 (0-15-671365-9, Harvest Bks) Harcourt.
Osborn, Kenton R., jt. auth. see Jenkins, Wilmer.
Osborn, Kenton R., jt. auth. see Jenkins, Wilmer A.
***Osborn, Kevin.** The Complete Idiot's Guide to Fatherhood. 352p. 1999. pap. text 16.95 (0-02-863189-7, Pub. by Macmillan Gen Ref) S&S Trade.
Osborn, Kevin. The Scholastic Encyclopedia of Sports in the United States. LC 96-39775. (Illus.). 224p. (J). (gr. 3-7). 1997. 17.95 (0-590-69264-X, Scholastic Ref) Scholastic Inc.
— Tolerance. rev. ed. (Values Library). (Illus.). 64p. (YA). (gr. 7-12). 1993. lib. bdg. 15.95 (0-8239-1508-5) Rosen Group.
Osborn, Kevin & Larson, Signe. Complete Idiot's Guide to Bringing up Your Baby. LC 97-73164. (Illus.). 352p. 1997. 16.95 (0-02-861957-9) Macmillan Gen Ref.
Osborn, Kevin, jt. auth. see Boyd, Keith.
Osborn, Kevin, jt. auth. see Neuwirth, Michael.
Osborn, Lawrence & Osborn, Diana. Celebrating Families: Ideas & Activities for Parents & Children. 176p. 1995. pap. 15.95 (0-687-06616-6) Abingdon.
Osborn, Linda. Good Liturgy, Small Parishes. 144p. (Orig.). 1996. pap. 12.00 (1-56854-150-3, GDLIT) Liturgy Tr Pubns.
Osborn, Linda, jt. auth. see Odenbach, Ginny.
Osborn, Lucy M. & Whitman, Neal A. Ward Attending: The Forty Day Month. 194p. 1991. text 30.00 (0-940193-09-4) Univ UT Sch Med.
Osborn, Lynn E., ed. Trenchless Pipeline Projects: Proceedings of the Conference, Boston, Massachusetts, June 8-11, 1997. LC 97-16274. 504p. 1997. 46.00 (0-7844-0244-2) Am Soc Civil Eng.
Osborn, M. & Weber, K., eds. Cytoskeletal Proteins in Tumor Diagnosis. (Current Communications in Molecular Biology Ser.). (Illus.). 244p. (C). 1989. pap. text 24.00 (0-87969-325-8) Cold Spring Harbor.
Osborn, M. Elizabeth, ed. On New Ground: Contemporary Hispanic-American Plays. LC 87-26734. 288p. (Orig.). 1987. reprint ed. pap. 13.95 (0-930452-68-2) Theatre Comm.
Osborn, M. Elizabeth & Richards, Gillian, eds. New Plays U. S. A. Two. 396p. 1984. 17.95 (0-930452-35-6) Theatre Comm.
Osborn, M. Elizabeth, ed. see Hoffman, William M., et al.
Osborn, M. Elizabeth, jt. ed. see Leverett, James.
Osborn, M. Livia, jt. auth. see Howells, John G.
Osborn, Marijane. Beowulf: A Verse Translation with Treasures of the Ancient North. LC 82-16135. (Illus.). 156p. reprint ed. pap. 48.40 (0-7837-4677-6, 204442400003) Bks Demand.
Osborn, Marijane, jt. auth. see Overing, Gillian R.
Osborn, Marijane, ed. & tr. see Chaucer, Geoffrey.
Osborn, Marvin S. Dynamic Devotions for Teens. Spear, Cindy G., ed. 108p. (Orig.). (YA). (gr. 7-12). 1993. pap., spiral bd. 11.95 (0-941005-90-9) Chrch Grwth VA.
Osborn, Marvin S. & Copeland, James. Women's Ministry: A Model for Mobilizing & Equipping Women for Ministry, Set, incl. audiocass. 1995. ring bd., vinyl bd. 99.95 (1-57052-023-2) Chrch Grwth VA.
Osborn, Marvin S. & Spear, Cindy G. Super Saturday: An Evangelistic Event Full of Exciting Activities for Teens. 105p. 1995. ring bd., vinyl bd. 89.95 incl. audio (1-57052-016-X) Chrch Grwth VA.
Osborn, Max. Die Teufelliteratur des 16 Jahrhunderts. vi, 236p. 1972. reprint ed. write for info. (0-318-71850-2); reprint ed. write for info. (3-487-00849-1) G Olms Pubs.
Osborn, Meredith B. Top 10 Guide to San Francisco. Nee, Patrick W. & Internationalist Staff, eds. (Top Ten Travel Guides Ser.). (Illus.). 224p. 2000. pap. 14.95 (1-891382-24-1, Pub. by Intrntnlst) BookWorld.
Osborn, Michael & Osborn, Suzanne. Public Speaking, 4 vols. 4th annot. ed. (C). 1996. text, teacher ed. 41.16 (0-395-80883-9) HM.
***Osborn, Michael & Osborn, Suzanne.** Public Speaking. 5th ed. 1999. pap. text 34.17 (0-395-96046-0) HM.
Osborn, Micheal. Public Speaking, 4 vols. 4th ed. LC 96-76943. (C). 1996. pap. text 39.16 (0-395-80882-0) HM.
Osborn, Nancy A. & Monroe, Martha C. Using Community Resources. (EEToolbox-Workshop Resource Manual Ser.). 44p. 1994. 8.00 (1-884782-08-6) Natl Consort EET.
Osborn, Nancy M., jt. auth. see Gradwohl, David M.
Osborn, Patricia. How Grammer Works: A Self- Teaching Guide. 2nd ed. LC 98-24402. 272p. 1999. pap. 16.95 (0-471-24388-4) Wiley.
— Poetry by Doing. 240p. 1991. pap. 22.59 (0-8442-5662-5) NTC Contemp Pub Co.
— Reading Smarter! More Than 200 Reproducible Activities to Build Reading Proficiency in Grades 7-12. LC 94-34552. 434p. 1994. pap. text 29.95 (0-87628-850-6) Ctr Appl Res.
— School Newspaper Adviser's Survival Guide. LC 97-23288. 320p. 1998. spiral bd. 29.95 (0-87628-891-3) Ctr Appl Res.
Osborn, Peggy. G. B. Giraldi's "Altile" The Birth of a New Dramatic Genre in Renaissance Ferrara. LC 91-47936. (Studies in Renaissance Literature: Vol. 12). 260p. 1992. 89.95 (0-7734-9445-6) E Mellen.
***Osborn, Peter & Benjamin, Andrew, eds.** Walter Benjamin's Philosophy: Destruction & Experience Reprint of 1993 Routledge Edition. 312p. 2000. pap. 29.95 (1-903083-08-7, Pub. by Clinamen Pr) Paul & Co Pubs.
Osborn, R. Applied Quantum Mechanics. 196p. 1988. text 48.00 (9971-5-0294-1); pap. text 32.00 (9971-5-0295-X) World Scientific Pub.
Osborn, R. R., ed. Grounds of Hope: Essays in Faith & Freedom. 184p. 1968. 6.50 (0-87921-055-9) Attic Pr.
Osborn, Richard. Introducing Eastern Philosophy. 176p. 1996. pap. text 9.95 (1-874166-34-X, Pub. by Totem Bks) Natl Bk Netwk.
Osborn, Richard K. & Yip, S. Foundations of Neutron Transport Theory. (U. S. Atomic Energy Commission Monographs). xii, 126p. 1966. text 216.00 (0-677-01170-9) Gordon & Breach.
Osborn, Richards C. Business Finance: The Management Approach. LC 65-15300. (Illus.). 1965. teacher ed. 5.00 (0-89197-054-1); text 22.95 (0-89197-053-3) Irvington.
Osborn, Robert. Osborn Festival of Phobias. LC 78-162432. (Illus.). 1971. pap. 2.95 (0-87140-250-5, Pub. by Liveright) Norton.
Osborn, Robert, ed. see Wordsworth, William.
Osborn, Robert T. The Barmen Declaration As a Paradigm for a Theology of the American Church. LC 91-44313. (Toronto Studies in Theology: Vol. 63). 168p. 1992. lib. bdg. 79.95 (0-7734-9472-3) E Mellen.
Osborn, Ronald E. The Faith We Affirm. LC 79-21079. 1979. pap. 4.99 (0-8272-1009-4) Chalice Pr.
— Folly of God: The Rise of Christian Preaching. LC 97-17416. (History of Christian Preaching Ser.: Vol. 1). 448p. 1998. boxed set 54.99 (0-8272-1429-4); pap. 39.99 (0-8272-1428-6) Chalice Pr.
Osborn-Ryan, Sharon. Cumulative Baptism Index to the Catholic Church Records of the Pacific Northwest, Vol. 3. vii, 412p. 1999. 30.00 (1-892650-02-9) Heritge Trail.
— Cumulative Death Index to the Catholic Church Records of the Pacific Northwest, Vol. 1. LC 98-204180. xvi, 144p. 1998. 15.00 (1-892650-00-2) Heritge Trail.
— Cumulative Marriage Index to the Catholic Church Records of the Pacific Northwest, Vol. 2. xii, 128p. 1998. 15.00 (1-892650-01-0) Heritge Trail.
Osborn, S., jt. auth. see Minder, W.
Osborn, Sherard. The Blockade of Kedah in 1838: A Midshipman's Exploits in Malayan Waters. (Oxford in Asia Hardback Reprints Ser.). (Illus.). 390p. 1987. 32.50 (0-19-588860-X) OUP.
Osborn, Sherard. Stray Leaves from an Arctic Journal: Or, Eighteen Months in the Polar Regions in Search of Sir John Franklin's Expedition in the Years 1850-1851. LC 74-5861. 1852. 27.50 (0-404-11667-1) AMS Pr.
Osborn, Sherard, ed. see McClure, Robert J.
***Osborn, Susan.** What's in a Name? LC 99-46877. (Illus.). 703p. 1999. per. 14.95 (0-671-02555-4, PB Trade Paper) PB.
Osborn, Susan, jt. auth. see Weiss, Jeffrey.
Osborn, Susan M. The System Made Me Do It! A Life Changing Approach to Office Politics. LC 96-94879. (Illus.). 176p. (Orig.). 1997. pap. 19.95 (0-9655368-0-7) LifeThread Pubns.
Osborn, Susan T., compiled by. The Complete Guide to Christian Writing & Speaking. 320p. 1994. pap. 9.95 (0-939497-35-2) Promise Pub.
Osborn, Susan T. & Tangvald, Christine H. Children Around the World Celebrate Christmas! (Illus.). 32p. (J). (gr. k-3). 1996. reprint ed. pap. 4.99 (0-7847-0356-6, 03822) Standard Pub.
Osborn, Susan T. & Weese, Wightman. Potpourri of Praise. LC 97-154583. 179p. (Orig.). 1995. pap. 9.95 (1-883893-27-5) WinePress Pub.
Osborn, Suzanne, jt. auth. see Osborn, Michael.
Osborn, T. L. The Best of Life. 2nd ed. (RUS.). (Orig.). 1995. mass mkt. write for info. (1-890863-10-6) Wrld Wide Print.
— God's Love Plan. 2nd ed. (RUS., Illus.). (Orig.). 1995. reprint ed. mass mkt. write for info. (1-890863-06-8) Wrld Wide Print.
— The Good Life. 2nd ed. (RUS., Illus.). (Orig.). 1995. mass mkt. write for info. (1-890863-11-4) Wrld Wide Print.
— Healing the Sick. 420p. 1981. pap. 14.99 (0-89274-187-2, HH-187) Harrison Hse.
— Healing the Sick: A Living Classic. 352p. 1993. 14.99 (0-89274-403-0, HH-403) Harrison Hse.
— 101 Divine Healing Facts. 32p. 1983. pap. 1.00 (0-89274-299-2, HH-299) Harrison Hse.
— Receive Miracle Healing. 2nd ed. (RUS., Illus.). 1995. mass mkt. write for info. (1-890863-08-4) Wrld Wide Print.
— Soul Winning. 2nd ed. (RUS., Illus.). (Orig.). 1995. mass mkt. write for info. (1-890863-09-2) Wrld Wide Print.
Osborn, T. L. & Osborn, Daisy. Receive Miracle Healing. Date not set. pap. 8.99 (0-89274-221-6) Harrison Hse.
— Soulwinning. Date not set. pap. 10.99 (0-89274-186-4) Harrison Hse.
***Osborn, Terry A.** Critical Reflection & the Foreign Language Classroom. LC 99-40323. (Critical Studies in Education & Culture Ser.). 143p. 2000. 49.95 (0-89789-681-5, Bergin & Garvey) Greenwood.
Osborn, Thomas C., jt. ed. see Beckmann, Jacques S.
Osborn, Thomas W. No Middle Ground: Thomas Ward Osborn's Letters from the Field (1862-1864) Crumb, Herb S. & Dhalle, Katherine, eds. LC 93-8590. (Illus.). 199p. 1993. 22.95 (0-9622393-4-8) Edmonston Publ.
Osborn, Tom & Gaye, Alphonse. Using Farmer Participatory Research to Improve Seed & Food Grain Production in Senegal. (Development Studies). 25p. (Orig.). 1991. pap. 6.00 (0-933595-57-3) Winrock Intl.
Osborn, Tom, tr. see Wedekind, Frank.
***Osborn, William M.** The Wild Frontier: Atrocities During the American-Indian War from Jamestown Colony. 2000. 24.95 (0-375-50374-9) Random.
Osborne. Coal Preparation Technology, Vol. 1. 1988. lib. bdg. write for info. (0-86010-995-X) Kluwer Academic.
— Coal Preparation Technology, Vol. 2. 1988. lib. bdg. write for info. (0-86010-996-8) Kluwer Academic.
— CPA Firm Communication Strategies. 96th ed. 1995. pap. text 79.00 (0-15-601919-1, Pub. by Harcourt Coll Pubs) Harcourt.
— MCSE Core Exams Test Yourself Personal Testing Center. (MCSE Certification Press Ser.). 1998. 99.00 (0-07-211926-8) Osborne-McGraw.
— 1989 Fall Consumer Catalog. 1989. write for info. (0-07-881569-X) McGraw.
— 1989 Fall International Catalog. 1989. write for info. (0-07-881571-1) McGraw.
— 1996 Human Resource Administration Handbook. 96th ed. 1995. 79.00 (0-15-601922-1); 79.00 (0-15-601923-X) Harcourt Legal.
***Osborne & Brown.** Critical Issues Life span. 128p. 2000. pap. text 26.67 (0-205-27105-7) Allyn.
Osborne, jt. auth. see Lambert, Kenneth.
Osborne, Adam & Dvorak, John C. Hypergrowth: The Rise & Fall of the Osborne Computer Corporations. 224p. 1985. mass mkt. 5.95 (0-380-69960-5, Avon Bks) Morrow Avon.
Osborne, Alan. The Merthyr Trilogy: Three Plays. 174p. 1998. pap. 14.95 (0-9521558-6-9) Parthian Bks.
Osborne, Algernon A. Speculation on the New York Stock Exchange, September, 1904-March, 1907. (Columbia University. Studies in the Social Sciences: No. 137). reprint ed. 37.50 (0-404-51137-6) AMS Pr.
Osborne, Alice. Alice Osborne's Alaska. LC 84-50652. (Illus.). 92p. 1984. pap. 5.95 (0-9610910-1-0) Western Gull Pub.
Osborne, Allan G., Jr. Disciplinary Options for Students with Disabilities. 83p. 1997. pap. text 20.00 (1-56534-096-5) Ed Law Assn.
Osborne, Allan G., Jr. Legal Issues in Special Education. LC 95-24024. 336p. 1995. 61.00 (0-205-18442-1) Allyn.
Osborne, Allan G., Jr. & DiMattia, Philip. Classroom Management: A Case Study Handbook for Teachers of Challenging Learners. LC 98-6539. 168p. 1998. pap. 19.95 (0-89089-873-1) Carolina Acad Pr.
Osborne, Allan G., et al. Effective Management of Special Education Programs: A Handbook for School Professionals. 160p. (C). 1993. text 36.00 (0-8077-3259-1); pap. text 16.95 (0-8077-3258-3) Tchrs Coll.
Osborne, Allen G., Jr. Complete Legal Guide to Special Education Services: A Handbook for Administrators, Counselors & Supervisors. 264p. 1988. text 34.95 (0-13-162025-8) P-H.
Osborne, Amy, ed. Multables, Inc. (Illus.). 3p. (J). (gr. 2-5). 13.99 (0-9645004-0-X) Multables.
Osborne, Annabelle & Weisiger, Benjamin B., prefs. Death Notices from Richmond, Virginia Newspapers 1821-1840. 347p. 1999. reprint ed. pap. 20.00 (1-888192-00-3) VA Geneal Soc.
— Marriage Notices from Richmond, Virginia, Newspapers, 1821-1840. 238p. 1999. reprint ed. pap. 20.00 (1-888192-01-1) VA Geneal Soc.
Osborne, Anne R. Reap the Whirlwind: Augusta & the Revolution. LC 89-10334. 1990. 4.95 (0-87844-087-9) Sandlapper Pub Co.
— The South Carolina Story. LC 87-37628. (Illus.). 168p. 1988. 12.95 (0-87844-083-6) Sandlapper Pub Co.
Osborne, Anthony. Complex Variables & Their Applications. LC 98-29672. 432p. (C). 1999. pap. text 82.00 (0-201-34290-1) Addison-Wesley.
Osborne, Arthur. For Those with Little Dust: Selected Writings of Arthur Osborne. (Insights on the Quest Ser.). 232p. 1990. pap. 12.95 (1-878019-03-1) Inner Drctns.
— Ramana Maharshi & the Path of Self-Knowledge. LC 76-18194. (Illus.). 208p. 1970. pap. 12.95 (0-87728-071-1) Weiser.
Osborne, Arthur, ed. Collected Works of Ramana Maharshi. 192p. 1997. pap. 12.95 (0-87728-907-7) Weiser.
— The Teachings of Ramana Maharshi. 2nd rev. ed. 200p. 1996. reprint ed. pap. 12.95 (0-87728-897-6) Weiser.
Osborne, Arthur, tr. see Guenon, Rene.
Osborne, B., jt. ed. see Armstrong, R.
Osborne, B. G., et al. Practical NIR Spectroscopy: With Applications in Food & Beverage Analysis. 2nd rev. ed. LC 92-36734. Orig. Title: Near Infrared Spectroscopy in Food Analysis. 1993. 144.15 (0-582-09946-3) Longman.
Osborne, Barbara, ed. see Seass, Robert P.
Osborne, Barbara A., jt. auth. see Matsudaira, Paul T.
Osborne, Brian. A Little Book of Scottish Heather. (Illus.). 60p. 1998. 9.95 (0-86281-705-6, Pub. by Appletree Pr) Irish Bks Media.
Osborne, Brian, jt. auth. see Reid, Alan.
Osborne, Brian D. The Ingenious Mr. Bell. LC 96-205616. 288p. 1995. 45.00 (1-874640-31-9, Pub. by Argyll Pubng) St Mut.
Osborne, Brian D. & Armstrong, Ronald. Scotch Obsessions. LC 97-130216. 208p. 1996. pap. 13.95 (1-874744-68-8, Pub. by Birlinn Ltd) Dufour.
— Scottish Dates. LC 98-130840. (Traditional Scotland Ser.). 188p. pap. 13.95 (1-874744-40-8, Pub. by Birlinn Ltd) Dufour.
Osborne, Bruce A., jt. auth. see Geider, Richard J.
Osborne, C. M., jt. auth. see Massey, W. C.
Osborne, Carl A. & Finco, Delmar R., eds. Canine & Feline Nephrology & Urology. LC 94-34694. (Illus.). 960p. 1995. 105.00 (0-683-06666-8) Lppncott W & W.
Osborne, Carol L., jt. auth. see Morrissey, Muriel E.
Osborne, Carol L., ed. see Mazzio, Skip & Veca, Donna.
Osborne, Carol M., et al. Museum Builders in the West: The Stanfords As Collectors & Patrons of Art, 1870-1906. LC 85-63383. (Illus.). 1986. pap. 9.95 (0-937031-10-0) Stanford Art.
— The Stanford Museum Centennial Handbook: One Hundred Works of Art. LC 90-72067. (Illus.). 128p. (Orig.). (C). 1991. 20.00 (0-937031-07-0); pap. 10.00 (0-937031-00-3) Stanford Art.
Osborne, Carol M., jt. auth. see Steadman, David W.
Osborne, Cary. Darkloom. 272p. 1998. pap. 5.99 (0-441-00569-1) Ace Bks.
— Deathweave. 304p. 1998. mass mkt. 5.99 (0-441-00498-9) Ace Bks.
— Glaive. 304p. 1996. mass mkt. 5.99 (0-441-00328-1) Ace Bks.
— Iroshi. 224p. (Orig.). 1995. mass mkt. 4.99 (0-441-00130-0) Ace Bks.
— Persea. 224p. 1996. mass mkt. 5.99 (0-441-00397-4) Ace Bks.
Osborne, Catherine. Eros Unveiled: Plato & the God of Love. 264p. 1995. text 59.00 (0-19-826761-4) OUP.
— Rethinking Early Greek Philosophy: Hippolytus of Rome & the Presocratics. LC 87-47719. 400p. (C). 1987. text 59.50 (0-8014-2103-9) Cornell U Pr.
Osborne, Cecil. Art of Understanding Your Mate: With Leader's Guide. 1979. pap. 4.95 (0-310-30602-7, 10476P) Zondervan.
Osborne, Cecil G. The Art of Getting along with People. 192p. 1982. pap. 3.95 (0-310-30612-4, 10477P) Zondervan.
— The Art of Getting Along with People. 192p. 1989. 8.95 (0-310-30611-6) Zondervan.
— The Art of Learning to Love Yourself. 160p. 1987. pap. 7.95 (0-310-30571-3, 10480P) Zondervan.
Osborne, Cecil G. The Art of Understanding Your Mate. 192p. 1988. mass mkt. 9.99 (0-310-30601-9, 10481P) Zondervan.
Osborne, Cecil G. The Art of Understanding Yourself. 1986. pap. 4.95 (0-310-30592-6, 10472P) Zondervan.
— The Art of Understanding Yourself. 224p. 1988. pap. 7.99 (0-310-30591-8, 10473P) Zondervan.
— How to Have a Happier Wife. LC 85-14255. 64p. (Orig.). 1985. pap. 3.95 (0-310-30622-1, 10478P) Zondervan.
— Psicologia del Matrimonio.Tr. of Art of Understanding Your Mate. (SPA.). 292p. 1989. pap. 4.99 (0-945792-83-2, 497704) Editorial Unilit.

O

An Asterisk (*) at the beginning of an entry indicates that the title is appearing for the first time.

Osborne, Charles. Bel Canto Operas: A Guide to the Operas of Rossini, Bellini, & Donizetti. 378p. 1994. pap. 19.95 (0-931340-84-5, Amadeus Pr) Timber.

— The Complete Operas of Mozart. LC 82-23639. (Quality Paperbacks Ser.). (Illus.). 349p. 1983. reprint ed. pap. 14.95 (0-306-80190-6) Da Capo.

— The Complete Operas of Puccini. LC 83-10142. (Quality Paperbacks Ser.). (Illus.). 282p. 1983. reprint ed. pap. 14.95 (0-306-80200-7) Da Capo.

— The Complete Operas of Richard Strauss. (Quality Paperbacks Ser.). (Illus.). 248p. 1991. reprint ed. pap. 13.95 (0-306-80459-X) Da Capo.

— The Complete Operas of Richard Wagner. LC 92-34417. (Illus.). 304p. 1992. pap. 13.95 (0-306-80522-7) Da Capo.

— The Complete Operas of Verdi: An Interpretive Study of the Librettos & Music & Their Relation to the Composer's Life. LC 77-23409. (Quality Paperbacks Ser.). 458p. 1977. pap. 14.95 (0-306-80072-1) Da Capo.

— The Dictionary of the Opera. rev. ed. (Illus.). 384p. 2000. pap. 16.95 (1-56649-108-8) Welcome Rain.

***Osborne, Charles.** The Importance of Being Earnest. 160p. 2000. text 21.95 (0-312-26177-2) St Martin.

Osborne, Charles. The Life & Crimes of Agatha Christie. large type ed. (Charnwood Library). (Illus.). 1991. 27.99 (0-7089-8583-1, Charnwood) Ulverscroft.

— W. H. Auden: The Life of a Poet. LC 95-34142. 352p. 1995. pap. 12.95 (0-87131-788-5) M Evans.

Osborne, Charles, ed. The Dictionary of Composers. LC 78-58291. (Illus.). 380p. 1981. pap. 19.95 (0-8008-2195-5) Taplinger.

Osborne, Charles, tr. see Leider, Frida.

Osborne, Charles C. Jubal: The Life & Times of General Jubal A. Early, CSA, Defender of the Lost Cause. LC 92-11982. (Illus.). 592p. 1992. 29.95 (0-945575-35-1) Algonquin Bks.

— Jubal: The Life & Times of General Jubal A. Early, CSA Defender of the Lost Cause. LC 92-11982. xvi, 592p. 1994. pap. 19.95 (0-8071-1913-X) La State U Pr.

Osborne, Chris. International Yearbook of Educational & Training Technology, 1994/95. 400p. 1994. 75.00 (0-7494-1334-4, Kogan Pg Educ) Stylus Pub VA.

Osborne, Christine. Jordan. (Travel Guides Ser.). (Illus.). 225p. 1987. pap. 9.95 (0-87052-465-8) Hippocrene Bks.

— Malaysia. (Essential Guides Ser.). (Illus.). 128p. 1994. 7.95 (0-8442-8921-3, 89213) NTC Contemp Pub Co.

— Middle Eastern Cooking: Over 100 Delicious Recipes. (Illus.). 152p. 1997. pap. 24.95 (1-85375-257-6, Pub. by Prion) Trafalgar.

Osborne, Claire G. Jackie: A Legend Defined. LC 96-6599. 240p. 1997. pap. 10.00 (0-380-79134-X, Avon Bks) Morrow Avon.

Osborne, Colin P., III. Day Dreaming-Night Thinking: Roaming in Two Worlds. LC 81-84497. (Illus.). 80p. 1982. 7.50 (0-9607332-2-1) Ololon Pubns.

Osborne, Colin P., III, ed. Aspirin: A Curriculum Resource for Post-16 Chemistry Courses. LC 98-223723. ii, 33 p. 1998. write for info. (1-870343-50-6) Royal Soc Chem.

Osborne, Craig. Civil Litigation: Legal Practice Course Guides. 424p. 1995. pap. 34.00 (1-85431-367-3, Pub. by Blackstone Pr) Gaunt.

— Civil Litigation: Legal Practice Course Guides. 452p. 1996. pap. 34.00 (1-85431-417-3, Pub. by Blackstone Pr) Gaunt.

— Civil Litigation, 1998-99. 6th ed. LC 99-199676. (Legal Practice Course Guides Ser.). 449p. 1998. pap. 40.00 (1-85431-784-9) Gaunt.

***Osborne, Craig.** Civil Litigation, 1999-2000. (Legal Practice Course Guides Ser.). 465p. 1999. pap. 38.00 (1-85431-968-X, Pub. by Blackstone Pr) Gaunt.

Osborne, Craig. Civil Litigation, 1996/97. 4th ed. (Legal Practice Course Guides Ser.). 430p. 1996. pap. 36.00 (1-85431-547-1, Pub. by Blackstone Pr) Gaunt.

— Civil Litigation, 1997/1998. 5th rev. ed. 436p. 1997. pap. 38.00 (1-85431-649-4, Pub. by Blackstone Pr) Gaunt.

***Osborne, Craig.** Criminal Litigation: Legal Practice Course Guides, 1999-2000. 7th ed. 374p. 1999. 38.00 (1-85431-971-X, Pub. by Blackstone Pr) Gaunt.

Osborne, Craig. Criminal Litigation, 1998-99. 6th ed. (Legal Practice Course Guides Ser.). 364p. 1998. pap. 40.00 (1-85431-785-7) Gaunt.

— Criminal Litigation 1996-97. 4th ed. (Legal Practice Course Guides Ser.). 347p. 1996. pap. 36.00 (1-85431-544-7, Pub. by Blackstone Pr) Gaunt.

— Criminal Litigation, 1997/98. 5th rev. ed. (Legal Practice Course Guides Ser.). 361p. 1997. pap. 38.00 (1-85431-648-6, Pub. by Blackstone Pr) Gaunt.

Osborne, Craig & Tighe, Maria. Civil Litigation. 200p. 1993. 34.00 (1-85431-292-8, Pub. by Blackstone Pr) Gaunt.

— Criminal Litigation. 200p. 1993. 34.00 (1-85431-294-4, Pub. by Blackstone Pr) Gaunt.

Osborne, Cynthia M. Litigation Guide for Paralegals: Research & Drafting, 2, Vol. 2. 2nd ed. 760p. 1995. boxed set 145.00 (0-471-01644-6) Wiley.

Osborne, D. G. Coal Preparation Technology, 2 vols., Set, Vols. 1 & 2. (C). 1988. lib. bdg. 955.50 (1-85333-092-2, Pub. by Graham & Trotman) Kluwer Academic.

Osborne, D. R. Scatter Me: Poems - Nineteen Eighty to Nineteen Eighty-Nine. Duthie, P. E., ed. 95p. (Orig.). 1990. pap. 8.00 (0-9626451-0-9) Laughing Coyote.

Osborne, David. Economic Competitiveness: The States Take the Lead. LC 87-82983. 85p. (Orig.). 1987. per. 12.00 (0-944826-00-8) Economic Policy Inst.

— Laboratories of Democracy: A New Breed of Governor Creates Models for National Growth. 407p. 1988. pap. 16.95 (0-87584-233-X) Harvard Busn.

— Reinventing Government Facilitator Guide. 1998. pap. text 89.95 (0-7879-4101-8) Jossey-Bass.

— Staff Training & Assessment. LC 95-31896. 1996. 80.00 (0-304-33119-8) Continuum.

— State Technology Programs: A Preliminary Analysis of Lessons Learned. 75p. 1989. 12.00 (0-934892-50-4) CSPA.

Osborne, David & Colon, Victor. Reinventing Government: Workbook. 1998. pap. text, wbk. ed. 19.95 (0-7879-4100-X) Jossey-Bass.

Osborne, David & Gaebler, Ted A. Reinventing Government: How the Entrepreneurial Spirit Is Transforming the Public Sector. 432p. 1992. 30.00 (0-201-52394-9) Addison-Wesley.

— Reinventing Government: How the Entrepreneurial Spirit Is Transforming the Public Sector. 432p. (C). 1993. pap. 15.95 (0-452-26942-3) Dutton Plume.

Osborne, David & Plastrik, Peter. Banishing Bureaucracy. 416p. 1998. pap. 14.95 (0-452-27980-1, Plume) Dutton Plume.

— Banishing Bureaucracy: The Five Strategies for Reinventing Government. 397p. 1996. 25.00 (0-201-62632-2) Addison-Wesley.

***Osborne, David & Plastrik, Peter.** The Reinventor's Fieldbook: Tools for Transforming Your Government. 2000. 35.00 (0-7879-4332-0) Jossey-Bass.

Osborne, David W. & Amann, Anton H. Topical Drug Delivery Formulations. (Drugs & the Pharmaceutical Sciences Ser.: Vol. 42). (Illus.). 352p. 1989. text 210.00 (0-8247-8183-X) Dekker.

Osborne, Denise. Cut To: Murder. LC 94-45808. (Mystery Ser.). 1995. 21.00 (0-8050-3114-6) H Holt & Co.

— Murder Offscreen. 1995. write for info. (0-8050-3113-8) H Holt & Co.

Osborne, Dorothy. The Temple of Love. large type ed. (Linford Romance Library). 304p. 1987. pap. 8.95 (0-7089-6379-X, Linford) Ulverscroft.

Osborne, Dorothy M. Naturally, Maine. LC 97-173839. 48p. 1997. pap. 9.95 (1-885206-46-1, Iliad Pr) Cader Pubng.

Osborne, Douglas. Excavations in the McNary Reservoir Basin Near Umatilla, Oregon, Paper No. 8. fac. ed. (Smithsonian Institution, Bureau of American Ethnology Ser.: Bulletin 166). (Illus.). 280p. (C). 1957. reprint ed. pap. text 33.75 (1-55567-713-4) Coyote Press.

Osborne, Douglas, et al. The Sheep Island Site & the Mid Columbia Valley, Vol. 24. fac. ed. (Smithsonian Institution, Bureau of American Ethnology Ser.: Bulletin 179). (Illus.). 70p. (C). 1961. reprint ed. pap. text 8.13 (1-55567-673-1) Coyote Press.

Osborne, Duncan E., ed. Asset Protection: Domestic & International Law & Tactics. LC 95-8267. 1995. write for info. (0-614-32280-4) West Group.

Osborne, Dwight A. All The Big Boys Do It. pap. 5.95 (0-9632817-6-3) Osborne Bks.

— Mojo. pap. 5.95 (0-9632817-7-1) Osborne Bks.

— Soul up for Sale. pap. 5.95 (0-9632817-8-X) Osborne Bks.

— The Squiggly Wiggly Head Family. (Illus.). 16p. (J). 1992. pap. 5.95 (0-9632817-0-4) Osborne Bks.

— Syreta. pap. 5.95 (0-9632817-5-5) Osborne Bks.

— Will. 93p. (Orig.). 1996. pap. 5.95 (0-9632817-9-8) Osborne Bks.

Osborne, E., jt. auth. see Van Alstyne, Dorothy.

Osborne, E. F. Global Timing Systems of Nanosecond Accuracy Using Satellite References. LC 70-131393. 189p. 1969. 19.00 (0-403-04526-6) Scholarly.

Osborne, Edward W. Biological Science Applications in Agriculture. 1994. 9.95 (0-8134-2958-7); text 58.75 (0-8134-2957-9) Interstate.

— Biological Science Applications in Agriculture I: Plant Science Teacher's Guide. 1998. teacher ed. 40.00 (0-8134-3035-6, 3035) Interstate.

— Biological Science Applications in Agriculture II: Animal Science Teacher's Guide. 1998. teacher ed. 40.00 (0-8134-3036-4, 3036) Interstate.

Osborne, Edward W., jt. auth. see Buriak, Philip.

Osborne, Elizabeth. The Distance Between. LC 99-30694. 256p. 2000. 24.00 (1-56947-180-0) Soho Press.

Osborne, Elsie, ed. see Bradley, Jonathan.

Osborne, Elsie, ed. see Bradley, Jonathan & Dubinsky, Helene.

Osborne, Elsie, jt. ed. see Dowling, Emilia.

Osborne, Elsie, ed. see Holditch, Lesley.

Osborne, Elsie, ed. see Lush, Dora.

Osborne, Elsie, ed. see Miller, Lisa.

Osborne, Elsie, ed. see Orford, Ellen.

Osborne, Elsie, ed. see Reid, Susan.

Osborne, Elsie, ed. see Sinason, Valerie.

Osborne, Elsie, ed. see Steiner, Deborah.

Osborne, Elsie, ed. see Trowell, Judith.

Osborne, Elsie, ed. see Williams, Gianna.

Osborne, Ernest L. & West, Victor. Men of Action: A History of the U. S. Life Saving Service on the Pacific Coast. LC 80-69563. (Illus.). 150p. (Orig.). 1981. pap. 10.00 (0-932368-05-0) Bandon Hist.

Osborne, Frank. Principles of Microbiology. 2nd ed. 144p. (C). 1997. spiral bd. 38.95 (0-7872-4413-9, 41441301) Kendall-Hunt.

Osborne, Frank & Goldstein, Judy. The New Book of Health. 402p. (Orig.). 1996. pap. 19.95 (0-9638596-7-6) Amer Pubng.

Osborne, Frank H. Principles of Microbiology. 136p. (C). 1996. spiral bd. 31.95 (0-8403-8606-0) Kendall-Hunt.

— Science & Technology. 80p. (C). 1994. pap. text, spiral bd. 17.95 (0-8403-9569-8) Kendall-Hunt.

Osborne, Frederick S., ed. The Fellowship of the Pennsylvania Academy of the Fine Arts: The Unbroken Line, 1897-1997 - A Centennial Exhibition. LC 97-61391. (Illus.). 68p. (Orig.). 1997. pap. 19.95 (0-9659340-0-4) Fellowship PA Acad.

Osborne, George E. Cases & Materials on Secured Transactions. 559p. (C). 1967. reprint ed. 45.50 (0-314-28264-5) West Pub.

Osborne, Gordon, ed. see Blewett, Mary H. & McKenna, Christine.

Osborne, Graeme & Lewis, Glen. Communication Traditions in 20th-Century Australia. (Australian Retrospectives). (Illus.). 206p. 1996. pap. text 24.00 (0-19-553511-1) OUP.

Osborne, Graham. Rainforest: Ancient Realm of the Pacific Northwest. (Illus.). 128p. Date not set. 34.95 (1-55054-620-1) Sterling.

Osborne, Graham, jt. auth. see Davis, Wade.

Osborne, Grant R. The Hermeneutical Spiral Vol. 7: A Comprehensive Introduction to Biblical Interpretation. 499p. 1997. pap. 22.99 (0-8308-1288-1, 1288) InterVarsity.

Osborne, Grant R., et al, eds. The IVP New Testament Commentary Series, 13 vols. including Revelation. 1997. 228.87 (0-8308-8092-5) InterVarsity.

Osborne, Harold. Aesthetics & Criticism. LC 73-3756. 341p. 1973. reprint ed. lib. bdg. 69.50 (0-8371-6847-3, OSAC, Greenwood Pr) Greenwood.

— Bolivia, a Land Divided. LC 85-24763. 193p. 1986. reprint ed. lib. bdg. 55.00 (0-313-24982-2, OSBO, Greenwood Pr) Greenwood.

Osborne, Harold, ed. The Oxford Companion to Art. (Illus.). 1,290p. 1970. 60.00 (0-19-866107-X) OUP.

Osborne, Harold F. Little City by the Sea. (Illus.). 136p. (Orig.). 1990. pap. 10.95 (0-9627567-0-9) Apple Tree Pr.

Osborne, Hilary, ed. see Calvin, John.

Osborne, Hilton. Line Dancing: Run to the Floor for Country Western . . . (Illus.). 192p. (Orig.). 1994. pap. 19.95 (1-882180-37-2) Griffin CA.

Osborne, J. E. Everything in Order! (Early Math Big Bks.). (Illus.). 16p. (J). (ps-2). Date not set. pap. 16.95 (1-58273-490-9) Newbridge Educ.

— Fact Families. (Early Math Big Bks.). (Illus.). 16p. (J). (ps-2). Date not set. pap. 16.95 (1-58273-142-X) Newbridge Educ.

— Give It a Guess! (Early Math Big Bks.). (Illus.). 16p. (J). (ps-2). Date not set. pap. 16.95 (1-58273-440-2) Newbridge Educ.

— Graph It! (Early Math Big Bks.). (Illus.). 16p. (J). (ps-2). Date not set. pap. 16.95 (1-58273-186-1) Newbridge Educ.

— Inventions. (Early Science Big Bks.). (Illus.). 16p. (J). (ps-2). Date not set. pap. 16.95 (1-58273-117-9) Newbridge Educ.

— Measuring Up. (Early Math Big Bks.). (Illus.). 16p. (J). (ps-2). Date not set. pap. 16.95 (1-56784-428-6) Newbridge Educ.

— The Money Book. (Early Math Big Bks.). (Illus.). 16p. (J). (ps-2). Date not set. pap. 16.95 (1-58273-141-1) Newbridge Educ.

— Solve It! (Early Math Big Bks.). (Illus.). 16p. (J). (ps-2). Date not set. pap. 16.95 (1-56784-432-4) Newbridge Educ.

— What Is Place Value? (Early Math Big Bks.). (Illus.). 16p. (J). (ps-2). Date not set. pap. 16.95 (1-58273-145-4) Newbridge Educ.

Osborne, J. L. & Wolfendale, Arnold W., eds. Origin of Cosmic Rays. LC 75-2436. (NATO Advanced Study Institutes Ser.: No. C14). x, 466p. 1975. lib. bdg. 146.00 (90-277-0585-2) Kluwer Academic.

Osborne, J. L., jt. auth. see Ginns, Patsy M.

Osborne, Jan, jt. ed. see Burns, Larry.

Osborne, Jane & Sugden, Chris. Luke. (Bible Study Commentaries Ser.). 1987. pap. 4.95 (0-87508-168-1) Chr Lit.

Osborne, Jayne E., ed. see PCPS Management of Accounting Practice Committee.

Osborne, Jean. Miracles with Love. 61p. (Orig.). 1982. write for info. (0-915631-02-4) Osborne.

— Notes on Notes. 101p. (C). 1974. write for info. (0-915631-01-6) Osborne.

Osborne, Jean, ed. Its Easier with Your Shoes Off. 50p. 1966. write for info. (0-915631-00-8) Osborne.

Osborne, Jeffrey J., jt. auth. see Beylarian, George.

Osborne, Jeffrey J., jt. auth. see Beylerian, George M.

Osborne, Jerry. Complete Library of American Phonograph Recordings, 1959. 256p. 1987. 45.95 (0-932117-06-6) Osborne Enterps.

— Complete Library of American Phonograph Recordings, 1960. 240p. 1987. 45.00 (0-932117-05-8) Osborne Enterps.

— Complete Library of American Phonograph Recordings, 1961. 249p. 1990. 45.00 (0-932117-16-3) Osborne Enterps.

— Country Music Buyers-Sellers Reference Book & Price Guide. (Illus.). 340p. 1984. pap. 14.95 (0-932117-00-7) Osborne Enterps.

***Osborne, Jerry.** Elvis: Word for Word. LC 00-38479. (Illus.). 320p. 2000. 29.95 (0-609-60803-7) Harmony Bks.

— Elvis - Word for Word: What He Said, Exactly As He Said It. (Illus.). 296p. 1999. (0-932117-29-5) Osborne Enterps.

Osborne, Jerry. Elvis, Like Any Other Soldier. (Illus.). 160p. 1989. pap. 19.95 (0-932117-11-2) Osborne Enterps.

— 1953 Humes Herald. (Illus.). 112p. 1988. 19.95 (0-932117-09-0) Osborne Enterps.

***Osborne, Jerry.** Offical Price Guide to Records: 2000 Edition. 14th ed. 2000. pap. 25.95 (0-676-60186-3) Hse Collectbls.

Osborne, Jerry. The Official Price Guide to Country Music Records. (Illus.). 512p. 1996. pap. 15.00 (0-676-60004-2) Random.

— Official Price Guide to Elvis. 2nd ed. 432p. 1998. pap. 17.00 (0-676-60141-3) Hse Collectbls.

— The Official Price Guide to Elvis Presley Records & Memorabilia. (Illus.). 384p. 1994. pap. 14.00 (0-87637-939-0) Hse Collectbls.

— Official Price Guide to Movie, TV Soundtracks & Original Cast Albums. 2nd ed. LC 97-210063. 1997. pap. 18.00 (0-676-60044-1) Random.

— The Official Price Guide to The Money Records: 1000 Most Valuable. LC 98-96064. 432p. 1998. pap. 17.95 (0-676-60140-5) Random.

— Official Records. 13th ed. 1999. 24.95 (0-676-60090-5) Hse Collectbls.

— Rockin' Records Buyers-Sellers Reference Book & Price Guide. 10th annot. ed. (Illus.). 648p. 1986. pap. 22.95 (0-932117-03-1) Osborne Enterps.

— Rockin' Records Buyers-Sellers Reference Book & Price Guide, 1989 Edition. (Illus.). 556p. 1989. pap. 24.95 (0-932117-12-0) Osborne Enterps.

— Rocking Records Buyers-Sellers Reference Guide, 1988. (Illus.). 480p. 1988. pap. 24.95 (0-932117-08-2) Osborne Enterps.

Osborne, Jill E. Dinosaur Dot-to-Dot: Fun-to-Learn Activity Book. 32p. (J). 1997. pap. 1.95 (0-89375-837-X) Troll Communs.

— Make & Color Halloween Decoration. (J). (ps-3). 1989. pap. 1.95 (0-89375-644-X) Troll Communs.

Osborne, Joan. Relish. 64p. 1996. otabind 14.95 (0-7935-6369-0) H Leonard.

Osborne, John. Deja Vu. 1994. pap. 5.95 (0-87129-237-8, D56) Dramatic Pub.

— The Entertainer. 100p. 1957. pap. 5.95 (0-87129-679-9, E15) Dramatic Pub.

— The Entertainer. LC 58-6810. 96p. 1994. 23.95 (0-87599-082-7) S G Phillips.

***Osborne, John.** Gerhart Hauptmann & the Naturalist Drama. (German Theatre Archive Ser.). 232p. 1998. text 42.00 (90-5755-005-9, Harwood Acad Pubs) Gordon & Breach.

— Gerhart Hauptmann & the Naturalist Drama. (German Theatre Archive Ser.). 232p. 1999. pap. text 23.00 (90-5755-006-7, Harwood Acad Pubs) Gordon & Breach.

Osborne, John. John Osborne Plays 2: The Entertainer-Hotel in Amsterdam-West of Suez. 1998. pap. text 16.95 (0-571-17846-4) Faber & Faber.

— John Osborne Plays 1 Plays 1: Look Back in Anger; Epitaph for George Dillion; The World of Paul... 400p. 1996. pap. 14.95 (0-571-17766-2) Faber & Faber.

— Look Back in Anger. 1987. pap. 5.95 (0-87129-222-X, L29) Dramatic Pub.

— Look Back in Anger. LC 57-9161. 96p. 1994. 23.95 (0-87599-081-9) S G Phillips.

— Look Back in Anger. 96p. 1982. pap. 8.95 (0-14-048175-3, Penguin Bks) Viking Penguin.

— Luther. 1961. pap. 5.95 (0-87129-208-4, L37) Dramatic Pub.

— The Meiningen Court Theatre, 1866-1890. (Illus.). 232p. 1988. text 69.95 (0-521-30394-X) Cambridge U Pr.

***Osborne, John.** Osborne: Four Plays. (Oberon Bks.). 240p. 2000. pap. 20.95 (1-84002-074-1) Theatre Comm.

— Osborne: Plays One. 240p. 1998. pap. 18.95 (1-84002-037-7, Pub. by Oberon Bks Ltd) Consort Bk Sales.

Osborne, John & Claridge, Amanda. Mosaics & Wallpaintings in Roman Churches. (Paper Museum of Cassiano Dal Pozzo Ser.: Ser. A, Pt. II, Vol. 1). (Illus.). 388p. 1996. text 150.00 (1-872501-62-1) Gordon & Breach.

Osborne, John, et al. Global Studies: A Competency Review Text. 3rd ed. Garnsey, Wayne & Stich, Paul, eds. (Illus.). 384p. (YA). (gr. 7-12). 1995. pap. text 12.95 (0-935487-37-9) N & N Pub Co.

— Global Studies: A Review Text. 7th ed. Garnsey, Wayne & Stich, Paul, eds. (Illus.). 448p. (YA). (gr. 7-12). 1998. pap. text 9.95 (0-935487-35-2) N & N Pub Co.

— Global Studies: Ten Day Competency Review. 2nd ed. Garnsey, Wayne & Stich, Paul, eds. (Illus.). 128p. (YA). (gr. 7-12). 1995. pap. text 7.95 (0-935487-53-0) N & N Pub Co.

— Global Studies: Ten Day Review. 2nd ed. Garnsey, Wayne & Stich, Paul, eds. (Illus.). 128p. (YA). (gr. 7-12). 1992. pap. text 7.95 (0-935487-48-4) N & N Pub Co.

Osborne, John, et al. Mosaics, Paintings, Sarcophagi & Small Objects, Vol. 2. (Paper Museum of Cassiano Dal Pozzo Ser.: Ser. A, Pt. II, Vol. 2). (Illus.). 304p. 1997. text 150.00 (1-872501-67-2) Gordon & Breach.

Osborne, John, jt. auth. see Wade, Ken.

Osborne, John C., tr. see Christoffel von Grimmelshausen, Hans J.

Osborne, John J., Jr. Paper Chase. 21.95 (0-8488-0185-7) Amereon Ltd.

Osborne, John M., jt. auth. see Petrowsky, Matthew.

Osborne, John T. Miracles. (Illus.). 90p. (J). 1988. pap. text 5.75 (0-929918-00-2) Midstates Pub.

Osborne, John W. William Cobbett: His Thoughts & His Times. LC 81-13231. (Illus.). 272p. 1982. reprint ed. lib. bdg. 52.50 (0-313-23222-9, OSWC, Greenwood Pr) Greenwood.

Osborne, John W. & Schweizer, Karl W. Cobbett & His Times. 192p. (C). 1990. text 61.00 (0-389-20932-5) B&N Imports.

***Osborne, Jonathan & Monk, Martin.** Good Practice in Science Teaching: What Research Has to Say? LC 99-29147. 2000. pap. 28.99 (0-335-20391-4) OpUniv Pr.

Osborne, Joseph F. Heirlooms of Ireland: An Easy Reference to Some Irish Surnames & Their Origins. rev. ed. LC 98-213234. 183p. 1998. pap. 29.95 (0-8063-4777-5, 9293) Clearfield Co.

Osborne, Judy. My Teacher Said Goodbye Today: Planning for the End of the School Year. 2nd ed. (Illus.). 39p. (J). (ps-6). 1987. reprint ed. pap. text 9.95 (0-9618303-8-7) Emijo Pubns.

An Asterisk (*) at the beginning of an entry indicates that the title is appearing for the first time.

***Osborne, Judy.** My Teacher Said Goodbye Today: Planning for the End of the School Year. 2nd rev. ed. (Illus.). (J). (ps-2). 1999. spiral bd. 9.95 (*0-9618303-7-9*) Emijo Pubns.

Osborne, Judy. Stepfamilies: The Restructuring Process. 24p. (Orig.). 1983. pap. 7.00 (*0-9618303-3-6*) Emijo Pubns.

Osborne, June. Cardinal. 1995. pap. 9.95 (*0-292-76043-4*) U of Tex Pr.

— John Piper & Stained Glass. LC 98-116037. (Illus.). 224p. 1997. 62.95 (*0-7509-1088-7*, Pub. by Sutton Pub Ltd) Intl Pubs Mktg.

— The Ruby-Throated Hummingbird. LC 98-4844. (Corrie Herring Hooks Ser.). (Illus.). 160p. 1998. pap. 17.95 (*0-292-76047-7*) U of Tex Pr.

— Stained Glass in England. LC 98-120867. (History Handbooks Ser.). (Illus.). 288p. 1997. pap. 26.95 (*0-7509-1613-3*, Pub. by Sutton Pub Ltd) Intl Pubs Mktg.

Osborne, Karen L. Carlyle Simpson. 25p. 1986. pap. 10.00 (*0-89733-204-0*) Academy Chi Pubs.

Osborne, Karen L. & Spurlin, William J., eds. Reclaiming the Heartland: Lesbian & Gay Voices from the Midwest. LC 95-46718. 256p. (C). 1996. 18.95 (*0-8166-2754-1*) U of Minn Pr.

Osborne, Kay. Do Cook for One. LC 84-90503. (Illus.). 216p. 1985. pap. 10.95 (*0-9613877-0-X*) K-D Enter.

Osborne, Kenan. History of Franciscan Theology. (Theology Ser.). 345p. 1994. pap. 25.00 (*1-57659-032-1*) Franciscan Inst.

***Osborne, Kenan B.** Christian Sacraments in a Postmodern World: A Theology for the Third Millennium. LC 99-44727. 320p. 2000. 18.95 (*0-8091-3904-9*) Paulist Pr.

Osborne, Kenan B. The Christian Sacraments of Initiation, Baptism, Confirmation, Eucharist. 256p. 1987. pap. 16.95 (*0-8091-2886-1*) Paulist Pr.

— Ministry: Lay Ministry in the Roman Catholic Church, Its History & Theology. LC 92-40299. 720p. 1993. pap. 29.95 (*0-8091-3371-7*) Paulist Pr.

— The Resurrection of Jesus: New Considerations for Its Theological Interpretation. LC 97-1669. 208p. (Orig.). 1997. pap. 14.95 (*0-8091-3703-8*) Paulist Pr.

— Sacramental Guidelines: A Companion to the New Catechism for Religious Educators. LC 95-3249. 160p. (Orig.). 1995. pap. 12.95 (*0-8091-3565-5*) Paulist Pr.

— Sacramental Theology: A General Introduction. 160p. 1988. pap. 9.95 (*0-8091-2945-0*) Paulist Pr.

Osborne, Larry N. & Nakamura, Margaret. Systems Analysis for Librarians & Information Professionals. 2nd ed. LC 99-39581. (Library & Information Science Text Ser.). 300p. 1999. pap. 50.00 (*1-56308-693-X*) Libs Unl.

Osborne, Laura, compiled by. The Rasta Cookbook: Vegetarian Cuisine - Eaten with the Salt of the Earth. LC 92-171760. (Illus.). 132p. (C). 1992. reprint ed. pap. 12.95 (*0-86543-133-7*) Africa World.

Osborne, Laurie E. The Trick of Singularity: "Twelfth Night" & the Performance Editions. LC 95-49374. (Studies in Theatre History & Culture). (Illus.). 226p. 1996. text 32.95 (*0-87745-544-9*) U of Iowa Pr.

Osborne, Laurie E., ed. & intro. see Shakespeare, William.

Osborne-LeBien, Lori, ed. see Smale, David.

Osborne, Lilly De Jongh, see De Jongh Osborne, Lilly.

Osborne, Linda B., jt. auth. see King, Casey.

Osborne, Linda Barrett, jt. auth. see Bisbort, Alan.

Osborne, Liz. Home Style: A Room-by-Room Guide to Giving Your Home a New Look. LC 97-222292. (Illus.). 192p. 1997. pap. 19.95 (*0-7063-7564-5*, Pub. by WrLock) Sterling.

— Resolving Patient Complaints: A Step-by-Step Guide to Effective Service Recovery. 212p. 1995. ring bd. 105.00 (*0-8342-0674-9*) Aspen Pub.

***Osborne, M. & Osborne, Will.** Dinosaurs: A Companion to Dinosaurs Before Dark. (Magic Tree House Research Guide Ser.: No. 1). (Illus.). 128p. (J). (gr. k-3). 2000. lib. bdg. 11.99 (*0-375-90296-1*, Pub. by Random Bks Yng Read) Random.

Osborne, M. F. The Stock Market & Finance from a Physicist's Viewpoint. LC 95-69502. (Illus.). 381p. (Orig.). 1996. pap. 19.95 (*0-9646292-0-8*) Crossgar Pr.

***Osborne, M. Scott.** Basic Homological Algebra. LC 99-46582. (Graduate Texts in Mathematics Ser.: Vol. 196). 384p. 2000. 49.95 (*0-387-98934-X*) Spr-Verlag.

Osborne, M. Scott & Warner, G. The Selberg Trace Formula III: Inner Product Formulae (Initial Considerations) LC 83-3918. (Memoirs of the American Mathematical Society Ser.: No. 44/283). 209p. 1983. pap. 26.00 (*0-8218-2283-7*, MEMO/44/283) Am Math.

Osborne, Maggie. The Best Man. 448p. (Orig.). 1998. mass mkt. 6.50 (*0-446-60527-1*, Pub. by Warner Bks); mass mkt. 148.50 (*0-446-16559-X*) Warner Bks.

***Osborne, Maggie.** I Do, I Do, I Do. 2000. mass mkt. 6.99 (*0-449-00517-8*) Ballantine Pub Grp.

Osborne, Maggie. The Promise of Jenny Jones. 384p. 1997. reprint ed. mass mkt. 6.50 (*0-446-60441-0*, Pub. by Warner Bks) Little.

— The Seduction of Samantha Kincade. 384p. (Orig.). 1995. reprint ed. mass mkt. 5.99 (*0-446-60093-8*, Pub. by Warner Bks) Little.

***Osborne, Maggie.** Silver Lining. 352p. 2000. mass mkt. 6.50 (*0-449-00516-X*) Ivy Books.

Osborne, Maggie. A Stranger's Wife. 384p. (Orig.). 1999. mass mkt. 6.50 (*0-446-60529-8*, Pub. by Warner Bks) Little.

— The Wives of Bowie Stone. 384p. (Orig.). 1994. reprint ed. mass mkt. 5.99 (*0-446-36533-5*, Pub. by Warner Bks) Little.

***Osborne, Margery D.** Examining Science Teaching in Elementary School from the Perspective of a Teacher & Learner. LC 99-25535. (Critical Education Practice Ser.: Vol. 18). 264p. 1999. 50.00 (*0-8153-2569-X*, SS1140) Garland.

Osborne, Martha S. Wilcox - Wilcoxson Families of New England & Their Descendants: A Genealogical Dictionary. 2nd rev. ed. LC 98-114323. x, 1179p. 1997. pap. 53.00 (*0-7884-0783-X*, 0705) Heritage Bk.

Osborne, Martin, jt. auth. see Lambert, Kenneth.

Osborne, Martin J. & Rubinstein, Ariel. Bargaining & Markets. (Economic Theory, Econometrics & Mathematical Economics Ser.). 216p. 1990. text 64.95 (*0-12-528631-7*); pap. text 24.95 (*0-12-528632-5*) Morgan Kaufmann.

— A Course in Game Theory. (Illus.). 420p. 1994. 40.00 (*0-262-15041-7*); pap. text 22.50 (*0-262-65040-1*) MIT Pr.

Osborne, Martin R. & Crosby, Neil T. Benzopyrene. (Monographs on Cancer Research). 352p. 1987. text 115.00 (*0-521-30122-X*) Cambridge U Pr.

Osborne, Mary, jt. auth. see Osborne, Will.

***Osborne, Mary Pope.** Adaline Falling Star. LC 99-30689. (Illus.). 208p. (gr. 7-12). 2000. 16.95 (*0-439-05947-X*, Scholastic Ref) Scholastic Inc.

Osborne, Mary Pope. Afternoon on the Amazon. LC 95-3237. (Magic Tree House Ser.: No. 6). (Illus.). 80p. (J). (gr. k-3). 1995. pap. 3.99 (*0-679-86372-9*) Random.

— Afternoon on the Amazon. LC 95-3237. (Magic Tree House Ser.: No. 6). (Illus.). (J). (gr. k-3). 1995. lib. bdg. 11.99 (*0-679-96372-3*) Random.

— Afternoon on the Amazon. (Magic Tree House Ser.: No. 6). (Illus.). (J). (gr. k-3). 1995. 9.19 (*0-606-08472-X*, Pub. by Turtleback) Demco.

— American Tall Tales. LC 89-37235. (Illus.). 128p. (J). (gr. 3-6). 1991. 22.00 (*0-679-80089-1*, Pub. by Knopf Bks Yng Read) Random.

— American Tall Tales. LC 89-37235. (Illus.). 128p. (J). (gr. 3-6). 1991. lib. bdg. 23.99 (*0-679-90089-6*, Pub. by Knopf Bks Yng Read) Random.

— Best Wishes, Joe Brady. 192p. (YA). (gr. 7 up). 1994. pap. 4.99 (*0-679-84560-7*, Bullseye Bks) Random Bks Yng Read.

— Buffalo Before Breakfast. LC 98-37089. (Magic Tree House Ser.: No. 18). (Illus.). 72p. (J). (gr. k-3). 1999. pap. 3.99 (*0-679-89064-5*); lib. bdg. 11.99 (*0-679-99064-X*) Random.

— Buffalo Before Breakfast. (Magic Tree House Ser.: No. 18). (Illus.). (J). (gr. k-3). 1999. 20.00 (*0-375-80041-7*, Pub. by Random Bks Yng Read) Random.

***Osborne, Mary Pope.** Civil War on Sunday. LC 99-54072. (Magic Tree House Ser.: No. 21). (Illus.). 96p. (J). (gr. k-3). 2000. pap. 3.99 (*0-679-89067-X*, Pub. by Random Bks Yng Read); lib. bdg. 11.99 (*0-679-99067-4*, Pub. by Random Bks Yng Read) Random.

— Civil War on Sunday. (Illus.). (J). 2000. 9.44 (*0-606-18852-5*) Turtleback.

Osborne, Mary Pope. Day of the Dragon King. LC 97-49199. (Magic Tree House Ser.: No. 14). (Illus.). (J). (gr. k-3). 1998. lib. bdg. 11.99 (*0-679-99051-8*, Pub. by Random Bks Yng Read) Random.

— Day of the Dragon King. (Magic Tree House Ser.). (Illus.). (J). 1998. 9.09 (*0-606-13958-3*, Pub. by Turtleback) Demco.

— Day of the Dragon King. 14th ed. LC 97-49199. (Magic Tree House Ser.: No. 14). (Illus.). (J). (gr. k-3). 1998. pap. 3.99 (*0-679-89051-3*) Random.

***Osborne, Mary Pope.** Dingoes at Dinnertime. LC 99-40598. (Magic Tree House Ser.: No. 20). (Illus.). 96p. (J). (gr. k-3). 2000. pap. 3.99 (*0-679-89066-1*, Pub. by Random Bks Yng Read) Random.

— Dingoes at Dinnertime. (Illus.). (J). 2000. 9.44 (*0-606-18491-0*) Turtleback.

— Dingoes at Dinnertime, Vol. 20. LC 99-40598. (Magic Tree House Ser.: No. 20). (Illus.). 96p. (J). (gr. k-3). 2000. lib. bdg. 11.99 (*0-679-99066-6*) Random.

— Dinosaurs Before Dark. (Magic Tree House Ser.: No. 1). (Illus.). (J). (gr. k-3). 1999. pap. 1.11 (*0-375-80598-2*) Random.

Osborne, Mary Pope. Dinosaurs Before Dark. LC 91-51106. (Magic Tree House Ser.: No. 1). (Illus.). 80p. (J). (gr. k-3). 1992. pap. 3.99 (*0-679-82411-1*, Pub. by Random Bks Yng Read) Random.

— Dinosaurs Before Dark. LC 91-51106. (Magic Tree House Ser.: No. 1). (Illus.). 80p. (J). (gr. k-3). 1992. lib. bdg. 11.99 (*0-679-92411-6*, Pub. by Random Bks Yng Read) Random.

Osborne, Mary Pope. Dinosaurs Before Dark. (Magic Tree House Ser.: No. 1). (Illus.). (J). (gr. k-3). 1992. 9.19 (*0-606-02319-4*, Pub. by Turtleback) Demco.

Osborne, Mary Pope. Dolphins at Daybreak. (Magic Tree House Ser.: No. 9). (Illus.). (J). (gr. k-3). 1997. pap. 3.99 (*0-614-28933-5*) Random Bks Yng Read.

Osborne, Mary Pope. Dolphins at Daybreak. (Magic Tree House Ser.: No. 9). (Illus.). (J). (gr. k-3). 1997. 8.94 (*0-606-11268-5*, Pub. by Turtleback) Demco.

Osborne, Mary Pope. Dolphins at Daybreak, No. 9. LC 96-30943. (Magic Tree House Ser.: No. 9). (Illus.). (J). (gr. k-3). 1997. pap. 3.99 (*0-679-88338-X*, Pub. by Random Bks Yng Read) Random.

— Dolphins at Daybreak, No. 9. LC 96-30943. (Magic Tree House Ser.: No. 9). (Illus.). (J). (gr. k-3). 1997. lib. bdg. 11.99 (*0-679-98338-4*, Pub. by Random Bks Yng Read) Random.

— Favorite Greek Myths. LC 87-32332. (Illus.). 96p. (J). (gr. 4-7). 1989. pap. 17.95 (*0-590-41338-4*) Scholastic Inc.

— Favorite Medieval Tales. LC 96-17285. (Illus.). 96p. (J). (gr. 3-7). 1997. 17.95 (*0-590-60042-7*) Scholastic Inc.

— Ghost Town at Sundown. LC 97-7298. (Magic Tree House Ser.: No. 10). (Illus.). (J). (gr. k-3). 1997. pap. 3.99 (*0-679-88339-8*, Pub. by Random Bks Yng Read) Random.

— Ghost Town at Sundown. (Magic Tree House Ser.: No. 10). (Illus.). (J). (gr. k-3). 1997. 9.09 (*0-606-12709-7*, Pub. by Turtleback) Demco.

— Ghost Town at Sundown, No. 10. LC 97-7298. (Magic Tree House Ser.: No. 10). (Illus.). (J). (gr. k-3). 1997. lib. bdg. 11.99 (*0-679-98339-2*, Pub. by Random Bks Yng Read) Random.

— Haunted Waters. LC 93-47566. 160p. (YA). (gr. 8-10). 1994. 14.95 (*1-56402-119-X*) Candlewick Pr.

— Haunted Waters. LC 93-47566. 160p. (YA). (gr. 7-12). 1996. pap. 4.99 (*1-56402-588-8*) Candlewick Pr.

— Haunted Waters. LC 93-47566. 1994. 10.09 (*0-606-09394-X*, Pub. by Turtleback) Demco.

— Hour of the Olympics. LC 98-24100. (Magic Tree House Ser.: No. 16). (Illus.). (J). (gr. k-3). 1998. lib. bdg. 11.99 (*0-679-99062-3*) Random.

— Hour of the Olympics, No. 16. LC 98-24100. (Magic Tree House Ser.: No. 16). (Illus.). (J). (gr. k-3). 1998. pap. 3.99 (*0-679-89062-9*) Random.

— Kate & the Beanstalk. LC 99-27029. (J). 2000. 16.00 (*0-689-82550-1*) S&S Childrens.

— The Knight at Dawn. LC 92-13075. (Magic Tree House Ser.: No. 2). (Illus.). 80p. (J). (gr. k-3). 1993. pap. 3.99 (*0-679-82412-X*, Pub. by Random Bks Yng Read) Random.

— The Knight at Dawn. LC 92-13075. (Magic Tree House Ser.: No. 2). (Illus.). 80p. (J). (gr. k-3). 1993. lib. bdg. 11.99 (*0-679-92412-4*, Pub. by Random Bks Yng Read) Random.

— The Knight at Dawn. LC 92-13705. (Magic Tree House Ser.: No. 2). (Illus.). (J). (gr. k-3). 1993. 9.19 (*0-606-09518-7*, Pub. by Turtleback) Demco.

— The Life of Jesus: In Masterpieces of Art. LC 98-60316. (Illus.). 48p. (J). (gr. 3-5). 1998. 17.99 (*0-670-87313-6*, Viking) Viking Penguin.

***Osborne, Mary Pope.** Lions at Lunchtime. (Magic Tree House Ser.: No. 11). (Illus.). (J). (gr. k-3). 1998. 9.09 (*0-606-12981-2*, Pub. by Turtleback) Demco.

Osborne, Mary Pope. Lions at Lunchtime, No. 11. LC 97-19885. (Illus.). (J). (gr. k-3). 1998. pap. 3.99 (*0-679-88340-1*, Pub. by Random Bks Yng Read) Random.

— Lions at Lunchtime, No. 11. LC 97-19885. (Magic Tree House Ser.: No. 11). (Illus.). (J). (gr. k-3). 1998. lib. bdg. 11.99 (*0-679-98340-6*, Pub. by Random Bks Yng Read) Random.

Osborne, Mary Pope. Magic Tree House Collection: Dinosaurs Before Dark; Knight at Dawn; Mummies in the Morning; Pirates Past Noon. (Magic Tree House Ser.: No. 1-4). (J). (gr. k-3). 1996. boxed set 4.00 (*0-679-88389-4*, Pub. by Random Bks Yng Read) Random.

— Magic Treehouse Bundle. (J). (ps-3). 1999. pap. 15.96 (*0-641-01436-8*) Random.

Osborne, Mary Pope. Magic Treehouse Goes to Am Rev. (J). 1999. pap. write for info. (*0-679-88608-7*, Bullseye Bks) Random Bks Yng Read.

— Magic Treehouse Visits America. (J). 1998. lib. bdg. 14.99 (*0-679-98542-5*, Pub. by Random Bks Yng Read) Random.

— The Many Lives of Benjamin Franklin. (Illus.). (J). (gr. 5 up). 1990. 13.95 (*0-685-31008-6*, Dial Yng Read) Peng Put Young Read.

— Mermaid Tales from Around the World. (Illus.). 96p. (J). (gr. 2-6). 1999. pap. 7.99 (*0-439-04781-1*) Scholastic Inc.

— Midnight on the Moon. (Magic Tree House Ser.: No. 8). (Illus.). (J). (gr. k-3). 1996. pap. 3.99 (*0-679-86374-5*) McKay.

— Midnight on the Moon. (Magic Tree House Ser.: No. 8). (Illus.). (J). (gr. k-3). 1996. lib. bdg. 11.99 (*0-679-96374-X*) McKay.

Osborne, Mary Pope. Midnight on the Moon. (Magic Tree House Ser.: No. 8). (Illus.). (J). (gr. k-3). 1996. 9.84 (*0-606-10876-9*, Pub. by Turtleback) Demco.

Osborne, Mary Pope. Mo & His Friends. (Easy-to-Read Bks.: Level 2). (Illus.). 48p. (J). (gr. k-3). 1996. pap. 3.99 (*0-14-036202-9*, PuffinBks) Peng Put Young Read.

— Mo & His Friends. (Puffin Easy-to-Read Ser.). 1996. 8.70 (*0-606-09623-X*, Pub. by Turtleback) Demco.

— Moonhorse. (Dragonfly Bks.). (Illus.). 40p. (J). (ps-2). 1994. pap. 6.99 (*0-679-86709-0*, Pub. by Knopf Bks Yng Read) Random.

Osborne, Mary Pope. Moonhorse. 1994. 12.19 (*0-606-06579-2*, Pub. by Turtleback) Demco.

Osborne, Mary Pope. Mummies in the Morning. (Magic Tree House Ser.: No. 3). (Illus.). 80p. (J). (gr. k-3). 1993. pap. 3.99 (*0-679-82424-3*, Pub. by Random Bks Yng Read) Random.

— Mummies in the Morning. (First Stepping Stone Bks.: Vol. 3). (Illus.). 80p. (J). (gr. k-3). 1993. lib. bdg. 11.99 (*0-679-92424-8*, Pub. by Random Bks Yng Read) Random.

— Mummies in the Morning. (Magic Tree House Ser.: No. 3). (Illus.). (J). (gr. k-3). 1993. 9.19 (*0-606-05932-6*, Pub. by Turtleback) Demco.

***Osborne, Mary Pope.** My Brother's Keeper: Virginia's Diary, Gettysburg, Pennsylvania, 1863. LC 00-20200. (My America Ser.). (Illus.). 112p. (J). (gr. 2-5). 2000. 8.95 (*0-439-15307-7*) Scholastic Inc.

— My Secret War: The World War II Diary of Madeline Beck. LC 00-21918. (Dear America Ser.). (Illus.). 208p. (YA). (gr. 4-7). 2000. 10.95 (*0-590-68715-8*) Scholastic Inc.

Osborne, Mary Pope. Night of the Ninjas. LC 94-29142. (Magic Tree House Ser.: No. 5). (Illus.). (J). (gr. k-3). 1995. pap. 3.99 (*0-679-86371-0*) Random.

— Night of the Ninjas. LC 94-29142. (Magic Tree House Ser.: No. 5). (Illus.). (J). (gr. k-3). 1995. lib. bdg. 11.99 (*0-679-96371-5*) Random.

— Night of the Ninjas. (Magic Tree House Ser.: No. 5). (Illus.). (J). (gr. k-3). 1995. 9.19 (*0-606-07947-5*, Pub. by Turtleback) Demco.

— One World, Many Religions. LC 96-836. 1996. 25.00 (*0-679-83930-5*) Random.

— One World, Many Religions. LC 96-836. (Illus.). 1996. lib. bdg. 26.99 (*0-679-93930-X*) Random.

— One World, Many Religions: The Ways We Worship. (J). (gr. 4-9). 1996. 25.00 (*0-614-19326-5*) Knopf.

— Pirates Past Noon. LC 93-2039. (Magic Tree House Ser.: No. 4). (Illus.). 80p. (J). (gr. k-3). 1994. pap. 3.99 (*0-679-82425-1*) Random.

— Pirates Past Noon. LC 93-2039. (Magic Tree House Ser.: No. 4). (Illus.). 80p. (J). (gr. k-3). 1994. lib. bdg. 11.99 (*0-679-92425-6*) Random.

Osborne, Mary Pope. Pirates Past Noon. (Magic Tree House Ser.). (Illus.). 1994. 9.19 (*0-606-07068-0*, Pub. by Turtleback) Demco.

Osborne, Mary Pope. Polar Bears Past Bedtime. LC 97-15624. (Magic Tree House Ser.: No. 12). (Illus.). (J). (gr. k-3). 1998. pap. 3.99 (*0-679-88341-X*, Pub. by Random Bks Yng Read); lib. bdg. 11.99 (*0-679-98341-4*, Pub. by Random Bks Yng Read) Random.

***Osborne, Mary Pope.** Polar Bears Past Bedtime, 12. (Magic Tree House Ser.: No. 12). (Illus.). (J). (gr. k-3). 1998. 9.09 (*0-606-13018-7*, Pub. by Turtleback) Demco.

— Revolutionary War on Wednesday. (Magic Tree House Ser.: No. 22). (Illus.). 96p. (J). (ps-3). 2000. pap. 3.99 (*0-679-89068-8*) Random.

— Revolutionary War on Wednesday, Vol. 22. (Magic Tree House Ser.: No. 22). (Illus.). 96p. (J). (ps-3). 2000. lib. bdg. 11.99 (*0-679-99068-2*) Random Bks Yng Read.

Osborne, Mary Pope. The Rocking Horse Christmas. LC 96-1993. (Illus.). 32p. (J). (ps-2). 1997. 15.95 (*0-590-92955-0*) Scholastic Inc.

— Spider Kane & the Mystery at Jumbo Nightcrawler's. LC 91-10983. (Stepping Stone Bks). (Illus.). 96p. (J). (gr. 3-5). 1999. pap. 3.99 (*0-679-80856-6*, Pub. by Random Bks Yng Read); lib. bdg. 11.99 (*0-679-90856-0*, Pub. by Random Bks Yng Read) Random.

— Spider Kane & the Mystery under the May-Apple. LC 90-33524. (Stepping Stone Bks). (Illus.). 96p. (J). (gr. 3-5). 1999. pap. 3.99 (*0-679-80855-8*, Pub. by Random Bks Yng Read); lib. bdg. 11.99 (*0-679-90855-2*, Pub. by Random Bks Yng Read) Random.

— Standing in the Light: The Captive Diary of Catherine Carey Logan, Delaware Valley, Pennsylvania, 1763. LC 97-40083. (Dear America Ser.). (Illus.). 184p. (YA). (gr. 3-9). 1998. 9.95 (*0-590-13462-0*, Dear America) Scholastic Inc.

— Sunset of the Sabertooth. LC 95-34697. (Magic Tree House Ser.: No. 7). (Illus.). (J). (gr. k-3). 1996. pap. 3.99 (*0-679-86373-7*, Pub. by Random Bks Yng Read); lib. bdg. 11.99 (*0-679-96373-1*, Pub. by Random Bks Yng Read) Random.

— Sunset of the Sabertooth. (Magic Tree House Ser.: No. 7). (Illus.). (J). (gr. k-3). 1996. 9.19 (*0-606-09913-1*, Pub. by Turtleback) Demco.

— Tigers at Twilight. LC 99-23493. (Magic Tree House Ser.: No. 19). (Illus.). 96p. (J). (gr. k-3). 1999. lib. bdg. 11.99 (*0-679-99065-8*, Pub. by Random Bks Yng Read) Random.

***Osborne, Mary Pope.** Tigers at Twilight. LC 99-23493. (Magic Tree House Ser.: No. 19). (Illus.). 96p. (J). (gr. k-3). 1999. pap. 3.99 (*0-679-89065-3*, Pub. by Random Bks Yng Read) Random.

Osborne, Mary Pope. Tonight on the Titanic. (Magic Tree House Ser.: No. 17). (Illus.). 71p. (J). (gr. k-3). 1999. pap. 3.99 (*0-679-89063-7*) Random.

— Tonight on the Titanic. (Magic Tree House Ser.: No. 17). (Illus.). 70p. (J). (gr. k-3). 1999. lib. bdg. 11.99 (*0-679-99063-1*) Random.

— Vacation under the Volcano. LC 97-39765. (Magic Tree House Ser.: No. 13). (Illus.). (J). (gr. k-3). 1998. pap. 3.99 (*0-679-89050-5*) Random.

— Vacation under the Volcano. LC 97-39765. (Magic Tree House Ser.: No. 135). (Illus.). (J). (gr. k-3). 1998. lib. bdg. 11.99 (*0-679-99050-X*, Pub. by Random Bks Yng Read) Random.

— Vacation under the Volcano, 13. (Magic Tree House Ser.: No. 13). (Illus.). (J). (gr. k-3). 1998. 9.09 (*0-606-13972-9*, Pub. by Turtleback) Demco.

— Viking Ships at Sunrise. LC 98-23602. (Magic Tree House Ser.: No. 15). (Illus.). 80p. (J). (gr. k-3). 1998. pap. 3.99 (*0-679-89061-0*); lib. bdg. 11.99 (*0-679-99061-5*) Random.

Osborne, Mary Pope, jt. auth. see Brookes, Diane.

Osborne, Mary Pope, jt. auth. see Osborne, Will.

Osborne, Mary T., ed. The Great Torch Race: Essays in Honor of Reginald Harvey Griffith. LC 61-10425. (Illus.). 1961. 10.00 (*0-87959-063-7*) U of Tex H Ransom Ctr.

***Osborne, Matthew.** Your Supernatural Healing Begins Now! 48p. 2000. pap. 7.95 (*0-9679739-0-2*) MDO Min.

***Osborne-McKnight, Juilene.** I Am of Irelaunde: A Novel of Patrick & Osian. LC 99-89863. 304p. 2000. 24.95 (*0-312-87320-4*, Pub. by Forge NYC) St Martin.

Osborne, Michael, jt. auth. see De Meza, David.

Osborne, Michael A. Nature, the Exotic, & the Science of French Colonialism. LC 93-21489. (Science, Technology, & Society Ser.). 244p. 1994. 35.00 (*0-253-34266-X*) Ind U Pr.

— Nature, the Exotic & the Science of French Colonialism. LC 93-21489. (Science, Technology, & Society Ser.). (Illus.). 232p. Date not set. reprint ed. pap. 72.00 (*0-608-20564-8*, 205447800002) Bks Demand.

Osborne, Michael J., et al, eds. A Lexicon of Greek Personal Names Vol. II: Attica. 532p. 1994. text 95.00 (*0-19-814990-5*) OUP.

O

An Asterisk (*) at the beginning of an entry indicates that the title is appearing for the first time.

Osborne, Michael R. Finite Algorithms in Optimization & Data Analysis. LC 84-11841. (Wiley Probability & Mathematical Statistics Ser.). 409p. 1985. reprint ed. pap. 126.80 (*0-608-02602-6*, 206326000004) Bks Demand.

Osborne, Mike. Twentieth Century Defence of Britain: Lincolnshire. Earle, James, ed. LC 97-30155. (Defense of Britain Ser.). (Illus.). 84p. 1998. pap. 14.95 (*1-85753-267-8*, Pub. by Brasseys) Brasseys.

Osborne, Mike, jt. auth. see Edom, Helen.

***Osborne, Milton.** The Mekong: Turbulent Past, Uncertain Future. LC 99-86337. 320p. 2000. 30.00 (*0-87113-806-9*, Pub. by Grove-Atltc) Publishers Group.

Osborne, Milton. River Road to China: The Search for the Source of the Mekong, 1866-73. LC 99-17643. (Illus.). 256p. 1999. pap. 16.00 (*0-87113-752-6*, Atlntc Mnthly) Grove-Atltic.

— Southeast Asia: An Introductory History. 7th ed. LC 97-223183. 263p. 1998. pap. 24.95 (*1-86448-479-9*, Pub. by Allen & Unwin Pty) Paul & Co Pubs.

Osborne, Milton E. Refugees: Four Political Case-Studies LC 83-124106. (Canberra Studies in World Affairs.). v, 119p. 1981. write for info. (*0-86784-061-7*) ANU Res Sch.

— Sihanouk: Prince of Light, Prince of Darkness. LC 93-48520. (C). 1994. 23.00 (*0-8248-1638-2*); pap. 14.25 (*0-8248-1639-0*) UH Pr.

— Singapore & Malaysia. LC 64-55818. (Cornell University, Southeast Asia Program, Data Paper Ser.: No. 53). 136p. reprint ed. pap. 42.20 (*0-8357-3535-4*, 203458600090) Bks Demand.

— Southeast Asia: An Illustrated Introductory History. 4th ed. (Illus.). 264p. 1989. pap. text 15.95 (*0-04-352238-6*) Routledge.

— Southeast Asia: An Illustrated Introductory History. 5th ed. (Illus.). 228p. 1994. pap. 19.95 (*0-04-442215-6*, Pub. by Allen & Unwin Pty) Paul & Co Pubs.

— Strategic Hamlets in South Vietnam: A Survey & Comparison. (Data Papers: Vol. 55). 66p. 1965. pap. 2.50 (*0-87727-055-4*) Cornell SE Asia.

— Strategic Hamlets in South Vietnam: A Survey & Comparison. LC 65-64732. (Cornell University, Southeast Asia Program, Data Paper Ser.: No. 55). 88p. reprint ed. pap. 30.00 (*0-8357-3668-7*, 203639400003) Bks Demand.

Osborne, Mitchel L. Official World's Fair Pictorial Photography. 48p. 1984. 3.95 (*0-317-12231-2*) Picayune Pr.

Osborne, Nancy M. Rubrics for Elementary Assessment: An Elementary School Teacher's Resource in Rubrics. rev. ed. (Illus.). 125p. 1999. ring bd. 27.95 (*1-928856-00-4*, 1-REA) Osborne Press.

Osborne, Nancy S. Crazy Quilt: Funky Smalltown Texas & Pieces of Life. LC 99-63629. 86p. 1999. pap. 15.00 (*0-9643477-5-X*) Hale Mary Pr.

Osborne, Neville N., ed. Biology of Serotonergic Transmission. LC 81-14671. (Illus.). 536p. reprint ed. pap. 166.20 (*0-8357-7242-X*, 202964600062) Bks Demand.

— Progress in Retinal Research, Vol. 2. (Illus.). 337p. 1983. 84.75 (*0-08-030773-6*, 07, Pergamon Pr) Elsevier.

O

Osborne, Neville N. & Chader, G. J., eds. Progress in Retinal Research, Vol. 3. (Illus.). 358p. 1984. 81.00 (*0-08-031701-4*, Pergamon Pr) Elsevier.

Osborne, Neville N. & Chader, Gerald J., eds. Progress in Retinal Research, Vol. 1. (Illus.). 245p. 1982. 95.75 (*0-08-028901-0*, Pergamon Pr) Elsevier.

— Progress in Retinal Research, Vol. 4. (Illus.). 330p. 1985. 120.00 (*0-08-031738-3*, Pergamon Pr) Elsevier.

Osborne, Neville N., jt. ed. see Weiler, R.

Osborne, Nigel, ed. see Clarke, Eric & Emmerson, Simon.

Osborne, Noel H. The Lytton Manuscripts. 79p. 1967. 65.00 (*0-900801-10-7*) St Mut.

***Osborne, P. & Van Ooijen, E.** Professional Effectiveness Through Supervision. (Illus.). 320p. 2000. pap. write for info. (*0-443-05842-3*, W B Saunders Co) Harcrt Hlth Sci Grp.

***Osborne, Patrick L.** Tropical Ecosystems & Ecological Concepts. LC 99-47853. 468p. (C). 2000. pap. write for info. (*0-521-64523-9*) Cambridge U Pr.

— Tropical Ecosystems & Ecological Concepts. LC 99-47853. (Illus.). 468p. (C). 2000. write for info. (*0-521-64251-5*) Cambridge U Pr.

Osborne, Peggy A. About Buttons: A Collector's Guide, A.D. 150 to the Present. (Illus.). 320p. 1993. 79.95 (*0-88740-555-X*) Schiffer.

Osborne, Peggy A. Button Button: Identification & Price Guide. rev. ed. LC 92-63104. (Illus.). 160p. (YA). (gr. 10 up). 1997. pap. 16.95 (*0-7643-0082-2*) Schiffer.

Osborne, Peggy A. Fun Buttons. LC 94-65981. (Illus.). 144p. 1994. 29.95 (*0-88740-691-2*) Schiffer.

***Osborne, Peter.** From an Aesthetic Point of View: Philosophy, Art & the Senses. (Illus.). 224p. 2001. pap. 20.00 (*1-85242-668-3*) Serpents Tail.

Osborne, Peter. The Politics of Time: Modernity & Avant-Garde. LC 95-30097. 224p. (C). (gr. 13 up). 1995. 65.00 (*0-86091-482-8*, Pub. by Verso) Norton.

***Osborne, Peter.** Traveling Light: Photography, Travel & Visual Culture. LC 99-42165. (Illus.). 260p. 2000. pap. 19.95 (*0-7190-4401-4*); text 69.95 (*0-7190-4400-6*) St Martin.

Osborne, Peter, ed. A Critical Sense: Interviews with Intellectuals. LC 96-3442. 216p. (C). 1996. 70.00 (*0-415-11505-1*); pap. 19.99 (*0-415-11506-X*) Routledge.

***Osborne, Phil.** The Law of Torts. (Essentials of Canadian Law Ser.). 350p. 2000. pap. 31.95 (*1-55221-035-9*, Pub. by Irwin Law) Gaunt.

Osborne, Philip. Parenting for the '90s. LC 89-2009. 314p. 1989. pap. 9.95 (*0-934672-73-3*) Good Bks PA.

Osborne, Philip & Koppenhaver, Karen W., eds. Great Short Stories about Parenting. LC 90-71116. 288p. (Orig.). 1990. pap. 9.95 (*1-56148-008-8*) Good Bks PA.

Osborne, Randall, jt. auth. see Weaver, Jeff.

***Osborne, Randall E.** Case Analyses for Abnormal Psychology. LC 99-39603. 192p. 1999. pap. text 24.95 (*0-86377-584-5*) L Erlbaum Assocs.

***Osborne, Randall E., et al.** Case Analyses for Abnormal Psychology: Learning to Look Beyond the Symptoms. LC 99-39603. 192p. 1999. 49.95 (*0-86377-583-7*, Pub. by Psychol Pr) Taylor & Francis.

Osborne, Rich, ed. see Feagler, Dick.

Osborne, Rich, ed. see Haynes, Marion E.

Osborne, Richard. Crime & the Media. 266p. (C). 1996. pap. 18.95 (*0-7453-0911-9*, Pub. by Pluto GBR); text 54.95 (*0-7453-0912-7*, Pub. by Pluto GBR) Stylus Pub VA.

***Osborne, Richard.** Herbert von Karajan: A Life in Music. LC 99-59108. (Illus.). 851p. 2000. 35.00 (*1-55553-425-2*) NE U Pr.

— Introducing Eastern Philosophy. (Illus.). 176p. 2000. pap. 10.95 (*1-84046-150-0*) Totem Bks.

Osborne, Richard. Philosophy for Beginners. 2nd ed. (Illus.). 186p. (Orig.). 1992. pap. 11.95 (*0-86316-157-X*) Writers & Readers.

— Talking To Your Children About God. LC 98-12649. (Illus.). 208p. 1998. pap. 12.00 (*0-06-066751-6*, Pub. by Harper SF) HarpC.

Osborne, Richard & Jansz, Litza. Introducing Sociology. (Illus.). 176p. 1999. pap. 10.95 (*1-874166-39-0*, Pub. by Icon Bks) Natl Bk Netwk.

Osborne, Richard, et al. A Guide to Marine Mammals of Greater Puget Sound. LC 87-3414. (Illus.). 200p. (Orig.). 1988. pap. 14.95 (*0-9615580-1-6*) Island Pubs WA.

Osborne, Richard, jt. auth. see Van der Maas, Ed M.

Osborne, Richard, ed. see Feagler, Richard H.

Osborne, Richard E. The Casablanca Companion: The Movie Classic & Its Place in History. (Illus.). 276p. (Orig.). 1997. pap. 18.95 (*0-9628324-3-X*) Riebel Roque.

— Tour Book for Antique Car Buffs. 3rd ed. (Illus.). 327p. (Orig.). 1999. pap. text 15.95 (*0-9628324-4-8*) Riebel Roque.

— World War II Sites in the United States: A Directory & Tour Guide. LC 91-68129. (Illus.). 303p. (Orig.). 1995. per. 19.95 (*0-9628324-1-3*) Riebel Roque.

Osborne, Rick. I Want to Know about Jesus: Who Jesus Is, What He Did, & Why He Died for Me. LC 97-38953. (I Want to Know Ser.). (Illus.). 32p. (J). (gr. 2-5). 1998. 9.99 (*0-310-22087-4*) Zondervan.

***Osborne, Rick.** I Want To Know about the Fruit of the Spirit. LC 98-51513. (I Want to Know Ser.). (Illus.). 32p. (J). 1999. 9.99 (*0-310-22096-3*) Zondervan.

Osborne, Rick. Kidcordance: Big Ideas from the Bible & Where to Find Them. LC 98-55702. (Illus.). 224p. (J). 1999. 14.99 (*0-310-22472-1*) Zondervan.

— Teaching Your Child How to Pray. LC 98-122621. 60p. 1997. pap. 11.99 (*0-8024-8489-1*, 14) Moody.

— Your Child & Jesus: A Family Activity Book. 1999. pap. 9.99 (*0-8024-2855-X*) Moody.

Osborne, Rick & Bowler, K. Christie. About the Ten Commandments. LC 98-11683. (I Want to Know Ser.). 2000. pap. 9.99 (*0-310-22095-5*) Zondervan.

— I Want to Know about God: Who God Is, What He Does, & Why He Cares about Me. LC 98-9633. (I Want to Know Ser.). (Illus.). 32p. (J). (gr. 2-5). 1998. 9.99 (*0-310-22090-4*) Zondervan.

***Osborne, Rick & Bowler, K. Christie.** I Want to Know about Prayer. LC 98-11306. (I Want to Know Ser.). (J). 1998. 9.99 (*0-310-22091-2*) Zondervan.

Osborne, Rick & Bowler, K. Christie. Your Child & the Christian Life: A Family Activity Book. (Learning for Life Ser.). (Illus.). 111p. 1999. pap. 9.99 (*0-8024-2853-3*) Moody.

Osborne, Rick & Miller, Kevin. Your Child & the Bible: A Family Activity Book. (Learning for Life Ser.). (Illus.). 111p. (J). 1999. pap. 9.99 (*0-8024-2852-5*) Moody.

Osborne, Rick, jt. auth. see Burkett, Larry.

Osborne, Rick, jt. ed. see Trent, John.

***Osborne, Robert.** Eternal Gift. LC 00-190653. 438p. 2000. 25.00 (*0-7388-1647-7*); pap. 18.00 (*0-7388-1648-5*) Xlibris Corp.

Osborne, Robert. 70 Years of the Oscar: The Official History of the Academy Awards. LC 99-195677. (Illus.). 384p. 1999. 65.00 (*0-7892-0484-3*) Abbeville Pr.

— 65 Years of the Oscar: The Official History of the Academy Awards. LC 94-198157. (Illus.). 352p. 1994. 69.95 (*1-55859-715-8*) Abbeville Pr.

Osborne, Robert A. Hardy Roses: An Organic Guide to Growing Frost- & Disease-Resistant Varieties. Art, Pam, ed. LC 91-55013. (Illus.). 144p. 1991. 24.95 (*0-88266-739-4*, Garden Way Pub) Storey Bks.

— Hardy Roses: An Organic Guide to Growing Frost & Disease-Resistant Varieties. 144p. 1995. pap. 18.95 (*0-88266-738-6*, Garden Way Pub) Storey Bks.

— Hardy Trees & Shrubs: A Guide to Disease-Resistant Varieties for the North. (Illus.). 176p. 1996. pap. 19.95 (*1-55013-760-3*) Firefly Bks Ltd.

Osborne, Robert D. Higher Education in Ireland: North & South. LC 96-157046. (Higher Education Policy Ser.: No. 33). 182p. 1996. 49.95 (*1-85302-379-5*, Pub. by Jessica Kingsley) Taylor & Francis.

Osborne, Robert D., jt. ed. see Cormack, Robert J.

Osborne, Robert H., ed. From Shoreline to Abyss: Contributions to Marine Geology in Honor of Francis Parker Shepard. (Special Publications: No. 46). (Illus.). 412p. 1991. 100.00 (*0-918985-92-7*) SEPM.

Osborne, Robin. Archaic & Classical Greek Art. LC 99-177295. (Oxford History of Art Ser.). (Illus.). 278p. 1998. pap. 16.95 (*0-19-284202-1*) OUP.

***Osborne, Robin.** Archaic & Classical Greek Art. LC 99-177295. (Oxford History of Art Ser.). (Illus.). 278p. 1998. 39.95 (*0-19-284264-1*) OUP.

Osborne, Robin. Classical Landscape with Figures: The Ancient Greek City & Its Countryside LC 87-141529. 216 p. 1987. 19.50 (*0-540-01111-8*) Philips Maps.

— Demos: The Discovery of Classical Attika. (Cambridge Classical Studies). (Illus.). 288p. 1985. text 65.00 (*0-521-26776-5*) Cambridge U Pr.

— Greece under Construction: From the Dark Ages to the Persian Wars. LC 96-4247. (Routledge History of the Ancient World Ser.). (Illus.). 416p. (C). 1996. pap. 29.99 (*0-415-03583-X*) Routledge.

***Osborne, Robin, ed.** Classical Greece. (Short Oxford History of Europe Ser.). (Illus.). 235p. 2000. pap. 17.95 (*0-19-873153-1*); text 60.00 (*0-19-873154-X*) OUP.

Osborne, Robin & Alcock, Susan E., eds. Placing the Gods: Sanctuaries & Sacred Space in Ancient Greece. (Illus.). 288p. 1994. 58.00 (*0-19-814947-6*) OUP.

Osborne, Robin, jt. ed. see Alcock, Susan E.

Osborne, Robin, jt. ed. see Goldhill, Simon.

Osborne, Roger, et al, eds. The Historical Atlas of the Earth: A Visual Exploration of the Earth's Physical Past. LC 95-79328. (Illus.). 208p. 1995. 45.00 (*0-8050-4552-X*) H Holt & Co.

Osborne, Roger & Freyberg, Peter. Learning in Science: The Implications of Children's Science. LC 84-27915. 198p. (Orig.). (C). (gr. 5). 1985. pap. text 22.00 (*0-435-57260-1*, 57260) Heinemann.

Osborne, Roger & Gray, Michael. The Elvis Atlas: A Journey Through Elvis Presley's America. LC 96-13313. (Illus.). 88p. 1995. 35.00 (*0-8050-4159-1*) H Holt & Co.

Osborne, Ronald E. Self: An Eclectic Approach. 300p. 1996. pap. text 38.00 (*0-205-20021-4*, T6020-6) Allyn.

Osborne, Ruby O. The Crisis Years: The College of William & Mary in Virginia, 1800-1827. (Illus.). 404, xxivp. 1990. 65.00 (*0-9645236-0-4*) Osborne Pr.

Osborne, Ruth F., jt. auth. see Kirkendall, Lester A.

Osborne, Sally E. Boost Your Health with Bovine Cartilage. 192p. 1998. pap. 14.95 (*0-87983-839-6*, Keats Publng) NTC Contemp Pub Co.

Osborne, Sandra. Windows NT Registry. 1998. pap. text 39.99 (*1-57870-061-2*) Macmillan Tech.

— Windows NT Registry. LC 98-86491. 1998. pap. 29.99 (*1-56205-941-6*) New Riders Pub.

Osborne, Seward R. Holding the Left at Gettysburg: The 20th New York State Militia on July 1, 1863. (Illus.). 36p. (Orig.). (C). 1990. pap. text 6.00 (*0-944413-14-5*) Longstreet Hse.

— The Saga of the Mountain Legion (156th N. Y. Vols.) & the "Modest Hero Who Saved Our Flag" (Illus.). 40p. 1994. pap. text 6.00 (*0-944413-31-5*) Longstreet Hse.

— The Three-Month Service of the 20th New York State Militia, April-August, 1861. (Illus.). 44p. 1998. pap. 9.00 (*0-944413-48-X*, 137) Longstreet Hse.

Osborne, Seward R., ed. The Civil War Diaries of Col. Theodore B. Gates, Twentieth New York State Militia. (Illus.). 197p. (C). 1992. 25.00 (*0-944413-21-8*) Longstreet Hse.

Osborne-Sheets, Carole. Pre & Perinatal Massage Therapy. (Illus.). 200p. 1998. pap. text 23.95 (*0-9665585-0-2*) Body Therapy.

Osborne, Sonny. Bluegrass Banjo Method. 40p. 1964. pap. 5.95 (*0-87166-578-6*, 93243) Mel Bay.

Osborne, Stephen. Ice & Fire: Dispatches from the New World. 220p. 1998. pap. 14.95 (*1-55152-061-3*, Pub. by Arsenal Pulp) LPC InBook.

Osborne, Stephen, jt. auth. see Luinenberg, Oline.

Osborne, Stephen, jt. auth. see Luinenburg, Oline.

***Osborne, Stephen P.** Public Private Partnerships: Theory & Practice in International Perspective. LC 00-38248. (Studies in the Management of Voluntary & Non-Profit Organizations). 2000. pap. write for info. (*0-415-21268-5*) Routledge.

Osborne, Stephen P. Voluntary Organizations & Innovation in Public Services. LC 98-18518. 304p. (C). 1998. 99.99 (*0-415-18256-5*) Routledge.

Osborne, Stephen P., ed. Managing in the Voluntary Sector: A Handbook for Managers in Voluntary & Non-Profit Organisations. (Management & Finance in the Public Services Ser.). 300p. 1997. mass mkt. 29.99 (*0-412-71840-5*) Chapman & Hall.

Osborne, Steven P. Looking for Angels: A Search for Truth about Heavenly Messengers. 126p. (Orig.). 1996. pap. 9.95 (*1-878423-23-1*) Morson Pub.

Osborne, Susan Titus, ed. Complete Guide to Writing for Publication. 224p. 1999. pap. 15.00 (*1-892525-09-7*, Pub. by ACW Press) Spring Arbor Dist.

Osborne, Susan Titus & Jensen, Sandra, compiled by. Beanie Baby Stories for the Heart. LC 98-83166. (Illus.). 208p. (YA). 1999. pap. 10.95 (*1-892016-04-4*) Starburst.

***Osborne, Susan Titus & Moses, Lucille.** Rest Stops for Single Moms: Encouragement for the Journey. rev. ed. LC 99-59902. (Illus.). 176p. 2000. 14.99 (*0-8054-2358-3*) Broadman.

Osborne, Susan Titus & Moses, Lucille. Rest Stops for Single Mothers: Devotions to Encourage You on Your Journey. 240p. 1985. pap. 9.99 (*0-8054-5385-7*, 4253-85) Broadman.

Osborne, Susan Titus, jt. auth. see Sanders, Nancy I.

Osborne, Susan Titus, ed. see Barnes-Rothmeier, Vicki.

Osborne, Theresa, jt. auth. see Haslam, Jonathan.

Osborne, Thomas. Aspects of Enlightenment: Social Theory & the Ethics of Truth. LC 98-5514. 232p. 1998. 69.00 (*0-8476-9077-6*); pap. 26.50 (*0-8476-9078-4*) Rowman.

— The Night the Mice Danced the Quadrille: Five Years in the Backwoods, 1875-1879. LC 95-190486. (Illus.). 192p. 1995. pap. 15.95 (*1-55046-135-4*, Pub. by Boston Mills) Genl Dist Srvs.

Osborne, Thomas J. Annexation Hawaii: Fighting American Imperialism. LC 81-8156. Orig. Title: Empire Can Wait. 182p. 1998. pap. 19.95 (*0-9633484-1-8*) Island Style.

— Empire Can Wait: American Opposition to Hawaiian Annexation, 1893 - 1898. LC 81-8156. 197p. reprint ed. pap. 61.10 (*0-7837-0501-8*, 204082500018) Bks Demand.

Osborne, Thomas L. Trial Handbook for Kentucky Lawyers. 2nd ed. LC 92-73548. 1992. 125.00 (*0-317-05373-6*) West Group.

Osborne, Thomas M. Society & Prisons: With Intro. Added. LC 72-172587. (Criminology, Law Enforcement, & Social Problems Ser.: No. 177). 1975. 22.00 (*0-87585-177-0*) Patterson Smith.

— Within Prison Walls: A Week in Auburn Prison. 328p. 1991. reprint ed. pap. 9.95 (*0-9625714-3-1*) Spruce Gulch Pr.

— Within Prison Walls, Being a Narrative of Personal Experience During a Week of Voluntary Confinement in the State Prison at Auburn, New York. LC 69-14940. (Criminology, Law Enforcement, & Social Problems Ser.: No. 72). 1969. reprint ed. 16.00 (*0-87585-072-3*) Patterson Smith.

Osborne, Thomas R. A Grande Ecole for the Grands Corps: Brooklyn College Studies on Society in Change; Social Science Monographs. (East European Monographs). 168p. 1983. text 51.00 (*0-88033-037-6*, Pub. by East Eur Monographs) Col U Pr.

Osborne-Thomason, Natalie. The Ghost Hunting Casebook. (Illus.). 192p. 1999. pap. 14.95 (*0-7137-2768-3*, Pub. by Blandford Pr) Sterling.

Osborne, Tom. Faith in the Game: Lessons on Football, Work & Life. LC 99-32557. 176p. 1999. 17.50 (*0-7679-0422-2*) Bantam.

***Osborne, Tom.** Faith in the Game: Lessons on Football, Work & Life. 160p. 2000. pap. 9.95 (*0-7679-0423-0*) Broadway BDD.

— Faith in the Game: Lessons on Football, Work & Life. LC 99-32557. 176p. 2000. pap. 9.95 (*1-57856-392-5*) Waterbrook Pr.

Osborne, Tom. Faith in the Game: Lessons on Football, Work, & Life. 176p. 1999. 17.50 (*1-57856-309-7*) Waterbrook Pr.

Osborne, Tom. On Solid Ground. 266p. 1996. 26.95 (*0-9648992-1-3*) Neb Bk Co.

Osborne, W. C. Fans. 1977. 111.00 (*0-08-021725-7*, Pub. by Pergamon Repr) Franklin.

— Running High/Looking Good. LC 95-62051. (Illus.). 270p. 1995. 27.95 (*0-9643126-3-8*) Woodburner Pr.

Osborne, W. Larry, et al. Career Development, Assessment, & Counseling: Applications of the Donald E. Super C-DAC Approach. LC 96-49704. 177p. (Orig.). (C). 1997. pap. text 25.95 (*1-55620-162-1*, 72633) Am Coun Assn.

Osborne, W. Larry, jt. auth. see Cohn, Benjamin.

Osborne, Will. Deadly Power of Medusa. 1988. 7.85 (*0-606-01809-3*, Pub. by Turtleback) Demco.

***Osborne, Will.** Dinosaurs: A Companion to Dinosaurs Before Dark. LC 99-43577. (Magic Tree House Research Guide Ser.: Vol. 1). 128p. (J). (gr. k-3). 2000. pap. 4.99 (*0-375-80296-7*, Pub. by Random Bks Yng Read) Random.

— Knights & Castles. (Magic Tree House Research Guide Ser.: Vol. 2). (Illus.). 128p. (J). (gr. k-3). 2000. pap. 4.99 (*0-375-80297-5*, Pub. by Random Bks Yng Read) Random.

— Mummies & Pyramids. (J). 2001. lib. bdg. 11.99 (*0-375-90298-8*) Random Bks Yng Read.

— Mummies & Pyramids. (Illus.). (J). 2001. pap. 4.99 (*0-375-80298-3*) Random Bks Yng Read.

***Osborne, Will & Osborne, Mary.** Knights & Castles. LC 99-49811. (Magic Tree House Research Guide Ser.: No. 2). (Illus.). 128p. (J). (gr. k-3). 2000. lib. bdg. 11.99 (*0-375-90297-X*, Pub. by Random Bks Yng Read) Random.

Osborne, Will & Osborne, Mary Pope. The Deadly Power of Medusa. 96p. (J). (gr. 4-6). 1992. pap. 2.75 (*0-590-45580-X*, Apple Paperbacks) Scholastic Inc.

Osborne, Will, jt. auth. see Osborne, M.

***Osborne, Will And Ma.** Pirates. (J). 2001. 11.99 (*0-375-90299-6*) Random.

— Pirates. (J). 2001. mass mkt. 4.99 (*0-375-80299-1*, Pub. by Random Bks Yng Read) Random.

Osborne, William. American Singing Societies & Their Partsongs: Ten Prominent American Composers of the Genre (1860-1940) & the Seminall Singing Societies That Performed the Repertory. (Monograph Ser.: No. 8). 112p. 1994. 15.00 (*0-614-05595-4*) Am Choral Dirs.

Osborne, William, ed. The Rape of the Powerless. vi, 208p. 1971. text 191.00 (*0-677-14720-1*) Gordon & Breach.

Osborne, William, ed. see O'Keefe, John & Shield, William.

Osborne, William L. Foundations: Covering the Time Frame from Creation to 400 B. C. Winter, Ralph D., ed. LC 93-44909. (World Christian Foundation Ser.). 1997. 75.00 (*0-87808-247-6*) William Carey Lib.

Osborne, William S., ed. see Kennedy, John P.

Osborne, William S., ed. see Kirkland, Caroline M.

Osbornova, J., et al, eds. Succession in Abandoned Fields: Studies in Central Bohemia, Czechoslovakia. (C). 1990. text 191.50 (*0-7923-0401-2*) Kluwer Academic.

Osborough, W. N. Law & the Emergence of Modern Dublin: A Litigation Topography for a Capital City. (Illus.). 256p. 1996. 39.50 (*0-7165-2583-6*, Pub. by Irish Acad Pr) Intl Spec Bk.

***Osborough, W. N.** Studies in Irish Legal History. LC 99-197157. 352p. 1999. boxed set 65.00 (*1-85182-447-2*, Pub. by Four Cts Pr) Intl Spec Bk.

Osborough, W. N., ed. Explorations in Law & History. (Irish Legal History Ser.: Vol. 4). 194p. 1995. 37.50 (*0-7165-2541-0*, Pub. by Irish Acad Pr) Intl Spec Bk.

Osborough, W. N., jt. ed. see Hogan, Daire H.

Osbourn. Mitchells Intro Building. (C). 1997. pap. 49.95 (*0-582-30200-5*, Pub. by Addison-Wesley) Longman.

Osbourn, Adeliese & Winter, Roger. Konversationen, Situationen. 1983. pap. text 8.55 (*0-582-22310-5*, 70916) Longman.

Osbourn, R. A. Ashlawn. LC 83-15773. 1986. pap. 14.95 (*0-87949-240-6*) Ashley Bks.

Osbourne, Alan. Modern Marine Engineer's Manual, Vol. II. 2nd ed. Hunt, Everett C., ed. LC 89-71201. (Illus.). 836p. 1991. text 55.00 (*0-87033-307-0*) Cornell Maritime.

Osbourne, Cynthia D. Between Heart & Mind. 12p. (Orig.). 1995. pap. write for info. (*1-885206-16-X*, Iliad Pr) Cader Pubng.

Osbourne, Elsie. Understanding Your 7 Year Old. (Understanding Your Child Ser.: Vol. 8). 96p. 1997. pap. 8.95 (*1-894020-07-3*) Warwick Publ.

***Osbourne, John.** I Want to Know about the Holy Spirit. LC 98-4012. (Illus.). 32p. (J). 1998. 9.99 (*0-310-22093-9*) Zondervan.

Osbourne, Lloyd. Love, the Fiddler. LC 73-103526. (Short Story Index Reprint Ser.). 1977. 20.95 (*0-8369-3268-4*) Ayer.

— Motormaniacs. LC 70-85692. (Short Story Index Reprint Ser.). 1977. 19.95 (*0-8369-3035-5*) Ayer.

— Queen Versus Billy & Other Stories. LC 70-101286. (Short Story Index Reprint Ser.). 1977. 20.95 (*0-8369-3223-4*) Ayer.

Osbourne, Lloyd, jt. auth. see Stevenson, Robert Louis.

Osbourne, Ozzy. Ozzmosis. 88p. 1996. otabind 22.95 (*0-7935-6371-2*) H Leonard.

Osbourne, Robert D., et al, eds. After the Reforms: Education & Policy in Northern Ireland. 304p. 1993. 72.95 (*1-85628-401-8*, Pub. by Avebry) Ashgate Pub Co.

Osbourne, Thomas R. A Grand Ecole for the Grands Corps: The Recruitment & Training of the French Administration. No. 29a. 1983. write for info. (*0-318-60317-9*) Brooklyn Coll Pr.

Osbun, Lee A. The Problem of Participation: A Radical Critique of Contemporary Democratic Theory. LC 85-5308. 146p. (Orig.). 1985. lib. bdg. 41.50 (*0-8191-4640-4*) U Pr of Amer.

Osbun, Lee A. & Schmidt, Steffen W., eds. Issues in Iowa Politics. LC 90-4829. (Illus.). 276p. (C). 1990. text 24.95 (*0-8138-0222-9*) Iowa St U Pr.

Osburn, A. E. Oklahoma Notes: Pediatrics. LC 92-49140. 280p. 1993. write for info. (*3-540-97955-7*) Spr-Verlag.

— Oklahoma Notes: Pediatrics. LC 92-49140. 280p. 1993. 16.95 (*0-387-97955-7*) Spr-Verlag.

Osburn, A. E., jt. ed. see Puls, Jane E.

Osburn, Bernice B., jt. auth. see Osburn, Burl N.

***Osburn, Brian.** Columbus Limo: The Adventure of the Friendship 7 A. E. V. LC 99-91761. 2000. 25.00 (*0-7388-1238-2*); pap. 18.00 (*0-7388-1239-0*) Xlibris Corp.

Osburn, Burl N. & Osburn, Bernice B. Measured Drawings of Early American Furniture. LC 74-79936. (Illus.). 82p. 1975. reprint ed. pap. 7.95 (*0-486-23057-0*) Dover.

Osburn, Burl N. & Wilber, Gordon O. Pewter-Working: Instructions & Projects. LC 78-74121. (Illus.). 160p. 1979. reprint ed. pap. 7.95 (*0-486-23786-9*) Dover.

Osburn, C. Dixon, et al. Conduct Unbecoming: Third Annual Report on "Don't Ask, Don't Tell, Don't Pursue" (Illus.). 53p. 1997. pap. text 25.00 (*0-7881-4678-5*) DIANE Pub.

Osburn, Carroll D., ed. Essays on Women in Earliest Christianity, Vol. I. LC 93-73234. 513p. (C). 1994. text 24.99 (*0-89900-618-3*) College Pr Pub.

— Essays on Women in Earliest Christianity, Vol. 2. 592p. (C). 1995. text 24.99 (*0-89900-734-1*) College Pr Pub.

Osburn, Charles B. Academic Research & Library Resources: Changing Patterns in America, 3. LC 78-20017. (New Directions in Librarianship Ser.: No. 3). (Illus.). 187p. 1979. 52.95 (*0-313-20722-4*, OAR/, Greenwood Pr) Greenwood.

— Present State of French Studies: A Collection of Research Reviews. LC 78-149990. 995p. 1971. 68.50 (*0-8108-0373-9*) Scarecrow.

— Research & Reference Guide to French Studies. 2nd ed. LC 81-5637. 570p. 1981. 45.00 (*0-8108-1440-4*) Scarecrow.

Osburn, Charles B. & Atkinson, Ross W., eds. Collection Management: A New Treatise, 2 Pt. Set. LC 91-33499. (Foundations in Library & Information Science: Vol. 26). 474p. 1992. 157.00 (*1-55938-231-7*) Jai Pr.

Osburn, Jesse. He's Waiting for You. 128p. (YA). (gr. 7 up). 1996. pap. 3.99 (*0-380-78042-9*, Avon Bks) Morrow Avon.

— Only Child. 256p. (Orig.). (YA). 1996. mass mkt. 3.99 (*0-380-78043-7*, Avon Bks) Morrow Avon.

— Prom Night. 160p. (Orig.). 1995. mass mkt. 3.99 (*0-380-77318-X*, Avon Bks) Morrow Avon.

Osburn, John D. Military Electromagnetic Compatibility Standards of the United States. LC 87-83430. (Electromagnetic Interference & Compatibility Ser.: Vol. 11). (Illus.). 340p. 1988. 45.00 (*0-944916-11-2*) emf-emi Control.

— Supporting & Unique Military Electromagnetic Compatibility Standards of the United States. LC 88-80526. (Electromagnetic Interference & Compatibility Ser.: Vol. 12). (Illus.). 276p. 1988. 39.00 (*0-944916-12-0*) emf-emi Control.

Osburn, Katherine. Southern Ute Women: Autonomy & Assimilation on the Reservation, 1887-1934. LC 97-40742. 165p. 1997. pap. 19.95 (*0-8263-1863-0*) U of NM Pr.

— Southern Ute Women: Autonomy & Assimilation on the Reservation, 1887-1934. LC 97-40742. 165p. 1998. 45.00 (*0-8263-1862-2*) U of NM Pr.

Osburn, LeaAnn A., tr. see Hutchinson, Hanna.

***Osburn, Tracy.** Gorp's Gift: Teacher's Guide. (J). 1999. pap., teacher ed. 7.95 (*0-9642160-1-9*) Roundtop Pr.

Osburn, William, Jr. A Hebrew & English Lexicon to the Old Testament. 287p. (C). 1981. reprint ed. pap. 9.95 (*0-310-20361-9*, 6264P) Zondervan.

Osburne, Adrea G. & Mulling, Sylvia S. Writing Together Set: A Project for Team Research. (Illus.). 216p. (C). 1998. pap. text 24.95 (*0-472-08461-5*, 08461) U of Mich Pr.

***Osburne, Andrea G. & Mulling, Sylvia S.** Anthology for Writing Together. LC 99-176061. (Illus.). 80p. (C). 1998. pap. text. write for info. (*0-472-08527-1*, 08527) U of Mich Pr.

— Writing Together: A Project For Team Research & Anthology for Writing Together. LC 99-176062. (Illus.). 216p. (C). 1998. pap. text 19.95 (*0-472-08526-3*, 08526) U of Mich Pr.

Oscar, Ina, jt. auth. see Andrew, Alice.

Oscard, Anne. Ghosts of the Self. Woodyard, Chris & Rasmer, Raymond, eds. (Illus.). 128p. (Orig.). 1995. pap. 9.95 (*0-9645166-0-8*) Hermit Pubns.

— Tristate Terrors: Famous, Historic, Female Ghosts of Ohio, Indiana & Kentucky. Rasmer, Raymond, ed. (Illus.). 137p. 1996. pap. 9.95 (*0-9645166-1-6*) Hermit Pubns.

Oscard, Anne L. Your Number's Up! Money, Romance & Predictions Through Numerology. Dawson, Kathleen et al, eds. LC 97-93161. (Illus.). 130p. (Orig.). 1997. mass mkt. 9.95 (*0-9645166-2-4*) Hermit Pubns.

***Oschman, James L.** Energy Medicine: The Scientific Basis. 272p. 2000. pap. 36.00 (*0-443-06261-7*) C Lvngstone UK.

***Oschmann, R.** Blow-Fill-Seal Technology. (Illus.). 1999. pap. text (*0-8493-1620-0*) CRC Pr.

Oschry, Leonard. The Story of the Vilna Gaon. 1.75 (*0-914131-62-1*, D520) Torah Umesorah.

Oschry, Leonard, tr. see Bachrach, Yehoshua.

Oschry, Leonard, tr. see Chaim, Chafetz, pseud.

Oschry, Leonard, tr. see Hayyim, Hafetz, pseud.

Oschry, Leonard, tr. see Kahana, Kalman.

Oschry, Leonard, tr. see Katz, Jacob.

Osco. Studies in Irish Cistercian History. 288p. 1998. pap. 29.95 (*1-85182-379-4*, Pub. by Four Cts Pr); boxed set 55.00 (*1-85182-378-6*, Pub. by Four Cts Pr) Intl Spec Bk.

Osdol. 400 Utilities. 1994. teacher ed. 20.93 (*0-07-047987-9*) McGraw.

Osdol, Louise Van, see Van Osdol, Louise.

O'Se, Diarmuid & Sheils, Joe. Teach Yourself Irish. (ENG & IRI.). 1993. pap. 18.95 (*0-7859-1059-X*, 0-340-564903); pap. 29.95 incl. audio (*0-7859-1060-3*, 0-340-56492-X) Fr & Eur.

O'Sean, Arlene A., jt. auth. see Swanson, Ellen.

Oseary, Guy. Jews Who Rock. 1999. pap. 0.00 (*0-375-75345-1*) Random.

***Oseary, Guy.** Jews Who Rock. 2001. pap. write for info. (*0-312-27267-7*, St Martin Griffin) St Martin.

Oseghale, Braimoh D. Political Instability, Interstate Conflict Adverse Changes in Host Government Policies & Foreign Direct Investment: A Sensitivity Analysis. LC 92-40969. (Foreign Economic Policy of the United States Ser.). 192p. 1993. text 10.00 (*0-8153-1254-7*) Garland.

***Osei, Akwasi.** Ghana: Recurrence & Change in a Post-Independence African State. LC 97-8538. (Society & Politics in Africa Ser.: Vol. 4). X, 167p. (C). 1999. text 44.95 (*0-8204-3391-8*) P Lang Pubng.

Osei, Akwasi O., compiled by. Reflections: Verses from the Bahai Teachings. 128p. 1994. pap. 11.95 (*0-85398-386-0*) G Ronald Pub.

Osei, G. K. The African Concept of Life & Death. Obaba, Al I., ed. (Illus.). 49p. (YA). 1991. pap. text 5.00 (*0-916157-64-4*) African Islam Miss Pubns.

Osei-Hwedie, Kwaku. A Search for Legitimate Social Development Education & Practice Models for Africa. LC 95-9138. (Studies in African Economic & Social Development: Vol. 7). 288p. 1996. text 89.95 (*0-7734-8887-1*, Mellen Biblical Pr) E Mellen.

Osei-Hwedie, Kwaku & Agyeman-Badu, Yaw. The Political Economy of Education in Ghana, 1920-1979: A Study of Education & National Development in Ghana. LC 84-61224. 189p. (Orig.). 1985. pap. 10.95 (*0-943324-13-0*) Omenana.

Osei-Hwedie, Kwaku & Ndulo, Muna, eds. Issues in Zambian Development. 200p. (Orig.). 1985. pap. 12.95 (*0-943324-17-3*) Omenana.

***Osei-Mensah, Michael Nana.** The Ghana Reform Case in African Technology & Telecommunications Policy. LC 99-45957. (Studies in African Economic & Social Development: Vol. 13). 352p. 1999. text 99.95 (*0-7734-7896-5*) E Mellen.

Osella, Caroline, jt. auth. see Osella, Filippo.

***Osella, Filippo & Osella, Caroline.** Social Mobility in Kerala: Modernity & Identity in Conflict. LC 00-9109. (Anthropolgy, Culture & Society Ser.). 2000. write for info. (*0-7453-1693-X*) Pluto GBR.

Oseman, Robert. Conferences & Their Literature: A Question of Value. LC 90-121875. 160p. 1989. reprint ed. pap. 49.60 (*0 7837-9263-8*, 206000200004) Bks Demand.

Osen, Diane. Royal Scandals: True Tales of Sex, Lust & Greed. LC 94-34641. 120p. 1995. 16.98 (*1-56799-161-0*, MetroBooks) M Friedman Pub Grp Inc.

Osen, Diane, ed. see Baldwin, Neil.

Osen, James L. Prophet & Peacemaker: The Life of Adolphe Monod. (Illus.). 420p. 1984. pap. text 31.00 (*0-8191-3826-6*); lib. bdg. 60.50 (*0-8191-3825-8*) U Pr of Amer.

— Royalist Political Thought During the French Revolution, 47. LC 94-25056. (Contributions to the Study of World History Ser.: Vol. 47). 168p. 1995. 57.95 (*0-313-29441-0*, Greenwood Pr) Greenwood.

Osen, Janet E. Mini Maestro Presents the Tic-Toc Clocks. large type ed. (Illus.). 30p. (J). (ps-k). 15.95 (*0-9700489-0-4*) Little Fiddle.

Osen, Lisa L. Creating the Future: A Business Guide to Visualization. LC 96-93051. (Illus.). 208p. (Orig.). Date not set. pap. 15.00 (*1-890282-20-0*) AeviVision.

— Visioning for Success! Using Probability-Based Thinking to 'Create' Your Life. 2nd ed. LC 96-93061. (Illus.). xvi, 152p. 1997. pap. 14.00 (*1-890282-21-9*) AeviVision.

Osen, Lynn M. Women in Mathematics. LC 73-19506. 224p. 1975. pap. text 16.50 (*0-262-65009-6*) MIT Pr.

Osen, Mary E. I'll Be Seeing You: World War II Diary & Correspondence of Cpl. Mary E. Osen, February 1943 - September 1945. Nielsen, Lynn E. & Nielsen, Mary T., eds. 143p. (Orig.). 1994. pap. 9.95 (*0-931209-54-4*) Mid-Prairie Bks.

Osenbach, Richard & Zeidman, Seth M. Infections of the Central Nervous System: Diagnosis & Management. LC 98-29117. 400p. 1998. text 129.00 (*0-397-51837-4*) Lppncott W & W.

Osenbaugh, Jack D. Heaven May Have Quills. LC 97-69234. 240p. 1998. 20.95 (*1-57197-085-1*) Pentland Pr.

Osenbaugh, Scott E. Love--or Mush? Six Action-Packed Lessons on 1 Corinthians 13: 1-6 to Use with Junior Highers. LC 87-80603. (Illus.). 96p. (gr. 4-7). 1988. pap., teacher ed. 7.95 (*0-88243-745-3*, 02-0745) Gospel Pub.

Osenberg, Craig W., jt. ed. see Schmitt, Russell J.

Osenberg, Jens B. & Brassington, David. Instrument Development for Atmospheric Research & Monitoring: Lidar Profiling, DOAS & Tunable Diode Laser Spectroscopy. LC 97-368. (Transport & Chemical Transformation of Pollutants in the Troposphere Ser.). 1997. 114.00 (*3-540-62516-X*) Spr-Verlag.

Osendal, Bernt. Stochastic Differential Equations: An Introduction with Applications. 4th ed. (Universitext Ser.). (Illus.). 271p. 1995. 36.00 (*3-540-60243-7*) Spr-Verlag.

Oseney Abbey Staff. The English Register of Oseney Abbey: Parts 1 & 2. (EETS, OS Ser.: No. 133, 144). 1972. reprint ed. 54.00 (*0-527-00130-9*) Periodicals Srv.

Osenkowsky, Tom. Broadcast Engineering. (Audio/Video Engineering Ser.). (Illus.). 350p. 1998. 85.95 incl. disk (*0-07-913742-3*) McGraw-Hill Prof.

Osenton, J., jt. auth. see Dorian, A.

Oser, Andrew. Star Power for Preschoolers: Learning Life Skills Through Physical Play. LC 97-29759. (Illus.). 1997. pap. 17.95 (*1-884834-35-3*, 3048) Redleaf Pr.

Oser, Fritz K., et al, eds. Effective & Responsible Teaching: The New Synthesis. LC 92-11511. (Education-Higher Education Ser.). 488p. 1992. text 50.00 (*1-55542-449-X*) Jossey-Bass.

Oser, Fritz K. & Gmunder, Paul. Religious Judgement: A Developmental Perspective. Hahn, Norbert F., tr. from GER. Orig. Title: Der Mensch: Stufen Seiner Religiosen Entwicklung. 235p. (Orig.). 1991. pap. 25.95 (*0-89135-081-0*) Religious Educ.

Oser, Fritz K. & Scarlett, W. George, eds. Religious Development in Childhood & Adolescence. LC 85-644581. (New Directions for Child Development Ser.: No. CD 52). 1991. 25.00 (*1-55542-788-X*) Jossey-Bass.

Oser, Fritz K., jt. ed. see Berkowitz, Marvin W.

Oser, Heinz, et al, eds. Life Sciences & Space Research XXIII (5) Gravitational Biology: Proceedings of the Topical Meeting of the COSPAR Interdisciplinary Scientific Commission F (Meetings F1, F3, F4 & F5) & of Workshops XVII & XVIII of the COSPAR 27th Plenary Meeting Held in Espoo, Finaldn, July, 1988. (Advances in Space Research Ser.: Vol. 9). 302p. 1989. pap. 92.75 (*0-08-040154-6*, 1702; 0201; 020, Pergamon Pr) Elsevier.

Oser, Helen, jt. auth. see Stewart, Mary.

Oser, Lee. T. S. Eliot & American Poetry. LC 98-21589. 192p. 1998. 29.95 (*0-8262-1181-X*) U of Mo Pr.

***Oser, Marie.** More Soy of Cooking: Healthful Renditions of Classic Traditional Meals. 304p. 2000. pap. 16.95 (*0-471-37761-9*) Wiley.

Oser, Marie. The Soy of Cooking: Easy to Make Vegetarian, Low-Fat, Fat-Free, & Antioxidant-Rich Gourmet Recipes. 304p. 1996. pap. 15.95 (*1-56561-086-5*) Wiley.

— Soy of Cooking: Easy to Make Vegetarian, Low-Fat, Fat-Free, & Antioxidant-Rich Gourmet Recipes. (Illus.). 304p. 1996. pap. 16.95 (*0-471-34705-1*) Wiley.

***Oser, Robert.** Chili! Mouth-Watering Meatless Recipes. LC 98-51404. 144p. 1999. 12.95 (*1-57067-070-6*) Book Pub Co.

Oser, Robert. Flavors of the Southwest. LC 97-46068. (Illus.). 192p. 1998. pap. 12.95 (*1-57067-049-8*) Book Pub Co.

Osers, Ewald. Arrive Where We Started. 48p. pap. write for info. (*3-7052-0935-3*, Pub. by Poetry Salzburg) Intl Spec Bk.

Osers, Ewald, ed. from MAC. Contemporary Macedonian Poetry. LC 91-70144. (Illus.). 223p. (Orig.). 1992. pap. 21.00 (*0-948259-67-1*, Pub. by Forest Bks) Dufour.

Osers, Ewald, tr. Contemporary German Poetry. (Modern Poets Ser.: Vol. 5). 1976. pap. 4.95 (*0-902675-69-9*) Oleander Pr.

Osers, Ewald, jt. auth. see Skelton, Raleigh A.

Osers, Ewald, tr. see Bernhard, Thomas.

Osers, Ewald, tr. see Boog, Hornst, et al, eds.

Osers, Ewald, tr. see Capek, Karel.

Osers, Ewald, tr. see Davidkov, Ivan.

Osers, Ewald, tr. see Haffner, Sebastian.

Osers, Ewald, tr. see Hanzlik, Josef.

Osers, Ewald, tr. see Heinrich, Harrer.

Osers, Ewald, tr. see Holub, Miroslav.

Osers, Ewald, tr. see Janovic, Vladimir.

Osers, Ewald, tr. see Klima, Ivan.

Osers, Ewald, tr. see Kroener, Bernhard R., et al, eds.

Osers, Ewald, tr. see Levchev, Lyubomir.

Osers, Ewald, tr. see Maier, Klaus A., et al.

Osers, Ewald, tr. see Milev, Geo.

Osers, Ewald, tr. see Piontek, Heinz.

Osers, Ewald, tr. see Safranski, Rudiger.

Osers, Ewald, tr. see Seifert, Jaroslav.

Oset, E., et al, eds. Pions in Nuclei: Proceedings of the International Workshop, Penyscola, Spain, 3-9 June 1991. 600p. (C). 1992. text 130.00 (*981-02-0732-8*) World Scientific Pub.

Oseth, John M. Regulating U. S. Intelligence Operations: A Study in Definition of the National Interest. LC 84-22105. 254p. reprint ed. pap. 78.80 (*0-7837-2421-7*, 204256700005) Bks Demand.

***Oseye, Ebele.** Hold That Thought! You Too Can Be a Simpleton. (Illus.). 30p. (YA). 2000. pap. 5.00 (*1-929454-05-8*, 917 863-6528) Eneke.

***Oseye, Ebele & Southerland, Ellease.** Opening Line: The Creative Writer. 39p. (YA). 2000. pap. text 10.00 (*1-929454-01-5*, 917 863-6528) Eneke.

— This Year in Nigeria. 100p. (YA). 2000. pap. 16.95 (*1-929454-02-3*, 917 863-6528) Eneke.

Oseye, Ebele, jt. auth. see Southerland, Ellease.

Osf Motif Series Staff. Motif User's Guide. (C). 1990. pap. text 27.00 (*0-13-640509-6*) P-H.

Osgerby, William. Youth in Britain since 1945. LC 97-17855. (Making Contemporary Britain Ser.). (Illus.). 256p. (C). 1997. text 62.95 (*0-631-19476-2*); pap. text 26.95 (*0-631-19477-0*) Blackwell Pubs.

Osgood. Como Amar Su Trabajo de Verdad.Tr. of How to Really Love Your Job. (SPA.). 116p. 1995. pap. write for info. (*0-614-27010-3*) Editorial Unilit.

— Como Amar Su Trabajo de Verdad - How to Really Love Your Job. (SPA.). 116p. 1995. write for info. (*0-614-24353-X*) Editorial Unilit.

Osgood, C. E. Lectures on Language Performance. (Language & Communication Ser.: Vol. 7). (Illus.). 368p. 1980. 90.95 (*0-387-09901-8*) Spr-Verlag.

Osgood, C. G. The Classical Mythology of Milton's English Poems. (Reprints in History Ser.). reprint ed. lib. bdg. 39.00 (*0-697-00014-1*) Irvington.

Osgood, Carl C. Fatigue Design. 2nd ed. (International Series on the Strength & Fracture of Materials & Structures). 500p. 1982. text 274.00 (*0-08-026167-1*, Pub. by Pergamon Repr) Franklin.

— Rafting to the Indies. (Illus.). 230p. 1997. pap. 19.00 (*0-9638587-2-6*) Vista Hse.

— The Travels of Frank Forrester. (Illus.). 198p. (Orig.). 1993. pap. 15.00 (*0-9638587-0-X*) Vista Hse.

— The Tunk Pond Episode. (Illus.). 203p. 1996. pap. 19.00 (*0-9638587-1-8*) Vista Hse.

Osgood, Charles. See You on the Radio. LC 99-26958. 272p. 1999. 23.95 (*0-399-14542-7*, G P Putnam) Peng Put Young Read.

***Osgood, Charles.** See You on the Radio. LC 99-55922. 2000. 29.95 (*0-7862-2312-X*) Thorndike Pr.

Osgood, Charles E. & Sebeok, Thomas A., eds. Psycholinguistics. LC 76-2579. (Indiana Univ. Studies in the History & Theory of Linguistics). (Illus.). 307p. 1976. reprint ed. lib. bdg. 55.00 (*0-8371-8730-3*, OSPS, Greenwood Pr) Greenwood.

Osgood, Charles E. & Tzeng, Oliver C., eds. Language, Meaning, & Culture: The Selected Papers of C. E. Osgood. LC 89-16055. (Centennial Psychology Ser.). 415p. 1990. 79.50 (*0-275-92521-8*, C2521, Praeger Pubs) Greenwood.

Osgood, Charles E., et al. Cross-Cultural Universals of Affective Meaning. LC 73-85570. (Illus.). 520p. 1975. pap. 17.50 (*0-252-00550-3*); text 44.95 (*0-252-00426-4*) U of Ill Pr.

— The Measurement of Meaning. LC 56-5684. (Illus.). 356p. 1967. reprint ed. pap. text 23.95 (*0-252-74539-6*) U of Ill Pr.

Osgood, Charles G. Classical Mythology of Milton's English Poems. LC 64-8180. 198p. 1964. reprint ed. 50.00 (*0-87752-080-1*) Gordian.

— Classical Mythology of Milton's English Poems. LC 65-15902. (Studies in Comparative Literature: No. 35). 1969. reprint ed. lib. bdg. 75.00 (*0-8383-0603-9*) M S G Haskell Hse.

— The Classical Mythology of Milton's English Poems. (BCL1-PR English Literature Ser.). 111p. 1992. reprint ed. lib. bdg. 69.00 (*0-7812-7387-0*) Rprt Serv.

— Concordance to the Poems of Edmund Spenser. 1990. 42.50 (*0-8446-1332-0*) Peter Smith.

— Poetry As a Means of Grace. LC 68-25106. 131p. 1965. reprint ed. 50.00 (*0-87752-081-X*) Gordian.

— Spenser's English Rivers. (Connecticut Academy of Arts & Sciences Ser., Trans.: Vol. 23). 1920. pap. 49.50 (*0-685-22835-5*) Elliots Bks.

Osgood, Charles G., Jr., ed. Pearl, a Middle English Poem. LC 78-144438. (Belles Lettres Ser. Section II: No. 4). reprint ed. 30.00 (*0-404-53614-X*) AMS Pr.

Osgood, Charles G., tr. see Boccaccio, Giovanni.

Osgood, Chas S. & Batchelder, H. M. Historical Sketch of Salem, Massachusetts, 1626-1879. (Illus.). 288p. 1998. reprint ed. lib. bdg. 35.00 (*0-8328-7126-5*) Higginson Bk Co.

Osgood, Cornelius. The Chinese: A Study of a Hong Kong Community, Vol. 1. LC 74-77207. (Illus.). 463p. 1975. pap. 143.60 (*0-608-05635-9*, 206609100001) Bks Demand.

— The Chinese: A Study of a Hong Kong Community, Vol. 2. LC 74-77207. (Illus.). 536p. 1975. pap. 166.20 (*0-608-05636-7*, 206609100002) Bks Demand.

O

— The Chinese: A Study of a Hong Kong Community, Vol. 3. LC 74-77207. (Illus.). 312p. 1975. pap. 96.80 (*0-608-05637-5*, 206609100003) Bks Demand.

— Contributions to the Ethnography of the Kutchin. LC 73-118247. (Yale University Publications in Anthropology Reprints Ser.: No. 14). 190p. 1970. pap. 22.00 (*0-87536-522-1*) HRAFP.

— The Han Indians: A Compilation of Ethnographic & Historical Data on the Alaska-Yukon Boundary Area. LC 76-156892. (Publications in Anthropology: No. 74). 1971. pap. 7.50 (*0-913516-07-4*) Yale U Anthro.

— Ingalik Material Culture. LC 77-118248. (Yale University Publications in Anthropology Reprints Ser.: No. 22). 500p. 1970. pap. 30.00 (*0-87536-516-7*) HRAFP.

— The Koreans & Their Culture. LC 51-271. (Illus.). 435p. reprint ed. 134.90 (*0-8357-9523-3*, 201584300097) Bks Demand.

— Village Life in Old China: A Community Study of Kao Yao Yhunnan. LC 63-19749. 415p. reprint ed. pap. 128.70 (*0-608-11806-0*, 201239000081) Bks Demand.

Osgood, D. Wayne, ed. NE Symposium on Motivation, 1996: Motivation & Delinquency. LC 53-11655. (Illus.). xiv, 295p. 1997. text 45.00 (*0-8032-3566-6*) U of Nebr Pr.

Osgood, D. Wayne, jt. auth. see Gold, Martin.

Osgood, Don. Como Amar Realmente Su Trabajo. (Serie Guia de Bolsillo - Pocket Guides Ser.).Tr. of How to Really Love Your Job. (SPA.). 109p. 1996. 2.79 (*1-56063-865-6*, 498072) Editorial Unilit.

— Formas Efectivas de Vencer Tension. (Serie Guia de Bolsillo - Pocket Guides Ser.).Tr. of Surefire Ways to Beat Stress. (SPA.). 2.79 (*1-56063-031-0*, 498058) Editorial Unilit.

Osgood, Don. Formas Efectivas de Vencer Tension. (Guia de Bosillo Ser.).Tr. of Surefire Ways to Beat Stress. (SPA.). 1994. 2.49 (*0-685-74937-1*, 498058); pap. write for info. (*0-614-27046-4*) Editorial Unilit.

Osgood, Ernest S. Day of the Cattleman. LC 57-7901. (Illus.). 1993. pap. 2.45 (*0-226-63555-4*, P13) U Ch Pr.

Osgood, Ernest S., ed. see Clark, William.

Osgood, Foster C. Building Healthy Gardens: A Safe & Natural Approach. rev. ed. Silva, Jeff, ed. LC 88-45486. Orig. Title: The Organic Gardener. (Illus.). 288p. 1989. reprint ed. pap. 11.95 (*0-88266-527-8*, Garden Way Pub) Storey Bks.

Osgood, Frank S. Gilmore. Robert & James Gilmore Who Settled in Southern New Hampshire & Their Descendants; also a Brief Account of Other Gilmores Not Related. (Illus.). 201p. 1997. reprint ed. pap. 31.00 (*0-8328-8748-X*); reprint ed. lib. bdg. 41.00 (*0-8328-8747-1*) Higginson Bk Co.

Osgood, Henry O. So This Is Jazz. LC 77-17859. (Roots of Jazz Ser.). (Illus.). 1978. reprint ed. lib. bdg. 32.50 (*0-306-77540-9*) Da Capo.

Osgood, I. A Genealogy of the Descendants of John, Christopher & William Osgood Who Settled in New England Early in the Seventeenth Century. Putnam, Eben, ed. 491p. 1989. reprint ed. pap. 74.00 (*0-8328-0925-X*); reprint ed. lib. bdg. 82.00 (*0-8328-0924-1*) Higginson Bk Co.

O

Osgood, Joseph B. Notes of Travel: Recollections of Majunga, Zanzibar, Musca, Aden, Mocha, & Other Eastern Ports. LC 72-5546. (Black Heritage Library Collection). 1977. reprint ed. 28.95 (*0-8369-9146-X*) Ayer.

Osgood, Judy, ed. Meditations for Alcoholics & Their Families. LC 92-41267. (Gilgal Meditations Ser.). 72p. 1993. pap. 6.95 (*0-916895-04-1*) Gilgal Pubns.

— Meditations for Bereaved Parents. LC 86-15003. (Gilgal Meditations Ser.). 72p. (Orig.). 1984. pap. 6.95 (*0-916895-00-9*) Gilgal Pubns.

— Meditations for the Divorced. LC 87-17687. (Gilgal Meditations Ser.). 72p. (Orig.). 1987. pap. 5.95 (*0-916895-02-5*) Gilgal Pubns.

— Meditations for the Terminally Ill & Their Families. LC 88-36326. (Gilgal Meditations Ser.). 72p. 1989. pap. 5.95 (*0-916895-05-X*) Gilgal Pubns.

— Meditations for the Widowed. LC 86-15002. (Gilgal Meditations Ser.). 72p. (Orig.). 1985. pap. 6.95 (*0-916895-01-7*) Gilgal Pubns.

Osgood, Lucile N. From My Mind's Eye: A Book of Haiku. 1997. pap. write for info. (*1-57553-564-5*) Watermrk Pr.

Osgood, Marcy & Ocorr, Karen. Principles of Biochemistry: Study Guide. 1993. pap., student ed. write for info. (*1-57259-100-5*) Worth.

Osgood, Mark. Ohio's Best in Amateur Wrestling: A Thorough Look at Ohio Wrestling from 1938-1997. 328p. (Orig.). Date not set. pap. 24.95 (*0-9659642-0-5*) Mark Osgood.

Osgood, Nancy J. Suicide in Later Life: Recognizing the Warning Signs. 168p. 1992. 23.95 (*0-669-21214-8*) Jossey-Bass.

Osgood, Nancy J., ed. Senior Settlers: Social Integration in Retirement Communities. LC 82-13352. 296p. 1982. 55.00 (*0-275-90873-9*, C0873, Praeger Pubs) Greenwood.

Osgood, Nancy J., et al, eds. Alcoholism & Aging: An Annotated Bibliography & Review, 24. LC 94-41371. (Bibliographies & Indexes in Gerontology Ser.: Vol. 24). 264p. 1995. lib. bdg. 69.50 (*0-313-28398-2*, Greenwood Pr) Greenwood.

Osgood, Nancy J. & McIntosh, John L., compiled by. Suicide & the Elderly: An Annotated Bibliography & Review, 3. LC 86-14935. (Bibliographies & Indexes in Gerontology Ser.: No. 3). 206p. 1986. lib. bdg. 69.50 (*0-313-24786-2*, OSE/, Greenwood Pr) Greenwood.

Osgood, Nancy J. & Sontz, Ann H. The Science & Practice of Gerontology: A Multidisciplinary Approach. 208p. 1989. write for info. (*1-85302-044-3*, Pub. by Jessica Kingsley) Taylor & Francis.

Osgood, Nancy J & Sontz, Ann H., eds. The Science & Practice of Gerontology: A Multidisciplinary Guide. LC 88-25100. 204p. 1989. lib. bdg. 59.95 (*0-313-26161-X*, OSP/, Greenwood Pr) Greenwood.

Osgood, Nancy J., et al. Suicide among the Elderly in Long-Term Care Facilities, 19. LC 90-36738. (Contributions to the Study of Aging Ser.: No. 19). 216p. 1990. 55.00 (*0-313-26522-4*, ODD, Greenwood Pr) Greenwood.

Osgood, Nancy J., jt. auth. see Clark, Patricia A.

Osgood, Rae G., jt. auth. see Meltz, Eva S.

Osgood, Rae Gunter, jt. auth. see Meltz, Eva Stolar.

Osgood, Robert E. Limited War: The Challenge to American Strategy. LC 57-5275. 326p. 1998. lib. bdg. 23.00 (*0-226-63779-4*) U Ch Pr.

— Limited War Revisited. LC 89-13427. (Special Studies). 124p. 1979. pap. text 49.00 (*0-89158-465-X*) Westview.

— NATO, the Engangling Alliance. LC 62-8348. 428p. reprint ed. pap. 132.70 (*0-608-30717-3*, 200727800063) Bks Demand.

— The Successor Generation: Its Challenges & Responsibilities. 45p. (C). 1983. pap. 21.95 (*0-87855-874-8*) Transaction Pubs.

— The Weary & the Wary: U. S. & Japanese Security Policies in Transition. LC 71-186510. (Washington Center of Foreign Policy Research. Studies in International Affairs: No. 16). 106p. reprint ed. pap. 32.90 (*0-608-11900-8*, 202313200031) Bks Demand.

Osgood, Robert E. & Tucker, Robert W. Force, Order & Justice. LC 67-16915. 384p. 1967. reprint ed. pap. 119.10 (*0-608-03740-0*, 206456500009) Bks Demand.

Osgood, Robert E., et al. America & the World: From the Truman Doctrine to Vietnam. LC 77-16133. 446p. 1970. reprint ed. pap. 138.30 (*0-608-04012-6*, 206474800011) Bks Demand.

— Japan & the United States in Asia. LC 68-9699. (Washington Center of Foreign Policy Research. Studies in International Affairs: No. 8). 75p. reprint ed. pap. 30.00 (*0-608-11899-0*, 202313300032) Bks Demand.

— Retreat from Empire? The First Nixon Administration. LC 72-12359. (America & the World Ser.: Vol. 2). 360p. reprint ed. pap. 111.60 (*0-608-06125-5*, 206645800008) Bks Demand.

Osgood, Robert E., jt. auth. see Hollick, Ann L.

*__Osgood, Robert L.__ "For Children Who Vary from the Normal Type" Special Education in Boston, 1838-1930. LC 99-59168. 2000. 49.95 (*1-56368-089-0*) Gallaudet Univ Pr.

Osgood, Russell K. The Law of Pensions & Profit-Sharing. LC 83-82690. 480p. 1984. suppl. ed. 80.00 (*0-316-66614-9*, Aspen Law & Bus) Aspen Pub.

— Pensions - Profit. 1984. 125.00 (*0-316-66612-2*, Aspen Law & Bus) Aspen Pub.

— Supplement Pensions - Profit '87. 1987. 35.00 (*0-316-66616-5*, Aspen Law & Bus) Aspen Pub.

Osgood, Russell K., ed. see Wiedenbeck, Peter J.

Osgood, Samuel. American Leaves: Familiar Notes of Thought & Life. LC 72-374. (Essay Index Reprint Ser.). 1977. reprint ed. 24.95 (*0-8369-2814-8*) Ayer.

Osgood, Wilfred H. Mammals of the Kelley-Roosevelts & Delacour Asiatic Expeditions. LC 33-22124. (Field Museum of Natural History, Publication 1362 Ser.: Vol. 18, No. 10). 149p. reprint ed. pap. 46.20 (*0-608-03780-X*, 206462700009) Bks Demand.

Osgood, William F. Funktionentheorie, 2 Vols, 1. LC 63-11319. 24.95 (*0-8284-0193-4*) Chelsea Pub.

— Funktionentheorie, 2 Vols, 2. LC 63-11319. 24.95 (*0-8284-0182-9*) Chelsea Pub.

Osgood, William R. Preparing Your Business Plan with Symphony. LC 84-18158. 1986. 19.95 (*0-13-698978-0*) P-H.

Osgood, William R. & Curtin, Dennis P. Preparing Your Business Plan with LOTUS 1-2-3. (Illus.). 176p. 1984. pap. 34.95 (*0-13-698424-X*); disk. write for info. (*0-318-58084-5*) P-H.

— Preparing Your Business Plan with MULTIPLAN. 44.95 (*0-685-09440-5*) P-H.

— Preparing Your Business Plan with SYMPHONY. 27.95 (*0-685-09442-1*) P-H.

Osgood, William R., jt. auth. see Curtin, Dennis P.

Osgoode Society for Canadian Legal History Staff, jt. auth. see Pound, Richard W.

Osguthorpe, Russell T. The Education of the Heart: Spiritual Foundations of Teaching & Learning. LC 96-26624. 1996. pap. 10.95 (*1-55503-985-5*, 01112430) Covenant Comms.

Osguthorpe, Russell T., et al, eds. Partner Schools: Centers for Educational Renewal. 348p. 1995. text 36.45 (*0-7879-0065-6*) Jossey-Bass.

Osguthorpe, Russell T. & Patterson, Robert S. Balancing the Tensions of Change: Eight Keys to Collaborative Educational Renewal. LC 98-8902. (1-Off Ser.). (Illus.). 152p. 1998. 49.95 (*0-8039-6699-7*); pap. 21.95 (*0-8039-6700-4*) Corwin Pr.

OSHA Staff. Chemical Information Manual. 3rd ed. 341p. 1995. pap. text 99.00 (*0-86587-469-7*) Gov Insts.

*__OSHA Staff.__ OSHA Technical Manual. 5th ed. 474p. 1999. pap. 89.00 (*0-86587-674-6*) Gov Insts.

Oshagan, Vahe, et al, eds. Armenia. (Review of National Literatures Ser.: Vol. 13). 260p. 1984. 12.00 (*0-918680-22-0*); pap. 6.95 (*0-918680-77-8*) Griffon House.

Oshagbemi, Titus. Leadership & Management in Universities: Britain & Nigeria. (Studies in Organization: No. 14). xx, 249p. (C). 1989. lib. bdg. 64.95 (*3-11-011514-X*) De Gruyter.

Oshana, Maryann. Women of Color: A Filmography of Minority & Third World Women. LC 82-49143. 350p. 1984. text 15.00 (*0-8240-9140-X*) Garland.

*__Oshana, Robert.__ DSP Software Development for Real-Time Systems. 352p. 2000. pap. 34.95 incl. cd-rom (*1-929629-12-5*, Pub. by C M P Books) Publishers Group.

Oshanahan Roca, A. Gran Diccionario del Habla Canaria. (SPA.). 1250p. 1995. 95.00 (*0-7859-9769-5*) Fr & Eur.

O'Shanick, G. J., jt. ed. see Peterson, Linda G.

Oshanin, L. V. Anthropological Composition of the Population of Central Asia, the Ethnogenesis of Its Peoples, 1 vol. in 3 nos. Field, Henry, ed. Maurin, Vladimir M., tr. LC 65-112085. (Harvard University, Peabody Museum of Archaeology & Ethnology, Russian Translation Ser.: Vol. 2, Nos. 1-3). reprint ed. 124.50 (*0-404-52650-0*) AMS Pr.

*__O'Shannon, Dan.__ Fan & the Flowers. 32p. (J). 2000. lib. bdg. 16.49 (*0-7868-2518-9*, Pub. by Hyperion) Little.

Oshaug, A., et al. Educational Handbook for Nutrition Trainers: How to Increase Your Skills & Make It Easier for Students to Learn. (ENG & FRE.). 322p. 1993. pap. text 58.50 (*0-614-32101-8*, 1930048) World Health.

O'Shaughnessey, John. Competitive Marketing. 2nd ed. LC 88-1886. (Illus.). 474p. (Orig.). (C). 1989. pap. 28.95 (*0-415-08429-6*) Thomson Learn.

— Competitive Marketing: A Strategic Approach. 3rd ed. LC 94-39927. 768p. (C). 1995. pap. 24.99 (*0-415-09317-1*, C0553) Thomson Learn.

— Competitive Marketing: A Strategic Approach. 3rd ed. LC 94-39927. 768p. (C). (gr. 13). 1995. pap. 72.00 (*0-415-12786-6*, D1000) Thomson Learn.

*__Oshaughnessy, Andrew J.__ Empire Divided: The American Revolution & the British Caribbean. 2000. 55.00 (*0-8122-3558-4*); pap. text. write for info. (*0-8122-1732-2*) U of Pa Pr.

O'Shaughnessy, Arthur. Poems. (BCL1-PR English Literature Ser.). 104p. 1992. reprint ed. lib. bdg. 69.00 (*0-7812-7611-X*) Rprt Serv.

O'Shaughnessy, Arthur E. Poems of Arthur O'Shaughnessy. Percy, William A., ed. LC 78-13947. 104p. 1979. reprint ed. lib. bdg. 49.50 (*0-313-21101-9*, OSPO, Greenwood Pr) Greenwood.

*__O'Shaughnessy, Brian.__ Consciousness & the World. LC 99-45064. 712p. 2000. write for info. (*0-19-823893-2*) OUP.

O'Shaughnessy, C. Vincent. Never the Same. 134p. 1997. pap. text 9.95 (*1-884920-11-X*) Jubilee Christian Ctr.

O'Shaughnessy, Charles O. To Comfort the Dying: Pain Control in Advanced Cancer. Kirschner, John R., ed. (Illus.). 250p. (Orig.). 1996. pap. 21.95 (*0-9654910-0-5*) Lovejoy Hospice.

O'Shaughnessy, Douglas. Speech Communications. (Electrical & Computer Engineering Ser.). (Illus.). 600p. (C). 1987. text 64.95 (*0-201-16520-1*) Addison-Wesley.

— Speech Communications: Human & Machine. 2nd ed. LC 99-28810. 560p. 1999. 99.95 (*0-7803-3449-3*, PC4194-QOE) Inst Electrical.

O'Shaughnessy, Edith L. Diplomat's Wife in Mexico. LC 73-111727. (American Imperialism: Viewpoints of United States Foreign Policy, 1898-1941 Ser.). 1970. reprint ed. 34.95 (*0-405-02042-2*) Ayer.

— Diplomat's Wife in Mexico. (American Biography Ser.). 355p. 1991. reprint ed. lib. bdg. 79.00 (*0-7812-8303-5*) Rprt Serv.

— Married Life. LC 71-52952. (Short Story Index Reprint Ser.). 1977. reprint ed. 20.95 (*0-8369-3867-4*) Ayer.

— Other Ways & Other Flesh. LC 70-150482. (Short Story Index Reprint Ser.). 1977. reprint ed. 18.95 (*0-8369-3823-2*) Ayer.

O'Shaughnessy, Ellen. Somebody Called Me a Retard Today - & My Heart Felt Sad. LC 92-10812. (Illus.). 24p. (YA). 1992. 13.95 (*0-8027-8196-9*); lib. bdg. 14.85 (*0-8027-8197-7*) Walker & Co.

O'Shaughnessy, Hugh. Latin Americans. LC 90-60713. (Illus.). 143p. 1990. 18.95 (*0-563-21393-0*) Parkwest Pubns.

*__O'Shaughnessy, Hugh.__ Pinochet: The Politics of Torture. LC 99-59431. 2000. 25.95 (*0-8147-6201-8*) NYU Pr.

O'Shaughnessy, James C., ed. Environmental Engineering. 1084p. 1985. 13.00 (*0-87262-468-4*) Am Soc Civil Eng.

O'Shaughnessy, James P. How to Retire Rich: Time-Tested Strategies to Beat the Market & Retire in Style. LC 97-28937. 288p. 1997. 25.00 (*0-7679-0072-3*) Broadway BDD.

— How to Retire Rich: Time-Tested Strategies to Beat the Market & Retire in Style. 272p. 1998. reprint ed. pap. 13.00 (*0-7679-0073-1*) Broadway BDD.

— Invest Like the Best. 244p. 1998. pap. 16.95 (*0-07-913754-7*) McGraw.

— Invest Like the Best: Using Your Computer to Unlock the Secrets of the Top Money Managers. (Illus.). 336p. 1998. pap. 16.95 (*0-07-048247-0*) McGraw.

— What Works on Wall Street. rev. ed. 1997. 49.95 incl. digital audio (*0-07-856644-4*) McGraw.

— What Works on Wall Street: A Guide to the Best Performing Investment Strategies of All Times. 2nd rev. ed. LC 98-5810. (Illus.). 325p. 1998. 29.95 (*0-07-048246-2*) McGraw.

O'Shaughnessy, John. Competitive Marketing: A Strategic Approach. 2nd ed. (Illus.). 352p. 1988. pap. text 27.95 (*0-04-445117-2*) Routledge.

— Competitive Marketing: A Strategic Approach. 3rd ed. 88p. 1995. pap., teacher ed. 62.65 (*0-415-12807-2*) Thomson Learn.

— Inquiry & Decision. LC 72-193562. 200p. 1972. write for info. (*0-04-658046-8*) Allen & Unwn AT.

— Why People Buy. (Illus.). 208p. (C). 1989. reprint ed. pap. text 21.95 (*0-19-504087-2*) OUP.

O'Shaughnessy, Laura & Serra, Luis. The Church & Revolution in Nicaragua. LC 82-92625. (Monographs in International Studies, Latin America Ser.: No. 11). 128p. 1986. pap. text 18.00 (*0-89680-126-8*) Ohio U Pr.

O'Shaughnessy, Laura N., jt. auth. see Dodson, Michael.

Oshaughnessy, Lynn. Unofficial Guide to Investing. LC 99-209435. 400p. 1998. pap. 16.00 (*0-02-862458-0*, Pub. by Macmillan) S&S Trade.

*__O'Shaughnessy, Margret.__ Das Todliche Dreieck: Die Familie Als Schauplatz des Nordirlandkonflikts in Funf Romanen Zeitgenossischer Autorinnen. 220p. 1998. 37.95 (*3-631-33983-6*) P Lang Pubng.

O'Shaughnessy, Martin. Jean Renoir. pap. write for info. (*0-7190-5063-4*, Pub. by Manchester Univ Pr); text. write for info. (*0-7190-5062-6*, Pub. by Manchester Univ Pr) St Martin.

O'Shaughnessy, Mary M. Feelings & Emotions in Christian Living. LC 87-21317. 152p. 1988. pap. 7.95 (*0-8189-0524-7*) Alba.

O'Shaughnessy, Michael. Media & Society: An Introduction. (Illus.). 328p. 2000. pap. text 24.95 (*0-19-550788-6*) OUP.

*__O'Shaughnessy, Michael.__ Millennium Woman: A Guideline to Personal Security & Financial Prosperity for Today's Woman. LC 99-95065. (Illus.). 200p. 2000. pap. 15.95 (*0-9674788-0-4*, 1000) M OShaughnessy.

O'Shaughnessy, Michael, photos by. A Kingdom of Saints: Early Bultos of New Mexico - A Postcard Collection. (Illus.). 22p. 1993. per. 8.95 (*1-878610-35-X*) Red Crane Bks.

— A Kingdom of Saints: Early Retablos of New Mexico - A Postcard Collection. (Illus.). 22p. 1993. per. 8.95 (*1-878610-36-8*) Red Crane Bks.

O'Shaughnessy, Michael J. Economic Democracy & Private Enterprise. LC 72-10848. (Essay Index Reprint Ser.). 1977. reprint ed. 18.95 (*0-8369-7235-X*) Ayer.

O'Shaughnessy, Patrick, ed. Lincoln Fair & Other Poems by Bernard Gilbert. (Illus.). 72p. (C). 1989. text 40.00 (*0-902662-34-1*, Pub. by R K Pubns); pap. text 30.00 (*0-902662-35-X*, Pub. by R K Pubns) St Mut.

O'Shaughnessy, Perri. Acts of Malice. LC 98-55253. 400p. 1999. 23.95 (*0-385-33276-9*) Delacorte.

*__O'Shaughnessy, Perri.__ Acts of Malice. 560p. 2000. mass mkt. 7.50 (*0-440-22581-7*) Dell.

— Acts of Malice. large type ed. LC 99-27783. 503p. 1999. 26.95 (*1-56895-766-1*, Compass) Wheeler Pub.

O'Shaughnessy, Perri. Breach of Promise. LC 98-5519. 448p. 1998. 23.95 (*0-385-31872-3*) Bantam.

— Breach of Promise. 535p. 1999. mass mkt. 7.50 (*0-440-22473-X*) Broadway BDD.

— Invasion of Privacy. 517p. 1997. mass mkt. 6.99 (*0-440-22069-6*, Island Bks) Dell.

— Motion to Suppress. 480p. 1996. mass mkt. 6.99 (*0-440-22068-8*, Island Bks) Dell.

— Motion to Suppress. LC 99-31988. 1999. write for info. (*1-56895-755-6*) Wheeler Pub.

*__O'Shaughnessy, Perri.__ Move to Strike. LC 00-37578. 416p. 2000. 23.95 (*0-385-33277-7*) Delacorte.

— Obstruction of Justice. large type ed. LC 99-86696. 2000. 26.95 (*1-56895-845-5*, Compass) Wheeler Pub.

O'Shaughnessy, Perri. Obstruction of Justice. 512p. 1998. reprint ed. mass mkt. 7.50 (*0-440-22472-1*) Dell.

O'Shaughnessy, Peter. Con's Fabulous Journey to the Land of Gobel O'Glug. rev. ed. (Illus.). 104p. (J). (gr. 6-10). 1992. reprint ed. pap. 5.95 (*0-947962-68-9*, Pub. by Anvil Books Ltd) Irish Bks Media.

O'Shaughnessy, Tim. Adoption, Social Work & Social Theory: Making the Connections. 288p. 1994. 67.95 (*1-85628-883-8*, Pub. by Avebry) Ashgate Pub Co.

*__O'Shaughnessy, William.__ Air Waves! A Collection. LC 99-21445. (Communications & Media Studies: No. 3). 250p. 1999. 25.00 (*0-8232-1904-6*) Fordham.

O'Shay, Tracey A., jt. ed. see Hoddinott, Keith B.

O'Shea. Intelligent Knowledge Based Systems. pap. 33.95 (*0-06-318366-8*) Sage.

O'Shea, Alan, jt. ed. see Nava, Mica.

O'Shea, B. P., jt. auth. see Taylor, R. B.

O'Shea, Bill. Questions Catholics Ask. enl. rev. ed. 344p. 1991. reprint ed. 12.95 (*0-85924-909-3*) Harper SF.

O'Shea, Brendan. Crisis at Bihac: Bosnia's Bloody Battlefield. LC 99-185447. (Illus.). 256p. 1998. 35.00 (*0-7509-1927-2*, Pub. by Sutton Pub Ltd) Intl Pubs Mktg.

*__O'Shea, Convadonga.__ La Armonia Vital. 1999. pap. 18.95 (*84-7880-972-4*) Planeta.

O'Shea, D. B. & Pollatsek, H., eds. Instructor's Manual for Mathematical Experimentation: A Laboratory Bridge Course. (TIMS - Texts in Mathematical Science Ser.). 150p. 1997. pap. 54.95 (*0-387-94998-4*) Spr-Verlag.

*__O'Shea, Donagh, comment.__ Bible Diary, 2000 The Jubilee Year. (Illus.). 456p. 1999. 19.95 (*0-8091-0506-3*) Paulist Pr.

Oshea, Donagh O. I Remember Your Name in the Night: Thinking about Death. LC 96-61628. 1997. pap. text 9.95 (*0-89622-718-9*) Twenty-Third.

O'Shea, Donal, jt. auth. see Pollatsek, Harriet S.

O'Shea, Donal, jt. auth. see Pontryagin, Lev S.

O'Shea, Donald C. Elements of Modern Optical Design. LC 84-19708. (Pure & Applied Optics Ser.). 416p. 1985. 118.00 (*0-471-07796-8*) Wiley.

O'Shea, Donald C. & Peckham, Donald C., eds. Lasers: Selected Reprints. 144p. 1982. per. 15.00 (*0-917853-74-1*, RB-36) Am Assn Physics.

O'Shea, Donald C., et al. Introduction to Lasers & Their Applications. (Physics Ser.). 276p. (C). 1977. 86.00 (*0-201-05509-0*) Addison-Wesley.

*__O'Shea, Elena Zamora.__ El Mesquite. (Rio Grande/Rio Bravo Ser.: Vol. 4). 160p. 2000. 27.95 (*0-89096-966-3*); pap. 15.95 (*1-58544-108-2*) Tex A&M Univ Pr.

O'Shea, Farrel. Advanced Windsurfing. (Adventure Sports Ser.). 1989. pap. 18.95 (*0-8117-2303-8*) Stackpole.

— Learn to Windsurf. (Illus.). 80p. 1997. pap. 9.95 (*0-7063-7541-6*, Pub. by WrLock) Sterling.

O'Shea, Francie J. Cooking at the Cafe: Lunch & Dinner Fare. (Illus.). 189p. (Orig.). 1992. pap. 15.95 (*0-9634342-0-9*, TXU 528 816) F OShea.

An Asterisk (*) at the beginning of an entry indicates that the title is appearing for the first time.

O'Shea, Gerald. Coaching Youth Basketball. 1999. pap. 8.95 (*0-8289-0588-6*) Viking Penguin.
— Youth Soccer: Amateur Coach. 1986. 10.95 (*0-317-54063-7*) Viking Penguin.
O'Shea, Harriet E. A Study of the Effect of the Interest of a Passage of Learning Vocabulary. LC 71-177138. reprint ed. 37.50 (*0-404-55351-6*) AMS Pr.
***O'Shea, J. B.** Deep Blood. LC 98-90417. 1999. 21.95 (*0-533-12797-1*) Vantage.
O'Shea, James. Dangerous Company: The Consulting Powerhouses & the Businesses They Save & Ruin. LC 96-38019. 1997. 27.50 (*0-8129-2634-X*, Times Bks) Crown Pub Group.
O'Shea, James & Madigan, Charles. Dangerous Company: Management Consultants & the Businesses They Save & Ruin. 368p. 1998. pap. 13.95 (*0-14-027685-8*) Viking Penguin.
O'Shea, Jim. Microsoft Access 97 for Windows Quickstart. LC 97-159619. 1996. pap. text 29.99 incl. cd-rom (*1-56276-473-X*, Ziff-Davis Pr) Que.
— Microsoft Word 97 for Windows Quickstart. LC 97-160191. 352p. 1996. pap. text 29.99 incl. cd-rom (*1-56276-471-3*, Ziff-Davis Pr) Que.
O'Shea, John. Priests, Politics & Society in Post-Famine Ireland. 368p. 1997. 27.95 (*0-905473-71-X*, Pub. by Wolfhound Press) Irish Amer Bk.
O'Shea, John, et al. Dyslexia: How Do We Learn? 108p. (Orig.). 1994. pap. 11.95 (*0-85572-236-3*, Pub. by Hill Content Pubng) Seven Hills Bk.
O'Shea, John, jt. ed. see Halstead, Paul.
O'Shea, John J. Index to Richmond County History: 1969-1983, Vols. 1-26. LC 86-63441. 88p. (Orig.). pap. 7.00 (*0-937044-11-3*) Richmond Cty Hist Soc.
O'Shea, John M. Villagers of the Maros: A Portrait of an Early Bronze Age Society. LC 96-30205. (Interdisciplinary Contributions to Archaeology Ser.). (Illus.). 384p. (C). 1996. 71.00 (*0-306-45322-3*, Plenum Trade) Perseus Pubng.
O'Shea, John M. & Ludwickson, John. Archaeology & Ethnohistory of the Omaha Indians: The Big Village Site. LC 89-35986. (Studies in the Anthropology of North American Indians). (Illus.). xviii, 374p. 1992. text 55.00 (*0-8032-3556-9*) U of Nebr Pr.
O'Shea, John M. & Shott, Michael J., eds. The Bridgeport Township Site: Archaeological Investigation at 20SA620, Saginaw County, Michigan. LC 89-48109. (Anthropological Papers Ser.: No. 81). (Illus.). xii, 304p. (Orig.). 1990. pap. 15.00 (*0-915703-19-X*) U Mich Mus Anthro.
O'Shea, Kate S. Healing Hip, Joint, & Knee Pain: A Mind-Body Guide to Recovery from Surgery & Injuries. LC 97-38017. Orig. Title: Finding Your Balance: (Illus.). 154p. 1998. reprint ed. pap. 14.95 (*1-55643-258-5*) North Atlantic.
***O'Shea, Kathleen.** Women on the Row: Revelations from Both Sides of the Bars. 160p. 2000. pap. 12.95 (*1-56341-124-5*, Pub. by Firebrand Bks); lib. bdg. 26.95 (*1-56341-125-3*, Pub. by Firebrand Bks) LPC InBook.
O'Shea, Kathleen A. Women & the Death Penalty in the United States, 1900-1998. LC 98-23550. 432p. 1999. 69.50 (*0-275-95952-X*, Praeger Pubs) Greenwood.
O'Shea, Kathleen A. & Fletcher, Beverly R. Female Offenders: An Annotated Bibliography, 5. LC 96-42163. (Research & Bibliographical Guides in Criminal Justice Ser.). 280p. 1997. lib. bdg. 79.50 (*0-313-29228-0*) Greenwood.
O'Shea, Kevin. Person in Analysis: Interpersonhood in Metaphysics & Analytic Theory. 175p. (C). 1996. text 40.00 (*1-55605-270-7*); pap. text 20.00 (*1-55605-269-3*) Wyndham Hall.
— Person in Cosmos: Metaphors of Meaning from Physics, Philosophy, & Theology. 225p. (C). 1995. text 40.00 (*1-55605-264-2*) Wyndham Hall.
— Person in Cosmos: Metaphors of Meaning from Physics, Philosophy & Theology. 225p. (C). 1995. pap. text 20.00 (*1-55605-263-4*) Wyndham Hall.
O'Shea, Lawrence J., et al. Learning Disabilities. LC 97-28717. 480p. 1997. text 62.00 (*0-02-389321-4*) Macmillan.
O'Shea, M. Lester. A Cure Worse Than the Disease: Fighting Discrimination Through Government. Hallberg, Charles, ed. LC 99-95190. 288p. 1999. 24.95 (*0-87319-048-3*) Hallberg Pub Corp.
O'Shea, M. V., ed. The Child: His Nature & His Needs. LC 74-21424. (Classics in Child Development Ser.). (Illus.). 576p. 1975. reprint ed. 56.95 (*0-405-06473-X*) Ayer.
O'Shea, Marese. The True Story of The Vice Queen. 192p. 1997. pap. 11.95 (*1-86023-055-5*, Pub. by Martello Bks) Irish Amer Bk.
***O'Shea, Maria.** Iran. LC 98-87494. (Illus.). 1999. pap. 12.95 (*1-55868-403-4*) Gr Arts Ctr Pub.
O'Shea, Maria. Kuwait, 6 vols., Set. LC 98-25833. (Cultures of the World Ser.). 128p. (J). 1999. lib. bdg. 35.64 (*0-7614-0871-1*) Marshall Cavendish.
O'Shea, Marie L., ed. see Field, Richard, et al.
O'Shea, Mark. Reptiles & Amphibians. (C). 1992. 21.00 (*0-907649-52-1*, Pub. by Expedit Advisory Ctr) St Mut.
O'Shea, Maureen, jt. auth. see Gustafson, Helen.
O'Shea, Michael J. James Joyce & Heraldry. LC 85-26260. 196p. (C). 1986. pap. text 21.95 (*0-88706-270-9*) State U NY Pr.
O'Shea-Noonan, Mary-Beth. Hungry Grass. 48p. 1998. pap. 12.00 (*0-941895-14-9*) Amherst Wri Art.
O'Shea, Pat. The Hounds of the Morrigan. LC 98-31280. 688p. (YA). (gr. 6-12). 1999. mass mkt. 6.95 (*0-06-447205-1*, HarpTrophy) HarpC Child Bks.
— The Hounds of the Morrigan. LC 85-16435. 469p. (J). (gr. 6-12). 1986. 16.95 (*0-8234-0595-8*) Holiday.
— Quantum Strength & Power Training: (Gaining the Winning Edge) (Illus.). Date not set. write for info. (*0-9648698-0-2*) Patricks Bks.
O'Shea, Patrick G. & Bennett, Harold E., eds. Free-Electron Laser Challenges, Vol. 2988. LC 97-194517. 302p. 1997. 80.00 (*0-8194-2399-8*) SPIE.
O'Shea, Paul, jt. auth. see Wood, Kieron.
O'Shea, Peter V. Guide to Adirondack Trails: Northern Region. 2nd rev. ed. Burdick, Neal S., ed. LC 93-28566. (Forest Preserve Ser.: Vol. II). (Illus.). 256p. 1997. reprint ed. pap. 16.95 (*0-935272-63-1*) ADK Mtn Club.
***O'Shea, Raymond.** The Sand Kings of Oman: Being the Experiences of an R. A. F. Officer in the Little Known Regions of Trucial Oman Arabia. 228p. 2000. text 110.00 (*0-7103-0675-X*) Col U Pr.
O'Shea, Sean & Walker, Meryl. The Millennium Myth: The Ever-Ending Story. Brand, Nancy, ed. LC 98-23167. (Illus.). (Orig.). 1998. lib. bdg. 26.95 (*0-89334-274-2*) Humanics Ltd.
O'Shea, Shad. Beware...the Song Shark! (Illus.). 400p. (Orig.). 1990. pap. write for info. (*0-918243-01-7*) Positive Feedback Comns.
O'Shea, Stephen. Back to the Front: An Accidental Historian Walks the Trenches of World War I. 1998. pap. 12.50 (*0-380-73167-3*, Avon Bks) Morrow Avon.
— Back to the Front: An Accidental Historian Walks the Trenches of World War I. LC 97-6255. 216p. 1997. 23.00 (*0-8027-1329-7*) Walker & Co.
***O'Shea, Stephen.** The Perfect Heresy: The Revolutionary Life & Spectacular Death of the Medieval Cathars. (Illus.). 224p. 2000. 24.00 (*0-8027-1350-5*) Walker & Co.
O'Shea, Tim, jt. ed. see Scanlon, Eileen.
O'Shea, Timothy J. The U. S.-Japanese Semiconductor Problem. (Pew Case Studies in International Affairs). 86p. (C). 1995. pap. text 3.50 (*1-56927-139-9*) Geo U Inst Dplmcy.
O'Shea, Tracy & LaLonde, Jane. Sexual Harassment: A Practical Guide to the Law, Your Rights, & Your Options for Taking Action. LC 98-21654. 256p. 1998. pap. 12.95 (*0-312-19524-9*) St Martin.
***O'Shei, Tim.** The Detroit Red Wings Hockey Team. LC 99-53163. (Great Sports Teams Ser.). (Illus.). 48p. (YA). (gr. 4-10). 2000. lib. bdg. 18.95 (*0-7660-1282-4*) Enslow Pubs.
O'Shei, Tim. The Duke Blue Devils Men's Basketball Team. LC 98-35037. (Great Sports Teams Ser.). 48p. (YA). (gr. 4-10). 1999. lib. bdg. 18.95 (*0-7660-1213-1*) Enslow Pubs.
***O'Shei, Tim.** Ulysses S. Grant. (Famous Figures of the Civil War Era Ser.). (Illus.). 2000. pap. 8.95 (*0-7910-6139-6*) Chelsea Hse.
— Ulysses S. Grant. LC 00-38393. (Famous Figures of the Civil War Era Ser.). (Illus.). 2000. 18.95 (*0-7910-6001-2*) Chelsea Hse.
***O'Sheilds, Dale.** Steps to Freedom. 192p. 2000. pap. 10.99 (*1-930027-10-9*, 921-026, Pub. by Insght Pub) BookWorld.
Osher & Ward. Learning for the 21st Century. 5th ed. 344p. (C). 1998. per. 32.95 (*0-7872-4742-1*, 41474201) Kendall-Hunt.
Osher, Bill & Ward, Joann. Engineering Success. 256p. (C). 1994. pap. text, spiral bd. 29.95 (*0-7872-0049-2*) Kendall-Hunt.
Osher-Kellogg. A Parent's Resource Guide to College. 192p. (C). 1998. per. 6.33 (*0-7872-5066-X*, 41506601) Kendall-Hunt.
Osher, Ron, jt. auth. see Shortz, Will.
Osher, S. J. Two Papers on Similarity of Certain Volterra Integral Operators. LC 52-42839. (Memoirs of the American Mathematical Society Ser.: No. 73). 47p. 1967. pap. 16.00 (*0-8218-1273-4*, MEMO/1/73C) Am Math.
Osherenko, Gail & Young, Oran R. The Age of the Arctic: Hot Conflicts & Cold Realities. (Studies in Polar Research). (Illus.). 336p. (C). 1989. text 85.00 (*0-521-36451-5*) Cambridge U Pr.
Osherenko, Gail, jt. auth. see Golovnev, Andrei V.
Osherenko, Gail, jt. ed. see Young, Oran R.
Osheroff, Neil, jt. auth. see Bjornsti, Mary-Ann.
Osherov, V. I., jt. auth. see Medvedev, E. S.
***Osherow, Jacqueline.** Dead Men's Praise: Poems. LC 99-25483. 112p. 1999. pap. 13.00 (*0-8021-3654-0*, Grove) Grove-Atltic.
Osherow, Jacqueline. Looking for Angels in New York. LC 88-4797. (Contemporary Poetry Ser.). 72p. 1988. 14.95 (*0-8203-1059-X*) U of Ga Pr.
— With a Moon in Transit. LC 96-18201. 96p. 1996. 18.00 (*0-8021-1599-3*, Grove) Grove-Atltic.
Osherson. Passions of Fatherhood. Date not set. pap. write for info. (*0-449-91071-7*) Fawcett.
Osherson, Daniel N., et al, eds. An Invitation to Cognitive Science Vol. 1: Language. 2nd ed. (Illus.). 500p. 1995. 55.00 (*0-262-15044-1*, Bradford Bks); pap. text 27.50 (*0-262-65044-4*, Bradford Bks) MIT Pr.
Osherson, Daniel N. & Kosslyn, Stephen M., eds. An Invitation to Cognitive Science Vol. 2: Visual Cognition. 2nd ed. (Illus.). 400p. 1995. 50.00 (*0-262-15042-5*, Bradford Bks); pap. text 25.00 (*0-262-65042-8*, Bradford Bks) MIT Pr.
Osherson, Daniel N. & Smith, Edward E., eds. An Invitation to Cognitive Science Vol. 3: Thinking. 2nd ed. (Illus.). 400p. 1995. 55.00 (*0-262-15043-3*, Bradford Bks); pap. text 27.50 (*0-262-65043-6*, Bradford Bks) MIT Pr.
Osherson, Samuel. The Hidden Wisdom of Parents. LC 99-35388. 352p. 1999. 22.95 (*1-58062-164-3*) Adams Media.
Osherson, Samuel D. Finding Our Fathers: How a Man's Life is Shaped by His Relationship with His Father. 1987. pap. 12.00 (*0-449-90247-1*, Columbine) Fawcett.
— Wrestling with Love: How Men Struggle with Intimacy. 496p. 1993. pap. 12.00 (*0-449-90826-7*, Columbine) Fawcett.
O'Shiel, Eda, tr. see Buytendijk, Frederik J.
O'Shields, French. Slaying the Giant: Practical Help for Understanding Preventing & Overcoming Depression. 145p. (Orig.). 1998. reprint ed. pap. 9.95 (*0-9641901-0-9*) Hem Of His Garment.
***Oshige, Kotaro.** Konvergenz der Interessenvertretungen Durch Globalisierung? Ein Vergleich der Funktionsmechanismen der Arbeitnehmer-interessenvertretungssysteme in Deutschland und Japan Am Beispiel der Elektroindustrie. (Arbeit - Technik - Organisation - Soziales Ser.: Bd. 8). 225p. 1999. 37.95 (*3-631-35580-7*) P Lang Pubng.
Oshii, Mamoru. Panzer Cops. (Hellhounds Ser.). (Illus.). 1997. pap. text 14.95 (*1-56971-256-5*) Dark Horse Comics.
Oshikoya, Temitope W. The Nigerian Economy: A Macroeconometric & Input-Output Model. LC 89-16352. 203p. 1990. 57.95 (*0-275-93417-9*, C317, Greenwood Pr) Greenwood.
Oshima, A., jt. ed. see Tominaga, S.
Oshima, Alice. Writing Academic English. 2nd ed. 288p. 1991. pap. text 25.73 (*0-201-51409-5*) Addison-Wesley.
Oshima, Alice & Hogue, Ann. Introduction to Academic Writing. 2nd ed. LC 96-36704. 240p. 1996. pap. text 27.18 (*0-201-69509-X*) Addison-Wesley.
— Writing Academic English: A Writing & Sentence Structure Handbook. 3rd ed. LC 98-23607. 288p. 1998. pap. text 26.00 (*0-201-34054-2*) Addison-Wesley.
Oshima, Alice, jt. auth. see Hogue, Oshimal A.
Oshima, E. & Van Rijn, C. F. Production Control in the Process Industry: Proceedings of the IFAC Workshop, Osaka, 29-31 October 1989 & Kariya, Japan, 1-2 November 1989. (IFAC Workshop Ser.: No. 9008). 258p. 1991. 142.00 (*0-08-036929-4*, Pergamon Pr) Elsevier.
Oshima, H., et al. Gastrokamera- und Roentgendiagnostik: Ein Atlas der kombinierten Magenuntersuchung mit histologischer Dokumentation. (Illus.). xii, 140p. (C). 1972. 226.95 (*3-11-001687-7*) De Gruyter.
Oshima, Harry T. Economic Growth in Monsoon Asia: A Comparative Study. 320p. 1987. 54.50 (*0-86008-402-7*, Pub. by U of Tokyo) Col U Pr.
— Strategic Processes in Monsoon Asia's Economic Development. LC 92-33545. (Studies in Development). 352p. (C). 1993. text 55.00 (*0-8018-4479-7*) Johns Hopkins.
Oshima, K., jt. ed. see Hafez, M.
Oshima, Mark, tr. see Nakamura, Matazo.
Oshima, Minoru. Ki Points: How to Enhance Your Daily Life from a Martial Artist's Perspective. LC 95-94877. (Illus.). 180p. (Orig.). 1996. pap. 14.00 (*0-9648172-0-9*) Kodokai Aikido.
Oshima, Nagisa. Cinema, Censorship, & the State: The Writings of Nagisa Oshima. Lawson, Dawn, tr. (October Bks.). (Illus.). 320p. 1992. 42.50 (*0-262-15040-9*) MIT Pr.
— Cinema, Censorship, & the State: The Writings of Nagisa Oshima. 320p. 1993. pap. text 21.00 (*0-262-65039-8*) MIT Pr.
Oshinsky, Carole. Young Children in Poverty: An Annotated Bibliography of Books & Reports, 1995. 80p. (Orig.). 1995. pap. text 12.00 (*0-926582-15-1*) NCCP.
Oshinsky, Carole J. & Goodman, Barbara. Building Bright Futures: An Annotated Bibliography of Substance Abuse Prevention for Families with Young Children. 51p. (C). 1999. reprint ed. pap. text 20.00 (*0-7881-8135-1*) DIANE Pub.
Oshinsky, Carole J., et al. Building Bright Futures: An Annotated Bibliography on Substance Abuse Prevention for Families with Young Children. LC 96-15063. 52p. 1996. pap. 8.00 (*0-926582-19-4*) NCCP.
Oshinsky, David M. The Darkest Corner of the South. 1996. 23.99 (*0-02-923495-6*) Free Pr.
— Worse Than Slavery: Parchman Farm & the Ordeal of Jim Crow Justice. 320p. 1997. per. 12.00 (*0-684-83095-7*) S&S Trade Pap.
Oshinsky, David M., et al. The Case of the Nazi Professor. LC 88-16895. 220p. (C). 1989. text 35.00 (*0-8135-1363-4*); pap. text 15.00 (*0-8135-1427-4*) Rutgers U Pr.
Oshinsky, Jerold & Howard, Theodore A. Practitioner's Guide to Litigating Insurance Coverage Actions, Set. 2nd ed. LC 97-39117. 1998. 360.00 (*1-56706-678-X*) Aspen Law.
Oshinsky, Jerold, et al. A Practitioner's Guide to Litigating Insurance Coverage Actions, 3 vols. LC 94-11950. 2254p. 1998. ring bd. 295.00 (*0-13-128166-6*) Aspen Law.
Oshiro, tr. see Ryokan.
Oshiro, Hide, tr. see Akiko, Yosano.
Oshiro, Kathy. Growing Fruits, Herbs, Nuts & Seeds in Hawaii: A How-To Guide for the Gardener. (Illus.). 80p. 2000. pap. 14.95 (*1-57306-109-3*) Bess Pr.
— Growing Vegetables in Hawaii: A How-To Guide for the Gardener. (Illus.). 96p. 1999. pap. 14.95 (*1-57306-080-1*) Bess Pr.
Oshiyama, O., jt. ed. see Kamimura, Hiroshi.
Osho. After Middle Age: A Limitless Sky. Amoore, Mary, ed. (Introduction to the Teachings of Osho Ser.). 96p. 1992. 6.95 (*0-918963-02-8*) Oshos.
— And Now, & Here. (Orig.). pap. 18.95 (*0-8464-4856-4*) Beekman Pubs.
— And Now, & Here, Vol. II. Vedant, Swami S., ed. LC 84-42798. (Early Writings & Discourses Ser.). 384p. (Orig.). 1985. pap. 4.95 (*0-88050-712-8*) Oshos.
— And Now, & Here: On Death, Dying & Past Lives. 181p. 1995. pap. 15.95 (*0-85207-286-4*, Pub. by C W Daniel) Natl Bk Netwk.
— And the Flowers Showered: Discourses on Zen. Nirgun, Ma A., ed. (Zen Ser.). 256p. 1992. 14.95 (*81-7261-002-5*, Pub. by Rebel Hse) Oshos.
— At the Feet of the Master. Sarito, Ma D., ed. (Initiation Talks Ser.). (Illus.). 404p. 1993. 24.95 (*3-89338-112-0*, Pub. by Rebel Hse) Oshos.
***Osho.** Autobiography of a Spiritually Incorrect Mystic. LC 00-26692. (Illus.). 288p. 2000. text 25.95 (*0-312-25457-1*) St Martin.
Osho. Be Still & Know. Anurag, Ma Y., ed. (Questions & Answers Ser.). (Illus.). 364p. (Orig.). 1981. pap. 14.95 (*0-88050-511-7*) Oshos.
— Behind a Thousand Names: Talks on the Nirvana Upanishad. LC 98-100803. 372p. 1996. 15.95 (*81-7261-015-7*, Pub. by Rebel Pub) Oshos.
— Bodhidharma, the Greatest Zen Master. Sarito, Ma D. & Gitika, Ma D., eds. LC 97-208510. (Zen Ser.). (Illus.). 780p. 1988. 21.95 (*3-89338-025-6*, Pub. by Rebel Hse) Oshos.
— A Book of Five Rings: Keys to Love & Meditation. abr. ed. 1990. pap. 10.95 incl. audio (*1-55927-088-8*) Audio Renaissance.
— A Book of Secrets. LC 98-14424. 1184p. 1998. pap. 35.00 (*0-312-18058-6*) St Martin.
— Book of Secrets: Keys to Love & Meditation. abr. ed. 1998. pap. text 16.95 incl. audio (*1-55927-486-7*) Audio Renaissance.
— The Book of the Books, Vol. 3. Karima, Ma P., ed. LC 82-50462. (Buddha Ser.). 352p. (Orig.). 1984. pap. 4.95 (*0-88050-515-X*) Oshos.
— The Book of the Books, Vol. 4. Krishna, P., ed. LC 82-50462. (Buddha Ser.). 384p. (Orig.). 1985. pap. 4.95 (*0-88050-516-8*) Oshos.
— The Book of the Secrets, Vol. IV. 2nd ed. Rajneesh Foundation International Staff, ed. LC 75-36733. (Tantra Ser.). 408p. 1982. pap. 3.95 (*0-88050-528-1*) Oshos.
— The Book of the Secrets: Discourses on "Vigyana Bhairava Tantra" LC 77-356775. 1976. write for info. (*0-500-27076-7*) Thames Hudson.
— The Book of Wisdom, Vol. 2. Prabhu, K., ed. LC 82-23142. (Atisha Ser.). 416p. (Orig.). 1984. pap. 5.95 (*0-88050-531-1*) Oshos.
— The Book of Wisdom: Discourses on Atisha's Seven Points of Mind Training. Prabhu, K., ed. (Atisha Ser.). 545p. 1993. 24.95 (*3-89338-117-1*, Pub. by Rebel Hse) Oshos.
***Osho.** Book of Wisdom: The Heart of Tibetan Buddhism. 2000. 27.50 (*1-86204-734-0*, Pub. by Element MA) Penguin Putnam.
Osho. The Buddha: The Emptiness of the Heart. Sarito, Deva & Ashik, Deva, eds. LC 97-221764. (Zen Ser.). (Illus.). 288p. 1989. 12.95 (*3-89338-055-8*, Pub. by Rebel Hse) Oshos.
— Christianity the Deadliest Poison & Zen the Antidote to All Poisons. Prabhu, Krishna, ed. (Zen Ser.). 340p. 1990. 21.95 (*3-89338-071-X*, Pub. by Rebel Hse) Oshos.
— Come, Come, Yet Again Come. Sagar, Ma D., ed. (Questions & Answers Ser.). 301p. 1991. 21.95 (*3-89338-108-2*, Pub. by Rebel Hse) Oshos.
— Communism & Zen Fire, Zen Wind. Ma Deva Sarito & Ma Shivam Suvarna, eds. LC 97-210575. (Zen Ser.). 338p. 1990. 21.95 (*3-89338-072-8*, Pub. by Rebel Hse) Oshos.
— Courage: The Joy of Living Dangerously. LC 99-16439. (Insights for a New Way of Living Ser.). 208p. 1999. pap. 11.95 (*0-312-20517-1*) St Martin.
— Creativity: Unleashing the Forces Within. LC 99-32895. (Insights for a New Way of Living Ser.). 208p. 1999. pap. 11.95 (*0-312-20519-8*) St Martin.
— A Cup of Tea. 4th rev. ed. LC 97-228306. (Illus.). 293p. 1980. 12.95 (*81-7261-013-0*, Pub. by Rebel Pub) Oshos.
— Death: The Greatest Fiction. LC 97-904070. (C). 1997. write for info. (*81-207-1951-4*) Sterling Pubs.
— The Dhammapada: The Way of the Buddha, 12 vols. Prabhu, Krishna, ed. Incl. 1991. (*3-89338-091-4*); 1991. (*3-89338-092-2*); 1991. (*3-89338-093-0*); 1991. (*3-89338-094-9*); 1991. (*3-89338-095-7*); 1991. (*3-89338-096-5*); 1991. (*3-89338-097-3*); 1991. (*3-89338-098-1*); 1991. (*3-89338-099-X*); 1991. 1991. (*3-89338-101-5*); 1991. (*3-89338-102-3*); (Buddha Ser.). 3149p. 1991. Set boxed set 99.00 (*0-685-50849-8*, Pub. by Rebel Hse) Oshos.
— Dimensions Beyond the Known. 2nd ed. Prem, Ananda, ed. Chit, Sadhu A. & Arup, Prem, trs. (Early Talks Ser.). 200p. 1990. 14.95 (*3-89338-061-2*, Pub. by Rebel Hse) Oshos.
— The Discipline of Transcendence, 4 vols. Anurag, Ma Y. et al, eds. LC 78-906087. (Buddha Ser.). (Illus.). (Orig.). 1978. 14.95 (*0-88050-047-6*); 14.95 (*0-88050-048-4*) Oshos.
— Dogen, the Zen Master: A Search & a Fulfillment. Burt, Anand, ed. LC 98-103007. (Zen Ser.). 204p. 1989. 14.95 (*3-89338-063-9*, Pub. by Rebel Hse) Oshos.
— Don't Let Yourself Be Upset by the Sutra: Rather Upset the Sutra Yourself. Prabhu, K., ed. LC 85-43054. (Initiation Talks Ser.). 560p. (Orig.). 1985. pap. 5.95 (*0-88050-584-2*) Oshos.
— Don't Look Before You Leap. Rajneesh Foundation International Staff, ed. LC 83-3282. (Initiation Talks Ser.). 480p. (Orig.). 1983. pap. 4.95 (*0-88050-554-0*) Oshos.
— The Empty Boat: Talks on the Sayings of Chuang Tzu. Prabhu, K., ed. (Tao Ser.). 326p. 1993. 18.95 (*3-89338-118-X*, Pub. by Rebel Hse) Oshos.
— Enlightenment: The Only Revolution: Discourses on the Great Mystic Ashtavakra. LC 98-100802. 405p. 1997. 15.95 (*81-7261-070-X*, Pub. by Rebel Pub) Oshos.
— Evening Contemplations. 2000. pap. 16.95 (*0-312-24562-9*) St Martin.
— The Everyday Meditator. (Illus.). 216p. 1993. pap. 16.95 (*0-8048-1976-9*) Tuttle Pubng.
— Finger Pointing to the Moon. 1994. pap. 13.95 (*1-85230-598-3*, Pub. by Element MA) Penguin Putnam.

O

An Asterisk (*) at the beginning of an entry indicates that the title is appearing for the first time.

— Finger Pointing to the Moon: Discourses on the Adhyatma Upanishad. 471p. 1994. 26.95 (*3-89338-138-4*, Pub. by Rebel Hse) Oshos.

— The First Principle. Chinmaya, P., ed. LC 83-179587. (Zen Ser.). (Illus.). 386p. (Orig.). 1979. 14.95 (*0-88050-061-1*) Oshos.

— From Bondage to Freedom: Answers to the Seekers of the Path. Devaraj, ed. (Talks in America Ser.). 512p. 1992. 24.95 (*3-89338-073-6*, Pub. by Rebel Hse) Oshos.

— From Darkness to Light. Devaraj, Sambuddha S. & Maneesha, Sambodhi M., eds. LC 97-208945. (Talks in America Ser.). 408p. 1988. 24.95 (*3-89338-020-5*, Pub. by Rebel Hse) Oshos.

— From Medication to Meditation. Date not set. pap. 29.95 (*0-8464-4390-2*) Beekman Pubs.

— From Medication to Meditation. LC 97-208522. 184p. 1995. pap. 19.95 (*0-85207-280-5*, Pub. by C W Daniel) Natl Bk Netwk.

— From Sex to Super Consciousness. 4th ed. (Illus.). 178p. Date not set. 12.95 (*81-7261-010-6*, Pub. by Rebel Pub) Oshos.

— From the False to the Truth: Answers to the Seekers of the Path. Sambodhi Ma Prem Maneesha & Ma Shivan Suvarna, eds. LC 97-208941. (Talks in America Ser.). 388p. 1988. 24.95 (*3-89338-022-1*, Pub. by Rebel Hse) Oshos.

— Glimpses of a Golden Childhood: The Rebellious Childhood of a Great Enlightened One. 3rd ed. (Illus.). 561p. 1997. 26.95 (*81-7261-072-6*, Pub. by Rebel Pub) Oshos.

— God Is Dead: Now Zen Is the Only Living Truth. Robin, Anand, ed. LC 98-102984. (Zen Ser.). 320p. 1992. 18.95 (*3-89338-081-7*, Pub. by Rebel Hse) Oshos.

— God's Got a Thing about You. Maneesha, Ma P., ed. LC 83-11237. (Initiation Talks Ser.). 576p. (Orig.). 1983. pap. 4.95 (*0-88050-568-0*) Oshos.

— The Golden Future. Bodhisattva Ma Nisango & Ma Prem Taranga, eds. (Mystery School Ser.). 414p. 1987. 24.95 (*3-89338-017-5*, Pub. by Rebel Hse) Oshos.

— The Goose Is Out. 2nd ed. 257p. (Orig.). 1982. 13.95 (*81-7261-014-9*, Pub. by Rebel Pub) Oshos.

— The Great Challenge. Robin, A., ed. (Early Talks Ser.). 220p. 1993. 11.95 (*81-7261-007-6*, Pub. by Rebel Pub) Oshos.

— The Great Pilgrimage: From Here to Here. Prabhu, Krishna & Taranga, Ma P., eds. LC 97-213738. (Questions & Answer Ser.). 356p. 1988. 21.95 (*3-89338-016-7*, Pub. by Rebel Hse) Oshos.

— Great Secret: Talks on the Songs of Kabir. Prem, Krishna, ed. LC 97-221809. (Kabir Ser.). 384p. 1992. 17.95 (*3-89338-087-6*, Pub. by Rebel Hse) Oshos.

— The Great Zen Master Ta Hui. Prabhu, Krishna et al, eds. LC 97-213903. (Zen Ser.). 544p. 1988. 24.95 (*3-89338-027-2*, Pub. by Rebel Hse) Oshos.

— Hari Om Tat Sat: The Divine Sound That Is the Truth. Suvarna, Ma S., ed. LC 97-210577. (Mantra Ser.). (Illus.). 328p. 1989. 21.95 (*3-89338-046-9*, Pub. by Rebel Hse) Oshos.

— The Heart Sutra: Discourse on Prajnaparamita Hridayam Sutra of Gautama the Buddha. LC 94-220966. 2000. pap. 16.95 (*1-85230-477-4*, Pub. by Element MA) Penguin Putnam.

— The Heart Sutra: Discourses on the Prajnaparamita Hridayam Suntra of Buddha. (Illus.). 285p. 1980. 26.95 (*3-89338-136-8*, Pub. by Rebel Hse) Oshos.

— Heartbeat of the Absolute: Commentaries on the Ishavasya Upanishad. 1994. pap. 13.95 (*1-85230-476-6*, Pub. by Element MA) Penguin Putnam.

— Heartbeat of the Absolute: Discourses on the Ishavasya Upanishad. 2nd ed. (Illus.). 321p. 1980. 26.95 (*3-89338-134-1*, Pub. by Rebel Hse) Oshos.

— The Hidden Harmony: Discourses on the Fragments of Heraclitus. Prabhu, K., ed. 233p. 1991. 21.95 (*3-89338-110-4*, Pub. by Rebel Hse) Oshos.

— Hidden Mysteries. LC 99-180529. (Illus.). 234p. 1997. 12.95 (*81-7261-008-4*, Pub. by Rebel Pub) Oshos.

— The Hidden Splendor. Ma Deva Sarito & Ma Prem Lisa, eds. (Mystery School Ser.). 332p. 1987. 21.95 (*3-89338-019-1*, Pub. by Rebel Hse) Oshos.

— Hsin Hsin Ming: The Book of Nothing. 3rd rev. ed. (Illus.). 276p. Date not set. 12.95 (*81-7261-003-3*, Pub. by Rebel Pub) Oshos.

— Hyakujo: The Everest of Zen: The Present Day Awakened One Speaks on the Ancient Masters of Zen. (Zen Ser.). 202p. 1989. 14.95 (*3-89338-066-3*, Pub. by Rebel Hse) Oshos.

— I Am That. Apa, Ma P., ed. LC 84-42809. (Upanishads Ser.). 416p. (Orig.). 1984. pap. 5.95 (*0-88050-580-X*) Oshos.

— I Am the Gate. Sagar, Ma D., ed. (Esoteric Ser.). 239p. 1991. 14.95 (*3-89338-088-4*, Pub. by Rebel Hse) Oshos.

— I Celebrate Myself: God Is No Where: Life Is Now Here. Sagar, Dhyan, ed. (Zen Ser.). 304p. 1992. 18.95 (*3-89338-079-5*, Pub. by Rebel Hse) Oshos.

— In Search of the Miraculous. 276p. write for info. (*0-85207-303-8*, Pub. by C W Daniel) Natl Bk Netwk.

— India My Love: Fragments of a Golden Past. LC 97-219132. (Illus.). 189p. 1997. 21.95 (*81-7261-006-8*, Pub. by Rebel Pub) Oshos.

— The Inner Journey. LC 98-103012. 270p. 1997. 13.95 (*81-7261-019-X*, Pub. by Rebel Pub) Oshos.

— The Invitation. Sagar, Ma D. & Robin, Anand, eds. (Mystery School Ser.). 384p. 1988. 21.95 (*3-89338-035-3*, Pub. by Rebel Hse) Oshos.

— Isan: No Footprints in the Blue Sky: The Present Day Awakened One Speaks on the Ancient Masters of Zen. Prabhu, Krishna, ed. LC 98-102999. (Zen Ser.). 202p. 1989. 14.95 (*3-89338-070-1*, Pub. by Rebel Hse) Oshos.

— Jesus Crucified Again, This Time in Ronald Reagan's America. Sarito, Ma D., ed. (Compilation Ser.). 320p. 1988. 18.95 (*3-89338-039-6*, Pub. by Rebel Hse) Oshos.

— Joshu: The Lion's Roar: The Present Day Awakened One Speaks on the Ancient Masters of Zen. Ma Deva Sarito & Sushil, Prem, eds. (Zen Ser.). 198p. 1989. 14.95 (*3-89338-068-X*, Pub. by Rebel Hse) Oshos.

— Journey to the Heart. 1994. pap. 13.95 (*1-85230-595-9*, Pub. by Element MA) Penguin Putnam.

— Journey to the Heart. 4th ed. 258p. 1976. 26.95 (*3-89338-141-4*, Pub. by Rebel Hse) Oshos.

— Just Around the Corner. Mahasattva, K., ed. LC 84-42870. (Initiation Talks Ser.). 224p. (Orig.). 1984. pap. 3.95 (*0-88050-588-5*) Oshos.

— Just Like That: Talks on Sufism. Prabhu, K., ed. (Sufi Ser.). 455p. 1993. 24.95 (*3-89338-113-9*, Pub. by Rebel Hse) Oshos.

— Krishna: The Man & His Philosophy. Sambuddha, A., ed. LC 85-43055. (Early Writings & Discourses Ser.). 880p. 1985. pap. 5.95 (*0-88050-713-6*) Oshos.

— Kyozan: A True Man of Zen. Robin, Anand, ed. (Zen Ser.). 95p. 1992. 14.95 (*3-89338-080-9*, Pub. by Rebel Hse) Oshos.

— The Language of Existence. Suvarna, Ma S., ed. LC 97-208506. (Zen Ser.). (Illus.). 288p. 1989. 12.95 (*3-89338-054-X*, Pub. by Rebel Hse) Oshos.

— The Last Testament, Vol. I. Prabhu, K. et al, eds. LC 85-63289. (Interview Ser.). (Illus.). 832p. (Orig.). (C). 1986. pap. 14.95 (*0-88050-250-9*) Oshos.

— Light on the Path. (Talks in the Himalayas Ser.). 416p. 1988. 24.95 (*3-89338-030-2*, Pub. by Rebel Hse) Oshos.

— The Long & the Short & the All. Prabhu, K., ed. LC 84-42806. (Early Writings & Discourses Ser.). 320p. 1984. pap. 4.95 (*0-88050-708-X*) Oshos.

— Ma Tzu: The Empty Mirror: The Present Day Awakened One Speaks on the Ancient Masters of Zen. Ashik, Deva, ed. LC 98-103005. (Zen Ser.). 202p. 1989. 14.95 (*3-89338-065-5*, Pub. by Rebel Hse) Oshos.

— Maturity: The Responsibilty of Being Oneself. LC 99-32893. 208p. 1999. pap. 11.95 (*0-312-20561-9*, St Martins Paperbacks) St Martin.

— Meditation: The Art of Ecstasy. Ma Prem Mangla, ed. 302p. 1992. 11.95 (*81-7261-000-9*, Pub. by Rebel Hse) Oshos.

— Meditation: The First & Last Freedom. LC 96-9227. 304p. 1996. text 22.95 (*0-312-14820-8*) St Martin.

— The Messiah: Commentaries on Kahlil Gibran's the Prophet, Vol. 1. Sarito, Dhyan, ed. 520p. (Orig.). 1987. 27.95 (*3-89338-002-7*, Pub. by Rebel Hse) Oshos.

— The Messiah: Commentaries on Kahlil Gibran's the Prophet, Vol. 1. Sarito, Dhyan, ed. (Mystery School Ser.). 520p. (Orig.). 1987. pap. 14.95 (*3-89338-009-4*, Pub. by Rebel Hse) Oshos.

— The Messiah: Commentaries on Kahlil Gibran's the Prophet, Vol. 2. Taranga, Ma P. & Melissa, Ma P., eds. (Mystery School Ser.). 519p. (Orig.). 1987. 27.95 (*3-89338-003-5*, Pub. by Rebel Hse); pap. 14.95 (*3-89338-010-8*, Pub. by Rebel Hse) Oshos.

— The Miracle. LC 97-208944. (Zen Ser.). 288p. 1989. 12.95 (*3-89338-053-1*, Pub. by Rebel Hse) Oshos.

— Morning Contemplations. 1999. pap. 16.95 (*0-312-24505-X*) St Martin.

— The Mustard Seed: Commentaries on the Fifth Gospel of St. Thomas. 6th ed. (Illus.). 498p. 1975. reprint ed. 26.95 (*3-89338-137-6*, Pub. by Rebel Hse) Oshos.

— Mustard Seed: Discourses on the Sayings of Jesus from the Gospel According to Thomas. 6th ed. 1994. pap. 14.95 (*1-85230-498-7*, Pub. by Element MA) Penguin Putnam.

— My Way, the Way of White Clouds. 192p. 1995. pap. 14.95 (*1-85230-699-8*, Pub. by Element MA) Penguin Putnam.

— The Mysteries of Life & Death. Bisen, Malini, tr. from HIN. 1978. reprint ed. pap. 3.50 (*0-89684-045-X*, Pub. by Motilal Bnarsidass) S Asia.

— Nansen: The Point of Departure: The Present Day Awakened One Speaks on the Ancient Masters of Zen. Robin, Anand, ed. (Zen Ser.). 206p. 1989. 14.95 (*3-89338-067-1*, Pub. by Rebel Hse) Oshos.

— The New Dawn. LC 97-214025. (Mystery School Ser.). 432p. 1989. 21.95 (*3-89338-023-X*, Pub. by Rebel Hse) Oshos.

— No Mind the Flowers of Eternity. Sarito, Deva & Robin, Anand, eds. LC 97-212702. (Zen Ser.). (Illus.). 276p. 1992. 21.95 (*3-89338-060-4*, Pub. by Rebel Hse) Oshos.

— No Water No Moon. 6th ed. (Illus.). 275p. 1977. reprint ed. 26.95 (*3-89338-135-X*, Pub. by Rebel Hse) Oshos.

— No Water, No Moon: Talks on Zen Stories. 1994. pap. 13.95 (*1-85230-490-1*, Pub. by Element MA) Penguin Putnam.

— Nowhere to Go but In. LC 97-220014. 373p. 1995. 15.95 (*81-7261-017-3*, Pub. by Rebel Pub) Oshos.

— Om Mani Padme Hum: The Sound of Silence: The Diamond in the Lotus. Sarito, Deva, ed. LC 97-220030. (Mantra Ser.). (Illus.). 242p. 1990. 21.95 (*3-89338-050-7*, Pub. by Rebel Hse) Oshos.

— Om Shantih Shantih Shantih: The Soundless Sound Peace, Peace, Peace. Sagar, Dhyan & Nirvesha, Deva, eds. LC 97-219998. (Mantra Ser.). (Illus.). 290p. 1990. 19.95 (*3-89338-048-5*, Pub. by Rebel Hse) Oshos.

— One Seed Makes the Whole Earth Green. Robin, Anand, ed. LC 97-221790. (Zen Ser.). 192p. 1992. 14.95 (*3-89338-077-9*, Pub. by Rebel Hse) Oshos.

— The Original Man. LC 97-208943. (Zen Ser.). xii, 231p. 1997. 12.95 (*3-89338-056-6*, Pub. by Rebel Hse) Oshos.

— Osho Neo Tarot. (Illus.). 85p. 1986. pap. 19.95 (*3-89338-129-5*, Pub. by Rebel Hse) Oshos.

— The OSHO No Book. 150p. 1989. 12.95 (*3-89338-047-7*, Pub. by Rebel Hse) Oshos.

— The Osho Transformation Tarot: Insights & Parables for Renewal in Everyday Life. LC 99-38828. 180p. 1999. text 24.95 (*0-312-24530-0*) St Martin.

— The Path of Love: Commentaries on the Songs of Kabir. 2nd ed. (Illus.). 306p. 1997. reprint ed. 13.95 (*81-7261-075-0*, Pub. by Rebel Pub) Oshos.

— The Path of Meditation: A Step by Step Guide to Meditation. Bharti, Pratap, tr. from HIN. Orig. Title: Dhyan Sutra. (Illus.). 262p. 1997. 12.95 (*81-7261-071-8*, Pub. by Rebel Pub) Oshos.

— The Perfect Master, 2 vols., Vol. 1. Anurag, Ma Y., ed. LC 83-172954. (Sufi Ser.). (Illus.). 1980. 14.95 (*0-88050-113-8*) Oshos.

— The Perfect Master, Vol. 2. Anurag, Ma Y., ed. LC 83-172954. (Sufi Ser.). (Illus.). 1980. 14.95 (*0-88050-114-6*) Oshos.

— The Psychology of the Esoteric. 3rd ed. Prem, Anand et al, eds. (Psychology Ser.). 184p. 1994. 12.95 (*3-89338-123-6*, Pub. by Rebel Hse) Oshos.

— The Rainbow Bridge. Prabhu, Krishna, ed. LC 85-42535. (Initiation Talks Ser.). 368p. (Orig.). (C). 1985. pap. 4.95 (*0-88050-618-0*) Oshos.

— The Rajneesh Bible, Vol. II. Rajneesh Academy Staff, ed. LC 85-42539. 839p. (Orig.). 1985. pap. 14.95 (*0-88050-201-0*) Oshos.

— The Rajneesh Bible, Vol. III. Rajneesh Academy Staff, ed. LC 85-42539. (Talks in America Ser.). 1072p. (Orig.). 1985. pap. 14.95 (*0-88050-202-9*) Oshos.

— The Rajneesh Bible, Vol. IV. LC 85-42539. (Illus.). 800p. (Orig.). (C). 1987. pap. 14.95 (*3-907757-02-5*) Oshos.

— The Razor's Edge. Bodhisattva Ma Deva Barkha, ed. (Mystery School Ser.). 374p. 1987. 21.95 (*3-89338-015-9*, Pub. by Rebel Hse) Oshos.

— The Rebel. Mahasattva Geet Govind, ed. LC 98-102986. (Questions & Answers Ser.). 358p. 1989. 21.95 (*3-89338-021-3*, Pub. by Rebel Hse) Oshos.

— The Rebellious Spirit. Prabhu, Krishna et al, eds. LC 87-42814. (Mystery School Ser.). 325p. (Orig.). 1987. pap. 14.95 (*3-907757-16-5*) Oshos.

— Returning to the Source: Talks on Zen. 192p. 1995. pap. 14.95 (*1-85230-700-5*, Pub. by Element MA) Penguin Putnam.

— Revolution, Rebellion & Religiousness. LC 89-82415. 176p. (Orig.). 1990. pap. 12.95 (*0-941404-63-3*) New Falcon Pubns.

— Rinzai: Master of the Irrational: The Present Day Awakened One Speaks on the Ancient Masters of Zen. Prabhu, Krishna, ed. LC 98-100354. (Zen Ser.). 202p. 1989. 14.95 (*3-89338-069-8*, Pub. by Rebel Hse) Oshos.

— Sacred Yes. Maneesha, Ma P., ed. LC 83-17665. (Initiation Talks Ser.). 448p. (Orig.). 1983. pap. 4.95 (*0-88050-624-5*) Oshos.

— Sat Chit Anand: Truth - Consciousness - Bliss. (Mantra Ser.). 416p. 1989. 21.95 (*3-89338-042-6*, Pub. by Rebel Hse) Oshos.

— Satyam Shivam Sundram: Truth - Godliness - Beauty. Prabhu, Krishna & Shabda, Ma V., eds. LC 97-219991. (Mantra Ser.). (Illus.). 368p. 1989. 21.95 (*3-89338-031-0*, Pub. by Rebel Hse) Oshos.

— The Search: Talks on the Ten Bulls of Zen. Anurag, Ma Yoga, ed. (Zen Ser.). 320p. 1993. 19.95 (*3-89338-116-3*, Pub. by Rebel Hse) Oshos.

— The Secrets, Bk. 4. 1981. pap. 5.95 (*0-06-090885-8*) HarpC.

— Seeds of Wisdom. rev. ed. LC 97-221796. 192p. 1997. 12.95 (*81-7261-018-1*, Pub. by Rebel Pub) Oshos.

— The Shadow of the Bamboo. Maneesha, Ma P., ed. LC 84-42807. (Initiation Talks Ser.). 240p. (Orig.). 1984. pap. 3.95 (*0-88050-630-X*) Oshos.

— Snap Your Fingers, Slap Your Face & Wake Up! Sarito, Ma D., ed. LC 84-43011. (Initiation Talks Ser.). 256p. (Orig.). 1984. pap. 3.95 (*0-88050-632-6*) Oshos.

— Socrates Poisoned Again after 25 Centuries. Lisa, M. P. & Sarar, M. D., eds. LC 97-220000. (Talks in Greece Ser.). 433p. 1988. 24.95 (*3-89338-018-3*, Pub. by Rebel Hse) Oshos.

— Straight to Freedom: Reflections on Sufi Stories. Anurag, Ma Yoga, ed. LC 78-318958. ix, 261p. 1977. write for info. (*0-85969-130-6*) Prof Commun Pr.

— The Sun Rises in the Evening. Asha, Ma P., ed. LC 83-181196. (Zen Ser.). (Illus.). 372p. (Orig.). 1980. 14.95 (*0-88050-139-1*) Oshos.

— The Supreme Doctrine: Discourses on the Ken Upanishad. 3rd ed. (Illus.). 388p. 1997. 14.95 (*81-7261-074-2*, Pub. by Rebel Pub) Oshos.

— The Sword & the Lotus. Ma Dhyan Sagar, ed. LC 97-217189. (Talks in the Himalayas Ser.). 338p. 1989. 21.95 (*3-89338-075-2*, Pub. by Rebel Hse) Oshos.

— Tantra: The Supreme Understanding: Discourses on the Tantric Way of Tilopa's Song of Mahamudra. 4th ed. Orig. Title: Only One Sky. (Illus.). 271p. Date not set. 17.95 (*81-7261-009-2*, Pub. by Rebel Pub) Oshos.

— The Tantra Experience. 2nd ed. (Discourses on the Royal Song of Saraha Ser.: Vol. 1). 296p. 1978. 26.95 (*3-89338-139-2*, Pub. by Rebel Hse) Oshos.

— Tantra Experience: Discoveries on the Royal Song of Saraha. 1994. pap. 13.95 (*1-85230-597-5*, Pub. by Element MA) Penguin Putnam.

— Tantra Spirituality & Sex. Anutoshen, D., ed. LC 94-7836. (Introduction to the Teachings of Osho Ser.). 160p. 1994. pap. 9.95 (*0-918963-03-6*) Oshos.

— Tantric Transformation. 2nd ed. (Discourses on the Royal Song of Saraha Ser.: Vol. 2). 298p. 1978. 26.95 (*3-89338-140-6*, Pub. by Rebel Hse) Oshos.

— Tantric Transformation: Discovering a Life of Total Freedom. 2000. pap. 16.95 (*1-85230-596-7*, Pub. by Element MA) Penguin Putnam.

— Tao: The Golden Gate, Vol. 2. Prabhu, K., ed. LC 84-42615. (Tao Ser.). 304p. (Orig.). 1985. pap. 4.95 (*0-88050-647-4*) Oshos.

— That Art Thou. Sagar, Ma D., ed. (Early Talks Ser.). (Illus.). (Orig.). 1987. pap. 17.95 (*3-89338-011-6*, Pub. by Rebel Hse) Oshos.

— Theologia Mystica. Asha, Ma P., ed. LC 83-11086. (Western Mystics Ser.). 400p. (Orig.). 1983. pap. 4.95 (*0-88050-655-5*) Oshos.

— The Transmission of the Lamp. Ashik, Deva, ed. (Talks in Uruguay Ser.). 464p. 1989. 24.95 (*3-89338-049-3*, Pub. by Rebel Hse) Oshos.

— Turning In. Sudha, Yoga & Shabda, Veet, eds. LC 97-208942. (Zen Ser.). (Illus.). 288p. 1989. 12.95 (*3-89338-059-0*, Pub. by Rebel Hse) Oshos.

— Vedanta: Seven Steps to Samadhi. 2nd ed. (Illus.). 427p. 1976. reprint ed. 14.95 (*81-7261-012-2*, Pub. by Rebel Pub) Oshos.

— The Way of Tao, Pt. II. Didi, Dolli, tr. 1979. 15.50 (*0-89684-056-5*, Pub. by Motilal Bnarsidass) S Asia.

— What Is Meditation? 128p. 1995. pap. 10.95 (*1-85230-726-9*, Pub. by Element MA) Penguin Putnam.

— When the Shoe Fits: Commentaries on the Stories of the Taoist Mystic, Chuang Tzu. (Illus.). 317p. 1997. reprint ed. 12.95 (*81-7261-073-4*, Pub. by Rebel Pub) Oshos.

— Won't You Join the Dance? Maneesha, Ma P., ed. LC 83-43217. (Initiation Talks Ser.). 320p. (Orig.). 1983. pap. 4.95 (*0-88050-676-8*) Oshos.

— Yaa-Hoo! The Mystic Rose. 2nd ed. (Illus.). 370p. Date not set. reprint ed. 19.95 (*81-7261-011-4*, Pub. by Rebel Pub) Oshos.

— Yakusan: Straight to the Point of Enlightenment. Robin, Anand, ed. LC 97-221958. (Zen Ser.). 224p. 1992. 14.95 (*3-89338-084-1*, Pub. by Rebel Hse) Oshos.

— Yoga: Science of the Soul, Vol. 3. 1984. pap. 4.95 (*0-88050-679-2*) Oshos.

— You Ain't Seen Nothing Yet. Maneesha, Ma P., ed. LC 84-42614. (Initiation Talks Ser.). 304p. (Orig.). 1984. pap. 4.95 (*0-88050-687-3*) Oshos.

— Zarathustra: The Laughing Prophet. Shanti, Ma A. & Suvarna, Ma M., eds. (Zarathustra Ser.). 548p. Date not set. 24.95 (*3-89338-008-6*, Pub. by Rebel Hse) Oshos.

— Zarathustra, a God That Can Dance: Talks on Friedrich Nietzsche's Thus Spoke Zarathustra. Shanti, Ma A. & Suvarna, Ma M., eds. LC 97-208350. (Zarathustra Ser.). 547p. Date not set. 24.95 (*3-89338-007-8*, Pub. by Rebel Hse) Oshos.

— Zarathustra, a God That Can Dance: Talks on Friedrich Nietzsche's Thus Spoke Zarathustra. Nityo, Prabodh & Agama, P., eds. (Zarathustra Ser.). 570p. pap. write for info. (*0-614-01947-8*, Pub. by Rebel Hse) Oshos.

— Zen: The Diamond Thunderbolt. LC 97-210578. (Illus.). 288p. 1988. 12.95 (*3-89338-043-4*, Pub. by Rebel Hse) Oshos.

— Zen: The Mystery & the Poetry of the Beyond. Prabhu, Krishna, ed. LC 98-103021. (Zen Ser.). 176p. 1992. 14.95 (*3-89338-082-5*, Pub. by Rebel Hse) Oshos.

— Zen: The Path of Paradox, 3 vols. Anurag, Ma Y. et al, eds. LC 82-246214. (Zen Ser.). (Illus.). 1978. 9.95 (*0-88050-189-8*); 9.95 (*0-88050-190-1*) Oshos.

— Zen: The Quantum Leap from Mind to No-Mind. Robin, Anand, ed. (Zen Ser.). (Illus.). 288p. 1988. 12.95 (*3-89338-045-0*, Pub. by Rebel Hse) Oshos.

— Zen: The Solitary Bird, Cuckoo of the Forest. Sarito, Ma D., ed. LC 98-100339. (Zen Ser.). (Illus.). 288p. 1988. 12.95 (*3-89338-044-2*, Pub. by Rebel Hse) Oshos.

— The Zen Manifesto: Freedom from Oneself. 2nd ed. Sagar, Ma D., ed. LC 97-221936. (Zen Ser.). xv, 296p. 1997. 18.95 (*3-89338-121-X*, Pub. by Rebel Hse) Oshos.

Osho & Ma Yoga Sudha. The Secret of Secrets, Vol. 2. LC 82-50464. (Tao Ser.). 528p. (Orig.). 1983. pap. 4.95 (*0-88050-629-6*) Oshos.

Osho & Sambuddha, D. Books I Have Loved. Mahasattva, D., ed. LC 85-43070. (Biography Ser.). 288p. (Orig.). 1985. pap. 3.95 (*0-88050-716-0*) Oshos.

Oshodi, John. Sex, Violence, Drugs & America: The Definition of A Culture. 114p. (Orig.). 1994. pap. 11.95 (*0-9644455-0-6*) Oshodi Fnd.

Oshodi, John E. Oshodi Sentence Completion Index (OSCI) 23p. (C). 1996. reprint ed. pap. text. write for info. (*0-9644455-1-4*) Oshodi Fnd.

Oshoosi, Michael. African Spirituality vs. the African American. 410p. 1997. pap. 15.00 (*0-9659203-0-5*) Ibi Koni.

Oshry, Barry. In the Middle. (Notes on Power Ser.). (Orig.). 1994. pap. text 18.95 (*0-910411-15-8*) Power & Sys.

— Leading Systems: Lessons from the Power Lab. LC 99-34616. (Illus.). 200p. 1999. pap. text 24.95 (*1-57675-072-8*) Berrett-Koehler.

— Organic Power. LC 80-4780. (Notes on Power Ser.). (Orig.). 1976. pap. text 7.50 (*0-910411-03-4*) Power & Sys.

— The Possibilities of Organization. 178p. (Orig.). (C). 1986. pap. text 19.95 (*0-910411-10-7*) Power & Sys.

— Power & Position. LC 88-8848. (Notes on Power Ser.). (Orig.). 1977. pap. text 13.50 (*0-910411-04-2*) Power & Sys.

— Seeing Systems: Unlocking the Mysteries of Organizational Life. LC 95-33582. (Illus.). 228p. 1996. reprint ed. pap. 22.95 (*1-881052-99-0*) Berrett-Koehler.

— Space Work. (Notes on Power Ser.). (Orig.). 1994. pap. text 13.95 (*0-910411-12-3*) Power & Sys.

— Take a Look at Yourself: Self-in-System Sensitizers. (Notes on Power Ser.). (Orig.). 1978. pap. text 10.50 (*0-910411-05-0*) Power & Sys.

Oshry, Ephraim & Churban, Lita. The Annihilation of Lithuanian Jewry: The Kovno Ghetto 1939-1944. Goldman, Bonnie, ed. Orig. Title: Churban Jita. (Illus.). 336p. 1996. 24.95 (*1-880582-18-X*) Judaica Pr.

Oshry, Harold L. & Winters, Kate. The Man in the Arena. 250p. 1995. write for info. (*1-888069-05-8*) Biography For Everyone.

Osiadacz, Andrzej J., ed. Simulation & Optimization of Large Systems. (Institute of Mathematics & Its Applications Conference Series, New Ser.: New Series 13). (Illus.). 352p. 1988. 79.00 (*0-19-853617-8*) OUP.

An Asterisk (*) at the beginning of an entry indicates that the title is appearing for the first time.

O'Siadhail, Michael. The Chosen Garden. (C). 1990. 23.00 (*0-948268-87-5*, Pub. by Dedalus) St Mut.
— Hail! Madam Jazz: New & Selected Poems. 160p. 1993. 30.00 (*1-85224-225-6*, Pub. by Bloodaxe Bks); pap. 18.95 (*1-85224-208-6*, Pub. by Bloodaxe Bks) Dufour.
— Our Double Time, 1. LC 98-189163. 1999. pap. text 17.95 (*1-85224-450-X*) Bloodaxe Bks.
***O'Siadhail, Michael.** Poems, 1975-1995: Hail! Madam Jazz & a Fragile City. 238p. 2000. pap. 22.95 (*1-85224-495-X*, Pub. by Bloodaxe Bks) Dufour.
O'Siadhail, Micheal. A Fragile City. 78p. 1996. pap. 16.95 (*1-85224-334-1*, Pub. by Bloodaxe Bks) Dufour.
Osiander, Andreas. The States System of Europe, 1640-1990: Peacemaking & the Conditions of International Stability. 368p. 1994. text 75.00 (*0-19-827887-X*) OUP.
Osiatinsky, Jerzy, ed. see Kalecki, Michal.
Osiatynski, Jerzy, ed. Socialism - Economic Growth & Efficiency of Investment. Jung, Bohdan, tr. LC 92-26359. (ENG & POL., Illus.). 382p. 1993. text 79.00 (*0-19-828666-X*, Clarendon Pr) OUP.
Osiatynski, Jerzy, ed. see Kalecki, Michal.
Osicka, V. & Poldauf, Ivan. English-Czech Dictionary. (CZE & ENG.). 640p. 1980. 75.00 (*0-569-06529-1*, Pub. by Collets) St Mut.
O'Sickey, Ingeborg M. A Case of Betrayal? Women in Marguerite Yourcenar's Early Work. LC 93-36531. (American University Studies: Vol. 36). 1994. write for info. (*0-8204-1311-9*) P Lang Pubng.
O'Sickey, Ingeborg M. & Von Zadow, Ingeborg, eds. Triangulated Visions: Women in Recent German Cinema. LC 97-34327. (SUNY Series in Feminist Criticism & Theory). 288p. (C). 1998. text 65.50 (*0-7914-3717-5*); pap. text 21.95 (*0-7914-3718-3*) State U NY Pr.
Osiecki, Henry. Food of the Gods. 199p. (C). 1989. pap. 65.00 (*0-7316-5821-3*, Pub. by Bio Concepts) St Mut.
— Nutrients in Profile. 120p. (C). 1990. pap. 45.00 (*1-875239-04-9*, Pub. by Bio Concepts) St Mut.
— The Physicians Handbook of Clinical Nutrition. 252p. (C). 1990. pap. 65.00 (*1-875239-03-0*, Pub. by Bio Concepts) St Mut.
Osiek, Carolyn. Philippians & Philemon. LC 99-40978. (New Testament Commentaries Ser.). 160p. 2000. pap. 19.95 (*0-687-05822-8*) Abingdon.
— The Shepherd of Hermas: A Commentary. Koester, Helmut, ed. LC 99-21999. 400p. 1998. 48.00 (*0-8006-6063-3*, 1-6063) Augsburg Fortress.
Osiek, Carolyn A. Beyond Anger: On Being a Feminist in the Church. LC 85-62936. 96p. 1986. pap. 10.95 (*0-8091-2777-6*) Paulist Pr.
— Rich & Poor in the Shepherd of Hermas: An Exegetical-Social Investigation. Vawter, Bruce, ed. LC 83-7385. (Catholic Biblical Quarterly Monographs: No. 15). xi, 184p. 1983. pap. 6.00 (*0-915170-14-0*) Catholic Bibl Assn.
— What Are They Saying about the Social Setting of the New Testament? enl. rev. ed. LC 92-16470. (What Are They Saying about...Ser.). 144p. (Orig.). 1992. pap. 7.95 (*0-8091-3339-3*) Paulist Pr.
Osiek, Carolyn A., et al, eds. Silent Voices, Sacred Lives: Women's Readings for the Liturgical Year. LC 92-26234. 448p. 1992. pap. 17.95 (*0-8091-3336-9*) Paulist Pr.
Osiek, Carolyn A. & Balch, David L. Families in the New Testament World: Households & House Churches. LC 96-37845. (Family, Religion, & Culture Ser.). 328p. 1997. pap. 25.00 (*0-664-25546-9*) Westminster John Knox.
Osiek, O. Galatians. 1989. pap. 21.00 (*0-86217-030-3*, Pub. by Veritas Pubns) St Mut.
Osieka, Rainhard, ed. Resistance to Antineoplastic Agents Is Multifaceted: 3rd International Meeting on Drug Resistance, Aachen 1993. (Journal Ser.: Vol. 19, Supplement 1, 1996). (Illus.). vi, 38p. 1996. pap. 28.75 (*3-8055-6429-5*) S Karger.
Osieke, E. Constitutional Law & Practice in the International Labour Organization. 1985. lib. bdg. 139.00 (*90-247-2985-8*) Kluwer Academic.
Osiel, Mark. Mass Atrocity, Collective Memory & the Law. LC 96-50097. 310p. 1997. text 34.95 (*1-56000-322-7*) Transaction Pubs.
— Mass Atrocity, Collective Memory & the Law. 317p. 1999. pap. 24.95 (*0-7658-0663-0*) Transaction Pubs.
Osiel, Mark J. Obeying Orders: Atrocity, Military Discipline & the Law of War. LC 98-38647. 398p. 1999. 34.95 (*1-56000-407-X*) Transaction Pubs.
Osier. In the Eye of the Garden. 176p. 1993. 15.00 (*0-685-70479-3*) Macmillan.
Osier, Dan. Teach Yourself Delphi 3 in 14 Days. 3rd ed. LC 97-66194. 624p. 1997. 29.99 (*0-672-31114-3*) Sams.
— Teach Yourself Delphi 2 in 21 Days. 2nd ed. (Illus.). 736p. 1996. 35.00 (*0-672-30863-0*) Sams.
Osier, Jeffrey, jt. auth. see Ochoa, George.
Osier, Tom. Ultra Marathoning. 1984. 14.95 (*0-02-499840-0*, Macmillan Coll) P-H.
Osifchin, Gary P., jt. ed. see Scouton, William A.
Osigweh, C. A. Organizational Science Abroad: Constraints & Perspectives. LC 88-28572. (Illus.). 364p. (C). 1989. 75.00 (*0-306-42969-1*, Plenum Trade) Perseus Pubng.
Osigweh, Chimezie A., ed. Communicating Employee Responsibilities & Rights: A Modern Management Mandate. LC 86-25281. 268p. 1987. 59.95 (*0-89930-200-9*, OSC/, Quorum Bks) Greenwood.
— Managing Employee Rights & Responsibilities. LC 88-38310. 321p. 1989. 69.50 (*0-89930-336-6*, OME/, Quorum Bks) Greenwood.
Osiko, V. V., ed. Selective Laser Spectroscopy of Activated Crystals & Glasses. (Proceedings of the Institute of General Physics of the Academy of Sciences of the U. S. S. R. Ser.: Vol. 9). (RUS.). 220p. 1990. text 165.00 (*0-941743-31-4*) Nova Sci Pubs.
Osilenker, B. Fourier Series in Orthogonal Polynomials. 250p. 1999. 48.00 (*981-02-3787-1*) World Scientific Pub.
***Osing, Gordon T.** Crossing Against the Sun. (Poetry New York Pamphlet Ser.: No. 27). 25p. 1999. pap. 5.00 (*0-923389-37-7*) Meet Eyes Bind.
Osing, Jurgen. The Carlsberg Papyri, 2: Hieratische Papri aus Tebtunis, I, 2 vols., Set. (Carsten Niebuhr Institute Publications (CNI): No. 17). 256p. 1998. 292.00 (*87-7289-280-3*, Pub. by Mus Tusculanum) Paul & Co Pubs.
Osing, Richard A. How to Love & Be Loved. 2nd ed. LC 98-55956. 1999. pap. 13.95 (*0-945213-37-9*) Rudi Pub.
— How to Love & Be Loved: Establishing & Maintaining Intimacy. 112p. 1992. pap. 11.95 (*0-945213-05-0*) Rudi Pub.
— Love at Midlife: Building & Re-Building Relationships at Midlife. LC 98-20707. 1998. pap. 13.95 (*0-945213-31-X*) Rudi Pub.
***Osinga, R., et al.** Marine Bioprocess Engineering: Proceedings of an International Symposium Organized under Auspices of the Working Party on Applied Biocatalysis of the European Federation of Biotechnology & the European Society for Marine Biotechnology, Noordwijkerhour, the Netherlands, Nobember 8-11, 1998. LC 99-89648. (Progress in Industrial Microbiology Ser.). 414p. 2000. write for info. (*0-444-50387-0*) Elsevier.
Osinski, A. Slownik Mitologiczny, 3 vols. 1993. reprint ed. 300.00 (*0-318-23358-4*) Szwede Slavic.
Osinski, Alice. Andrew Jackson. LC 86-29983. (Encyclopedia of Presidents Ser.). (Illus.). 100p. (J). (gr. 3 up). 1987. lib. bdg. 24.00 (*0-516-01387-4*) Childrens.
— The Chippewa. LC 86-32687. (New True Books Ser.). (Illus.). 48p. (J). (gr. k-4). 1987. pap. 5.50 (*0-516-41230-2*) Childrens.
— The Chippewa. LC 86-32687. (New True Books Ser.). (Illus.). 48p. (J). (ps-3). 1987. lib. bdg. 21.00 (*0-516-01230-4*) Childrens.
— The Eskimo: Inuit & Yupik. LC 85-9691. (New True Books Ser.). (Illus.). 45p. (J). (gr. 3-5). 1985. pap. 5.50 (*0-516-41267-1*); lib. bdg. 21.00 (*0-516-01267-3*) Childrens.
— Franklin D. Roosevelt. (Encyclopedia of Presidents Ser.). (Illus.). 100p. (J). (gr. 5-8). 1987. lib. bdg. 24.00 (*0-516-01395-5*) Childrens.
— The Navajo. (New True Books Ser.). (Illus.). (J). (gr. 2-4). 1987. pap. 5.50 (*0-516-41236-1*) Childrens.
— The Navajo. LC 86-30978. (New True Books Ser.). (Illus.). 48p. (J). (ps-3). 1987. lib. bdg. 21.00 (*0-516-01236-3*) Childrens.
— The Nez Perce. LC 88-11822. (New True Books Ser.). (Illus.). 48p. (J). (gr. 2-4). 1988. pap. 5.50 (*0-516-41154-3*); lib. bdg. 21.00 (*0-516-01154-5*) Childrens.
— The Sioux. LC 84-7629. (New True Books Ser.). (Illus.). 48p. (J). (gr. k-4). 1984. lib. bdg. 21.00 (*0-516-01929-5*) Childrens.
— The Sioux. LC 84-7629. (New True Books Ser.). (Illus.). 48p. (J). (gr. 2-4). 1984. pap. 5.50 (*0-516-41929-3*) Childrens.
— The Tlingit. LC 89-25345. (New True Books Ser.). (Illus.). 48p. (J). (gr. 3-5). 1990. pap. 5.50 (*0-516-41189-6*) Childrens.
— Woodrow Wilson. LC 88-8678. (Encyclopedia of Presidents Ser.). (Illus.). 100p. (J). (gr. 5-8). 1989. lib. bdg. 24.00 (*0-516-01367-X*) Childrens.
Osinski, Christine, ed. & illus. see Flanagan, Alice K.
Osinski, F. W., et al, eds. Toward Gog & Magog Or? A Critical Review of the Literature of Adult Group Discussion. LC 72-6475. (Occasional Papers: No. 30). 80p. (Orig.). 1972. pap. 2.00 (*0-87060-053-2*, OCP 30) Syracuse U Cont Ed.
***Osinski, Marek, et al, eds.** Advanced High-Power Lasers. 1999. pap. text 163.00 (*0-8194-3487-6*) SPIE.
— Design, Fabrication & Characterization of Photonic Devices. 1999. pap. text 145.00 (*0-8194-3498-1*) SPIE.
Osinski, Marek, et al, eds. Physics & Simulation of Optoelectronic Devices VI. (Proceedings of SPIE Ser.: Vol. 3283). 1037p. 1998. 149.00 (*0-8194-2722-5*) SPIE.
Osinski, Marek & Chow, Weng W., eds. Physics & Simulation of Optoelectronic Devices V, Vol. 2994. 890p. 1997. 132.00 (*0-8194-2405-6*) SPIE.
Osinski, Marek & Su, Yan K., eds. Optoelectronic Materials & Devices. (Proceedings of SPIE Ser.: Vol. 3419). 474p. 1998. 107.00 (*0-8194-2873-6*) SPIE.
Osinski, Z., ed. Damping of Vibrations. (Illus.). 562p. (C). 1998. text 104.00 (*90-5410-676-X*, Pub. by A A Balkema); pap. text 61.00 (*90-5410-677-8*, Pub. by A A Balkema) Ashgate Pub Co.
Osio, Antonio M. The History of Alta California: A Memoir of Mexican California. Beebe, Rose M. & Senkewicz, Robert M., eds. & trs. by. from SPA. LC 95-25695. (Illus.). 400p. 1996. 45.00 (*0-299-14970-6*) U of Wis Pr.
— The History of Alta California: A Memoir of Mexican California. Beebe, Rose M. & Senkewicz, Robert M., eds. & trs. by. from SPA. LC 95-25695. 400p. 1996. pap. 21.95 (*0-299-14974-9*) U of Wis Pr.
O'Siochain, Padraig A. A Journey into Lost Time. 184p. 1985. 14.95 (*0-685-09679-3*) Devin.
Osip, Anna Mae. Tanning Moosehide & Making Babish. (Illus.). 22p. 1994. reprint ed. pap. 4.95 (*1-878051-26-1*) Circumpolar Pr.
***Osipenko, K. Yu.** Optimal Recovery of Analytic Functions. 220p. 2000. lib. bdg. 89.00 (*1-56072-821-3*) Nova Sci Pubs.
Osipow, Lloyd I. Surface Chemistry: Theory & Industrial Applications. LC 62-20782. (ACS Monograph Ser.: Vol. 153). (Illus.). 487p. reprint ed. pap. 151.00 (*0-608-06933-7*, 206714100009) Bks Demand.
Osipow, Samuel H. & Fitzgerald, Louise F. Theories of Career Development. 4th ed. LC 95-9133. 416p. 1995. 79.00 (*0-205-18391-3*) Allyn.
Osipow, Samuel H., ed. see Campbell, Vicki L. & Watkins, C. Edward, Jr.
Osipow, Samuel H., jt. ed. see Walsh, W. Bruce.
Osip'Yan, Yu A. Interference Phenomena in X-Ray Scattering. 250p. 1997. pap. text 108.00 (*90-5699-084-5*) Gordon & Breach.
Osis, Karlis. Deathbed Observations by Physicians & Nurses. 4th ed. LC 61-18247. (Parapsychological Monographs: No. 3). 1961. pap. 7.00 (*0-912328-06-1*) Parapsych Foun.
— Dosage Calculations in SI Units, No. 2. (Illus.). 192p. 1990. spiral bd. 15.95 (*0-8016-3753-8*) Mosby Inc.
Osis, Maureen J. Dosage Calculations in SI Units. 3rd ed. (Illus.). 192p. (C). (gr. 13). 1995. spiral bd. 17.00 (*0-8151-6549-8*, 23838) Mosby Inc.
Oskai, S. & Hatoyama, Y., eds. Stochastic Models in Reliability Theory. (Lecture Notes in Economics & Mathematical Systems Ser.: Vol. 235). vii, 212p. 1984. 36.00 (*0-387-13888-9*) Spr-Verlag.
***Oskam, A. J.** Additional Eu Policy Instruments for Plant Protection Products. (Illus.). 290p. 1999. pap. 51.00 (*90-74134-55-6*) Wageningen Pers.
Oskam, B., jt. auth. see Polto, Pearl B.
Oskam, Bob, jt. ed. see Choron, Sandra.
Oskamp, A., jt. ed. see Kaspersen, H. W.
Oskamp, Stuart. Attitudes & Opinions. 2nd ed. 496p. (C). 1990. text 50.20 (*0-13-050592-7*) P-H.
Oskamp, Stuart, ed. Family Processes & Problems: Social Psychological Aspects. LC 80-645341. (Applied Social Psychology Annual Ser.: Vol. 7). 328p. (Orig.). 1987. reprint ed. pap. 101.70 (*0-608-02788-X*, 206385500007) Bks Demand.
— International Conflict & National Public Policy Issues. LC JX1255.I65. (Applied Social Psychology Annual Ser.: No. 6). (Illus.). 312p. 1985. reprint ed. pap. 96.80 (*0-608-01156-8*, 205945600001) Bks Demand.
— People's Reactions to Technology: In Factories, Offices, & Aerospace. (Claremont Symposium on Applied Social Psychology Ser.). 296p. (C). 1990. text 39.95 (*0-8039-3852-7*) Sage.
— People's Reactions to Technology: In Factories, Offices, & Aerospace, No. 4. (Claremont Symposium on Applied Social Psychology Ser.). 296p. (C). 1990. pap. text 18.95 (*0-8039-3853-5*) Sage.
***Oskamp, Stuart, ed.** Reducing Prejudice & Discrimination. (A Volume in Claremont Symposium on Applied Social Psychology). 352p. 2000. write for info. (*0-8058-3481-8*); pap. write for info. (*0-8058-3482-6*) L Erlbaum Assocs.
Oskamp, Stuart & Costanzo, Mark, eds. Gender Issues in Social Psychology. (Claremont Symposium on Applied Social Psychology Ser.: Vol. 6). (Illus.). 164p. (C). 1993. text 39.95 (*0-8039-5229-5*) Sage.
— Gender Issues in Social Psychology, No. 6. (Claremont Symposium on Applied Social Psychology Ser.: Vol. 6). (Illus.). 164p. (C). 1993. pap. text 18.95 (*0-8039-5230-9*) Sage.
Oskamp, Stuart & Thompson, Suzanne. Understanding & Preventing HIV Risk Behavior. LC 96-10121. (Claremont Symposium on Applied Social Science Ser.: Vol. 9). 248p. 1996. 45.00 (*0-8039-7424-8*) Sage.
— Understanding & Preventing HIV Risk Behavior, No. 9. LC 96-10121. (Claremont Symposium on Applied Social Science Ser.: Vol. 9). 248p. 1996. pap. 21.95 (*0-8039-7425-6*) Sage.
Oskamp, Stuart, et al. Applied Social Psychology. 2nd ed. LC 97-15004. 450p. 1997. 74.00 (*0-13-533837-9*) P-H.
Oskamp, Stuart, jt. auth. see Arriaga, Ximena B.
Oskamp, Stuart, jt. auth. see Costanzo, Mark.
Oskamp, Stuart, jt. auth. see Granrose, Cherlyn S.
Oskamp, Stuart, jt. auth. see Spacapan, Shirlynn.
Oskamp, Stuart, jt. ed. see Arriaga, Ximena B.
Oskamp, Stuart, ed. see Claremont Graduate School, Symposium on Applied So.
Oskamp, Stuart, ed. see Claremont Symposium on Applied Social Psychology S.
Oskamp, Stuart, jt. ed. see Spacapan, Shirlynn.
Oskarsson, Karin, et al. A Planner's Guide for Selecting Clean-Coal Technologies for Power Plants. LC 97-38022. (World Bank Technical Papers: No. 387). 176p. 1997. pap. 22.00 (*0-8213-4065-4*, 14065) World Bank.
***Oskey, Waren.** Spiritual Awareness: Pathway to Enlightenment. LC 99-91794. 2000. 25.00 (*0-7388-1262-5*); pap. 18.00 (*0-7388-1263-3*) Xlibris Corp.
Oski, Frank A. Don't Drink Your Milk. 9th rev. ed. LC 77-8102. 96p. 1994. per. 7.95 (*0-945383-34-7*, 945-5807) Teach Servs.
— Essentials of Pediatrics. LC 96-38508. 761p. 1996. pap. text 34.95 (*0-397-51514-6*) Lppncott W & W.
— Principles & Practice of Pediatrics. 2nd ed. 2,400p. (C). 1993. text 99.50 (*0-397-51221-X*) Lppncott W & W.
Oski, Frank A. & Tinkelman, David G. Allergies in Childhood: A Guide for Parents. (Pediatrics Ser.). (Illus.). 32p. 1999. pap. 2.95 (*1-885274-07-6*) Health InfoNet Inc.
Oski, Frank A., et al. Principles & Practice of Pediatrics. (Illus.). 2155p. 1989. text 99.50 (*0-397-50707-0*) Lppncott W & W.
Oski, Frank A., jt. auth. see Markel, Howard.
Oski, Frank A., jt. auth. see McMillan, Julia A.
Oski, Frank A., jt. auth. see Starfield, Barbara H.
Oski, Frank A., ed. see Barnesa, Lewis.
Oski, Frank A., ed. see David & Cohen, Bernard.
Oski, Frank A., ed. see Paradise, Jack.
Oski, Frank A., ed. see Wilson, Modena.
Oski, Frank A., ed. see Year Book of Pediatrics Staff.
Oslance, Michael, jt. auth. see Markuly, Mark S.
Osland, Birger. A Long Pull from Stavanger: The Reminiscences of a Norwegian Immigrant. 263p. 1945. 15.00 (*0-87732-027-6*) Norwegian-Am Hist Assn.
***Osland, Joyce S., et al.** Organizational Behavior: An Experiential Approach. 7th ed. LC 00-27648. 592p. 2000. pap. 61.33 (*0-13-017610-9*) P-H.
Osland, Joyce S., jt. auth. see Kolb, David A.
Osleeb, Jeffrey P., jt. auth. see ZumBrunnen, Craig.
Osler, et al. Corporate Environmental Responsibilities. 256p. 130.00 (*0-409-89718-3*, MICHIE) LEXIS Pub.
Osler, A. Education & Career Black Teach: Changing Identities, Changing Lives. LC 97-9041. 1997. pap. 32.95 (*0-335-19775-2*) OpUniv Pr.
Osler, Andrew M. News - the Evolution of Journalism in Canada. pap. text. write for info. (*0-7730-5193-7*) Addison-Wes.
Osler, Audrey. Development Education: Global Perspectives in the Curriculum. (Council of Europe Ser.). 224p. 1994. text 90.00 (*0-304-32567-8*); pap. text 33.95 (*0-304-32565-1*) Continuum.
— The Education & Careers of Black Teachers: Changing Identities, Changing Lives. LC 97-9041. 1997. 108.00 (*0-335-19776-0*) OpUniv Pr.
Osler, Audrey & Starkey, Hugh, eds. Teacher Education & Human Rights. LC 96-227997. 192p. 1996. pap. 25.95 (*1-85346-406-6*, Pub. by David Fulton) Taylor & Francis.
Osler-Brooks, Ethel. Signs of Time in Black Poetry Yesterday Today Tomorrow. 1998. pap. write for info. (*1-57553-539-4*) Watermrk Pr.
Osler, Dorothy. Quilting Design Sourcebook. Hoffman, Kerry, ed. LC 96-16464. (Illus.). 96p. (Orig.). 1996. pap., spiral bd. 19.95 (*1-56477-152-0*, B269) Martingale & Co.
Osler, Jack M. Fifty Great Mini-Trips for Indiana. (Illus.). 1978. pap. 2.95 (*0-89645-005-8*) Media Ventures.
— Fifty Great New Mini-Trips for Ohio. (Jack Osler's Mini-Trips Ser.). (Illus.). (Orig.). 1980. pap. 3.50 (*0-89645-013-9*) Media Ventures.
Osler, Margaret J. Divine Will & the Mechanical Philosophy: Gassendi & Descartes on Contingency & Necessity in the Created World. LC 93-37129. 298p. (C). 1994. text 59.95 (*0-521-46104-9*) Cambridge U Pr.
Osler, Margaret J., ed. Atoms, Pneuma, & Tranquillity: Epicurean & Stoic Themes in European Thought. 316p. (C). 1991. text 69.95 (*0-521-40048-1*) Cambridge U Pr.
***Osler, Margaret J., ed.** Rethinking the Scientific Revolution. (Illus.). 352p. (C). 2000. text 69.95 (*0-521-66101-3*); pap. text 24.95 (*0-521-66790-9*) Cambridge U Pr.
Osler, Mirabel. Breath from Elsewhere. LC 98-74908. 224p. 1999. 21.95 (*1-55970-454-3*, Pub. by Arcade Pub Inc) Time Warner.
— A Gentle Plea for Chaos. LC 98-10350. 192p. 1998. 19.45 (*1-55970-439-X*, Pub. by Arcade Pub Inc) Time Warner.
Osler, Sonia F. & Cooke, Robert E., eds. The Biosocial Basis of Mental Retardation. LC 65-17078. 168p. reprint ed. pap. 52.10 (*0-8357-7255-1*, 202073100018) Bks Demand.
Osler, Tom. The Serious Runner's Handbook. LC 78-367. (Illus.). 187p. 1978. pap. 5.95 (*0-89037-126-1*) Anderson World.
— The Serious Runner's Handbook. 1978. pap. 5.95 (*0-02-499770-6*, Macmillan Coll) P-H.
Osler, Tom & Dodd, Ed. Ultramarathoning: The Next Challenge. LC 78-68612. (Illus.). 240p. 1980. 14.95 (*0-89037-169-5*) Anderson World.
Osler, William. Aequanimitas: With Other Addresses to Medical Students, Nurses & Practitioners of Medicine. 3rd ed. 421p. 1932. text 60.00 (*0-07-047915-1*) McGraw-Hill HPD.
— Bibliotheca Osleriana: A Catalogue of Books Illustrating the History of Medicine & Science. Francis, W. W. et al, eds. 822p. 1997. reprint ed. 95.00 (*1-57898-015-1*) Martino Pubng.
Osler, William. The Cerebral Palsies of Children: A Clinical Study from the Infirmary for Nervous Diseases, Philadelphia. (Classics in Developmental Medicine Ser.: No. 1). (Illus.). 92p. (C). 1991. text 19.95 (*0-521-41326-5*, Pub. by Mc Keith Pr) Cambridge U Pr.
Osler, William. The Evolution of Modern Medicine: A Series of Lectures Delivered at Yale University on the Silliman Foundation in April, 1913. LC 77-140610. (Medicine & Society in America Ser.). (Illus.). 264p. 1980. reprint ed. 24.95 (*0-405-02805-9*) Ayer.
— Incunabula Medica: A Study of the Earliest Printed Medical Books 1467-1480. (Illus.). 152p. 1994. reprint ed. 60.00 (*1-888262-56-7*) Martino Pubng.
— Science & Immortality. Kastenbaum, Robert J., ed. LC 76-19586. (Death & Dying Ser.). 1977. reprint ed. lib. bdg. 17.95 (*0-405-09581-3*) Ayer.
— Student Life, & Other Essays. LC 67-23256. (Essay Index Reprint Ser.). 1977. 18.95 (*0-8369-0756-6*) Ayer.
— A Way of Life. 1937. text 11.95 (*0-06-141860-9*) Lppncott W & W.
— A Way of Life: An Address Delivered to Yale Students Sunday Evening, April 20, 1913. (Illus.). 54p. 1969. 19.95 (*0-398-01433-7*) C C Thomas.
Osler, William, jt. auth. see Beaumont, William.
Osler, William, jt. auth. see McKusick, Victor A.
Osley, A. S. Calligraphy & Palaeography. (Illus.). 1966. 25.00 (*0-8079-0020-6*) October.
Osley, Anthony. Persuading the People: Government Publicity in the Second World War. LC 96-137994. 92p. 1995. pap. 30.00 (*0-11-701885-6*, Pub. by Statnry Office) Balogh.

O

Osley, Carol A. Beyond the Storm. (Orig.). 1985. write for info. (*0-910119-13-9*) SOCO Pubns.
— Computing to Success. (Orig.). 1985. write for info. (*0-910119-14-7*) SOCO Pubns.
— Creative Writing Workbook: Instructor's Manual. 180p. (Orig.). (C). 1983. 15.00 (*0-910119-10-4*) SOCO Pubns.
— Creative Writing Workbook: Student's Manual. 180p. (Orig.). (C). 1983. 15.00 (*0-910119-09-0*) SOCO Pubns.
— Getting Around Writer's Block. 1982. pap. 2.50 (*0-910119-04-X*) SOCO Pubns.
— Helpful Hints for Writers. (Orig.). (C). 1983. pap. 3.00 (*0-910119-06-6*) SOCO Pubns.
— How Not to Get Published. (Orig.). (C). 1983. pap. 2.75 (*0-910119-08-2*) SOCO Pubns.
— How to Properly Prepare Poems. (Orig.). 1983. 4.25 (*0-910119-11-2*) SOCO Pubns.
— How to Set up Secretarial Inservice Classes. (Illus.). 1982. pap. 4.25 (*0-910119-02-3*) SOCO Pubns.
— My Personal Tribute to President Ronald Reagan: The President in Verse. (Orig.). (C). 1983. pap. 4.00 (*0-910119-07-4*) SOCO Pubns.
— Reflections of Love. 42p. (Orig.). 1982. pap. 4.25 (*0-910119-01-5*) SOCO Pubns.
— The Soldier, America & Me. 1982. pap. 4.50 (*0-910119-00-7*) SOCO Pubns.
— The Tender Beguilement. (Orig.). 1985. write for info. (*0-910119-12-0*) SOCO Pubns.
— Writer's Do's & Don'ts. (Orig.). (C). 1982. pap. 2.00 (*0-910119-03-1*) SOCO Pubns.
Oslie, Pamala. Life Colors. LC 91-40295. 380p. 1991. pap. 14.95 (*0-931432-81-2*) New Wrld Lib.
***Oslie, Pamala.** Life Colors: What the Colors in Your Aura Reveal. rev. ed. 384p. 2000. pap. 16.95 (*1-57731-169-8*, Pub. by New Wrld Lib) Publishers Group.
Oslie, Pamala. Make Your Dreams Come True: Simple Steps for Changing the Beliefs That Limit You. LC 98-15626. 176p. 1998. pap. 12.95 (*1-878424-33-5*) Amber-Allen Pub.
Oslin, George P. One Man's Century: From the Deep South to the Top of the Big Apple. LC 98-43917. 144p. 1999. 20.00 (*0-86554-647-9*) Mercer Univ Pr.
— The Story of Telecommunications: From the Deep South to the Top of the Big Apple. 1999. pap. 30.00 (*0-86554-659-2*) Mercer Univ Pr.
Oslow, Darlene & Shilling, Dana, eds. Hiring Handbook. 400p. 1991. reprint ed. text 96.00 (*1-878375-85-7*) Panel Pubs.
Oslund, Clayton & Oslund, Michele. Hawaiian Gardens Are to Go to: A Pictoral History of Hawaiian Gardens Based on Our Experience of Guiding Tours Through These Gardens. (Illus.). 106p. 1998. pap. 19.95 (*0-9667399-0-6*) Plant Pics.
Oslund, Michele, jt. auth. see Oslund, Clayton.
Osmak, Karen A. Take Your Students to Spring Training Vol. 1: A Leadership Training Manual. unabridged ed. (Illus.). 118p. 1997. ring bd. 175.00 (*0-9659301-0-6*, LT100) Adair Bus.
— Take Your Students to Spring Training Vol. 2: An Interpersonal Skills Training Manual. unabridged ed. (Illus.). 100p. 1997. ring bd. 175.00 (*0-9659301-1-4*, IS100) Adair Bus.
Osman, A. E., et al, eds. The Role of Legumes in the Farming Systems of the Mediterranean Areas. (C). 1990. lib. bdg. 137.50 (*0-7923-0419-5*) Kluwer Academic.
Osman, Ahmed. Idegen a Kiralyok Volgyeben: Egy Mumia Titka. Gaal, Violetta, tr. from ENG. (HUN.). 160p. 1993. 25.00 (*0-9637584-0-3*) Violetta Gaal.
***Osman, Ahmed.** Out of Egypt. 1998. 35.00 (*0-7126-7962-6*, Pub. by Random) Trafalgar.
— Out of Egypt. 1999. mass mkt. 13.95 (*0-09-927765-4*, Pub. by Random) Trafalgar.
Osman, Beshir M. Regionalisation in the Sudan. (C). 1986. 29.00 (*0-7855-3832-1*, Pub. by Oxford Polytechnic) St Mut.
Osman, Betty. Learning Disabilities & ADHD: A Family Guide to Living & Learning Together. 2nd ed. LC 97-1211. 228p. 1997. pap. 14.95 (*0-471-15510-1*) Wiley.
Osman, Betty B. Learning Disabilities. 1988. mass mkt. 4.95 (*0-446-35554-2*, Pub. by Warner Bks) Little.
— No One to Play With. rev. ed. 1996. pap. 15.00 (*0-87879-687-8*) Acad Therapy.
Osman, Betty B., jt. auth. see Greenhill, Laurence L.
Osman, Christopher C., ed. see McMullen, John, et al.
Osman, Colin. Egypt: Caught in Time. (Illus.). 160p. 1998. 30.00 (*1-873938-95-0*, Pub. by Garnet-Ithaca) LPC InBook.
***Osman, Colin.** Jerusalem: Caught in Time. LC 99-53019. (Illus.). 148p. 2000. text 35.00 (*0-8147-6200-X*) NYU Pr.
Osman, Elizabeth M., jt. ed. see Dupont, Jacqueline.
Osman, Fathi. Jihad: A Legitimate Struggle for Human Rights. 60p. 1991. pap. text 3.00 (*1-881504-05-0*) Minaret Pubns.
— Muslim Women: In the Family & the Society. 60p. 1991. pap. text 3.00 (*1-881504-02-6*) Minaret Pubns.
— Muslim World Issues & Challenges. 510p. 1989. pap. text 10.00 (*1-881504-06-9*) Minaret Pubns.
Osman, Ibrahim H., ed. Meta-Heuristics: Theory & Applications. 704p. (C). 1996. lib. bdg. 212.00 (*0-7923-9700-2*) Kluwer Academic.
Osman, Jack D. Fat Fat Fat: A Threefold Look at Fat Control. LC 84-81813. (Illus.). 134p. (Orig.). 1985. 14.95 (*0-685-09743-9*); pap. 7.95 (*0-918275-00-8*) Fat Control.
Osman, Jena. Amblyopia. 48p. (Orig.). (C). 1993. pap. text 8.00 (*0-939691-09-4*) Avenue B.
— The Character. LC 98-48252. 128p. 1999. pap. 15.00 (*0-8070-6847-0*) Beacon Pr.
— Twelve Parts of Her. (Burning Deck Poetry Chapbooks Ser.). 24p. 1989. pap. 4.00 (*0-930901-63-0*) Burning Deck.
— Underwater Dive, Version One. (Illus.). 24p. (Orig.). 1990. pap. 4.00 (*0-945926-22-7*) Paradigm RI.
***Osman, Jena, et al, eds.** Chain 6: Letters. (Illus.). 271p. 1999. pap. 12.00 (*0-9666303-4-3*, Pub. by A A Arts) SPD-Small Pr Dist.
Osman, Jena & Spahr, Juliana, eds. Gender & Editorial Practice. 288p. (C). 1994. pap. 7.95 (*0-922668-12-4*) SUNYB Poetry Rare Bks.
Osman, Joseph H., jt. auth. see Habegger, Jerryll.
Osman, Karen. The Italian Renaissance. LC 95-31679. (World History Ser.). (Illus.). 112p. (J). (gr. 4-12). 1997. lib. bdg. 18.96 (*1-56006-237-1*) Lucent Bks.
Osman, Loren H. W. D. Hoard: A Man for His Time. LC 84-62450. (Illus.). 451p. 1985. 14.95 (*0-932147-00-3*) Hoard & Sons Co.
Osman, Madina M., jt. auth. see Zorc, R. David.
Osman, Michael, jt. ed. see Whitten, Theodore.
Osman, Mohamed F. The Children of Adam: An Islamic Perspective on Pluralism. (Occasional Papers). v, 74p. 1996. pap. 5.95 (*1-929218-02-8*, 1) Georgetwn U Ctr Muslim.
Osman, Mohamed M. Successful C for Commercial UNIX Developers. LC 96-46060. 368p. 1996. pap. text 29.00 incl. disk (*0-89006-642-6*) Artech Hse.
Osman, Osman M. & Robinson, Enders A., eds. Seismic Source Signature Estimation & Measurement. LC 96-38275. (Geophysics Reprints Ser.: Vol. 18). (Illus.). 732p. (Orig.). 1996. pap. text 69.00 (*1-56080-040-2*, 192A) Soc Expl Geophys.
Osman, Osman M., jt. ed. see Robinson, Enders A.
Osman, Shaukat. Janani. (Asian Writers Ser.). 213p. 1994. pap. 9.95 (*0-435-95083-5*, 95083) Heinemann.
Osmanczyk, Edmund J. The Encyclopedia of the United Nations & International Agreements. 2nd rev. ed. 1059p. 1990. 310.00 (*0-85066-833-6*) Intl Pubns Serv.
Osmani, Siddiqur R., ed. Nutrition & Poverty. (WIDER Studies in Development Economics). (Illus.). 382p. 1993. text 69.00 (*0-19-828396-2*) OUP.
Osmania University, Dept. of English Staff. Critical Responses Vol. II: British & American Literature. (C). 1993. write for info. (*81-207-1636-1*) Sterling Pubs.
Osmanov, M. Persian-Russian Dictionary, 2 vols., Set. (PER & RUS.). 1600p. 1983. 95.00 (*0-8288-0800-7*, F46360) Fr & Eur.
Osmanski, Elaine C. The College Parent's Guide to Savings...of Time, Money & Aggravation. iv, 52p. 1997. pap. 19.95 (*0-9660701-0-0*) Appletree PA.
Osmanston, V. C. Management of Forests. 384p. (C). 1985. reprint ed. pap. 175.00 (*81-7089-031-4*, Pub. by Intl Bk Distr) St Mut.
Osmar, Nils. The Hungry Time: Eight Science Fiction Fables. pap. 7.95 (*1-889610-00-3*) Wonder Publng.
Osmaston, A. E. Forest Flora for Kumaon. 605p. (C). 1976. 250.00 (*0-7855-3126-2*, Pub. by Intl Bk Distr) St Mut.
Osmaston, F. B., tr. see Hegel, Georg Wilhelm Friedrich.
Osmaston, Henry & Tsering, Nawang, eds. Recent Research on Ladakh 6: Proceedings of the 6th International Colloquium on Ladakh Leh, 1993. (C). 1997. 28.00 (*81-208-1432-0*, Pub. by Motilal Bnarsidass) S Asia.
Osment, Philip. The Undertaking. (Oberon Bks.). 128p. 1997. pap. 12.95 (*1-870259-87-4*) Theatre Comm.
Osmer, et al. Making Connections: The Minister As Practical Theologian. 192p. 1997. pap. 16.95 (*0-687-01729-7*) Abingdon.
***Osmer, Harold.** Where They Raced - Lap 2: Auto Racing Venues in Southern California 1900-2000. (Illus.). 140p. 2000. pap. write for info. (*0-9659533-3-5*) H L Osmer.
Osmer, Harold & Harms, Phil. Real Road Racing: The Santa Monica Road Races. (Illus.). 144p. 1999. pap. 29.95 (*0-9659533-1-9*) H L Osmer.
Osmer, Harold L. Where They Raced: Auto Racing Venues in Los Angeles, 1900-1990. (Illus.). 64p. (Orig.). 1996. pap. 24.95 (*0-9659533-0-0*) H L Osmer.
Osmer-Newhouse, Carol, jt. auth. see Kaufer, Nelly.
Osmer, Patrick, et al, eds. Proceedings of a Workshop on Optical Surveys for Quasars. LC 88-71919. (Astronomical Society of the Pacific Conference Ser.: Vol. 2). (Illus.). 394p. 1988. 34.00 (*0-937707-19-8*) Astron Soc Pacific.
Osmer, Richard R. Confirmation: Presbyterian Practices in Ecumenical Perspective. 1996. pap. 21.95 (*0-664-50000-5*) Geneva Press.
— A Teachable Spirit: Recovering the Teaching Office in the Church. 340p. (Orig.). 1990. pap. 24.95 (*0-664-25079-3*) Westminster John Knox.
— Teaching for Faith: A Guide for Teachers of Adult Classes. 224p. (Orig.). 1992. pap. 19.95 (*0-664-25217-6*) Westminster John Knox.
Osmers, R. & Kurjak, Asim. Ultrasound & the Uterus. (Progress in Obstetric & Gynecological Sonography Ser.). (Illus.). 138p. (C). 1995. text 78.00 (*1-85070-613-1*) Prthnon Pub.
***Osmick, Mary J. & Varner, Linnea Smith.** Chronic Care Management, a Toolbox for Action. (Illus.). xiv, 528p. 1999. pap. 130.00 (*0-9677724-0-0*) Natl Resource Ctr.
Osmolovskii, N. P., jt. auth. see Miliutin, A. A.
Osmolovskii, V. G. Linear & Nonlinear Perturbations of the Operator. Rozhkovskaya, Tamara, tr. from RUS. LC 96-40489. (Translations of Mathematical Monographs: Vol. 160). 104p. 1997. text 59.00 (*0-8218-0586-X*, MMONO/160) Am Math.
Osmond & Hoffer. New Hope for Alcoholics. 7.50 (*0-8216-0007-9*) Carol Pub Group.
***Osmond, Alan.** Huff N' Puff. LC 98-48018. (Twice Upon a Time Tales Ser.). (Illus.). 32p. (J). (ps-3). 1999. 11.95 (*1-57102-147-7*, Ideals Child) Hambleton-Hill.
Osmond, Alan. If the Shoe Fits. LC 98-19244. (Twice upon a Time Tales Ser.). 32p. (J). 1998. 11.95 (*1-57102-133-7*) Hambleton-Hill.
— Just Right. LC 98-16586. (Twice upon a Time Ser.). (Illus.). (J). 1998. 11.95 (*1-57102-132-9*, Ideals Child) Hambleton-Hill.
Osmond, D. S., tr. see Steiner, Rudolf.
Osmond, Donny & Romanowski, Patricia. Life Is Just What You Make It: My Story So Far. LC 99-24543. (Illus.). 304p. 1999. 22.95 (*0-7868-6494-X*, Pub. by Disney Pr) Time Warner.
Osmond, Donny & Romanowski, Patty. Life Is Just What You Make It: My Story So Far. 2000. mass mkt. 6.99 (*0-7868-8971-3*, Pub. by Hyperion) Time Warner.
Osmond, Dorothy S., tr. see Steiner, Rudolf.
Osmond, Hazel M. Mollie & Company: And Gussie Too. (Illus.). (J). (ps up). 1996. write for info. (*1-86106-083-1*, Pub. by Minerva Pr) Unity Dist.
Osmond, J. K. & Cowart, J. B. Natural Uranium & Thorium Series Disequilibrium: New Approaches to Geochemical Problems, Vol.1. (Nuclear Science Applications Ser.: Section B). 50p. 1982. pap. text 98.00 (*3-7186-0131-1*) Gordon & Breach.
Osmond, John. Changing Wales Vol. III: The Democratic Challenge. 1993. pap. 21.00 (*0-86383-927-4*, Pub. by Gomer Pr) St Mut.
— The Democratic Challenge. Stephens, Meic, ed. (Changing Wales Ser.). 44p. 1998. pap. 11.95 (*0-8464-4718-5*) Beekman Pubs.
— The Reality of Dyslexia. (Education Ser.). (Illus.). 160p. 1993. 60.00 (*0-304-32762-X*); pap. 35.00 (*0-304-32763-8*) Weidner & Sons.
— The Reality of Dyslexia. rev. ed. 150p. 1995. pap. text 14.95 (*1-57129-017-6*) Brookline Bks.
Osmond, John, ed. The National Question Again. 323p. (C). 1985. pap. 20.00 (*0-86383-132-X*, Pub. by Gomer Pr) St Mut.
— A Parliament for Wales. LC 95-233324. 288p. 1994. pap. 30.00 (*1-85902-173-5*, Pub. by Gomer Pr) St Mut.
Osmond, Margaret, et al. Treating the Aftermath of Sexual Abuse: A Handbook for Working with Children in Care. LC 97-52025. 176p. 1998. pap. 18.95 (*0-87868-693-2*, 6932) Child Welfare.
Osmond, Mark, jt. ed. see Bellairs, Ruth.
Osmond, Nick, ed. see Rimbaud, Arthur.
Osmond, Olive, jt. ed. see Kinsella, Cathy.
Osmond, Olive D. Let's Be Organized: How to Organize Your Entire Life with 5 x 8 Cards. (Illus.). (Orig.). 1990. pap. text 5.95 (*0-929786-00-9*) Know Unltd UT.
— Mother Osmond's Favorite Recipes, Vol. I. 150p. 1990. pap. text. write for info. (*0-929786-01-7*) Know Unltd UT.
Osmond, P. The Mystical Poets of the English Church. 1972. 59.95 (*0-8490-0696-1*) Gordon Pr.
Osmond, Rosalie. Mutual Accusation: Seventeenth-Century Body & Soul Dialogues in Their Literary & Theological Context. 272p. 1970. text 50.00 (*0-8020-5843-4*) U of Toronto Pr.
Osmond-Smith, David, ed. & tr. see Berio, Luciano, et al.
***Osmondson, Eugene.** Odd Ones Never Quit: 2500 Miles Solo on the Mighty Mississippi. (Illus.). 336p. 1999. 20.00 (*0-8059-4720-5*) Dorrance.
Osmont, Kelly. More Than Surviving: Caring for Yourself While You Grieve. (Illus.). 52p. (Orig.). 1990. pap. 3.75 (*1-56123-004-9*) Centering Corp.
— What Can I Say? How to Help Someone Who Is Grieving: A Guide. McFarlane, Marilyn, ed. 34p. 1988. pap. 3.95 (*0-941211-02-9*) Nobility Pr.
Osmont, Kelly & McFarlane, Marilyn. Parting Is Not Goodbye. LC 86-63796. 144p. (Orig.). 1987. 10.95 (*0-941211-00-2*); pap. 9.95 (*0-941211-01-0*) Nobility Pr.
Osmowej, M. N. Polish-Russian Dictionary of Economics. deluxe ed. (POL & RUS.). 494p. 1977. 35.00 (*0-8288-5511-0*, M9121) Fr & Eur.
Osmun, Mark H. Marley's Ghost. LC 99-64220. 336p. 2000. pap. 12.99 (*0-9673079-0-2*, 1225) Twelfth Ngt Pr.
Osmun, Richard, et al. Discoveries in Earth Science. (Upco's Science Ser.). (Illus.). (Orig.). 1987. teacher ed. 9.95 (*0-937323-07-1*); student ed. 5.95 (*0-937323-06-3*) United Pub Co.
— Discoveries in Earth Science: Testing Program Master Sheets. 56p. (Orig.). 1990. 49.95 (*0-937323-10-1*) United Pub Co.
Osmundson, Theodore. Roof Garden Design & Implementation. 1985. text. write for info. (*0-442-27297-9*, VNR) Wiley.
— Roof Gardens: History, Design & Construction. LC 98-50595. 320p. 1999. 75.00 (*0-393-73012-3*) Norton.
Osmus, Kathy, ed. see Echaore-Yoon, Susan.
Osmus, Mary R. Machine Embroidery: Stitches & Techniques Instruction Workbook. 130p. 1990. student ed., spiral bd. 22.95 (*1-883118-01-8*) MRayOs Fiberwrks.
— Machine Embroidery Vol. I: Beginning & Intermediate Patterns. 64p. 1992. student ed. 15.95 (*1-883118-02-6*) MRayOs Fiberwrks.
— Machine Embroidery Vol. II: Intermediate & Advanced Patterns. 106p. 1992. student ed. 19.95 (*1-883118-03-4*) MRayOs Fiberwrks.
***Osner, Dorothy Faye.** Evergreen & Bittersweet. 112p. 2000. 9.95 (*1-56167-603-9*) Am Literary Pr.
Osnes, E., jt. auth. see Kuo, T. T.
***Osnes, Russell E. & Gesme, Carole.** Life is a Celebration: Are You Celebrating, Just Getting Along, Suffering? (Illus.). 304p. 2000. pap. 14.95 (*1-890676-53-5*, Pub. by Beavers Pond) Bookman Bks.
Osness, Ken, jt. auth. see York, Gary.
O'Snodaigh, Padraig, jt. auth. see Mitchell, A.
Osnos, Peter, ed. see Birnbaum, Jeffrey H. & Murray, Alan S.
Osoba, David. Effect of Cancer on Quality of Life. 368p. 1991. lib. bdg. 139.00 (*0-8493-6977-0*, SB324) CRC Pr.
***Osofisan, Femi.** The Nostalgic Drum. LC 99-50317. 1999. pap. write for info. (*0-86543-806-4*) Africa World.
Osofisan, Femi. The Oriki of a Grasshopper, & Other Plays. LC 95-6636. 195p. 1995. pap. 19.95 (*0-88258-181-3*) Howard U Pr.
Osofskey, Joy D., ed. see Zero to Three Violence Study Group.
Osofsky, Audrey. Dreamcatcher. LC 91-20029. (Illus.). 32p. (J). (ps-3). 1992. 15.95 (*0-531-05988-X*); lib. bdg. 16.99 (*0-531-08588-0*) Orchard Bks Watts.
— Dreamcatcher. LC 91-20029. (Illus.). 32p. (J). (ps-2). 1999. pap. 5.95 (*0-531-07113-8*) Orchard Bks Watts.
— Free to Dream: The Making of a Poet, Langston Hughes. LC 95-17354. (Illus.). 112p. (YA). (gr. 4-7). 1996. 16.00 (*0-688-10605-6*) Lothrop.
— My Buddy. LC 92-3028. (Illus.). 32p. (J). (gr. k-3). 1995. 14.95 (*0-8050-1747-X*, Bks Young Read) H Holt & Co.
— My Buddy. (Illus.). (J). (gr. 3). 1995. pap. 5.95 (*0-8050-3546-X*) H Holt & Co.
— My Buddy. (Illus.). (J). (gr. 3). 1995. 8.60 (*0-395-73228-X*) HM.
— My Buddy. large type ed. (Illus.). 54p. (J). (gr. 3). 13.50 (*0-614-20607-3*, L-38215-00 APHB) Am Printing Hse.
Osofsky, Barbara L. Homological Dimensions of Modules. LC 72-6826. (CBMS Regional Conference Series in Mathematics. No. 12). 89p. 1973. reprint ed. pap. 17.00 (*0-8218-1662-4*, CBMS/12) Am Math.
Osofsky, Gilbert. Harlem - The Making of a Ghetto: Negro New York, 1890-1930. 300p. 1996. pap. 14.95 (*1-56663-104-1*, EL133, Elephant Paperbacks) I R Dee.
Osofsky, Howard J. & Blumenthal, Susan J., eds. Premenstrual Syndrome: Current Findings & Future Directions. LC 85-6100. (Progress in Psychiatry Ser.). (Illus.). 111p. 1985. reprint ed. pap. 34.50 (*0-608-06671-0*, 206686800009) Bks Demand.
Osofsky, Joy D., ed. Children in a Violent Society. LC 97-1893. 338p. 1997. lib. bdg. 40.00 (*1-57230-183-X*, 0183) Guilford Pubns.
— Children in a Violent Society. 338p. 1998. pap. text 22.00 (*1-57230-387-5*) Guilford Pubns.
— Handbook of Infant Development. 2nd ed. LC 86-28906. (Personality Processes Ser.). 1424p. 1987. 299.95 (*0-471-88565-7*) Wiley.
***Osofsky, Joy D. & Fitzgerald, Hiram E., eds.** Handbook of Infant Mental Health, 4 vols. Incl. Early Intervention, Evaluation, & Assessment. LC 99-11893. 2000p. 1999. 125.00 (*0-471-18944-8*); Infant Mental Health Groups at High Risk. LC 99-11893. 2000p. 1999. 125.00 (*0-471-18947-2*); Parenting & Child Care. LC 99-11893. Orig. Title: Christian Parenting & Child Care. 425p. 1999. 125.00 (*0-471-18946-4*); Perspectives on Infant Mental Health. LC 99-11893. 2000p. 1999. 125.00 (*0-471-18941-3*); LC 99-11893. (Parenting & Child Care Ser.). 2432p. 2000. 500.00 (*0-471-18988-X*) Wiley.
***Osokina, Elena, et al, eds.** Our Daily Bread: Socialist Distribution & the Art of Survival in Stalin's Russia, 1927-1941. LC 99-86153. (The New Russian History Ser.). (Illus.). 288p. 2000. 64.95 (*1-56324-904-9*) M E Sharpe.
Osor Productions Staff, ed. see Ortiz, Oscar F.
Osorio, Fernando C., jt. auth. see Glorioso, Robert M.
Osorio, Jonathan K. & Young, Kanalu G. Music, Past & Present, at Kamehameha Schools: Lei Mele No Pauahi. LC 98-165854. Orig. Title: Lei Mele No Pauahi. (Illus.). 96p. 1997. pap. 16.95 (*0-87336-050-8*) Kamehameha Schools.
Osorio, Lizaraza J. The Illuminated Island. Nolan, James I., tr. 1976. lib. bdg. 59.95 (*0-8490-2034-4*) Gordon Pr.
Osorio, Marta. Romanies/Gypsies. 1997. pap. text 7.95 (*84-207-3103-X*) Lectorum Pubns.
***Osoroma, Drachir S.** The Scientific Origins of Sexual Preference: A Vanguard of Millennial Cosmology. LC 00-100694. (Illus.). (C). 2000. pap. 17.95 (*0-9678687-0-X*) Noetic Pr CA.
Osostowicz, Krysia, tr. see Eigeldinger, Jean-Jacques.
O'Souza, Philip. Of Human Phenomena. 136p. 1985. 13.95 (*0-318-37151-0*) Asia Bk Corp.
Ospina, Clara, jt. auth. see Dorland, Gil.
Ospina, Hernando C. Salsa! (Illus.). 180p. 1995. pap. 19.00 (*0-85345-956-8*, PB9568, Pub. by Monthly Rev) NYU Pr.
Ospina, Martha. Parchment Craft: Over 15 Original Projests Plus Dozens of New Design Ideas. LC 98-41226. 80p. 1998. 18.95 (*1-57990-095-X*, Pub. by Lark Books) Random.
Ospina, Sonia M. Illusions of Opportunity: Employee Expectations & Workplace Inequality. LC 95-44709. (Illus.). 288p. (C). 1996. 39.95 (*0-87546-356-8*, ILR Press); pap. 16.95 (*0-87546-357-6*, ILR Press) Cornell U Pr.
***Ospina, William.** Mestizo America: The Country of the Future. (Illus.). 344p. 2000. 75.00 (*958-9393-87-X*, Pub. by Villegas Ed) Rizzoli Intl.
Ospina, William. Too Late for Man: Essays. Budoff, Nathan, tr. from SPA. (New Voices from Latin America Ser.). 108p. 1995. pap. 13.95 (*1-57129-018-4*) Brookline Bks.
Ospiov, Yu S. Inverse Problems for Ordinary Differential Equations: Dynamical Solutions. 762p. 1995. text 198.00 (*2-88124-944-2*) Gordon & Breach.
Osprey. Afrikakorps 1941-43, 34. 1999. pap. text 14.95 (*1-85532-938-7*) Osprey.
— Crusader Knight, 18. 1999. pap. text 14.95 (*1-85532-934-4*) Osprey.
— Culloden 1746, Vol. 12. 1999. pap. text 17.95 (*1-85532-629-9*) Greenhill Bks.
— English Longbowman 1250-1513, Vol. 11. (Warrior Ser.). 1999. pap. text 14.95 (*1-85532-932-8*) Greenhill Bks.
— German U-Boat Crews 1914-45, Vol. 60. (Elite Ser.). 1999. pap. text 14.95 (*1-85532-940-9*) Greenhill Bks.
— Gettysburg 1863, Vol. 52. (Campaign Ser.). 1999. pap. text 17.95 (*1-85532-953-0*) Greenhill Bks.
— Guardians of the Roman Empire, Vol. 50. (Elite Ser.). 1999. pap. text 14.95 (*1-85532-941-7*) Greenhill Bks.

An Asterisk (*) at the beginning of an entry indicates that the title is appearing for the first time.

— Hastings 1066, Vol.13. 1999. pap. text 17.95 (*1-85532-630-2*) Greenhill Bks.
— Highland Clansman 1689-1746, Vol. 21. (Warrior Ser.). 1999. pap. text 14.95 (*1-85532-935-2*) Greenhill Bks.
— Normandy 1944, 1. 1999. pap. text 17.95 (*1-85532-949-2*) Osprey.
— Pirates!, 67. 1999. pap. text 14.95 (*1-85532-837-2*) Osprey.
— Samurai, Vol. 23. (Elite Ser.). 1999. pap. text 14.95 (*1-85532-946-8*, Osprey Bks) Chapman & Hall.
— Spartan Army, Vol. 66. (Elite Ser.). 1999. pap. text 14.95 (*1-85532-948-4*) Greenhill Bks.
— Vikings, Vol. 3. (Elite Ser.). 1999. pap. text 14.95 (*1-85532-943-3*, Osprey Bks) Chapman & Hall.
— Waffen SS Soldier 1940-45, Vol. 2. 1999. pap. text 14.95 (*1-85532-931-X*) Greenhill Bks.
— Warriors of Ancient Greece, Vol. 7. (Elite Ser.). 1999. pap. text 14.95 (*1-85532-936-0*) Greenhill Bks.
— Yorktown, 1781, Vol. 47. 1999. pap. text 17.95 (*1-85532-956-5*, Osprey Bks) Chapman & Hall.
— Zulus. Vol. 21. (Illus.). 64p. 1999. pap. text 14.95 (*1-85532-942-5*) Greenhill Bks.

Osprey Staff. Agincourt 1415, 9. 1999. pap. text 17.95 (*1-85532-950-6*) Osprey.
— Ardennes Northern Front 1944: German Forces, 4. (Order of Battle Ser.). 1999. pap. text 19.95 (*1-85532-853-4*) Osprey.
— Armies of the Pharaohs (New Kingdom Egypt), 40. 1999. pap. text 14.95 (*1-85532-939-5*) Osprey.
— Austerlitz 1805, 2. 1999. pap. text 17.95 (*1-85532-954-9*) Osprey.
— Crusades, 19. 1999. pap. text 14.95 (*1-85532-945-X*) Osprey.
— Knights at Tournament, 17. 1999. pap. text 14.95 (*1-85532-937-9*) Osprey.
— Malta 1565, 50. 1999. pap. text 17.95 (*1-85532-830-5*) Osprey.
— Medieval Siege Warfare, 28. 1999. pap. text 14.95 (*1-85532-947-6*) Osprey.
— Osprey Illustrated Military Diary, 2000. (Illus.). 72p. 1999. 18.95 (*1-85532-869-0*, Pub. by Osprey) Stackpole.
— Rorke's Drift 1879, 41. 1999. pap. text 17.95 (*1-85532-951-4*) Osprey.
— Waterloo, 1815, Vol. 15. (Campaign Ser.). 1999. pap. text 17.95 (*1-85532-955-7*, Osprey Bks) Chapman & Hall.

Osprey Staff, et al. Confederate: The Army of Northern Virginia. (Order of Battle Ser.: Vol. 1). (Illus.). 96p. 1999. pap. text 19.95 (*1-85532-834-8*, Pub. by Osprey) Stackpole.

Oss, Kathleen A., jt. auth. see Bean, Barton A.

***Oss, Monica E.** Readings on Trends in Social Service Financing. (Illus.). 87p. 1999. spiral bd. 39.00 (*1-878586-49-1*, M-22) Open Minds PA.

***Oss, Monica E., ed.** Readings in Managed Care Readings. (Illus.). 121p. 1999. spiral bd. 39.00 (*1-878586-36-X*, M-9) Open Minds PA.
— Readings on Behavioral Health & Social Service Industry Market Trends. 64p. 1999. spiral bd. 39.00 (*1-878586-42-4*, M-15) Open Minds PA.
— Readings on Behavioral Health & Social Service Management. (Illus.). 110p. 1999. spiral bd. 39.00 (*1-878586-44-0*, M-17) Open Minds PA.

Oss, Monica E., ed. Readings on Behavioral Health & Social Service Outcomes Measurement & Performance Standards. (Illus.). 65p. 1999. spiral bd. 39.00 (*1-878586-39-4*, M12/21) Open Minds PA.

***Oss, Monica E., ed.** Readings on Employee Assistance & Workplace Issues. (Illus.). 73p. 1999. spiral bd. 39.00 (*1-878586-37-8*, M-10) Open Minds PA.
— Readings on Information Systems & Technology. (Illus.). 48p. 1999. spiral bd. 39.00 (*1-878586-35-1*, M-8/24) Open Minds PA.
— Readings on Marketing. (Illus.). 91p. 1999. spiral bd. 39.00 (*1-878586-34-3*, M-7) Open Minds PA.
— Readings on Mental Health Parity & the Medical Care Offset of Mental Health & Chemical Dependency Treatment. (Illus.). 60p. 1999. spiral bd. 39.00 (*1-878586-46-7*, M-19) Open Minds PA.
— Readings on Pricing Models & Unit Costing. (Illus.). 97p. 1999. spiral bd. 39.00 (*1-878586-38-6*, M-11) Open Minds PA.
— Readings on Risk Management. (Illus.). 72p. 1999. spiral bd. 39.00 (*1-878586-75-0*, M-23) Open Minds PA.
— Readings on Strategic Planning. (Illus.). 89p. 1999. spiral bd. 39.00 (*1-878586-33-5*, M-6) Open Minds PA.

***Oss, Monica E. & Clary, John.** Child Welfare Management & Financing Institute. (Illus.). 1999. spiral bd. 195.00 (*1-878586-24-6*, HB-31) Open Minds PA.

Oss, Monica E. & Clary, John H. Managed Behavioral Health Market Share in the United States, 1998-1999. 5th rev. ed. (Illus.). 50p. 1998. spiral bd. 65.00 (*1-878586-15-7*, DR-1) Open Minds PA.
— Managed Behavioral Health Readiness Audit Tool. 38p. 1998. spiral bd. 39.00 (*1-878586-29-7*, M-2) Open Minds PA.
— Marketing Institute Chartbook: Succeeding in an Increasingly Competitive Market: Marketing Tools for the Behavioral Health & Social Services Fields. (Illus.). 258p. 1998. spiral bd. 295.00 (*1-878586-26-2*, HB-33) Open Minds PA.

***Oss, Monica E. & Clary, John H.** Strategic Cost Management Institute Chartbook: Cost Accounting & Pricing Issues for Succeeding in the Behavioral Health & Social Services Fields. (Illus.). 180p. 1999. spiral bd. 195.00 (*1-878586-27-0*, HB-35) Open Minds PA.
— Strategic Planning & Strategic Collaborations Institute Chartbook: Strategic Options for Behavioral Health & Social Service Organizations. (Illus.). 154p. 1999. spiral bd. 195.00 (*1-878586-25-4*, HB-30) Open Minds PA.

***Oss, Monica E. & Fox, Aleta.** Discussion Guide on Mergers, Alliances & Joint Ventures: Should You Collaborate? What Makes a Collaboration Competitive & Successful. (Illus.). 39p. 1999. spiral bd. 44.00 (*1-878586-31-9*, M-1/5) Open Minds PA.

Oss, Monica E. & Yennie, Henry. Risk Management Institute Chartbook: Succeeding with Case Rate & Capitation Contracts. (Illus.). 1998. spiral bd. 195.00 (*1-878586-28-9*, HB-32) Open Minds PA.

Oss, Monica E., ed. see Fox, Aleta & Garris, Keith.

Oss, O. T. & Oeric, O. N. Psilocybin: Magic Mushroom Grower's Guide. 2nd ed. (Illus.). 81p. 1986. reprint ed. pap. 16.95 (*0-932551-06-8*) Quick Am Pub.

Ossa, Mikka. The Serpentine Rouletted Stamps of Finland: Issues of 1860 & 1866, Vol. 2. Koplowitz, George B., ed. Aro, Kauko I., tr. from FIN. (Illus.). 116p. (Orig.). 1985. pap. text 18.50 (*0-936493-08-9*) Scand Philatelic.

Ossa, Pat, jt. auth. see Nieto, Zoilo C.

Ossana, Diana, jt. auth. see McMurtry, Larry.

***Osseiran, Adam.** Analog & Mixed-Signal Boundary-Scan: A Guide to the IEEE 1149.4 Test Standard. LC 99-51735. (Frontiers in Electronic Testing Ser.). 1999. write for info. (*0-7923-8686-8*) Kluwer Academic.

Osselton, John W., et al. Clinical Neurophysiology: Electroencephalography, Paediatric Neurophysiology, Special Techniques & Applications. (Illus.). 448p. 2000. text 140.00 (*0-7506-1663-6*) Buttrwrth-Heinemann.

Osselton, John W., ed. see Binnie, Colin D., et al.

Osselton, N. E. Chosen Words: Past & Present Problems for Dictionary Makers. (Linguistic Studies). (Illus.). 192p. 1995. text 49.95 (*0-85989-419-3*, Pub. by Univ Exeter Pr) Northwestern U Pr.

Ossenbruggen, Paul J. Fundamental Principles of Systems Analysis & Decision-Making. 412p. 1994. pap. 80.95 (*0-471-52156-6*) Wiley.
— Systems Analysis for Civil Engineers. 328p. 1984. pap. text, suppl. ed. 20.00 (*0-471-89118-5*) Wiley.

Ossenfort, Cynthia. Cruise Ship Jobs! Where They Are & How to Get Them. 80p. Date not set. pap. 24.95 (*0-9670923-0-2*) Exciting Travel.

Ossenkopp, Klaus-Peter. Measuring Movement & Locomotion: From Invertebrates to Humans. Kavaliers, Martin & Sanberg, Paul R., eds. (Neuroscience Intelligence Unit Ser.). 261p. 1996. 99.00 (*1-57059-322-1*) Landes Bioscience.

Ossenkopp, Klaus-Peter, et al, eds. Motor Activity & Movement Disorders: Research Issues & Applications. LC 95-40459. (Contemporary Neuroscience Ser.). (Illus.). 392p. 1995. 119.50 (*0-89603-327-9*, RC376) Humana.

Osseo-Asare, Fran. Good Soup Attracts Chairs: A First African Cookbook for American Kids. LC 92-42982. (Illus.). 160p. 1993. 18.95 (*0-88289-816-7*) Pelican.

Osseo-Asare, K., ed. see International Symposium on Hydrometallurgy Staff.

Osser, Caren. Infinity. (Orig.). 1997. pap. write for info. (*1-57553-481-9*) Watermrk Pr.

Osserman, Richard A., jt. auth. see Ruskay, Joseph A.

Osserman, Robert. Poetry of the Universe: The Mathematical Imagination & the Nature of the Cosmos. (Illus.). 224p. 1996. pap. 11.95 (*0-385-47429-6*, Anchor NY) Doubleday.
— A Survey of Minimal Surfaces. 192p. 1986. reprint ed. pap. 8.95 (*0-486-64998-9*) Dover.

Osserman, Robert, ed. Geometry Vol. V: Minimal Surfaces. 270p. 1996. 102.00 (*3-540-60523-1*) Spr-Verlag.

Osserman, Robert & Hoffman, D. A. The Geometry of the Generalized Gauss Map. LC 80-23014. (Memoirs Ser.: No. 28/236). 105p. 1980. pap. 17.00 (*0-8218-2236-5*, MEMO/28/236) Am Math.

Osserman, Robert & Weinstein, Alan, eds. Geometry of the LaPlace Operator. LC 79-26934. (Proceedings of Symposia in Pure Mathematics Ser.: Vol. 36). 323p. 1982. reprint ed. pap. 42.00 (*0-8218-1439-7*, PSPUM/36) Am Math.

Osserman, Robert, ed. see Pure Mathematics Symposium Staff.

Ossian. Poems of Ossian. 492p. reprint ed. lib. bdg. 79.00 (*0-7812-0259-0*) Rprt Serv.
— Poems of Ossian. Macpherson, James, ed. LC 76-107180. 1970. reprint ed. 49.00 (*0-403-00036-X*) Scholarly.

Ossian, jt. auth. see Macpherson, James.

Ossianic Society of Dublin Staff. Transactions, 6 vols. LC 78-144462. reprint ed. 72.50 (*0-404-09070-2*) AMS Pr.

Ossiannilsson, F. The Auchenorrhyncha (Homoptera) of Fennoscandia & Denmark Pt. 1: Introduction, Infraorder Fulgoromorpha. (Fauna Entomologica Scandinavica Ser.: No. 7-1). (Illus.). 222p. 1978. text 42.00 (*87-87491-24-9*) Lubrecht & Cramer.
— The Auchenorrhyncha (Hompotera) of Fennoscandia & Denmark Pt. 2z: The Families Cicadidae, Cercopidae, Membracidae, & Cicadellidae (Excluding Deltocephalinae) (Fauna Entomologica Scandinavica Ser.: No. 7-2). (Illus.). 408p. 1981. text 53.00 (*87-87491-36-2*) Lubrecht & Cramer.
— The Psylloidea (Homoptera) of Fennoscandia & Demark. LC 92-16949. (Fauna Entomologica Scandinavica Ser.: Vol. 26). (Illus.). 348p. 1992. lib. bdg. 142.00 (*90-04-09610-8*) Brill Academic Pubs.

Ossin, Archie & Ossin, Myrna. How to Start & Run a Profitable Craft Business. LC 77-88745. (Illus.). (C). 1977. pap. 7.95 (*0-930912-00-4*) Ossi Pubns.

Ossin, Myrna, ed. Culinary Arts & Crafts, a Cookbook for Moms, Dads & Kids. (Illus.). 1984. pap. 12.00 (*0-9613532-0-1*) Park Maitland.

Ossin, Myrna, jt. auth. see Ossin, Archie.

Ossip, Kathleen. Living English for Spanish Speakers: Conversational Manual. rev. ed. (Complete Living Language Course Ser.). (ENG & SPA.). 1993. pap. 6.00 (*0-517-59046-8*) Liv Lang.
— Living Language English for Spanish Speaker: Dictionary. rev. ed. (Complete Living Language Course Ser.). (ENG & SPA.). 1993. pap. 5.00 (*0-517-59047-6*) Liv Lang.

Ossipova, Victoria. Introduction to Discrete Mathematics. LC 94-44215. 1994. write for info. (*1-885978-00-6*); pap. write for info. (*1-885978-01-4*) Wrld Fed Pubs.

Ossman, Bruce. Violin Making: A Guide for the Amateur. (Illus.). 67p. 1997. pap. 14.95 (*1-56523-091-4*) Fox Chapel Pub.

Ossman, David. The Rainbow Cafe. limited ed. (Illus.). 20p. 1982. 40.00 (*0-918824-37-0*) Turkey Pr.

Ossman, Susan. Picturing Casablanca: Portraits of Power in a Modern City. LC 93-36561. 1994. 48.00 (*0-520-08402-0*, Pub. by U CA Pr); pap. 16.95 (*0-520-08403-9*, Pub. by U CA Pr) Cal Prin Full Svc.

Osso, Rafael. The Handbook of Communications Technologies Next Decade. LC 99-25427. (Advanced & Emerging Communications Technologies Ser.). 400p. 1999. boxed set 79.95 (*0-8493-9594-1*) CRC Pr.

Ossoff, Jon. In the Cavern of the Demon of the Black Mountain: A Meditation on Oppression, Betrayal & the Tyranny of Control. LC 95-80219. 135p. (C). 1995. pap. text 12.00 (*0-9648850-6-9*) L Canyon Bks.

Ossoff, Robert H. Atlas of Head & Neck Surgery. Date not set. text. write for info. (*0-7216-4922-X*, W B Saunders Co) Harcrt Hlth Sci Grp.

Ossoff, Robert H., jt. auth. see Krespi, Yosef P.

Ossoinig, K. C., ed. Ophthalmic Echography. (Documenta Ophthalmologica Proceedings Ser.). (C). 1987. text 389.50 (*0-89838-873-2*) Kluwer Academic.

Ossoli, Margaret F. Summer on the Lakes. LC 68-24991. (Concordance Ser.: No. 37). 1969. reprint ed. lib. bdg. 75.00 (*0-8383-0225-4*) M S G Haskell Hse.
— Woman in the Nineteenth Century: And Kindred Papers Relating to the Sphere, Condition & Duties, of Woman. Fuller, Arthur B., ed. LC 72-312. (Essay Index Reprint Ser.). 1977. reprint ed. 26.95 (*0-8369-2815-6*) Ayer.
— Woman in the Nineteenth Century & Kindred Papers. 1972. 59.95 (*0-8490-1315-1*) Gordon Pr.

Ossoli, Margaret S. Love Letters of Margaret Fuller, 1845-1846. LC 72-122592. reprint ed. 41.50 (*0-404-04835-8*) AMS Pr.
— Papers on Literature & Art, 2 pts. in 1. LC 76-144668. reprint ed. 49.50 (*0-404-04836-6*) AMS Pr.

Ossoli, Sarah M. Love-Letters of Margaret Fuller, 1845-1846. (BCL1-PS American Literature Ser.). 228p. 1992. reprint ed. lib. bdg. 79.00 (*0-7812-6817-6*) Rprt Serv.
— Marchesa D'. Summer on the Lakes in 1843. (BCL1 - United States Local History Ser.). 256p. 1991. reprint ed. lib. bdg. 79.00 (*0-7812-6320-4*) Rprt Serv.
— Papers on Literature & Art. (BCL1-PS American Literature Ser.). 1992. reprint ed. lib. bdg. 99.00 (*0-7812-6816-8*) Rprt Serv.
— Writings of Margaret Fuller. (BCL1-PS American Literature Ser.). 608p. 1993. reprint ed. lib. bdg. 129.00 (*0-7812-6996-2*) Rprt Serv.
— The Writings of Margaret Fuller. Wade, Mason, ed. LC 72-122079. xi, 608p. 1973. reprint ed. lib. bdg. 49.50 (*0-678-03177-0*) Kelley.

Ossorio, Joseph D., et al. The Little Duke. (Under Twenty Writing Society Ser.). (Illus.). 48p. (J). (gr. 3-5). 1994. pap. 6.95 (*1-56721-049-X*) Twnty-Fifth Cent Pr.
— Poor, Rich & Happy. (Life's Roadmap Ser.). (Illus.). 60p. (J). (gr. 4-6). 1994. pap. 6.95 (*1-56721-043-0*) Twnty-Fifth Cent Pr.
— Truth about the Chase. (Life's Roadmap Ser.). (Illus.). 60p. (J). (gr. 4-6). 1994. pap. 6.95 (*1-56721-044-9*) Twnty-Fifth Cent Pr.

Ossorio, Nelson A. Danger in the Land of Mavericks. (Orig.). 1995. pap. 11.95 (*1-56721-124-0*) Twnty-Fifth Cent Pr.
— Insights from the Other Side of Life. (Orig.). 1995. pap. 10.95 (*1-56721-123-2*) Twnty-Fifth Cent Pr.
— Journeys Through Time. (Orig.). 1995. pap. 8.95 (*1-56721-113-5*) Twnty-Fifth Cent Pr.
— The Myth of Teaching. (Orig.). 1995. pap. 8.95 (*1-56721-122-4*) Twnty-Fifth Cent Pr.
— Power of the Shadow. (Orig.). 1995. pap. 11.95 (*1-56721-119-4*) Twnty-Fifth Cent Pr.
— Selections from the Journeys - Selecciones de las Jornadas. 3rd ed. (ENG & SPA., Illus.). 140p. (Orig.). 1994. 14.95 (*1-56721-088-0*) Twnty-Fifth Cent Pr.
— A Stroll Through Life. (Orig.). 1995. pap. 11.95 (*1-56721-111-9*) Twnty-Fifth Cent Pr.

Ossorio, Nelson A. & Bolinger, Loren, eds. Multilingual Computer Advisor. (ENG, GER & SPA.). (Orig.). 1995. pap. 29.95 (*1-56721-089-9*) Twnty-Fifth Cent Pr.

Ossorio, Nelson A. & Eisberg, George L. The Caves of Amanao. (Orig.). 1995. pap. 12.95 (*1-56721-120-8*) Twnty-Fifth Cent Pr.
— To Tread Gently. (Orig.). 1995. pap. 8.95 (*1-56721-098-8*) Twnty-Fifth Cent Pr.
— To Walk in Silence. (Orig.). 1995. pap. 9.95 (*1-56721-131-3*) Twnty-Fifth Cent Pr.

Ossorio, Nelson A. & Salvadeo, Michele B. Boy of la Mancha. (Spark of Life Ser.). (Illus.). 60p. (J). (gr. 4-6). 1994. pap. 6.95 (*1-56721-068-6*) Twnty-Fifth Cent Pr.
— The Song No One Liked. (To Be Your Own Ser.). (Illus.). 48p. (J). (gr. 3-5). 1994. pap. 6.95 (*1-56721-050-3*) Twnty-Fifth Cent Pr.

Ossorio, Nelson A., et al. Tiger's New Prey. (Wildlife among Us Ser.). (Illus.). 48p. (J). (gr. 4-6). 1994. pap. 6.95 (*1-56721-074-0*) Twnty-Fifth Cent Pr.
— To Run Like the Wind: or The Wisdom of the Cheetah. (To Be Your Own Ser.). (Illus.). 48p. (J). (gr. 4-6). 1994. pap. 6.95 (*1-56721-047-3*) Twnty-Fifth Cent Pr.

Ossorio, Nelson A., jt. auth. see Eisberg, George L.

Ossorio, Peter G. The Collected Works of Peter G. Ossorio Vol. I: Persons. 289p. 1995. text 70.00 (*0-9625661-8-7*) Descriptive Psych Pr.
— Collected Works of Peter G. Ossorio Vol. II: Essays on Clinical Topics. 1997. 70.00 (*0-9625661-9-5*) Descriptive Psych Pr.
— The Collected Works of Peter G. Ossorio Vol. III: Place. 1998. 70.00 (*1-891700-00-6*) Descriptive Psych Pr.

Ossowski, Liliana & Lopez, R. M., eds. Proteolytic Enzymes in Cancer Invasion. (Journal Ser.: Vol. 49, No. 1-3, 1996). (Illus.). 182p. 1996. pap. 62.75 (*3-8055-6318-3*) S Karger.

Ossowski, S. The Foundations of Aesthetics. 416p. 1978. text 138.00 (*90-277-0551-8*) Kluwer Academic.

Ossowski, Sascha. Co-Ordination in Artificial Agent Societies: Social Structures & Its Implications for Autonomous Problem-Solving Agents. Carbonell, J. G. & Siekmann, J., eds. LC 98-55550. (Lecture Notes in Computer Science Ser.: Vol. 1535). xvi, 221p. 1999. pap. 39.00 (*3-540-65495-X*) Spr-Verlag.

Ossulton, M. David. Forensic Toxicology. 200p. 1996. 99.00 (*0-7484-0336-1*) Taylor & Francis.

Osswald, Reiner. Pactane Sunt Servanda? Hattenbauer, Hans, ed. (Rechtshistorische Reihe Ser.: Vol. 175). XXI, 473p. 1998. pap. 67.95 (*3-631-32043-4*) P Lang Pubng.

Osswald, Tim A. Polymer Processing Fundamentals. LC 98-33644. 229p. 1998. pap. 34.95 (*1-56990-262-3*) Hanser-Gardner.

Osswald, Tim A. & Menges, Georg. Materials Science of Polymers for Engineers. LC 95-33357. 512p. (C). 1995. pap. 49.95 (*1-56990-192-9*) Hanser-Gardner.

Osswald, W., ed. Problems of Adrenergic Mechanisms in Blood Vessel. (Journal: Blood Vessels: Vol. 21, No. 3, 1984). (Illus.). 44p. 1984. pap. 35.00 (*3-8055-3927-4*) S Karger.

Ost, B. W., jt. auth. see Burg, R. G.

Ost, David. Solidarity & the Politics of Anti-Politics: Opposition & Reform in Poland since 1968. (Labor & Social Change Ser.). 272p. (C). 1990. 39.95 (*0-87722-655-5*) Temple U Pr.
— Solidarity & the Politics of Anti-Politics: Opposition & Reform in Poland since 1968. (Labor & Social Change Ser.). 272p. (C). 1991. pap. 18.95 (*0-87722-900-7*) Temple U Pr.

Ost, David, ed. see Michnik, Adam.

Ost, Francois & Van de Kerchove, Michel. The Legal System: Between Order & Disorder. Stewart, Iain, tr. 216p. 1994. text 48.00 (*0-19-825692-2*) OUP.

Ost, Hans. Leonardo-Studien. (Beitraege zur Kunstgeschichte Ser.: Vol. 11). (GER., Illus.). xii, 750p. (C). 1975. 165.40 (*3-11-005727-1*) De Gruyter.

Ostacher, Joan, ed. see Rothstein, Evelyn, et al.

Ostacher, Joan, ed. see Waters, Michelle & Mehlmann, Marybeth A.

Ostadal, Bohuslav & Dhalla, Naranjan S., eds. Heart Function in Health & Disease: Proceedings of the Cardiovascular Program Sponsored by the Council of Cardiac Metabolism of the International Society & Federation of Cardiology During the Regional Meeting of the International Union of Physiological Sciences, Prague, Czechoslovakia, June 30 - July 5, 1991. LC 92-48911. (Developments in Cardiovascular Medicine Ser.: Vol. DICM 140). 352p. (C). 1993. text 172.50 (*0-7923-2052-2*) Kluwer Academic.

Ostade, Ingrid Tieken-Boon Van, see Tieken-Boon Van Ostade, Ingrid.

Ostaijen, Paul Van, see Van Ostaijen, Paul.

Ostapenko, N. I., et al. Spectroscopy of Defects in Organic Crystals. Onipko, Alexander I., tr. from RUS. LC 93-3224.Tr. of Spektraskopiia Defektov V Molekuliarnykh Kristallakh. 272p. (C). 1993. text 178.50 (*0-7923-2230-4*) Kluwer Academic.

***Ostapski.** Business Law: The Game. 2000. pap. 10.00 (*0-324-07059-4*) Sth-Wstrn College.

Ostar, Allan W., jt. auth. see Harcleroad, Fred F.

Ostaro, Dhruv. The Art & Craft of Success: Ten Steps. 180p. 2000. pap. 15.00 (*1-58151-051-9*, Pub. by BookPartners) Midpt Trade.

Ostashev, Vladimir. Acoustics in Moving Inhomogeneous Media. LC 97-66370. (Illus.). 272p. (C). (gr. 13). 1998. 150.00 (*0-419-22430-0*, D5612, E & FN Spon) Routledge.

Ostaszewski, Adam. Advanced Mathematical Methods. (London School of Economics Mathematics Ser.). (Illus.). 559p. (C). 1991. pap. text 52.95 (*0-521-28964-5*) Cambridge U Pr.
— Mathematics in Economics: Models & Methods. LC 92-32454. 1993. 64.95 (*0-631-18055-9*); pap. 31.95 (*0-631-18056-7*) Blackwell Pubs.

Ostaszewski, Krzysztof. Henstock Integration in the Plane. LC 86-17399. (Memoirs of the American Mathematical Society Ser.: No. 63/353). 106p. 1986. pap. 21.00 (*0-8218-2416-3*, MEMO/63/353) Am Math.
— An Investigation into Possible Applications of Fuzzy Set Methods in Actuarial Science. 1993. text 20.00 (*0-938959-27-1*) Soc Actuaries.

Ostberg, Donald R., jt. auth. see Lynch, Ransom V.

Ostberg, Kay. The Easy Way Probate: A Step-by-Step Guide to Settling an Estate. 173p. 1994. 10.00 (*0-910073-21-X*) HALT DC.
— If You Want to Sue a Lawyer: A Directory of Legal Malpractice Attorneys. 130p. 1995. 10.00 (*0-910073-22-8*) HALT DC.

Ostberg, Kay A., et al. Your Guide to Living Trusts & Other Trusts: How Trusts Can Help You Avoid Probate & Taxes. 214p. 1994. pap. 10.00 (*0-910073-19-8*) HALT DC.

Ostberg, Wilhelm. The Kondoa Transformation: Coming to Grips with Soil Erosion in Central Tanzania. (Research Report Ser.: No. 76). 99p. 1986. write for info. (*91-7106-251-3*, Pub. by Nordic Africa) Transaction Pubs.
— Land Is Coming Up: The Berunge of Central Tanzania &

O

Their Environments. (Stockholm Studies in Social Anthropology: No. 34). (Illus.). 258p. (Orig.). 1995. pap. 67.50 (*91-7153-404-0*) Coronet Bks.

Ostblom, Svante, jt. auth. see Karlof, Bengt.

Ostbo, Johannes, jt. auth. see Fabricius Hansen, Cathrine.

Osthy, Marnald. Matching Up: Winning with Team Defense. 57p. (Orig.). 1985. pap. 9.95 (*0-932741-03-7*) Championship Bks & Vid Prodns.

***Ostdeutsche Sparkassenstiftung Foundation.** Vitale Module: Gegenwartskunst aus Sachsen. (GER., Illus.). 192p. 1998. pap. text 25.00 (*90-5705-079-X*, Verlag Kunst) Gordon & Breach.

Ostdiek. Inquiry into Physics with Infotrac. 4th ed. LC 99-38917. (Physics). 1999. 62.00 (*0-534-36461-6*) Brooks-Cole.

— Inquiry Physics. 2nd ed. Date not set. pap. text, teacher ed. write for info. (*0-314-83973-9*) West Pub.

Ostdiek, Gilbert. Catechesis for Liturgy. 1986. 12.95 (*0-912405-23-6*, Pastoral Press) OR Catholic.

Ostdiek, Gilbert, jt. auth. see Hughes, Kathleen.

***Ostdiek, Vernon J. & Bord, Donald J.** Inquiry into Physics. 4th ed. LC 99-38917. 504p. 1999. 78.95 (*0-534-37311-9*) Brooks-Cole.

Ostdiek, Vernon J., jt. auth. see Bord, Donald J.

Osteaux, M., et al, eds. Hospital Integrated Picture Archiving & Communication Systems: A Second Generation PACS Concept. (Illus.). 384p. 1992. 255.00 (*0-387-54592-1*) Spr-Verlag.

Osteaux, M. & Meirleir, K., eds. Magnetic Resonance Imaging & Spectroscopy in Sports Medicine. (Illus.). 216p. 1991. 123.00 (*0-387-52548-3*) Spr-Verlag.

Ostebee. Calc from G, N, S Vols. 1,2 1e (Sch Bndg) 1997. 86.00 (*0-03-052659-0*) H Holt & Co.

— Calc from Graph, Num, & Sym Points View: Volume II, Vol. 2. LC 96-67893. (C). 1996. text 44.50 (*0-03-016977-1*) Harcourt Coll Pubs.

— Calc Graph Num & Sym, Vol. 2. 1997. teacher ed. 4.00 (*0-03-017429-5*) Dryden Pr.

— Calculus: Explained Using Graphs & Calculators, 2 vols., Vols. 1 & 2. (C). 1996. pap. text, lab manual ed. 20.50 (*0-03-017423-6*) Harcourt Coll Pubs.

— Calculus: Points of View. 2nd ed. (C). 1999. pap. text 44.50 (*0-03-025664-X*) Harcourt Coll Pubs.

— Calculus: Principles in Practice. (C). 2000. pap. text 44.50 (*0-03-025712-3*) Harcourt Coll Pubs.

— Calculus: Student Answer Book, Vol. 1. (C). 1996. pap. text, student ed. 3.00 (*0-03-017432-5*) Harcourt Coll Pubs.

— Calculus & Mathematics. (C). 1996. pap. text, lab manual ed. 20.50 (*0-03-017424-4*) Harcourt Coll Pubs.

— Calculus Expl Usg Derive -CALC. (C). 1996. pap. text, lab manual ed. 20.50 (*0-03-017428-7*) Harcourt Coll Pubs.

— Calculus explorations using Maple, Vol. 1 & 2. LC 96-148789. (C). 1996. pap. text, lab manual ed. 20.50 (*0-03-017434-1*) Harcourt Coll Pubs.

— Calculus for G, N, S, Vol. 2. 1997. 92.50 (*0-03-017417-1*, Pub. by Harcourt Coll Pubs) Harcourt.

— Calculus from Graphs, Numbers, & Symbols, Vol. 1. (C). 1996. pap. text, student ed. 17.00 (*0-03-017404-X*, Pub. by Harcourt Coll Pubs) Harcourt.

— Calculus from Graphs, Numbers, & Symbols, Vol. 2. (C). 1997. pap. text, student ed. 17.00 (*0-03-017433-3*, Pub. by Harcourt Coll Pubs) Harcourt.

— Calculus from Graphs, Numbers, & Symbols, Vols. 1 & 2. (C). 1997. text, lab manual ed. 86.00 (*0-03-019587-X*) Harcourt Coll Pubs.

— Calculus Graphs, Numbers & Symbols, Vol. 1. 1996. 92.50 (*0-03-017407-4*) Harcourt Coll Pubs.

— Calculus, Graphs, Numbers & Symbols, Vols. 1 & 2. 1997. 33.50 (*0-03-017418-X*) Harcourt Coll Pubs.

— Calculus, Graphs, Numbers, Symbols with ABK, Vol. 2. (C). 1997. 35.00 (*0-03-018107-0*) Harcourt.

— Calc Graph Number & System Points, Vol. 1. 1996. teacher ed. 17.00 (*0-03-017409-0*, Pub. by Harcourt Coll Pubs) Harcourt.

— Lecture Guide & Student Notes for Calculus, Vol. 2. 1996. teacher ed. 17.00 (*0-03-017408-2*, Pub. by Harcourt Coll Pubs) Harcourt.

— Multivariable Calculus. (C). 1998. text 39.00 (*0-03-018903-9*); pap. text, teacher ed. 28.00 (*0-03-018904-7*) Harcourt Coll Pubs.

— Multivariable Calculus: Solutions Manual. (C). 1998. pap. text, student ed. 12.50 (*0-03-018908-X*) Harcourt Coll Pubs.

— Multivariable Calculus: Student Answer Book. 1998. pap. text, student ed. 3.50 (*0-03-018907-1*) Harcourt.

Ostebee, jt. auth. see Zorn.

Ostebee, Arnold. Multivariable Calculus from Graphical, Numerical, & Symbolic Points of View. 80p. (C). 1997. pap. text, student ed. 14.00 (*0-03-023787-4*) SCP.

Ostebee, Arnold & Zorn, Paul. Multivariable Calculus from Graphical, Numerical, & Symbolic Points of View. 2nd ed. (C). 1997. pap. text 20.00 (*0-03-023786-6*) SCP.

Osteen, D. Healed of Cancer. 96p. 1986. mass mkt. 4.00 (*0-912631-33-3*) J O Pubns.

O'Steen, Darlene, jt. auth. see Needle's Prayse Staff.

Osteen, Joh. How to Release Power of God. 64p. 1968. mass mkt. 2.00 (*0-912631-06-6*) J O Pubns.

Osteen, John. El ABC de la Fe.Tr. of ABC's of Faith. (SPA.). 32p. 1996. mass mkt. 0.75 (*0-912631-67-8*) J O Pubns.

— ABC's of Faith. 32p. 1981. mass mkt. 0.75 (*0-912631-26-0*) J O Pubns.

— Amor & Matrimonio.Tr. of Love & Marriage. (SPA.). 32p. 1996. mass mkt. 0.75 (*0-912631-73-2*) J O Pubns.

— The Believer's #1 Need. 48p. 1980. mass mkt. 2.00 (*0-912631-09-0*) J O Pubns.

— Believing God for Your Loved Ones. 32p. 1988. mass mkt. 1.50 (*0-912631-39-2*) J O Pubns.

— The Bible Way to Spiritual Power. 80p. 1970. mass mkt. 2.00 (*0-912631-10-4*) J O Pubns.

— Como Demostrar la Derrota de Satanas.Tr. of How to Demonstrate Satan's Defeat. (SPA.). 32p. 1996. mass mkt. 1.50 (*0-912631-69-4*) J O Pubns.

— Como Recibir la Vida Eterna.Tr. of How to Receive Life Eternal. (SPA.). 48p. 1986. mass mkt. 0.75 (*0-912631-61-9*) J O Pubns.

— Como Reclamar los Beneficios del Testamento.Tr. of How to Claim the Benefits of the Will. (SPA.). 64p. 1984. mass mkt. 2.00 (*0-912631-55-4*) J O Pubns.

— The Confessions of a Baptist Preacher. 112p. 1978. pap. 5.00 (*0-912631-00-7*) J O Pubns.

— Creyendo en Dios por Sus Seres Queridos.Tr. of Believing God for Your Loved Ones. (SPA.). 32p. 1996. mass mkt. 1.50 (*0-912631-70-8*) J O Pubns.

— Deception! Recognizing True & False Ministries. 48p. 1986. mass mkt. 0.75 (*0-912631-32-5*) J O Pubns.

— Destruyendo Fortalezas.Tr. of Pulling down Strongholds. (SPA.). 40p. 1981. mass mkt. 1.50 (*0-912631-52-X*) J O Pubns.

— The Divine Flow. 32p. 1978. mass mkt. 1.50 (*0-912631-11-2*) J O Pubns.

— El Divino Fluir.Tr. of Divine Flow. (SPA.). 32p. 1979. mass mkt. 1.50 (*0-912631-53-8*) J O Pubns.

— Four Principles in Receiving from God. 32p. 1981. mass mkt. 0.75 (*0-912631-20-1*) J O Pubns.

— Hay un Milagro en Tu Boca.Tr. of There Is a Miracle in Your Mouth. (SPA.). 32p. 1979. mass mkt. 1.50 (*0-912631-56-2*) J O Pubns.

— How to Claim the Benefits of the Will. 48p. 1978. mass mkt. 2.00 (*0-912631-03-1*) J O Pubns.

— How to Demonstrate Satan's Defeat. 32p. 1978. mass mkt. 1.50 (*0-912631-30-9*) J O Pubns.

— How to Flow in the Super Supernatural. 64p. 1978. mass mkt. 2.00 (*0-912631-05-8*) J O Pubns.

— How to Minister Healing to the Sick. 32p. 1981. mass mkt. 0.75 (*0-912631-28-7*) J O Pubns.

— How to Receive Life Eternal. 48p. 1985. mass mkt. 0.75 (*0-912631-31-7*) J O Pubns.

— Keep What God Gives. 32p. 1980. mass mkt. 0.75 (*0-912631-22-8*) J O Pubns.

— Love & Marriage. 32p. 1980. mass mkt. 0.75 (*0-912631-23-6*) J O Pubns.

— Un Lugar Llamado Alli.Tr. of Place Called There. (SPA.). 32p. 1996. mass mkt. 0.75 (*0-912631-76-7*) J O Pubns.

— Un Milagro para su Matrimonio.Tr. of A Miracle for Your Marriage. (SPA.). 32p. 1996. mass mkt. 1.50 (*0-912631-72-4*) J O Pubns.

— A Miracle for Your Marriage. 32p. 1988. mass mkt. 1.50 (*0-912631-38-4*) J O Pubns.

— La Necesidad No. 1 del Creyente.Tr. of Believer's #1 Need. (SPA.). 48p. 1996. mass mkt. 2.00 (*0-912631-71-6*) J O Pubns.

— Overcoming Hindrances to Receiving the Baptism in the Holy Spirit. 56p. 1987. mass mkt. 2.00 (*0-912631-37-6*) J O Pubns.

— A Place Called There. 32p. 1982. mass mkt. 0.75 (*0-912631-19-8*) J O Pubns.

— Pulling down Strongholds. 40p. 1972. mass mkt. 1.50 (*0-912631-07-4*) J O Pubns.

— Que Hacer Cuando Nada Parece Dar Resultado.Tr. of What to Do When Nothing Seems to Work. (SPA.). 32p. 1986. mass mkt. 0.75 (*0-912631-60-0*) J O Pubns.

— Que Hacer Cuando Viene el Tentador.Tr. of What to Do When the Tempter Comes. (SPA.). 32p. 1996. mass mkt. 1.50 (*0-912631-65-1*) J O Pubns.

— Receive the Holy Spirit. 32p. 1980. mass mkt. 0.75 (*0-912631-24-4*) J O Pubns.

— Reciba al Espiritu Santo.Tr. of Receive the Holy Spirit. (SPA.). 48p. 1986. mass mkt. 0.75 (*0-912631-63-5*) J O Pubns.

— Reigning in Life As a King. 144p. 1984. pap. 5.00 (*0-912631-01-5*) J O Pubns.

— Rivers of Living Water. 96p. 1978. mass mkt. 2.50 (*0-912631-08-2*) J O Pubns.

— Sanada de Cancer.Tr. of Healed of Cancer. (SPA.). 104p. 1986. mass mkt. 4.00 (*0-912631-64-3*) J O Pubns.

Osteen, John. Saturday's Coming. 32p. 1980. mass mkt. 0.75 (*0-912631-25-2*) J O Pubns.

Osteen, John. Seven Facts about Prevailing Prayer. 24p. 1990. mass mkt. 0.75 (*0-912631-41-4*) J O Pubns.

— Seven Qualities of a Man of Faith. 34p. 1990. mass mkt. 0.75 (*0-912631-42-2*) J O Pubns.

Osteen, John. El Sexto Sentido... Fe.Tr. of Sixth Sense... Faith. (SPA.). 48p. 1985. mass mkt. 1.50 (*0-912631-54-6*) J O Pubns.

Osteen, John. Six Lies the Devil Uses to Destroy Marriages. 48p. 1989. mass mkt. 2.00 (*0-912631-98-8*) J O Pubns.

— The Sixth Sense... Faith. 32p. 1980. mass mkt. 1.50 (*0-912631-12-0*) J O Pubns.

Osteen, John. Spiritual Food for Victorious Living. 48p. 1985. mass mkt. 0.75 (*0-912631-96-1*) J O Pubns.

Osteen, John. There Is a Miracle in Your Mouth. 32p. 1978. pap. 1.50 (*0-912631-14-7*) J O Pubns.

— This Awakening Generation. 96p. 1964. mass mkt. 2.50 (*0-912631-15-5*) J O Pubns.

— The Truth Shall Set You Free. 48p. 1978. mass mkt. 2.00 (*0-912631-13-9*) J O Pubns.

— Unraveling the Mystery of the Blood Covenant. 80p. 1987. mass mkt. 2.50 (*0-912631-34-1*) J O Pubns.

— What to Do When Nothing Seems to Work. 32p. 1981. mass mkt. 0.75 (*0-912631-27-9*) J O Pubns.

— What to Do When the Tempter Comes. 32p. 1981. mass mkt. 1.50 (*0-912631-16-3*) J O Pubns.

— You Can Change Your Destiny. 64p. 1968. mass mkt. 2.00 (*0-912631-17-1*) J O Pubns.

Osteen, Kevin G., jt. auth. see Diamond, Michael P.

***Osteen, Louis.** Louis Osteen's Charleston Cuisine: Recipes from a Lowcountry Chef. LC 99-32156. 320p. 1999. 24.95 (*1-56512-087-6*) Algonquin Bks.

***Osteen, Mark.** American Magic & Dread: The Fiction of Don DeLillo. LC 00-24546. 288p. 2000. write for info. (*0-8122-3551-7*) U of Pa Pr.

Osteen, Mark. The Economy of Ulysses: Making Both Ends Meet. (Irish Studies). 416p. 1995. text 49.95 (*0-8156-2653-3*); pap. text 19.95 (*0-8156-2661-4*) Syracuse U Pr.

Osteen, Mark & Woodmansee, Martha. The New Economic Criticism. LC 98-20146. 320p. (C). 1998. 100.00 (*0-415-14944-4*); pap. 29.99 (*0-415-14945-2*) Routledge.

Osteen, Mark, ed. see DeLillo, Don.

Osteen, Marlene & Cumberland House Publishing Staff. Great Chefs of the South. LC 97-39902. (Illus.). 224p. 1997. 24.95 (*1-888952-45-8*) Cumberland Hse.

O'Steen, Neal. Making Heroes of Scholars: The Honor Society of Phi Kappa Phi, 1971-1983. (Illus.). 142p. 1985. 10.00 (*0-9614651-0-7*); pap. 6.00 (*0-9614651-1-5*) Honor Soc P K P.

Osteen, Robert T., jt. ed. see Steele, Glenn, Jr.

Ostell, Alistair & Oakland, Susan. Headteacher Stress, Coping & Health: A Research Monograph. 272p. 1995. 72.95 (*1-85972-164-8*, Pub. by Avebry) Ashgate Pub Co.

Osten, Gert Von Der, see Von Der Osten, Gert.

***Osten, H. J.** Carbon-Containing Layers on Silicon: Growth, Properties & Applications. (Materials Science Foundations Ser.: Vol. 7). (Illus.). 77p. (C). 1999. pap. 48.00 (*0-87849-834-6*, Pub. by Trans T Pub) Enfield Pubs NH.

Osten, James, ed. see Hassall, Kevin & Siembieda, Kevin.

Osten, James, ed. see Siembieda, Kevin.

Osten, James, ed. see Siembieda, Kevin & Bartold, Thomas.

Osten, James, ed. see Siembieda, Kevin & Breaux, Wayne, Jr.

Osten, James, ed. see Siembieda, Kevin & Carella, C. J.

Osten, James, ed. see Siembieda, Kevin & Kornmann, Chris.

Osten, James, ed. see Siembieda, Kevin & Nowak, Patrick.

Osten, James, ed. see Siembieda, Kevin & Zeleznik, John.

Osten, James, ed. see Siembieda, Kevin, et al.

Osten-Sacken, C. R. & Smith, K. G. Record of My Life-Work in Entomology. 1978. 50.00 (*0-7855-0672-1*) St Mut.

Osten, Wolfgang. Fringe '97. Juptner, Werner, ed. 300p. 1998. 149.95 (*3-527-40126-1*) Wiley.

Osten, Wolfgang, et al, eds. Fringe, '89: Automatic Processing of Fringe Patterns. (Chemical Research Ser.: Vol. 10). 168p. 1989. pap. 27.00 (*3-05-500682-8*, Wiley-VCH) Wiley.

Osten, Wolfgang, ed. see Kreis, Thomas.

Osten, Wolfgang, jt. ed. see Kujawinska, Malgorzata.

Ostendarp, Carol, jt. auth. see Hekelman, Francine.

Ostendorf, Lloyd. Photographs of Mary Todd Lincoln. 64p. 1989. reprint ed. pap. text 5.00 (*0-942579-05-4*) IHPA.

Ostendorf, Wim, jt. ed. see Musterd, Sako.

Ostenfeld, E. N. Forms, Matter & Mind: Three Strands in Plato's Metaphysics. 360p. 1982. text 141.50 (*90-247-3051-1*) Kluwer Academic.

Ostenfeld, Erik. Ancient Greek Psychology & the Modern Mind-Body Debate. 120p. (Orig.). (C). 1986. pap. text 16.95 (*87-7288-010-4*, Pub. by Aarhus Univ Pr) David Brown.

***Ostenfeld, Erik & Blomquist, Karin, eds.** Greek Romans & Roman Greeks: Studies in Cultural Interaction. (Studies in Mediterranean Antiquity: Vol. 3). (Illus.). 196p. 2000. 29.95 (*87-7288-796-6*, Pub. by Aarhus Univ Pr) David Brown.

Ostenfeld, Erik Nis, ed. Essays on Plato's Republic. (Studies in Mediterranean Antiquity: Vol. 2). 120p. 1998. 26.95 (*87-7288-785-0*, Pub. by Aarhus Univ Pr) David Brown.

Ostenso, Martha. Wild Geese. 1996. pap. 7.95 (*0-7710-9994-0*) McCland & Stewart.

Ostenso, Martha, jt. auth. see Kenny, Elizabeth.

Ostenson, C. G., et al. New Concepts in the Pathogenesis of NIDDM. LC 93-29031. (Advances in Experimental Medicine & Biology Ser.: Vol. 334). (Illus.). 326p. (C). 1993. text 89.50 (*0-306-44563-8*, Kluwer Plenum) Kluwer Academic.

Ostenstad, Gunnar H. Patterns of Redemption in the Fourth Gospel: An Experiment in Structural Analysis. LC 98-18598. (Studies in the Bible & Early Christianity: Vol. 38). 404p. 1998. 109.95 (*0-7734-8396-9*) E Mellen.

Oster, Andrew G., tr. see Burghardt, Erich.

Oster, Clinton V., Jr., et al. Why Airplanes Crash: Aviation Safety in a Changing World. (Illus.). 224p. 1992. text 45.00 (*0-19-507223-5*) OUP.

Oster, Clinton V., Jr., jt. auth. see Meyer, John R.

Oster, Don. Largemouth Bass. LC 83-166989. (Hunting & Fishing Library). (Illus.). 160p. 1983. 19.95 (*0-86573-005-9*) Creat Pub Intl.

Oster, Eileen F. The Healing Mind: Your Guide to the Power of Meditation, Prayer, & Reflection. LC 96-2170. (Illus.). 208p. 1996. pap. 14.00 (*0-7615-0488-5*) Prima Pub.

Oster, Ernst, tr. see Schenker, Heinrich.

Oster, George F., ed. Some Mathematical Questions in Biology. LC 77-25086. (Lectures on Mathematics in the Life Sciences: Vol. 13). 174p. 1980. pap. 37.00 (*0-8218-1163-0*, LLSCI/13) Am Math.

Oster, George F., et al, eds. Irreversible Thermodynamics & the Origin of Life. xii, 70p. 1974. text 184.00 (*0-677-14270-6*) Gordon & Breach.

Oster, George F. & Wilson, Edward O. Caste & Ecology in the Social Insects. LC 78-51185. (Monographs in Population Biology: Vol. 12). 371p. 1978. reprint ed. pap. 115.10 (*0-608-02947-5*, 206401300008) Bks Demand.

Oster, Gerald D. & Caro, Janice E. Understanding & Treating Depressed Adolescents & Their Families. LC 89-37665. (Personality Processes Ser.). 228p. 1990. 105.00 (*0-471-60897-1*) Wiley.

Oster, Gerald D. & Gould, Patricia. Using Drawings in Assessment & Therapy: A Guide for Mental Health Professionals. LC 86-30958. (Illus.). 208p. 1987. pap. text 24.95 (*0-87630-478-1*) Brunner-Mazel.

Oster, Gerald D. & Montgomery, Sarah. Helping Your Depressed Teenager: A Guide for Parents & Caregivers. 208p. 1994. pap. 18.95 (*0-471-62184-6*) Wiley.

Oster, Judith. Toward Robert Frost: The Reader & the Poet. LC 90-11277. 352p. 1993. pap. 19.95 (*0-8203-1621-0*) U of Ga Pr.

Oster, Kurt A., et al. Homogenized Milk May Cause Your Heart Attack: The XO Factor. (Advances in Preventive Health Ser.). (Illus.). 312p. (Orig.). 1983. 14.95 (*0-943550-01-7*); pap. 10.95 (*0-943550-02-5*) Park City Pr.

Oster, M. 10 Steps to Beautiful Roses. 1989. pap. 2.95 (*0-88266-553-7*, Storey Pub) Storey Bks.

Oster, Maggie. All about Herbs. LC 98-66920. (Ortho's All about Ser.). (Illus.). 96p. 1998. pap. 11.95 (*0-89721-420-X*, Ortho Bks) Meredith Bks.

— Bamboo Baskets: Japanese Art & Culture Interwoven with the Beauty of Ikebana. (Illus.). 144p. 1998. pap. text 23.00 (*0-7881-5455-9*) DIANE Pub.

— Herbal Palate Cookbook: Delicious Recipes That Showcase the Versatility & Magic of Fresh Herbs. 1998. pap. 19.95 (*1-58017-025-0*) Storey Bks.

— Herbal Vinegar. Steege, Gwen, ed. LC 93-20858. (Illus.). 176p. 1994. 18.95 (*0-88266-876-5*, Storey Pub); pap. 12.95 (*0-88266-843-9*) Storey Bks.

— Making Ice Cream & Frozen Yogurt. LC 95-30536. (Storey Publishing Bulletin Ser.: Vol. A-142). 1995. pap. 2.95 (*0-88266-414-X*) Storey Bks.

Oster, Maggie. Perennials. LC 99-216600. (Illus.). 1997. write for info. (*0-914697-89-7*) N Amer Outdoor Grp.

Oster, Maggie & Gilbertie, Sal. Growing Herbs in Containers. LC 98-4598. (Country Wisdom Bulletins Ser.: Vol. A-179). 1998. 2.95 (*1-58017-014-5*) Storey Bks.

— The Herbal Palate Cookbook. LC 96-3203. (Illus.). 176p. 1996. 29.95 (*0-88266-915-X*) Storey Bks.

***Oster, Maggie & Gilbertie, Sal.** The Herbal Palate Cookbook: Delicious Recipes That Showcase the Versatility & Magic of Fresh Herbs. (Illus.). 172p. 2000. reprint ed. text 30.00 (*0-7881-9096-2*) DIANE Pub.

***Oster, Maggie & Reilly, Ann.** How to Plant & Grow Annuals & Perennials. (Illus.). 192p. 1999. 24.95 (*2-921556-87-1*, Pub. by Modus Viv) ACCESS Pubs Network.

***Oster, Merrill & Hamel, Mike.** The Entrepreneur's Creed: The Principles & Passions of 20 Successful Entrepreneurs. 2000. 19.99 (*0-8054-2357-5*) Broadman.

Oster, Merrill J. Commodity Futures for Profit. LC 77-92119. 1983. 30.00 (*0-914230-04-2*) Investor Pubns.

— How to Multiply Your Money. LC 78-14888. 1985. 14.95 (*0-914230-03-4*) Investor Pubns.

Oster, Merrill J., et al. Multiply Your Money Trading Soybeans: A Beginner's Guide to Speculating in Soybean Futures. 198p. 1981. 14.95 (*0-914230-10-7*) Investor Pubns.

***Oster, Nancy, et al.** Making Informed Medical Decisions: Where to Look & How to Use What You Find. 280p. 2000. pap. 17.95 (*1-56592-459-2*, Patient-Centered) OReilly & Assocs.

Oster, P. Robert Dictionnaire des Citations Francaises. (FRE.). 934p. 1997. 69.95 (*0-320-00489-9*) Fr & Eur.

Oster, P., jt. auth. see Winter, Hans.

Oster, Patrick. The Mexicans: A Personal Portrait of a People. LC 89-45843. 336p. 1990. reprint ed. pap. 14.00 (*0-06-097310-2*, Perennial) HarperTrade.

Oster, Pierre. Dictionnaire de Citations Francaises. (FRE.). 934p. 1992. 110.00 (*0-7859-9219-7*) Fr & Eur.

— Dictionnaire de Citations Francaises de Villon a Beaumarchais, Vol. 1. (FRE.). 818p. 1990. 34.95 (*0-7859-9215-4*) Fr & Eur.

Oster, Richard E. The Acts of the Apostles, Pt. 2. LC 79-63269. 180p. 1984. 12.95 (*0-915547-25-2*) Abilene Christ U.

— A Bibliography of Ancient Ephesus. LC 87-12617. (American Theological Library Association Monograph: No. 19). 181p. 1987. 26.50 (*0-8108-1996-1*) Scarecrow.

Oster, Sharon M. Modern Competitive Analysis. 2nd ed. LC 93-9826. (Illus.). 424p. 1994. text 51.95 (*0-19-507579-X*) OUP.

— Modern Competitive Analysis. 3rd ed. LC 98-38221. (Illus.). 448p. (C). 1999. text 54.00 (*0-19-511941-X*) OUP.

— Strategic Management for Nonprofit Organizations: Theory & Cases. (Illus.). 360p. 1995. text 39.95 (*0-19-508503-5*) OUP.

Oster, Sharon M., ed. Management of Non-Profit Organizations. (International Library of Management). 544p. 1994. 235.95 (*1-85521-465-2*, Pub. by Dartmth Pub) Ashgate Pub Co.

Osterberg, Arvid, et al, eds. Design Research Interactions. (EDRA Proceedings Ser.). 600p. 1981. pap. text 30.00 (*0-939922-03-7*) EDRA.

Osterberg, E. & Saila, S. L. Natural Experiments with Decreased Availability of Alcoholic Beverages: Finnish Alcohol Strikes in 1972 & 1985. (Finnish Foundation for Alcohol Studies: Vol. 40). 1991. pap. 35.00 (*951-9192-49-2*) Rutgers Ctr Alcohol.

An Asterisk (*) at the beginning of an entry indicates that the title is appearing for the first time.

Osterberg, Jan. Self & Others: A Study of Ethical Egoism. 266p. (C). 1988. lib. bdg. 147.00 (*90-277-2648-5*, Pub. by Kluwer Academic) Kluwer Academic.

Osterberg, Matthew. Matamora to Shohola. LC 98-87321. (Images of America Ser.). (Illus.). 128p. 1998. pap. 18.99 (*0-7524-1297-3*) Arcadia Publng.

Osterberg, Richard. Silver Hollowware for Dining Elegance. (Illus.). 256p. 1996. 39.95 (*0-88740-955-5*) Schiffer.

— Sterling Silver Flatware for Dining Elegance. LC 94-65622. (Illus.). 204p. 1994. 39.95 (*0-88740-630-0*) Schiffer.

— Sterling Silver Flatware for Dining Elegance. 2nd rev. ed. (Illus.). 204p. 1999. 39.95 (*0-7643-0890-4*) Schiffer.

Osterberg, Susan S., jt. auth. see Jackson, R. Eugene.

Osterbind, Carter C. & O'Rand, Angela M., eds. Older People in Florida: A Statistical Abstract 1978. 2nd ed. LC HQ1064.46. 277p. reprint ed. pap. 85.90 (*0-7837-0597-2*, 204094500019) Bks Demand.

Osterbind, Carter C., jt. ed. see Kraft, John.

Osterbind, Carter C., ed. see Southern Conference on Gerontology Staff.

Osterbrock, Donald E. Astrophysics of Gaseous Nebulae & Active Galactic Nuclei. (Illus.). 325p. (C). 1989. text 36.00 (*0-935702-22-9*) Univ Sci Bks.

— Pauper & Prince: Ritchey, Hale, & Big American Telescopes. LC 92-42704. (Illus.). 350p. 1993. 46.00 (*0-8165-1199-3*) U of Ariz Pr.

— Yerkes Observatory, 1892-1950. LC 96-25450. 1996. 40.00 (*0-226-63945-2*) U Ch Pr.

— Yerkes Observatory, 1892-1950: The Birth, Near Death, & Resurrection of a Scientific Research Institution. LC 96-25450. 1999. pap. text 25.00 (*0-226-63946-0*) U Ch Pr.

Osterbrock, Donald E. & Miller, Joseph S., eds. Active Galactic Nuclei. (C). 1989. pap. text 97.00 (*0-7923-0257-5*); lib. bdg. 220.50 (*0-7923-0256-7*) Kluwer Academic.

Osterbrock, Donald E. & Raven, Peter H. Origins & Extinctions. LC 88-1396. (C). 1988. 25.00 (*0-300-04260-4*) Yale U Pr.

Osterbrock, Donald E., ed. see International Astronomical Union Staff.

***Osterburg, Bertil O.** Colonial America on Film & Television: A Filmography. (Illus.). 240p. 2000. 48.50 (*0-7864-0862-6*) McFarland & Co.

Osterburg, J., jt. ed. see Haile, D.

Osterburg, James W. The Crime Laboratory: Case Studies of Scientific Investigation. 2nd ed. LC 81-7694. 1982. pap. 19.95 (*0-87632-364-6*) West Group.

Osterburg, James W. & Ward, Richard H. Criminal Investigation: A Method for Reconstructing the Past. 2nd ed. LC 96-83683. (Illus.). 843p. (C). 1996. pap. text 54.95 (*0-87084-237-4*) Anderson Pub Co.

***Osterburg, James W. & Ward, Richard H.** Criminal Investigation: A Method for Reconstructing the Past. 3rd ed. LC 99-88637. 2000. pap. 65.95 (*0-87084-330-3*) Anderson Pub Co.

Osterdahl, Inger. La France dans l'Afrique de l'Apres-Guerre Froide: Interventions et Justifications. (Document de Recherche Ser.: No. 2). 87p. 1997. 14.95 (*91-7106-410-9*, Pub. by Nordic Africa) Transaction Pubs.

— Threat to the Peace: The Interpretation by the Security Council of Article 39 of the UN Charter. (Studies in International Law: No. 13). 176p. 1998. pap. 69.50 (*91-7678-373-1*, Pub. by Almqvist Wiksell) Coronet Bks.

Osterfeld, David. Prosperity Versus Planning: How Government Stifles Economic Growth. (Illus.). 288p. (C). 1992. pap. text 26.95 (*0-19-507614-1*) OUP.

Osterfind, Steven J. Constructing Test Items: Multiple-Choice, Constructed-Response, Performance & Other Formats. 2nd ed. LC 97-35134. (Evaluation in Education & Human Services Ser.: 7). 352p. 1998. 89.95 (*0-7923-8077-0*) Kluwer Academic.

Ostergaard, Bernt S., ed. see Euromedia Research Group Staff.

Ostergaard, D. Eugene. Basic Diemaking. (Diemaking Ser.). 208p. (Orig.). 1982. pap. 37.95 (*0-910399-34-4*) McGraw.

Ostergaard, J. M. Fossil Marine Mollusks of Oahu. (BMB Ser.: No. 51). 1969. reprint ed. pap. 25.00 (*0-527-02157-1*) Periodicals Srv.

— Recent & Fossil Marine Molluska of Tongatabu. (BMB Ser.). 1974. reprint ed. pap. 25.00 (*0-527-02237-3*) Periodicals Srv.

Ostergaard, Lise, ed. Gender & Development: A Practical Guide. LC 91-16824. 224p. (C). 1992. pap. 25.99 (*0-415-07132-1*, A6689) Routledge.

Ostergaard, Svend. The Mathematics of Meaning. 224p. (C). 1997. pap. 27.00 (*87-7288-515-7*, Pub. by Aarhus Univ Pr) David Brown.

Ostergaard, Tom. SADCC - Beyond Transportation: The Challenge of Industrial Cooperation in Southern Africa. (Scandinavian Institute of African Studies). 136p. (Orig.). 1989. pap. 48.00 (*91-7106-294-7*, Pub. by Umea U Bibl) Coronet Bks.

Ostergard, Carey. A Trunk Full of Adventure. 24p. (J). (gr. 4-12). 1992. pap. 5.00 (*1-886210-08-X*) Tyketoon Yng Author.

Ostergard, Derek E. George Nakashima: Full Circle. (Illus.). 192p. 1997. reprint ed. pap. text 25.00 (*0-7881-5076-6*) DIANE Pub.

— Porcelain Manufactory at Sevres, 1800-1847. LC 97-61445. 416p. 1997. 75.00 (*0-300-07338-0*) Yale U Pr.

Ostergard, Derek E. & Hoff, Marlise. Along the Royal Road: Berlin & Potsdam in KPM Porcelain. (Illus.). 251p. 1993. pap. 45.00 (*0-614-07358-8*) Bard Grad Ctr.

Ostergard, Derek E., et al. Along the Royal Road: Berlin & Potsdam in KPM Porcelain & Painting 1815-1848. (Illus.). 251p. 1993. pap. 45.00 (*1-887506-00-4*) Bard Grad Ctr.

— The Brilliance of Swedish Glass, 1918-1939: An Alliance of Art & Industry. LC 96-78504. (Illus.). 336p. 1996. pap. 45.00 (*0-300-07044-6*) Yale U Pr.

Ostergard, Derek E., et al. The Brilliance of Swedish Glass, 1918-1939: An Alliance of Art & Industry. LC 96-78504. (Illus.). 336p. 1996. 70.00 (*0-300-07005-5*) Yale U Pr.

Ostergard, Derek E., et al. Cast Iron from Central Europe 1800-1850. (Illus.). 351p. 1995. pap. 50.00 (*1-887506-01-2*) Bard Grad Ctr.

Ostergard, Donald R. & Bent, Alfred E. Urogynecology & Urodynamics. 3rd ed. (Illus.). 692p. 1991. 98.00 (*0-683-06647-1*) Lppncott W & W.

Ostergard, Donald R. & Bent, Alfred E., eds. Urogynecology & Urodynamics: Theory & Practice. 4th ed. LC 95-47708. (Illus.). 658p. 1996. 109.00 (*0-683-06648-X*) Lppncott W & W.

Ostergard, Donald R., et al. Atlas of Gynecologic Surgery. Schmitt, William, ed. LC 99-19761. (Illus.). 605p. 1999. text. write for info. (*0-7216-5307-3*, W B Saunders Co) Harcrt Hlth Sci Grp.

Ostergard, Donald R., jt. auth. see Sand, Peter K.

Ostergren, Robert C. A Community Transplanted: The Trans-Atlantic Experience of a Swedish Immigrant Settlement in the Upper Middle West, 1835-1915. LC 88-211. (Illus.). 416p. (Orig.). (C). 1988. text 45.00 (*0-299-11320-5*); pap. text 19.95 (*0-299-11324-8*) U of Wis Pr.

Ostergren, Robert C. & Vale, Thomas R., eds. Wisconsin Land & Life. LC 96-36447. (North Coast Bks.). (Illus.). 626p. 1997. 69.95 (*0-299-15350-9*); pap. 29.95 (*0-299-15354-1*) U of Wis Pr.

Ostergren, Robert C., jt. auth. see Tanner, Helen H.

Osterhammel, Jurgen. Colonialism: A Theoretical Overview. Frisch, Shelley L., tr. from GER. LC 95-53736.Tr. of Kolonialismus: Geschichte, Formen, Folgen. (Illus.). 146p. (C). 1997. text 42.95 (*1-55876-129-2*); pap. text 18.95 (*1-55876-130-6*) Wiener Pubs Inc.

Osterhaus, A. D., ed. Virus Infections of Rodents & Lagomorphs. LC 94-21040. (Virus Infections of Vertebrates Ser.: Vol. 5). 432p. 1994. 256.25 (*0-444-81909-6*) Elsevier.

Osterhaus, A. D. & Uytedehaag, F. G., eds. Idiotype Networks in Biology & Medicine: Proceedings of the International Congress on Idiotype Networks in Biology & Medicine, 17-20 April, 1989. (International Congress Ser.: No. 862). 310p. 1990. 92.50 (*0-685-45393-6*) Elsevier.

Osterhaus, Ellen. Effigy Mounds: Monuments of the Earth. (Illus.). 90p. (J). (gr. 4-12). 1998. pap. 9.95 (*0-9664517-1-6*, 1951) Out Box.

Osterhaus, J. Como Establecer Relaciones Masculinas. (Hombres de Integridad Ser.).Tr. of Building Strong Male Relationships. (SPA.). 40p. 1995. 2.99 (*1-56063-576-2*) Editorial Unilit.

Osterhaus, James P. Bonds of Iron: Forging Lasting Male Relationships. Oliver, Gary J., ed. LC 97-147231. 224p. 1997. pap. 11.99 (*0-8024-7134-X*, 95) Moody.

— Family Tales: Rewriting the Stories That Made You Who You Are. LC 96-36846. 216p. (Orig.). 1997. pap. 11.99 (*0-8308-1996-7*, 1996) InterVarsity.

— Family Ties Don't Have to Bind. LC 93-37373. 1994. 15.99 (*0-8407-7805-8*) Nelson.

Osterhausen, Fritz Von, see Von Osterhausen, Fritz.

Osterhaven, M. Eugene, jt. tr. see Miller, Allen O.

Osterheld, Albert L. & Goldstein, William H., eds. Atomic Processes in Plasmas: Tenth Topical Conference. (AIP Conference Proceedings Ser.: No. 381). 310p. 1996. 135.00 (*1-56396-552-6*, AIP Pr) Spr-Verlag.

Osterhoff, Robert J., jt. auth. see Weaver, Alan T.

Osterholm, J. Roger. Bing Crosby: A Bio-Bibliography. 58. LC 94-28690. (Bio-Bibliographies in the Performing Arts Ser.: Vol. 58). 504p. 1994. lib. bdg. 79.50 (*0-313-27726-5*, Greenwood Pr) Greenwood.

Osterholm, J. Roger, jt. auth. see Kum-Sok, No.

Osterholm, Michael, et al, eds. Infectious Diseases in Child Day Care: Management & Protection. viii, 185p. 1996. lib. bdg. 36.00 (*0-226-63947-9*) U Ch Pr.

***Osterholm, Michael T.** Living Terrors: What America Needs to Know to Survive the Coming Bio-Terror Catastrophe. 2000. write for info. (*0-385-33480-X*) Delacorte.

Osterhoudt, Elmer G. Crystal Detectors. 2nd ed. (MRL Handbook Ser.: Vol. HB-3). (Illus.). 24p. 1999. reprint ed. pap. write for info. (*1-891501-02-X*) Modern Radio.

— Crystal Set Circuits, MRL 18. (MRL Handbook Ser.: Vol. HB-25). (Illus.). 24p. 1999. reprint ed. pap. write for info. (*1-891501-14-3*) Modern Radio.

— Crystal Set Circuits, MRL 20. (MRL Handbook Ser.: Vol. HB-17). (Illus.). 24p. 1999. reprint ed. pap. write for info. (*1-891501-13-5*) Modern Radio.

— Crystal Set Construction. (MRL Handbook Ser.: Vol. HB-5). (Illus.). 24p. 1999. reprint ed. pap. write for info. (*1-891501-04-6*) Modern Radio.

— Experiments with Magnetism & Coils. (MRL Handbook Ser.: Vol. HB-7). (Illus.). 24p. 1999. reprint ed. pap. write for info. (*1-891501-06-2*) Modern Radio.

— Facts for Crystal Experimenters. (MRL Handbook Ser.: Vol. HB-10). (Illus.). 24p. 1999. reprint ed. pap. write for info. (*1-891501-09-7*) Modern Radio.

— Headphones: Operation & Repair. (MRL Handbook Ser.: Vol. HB-1). (Illus.). 24p. 1999. reprint ed. pap. write for info. (*1-891501-00-3*) Modern Radio.

— How to Wind Coils. (MRL Handbook Ser.: Vol. HB-6). (Illus.). 24p. 1999. reprint ed. pap. write for info. (*1-891501-05-4*) Modern Radio.

— Long Distance Crystal Set, MRL 2. (MRL Handbook Ser.: Vol. HB-2). (Illus.). 24p. 1999. pap. write for info. (*1-891501-01-1*) Modern Radio.

— MRL Detail Print File, No. 1. (Illus.). 17p. 1999. reprint ed. pap. write for info. (*1-891501-15-1*) Modern Radio.

— MRL Detail Print File, No. 2. (Illus.). 17p. 1999. reprint ed. pap. write for info. (*1-891501-16-X*) Modern Radio.

— Radio Kinks & Quips. (MRL Handbook Ser.: Vol. HB-8). (Illus.). 24p. 1999. reprint ed. pap. write for info. (*1-891501-07-0*) Modern Radio.

— Radio Notes. (MRL Handbook Ser.: Vol. HB-9). (Illus.). 24p. 1999. reprint ed. pap. write for info. (*1-891501-08-9*) Modern Radio.

— Radio Notes, No. 2. (MRL Handbook Ser.: Vol. HB-13). (Illus.). 24p. 1999. reprint ed. pap. write for info. (*1-891501-12-7*) Modern Radio.

— Radio Operating As a Career. (MRL Handbook Ser.: Vol. HB-11). (Illus.). 24p. 1999. reprint ed. pap. write for info. (*1-891501-10-0*) Modern Radio.

— Radio Workbench Tips. (MRL Handbook Ser.: Vol. HB-12). (Illus.). 24p. 1999. reprint ed. pap. write for info. (*1-891501-11-9*) Modern Radio.

— Tube D. C. All-Wave Receiver, MRL 1. (MRL Handbook Ser.: Vol. HB-4). (Illus.). 24p. 1999. reprint ed. pap. write for info. (*1-891501-03-8*) Modern Radio.

Osterhout, Marilyn M., ed. Decontamination & Decommissioning of Nuclear Facilities. LC 80-10223. (Illus.). 819p. 1980. reprint ed. pap. 200.00 (*0-608-05435-6*, 206590400006) Bks Demand.

Osterhues, Hans-H., ed. see Hombach, V., et al.

Osterink, Carole. My First Word Book. (Illus.). 64p. (Orig.). (J). (ps-3). 1996. pap. 6.95 (*1-56293-845-2*, McClanahan Book) Learn Horizon.

— Search for Delicious: A Study Guide. Friedland, J. & Kessler, R., eds. (Novel-Ties Ser.). (J). (gr. 3-5). 1994. pap. text, student ed. 15.95 (*1-56982-061-9*) Lrn Links.

Osterink, Carole & Spencer, Beth. Sounds in Stories - Long Vowel Sounds: A Study Guide. Friedland, J. & Kessler, R., eds. (Novel-Ties Ser.). 1993. pap. text, student ed. 20.95 (*1-56982-031-7*) Lrn Links.

— Sounds in Stories - Short Vowel Sounds: A Study Guide. Friedland, J. & Kessler, R., eds. (Novel-Ties Ser.). 1993. pap. text, student ed. 20.95 (*1-56982-033-3*) Lrn Links.

Osterink, Marcia. Arts Attack, Grade 1 - Teacher's Handbook. (Illus.). iv, 110p. 1996. ring bd. write for info. (*1-890745-50-2*) Arts Attack.

— Arts Attack, Grade 2 - Teacher's Handbook. (Illus.). iv, 110p. 1996. ring bd. write for info. (*1-890745-51-0*) Arts Attack.

— Arts Attack, Grade 3 - Teacher's Handbook. (Illus.). iv, 124p. 1996. ring bd. write for info. (*1-890745-52-9*) Arts Attack.

— Arts Attack, Grade 4 - Teacher's Handbook. (Illus.). iv, 162p. 1996. ring bd. write for info. (*1-890745-53-7*) Arts Attack.

— Arts Attack, Grade 5 - Teacher's Handbook. (Illus.). iv, 164p. 1996. ring bd. write for info. (*1-890745-54-5*) Arts Attack.

— Arts Attack, Grade 6 - Teacher's Handbook. (Illus.). iv, 152p. 1996. ring bd. write for info. (*1-890745-55-3*) Arts Attack.

Osterkamp, Ernst. Lucifer Stationen eines Motivs. (Komparatistische Studien: Vol. 9). (C). 1979. 104.60 (*3-11-007804-X*) De Gruyter.

Osterkamp, Ernst, ed. Rudolf Borchardt und Seine Zeitgenossen. (Quellen und Forschungen zur Literatur- und Kutlurgeschichte Ser.: Vol. 10). (GER.). xii, 406p. (C). 1997. lib. bdg. 129.65 (*3-11-015603-2*) De Gruyter.

Osterkamp, Lynn & Press, Allan N. Stress? Find Your Balance. rev. ed. 160p. 1988. reprint ed. pap. 6.95 (*0-9620725-0-8*) Preventive Measures.

Osterkamp, Peggy. Warping Your Loom & Tying on New Warps. 2nd rev. ed. (Peggy Osterkamp's New Guide to Weaving Ser.: No. 2). (Illus.). 188p. 1997. pap. 34.95 (*0-9637793-2-X*) Lease Sticks.

— Weaving & Designing Woven Fabrics. (Peggy Osterkamp's New Guide to Weaving Ser.: No. 3). (Illus.). 200p. (Orig.). 2000. pap. write for info. (*0-9637793-3-8*) Lease Sticks.

— Winding a Warp & Using a Paddle. 2nd rev. ed. (Peggy Osterkamp's New Guide to Weaving Ser.: Vol. 1). (Illus.). 175p. 1998. pap. 39.95 (*0-9637793-4-6*) Lease Sticks.

Osterle, Heinz D., ed. Amerika! New Images in German Literature. (German Life & Civilization Ser.). 355p. (C). 1989. text 54.95 (*0-8204-1058-6*) P Lang Pubng.

Osterle, Hubert. Business in the Information Age: Heading for New Processes. LC 95-20733. (Illus.). 318p. 1995. 89.00 (*3-540-60023-X*) Spr-Verlag.

***Osterle, Hubert, et al, eds.** Business Networking: Shaping Enterprise Relationship on the Internet. LC 99-54443. (Illus.). xvi, 376p. 1999. 59.95 (*3-540-66612-5*) Spr-Verlag.

Osterle, Hubert, et al. Total Information Systems Management: A European Approach. LC 93-12283. (Series in Information Systems). 322p. 1993. 115.00 (*0-471-93932-3*) Wiley.

Osterlin, Lars. Churches of Northern Europe in Profile: A Thousand Years of Anglo-Nordic Relations. 317p. 1996. pap. 19.95 (*1-85311-128-7*, 6324, Pub. by Canterbury Press Norwich) Morehouse Pub.

Osterlind, Steven J. A National Review of Scholastic Achievement in General Education: How Are We Doing & Why Should We Care. Fife, Jonathan D., ed. (ASHE-ERIC Higher Education Reports: Vol. 25-8). 100p. 1997. pap. 24.00 (*1-878380-80-X*) GWU Grad Schl E&HD.

— Test Item Bias. (Quantitative Applications in the Social Sciences Ser.: Vol. 30). 88p. 1983. pap. 10.95 (*0-8039-1989-1*) Sage.

Osterling, Jorge P. Democracy in Colombia: Clientelistic Politics & Guerrilla Warfare. 350p. 1989. 44.95 (*0-88738-229-0*) Transaction Pubs.

Osterloh, Karl-Heinz, jt. auth. see Cohen.

Osterloh, Karl-Heinz, jt. auth. see Cohen, Ulrike.

***Osterlund, Carol & Sellers, Robert.** Arrival Time: A Journal of Love. LC 99-50459. 112p. 2000. pap. 12.00 (*1-56474-329-2*) Fithian Pr.

Osterman, Bernt. Value & Requirements: An Inquiry Concerning the Origin of Value. 202p. 1995. text 66.95 (*1-85972-028-5*, Pub. by Avebry) Ashgate Pub Co.

Osterman, Eurydice. What God Says about Music. Davis, Oliver J., ed. Ward, Eric C., tr. LC 97-94873. 1997. pap. 12.95 (*0-9661690-0-X*) Awsahm.

Osterman, Fred. Buying a Used Shortwave Receiver: A Market Guide to Modern Shortwave Radios. 4th ed. LC 98-75112. (Illus.). 78p. 1998. pap. 5.95 (*1-882123-14-X*) Universal Radio Rsch.

Osterman, Fred J. Shortwave Receivers Past & Present: Communications Receivers, 1942-1997. 3rd ed. LC 98-60282. (Illus.). 473p. 1998. pap. 24.95 (*1-882123-07-7*) Universal Radio Rsch.

Osterman, Fred J. & Gorka, Gary. The Soviet Maritime Radioteletype Dictionary. (Illus.). 102p. (Orig.). 1988. pap. 9.95 (*1-882123-20-4*) Universal Radio Rsch.

Osterman, H., ed. see Rasmussen, Knud J.

Osterman, Helen. Things Hidden. Picariello, Gloria, ed. LC 98-60716. 128p. 1998. pap. 12.95 (*1-880254-55-7*) Vista.

Osterman, Helen M. The Web. Zagury, Carolyn S., ed. LC 96-61492. 184p. 1997. pap. 12.95 (*1-880254-41-7*) Vista.

Osterman, Joe. Fifty Years in "Old" El Toro: A Family, a Time, a Place. 3rd ed. LC 81-85994. (Illus.). 290p. 1992. reprint ed. 14.95 (*1-881129-00-4*) Old El Toro Pr.

— The "Old" El Toro Reader: A Guide to the Past. Walker, Doris & Osterman, Tim, eds. LC 92-96902. (Illus.). 112p. (J). (gr. 3-6). 1992. pap. 9.95 (*1-881129-02-0*) Old El Toro Pr.

— Stories of Saddleback Valley. LC 85-63697. (Illus.). 160p. (Orig.). 1992. pap. 7.95 (*1-881129-01-2*) Old El Toro Pr.

Osterman, Karen F. & Kottkamp, Robert B. Reflective Practice for Educators: Improving Schooling Through Professional Development. LC 92-37083. 224p. 1993. pap. 24.95 (*0-8039-6047-6*) Corwin Pr.

Osterman, L. A. Methods of Protein & Nucleic Acid Research: Electrophoresis, Isoelectric Focusing, Ultracentrifugation, Vol. 1. (Illus.). 370p. 1985. 219.95 (*0-387-12735-6*) Spr-Verlag.

— Methods of Protein & Nucleic Acid Research: Immunoelectrophoresis - Application of Radioisotopes. (Illus.). 220p. 1988. 158.95 (*0-387-13094-2*) Spr-Verlag.

— Methods of Protein & Nucleic Acid Research Vol. 3: Chromatography. (Illus.). 520p. 1986. 278.95 (*0-387-16855-9*) Spr-Verlag.

Osterman, Marilyn & Kluge, Marilyn. The Dancing Spider. 1979. 3.95 (*0-87129-238-6*, D29) Dramatic Pub.

Osterman, Mark. Justifiable Homicide. LC 93-11988. 288p. (Orig.). 1993. pap. 5.95 (*1-877633-17-8*) Luthers.

Osterman, Paul. Securing Prosperity: The American Labor Market: How It Has Changed & What to Do about It. LC 99-17488. (Illus.). 244p. 1999. 24.95 (*0-691-01011-0*, Pub. by Princeton U Pr) Cal Prin Full Svc.

Osterman, Paul, ed. Broken Ladders: Managerial Careers in the New Economy. (Illus.). 272p. 1996. 45.00 (*0-19-509353-4*) OUP.

Osterman, Paul, jt. auth. see Kochan, Thomas A.

Osterman, Paul, jt. auth. see Marshall, Ray.

Osterman, Peg. Concise Illustrator's Reference Manual: Figures. 128p. 1996. 9.98 (*0-7858-0515-X*) Bk Sales Inc.

— Concise Illustrator's Reference Manual: Nudes. 1996. 9.98 (*0-7858-0514-1*) Bk Sales Inc.

Osterman, Susan. Strip Mining. (Cambric Poetry Ser.). 72p. (Orig.). 1987. pap. 7.00 (*0-918342-26-0*) Cambric.

Osterman, Tim, ed. see Osterman, Joe.

***Ostermann, Matthias.** The New Maiolica: Contemporary Approaches to Colour & Technique. (Illus.). 160p. 1999. text. write for info. (*90-5703-562-6*, Pub. by Craftsman House) Gordon & Breach.

— The New Maiolica: Contemporary Approaches to Colour & Technique. LC 99-20674. 1999. 39.95 (*0-8122-3513-4*) U of Pa Pr.

Ostermann, R., jt. ed. see Dirschedl, P.

Ostermann, Tricia, ed. see Turechek, Alma A.

Ostermann, Ursula, jt. auth. see Ackermans, Gian.

Ostermark-Johansen, Lene. Sweetness & Strength: The Reception of Michelangelo in Late Victorian England. LC 98-29299. (Illus.). 16p. 1998. text 50.95 (*1-85928-452-3*, Pub. by Scolar Pr) Ashgate Pub Co.

Ostermiller, Lillian. Bernese Mountain Dogs. (Illus.). 192p. Date not set. pap. 9.95 (*0-7938-2303-X*, KW-202S) TFH Pubns.

Ostermiller, R. Kenneth. Talking with Your Child about Sexuality. LC 90-21702. (Growing Together Ser.). (Orig.). 1991. pap. 2.25 (*0-8298-0863-9*) Pilgrim OH.

Ostermiller, R. Kenneth, jt. auth. see Monkres, Peter R.

Ostermoller, Wolfgang. Aquariums. (Illus.). 80p. 1984. pap. 6.95 (*0-86622-845-4*, PB-101) TFH Pubns.

Osternick, Carole. Auditory-Visual Discrimination. (Fun with Phonics Ser.). 1997. pap. text 6.95 (*0-590-76488-8*) Scholastic Inc.

Osterode. Welfensitz und Burgerstadt Im Wandel der Jahrhunderte. (GER.). 784p. 1993. write for info. (*3-487-09808-3*) G Olms Pubs.

Osterreich, Shelley A., compiled by. The American Indian Ghost Dance, 1870 & 1890: An Annotated Bibliography, Vol. 19. LC 91-7957. (Bibliographies & Indexes in American History Ser.: No. 19). 296p. 1991. lib. bdg. 49.95 (*0-313-27469-X*, OGD, Greenwood Pr) Greenwood.

O

Osterreich, Shelley Anne, compiled by. Native North American Shamanism: An Annotated Bibliography, 38. LC 98-28015. (Bibliographies & Indexes in American History: Vol. 38). 128p. 1998. lib. bdg. 55.00 (*0-313-30168-9*, Greenwood Pr) Greenwood.

Osterreicher, John M. The Unfinished Dialogue: Martin Buber & the Christian Way. 136p. 1987. reprint ed. pap. 5.95 (*0-8065-1050-1*, Citadel Pr) Carol Pub Group.

Ostertag, C., et al, eds. Advances in Stereotactic & Functional Neurosurgery, Vol. 10. LC 93-41431. 200p. 1993. 158.00 (*0-387-82478-2*) Spr-Verlag.

Ostertag, C., jt. ed. see Meyerson, B.

Ostertag, C. B., et al, eds. Advances in Stereotactic & Functional Neurosurgery 12. LC 97-20848. (Acta Neurochirurgica Ser.: Suppl. 68). (Illus.). 200p. 1997. 73.00 (*3-211-82978-4*) Spr-Verlag.

Ostertag, Gary, ed. Definite Descriptions: A Reader. LC 97-47000. (Illus.). 423p. 1998. 30.00 (*0-262-65049-5*, Bradford Bks) MIT Pr.

***Ostertag, George & Ostertag, Rhonda.** 100 Hikes in Oregon. 2nd ed. LC 99-50629. (100 Hikes in Ser.). (Illus.). 352p. 2000. pap. 14.95 (*0-89886-619-7*) Mountaineers.

Ostertag, George, jt. auth. see Ostertag, Rhonda.

Ostertag, Heinrich. Der Philosophische Gehalt des Wolff-Manteuffelschen Briefwechsels. (Materialien und Dokumente Ser.: Bd. 14). (GER.). 189p. 1980. reprint ed. write for info. (*3-487-06967-9*) G Olms Pubs.

Ostertag, Rhonda. Fifty Hikes in Oregon's Coast Range & Siskiyous. LC 89-3150. (Illus.). 184p. (Orig.). 1989. pap. 10.95 (*0-89886-200-0*) Mountaineers.

***Ostertag, Rhonda.** Oregon. LC 99-29579. (Camping Guides Ser.). 1999. pap. 16.95 (*1-56044-707-9*) Falcon Pub Inc.

Ostertag, Rhonda & Ostertag, George. California State Parks: A Complete Recreation Guide. (Illus.). 400p. 1995. pap. 16.95 (*0-89886-419-4*) Mountaineers.

— 50 Hikes in Hells Canyon & Oregon's Wallowas. LC 97-26102. (One Hundred Hikes in Ser.). (Illus.). 160p. 1997. pap. 14.95 (*0-89886-521-2*) Mountaineers.

— Hiking New York State. LC 96-26273. (Illus.). 304p. (Orig.). 1996. pap. 14.95 (*1-56044-396-0*) Falcon Pub Inc.

— Hiking Pennsylvania. LC 97-28394. 312p. 1998. pap. 15.95 (*1-56044-592-0*) Falcon Pub Inc.

— Hiking Southern New England. LC 97-627. (Illus.). 256p. (Orig.). 1997. pap. 14.95 (*1-56044-507-6*) Falcon Pub Inc.

— Oregon Campgrounds Hiking Guide. LC 97-24352. 256p. 1997. 14.95 (*0-89886-547-6*) Mountaineers.

— Scenic Driving Pennsylvania. LC 98-44269. (Illus.). 296p. 1999. pap. 15.95 (*1-56044-732-X*) Falcon Pub Inc.

Ostertag, Rhonda, jt. auth. see Ostertag, George.

Ostertag, Robert L. Structuring, Financing & Representing the Small Business, 1997. LC 98-106652. (Litigation Course Handbook Ser.). 376p. 1997. write for info. (*0-87224-380-X*) PLI.

— Structuring, Financing, & Representing the Small Business, 1998 LC 98-194513. (Corporate Law & Practice Course Handbook Ser.). 216 p. 1998. write for info. (*0-87224-494-6*) PLI.

Osterud, Erik. Theatrical & Narrative Space: Studies in Ibsen, Strindberg & J. P. Jacobsen. 160p. 1998. 25.95 (*87-7288-658-7*, Pub. by Aarhus Univ Pr) David Brown.

Osterud, Nancy G. Bonds of Community: The Lives of Farm Women in Nineteenth-Century New York. LC 90-41814. (Illus.). 320p. 1991. text 47.50 (*0-8014-2510-7*); pap. text 16.95 (*0-8014-9798-1*) Cornell U Pr.

Osterwald, Doris B. Beyond the Third Rail with Monte Ballough & His Camera. (Illus.). 216p. 1994. 34.95 (*0-931788-40-4*) Western Guideways.

— Cinders & Smoke: A Mile by Mile Guide for the Durango & Silverton Narrow Gauge Railroad. 7th rev. ed. LC 68-4969. (Illus.). 168p. 1995. pap. 7.95 (*0-931788-95-1*) Western Guideways.

— High Line to Leadville: A Mile by Mile Guide for the Leadville, Colorado & Southern Railroad. (Illus.). 160p. (Orig.). 1991. pap. 9.95 (*0-931788-70-6*) Western Guideways.

— Ticket to Toltec: A Mile by Mile Guide for the Cumbres & Toltec Scenic Railroad. (Illus.). 128p. 1992. pap. 9.95 (*0-931788-26-9*) Western Guideways.

Osterwalder, Fritz, jt. auth. see Oelkers, Jurgen.

***Osterwalder, Anja.** Space Manual. (Illus.). 40p. 1999. pap. 39.99 (*3-931126-26-9*, Pub. by Die Gestalten) Consort Bk Sales.

Osterwalder, Jurg & Aebi, Philipp. Photoelectron Diffraction & Fermi Surface Mapping. 200p. 1997. pap. text 26.00 (*981-02-3207-1*) World Scientific Pub.

Osterwalder, Marcus. Dictionnaire des Illustrateurs: 1890-1945, No. 2. (FRE.). 1384p. 1989. text 325.00 (*0-7859-8038-5*, 2825800392) Fr & Eur.

— Dictionnaire des Illustrateurs Vol. 1: 1800-1914. (FRE.). 1223p. 1989. 325.00 (*0-7859-8037-7*, 2825800309) Fr & Eur.

Osterweil. Geriatric Assessment. 2000. 69.00 (*0-07-134725-9*) McGraw.

***Osterweil, Adam.** Comic Book Kid. 2000. 15.95 (*1-886910-62-6*, Front Street) Front Str.

Osterweil, Michael. Alexa. 296p. 1998. pap. 17.95 (*0-9649210-5-7*) Motivo Pubng.

Osterweis, Marian, et al, eds. Promoting Health & Preventing Disease. LC 92-7351. (Health Policy Annual Ser.: Vol. II). 250p. (Orig.). 1992. 20.00 (*1-879694-04-2*) AAH Ctrs.

Osterweis, Marian & Garfinkel, Stephen, eds. The Roles of Physician Assistants & Nurse Practitioners in Primary Care. (Orig.). 1993. pap. write for info. (*1-879694-07-7*) AAH Ctrs.

Osterweis, Marian, et al. The U. S. Health Workforce: Power, Politics & Policy. 300p. 1996. pap. 25.00 (*1-879694-11-5*) AAH Ctrs.

Osterweis, Marian, jt. ed. see Holmes, Denise E.

Osterweis, Marian, ed. see Institute of Medicine Staff.

Osterweis, Marian, jt. ed. see Skelton, W. Douglas.

Osterweis, Rollin G. The Sesquicentennial History of the Connecticut Academy of Arts & Sciences. (Connecticut Academy of Arts & Sciences Ser., Trans.: Vol. 38, Pt. 2). 1949. pap. 29.50 (*0-685-22901-7*) Elliots Bks.

— Three Centuries of New Haven, 1638-1938. LC 52-12064. (Illus.). 559p. reprint ed. pap. 173.30 (*0-8357-8351-0*, 203384900087) Bks Demand.

Osterwiel, Leon, jt. auth. see Song, Xiping.

Osterwold, Tilman. Pop Art. 1994. pap. 19.99 (*3-8228-0294-8*) Taschen Amer.

— Pop Art. (SPA.). 1996. pap. 19.99 (*3-8228-0667-6*) Taschen Amer.

***Osterwold, Tilman.** Pop Art. 1999. 19.99 (*3-8228-7014-5*) Taschen Amer.

— Pop Art. (Big Art Ser.). (Illus.). 240p. 1999. reprint ed. 19.99 (*3-8228-7021-8*) Taschen Amer.

Osterwold, Tilman, jt. auth. see Felix, Zdenek.

Osteryoung. Pocket Handbook of Electroanalytical Instrumental Techniques for Analytical Chemistry. (C). 2001. 14.95 (*0-13-738907-8*, Macmillan Coll) P-H.

— Small Firm Finance. (C). 1997. pap. text, teacher ed. 42.00 (*0-03-018634-X*) Harcourt Coll Pubs.

Osteryoung, J. G., et al. Intermetallic Compounds in Mercury. (IUPAC Solubility Data Ser.: Vol. 51). 289p. 1992. 121.75 (*0-08-037206-6*, Pergamon Pr) Elsevier.

Osteryoung, Jerome S., et al. Small Firm Finance: An Entrepreneurial Analysis. LC 95-67390. 416p. (C). 1997. pap. text 61.50 (*0-03-098220-0*) Dryden Pr.

Osteyee, Carol H., jt. auth. see Hoffman, Preston.

Ostfeld, Adrian M., et al. Stress, Crowding & Blood Pressure in Prison. (Health Environment Ser.). 256p. 1987. text 49.95 (*0-89859-574-6*) L Erlbaum Assocs.

Ostgarden, Jo, ed. see Hill, Deborah A.

Osthaus, Carl R. Freedmen, Philanthropy & Fraud: A History of the Freedman's Savings Bank. LC 75-23214. (Blacks in the New World Ser.). 276p. 1976. text 29.95 (*0-252-00305-5*) U of Ill Pr.

— Partisans of the Southern Press: Editorial Spokesmen of the Nineteenth Century. LC 94-16880. 288p. 1994. 39.95 (*0-8131-1875-1*) U Pr of Ky.

Osthecker, Sonja, jt. auth. see Nash, Rod.

Ostheeren, Klaus, contrib. by. The Erl of Tolous & the Emperes of Almayn. (GER.). x, 322p. 1970. write for info. (*3-296-25110-3*, Pub. by Weidmann) Lubrecht & Cramer.

Osthoff, Hermann & Brugman, Karl. Morphologische Untersuchungen Auf Dem Gebiete der Indogermanischen Sprachen, 3 vols., Set. (Documenta Semiotica, Ser. Linguistica). lxxx, 1810p. 1974. reprint ed. write for info. (*3-487-05079-X*) G Olms Pubs.

Osthoff, Rich. Fly-Fishing the Rocky Mountain Backcountry. LC 98-26356. 1998. pap. 19.95 (*0-8117-2766-1*) Stackpole.

Osthols, E., jt. ed. see Sandino, M. C. Amaia.

Osthovener, Claus-Dieter. Die Lehre von Gottes Eigenschaften Bei Friedrich Schleiermacher und Karl Barth. (Theologische Bibliothek Toepelmann Ser.: Vol. 76). (GER.). ix, 232p. (C). 1996. lib. bdg. 124.45 (*3-11-015055-7*) De Gruyter.

***Osti, Gian Lupo.** Book of Tree Peonies. (Illus.). 2000. 45.00 (*88-422-0750-0*) U Allemandi.

Ostianu, N. M., jt. ed. see Pontryagin, Lev S.

O'Stick, Stephen. Superman's Song: The Story of the Crash Test Dummies. LC 96-105815. (Illus.). 203p. 1995. pap. 15.95 (*1-55082-130-X*, QP00805, Pub. by Quarry Pr) LPC InBook.

Ostile, Dale A. & Carroll, Bradley W. Introduction to Modern Stellar Astrophysics. LC 95-45143. 752p. (C). 1995. 97.00 (*0-201-59880-9*) Addison-Wesley.

Ostle, Bernard & Malone, Linda C. Statistics in Research: Basic Concepts & Techniques for Research Workers. 4th ed. (Illus.). 682p. 1987. text 64.95 (*0-8138-1569-X*) Iowa St U Pr.

Ostle, Bernard & Turner, Kenneth V., Jr. Engineering Statistics: The Industrial Experience. 1997. pap. 16.75 (*0-534-26541-3*) Brooks-Cole.

Ostle, Bernard, et al. Engineering Statistics: The Industrial Experience. LC 95-24044. 1996. text 104.95 incl. 3.5 hd (*0-534-26538-3*) Wadsworth Pub.

Ostler, Barbara F. & Featherston, Phyllis. Bed & Breakfast Guide - Official: 1993-1994. 6th ed. 1993. pap. 16.95 (*0-9611298-5-9*) Natl Bed.

Ostler, Barbara F., jt. auth. see Featherston, Phyllis.

Ostler, Elliott, jt. auth. see Mooney, Pamela J.

Ostler, H. Bruce. Diseases of the External Eye & Adnexa: A Text & Atlas. (Illus.). 864p. 1993. 250.00 (*0-683-06651-X*) Lppncott W & W.

Ostler, H. Bruce, et al. Color Atlas of Infectious & Inflammatory Diseases of the External Eye. LC 86-15941. (Illus.). 166p. 1987. 145.00 (*0-683-06650-1*) Lppncott W & W.

— Diseases of the Eye & Skin: A Color Atlas. (Illus.). 352p. 1996. write for info. (*0-683-06653-6*) Lppncott W & W.

Ostler, James, et al. Zuni: A Village of Silversmiths. LC 95-70836. 143p. 1996. 45.00 (*0-912535-11-3*); pap. 29.95 (*0-912535-08-3*) Zuni Ashiwi.

Ostler, James, jt. auth. see Rodee, Marian.

Ostler, James, jt. auth. see Rodes, Marian E.

Ostler, Jeffrey. Prairie Populism: The Fate of Agrarian Radicalism in Kansas, Nebraska, & Iowa, 1880-1892. LC 93-14828. (Rural America Ser.). 272p. 1993. 29.95 (*0-7006-0606-8*) U Pr of KS.

Ostler, Larry J., et al. The Closing of American Library Schools: Problems & Opportunities, 85. LC 94-46942. (Contributions in Librarianship & Information Science Ser.: No. 85). 176p. 1995. 57.95 (*0-313-28461-X*, Greenwood Pr) Greenwood.

Ostler, Neal K. Prentice Hall Enviromental Technology. (Environmental Technology Ser.: Vol. 2). 220p. (C). 1995. 70.00 (*0-02-389542-X*, Macmillan Coll) P-H.

Ostler, Neal K. Prentice Hall Enviromental Technology. (Environmental Technology Ser.: Vol. 3). 256p. (C). 1996. 70.00 (*0-02-389551-9*, Macmillan Coll) P-H.

Ostler, Neal K., ed. Industrial Waste, Vol. 6. LC 97-31973. (Environmental Technology Ser.: Vol. VI). 343p. (C). 1998. 61.00 (*0-13-238569-4*) P-H.

Ostler, Neal K., ed. Prentice Hall Enviromental Technology. LC 95-30512. (Prentice Hall Environmental Technology Ser.: Vol. 1). 334p. 1995. 70.00 (*0-02-389532-2*, Macmillan Coll) P-H.

Ostler, Neal K. & Nielsen, John T. Prentice Hall Eviromental Technology Service. LC 97-22365. (Prentice Hall's Environmental Technology Ser.: Vol. 5). 356p. 1997. 63.00 (*0-02-389545-4*) P-H.

Ostler, Neil K. & Holley, Patrick. Prentice Hall Enviromental Technology. LC 96-48897. (Prentice Hall Technology Ser.: Vol. 4). 272p. 1997. 68.00 (*0-02-389534-9*, Macmillan Coll) P-H.

Ostler, Rosalyn, ed. see Lebeda, Guy & Neibaur, Alexander.

Ostler, Rosemarie. Theoretical Syntax, 1980-1990: An Annotated & Classified Bibliography. LC 91-42086. (Library & Information Sources in Linguistics: No. 21). viii, 192p. 1992. 53.00 (*1-55619-251-7*) J Benjamins Pubng Co.

Ostler, Scott, jt. auth. see Haywood, Spencer.

Ostlie, Dale A., jt. auth. see Carroll, Bradley W.

Ostling, Acton, jt. auth. see Whitwell, David.

Ostling, Joan K., jt. auth. see Christopher, Joe R.

Ostling, Joan K., jt. auth. see Ostling, Richard N.

Ostling, Richard N. & Ostling, Joan K. Mormon America: The Power & the Promise. LC 99-28516. (Illus.). 480p. 1999. 26.00 (*0-06-066371-5*) HarpC.

***Ostling, Richard N. & Ostling, Joan K.** Mormon America: The Power & the Promise. LC 99-28516. 480p. 2000. reprint ed. pap. 17.00 (*0-06-066372-3*) HarpC.

Ostling, Richard N., jt. auth. see Nathanson, Bernard N.

Ostlund, DeLys. The Re-Creation of History in the Fernando & Isabel Plays of Lope de Vega. (Iberica Ser.: Vol. 18). 129p. (C). 1998. text 36.95 (*0-8204-2894-9*) P Lang Pubng.

Ostlund, Karen. Sciences Process Skills. 144p. (J). 1995. pap. text. write for info. (*0-201-29092-8*) Addison-Wesley.

Ostlund, Karen L. & Mercier, Sheryl A. Rising to the Challenge of the National Science Education Standards: The Processes of Science Inquiry. (Illus.). 90p. (J). (gr. 4-8). 1996. pap. text, teacher ed. 20.00 (*0-9658768-0-2*) S & K Assocs.

***Ostlund, Krister.** Johan Ihre on the Origins & History of the Runes: Three Latin Dissertations from the Mid 18th Century - Edited with Translation & Commentary. (Studia Latina Upsaliensia Ser.: Vol. 25). (ENG & LAT.). 392p. 2000. pap. 57.50 (*91-554-4642-6*, Pub. by Uppsala Univ Acta Univ Uppsaliensis) Coronet Bks.

Ostlund, Neil S., jt. auth. see Szabo, Attila.

Ostlund, S., jt. ed. see Steinhardt, P.

Ostman, Eleanor. Always on Sunday. LC 98-153336. 1998. pap. text 19.95 (*0-9662614-0-2*) Sunday Pr.

Ostman, Hans. Swedish Non-Academic Criticism in the Era of Freedom, 1718-1772. (Stockholm Studies in the History of Literature: No. 32). 106p. (Orig.). 1993. pap. 36.50 (*91-22-01563-9*) Coronet Bks.

Ostman, Jan-Ola. You Know: A Discourse-Functional Study. (Pragmatics & Beyond Ser.: II: 7). ix, 91p. (Orig.). 1981. pap. 29.00 (*90-272-2516-8*) J Benjamins Pubng Co.

Ostman, Lars, jt. auth. see Johansson, Sven-Erik.

Ostman, Leif, jt. auth. see Roberts, Douglas A.

Ostman, Ronald E., ed. Communication & Indian Agriculture. 320p. (C). 1989. text 25.00 (*0-8039-9599-7*) Sage.

Ostmann, Barbara G. The Recipe Writer's Handbook. LC 96-48845. 288p. 1997. 34.95 (*0-471-17294-4*) Wiley.

Ostmann, Spike. Spectrum Dancer. LC 97-91928. 210p. 1997. pap. 11.95 (*0-9658711-0-X*, 001) Qumoy Pub.

Ostoby, Willard G., ed. World Religions: Eastern Traditions. (Illus.). 500p. 1996. pap. text 34.95 (*0-19-540750-4*) OUP.

Ostoia, Vera K., tr. see D'Allemagne, Henry R.

Ostoja-Starzewski, Martin & Jasiuk, Iwona, eds. Micromechanics of Random Media: Selected & Revised Proceedings of the Symposium on Micromechanics of Random Media, MEET'N '93. 240p. 1994. pap. 170.00 (*0-614-32147-6*) ASME.

Ostolaza, Margarita. Politica Sexual en Puerto Rico. LC 88-83952. 204p. 1989. pap. 12.50 (*0-929157-00-1*) Ediciones Huracan.

Ostor, Akos. The Play of the Gods: Locality, Ideology, Structure & Time in the Festivals of a Bengali Town. LC 79-25661. 264p. 1993. 27.00 (*0-226-63954-1*) U Ch Pr.

— Vessels of Time: An Essay on Temporal Change & Social Transformation. 120p. 1994. 15.95 (*0-19-563285-0*) OUP.

Ostor, Akos, et al, eds. Concepts of Person: Kinship, Caste & Marriage in India. (Oxford India Paperbacks Ser.). (Illus.). 304p. 1993. pap. text 12.95 (*0-19-563033-5*) OUP.

Ostor, Akos, et al. Concepts of Person: Kinship, Caste, & Marriage in India. (Harvard Studies in Cultural Anthropology: Vol. 5). (Illus.). 288p. 1982. 51.50 (*0-674-15765-6*) HUP.

Ostor, Andrew G., tr. see Burghardt, E., et al.

Ostosky-Solis, Peggy, jt. auth. see Ardila, Alfredo.

Ostovic, Vlado. Dynamics of Saturated Electric Machines. (Illus.). xiii, 445p. 1989. 107.95 (*0-387-97079-7*, 3103) Spr-Verlag.

Ostovich, Helen, ed. Ben Johnson Four Comedies. annot. ed. LC 96-2274. (Annotated Texts Ser.). 688p. (C). 1997. pap. text 44.00 (*0-582-07066-X*) Addison-Wesley.

***Ostovich, Helen, et al, eds.** Other Voices, Other Views: Expanding the Canon in English Renaissance Studies. LC 99-18368. (Illus.). 328p. 1999. 47.50 (*0-87413-680-6*) U Delaware Pr.

Ostow, M. Judaism & Psychoanalysis. 320p. 1997. pap. 30.00 (*1-85575-180-1*, Pub. by H Karnac Bks Ltd) Other Pr LLC.

Ostow, Miriam, jt. auth. see Ginzberg, Eli.

Ostow, Mortimer. Myth & Madness: The Psychodynamics of Antisemitism. LC 95-36973. 208p. 1995. 34.95 (*1-56000-224-7*) Transaction Pubs.

— Ultimate Intimacy: The Psychodynamics of Jewish Mysticism. 432p. 1995. pap. text 50.00 (*1-85575-105-4*, Pub. by H Karnac Bks Ltd) Other Pr LLC.

Ostow, Mortimer, ed. Ultimate Intimacy: The Psychodynamics of Jewish Mysticism. 432p. 1996. 62.50 (*0-8236-6686-7*, BN 06686) Intl Univs Pr.

Ostow, Mortimer & Scharfstein, Ben-Ami. The Need to Believe: The Psychology of Religion. 1969. reprint ed. pap. 24.95 (*0-8236-8159-9*, 23520) Intl Univs Pr.

Ostrager, Barry R. & Newman, Thomas. Handbook on Insurance Coverage Disputes. 1989. write for info. (*0-318-66843-2*) P-H.

Ostrager, Barry R. & Newman, Thomas R. Handbook on Insurance Coverage Disputes. 6th ed. LC 93-35775. 1028p. 1993. 150.00 (*0-13-109141-7*) Aspen Law.

— Handbook on Insurance Coverage Disputes. 8th ed. 1148p. ring bd. 174.00 (*1-56706-287-3*, 62873) Panel Pubs.

— Handbook on Insurance Coverage Disputes. annuals 9th ed. 1148p. ring bd. 180.00 (*1-56706-722-0*, 67220) Panel Pubs.

Ostrager, Barry R. & Vyskocil, Mary K. Modern Reinsurance Law & Practice. 1996. ring bd. 119.20 (*1-888075-50-3*) Glasser LegalWrks.

Ostrand, Kenneth D. As I Recall: Sources in Western Civilization (Renaissance to the Present) 2nd ed. 284p. (C). 1992. pap. text 32.00 (*0-9627173-5-5*) Intl Horizons.

— As I Recall: Sources in Western Civilization (to the Renaissance) 2nd ed. 300p. (C). 1992. pap. text 32.00 (*0-9627173-4-7*) Intl Horizons.

— As I Recall...Sources in Western Civilization: Ancient Times to the Renaissance, Vol. 1. 212p. (C). 1989. pap. text 18.00 (*0-318-41279-9*) Intl Horizons.

— As I Recall...Sources in Western Civilization, Vol. 2: Renaissance to Napoleon. 164p. 1989. pap. text 18.00 (*0-317-01806-X*) Intl Horizons.

— Dinner Lectures. 21p. 9.95 (*0-914951-16-5*) LERN.

— Trips & Tours Manual. 147p. 29.95 (*0-914951-04-1*) LERN.

Ostrand, Kenneth P. Egypt: Beneath the Surface. 2nd ed. 234p. (C). 1993. pap. text 35.00 (*0-9627173-3-9*) Intl Horizons.

Ostrander, Arthur E. & Wilson, Dana. Contemporary Choral Arranging. LC 85-17000. 352p. (C). 1986. 80.00 (*0-13-169756-0*) P-H.

Ostrander, Betty. Woman's Guide to Autos. 2nd ed. (Illus.). 85p. 1993. 49.00 (*1-56216-153-9*); pap. 29.00 (*1-56216-154-7*) Systems Co.

— A Woman's Guide to Autos: Basics, Operation, Safety & Maintenance. (Illus.). 60p. 1991. 45.00 (*1-56216-015-X*); pap. 25.00 (*1-56216-016-8*) Systems Co.

Ostrander, Dan. The Herbal Connection. 145p. (Orig.). 1996. pap. 9.95 (*0-9653302-0-6*) D Ostrander.

Ostrander, Edgar A. Evidence That Ancient Mayan Cosmology Incorporated the Internal Functioning of the Human Brain. LC 83-72070. (Illus.). 56p. 1983. 10.00 (*0-9611638-0-1*) Bks of New Univ.

Ostrander, Gary K. Techniques in Aquatic Toxicology. LC 96-6037. (Illus.). 704p. 1996. lib. bdg. 95.00 (*1-56670-149-X*, L1149) Lewis Pubs.

***Ostrander, Gary K., ed.** The Laboratory Fish. (Handbook of Experimental Animals Ser.). (Illus.). 500p. 2000. 199.95 (*0-12-529650-9*) Acad Pr.

Ostrander, Gary K. & Brocksmith, Richard. The Fishes of San Salvador Island: The Bahamas. (Illus.). 53p. (C). 1997. pap. text 20.00 (*0-935909-64-8*) Bahamian.

Ostrander, Gary K., jt. ed. see Malins, Donald C.

Ostrander, Gilman H. Early Colonial Thought. 1970. pap. text 3.25 (*0-88273-221-8*) Forum Pr IL.

Ostrander, Gilman M. Republic of Letters: The American Intellectual Community, 1776-1865. LC 98-37077. 1999. 35.95 (*0-945612-63-X*) Madison Hse.

Ostrander, John. Bishop: Mountjoy Crisis. 1996. pap. text 12.95 (*0-7851-0191-8*) Marvel Entrprs.

— Kents. 272p. 2000. pap. text 19.95 (*1-56389-513-7*, Pub. by DC Comics) Time Warner.

— Onslaught: The Front Line, Vol. 5. (Illus.). 112p. 1997. pap. text 9.95 (*0-7851-0284-1*) Marvel Entrprs.

— Penguin Triumphant. O'Neil, Dennis, ed. (Illus.). 48p. 1992. pap. 4.95 (*1-56389-030-5*) DC Comics.

— The Spectre: Crimes & Punishments. deluxe ed. Kahan, Bob, ed. (Illus.). 104p. (J). 1993. pap. 9.95 (*1-56389-127-1*, Pub. by DC Comics) Warner Bks.

Ostrander, John & Wein, Len. Legends: The Collected Edition. Kahan, Bob, ed. (Illus.). 160p. 1993. pap. 9.95 (*1-56389-095-X*, Pub. by DC Comics) Warner Bks.

Ostrander, John, jt. auth. see Shooter, Jim.

An Asterisk (*) at the beginning of an entry indicates that the title is appearing for the first time.

Ostrander, Kenneth H. The Legal Structure of Collective Bargaining in Education. 23. LC 87-8470. (Contributions to the Study of Education Ser.). 164p. 1987. 49.95 (*0-313-24474-X*, OLS/, Greenwood Pr) Greenwood.

Ostrander, Norma. Ivanhoe Notes. (Cliffs Notes Ser.). 72p. 1962. pap. 4.95 (*0-8220-0663-4*, Cliff) IDG Bks.

— A Passage to India. (Cliffs Notes Ser.). 72p. 1964. pap., student ed. 4.95 (*0-8220-0985-4*, Cliff) IDG Bks.

***Ostrander, Rick.** The Life of Prayer in a World of Science: Protestants, Prayer & American Culture, 1870-1930. (Religion in America Ser.). 240p. 2000. text 39.95 (*0-19-513610-1*) OUP.

Ostrander, Sheila. Psychic Discoveries: The Iron Curtain Lifted. 2nd ed. 384p. 1997. pap. text 14.95 (*1-56924-750-1*) Marlowe & Co.

Ostrander, Sheila & Schroeder, Lynn. Superlearning. abr. ed. 1987. 12.00 incl. audio (*0-394-29824-1*) Random.

***Ostrander, Stephen.** Great Natural Areas in Western Pennsylvania. LC 99-45680. 2000. 19.95 (*0-8117-2778-5*) Stackpole.

Ostrander, Stephen J. Great Natural Areas in Eastern Pennsylvania. (Illus.). 256p. 1996. pap. 19.95 (*0-8117-2574-X*) Stackpole.

Ostrander, Susan A. Money for Change: Social Movement Philanthropy at the Haymarket People's Fund. LC 95-12095. 256p. (C). 1995. lib. bdg. 69.95 (*1-56639-363-9*) Temple U Pr.

— Money for Change: Social Movement Philanthropy at the Haymarket People's Fund. LC 95-12095. 256p. (C). 1997. pap. text 22.95 (*1-56639-364-7*) Temple U Pr.

— Women of the Upper Class. LC 83-18214. (Women in the Political Economy Ser.). 256p. 1986. pap. 19.95 (*0-87722-475-7*) Temple U Pr.

Ostransky, Leroy. The Anatomy of Jazz. LC 73-11857. (Illus.). 362p. 1973. reprint ed. lib. bdg. 35.00 (*0-8371-7092-3*, OSAJ, Greenwood Pr) Greenwood.

Ostreiko, V. N. Calculation of Electromagnetic Fields in Multilayer Media. xiv, 156p. 1989. text 218.00 (*2-88124-674-5*) Gordon & Breach.

***Ostreng, Willy.** The Impact of International Law on the Practice of Law. 164p. 1999. 60.00 (*90-411-9779-6*) Kluwer Law Intl.

— Recueil Des Cours. 432p. 1999. 129.00 (*90-411-1315-0*) Kluwer Law Intl.

Ostreng, Willy. The Soviet Union in Arctic Waters. (Law of the Sea Occasional Papers: No. 36). 87p. (Orig.). 1987. pap. 10.00 (*0-911189-15-7*) Law Sea Inst.

***Ostreng, Willy, ed.** National Security & International Environmental Cooperation in the Arctic: The Case of the Northern Sea Route. LC 98-49748. (Environment & Policy Ser.: Vol. 16). 367p. 1999. 198.00 (*0-7923-5528-8*) Kluwer Academic.

Ostreng, Willy, jt. ed. see Andresen, S.

Ostrer, Harry. Non Mendelian Genetics in Humans: Medelian & Non-Mendelian. LC 97-20620. (Oxford Monographs on Medical Genetics: No. 35). (Illus.). 216p. 1998. text 42.50 (*0-19-506877-7*) OUP.

Ostria, Gutierrez A. The Tragedy of Bolivia: A People Crucified. Golden, Eithne, tr. from SPA. LC 81-2424. Orig. Title: Un Pueblo en la Cruz. 224p. 1981. reprint ed. lib. bdg. 35.00 (*0-313-22935-X*, GUTB, Greenwood Pr) Greenwood.

Ostriker, Alicia S. The Crack in Everything. LC 95-43297. (Pitt Poetry Ser.). 100p. (C). 1996. pap. 10.95 (*0-8229-5593-8*) U of Pittsburgh Pr.

***Ostriker, Alicia S.** Dancing at the Devil's Party: Essays on Poetry, Politics & the Erotic. LC 99-47945. (Poets on Poetry Ser.). 136p. 2000. pap. 13.95 (*0-472-06696-X*, 06696); text 39.50 (*0-472-09696-6*, 09696) U of Mich Pr.

Ostriker, Alicia S. Green Age. LC 89-32020. (Poetry Ser.). 72p. 1989. pap. 10.95 (*0-8229-5421-4*); text 19.95 (*0-8229-3624-0*) U of Pittsburgh Pr.

— The Imaginary Lover. LC 86-7005. (Poetry Ser.). 110p. 1986. pap. 10.95 (*0-8229-5385-4*); text 19.95 (*0-8229-3543-0*) U of Pittsburgh Pr.

— The Little Space: Poems Selected & New, 1968-1998. LC 98-25458. (Pitt Poetry Ser.). 264p. 1998. pap. 16.95 (*0-8229-5680-2*); text 30.00 (*0-8229-4080-9*) U of Pittsburgh Pr.

— The Nakedness of the Fathers: Biblical Visions & Revisions. LC 94-14616. 225p. (Orig.). (C). 1994. 35.00 (*0-8135-2125-4*) Rutgers U Pr.

— The Nakedness of the Fathers: Biblical Visions & Revisions. LC 94-14616. 225p. (Orig.). (C). 1997. pap. text 16.95 (*0-8135-2447-4*) Rutgers U Pr.

— Once More Out of Darkness. 32p. 1974. pap. 9.95 (*0-917658-00-0*) BPW & P.

— Stealing the Language: The Emergence of Women's Poetry in America. LC 85-73368. 336p. 1987. pap. 18.50 (*0-8070-6303-7*, BP 763) Beacon Pr.

— A Woman under the Surface: Poems & Prose Poems. LC 81-47938. (Contemporary Poets Ser.). 77p. 1982. pap. 10.95 (*0-691-01390-X*, Pub. by Princeton U Pr) Cal Prin Full Svc.

— Writing Like a Woman. (Poets on Poetry Ser.). 160p. 1983. pap. 13.95 (*0-472-06347-2*, 06347) U of Mich Pr.

Ostriker, Alicia S., ed. see Blake, William.

Ostriker, J. P., ed. see Zeldovich, Yakov B.

Ostriker, Jeremiah P. Development of Large Scale Structure in the Universe. (Lezione Fermiane Ser.). (Illus.). 77p. (C). 1992. pap. text 25.95 (*0-521-42361-9*) Cambridge U Pr.

Ostriker, Jeremiah P., ed. Selected Works of Yakov Borisovich Zeldovich, 2 vols. 1144p. 1993. text 150.00 (*0-691-08743-1*, Pub. by Princeton U Pr) Cal Prin Full Svc.

— Selected Works of Yakov Borisovich Zeldovich Vol. I: Chemical Physics & Hydrodynamics. 500p. 1992. text 99.50 (*0-691-08594-3*, Pub. by Princeton U Pr) Cal Prin Full Svc.

Ostriker, Jeremiah P. & Granik, A., eds. Selected Works of Yakov Borisovich Zeldovich Vol. II: Particles, Nuclei, & the Universe. Jackson, E., tr. 644p. 1993. text 99.50 (*0-691-08742-3*, Pub. by Princeton U Pr) Cal Prin Full Svc.

Ostriker, Jeremiah P., jt. auth. see Bahcall, John N.

Ostriker, Jeremiah P., jt. ed. see Dekel, Avishai.

Ostriker, Rebecca, ed. Vaccines: New Advances in Technologies & Applications. (Biomedical Library). 356p. 1996. pap. 795.00 (*1-57936-013-0*) IBC USA.

Ostrikova, O., jt. auth. see Bezborodova, V.

Ostrikova, O., jt. ed. see Bezborodova, V.

Ostro, Marc J., ed. Liposomes: From Biophysics to Therapeutics. (Illus.). 418p. 1987. text 225.00 (*0-8247-7762-X*) Dekker.

Ostroff, Anthony & Van Loen, Alfred. The Endless Line. 64p. 1985. pap. 7.00 (*0-913057-05-3*) Confront Mag Pr.

— The Endless Line. deluxe limited ed. 64p. 1985. 20.00 (*0-913057-06-1*) Confront Mag Pr.

Ostroff, David J., jt. auth. see Krishnamurty, G. B.

Ostroff, Earl. Reflections. 608p. 1999. pap. 32.00 (*0-8059-4546-6*) Dorrance.

Ostroff, Edward D., et al. Solid-State Radar Transmitters. LC 85-73318. 280p. 1985. reprint ed. pap. 86.80 (*0-608-01416-8*, 206217900002) Bks Demand.

Ostroff, Frank. The Horizontal Organization: How to Use Structure to Boost Business & Employee Performance. LC 98-9781. (Illus.). 272p. 1999. 27.50 (*0-19-512138-4*) OUP.

Ostroff, Harriet & Nichols, Tom. Specialty Cookbooks: A Bibliography. LC 91-37398. 672p. 1992. text 30.00 (*0-8240-6947-1*, H1297) Garland.

Ostroff, Monika, jt. auth. see Hall, Lindsey.

Ostrogorski, Moisei A. Democracy & the Organization of Political Parties, 2 vols. abr. ed. LC 81-2862. (Social Science Classics Ser.). 350p. (C). 1982. reprint ed. pap. 29.95 (*0-87855-877-2*); reprint ed. pap. 29.95 (*0-87855-878-0*) Transaction Pubs.

— Democracy & the Organization of Political Parties, 2 Vols. LC 72-122620. (World History Ser.: No. 48). 1970. reprint ed. lib. bdg. 150.00 (*0-8383-1003-6*) M S G Haskell Hse.

— Democracy & the Organization of Political Parties, 2 vols., Set. abr. ed. LC 81-2862. (Social Science Classics Ser.). (C). 1982. reprint ed. pap. 44.95 (*0-87855-921-3*) Transaction Pubs.

— Democracy & the Party System in the United States: A Study in Extra Constitutional Government. LC 73-19166. (Politics & People Ser.). 480p. 1974. reprint ed. 35.95 (*0-405-05888-8*) Ayer.

— The Rights of Women: A Comparative Study in History & Legislation. LC 80-21262. xv, 232p. 1980. reprint ed. lib. bdg. 37.50 (*0-87991-960-4*) Porcupine Pr.

Ostrogorsky, George. History of the Byzantine State. 624p. 1986. pap. text 25.00 (*0-8135-1198-4*) Rutgers U Pr.

Ostrom. Ecosystemes Forestiers Tropicaux D'Afrique (Tropical Forest Ecosystems of Africa)Tr. of Tropical Forest Ecosytems of Africa. (FRE.). 474p. 1983. pap. 30.00 (*2-7099-0681-3*, Pub. by LInstitut Francais) Balogh.

Ostrom, ed. Metro. LC 99-86070. (C). 1999. text. write for info. (*0-321-01132-5*) Addson-Wesley Educ.

Ostrom, Bob. Open Up. LC 98-224670. 1998. 4.99 (*0-679-89244-3*, Pub. by Random Bks Yng Read) Random.

Ostrom, Brian J. & Kauder, Neal B. Examining the Work of State Courts, 1995: A National Perspective from the Court Statistics Project. (Illus.). 108p. 1996. pap. 20.00 (*0-89656-172-0*, R-191) Natl Ctr St Courts.

Ostrom, Carl. Video Compression. 1992. text. write for info. (*0-442-01422-8*, VNR) Wiley.

Ostrom, Carol. Archbishop Hunthausen. 1992. write for info. (*0-201-09248-4*) Addison-Wesley.

Ostrom, Charles W., Jr. Time Series Analysis: Regression Techniques, No. 9. 2nd ed. (Quantitative Applications in the Social Sciences Ser.: Vol. 9). (Illus.). 96p. (C). 1990. pap. 10.95 (*0-8039-3135-2*) Sage.

Ostrom, Elinor. Crafting Institutions for Self-Governing Irrigation Systems. 1992. pap. 19.95 (*1-55815-168-0*) ICS Pr.

— Decision-Related Research on the Organization of Service Delivery Systems in Metropolitan Areas: Police Protection. LC 79-83821. 1979. write for info. (*0-89138-983-0*) ICPSR.

— Governing the Commons: The Evolution of Institutions for Collective Action. (Political Economy of Institutions & Decisions Ser.). (Illus.). 298p. (C). 1990. pap. text 18.95 (*0-521-40599-8*) Cambridge U Pr.

Ostrom, Elinor, ed. Strategies of Political Inquiry. LC 82-852. (Sage Focus Editions Ser.: No. 48). 224p. 1982. reprint ed. pap. 69.50 (*0-608-01483-4*, 205952700001) Bks Demand.

Ostrom, Elinor, et al. Rules, Games, & Common-Pool Resources. LC 93-44406. 392p. (C). 1994. text 75.00 (*0-472-09546-3*, 09546); pap. text 24.95 (*0-472-06546-7*, 06546) U of Mich Pr.

Ostrom, Elinor, jt. auth. see Keohane, Robert O.

Ostrom, George. Glacier's Secrets: Above the Clouds & Beyond the Trails. LC 99-195853. (Illus.). 96p. (Orig.). 1997. pap. 15.95 (*1-56037-122-6*) Am Wrld Geog.

— Wondrous Wildlife. 1998. pap. 15.95 (*1-56037-132-3*) Am Wrld Geog.

Ostrom, Hans A. Lives & Moments: An Introduction to Short Fiction. 900p. (C). 1991. pap. text 48.00 (*0-03-030374-5*, Pub. by Harcourt Coll Pubs); pap. text 34.00 (*0-03-030377-X*) Harcourt Coll Pubs.

Ostrom, Hans A., et al. Spectrum: A Reader. 552p. (C). 1987. teacher ed. write for info. (*0-15-583187-9*) Harcourt Coll Pubs.

Ostrom, John & Cook, William. Paragraph Writing Simplified. LC 92-17962. (Simplified Ser.). 160p. (C). 1997. pap. text 14.66 (*0-06-501150-3*) Addson-Wesley Educ.

Ostrom, John, ed. see Poe, Edgar Allan.

***Ostrom, John H. & McIntosh, John S.** Marsh's Dinosaurs: The Collections from Como Bluff LC 99-32467. (Illus.). 416p. 2000. 85.00 (*0-300-08208-8*) Yale U Pr.

Ostrom, John S. Accounting for Contributions: Understanding the Requirements of FASB Statement, No. 116. Kendrick, Anne, ed. LC 96-3020. 66p. 1996. 47.95 (*1-56972-003-7*) NACUBO.

— Selecting an Auditor. Greene, Deirdre M., ed. LC 92-23093. 184p. 1992. 60.00 (*0-915164-86-8*) NACUBO.

Ostrom, Joseph. You & Your Aura. (Illus.). 124p. (Orig.). 1989. pap. 10.95 (*0-85030-549-7*, Pub. by Aqrn Pr) HarpC.

Ostrom, Lee T. Creating the Ergonomically Sound Workplace. LC 93-41614. (The Management Ser.). 219p. 1994. pap. 41.95 (*1-55542-621-2*) Jossey-Bass.

Ostrom, Neenyah. Fifty Things You Should Know about the Chronic Fatigue Symdrome Epidemic. 1993. mass mkt. 4.99 (*0-312-95043-8*) St Martin.

Ostrom, Stanley. Celebrating 100 Years of God's Blessings. LC 99-93149. 90p. 1999. pap. 10.00 (*0-7392-0201-4*, PO3198) Morris Pubng.

Ostrom, T. G. & Johnson, Normal L. Mostly Finite Geometries: In Celebration of T. G. Ostrom's 80th Birthday. LC 97-10208. (Lecture Notes in Pure & Applied Mathematics Ser.). (Illus.). 456p. 1997. pap. text 175.00 (*0-8247-0035-X*) Dekker.

Ostrom, T. G., ed. see International Conference on Projective Planes Staf.

Ostrom, Vincent. The Intellectual Crisis in American Public Administration. 2nd ed. LC 88-15677. 232p. (C). 1989. pap. text 19.95 (*0-8173-0418-5*) U of Ala Pr.

— The Meaning of American Federalism: Constituting a Self-Governing Society. 301p. 1991. 24.95 (*1-55815-076-5*); pap. 19.95 (*1-55815-393-4*) ICS Pr.

— The Meaning of Democracy & the Vulnerability of Democracies: A Response to Tocqueville's Challenge. LC 96-51299. 360p. (C). 1997. text 44.50 (*0-472-10797-6*, 10797); pap. text 19.95 (*0-472-08456-9*, 08456) U of Mich Pr.

— The Political Theory of a Compound Republic: Designing the American Experiment. 2nd ed. LC 86-7063. xxx, 240p. 1987. 24.95 (*0-8032-3554-2*) ICS Pr.

Ostrom, Vincent, et al, eds. Rethinking Institutional Analysis & Development: Issues, Alternatives & Choices. LC 88-28421. 480p. 1988. text 34.95 (*1-55815-024-2*) ICS Pr.

— Rethinking Institutional Analysis & Development: Issues, Alternatives & Choices. rev. ed. LC 93-16940. 1993. pap. 19.95 (*1-55815-264-4*) ICS Pr.

Ostrom, Warren. In God We Live. LC 86-61674. (Orig.). 1986. pap. 1.00 (*0-87574-268-8*) Pendle Hill.

Ostroot, Gerald. The Consistency Control Book. 176p. 1993. pap. 99.00 (*0-89852-308-7*, 0101R215) TAPPI.

Ostroske, Walter & Devaney, John. Correct the Ten Most Common Golf Problems in Ten Days. (Illus.). 128p. 1991. pap. 10.00 (*0-399-51656-5*, Perigee Bks) Berkley Pub.

— Master Your Short Game in 16 Days: A How-To Guide for the Weekend Golfer. LC 93-36213. (Illus.). 128p. (Orig.). 1994. pap. 9.95 (*0-399-51861-4*, Perigee Bks) Berkley Pub.

— Two-Putt Greens in Eighteen Days: A How-To Guide for the Weekend Golfer. (Illus.). 128p. (Orig.). 1992. pap. 10.00 (*0-399-51747-2*, Perigee Bks) Berkley Pub.

Ostrosky, Michaelene, jt. ed. see Sandall, Susan R.

Ostrosky-Solis, F., jt. auth. see Ardila, A.

Ostroumoff, Ivan N. The History of the Council of Florence. 189p. 1972. pap. 8.00 (*0-913026-03-4*) St Nectarios.

Ostroumov, S. A., jt. auth. see Yablokov, A. V.

Ostrov, Benjamin C. Conquering Resources: The Growth & Decline of the PLA's Science & Technology Commission for National Defense. LC 90-26809. (Studies on Contemporary China). 176p. (C). (gr. 13). 1991. text 79.95 (*0-87332-654-7*, East Gate Bk) M E Sharpe.

Ostrov, Rick. Power Reading. 1978. pap. write for info. (*0-9601706-2-6*) Educ Pr CA.

Ostrov, Ricki. Solving Skin Problems. LC 99-27330. (Health Factfiles Ser.). (Illus.). 112p. (J). (gr. 11). 1999. pap. 12.95 (*0-7370-1614-0*) T-L Custom Pub.

Ostrove, S., jt. ed. see Henon, B. K.

Ostrove, Stephanie, ed. California Legal Assistant Handbook. 600p. 1996. ring bd. 89.98 incl. disk (*0-938065-95-5*) James Pub Santa Ana.

— Texas Torts. 1998. ring bd. 119.00 (*1-58012-025-3*) James Pub Santa Ana.

Ostrove, Stephanie, ed. see Turano, Thomas A.

Ostrovskii, Aleksandr N. Easy Money, & Two Other Plays: Even a Wise Man Stumbles, & Wolves & Sheep. Magarshack, David, tr. LC 78-110861. 296p. 1970. reprint ed. lib. bdg. 69.50 (*0-8371-4532-5*, OSEM) Greenwood.

Ostrovskii, Alexander G., jt. auth. see Piterbarg, Leonid I.

Ostrovskii, B. I. Physics Reviews: X-Ray Diffraction Study of Nematic, Smectic A & C Liquid Crystals, Vol. 12. Gol'danskii, V. I. et al, eds. (Soviet Scientific Reviews Ser.: Vol. 12, Pt. 2). ii, 68p. 1989. pap. text 74.00 (*3-7186-4907-1*) Gordon & Breach.

Ostrovskii, I. A., jt. ed. see Shapiro, Leonid B.

Ostrovskii, I. V., jt. auth. see Linnik, Iuril V.

Ostrovskii, I. V., ed. see Govorov, N. V.

Ostrovskii, Iosif V., jt. auth. see Linnik, Jurii V.

Ostrovskii, L. A. Modulated Waves: Theory & Applications. LC 98-20381. (Series in the Mathematical Sciences). 376p. 1998. 60.00 (*0-8018-5870-4*) Johns Hopkins.

Ostrovskii, V. N., jt. auth. see Demkov, Yu N.

Ostrovsky. Mathematical Modeling of Chemical Processes. 1991. 104.00 (*0-8493-7132-5*, TP155) CRC Pr.

Ostrovsky, Alexander. Ostrovsky: Four Plays. Mulrine, Stephen, tr. (Absolute Classics Ser.). 128p. 1997. pap. 16.95 (*1-899791-05-1*) Theatre Comm.

— Plays. Noyes, George R., ed. LC 70-98632. reprint ed. 41.50 (*0-404-04837-4*) AMS Pr.

— The Storm. Magarshack, David, tr. from RUS. 120p. 1988. pap. 5.00 (*0-88233-551-0*) Ardis Pubs.

— Too Clever by Half: or The Diary of a Scoundrel. Ackland, Rodney & Gerould, Daniel, trs. from RUS. (Old Vic Theatre Collection Ser.: Vol. 3). 120p. 1988. pap. 7.95 (*1-55783-023-1*) Applause Theatre Bk Pubs.

— Without a Dowry & Other Plays. Henley, Norman, ed. & tr. by. from RUS. 1997. 37.95 (*0-88233-933-8*) Ardis Pubs.

Ostrovsky, Erika. A Constant Journey: The Fiction of Monique Wittig. LC 89-49482. 208p. (C). 1991. 26.95 (*0-8093-1642-0*) S Ill U Pr.

Ostrovsky, L. A., jt. auth. see Naugolnykh, K. A.

Ostrovsky, Yu I., et al. Holographic Interferometry in Experimental Mechanics. (Optical Sciences Ser.: Vol. 60). (Illus.). 272p. 1991. 86.95 (*0-387-52604-8*) Spr-Verlag.

— Interferometry by Holography. (Optical Sciences Ser.: Vol. 20). (Illus.). 280p. 1980. 59.95 (*0-387-09886-0*) Spr-Verlag.

Ostrow, Andrew C., ed. Directory of Psychological Tests in the Sport & Exercise Sciences. 2nd ed. LC 96-86376. 570p. (C). 1996. text 46.00 (*1-885693-06-0*) Fit Info Tech.

***Ostrow, Ann K.** Naked Truths: Women, Sexuality & Gender in Classical Art & Archaeology. (Illus.). 2000. pap. 27.99 (*0-415-21752-0*) Routledge.

Ostrow, Bridget & Ostrow, Louis B. Veins: Everything You Need to Know for Health & Beauty. LC 99-74176. (Illus.). 183p. 1999. pap. 15.95 (*0-9670025-3-2*, Pub. by Drs Bk Pr) BookWorld.

Ostrow, D. G. Behavioral Aspects of AIDS. LC 90-7242. (Illus.). 430p. (C). 1990. 78.00 (*0-306-43452-0*, Plenum Trade) Perseus Pubng.

Ostrow, D. G. & Kalichman, S. C., eds. Psychosocial & Public Health Impacts of New HIV Therapies. LC 98-56536. (AIDS Prevention & Mental Health Ser.). (Illus.). 240p. (C). 1999. text 75.00 (*0-306-45973-6*, Kluwer Plenum) Kluwer Academic.

Ostrow, D. G. & Kessler, R. C. Methodological Issues in AIDS Behavioral Research. (AIDS Prevention & Mental Health Ser.). (Illus.). 374p. (C). 1993. text 59.00 (*0-306-44439-9*, Kluwer Plenum) Kluwer Academic.

Ostrow, David G., ed. Biobehavioral Control of AIDS. (Illus.). 250p. (C). 1987. text 29.50 (*0-8290-2354-2*) Irvington.

Ostrow, David G., et al, eds. Sexually Transmitted Diseases in Homosexual Men: Diagnosis, Treatment, & Research. LC 83-10957. (Illus.). 292p. 1983. 65.00 (*0-306-41337-X*, Plenum Trade) Perseus Pubng.

Ostrow, David G., jt. ed. see Nichols, Stuart E.

Ostrow, Eileen J., ed. Center Stage: An Anthology of Twenty-One Contemporary Black-American Plays. (Illus.). 328p. (Orig.). 1991. pap. text 19.95 (*0-252-06178-0*) U of Ill Pr.

— Center Stage: An Anthology of Twenty-One Contemporary Black-American Plays. num. ed. LC 80-53143. (Illus.). 328p. (Orig.). 1981. pap. 29.95 (*0-9605208-0-5*) Sea Urchin.

Ostrow, Gail, ed. see Chapman, Merrill R.

***Ostrow, James, et al, eds.** Cultivating the Sociological Imagination: Concepts & Models for Service - Learning in Sociology. (AAHE'S Series on Service - Learning in the Discipline). 246p. 1999. pap. 28.50 (*1-56377-017-2*, SL15DS) Am Assn Higher Ed.

Ostrow, James M. Social Sensitivity: A Study of Habit & Experience. LC 89-35027. (SUNY Series in Philosophy of the Social Sciences). 137p. (C). 1990. pap. text 21.95 (*0-7914-0216-9*) State U NY Pr.

— Social Sensitivity: A Study of Habit & Experience. LC 89-35027. (SUNY Series in Philosophy of the Social Sciences). 137p. (C). 1990. text 64.50 (*0-7914-0215-0*) State U NY Pr.

Ostrow, Jill. Making Problems, Creating Solutions: Challenging Young Mathematicians. LC 98-26806. 176p. 1998. pap. text 19.50 (*1-57110-041-5*) Stenhse Pubs.

— A Room with a Different View: First Through Third Graders Build Community & Create Curriculum. (Illus.). 168p. (Orig.). (C). 1995. pap. text 20.00 (*1-57110-009-1*) Stenhse Pubs.

***Ostrow, Joel M.** Comparing Post-Soviet Legislatures: A Theory of Institutional Design & Political Conflict. LC 99-59121. (Parliaments & Legislatures Ser.). 288p. (C). 2000. text 65.00 (*0-8142-0841-X*); pap. text 26.95 (*0-8142-5044-0*) Ohio St U Pr.

Ostrow, Kim. Colorful Christmas. 10p. 1999. pap. 7.99 (*0-8431-7551-6*, Price Stern) Peng Put Young Read.

Ostrow, Lauren S., jt. auth. see Carter, Lanie.

Ostrow, Louis B., jt. auth. see Ostrow, Bridget.

Ostrow, Marshall E. Bettas. (Illus.). 96p. 1989. 9.95 (*0-86622-745-8*, KW-052) TFH Pubns.

— A Complete Introduction to Gerbils. (Complete Introduction to...Ser.). (Illus.). 128p. (Orig.). 1987. pap. 8.95 (*0-86622-299-5*, CO-018S) TFH Pubns.

— Goldfish. 2nd ed. Vriends, Matthre M., ed. LC 95-18370. (Complete Pet Owner's Manual Ser.). (Illus.). 1995. pap. 6.95 (*0-8120-9016-0*) Barron.

O

Ostrow, Rona & Smith, Sweetman R. The Dictionary of Marketing. LC 87-82654. (Illus.). 258p. 1987. 42.00 (*0-87005-573-9*) Fairchild.

— Fairchild's Dictionary of Retailing. LC 84-82074. (Illus.). 264p. (C). 1984. 42.00 (*0-87005-437-6*) Fairchild.

***Ostrow, Saul.** Painting Function: Making It Real. (Illus.). 24p. 2000. pap. 3.00 (*0-9667008-2-1*) SPACES.

***Ostrow, Scott.** The Insider's Guide to Joining the Military. 2000. pap. 15.99 (*0-7645-6189-8*, Arco) Macmillan Gen Ref.

Ostrow, Stephen. Digitizing Historical Pictorial Collections for the Internet. (Illus.). 36p. 1998. pap. 20.00 (*1-887334-57-2*) Coun Lib & Info.

Ostrow, Stephen E., ed. Visions & Revisions. LC 68-56466. (Illus.). 1968. pap. 2.00 (*0-911517-42-1*) Mus of Art RI.

Ostrow, Stephen E., pref. Library of Congress Prints & Photographs: An Illustrated Guide. LC 94-17438. (Illus.). 80p. 1994. pap. 7.50 (*0-8444-0816-6*) Lib Congress.

Ostrow, Steven A. Bridges. LC 96-40509. 1997. 14.98 (*1-56799-445-8*, Friedman-Fairfax) M Friedman Pub Grp Inc.

Ostrow, Stuart. A Producer's Broadway Journey. LC 97-46533. 232p. 1999. 19.95 (*0-275-95866-3*, Praeger Pubs) Greenwood.

Ostrow, Vivian. My Brother Is from Outer Space: The Book of Proof. LC 95-38321. (Illus.). 32p. (J). (gr. k-4). 1996. lib. bdg. 14.95 (*0-8075-5325-5*) U Ch Pr. A Whitman.

— My Brother Is from Outer Space: (The Book of Proof) (Illus.). 32p. (J). (gr. k-4). 1999. pap. 6.95 (*0-8075-5326-3*) A Whitman.

Ostrow, Vivian, jt. auth. see Ostrow, William.

Ostrow, William & Ostrow, Vivian. All about Asthma. Levine, Abby, ed. LC 89-5254. (Illus.). 32p. (J). (gr. 2-6). 1989. pap. 4.95 (*0-8075-0275-8*) A Whitman.

Ostrower. The United Nations & the United States. 317p. 1998. 29.95 (*0-8057-7937-X*) Mac Lib Ref.

Ostrower, Francie. Why the Wealthy Give: The Culture of Elite Philanthropy. 203p. 1996. pap. text 14.95 (*0-691-01588-0*, Pub. by Princeton U Pr) Cal Prin Full Svc.

— Why the Wealthy Give: The Culture of Elite Philanthropy. LC 95-2854. 208p. 1996. text 35.00 (*0-691-04434-1*, Pub. by Princeton U Pr) Cal Prin Full Svc.

Ostrower, Francie, jt. auth. see DiMaggio, Paul.

Ostrower, Gary B. Collective Insecurity: The United States & the League of Nations During the Early Thirties. LC 76-754. 287p. 1979. 37.50 (*0-8387-1799-3*) Bucknell U Pr.

— League of Nations from 1919-1929. LC 94-8337. (Partners for Peace Ser.: Vol. 1). 192p. pap. 25.00 (*0-89529-636-5*, Avery) Penguin Putnam.

Ostrowitz, Judith. Privileging the Past: Reconstructing History in Northwest Coast Art. (Illus.). 264p. 1999. 35.00 (*0-295-97814-7*) U of Wash Pr.

Ostrowky, Nicole, jt. ed. see Stanley, H. Eugene.

Ostrowskaja, Rita. Jews in the Ukraine. 1996. pap. 55.00 (*3-89322-852-7*, Pub. by Edition Cantz) Dist Art Pubs.

Ostrowski, Alexander. Aufgabensammlung zur Infinitesimalrechnung. Incl. Vol. 1. Funktionen Einer Variablen. 341p. 1980. 80.50 (*0-8176-0290-9*); Vol. 3. Integralrechnung Auf Dem Gebiete Mehrerer Variablen: Differentialrechnung Auf Dem Gebiete Mehrerer Variablen, Losungen. (GER.). 398p. 1977. 53.95 (Mathematische Reihe Ser.: Vols. 28, 38, 47 & 56). (GER.). write for info. (*0-8176-0785-4*) Birkhauser.

— Collected Papers, 6 vols., Set, Vol. 4, X-XII. (ENG, FRE & GER.). 600p. 1983. 625.50 (*0-8176-1512-1*) Birkhauser.

— Collected Papers, Vol. 4, X-XII. (ENG, FRE & GER.). 600p. 1984. 91.00 (*0-8176-1509-1*) Birkhauser.

— Collected Papers, Vol. 5. (Contemporary Mathematicians Ser.). 560p. 1985. 85.00 (*0-8176-1510-5*) Birkhauser.

— Collected Papers: Alexander Ostrowski, Vol. 6. (Contemporary Mathematicians Ser.). 720p. 1985. 110.00 (*0-8176-1511-3*) Birkhauser.

Ostrowski, Donald. Muscovy & the Mongols: Cross-Cultural Influences on the Steppe Frontier, 1304-1589. LC 97-21385. 300p. (C). 1998. 59.95 (*0-521-59085-X*) Cambridge U Pr.

***Ostrowski, Donald & Birnbaum, David J., eds.** The Povest' vremennykh Let: An Interlinear Collation & Paradosis, 3 vols. (Library of Early Ukrainian Literature: Vol. 10, Pts. 1-3). (SLO.). 2100p. 1999. text 125.00 (*0-916458-91-1*) Harvard Ukrainian.

Ostrowski, Jan K. Land of the Winged Horseman: Art in Poland, 1572-1764. (Illus.). 380p. 1999. 65.00 (*0-300-07918-4*) Yale U Pr.

Ostrowski, Jan K., et al. Land of the Winged Horseman: Art in Poland, 1572-1764. LC 98-37979. 380p. 1999. 60.00 (*0-88397-131-3*) Art Srvc Intl.

Ostrowski, Mary. Far Out & from the Heart. 64p. 1996. pap. 16.95 (*0-9641973-8-3*) Genie Pubng.

— Far Out & from the Heart. LC 96-75858. (Illus.). 50p. 1996. reprint ed. 19.95 (*1-889137-00-6*) Genie Pubng.

Ostrowsky, Daniel B. & Reinisch, Raymond, eds. Guided Wave Nonlinear Optics: Proceedings of the NATO Advanced Study Institute, Cargese, France, August 12-24, 1991. LC 92-10359. (NATO Advanced Science Institutes Series C: Mathematical & Physical Sciences: Vol. 214). 672p. (C). 1992. text 288.00 (*0-7923-1727-0*) Kluwer Academic.

Ostrowsky, Daniel B. & Spitz, E., eds. New Directions in Guided Wave & Coherent Optics, 2 vols., Set. 1984. text 321.50 (*90-247-2938-6*) Kluwer Academic.

Ostrowsky, Nicole, jt. ed. see Stanley, H. Eugene.

Ostrum, Gus, jt. ed. see Parker, Janet.

Ostrum, Hans, jt. ed. see Bishop, Wendy.

Ostrum, Meg, ed. see Miller, John M.

Ostrum, Meg, jt. ed. see Sharrow, Gregory.

***Ostrup, Finn.** Money & the Natural Rate of Unemployment. LC 99-29143. 318p. (C). 2000. 74.95 (*0-521-66139-0*); pap. 27.95 (*0-521-66739-9*) Cambridge U Pr.

Ostry, Bernard, jt. auth. see Ferns, Henry.

Ostry, Sylvia. Authority & Academic Scribblers: The Role of Research in East Asian Policy Reform. 181p. 1991. pap. 19.95 (*1-55815-132-X*); 6.95 (*1-55815-141-9*) ICS Pr.

— L' Interdependance, Vulnerabilite et Possibilites. LC HF1411.O77. (Fondation Per Jacobsson Conference de 1990 Ser.). (FRE.). 36p. reprint ed. pap. 30.00 (*0-608-08784-X*, 206942300004) Bks Demand.

— Interdependence, Vulnerability & Opportunity. LC HF1411.O77. (Per Jacobsson Lecture Ser.: Vol. 1987). 30p. reprint ed. pap. 30.00 (*0-608-08782-3*, 206942100004) Bks Demand.

— La Interdependencia, Vulnerabilidad y Posibilidades. LC HF1411.O77. (Conferencia Per Jacobsson de 1987 Ser.). (SPA.). 44p. reprint ed. pap. 30.00 (*0-608-08783-1*, 206942200004) Bks Demand.

— New Dimensions of Market Access. (Occasional Paper Ser.: No. 49). 32p. (Orig.). 1995. pap. 10.00 (*1-56708-049-9*) Grp of Thirty.

— A New Regime for Foreign Direct Investment. (Occasional Paper Ser.: No. 53). 30p. 1997. pap. 10.00 (*1-56708-102-9*) Grp of Thirty.

— The Post-Cold War Trading System: Who's on First. LC 96-42495. 1997. pap. 17.95 (*0-226-63790-5*) U Ch Pr.

— The Post-Cold War Trading System: Who's on First. LC 96-42495. 296p. 1999. lib. bdg. 48.00 (*0-226-63789-1*) U Ch Pr.

— Reinforcing the WTO. (Occasional Paper Ser.: Vol. 56). 37p. 1998. pap. 10.00 (*1-56708-105-3*) Grp of Thirty.

— The Threat of Managed Trade to Transforming Economics. (Occasional Paper Ser.: No. 41). (Orig.). 1993. pap. text 10.00 (*1-56708-088-X*) Grp of Thirty.

Ostry, Sylvia & Nelson, Richard R. Techno-Nationalism & Techno-Globalism: Conflict & Cooperation. (Integrating National Economies Ser.). 160p. (C). 1995. 34.95 (*0-8157-6674-2*); pap. 14.95 (*0-8157-6673-4*) Brookings.

Ostrzenski, Adam. Laproscopic Panhysterectomy with Reconstructive Posterior Culdeplasty & Vaginal Vault Suspension. (Illus.). 126p. (C). 1994. 78.00 (*0-9638210-0-8*) Med Sci Pub.

Ostuni, Elizabeth E. & Santo Pietro, Mary J. Successful Communication with Alzheimer's Disease Patients: An In-Service Training Manual. LC 96-54719. 288p. 1997. text 39.50 (*0-7506-9564-1*) Buttrwrth-Heinemann.

Ostuni, Elizabeth E. & Silver, Elaine N. I'm Good at Speech: Music & Activities to Teach Children Good Communication Skills. (Illus.). 112p. (Orig.). 1990. pap. text 14.95 (*1-879267-00-4*); audio 9.95 (*1-879267-01-2*) Accent Pub NJ.

Ostuni, Elizabeth E., jt. auth. see Santo Pietro, Mary J.

Ostwald, Martin. Anarke in Thucydides. LC 88-32781. (American Philological Association, American Classical Studies). 82p. 1989. pap. 12.95 (*1-55540-280-1*) OUP.

— Autonomia: Its Genesis & Early History. (American Classical Studies). 82p. 1982. pap. 15.95 (*0-89130-572-6*, 40 04 11) OUP.

— From Popular Sovereignty to the Sovereignty of Law: Law, Society, & Politics in Fifth Century Athens. LC 85-690. 500p. 1986. pap. 22.50 (*0-520-06798-3*, Pub. by U CA Pr) Cal Prin Full Svc.

Ostwald, Martin, et al. The Meters of Greek & Latin Poetry. LC 93-47104. 152p. (C). 1994. reprint ed. pap. text 9.95 (*0-87220-243-7*); reprint ed. lib. bdg. 29.95 (*0-87220-244-5*) Hackett Pub.

Ostwald, Martin, ed. see Aristotle.

Ostwald, Martin, ed. see Plato.

Ostwald, Peter F. Glenn Gould: The Ecstasy & Tragedy of Genius. (Illus.). 368p. 1998. pap. 15.00 (*0-393-31847-8*) Norton.

— Schumann: The Inner Voices of a Musical Genius. (Illus.). 390p. 1987. reprint ed. pap. text 18.95 (*1-55553-014-1*) NE U Pr.

— Vaslav Nijinsky: A Leap into Madness. 1990. 19.95 (*0-8184-0535-X*) Carol Pub Group.

— Vaslav Nijinsky: A Leap into Madness. rev. ed. LC 95-9381. (Illus.). 400p. 1996. pap. 14.95 (*0-8065-1681-X*, Citadel Pr) Carol Pub Group.

Ostwald, Peter F. & Zegans, Leonard S. The Threat to the Cosmic Order: Psychological, Social & Health Implications of Richard Wagner's Ring of the Nibelung. LC 96-24652. (Mental Health Library Series). 1997. 32.50 (*0-8236-6528-3*) Intl Univs Pr.

Ostwald, Peter F. & Zegans, Leonard S., eds. The Pleasures & Perils of Genius: Mostly Mozart. LC 93-24461. (Mental Health Library: Monograph 2). 228p. (C). 1993. 35.00 (*0-8236-4162-7*) Intl Univs Pr.

Ostwald, Peter F., tr. & pref. see Nauhaus, Gerd.

Ostwald, Phillip F. A M Cost Estimator. (Illus.). 560p. 1989. reprint ed. 119.50 (*0-932905-06-4*) Penton Pub.

***Ostwald, Phillip F.** Construction Cost Analysis & Estimating. 504p. 2000. 95.00 (*0-13-083207-3*) P-H.

Ostwald, Phillip F. Engineering Cost Estimating. 3rd ed. 576p. 1991. 95.00 (*0-13-276627-2*) P-H.

Ostwald, Phillip F., ed. Manufacturing Cost Estimating. LC 79-67648. 266p. reprint ed. pap. 82.50 (*0-608-13390-6*, 205573800034) Bks Demand.

Ostwald, Phillip F. & Munoz, Jairo. Manufacturing Processes & Systems. 9th ed. LC 96-47300. 800p. 1997. text 106.95 (*0-471-04741-4*) Wiley.

Ostwalt, Conrad E., Jr. After Eden: The Secularization of American Space in the Fiction of Willa Cather & Theodore Dreiser. LC 89-42505. 160p. 1990. 32.50 (*0-8387-5168-7*) Bucknell U Pr.

Ostwalt, Conrad E. Love Valley: An American Utopia. LC 98-23595. 202p. 1998. 45.95 (*0-87972-759-4*); pap. 21.95 (*0-87972-760-8*) Bowling Green Univ Popular Press.

Ostwinkle, Pamela S. The Little Teardrop. (Illus.). 27p. (J). (ps-4). 1999. 15.99 (*1-889406-16-3*) Prell Pub.

Osuchowska, Isia. The Gift: A Magical Story about Caring for the Earth. LC 96-5889. (Illus.). 32p. (J). 1996. 14.95 (*0-86171-116-5*) Wisdom MA.

Osuchukwu, Peter. The Spirit of Umunna & the Development of Small Christian Communities in Igboland. (European University Studies: Series 23, Vol. 544). (Illus.). 289p. 1995. pap. 54.95 (*3-631-49301-0*) P Lang Pubng.

— The Spirit of Umunna & the Development of Small Christian Communities in Igboland. LC 95-39195. (European University Studies, Series 23: Vol. 544). (Illus.). 289p. 1995. pap. 54.95 (*0-8204-2933-3*, 68721) P Lang Pubng.

O'Suilleabhain, Michael. Bodhran Tutor Book. 25p. 1984. pap. 10.95 (*0-7866-1594-X*, 95179WW) Mel Bay.

O'Suilleabhain, Michael, jt. auth. see O'Sullivan, Donal.

O'Suilleahain, Sean. Storytelling in Irish Tradition LC 79-110949. (Irish Life & Culture Ser.). 53p. 1973. write for info. (*0-85342-306-7*) Mercier Pr.

O'Sullevan, Peter, ed. see Magee, Sean.

Osullivan. Economics: Principles & Tools D-CART. 1998. 69.00 (*0-13-011084-1*) P-H.

O'Sullivan. Economics & Macroeconomics Study Guide, 2 bks. 1998. text 78.63 (*0-13-080542-4*) P-H.

— Meaning of Famine. LC 96-44980. 1997. write for info. (*0-7185-1426-2*) St Martin.

O'Sullivan & Hunter. Law Business & Regulation. 658p. (C). 1998. pap. text 56.75 (*0-536-01523-6*) Pearson Custom.

Osullivan & Sheffrin. Macroeconomics. 1997. pap. text, student ed. 21.33 (*0-13-855172-3*) P-H.

— Microeconomics. 1997. pap. text, student ed. 21.33 (*0-13-855602-4*) P-H.

— Practicum Economics. (C). 1998. pap. text 30.60 (*0-13-975269-2*) P-H.

O'Sullivan & Sheffrin, Steven M. Microeconomics: Principles & Tools. LC 97-24097. 448p. (C). 1997. pap. text 63.00 (*0-13-742859-6*) P-H.

O'Sullivan, jt. auth. see Eber, Christine.

O'Sullivan, jt. auth. see McKenna.

O'Sullivan, A. W., tr. see Hurgronje, Christian S.

O'Sullivan, Ann & Sheehan, John, eds. The Iveragh Peninsula: Suirbhe Seandalaiochta Uibh Rathaigh. (Illus.). 484p. 1996. 39.95 (*0-902561-84-7*, Pub. by Cork Univ) Stylus Pub VA.

***O'Sullivan, Arthur.** Urban Economics. LC 99-30311. 1999. write for info. (*0-256-26331-0*, Irwn McGrw-H) McGrw-H Hghr Educ.

— Urban Economics. 4th ed. LC 99-30311. (Illus.). 2000. write for info. (*0-07-116974-1*, Irwn Prfssnl) McGraw-Hill Prof.

O'Sullivan, Arthur & Sheffrin, Steven M. Economics: Principles & Tools. LC 97-26468. 684p. 1997. 89.00 (*0-13-206368-9*) P-H.

***O'Sullivan, Arthur & Sheffrin, Steven M.** Economics: Principles & Tools. 2nd ed. 768p. 2000. 88.00 incl. cd-rom (*0-13-027383-X*) P-H.

— Macroeconomics: Principles & Tools. 2nd ed. 448p. 2000. pap. 61.33 (*0-13-018975-8*) P-H.

— Microeconomics: Principles & Tools. 2nd ed. 480p. 2000. pap. 61.33 (*0-13-018982-0*, Prentice Hall) P-H.

O'Sullivan, Arthur, et al. Property Taxes & Tax Revolts: The Legacy of Proposition 13. (Illus.). 171p. (C). 1995. text 47.95 (*0-521-46159-6*) Cambridge U Pr.

O'Sullivan, Arthur M. Urban Economics. 3rd ed. LC 95-37278. (Irwin Series in Economics). 768p. (C). 1995. text 67.50 (*0-256-16072-4*, Irwn McGrw-H) McGrw-H Hghr Educ.

O'Sullivan, Authur & Sheffrin, Steven M. Macroeconomics. LC 97-24092. 384p. 1997. pap. text 63.00 (*0-13-742842-1*) P-H.

O'Sullivan, Bill. Precious Blood. LC 91-47500. 202p. 1992. 18.95 (*0-939149-67-2*) Soho Press.

O'Sullivan, Brad. Pointing at the Direction of Sound. 44p. (Orig.). 1996. pap. 5.00 (*1-887289-12-7*) Rodent Pr.

O'Sullivan, Carol. Alcohol: Understanding Words in Context. LC 89-11712. (Opposing Viewpoints Juniors Ser.). (Illus.). 36p. (J). (gr. 3-6). 1990. lib. bdg. 16.20 (*0-89908-634-9*) Greenhaven.

— Drugs & Sports: Locating the Author's Main Idea. LC 89-36322. (Opposing Viewpoints Juniors Ser.). (Illus.). 36p. (J). (gr. 3-6). 1990. lib. bdg. 16.20 (*0-89908-637-3*) Greenhaven.

— Gun Control: Distinguishing Between Fact & Opinion. LC 89-2226. (Opposing Viewpoints Juniors Ser.). (Illus.). 36p. (J). (gr. 3-6). 1990. lib. bdg. 16.20 (*0-89908-638-1*) Greenhaven.

O'Sullivan, Christine Y. NAEP 1996 Science Report Card for the Nation & States: Findings from the National Assessment of Educational Progress. 131p. 1997. pap. 14.00 (*0-16-063616-7*) USGPO.

O'Sullivan, Christine Y. Students Learning Science: A Report on Policies & Practices in United States Schools. LC 98-214791. (Education Department Publication Ser.: No. NCES 98-493). (Illus.). 143p. 1998. pap. 15.00 (*0-16-049733-7*) USGPO.

***O'Sullivan, Christine Y., et al.** Student Work & Teacher Practices in Science: A Report on What Students Know & Can Do. LC 99-237003. (Illus.). 387p. 1999. write for info. (*0-16-050036-2*) USGPO.

O'Sullivan, Colm, jt. auth. see Mansfield, Mike.

O'Sullivan, D. & Ramadurai, S., eds. Charge Composition of Ultra Heavy Nuclei. (Advances in Space Research Ser.: Vol. 15). 88p. 1995. pap. 97.75 (*0-08-042556-9*, Pergamon Pr) Elsevier.

O'Sullivan, Dan, jt. auth. see Lockyer, Roger.

O'Sullivan, Denis. Commitment, Educative Action & Adults: Learning Programmes with a Social Purpose. 224p. 1993. 72.95 (*1-85628-292-9*, Pub. by Avebry) Ashgate Pub Co.

O'Sullivan, Denis, jt. ed. see Peache, Robert J.

O'Sullivan, Donal. The Irish Free State & Its Senate: A Study in Contemporary Politics. LC 72-4286. (World Affairs Ser.: National & International Viewpoints). 696p. 1972. reprint ed. 44.95 (*0-405-04579-4*) Ayer.

O'Sullivan, Donal, ed. Songs of the Irish. 199p. 1981. pap. 16.95 (*0-85342-653-8*) Dufour.

O'Sullivan, Donal & O'Suilleabhain, Michael. Bunting's Ancient Music of Ireland. 1983. 39.95 (*0-902561-25-1*, Pub. by Cork Univ) Stylus Pub VA.

***O'Sullivan, Donal J.** The Irish Constabularies, 1822-1922. (Illus.). 416p. 1999. pap. 59.95 (*0-86322-257-9*, Pub. by Brandon Bk Pubs) Irish Bks Media.

O'Sullivan, Doreen. Dairying History of the Darling Downs. (Illus.). xiv, 102p. (Orig.). 1992. pap. 14.95 (*0-949414-82-4*, Pub. by U Sthrn Queenslnd) Accents Pubns.

***O'Sullivan, Edmund.** Transformative Learning: Educational Vision for the 21st Century. LC 99-17550. 1999. pap. 22.50 (*1-85649-699-6*) St Martin.

O'Sullivan, Elizabethann. Research Methods for Public Administrators. 3rd ed. (C). 1998. text. write for info. (*0-8013-1851-3*) Addison-Wesley.

— Research Methods for Public Administrators. 3rd ed. LC 98-38583. 512p. (C). 1998. pap. text 77.00 (*0-8013-1850-5*) Addson-Wesley Educ.

O'Sullivan, Elizabethann & Rassel, Gary R. Research Methods for Public Administrators. 372p. 1989. text 39.33 (*0-582-28567-4*, 71594) Longman.

— Research Methods for Public Administrators. 2nd ed. 576p. (C). 1995. text 63.75 (*0-8013-1172-1*) Longman.

O'Sullivan, Ellen L. Marketing for Parks, Recreation, & Leisure. LC 91-65916. 275p. 1991. 28.95 (*0-910251-43-6*) Venture Pub PA.

O'Sullivan, Ellen L. & Spangler, Kathy J. Experience Marketing: Strategies for the New Millenium. LC 98-86937. 430p. (C). 1998. text 34.95 (*0-910251-98-3*) Venture Pub PA.

O'Sullivan, Fergus, jt. auth. see West-Burnham, John.

O'Sullivan, George, jt. auth. see Bancroft, Gordon.

***O'Sullivan, Harold.** John Bellew, a Seventeenth Century Man of Many Parts. LC 99-36754. (Social Sciences Research Centre Ser.). (Illus.). 224p. 2000. 49.50 (*0-7165-2622-0*, Pub. by Irish Acad Pr) Intl Spec Bk.

O'Sullivan, Helene, jt. ed. see Jenkinson, William R.

O'Sullivan, Ivo, tr. see Giles.

O'Sullivan, James N. Xenophon of Ephesus: His Compositional Technique & the Birth of the Novel. (Untersuchungen zur Antiken Literatur und Geschichte Ser.: Vol. 44). 227p. (C). 1994. lib. bdg. 107.70 (*3-11-014310-0*) De Gruyter.

O'Sullivan, James N., ed. Lexicon to Achilles Tatius. (Untersuchungen zur Antiken Literatur und Geschichte Ser.: Vol. 18). (GER.). 442p. (C). 1980. text 176.95 (*3-11-007844-9*) De Gruyter.

O'Sullivan, Jan. Journeys Through Microsoft Excel 4.0. LC 92-43204. (Macintosh Guide Ser.). 1993. pap. text. write for info. (*0-201-63157-1*) Addison-Wesley.

— The MacIntosh Guide: Journeys Through Microsoft Excel 4.0. (C). 1993. pap. text. write for info. (*0-201-59487-0*) Addison-Wesley.

O'Sullivan, Jeremiah F. Cistercian Settlements in Wales & Monmouthshire, 1140-1540. LC 48-6318. (Fordham University Studies. History Ser.: No. 2). 151p. reprint ed. pap. 46.90 (*0-7837-5577-5*, 204535900005) Bks Demand.

O'Sullivan, Jeremiah F., tr. see Idung Of Prufening.

O'Sullivan, Jeremiah F., tr. see Lackner, Bede K., ed.

O'Sullivan, Jeremiah F., tr. see Salvian the Presbyter.

O'Sullivan, Jerry. Teaching English in Japan: Finding Work, Teaching & Living in Japan. LC 95-68430. (Illus.). 228p. 1995. pap. 14.95 (*0-8442-0875-2*, 08752) NTC Contemp Pub Co.

O'Sullivan, John & Meckler, Alan M., eds. The Draft & Its Enemies: A Documentary History. LC 74-10979. 309p. reprint ed. pap. 95.80 (*0-608-30760-2*, 202226200026) Bks Demand.

O'Sullivan, John, jt. auth. see Frazer, Heather T.

O'Sullivan, John C. Joyce's Use of Colors: Finnegans Wake & the Earlier Works. LC 87-13741. (Studies in Modern Literature: No. 75). 216p. reprint ed. pap. 67.00 (*0-8357-1816-6*, 207064700012) Bks Demand.

O'Sullivan, John L. Report in Favor of the Abolition of the Punishment of Death by Law, Made to Legislature of the State of New York April 14, 1841. LC 74-3846. (Criminal Justice in America Ser.). 1974. reprint ed. 20.95 (*0-405-06162-5*) Ayer.

O'Sullivan, Judy. The Pasadena Playhouse: A Celebration of One of the Oldest Theatrical Organizations in America. (Orig.). 1992. 89.95 (*0-9633603-0-2*); pap. 39.95 (*0-9633603-1-0*) Theatre Corp Am.

O'Sullivan, Kathleen. A Way of Life: A Human-Spiritual Growth Series for Lay Groups. 126p. 1989. pap. 22.00 (*0-86217-203-9*, Pub. by Veritas Pubns) St Mut.

O'Sullivan, Kathleen F. One Impulsive Black Rose. Danbury, Richard S., III, ed. LC 94-66579. 160p. (Orig.). 1994. pap. 8.95 (*0-89754-089-1*) Dan River Pr.

O'Sullivan, Kevin. Living Parables. 120p. 1979. 7.50 (*0-8199-0780-4*, Frncscn Herld) Franciscan Pr.

— The Sunday Readings: An Explanation & Application of the Sunday Readings, Cycle C. 2nd ed. LC 74-141766. (Sunday Readings Ser.). 437p. (C). 1996. reprint ed. pap. 15.00 (*0-8199-0482-1*, 0482-1, Frncscn Herld) Franciscan Pr.

— The Sunday Readings: An Explanation & Application of

O

the Sunday Readings, Cycle A. 2nd ed. LC 74-141766. (Sunday Readings Ser.). 419p. (C). 1996. reprint ed. pap. 15.00 (0-8199-0436-8, 0436-8, Frncscn Herld) Franciscan Pr.

— The Sunday Readings: An Explanation & Application of the Sunday Readings, Cycle B. 2nd ed. LC 74-141766. (Sunday Readings Ser.). (Illus.). 482p. (C). 1996. reprint ed. pap. 15.00 (0-8199-0433-3, 0433-3, Frncscn Herld) Franciscan Pr.

O'Sullivan, Lucia F., jt. ed. see Byers, E. Sandra.

O'Sullivan, Maggie, ed. Out of Everywhere: Linguistically Innovative Poetry by Women in North America & the U. K. 254p. 1996. 15.00 (1-874400-08-3, Pub. by Reality St Edits) SPD-Small Pr Dist.

O'Sullivan, Marie, jt. ed. see Steen, Sara J.

O'Sullivan, Mark. Melody For Nora: One Girl's Story in The Civil War. LC 94-204224. 192p. (J). (gr. 4-7). 1997. pap. 6.95 (0-86327-425-0, Pub. by Wolfhound Press) Irish Amer Bk.

— Wash Basin Street Blues: Nora in New York. 222p. (J). (gr. 4-7). 1998. pap. 6.95 (0-86327-467-6, Pub. by Wolfhound Press) Irish Amer Bk.

***O'Sullivan, Mary.** Contests for Corporate Control: Corporate Governance & Economic Performance in the United States & Germany. (Illus.). 300p. 2000. text 70.00 (0-19-829346-1) OUP.

O'Sullivan, Mary. Corporate Governance in Germany. (Public Policy Briefs Highlights Ser.: Vol. 49A). 6p. 1998. pap. write for info. (0-941276-62-7) J Levy.

— Corporate Governance in Germany: Productive & Financial Challenges. (Public Policy Briefs Ser.: Vol. 49). 51p. 1998. pap. write for info. (0-941276-61-9) J Levy.

O'Sullivan, Mary, jt. auth. see Lazonick, William.

O'Sullivan, Mary I. The Gift of Sleep: A Program for Reducing Stress & Improving Sleep. (Illus.). 34p. 1997. 29.95 incl. cd-rom (0-9662254-0-6) Quanta Dynamics.

O'Sullivan, Maurice. Twenty Years A-Growing. unabridged ed. Davies, Moya L. & Thomson, George, trs. from IRI. LC 98-34555. (Illus.). 288p. 1998. reprint ed. pap. 15.95 (1-879941-39-2, Pub. by J S Sanders) Natl Bk Netwk.

O'Sullivan, Maurice & Lane, Jack, eds. Florida Reader: Visions of Paradise. LC 84-42772. 274p. 1991. pap. 16.95 (1-56164-062-X) Pineapple Pr.

O'Sullivan, Maurice, jt. ed. see Glassman, Steve.

O'Sullivan, Maurice, jt. ed. see Jones, Jane A.

O'Sullivan, Maurice J. Shakespeare's Other Lives. LC 91-3473. 1995. text 35.00 (0-89341-680-0, Longwood Academic) Hollowbrook.

O'Sullivan, Maurice J., Jr., ed. Shakespeare's Other Lives: An Anthology of Fictional Depictions of the Bard. LC 97-1050. 231p. 1997. lib. bdg. 39.95 (0-7864-0335-7) McFarland & Co.

***O'Sullivan, Maurice J. & Glassman, Steve, eds.** Orange Pulp: Stories of Mayhem, Murder, & Mystery. 2000. 24.95 (0-8130-1803-X) U Press Fla.

O'Sullivan, Michael. Boiling Water: The World's Best Vegetarian Recipes from America's Premier Vegetarian Chef - Fast, Simple, Filling. 114p. 1995. pap. 10.95 (0-9636867-0-4) Leichman Assocs.

— Brendan Behan: A Life. 354p. 1999. reprint ed. 28.00 (1-57098-274-0) Roberts Rinehart.

***O'Sullivan, Miko.** HTML Toolbox. Koman, Richard, ed. (Illus.). 300p. 2000. pap. 29.95 (1-56592-541-6) OReilly & Assocs.

O'Sullivan, Muiris. Megalithic Art in Ireland. (Treasures of the National Museum of Ireland Ser.). (Illus.). 48p. (Orig.). 1995. pap. 7.95 (0-946172-36-6, Pub. by Town Hse) Roberts Rinehart.

O'Sullivan, Nadine. Dysphagia Care: Team Approach. (Team Approach with Acute & Long Term Patients). (Illus.). 112p. (Orig.). (C). 1990. pap. 29.95 (0-9633234-0-7) Cottage Sq Pr.

— Dysphagia Care Team Approach with Acute & Long Term Patients. 2nd ed. Turner, Arthur C., ed. (Illus.). 212p. (C). 1995. pap. 20.97 (0-9633234-1-5) Cottage Sq Pr.

***Osullivan, Natalia.** Soul Rescuers: A 21st Century Guide to the Spirit World. 2000. 24.00 (0-7225-3859-6) Thorsons PA.

O'Sullivan, Neal. Santayana. 112p. 1993. 19.95 (1-870626-33-8, Pub. by Claridge Pr); pap. 12.95 (1-870626-38-9, Pub. by Claridge Pr) Paul & Co Pubs.

O'Sullivan, Noel, ed. The Structure of Modern Ideology: Critical Perspectives on Social & Political Theory. 232p. 1989. text 95.00 (1-85278-036-3) E Elgar.

***O'Sullivan, Nohel.** Political Theory in Transition. LC 99-52540. 2000. pap. write for info. (1-85728-855-6) Taylor & Francis.

***O'Sullivan, Orlaith & Herron, Ellen N.** The Bible as Book: The Reformation. LC 00-39138. 2000. write for info. (1-58456-025-8) Oak Knoll.

O'Sullivan, Owen. A Basic Catholic Dictionary. (C). 1988. 50.00 (0-7855-3221-8, Pub. by St Paul Pubns) St Mut.

O'Sullivan, Paddy. The Lusitania: Unraveling the Mysteries. LC 98-235776. (Illus.). 144p. 1998. 49.95 (1-898256-51-9, Pub. by Collins Press) Dufour.

O'Sullivan, Paddy, jt. ed. see Coleman, Stephen.

O'Sullivan, Patrick. A Country Diary: The Year in Kerry. (Illus.). 160p. (Orig.). 1993. pap. 13.95 (0-947962-76-X, Pub. by Anvil Books Ltd) Irish Bks Media.

— Elsie & The Seal Boy. 160p. 1997. pap. 6.95 (0-86327-558-3, Pub. by Wolfhound Press) Irish Amer Bk.

— A Girl & A Dolphin. 112p. (J). (gr. 4-7). 1997. pap. 6.95 (0-86327-426-9, Pub. by Wolfhound Press) Irish Amer Bk.

— I Heard the Wild Birds Sing: A Kerry Childhood. (Illus.). 208p. (Orig.). 1991. pap. 9.95 (0-947962-55-7, Pub. by Anvil Books Ltd) Irish Bks Media.

— Irish Women & Irish Migration. LC 94-24613. (Irish World Wide Ser.: Vol. 4). 240p. 1995. 79.90 (0-7185-1425-4) Bks Intl VA.

***O'Sullivan, Patrick.** The Lusitania: Unraveling the Mysteries. (Illus.). 144p. 2000. 34.95 (1-86227-086-4, Pub. by Spellmnt Pubs) St Mut.

— The Lusitania: Unravelling the Mysteries. LC 99-48198. 240p. 2000. pap. 16.50 (1-57409-094-1) Sheridan.

— Meaning of the Famine. (Irish Worldwide Ser.). 2000. pap. text 24.95 (0-7185-0232-9) Leicester U Pr.

— Religion & Identity. (Irish Worldwide Ser.). 2000. pap. text 22.95 (0-7185-0233-7) Leicester U Pr.

O'Sullivan, Patrick. Terrain & Tactics, 115. LC 91-12223. (Contributions in Military Studies Ser.: No. 115). 192p. 1991. 52.95 (0-313-27923-3, OTT, Greenwood Pr) Greenwood.

O'Sullivan, Patrick, ed. The Creative Migrant. (Irish World Wide Ser.). 256p. 1997. pap. 24.95 (0-7185-0114-4) Bks Intl VA.

— The Creative Migrant. 256p. 1994. text 69.00 (0-7185-1423-8, Pub. by Leicester U Pr) Cassell & Continuum.

— The Irish in the New Communities. (Irish World Wide Ser.). (Illus.). 280p. 1997. pap. 24.95 (0-7185-0116-0) Bks Intl VA.

— The Irish in the New Communities. 256p. (C). 1992. text 59.00 (0-7185-1427-0, Pub. by Leicester U Pr) Cassell & Continuum.

— Irish Women & Irish Migration. (Irish World Wide Ser.). 240p. 1997. pap. 24.95 (0-7185-0115-2) Bks Intl VA.

— Patterns of Migration. (Irish World Wide Ser.). (Illus.). 256p. 1997. 24.95 (0-7185-0118-7) Bks Intl VA.

— Patterns of Migration. 240p. (C). 1992. text 59.00 (0-7185-1422-X, Pub. by Leicester U Pr) Cassell & Continuum.

— Religion & Identity. (Irish Studies). 240p. 1996. 84.95 (0-7185-1424-6) Bks Intl VA.

O'Sullivan, Patrick, et al, eds. Azerbaijani-English Dictionary. LC 94-69717. 400p. 1995. 74.00 (1-881265-18-8) Dunwoody Pr.

O'Sullivan, Patrick, ed. see Matsov, Akhmat G.

O'Sullivan, Patrick V. Irish Superstitions & Legends of Animals & Birds. 1991. pap. 11.95 (0-85342-957-X) Dufour.

O'Sullivan, Paul. All about the Angels. LC 90-70122. 148p. 1990. reprint ed. pap. 6.00 (0-89555-388-0) TAN Bks Pubs.

— An Easy Way to Become a Saint. LC 90-70237. 105p. 1993. reprint ed. pap. 5.00 (0-89555-398-8) TAN Bks Pubs.

— The Holy Ghost, Our Greatest Friend - He Who Loves Us Best. LC 91-75171. 72p. 1994. reprint ed. pap. 2.00 (0-89555-448-8) TAN Bks Pubs.

— How to Avoid Purgatory. LC 92-64438. 39p. 1992. pap. 1.50 (0-89555-477-1) TAN Bks Pubs.

— How to Be Happy, How to Be Holy. LC 89-51901. 234p. 1989. reprint ed. pap. 8.00 (0-89555-386-4) TAN Bks Pubs.

— Read Me or Rue It. LC 92-61256. 48p. 1992. pap. 1.50 (0-89555-458-5) TAN Bks Pubs.

— St. Philomena, the Wonder-Worker. LC 93-61563. 155p. 1993. pap. 7.00 (0-89555-501-8) TAN Bks Pubs.

— The Secret of Confession Including the Wonders of Confession. LC 92-61255. 96p. 1992. reprint ed. pap. 5.00 (0-89555-459-3) TAN Bks Pubs.

— The Wonders of the Holy Name. LC 93-60345. 45p. 1993. pap. 1.50 (0-89555-490-9) TAN Bks Pubs.

— The Wonders of the Mass. LC 93-60344. 42p. 1993. pap. 1.25 (0-89555-491-7) TAN Bks Pubs.

Osullivan, Penelope. Birdhouses & Birdbaths. (For Your Garden Ser.). 1999. pap. 12.95 (1-56799-644-2, Friedman-Fairfax) M Friedman Pub Grp Inc.

***Osullivan, Penelope.** A Garden Almanac: A Month-by-Month Guide. LC 99-37598. 2000. 25.00 (0-688-16619-9, Hearst) Hearst Commns.

Osullivan, Penelope. Garden Sheds & Potting Areas. LC 99-32413. (For Your Garden Ser.). 1998. pap. text 12.95 (1-56799-698-1, Friedman-Fairfax) M Friedman Pub Grp Inc.

O'Sullivan, Penelope. Ortho's Shrubs & Hedges. LC 98-66912. (Ortho's All about Ser.). (Illus.). 96p. 1998. pap. 11.95 (0-89721-432-3, Ortho Bks) Meredith Bks.

***Osullivan, Penelope.** Stone & Marble. LC 99-18454. (For Your Home Ser.). 1999. pap. text 12.95 (1-56799-786-4, Friedman-Fairfax) M Friedman Pub Grp Inc.

O'Sullivan, Richard. Fifty-Fifth Virginia Infantry. (Virginia Regimental Histories Ser.). (Illus.). 160p. 1989. 19.95 (0-930919-73-4) H E Howard.

O'Sullivan, Richard, tr. see Maritain, Jacques.

O'Sullivan, Rita G. & Tennant, Cheryl V. Programs for At-Risk Students: A Guide to Evaluation. (Essential Tools for Educators Ser.). 96p. 1993. pap. 24.95 (0-8039-6043-3) Corwin Pr.

O'Sullivan, Rosaleen. Enneagram Dialogs on Prayer. 1998. pap. 15.95 (0-941037-71-1, BIBAL Press) D & F Scott.

O'Sullivan, Sean. Folktales of Ireland. (Folktales of the World Ser.). 1999. pap. 15.00 (0-226-63998-3) U Ch Pr.

O'Sullivan, Sean, tr. Folktales of Ireland. LC 66-11885. (Folktales of the World Ser.). 363p. 1968. pap. text 17.95 (0-226-64000-0, FW4) U Ch Pr.

O'Sullivan See, Katherine, jt. auth. see Racioppi, Linda.

O'Sullivan, Sheryl. Early Childhood Education: Professional Guide. LC 96-169170. 1997. pap. text 9.95 (1-55734-889-8) Tchr Create Mat.

***O'Sullivan, St. John.** Little Chapters about Mission San Juan Capistrano. 42nd ed. (Special Bks.: Vol. 4). (Illus.). v, 33p. 1998. reprint ed. pap. 9.95 (1-891030-05-1) Paragon Agency.

O'Sullivan, St. John, ed. see Saunders, Charles F.

***O'Sullivan, Steffan.** GURPS Fantasy Bestiary: Fantastic Creatures for Fantasy Roleplaying. Jackson, Steve, ed. 128p. 1999. pap. 19.95 (1-55634-184-9, Pub. by S Jackson Games) BookWorld.

O'Sullivan, Sue. I Used to Be Nice: Reflections on Feminist & Lesbian Politics. (Sexual Politics Ser.). 224p. 1997. 69.95 (0-304-33571-1) Continuum.

— I Used to Be Nice: Reflections on Feminist & Lesbian Politics. LC 96-208607. (Sexual Politics Ser.). 224p. 1997. pap. 21.95 (0-304-33572-X) Continuum.

— Positively Women: Living with AIDS. 336p. 1996. pap. 18.00 (0-04-440943-5, Pub. by Pandora) NYU Pr.

O'Sullivan, Sue & Parmar, Pratibha. Lesbians Talk (Safer) Sex. 64p. (Orig.). 1992. pap. 8.50 (1-85727-020-7, Pub. by Scarlet Pr) LPC InBook.

O'Sullivan, Susan B. & Schmitz, Thomas J. Physical Rehabilitation: Assessment & Treatment. 4th ed. (Illus.). 1296p. 2000. text 65.00 (0-8036-0533-1) Davis Co.

— Physical Rehabilitation Laboratory Manual: Focus on Functional Training. LC 98-205026. (Illus.). 388p. 1998. pap. 24.95 (0-8036-0257-X) Davis Co.

O'Sullivan, T. D. The De Excidio of Gildas. 1978. 27.00 (90-04-05793-5, CSCT, 7) Brill Academic Pubs.

O'Sullivan, Terry. Did I Miss Anything? Memoirs of a Soap Opera Star. LC 97-29183. (Illus.). 256p. 1997. pap. 16.95 (1-880090-56-2) Galde Pr.

O'Sullivan, Terry, jt. auth. see Hill, Elizabeth.

O'Sullivan, Thomas. North Star Statehouse: An Armchair Guide to the Minnesota State Capitol. LC 94-66863. (Illus.). 124p. (Orig.). 1995. pap. 16.95 (1-880654-07-5) Pogo Pr.

O'Sullivan, Thomas, ed. The Prints of Adolf Dehn: A Catalogue Raisonne. LC 87-7776. (Illus.). viii, 268p. 1987. 75.00 (0-87351-203-0) Minn Hist.

O'Sullivan, Thomas J. Pioneer Airplane Mails of the United States. 346p. 1986. 25.00 (0-939429-13-6) Am Air Mail.

O'Sullivan, Tim & Jewkes, Yvonne, eds. The Media Studies Reader. LC 97-208. (An Arnold Publication). 480p. 1997. text 65.00 (0-340-64526-1); pap. text 19.95 (0-340-64547-4) OUP.

O'Sullivan, Tim, et al. Key Concepts in Communication & Cultural Studies. 2nd ed. LC 93-7405. (Studies in Culture & Communication). 1993. write for info. (0-415-01411-5) Routledge.

— Key Concepts in Communication & Cultural Studies. 2nd ed. LC 93-7405. (Studies in Culture & Communication). 272p. (C). 1993. pap. 18.99 (0-415-06173-3) Routledge.

— Studying Media. 2nd ed. LC 99-210720. (Arnold Publications). (Illus.). 300p. 1998. pap. text 24.95 (0-340-67685-X) OUP.

— Studying the Media: An Introduction. LC 94-14195. (An Arnold Publication). (Illus.). 256p. 1995. pap. text 16.95 (0-340-59828-X, Pub. by E A) OUP.

O'Sullivan, Tim, ed. see Hartley, John, et al.

***O'Sullivan, Valerie.** Inner Thoughts: Reflections of Contemporary Celtic Women. 134p. 1999. 24.95 (1-85390-448-1, Pub. by Veritas Pubns) Irish Bks Media.

O'Sullivan, Vincent. Aspects of Wilde. 1976. lib. bdg. 59.95 (0-8490-1460-3) Gordon Pr.

— The Houses of Sin, 1897: With Poems, 1896. LC 93-41352. (Decadents, Symbolists, Anti-Decadents Ser.). 1994. 49.50 (1-85477-153-1) Continuum.

***O'Sullivan, Vincent.** Seeing You Asked. (Illus.). 88p. 2000. pap. 14.95 (0-86473-352-6, Pub. by Victoria Univ Pr) Paul & Co Pubs.

O'Sullivan, Vincent. The Unsparing Scourge: Australian Satirical Texts. pap. 12.95 (0-86422-056-1, Pub. by Univ of West Aust Pr) Intl Spec Bk.

O'Sullivan, Vincent, ed. An Anthology of Twentieth Century New Zealand Poetry. 3rd ed. (Illus.). 460p. 1987. pap. text 29.95 (0-19-558163-6) OUP.

O'Sullivan, Vincent, selected by. The Oxford Book of New Zealand Short Stories. 464p. 1994. pap. text 19.95 (0-19-558291-8) OUP.

O'Sullivan, Vincent & Scott, Margaret, eds. The Collected Letters of Katherine Mansfield Vol. 4: 1920 - 1921, Vol. 4. (Illus.). 392p. (C). 1996. text 85.00 (0-19-818532-4) OUP.

O'Sullivan, Vincent, jt. auth. see Bethell, Ursula.

O'Sullivan, Vincent, ed. see Bethell, Ursula.

O'Sullivan, Vincent, ed. see Mansfield, Katherine.

O'Sullivan, William. Captain Satan - Parole for the Dead. Gunnison, John P., ed. & intro. by. (High Adventure Ser.: 45). (Illus.). 96p. (C). 1999. pap. 6.00 (1-886937-32-X) Adventure Hse.

***Osumi, Ikuko.** Ikuko Osumi, Japanese Master of Seiki Jutsu. Keeney, Bradford, ed. 2000. 39.95 (0-9666509-1-3) Ringing Rocks.

Osumi, Midori. Tinrin Grammar. (Oceanic Linguistics Special Publications: No. 25). 340p. (C). 1994. pap. text 35.00 (0-8248-1629-3) UH Pr.

Osumi, Yuichi. Die Kompositionsgeschichte des Bundesbuches Exodus 20, 22b-23, 33. (Orbis Biblicus et Orientalis Ser.: Vol. 105). (GER.). 1991. text 59.00 (3-7278-0744-X, Pub. by Presses Univ Fribourg) Eisenbrauns.

Osuna, Juan J. A History of Education in Puerto Rico. LC 74-14239. (Puerto Rican Experience Ser.). (Illus.). 686p. 1975. reprint ed. 56.95 (0-405-06227-3) Ayer.

***Osuna, Montse.** El Libro De Magia De La Bruja Moderna. 1999. pap. 17.95 (84-270-2418-5) Planeta.

***Osundare, Niyi.** Pages from the Book of the Sun: New & Selected Poems. LC 00-33217. 2000. pap. write for info. (0-86543-868-4) Africa World.

— Selected Poems. (African Writers Ser.). 116p. (C). 1992. pap. 8.95 (0-435-91195-3, 91195) Heinemann.

— Thread in the Loom: Essays on African Literature & Culture. LC 00-34865. 2000. pap. write for info. (0-86543-866-8) Africa World.

***Osunde, Egerton O.** Understanding Student Teaching: Case Studies of Experiences & Suggestions for Survival. LC 99-41525. (Illus.). 160p. 1999. 48.00 (0-7618-1498-1); pap. 26.50 (0-7618-1499-X) U Pr of Amer.

***Osundeko, Teniola A.** Enchantment & Fun in Yoruba Kingdom. (J). (gr. k-3). 1999. pap. 6.95 (0-533-12619-3) Vantage.

Osuntogun & Adewunm. Rural Banking Nigeria. 1983. pap. text. write for info. (0-582-64419-4, Pub. by Addison-Wesley) Longman.

Osuntogun, Adeniyi & Adewunmi, Wole, eds. Rural Banking in Nigeria. LC 82-176. (Illus.). 144p. reprint ed. pap. 44.70 (0-8357-2964-8, 203922600011) Bks Demand.

Osuntoki, Chief. The Book of African Names. LC 90-82690. 32p. 1991. reprint ed. pap. 5.95 (0-933121-24-5) Black Classic.

Osuntokun, Akinjide. Chief S. Ladoke Akintola: His Life & Times. (Illus.). 212p. 1984. text 29.50 (0-7146-3219-8, BHA-00169, Pub. by F Cass Pubs) Intl Spec Bk.

Osunwa-Oguamanam, A. C. Folktales from Our Ancestors: An African Folkstories of Wisdom, Spirituality & Morality. 176p. 1997. pap. 15.00 (0-9656642-2-8) PalmTree Pubs.

— Once upon a Time in the Motherland: An African Storybook for Children. LC 97-91446. (Illus.). 80p. (J). (ps-12). 1997. pap. 8.00 (0-9656642-0-1) PalmTree Pubs.

Osur, Alan M. Blacks in the Army Air Forces During World War II: The Problem of Race Relations. Gilbert, James B., ed. LC 79-7291. (Flight: Its First Seventy-Five Years Ser.). (Illus.). 1980. reprint ed. lib. bdg. 30.95 (0-405-12199-7) Ayer.

Oswald. The Law of Marketing. (SWC-Business Law Ser.). 2000. pap. 50.00 (0-324-00902-X) Thomson Learn.

Oswald, jt. auth. see Krar, Steve F.

Oswald, A. J. & Mascarenhas, S. J. New Product Development: Its Marketing Research & Management. (C). 1987. 17.50 (81-204-0231-6, Pub. by Oxford IBH) S Asia.

Oswald, Alice. The Thing in the Gap-Stone Stile. 64p. (C). 1996. pap. 12.95 (0-19-282513-5) OUP.

***Oswald, Allan.** The History & Practice of Falconry. (Illus.). 119p. 1999. pap. 17.95 (0-8464-4968-4) Beekman Pubs.

Oswald, Andrew J., jt. auth. see Blanchflower, David G.

Oswald, Andrew J., jt. auth. see Carruth, Alan A.

Oswald, Brian P., jt. auth. see Walker, Laurence C.

Oswald, David, tr. see Rilke, Rainer Maria.

Oswald, Debra. Dags. 57p. 1990. pap. 5.50 (0-87129-012-X, D48) Dramatic Pub.

***Oswald, Diane.** Aggies Are We: Coloring & Activity Book. (Illus.). 40p. (J). (ps-4). 1999. pap. 9.95 (0-9659698-3-5, LW5004) Lacewing Pr.

— A Practical Guide to Bryan-College Station. 2nd rev. ed. Maxwell, Alma, ed. (Illus.). 1999. pap. 8.95 (0-9659698-2-7, LW5003) Lacewing Pr.

Oswald, Diane L. Fire Insurance Maps, Their History & Applications. unabridged ed. LC 97-94262. (Illus.). 100p. 1997. pap. 9.95 (0-9659698-0-0) Lacewing Pr.

— 101 Great Collectibles for Kids. (Illus.). 192p. (Orig.). (J). 1997. pap. 16.95 (0-930625-75-7) Krause Pubns.

— A Practical Guide to Bryan-College Station: Your Indespensable Reference. (Illus.). 112p. 1998. pap. 7.95 (0-9659698-1-9, LW5002) Lacewing Pr.

Oswald, Franz. The Political Psychology of the White Collar Worker in Martin Walser's Novels: The Impact of Work Ideology on the Reception of Martin Walser's Novels, 1957-1978. LC 98-36233. 238p. 1998. pap. text 39.95 (0-8204-3559-7) P Lang Pubng.

— The Political Psychology of the White Collar Worker In Martin Walser's Novels: The Impact of Work Ideology on the Reception of Martin Walser's Novels 1957-1978. 238p. 1998. 39.95 (3-631-32838-9) P Lang Pubng.

Oswald, Gert. Lexikon der Heraldik. (GER.). 478p. 1985. 79.95 (0-7859-8349-X, 3411021497) Fr & Eur.

Oswald, Helene, jt. auth. see Carraze, Alain.

Oswald, Hilton C., ed. see Luther, Martin.

Oswald, Hilton C., ed. see Luther, Martin H.

Oswald, Hilton C., tr. see Hans-Joachim, Kraus.

Oswald, I., ed. see International Congress of Pharmacology Staff.

Oswald, J. W., jt. auth. see Krar, Stephen F.

Oswald, James F. Contempt of Court: Committal, & Attachment & Arrest upon Civil Process, in the Supreme Court of Judicature with the Practice & Forms. LC 97-74175. xxiv, 214p. 1997. reprint ed. 72.00 (1-56169-321-9, 14641) Gaunt.

Oswald, James W., jt. auth. see Krar, Stephen F.

Oswald, Jean A. Yours for Health: The Life & Times of Herbert M. Shelton. (Illus.). 168p. (Orig.). 1989. pap. 9.95 (0-9620490-0-X) Franklin Bks.

Oswald, Laura. Jean Genet & the Semiotics of Performance. LC 88-45447. (Advance in Semiotics Ser.). 189p. reprint ed. pap. 58.60 (0-608-09357-2, 205410300002) Bks Demand.

Oswald, Lee Harvey. Stretching for Fitness, Health & Performance. LC 97-50476. (Illus.). 192p. 1998. 14.95 (0-8069-0985-4) Sterling.

Oswald, Martin & Friedenberg Lutheran Historical Society Book Commi. Friedenberg Remembrances: A Story of Peace, Faith & Life. LC 98-65620. (Illus.). 1998. 27.95 (0-9659555-0-8) Concordia Hist.

Oswald, Martin, jt. auth. see Jowett, Benjamin E.

Oswald, Peter. Fair Ladies at a Game of Poem Cards. 1997. pap. 10.95 (0-413-71510-8) Methn.

Oswald, Peter, tr. see Schiller, Friedrich.

Oswald, Roy M. Clergy Self-Care: Finding a Balance for Effective Ministry. LC 90-86201. 234p. (Orig.). 1991. pap. 18.25 (1-56699-044-0, AL125) Alban Inst.

— Crossing the Boundary Between Seminary & Parish. pap. 10.50 (1-56699-182-X, OD122) Alban Inst.

O

An Asterisk (*) at the beginning of an entry indicates that the title is appearing for the first time.

— Ending Well, Starting Strong: Your Personal Pastorate Start-up Workshop. pap. 89.95 (*1-56699-143-9*, AL157) Alban Inst.

— Getting a Fix on Your Ministry: A Practical Guide to Clergy Performance Appraisal. 8.00 (*1-56699-072-6*) Alban Inst.

— Making Your Church More Inviting: A Step-by-Step Guide for In-Church Training. LC 92-72456. (Orig.). 1992. pap. 14.95 (*1-56699-055-6*, AL134) Alban Inst.

— New Beginnings: The Pastorate Start up Workbook. rev. ed. 90p. 1989. pap. 13.25 (*1-56699-032-7*, AL111) Alban Inst.

— The Pastor As Newcomer. pap. 7.25 (*1-56699-188-9*, OD123) Alban Inst.

— Power Analysis of a Congregation. pap. 6.25 (*1-56699-008-4*) Alban Inst.

— Running Through the Thistles: Terminating a Ministerial Relationship with a Parish. pap. 6.95 (*1-56699-004-1*) Alban Inst.

Oswald, Roy M. & Friedrich, Robert E., Jr. Discerning Your Congregation's Future: A Strategic & Spiritual Approach. LC 96-85703. 192p. 1996. pap. 18.25 (*1-56699-174-9*, AL176) Alban Inst.

Oswald, Roy M. & Kroeger, Otto. Personality Type & Religious Leadership. LC 88-70758. 183p. (Orig.). 1988. pap. 17.95 (*1-56699-025-4*, AL103) Alban Inst.

Oswald, Roy M. & Leas, Speed B. The Inviting Church: A Study of New Member Assimilation. LC 87-71965. 119p. (Orig.). 1987. pap. 12.25 (*1-56699-020-3*, AL99) Alban Inst.

Oswald, Roy M., et al. New Visions for the Long Pastorate. LC 83-73205. 111p. (Orig.). 1983. pap. 10.95 (*1-56699-010-6*, AL73) Alban Inst.

Oswald, Sally, et al. Plays from the Philadelphia Young Playwrights Festival. 96p. 1998. pap. 5.00 (*0-87440-057-0*) Bakers Plays.

Oswald, Tom. Bicycling in Florida: The Cyclist's Road & Off-Road Guide. LC 98-33189. 144p. 1999. pap. 12.95 (*1-56164-161-8*) Pineapple Pr.

***Oswald, W. D. & Fleischmann, U. M.** Neuropsychological Aging Inventory (NAI) 300p. 2001. 79.00 (*0-88937-215-2*) Hogrefe & Huber Pubs.

Oswald, Wolfgang. Israel am Gottesberg: Eine Untersuchung zur Literargeschichte der Vorderen Sinaiperikope Ex 19-24 und Deren Historischem Hintergurnd. (Orbis Biblicus et Orientalis Ser.: Vol. 159). (GER.). vii, 286p. 1998. text 62.50 (*3-7278-1161-7*, Pub. by Ed Univ Fri) Eisenbrauns.

Oswalt, Brenda K. Daily Prescription for Happiness. (Illus.). 88p. 1995. 19.95 (*0-9644118-1-4*) Dixie USA.

Oswalt, Jerry E. Proclaiming the Whole Counsel of God: Suggestions for Planning & Preparing Doctrinal Sermons. 66p. (Orig.). (C). 1993. pap. text 18.00 (*0-8191-9011-X*) U Pr of Amer.

Oswalt, John. The Book of Isaiah. LC 97-24215. (New International Commentary on the Old Testament Ser.). 786p. 1998. 48.00 (*0-8028-2534-6*) Eerdmans.

Oswalt, John N. Called to Be Holy: A Biblical Perspective. LC 98-72661. 160p. 1999. pap. 12.95 (*0-916035-92-1*, Ausbury Press) Evangel Indiana.

Oswalt, John N. Isaiah 1-39. (New International Commentary on the Old Testament Ser.). 759p. 1986. 44.00 (*0-8028-2529-X*) Eerdmans.

— Where Are You, God? Malachi's perspectives on Injustice & Suffering. LC 98-72655. 156p. 1999. reprint ed. pap. 12.95 (*0-916035-90-5*) Evangel Indiana.

Oswalt, John N. & Lane, William L. Newell Lectureships, Vol. 3. Dwyer, Timothy, ed. 1996. 19.95 (*0-87162-678-0*) Warner Pr.

Oswalt, Robert L. Kashaya Texts. fac. ed. (University of California Publications in American Archaeology & Ethnology: Vol. 36). (Illus.). 341p. (C). 1964. pap. text 36.25 (*1-55567-663-4*) Coyote Press.

Oswalt, Wendell H. Bashful No Longer: An Alaskan Eskimo Ethnohistory, 1778-1988. LC 89-37036. (Civilization of the American Indian Ser.: No. 199). (Illus.). 288p. 1990. 24.95 (*0-8061-2256-0*) U of Okla Pr.

— Eskimos & Explorers. 2nd ed. LC 99-13969. (Illus.). 368p. 1999. pap. 19.95 (*0-8032-8613-9*, Bison Books) U of Nebr Pr.

Oswalt, Wendell H. & Neely, Sharlotte. This Land Was Theirs: A Study of Native Americans. 6th ed. LC 98-25731. (Illus.). xv, 537p. 1998. pap. text 38.95 (*0-7674-0504-8*, 0504-8) Mayfield Pubns.

***Oswalt, Wendell H. & Neely, Sharlotte.** This Land Was Theirs Instructor's Manual. 6th rev. ed. v, 133p. 1998. pap. text, teacher ed. write for info. (*0-7674-0652-4*, 0652-4) Mayfield Pub.

Oswatitsch, K. & Rues, D., eds. Symposium Transsonicum 2. (International Union of Theoretical & Applied Mechanics Symposia Ser.). 1976. 86.95 (*0-387-07526-7*) Spr-Verlag.

Osweiler, Gary D. Toxicology. LC 94-49123. (National Veterinary Medical Series for Independent Study). 508p. 1996. 24.50 (*0-683-06664-1*) Lppncott W & W.

Oswick, Cliff, jt. auth. see Grant, David.

Oswood, M. W., jt. ed. see Milner, A. M.

Oszkay, Zulay, tr. see Rinder, Lenore.

Oszko, Beatrix, jt. auth. see Hegedus, Rita.

Oszuscik, Philippe. Louisiana's Gothic Revival Architecture. 1973. 15.00 (*0-87511-093-2*) Claitors.

Oszustowicz, John, jt. auth. see Oszustowicz, Len.

Oszustowicz, Len. Death at Sea: A Murder Mystery in 3-D. Towle, Mike, ed. (Illus.). 80p. (YA). (gr. 6 up). 1994. 12.95 (*1-56530-165-X*) Summit TX.

Oszustowicz, Len & Oszustowicz, John. Life's Lessons from Mayberry. LC 97-4918. 128p. 1997. 9.99 (*1-56530-250-8*, Pub. by Summit TX) BookWorld.

Oszustowicz, Len, et al. Barney Fife's Guide to Life, Love & Self-Defense. LC 93-42332. (Illus.). vii, 167 p. 1993. 12.95 (*1-56530-103-X*, Pub. by Summit TX) BookWorld.

Oszustowicz, Len, jt. auth. see Colf, Mary K.

Ota. World Transplantation 1995. (C). 1995. 200.00 (*0-8385-9835-8*) Appleton & Lange.

Ota, Inazo N., see Nitobe, Inazo, pseud.

Ota, K., jt. ed. see Rudd, E. J.

Ota, Masako, tr. see Mangus, Donald J.

Ota, Mitchell. Pinshooting: A Complete Guide. 1991. 14.95 (*1-879356-04-X*) Wolfe Pub Co.

OTA Staff. Protecting the Nation's Ground Water from Contamination. (C). 1987. text 125.00 (*81-85046-52-2*, Pub. by Scientific Pubs) St Mut.

Ota, Yasuto, et al. Setsuko Migishi: A Retrospective. LC 91-7707. (Illus.). 136p. 1991. pap. 21.95 (*0-940979-16-0*) Natl Museum Women.

Ota, Yuzo. Basil Hall Chamberlain: Portrait of a Japanologist. (Meiji Ser.: Vol. 4). 240p. 1998. text 45.00 (*1-873410-73-5*, Pub. by Curzon Pr Ltd) UH Pr.

Otabil, Kwesi. Agonistic Imperative: The Rational Burden of Africa-Centeredness. 250p. (C). text 32.00 (*1-55605-245-6*); pap. text 20.00 (*1-55605-244-8*) Wyndham Hall.

Otabil, Mensa. Beyond the Rivers of Ethiopia. 1995. pap. 7.99 (*1-56229-404-0*) Pneuma Life Pub.

— Four Laws of Productivity. pap. 7.99 (*1-56229-405-9*) Pneuma Life Pub.

Otaka, Terumi. Lovable Mini Dolls. (Illus.). 96p. 1982. pap. 17.00 (*0-87040-518-7*) Japan Pubns USA.

Otake, Ken, tr. see Odell, Bob.

Otake, Takashi & Cutler, Anne, eds. Phonological Structure & Language Processing: Cross-Linguistic Studies. (Speech Research Ser.: Vol. 12). xii, 254p. (C). 1996. lib. bdg. 117.05 (*3-11-014967-2*) Mouton.

Otaki, Tadao, jt. auth. see Draeger, Donn F.

Otani, I. & Pham, C. Do, eds. The Lao PDR Economy: Experience with Systemic Transformation & Adjustment. LC 96-167536. (Occasional Papers: No. 137). 1996. pap. 15.00 (*1-55775-560-4*) Intl Monetary.

Otani, Kosho K. The Successor: My Life. LC 84-23016. (Illus.). 114p. 1985. 18.95 (*0-914910-50-7*) Buddhist Bks.

Otani, Kosho Ko-nyo, see Kosho Ko-nyo Otani.

Otani, Ryuji. Ready-to-Use Gourmet Food Illustrations. (Clip Art Ser.). (Illus.). 64p. (Orig.). 1991. pap. 5.95 (*0-486-26652-4*) Dover.

Otani, Shin. Cats of Venice. 96p. 1998. 12.95 (*0-8118-1937-X*) Chronicle Bks.

Otani, Y. & El-Hodiri, M. A. Microeconomic Theory. (Illus.). 310p. 1987. 47.95 (*0-387-17994-1*) Spr-Verlag.

Otaola, Javier. El Sol y la Tierra. (Ciencia para Todos Ser.). (SPA.). pap. 6.99 (*968-16-3741-0*, Pub. by Fondo) Continental Bk.

Otaola, Javier A. Los Rayos Cosmicos: Mensajeros de las Estrellas. (Ciencia para Todos Ser.). (SPA.). pap. 6.99 (*968-16-3739-9*, Pub. by Fondo) Continental Bk.

Otaola, Jose R. Freddie: Story of a Pebble. (J). (gr. 1-3). 1996. 7.95 (*0-533-11548-5*) Vantage.

Otawa, Toru, et al. Indiana Wind Energy: A Guide to Harnessing Hoosier Wind Power. (Illus.). 108p. (Orig.). 1982. pap. 7.00 (*0-912431-00-8*) Ctr Env Des Res.

Otayahuk, J. & Kaneshiro, V. Otayahuk Ungazimi (Otayahuk in Siberia) (ESK.). 17p. 1973. pap. 2.00 (*0-933769-72-5*) Alaska Native.

Otchere, Freda E. African Studies Thesaurus: Subject Headings for Library Users, 29. LC 92-12523. (Bibliographies & Indexes in Afro-American & African Studies: No. 29). 480p. 1992. lib. bdg. 85.00 (*0-313-27437-1*, OAB/, Greenwood Pr) Greenwood.

Otega, Jose, jt. auth. see Ferres, Antonio.

***Otegui, Maria Elena & Slafer, Gustavo A., eds.** Physiological Bases for Maize Improvement. LC 00-22372. (Illus.). 265p. (C). 2000. lib. bdg. 69.95 (*1-56022-889-X*, Food Products) Haworth Pr.

Otegui, Miguel, et al. Diccionario Espanol de la Lengua China: Spanish Dictionary of the Chinese Language. 2nd ed. (CHI & SPA.). 1381p. 1979. 350.00 (*0-8288-5339-8*, S31804) Fr & Eur.

Oteiza, Esther J., jt. ed. see Balado, Carl R.

Otenasek, Mildred B. Alexander Hamilton's Financial Policies. Bruchey, Stuart, ed. LC 76-39837. (Nineteen Seventy-Seven Dissertations Ser.). 1977. lib. bdg. 20.95 (*0-405-09917-7*) Ayer.

Otera, Corazon. Manuel M. Ponce & the Guitar. Roberts, J. D., tr. (Illus.). 96p. 1995. reprint ed. 24.95 (*0-933224-84-2*, T320) Bold Strummer Ltd.

Oteri, Laura, ed. see International Conference, Geneva Staff.

Otero, Aurora, jt. ed. see Schildkraut, Joseph J.

Otero, Carlos, ed. Noam Chomsky: Critical Assessments, 4 vols., Set. (cr). (Illus.). 1600p. (C). 1994. 660.00 (*0-415-10692-3*) Routledge.

— Noam Chomsky: Critical Assessments, 8 vols., Set. (Illus.). 3408p. (C). 1994. 1195.00 (*0-415-10697-4*) Routledge.

Otero, Carlos, ed. see Chomsky, Noam.

Otero, Carlos P. Letras, I. (Monagrafias A Ser.: Vol. VIII). (SPA.). 202p. (Orig.). (C). 1966. pap. 51.00 (*0-900411-47-3*, Pub. by Tamesis Bks Ltd) Boydell & Brewer.

Otero, Carlos P., ed. Noam Chomsky: Critical Assessments, 4 vols., Set. LC 92-47084. 1600p. (C). (gr. 13). 1994. 660.00 (*0-415-01005-5*, B2431) Routledge.

Otero, Carlos P., ed. see Chomsky, Noam.

Otero, Clara R. La Cene de Tio Tigre y Otras Obras de Teatro Para Ninos (Uncle Tiger's Supper & Other Plays for Children) (SPA., Illus.). 88p. (J). (gr. 3-7). 7.95 (*980-257-135-0*, Pub. by Ediciones Ekare) Kane-Miller Bk.

Otero, Corazon. Manuel Ponce & the Guitar. Roberts, J. D., tr. from SPA. (Guitar Study Ser.). (Illus.). 90p. 1995. pap. 19.95 (*0-933224-85-0*, T321) Bold Strummer Ltd.

Otero, Francisco M. Cinquenta Anos de Periodismo. (SPA.). 108p. (Orig.). 1985. pap. 6.00 (*0-89729-376-2*) Ediciones.

Otero, George G. & Harris, Zoanne. Death: A Part of Life. rev. ed. (Illus.). 147p. (gr. 4-12). 1981. pap. 15.00 (*0-943804-10-8*) U of Denver Teach.

Otero, George G., Jr. & Moeller, Carol. Teaching Reading: A Global Approach. rev. ed. (Illus.). 191p. (Orig.). (gr. 6-12). 1994. pap. 26.95 (*0-943804-30-2*) U of Denver Teach.

Otero, George G. & Smith, Gary R. Teaching about Cultural Awareness with Student Handouts in Spanish. Espinosa, Ann L. & Espinosa, Ismael E., trs. (Illus.). 235p. (gr. 4-12). 1982. pap. 8.50 (*0-943804-26-4*) U of Denver Teach.

— Teaching about Ethnic Heritage. rev. ed. (Illus.). 135p. (Orig.). (gr. k-12). 1979. pap. 9.95 (*0-943804-06-X*) U of Denver Teach.

Otero, Gerardo. Farewell to the Peasantry? Political Class Formation in Rural Mexico. LC 99-10741. 200p. 1999. text 60.00 (*0-8133-3645-7*, Pub. by Westview) HarpC.

Otero, Jesus. Schoolmaster's Son. (American Autobiography Ser.). 130p. 1995. reprint ed. lib. bdg. 69.00 (*0-7812-8605-0*) Rprt Serv.

Otero, Manuel R. Invitacion al Polvo. (Biblioteca de Autores de Puerto Rico Ser.). (SPA.). 74p. (Orig.). 1991. pap. text 5.95 (*1-56328-005-1*) Edit Plaza Mayor.

Otero, Maria & Rhyne, Elisabeth H., eds. The New World of Microenterprise Finance: Building Healthy Financial Institutions for the Poor. LC 93-47513. (Library of Management for Development). (Illus.). 318p. 1994. 37.00 (*1-56549-031-2*); pap. 26.95 (*1-56549-030-4*) Kumarian Pr.

Otero, Miguel A. Otero, 3 vols. LC 73-14420. (Mexican American Ser.). 1036p. 1977. reprint ed. 75.95 (*0-405-05685-0*) Ayer.

Otero, Muguel A. The Real Billy the Kid. LC 98-3220. 144p. 1998. pap. 12.95 (*1-55885-234-4*) Arte Publico.

Otero, Rodolfo. El Camino de Santa Fe (The Route to Santa Fe) (SPA.). 232p. (YA). 1994. pap. 6.99 (*968-16-4070-5*, Pub. by Fondo) Continental Bk.

Otero, Rosa V. En el Fondo del Cano (Genealogia) (Aqui y Ahora Ser.). (Illus.). 73p. 1997. pap. 6.95 (*0-8477-0311-8*) U of PR Pr.

Otero, Rosalie. Guide to American Drama Explication. 1995. 65.00 (*0-8161-7351-6*, G K Hall & Co) Mac Lib Ref.

Otey, Don, jt. auth. see Sehlinger, Bob.

Otey, Elizabeth L. The Beginnings of Child Labor Legislation in Certain States: A Comparative Study. Bremner, Robert H., ed. LC 74-1697. (Children & Youth Ser.). 230p. 1974. reprint ed. 23.95 (*0-405-05974-4*) Ayer.

Otey, Frank M. & Grant, Alice M. Eatonville, Florida: A Brief History of One of America's First Freedmen's Towns. 92p. (Orig.). 1991. pap. 8.95 (*0-9625423-0-X*) Four-G Pubs.

Otey-Little, Mimi. Yoshiko & the Foreigner. LC 95-33512. 40p. (J). (ps-3). 1996. 16.00 (*0-374-32448-4*) FS&G.

Otey, Michael. Building AS/400 Client Server Applications: Put ODBC & Client Access APIs to Work. LC 97-33780. 505p. 1997. pap. 89.00 incl. cd-rom (*1-882419-69-3*) News Four-Hund.

***Otey, Michael.** SQL Server 2000 Developer's Guide. (Database Professional's Library). (Illus.). 2000. pap. 59.99 (*0-07-212569-1*) Osborne-McGraw.

Otey, Michael. SQL Server 7: Developer's Guide. LC 99-191106. (SQL Server Professional Library). 1998. pap. text 49.99 incl. cd-rom (*0-07-882548-2*) Osborne-McGraw.

— Visual Basic Answers! Certified Tech Support. 574p. 1999. pap. 29.99 (*0-07-211895-4*) McGraw.

Otey, Michael & Conte, Paul. Windows NT Database Developer's Guide. (Windows NT Professional Library). (Illus.). 656p. (Orig.). 1997. pap. 44.99 incl. cd-rom (*0-07-882384-6*, Oracle Press) Osborne-McGraw.

Otfinoski, Paul. Blasting Off: Rockets Then & Now. LC 97-15444. (Here We Go! Ser.). (Illus.). 32p. (J). (gr. 1-4). 1998. lib. bdg. 22.79 (*0-7614-0611-5*, Benchmark NY) Marshall Cavendish.

— Here We Go! - Group 2, 4 bks. Incl. Around the Track: Race Cars Then & Now. LC 97-11548. (Illus.). 32p. (J). (gr. 1 up). 1997. lib. bdg. 22.79 (*0-7614-0608-5*, Benchmark NY); On the High Seas: Ships Then & Now. LC 97-6039. (Illus.). 32p. (J). (gr. 4-7). 1997. lib. bdg. 22.79 (*0-7614-0609-3*, Benchmark NY); On the Road: Trucks Then & Now. LC 97-11562. (Illus.). 32p. (J). (gr. 1 up). 1997. lib. bdg. 22.79 (*0-7614-0606-9*, Benchmark NY); Wild on Wheels: Motorcycles Then & Now. LC 97-3540. (Illus.). 32p. (J). (gr. 4-7). 1997. lib. bdg. 22.79 (*0-7614-0607-7*, Benchmark NY); (J). 91.14 (*0-7614-0605-0*) Marshall Cavendish.

Otfinoski, Steve. The Golden Age of Novelty Songs. LC 99-50263. (Illus.). 256p. 1999. pap. 18.95 (*0-8230-7694-6*) Watsn-Guptill.

— Whirling Around: Helicopters Then & Now. LC 97-13163. (Here We Go! Ser.). (Illus.). 32p. (J). (gr. 1-4). 1998. lib. bdg. 22.79 (*0-7614-0610-7*, Benchmark NY) Marshall Cavendish.

Otfinoski, Steven. Blizzards. (When Disaster Strikes Ser.). (Illus.). 64p. (J). (gr. 5-8). 1995. lib. bdg. 18.90 (*0-8050-3093-X*) TFC Bks NY.

***Otfinoski, Steven.** Bugsy Siegel & the Post-War Boom. LC 00-9074. (Notorious Americans & Their Times Ser.). (Illus.). 112p. 2000. 19.95 (*1-56711-224-2*) Blackbirch.

Otfinoski, Steven. Bulgaria. LC 98-10577. (Nations In Transition Ser.). (J). 1998. 19.95 (*0-8160-3705-1*) Facts on File.

— The Czech Republic. LC 95-32706. (Nations in Transition Ser.). 128p. 1997. 19.95 (*0-8160-3080-4*) Facts on File.

— The Golden Age of Rock Instrumentals: A Loving Tribute to the Pioneers of the Instrumental Era, from Dick Dale & Sandy Nelson to Booker T. & the MGs & the Ventures. LC 97-21919. (Illus.). 224p. 1997. 19.95 (*0-8230-7639-3*, Billboard Bks) Watsn-Guptill.

— Great Black Writers. LC 93-39871. (American Profiles Ser.). (Illus.). 128p. (YA). (gr. 5-12). 1994. 19.95 (*0-8160-2906-7*) Facts on File.

— Igor Sikorsky: Father of the Helicopter. LC 93-2822. (Masters of Invention Ser.). 48p. (J). (gr. 4-8). 1993. lib. bdg. 21.27 (*0-86592-100-8*) Rourke Enter.

— John Wilkes Booth & the Civil War. LC 98-11571. (Notorious Americans & Their Times Ser.). (Illus.). 80p. (YA). (gr. 5 up). 1998. lib. bdg. 19.45 (*1-56711-222-6*) Blackbirch.

— The Kid's Guide to Money: Earning It, Saving It, Spending It, Growing It, Sharing It. (J). (gr. 3 up). 1996. 12.95 (*0-614-15778-1*) Scholastic Inc.

— The Kid's Guide to Money: Earning It, Saving It, Spending It, Growing It, Sharing It. LC 96-156454. 128p. (J). (gr. 4-7). 1996. pap. 4.95 (*0-590-53853-5*, Cartwheel) Scholastic Inc.

— The Kid's Guide to Money: Earning It, Saving It, Spending It, Growing It, Sharing It. (Scholastic Reference Ser.). 1996. 10.15 (*0-606-09512-8*, Pub. by Turtleback) Demco.

— Marian Wright Edelman: Defender of Children's Rights. LC 91-598. (Famous Women Ser.). (Illus.). 64p. (J). (gr. 4-6). 1992. lib. bdg. 14.95 (*0-8239-1206-X*) Rosen Group.

— Mikhail Gorbachev, the Soviet Innovator. (Great Lives Ser.). (J). 1989. 9.05 (*0-606-01927-8*, Pub. by Turtleback) Demco.

— New Hampshire, 5 vols., Set. LC 97-50379. (Celebrate the States Ser.). 144p. (J). 1999. 35.64 (*0-7614-0669-7*, Benchmark NY) Marshall Cavendish.

— Oprah Winfrey: Television Star. LC 93-21540. (Library of Famous Women). (Illus.). 64p. (J). (gr. 4-7). 1993. lib. bdg. 17.95 (*1-56711-015-0*) Blackbirch.

— Poland. LC 95-17252. (Nations in Transition Ser.). (Illus.). 144p. (YA). (gr. 7-12). 1995. 19.95 (*0-8160-3063-4*) Facts on File.

— Putting It in Writing. 144p. (YA). (gr. 7-12). 1994. pap. 4.95 (*0-590-49459-7*) Scholastic Inc.

— Scott Joplin: A Life in Ragtime. LC 95-8526. (Impact Biographies Ser.). (Illus.). 112p. (YA). (gr. 7-12). 1995. lib. bdg. 24.00 (*0-531-11244-6*) Watts.

— Speaking up, Speaking Out: A Kid's Guide to Making Speeches, Oral Reports, & Conversation. LC 96-509. (Illus.). 80p. (J). (gr. 5-8). 1996. lib. bdg. 23.90 (*1-56294-345-6*) Millbrook Pr.

— Speaking up, Speaking Out: A Kid's Guide to Making Speeches, Oral Reports, & Conversation. (Illus.). 80p. (J). (gr. 4-8). 1997. pap. 8.95 (*0-7613-0138-0*) Millbrook Pr.

***Otfinoski, Steven.** Triumph & Terror: The French Revolution. (Illus.). 128p. (YA). (gr. 6-9). 1999. 24.95 (*0-7351-0213-9*) Replica Bks.

Otfinoski, Steven. The Truth about Three Billy Goats Gruff. LC 93-42391. (Illus.). 32p. (J). (gr. k-3). 1997. pap. 3.95 (*0-8167-3013-X*) Troll Communs.

— Truth about Three Billy Goats Gruff. LC 93-42391. (Illus.). 32p. (J). (gr. k-3). 1994. lib. bdg. 15.85 (*0-8167-3012-1*) Troll Communs.

Otfinoski, Steven. Truth About Three Billy Goats Gruff. (J). 1994. 8.15 (*0-606-06829-5*, Pub. by Turtleback) Demco.

Otfinoski, Steven. Who Stole Home Plate? (Southside Sluggers Ser.). (Illus.). 112p. (J). (gr. 2-6). 1992. pap. 2.95 (*0-671-72932-2*) S&S Bks Yung.

— William Gaines: MAD Man. LC 93-16177. (Made in America Ser.). 48p. (J). (gr. 4-8). 1993. lib. bdg. 21.27 (*0-86592-080-X*) Rourke Enter.

***Otfinoski, Steven & World Book, Inc. Staff.** Hammerheads & Other Sharks. LC 00-22450. (Animals of the World Ser.). (Illus.). 64p. (J). (gr. 1-4). 2000. write for info. (*0-7166-1210-0*) World Bk.

— Hedgehogs & Other Insectivores. LC 00-21638. (Animals of the World Ser.). (Illus.). 64p. (J). (gr. 1-4). 2000. write for info. (*0-7166-1208-9*) World Bk.

— Ladybugs & Other Beetles. LC 00-21637. (Illus.). 64p. (J). (gr. 1-4). 2000. write for info. (*0-7166-1207-0*) World Bk.

Otger, Neufang. Elektronik-Woerterbuch: English-German. 4th ed. (ENG & GER.). 369p. 1993. 75.00 (*0-7859-8553-0*, 3922410294) Fr & Eur.

Otha L. Co. Staff. FCC Radar Endorsement Examination. (FCC Radio Operators Examination Study Guide Ser.). 60p. (C). 1994. pap. text, student ed. write for info. (*0-9642235-1-1*) OC Communs.

Otheguy, Ricardo, jt. auth. see Garcia, Ofelia.

Other, A. N. ABC American Airlines. (Illus.). 96p. (Orig.). 1997. pap. 12.95 (*1-882663-21-7*) Plymouth VT.

— ABC United Airlines. (Illus.). 96p. 1997. pap. 12.95 (*1-882663-20-9*) Plymouth VT.

Othersen. The Pediatric Airway. (Illus.). 256p. 1991. text 110.00 (*0-7216-2778-1*, W B Saunders Co) Harcrt Hlth Sci Grp.

Othman, Abdul H. & Awang, Amir, eds. Counseling in the Asia-Pacific Region, 20. LC 92-45074. (Contributions in Psychology Ser.: No. 20). 168p. 1993. 62.95 (*0-313-28799-6*, GM8799, Greenwood Pr) Greenwood.

Othman, Datohaji S. Crafts of Malaysia. 1997. 39.95 (*981-3018-07-0*) Archipelago.

Othman, Haroub, jt. ed. see Oden, Bertil.

Othman, Rafiqa, jt. auth. see Gorkin, Michael.

Othman, Zaharah & Atmosumarto, Sutanto. Colloquial Malay: A Complete Language Course. (Colloquials Ser.). 1995. 22.95 incl. audio (*0-415-11013-0*, B4028) Routledge.

— Colloquial Malay: A Complete Language Course. LC 95-5663. (Colloquials Ser.). 288p. (gr. 13). 1995. pap. 22.99 (*0-415-11012-2*, B4538) Routledge.

— Colloquial Malay: A Complete Language Course. (Colloquials Ser.). 288p. (gr. 13). 1995. 45.00 incl. audio (*0-415-11014-9*, B4024) Routledge.

Othmer, Ekkehard & Othmer, Sieglinde C. The Clinical Interview Using DSM-III-R. LC 88-16781. 531p. 1989. reprint ed. pap. 164.70 (*0-608-02013-3*, 206266900003) Bks Demand.

— The Clinical Interview Using DSM-IV: Fundamentals, Vol. 1. 544p. 1998. pap. text 36.00 (*0-88048-825-5*, 8825) Am Psychiatric.

— The Clinical Interview Using DSM-IV: The Difficult Patient, Vol. 2. 576p. 1994. text 51.95 (*0-88048-520-5*, 8520) Am Psychiatric.

Othmer, H. G., et al. Experimental & Theoretical Advances in Biological Pattern Formation. (NATO ASI Ser.: Vol. 259). (Illus.). 398p. (C). 1994. text 130.00 (*0-306-44661-8*, Kluwer Plenum) Kluwer Academic.

Othmer, H. G., jt. auth. see Maini, Philip K.

Othmer, Hans G., ed. Nonlinear Oscillations in Biology & Chemistry. (Lecture Notes in Biomathematics Ser.: Vol. 66). vi, 289p. 1986. 51.95 (*0-387-16481-2*) Spr-Verlag.

— Some Mathematical Questions in Biology: The Dynamics of Excitable Media. LC 89-17794. (Lectures in Mathematics in the Life Sciences: Vol. 21). 181p. 1989. pap. 37.00 (*0-8218-1171-1*, LLSCI/21) Am Math.

Othmer, Hans G., et al. Case Studies of Mathematical Modeling. LC 96-47909. 416p. (C). 1996. pap. text 45.33 (*0-13-574039-8*) P-H.

Othmer, Konstantin. Debugging Macintosh Software with MacSbug: Includes MacsBug 6.2 on Disc & Book. 576p. 1991. pap. text 34.95 (*0-201-57049-1*) Addison-Wesley.

Othmer, Sieglinde C., jt. auth. see Othmer, Ekkehard.

Othonos, Andreas. Fiber Bragg Gratings: Fundamentals & Applications in Telecommunications & Sensing. LC 99-21679. 1999. 99.00 (*0-89006-344-3*) Artech Hse.

***Othow, Helen Chavis.** John Chavis: African American Patriot, Preacher, Teacher & Mentor (1783-1838) (Illus.). 176p. 2000. per. 32.00 (*0-7864-0818-9*) McFarland & Co.

Oti, M. N., jt. auth. see Postma, G.

Otieno, Nicholas. A Flight into the Unknown: Contemplating the Hidden Meaning of Life. 112p. 1999. pap. 14.95 (*1-55805-994-6*, Pub. by Franc Pubs WI) Multi Media Design.

***Otieno, Wambui.** Complete Book of C Programming. LC 99-30447. 1005p. (C). 1999. pap. text 85.00 incl. audio compact disk (*0-13-096093-4*, Prentice Hall) P-H.

Otieno, Wambui. Mau Mau's Daughter: The Life History of Wambui Waiyaki Otieno. Presley, Cora A., ed. & intro. by. LC 98-10980. 255p. 1998. lib. bdg. 49.95 (*1-55587-722-2*) L Rienner.

Otilia, Meza. Moctezuma Xocoyotzin. (SPA.). 1997. pap. 11.98 (*968-409-586-4*) Edamex.

Otim-Nape, G. W., et al. Cassava Mosaic Virus Disease in Uganda: The Current Pandemic & Approaches to Control. 1997. pap. 60.00 (*0-85954-466-4*, Pub. by Nat Res Inst) St Mut.

Otis, Alicia. The First Koshare: Legends. Smith, James C., Jr., ed. LC 90-35788. (Illus.). 128p. (Orig.). 1991. pap. 8.95 (*0-86534-144-3*) Sunstone Pr.

— Spiderwoman's Dream: Legends. LC 87-1944. 64p. (Orig.). 1987. pap. 7.95 (*0-86534-099-4*) Sunstone Pr.

Otis, Brooks. Virgil: A Study in Civilized Poetry. LC 95-17062. (Oklahoma Classical Culture Ser.: Vol. 20). 456p. 1995. pap. 17.95 (*0-8061-2782-1*) U of Okla Pr.

***Otis, Carol L. & Goldingay, Roger.** The Athletic Woman's Survival Guide. LC 99-55550. (Illus.). 272p. 2000. pap. write for info. (*0-7360-0121-2*) Human Kinetics.

Otis, Carol L. & Goldingay, Roger. Campus Health Guide: The College Student's Handbook for Healthy Living. 460p. (C). 1989. pap. 14.95 (*0-87447 317 9*) College Bd.

Otis, Caroline, ed. see Brown, Christopher.

Otis, Caroline H. The Cone with the Curl on Top: The "Dairy Queen" Story. Mundale, Susan et al, eds. 160p. (Orig.). 1990. pap. 29.95 (*0-9629040-0-7*) Intl Dairy Queen.

Otis, Charles E. Aircraft Gas Turbine Powerplants. 2nd ed. LC 91-14478. (Aviation Maintenance Training Course Ser.). (Illus.). 468p. 1989. reprint ed. pap. 28.00 (*0-89100-255-3*, JS312648) Jeppesen Sanderson.

— Aircraft Gas Turbine Powerplants Workbook. IAP, Inc. Staff, ed. (Illus.). 188p. (Orig.). (C). 1989. pap., wbk. ed. 12.45 (*0-89100-342-8*, JS322706) Jeppesen Sanderson.

Otis, Charles E. & Vosbury, Peter A. Encyclopedia of Jet Aircraft & Engines. LC 91-28478. (Illus.). 520p. 1997. pap. text 26.95 (*0-89100-390-8*, JS312626) Jeppesen Sanderson.

Otis, Delos S. The Dawes Act & the Allotment of Indian Lands. LC 72-3597. (Civilization of the American Indian Ser.: No. 123). 226p. reprint ed. pap. 70.10 (*0-8357-8088-0*, 203396500087) Bks Demand.

Otis, Denise, jt. auth. see Maia, Ronaldo.

***Otis, Don S.** Teach Your Children Well: Helping Kids Make Moral Choices. LC 00-21687. 192p. (gr. 13). 2000. pap. 12.99 (*0-8007-5723-8*) Chosen Bks.

Otis, Don S. Trickle-Down Morality: Returning to Truth in a World of Compromise. LC 97-38084. 256p. 1998. pap. 12.99 (*0-8007-9257-2*) Chosen Bks.

***Otis, Eliza A., et al.** Architects of Our Fortunes: The Journal of Eliza A. W. Otis, 1860-1863 with Letters & Civil War Journal of Harrison Gray Otis. LC 00-35048. 2000. write for info. (*0-87328-181-0*) Huntington Lib.

Otis, Fessenden N. Illustrated History of the Panama Railroad. LC 77-184965. 150p. 45.00 (*0-87026-045-6*) Westernlore.

— Illustrated History of the Panama Railroad. enl. rev. ed. LC 72-128415. reprint ed. write for info. (*0-404-04838-2*) AMS Pr.

***Otis, George.** God's Trademark. 2001. pap. 11.99 (*0-8007-9281-5*) Chosen Bks.

Otis, George. The Guns of God. LC 97-169122. 140p. 1997. pap. 9.99 (*1-56043-281-0*, Treasure Hse) Destiny Image.

Otis, George, Jr. Informed Intercession: Transforming Your Community Through Spiritual Mapping & Strategic Prayer. LC 99-13577. 204p. (Orig.). 1999. pap. 11.99 (*0-8307-1937-7*, Regal Bks) Gospel Lght.

— The Last of the Giants. LC 91-21233. 272p. 1991. pap. 12.99 (*0-8007-9192-4*) Chosen Bks.

***Otis, George.** Millennium: The Thousand Year Reign of King Jesus. 2000. 18.99 (*1-57778-127-9*) Albury Pub.

Otis, George, Jr. The Twilight Labyrinth: Why Does Spiritual Darkness Linger Where It Does? LC 97-15171. (Spiritual Mapping Ser.). 416p. 1997. pap. 16.99 (*0-8007-9255-6*) Chosen Bks.

Otis, George, Jr. & Brockman, M., eds. Strongholds of the 10/40 Window: Intercessor's Guide to the World's Least Evangelized Nations. 274p. 1995. pap. 12.99 (*0-927545-86-1*) YWAM Pub.

Otis, Harry B., ed. The Best of the Cockle Bur: A Collection of Wit, Wisdom, Humor & Beauty. (Illus.). 241p. 1987. pap. 11.95 (*0-9619994-0-3*) Bur Inc.

***Otis, Harry B. & Erickson, Donald H.** E Pluribus Omaha: Immigrants All. (Illus.). 332p. 2000. pap. 17.50 (*1-930644-04-3*) Lamplighter Pr.

— A Journey with Seymour. (Illus.). 194p. 1993. pap. 15.95 (*1-930644-03-5*) Lamplighter Pr.

***Otis, James.** Mary of Plymouth. (Illus.). 160p. (YA). 1999. 10.00 (*1-889128-60-0*) Mantle Ministries.

Otis, James. Mary of Plymouth: A Story of the Pilgrim Settlement. LC 97-71254. (Illus.). 178p. (J). (gr. 3-6). 1997. reprint ed. 14.95 (*0-9652735-9-8*) Lost Classics.

— Some Political Writings of James Otis, 2 vols. in 1. LC 75-31099. reprint ed. 34.50 (*0-404-13516-1*) AMS Pr.

— The Story of Old Falmouth. (Illus.). 127p. 1997. reprint ed. pap. 19.50 (*0-8328-5836-6*); reprint ed. lib. bdg. 27.50 (*0-8328-5835-8*) Higginson Bk Co.

— The Story of Pemaquid. (Illus.). 181p. 1997. reprint ed. lib. bdg. 26.00 (*0-8328-5889-7*) Higginson Bk Co.

— Toby Tyler. 239p. Date not set. 21.95 (*0-8488-2378-8*) Amereon Ltd.

— Toby Tyler. 152p. (J). 1981. reprint ed. lib. bdg. 25.95 (*0-89966-363-X*); reprint ed. lib. bdg. 19.95 (*0-89967-037-7*, Harmony Rain) Buccaneer Bks.

— Toby Tyler: or Ten Weeks with a Circus. unabridged ed. LC 97-2078. (Illus.). 135p. (J). 1996. reprint ed. pap. text 2.00 (*0-486-29349-1*) Dover.

Otis, Johnny. Red Beans & Rice & Other Rock 'n Roll Recipes. LC 97-17359. (Illus.). 128p. (Orig.). 1997. pap. 16.00 (*0-7649-0361-6*, A902) Pomegranate Calif.

— Upside Your Head! Rhythm & Blues on Central Avenue. LC 93-13611. (Music - Culture Ser.). (Illus.). 212p. 1993. pap. 17.95 (*0-8195-6287-4*, Wesleyan Univ Pr) U Pr of New Eng.

Otis, Ken. Puzzle Pieces. unabridged ed. (Illus.). 160p. 1998. pap. 12.95 (*0-9666106-0-1*) K Otis.

Otis, Laura. Membranes: Metaphors of Invasion in Nineteenth-Century Literature, Science, & Politics. LC 98-29763. (Medicine & Culture Ser.). 248p. 1999. 45.00 (*0-8018-5996-4*) Johns Hopkins.

***Otis, Laura.** Membranes: Metaphors of Invasion in Nineteenth-Century Literature, Science & Politics. (Medicine & Culture Ser.). 224p. 2000. pap. 17.95 (*0-8018-6527-1*) Johns Hopkins.

Otis, Laura. Organic Memory: History & the Body in the Late Nineteenth & Early Twentieth Centuries. LC 93-47280. (Texts & Contexts Ser.: No. 11). xiii, 300p. 1994. text 50.00 (*0-8032-3561-5*) U of Nebr Pr.

Otis, Leah L. Prostitution in Medieval Society: The History of an Urban Institution in Languedoc. LC 84-16184. (Women in Culture & Society Ser.). (Illus.). 240p. 1987. pap. text 11.95 (*0-226-64033-7*) U Ch Pr.

— Prostitution in Medieval Society: The History of an Urban Institution in Languedoc. LC 84-16184. (Women in Culture & Society Ser.). (Illus.). 240p. 1993. lib. bdg. 22.50 (*0-226-64032-9*) U Ch Pr.

Otis, Margaret R. Relics Recycled on Cloud Nine. LC 81-18286. (Illus.). 96p. 1981. pap. 4.95 (*0-915010-30-5*) Sutter House.

Otis, Pauletta. The Pacific Century. 2nd ed. LC 98-32337. 128p. 1998. pap., student ed. 15.00 (*0-8133-3605-8*, Pub. by Westview) HarpC.

Otis, Pauletta, jt. auth. see Benson, Paul.

Otis, Pauletta J. & Kaplan, Stephen H., eds. Between the Lines: International Short Stories of War. LC 94-650. 438p. (C). 1994. pap. 19.95 (*0-87081-329-3*) Univ Pr Colo.

Otis, Pauletta J. & Kaplan, Steven A., eds. Between the Lines: International Short Stories of War. LC 94-650. 438p. (C). 1994. 26.95 (*0-87081-328-5*) Univ Pr Colo.

Otis, Philo A. The Chicago Symphony Orchestra. LC 79-37904. (Select Bibliographies Reprint Ser.). 1977. reprint ed. 35.95 (*0-8369-6742-9*) Ayer.

Otis Public Library Staff. Washington County, Colorado. (Illus.). 323p. 1989. 45.00 (*0-88107-140-4*) Curtis Media.

Otis, Rebecca, jt. auth. see Hurst, Carol Otis.

Otis, Rose. Listening Heart 426p. 1993. 14.99 (*0-8280-0769-1*) Review & Herald.

Otis, Rose, ed. Close to Home: A Daily Devotional for Women by Women. LC 96-218454. 416p. 1998. 14.99 (*0-8280-1109-5*) Review & Herald.

— Gift of Love: A Daily Devotional for Women by Women. 426p. 1994. 14.99 (*0-8280-0883-3*) Review & Herald.

— A Moment of Peace: A Daily Devotional for Women by Women. LC 95-33463. 399p. 1995. 14.99 (*0-8280-0979-1*) Review & Herald.

— A Touch of Joy: Devotional Thoughts for Women by Women. 1995. pap. 5.99 (*0-8280-1038-2*) Review & Herald.

Otis, Rose M., ed. From the Heart: A Daily Devotional for Women by Women. LC 97-25839. 1997. 14.99 (*0-8280-1288-1*) Review & Herald.

Otis, S. U. S. vs. Steven F. Soliah. (Monographs: No. CR-6). 1975. 4.00 (*1-55524-006-2*) Ctr Respon Psych.

Otis, Sharon. My Kid Won't Eat Cookbook. (Orig.). 1986. pap. 5.00 (*0-9617737-1-5*) Total Lrn.

Otis, Sharon & Walker, Lois. Jeffrey's Laugh. (Illus.). (Orig.). (J). (ps-6). 1987. student ed. 6.50 (*0-9617737-2-3*) Total Lrn.

— Tammy's Smile. (Illus.). (Orig.). (J). (ps-7). 1985. student ed. 6.00 (*0-9617737-0-7*) Total Lrn.

Otis, William B. American Verse, 1625-1807: A History. 303p. (C). 1966. lib. bdg. 75.00 (*0-8383-0605-5*) M S G Haskell Hse.

Otken, Charles H. The Ills of the South. LC 72-11345. (American South Ser.). 1973. reprint ed. 28.95 (*0-405-05061-5*) Ayer.

Otlewis, Julie. Hooked on Golf. (Illus.). 168p. (Orig.). 1994. pap. 5.95 (*1-56245-082-4*) Great Quotations.

— A Lifetime of Love. 168p. (Orig.). 1994. pap. 5.95 (*1-56245-087-5*) Great Quotations.

— Love, Honor, Cherish. (Orig.). 1994. pap. 7.95 (*1-56245-081-6*) Great Quotations.

— Many Thanks to You. Caton, Patrick, ed. 80p. (Orig.). 1996. pap. 7.95 (*1-56245-249-5*) Great Quotations.

— Simply the Best Mom. 366p. 1993. pap., spiral bd. 8.95 (*1-56245-076-X*) Great Quotations.

Otley, jt. auth. see Emmanuel.

Otley, David T., jt. auth. see Emmanuel, C.

Otlowski, Margaret. Voluntary Euthanasia & the Common Law. LC 97-5641. (Illus.). 598p. 1997. text 135.00 (*0-19-825996-4*) OUP.

***Otlowski, Margaret.** Voluntary Euthanasia & the Common Law. 600p. 2000. pap. text 45.00 (*0-19-829868-4*) OUP.

Otman, G. Dictionary of Artifical Intelligence Terms French-English. Orig. Title: Terminologie de l'Intelligence Artificielle. 286p. 1997. pap. 57.00 (*2-85608-087-1*) IBD Ltd.

— Dictionary of Artificial Intelligence Terms, French-English. (ENG & FRE.). 1997. 57.00 (*0-7859-9720-2*) Fr & Eur.

— Terms, Artificial Intelligence: French/English/French. (ENG & FRE.). 286p. 1997. 105.00 (*0-320-00455-4*) Fr & Eur.

Otmishi, Abe. The Book of Formulas. LC 99-63919. (Illus.). 175p. 1999. pap. write for info. (*1-893181-19-7*) Le Gesse Stevens.

Otnes, Cele, et al, eds. Gift Giving: A Research Anthology. 235p. 1995. 39.95 (*0-87972-705-5*); pap. 19.95 (*0-87972-706-3*) Bowling Green Univ Popular Press.

Otnes, Per. Other-Wise: Alterity, Materiality & Meditation. 202p. (C). 1997. text 33.00 (*82-00-22558-5*) Scandnvan Univ Pr.

Otness, Harold M. Index to Early Twentieth Century City Plans Appearing in Guidebooks: Baedeker, Muirhead-Blue Guides, Murray, I. J. G. R., Etc., Plus Selected Other Works to Provide Worldwide Coverage of Over 2,000 Plans to Over 1,200 Communities, Found in 74 Guidebooks. LC 78-15094. (Occasional Papers: No. 4). (Illus.). 124p. (Orig.). 1978. pap. 6.00 (*0-939112-05-1*) Western Assn Map.

— Index to Nineteenth Century City Plans Appearing in Guidebooks: Baedeker, Murray, Joanne, Black, Appleton, Meyer, Plus Selected Other Works to Provide Coverage of Over 1,800 Plans to Nearly 600 Communities Found in 164 Guidebooks. LC 80-24483. (Occasional Papers: No. 7). (Illus.). 108p. (Orig.). 1980. pap. 6.00 (*0-939112-08-6*) Western Assn Map.

Otness, Harold M., compiled by. The Shakespeare Folio Handbook & Census: Bibliographies & Indexes in World Literature, 25. LC 89-28650. 146p. 1990. lib. bdg. 55.00 (*0-313-27257-3*, OSA/, Greenwood Pr) Greenwood.

Oto, Ali M., ed. Practice & Progress in Cardiac Pacing & Electrophysiology. LC 96-116. (Developments in Cardiovascular Medicine Ser.: Vol. 183). 416p. (C). 1996. text 217.50 (*0-7923-3950-9*) Kluwer Academic.

Otobe, S. Oral Implantology. 1990. text 80.00 (*1-57235-013-X*) Piccin Nuova.

Otobe, S. Oral Implantology. (Illus.). 264p. 1990. text 88.00 (*88-299-0263-2*, Pub. by Piccin Nuova) Gordon & Breach.

Otomo, Kat S. Legend of Mother Sarah: Tunnel Town. unabridged ed. Lewis, Dana & Smith, Toren, trs. from JPN. (Illus.). 224p. (Orig.). (YA). (gr. 7 up). 1996. pap. 18.95 (*1-56971-145-3*) Dark Horse Comics.

Otomo, Katsuhiro. Domu: A Child's Dream. (Illus.). 240p. 1996. pap. 17.95 (*1-56971-140-2*) Dark Horse Comics.

Oton, Jose M. Smart Cards. LC 94-7671. 1994. 79.00 (*0-89006-687-6*) Artech Hse.

Otoo, David & Otoo, Tamminay. Authentic African Cuisine from Ghana LC 99-173583. v, 107p. 1997. write for info. (*0-9659209-0-9*) Sankofa.

Otoo, Tamminay, jt. auth. see Otoo, David.

***O'Tool, Martha N. & Payne, Mary B.** Long-Term Caring for Your Parents. iv, 44p. 1998. pap. 9.95 (*0-9664247-1-9*) Sndwch Pr.

O'Toole. Irish Art Now. pap. 24.95 (*1-85894-089-3*, Pub. by Merrell Holberton) U of Wash Pr.

O'Toole. Nostalgia Street Rods. 1998. 19.95 (*0-949398-57-8*, 861701Q, Pub. by Graffiti) Motorbooks Intl.

***O'Toole, Andrew.** Branch Rickey in Pittsburgh: Baseball's Trailblazing General Manager for the Pirates, 1950-1955. (Illus.). 223p. 2000. per. 29.95 (*0-7864-0839-1*) McFarland & Co.

O'Toole, Anita W. & Welt, Sheila R. Interpersonal Theory in Nursing Practice: Selected Works of Hildegard E. Peplau. 400p. 1989. 45.95 (*0-8261-6060-3*) Springer Pub.

O'Toole, Barry & Jordan, A. Grant, eds. Next Steps: Improving Management in Government. 224p. 1995. 77.95 (*1-85521-491-1*) Ashgate Pub Co.

O'Toole, Barry, jt. ed. see Hunt, Michael.

O'Toole, Brian & McConkey, Roy, eds. Innovations in Developing Countries for People with Disabilities. LC 96-116266. 284p. 1995. pap. 28.00 (*1-870335-18-X*, 18X, Pub. by Lisieux Hall) P H Brookes.

O'Toole, Christopher. Bees of the World. 192p. 1999. pap. text 19.95 (*0-7137-2472-2*) Blandford Pr.

O'Toole, Christopher, ed. The Encyclopedia of Insects. (Illus.). 160p. 1986. 29.95 (*0-8160-1358-6*) Facts on File.

O'Toole, Christopher & Raw, Anthony. Bees of the World. (Of the World Ser.). (Illus.). 192p. 1991. lib. bdg. 29.95 (*0-8160-1992-4*) Facts on File.

O'Toole, Coleen. The Search for Purity: A Retrospective Policy Analysis of Decision to Chlorinate Cincinnati's Public Water Supply, 1890-1920. LC 90-13865. (Environment: Problems & Solutions Ser.: Vol. 26). 150p. 1990. text 15.00 (*0-8240-9792-0*) Garland.

O'Toole, Donna R. Aarvy Aardvark Finds Hope: A Read-Aloud Story for People of All Ages. (Illus.). 80p. (Orig.). (J). (ps up). 1989. audio 10.95 (*1-878321-28-5*, Compassion Pr) Compassion Bks.

— Facing Change: Falling Apart & Coming Together Again in the Teen Years. (Illus.). 48p. (Orig.). (YA). (gr. 7 up). 1995. pap. 6.95 (*1-878321-11-0*) Compassion Bks.

— Growing Through Grief: A K-Twelve Curriculum to Help Young People Through All Kinds of Loss. rev. ed. (Illus.). 392p. (J). (gr. k-12). 1989. ring bd. 59.95 (*1-878321-00-5*, Compassion Pr) Compassion Bks.

— Healing & Growing Through Grief. (Illus.). 20p. (J). 1986. pap. 4.25 (*1-878321-10-2*, HG-02-4) Compassion Bks.

O'Toole, Donna R., jt. auth. see Mcwhirter, Kore L.

O'Toole, Eamonn. Decorations & Medals of the Republic of Ireland. enl. rev. ed. (Illus.). 1990. pap. 13.95 (*0-685-54342-0*) Medallic Pub.

— Medals of the Republic of Ireland. (Illus.). 86p. 1990. pap. 14.00 (*0-9624663-5-2*) Medallic Pub.

O'Toole, Edward. Opportunities in Securities Industry. (Opportunities In . . . Ser.). (Illus.). 160p. pap. 12.95 (*0-8442-6642-6*, 297OISI, VGM Career) NTC Contemp Pub Co.

— Opportunities in Securities Industry. (Illus.). 160p. 1987. 13.95 (*0-8442-6641-8*, VGM Career) NTC Contemp Pub Co.

O'Toole, Faith A. Astrological Mandala Meditations, Vol. 1. (Illus.). 20p. 1997. 25.00 (*0-9661373-7-X*) Munbo Pub.

O'Toole, Fintan. Black Hole, Green Card: The Disappearance of Ireland. 223p. (Orig.). 1994. reprint ed. pap. 13.95 (*1-874597-01-4*, Pub. by New Island Books) Irish Bks Media.

— Democracy Blindfolded: The Case for a Freedom of Information Act in Ireland. LC 94-236060. 1994. pap. 7.50 (*1-85918-040-X*, Pub. by Cork Univ) Intl Spec Bk.

— The Ex-Isle of Erin: Images of a Global Ireland. LC 97-161118. 236p. 1997. pap. 15.95 (*1-874597-49-9*) Dufour.

***O'Toole, Fintan.** The Irish Times Book of the Century. (Illus.). 368p. 1999. 39.95 (*0-7171-2749-4*, Pub. by Gill & MacMill) Irish Bks Media.

O'Toole, Fintan. The Lie of the Land: Irish Identities. 172p. (C). 1998. 23.00 (*1-85984-821-4*, Pub. by Verso) Norton.

— The Lie of the Land: Irish Identities. LC 97-42223. 192p. 1998. pap. 14.00 (*1-85984-132-5*, Pub. by Verso) Norton.

— Mass for Jesse James. 1996. pap. 12.95 (*1-85186-078-9*) Dufour.

— The Politics of Magic: Tom Murphy. LC 94-184679. 121994p. 1994. pap. 21.00 (*1-874597-75-8*) Dufour.

— A Radical Guide to Macbeth & Hamlet. 78p. 1994. pap. 5.95 (*1-874597-19-7*, Pub. by New Island Books) Irish Bks Media.

— A Traitor's Kiss: The Life of Richard Brinsley Sheridan. LC 98-23261. xxi, 519p. 1998. 30.00 (*0-374-27931-4*) FS&G.

— Women & the New Reproductive Technologies in Ireland. LC 95-178445. (Undercurrents Ser.). 1994. pap. 7.50 (*1-85918-030-2*, Pub. by Cork Univ) Intl Spec Bk.

O'Toole, Fintan, ed. see Hanafin, Patrick.

O'Toole, Fintan, ed. see Murphy, Tim.

O'Toole, Frederick J. 30 Days to the LSAT. 240p. 1998. pap. 11.95 (*0-02-862176-X*) Macmillan.

O'Toole, Frederick J., jt. auth. see Stewart, Mark A.

O'Toole, Frederick J., jt. auth. see Stewart, Mark Alan.

O'Toole, G. J. The Encyclopedia of American Intelligence & Espionage: From the Revolutionary War to the Present. (Illus.). 560p. 1988. 55.00 (*0-8160-1011-0*) Facts on File.

— Honorable Treachery. LC 91-13203. 591p. 1993. pap. 15.00 (*0-87113-492-6*, Atlntc Mnthly) Grove-Atltic.

— The Spanish War: An American Epic, 1898. (Illus.). 448p. 1986. reprint ed. pap. 16.95 (*0-393-30304-7*) Norton.

O'Toole, Jack. Forming the Future: Lessons from the Saturn Corporation. LC 96-7504. (Illus.). 192p. 1996. 17.95 (*1-55786-836-0*) Blackwell Pubs.

O'Toole, James. The Executive's Compass: Business & the Good Society. (Illus.). 176p. 1995. pap. 11.95 (*0-19-509644-4*) OUP.

— Leadership A to Z: A Guide for the Appropriately Ambitious. LC 99-6416. 352p. 1999. text 22.00 (*0-7879-4658-3*) Jossey-Bass.

O

An Asterisk (*) at the beginning of an entry indicates that the title is appearing for the first time.

— Leading Change: Overcoming the Ideology of Comfort & the Tyranny of Custom. LC 94-39421. (Management Ser.). 302p. 1995. mass mkt. 27.00 (1-55542-608-5) Jossey-Bass.

— Leading Change: The Argument for Values-Based Leadership. 304p. 1996. pap. 12.50 (0-345-40254-5) Ballantine Pub Grp.

— Work, Learning & the American Future. LC 76-50726. 256p. reprint ed. pap. 79.40 (0-8357-4956-8, 203788800009) Bks Demand.

O'Toole, James, et al, eds. Working: Changes & Choices. LC 81-6773. 525p. (C). 1981. pap. 24.95 (0-89885-111-4, Kluwer Acad Hman Sci); pap. 18.95 (0-89885-113-0, Kluwer Acad Hman Sci); pap., student ed. 18.95 (0-89885-112-2, Kluwer Acad Hman Sci) Kluwer Academic.

O'Toole, James, et al. Three Views: Tenure. 56p. 1979. pap. text 14.95 (0-915390-21-3) Transaction Pubs.

O'Toole, James M. Militant & Triumphant: William Henry O'Connell & the Catholic Church in Boston, 1859-1944. LC 91-50570. (C). 1993. pap. text 17.50 (0-268-01403-5) U of Notre Dame Pr.

— Understanding Archives & Manuscripts. (Archival Fundamentals Ser.). 76p. 1990. pap. 27.00 (0-931828-77-5) Soc Am Archivists.

O'Toole, James M., ed. The Records of American Business. LC 97-24781. 411p. 1997. 39.95 (0-931828-45-7) Soc Am Archivists.

O'Toole, James M., jt. ed. see Sullivan, Robert E.

O'Toole, John. Caribbean Home Ownership: A Dummie's Handbook. LC 97-215732. (Illus.). 144p. (Orig.). 1997. pap. 13.95 (0-9658026-6-3) Pooka Pub.

— The Process of Drama. LC 92-7785. (Illus.). 272p. (C). 1992. pap. 25.99 (0-415-08244-7, A9664) Routledge.

O'Toole, John. Tornado! Eighty-Four Minutes, Ninety-Four Lives. LC 93-70976. (Illus.). 276p. 1993. pap. 16.95 (0-9636277-0-8) Chandler Hse.

O'Toole, John, ed. The Wisdom of Buddha. LC 96-21499. (Illus.). 56p. 1996. 8.95 (0-7892-0238-7) Abbeville Pr.

O'Toole, John & Richmond, Marvin. Tornado! Eighty-Four Minutes Ninety-Four Lives, Set. LC 93-70976. (Illus.). 288p. 1993. pap. 34.95 incl. audio, VHS (0-9636277-2-4) Chandler Hse.

O'Toole, John, jt. auth. see Haseman, Brad.

O'Toole, John, tr. see Del Todesco, Charles.

O'Toole, Judith H. George Luks: Expressionist Master of Color - the Watercolors Rediscovered. 2nd ed. LC 94-69203. (Illus.). 65p. 1994. pap. write for info. (0-9644071-0-8) Canton Art Inst.

O'Toole, Judith H., et al. Scavnicky: Portrait of an Anthracite Family Nelson Morris, Photographer. (Illus.). 47p. (Orig.). (C). 1992. pap. 5.00 (0-942945-02-6) Sordoni Gal.

***O'Toole, Julie.** Anorexia & Bulimia Cookbook. 36p. 1999. spiral bd. 18.50 (0-9672060-3-0) Nine Lights.

***O'Toole, Karen, ed.** Massachusetts Attorney Discipline Reports, Vol. 14. 850p. 1999. write for info. (0-327-04957-X, 8144110) LEXIS Pub.

***O'Toole, Katherine.** A Time for Heroes. Wise, Noreen, ed. (Lemonade Collection). 208p. (YA). (gr. 5 up). 2000. pap. 9.95 (1-58584-275-3) Huckleberry CT.

O

O'Toole, L., ed. Chekhov: Three Farces (Tri Shutki) (Bristol Russian Texts Ser.). (RUS.). 126p. 1993. pap. 18.95 (1-85399-360-3, Pub. by Brist Class Pr) Focus Pub-R Pullins.

***O'Toole, Larry.** Chopping Tops: Practical Hot Rodder's Guide. (Illus.). 160p. 2000. pap. 19.95 (0-949398-18-7, 130730AE, Pub. by Graffiti) Motorbooks Intl.

O'Toole, Larry. The Colorful World of Street Rods. (Illus.). 112p. 1996. 19.95 (0-949398-17-9, Pub. by Graffiti) Motorbooks Intl.

— Engineering Street Rods. 1998. pap. text 19.95 (0-949398-81-0) Graffiti.

— Styling Street Rods: Practical Hot Rodders Guide. (Illus.). 144p. 1997. pap. 19.95 (0-949398-49-7, Pub. by Graffiti) Motorbooks Intl.

O'Toole, Laura L. & Schiffman, Jessica. Gender Violence: Interdisciplinary Perspectives. LC 96-49903. 432p. (C). 1997. text 65.00 (0-8147-8040-7); pap. text 25.00 (0-8147-8041-5) NYU Pr.

O'Toole, Laurence. The Cornish Captain's Tale. (C). 1989. 50.00 (1-85022-011-5, Pub. by Dyllansow Truran) St Mut.

O'Toole, Laurence J. Institutions, Policy & Outputs for Acidification: The Case of Hungary. (Studies in Green Research). (Illus.). 174p. 1998. text 55.95 (1-85972-611-9, Pub. by Ashgate Pub) Ashgate Pub Co.

***O'Toole, Laurence J.** Pornocopia: Porn, Sex, Technology & Desire. 2000. pap. 15.00 (1-85242-720-5) Serpents Tail.

O'Toole, Laurence J., Jr., ed. American Intergovernmental Relations: Foundations, Perspectives, & Issues. 2nd ed. LC 92-30912. 430p. 1992. 26.95 (0-87187-718-X) Congr Quarterly.

***O'Toole, Laurence J., Jr., ed.** American Intergovernmental Relations: Foundations, Perspectives & Issues. 3rd ed. LC 99-37623. 425p. 1999. pap. 31.95 (1-56802-405-3) CQ Pr.

O'Toole, Laurence J. & Montjoy, Robert S. Regulatory Decision Making: The Virginia State Corporation Commission. LC 84-5146. 405p. reprint ed. pap. 125.60 (0-8357-2715-7, 203982900013) Bks Demand.

O'Toole, Lela, ed. The International Heritage of Home Economics in the United States. 1988. 20.00 (0-318-62843-0) AAFCS.

O'Toole, Margarette. Jesus, the Word of God. 96p. (Orig.). 1993. pap. text 9.95 (0-8146-2235-6) Liturgical Pr.

***O'Toole, Martha N. & Payne, Mary B.** Legal Planning for Your Parents. LC 98-170423. vi, 36p. 1998. pap. 9.95 (0-9664247-0-0) Sndwch Pr.

O'Toole, Maureen A. Ama & the White Crane. (J). 1991. pap. 7.00 (0-87602-295-6) Anchorage.

O'Toole, Michael. The Language of Displayed Art. 1995. pap. 24.95 (0-7185-1940-X) Bks Intl VA.

— The Language of Displayed Art. (Illus.). 300p. 1994. 38.50 (0-8386-3604-7) Fairleigh Dickinson.

— The Language of Displayed Art. LC 93-41668. (Illus.). 280p. 1994. write for info. (0-7185-1632-X) St Martin.

— More Kicks Than Pence: A Life in Irish Journalism. 200p. 1992. pap. 17.95 (1-85371-143-8, Pub. by Poolbeg Pr) Dufour.

O'Toole, Michael, jt. ed. see Birch, David.

***O'Toole, Michael P.** The Payroll Source: 2000 Edition, 2 vols. 7th rev. ed. 1200p. 2000. 162.95 (1-930471-04-1, 0700) American Payroll.

O'Toole, Michael P., ed. see APA Automated Clearing House Committee.

O'Toole, Michael P., ed. see Haug, Leonard A.

O'Toole, Mo. Regulation Theory & the British State: The Case of the Urban Development Corporation. LC 96-83250. 256p. 1996. 68.95 (1-85972-305-5, Pub. by Avebry) Ashgate Pub Co.

O'Toole, Oliver. Baseball's Best Kept Secret: Al Oliver & His Time in Baseball. 200p. 1997. 24.95 (0-9649311-6-8) City of Champns.

O'Toole, Patricia. Money & Morals in America: A History. LC 97-50263. 432p. 1998. 30.00 (0-517-58693-2) C Potter.

O'Toole, Peter. Loitering with Intent. large type ed. 237p. 1995. 25.95 (1-85695-051-4, Pub. by ISIS Lrg Prnt) Transaction Pubs.

— Loitering with Intent: The Apprentice. (Illus.). 448p. (J). 1997. 24.45 (0-7868-6065-0, Pub. by Hyperion) Time Warner.

— Loitering with Intent: The Child. (Illus.). 224p. (J). 1997. pap. 12.45 (0-7868-8196-8, Pub. by Hyperion) Time Warner.

— Loitering with Intent Vol. 2: The Apprentice. (Illus.). 256p. (Orig.). 1997. pap. 19.95 (0-330-35208-3, Pub. by Pan) Trans-Atl Phila.

O'Toole, Randal. Reforming the Forest Service. (Illus.). 248p. 1988. text 40.00 (0-933280-49-1); pap. text 25.00 (0-933280-45-9) Island Pr.

O'Toole, Richard, ed. The Organization, Management, & Tactics of Social Research. LC 77-138996. 330p. 1971. reprint ed. pap. 102.30 (0-608-05345-7, 206505000012) Bks Demand.

O'Toole, Richard, jt. auth. see Trela, James E.

O'Toole, Roger, ed. Sociological Studies in Roman Catholic Religion: Historical & Contemporary Perspectives. LC 89-37719. (Studies in Religion & Society: Vol. 24). 192p. 1989. lib. bdg. 79.95 (0-88946-850-8) E Mellen.

O'Toole, Sean M., jt. auth. see McManus, Robert A.

O'Toole, Shirley, ed. see Topeka Genealogical Society Staff.

O'Toole, Simon. Confessions of an American Scholar. LC 71-123152. 117p. reprint ed. pap. 36.30 (0-608-14130-5, 205589500039) Bks Demand.

O'Toole, Terence M. Successful Private Equity Investing: Legal, Financial & Strategic Techniques. LC 99-170051. (Corporate Law & Practice Course Handbook Ser.). 272p. 1998. 129.00 (0-87224-541-1) PLI.

O'Toole, Tess. Genealogy & Fiction in Hardy: Family Lineage & Narrative Lines. LC 97-1763. 224p. 1997. text 55.00 (0-312-17462-4) St Martin.

O'Toole, Thomas. Understanding Humankind: A Global Introduction to Social Science. Davies Group Staff, ed. & illus. by. 288p. (C). 1996. pap. 22.75 (1-888570-10-5) Davies Grp.

O'Toole, Thomas E., jt. auth. see Bah-Lalya, Ibrahima.

O'Toole, Thomas E., tr. see Kalck, Pierre.

Otooni, M. A., et al, eds. Elements of Rapid Solidification: Fundamentals & Applications. LC 96-53989. (Series in Materials Science: No. 29). (Illus.). xvii, 320p. 1997. 96.00 (3-540-61791-4) Spr-Verlag.

Otooni, Monde A., ed. Science & Technology of Rapid Solidification & Processing: Proceedings of the NATO Advanced Research Workshop, West Point Military Academy, New York, NY, U. S. A., June 21-24, 1994. (NATO Advanced Science Institutes: Series E). 392p. (C). 1994. text 234.00 (0-7923-3203-2) Kluwer Academic.

***Ototake, Hirotada.** No One's Perfect. LC 00-33074. 2000. 19.95 (4-7700-2500-9) Kodansha Intl.

Ototani, T. Calcium Clean Steel. (Materials Research & Engineering Ser.). (Illus.). 160p. 1986. 128.95 (0-387-16346-8) Spr-Verlag.

Otrakul, Ampha. Thai-German Dictionary: Thai-Deutsches Woerterbuch. (GER & THA.). 779p. 1986. write for info. (0-8288-1722-7, F65790) Fr & Eur.

Otsamo, Pentti. Homunculus: A Picture Novella in Six Parts. 80p. 1998. pap. 9.95 (1-896597-15-7) LPC InBook.

Otschl, Johann G., ed. Revolutionary Changes in Understanding Man & Society: Scopes & Limits. (Theory & Decision Library Series A: Vol. 21). 1995. lib. bdg. 161.50 (0-7923-3627-5, Pub. by Kluwer Academic) Kluwer Academic.

Otstot, Charles M. The Descendants & Antecedents of Alfred & Catherine (Dawley) Fellows. LC 87-80062. 140p. (Orig.). 1987. pap. 15.00 (0-9603808-1-7) C M Otstot.

— A History of the Otstot Family in America 1988: Also Being a Guide to the Descendents of Jost & Katherine Otstadt. LC 72-97229. (Illus.). 1459p. 1988. pap. 25.00 (0-9603808-0-9) C M Otstot.

Otsuka, K., et al, eds. Materials for Smart Systems II. LC 97-6489. (Materials Research Society Symposium Proceedings Ser.: No. 459). 588p. 1997. text 68.00 (1-55899-363-0) Materials Res.

***Otsuka, K. & Wayman, C. M., eds.** Shape Memory Materials. (Illus.). 284p. (C). 1999. pap. 39.95 (0-521-66384-9) Cambridge U Pr.

Otsuka, K., jt. ed. see Hattori, H.

Otsuka, Katsuo, jt. auth. see Kazushi, Ohkawa.

Otsuka, Keijiro, et al. Industrial Reform in China: Past Performance & Future Prospects. (Studies on Contemporary China). (Illus.). 282p. 1999. text 65.00 (0-19-829408-5) OUP.

Otsuka, Keijiro, jt. ed. see David, Christina C.

Otsuka, Masanori & Hall, Zach W., eds. Neurobiology of Chemical Transmission. LC 78-24602. 336p. reprint ed. 104.20 (0-8357-9940-9, 201571100097) Bks Demand.

Otsuka, Ronald Y., jt. auth. see White, Julia M.

Otsuka, Sei, jt. ed. see Eliel, Ernest L.

Otsuka, T., jt. auth. see Gruber, B.

Otsuki, Hiroshi, jt. auth. see Grindstaff, Bradley.

Otsuki, R., et al. Silkworm Egg Production. (Illus.). 200p. 1997. 38.00 (1-57808-009-6, V096) Science Pubs.

Ott. Statistics. 4th ed. (Business Statistics Ser.). 1987. 14.25 (0-87150-024-8) PWS Pubs.

— Understanding Statistics. 4th ed. (Statistics Ser.). Date not set. 34.25 (0-87150-855-9) PWS Pubs.

— Understanding Statistics. 4th ed. (Statistics Ser.). 1985. 4.00 (0-87150-001-9); teacher ed. 4.00 (0-87150-856-7) PWS Pubs.

Ott & Mendenhall. S.g. Understanding Statistics. 5th ed. (Statistics). 1990. student ed. 16.50 (0-534-92385-2) Brooks-Cole.

— Statistics: Tool For Social Sciences. 3rd ed. (Business Statistics Ser.). 1983. 10.50 (0-87150-402-2) PWS Pubs.

— Statistics: Tool for Social Sciences. 4th ed. (Business Statistics Ser.). 1987. 9.50 (0-87150-035-3) PWS Pubs.

— Understanding Statistics. 4th ed. (Statistics Ser.). 1985. teacher ed. 14.00 (0-87150-891-5) PWS Pubs.

Ott & Mendenhall, William. Understanding Statistics. 6th ed. (Statistics Ser.). 1994. pap., student ed. 20.95 (0-534-20924-6) Wadsworth Pub.

Ott, et al. Process Quality Control. 3rd ed. LC 00-37255. (Illus.). 500p. 2000. pap. 74.95 (0-07-135010-1) McGraw-Hill Prof.

Ott, jt. auth. see Hildebrand, David K.

***Ott, William J.** Clinical Obstetrical Ultrasound. LC 98-32454. 416p. 1999. 159.95 incl. cd-rom (0-471-32927-4) Wiley.

***Ott, Alice M.** A Secure Place. 128p. 1999. pap. 7.95 (1-57258-148-4) Teach Servs.

Ott, Anneliese. The Art of Dried & Scented Flowers. LC 96-170976. (Illus.). 160p. 1995. pap. 16.95 (0-304-34661-6, Pub. by Cassell) Sterling.

Ott, Attiat F., ed. Public Sector Budgets: A Comparative Study. (Illus.). 304p. 1993. 95.00 (1-85278-618-3) E Elgar.

Ott, Attiat F. & Gray, Wayne B. The Massachusetts Health Plan: The Right Prescription? LC 88-62773. (Pioneer Paper Ser.: No. 1). 123p. (Orig.). 1988. pap. 10.00 (0-929930-00-2) Pioneer Inst.

Ott, Attiat F. & Hartley, Keith, eds. Privatization & Economic Efficiency: A Comparative Analysis of Developed & Developing Countries. 288p. 1991. text 100.00 (1-85278-414-8) E Elgar.

Ott, Attiat F., jt. auth. see Ott, David J.

Ott, Bertrand. Lisztian Keyboard Energy - Liszt et la Pedagogie du Piano: An Essay on the Pianism of Franz Liszt. Windham, Donald H., tr. LC 92-25796. (FRE., Illus.). 308p. 1992. reprint ed. text 99.95 (0-7734-9589-4) E Mellen.

Ott, C. & Von Wangenheim, G. Essays in Law & Economics Vol. IV: Public Law, Private Law & Adjudication. LC 98-187113. 282p. 1998. 90.00 (90-6215-586-3) Gaunt.

***Ott, Christopher.** Global Solutions for Multilingual Applications: Real World Techniques for Developers & Designers. LC 99-35174. 248p. 1999. pap. 34.99 (0-471-34827-9) Wiley.

Ott, Christopher, jt. auth. see Sanborn, Robert.

***Ott, Dana.** Small is Democratic: An Examination of State Size & Democratic Development. LC 00-21539. (Comparative Studies of Democratization). 2000. write for info. (0-8153-3910-0) Garland.

Ott, Darlene, ed. see Massie, Gabriele.

Ott, David H. Palestine in Perspective: Politics, Human Rights & the West Bank. 14.95 (0-7043-2263-3, Pub. by Quartet) Charles River Bks.

Ott, David J. & Fayez, Jamil A. Hysterosalpingography: A Text & Atlas. (Illus.). 144p. 1991. text 82.00 (0-683-06658-7) Lppncott W & W.

Ott, David J. & Meltzer, Allan H. Federal Tax Treatment of State & Local Securities. LC 79-27915. (Brookings Institution, National Committee on Government Finance, Studies of Government Finance). (Illus.). 146p. 1980. reprint ed. lib. bdg. 59.50 (0-313-22306-8, OTFT) Greenwood.

Ott, David J. & Ott, Attiat F. Federal Budget Policy. 3rd ed. LC 77-24198. (Studies of Government Finance). 178p. 1977. 26.95 (0-8157-6710-2); pap. 9.95 (0-8157-6709-9) Brookings.

Ott, David J., et al. Hysterosalpingography: A Text & Atlas. 2nd ed. LC 98-10427. (Illus.). 160p. 1998. 89.00 (0-683-30378-3) Lppncott W & W.

— Manual of Gastrointestinal Fluoroscopy: Performance of Procedures. (Illus.). 212p. (C). 1996. text 52.95 (0-398-06555-1) C C Thomas.

Ott, David J., jt. auth. see Meschan, Isadore.

Ott, Douglas E. & Wilderotter, Thomas J. A Designer's Guide to VHDL Synthesis. LC 94-20003. 336p. (C). 1994. reprint ed. text 121.50 (0-7923-9472-0) Kluwer Academic.

Ott, E. Revision der Sektion Chronopus Bge. der Gattung Astragalus. L. (Phanerogamarum Monographiae: No. 9). (Illus.). 1979. lib. bdg. 40.00 (3-7682-1187-8) Lubrecht & Cramer.

Ott, E. Stanley. The Joy of Discipling: Friend with Friend, Heart with Heart. 144p. 1989. pap. 5.99 (0-310-24821-3) Zondervan.

— Small Group Life: A Guide for Members & Leaders. 40p. 1994. pap. 2.50 (1-885121-04-0) CTS Press.

— Vision for a Vital Church: Shaping Ministry for Today's Church. 40p. 1994. pap. 2.50 (1-885121-01-6) CTS Press.

Ott, Edgar A. & Sharp, Daniel C. Horse Enterprise Management. 1999. 45.00 (0-8493-8759-0) CRC Pr.

Ott, Edward. Chaos in Dynamical Systems. LC 93-9344. (Illus.). 397p. (C). 1993. pap. text 38.95 (0-521-43799-7) Cambridge U Pr.

Ott, Edward, et al, eds. Coping with Chaos: Analysis of Chaotic Data & the Exploitation of Chaotic Systems. 432p. 1994. 84.95 (0-471-02556-9) Wiley.

Ott, Ernst, jt. auth. see Lachner, Bert.

Ott, Franziska C. Cincinnati German Imprints: A Checklist. LC 92-15690. (New German-American Studies: Vol. 7). XXI, 378p. 1994. 58.95 (0-8204-1900-1) P Lang Pubng.

Ott, Frederick W. The Great German Films. LC 85-29068. (Illus.). 304p. (C). 1986. 24.94 (0-8065-0961-9, Citadel Pr) Carol Pub Group.

— Great German Films. 1991. pap. 15.95 (0-8065-1218-0, Citadel Pr) Carol Pub Group.

Ott, Gil. Public Domain. 84p. (Orig.). 1989. pap. 8.50 (0-937013-29-3) Potes Poets.

***Ott, Gil.** Traffic. LC 00-25915. 2000. write for info. (0-925904-31-7) Chax Pr.

Ott, Gil. Traffic. 24p. 1985. pap. 2.50 (0-935162-06-2) Singing Horse.

— Within Range: Poems. (Poetry Chapbooks). 28p. 1986. pap. 4.00 (0-930901-38-X) Burning Deck.

Ott, Gil, ed. see Brutus, Dennis.

Ott, H., jt. ed. see L'Hermite, P. L.

Ott, H., jt. ed. see Versino, B.

Ott, H. R., ed. Ten Years of Superconductivity, 1980-1990. LC 92-38477. (Perspectives in Condensed Matter Physics Ser.: Vol. 7). 328p. (C). 1993. text 188.00 (0-7923-2067-0) Kluwer Academic.

Ott, Henry W. Noise Reduction Techniques in Electronic Systems. 2nd ed. 448p. 1988. 94.95 (0-471-85068-3) Wiley.

Ott, Hermann, jt. auth. see Oberthhur, Sebastian.

Ott, J., ed. Models & Methods for the Genetic Analysis of Pedigree Data. (Journal: Reprint from Human Heredity Ser.: Vol. 42, No. 1, 1992). (Illus.). 92p. 1993. 39.25 (3-8055-5762-0) S Karger.

***Ott, J. & Lehner, T., eds.** Recent Advances in Genetic Epidemiology: Published in Honor of Professor Newton Morton's 70th Birthday. (Human Heredity Ser.: Vol. 50, No. 1). (Illus.). 90p. 2000. pap. 34.00 (3-8055-6984-X) S Karger.

***Ott, J. Bevan & Boerio-Goates, Juliana.** Chemical Thermodynamics: Advanced Applications. 260p. 2000. 79.95 (0-12-530985-6) Acad Pr.

— Chemical Thermodynamics: Principles & Applications. 360p. 2000. 79.95 (0-12-530990-2) Acad Pr.

***Ott, J. Steven.** Nonprofit Organizations: Their Leadership, Management & Functions. 2000. pap. 38.00 (0-8133-6787-5) Westview.

— Nonprofit Sector: An Overview. 600p. 2000. pap. 38.00 (0-8133-6785-9) Westview.

Ott, J. Steven, ed. Classic Readings in Organizational Behavior. 2nd ed. LC 95-18087. 519p. (C). 1995. pap. text 57.50 (0-534-50413-2) Harcourt.

Ott, Jack. Digital Mathematics, Infinity & Revival. (Illus.). 130p. (Orig.). 1988. pap. 7.95 (0-9621493-0-6) J Appleseed Pr.

Ott, Jackie, et al, eds. The Heritage of Bibb County, Alabama. LC 98-70287. (Heritage of Alabama Ser.: No. 4). (Illus.). 240p. 1998. 55.00 (1-891647-08-3) Herit Pub Consult.

Ott, James & Neidl, Raymond E. Airline Odyssey: The Airline Industry's Turbulent Flight into the Future. (Illus.). 269p. 1998. reprint ed. lib. bdg. 34.95 (0-7351-0030-6) Replica Bks.

***Ott, Jeff.** My World: Ramblings of an Aging Gutter Punk. 2000. pap. 15.00 (0-9677287-0-3) Sub City.

Ott, Johann, jt. ed. see Eitner, Robert.

Ott, John. M. D. Geist Data Album 1. (Illus.). 96p. 1996. pap. 9.95 (1-56219-903-X, CMX 0601) Central Pk Media.

Ott, John N. Health & Light. 232p. 1990. pap. 10.95 (0-89804-098-1) Ariel GA.

— Health & Light. (Illus.). 225p. 1988. 12.95 (0-8159-5703-3) Devin.

— Light, Radiation & You: How to Stay Healthy. LC 81-69951. (Illus.). 175p. 1990. pap. 11.95 (0-8159-6121-9) Devin.

— My Ivory Cellar. (Illus.). 12.95 (0-8159-6217-7) Devin.

Ott, John S. Not As Long but Just As Wide: The Story of Tacoma's Municipal Belt Line Railway. 300p. (Orig.). 1996. pap. write for info. (0-9637684-2-5) Tacoma Pub Util.

Ott, John S. & Malloy, Dick. The Tacoma Public Utilities Story: The First 100 Years. LC 93-60904. (Illus.). 300p. 1993. 30.00 (0-9637684-0-9); pap. 20.00 (0-9637684-1-7) Tacoma Pub Util.

Ott, Jonathan. The Age of Entheogens & the Angels' Dictionary. (Illus.). 160p. (Orig.). 1995. 36.00 (0-9614234-6-3); pap. 18.00 (0-9614234-7-1) Natural Prod.

— Ayahuasca Analogues - Pangaean Entheogens. 128p. 1994. 24.00 (0-9614234-4-7) Natural Prod.

— Ayahuasca Analogues - Pangaean Entheogens. deluxe limited ed. 128p. 1994. boxed set 60.00 (0-614-00875-1) Natural Prod.

— The Cacahuatl Eater: Ruminations of an Unabashed Chocolate Addict. (Illus.). 128p. (Orig.). 1985. 20.00 (0-9614234-0-4); pap. 10.00 (0-9614234-1-2) Natural Prod.

— Pharmacophilia: or The Natural Paradises. LC 98-163754. (Illus.). 192p. 1997. 36.00 (*1-888755-00-8*); pap. 18.00 (*1-888755-01-6*) Natural Prod.

— Pharmacotheon - Entheogenic Drugs, Their Plant Sources & History. 640p. 1993. 70.00 (*0-9614234-2-0*) Natural Prod.

Ott, Jonathan & Hofmann, Albert. Pharmacotheon: Entheogenic Drugs, Their Plant Sources & History. rev. ed. 640p. 1997. pap. 40.00 (*0-9614234-9-8*); boxed set 100.00 (*0-9614234-8-X*) Natural Prod.

Ott, Jurg. Analysis of Human Genetic Linkage. 2nd rev. ed. LC 91-7048. (Series in Contemporary Medicine & Public Health). (Illus.). 320p. 1991. text 47.50 (*0-8018-4257-3*) Johns Hopkins.

— Analysis of Human Genetic Linkage. 3rd ed. LC 98-37347. 1999. 55.00 (*0-8018-6140-3*) Johns Hopkins.

Ott, Jurg, jt. auth. see Terwilliger, Joseph D.

Ott, Karl O. & Spnrad, Bernard I., eds. Nuclear Energy: A Sensible Alternative. 408p. 1985. 49.50 (*0-306-41441-4*, Plenum Trade) Perseus Pubng.

Ott, Karl O., jt. auth. see Bezella, Winfred A.

Ott, Karl Otto & Neuhold, Roberty J. Introductory Nuclear Reactor Dynamics. 362p. 1985. 47.00 (*0-89448-029-4*, 350011) Am Nuclear Soc.

Ott, Katarina, jt. ed. see Feige, Edgar L.

Ott, Katherine. Fevered Lives: Tuberculosis in American Culture since 1870. (Illus.). 256p. 1996. 27.95 (*0-674-29910-8*) HUP.

***Ott, Katherine.** Fevered Lives: Tuberculosis in American Culture since 1870. 1999. pap. text 16.95 (*0-674-29911-6*) HUP.

Ott, Leonard. Orchestration & Orchestral Style of Major Symphonic Works: Analytical Perspectives. LC 97-25667. (Studies in the History & Interpretation of Music). 344p. 1997. 99.95 (*0-7734-8601-1*) E Mellen.

Ott, Linda M., jt. auth. see Rauscher, Tomlinson G.

Ott, Longnecker. An Introduction to Statistical Methods & Data Analysis. 5th ed. (Statistics Ser.). 2000. pap. text, student ed. write for info. (*0-534-37123-X*) Brooks-Cole.

Ott, Ludwig. Fundamentals of Catholic Dogma. Bastible, James C., ed. Lynch, Patrick, tr. from GER. Orig. Title: Grundriss der Katholischen Dogmatik. 1994. reprint ed. pap. 21.00 (*0-89555-009-1*) TAN Bks Pubs.

Ott, Lyman, et al. Statistics: A Tool for the Social Sciences. 3rd ed. 512p. (C). 1983. pap. 28.75 (*0-87150-400-6*, 6084) PWS Pubs.

Ott, Lyman, jt. auth. see Mendenhall, William.

Ott, Lyman R. An Introduction to Statistical Methods & Data Analysis. 4th ed. (Statistics Ser.). 1993. pap., student ed. 20.95 (*0-534-93266-5*) Wadsworth Pub.

Ott, Margaret V., jt. auth. see Swanson, Gloria M.

Ott, Martin. Misery Loves. 32p. (Orig.). 1994. pap. 4.00 (*1-881168-49-2*) Red Danceflr.

Ott, N. & Sinn, Hans-Werner. Intrafamily Bargaining & Household Decisions. Guth, Wilfried et al, eds. (Microeconomic Studies). (Illus.). viii, 242p. 1992. 82.95 (*0-387-55061-5*) Spr-Verlag.

Ott, N. & Wagner, G. G., eds. Income Inequality & Poverty in Eastern & Western Europe. LC 97-151932. (Contributions to Economics Ser.). (Illus.). x, 253p. 1996. pap. 71.00 (*3-7908-0974-8*) Spr-Verlag.

***Ott, Pamela.** Dancing 'Round the World: Song-Stretching Activities for Children's Favorite Tunes. (Illus.). 96p. 1999. pap. 14.95 (*0-7619-7549-7*) Corwin Pr.

— Father's Whiskers: Song-Stretching Activities for Children's Favorite Tunes. (Illus.). 96p. 1999. pap. 14.95 (*0-7619-7550-0*) Corwin Pr.

— Happy Tunes & More! Song-Stretching Activities for Children's Favorite Tunes. (Illus.). 96p. 1999. pap. 14.95 (*0-7619-7547-0*) Corwin Pr.

— Hushhh-- 54 More Activities for Quiet Times & Rainy Days. LC 00-29045. (Teaching Tunes Ser.). 2000. pap. write for info. (*0-7619-7661-2*) Corwin Pr.

— Laugh a Lot! Song-Stretching Activities for Children's Favorite Tunes. (Illus.). 96p. 1999. pap. 14.95 (*0-7619-7546-2*) Corwin Pr.

— Peek-a-Boogie: Song-Stretching Activities for Children's Favorite Tunes. (Illus.). 96p. 1999. pap. 14.95 (*0-7619-7543-8*) Corwin Pr.

— Shhh. . . Song-Stretching Activities for Children's Favorite Tunes. (Illus.). 96p. 1999. pap. 14.95 (*0-7619-7544-6*) Corwin Pr.

— Teaching Tune Kit: Song-Stretching Activities for Children's Favorite Tunes, 8 vols. (Illus.). 999p. 1999. 109.95 (*0-7619-7551-9*) Corwin Pr.

— The Three B's: Boogie & Rock to Beethoven, Brahams & Bach. (Illus.). 96p. 1999. pap. 14.95 (*0-7619-7548-9*) Corwin Pr.

— Waddley Ah Cha: Song-Stretching Activities for Children's Favorite Tunes. (Illus.). 96p. 1999. pap. 14.95 (*0-7619-7545-4*) Corwin Pr.

Ott, Peggy J., et al, eds. Sourcebook on Substance Abuse: Etiology, Epidemiology, Assessment, & Treatment. LC 98-35240. 472p. 1999. 79.50 (*0-205-19802-3*) Allyn.

Ott, R. Lyman. Intro To Stat Methods & Data Analysis. 3rd ed. (Statistics). 912p. (C). 1988. pap. 47.50 (*0-534-91926-X*) Wadsworth Pub.

— An Introduction to Statistical Methods & Data Analysis. 2nd ed. LC 92-31934. (C). 1984. pap. 33.75 (*0-87150-473-1*) PWS Pubs.

— An Introduction to Statistical Methods & Data Analysis 4th ed. LC 92-31934. 1051p. 1998. pap. 72.95 (*0-534-93150-2*) Wadsworth Pub.

Ott, R. Lyman & Mendenhall, William. Understanding Statistics. 5th ed. (Statistics). 608p. (C). 1990. pap. 49.25 (*0-534-92154-X*) Wadsworth Pub.

Ott, R. Lyman, et al. Statistics: A Tool for the Social Sciences. 5th ed. 634p. (C). 1992. pap. 54.25 (*0-534-92931-1*) Wadsworth Pub.

Ott, R. Lyman, jt. auth. see Hildebrand, David K.

Ott, R. Lyman, jt. auth. see Mendenhall, William.

Ott, Richard. Creating Demand: Powerful Tips & Tactics for Marketing Your Product or Service. 250p. 1991. text 30.00 (*1-55623-560-7*, Irwn Prfssnl) McGraw-Hill Prof.

— Oriental Design Stained Glass Pattern Book. 64p. 1986. pap. 4.95 (*0-486-25229-9*) Dover.

— Unleashing Your Productivity: Secrets of Getting Things Done. 1995. 16.00 incl. audio (*0-671-52976-5*) S&S Trade.

Ott, Richard, et al, eds. Managed Care & the Cardiac Patient. LC 94-40714. (Illus.). 334p. 1995. text 54.00 (*1-56053-122-3*) Hanley & Belfus.

***Ott, Rick.** Creating Demand: Move the Masses to Buy Your Product, Service, or Idea. rev. ed. (Illus.). 258p. 1999. pap. 22.00 (*0-9663491-1-3*) Ocean View.

Ott, Riki. Alaska's Copper River Delta. LC 98-25746. (Illus.). 144p. 1998. pap. 29.95 (*0-295-97743-4*) U of Wash Pr.

Ott, Robert W. & Hurwitz, Al, eds. Art in Education: An International Perspective. LC 83-43226. (Illus.). 336p. 1984. 35.00 (*0-271-00372-3*) Pa St U Pr.

Ott, Sandra. The Circle of Mountains: A Basque Shepherding Community. (Illus.). 254p. 1981. text 55.00 (*0-19-823199-7*) OUP.

— The Circle of Mountains: A Basque Shepherding Community. LC 93-13842. (Basque Ser.). (Illus.). 272p. 1993. pap. text 12.95 (*0-87417-224-1*) U of Nev Pr.

Ott, Thomas O. The Haitian Revolution, 1789-1804. LC 72-85085. (Illus.). 246p. 1973. pap. 16.95 (*0-87049-545-3*) U of Tenn Pr.

Ott, Ulrich. Die Kunst Des Gegensatzes in Theokrits Hirtengedichten. x, 231p. 1969. write for info. (*0-318-70993-7*) G Olms Pubs.

Ott, Wayne R. Environmental Statistics & Data Analysis. 336p. 1994. lib. bdg. 85.00 (*0-87371-848-8*, L848) Lewis Pubs.

Ott, Wendell L., frwd. Director's Invitational, September 16-November 6, 1988. (Illus.). 14p. (Orig.). 1988. pap. 2.00 (*0-924335-06-8*) Tacoma Art Mus.

Ott, William H. California College Review. 80p. (C). 1994. 7.95 (*0-8403-9217-6*) Kendall-Hunt.

Ottanelli, Fraser M. The Communist Party of the United States from the Depression to World War II. LC 90-34391. 300p. (C). 1991. text 45.00 (*0-8135-1612-9*) Rutgers U Pr.

Ottar, Brynjulf, jt. ed. see Pacyna, Jozef M.

Ottariano, Steven G. Medicinal Herbal Therapy: A Pharmacist's View Point. LC 98-22339. (Illus.). 192p. 1999. pap. 14.95 (*0-9637077-6-0*) Nicolin Flds.

Ottati, Douglas F. Hopeful Realism: Reclaiming the Poetry of Theology. LC 98-37473. 144p. 1999. pap. 14.95 (*0-8298-1322-5*) Pilgrim OH.

— Jesus Christ & Christian Vision. 192p. 1996. pap. 19.95 (*0-664-25662-7*) Westminster John Knox.

— Reforming Protestantism: Christian Commitment in Today's World. LC 95-10454. 192p. (Orig.). 1995. pap. 22.95 (*0-664-25604-X*) Westminster John Knox.

Ottaviani, Alfredo C. Duties of the Catholic State in Regard to Religion. Fahey, Denis, tr. from ITA. & frwd. by. 26p. 1993. reprint ed. pap. 5.45 (*0-935952-89-6*) Angelus Pr.

Ottaviani, Alfredo C. & Bacci, Antonio C. The Ottaviani Intervention: Short Critical Study of the New Order of Mass. Cekada, Anthony, tr. LC 92-60956. 63p. (Orig.). 1992. pap. 7.00 (*0-89555-470-4*) TAN Bks Pubs.

Ottaviani, G., ed. Financial Risk in Insurance. LC 94-46824. 1997. 95.00 (*0-387-57054-3*) Spr-Verlag.

***Ottaviani, G., ed.** Financial Risk in Insurance. LC 99-45871. (Illus.). xii, 112p. 1999. pap. 42.00 (*3-540-66143-3*) Spr-Verlag.

Ottaviani, G., jt. ed. see Matacotta, F. C.

Ottaviani, Jim. Dignifying Science: Stories about Women Scientists. (Illus.). 142p. 2000. pap. 16.95 (*0-9660106-1-2*, Pub. by G T Labs) Koen Bk Distributors.

— Two-Fisted Science. (Illus.). 128p. 1997. pap. 10.00 (*0-9660106-0-4*) G T Labs.

Ottaviani, Maurizio, jt. auth. see Maino, Giuseppe.

Ottavianni, Aldo & Fanale, Lawrence. The Magic of Chef Aldo: His "True Taste of Italy" Favorites. (Illus.). 94p. (Orig.). 1996. pap. 21.95 (*0-9629299-1-3*) B A Perry & Assocs.

Ottaviano, E., et al, eds. Angiosperm Pollen & Ovules. LC 92-1605. (Illus.). xxvi, 465p. 1992. 128.00 (*0-387-97888-7*) Spr-Verlag.

Ottaviano, Victor B. National Mechanical Estimator. 23rd ed. LC 93-17560. 1993. write for info. (*0-88173-186-2*) Fairmont Pr.

— National Mechanical Estimator. 23rd ed. 1993. pap. 85.00 (*1-878656-04-X*) Ottaviano Tech Serv.

— National Mechanical Estimator. 24th ed. LC 95-37046. 950p. 1995. 98.50 (*0-88173-235-4*) Fairmont Pr.

— National Mechanical Estimator. 24th ed. (Illus.). 850p. 1995. pap. 95.00 (*1-878656-05-8*) Ottaviano Tech Serv.

— National Plumbing Estimator. 8th ed. (Illus.). 792p. 1992. pap. 85.00 (*1-878656-01-5*) Ottaviano Tech Serv.

Ottaway. The Technology of Vitamins in Food. 1994. text 99.95 (*0-442-30864-7*, VNR) Wiley.

Ottaway, Barbara, ed. Archaeology, Dendrochronology & the Radiocarbon Calibration Curve. (Illus.). 100p. 1993. pap. 14.00 (*0-614-21826-8*) David Brown.

Ottaway, C. W., ed. see Stubbs, George.

Ottaway, David B. & Ottaway, Marina. Afrocommunism. 2nd ed. (Illus.). 280p. (C). 1986. pap. text 20.00 (*0-8419-1035-9*) Holmes & Meier.

— Afrocommunism. 2nd ed. (Illus.). 280p. (C). 1986. text 39.50 (*0-8419-1034-0*) Holmes & Meier.

— Ethiopia: Empire in Revolution. LC 77-28370. (Illus.). 250p. 1978. 39.95 (*0-8419-0362-X*, Africana) Holmes & Meier.

Ottaway, Hugh. Mozart. LC 79-91954. (Illus.). 208p. reprint ed. pap. 64.50 (*0-7837-3642-8*, 204351000009) Bks Demand.

Ottaway, J. H. Regulation of Enzyme Activity: In Focus. (In Focus Ser.). (Illus.). 100p. 1988. pap. text 17.95 (*1-85221-072-9*) OUP.

Ottaway, John R., jt. auth. see Baer, Charles J.

Ottaway, Marina. Africa's New Leaders: Democracy or State Reconstruction? LC 98-55067. vi, 138 p. 1999. pap. 10.95 (*0-87003-134-1*) Carnegie Endow.

— Democratization & Ethnic Nationalism: African & Eastern European Experiences. LC 94-36131. (Policy Essay Ser.: Vol. 14). 1994. pap. 13.95 (*1-56517-019-9*) Overseas Dev Council.

— South Africa: The Struggle for a New Order. 1993. 36.95 (*0-8157-6716-1*); pap. 16.95 (*0-8157-6715-3*) Brookings.

Ottaway, Marina, ed. Democracy in Africa: The Hard Road Ahead. LC 96-39895. (Sais African Studies Library). 1997. 45.00 (*1-55587-312-X*) L Rienner.

— The Political Economy of Ethiopia. LC 89-77108. (SAIS Studies of Africa). 264p. 1990. 59.95 (*0-275-93472-1*, C3472, Greenwood Pr) Greenwood.

Ottaway, Marina, jt. auth. see Ottaway, David B.

Ottaway, Mark. The Most Beautiful Villages of Greece. LC 97-61611. (Illus.). 224p. 1998. 40.00 (*0-500-01834-0*, Pub. by Thames Hudson) Norton.

Ottaway, P. Berry. The Technology of Vitamins in Food. 280p. 1993. 155.00 (*0-8342-1681-7*) Aspen Pub.

Ottaway, Richard N. Change Agents at Work, 27. LC 79-24. (Contributions in Economics & Economic History Ser.: No. 27). 169p. 1979. 55.00 (*0-313-21252-X*, OCA/, Greenwood Pr) Greenwood.

Ottaway, Susan. Dambuster: A Life of Guy Gibson, VC, DSO*, DFC* (Illus.). 208p. 1996. pap. 16.95 (*0-85052-503-9*, Pub. by Leo Cooper) Trans-Atl Phila.

Ottchen, Cynthia J. & Hill, Wayne F. Shakespeare's Love Kit: Create Your Own Shakespearean Love Rhymes. 436p. 1995. boxed set 19.95 (*0-9518684-5-4*) MainSail Pr.

— Shakespeare's Seduction Kit: Unveil Your Powers of Attraction. 450p. Date not set. boxed set 19.95 (*0-9518684-7-0*) MainSail Pr.

— Shakespeare's Sex Kit: Unleash Your Powers of Seduction. 450p. 1998. boxed set 19.95 (*0-9518684-6-2*) MainSail Pr.

— Williams Wit Kit: Create Your Own Shakespearean Insults. 416p. 1995. boxed set 19.95 (*0-9518684-4-6*) MainSail Pr.

Ottchen, Cynthia J., jt. auth. see Hill, Wayne F.

Otte. Rising Middle Power. LC 99-55259. 1999. text 49.95 (*0-312-22653-5*) St Martin.

Otte, Alfred. The HG Panzer Division. LC 89-63360. (Illus.). 176p. 1989. 24.95 (*0-88740-206-2*) Schiffer.

Otte, Arie P., jt. ed. see Van Driel, Roel.

Otte, Beate C. Zeit in der Spannung von Werden und Handeln Bei Victor Emil Freiherr V. Gebsattel: Zur Psychologischen und Ethischen Bedeutung von Zeit. (Europaische Hochschulschriften Ser.: Reihe 23, Bd. 574). (GER.). 234p. 1996. 44.95 (*3-631-30214-2*) P Lang Pubng.

Otte, Daniel. The Crickets of Hawaii: Origin, Systematics & Evolution. (Publications on Orthopteran Diversity). (Illus.). 396p. (Orig.). 1994. pap. text 75.00 (*0-9640101-0-0*) Orthopterists.

— The North American Grasshoppers: Acrididae - Gomphocerinae & Acridinae, Vol. 1. (Illus.). 304p. (C). 1981. 86.95 (*0-674-62660-5*) HUP.

— The North American Grasshoppers: Acrididae, Oedipodinae, Vol. 2. (Illus.). 352p. 1985. 88.95 (*0-674-62661-3*) HUP.

— Orthoptera Species File No. 1: Crickets (Grylloidea) 120p. (Orig.). 1994. pap. 55.00 (*0-9640101-2-7*) Orthopterists.

— Orthoptera Species File No. 2: Grasshoppers (Acridomorpha) A. 162p. (Orig.). 1994. pap. 35.00 (*0-9640101-3-5*) Orthopterists.

— Orthoptera Species File No. 3: Grasshoppers (Acridomorpha) B. 241p. (Orig.). 1994. pap. 45.00 (*0-9640101-4-3*) Orthopterists.

— Orthoptera Species File No. 4: Grasshoppers (Acridomorpha) C. 518p. (Orig.). 1995. pap. 65.00 (*0-9640101-5-1*) Orthopterists.

— Orthoptera Species File No. 5: Grasshoppers (Acridomorpha) D. 630p. (Orig.). 1995. pap. 65.00 (*0-9640101-6-X*) Orthopterists.

— Orthoptera Species File No. 6: Tetrigoidea & Tridactyloidea: (Orthoptera: Caelifera) & Addenda to OSF Vols. 1-5. 261p. 1997. pap. 25.00 (*0-9640101-7-8*) Orthopterists.

— Orthoptera Species File No. 7: Tettigonioidea. 373p. 1997. pap. 50.00 (*0-9640101-8-6*) Orthopterists.

— Orthoptera Species File Series, Set, Nos. 1-5. (Illus.). (Orig.). 1995. pap. text 265.00 (*0-9640101-1-9*) Orthopterists.

Otte, Daniel & Alexander, Richard D. The Australian Crickets (Orthoptera: Gryllidae) (Monograph: No. 22). (Illus.). 477p. 1983. lib. bdg. 20.00 (*0-910006-52-0*) Acad Nat Sci Phila.

— The Australian Crickets (Orthoptera: Gryllidae) (Monograph: No. 22). (Illus.). 477p. 1983. pap. 15.00 (*0-910006-30-X*) Acad Nat Sci Phila.

Otte, E., jt. auth. see Lockhart, James.

Otte, E. C., tr. see Von Humboldt, Alexander.

Otte, Elmer. I Remember the Day of My Hanging: A Collection of Poems. 72p. 1995. write for info. (*0-9648628-3-2*) Folklore Hse.

— I Remember the Day of My Hanging: A Collection of 66 Poems. LC 95-90763. 72p. 1995. pap. write for info. (*0-9648628-0-8*) Folklore Hse.

— Stuff I Remember: I Saw It, I Heard It, I Lived It. 128p. 1995. write for info. (*0-9648628-5-9*) Folklore Hse.

— Wise & Otherwise: Fables, Myths, Fairy Tales & Other Jolly Nonsense. 72p. 1995. write for info. (*0-9648628-4-0*); pap. write for info. (*0-9648628-1-6*) Folklore Hse.

Otte, Enrique. Cartas Privadas de Emigrantes a Indias, 1540-1616 (Private Letters from Immigrants to the Indies, 1540-1616) (SPA.). 611p. 1988. pap. 20.99 (*968-16-3975-8*, Pub. by Fondo) Continental Bk.

Otte, George & Palumbo, Linda J. Casts of Thought. 530p. (C). 1989. pap. text 29.00 (*0-02-389961-1*, Macmillan Coll) P-H.

— Casts of Thought: Writing in & Against Tradition. (C). 1989. pap., teacher ed. write for info. (*0-02-389962-X*, U5247-4) Allyn.

Otte, George, jt. auth. see Mason, Nondita.

Otte, Heinrich. Archaologisches Worterbuch Zur Erklarung der in Den Schriften Uber Christliche Kunstalterthumer Vorkommenden Kunstausdrucke. viii, 488p. 1978. reprint ed. write for info. (*3-487-06455-3*) G Olms Pubs.

Otte, Henry M., ed. see Southern Metals/Materials Conference on Advances i.

Otte, James K., jt. auth. see Alfred.

***Otte, Jean-Pierre.** Love in the Garden. Black, Moishe & Green, Maria, trs. 2000. 20.00 (*0-8076-1467-X*) Braziller.

Otte, Linda, ed. see King, Robert L.

Otte, M., jt. ed. see Jahnke, H. N.

***Otte, Marc.** Hide & Seek: On the Trail with Orrin Porter Rockwell. LC 99-69007. (Illus.). 176p. 1999. pap. 12.95 (*1-888125-53-5*) Publ Consult.

Otte, Marc. Pray for Justice: On the Trail with Ornin Porter Rockwell. LC 97-69007. (Illus.). 172p. 1997. pap. 12.95 (*1-888125-19-5*) Publ Consult.

Otte, Miriam. Marketing with Speeches & Seminars: Your Key to More Clients & Referrals. LC 98-96086. ix, 200p. 1998. pap. 16.95 (*0-9663131-0-0*) Zest Pr.

Otte, Peter. Cyberia: The Official Strategy Guide. 1995. pap. 19.95 (*1-55958-795-4*) Prima Pub.

— Cyberia No. 2: Resurrection: The Official Strategy Guide. 1996. pap. 19.99 (*0-7615-0411-7*) Prima Pub.

Otte, Randy, et al. Understanding CORBA: The Common Object Request Broker Architecture. LC 95-37455. 288p. (C). 1995. pap. 55.00 (*0-13-459884-9*) P-H.

Otte, Rob. Low-Power Wireless Optical Transmission: Systems for Communications, Telemetry & Control. (Illus.). 167p. 1998. pap. 44.50 (*90-407-1609-9*, Pub. by Delft U Pr) Coronet Bks.

***Otte, Rob, et al.** Low-Power Wireless Infrared Communications. LC 99-45811. 1999. text 105.00 (*0-7923-8643-4*) Kluwer Academic.

***Otte, Ronald K.** Checkbook 9-1-1: Emergency Help for Your Checkbook. (Illus.). 52p. 1999. pap. 6.50 (*0-615-11243-9*) R K Otte.

Otte, Steven W. Trinity Field Report: Oceania. (Trinity Ser.). (Illus.). 24p. 1999. pap. 4.95 (*1-56504-606-4*, 9205) White Wolf.

Otte, Thomas G. & Pagedas, C., eds. Personalities, War & Diplomacy: Essays on International History. LC 97-16760. 291p. 1997. 59.95 (*0-7146-4818-3*, Pub. by F Cass Pubs) Intl Spec Bk.

Otte, Thomas G., jt. auth. see Dorman, Andrew M.

***Otte, Tina.** The Illustrated Guide to Pregnancy & Birth. (Illus.). 160p. 2000. pap. 16.95 (*0-7373-0413-8*, 04138W, Pub. by Lowell Hse) NTC Contemp Pub Co.

Ottemoeller, Sylvia, ed. see Barbasiewicz, Robert.

Otten, jt. ed. see Lane.

***Otten, Alan L.** The Health Sector & Y2K: The Status of Preparation in the New York - New Jersey - Connecticut Metropolitan Area. 28p. 1999. pap. write for info. (*1-887748-31-8*) Milbank Memorial.

Otten, Alan L. Mental Health Parity: What Can It Accomplish in a Market Dominated by Managed Care? (Illus.). 44p. 1998. pap. write for info. (*1-887748-21-0*) Milbank Memorial.

Otten, Almar, et al. In Situ Soil Remediation. LC 97-29156. (Soil & Environment Ser.: No. 6). 120p. 1997. text 84.00 (*0-7923-4635-1*) Kluwer Academic.

Otten, Anna, ed. Mensch und Zeit: An Anthology of German Radio Plays. LC 66-19203. (GER., Illus.). 1966. pap. 1.00 (*0-89197-301-X*); pap. text 8.95 (*0-89197-300-1*) Irvington.

Otten, Carol C. Cross Roads. (Our Town Ser.). 288p. 1996. mass mkt. 5.99 (*0-515 11985-7*, Jove) Berkley Pub.

— Dream Weaver. 304p. 1997. mass mkt. 5.99 (*0-515-12141-X*, Jove) Berkley Pub.

— Pieces of Yesterday. 1999. mass mkt. 5.99 (*0-515-12524-5*, Jove) Berkley Pub.

Otten, Catherine. The Corner Grocery Store. (Illus.). 148p. (Orig.). 1980. pap. 4.95 (*0-937816-02-7*) Tech Data.

Otten, Charlotte. January Rides the Wind: A Book of Months. LC 92-44159. (Illus.). 32p. (J). (ps-3). 1997. 16.00 (*0-688-12556-5*); lib. bdg. 15.93 (*0-688-12557-3*) Lothrop.

Otten, Charlotte F. Environ'd with Eternity: God, Poems, & Plants in Sixteenth & Seventeenth Century England. (Illus.). 200p. 1984. 25.00 (*0-87291-168-3*) Coronado Pr.

— A Lycanthropy Reader: Werewolves in Western Culture. LC 86-14443. (Illus.). 357p. 1986. reprint ed. pap. 110.70 (*0-608-06965-5*, 206717300009) Bks Demand.

Otten, Charlotte F., ed. English Women's Voices, 1540-1700. 448p. (C). 1991. 49.95 (*0-8130-1083-7*); pap. 24.95 (*0-8130-1099-3*) U Press Fla.

— A Lycanthropy Reader: Werewolves in Western Culture. (Illus.). 352p. 1986. pap. text 24.95 (*0-8156-2384-4*) Syracuse U Pr.

Otten, Charlotte F. & Schmidt, Gary D., eds. The Voice of the Narrator in Children's Literature: Insights from Writers & Critics, 28. LC 88-7709. (Contributions to the Study of World Literature Ser.). 432p. 1989. 65.00 (*0-313-26370-1*, OVN) Greenwood.

Otten, D., jt. auth. see Karpe, H. J.

Otten, E. W. Investigation of Short-Lived Isotopes by Laser Spectroscopy. Letokhov, V. S., ed. (Laser Science & Technology Ser.: Vol. 5). viii, 76p. 1989. pap. text 85.00 (*3-7186-4892-X*) Gordon & Breach.

Otten, Fred W. The Humorous World of Animals & Insects. LC 97-67439. 1997. mass mkt., per. 10.95 (*1-889131-14-8*) CasAnanda.

Otten, G., jt. ed. see Lane, R. W.

Otten, George A. Van, see Lew, Alan A. & Van Otten, George A., eds.

Otten, Gerard A., jt. auth. see Cannan, Stephen J.

Otten, Lambert, jt. ed. see Fayed, Mohammed E.

Otten, Laura A. Women & the Law. (Contemporary Legal Issues Ser.). 1998. lib. bdg. 39.50 (*0-87436-878-2*) ABC-CLIO.

— Women's Rights & the Law. LC 93-20127. 264p. 1993. 69.50 (*0-275-93184-6*, C3184, Praeger Pubs); pap. 19.95 (*0-275-93185-4*, B3185, Praeger Pubs) Greenwood.

Otten, Leaun G. & Caldwell, C. Max. Sacred Truths of the Doctrine & Covenants, Vol. 1. LC 82-71971. xi, 355p. 1993. 19.95 (*0-87579-783-0*) Deseret Bk.

— Sacred Truths of the Doctrine & Covenants, Vol. 2. LC 82-71791. xii, 412p. 1993. 19.95 (*0-87579-784-9*) Deseret Bk.

Otten, Linda. Curriculum for Personal & Social Education. (Resource Materials for Teachers Ser.). 1999. pap. 27.95 (*1-85346-596-8*) David Fulton.

Otten, Mariel. Transmigrasi - Indonesian Resettlement Policy, 1965-1985: Myths & Realities. (IWGIA Document Ser.: No. 57). (Illus.). 254p. (Orig.). 1986. pap. text 49.00 (*0-317-65617-1*) Coronet Bks.

Otten, R. H. & Van Ginneken, L. P. The Annealing Algorithm. (International Series in Engineering & Computer Science, VLSI, Computer Architecture, & Digital Screen Processing). 224p. (C). 1989. text 121.00 (*0-7923-9022-9*) Kluwer Academic.

Otten, Willemien. The Anthropology of Johannes Scottus Eriugena. LC 90-42391. (Brill's Studies in Intellectual History: Vol. 20). viii, 242p. 1990. 71.00 (*90-04-09302-8*) Brill Academic Pubs.

Otten, Willemien, jt. ed. see McGinn, Bernard.

Otten, William L., Jr. Colonel J. F. Hamtramck - His Life & Times, 1756-1783: Captain of the Revolution, 2 vols., Vol. 1. LC 97-91610. (Illus.). 400p. (Orig.). 1997. pap. 23.95 (*0-9657423-0-X*) W L Otten.
COLONEL J. F. HAMTRAMCK - VOLUME 1: CAPTAIN OF THE REVOLUTION. Hamtramck, truly a forgotten hero of American history, was a career officer in the post-Revolutionary army. A major player in the Indian battles of 1790, 1791 & 1794, he was the first American commander at Vincennes, Fort Wayne & Detroit & second in command of the army when he died in 1803. Vol. 1 chronicles his early military career through 1783, which prepared him for leadership on the western frontier. Born in Quebec, he joined the Continental Army during the Canadian invasion (1775); was promoted to captain & caught at the Cedars (1776); fought with the 5th New York Regiment at the Highlands (1777); & Sullivan-Clinton Expedition against the Iroquois (1779). Retained in the 2nd New York Regiment after reorganization he served in Lafayette's Light Infantry at Yorktown during the assault of Redoubt 10. Priced at $23.95 order should be sent to Otten Publishing, P.O. Box 1488, Port Aransas, TX 78373. Phone: 361-749-5855. (PA)
Publisher Paid Annotation.

O

Ottenbacher, Kenneth J. & Short-DeGraff, Margaret A., eds. Collaborative Research in Developmental Therapy: A Model with Studies of Learning Disabled Children. LC 86-11978. 157p. 1986. text 49.95 (*0-86656-570-1*) Haworth Pr.

Ottenbacher, Kenneth J. & Short, Margaret A., eds. Vestibular Processing Dysfunction in Children. LC 85-8636. (Physical & Occupational Therapy in Pediatrics Ser.: Vol. 5, Nos. 2 & 3). 152p. 1985. text 49.95 (*0-86656-431-4*) Haworth Pr.

— Vestibular Processing Dysfunction in Children. LC 85-8636. (Physical & Occupational Therapy in Pediatrics Ser.: Vol. 5, Nos. 2 & 3). 152p. 1985. pap. text 14.95 (*0-86656-432-2*) Haworth Pr.

Ottenberg, Hans-Gunter. C. P. E. Bach. Whitmore, Philip J., tr. (Illus.). 296p. 1988. 85.00 (*0-19-315246-0*) OUP.

Ottenberg, June C. Opera Odyssey: Toward History of Opera in Nineteenth Century America, 32. LC 93-35861. (Contributions to the Study of Music & Dance Ser.: No. 32). 224p. 1994. 57.95 (*0-313-27841-5*, Greenwood Pr) Greenwood.

Ottenberg, Simon. Boyhood Rituals in an African Society: An Interpretation. LC 87-21701. (Illus.). 368p. 1989. pap. 30.00 (*0-295-96575-4*) U of Wash Pr.

— Double Descent in an African Society. LC 84-45540. (American Ethnological Society Monographs: No. 47). 1988. reprint ed. 36.00 (*0-404-62945-8*) AMS Pr.

— New Traditions from Nigeria: Seven Artists of the Nsukka Group. LC 97-7666. 1997. text 49.95 (*1-56098-800-2*) Smithsonian.

— Seeing with Music: Three Blind. LC 95-49962. (Illus.). 232p. 1996. 35.00 (*0-295-97525-3*) U of Wash Pr.

Ottenbreit, Gerald E., Jr. A State of the Society Address: Selected Writings, Musings & Poetry of a Curmudgeon (Including Armenia & Kuwait) 113p. 1992. pap. 12.00 (*0-9634509-0-5*) Bookshelf Pubs.

Ottenbrite, Raphael M., ed. Frontiers in Biomedical Polymer Applications, 1. LC 97-62207. 325p. 1998. 169.95 (*1-56676-577-3*) Technomic.

— Polymeric Drugs & Drug Administration. LC 93-48086. (ACS Symposium Ser.: No. 545). 278p. 1994. text 78.00 (*0-8412-2744-6*, Pub. by Am Chemical) OUP.

Ottenbrite, Raphael M., et al, eds. Hydrogels & Biodegradable Polymers for Bioapplications. LC 96-33785. (ACS Symposium Ser.: No. 627). (Illus.). 280p. 1996. text 105.00 (*0-8412-3400-0*, Pub. by Am Chemical) OUP.

Ottenbrite, Raphael M. & Chiellini, Emo, eds. Polymers in Medicine: Biomedical & Pharmaceutical Applications. LC 92-60021. 265p. 1992. text 69.95 (*0-87762-929-3*) Technomic.

Ottenbrite, Raphael M., jt. ed. see Dunn, Richard L.

Ottenheimer. Dreams: Hidden Meanings & Secrets. 288p. 1983. pap. 11.00 (*0-671-76268-0*, Fireside) S&S Trade Pap.

***Ottenheimer, Fritz.** Escape & Return: Memories of Nazi Germany. LC 99-41302. (Illus.). 178p. 1999. pap. 14.95 (*1-887969-11-X*) Cathedral PA.

Ottenheimer, Harriet, jt. auth. see Ottenheimer, Martin.

Ottenheimer, Harriet J., jt. auth. see Joseph, Pleasant.

Ottenheimer, Laurence. Japan: Land of Samurai & Robots. LC 87-34524. (Illus.). 38p. (J). (gr. k-5). 1988. 5.95 (*0-944589-11-1*, 111) Young Discovery Lib.

— Livre de l'Automne. (Gallimard - Decouverte Cadet Ser.: No. 6). (FRE., Illus.). 90p. (J). (gr. 4-9). 1983. 8.95 (*2-07-039506-5*) Schoenhof.

— Livre de l'Ete. (Gallimard - Decouverte Cadet Ser.: No. 8). (FRE., Illus.). 88p. (J). (gr. 4-9). 1983. 15.95 (*2-07-039508-1*) Schoenhof.

— Livre de L'Hiver. (Gallimard - Decouverte Cadet Ser.: No. 5). (FRE., Illus.). 93p. (J). (gr. 4-9). 1983. 15.95 (*2-07-039505-7*) Schoenhof.

— Livre du Printemps. (Gallimard - Decouverte Cadet Ser.: No. 7). (FRE.). 96p. (J). (gr. 4-9). 1983. 15.95 (*2-07-039507-3*) Schoenhof.

Ottenheimer-Maquet, L. How Things Are Made. LC 97-27526. Orig. Title: What Are Things Made Of?. (Illus.). 80p. (J). (gr. 2-9). 1998. lib. bdg. 23.95 (*0-88682-955-0*, Creat Educ) Creative Co.

— World Agriculture. Gibson, Sarah et al, trs. LC 97-27524. Orig. Title: Our Food. (Illus.). 80p. (J). (gr. 2-9). 1998. lib. bdg. 23.95 (*0-88682-952-6*, Creat Educ) Creative Co.

Ottenheimer, Martin. Forbidden Relatives: The American Myth of Cousin Marriage. LC 95-41800. 192p. 1996. pap. text 14.95 (*0-252-06540-9*) U of Ill Pr.

— Marriage in Domoni: Husbands & Wives in an Indian Ocean Community. 106p. (C). 1994. reprint ed. pap. text 11.50 (*1-879215-23-3*) Sheffield WI.

Ottenheimer, Martin & Ottenheimer, Harriet. Historical Dictionary of Comoro Islands. LC 93-42244. (African Historical Dictionaries Ser.). 1994. 30.00 (*0-8108-2819-7*) Scarecrow.

Ottenheimer, Peter. Toy Autos, 1890-1939. Levy, Allen, ed. (Illus.). 168p. pap. 25.00 (*1-872727-61-1*, Pub. by New Cavendish) Pincushion Pr.

Ottenheimer Publishing Staff, Kelly. Baby's Bible Alphabet Board Book, 1. (Illus.). 24p. (J). 1998. bds. 9.99 (*0-8499-5903-9*) Tommy Nelson.

Ottenhoff, Tom & De Vries, Rene. Recognition of M. Leprae Antigens. (Development in Hematology & Immunology Ser.). (C). 1987. text 122.00 (*0-89838-887-2*) Kluwer Academic.

Ottenjann, R., jt. ed. see Maratka, Zdenek.

Ottens, Allen J. Coping with Academic Anxiety. rev. ed. (Coping Ser.). 140p. (YA). (gr. 7-12). 1991. lib. bdg. 17.95 (*0-8239-1337-6*) Rosen Group.

***Ottens, Allen J. & Hotelling, Kathy.** Sexual Violence on Campus: Policies, Programs & Perspectives for the 21st Century. LC 00-30140. (Family Violence Ser.). 2001. write for info. (*0-8261-1374-5*) Springer Pub.

Ottensmann, John R. & Neuenschwander, Jan. Working with Lotus Agenda. (Illus.). 256p. 1989. pap. 24.95 (*0-8306-3161-5*, 3161) McGraw-Hill Prof.

Ottensmeyer, Edward J. & McCarthy, Gerald D. Ethics in the Workplace. LC 95-82014. 512p. (C). 1996. pap. 50.00 (*0-07-048160-1*) McGraw.

Ottensmeyer, Edward J., jt. ed. see McGowan, Robert.

Ottensoser, Max & Roberg, Alex, eds. Israelitische Lehrerbildungsanstalt Wurzburg. LC 81-81930. (Illus.). 256p. 1982. 12.95 (*0-8187-0046-7*) Harlo Press.

Ottenstein, Claire. Catch a Whiffle-Poofle! (Illus.). 64p. (Orig.). (J). 1991. lib. bdg. 8.95 (*1-878149-03-2*) Counterpoint Pub.

— The Healing Touch of Poetry. (Illus.). 52p. (Orig.). 1990. lib. bdg. 6.95 (*1-878149-07-5*) Counterpoint Pub.

— In the Shadow of His Wings. (Illus.). 28p. (Orig.). 1995. pap. 5.00 (*1-878149-32-6*) Counterpoint Pub.

— The Poetry Fun Book. (Illus.). 40p. (Orig.). (J). 1992. pap. 7.95 (*1-878149-20-2*) Counterpoint Pub.

— Seven Steps to Getting Published. LC 92-73827. 56p. (Orig.). 1992. pap. 6.00 (*1-878149-14-8*) Counterpoint Pub.

Ottenstein, Claire, ed. Anthology of Children's Poetry, 1992. (Illus.). 36p. (Orig.). 1992. pap. 4.00 (*1-878149-15-6*) Counterpoint Pub.

— Anthology of Children's Poetry, 1994. (Illus.). 36p. (Orig.). (J). (gr. 1-5). 1994. pap. 4.00 (*1-878149-30-X*) Counterpoint Pub.

— A Book of the Year, 1996: The Poetry Society of Texas. (Illus.). 176p. (Orig.). 1996. pap. 7.50 (*1-878149-35-0*) Counterpoint Pub.

— Texas Rib-Ticklers! (Illus.). 84p. 1990. lib. bdg. 7.95 (*1-878149-00-8*) Counterpoint Pub.

Ottenstein, Claire, ed. Anthology of Children's Poetry. (Illus.). 36p. (Orig.). (J). (gr. 1-5). 1993. pap. 4.00 (*1-878149-23-7*) Counterpoint Pub.

Ottenstein, Claire & Newton, Violette. Because We Dream. LC 94-70819. (Illus.). 68p. 1994. lib. bdg. 8.00 (*1-878149-25-3*) Counterpoint Pub.

Ottenstein, Claire, ed. see Anthology of Winning Poets Staff.

Ottenstein, Claire, jt. ed. see Braud, Janice.

Ottenstein-Ross, Claire. The Singing Bird. 32p. 1998. pap. 5.00 (*1-878149-41-5*) Counterpoint Pub.

Otter, A. A. Den, see Den Otter, A. A.

Otter, Casten Von, see Saltman, Richard B. & Von Otter, Casten.

Otter, Casten Von, see Von Otter, Casten, ed.

Otter, Casten Von, see Naschold, Frieder & Von Otter, Casten.

***Otter, Charlotte, et al.** SAP Employee Self-Service Release 4.6: Installation Guide. 276p. 1999. pap. write for info. (*1-893570-99-1*) SAP Labs.

Otter, Floyd L. Men of Mammoth Forest. (Illus.). 169p. 1995. reprint ed. 21.95 (*0-9614459-1-2*) Otter Veterinary.

Otter, P. W. Dynamic Feature Space Modelling, Filtering & Self-Tuning Control of Stochastic Systems. (Lecture Notes in Economics & Mathematical Systems Ser.: Vol. 246). xiv, 177p. 1985. 31.00 (*0-387-15654-2*) Spr-Verlag.

Otter, Samuel. Melville's Anatomies. LC 97-50369. 418p. 1998. 48.00 (*0-520-20581-2*, Pub. by U CA Pr) Cal Prin Full Svc.

— Melville's Anatomies. LC 97-50369. 418p. 1999. pap. 22.50 (*0-520-20582-0*, Pub. by U CA Pr) Cal Prin Full Svc.

Otter, Sandra D. British Idealism & Social Explanation: A Study in Late Victorian Thought. LC 95-34291. (Oxford Historical Monographs). (Illus.). 262p. (C). 1996. text 68.00 (*0-19-820600-3*) OUP.

***Otter Tail County Historical Society Staff, ed.** Reaching the Millennium: Events & Inventions That Changed Our Lives. LC 99-76058. 80p. 1999. spiral bd. 6.95 (*0-9670516-2-2*) Annika Pubns.

Otter, William. History of My Own Times: Or, the Life & Adventures of William Otter, Sr., Comprising a Series of Events, & Musical Incidents Altogether Original. Stott, Richard B., ed. (Documents in American Social History Ser.). (Illus.). 256p. 1995. text 42.50 (*0-8014-2667-7*); pap. text 15.95 (*0-8014-9961-5*) Cornell U Pr.

***Otterbein.** When War Began & Evolution. 2000. 27.00 (*0-8133-3778-X*, Pub. by Westview) HarpC.

Otterbein, Angelo F. We Have Kept the Faith: The First 150 Years of the Boys' School of St. Paul's Parish. (Illus.). iv, 268p. 1999. 40.00 (*0-9671824-0-9*); 150.00 (*0-9671824-1-7*) St Pauls MD.

Otterbein College Staff, ed. see Humesky, Assya, et al.

Otterbein, Keith F. Evolution of War: A Cross-Cultural Study. 3rd ed. LC 79-87852. (Comparative Studies). 184p. 1989. pap. 20.00 (*0-87536-324-5*) HRAFP.

— The Ultimate Coercive Sanction: A Cross-Cultural Study of Capital Punishment. LC 86-80163. 164p. (C). 1987. pap. 10.00 (*0-87536-346-6*) HRAFP.

Otterbein, Keith F., ed. Feuding & Warfare: Selected Works of Keith F. Otterbein. LC 93-11752. 216p. 1993. pap. text 27.00 (*2-88124-621-4*) Gordon & Breach.

— Feuding & Warfare: Selected Works of Keith F. Otterbein, Vol. 1. LC 93-11752. 216p. 1993. text 55.00 (*2-88124-620-6*) Gordon & Breach.

***Otterbourg, Robert K.** Careers in the Food Service Industry. LC 98-50282. (Success Without College Ser.). (Illus.). 136p. 1999. pap. 9.95 (*0-7641-0739-9*) Barron.

Otterbourg, Robert K. It's Never Too Late: One Hundred-Fifty Men & Women Who Changed Their Careers. 240p. 1993. pap. 9.95 (*0-8120-1464-2*) Barron.

— Retire & Thrive: Remarkable People Share Their Creative, Productive & Profitable Retirement Strategies. 2nd rev. ed. LC 99-10133. (Illus.). 283p. 1999. 22.50 (*0-938721-64-X*) Kiplinger Bks.

Otterbourg, Susan D. School Partnerships Handbook: How to Set up & Administer Programs with Business, Government & Your Community. 336p. 1986. 29.95 (*0-13-793852-7*) P-H.

Otterbrandt, T. & Lodhi, A. Kortfattad Swahili-Svensk. (SWA & SWE.). 1980. 59.95 (*0-8288-1101-6*, M 2174) Fr & Eur.

Otterbrandt, Tommy & Lodhi, Abdulaziz Y. Kortfattad Swahili-Svensk Ordbok. 195p. 1980. write for info. (*91-7106-165-7*, Pub. by Nordic Africa) Transaction Pubs.

Otterbrandt, Tommy, jt. auth. see Lodhi, Abdulaziz Y.

Otterholt, Howard V. How to Be Your Own Good Samaritan. LC 81-3465. 1982. 22.95 (*0-87949-195-7*) Ashley Bks.

Otterman, George R., jt. ed. see Lima, Joseph A.

Otterman, J., jt. ed. see Godby, E. A.

Ottermann, Christian. Initiatisches Christentum: Karlfried Graf Durckheims Lehre Vom "Initiatischen Weg" Als Herausforderung an die Evangelische Theologie. (Europaische Hochschulschriften Ser.: Reihe 23, Bd. 402). (GER., Illus.). VIII, 639p. 1990. 101.80 (*3-631-43110-4*) P Lang Pubng.

Otterness, Ivan, et al, eds. Advances in Inflammation Research, Vol. 11. LC 78-55804. 359p. 1986. reprint ed. pap. 111.30 (*0-7837-9250-6*, 204715600011) Bks Demand.

— Therapeutic Control of Inflammatory Diseases. LC 82-48972. (Advances in Inflammation Research Ser.: Vol. 7). 327p. 1984. reprint ed. pap. 101.40 (*0-608-00437-5*, 206115200007) Bks Demand.

***Ottersen, O. P. & Storm-Mathisen, J., eds.** Glutamate. 2000. write for info. (*0-444-50286-6*, Excerpta Medica) Elsevier.

Ottersen, Ole P., ed. see Storm-Mathisen, Jon, et al.

Ottersen, Signe R., ed. see International Institute for Environment & Developm.

Otterson, Lynn, ed. see Cottingham, Carl D., et al.

Otterspeer, Willem, ed. Leiden Oriental Connections, 1850 to 1940. (Studies in the History of Leiden University: Vol. 5). (Illus.). viii, 391p. 1989. pap. 110.50 (*90-04-09022-3*) Brill Academic Pubs.

Otterstatter, Gisbert. Coloring of Food, Drugs & Cosmetics. LC 98-50964. (Illus.). 488p. 1999. text 185.00 (*0-8247-0215-8*) Dekker.

Otterstedt, Jan-Erik & Brandreth, Dale A. Small Particles Technology. 528p. 1998. 110.00 (*0-306-45935-3*, Plenum Trade) Perseus Pubng.

Otterstrom, Thorvald. A Theory of Modulation. LC 74-34379. (Music Reprint Ser.).Tr. of Eine/Modulations Theorie. (ENG & GER., Illus.). viii, 162p. 1975. reprint ed. lib. bdg. 29.50 (*0-306-70721-7*) Da Capo.

Ottervanger, Tom, et al. Competition Law of the European Community, The Netherlands & Belgium. LC 98-12723. (Loeff Legal Ser.). 1998. pap. 46.00 (*90-411-0577-8*) Kluwer Academic.

Ottery, Rudi, jt. auth. see Ottery, Will.

Ottery, Will & Ottery, Rudi. A Man Called Sampson, 1580-1989: The Ancestry & Progeny of Sampson, a Mashantucket Pequot Indian. 432p. 1989. 150.00 (*0-929539-51-6*, 1151) Picton Pr.

***Ottesen, Otto.** Market Communication: A Holistic Approach for Increased Profitability. 2000. Price not set. (*87-16-13335-8*, Pub. by Copenhagen Busn Schl) Bks Intl VA.

Ottesen, B. & Tabor, A., eds. New Insights in Gynecology & Obstetrics: Research & Practice. LC 98-15899. (Illus.). 336p. 1998. 125.00 (*1-85070-966-1*) Prthnon Pub.

Ottesen, Carol C. L. A. Stories: The Voices of Cultural Diversity. LC 99-14679. 184p. 1999. pap. 24.50 (*0-7618-1402-7*) U Pr of Amer.

Ottesen, Carole. Ornamental Grasses: The Amber Wave. 2nd ed. 288p. 1995. pap. 24.95 (*0-07-048021-4*) McGraw.

Ottesen, Frances. Speak Like Rain. (Illus.). 50p. (Orig.). 1986. pap. 6.00 (*0-9605220-1-8*) Otafra.

— Sun-Spaces. (Illus.). 76p. 1981. 7.95 (*0-9605220-0-X*) Otafra.

Ottesen, Johnny T. Infinite Dimensional Groups & Algebras in Quantum Physics. LC 95-7866. (Lecture Notes in Physics: New Series M; Monographs: Vol. 27). 227p. 1996. 49.00 (*3-540-58914-7*) Spr-Verlag.

Otteson, Orlo, jt. auth. see Patee, James.

Otteson, Orlo J., jt. auth. see Pattee, James J.

Otteson, Orlo J., jt. auth. see Seifert, Milton H., Jr.

***Otteson, Paul.** Adventures in Nature: Alaska. 2nd ed. LC 97-31273. (Illus.). 408p. 2000. pap. 18.95 (*1-56261-487-8*) Avalon Travel.

Otteson, Paul. Kids Who Walk on Volcanoes. LC 96-26513. 32p. (J). (gr. 4-7). 1996. pap. 6.95 (*1-56261-308-1*, J Muir) Avalon Travel.

***Otteson, Paul.** Travel Smart: Alaska. 2nd ed. (Illus.). 256p. 2000. pap. 16.95 (*1-56261-448-7*, Travel Smart) Avalon Travel.

Otteson, Paul. Travel Smart: Northern California. 2nd ed. (Travel Smart Ser.). (Illus.). 272p. 1998. pap. text 16.95 (*1-56261-422-3*, Travel Smart) Avalon Travel.

— The World Awaits: A Comprehensive Guide to Extended Backpack Travel. (Illus.). 280p. 1996. pap. 16.95 (*1-56261-277-8*) Avalon Travel.

Ottestad, P. Statistical Models & Their Experimental Applications. (Griffin's Statistical Monographs: No. 25). 88p. 1970. pap. text 25.00 (*0-85264-166-4*) Lubrecht & Cramer.

Ottewell, David J. Nottinghamshire at Work. LC 97-172902. (Britain in Old Photographs Ser.). (Illus.). 125p. 1996. write for info. (*0-7509-1278-2*) Sutton Pub Ltd.

***Ottewell, Guy.** The Arithmetic of Voting. rev. ed. 8p. 1999. pap. 2.00 (*0-934546-42-8*) Univ Wrkshop.

— Plurry: A Scheme for a Musical Instrument. (Illus.). 36p. 1992. 6.00 (*0-934546-45-2*) Univ Wrkshop.

Ottewell, Guy. Stripe Latin. (Illus.). 17p. 1994. pap. 7.00 (*0-934546-29-0*) Univ Wrkshop.

Ottewell, Guy. A Ten-Minute History of the World: From a Zoroastrian Perspective. rev. ed. 15p. 1997. pap. 3.00 (*0-934546-43-6*) Univ Wrkshop.

Ottewell, Guy. The Troy Town Tale. (Illus.). 408p. 1999. 29.00 (*0-934546-38-X*) Univ Wrkshop.

***Ottewell, Guy.** Turkey: A Very Short History. 1999. pap. 4.00 (*0-934546-39-8*) Univ Wrkshop.

Ottewell, Guy V. Albedo to Zodiac. (Illus.). 64p. (Orig.). 1996. pap. text 11.00 (*0-934546-34-7*) Univ Wrkshop.

***Ottewell, Guy V.** Astronomical Calendar 2000. annuals (Illus.). 77p. 1999. pap. 22.00 (*0-934546-40-1*) Univ Wrkshop.

Ottewell, Guy V. Astronomical Companion. (Illus.). 73p. (C). 1979. pap. 22.00 (*0-934546-01-0*) Univ Wrkshop.

— Language. 97p. 1987. pap. text 9.00 (*0-934546-17-7*) Univ Wrkshop.

— Spiral Library. (Illus.). 20p. 1991. pap. 5.00 (*0-934546-25-8*) Univ Wrkshop.

— Think Like a Mother. (Illus.). 48p. 1995. pap. 8.00 (*0-934546-31-2*) Univ Wrkshop.

— The Thousand-Yard Model: or The Earth as a Peppercorn. (Illus.). 16p. 1989. pap. 6.00 (*0-934546-21-5*) Univ Wrkshop.

— To Know the Stars. (Illus.). 41p. (J). (gr. 3 up). 1984. pap. 8.00 (*0-934546-12-6*) Univ Wrkshop.

— The Under-Standing of Eclipses. (Illus.). 96p. (Orig.). 1991. pap. 14.00 (*0-934546-24-X*) Univ Wrkshop.

— Winged Velocipede. (Illus.). 48p. 1995. pap. 5.00 (*0-934546-32-0*) Univ Wrkshop.

Ottewell, O. Wildlife Walks in the North Cotswolds. (C). 1988. pap. 29.00 (*0-946328-00-5*, Pub. by Thornhill Pr) St Mut.

Ottewill, David. The Edwardian Garden. LC 88-50427. 240p. (C). 1989. 60.00 (*0-300-04338-4*) Yale U Pr.

Ottewill, Ronald H. Colloids. text. write for info. (0-471-48926-3); pap. text. write for info. (0-471-48927-1) Wiley.

Ottewill, Ronald H. & Rennie, A. R., eds. Trends in Colloid & Interface Science VIII. (Progress in Colloid & Polymer Science Ser.: Vol. 97). 340p. 1994. 152.95 (3-7985-0984-0) Spr-Verlag.

Ottewill, Ronald H., jt. ed. see Candau, Francoise.

Ottewitte, E. H. & Kells, W., eds. Intense Position Beams: 1987 Workshop. 300p. 1988. text 86.00 (9971-5-0593-2) World Scientific Pub.

Ottewitte, Eric & Weiss, Alex, eds. Slow Positron Beam Techniques for Solids & Surfaces. LC 94-71036. (AIP Conference Proceedings Ser.: No. 303). 640p. 1994. pap. text 165.00 (1-56396-267-5) Am Inst Physics.

Ottina, Theresa. A Financial Profile of Television Stations by Network Affiliation. (Illus.). 1997. pap. 225.00 (0-89324-304-3, 3854) Natl Assn Broadcasters.

Ottina, Theresa J. 1997 Ad Revenue for TV Household: A Market by Market Analysis. 62p. 1997. pap. 225.00 (0-89324-305-1, 3853) Natl Assn Broadcasters.

— 1997 NAB/BCFM Television Market Analysis. 140p. 1997. pap. 475.00 (0-89324-303-5) Natl Assn Broadcasters.

— 1997 TV Employee Compensation & Fringe Benefits Report. 65p. 1997. pap. 225.00 (0-89324-302-7, 3857) Natl Assn Broadcasters.

— 1997 TV Financial Report. 179p. 1997. pap. 375.00 (0-89324-301-9, 3851) Natl Assn Broadcasters.

— 1997 TV Regional Report. (Illus.). 81p. 1997. pap. 225.00 (0-89324-309-4, 3856) Natl Assn Broadcasters.

Otting, Rae. When Jesus Was a Lad. (Illus.). (J). (gr. 1-2). 1978. pap. 1.25 (0-89508-055-9) Rainbow Bks.

Ottinger, Bill. Napoleonic Plastic Figure Modeling: Bill Ottinger's Masterclass. (Illus.). 128p. 1997. 29.95 (1-85915-019-5, Pub. by W & G) Motorbooks Intl.

Ottinger, Cecelia, ed. Community, Technical & Junior College Fact Book. 1988. write for info. (0-318-63184-9, 2004) Macmillan.

Ottinger, Cecilia, ed. Fact Book on Higher Education, 1986-1987. (ACE-Oryx Series on Higher Education). 224p. 1986. text. write for info. (0-318-62001-4) Macmillan.

Ottinger, H. C. Stochastic Processes in Polymeric Fluids: Tools & Examples for Developing Simulation Algorithms. LC 95-44913. 386p. 1995. 75.00 incl. 3.5 hd (0-387-58353-X) Spr-Verlag.

Ottinger, Richard L. & Hohmeyer, Olav, eds. External Environmental Costs of Electric Power: Analysis & Internalization, Proceedings of a German-American Workshop Held at Ladenburg, FRG, October 23-25, 1990. (Illus.). ix, 497p. 1991. 130.95 (0-387-54184-5) Spr-Verlag.

Ottinger, Richard L., jt. ed. see Hohmeyer, Olav.

Ottino, J. M. The Kinetics of Mixing: Stretching, Chaos & Transport. (Cambridge Texts in Applied Mathematics Ser.: No. 4). (Illus.). 378p. 1989. pap. text 49.95 (0-521-36878-2) Cambridge U Pr.

Ottino, P. L' Etrangere Intime. (Ordres Sociaux Ser.). 1986. text 153.00 (2-88124-088-7) Gordon & Breach.

— L' Etrangere Intime, 2 vols., Set. (FRE.). 280/630p. 1986. pap. text 56.00 (2-88124-095-X) Gordon & Breach.

Ottis, Kenneth, et al. Experimental Animal Physiology: A Contemporary Systems Approach. 4th ed. 236p. (Orig.). (C). 1996. spiral bd. 25.95 (0-8403-7127-6) Kendall-Hunt.

Ottlelart, Lydie. Painting Flowers on Silk. 64p. pap. 14.95 (0-85532-706-5, 706-5, Pub. by Srch Pr) A Schwartz & Co.

***Ottley & Decker.** The Investigation & Prosecution of Arson. 900p. 1999. write for info. (0-327-01766-X, 6433810) LEXIS Pub.

Ottley, Allan R., ed. John A Sutter's Last Days: The Bidwell Letters. LC 86-61877. (Illus.). 72p. 1986. lib. bdg. 37.50 (0-9617334-0-3) Sacto Bk Collectors.

Ottley, Bruce L. & Polelle, Michael J. Illinois Tort Law, 2 vols., Set. 2nd ed. LC 93-32151. 800p. 1994. spiral bd. 165.00 (1-56257-680-1, 81155-10, MICHIE) LEXIS Pub.

Ottley, Bruce L., jt. auth. see Polelle, Michael J.

Ottley, Erika & Southern-Roberts, Heulwen. Acquired Communication Disorders. 224p. 2000. pap. text 32.50 (0-7506-2937-1) Buttrwrth-Heinemann.

Ottley, Roi. New World A-Coming: Inside Black America. LC 68-29014. (American Negro: His History & Literature. Series 1). 1969. reprint ed. 17.95 (0-405-01833-9) Ayer.

Ottlik, Geza. Adventures in Card Play. 288p. 1997. pap. 24.95 (0-575-06436-6, Pub. by V Gollancz) Trafalgar.

Ottlinger, Claudia. Death-Motif in the Poetry of Emily Dickinson & Christina Rossetti. LC 96-23197. (Studien Zur Englischen Und Amerikanische). 194p. 1996. 42.95 (0-8204-3183-4) P Lang Pubng.

Ottman. Elementary Harmony. 5th ed. 480p. 1997. pap. text 56.00 (0-13-281610-5) P-H.

Ottman & Mainous, Frank D. The Rudiments of Music. 2nd ed. 304p. (C). 1987. pap. text 52.00 (0-13-783671-6) P-H.

Ottman, Jacquelyn A. Green Marketing: Challenges & Opportunities for the New Marketing Age. 208p. 1994. pap. 14.95 (0-8442-3290-4) NTC Contemp Pub Co.

— Green Marketing: Opportunities for Innovation in the New Marketing Age. 2nd ed. (Illus.). 224p. 1997. 24.95 (0-8442-3239-4, NTC Business Bks) NTC Contemp Pub Co.

— Green Marketing: Responding to Environmental Consumer Demands. 208p. 1994. 24.95 (0-8442-3250-5, NTC Business Bks) NTC Contemp Pub Co.

***Ottman, Robert W.** Advanced Harmony: Theory & Practice. 5th ed. 1999. text 58.67 (0-13-083339-8) P-H.

— Advanced Harmony: Theory & Practice. 5th ed. LC 99-42122. 504p. 2000. pap. text 66.00 (0-13-086237-1) P-H.

Ottman, Robert W. Advanced Harmony, Theory & Practice. 4th ed. 1992. pap. text, wbk. ed. 44.00 (0-13-006818-7) P-H.

— Elementary Harmony. 4th ed. 1989. pap. text, student ed., wbk. ed. 41.00 (0-13-257312-1) P-H.

— Music for Sight Singing. 4th ed. 360p. 1996. spiral bd. 48.00 (0-13-234360-6) P-H.

— Theory & Practice With CD. 5th ed. 468p. 1997. pap. text 67.67 (0-13-775503-1) P-H.

Ottman, Robert W. & Dworak, Paul. Basic Ear Training Skills. 352p. 1991. pap. text 45.00 (0-13-058926-8, 650202) P-H.

Ottman, Robert W. & Mainous, Frank D. Programmed Rudiments of Music. 2nd ed. LC 92-46702. 352p. (C). 1993. pap. text 65.00 (0-13-138042-7) P-H.

— The Rudiments of Music. 2nd ed. (Illus.). 320p. (C). 1987. write for info. (0-318-61355-7) P-H.

— The Rudiments of Music. 3rd ed. LC 94-41687. 320p. 1995. pap. text 52.00 (0-13-706740-2) P-H.

Ottmann, Henning. Individuum und Gemeinschaft bei Hegel: Hegel im Spiegel der Interpretationen, Vol. 1. (Quellen und Studien zur Philosophie). (C). 1977. 106.95 (3-11-007134-7) De Gruyter.

— Philosophie und Politik Bei Nietzsche Vol. 2: Durchgesehene & Um ein Vorwort Erweiterte Auflage. 444p. 1997. 124.00 (3-11-014770-X) De Gruyter.

Ottmann, Klaus. Astrid Klein. (Illus.). 12p. 1991. pap. 6.00 (0-929687-08-6) E & C Zilkha Gal.

— Mark Morrisroe. (Illus.). 220p. 1999. 60.00 (0-944092-62-4) Twin Palms Pub.

— Mary Kelly: Gloria Patri. (Illus.). 38p. (Orig.). (C). 1992. 12.00 (0-929687-11-6) E & C Zilkha Gal.

***Ottmann, Klaus.** Michelangelo. (Essential Ser.). 2000. pap. 12.95 (0-8109-5817-1) Abrams.

— Michelangelo. (Essential Ser.). (Illus.). 112p. 2000. 12.95 (0-7407-0728-0, Abrams Essential) Andrews & McMeel.

Ottmann, Klaus. Otto Kunzli: Oh, Say. (Illus.). 32p. (C). 1992. 10.00 (0-929687-10-8) E & C Zilkha Gal.

— Rotraut Uecker Klein. (Illus.). 32p. (Orig.). (C). 1989. pap. 12.00 (0-929687-02-7) E & C Zilkha Gal.

Ottmann, Klaus, ed. Jessica Stockholder Pt. 3: The Broken Mirror. (Illus.). 4p. (C). 1991. 5.00 (0-929687-07-8) E & C Zilkha Gal.

Ottmann, Klaus & Bleckner, Ross. David Deutsch. Cunnick, Elizabeth, ed. (Illus.). 36p. (Orig.). 1989. pap. 10.00 (0-924008-02-4) Blum Helman.

Ottmann, Klaus & Lowe, Celia. Exotism: Art of Incorporation. (Illus.). 20p. (Orig.). (C). 1990. pap. text 8.00 (0-929687-03-5) E & C Zilkha Gal.

***Ottmann, Klaus, et al.** Wolfgang Laib: A Retrospective. LC 00-36269. 2000. write for info. (1-885444-14-1) Am Fed Arts.

Ottmann, Klaus, ed. see Laramee, Eve A.

Ottmann, Klaus, ed. see Restany, Pierre.

Ottmann, T., ed. Automata, Languages & Programming. (Lecture Notes in Computer Science Ser.: Vol. 267). (Illus.). x, 565p. 1987. 57.00 (0-387-18088-5) Spr-Verlag.

Ottmar, Roger D., jt. auth. see Reinhardt, Timothy E.

Otto. Die Deutsche Grammar. 1995. pap. text 14.20 (0-13-328154-X) P-H.

***Otto.** Enfermeria Oncologica. 3rd ed. (C). 1999. text 80.28 (84-8174-427-1) Mosby Inc.

— Oncology Nursing. 4th ed. 2001. pap. text. write for info. (0-323-01217-5) Mosby Inc.

Otto, et al. Werkboek vir Kommersiele Reg, Vol. 1. 3rd ed. (AFR.). 1997. wbk. ed. write for info. (0-409-06131-X, MICHIE) LEXIS Pub.

— Werkboek vir Kommersiele Reg, Vol. 2. 3rd ed. (AFR.). 1997. wbk. ed. write for info. (0-409-06132-8, MICHIE) LEXIS Pub.

— Workbook for Commerical Law, Vol. 1. 3rd ed. 1997. wbk. ed. write for info. (0-409-06133-6, MICHIE) LEXIS Pub.

— Workbook for Commerical Law, Vol. 2. 3rd ed. 1997. wbk. ed. write for info. (0-409-06134-4, MICHIE) LEXIS Pub.

Otto, A. S., ed. Chairman's Chat-Life Lines. 120p. 1981. vinyl bd. 24.95 (0-912132-11-6) Dominion Pr.

— Comprehensive Immortalist Primer. 1975. 24.95 (0-912132-06-X) Dominion Pr.

— Invisible Ministry Annual Reports. 120p. 1989. vinyl bd. 19.95 (0-912132-12-4) Dominion Pr.

— Theologia Twenty-One, 3 vols. 150p. 1991. vinyl bd. 69.95 (0-912132-08-6) Dominion Pr.

— The Theologia Twenty-One Encyclopedia, 3 vols. 700p. 1991. vinyl bd. 54.95 (0-912132-16-7) Dominion Pr.

Otto, August. Die Sprichworter und Sprichwortlichen Redensarten der Romer. xlv, 436p. 1988. reprint ed. write for info. (3-487-00240-X) G Olms Pubs.

***Otto, Beatrice K.** Global Jokers. 2000. 34.00 (0-226-64091-4) U Ch Pr.

Otto, Bridget, ed. see PGE Chef's Night Out Committee.

Otto, C., ed. Proceedings of the 7th International Symposium on Trichoptera, Ume, Sweden, 3-8 August 1992. (Illus.). 312p. 1993. 105.00 (90-73348-27-7, Pub. by Backhuys Pubs) Balogh.

Otto, Carolyn. I Can Tell by Touching. LC 93-18630. (Let's Read-&-Find-Out Science Ser.). 1994. 10.15 (0-606-06485-0, Pub. by Turtleback) Demco.

— Mighty Joe Young. LC 97-80191. (Junior Novelization Ser.). (Illus.). 96p. (J). (gr. 3 7). 1998. pap. 4.95 (0-7868-4137-0, Pub. by Disney Pr) Time Warner.

— Our Puppies Are Growing. LC 97-27697. (Let's-Read-&-Find-Out Science Ser.). (Illus.). 32p. (J). (ps-1). 1998. 15.95 (0-06-027271-6); lib. bdg. 15.89 (0-06-027272-4) HarpC.

— Our Puppies Are Growing. (Let's Read-&-Find-Out Science Ser.). (J). 1998. 10.15 (0-606-13684-3, Pub. by Turtleback) Demco.

— Ruby Bridges. LC 97-80134. (Wonderful World of Disney Ser.). 80p. (J). (gr. 3-7). 1997. pap. 3.95 (0-7868-4210-5, Pub. by Disney Pr) Time Warner.

***Otto, Carolyn.** Shadows. LC 00-36241. (Science Readers Ser.). (Illus.). (J). 2000. write for info. (0-439-20548-4) Scholastic Inc.

Otto, Carolyn. What Color Is Camouflage? LC 95-32173. (Let's-Read-And-Find-Out Science. Stage 2 Ser.). 1996. 10.15 (0-606-10041-5, Pub. by Turtleback) Demco.

***Otto, Carolyn.** Wolves. LC 00-25359. (Science Reader Ser.). (Illus.). (J). 2000. write for info. (0-439-16295-5) Scholastic Inc.

Otto, Carolyn B. Ducks, Ducks, Ducks. LC 90-42089. (Illus.). 32p. (J). (ps-1). 1991. 14.95 (0-06-024637-5); lib. bdg. 14.89 (0-06-024639-1) HarpC Child Bks.

— One Dog Twenty Stars. (J). 1995. 14.95 (0-8050-2369-0) H Holt & Co.

— Pioneer Church. LC 95-42007. 32p. (J). (gr. k-4). 2000. 16.95 (0-8050-2554-5) H Holt & Co.

— Raccoon at Clear Creek Road. (Smithsonian's Backyard Ser.). (Illus.). 32p. (J). (ps-2). 1995. 15.95 (1-56899-175-4) Soundprints.

Otto, Carolyn B. Raccoon at Clear Creek Road. (Smithsonian's Backyard Ser.). (Illus.). 32p. (J). (ps-2). 1995. 19.95 incl. audio (1-56899-179-7, BC5008) Soundprints.

Otto, Carolyn B. Raccoon at Clear Creek Road, Incl. 12" toy. (Smithsonian's Backyard Ser.). (Illus.). 32p. (J). (ps-2). 1995. 37.95 incl. audio (1-56899-181-9); 32.95 (1-56899-177-0) Soundprints.

— Raccoon at Clear Creek Road, Micro bk. (Smithsonian's Backyard Ser.). (Illus.). 32p. (J). (ps-2). 1995. 4.95 (1-56899-176-2) Soundprints.

— Raccoon at Clear Creek Road, Micro bk., incl. 6" toy. (Smithsonian's Backyard Ser.). (Illus.). 32p. (J). (ps-3). 1995. 12.95 (1-56899-178-9) Soundprints.

— That Sky, That Rain. LC 89-36582. (Illus.). 32p. (J). (ps-3). 1990. 12.95 (0-690-04763-0); lib. bdg. 12.89 (0-690-04765-7) HarpC Child Bks.

— What Color Is Camouflage? LC 95-32173. (Let's-Read-&-Find-Out-Science Bks.). (Illus.). 32p. (J). (gr. k-4). 1996. lib. bdg. 14.89 (0-06-027099-3) HarpC Child Bks.

— What Color Is Camouflage. LC 95-32173. (Illus.). 32p. (J). (ps-3). 1996. pap. 4.95 (0-06-445160-7) HarpC.

Otto, Catherine M. Clinical Echocardiography. Zorab, Ricahrd, ed. (Illus.). 832p. 1996. text 173.00 (0-7216-6019-3, W B Saunders Co) Harcrt Hlth Sci Grp.

— Valvular Heart Disease. Zorab, Richard, ed. LC 98-47450. (Illus.). 575p. 1999. text. write for info. (0-7216-7139-X, W B Saunders Co) Harcrt Hlth Sci Grp.

Otto, Catherine M. & Pearlman, Alan S. Textbook of Clinical Echocardiography. LC 94-6846. (Illus.). 416p. 1994. text. write for info. (0-7216-6634-5, W B Saunders Co) Harcrt Hlth Sci Grp.

— Textbook of Clinical Echocardiography. 2nd ed. LC 99-23054. (Illus.). 460p. (C). 1999. text 105.00 (0-7216-7669-3, W B Saunders Co) Harcrt Hlth Sci Grp.

Otto, Christian F., jt. auth. see Pommer, Richard.

Otto, Christian F., ed. see Klingensmith, Samuel J.

Otto, Crolyn. Our Puppies Are Growing. LC 97-27697. (Let's-Read-&-Find-Out Science Ser.). (Illus.). 32p. (J). (ps-1). 1998. pap. 4.95 (0-06-445169-0) HarpC.

Otto, David, jt. auth. see Knops, Robert D.

Otto, Dixon P. On Orbit: The First Space Shuttle Era. (Illus.). 112p. (Orig.). pap. text 9.95 (0-936447-00-1) Main Stage.

Otto, Don H. Finding Your Church. 116p. (Orig.). 1994. pap. 4.95 (1-886349-00-2) D H Otto.

Otto, Donna. Between Women of God: The Gentle Art of Mentoring. (Orig.). 1995. pap. 8.99 (1-56507-365-7) Harvest Hse.

— The Gentle Art of Mentoring. LC 97-2658. 108p. 1997. pap. 7.99 (1-56507-757-1) Harvest Hse.

— Get More Done in Less Time: And Get on with the Good Stuff! (Orig.). 1994. pap. 8.99 (1-56507-253-7) Harvest Hse.

— Mentors for Mothers. 1999. pap. text, teacher ed. 34.99 (0-8474-1331-4) Back to Bible.

— The Stay-at-Home Mom: For Women at Home & Those Who Want to Be. expanded rev. ed. LC 96-45434. 224p. (Orig.). 1997. pap. 8.99 (1-56507-638-9) Harvest Hse.

Otto, Donna, jt. auth. see Barnes, Emilie.

Otto-Dorn, Katerina. Art & Architecture of the Islamic World. 490p. 1996. 65.00 (0-614-21567-6, 70) Kazi Pubns.

Otto, E. & Smolska, J. Nomography. LC 63-10028. (International Series of Monographs on Pure & Applied Mathematics: Vol. 42). 1963. 140.00 (0-08-010164-X, Pub. by Pergamon Repr) Franklin.

Otto, Eberhard, jt. auth. see Helck, Wolfgang.

Otto, Eckart. Rechtsgeschichte der Redaktionen Im Kodex Esnunna und Im Bundesbuch: Eine Redaktionsgeschichtliche und Rechtsvergleichende Studie Zu Altbabylonischen und Altisraelitischen Rechtsuberlieterungen. (Orbis Biblicus et Orientalis Ser.: Vol. 85). (GER.). 209p. 1989. text 41.50 (3-7278-0602-8, Pub. by Presses Univ Fribourg) Eisenbrauns.

Otto, Ernst. Zur Grundlegung der Sprachwissenschaft. vi, 39p. reprint ed. write for info. (0-318-71464-7) G Olms Pubs.

Otto et al & Bryant. Alles Klar. (GER.). 1996. pap. text, wbk. ed., lab manual ed. 31.20 (0-13-249939-8) P-H.

***Otto, Frei.** Occupying & Connecting. (Illus.). 112p. 2001. 29.90 (3-932565-11-8) Edition A Menges.

Otto, Friedrich, jt. auth. see Book, Ronald V.

Otto, Gilbert, ed. Proceedings of the Heartworm Symposium, '89. 1990. text 43.00 (0-940275-01-5) Am Heartworm Soc.

Otto, Gordon H. & Soules, James G. Statistical Tools for Total Quality Management: Using Lotus 1-2-3, Version D-1.0. LC 94-60523. (Illus.). 140p. (Orig.). 1994. pap. 29.00 (0-9639553-2-2) Verenikia Pr.

Otto, Gordon H., jt. auth. see Otto, Helen Tzima.

Otto, Gordon H., ed. see Otto, Helen Tzima.

Otto, Gottlieb F. Lexicon der Seit Dem 15: Jahrhundert Verstorbenen und Jezt Lebenden Oberlausitzischen Schriftsteller und Kunstler, 3 vols., Set. 1983. write for info. incl. fiche (0-318-71937-1) G Olms Pubs.

Otto, Hans-Uwe & Flosser, Gaby, eds. How to Organize Prevention: Political, Organizational & Professional Challenges to Social Services. (Prevention & Intervention in Childhood & Adolescence Ser.: No. 12). xvi, 424p. (C). 1992. lib. bdg. 84.95 (3-11-013536-1, 45-92) De Gruyter.

Otto, Hans-Uwe, jt. auth. see Sunker, Heinz.

Otto, Hans-Uwe, jt. ed. see Albrecht, Gunter.

Otto, Hans-Uwe, jt. ed. see Flosser, Gaby.

Otto, Helen T. Our Revelationary Age. Myers, Gene & Meyers, Jim, eds. 576p. 1993. text 39.95 (1-884332-08-0); pap. text 29.95 (1-884332-09-9) Netwrk Pr TX.

— Our Revelationary Age: The Prophecies for WWIII & the Year 2000. LC 94-60322. 526p. (Orig.). 1994. 34.00 (0-9639553-0-6); pap. 20.00 (0-9639553-1-4) Verenikia Pr.

— Their Earthshaking News: When Science & Theology Speak the Same Urgent Language. 437p. 1996. pap. 18.00 (0-9639553-4-9) Verenikia Pr.

Otto, Helen T., tr. see O'Dowd, Leonard.

***Otto, Helen Tzima.** Orthodox Prophecy on the Pontificate of John Paul II & the Oracle of Kremna: The WWIII. Otto, Gordon H., ed. LC 98-90545. (Orthodox Prophecy on the End Times: Vol. 1). (Illus.). 216p. 2000. pap. 12.00 (1-891663-00-3) Verenikia Pr.

***Otto, Helen Tzima & Otto, Gordon H.** When Heaven Broke the Seals & Opened the Scrolls. LC 98-90482. 488p. 1998. pap. 15.00 (0-9639553-7-3) Verenikia Pr.

Otto, Herbert A. Liberated Orgasm: The Orgasmic Revolution. 268p. 1999. pap. 23.95 (0-9671181-3-1) Liberating Creations.

Otto, Herbert A., ed. Human Potentialities: The Challenge & the Promise. LC 67-26016. 231p. reprint ed. pap. 71.70 (0-608-11219-4, 201219300081) Bks Demand.

Otto, Herbert A. & Knight, James W., eds. Dimensions in Wholistic Healing: New Frontiers in the Treatment of the Whole Person. LC 78-27071. 568p. 1979. text 46.95 (0-88229-513-6) Burnham Inc.

Otto, Herbert A. & Tuedio, James, eds. Perspectives on Mind. 430p. (C). 1987. text 176.50 (90-277-2640-X, D Reidel) Kluwer Academic.

Otto, Jacob A. Treatise of the Structure & Preservation of the Violin. 1976. lib. bdg. 45.00 (0-403-03760-3) Scholarly.

— Treatise of the Structure & Preservation of the Violin. 1988. reprint ed. lib. bdg. 59.00 (0-7812-0345-7) Rprt Serv.

Otto, Jacob A. & Hanks, J. F. Treatise on the Construction, Preservation, Repair, & Improvement of the Violin: Supplement by J. F. Hanks. 48p. 1995. reprint ed. pap. 9.95 (0-931877-26-1) Captain Fiddle Pubns.

Otto, James. Taxation of Mineral Enterprises. (International Energy & Resources Law & Policy Ser.). 1995. lib. bdg. 139.00 (1-85966-105-X) Kluwer Academic.

Otto, Jim & Newhouse, Dave. Jim Otto: The Pain of Glory. (Illus.). 200p. 1999. 22.95 (1-58261-066-5) Sprts Pubng.

Otto, John, tr. see Oury, Guy-Marie.

Otto, John S. Cannon's Point Plantation, 1794-1860: Living Conditions & Status Patterns in the Old South. LC 83-15784. (Studies in Historical Archaeology). 1984. text 59.95 (0-12-531060-9) Acad Pr.

— Southern Agriculture During the Civil War Era, 1860-1880, 153. LC 93-32981. (Contributions in American History Ser.: No. 153). 184p. 1994. 55.00 (0-313-26714-6, Greenwood Pr) Greenwood.

— The Southern Frontiers, 1607-1860: The Agricultural Frontiers of the Colonial & Antebellum South, 133. LC 88-32793. (Contributions in American History Ser.: No. 133). 190p. 1989. 52.95 (0-313-26092-3, OSF, Greenwood Pr) Greenwood.

***Otto, John Solomon.** The Final Frontiers, 1880-1930: Settling the Southern Bottomlands, Vol. 183. LC 99-21710. (Contributions in American History Ser.: Vol. 183). 208p. 1999. 59.95 (0-313-28963-8) Greenwood.

Otto, Jonathan. NGOs in the Sahel: Issues in Cooperation for Natural Resources Management. (Occasional Paper Ser.). 1991. 3.00 (0-932288-86-3) Ctr Intl Ed U of MA.

Otto, Joseph & Nordenstam, Garry L. PowerUp with Excel 5 for Windows. 5th ed. 448p. 1994. text 28.95 incl. 3.5 hd (1-56118-617-1) Paradigm MN.

— PowerUp with Lotus 5 for Windows. 5th ed. 428p. 1996. text 28.95 incl. 3.5 hd (1-56118-615-5) Paradigm MN.

Otto, Joseph C. Spreadsheet Applications: Job-Based Tasks. 5th ed. 160p. (C). 1993. pap. text 13.95 (1-56118-448-9) Paradigm MN.

— Spreadsheet Applications: Job-Based Tasks. 25th ed. 160p. (C). 1993. pap. text 13.95 (1-56118-447-0) Paradigm MN.

Otto, Joseph C. Spreadsheet Prod EX/APPS IG/SP: Instructor's guide with Instructor's disks, 3.5 IBM. 5th ed. text 69.00 (1-56118-389-X) EMC-Paradigm.

Otto, Joseph C. & Nordenstam, Garry L. Power up with Lotus 5 for Windows. 1996. pap. text 28.95 (1-56118-808-5) Paradigm MN.

Otto, Karl F. Alles Klar? Beginning German in a Global Context with Handbook. 1996. 58.67 (0-13-575036-9) P-H.

O

— Bibliographia Kleschiana: The Writings of a Baroque Family. Clark, Jonathan P., Jr., ed. LC 96-10277. (GERM Ser.). xxix, 191p. 1996. 60.00 (*1-57113-012-8*) Camden Hse.

Otto, Karl F., Jr. & Von Schmidt. Alles Klar Begin Germany: German Within. 544p. 1996. 58.67 (*0-13-249905-3*) P-H.

***Otto, Kevin & Wood, Kristin.** Product Design. 800p. 2000. 81.00 (*0-13-021271-7*, Prentice Hall) P-H.

Otto, Lon. Cover Me. LC 88-11817. 144p. (Orig.). 1988. pap. 9.95 (*0-918273-40-4*) Coffee Hse.

— A Nest of Hooks. LC 78-16507. (Iowa Short Fiction Award Ser.). 152p. 1978. pap. 3.25 (*0-87745-090-0*) U of Iowa Pr.

Otto, Lorraine. Parables of the Baskets. 84p. 1995. pap. 14.95 (*0-9648543-0-9*) L Otto.

Otto, Luther B. Helping Your Child Choose a Career. 342p. (Orig.). 1995. pap. 14.95 (*1-56370-184-7*, J1847) JIST Works.

Otto, Martin. Bounded Variable Logics & Counting: A Study in Finite Models, Vol. IX. LC 96-51089. (Lectures Notes in Logic Ser.). 183p. 1997. pap. 49.00 (*3-540-62037-0*) Spr-Verlag.

Otto, Maryleah. Never, No Matter What. (Illus.). 24p. (J). (ps-3). pap. 4.95 (*0-88961-133-5*, Pub. by Womens Pr) LPC InBook.

— Tom Doesn't Visit Us Anymore. (Illus.). 24p. (J). reprint ed. pap. 4.95 (*0-88961-117-3*, Pub. by Womens Pr) LPC InBook.

***Otto, Michael W.** Stopping Anxiety Medication: Panic Control Therapy for Benzodiazepine Discontinuation (PCT-BD) 157p. 2000. pap. 32.00 (*0-12-784451-1*); pap. 26.00 (*0-12-784452-X*) Acad Pr.

Otto, Nancy. Almanac of America Cook Book. LC 86-90559. (Illus.). 263p. 1986. 16.95 (*0-9617435-0-6*) N L Otto.

Otto, Pat H. I Hate Divorce: I Love My Parents, but... I Hate Divorce. large type ed. (Illus.). (J). (gr. k-6). 1997. 6.95 (*0-9657854-1-6*) Wild Water.

Otto, Peter. Constructive Vision & Visionary Deconstruction: Loss, Eternity & the Productions of Time in the Later Poetry of William Blake. (Illus.). 256p. 1991. text 72.00 (*0-19-811751-5*) OUP.

Otto, Peter, jt. ed. see Coleman, Deirdre.

Otto, Ramona & Balaban, Jocelyn. The Box Book: Creative Projects to Make Using Boxes. Clark Editorial & Design Staff, ed. (Illus.). 120p. (J). (gr. 3-6). 1998. pap. 14.95 (*0-88160-289-2*, LW359) Learning Wks.

Otto, Randall E. Coming in the Clouds: An Evangelical Case for the Invisibility of Christ at His Second Coming. LC 93-49434. 308p. (Orig.). (C). pap. text 26.50 (*0-8191-9443-3*); lib. bdg. 55.00 (*0-8191-9442-5*) U Pr of Amer.

— The God of Hope: The Trinitarian Vision of Jurgen Moltman. 260p. (C). 1992. lib. bdg. 48.50 (*0-8191-8290-7*) U Pr of Amer.

Otto, Randy K. & Petrila, John. Law & Mental Health Professionals: Florida. LC 95-40356. 373p. (C). 1996. text 59.95 (*1-55798-322-4*, 431-5120) Am Psychol.

Otto, Robert C. Publishing for the People: The Firm Posrednik, 1885-1905. LC 87-240. (Modern European History Ser.). 264p. 1987. text 15.00 (*0-8240-8060-2*) Garland.

Otto, Rudiger. Studien zur Spinozarezeption in Deutschland Im 18. Jahrhundert. (Europaische Hochschulschriften Ser.: Reihe 23, Bd. 451). (GER.). 463p. 1994. 59.95 (*3-631-43579-7*) P Lang Pubng.

Otto, Rudolf. Autobiographical & Social Essays. Alles, Gregory D., ed. LC 96-12907. (History of Religions in Translation Ser.: Vol. 2). viii, 317p. (C). 1996. text 80.00 (*3-11-014519-7*); pap. text 48.60 (*3-11-014518-9*) Mouton.

— Idea of the Holy. 2nd ed. Harvey, John W., tr. 254p. 1958. pap. text 12.95 (*0-19-500210-5*) OUP.

Otto, S., jt. ed. see Albertz, R.

Otto, Shirley. Chemotherapy Quick Reference. 2nd ed. (Illus.). 64p. (C). (gr. 13). 1996. pap. text 8.95 (*0-8151-8956-7*, 29033) Mosby Inc.

Otto, Shirley & Orford, Jim. Not Quite Like Home: Small Hostels for Alcoholics & Others. LC 77-12664. 234p. reprint ed. pap. 72.60 (*0-608-13422-8*, 202428200035) Bks Demand.

Otto, Shirley E. Oncology Nursing. 3rd ed. (Illus.). 928p. (C). (gr. 13). 1996. pap. text 54.95 (*0-8151-8955-9*, 29032) Mosby Inc.

— Pocket Guide to Oncology Nursing. (Illus.). 640p. (C). (gr. 13). 1995. text 22.95 (*0-8151-6547-1*, 23768) Mosby Inc.

Otto, Shirley E., jt. auth. see LaRocca, Joanne C.

Otto, Simon. Ah Soo Can Nah Nah. unabridged ed. (Illus.). 100p. (Orig.). 1997. pap. 12.95 (*0-9658411-0-3*) Talking Leaves Pub.

— Grandmother Moon Speaks. (Illus.). 1995. pap. 12.95 (*1-882376-10-2*) Thunder Bay Pr.

— Walk in Peace: Legends & Stories of the Michigan Indians. 2nd ed. Bussey, M. T., ed. (Illus.). 56p. (J). (gr. 3-4). 1992. pap. 9.95 (*0-9617707-5-9*) Grnd Rpds Intertribal.

Otto, Stella B. The Backyard Orchardist: A Complete Guide to Growing Fruit Trees in the Home Garden. 2nd rev. ed. LC 92-96980. (Illus.). 264p. 1995. pap. 14.95 (*0-9634520-3-7*, Pub. by OttoGraphics) Chelsea Green Pub.

Otto, Steve. War on Drugs, War on People. LC 95-46098. x, 203p. (Orig.). 1995. pap. 15.00 (*0-86663-249-2*) Ide Hse.

Otto, Steve & Fay, Michael. Treasures on Tampa Bay: Tampa, Saint Petersburg, Clearwater. LC 96-277. (Urban Tapestry Ser.). (Illus.). 224p. 1996. 39.50 (*1-881096-31-9*) Towery Pub.

Otto, Steve, jt. auth. see Moline, Judi.

Otto, Sylvia, tr. see Bishop, Jacqueline.

Otto, Ton & Borsboom, Ad, eds. Cultural Dynamics of Religious Change in Oceania. (Verhandelingen Ser.: Vol. 176). 152p. 1998. pap. 33.50 (*90-6718-119-6*, Pub. by KITLV Pr) Cellar.

Otto, Ton & Thomas, Nicholas, eds. Narratives of Nation in the South Pacific. (Studies in Anthropology & History: Vol. 19). 245p. 1997. text 37.00 (*90-5702-085-8*, Harwood Acad Pubs); pap. text 16.00 (*90-5702-086-6*, Harwood Acad Pubs) Gordon & Breach.

Otto, Ton, jt. ed. see Driessen, Henk.

Otto, Walter F. Gestez Urbild & Mythos. Bolle, Kees W., ed. LC 77-82281. (Mythology Ser.). (GER.). 1978. reprint ed. lib. bdg. 19.95 (*0-405-10572-X*) Ayer.

— The Homeric Gods: The Spiritual Significance of Greek Religion. Bolle, Kees W., ed. LC 77-79149. (Mythology Ser.). 1978. reprint ed. lib. bdg. 24.95 (*0-405-10558-4*) Ayer.

Otto, Walter F, et al. Dionysus: Myth & Cult. LC 65-11792. 266p. 1995. per. 14.95 (*0-253-20891-2*) Ind U Pr.

Otto, Walter G. Priester und Tempel Im Hellenistischen Agypten: Ein Beitrag Zur Kulturgeschichte Des Hellenismus, 2 vols. LC 75-10645. (Ancient Religion & Mythology Ser.). (GER.). 1976. reprint ed. 68.95 (*0-405-07278-3*) Ayer.

Otto, Wayne, et al. Focused Reading Instruction. (C). 1974. text 12.00 (*0-201-05511-2*) Addison-Wesley.

Otto, Whitney. How to Make an American Quilt. (Illus.). (J). 1992. 12.34 (*0-606-17988-7*) Turtleback.

Otto, Whitney. How to Make an American Quilt. large type ed. LC 91-31109. 294p. 1992. lib. bdg. 19.95 (*0-8161-5338-8*, G K Hall Lrg Type) Mac Lib Ref.

— How to Make an American Quilt. 256p. 1992. reprint ed. mass mkt. 6.99 (*0-345-37080-5*) Ballantine Pub Grp.

— How to Make an American Quilt: A Novel. 256p. 1994. pap. 10.00 (*0-345-38896-8*) Ballantine Pub Grp.

— Now You See Her. 320p. 1995. pap. 12.00 (*0-345-37826-1*) Ballantine Pub Grp.

— Now You See Her. large type ed. LC 94-18646. 388p. 1994. lib. bdg. 23.95 (*0-8161-7407-5*, G K Hall Lrg Type) Mac Lib Ref.

— The Passion Dream Book: A Novel. LC 97-3563. 288p. 1998. pap. 13.00 (*0-06-109623-7*, Harp PBks) HarpC.

— The Passion Dream Book: A Novel. large type ed. LC 97-36730. (Americana Series). 432p. 1997. lib. bdg. 23.95 (*0-7862-1247-0*) Thorndike Pr.

Otto, Wolfgang, jt. auth. see Radinger, Willy.

Ottoboni, Alice M. The Dose Makes Poison: A Plain Language Guide. 2nd ed. (Occupational Health & Safety Ser.). 256p. 1997. pap. 26.95 (*0-442-02556-4*, VNR) Wiley.

Ottoboni, Fred. Korea Between the Wars: A Soldier's Story. LC 96-34188. (Illus.). 324p. (Orig.). 1997. pap. 19.95 (*0-915241-02-1*) Vincente Bks.

Ottoboni, M. Alice. The Dose Makes the Poison: A Plain-Language Guide to Toxicology. 2nd ed. 256p. 1997. pap. 39.95 (*0-471-28837-3*, VNR) Wiley.

Ottokar, Peter. Diccionario Rioduero: Quimica. 3rd ed. (SPA.). 272p. 1982. 35.00 (*0-7859-5071-0*) Fr & Eur.

Ottomanelli, Gennaro. Children & Addiction. LC 95-11274. 152p. 1995. 47.95 (*0-275-95171-5*, Praeger Pubs) Greenwood.

— HIV Infection & Intravenous Drug Use. LC 92-3260. 160p. 1992. 47.95 (*0-275-94301-1*, C4301, Praeger Pubs) Greenwood.

Ottomeyer, Hans. Friedrich Adler: Zwischen Jugendstil und Art Deco. (GER., Illus.). 448p. 95.00 (*3-925369-34-1*, Pub. by Arnoldsche Art Pubs) Antique Collect.

Otton, Frei. Finding Form: Towards an Architecture of the Minimal. LC 96-224568. (Illus.). 240p. 1995. 58.00 (*3-930698-66-8*, Pub. by E J Wasmuth) Dist Art Pubs.

Otton, William G., et al. Celebration! A History of the Art Museum of South Texas. (Illus.). 125p. 1997. pap. 25.00 (*1-888581-01-8*) Art Museum So TX.

Ottonello, Giulio. Principles of Geochemistry. LC 96-23987. 1997. 95.00 (*0-231-09984-3*) Col U Pr.

***Ottonello, Giulio.** Principles of Geochemistry. (Illus.). 2000. pap. text 40.00 (*0-231-09985-1*) Col U Pr.

Ottosen, Garry K. Making American Government Work: A Proposal to Reinvigorate Federalism. 191p. (Orig.). (C). 1992. pap. text 26.00 (*0-8191-8793-3*); lib. bdg. 49.00 (*0-8191-8792-5*) U Pr of Amer.

— Monopoly Power: How It Is Measured & How It Has Changed. LC 89-81840. 125p. 1990. pap. 9.95 (*0-9624038-1-4*) Crossroads Rsch.

Ottosen, Garry K. & Thompson, Douglas N. Reducing Unemployment: A Case for Government Deregulation. LC 95-30555. 184p. 1996. 52.95 (*0-275-95360-2*, Praeger Pubs) Greenwood.

Ottosen, Joleen. The Blood Conspiracy: How to Avoid Getting AIDS & Hepatitis in a Transfusion. Ross, Marilyn, ed. LC 92-71818. 326p. 1993. 24.95 (*0-9632963-3-7*) Aspen Leaf Pr.

Ottosen, Knud. The Responsories & Versicles of the Latin Office of the Dead. (Illus.). 512p. (C). 1993. 40.00 (*87-7288-315-4*, Pub. by Aarhus Univ Pr) David Brown.

Ottoson, David, ed. Duality & Unity of the Brain: Unified Functioning & Specialization of the Hemispheres. LC 87-42720. (Wenner-Gren International Symposia Ser.: Vol. 47). 516p. 1987. 125.00 (*0-306-42720-6*, Plenum Trade) Perseus Pubng.

Ottoson, David, et al, eds. Challenges & Perspectives in Neuroscience. LC 95-22622. (Wenner-Gren International Ser.: Vol. 66). 312p. 1995. 168.00 (*0-08-042515-1*, Pergamon Pr) Elsevier.

Ottoson, David, jt. ed. see Bartfai, Tamas.

Ottoson, Howard W., et al. Land & People in the Northern Plains Transition Area. Bruchey, Stuart, ed. LC 78-56708. (Management of Public Lands in the U. S. Ser.). (Illus.). 1979. reprint ed. lib. bdg. 31.95 (*0-405-11349-8*) Ayer.

Ottoson, Howard W., ed. see Homestead Centennial Symposium Staff.

Ottoson, Owen O. Animal Physiology: Index of New Information with Authors, Subjects & Bibliography. rev. ed. 1994. 47.50 (*0-7883-0166-7*); pap. 44.50 (*0-7883-0167-5*) ABBE Pubs Assn.

Ottosson, Jan, jt. ed. see Magnusson, Lars.

Ottova, A., jt. auth. see Ti Tien, H.

Ottow, E., et al, eds. Stereoselective Synthesis: Lectures Honouring Rudolf Wiechert. LC 93-34943. 160p. 1994. 123.95 (*0-387-57202-3*) Spr-Verlag.

Ottoway, Patrick. Archaeology in British Towns: From the Emperor Claudius to the Black Death. (Illus.). 264p. (C). 1996. pap. 27.99 (*0-415-14420-5*) Routledge.

Otts, Lee M., jt. auth. see Egger, Bruce E.

Ottum, Bob, ed. A Day in an Amish Kitchen. LC 95-69388. 100p. 1995. 14.95 (*0-89821-147-6*, 20107) Reiman Pubns.

— A Day in Cowboy Country. LC 96-68257. 100p. 1996. 14.95 (*0-89821-173-5*, 20408) Reiman Pubns.

— A Day in the Life of the Amish. LC 94-67583. 102p. 1994. 14.95 (*0-89821-126-3*, 19502) Reiman Pubns.

Ottum, Bob & Wood, JoAnne. Santa's Beard Is Soft & Warm. (Golden Touch & Feel Bks.). (Illus.). 24p. (J). (ps-3). 1974. 7.99 (*0-307-12148-8*, 12148, Goldn Books) Gldn Bks Pub Co.

O'Tuairisc, Eoghan. L' Attaque. 140p. 1997. reprint ed. pap. 9.95 (*0-85342-545-0*, Pub. by Mercier Pr) Irish Amer Bk.

Otuathail, Gearoid, et al. The Geopolitics Reader. LC 97-13460. (Illus.). 344p. (C). 1998. 100.00 (*0-415-16270-X*); pap. 29.99 (*0-415-16271-8*) Routledge.

Otubusin, Paul O. Exploitation, Unequal Exchange & Dependency: A Dialectical Development. LC 90-6019. (American University Studies: Philosophy: Ser. V, Vol. 88). IX, 165p. (C). 1993. text 23.95 (*0-8204-1234-1*) P Lang Pubng.

Otubusin, Paul O., ed. Battered Women Syndrome: Critical Study & Assessment. LC 96-157743. 160p. (Orig.). (C). 1996. pap. text 14.95 (*0-943025-71-0*) Cummngs & Hath.

O'Tuel, Frances S. & Bullard, Ruth K. Developing Higher Order Thinking in the Content Areas K-12. 280p. 1993. pap. 34.95 (*0-89455-499-9*, MP2101) Crit Think Bks.

O'Tuel, Muriel. Footprints on the Heart: The Caring Path to Prosperity. 247p. 1992. 24.95 (*0-939975-07-6*) Exec Pr NC.

Otugen, M. V., et al, eds. Separated & Complex Flows, 1995. LC 95-78761. (1995 ASME/JSME Fluids Engineering Conference Ser.: FED-Vol. 217). 288p. 1995. 130.00 (*0-7918-1472-6*, G00967) ASME.

Otugen, M. V., jt. ed. see Huang, T. T.

Otunnu, Olara A. & Doyle, Michael W., eds. Peacemaking & Peacekeeping for the New Century. LC 97-13387. 368p. (C). 1998. 69.00 (*0-8476-8726-0*); pap. 26.95 (*0-8476-8727-9*) Rowman.

Otway, Harry J. & Peltu, Malcolm. New Office Technology. LC 82-24473. 248p. 1983. text 73.25 (*0-89391-198-4*) Ablx Pub.

Otway, Thomas. Complete Works, 3 vols. Summers, Montague, ed. LC 27-20965. (Chertsey Worthies' Library). reprint ed. 210.00 (*0-404-04860-9*) AMS Pr.

— The Orphan. Taylor, Aline M., ed. LC 75-13067. (Regents Restoration Drama Ser.). 148p. 1976. reprint ed. pap. 45.90 (*0-7837-8910-6*, 204962100002) Bks Demand.

— Venice Preserved. Kelsall, Malcolm, ed. LC 69-12902. (Regents Restoration Drama Ser.). 138p. reprint ed. pap. 42.80 (*0-8357-4080-3*, 203677000005) Bks Demand.

Otway, Thomas, et al. Four Restoration Marriage Plays: The Soldier's Fortune, The Princess of Cleves, Amphitryon or The Two Sosias, & The Wives' Excuse or Cuckolds Make Themselves. Cordner, Michael & Clayton, Ronald, eds. (Oxford Drama Library). 499p. 1995. text 65.00 (*0-19-812163-6*) OUP.

Otwell, Steven & Rodrick, Gary E. Molluscan Shellfish Depuration. (Illus.). 380p. 1991. lib. bdg. 159.00 (*0-8493-4295-3*, SH) CRC Pr.

Otypka, Sylvia J. Flying the Big Birds: On Becoming an Airline Pilot. LC 96-95011. (Illus.). 100p. (Orig.). 1997. pap. 14.95 (*0-9655102-0-4*) Leadng Edge.

— Flying the Big Birds: On Becoming an Airline Pilot. 2nd rev. ed. (Illus.). 100p. (Orig.). 1998. pap. 14.95 (*0-9655102-1-2*) Leadng Edge.

Otze, Heinz, jt. auth. see Sarkowski, Heinz.

Otzen, Benedikt. Judaism in Antiquity: Political Developments & Religious Currents from Alexander to Hadrian. (Biblical Seminar Ser.: No. 7). 243p. 1990. 70.00 (*1-85075-197-8*, Pub. by Sheffield Acad) CUP Services.

Otzen, Benedikt, jt. auth. see Jeppesen, Knud.

Ou, S. H. Rice Diseases. 2nd ed. (Illus.). 380p. 1985. text 105.00 (*0-85198-545-9*) OUP.

***OU Spanish Course Staff.** En Rumbo Pack 1: Fresh Start In Spanish. (C). (gr. 13). 1999. text 39.99 (*0-415-20598-0*) Routledge.

***Ou Spanish Course Team Staff.** En Rumbo, Bk. 1.Tr. of Fresh Start. (SPA.). 160p. (Orig.). (C). 1999. pap. text 24.99 (*0-415-20324-4*) Routledge.

— En Rumbo, Bk. 2.Tr. of Fresh Start. (SPA.). 160p. (Orig.). (C). 1999. pap. text 24.99 (*0-415-20325-2*) Routledge.

— En Rumbo, Bk. 3.Tr. of Fresh Start. (SPA.). 160p. (Orig.). (C). 1999. pap. text 24.99 (*0-415-20326-0*) Routledge.

— En Rumbo, Bk. 4.Tr. of Fresh Start. 160p. (Orig.). (C). 1999. pap. text 24.99 (*0-415-20327-9*) Routledge.

— En Rumbo Cassette & Transcript 1: Fresh Start in Spanish. (C). 1999. 16.99 (*0-415-20600-6*) Routledge.

— En Rumbo Cassette & Transcript 2: Fresh Start in Spanish. (C). 1999. 16.99 (*0-415-20603-0*) Routledge.

— En Rumbo Cassette & Transcript 3: Fresh Start in Spanish. (C). 1999. 16.99 (*0-415-20606-5*) Routledge.

— En Rumbo Cassette & Transcript 4: Fresh Start in Spanish. (SPA.). (C). 1999. 16.99 (*0-415-20609-X*) Routledge.

— En Rumbo Pack 2: Fresh Start in Spanish. (C). 1999. text 39.99 (*0-415-20601-4*) Routledge.

— En Rumbo Pack 3: Fresh Start in Spanish. (C). 1999. text 39.99 (*0-415-20604-9*) Routledge.

— En Rumbo Pack 4: Fresh Start in Spanish. (SPA.). (C). 1999. text 39.99 (*0-415-20607-3*) Routledge.

— En Rumbo Pronunciation Cassettes & Transcript. (C). 1999. audio 24.99 (*0-415-20745-2*) Routledge.

— En Rumbo Video: Fresh Start in Spanish. (C). (gr. 13). 1999. 32.99 (*0-415-20610-3*) Routledge.

Ou-Yang, Geng Hau, tr. see Boice, James M.

Ouahib. Understanding & Using Corel Wp 8.0. (DF - Computer Applications Ser.). (C). 1998. pap. 79.95 (*0-538-71975-3*) S-W Pub.

Ouaki, Fabien, jt. auth. see Dalai Lama XIV.

Ouaknin, Marc-Alain. The Burnt Book: Reading the Talmud. Brown, Llewellyn, tr. from FRE. LC 94-39674.Tr. of Livre Brule. (ENG & FRE.). 272p. 1995. text 45.00 (*0-691-03729-9*, Pub. by Princeton U Pr) Cal Prin Full Svc.

— Burnt Book: Reading the Talmud. 272p. 1995. pap. text 18.95 (*0-691-05920-9*, Pub. by Princeton U Pr) Cal Prin Full Svc.

— Mysteries of the Alphabet. LC 98-44840. (Illus.). 384p. 1999. 39.95 (*0-7892-0523-8*); pap. 24.95 (*0-7892-0521-1*) Abbeville Pr.

***Ouaknin, Marc-Alain.** Mysteries of the Kabbalah. 2000. 39.95 (*0-7892-0654-4*) Abbeville Pr.

Oualline, Steve. C Elements of Style: The Programming Guide to Developing Well-Written C & C Plus Plus Programs. LC 92-33734. 200p. (Orig.). 1995. pap. 21.95 (*1-55851-291-8*, M&T Bks) IDG Bks.

— Discover Linux. LC 97-74805. 464p. 1997. pap. 24.99 (*0-7645-3105-0*) IDG Bks.

— Practical C++ Programming. Nye, Adrian, ed. LC 96-137928. 584p. 1995. reprint ed. pap. 34.95 (*1-56592-139-9*) Thomson Learn.

— Practical C Programming. 3rd rev. ed. Oram, Andy, ed. (Illus.). 454p. (Orig.). 1997. pap. 34.95 (*1-56592-306-5*) OReilly & Assocs.

Ouazar, D., et al, eds. Computational Hydraulics. (Computer Methods & Water Resources Ser.: Vol. 2). 470p. 1988. 129.95 (*0-387-18854-1*) Spr-Verlag.

— Computer Methods & Water Resources Vol. 2: Computational Hydraulics. LC 87-73387. (Computer Methods in Water Resources Ser.: Vol. 1). 500p. 1988. 108.00 (*0-931215-90-0*) Computational Mech MA.

— Water Quality, Planning & Management. (Computer Methods & Water Resources Ser.: Vol. 6). 310p. 1988. 128.95 (*0-387-18858-4*) Spr-Verlag.

Ouazar, D. & Brebbia, Carlos A., eds. Computational Transport Phenomena. (Computer Methods & Water Resources Ser.: Vol. 5). 270p. 1988. 79.95 (*0-387-18857-6*) Spr-Verlag.

— Computer Methods & Water Resources Vol. 1: Groundwater & Aquifer Modelling. LC 87-73387. (Computer Methods & Water Resources Ser.: Vol. 1). 210p. 1988. 51.00 (*0-931215-89-7*) Computational Mech MA.

— Computer Methods & Water Resources Vol. 4: Computer Aided Engineering in Water Resources. LC 87-73387. (Computer Methods in Water Resources Ser.: Vol. 1). 500p. 1988. 108.00 (*0-931215-92-7*) Computational Mech MA.

— Computer Methods & Water Resources Vol. 5: Computational Transport Phenomena. LC 87-73387. (Computer Methods in Water Resources Ser.: Vol. 1). 250p. 1988. 60.00 (*0-931215-93-5*) Computational Mech MA.

— Groundwater & Aquifer Modeling. (Computer Methods & Water Resources Ser.: Vol. 1). 210p. 1988. 68.95 (*0-387-18852-5*) Spr-Verlag.

Ouazar, D., jt. ed. see Blain, W. R.

Ouboter, P. E. Ecological Studies on Crocodilians in Suriname: Niche Segregation & Competition in Predators. (Illus.). viii, 140p. 1996. pap. 55.00 (*90-5103-131-9*, Pub. by SPB Acad Pub) Balogh.

Ouboter, Paul E., ed. The Freshwater Ecosystems of Suriname. LC 93-5180. (Monographiae Biologicae: Vol. 70). 292p. (C). 1993. text 223.00 (*0-7923-2408-0*) Kluwer Academic.

Oubre, Alondra Y. Instinct & Revelation: Reflections on the Origins of Numinous Perception. (World Futures' General Evolution Studies). 320p. 1997. pap. text 19.00 (*90-5699-528-6*) Gordon & Breach.

— Instinct & Revelation: Reflections on the Origins of Numinous Perception. (World Futures General Evolution Studies: Vol. 10). 320p. 1997. text 52.00 (*90-5699-527-8*) Gordon & Breach.

Oubre, Elton J. Vacherie, St. James Parish, Louisiana: History & Genealogy. LC 86-62380. (Illus.). 576p. 1986. 30.00 (*0-9617559-0-3*) Oubres Bks.

Ouby, Ian. Literary Britain & Ireland. 2nd ed. (Blue Guide Ser.). 1990. pap. 19.95 (*0-393-30490-6*) Norton.

Ouches, Thierry Des, see Des Ouches, Thierry.

Ouchi, Glenn I. Lotus in the Lab: Spreadsheet Applications for Scientists & Engineers. 196p. (C). 1988. pap. 24.95 (*0-201-14307-0*) Addison-Wesley.

— Personal Computers for Scientists. LC 86-24846. (Illus.). x, 250p. 1986. 34.95 (*0-8412-1000-4*); pap. 22.95 (*0-8412-1001-2*) Am Chemical.

— Personal Computers for Scientists: A Byte at a Time. LC 86-25846. 288p. 1987. reprint ed. pap. 89.30 (*0-608-03843-1*, 206429000008) Bks Demand.

Ouchi, Hajime. Japanese Optical & Geometrical Art. LC 77-82360. 170p. (Orig.). 1977. pap. 9.95 (*0-486-23553-X*) Dover.

Ouchl, K., jt. ed. see Gorbaty, Martin L.

O

An Asterisk (*) at the beginning of an entry indicates that the title is appearing for the first time.

Ouchi, William G. M-Form Society. 352p. 1986. mass mkt. 4.95 (0-380-69914-1, Avon Bks) Morrow Avon.
— Theory Z: How American Business Can Meet the Japanese Challenge. 1982. mass mkt. 5.99 (0-380-59451-X, Avon Bks) Morrow Avon.
Ouchley, jt. auth. see Findley.
Ouchley, Amy, jt. auth. see Findley, Ann.
Ouchterlony, O., ed. see WHO, 43rd Nobel Symposium, Stockholm, August 1978.
Oudar, J. & Wise, H. Deactivation & Poisoning of Catalysts. (Chemical Industries Ser.: Vol. 20). (Illus.). 344p. 1985. text 199.00 (0-8247-7338-1) Dekker.
Oudar, Jacques L., jt. ed. see Marcus, P.
Oude Essink, Gaulbert H. Impact of Sea Level Rise on Groundwater Flow Regimes: A Sensitivity Analysis for the Netherlands. (Illus.). 411p. (Orig.). 1996. pap. 54.50 (90-407-1330-8, Pub. by Delft U Pr) Coronet Bks.
Oude, N. T. De, see De Oude, N. T., ed.
Oudega, Martin, et al. Development of the Rat Spinal Cord: Immuno- & Enzyme Histochemical Approaches. LC 93-44601. 1994. 108.00 (0-387-57173-6) Spr-Verlag.
— Development of the Rat Spinal Cord: Immuno- & Enzyme Histochemical Approaches. LC 93-44601. (Advances in Anatomy, Embryology & Cell Biology Ser.: Vol. 129). viii, 166p. 1994. pap. write for info. (3-540-57173-6) Spr-Verlag.
Oudejans, J. H. Studies on IPM Policy in SE Asia: Two Centuries of Plant Protection in Indonesia, Malaysia & Thailand. (Wageningen Agricultural University Papers: Vol. 99.1). (Illus.). 334p. 1999. pap. 78.00 (90-5782-020-X) Backhuys Pubs.
Oudel, Solomon & Barfield, Owen. Reminiscences And . . . 1986. pap. 3.95 (0-916786-89-7, Saint George Pubns) R Steiner Col.
Oudemans, T. C. & Lardinois, A. P. Tragic Ambiguity: Anthropology, Philosophy & Sophocles' Antigone. (Brill's Studies in Intellectual History: Vol. 4). 280p. 1987. 93.00 (90-04-08417-7) Brill Academic Pubs.
Ouden, Bernard D. Den, see Den Ouden, Bernard D.
Ouden, C. Den, see Den Ouden, C., ed.
Ouden, C. Den, see Steemers, Theo C. & Den Ouden, C., eds.
Ouden, Den C. & Nicolay, D., eds. First E. C. Conference on Solar Heating. 1984. text 364.50 (90-277-1875-X) Kluwer Academic.
Oudenaarden, Alexander Van, see Van Oudenaarden, Alexander.
Oudenaren, John Van, see Van Oudenaren, John.
Oudenhoven, Nico Van, see Wazir, Rekha & Van Oudenhoven, Nico.
Oudheusden, B. W. Van, see Van Oudheusden, B. W.
Oudheusden, Susan. Go for It! A Student's Guide to Independent Projects. 75p. (J). 1989. pap. 14.95 (0-936386-51-7) Creative Learning.
Oudin, Bernard. Dictionnaire des Architectes de l'Antiquite a nos Jours. (FRE.). 568p. 1983. pap. 34.95 (0-7859-7796-1, 2221010906) Fr & Eur.
Oudin, Cesar. Refranes O Proverbios Castellanos Traduzidos en Lingua Francesca. 256p. reprint ed. write for info. (0-318-71627-5) G Olms Pubs.
Ouditt, Sharon. Fighting Forces, Writing Women: Identity & Ideology in the First World War. (Illus.). 240p. (C). 1993. pap. 29.99 (0-415-04705-6) Routledge.
— Fighting Forces, Writing Women: Identity & Ideology in the First World War. LC 93-15511. (Illus.). 240p. (C). (gr. 13). 1993. 90.00 (0-415-04704-8, A7955) Routledge.
***Ouditt, Sharon.** Women Writers of the First World War: An Annotated Bibliography. LC 99-20102. 288p. (C). (gr. 13). 1999. 85.00 (0-415-04752-8, E & FN Spon) Routledge.
Oudkerk, M. High-Power Gradient MR-Imaging: Advances in MRI II. (Illus.). 1997. 159.00 (0-632-04861-1) Blackwell Sci.
***Oudkerk, Matthijs.** Pulmonary Embolism: Epidemiology, Diagnosis & Treatment. (Illus.). 430p. 1998. 160.00 (0-632-04223-0) Blackwell Sci.
***Oudolf, Piet & Gerritsen, Henk.** Dream Plants for the Natural Garden. (Illus.). 144p. 2000. 34.95 (0-88192-493-8) Timber.
Oudolf, Piet & Kingsbury, Noel. Designing with Plants. LC 99-40854. (Illus.). 160p. 1999. 34.95 (0-88192-437-7) Timber.
Oudolf, Piet, jt. auth. see King, Michael.
Oudot, J. S. Guide to Correspondence in French. (Guides to Correspondence Ser.). (ENG & FRE., Illus.). 144p. (C). 1984. pap. 8.95 (0-8442-1501-5, 15014) NTC Contemp Pub Co.
Oudot, Simone. French Verbs & Essentials of Grammar. LC 99-86850. (...Verbs & Essentials of Ser.). (FRE., Illus.). 136p. (C). 2000. pap. 7.95 (0-8442-1500-7, 15007) NTC Contemp Pub Co.
Oudot, Simone & Gobert, David. Conversational French: A Functional Approach to Building Oral Proficiency. (FRE.). (C). pap., teacher ed. 11.25 (0-8442-1506-6, VF1506-6) NTC Contemp Pub Co.
Oudot, Simone & Gobert, David L. Conversational French. (FRE., Illus.). 320p. 1995. pap. 23.95 (0-8442-1505-8, 15058, Passprt Bks) NTC Contemp Pub Co.
***Oudshoorn, Henk, et al, eds.** Sustainable Development of Deltas: Proceedings International Conference at the Occasion of 200 Year Dictorate-General for Public Works & Water Management, Amsterdam, the Netherlands 23-27 November 1998. LC 99-237547. (Illus.). 484p. 1999. 62.50 (90-407-1856-3, Pub. by Delft U Pr) Coronet Bks.
Oudshoorn, Nelly. Beyond the Natural Body: An Archaeology of Sex Hormones. LC 94-4945. (Illus.). 224p. (C). 1994. pap. 25.99 (0-415-09191-8, A9982) Routledge.
Oudtshoorn, Lyn Van, see Summerfield, Jenny & Van Oudtshoorn, Lyn.
***Oueijan, Naji B.** A Compendium of Eastern Elements in Byron's Oriental Tales. LC 98-37894. (Studies in Nineteenth-Century British Literature: Vol. 13). 200p. (C). 1999. text 47.95 (0-8204-4173-2) P Lang Pubng.
Oueijan, Naji B. The Progress of an Image: The East in English Literature, Vol. 181. (American University Studies: Ser. IV). 152p. (C). 1996. 39.95 (0-8204-2712-8) P Lang Pubng.
Oueijan, Naji B., et al, eds. Kahlil Gibran & Ameen Rihani: Prophets of Lebanese-American Literature. 247p. 1999. 15.00 (0-9634349-4-2, Pub. by Notre Dame Univ) Platform Intl.
Oueinaught, R. Louis. The AESA: Accelerated Evolution Species Adjustment. LC 97-97196. 268p. 1998. 27.95 (1-891842-02-1); mass mkt. 9.95 (1-891842-03-X) Wash Oaks Pubg.
— IRkS: Internal Revenue (killing) Service. LC 97-97198. 264p. 1998. 27.95 (1-891842-04-8); mass mkt. 9.95 (1-891842-05-6) Wash Oaks Pubg.
— A Tiger Tail's Tales: Looking for the Perfect Woman - One with the Right Set of Imperfections. LC 97-97195. 272p. 1998. 27.95 (1-891842-00-5); mass mkt. 9.95 (1-891842-01-3) Wash Oaks Pubg.
Ouellet, Denis, tr. see Brown, H. Jackson, Jr.
Ouellet, Denis, tr. see Hay, Louise L.
Ouellet, Denis, tr. see Millman, Dan.
Ouellet, Denis, tr. see Williamson, Marianne.
Ouellet, Fernand, et al. Constitutionalism & Nationalism in Lower Canada: Essays. LC 75-431747. (Canadian Historical Readings Ser.: No. 5). 106p. reprint ed. pap. 32.90 (0-8357-6377-3, 203573100096) Bks Demand.
Ouellet, Jean-Claude. Repertoire des Deces et Sepultures No. 3: L'Isle Verte (1783-1993) 6th rev. ed. LC 96-7218. (FRE.). 131p. 1992. 16.00 (2-9803120-2-9) SGEQ.
Ouellet, Lawrence J. Pedal to the Metal: The Work Life of Truckers. LC 93-38954. 336p. (C). 1994. pap. 22.95 (1-56639-176-8); text 59.95 (1-56639-175-X) Temple U Pr.
Ouellete-Michalska, Madeleine. The Sandwoman. 96p. 1990. pap. 8.00 (0-920717-24-1) Guernica Editions.
Ouellette. Experiments in General, Organic & Biological Chemistry, Introduction to General Organ Chemistry. 4th ed. 320p. 1996. pap. text 47.00 (0-13-286758-3) P-H.
Ouellette, B. F., jt. auth. see Baxevanis, Andreas.
Ouellette, Daniel. The Volkswagen Bug Book: A Celebration of Beetle Culture. LC 99-6082. (Illus.). 144p. 1999. 30.00 (1-883318-00-9) Angel City Pr.
Ouellette, Dean C., ed. see Rockman, Richard G., Jr.
Ouellette, Deborah. Getting Started in the Modeling-Talent Industry. Neumann, Sarah, ed. LC 90-80008. (Illus.). 200p. (Orig.). 1990. pap. 24.95 (0-9625405-0-1) Aries MI.
Ouellette, Frances, jt. auth. see Redmond, Gertrude T.
Ouellette, Francois, jt. ed. see Dignonet, Michael J.
Ouellette, Francois, jt. ed. see Dignonet, Michel J.
Ouellette, Guillemond B., jt. ed. see Petrini, Orlando.
Ouellette, Helen T., ed. William of Malmesbury - Polyhistor: A Critical Edition. LC 81-18918. (Medieval & Renaissance Texts & Studies: Vol. 10). 176p. 1982. 30.00 (0-86698-017-2, MR10) MRTS.
Ouellette, Hughe & Tetreault, Patrice. Clinical Radiology Made Ridiculously Simple. (Illus.). 110p. 2000. pap. text 24.95 (0-940780-41-0) MedMaster.
Ouellette, L. Paul. How to Market the I/S Department Internally: Gaining the Recognition & Strategic Position You Merit. 224p. 1992. 28.95 (0-8144-5997-8) AMACOM.
Ouellette, Paul. I-S at Your Service: Knowing & Keeping Your Clients. 224p. 1998. 29.95 (0-7872-3408-7) Kendall-Hunt.
Ouellette, Pierre. The Deus Machine. 1996. mass mkt. 5.99 (0-671-53649-4, PB Trade Paper) PB.
— The Third Pandemic. 1997. per. 6.99 (0-671-52536-0) PB.
Ouellette, Raymond. Holistic Healing & the Edgar Cayce Readings. LC 80-80446. 384p. 1980. 11.95 (0-936450-07-X); pap. 7.75 (0-936450-08-8) Aero Pr.
— Life & Death & the Edgar Cayce Readings. LC 82-70682. 256p. 1982. 8.95 (0-936450-09-6) Aero Pr.
— 1998: The Year of Destiny, 2 bks., Bk. 1. LC 77-89344. (Illus.). 1978. 9.95 (0-936450-27-4) Aero Pr.
— 1998: The Year of Destiny, 2 bks., Bk. 2. LC 77-89344. (Illus.). 1978. 8.95 (0-936450-29-0) Aero Pr.
— 1998: The Year of Destiny, 2 bks., Set. LC 77-89344. (Illus.). 1978. write for info. (0-936450-28-2) Aero Pr.
— Psychic Magic. LC 74-78491. (Illus.). 343p. 1974. 12.95 (0-936450-00-2) Aero Pr.
Ouellette, Robert J. Introduction to General, Organic & Biological Chemistry. 4th ed. LC 95-32247. 782p. 1996. 95.00 (0-02-389670-1, Macmillan Coll) P-H.
— Organic Chemistry: A Brief Introduction. (Illus.). 624p. (C). 1994. write for info. (0-318-69913-3) Macmillan.
— Organic Chemistry: A Brief Introduction. 2nd ed. LC 97-25850. 559p. (C). 1997. pap. text 79.67 (0-13-841933-7) P-H.
Ouellette, Roland. Management of Aggressive Behavior: A Comprehensive Guide to Learning How to Recognize, Reduce, Manage, & Control Aggressive Behavior. LC 92-44600. 1993. 14.95 (1-879411-22-9) Perf Dimensions Pub.
Ouellette, Sylvie. Healing Passion. (Black Lace Ser.). 1995. mass mkt. 5.95 (0-352-32998-X, Pub. by Virgin Bks) London Brdge.
— Jasmine Blossoms. (Orig.). 1997. mass mkt. 5.95 (0-352-33157-7, Pub. by BLA4) London Brdge.
— The King's Girl. (Black Lace Ser.). 320p. 1996. mass mkt. 5.95 (0-352-33095-3, Pub. by Virgin Bks) London Brdge.
Ouette, Joseph. Practical Telepathy (1924) 116p. 1998. reprint ed. pap. 14.95 (0-7661-0634-9) Kessinger Pub.
***Ouffy, Jan.** Recuerdos de las Montanas. (SPA.). (J). (gr. 8-12). 2000. mass mkt. 3.99 (0-7899-0804-2) Spanish Hse Distributors.
Ough, C. S. & Amerine, Maynard A. Methods Analysis of Musts & Wines. 2nd ed. LC 87-28004. 400p. 1988. 185.00 (0-471-62757-7) Wiley.
Ough, Cornelius S. Winemaking Basics. LC 91-2253. (Illus.). 340p. 1992. pap. 29.95 (1-56022-006-6); lib. bdg. 59.95 (1-56022-005-8) Haworth Pr.
Ough, R. & McClelland, Alan M. Child Abuse: The Legal Approach to Medical Evidence. Matheson, Duncan et al, eds. 258p. 1995. pap. write for info. (0-406-04980-7, OCAL, MICHIE) LEXIS Pub.
Ough, Stuart, jt. auth. see Graham, John.
Oughourlian, Jean-Michel. The Puppet of Desire: The Psychology of Hysteria, Possession & Hypnosis. Webb, Eugene, tr. from FRE. LC 90-42448. 289p. 1991. 37.50 (0-8047-1823-7) Stanford U Pr.
Oughstun, K. E., et al. Electromagnetic Pulse Propagation in Causal Dielectrics, 16. Brekhovskikh, L. M. & Felsen, L. B., eds. (Wave Phenomena Ser.). 479p. 1997. 99.95 (0-387-57892-7) Spr-Verlag.
Oughstun, Kurt E., ed. Scalar Wave Diffraction. 652p. 1992. 65.00 (0-8194-0832-8); pap. 50.00 (0-8194-0833-6) SPIE.
Oughstun, Kurt E. & Sherman, G. C. Electromagnetic Pulse Propagation in Causal Dielectrics. LC 97-20903. (Springer Series on Wave Phenomena Ser.). 1997. write for info. (3-540-57892-7) Spr-Verlag.
Oughten, Jerrie. The Magic Weaver of Rugs. LC 93-4850. (Illus.). 32p. (J). 1994. 16.00 (0-395-66140-4) HM.
Oughton. Great African-American Athletes. 1998. pap. 2.95 (0-486-29319-X) Dover.
Oughton, jt. auth. see Martin.
Oughton, David & Lowry, John. Blackstone's Law Questions & Answers: Q&A Law of Torts. 2nd ed. 252p. 1999. pap., student ed. 24.00 (1-85431-810-1, Pub. by Blackstone Pr) Gaunt.
Oughton, David W. Consumer Law: Text, Cases & Materials. xxxii, 436p. (C). 1991. pap. 54.00 (1-85431-173-5, Pub. by Blackstone Pr) Gaunt.
Oughton, David W. & Lowry, John. Textbook on Consumer Law. 530p. 1997. pap. 54.00 (1-85431-538-2, Pub. by Blackstone Pr) Gaunt.
Oughton, David W., jt. auth. see Davis, Martin.
Oughton, Frederick. Grinling Gibbons & the English Woodcarving Tradition. LC 98-48735. (Illus.). 224p. 1999. reprint ed. pap. 45.00 (0-941936-52-X) Linden Pub Fresno.
Oughton, Jerrie. How the Stars Fell into the Sky. (Illus.). 32p. (J). (gr. k-3). 1992. 16.00 (0-395-58798-0) HM.
— How the Stars Fell into the Sky: A Navajo Legend. LC 91-17274. (Illus.). 32p. (J). (ps-3). 1996. pap. 5.95 (0-395-77938-3, Sandpiper) HM.
Oughton, Jerrie. How the Stars Fell into the Sky: A Navajo Legend. LC 91-17274. 1992. 11.15 (0-606-09438-5, Pub. by Turtleback) Demco.
Oughton, Jerrie. Music from a Place Called Half Moon. LC 94-25368. 176p. (YA). (gr. 5-9). 1997. mass mkt. 3.99 (0-440-21999-X, YB BDD) BDD Bks Young Read.
— Music from a Place Called Half Moon. LC 94-25368. 176p. (J). (gr. 5-8). 1995. 15.00 (0-395-70737-4) HM.
Oughton, Jerrie. Music from a Place Called Half Moon. 1997. 9.09 (0-606-11003-8, Pub. by Turtleback) Demco.
Oughton, Jerrie. The War in Georgia. 192p. (YA). (gr. 7). 1999. mass mkt. 4.50 (0-440-22752-6) BDD Bks Young Read.
— The War in Georgia. LC 96-22029. 192p. (J). 1997. 14.95 (0-395-81568-1) HM.
Oughton, John. Counting Out the Millennium. 84p. 1997. pap. 10.00 (1-87603-37-6) Pecan Grove.
Oughton, R. D. & Tyler, E. L. Tyler's Family Provision. 2nd ed. 1984. 90.00 (0-86205-075-8, MICHIE) LEXIS Pub.
***Oughtred, Iain.** Clinker Plywood Boatbuilding Manual. (Illus.). 174p. 2000. pap. 29.95 (0-937822-61-2) WoodenBoat Pubns.
Ougizawa, Toshiaki, jt. auth. see Rudolf, Bernd.
Ouhalla, Jamal. Introducing Transformational Grammar: From Rules to Principles & Parameters. 384p. 1995. pap. text 24.95 (0-340-55630-7, Pub. by E A) OUP.
— Introducing Transformational Grammer: From Principles & Parameters to Minimalism. 2nd ed. (An Arnold Publication). 496p. 1999. pap. text 24.95 (0-340-74036-1) OUP.
Ouida, pseud. A Dog of Flanders. (Illus.). 80p. (J). 1992. reprint ed. pap. 1.00 (0-486-27087-4) Dover.
— Under Two Flags, 3 vols., 2 bks. LC 79-8187. reprint ed. 84.50 (0-404-62088-4) AMS Pr.
Ouimet, Donald P. Woodcraft Gift Projects. LC 79-15909. (Illus.). 1979. 12.50 (0-8246-0243-9) Jonathan David.
Ouimette, Helen E. Country Catalog of Memories: A Childhood on a German-American Farm in the Late 1920s & Early 1930s. rev. ed. (Illus.). 204p. (Orig.). 1987. pap. 14.95 (0-9617116-1-2) H Ouimette.
Ouimette, Janice. Perinatal Nursing: Care of the High Risk Infant. 461p. (C). 1986. 56.25 (0-86720-356-0) Jones & Bartlett.
Ouimette, Victor. Reason Aflame: Unamuno & the Heroic Will. (Romantic Studies: No. 24). 237p. 1974. 35.00 (0-300-01666-2) Yale U Pr.
Ouk, Mory, tr. see Burns Knight, Margy.
Oukada, Larbi, jt. auth. see Oates, Michael D.
Oukah. Cherokee Bibliography. 145p. (Orig.). 1994. pap. 25.00 (1-890174-02-5) Triskelion Pr.
— Hawaiian Royal & Noble Genealogies: Who Is Who in Hawaii Today. 380p. 1998. pap. 25.00 (1-890174-05-X) Triskelion Pr.
— Hawaiian Royal Genealogies: Charts & Comments. 84p. (Orig.). 1994. pap. 25.00 (1-890174-01-7) Triskelion Pr.
— So Love Me Now. 74p. (Orig.). 1989. pap. 12.00 (1-890174-00-9) Triskelion Pr.
— The Ultimate Cherokee Cookbook. (Illus.). 72p. (Orig.). 1996. pap. 12.00 (1-890174-03-3) Triskelion Pr.
Oulanoff, Hongor. The Prose Fiction of Veniamin A. Kaverin. v, 203p. 1976. pap. 19.95 (0-89357-032-X) Slavica.
***Ould-Abdallah, Ahmedou.** Burundi on the Brink, 1993-95: A UN Special Envoy Reflects on Preventive Diplomacy. 192p. 2000. pap. 8.95 (1-929223-00-5) US Inst Peace.
Ould, Alan & Maycock, Stephen. The Beatles Collectibles. (Illus.). 144p. 1997. 17.98 (0-7858-0735-7) Bk Sales Inc.
Ould, Martyn A. Business Processes: Modelling & Analysis for Re-Engineering & Improvement. LC 95-3608. 224p. 1995. 109.95 (0-471-95352-0) Wiley.
— Managing Software Quality & Business Risk. LC 99-32078. 392p. 1999. pap. 64.99 (0-471-99782-X) Wiley.
Ould, Martyn A. & Unwin, Charles, eds. Testing in Software Development. (British Computer Society Monographs in Informatics). 134p. 1987. pap. text 30.95 (0-521-33786-0) Cambridge U Pr.
Ould, Martyn A., jt. auth. see Birrell, N. D.
Ould-Mey, Mohameden. Global Restructuring & Peripheral States: The Carrot & the Stick in Mauritania. 330p. (C). 1996. pap. text 24.95 (0-8226-3051-6); lib. bdg. 67.50 (0-8226-3050-8) Littlefield.
Oulette, Benoit, tr. see Martin, Michele.
Oulton, Derek, ed. see Lewis, David.
Oulton, J. E., tr. Ecclesiastical History, 2 vols., 2. (Loeb Classical Library: No. 153, 265). 500p. 1932. 18.95 (0-674-99293-8) HUP.
Oulton, Nicholas & O'Mahony, Mary. Productivity & Growth. (National Institute of Economic & Social Research Occasional Papers: No. 46). (Illus.). 333p. (C). 1994. text 64.95 (0-521-45345-3) Cambridge U Pr.
***Oum, et al.** Strategic Alliances of the World's Major Airlines. 2000. 65.00 (0-08-043596-3, Pergamon Pr) Elsevier.
Oum, Tae H., et al, eds. Transport Economics: Selected Readings. 710p. 1997. pap. text 26.00 (90-5702-186-2, Harwood Acad Pubs) Gordon & Breach.
Oum, Tae H. & Yu, Chunyan. Winning Airlines: Productivity & Cost Competitiveness of the World's Major Airlines. LC 97-41219. (Transportation Research, Economics & Policy Ser.: No. 8). 240p. 1997. 104.50 (0-7923-8010-X) Kluwer Academic.
Ouma-Onyango, Richard. Information Resources & Technology Transfer Management in Developing Countries. LC 97-6092. (Studies in Information & Library Management Systems Ser.). 240p. (C). 1997. 75.00 (0-415-09156-X) Routledge.
Oumano, Elena. A Handbook of Natural Folk Remedies. LC 96-96920. 256p. (Orig.). 1997. mass mkt. 5.99 (0-380-78448-3, Avon Bks) Morrow Avon.
— Natural Sex: How to Use Natural & Ancient Techniques to Create a More Passionate Love Life. LC 98-42311. 1999. pap. 13.95 (0-452-28048-6, Plume) Dutton Plume.
Oumano, Elena, jt. auth. see Esposito, Joe.
Oumano, Elena, jt. auth. see Gold, Aviva.
Oumlil, A. Ben, ed. see Academy of Marketing Science Staff.
Ounsted, Christopher, et al. Temporal Lobe Epilepsy, 1948-1986. (Clinics in Developmental Medicine Ser.: No. 103). (Illus.). 129p. (C). 1987. text 49.50 (0-685-41924-X, Pub. by Mc Keith Pr) Cambridge U Pr.
— Temporal Lobe Epilepsy, 1948 to 1986. (Clinics in Developmental Medicine Ser.: No. 103). 129p. 1991. text 49.95 (0-521-41220-X) Cambridge U Pr.
Ouologuem, Yambo. Bound to Violence. (African Writers Ser.). 182p. (C). 1971. pap. 9.95 (0-435-90099-4, 90099) Heinemann.
Our Lady of Perpetual Help Church Women's Guild St & Leonard, Rita. Simple Elegance: A Culinary Collection of Simple to Elegant Recipes. LC 92-60860. 288p. 1997. reprint ed. 18.95 (0-9633165-0-8) Our Lady Perpet HCWG.
Our Square Members. Inside the Square: Our Secrets to Success. Grossberg, Blythe, ed. 136p. 1999. pap. 12.95 (0-9670835-0-8, Our Square) Desiderata Alli.
***Our Sunday Visitor Staff.** Cantate et Jubilate Des: A Devotional & Liturgical Hymnal.Tr. of Devotional & Liturgical Hymnal. (ENG & SPA.). 1999. 29.95 (0-87973-971-1) Our Sunday Visitor.
— Catechism of the Catholic Church. 2nd ed. 928p. 2000. 24.95 (0-87973-977-0); pap. text 14.95 (0-87973-976-2) Our Sunday Visitor.
Our Sunday Visitor Staff. Our Sunday Visitors Christmas Memories. LC 97-67611. 104p. 1997. pap. text 5.95 (0-87973-919-3) Our Sunday Visitor.
Our Town Revision Committee Staff. Our Town, Mesa, Arizona: The Story of Mesa. 6th rev. ed. (Illus.). 208p. 1991. 24.95 (0-9629563-0-9) Mesa Pub Schl.
Oura, Eleanor N., jt. ed. see Chiogioji, Melvin H.
Ourada, Joanne, jt. compiled by see Hough-Savage, Melissa.
Ourcharacter.com Technical Advisory Committee, ed. see Abdian, Geoffrey & Arvidson, P. Sven.
Ourcharacter.com Technical Advisory Committee, ed. see Arvidson, P. Sven & Abdian, Geoffrey.
Ourdan, J. P. The Art of Retouching by Burrows & Colton. LC 72-9187. (Literature of Photography Ser.). 1973. reprint ed. 17.95 (0-405-04898-X) Ayer.
Ouren, Dallas L. A Reexamination of Sir William Hamilton's Philosophy: Mill on Hamilton. LC 91-44634. (Illus.). 216p. 1992. lib. bdg. 89.95 (0-7734-9940-7) E Mellen.
Ouriel, Kenneth, ed. Lower Extremity Vascular Disease. LC 95-6842. 1995. text 152.00 (0-7216-4749-9, W B Saunders Co) Harcrt Hlth Sci Grp.

O

Ouriel, Kenneth & Rutherford, Robert B. Atlas of Vascular Surgery: Operative Procedures. Bralow, Lisette, ed. LC 97-22033. (Illus.). 384p. 1998. text 95.00 (*0-7216-6994-8*, W B Saunders Co) Harcrt Hlth Sci Grp.

Ouriou, Katie. Love Ya Like a Sister: A Story of Friendship from the Journals of Katie Ouriou. Johnston, Julie, ed. 208p. (YA). (gr. 5 up). 1999. pap. 7.95 (*0-88776-454-1*) Tundra Bks.

Ouriou, Susan, tr. see Marineau, Michele.

Ouriou, Susan, tr. see Olaizola, Jose L.

*__Ourisman, David J.__ From Gospel to Sermon: Preaching Synoptic Texts. 1999. pap. 17.99 (*0-8272-1026-4*) Chalice Pr.

Ours, Frank. Cold Weather Gardening. (Illus.). 30p. 1994. pap. 5.00 (*0-87012-526-5*) McClain.
This book is a step-by-step account of gardening in cold temperatures with alternate energy resources, plant protectors, storage, mulchers & greenhouses. Graphic artwork & photos assist the cold weather gardener. *Publisher Paid Annotation.*

Ours, Jan C. Van, see Van Ours, Jan C.

*__Ours, Robert M.__ College Football Encyclopedia. 3rd rev. ed. (Illus.). 1500p. 2000. 49.95 (*0-9675534-1-5*) R M Ours.

Ours, Robert M. Journalism at West Virginia University. LC 77-84188. (Illus.). 1977. pap. 3.00 (*0-930362-01-2*) Sch Journal WVU.

*__Oursler, Bill.__ Porsche Racing Cars. (Illus.). 192p. 2000. 39.95 (*0-7603-0727-X*, 129811AP, Pub. by MBI Pubg) Motorbooks Intl.

Oursler, Fulton. A Child's Life of Jesus. (Illus.). 96p. (J). (gr. k-3). 1997. 15.95 (*0-687-02910-4*) Abingdon.
— A Child's Story of Christmas. LC 97-185335. 24p. 1996. pap. 1.95 (*0-687-02200-2*) Abingdon.
— The Greatest Story Ever Told. 1994. reprint ed. lib. bdg. 21.95 (*1-56849-555-2*) Buccaneer Bks.
— The Greatest Story Ever Told. 320p. 1989. reprint ed. pap. 11.95 (*0-385-08028-X*, D121, Image Bks) Doubleday.
— The Greatest Story Ever Told: The Timeless Story of the Life of Jesus Christ. LC 97-8109. 1998. write for info. (*0-05-171786-7*) Random Hse Value.

Oursler, Henry. Satisfaction Guaranteed: Contentment. (Inter Acta Ser.). (Illus.). 6p. (C). 1994. teacher ed., ring bd. 1.25 (*1-885702-71-X*, 741-051t, Inter Acta); student ed., ring bd. 3.25 (*1-885702-70-1*, 741-051s, Inter Acta) WSN Pr.

*__Oursler, Tony, et al.__ Introjection: Tony Oursler, Mid-Career Survey, 1976-1999. LC 99-57569. (Illus.). 128p. 2000. write for info. (*0-913697-25-7*, Pub. by Williams Art) Dist Art Pubs.

Ourth, John & Tamarri, Kathie T. Career Caravan. 64p. (J). (gr. 4-8). 1979. 8.99 (*0-916456-52-8*, GA121) Good Apple.

Ourth, John, jt. auth. see McCrory, Rosemary.

Ourusoff de Fernandez-Gemenez, Elizabeth & Mundy, E. James. Multilateralism vs. Regionalism: Trade Issues after the Uruguay Round. LC 89-12920. (Illus.). 315p. 1990. text 119.95 (*0-521-39095-8*) Cambridge U Pr.

O

Oury, Guy-Marie. Dictionnaire de la Foi Catholique. (FRE.). 267p. 1986. 59.95 (*0-7859-8088-1*, 2854431162) Fr & Eur.
— Dictionnaire de la Priere. (FRE.). 236p. 1990. 75.00 (*0-7859-8091-1*, 2854432169) Fr & Eur.

Oury, Guy-Marie. The Mass: Spirituality, History, & Practice. Otto, John, tr. from FRE.Tr. of La/Messe: Spiritualite, Historie, Pratique. 126p. 1988. pap. 3.95 (*0-89942-126-1*, 126/04) Catholic Bk Pub.

Oury, Guy-Marie. A Monastic Pilgrimage: Following in the Steps of Saint Benedict. LC 98-6250. 184p. 1998. pap. 15.95 (*1-879007-28-2*, MONA) St Bedes Pubns.

Ousaka, Yumi, jt. compiled by see Yamazaki, Moriichi.

Ousby. Companion to English Literature. 1036p. 1997. pap. 7.95 (*1-85326-336-2*, 3362WW, Pub. by Wrdsworth Edits) NTC Contemp Pub Co.

Ousby, Ian. Blue Guide: Burgundy. (Illus.). 212p. 1992. pap. 19.95 (*0-393-30886-3*) Norton.
— Cambridge Guide to Fiction in English. (Illus.). 332p. (C). 1998. pap. 18.95 (*0-521-57617-2*); text 44.95 (*0-521-63138-6*) Cambridge U Pr.
— England. 11th ed. (Blue Guide Ser.). (Illus.). 784p. 1995. pap. 24.00 (*0-393-31340-9*, Norton Paperbks) Norton.
— Guilty Parties: A Mystery Lover's Companion. LC 97-60242. (Illus.). 224p. (Orig.). 1997. pap. 24.95 (*0-500-27978-0*, Pub. by Thames Hudson) Norton.

*__Ousby, Ian.__ Occupation: The Ordeal of France, 1940-1944. LC 00-22779. 2000. 18.95 (*0-8154-1043-3*) Cooper Sq.

Ousby, Ian. Occupation: The Ordeal of France, 1940-1944. LC 98-11229. 352p. 1998. text 25.95 (*0-312-18148-5*) St Martin.

Ousby, Ian, ed. The Cambridge Guide to Literature in English. 2nd ed. (Illus.). 1067p. (C). 1994. 49.95 (*0-521-44086-6*) Cambridge U Pr.
— Cambridge Paperback Guide to Literature in English. 444p. (C). 1996. pap. 19.95 (*0-521-43627-3*) Cambridge U Pr.

Ouseg, H. L. The International Dictionary: The Words You Need in Twenty One Languages. 368p. 1995. pap. 14.95 (*0-8065-1677-1*, Citadel Pr) Carol Pub Group.

Ouseley, S. G. Colour Meditations. 90p. 1996. reprint ed. pap. 11.50 (*0-7873-1175-8*) Hlth Research.
— The Power of the Rays. 99p. 1996. reprint ed. pap. 11.00 (*0-7873-0648-7*) Hlth Research.

Ouseley, William G. Remarks on the Statistics & Political Institutions of the United States. LC 70-117887. (Select Bibliographies Reprint Ser.). 1977. reprint ed. 21.95 (*0-8369-5340-1*) Ayer.

Ouseley, William G., tr. see Hawqal, Ibn.

Ouslander, Joseph G., et al. Medical Care in the Nursing Home. 461p. 1991. text 58.00 (*0-07-047949-6*) McGraw-Hill HPD.
— Medical Care in the Nursing Home. 2nd ed. LC 96-43576. (Illus.). 480p. 1996. text 60.00 (*0-07-048209-8*) McGraw-Hill HPD.

Ousler, Will. The Healing Power of Faith. 366p. 1989. reprint ed. pap. 9.95 (*0-930298-14-4*) Westwood Pub Co.

Ousley, Pamela D. The Law & Mercury-Free Dentistry. 260p. (Orig.). 1994. pap. 19.65 (*0-941011-11-9*) Bio-Probe.

Ousmane, Sembene. God's Bits Of Wood. 256p. 1996. pap. 11.95 (*0-435-90959-2*) Heinemann.
— God's Bits of Wood. Price, Francis, tr. from FRE. (African Writers Ser.). 256p. (C). 1987. reprint ed. pap. 10.95 (*0-435-90892-8*, 90892) Heinemann.

Ousmane, Sembene. The Last of the Empire. Adams, Adrian, tr. from FRE. (African Writers Ser.). Orig. Title: Le Dernier de L'Empire. 238p. (Orig.). (C). 1983. pap. 11.95 (*0-435-90250-4*, 90250) Heinemann.

Ousmane, Sembene. The Money-Order with White Genesis. Wake, Clive, tr. from FRE. (African Writers Ser.). 138p. (C). 1987. pap. 9.95 (*0-435-90894-4*, 90894) Heinemann.
— Niiwam & Taaw. Glenn-Lauga, Catherine, tr. (African Writers Ser.). 110p. (C). 1992. pap. 8.95 (*0-435-90671-2*, 90671) Heinemann.

Ousmane, Sembene. Tribal Scars & Other Stories. Ortzen, Len, tr. LC 87-25035. (African Writers Ser.). 117p. (C). 1987. pap. 8.95 (*0-435-90142-7*, 90142) Heinemann.

Ousmane, Sembene. Xala. Wake, Clive, tr. from FRE. LC 75-41811. (Illus.). 110p. 1983. pap. 9.95 (*1-55652-070-0*, Lawrence Hill) Chicago Review.

Ousnamer, Mark A. OFE & M: The Only Acronym You'll Ever Need. LC 97-11359. (Illus.). 118p. (Orig.). 1997. pap. 25.00 (*0-89806-175-X*, OUSNAM) Eng Mgmt Pr.
— Practical Ergonomics. LC 98-2851. (Illus.). 1998. 29.95 (*0-89806-184-9*, PRERGO) Eng Mgmt Pr.

Ouspensky, Leonid. Theology of the Icon, 2 vols. Gythiel, Anthony P. & Meyendorff, Elizabeth, trs. from FRE. LC 92-12323. (Illus.). 728p. (C). 1992. pap. 26.95 (*0-88141-124-8*) St Vladimirs.
— Theology of the Icon, 2 vols., 1. Gythiel, Anthony P. & Meyendorff, Elizabeth, trs. from FRE. LC 92-12323. (Illus.). 728p. (C). 1992. pap. 12.95 (*0-88141-122-1*) St Vladimirs.
— Theology of the Icon, 2 vols., 2. Gythiel, Anthony P. & Meyendorff, Elizabeth, trs. from FRE. LC 92-12323. (Illus.). 728p. (C). 1992. pap. 13.95 (*0-88141-123-X*) St Vladimirs.

Ouspensky, Leonid, jt. auth. see Lossky, Vladimir.

Ouspensky, P. D. Fourth Way. 1971. pap. 15.00 (*0-394-71672-8*) Vin Bks.
— In Search of the Miraculous: Fragments of an Unknown Teaching. 416p. 1965. pap. 14.00 (*0-15-644508-5*, Harvest Bks) Harcourt.
— A New Model of the Universe. LC 97-6291. 576p. 1997. reprint ed. pap. text 12.95 (*0-486-29701-2*) Dover.
— New Model of the Universe (1931) 570p. 1999. reprint ed. pap. 27.50 (*0-7661-0822-8*) Kessinger Pub.
— Psychology of Man's Possible Evolution. 2nd ed. 1973. pap. 8.00 (*0-394-71943-3*) Knopf.
— The Symbolism of the Tarot. Pogossky, A. L., tr. from RUS. (Illus.). 63p. 1976. reprint ed. pap. 2.95 (*0-486-23291-3*) Dover.
— The Symbolism of the Tarot: A Long-Lost Classic Resurrected. 75p. 1995. pap. 18.95 (*0-87877-229-4*) Newcastle Pub.
— The Symbolism of the Tarot (1913) Philosophy of Occultism in Pictures & Numbers. 68p. 1998. reprint ed. pap. 12.95 (*0-7661-0478-8*) Kessinger Pub.

*__Ouspensky, P. D.__ Talks with a Devil. Bennett, J. G., tr. from RUS. LC 99-58155. 192p. 2000. pap. 14.95 (*1-57863-164-5*) Weiser.

Ouspensky, P. D. Tertium Organum. 350p. 1998. reprint ed. pap. 24.95 (*0-7661-0422-2*) Kessinger Pub.
— Tertium Organum: A Key to the Enigmas of the World, Vol. 168. Kadloubovsky, E., tr. from RUS. LC 81-52264. 320p. 1982. pap. 15.00 (*0-394-75168-X*) Vin Bks.

Oussaid, Brick. The Mountains Forgotten by God: The Story of a Moroccan Berber Family. Woollcombe, Ann, tr. from FRE. 129p. 1989. 10.95 (*0-89410-481-0*, Three Contnts) L Rienner.

Oussiemi, Maria & Abuhaidar, Lamia. Caught in the Crossfire: Young Victims of War Speak Out. 128p. (YA). (gr. 5 up). 1995. lib. bdg. 20.85 (*0-8027-8364-3*) Walker & Co.

Oussiemi, Maria, et al. Caught in the Crossfire: Young Victims of War Speak Out. LC 94-44457. (Illus.). 128p. (YA). (gr. 4-7). 1995. 19.95 (*0-8027-8363-5*) Walker & Co.

Ousterhou. Aesthetic Contouring of the Craniofacial Skeleton. 1991. 350.00 (*0-316-67410-9*, Little Brwn Med Div) Lppncott W & W.

Ousterhout. Atlas Facial Aesthetic Skeletal Contouring. 1997. write for info. (*0-7216-5460-6*, W B Saunders Co) Harcrt Hlth Sci Grp.

Ousterhout, Anne M. A State Divided: Opposition in Pennsylvania to the American Revolution, 123. LC 86-29573. (Contributions in American History Ser.: No. 123). 358p. 1987. 59.95 (*0-313-25728-0*, OUS/, Greenwood Pr) Greenwood.

Ousterhout, John K. TCL & the TK Toolkit. 480p. (C). 1994. pap. text 46.95 (*0-201-63337-X*) Addison-Wesley.
— The TCL & TK Reference Manual. 600p. 1996. pap. write for info. (*0-201-63443-0*) Addison-Wesley.

Ousterhout, Robert G. Architecture of the Kariye Camii in Istanbul. LC 87-22279. (Dumbarton Oaks Studies: Vol. 25). (Illus.). 292p. 1988. 45.00 (*0-88402-165-3*) Dumbarton Oaks.

*__Ousterhout, Robert G.__ Master Builders of Byzantium. LC 99-29652. 320p. 2000. 65.00 (*0-691-00535-4*, Pub. by Princeton U Pr) Cal Prin Full Svc.

Ousterhout, Robert G. & Basgelen, Nezih. Monuments of Unaging Intellect: Historic Postcards of Byzantine Istanbul. (Illus.). 136p. (C). 1995. pap. text 29.95 (*0-252-06473-9*) U of Ill Pr.

Ousterhout, Robert G. & Brubaker, Leslie, eds. The Sacred Image East & West. LC 93-43343. (Illinois Byzantine Studies: Vol. 4). 320p. 1994. text 29.95 (*0-252-02096-0*) U of Ill Pr.

Ouston, Janet, et al, eds. OFSTED Inspections: The Early Experience. 176p. 1996. pap. 27.95 (*1-85346-408-2*, Pub. by David Fulton) Taylor & Francis.

Ouston, Julie E. Veterinary Nursing: Self-Assessment Questions & Answers, Vol. 1. 128p. 1997. pap. text 20.00 (*0-7506-3731-5*) Buttrwrth-Heinemann.
— Veterinary Nursing: Self-Assessment Questions & Answers, Vol. 2. 148p. 1997. pap. text 20.00 (*0-7506-3732-3*) Buttrwrth-Heinemann.

*__Ouston, Julie Elizabeth.__ Veterinary Nursing Self-Assessment Questions & Answers. 2nd ed. 256p. 2000. pap. text 25.00 (*0-7506-4803-1*) Buttrwrth-Heinemann.

Ouston, Rick. Finding Family. 214p. 1994. pap. 11.00 (*0-921586-31-0*, Pub. by New Star Bks) Genl Dist Srvs.

Out el Kouloub. Ramza. Atiya, Nayra, tr. from FRE. (Contemporary Issues in the Middle East Ser.). (Illus.). 128p. 1994. pap. 16.95 (*0-8156-0280-4*); text 34.95 (*0-8156-2618-5*) Syracuse U Pr.
— Zanouba: A Novel. Atiya, Nayra, tr. & intro. by. LC 96-21142. (Middle East Literature in Translation Ser.). 192p. 1996. 39.95 (*0-8156-2718-1*, ATZA); pap. 17.95 (*0-8156-0408-4*, ATZAP) Syracuse U Pr.

Out, H. J. & Bennink, H. J., eds. Recombinant FSH (Puregon) Preclinical & Clinical Experience. LC 96-20463. (Studies in Profertility Ser.: Vol. 5). 190p. 1996. 65.00 (*1-85070-746-4*) Prthnon Pub.

Out Magazine Editors Staff. The Gay & Lesbian Address Book. LC 94-44475. 288p. 1995. pap. 13.00 (*0-399-51933-5*, Perigee Bks) Berkley Pub.

Out Magazine Staff, jt. auth. see Fitch, James.

Out of Control: Lesbian Committee to Support Women Political Prisoners, ed. see Whitehorn, Laura, et al.

Outaiba Elhuwaib, tr. see Abdulhamid Jodah Al Sahhar.

Outcalt, Charles L., ed. see McMahon, Kathleen N.

Outcalt, Todd. Before You Say "I Do" Loving Questions for couples. LC 97-16804. 288p. 1998. pap. 12.95 (*0-399-52375-8*, Perigee Bks) Berkley Pub.
— The Best Things in Life Are Free. LC 98-16010. 250p. 1998. pap. 11.95 (*1-55874-607-2*) Health Comm.
— The Heat is On: 100 Cool Ideas for Summertime Youth Events. LC 98-40762. 112p. 1998. pap. 12.95 (*0-687-08214-5*) Abingdon.

*__Outcalt, Todd.__ Holidays, Holy Days & Other Big Days for Youth. (J). 1999. 13.00 (*0-687-08204-8*) Abingdon.

Outcalt, Todd. Meeting-Space Ideas for Youth Ministry: 80 Fun Options to Create a Faith-Building Place Kids Want to Be. Simpson, Amy, ed. LC 97-39561. 176p. 1998. per. 15.99 (*0-7644-2026-7*) Group Pub.
— Seeing Is Believing! 100 Youth Talks for Every Occasion. LC 98-25979. 112p. 1998. pap. 12.95 (*0-687-07182-8*) Abingdon.

Outcault, Richard F. The Yellow Kid: A Centennial Celebration of the Kid Who Started the Comics. Blackbeard, Bill, ed. (Illus.). 1995. 55.00 (*0-87816-380-8*) Kitchen Sink.

Outdoor Books & Maps, Inc. Staff. Arapaho & Roosevelt National Forest Recreation Guide. rev. ed. 96p. 1998. pap. 12.95 (*0-930657-08-X*) Outdr Bks & Maps.
— The Best of Colorado Biking Trails. rev. ed. LC 96-675618. 96p. 1998. pap. 9.95 (*0-930657-28-4*) Outdr Bks & Maps.
— Best of Northern Colorado Hiking Trails. rev. ed. 112p. 1998. pap. 12.95 (*0-930657-18-7*) Outdr Bks & Maps.
— Best of Western Colorado Hiking Trails. rev. ed. 72p. 1998. pap. 9.95 (*0-930657-17-9*) Outdr Bks & Maps.

Outdoor Books & Maps Inc. Staff. Colorado Lakes & Reservoirs Guide. rev. ed. 160p. 1998. 14.95 (*0-930657-00-4*, CO5) Outdr Bks & Maps.
— The Complete Colorado Campground Guide. rev. ed. 160p. 1999. 14.95 (*0-930657-23-3*, CO4) Outdr Bks & Maps.
— Fishing Close to Home. rev. ed. 32p. 1999. 5.95 (*0-930657-05-5*, CO6) Outdr Bks & Maps.
— Front Range Lake Bottom Book. 31p. 1991. 4.95 (*0-930657-06-3*, CO7) Outdr Bks & Maps.
— Grand Mesa National Forest Recreation Guide. 48p. 1996. pap. 6.95 (*0-930657-09-8*) Outdr Bks & Maps.

Outdoor Books & Maps, Inc. Staff. Gunnison National Forest Recreation Guide. 160p. 1995. pap. 12.95 (*0-930657-10-1*) Outdr Bks & Maps.
— Pike National Forest Recreation Guide. rev. ed. 64p. 1998. pap. 12.95 (*0-930657-11-X*) Outdr Bks & Maps.

Outdoor Books & Maps Inc. Staff. Rio Grande National Forest. 96p. 1997. 9.95 (*0-930657-15-2*) Outdr Bks & Maps.
— Routt National Forest. 64p. 1997. 9.95 (*0-930657-12-8*) Outdr Bks & Maps.

Outdoor Books & Maps, Inc. Staff. San Isabel National Forest Recreation Guide. 160p. 1995. pap. 12.95 (*0-930657-14-4*) Outdr Bks & Maps.

Outdoor Books & Maps Inc. Staff. San Juan National Forest. 72p. 1997. 9.95 (*0-930657-13-6*) Outdr Bks & Maps.
— White River National Forest. 96p. 1997. 9.95 (*0-930657-16-0*) Outdr Bks & Maps.

Outdoor Life (Times Mirror Magazine, Inc.) Staff, jt. auth. see Cowles Creative Publishing Staff.

*__Outdoor Life Magazine Staff.__ Best of Outdoor Life: The Greatest Hunting, Fishing & Survival Stories from America's Favorite Outdoors Magazine. 2000. 27.95 (*1-58574-119-1*) Lyon Press.

Outdoor Life Staff. Deer Hunter's Yearbook, 1987. 1987. 19.95 (*0-943822-77-7*) Times Mir Mag Bk Div.
— Guns & Shooting Yearbook, 1987. 1987. 19.95 (*0-943822-84-X*) Times Mir Mag Bk Div.

*__Outdoor Life Staff.__ Outdoor Life Hunting Big Game in North America: Outdoor Life's Experts Reveal Their Secrets. (Outdoor Life Ser.). (Illus.). 224p. 2000. pap. 14.95 (*0-86573-123-3*) Creat Pub Intl.

Outdoor Scotland Series Staff. Edinburgh-Lothians, Fife, Around Glasgow: Outdoor Scotland Pack. (Outdoor Scotland Ser.). (Illus.). 150p. 1997. pap. 38.00 (*0-11-702196-2*, Pub. by Statnry Office) Balogh.

Outdoor Writers Association of America Staff. Outdoor Writers Association of America Outdoor Style Manual. Brown, Jack et al, eds. LC 91-61065. 88p. (Orig.). 1991. pap. 10.00 (*0-944973-00-0*) Outdoor Writ.

Outerbridge, David. Champion in a Man's World: The Biography of Marion Hollins. LC 98-11410. (Illus.). 208p. 1998. 24.95 (*1-886947-40-6*) Sleepng Bear.

*__Outerbridge, Graeme.__ Trains: A Photographer's Journey. LC 99-41258. (Illus.). 152p. 2000. 35.00 (*0-8109-4481-2*, Pub. by Abrams) Time Warner.

Outhoefer, Frank. Lecithin & Health: Featuring Phosphatidylcholine & Serine. LC 99-212483. (Illus.). 84p. 1998. pap. 8.95 (*1-890612-03-0*, 58604) Vital Health.

Outhwaite, Lucille C. Flowers in the Wind. LC 94-92291. (Illus.). 88p. (Orig.). 1994. pap. 19.95 (*0-9631722-3-9*) Hamilton Print.
— To the Ends of the Earth. (Illus.). 132p. (Orig.). 1997. pap. 19.95 (*0-9631722-7-1*) Hamilton Print.

Outhwaite, R. B. Clandestine Marriage in England, 1500-1850. LC 95-13102. 1995. 45.00 (*1-85285-130-9*) Hambledon Press.
— Dearth, Public Polity & Social Disturbance in England, 1550-1800. (New Studies in Economic & Social History: Vol. 14). 72p. (C). 1995. text 34.95 (*0-521-55273-7*); pap. text 10.95 (*0-521-55780-1*) Cambridge U Pr.
— Scandal in the Church: Dr. Edward Drax Free, 1764-1843. LC 97-22833. 208p. 1997. 40.00 (*1-85285-165-1*) Hambledon Press.

Outhwaite, William. Habermas: A Critical Introduction. (Key Contemporary Thinkers Ser.). 165p. (C). 1995. 35.00 (*0-8047-2478-4*); pap. 14.95 (*0-8047-2479-2*) Stanford U Pr.

Outhwaite, William & Bottomore, Tom, eds. The Blackwell Dictionary of Twentieth-Century Social Thought. 880p. (C). 1994. pap. text 38.95 (*0-631-19575-0*) Blackwell Pubs.

Outhwaite, William & Martell, Luke, eds. The Sociology of Politics, 3 vols. LC 97-37216. (International Library of Critical Writings in Economics Ser.: Series 10). 1976p. (C). 1998. 690.00 (*1-85278-901-8*) E Elgar.

Outhwaite, William & Mulkay, Michael, eds. Social Theory & Social Criticism: Essays for Tom Bottomore. (Modern Revivals in Sociology Ser.). 273p. 1992. 61.95 (*0-7512-0073-5*, Pub. by Gregg Revivals) Ashgate Pub Co.

*__Outing, Steve.__ Newspapers & New Media: The Digital Awakening of the Newspaper Industry. LC 99-68450. (Illus.). 72p. (C). 2000. pap. text 25.00 (*0-88362-302-1*) GATFPress.

Outka, Gene. Agape: An Ethical Analysis. LC 78-88070. (Publications in Religion Ser.: No. 17). 336p. 1977. pap. 18.00 (*0-300-02122-4*) Yale U Pr.

Outka, Gene & Reeder, John P., Jr., eds. Prospects for a Common Morality. LC 92-5681. 296p. 1992. text 65.00 (*0-691-07418-6*, Pub. by Princeton U Pr); pap. text 18.95 (*0-691-02093-0*, Pub. by Princeton U Pr) Cal Prin Full Svc.

Outland, Barbara. Reading! 3rd ed. 288p. (C). 1995. pap. text, per. 52.95 (*0-7872-0409-9*, 41040901) Kendall-Hunt.

Outland, Breck, et al. Three Myths: Of Gods, Devils & Beasts. Rhipidon Society Staff, ed. (Illus.). 142p. 1997. 30.00 (*0-9659512-2-7*); pap. 10.00 (*0-9659512-3-5*) Pentaradial.

Outland, Charles F. Mines, Murders, & Grizzlies: Tales of California's Ventura Back Country. rev. ed. LC 69-19561. (Illus.). 151p. 1986. pap. 17.50 (*0-87062-173-4*) A H Clark.

*__Outland, Orland.__ Coming Out: A Handbook for Men. LC 00-27274. 256p. 2000. pap. 13.95 (*1-55583-514-7*, Pub. by Alyson Pubns) Consort Bk Sales.

Outland, Orland. Death Wore a Fabulous New Fragrance. 1998. mass mkt. 5.99 (*0-425-16197-8*, Prime Crime) Berkley Pub.
— Death Wore a Smart Little Outfit. 224p. 1997. mass mkt. 5.50 (*0-425-15855-1*, Prime Crime) Berkley Pub.

*__Outland, Orland.__ Death Wore the Emperors New Clothes, Vol. 1. 1999. mass mkt. 5.99 (*0-425-17263-5*) Berkley Pub.

Outland, Orland. Every Man for Himself. 272p. 1999. text 22.00 (*1-57566-418-6*) Kensgtn Pub Corp.

*__Outland, Orland.__ Every Man for Himself. 2000. pap. text 13.00 (*1-57566-553-0*, Knsington) Kensgtn Pub Corp.
— Principles: The Gay Man's Guide Getting & Keeping. 2000. pap. text 12.00 (*1-57566-626-X*, Knsington) Kensgtn Pub Corp.

Outland, Orland. The Principles: The Gay Man's Guide to Getting & Keeping Mr. Right. 112p. 1998. pap. 6.99 (*1-57566-281-7*) Kensgtn Pub Corp.

Outland, Wendy, ed. see Duval, Cynthia.

Outlaw, Alain C. Governor's Land: Archaeology of Early Seventeenth-Century Virginia Settlements. LC 80-20340. (Illus.). 205p. 1990. pap. text 30.00 (*0-8139-0875-2*) U Pr of Va.

An Asterisk (*) at the beginning of an entry indicates that the title is appearing for the first time.

Outlaw, Doris C. Croom Family. 332p. 1997. reprint ed. pap. 51.00 (*0-8328-8148-1*); reprint ed. lib. bdg. 61.00 (*0-8328-8147-3*) Higginson Bk Co.

Outlaw, Larry A., jt. auth. see Hetrick, Patrick K.

Outlaw, Lucius. On Race & Philosophy. LC 96-25170. 256p. (C). 1996. pap. 20.99 (*0-415-91535-X*) Routledge.

— On Race & Philosophy. LC 96-25170. 264p. (C). 1996. 65.00 (*0-415-91534-1*) Routledge.

Outlaw, W. Stanley. Questions from Text of Old Testament. 1977. pap. 4.95 (*0-89265-049-4*) Randall Hse.

— Questions from the Text of the New Testament. 36p. 1977. pap. 4.95 (*0-89265-050-8*) Randall Hse.

Outlaw, W. Stanley & O'Donnell, J. D. A Survey of the Pentateuch. 93p. 1975. pap. 3.95 (*0-89265-027-3*) Randall Hse.

Outlaw, W. Stanley, et al. A Survey of the General Epistles & Revelation. 1976. pap. 3.95 (*0-89265-036-2*) Randall Hse.

Outlaw, Wayne. Smart Staffing: How to Hire, Reward & Keep Top Employees for Your Growing Company. LC 98-9935. 256p. 1998. pap. 19.95 (*1-57410-095-5*, 61013501) Dearborn.

Outler, Albert, ed. John Wesley. 532p. 1980. pap. text 17.95 (*0-19-502810-4*) OUP.

Outler, Albert C. Evangelism & Theology in the Wesleyan Spririt. LC 95-83588. 148p. 1996. pap. 15.95 (*0-88177-151-1*) Discipleship Res.

Outler, Albert C., ed. see Wesley, John.

Outlet Book Co. Staff. History of the Confederate. 1988. 12.99 (*0-517-23913-2*) Random.

— Hot & Spicy Cooking. 9.99 (*0-685-65127-4*) Random Hse Value.

— Instant Guide to Reptiles & Amphibians. LC 98-29083. (Illus.). 128p. 1988. 4.99 (*0-517-61800-1*) Random Hse Value.

Outlet Staff. Blue Blank Book. (Classic Executive Bks.). 1991. 5.99 (*0-517-06649-1*) Random Hse Value.

Outlet Staff. Quilling Paper Art for Everyone. 1988. 3.99 (*0-517-19253-5*) Random Hse Value.

— Websters Treasures of Relevant Quotations. LC 82-25132. 672p. 1988. 9.99 (*0-517-40879-1*) Random Hse Value.

Outlet Staff, creator. Anything Book: Burgundy Classic Executive. 160p. 1991. 5.99 (*0-517-06648-3*) Random Hse Value.

— Brown: Brown Classic Executive. 160p. 1991. 5.99 (*0-517-06647-5*) Random Hse Value.

Outlet Staff, des. Anything Book. (Classic Executive Bks.). 160p. 1991. 5.99 (*0-517-06646-7*) Random Hse Value.

Outman, Tim. Remote Network Administrator's Guide. 608p. 1997. 49.99 (*0-7897-1236-9*) Que.

Outram. Social Policy. 1990. pap. text. write for info. (*0-582-35533-8*, Pub. by Addison-Wesley) Longman.

Outram, Dorinda. The Body & the French Revolution: Sex, Class & Political Culture. LC 89-50070. (Illus.). 207p. reprint ed. pap. 64.20 (*0-608-07842-5*, 205401800011) Bks Demand.

— The Enlightenment. (New Approaches to European History Ser.: Vol. 6). 157p. 1995. text 54.95 (*0-521-41522-5*); pap. text 16.95 (*0-521-42534-4*) Cambridge U Pr.

Outram, Dorinda, jt. ed. see Abir-Am, Pnina G.

Outram, Quentin, jt. auth. see Church, Roy.

Outram, Richard Daley. Hiram & Jenny. 136p. 1988. pap. write for info. (*0-88984-118-7*, Pub. by Porcup Quill) Genl Dist Srvs.

— Man in Love. (Illus.). 64p. 1985. pap. write for info. (*0-88984-069-5*, Pub. by Porcup Quill) Genl Dist Srvs.

— Mogul Recollected. LC 94-149500. (Illus.). 96p. 1993. pap. write for info. (*0-88984-174-8*, Pub. by Porcup Quill) Genl Dist Srvs.

Outrata, Jiri V., et al. Nonsmooth Approach to Optimization Problems with Equilibrium Constraints: Theory, Applications & Numerical Results. LC 98-24596. 273p. 1998. write for info. (*0-7923-5170-3*) Kluwer Academic.

Outreville, J. Fran Cois. Theory & Practice of Insurance. LC 97-37191. 352p. 1997. lib. bdg. 115.50 (*0-7923-9996-X*) Kluwer Academic.

Outside Magazine Editors. The Best of Outside: The First Twenty Years. LC 98-231778. 420p. 1998. pap. 14.00 (*0-375-70313-6*) Vin Bks.

— Exposure. (Illus.). 144p. 1992. 45.00 (*0-671-75464-5*) S&S Trade.

Outside Magazine Editors, compiled by. Out of the Noosphere: Adventure, Sports, Travel & the Environment - The Best of Outside Magazine. 480p. 1998. per. 15.00 (*0-684-85233-0*, Fireside) S&S Trade Pap.

Outside Magazine Editors, ed. The Best of Outside: The First Twenty Years. LC 97-22666. 304p. 1997. 24.95 (*0-375-50064-2*) Villard Books.

Outside Magazine Staff, ed. Exposure: 20 Years of Photographing the World. LC 98-125204. (Illus.). 128p. 1997. 40.00 (*1-56579-242-4*) Westcliffe Pubs.

Outslay, Edmund, jt. auth. see Moore, Michael L.

Outten, Wayne N., et al. The Rights of Employees & Union Members: A Basic Guide to the Legal Rights of Non-Government Employees. rev. ed. LC 93-16895. (American Civil Liberties Union Handbook Ser.). 605p. (C). 1994. pap. 15.95 (*0-8093-1914-4*) S Ill U Pr.

Outteridge, Peter M. Veterinary Immunology. 280p. 1986. pap. text 52.00 (*0-12-531131-1*) Acad Pr.

Outtz, Janice H. Demographics of American Families. 24p. 1993. 12.00 (*0-937846-54-6*) Inst Educ Lead.

— Shattering Stereotypes: A Demographic Look at the Facts about Children in the United States. 52p. 1994. 12.00 (*0-937846-45-7*) Inst Educ Lead.

Outtz, Janice H., jt. auth. see Hodgkinson, Harold L.

Outward Bound, Inc. Staff. Field Work: Expeditionary. 192p. 1996. pap. text, per. 14.50 (*0-7872-0229-0*) Kendall-Hunt.

— Fieldwork: An Expeditionary Learning Outward Bound Reader, Vol. II. LC 94-79896. 176p. 1996. pap. text, per. 17.95 (*0-7872-2308-5*) Kendall-Hunt.

— Guide to Planning a Learning Expedition. 17p. 1998. per. 4.95 (*0-7872-4979-3*) Kendall-Hunt.

— Journeys Through Our Classrooms. LC 96-77199. 180p. 1996. pap. text, per. 14.95 (*0-7872-2309-3*) Kendall-Hunt.

***Outward Bound, Inc. Staff.** Literacy All Day Long. 250p. (C). 2000. per. 19.95 (*0-7872-7272-8*) Kendall-Hunt.

Outward Bound, Inc. Staff. Reflections on Design Principles. LC 98-228474. 80p. 1998. per. 4.95 (*0-7872-4978-5*, 41497801) Kendall-Hunt.

***Outward Bound, Inc. Staff.** Service at the Heart of Learning: Teacher's Writings. LC 99-62811. 304p. 1999. per. 19.95 (*0-7872-6030-4*) Kendall-Hunt.

Outwater, Alice. Reuse of Sludge & Minor Wastewater Residuals. 192p. 1994. lib. bdg. 75.00 (*0-87371-677-9*, L677) Lewis Pubs.

— Water: A Natural History. 224p. 1997. pap. 13.00 (*0-465-03780-1*, Pub. by Basic) HarpC.

Outwater, Alice, jt. auth. see Gonick, Larry.

Outwater, Eric & Outwater, Myra. Florida Kitsch. (Illus.). 112p. 1999. pap. 19.95 (*0-7643-0944-7*) Schiffer.

Outwater, Eric B., jt. auth. see Outwater, Myra Yellin.

Outwater, Eric Boe, jt. auth. see Outwater, Myra Yellin.

Outwater, Lynn & Lotito, Michael. Minding Your Business: Legal Issues & Practical Answers for Managing Workplace Privacy. 160p. 1997. pap. 35.00 (*0-939900-57-2*) Soc Human Resc Mgmt.

Outwater, Myra, jt. auth. see Outwater, Eric.

Outwater, Myra Y. Advertising Dolls. LC 97-67383. (Schiffer Book for Collectors Ser.). (Illus.). 160p. 1997. pap. 29.95 (*0-7643-0303-1*) Schiffer.

Outwater, Myra Yellin. Ocean Liner Collectibles. LC 98-84404. 160p. 1998. pap. 29.95 (*0-7643-0581-6*) Schiffer.

***Outwater, Myra Yellin & Outwater, Eric B.** Floridiana, Collecting Florida's Best. (Illus.). 160p. 1999. pap. 29.95 (*0-7643-0973-0*) Schiffer.

Outwater, Myra Yellin & Outwater, Eric B. Judaica. LC 98-55102. (Illus.). 189p. 1999. 49.95 (*0-7643-0785-1*) Schiffer.

***Outwater, Myra Yellin & Outwater, Eric Boe.** Cast Iron Automotive Toys. LC 99-59468. 264p. 2000. 69.95 (*0-7643-1077-1*) Schiffer.

Ouverson, Martin. Macintosh for Kids. write for info. (*0-318-58226-0*) P-H.

Ouvrier, R. A., et al. Peripheral Neuropathy in Childhood. 2nd rev. ed. (International Review of Child Neurology Ser.). 300p. (C). 1998. text 69.95 (*1-898683-17-4*, Pub. by Mc Keith Pr) Cambridge U Pr.

Ouvrier, Robert A., et al. Peripheral Neuropathy in Childhood. LC 90-8677. (International Review of Child Neurology Ser.). (Illus.). 251p. 1990. reprint ed. pap. 77.90 (*0-608-05873-4*, 205984000007) Bks Demand.

Ouvry, Philip, jt. auth. see Langley-Price, Pat.

Ouvry, Philip, jt. auth. see Price, Pat L.

Ouwehand, Terre. Voices from the Well. (Illus.). 1986. pap. 8.95 (*0-914598-44-9*) Pr MacDonald & Reinecke.

— Voices from the Well. deluxe ed. (Illus.). 1986. 12.95 (*0-914598-41-4*) Pr MacDonald & Reinecke.

— Writing Your Way to Wholeness: Creative Exercises for Personal Growth. LC 94-24332. 205p. (Orig.). (C). 1995. pap. 17.95 (*0-89390-312-4*) Resource Pubns.

Ouwendijk, George. Santas of the World. LC 97-26802. (Looking into the Past). (Illus.). 64p. (YA). (gr. 5 up). 1999. lib. bdg. 16.95 (*0-7910-4678-8*) Chelsea Hse.

Ouweneel, Arij. Shadows over Anahuac: An Ecological Interpretation of Crisis & Development in Central Mexico, 1730-1800. LC 95-41814. 431p. (C). 1996. 60.00 (*0-8263-1731-6*) U of NM Pr.

Ouweneel, W. J. Creation or Evolution-What Is the Truth? 58p. pap. 3.95 (*0-88172-143-X*) Believers Bkshelf.

— What Is Election? pap. 2.25 (*0-88172-162-X*) Believers Bkshelf.

— What Is Eternal Life? pap. 2.50 (*0-88172-149-2*) Believers Bkshelf.

— What Is the Christian's Hope? 53p. pap. 2.95 (*0-88172-116-6*) Believers Bkshelf.

— What Is the Sonship of Christ? pap. 2.25 (*0-88172-167-0*) Believers Bkshelf.

Ouwerkerk, C. Theory of Macroscopic Systems. (Illus.). 288p. 1991. pap. 34.00 (*0-387-51575-5*) Spr-Verlag.

Ouwerkerk, C. van, jt. ed. see Soane, B. D.

Ouwerkerk, Louise. No Elephants for the Maharaja: Social & Political Change in Travancore 1921-1947. (C). 1994. text 27.50 (*81-7304-068-0*, Pub. by Manohar) S Asia.

Ouwerkerk, Patsy Van, see Van Ouwerkerk, Patsy.

Ouyang, Wen-Chin. Literary Criticism in Medieval Arabic Islamic Culture: The Making of a Tradition. LC 98-179549. 256p. 1998. 68.00 (*0-7486-0897-4*, Pub. by Edinburgh U Pr) Col U Pr.

Ouzts, Susan B. Global Voices: Using Historical Fiction to Teach Social Studies. (Illus.). 1998. pap. 11.95 (*0-673-36395-3*, GoodYrBooks) Addson-Wesley Educ.

Ovacik, Irfan M. & Uzsoy, Reha. Decomposition Methods for Complex Factory Scheduling Problems. LC 96-37136. 232p. (C). 1996. lib. bdg. 133.00 (*0-7923-9835-1*) Kluwer Academic.

Ovadal, Ralph. Answering Sodom. LC 98-93183. (Illus.). 1998. pap. 11.00 (*0-9665251-0-8*) Hrt of Mattr.

Ovadia, Tali, jt. auth. see Kramer, Jackie.

Ovando. Capacitacion del Liderazgo - Leadership Training. pap. write for info. (*0-7899-0245-1*) Editorial Unilit.

— Fundamentos para una Iglesia Viva - Foundations of the Church Revival. pap. write for info. (*1-56063-392-1*) Editorial Unilit.

Ovando, jt. auth. see Larson.

Ovando, Carlos & Collier, Virginia. Bilingual & ESL Classrooms: Teaching in Multicultural Contexts. 354p. 1987. 25.95 (*0-07-047951-8*) McGraw.

***Ovando, Carlos & McLaren, Peter.** The Politics of Multiculturalism & Bilingual Education: Students & Teachers Caught in the Cross Fire. 264p. (C). 1999. pap. 28.75 (*0-07-366076-0*) McGrw-H Hghr Educ.

Ovando, Carlos J. & Collier, Virginia P. Bilingual & ESL Classrooms: Teaching in Multicultural Contexts. 2nd ed. LC 97-23752. 408p. 1997. pap. 40.31 (*0-07-047959-3*) McGraw.

Ovando, Jorge. El Ministerio de Liberacion.Tr. of Liberation Ministry. (SPA.). 80p. 1996. 2.99 (*0-89922-294-3*, C033-2943) Caribe Betania.

— El Sentido Profetico del Predicador.Tr. of Prophetic & the Preacher. (SPA.). 64p. 1996. 2.99 (*0-89922-496-2*, C071-4962) Caribe Betania.

***Ovando, Jorge A.** Como Dejar de Ser Pobres.Tr. of How to Overcome Poverty. (SPA.). 112p. 1998. pap. text 6.50 (*0-311-46162-X*, Edit Mundo) Casa Bautista.

Ovando, Jorge A. El Mejor Regalo para un Soltero.Tr. of Best Gift for a Single Person. (SPA.). 122p. 1992. pap. 3.99 (*1-56063-107-4*, 498539) Editorial Unilit.

Ovando, Jorge A. Posesion Demoniaca: Un Manual Practico para la Iglesia de Hoy.Tr. of Demonic Possession: Handbook for Today's Church. (SPA.). 96p. 1997. pap. text 7.99 (*0-311-05770-5*) Casa Bautista.

Ovando, Jorge A. Sanidad Interior. (Serie Guia de Bolsillo - Pocket Guides Ser.).Tr. of Inner Healing. (SPA.). 2.79 (*0-7899-0207-9*, 498069) Editorial Unilit.

— Seras Tu el Lider Que Dios Necesita? (Serie Guia de Bolsillo - Pocket Guides Ser.).Tr. of Are You the Leader God Needs?. (SPA.). 120p. 1990. pap. 2.79 (*1-56063-017-5*, 498054) Editorial Unilit.

Ovando, Martha N., jt. auth. see Owen, Jane C.

***Ovanessian, Vahik.** Symbols & Deception & the Social Murder of Identity. LC 99-65367. 195p. 1999. pap. 13.50 (*0-9673617-0-2*) Human View.

***Ovanesyan, Oleg.** Professional Visual Basic SAP R/3 Programming. (Professional Ser.). 500p. 1999. pap. 59.99 (*1-86100-278-5*) Wrox Pr Inc.

Ovange, Sheila, ed. see Dunn, Charles.

Ovard, Glen F. Administration of the Changing Secondary School. 1966. text. write for info. (*0-685-14568-9*) Macmillan.

Ovard, Glen F., jt. auth. see Davies, J. Kenneth.

Ovard, Glen F., jt. auth. see Kapfer, Philip G.

Ovary, Zoltan. Souvenirs: Around the World in Ninety Years. LC 98-92391. 290p. 1999. 18.95 (*0-9662878-1-9*) India Ink Pr.

Ovaska, jt. auth. see Jones, Grahame.

***Ovason, David.** The Secret Architecture Of Our Nation's Capital: The Masons & the Building of Washington, D.C. 512p. 2000. 27.50 (*0-06-019537-1*) HarpC.

Ovason, David. Los Secretos de Nostradamus. (SPA.). 520p. 1998. pap. 17.95 (*0-553-06092-9*) Bantam.

***Ovason, David.** Secrets of Nostradamus. 2000. 27.50 (*0-06-019671-8*) HarpC.

Ovason, David. The Secrets of Nostradamus: The Medieval Code of the Master Revealed in the Age of Computer Science. (Illus.). 512p. 1997. 29.95 (*0-7126-7710-0*, Pub. by CEN3) Trafalgar.

Ovason, David, ed. see Hedsel, Mark.

Ovassapian, Andranik, ed. Fiberoptic Endoscopy & the Difficult Airway. 2nd rev. ed. LC 96-4639. Orig. Title: Fiberoptic Airway Endoscopy in Anesthesia & Critical Care. 304p. 1996. text 150.00 (*0-7817-0272-0*) Lppncott W & W.

Ovchinnikov, A. A. & Timashev, S. F., eds. Kinetics of Diffusion Controlled Chemical Processes. 227p. (C). 1989. text 175.00 (*0-941743-52-7*) Nova Sci Pubs.

Ovchinnikov, A. A. & Ukrainskii, I. I., eds. Low-Dimensional Conductors & Superconductors: Electron-Electron Correlation Effects In. (Research Reports in Physics). (Illus.). ix, 161p. 1991. pap. 69.00 (*0-387-54248-5*) Spr-Verlag.

Ovchinnikov, V. I., ed. The Method of Orbits in Interpolation Theory, Vol. 1. (Mathematical Reports: Vol. 1, Pt. 2). x, 166p. 1984. text 123.00 (*3-7186-0259-8*) Gordon & Breach.

Ovchinnikov, Vsevolod. The Road to Shambala. (Illus.). 101p. 1995. pap. 9.95 (*7-80005-295-8*, Pub. by New World Pr) China Bks.

Ovchinnikov, Y. A. & Hucho, F. Receptors & Ion Channels: Proceedings of the Symposium, Tashkent, U. S. S. R., October 2-5, 1986. xi, 351p. 1987. lib. bdg. 169.25 (*3-11-010346-X*) De Gruyter.

Ovchinnikov, Y. A., jt. ed. see Hucho, F.

Ovchinnikov, Yu A., ed. FEBS: Proceedings of the 16th Congress, Moscow, 1986, 3 vols., Set. (Illus.). 1589p. 1985. lib. bdg. 287.50 (*90-6764-044-1*, Pub. by VSP) Coronet Bks.

— Retinal Proteins. 590p. 1987. lib. bdg. 155.00 (*90-6764-102-2*, Pub. by VSP) Coronet Bks.

Ovchinnikov, Yu A., jt. auth. see Ivanov, V. T.

Ove, Robert S. & Stockel, H. Herietta. Geronimo's Kids: A Teacher's Lessons on the Apache Reservation. LC 97-18561. (Elma Dill Russell Spencer Series in the West & Southwest: 16). (Illus.). 200p. 1997. 26.95 (*0-89096-774-1*) Tex A&M Univ Pr.

Ovechka, Greg. Ferrets As a New Pet. (Illus.). 64p. 1991. pap. 6.95 (*0-86622-622-2*, TU-014) TFH Pubns.

— Hamsters As a Hobby. (Illus.). 96p. 1993. 8.95 (*0-86622-412-2*, TT006) TFH Pubns.

— Kittens Today. (Illus.). 64p. 1996. 12.95 (*0-7938-0102-8*, WW003) TFH Pubns.

Ovechka, Greg & American Society for the Prevention of Cruelty to. Kittens Today: A Complete & Up-to-Date Guide. LC 97-3627. (Basic Domestic Pet Library). 76p. (J). (gr. 3 up). 1997. 19.95 (*0-7910-4613-3*) Chelsea Hse.

Ovecka, Janice. Captive of Pittsford Ridge. LC 94-24533. 96p. (Orig.). (YA). 1994. pap. 10.95 (*1-881535-11-8*) New Eng Pr VT.

— Cave of Falling Water. LC 92-56713. (Illus.). (J). 1992. pap. 10.95 (*0-933050-98-4*) New Eng Pr VT.

Oved, Yaacov. Two Hundred Years of American Communes. Lash, Hannah, tr. 419p. 1988. 49.95 (*0-88738-113-8*) Transaction Pubs.

— Two Hundred Years of American Communes. 516p. (C). 1992. pap. 24.95 (*1-56000-647-1*) Transaction Pubs.

— Witness of the Brothers: A History of the Bruderhof. Berris, Anthony, tr. 350p. (C). 1996. text 44.95 (*1-56000-203-4*) Transaction Pubs.

Ovedovitz, Albert. Brief Business Statistics: Data, Tools & Analysis. LC 98-50440. 576p. 1999. pap. text. write for info. (*0-471-05582-4*) Wiley.

***Ovedovitz, Albert C.** Business Statistics in Brief. LC 99-88981. 507p. 2001. 72.95 (*0-324-04868-8*) Sth-Wstrn College.

Oveido, Jose M. Nina de Nueva York. (SPA.). pap. 7.99 (*968-16-3247-8*, Pub. by Fondo) Continental Bk.

***Ovellet, Jean-Claude.** Annotations Marginales de Isle-Verte, Vol.18. (FRE.). 220p. 1999. pap. 34.00 (*2-921848-09-0*) SGEQ.

— Nussances et Baptemes St. Paul le la Craine: Notre-Dame-des-Sept-Donteurs. (FRE.). 140p. 1999. pap. 29.00 (*2-921848-10-4*) SGEQ.

Ovellette, Daryl. Dancing in Circles. 740p. mass mkt. 6.99 (*1-896329-35-7*) Picasso Publ.

Ovello, A. C. Building Blocks of Nuclear Structure: The Fourth International Spring Seminar on Nuclear Physics. 648p. 1993. text 135.00 (*981-02-1069-8*) World Scientific Pub.

Ovelmen-Levitt, Janice. Deafferentation Pain Syndromes: Pathophysiology & Treatment. Nashold, Blaine S., Jr., ed. (Advances in Pain Research & Therapy Ser.: Vol. 19). 368p. 1991. text 118.00 (*0-88167-823-6*) Lppncott W & W.

Ovelmen-Levitt, Janice, jt. ed. see Nashold, Blaine S., Jr.

***Ovendale.** Longman Companion to the Middle East since 1914. 2nd ed. LC 98-14432. (Longman Companions to History Ser.). 408p. (C). 1998. pap. text, suppl. ed. 29.50 (*0-582-31555-7*) Longman.

Ovendale, Ritchie. Anglo-American Relations in the Twentieth Century. LC 98-11479. (British History in Perspective Ser.). 216p. 1998. text 45.00 (*0-312-21454-5*) St Martin.

— Britain, the U. S. & the Transfer of Power in the Middle East 1945-1962. 288p. 1996. text 110.00 (*0-7185-1438-6*) Bks Intl VA.

— Britain, the United States & the End of the Palestine Mandate 1942-1948. (RHS Studies in Celtic History: No. 57). 340p. (C). 1989. 75.00 (*0-86193-214-5*) Boydell & Brewer.

— British Defence Policy since 1945. LC 94-12637. (Documents in Contemporary History Ser.). 1994. text 21.95 (*0-7190-4015-9*, Pub. by Manchester Univ Pr) St Martin.

— The English Speaking Alliance: Britain, the United States, the Dominions & Cold War, 1945-1951. LC 85-11075. 280p. 1985. text 60.00 (*0-04-327078-6*) Routledge.

— The Origins of the Arab Israeli Wars. 3rd ed. LC 99-12400. (Origins of Modern Wars Ser.). 360p. 1999. pap. 30.73 (*0-582-36895-2*) Longman.

— The Origins of the Arab-Israeli Wars: Origins of Modern Wars. 2nd ed. (Origins of Modern Wars Ser.). (Illus.). 264p. (C). 1992. pap. text 33.25 (*0-582-06369-8*) Longman.

Ovenden, Graham. Childhood Streets. LC 98-22759. 1998. 35.00 (*1-888425-10-5*) Ophelia Edits.

Ovenden, Graham, ed. Pre-Raphaelite Photography. (Illus.). 84p. 1984. pap. 14.95 (*0-312-63736-5*) St Martin.

— A Victorian Album: Julia Margaret Cameron & Her Circle. LC 75-18728. (Photography Ser.). (Illus.). 119p. 1975. lib. bdg. 45.00 (*0-306-70749-7*) Da Capo.

Ovenden, Keith. A Fighting Withdrawal, the Life of Dan Davin: Writer, Soldier, Publisher. (Illus.). 492p. (C). 1996. text 45.00 (*0-19-212335-1*) OUP.

Ovenden, Richard. John Thomson (1837-1921) Photographer. (Illus.). 128p. 1997. 40.00 (*0-11-495833-5*, Pub. by Statnry Office) Seven Hills Bk.

Ovenell-Carter, Julie. Adam's Daycare. (Illus.). 32p. (J). (ps-3). 1997. pap. 5.95 (*1-55037-444-3*, Pub. by Annick); lib. bdg. 15.95 (*1-55037-445-1*, Pub. by Annick) Firefly Bks Ltd.

— The Butterflies' Promise. (Illus.). 32p. (J). (gr. k-3). 1999. pap. 6.95 (*1-55037-566-0*, Pub. by Annick Pr) Firefly Bks Ltd.

***Ovenell-Carter, Julie.** The Butterflies' Promise. (Illus.). 32p. (J). (gr. k-3). 1999. lib. bdg. 15.95 (*1-55037-567-9*, Pub. by Annick Pr) Firefly Bks Ltd.

Ovenell, R. F. The Ashmolean Museum, 1683-1894. (Illus.). 304p. 1986. 55.00 (*0-19-951542-5*) OUP.

Ovens, Peter. Reflective Teacher Development in Primary Science. LC 99-36839. (Illus.). 192p. 1999. 77.00 (*0-7507-0863-8*, Pub. by Falmer Pr UK); pap. 23.95 (*0-7507-0862-X*, Pub. by Falmer Pr UK) Taylor & Francis.

Ovens, William G. Design Manual for Water Wheels. 77p. 1988. 9.50 (*0-86619-045-7*) Vols Tech Asst.

Over, jt. auth. see Evans, Jonathan.

Over, Carol. Newfoundland Recipes: Recipes From The Kitchens Of Newfoundland. 56p. 1979. reprint ed. pap. 3.15 (*0-920021-69-7*) Creative Bk Pub.

Over, Charles Van, see Van Over, Charles.

Over, Mead. Economics for Health Sector Analysis: Concepts & Cases. (EDI Seminar Ser.). 224p. 1992. pap. 22.00 (*0-8213-1335-5*, 11335) World Bank.

O

Over, Naomi L. Ruby Glass of the Twentieth Century. Klopp, Tom, ed. (Illus.). 128p. 1990. 29.95 (*0-915410-67-2*, 3085); pap. 21.95 (*0-915410-68-0*, 3084) Antique Pubns.
— Ruby Glass of the Twentieth Century, Bk. II. (Illus.). 128p. 1999. 39.95 (*1-57080-055-3*); pap. 29.95 (*1-57080-054-5*) Antique Pubns.

Over, Raymond Van, see Van Over, Raymond.

***Over, William.** Human Rights in the International Public Sphere: Civic Discourse for the 21st Century. LC 99-17575. (Civic Discourse for the Third Millenium Ser.: Vol. 6). 300p. 1999. 48.50 (*1-56750-446-9*) Ablx Pub.
— Human Rights in the International Public Sphere: Civic Discourse for the 21st Century. LC 99-17575. (Civic Discourse for the Third Millenium Ser.). 300p. 1999. pap. 29.95 (*1-56750-447-7*) Ablx Pub.

Overacker, Ingrid. The African American Church Community in Rochester, New York, 1900-1940. LC 98-7283. 256p. 1998. 65.00 (*1-878822-89-6*, Pub. by Univ Rochester Pr) Boydell & Brewer.

Overacker, Louise. Money in Elections. LC 73-19167. (Politics & People Ser.). (Illus.). 490p. 1974. reprint ed. 36.95 (*0-405-05889-6*) Ayer.
— Presidential Campaign Funds. LC 76-29407. reprint ed. 29.50 (*0-404-15341-0*) AMS Pr.
— The Presidential Primary. LC 73-19168. (Politics & People Ser.). (Illus.). 318p. 1974. reprint ed. 26.95 (*0-405-05890-X*) Ayer.

Overacker, Roger, ed. & illus. see Adkins, Gregory.

***Overall, Carol.** The Best of Carol Cape Overall's a Catered Affair San Mateos Texas. (Illus.). 1999. pap. 18.50 (*0-9676559-0-0*) C Overall.

Overall, Christine. Ethics & Human Reproduction: A Feminist Analysis. 256p. 1987. text 39.95 (*0-04-497009-9*); pap. text 19.95 (*0-04-497010-2*) Routledge.
— A Feminist I: Reflections from Academia. LC 99-166528. 200p. 1998. pap. 14.95 (*1-55111-219-1*) Broadview Pr.
— Human Reproduction: Principles, Practices, Policies. 184p. 1993. pap. text 24.95 (*0-19-540961-2*) OUP.

Overall, Christine & Zion, William P., eds. Perspectives on Aids: Ethical & Social Issues. 240p. 1991. pap. text 24.95 (*0-19-540749-0*) OUP.

Overall, John. Convocation Book of Sixteen Six. LC 77-173482. (Library of Anglo-Catholic Theology: No. 15). reprint ed. 27.50 (*0-404-52107-X*) AMS Pr.

Overall, John E. & Klett, C. James. Applied Multivariate Analysis. LC 81-20944. 522p. (C). 1983. reprint ed. lib. bdg. 52.50 (*0-89874-325-7*) Krieger.

Overall, Karen L. Clinical Small Animal Behavior. LC 96-18753. (Illus.). 560p. (C). (gr. 13). 1997. text 52.95 (*0-8016-6820-4*, 06820) Mosby Inc.

Overall, Kitty, ed. see Van Duyne, Marie A.

Overall, Lyn, jt. auth. see Cashdan, Asher.

Overback. Major Principles of Media Law. (C). 1998. pap. text 56.00 (*0-15-507293-5*, Pub. by Harcourt Coll Pubs) Harcourt.

Overbeck, Bernhard H., jt. auth. see Burns, Thomas S.

Overbeck, Buz. Introduction to the New Astrology. LC 81-66053. (Matrix Seminar Ser.). 64p. 1981. 13.00 (*0-86690-130-2*, 01329-014) Am Fed Astrologers.

Overbeck, Cynthia. Ants. LC 81-17216. (Lerner Natural Science Ser.). (Illus.). 48p. (J). (gr. 4-6). 1982. pap. 5.95 (*0-8225-9525-7*, First Ave Edns) Lerner Pub.
— Ants. LC 81-17216. (Lerner Natural Science Ser.). (Illus.). 48p. (J). (gr. 4 up). 1982. lib. bdg. 22.60 (*0-8225-1468-0*, Lerner Publctns) Lerner Pub.
— Cactus. LC 82-211. (Natural Science Bks.). (Illus.). 48p. (J). (gr. 4 up). 1982. pap. 5.95 (*0-8225-9556-7*, Lerner Publctns) Lerner Pub.
— Carnivorous Plants. LC 81-17234. (Natural Science Bks.). (Illus.). 48p. (J). (gr. 4 up). 1982. lib. bdg. 22.60 (*0-8225-1470-2*, Lerner Publctns) Lerner Pub.
— Cats. LC 83-17530. (Lerner Natural Science Bks.). (Illus.). 48p. (J). (gr. 4 up). 1983. lib. bdg. 22.60 (*0-8225-1480-X*, Lerner Publctns) Lerner Pub.
— Elephants. LC 80-27550. (Lerner Natural Science Bks.). (Illus.). 48p. (J). (gr. 4 up). 1981. lib. bdg. 22.60 (*0-8225-1452-4*, Lerner Publctns) Lerner Pub.
— How Seeds Travel. LC 81-17217. (Lerner Natural Science Bks.). (Illus.). 48p. (J). (gr. 4 up). 1982. lib. bdg. 22.60 (*0-8225-1474-5*, Lerner Publctns) Lerner Pub.
— How Seeds Travel. (Illus.). 48p. (J). (gr. 4 up). 1982. reprint ed. pap. 5.95 (*0-8225-9569-9*, Lerner Publctns) Lerner Pub.

Overbeck, John C. Ayia Irini, Period IV, Pt. 1: The Stratigraphy & the Find Deposits. (Illus.). 216p. 1989. write for info. (*3-8053-1024-2*, DM160, Pub. by P Zabern) Eisenbrauns.
— The Bronze Age Pottery from the Kastro at Paros. (Studies in Mediterranean Archaeology & Literature: No. 78). (Illus.). 85p. (Orig.). 1989. pap. 39.50 (*91-85058-09-2*, Pub. by P Astroms) Coronet Bks.

Overbeck, John C. & Swiny, Stuart. Two Cypriot Bronze Age Sites at Kafkallia (Dhali) (Studies in Mediterranean Archaeology: Vol. XXXIII). (Illus.). 50p. 1972. pap. 26.50 (*91-85058-51-3*, Pub. by P Astroms) Coronet Bks.

Overbeck, Joy, jt. auth. see Pogzeba, Wolfgang.

Overbeck, Juergen, ed. Proceedings of the Workshop on Measurement of Microbial Activities in the Carbon Cycle of Freshwaters. (Advances in Limnology Ser.: Vol. 12). (GER., Illus.). vi, 170p. (Orig.). 1979. 38.00 (*3-510-47010-9*, Pub. by E Schweizerbartsche) Balogh.

Overbeck, Juergen, et al, eds. Proceedings of the Second Workshop on Measurement of Microbial Activity in the Carbon Cycle of Aquatic Ecosystems. (Advances in Limnology Ser.: Vol. 19). (GER., Illus.). xii, 316p. 1984. pap. text 82.00 (*3-510-47017-6*, Pub. by E Schweizerbartsche) Balogh.

Overbeck, Jurgen, et al, eds. Aquatic Microbial Ecology: Biochemical & Molecular Approaches. (Contemporary Bioscience Ser.). 224p. 1990. 49.00 (*0-387-97222-6*) Spr-Verlag.

Overbeck, Jurgen & Chrost, Ryszard J., eds. Microbial Ecology of Lake Plusssee. LC 93-5258. (Ecological Studies: Vol. 105). 1993. 118.00 (*0-387-94120-7*) Spr-Verlag.

Overbeck, Konrad. Uber Den Ursprung der Menschlichen Sinnerfahrung: Eine Untersuchung Zu Anthropologischen Grundannahmenin der Strukturpsychologie von August Vetter. (Moraltheologie - Anthropologie - Ethik Ser.: Bd. 1). (GER., Illus.). XII, 358p. 1997. 63.95 (*3-631-31176-1*) P Lang Pubng.

Overbeck, Peter, ed. see Linley, Thomas, Jr.

Overbeck, T. Jerome. Ancient Fonts, Modern Lessons. Philippart, David, ed. (Meeting House Essays Ser.: Vol. 9). 32p. 1998. pap. 6.00 (*1-56854-091-4*) Liturgy Tr Pubns.

Overbeck, Werner & Bohm, Dieter, eds. Body Composition - Research Techniques & Nutritional Assessment. (Internationale Zeitschrift fuer Infusionstherapie, Klinische Ernahrung und Transfusionsmedizin Ser.: Supplement 3 zu Band 17, April 1990). 1990. 18.50 (*3-8055-5228-9*) S Karger.

Overbeck, Winfried. Menschwerdung: Eine Untersuchung zur Literarischen und Theologischen Einheit des Funften Buches "Adversus Haereses" des Irenaus von Lyon. (Basler und Berner Studien zur Historischen und Systematischen Theologie: Bd. 61). (GER.). xvi, 634p. 1995. 76.95 (*3-906755-40-1*, Pub. by P Lang) P Lang Pubng.

Overbeek, Henk. Global Capitalism & National Decline: The Thatcher Decade in Perspective. 272p. 1990. text 60.00 (*0-04-445413-9*) Routledge.

Overbeek, Johannes. Free Trade vs. Protectionism: A Source Book of Essays & Readings. LC 98-42879. 656p. 1999. 120.00 (*1-85898-971-X*) E Elgar.
— The Modern World Economy: Theories & Policies. 480p. (Orig.). (C). 1993. text 69.50 (*0-8191-9131-0*); pap. text 47.50 (*0-8191-9132-9*) U Pr of Amer.
— The Population Challenge: A Handbook for Non-Specialists, 19. LC 76-5328. (Contributions in Sociology Ser.: No. 19). (Illus.). 214p. 1976. 57.95 (*0-8371-8896-2*, OPC/, Greenwood Pr) Greenwood.

Overbeek, Johannes, ed. The Evolution of Population Theory: A Documentary Sourcebook, 23. LC 76-43138. (Contributions in Sociology Ser.: No. 23). 277p. 1977. 47.95 (*0-8371-9313-3*, OVP/, Greenwood Pr) Greenwood.

Overbeek, Johannes, intro. Two Essays by Wilhelm Roepke: The Problem of Economic Order, Welfare, Freedom & Inflation. LC 86-33982. 114p. (Orig.). (C). 1987. pap. text 14.00 (*0-8191-6126-8*) U Pr of Amer.

Overbeek, R., jt. ed. see Lusk, Ewing L.

Overbeek, Ross A. Assembler Language with Assist & Assist I. 4th ed. 572p. (C). 1990. text 52.51 (*0-02-390005-9*, Macmillan Coll) P-H.

Overbeek, Ross A. & Singletary, Wilson E. Introduction to COBOL. 400p. (C). 1986. pap. text. write for info. (*0-318-59748-9*); 8.00 (*0-201-16316-0*) Addison-Wesley.
— Introduction to COBOL: A Primer & a Programmer's Guide. LC 84-14491. 408p. 1985. pap. write for info. (*0-201-16310-1*); 5.50 (*0-685-10456-7*) Addison-Wesley.

Overberg, Henk, tr. see Herzl, Theodor.

Overberg, Kenneth. Journey to Jerusalem. (Illus.). 64p. (Orig.). 1991. pap. text 10.95 (*0-932506-76-3*, 6763) St Bedes Pubns.

Overberg, Kenneth R. Conscience in Conflict: How to Make Moral Choices. 168p. 1997. pap. text 10.95 (*0-86716-313-5*) St Anthony Mess Pr.
— Roots & Branches: Grounding Religion in Human Experience. rev. ed. LC 91-61103. 160p. (C). 1991. pap. 10.95 (*1-55612-457-0*, LL1457) Sheed & Ward WI.

Overberg, Kenneth R., ed. Mercy or Murder? Euthanasia, Morality & Public Policy. 300p. (Orig.). 1993. pap. 15.95 (*1-55612-609-3*) Sheed & Ward WI.

Overbey, Daniel L. Railroads: The Free Enterprise Alternative. LC 82-7503. (Illus.). 225p. 1982. 55.00 (*0-89930-031-6*, OVR/, Quorum Bks) Greenwood.

Overbey, James & Overbey, Taylor. Straight White American Male: A Politically Incorrect Illustrated Survival Guide. LC 96-75032. (Illus.). 21.95 (*0-9651198-0-7*) Marina Pubs.

Overbey, Scot. Vladimir Zhirinovsky: The Man Who Would Be God. (Illus.). 150p. (Orig.). 1994. pap. 9.95 (*1-879366-74-6*) Hearthstone OK.

Overbey, Scott, jt. auth. see Hitchcock, Mark.

Overbey, Taylor, jt. auth. see Overbey, James.

Overbury, Thomas. Conceited News of Sir Thomas Overbury & His Friends: With Sir Thomas Overbury His Wife. Savage, James E., ed. LC 68-29084. 408p. 1968. 60.00 (*0-8201-1039-6*) Schol Facsimiles.
— The Overburian Characters, to Which Is Added, a Wife. Paylor, W. J., ed. LC 75-41207. reprint ed. 32.50 (*0-404-14580-9*) AMS Pr.
— Sir T. Overbury His Observations in His Travailes. LC 70-26399. (English Experience Ser.: No. 154). 28p. 1969. reprint ed. 25.00 (*90-221-0154-1*) Walter J Johnson.

Overby, A. J., jt. ed. see Cross, H. R.

Overby, Charles M. A Call for Peace: The Implications of Japan's War-Renouncing Constitution. (Illus.). 1998. 18.00 (*4-7700-2062-7*, Pub. by Kodansha Intl) Kodansha.

Overby, James O., jt. auth. see O'Brien, Dianne B.

Overby, L. Marvin, jt. auth. see Burns, James M.

Overby, Lacy R., ed. see International Max von Pettenkofer Symposium Ster.

Overby, Lynette Y. & Humphrey, James H., eds. Dance, Vol. 3. LC 87-47814. (Illus.). 310p. 1992. 37.50 (*0-404-63853-8*) AMS Pr.
— Dance: Current Selected Research, Set, Vols. 1-4. LC 87-47814. 1993. 37.50 (*0-404-63850-3*) AMS Pr.

***Overby, Osmund.** William Adair Bernoudy, Architect: Bringing the Legacy of Frank Lloyd Wright to St. Louis. LC 99-11930. 328p. 1999. 49.95 (*0-8262-1224-7*) U of Mo Pr.

Overby, Osmund & Larson, Sidney. Fred Shane Paintings, 1923-1979. 48p. (Orig.). 1982. pap. 7.50 (*0-910501-00-9*) U of Missouri Mus Art Arch.

Overby, Paul. Holy Blood: An Inside View of the Afghan War. LC 93-20126. 248p. 1993. 65.00 (*0-275-94622-3*, C4622, Praeger Pubs) Greenwood.

Overby, Robert, jt. auth. see Myers, Terry R.

Overbye, Dennis. Einstein in Love: A Scientific Romance. 1999. write for info. (*0-316-64946-5*) Little.
— Einstein in Love: A Scientific Romance. 416p. (gr. 8). 2000. 27.95 (*0-316-64218-5*) Little.

***Overbye, Dennis.** Einstein in Love: A Scientific Romance. 416p. 2000. 27.95 (*0-670-89430-3*, Viking) Viking Penguin.
— Lonely Hearts of the Cosmos: The Story of the Scientific Quest for the Secret of the Universe. LC 99-45792. 464p. 1999. pap. 16.95 (*0-316-64896-5*, Back Bay) Little.

Overcash, Michael R. Techniques for Industrial Pollution Prevention. 203p. 1986. 10.00 (*0-317-05673-5*, P89004HAZ); 10.00 (*0-317-05691-3*, P93002WAT) Assn Bay Area.
— Techniques for Industrial Pollution Prevention. (Illus.). 200p. 1986. 124.00 (*0-87371-071-1*, TD897, CRC Reprint) Franklin.

Overcash, Michael R., et al. Livestock Waste Management, 2 vols., I. 512p. 1983. 144.00 (*0-8493-5595-8*, TD930) CRC Pr.
— Livestock Waste Management, 2 vols., II. 512p. 1983. 146.00 (*0-8493-5596-6*, TD930, CRC Reprint) Franklin.
— Livestock Waste Management, 2 vols., Set. 512p. 1983. write for info. (*0-318-57538-8*, TD930) CRC Pr.

Overcast, Thomas D., et al, eds. Law & Mental Health Professionals: Washington. LC 95-5363. 492p. 1995. text 59.95 (*1-55798-278-3*, 431-5110) Am Psychol.

Overcast, Thomas D., jt. auth. see Edelhertz, Herbert.

Overdieck, D., jt. auth. see Esser, D. G.

Overdorf, D. G. & Kotnik, R. L. AC Polyphase Motors. (Technical Papers: Vol. P109.23B). (Illus.). 19p. 1970. pap. text 30.00 (*1-55589-426-7*) AGMA.

Overdorf, Scot W., jt. ed. see Randall, Richard L.

***Overduin, Dee.** The Paper Tole Book. large type ed. (Illus.). 94p. 1998. 23.95 (*0-9669185-0-9*) Tole Way.

Overduin, Jan. Making Music: Improvisation for Organists. LC 97-46196. (Illus.). 224p. 1998. pap. text 29.95 (*0-19-386075-9*) OUP.

Overduin, Nick. Job: Challenging a Silent God. (Revelation Ser.). 1994. pap., student ed. 4.95 (*1-56212-065-4*) CRC Pubns.
— Voice from the Cloud: A Fresh Look at the Gospel of Mark. LC 96-28194. (Fresh Look Ser.). 100p. (Orig.). 1996. pap., student ed. 9.95 (*1-56212-192-8*, 1315-2020) CRC Pubns.

Overdurf, John & Silverthorn, Julie. Dreaming Realities: A Spiritual System to Create Inner Alignment Through Dreams. 189p. 1999. pap. 15.95 (*1-899836-30-6*, Pub. by Crown Hse) LPC Group.

Overeaters Anonymous, Inc. Staff. Abstinence: Members of Overeaters Anonymous Share Their Experience, Strength, & Hope. LC 94-67576. 1994. pap. 8.35 (*0-9609898-7-0*) Overeaters Anym.
— Journal to Recovery. LC 95-67547. 1995. pap. 4.99 (*0-9609898-8-9*) Overeaters Anym.
— A New Beginning: Stories of Recovery from Relapse. LC 97-76416. 129 p. 1998. pap. 8.35 (*1-889681-01-6*) Overeaters Anym.
— The Twelve-Step Workbook of Overeaters Anonymous. LC 93-83640. 1993. pap. 8.35 (*0-9609898-5-4*) Overeaters Anym.
— The Twelve Steps & Twelve Traditions of Overeaters Anonymous. LC 93-85052. 1993. pap. 10.99 (*0-9609898-6-2*) Overeaters Anym.

Overend. Making a Business from Biomass in Energy Environment, Chemicals, Fibres & Materials. LC 97-221334. 1770p. 1997. 400.00 (*0-08-042996-3*, Pergamon Pr) Elsevier.

***Overend, Jenni.** Welcome with Love. (Illus.). 32p. (J). (ps-3). 2000. 15.95 (*0-916291-96-0*, Cranky Nell Bks) Kane-Miller Bk.

Overend, Jennifer. Best of Teachers Helper 1994. pap. 20.76 (*1-56234-109-X*) Educ Ctr.

***Overend, Ned & Pavelka, Ed.** Mountain Bike Like a Champion: Master All the Skills to Tackle the Toughest Terrain. LC 99-28633. (Illus.). 240p. 1999. pap. 16.95 (*1-57954-081-3*) Rodale Pr Inc.

***Overend, R. P. & Chornet, E.** Biomass: A Growth Opportunity in Green Energy & Value-Added Products. (Illus.). 1892p. 1999. 404.50 (*0-08-043019-8*, Pergamon Pr) Elsevier.

Overend, Ralph P. & Hall, David O., eds. Biomass Regenerable Energy. fac. ed. LC 86-15685. (World Energy Options Ser.). (Illus.). 514p. 1994. pap. 159.40 (*0-7837-7661-6*, 204741400007) Bks Demand.

Overesch, Manfred. Machtergreifung von Links - Thuringen, 1945/46. (GER.). 198p. 1993. write for info. (*3-487-09786-9*) G Olms Pubs.

Overfelt, Kathy & Overfelt, Tony. No Thanks - I'll Sell It Myself. 128p. 1991. pap. 3.95 (*0-380-76186-6*, Avon Bks) Morrow Avon.

Overfelt, Tony, jt. auth. see Overfelt, Kathy.

***Overfield, J., et al.** Transfusion Science. LC 99-33335. (BMS Explained Ser.). 202p. 1999. pap. text 36.00 (*0-7506-3415-4*) Buttrwrth-Heinemann.

Overfield, James H. Humanism & Scholasticism in Late Medieval Germany. LC 84-42568. 363p. 1984. reprint ed. pap. 112.60 (*0-7837-9410-X*, 20601550004) Bks Demand.

Overfield, James H., jt. auth. see Andrea, Alfred J.

Overfield, Joan. Exquisite. 304p. 1998. mass mkt. 5.50 (*0-8217-5894-2*, Zebra Kensgtn) Kensgtn Pub Corp.
— Exquisite. 304p. 1999. mass mkt. 5.99 (*0-8217-6110-2*, Zebra Kensgtn) Kensgtn Pub Corp.
— Lady Cat. 304p. 1999. mass mkt. 5.99 (*0-8217-6096-3*) Kensgtn Pub Corp.
— Rose in Scotland. LC 97-93795. 384p. 1998. mass mkt. 5.99 (*0-380-78007-0*, Avon Bks) Morrow Avon.

Overfield, Joan E. Belle of the Ball. 224p. (Orig.). 1993. mass mkt. 3.99 (*0-380-76923-9*, Avon Bks) Morrow Avon.
— The Dutiful Duke. 224p. (Orig.). 1994. mass mkt. 3.99 (*0-380-77400-3*, Avon Bks) Morrow Avon.
— The Learned Lady. 192p. (Orig.). 1996. mass mkt. 3.99 (*0-380-78005-4*, Avon Bks) Morrow Avon.
— A Proper Taming. 224p. (Orig.). 1994. mass mkt. 3.99 (*0-380-77401-1*, Avon Bks) Morrow Avon.
— A Spirited Bluestocking. 1992. mass mkt. 3.50 (*0-8217-3727-9*, Zebra Kensgtn) Kensgtn Pub Corp.
— Time's Tapestry. 304p. 1996. mass mkt. 4.99 (*0-8217-5381-9*, Zebra Kensgtn) Kensgtn Pub Corp.
— The Viscount's Vixen. 224p. (Orig.). 1992. mass mkt. 3.99 (*0-380-76922-0*, Avon Bks) Morrow Avon.

Overfield, Karen. Developing & Managing Organizational Learning: A Guide to Effective Training Project Management. LC 98-73225. v, 148p. 1998. 26.95 (*1-56286-090-9*) Am Soc Train & Devel.

Overfield, Richard A. Science with Practice: Charles E. Bessey & the Maturing of American Botany. LC 91-16180. (History of Technology & Science Ser.). (Illus.). 276p. 1993. text 44.95 (*0-8138-1822-2*) Iowa St U Pr.

Overfield, Theresa. Biological Variation in Health & Illness: Race, Age, & Sex Differences. 2nd ed. LC 94-42293. 220p. 1995. boxed set 149.95 (*0-8493-4577-4*, 4577) CRC Pr.

Overgaard, B., ed. see Hermodsson, Ivan.

Overgaard, Gerd. The Mandative Subjunctive in American & British English in the 20th Century. LC 96-226108. (Studia Anglistica Upsaliensia Ser.: No. 94). 139p. (Orig.). 1995. pap. 37.50 (*91-554-3676-5*) Coronet Bks.

Overgaard, Jens, ed. Hyperthermic Oncology: Proceedings of the Fourth International Conference on Hyperthermic Oncology, 1984, 2 vols., Set. 1270p. 1984. 209.00 (*0-8002-3824-9*) Taylor & Francis.
— Hyperthermic Oncology, Vol. 1: Summary Papers. 870p. 1984. 154.00 (*0-85066-273-7*) Taylor & Francis.
— Hyperthermic Oncology, Vol. 2: Review Lectures, Symposium Summaries & Workshop Summaries. 400p. 1984. 88.00 (*0-85066-281-8*) Taylor & Francis.

Overgard, Zeta, ed. The Best of Quick 'n Easy Cookin', 1986-87. 82p. 1987. pap. 6.95 (*0-9618379-0-X*) Parkside Pubns.
— The Best of Quick 'n Easy Cookin', 1988-89. 124p. 1989. pap. 6.95 (*0-9618379-1-8*) Parkside Pubns.

Overhage, Carl. Six One-Day Walks in the Pecos Wilderness: A Guide. rev. ed. LC 80-20061. 60p. 1984. pap. 4.95 (*0-86534-044-7*) Sunstone Pr.

Overhauser, David, jt. auth. see Kong, Jeong-Taek.

Overheim, R. Daniel & Wagner, David L. Light & Color. LC 81-21955. 288p. (C). 1982. text 81.95 (*0-471-08348-8*) Wiley.

Overhill, Heidi. The Only Baby Name Book You'll Ever Need. (Illus.). 232p. 1996. pap. 14.95 (*1-55013-754-9*) Firefly Bks Ltd.

Overhof, H. & Thomas, P. Electronic Transport in Hydrogenated Amorphous Semiconductors. (Tracts in Modern Physics Ser.: Vol. 114). (Illus.). 190p. 1989. 91.95 (*0-387-50186-X*) Spr-Verlag.

***Overhoff, Jurgen.** Hobbes's Theory of Will: Ideological Reasons & Historical Circumstances. LC 99-45646. 288p. 2000. text 75.00 (*0-8476-9648-0*) Rowman.
— Hobbes's Theory of Will: Ideological Reasons & Historical Circumstances. LC 99-45646. 288p. 2000. pap. 24.95 (*0-8476-9649-9*) Rowman.

Overholder, Marguariete. On the Oregon Trail: With the Ira Hooker Family - 1848. LC 96-79729. (Illus.). 96p. 1993. pap. 6.95 (*0-8323-0519-7*) Binford Mort.

Overholdt, William H. The Rise of China: How Economic Reform Is Creating a New Superpower. 1994. pap. 14.00 (*0-393-31245-3*) Norton.

***Overholsen, Stephen.** Hanging in Sweetwater. 1999. 19.00 (*0-7540-8049-8*) Chivers N Amer.

Overholser. Embers at Dawn. LC 98-22722. 222p. 1998. 18.95 (*0-7862-1163-6*) Thorndike Pr.
— The Judas Gun. large type ed. LC 98-33777. Date not set. 19.95 (*0-7838-0355-9*, G K Hall Lrg Type) Mac Lib Ref.

Overholser, Dennis & Remus, Timothy. Hot Rod Wiring: Painless Wiring for Your Hot Rod or Truck. (Illus.). 144p. 1997. pap. 19.95 (*0-9641358-6-8*) Wolfgang Pubns.

Overholser, Lee C. Ericksonian Hypnosis. LC 82-6627. 1982. pap. 32.95 (*0-8290-0738-5*) Irvington.
— Ericksonian Hypnosis: A Handbook of Clinical Practice. rev. ed. 324p. 1994. reprint ed. pap. 29.95 (*0-8290-2635-5*) Irvington.

Overholser, Lee C., jt. auth. see Pelton, Ross.

Overholser, Marguariete. A Man Is a Man: Hooker Family Saga. LC 93-70835. (Illus.). 344p. 1993. pap. 19.95 (*0-8323-0500-6*) Binford Mort.

***Overholser, Stephen.** Cold Wind. LC 99-41702. 1999. 19.95 (*0-7862-1896-7*) Five Star.
— Dark Embers at Dawn. 208p. 1999. mass mkt. 4.50 (*0-8439-4657-1*, Leisure Bks) Dorchester Pub Co.

An Asterisk (*) at the beginning of an entry indicates that the title is appearing for the first time.

Overholser, Stephen. Dark Embers at Dawn. large type ed. LC 99-21874. 1999. pap. 30.00 (*0-7862-1175-X*) Mac Lib Ref.

— Field of Death. large type ed. LC 96-53969. 1997. lib. bdg. 17.95 (*1-57490-058-7*, Sagebrush LP West) T T Beeler.

***Overholser, Stephen.** A Hanging in Sweetwater. large type ed. LC 99-41164. (Thorndike Western Ser.). 1999. 23.95 (*0-7862-2206-9*) Thorndike Pr.

Overholser, Stephen. Molly on the Outlaw Trail, Vol. 1. LC 99-21838. 1999. pap. 22.95 (*0-7838-8615-2*) Thorndike Pr.

***Overholser, Stephen.** Search for the Fox. 192p. 2000. mass mkt. 3.99 (*0-8439-4745-4*, Leisure Bks) Dorchester Pub Co.

Overholser, Stephen. Track of a Killer. large type ed. (Sagebrush Large Print Westerns Ser.). 168p. 1996. lib. bdg. 17.95 (*1-57490-016-1*) T T Beeler.

Overholser, Wayne D. The Best Western Stories of Wayne D. Overholser. Pronzini, Bill & Greenberg, Martin H., eds. LC 83-20111. (Best Western Stories Ser.). 220p. 1989. reprint ed. pap. 12.95 (*0-8040-0913-9*) Swallow.

— Buckaroo's Code. 192p. (Orig.). 1992. reprint ed. pap. text, mass mkt. 3.50 (*0-8439-3290-2*) Dorchester Pub Co.

— Bunch Grass - Sun on the Wall, 2 bks. in 1. 384p. 1996. reprint ed. pap. text, mass mkt. 4.99 (*0-8439-3949-4*) Dorchester Pub Co.

***Overholser, Wayne D.** By Gun & Spur. large type ed. LC 99-462296. 248p. 2000. 21.95 (*0-7838-8996-8*, G K Hall & Co) Mac Lib Ref.

Overholser, Wayne D. Cast a Long Shadow. large type ed. LC 98-11018. 247p. 1998. 21.95 (*0-7838-8446-X*, G K Hall & Co) Mac Lib Ref.

— Cast a Long Shadow. large type ed. (Sagebrush Large Print Westerns Ser.). 248p. 1995. lib. bdg. 17.95 (*1-57490-005-6*) T T Beeler.

— Chumley's Gold: A Western Duo. LC 98-54653. 250p. 1999. 30.00 (*0-7862-1571-2*) Thorndike Pr.

— Chumley's Gold: A Western Duo. large type ed. LC 99-58961. 275p. 2000. 30.00 (*0-7862-1583-6*) Thorndike Pr.

— Day of Judgment. large type ed. 1996. lib. bdg. 17.95 (*1-57490-044-7*, Sagebrush LP West) T T Beeler.

— Desperate Man. large type ed. LC 97-35648. 280p. 1998. 19.95 (*0-7838-8294-7*, G K Hall Lrg Type) Mac Lib Ref.

— Fabulous Gunman. large type ed. LC 98-26419. 1998. 21.95 (*0-7838-0304-4*, G K Hall Lrg Type) Mac Lib Ref.

— Fabulous Gunman. 192p. 1991. reprint ed. pap. 3.50 (*0-8439-3168-X*) Dorchester Pub Co.

— Hearn's Valley - Tough Hand, 2 bks. in 1. 384p. 1995. pap. text, mass mkt. 4.99 (*0-8439-3831-5*) Dorchester Pub Co.

— Judas Gun. LC 98-33777. 196 p. 1999. write for info. (*0-7540-3544-1*) Chivers N Amer.

— Land of Promises. 176p. 1989. pap. 2.75 (*0-380-70679-2*, Avon Bks) Morrow Avon.

— The Lone Deputy - Desperate Man. 384p. 1995. pap. text, mass mkt. 4.99 (*0-8439-3782-3*) Dorchester Pub Co.

— Nightmare in Broken Bow. large type ed. LC 98-10488. 238p. 1998. pap. 18.95 (*0-7838-8456-7*, G K Hall & Co) Mac Lib Ref.

— Nightmare in Broken Bow large type ed. LC 98-10488. (A Large Print Western Ser.). 194p. 1998. write for info. (*0-7540-3292-2*) Chivers N Amer.

— Nightmare in Broken Bow - Day of Judgment. 384p. 1996. pap. text, mass mkt. 4.99 (*0-8439-3910-9*) Dorchester Pub Co.

— Nugget City. 224p. 1998. mass mkt. 4.40 (*0-8439-4454-4*, Leisure Bks) Dorchester Pub Co.

— Nugget City. LC 96-43959. (Five-Star Western Ser.). 218p. 1997. 17.95 (*0-7862-0733-7*) Five Star.

— Nugget City. large type ed. LC 97-45667. 1998. 18.95 (*0-7862-0756-6*) Thorndike Pr.

— Oregon Trunk. large type ed. LC 98-15050. (Sagebrush Large Print Westerns Ser.). 1998. 18.95 (*1-57490-127-3*) T T Beeler.

***Overholser, Wayne D.** The Outlaws. LC 00-23521. 208p. 2000. 30.00 (*0-7862-2102-X*) Mac Lib Ref.

Overholser, Wayne D. Proud Journey. 176p. 1989. pap. 2.75 (*0-380-70678-4*, Avon Bks) Morrow Avon.

— Red Is the Valley. 160p. 1988. pap. 2.75 (*0-380-70680-6*, Avon Bks) Morrow Avon.

***Overholser, Wayne D.** Riders of the Sundowns. 208p. 1999. mass mkt. 4.50 (*0-8439-4530-3*, Leisure Bks) Dorchester Pub Co.

Overholser, Wayne D. Riders of the Sundowns. LC 97-9306. 204p. 1997. lib. bdg. 17.95 (*0-7862-0749-3*) Five Star.

— Riders of the Sundowns. LC 98-24419. 304 p. 1998. write for info. (*0-7540-3466-6*) Mac Lib Ref.

— Steel to the South. large type ed. LC 97-43617. 234p. 1998. 21.95 (*0-7838-8390-0*, G K Hall & Co) Mac Lib Ref.

— Tough Hand. 192p. 1992. reprint ed. pap. 3.50 (*0-8439-3279-1*) Dorchester Pub Co.

— The Violent Land. large type ed. LC 95-11097. (Nightingale Ser.). 365p. 1995. pap. 17.95 (*0-7838-1385-6*, G K Hall Lrg Type) Mac Lib Ref.

Overholt, Bergin F. & Chobanian, Sarkis J. Office Endoscopy. 216p. 1990. 49.00 (*0-683-06660-9*) Lppncott W & W.

Overholt, Catherine, et al, eds. Gender Roles in Development Projects: A Case Book. fac. ed. LC 84-23325. (Kumarian Press Case Studies). (Illus.). 340p. 1994. pap. 105.40 (*0-7837-7574-1*, 204732700007) Bks Demand.

Overholt, Catherine A. & Saunders, Margaret K., eds. Policy Choices & Practical Problems in Health Economics: Cases from Latin America & the Caribbean. LC 94-29559. (EDI Learning Resources Ser.: Vol. 3). 242p. 1997. pap. 22.00 (*0-8213-3012-8*, 13012) World Bank.

Overholt, Dorothy. Exchanging Real Estate Made Simple. 112p. (Orig.). 1992. pap. 24.95 (*0-9631409-0-6*) Invest Realty.

Overholt, James L. Math Wise: Hands-On Activities & Worksheets for Elementary Students. LC 95-6989. 251p. 1995. pap. text 29.95 (*0-87628-555-8*) Ctr Appl Res.

Overholt, James L., et al. Big Math Activities for Young Children. LC 98-3263. 256p. (C). 1998. text 32.95 (*0-7668-0018-0*) Delmar.

— Math Problem Solving for Grades 4 Through 8. 428p. (gr. 4-8). 1983. pap. text 36.00 (*0-205-08024-3*, H80245) Allyn.

— Math Stories for Problem Solving Success: Ready-to-Use Activities for Grades 7-12. 256p. 1989. pap. text 28.95 (*0-87628-570-1*) Ctr Appl Res.

Overholt, James L., jt. auth. see Foster, David.

Overholt, James L., jt. auth. see Foster, David R.

Overholt, Jim, ed. These Are Our Voices: The Story of Oak Ridge, 1942-1970. (Illus.). 535p. 1987. 19.95 (*0-9606832-4-0*) Chldrns Mus.

Overholt, Mary K., ed. American Cooperation, 1984. LC 26-276. (Illus.). 375p. 1984. write for info. (*0-938868-07-1*); pap. 12.00 (*0-938868-06-3*) Nat Coun of Farmer.

Overholt, Miles. Building Organizations. 128p. 1995. per., boxed set 25.00 (*0-7872-1756-5*) Kendall-Hunt.

Overholt, Thomas W. Cultural Anthropology & the Old Testament. LC 95-43457. (Guides to Biblical Scholarship Ser.). 112p. 1996. pap. 14.00 (*0-8006-2889-6*, 1-2889, Fortress Pr) Augsburg Fortress.

Overholt, Thomas W. & Callicott, J. Baird. Clothed-in-Fur & Other Tales: An Introduction to an Ojibwa World View. LC 81-43673. 198p. (Orig.). 1982. pap. text 22.50 (*0-8191-2365-X*); lib. bdg. 57.00 (*0-8191-2364-1*) U Pr of Amer.

Overholt, Thomas W., jt. ed. see Merrill, Arthur L.

Overholt, William H. The Rise of China: How Economic Reform Is Creating a New Superpower. (Illus.). 434p. 1998. reprint ed. lib. bdg. 30.00 (*0-7351-0024-1*) Replica Bks.

Overholtzer, Ruth P. From Then Till Now. (CEF History Ser.). 155p. 1990. pap. 6.99 (*1-55976-122-9*) CEF Press.

Overing, Gillian R. Language, Sign, & Gender in Beowulf. LC 89-5922. 160p. (C). 1990. 26.50 (*0-8093-1563-7*) S Ill U Pr.

Overing, Gillian R. & Osborn, Marijane. Landscape of Desire: Partial Stories of the Northern Medieval World. LC 93-32773. 1994. pap. 16.95 (*0-8166-2375-9*); text 42.95 (*0-8166-2374-0*) U of Minn Pr.

Overing, Gillian R., jt. ed. see Caywood, Cynthia.

Overing, Gillian R., jt. ed. see Harwood, Britton J.

Overing, Joanna, ed. Reason & Morality. (ASA Monographs). 240p. (C). 1985. pap. text 15.95 (*0-422-79810-X*, 9605, Pub. by Tavistock) Routldge.

***Overing, Joanna & Passes, Alan.** The Anthropology of Love & Anger: The Aesthetics of Conviviality in Native Amazonia. LC 00-32835. 2000. pap. write for info. (*0-415-22418-7*) Routledge.

Overington, I. Computer Vision: A Unified, Biologically-Inspired Approach. 424p. 1991. 212.50 (*0-444-88972-8*, North Holland) Elsevier.

Overington, Michael A., jt. auth. see Mangham, Iain L.

Overkleeft, D. & Groosman, L. E., eds. The Dekker Perspective. (C). 1988. lib. bdg. 41.50 (*1-85333-108-2*, Pub. by Graham & Trotman) Kluwer Academic.

Overlach, Theodore W. Foreign Financial Control in China. Bruchey, Stuart & Bruchey, Eleanor, eds. LC 76-5027. (American Business Abroad Ser.). 1976. reprint ed. 30.95 (*0-405-09293-8*) Ayer.

***Overlaet, B. & Haerinck, E.** Luristan Excavation Documents: Djub-i Gauhar & Gul Khanan Murdah Iron Age III--Graveyards in the Aivan Plain. Vol. 3. 1999. 81.50 (*90-429-0718-5*, Pub. by Peeters Pub) Bks Intl VA.

Overlake School Staff. The Overlake School Cookbook. 3rd ed. Mickelson, Bonnie S., ed. LC 89-63118. (Illus.). 190p. 1984. 11.95 (*0-9612946-0-4*) Overlake Schl.

Overland. Java in Plain English. 2nd ed. 1997. 19.95 (*0-8052-8563-6*, M&T Bks) IDG Bks.

***Overland, Brian.** C++ in Plain English. 2nd ed. LC 99-47115. 608p. 1999. pap. 19.99 (*0-7645-4572-8*) IDG Bks.

Overland, Brian. Java in Plain English. 2nd ed. LC 97-30978. 704p. 1997. pap. 19.95 (*1-55828-563-6*, MIS Pr) IDG Bks.

***Overland, Brian R.** Visual Basic 6 in Plain English. LC QA76.73.B3O94 1999. 592p. 1998. pap. text 24.99 (*0-7645-7007-2*, MIS Pr) IDG Bks.

Overland, Carlton, jt. auth. see Cox, Richard.

Overland, Larry. Early Settlement of Lake Cushman. 2nd ed. (Illus.). 46p. (Orig.). 1981. reprint ed. pap. 3.75 (*0-935693-02-5*) Mason Cty Hist.

Overland, Orm. The Western Home: A Literary History of Norwegian America. Lovoll, Odd Sverre, ed. (Authors Ser.: Vol. 8). (Illus.). 442p. 1996. 44.95 (*0-87732-085-3*) Norwegian-Am Hist Assn.

Overland, Orm, ed. from NOR. Johan Schrxder's Travels in Canada, 1863. (McGill-Queen's Studies in Ethnic History). (Illus.). 192p. (C). 1989. text 65.00 (*0-7735-0718-3*, Pub. by McG-Queens Univ Pr) CUP Services.

Overlee, Edye, jt. auth. see Overlee, Vern.

Overlee, Vern. The Psychic. 3rd rev. ed. Orig. Title: Let the Dead Speak of Their Lives. (Illus.). 204p. 1983. 11.95 (*0-9645230-1-9*) Mora Pr.

Overlee, Vern & Overlee, Edye. The Great Beyond. (Illus.). 224p. 1995. 19.95 (*0-9645230-2-7*) Mora Pr.

Overlie, George. Match Wits with Sherlock Holmes, Vol. 3. (Match Wits with Sherlock Holmes Ser.: Vol. III). (J). (gr. 4-7). 1993. pap. 4.95 (*0-87614-530-6*, Carolrhoda) Lerner Pub.

Overlin, Eloise, jt. auth. see Vujovich-LaBarre, Mila.

Overlin, Trudy K. & Stevens, Kathryn J., eds. Training, Education & Liability Issues for Law Enforcement Scientists & Engineers, Vol. 2939. LC 96-69889. 120p. 1997. 46.00 (*0-8194-2341-6*) SPIE.

Overlock, Leland. Windships of Warren, Maine, Seventeen Seventy to Eighteen Sixty-Seven. LC 88-90850. (Illus.). 306p. 1988. pap. 15.50 (*0-941216-41-1*); lib. bdg. 24.95 (*0-941216-42-X*) Cay-Bel.

Overlook Hospital Auxilary Staff. Cooking is Our Bag. Lamberto, Charlanne & Morrow, Nancy, eds. (Illus.). 250p. 1980. 9.95 (*0-9604560-0-7*) Overlook Hosp.

Overly, Michael R. E-Policy: How to Develop Computer, E-mail, & Internet Guidelines to Protect Your Company & Its Assets. LC 98-26077. 144p. 1998. pap. 24.95 (*0-8144-7996-0*) AMACOM.

— Overly on Electronic Evidence in California LC 98-55952. (Expert Ser.). 1999. write for info. (*0-314-23371-7*) West Pub.

Overly, Mike. Fretboard Flashcards: Learn Guitar in a Flash. (Illus.). 148p. 1998. ring bd. 10.95 (*0-9658086-1-0*) Twelve Tone.

— Fretboard Flashcards - Bass Edition: The Fastest Way to Learn 12 Pitches on 4 Strings. (Illus.). 102p. 1999. 11.95 (*0-9658086-2-9*) Twelve Tone.

— Guitar EncycloMedia: How to Visualize the Whole Fretboard & Easily See Its Many Chord, Scale & Arpeggio Fragments. LC 96-94808. (Illus.). xxi, 313p. 1996. spiral bd. 39.95 (*0-9658086-0-2*) Twelve Tone.

Overly, Philip. Poems for My Family. 116p. (Orig.). 1996. pap. write for info. (*1-57502-216-8*, P0869) Morris Pubng.

Overly, Philip R. More Poems for My Family. 120p. 1998. pap. write for info. (*1-57502-873-5*, PO2376) Morris Pubng.

Overman, Andrew, ed. see Sloyan, Gerard S.

Overman, Christian. Assumptions That Affect Our Lives LC 97-172719. 273p. 1996. write for info. (*1-883035-50-3*) Grow Families.

Overman, Dean L. A Case Against Accident & Self-Organization. LC 97-25885. 240p. 1997. 24.95 (*0-8476-8966-2*) Rowman.

Overman, E. Samuel, jt. auth. see Garson, G. David.

Overman, E. Samuel, ed. see Campbell, Donald T.

Overman, J. Andrew. Church & Community in Crisis: The Gospel According to Matthew. LC 96-12471. (New Testament in Context Ser.). 448p. 1996. pap. 28.00 (*1-56338-101-X*) TPI PA.

Overman, J. Andrew, ed. see Johnson, Luke T.

Overman, Larry. Organic Syntheses, Vol. 71. 320p. 1993. 69.95 (*0-471-30531-6*) Wiley.

Overman, Marjorie. The Edge of Forever. (Illus.). 80p. (Orig.). pap. 8.95 (*0-9614853-0-2*) Overman Pub.

Overman, Marvin, jt. auth. see Henderson, R. Winn.

Overman, Steven J. The Influence of the Protestant Ethic on Sport & Recreation. LC 96-78545. 408p. 1997. text 83.95 (*1-85972-387-X*, Pub. by Avebry) Ashgate Pub Co.

Overmars, M. H. The Design of Dynamic Data Structures. (Lecture Notes in Computer Science Ser.: Vol. 156). 181p. 1987. 30.00 (*0-387-12330-X*) Spr-Verlag.

Overmars, Mark, jt. ed. see Laumond, Jean-Paul.

Overmeyer, Daniel. Precious Volumes: An Introduction to Chinese Sectarian Scriptures from the 16th & 17th Centuries, Vol.49. LC 99-19188. (Harvard-Yenching Institute Monograph Ser.). 1999. 55.00 (*0-674-69838-X*) HUP.

Overmier, Bruce J., jt. auth. see Brush, Robert.

Overmier, J. Bruce & Burke, Patricia D., eds. Animal Models of Human Pathology: A Bibliography of a Quarter Century of Behavioral Research, 1967-1992. 322p. 1992. pap. 19.95 (*1-55798-184-1*) Am Psychol.

Overmier, Judith A. & Senior, John E. Books & Manuscripts of the Bakken. LC 92-8512. (Illus.). 525p. 1992. 83.50 (*0-8108-2570-8*) Scarecrow.

Overmyer, Allen, jt. auth. see Shook, Hal.

Overmyer, Daniel L. Folk Buddhist Religion: Dissenting Sects in Late Traditional China. LC 75-23467. (Harvard East Asian Ser.: No. 83). 311p. reprint ed. pap. 96.50 (*0-608-15243-9*, 202917200059) Bks Demand.

— Religions of China: The World As a Living System. (Illus.). 125p. (C). 1998. reprint ed. pap. text 10.50 (*1-57766-000-5*) Waveland Pr.

Overmyer, Daniel L., jt. auth. see Jordan, David K.

Overmyer, Eric. Don Quixote de la Jolla. 1993. pap. 6.95 (*0-88145-109-6*) Broadway Play.

— Eric Overmyer: Collected Plays. (Contemporary Playwrights Ser.). 336p. 1993. 35.00 (*1-880399-40-7*); pap. 19.95 (*1-880399-33-4*) Smith & Kraus.

— The Heliotrope Bouquet. 1993. pap. 6.95 (*0-88145-108-8*) Broadway Play.

— Mi Vida Loca. 1991. pap. 6.95 (*0-88145-100-2*) Broadway Play.

— Native Speech. 96p. 1984. pap. 5.95 (*0-88145-017-0*) Broadway Play.

— On the Verge. 76p. (Orig.). 1986. pap. 6.95 (*0-88145-046-4*) Broadway Play.

Overmyer, Grace. America's First Hamlet. LC 75-31964. (Illus.). 439p. 1976. reprint ed. lib. bdg. 49.75 (*0-8371-8446-0*, OVAH, Greenwood Pr) Greenwood.

Overmyer, Jack K. A Stupendous Effort: The 87th Indiana in the War of the Rebellion. LC 96-54581. 1997. 29.95 (*0-253-33301-6*) Ind U Pr.

Overmyer, James. Queen of the Negro Leagues: Effa Manley & the Newark Eagles. LC 97-49909. (Illus.). 298p. 1998. pap. 16.95 (*1-57886-001-6*) Scarecrow.

Overmyer, John C. Hasselbach. History & Genealogy of the Hasselbach Family, Being a Record of the John Peter, John Phillip, Regina Elizabeth & Elizabeth Margaret; Four Children of John Jacob Hasselbach & Their Descendants, 1781-1910. (Illus.). 159p. 1997. reprint ed. pap. 26.00 (*0-8328-9036-7*); reprint ed. lib. bdg. 36.00 (*0-8328-9035-9*) Higginson Bk Co.

***Overmyer, Leonard G., III.** Forest Haven Soldiers: The Civil War Veterans of Glen Lake & Surrounding Leelanau. LC 00-131665. (Illus.). 194p. 2000. pap. 17.95 (*0-9679259-0-8*) Overmyer Hist.

Overney, Rene M., jt. ed. see Frommer, Jane E.

Oversby, V. M. & Brown, Paul W., eds. Scientific Basis for Nuclear Waste Management XIII Vol. 176: Materials Research Society Symposium Proceedings. 804p. 1990. text 17.50 (*1-55899-064-X*) Materials Res.

Overschee, Peter Van, see Van Overschee, Peter.

Overseas Development Council Staff & McLaughlin, Martin M. The United States & World Development: Agenda 1979. LC 78-71589. 348p. 1979. 65.00 (*0-275-90392-3*, C0392, Praeger Pubs) Greenwood.

Overshiner, Elwyn E. Course 095 to Eternity. 2nd ed. LC 80-82005. (Illus.). 256p. 1989. 10.95 (*0-936940-07-7*) Helm Pub.

Overshott, K. J., jt. auth. see Boll, Richard.

Overstein, Peggy. Pressure Points. 1999. write for info. (*0-679-45288-5*) McKay.

Overstone, Samuel J. The Evidence Given by Lord Overstone on Bank Acts. LC 68-30538. (Library of Money & Banking History). x, 306p. 1973. reprint ed. 45.00 (*0-678-00955-4*) Kelley.

— Tracts & Other Publications on Metallic & Paper Currency: With Further Reflections on the State of the Currency (1837), 2 vols. in 1. LC 67-20089. (Library of Money & Banking History). viii, 649p. 1972. reprint ed. 57.50 (*0-678-00902-3*) Kelley.

Overstraeten, R. J. Van, see Van Overstraeten, R. J.

Overstreet, Alfred T. Are Men Born Sinners? The Myth of Original Sin. vi, 275p. (Orig.). 1995. pap. 9.95 (*0-9644832-0-3*) Evangel Bks Pub.

Overstreet, Bonaro W., jt. auth. see Overstreet, Harry A.

Overstreet, Charles W. Plains Indian & Mountain Man Arts & Crafts: An Illustrated Guide. Smith, Monte & Knight, Denise, eds. LC 93-74239. (Illus.). 160p. (Orig.). 1994. pap., per. 13.95 (*0-943604-41-9*, BOO/34) Eagles View.

— Plains Indian & Mountain Man Arts & Crafts II: An Illustrated Guide, Vol. II. Knight, Denise, ed. LC 95-83908. (Illus.). 144p. (Orig.). 1996. pap., per. 12.95 (*0-943604-51-6*, BOO40) Eagles View.

— Toys & Games of Early America: A How-To Book. Knight, Denise, ed. (Illus.). 220p. 2000. pap. 15.95 (*0-943604-54-0*, BOO/31) Eagles View.

Overstreet, Daphne. Arizona Territory Cookbook. LC 96-37279. 1997. ring bd. 6.95 (*0-914846-75-2*) Golden West Pub.

Overstreet, David F. Chesrow: A Paleoindian Complex in the Southern Lake Michigan Basin. (Case Studies in Great Lakes Archaeology). (Illus.). 183p. (C). 1993. pap. 15.00 (*1-881354-02-4*) Gt Lks Archaeol.

Overstreet, David F., et al. Archaeological Studies on the Southeast Wisconsin Uplands, Kenosha County. (Case Studies in Great Lakes Archaeology). 143p. (C). 1992. pap. 15.00 (*1-881354-00-8*) Gt Lks Archaeol.

Overstreet, Deborah W. Unencumbered by History: The Vietnam Experience in Young Adult Fiction. LC 98-22140. 328p. 1998. 48.00 (*0-8108-3535-5*) Scarecrow.

Overstreet, Dennis & Gibbons, David. Overstreet's New Wine Guide: Celebrating the New Wave in Winemaking. LC 99-13373. 272p. 1999. 40.00 (*0-517-70784-5*) C Potter.

***Overstreet Editors, et al.** Overstreet's New Wine Guide: Celebrating the New Wave in Winemaking. 272p. 1999. pap. 27.50 (*0-609-80518-5*) Crown.

Overstreet, George A., Jr. & Rubin, Geoffrey M. Blurred Vision: Challenges in Credit Union Research & Modeling. 45p. 1991. pap. 100.00 (*1-880572-00-1*) Filene Res.

Overstreet, George A., jt. auth. see Fried, Harold O.

Overstreet, George A., jt. auth. see Rubin, Geoffrey M.

Overstreet, Harry A. Guide to Civilized Leisure. LC 73-84357. (Essay Index Reprint Ser.). 1977. 20.95 (*0-8369-1151-2*) Ayer.

Overstreet, Harry A. & Overstreet, Bonaro W. Communism. 1958. 6.50 (*0-393-05277-X*) Norton.

— Iron Curtain. 1963. 4.50 (*0-393-05303-2*) Norton.

— War Called Peace: Khrushchev's Communism. 1961. 4.95 (*0-393-05286-9*) Norton.

***Overstreet, Kris.** In Nomine Corporeal Player's Guide. Dawson, Alain H., ed. 128p. 1999. 19.95 (*1-55634-389-2*, Pub. by S Jackson Games) BookWorld.

Overstreet, Larry C. Morals & Issues: Index of Modern Information. rev. ed. 145p. 1994. 47.50 (*0-7883-0466-6*); pap. 44.50 (*0-7883-0467-4*) ABBE Pubs Assn.

Overstreet, Mark R., et al. Debtor/Creditor Relations in Kentucky. xiv, 590p. 1991. 83.75 (*1-58757-000-9*, PH017) Univ of KY.

Overstreet, Mark R., ed. see Bucknam, Kevin P., et al.

Overstreet, Maryann. Whales, Candlelight & Stuff Like That: General Extenders in English Discourse. LC 98-45489. (Oxford Studies in Sociolinguistics). (Illus.). 184p. 2000. text 39.95 (*0-19-512574-6*) OUP.

Overstreet, Paul. Paul Overstreet - Heroes. Okun, Milton, ed. pap. 14.95 (*0-89524-626-0*) Cherry Lane.

— Paul Overstreet - Sowin' Love. Okun, Milton, ed. pap. 12.95 (*0-89524-485-3*) Cherry Lane.

O

An Asterisk (*) at the beginning of an entry indicates that the title is appearing for the first time.

Overstreet, Robert M. The Official Overstreet Comic Book Price Guide. 18th ed. (Illus.). 740p. pap. 12.95 (*0-685-07938-4*) Overstreet.
— The Official Overstreet Comic Book Price Guide. 22nd ed. 1992. pap. write for info. (*0-87637-891-2*) Hse Collectbls.
— The Official Overstreet Guide to Indian Arrowheads. 2nd ed. (Illus.). 768p. pap. 19.00 (*0-685-60183-8*) Overstreet.
— The Overstreet Comic Book Companion: Identification & Price Guide. 6th ed. (Confident Collector Ser.). (Illus.). 608p. 1992. mass mkt. 6.00 (*0-380-76911-5*, Avon Bks) Morrow Avon.
***Overstreet, Robert M.** Overstreet Comic Book Price Guide. 2000. pap. 15.00 (*0-380-77307-4*) Morrow Avon.
Overstreet, Robert M. The Overstreet Comic Book Price Guide. 22nd ed. 544p. 1992. pap. 15.00 (*0-380-76912-3*, Avon Bks) Morrow Avon.
— The Overstreet Comic Book Price Guide. 23rd ed. 760p. 1993. pap. 15.00 (*0-380-77220-5*, Avon Bks) Morrow Avon.
— The Overstreet Comic Book Price Guide. 25th ed. (Illus.). 816p. 1995. pap. 17.00 (*0-380-78210-3*, Avon Bks) Morrow Avon.
— The Overstreet Comic Book Price Guide. 27th ed. 896p. 1997. pap. 18.00 (*0-380-79463-2*, Avon Bks) Morrow Avon.
— The Overstreet Comic Book Price Guide. 28th ed. 960p. 1998. pap. 18.00 (*0-380-80075-6*, Avon Bks) Morrow Avon.
***Overstreet, Robert M.** The Overstreet Comic Book Price Guide. 30th rev. ed. (Illus.). 992p. 2000. pap. 22.00 (*0-06-095734-4*) HarpC.
Overstreet, Robert M. The Overstreet Comic Book Price Guide, Vol. 26. 26th rev. ed. (Illus.). 832p. 1996. pap. 17.00 (*0-380-78778-4*, Avon Bks) Morrow Avon.
— The Overstreet Comic Book Price Guide: 29th Edition Collectibles. 29th ed. (Illus.). 1008p. 1999. pap. 20.00 (*0-380-80780-7*, Avon Bks) Morrow Avon.
— The Overstreet Comic Book Price Guide Companion. 7th ed. 464p. 1995. pap. 6.00 (*0-380-78229-4*, Avon Bks) Morrow Avon.
— The Overstreet Comic Price Guide. 24th ed. 1994. pap. 15.00 (*0-380-77854-8*, Avon Bks) Morrow Avon.
— The Overstreet Comics & Cards Price Guide. 464p. (Orig.). 1993. mass mkt. 6.00 (*0-380-77310-4*, Avon Bks) Morrow Avon.
***Overstreet, Robert M.** The Overstreet Indian Arrowheads Identification & Price Guide. 6th ed. (Confident Collector Ser.). (Illus.). 972p. (Orig.). 1999. pap. 24.00 (*0-380-80781-5*, Avon Bks) Morrow Avon.
Overstreet, Robert M. & Carter, Gary. The Overstreet Comic Book Grading Guide. 320p. (Orig.). 1992. pap. 12.00 (*0-380-76910-7*, Avon Bks) Morrow Avon.
Overstreet, Robert M. & Peake, Howard. The Overstreet Indian Arrowheads: Identification & Price Guide. 3rd ed. xvi, 784p. (Orig.). 1993. pap. 20.00 (*0-380-77186-1*, Avon Bks) Morrow Avon.
— The Overstreet Indian Arrowheads: Identification & Price Guide. 4th ed. (Illus.). 816p. (Orig.). 1995. pap. 20.00 (*0-380-78211-1*, Avon Bks) Morrow Avon.
Overstreet, Thomas R., Jr., jt. auth. see Ippolito, Pauline M.
Overthrow, David. Beginning Electric Bass. Date not set. pap. write for info. (*0-7390-0688-6*, 19361); pap. write for info. incl. audio compact disk (*0-7390-0689-4*, 19362) Alfred Pub.
— Intermediate Electric Bass. Date not set. pap. write for info. (*0-7390-0685-1*, 19358); pap. write for info. incl. audio compact disk (*0-7390-0686-X*, 19359) Alfred Pub.
— Mastering Electric Bass. Date not set. pap. write for info. (*0-7390-0682-7*, 19355); pap. write for info. incl. audio compact disk (*0-7390-0683-5*, 19356) Alfred Pub.
Overton. Assessment in Special Education: An Applied Approach. 3rd ed. LC 99-29667. (Illus.). 541p. 1999. pap. text 56.00 (*0-13-082654-5*) P-H.
Overton, Barbara, jt. auth. see Carroll, James.
Overton, Barbara, jt. auth. see Carroll, James M.
Overton, Basil. Gems from Greek. 1991. 12.05 (*0-89137-125-7*); pap. 8.50 (*0-685-51733-0*) Quality Pubns.
— Highest Peak of Human Performance. 1990. pap. 6.95 (*0-89137-118-4*) Quality Pubns.
— Mule Musings. 1983. 8.75 (*0-89137-106-0*); pap. 6.15 (*0-89137-105-2*) Quality Pubns.
— When Christ Was Preached to Christ. 1983. pap. 7.75 (*0-89137-545-7*) Quality Pubns.
Overton, Bruce. Executive Compensation Answer Book. annuals 2nd ed. 360p. 1994. 118.00 (*1-56706-134-6*, S69) Panel Pubs.
***Overton, Bruce.** Executive Compensation Answer Book: 1999 Supplement. LC 99-198641. 1999. pap. text 89.00 (*1-56706-870-7*) Panel Pubs.
Overton, Bruce, jt. auth. see Stoffer, Sue.
Overton, Bruce B. & Steele, Mary T. Designing Management Incentive Plans: An Approach to Developing a Short-Term Incentive Plan for Managers. (Building Blocks Ser.: Vol. 5). (Illus.). 4p. (Orig.). 1992. pap. 24.95 (*1-57963-008-1*, A0005) Am Compensation.
Overton, C. Kerry, et al. Fish & Fish Habitat Standard Inventory Procedures Handbook. (Illus.). 73p. (C). 1998. pap. text 25.00 (*0-7881-7180-1*) DIANE Pub.
— Northern/Intermountain Regions' Fish Habitat Inventory: Grazed, Rested, & Ungrazed Reference Stream Reaches, Silver King Creek, California. (Illus.). 32p. 1997. reprint ed. 10.00 (*0-89904-600-2*, Bear Meadows Resrch Grp); reprint ed. pap. 4.20 (*0-89904-601-0*, Bear Meadows Resrch Grp) Crumb Elbow Pub.
Overton, Charles E. Studies of Narcosis. Lipnick, Robert L., ed. xi, 203p. (C). 1990. text 65.00 (*0-412-35240-0*) Chapman & Hall.
Overton, David. Common Market Digest: An Information Guide to the European Communities. LC 83-105101. (Illus.). 435p. reprint ed. pap. 134.90 (*0-7837-5294-6*, 204504800005) Bks Demand.
Overton, George W., jt. ed. see Futter, Victor.
Overton, Grant M. Authors of the Day: Studies in Contemporary Literature. LC 75-156700. (Essay Index Reprint Ser.). 1977. reprint ed. 28.95 (*0-8369-2289-1*) Ayer.
— Cargoes for Crusoes. LC 72-1316. (Essay Index Reprint Ser.). 1977. reprint ed. 30.95 (*0-8369-2851-2*) Ayer.
— When Winter Comes to Main Street. LC 72-37798. (Essay Index Reprint Ser.). 1977. reprint ed. 26.95 (*0-8369-2616-1*) Ayer.
— Why Authors Go Wrong, & Other Explanations. LC 68-22936. (Essay Index Reprint Ser.). 1977. 19.95 (*0-8369-0757-4*) Ayer.
— The Women Who Make Our Novels. rev. ed. LC 67-23257. (Essay Index Reprint Ser.). 1977. 23.95 (*0-8369-0758-2*) Ayer.
Overton, Gwedolen. The Heritage of Unrest. LC 68-57544. 329p. reprint ed. lib. bdg. 30.00 (*0-8398-1454-2*) Irvington.
Overton, J. Strategies for Sustainable Development: Local Agendas for the Southern Hemisphere. 1999. 69.95 (*1-85649-641-4*) Zed Books.
Overton, James B. Rolling Thunder: January, 1967-November, 1968. 53p. 1993. reprint ed. pap. 10.00 (*0-923135-71-5*) Dalley Bk Service.
Overton, John. Colonial Green Revolution? Food, Irrigation & the State in Colonial Malaya. (Illus.). 256p. 1994. text 70.00 (*0-85198-912-8*) OUP.
***Overton, John & Scheyvens, Regina, eds.** Strategies for Sustainable Development: Experiences from the Pacific. (Illus.). 306p. 1999. pap. 29.95 (*0-86840-689-9*, Pub. by New South Wales Univ Pr) Intl Spec Bk.
Overton, John H. & Relton, Frederic. English Church from the Accession of George First to the End of the Eighteenth Century, 1714-1800. (History of the English Church Ser.: No. 7). reprint ed. 62.50 (*0-404-50757-3*) AMS Pr.
Overton, John R., ed. see Ettinger, Karl E.
Overton, Joice. Cowboy Equipment. LC 97-29686. 160p. 1998. 39.95 (*0-7643-0405-4*) Schiffer.
Overton, Joice I. Cowboy Bits & Spurs. LC 96-33430. 160p. (gr. 10). 1997. 39.95 (*0-7643-0104-7*) Schiffer.
Overton, Joseph P., jt. auth. see Steelman, Aaron.
Overton, Lois A. Out of the Golden Cage. LC 98-94831. (Illus.). 1999. pap. 12.00 (*0-9661040-1-3*) Cedar Tr Pr.
— The Winter Girls: When Joys Were Vivid. LC 97-92486. (Illus.). 250p. 1997. pap. 13.00 (*0-9661040-0-5*) Cedar Tr Pr.
Overton, Mark. Agricultural Revolution in England: The Transformation of the Agrarian Economy 1500-1850. (Cambridge Studies in Historical Geography: No. 23). 272p. (C). 1996. pap. text 20.95 (*0-521-56859-5*) Cambridge U Pr.
Overton, Mary. The Wine of Astonishment. LC 97-65055. 180p. (Orig.). 1997. pap. 12.00 (*0-9644348-1-4*) La Questa Pr.
Overton, Meredith H. & Lukert, Barbara P. Clinical Nutrition: A Physiologic Approach. LC 77-81527. (Illus.). 181p. 1977. reprint ed. pap. 56.20 (*0-8357-7626-3*, 205694900096) Bks Demand.
Overton, Patrick, intro. Grassroots & Mountain Wings: The Arts in Rural & Small Communities. 135p. reprint ed. pap. write for info. (*0-9639060-1-1*) CC CC&CS.
Overton, R. K. Letters to Rollins. (Illus.). 96p. (Orig.). 1994. pap. 10.00 (*1-880985-20-9*) Two Thirteen Sixty-one.
Overton, R. K., compiled by. More Letters to Rollins. 180p. 2000. pap. 12.00 (*1-880985-68-3*) Two Thirteen Sixty-one.
Overton, Ray. Main Course Salads. LC 99-60107. (Illus.). 122p. 1999. 15.95 (*1-56352-512-7*) Longstreet.
***Overton, Ray.** Main-Course Sandwiches. LC 99-61760. (Illus.). 128p. 1999. 15.95 (*1-56352-576-3*) Longstreet.
Overton, Ray. Main-Course Soups. LC 97-73570. (Illus.). 124p. 1998. 15.95 (*1-56352-445-7*) Longstreet.
Overton, Ray L. Dutch Oven Cookbook. LC 98-66371. 128p. 1998. 15.95 (*1-56352-527-5*) Longstreet.
— Layers of Flavors. LC 97-76260. (Illus.). 170 p. 1998. 18.95 (*1-56352-464-3*) Longstreet.
***Overton, Ray L. & Williams, Chuck.** The South. LC 99-43383. (Williams-Sonoma New American Cooking Ser.). (Illus.). 144p. (YA). (gr. 8). 2000. 22.95 (*0-7370-2040-7*) Time-Life.
Overton, Richard C. Perkins-Budd: Railway Statesmen of the Burlington, 45. LC 81-6961. (Contributions in Economics & Economic History Ser.: No. 45.). (Illus.). 271p. 1982. 59.95 (*0-313-23173-7*, OPB/, Greenwood Pr) Greenwood.
Overton, Ron. Hotel Me: Poems for Gil Evans & Others. LC 93-47147. 1994. 18.00 (*1-882413-09-1*); pap. 10.00 (*1-882413-08-3*) Hanging Loose.
— Love on the Alexander Hamilton. 88p. 1985. pap. 6.00 (*0-914610-39-2*) Hanging Loose.
Overton, Sadie W. The House of the Lord: Lake Providence Missionary Baptist Church, Nashville, Tennessee 1868-19. (Illus.). 192p. 1997. write for info. (*1-57736-033-8*) Providence Hse.
Overton, Ted. Sports after Fifty: Fit Yourself into Fun Sports. LC 88-70544. (Illus.). 224p. 1988. 17.95 (*0-913179-20-5*) Azimuth Pr.
***Overton, Theodora.** Loose Diamonds: A Novel. 304p. 2001. pap. 14.95 (*1-56474-355-1*) Fithian Pr.
Overton, Valerie, jt. auth. see Applegate, April.
Overton, Volma & Jones, Carolyn L. Volma, My Journey: One Man's Impact on the Civil Rights Movement in Austin, Texas. LC 98-10628. (Illus.). (Orig.). 1998. pap. 18.95 (*1-57168-218-X*, Eakin Pr) Sunbelt Media.
Overton, W. F., ed. Reasoning, Necessity & Logic: Developmental Perspectives. (Jean Piaget Symposia Ser.). 344p. (C). 1990. text 89.95 (*0-8058-0090-5*) L Erlbaum Assocs.
Overton, Willis F., ed. The Relationship Between Social & Cognitive Development. (Jean Piaget Society Ser.). 272p. (C). 1983. text 49.95 (*0-89859-249-6*) L Erlbaum Assocs.
Overton, Willis F. & Palermo, David S., eds. The Nature & Ontogenesis of Meaning. (Jean Piaget Symposia Ser.). 320p. 1994. text 69.95 (*0-8058-1211-3*) L Erlbaum Assocs.
Overton, Yvonne. Romantic Applique. (Illus.). 96p. 1995. pap. 12.95 (*0-614-07136-4*, Pub. by Sally Milner) Sterling.
— Romantic Applique. (Illus.). 72p. 1995. pap. 14.95 (*1-86351-140-7*, Pub. by Sally Milner) Sterling.
Overturf. Money & European Union. LC 99-58619. 1999. pap. 19.95 (*0-312-22460-5*) St Martin.
Overturf, Stephen F. The Economic Principles of European Integration. LC 86-21271. 196p. 1986. pap. 21.95 (*0-275-92277-4*, B2277, Praeger Pubs) Greenwood.
— The Economic Principles of European Integration. LC 86-21271. 196p. 1986. 57.95 (*0-275-92276-6*, C2276, Praeger Pubs) Greenwood.
— Money & European Union. LC 96-53464. 352p. 1997. text 45.00 (*0-312-17301-6*) St Martin.
Overvold, Mark C. & Heil, John. Rationality, Morality & Self-Interest: Essays Honoring Mark Carl Overvold. LC 92-36825. (Studies in Epistemology & Cognitive Theory). xi, 304p. 1993. write for info. (*0-8476-7767-2*) Rowman.
Overvoorde, Chris S. So You've Been Asked To... Design Visuals for Worship. (Illus.). 22p. 1999. mass mkt. 1.25 (*1-56212-428-5*, 2270-0090) CRC Pubns.
Overwater, R. M. The Physics of Big Sample Instrumental Neutron Activation Analysis. (Delft Studies in Integrated Water Management: No. 5). 192p. 1994. pap. 57.50 (*90-407-1048-1*, Pub. by Delft U Pr) Coronet Bks.
Overy, Angela. Sex in Your Garden. LC 96-42380. (Illus.). 120p. 1997. pap. 19.95 (*1-55591-335-0*) Fulcrum Pub.
Overy, Paul. DeStijl. LC 90-72120. (World of Art Ser.). (Illus.). 216p. (Orig.). 1991. pap. 14.95 (*0-500-20240-0*, Pub. by Thames Hudson) Norton.
Overy, R. J. The Air War, 1939-1945. LC 80-6200. (Illus.). 288p. 1981. pap. 12.95 (*0-8128-6156-6*, Scrbrough Hse) Madison Bks UPA.
— The Inter-War Crisis, 1919-1939. LC 94-359. (Seminar Studies in History). (C). 1995. pap. text 13.50 (*0-582-35379-3*, Pub. by Addison-Wesley) Longman.
— The Nazi Economic Recovery 1932-1938. 2nd ed. (New Studies in Economic & Social History: No. 27). (Illus.). 84p. (C). 1996. text 34.95 (*0-521-55286-9*); pap. text 10.95 (*0-521-55767-4*) Cambridge U Pr.
— The Origins of the Second World War. 2nd ed. LC 97-38405. (Seminar Studies in History). (C). 1998. pap. text 13.13 (*0-582-29085-6*, Drumbeat) Longman.
— War & Economy in the Third Reich. (Illus.). 404p. 1995. pap. text 26.00 (*0-19-820599-6*) OUP.
Overy, Richard. The Penguin Historical Atlas of the Third Reich. 144p. 1997. pap. 16.95 (*0-14-051330-2*) Viking Penguin.
***Overy, Richard.** Road to War. rev. ed. (Illus.). 388p. 1999. pap. 14.95 (*0-14-028530-X*) Viking Penguin.
Overy, Richard. Russia's War: A History of the Soviet War Effort, 1941-1945. LC D765.O84 1997. (Illus.). 432p. 1998. pap. 14.95 (*0-14-027169-4*) Viking Penguin.
— Russia's War: Blood upon the Snow. LC 97-213178. (Illus.). 384p. 1997. 29.95 (*1-57500-051-2*, Pub. by TV Bks) HarpC.
— Why the Allies Won. (Illus.). 396p. 1998. text 30.00 (*0-7881-5869-4*) DIANE Pub.
— Why the Allies Won. 416p. 1996. 29.95 (*0-393-03925-0*) Norton.
— Why the Allies Won. 428p. 1997. pap. 15.95 (*0-393-31619-X*) Norton.
Overy, Richard, ed. see Black.
Overy, Richard, ed. see Geary, Dick.
Overy, Richard, ed. see Hammond World Publishing Staff.
***Overy, Ronald & Lecanuet, Jacqueline.** French in Three Months. LC 97-47225. (FRE.). 1998. pap. 29.95 incl. audio (*0-7894-3227-7*) DK Pub Inc.
Overzee, Anne H. The Body Divine: The Symbol of the Body in the Works of Teilhard de Chardin & Ramanuja. (Studies in Religious Traditions: No. 2). 234p. (C). 1992. text 69.95 (*0-521-38516-4*) Cambridge U Pr.
Ovesen, Ellis. Memories of South Dakota. Leih, Janet, ed. LC 93-60173. 60p. (Orig.). 1993. 7.00 (*1-877649-19-8*); per. 2.50 (*1-877649-18-X*) Tesseract SD.
— The Year of the Horse, Poems of Prophesy & the Human Predicament. (Illus.). 63p. 1991. 4.50 (*0-8233-0472-8*) Tesseract SD.
Ovesen, Jan, jt. auth. see Michaud, Jean.
Oveson, W. V., jt. auth. see Utah Staff.
Oviatt, Charles G. Quaternary Geology of Fish Springs Flat, Juab County, Utah. LC TN24.U8 A322. (Special Study Ser.: Vol. 77). (Illus.). 16p. 1991. pap. 6.00 (*1-55791-196-7*, SS-77) Utah Geological Survey.
— Quaternary Geology of Part of the Sevier Desert, Millard County, Utah. LC TN24.U8A322. (Special Study Ser.: Vol. 70). (Illus.). 41p. 1989. pap. 7.50 (*1-55791-189-4*, SS-70) Utah Geological Survey.
— Quaternary Geology of the Black Rock Desert, Millard County, Utah. LC TN24.U8 A322. (Special Study Ser.: Vol. 73). (Illus.). 23p. 1991. pap. 6.00 (*1-55791-192-4*, SS-73) Utah Geological Survey.
— Quaternary Geology of the Scipio Valley Area, Millard & Juab Counties, Utah. LC TN24.U8 A322. (Special Study Ser.: Vol. 79). (Illus.). 16p. 1992. pap. 6.00 (*1-55791-198-3*, SS-79) Utah Geological Survey.
Oviatt, Charles G., et al. Quaternary Geologic Map of the Old River Bed & Vicinity, Millard, Juab, & Tooele Counties, Utah. (Map of the Utah Geological Survey Ser.: Vol. 161). (Illus.). 24p. 1994. pap. 6.00 (*1-55791-563-6*, M-161) Utah Geological Survey.
Oviatt, Denise K., ed. see Corts, C. Mark.
Oviatt, Edwin. Beginnings of Yale, Seventeen Hundred One to Seventeen Twenty-Six. LC 70-89214. (American Education: Its Men, Institutions, & Ideas. Series 1). 1978. reprint ed. 23.95 (*0-405-01453-8*) Ayer.
Oviatt, Joan. Amazing but True Mormon Stories. 144p. 1994. 11.98 (*0-88290-507-4*, 1050) Horizon Utah.
— More Amazing but True Mormon Stories. 176p. (Orig.). 1996. pap. 13.98 (*0-88290-578-3*, 1043) Horizon Utah.
Oviatt, Mark D. & Miller, Richard K. Industrial Pneumatic Systems: Noise Control & Energy Conservation. 39.00 (*0-915586-19-3*) Fairmont Pr.
Oviatt, Ross H. South Dakota Justice: The Judges & the System. 67p. 1989. per. 7.95 (*0-614-24800-0*) Tesseract SD.
Ovid. Amores. Kenney, Edwin J., ed. Incl. Ars Amatoria. 1961. Medicamina Faciei Femineae. 1961. Remedia Amoria. 1961. (Oxford Classical Texts Ser.). 1961. 21.00 (*0-19-814642-6*) OUP.
Ovid. Amores, Medicamina Faciei Femineae, Ars Amatoria, Remedia Amoris. 2nd ed. Kenney, E. J., ed. (Classical Texts Ser.). (Illus.). 288p. 1994. text 24.94 (*0-19-814969-7*) OUP.
Ovid. Ars Amatoria, Bk. 1. (Illus.). 196p. 1989. reprint ed. pap. text 27.00 (*0-19-814736-8*) OUP.
— L' Art de l'Aimer, Les Remedes a l'Amour, Les Produits de Beaute. (FRE.). 1974. pap. 10.95 (*0-7859-4024-3*) Fr & Eur.
— The Art of Beauty - De Medicamine Faciei Femihae. limited ed. (Illus.). 18p. 1990. 350.00 (*0-923980-28-8*) Arundel Pr.
— The Art of Love. Humphries, Rolfe T., tr. LC 57-7706. (Greek & Latin Classics Ser.). 208p. 1957. pap. 12.95 (*0-253-20002-4*, MB-2) Ind U Pr.
— A Choice of Ovid: Selections from Metamorphoses, Fasti & Tristia. Kennedy, Eberhard C., ed. (College Classical Ser.). (LAT.). (C). 1984. pap. text 16.00 (*0-89241-472-3*) Caratzas.
— De Arte Amatoria Libri Tres. Brandt, Paul, ed. xxiii, 255p. 1991. reprint ed. write for info. incl. 3.5 hd (*3-487-05033-1*) G Olms Pubs.
— Fasti. Fantham, Elaine, ed. (Greek & Latin Classics: Bk. IV). (Illus.). 302p. (C). 1998. text 64.95 (*0-521-44538-8*); pap. text 24.95 (*0-521-44996-0*) Cambridge U Pr.
— Fasti. Frazer, James George, tr. (Loeb Classical Library: No. 253). 494p. 1931. text 18.95 (*0-674-99279-2*) HUP.
***Ovid.** Fasti. (Penguin Classics Ser.). 432p. 2000. pap. 14.00 (*0-14-044690-7*, Penguin Bks) Viking Penguin.
Ovid. Fastorum Libri Sex. Merkelio, R., ed. ccxciv, 320p. 1971. reprint ed. write for info. (*3-487-04087-5*) G Olms Pubs.
— Fastorum Libri Sex, 5 vols., Set. Frazer, James George, tr. & comment by. xlii, 1855p. 1973. reprint ed. write for info. (*3-487-04612-1*) G Olms Pubs.
— The XV Bookes Entytuled Metamorphosis. Golding, Arthur, tr. LC 77-7418. (English Experience Ser.: No. 881). 1977. reprint ed. lib. bdg. 70.00 (*90-221-0881-3*) Walter J Johnson.
— Heroides: Select Epistles. Knox, Peter E., ed. (Greek & Latin Classics Ser.). 339p. (C). 1996. text 64.95 (*0-521-36279-2*) Cambridge U Pr.
Ovid. The Love Books of Ovid. 20.00 (*0-8196-2769-0*) Biblo.
Ovid. The Love Poems. Melville, A. D., tr. 304p. 1999. pap. 10.95 (*0-19-283633-1*) OUP.
— Metamorphosen, Bd. I, Buch 1-7. Haupt, Moritz et al, eds. viii, 502p. 1966. write for info. (*3-296-14811-6*) G Olms Pubs.
— Metamorphosen, Bd. I, Buch 8-15. Haupt, Moritz et al, eds. viii, 559p. 1975. write for info. (*3-296-14812-4*) G Olms Pubs.
— Metamorphoses. Humphries, Rolfe, tr. LC 55-6269. (Greek & Latin Classics Ser.). 416p. (C). 1955. 31.95 (*0-253-33755-0*); pap. 8.95 (*0-253-20001-6*, MB-1) Ind U Pr.
— Metamorphoses. Gregory, Horace, tr. 1960. mass mkt. 6.99 (*0-451-62622-2*, Ment) NAL.
— Metamorphoses. Melville, A. D., tr. (Oxford World's Classics Ser.). 520p. 1998. reprint ed. pap. 8.95 (*0-19-283472-X*) OUP.
***Ovid.** Metamorphoses, Bk. XIII. Hopkinson, Neil, ed. (Cambridge Greek & Latin Classics Ser.). (Illus.). 264p. 2001. write for info. (*0-521-55421-7*); pap. write for info. (*0-521-55620-1*) Cambridge U Pr.
— Metamorphoses of Ovid. (Penguin Classics). (J). 1955. 15.05 (*0-606-03857-4*, Pub. by Turtleback) Demco.
Ovid. Ovid: The Art of Love & Remedies for Love. Shapiro, Jack, tr. LC 66-22893. (Orig.). 1967. pap. 7.95 (*0-934810-09-5*) Carissimi Laurida.
— Ovid I-IV: Metamorphoses. Hill, D. E., ed. (Classical Texts Ser.). 1985. 59.99 (*0-85668-256-X*, Pub. by Aris & Phillips) David Brown.
— Ovid I-IV: Metomorphoses. Hill, D. E., ed. (Classical Texts Ser.). 1985. pap. 28.00 (*0-85668-257-8*, Pub. by Aris & Phillips) David Brown.
— Ovid II: Amores. Booth, Joan Booth, ed. (Classical Texts Ser.). 1991. 59.99 (*0-85668-174-1*, Pub. by Aris & Phillips); pap. 28.00 (*0-85668-175-X*, Pub. by Aris & Phillips) David Brown.
— Ovid V-VIII: Metamorphoses. Hill, D. E., ed. (Classical Texts Ser.). 1992. pap. 28.00 (*0-85668-395-7*, Pub. by Aris & Phillips) David Brown.
— Ovid V-VIII: Metomorphoses. Hill, D. E., ed. (Classical Texts Ser.). 1992. 59.99 (*0-85668-394-9*, Pub. by Aris & Phillips) David Brown.

O

An Asterisk (*) at the beginning of an entry indicates that the title is appearing for the first time.

Ovid. Ovid's Art of Love, 3 vols. Dryden, John et al, trs. LC 73-161789. (Augustan Translators Ser.). reprint ed. 49.50 (*0-404-54127-5*) AMS Pr.

Ovid. Ovid's Fasti: Roman Holidays. Nagle, Betty R., tr. from LAT. & notes by. LC 94-21660. Orig. Title: Fasti. (ENG.). 224p. 1995. 25.00 (*0-253-33967-7*) Ind U Pr.

— Ovid's Metamorphoses: Susanna's Selections. large type unabridged ed. (Illus.). 216p. (Orig.). 1997. pap. 15.00 (*0-9612018-9-4*) B RUGGED.

— P. Ovidi Nasonis Metamorphoseon: Ovid's Metamorphoses, 15 bks., Set. lib. bdg. write for info. (*0-318-50866-4*) Ayer.

— P. Ovidi Nasonis Metamorphoseon Liber I. Lee, A. G., ed. LC 78-67140. 170p. reprint ed. pap. 48.50 (*0-608-13034-6*, 2024505) Bks Demand.

Ovid & Dryden, H. Ovid's Metamorphoses in Fifteen Books. Dryden, Joan et al, trs. LC 70-158323. (Augustan Translators Ser.). reprint ed. 105.00 (*0-404-54128-3*) AMS Pr.

Ovid & Lee, Guy. Ovid's Amores. LC 68-135400. vii, 202 p. 1968. write for info. (*0-7195-1796-6*) John Murray.

***Ovid & Musgrove, Margaret Worsham.** The Student's Ovid: Selections from the Metamorphoses. LC 99-45081. (Oklahoma Series in Classical Culture). 224p. 2000. 29.95 (*0-8061-3219-1*) U of Okla Pr.

Ovid, jt. auth. see Lafleur, Richard A.

***Ovide, Stephanie.** Cooking in the French Fashion. LC 99-38296. (Hippocrene Bilingual Cookbks.). (Illus.). 93p. 1999. 11.95 (*0-7818-0739-5*) Hippocrene Bks.

Ovide, Stephanie. Creole (Caribbean)-English - English-Creole (Caribbean) Concise Dictionary. LC 96-17265. (CRP & ENG.). 200p. (Orig.). 1996. pap. 11.95 (*0-7818-0455-8*) Hippocrene Bks.

Oviedo, Jose M. Soledad y Compania. (SPA.). 236p. 1988. pap. 12.00 (*0-910061-34-3*, 1118) Ediciones Norte.

Ovilo y Otero, Manuel. Manual de Biografia y de Bibliografia de los Escritores Espanoles del Siglo, No. XIX. vii, 540p. 1976. reprint ed. write for info. (*3-487-05861-8*) G Olms Pubs.

Oving, Maud & Joiner, Tricia. Hindeloopen: A Traditional Dutch Folk Painting, Vol. 1. (Illus.). 56p. 1986. pap. 10.95 (*0-941284-34-4*) J Shaw Studio.

Ovington, J. Essay upon the Nature & Qualities of Tea: The Earliest Tea Book in English. 1998. reprint ed. pap. 7.50 (*0-89979-103-4*) British Am Bks.

— Voyage to Surat in the Year 1689. Rawlinson, H. G., ed. (C). 1994. reprint ed. 24.00 (*81-206-0945-X*, Pub. by Asian Educ Servs) S Asia.

Ovington, J. D., ed. Temperate Broad-Leaved Evergreen Forests. (Ecosystems of the World Ser.: Vol. 10). 242p. 1983. 182.25 (*0-444-42091-6*, I-399-83) Elsevier.

Ovington, J. D., jt. auth. see Australian National University Staff.

Ovington, Mary W. The Awakening. LC 70-39096. (Black Heritage Library Collection). 1977. reprint ed. 15.95 (*0-8369-9034-X*) Ayer.

— Black & White Sat Down Together: Reminiscences of an NAACP Founder. Luker, Ralph E., ed. LC 94-41363. (Illus.). 174p. 1995. 19.95 (*1-55861-099-5*) Feminist Pr.

— Black & White Sat down Together: The Reminiscences of an NAACP Founder. Luker, Ralph E., ed. LC 94-41363. (Illus.). 174p. 1996. pap. text 10.95 (*1-55861-156-8*) Feminist Pr.

— Half a Man: The Status of the Negro in New York. LC 79-84692. 236p. 1970. reprint ed. lib. bdg. 45.00 (*0-8371-1263-X*, OVH&) Greenwood.

— Hazel. LC 72-4639. (Black Heritage Library Collection). (Illus.). 1977. reprint ed. 23.95 (*0-8369-9117-6*) Ayer.

— Portraits in Color. 241p. 1977. 18.95 (*0-8369-2516-5*) Ayer.

— The Shadow. LC 72-4736. (Black Heritage Library Collection). 1977. reprint ed. 31.95 (*0-8369-9118-4*) Ayer.

— Walls Came Tumbling Down. LC 69-18543. (American Negro: His History & Literature. Series 2). 1969. reprint ed. 29.95 (*0-405-01884-3*) Ayer.

Ovington, Ray. Birds of Prey. 2nd rev. ed. 1995. pap. 3.95 (*0-8200-0908-3*) Great Outdoors.

— Commonsense Fly Fishing. LC 82-17029. (Illus.). 192p. 1983. pap. 12.95 (*0-8117-2167-1*) Stackpole.

— How to Take Trout on Wet Flies & Nymphs. 1974. 9.95 (*0-88395-020-0*) Freshet Pr.

— Pelican. LC 76-3763. (Illus.). 32p. 1977. pap. 2.95 (*0-8200-0905-9*) Great Outdoors.

Ovist, Daniel. Second Chance. (Orig.). 1997. pap. write for info. (*0-9655772-0-1*) D Ovist.

Ovist, Howard E. Why Change? Making Changes to Get Ahead. LC 97-91527. 146p. (Orig.). 1997. pap. 7.50 (*1-57502-431-4*, PO1316) Morris Pubng.

Ovnick, Merry. Los Angeles: The End of the Rainbow. LC 94-7219. (Illus.). 384p. (Orig.). 1995. pap. 34.95 (*0-9643119-0-9*) Balcony Pr.

Ovretveit, John. Evaluating Health Interventions: An Introduction to Evaluation of Health Treatments, Services, Policies & Organizational Interventions. LC 97-8733. 1997. 109.00 (*0-335-19965-8*); pap. 34.95 (*0-335-19964-X*) OpUniv Pr.

— Health Service Quality. (Illus.). 200p. 1991. pap. 32.50 (*0-632-03279-0*) Blackwell Sci.

— Therapy Services: Organisation, Management & Autonomy. 222p. 1992. text 74.00 (*3-7186-5245-5*, Harwood Acad Pubs); pap. text 38.00 (*3-7186-5246-3*, Harwood Acad Pubs) Gordon & Breach.

Ovsenbury, M. Descendants of Thomas Carhart. (Illus.). 142p. 1989. reprint ed. pap. 25.00 (*0-8328-1311-7*); reprint ed. lib. bdg. 35.00 (*0-8328-1310-9*) Higginson Bk Co.

Ovshinsky, S. R., et al. Disordered Materials: Science & Technology. (Institute for Amorphous Studies). (Illus.). 410p. (C). 1991. text 114.00 (*0-306-43385-0*, Kluwer Plenum) Kluwer Academic.

Ovsiew, Fred, ed. Neuropsychiatry & Mental Health Services. 1999. 61.95 (*0-88048-730-5*, 8730) Am Psychiatric.

Ovsiyenko, Y. G. Russian for Beginners. 448p. (C). 1992. 17.95 (*0-8285-4999-0*) Firebird NY.

Ovsyanikov, Nikita. Polar Bears. LC 98-3431. (Worldlife Library). 72p. (YA). 1998. pap. 16.95 (*0-89658-358-9*) Voyageur Pr.

— Polar Bears: Living with the White Bear. LC 96-33764. (Illus.). 144p. 1996. 29.95 (*0-89658-323-6*) Voyageur Pr.

— Polar Bears: Living with the White Bear. LC 96-33764. (Illus.). 144p. 1999. pap. 19.95 (*0-89658-426-7*) Voyageur Pr.

Ovsyannikov, A. A., et al. Thermal Plasma Diagnostics. 450p. 1995. boxed set 130.00 (*1-898326-23-1*, Pub. by CISP) Balogh.

Ovsyannikov, A. J., jt. auth. see Shevrin, L. N.

***Ovsyshcher, I. Eli, ed.** Cardiac Arrhythmias & Device Therapy: Results & Perspectives for the New Century. 448p. 2000. 115.00 (*0-87993-455-7*) Futura Pub.

Ovtscharoff, W. A., jt. auth. see Bozhilova-Pastirova, A.

Ovunc, B. A., et al, eds. Structural Dynamics & Vibration, 1994, Vol. 63. LC 93-74684. 168p. 1994. pap. 42.50 (*0-7918-1191-3*) ASME.

— Structural Dynamics & Vibration, 1995: Proceedings: The Energy & Environmental EXPO '95 - the Energy-Sources Technology Conference & Exhibition (1995: Houston, TX) LC 93-74684. (PD Ser.: Vol. 70). 245p. 1995. pap. 94.00 (*0-7918-1293-6*, H00925) ASME.

Ow, Francis M. Origami Hearts. (Illus.). 112p. (Orig.). 1996. pap. 15.00 (*0-87040-957-3*) Japan Pubns USA.

Owa, Shigeyoshi, jt. ed. see Srivastava, H. M.

Owa, Shiseyoshi, jt. auth. see Srivastava, H. M.

Owago, Naohiro, jt. ed. see Ermisch, John F.

Owaida, Mohammad T. Glimpses of Islam. Obaba, Al I., ed. 49p. (Orig.). 1977. pap. text 1.50 (*0-916157-70-9*) African Islam Miss Pubns.

Owall, Bengt, et al. Prosthetic Dentistry: Principles & Treatment Strategies. (Illus.). 256p. 1995. text 96.95 (*0-7234-2046-7*, Pub. by Martin Dunitz) Mosby Inc.

Owan-McMenainin, Jan, jt. auth. see Spaude, Pam.

Owcharuk, Volodymyr. From Genesis to Christ's Gennesis: Was Christ Really Born December 25th? 96p. 1998. pap. text 10.00 (*1-893760-00-6*) Eliopoulos.

— Procession of Holy Spirit: An Insight to the Triadic Relationship of the Divinity. Masterjohn, Raphael & Eliopoulos, Nicholas C., eds. 112p. 1999. pap. text 12.00 (*1-893760-01-4*) Eliopoulos.

Oweida, A. M. The New Medical-Pharmaceutical Dictionary. (ARA & ENG.). 2404p. 1970. 150.00 (*0-8288-6550-7*, M-9766) Fr & Eur.

Oweis, I. S. Geotechnology of Waste Management. 2nd ed. LC 97-31813. (Civil Engineering Ser.). (Illus.). 608p. (C). 1998. 102.95 (*0-534-94524-4*) PWS Pubs.

Oweiss, Ibrahim M., ed. The Political Economy of Contemporary Egypt. 330p. (Orig.). 1990. text 34.95 (*0-932568-20-3*); pap. text 16.95 (*0-932568-21-1*) GU Ctr CAS.

Oweiss, Ibrahim M., jt. auth. see Al-Qazzaz, Ayad.

Oweiss, Ibrahim M., jt. ed. see Atiyeh, George Nicholas.

Owen. Dialysis & Transplantation. LC 98-53548. 1999. text. write for info. (*0-7216-7687-1*, W B Saunders Co) Harcrt Hlth Sci Grp.

— Poverty in World Politics. LC 99-11276. 272p. 1999. text 68.00 (*0-312-22314-5*) St Martin.

***Owen.** Quickbooks Pro 99 for Accounting. LC 99-45954. (SWC-Accounting Ser.). 1999. 55.95 (*0-324-02831-8*) Thomson Learn.

— Say Cheese. 2000. pap. 4.95 (*0-552-52975-3*, Pub. by Transworld Publishers Ltd) Trafalgar.

Owen. Today's Technician: Basic Services. 2nd ed. LC 99 35374. (Automotive Technology). 781p. (C). 1999. 82.95 (*0-8273-8544-7*) Delmar.

Owen & Solomon Communications Staff. Using Quickbooks 4.0: First Accounting Course. 1997. write for info. (*0-538-86603-9*) Sth-Wstrn College.

Owen, jt. auth. see Cummins/Owen.

Owen, A. D., jt. auth. see Campbell, H. F.

Owen, A. E. Flexible Assembly Systems: Assembly by Robots & Computerized Integrated Systems. LC 84-4852. (Illus.). 242p. (C). 1984. 107.00 (*0-306-41527-5*, Plenum Trade) Perseus Pubng.

— The Medieval Lindsey Marsh: Select Documents. LC 97-137111. (Publications of the Lincoln Record Society: No. 85). (Illus.). 208p. 1997. 75.00 (*0-901503-58-4*) Boydell & Brewer.

Owen, A. J., tr. see De Aldama, A. M.

Owen, A. L. Conservation under FDR. LC 83-3966. 268p. 1983. 55.00 (*0-275-91055-5*, C1055, Praeger Pubs) Greenwood.

— The Famous Druids: A Survey of Three Centuries of English Literature in the Druids. LC 78-13614. (Illus.). 264p. 1979. reprint ed. lib. bdg. 35.00 (*0-313-20629-5*, OWFD, Greenwood Pr) Greenwood.

Owen, A. S. Euripides: Ion. (GRE.). 196p. 1987. reprint ed. 29.95 (*0-86292-039-6*, Pub. by Brist Class Pr) Focus Pub-R Pullins.

Owen, Albert K. Integral Cooperation: Its Practical Application. LC 74-32103. (American Utopian Adventure Ser.). (Illus.). 208p. 1975. reprint ed. lib. bdg. 39.50 (*0-87991-019-4*) Porcupine Pr.

Owen, Allison, jt. auth. see Miami Herald Staff.

Owen, Aloysius, tr. see Alessio, Luis & Munoz, Hector.

Owen, Aloysius, tr. see Bojorge, Horacio.

Owen, Aloysius, tr. see Philipon, M. M.

Owen, Alun. A Hard Day's Night: A Screen Adaptation from an Original Screenplay, Directed by Richard Lester. Garrett, George P. et al, eds. LC 71-135273. (Film Scripts Ser.). pap. text 19.95 (*0-89197-782-1*) Irvington.

Owen, Andy. Snow. LC 98-42814. (What Is Weather? Ser.). 32p. (J). 1999. lib. bdg. write for info. (*1-57572-790-0*) Heinemann Lib.

Owen, Andy & Ashwell, Miranda. Deserts. LC 97-34421. (Geography Starts Ser.). (Illus.). 32p. (J). 1998. write for info. (*1-57572-605-X*) Heinemann.

— Forests. LC 97-34418. (Geography Starts Ser.). (J). 1998. (*1-57572-610-6*) Heinemann Lib.

— Lakes. LC 97-34417. (Geography Starts Ser.). (J). 1998. (*1-57572-606-8*) Heinemann.

— Mountains. LC 97-34420. (Geography Starts Ser.). (J). 1998. (*1-57572-607-6*) Heinemann.

— Rain. LC 98-42818. (What Is Weather? Ser.). (Illus.). 32p. (J). 1999. write for info. (*1-57572-789-7*) Heinemann Lib.

— Rivers. LC 97-34419. (Geography Starts Ser.). (J). 1998. (*1-57572-609-2*) Heinemann.

***Owen, Andy & Ashwell, Miranda.** Science Topics Series, 5 bks. 32p. 1999. 113.95 (*1-57572-771-4*) Heinemann Lib.

Owen, Andy & Ashwell, Miranda. Seas & Oceans. LC 97-34422. (Geography Starts Ser.). (J). 1998. write for info. (*1-57572-608-4*) Heinemann.

***Owen, Andy & Ashwell, Miranda.** Sunshine. LC 98-42815. (What Is Weather? Ser.). 32p. (J). 1999. write for info. (*1-57572-791-9*) Heinemann Lib.

Owen, Andy & Ashwell, Miranda. Watching the Weather. LC 98-42817. (What Is Weather? Ser.). 32p. (J). 1999. write for info. (*1-57572-792-7*) Heinemann Lib.

***Owen, Andy & Ashwell, Miranda.** What Is Weather?, 5 bks. 32p. 1999. 99.60 (*1-57572-794-3*) Heinemann Lib.

— Wind. LC 98-42816. (What Is Weather? Ser.). 32p. (J). 1999. lib. bdg. write for info. (*1-57572-793-5*) Heinemann Lib.

Owen, Anna. Pocket Guide to Critical Care Monitoring. 2nd ed. (Illus.). 288p. (C). (gr. 13). 1996. text 22.95 (*0-8151-7374-1*, 28101) Mosby Inc.

Owen, Annie. From Snowflakes to Sandcastles: A Child's Year in Words & Pictures. (Illus.). 24p. (J). 16.99 (*0-590-24749-2*) Scholastic Inc.

Owen, Anthony D. Economics of Uranium. LC 85-3583. 240p. 1985. 59.95 (*0-275-90151-3*, C0151, Praeger Pubs) Greenwood.

Owen, Barbara. God Hears Me. LC 94-71288. (Illus.). 32p. (J). (ps-3). 1994. pap. 5.99 (*0-8066-2696-8*, 9-2696, Augsburg) Augsburg Fortress.

— In the Mix: Struggle & Survival in a Women's Prison. LC 97-9013. (SUNY Series in Women, Crime, & Criminology). 219p. (C). 1998. pap. text 19.95 (*0-7914-3608-X*) State U NY Pr.

— Jesus, Remember Me: Words of Assurance from Martin Luther. LC 98-9838. 1998. pap. text 10.99 (*0-8066-3610-6*, 9-3610, Augsburg) Augsburg Fortress.

Owen, Barbara. The Mormon Tabernacle Organ. 19.95 (*1-55517-054-4*) CFI Dist.

Owen, Barbara. The Registration of Baroque Organ Music. LC 96-33081. 296p. 1997. text 39.95 (*0-253 33240-0*) Ind U Pr.

— Timeline of the Organ: 2600 Years of History. (Illus.). 16p. 1995. pap. 2.25 (*0-9616755-6-X*) Westfield Ctr.

Owen, Barbara, intro. The American Musical Directory. LC 80-16490. (Music Reprint Ser.). (Illus.). 260p. 1980. reprint ed. lib. bdg. 35.00 (*0-306-76037-1*) Da Capo.

Owen, Barbara, ed. see Luther, Martin.

Owen, Barbara A. The Reproduction of Social Control: A Study of Prison Workers at San Quentin. LC 87-36113. 168p. 1988. 52.95 (*0-275-92818-7*, C2818, Praeger Pubs) Greenwood.

Owen, Betty. Typing for Beginners. rev. ed. (Practical Handbook Ser.). 80p. 1985. pap. 8.95 (*0-399-51147-4*, Perigee Bks) Berkley Pub.

Owen, Bill. Summer Wine, Vintage Years: A Cluttered Life. large type ed. 22.95 (*1-85695-153-7*, Pub. by ISIS Lrg Prnt) Transaction Pubs.

Owen, Bill, jt. auth. see Buxton, Frank.

Owen, Bob, ed. see Waldman, David.

Owen, Bob L. Roger's Recovery from AIDS: How One Man Defeated the Dread Disease. 6th rev. ed. LC 87-71065. (Illus.). 214p. 1997. reprint ed. pap. 12.95 (*0-937831-01-8*) Hlth Hope Pub.

Owen, Bob L. & Johnson, Thomas. The Pure Cure for Arthritis & Other Auto-Immune & Inflammatory Diseases. LC 97-93664. (Illus.). 112p. (Orig.). 1997. pap. 14.00 (*1-882657-14-4*) Health Digest.

Owen, Bobbi. Costume Design on Broadway: Designers & Their Credits, 1915-1985, 5. LC 87-7515. (Bibliographies & Indexes in the Performing Arts Ser.: No. 5). (Illus.). 269p. 1987. lib. bdg. 85.00 (*0-313-25524-5*, OCD/, Greenwood Pr) Greenwood.

— Lighting Design on Broadway: Designers & Their Credits, 1915-1990, 11. LC 91-24007. (Bibliographies & Indexes in the Performing Arts Ser.: No. 11). 176p. 1991. lib. bdg. 49.95 (*0-313-26533-X*, OLD, Greenwood Pr) Greenwood.

— Scenic Design on Broadway: Designers & Their Credits, 1915-1990, 10. LC 91-25254. (Bibliographies & Indexes in the Performing Arts Ser.: No. 10). 320p. 1991. lib. bdg. 69.50 (*0-313-26534-8*, OSN, Greenwood Pr) Greenwood.

Owen, Brooks. How to Make PVC Furniture for Profits. (Illus.). 151p. (Orig.). 1994. pap. text 19.00 (*0-939349-00-0*) Owen Pub.

Owen, Bruce M. The Internet Challenge to Television. LC 98 39236. (Illus.). xii, 372 p. 1999. 29.95 (*0-674-87299-1*) HUP.

***Owen, Bruce M.** Internet Challenge to Television. 384p. 2000. pap. 17.95 (*0-674-00389-6*) HUP.

Owen, Bruce M. & Wildman, Steven S. Video Economics. (Illus.). 384p. (C). 1992. 46.50 (*0-674-93716-3*) HUP.

Owen, Bruce M., et al. The Economics of a Disaster: The Exxon Valdez Oil Spill. LC 95-3782. 216p. 1995. 62.95 (*0-89930-987-9*, Quorum Bks) Greenwood.

Owen, Bruce M., jt. auth. see Frankena, Mark W.

Owen, Bryn, et al. Achieving ISO Registration. 416p. 1994. text 30.00 (*0-945320-41-8*) Stat Process Contrl.

Owen, C. Everything You Ever Wanted to Know about Periods. 1995. mass mkt. 7.95 (*0-340-63604-1*, Pub. by Hodder & Stought Ltd) Trafalgar.

Owen, Carol Ann. Death by Charity. 178p. mass mkt. 4.99 (*1-55197-010-4*) Picasso Publ.

Owen, Carole. Bellefontaine: An Historical Narrative. (Illus.). 120p. (Orig.). 1989. pap. 14.95 (*0-9624102-1-7*) Canyon Ranch.

Owen, Charles. Plain Yarns from the Fleet: The Spirit of the Royal Navy During Its Twentieth Century Heyday. LC 97-160012. (Illus.). 224p. 1997. 33.95 (*0-7509-0770-3*, Pub. by Sutton Pub Ltd) Intl Pubs Mktg.

Owen, Charles A., ed. Discussions of the Canterbury Tales. LC 77-20278. (Illus.). 110p. 1978. reprint ed. lib. bdg. 35.00 (*0-313-20012-2*, OWDC, Greenwood Pr) Greenwood.

***Owen, Charles B. & Makedon, F.** Computed Synchronization for Multimedia Applications. LC 99-27711. (International Series in Engineering & Computer Science). 226p. 1999. write for info. (*0-7923-8565-9*, Kluwer Acad) Kluwer Academic.

Owen, Cheryl. Dough Folk Art. (Illus.). 160p. 1998. pap. 14.95 (*0-8069-8651-4*) Sterling.

— My Nature Crafts Book. LC 92-10187. (Illus.). 96p. (J). 1993. 15.95 (*0-316-67715-9*) Little.

***Owen, Cheryl.** Sand Art. 1999. 9.95 (*1-56010-477-5*) W Foster Pub.

— Simple Glass Painting: 25 Beautiful Step-by-Step Glass Painting Projects. (Illus.). 2000. 27.95 (*0-7153-0954-4*) D & C Pub.

Owen, Cheryl. Spirit Crafts: Over 30 Mystical Projects to Make. 1997. 12.99 (*1-85833-660-0*, Pub. by CLib Bks) Whitecap Bks.

— Step by Step Art of Floral Paper Crafts. 1994. 12.98 (*0-7858-0073-5*) Bk Sales Inc.

— Step by Step Art of Making Soft Toys. 1994. 14.98 (*0-7858-0075-1*) Bk Sales Inc.

— Step by Step Art of Papercrafts. 1993. 12.98 (*1-55521-884-9*) Bk Sales Inc.

— Storage Solutions. 1998. 14.99 (*1-85833-967-7*) Quadrillion Pubng.

Owen, Chris. Urban Rock: Stoney Point Top Rope Guide. 2nd rev. ed. (Illus.). 84p. 1994. pap. 12.95 (*0-9654448-0-5*) C Owen.

Owen, Chris, ed. Lara Croft Cybermodel. (Illus.). 96p. 1998. 22.50 (*0-7893-0244-6*, Pub. by Universe) St Martin.

Owen, Christopher H. The Sacred Flame of Love: Methodism & Society in Nineteenth-Century Georgia. LC 97-38487. 312p. 1998. text 50.00 (*0-8203-1963-5*) U of Ga Pr.

***Owen, Cindy.** Abdominal Sonography Review. Grant, Edward G., ed. (Illus.). 214p. 2000. 55.00 (*0-941022-46-3*) Davies Pubng.

Owen Courtois, Suzanne, jt. auth. see EMC-Paradigm Publishing Staff.

Owen-Crocker. Medieval Art-Recent Perspectives: A Memorial Tribute to C. R. Dodwell. LC 98-17826. (Illus.). 304p. 1998. text 79.95 (*0-7190-4992-X*, Pub. by Manchester Univ Pr) St Martin.

***Owen-Crocker, Gale R.** The Four Funerals in Beowulf: And the Structure of the Poem. LC 99-51312. 2000. write for info. (*0-7190-5497-4*, Pub. by Manchester Univ Pr) St Martin.

Owen, D., ed. Green Reporting: Accountancy & the Challenge of the 90s. 620p. (gr. 13). 1991. mass mkt. 34.95 (*0-412-40130-4*, A5789) Chapman & Hall.

Owen, D. B., jt. auth. see Odeh, Robert E.

Owen, D. D. Arthurian Romance: Seven Essays. LC 70-571764. 102p. 1970. write for info. (*0-7011-1662-5*, Pub. by Chatto & Windus) Trafalgar.

Owen, D. D. Eleanor of Aquitaine: Queen & Legend. (Illus.). 272p. 1996. pap. 25.95 (*0-631-20101-7*) Blackwell Pubs.

Owen, D. D., jt. ed. see Monks, Peter R.

Owen, D. D., ed. & tr. see De Troyes, Chretien.

Owen, D. I. & Morrison, M. A., eds. General Studies & Excavations at Nuzi 9/1, No. 2. LC 81-15123. (Studies on the Civilization & Culture of Nuzi & the Hurrians Ser.). (Illus.). ix, 723p. 1987. text 79.50 (*0-931464-37-4*) Eisenbrauns.

Owen, D. I., jt. ed. see Morrison, M. A.

Owen, D. R. A First Course in the Mathematical Foundations of Thermodynamics. (Undergraduate Texts in Mathematics Ser.). (Illus.). 190p. 1983. 54.95 (*0-387-90897-8*) Spr-Verlag.

Owen, D. R., jt. auth. see Hinton, E.

Owen, D. R., jt. ed. see Wilshire, B.

Owen, D. W., jt. auth. see Green, A. E.

Owen, Dan. Vintage & Historic Indianapolis Race Cars. LC 98-13186. (Illus.). 96p. 1998. pap. 13.95 (*0-7603-0347-9*) MBI Pubg.

Owen, Dan R. That You May Believe. 1993. pap. 8.25 (*0-89137-337-3*) Quality Pubns.

Owen, David. Alfa Romeo: Always with Passion. (Illus.). 160p. 1999. 34.95 (*1-85960-628-8*, Pub. by J H Haynes & Co) Motorbooks Intl.

— Balkan Odyssey. LC 97-5119. 432p. (C). 1997. pap. 15.00 (*0-15-600521-2*, Harvest Bks) Harcourt.

***Owen, David.** The Complete Office Golf. (Illus.). 96p. 1999. pap. 14.95 (*0-7611-1593-5*) Workman Pub.

Owen, David. The Complete Wedding Video Organiser. 192p. (Orig.). 1993. pap. 19.95 (*0-572-01817-7*, Pub. by W Foulsham) Trans-Atl Phila.

— Facilities Planning & Relocation, 2 vols., Set. 1993. 109.95 (*0-87629-281-3*, 67301) R S Means.

— Golf. 1998. write for info. (*0-679-45654-6*) Villard Books.

O

An Asterisk (*) at the beginning of an entry indicates that the title is appearing for the first time.

— The Government of Victorian London, 1855-1889: The Metropolitan Board of Works, the Vestries, & the City Corporation. LC 81-7173. (Illus.). 480p. 1990. 44.50 (*0-674-35885-6*) Belknap Pr.

***Owen, David.** Hidden Evidence: Forty True Crimes & How Forensic Science Helped Solve Them. (Illus.). 240p. 2000. 35.00 (*1-55209-492-8*); pap. 24.95 (*1-55209-483-9*) Firefly Bks Ltd.

Owen, David. Hume's Reason. LC 99-51897. 248p. 2000. 45.00 (*0-19-823831-2*) OUP.

***Owen, David.** Into Outer Space: An Exploration of Man's Obsession & Interaction with the Cosmos - Fact & Fiction. LC 00-26964. 144p. 2000. pap. 19.95 (*0-7373-0469-3*, 04693W, Pub. by Lowell Hse) NTC Contemp Pub Co.

Owen, David. JVC Make Your Home Video More Professional. 144p. 1995. 17.95 (*0-572-01151-2*, Pub. by Foulsham UK) Assoc Pubs Grp.

***Owen, David.** Life under a Leaky Roof: Reflections on Home, Tools & Country Living. LC 99-55760. 208p. 2000. pap. 12.95 (*0-86730-799-4*) Lebhar Friedman.

Owen, David. Lighter Than Air. 1999. 17.99 (*0-7858-1045-5*) Bk Sales Inc.

— Make Better Home Videos. 192p. (Orig.). 1993. pap. 12.95 (*0-572-01933-5*, Pub. by W Foulsham) Trans-Atl Phila.

— The Making of the Masters: Clifford Roberts, Augusta National & Golf's Most Prestigious Tournament. LC 98-55532. (Illus.). 277p. 1999. 25.00 (*0-684-85729-4*) S&S Trade.

— Maturity & Modernity: Nietzsche, Weber, Foucault, & the Ambivalence of Reason. 272p. 1997. pap. 18.95 (*0-415-15343-3*) Routledge.

— Maturity & Modernity: Nietzsche, Weber, Foucault, & the Ambivalence of Reason. 272p. (C). 1997. pap. 24.99 (*0-415-15352-2*) Routledge.

— My Usual Game: Adventures in Golf. 288p. 1996. pap. 14.95 (*0-385-48338-4*) Doubleday.

— Nietzsche, Politics & Modernity: A Critique of Liberal Reason. 192p. 1995. 69.95 (*0-8039-7766-2*); pap. 26.95 (*0-8039-7767-0*) Sage.

— The Walls Around Us: The Thinking Person's Guide to How a House Works. LC 92-50070. (Illus.). 1992. pap. 14.00 (*0-679-74144-5*) Vin Bks.

***Owen, David, compiled by.** Hidden Evidence: 41 True Crimes & How Forensic Science Helped Solve Them. 1999. 24.95 (*0-7621-0231-4*) RD Assn.

Owen, David, ed. Sociology after Postmodernism. LC 97-66126. 224p. 1997. 75.00 (*0-8039-7514-7*); pap. 25.95 (*0-8039-7515-5*) Sage.

Owen, David & Bingham, Joan, eds. Lure of the Links: Great Golf Stories. LC 97-2979. 400p. 1997. 23.00 (*0-87113-685-6*, Atlntc Mnthly) Grove-Atltic.

— Lure of the Links: Great Golf Stories. 400p. 1999. reprint ed. pap. 14.00 (*0-87113-749-6*, Atlntc Mnthly) Grove-Atltic.

Owen, David & Doerr, Marilyn. None of the Above: The Truth Behind the SATs. LC 99-16334. 352p. 1999. 60.00 (*0-8476-9506-9*) Rowman.

— None of the Above: The Truth Behind the SATs. rev. ed. LC 99-16334. 352p. 1999. pap. 17.95 (*0-8476-9507-7*, Pub. by Rowman) Natl Bk Netwk.

Owen, David, et al. Democracy Must Work: A Trilateral Agenda for the Decade. (Triangle Papers: Vol. 28). 1984. pap. 6.00 (*0-685-70506-4*) Trilateral Comm.

Owen, David, jt. auth. see Cummins, Robert.

Owen, David, jt. auth. see Hahn, Cynthia T.

Owen, David A. & Kelly, James. Pathology of the Gallbladder, Biliary Tract & Pancreas. (Illus.). Date not set. text. write for info. (*0-7216-1910-X*, W B Saunders Co) Harcrt Hlth Sci Grp.

Owen, David A. & Kelly, James K. Atlas of Gastrointestinal Pathology. LC 94-989. 1994. text 210.00 (*0-7216-6730-9*, W B Saunders Co) Harcrt Hlth Sci Grp.

Owen, David G., ed. The Philosophical Foundations of Tort Law. 526p. 1996. text 75.00 (*0-19-825847-X*, Clarendon Pr) OUP.

— The Philosophical Foundations of Tort Law. 526p. 1997. reprint ed. pap. text 26.00 (*0-19-826579-4*) OUP.

Owen, David G. & Davis, Mary J. 1998 Cases & Statutory Supplement to Products Liability & Safety, Cases & Materials. 3rd ed. (University Casebks.). 600p. 1998. pap. text 16.95 (*1-56662-678-1*) Foundation Pr.

— Product Liability & Safety. 3rd ed. (University Casebook Ser.). 204p. (C). 1997. pap. text, teacher ed. write for info. (*1-56662-580-7*) Foundation Pr.

— Products Liability & Safety, Cases & Materials, 1997 Case & Statutory Supplement To. (University Casebook Ser.). 589p. 1997. pap. text. write for info. (*1-56662-567-X*) Foundation Pr.

Owen, David G., et al. Product Liability Problems, 1996 Edition for Use with Products Liability & Safety, Cases & Materials. 3rd ed. (University Casebook Ser.). 243p. 1996. pap. text. write for info. (*1-56662-426-6*) Foundation Pr.

— Products Liability & Safety, Cases & Materials: Statutory Supplement. 3rd ed. (University Casebook Ser.). 469p. 1996. pap. text. write for info. (*1-56662-419-3*) Foundation Pr.

— PRODUCTS LIABILITY & SAFETY 3E. 3rd ed. LC 96-5863. (Paralegal). 1105p. (C). 1996. text 42.00 (*1-56662-341-3*) Foundation Pr.

Owen, David I. Neo-Sumerian Archival Texts: Primarily from Nippur in the University Museum, the Oriental Institute, & the Iraq Museum. LC 82-1358. (Illus.). xiii, 85p. 1982. text 50.00 (*0-931464-09-9*) Eisenbrauns.

Owen, David I. & Lacheman, Ernest R., eds. General Studies & Excavations at Nuzi 9/3, No. 5. (Studies on the Civilization & Culture of Nuzi & the Hurrians: Bk. 5). 1x, 357p. 1995. text 79.50 (*0-931464-67-6*) Eisenbrauns.

Owen, David I. & Wilhelm, Gernot. General Studies & Excavations at Nuzi. LC 98-22844. (Studies on the Civilization & Culture of Nuzi & the Hurrians: 9). 1998. 60.00 (*1-883053-26-9*) CDL Pr.

Owen, David I. & Wilhelm, Gernot, eds. Edith Porada Memorial Volume. LC 95-35. (Studies on the Civilization & Culture of Nuzi & the Hurrians: Vol. 7). x, 159p. (C). 1995. 50.00 (*1-883053-07-2*) CDL Pr.

***Owen, David I. & Wilhelm, Gernot, eds.** Nuzi at Seventy-Five. LC 99-52665. (Studies on the Civilization & Culture of Nuzi & the Hurrians: Vol. 10). (Illus.). 454p. 2000. 60.00 (*1-883053-50-1*) CDL Pr.

Owen, David I. & Wilhelm, Gernot, eds. Richard F. S. Starr Memorial Volume. LC 96-8532. (Studies on the Civilization & Culture of Nuzi & the Hurrians: 8). viii, 478p. (C). 1996. 60.00 (*1-883053-10-2*) CDL Pr.

Owen, David I., jt. auth. see Stone, Elizabeth C.

Owen, David I., ed. see Rabinowitz, Isaac.

***Owen, David Lloyd.** The History of the Long Range Desert Group: Providence Their Guide. (Illus.). 2000. 39.95 (*0-85052-712-0*, Pub. by Leo Cooper) Combined Pub.

Owen, David R. & Tolley, Michael C. Courts of Admiralty in Colonial America: The Maryland Experience, 1634-1776. LC 95-68702. (Illus.). 446p. (C). 1995. 45.00 (*0-89089-856-1*) Carolina Acad Pr.

Owen, Dean. The Gunpointer. large type ed. (Linford Western Library). 320p. 1989. pap. 16.99 (*0-7089-6674-8*, Linford) Ulverscroft.

— Guns of Spring. 1993. 17.50 (*0-7451-4559-0*, Gunsmoke) Chivers N Amer.

— Guns of Spring. large type ed. (Linford Western Library). 1989. pap. 16.99 (*0-7089-6771-X*) Ulverscroft.

— A Killer's Bargain. large type ed. (Linford Western Library). 1989. pap. 16.99 (*0-7089-6681-0*) Ulverscroft.

— Last-Chance Range. large type ed. (Linford Western Library). 1989. pap. 16.99 (*0-7089-6723-X*, Linford) Ulverscroft.

Owen, Deborah & Cole, Peter. EMU in Perspective: Understanding Monetary Union. (Illus.). 191p. 1999. 35.00 (*0-273-63302-3*) F T P H.

Owen, Denis F. Animal Ecology in Tropical Africa. 2nd ed. LC 75-46586. (Tropical Ecology Ser.). (Illus.). 140p. reprint ed. pap. 43.40 (*0-8357-6016-2*, 203450200090) Bks Demand.

— Camouflage & Mimicry. LC 82-2566. (Phoenix Ser.). (Illus.). 158p. (C). 1982. pap. text 14.95 (*0-226-64188-0*) U Ch Pr.

Owen, Diana. Media Messages in American Presidential Elections, 25. LC 90-43384. (Contributions to the Study of Mass Media & Communications Ser.: No. 25). 216p. 1991. 55.00 (*0-313-26362-0*, OMD/, Greenwood Pr) Greenwood.

Owen, Diana, jt. auth. see Davis, Richard.

Owen, Diana M. Political Socialization. (C). 1998. pap. 34.00 (*0-205-19433-8*, Macmillan Coll) P-H.

Owen, Diane & Davis, Moya. Help with Your Project. 2nd rev. ed. (Illus.). 80p. 1996. pap. text 24.95 (*1-56593-801-1*, 1566) Thomson Learn.

Owen, Dolores B. Abstracts & Indexes in Science & Technology: A Descriptive Guide. 2nd ed. LC 84-10902. 252p. 1984. 27.50 (*0-8108-1712-8*) Scarecrow.

— Directory of Associations in Louisiana. 3rd rev. ed. 414p. 1996. pap. text 25.00 (*0-9630719-1-2*) Owen Hse.

— Guide to Genealogical Resources in the British Isles. LC 88-22574. (Illus.). 409p. 1989. 41.50 (*0-8108-2153-2*) Scarecrow.

Owen, Donald B., ed. The Search for Oil: Some Statistical Methods & Techniques. LC 75-25162. (Statistics, Textbooks & Monographs: No. 13). (Illus.). 208p. reprint ed. pap. 64.50 (*0-7837-0975-7*, 204128100019) Bks Demand.

Owen, Donald Bruce. Beating Your Competition Through Quality. (Illus.). 144p. 1988. text 55.00 (*0-8247-8065-5*) Dekker.

Owen, Dorothy M. The Making of King's Lynn: A Documentary Survey. (Records of Social & Economic History Ser.: Vol. IX). 1984. 69.00 (*0-19-726027-6*) OUP.

Owen, Dwayne G., jt. auth. see Ruhl, Roland A.

Owen, E. A. Norfolk County Pioneer Sketches of Long Point Settlement: or Norfolk's Foundation Builders & Their Family Genealogies. (Illus.). 578p. 1996. reprint ed. lib. bdg. 59.50 (*0-8328-5157-4*) Higginson Bk Co.

Owen, E. T. The Story of the Iliad. Betts, John H., ed. (Illus.). 248p. (C). 1989. reprint ed. pap. 15.00 (*0-86516-235-2*) Bolchazy-Carducci.

Owen, Ed. Playing & Coaching Wheelchair Basketball. LC 81-10456. (Illus.). 320p. 1982. pap. text 18.95 (*0-252-00867-7*) U of Ill Pr.

Owen, Edward R. & Pamuk, Sevket. A History of Middle East Economies in the Twentieth Century. LC 98-29099. 1999. pap. 24.95 (*0-674-39831-9*) HUP.

Owen, Edward R. & Pamuk, Svket. A History of Middle East Economies in the Twentieth Century. LC 98-29099. 1999. 60.00 (*0-674-39830-0*) HUP.

Owen, Eileen, ed. see Steves, Rick.

Owen, Eleanor. Connections: A Self-Help & Resource Guide for Individuals with Mental Illness, Their Families & Social Service Professionals. 9th rev. ed. 225p. (C). 1996. pap. text 33.00 (*0-926980-00-9*) WA Advocates.

Owen, Elizabeth, jt. auth. see Bellingham, Brenda.

Owen, Eric, jt. auth. see Fiedelholz, Sara.

Owen, Felicity, et al. Noble & Patriotic: The Beaumont Gift, 1828. (Illus.). 64p. 1988. pap. 14.95 (*0-295-96898-2*) U of Wash Pr.

Owen, Frank F. The Purple Sea: More Splashes of Chinese Color. Reginald, R. & Melville, Douglas, eds. LC 77-84262. (Lost Race & Adult Fantasy Ser.). 153 p. 1978. reprint ed. lib. bdg. 19.95 (*0-405-11003-0*) Ayer.

— The Wind That Tramps the World: Splashes of Chinese Color, Vol. 1. LC 72-4426. (Short Story Index Reprint Ser.). 1977. reprint ed. 18.95 (*0-8369-4186-1*) Ayer.

Owen, Frank F., ed. Campaign in Burma. 192p. (C). 1987. pap. 35.00 (*81-7002-052-2*, Pub. by Himalayan Bks) St Mut.

Owen, Frank F., jt. auth. see Jones, Ron.

Owen, Fred & Maidment, Derek, eds. Quality Assurance. 2nd ed. 64p. 1996. pap. 30.00 (*0-85295-372-0*, 53720) Gulf Pub.

Owen, G., jt. ed. see Grofman, Bernard N.

Owen, G. Dyfnallt. Wales in the Reign of James I. (Royal Historical Society: Studies in History: No. 53). 1988. 75.00 (*0-86193-210-2*) Boydell & Brewer.

Owen, G. Dyfnallt, ed. Manuscripts of the Marquess of Salisbury, Addenda 1562-1605. (Reports & Calendars, Series 9: Vol. 23). 294p. 1973. 7.00 (*0-11-440042-3*, HM00423, Pub. by Statnry Office) Bernan Associates.

Owen, G. Dynfallt, ed. Manuscripts of the Marquess of Salisbury, Addenda 1605-1668. (Reports & Calendars, Series 9: Vol. 24). 417p. 1976. 19.00 (*0-11-440062-8*, HM00628, Pub. by Statnry Office) Bernan Associates.

Owen, G. Dynfallt, jt. ed. see Anderson, Sonia P.

Owen, G. E. Logic, Science, & Dialectic: Collected Papers in Greek Philosophy. LC 85-17479. 394p. pap. text 27.50 (*0-8014-9359-5*) Cornell U Pr.

— Logic, Science & Dialectic In Greek Collected Papers 394p. 1986. text 57.50 (*0-8014-1726-0*) Cornell U Div Nutrit Scis.

Owen, G. Frederick. Abraham Lincoln: The Man & His Faith. LC 81-52112. 232p. 1981. pap. 9.99 (*0-8423-0000-7*) Tyndale Hse.

Owen, G. Vale. Problems Which Perplex (Mainly Psychic) Explained by Question & Answer (1890) 156p. 1998. reprint ed. pap. 17.95 (*0-7661-0641-1*) Kessinger Pub.

Owen, Gareth. Accounting for Hospitality, Tourism & Leisure. 352p. (Orig.). 1994. pap. 49.50 (*0-273-60263-2*, Pub. by Pitman Pub) Trans-Atl Phila.

Owen, Gay, jt. auth. see Babb, Paul.

***Owen, Geoff.** Turning Back the Clock. (Illus.). 256p. 2000. pap. 17.95 (*0-948358-06-8*, 130541AE, Pub. by Motor Racing) Motorbooks Intl.

Owen, George E. Fundamentals of Scientific Mathematics. LC 61-12287. 286p. reprint ed. pap. 88.70 (*0-608-12101-0*, 202414000035) Bks Demand.

— The Universe of the Mind. LC 76-125674. (Seminars in the History of Ideas Ser.). (Illus.). 367p. 1971. reprint ed. pap. 113.80 (*0-608-06111-5*, 206644400008) Bks Demand.

Owen, Glen. QuickBooks 5.0 for Accounting. 2nd ed. LC 98-24635. 224p. 1999. pap. 54.95 (*0-324-00402-8*) Sth-Wstrn College.

Owen, Glen & Solomon, Paul. Using Quickbooks 4.0 in the First Accounting Course. LC 97-12692. 1997. write for info. (*0-538-86559-8*) S-W Pub.

Owen, Glenn. Owen Bus Studnts Internet W/I. 160p. (C). 1996. pap. text 19.96 (*0-395-76714-8*) HM.

Owen, Glenn & Solomon, Paul. Quickbooks 5.0 for Accounting. LC 98-24635. 1998. write for info. (*0-324-00357-9*) Sth-Wstrn College.

Owen, Goodwin & Bickersteth, Warfield. Classics on the Trinity. abr. rev. ed. Green, Jay P., Sr., ed. (Fifty Greatest Christian Classics Ser.). 672p. 1991. 29.95 (*1-878442-61-9*) Sovreign Grace Pubs.

Owen, Gordon. Bonsai. LC 99-175704. (Growing Classic Ser.). (Illus.). 128p. 1998. pap. 12.95 (*0-8069-3772-6*) Sterling.

Owen, Gordon R. The Two Alberts: Fountain & Fall. LC 95-61955. (Illus.). 576p. 1996. 28.95 (*1-881325-20-2*) Yucca Tree Pr.

Owen, Guillermo. Discrete Mathematics & Game Theory LC 99-25666. (Theory & Decision Library). 1999. write for info. (*0-7923-8511-X*) Kluwer Academic.

— Game Theory. 3rd ed. LC 95-12397. (Illus.). 447p. 1995. text 49.95 (*0-12-531151-6*) Acad Pr.

Owen, Guy. The Ballad of the Flim-Flam Man. LC 84-45411. reprint ed. 29.50 (*0-404-19939-9*) AMS Pr.

— Flim-Flam Man & the Apprentice Grifter. LC 84-45575. reprint ed. 28.00 (*0-404-19940-2*) AMS Pr.

Owen, Guy & Willams, Mary C., eds. Contemporary Poetry of North Carolina. LC 77-20809. 171p. 1977. 12.95 (*0-910244-98-7*) Blair.

***Owen, Guy, et al.** The Ballad of the Flim-Flam Man. 2nd ed. LC 99-88835. 304p. 2000. reprint ed. pap. 13.95 (*1-928556-05-1*) Coastal NC.

Owen, H. Kids Musical Year-Junior: Director. 1993. pap. 8.95 (*1-55897-413-X*) Brentwood Music.

— Miracle at the Manger. 1990. pap. 6.95 (*1-55897-038-X*) Brentwood Music.

Owen, H. Goddard. A Recollection of Marcella Sembrich. LC 81-22197. (Music Reprint Ser.). (Illus.). 80p. 1982. reprint ed. lib. bdg. 21.50 (*0-306-76141-6*) Da Capo.

***Owen, Harold.** Music Theory Resource Book. LC 99-21158. (Illus.). 272p. (C). 2000. spiral bd. 35.00 (*0-19-511539-2*) OUP.

Owen, Harrison. Expanding Our Now: The Story of Open Space Technology. LC 97-17806. 178p. (Orig.). 1997. pap. 24.95 (*1-57675-015-9*) Berrett-Koehler.

— The Millennium Organization. LC 94-94260. (Illus.). 174p. (Orig.). 1994. pap. 20.00 (*0-9618205-4-3*) Abbott Pub.

— Open Space Technology: A User's Guide. 2nd rev. ed. LC 97-17807. 200p. 1997. pap. 24.95 (*1-57675-024-8*) Berrett-Koehler.

***Owen, Harrison.** The Power of Spirit: How Organizations Transform. 260p. 2000. pap. 19.95 (*1-57675-090-6*, Pub. by Berrett-Koehler) Publishers Group.

Owen, Harrison. Riding the Tiger: Doing Business in a Transforming World. LC 91-76873. 216p. (Orig.). 1992. pap. 20.00 (*0-9618205-2-7*) Abbott Pub.

***Owen, Harrison.** The Spirit of Leadership: Liberating the Leader in Each of Us. LC 99-11598. 180p. 1999. pap. 15.95 (*1-57675-056-6*) Berrett-Koehler.

Owen, Harrison, ed. Tales from Open Space. LC 95-75969. 156p. 1995. pap. 20.00 (*0-9618205-5-1*) Abbott Pub.

Owen, Henry, ed. The Next Phase in Foreign Policy. LC 73-1077. 357p. reprint ed. pap. 110.70 (*0-608-12460-5*, 202539700043) Bks Demand.

Owen, Henry & Smith, John T., II, eds. Gerard C. Smith: A Career in Progress. LC 89-5774. (Illus.). 152p. (C). 1989. lib. bdg. 22.50 (*0-8191-7444-0*) U Pr of Amer.

Owen, Henry D., jt. ed. see Fried, Edward R.

Owen, Henry W. The Edward Clarence Plummer History of Bath. (Illus.). 575p. 1995. reprint ed. lib. bdg. 61.00 (*0-8328-4687-2*) Higginson Bk Co.

Owen, Herb. Clubhouse Ministries Camping Guide: Planning A Totally Awesome Summer Camp for Kids. (Illus.). 64p. (Orig.). 1994. pap., wbk. ed. 10.95 (*0-89827-136-3*, CHC20) Wesleyan Pub Hse.

— Clubhouse Ministries Champion Camper. (Illus.). 24p. (Orig.). 1995. pap., teacher ed. 2.95 (*0-89827-145-2*, CHB45) Wesleyan Pub Hse.

— Clubhouse Ministries Champion Camper's Guide. (Illus.). 30p. (Orig.). (J). (gr. 5-6). 1995. pap. 1.95 (*0-89827-146-0*, CHB46) Wesleyan Pub Hse.

— Clubhouse Ministries Discovery Camper. (Illus.). 16p. 1995. pap., teacher ed. 2.95 (*0-89827-143-6*, CHA88) Wesleyan Pub Hse.

— Clubhouse Ministries Discovery Camper's Guide. (Illus.). 16p. (Orig.). (J). (gr. 1-4). 1995. pap. 1.95 (*0-89827-144-4*, CHA89) Wesleyan Pub Hse.

— The Complete Guide to Starting or Evaluating a Children's Ministry. Spear, Cindy G., ed. 144p. 1993. ring bd. 99.95 incl. audio (*0-941005-67-4*) Chrch Grwth VA.

— How to Shepherd Children in a World Full of Wolves. Spear, Cindy G., ed. 156p. 1993. pap. text 9.95 (*0-941005-66-6*) Chrch Grwth VA.

Owen, Hilarie. Creating Top Flight Teams. 1997. 17.95 (*0-7494-1828-1*) Kogan Page Ltd.

— Creating Top Flight Teams. 1997. pap. text 14.95 (*0-7494-1829-X*, Pub. by Kogan Pg) Nichols Pub.

Owen, Hilary, ed. Gender, Ethnicity & Class in Modern Portuguese-Speaking Culture. 240p. 1996. text 89.95 (*0-7734-8849-9*) E Mellen.

Owen, Hilary & Pritchard, Jacki, eds. Good Practice in Child Protection: A Training Manual for Professionals. 240p. 1993. pap. 27.00 (*1-85302-205-5*) Taylor & Francis.

Owen, Howard. Answers to Lucky. 1996. write for info. (*0-614-14720-4*) HarpC.

— Answers to Lucky: A Novel. 224p. 1997. pap. 12.00 (*0-06-092809-3*, Perennial) HarperTrade.

— Fat Lightning. LC 93-6339. 181p. 1994. 22.00 (*1-877946-41-9*) Permanent Pr.

***Owen, Howard.** Harry & Ruth. LC 99-34819. 288p. 2000. 25.00 (*1-57962-066-3*) Permanent Pr.

Owen, Howard. Littlejohn. large type ed. LC 92-45722. (Americana Series). 306p. 1993. reprint ed. lib. bdg. 20.95 (*1-56054-658-1*) Thorndike Pr.

Owen, Huw P. Christian Theism: A Study in Its Basic Principles. 184p. 1984. 29.95 (*0-567-09336-0*, Pub. by T & T Clark) Bks Intl VA.

Owen, Hylda. Bloodhounds. (Illus.). 192p. 1990. 9.95 (*0-86622-675-3*, KW166) TFH Pubns.

Owen, Hywel W. The Place-Names of East Flintshire. LC 94-202940. xxxvi, 428p. 1994. write for info. (*0-7083-1242-X*, Pub. by Univ Wales Pr) Paul & Co Pubs.

— Pocket Guide to the Place-Names of Wales. LC 98-217939. (Pocket Guides Ser.). 120p. 1998. pap. 9.95 (*0-7083-1458-9*, Pub. by Univ Wales Pr) Paul & Co Pubs.

Owen, J. Hannah's House. (J). (gr. 4-8). 4.99 (*1-85792-131-3*, Pub. by Christian Focus) Spring Arbor Dist.

— Life by His Death. 1998. pap. text 5.99 (*0-9505476-3-8*) P & R Pubng.

***Owen, J.** Living with the Living God. 1998. pap. text 4.99 (*0-946462-53-4*) Grace Pubns Trust.

— What Every Child Needs. 1998. pap. text 6.99 (*0-946462-47-X*) Grace Pubns Trust.

Owen, J., ed. see Brambilla, R. & Crotti, A.

Owen, J. G. The Management of Curriculum Development. LC 72-97876. 186p. reprint ed. pap. 53.10 (*0-608-13035-4*, 2024506) Bks Demand.

Owen, J. Glyn. From Simon to Peter. 1985. pap. 13.99 (*0-85234-195-4*, Pub. by Evangelical Pr) P & R Pubng.

Owen, J. I., ed. Brassey's Infantry Weapons of the World. 2nd ed. 488p. 1979. 170.00 (*0-08-027013-1*, Pergamon Pr) Elsevier.

— Infantry Weapons of the Armies of Africa, the Orient & Latin America. 196p. 1980. pap. 35.95 (*0-08-027017-4*, Pergamon Pr) Elsevier.

— Infantry Weapons of the NATO Armies. 2nd ed. 192p. 1979. pap. 35.95 (*0-08-027015-8*, Pergamon Pr) Elsevier.

— Infantry Weapons of the Warsaw Pact Armies. 2nd ed. 160p. 1979. pap. 35.95 (*0-08-027016-6*, Pergamon Pr) Elsevier.

Owen, Jack. Palm Beach - An Irreverent Guide. (Illus.). 52p. (Orig.). 1986. pap. 6.95 (*0-938673-00-9*) Old Bk Shop Pubn.

Owen, Jackie. Early Settlers on the Poor Fork of the Cumberland River, Harlan County, Kentucky & Adjoining Counties. LC 89-69853. (Illus.). 176p. 1990. 32.00 (*0-9625700-0-1*) J Owen.

Owen, Jackie, jt. auth. see Laemmlen, Ann.

An Asterisk (*) at the beginning of an entry indicates that the title is appearing for the first time.

***Owen-Jackson, Gwyneth.** Learning to Teach Design & Technology in the Secondary School: A Companion to School Experience. LC 99-87308. (Learning to Teach Subjects in the Secondary School Ser.). 2000. pap. write for info. (*0-415-21693-1*) Routledge.

***Owen, James.** No Time for Pilots. LC 99-74222. 368p. 2000. 26.95 (*1-57197-186-6*) Pentland Pr.

— The Prudent Investor's Guide to Hedge Funds: Profiting from Uncertainty & Volatility. 288p. 2000. 49.95 (*0-471-32336-5*) Wiley.

Owen, James D. Christian Psychology's War on God's Word: The Victimization of the Believer. LC 93-70361. 218p. (Orig.). 1993. pap. 12.00 (*0-941717-08-9*) EastGate Pubs.

Owen, James L. Context & Communication Behavior. LC 97-7147. 1997. 49.95 (*1-878978-28-4*) Context Pr.

Owen, James P. The Prudent Investor: The Definitive Guide to Professional Investment Management. 1990. text 32.50 (*1-55738-106-2*, Irwn Prfssnl) McGraw-Hill Prof.

— The Prudent Investor: The Definitive Guide to Professional Investment Management. 200p. 1993. reprint ed. per. 21.95 (*1-55738-490-8*, Irwn Prfssnl) McGraw-Hill Prof.

Owen, Jan. Guidebook to Adventure, Vol. II. 2nd ed. (Illus.). 112p. 1985. pap. 16.95 (*0-13-368846-1*) P-H.

— Guidebook to Adventure, Volume 2. write for info. (*0-318-59626-1*) S&S Trade.

***Owen, Jane C. & Ovando, Martha N.** A Superintendent's Guide to Community. 150p. 2000. pap. text 27.95 (*0-8108-3764-1*) Scarecrow.

— A Superintendent's Guide to Community. 150p. 2000. text 45.00 (*0-8108-3763-3*) Scarecrow.

Owen, Jennie S. The Annals of Kansas, 1886-1925, 2 vols., Set. Mechem, Kirke, ed. Incl. Vol. 1. LC 55-62029. 526p. 1954. 4.00 (*0-87726-009-5*); Vol. 2. LC 55-62029. 551p. 1956. 7.00 (*0-87726-010-9*); LC 55-62029. (Illus.). 12.50 (*0-87726-008-7*) Kansas St Hist.

Owen, Jennifer. The Ecology of a Garden: The First Fifteen Years. (Illus.). 415p. (C). 1991. text 115.00 (*0-521-34335-6*) Cambridge U Pr.

— Feeding Strategy. LC 82-2569. (Phoenix Ser.). (Illus.). 158p. (C). 1982. pap. text 14.95 (*0-226-64186-4*) U Ch Pr.

— Insect Life. (Mysteries & Marvels Ser.). (Illus.). 32p. (J). (gr. 3-7). 1985. pap. 5.95 (*0-86020-843-5*, Usborne) EDC.

— Insect Life. (Mysteries & Marvels Ser.). (Illus.). 32p. (J). (gr. 4-7). 1999. lib. bdg. 14.95 (*0-88110-173-7*, Usborne) EDC.

Owen, Jill. Shades of Comfort: Decorative Window Treatments for an Energy Efficient Home. Weiland, Barbara, ed. (Illus.). 88p. (Orig.). 1996. pap. 9.95 (*0-9654466-0-3*) Warm Co.

Owen, John. Apostasy from the Gospel. 184p. 1992. reprint ed. pap. 6.99 (*0-85151-609-2*) Banner of Truth.

— Biblical Theology. Kistler, Don, ed. Westcott, Stephen, tr. 911p. 1994. 50.00 (*1-877611-83-2*) Soli Deo Gloria.

— Cattle Feeding. 2nd ed. (Illus.). 182p. 1991. 29.95 (*0-85236-220-X*, Pub. by Farming Pr) Diamond Farm Bk.

— Christians Are for Ever! 1987. pap. 4.99 (*0-946462-14-3*, Pub. by Evangelical Pr) P & R Pubng.

— Communion with God. Law, R. J., ed. 224p. 1991. pap. text 6.99 (*0-85151-607-6*) Banner of Truth.

— The Correspondence: With an Account of His Life & Work. Toon, Peter, ed. 215p. 1970. 14.00 (*0-227-67746-3*) Attic Pr.

— Death of Death. 1983. pap. 13.99 (*0-85151-382-4*) Banner of Truth.

— The Five Great Skeptical Dramas of History. LC 72-295. (Essay Index Reprint Ser.). 1977. reprint ed. 24.95 (*0-8369-2816-4*) Ayer.

***Owen, John.** La Gloria de Cristo. abr. ed. Mockford, Hervey, ed. Montgomery, Thomas & Negrete, Omar Ibanez, trs. Orig. Title: The Glory of Christ. (SPA.). 96p. 1999. pap. 2.15 (*1-928980-05-8*) Pub Faro.

Owen, John. Glory of Christ. 1987. pap. 4.99 (*0-946462-13-5*, Pub. by Evangelical Pr) P & R Pubng.

— The Glory of Christ. abr. ed. 168p. 1994. pap. 6.99 (*0-85151-661-0*) Banner of Truth.

Owen, John. Gluttony Without Guilt. (Illus.). 78p. 1997. pap. 14.95 (*0-9624559-6-2*) Seattle Post.

Owen, John. Hebrews. abr. ed. LC 98-33632. (Crossway Classic Commentaries Ser.). 272p. 1998. pap. text 15.99 (*1-58134-026-5*) Crossway Bks.

— Hebrews, 7 vols., Set. 1991. reprint ed. 174.99 (*0-85151-619-X*) Banner of Truth.

— Hebrews: The Epistle of Warning. LC 68-57719. 288p. 1973. pap. 13.99 (*0-8254-3407-6*, Kregel Class) Kregel.

— Life by His Death. 1992. pap. 4.99 (*0-85234-763-4*, Pub. by Evangelical Pr) P & R Pubng.

***Owen, John.** La Mortification del Pecado: Lo Que Cada Creyente Deberia Saber Acerca de la Mortificacion del Pecado. Swanson, Andrew, ed. Montgomery, Thomas & Negrete, Omar Ibanez, trs. Orig. Title: What Every Christian Needs to Know about Temptation & Putting Sin to Death. (SPA.). 80p. 1999. pap. 1.80 (*1-928980-09-0*) Pub Faro.

Owen, John. Seattle Cookbook. (Illus.). 105p. 1993. pap. 14.95 (*0-9624559-1-1*) Seattle Post.

— The Skeptics of the French Renaissance. 1972. 59.95 (*0-8490-1058-6*) Gordon Pr.

— The Skeptics of the Italian Renaissance. 1972. 59.95 (*0-8490-1059-4*) Gordon Pr.

***Owen, John.** Sobre la Tentacion: Lo Que Cada Creyente Debe Saber Sobre la Tentacion. abr. ed. Swanson, Andrew, ed. Montgomery, Thomas & Negrete, Omar Ibanez, trs. Orig. Title: What Every Christian Needs to Know about Temptation. (SPA.). 68p. 1999. pap. 1.56 (*1-928980-08-2*) Pub Faro.

— Vida por Su Muerte. Appleby, H. J., ed. Montgomery, Thomas & Negrete, Omar Ibanez, trs. Orig. Title: Life by His Death. (SPA.). 82p. 1999. pap. 1.84 (*1-928980-11-2*) Pub Faro.

— Walking Seattle. (Falcon Guides Walking Ser.). (Illus.). 2000. pap. 12.95 (*1-56044-863-6*) Falcon Pub Inc.

Owen, John. Works of John Owen, 16 vols., Set. 1980. 429.99 (*0-85151-392-1*) Banner of Truth.

— Works of John Owen, Vol. I. 1980. 29.99 (*0-85151-123-6*) Banner of Truth.

— Works of John Owen, Vol. II. 1980. 29.99 (*0-85151-124-4*) Banner of Truth.

— Works of John Owen, Vol. III. 1980. 29.99 (*0-85151-125-2*) Banner of Truth.

— Works of John Owen, Vol. IV. 1980. 29.99 (*0-85151-068-X*) Banner of Truth.

— Works of John Owen, Vol. V. 1980. 29.99 (*0-85151-067-1*) Banner of Truth.

— Works of John Owen, Vol. VI. 1980. 29.99 (*0-85151-126-0*) Banner of Truth.

— Works of John Owen, Vol. VII. 1980. 29.99 (*0-85151-127-9*) Banner of Truth.

— Works of John Owen, Vol. VIII. 1980. 29.99 (*0-85151-066-3*) Banner of Truth.

— Works of John Owen, Vol. IX. 1980. 29.99 (*0-85151-065-5*) Banner of Truth.

— Works of John Owen, Vol. X. 1980. 29.99 (*0-85151-064-7*) Banner of Truth.

— Works of John Owen, Vol. XI. 1980. 29.99 (*0-85151-128-7*) Banner of Truth.

— Works of John Owen, Vol. XII. 1980. 29.99 (*0-85151-129-5*) Banner of Truth.

— Works of John Owen, Vol. XIII. 1980. 29.99 (*0-85151-063-9*) Banner of Truth.

— Works of John Owen, Vol. XIV. 1980. 29.99 (*0-85151-062-0*) Banner of Truth.

— Works of John Owen, Vol. XV. 1980. 29.99 (*0-85151-130-9*) Banner of Truth.

— Works of John Owen, Vol. XVI. 1980. 29.99 (*0-85151-061-2*) Banner of Truth.

Owen, John & Law, R. J. The Holy Spirit: The Treasures of John Owen for Today's Readers. abr. ed. (Treasures of John Owen for Today's Readers Ser.). 208p. 1998. pap. 6.99 (*0-85151-698-X*) Banner of Truth.

Owen, John, tr. see Calvin, John.

Owen, John, tr. see John, Calvin.

Owen, John B. The Rise of the Pelhams. LC 76-24488. x, 357 p. 1971. write for info. (*0-389-04145-9*) B&N Imports.

Owen, John C. Budapest 1896 International Chess Tournament: The First Great Chess Tournament in Hungary. LC 95-145595. (Great Tournaments Ser.). (Illus.). 205p. 1994. 30.00 (*0-939433-20-6*) Caissa Edit.

— The Match Tournament at St. Petersburg, 1895-6. (World's Greatest Chess Tournaments Ser.). (Illus.). 118p. 1989. 26.00 (*0-939433-10-9*) Caissa Edit.

Owen, John C., ed. Nuremberg 1896 International Chess Tournament. (Great Tournaments Ser.: Vol. 9). (Illus.). 413p. Date not set. 45.00 (*0-939433-54-0*) Caissa Edit.

Owen, John D. Reduced Working Hours: Cure for Unemployment or Economic Burden? LC 88-30352. (Illus.). 195p. reprint ed. pap. 60.50 (*0-608-06178-6*, 206651000008) Bks Demand.

— School Inequality & the Welfare State. LC 74-6834. 222p. reprint ed. pap. 68.90 (*0-608-18043-2*, 202790100057) Bks Demand.

— Why Our Kids Don't Study: An Economic Analysis of Causes & Proposed Remedies. LC 94-21829. 136p. 1995. text 32.50 (*0-8018-4925-X*) Johns Hopkins.

Owen, John M. Liberal Peace, Liberal War: American Politics & International Security. LC 97-29419. (Studies in Security Affairs). 224p. 1997. 35.00 (*0-8014-3319-3*) Cornell U Pr.

***Owen, John M., IV.** Liberal Peace, Liberal War: American Politics & International Security. 2000. reprint ed. pap. 17.95 (*0-8014-8690-4*) Cornell U Pr.

Owen, John M. Program Evaluation: Forms & Approaches. 176p. 1994. pap. 22.95 (*1-86373-462-7*, Pub. by Allen & Unwin Pty) Paul & Co Pubs.

Owen, John M. & Rogers, Patricia. Program Evaluation. 2nd ed. 272p. 1998. pap. 35.00 (*1-86448-784-4*, Pub. by Allen & Unwin Pty) Paul & Co Pubs.

Owen, Jon, jt. auth. see Bloor, Susan.

Owen-Jones, Peter. Bed Of Nails. 1996. 22.95 (*0-7459-3627-X*, Pub. by Lion Pubng) Trafalgar.

— Bed Of Nails. 1997. pap. 10.95 (*0-7459-3628-8*, Pub. by Lion Pubng) Trafalgar.

Owen, Joseph R. Colder Than Hell: A Marine Rifle Company at Chosin Reservoir. LC 97-93361. 1997. mass mkt. 5.99 (*0-8041-1697-0*) Ivy Books.

— Colder Than Hell: A Marine Rifle Company at Chosin Reservoir. LC 96-17124. (Illus.). 272p. 1996. 29.95 (*1-55750-660-4*) Naval Inst Pr.

***Owen, Joseph R.** Colder Than Hell: A Marine Rifle Company at Chosin Reservoir. (Bluejacket Book Ser.). (Illus.). 272p. 2000. pap. 16.95 (*1-55750-416-4*) Naval Inst Pr.

Owen, Josylyn. Managing Education. 1992. pap. text. write for info. (*0-582-08504-7*, Pub. by Addison-Wesley) Longman.

Owen, Julia. Hold on Hannah. (J). (gr. 4-8). 1996. 3.99 (*1-85792-187-9*, Pub. by Christian Focus) Spring Arbor Dist.

Owen, Keeton, jt. auth. see Owen, Montgomery.

Owen, Keith & Coley, Trevor. Automotive Fuels Reference Book. 2nd ed. 980p. 1995. 129.00 (*1-56091-589-7*, R151) Soc Auto Engineers.

Owen, Keith & Marshall, E. L., eds. Motor Gasoline. 282p. 1995. 156.00 (*0-85404-409-4*, TJ751) CRC Pr.

Owen, Keith, et al. Developing High Performance People. (Illus.). 208p. 1993. pap. 27.00 (*0-201-56313-4*) Addison-Wesley.

— Groups at Work. LC 87-9081. (Techniques in Training & Performance Development Ser.). (Illus.). 279p. (C). 1987. 42.95 (*0-87778-196-6*) Educ Tech Pubns.

Owen, Kenneth. Concorde & the Americans: International Politics of the Supersonic Transport. LC 96-42415. (History of Aviation Ser.). (Illus.). 288p. 1997. text 37.95 (*1-56098-736-7*) Smithsonian.

Owen, L. A., et al. Neotectonics No. 3: Recent Advances. 118p. 1996. pap. 75.00 (*0-471-95702-X*) Wiley.

Owen, L. A., jt. ed. see Derbyshire, Edward D.

***Owen, Lara.** Pain-Free Magnet Therapy: Discover How Magnets Can Work to Help Relieve Your Arthritis, Sports Injuries, Fibromyalgia & Much More. LC 00-26820. 240p. 2000. pap. text 14.95 (*0-7615-2086-4*) Prima Pub.

Owen, Lewis. The Running Register: Recording the State of the English Colledges in All Forraine Parts. LC 68-54654. (English Experience Ser.: No. 19). 118p. 1968. reprint ed. 20.00 (*90-221-0019-7*) Walter J Johnson.

Owen, Lewis A. & Unwin, P. Tim, eds. Environmental Management: Readings & Case Studies. LC 96-47639. (Readers on the Natural Environment Ser.). (Illus.). 448p. 1997. text 83.95 (*0-631-20116-5*); pap. text 36.95 (*0-631-20117-3*) Blackwell Pubs.

Owen, Lewis A., jt. auth. see Pickering, K. T.

Owen, Lewis A., jt. auth. see Pickering, Kevin T.

Owen, Lewis J. & Owen, Nancy H., eds. Middle English Poetry: An Anthology. LC 76-138662. (Library of Literature). 1971. pap. 7.50 (*0-672-60984-3*, LL-12, Bobbs) Macmillan.

Owen, Lisa B. & Lamb, Charles E. Bringing the NCTM Standards to Life: Best Practices from Elementary Educators. 168p. 1996. pap. 17.95 (*1-883001-20-X*) Eye On Educ.

Owen, Lyla H. & Murphy, Owen. Creoles of New Orleans: People of Color. 102p. (Orig.). 1987. pap. 15.95 (*0-940835-00-2*) First Quarter Pub.

Owen, Lynette. Selling Rights. 3rd ed. LC 97-9444. 312p. (C). 1997. 60.00 (*0-415-16854-6*) Routledge.

Owen, M., jt. auth. see Burr, A.

Owen, M. C. Sewell: The Sewells of the Isle of Wight, England, with an Account of Some of the Families Connected by Marriage. 204p. 1993. reprint ed. pap. 32.00 (*0-8328-3749-0*); reprint ed. lib. bdg. 42.00 (*0-8328-3748-2*) Higginson Bk Co.

***Owen, M. J., et al, eds.** Intergrated Design & Manufacture Using Fibre-Reinforced Composites. 2000. 170.00 (*1-85573-453-2*, Pub. by Woodhead Pubng) Am Educ Systs.

Owen, M. J. & Lamb, J. R. Immune Recognition: In Focus. (In Focus Ser.). (Illus.). 84p. 1988. pap. text 14.95 (*1-85221-062-1*) OUP.

***Owen, M. J., et al.** Integrated Design & Manufacture Using Fibre Reinforced Polymeric Composites. LC 00-39838. 2000. write for info. (*0-8493-0858-5*) CRC Pr.

Owen, M. J., jt. ed. see Bodmer, W. F.

Owen, M. Trefor. Welsh Folk Customs. 4th ed. 197p. 1987. pap. 14.95 (*0-8464-4703-7*) Beekman Pubs.

Owen, Mac & Lagoe, J. Arthur. Reaching the Heart of God: The Key to Revival. LC 96-85872. 192p. (Orig.). 1996. pap. 8.00 (*0-9641761-1-4*) Aletheia WA.

Owen, Malcolm. SPC in the Office: A Practical Guide to Continuous Improvement. 1998. 59.95 (*0-7134-8368-7*, Pub. by B T B) Branford.

Owen, Margaret. A World of Widows. 240p. (C). 1996. pap. 19.95 (*1-85649-420-9*, Pub. by Zed Books) St Martin.

Owen, Margaret, jt. auth. see Gustafson, Monica.

Owen, Marion. Apologies & Remedial Interchanges: A Study of Language Use in Social Interaction. LC 83-13375. (Linguistic Supplementary Studies). x, 192p. 1983. 70.00 (*90-279-3360-X*); pap. 21.55 (*90-279-3370-7*) Mouton.

Owen, Marna. Animal Rights: Yes or No? (YA). (gr. 6 up). 1993. lib. bdg. 21.27 (*0-8225-2603-4*, Lerner Publctns) Lerner Pub.

Owen-Martin, Lydi. Don't Take My Baby Away! The Unexplored Cause Of Child Abuse in America. 295p. (Orig.). 1995. 23.95 (*0-9646739-1-6*); pap. 14.95 (*0-9646739-0-8*) Home Birthing Serv.

Owen, Mary A. Voodoo Tales, As Told among the Negroes of the Southwest. LC 70-149874. (Black Heritage Library Collection). (Illus.). 1977. 30.95 (*0-8369-8754-3*) Ayer.

Owen, Maureen. Hearts in Space. (Illus.). 7.00 (*0-686-73477-7*); pap. 3.50 (*0-686-73478-5*) Kulchur Foun.

— Hearts in Space. 1980. pap. 5.00 (*0-936538-01-5*) Kulchur Foun.

— Imaginary Income. 1992. 16.00 (*0-914610-98-8*); pap. 9.00 (*0-914610-97-X*) Hanging Loose.

— Untapped Maps. 96p. (Orig.). 1993. pap. 9.50 (*0-937013-44-7*) Potes Poets.

Owen, Maureen, ed. see Bennett, Will.

Owen, Maureen, jt. ed. see Beresford, Jon.

Owen, Maureen, ed. see Cataldo, Susan.

Owen, Maureen, ed. see Dawson, Fielding.

Owen, Maureen, ed. see Friedman, Ed.

Owen, Maureen, ed. see Hamill, Janet.

Owen, Maureen, ed. see Hartman, Yuki.

Owen, Maureen, ed. see Schneeman, Elio.

Owen, Maureen, ed. see Vega, Janine P.

Owen, Maureen, ed. see Weigel, Tom.

Owen, Maureen, ed. see Wright, Rebecca.

Owen, Max. In the Minds of Men. 256p. 1989. 21.95 (*0-8027-1071-9*) Walker & Co.

Owen, May A. Folk-Lore of the Musquakie Indians of North America & Catalogue of Musquakie Beadwork & Other Objects in the Collection of the Folk-Lore Society. (Folk-Lore Society, London Monographs: Vol. 51). 1972. reprint ed. pap. 25.00 (*0-8115-0523-5*) Periodicals Srv.

Owen, Meran R. & Pen, J. Transgenic Plants: A Production System for Industrial & Pharmaceutical Proteins. LC 96-21457. 360p. 1996. 240.00 (*0-471-96443-3*); pap. 99.95 (*0-471-96444-1*) Wiley.

***Owen, Michael.** I Hate Giving Presentations. 122p. 1998. ring bd. 32.50 (*0-7494-2744-2*, Kogan Pg Educ) Stylus Pub VA.

Owen, Michael & Kinzie, Jan J. Model Employment Contracts. (Executive Performance Ser.). 40p. (Orig.). 1993. pap. 69.00 (*1-889394-04-1*) Credit Union Execs.

Owen, Michael, jt. auth. see Murphy, Michael.

Owen, Michael G. Master Electrician Examinations: Based on 1999 NEC. 6th rev. ed. 60p. 1999. pap. text 19.95 (*1-888512-08-3*) Elect Trnging.

— Sample Exams for Electrical Licensing: Based on 1999 NEC. 6th rev. ed. 42p. 1999. pap. text 19.95 (*1-888512-07-5*) Elect Trnging.

— Sample Exams for Master Electricians: Based on 1999 NEC. 6th rev. ed. 52p. 1999. pap. text 19.95 (*1-888512-06-7*) Elect Trnging.

— Study Guide for Electrical Examinations: Based on the 1999 NEC. 6th rev. ed. (Illus.). 140p. 1999. pap. text 39.95 (*1-888512-10-5*) Elect Trnging.

— Study Guide for Electrical Examinations: Instructor's Solution Manual Based on 1999 NEC. 6th rev. ed. 45p. 1999. pap. text, teacher ed. 19.95 (*1-888512-11-3*) Elect Trnging.

— Working with the Code: A Journeyman Electrician's Exam Preparation Based on 1999 NEC. 6th rev. ed. (Illus.). 135p. 1999. pap. text 39.95 (*1-888512-09-1*) Elect Trnging.

Owen, Michael G. & Armstrong, Jeff. A Complete 1999 Electrical Code Exam Preparation Guide Covering Most Commonly Asked Questions on Exams. 250p. 1999. pap. text 69.95 (*1-888512-12-1*) Elect Trnging.

Owen, Michael S., jt. auth. see Newman, Sandra J.

Owen, Mildred. Cook's Guide to Growing Herbs, Greens & Aromatics. 368p. 1999. pap. text 16.95 (*1-55821-917-X*) Lyons Pr.

— A Cook's Guide to Growing Herbs, Greens, & Aromatics. (Cook's Classic Library). (Illus.). 368p. 1999. reprint ed. pap. 16.95 (*1-55821-110-1*) Lyons Pr.

Owen, Montgomery & Owen, Keeton. Products Liability & Safety, Cases & Materials, Products Liability Problems 1996 Edition for Use in Conjunction With. 3rd ed. LeBel, Paul A., ed. (University Casebook Ser.). 164p. Date not set. pap. text. write for info. (*1-56662-422-3*) Foundation Pr.

Owen, Morag, jt. auth. see Farmer, Elaine.

Owen, Myrfyn. The Barnacle Goose. (Natural History Ser.: No. 51). (Illus.). 24p. 1989. pap. 5.25 (*0-7478-0053-7*, Pub. by Shire Pubns) Parkwest Pubns.

Owen, Myrfyn & Black, Jeffrey M. Waterfowl Ecology. (Tertiary Level Biology Ser.). (Illus.). 200p. (gr. 13). 1990. mass mkt. 34.95 (*0-412-02201-X*, A3621, Chap & Hall NY) Chapman & Hall.

Owen, N. Tattenham Corner Branch. (C). 1985. 39.00 (*0-85361-224-2*) St Mut.

***Owen, Nancy E.** Rookwood & the Industry of Art: Women, Culture, & Commerce, 1880-1913. (Illus.). 320p. 2000. 49.95 (*0-8214-1337-6*); pap. 24.95 (*0-8214-1338-4*) Ohio U Pr.

Owen, Nancy H., jt. ed. see Owen, Lewis J.

Owen, Nancy R., jt. auth. see Combs, Richard E.

Owen, Natasha, tr. see Kokoshvili, Simon, et al.

Owen, Neville, jt. auth. see Sallis, James F.

Owen, Nicholas. Diana: The People's Princess. LC 97-44321. 1997. write for info. (*0-7621-0079-6*) RD Assn.

Owen, Norman G., ed. Death & Disease in Southeast Asia: Explorations in Social, Medical & Demographic History. (Illus.). 298p. 1987. pap. text 29.95 (*0-19-588853-7*) OUP.

— The Philippine Economy & the United States: Studies in Past & Present Interactions. LC 82-74314. (Michigan Papers on South & Southeast Asia: No. 22). xvi, 208p. (Orig.). 1984. pap. 16.95 (*0-89148-025-0*); text 16.95 (*0-89148-024-2*) Ctr S&SE Asian.

Owen, Oliver S. Acorn to Oak Tree. LC 94-6302. 32p. (J). (gr. 2-8). 1994. lib. bdg. 14.98 (*1-56239-289-1*) ABDO Pub Co.

— Bulb to Tulip. (Lifewatch Ser.). 32p. (J). (gr. 2-8). 1996. lib. bdg. 14.98 (*1-56239-488-6*) ABDO Pub Co.

— Calf to Dolphin. LC 94-19967. (Lifewatch Ser.). (Illus.). 32p. (J). (gr. 2-8). 1994. lib. bdg. 14.98 (*1-56239-292-1*) ABDO Pub Co.

— Caterpillar to Butterfly. LC 94-14306. (Lifewatch Ser.). 32p. (J). (gr. 2-8). 1994. lib. bdg. 14.98 (*1-56239-290-5*) ABDO Pub Co.

— Doctors, Dollars & Death: Bad Medicine in America. 115p. (Orig.). (C). 1994. pap. text 17.50 (*0-87527-508-7*) Green.

— Eco-Solutions: It's in Your Hands. LC 93-19132. (Target Earth Ser.). (J). 1993. pap. 7.49 (*1-56239-426-6*) ABDO Pub Co.

— Eco-Solutions: It's in Your Hands. LC 93-19132. (Target Earth Ser.). 64p. (J). (ps-7). 1993. lib. bdg. 15.98 (*1-56239-203-4*) ABDO Pub Co.

— Egg to Snake. LC 94-12943. (Lifewatch Ser.). 32p. (J). (gr. 2-8). 1994. lib. bdg. 14.98 (*1-56239-294-8*) ABDO Pub Co.

— From Egg to Robin. LC 94-7793. (Life Watch Ser.). 32p. (J). (gr. 2-8). 1994. lib. bdg. 14.98 (*1-56239-293-X*) ABDO Pub Co.

An Asterisk (*) at the beginning of an entry indicates that the title is appearing for the first time.

O

— Intro to Your Environment. Italia, Bob, ed. LC 93-7746. (Target Earth Ser.). (J). 1993. pap. 7.49 (*1-56239-418-5*) ABDO Pub Co.

— Intro to Your Environment. Italia, Bob, ed. LC 93-7746. (Target Earth Ser.). 48p. (J). (ps-7). 1993. lib. bdg. 15.98 (*1-56239-204-2*) ABDO Pub Co.

— Pup to Grizzly Bear. LC 95-3317. (Lifewatch Ser.). 32p. (J). (gr. 2-8). 1995. lib. bdg. 14.98 (*1-56239-486-X*) ABDO Pub Co.

— Pup to Timber Wolf. LC 95-1172. (Lifewatch Ser.). 32p. (J). (gr. 2-8). 1995. lib. bdg. 14.98 (*1-56239-487-8*) ABDO Pub Co.

— Seed to Peanut. LC 95-10523. (Lifewatch Ser.). 32p. (J). (gr. 2-8). 1996. lib. bdg. 14.98 (*1-56239-489-4*) ABDO Pub Co.

— Tadpole to Frog. LC 94-11370. (Lifewatch Ser.). 32p. (J). (gr. 2-8). 1994. lib. bdg. 14.98 (*1-56239-291-3*) ABDO Pub Co.

Owen, Oliver S. & Chiras, Daniel D. Natural Resource Conservation: Management for a Sustainable Future. 7th ed. LC 97-7765. 594p. (C). 1997. 90.00 (*0-13-840133-0*) P-H.

Owen, Orville W. Sir Francis Bacon's Cipher Story. 218p. 1996. reprint ed. pap. 19.95 (*1-56459-591-9*) Kessinger Pub.

Owen, P. E., jt. auth. see Lewis, G. P.

Owen, Pamela & Pumfrey, Peter D., eds. Children Learning to Read - International Concerns: Curriculum & Assesment Issues, 2 vols., Vol. 2. LC 49-37967. 210p. 1995. 85.00 (*0-7507-0365-2*, Falmer Pr); pap. 27.95 (*0-7507-0366-0*, Falmer Pr) Taylor & Francis.

— Children Learning to Read - International Concerns: Emergent & Developing Reading, 2 vols., Vol. 1. LC 94-37967. 210p. 1995. 85.00 (*0-7507-0363-6*, Falmer Pr); pap. 27.95 (*0-7507-0364-4*, Falmer Pr) Taylor & Francis.

Owen, Pat. Bing & Grondahl Christmas Plates: The First Hundred Years. (Illus.). 256p. 1995. 35.00 (*0-913428-76-0*) Landfall Pr.

— Story of Bing & Grondahl Christmas Plates. (Illus.). 1998. ring bd. 25.00 (*0-911576-02-9*) Viking Import.

— Story of Royal Copenhagen Christmas Plates. (Illus.). 1998. ring bd. 25.00 (*0-911576-01-0*) Viking Import.

*__Owen, Patricia.__ I Can See Tomorrow: A Guide for Living with Depression. 200p. 2000. pap. 13.00 (*1-56838-568-4*) Hazelden.

Owen, Patricia, jt. auth. see Drake, Pat.

Owen, Patricia, jt. ed. see Griffiths, Vivienne.

Owen, Patricia Hershey. Seven Styles of Parenting. LC 93-80895. 96p. 1994. pap. 10.00 (*1-882657-08-X*) Health Digest.

Owen, Patricia L. I Can See Tomorrow: A Guide for Living with Depression. LC 95-30883. 183p. pap. 11.95 (*1-56838-087-9*) Hazelden.

Owen, Patricia M. Sudden Cardiac Death: Theory & Practice. LC 90-14506. 272p. 1991. text 62.00 (*0-8342-0200-X*) Aspen Pub.

*__Owen, Paula S.__ How to Find Information: Environment. 36p. 1998. pap. 14.50 (*0-7123-0808-3*) L Erlbaum Assocs.

O

Owen, Peter. Book of Camping Knots. 1999. pap. text 12.95 (*1-55821-927-7*) Lyons Pr.

— Book of Climbing Knots. 1999. pap. text 12.95 (*1-55821-928-5*) Lyons Pr.

— The Book of Decorative Knots. LC 94-5176. (Illus.). 144p. 1994. pap. 12.95 (*1-55821-304-X*) Lyons Pr.

— The Book of Outdoor Knots. (Illus.). 144p. 1993. pap. 12.95 (*1-55821-225-6*) Lyons Pr.

— The Book of Sailing Knots. LC 98-40920. (Illus.). 144p. 1999. pap. 12.95 (*1-55821-872-6*) Lyons Pr.

— The Craft & Hobby Airbrush Book. (Illus.). 96p. 1995. pap. 17.95 (*1-55821-333-3*) Lyons Pr.

— The Field & Stream Fishing Knots Handbook. LC 98-54586. (Field & Stream Fishing & Hunting Library). (Illus.). 128p. 1999. pap. 9.95 (*1-55821-868-8*) Lyons Pr.

*__Owen, Peter.__ Knots: More Than 50 of the Most Useful Knots for Camping, Sailing, Fishing & Climbing. (Illus.). 2000. 9.99 (*0-7858-1174-5*) Bk Sales Inc.

— L. L. Bean Outdoor Knots Handbook. LC 99-23385. (Illus.). 144p. 1999. pap. 14.95 (*1-55821-871-8*) Lyons Pr.

— The Pocket Guide to Fishing Knots. LC 98-21947. (Illus.). 80p. 1998. 9.95 (*1-58080-064-5*) Burford Bks.

Owen, Peter. Publishing Now. 2nd ed. LC 97-180158. 176p. 1997. pap. 26.00 (*0-7206-1009-5*, Pub. by P Owen Ltd) Dufour.

Owen, Peter, ed. Publishing: The Future. LC 88-61919. 128p. 1988. pap. 14.95 (*0-7206-0721-3*) Dufour.

— Publishing: The Future. LC 88-61919. 128p. 1988. 21.00 (*0-7206-0720-5*, Pub. by P Owen Ltd) Dufour.

Owen, Peter, intro. The Peter Owen Anthology: Forty Years of Independent Publishing. 231p. 1991. 35.00 (*0-7206-0810-4*, Pub. by P Owen Ltd) Dufour.

Owen, Peter & Hackett, Phil. The Juggling Book. LC 97-130. (Illus.). 96p. 1997. pap. 12.95 (*1-55821-326-0*) Lyons Pr.

Owen, R. Anatomy of Vertebrates Fishes & Reptiles. 650p. 1984. pap. 175.00 (*0-7855-0340-4*, Pub. by Intl Bks & Periodicals) St Mut.

*__Owen, Ray.__ Each One Disciple One: The Essentials. LC 99-71090. 56p. 1999. pap. 2.50 (*0-9662905-0-X*, J Wesley Pr) United Meth Church.

— Second Thoughts: Ideas Recycled. LC 00-132160. (Illus.). 168p. 2000. pap. 6.95 (*0-9662905-1-8*, J Wesley Pr) United Meth Church.

— The Witness We Make: To Heal Our Dividedness. 4.00 (*0-687-08561-6*) Abingdon.

Owen, Raymond S. Fred K. Owen, Newspaper Man. LC 83-50687. (Illus.). 128p. (Orig.). 1984. pap. 7.95 (*0-931474-27-2*) TBW Bks.

Owen, Richard. Essential Europe Community Law. Bourne, Nicholas, ed. (Essential Law Ser.). 192p. 1995. pap. write for info. (*1-85941-120-7*, Pub. by Cavendish Pubng) Gaunt.

— Essential Tort. Bourne, Nicholas, ed. (Essential Law Ser.). 207p. 1995. pap. write for info. (*1-85941-121-5*, Pub. by Cavendish Pubng) Gaunt.

*__Owen, Richard.__ The First "Dinosaur" Book: Richard Owen on British Fossil Reptiles (1842) Dean, Dennis R., ed. LC 99-30427. (Scholars' Facsimiles & Reprints Ser.: Vol. 526). 1999. 75.00 (*0-8201-1526-6*) Schol Facsimiles.

Owen, Richard. Generals at Rest: The Grave Sites of the 425 Official Confederate Generals. LC 97-22958. 352p. 1998. 65.00 (*1-57249-045-4*) White Mane Pub.

— A History of British Fossil Mammals & Birds. LC 72-1705. (Illus.). reprint ed. 52.50 (*0-404-07991-1*) AMS Pr.

— The Hunterian Lectures in Comparative Anatomy. Sloan, Phillip R., ed. (Illus.). 356p. 1992. pap. text 18.95 (*0-226-64190-2*) U Ch Pr.

— The Hunterian Lectures in Comparative Anatomy. Sloan, Phillip R., ed. (Illus.). 356p. 1992. lib. bdg. 48.50 (*0-226-64189-9*) U Ch Pr.

— Memoir on the Pearly Nautilus. LC 72-1700. (Illus.). reprint ed. 27.50 (*0-404-07978-4*) AMS Pr.

— On the Anatomy of Vertebrates, 3 vols. LC 72-1701. (Illus.). reprint ed. 225.00 (*0-404-08300-5*) AMS Pr.

— Paleontology: Or, a Systematic Summary of Extinct Animals & Their Geological Relations. Gould, Stephen Jay, ed. LC 79-8342. (History of Paleontology Ser.). (Illus.). 1980. reprint ed. lib. bdg. 40.95 (*0-405-12732-4*) Ayer.

— The Times Guide to World Organizations: Their Role & Reach in the New World Order. LC 96-164725. (C). 1996. text 75.00 (*0-8133-6967-3*, Pub. by Westview) HarpC.

Owen, Richard S. The Life of Richard Owen, 2 vols. LC 72-1697. (Illus.). reprint ed. 124.50 (*0-404-07995-4*) AMS Pr.

Owen, Robert. A Development of the Principles & Plans on Which to Establish Self-Supporting Home Colonies. LC 72-2941. reprint ed. 34.50 (*0-404-10707-9*) AMS Pr.

— Gen X TV: "The Brady Bunch" to "Melrose Place" LC 96-39043. (Television Ser.). (Illus.). 238p. 1997. 29.95 (*0-8156-0443-2*) Syracuse U Pr.

— Gen X TV: "The Brady Bunch" to "Melrose Place" (Television Ser.). 240p. 1999. pap. text 17.95 (*0-8156-0585-4*) Syracuse U Pr.

— The Life & Ideas of Robert Owen. 256p. 1969. pap. 1.95 (*0-7178-0115-2*) Intl Pubs Co.

— The Life of Robert Owen: With Selections from His Writings & Correspondence, 2 vols. i. LC 66-21690. 1977. 75.00 (*0-678-00271-1*) Kelley.

— A New View of Society, 1816. Stern, Jeffrey, ed. & intro. by. (Classics in Education Ser.). 184p. 1996. reprint ed. 75.00 (*1-85506-300-X*) Bks Intl VA.

— A New View of Society. LC 70-134407. reprint ed. 36.00 (*0-404-08453-2*) AMS Pr.

— A New View of Society. LC 91-31814. 194p. 1991. reprint ed. 48.00 (*1-85477-077-2*) Continuum.

— Report of the County of Lanark of a Plan for Relieving Public Distress & Removing Discontent by Giving Permanent, Productive Employment to the Poor & Working Classes. LC 72-2942. reprint ed. 34.50 (*0-404-10708-7*) AMS Pr.

— Robert Owen's Millennial Gazette, Nos. 1-16. LC 74-134408. reprint ed. 115.00 (*0-404-08454-0*) AMS Pr.

— Selected Works of Robert Owen, 4 vols., Set. Claeys, Gregory, ed. LC 99-28820. 1577p. 1993. 395.00 (*1-85196-088-0*, Pub. by Pickering & Chatto) Ashgate Pub Co.

Owen, Robert & Dale, David. The Story of New Lanark. (C). 1989. 50.00 (*0-948473-02-9*) St Mut.

Owen, Robert, et al. European Economic Integration. LC 97-52273. 1998p. 1998. pap. 30.95 (*0-631-20855-0*) Blackwell Pubs.

Owen, Robert, jt. ed. see Surawicz, Christina.

*__Owen, Robert C.__ Deliberate Force: A Case Study in Effective Air Campaigning: Final Report of the Air University Balkans Air Campaign Study. LC 99-87096. 2000. write for info. (*1-58566-076-0*) Air Univ.

Owen, Robert C. The Modern Gaelic-English Dictionary. 139p. 1993. pap. 29.95 (*1-871901-29-4*) Colton Bk.

Owen, Robert D. Beyond the Breakers. (Notable American Authors Ser.). 1999. reprint ed. lib. bdg. 125.00 (*0-7812-4687-3*) Rprt Serv.

— The Debatable Land Between This World & the Next. (Notable American Authors Ser.). 1999. reprint ed. lib. bdg. 125.00 (*0-7812-4685-7*) Rprt Serv.

— Divorce: Being a Correspondence Between Horace Greeley & Robert Dale Owen. (Notable American Authors Ser.). 1999. reprint ed. lib. bdg. 125.00 (*0-7812-4683-0*) Rprt Serv.

— Footfalls on the Boundary of Another World. 529p. 1998. reprint ed. pap. 32.00 (*0-7873-0649-5*) Hlth Research.

— Footfalls on the Boundary of Another World. (Notable American Authors Ser.). 1999. reprint ed. lib. bdg. 125.00 (*0-7812-4684-9*) Rprt Serv.

— Hints on Public Architecture. LC 77-17509. (Architecture & Decorative Art Ser.). (Illus.). 1978. reprint ed. lib. bdg. 85.00 (*0-306-77545-X*) Da Capo.

— Hints on Public Architecture. (Notable American Authors Ser.). 1999. reprint ed. lib. bdg. 125.00 (*0-7812-4682-2*) Rprt Serv.

— Hints on Public Architecture. LC 77-17509. (Illus.). 120p. 1978. reprint ed. text 55.00 (*0-87474-736-8*, OWHP) Smithsonian.

— An Outline of the System of Education at New Lanark. (Notable American Authors Ser.). 1999. reprint ed. lib. bdg. 125.00 (*0-7812-4680-6*) Rprt Serv.

— Pocahontas: An Historical Drama. (Notable American Authors Ser.). 1999. reprint ed. lib. bdg. 125.00 (*0-7812-4681-4*) Rprt Serv.

— Political - The Policy of Emanicipation. (Notable American Authors Ser.). 1999. reprint ed. lib. bdg. 125.00 (*0-7812-4678-4*) Rprt Serv.

— Threading My Way. (Notable American Authors Ser.). 1999. reprint ed. lib. bdg. 125.00 (*0-7812-4686-5*) Rprt Serv.

— Threading My Way: Twenty-Seven Years of Autobiography. LC 67-18582. 360p. 1967. reprint ed. 45.00 (*0-678-00261-4*) Kelley.

— The Wrong of Slavery. (Notable American Authors Ser.). 1999. reprint ed. lib. bdg. 125.00 (*0-7812-4679-2*) Rprt Serv.

Owen, Robert D. & Schnell, Gary D. Oklahoma Mammalogy: An Annotated Bibliography & Checklist. LC 88-27959. (Oklahoma Museum of Natural History Publications). 240p. 1989. 28.95 (*0-8061-2185-8*) U of Okla Pr.

Owen, Robert D., jt. auth. see Knowlton, Charles.

Owen, Robert L. Dr. Anne's Cancer Journal. LC 90-81824. 414p. 1990. pap. 14.00 (*1-882657-06-3*) Health Digest.

Owen, Rodrick. Braids: 250 Patterns from Japan, Peru & Beyond. (Illus.). 160p. 1995. 24.95 (*1-883010-06-3*) Interweave.

Owen, Roger. The Middle East in the World Economy, 1800-1914. 378p. 1993. text 19.95 (*1-85043-658-4*, Pub. by I B T) St Martin.

— The Middle East in the World Economy, 1800-1914. 400p. 1987. pap. 25.00 (*0-416-03272-9*) Routledge.

*__Owen, Roger.__ State Power & Politics in the Making of the Modern Middle East. 2nd ed. LC 99-47864. 272p. 2000. pap. write for info. (*0-415-19674-4*) Routledge.

Owen, Roger. State, Power & Politics in the Making of the Modern Middle East. LC 91-41501. (Illus.). 288p. (C). 1997. pap. 24.99 (*0-415-07591-2*, A7080) Routledge.

Owen, Roger, ed. Studies in the Economic & Social History of Palestine in the 19th & 20th Centuries. LC 82-80662. 271p. 1982. 31.95 (*0-8093-1089-9*) S Ill U Pr.

Owen, Roger, jt. ed. see Asad, Talal.

Owen, Rosamund. The Art of Side Saddle: History, Etiquette, Showing. 176p. 1989. 110.00 (*0-9509663-0-4*) St Mut.

Owen, Roy. My Night Forest. LC 93-45666. (Illus.). 32p. (J). (ps-2). 1994. mass mkt. write for info. (*0-02-769005-9*) S&S Bks Yung.

Owen, Ruth. Gambler's Daughter. 352p. 1999. mass mkt. 5.99 (*0-553-57742-5*) Bantam.

*__Owen, Ruth.__ Midnight Mistress. (Meet Me at Midnight Ser.). 320p. 2000. mass mkt. 5.99 (*0-553-57746-8*) Bantam.

Owen, S. A Guide to Modern Inorganic Chemistry. 1991. pap. text 34.95 (*0-582-06439-2*) P Lngmn NZ.

Owen, S. 69 Club. mass mkt. 11.95 (*0-340-68573-5*, Pub. by Hodder & Stought Ltd) Trafalgar.

Owen, S. G. Electrocardiography: A Programmed Text. rev. ed. 180p. 1973. pap. 18.00 (*0-316-67724-8*, Little Brwn Med Div) Lppncott W & W.

Owen, S. G., ed. Tristia, Ibis, Ex Ponto, Halieutica, Fragmenta. (Oxford Classical Texts Ser.). 365p. 1922. text 29.95 (*0-19-814626-4*) OUP.

Owen, Sandy & McNeil, Dani. Divorce Can Be Fun. 128p. (Orig.). pap. 7.00 (*0-317-57794-8*) Triumph Pr.

*__Owen, Sir Geoffrey.__ From Empire to Europe. 1999. 35.00 (*0-00-255682-0*, Pub. by HarpC) Trafalgar.

Owen-Smith, Eric. The German Economy. LC 93-34911. 560p. (C). 1994. pap. 39.99 (*0-415-06289-6*, B3920) Routledge.

Owen-Smith, R. Norman. Megaherbivores: The Influence of Very Large Body Size on Ecology. (Studies in Ecology). (Illus.). 384p. (C). 1992. pap. text 39.95 (*0-521-42637-5*) Cambridge U Pr.

Owen-Smith, Rhonda. No Compromises: Encouragement for the Workplace. LC 99-179222. 224p. 1998. lthr. 4.97 (*1-57748-182-8*) Barbour Pub.

Owen, Sri. Classic Asian Cookbook. LC 97-13893. (Illus.). 160p. 1998. 24.95 (*0-7894-1971-8*) DK Pub Inc.

— Exotic Feasts: Sri Owen's Book of Seasonal Menus. (Illus.). 224p. 1994. pap. 17.95 (*1-85626-100-X*) Trafalgar.

— Healthy Thai Cooking. LC 96-49512. (Illus.). 100p. 1997. 29.95 (*1-55670-539-5*) Stewart Tabori & Chang.

— Homestyle Thai & Indonesian Cooking. LC 97-11512. (Homestyle Cooking Ser.). (Illus.). 160p. 1997. pap. 16.95 (*0-89594-859-1*) Crossing Pr.

— Indonesian Food & Cookery. 268p. 1986. 21.50 (*0-907325-28-9*) Food Words.

— Indonesian Regional Cooking. 1995. text 18.95 (*0-312-11832-5*) St Martin.

*__Owen, Sri.__ Noodles: The New Way. LC 00-27532. (Illus.). 144p. 2000. 24.95 (*0-375-50436-2*) Villard Books.

Owen, Sri. The Rice Book: The Definitive Book on the Magic of Rice, with Hundreds of Exotic Recipes from Around the World. (Illus.). 416p. 1996. pap. 15.95 (*0-312-14132-7*, St Martin Griffin) St Martin.

Owen, Stephanie. Law for the Construction Industry. 2nd ed. xxii, 289p. 1997. pap. 31.00 (*0-582-28708-1*, 15706) Gaunt.

Owen, Stephen. Analogy for Automated Reasoning. (Perspectives in Artificial Intelligence Ser.: Vol. 9). (Illus.). 234p. 1990. text 62.00 (*0-12-531715-8*) Acad Pr.

Owen, Stephen. Anthology of Chinese Literature: Beginnings to 1911. 1997. 46.75 (*0-393-97106-6*) Norton.

Owen, Stephen. The End of the Chinese 'Middle Ages' Essays in Mid-Tang Literary Culture. 1996. 39.50 (*0-8047-2666-3*); pap. 14.95 (*0-8047-2667-1*) Stanford U Pr.

— Mi-Lou: Poetry & the Labyrinth of Desire. LC 88-28393. (Studies in Comparative Literature: No. 39). 240p. 1989. 39.50 (*0-674-57275-0*) HUP.

— Planning Settlements Naturally. (Illus.). 154p. (C). 1994. text 175.00 (*1-85341-029-2*, Pub. by Surrey Beatty & Sons) St Mut.

— The Poetry of Meng Chiao & Han Yu. LC 74-29732. 304p. reprint ed. pap. 94.30 (*0-8357-8273-5*, 203385000087) Bks Demand.

— Readings in Chinese Literary Thought. (Harvard-Yenching Institute Monographs: No. 30). 674p. 1996. pap. 25.00 (*0-674-74921-9*) HUP.

— Remembrances: The Experience of the Past in Classical Chinese Literature. 159p. 1986. 24.50 (*0-674-76015-8*) HUP.

— Traditional Chinese Poetry & Poetics: Omen of the World. LC 83-40269. 313p. reprint ed. pap. 97.10 (*0-608-20465-X*, 207171700002) Bks Demand.

Owen, Stephen, jt. ed. see Lin, Shuen-Fu.

Owen, Sue. My Doomsday Sampler. LC 99-14900. 72p. 1999. pap. 12.95 (*0-8071-2403-6*); text 19.95 (*0-8071-2402-8*) La State U Pr.

— Nursery Rhymes for the Dead. LC 80-18778. 61p. 1980. pap. 4.00 (*0-87886-112-2*, Greenfld Rev Pr) Greenfld Rev Lit.

Owen, Sue, jt. auth. see Jamieson, Anne.

Owen, Susan & Haine, Angela. Discovering Country Walks in South London. 1989. pap. 35.00 (*0-7478-0114-2*, Pub. by Shire Pubns) St Mut.

Owen, Susan, jt. auth. see Haine, Angela.

Owen, Susan J. Restoration Theatre & Crisis. 356p. 1997. text 76.00 (*0-19-818387-9*) OUP.

Owen, Susan J., jt. ed. see Nicholls, James.

Owen, Susanne, et al. Biofeedback in Neuromuscular Re-Education: History, Uses, Procedures. LC 27-954. (Illus.). 1975. pap. 5.50 (*0-685-64751-X*) Biofeedback Research.

Owen, Suzanne, ed. see Alpert, Gerri.

Owen, T. C. Characterization of Organic Compounds by Chemical Methods: An Introductory Laboratory Textbook. (Illus.). 256p. 1969. text 59.75 (*0-8247-1510-1*) Dekker.

Owen, Ted & Dickson, Denise. High Art: A History of the Psychedelic Poster. (Illus.). 1999. pap. 30.00 (*1-86074-256-4*) Sanctuary Pub.

Owen, Terry, jt. auth. see Chall, Miriam.

Owen, Thomas. Wine, Beer & Spirits: The Concise Guide. LC 96-85517. (Illus.). 152p. (Orig.). 1997. pap. 5.95 (*0-9653295-1-8*) Copacetic Publns.

Owen, Thomas C. The Corporation under Russian Law, 1800-1917: A Study in Tsarist Economic Policy. 254p. (C). 1991. text 74.95 (*0-521-39126-1*) Cambridge U Pr.

— Russian Corporate Capitalism from Peter the Great to Perestroika. (Illus.). 272p. 1995. text 70.00 (*0-19-509677-0*) OUP.

Owen, Thomas C., ed. & frwd. see Roosa, Ruth A.

Owen, Thomas M. Revolutionary Soldiers in Alabama. 131p. 1997. reprint ed. 16.50 (*0-8063-0269-0*, 4350) Clearfield Co.

*__Owen, Tim.__ For Glory & Virtue: On the Trail of a Disciple. (Illus.). 180p. 2000. pap. 12.95 (*1-929301-00-6*) Coach Corner.

Owen, Tim, jt. auth. see Livingstone, Stephen.

Owen, Tobias, jt. auth. see Goldsmith, Donald.

Owen, Tobias, tr. see Marov, Mikhail Y. & Grinspoon, David H.

Owen, Tobias C., jt. auth. see Morrison, David.

Owen, Tom. Feed the Muscle Starve the Fat: Get Lean, Fit, Healthy & Strong at Any Age. 1999. pap. text 17.95 (*0-9632905-1-7*) T Owen.

Owen-Towle, Tom. Brother-Spirit: Men Joining Together in the Quest for Intimacy & Ultimacy. 180p. 1991. pap. 11.95 (*0-9630636-0-X*) Bald Eagle Mtn.

— Freethinking Mystics with Hands: Exploring the Heart of Unitarian Universalism. 104p. 1998. pap. 12.00 (*1-55896-367-7*, Skinner Hse Bks) Unitarian Univ.

— Generation to Generation: A Father Writes His Kids about Choosing the Good Life. LC 86-61696. (Illus.). 112p. (Orig.). 1986. pap. 7.95 (*0-931104-19-X*) SunInk Pubn.

— The Gospel of Universalism: Hope, Courage, & the Love of God. LC 93-8307. 1993. pap. 10.00 (*1-55896-315-4*, Skinner Hse Bks) Unitarian Univ.

*__Owen-Towle, Tom.__ Hard Blessings: Doing the Work of Love. 152p. 1999. pap. 12.95 (*0-931104-48-3*) SunInk Pubn.

Owen-Towle, Tom. Love Meets the Dragon: A Field Manual for Ministers. LC 97-69514. 174p. 1997. pap. 12.95 (*0-931104-46-7*) SunInk Pubn.

— New Men - Deeper Hungers. LC 88-63742. (Illus.). 146p. (Orig.). (C). 1988. pap. 7.95 (*0-931104-25-4*) SunInk Pubn.

— O. Eugene Pickett: Borne on a Wintry Wind. 240p. (Orig.). 1996. pap. 14.00 (*1-55896-344-8*, 5231, Skinner Hse Bks) Unitarian Univ.

— Sauntering: A Soul-Journey in the Woods with Thoreau As My Guide. (Illus.). 180p. 1996. pap. 12.95 (*0-9630636-2-6*) Bald Eagle Mtn.

— Spiritual Fitness. LC 89-63710. 394p. (Orig.). 1989. pap. 12.00 (*0-931104-27-0*) SunInk Pubn.

— Staying Together: Forty Ways to Make your Marriage Work. LC 87-62585. (Illus.). 108p. (Orig.). 1987. pap. 7.95 (*0-931104-21-1*) SunInk Pubn.

Owen-Towle, Tom, jt. auth. see Hassett, Chris.

Owen, Trefor M. Welsh Folk Customs. 197p. 1987. pap. 30.00 (*0-85088-347-4*, Pub. by Gomer Pr) St Mut.

— Welsh for Customs. 197p. (C). 1987. pap. 50.00 (*0-7855-6764-X*, Pub. by Gomer Pr) St Mut.

Owen, Trevor, et al. The Learning Highway: Smart Students & the Net. 2nd rev. ed. (Illus.). 210p. (YA). (gr. 9 up). 1997. pap. 16.95 (*1-55013-878-2*) Firefly Bks Ltd.

An Asterisk (*) at the beginning of an entry indicates that the title is appearing for the first time.

Owen, Trevor A. Troilus & Cressida: An Annotated Bibliography. (Garland Shakespeare Bibliographies Ser.). Date not set. text 120.00 (0-8240-8514-0) Garland.
Owen, V. The Adventures of a Quiet Soul: A Scrapbook of Memories. limited ed. LC 96-92449. (Illus.). 168p. (Orig.). 1996. pap. 24.95 (0-9653334-0-X) V Owen.
***Owen Vandersluis, Sarah.** The State & Identity Construction in International Relations. LC 99-54959. (Millennium Ser.). 2000. text 69.95 (0-312-23118-0) St Martin.
***Owen, Vi.** So You Want to Write a Baseball Book: A Manual for Rookie Writers. limited ed. (Illus.). 72p. 1999. pap. 9.95 (0-9653334-1-8) V Owen.
Owen, Virginia L. & Tinkler, Sarah. Economics: Instructor's Resource Manual. 1996. teacher ed., ring bd. write for info. (1-57259-046-7); teacher ed., ring bd. write for info. (1-57259-047-5) Worth.
Owen, W. G., jt. ed. see Machovich, R.
Owen, W. J., ed. see Wordsworth, William.
Owen, W. J., ed. see Wordsworth, William & Coleridge, Samuel Taylor.
Owen, W. M. Camp & Battle with Washington Artillery. 38.50 (0-8488-1120-8) Amereon Ltd.
Owen, W. R. & Goodman, Lizbeth, eds. Shakespeare, Aphra Behn, & the Canon. LC 96-16360. (Approaching Literature Ser.: Bk. 3). (Illus.). 352p. (C). 1996. 90.00 (0-415-13575-3); pap. 22.99 (0-415-13576-1) Routledge.
Owen, W. S., ed. see Cohen, Morris.
Owen, Wanda. Forever My Fancy. 448p. 1997. mass mkt. 5.50 (0-8217-5705-9, Zebra Kensgtn) Kensgtn Pub Corp.
— Golden Gypsy. (Orig.). 1983. mass mkt. 3.75 (0-8217-1188-1, Zebra Kensgtn) Kensgtn Pub Corp.
— Reckless Ecstasy. mass mkt. 3.95 (0-317-43144-7, Zebra Kensgtn) Kensgtn Pub Corp.
— Sea Princess. 400p. 1995. mass mkt. 4.99 (0-8217-5084-4, Zebra Kensgtn) Kensgtn Pub Corp.
— Sweet Seduction. 448p. 1996. mass mkt. 4.99 (0-8217-5402-5, Zebra Kensgtn) Kensgtn Pub Corp.
Owen, Warwick J. Wordsworth As Critic. LC 73-398699. 254p. reprint ed. pap. 78.80 (0-8357-8381-2, 203400900088) Bks Demand.
***Owen, Weldon & Kager, Pac.** Birds. (Pathfinder Ser.). (Illus.). 64p. (J). (gr. 3-9). 2000. write for info. (1-57584-376-5, RDYF) Rdrs Digest.
Owen, Wendy. Cat Lover & Other Stories. 128p. 1976. 24.00 (0-7206-0104-5, Pub. by P Owen Ltd) Dufour.
Owen, Wilfred. Collected Poems. rev. ed. Day Lewis, Cecil, ed. LC 64-10290. 1965. pap. 9.95 (0-8112-0132-5, NDP210, Pub. by New Directions) Norton.
— Disabled & Other Poems. 1995. pap. 12.95 (1-900022-01-X, Pub. by Hrthstone Pubns) Intl Spec Bk.
— Disabled & Other Poems. limited ed. 44p. 1995. text 24.95 (1-900022-00-1, Pub. by Hrthstone Pubns) Intl Spec Bk.
— The Metropolitan Transportation Problem. rev. ed. LC 66-21151. 280p. reprint ed. pap. 86.80 (0-608-12463-X, 202539800043) Bks Demand.
— Strategy for Mobility. LC 78-17067. 249p. 1978. reprint ed. lib. bdg. 65.00 (0-313-20571-X, OWSM, Greenwood Pr) Greenwood.
— Transportation & World Development. LC 87-4154. (Illus.). 174p. reprint ed. pap. 54.00 (0-608-06179-4, 206651100008) Bks Demand.
— Transportation for Cities: The Role of Federal Policy. LC 75-44508. 70p. 1976. pap. 8.95 (0-8157-6773-0) Brookings.
Owen, Wilfred, jt. auth. see Dearing, Charles L.
Owen, Wilfred, ed. see Carpenter, Allan.
Owen, William. Diary: From November 10, 1824 to April 20, 1825. (American Biography Ser.). 134p. 1991. reprint ed. lib. bdg. 59.00 (0-7812-8304-3) Rprt Serv.
— Diary of William Owen from Nov. 10, 1824 to April 20, 1825. Hiatt, Joel W., ed. LC 72-77057. xi, 134p. 1973. reprint ed. lib. bdg. 29.50 (0-678-00918-X) Kelley.
— Magazine Design. 272p. (C). 1991. text. write for info. (0-697-14791-6) Brown & Benchmark.
— Magazine Design LC 91-199134. 240p. 1991. write for info. (1-85669-003-2) L King Pubng.
Owen, William, jt. auth. see Brown, Tom, Jr.
Owen, William B., jt. auth. see Goodspeed, Edgar J.
Owen, William C. Economics of Herbert Spencer. 1977. lib. bdg. 59.95 (0-8490-1747-5) Gordon Pr.
— Selected Writings of William C. Owen. 1977. lib. bdg. 69.95 (0-8490-2591-5) Gordon Pr.
Owen, William M. Autopsy of a Merger: Trans Union: The Deal That Rocked the Corporate World, Vol. 1. LC 83-91307. 341p. 1986. 19.95 (0-9613247-0-8) W M Owen.
— In Camp & Battle with the Washington Artillery of New Orleans. LC 98-55142. (Illus.). 512p. 1999. pap. 22.95 (0-8071-2385-4) La State U Pr.
— In Camp & Battle with the Washingtons Artillery of New Orleans. 467p. 1983. reprint ed. 32.50 (0-942211-86-3) Olde Soldier Bks.
Owen, William P., jt. auth. see Culp, Wesner, Clup, Inc.
Owens. Canticle of Brother Sun. (J). 1996. 15.00 (0-671-90016-1) S&S Bks Yung.
— The Developing Child. (Psychology Ser.). 2000. pap. 52.00 (0-534-36618-X) Brooks-Cole.
— Examaster Nuclear Medicine Image. 1998. write for info. (0-7216-6153-X, W B Saunders Co) Harcrt Hlth Sci Grp.
— Finance Marketing Ins. 1997. student ed. 18.00 (0-02-390285-X) P-H.
— Nuclear Medicine Imaging. 1999. text. write for info. (0-7216-6089-4, W B Saunders Co) Harcrt Hlth Sci Grp.
— Psychological Aspects of Terminal Care. pap. 30.00 (0-471-96621-5) Wiley.
— The World of the Child. (C). 1993. pap. text, student ed. 21.00 (0-675-21337-1, Merrill Coll) P-H.

Owens, Adrian. Introductory Technology: A Resource Book for Teachers. (Illus.). 142p. 1990. pap. 19.50 (1-85339-064-X, Pub. by Intermed Tech) Stylus Pub VA.
Owens, Amanda, ed. see Johnston, Paul.
Owens, Amanda, ed. see Tullock, Gordon.
Owens, Amanda J., jt. auth. see Rubin, Haya R.
Owens, Ann-Maureen & Yealland, Jane. Forts of Canada. (Illus.). 64p. (J). 1996. 19.90 (1-55074-316-3); pap. 14.99 (1-55074-271-X) Kids Can Pr.
Owens, Ann-Maureen, et al. Canada's Maple Leaf: The Story of Our Flag. (J). 14.95 (1-55074-459-3) Kids Can Pr.
— Canada's Maple Leaf: The Story of our Flag. (J). 1999. pap. 9.95 (1-55074-516-6) Kids Can Pr.
Owens, Anthony. Assessment in Specific Circumstances. (C). 1991. pap. 45.00 (0-7300-1336-7, ECT338, Pub. by Deakin Univ) St Mut.
Owens, April, ed. see Owens, Vivian.
Owens, April U., ed. see Owens, Vivian W.
Owens, B. B. Batteries for Implantable Biomedical Devices. LC 86-582. (Illus.). 380p. (C). 1986. text 107.00 (0-306-42148-8, Kluwer Plenum) Kluwer Academic.
***Owens, Barcley.** Cormac McCarthy's Western Novels. LC 00-8080. 155p. 2000. 35.00 (0-8165-1927-7) U of Ariz Pr.
— Cormac McCarthy's Western Novels. LC 00-8080. 2000. pap. write for info. (0-8165-1928-5) U of Ariz Pr.
***Owens, Beth.** Contemporary Fashion Dolls: The Next Generation. (Illus.). 2000. pap. 24.95 (0-87588-576-4) Hobby Hse.
Owens, Bill. How to Build a Small Brewery: Draught Beer in Ten Days. (Illus.). 50p. (Orig.). 1994. pap. 10.95 (0-9619072-7-4) G W Kent.
— The Magnetic Music Ministry: Ten Productive Goals. Miller, Herb, ed. (Effective Church Ser.). 144p. (Orig.). 1996. pap. 12.95 (0-687-00731-3) Abingdon.
***Owens, Bill, photos by.** Suburbia. rev. ed. LC 99-63905. (Illus.). 120p. 1999. 29.95 (1-881270-40-8) FotoFolio.
Owens, Bobby. The Command Sergeant Major's Interventions. LC 93-73657. (Illus.). 1995. 40.00 (1-884308-07-4); pap. text 25.95 (1-884308-08-2) Enlisted Ldrship.
— The Diamond. LC 93-90791. 217p. 1993. 34.00 (1-884308-01-5); pap. text 10.95 (1-884308-02-3) Enlisted Ldrship.
— The Military Years. LC 93-90793. 80p. 1994. 25.00 (1-884308-09-0); pap. text 15.00 (1-884308-10-4) Enlisted Ldrship.
— Platoon Sergeant. LC 93-90792. (Illus.). 224p. 1994. 25.00 (1-884308-03-1); pap. text 14.95 (1-884308-04-X) Enlisted Ldrship.
— Squad Leader. LC 93-93623. 147p. 1993. pap. text 25.00 (1-884308-05-8); pap. text 14.95 (1-884308-06-6) Enlisted Ldrship.
— The Star & the Wreath. 227p. (Orig.). 1993. 33.95 (1-884308-00-7) Enlisted Ldrship.
Owens, Bobby & Wright, David B. First Sergeant Spouse's Notes. (Illus.). (Orig.). 1995. pap. text 8.95 (1-884308-27-9) Enlisted Ldrship.
— First Sergeant Spouse's Notes. (Illus.). (Orig.). 1995. 16.95 (1-884308-26-0) Enlisted Ldrship.
Owens, Boone B., ed. see Symposium on Power Sources for Biomedical Implanta.
Owens, Caleb. Coral Reefs. LC 97-30407. (Biomes of Nature Ser.). (Illus.). 32p. (J). (gr. 2-6). 1998. lib. bdg. 22.79 (1-56766-467-9) Childs World.
— Deforestation. LC 97-31353. (Illus.). 32p. (J). 1998. lib. bdg. 22.79 (1-56766-507-1) Childs World.
— Pluto. LC 97-31356. Date not set. write for info. (1-56766-512-8) Childs World.
Owens, Carole. The Berkshire Cottages: A Vanishing Era. (Illus.). 240p. (Orig.). 1996. reprint ed. pap. 32.50 (0-918343-00-3) Cottage Pr Inc.
— The Lost Days of Agatha Christie. 1996. pap. 12.95 (0-918343-03-8) Cottage Pr Inc.
Owens, Carole, ed. see Kerness, Elton J.
Owens, Carolyn. God Loves My Family. (J). (ps-2). 1995. wbk. ed. 3.99 (0-570-04784-6, 56-1804) Concordia.
— My Christmas Activity Book. 32p. 1995. pap. text 3.99 (0-570-04785-4, 56-1805) Concordia.
— What Will You Be? (Illus.). 32p. (J). (ps-2). 1996. 3.99 (0-570-04795-1, 56-1815) Concordia.
Owens, Carolyn, jt. auth. see Roggow, Linda.
***Owens, Carrie.** Working Dogs. LC 99-40940. (Illus.). 144p. 1999. 25.00 (0-7615-1978-5) Prima Pub.
Owens-Celli, Morgyn G. The Book of Wheat Weaving & Straw Craft: From Simple Plaits to Exquisite Designs. Rich, Chris, ed. LC 93-35514. (Illus.). 144p. 1997. 24.95 (1-887374-20-5) Lark Books.
— The Book of Wheat Weaving & Straw Craft: From Simple Plaits to Exquisite Designs. Rich, Chris, ed. LC 96-35514. (Illus.). 144p. 1998. pap. 18.95 (1-57990-078-X) Lark Books.
Owens, Claire M. The Unpredictable Adventure: A Comedy of Women's Independence. (Utopianism & Communitarianism Ser.). (Illus.). 511p. 1992. reprint ed. pap. 17.95 (0-8156-2583-9) Syracuse U Pr.
Owens, Claire M. Zen & the Lady: Memoirs--Personal & Transpersonal in a World in Transition LC 79-50288. v, 306 p. 1979. write for info. (0-88238-996-3) Law Arts.
Owens, Coilin D. & Radner, Joan N., eds. Irish Drama, 1900-1980. LC 89-727. 754p. 1989. pap. 24.95 (0-8132-0705-3) Cath U Pr.
Owens, Colodia. Managed Care Organizations: Practical Implications for Medical Practices & other Providers. 185p. 1996. pap. text 44.95 (1-57066-094-8) Practice Mgmt Info.
Owens, Craig. Beyond Recognition: Representation, Power, & Culture. 1992. 45.00 (0-520-07739-3, Pub. by U CA Pr) Cal Prin Full Svc.

— Beyond Recognition: Representation, Power, & Culture. LC 92-5314. 1994. pap. 19.95 (0-520-07740-7, Pub. by U CA Pr) Cal Prin Full Svc.
Owens, D. Alfred & Wagner, Mark, eds. Progress in Modern Psychology: The Legacy of American Functionalism. LC 92-15990. 352p. 1992. 69.50 (0-275-93055-6, C3055, Praeger Pubs) Greenwood.
Owens, D. G. A Guide to the Extrapyramidal Side Effects of Antipsychotic Drugs. LC 98-7142. (Illus.). 300p. (C). 1999. pap. text 49.95 (0-521-63353-2) Cambridge U Pr.
Owens, D. H., jt. auth. see Edwards, J. B.
Owens, D. H., jt. auth. see Rogers, E. T.
Owens, D. H., jt. ed. see Nichols, N. K.
Owens, D. R. Human Insulin. 1986. text 206.50 (0-85200-951-8) Kluwer Academic.
Owens, Dan & Platt, John. Kids Study Groups: From Classroom Meetings to Peer Counseling. LC 81-67380. 112p. (Orig.). (C). 1981. pap. text 6.00 (0-918560-26-8) Adler Sch Prof Psy.
***Owens, Daniel.** In God We Trust, but Only As a Last Resort. 160p. 2000. pap. 9.99 (1-58134-213-6) Crossway Bks.
Owens, Daniel. Sharing Christ When You Feel You Can't: Making It Easier to Tell Your Friends & Family about Your Faith in Christ. LC 96-52236. 192p. 1997. pap. 10.99 (0-89107-935-1) Crossway Bks.
Owens, David. Causes & Coincidences. (Studies in Philosophy). (Illus.). 200p. (C). 1992. text 52.95 (0-521-41650-7) Cambridge U Pr.
***Owens, David.** Reason Without Freedom: The Problem of Epistemic Normativity. LC 99-87518. (International Library of Philosophy). 2000. pap. write for info. (0-415-22389-X) Routledge.
Owens, David. A Tribute to Toshiro Mifune. (Illus.). 32p. 1984. pap. 3.50 (0-317-65759-3) Japan Soc.
Owens, David W. Conflicts of Interest in Land Use Management Decisions. 105p. (Orig.). (C). 1990. pap. text 10.00 (1-56011-175-5) Institute Government.
— The Gods of Man: A Small Dictionary of Pagan Gods & Godesses. 60p. 1994. pap. 5.00 (1-57353-103-0) Eschaton Prods.
— The Gods of Man: A Small Dictionary of Pagan Gods & Godesses. 2nd ed. 96p. 1999. pap. 7.50 (1-57353-503-6) Eschaton Prods.
— Introduction to Zoning. 120p. (Orig.). (C). 1995. pap. text 15.00 (1-56011-275-1, 95.18) Institute Government.
— Legislative Zoning Decisions: Legal Aspects. 2nd ed. LC 99-229827. (C). 1999. text 42.00 (1-56011-341-3); pap. text 36.00 (1-56011-336-7) Institute Government.
— Public Rights in Shoreline Recreation Areas: A Selectively Annotated Bibliography, No. 894. 1975. 5.00 (0-686-20369-0, Sage Prdcls Pr) Sage.
— Regulating Sexually Oriented Businesses. LC 97-128141. (Special Ser.: Vol. 15). 15p. (Orig.). 1997. pap. text 15.00 (1-56011-304-9) Institute Government.
Owens, David W., compiled by. Planning Legislation in North Carolina. 18th ed. 386p. (C). 1996. pap. text 30.00 (1-56011-283-2) Institute Government.
***Owens, David W., ed.** North Carolina Legislation 1999: A Summary of Legislation in the 1999 General Assembly. (C). 1999. pap. 30.00 (1-56011-361-8) Institute Government.
— North Carolina Legislation, 2000: A Summary of Legislation in the 2000 General Assembly of Interest to North Carolina Public Officials. (C). 2000. pap. 25.00 (1-56011-381-2) Institute Government.
***Owens, David W., ed.** Hume: General Philosophy. LC 99-43341. (International Library of Critical Essays in the History of Philosophy). 510p. 2000. text 166.95 (1-84014-711-3, Pub. by Ashgate Pub) Ashgate Pub Co.
Owens, Dean L. Practical Principles of Ion-Exchange Water Treatment. 2nd rev. ed. LC 85-51869. 210p. 1995. 55.00 (0-927188-00-7) Tall Oaks Pub.
Owens, DeDe & Bunker, Linda. Coaching Golf Effectively: The American Coaching Effectiveness Program, Leader Level 1 Golf Book. LC 88-13843. (Illus.). 194p. 1989. reprint ed. pap. 60.20 (0-608-07055-6, 206726100009) Bks Demand.
Owens, DeDe & Bunker, Linda K. Advanced Golf: Steps to Success. LC 92-5940. (Steps to Success Activity Ser.). (Illus.). 176p. 1992. pap. 15.95 (0-88011-464-9, POWE0464) Human Kinetics.
— Golf: Steps to Success. 2nd ed. LC 95-1518. (Steps to Success Activity Ser.). (Illus.). 168p. 1995. pap. 15.95 (0-87322-578-3, POWE0578) Human Kinetics.
Owens, DeDe, jt. auth. see Kirchenbaum, Daniels.
Owens, Delia. Eye of the Elephant: An Epic Adventure in the African Wilderness. 320p. 1993. pap. 14.00 (0-395-68090-5) HM.
Owens, Delia, jt. auth. see Owens, Mark.
Owens, Derek. Resisting Writings (And the Boundaries of Composition) LC 93-18752. (SMU Studies in Composition & Rhetoric). 212p. 1994. text 24.95 (0-87074-343-0) SMU Press.
Owens, Derrick, jt. auth. see Owens, Thomas.
***Owens, DeWayne.** How to Get Rich on Purpose. LC 00-103490. 215p. 2000. pap. 15.99 (0-9700798-0-X, 00-0861-1000) N Harmony.
Owens, Diana, jt. auth. see Lee, William.
Owens, Doreen. Jardee: The Mill That Cheated Time. pap. 19.95 (1-875560-31-9, Pub. by Staples) Intl Spec Bk.
***Owens, Dorothy M.** Hospitality to Strangers: Empathy in the Physician-Patient Relationship. LC 99-56413. (American Academy of Religion Academy Ser.). 163p. 1999. pap. 24.95 (0-7885-0603-X, 012000) OUP.
Owens, Dorothy V. Command Sergeant Major's Spouse's Notes. (Illus.). 190p. (Orig.). 1995. pap. text 6.95 (1-884308-25-2) Enlisted Ldrship.
— Command Sergeant Major's Spouse's Notes. (Illus.). 190p. (Orig.). 1995. 15.95 (1-884308-24-4) Enlisted Ldrship.

— D. V. O. Models. LC 93-90794. (Illus.). 100p. 1993. write for info. (1-884308-11-2); pap. write for info. (1-884308-12-0) Enlisted Ldrship.
Owens, E. J. The City in the Greek & Roman World. (Illus.). 224p. (C). 1992. pap. 25.99 (0-415-08224-2, A7630) Routledge.
Owens, Edgar. The Future of Freedom in the Developing World: Economic Development As Political Reform. LC 86-25568. 1987. 32.00 (0-08-034697-9, Pergamon Pr); pap. 17.95 (0-08-034696-0, Pergamon Pr) Elsevier.
Owens, Elisabeth A. Bibliography on Taxation of Foreign Operations & Foreigners. LC 68-23792. 112p. (Orig.). 1968. pap. 5.00 (0-915506-09-2) Harvard Law Intl Tax.
Owens, Elisabeth A. & Ball, Gerald T. Indirect Credit: A Study of Various Foreign Tax Credits Granted to Domestic Shareholders Under U. S. Income Tax Law, Vol. 2. LC 75-14037. (Illus.). 404p. 1979. 50.00 (0-915506-18-1) Harvard Law Intl Tax.
Owens, Elisabeth A. & Hovemeyer, Gretchen A. Bibliography on Taxation of Foreign Operations & Foreigners, 1968-1975. LC 76-14456. 122p. (Orig.). 1976. pap. 7.50 (0-915506-21-1) Harvard Law Intl Tax.
— Bibliography on Taxation of Foreign Operations & Foreigners, 1976-1982. LC 83-18402. 206p. (Orig.). 1983. pap. text 12.50 (0-915506-27-0) Harvard Law Intl Tax.
***Owens, Elizabeth.** Woman Celebrating Life: A Guide to Growth & Transformation. 2000. pap. write for info. (1-56718-508-8) Llewellyn Pubns.
Owens, Elmer & Kessler, Dorcas K. Cochlear Implants in Young Deaf Children. LC 90-21332. (Orig.). write for info. (0-89079-395-6) PRO-ED.
Owens, Everett. Out of My League. (Love Stories Super Edition Ser.). 208p. (YA). (gr. 7-12). 1998. mass mkt. 4.50 (0-553-48594-6) BDD Bks Young Read.
Owens, Everett. X Files: Control, No. 7. (X Files Young Adult Ser.: No. 7). 144p. (YA). (gr. 12 up). 1997. pap. 4.50 (0-06-447177-2, HarpTrophy) HarpC Child Bks.
— X Files: Howlers, No. 11. (X Files Ser.: Vol. 11). 128p. (J). (gr. 12 up). 1999. pap. 4.50 (0-06-447185-3, HarpEntertain) Morrow Avon.
— X Files: Regeneration, No. 14. (X-Files Ser.: Vol. 14). 144p. (J). (gr. 7 up). 1999. 13.95 (0-06-447190-X) HarpC Child Bks.
— X Files: Regeneration, Vol. 14. 128p. (YA). 2000. mass mkt. 4.50 (0-06-106619-2) Morrow Avon.
Owens, F. J. & Poole, C. P., Jr. Electromagnetic Absorption in the Copper Oxide Superconductors. LC 98-48669. (Selected Topics in Superconductivity Ser.). (Illus.). 212p. (C). 1999. 82.50 (0-306-45948-5, Plenum Trade) Perseus Pubng.
Owens, F. J. & Poole, C. P. The New Superconductors. LC 96-43014. (Selected Topics in Superconductivity Ser.). (Illus.). 215p. (C). 1996. text 47.00 (0-306-45453-X, Kluwer Plenum) Kluwer Academic.
Owens, Fed, et al. Careers for Chemists: A World Outside the Lab. LC 96-44772. 1996. pap. write for info. (0-8412-3479-5) Am Chemical.
Owens, Gail. The Down & Up Fall. LC 96-5388. 128p. (J). (gr. 3-7). 1996. 15.00 (0-688-14568-X, Wm Morrow) Morrow Avon.
Owens, Gareth A. Kritika Daidalika: Evidence for the Minoan Language, Selected Essays in Memory of James Hooker on the Archaeology, Epigraphy & Philology of Minoan & Mycenaean Crete. (Illus.). 304p. 1997. pap. 82.00 (90-256-1096-X, Pub. by AM Hakkert) BookLink Distributors.
Owens, Garland C., jt. auth. see Cashin, James A.
Owens, Gene, ed. see Elliott, Ryan.
Owens, Genevieve S., ed. Electronic Resources: Implications for Collection Management. LC 96-9554. (Collection Management Ser.: Vol. 21, No. 1). 104p. (C). 1996. 24.95 (1-56024-824-6) Haworth Pr.
Owens, Georgette. International Women Artists. LC 97-225422. (Illus.). 192p. (Orig.) 1997. pap. text. write for info. (0-9658412-0-0) Alliance Women.
Owens, Graham W. & Cheal, Brian. Structural Steelwork Connections. (Illus.). 330p. 1989. 170.00 (0-408-01214-5) Buttrwrth-Heinemann.
Owens, Greg & Staples, David. The Third Suspect: The Shocking True Story of a Bitter Labor Struggle & the Cold-Blooded Murder of Nine Yellowknife Miners. LC 96-142669. 480p. 1995. pap. 17.95 (0-88995-131-4, Pub. by Red Deer) Genl Dist Srvs.
Owens, Guinn, jt. auth. see Blumberg, Stanley.
Owens, Gwendolyn, jt. auth. see Milroy, Elizabeth.
Owens, Gwinn, ed. see Gabler, James M.
Owens, I. F., ed. Recent Research in Australasian Geomorphology. (Zeitschrift fuer Geomorphologie - Annals of Geomorphology Ser.: Supplementband 105). (Illus.). iv, 164p. 1996. pap. 70.00 (3-443-21105-4, Pub. by Gebruder Borntraeger) Balogh.
Owens, Ian, et al. Information & Business Performance: A Study of Information Systems & Services in High Performing Companies. LC 96-213177. 206p. 1996. 60.00 (1-85739-108-X) Bowker-Saur.
Owens, Irene, ed. Acquisitions & Collection Development in the Humanities. LC 97-36871. (Acquisitions Librarian Monograph Ser.: Vol. 9, Nos. 17 & 19). 194p. 1997. 34.95 (0-7890-0368-6) Haworth Pr.
Owens, J., et al. The New Consumer Credit Code. LC 94-238078. 260p. 1994. pap. write for info. (0-409-31089-1, MICHIE) LEXIS Pub.
Owens, J. E. Revolutionary Soul. 51p. 1994. pap. text 11.95 (0-9642191-0-7) Promiseland.
Owens, J. F., jt. ed. see Duke, D. W.
Owens, J. J., jt. auth. see Yates, Kyle M.
Owens, Jack A. & Tennenhouse, Dan J. Dental Risk Prevention: Communicating & Record Keeping in Dental Practice. 171p. 1990. pap. 75.00 (1-930548-02-8) Tennenhouse Prof Pubns.

O

An Asterisk (*) at the beginning of an entry indicates that the title is appearing for the first time.

Owens, James. Loan of the Quick: Poems. 40p. 1998. pap. 7.00 (*1-885912-18-8*) Sows Ear Pr.

Owens, James, ed. see Briscoe, Jack, Jr.

*Owens, Janette. A Swan Song: A Intimate Collection of Poems & Short Stories. Bentley, Nicole, ed. 103p. 2000. pap. 12.00 (*0-9677312-0-8*) Oneswan.

Owens, Janis. My Brother Michael. LC 96-51172. 304p. 1997. 18.95 (*1-56164-124-3*) Pineapple Pr.

— Myra Sims. LC 98-24079. 480p. 1999. 21.95 (*1-56164-177-4*) Pineapple Pr.

Owens, Jeff. The One Thing Money Can't Buy - The One Thing You Can't Afford to Be Without! Character. Date not set. write for info. (*0-9649393-0-4*) Owens Pubns.

Owens, Jeffery A. Practical Counseling Principles for the Christian: Biblical Counseling & How to Give It. Stubbelfield, Linda, ed. LC 97-95058. 384p. 1998. pap. 13.95 (*0-9649393-1-2*) Owens Publns.

*Owens, Jeffrey A. The Ant That Tunrned His Burden into a Bridge. 44p. 1999. pap. 5.00 (*0-9649393-2-0*) Owens Publns.

Owens, Jerry M. & Biery, Darryl N. Radiographic Interpretation for the Small Animal Clinician. 2nd ed. LC 98-41669. (Illus.). 308p. 1998. 49.95 (*0-683-06684-6*) Lppncott W & W.

Owens, Jesse, ed. Francesco Portinaro: Il Quarto Libro de Madrigali a Cinque Voci (Venice, 1560) LC 91-760708. (Sixteenth-Century Madrigal Ser.: Vol. 24). 320p. 1992. text 99.00 (*0-8240-5524-1*) Garland.

Owens, Jessie A. Claudio Merulo Il Primo Libro de Madrigali a Cinque Voci (Venice, 1566) LC 93-33356. (Sixteenth-Century Madrigal Ser.: Vol. 18). 232p. 1994. text 94.00 (*0-8240-5518-7*) Garland.

— Francesco Orso: Il Primo Libro de' Madrigali...Con Due Madrigali Cromatici Nel Fine (Venice, 1567) (Sixteenth-Century Madrigal Ser.: Vol. 22). 272p. 1996. text 105.00 (*0-8240-5522-5*) Garland.

— Giulio Fiesco: Il Primo Libro di Madrigali a Quattro Voci (Venice, 1554) (Sixteenth-Century Madrigal Ser.: Vol. 12). 152p. 1996. text 79.00 (*0-8240-5512-8*) Garland.

— Hoste da Reggio II Se. LC 88-752049. (Italian Madrigal Sixteenth Century Ser.: Vol. 9). 147p. 1989. text 30.00 (*0-8240-5509-8*) Garland.

— Music in Renaissance Cities & Courts: Studies in Honor of Lewis Lockwood. Cummings, Anthony, ed. LC 96-41999. (Detroit Monographs in Musicology: No. 18). 533p. 1996. 65.00 (*0-89990-102-6*) Harmonie Park Pr.

— Philippe Verdelot: Madrigals for Four & Five Voices, Vol. 2. LC 88-32982. (Italian Madrigal Sixteenth Century Ser.: Vol. 29). 1989. text 30.00 (*0-8240-5531-4*) Garland.

— Philippe Verdelot: Madrigals for Four & Five Voices, Vol. 3. LC 88-32982. (Italian Madrigal Sixteenth Century Ser.: Vol. 30). 148p. 1989. text 30.00 (*0-8240-5532-2*) Garland.

Owens, Jessie A., ed. Alfonso Dalla Viola: Primo Libro Di Madrigali (4) (Ferrara, 1539) LC 90-750439. (Sixteenth-Century Madrigal Ser.: Vol. 5). 275p. 1990. text 30.00 (*0-8240-5505-5*) Garland.

— Claudio Merulo: Il Secondo Libro de Madrigali a Cinque Voci (Venice, 1604) LC 93-49757. (Sixteenth-Century Madrigal Ser.: Vol. 19). 208p. 1994. text 83.00 (*0-8240-5519-5*) Garland.

— Claudio Veggio: Madrigali a Guattro Voci (Venice, 1540) LC 92-772058. (Sixteenth-Century Madrigal Ser.: Vol. 4). (Illus.). 216p. 1992. text 83.00 (*0-8240-5504-7*) Garland.

— Francesco Dalla Viola (d. 1568), Vol. 7. LC 88-751231. (Italian Madrigal in the Sixteenth Century Ser.). 219p. 1988. text 30.00 (*0-8240-5507-1*) Garland.

— Francesco Manara: Il Primo Libro di Madrigali a Quattro Voci (Venice, 1555) LC 94-295. (Sixteenth-Century Madrigal Ser.: Vol. 17). (Illus.). 176p. 1994. text 83.00 (*0-8240-5517-9*) Garland.

— Giachet de Berchem: Madrigali a Cinque Voci. . . Libro Primo (Venice, 1546) LC 93-9142. (Sixteenth-Century Madrigal Ser.: Vol. 1). 280p. 1993. text 99.00 (*0-8240-5501-2*) Garland.

— Giacomo Fogliano: Madrigali a Cinque Voci il Primo Libro (Padua, 1547) LC 94-294. (Sixteenth-Century Madrigal Ser.: Vol. 13). 268p. 1994. text 105.00 (*0-8240-5513-6*) Garland.

— Hoste Da Regio Primo. LC 87-733554. (Italian Madrigal in the Sixteenth Century Ser.: Vol. 8). 188p. 1988. text 30.00 (*0-8240-5508-X*) Garland.

— Jan Nasco: Il Primo Libro de Madrigali a Quatro Voci (Venice, 1554) LC 91-755866. (Sixteenth-Century Madrigal Ser.: Vol. 20). 176p. 1992. text 83.00 (*0-8240-5520-9*) Garland.

— Jan Nasco: Il Secondo Libro d'I Madrigali a Cinque Voci (Venice, 1557) LC 92-755826. (Sixteenth-Century Madrigal Ser.: Vol. 21). 272p. 1992. text 94.00 (*0-8240-5521-7*) Garland.

— Marc'Antonio Ingegneri: Il Secondo Libro de Madrigali a Quattro Voci (Venice, 1579) LC 93-18257. (Sixteenth-Century Madrigal Ser.: Vol. 16). 104p. 1993. text 61.00 (*0-8240-5516-0*) Garland.

— Perissone Cambio. LC 90-751362. (Sixteenth-Century Madrigal Ser.: Vol. 2). 232p. 1990. reprint ed. text 30.00 (*0-8240-5502-0*) Garland.

— Philippe Verdelot Vol. 1: Madrigals for Four & Five Voices. LC 88-32982. (16th Century Madrigal Ser.: Vol. 28). 152p. 1989. text 30.00 (*0-8240-5530-6*) Garland.

— Vincenzo Ruffo (c. 1508-1587) Madrigali a sei, sette e otto voci--Venice: Girolamo Scotto, 1554, Vol. 26. (Italian Madrigal in the Sixteenth Century Ser.). 1988. text 30.00 (*0-8240-5528-4*) Garland.

— Vincenzo Ruffo (c. 1508-1587) Primo Libro di madrigali a cinque voci--Venice: Girolamo Scotto 1533, Vol. 25. (Italian Madrigal in the Sixteenth Century Ser.). 1989. text 30.00 (*0-8240-5527-6*) Garland.

Owens, Jessie A. & Nagaoka, Megumi, eds. Guglielmo Gonzaga: Madrigali a Cinque Voci (Venice, 1583) LC 95-700102. (Sixteenth-Century Madrigal Ser.: Vol. 14). (Illus.). 320p. 1995. text 105.00 (*0-8240-5514-4*) Garland.

Owens, Jessie A., jt. auth. see Archetto, Macia.

Owens, Jessie A., ed. see Ferrabosco, Domenico M.

Owens, Jessie A., ed. see Moll, Kevin N.

Owens, Jessie A., ed. see Pietro, Taglia.

Owens, Jessie Ann. Composers at Work: The Craft of Musical Composition 1450-1600. (Illus.). 368p. 1998. pap. 24.95 (*0-19-512904-0*) OUP.

Owens, Joanne. The Official Sunday School Teacher's Handbook. LC 87-43102. (Illus.). 240p. 1987. pap., teacher ed. 12.95 (*0-916260-42-9*, B152) Meriwether Pub.

Owens, John, tr. see Calvin, John.

Owens, John E., jt. auth. see Foley, Michael.

Owens, John G., jt. auth. see Fewkes, Jesse W.

*Owens, John J. 255 ATE: Recipes from the Staff of Barnes & Noble 2558. 28p. 1999. pap. 5.00 (*1-884416-30-6*) A Press.

*Owens, Jonathan. Arabic As a Minority Language. LC 99-54417. (Contributions to the Sociology of Language Ser.). 1999. write for info. (*3-11-016578-3*) De Gruyter.

Owens, Jonathan. Early Arabic Grammatical Theory: Heterogeneity & Standardization. LC 90-57. (Studies in the History of the Language Sciences: Vol. 53). xvi, 294p. 1990. 65.00 (*90-272-4538-X*) J Benjamins Pubng Co.

— The Foundations of Grammar: An Introduction to Medieval Arabic Grammatical Theory. LC 87-897. (Studies in the History of the Language Sciences: No. 45). xii, 371p. (C). 1988. 71.00 (*90-272-4528-2*) J Benjamins Pubng Co.

— Neighborhood & Ancestry: Variation in the Spoken Arabic of Maiduguri, Nigeria. LC 98-29002. (Impact: Studies in Language & Society: Vol. 4). xiv, 390p. 1998. 120.00 (*1-55619-853-1*) J Benjamins Pubng Co.

Owens, Joseph. Aristotle: The Collected Papers of Joseph Owens. Catan, John R., ed. LC 81-7602. 264p. (C). 1981. text 24.50 (*0-87395-534-X*) State U NY Pr.

— Cognition: An Epistemological Inquiry. LC 92-70254. (C). 1992. text 34.50 (*0-268-00792-6*); pap. text 17.50 (*0-268-00791-8*) U of Notre Dame Pr.

— An Elementary Christian Metaphysics. LC 84-23888. 399p. (C). 1985. reprint ed. pap. text 15.00 (*0-268-00916-3*) U of Notre Dame Pr.

— An Interpretation of Existence. LC 84-23805. 153p. 1987. pap. 7.95 (*0-685-31941-5*) Ctr Thomistic.

— An Interpretation of Existence. LC 84-23805. 162p. (C). 1987. reprint ed. pap. text 9.50 (*0-268-01157-5*) U of Notre Dame Pr.

— Saint Thomas Aquinas on the Existence of God: The Collected Papers of Joseph Owens. Catan, John R., ed. LC 79-13885. 291p. 1980. text 21.50 (*0-87395-401-7*) State U NY Pr.

— Towards a Christian Philosophy. LC 96-33318. (Studies in Philosophy & the History of Philosophy). (Illus.). 332p. 1990. 44.95 (*0-8132-0708-8*) Cath U Pr.

Owens, Joseph, jt. auth. see Anderson, C. Anthony.

Owens, Joseph C. St. Thomas & the Future of Metaphysics. LC 57-7374. (Aquinas Lectures). 1957. 15.00 (*0-87462-122-4*) Marquette.

Owens, Judith. Divine Passage: Confessions of a Menopausal Woman. rev. ed. 115p. 1999. per. 12.99 (*0-9672444-0-4*) W E L L Pubns.

— Happy at Work: How to Enjoy Your Job. 27p. 1998. pap. 6.99 (*0-9672444-1-2*) W E L L Pubns.

*Owens, Judith. Your Love: Songs of the Beloved. large type ed. 42p. 1999. pap. 9.99 (*0-9672444-3-9*) W E L L Pubns.

*Owens, June. The Mask of Agamemnon: Poems by June Owens. 24p. 1999. pap. 7.00 (*0-916897-40-0*) Andrew Mtn Pr.

Owens, June. Tree Line. LC 98-67224. 96p. 1998. pap. 14.95 (*1-892668-05-X*) Prospect Pr.

Owens, Karen B. Raising Your Child's Inner Self-Esteem: The Authoritative Guide from Infancy Through the Teen Years. (Illus.). 372p. (C). 1995. 24.95 (*0-306-45084-4*, Plenum Trade) Perseus Pubng.

— The World of the Child. 2nd ed. LC 92-9837. 752p. (C). 1992. text 86.00 (*0-675-21336-3*, Merrill Coll) P-H.

Owens, Kathy, jt. auth. see Whitlock, Betty.

Owens, Keith. Law for Business Studies Students. 536p. 1995. pap. 28.00 (*1-85941-133-9*, Pub. by Cavendish Pubng) Gaunt.

Owens, Kenneth N., ed. John Sutter & a Wider West. LC 93-36522. (Illus.). x, 138p. (C). 1994. text 35.00 (*0-8032-3560-7*) U of Nebr Pr.

*Owens, Kenneth N., ed. The Wreck of the Sv. Nikolai. (Illus.). 126p. 2001. pap. 12.95 (*0-8032-8615-5*, Bison Books) U of Nebr Pr.

Owens, Kenneth N., ed. see Purple, Edwin R.

Owens, Kevin T. Building Intelligent Databases with Oracle PL/SQL, Triggers, & Stored Procedures. 2nd ed. LC 97-42086. (Oracle Bks.). (Illus.). 560p. (YA). 1997. pap. 49.95 incl. cd-rom (*0-13-794314-8*) P-H.

Owens-Kristenson, Jodi, jt. auth. see Ross, Patricia.

Owens, L., ed. Black Beauty & Other Horse Stories. (Illus.). 1983. 7.98 (*0-685-07113-8*) Random Hse Value.

*Owens, L. L. Tales of Greek Mythology II: Retold Timeless Classics. (Cover-to-Cover Timeless Classics Bks.). (Illus.). 58p. (YA). (gr. 5 up). 2000. 10.60 (*0-7807-9035-9*, Covercraft); pap. 5.60 (*0-7891-5064-6*) Perfection Learn.

Owens, Larry. How to Keep Your Subaru Alive: A Manual of Step-by-Step Procedures for the Compleat Idiot. 2nd ed. LC 89-9457. 480p. 1989. pap. 21.95 (*0-945465-11-4*, J Muir) Avalon Travel.

— How to Keep Your Toyota Pick-Up Alive: A Manual of Step by Step Procedures for the Compleat Idiot. (Illus.). 392p. 1988. pap. 21.95 (*0-912528-89-3*) Avalon Travel.

*Owens, Laura Gwen. Warm Places in the Shade. 2000. 18.95 (*0-9667634-1-6*) Whats Inside CA.

Owens, Laurella, jt. auth. see Brown, Virginia P.

Owens, Laurella, jt. ed. see Brown, Virginia P.

Owens, Lee & Barnes, Jenny. Learning Preference Skills. (C). 1992. 90.00 (*0-86431-113-3*, Pub. by Aust Council Educ Res) St Mut.

Owens, Leslie H. This Species of Property: Slave Life & Culture in the Old South. LC 75-38110. 291p. 1977. pap. text 14.95 (*0-19-502245-9*) OUP.

Owens, Letha. Life Is Good. 56p. 1999. pap. 12.95 (*1-892668-07-6*) Prospect Pr.

Owens, Lily, ed. see Andersen, Hans Christian.

Owens, Linda. Residential Lighting: Use & Potential Savings. (Illus.). 77p. (C). 1998. reprint ed. pap. text 25.00 (*0-7881-4719-6*) DIANE Pub.

Owens, Louis. Bone Game: A Novel. LC 94-13882. (American Indian Literature & Critical Studies: Vol. 10). 256p. 1994. 19.95 (*0-8061-2664-7*) U of Okla Pr.

— Bone Game: A Novel. LC 94-13882. (American Indian Literature & Critical Studies Ser.: Vol. 10). 250p. 1996. pap. 11.95 (*0-8061-2841-0*, 2841) U of Okla Pr.

*Owens, Louis. Dark River. 296p. 2000. pap. 12.95 (*0-8061-3282-5*) U of Okla Pr.

Owens, Louis. Dark River: A Novel. LC 98-37695. (American Indian Literature & Critical Studies Ser.: Vol. 30). 296p. 1999. 23.95 (*0-8061-3115-2*) U of Okla Pr.

— Mixedblood Messages: Literature, Film, Family, Place. LC 98-5361. (American Indian Literature & Critical Studies: No. 26). (Illus.). 252p. 1998. 27.95 (*0-8061-3051-2*) U of Okla Pr.

— Other Destinies: Understanding the American Indian Novel. LC 92-3507. (American Indian Literature & Critical Studies: Vol. 3). 302p. (Orig.). 1994. pap. 13.95 (*0-8061-2673-6*) U of Okla Pr.

— The Sharpest Sight: A Novel. LC 91-33072. (American Indian Literature & Critical Studies Ser.: Vol. 1). 272p. 1995. pap. 12.95 (*0-8061-2574-8*) U of Okla Pr.

— Wolfsong: A Novel. LC 94-36435. (American Indian Literature & Critical Studies Ser.: Vol. 17). 256p. 1995. pap. 12.95 (*0-8061-2737-6*) U of Okla Pr.

Owens, Louis, ed. American Literary Scholarship: An Annual, 1990. LC 65-19450. 545p. 1992. text 56.00 (*0-8223-1234-4*) Duke.

Owens, Louis D. The Grapes of Wrath: Trouble in the Promised Land. (Masterwork Studies). 128p. (C). 1989. 29.00 (*0-8057-7998-1*) Macmillan.

— The Grapes of Wrath: Trouble in the Promised Land. (Twayne's Masterworks Ser.: No. 27). 144p. 1989. pap. 18.00 (*0-8057-8047-5*) Macmillan.

Owens, Loulie L. Dramatizing Your Church's History. Deweese, charles W., ed. (Resource Kit for Your Church's History Ser.). 8p. 1984. pap. 0.60 (*0-939804-21-2*) Hist Comm S Baptist.

Owens, M., ed. see Wu, Tai T., et al.

Owens, Maire. The Acquisition of Irish: A Case Study. (Multilingual Matters Ser.: No. 72). 300p. 1992. 99.00 (*1-85359-114-9*, Pub. by Multilingual Matters); pap. 39.95 (*1-85359-113-0*, Pub. by Multilingual Matters) Taylor & Francis.

Owens, Marilyn A. & Loken, Michael R. Flow Cytometry Principles for Clinical Laboratory Practice: Quality Assurance for Quantitative Immunophenotyping. LC 94-35038. (Illus.). 224p. 1994. pap. 65.00 (*0-471-02176-8*, Wiley-Liss) Wiley.

Owens, Marion D. Time to Go. 160p. (Orig.). 1995. pap. 4.95 (*1-56794-085-4*, C-2381) Star Bible.

Owens, Mark & Owens, Delia. Cry of the Kalahari. (Illus.). 352p. 1992. pap. 15.00 (*0-395-64780-0*) HM.

Owens, Martha & Rockett, Susan. Every Child a Winner: Movement from Preschool. 196p. (C). 1996. per. 32.95 (*0-7872-2295-X*, 41229501) Kendall-Hunt.

*Owens, Martha Galyon. A Tennessee Journey: An Interactive Student Workbook. (Illus.). 24p. (J). (gr. k-7). 1999. pap., wbk. ed. 9.95 (*1-57072-142-4*) Overmountain Pr.

Owens, Martin. Legal Eagles. (Illus.). 192p. (Orig.). 1986. pap. 7.95 (*0-918432-74-X*) Baseline Bks.

Owens, Mary B. A Caribou Alphabet. LC 88-70631. (Illus.). 40p. (J). (ps-3). 1990. pap. 4.95 (*0-374-41043-7*) FS&G.

Owens, Mary Beth. Be Blest: A Celebration of Seasons. LC 98-49038. (Illus.). 40p. (J). (gr. 2-6). 1999. 17.00 (*0-689-80546-2*) S&S Childrens.

Owens, Maureen C. American Rush: Selected Poems. LC 98-16329. 160p. 1998. 33.95 (*1-883689-70-8*); pap. 13.95 (*1-883689-69-4*) Talisman Hse.

*Owens, Michael. Michael Owens Soccer Skills. 2000. pap. 17.95 (*0-00-218935-6*) HarpC.

Owens, Michael E. A Key Lost in Time: The Return of the Past. 233p. 1998. pap. 13.95 (*0-9665404-0-9*) S A L Prods.

Owens, Mig, ed. see Lathim, Marie.

Owens, Milton E., Jr., ed. Outstanding Black Sermons, Vol. 3. 80p. 1982. pap. 12.00 (*0-8170-0973-6*) Judson.

Owens, Nancy. 27. 97p. 1998. pap. 12.97 (*0-9668737-0-X*) Ocean Beach Pubg.

*Owens-Navslar, JoAnne & Sime, Wes. Making Do Out of Doo Doo: Lessons in Life for Hardiness, Health & Fitness. Dageforde, Linda J., ed. LC 99-25909. 100p. 1999. pap. 12.95 (*1-886225-44-3*, 5000) Dageforde Pub.

Owens, Nina. Another Holiday Medley. 76p. 1994. pap. 10.50 (*1-56770-296-1*) S Scheewe Pubns.

— Holiday Medley. 82p. 1993. pap. 10.50 (*1-56770-265-1*) S Scheewe Pubns.

Owens, Owen. Living Waters: How to Save Your Local Stream. LC 93-7641. (Illus.). 220p. (C). 1993. pap. 14.95 (*0-8135-1998-5*); text 35.00 (*0-8135-1997-7*) Rutgers U Pr.

*Owens, Patti. Early Childhood Education & Care. 250p. 1998. pap. 27.50 (*1-85856-080-2*, Trentham Bks) Stylus Pub VA.

Owens, Paul & Eckroate, Norma. The Dog Whisperer. LC 99-15824. 256p. 1999. pap. 10.95 (*1-58062-203-8*) Adams Media.

Owens, Peggy, ed. When Maize & Tobacco Are Not Enough: A Church Study of Malawi's Agro-Economy. 66p. 1997. 54.95 (*1-57309-230-4*, U Pr W Africa) Intl Scholars.

Owens, Peter L., jt. auth. see Owens, Susan.

Owens, Philip. Look, Christ. (C). 1979. pap. 33.00 (*0-85088-601-5*, Pub. by Gomer Pr) St Mut.

*Owens, R. G. Techniques of Computational Rheology. 300p. 1999. 51.00 (*1-86094-186-9*) World Scientific Pub.

*Owens, Ray. If You Beat Your Fish It Will Die. LC 99-66850. (Illus.). xxi, 219p. 1999. pap. 9.95 (*0-9659152-0-4*) Joke a Day.

Owens, Richard. Peaceful Warrior: A Biography of Horace Porter, 1837-1921. LC 90-48478. (Dissertations in Nineteenth-Century American Political & Social History: Vol. 1). 300p. 1990. 20.00 (*0-8240-8195-1*) Garland.

Owens, Richard, ed. see International Joint Conference on Artificial Intel.

*Owens, Richard Wilson. A Teachable Spirit: Talking with My "Self" xvi, 173p. 1999. pap. 14.95 (*0-9678377-0-7*) Protheus Pr.

Owens, Robert E. Language Development: An Introduction. 4th ed. 576p. 1995. pap. 63.00 (*0-02-390191-8*, Macmillan Coll) P-H.

— Language Disorders: A Functional Approach to Assessment & Intervention. 3rd ed. LC 98-34366. 596p. 1998. 71.00 (*0-205-28703-4*) P-H.

Owens, Robert E., Jr. Queer Kids: The Challenges & Promise for Lesbian, Gay, & Bisexual Youth. LC 97-39230. 355p. 1998. 49.95 (*0-7890-0439-9*, Harrington Park); pap. 24.95 (*1-56023-929-8*, Harrington Park) Haworth Pr.

Owens, Robert E., et al. Introduction to Communication Disorders. LC 99-40706. 558p. (C). 1999. 61.00 (*0-205-27458-7*) Allyn.

Owens, Robert G. Organizational Behavior in Education. 6th ed. LC 97-23120. 368p. 1997. 71.33 (*0-205-26909-5*) P-H.

*Owens, Robert G. Organizational Behavior in Education: Instructional Leadership & School Reform. 7th ed. 368p. 2000. 71.33 (*0-205-32198-4*) Allyn.

Owens, Robert R. Speak to the Rock: The Azusa Street Revival: Its Roots & Its Message. LC 98-15716. 148p. (C). 1998. 34.50 (*0-7618-1101-X*) U Pr of Amer.

Owens, Rochelle. I Am the Babe of Joseph Stalin's Daughter. pap. 3.50 (*0-686-09754-8*) Kulchur Foun.

— New & Selected Poems, 1961-1996. LC 97-70510. 192p. 1997. pap. 20.00 (*1-881523-06-3*) Junction CA.

— Rubbed Stones: Collected Poems, 1960-1990. (Illus.). 108p. (Orig.). 1994. pap. 8.00 (*0-9641837-0-6*) Texture Pr.

— W. C. Fields in French Light. Gosciak, Josh & Kenny, Maurice, eds. LC 86-16843. 60p. (Orig.). 1986. pap. 4.50 (*0-936556-14-5*) Contact Two.

— The Widow & the Colonel. 1977. pap. 3.25 (*0-8222-1252-8*) Dramatists Play.

Owens, Ron. Oklahoma Justice: A Century of Gunfighters, Gangsters & Terrorists. LC 95-62081. 336p. 1995. 29.95 (*1-56311-280-9*) Turner Pub KY.

— Return to Worship: Letters to the Church. LC 99-20606. 224p. 1999. pap. 12.99 (*0-8054-1888-1*) Broadman.

Owens, Ron, frwd. Finding What's Missing: Keys to Full-Color Living in a Spiritually Colorless World. 1995. pap. 7.99 (*1-886797-20-X*) Fresh Springs.

Owens, Ron, jt. auth. see Wodak, Alex.

Owens, Rosemary, jt. ed. see Naffine, Ngaire.

*Owens, Russell L. How to Evaluate a School: A Black & White Primer for the Fortunate Half of America That Can Still Read. 262p. 2000. pap. 19.95 (*0-9676953-0-9*) Berean Pubng.

Owens, Russell L. & Rollins, Kyle M., eds. Collapsible Soil Hazard Map for the Southern Wasatch Front, Utah. (Miscellaneous Publication Ser.: Vol. 90-1). (Illus.). 38p. 1991. pap. 6.75 (*1-55791-308-0*, MP-90-1) Utah Geological Survey.

*Owens, S. J. & Rudall, P. J. Reproductive Biology in Systematics, Conservation & Economic Botany. (Illus.). 491p. 1999. pap. 99.00 (*1-900347-62-8*, Pub. by Royal Botnic Grdns) Balogh.

Owens, S. P., ed. see De Larkin, E. Martin, Jr.

Owens, Sabra. Criminal Responsibility & Multiple Personality Defendants. Parry, John W. & Lichtenstein, Elissa C., eds. LC 97-73199. 64p. 1997. pap. 15.00 (*1-57073-460-7*, 231-0015) Amer Bar Assn.

Owens, Sally L. Compact Dish: The Bread & Breakfast Cookbook. LC 93-71980. (Compact Dish Cookbooks Ser.). 60p. (Orig.). 1993. spiral bd. write for info. (*1-883810-06-X*) Compact Ckbk.

— Compact Dish: The Casual Chic Cookbook. LC 93-71980. (Compact Dish Cookbooks Ser.). 60p. (Orig.). 1993. spiral bd. write for info. (*1-883810-02-7*) Compact Ckbk.

— Compact Dish: The Cuisine with Kids Cookbook. LC 93-71980. (Compact Dish Cookbooks Ser.). 60p. (Orig.). 1993. spiral bd. write for info. (*1-883810-04-3*) Compact Ckbk.

— Compact Dish: The Double Income, No Kids Cookbook. LC 93-71980. (Compact Dish Cookbooks Ser.). 60p. (Orig.). 1993. spiral bd. write for info. (*1-883810-03-5*) Compact Ckbk.

— Compact Dish: The Rush Hour Cookbook. LC 93-71980. (Compact Dish Cookbooks Ser.). 60p. (Orig.). 1993. spiral bd. write for info. (*1-883810-01-9*) Compact Ckbk.

O

An Asterisk (*) at the beginning of an entry indicates that the title is appearing for the first time.

— Compact Dish Cookbook Series, 6 vols., Set. LC 93-71980. 360p. (Orig.). 1993. spiral bd. write for info. (*1-883810-00-0*) Compact Ckbk.

Owens, Sally L., jt. auth. see Atkins, Cary C.

Owens, Selena, ed. see Owens, William.

Owens, Selena M. Helpmate, Not Hellmate: Give Your Husband Help Not Hell. Owens, William G., ed. (Illus.). 64p. 1997. pap. 6.99 (*0-9658629-1-7*) Higher Stand.

— Keep the Vision Alive: Make, Don't Break the Man of Vision. Owens, William, ed. (Illus.). (Orig.). Date not set. pap. text. write for info. (*0-9658629-3-3*) Higher Stand.

Owens, Selena M., jt. ed. see Owens, William G.

Owens, Shelby. About That Hair. LC 89-91010. (Illus.). 144p. (Orig.). 1989. pap. 8.95 (*0-9622542-0-7*) S Owens.

Owens, Sherman. Ladder to the Top! Date not set. 7.99 (*1-57778-039-6*, SO-001) Albury Pub.

— Why Don't They Teach This in Bible School? 31 Master Secrets Rarely Discovered. 2nd ed. LC 94-96199. 68p. (Orig.). 1994. reprint ed. pap. 7.00 (*0-9642305-0-X*) Ldrship Pubng.

***Owens, Sherrie.** Falling in Love, off Cliffs, into Ravines... & Other Hazards. 1999. pap. 5.95 (*1-56245-382-3*) Great Quotations.

Owens, Sherwood, III. All Our Works Begun: Reflections on Being a Working Parent. 117p. 1999. pap. 5.95 (*0-87946-203-5*, 286) ACTA Pubns.

***Owens, Stephen, et al.** Classification Evaluation of the 1994-95 Common Core of Data: Public/Elementary/ Secondary Education Agency Universe Survey. LC 99-187596. (Technical Report/National Center for Education Statistics Ser.). 70 p. 1999. write for info. (*0-16-049942-9*) USGPO.

Owens, Susan & Owens, Peter L. Environment, Resources & Conservation. (Topics in Geography Ser.: No. 2). (Illus.). 112p. (C). 1991. pap. text 21.95 (*0-521-31378-3*) Cambridge U Pr.

***Owens, Susie.** Unless Two Agree. (Illus.). 110p. 2000. pap. 10.00 (*0-9667850-6-1*) Black Pearl Pub.

***Owens, Suzanne.** The Daughters of Discordia. (A. Poulin, Jr., New Poets of America Ser.: Vol. 21). 75p. 2000. pap. 12.50 (*1-880238-89-6*) BOA Edns.

Owens, Terry W., jt. auth. see King, C. Daly.

Owens, Thomas. Collecting Basketball Cards. LC 98-4432. (Illus.). 78p. (YA). (gr. 3-8). 1998. 23.90 (*0-7613-0418-5*, Copper Beech Bks) Millbrook Pr.

— Nascar: Owens, Tom, Game Plan. LC 99-10859. (Game Plan Ser.). 64p. (J). (gr. 5-8). 1999. 23.40 (*0-7613-1374-5*) TFC Bks NY.

— Soccer. LC 99-41541. (Game Plan Ser.). 64p. (J). (gr. 5-8). 2000. lib. bdg. 23.40 (*0-7613-1400-8*) TFC Bks NY.

Owens, Thomas & Owens, Derrick. Seven Days. Reed, Douglas, ed. (Orig.). 1997. pap. write for info. (*1-889732-08-7*) Word-For-Word.

Owens, Thomas S. The Atlanta Braves Baseball Team. LC 97-19145. (Great Sports Teams Ser.). (Illus.). 48p. (J). (gr. 4-10). 1998. lib. bdg. 18.95 (*0-7660-1021-X*) Enslow Pubs.

— The Chicago Bulls Basketball Team. LC 96-26415. (Great Sports Teams Ser.). (Illus.). 48p. (J). (gr. 4-10). 1997. lib. bdg. 18.95 (*0-89490-793-X*) Enslow Pubs.

Owens, Thomas S. The Chicago Bulls Basketball Team. LC 96-26415. (Great Sports Teams Ser.). (Illus.). 48p. (YA). (gr. 4-10). 1997. pap. 9.95 (*0-7660-1748-6*) Enslow Pubs.

Owens, Thomas S. Collecting Baseball Cards. LC 92-18166. (Illus.). 80p. (J). (gr. 3-6). 1993. lib. bdg. 22.40 (*1-56294-254-9*) Millbrook Pr.

— Collecting Baseball Memorabilia. (Illus.). 96p. (J). (gr. 5-8). 1996. lib. bdg. 23.40 (*1-56294-579-3*) Millbrook Pr.

— Collecting Comic Books: A Young Person's Guide. LC 94-48117. (Illus.). 80p. (J). (gr. 4 up). 1995. lib. bdg. 25.90 (*1-56294-580-7*) Millbrook Pr.

Owens, Thomas S. Ellis Island. LC 97-11538. (Library of American Landmarks). (Illus.). 24p. (J). (gr. k-4). 1997. lib. bdg. 13.95 (*0-8239-5020-4*, PowerKids) Rosen Group.

Owens, Thomas S. The Golden Gate Bridge. LC 97-11547. (Library of American Landmarks). (Illus.). 24p. (J). (gr. k-4). 1997. lib. bdg. 15.93 (*0-8239-5016-6*, PowerKids) Rosen Group.

— Great Catchers. LC 96-3465. 1997. 14.98 (*1-56799-417-2*, MetroBooks) M Friedman Pub Grp Inc.

— Mount Rushmore. LC 97-11539. (Library of American Landmarks). (Illus.). 24p. (J). (gr. k-4). 1997. lib. bdg. 15.93 (*0-8239-5017-4*, PowerKids) Rosen Group.

Owens, Thomas S. Remember When: A Nostalgic Look at America's National Pastime. 176p. 1996. 22.98 (*1-56799-392-3*, MetroBooks) M Friedman Pub Grp Inc.

***Owens, Thomas S.** Remember When: A Nostalgic Look at America's National Pastime. (Illus.). 176p. 2000. 15.98 (*1-56799-995-6*) Magnolia Edtns.

Owens, Thomas S. & Helmer, Diana S. The Charlotte Sting: Teamwork. LC 98-16493. (Women's Professional Basketball Ser.). 24p. (J). 1999. 18.60 (*0-8239-5242-8*, PowerKids) Rosen Group.

— The Cleveland Rockers: Teamwork. LC 98-5640. (Women's Professional Basketball Ser.). 24p. (J). 1999. 18.60 (*0-8239-5241-X*, PowerKids) Rosen Group.

— Inside Collectible Card Games. (Illus.). 144p. (J). (gr. 4-8). 1996. lib. bdg. 22.90 (*1-56294-581-5*) Millbrook Pr.

— The Los Angeles Sparks: Teamwork. LC 98-16492. (Women's Professional Basketball Ser.). 24p. (J). 1999. 18.60 (*0-8239-5240-1*, PowerKids) Rosen Group.

— The New York Liberty: Teamwork. LC 98-16487. (Women's Professional Basketball Ser.). 24p. (J). 1999. 18.60 (*0-8239-5239-8*, PowerKids) Rosen Group.

Owens, Tom. Collecting Sports Autographs: Fun & Profit from This Easy-to-Learn Hobby. 131p. (Orig.). (YA). (gr. 7 up). 1989. pap. 6.95 (*0-933893-79-5*) Bonus Books.

— Dan Marino: Record-Setting Quarterback. LC 97-4152. (Sports Greats Ser.). (J). 1997. lib. bdg. 17.27 (*0-8239-5092-1*, PowerKids) Rosen Group.

— David Robinson: All-Star Center. LC 97-4153. (Sports Greats Ser.). (J). 1997. lib. bdg. 17.27 (*0-8239-5091-3*, PowerKids) Rosen Group.

***Owens, Tom.** Football Stadiums. LC 00-20413. (Sports Palaces Ser.). (Illus.). 2000. lib. bdg. write for info. (*0-7613-1764-3*) Millbrook Pr.

— Insiders' Guide to the Monterey Peninsula. 2nd ed. 496p. 2000. pap. text 16.95 (*1-57380-117-8*) IPBI.

Owens, Tom. Jerry Rice: Record-Setting Wide Receiver. LC 97-4151. (Sports Greats Ser.). (J). 1997. lib. bdg. 17.27 (*0-8239-5093-X*, PowerKids) Rosen Group.

— Ken Griffey, Jr. Extraordinary Center Fielder. LC 96-39986. (Sports Greats Ser.). (J). 1997. lib. bdg. 17.27 (*0-8239-5088-3*, PowerKids) Rosen Group.

— Michael Jordan: Legendary Guard. LC 97-3864. (Sports Greats Ser.). (J). 1997. lib. bdg. 17.27 (*0-8239-5090-5*, PowerKids) Rosen Group.

— Mike Piazza: Phenomenal Catcher. LC 97-506. (Sports Greats Ser.). (J). 1997. lib. bdg. 17.27 (*0-8239-5089-1*, PowerKids) Rosen Group.

Owens, Tom & Helmer, Diana S. Teamwork, the Houston Comets in Action. LC 98-17891. (Women's Professional Basketball Ser.). 24p. (J). 1999. 18.60 (*0-8239-5246-0*, PowerKids) Rosen Group.

— Teamwork, the Phoenix Mercury in Action. LC 98-5639. (Women's Professional Basketball Ser.). 24p. (J). 1999. 18.60 (*0-8239-5243-6*, PowerKids) Rosen Group.

— Teamwork, the Sacramento Monarchs in Action. LC 98-16488. (Women's Professional Basketball Ser.). 24p. (J). 1999. 18.60 (*0-8239-5245-2*, PowerKids) Rosen Group.

— The Utah Starzz: Teamwork. LC 97-41101. (Women's Professional Basketball Ser.). 24p. (J). 1999. 18.60 (*0-8239-5244-4*, PowerKids) Rosen Group.

Owens, Tom, jt. auth. see Craft, David.

Owens, Tom, jt. auth. see Helmer, Diana S.

Owens, Tom, ed. see Dixon, Sheila A. & Crowell, Richard D.

Owens, Tony, jt. auth. see Johanson, Chris E.

Owens, Tuppy. High Teas: Twelve Easy to Feed Each Other Recipes. (Illus.). 28p. 1993. 8.00 (*1-872819-01-X*, Pub. by Tuppy Owens) AK Pr Dist.

— Safer Planet Sex: The Handbook. (Illus.). 270p. (Orig.). 1994. pap. 14.95 (*1-872819-11-7*, Pub. by Tuppy Owens) AK Pr Dist.

— Sensations. (Orig.). 1993. mass mkt. 6.95 (*1-56333-081-4*, Rhinoceros) Masquerade.

— Shaggy Birthday. (Illus.). 28p. 1993. 5.00 (*1-872819-02-8*, Pub. by Tuppy Owens) AK Pr Dist.

Owens-Viani, Lisa, et al. Sustainable Use of Water: California Success Stories. (Illus.). xxvi, 372p. (C). 1998. pap. 20.00 (*1-893790-00-2*) Pcfc Inst.

Owens, Virginia S. Daughters of Eve: Women of the Bible Speak to Women of Today. 200p. 1995. pap. 12.00 (*0-89109-824-0*); mass mkt., student ed. 6.00 (*0-89109-825-9*) NavPress.

Owens, Virginia S. If You Do Love Old Men. LC 90-31158. 217p. reprint ed. pap. 67.30 (*0-7837-6566-5*, 204613100011) Bks Demand.

— Wind River Winter. 221p. (C). 1995. reprint ed. pap. 19.95 (*1-57383-051-8*) Regent College.

— Wind River Winter: How the World Dies. 288p. 1987. pap. 10.95 (*0-310-45861-7*, 12469P) Zondervan.

Owens, Virginia Stem. Assault on Eden: A Memoir of Communal Life in the Early '70's. LC 95-3452. 168p. (YA). (gr. 10). 1995. reprint ed. 15.99 (*0-8010-5241-6*) Baker Bks.

— Looking for Jesus. 1997. 16.00 (*0-06-066399-5*) HarpC.

Owens, Vivian. Chemistry Quickies: Fun Questions to Rouse Your Chemistry Instincts. unabridged ed. LC 97-77828. (Illus.). 164p. 1998. pap. 13.95 (*0-9623839-7-X*) Eschar Pubns.

— I Met a Great Lady: Ivy Meets Mary McLeod Bethune. unabridged ed. Maxwell, Carolyn, ed. LC 97-77829. (Illus.). 80p. (J). (gr. 4-11). 1998. pap. 8.95 (*0-9623839-5-3*) Eschar Pubns.

— I Met a Great Man: John Meets Dr. Carver of Tuskegee. unabridged ed. Owens, April, ed. LC 97-77830. (Illus.). 64p. (J). (gr. 4-10). 1998. pap. 8.95 (*0-9623839-6-1*) Eschar Pubns.

Owens, Vivian W. Create a Math Environment: Arithmetic Made Touchable. LC 92-71252. (Illus.). 192p. (Orig.). 1992. pap. 11.95 (*0-9623839-1-0*) Eschar Pubns.

***Owens, Vivian W.** How Oswa Came to Own All Music: Oswa Gremla of Florida. Owens, April U., ed. LC 99-93879. (Illus.). 64p. (J). (gr. k-6). 2000. 11.95 (*0-9623839-9-6*, Pub. by Eschar Pubns) Baker & Taylor.

— The Mount Dorans: African American History Notes of a Florida Town. LC 99-93878. (Illus.). 248p. 2000. 18.95 (*0-9623839-8-8*, Pub. by Eschar Pubns) Baker & Taylor.

Owens, Vivian W. Nadanda, the Wordmaker: Hide the Doll. Maxwell, Carolyn, ed. LC 93-74671. (Illus.). 248p. (YA). (gr. 5 up). 1994. 14.95 (*0-9623839-3-7*) Eschar Pubns.

— Parenting for Education. LC 89-80830. 112p. (Orig.). 1989. pap. 6.00 (*0-9623839-0-2*) Eschar Pubns.

— The Rosebush Witch. LC 96-83179. (Illus.). 112p. (Orig.). (J). (gr. 3-9). 1996. pap. 8.95 (*0-9623839-4-5*) Eschar Pubns.

Owens, Vivian W., ed. see Tarry, Tarnie G.

***Owens, W. R. & Furbank, P. N.** Political & Economic Writings of Daniel Defoe, 8 vols. (Pickering Masters Ser.). 3200p. 2000. 880.00 (*1-85196-465-7*, Pub. by Pickering & Chatto) Ashgate Pub Co.

— Travel & Historical Writings of Daniel Defoe, Vols. 1-4. (Pickering Masters Ser.). 3200p. 2001. 530.00 (*1-85196-718-4*, Pub. by Pickering & Chatto) Ashgate Pub Co.

— Travel & Historical Writings of Daniel Defoe, Vols. 5-8. (Pickering Masters Ser.). 3200p. 2002. 530.00 (*1-85196-723-0*, Pub. by Pickering & Chatto) Ashgate Pub Co.

Owens, W. R. & Furbank, Philip N. Critical Bibliography of Daniel DeFoe. LC 97-47584. 1998. 190.00 (*1-85196-389-8*, Pub. by Pickering & Chatto) Ashgate Pub Co.

Owens, W. R., jt. auth. see Furbank, P. N.

Owens, W. R., ed. see Bunyan, John.

Owens, W. R., ed. & intro. see Bunyan, John.

Owens, William. Black Mutiny. LC 97-39750. (Illus.). 352p. 1997. reprint ed. pap. 12.95 (*0-452-27935-6*, Plume) Dutton Plume.

— Divine Protocol for the Next Millennium: God's Official Order That Is Correct in the Dealings of His Kingdom. Owens, Selena, ed. (Illus.). 150p. 1997. pap. 9.95 (*0-9658629-2-5*) Higher Stand.

— The Goblin Vol. 1: A True Tale of the Paranormal. LC 96-201980. (Illus.). 285p. (Orig.). 1996. pap. 22.00 (*0-9619127-1-5*) King Wales.

Owens, William, ed. see Owens, Selena M.

Owens, William A. Black Mutiny: The Revolt on the Schooner Amistad. LC 97-74501. (Illus.). 322p. 1997. reprint ed. 22.00 (*1-57478-004-2*) Black Classic.

— Eye-Deep in Hell: A Memoir of the Liberation of the Philippines, 1944-45. LC 88-42637. (Illus.). 260p. 1989. 24.95 (*0-87074-279-5*) SMU Press.

— High Seas: The Naval Passage to an Uncharted World. LC 94-38465. (Illus.). 224p. 1995. 29.95 (*1-55750-661-2*) Naval Inst Pr.

— Look to the River. LC 87-40267. (Texas Tradition Ser.: No. 8). 134p. 1988. reprint ed. pap. 11.95 (*0-87565-026-0*) Tex Christian.

— Tell Me a Story, Sing Me a Song: A Texas Chronicle. 336p. 1983. pap. 17.95 (*0-292-78056-7*) U of Tex Pr.

— This Stubborn Soil. 312p. 1992. 19.95 (*0-941130-19-3*) Lyons Pr.

***Owens, William A.** This Stubborn Soil: A Frontier Boyhood. 1999. pap. 16.95 (*1-55821-989-7*) Lyons Pr.

Owens, William A. Three Friends, Roy Bedichek, J. Frank Dobie, Walter Prescott Webb. LC 75-304951. 335p. reprint ed. pap. 103.90 (*0-608-20868-X*, 207196700003) Bks Demand.

— Walking on Borrowed Land. LC 87-40266. (Texas Tradition Ser.: No. 9). 320p. 1988. reprint ed. pap. 11.95 (*0-87565-028-7*) Tex Christian.

Owens, William A., compiled by. Texas Folk Songs. rev. ed. LC 76-43005. (Texas Folklore Society Publications: No. 23). (Illus.). 210p. 1976. reprint ed. 15.00 (*0-87074-157-8*) UNTX Pr.

Owens, William A. & Grant, Lyman, eds. Letters of Roy Bedichek. 600p. 1985. 24.95 (*0-292-70742-8*) U of Tex Pr.

***Owens, William A. & Offley, Ed.** Lifting the Fog of War. LC 99-53312. 256p. 2000. text 25.00 (*0-374-18627-8*) FS&G.

Owens, William A., jt. auth. see Frary, Michael.

Owens, William F. Doctor Shakspear: A Tale of Lust, Love, & Horrible Slander. 2nd ed. (Illus.). 347p. 1997. reprint ed. pap. 22.00 (*0-9619127-0-7*) King Wales.

Owens, William G. & Owens, Selena M., eds. Without Father: Bastards in the Pulpit. (Illus.). 96p. (Orig.). 1997. pap. 7.99 (*0-9658629-0-9*) Higher Stand.

Owens, William G., ed. see Owens, Selena M.

Owens, William J. Green Hell: The Battle for Guadacanal. LC 98-54597. (Illus.). 276p. 1999. pap. 18.95 (*1-55571-498-6*) PSI Resch.

Owens, William L., ed. see American Society of Mechanical Engineers Staff.

Owens, Yvonne. Journey of the Bard: Celtic Initiatory Magic. (Illus.). 1997. pap. 14.95 (*0-9696066-2-1*, Pub. by Horned Owl) Abyss Dist.

Owensby, Brian Philip. Intimate Ironies: Modernity & the Making of Middle-Class Lives in Brazil. LC 98-46129. xiii, 332p. 1999. 45.00 (*0-8047-3360-0*) Stanford U Pr.

Owensby, Clenton E. Kansas Prairie Wildflowers. LC 80-17791. (Illus.). 124p. 1980. pap. 19.95 (*0-8138-1160-0*) Iowa St U Pr.

Owensby, Craig, ed. see Davis, Flora P. & Lane, Lauree.

Owensby, Craig, ed. see Womack, Tommy.

Owensby, Jacob. Dilthey & the Narrative of History. 208p. 1994. text 35.00 (*0-8014-3011-9*) Cornell U Pr.

Owensby, Jean, et al. Apple Pie: Delta's Beginning ESL Program, Bk. 1A. rev. ed. Iwataki, Adae, ed. (Illus.). 120p. 1995. pap. text, teacher ed. 12.95 (*0-937354-60-0*); audio 10.95 (*0-937354-99-6*) Delta Systems.

— Apple Pie: Delta's Beginning ESL Program, Bk. 1A. rev. ed. Iwataki, Adae, ed. (Illus.). 222p. (YA). 1995. pap. text, student ed. 7.95 (*0-937354-56-2*) Delta Systems.

— Apple Pie: Delta's Beginning ESL Program, Bk. 1A Visuals. rev. ed. Iwataki, Adae, ed. (Illus.). 123p. 1995. pap. text 24.95 (*0-937354-64-3*) Delta Systems.

— Apple Pie: Delta's Beginning ESL Program, Bk. 1B. rev. ed. Iwataki, Sadae, ed. (Illus.). 112p. 1995. pap. text, teacher ed. 12.95 (*0-937354-61-9*) Delta Systems.

— Apple Pie: Delta's Beginning ESL Program, Bk. 1B. rev. ed. Iwataki, Sadae, ed. (Illus.). 238p. (YA). 1995. pap. text, student ed. 7.95 (*0-937354-57-0*) Delta Systems.

— Apple Pie: Delta's Beginning ESL Program, Bk. 1B Visuals. rev. ed. Iwataki, Sadae, ed. (Illus.). 133p. 1995. pap. text 24.95 (*0-937354-65-1*) Delta Systems.

— Apple Pie: Delta's Beginning ESL Program, Bk. 2A. rev. ed. Iwataki, Sadae, ed. (Illus.). 120p. 1995. pap. text, teacher ed. 12.95 (*0-937354-62-7*) Delta Systems.

— Apple Pie: Delta's Beginning ESL Program, Bk. 2A. rev. ed. Iwataki, Sadae, ed. (Illus.). 248p. (YA). 1995. pap. text, student ed. 7.95 (*0-937354-58-9*) Delta Systems.

— Apple Pie: Delta's Beginning ESL Program, Bk. 2A Visuals. rev. ed. Iwataki, Sadae, ed. (Illus.). 187p. 1995. pap. text 24.95 (*0-937354-66-X*) Delta Systems.

— Apple Pie: Delta's Beginning ESL Program, Bk. 2B. rev. ed. Iwataki, Sadae, ed. (Illus.). 136p. 1995. pap. text, teacher ed. 12.95 (*0-937354-63-5*) Delta Systems.

— Apple Pie: Delta's Beginning ESL Program, Bk. 2B. rev. ed. Iwataki, Sadae, ed. (Illus.). 240p. (YA). 1995. pap. text, student ed. 7.95 (*0-937354-59-7*) Delta Systems.

— Apple Pie: Delta's Beginning ESL Program, Bk. 2B Visuals. rev. ed. Iwataki, Sadae, ed. (Illus.). 141p. 1995. pap. text 24.95 (*0-937354-67-8*) Delta Systems.

— Apple Pie: Delta's Beginning ESL Program, No. 1B. rev. ed. Iwataki, Sadae, ed. (Illus.). 1995. audio 10.95 (*0-937354-50-3*) Delta Systems.

— Apple Pie: Delta's Beginning ESL Program, No. 2A. rev. ed. Iwataki, Sadae, ed. (Illus.). 1995. audio 10.95 (*0-937354-51-1*) Delta Systems.

— Apple Pie: Delta's Beginning ESL Program, No. 2B. rev. ed. Iwataki, Sadae, ed. (Illus.). 1995. audio 10.95 (*0-937354-52-X*) Delta Systems.

Owensby, Phil. Sun 'n' Soak: Clothing Optional Naturally. (Illus.). 144p. 1994. 19.95 (*0-9643762-0-2*) Solavescence.

Owensby, Walter L. Economics for Prophets: A Primer on Concepts, Realities, & Values in Our Economic System. fac. ed. LC 88-1402. (Illus.). 219p. 1988. reprint ed. pap. 67.90 (*0-7837-7969-0*, 204772500008) Bks Demand.

Owenson, Sydney. The Wild Irish Girl, 1807: A National Tale. Kirkpatrick, Kathryn, ed. LC 98-47831. (Oxford World's Classics Ser.). 290p. 1999. pap. 10.95 (*0-19-283283-2*) OUP.

Ower, Ernest & Pankhurst, F. C. Measurement of Air Flow: In SI-Metric Units. 5th ed. 1977. 167.00 (*0-08-021282-4*, Pub. by Pergamon Repr) Franklin.

Owers, Elizabeth A. Whispers in the Peepul Tree. 1997. pap. 56.95 (*1-57553-541-6*) Watermrk Pr.

***Owhonda, John.** Musa the Mouse. large type ed. (Illus.). 27p. (J). (gr. 1-4). 1999. 19.95 (*0-9650505-3-X*) CGS Communs.

Owhonda, John. Nigeria: A Nation of Many Peoples. LC 96-26165. (Discovering Our Heritage Ser.). 128p. (J). (gr. 4-8). 1997. lib. bdg. 14.95 (*0-382-39454-2*, Dillon Silver Burdett) Silver Burdett Pr.

Owicki, Jack C., jt. ed. see Cohn, Gerald E.

Owileya. Frank Lloyd Wright Domestic Architecture & Objects: Postcard Book. 44p. 1995. pap. 8.95 (*0-471-14501-7*) Wiley.

— Kirk-Othmer Encyclopedia of Chemical Technology, Vol. 21. 4th ed. LC 91-16789. 1122p. 1996. 350.00 (*0-471-52690-8*) Wiley.

— Kirk-Othmer Encyclopedia of Chemical Technology: Silicon Compounds to Succinic Acid & Succinic Anhydride, Vol. 22. 4th ed. LC 91-16789. 1102p. 1997. 350.00 (*0-471-52691-6*) Wiley.

Owings. Introduction to Psychobiology. 458p. (C). 1997. 45.00 (*0-536-00763-2*) S&S Trade.

Owings, Alison. Frauen: German Women Recall the Third Reich. LC 92-42097. 550p. (C). 1993. 45.00 (*0-8135-1992-6*) Rutgers U Pr.

— Frauen: German Women Recall the Third Reich. 494p. 1995. pap. text 16.95 (*0-8135-2200-5*) Rutgers U Pr.

Owings, Chloe. Women Police, a Study of the Development & Status of the Women Police Movement. LC 69-14941. (Criminology, Law Enforcement, & Social Problems Ser.: No. 28). 1969. reprint ed. 24.00 (*0-87585-028-6*) Patterson Smith.

Owings, Donald H., et al, eds. Perspectives in Ethology Vol. 12: Communication, Vol. 12. (Illus.). 446p. (C). 1998. text 138.00 (*0-306-45764-4*, Kluwer Plenum) Kluwer Academic.

Owings, Donald H. & Morton, Eugene S. Animal Vocal Communication: A New Approach. LC 97-27049. (Illus.). 296p. (C). 1998. text 64.95 (*0-521-32468-8*) Cambridge U Pr.

Owings, Loren C. Quest for Walden: A Study of the "Country Book" in American Popular Literature, with an Annotated Bibliography, 1863-1995. LC 97-18932. 282p. 1997. pap. 55.00 (*0-7864-0354-3*) McFarland & Co.

Owings, Margaret. Voice from the Sea: And Other Reflections on Wildlife & Wilderness. LC 98-51930. 230p. 1998. 19.95 (*1-878244-23-X*) Monterey Bay Aquarium.

***Owings, Maria F.** Ambulatory & Inpatient Procedures in the United States, 1996. 123p. 1998. per. 13.00 (*0-16-061500-3*) USGPO.

— Detailed Diagnoses & Procedures, National Hospital Discharge Survey, 1997. 161p. 2000. per. 16.00 (*0-16-050251-9*) USGPO.

***Owings, Marty.** Wings of Words. 1999. pap. write for info. (*1-58235-361-1*) Watermrk Pr.

Owings, Richard. Non-Operative Aspects of Pediatric Surgery. LC 72-176176. 160p. 1973. 10.00 (*0-87527-118-9*) Green.

Owings, Stephanie & Gilbertie, James L. Principles of Macroeconomics. 2nd ed. 308p. (C). 1996. pap. text 39.95 (*1-56226-342-0*) CAT Pub.

Owings, Timothy. Hearing God in a Noisy World: Prayer As Listening. LC 97-50020. 128p. 1998. 16.00 (*1-57312-175-4*) Smyth & Helwys.

***Owl & Chikadee Magazines Editors.** The Anti-Boredom Book: 133 Completely Unboring Things to Do! (Illus.). 128p. (J). (gr. k-4). 2000. pap. 12.95 (*1-895688-99-X*, Pub. by Owl Bks) Firefly Bks Ltd.

Owl, Grey. Sajo & the Beaver People. 188p. (YA). (gr. 7-11). 1991. reprint ed. pap. 5.95 (*0-7736-7341-5*) Stoddart Publ.

An Asterisk (*) at the beginning of an entry indicates that the title is appearing for the first time.

Owl, Grey. Tales of an Empty Cabin. (Illus.). 296p. 1999. pap. 14.95 (*1-55263-030-7*, Pub. by Key Porter) Firefly Bks Ltd.

Owl Magazine Editors. Amazing but True, Mini-Bk. (Illus.). 96p. (J). (gr. 3 up). 1992. pap. 4.95 (*0-920775-69-1*, Pub. by Owl Bks) Firefly Bks Ltd.

— Jokes & Riddles, Mini-Bk. (Illus.). 96p. (J). (gr. 3 up). 1992. pap. 4.95 (*0-919872-85-9*, Pub. by Owl Bks) Firefly Bks Ltd.

— The Kids' Horse Book. (Illus.). 72p. (YA). (gr. 3 up). pap. 9.95 (*1-895688-07-8*, Pub. by Greey dePencier) Firefly Bks Ltd.

— The New Kids' Question & Answer Book. (Illus.). 64p. 1993. pap. 9.95 (*1-895688-05-1*, Pub. by Greey dePencier) Firefly Bks Ltd.

— Puzzles & Puzzlers, Mini-Bk. (Illus.). 96p. (J). (gr. 3 up). 1992. pap. 4.95 (*0-920775-67-5*, Pub. by Owl Bks) Firefly Bks Ltd.

— Singing Fish & Flying Rhinos: Amazing Animal Habits. (Illus.). 48p. (J). (gr. 2 up). 1992. pap. 6.95 (*0-920775-45-4*, Pub. by Greey dePencier) Firefly Bks Ltd.

— Summer Fun: A Book Full of Things to Do in Good Weather. (Illus.). 128p. (YA). (gr. 4 up). 1992. pap. 8.95 (*0-919872-87-5*, Pub. by Greey dePencier) Firefly Bks Ltd.

— Weird & Wonderful, Mini-Bk. (Illus.). 96p. (J). (gr. 2-12). 1992. pap. 4.95 (*0-919872-81-6*, Pub. by Owl Bks) Firefly Bks Ltd.

— You Asked? Over 300 Great Questions & Astounding Answers. (Illus.). 160p. (YA). (gr. 3 up). 1996. pap. 14.95 (*1-895688-59-0*, Pub. by Owl Bks) Firefly Bks Ltd.

— You Asked? Over 300 Great Questions & Astounding Answers. (Illus.). 160p. (YA). (gr. 4-7). 1996. 24.95 (*1-895688-58-2*, Pub. by Owl Bks) Firefly Bks Ltd.

Owl Magazine Editors, ed. The Kids' Cat Book. (Illus.). 96p. (YA). (gr. 3 up). 1992. pap. 9.95 (*0-920775-51-9*, Pub. by Owl Bks) Firefly Bks Ltd.

— The Kids' Dog Book. (Illus.). 96p. (YA). (gr. 3 up). 1992. pap. 9.95 (*0-920775-50-0*, Pub. by Greey dePencier) Firefly Bks Ltd.

Owl Magazine Editors & Chicadee Magazine Editors. Outdoor Fun. (Illus.). 32p. (J). (gr. 2 up). 1996. pap. 7.95 (*0-920775-37-3*, Pub. by Greey dePencier) Firefly Bks Ltd.

Owl Magazine Editors & Dinosaur Project Editors. The Dinosaur Question & Answer Book. (Illus.). 64p. (YA). (gr. 3 up). 1996. 16.95 (*0-920775-79-9*, Pub. by Greey dePencier); pap. 9.95 (*0-920775-77-2*, Pub. by Greey dePencier) Firefly Bks Ltd.

Owl Magazine Staff. Dinosaur Question & Answer Book: Everything Kids Want to Know about Dinosaurs, Fossils & Pa. (J). 1998. 13.15 (*0-606-13333-X*, Pub. by Turtleback) Demco.

Owl, Michael W. Flat Peyote Stitch. Aberbach, Jason & McCluhan, Michael, eds. (Illus.). 70p. (Orig.). 1993. 19.95 (*0-9643662-0-7*) White Owl Pubns.

Owles, Clementina. Growing up Yesterday. 130p. (C). 1988. 35.00 (*0-7212-0692-1*, Pub. by Regency Pr GBR) St Mut.

— Salad Days in Baghdad. 130p. 1986. 45.00 (*0-7212-0712-X*, Pub. by Regency Pr GBR) St Mut.

Owles, Derrick. Avoiding Liability for Defective Products. (C). 1987. 155.00 (*0-7855-4316-3*, Pub. by Witherby & Co) St Mut.

Owles, Derrick & Owles, Margot. Independent Taxation of the Husband & Wife. (C). 1991. lib. bdg. 57.50 (*1-85333-384-0*, Pub. by Graham & Trotman) Kluwer Academic.

Owles, Margot, jt. auth. see Owles, Derrick.

Owlett, Steven E. Seasons along the Tiadaghton: An Environmental History of the Pine Creek Gorge. 104p. 1993. 39.95 (*0-9635905-0-2*); pap. 23.95 (*0-9635905-1-0*) S E Owlett.

Own, Stephanie. Law for the Builder. (C). 1987. pap. text. write for info. (*0-582-41619-1*, Pub. by Addison-Wesley) Longman.

Ownbey, Gerald B. & Morley, Thomas. Vascular Plants of Minnesota: A Checklist & Atlas. 307p. 1993. pap. 29.95 (*0-8166-2354-6*) U of Minn Pr.

Ownby, David. Brotherhoods & Secret Societies in Early & Mid-Qing China: The Formation of a Tradition. LC 95-31759. 1996. 39.50 (*0-8047-2651-5*) Stanford U Pr.

Ownby, David & Heidhues, Mary S., eds. Secret Societies Reconsidered: Perspectives on the Social History of Early Modern South China & Southeast Asia. LC 93-26121. (Studies on Modern China Ser.). (Illus.). 270p. (C). (gr. 13). 1993. text 85.95 (*1-56324-198-6*, East Gate Bk); pap. text 30.95 (*1-56324-199-4*, East Gate Bk) M E Sharpe.

***Ownby, Karen.** Half Way up the Mountain: The Fight to the Top. (Illus.). 59p. 1999. pap. 14.95 (*1-930002-00-9*) I&L Pubs.

Ownby, Raymond L. Psychological Reports: A Guide to Report Writing in Professional Psychology. 2nd rev. ed. LC 91-70437. (Illus.). 198p. (C). 1991. pap. text 21.95 (*0-88422-019-2*) Clinical Psych.

— Psychological Reports: A Guide to Report Writing in Professional Psychology. 3rd ed. LC 96-20539. 209p. 1997. pap. 39.95 (*0-471-16887-4*) Wiley.

Ownby, Ted. American Dreams in Mississippi: Consumers, Poverty & Culture, 1830-1998. LC 98-30825. (Illus.). 248p. 1999. pap. 18.95 (*0-8078-4806-9*); lib. bdg. 45.00 (*0-8078-2479-8*) U of NC Pr.

— Subduing Satan: Religion, Recreation, & Manhood in the Rural South, 1865-1920. LC 89-48578. (Fred W. Morrison Series in Southern Studies). (Illus.). xiv, 286p. (C). 1990. 45.00 (*0-8078-1913-1*) U of NC Pr.

— Subduing Satan: Religion, Recreation, & Manhood in the Rural South, 1865-1920. LC 89-48578. (Fred W. Morrison Series in Southern Studies). (Illus.). xxii, 286p. 1993. reprint ed. pap. 17.95 (*0-8078-4429-2*) U of NC Pr.

Ownby, Ted, ed. Black & White: Cultural Interaction in the Antebellum South. LC 92-45586. (Chancellor's Symposium on Southern History Ser.). 264p. 1993. text 42.00 (*0-87805-620-3*) U Pr of Miss.

Owne, David. Air Accident Investigation - The Detection & Prevention of the Factors Contributing to Aviation Disasters. (Illus.). 192p. 1998. pap. 25.95 (*1-85260-583-9*, Pub. by P Stephens) Haynes Manuals.

Owne, Trefor M. Welsh Folk Customs. 197p. (C). 1987. text 40.00 (*0-7855-6570-1*, Pub. by Gomer Pr) St Mut.

Ownen, John. Sin & Temptation: The Challenge of Personal Godliness. (Classics Faith & Devotion Ser.: Bk. 2). 28p. 1996. pap. 9.99 (*1-55661-830-1*) Bethany Hse.

Owner Builder Center Staff, jt. auth. see Roskind, Robert.

Ownes, Glynn R. Psychological Aspects of Terminal Care. (Clinical Psychology Ser.). 300p. 1998. 65.00 (*0-471-95291-5*) Wiley.

Ownsbey, Betty J. Alias "Paine" Lewis Thornton Powell, the Mystery Man of the Lincoln Conspiracy. LC 92-56677. (Illus.). 247p. 1993. lib. bdg. 35.00 (*0-89950-874-X*) McFarland & Co.

Owoahene-Acheampong, Stephen. Inculturation & African Religion: Indigenous & Western Approaches to Medical Practice. LC 96-478. (American University Studies XXI: Vol. 16). XV, 225p. (C). 1998. text 43.95 (*0-8204-3129-X*) P Lang Pubng.

***Owocki, Gretchen.** Literacy, Inquiry & Teaching. 2001. pap. text. write for info. (*0-325-00270-3*) Heinemann.

Owocki, Gretchen. Literacy Through Play. LC 98-54827. 126p. 1999. pap. text 17.00 (*0-325-00127-8*) Heinemann.

Owoeye, Jide. Japan's Policy in Africa. LC 92-41579. 200p. 1993. text 79.95 (*0-7734-9236-4*) E Mellen.

Owolabi, Kola. Language in Nigeria: Essays in Honor of Ayo Bamgbose. 530p. 1998. 89.95 (*0-86543-654-1*); pap. 29.95 (*0-86543-655-X*) Africa World.

Owolabi, Robert O. An African's View of the American Society: An Eyewitness Account of over 15 Years of Living, Studying & Working in the United States of America. LC 95-73137. viii, 144p. (Orig.). 1996. pap. 12.00 (*1-57087-227-9*) Prof Pr NC.

— Effective Parenting: Strategies That Work & Mistakes to Avoid. LC 98-43440. 100p. 1999. pap. 4.95 (*0-9666450-0-6*) Bob & Bob Pub.

Owomoyela, Oyekan. The African Difference: Discourses on Africanity & the Relativity of Cultures. (Studies in African & African-American Culture: Vol. 10). XII, 236p. (C). 1996. pap. text 29.95 (*0-8204-2881-7*) P Lang Pubng.

— Amos Tutuola Revisited. LC 99-14327. 1998. 22.95 (*0-8057-4610-2*, Twyne) Mac Lib Ref.

— A Ki I: Yoruba Proscriptive & Prescriptive Proverbs. (Yoruba Proverbs: A Comprehensive Standard Source Ser.). 398p. (C). 1988. lib. bdg. 53.00 (*0-8191-6502-6*) U Pr of Amer.

— Visions & Revisions: Essays on African Literature & Criticism. LC 91-6763. (American University Studies: African Literature: Ser. XVIII, Vol. 3). XII, 239p. (C). 1991. text 41.95 (*0-8204-1471-9*) P Lang Pubng.

— Yoruba Trickster Tales. LC 96-37321. xviii, 218p. 1997. pap. 15.00 (*0-8032-8611-2*); text 45.00 (*0-8032-3563-1*) U of Nebr Pr.

Owomoyela, Oyekan, ed. A History of Twentieth-Century African Literatures. LC 92-37874. x, 411p. (C). 1993. pap. text 25.00 (*0-8032-8604-X*, Bison Books) U of Nebr Pr.

Owram, Doug. Born at the Right Time: A History of the Baby Boom Generation. (Illus.). 559p. 1996. reprint ed. text 34.95 (*0-8020-5957-0*) U of Toronto Pr.

— Born at the Right Time: A History of the Baby Boom Generation. (Illus.). 416p. 1997. reprint ed. pap. text 19.95 (*0-8020-8086-3*) U of Toronto Pr.

— The Government Generation: Canadian Intellectuals & the State, 1900-1945. 402p. 1986. text 45.00 (*0-8020-2581-1*) U of Toronto Pr.

— Promise of Eden: The Canadian Expansionist Movement & the Idea of the West, 1856-1900. LC 80-491231. 276p. reprint ed. pap. 85.60 (*0-608-12873-2*, 202365800033) Bks Demand.

— Promise of Eden: The Canadian Expansionist Movement & the Idea of the West, 1856-1900. (Reprints in Canadian History Ser.). 288p. 1992. reprint ed. pap. text 22.95 (*0-8020-7390-5*) U of Toronto Pr.

Owram, Doug, jt. auth. see Moyles, R. G.

Owram, Doug, jt. ed. see Taylor, M. Brook.

Owre, J. R., ed. see Miami University, Hispanic American Institute Staf.

Owre, J. Riis, ed. see Casona, Alejandro.

Owre, Oscar T. Adaptations for Locomotion & Feeding in the Anhinga & the Double-Crested Cormorant. 138p. 1967. 10.00 (*0-943610-06-0*) Am Ornithologists.

Owsia, Parviz. Formation of Contract: A Comparative Study under English, French, Islamic, & Iranian Law. LC 93-19096. 640p. (C). 1994. lib. bdg. 317.00 (*1-85333-263-1*, Pub. by Graham & Trotman) Kluwer Academic.

***Owsinski, Bobby.** Mastering Engineer's Handbook. 2000. pap. 29.95 (*0-87288-741-3*) Intertec Pub.

Owsinski, Bobby. Mixing Engineer's Handbook. LC 99-62534. 180p. 1999. pap. text 34.95 (*0-87288-723-5*) Intertec Pub.

Owsley, Beatrice R. Hispanic Americans: An Oral History of the American Dream. (Twayne's Oral History Ser.). 200p. 1992. pap. 14.95 (*0-8057-9115-9*) Macmillan.

— Hispanic Americans: An Oral History of the American Dream. (Twayne's Oral History Ser.). 200p. 1993. 26.95 (*0-8057-9107-8*) Macmillan.

Owsley, Douglas W. & Jantz, Richard L., eds. Skeletal Biology in the Great Plains: Migration, Warfare, Health, & Subsistence. LC 91-14388. (Illus.). 408p. (C). 1994. text 45.00 (*1-56098-093-1*) Smithsonian.

Owsley, Douglas W., et al. Bioarcheology of the North Central United States: A Volume in the Central & Northern Plains Archeological Overview. LC 96-40046. (Usacerl Special Report ;Urvey Research Series ;). 1997. pap. 30.00 (*1-56349-080-3*, RS49) AR Archaeol.

— Bioarcheology of the South Central United States. Rose, Jerome C., ed. LC 99-18382. (Arkansas Archeological Survey Research Ser.: Vol. 55). (C). 1999. pap. 30.00 (*1-56349-086-2*) AR Archaeol.

Owsley, Frank L., Jr. The C.S.S. Florida: Her Building & Operations. LC 86-19362. 224p. 1987. 24.95 (*0-8173-0336-7*) U of Ala Pr.

Owsley, Frank L. King Cotton Diplomacy: Foreign Relations of the Confederate States of America. LC 58-11952. 637p. reprint ed. pap. 197.50 (*0-8357-8931-4*, 205676700085) Bks Demand.

— Plain Folk of the Old South. LC 82-9903. (Walter Lynwood Fleming Lectures in Southern History). 234p. (C). 1982. pap. text 17.95 (*0-8071-1063-9*) La State U Pr.

— State Rights in the Confederacy. 1990. 16.50 (*0-8446-1337-1*) Peter Smith.

Owsley, Frank L., Jr. The Struggle for the Gulf Borderlands: The Creek War & the Battle of New Orleans, 1812-1815. LC 80-11109. (Illus.). vii, 255p. 1981. 34.95 (*0-8130-0662-7*) U Press Fla.

Owsley, Frank L., Jr. & Smith, Gene A. Filibusters & Expansionists: Jeffersonian Manifest Destiny, 1800-1821. LC 96-51196. 256p. 1997. text 29.95 (*0-8173-0880-6*) U of Ala Pr.

Owsley, Frank L., Jr., ed. see Reid, John & Eaton, John.

***Owsley, Frank Lawrence, Jr.** The Struggle for the Gulf Borderlands: The Creek War & the Battle of New Orleans, 1812-1815. 2000. pap. 22.95 (*0-8173-1062-2*) U of Ala Pr.

Owsley, Harriet C. Frank Lawrence Owsley: Historian of the Old South: A Memoir. LC 90-46836. (Illus.). xvi, 223p. (Orig.). (C). 1990. 29.95 (*0-8265-1242-9*); pap. 15.95 (*0-8265-1243-7*) Vanderbilt U Pr.

Owsley, Harriet C., jt. ed. see Smith, Sam B.

Owsley, John Q. Aesthetic Facial Surgery. LC 93-2826. (Illus.). 416p. 1993. text 185.00 (*0-7216-3364-1*, W B Saunders Co) Harcrt Hlth Sci Grp.

Owsley, Pat, jt. auth. see Gayle, Shaun.

Owsley, rank L., Jr., ed. see Ball, T. H. & Halbert, H. S.

Owst, Ken. Laurel & Hardy in Hull. (C). 1989. text 40.00 (*0-948929-34-0*) St Mut.

Owston, Ronald D. Making the Link: Teacher Professional Development on the Internet. LC 97-50314. 174p. 1998. pap. 24.00 (*0-325-00077-8*) Heinemann.

Owuso, Maxwell, ed. Colonialism & Change: Essays Presented to Lucy Mair. LC 74-83128. (Studies in Anthropology: No. 4). (Illus.). 264p. 1975. pap. text 44.65 (*90-279-3187-9*) Mouton.

Owusu-Ansah, David. Islamic Talismanic Tradition in Nineteenth Century Asante. LC 91-27337. (African Studies: Vol. 21). (Illus.). 268p. 1991. lib. bdg. 89.95 (*0-7734-9726-9*) E Mellen.

Owusu-Ansah, David & McFarland, Daniel M. Historical Dictionary of Ghana. 2nd ed. LC 94-18978. (African Historical Dictionaries Ser.: No. 63). 1994. 60.00 (*0-8108-2919-5*) Scarecrow.

Owusu-Bempah, J., jt. auth. see Howitt, Dennis.

***Owusu, Heike.** Symbols of Africa. (Illus.). 320p. 2000. pap. 13.95 (*0-8069-2871-9*) Sterling.

— Symbols of Egypt. 2000. pap. 13.95 (*0-8069-3545-6*) Sterling.

Owusu, Heike. Symbols of Native America. LC 98-51478. 1999. pap. text 13.95 (*0-8069-6347-6*) Sterling.

Owusu, Kewsi. Black British Culture & Society: A Text-Reader. LC 99-89998. (Comedia Ser.). 1999. 75.00 (*0-415-17845-2*); pap. 27.99 (*0-415-17846-0*) Routledge.

Owusu, Martin. Drama of the Gods: A Study of Seven African Plays. 175p. (Orig.). 1983. pap. 8.95 (*0-685-06783-1*) Omenana.

Owusu, Maxwell. Uses & Abuses of Political Power: A Case Study of Continuity & Change in the Politics of Ghana. LC 73-121354. 1993. lib. bdg. 21.00 (*0-226-64240-2*) U Ch Pr.

Owusu-Mensa, Kofi. Saturday God & Adventism in Ghana. LC 93-7935. (Archives of International Adventist History Ser.: No. 6). (Illus.). III, 102p. 1993. 19.00 (*3-631-45646-8*) P Lang Pubng.

Owusu, N., jt. auth. see Redden, J. E.

Owusu, Vincent L. Temperature - Effects on Life, Health, Disease, Behavior & Emotions: Index of New Information. (Illus.). 160p. 1998. 47.50 (*0-7883-2046-7*); pap. 44.50 (*0-7883-2047-5*) ABBE Pubs Assn.

Owyang, G. H. Foundations for Microwave Circuits. (Illus.). 904p. 1989. 109.95 (*0-387-96989-6*) Spr-Verlag.

Owyang, Gregory R. Taking a Stand for God. 226p. (Orig.). 1987. pap. 3.50 (*0-945304-00-5*) FCBC.

Owyong & Chan, Laurence. Handbook of Singapore Tax Statutes. 954p. 1989. pap. 180.00 (*0-409-99571-1*, MICHIE) LEXIS Pub.

Owyoung, Stephen D., tr. see Conant, Ellen P.

Oxaal, Ivar. Black Intellectuals & the Dilemmas of Race & Class in Trinidad. LC 81-13590. 334p. 1982. pap. text 22.95 (*0-87073-417-2*) Schenkman Bks Inc.

— Race & Revolutionary Consciousness: A Documentary Interpretation of the 1970 Black Revolt in Trinidad. 96p. 1971. boxed set 32.95 (*0-87073-066-5*) Transaction Pubs.

Oxborrow, Mike. A Practical Reference to SNA. LC 92-43138. 1993. 24.95 (*0-07-707791-1*) McGraw.

Oxbridge Staff. National Directory of Magazines, 1998. 1692p. 1997. pap. 595.00 incl. cd-rom (*0-917460-90-1*) Oxbridge Comm.

Oxelheim, Lars. Corporate Strategies to Internationalise the Cost of Capital. LC 98-140746. (Copenhagen Studies in Economics & Management: No. 12). (Illus.). 334p. 1998. 97.50 (*87-16-13271-8*, Pub. by Almqvist Wiksell) Coronet Bks.

— Financial Markets in Transition: Globalization of National Financial Markets. LC 95-22957. 450p. 1996. pap. 69.00 (*0-415-10816-0*) Thomson Learn.

— Financial Markets in Transition: The Globalization of National Financial Markets. 416p. 1997. pap. 26.99 (*1-86152-099-9*) Thomson Learn.

— International Financial Integration. xviii, 389p. 1990. 87.95 (*0-387-52629-3*) Spr-Verlag.

Oxelheim, Lars, ed. The Global Race for Foreign Direct Investment: Prospects for the Future. LC 93-5807. (Illus.). xiv, 273p. 1993. 101.95 (*0-387-56846-8*) Spr-Verlag.

Oxelheim, Lars & Wihlborg, Clas. Strategies for Managing Macroeconomic Risk: Corporate Performance & Exposure Assessments. LC 97-1101. 236p. 1997. 61.50 (*0-471-97474-9*) Wiley.

Oxelheim, Lars, jt. auth. see Wihlborg, Clas G.

Oxenberg, Christina. Taxi. (Illus.). 208p. 1988. 14.95 (*0-7043-2517-9*, Pub. by Quartet) Interlink Pub.

Oxenbury, Helen. All Fall Down. (Illus.). 10p. (J). (ps-k). 1999. bds. 6.99 (*0-689-81985-4*) Litle Simon.

***Oxenbury, Helen.** Clap Hands. (Illus.). 10p. (J). (ps-k). 1999. bds. 6.99 (*0-689-81984-6*) Litle Simon.

Oxenbury, Helen. Dancing Class. (Out-&-About Bks.). (J). 1993. 9.19 (*0-606-05798-6*, Pub. by Turtleback) Demco.

— Dressing. (Oxenbury Board Bks.). (Illus.). 14p. (J). (ps up). 1981. bds. 4.95 (*0-671-42113-1*) Litle Simon.

— Family. (Oxenbury Board Bks.). (Illus.). 14p. (J). (ps up). 1981. pap. 4.95 (*0-671-42110-7*) Litle Simon.

— Favorite Nursery Stories. (Illus.). 32p. (J). (ps-k). 1994. mass mkt. 4.95 (*0-689-71879-9*) S&S Childrens.

— Grandma & Grandpa. (Out-&-About Bks.). (J). 1993. 9.19 (*0-606-05849-4*, Pub. by Turtleback) Demco.

— Helen Oxenbury Favorite Nursery. (J). 1994. pap. 47.40 (*0-689-71882-9*) Aladdin.

— Helen Oxenbury's ABC of Things. (Illus.). 28p. (J). (ps-k). 1993. mass mkt. 3.95 (*0-689-71761-X*) Aladdin.

— Helen Oxenbury's First Nursery Stories. (Illus.). 32p. (J). (ps-k). 1994. mass mkt. 4.95 (*0-689-71825-X*) S&S Childrens.

— Helen Oxenbury's Little Baby Books. (Illus.). (J). 1996. bds. 5.99 (*1-56402-691-4*) Candlewick Pr.

— I Can. (Baby Beginner Board Bks.). (Illus.). (J). (ps). 1995. 3.95 (*1-56402-547-0*) Candlewick Pr.

— I Hear. (Baby Beginner Board Bks.). (Illus.). (J). (ps). 1995. 3.95 (*1-56402-548-9*) Candlewick Pr.

— I See. 2nd ed. (Baby Beginner Board Bks.). (Illus.). (J). (ps). 1995. 3.95 (*1-56402-549-7*) Candlewick Pr.

— I Touch. 2nd ed. (Baby Beginner Board Bks.). (Illus.). (J). (ps). 1995. 3.95 (*1-56402-550-0*) Candlewick Pr.

— It's My Birthday. LC 93-39667. (Illus.). 24p. (J). (ps up). 1994. 9.95 (*1-56402-412-1*) Candlewick Pr.

— It's My Birthday. LC 93-39667. (Illus.). (J). (ps-3). 1996. pap. 3.99 (*1-56402-602-7*) Candlewick Pr.

— Oxenbury Boxed Set 4 Baby Board Books. (J). 1996. 8.99 (*0-689-80608-6*) S&S Bks Yung.

— Pippo Gets Lost. (Tom & Pippo Ser.). (Illus.). 16p. (J). (ps). 1998. mass mkt. 4.99 (*0-689-81957-9*) S&S Childrens.

— Playing. (Oxenbury Board Bks.). (Illus.). 14p. (J). (ps up). 1981. bds. 4.95 (*0-671-42109-3*) Litle Simon.

— Puzzle People. LC 94-68898. (Illus.). 18p. (J). (ps up). 1995. pap. 4.99 (*1-56402-572-1*) Candlewick Pr.

— Say Goodnight. (Illus.). 10p. (J). (ps-k). 1999. 6.99 (*0-689-81987-0*) S&S Childrens.

— Tickle Tickle. (Illus.). 10p. (J). (ps-k). 1999. 6.99 (*0-689-81986-2*) Litle Simon.

— Tom & Pippo & the Bicycle. LC 92-42379. (Illus.). 24p. (J). (ps). 1997. reprint ed. pap. 3.99 (*0-7636-0162-4*) Candlewick Pr.

— Tom & Pippo at the Beach. LC 92-53130. (Illus.). 24p. (J). (ps). 1997. reprint ed. pap. 3.99 (*0-7636-0163-2*) Candlewick Pr.

— Tom & Pippo Go for a Walk. (Tom & Pippo Ser.: No. 2). (Illus.). 16p. (J). (ps). 1998. mass mkt. 4.99 (*0-689-81956-0*) S&S Childrens.

— Tom & Pippo Go Shopping. LC 88-10497. (Tom & Pippo Bks.). (Illus.). 14p. (J). (ps-1). 1989. reprint ed. mass mkt. 5.95 (*0-689-71278-2*) Aladdin.

— Tom & Pippo in the Garden. LC 88-9145. (Tom & Pippo Bks.). (Illus.). 14p. (J). (ps-1). 1989. reprint ed. mass mkt. 5.95 (*0-689-71275-8*) Aladdin.

— Tom & Pippo Read a Story. (Tom & Pippo Ser.). (Illus.). 16p. (J). (ps). 1998. mass mkt. 4.99 (*0-689-81958-7*) S&S Childrens.

— Tom & Pippo See the Moon. (Tom & Pippo Bks.). (Illus.). 14p. (J). (ps-1). 1989. reprint ed. mass mkt. 5.95 (*0-689-71277-4*) Aladdin.

— Tom & Pippo's Day. (Tom & Pippo Ser.: No. 1). (Illus.). 16p. (J). (ps). 1998. mass mkt. 4.99 (*0-689-81955-2*) S&S Childrens.

— Vamos a Cazar un Oso (We're Going on a Bear Hunt) (Illus.). 36p. (J). (ps-1). 1999. 17.95 (*980-257-107-5*, Pub. by Ediciones Ekare) Kane-Miller Bk.

— Working. (Oxenbury Board Bks.). (Illus.). 7p. (J). (ps up). 1981. pap. 4.95 (*0-671-42112-3*) Litle Simon.

***Oxender, D. L. & Post, L. E., eds.** Novel Therapeutics from Modern Biotechnology: From Laboratory to Human Testing. LC 99-16259. (Illus.). 250p. 1999. pap. 106.00 (*3-540-65927-7*) Spr-Verlag.

Oxender, Dale L. & Fox, C. Fred, eds. Protein Engineering. LC 86-27741. 392p. 1987. 149.95 (*0-471-63066-7*) Wiley.

O

An Asterisk (*) at the beginning of an entry indicates that the title is appearing for the first time.

Oxendine, Joseph B. American Indian Sports Heritage. LC 95-22729. (Illus.). xxv, 334p. 1995. pap. 16.95 (*0-8032-8609-0*, Bison Books) U of Nebr Pr.

Oxendine, Reginald. An Educational American Indian Coloring Book. (Illus.). 31p. 1994. pap. text 5.95 (*0-944049-05-2*) Arrow Pub NC.

— An Educational American Leaders Coloring Book. (Illus.). 39p. 1994. pap. text 5.95 (*0-944049-04-4*) Arrow Pub NC.

— Great African American Leaders. (Illus.). 34p. (Orig.). 1994. pap. text 5.95 (*0-944049-03-6*) Arrow Pub NC.

— Our Family Can Read, 2 bks. (Illus.). 76p. (Orig.). (J). (gr. k up). 1992. 29.95 (*0-944049-01-X*); 29.95 (*0-944049-02-8*) Arrow Pub NC.

— Our Family Can Read, 2 bks., Set. (Illus.). 76p. (Orig.). (J). (gr. k up). 1992. pap. text 29.95 incl. audio (*0-944049-00-1*) Arrow Pub NC.

Oxenfeldt, A. R., jt. auth. see Brown, F. E.

Oxenfeldt, Alfred R. Cost-Benefit Analysis for Executive Decision Making: The Danger of Plain Common Sense. LC 79-14617. 442p. reprint ed. pap. 137.10 (*0-608-13414-7*, 205574800036) Bks Demand.

— Decision Economics. Christopher, Bill, ed. LC 97-65794. (Management Library). (Illus.). 90p. (Orig.). 1997. pap. 12.95 (*1-56052-434-0*) Crisp Pubns.

— Pricing Strategies. LC 74-78207. 267p. reprint ed. pap. 82.80 (*0-608-13027-3*, 202352700033) Bks Demand.

Oxenfeldt, Alfred R. & Schwartz, Jonathan E. A Competitive Analysis. LC HD0041.O9. (Special Study-Presidents Association Ser.: No. 75). 96p. reprint ed. pap. 30.00 (*0-608-13721-9*, 205161000097) Bks Demand.

Oxenford, John, tr. see Eckermann, Johann P.

Oxenford, Lyn. Design for Movement. 1951. pap. 9.95 (*0-87830-561-0*, Thtre Arts Bks) Routledge.

Oxenford, Rosalind. Discover Reflexology: A First-Step Handbook to Better Health. LC 97-60159. (Discover Ser.). Orig. Title: Healing with Reflexology. (Illus.). 132p. 1997. pap. 8.95 (*1-56975-112-9*) Ulysses Pr.

— Instant Reflexology: A Step-by-Step Guide to Relieving, Relaxing & Enhancing the Mind & Body. (New Life Library). (Illus.). 64p. 1997. 9.95 (*1-85967-342-2*, Lorenz Bks) Anness Pub.

Oxenham, J., jt. ed. see Watson, K.

Oxenham, John. Selected Poems of John Oxenham. Wallis, Charles L., ed. LC 71-179735. (Biography Index Reprint Ser.). 1977. reprint ed. 18.95 (*0-8369-8103-0*) Ayer.

Oxenham, John, ed. Education & Values in Developing Nations. 170p. 1988. 24.95 (*0-89226-050-5*) Paragon Hse.

Oxenham, Larry. The Million Dollar Book Writing Formula: It Can Make You Rich (Even if You Can't Write!) (Illus.). 156p. (Orig.). 1988. 14.95 (*0-943813-02-6*) Page One Pub.

— What You Must Know about Home Lenders: Seventeen Answers - The Answer Book, Vol. I. (Illus.). 40p. (Orig.). 1987. pap. 4.75 (*0-943813-00-X*) Page One Pub.

— You Should Not Get a Home Equity Line of Credit: Thirteen Reasons - The Answer Book. (Answer Bk.: Vol. II). (Illus.). 40p. 1987. 4.75 (*0-943813-01-8*) Page One Pub.

Oxenhandler, Neal, jt. ed. see Nelson, Robert J.

Oxenhorn, Douglas, ed. Money for Film & Video Artists: A Comprehensive Resource Guide. 2nd ed. LC 93-38044. 304p. 1993. pap. 15.95 (*1-879903-09-1*) Am for the Arts.

— Money for Visual Artists: A Comprehensive Resource Guide. 2nd ed. LC 93-25366. 317p. 1993. pap. 14.95 (*1-879903-05-9*) Am for the Arts.

***Oxenhorn, Harvey.** Tuning the Rig: A Journey to the Arctic. 288p. 2000. pap. 16.00 (*1-58195-020-9*) Zoland Bks.

Oxenius, J. Kinetic Theory of Particles & Photons. (Electrophysics Ser.: Vol. 20). (Illus.). 370p. 1986. 97.95 (*0-387-15809-X*) Spr-Verlag.

Oxenstierna, Susanne. From Labour Shortage to Unemployment? The Soviet Labour Movement in the 1980s. (Swedish Institute for Social Research Ser.: No. 12). 311p. (Orig.). 1990. pap. 59.50 (*91-7604-033-X*) Coronet Bks.

Oxerrmann, Alfred. Halloween '97 or Theater of Absurdity. (Illus.). 132p. 1998. pap. write for info. (*1-57502-003-3*, PO2093) Morris Pubng.

OXF BIBLE. Holy Communion Rite A. 128p. 1991. pap. 7.00 (*0-19-145952-6*) OUP.

***OXF, PCKT.** The Oxford Pocket Bible. 1200p. 1998. pap. 39.99 (*0-19-528209-4*); pap. 44.99 (*0-19-528210-8*); pap. 44.99 (*0-19-528211-6*) OUP.

— Oxford Pocket Bible: Bonded Leather. 1200p. 1998. pap. 39.99 (*0-19-528208-6*) OUP.

Oxfam Images Working Group Staff. How Does the World Look to You? (Illus.). 34p. (C). 1992. 9.95 (*0-85598-156-3*, Pub. by Oxfam Pub) Stylus Pub VA.

Oxfam Policy Department Staff. A Case for Reform: Fifty Years of the IMF & World Bank. (Insight Ser.). 64p. (C). 1995. pap. 7.95 (*0-85598-301-9*, Pub. by Oxfam Pub) Stylus Pub VA.

Oxfam Publications Staff. Art for a Fairer World. (C). 1992. pap. text 35.00 (*0-85598-208-X*, Pub. by Oxfam Pubns) St Mut.

— The Kei Road Eviction. (C). 1990. pap. text 24.00 (*0-85598-167-9*, Pub. by Oxfam Pubns) St Mut.

Oxfam Staff. Africa: Make or Break Report: Action for Recovery; Trade, Aid & Debt. (Trade, Aid & Debt Ser.). 44p. (C). 1993. pap. 6.95 (*0-85598-245-4*, Pub. by Oxfam Pub) Stylus Pub VA.

— Development in Papua New Guinea: Alternative Perspectives. (Books from Community Aid Abroad). 40p. (C). 1993. pap. 14.95 (*0-646-14299-2*, Pub. by Oxfam Pub) Stylus Pub VA.

— Learning the Lessons. 1995. pap. 15.95 (*0-614-11370-9*, Pub. by Oxfam Pub) Stylus Pub VA.

— Oxfam Emergency Water Supplies Manuals, Set. (C). 1995. pap. 47.50 (*0-85598-239-X*, Pub. by Oxfam Pub) Stylus Pub VA.

— Oxfam Emergency Well Digging Manuals. (C). 1995. pap. 47.50 (*0-85598-238-1*, Pub. by Oxfam Pub) Stylus Pub VA.

— The Oxfam Handbook Resource Directory. LC 96-155609. 216p. 1996. pap. 15.00 (*0-85598-309-4*, Pub. by Oxfam Pub) Stylus Pub VA.

— Trade-Offs: The Impact of New Trade Rules on Developing Countries. (Books from Community Aid Abroad). (C). 1994. pap. 11.95 (*1-875870-04-0*, Pub. by Oxfam Pub) Stylus Pub VA.

— The World, 1997-1998: A Third World Guide. (C). 1997. pap. 39.95 (*0-85598-360-4*, Pub. by Oxfam Pub) Stylus Pub VA.

Oxfam Staff, jt. auth. see Simmons, Pat.

Oxfam Staff, jt. auth. see Sweetman, Caroline.

Oxfeld, Ellen. Blood, Sweat, & Mahjong: Family & Enterprise in an Overseas Chinese Community. LC 92-56779. (Anthropology of Contemporary Issues Ser.). (Illus.). 320p. 1993. text 45.00 (*0-8014-2593-X*); pap. text 17.95 (*0-8014-9908-9*) Cornell U Pr.

Oxford. Oxford-Hachette Concise French/English/French Dictionnaire. (ENG & FRE.). 1997. 59.95 (*0-320-00427-9*) Fr & Eur.

— The Tapestry of Language Learning. 2nd ed. (C). 2001. pap. text 26.95 (*0-8384-0994-6*) Heinle & Heinle.

Oxford & Scarcella, Robin C. The Tapestry of Language Learning. 228p. (J). 1992. mass mkt. 26.95 (*0-8384-2359-0*) Heinle & Heinle.

Oxford, A. W., jt. ed. see King, F. D.

Oxford Analytica Staff. Latin America in Perspective. (C). 1991. pap. text. write for info. (*0-395-52583-7*) HM Soft Schl Col Div.

Oxford, Arnold W. English Cookery Books: To the Year 1850. 199p. 1996. reprint ed. 45.00 (*1-888262-51-6*) Martino Pubng.

Oxford Brookes University Staff. Buildings Design & the Delivery of Day Care Services to Elderly People. 152p. 1994. pap. 75.00 (*0-11-321622-X*, HM21622X, Pub. by Statnry Office) Bernan Associates.

Oxford Center for Tourism & Leisure Studies, Oxfor. Cassell Directory of U. K. Visitor Attractions. (Illus.). 256p. 1994. pap. text 400.00 (*0-304-32694-1*) Continuum.

Oxford Conference on Microscopy of Semiconducting. Microscopy of Semiconducting Materials, 1981: Proceedings of the Royal Microscopical Society Conference Held in St. Catherine's College, Oxford, 6-10 April 1981. Cullis, A. G. & Joy, D. C., eds. LC QC0611.6.M5M. (Conference Ser.: No. 60). 476p. reprint ed. pap. 147.60 (*0-7837-3255-4*, 204327400007) Bks Demand.

Oxford, Earl. Physics Lab Manual No. I: Mechanics, Waves & Heat. 3rd ed. 154p. 1998. spiral bd. 28.95 (*0-7872-4892-4*, 41489201) Kendall-Hunt.

— Physics Lab Manual Vol. II: Electricity, Magnetism & Light. 2nd ed. 180p. (C). 1998. spiral bd. 28.95 (*0-7872-5177-1*, 41517701) Kendall-Hunt.

Oxford, Gerry S. & Armstrong, Clay M., eds. Secretion & Its Control. 347p. 1989. 50.00 (*0-87470-045-0*) Rockefeller.

Oxford, Jeffrey. Vicente Blasco Ibanez: Color Symbolism in Slected Novels. LC 96-22421. (American University Studies II: No. 223). 100p. (C). 1997. text 29.95 (*0-8204-3358-6*) P Lang Pubng.

Oxford, John S., ed. Chemoprophylaxis & Virus Infections of the Respiratory Tract, 1. (Uniscience Ser.). 1977. 133.00 (*0-8493-5136-7*, RC732, CRC Reprint) Franklin.

— Chemoprophylaxis & Virus Infections of the Respiratory Tract, 2. (Uniscience Ser.). 1977. 139.00 (*0-8493-5137-5*, RC732, CRC Reprint) Franklin.

Oxford, John S. & Stuart-Harris, Charles H., eds. Problems of Antiviral Therapy. (Beecham Colloquia Ser.). 360p. 1984. text 94.00 (*0-12-674760-1*) Acad Pr.

Oxford, John S., jt. auth. see Collier, Leslie.

Oxford, John S., ed. see Collier, Leslie.

Oxford, June. The Capital That Couldn't Stay Put: The Complete Book of California's Capitols. (Illus.). 102p. (Orig.). 1995. pap. 12.95 (*1-885852-04-5*) J D Stevenson.

Oxford, Peter, jt. auth. see Horwell, David.

Oxford Polytechnic Staff. The Socio-Economic Effects of Power Stations on Their Localities. (C). 1989. write for info. (*0-7855-2603-X*, Pub. by Oxford Polytechnic) St Mut.

Oxford, Rebecca L. Language Learning Strategies. 342p. (J). 1990. mass mkt. 27.95 (*0-8384-2862-2*, Newbury) Heinle & Heinle.

— Language Learning Strategies: Conversation Skills Through Oral Histories. (C). 1990. pap. 18.00 (*0-06-632607-9*) Addson-Wesley Educ.

— Patterns of Cultural Identity: Advanced Culture-Tapestry. (College ESL Ser.). (J). 1995. mass mkt. 22.95 (*0-8384-4123-8*) Heinle & Heinle.

Oxford, Rebecca L., ed. Language Learning Motivation: Pathways to the New Century. (Technical Report Ser.: No. 11). 232p. 1996. pap. text 20.00 (*0-8248-1849-0*) Sec Lang Tching.

— Language Learning Strategies Around the World: Cross-Cultural Perspectives. (Technical Reports: No. 13). 320p. 1996. pap. text 20.00 (*0-8248-1910-1*) Sec Lang Tching.

Oxford Reference Staff. Oxford Reference Bible. 1578p. 1997. 85.00 (*0-19-111603-3*) OUP.

Oxford Staff. Atlas of Exploration. (Illus.). 248p. (C). 1997. 45.00 (*0-19-521353-X*) OUP.

— Atlas of the World. 5th ed. (Illus.). 390p. 1997. 75.00 (*0-19-521368-8*) OUP.

— Interactive American WordPower. 1999. 49.95 (*0-19-431504-5*) OUP.

— Myths & Legends, 4 vols. 1995. 80.00 (*0-19-521154-5*) OUP.

— Oxford Global Science Library, 4 vols. 1995. 149.95 (*0-19-521147-2*) OUP.

Oxford Staff & Asquith, Herbert H. Studies & Sketches. LC 68-54366. (Essay Index Reprint Ser.). 1977. 18.95 (*0-8369-0759-0*) Ayer.

Oxford University, British Commonwealth Group Staf. Germany's Colonial Demands. Bullock, Alan, ed. LC 75-8482. (Illus.). 274p. 1975. reprint ed. lib. bdg. 49.75 (*0-8371-8154-2*, BUGC, Greenwood Pr) Greenwood.

Oxford University Press. Dictionary Dept. German Section, jt. auth. see Dudenredaktion (Bibliographisches Institut).

Oxford University Press, English Language Teaching, jt. auth. see Donovan, Peter.

Oxford University Press Incorporated Staff, ed. Economics. 138p. 1997. 12.95 (*0-19-437606-0*) OUP.

***Oxford University Press Incorporated Staff, ed.** Language & Culture. LC 99-169749. 144p. 1998. pap. text 11.95 (*0-19-437214-6*) OUP.

Oxford University Press Staff. Business Map of the Arab World. 1980. pap. text 20.50 (*0-86010-211-4*) G & T Inc.

***Oxford University Press Staff.** Concise Atlas of the World. 5th ed. (Illus.). 182p. 1999. 45.00 (*0-19-521564-8*) OUP.

— Dictionary of Biology. 4th ed. (Oxford Paperback Reference Ser.). (Illus.). 2000. pap. text 14.95 (*0-19-280102-3*) OUP.

Oxford University Press Staff. Dictionary of English Idioms. 748p. 1994. text 32.95 (*0-19-431286-0*) OUP.

— Dictionary of English Idioms. 748p. 1994. pap. text 17.95 (*0-19-431287-9*) OUP.

— Dictionary of Phrasal Verbs. 2nd ed. 536p. 1993. pap. text 17.95 (*0-19-431285-2*) OUP.

***Oxford University Press Staff.** Dictionary of Physics. 4th ed. Issacs, Alan, ed. (Oxford Paperback Reference Ser.). (Illus.). 2000. pap. text 16.95 (*0-19-280103-1*) OUP.

Oxford University Press Staff. Dictionary of Scientists. (Oxford Paperback Reference Ser.). 592p. 1999. pap. 16.95 (*0-19-280086-8*) OUP.

***Oxford University Press Staff.** Dictionary of World History. (Illus.). 736p. 2000. pap. 16.95 (*0-19-280105-8*) OUP.

— Encyclopedic World Atlas. 5th ed. (Illus.). 288p. 2000. 45.00 (*0-19-521589-3*) OUP.

Oxford University Press Staff. Lerner's Dictionary of English Idioms. 2nd ed. 350p. 1995. pap. text 10.95 (*0-19-431277-1*) OUP.

— New Shorter Oxford English Dictionary. 1997. disk 110.00 (*0-19-268302-0*) OUP.

***Oxford University Press Staff.** Old Scofield Readers Study Bible. 1616p. 1998. 39.99 (*0-19-527414-8*) OUP.

Oxford University Press Staff. The Old Scofield Study Bible. 1632p. 1998. 39.99 (*0-19-527452-0*); 39.99 (*0-19-527453-9*); 39.99 (*0-19-527454-7*); 39.99 (*0-19-527455-5*); 39.99 (*0-19-527456-3*); 39.99 (*0-19-527457-1*) OUP.

— The Oxford Children's Book of Famous People. LC 99-461930. (Illus.). 384p. (J). (gr. 4-7). 1999. 37.50 (*0-19-521517-6*) OUP.

***Oxford University Press Staff.** Oxford Dictionary of American Usage & Style. (Essential Resource Library). 2000. mass mkt. 5.99 (*0-425-17598-7*) Berkley Pub.

Oxford University Press Staff. Oxford-Duden Pictorial Spanish & English Dictionary. 2nd ed. (SPA & ENG., Illus.). 884p. 1995. pap. 21.95 (*0-19-864515-5*) OUP.

— The Oxford Essential Dictionary. (Illus.). 810p. 1998. mass mkt. 6.99 (*0-425-16420-9*) Berkley Pub.

***Oxford University Press Staff.** Oxford Essential Guide for Puzzle Solvers. (Essential Resource Library). 2000. mass mkt. 5.99 (*0-425-17599-5*) Berkley Pub.

— Oxford Essential Guide to the U. S. Government. (Essential Resource Library). 2000. mass mkt. 6.99 (*0-425-17615-0*) Berkley Pub.

— Oxford Essential Guide to Writing. (Essential Resource Library). 2000. mass mkt. 5.99 (*0-425-17640-1*) Berkley Pub.

Oxford University Press Staff. The Oxford Essential Spelling Dictionary: American Edition. 433p. 1998. mass mkt. 5.99 (*0-425-16388-1*) Berkley Pub.

— Oxford Essential Thesaurus. 1998. mass mkt. 6.99 (*0-425-16421-7*) Berkley Pub.

***Oxford University Press Staff.** Oxford Greek Dictionary. (Essential Resource Library). (GRE & ENG.). 2000. mass mkt. 5.99 (*0-425-17600-2*) Berkley Pub.

— Oxford Pocket Bible. 1998. bond lthr. 44.99 (*0-19-528207-8*) OUP.

Oxford University Press Staff. Oxford Portuguese Dictionary. (POR.). 1998. mass mkt. 4.99 (*0-425-16389-X*) Berkley Pub.

***Oxford University Press Staff.** Pocket World Atlas. 3rd ed. (Illus.). 224p. 2000. 15.95 (*0-19-521588-5*) OUP.

Oxford University Press Staff. Revised English. 1088p. 1997. 22.99 (*0-19-101208-4*) OUP.

— Revised English Bible. 1998. 24.99 (*0-19-101213-0*) OUP.

— Scofield Study Bible. 1760p. 1998. 76.99 (*0-19-528156-X*) OUP.

***Oxford University Press Staff.** Scofield Study Bible. 1616p. 1998. lthr. 86.99 (*0-19-527443-1*) OUP.

Oxford University Press Staff. Scofield Study Pocket Bible. 1760p. 1998. 44.99 (*0-19-528133-0*); 44.99 (*0-19-528175-6*) OUP.

***Oxford University Press Staff, ed.** Book of Common Prayer. 1999. 29.99 (*0-19-528761-4*); 29.99 (*0-19-528762-2*); 39.99 (*0-19-528763-0*); 39.99 (*0-19-528764-9*); 54.99 (*0-19-528765-7*); 54.99 (*0-19-528766-5*) OUP.

Oxford University Press Staff, ed. Book of Common Prayer: Personal Edition. 1998. 42.99 (*0-19-528708-8*); 42.99 (*0-19-528709-6*); 42.99 (*0-19-528710-X*); 42.99 (*0-19-528711-8*); 42.99 (*0-19-528712-6*) OUP.

Oxford University Press Staff, ed. New Oxford Bible Maps. 1996. pap. 49.99 incl. cd-rom (*0-19-528465-8*) OUP.

Oxford University Press Staff, ed. New Oxford Picture Dictionary. 1988. 6.95 (*0-19-434296-4*) OUP.

— The Oxford Children's Science Library, 3 vols., Set. (Illus.). 160p. (J). (gr. 3-9). 1995. 120.00 (*0-19-521142-1*) OUP.

— The Oxford Italian Minidictionary. 2nd rev. ed. 630p. 1999. vinyl bd. 6.50 (*0-19-860253-7*) OUP.

Oxford University Press Staff & Graham & Trotman, Ltd. Staff. Business Map of Nigeria. 1980. pap. text 20.50 (*0-86010-194-0*) G & T Inc.

***Oxford University Staff.** Oxford Pocket Bible. 1998. 49.99 (*0-19-528214-0*); bond lthr. 44.99 (*0-19-528206-X*) OUP.

— Oxford Pocket Bible: Berkshire Leather. 1998. lthr. 49.99 (*0-19-528215-9*) OUP.

Oxford University. Taylor Institution Staff. Studies in European Literature, Being the Taylorian Lectures 1920-1930. LC 76-90673. (Essay Index Reprint Ser.). 1977. 26.95 (*0-8369-1232-2*) Ayer.

Oxford, William. The Ferry Steamers. (Illus.). 128p. (Orig.). 1992. pap. 14.95 (*1-55046-078-1*, Pub. by Boston Mills) Genl Dist Srvs.

Oxhorn, Philip. Organizing Civil Society: The Popular Sectors & the Struggle for Democracy. LC 94-34682. 448p. 1995. 60.00 (*0-271-01435-0*); pap. 19.95 (*0-271-01436-9*) Pa St U Pr.

Oxhorn, Philip & Ducatenzeiler, Graciela. What Kind of Democracy? What Kind of Market? Latin America in the Age of Neoliberalism. LC 97-49899. 270p. 1998. 45.00 (*0-271-01799-6*); pap. 17.95 (*0-271-01800-3*) Pa St U Pr.

Oxhorn, Philip & Starr, Pamela K., eds. Markets & Democracy in Latin America: Conflict or Convergence? LC 98-7421. 290p. 1998. lib. bdg. 55.00 (*1-55587-716-8*) L Rienner.

Oxlad, Melissa, jt. auth. see Baldwin, Steve.

Oxlade & Dewar. Virtual Reality. 1996. mass mkt. 8.95 (*0-340-65591-7*, Pub. by Hodder & Stought Ltd) Trafalgar.

Oxlade, C. Science Museum Book Construction. (J). mass mkt. 8.95 (*0-340-68994-3*, Pub. by Hodder & Stought Ltd) Trafalgar.

Oxlade, C. & Stockley, Corinne. The World of the Microscope. (Science & Experiments Ser.). (Illus.). 48p. (YA). (gr. 5-11). 1989. pap. 7.95 (*0-7460-0289-0*) EDC.

— The World of the Microscope. (Science & Experiments Ser.). (Illus.). 48p. (YA). (gr. 5-11). 1999. lib. bdg. 15.95 (*0-88110-364-0*) EDC.

Oxlade, C., jt. auth. see Wertheim, J.

Oxlade, Chris. Air. LC 94-5547. (Science Magic Ser.). (Illus.). 32p. (J). (gr. 2-5). 1994. 9.95 (*0-8120-6444-5*); pap. 4.95 (*0-8120-1983-0*) Barron.

***Oxlade, Chris.** Bicycles. LC 00-25764. (Transportation Around the World Ser.). (Illus.). (J). 2000. pap. write for info. (*1-57572-300-X*) Heinemann Lib.

— Boats & Ships. LC 00-23617. (Transportation Around the World Ser.). (Illus.). 2000. lib. bdg. write for info. (*1-57572-301-8*) Heinemann Lib.

— Bridges. LC 00-26987. (Building Amazing Structures Ser.). (Illus.). 2000. lib. bdg. write for info. (*1-57572-275-5*) Heinemann Lib.

Oxlade, Chris. Bridges. LC 96-10849. (Superstructures Ser.). (Illus.). 48p. (J). (gr. 4-8). 1997. lib. bdg. 24.26 (*0-8172-4331-3*) Raintree Steck-V.

— Cameras. (Learn about Ser.). (Illus.). 64p. (J). (gr. 3-7). 1997. 7.95 (*1-85967-312-0*, Lorenz Bks) Anness Pub.

***Oxlade, Chris.** Canals. LC 00-26967. (Building Amazing Structures Ser.). (Illus.). 2000. lib. bdg. write for info. (*1-57572-276-3*) Heinemann Lib.

Oxlade, Chris. Car. LC 96-26574. (Take It Apart Ser.). (Illus.). 32p. (J). (gr. 1-2). 1997. pap. 5.95 (*0-382-39666-9*, Silver Pr NJ); lib. bdg. 12.95 (*0-382-39665-0*, Silver Pr NJ) Silver Burdett Pr.

***Oxlade, Chris.** Cars. LC 00-27548. 2000. write for info. (*1-57572-302-6*) Heinemann Lib.

Oxlade, Chris. Cars. LC 97-19068. (Twentieth Century Inventions Ser.). (Illus.). 48p. (J). (gr. 4-9). 1998. 24.26 (*0-8172-4835-8*) Raintree Steck-V.

— Chemistry. LC 97-46796. (Science Projects Ser.). (Illus.). (J). 1998. write for info. (*0-7502-2160-7*); 24.26 (*0-8172-4948-6*) Raintree Steck-V.

— Crime Detection. LC 96-32567. (Science Encounters Ser.). (J). 1998. 21.36 (*1-57572-090-6*) Heinemann Lib.

***Oxlade, Chris.** Dams. LC 00-25727. (Building Amazing Structures Ser.). (Illus.). (J). 2000. lib. bdg. write for info. (*1-57572-277-1*) Heinemann Lib.

Oxlade, Chris. Digger. LC 96-27529. (Take It Apart Ser.). 32p. (J). (gr. 1-2). 1997. pap. 5.95 (*0-382-39672-3*, Silver Pr NJ); lib. bdg. 12.95 (*0-382-39671-5*, Silver Pr NJ) Silver Burdett Pr.

***Oxlade, Chris.** The Earth & Beyond. LC 98-11591. (Science Topics Ser.). (Illus.). 32p. (J). 1999. write for info. (*1-57572-770-6*) Heinemann Lib.

Oxlade, Chris. Electricity & Magnetism. LC 99-12880. (Science Topics Ser.). 1999. write for info. (*1-57572-773-0*) Heinemann Lib.

— Electronic Communication. (Hello Out There Ser.). (Illus.). 32p. 1998. pap. 6.95 (*0-531-15350-9*) Watts.

***Oxlade, Chris.** Energy. LC 98-11587. (Science Topics Ser.). (Illus.). 32p. (J). 1999. write for info. (*1-57572-766-8*) Heinemann Lib.

O

Oxlade, Chris. Energy & Movement. LC 98-4501. (Step-by-Step Science Ser.). (Illus.). 32p. (J). (gr. 1-4). 1999. 18.00 (*0-516-20988-4*) Childrens.

***Oxlade, Chris.** Fantastic Facts: Cameras. 64p. (J). 2000. pap. 6.95 (*1-84215-118-5*) Anness Pub.

— Fantastic Facts - Machines. (J). 2000. pap. 6.95 (*1-84215-085-5*) Anness Pub.

Oxlade, Chris. Fantastic Transport Machines. LC 94-30820. (X-Ray Picture Bks.). (Illus.). 48p. (J). (gr. 5-8). 1995. lib. bdg. 24.00 (*0-531-14351-1*) Watts.

— Fantastic Transport Machines. LC 94-30820. (X-Ray Picture Bks.). (Illus.). 48p. (J). (gr. 5-8). 1995. pap. 8.95 (*0-531-15733-4*) Watts.

— Fire Engine. LC 98-34531. (Take It Apart Ser.). (Illus.). (J). 1999. lib. bdg. 22.00 (*0-382-42069-1*) Silver.

— Flight. LC 95-23171. (Through Time Ser.). (Illus.). 48p. (J). (gr. 4-8). 1996. lib. bdg. 24.26 (*0-8172-4140-X*) Raintree Steck-V.

— Flowering Plants. LC 98-3476. (Step-by-Step Science Ser.). (Illus.). 32p. (J). (gr. 2-5). 1999. 18.00 (*0-516-20989-2*) Childrens.

— Forces: A BBC Fact Finders Book. (Illus.). 48p. (J). (gr. 3-5). 1996. 14.95 (*0-563-39783-7*, BBC-Parkwest); pap. 8.95 (*0-563-39655-5*, BBC-Parkwest) Parkwest Pubns.

— Helicopter. LC 96-26575. (Take It Apart Ser.). (Illus.). 32p. (J). (gr. 1-2). 1997. pap. 5.95 (*0-382-39670-7*, Silver Pr NJ); lib. bdg. 12.95 (*0-382-39669-3*, Silver Pr NJ) Silver Burdett Pr.

— Houses & Homes. LC 94-15514. (Technology Craft Topics Ser.). (Illus.). 32p. (J). (gr. 5-7). 1994. lib. bdg. 20.00 (*0-531-14330-9*) Watts.

— Light & Dark. LC 99-179636. (Step-by-Step Science Ser.). 32p. (J). (gr. 2-5). 1999. 18.00 (*0-516-20990-6*) Childrens.

— Light & Sound. LC 99-12884. (Science Topics Ser.). 1999. write for info. (*1-57572-774-9*) Heinemann Lib.

— The Mystery of Black Holes. LC 99-17399. (Can Science Solve Ser.). (Illus.). 32p. (J). (gr. 4-6). 1999. lib. bdg. 15.95 (*1-57572-808-7*) Heinemann Lib.

— The Mystery of Crop Circles. LC 98-54489. (Can Science Solve Ser.). 32p. (J). 1999. 22.79 (*1-57572-804-4*) Heinemann Lib.

— The Mystery of the Bermuda Triangle. LC 99-18042. (Can Science Solve Ser.). (Illus.). 32p. (J). (gr. 4-6). 1999. lib. bdg. 15.95 (*1-57572-811-7*) Heinemann Lib.

— The Mystery of UFOs. LC 98-54488. 32p. (YA). 1999. 22.79 (*1-57572-806-0*) Heinemann Lib.

***Oxlade, Chris.** Olympic Games. (Eyewitness Books). (Illus.). (J). (gr. 4-7). 2000. 19.99 (*0-7894-6628-7*) DK Pub Inc.

— Olympic Games. (Eyewitness Books). (J). (gr. 4-7). 2000. 15.95 (*0-7894-6292-3*) DK Pub Inc.

Oxlade, Chris. Olympics, No. 79. LC 99-22807. 1999. lib. bdg. 20.99 (*0-375-90222-8*) Random.

— Olympics, No. 79. LC 99-22807. 60p. (J). (gr. 4-8). 1999. 19.00 (*0-375-80222-3*) Random.

— Plane. (Take It Apart Ser.). (Illus.). (J). (gr. 1-2). 1997. pap. 5.95 (*0-382-39668-5*, Silver Pr NJ); lib. bdg. 12.95 (*0-382-39667-7*, Silver Pr NJ) Silver Burdett Pr.

***Oxlade, Chris.** Planes. LC 00-27549. 2000. write for info. (*1-57572-303-4*) Heinemann Lib.

— Science Magic with Air. (Science Magic Ser.). 1994. 10.15 (*0-606-07079-6*, Pub. by Turtleback) Demco.

Oxlade, Chris. Science Magic with Forces. LC 94-32052. (Science Magic Ser.). (Illus.). 32p. (J). (gr. 2-5). 1995. 10.95 (*0-8120-6502-6*) Barron.

Oxlade, Chris. Science Magic with Forces. (Science Magic Ser.). 1995. 10.15 (*0-606-08865-2*, Pub. by Turtleback) Demco.

Oxlade, Chris. Science Magic with Light. LC 94-5549. (Science Magic Ser.). (Illus.). 32p. (J). (gr. 2-5). 1994. 9.95 (*0-8120-6445-3*); pap. 4.95 (*0-8120-1984-9*) Barron.

— Science Magic with Light. (Science Magic Ser.). 1994. 10.15 (*0-606-07080-X*, Pub. by Turtleback) Demco.

Oxlade, Chris. Science Magic with Machines. (Science Magic Ser.). 1995. 10.15 (*0-606-08866-0*, Pub. by Turtleback) Demco.

Oxlade, Chris. Science Magic with Magnets. LC 94-32055. (Science Magic Ser.). (Illus.). 32p. (J). (gr. 2-5). 1995. 10.95 (*0-8120-6501-8*); pap. 4.95 (*0-8120-9190-6*) Barron.

Oxlade, Chris. Science Magic with Magnets. (Science Magic Ser.). 1995. 10.15 (*0-606-08867-9*, Pub. by Turtleback) Demco.

Oxlade, Chris. Science Magic with Shapes & Materials. LC 94-40701. (Science Magic Ser.). (Illus.). 32p. (J). (gr. 2-5). 1995. pap. 4.95 (*0-8120-9369-0*); lib. bdg. 10.95 (*0-8120-6518-2*) Barron.

Oxlade, Chris. Science Magic with Shapes & Materials. (Science Magic Ser.). 1995. 10.15 (*0-606-08868-7*, Pub. by Turtleback) Demco.

Oxlade, Chris. Science Magic with Sound. LC 94-5550. (Science Magic Ser.). (Illus.). 30p. (J). (gr. 2-5). 1994. pap. 4.95 (*0-8120-1985-7*) Barron.

Oxlade, Chris. Science Magic with Sound. (Science Magic Ser.). 1994. 10.15 (*0-606-07081-8*, Pub. by Turtleback) Demco.

Oxlade, Chris. Science Magic with Water. LC 94-5548. (Science Magic Ser.). (Illus.). 32p. (J). (gr. 2-5). 1994. pap. 4.95 (*0-8120-1986-5*); lib. bdg. 9.95 (*0-8120-6448-8*) Barron.

Oxlade, Chris. Science Magic with Water. (Science Magic Ser.). 1994. 10.15 (*0-606-07082-6*, Pub. by Turtleback) Demco.

Oxlade, Chris. Ships: A Fascinating Fact File & Learn-It-Yourself Book. 1999. 12.95 (*1-85967-913-7*, Lorenz Bks) Anness Pub.

***Oxlade, Chris.** Skyscrapers. LC 00-25699. (Illus.). (J). 2000. lib. bdg. write for info. (*1-57572-278-X*) Heinemann Lib.

Oxlade, Chris. Skyscrapers & Towers. LC 96-5166. (Superstructures Ser.). (Illus.). 48p. (J). (gr. 4-8). 1996. lib. bdg. 24.26 (*0-8172-4329-1*) Raintree Steck-V.

— Space. LC 98-17935. (Step-by-Step Science Ser.). 32p. (J). (gr. 2-5). 1999. 18.00 (*0-516-20991-4*) Childrens.

— Space Shuttle. LC 98-34532. (Take It Apart Ser.). (Illus.). (J). 1999. lib. bdg. 22.00 (*0-382-42071-3*) Silver.

— Telecommunications. LC 96-46005. (20th Century Inventions Ser.). (Illus.). 48p. (J). (gr. 4-9). 1997. lib. bdg. 24.26 (*0-8172-4813-7*) Raintree Steck-V.

— Toys. LC 95-23173. (Through Time Ser.). (Illus.). 48p. (J). (gr. 4-6). 1996. lib. bdg. 24.26 (*0-8172-4139-6*) Raintree Steck-V.

— Train. LC 98-35965. (Take It Apart Ser.). (Illus.). (J). 1999. 22.00 (*0-382-42075-6*) Silver.

— Traveling on Water. (Launch Pad Library). (Illus.). 32p. (J). (gr. k-4). 1998. 11.95 (*1-58087-001-5*) C D Stampley Ent.

— Trees. (Learn about Ser.). (Illus.). 64p. (J). (gr. 3-7). 1997. 7.95 (*1-85967-313-9*, Lorenz Bks) Anness Pub.

***Oxlade, Chris.** Tunnels: Chris Oxlade. LC 00-26988. (Building Amazing Structures Ser.). (Illus.). 2000. lib. bdg. write for info. (*1-57572-280-1*) Heinemann Lib.

Oxlade, Chris. Viajes por Agua. Sanz, Maria T., tr. (Biblioteca de Descubrimientos Ser.). (SPA., Illus.). 32p. (J). (gr. k-4). 1998. 11.95 (*1-58087-008-2*) C D Stampley Ent.

— The Weather. LC 97-41171. (Science Projects Ser.). (Illus.). 48 p. (J). 1999. 24.26 (*0-8172-4949-4*) Raintree Steck-V.

***Oxlade, Chris.** Weather. (Illus.). (J). 2000. 27.12 (*0-7398-1008-1*) Raintree Steck-V.

***Oxlade, Chris, et al, eds.** Illustrated Dictionary of Chemistry. rev. ed. (Illustrated Dictionaries Ser.). (Illus.). 128p. (YA). (gr. 5-9). 2000. pap. 12.95 (*0-7460-3794-5*, Pub. by Usbrne Pbng UK) EDC.

— Illustrated Dictionary of Physics. rev. ed. (Illustrated Dictionaries Ser.). (Illus.). 128p. (YA). (gr. 4-7). 2000. pap. 12.95 (*0-7460-3796-1*, Pub. by Usbrne Pbng UK) EDC.

— The Usborne Illustrated Dictionary of Science: Physics, Chemistry & Biology Facts. rev. ed. (Illustrated Dictionaries Ser.). (Illus.). 384p. (gr. 4-7). 2000. pap. 29.95 (*0-7460-3485-7*, Pub. by Usbrne Pbng UK) EDC.

Oxlade, Chris & Rowe, Julian. Movies. LC 96-27563. (Science Encounters Ser.). (J). 1998. 19.92 (*1-57572-088-4*) Heinemann Lib.

Oxlade, Chris & Wallace, Holly. The Mystery of the Loch Ness Monster. LC 98-54481. (Can Science Solve Ser.). 32p. (J). 1999. write for info. (*1-57572-805-2*) Heinemann Lib.

Oxlade, Chris, jt. auth. see Clemmet, Mike.

Oxlade, Chris, jt. auth. see Ganeri, Anita.

Oxlee, G. J. Aerospace Reconnaissance. LC 96-33621. (Air Power: Aircraft, Weapons Systems & Technology Ser.). (Illus.). 200p. 1996. 32.95 (*1-85753-138-8*, Pub. by Brasseys) Brasseys.

Oxlet, Jolyon, et al, eds. Chronic Toxicity of Antiepileptic Drugs. LC 83-3411. (Illus.). 318p. 1983. reprint ed. pap. 98.60 (*0-608-00585-1*, 206117200007) Bks Demand.

Oxley. Housing in Europe. (Illus.). 232p. (C). 1996. pap. 45.00 (*0-419-20720-1*, E & FN Spon) Routledge.

***Oxley, Alan.** Seize the Future: How Australia Can Prosper in the New Century. 276p. 2000. pap. 19.95 (*1-86508-205-8*, Pub. by Allen & Unwin Pty) Paul & Co Pubs.

Oxley, Beverly, jt. auth. see Duewel, Wesley L.

Oxley, Connie, ed. see Barrett, Patricia R.

Oxley, Connie, ed. see Hart, Rhonda M.

Oxley, Connie, ed. see Hobson, Phyllis.

Oxley, Constance, ed. see Anton, Liz & Dooley, Beth.

Oxley, Constance, ed. see Bennett, Bob.

Oxley, Constance, ed. see Dooley, Beth.

Oxley, Constance, ed. see Harrington, Geri.

Oxley, Constance, ed. see Hendrickson, Audra & Hendrickson, Jack.

Oxley, Constance, ed. see Johnson, Pam.

Oxley, Constance, ed. see Stovel, Edith.

Oxley, Constance, tr. see Reavis, Charles.

Oxley, Debra F. Glass Elegance. (Illus.). 40p. 1989. pap. 14.95 (*0-935133-27-5*) CKE Pubns.

***Oxley, Debra F.** Gorgeous in Glass. (Illus.). 36p. 1999. pap. 14.95 (*0-935133-76-3*) CKE Pubns.

Oxley, Debra F. & Dobbins, Norman. Glass Etching 2 - Carving Techniques & Designs. 72p. 1994. pap. text 19.95 (*0-935133-47-X*) CKE Pubns.

Oxley, Debra F., jt. auth. see Dobbins, Norman.

Oxley, H. G. Mateship in Local Organization: A Study of Egalitarianism, Stratification, Leadership & Amenities Projects in a Semi-industrial Community of Inland New South Wales. LC 74-174424. xvi, 240p. 1974. write for info. (*0-7022-0820-5*) Intl Spec Bk.

Oxley, J. Handbook of Logistic & Distribution Management. 339p. (C). 1989. 320.00 (*0-7855-5727-X*, Pub. by Inst Pur & Supply) St Mut.

Oxley, J., jt. auth. see Rushton, A.

Oxley, James G. Matroid Theory. LC 92-20802. (Oxford Graduate Texts in Mathematics Ser.). (Illus.). 544p. (C). 1993. text 98.00 (*0-19-853563-5*) OUP.

***Oxley, Joanne E.** Governance of International Strategic Alliances: Technology & Transaction Costs. (Studies in Global Competition Ser.: Vol. 7). 144p. 1999. text 45.00 (*90-5702-591-4*, Harwood Acad Pubs) Gordon & Breach.

Oxley, Joanne E., et al, eds. Structural Change, Industrial Location & Competitiveness. LC 98-17081. (Globalization of the World Economy Ser.: Vol. 3). 680p. 1998. 240.00 (*1-85898-688-5*) E Elgar.

***Oxley, John M.** New Seasons of Happiness: The Ultimate Dimension of Life. LC 99-90597. 1999. 25.00 (*0-7388-0488-6*); pap. 18.00 (*0-7388-0489-4*) Xlibris Corp.

Oxley, L., et al, eds. Surveys in Econometrics. (Illus.). 400p. (C). 1995. pap. 40.95 (*0-631-19065-1*) Blackwell Pubs.

Oxley, Leslie & McAleer, Michael, eds. Practical Issues in Cointegration Analysis. LC 99-19757. (Journal of Economic Surveys Ser.). 274p. 1998. pap. 39.95 (*0-631-21198-5*) Blackwell Pubs.

Oxley, Mat. Mick Doohan: Thunder from Down Under. LC 98-75398. (Illus.). 160p. 1999. 29.95 (*1-85960-635-0*) J H Haynes & Co.

Oxley, Michael, jt. auth. see King, Peter.

Oxley, Michael G., ed. Federal Barriers to Common Sense Cleanups: Hearings Before the Committee on Commerce, U. S. House of Representatives. 121p. 1998. pap. text 25.00 (*0-7881-4972-5*) DIANE Pub.

— Financial Services Reform: Congressional Hearing. 163p. (C). 1999. reprint ed. pap. text 30.00 (*0-7881-8111-4*) DIANE Pub.

***Oxley, Michael G., ed.** Improving Price Competition for Mutual Funds & Bonds: Congressional Hearing. 152p. (C). 2000. reprint ed. pap. text 30.00 (*0-7881-8959-X*) DIANE Pub.

Oxley, Michael R., ed. The Common Cents Stock Pricing Act of 1997. (Illus.). 256p. 1999. reprint ed. pap. text 35.00 (*0-7881-8061-4*) DIANE Pub.

Oxley-Oxland, J. Federal Constitutional Law. 2nd ed. (LBC Nutshell Ser.). xi, 100p. 1989. pap. 11.95 (*0-455-20905-7*, Pub. by LawBk Co) Gaunt.

— New South Wales Police Law Handbook. 1988. pap. 33.00 (*0-409-49319-8*, A.T., MICHIE) LEXIS Pub.

— Principles of Criminal Law in New South Wales. 1985. pap. 54.00 (*0-409-49135-7*, AT, MICHIE) LEXIS Pub.

Oxley-Oxland, J. & Freilich, A. Y. Butterworths Student Companions: Commercial Law, 2 vols., Set. (Student Companion Ser.). 90p. 1986. pap. 14.00 (*0-409-49095-4*, Austral, MICHIE) LEXIS Pub.

Oxley, P. L. The Mechanics of Machining: An Analytical Approach to Assessing Machinability. 1989. text 72.95 (*0-470-21382-5*) P-H.

Oxley, R. & Poskitt, R. Management Techniques Applied to the Construction Industry. 5th ed. LC 96-13801. 400p. 1996. pap. text 39.95 (*0-632-03862-4*) Blackwell Sci.

Oxley, Richard. Love Is an Awesome Thing. Ohr, Tim, ed. (Illus.). 1996. 12.95 (*1-884942-01-6*) Wrld Tampa.

Oxley, Robert. How to Increase Your Sales Immediately. 8p. 1994. 34.95 incl. audio (*0-8403-9785-2*, 40978501) Kendall-Hunt.

***Oxley, Robert.** How to Increase Your Sales Immediately: Interior Design, Kitchen, Bath & Remodeling, Set. 2nd ed. 12p. 2000. reprint ed. pap., wbk. ed. 34.95 incl. audio (*0-9678289-1-0*) R Oxley Trng.

Oxley, Robert M., tr. see Pastore, Jose.

Oxley, Robert R. The Brandom Collection, Cabinetry for the Home Furniture: The Brandom Furniture Design Portfolio. Montgomery, Becky & Bailey, L. Charles, eds. (Illus.). 120p. 1997. 29.95 (*0-9648659-1-2*) Brandom Mfg.

Oxley, T. A., ed. see International Biodeterioration Symposium Staff.

Oxley, William. Collected Longer Poems. 416p. pap. write for info. (*3-7052-0627-3*, Pub. by Poetry Salzburg) Intl Spec Bk.

— The Playboy. 109p. pap. write for info. (*3-7052-0223-5*, Pub. by Poetry Salzburg) Intl Spec Bk.

— Three Plays. 246p. pap. write for info. (*3-7052-0781-4*, Pub. by Poetry Salzburg) Intl Spec Bk.

Oxman, Bernard, ed. The Law of the Sea: U. S. Policy Dilemma. LC 83-107880. 184p. (C). 1983. pap. 24.95 (*0-917616-53-7*); text 44.95 (*0-917616-59-6*) Transaction Pubs.

Oxman, Fannie-Rose, jt. auth. see Harnett, Juli O.

Oxman, Jeff, jt. auth. see Fey, Michael S.

Oxman, Jeff, ed. see Fey, Michael S.

Oxman, Michael, ed. see Shrayer, Daivd.

Oxman, Murray. The How to Handle Difficult People Handbook: Everything Problem-People Don't Want You to Know. 24p. 1998. pap. 4.95 (*0-9669202-0-1*) Success Without Stress.

Oxman, Thomas E., jt. ed. see Emery, V. Olga.

***Oxmoor House Publishing Staff.** Quick Cooking for Two. (Illus.). 240p. 2000. pap. 21.95 (*0-376-02336-8*) Sunset Books.

— Sunset Appetizers. (Illus.). 96p. 2000. pap. 12.95 (*0-376-02027-X*) Sunset Books.

— Sunset Cookbook Classics. (Illus.). 832p. 2000. 24.95 (*0-376-02308-2*) Sunset Books.

— Sunset Fresh Ways with Pasta. (Illus.). 96p. 2000. pap. 12.95 (*0-376-02524-7*) Sunset Books.

— Sunset Homemade Soups. (Illus.). 96p. 2000. pap. 12.95 (*0-376-02627-8*) Sunset Books.

— Sunset Low Cholesterol Cookbook. (Illus.). 96p. 2000. pap. 12.95 (*0-376-02515-8*) Sunset Books.

— Sunset Recipe Annual 2001. (Illus.). 312p. 2000. pap. 21.95 (*0-376-02708-8*) Sunset Books.

— Sunset Vegetarian Cooking. (Illus.). 96p. 2000. pap. 12.95 (*0-376-02912-9*) Sunset Books.

— Sunset Wok Cookbook. (Illus.). 96p. 2000. pap. 12.95 (*0-376-02965-X*) Sunset Books.

Oxmoor House Staff. Afghans on the Double. 128p. 1996. pap. 14.95 (*0-942237-90-0*) Leisure AR.

— Aleene's Prizewinning Crafts from Readers & Viewers. LC 96-71091. 144p. 1997. pap. 14.95 (*0-8487-1539-X*) Oxmoor Hse.

— American Country Christmas, Bk. 1. LC 89-61909. 160p. 1993. pap. 14.95 (*0-8487-1174-2*) Oxmoor Hse.

— American Country Christmas Bk. 2, Bk. 4. 160p. 1994. pap. 14.95 (*0-8487-1186-6*) Oxmoor Hse.

— American Country Christmas Bk. 3, Bk. 3. 160p. 1995. pap. 14.95 (*0-8487-1423-7*) Oxmoor Hse.

— American Country Christmas Bk. 4, Bk. 4. 160p. 1996. pap. text 14.95 (*0-8487-1444-X*) Oxmoor Hse.

— America's Best Recipes, Vol. 3. 336p. 1997. pap. 19.95 (*0-8487-1640-X*) Oxmoor Hse.

— America's Best Recipes Vol. 1: A Hometown Collection, Vol. 1. 336p. 1993. pap. 19.95 (*0-8487-1474-1*) Oxmoor Hse.

— America's Best Recipes Vol. 2: A Hometown Collection, Vol. 2. 336p. 1996. pap. text 19.95 (*0-8487-1499-7*) Oxmoor Hse.

— At Home with Crochet. 144p. 1995. pap. 14.95 (*0-942237-59-5*) Leisure AR.

— Best Selling Bazaar Patchwork. 160p. 1992. 24.99 (*0-8487-1092-4*) Oxmoor Hse.

— Biltmore Estate Specialities of the House. LC 94-67754. 160p. 1994. 22.95 (*0-8487-1246-3*) Oxmoor Hse.

— Bubba Gump Shrimp Co. Cookbook: Recipes & Reflections from Forrest Gump. 108p. 1994. 14.95 (*0-8487-1479-2*) Oxmoor Hse.

— Christmas Is Coming, Vol. 2. 144p. 1992. pap. 9.99 (*0-8487-1110-6*) Oxmoor Hse.

— Christmas Is Coming, 1994 Vol. 4: Holiday Projects for Children & Parents. 144p. 1994. pap. 14.95 (*0-8487-1414-8*) Oxmoor Hse.

— Christmas with Southern Living - 1994. 1994. 24.95 (*0-8487-1190-4*) Oxmoor Hse.

— Christmas with Southern Living, 1992. 160p. 1992. 24.99 (*0-8487-1091-6*) Oxmoor Hse.

— Christmas with Southern Living 1993. LC 84-63032. 160p. 1993. 24.99 (*0-8487-1133-5*) Oxmoor Hse.

— Christmas with Southern Living 1995. 160p. 1995. 24.95 (*0-8487-1445-8*) Oxmoor Hse.

— Christmas with Southern Living 1996. 160p. 1996. 29.95 (*0-8487-1509-8*) Oxmoor Hse.

— Christmas With Southern Living 1997. LC 96-68891. 160p. 1997. 29.95 (*0-8487-1556-X*) Oxmoor Hse.

— Classic Blue Quilts. LC 97-73654. (Illus.). 160p. 1997. pap. 19.95 (*1-57486-068-2*, 108009) Leisure AR.

— The Complete Step-By-Step Diabetic Cookbook. 368p. 1995. 17.95 (*0-8487-1431-8*) Oxmoor Hse.

— Cook Healthy Cook Quick. 240p. 1995. 29.95 (*0-8487-1424-5*) Oxmoor Hse.

— Cooking Light Cookbook, 1993. 272p. 1993. 24.99 (*0-8487-1104-1*) Oxmoor Hse.

— Cooking Light Cookbook, 1995. 272p. 1995. 24.95 (*0-8487-1408-3*) Oxmoor Hse.

— Cooking Light Cookbook, 1996. 272p. 1996. 24.95 (*0-8487-1456-3*) Oxmoor Hse.

— Cooking Light, 1994. LC 87-61020. 272p. 1993. 24.95 (*0-8487-1144-0*) Oxmoor Hse.

— Creative Crochet. LC 95-81458. 144p. 1996. pap. 14.95 (*0-942237-63-3*) Leisure AR.

Oxmoor House Staff. Crochet Collection. 144p. 1995. pap. 14.95 (*0-942237-55-2*) Leisure AR.

Oxmoor House Staff. Crochet for Today. (Illus.). 144p. 1996. pap. 14.95 (*1-57486-022-4*) Leisure AR.

— EatRight Heart Smart. (Illus.). 144p. 1998. 24.95 (*0-8487-1599-3*) Oxmoor Hse.

— Great American Holiday Iron-On Transfer. 1998. pap. text 15.95 (*1-57486-101-8*) Oxmoor Hse.

— Great American Quilts, Bk. 1. LC 86-62283. 144p. 1993. pap. 19.95 (*0-8487-1179-3*) Oxmoor Hse.

— Great American Quilts, Bk. 2. 144p. 1994. pap. 19.95 (*0-8487-1401-6*) Oxmoor Hse.

— Great American Quilts, Bk. 3. LC 87-641817. 144p. 1995. pap. 19.95 (*0-8487-1461-X*) Oxmoor Hse.

— Great American Quilts, Bk. 4. Vol. 4. 144p. 1997. pap. 19.95 (*0-8487-1526-8*, 102673) Oxmoor Hse.

— Great American Quilts, Bk. 5. (Illus.). 144p. 1997. pap. 19.95 (*0-8487-1617-5*, 108052) Oxmoor Hse.

— Great American Quilts, 1993. 144p. 1993. 24.99 (*0-8487-1098-3*) Oxmoor Hse.

— Great American Quilts 1993. LC 86-62283. 144p. 1993. pap. 14.95 (*0-8487-1151-3*) Oxmoor Hse.

— Healthy Heart Cookbook. 256p. 1992. 24.99 (*0-8487-0797-4*) Oxmoor Hse.

— Heartfelt Iron-On Transfers. 1998. pap. text 15.95 (*1-57486-103-4*) Oxmoor Hse.

— Herrschner's Blue Ribbon Afghans. LC 98-65197. (Illus.). 160p. 1998. pap. 14.95 (*0-8487-1460-1*) Oxmoor Hse.

— Home for the Holidays Cookbook. (Illus.). 108p. 1995. 14.95 (*0-8487-1518-7*) Oxmoor Hse.

— Home Sweet Home Afghans. LC 97-73648. 1998. pap. text 14.95 (*1-57486-053-4*) Oxmoor Hse.

— In Love with Crochet. LC 96-78952. 144p. 1997. pap. 14.95 (*1-57486-021-6*) Leisure AR.

— Jenny Craig Diabetes Cookbook. (Illus.). 372p. 1997. 24.95 (*0-8487-1803-8*) Oxmoor Hse.

— Lazy Gourmet Cookbook. LC 97-65857. 240p. 1997. 29.95 (*0-8487-1544-6*) Oxmoor Hse.

— Light & Luscious Cookbook. LC 93-87339. 326p. 1994. 29.95 (*0-8487-1150-5*) Oxmoor Hse.

— Light Cooking for Two. 240p. 1995. 29.95 (*0-8487-1434-2*) Oxmoor Hse.

— Low-Fat, High-Flavor Cookbook. 240p. 1996. 29.95 (*0-8487-1454-7*) Oxmoor Hse.

— The Low-Fat Way to Cook. LC 93-84154. 256p. 1993. 29.99 (*0-8487-1125-4*) Oxmoor Hse.

— Low-Fat Way to Cook Chicken. LC 94-74793. (Illus.). 144p. 1995. spiral bd. 18.95 (*0-8487-2200-0*) Oxmoor Hse.

— Low-Fat Way to Cook Pasta. LC 94-62126. (Illus.). 144p. 1995. spiral bd. 18.95 (*0-8487-2201-9*) Oxmoor Hse.

— Low-Fat Ways to Cook Desserts. LC 95-74600. 144p. 1995. spiral bd. 18.95 (*0-8487-2204-3*) Oxmoor Hse.

— Low Fat Ways to Cook Fish & Shellfish. LC 96-71083. 144p. 1997. spiral bd. 18.95 (*0-8487-2207-8*) Oxmoor Hse.

An Asterisk (*) at the beginning of an entry indicates that the title is appearing for the first time.

— Low-Fat Ways to Cook Meats. LC 95-74601. 144p. 1996. spiral bd. 18.95 (*0-8487-2205-1*) Oxmoor Hse.

— Low-Fat Ways to Cook One-Dish Meals. LC 95-97712. 144p. 1995. spiral bd. 18.95 (*0-8487-2202-7*) Oxmoor Hse.

— Low-Fat Ways to Cook Quick & Easy. LC 95-67713. 144p. 1995. spiral bd. 18.95 (*0-8487-2203-5*) Oxmoor Hse.

— Low Fat Ways to Cook Regional Fare. LC 96-71084. 144p. 1997. spiral bd. 18.95 (*0-8487-2213-2*) Oxmoor Hse.

— Low-Fat Ways to Stir-Fry. LC 96-67711. 144p. 1996. spiral bd. 18.95 (*0-8487-2209-4*, 104008) Oxmoor Hse.

— Mountain Mist Quilt Favorites. LC 97-75544. (Illus.). 160p. 1998. pap. 19.95 (*0-8487-1669-8*) Oxmoor Hse.

— Quick & Cozy Afghans. 128p. 1994. pap. 14.95 (*0-942237-48-X*) Leisure AR.

— Quick & Easy Scrap Quilts. 160p. 1996. pap. 19.95 (*0-8487-1462-8*) Oxmoor Hse.

***Oxmoor House Staff.** Quick Cooking for Two. 2000. pap. 21.95 (*0-376-02337-6*) Sunset Books.

Oxmoor House Staff. Quick Method Favorite Quilts. 160p. 1995. pap. 19.95 (*0-942237-61-7*) Leisure AR.

Oxmoor House Staff. Quick Method Quilts, Bk. 1. 160p. 1994. 19.95 (*0-942237-54-4*) Leisure AR.

Oxmoor House Staff. Quick Method Quilts Galore. LC 94-74354. 160p. 1995. pap. 19.95 (*0-942237-57-9*) Leisure AR.

— Quilt with the Best. LC 91-68146. 160p. 1992. 24.99 (*0-8487-1078-9*, 100350) Oxmoor Hse.

— Quilt with the Best. LC 91-68146. 160p. 1993. pap. 14.95 (*0-8487-1175-0*) Oxmoor Hse.

— Quilter's Complete Guide. LC 92-60992. 256p. 1992. pap. 19.95 (*0-8487-1152-1*) Oxmoor Hse.

— Quilts for All Seasons. LC 93-83737. 160p. 1993. pap. 19.95 (*0-8487-1176-9*) Oxmoor Hse.

— Santa's Great Book. LC 96-75335. 144p. 1996. pap. text 19.95 (*1-57486-039-9*) Oxmoor Hse.

— Scrap Quilts Fast & Fun. LC 97-68506. (Illus.). 160p. 1998. pap. 19.95 (*0-8487-1671-X*) Oxmoor Hse.

— Southern Living: Our Best Christmas Recipes. 256p. 1994. 24.95 (*0-8487-1183-1*) Oxmoor Hse.

— Southern Living All Time Favorite Dessert Recipes. 1996. pap. text 14.95 (*0-8487-2226-4*) Leisure AR.

— Southern Living All-Time Favorite Light Meals. LC 96-68033. 144p. pap. 14.95 (*0-8487-2229-9*) Oxmoor Hse.

— Southern Living All-Time Favorite Soups & Stews Recipes. LC 96-67713. 144p. 1996. pap. 14.95 (*0-8487-2225-6*) Oxmoor Hse.

— Southern Living Annual Recipes, 1996. 368p. 1996. 29.95 (*0-8487-1523-3*, 102572) Oxmoor Hse.

— Southern Living Garden Guide Annuals. LC 95-74602. 128p. 1996. pap. 12.95 (*0-8487-2240-X*) Oxmoor Hse.

— Southern Living Garden Guide Perennials. LC 95-74603. 128p. 1996. pap. 12.95 (*0-8487-2241-8*) Oxmoor Hse.

— Southern Living Garden Guide Shrubs. LC 95-74605. 128p. 1996. pap. 12.95 (*0-8487-2243-4*) Oxmoor Hse.

— Southern Living Garden Guide to Houseplants. LC 96-67716. 128p. 1996. pap. 12.95 (*0-8487-2244-2*) Oxmoor Hse.

— Southern Living Garden Guide Trees. LC 95-74604. 128p. 1996. pap. 12.95 (*0-8487-2242-6*) Oxmoor Hse.

— Southern Living Garden Low Maintenance Gardening. LC 96-67717. 128p. 1997. 12.95 (*0-8487-2246-9*) Oxmoor Hse.

— Southern Living, Our Best Recipes Made Lighter. LC 98-66268. 160p. 1998. write for info. (*0-8487-1850-X*) Oxmoor Hse.

— Trash to Treasure-The Year's Best Creative Crafts, Vol. 1. 1998. 19.95 (*1-57486-078-X*) Oxmoor Hse.

— Wonder-Under Sew No More Christmas Decor. LC 97-75836. (Illus.). 144p. 1998. pap. 14.95 (*0-8487-1683-3*) Oxmoor Hse.

— Year of Afghans, Bk. 2. 144p. 1997. pap. 14.95 (*1-57486-045-3*) Leisure AR.

— A Year of Afghans, Bk. 4. Childs, Ann, ed. Vol. 4. (Illus.). 144p. 1999. pap. 14.95 (*1-57486-127-1*) Leisure AR.

Oxmoor House Staff, ed. The Best of Vanessa-Ann's Cross-Stitch Collection: Cross-Stitch Collection. (Illus.). 160p. 1992. 24.99 (*0-8487-1112-2*) Oxmoor Hse.

— 75 Great American Garden Plants. LC 97-75804. (Illus.). 160p. 1998. pap. 14.95 (*0-8487-1620-5*, 102453) Oxmoor Hse.

Oxnam, Garfield B. Preaching in a Revolutionary Age. LC 75-142687. (Essay Index Reprint Ser.). 1977. reprint ed. 20.95 (*0-8369-2421-5*) Ayer.

Oxnam, Robert B. Ruling from Horseback: Manchu Politics in the Oboi Regency, 1661-1669. LC 74-10343. xii, 250p. 1994. lib. bdg. 20.00 (*0-226-64244-5*) U Ch Pr.

Oxnard, Charles & Freedman, Leonard, eds. Human Adaptability: Future Trends & Lessons from the Past. (Perspectives in Human Biology Ser.: Vol. 3). 128p. 1998. 32.00 (*981-02-3354-X*); pap. 16.00 (*981-02-3356-6*) World Scientific Pub.

Oxnard, Charles E. Form & Pattern in Human Evolution. 228p. 1998. lib. bdg. 20.50 (*0-226-64251-8*) U Ch Pr.

— Humans, Apes & Chinese Fossils: New Implications for Human Evolution. 52p. (C). 1985. pap. text 20.00 (*962-209-073-7*, Pub. by HK Univ Pr) Coronet Bks.

— Uniqueness & Diversity in Human Evolution: Morphometric Studies of Australopithecines. LC 74-16689. viii, 144p. 1975. lib. bdg. 21.00 (*0-226-64253-4*) U Ch Pr.

Oxner, Edwin S. FET Technology & Application. (Electrical Engineering & Electronics Ser.: Vol. 54). (Illus.). 288p. 1988. text 125.00 (*0-8247-8050-7*) Dekker.

Oxorn, Harry. The First Fifty Years, 1944-1994, Society of Obstetricians & Gynaecologists of Canada. 362p. 1994. 58.00 (*1-85070-562-3*) Prthnon Pub.

— Oxorn-Foote Human Labor & Birth. 5th ed. (Illus.). 918p. (C). 1998. pap. text 55.00 (*0-8385-7665-6*, A7665-1, Apple Lange Med) McGraw.

Oxrieder, C. A. Your Number's Up: A Calculus Approach to Successful Math Study. 1982. text. write for info. (*0-201-05526-0*) Addison-Wesley.

Oxrieder, Julia W. Kiss the Doorknob: Folk Ways & Folklore of Floyd County, Virginia. LC 96-83605. (Illus.). 300p. (Orig.). 1996. pap. 20.00 (*0-9633240-2-0*, 101521) Dory Pr.

Oxtoby. Chemistry: Science of Change. 2nd ed. (C). 1994. pap. text, teacher ed. 33.75 (*0-03-096802-X*) Harcourt Coll Pubs.

— Chemistry: Science of Change. 3rd ed. (C). 1997. pap. text 31.00 (*0-03-020474-7*) Harcourt Coll Pubs.

— Chemistry: Science of Change. 3rd ed. LC 97-67375. (Illus.). 1120p. (C). 1997. text 113.00 (*0-03-020088-1*, Pub. by SCP) Harcourt.

— Ohts T/a Chemistry:sci Of Change 3/e. 3rd ed. (C). 1997. pap. text 441.50 (*0-03-020478-X*) Harcourt Coll Pubs.

— Principles Modern Chemistry. 2nd ed. (C). 1991. pap. text, teacher ed. 28.00 (*0-03-053502-6*) Harcourt Coll Pubs.

— Principles of Modern Chemistry. 3rd ed. (C). 1995. student ed. 124.00 (*0-03-018402-9*) Harcourt.

— Principles of Modern Chemistry. 3rd ed. (C). 1995. pap. text, teacher ed. 28.00 (*0-03-015649-1*); trans. 261.00 (*0-03-015653-X*, Pub. by Harcourt Coll Pubs) Harcourt.

— Principles of Modern Chemistry. 4th ed. (C). 1998. pap. text, teacher ed. 26.75 (*0-03-024752-7*) Harcourt Coll Pubs.

— Principles of Modern Chemistry. 4th ed. (C). 1998. text 138.50 incl. cd-rom (*0-03-027392-7*, Pub. by Harcourt Coll Pubs) Harcourt.

— Science of Change: Student Solutions Manual to Accompany Chemistry. 3rd ed. 1997. pap. text, teacher ed. 28.50 (*0-03-020472-0*) H Holt & Co.

Oxtoby, et al. Principles of Modern Chemistry: Study Guide & Student Solutions Manual to Accompany. 4th ed. 624p. 1998. pap., student ed. 37.50 (*0-03-024751-9*) SCP.

Oxtoby, David W. Chemistry: Science of Change. 3rd ed. 376p. (C). 1997. pap. text, student ed. 35.50 (*0-03-020477-1*) SCP.

— Principles of Modern Chemistry. 3rd ed. (C). 1995. text 107.00 (*0-03-005904-6*) Harcourt Coll Pubs.

— Principles of Modern Chemistry. 4th ed. LC 98-84384. 1008p. (C). 1998. text 124.00 (*0-03-024427-7*, Pub. by SCP) Harcourt.

Oxtoby, J. C. Measure & Category: A Survey of the Analogies Between Topological & Measure Spaces. 2nd rev. ed. LC 73-149248. (Graduate Texts in Mathematics Ser.: Vol. 2). (C). 1996. 47.95 (*0-387-90508-1*) Spr-Verlag.

Oxtoby, J. C., et al, eds. John Von Neumann, 1903-1957 - JVNM. (Bulletin Ser.: Vol. 64, No. 3). 129p. 1988. reprint ed. pap. 38.00 (*0-8218-0021-3*, JVN) Am Math.

Oxtoby, L., tr. see Denecke, H. J. & Meyer, R.

Oxtoby, M., ed. Children in Care: The Medical Contribution. (C). 1989. 50.00 (*0-903534-81-9*, Pub. by Brit Ag for Adopt & Fost) St Mut.

— Genetics in Adoption & Fostering: Guidelines & Resources. (C). 1989. 50.00 (*0-903534-41-X*, Pub. by Brit Ag for Adopt & Fost) St Mut.

Oxtoby, Willard G., ed. World Religions: Western Traditions. (Illus.). 500p. 1996. pap. text 34.95 (*0-19-540751-2*) OUP.

Oxtoby, Willard G., jt. ed. see Ching, Julia.

Oxton, John R., jt. auth. see Collins, D. Ray.

Oxtopcu, Kurtulus, jt. auth. see Abouv, Zhoumagaly.

Oxtot, Dick & Goggin, Jim. Jazz Scrapbook. LC 97-65994. (Illus.). 108p. 1998. pap. 18.50 (*0-88739-150-8*) Creat Arts Bk.

Oya, H., jt. ed. see Tsurutani, B. T.

***Oyague, Maria Amparo.** Do Options Exist? The Reform of Pensions & Health Care Systems in Latin America. LC 99-211612. (Latin American Ser.). 404p. (C). 1999. text 60.00 (*0-8229-4079-5*) U of Pittsburgh Pr.

Oyaide, William J., et al. Presidentialism: New Recipes for Nigeria's Political System. LC 88-114523. 133p. 1987. write for info. (*978-30055-0-2*) Adelekan Pub Co.

Oyama, Mas. Mas Oyama's Complete Karate Course. LC 99-187442. (Illus.). 256p. 1998. pap. 14.95 (*0-8069-8845-2*) Sterling.

***Oyama, N. & Birss, V., eds.** Molecular Functions of Electroactive Thin Films. LC 99-62295. 274p. 1999. 46.00 (*1-56677-220-6*, PV 98-26) Electrochem Soc.

Oyama, S. T. Chemistry of Transition Metal Carbides & Nitrides. 576p. 1996. write for info. (*0-7514-0365-2*) Kluwer Academic.

Oyama, S. Ted & Hightower, Joe W., eds. Catalytic Selective Oxidation: Developed from a Symposium. LC 92-45894. (ACS Symposium Ser.: No. 523). (Illus.). 460p. 1993. text 120.00 (*0-8412-2637-7*, Pub. by Am Chemical) OUP.

Oyama, S. Ted & Hunter, Paige. Control of Volatile Organic Compound Emissions: Conventional & Emerging Technologies. LC 99-43060. 330p. 2000. text 89.95 (*0-471-33369-7*) Wiley.

***Oyama, Susan.** Evolution's Eye: Biology, Culture & Developmental Systems. LC 99-38175. (Science & Cultural Theory Ser.). 272p. 2000. pap. 18.95 (*0-8223-2472-5*) Duke.

— The Ontogeny of Information: Developmental Systems & Evolution. 2nd rev. enl. ed. LC 99-34735. (Science & Cultural Theory Ser.). 280p. 2000. pap. text 19.95 (*0-8223-2466-0*) Duke.

***Oyama, Susan, et al, eds.** Cycles of Contingency: Developmental Systems & Evolution. LC 00-26951. (Illus.). 484p. (C). 2001. 60.00 (*0-262-15053-0*, Bradford Bks) MIT Pr.

Oyama, T. & Smith, G., eds. Pain & Kampo: The Use of Japanese Herbal Medicine in Management of Pain. LC 93-47603. 1994. write for info. (*4-431-70135-4*); write for info. (*3-540-70135-4*); write for info. (*0-387-70135-4*) Spr-Verlag.

Oyama, Toshikazu, et al, eds. Shakespeare Translation: Annual Publication, 13 vols. 1980. write for info. (*0-404-19572-5*) AMS Pr.

Oyamo. I Am a Man: A New Play. 128p. 1995. pap. 6.95 (*1-55783-211-0*) Applause Theatre Bk Pubs.

***Oyamo.** Resurrection of Lady Lester Vol. 59: A Poetic Mood Song Based on the Legend of Lester Young. 109p. 2000. pap. 8.95 (*1-892295-51-2*, Pub. by Green Integer) SPD-Small Pr Dist.

Oyatieva, E. The Dawn of Art: Palaeolithic, Neolithic, Bronze Age & Iron Age Remains Found in the Territory of the Soviet Union. (Hermitage Collection). 196p. 1974. 35.00 (*0-7855-0698-5*) St Mut.

Oye, Kenneth A. Economic Discrimination & Political Exchange: World Political Economy in the 1930s & 1980s. (Studies in International History & Politics). 244p. 1992. text 45.00 (*0-691-07849-1*, Pub. by Princeton U Pr); pap. text 18.95 (*0-691-00083-2*, Pub. by Princeton U Pr) Cal Prin Full Svc.

Oye, Kenneth A., ed. Cooperation under Anarchy. LC 85-42936. 330p. 1985. pap. text 16.95 (*0-691-02240-2*, Pub. by Princeton U Pr) Cal Prin Full Svc.

Oyebade, Adebayo. Africa after the Cold War: The Changing Perspectives on Security. LC 98-14115. 250p. 1998. 79.95 (*0-86543-650-9*); pap. 21.95 (*0-86543-651-7*) Africa World.

Oyejide. Regional Integration, Vol. 1. LC 96-49387. 489p. 1997. text 69.95 (*0-312-17321-0*) St Martin.

Oyejide, Ademola. Regional Integration & Trade Liberalization in Subsaharan Africa: Regional Case-Studies, Vol. 3. 240p. 1999. text 75.00 (*0-312-21771-4*) St Martin.

— Regional Integration & Trade Liberalization in Subsaharan Africa: Vol. 4, Synthesis & Review. 240p. 1999. text 75.00 (*0-312-21772-2*) St Martin.

***Oyejide, Ademola.** Regional Integration & Trade Liberalization in Subsaharan African: County Case-studies. 1999. text 75.00 (*0-312-21769-2*) St Martin.

Oyemade, Ura J. & Brandon-Monye, Deloris, eds. Ecology of Alcohol & Other Drug Use: Helping Black High-Risk Youth. 228p. (Orig.). (C). 1996. pap. text 30.00 (*0-7881-2640-7*) DIANE Pub.

Oyen, Duane B. Business Fluctuations & Forecasting. LC 85-183986. 600p. 1991. text 59.95 (*0-88462-922-8*, 4106-3501) Dearborn.

Oyen, Else. Comparative Methodology: Theory & Practice in International Social Research. (Studies in International Sociology). (Illus.). 224p. (C). 1990. 45.00 (*0-8039-8325-5*); pap. 18.95 (*0-8039-8326-3*) Sage.

Oyen, Else, ed. Comparing Welfare States & Their Futures. 243p. 1986. text 72.95 (*0-566-00910-2*, Pub. by Avebry) Ashgate Pub Co.

Oyen, Else, et al, eds. Poverty a Global Review: Handbook on Poverty Research. LC 97-105691. 600p. 1996. 54.00 (*82-00-22649-2*) Scandnvan Univ Pr.

Oyen, L. P. & Nguyen Xuan Dung, eds. Prosea Plant Resources of South-East Asia: Essential-Oil Plants. (Illus.). 277p. 1999. 95.00 (*90-5782-010-2*, Pub. by Backhuys Pubs) Balogh.

Oyen, Wenche. The Snowstorm. (J). 1985. pap. 7.95 (*0-919519-98-9*, Pub. by Breakwater Bks) BookWorld.

***Oyer, Darrell J.** Pricing & Cost Accounting: A Handbook for Goverment Contractors. 250p. 1999. 125.00 (*1-56726-089-6*) Mgmt Concepts.

Oyer, Elizabeth, jt. auth. see Ravid, Ruth.

Oyer, Herbert J. Pastor Amos: Tragedy & Triumph. 1997. pap. 12.95 (*0-7880-0916-8*, Fairway Pr) CSS OH.

Oyer, Herbert J., ed. Current Trends in Audiology. (Journal Ser.: Vol. 48, No. 3, 1996). (Illus.). 58p. 1996. pap. 36.50 (*3-8055-6362-0*) S Karger.

Oyer, Herbert J., et al. Speech, Language, & Hearing Disorders: A Guide for the Teacher. 2nd ed. LC 93-22943. 256p. (C). 1993. pap. 42.95 (*0-205-14908-1*) Allyn.

Oyer, John S. & Kreider, Robert S. Mirror of the Martyrs. LC 90-71117. (Illus.). 96p. 1999. pap. 9.95 (*1-56148-003-7*) Good Bks PA.

Oyer, Ken & Erdos, Dawn. Photoshop Tech Support. LC 96-76252. 296p. 1997. pap. 29.99 (*0-7645-4000-9*) IDG Bks.

Oyer, Phyllis S. Oyer & Allied Families: Their History & Genealogy. (Illus.). 400p. 1988. 30.00 (*0-9620297-0-X*) P S Oyer.

Oyewole, Abiodun, et al. On a Mission: Selected Poems & a History of the Last Poets. 1996. pap. 12.95 (*0-614-20811-4*, Owl) H Holt & Co.

Oyewole, Anthony & Lucas, John. Historical Dictionary of Nigeria. 2nd ed. LC 97-9168. (African Historical Dictionaries Ser.: No. 40). (Illus.). 480p. 1998. 85.00 (*0-8108-3262-3*) Scarecrow.

Oyewumi, Oyeronke. The Invention of Women: Making an African Sense of Western Gender Discourses. LC 97-36162. 240p. 1997. pap. 21.95 (*0-8166-2441-0*); text 54.95 (*0-8166-2440-2*) U of Minn Pr.

Oyewumi, Oyeronke, ed. African Women & Feminism: Reflecting on the Politics of Sisterhood. 300p. 1997. 79.95 (*0-86543-627-4*); pap. 21.95 (*0-86543-628-2*) Africa World.

***Oyeyemi, Remi.** Songs from Exile. 1999. pap. write for info. (*1-58235-291-7*) Watermrk Pr.

Oyhamburu, Philippe. Dictionnaire des Patronymes Basques: Euskal Deiruren Hiztegia, Vol. 1. (BAQ & FRE.). 788p. 1991. 75.00 (*0-7859-8242-6*, 2908132028) Fr & Eur.

***Oyibo, Gabriel A.** Grand Unified Theorem. 351p. 1999. lib. bdg. 79.00 (*1-56072-689-X*) Nova Sci Pubs.

Oyibo, Gabriel A. New Group Theory for Mathematical Physics Gas Dynamics & Turbulence. 187p. 1993. lib. bdg. 145.00 (*1-56072-123-5*) Nova Sci Pubs.

Oyibo, Gabriel A., ed. Applied Mathematics: Methods & Applications. LC 95-47614. 450p. (C). 1997. lib. bdg. 175.00 (*1-56072-293-2*) Nova Sci Pubs.

***Oyibo, Papa.** Big Brother, Little Sister. (Illus.). 40p. (J). (ps-3). 2000. 15.95 (*1-84148-117-3*) Barefoot Bks NY.

Oyler, Celia. Making Room for Students: Sharing Teacher Authority in Room 104. 192p. (C). 1996. text 40.00 (*0-8077-3546-9*); pap. text 18.95 (*0-8077-3545-0*) Tchrs Coll.

Oyler, Phyllis. Sandyvale Cemetery, Johnstown, PA: A Recreation of Burials, 1850-1906. 363p. 1989. pap. text 30.00 (*0-933227-72-8*, 182) Closson Pr.

Oyler, Richard F. Ancestors (& Some Descendents) of Grant Oyler & Susan Ferguson. LC 98-110248. 784p. 1997. write for info. (*0-9654355-2-0*) Fmly History.

Oyola, Eliezer, tr. see Hayford, Jack W.

Oyola, Jose. Social Security Financing: Implications of Government Stock Investing for the Trust Fund, the Federal Budget & the Economy. (Illus.). 82p. (C). 1999. pap. text 20.00 (*0-7881-7781-8*) DIANE Pub.

Oyono, Eric. Gollo & the Lion. LC 94-7276. (Illus.). 32p. (J). (gr. 3-5). 1995. lib. bdg. 14.89 (*0-7868-2034-9*, Pub. by Hyprn Child) Little.

— Gollo & the Lion. LC 94-7276. (Illus.). 32p. (J). (ps-3). 1995. 14.95 (*0-7868-0041-0*, Pub. by Hyprn Child) Little.

Oyono, Ferdinand. Chemin d'Europe. (FRE.). 1973. pap. 14.95 (*0-7859-3183-X*, 2264004304) Fr & Eur.

— Houseboy. Reed, John, tr. from FRE. (African Writers Ser.). 122p. (Orig.). (C). 1991. pap. 9.95 (*0-435-90532-5*) Heinemann.

— The Old Man & the Medal. Reed, John, tr. from FRE. (African Writers Ser.).Tr. of Le Vieux Negre et la Medaille. 167p. (Orig.). (C). 1969. reprint ed. pap. 8.95 (*0-435-90039-0*, 90039) Heinemann.

— Road to Europe. Bjornson, Richard, tr. from FRE. LC 86-51301.Tr. of Chemin d'Europe. 103p. (Orig.). 1989. 20.00 (*0-89410-590-6*, Three Contnts); pap. 10.00 (*0-89410-591-4*, Three Contnts) L Rienner.

— Une Vie de Boy. (FRE.). 1970. pap. 9.95 (*0-7859-3430-8*) Fr & Eur.

— Le Vieux Negre et la Medaille. (FRE.). 1972. pap. 14.95 (*0-7859-3195-3*, 2264009624) Fr & Eur.

Oyono-Mbia, Guillaume, et al. Faces of African Independence: Three Plays. Arnold, A. J. & Drame, K., eds. Blair, Dorothy & Wake, Clive, trs. from FRE. LC 88-6976. (CARAF Bks.). 127p. 1988. text 25.00 (*0-8139-1186-9*); pap. text 14.95 (*0-8139-1187-7*) U Pr of Va.

***Oyos, Lynwood E.** History of the South Dakota Farmers Union. (Illus.). 200p. 1999. 24.95 (*0-931170-71-0*); pap. 15.95 (*0-931170-72-9*) Ctr Western Studies.

Oyos, Lynwood E. A Noble Calling: Teacher Education at Lutheran Normal School & Augustana College, 1889-1989. LC 90-30516. 100p. (Orig.). 1990. pap. 2.00 (*0-931170-45-1*) Ctr Western Studies.

— Over a Century of Leadership: South Dakota Territorial & State Governors. LC 87-71833. (Illus.). 250p. 1987. 9.95 (*0-931170-34-6*) Ctr Western Studies.

— Over a Century of Leadership: South Dakota Territorial & State Governors. deluxe ed. LC 87-71833. (Illus.). 250p. 1987. 25.00 (*0-931170-35-4*) Ctr Western Studies.

O'Young, Bryan, jt. ed. see Young, Mark.

O'Young, Leoung. Mike & the Bike. (Kids of Canada Ser.). 32p. (J). 1980. 12.95 (*0-88862-257-0*, Pub. by J Lorimer); pap. 5.95 (*0-88862-258-9*, Pub. by J Lorimer) Formac Dist Ltd.

Oystaeyen, F. M., ed. Ring Theory. (Lecture Notes in Mathematics Ser.: Vol. 1197). v, 231p. 1986. 32.95 (*0-387-16496-0*) Spr-Verlag.

Oystaeyen, Freddy Van, see Nastasescu, Constantin & Van Oystaeyen, Freddy.

Oystaeyen, Freddy Van, see Van Oystaeyen, Freddy, ed.

Oyster. Group Dynamics. LC 99-47177. 384p. 1999. pap. 40.94 (*0-07-048245-4*) McGraw.

Oyster, et al. Introduction to Research: A Guide for the Health Science Professional. LC 64-4347. 1987. text 21.50 (*0-397-54626-2*, Lippncott) Lppncott W & W.

Oyster Books Staff. My Ballet Collection: Sleeping Beauty. (Illus.). 32p. (J). 1995. 4.95 (*0-8362-0769-6*) Andrews & McMeel.

— My Ballet Collection: Swan Lake. (Illus.). 32p. (J). 1995. 4.95 (*0-8362-0771-8*) Andrews & McMeel.

Oyster, Carol K., jt. auth. see Stange, Mary Zeiss.

Oyster, Clyde W. The Human Eye: Structure & Function. LC 99-25402. (C). 1999. text 84.95 (*0-87893-645-9*) Sinauer Assocs.

Oyster, Esther M., jt. auth. see Moench, John O.

Oyston, Mildred V. Joseph's Sojourn in Egypt. 60p. 4.95 (*0-89036-153-3*) Liahona Pub Trust.

Oyuela-Caycedo, Augusto. History of Latin American Archaeology. LC 94-4854. (Worldwide Archaeology Ser.: Vol. 15). 1994. 85.95 (*1-85628-714-9*, Pub. by Avebry) Ashgate Pub Co.

Oyuela-Caycedo, Augusto & Raymond, J. Scott, eds. Recent Advances in the Archaeology of the Northern Andes: In Memory of Gerardo Reichel-Dolmatoff. LC 97-53049. (Monograph Ser.: No. 39). (Illus.). 176p. 1998. pap. 30.00 (*0-917956-90-7*) UCLA Arch.

Oyugi, Walter O., et al. Democratic Theory & Practice in Africa. LC 88-21101. 237p. (Orig.). (C). 1988. pap. text 18.50 (*0-435-08026-1*, 08026) Heinemann.

Oz. Management Information Systems. (C). 1997. pap. 48.00 (*0-7600-4946-7*) Course Tech.

***Oz.** The Same Sea. 2001. write for info. (*0-15-100572-9*) Harcourt.

Oz, Amos. Black Box. De Lange, Nicholas, tr. LC 87-33525. 320p. 1988. 19.95 (*0-15-112888-X*) Harcourt.

O

— Black Box. De Lange, Nicholas, tr. (Vintage International Ser.). 1989. pap. 12.00 (*0-679-72185-1*) Vin Bks.

— Don't Call It Night. DeLange, Nicholas, tr. 1997. pap. 11.00 (*0-15-600557-3*) Harcourt.

— Elsewhere, Perhaps. De Lange, Nicholas, tr. LC 73-8628. (Helen & Kurt Wolff Bk.). 324p. 1985. pap. 13.00 (*0-15-628475-8*, Harvest Bks) Harcourt.

— Fima. LC 92-44200. 322p. 1993. 22.95 (*0-15-189851-0*) Harcourt.

— Fima. 336p. (C). 1994. pap. 13.00 (*0-15-600143-8*) Harcourt.

— The Hill of Evil Counsel. 216p. 1991. pap. 7.95 (*0-15-640275-0*, Harvest Bks) Harcourt.

— In the Land of Israel. 304p. (C). 1993. pap. 13.00 (*0-15-648114-6*) Harcourt.

— Israel, Palestine, & Peace. 162p. 1995. pap. 11.00 (*0-15-600192-6*) Harcourt.

— My Michael. 1999. pap. 7.95 (*0-14-011729-6*, Viking) Viking Penguin.

— Panther in the Basement. De Lange, Nicholas, tr. from HEB. LC 97-20577. 160p. 1997. 21.00 (*0-15-100287-8*) Harcourt.

— Panther in the Basement. 160p. 1998. pap. 11.00 (*0-15-600630-8*, Harvest Bks) Harcourt.

— A Perfect Peace. Halkin, Hillel, tr. from HEB. LC 84-25171. (Helen & Kurt Wolff Bk.). 400p. 1985. 16.95 (*0-15-171696-X*) Harcourt.

Oz, Amos. A Perfect Peace. 384p. 1993. pap. 13.00 (*0-15-671683-6*) Harcourt.

— Silence of Heaven: Agnon's Fear of God. 2000. 29.95 (*0-691-03692-6*, Pub. by Princeton U Pr) Cal Prin Full Svc.

Oz, Amos. The Slopes of Lebanon. Goldberg-Bartura, Maurie, tr. 1989. 18.95 (*0-15-183090-8*) Harcourt.

— The Story Begins: Essays on Literature. Bar-Tura, Maggie, tr. from HEB. LC 98-35353. 118p. 1999. 20.00 (*0-15-100297-5*) Harcourt.

— To Know a Woman. 1991. 19.95 (*0-15-190499-5*) Harcourt.

— To Know a Woman. 272p. 1992. pap. 10.00 (*0-15-690680-5*, Harvest Bks) Harcourt.

— Touch the Water, Touch the Wind. 180p. (C). 1991. pap. 11.00 (*0-15-690772-0*, Harvest Bks) Harcourt.

— Under This Blazing Light. De Lange, Nicholas, tr. 219p. (C). 1995. 27.95 (*0-521-44367-9*) Cambridge U Pr.

— Under This Blazing Light. De Lange, Nicholas, tr. (Canto Book Ser.). 224p. (C). 1996. pap. 10.95 (*0-521-57622-9*) Cambridge U Pr.

Oz, Amos & Farah, Nuruddin. Suitcase Vol. 3: A Journal of Transcultural Traffic. (Illus.). 420p. 1998. pap. 19.95 (*0-9659565-2-0*) Suitcase.

Oz, Avraham. The Yoke of Love: Prophetic Riddles in The Merchant of Venice. LC 93-31278. 264p. 1995. 39.50 (*0-87413-490-0*) U Delaware Pr.

Oz, Avraham, ed. Strands Afar Remote: Israeli Perspectives on Shakespeare. LC 97-19193. (Illus.). 312p. 1998. 48.50 (*0-87413-597-4*) U Delaware Pr.

Oz, Charles & Messner, Julian. How Does Soda Get into the Bottle? 32p. (J). 1996. pap. 4.95 (*0-382-24375-7*) Silver Burdett Pr.

Oz, Effy. Ethics for an Information Age. 336p. (C). 1993. per. 16.87 (*0-697-20463-4*) Bus & Educ Tech.

— Ethics for an Information Age. 336p. (C). 1993. per. 33.12 (*0-697-20462-6*) Bus & Educ Tech.

Oz, Effy. Management Information Systems. 2nd ed. 700p. boxed set 72.95 (*0-7600-1091-9*, Pub. by Course Tech) Thomson Learn.

Oz, Mehmet. Healing from the Heart: A Leading Heart Surgeon Explores the Cutting Edge of Alternative Medicine. LC 98-4573. 224p. 1998. 23.95 (*0-525-94410-9*) NAL.

Oz, Mehmet, et al. Healing from the Heart: A Leading Surgeon Combines Eastern & Western Traditions to Create the Medicine of the Future. 224p. 1999. pap. 12.95 (*0-452-27955-0*) NAL.

Oz, Mehmet, jt. ed. see Goldstein, Daniel J.

Oz, Mehmet C. & Goldstein, Daniel. Minimally Invasive Cardiac Surgery, Vol. II. LC 98-30788. (Contemporary Cardiology Ser.: Vol. 2). 256p. 1998. 125.00 (*0-89603-635-9*) Humana.

Oz, Ozlem. The Competitive Advantage of Nations: The Case of Turkey. LC HF3756.5.Z5O98 1999. 226p. 1999. text 69.95 (*1-84014-982-5*) Ashgate Pub Co.

Oz, Robin. Peanut Butter. 2nd ed. (Let Me Read Ser.). 16p. (J). (ps-1). 1995. bds. 2.95 (*0-673-36271-X*, GoodYrBooks) Addson-Wesley Educ.

Oz-Salzberger, Fania. Translating the Enlightenment: Scottish Civic Discourse in Eighteenth-Century Germany. (Oxford Historical Monographs). 366p. 1995. text 59.00 (*0-19-820519-8*) OUP.

Oz-Salzberger, Fania, ed. see Ferguson, Adam.

***Oz, Tony.** The Stock Trader: How I Make a Living Trading Stocks. 279p. 2000. 55.00 (*0-9679435-0-7*) Goldman Brown.

— Stock Trading Wizard: Advanced Short-Term Trading Strategies. (Illus.). 189p. 1999. 96.00 (*0-9673862-0-9*) Tony Oz Pubns.

Oza, B. M. Bofors, the Ambassador's Evidence LC 97-901355. x, 176 p. 1997. write for info. (*81-220-0494-6*, Pub. by Konark Pubs Pvt Ltd) S Asia.

Oza, S. S. & Bhatt, R. G. Modern Combined Dictionary: English - Gujarti & Gujarti - English. 103p. 1992. reprint ed. 29.95 (*0-8288-8471-4*) Fr & Eur.

Ozaeta, Pablo. Mis Primeros Cuentos. Frank, Marjorie & Lono, Luz P., eds. LC 75-16546. (Illus.). (J). (gr. 4-8). 1991. pap., teacher ed. 10.60 (*0-8325-9641-8*, Natl Textbk Co) NTC Contemp Pub Co.

— Mis Primeros Cuentos. Frank, Marjorie & Lono, Luz P., eds. LC 75-16546. (Illus.). (J). (gr. 4-8). 1994. pap., student ed. 6.60 (*0-8325-9642-6*, Natl Textbk Co) NTC Contemp Pub Co.

— Mis Primeros Cuentos. Frank, Marjorie & Lono, Luz P., eds. LC 75-16546. (Illus.). (J). (gr. 4-8). 1995. 76.60 (*0-8325-9640-X*, Natl Textbk Co) NTC Contemp Pub Co.

Ozaga, John. Whitetail Country. (Illus.). 1993. pap. 19.95 (*1-55971-207-4*, NorthWord Pr) Creat Pub Intl.

Ozaki, Hosai. Right under the Big Sky, I Don't Wear a Hat: The Haiku & Prose of Hosai Ozaki. Sato, Hiroaki, tr. from JPN. LC 93-3814. 144p. (Orig.). 1993. pap. 12.00 (*1-880656-05-1*) Stone Bridge Pr.

Ozaki, Kazuo. Rosy Glasses. Epp, Robert, tr. 150p. (C). 1996. text 29.00 (*0-904404-52-8*, Pub. by Curzon Pr Ltd) UH Pr.

Ozaki, Muneto, et al. Labour Relations in the Public Service: Developing Countries. xv, 205p. (Orig.). 1988. pap. 24.75 (*92-2-106394-1*) Intl Labour Office.

— Technological Change & Labour Relations. xiv, 205p. 1992. pap. 27.00 (*92-2-107753-5*) Intl Labour Office.

Ozaki, Muneto, jt. ed. see Gladstone, Alan.

***Ozaki, Y. & Noda, I., eds.** Two-Dimensional Correlation Spectroscopy: Kobe-Sanda, Japan, 29 August-1 September 1999. LC 00-100066. (AIP Conference Proceedings Ser.: Vol. 503). (Illus.). xiii, 343p. 2000. 105.00 (*1-56396-916-5*) Am Inst Physics.

Ozaki, Yei T., concept. The Japanese Fairy Book. LC 70-109415. (Illus.). 320p. (J). (gr. 3-8). 1970. pap. 12.95 (*0-8048-0885-6*) Tuttle Pubng.

Ozaki, Yei T., ed. Japanese Fairy Tales. 1977. lib. bdg. 250.00 (*0-8490-2091-3*) Gordon Pr.

***Ozaktas.** The Fractional Fourier Transform. 376p. 2000. text 95.00 (*0-471-96346-1*) Wiley.

Ozan, Ozcan. The Sultan's Kitchen: A Turkish Cookbook. LC 97-52132. (Illus.). 160p. 1998. 29.95 (*962-593-223-2*) Periplus.

Ozanam, Frederic & Lattey, Cuthbert. Back to the Bible. 128p. 1996. reprint ed. 16.95 (*0-912141-41-7*) Roman Cath Bks.

Ozand, Pinar T., jt. auth. see Nyhan, William L.

***Ozaniec, Naomi.** Chakras: An Introductory Guide to Your Energy Centers for Total Health. (New Perspectives (Element) Ser.). (Illus.). 128p. 2000. pap. 9.95 (*1-86204-765-0*, Pub. by Onewrld Pubns) Penguin Putnam.

Ozaniec, Naomi. Chakras for Beginners. (Headway Guide for Beginners Ser.). (Illus.). 112p. 1995. pap. 11.95 (*0-340-62082-X*, Pub. by Headway) Trafalgar.

— Daughter of the Goddess: The Sacred Priestess. (Illus.). 1994. 16.00 (*1-85538-280-6*, Pub. by Aqrn Pr) Harper SF.

— Dowsing for Beginners. (Headway Guide for Beginners Ser.). (Illus.). 128p. 1995. pap. 11.95 (*0-340-60882-X*, Pub. by Headway) Trafalgar.

— Element Tarot Handbook: Initiation into the Key Elements of the Tarot. (Illus.). 190p. 1994. pap. 14.95 (*1-85230-488-X*, Pub. by Element MA) Penguin Putnam.

— Elements of Chakras. LC 98-196189. (Illus.). 144p. 1997. pap. 9.95 (*1-86204-029-X*, Pub. by Element MA) Penguin Putnam.

— Elements of Egyptian Wisdom. 1994. pap. 9.95 (*1-85230-497-9*, Pub. by Element MA) Penguin Putnam.

— Illustrated Guide to the Tarot. LC 99-14070. (Illus.). 1999. 21.95 (*0-8069-7091-X*) Sterling.

***Ozaniec, Naomi.** Illustrated Guide to the Tarot. (Illus.). 2000. pap. 14.95 (*0-8069-7132-0*) Sterling.

Ozaniec, Naomi. Meditation: Meditation. (Teach Yourself Ser.). (Illus.). 192p. 1998. pap. 9.95 (*0-8442-0018-2*, 00182) NTC Contemp Pub Co.

— Meditation for Beginners. (Headway Guide for Beginners Ser.). (Illus.). 88p. 1996. mass mkt. 11.95 (*0-340-64835-X*, Pub. by Headway) Trafalgar.

— Teach Yourself Tarot. (Teach Yourself Ser.). 192p. 1998. pap. 11.95 (*0-8442-3112-6*, Teach Yrslf) NTC Contemp Pub Co.

Ozaniec, Naomi, compiled by. The Little Book of Egyptian Wisdom. LC 97-9024. (Little Bks.). (Illus.). 48p. 1997. 5.95 (*1-86204-110-5*, Pub. by Element MA) Penguin Putnam.

Ozanne, Adam. Perverse Supply Response in Agriculture: The Importance of Produced Means of Production & Uncertainty. 188p. 1992. 82.95 (*1-85628-375-5*, Pub. by Avebry) Ashgate Pub Co.

Ozanne, Charles. Life & Soul of Mortal Man. 32p. (Orig.). 1995. pap. 3.00 (*1-880573-21-0*) Bible Search Pubns.

— The Pastorals in Perspective. 40p. (Orig.). 1993. pap. 3.00 (*1-880573-10-5*) Bible Search Pubns.

***Ozanne, Charles.** The Priority of Philippians. 36p. 2000. pap. 4.00 (*1-880573-56-3*) Bible Search Pubns.

Ozanne, Charles. Samuel, Saul & the Son of Jesse. 32p. (Orig.). 1997. pap. 3.00 (*1-880573-37-7*) Bible Search Pubns.

Ozanne-Rivierre, Francoise. Dictionnaire Iaai. (FRE.). 1984. 59.95 (*0-7859-8078-4*, 2-85297-126-7) Fr & Eur.

Ozanne, Robert W. Wages in Practice & Theory: McCormick & International Harvester, 1860-1960. LC 68-19572. (Illus.). 195p. reprint ed. pap. 60.50 (*0-8357-6778-7*, 203545400095) Bks Demand.

***Ozar, David T. & Sokol, David J.** Dental Ethics at Chairside: Professional Principles & Practical Applications. 2nd ed. LC 99-37080. 288p. 1999. pap. text 38.00 (*0-87840-759-6*) Georgetown U Pr.

Ozar, Lorraine A. Creating a Curriculum That Works. LC 95-163195. (Illus.). 172p. (Orig.). 1994. pap. 12.50 (*1-55833-143-3*) Natl Cath Educ.

Ozar, Lorraine A., ed. By Their Fruits You Shall Know Them. 27p. (Orig.). 1995. pap. 10.60 (*1-55833-145-X*) Natl Cath Educ.

Ozarowski, Filip. Gdy Plonal Wolyn. 2nd rev. unabridged ed. (POL., Illus.). v, 240p. 1996. reprint ed. pap. 9.99 (*0-9655488-0-5*) F Ozarowski.

— Wolyn Aflame. (Illus.). 357p. 1997. pap. 12.00 (*0-9655488-1-3*) F Ozarowski.

Ozarowski, Joseph S. To Walk in God's Ways: Jewish Pastoral Perspectives on Illness & Bereavement. LC 94-40782. 232p. 1995. 30.00 (*1-56821-388-3*) Aronson.

Ozarowski, Joseph S., et al. Common Ground: The Weekly Torah Portion Through the Eyes of a Conservative, Orthodox & Reform Rabbi. Lipman, Steve, ed. & intro. by. LC 97-13609. 416p. 1997. 40.00 (*0-7657-5992-6*) Aronson.

Ozawa. Analog Methods for Computer-Aided Circuit Analysis & Diagnosis. (Electrical Engineering & Electronics Ser.: No. 48). 448p. 1988. 150.00 (*0-8247-7843-X*) Dekker.

Ozawa, E., jt. ed. see Ebashi, Setsuro.

Ozawa, H., ed. see Nihón Seishin Shinkei Gakkai.

Ozawa, Hiroshi. Kendo: The Definitive Guide. 1997. 35.00 (*4-7700-2119-4*, Pub. by Kodansha Int) OUP.

Ozawa, Hiroyuki. The Great Festivals of Japan: Spectacle & Spirit. Bester, John, tr. (Illus.). 120p. 1999. 30.00 (*4-7700-2394-4*, Pub. by Kodansha Intl) Kodansha.

Ozawa, Ichiro. Blueprint for a New Japan: The Rethinking of a Nation. Rubenfein, Louisa, tr. 208p. pap. 10.00 (*4-7700-2034-1*) FS&G.

— Blueprint for a New Japan: The Rethinking of a Nation. Rubinfien, Louisa, tr. 208p. 1994. 25.00 (*4-7700-1871-1*) Kodansha.

Ozawa, K. Liver Surgery Approached Through the Mitochondria. (Illus.). 222p. 1993. 132.25 (*3-8055-5716-7*) S Karger.

— Living Related Donor Liver Transplantation: Assessment of Graft Viability Based on the Redox Theory. (Illus.). xii, 212p. 1994. 195.00 (*3-8055-5800-7*) S Karger.

Ozawa, K. A. High Density Magnetic Recording for Home Vtr, Vol. 4. (Japanese Technology Reviews Ser.). 138p. 1993. pap. text 61.00 (*2-88124-887-X*) Gordon & Breach.

Ozawa, Martha N., ed. Women's Life Cycle & Economic Insecurity: Problems & Proposals. LC 89-32804. (Contributions in Women's Studies: No. 108). 242p. 1989. pap. 21.95 (*0-275-93348-2*, B3348, Praeger Pubs) Greenwood.

— Women's Life Cycle & Economic Insecurity: Problems & Proposals, 108. LC 89-7505. (Contributions in Women's Studies: No. 108). 242p. 1989. 55.00 (*0-313-26753-7*, OWC/, Praeger Pubs) Greenwood.

Ozawa, Osamu, jt. auth. see Hassell, Randall G.

Ozawa, T., ed. New Trends in Biological Chemistry. (Illus.). 440p. 1991. 149.95 (*0-387-53935-2*) Spr-Verlag.

Ozawa, T., et al, eds. Biodefence Mechanisms Against Environmental Stress. 208p. 1998. 109.00 (*3-540-63899-7*) Spr-Verlag.

Ozawa, T., jt. ed. see Kim, C. H.

Ozawa, Tadashi. Anime Character Designs Made Easy, 1. 1999. pap. text 19.95 (*4-7661-1070-6*) Graphic-Sha.

Ozawa, Terutomo. People & Productivity in Japan. (Studies in Productivity: Vol. 25). 42p. 1982. pap. 55.00 (*0-08-029506-1*) Work in Amer.

Ozawa, Terutomo, jt. auth. see Castello, Sergio.

Ozbalkan, N. German-Turkish Technical Dictionary. 6th ed. (TUR & GER.). 934p. 1993. 95.00 (*0-320-03100-4*) Fr & Eur.

Ozbalkan, Nuri. English-Turkish Dictionary of Technical Terms. 7th ed. (ENG & TUR.). 1989. 117.00 (*0-7859-8973-0*) Fr & Eur.

— English-Turkish Dictionary of Technical Terms. 7th ed. 960p. 1989. 112.00 (*975-7609-02-1*) IBD Ltd.

— Ingilizce-Turkce Teknik Terimler Sozlugu. 7th ed. (ENG & TUR.). 976p. 1989. write for info. (*0-7859-6786-9*) Fr & Eur.

— Textile Dictionary in Four Languages. (ENG, FRE, GER & TUR.). 1053p. 87.95 (*0-88431-308-5*) IBD Ltd.

— Turkish-English Dictionary of Technical Terminology. (ENG & TUR.). 1152p. 1984. 150.00 (*0-8288-0672-1*, M1980) Fr & Eur.

— Turkish-English Dictionary of Technical Terms. 2nd rev. ed. 1152p. 1989. 105.00 (*975-7368-19-9*) IBD Ltd.

***Ozbay, Hitay.** Introduction to Feedback Control Theory. LC 99-33365. 232p. (C). 1999. boxed set 69.95 (*0-8493-1867-X*) CRC Pr.

Ozbay, K., jt. auth. see Kachroo, P.

Ozbay, Kaan. Incident Management in Intelligent Transportation Systems. LC 99-17751. 267p. 1999. 85.00 (*0-89006-774-0*) Artech Hse.

Ozben, Tomris, ed. Free Radicals, Oxidative Stress & Antioxidants: Pathological & Physiological Significance. LC 98-18042. (NATO ASI Ser.: No. 296). (Illus.). 406p. (C). 1998. text 129.50 (*0-306-45813-6*, Kluwer Plenum) Kluwer Academic.

Ozbudum, Ergun, jt. auth. see Weiner, Myron.

***Ozbudun, Ergun.** Contemporary Turkish Politics: Challenges to Democratic Consolidation. LC 99-38717. 174p. 1999. 49.95 (*1-55587-735-4*) L Rienner.

Ozbudun, Ergun & Ulusan, Aydin, eds. The Political Economy of Income Distribution in Turkey. LC 79-2781. (Political Economy of Income Distribution in Developing Countries Ser.: Vol. III). 1980. 85.00 (*0-8419-0563-0*) Holmes & Meier.

Ozcan, Azmi. Pan-Islamism: Indian Muslims, the Ottomans & Britain (1877-1924) LC 97-5470. (Ottoman Empire & Its Heritage Ser.: No. 12). 260p. 1997. 90.50 (*90-04-10632-4*, NLG 143) Brill Academic Pubs.

Ozcan, Gul B. Small Firms & Local Economic Developments: Entrepreneurship in Southern Europe & Turkey. 240p. 1995. 72.95 (*1-85972-117-6*, Pub. by Avebry) Ashgate Pub Co.

Ozcubukcu, Koray, jt. auth. see Gascoyne, Richard J.

Ozdalga, Elisabeth. The Veiling Issue, Official Secularism & Popular Islam in Modern Turkey. 128p. 1998. 45.00 (*0-7007-0983-5*, Pub. by Curzon Pr Ltd) Paul & Co Pubs.

***Ozdalga, Elisabeth, ed.** The Nakshibendis in Western & Central Asia: Change & Continuity. 180p. 1999. pap. (*0-7007-1147-3*, Pub. by Curzon Pr Ltd) Paul & Co Pubs.

Ozdalga, Elisabeth & Persson, Sune, eds. Civil Society, Democracy & the Muslin World. 145p. 1998. pap. 29.95 (*0-7007-1053-1*, Pub. by Curzon Pr Ltd) Paul & Co Pubs.

Ozdemir. North American Tunneling '96, Vol. 1. 529p. 1996. 97.00 (*90-5410-803-7*) Ashgate Pub Co.

— North American Tunneling '96, Vol. 2. 270p. 1996. 97.00 (*90-5410-804-5*) Ashgate Pub Co.

Ozdemir, Levent, ed. North American Tunneling '98: Proceedings of the North American Tunneling '98 Conference, Newport Beach, California, 21-25.02.1998. LC 99-496418. (Illus.). 275p. (C). 1998. text 98.00 (*90-5410-931-9*, Pub. by A A Balkema) Ashgate Pub Co.

— North American Tunneling, '96: Proceedings of the North American Conference NAT '96 & 22nd General Assembly International, vols. 2. (Illus.). 863p. (C). 1996. text 188.00 (*90-5410-802-9*, Pub. by A A Balkema) Ashgate Pub Co.

Ozdemir, Ozden, jt. auth. see Dunlop, David J.

Ozdemir, T., et al. Modeling of Conformal Antennas on Doubly Curved Platforms & Their Interactions with Aircraft Platforms: Annual Progress Report. LC TL0694.A6. (University of Michigan Reports: No. 031307-5-T). 96p. 1995. reprint ed. pap. 30.00 (*0-608-02396-5*, 206303700004) Bks Demand.

Ozee, Carol, jt. auth. see Carter, Carol.

Ozegovic, Jack. Northern Spirits Distilled: Memories of the Upper Midwest. Semken, Steven H., ed. LC 99-71800. 252p. 2000. pap. 16.95 (*1-888160-53-5*, Pub. by Ice Cube) SPD-Small Pr Dist.

Ozeki, Kazuo, jt. ed. see Asaka, Tetsuichi.

Ozeki, Ruth L. My Year of Meats: A Novel. LC 97-52319. 364p. 1998. 23.95 (*0-670-87904-5*, Viking) Viking Penguin.

***Ozeki, Ruth L.** My Year of Meats: A Novel. LC 97-52319. 384p. 1999. pap. 12.95 (*0-14-028046-4*) Viking Penguin.

Ozeki, Yuzuru, jt. auth. see Tavlas, George S.

Ozekici, S., ed. Reliability & Maintenance of Complex Systems. LC 96-13936. (NATO ASI Ser.: Vol. 154). 587p. 1996. 173.00 (*3-540-61109-6*) Spr-Verlag.

Ozelsel, Michaela. Forty Days: The Diary of a Traditional Solitary Sufi Retreat. 240p. 1996. pap. text 18.95 (*0-939660-52-0*) Threshold CA.

Ozen, Alf, ed. Historische Wahrheit und Theologische Wissenschaft: Gerd Ludemann Zum 50. Geburtstag. (GER., Illus.). 148p. 1996. 32.95 (*3-631-30427-7*) P Lang Pubng.

Ozen, Alf, jt. auth. see Ludemann, Gerd.

Ozenbaugh, Richard Lee. EMI Filter Design. (Electrical Engineering & Electronics Ser.: Vol. 95). (Illus.). 272p. 1995. text 125.00 (*0-8247-9631-4*) Dekker.

Ozenda, P. Lichens. (Handbuch der Pflanzenanatomie Encyclopedia of Plant Anatomy - Traite d' Anatomie Vegetale Ser.: Vol. 6, Pt. 9). (GER., Illus.). xii, 200p. 1963. 62.00 (*3-443-39010-2*, Pub. by Gebruder Borntraeger) Balogh.

Ozer, D. J. Consistency in Personality. (Recent Research in Psychology Ser.). (Illus.). 82p. 1986. 50.95 (*0-387-96299-9*) Spr-Verlag.

Ozer, Daniel J., jt. auth. see Funder, David Charles.

Ozer, Elizabeth M., ed. The Impact of Work-Family Systems on Women's Psychological Health: A Special Issue of Women's Health. 114p. 1998. pap. write for info. (*0-8058-9791-7*) L Erlbaum Assocs.

Ozer, Jan. Publishing Digital Video. 2nd ed. LC 97-10922. (Illus.). 557p. 1997. pap., pap. text 34.95 incl. cd-rom (*0-12-531942-8*) Morgan Kaufmann.

***Ozer, Jerome S., ed.** Film Review Annual, 1998. (Film Review Annual Ser.: Vol. 18). xiv, 1642p. 2000. lib. bdg. 140.00 (*0-89198-152-7*, Film Review Pubns) Ozer.

Ozer, Jerome S., ed. Film Review Annual, 1997. (Film Review Annual Ser.). xiv, 1742p. 1998. lib. bdg. 140.00 (*0-89198-150-0*, Film Review Pubns) Ozer.

— Film Review Annual, 1981. xiii, 1153p. 1982. lib. bdg. 140.00 (*0-89198-125-X*) Ozer.

— Film Review Annual, 1982. xiii, 1362p. 1983. 140.00 (*0-89198-126-8*) Ozer.

— Film Review Annual, 1983. xiii, 1538p. 1984. lib. bdg. 140.00 (*0-89198-131-4*) Ozer.

— Film Review Annual, 1984. (Film Review Annual Ser.). xiii, 1548p. 1985. 140.00 (*0-89198-133-0*) Ozer.

— Film Review Annual, 1985. xiii, 1554p. 1986. 140.00 (*0-89198-134-9*) Ozer.

— Film Review Annual, 1986. 6th ed. xiii, 1650p. 1987. 140.00 (*0-89198-135-7*) Ozer.

— Film Review Annual, 1987. xiii, 1656p. 1988. 140.00 (*0-89198-136-5*) Ozer.

— Film Review Annual, 1988. xiii, 1773p. 1989. 140.00 (*0-89198-138-1*) Ozer.

— Film Review Annual, 1989. xiii, 1788p. 1991. 140.00 (*0-89198-139-X*) Ozer.

— Film Review Annual, 1990: With Ten-Year Cumulative Title Index. xiv, 1658p. 1991. 140.00 (*0-89198-142-X*) Ozer.

— Film Review Annual, 1991. xvi, 1744p. 1992. lib. bdg. 140.00 (*0-89198-144-6*) Ozer.

— Film Review Annual, 1992, Vol. 12. xiv, 1714p. 1993. 140.00 (*0-89198-145-4*) Ozer.

— Film Review Annual, 1993, Vol. 13. xvi, 1732p. 1994. 140.00 (*0-89198-146-2*, Film Review Pubns) Ozer.

— Film Review Annual, 1994 Vol. 14. xiv, 1747p. 1995. 140.00 (*0-89198-147-0*, Film Review Pubns) Ozer.

— Film Review Annual, 1995, Vol. 15. xiv, 1720p. 1996. 140.00 (*0-89198-148-9*, Film Review Pubns) Ozer.

— Film Review Annual, 1996: Films of 1995. (Film Review Annual Ser.: Vol. 16). xiv, 1640p. 1997. 140.00 (*0-89198-149-7*) Ozer.

An Asterisk (*) at the beginning of an entry indicates that the title is appearing for the first time.

P

P

An Asterisk (*) at the beginning of an entry indicates that the title is appearing for the first time.

-M in Defense Technology Seminar Staff. Powder Metallurgy in Defense Technology: Proceedings of the P-M in Defense Technology Seminar, Held at Yuma, AZ, November 13 & 14, 1979, Vol. 5. LC TN0695.P66. (Illus.). 128p. reprint ed. pap. 39.70 (*0-7837-1561-7*, 20418530005) Bks Demand.

P. M. Staff. Bolo' Bolo. 192p. Date not set. 7.00 (*0-936756-08-X*) Autonomedia.

P., Maingot Joseph. Le Privilege Parliamentaire au Canada. 2nd ed. (FRE.). 1997. text 65.00 (*0-7735-1720-0*, Pub. by McG-Queens Univ Pr) CUP Services.

P., Mark, jt. auth. see Echenberg, Erica.

P., Pevet, ed. Adaptations to Climatic Changes. (Limited Volume Series: Comparative Physiology of Environmental Adaptations: Vol. 3). (Illus.). vii, 188p. 1987. 155.00 (*3-8055-4472-3*) S Karger.

P. S. Associates Staff & Van Den Heuvel, Edward P. The Nature & Evolutionary Status of Herbig Ae/Be Stars, No. 62. LC 94-72188. 464p. 1994. 34.00 (*0-937707-81-3*) Astron Soc Pacific.

P., Wally. But for the Grace of God: How Intergroups & Central Offices Carried the Message of Alcoholics Anonymous. LC 96-178444. (Illus.). 226p. (Orig.). 1995. pap. 15.00 (*1-877686-08-5*) Bishop Bks.

P-51 Mustang Pilots Association Staff. The P-51 Mustang. 2nd rev. ed. LC 87-51161. (Illus.). 192p. 1987. 49.95 (*1-56311-080-6*) Turner Pub KY.

P/M in Aerospace & Defense Technologies Symposium. P/M in Aerospace & Defense Technologies, 1991: Proceedings of the P/M in Aerospace & Defense Technologies Symposium, Sponsored by the Metal Powder Industries Federation, Held in Tampa, FL, March 4-6, 1991. LC 91-19049. 424p. 1991. reprint ed. pap. 131.50 (*0-608-01820-1*, 206246900003) Bks Demand.

Pa Chin. Family. 332p. (C). 1988. reprint ed. pap. text 7.50 (*0-88133-373-5*) Waveland Pr.

Pa, Chin, ed. see Li, Fei-Kan.

Pa Kin. Le Jardin de Repos. (FRE.). 1981. pap. 10.95 (*0-7859-4147-9*) Fr & Eur.

— Nuit Glacee. (FRE.). 1983. pap. 15.95 (*0-7859-4195-9*) Fr & Eur.

Pa. Public Utility Commission Staff. Pa. Public Utility Commission Decisions July 1995 to December 1995, Vol. 85. Leming, Shirley, ed. 719p. 1995. 235.62 (*0-8182-0219-X*) Commonweal PA.

PA State Data Staff. The Pennsylvania Source Book. 70p. 1998. 20.00 (*1-58036-054-8*) Penn State Data Ctr.

Paakkanen, Lisa. Jipemoyo 4. 156p. 1981. write for info. (*951-46-5316-5*, Pub. by Nordic Africa) Transaction Pubs.

Paal, E. & Menon, P. G. Hydrogen Effects in Catalysis: Fundamentals & Practical Applications. (Chemical Industries Ser.: Vol. 31). (Illus.). 784p. 1987. text 285.00 (*0-8247-7774-3*) Dekker.

Paalman, Anthony. Training Showjumpers. 352p. 1990. 62.00 (*0-85131-260-8*, Pub. by J A Allen) St Mut.

***Paalman, Anthony.** Training Showjumpers. 2000. 55.00 (*0-85131-548-8*, Pub. by J A Allen) Trafalgar.

Paalman, Anthony. Training Showjumpers. rev. ed. (Illus.). 160p. 1998. 150.00 (*0-85131-549-6*, Pub. by J A Allen) Trafalgar.

Paalman, M., ed. Promoting Safer Sex. x, 252p. 1990. 30.00 (*90-265-1012-8*) Swets.

Paananen, Lauri, jt. auth. see Engle, Eloise.

Paananen, Victor N. British Marxist Criticism. Cain, William, ed. LC 99-29365. (Bibliographies of Modern Critics & Critical Schools Ser.). 500p. 1999. 65.00 (*0-8153-0385-8*) Garland.

— William Blake. (English Authors Ser.: No. 202). 176p. 1977. 22.95 (*0-8057-6672-3*) Macmillan.

— William Blake. rev. ed. 1996. 32.00 (*0-8057-7053-4*, Twyne) Mac Lib Ref.

Paap, Carolin. Die Josephsgeschichte Genesis 37-50: Bestimmungen Ihrer Literarischen Gattung in der Zweiten Halfte des 20. Jahrhunderts. (Europaische Hochschulschriften Ser.: Reihe 23, Bd. 534). (GER.). 193p. 1995. 42.95 (*3-631-48571-9*) P Lang Pubng.

Paap, David A. Biblical Equipping: God's Word in Your World. rev. ed. LC 96-69292. 96p. 1996. pap. text 8.95 (*0-9633831-5-9*) Stephen Minist.

Paap, David A., ed. see McKay, William J. & Haugk, Kenneth C.

Paar, C., jt. ed. see Koc, C. K.

Paar, H. P., jt. auth. see Caldwell, D. O.

Paar, Vladimir, jt. auth. see Meyer, Richard A.

Paar, Vladimir, jt. ed. see Meyer, R. A.

Paardt, R. T. Van der, see Van der Paardt, R. T.

Paardt, R. T. Van Der, see Hijmans, B. L., Jr.

Paardt, R. T. Van Der, see Hijmans, B. L.

Paarlberg, Don. An Analysis & History of Inflation. LC 92-17815. 208p. 1992. 55.00 (*0-275-94416-6*, C4416, Praeger Pubs) Greenwood.

— Farm & Food Policy: Issues of the 1980s. LC 79-17496. 348p. 1980. reprint ed. pap. 107.90 (*0-608-01843-0*, 206249300003) Bks Demand.

— Farmers of Five Continents. LC 83-17090. 124p. reprint ed. pap. 38.50 (*0-7837-1825-X*, 204202500001) Bks Demand.

— Toward a Well-Fed World. LC 87-36152. (Henry A. Wallace Series on Agricultural History & Rural Studies). 288p. 1988. reprint ed. pap. 89.30 (*0-608-00113-9*, 206087800006) Bks Demand.

***Paarlberg, Don & Paarlberg, Phillip.** The Agricultural Revolution of the 20th Century. 176p. 2000. 54.95 (*0-8138-2198-3*) Iowa St U Pr.

Paarlberg, Phillip, jt. auth. see Paarlberg, Don.

Paarlberg, Robert L. Countrysides at Risk: The Political Geography of Sustainable Agriculture. LC 94-43973. (Policy Essay Ser.: Vol. 16). (Orig.). 1994. pap. 13.95 (*1-56517-021-0*) Overseas Dev Council.

— Fixing Farm Trade: Policy Options for the United States. LC 87-24118. (Council on Foreign Relations Series on International Trade). 176p. 1987. text 19.95 (*0-88730-196-7*, HarpBusn) HarpInfo.

— Leadership Abroad Begins at Home: U. S. Foreign Economic Policy after the Cold War. (Integrating National Economies Ser.). 144p. (C). 1995. 34.95 (*0-8157-6804-4*); pap. 14.95 (*0-8157-6803-6*) Brookings.

Paarlberg, Robert L., et al, eds. Diplomatic Dispute: U. S. Conflict with Iran, Japan & Mexico. (Harvard Studies in International Affairs: No. 39). 174p. 1984. reprint ed. pap. text 24.00 (*0-8191-4063-5*) U Pr of Amer.

Paas, Martha W. Population Change, Labor Supply, & Agriculture in Ausburg, 1480-1618: A Study of Early Demographic-Economic Interactions. Bruchey, Stuart, ed. LC 80-2821. (Dissertations in European Economic History Ser.). (Illus.). 1981. lib. bdg. 29.95 (*0-405-14005-3*) Ayer.

Paasch, Henri. Dictionnaire Anglais-Francais et Francais-Anglais des Termes et Locutions Maritimes. 2nd ed. (ENG & FRE.). 320p. 1974. pap. 23.50 (*0-7859-0749-1*, M-6437) Fr & Eur.

Paasch, Henry. Paasch's Illustrated Marine Dictionary: An Authentic Document of the Age of Steam & Sail. LC 97-201662. Orig. Title: From Keel to Truck. (Illus.). 408p. 1997. reprint ed. 25.00 (*1-55821-650-2*) Lyons Pr.

Paashuis, Victor. The Organisation of Integrated Product Development. Pham, D. T., ed. LC 97-44699. (Advanced Manufacturing Ser.). (Illus.). xi, 266p. 1997. 84.95 (*3-540-76225-6*) Spr-Verlag.

Paasi, Annsi, ed. see Grano, Johannes G.

Paasi, Anssi. Territories, Boundaries & Consciousness: The Changing Geographies of the Finnish-Russian Border. LC 95-31384. (Studies in Political Geography). 376p. 1997. 85.00 (*0-471-96119-1*, Belhaven) Halsted Pr.

Paasilinna, Arto. The Year of the Hare. Lomas, Herbert, tr. from FIN. 135p. 1995. 29.00 (*0-7206-0949-6*, Pub. by P Owen Ltd) Dufour.

— The Year of the Hare. Lomas, Herbert, tr. from FIN. 136p. 1996. pap. 17.95 (*0-7206-1017-6*, Pub. by P Owen Ltd) Dufour.

Paasivirta, Esa. Participation of States in International Contracts & Arbitral Settlement of Disputes. 346p. (Orig.). 1990. pap. 147.50 (*951-640-519-3*) Coronet Bks.

***Paasivirta, J., ed.** New Types of Persistent Halogenated Compounds. (Handbook of Environmental Chemistry Ser.: Vol. 3, Pt. K). (Illus.). 336p. 2000. 175.00 (*3-540-65838-6*) Spr-Verlag.

Paasivirta, Jaakko. Chemical Ecotoxicology. 232p. 1991. lib. bdg. 95.00 (*0-87371-366-4*, L366) Lewis Pubs.

Paasivirta, Juhani. Finland & Europe: International Crises in the Period of Autonomy, 1808-1914. Kirby, D. G., ed. Upton, Anthony F. & Upton, Sirkka R., trs. from FIN. LC 82-133218. (Nordic Ser.: No. 7). 282p. reprint ed. pap. 87.50 (*0-7837-2931-6*, 205752300006) Bks Demand.

Paasonen, M., jt. auth. see Tuomisto, J.

Paaswell, Robert E., et al, eds. Site Impact Traffic Assessment: Problems & Solutions, Proceedings of the Conference Sponsored by the Urban Transportation Division of the American Society of Civil Engineers in Cooperation with Institute of Transportation Engineers, Urban Land Institute, National Association of Regional Councils. LC 92-13902. 256p. 1992. pap. text 29.00 (*0-87262-870-1*) Am Soc Civil Eng.

Paaswell, Robert E. & Recker, Wilfred W. Problems of the Carless. LC 77-13730. (Praeger Special Studies). 190p. 1978. 49.95 (*0-275-90308-7*, C0308, Praeger Pubs) Greenwood.

Paat, Jude B. Stardust to Twilight: A Collection of Poems. (Illus.). 75p. (Orig.). 1992. pap. 7.50 (*971-10-0495-X*, Pub. by New Day Pub) Cellar.

Paat, Laurens H. Die Theologisch-Okumenischen Partneschaftsgrundgedanken der Kirchen Indonesiens: Am Beispiel der Evangelischen Kirche in der Minahasa. (Europaische Hochschulschriften Ser.: Reihe 23, Bd. 429). (GER.). XIV, 252p. 1991. 51.80 (*3-631-44098-7*) P Lang Pubng.

Paatalo, Kalle. Storm over the Land: A Novel about War. Impola, Richard A., tr. from FIN. & frwd. by. 579p. (Orig.). 1993. pap. 15.00 (*1-880474-06-9*) FATA.

Paau, Danny S. L., jt. ed. see Mak, Ricardo K. S.

Paauwe, Jac, jt. auth. see Spain, Ian L.

Paauwe, Theresia, jt. auth. see Gilkeson, Linda.

Paavilainen, E. & Paivanen, J. Peatland Forestry: Ecology & Principles. LC 95-2115. (Ecological Studies: Vol. 111). (GER.). 1995. write for info. (*3-540-58252-5*) Spr-Verlag.

— Peatland Forestry: Ecology & Principles. LC 95-2115. (Ecological Studies: Vol. 111). 1995. 117.95 (*0-387-58252-5*) Spr-Verlag.

Paavo Nurmi Symposium Staff. Early Diagnosis of Coronary Heart Disease: Proceedings of the Paavo Nurmi Symposium, 2nd, Porvoo, September 1971. Halonen, P. I. & Louhija, A., eds. (Advances in Cardiology Ser.: Vol. 8). 1972. 68.00 (*3-8055-1352-6*) S Karger.

— Physical Activity & Coronary Heart Disease: Proceedings of the Paavo Nurmi Symposium, 2nd, Helsinki, 1975. Manninen, V., ed. (Advances in Cardiology Ser.: Vol. 18). (Illus.). 240p. 1976. 104.50 (*3-8055-2356-4*) S Karger.

— Sudden Coronary Death: Proceedings of the Paavo Nurmi Symposium, 4th, Helsinki, September 15-17, 1977. Manninen, V., ed. (Advances in Cardiology Ser.: Vol. 25). (Illus.). 1978. 102.75 (*3-8055-2881-7*) S Karger.

— Thrombosis & Coronary Heart Disease: Proceedings of the Paavo Nurmi Symposium, 1st, Finland, 1969. Halonen, P. I. & Louhija, A., eds. (Advances in Cardiology Ser.: Vol. 4). 1970. 78.50 (*3-8055-0727-5*) S Karger.

Pabalan, R. T., jt. ed. see Interrante, C. G.

Pabbisetty, Seshu V., jt. ed. see Lee, Thomas W.

Pabel, Andrea, jt. auth. see Tellington-Jones, Linda.

Pabel, Hilma M. Conversing with God: Prayer in Erasmus' Pastoral Writings. LC 97-185134. (Erasmus Studies: Vol. 13). 264p. 1997. text 60.00 (*0-8020-4101-9*, BV207) U of Toronto Pr.

Pabel, Hilmar M., ed. Erasmus' Vision of the Church. LC 95-37531. (Sixteenth Century Essays & Studies: Vol. 33). 170p. 1995. 40.00 (*0-940474-35-2*, SCJP) Truman St Univ.

Pabellon, Edwin. Los Hijos De la Noche. 85p. 1995. pap. text. write for info. (*1-56758-037-8*) Edit Cultl.

Paber, Stanley W., ed. Callville: Head of Navigation, Arizona Territory. (Illus.). 40p. 1981. pap. 5.95 (*0-913814-39-3*) Nevada Pubns.

Pabich, Jill, tr. & illus. see Ross, Steven.

Pabis, Stanislaw, et al. Grain Drying: Theory & Practice. LC 97-22339. 303p. 1998. 200.00 (*0-471-57387-6*) Wiley.

Pabisch, Peter. Sante Fe Etc. Etc. Etc. Gedichte & Skizzen - Poems & Sketches. large type ed. Genger, Michael & Willson, A. Leslie, trs. (Illus.). 78p. 1990. 11.95 (*0-911173-03-X*) Dimension Pr.

Pabisch, Peter, ed. From Wilson to Waldheim: Proceedings of a Workshop on Austrian-American Relations, 1917-1987. (Studies in Austrian Literature, Culture, & Thought). (Illus.). 354p. 1989. 37.50 (*0-929497-04-X*); pap. 25.00 (*0-929497-09-0*) Ariadne CA.

Pabla, B. S. & Adithan, M. CNC Machines. 1994. write for info. (*81-224-0669-6*, Pub. by Wiley Estrn) Franklin.

Pabla, B. S., jt. auth. see Adithan, M.

Pable, Martin. Catholics & Fundamentalists: Understanding the Difference. 2nd ed. 96p. 1997. pap. 5.95 (*0-87946-167-5*, 263) ACTA Pubns.

— Catolicos y Fundamentalistas. 128p. 1998. pap. 5.95 (*0-87946-188-8*, 264) ACTA Pubns.

Pable, Martin W. The Quest for the Male Soul: In Search of Something More. LC 96-31129. 144p. 1996. pap. 8.95 (*0-87793-580-7*) Ave Maria.

Pablico, Manuel B., et al. The Sound of the Seventh Trumpet. 112p. (Orig.). 1996. pap. 19.95 (*0-9654861-1-7*) Svnth Trumpet CA.

Pablo, et al, eds. Presynaptic Inhibition & Neural Control. LC 97-2286. (Illus.). 466p. 1997. text 85.00 (*0-19-510516-8*) OUP.

Pablo, Flora De, see De Pablo, Flora.

Pablo, Garcia Rodriguez. Salve Su Matrimonio. (SPA.). 1997. pap. text 8.98 (*968-409-725-5*) Edamex.

Pablo, Juan, II. Mensajero de la Paz y la Esperanza: Textos y Documentos de la Visita de Su Santidad Juan Pablo II a Cuba. (Coleccion Felix Varela Ser.). (Illus.). 183p. 1998. pap. 15.00 (*0-89729-867-5*) Ediciones.

***Pablo, Juan, II.** Orar. 1999. 19.95 (*84-08-02482-5*) Planeta Edit.

Pablo, Mary, jt. auth. see Rozell, Erik.

Pablos, Julia T. Women in Mexico: A Past Unveiled. Hynds, Alan, tr. LC 98-51647. Orig. Title: Mujeres en Mexico: Una Historia Olvidada. (Illus.). 120p. 1999. 20.00 (*0-292-78160-1*) U of Tex Pr.

Pablos, Julia Tunon. Women in Mexico: A Past Unveiled. Hynds, Alan, tr. LC 98-51647. (Translations from Latin America Ser.). Orig. Title: Mujeres en Mexico: Una Historia Olvidada. (Illus.). 144p. 1999. pap. 9.95 (*0-292-78161-X*) U of Tex Pr.

Pabon, Jose M. Vox-Diccionario Manual Griego-Espanol: Greek-Spanish. 11th ed. (GRE & SPA.). 724p. 1979. 39.95 (*0-8288-4854-8*, S12136) Fr & Eur.

Pabrai, Uday. TCP-IP Networks: Performance Analysis & Fine Tuning. (McGraw Hill Series on Computer Communication). (Illus.). 400p. 1997. pap. text 44.95 incl. cd-rom (*0-07-913624-9*) McGraw.

Pabrai, Uday O. Internet & TCP/IP Security for UNIX Administrators. LC 96-22133. (Illus.). 357p. 1996. pap. 39.95 (*0-07-048215-2*) McGraw.

— UNIX Internetworking. LC 93-7164. 1993. text 69.00 (*0-89006-685-X*) Artech Hse.

Pabrai, Uday O. & Shah, Hemant. X Window System User's Guide. LC 93-39579. 236p. 1994. 19.00 (*0-89006-740-6*) Artech Hse.

Pabst, Beverly. Paris Lights. (Illus.). 40p. (Orig.). 1986. pap. 10.95 (*0-87663-504-4*, Pub. by Universe) St Martin.

Pabst, H. W., jt. ed. see Hor, Gustav.

Pabst, Janet, jt. ed. see Henke, Russell.

Pabst, Margery & Goldhammer, Rita. A Moving Experience: Coping with the Challenge of Moving. (Illus.). (Orig.). 1996. pap. 12.95 (*0-9650260-0-0*) Goldhammer.

Pabst, Martin. Technologisches Woerterbuch Franzoisisch. (FRE & GER.). 550p. 1971. 175.00 (*0-8288-6482-9*, M-7662) Fr & Eur.

Pabst, Nick, ed. see Weber, William J.

Pabst, R., jt. ed. see Putz, R.

Pabst, Thomas. Tom's Hardware Guide: High Performance PC Secrets. LC 98-84862. 1998. 29.99 (*0-7897-1686-0*) Que.

Pabst, W. R., Jr. Butter & Oleomargarine. LC 70-76644. (Columbia University. Studies in the Social Sciences: No. 427). reprint ed. 20.00 (*0-404-51427-8*) AMS Pr.

Pabst, William R. Jury Manual: A Guide for Prospective Jurors. Carson, Christopher et al, eds. (Illus.). 108p. (Orig.). 1985. 19.95 (*0-933745-00-1*); pap. 9.65 (*0-933745-01-X*) Metro Pub.

Pacak-Carroll, Darice K. & Schierling, Janelle. Radiology Basics for Dental Auxiliaries. (Illus.). 400p. pap. text 37.95 (*0-8036-0555-2*) Davis Co.

Pacak, Mike. Flipper Pinball Flyer Book, 3 vols. Schelberg, Jim, ed. (Illus.). 1400p. 1997. pap. 150.00 (*0-9661333-9-0*) Pingame Jrnl.

Pacala, Leon. The Role of ATS in Theological Education, 1980-1990. LC 98-16150. 200p. 1998. write for info. (*0-7885-0448-7*) Assn of Theol Schls.

***Pacard, Frank & Riviere, T.** Linear & Nonlinear Aspects of Vortices: The Ginzburg-Landau Model. (Progress in Nonlinear Differential Equations & Their Applications Ser.: Vol. 39). 360p. 2000. 79.95 (*0-8176-4133-5*) Birkhauser.

***Pacard, Frank & Riviere, Tristan.** Linear & Non-Linear Aspects of Vortices: The Ginzburg--Landau Model. LC 00-36108. (Progress in Nonlinear Differential Equations & Their Applications Ser.). 2000. write for info. (*3-7643-4133-5*) Birkhauser.

Pacault, A., jt. ed. see Vidal, C.

Pacaut, Marcel. Doctrines Politiques et Structures Ecclesiastiques dans l'Occident Medieval. (Collected Studies: No. CS 223). (FRE.). 304p. (C). 1985. reprint ed. lib. bdg. 115.95 (*0-86078-171-2*, Pub. by Variorum) Ashgate Pub Co.

Paccagnwll. In the Balance. 1989. pap. text. write for info. (*0-582-66360-1*, Pub. by Addison-Wesley) Longman.

Paccaud, F., et al, eds. Assessing AIDS Prevention: Selected Papers Presented at the International Conference Held in Montreux (Switzerland), October 29-November 1, 1990. x, 305p. 1992. 174.50 (*0-8176-2722-7*) Birkhauser.

Pacchione, Diane, jt. ed. see Ikonomou, Charlene.

Pacchioni, G., et al. Cluster Models for Surface & Bulk Phenomena. (NATO ASI Ser.: Vol. 283). (Illus.). 712p. (C). 1992. text 159.50 (*0-306-44102-0*, Kluwer Plenum) Kluwer Academic.

Pacchioni, Gianfranco, et al, eds. Elemental & Molecular Clusters. (Materials Science Ser.: Vol. 6). (Illus.). 377p. 1988. 74.00 (*0-387-19048-1*, 1687) Spr-Verlag.

Pacchioni, Gianfranco, jt. ed. see Lambert, Richard M.

Paccia-Cooper, Jeanne, jt. auth. see Cooper, William E.

Pace. F-22 Raptor. (The Walter J. Boyne Military Aircraft Series). 144p. 1999. 36.95 (*0-07-134271-0*) McGraw.

— Introduction to Algebra. 2nd ed. 1994. pap. text, student ed. 27.80 (*0-13-503756-5*) P-H.

Pace, jt. auth. see Ethell, Jeffrey L.

Pace, Anita L. If You Want to Soar You've Got to Learn How to Fly. (Illus.). 256p. (Orig.). 1993. pap. 10.95 (*0-9631666-1-1*) Baby Steps Pr.

— Pets' Peeves: Dogs Speak Out! (Illus.). 104p. (Orig.). 1997. pap. 6.95 (*0-9631666-5-4*) Baby Steps Pr.

Pace, Anita L., et al. From Grief to Action: Caring on the Spirits of Princess Diana & Mother Teresa. LC 97-94751. 160p. 1998. pap. text 7.95 (*0-9631666-6-2*) Baby Steps Pr.

— Life Isn't Just a Panic: Stories of Hope by Recovering Agoraphobics. (Illus.). 256p. (Orig.). 1996. pap. 13.95 (*0-9631666-3-8*) Baby Steps Pr.

— Write from the Heart: Lesbians Healing from Heartache. rev. ed. 256p. 1996. pap. 13.95 (*0-9631666-4-6*) Baby Steps Pr.

— Write from the Heart - Lesbians Healing from Heartache: An Anthology. 226p. 1992. pap. 10.95 (*0-9631666-0-3*) Baby Steps Pr.

Pace-Asciak, Cecil. Mass Spectra of Prostaglandins & Related Products. LC 83-645438. (Advances in Prostaglandin, Thromboxane, & Leukotriene Research Ser.: Vol. 18). 586p. 1989. reprint ed. pap. 181.70 (*0-608-04669-8*, 206539000004) Bks Demand.

Pace-Asciak, Cecil R., jt. ed. see Nigam, S.

Pace-Asciak, Cecil R., jt. ed. see Schror, K.

Pace, Barney. Family Papers: A Reader for Writers. 544p. (C). 1997. pap. text 47.00 (*0-06-501222-4*) Addson-Wesley Educ.

Pace, Betty. Chris Gets Ear Tubes. LC 87-26759. (Illus.). 48p. (J). (ps-2). 1987. pap. 7.95 (*0-930323-36-X*, Pub. by K Green Pubns) Gallaudet Univ Pr.

Pace, Bill, jt. auth. see Saxton, Paul.

Pace, Charles R. Measuring Outcomes of College: Fifty Years of Findings & Recommendations for the Future. LC 79-88774. (Jossey-Bass Series in Higher Education). 200p. reprint ed. pap. 62.00 (*0-8357-4957-6*, 203788900009) Bks Demand.

Pace, Claire. Felibien's Life of Poussin. (Illus.). 160p. pap. 29.95 (*0-302-00542-0*, Pub. by Zwemmer Bks) Intl Spec Bk.

Pace, Dale K. & Fayek, Abdel-Moaty, eds. Proceedings, 1994 Summer Computer Simulation Conference. 972p. 1994. 180.00 (*1-56555-029-3*, SCSC-94) Soc Computer Sim.

***Pace, David.** Rock-a-Bye-Baby: With Doll & Cradle. (Illus.). 11p. (ps). 1999. 14.99 (*0-448-41958-0*) Putnam Pub Group.

— Shouting Sharon: A Riotous Counting Rhyme. (Illus.). (J). 1999. pap. text 6.99 (*0-7112-0896-4*) F Lincoln.

Pace, David. The Three Billy Goats Gruff. (Fairy Tale Pop-ups Ser.). 16p. (J). 1994. 3.95 (*0-7214-9418-8*, Ladybrd) Penguin Putnam.

— The Three Little Pigs. (Fairy Tale Pop-ups Ser.). 16p. (J). 1994. 3.95 (*0-7214-9419-6*, Ladybrd) Penguin Putnam.

Pace, David & Pugh, Sharon L. Studying for History. Smith, Brenda D., ed. LC 95-12331. (Studying for Ser.). (Illus.). 208p. (C). 1997. pap. text 22.26 (*0-06-500649-6*) Addson-Wesley Educ.

Pace, David P. & Barksdale, E. C. As Dreams Are Made On: Previews of the Human Mind. LC 87-91102. 1988. 18.95 (*0-87212-209-3*) Libra.

Pace, Deborah L. Been There . . . Teenage Moms Who Beat the Odds. LC 98-66744. xviii, 121p. 1998. pap. 9.95 (*0-9665182-0-9*) One Womans.

Pace, Denny F. Community Relations Concepts. 3rd ed. LC 92-58119. (Illus.). 273p. (Orig.). (C). 1993. pap. 31.95 (*0-942728-54-8*) Copperhouse.

— Concepts of Vice, Narcotics & Organized Crime. 3rd ed. 320p. (C). 1990. pap. text 26.80 (*0-13-173691-4*) P-H.

Pace, DeWanna. Beckoning Shore. 272p. 1997. mass mkt. 5.99 (*0-515-12101-0*, Jove) Berkley Pub.

Pace, Dewanna. Sugar & Spice. (Our Town Ser.). 288p. 1996. mass mkt. 5.99 (*0-515-11970-9*, Jove) Berkley Pub.

P

An Asterisk (*) at the beginning of an entry indicates that the title is appearing for the first time.

— Surrender Sweet Stranger. 1988. 3.95 (*0-517-00652-9*) Random Hse Value.

Pace, DeWanna. A Taste of Honey. (Friends Romance Ser.). 304p. 1998. pap. 5.99 (*0-515-12387-0*, Jove) Berkley Pub.

***Pace, Dewanna.** Where Heroes Sleep. 1999. mass mkt. 5.99 (*0-515-12702-7*, Jove) Berkley Pub.

***Pace, Diana.** The Career Fix-It Book. 2000. pap. 14.95 (*1-57071-562-9*) Sourcebks.

Pace, Edmond E., et al. Developing a Basic Loan Training Program. 2nd ed. LC 87-7936. 108p. 1987. pap. 45.00 (*0-936742-41-0*) Robt Morris Assocs.

Pace, Franco. William Fife: Master of the Classic Yacht. (Illus.). 160p. 1998. 69.95 (*0-937822-49-3*) WoodenBoat Pubns.

Pace, Frank J., jt. auth. see Mosier, Alice.

Pace-Fritz, Angela D. Thought & Vision: A Critical Reading of H. D.'s Poetry. LC 87-13193. 245p. 1988. reprint ed. pap. 76.00 (*0-7837-9119-4*, 204992000004) Bks Demand.

Pace, George. Bishophill, York. (Illus.). 1999. pap. 21.00 (*0-900657-22-7*, Pub. by W Sessions) St Mut.

Pace, George B., ed. see Chaucer, Geoffrey.

Pace, George W. Knowing Christ. pap. 11.98 (*1-55517-261-X*) CFI Dist.

Pace, Glenn L. Spiritual Revival. LC 93-9902. viii, 198p. 1993. 12.95 (*0-87579-733-4*) Deseret Bk.

Pace, Glennellen, ed. Whole Learning in the Middle School: Evolution & Transition. 296p. 1995. pap. text 36.95 (*0-926842-44-7*) CG Pubs Inc.

Pace, Guiseppe. Mushrooms of the World. (Illus.). 310p. 1998. text 35.00 (*1-55209-212-7*) Firefly Bks Ltd.

Pace International Research, Inc. Staff. ABC (Active Basic Communication), Program 1. (ABC Video Ser.). (Illus.). 157p. 1984. text 8.95 (*0-89209-215-7*); pap. text 4.25 (*0-89209-326-9*); audio 4.00 (*0-89209-327-7*); VHS 115.00 (*0-89209-178-9*) Pace Grp Intl.

— ABC (Active Basic Communication), Program 10. (ABC Video Ser.). (Illus.). 171p. 1984. text 8.95 (*0-89209-224-6*); pap. text 4.25 (*0-89209-344-7*); audio 4.00 (*0-89209-345-5*); VHS 115.00 (*0-89209-187-8*) Pace Grp Intl.

— ABC (Active Basic Communication), Program 11. (ABC Video Ser.). (Illus.). 151p. 1984. text 8.95 (*0-89209-225-4*); pap. text 4.25 (*0-89209-346-3*); audio 4.00 (*0-89209-347-1*); VHS 115.00 (*0-89209-188-6*) Pace Grp Intl.

— ABC (Active Basic Communication), Program 12. (ABC Video Ser.). (Illus.). 173p. 1984. text 8.95 (*0-89209-226-2*); pap. text 4.25 (*0-89209-348-X*); audio 4.00 (*0-89209-349-8*); VHS 115.00 (*0-89209-189-4*) Pace Grp Intl.

— ABC (Active Basic Communication), Program 13. (ABC Video Ser.). (Illus.). 153p. 1984. text 8.95 (*0-89209-227-0*); pap. text 4.25 (*0-89209-375-7*); audio 4.00 (*0-89209-376-5*); VHS 115.00 (*0-89209-190-8*) Pace Grp Intl.

— ABC (Active Basic Communication), Program 14. (ABC Video Ser.). (Illus.). 153p. 1984. text 8.95 (*0-89209-228-9*); pap. text 4.25 (*0-89209-377-3*); audio 4.00 (*0-89209-378-1*); VHS 115.00 (*0-89209-191-6*) Pace Grp Intl.

— ABC (Active Basic Communication), Program 15. (ABC Video Ser.). (Illus.). 177p. 1984. text 8.95 (*0-89209-229-7*); pap. text 4.25 (*0-89209-379-X*); audio 4.00 (*0-89209-380-3*); VHS 115.00 (*0-89209-192-4*) Pace Grp Intl.

— ABC (Active Basic Communication), Program 16. (ABC Video Ser.). (Illus.). 145p. 1984. text 8.95 (*0-89209-230-0*); pap. text 4.25 (*0-89209-381-1*); audio 4.00 (*0-89209-382-X*); VHS 115.00 (*0-89209-193-2*) Pace Grp Intl.

— ABC (Active Basic Communication), Program 2. (ABC Video Ser.). (Illus.). 177p. 1984. text 8.95 (*0-89209-216-5*); pap. text 4.25 (*0-89209-328-5*); audio 4.00 (*0-89209-329-3*); VHS 115.00 (*0-89209-179-7*) Pace Grp Intl.

— ABC (Active Basic Communication), Program 3. (ABC Video Ser.). (Illus.). 149p. 1984. text 8.95 (*0-89209-217-3*); pap. text 4.25 (*0-89209-330-7*); audio 4.00 (*0-89209-331-5*); VHS 115.00 (*0-89209-180-0*) Pace Grp Intl.

— ABC (Active Basic Communication), Program 4. (ABC Video Ser.). (Illus.). 167p. 1984. text 8.95 (*0-89209-218-1*); pap. text 4.25 (*0-89209-332-3*); audio 4.00 (*0-89209-333-1*); VHS 115.00 (*0-89209-181-9*) Pace Grp Intl.

— ABC (Active Basic Communication), Program 5. (ABC Video Ser.). (Illus.). 147p. 1984. text 8.95 (*0-89209-219-X*); pap. text 4.25 (*0-89209-334-X*); audio 4.00 (*0-89209-335-8*); VHS 115.00 (*0-89209-182-7*) Pace Grp Intl.

— ABC (Active Basic Communication), Program 6. (ABC Video Ser.). (Illus.). 167p. 1984. text 8.95 (*0-89209-220-3*); pap. text 4.25 (*0-89209-336-6*); audio 4.00 (*0-89209-337-4*); VHS 115.00 (*0-89209-183-5*) Pace Grp Intl.

— ABC (Active Basic Communication), Program 8. (ABC Video Ser.). (Illus.). 195p. 1984. text 8.95 (*0-89209-222-X*); pap. text 4.25 (*0-89209-340-4*); audio 4.00 (*0-89209-341-2*); VHS 115.00 (*0-89209-185-1*) Pace Grp Intl.

— ABC (Active Basic Communication), Program 9. (ABC Video Ser.). (Illus.). 157p. 1984. text 8.95 (*0-89209-223-8*); pap. text 4.25 (*0-89209-342-0*); audio 4.00 (*0-89209-343-9*); VHS 115.00 (*0-89209-186-X*) Pace Grp Intl.

— E-2, 3. (E-2 Video Ser.). (Illus.). 103p. 1984. write for info. (*0-89209-255-6*) Pace Grp Intl.

— E-2, 4. (E-2 Video Ser.). (Illus.). 103p. 1984. write for info. (*0-89209-256-4*) Pace Grp Intl.

— E-2, 5. (E-2 Video Ser.). (Illus.). 110p. 1984. write for info. (*0-89209-258-0*) Pace Grp Intl.

— E-2, 6. (E-2 Video Ser.). (Illus.). 110p. 1984. write for info. (*0-89209-257-2*) Pace Grp Intl.

— E-2, 11. (E-2 Video Ser.). (Illus.). 102p. 1984. write for info. (*0-89209-259-9*) Pace Grp Intl.

— E-2, 12. (E-2 Video Ser.). (Illus.). 102p. 1984. write for info. (*0-89209-260-2*) Pace Grp Intl.

— E-2, 13. (E-2 Video Ser.). (Illus.). 108p. 1984. write for info. (*0-89209-261-0*) Pace Grp Intl.

— E-2, 14. (E-2 Video Ser.). (Illus.). 108p. 1984. write for info. (*0-89209-262-9*) Pace Grp Intl.

— E-2, 17. (E-2 Video Ser.). (Illus.). 113p. 1984. write for info. (*0-89209-263-7*) Pace Grp Intl.

— E-2, 18. (E-2 Video Ser.). (Illus.). 113p. 1984. write for info. (*0-89209-264-5*) Pace Grp Intl.

— E-2, Vol. 1. (E-2 Video Ser.). (Illus.). 103p. 1984. text 8.95 (*0-89209-250-5*); pap. text 4.25 (*0-89209-295-5*) Pace Grp Intl.

— E-2, Vol. 2. (E-2 Video Ser.). (Illus.). 110p. 1984. text 8.95 (*0-89209-251-3*); pap. text 4.25 (*0-89209-296-3*) Pace Grp Intl.

— E-2, 2 vols., Vol. 7. (E-2 Video Ser.). (Illus.). 103p. 1984. audio 8.00 (*0-89209-265-3*) Pace Grp Intl.

— E-2, Vol. 8. (E-2 Video Ser.). (Illus.). 110p. 1984. audio 8.00 (*0-89209-266-1*) Pace Grp Intl.

— E-2, Vol. 9. (E-2 Video Ser.). (Illus.). 102p. 1984. text 8.95 (*0-89209-252-1*); pap. text 4.25 (*0-89209-297-1*) Pace Grp Intl.

— E-2, Vol. 10. (E-2 Video Ser.). (Illus.). 108p. 1984. text 8.95 (*0-89209-253-X*); pap. text 4.25 (*0-89209-298-X*) Pace Grp Intl.

— E-2, 2 vols., Vol. 15. (E-2 Video Ser.). (Illus.). 108p. 1984. audio 8.00 (*0-89209-267-X*); audio 8.00 (*0-685-55708-1*) Pace Grp Intl.

— E-2, Vol. 16. (E-2 Video Ser.). (Illus.). 113p. 1984. text 8.95 (*0-89209-254-8*); pap. text 4.25 (*0-89209-299-8*) Pace Grp Intl.

— E-2, 2 vols., Vol. 19. (E-2 Video Ser.). (Illus.). 113p. 1984. audio 8.00 (*0-89209-268-8*) Pace Grp Intl.

— E-2, 2 vols., Vols. 3 & 4. (E-2 Video Ser.). (Illus.). 103p. 1984. VHS 230.00 (*0-89209-280-7*) Pace Grp Intl.

— E-2, 2 vols., Vols. 5 & 6. (E-2 Video Ser.). (Illus.). 110p. 1984. VHS 230.00 (*0-89209-281-5*) Pace Grp Intl.

— E-2, 2 vols., Vols. 11 & 12. (E-2 Video Ser.). (Illus.). 102p. 1984. VHS 230.00 (*0-89209-284-X*) Pace Grp Intl.

— E-2, 2 vols., Vols. 13 & 14. (E-2 Video Ser.). (Illus.). 108p. 1984. VHS 230.00 (*0-89209-285-8*) Pace Grp Intl.

— E-2, 2 vols., Vols. 17 & 18. (E-2 Video Ser.). (Illus.). 113p. 1984. VHS 230.00 (*0-685-09187-2*) Pace Grp Intl.

— Life in Western America. (AAA Video Ser.). (Illus.). 132p. 1984. text 8.95 (*0-89209-049-9*); pap. text 4.25 (*0-89209-080-4*); digital audio 3.25 (*0-89209-081-2*); VHS 60.00 (*0-89209-046-4*) Pace Grp Intl.

— San Francisco--I Love It! (AAA Video Ser.). (Illus.). 144p. 1984. text 8.95 (*0-89209-047-2*); pap. text 4.25 (*0-89209-076-6*); audio 3.25 (*0-89209-077-4*); VHS 60.00 (*0-89209-044-8*) Pace Grp Intl.

— Seattle & Its People. (AAA Video Ser.). (Illus.). 135p. 1984. text 8.95 (*0-89209-048-0*); pap. text 4.25 (*0-89209-078-2*); audio 3.25 (*0-89209-079-0*); VHS 60.00 (*0-89209-045-6*) Pace Grp Intl.

Pace International Research, Inc. Staff & Cornelius, Edwin T., Jr. Encounters, Bk. 1, Tasks 1-24. (Encounters Video Ser.). (Illus.). 150p. 1988. student ed. 6.95 (*0-89209-656-X*); pap. text 7.95 (*0-89209-650-0*); VHS 59.95 (*0-89209-675-6*); VHS 59.95 (*0-89209-676-4*) Pace Grp Intl.

— Encounters, Bk. 2, Tasks 24-48. (Encounters Video Ser.). (Illus.). 155p. 1988. student ed. 6.95 (*0-89209-657-8*); pap. text 7.95 (*0-89209-651-9*); VHS 59.95 (*0-89209-677-2*); VHS 59.95 (*0-89209-678-0*) Pace Grp Intl.

— Encounters, Bk. 3, Tasks 49-72. (Encounters Video Ser.). (Illus.). 171p. 1988. student ed. 6.95 (*0-89209-658-6*); pap. text 7.95 (*0-89209-652-7*); VHS 59.95 (*0-89209-679-9*); VHS 59.95 (*0-89209-680-2*) Pace Grp Intl.

— Encounters, Bk. 4, Tasks 73-96. (Encounters Video Ser.). (Illus.). 181p. 1988. student ed. 6.95 (*0-89209-659-4*); pap. text 7.95 (*0-89209-653-5*); VHS 59.95 (*0-89209-681-0*); VHS 59.95 (*0-89209-682-9*) Pace Grp Intl.

Pace, James O. Amendment to the Constitution: Averting the Decline & Fall of America. 179p. (Orig.). 1985. pap. text 10.00 (*0-9615268-0-7*) JP SF.

Pace, Jeansonne S. The Old Greek Translation of Daniel 7-12. Karris, Robert J., ed. LC 87-15865. (Catholic Biblical Quarterly Monographs: No. 19). x, 147p. 1988. pap. 5.00 (*0-915170-18-3*) Catholic Bibl Assn.

Pace, Jessica & Talbert, Jane H. A Will to Live: The Story of a Transplant Kid. 92p. (J). 1998. pap. 15.00 (*0-9615704-9-0*) Fawn Grove Pr.

Pace, Jill H., jt. auth. see Teich, Albert H.

Pace, John & Erickson, John. On the Go! (Illus.). 116p. (Orig.). 1995. pap. 15.00 (*0-9649297-0-8*) J Erickson.

Pace, Joseph, II. Admissions & Enrollment Management: A Computerized Management System for Independent Schools & Colleges, Version 3.1. 1987. 995.00 (*0-471-85524-3*) P-H.

Pace, Kathleen, jt. auth. see Robinson, Myles.

Pace, Kathy L. A Ribbon Bouquet: A Guide to French Ribbon Flowers & Silk Ribbon Embroidery. Sargent, Amber, ed. (Illus.). 96p. (Orig.). 1995. pap. 11.50 (*1-887820-00-0*) Gooseberry Hill.

— Ribbon Work Gifts. (Illus.). 96p. 1996. pap. 21.95 (*1-887820-02-7*, 224) Gooseberry Hill.

Pace, Larry, jt. auth. see Pace, Philip.

Pace, Larry A., jt. auth. see Smits, Stanley.

Pace, Laurel. Blood Ties. (Intrigue Ser.). 1993. per. 2.99 (*0-373-22247-5*, 1-22247-0) Harlequin Bks.

— Destiny's Promise. (Historical Ser.). 1993. per. 3.99 (*0-373-28772-0*, 1-28772-1) Harlequin Bks.

— Winds of Destiny. LC 95-16473. 297p. 1994. per. 3.99 (*0-373-28842-5*, 1-28842-2) Harlequin Bks.

Pace, Lee. Sandhills Classic: The Stories of Mid Pines & Pine Needles. (Illus.). 144p. 1996. write for info. (*0-9651076-0-4*) Pine Needles.

***Pace, Lorenzo.** Jalani & the Lock. LC 00-9274. (Illus.). (J). 2001. lib. bdg. write for info. (*0-8239-9700-6*, PowerKids) Rosen Group.

Pace, M. O., jt. ed. see Christophorou, Loucas G.

Pace, Maria & Scaini-Jojic, Louisa. The Little Italy Cookbook: Recipes from North American's Italian Communities. (Illus.). 220p. (Orig.). 1996. pap. 16.95 (*1-895629-72-1*) Warwick Publ.

Pace, Michael L. & Groffman, Peter M., eds. Successes, Limitations, & Frontiers in Ecosystem Science. LC 98-4683. (Illus.). 528p. 1998. 99.95 (*0-387-98476-3*); pap. 49.95 (*0-387-98475-5*) Spr-Verlag.

Pace, Mildred M. Friend of Animals: The Story of Henry Bergh. 2nd ed. Miller, Danny L., ed. & intro. by. LC 94-2193. (Illus.). (J). (gr. 4 up). 1995. reprint ed. 12.00 (*0-945084-47-1*) J Stuart Found.

— Juliette Low. Miller, Danny L., ed. & intro. by. LC 97-2456. (Illus.). 208p. 1997. reprint ed. 20.00 (*0-945084-61-7*) J Stuart Found.

— Kentucky Derby Champion. rev. ed. Gifford, James M. et al, eds. LC 93-18595. (Illus.). 144p. (J). (gr. 3 up). 1993. reprint ed. 12.00 (*0-945084-36-6*) J Stuart Found.

— Pyramids: Tombs for Eternity. LC 97-46032. (Illus.). 192p. (J). 1998. pap. 10.95 (*0-87226-548-X*, 6548XB, P Bedrick Books) NTC Contemp Pub Co.

— Wrapped for Eternity: The Story of the Egyptian Mummy. LC 97-46030. (Illus.). 192p. (J). (gr. 7-12). 1998. pap. 10.95 (*0-87226-549-8*, 65498B, P Bedrick Books) NTC Contemp Pub Co.

Pace, Nicholas A. & McLean, Sheila. Ethics & the Law in Intensive Care. (Illus.). 208p. (C). 1996. text 69.50 (*0-19-262520-9*) OUP.

Pace, Nicholas M., jt. auth. see Kakalik, James S.

Pace, Philip & Pace, Larry. Logic Tools for Programming. 320p. (C). 1987. pap. 31.95 (*0-8273-2582-7*) Delmar.

— Logic Tools for Programming. 320p. (C). 1987. teacher ed. 10.00 (*0-8273-2583-5*) Delmar.

***Pace, Phillip E.** Advanced Techniques for Digital Receivers. (Radar Library). 2000. write for info. (*1-58053-053-2*) Artech Hse.

Pace Products Staff & Miller, Raymond. Native American Masks: Create 5 Genuine Native American Designs. (Illus.). 16p. (Orig.). (J). 1996. pap. 10.95 (*0-8362-2201-6*) Andrews & McMeel.

Pace, R. Daniel. Limitations on the Business of Banking: An Analysis of Expanded Securities, Insurance, & Real Estate Activities. LC 95-23787. (Financial Sector of the American Economy Ser.). 154p. 1995. text 20.00 (*0-8153-2176-7*) Garland.

Pace, R. P. & Van Der Westhuizen, W. Wills & Trusts. 1996. ring bd. write for info. (*0-409-04780 5*, MICHIE) LEXIS Pub.

Pace, R. Wayne & Faules, Don F. Organizational Communication. 3rd ed. LC 93-31436. 386p. 1993. 63.00 (*0-13-643800-8*) P-H.

Pace, Richard. De Fructu Qui Ex Doctrina Percipitur (The Benefit of a Liberal Education, 1517) Manley, Francis & Sylvester, Richard S., eds. LC 66-21029. (Renaissance Text Ser.: No. 2). xxvi, 190p. 1967. 8.50 (*0-9602696-1-4*) Renaiss Society Am.

— The Struggle for Amazon Town: Gurupa Revisited. LC 97-242. 244p. 1998. pap. 18.95 (*1-55587-352-9*); lib. bdg. 49.95 (*1-55587-339-1*) L Rienner.

— Talos: Crossroads of the Galaxy. 371p. (Orig.). 1992. mass mkt. 5.95 (*0-9632819-0-9*) RASP Pubns.

Pace, Richard, jt. auth. see Mixon, Will.

Pace, Richard, ed. see Lowder, James.

Pace, Robert. Creative Keyboard, Bk. 1B. 32p. 1995. pap. 5.95 (*0-7935-4940-X*, 00372368) H Leonard.

— Creative Music, Bk. 1. (Basic Piano Ser.). 48p. 1988. pap. 5.95 (*0-7935-2693-0*, 00372311) H Leonard.

— Creative Music, Bk. 2. (Basic Piano Ser.). 48p. 1988. pap. 5.95 (*0-7935-3326-0*, 00372314) H Leonard.

— Creative Music, Bk. 3. (Basic Piano Ser.). 48p. 1988. pap. 5.95 (*0-7935-3576-X*, 00372321) H Leonard.

— Finger Builders, Bk. 1. 48p. 1988. pap. 5.95 (*0-7935-3705-3*, 00372310) H Leonard.

— Finger Builders, Bk. 2. 48p. 1988. pap. 5.95 (*0-7935-3581-6*, 00372316) H Leonard.

— Finger Builders, Bk. 3. 48p. 1988. pap. 5.95 (*0-7935-3871-8*, 00372323) H Leonard.

— Finger Builders, Bk. 4. 48p. 1988. pap. 5.95 (*0-7935-3116-0*, 00372334) H Leonard.

— Kinder Keyboard Basic Piano. (Pace Piano Education Ser.). 1988. pap., teacher ed. 5.00 (*0-7935-8071-4*) H Leonard.

— Music for Keyboard, Bk. 1A. 32p. 1994. pap. 5.95 (*0-7935-3992-7*, 00372365) H Leonard.

— Music for Keyboard, Bk. 1B. 1995. pap. 5.95 (*0-7935-4939-6*, 00372367) H Leonard.

— Music For Piano. (Pace Piano Education Ser.: Bk. 4). 1988. pap. 6.95 (*0-7935-8378-0*) H Leonard.

— Music for Piano, Bk. 1. 48p. 1988. pap. 5.95 (*0-7935-2787-2*, 00372121) H Leonard.

— Theory Papers, Bk. 4. 48p. 1988. pap. 5.95 (*0-7935-3791-6*, 00372333) H Leonard.

— The Way to Play, Bk. 1. 32p. 1988. pap. 4.50 (*0-7935-3704-5*, 00371214) H Leonard.

Pace, Rosella. Portugal: The Villages. 1977. 2.00 (*0-88031-039-1*) Invisible-Red Hill.

Pace, Ruth & McGee, Mary P. The Life & Times of Ridgeway, Virginia, 1728-1990. LC 90-37899. (Illus.). 292p. 1990. 42.00 (*0-936015-25-X*) Pocahontas Pr.

Pace, S. & Acquarone, M., eds. Superconductivity - Prog in Hts Vol. 27: Proceedings of the Twenty-Fourth Italian National School on Condensed Matter. 550p. (C). 1991. text 129.00 (*981-02-0328-4*) World Scientific Pub.

Pace, Scott, et al. Data Policy Issues & Barriers to Using Commercial Resources for Mission to Planet Earth. 263p. 1999. pap. 20.00 (*0-8330-2701-8*, DB-247NASA/OSTP) Rand Corp.

— The Global Positioning System: Assessing National Policies. LC 95-51394. 400p. (Orig.). 1996. pap. text 30.00 (*0-8330-2349-7*, MR-614-OSTP) Rand Corp.

— Using Intelligence Data for Environmental Needs: Balancing National Interests. LC 96-51134. xviii, 75p. 1997. pap. 15.00 (*0-8330-2476-0*, MR-799-CMS) Rand Corp.

***Pace, Steve.** Airforce Legends Number 205 McDonnell XF-88 VOODOO. Ginter, Steve, ed. (Air Force Legends Ser.: 205). (Illus.). 56p. 2000. pap. 12.95 (*0-942612-96-5*, NFAF205) Naval Fighters.

— B-2 Spirit: The Most Capable War Machine on the Planet LC 99-29342. 1999. write for info. (*0-07-134433-0*) McGraw.

— B-2 Spirit: The Most Capable War Machine on the Planet. (The Walter J. Boyne Military Aircraft Series). 160p. 1999. 36.95 (*0-07-134434-9*) McGraw.

— Boeing North American B-1 Lancer. (WarbirdTech Ser.: Vol. 19). (Illus.). 100p. 1999. pap. 16.95 (*1-58007-012-4*, Pub. by Specialty Pr) Voyageur Pr.

Pace, Steve. F-22 Raptor: America's Next Lethal War Machine LC 99-17914. 1999. write for info. (*0-07-134209-5*) McGraw.

— The Grumman X-29. (Illus.). 86p. 1998. pap. text 10.00 (*0-7881-5308-0*) DIANE Pub.

— The Grumman X-29. (Aero Ser.: Vol. 4). (Illus.). 96p. 1990. pap. 10.95 (*0-8306-3498-3*, 3498) McGraw-Hill Prof.

— Lockheed P-38 Lightning. (Illus.). 120p. (YA). 1996. pap. 14.98 (*0-7603-0151-4*) MBI Pubg.

— Lockheeds Constellation. LC 97-45037. (Illus.). 96p. 1998. pap. 13.95 (*0-7603-0303-7*) MBI Pubg.

— Vought's F-8 Crusader Pt. 1: Development & Testing Foreign Users & F8U-3. (Naval Fighters Ser.: No. 16). 114p. 1988. pap. 17.95 (*0-942612-16-7*) Naval Fighters.

— X-Planes at Edwards. (Enthusiast Color Ser.). (Illus.). 96p. 1995. pap. 13.95 (*0-87938-985-0*) MBI Pubg.

Pace, Tony. Fightin' Irish: The A-to-Z Notre Dame Football Trivia Book. 1997. per. 12.00 (*0-671-00952-4*) PB.

Pace, Tony & Spellen, Mark. Fightin' Irish: A to Z Notre Dame Trivia Book. 1997. pap. 12.00 (*0-614-27669-1*) PB.

***Pace University International Law Journal Staff, ed.** Review of the Convention on Contracts for the International Sale of Goods (CISG) - 1998. LC 99-37968. 300p. 1999. write for info. (*90-411-9352-9*) Kluwer Law Intl.

Pace, William G. & Ernst, Frederick W. Now They Lay Me down to Sleep: What You Don't Know about Anesthesia & Surgery May Harm You. LC 96-19515. 180p. 1996. pap. 12.00 (*0-9651454-0-9*, Pub. by F W Ernst) Partners Pubs Grp.

Pacejka, Hans B., ed. Tyre Models for Vehicle Dynamic Analysis: Proceedings of the First International Colloquium on Tyre Models for Vehicle Dynamics Analysis, Held in Delft, The Netherlands, Oct. 21-22, 1991. LC 92-46188. viii, 192p. 1993. 116.00 (*90-265-1332-1*) Swets.

Pacejka, Hans B., jt. auth. see De Pater, A. D.

Pacejka, Hans B., jt. ed. see Pauwelussen, J. P.

Pacela, Allan F. How to Successfully Value & Sell Your Publishing Property. (Illus.). 74p. 1997. pap. 200.00 (*1-891549-00-6*) Publ Mgmt.

— Valuing Publishing Properties Vol. I: How Buyers & Sellers Adjust Financial Statements to Determine True Value. (Illus.). 49p. 1997. pap. 40.00 (*1-891549-01-4*) Publ Mgmt.

— Valuing Publishing Properties Vol. II: How to Detect "Creative Accounting" & "Earnings Management" That Falsely Inflate Value. (Illus.). 49p. 1997. pap. 40.00 (*1-891549-02-2*) Publ Mgmt.

***Pacelle, Richard L., Jr.** Supreme Court in American Politics: New Subtitle. 180p. 2000. write for info. (*0-8133-6752-2*, Pub. by Westview) HarpC.

— Supreme Court in Americann Politics. 2000. pap. 15.95 (*0-8133-6753-0*, Pub. by Westview) HarpC.

Pacelli, Albert P. The Speculator's Edge: Strategies for Profit in the Futures Market. LC 88-37862. 304p. 1989. 29.95 (*0-471-50360-6*) Wiley.

Pacelli, Eugenio, see Pius XII, pseud.

Pacelli, Joseph G., jt. auth. see Allen, George H.

Pacelli, Maria, jt. auth. see Bevan, Joan.

Pacelli, Maria A., jt. auth. see Bevan, Joan C.

Pacelli, William M. Radio Advertising Sales Success - The Game Plan. 176p. 1988. 19.95 (*0-945664-00-1*) Cambridge Hse Assocs.

Pacepa, Ion M. Red Horizons: Chronicles of a Communist Spy Chief. LC 87-26378. (Illus.). 396p. 1987. lib. bdg. 19.95 (*0-89526-570-2*) Regnery Pub.

— Red Horizons: The True Story of Nicolae & Elena Ceausescus' Crimes, Lifestyle, & Corruption. LC 87-26378. (Illus.). 456p. 1990. pap. 12.95 (*0-89526-746-2*) Regnery Pub.

Pacer, Leonard A., jt. auth. see Pfeister, Joseph L.

Pacernick, Gary. The Jewish Poems. 70p. (Orig.). 1985. pap. 6.50 (*0-932429-00-9*) Univ Monographs.

— Memory & Fire: Ten American Jewish Poets. (Twentieth Century American Jewish Writers Ser.). XII, 259p. (C). 1989. text 45.70 (*0-8204-0419-5*) P Lang Pubng.

— Something Is Happening: Poems. LC 91-48235. 60p. 1992. pap. 14.95 (*0-7734-9439-1*, Mellen Poetry Pr) E Mellen.

P

An Asterisk (*) at the beginning of an entry indicates that the title is appearing for the first time.

***Pacetta, Frank.** Stop Whining--and Start Winning: Recharging People, Re-igniting Passion, & PUMPING UP Profits. 304p. 2000. 25.00 (0-06-662005-8) HarpC.

Pacetta, Frank & Gittines, Roger. Don't Fire Them, Fire Them Up: Motivate Yourself & Your Team. 288p. 1995. per. 13.00 (0-684-80050-0) S&S Trade.

Pacetti, David. Sozo What It Means to Be Saved. 62p. 1985. pap. 2.95 (0-88144-041-8) Christian Pub.

Pacey, Arnold. The Culture of Technology. (Illus.). 224p. 1985. pap. text 14.00 (0-262-66056-3) MIT Pr.

— Gardening for Better Nutrition. 64p. 1978. reprint ed. pap. 12.00 (0-903031-50-7, Pub. by Intermed Tech) Stylus Pub VA.

— The Maze of Ingenuity: Ideas & Idealism in the Development of Technology. LC 74-18380. 337p. 1975. 37.95 (0-8419-0181-3) Holmes & Meier.

— The Maze of Ingenuity: Ideas & Idealism in the Development of Technology. 2nd ed. (Illus.). 320p. 1992. 35.00 (0-262-16128-1); pap. text 17.50 (0-262-66075-X) MIT Pr.

— Meaning in Technology. LC 98-49287. (Illus.). 264p. 1999. 27.50 (0-262-16182-6) MIT Pr.

— Technology in World Civilization: A Thousand-Year History. (Illus.). 256p. 1991. pap. text 14.50 (0-262-66072-5) MIT Pr.

Pacey, Arnold, compiled by. Hand Pump Maintenance in the Context of Community Well Projects. rev. ed. (Illus.). 44p. 1980. pap. 12.00 (0-903031-70-1, Pub. by Intermed Tech) Stylus Pub VA.

Pacey, Arnold, ed. Sanitation in Developing Countries. LC 78-4215. 252p. reprint ed. pap. 78.20 (0-8357-6942-9, 203900100009) Bks Demand.

— Water for the Thousand Millions, Vol. 4. LC 77-23127. 1977. pap. 8.00 (0-08-021805-9, Pergamon Pr) Elsevier.

Pacey, Arnold & Thrupp, Lori A. Farmer First: Farmer Innovation & Agricultural Research. Chambers, Robert, ed. (Illus.). 192p. 1989. pap. 13.50 (0-942850-20-3) Bootstrap Pr.

Pacey, Arnold, jt. auth. see Cullis, Adrian.

Pacey, Desmond. Essays in Canadian Criticism, 1938-1968. LC 74-93870. 294p. 1969. write for info. (0-7700-0289-7) McG-H Ryerson.

Pacey, G. E., jt. auth. see Karlberg, B.

Pacey, Lorene M., ed. Readings in the Development of Settlement Work. LC 79-142688. (Essay Index Reprint Ser.). 1977. 23.95 (0-8369-2198-4) Ayer.

Pacey, Philip. David Jones & Other Wonder Voyagers: Essays. 134p. 1982. 35.00 (0-907476-14-7) Dufour.

Pach, Chester J., Jr. Arming the Free World: The Origins of the United States Military Assistance Program, 1945-1950. LC 90-41120. x, 322p. 1991. pap. text 22.50 (0-8078-1943-3) U of NC Pr.

Pach, Chester J., Jr. & Richardson, Elmo. The Presidency of Dwight D. Eisenhower. rev. ed. LC 90-45952. (American Presidency Ser.). xiv, 290p. 1991. 29.95 (0-7006-0436-7); pap. 15.95 (0-7006-0437-5) U Pr of KS.

Pach, Jacqueline S. & Wilhelm, Robert M. An Alphabet Book for Spoon Collectors & Children: "Baby Spoon's New Handle" & a Compendium of Souvenir Spoons. (Illus.). 240p. 1998. pap. 40.00 (0-9662763-0-2, 1671998) Campanian Soc.

Pach, Janos, ed. New Trends in Discrete & Computational Geometry. LC 92-23684. (Algorithms & Combinatorics Ser.: Vol. 10). 1993. 89.00 (0-387-55713-X) Spr-Verlag.

Pach, Janos & Agarwal, Pankaj K. Combinatorial Geometry. LC 94-48203. (Discrete Mathematics & Optimization Ser.). 376p. 1995. 79.95 (0-471-58890-3) Wiley.

Pach, Paul S. Studies on the Hungarian Economy in Early Modern Times. (Collected Studies: No. CS469). 320p. 1994. 117.95 (0-86078-462-2) Ashgate Pub Co.

Pach, Walter. Ingres. LC 83-45830. (Illus.). reprint ed. 84.50 (0-404-20195-4) AMS Pr.

— Masters of Modern Art. LC 72-5633. (Essay Index Reprint Ser.). 1977. reprint ed. 27.95 (0-8369-7295-3) Ayer.

— Queer Thing, Painting: Forty Years in the World of Art. LC 79-156701. (Essay Index Reprint Ser.). 1977. reprint ed. 27.95 (0-8369-2328-6) Ayer.

— Renoir. (Masters of Art Ser.). (Illus.). 128p. 1983. 24.95 (0-8109-1593-6, Pub. by Abrams) Time Warner.

— Vincent Van Gogh, 1853-1890. LC 78-99666. (Select Bibliographies Reprint Ser.). 1977. 21.95 (0-8369-5095-X) Ayer.

Pach, Z. P. Eighth International Economic History Congress, Budapest, 1982. International Economic History Assoc. Staff, ed. (ENG & FRE.). 190p. (C). 1982. pap. 45.00 (963-05-3104-6, Pub. by Akade Kiado) St Mut.

Pach, Zsigmond P. Levantine Trade & Hungary in the Middle Ages: Theses, Controversies, Arguments. LC 84-672719. (Studia Historica Academiae Scietiarum Hungaricae). (ENG & RUS.). 27p. 1975. write for info. (963-05-0810-9, Pub. by Akade Kiado) Intl Spec Bk.

Pacha, Sergio, jt. ed. see Williams, Frederick G.

Pachai, Bridglal. Malawi: The History of the Nation. LC 73-173415. (Illus.). 336p. reprint ed. pap. 104.20 (0-8357-6200-9, 203447200090) Bks Demand.

Pachauri, R. K. The Political Economy of Global Energy. LC 84-21825. (Illus.). 207p. reprint ed. pap. 64.20 (0-608-06112-3, 206644500008) Bks Demand.

Pachauri, Rajendra K. Contemporary India. 192p. 1992. 27.50 (0-7069-6078-5, Pub. by Vikas) S Asia.

***Pachauri, S. K.** Women & Human Rights. 1999. 36.00 (81-7648-077-0, Pub. by Ashish Pub Hse) S Asia.

Pachauri, Saroj, ed. Reaching India's Poor: Non-Governmental Approaches to Community Health. LC 94-4731. 420p. 1994. 29.95 (0-8039-9172-X) Sage.

Pache, Corinne, tr. see Loraux, Nicole.

Pache, Rene. The Inspiration & Authority of Scripture. 349p. (C). 1992. reprint ed. pap. text 18.50 (1-879215-11-X) Sheffield WI.

Pacheco. Academic Reading & Study Skills. (C). 1985. pap. text, teacher ed. 27.50 (0-03-001484-0) Harcourt Coll Pubs.

Pacheco, Anita. Early Women Writers. LC 97-12383. (Critical Readers Ser.). (C). 1997. 68.44 (0-582-30462-8); pap. 27.40 (0-582-30463-6) Addison-Wesley.

Pacheco, Anita, ed. see Bunyan, John.

Pacheco, Beth M. Academic Reading & Study Skills: A Theme-Centered Approach. 2nd ed. 332p. (C). 1992. pap. text 39.00 (0-03-055533-7, Pub. by Harcourt Coll Pubs); pap. text, teacher ed. write for info. (0-03-055867-0) Harcourt Coll Pubs.

Pacheco, Blanca Silvestrini De, see Silvestrini De Pacheco, Blanca.

Pacheco, Christine. A Husband in Her Stocking. (Desire Ser.: No. 1113). 1997. per. 3.50 (0-373-76113-9, 1-76113-9) Harlequin Bks.

— Lovers Only. (Desire Ser.). 1997. per. 3.50 (0-373-76054-X, 1-76054-5) Silhouette.

— The Rogue & the Rich Girl. 1995. per. 3.25 (0-373-05960-4, 1-05960-9) Silhouette.

Pacheco, Cristina. La Luz de Mexico (The Light of Mexico) (SPA.). 355p. 1995. pap. 10.99 (968-16-4308-9, Pub. by Fondo) Continental Bk.

Pacheco, Ernesto V. Tulum: Organizacion Politico-Territorial de la Costa Oriental de Quintana Roo. (SPA., Illus.). 254p. 1997. pap. 27.50 (968-36-6326-5, UN062, Pub. by Instit de Invest) UPLAAP.

Pacheco, F. H., ed. see Menendez Pidal, Ramon.

Pacheco, Ferdie. Muhammad Ali: A View from the Corner. (Illus.). 256p. 1992. 21.95 (1-55972-100-6, Birch Ln Pr) Carol Pub Group.

— Pacheco's Art of Ybor City. LC 97-11190. (Illus.). 112p. 1997. 39.95 (0-8130-1517-0) U Press Fla.

***Pacheco, Ferdie.** The 12 Greatest Rounds of Boxing: The Untold Stories. (Illus.). 224p. 2000. 24.95 (1-892129-37-X) Total Sprts.

Pacheco, Ferdie. Ybor City Chronicles: A Memoir. LC 94-822. (Illus.). 320p. 1994. 24.95 (0-8130-1296-1) U Press Fla.

Pacheco, Ferdie & Pacheco, Luisita S. The Christmas Eve Cookbook: With Tales of Nochebuena & Chanukah. LC 98-15243. (Illus.). 192p. 1998. 19.95 (0-8130-1624-X) U Press Fla.

Pacheco, Ferdie, jt. auth. see Gonzmart, Adela H.

Pacheco, James E., jt. ed. see Claridge, David E.

Pacheco, Jorge M. Conflitos Da Ultima Geracao. (POR.). 150p. 1997. pap. 7.00 (0-9659619-0-7) G Pacheco.

Pacheco, Jose E. An Ark for the Next Millennium: Poems. LC 92-41086. (Texas Pan American Ser.).Tr. of Album de Zoologia. (SPA., Illus.). 152p. (C). 1993. pap. 9.95 (0-292-76548-7); text 19.95 (0-292-76547-9) U of Tex Pr.

— Battles in the Desert & Other Stories. Silver, Katherine, tr. from SPA. LC 86-28596. 128p. 1987. 19.95 (0-8112-1019-7, Pub. by New Directions); pap. 8.95 (0-8112-1020-0, NDP637, Pub. by New Directions) Norton.

— City of Memory & Other Poems. Steele, Cynthia & Lauer, David, trs. from SPA. LC 96-9670. 180p. (Orig.). 1997. pap. 10.95 (0-87286-324-7) City Lights.

— Moriras Lejos. (SPA.). 154p. 1980. pap. 8.00 (84-85859-00-6, 2011) Ediciones Norte.

— Selected Poems. McWhirter, George, ed. Hoeksema, Thomas et al, trs. from SPA. LC 86-31075. 224p. 1987. pap. 11.95 (0-8112-1022-7, NDP638, Pub. by New Directions) Norton.

Pacheco, Jose E. & Foster, David W. Proceedings/Memoria Conference on Books in Spanish for Young Readers, Fourth Annual. Schon, Isabel, ed. 23p. (Orig.). (C). 1994. pap. 5.00 (0-9639354-3-7) Ctr Bks Spanish.

Pacheco, Josephine F., ed. Antifederalism: The Legacy of George Mason. LC 92-9206. (George Mason Lectures). 144p. (C). 1992. 47.50 (0-913969-47-8) Univ Pub Assocs.

Pacheco, Josephine F., jt. auth. see Foner, Philip S.

Pacheco, Larry. Nashville Redbook: The Complete & Unparalleled Source Directory for Nashville's Music & Entertainment, Vol. 1. 1999. pap. 9.99 (0-927089-01-7) Nashvll Red Bk.

Pacheco, Larry & Post, Alan, eds. Nashville Red Book: The Complete Directory of Nashville's Music & Entertainment Industry 1988-89. 108p. 1989. write for info. (0-318-64828-8) Nashvll Red Bk.

Pacheco, Laura E., tr. see Howker, Janni.

Pacheco, Luisita S., jt. auth. see Pacheco, Ferdie.

Pacheco, M. Economic Terminology English-Spanish. (ENG & SPA.). 480p. 1967. 19.95 (0-7859-0832-3, M-7354) Fr & Eur.

Pacheco, M. A., jt. auth. see Sanchez, J. L.

***Pacheco-Matos, Armando.** Biografia del Dr. Ramon Emeterio Betances. Iztaccihuatl, Bomexi, ed. (ENG & SPA.). 240p. 1998. pap. text 14.99 (1-929183-00-3) Edit Fundacion.

— Padre Nuestro Que Te Escondes en el Cielo: De San Anton Al Bronx. Iztaccihuatl, Bomexi, ed. (SPA.). 70p. 1990. mass mkt. 6.99 (1-929183-01-1) Edit Fundacion.

Pacheco, Paul J. & Ohio Archaeological Council. A View From the Core: A Synthesis of Ohio Hopewell Archaeology. LC 98-116946. vii, 427p. 1996. write for info. (0-9626931-9-7) Muskingum Val Arch.

Pacheco, Paul J., jt. ed. see Dancey, William S.

Pacheco, Peter. Parallel Programming with MPI. LC 96-39324. 419p. 1996. pap. text 47.95 (1-55860-339-5) Morgan Kaufmann.

Pacheco, Richard, et al. Winning Career Strategies: Teaching - K-12. Parkerson, Janet, ed. (C). 1989. pap. text. write for info. (0-935423-07-9) Educ Pubns.

Pacheco, Teixiera & Pacheco, Xavier. Borland C++ Builder Developer's Guide. 1200p. 1997. 59.99 (0-672-31023-6) Sams.

Pacheco, Victor, et al. Lista Anotada de los Mamiferos Peruanos. (SPA.). 32p. 1994. pap. 7.00 (1-881173-06-2) Conser Intl.

***Pacheco, Xavier.** Delphi 5 Developer's Guide. (Illus.). 1200p. 1999. pap. 59.99 (0-672-31781-8) Sams.

Pacheco, Xavier. Delphi 4 Developer's Guide. LC 98-84680. 1600p. 1998. 59.99 (0-672-31284-0, Pub. by Macmillan) S&S Trade.

Pacheco, Xavier & Teixeira, Steve. Delphi 2 Developer's Guide. 2nd ed. 1996. 49.99 incl. cd-rom (0-614-14447-7) Macmillan.

Pacheco, Xavier, jt. auth. see Pacheco, Teixiera.

Pacheko, Pedro. The Correspondence of Pedro Pacheko. 160p. 1992. pap. write for info. (0-9634659-0-2) Av-Garde Bks.

Pachel, Peter, et al. Voices from the Third Reich: An Oral History. LC 88-32195. 512p. 1989. 24.95 (0-89526-766-7) Regnery Pub.

Pachelbel, Johann. The Fugues on the Magnificat for Organ or Keyboard. 100p. pap. 8.95 (0-486-25037-7) Dover.

— Magnificat in C. Score for Orchestral Accompaniment. Woodward, Henry, ed. LC M 2020.P3. 148p. reprint ed. pap. 45.90 (0-608-10793-X, 200345000030) Bks Demand.

— Organ Works. 160p. pap. text 10.95 (0-486-27858-1) Dover.

Pacheleke, Calisto, jt. auth. see Darch, Colin.

Pachell, Michael, jt. auth. see Sabella, Tom.

Pachen, Ani & Donnelley, Adelaide. Sorrow Mountain: The Journey of a Tibetan Warrior Nun. LC 99-46761. 324p. 1999. 24.00 (1-56836-294-3) Kodansha.

***Pachepsky, Y., et al.** Fractals in Soil Science. LC 00-42992. (Developments in Soil Science Ser.). (Illus.). 2000. write for info. (0-444-50530-X) Elsevier.

Pacher, Sara & Richards, Constance. The Insiders' Guide to North Carolina's Mountains. 4th ed. (Insiders' Guide Travel Ser.). 1999. pap. 16.95 (1-57380-095-3, The Insiders Guide) Falcon Pub Inc.

***Pachero, Jose Antonio Anton.** Visionary Consciousness: Emanuel Swedenb er & the Immanence of Spiritual Reality. Fox, Leonard, ed. Shillenn, Robert E., tr. from SPA. Orig. Title: Un Libro Sobre Swedenb. 104p. (C). 2000. 9.95 (1-883270-17-0, Arcana Bks) Swedenborg Assn.

Pachinko, Joe. Swamp! 216p. 1998. pap. 12.50 (0-9665313-0-2) Superstition Street.

***Pachkowski, John.** CCH Guide to BSA & OFAC. Bond, Kris, ed. LC 99-202768. 559p. 1998. pap. 129.00 (0-8080-0299-6) CCH INC.

Pachkowski, John. CCH Guide to RESPA. Bond, Kris, ed. (Financial Institutions Management & Compliance Ser.). 276p. Date not set. pap. text 75.00 (0-8080-0335-6) CCH INC.

Pachl, Jarmila. Dreams upon the Stars: A Memoir of a Century. Gerding, Susan B. & Hoffmann, Candace, eds. (Illus.). 284p. 1997. text 24.95 (1-884886-03-5) Star Group.

Pachlatko & Beran, R. G., eds. Economic Evaluation of Epilepsy Management. 112p. 1996. 35.00 (0-86196-556-6, Pub. by J Libbey Med) Bks Intl VA.

***Pachler, Norbert.** Teaching Modern Foreign Languages at Advanced Level. LC 99-22622. 1999. pap. write for info. (0-415-20314-7) Routledge.

Pachler, Norbert & Field, Kit. Learning to Teach Modern Foreign Languages in the Secondary School: A Companion for the Student Modern Foreign Languages Teacher. LC 97-18728. (Learning to Teach Subjects in the Secondary School Ser.). 416p. (C). 1997. pap. 25.99 (0-415-16281-5) Routledge.

Pachler, Norbert, jt. auth. see Leask, Marilyn.

Pachlke, Robert C., ed. Conservation & Environmentalism: An Encyclopedia. 1996. 125.00 (1-884964-14-1) Fitzroy Dearborn.

Pachman, Ludek. Decisive Games in Chess History. 266p. 1987. reprint ed. pap. 8.95 (0-486-25323-6) Dover.

— Modern Chess Strategy. Russell, Allen S., tr. from CZE. (Illus.). 314p. 1971. reprint ed. pap. 8.95 (0-486-20290-9) Dover.

Pachman, Stuart L. & Conover, John L. New Jersey Corporate Forms, 2 vols. 1993. ring bd., suppl. ed. 75.00 (0-685-74626-7, MICHIE) LEXIS Pub.

— New Jersey Corporate Forms, 2 vols., Set. 1260p. 1990. ring bd. 250.00 incl. disk (0-8342-0155-0, 82080-10, MICHIE); disk 75.00 (0-685-74627-5, MICHIE) LEXIS Pub.

Pachmuss, Temira. D. S. Merezhkovsky in Exile: The Master of the Genre of Biographie Romancee. LC 89-13253. (American University Studies: Slavic Languages & Literature: Ser. XII, Vol. 12). (Illus.). XVI, 338p. (C). 1990. text 64.00 (0-8204-1254-6) P Lang Pubng.

— A Moving River of Tears: Russia's Experience in Finland. LC 92-25217. (American University Studies: Slavic Languages & Literature: Ser. XII, Vol. 15). (Illus.). XIII, 289p. (C). 1993. text 49.95 (0-8204-1956-7) P Lang Pubng.

— Russian Literature in the Baltic Between the World Wars. 448p. 1988. 29.95 (0-89357-181-4) Slavica.

Pachmuss, Temira, ed. see Hippius, Zinaida.

Pachmuss, Temira, ed. see Hippius, Zinaida N.

Pachner, Edmond. Architectural Contract Administration. LC 91-29761. 248p. 1992. pap. 90.00 (0-471-55004-3) Wiley.

***Pachner, Joan, contrib. by.** David Smith: Photographs, 1931-1965. (Illus.). 125p. 1998. 39.95 (1-881337-04-9) M Marks.

Pachner, Joan, jt. contrib. by see Kertess, Klaus.

Pachocinski, Ryszard, ed. Proverbs of Africa: Human Nature in the Nigerian Oral Tradition. 424p. 1996. 29.95 (1-885118-01-5); pap. 19.95 (1-885118-02-3) Prof World Peace.

Pacholczyk, A. G. The Catastrophic Universe: An Essay in the Philosophy of Cosmology. LC 83-62523. (Philosophy in Science Library: Vol. 2). (Illus.). 128p. 1984. pap. 9.95 (0-88126-702-3) Pachart Pub Hse.

— Central Lithuania: Specialized Stamp Catalogue. LC 90-70422. (Illus.). 208p. 1990. pap. 67.50 (1-878543-01-6) Stochastic Pr.

Pacholczyk, A. G., jt. ed. see Ferrari, Attilio.

Pacholski, Leszek & Tiuryn, Jerzy, eds. Computer Science Logic: 8th Workshop, CSL '94, Kazimierz, Poland, September 28-30, 1994: Proceedings. (Lecture Notes in Computer Science Ser.: No. 933). 1995. write for info. (0-387-60017-5) Spr-Verlag.

— Computer Science Logic: 8th Workshop, CSL '94, Kazimierz, Poland, September 28-30, 1994: Proceedings. (Lecture Notes in Computer Science Ser.: No. 933). 543p. 1995. 87.00 (3-540-60017-5) Spr-Verlag.

Pachomius. History of the Monks at Tabenna. 1975. pap. 2.95 (0-89981-029-2) Eastern Orthodox.

— Instructions of St. Pachomius. Budge, E. A. Wallis, tr. 1975. pap. text 2.95 (0-89981-036-5) Eastern Orthodox.

— Rule of St. Pachomius. Budge, E. A. Wallis, tr. from COP. 1975. reprint ed. pap. 2.95 (0-89981-078-0) Eastern Orthodox.

Pachon, Harry, jt. auth. see Moore, Joan W.

Pachon, Harry, pref. see Tomas's Rivera Center Staff.

Pachonski, Jan & Wilson, Reuel K. Poland's Caribbean Tragedy: A Study of Polish Legions in the Haitian War of Independence 1802-1803. (East European Monographs: No. 199). (Illus.). 386p. 1986. text 63.00 (0-88033-093-7, Pub. by East Eur Monographs) Col U Pr.

Pachori, L. N. The Erotic Sculpture of Khajuraho. (C). 1989. 27.00 (81-85109-79-6, Pub. by Naya Prokash) S Asia.

Pachori, Satya S., ed. see Jones, William.

Pachovsky, Vasyl. Collected Poems, Vol. 1. 420p. 1984. 12.00 (0-930013-00-X) Assn Ukrainian Writers.

Pachpatte, B. G. Inequalities for Differential & Integral Equations. LC 97-45610. (Mathematics in Science & Engineering Ser.: Vol. 197). (Illus.). 624p. 1997. text 69.95 (0-12-543430-8) Morgan Kaufmann.

Pacht, Judith. Lean or Lavish: Two Tempting Versions of Each Dish. 1991. pap. 12.95 (0-446-39221-9) Warner Bks.

Pacht, Otto. Book Illumination in the Middle Ages. (Illus.). 224p. 1994. pap. text 39.95 (1-872501-76-1) Gordon & Breach.

— Early Netherlandish Painting: From Rogier van der Weyden to Gerard David. (Illus.). 264p. 1997. 78.00 (1-872501-84-2, Pub. by Harvey Miller) Gordon & Breach.

— The Practice of Art History: Reflections on Method. Britt, David, tr. (Illus.). 152p. 1999. text 29.95 (1-872501-26-5); pap. text 14.95 (1-872501-31-1) Gordon & Breach.

— Van Eyck & the Founders of Early Netherlandish Painting. Schmidt-Dengler, Maria, ed. Britt, David, tr. from GER. (Illus.). 224p. 1995. text 65.00 (1-872501-81-8, Pub. by Harvey Miller) Gordon & Breach.

Pachter, Barbara. Prentice Hall Complete Business Etiquette Handbook. 350p. (C). 1994. text 29.95 (0-13-156951-1) P-H.

Pachter, Barbara & Brody, Marjorie. Climbing the Corporate Ladder: What You Need to Know & Do to Be a Promotable Person. Scanlon, Kelly, ed. LC 95-69804. (Self Study Sourcebook Ser.). (Illus.). 140p. (Orig.). 1995. 15.95 (1-878542-85-0, 13-0009) SkillPath Pubns.

***Pachter, Barbara & Magee, Susan F.** The Power of Positive Confrontation. LC 99-40096. 224p. 1999. 22.95 (1-56924-679-3) Marlowe & Co.

Pachter, Barbara, jt. auth. see Brody, Marjorie.

Pachter, Henry. Socialism & History: The Political Essays of Henry Pachter. Bronner, Stephen E., ed. LC 83-18904. (Illus.). 300p. 1984. text 63.00 (0-231-05660-5) Col U Pr.

— The Weimar Etudes. Bronner, Stephen E., ed. LC 82-1122. (Illus.). 360p. 1982. text 52.50 (0-231-05360-6) Col U Pr.

Pachter, Josh, tr. see Luitjters, Guus & Timmer, Gerard.

Pachter, L. M. Latino Folk Illness. 110p. 1993. pap. text 82.00 (2-88124-636-2) Gordon & Breach.

Pachter, M., jt. ed. see Yavin, Y.

Pachuta, Jack. Ideas That Work in Today's Business World. 96p. (Orig.). Date not set. pap. 9.95 (1-888475-00-5) Mangmt Stratgies.

— No-Nonsense Negotiations: A Practical, Easy Method for Getting What You Want. 180p. 1999. pap. 12.95 (1-888475-09-9) Mangmt Stratgies.

Pachuta, Jack, jt. auth. see Skibosh, Tom S.

Paci, Enzo. The Function of the Sciences & the Meaning of Man. Piccone, Paul & Hansen, James, trs. (Studies in Phenomenology & Existential Philosophy). 475p. 1972. pap. 19.95 (0-8101-0618-3) Northwestern U Pr.

Paci, F. G. Sex & Character. 196p. 1993. write for info. (0-88750-913-4) Oberon Pr.

Paci, Frank. La Famille Gaetano. 1989. pap. write for info. (2-89135-018-9) Guernica Editions.

Paci, M., jt. auth. see Hallsteinsen, S.

***Paciello, Michael G.** WebAble: Making Web Sites Accessible to People with Disabilities. LC 99-15715. 300p. 1999. 24.99 (0-7645-3323-1) IDG Bks.

***Paciello, Mike.** Web Accessibility for People with Disabilities. 384p. 2000. pap. 34.95 (1-929629-08-7, Pub. by C M P Books) Publishers Group.

P

Paciesas, W. & Fishman, G. Gamma-Ray Bursts. (AIP Conference Proceedings Ser.: No. 265). 500p. 1992. 115.00 (*1-56396-018-4*) Am Inst Physics.

Pacific Asia Resource Center Staff. The People vs. Global Capital - the G-7, TNCs, SAPs, & Human Rights: Report of the International Peoples Tribunal to Judge the G-7, Tokyo, July 1994. LC 95-902853. 184p. (Orig.). 1995. pap. 14.95 (*0-945257-23-6*) Apex Pr.

***Pacific Asia Travel Association Staff.** German Outbound Report. (Illus.). 106p. 1999. pap. 500.00 (*1-882866-14-2*) Pac Asia Trvl.

Pacific Asia Travel Association Staff, jt. auth. see Oelrichs, Ian.

Pacific Basin Research Center Staff & Heffron, John M. Values in Education: Social Capital Formation in Asia & the Pacific. Montgomery, John D., ed. LC 97-41370. 210p. 1997. 29.95 (*1-884186-07-6*) Hollis Pub.

Pacific Circle Consortium Staff, jt. auth. see University of Hawaii, Honolulu Staff.

Pacific Conference on Gravitation & Cosmology Staff, et al. Pacific Conference on Gravitation & Cosmology: February 1-6, 1996, Sheraton Walker-Hill, Seoul, Korea. LC 98-45010. 348p. 1999. 78.00 (*981-02-3698-0*) World Scientific Pub.

Pacific Economic Cooperation Council Staff. Pacific Economic Development Report, 1995. Borthwick, E. Mark, ed. (Illus.). 192p. (Orig.). 1994. pap. text. write for info. (*1-886418-00-4*) US Natl Committee.

Pacific Entomological Survey Publications Staff. Society Islands Insects. (BMB Ser.). 1935. 21.00 (*0-527-02219-5*) Periodicals Srv.

Pacific Fast Mail Staff, ed. see Austin, Ed & Dill, Tom.

Pacific Fast Mail Staff, ed. see Dill, Tom & Grande, Walter R.

Pacific Fast Mail Staff, ed. see Ferrell, Mallory H.

Pacific Fast Mail Staff, ed. see Garmany, John B.

Pacific Fast Mail Staff, ed. see Kohl, Phil & Kohl, Ruth.

Pacific Fast Mail Staff, ed. see Pfeifer, Jack A.

Pacific Fast Mail Staff, ed. see Riegger, Hal.

Pacific Fast Mail Staff, ed. see Wing, Warren W.

Pacific, G. M. & Fracchia, G. N. Advances in Drug Metabolism in Man. 1044p. 1995. 85.00 (*92-827-3982-1*, Pub. by Comm Europ Commun) Bernan Associates.

Pacific Gold Coast Staff. PGC Case Graphics Software Users Handbook with IBM 3.5. (C). 1995. text 154.50 (*0-256-21525-1*, Irwn McGrw-H) McGrw-H Hghr Educ.

Pacific Historian Staff, ed. John Muir: Life & Legacy. (Illus.). 192p. 1986. pap. 10.00 (*0-317-46609-7*) Holt-Atherton.

Pacific Information Management, Inc. Staff. Information Engineering Management Guide. LC 89-64246. (Illus.). 280p. 1989. 95.00 (*0-9624554-0-7*) Pac Info Mgmt.

Pacific Northwest National Parks & Forests Associa, jt. auth. see Gibson, William.

Pacific Northwest Research Station Staff. Recent Publications of the Pacific Northwest Research Station, First Quarter, 1996. 20p. 1998. reprint ed. pap. 3.00 (*0-89904-707-6*, Cascade Geog Soc) Crumb Elbow Pub.

— Recent Publications of the Pacific Northwest Research Station, First Quarter, 1997. 24p. 1998. reprint ed. pap. 3.40 (*0-89904-726-2*, Cascade Geog Soc) Crumb Elbow Pub.

— Recent Publications of the Pacific Northwest Research Station, Second Quarter, 1997. (Illus.). 24p. 1998. reprint ed. pap. 3.40 (*0-89904-769-6*) Crumb Elbow Pub.

— Recent Publications of the Pacific Northwest Research Station, Third Quarter, 1997. 24p. 1998. reprint ed. pap. 3.40 (*0-89904-725-4*, Cascade Geog Soc) Crumb Elbow Pub.

— Research Priorities for Entering the 21st Century: Pacific Northwest Research Station. (Illus.). 24p. 1997. reprint ed. pap. 4.00 (*0 89904-571-5*, Bear Meadows Resrch Grp) Crumb Elbow Pub.

Pacific Press Staff. Before I Was a Kid. (J). 1991. pap. 1.97 (*0-8163-1043-2*) Pacific Pr Pub Assn.

Pacific Rim Institute for Development & Education Staff, jt. auth. see International Symposium on Religious Culture & Ethics Staff.

Pacific Rim International Conference on Advanced M. The First Pacific Rim International Conference on Advanced Materials & Processing (PRICM-1) Proceedings of a Meeting Held in Hangzhou, China, June 23-27, 1992. Shi, Changxu et al, eds. LC 92-63405. (Illus.). 1059p. 1993. pap. 200.00 (*0-608-04898-4*, 206559000004) Bks Demand.

***Pacific Rim International Workshop on Multi-Agents Staff.** Approaches to Intelligent Agents: Proceedings of the 2nd Pacific Rim International Workshop on Multi-Agents, Prima '99, Kyoto, Japan, December 2-3, 1999. Nakashima, Hideyuki & Zhang, Chengqi, eds. LC 99-88052. (Lecture Notes in Artificial Intelligence Ser.: Vol. 1733). xii, 241p. 1999. 52.00 (*3-540-66823-3*) Spr-Verlag.

Pacific Rim/ASME Staff. Proceedings of the Pacific Rim/ASME International Intersociety Electronic & Photonic Packaging Conference, Kohala Coast, Hawaii, 1997: Advances in Electronic Packaging 1997, 2 vols. Suhir, E. et al, eds. LC 97-73292. 2223p. 1997. pap. 500.00 (*0-7918-1559-5*) ASME.

Pacific School of Religion Staff. Religious Progress on the Pacific Slope: Addresses & Papers at the Celebration of the Semi-Centennial Anniversary of Pacific School of Religion, Berkeley, California. LC 68-22941. (Essay Index Reprint Ser.). 1977. reprint ed. 21.95 (*0-8369-0820-1*) Ayer.

Pacific Science Congress Staff. Ryukyuan Culture & Society: Proceedings of the Pacific Science Congress, 10th, Honolulu, 1961. LC 63-19525. 121p. reprint ed. pap. 37.60 (*0-608-30854-4*, 200007300025) Bks Demand.

— Society & Non-Timber Products in Tropical Asia. Fox, Jefferson, ed. LC 94-48590. (Occasional Papers: No. 19). 1995. write for info. (*0-86638-169-4*) EW Ctr HI.

Pacific Trade & Development Conference Staff. Trade & Employment in Asia & the Pacific: Proceedings of the Eighth Pacific Trade & Development Conference, Pattaya, Thailand, July 10-14, 1976. Akrasanee, Narongchai et al, eds. LC HF3762.P3.. 469p. reprint ed. pap. 145.40 (*0-7837-1304-5*, 204145200020) Bks Demand.

Pacific War Research Society Staff. The Day Man Lost: Hiroshima, 6 August 1945. LC 80-85386. (Illus.). 344p. 1981. reprint ed. pap. 12.00 (*0-87011-471-9*) Kodansha.

Pacific War Research Society Staff, ed. Japan's Longest Day: Surrender - The Last 24 Hours Through Japanese Eyes. LC 68-17573. (Illus.). 340p. 1980. pap. 13.00 (*0-87011-422-0*) Kodansha.

Pacifici, Sergio. From Verismo to Experimentalism: Essays on the Modern Italian Novel. LC 74-98980. (Midland Bk.: MB 134). 316p. reprint ed. pap. 98.00 (*0-608-13656-5*, 205520400011) Bks Demand.

Pacifico, Carl. Think Better, Feel Better. LC 89-91280. 1990. 20.00 (*0-87212-224-7*) Libra.

Pacifico, James J. Four Philosophical Dialogues: Dynamiedes; Greater Dynamiedes; Metacosmologion; Heterochopdeis. 40p. (Orig.). (C). 1996. pap. 12.95 (*0-614-18960-8*) Holy Grail.

— The Synermergency: A Clarion Call to Anything But Arms. rev. ed. LC 91-92488. 184p. 1992. 8.95 (*0-9632022-4-3*); lib. bdg. 24.95 (*0-9632022-1-9*); 13.00 (*0-9632022-3-5*) Holy Grail.

— The Synermergency: A Clarion Call to Anything But Arms. 2nd rev. ed. LC 91-92488. 184p. 1992. 24.95 (*0-9632022-0-0*) Holy Grail.

— The Synermergency: A Clarion Call to Anything But Arms. 2nd rev. ed. LC 91-92488. (Illus.). 212p. (C). 1997. pap. 24.95 (*0-9632022-2-7*) Holy Grail.

Pacilio, Nicola. Reactor-Noise Analysis in the Time Domain. LC 79-600321. (AEC Critical Review Ser.). 102p. 1969. pap. 10.50 (*0-87079-335-7*, TID-24512); fiche 9.00 (*0-87079-336-5*, TID-24512) DOE.

Pacilio, V. J. Ling Cho & His Three Friends. LC 97-50210. (Illus.). 32p. (YA). (ps-3). 2000. 16.00 (*0-374-34545-7*) FS&G.

Pacini, Andrea, ed. Christian Communities in the Arab Middle East: The Challenge of the Future. (Illus.). 380p. 1999. text 80.00 (*0-19-829388-7*) OUP.

Pacini, Deborah & Franquemont, Christine, eds. Coca & Cocaine: Effects on People & Policy in Latin America. (Cultural Survival Reports: No. 23). 170p. 1986. pap. 8.00 (*0-939521-24-5*) Cultural Survival.

Pacini, F., ed. High Energy Phenomena Around Collapsed Stars. 1987. text 176.50 (*90-277-2453-9*) Kluwer Academic.

Pacini, Giovanni. Il Corsaro. Gossett, Philip, ed. (Italian Opera 1810-1840 Ser.: Vol. 34). 330p. 1985. text 30.00 (*0-8240-6583-2*) Garland.

— Saffo & Excerpts from Furio Cammila. (Italian Opera 1810-1840 Ser.). 330p. 1986. text 30.00 (*0-8240-6585-9*) Garland.

Pacini-Hernandez, Deborah. Bachata: Social History of a Dominican Popular Music. LC 94-29477. (Illus.). 288p. (C). 1995. pap. text 22.95 (*1-56639-300-0*) Temple U Pr.

***Paciocco, David M.** Getting Away with Murder: The Canadian Criminal Justice System. (Law & Public Policy Ser.). 2000. pap. 19.95 (*1-55221-043-X*, Pub. by Irwin Law) Gaunt.

***Paciocco, David M., contrib. by.** Getting Away with Murder: The Canadian Criminal Justice System. LC 99-175323. (Law & Public Policy Ser.). 1999. 23.95 (*1-55221-032-4*, Pub. by Irwin Law) Gaunt.

***Paciocco, David M. & Stuesser, Lee.** The Law of Evidence. 2nd ed. (Essentials of Canadian Law Ser.). xx, 388p. 1999. pap. 31.95 (*1-55221-038-3*, Pub. by Irwin Law) Gaunt.

Pacioli, Luca. De Divina Proportione. (Janus Ser.).Tr. of Divine Proportion. (C). Date not set. 35.00 (*0-89835-065-4*) Abaris Bks.

— Particularis de Computis: Accounting Books & Records. Thompson, Marianne, ed. Cripps, Jeremy, tr. (Illus.). 109p. 1995. 45.00 (*0-9647778-0-0*) Pacioli Soc.

Pacione, Michael. Applied Geography: Principles & Practice LC 98-53104. 1999. text. write for info. (*0-415-18268-9*) Routledge.

— Britain's Cities: Geographies of Division in Urban Britain. LC 96-9722. (Illus.). 384p. (C). 1997. pap. 27.99 (*0-415-13775-6*) Routledge.

— Britain's Cities: Geographies of Division in Urban Britain. LC 96-9722. (Illus.). 384p. (C). 1997. 85.00 (*0-415-13774-8*) Routledge.

— Glasgow: The Socio-Spatial Development of the City. LC 94-46872. (Belhaven World Cities Ser.). 296p. 1995. 100.00 (*0-471-94947-7*) Wiley.

Pacione, Michael, ed. The Geography of the Third World: Progress & Prospect. 416p. 1988. lib. bdg. 62.50 (*0-415-00467-5*) Routledge.

— Population Geography: Progress & Prospects. (Progress in Geography Ser.). 336p. 1987. 49.95 (*0-7099-4045-9*, Pub. by C Helm) Routldge.

— Progress in Agricultural Geography. (Progress in Geography Ser.). 288p. 1986. 55.00 (*0-7099-2095-4*, Pub. by C Helm) Routldge.

— Progress in Rural Geography. LC 82-22756. (Illus.). 268p. (C). 1983. text 41.50 (*0-389-20358-0*, N7218) B&N Imports.

— Progress in Urban Geography. LC 82-22757. (Illus.). 296p. (C). 1983. text 46.00 (*0-389-20357-2*, N7217) B&N Imports.

— Social Geography: Progress & Prospect. LC 87-506. 328p. 1987. 57.50 (*0-7099-4026-2*, Pub. by C Helm) Routldge.

Pacione, Sharon. Winking at Destiny: A Journey into Consciousness. LC 97-93837. (Illus.). 248p. (Orig.). 1997. pap. 14.00 (*0-9658394-0-0*) Lotus Hse OH.

Paciorek. Sources of Early Childhood Education. 2nd ed. 1998. pap. 20.94 (*0-697-34334-0*) McGraw.

Paciorek & Munro. Early Childhood 1996/97. 17th annot. ed. 1996. teacher ed. 13.12 (*0-697-31551-7*, WCB McGr Hill) McGrw-H Hghr Educ.

***Paciorek, Karen M.** Early Childhood Education 1999-2000. 20th ed. (Illus.). 1999. pap., student ed. 16.56 (*0-07-039784-8*) McGraw.

Paciorek, Karen M. & Munro, Joyce H. Annual Editions: Early Childhood Education, 97-98. 18th ed. 256p. (C). 1997. text 12.25 (*0-697-37251-0*) Brown & Benchmark.

— Early Childhood Education: 1996-1997. annuals 17th ed. 256p. (C). 1996. text. write for info. (*0-697-31550-9*) Brown & Benchmark.

— Early Childhood Education, 98-99. 19th ed. (Annual Ser.). (Illus.). 240p. 1998. pap. text 12.25 (*0-697-39129-9*, Dshkn McG-Hill) McGrw-H Hghr Educ.

— Sources: Notable Selections in Early Childhood Education. 400p. (C). 1995. per. write for info. (*1-56134-321-8*, Dshkn McG-Hill) McGrw-H Hghr Educ.

Paciorek, Karen M. & Munro, Joyce H., eds. Annual Editions: Early Childhood Edition, 95-96. 16th rev. ed. (Illus.). 256p. (C). 1995. text 12.95 (*1-56134-351-X*, Dshkn McG-Hill) McGrw-H Hghr Educ.

Paciorek, Michael J. & Jones, Jeffery A. Sports & Recreation for the Disabled. LC 94-16013. (Illus.). 468p. 1994. reprint ed. pap. 19.95 (*1-57028-012-6*, Mstrs Pr) NTC Contemp Pub Co.

***Paciorek, Michael J. & Jones, Jeffrey A.** Disability Sport & Recreation Resources. 3rd ed. 2000. write for info. (*1-884125-75-1*) Cooper Pubng.

Pacis, Vicente A., jt. auth. see Aguinaldo, Emilio.

Pacitti, Aleen M., ed. see Busa, Marie.

Pacitti, Aleen M., ed. see Morrison, Golda L.

Pacius, Julius. In Porphyrii Isagogen et Aristotelis Organum, Commentarius Analyticus. xii, 536p. 1966. reprint ed. write for info. (*0-318-71270-9*) G Olms Pubs.

Pack, A. J. The Man Who Burned the White House: The Story of Admiral of the Fleet Sir George Cockburn (1772-1853) (Maritime) 288p. 1987. 65.00 (*0-85937-332-0*, Pub. by K Mason Pubns Ltd) St Mut.

— Nelson's Blood. 160p. 1987. 45.00 (*0-85937-279-0*, Pub. by K Mason Pubns Ltd) St Mut.

Pack, Allan I., jt. ed. see Dempsey, Jerome A.

Pack, Arthur N. The Challenges of Leisure. 1982. 20.95 (*0-8434-0438-8*) McGrath NH.

Pack-Brown, Sherlon P., et al. Images of Me: A Guide to Group Work with African-American Women. LC 97-37714. 286p. (C). 1997. 45.00 (*0-205-17184-2*) Allyn.

Pack, Clare, jt. auth. see Kenen, Peter.

Pack, Frank. The Gospel According to John, Pt. 1. LC 79-632639. 1984. 12.95 (*0-915547-22-8*) Abilene Christ U.

— The Gospel According to John, Pt. 2. LC 79-63269. 1984. 12.95 (*0-915547-23-6*) Abilene Christ U.

— Message of the New Testament: Revelations, 2 vols., 176. (Way of Life Ser.: Nos. 176 & 177). 1984. pap. 6.95 (*0-89112-176-5*) Abilene Christ U.

— Message of the New Testament: Revelations, 2 vols., 177. (Way of Life Ser.: Nos. 176 & 177). 1984. pap. 6.95 (*0-89112-177-3*) Abilene Christ U.

Pack, Greta, jt. auth. see Davis, Mary L.

Pack, Howard, jt. ed. see Heston, Alan W.

Pack, James. Nelson's Blood: The Story of Naval Rum. (Illus.). 208p. 1996. pap. 15.95 (*1-55750-666-3*) Naval Inst Pr.

Pack, Janet R. Urban Models. (Monographs: No. 7). 1978. 27.50 (*1-55869-129-4*) Regional Sci Res Inst.

Pack, Jay J., jt. auth. see Dunnan, Nancy.

Pack, Nancy C., jt. ed. see Foos, Donald D.

Pack, Phillip. AP Biology Preparation Guide. (Illus.). 558p. 1994. pap. 14.95 (*0-8220-2301-6*, Cliff) IDG Bks.

Pack, Phillip E. Anatomy & Physiology Quick Review. LC 97-220104. (Cliffs Quick Reviews Ser.). (Illus.). 101p. 1997. pap. text 9.95 (*0-8220-5301-2*, Cliff) IDG Bks.

Pack, Richard. Affairs: Is Your Partner Having One? 110p. 1998. pap. 9.95 (*0-9659231-0-X*) R Pack.

— Close Contact. large type ed. (Illus.). 54p. 1998. 9.95 (*0-9659231-1-8*) R Pack.

Pack, Robert. Affirming Limits: Essays on Mortality, Choice, & Poetic Form. LC 85-2768. 272p. (Orig.). 1985. 32.50 (*0-87023-483-8*); pap. 17.95 (*0-87023-653-9*) U of Mass Pr.

— Clayfeld Rejoices, Clayfeld Laments: A Sequence of Poems. LC 87-7414. 112p. 1987. 14.95 (*0-87923-695-7*); pap. 9.95 (*0-87923-696-5*) Godine.

— Faces in a Single Tree: A Cycle of Monologues. LC 83-49005. 96p. 1984. 13.95 (*0-87923-521-7*); pap. 8.95 (*0-87923-525-X*) Godine.

— Fathering the Map: New & Selected Later Poems. LC 93-3689. 312p. 1993. 24.95 (*0-226-64405-7*) U Ch Pr.

— The Long View: Essays on the Discipline of Hope & Poetic Craft. LC 91-13598. 296p. (C). 1991. lib. bdg. 32.50 (*0-87023-761-6*) U of Mass Pr.

— Minding the Sun. LC 95-31080. 112p. 1996. pap. 11.95 (*0-226-64408-1*); lib. bdg. 35.00 (*0-226-64407-3*) U Ch Pr.

— The Octopus Who Wanted to Juggle. (Illus.). (Orig). (J). (ps-7). 1990. text 13.95 (*0-913123-26-9*) Galileo.

— Rounding It Out: A Cycle of Sonnetelles. LC 98-35253. 64p. 1999. pap. 10.00 (*0-226-64411-1*); lib. bdg. 28.00 (*0-226-64410-3*) U Ch Pr.

— Waking to My Name: New & Selected Poems. LC 79-3651. 272p. 1980. 25.00 (*0-8018-2357-9*) Johns Hopkins.

— Wallace Stevens: An Approach to His Poetry & Thought. LC 68-24044. 203p. 1967. reprint ed. 50.00 (*0-87752-082-8*) Gordian.

Pack, Robert, et al, eds. The Bread Loaf Anthology of Contemporary American Poetry. LC 85-40489. (Bread Loaf Anthology Ser.). 367p. 1985. pap. 19.95 (*0-87451-350-2*) U Pr of New Eng.

Pack, Robert & Lelash, Marjorie, trs. Three Mozart Libretti: The Marriage of Figaro, Don Giovanni & Cosi Fan Tutte. LC 93-1233. (ENG & ITA.). 320p. 1993. reprint ed. pap. 8.95 (*0-486-27726-7*) Dover.

Pack, Robert & Parini, Jay, eds. American Identities: Contemporary Multicultural Voices. LC 94-8809. (Bread Loaf Anthology Ser.). 389p. 1994. pap. 17.95 (*0-87451-759-1*) U Pr of New Eng.

Pack, Robert & Parini, Jay, eds. The Bread Loaf Anthology of Contemporary American Essays. LC 88-40352. (Bread Loaf Anthology Ser.). 389p. 1989. pap. 19.95 (*0-87451-475-4*) U Pr of New Eng.

Pack, Robert & Parini, Jay, eds. Introspections: American Poets on One of Their Own Poems. LC 97-19542. 337p. 1997. pap. 19.95 (*0-87451-773-7*); text 45.00 (*0-87451-772-9*) U Pr of New Eng.

— Poems for a Small Planet: Contemporary American Nature Poetry. LC 92-56909. (Bread Loaf Anthology Ser.). 320p. 1993. pap. 19.95 (*0-87451-621-8*) U Pr of New Eng.

— Touchstones: American Poets on a Favorite Poem. LC 95-32557. (Bread Loaf Anthology Ser.). 346p. 1996. pap. 19.95 (*0-87451-723-0*) U Pr of New Eng.

— Writers on Writing. LC 91-50372. (Bread Loaf Anthology Ser.). 306p. 1991. pap. 19.95 (*0-87451-560-2*); text 45.00 (*0-87451-559-9*) U Pr of New Eng.

Pack, Robert, jt. auth. see Speakes, Larry.

Pack, S. W. Invasion North Africa, 1942. (Illus.). 1981. 4.95 (*0-684-15921-X*, Scribners Ref) Mac Lib Ref.

Pack, Sandy, ed. see Bell, Laurie L.

Pack, Spencer L. Reconstructing Marxian Economics: Marx Based upon a Sraffian Commodity Theory of Value. LC 84-26279. 174p. 1985. 49.95 (*0-275-90152-1*, C0152, Praeger Pubs) Greenwood.

Pack, Susan. Film Posters of the Russian Avant-Garde. LC 96-134594. (Illus.). 360p. 1996. 39.99 (*3-8228-8928-8*) Taschen Amer.

Pack, Thomas. 10 Minute Guide to Business Research on the Net. LC 97-65008. 208p. 1997. 14.99 (*0-7897-1170-2*) Que.

Packa, Sheila J. Always Saying Good-Bye. unabridged ed. 28p. 1998. pap. 4.95 (*1-886895-12-0*) Poetry Harbor.

Packaged Facts (Firm) Staff. The Foot Care Market. LC 98-226716. 1996. write for info. (*1-56241-374-0*) FIND-SVP.

Packaged Facts (Firm) Staff. The International Market for Chilled Foods. LC 99-170764. xv, 206 p. 1996. write for info. (*1-56241-409-7*) FIND-SVP.

— The International Soup Market. LC 99-170775. 1996. write for info. (*1-56241-403-8*) FIND-SVP.

Packaged Facts (Firm) Staff. The Market for Fortified Foods & Beverages. LC 98-186522. xi, 144 p. 1996. write for info. (*1-56241-373-2*) FIND-SVP.

— The U. S. Footwear Market. LC 99-165445. 1997. 2750.00 (*1-56241-415-1*) FIND-SVP.

— The U. S. Home Fragrance Market. LC 99-204246. 1997. write for info. (*1-56241-423-2*) FIND-SVP.

— The U.S. Market for Distance Learning Systems & Services. LC 99-184111. xi, 136p. 1997. write for info. (*1-56241-323-6*) FIND-SVP.

Packaged Facts (Firm) Staff & Scenehouse Productions Staff. The Kids Market. LC 99-159844. 181 p. 1997. write for info. (*1-56241-419-4*) FIND-SVP.

Packaged Facts, Inc. Staff. The Electronic Retailing Market. LC 95-25741. (National Retail Federation Ser.). 176p. 1996. 125.00 (*0-471-13358-2*) Wiley.

Packaged Facts Staff & Apenehouse Productions Staff. The U. S. Market for Powermerchants: Warehouse Clubs & Supercenters. LC 99-182759. 1997. write for info. (*1-56241-417-8*) FIND-SVP.

Packaged Facts Staff & Scenehouse Productions Staff. Marketing to Americans with Disabilities. LC 99-182782. 1997. write for info. (*1-56241-422-4*) FIND-SVP.

— The U.S. Market for Vitamins, Supplements & Minerals. LC 99-182777. 1997. write for info. (*1-56241-324-4*) FIND-SVP.

— The Vended Foods Market. LC 99-182768. 1997. write for info. (*1-56241-451-8*) FIND-SVP.

Packaged Facts Staff & Scenehouse Productions Staff. The U.S. Italian Foods Market. LC 99-182763. 1997. write for info. (*1-56241-380-5*) FIND-SVP.

Packaging & Manufacturing Technology Society Components Staff, jt. auth. see IEEE International Workshop on Integrated Power Packaging Staff.

Packam, Jo. Making Fabulous Pincushions: 93 Designs for Spectacular & Unusual Projects. (Illus.). 144p. 1996. pap. 14.95 (*0-8069-0995-1*, Chapelle) Sterling.

Packan, N. H., et al, eds. Effects of Radiation on Materials: 14th International Symposium, Vol. I. LC 89-18449. (Special Technical Publication Ser.: No. 1046). (Illus.). 700p. 1990. text 127.00 (*0-685-33032-X*, STP1046) ASTM.

Packan, Nicholas H., et al, eds. Effects of Radiation on Materials: 14th International Symposium, Vol. 1. LC 89-18449. (ASTM Special Technical Publication Ser.: No. 1046). (Illus.). 687p. reprint ed. pap. 200.00 (*0-608-10485-X*, 207111500001) Bks Demand.

— Effects of Radiation on Materials: 14th International Symposium, Vol. 2. LC 89-18449. (ASTM Special Technical Publication Ser.: No. 1046). 834p. reprint ed. pap. 200.00 (*0-608-10486-8*, 207111500002) Bks Demand.

Packard. Victoria's Daughters. (Illus.). 384p. (J). 1999. pap 15.95 (*0-312-24496-7*) St Martin.

P

— Woman As Is: Anthology/20th Century Woman's Poetry. 480p. 1995. mass mkt. 5.99 (0-440-21779-2) Dell.

Packard, Alpheus S. The Cave Fauna of North America: Remarks on the Anatomy of the Brain & Origin of the Blind Species. Egerton, Frank N., 3rd, ed. LC 77-74244. (History of Ecology Ser.). (Illus.). 1978. reprint ed. lib. bdg. 18.95 (0-405-10413-8) Ayer.

— The Labrador Coast: A Journal of Two Summer Cruises to That Region. LC 74-5862. reprint ed. 65.00 (0-404-11668-X) AMS Pr.

— Lamarck: The Founder of Evolution; His Life & Work; with Translations of His Writings on Organic Evolution. Cohen, I. Bernard, ed. LC 79-7980. (Three Centuries of Science in America Ser.). (Illus.). 1980. reprint ed. lib. bdg. 42.95 (0-405-12562-3) Ayer.

Packard, Andrea, jt. auth. see Packard, Edward.

Packard, Ann & Stafford, Shirley. Holidays. (Learning Experiences for Young Children Ser.). 116p. (J). 1983. write for info. (0-9607580-4-6) S Stafford.

— Space. (Learning Experiences for Young Children Ser.). 58p. (J). (ps-3). 1981. write for info. (0-9607580-2-X) S Stafford.

— Time of the Dinosaurs. (Learning Experiences for Young Children Ser.). 92p. (J). (ps-3). 1981. write for info. (0-9607580-1-1) S Stafford.

Packard, Candis C. Pocket Guide to Ayurvedic Healing. (Crossing Press Pocket Ser.). (Illus.). 144p. (Orig.). 1996. pap. text 6.95 (0-89594-764-1) Crossing Pr.

Packard, Dane. The Church Becoming Christ's Body: The Small Church's Manual of Dances for Holy Seasons. Adams, Doug, ed. 110p. (Orig.). 1985. pap. 7.95 (0-941500-35-7) Sharing Co.

Packard, Dave. Crystals. (Illus.). 16p. (Orig.). (J). (gr. 2-7). 1996. pap. 6.95 (0-8167-4129-8) Troll Communs.

— Grow Your Own Crystals. (J). (gr. 4-7). 1995. pap. 6.95 (0-8167-3525-5) Troll Communs.

Packard, David. Ball Game, 1. LC 92-36007. (Illus.). 32p. (J). (ps-3). 1993. pap. 3.95 (0-590-46190-7) Scholastic Inc.

— Grow Your Own Crystal Geode. 1997. pap. 6.95 (0-8167-4210-3) Troll Communs.

— The HP Way: How Bill Hewlett & I Built Our Company. Kirby, David & Lewis, Karen, eds. (Illus.). 212p. 1998. pap. text 12.00 (0-7881-5329-3) DIANE Pub.

— The HP Way: How Bill Hewlett & I Built Our Company. 224p. 1996. pap. 13.00 (0-88730-817-1, HarpBusn) HarpInfo.

Packard, David W. Concordance to Livy, 4 Vols, Set. LC 68-29181. 5395p. 1968. 400.00 (0-674-15890-3) HUP.

Packard, E. P. Martial Power Exemplified in Mrs. Packard's Trial: And Self-Defense from the Charge of Insanity; or Three Years' Imprisonment for Religious Beliefs by the Arbitrary Will of a Husband, with an Appeal to the Government to So Change the Laws As to Protect the Rights of Married Women. (Women & the Law Reprint Ser.). xxiv, 137p. 1994. reprint ed. 37.50 (0-8377-2552-6, Rothman) W S Hein.

***Packard, Edward.** Big Numbers. LC 99-32242. (Illus.). 32p. (J). (gr. k-3). 2000. 22.40 (0-7613-1570-5) Millbrook Pr.

Packard, Edward. Biting for Blood. (Choose Your Own Adventure Ser.: No. 7). (J). (gr. 4-8). 1996. pap. 4.75 (0-553-54263-X) BDD Bks Young Read.

— Biting for Blood. (Choose Your Own Nightmare Ser.: No. 7). 96p. (J). (gr. 4-7). 1996. pap. 3.50 (0-553-48359-5) Bantam.

— Biting for Blood. (Choose Your Own Nightmare Ser.: No. 7). (J). (gr. 4-8). 1996. 8.60 (0-606-09141-6, Pub. by Turtleback) Demco.

— The Cave of Time. (Choose Your Own Adventure Ser.: No. 1). (J). (gr. 4-8). 1979. 8.35 (0-606-01154-4, Pub. by Turtleback) Demco.

— Choose Your Own Adventure, 20 bks. Incl. Worst Day of Your Life. large type ed. LC 94-44199. (Illus.). 128p. (J). (gr. 4-8). 1995. lib. bdg. 21.27 (0-8368-1312-X); (J). 1995. Set pap. 425.33 (0-8368-1491-6) Gareth Stevens Inc.

— The Computer Takeover. (Choose Your Own Adventure Ser.: No. 160). (J). (gr. 4-8). 1995. 8.60 (0-606-07387-6, Pub. by Turtleback) Demco.

— Curse of the Haunted Mansion. (Choose Your Own Adventure Ser.). (J). 1980. 8.60 (0-606-01773-9, Pub. by Turtleback) Demco.

— A Day with the Dinosaurs. (Choose Your Own Adventure Ser. (For Younger Readers): No. 46). (J). (gr. 2-4). 1988. 8.70 (0-606-03766-7, Pub. by Turtleback) Demco.

— Deadwood City. LC 77-17501. (Choose Your Own Adventure Ser.: No. 8). (Illus.). 96p. (J). (gr. 4-8). 1978. pap. 3.95 (0-397-31798-0) HarpC Child Bks.

— Fire on Ice. (Choose Your Own Adventure Ser.: No. 181). (Illus.). 112p. (Orig.). (J). (gr. 4-8). 1997. pap. 3.50 (0-553-56749-7) BDD Bks Young Read.

— Fright Night. (Choose Your Own Adventure Ser.: No. 164). (J). (gr. 4-8). 1995. 8.60 (0-606-07546-1) Turtleback.

— Fugitive. (Choose Your Own Adventure Ser.: No. 182). (Illus.). 112p. (J). (gr. 3-7). 1998. pap. 3.50 (0-553-56752-7, Choose) BDD Bks Young Read.

— Greed, Guns & Gold. (Choose Your Own Adventure Ser.: No. 170). (J). (gr. 4-8). 1996. 8.60 (0-606-09362-1, Pub. by Turtleback) Demco.

— Hostage! (Choose Your Own Adventure Ser.: No. 168). (J). (gr. 4-8). 1996. 8.60 (0-606-09433-4, Pub. by Turtleback) Demco.

— Imagining the Universe: A Visual Journey. LC 94-17980. 160p. (Orig.). 1994. pap. 15.00 (0-399-52124-0, Perigee Bks) Berkley Pub.

— Journey to the Year 3000. (Choose Your Own Adventure: No. 1). (J). (gr. 4-8). 1987. 8.60 (0-606-02259-7, Pub. by Turtleback) Demco.

— The Luckiest Day of Your Life. (Choose Your Own Adventure Ser.: No. 132). (Illus.). (J). (gr. 4-8). 1993. 16.25 (0-553-63484-4) Bantam.

— The Luckiest Day of Your Life. (Choose Your Own Adventure Ser.: No. 132). (J). (gr. 4-8). 1993. 8.60 (0-606-02732-7, Pub. by Turtleback) Demco.

— Mountain Biker. (Choose Your Own Adventure Ser.: No. 172). (Illus.). 128p. (J). (gr. 4-8). 1996. pap. 3.50 (0-553-56625-3, Choose) BDD Bks Young Read.

— Mountain Biker. (Choose Your Own Adventure Ser.: No. 172). (J). (gr. 4-8). 1996. 8.60 (0-606-09633-7, Pub. by Turtleback) Demco.

— Night of the Werewolf. (Choose Your Own Nightmare Ser.: No. 1). (J). (gr. 4-8). 1995. 8.70 (0-606-07365-5, Pub. by Turtleback) Demco.

— The Power Dome. (Choose Your Own Adventure Ser.: No. 174). (J). (gr. 4-8). 1996. 8.60 (0-606-09764-3, Pub. by Turtleback) Demco.

— Reality Machine. (Choose Your Own Adventure Ser.: No. 142). (J). (gr. 4-8). 1993. 8.60 (0-606-05985-7, Pub. by Turtleback) Demco.

— River of No Return. (Choose Your Own Adventure Ser.: No. 178). (Illus.). 112p. (J). (gr. 4-8). 1997. pap. 3.50 (0-553-56755-1) BDD Bks Young Read.

— Secret of the Dolphins. (Choose Your Own Adventure Ser.: No. 134). (J). (gr. 4-8). 1993. 8.60 (0-606-05587-8, Pub. by Turtleback) Demco.

— Soccer Star. LC 95-59925. (Choose Your Own Adventure Ser.: No. 146). 128p. (J). (gr. 5 up). 1994. pap. 3.50 (0-553-56011-5) Bantam.

— Soccer Star. (Choose Your Own Adventure Ser.: No. 146). (J). (gr. 4-8). 1994. 8.60 (0-606-06009-X, Pub. by Turtleback) Demco.

— Through the Black Hole. (Choose Your Own Adventure Ser.: No. 97). 128p. (J). (gr. 4-8). 1989. pap. 3.50 (0-553-28440-1) Bantam.

— Through the Black Hole. (Choose Your Own Adventure Ser.: No. 97). (J). (gr. 4-8). 1990. 8.60 (0-606-04411-6, Pub. by Turtleback) Demco.

— Vampire Invaders. (Choose Your Own Adventure Ser.: No. 118). (J). (gr. 4-8). 1991. 8.60 (0-606-00816-0, Pub. by Turtleback) Demco.

— War with the Mutant Spider Ants. (Choose Your Own Adventure Ser.: No. 152). 128p. (J). (gr. 4-8). 1994. pap. 3.50 (0-553-56399-8) Bantam.

— Who Are You? (Choose Your Own Adventure Ser.: No. 150). (J). (gr. 4-8). 1994. 8.60 (0-606-06875-9, Pub. by Turtleback) Demco.

— The Worst Day of Your Life. (Choose Your Own Adventure Ser.: No. 100). (J). (gr. 4-8). 1990. 8.60 (0-606-04594-5, Pub. by Turtleback) Demco.

***Packard, Edward & Murdocca, Sal.** Big Numbers: And Pictures That Show Just How Big They Are! LC 99-32242. 32p. (J). (gr. k-3). 2000. lib. bdg. 14.95 (0-7613-1280-3, Copper Beech Bks) Millbrook Pr.

Packard, Edward & Packard, Andrea. Mayday! (Choose Your Own Adventure Ser.: No. 184). (Illus.). 112p. (J). (gr. 3-7). 1998. mass mkt. 2.99 (0-553-56758-6, Choose) BDD Bks Young Read.

Packard, Elisabeth, jt. auth. see Zeri, Federico.

Packard, Elizabeth P. Great Disclosure of Spiritual Wickedness in High Places: With Appeal to the Government to Protect the Inalienable Rights of Married Women. LC 74-3965. (Women in America Ser.). (Illus.). 162p. 1974. reprint ed. 18.95 (0-405-06114-5) Ayer.

— Modern Persecution: or Insane Asylums Unveiled, As Demonstrated by the Report of the Investigating Committee of the Legislature of Illinois, 2 vols. LC 73-2410. (Mental Illness & Social Policy; the American Experience Ser.). 1973. reprint ed. 57.95 (0-405-05220-0) Ayer.

***Packard, Emma, et al.** 500 Tips for Primary Teachers. 160p. 1998. pap. 25.00 (0-7494-2371-4, Kogan Pg Educ) Stylus Pub VA.

Packard, Francis R. Guy Patin & the Medical Profession in Paris in the XVIIth Century. LC 78-95624. (Illus.). xxii, 344p. 1970. reprint ed. 45.00 (0-678-03759-0) Kelley.

Packard, Francis R., ed. see Pare, Ambroise.

Packard, Frank L. Jimmie Dale & the Blue Envelope Murder. reprint ed. lib. bdg. 23.95 (0-88411-582-8) Amereon Ltd.

— Tiger Claws. reprint ed. lib. bdg. 24.95 (0-88411-581-X) Amereon Ltd.

Packard, Frederic A. Daily Public School in the United States. LC 73-89215. (American Education: Its Men, Institutions, & Ideas. Series 1). 1974. reprint ed. 16.95 (0-405-01454-6) Ayer.

Packard, George R., jt. auth. see Johnson, U. Alexis.

Packard, Gwen. Coping with Stress. (Coping Skills Library). 128p. (gr. 7-12). 1997. pap. 6.95 (1-56838-176-X, 1151 A) Hazelden.

Packard, Gwen K. Coping in an Interfaith Family. LC 92-39454. (YA). (gr. 7-12). 1993. lib. bdg. 17.95 (0-8239-1452-6) Rosen Group.

— Coping When a Parent Goes Back to Work. LC 94-13198. (YA). (gr. 7-12). 1995. lib. bdg. 16.95 (0-8239-1698-7) Rosen Group.

— Coping with Stress. LC 96-52137. (Coping Ser.). 192p. (YA). (gr. 7-12). 1997. lib. bdg. 17.95 (0-8239-2081-X, D2081-X) Rosen Group.

Packard, Helen C. Prozac: The Controversial Cure. LC 97-44529. (Drug Abuse Prevention Library). (Illus.). 64p. (YA). (gr. 7-9). 1998. lib. bdg. 17.95 (0-8239-2551-X) Rosen Group.

Packard, Helen C. & Wirths, C. A Day in the Life of a Dancer. LC 97-13940. (Kids' Career Library). (Illus.). 24p. (J). (gr. k-4). 1997. lib. bdg. 15.93 (0-8239-5098-0) Rosen Group.

Packard, Helen C., ed. see La Civita, Michael J. L., et al.

Packard, Jarver. Enfermedades del Higado, Su Cura Natural. (SPA.). 1997. pap. text 3.98 (968-15-0543-3) Ed Mex.

Packard, Jasper. History of La Porte County, Indiana. 467p. 1993. reprint ed. lib. bdg. 47.50 (0-8328-3452-1) Higginson Bk Co.

Packard, Jerome L. A Linguistic Investigation of Aphasic Chinese Speech. LC 93-28051. (Studies in Theoretical Psycholinguistics: Vol. 18). 344p. (C). 1993. text 179.50 (0-7923-2466-8) Kluwer Academic.

***Packard, Jerome L.** The Morphology of Chinese: A Linguistic & Cognitive Approach. 300p. (C). 2000. 59.95 (0-521-77112-9) Cambridge U Pr.

Packard, Jerome L., ed. New Approaches to Chinese Word Formation: Morphology, Phonology, & the Lexicon in Modern & Ancient Chinese. LC 97-33206. (Trends in Linguistics, Studies & Monographs). 304p. 1997. lib. bdg. 137.00 (3-11-015109-X) Mouton.

Packard, Jerrold M. Neither Friend nor Foe: The European Neutrals. 544p. 1992. text 30.00 (0-684-19248-9, Scribners Ref) Mac Lib Ref.

Packard, Joan, ed. see Bellissino, Charles A.

Packard, John H. A Manual of Minor Surgery. LC 88-60670. (American Civil War Surgery Ser.: No. 10). 288p. 1989. reprint ed. 45.00 (0-930405-08-0) Norman SF.

Packard, Kathleen W. La Guardia's Fire Chief. rev. ed. (Illus.). 206p. 1993. reprint ed. pap. 9.95 (0-925165-11-5) Fire Buff Hse.

Packard, Laurence B. The Age of Louis the Fourteenth. rev. ed. (Illus.). 64p. (C). 1991. pap. text 2.25 (1-877891-04-5) Paperbook Pr Inc.

Packard, Mary. Barbie & the Scavenger Hunt. (Little Golden Storybks.). (J). (ps-3). 1997. 3.99 (0-307-16179-X, 16179) Gldn Bks Pub Co.

— Barbie & the Scavenger Hunt. (Little Golden Bks.). (Illus.). 24p. (J). (ps-3). 1996. 2.29 (0-307-30199-0, 98767) Gldn Bks Pub Co.

— Best Friends. LC 95-78236. (Look-Look Bks.). (J). 1996. pap. text 3.29 (0-307-12939-X, 12939, Goldn Books) Gldn Bks Pub Co.

— Big City Dump Truck Package (incl. toy) (Tonka Action Storybook Ser.). (Illus.). 32p. (J). (ps). 1997. pap. 6.95 (0-590-04464-8) Scholastic Inc.

***Packard, Mary.** Big City Rescue. (Fisher-Price Magic Wheels Ser.). (Illus.). 12p. (J). (gr. k-3). 1999. bds. 7.99 (1-57584-323-4, Pub. by Rdrs Digest) Random.

Packard, Mary. Big Farm Tractor Package, Incl. toy. LC 97-177451. (Tonka Action Storybook Ser.). (Illus.). 32p. (J). (ps). 1997. pap. 6.95 (0-590-04458-3) Scholastic Inc.

— Bubble Trouble. LC 94-16975. (My First Hello Reader Ser.). (Illus.). 32p. (J). (ps-3). 1995. 3.95 (0-590-48513-X, Cartwheel) Scholastic Inc.

***Packard, Mary.** Chopsticks. Nichols, Cathy, ed. (Illus.). 16p. (J). 2000. write for info. (1-884270-19-0) Nancy Hall.

Packard, Mary. David & Goliath. (Super Shape Bks.). 24p. (J). (ps-k). 1998. pap. text 3.29 (0-307-10207-6, 10207) Gldn Bks Pub Co.

— Dinosaurs. LC 81-16870. (Illus.). 48p. (J). (ps-3). 1981. pap. 12.00 (0-671-43040-8) S&S Bks Yung.

— Disney's Bambi: Opossum Problems. LC 97-70397. (Little Super Shape Bks.). (Illus.). (J). (ps). 1997. pap. text 1.79 (0-307-10581-4, 10581, Goldn Books) Gldn Bks Pub Co.

— The Great Easter Egg Hunt. LC 98-235688. (Illus.). 4p. 1998. 12.95 (0-7611-0900-5) Workman Pub.

— The Happy Trick-or-Treaters. LC 96-18434. (Read with Me Paperback Ser.). (Illus.). 32p. (J). (ps-3). 1997. 2.99 (0-590-94957-8) Scholastic Inc.

Packard, Mary. The Happy Trick-or-Treaters. (Read with Me Ser.). 1997. 8.19 (0-606-11427-0, Pub. by Turtleback) Demco.

Packard, Mary. I Am King! (My First Reader Ser.). (Illus.). 28p. (J). (gr. k-2). 1994. pap. 3.95 (0-516-45365-3) Childrens.

— I Am Not a Dinosaur. LC 96-75. (My First Hello Reader Ser.). (Illus.). 32p. (J). (ps-1). 1997. 3.99 (0-590-68997-5) Scholastic Inc.

Packard, Mary. I Am Not a Dinosaur, with Flash Cards. (My First Hello Reader! Ser.). (J). 1997. 9.19 (0-606-11492-0, Pub. by Turtleback) Demco.

Packard, Mary. I Know Karate. (Hello Reader! Ser.). (Illus.). 32p. (J). (ps-1). 1996. pap. 3.95 (0-590-25498-7, Cartwheel) Scholastic Inc.

— I'm a Fire Fighter. LC 96-104033. (Hello Reader! Ser.). (Illus.). 32p. (J). (ps-k). 1995. pap. 3.95 (0-590-25497-9, Cartwheel) Scholastic Inc.

Packard, Mary. I'm a Fire Fighter. (My First Hello Reader! Ser.). (J). 1995. 9.19 (0-606-09452-0, Pub. by Turtleback) Demco.

Packard, Mary. Jonah & the Whale. (Super Shape Bks.). (Illus.). 24p. (J). (ps-3). 1996. pap. text 3.29 (0-307-10013-8, 10013) Gldn Bks Pub Co.

— Little Star. (J). 1995. 12.95 (0-590-54425-X) Scholastic Inc.

— Make Your Own Time Capsule. (Illus.). (J). (gr. 2-7). 1999. pap. 6.95 (0-8167-4976-0) Troll Communs.

— Mickey Mouse & the Pet Shop. (Super Shape Bks.). (Illus.). 24p. (J). (ps-3). 1996. pap. text 3.29 (0-307-10008-1, 10008) Gldn Bks Pub Co.

***Packard, Mary.** Morse Code. Nichols, Cathy, ed. (Illus.). 16p. (YA). 2000. write for info. (1-884270-14-X) Nancy Hall.

Packard, Mary. My Messy Room. LC 92-36006. (Illus.). 32p. (J). 1993. pap. 3.95 (0-590-46191-5) Scholastic Inc.

— Noah's Ark. (Illus.). 24p. (J). (ps). 1997. pap. text 1.29 (0-307-98783-3, Goldn Books) Gldn Bks Pub Co.

— The Pet That I Want. LC 94-16976. (My First Hello Reader Ser.). (Illus.). 32p. (J). (ps-1). 1995. 3.95 (0-590-48512-1, Cartwheel) Scholastic Inc.

— Rocks & Minerals. (J). (gr. 4-7). 1997. pap. 6.95 (0-8167-3527-1) Troll Communs.

— Scaredy Ghost. LC 93-24845. (Illus.). 24p. (J). (gr. k-2). 1994. pap. 1.50 (0-8167-3246-9) Troll Communs.

— Sleep-over Mouse. (My First Reader Ser.). (Illus.). 28p. (J). (ps-2). 1994. pap. 3.95 (0-516-45367-X) Childrens.

— Spooky Stories & Other Scary Stuff. (Illus.). 32p. (Orig.). (J). (gr. k-3). 1996. pap. 6.95 (0-8167-3833-5) Troll Communs.

— Stars & Planets. (J). (ps-3). 1995. pap. 6.95 (0-8167-3563-8) Troll Communs.

— Surprise! (My First Reader Ser.). (Illus.). 28p. (J). (ps-2). 1990. pap. 3.95 (0-516-45360-2) Childrens.

— We Are Monsters. LC 96-1466. (My First Hello Reader Ser.). (Illus.). 32p. (J). (ps-3). 1996. 3.99 (0-590-68995-9, Cartwheel) Scholastic Inc.

***Packard, Mary.** What's My Job? (Window Surprise Ser.). (Illus.). 12p. (J). (ps-k). 2000. bds. write for info. (1-57584-654-3, Pub. by Rdrs Digest) S&S Trade.

— When I Am Big, Level 1. LC 98-49565. (Fisher-Price All-Star Readers Ser.: Vol. 3). (Illus.). 32p. (J). (gr. k-3). 1999. mass mkt. 3.99 (1-57584-294-7, Pub. by Rdrs Digest) Random.

Packard, Mary. When I Grow Up: Learning about Animals. (Fisher-Price Puzzle Playbks.: Vol. 1). (Illus.). 12p. (J). (gr. k-3). 1999. bds. 6.99 (1-57584-272-6, Pub. by Rdrs Digest) Random.

— Where Is Jake? (My First Reader Ser.). (Illus.). 28p. (J). (gr. k-2). 1990. pap. 3.95 (0-516-45361-0) Childrens.

***Packard, Mary.** Who Lives Here? (Window Surprise Ser.). (Illus.). 12p. (J). (ps-k). 2000. bds. write for info. (1-57584-655-1, Pub. by Rdrs Digest) S&S Trade.

Packard, Mary. World up Close. (Illus.). 16p. (J). (gr. 4-7). 1997. pap. 6.95 (0-8167-3524-7) Troll Communs.

Packard, Mary & Reader's Digest Editors. Heather Hops to It! A Book about Helping Out. (Refrigerator Bks.: Vol. 2). (Illus.). 12p. (J). (gr. k-3). 1999. bds. 3.50 (1-57584-265-3, Pub. by Rdrs Digest) Random.

***Packard, Mary & Regan, Dana.** Fall Leaves. LC 99-31456. (My First Hello Reader Ser.). 32p. (J). (ps-1). 1999. 3.99 (0-439-09911-0) Scholastic Inc.

Packard, Mary E. The Witch Who Couldn't Fly. LC 93-2212. (Glow-in-the-Dark Bk.). (Illus.). 24p. (J). (gr. k-3). 1996. pap. 2.95 (0-8167-3256-6) Troll Communs.

Packard, Michael E. Choosing a Management Company No. 8: Choosing a Management Company. 3rd rev. ed. (GAP Reports: No. 8). 16p. (C). 1994. pap. 17.50 (0-944715-33-8) CAI.

Packard, Mike, et al. Community First! Emerging Visions Reshaping America's Condominium & Homeowner Associations. LC 99-25145. 140p. 1999. pap. text 14.95 (0-941301-43-5, 6081) CAI.

***Packard, Nick & Race, Phil.** 2000 Tips for Teachers. 300p. 2000. pap. 32.50 (0-7494-3081-8, Kogan Pg Educ) Stylus Pub VA.

Packard, Peter, jt. auth. see Slater, John.

Packard, Philip C. Critical Path Analysis for Development Administration. LC 72-85842. (Institute of Social Studies Publications: No. 7). (Illus.). 84p. (Orig.). 1972. pap. text 12.35 (90-279-2174-1) Mouton.

— Project Appraisal for Development Administration. LC 74-75576. (Publications of the Institute of Social Studies: No. 12). 158p. 1974. pap. text 24.65 (90-279-3452-5) Mouton.

Packard, Randall M. Chiefship & Cosmology: An Historical Study of Political Competition. LC 81-47013. (African Systems of Thought Ser.). 255p. 1981. reprint ed. pap. 79.10 (0-608-01069-3, 205937700001) Bks Demand.

— White Plague, Black Labor: Tuberculosis & the Political Economy of Health & Disease in South Africa. 1989. pap. 19.95 (0-520-06575-1, Pub. by U CA Pr) Cal Prin Full Svc.

— White Plague, Black Labor: Tuberculosis & the Political Economy of Health & Disease in South Africa. 416p. 1990. pap. write for info. (0-86980-733-1, Pub. by Univ Natal Pr) Intl Spec Bk.

Packard, Randall M., jt. auth. see Cooper, Frederick.

Packard, Richard B. & Kinear, Fiona C. Manual of Cataract & Intraocular Lens Surgery. (Illus.). 144p. 1991. 90.00 (0-443-04091-5) Church.

Packard, Robert T., jt. ed. see Wilkes, Joseph A.

Packard, Rosa C. The Hidden Hinge. LC 74-188958. 1995. pap. text 19.95 (0-8190-0074-4) R C Packard.

Packard, Sidney. Strategies & Tactics in Fashion Marketing: Selected Readings. LC 82-70063. (Illus.). 143p. reprint ed. pap. 44.40 (0-8357-3714-4, 203643600003) Bks Demand.

Packard, Sidney, et al. Fashion Buying & Merchandising. 2nd ed. (Illus.). 404p. (C). 1983. 50.00 (0-87005-445-7) Fairchild.

Packard, Stephen & Mutel, Cornelia F. The Tallgrass Restoration Handbook: For Prairies, Savannas, & Woodlands. 432p. (C). 1997. text 50.00 (1-55963-319-0) Island Pr.

Packard, Stephen & Mutel, Cornelia F., eds. The Tallgrass Restoration Handbook: For Prairies, Savannas, & Woodlands. (C). 1997. pap. text 25.00 (1-55963-320-4) Island Pr.

Packard, Vance & Horowitz, Daniel, eds. The Status Seekers. 224p. 1995. pap. text 12.95 (0-312-11180-0) St Martin.

Packard, Vernal S. Processed Foods & the Consumer: Additives, Labeling, Standards, & Nutrition. LC 75-32670. 367p. reprint ed. pap. 113.80 (0-7837-2930-8, 205752400006) Bks Demand.

Packard, Wellman. Early Emigration to California. 32p. 1971. reprint ed. pap. 3.95 (0-87770-068-0) Ye Galleon.

Packard, William. The Art of Poetry Writing: A Guide for Poets, Students, & Readers. 240p. 1992. text 19.95 (0-312-07641-X) St Martin.

P

An Asterisk (*) at the beginning of an entry indicates that the title is appearing for the first time.

— The Art of Screenwriting. 2nd ed. LC 98-164002. 200p. 1997. pap. 13.95 (*1-56025-141-7*, Thunders Mouth) Avalon NY.

— The Art of the Playwright. 2nd ed. 200p. 1997. pap. 13.95 (*1-56025-117-4*, Thunders Mouth) Avalon NY.

— Evangelism in America: From Tents to TV. LC 87-2230. (Illus.). 275p. 1988. pap. 10.95 (*1-55778-179-6*) Paragon Hse.

— The Poet's Dictionary: A Handbook of Prosody & Poetic Devices. LC 88-45899. 240p. 1994. reprint ed. pap. 15.00 (*0-06-272045-7*, Harper Ref) HarpC.

— Shipping Pools. 2nd ed. 200p. 1995. 85.00 (*1-85044-512-5*) LLP.

Packard, William & Mitchell, John D. Women - Men (Femmes - Hommes) The Erotic Poetry of Paul Verlaine. LC 77-23853. (ENG & FRE., Illus.). 150p. (Orig.). (C). 1991. reprint ed. pap. 24.95 (*1-882763-01-7*) IASTA.

Packard, Wyman H. A Century of United States Naval Intelligence. LC 94-35197. 1996. text 42.00 (*0-945274-25-4*) Naval Hist Ctr.

Packe, Michael. King Edward III. Seaman, L. C., ed. 336p. 1984. pap. 8.95 (*0-7448-0023-4*) Routledge.

Packel, Ed. Mathematica for Mathematics Teachers. (Illus.). 96p. 1996. pap. 25.00 (*0-9631678-4-7*) Inst Computation.

Packel, Edward W. Animating Calculus: Mathematics Notebooks for the Laboratory. 292p. 1996. pap. text 34.95 incl. disk (*0-387-94748-5*) Spr-Verlag.

— The Mathematics of Games & Gambling. LC 80-85037. (New Mathematical Library: No. 28). 141p. 1981. pap. text 22.00 (*0-88385-628-X*, NML-28) Math Assn.

***Packel, Jackie Day.** Sams Teach Yourself E-Retirement Planning Today: Using the Internet to Help Plan Now for Your Finances. (Illus.). 300p. 2000. pap. 17.99 (*0-672-31980-2*) Sams.

Packel, Leonard & Spina, Delores B. Trial Advocacy: A Systematic Approach. LC 84-70166. 207p. 1995. reprint ed. pap. text 35.00 (*0-8318-0453-X*, B548) Am Law Inst.

Packenham, Robert A. The Dependency Movement: Scholarship & Politics in Development Studies. 400p. (C). 1992. 55.50 (*0-674-19810-7*) HUP.

— Dependency Movement: Scholarship & Politics in Development Studies. 384p. 1998. pap. text 21.00 (*0-674-19811-5*) HUP.

Packer. The Way of Wisdom. 2000. pap. 24.99 (*0-310-22728-3*) Zondervan.

Packer & Yodoi, eds. Redox Regulation of Cell Signaling & Clinical Applications. LC 99-17629. (Oxidative Stress & Disease Ser.). (Illus.). 344p. 1999. text 150.00 (*0-8247-1961-1*) Dekker.

Packer, Alan. Hey Kid: Letters from a Dad. Packer, Dawn, ed. 116p. 1999. pap. 9.95 (*0-9672770-0-0*) Integrity House.

Packer, Alex J. Bringing up Parents: The Teenager's Handbook. LC 92 36625. (Illus.). 272p. (YA). (gr. 8 up). 1993. reprint ed. pap. 14.95 (*0-915793-48-2*) Free Spirit Pub.

***Packer, Alex J.** Highs! Over 150 Ways to Feel Really, Really Good... Without Alcohol or Other Drugs. LC 99-57189. (Illus.). 264p. (YA). (gr. 8 up). 2000. pap. 14.95 (*1-57542-074-0*) Free Spirit Pub.

Packer, Alex J. How Rude! The Teenagers' Guide to Good Manners, Proper Behavior, & Not Grossing People Out. LC 97-13015. (Illus.). 480p. (YA). (gr. 6 up). 1997. pap. text 19.95 (*1-57542-024-4*) Free Spirit Pub.

— Parenting One Day at a Time: Using the Tools of Recovery to Become Better Parents & Raise Better Kids. LC 98-48414. 290p. 1999. pap. 14.95 (*1-56838-323-1*, 1123) Hazelden.

***Packer, Andrew J.** Manual of Retinal Surgery. 2nd ed. (Illus.). 144p. 2000. pap. 45.00 (*0-7506-7106-8*) Buttrwrth-Heinemann.

Packer, Anthony, tr. see Landsbergis, Vytautas.

***Packer, Arnold & Brainard, Scott.** Teaching Workplace Competencies, Vol. 4. Ries, Eric, ed. (Illus.). 36p. 2000. pap. 6.50 (*0-89514-008-X*) ACTE.

Packer, Arnold E., jt. auth. see Johnston, William B.

Packer, Arnold H. & Pines, Marion W. School-to-Work. (Illus.). 280p. (C). 1996. 42.95 (*1-883001-18-8*) Eye On Educ.

Packer, Barlow. The Soft Reply. 1997. pap. 8.95 (*1-57008-316-9*) Bookcraft Inc.

Packer, Barry & Matheson, Boyd C. Put Yourself on Paper! The Warmth, Power & Influence of Handwritten Expression. 96p. 1995. pap. text 12.95 (*1-882441-12-5*) InANutshell Bks.

Packer, Bevill. Appropriate Paper-Based Technology (APT) 176p. 1995. pap. 19.95 (*1-85339-268-5*, Pub. by Intermed Tech) Stylus Pub VA.

Packer, Bill. Butterworths Personal Tax Service. 1991. ring bd. write for info. (*0-406-99653-9*, BPTSASET, MICHIE) LEXIS Pub.

Packer, Billy & Lazenby, Roland. Why We Win: Strategies for Success in Sports, Business & Life. LC 97-47382. (Illus.). 352p. 1998. 24.00 (*1-57028-184-X*, 8184XH, Mstrs Pr) NTC Contemp Pub Co.

Packer, Boyd K. A Christmas Parable. 1993. 12.95 (*0-88494-901-X*) Bookcraft Inc.

— The Holy Temple. 1980 16.95 (*0-88494-411-5*) Bookcraft Inc.

— Let Not Your Heart Be Troubled. 1991. 19.95 (*0-88494-787-4*) Bookcraft Inc.

— Memorable Stories & Parables by Boyd K. Packer. LC 97-74251. 1997. 14.95 (*1-57008-336-3*) Bookcraft Inc.

— Our Father's Plan. rev. ed. LC 84-72516. 62p. 1994. 12.95 (*0-87579-820-9*) Deseret Bk.

— Teach Ye Diligently. rev. ed. LC 75-22704. x, 388p. 1991. reprint ed. pap. 14.95 (*0-87579-476-9*) Deseret Bk.

— That All May Be Edified. 1982. 12.95 (*0-88494-473-5*) Bookcraft Inc.

— The Things of the Soul. 1996. 15.95 (*0-88494-951-6*) Bookcraft Inc.

Packer, Cathy. Freedom of Expression in the American Military: A Communication Modeling Analysis. LC 88-27508. (Illus.). 279p. 1989. 65.00 (*0-275-93028-9*, C3028, Greenwood Pr) Greenwood.

Packer, Corinne A. The Right to Reproductive Choice: A Study in International Law. 213p. 1996. pap. 32.00 (*951-650-546-5*) Women Ink.

Packer, Craig. Into Africa. LC 94-8428. 292p. 1994. 24.95 (*0-226-64429-4*) U Ch Pr.

— Into Africa. LC 96-17889. (Illus.). viii, 288p. 1996. pap. 14.95 (*0-226-64430-8*) U Ch Pr.

Packer, Dawn, ed. see Packer, Alan.

Packer, Donna S. On Footings from the Past. 1988. 19.95 (*0-88494-681-9*) Bookcraft Inc.

Packer, Duane, jt. auth. see Roman, Sanaya.

Packer, Eve. Skulls Head Samba. 60p. 1994. 8.00 (*0-9639585-0-X*) Fly by Nght.

Packer-Fletcher, Dorothy G. Basic Code Enforcement. 289p. write for info. (*0-318-61820-6*) Bldg Code Admins.

***Packer, George.** Blood of the Liberals. 2000. 26.00 (*0-374-25142-8*) FS&G.

Packer, George. Central Square. LC 98-84450. 304p. 1998. 24.95 (*1-55597-277-2*) Graywolf.

— The Village of Waiting. LC 87-45912. (Departures Ser.). 352p. (Orig.). 1988. pap. 12.00 (*0-394-75754-8*) Vin Bks.

Packer, Herbert L. The Limits of the Criminal Sanction. LC 68-26780. 397p. reprint ed. pap. 30.00 (*0-608-08907-9*, 2069542) Bks Demand.

Packer, Ian. Lloyd George. LC 98-21674. 144p. 1998. text 55.00 (*0-312-21707-2*) St Martin.

***Packer, J. I.** Collected Shorter Writings of J. I. Packer No. 1: Celebrating the Saving Work of God. 235p. 1998. reprint ed. 25.00 (*0-85364-896-4*, Pub. by Paternoster Pub) OM Literature.

— Collected Shorter Writings of J. I. Packer No. 2: Serving the People of God. (Collected Shorter Writings of J. I. Packer: Vol. 2). 392p. 1998. reprint ed. 25.00 (*0-85364-904-9*, Pub. by Paternoster Pub) OM Literature.

Packer, J. I. Concise Theology: A Guide to Historic Christian Beliefs. LC 92-37771. 267p. 1993. 16.99 (*0-8423-1111-4*) Tyndale Hse.

— Decisions: Finding God's Will. (Christian Basics Bible Studies). 64p. (Orig.). 1996. pap., wbk. ed. 4.99 (*0-8308-2014-0*, 2014) InterVarsity.

— Evangelism & the Sovereignty of God. 2nd ed. LC 67-28875. 126p. 1991. reprint ed. pap. 9.99 (*0-8308-1339-X*, 1339) InterVarsity.

— Freedom & Authority. (ICBA Foundation Ser.). 32p. 1995. reprint ed. pap. 2.99 (*1-57383-035-6*) Regent College.

— Fundamentalism & the Word of God. 1958. pap. 8.00 (*0-8028-1147-7*) Eerdmans.

— God Has Spoken: Revelation & the Bible. 3rd ed. 176p. 1994. pap. 11.99 (*0-8010-7128-3*) Baker Bks.

— God's Words: Studies of Key Bible Themes. LC 96-20836. 223p. 1998. pap. 9.99 (*0-8010-7105-4*) Baker Bks.

— Growing in Christ. LC 93-50566. 288p. 1994. pap. 15.99 (*0-89107-794-4*) Crossway Bks.

Packer, J. I. Hacia el Conocimiento de Dios.Tr. of Knowing God. 9.99 (*0-7899-0463-2*, 495028) Editorial Unilit.

— J. I. Packer, 4 vols., Set. (Collected Writings of J. I. Packer Ser.). 1999. 99.00 (*0-85364-760-7*, Pub. by Paternoster Pub) Eisenbrauns.

— J. I. Packer Vol. 3: Honouring the Written Word of God, (Collected Writings of J. I. Packer Ser.). 1999. 25.00 (*0-85364-882-4*, Pub. by Paternoster Pub) Eisenbrauns.

— J. I. Packer Vol. 4: Honouring the People of God. 1999. 25.00 (*0-85364-905-7*, Pub. by Paternoster Pub) Eisenbrauns.

Packer, J. I. Keep in the Step with the Spirit. LC 84-1304. 302p. (gr. 13). 1987. pap. 9.99 (*0-8007-5235-X*) Revell.

***Packer, J. I.** Knowing & Doing the Will of God. 2000. pap. 9.99 (*1-56955-220-7*) Servant.

— Knowing Christianity. LC 99-29790. 180p. 1999. pap. 10.99 (*0-8308-2216-X*) InterVarsity.

Packer, J. I. Knowing Christianity. 264p. 1995. 15.99 (*0-87788-058-1*, H Shaw Pubs) Waterbrook Pr.

— Knowing God. 20th rev. annot. ed. LC 73-81573. 288p. 1993. reprint ed. pap. 12.99 (*0-8308-1650-X*, 1650) InterVarsity.

— Knowing God: Twentieth Anniversary Edition. 20th rev. anniversary ed. LC 73-81573. 312p. 1993. student ed. 22.99 (*0-8308-1651-8*, 1651) InterVarsity.

— Life in the Spirit: A 30 Day Personal Bible Study. abr. ed. LC 96-13990. 144p. 1996. pap. 9.99 (*0-89107-892-4*) Crossway Bks.

— Meeting God. (LifeGuide Bible Studies). 64p. (Orig.). 1986. pap., wbk. ed. 4.99 (*0-8308-1057-9*, 1057) InterVarsity.

— Mundo Del Antiguo Testamento.Tr. of World of the Old Testament. (SPA.). 192p. 1985. pap. 8.99 (*0-8297-1416-2*) Vida Pubs.

— Mundo Del Nuevo Testamento.Tr. of World of the New Testament. (SPA.). 192p. 1985. pap. 8.99 (*0-8297-1418-9*) Vida Pubs.

— A Passion for Faithfulness: Wisdom from the Book of Nehemiah. LC 94-24366. (Living Insights Ser.). 224p. 1994. 14.99 (*0-89107-733-2*) Crossway Bks.

— A Quest for Godliness: The Puritan Vision of the Christian Life. LC 94-10535. 368p. 1994. pap. 17.99 (*0-89107-819-3*) Crossway Bks.

— Rediscovering Holiness. 300p. 1999. pap. text 12.99 (*1-56955-045-X*, Vine Bks) Servant.

— Renacer de la Santidad.Tr. of Rediscovering Holiness. (SPA.). 271p. 1995. 11.99 (*0-89922-509-8*, C067-5098) Caribe Betania.

Packer, J. I. Teologia Concisa.Tr. of Concise Theology. (SPA.). 9.99 (*1-56063-949-0*, 498209) Editorial Unilit.

***Packer, J. I.** Truth & Power: The Place of Scripture in the Christian Life. LC 99-23124. 192p. 1999. pap. 11.99 (*0-8308-2215-1*) InterVarsity.

Packer, J. I. Truth & Power: The Place of Scripture in the Christian Life. 250p. 1996. 14.99 (*0-87788-815-9*, H Shaw Pubs) Waterbrook Pr.

***Packer, J. I. & Nystrom, Carolyn.** Knowing God Journal. rev. ed. 120p. 2000. pap. 7.99 (*0-8308-1185-0*) InterVarsity.

— Never Beyond Hope: How God Touches & Uses Imperfect People. 144p. 2000. 14.99 (*0-8308-2232-1*) InterVarsity.

Packer, J. I. & Wilkinson, Loren, eds. Alive to God: Studies in Spirituality. 314p. 1992. pap. 29.95 (*1-57383-167-0*, Regent Coll Pub) Regent College.

Packer, J. I. & Wilkinson, Loren, eds. Alive to God: Studies in Spirituality Presented to James M. Houston. LC 92-31340. 320p. (Orig.). 1992. pap. 19.99 (*0-8308-1767-0*, 1767) InterVarsity.

***Packer, J. I. & Zoba, Wendy Murray.** J. I. Packer Answers Questions for Today. LC 00-36379. 2000. pap. 8.99 (*0-8423-3615-X*) Tyndale Hse.

Packer, J. I., et al. Knowing God: Study Guide. anniversary ed. LC 73-81573. 1993. pap., student ed. 4.99 (*0-8308-1649-6*, 1649) InterVarsity.

— O Mundo do Novo Testamento.Tr. of World of the New Testament. (POR.). 192p. 1990. pap. 8.95 (*0-8297-1590-8*) Vida Pubs.

Packer, J. I., ed. see White, William, Jr.

Packer, James E. The Forum of Trajan in Rome: A Study of the Monuments, 3 vols., Vol. Set. LC 95-41139. (California Studies in the History of Art: Vol. 31). (Illus.). 3p. 1997. 675.00 (*0-520-07493-9*, Pub. by U CA Pr) Cal Prin Full Svc.

***Packer, James E.** The Forum of Trajan in Rome: A Study of the Monuments in Brief. (Illus.). 264p. 2000. pap. 39.95 (*0-520-22673-9*, Pub. by U CA Pr) Cal Prin Full Svc.

Packer, James I., jt. auth. see Dart, Ron.

Packer, Jane. The Complete Guide To Flower Arranging. LC 98-202235. 192p. 1999. 13.95 (*0-7894-3752-X*) DK Pub Inc.

— Fast Flower Arranging. 1998. 19.95 (*0-676-57289-8*) Random.

— Fast Flower Arranging: Create Stunning Displays in Minutes. LC 97-38653. 128p. 1998. 19.95 (*0-7894-2394-4*) DK Pub Inc.

***Packer, Jane.** Fast Flowers. (Illus.). 128p. 2000. pap. 13.95 (*0-7894-6144-7*) DK Pub Inc.

Packer, Jane. Jane Packer's New Flower Arranging. (Illus.). 128p. 1996. reprint ed. pap. 17.95 (*1-57076-037-3*, Trafalgar Sq Pub) Trafalgar.

— Living with Flowers. LC 96-61471. (Illus.). 160p. 1997. 29.95 (*1-57076-079-9*, Trafalgar Sq Pub) Trafalgar.

Packer, Jo, jt. auth. see McReynolds, Anne.

Packer, Joan G. Rebecca West: An Annotated Bibliography. LC 91-11183. 164p. 1991. text 10.00 (*0-8240-5692-2*, H1158) Garland.

Packer, John G., jt. auth. see Moss, Ezra H.

Packer, John W. Acts of the Apostles. (Cambridge Bible Commentary on the New English Bible, New Testament Ser.). 234p. (Orig.). (C). 1966. pap. text 20.95 (*0-521-09383-X*) Cambridge U Pr.

Packer, Jonathan. Live & Work in Spain & Portugal. 2nd ed. (Live & Work Abroad Guides Ser.). 288p. 1998. pap. 17.95 (*1-85458-186-4*, Pub. by Vac Wrk Pubns) Seven Hills Bk.

Packer, Kathryn, jt. auth. see Webster, Andrew.

Packer, Kenneth J., jt. auth. see McBrierty, Vincent J.

Packer, Kenneth L. HIV Infection: The Facts You Need to Know. LC 97-13755. (Venture Ser.). 160p. (J). 1998. lib. bdg. 24.00 (*0-531-11333-7*) Watts.

— HIV Infection: The Facts You Need to Know. (Venture-Health & the Human Body Ser.). (Illus.). (YA). (gr. 7 up). 1998. pap. 9.95 (*0-531-15899 3*) Watts.

***Packer, Lester.** The Antioxidant Miracle: Put Lipoic Acid, Pycogenol & Vitamins E & C to Work for You. LC 99-52442. 256p. 1999. pap. 14.95 (*0-471-35311-6*) Wiley.

***Packer, Lester, ed.** Antioxidants in Diabetes Management. (Oxidative Stress & Disease Ser.: Vol. 4). 349p. 2000. 150.00 (*0-8247-8844-3*) Dekker.

Packer, Lester, ed. Oxygen Radicals in Biological Systems, Pt. D. (Methods in Enzymology Ser.: Vol. 234). 704p. 1994. text 115.00 (*0-12-182135-8*) Acad Pr.

Packer, Lester, et al, eds. Cyanobacteria, Vol. 167. (Methods in Enzymology Ser.). 750p. 1988. text 139.00 (*0-12-182068-8*) Acad Pr.

— Free Radicals in Brain Physiology & Disorders. (Illus.). 474p. 1996. text 95.00 (*0-12-543445-6*) Acad Pr.

— Methods in Enzymology Vol. 299: Oxidants & Antioxidants. (Illus.). 506p. (C). 1998. boxed set 99.95 (*0-12-182200-1*) Acad Pr.

— Nitric Oxide Pt. A: Sources & Detection of NO; NO Synthase. LC 97-132273. (Methods in Enzymology Ser.: Vol. 268). (Illus.). 555p. 1996. text 95.00 (*0-12-182169-2*) Acad Pr.

— Nitric Oxide Pt. B: Physiological & Pathological Processes. (Methods in Enzymology Ser.: Vol. 269). (Illus.). 528p. 1996. text 85.00 (*0-12-182170-6*) Acad Pr.

— Oxygen Radicals in Biological Systems, Pt. C. (Methods in Enzymology Ser.: Vol. 233). (Illus.). 711p. 1994. text 115.00 (*0-12-182134-X*) Acad Pr.

— Oxygen Radicals in Biological Systems Pt. B: Oxygen Radicals & Antioxidants. (Methods in Enzymology Ser.: Vol. 186). 855p. 1990. text 142.00 (*0-12-182087-4*) Acad Pr.

— Proceedings of the International Symposium on Natural Antioxidants: Molecular Mechanisms & Health Effects. LC 96-15468. (Illus.). xiii, 705 p. 1996. 150.00 (*0-935315-69-1*) Am Oil Chemists.

— Retinoids Pt. A: Molecular & Metabolic Aspects. (Methods in Enzymology Ser.: Vol. 189). 583p. 1990. text 121.00 (*0-12-182090-4*) Acad Pr.

— Retinoids Pt. B: Cell Differentiation & Clinical Applications. (Methods in Enzymology Ser.: Vol. 190). 488p. 1990. text 121.00 (*0-12-182091-2*) Acad Pr.

Packer, Lester & Cadenas, Enrique, eds. Biothiols in Health & Disease, No. 2. (Antioxidants in Health & Disease Ser.: Vol. 2). (Illus.). 552p. 1995. text 180.00 (*0-8247-9654-3*) Dekker.

— Handbook of Synthetic Antioxidants. LC 96-53380. (Antioxidants in Health & Disease Ser.). (Illus.). 464p. 1997. text 150.00 (*0-8247-9810-4*) Dekker.

***Packer, Lester & Coleman, Carol.** Antioxidant. LC 98-34992. 272p. 1999. 24.95 (*0-471-29768-2*) Wiley.

Packer, Lester & Fleischer, Sidney, eds. Biomembranes. LC 97-125863. (Selected Methods in Enzymology Ser.). (Illus.). 1096p. 1997. pap. 99.00 (*0-12-543565-7*) Morgan Kaufmann.

Packer, Lester & Fuchs, Jurgen, eds. Vitamin C in Health & Disease. LC 97-7703. (Antioxidants in Health & Disease Ser.: Vol. 5). (Illus.). 560p. 1997. text 150.00 (*0-8247-9313-7*) Dekker.

— Vitamin E in Health & Disease: Biochemistry & Clinical Applications. LC 92-49976. (Illus.). 1024p. 1992. text 255.00 (*0-8247-8692-0*) Dekker.

Packer, Lester & Ong, Augustine S., eds. Biological Oxidants & Antioxidants: Molecular Mechanisms & Health Effects. LC 98-6432. (Illus.). 1998. 130.00 (*0-935315-91-8*, PC120) Am Oil Chemists.

Packer, Lester & Wirtz, Karel W., eds. Signalling Mechanisms: From Transcription Factors to Oxidative Stress. LC 95-10171. (NATO ASI Series H: Vol. 92). (Illus.). 472p. 1995. 217.95 (*3-540-59127-3*) Spr-Verlag.

Packer, Lester, jt. auth. see Cadenas, Enrique.

Packer, Lester, jt. ed. see Cadenas, Enrique.

Packer, Lester, jt. ed. see Colowick, Sidney P.

Packer, Lester, ed. see Cutler, R. G., et al.

Packer, Lester, jt. ed. see Fuchs, Jurgen.

Packer, Lester, ed. see Livrea, M. A.

Packer, Lester, jt. ed. see Ohya-Nishiguchi, H.

Packer, Lester, jt. ed. see Ong, A. S.

Packer, Lester, jt. ed. see Rajamanickam, C.

Packer, Lester, jt. ed. see Rice-Evans, Catherine T.

Packer, Lester, ed. see Simon, Melvin I.

***Packer, Martin J.** Changing Classes: School Reform & the New Economy. (Learning in Doing Ser.). 336p. (C). 2000. Price not set. (*0-521-64234-5*); pap. Price not set. (*0-521-64540-9*) Cambridge U Pr.

Packer, Martin J. The Structure of Moral Action: A Hermeneutic Study of Moral Conflict. (Contributions to Human Development Ser.: Vol. 13). (Illus.). xii, 164p. 1985. 84.50 (*3-8055-3999-1*) S Karger.

Packer, Martin J. & Addison, Richard B., eds. Entering the Circle: Hermeneutic Investigation in Psychology. LC 88-24908. 329p. (C). 1989. pap. text 24.95 (*0-7914-0015-8*) State U NY Pr.

***Packer, Michael.** Feet Don't Fail Me Now! Studies for Developing Drumset Independence over Foot Ostinatos. 72p. 1999. pap. 12.95 (*0-7935-9837-0*) H Leonard.

Packer, Miriam. Piece Work. LC 95-81761. (Drama Ser.: No. 14). 160p. Date not set. pap. 10.00 (*1-55071-038-9*) Guernica Editions.

— Take Me to Coney Island, Vol. 1. (Prose Ser.: No. 25). 191p. 1993. pap. 13.00 (*0-920717-92-6*) Guernica Editions.

***Packer, Mirium.** Us Fools Believing: Short Stories. 128p. 2000. pap. 13.00 (*1-55071-056-7*, Pub. by Guernica Editions) Paul & Co Pubs.

Packer, Nancy E. White Gloves & Red Bricks: APVA, 1889-1989. (Illus.). 87p. 1989. pap. 9.95 (*0-917565-02-9*) Assn Preserv VA.

Packer, Nancy H. Jealous-Hearted Me: Stories. LC 96-9621. 144p. 1997. pap. 10.00 (*1-880284-20-0*) J Daniel.

— Women Who Walk: Stories. LC 88-28617. x, 184p. 1989. 17.95 (*0-8071-1458-8*) La State U Pr.

Packer, Nancy H. & Timpane, John. Writing Worth Reading: The Critical Process. 3rd ed. LC 96-86778. 596p. 1997. pap. text 32.95 (*0-312-06101-3*) St Martin.

Packer, Nancy H., jt. auth. see Stone, Wilfred.

Packer, Paul C. Housing of High School Programs. LC 70-177140. (Columbia University. Teachers College. Contributions to Education Ser.: No. 159). reprint ed. 37.50 (*0-404-55159-9*) AMS Pr.

Packer, Randall. Multimedia. 26.95 (*0-393-04979-5*) Norton.

Packer, Robert B. Financial Liberalization & the Reconstruction of State-Market Relations. rev. ed. LC 98-37933. (Financial Sector of the American Economy Ser.). 225p. 1998. 57.00 (*0-8153-3161-4*) Garland.

Packer, Roger J., et al, eds. Pediatric Neuro-Oncology: New Trends in Clinical Research. LC 90-4990. (Monographs in Clinical Pediatrics: Vol. 3). 320p. 1991. text 143.00 (*3-7186-0524-4*) Gordon & Breach.

Packer, Steve, jt. auth. see Bray, Mark.

Packer, Thane. On My Honor. LC 98-72460. 1998. pap. 9.95 (*1-57008-439-4*) Bookcraft Inc.

Packer, Tina, jt. auth. see Whitney, John.

Packer, Toni. The Light of Discovery. LC 95-23229. 160p. 1995. 17.95 (*0-8048-3063-0*) Tuttle Pubng.

— The Light of Discovery. 1999. pap. 12.95 (*0-8048-3196-3*) Tuttle Pubng.

— The Work of This Moment. 128p. (Orig.). 1995. pap. 12.95 (*0-8048-3062-2*) Tuttle Pubng.

Packer, William. Fashion Drawing in Vogue. LC 88-51325. (Illus.). 240p. 1997. pap. 34.95 (*0-500-27528-9*, Pub. by Thames Hudson) Norton.

Packer, William A., tr. see Medvedev, Roy A.

P

An Asterisk (*) at the beginning of an entry indicates that the title is appearing for the first time.

cker, William A., tr. see Zevi, Bruno.

Packet. Antioxidant Food Supplements in Human Health. LC 98-48062. 500p. 1999. 99.95 (*0-12-543590-8*) Acad Pr.

Packham, D. E., ed. Handbook of Adhesion. 1992. 232.50 (*0-582-04423-5*, Pub. by Addison-Wesley) Longman.

Packham, Eric. Success or Failure: The UN Intervention in the Congo after Independence. 326p. 1998. pap. 24.00 (*1-56072-566-4*) Nova Sci Pubs.

Packham, Eric S. Freedom & Anarchy. LC 95-9958. 187p. 1996. lib. bdg. 95.00 (*1-56072-232-0*) Nova Sci Pubs.

Packham, Jo. The Complete Book of Scarves. (Illus.). 1999. pap. 14.95 (*0-8069-7781-7*) Sterling.

— The Complete Book of Scarves: All You Need to Make, Decorate, Embellish, Tie & Wear. LC 97-35570. (Illus.). 128p. 1997. write for info. (*0-8069-0428-3*) Sterling.

— Glue Crafts: More Things to Do with Glue Than You Ever Imagined. LC 95-11240. (Illus.). 144p. 1995. 24.95 (*0-8069-3187-6*, Chapelle) Sterling.

— Moments to Remember: The Art of Creating Scrapbook Memories. LC 98-33643. 1998. 24.95 (*0-8362-5255-1*) Andrews & McMeel.

— Wedding Receptions: Arranging a Joyous Celebration. LC 93-25930. (Wedding Ser.). (Illus.). 112p. 1993. pap. 5.95 (*0-8069-8833-9*, Chapelle) Sterling.

***Packham, Jo.** Wedding Toasts: Finding the Perfect Words. LC 00-37196. 2000. pap. write for info. (*0-8069-7387-0*) Sterling.

Packham, Jo. Wedding Toasts & Speeches: Finding the Perfect Words. LC 92-41319. (Illus.). 96p. 1993. pap. 5.95 (*0-8069-8832-0*, Chapelle) Sterling.

— Wedding Vows: Finding the Perfect Words. LC 98-44564. 1999. pap. 7.95 (*0-8069-0639-1*) Sterling.

Packham, John R., et al. Functional Ecology of Woodlands. (Illus.). 384p. (C). 1992. text 85.00 (*0-412-44390-2*, A7417) Chapman & Hall.

Packman, Ann, jt. ed. see Onslow, Mark.

Packman, Brenda, tr. see Scala, Giambattista.

Packman, Eric, jt. auth. see Croll, Alistair.

Packman, Jean. From Care to Accommodation: Support, Protection & Control in Child Care Services. LC 98-209156. (Studies in Evaluating the Children Act 1989). xii, 289p. 1998. 25.00 (*0-11-321869-9*, HM18699, Pub. by Statnry Office) Bernan Associates.

Packo, John E. Coping with Cancer: Twelve Creative Choices. LC 90-62157. 225p. 1991. pap. 9.99 (*0-87509-438-4*) Chr Pubns.

— Find & Use Your Spiritual Gifts. LC 80-69967. 117p. (Orig.). 1980. pap. 9.99 (*0-87509-293-4*) Chr Pubns.

Packull, Werner O. Hutterite Beginnings: Communitarian Experiments During the Reformation. LC 98-6330. (Illus.). 488p. 1996. text 59.95 (*0-8018-5048-7*) Johns Hopkins.

— Hutterite Beginnings: Communitarian Experiments During the Reformation. 488p. 1999. pap. 24.95 (*0-8018-6256-6*) Johns Hopkins.

— Mysticism & the Early South German-Austrian Anabaptist Movement, 1525-1531. LC 76-46557. (Studies in Anabaptist & Mennonite History: No. 19). 254p. reprint ed. pap. 72.40 (*0-608-06024-0*, 2066353) Bks Demand.

***Packull, Werner O., et al.** Radical Reformation Studies: Essays Presented to James M. Stayer. Stayer, James M. & Dipple, Geoffrey, eds. LC 99-40592. (St. Andrews Studies in Reformation History). 201p. 2000. text 86.95 (*0-7546-0032-7*, Pub. by Ashgate Pub) Ashgate Pub Co.

Packwood, Bob, ed. Medicare: The Next 30 Years. 50p. (C). 1999. reprint ed. pap. text 20.00 (*0-7881-8143-2*) DIANE Pub.

***Packwood, Bob, ed.** Medicare Fraud & Abuse: Congressional Hearing. 108p. (C). 1999. reprint ed. pap. text 25.00 (*0-7881-8090-8*) DIANE Pub.

Packwood, Burley. Bird Turd Peppers & Other Delights. (Illus.). 313p. (Orig.). 1993. pap. 7.95 (*0-9624358-1-3*) Quantum Pr AZ.

— Quail in My Bed. LC 89-92060. (Illus.). 195p. (Orig.). 1989. pap. 6.95 (*0-9624358-0-5*) Quantum Pr AZ.

Paclisanu, Zenobius. Hungary's Struggle to Annihilate Its National Minorities: Based on Secret Hungarian Documents. 182p. 1985. write for info. (*0-937019-00-3*); pap. 18.00 (*0-937019-01-1*) Romanian Hist.

Paco, Mariano D., ed. see Benavente, Jacinto.

Paco, Mariano D., ed. see Vallejo, Antonio B.

Pacolet, Jozef. Social Protection & the European Economic & Monetary Union. 320p. 1996. text 82.95 (*1-85628-581-2*, Pub. by Avebry) Ashgate Pub Co.

Pacolet, Jozef & Wilderom, Celeste. Economics of Care of the Elderly. 240p. 1991. 83.95 (*1-85628-196-5*, Pub. by Avebry) Ashgate Pub Co.

Pacosz, Christina. This Is Not a Place to Sing. 48p. (Orig.). (C). 1987. pap. 4.95 (*0-931122-47-3*) West End.

Pacosz, Christina V. Some Winded, Wild Beast. 1985. pap. 2.50 (*0-934868-28-X*) Black & Red.

Pacotti, Pamela. Legacy of Secrets. 1988. 3.95 (*0-517-00036-9*) Random Hse Value.

Pacovska, Kveta. Flying. LC 95-8327.Tr. of Turme. (Illus.). 48p. (J). (gr. k-3). 1995. 28.00 (*1-55858-496-X*, Pub. by North-South Bks NYC) Chronicle Bks.

— The Little Flower King. Bell, Anthea, tr. LC 95-23866. (Illus.). 40p. (J). (gr. k-3). 1996. 15.95 (*1-55858-532-X*, Pub. by North-South Bks NYC) Chronicle Bks.

— The Midnight Play. Clements, Andrew, tr. from GER. LC 94-26546.Tr. of Mitternacht Spiel. (Illus.). 48p. (J). (gr. k-3). 1994. 28.00 (*1-55858-252-5*, Pub. by North-South Bks NYC) Chronicle Bks.

— The Midnight Play. LC 93-16258.Tr. of Mitternacht Spiel. (Illus.). (J). (ps-8). 1993. 15.95 (*0-88708-317-X*, Picture Book Studio) S&S Childrens.

— One Five Many. (J). (ps-3). 1990. 16.95 (*0-685-54064-2*, Clarion Bks) HM.

— Pacovska's Art Pack, Vol. 1. (J). 1996. pap. text 5.99 (*1-55858-533-8*, Pub. by North-South Bks NYC) Chronicle Bks.

— El Pequeno Rey de las Flores. LC 95-38557. (SPA., Illus.). 40p. (J). (gr. k-3). 1996. 15.95 (*1-55858-538-9*, Pub. by North-South Bks NYC) Chronicle Bks.

Pacquement, Alfred, jt. text see Bordeaux, Jean-Luc.

Pacquet, Marcel. Magritte. 1994. pap. 9.99 (*3-8228-9648-9*) Taschen Amer.

Pact, Virginia, et al. The Muscle Testing Handbook. 194p. 1984. 36.95 (*0-316-68768-5*, Little Brwn Med Div) Lppncott W & W.

Pacteau, Francette. The Symptom of Beauty. LC 93-38507. (Essays in Art & Culture Ser.). 192p. 1994. 41.00 (*0-674-85987-1*) HUP.

— The Symptom of Beauty: Essays in Art & Culture. (Essays in Art & Culture Ser.). (Illus.). 232p. (Orig.). (C). 1995. pap. text 20.50 (*0-674-85988-X*) HUP.

Pacter, Paul. Reporting Disaggregated Information. LC 93-70113. (Financial Accounting Standards Board Research Report Ser.). 423p. 1993. pap. 25.00 (*0-910065-54-3*) Finan Acct Found.

Pactor, Howard S., compiled by. Colonial British Caribbean Newspapers: A Bibliography & Directory, 19. LC 90-35630. (Bibliographies & Indexes in World History Ser.: No. 19). 160p. 1990. lib. bdg. 69.50 (*0-313-27232-8*, PBC/, Greenwood Pr) Greenwood.

Pactor, Peter A. The Day the Pig Got Loose in School (& Other Strange Stories) 139p. 1993. pap. 10.95 (*0-9638569-0-1*) P A Pactor.

— Thoughts to Hold Onto: Just for Teenagers. 48p. (Orig.). (YA). 1995. pap. 5.95 (*0-9638569-1-X*) P A Pactor.

Pacuilla, Nicholas. Artificer Asylum. 260p. 1993. pap. 7.95 (*0-9638757-0-1*) Asylum Pubns.

Pacult, F. Paul. Kindred Spirits: The Spirit Journal Guide to the World's Distilled Spirits & Fortified Wines. LC 96-39289. 480p. (J). 1997. pap. 16.95 (*0-7868-8172-0*, Pub. by Hyperion) Time Warner.

Pacwa, Mitch. Catholics & the New Age: How Good People Are Being Drawn into Jungian Psychology, the Enneagram, & the Age of Aquarius. 236p. (Orig.). 1992. pap. 10.99 (*0-89283-756-X*, Charis) Servant.

Pacwa, Mitch. Father, Forgive Me, for I Am Frustrated: Growing in Your Faith Even When It Isn't Easy Being Catholic. LC 96-40845. 220p. 1997. pap. 10.99 (*0-89283-840-X*, Charis) Servant.

Pacyga, Dominic & Sellers, Rod. Chicago's Southeast Side. LC 98-87775. (Images of America Ser.). (Illus.). 128p. 1998. pap. 16.99 (*0-7524-1315-5*) Arcadia Publng.

Pacyga, Dominic A. Polish Immigrants & Industrial Chicago: Workers on the South Side, 1880-1922. LC 90-25391. (Urban Life & Urban Landscape Ser.). 298p. 1991. text 21.50 (*0-8142-0541-0*) Ohio St U Pr.

Pacyna, Jozef M. & Ottar, Brynjulf, eds. Control & Fate of Atmospheric Trace Metals. (C). 1989. text 196.50 (*0-7923-0152-8*) Kluwer Academic.

Paczkowski. Learning Guide Marketing. 4th ed. 1996. pap. text 27.20 (*0-13-271768-9*) St Martin.

Paczkowski, Thomas. A Learning Guide to Marketing. 3rd ed. (C). 1993. pap. text 25.20 (*0-13-562778-8*) P-H.

***Paczkowski, Thomas J.** Principles of Marketing. 8th ed. (Illus.). 1999. pap. 25.00 (*0-13-099816-8*) P-H.

Paczolay, Gy. Comparative Dictionary of Proverbs. 300p. (C). 1987. 99.00 (*0-7855-6680-5*, Pub. by Collets) St Mut.

Paczuska, Anna & Grillet, Sophie. Socialism for Beginners. (Writers & Readers Documentary Comic Bks.). (Illus.). (C). 1986. pap. 6.95 (*0-906495-92-X*) Writers & Readers.

Paczyriski. Poland's Financial Services. (Euromoney Country Guide Ser.). 183p. 1997. 170.00 (*1-85564-569-6*, Pub. by Euromoney) Am Educ Systs.

Pada Das, Bishnu. Some Aspects of Socio-Economic Changes in South-Western Frontier Bengal since Introduction of Neo-Vaisnavism. 1996. 34.00 (*81-7102-049-6*, Pub. by Firma KLM) S Asia.

Pada, James, Jr. My Little Angel. 76p. 1997. pap. write for info. (*1-57502-561-2*, PO1624) Morris Pubng.

Padadoyannis, I. N. HPLC in Clinical Chemistry. (Chromatographic Science Ser.: Vol. 54). (Illus.). 504p. 1990. text 185.00 (*0-8247-8139-2*) Dekker.

Padak, Nancy, jt. auth. see Rasinski, Timothy.

Padak, Nancy, jt. auth. see Rasinski, Timothy V.

Padaki, Vijay. Development Intervention & Programme Evaluation: Concepts & Cases. LC 95-8277. 216p. (C). 1995. 29.95 (*0-8039-9240-8*); pap. 14.95 (*0-8039-9241-6*) Sage.

Padam, Sundarsanam. Bus Transport in India: The Structure, Management & Performance of Road Transport Corporation. 1990. 32.50 (*81-202-0222-8*, Pub. by Ajanta) S Asia.

***Padamsee, Alyque & Prabhu, Arun.** A Double Life: My Exciting Years in Theatre & Advertising. LC 99-932835. 320p. 1999. 23.50 (*0-14-024071-3*, Penguin Classics) Viking Penguin.

Padamsee, Hasan, et al. RF Superconductivity for Accelerators. LC 97-22367. (Series in Beam Physics & Accelerator Technology). 544p. 1998. 89.95 (*0-471-15432-6*) Wiley.

Padavic, Irene, jt. auth. see Reskin, Barbara F.

Padawer, Patricia, jt. auth. see Goldstein, Joan.

Padawitz, P. Computing in Horn Clause Theories. (EATCS Monographs on Theoretical Computer Science). (Illus.). xi, 322p. 1988. 65.95 (*0-387-19427-4*) Spr-Verlag.

— Deductive & Declarative Programming. (Tracts in Theoretical Computer Science Ser.: No. 28). (Illus.). 285p. (C). 1992. text 54.95 (*0-521-41723-6*) Cambridge U Pr.

Padberg, D. I., et al, eds. Agro-Food Marketing. LC 96-2755. (A CAB International Publication). 512p. 1997. pap. text 49.95 (*0-85199-144-0*) OUP.

— Agro-Food Marketing. LC 96-2755. (A CAB International Publication). 512p. (C). 1997. text 100.00 (*0-85199-143-2*) OUP.

Padberg, John W. Colleges in Controversy: The Jesuit Schools in France from Revival to Suppression, 1815-1880. LC 75-78523. (Historical Studies: No. 83). 347p. 1969. 25.00 (*0-674-14160-1*) HUP.

— Together As a Companionship: A History of the Thirty-First, Thirty-Second, & Thirty-Third General Congregations of the Society of Jesus. (Series IV: No. 15). viii, 145p. (Orig.). 1994. 14.95 (*1-880810-08-5*) Inst Jesuit.

Padberg, John W., ed. Documents of the Thirty-First & Thirty-Second General Congregations of the Society of Jesus: An English Translation of the Official Latin Texts of the General Congregations & of the Accompanying Papal Documents. LC 77-70881. (Jesuit Primary Sources in English Translation Series I: No. 2). x, 598p. 1977. pap. 6.00 (*0-912422-26-2*) Inst Jesuit.

***Padberg, M.** Linear Optimization & Extensions. 2nd expanded rev. ed. Graham, R. L. et al, eds. LC 99-23776. (Algorithms & Combinatorics Ser.: Vol. 12). (Illus.). xxi, 501p. 1999. 106.00 (*3-540-65833-5*) Spr-Verlag.

Padberg, Manfred. Linear Optimization & Extensions. LC 94-47365. (Algorithms & Combinatorics Ser.: Vol. 12). 1995. 109.95 (*3-540-58734-9*) Spr-Verlag.

Padbury, Andy, ed. My War: or How I Survived in the Royal Air Force. (C). 1989. 45.00 (*0-7855-6629-5*) St Mut.

PADC Environmental Impact Assessment & Planning Un. Environmental Impact Assessment: University of Aberdeen, Dept. of Geography, Old Aberdeen, U. K. 1983. text 225.50 (*90-247-2765-0*) Kluwer Academic.

Padda, Darshan S. Selected Essays on Food & Agriculture in the Virgin Islands. (Illus.). 700p. (Orig.). 1991. pap. text. write for info. (*0-9628909-0-1*) U VI CES.

Padden, Carol A. & Humphries, Tom L. Deaf in America: Voices from a Culture. LC 88-11769. (Illus.). 160p. 1988. 24.00 (*0-674-19423-3*) HUP.

— Deaf in America: Voices from a Culture. (Illus.). 448p. 1988. pap. text 13.95 (*0-674-19424-1*) HUP.

Padden, Carol A., jt. auth. see Humphries, Tom L.

Padden, Michael. May the Road Rise to Meet You: Everything You Need to Know about Irish American History. LC 98-42360. 320p. 1999. pap. 13.95 (*0-452-27853-8*) NAL.

Padden, R. C., ed. see Arzans de Orsua y Vela, Bartolome.

Paddie, Dennis. Morning Wounds in the Warehouse. (Illus.). 64p. (Orig.). 1993. pap. 12.00 (*0-9631569-1-8*) Backyard Pr.

Paddington Bear. Childhood Memories. large type ed. 212p. (J). 1991. 21.95 (*1-85089-456-6*, Pub. by ISIS Lrg Prnt) Transaction Pubs.

Paddio-Johnson, Eunice. Pat's First Book of Thoughts in Poetry & Prose. 1991. write for info. (*1-880143-00-3*) Paddio-Johnson.

Paddison, Joshua, ed. A World Transformed: Firsthand Accounts of California Before the Gold Rush. (Illus.). 368p. 1998. pap. 16.95 (*1-890771-13-9*) Heyday Bks.

Paddison, Max. Adorno, Modernism & Mass Culture: Essays on Critical Theory & Music. 149p. 1997. pap. 24.95 (*1-871082-61-7*, Pub. by Kahn & Averill) Paul & Co Pubs.

— Adorno's Aesthetics of Music. (Illus.). 390p. (C). 1998. pap. text 24.95 (*0-521-62608-0*) Cambridge U Pr.

Paddison, Patricia L., ed. Treatment of Adult Survivors of Incest. LC 92-17653. (Clinical Practice Ser.: No. 27). 148p. 1993. text 12.95 (*0-88048-469-1*, 8469) Am Psychiatric.

Paddison, Ronan. Marketing & Distribution in the Third World. (Routledge Introductions to Development Ser.). (Illus.). 128p. (C). 1998. pap. 14.99 (*0-415-05583-0*) Routledge.

Paddison, Ronan, et al, eds. International Perspective in Urban Studies, Vol. 5. 240p. 1997. pap. 34.95 (*1-85302-443-0*, Pub. by Jessica Kingsley) Taylor & Francis.

— International Perspectives in Urban Studies. 163p. 1993. pap. 42.00 (*1-85302-163-6*) Taylor & Francis.

— International Perspectives in Urban Studies, No. 2. 328p. 1994. pap. 37.50 (*1-85302-216-0*) Taylor & Francis.

— International Perspectives in Urban Studies, Vol. 4. 276p. 1996. pap. text 34.95 (*1-85302-383-3*, Pub. by Jessica Kingsley) Taylor & Francis.

Paddison, Ronan & Bailey, Stephen, eds. Local Government Finance: International Perspectives. LC 89-113801. 277p. reprint ed. pap. 85.90 (*0-608-20311-4*, 207156400002) Bks Demand.

Paddison, Ronan & Money, John, eds. International Perspectives in Urban Studies, No. 3. 276p. 1995. pap. 37.50 (*1-85302-311-6*) Taylor & Francis.

Paddison, Ronan, jt. auth. see Muir, Richard.

Paddison, Ronan, jt. ed. see Bailey, S. J.

Paddison, Sara. The Hidden Power of the Heart: Discovering an Unlimited Source of Intelligence. 2nd rev. ed. LC 98-33702. Orig. Title: The Hidden Power of the Heart: Achieving Balance & Fulfillment in a Stressful World. 294p. 1998. 23.00 (*1-879052-43-1*) Planetary Pubns.

Paddison, Sara, jt. auth. see Childre, Doc Lew.

Paddison, Sara H. The Hidden Power of the Heart: Achieving Balance & Fulfillment in a Stressful World. LC 92-32852. 280p. 1992. pap. 14.95 (*1-879052-35-0*) Planetary Pubns.

Paddison, Sara H., ed. see Childre, Doc Lew.

Paddison, Valda, jt. auth. see Cave, Yvonne.

***Paddleford, Robert R.** The Last Tasmanian Tiger: The History & Extinction of the Thylacine. (Illus.). 336p. (C). 2000. text Price not set. (*0-521-78219-8*) Cambridge U Pr.

Paddleford, Robert R. Manual of Small Animal Anesthesia. 2nd ed. Kersey, Ray, ed. LC 98-15368. (Illus.). 320p. (C). 1998. pap. text 39.95 (*0-7216-4060-5*, W B Saunders Co) Harcrt Hlth Sci Grp.

Paddock, Bruce. Victorian Christmas. LC 94-78179. (Traditional Country Life Recipe Ser.). (Illus.). 96p. 1994. pap. 9.95 (*1-883283-06-X*) Brick Tower.

Paddock, Charles E. Structured FORTRAN for Business. LC 84-18377. (Illus.). 272p. (C). 1985. pap. text 32.00 (*0-13-854233-3*) P-H.

Paddock, Charles L. Life's Detours. 32p. 1952. pap. 0.99 (*0-8163-0074-7*, 12225-9) Pacific Pr Pub Assn.

Paddock, Craig, ed. see Landolphi, Suzi.

Paddock, Eric. Belonging to the West. LC 95-50044. (Illus.). 136p. 1996. pap. 29.95 (*0-8018-5323-0*); text 49.95 (*0-8018-5322-2*) Johns Hopkins.

Paddock, G. J. The Sectional Title Handbook. 2nd ed. 216p. 1990. pap. write for info. (*0-7021-2346-3*, Pub. by Juta & Co) Gaunt.

Paddock, Harold. A Dialect Survey of Carbonear, Newfoundland. (Publications of the American Dialect Society: No. 68). (Illus.). 85p. 1982. pap. text 8.50 (*0-8173-0093-7*) U of Ala Pr.

Paddock, Joe. Boars' Dance: Poems. LC 92-54183. 85p. 1993. pap. 8.95 (*0-930100-51-4*) Holy Cow.

— Earth Tongues: Poems. LC 85-61268. (Illus.). 72p. (Orig.). 1985. pap. 6.00 (*0-915943-07-7*) Milkweed Ed.

Paddock, John. Oaxacans in Mesoamerica. Date not set. pap. write for info. (*0-939923-23-8*) M & W Pub Co.

Paddock, John, ed. Ancient Oaxaca: Discoveries in Mexican Archeology & History. (Illus.). xvi, 416p. 1966. 49.50 (*0-8047-0170-9*) Stanford U Pr.

Paddock, John R. Colorado Employment Law & Practice Handbook. LC 99-184222. (Colorado Practice Ser.). 659 p. 1998. write for info. (*0-314-23825-5*) West Pub.

Paddock, Lisa. Facts about the Supreme Court of the United States. LC 95-53202. (Illus.). 512p. 1996. 65.00 (*0-8242-0896-X*) Wilson.

Paddock, Lisa, jt. auth. see Rollyson, Carl.

Paddock, Lisa, jt. auth. see Rollyson, Carl E.

Paddock, Lisa O. Contrapuntal in Integration: A Study of Three Faulkner Short Story Volumes. LC 98-12454. 232p. 1998. 74.95 (*1-57309-281-9*, Pub. by Intl Scholars); pap. 54.95 (*1-57309-280-0*, Pub. by Intl Scholars) U Pr of Amer.

Paddock, Lowell C., jt. auth. see Friedman, Dave.

Paddock, Maria A. Where Do We Go from Here? large type ed. (Illus.). 85p. 1999. pap. 16.95 (*0-9672023-0-2*, 1-WDG) EarthWild.

***Paddock, Rob.** Hands on VB6 for Web Development. LC 98-66119. (Illus.). 471p. 1998. pap. 40.00 (*0-7615-1647-6*) Prima Pub.

Paddock, Rod. Mastering Visual FoxPro X. 1996. pap. text 39.99 incl. audio compact disk (*0-7821-1940-9*) Sybex.

Paddock, Rod, et al. Visual FoxPro 6.0 Enterprise Development. LC 97-75920. 736p. 1998. boxed set 55.00 (*0-7615-1381-7*) Prima Pub.

Paddock, Stephen W. Confocal Microscopy: Methods & Protocols. LC 98-38205. (Methods in Molecular Biology Ser.: No. 122). (Illus.). 464p. 1998. 99.50 (*0-89603-526-3*) Humana.

Paddock, T. B. Plagiotropis Pfitzer & Tropidoneis Cleve, a Summary Account. (Bibliotheca Diatomologica Ser.: Vol. 16). (Illus.). 190p. 1988. pap. 65.00 (*3-443-57007-0*, Pub. by Gebruder Borntraeger) Balogh.

Paddock, Todd & Patrick, Ruth, eds. Proceedings of the 4th National Conference: Solid Waste Management. LC 90-82564. (Illus.). 355p. (Orig.). 1990. pap. 15.00 (*0-910006-50-4*) Acad Nat Sci Phila.

Paddon, Anthony. Labrador Doctor: My Life with the Grenfell Mission. 279p. 1989. mass mkt. 6.95 (*0-88780-160-9*, Pub. by Formac Publ Co) Formac Dist Ltd.

Paddon, D. J., ed. Supercomputers & Parallel Computations. (Institute of Mathematics & Its Applications Conference Series, New Ser.). (Illus.). 268p. 1984. 78.00 (*0-19-853601-1*) OUP.

Paddon, Michael, jt. auth. see Busfield, Joan.

Paddon, Peter. The Book of the Veil. (Illus.). 1995. pap. 22.95 (*1-898307-38-5*) Holmes Pub.

— Passing Through the Veil. 240p. (Orig.). 1996. pap. 22.95 (*1-898307-42-3*, Pub. by Capall Bann Pubng) Holmes Pub.

— Through the Veil. (Illus.). (Orig.). 1997. pap. 22.95 (*1-898307-49-0*) Holmes Pub.

Pade, Victoria. Baby Love: That's My Baby! & A Ranching Family. (Special Edition Ser.: No. 1249). 1999. per. 4.25 (*0-373-24249-2*, 1-24249-4) Silhouette.

— Baby My Baby: (A Ranching Family) (Special Edition Ser.). 1995. per. 3.75 (*0-373-09946-0*, 1-09946-4) Silhouette.

— The Case of the Accidental Heiress. LC 95-23278. (American Romance Ser.). 250p. 1995. per. 3.50 (*0-373-16594-3*, 1-16594-3) Harlequin Bks.

— The Case of the Borrowed Bride. LC 95-13578. (American Romance Ser.). 251p. 1995. per. 3.50 (*0-373-16588-9*, 1-16588-5) Harlequin Bks.

— The Case of the Maybe Babies. LC 95-13711. (American Romance Ser.). 249p. 1995. per. 3.50 (*0-373-16590-0*, 1-16590-1) Harlequin Bks.

***Pade, Victoria.** Cowboy's Caress. (Special Edition Ser.). 2000. per. 4.50 (*0-373-24311-1*) Silhouette.

— The Cowboy's Gift-Wrapped Bride. 2001. mass mkt. 4.50 (*0-373-24365-0*, 1-24365-8) Silhouette.

Pade, Victoria. The Cowboy's Ideal Wife. (Special Edition Ser.). 1998. per. 4.25 (*0-373-24185-2*, 1-24185-0) Silhouette.

— Cowboy's Kin: A Ranching Family. 1994. per. 3.50 (*0-373-09923-1*, 1-09923-3) Harlequin Bks.

— Cowboy's Kiss. (Special Edition Ser.). 1995. per. 3.75 (*0-373-09970-3*, 1-09970-4) Silhouette.

— Cowboy's Lady. (Special Edition Ser.: No. 1106). 1997. per. 3.99 (*0-373-24106-2*, 1-24106-6) Silhouette.

***Pade, Victoria.** Cowboy's Lady. large type ed. 2000. 22.95 (*0-373-59687-1*) Silhouette.

An Asterisk (*) at the beginning of an entry indicates that the title is appearing for the first time.

Pade, Victoria. Cowboy's Love. 1998. per. 4.25 (*0-373-24159-3*, 1-24159-5) Silhouette.
— Dating Can Be Deadly. 336p. 1999. mass mkt. 5.99 (*0-440-22642-2*) Dell.
— Divorce Can Be Murder. (Jimi Plain Mystery Ser.: Bk. 1). 1999. mass mkt. 5.99 (*0-440-22646-5*) Dell.
***Pade, Victoria.** The Doubletree. 2000. mass mkt. 4.50 (*0-373-82214-6*, 1-82214-7) Harlequin Bks.
Pade, Victoria. Ladylight. 368p. (Orig.). 1987. pap. 3.95 (*0-380-75320-0*, Avon Bks) Morrow Avon.
***Pade, Victoria.** The Marriage Bargain. (Montana Mavericks Ser.: Vol. 4). 256p. 2000. mass mkt. 4.50 (*0-373-65049-3*, 1-65049-8) Harlequin Bks.
Pade, Victoria. Mom for Hire. 1996. per. 3.99 (*0-373-24057-0*, 1-24057-1) Silhouette.
— Mum for Hire. (Silhouette Ser.). 1999. 21.95 (*0-373-59596-4*) Silhouette.
— Red-Hot Ranchman. (American Romance Ser.: No. 656). 1996. per. 3.75 (*0-373-16656-7*, 1-16656-0) Harlequin Bks.
— Unmarried with Children. (Special Edition Ser.). 1993. per. 3.50 (*0-373-09852-9*, 5-09852-0) Silhouette.
***Pade, Victoria.** Wyoming Wrangler: (Worlds Most Eligible Bachelors) (World's Most Eligible Bachelors Ser.: Bk. 9). 1999. per. 4.50 (*0-373-65026-4*, 1-65026-6, Harlequin) Harlequin Bks.
Pade, Victoria & Ireland, Liz. Downhome Darlin' The Best Man Switch. Vol. 5. 1999. per. 5.99 (*0-373-44071-5*) Harlequin Bks.
Padeh, Zwe, jt. auth. see Menzi, Donald W.
Padel, Felix. The Sacrifice of Human Being: British Rule & the Konds of Orissa. LC 95-910546. (Illus.). 446p. 1996. text 35.00 (*0-19-563640-6*) OUP.
Padel, Ruth. Angel. 80p. 1994. pap. 14.95 (*1-85224-278-7*, Pub. by Bloodaxe Bks) Dufour.
— In & Out of the Mind: Greek Images of the Tragic Self. 215p. 1992. text 39.50 (*0-691-07379-1*, Pub. by Princeton U Pr); pap. text 13.95 (*0-691-03766-3*, Pub. by Princeton U Pr) Cal Prin Full Svc.
— Whom Gods Destroy: Elements of Greek & Tragic Madness. LC 94-25529. 276p. 1995. text 42.50 (*0-691-03360-9*, Pub. by Princeton U Pr); pap. text 14.95 (*0-691-02588-6*, Pub. by Princeton U Pr) Cal Prin Full Svc.
Padel, S., jt. ed. see Lampkin, N. H.
Padelford, Frederick M. Early Sixteenth-Century Lyrics. LC 70-144436. (Belles Lettres Ser., Section 2: No. 3). reprint ed. 30.00 (*0-404-53613-1*) AMS Pr.
— Political & Ecclesiastical Allegory of the First Book of the Fairie Queen. LC 70-111785. reprint ed. 20.00 (*0-404-04856-0*) AMS Pr.
Padelford, Philip, ed. see Honyman, Robert.
Padelsky, Londie G., et al. Outhouses. LC 98-39588. 112p. 1998. pap. 25.95 (*1-56313-927-8*) BrownTrout Pubs Inc.
Paden, Ann. I Bought It at Polk Bros. The Story of an American Retailing Phenomenon. (Illus.). 360p. 1996. 22.95 (*1-56625-073-0*) Bonus Books.
Paden, Ann, jt. ed. see Carter, Gwendolen M.
Paden, Donald W. An Introduction to Economic Analysis. LC 74-28440. 470p. reprint ed. pap. 145.70 (*0-608-12018-9*, 202284400030) Bks Demand.
Paden, Elaine P., jt. auth. see Hodson, Barbara W.
Paden, Irene D. Prairie Schooner Detours. 2nd ed. (Illus.). 310p. 1990. reprint ed. pap. 12.95 (*0-935284-77-X*) Patrice Pr.
Paden, Irene D. & Schlichtmann, Margaret M. Big Oak Flat Road to Yosemite. 1986. pap. 15.00 (*0-915266-17-2*) Awani Pr.
Paden, John N., ed. Ahmadu Bello: Sardauna of Sokoto: Values & Leadership in Nigeria. 800p. (C). 1986. pap. 13.50 (*0-340-38967-2*, 00589) Heinemann.
Paden, John N. & Soja, Edward W., eds. The African Experience, Vol. 3-A, Bibliography. LC 70-98466. 1123p. 1970. reprint ed. pap. 200.00 (*0-8357-5233-X*, 201672000003) Bks Demand.
— The African Experience, Vol. 3-B, Guide to Resources. LC 70-98466. 149p. 1970. reprint ed. pap. 46.20 (*0-8357-5234-8*, 201672000004) Bks Demand.
— The African Experience Vol. 3B: Guide to Resources. 141p. 1970. 45.00 (*0-89771-005-3*) St Mut.
Paden, Joseph. Sarcosomataceae (Pezizales Sarcosyphgineae) LC 83-8056. (Flora Neotropica Monographs: No. 37). (Illus.). 17p. (Orig.). 1983. pap. 5.50 (*0-89327-250-7*) NY Botanical.
Paden, Margaret S., tr. see Rulfo, Juan.
Paden, Mary, ed. see Snyder, Sarah A.
Paden, Ross. The Cottonwood Stage. large type ed. (Linford Western Library). 1995. pap. 16.99 (*0-7089-7766-9*, Linford) Ulverscroft.
Paden, William D. An Introduction to Old Occitan. LC 97-24074. (Introductions to Older Languages Ser.: No. 4). 600p. (C). 1998. lib. bdg. 35.00 incl. audio compact disk (*0-87352-293-1*, Z103C) Modern Lang.
***Paden, William D.** Medieval Lyric: Genres in Historical Context. LC 99-50897. (Medieval Studies). 2000. 39.95 (*0-252-02536-9*) U of Ill Pr.
Paden, William D., ed. The Future of the Middle Ages: Medieval Literature in the 1990s. (Illus.). 200p. (C). 1994. 49.95 (*0-8130-1278-3*); pap. 19.95 (*0-8130-1279-1*) U Press Fla.
— The Voice of the Trobairitz: Perspectives on the Women Troubadours. LC 89-4920. (Middle Ages Ser.). (Illus.). 274p. (C). 1989. text 36.50 (*0-8122-8167-5*) U of Pa Pr.
Paden, William D., tr. see Dinesen, Isak.
Paden, William D., tr. see Dinsen, Isak.
Paden, William E. Interpreting the Sacred: Ways of Viewing Religion. LC 91-12152. 176p. 1992. pap. 16.00 (*0-8070-7707-0*) Beacon Pr.
— Religious Worlds: The Comparative Study of Religion. 2nd ed. LC 93-43025. 208p. (C). 1994. pap. 15.50 (*0-8070-1229-7*) Beacon Pr.
Pader, Olga F. Oral Hygiene: Products & Practice. (Cosmetic Science & Technology Ser.: Vol. 6). (Illus.). 552p. 1987. text 250.00 (*0-8247-7701-8*) Dekker.
Paderewski, Ignacy J., ed. see Chopin, Frederic.
Paderewski, Ignance Jan. Polish Piano Music: Works by Paderewski, Scharwenka, Moszkowski. Date not set. pap. text 12.95 (*0-486-40624-5*) Dover.
Paderewski, Jan I. & Lawton, Mary. The Paderewski Memoirs. LC 80-21323. (Music Ser.). 1980. reprint ed. 45.00 (*0-306-76046-0*) Da Capo.
Padesky, Christine A. & Greenberger, Dennis. Clinician's Guide to Mind over Mood. 276p. 1995. pap. text 21.00 (*0-89862-821-0*) Guilford Pubns.
Padesky, Christine A., jt. auth. see Dattilio, Frank M.
Padesky, Christine A., jt. auth. see Greenberger, Dennis.
Padfield, Gareth. Helicopter Flight Dynamics: The Theory & Application of Flying Qualities & Simulation Modeling. LC 95-657. 514p. (C). 1996. text 99.95 (*1-56347-205-8*) AIAA.
Padfield, Harland & Martin, William E. Farmers, Workers & Machines: Technological & Social Change in Farm Industries of Arizona. LC 65-25018. 341p. reprint ed. pap. 105.80 (*0-608-15196-3*, 202738500055) Bks Demand.
Padfield, K. Randall. Flying in Adverse Conditions. (Illus.). 312p. 1994. 29.95 (*0-07-048139-3*) McGraw.
— Flying in Adverse Conditions. (Illus.). 312p. 1994. pap. 22.95 (*0-07-048140-7*) McGraw.
Padfield, Maureen, jt. auth. see Procter, Ian.
***Padfield, Nicholas L.** Total Intravenous Anaesthesia. (Illus.). 304p. 2000. 75.00 (*0-7506-4171-1*) Buttrwrth-Heinemann.
Padfield, Nicola. Padfield: Criminal Law. (Butterworths Core Text Ser.). 1997. pap. write for info. (*0-406-03310-2*, PCL, MICHIE) LEXIS Pub.
Padfield, Nicola, jt. auth. see Walker, Nigel.
Padfield, Paul L., jt. ed. see Baylis, Peter H.
Padfield, Peter. Himmler. LC 96-76464. (Illus.). 656p. 1996. reprint ed. 12.98 (*1-56731-118-0*, MJF Bks) Fine Comms.
— Himmler Reichsfuhrer-SS: A Biography. 664p. 1995. pap. 19.95 (*0-8050-2699-1*) H Holt & Co.
***Padfield, Peter.** Maritime Supremacy & the Opening of the Western Mind: Naval Campaign That Shaped the Modern World, 1588-1782. LC 99-58999. (Illus.). 340p. 2000. 35.00 (*1-58567-002-2*, Pub. by Overlook Pr) Penguin Putnam.
— Nelson's War. (Illus.). 2000. pap. 12.99 (*1-84022-225-5*, Pub. by Wrdsworth Edits) Combined Pub.
Padfield, Peter. War Beneath the Sea: Submarine Conflict During World War II. 560p. 1998. pap. 19.95 (*0-471-24945-9*) Wiley.
Padfield, R. Randall. Learning to Fly Helicopters. 368p. 1992. pap. 24.95 (*0-07-157724-6*) McGraw.
— Learning to Fly Helicopters. 368p. 1992. 29.95 (*0-8306 2113-X*) McGraw-Hill Prof.
— Learning to Fly Helicopters. (Illus.). 354p. 1992. pap. 19.95 (*0-8306-2092-3*) McGraw-Hill Prof.
Padgaonkar, Dileep, ed. When Bombay Burned: Reportage & Comments on the Riots & Blasts from the Times of India. (C). 1993. 22.50 (*81-85944-55-5*, Pub. by UBS Pubs Dist) S Asia.
Padgaonkar, Latika, tr. see Vincent, Rose, ed.
***Padgelek, Mary G.** In the Hand of the Holy Spirit: The Visionary Art of J. B. Murray. (Illus.). 160p. 2000. 30.00 (*0-86554-699-1*) Mercer Univ Pr.
Padgen, Anthony. The Uncertainties of Empire: Essays in Iberian & Ibero-American Intellectual History. (Collected Studies: No. CS468). 320p. 1994. 101.95 (*0-86078-461-4*, Pub. by Variorum) Ashgate Pub Co.
***Padget, Julian A., ed.** Collaboration Between Human & Artificial Societies: Coordination & Agent-Based Distributed Computing. LC 99-88777. (Lecture Notes in Computer Science Ser.: Vol. 1624). viii, 301p. 2000. pap. 56.00 (*3-540-66930-2*) Spr-Verlag.
Padgett, et al. Windmore Writers Anthology. 1993 pap. 8.50 (*0-9636786-0-4*) Blue Rdge Mntns.
Padgett, jt. ed. see Karplus.
Padgett, Abigail. Blue. LC 98-16067. 288p. 1998. 22.00 (*0-89296-671-8*, Pub. by Mysterious Pr) Little.
— Blue. 1999. mass mkt. write for info. (*0-446-60763-0*) Warner Bks.
— Child of Silence. 208p. 1993. 17.95 (*0-89296-488-X*) Mysterious Pr.
— The Dollmaker's Daughters. 320p. 1998. mass mkt. 6.50 (*0-446-40536-1*, Pub. by Warner Bks) Little.
***Padgett, Abigail.** The Last Blue Plate Special. 256p. 2001. 23.95 (*0-89296-731-5*) Mysterious Pr.
Padgett, Abigail. Turtle Baby. large type ed. (Large Print Ser.). 496p. 1996. 27.99 (*0-7089-3560-5*) Ulverscroft.
Padgett, Alan G., ed. The Mission of the Church in Methodist Perspective: The World Is My Parish. LC 92-34032. (Studies in the History of Missions: Vol. 10). 196p. 1992. text 79.95 (*0-7734-9157-0*) E Mellen.
— Reason & the Christian Religion: Essays in Honour of Richard Swinburne. (Illus.). 376p. 1995. text 69.00 (*0-19-824042-2*) OUP.
Padgett, Alan G., jt. auth. see Wilkens, Steven.
Padgett, Allen & Smith, Bruce. On Rope. 2nd ed. (Illus.). 382p. 1996. 32.00 (*1-879961-05-9*, 07-0010) Natl Speleological.
Padgett, Barbara, jt. auth. see Denver Parent, Inc. Staff.
Padgett, Bill. Dragons. (Illus.). 174p. 1984. 17.95 (*0-934073-00-7*) Rountree Pub NC.
— In Search of the Big Cookie. (Illus.). 1986. 9.50 (*0-934073-02-3*) Rountree Pub NC.
— Juliet. (Illus.). 52p. 1986. write for info. (*0-934073-03-1*) Rountree Pub NC.
— Sippin' (Illus.). 52p. 1988. 12.95 (*0-934073-04-X*) Rountree Pub NC.
Padgett, Deborah. Qualitative Methods in Social Work Research: Challenges & Rewards. LC 97-33908. (Sage Sourcebooks for the Human Services Ser.). 1998. write for info. (*0-7619-0200-7*); pap. write for info. (*0-7619-0201-5*) Sage.
— Settlers & Sojourners: A Study of Serbian Adaptation in Milwaukee, Wisconsin. LC 88-46193. (Immigrant Communities & Ethnic Minorities in the U. S. & Canada Ser.: No. 39). 1989. 57.50 (*0-404-19449-4*) AMS Pr.
Padgett, Deborah K., ed. Handbook on Ethnicity, Aging & Mental Health. LC 94-11220. 376p. 1995. lib. bdg. 99.50 (*0-313-28204-8*, Greenwood Pr) Greenwood.
Padgett, Douglas E. & Pellicci, Paul M. Atlas of Total Hip Replacement. LC 95-9614. (Orthopaedic Surgical Skills Ser.). (Illus.). 1995. text 168.00 (*0-443-08902-7*) Church.
Padgett, George A. Control of Canine Genetic Diseases. 256p. 1998. 27.95 (*0-87605-004-6*) Howell Bks.
Padgett, Hilda. The Erwin Nine. (Illus.). 154p. 1993. pap. 9.95 (*0-932807-97-6*) Overmountain Pr.
***Padgett, James.** Learn AutoCAD LT 2000 for Architects. (Illus.). 400p. (C). 2000. pap. 42.95 (*1-55622-754-X*) Wordware Pub.
Padgett, James E. Angelic Revelations of Divine Truth, Set, Vols. I & II. 1989. pap. 30.00 (*1-887621-02-4*) Found Ch Divine Truth.
— Angelic Revelations of Divine Truth. Vol. I. 437p. 1989. pap. 17.00 (*1-887621-00-8*) Found Ch Divine Truth.
— Angelic Revelations of Divine Truth, Vol. II. 457p. 1989. pap. 17.00 (*1-887621-01-6*) Found Ch Divine Truth.
***Padgett, James E.** Celestial Messages: A Chronicle of the Progression & Transformation of the Soul. Boster, Gregory, ed. (Illus.). 232p. 1999. 14.95 (*0-9673600-0-5*) New Heart Prodns.
Padgett, James E. Important Truths That All Mankind Should Know. 1989. pap. 0.50 (*1-887621-15-6*) Found Ch Divine Truth.
— Jesus' Birth & Youth, As Known by Mary, Mother of Jesus. 1989. pap. 3.50 (*1-887621-08-3*) Found Ch Divine Truth.
— The Prayer for Divine Love, by Jesus of Nazareth. 1989. pap. write for info. (*1-887621-18-0*) Found Ch Divine Truth.
— True Gospel Revealed Anew by Jesus, Vol. III. 443p. 1989. 10.00 (*1-887621-03-2*) Found Ch Divine Truth.
— Truths in Miniature. 1989. pap. 0.50 (*1-887621-23-7*) Found Ch Divine Truth.
— What Is Divine Love? 1989. pap. 0.50 (*1-887621-16-4*) Found Ch Divine Truth.
— Who & What Is God? 1989. pap. 0.50 (*1-887621-05-9*) Found Ch Divine Truth.
Padgett, James E. & Samuels, Daniel G. The Jeremiah Sermons by Jesus. 1989. pap. 7.50 (*1-887621-12-1*) Found Ch Divine Truth.
— New Testament Revelations of Jesus of Nazareth. 555p. 1995. pap. 20.00 (*1-887621-04-0*) Found Ch Divine Truth.
Padgett, James R. Paper Mansions. LC 86-13628. (Illus.). 256p. 1986. 14.95 (*0-914875-12-4*) Bright Mtn Bks.
Padgett, Jaye. Stricture in Feature Geometry: Dissertations in Linguistics. 230p. (Orig.). 1995. 49.95 (*1-881526-67-4*); pap. 22.95 (*1-881526-66-6*) CSLI.
Padgett, Jim. Jesus, God's Gift of Love. 16p. 1999. pap. 3.95 (*0-687-08449-0*) Abingdon.
Padgett, Jo A. Craft School: Over 90 Step-by-Step Craft Projects. LC 97-169. (Illus.). 320p. 1997. 14.99 (*1-57145-041-6*, Thunder Bay) Advantage Pubs.
Padgett, JoAnn, ed. Ballet Diary. (YA). (gr. 2 up). 1997. 14.95 (*1-57145-310-5*, Silver Dolph) Advantage Pubs.
— Start Your Own: One Hundred One Extra Income Ideas. LC 94-6928. (Start Your Own Ser.). 144p. 1996. pap. text 12.95 (*0-89384-265-6*, Pfffr & Co) Jossey-Bass.
— Start Your Own Coffee & Tea Store. LC 94-8601. (Start Your Own Ser.). 272p. 1996. pap. text 12.95 (*0-89384-262-1*, Pfffr & Co) Jossey-Bass.
— Start Your Own Gift Basket Business. LC 94-4935. (Start Your Own Ser.). 256p. 1994. pap. text 12.95 (*0-89384-261-3*, Pfffr & Co) Jossey-Bass.
— Start Your Own Temporary Help Agency. LC 94-4494. (Start Your Own Ser.). 224p. 1996. pap. text 12.95 (*0-89384-264-8*, Pfffr & Co) Jossey-Bass.
Padgett, JoAnn, ed. see Hopson, Barrie & Scally, Mike.
Padgett, JoAnn, ed. see Nolan, Timothy M., et al.
Padgett, Julianna D., jt. auth. see Graubarth-Szyller, Bobbie R.
Padgett, Mark E. A Contemporary Approach to Permanent Waving Course Guide. (Cosmetology Ser.). (Illus.). 142p. 1997. 49.95 (*1-56253-309-6*) Milady Pub.
— Milady's a Contemporary Approach to Permanent Waving. LC 93-28020. 142p. 1994. pap. 19.95 (*1-56253-101-8*) Milady Pub.
Padgett, Mary L., ed. International Simulation Technology Conference, 1991. 632p. 1991. 80.00 (*0-911801-98-7*, SIMTEC 91) Soc Computer Sim.
— Proceedings of the First Workshop on Neural Networks, 1990: Academic-Industrial-NASA-Defense. 516p. 1990. pap. 80.00 (*0-911801-66-9*, WNN90-1) Soc Computer Sim.
— Proceedings of the 2nd Workshop on Neural Networks, 1991: Academic-Industrial-NASA-Defense. 816p. 1991. pap. 100.00 (*0-911801-77-4*, WNN91-1) Soc Computer Sim.
— Proceedings of the 3rd Workshop on Neural Networks. 662p. 1993. pap. 90.00 (*1-56555-007-2*, WNN92-1) Soc Computer Sim.
Padgett, Mary L. & Lindblad, Thomas, eds. Sixth, Seventh & Eighth Workshops on Virtual Intelligence, Vol. 2878. 608p. 1996. 110.00 (*0-8194-2276-2*) SPIE.
Padgett, Mary Lou & Karayiannis, Nicolaos B. Handbook of Applied Computational Intelligence. 1999. 110.00 (*0-8493-7334-4*) CRC Pr.
Padgett, Michael. A Goodly Heritage: A History of the Church of God Mountain Assembly, Inc. LC 95-192782. 180p. 1995. pap. 10.00 (*0-9646344-0-6*) M Padgett.
Padgett, Ron. Albanian Diary. 72p. 1999. pap. 10.00 (*0-935724-95-8*) Figures.
— The Big Something. 64p. 1990. per. 7.50 (*0-935724-38-9*) Figures.
— Blood Work. 104p. 1993. pap. 12.00 (*0-917453-26-3*) Bamberger.
— Creative Reading: What It Is, How to Do It, & Why. LC 96-38010. 161p. 1997. pap. 22.95 (*0-8141-0906-3*) NCTE.
— Great Balls of Fire. rev. ed. LC 90-2457. 96p. 1990. reprint ed. pap. 8.95 (*0-918273-80-3*) Coffee Hse.
— New & Selected Poems, 1963-1992. LC 95-15239. 120p. 1995. 14.95 (*1-56792-038-1*) Godine.
— Scribners Poets for Students. 2000. 100.00 (*0-684-80592-8*); 100.00 (*0-684-80609-6*) S&S Trade.
— Scribners Poets for Students. 3rd ed. 2000. 100.00 (*0-684-80610-X*) S&S Trade.
***Padgett, Ron.** The Straight Line: Writings on Poetry & Poets. (Poets on Poetry Ser.). 168p. 2000. pap. 14.95 (*0-472-06726-5*, 06726); text 39.50 (*0-472-09726-1*, 09726) U of Mich Pr.
— The Teachers & Writers Handbook of Poetic Forms. 2nd ed. LC 00-30248. 2000. write for info. (*0-915924-60-9*) Tchrs & Writers Coll.
Padgett, Ron. Ted: A Personal Memoir of Ted Berrigan. 1993. pap. 10.00 (*0-935724-60-5*) Figures.
— Tulsa Kid. Elmslie, Kenward, ed. (Illus.). (Orig.). 1980. 10.00 (*0-915990-16-4*); pap. 5.00 (*0-915990-17-2*) Z Pr.
— The Writing Book: Teachers' Manual. 12p. (J). (gr. 3-6). 1986. pap., teacher ed. 5.95 (*0-915924-70-6*) Tchrs & Writers Coll.
Padgett, Ron, ed. The Teachers & Writers Guide to Walt Whitman. (Illus.). 210p. (Orig.). 1991. pap. 14.95 (*0-915924-36-6*) Tchrs & Writers Coll.
— The Teachers & Writers Handbook of Poetic Forms. 2nd rev. ed. 230p. (J). 2000. 27.95 (*0-915924-24-2*); pap. 16.95 (*0-915924-23-4*) Tchrs & Writers Coll.
— White Dove Review, Nos. 1[00ad]5. (Avant-Garde Magazines Ser.). 1974. reprint ed. 18.95 (*0-405-01757-X*) Ayer.
***Padgett, Ron, ed.** World Poets. LC 00-24801. 1400p. 2000. boxed set 225.00 (*0-684-80591-X*) Gale.
Padgett, Ron & Coolidge, Clark. Supernatural Overtones. 1990. pap. 7.50 (*0-935724-40-0*) Figures.
Padgett, Ron & Roussel, Raymond. Among the Blacks. LC 88-70205. 64p. (Orig.). 1988. pap. 7.50 (*0-939691-02-7*) Avenue B.
Padgett, Ron, ed. see Ceravolo, Joseph.
Padgett, Ron, jt. ed. see Edgar, Christopher.
Padgett, Ron, jt. ed. see Shapiro, Nancy Larson.
Padgett, S. T. The Christian Philosophy of William Temple. 324p. 1974. pap. text 106.00 (*90-247-1610-1*, Pub. by M Nijhoff) Kluwer Academic.
Padgett, Stephen. A History of Social Democracy in Postwar Europe: The Postwar World. (Post War World Ser.). (C). 1991. text 63.50 (*0-582-49173-8*, 789602); pap. text 33.50 (*0-582-49174-6*, 78961) Longman.
— Organizing Democracy in Eastern Germany: Interest Groups in Post-Communist Society. LC 99-12130. (Illus.). 216p. (C). 2000. 57.95 (*0-521-65170-0*); pap. 21.95 (*0-521-65703-2*) Cambridge U Pr.
***Padgett, Stephen & Saalfeld, Thomas, eds.** Bundestagswahl '98: The End of an Era. LC 99-36580. (German Politics Ser.). 200p. 1999. 52.50 (*0-7146-5019-6*, Pub. by F Cass Pubs); pap. 24.50 (*0-7146-8076-1*, Pub. by F Cass Pubs) Intl Spec Bk.
Padgett, Stephen, ed. see Abromeit, Heidrun, et al.
Padgett, Thomas J. Norfork Lake: A Cultural Resources Management Study with Implications for Prehistoric Settlement-Subsistence Patterns in the Ozarks. (Illus.). 72p. 1979. pap. 1.50 (*1-56349-027-7*, RR15) AR Archaeol.
Padgham, Lin, et al, eds. International Description Logics: Papers from the 1996 Workshop. (Technical Reports). (Illus.). 204p. 1996. spiral bd. 30.00 (*1-57735-014-6*) AAAI Pr.
Padgitt, Donald L. A Short History of the Early American Microscopes, Vol. 12. LC 74-30750. (Illus.). 1975. 30.00 (*0-904962-04-0*) Microscope Pubns.
Padhi, B. C. Socioeconomic Conditions of the Tribal under British Rule (1803-1936) (C). 1992. 30.00 (*0-685-61701-7*, Pub. by Punthi Pus) S Asia.
Padhi, Bibhu. D. H. Lawrence: Modes of Fictional Style. LC 87-50832. Orig. Title: Modes of Style in Lawrence's Fiction. x, 223p. 1988. 45.00 (*0-87875-354-0*) Whitston Pub.
— Painting the House: Poems LC 99-934542. 79p. 1999. write for info. (*81-250-1543-4*, Pub. by Orient Longman Ltd) S Asia.
***Padhi, Bidhu & Padhi, Minakshi.** Indian Philosophy & Religion: A Reader's Guide. 1998. 34.00 (*81-246-0116-X*, Pub. by D K Printwrld) S Asia.
Padhi, G. S., ed. Forestry in India, a Critical Study. 170p. (C). 1982. 140.00 (*81-7089-008-X*, Pub. by Intl Bk Distr) St Mut.
Padhi, Minakshi, jt. auth. see Padhi, Bidhu.
Padhy, Drushna S. Indian Press Role & Responsibility. (C). 1994. text 27.50 (*81-7024-636-9*, Pub. by Ashish Pub Hse) S Asia.
Padhy, K. P. Orissa: Its Golden Epoch. (C). 1994. 50.00 (*81-85151-85-7*) S Asia.
Padhy, K. S. & Muni, P. K. Corruption in Indian Politics. 221p. 1987. 29.95 (*0-318-37295-9*) Asia Bk Corp.
Padhy, K. S. & Satapathy, P. C. Tribal India. (C). 1988. 18.00 (*81-7024-225-8*, Pub. by Ashish Pub Hse) S Asia.
Padhye, A. M. The Framework of Nagarjuna's Philosophy. (Bibliotheca Indo-Buddhica Ser.: No. 35). 1988. text 15.00 (*81-7030-124-6*) S Asia.

P

An Asterisk (*) at the beginning of an entry indicates that the title is appearing for the first time.

...I Staff, ed. see Tackett, Eric.

Padian, Kevin. Beginning of the Age of Dinosaurs. 390p. 1988. pap. text 52.95 (*0-521-36779-4*) Cambridge U Pr.

Padian, Kevin, ed. The Origin of Birds & the Evolution of Flight. (Memoirs of the California Academy of Sciences Ser.: No. 8). 98p. 1986. pap. text 13.00 (*0-940228-14-9*) Calif Acad Sci.

Padian, Kevin, jt. ed. see Currie, Philip.

Padian, Kevin, tr. see Taquet, Philippe.

Padilla, Amado M. Public Library Services for Immigrant Populations in California. (Partnerships for Change Ser.: No. 4). 48p. 1992. pap. text 8.50 (*0-929722-49-3*) CA State Library Fndtn.

Padilla, Amado M., ed. Hispanic Psychology: Critical Issues in Theory & Research. 336p. 1994. 58.00 (*0-8039-5552-9*); pap. 26.00 (*0-8039-5553-7*) Sage.

Padilla, Amado M., et al, eds. Bilingual Education: Issues & Strategies. (Focus Editions Ser.: Vol. 112). (Illus.). 264p. (C). 1990. pap. 27.95 (*0-8039-3639-7*, D1478) Corwin Pr.

— Foreign Language Education: Issues & Strategies. LC 89-27827. (Sage Focus Edition Ser.: No. 113). 256p. 1990. pap. 79.40 (*0-608-05603-0*, 206606100006) Bks Demand.

Padilla, Armando M., jt. auth. see Keefe, Susan E.

Padilla, Barbara, ed. see Cuza-Male, Belkis.

Padilla, Barbara, tr. see Welsh, Patricia A.

Padilla, Carlos E. Optimizing Jet Transport Efficiency: Performance, Operations, & Economics. LC 96-16573. (Illus.). 205p. 1996. pap. 49.95 (*0-07-048208-X*) McGraw.

Padilla, Carmella. The Chile Chronicles: Tales of a New Mexico Harvest. LC 97-35693. (Illus.). 136p. 1997. pap. 29.95 (*0-89013-350-6*) Museum NM Pr.

Padilla, Carmella & Parsons, Jack. Low 'n Slow: Lowriding in New Mexico. LC 98-31198. (Illus.). 120p. 1999. 39.95 (*0-89013-372-7*) Museum NM Pr.

Padilla, Efren. Pak: American Urban & Regional Experience. 390p. (C). 1996. 61.95 (*0-7872-2874-5*) Kendall-Hunt.

— Pak: The New Filipino Story. 336p. (C). 1997. pap. text 58.95 (*0-7872-4565-8*, 41456501) Kendall-Hunt.

Padilla, Ernest. Ambulatory Thought. 2nd ed. 1998. 18.50 (*0-07-039654-X*) McGraw.

Padilla, Ernesto, ed. & pref. see Serros, Michele M.

Padilla, Ezequiel. Free Men of America. LC 72-4624. (Essay Index Reprint Ser.). 1977. reprint ed. 19.95 (*0-8369-2965-9*) Ayer.

***Padilla, Felix.** Mis Dos Luces. Padilla, Rebecca, ed. (SPA., Illus.). 32p. 1999. 16.00 (*0-9675413-1-X*) Libros Latin Treas.

— My Two Lights. Padilla, Rebecca, ed. (Illus.). 32p. 2000. 16.00 (*0-9675413-0-1*) Libros Latin Treas.

Padilla, Felix, ed. see Padilla, Rebecca.

Padilla, Felix M. Latino Ethnic Consciousness: The Case of Mexican Americans & Puerto Ricans in Chicago. LC 85-8576. 196p. 1986. pap. 14.00 (*0-268-01275-X*); text 29.00 (*0-268-01274-1*) U of Notre Dame Pr.

— The Struggle of Latino/Latina University Students: In Search of a Liberating Education. LC 96-50207. 256p. (C). 1997. 80.00 (*0-415-91293-8*); pap. 23.99 (*0-415-91294-6*) Routledge.

Padilla, Felix M., ed. The Handbook of Hispanic Cultures in the United States: Sociology. LC 93-13348. 368p. 1994. 60.00 (*1-55885-101-1*) Arte Publico.

Padilla, Gail, see Greene, Ellen, pseud.

Padilla, Gail, ed. see Greene, Ellen, pseud.

Padilla, Genaro, jt. ed. see Gutierrez, Ramon.

Padilla, Genaro M. My History, Not Yours: The Formation of Mexican American Autobiography. LC 93-3457. (Studies in American Autobiography). (Illus.). 224p. (Orig.). (C). 1993. pap. 18.95 (*0-299-13974-3*); lib. bdg. 40.00 (*0-299-13970-0*) U of Wis Pr.

Padilla, Gilbert. Refreshment in the Desert: Spiritual Connections in Daily Life. LC 85-50663. 128p. (Orig.). 1992. pap. 7.95 (*0-89622-228-4*) Twenty-Third.

Padilla, Heberto. Fountain, a House of Stone. Reid, Alastair & Coleman, Alexander, trs. 1992. pap. 10.00 (*0-374-52364-9*, Noonday) FS&G.

— A Fountain, a House of Stone: Poems. Reid, Alastair & Coleman, Alexander, trs. (ENG & SPA.). 128p. 1991. text 19.95 (*0-374-15781-2*) FS&G.

— Fuera del Juego: Premio Julian des Casal, 1968, Edicion Conmemorativa 1968-1998. LC 98-87652. (Coleccion Clasicos Cubanos: 19). (SPA.). 199p. (Orig.). 1998. pap. 19.95 (*0-89729-881-0*) Ediciones.

— Self-Portrait of the Other: A Memoir. Coleman, Alexander, tr. from SPA. 220p. 1990. 19.95 (*0-374-26086-9*) FS&G.

Padilla, Herberto. Fuera del Juego. (SPA.). 1998. 50.00 (*0-89729-887-X*) Ediciones.

Padilla, Jaime & Taylor, Maurie. Easy Spanish Word Games. (SPA., Illus.). 64p. (J). (ps up). 1994. pap. 4.95 (*0-8442-7242-6*, 72426, Natl Textbk Co) NTC Contemp Pub Co.

Padilla, Jose A. On the Definition of Binding Domains in Spanish: Evidence from Child Language. (C). 1990. text 118.00 (*0-7923-0744-5*) Kluwer Academic.

Padilla, Mario R. Reaching Back for the Neverendings. 100p. 1993. 8.95 (*1-881168-32-8*) Red Danceflr.

Padilla, Mark W. The Myths of Herakles in Ancient Greece: Survey & Profile. LC 98-2650. 112p. (C). 1998. 40.00 (*0-7618-1050-1*); pap. 21.50 (*0-7618-1051-X*) U Pr of Amer.

***Padilla, Mark W., ed.** Rites of Passage in Ancient Greece: Literature, Religion, Society. (Bucknell Review Ser.: Vol. 43, No. 1). 312p. 1999. 28.00 (*0-8387-5418-X*) Fairleigh Dickinson.

Padilla, Mary R. Celebration: The Life of Father Ramon Estivill, a Renaissance Man of God. 200p. 1998. spiral bd. 24.95 (*0-9637606-2-9*) Nornel Assocs.

Padilla, Michelle, ed. see Desmarais, Charles.

***Padilla, Mike.** Hard Language. 192p. 2000. pap. 12.95 (*1-55885-298-0*) Arte Publico.

Padilla, Napoleon S. Memorias de un Cubano Sin Importancia. 328p. 1988. pap. 10.00 (*0-9620495-0-6*) N S Padilla.

Padilla, Raymond V., ed. Ethnoperspectives in Bilingual Education Research Vol. I: Bilingual Education & Public Policy in the United States. LC 79-9265. 507p. 1979. pap. 25.00 (*0-916950-43-3*) Biling Rev-Pr.

— Ethnoperspectives in Bilingual Education Research Vol. II: Theory in Bilingual Education. LC 80-68525. 430p. 1980. pap. 25.00 (*0-916950-44-1*) Biling Rev-Pr.

— Ethnoperspectives in Bilingual Education Research Vol. III: Bilingual Education Technology. LC 81-68614. 482p. 1981. pap. 25.00 (*0-916950-45-X*) Biling Rev-Pr.

Padilla, Raymond V. & Benavides, Alfredo H., eds. Critical Perspectives on Bilingual Education Research. LC 91-21873. 432p. 1992. pap. 25.00 (*0-927534-20-7*) Biling Rev-Pr.

Padilla, Raymond V. & Chavez, Rudolfo C., eds. The Leaning Ivory Tower: Latino Professors in American Universities. LC 94-28756. (SUNY Series, United States Hispanic Studies). 224p. (C). 1995. text 54.50 (*0-7914-2427-8*); pap. text 19.95 (*0-7914-2428-6*) State U NY Pr.

Padilla, Raymond V. & Montiel, Miguel. Debatable Diversity: Critical Dialogues on Change in American Universities. LC 97-4397. (Freire & Macedo, Critical Perspectives Ser.). 316p. 1998. 55.00 (*0-8476-8730-9*); pap. 19.95 (*0-8476-8731-7*) Rowman.

Padilla, Raymond V., jt. ed. see Garcia, Eugene E.

***Padilla, Rebecca.** Cuentitos de Mami Amor. Padilla, Felix, ed. (Illus.). 34p. 1999. 16.00 (*0-9675413-3-6*) Libros Latin Treas.

— Mami Amor's Little Stories. Padilla, Felix, ed. (Illus.). 34p. 1999. 16.00 (*0-9675413-2-8*) Libros Latin Treas.

Padilla, Rebecca, ed. see Padilla, Felix.

Padilla, Salvador M., ed. see Tugwell, Rexford G.

Padilla, Stan. Deer Dancer. LC 98-16757. 80p. 1998. pap. 11.95 (*1-57067-057-9*) Book Pub Co.

— A Natural Education. rev. ed. LC 94-5479. (Illus.). 80p. (YA). (gr. 7-12). 1994. pap. text 8.95 (*0-913990-14-0*) Book Pub Co.

— Yaqui Coloring Book. (Illus.). 28p. (J). 1999. pap. 4.95 (*1-57067-068-4*) Book Pub Co.

Padilla, Stan. Chants & Prayers: A Native American Circle of Beauty. 112p. (Orig.). 1996. pap. text 9.95 (*1-57067-020-X*) Book Pub Co.

Padilla, William. Hunting the Comeback Trail. (Illus.). 144p. 1999. pap. 15.00 (*0-8059-4684-5*) Dorrance.

Padilla, Yolanda C. Reflexiones 1998. 176p. 1999. pap. 12.95 (*0-292-76588-6*) U of Tex Pr.

Padin Zamot, William. Manual de Teatro Escolar. (SPA.). 168p. 1995. 17.95 (*0-8477-0227-8*) U of PR Pr.

Padinjarekuttu, Isaac. The Missionary Movement of the 19th & 20th Centuries & Its Encounter with India: A Historico-Theological Investigation with Three Case Studies. LC 95-139262. (European University Studies: Series 23, Vol. 527). XIII, 305p. 1995. pap. 52.95 (*3-631-47415-6*) P Lang Pubng.

Padirac, Bruno de, see de Padirac, Bruno.

Padiyar, K. Analysis of Subsynchronous Resonance in Power Systems, Vol. 471. LC 98-39845. (Power Electronics & Power System Engineering & Computer Science Ser.). 1998. 138.00 (*0-7923-8319-2*) Kluwer Academic.

Padiyar, K. R. Power System Dynamics: Stability & Control. LC 95-48240. 1999. pap. 45.00 (*0-471-19002-0*) Wiley.

***Padjen, Robert.** CCDP: Cisco Internetwork Design Study Guide. (Illus.). 704p. 2000. 49.99 (*0-7821-2639-1*, Network Pr) Sybex.

— CCDP Exam Notes. (CCDP Exam Notes Ser.). 400p. 2000. pap. 19.99 (*0-7821-2640-5*) Sybex.

***PADL 2000 Staff, et al, eds.** Practical Aspects of Declarative Languages: Proceedings of Second International Workshop, PADL 2000, Boston, MA, U. S. A., January 17-18, 2000. LC 00-20529. (Lecture Notes in Computer Science Ser.: Vol. 1753). x, 323p. 2000. pap. 56.00 (*3-540-66992-2*) Spr-Verlag.

Padley, Fred B., ed. Advances in Applied Lipid Research, Vol. 1. 271p. 1992. 109.50 (*1-55938-317-8*) Jai Pr.

— Advances in Applied Lipid Research, Vol. 2. 1996. 109.50 (*1-55938-534-0*) Jai Pr.

— Advances in Applied Lipid Research, Vol. 3. Date not set. 109.50 (*0-7623-0207-0*) Jai Pr.

Padley, Fred B., jt. ed. see Gunstone, F. D.

Padley, G. A. Grammatical Theory in Western Europe, 1500-1700: Trends in Vernacular Grammar II. 544p. 1988. text 99.95 (*0-521-33514-0*) Cambridge U Pr.

Padma, B. Costumes, Coiffure & Ornaments in the Temple Sculpture of Northern Andhra. (C). 1991. 56.00 (*0-8364-2640-1*, Pub. by Agam Kala Prakashan) S Asia.

Padma-Chos-Phel & Semendra, K. Leaves of the Heaven Tree: The Great Compassion of the Buddha. Black, Deborah, tr. from TIB. LC 97-416. (Tibetan Translation Ser.). 1997. 40.00 (*0-89800-283-4*); pap. 25.00 (*0-89800-285-0*) Dharma Pub.

***Padma-Nathan, Harin.** Medical Management of Erectile Dysfunction: A Primary-Care Manual. 153p. 1999. pap. text 19.95 (*1-884735-40-1*) Prof Comms.

Padmakara Translation Group Staff, tr. see Dalai Lama XIV.

Padmakara Translation Group Staff, tr. see Rinpeche, Dilgo K.

Padmakara Translation Group Staff, tr. see Rinpoche, Dilgo K.

Padmakara Translation Group Staff, tr. see Shantideva.

Padmanabha, K. P. History of Kerala, 4 vols., Set, Vols. 1-4. Menon, T. K., ed. (C). 1982. reprint ed. 130.00 (*0-8364-2401-8*, Pub. by Asian Educ Servs) S Asia.

— Hosala Sculptures: A Cultural Study. (C). 1989. 96.00 (*81-85067-17-1*, Pub. by Sundeep Prak) S Asia.

***Padmanabhan, Chandra.** Dakshin: Vegetarian Cuisine from South India. (Illus.). 176p. 1999. pap. text 18.95 (*962-593-527-4*) Periplus.

Padmanabhan, Manjula. Hot Death, Cold Soup: Twelve Short Stories. 192p. 1997. pap. 13.95 (*1-85964-111-3*) Garnet-Ithaca.

Padmanabhan, Mukund, et al. Feedback-Based Orthogonal Digital Filters: Theory, Applications & Implementation. (International Series in Engineering & Computer Science, Natural Language Processing & Machine Translation: Vol. 343). 280p. (C). 1995. text 111.00 (*0-7923-9655-3*) Kluwer Academic.

Padmanabhan, R., jt. auth. see McCune, W.

Padmanabhan, S. Y., jt. auth. see Gangopadhyay, S.

Padmanabhan, T. After the First Three Minutes: The Story of Our Universe. LC 97-11060. (Illus.). 228p. (C). 1998. pap. 20.95 (*0-521-62972-1*); text 59.95 (*0-521-62039-2*) Cambridge U Pr.

— Cosmology & Astrophysics Through Problems. (Illus.). 511p. (C). 1996. text 85.00 (*0-521-46230-4*); pap. text 37.95 (*0-521-46783-7*) Cambridge U Pr.

***Padmanabhan, T.** Theoretical Astrophysics: Astrophysical Processes. (Illus.). 390p. 2000. pap. write for info. (*0-521-56632-0*) Cambridge U Pr.

— Theoretical Astrophysics: Astrophysical Processes, Vol. 1. (Illus.). 390p. 2000. write for info. (*0-521-56240-6*) Cambridge U Pr.

Padmanabhan, T., jt. auth. see Dhurandhar, Sanjeev.

Padmanabhan, T., jt. auth. see Narlikar, Jayant V.

***Padmanabhan, Tattamangalam R.** Industrial Instumentation: Principles & Design. LC 99-41995. (Illus.). xxii, 650p. 1999. pap. 119.00 (*1-85233-208-5*) Spr-Verlag.

Padmarajiah, Y. J. A Comparative Study of the Jaina Theories of Reality & Knowledge. 432p. 1986. reprint ed. 22.00 (*81-208-0036-2*, Pub. by Motilal Bnarsidass) S Asia.

Padmasambhava. Advice from the Lotus-Born. 184p. 1996. pap. 18.00 (*962-7341-20-7*) Bookpeople.

— Natural Liberation: Padmasambhava's Teachings in the Six Bardos. Wallace, B. Alan, tr. LC 97-2608. 272p. 1997. pap. 16.95 (*0-86171-131-9*) Wisdom MA.

— Self-Liberation Through Seeing with Naked Awareness: An introduction to the Nature of One's Own Mind in the Tibetan Dzogchen Tradition. Quasha, George, ed. Reynolds, John M., tr. from TIB. (Illus.). 240p. (C). 1989. pap. 14.95 (*0-88268-050-1*) Station Hill Pr.

Padmasambhava, Guru. The Legend of the Great Stupa. LC 73-79059. (Tibetan Translation Ser.: Vol. 2). (Illus.). 140p. 1973. pap. 12.95 (*0-913546-03-8*) Dharma Pub.

Padmasri, jt. auth. see Adiccabandhu.

Padmasuri. But Little Dust: Life Amongst the Ex-Untouchables of India. LC 99-205240. (Illus.). 216p. 1998. pap. 19.95 (*0-904766-85-3*) Windhorse Pubns.

Padmore, George. Africa & World Peace. 285p. 1972. reprint ed. 37.50 (*0-7146-1764-4*, BHA-01764, Pub. by F Cass Pubs) Intl Spec Bk.

Padmore, George A. The Memoirs of a Liberian Ambassador, George Arthur Padmore. LC 96-21538. (Illus.). 212p. 1996. 89.95 (*0-7734-8744-1*) E Mellen.

Padoa-Schioppa, Antonio, ed. Legislation & Justice. (The Origins of the Modern State in Europe Ser.). 454p. 1997. text 95.00 (*0-19-820546-5*) OUP.

Padoa-Schioppa, Tommaso. Europe after 1992: Three Essays. Riccardi, Margaret B., ed. LC 91-18803. (Essays in International Finance Ser.: No. 182). 52p. 1991. pap. text 10.00 (*0-88165-089-7*) Princeton U Int Finan Econ.

— Financial & Monetary Integration in Europe: 1990, 1992 & Beyond. (Occasional Paper Ser.: No. 28). 36p. 1990. pap. 10.00 (*1-56708-027-8*) Grp of Thirty.

— The Road to Monetary Union in Europe. (Illus.). 294p. 1995. text 55.00 (*0-19-828843-3*) OUP.

— Tripolarism: Regional & Global Economic Cooperation. (Occasional Paper Ser.: No. 42). (Orig.). 1993. pap. 10.00 (*1-56708-089-8*) Grp of Thirty.

Padoan, Gianni. Danger Kid. LC 90-48381. 28p. (J). 1989. 11.99 (*0-85953-312-3*) Childs Play.

— Remembering Grandad. 28p. (J). 1989. 11.99 (*0-85953-311-5*) Childs Play.

Padoan, Gianni & Collini, Emanuela. Follow My Leader. 28p. (J). (gr. 4 up). 1989. 11.99 (*0-85953-313-1*) Childs Play.

Padoan, Pier C. The Political Economy of International Financial Instability. 240p. 1986. 45.00 (*0-7099-4003-3*, Pub. by C Helm) Routldge.

Padoan, Pier C., ed. The International Impact of 1992: Toward Regionalisation in the International Economy. 200p. 1992. 69.95 (*0-7103-0431-5*, A7588) Routledge.

Padoan, Pier C., jt. ed. see Guerrieri, Paolo.

Padoan, Pier C., jt. ed. see Lombardini, Siro.

***Padoan, Pier Carlo.** Monetary Union, Employment & Growth: The Impact of the Euro as a Global Currency. LC 00-29414. 2000. write for info. (*1-84064-372-2*) E Elgar.

Padoan, Pier Carlo, jt. auth. see Henning, C. Randall.

Padoch, et al. Varzea: Diversity, Development & Conservation of Amazonia's Whitewater Floodplains. LC 98-55089. (Advances in Economic Botany Ser.: Vol. 13). 1998. pap. 39.50 (*0-89327-419-4*, AEB13) NY Botanical.

Padoch, Christine & Peluso, Nancy L., eds. Borneo in Transition: People, Forests, Conservation, & Development. (South-East Asian Social Science Monographs). (Illus.). 312p. (C). 1996. text 55.00 (*967-65-3110-3*) OUP.

Padoch, Christine, jt. ed. see Denevan, W. M.

Padoch, Christine, jt. ed. see Denslow, Julie S.

Padoch, Christine, jt. ed. see Redford, Kent H.

Padol, Brian A. A-Z Crossword Puzzle Sol. 1408p. 1995. mass mkt. 7.99 (*0-380-77518-2*, Avon Bks) Morrow Avon.

Padol, Brian A., tr. see Housman, Mordechai.

Padon, Thomas. Nancy Graves: Excavations in Print: a Catalogue Raisonne. LC 95-23940. (Illus.). 208p. 1996. 49.50 (*0-8109-3391-8*, Pub. by Abrams) Time Warner.

***Padova, Ted.** Acrobat PDF Bible. LC 99-14030. (Bible Ser.). 744p. 1999. pap. 39.99 (*0-7645-3242-1*) IDG Bks.

Padova, Ted. Photoshop 4 One Step at a Time. (New Tutorial Ser.). 400p. 1999. pap. 29.99 (*0-7645-3127-1*) IDG Bks.

Padovan, Richard. Proportion: Philosophy, Science & Architecture. LC 98-49274. 1999. pap. 39.99 (*0-419-22780-6*, E & FN Spon) Routledge.

Padovani, Giuseppe. Dictionnaire Bilingue: French-Italian, Italian-French. (FRE & ITA.). 536p. 1987. pap. 14.95 (*0-7859-7846-1*, 2253002798) Fr & Eur.

Padovani, Martin H. Healing Wounded Emotions. LC 86-51614. 128p. (YA). (gr. 9 up). 1987. pap. 7.95 (*0-89622-333-7*) Twenty-Third.

Padovano, Anthony. Dawn Without Darkness: A Trilogy on the Spiritual Life, Including Belief in Human Life & Freedom, 3 vols. LC 82-45117. 1982. pap. 4.95 (*0-385-18183-3*) Doubleday.

Padovano, Anthony T. The Church Today: Belonging & Believing. (Catholic Home Library). (Illus.). 128p. 1989. 4.95 (*1-55944-001-5*) Franciscan Comns.

— Hope Is a Dialogue. Gawlik, David A., ed. 267p. (Orig.). 1998. pap. 14.95 (*0-9668228-0-3*) Caritas Commns.

— The Process of Sculpture. (Illus.). 352p. 1986. pap. 17.95 (*0-306-80273-2*) Da Capo.

— Reform & Renewal: Essays on Authority, Ministry & Social Justice in the American Church. LC 89-63119. 144p. (Orig.). (C). 1990. pap. 9.95 (*1-55612-266-7*) Sheed & Ward WI.

— A Retreat with Thomas Merton: Becoming Who We Are. 120p. 1996. pap. text 7.95 (*0-86716-229-5*) St Anthony Mess Pr.

Padovano, Romy. Hit Parade: Classifiche, Dischi, Artisti Dagli Anni '50 Ai Nostri Giorni. LC 98-213885. (Guide Oro Ser.). 383p. 1997. write for info. (*88-04-42563-6*) Mondadori & II.

Padover, Saul K. Jefferson: A Great American's Life & Ideas. 192p. 1952. mass mkt. 6.99 (*0-451-62797-0*, Ment) NAL.

— The Living U. S. Constitution. 3rd rev. ed. 416p. (C). 1995. pap. 14.95 (*0-452-01147-7*) NAL.

Padover, Saul K., ed. Confessions & Self-Portraits. LC 68-58807. (Essay Index Reprint Ser.). 1977. 23.95 (*0-8369-1048-6*) Ayer.

Padover, Saul K., ed. see Jefferson, Thomas.

Padrick, Jeff, jt. auth. see Student, Annette L.

Padro, Alexander M., jt. auth. see Moran, Mark M.

Padron, Consuelo E. Flora y Vegetacion Liquenica Epifita de los Sabinares Herrenos. Wirth, Volkmar et al, eds. (Bibliotheca Lichenologica: Vol. 27). (GER., Illus.). 341p. 1987. pap. 83.00 (*3-443-58006-8*, Pub. by Gebruder Borntraeger) Balogh.

Padron, Francisco M., ed. The Journal of Don Francisco de Saavedra, 1780-1783. Topping, Aileen M., tr. LC 88-14260. 424p. (Orig.). 1989. 49.95 (*0-8130-0877-8*) U Press Fla.

Padron, Justo J. On the Cutting Edge: Selected Poems. Bourne, Louis, tr. from SPA. & intro. by. LC 87-82774. 156p. (Orig.). 1988. pap. 19.95 (*0-948259-42-6*, Pub. by Forest Bks) Dufour.

— Solo Muere la Mano Que Te Escribe. (Nueva Austral Ser.: Vol. 98). (SPA.). 1991. pap. text 24.95 (*84-239-1898-X*) Elliots Bks.

Padron, Mary E. A Magical Christmas Dream. LC 95-92595. (Illus.). 32p. (Orig.). (J). (ps-2). 1996. pap. 12.95 (*0-9648284-0-5*) Pink Hse Pr.

Padron, Victor A., ed. see Aruna, Augustine S.

Padt, Maartje. Shanti. LC 98-188290. (Illus.). 32p. (J). (ps-2). 1998. 14.95 (*0-7894-2520-3*) DK Pub Inc.

***Padua, L. S., et al.** PROSEA (Plant Resources of South-East Asia 12 (1) Medicinal & Poisonous Plants (1) (Illus.). 711p. 1999. 185.00 (*90-5782-042-0*, Pub. by Backhuys Pubs) Balogh.

Padua, Nancy, ed. see Ahern, Jerry.

Padua, Nancy, ed. see Waters, Kenneth.

Paduano, Joseph. Art of Infrared Photography: A Comprehensive Guide to the Use of Black & White Infrared Film. 4th ed. LC 97-75204. (Illus.). 112p. 1997. pap. 29.95 (*0-936262-50-8*) Amherst Media.

— Infrared Nude Photography. 2nd ed. LC 98-77821. (Illus.). 104p. 1998. pap. 29.95 (*0-936262-67-2*) Amherst Media.

— Seascapes: A Collection of Photographs of the Jersey Shore. LC 83-91284. (Illus.). 48p. (Orig.). 1983. pap. 9.95 (*0-9612590-0-0*, TR 24.N5) J Paduano.

— Wide-Angle Lens Photography. LC 95-80949. (Illus.). 112p. 1996. pap. 15.95 (*0-936262-43-5*) Amherst Media.

***Padubidri, V.** Principles & Practice of Obstetrics. (Illus.). 400p. 2000. text 39.95 (*0-19-564951-6*) OUP.

Paduda, Joe, ed. The Art of Sculling. (Illus.). 144p. 1991. pap. 15.95 (*0-07-158010-7*) McGraw.

Paduda, Joe & Henig, Les. Art of Sculling. (Illus.). 160p. 1992. pap. 14.95 (*0-87742-308-3*) Intl Marine.

Padula, Alfred, jt. auth. see Smith, Lois M.

Padula, Robert. Building Custodian, Building Superintendent, Custodial. 8th ed. 192p. 1992. per. 15.95 (*0-671-86851-9*, Arc) IDG Bks.

Padula, William V. Neuro-Optometric Rehabilitation. 3rd rev. ed. Corngold, Sally M., ed. 212p. 2000. reprint ed. lib. bdg. 29.50 (*0-943599-65-2*) OEPF.

Padva, F. De, see MacFarlane, P. W. & De Padva, F.

Padwa, Albert. One, Three-Dipolar Cycloaddition Chemistry, 2 vols., Vol. 2. (General Heterocyclic Chemistry Ser.: No. 1-128). 1521p. 1984. 899.00 (*0-471-08364-X*) Wiley.

P

Padwa, Albert, ed. Organic Photochemistry, Vol. 11. (Illus.). 456p. 1991. text 225.00 (*0-8247-8561-4*) Dekker.

Padwa, Lynette. Everything You Pretend to Know & Are Afraid Someone Will Ask. LC 95-15763. 224p. 1996. pap. 10.95 (*0-14-051322-1*, Penguin Bks) Viking Penguin.

Padwa, Lynette & Scheman, Lani. Dogs! A Fun & Care Book. LC 97-32166. (Fun & Care Bks.). (Illus.). 112p. 1998. pap. 16.95 (*1-889540-03-X*) Bowtie Press.

Padwa, Lynette, jt. auth. see Baron, David.

Padwa, Lynette, jt. auth. see Herst, Charney W.

Padwee, Howard. The Cat Who Couldn't See in the Dark: Veterinary Mysteries & Advice on Feline Care & Behavior. LC 98-36078. 240p. 1998. pap. 11.00 (*0-395-93524-5*) HM.

Padwick, Constance E. Muslim Devotions: A Study of Prayer-Manuals in Common Use. 313p. 1996. pap. 19.95 (*1-85168-115-9*, 574, Pub. by Onewrld Pubns) Penguin Putnam.

Padwick, Gordon. Microsoft Outlook Quick Reference. 300p. 1997. 19.99 (*0-7897-1267-9*) Que.

— Special Edition Using Outlook 9X. LC 98-84841. 656p. 1998. pap. 29.99 (*0-7897-1516-3*) Que.

— Special Edition Using Microsoft Outlook 97. 888p. 1997. 34.99 (*0-7897-1096-X*) Que.

Padwick, Gordon & Feddema, Helen. Using Microsoft Outlook 2000: Special Edition. (Using ... / Que Ser.). (Illus.). 1452p. 1999. pap. 39.99 (*0-7897-1909-6*) Que.

Padys, Diane, jt. tr. see Herman, Anne.

Padzik, Alicja, ed. At Babci's Knee. Zurawiecka, Aska, tr. LC 85-51371. (Little La Ser.). (ENG & POL., Illus.). 165p. (Orig.). (J). (ps). 1985. audio. write for info. (*0-935003-00-2*) Talent-Ed.

— At Babci's Knee. unabridged ed. Zurawiecka, Aska, tr. LC 85-51371. (Little La Ser.). (ENG & POL., Illus.). 165p. (Orig.). (J). (ps up). 1985. pap. 25.00 incl. audio (*0-935003-01-0*) Talent-Ed.

Pae, K. D., ed. U. S. - Japan Seminar of Piezoelectric Polymers: Proceedings: Honolulu, Hawaii, July 1983: Special Issue of Journal Ferroelectrics. (Ferroelectricity & Related Materials Ser.). 354p. 1984. text 149.00 (*0-677-16555-2*) Gordon & Breach.

Pae, Sung M. Korea Leading Developing Nations: Economy, Democracy & Welfare. LC 92-16787. 536p. (Orig.). (C). 1992. pap. text 44.00 (*0-8191-8743-7*) U Pr of Amer.

— Korea Leading Developing Nations: Economy, Democracy & Welfare. LC 92-16787. 536p. (Orig.). (C). 1992. lib. bdg. 75.00 (*0-8191-8742-9*) U Pr of Amer.

Paechter, Carrie. Educating the Other: Gender, Power & Schooling. LC 98-149680. (Master Classes In Education Ser.). 1998. 79.00 (*0-7507-0774-7*, Falmer Pr); pap. 24.95 (*0-7507-0773-9*, Falmer Pr) Taylor & Francis.

***Paechter, Carrie F.** Changing School Subjects: Power, Gender & Curriculum. LC 00-35991. (Changing Education Ser.). 2000. pap. write for info. (*0-335-20119-9*, Pub. by OpUniv Pr) Taylor & Francis.

***Paeen, Bernard M.** One or Two Things I Remember about Her. 89p. 1999. pap. 10.95 (*0-7414-0007-3*) Buy Books.

Paefeny, Starets. Spiritual Counsels of Starets Parfeny. 1991. pap. 1.00 (*0-89981-135-3*) Eastern Orthodox.

Paehlke, Robert & Torgerson, Douglas, eds. Managing Leviathan: Environmental Politics & the Administrative State. 310p. 1990. pap. 22.95 (*0-921149-54-9*) Broadview Pr.

Paehlke, Robert C. Environmentalism & the Future of Progressive Politics. LC 88-27529. 320p. (C). 1989. 45.00 (*0-300-04021-0*) Yale U Pr.

Paehlke, Robert C., ed. Conservation & Environmentalism: An Encyclopedia. LC 94-49708. (Illus.). 808p. 1995. text 125.00 (*0-8240-6101-2*) Garland.

Paek, Min. Aekyung's Dream. rev. ed. LC 88-18928. (ENG & KOR., Illus.). 24p. (YA). (gr. 2-4). 1988. 14.95 (*0-89239-042-5*) Childrens Book Pr.

Paek, Seung M., ed. see Lee, Seung H.

Paelian, Frances. The Mystical Marriage of Science & Spirit. LC 81-70272. (Illus.). 200p. 1981. pap. 11.95 (*0-918936-11-X*) Astara.

Paelian, Frances, ed. see New Age Bible Interpretation Staff.

Paelian, G. Nicholas Roerich. 2nd ed. LC 74-11757. 1996. pap. 12.00 (*0-911794-34-4*) Saraydarian Inst.

Paelinck, J. H. Qualitative & Quantitative Mathematical Economics. 1982. lib. bdg. 112.50 (*90-247-2623-9*) Kluwer Academic.

Paelinck, Jean H., et al. Spatial Econometrics of Services. 109p. 1992. 82.95 (*1-85628-297-X*, Pub. by Avebry) Ashgate Pub Co.

Paenson, Isaac. Abridged Economics Glossary. (ENG, FRE, RUS & SPA.). 1983. write for info. (*0-8288-0152-5*, M 15495) Fr & Eur.

— Environment in Key Words: A Multilingual Handbook of the Environment, 2 vols. rev. ed. (ENG, FRE, GER & RUS., Illus.). 930p. 1990. 419.75 (*0-08-024524-2*, Pergamon Pr) Elsevier.

— Manual of the Terminology of Public International Law & International Organizations. 1983. text 301.00 (*90 6544-052-6*) Kluwer Law Intl.

— Manual of the Terminology of Public International Law & Organizations. (ENG, FRE, RUS & SPA.). 846p. 1983. 295.00 (*0-8288-0413-3*, M6435) Fr & Eur.

— Manual of the Terminology of Public International Law (Law of Peace) & of International Organizations. (ENG, FRE & SPA.). xlviii, 846p. 1983. write for info. (*3-598-07558-8*) K G Saur Verlag.

— Manual of the Terminology of the Law of Armed Conflicts & of International Humanitarian Organizations. (ENG, FRE & SPA.). xxxviii, 844p. 1989. write for info. (*3-598-07559-6*) K G Saur Verlag.

— Manual of the Terminology of the Law of Armed Conflicts & of International Humanitarian Organizations. (ENG, FRE, RUS & SPA.). 864p. 1989. lib. bdg. 359.00 (*90-247-3466-5*) Kluwer Academic.

— Systematic Glossary of Selected Economics & Social Terms. (ENG, FRE, RUS & SPA.). 450p. 1982. 175.00 (*0-8288-0153-3*, M 8172) Fr & Eur.

— Systematic Glossary of Terminology of Statistical Methods: English, French, Spanish & Russian. LC 63-10029. (ENG, FRE, RUS & SPA.). 1970. 235.00 (*0-08-012285-X*) Franklin.

— Systematic Glossary of the Terminology of Statistical Methods. (ENG, FRE, RUS & SPA.). 544p. 1982. 295.00 (*0-8288-2354-5*, M8173) Fr & Eur.

Paepe, Roland, et al, eds. Greenhouse Effect, Sea Level & Drought. (NATO Advanced Science Institutes Series C: Mathematical & Physical Sciences). 736p. (C). 1990. text 330.00 (*0-7923-1017-9*) Kluwer Academic.

Paepke, Andreas, jt. auth. see Kiczales, Gregor.

***Paepke, Hans-Joachim, ed.** Bloch's Ficsh Collection in the Museum Fuer Naturkunde der Humboldt Universitat zuBerlin. (Illus.). 280p. 2000. 50.00 (*3-904144-16-2*, Pub. by Gantner) Lubrecht & Cramer.

Paeplow, Betty J. Help: For Bible Studies - Devotionals & Discipleship. (Illus.). 116p. 1998. pap. 5.99 (*0-9663159-0-1*) Pine Ridge FL.

Paerregaard, Karsten. Linking Separate Worlds: Urban Migrants & Rural Lives in Peru. LC 97-202655. (Explorations in Anthropology Ser.). (Illus.). 256p. 1997. 55.00 (*1-85973-103-1*, Pub. by Berg Pubs); pap. 19.50 (*1-85973-108-2*, Pub. by Berg Pubs) NYU Pr.

Paes, H., jt. ed. see Klapdor-Kleingrothaus, H. V.

Paese, Paul. Student Teaching Handbook. 12th ed. 136p. (C). 1998. per. 14.95 (*0-7872-5266-2*) Kendall-Hunt.

— Student Teaching Handbook for Student Teachers. 11th ed. 112p. (C). 1997. per. 13.95 (*0-7872-4432-5*) Kendall-Hunt.

Paesler, Michael & Moyer, Patrick. Near-Field Optics: Theory, Instrumentation, & Applications. LC 95-46171. (Illus.). 355p. 1996. 89.95 (*0-471-04311-7*, Wiley-Interscience) Wiley.

Paeth, Alan W., ed. Graphics Gems, Vol. 5. (Illus.). 438p. 1995. text 59.00 (*0-12-543455-3*); text 49.95 (*0-12-543457-X*) Acad Pr.

Paetow, Julie Rae & Wood, Toni Lynn. Living in Both Worlds Vol. 1: A Healer & Her Journey with Spirit. unabridged ed. LC 97-222612. (Illus.). 312p. (Orig.). 1997. pap., per. 18.95 (*0-9657037-0-3*) Paewood Ent.

Paetow, Louis J. Guide to the Study of Medieval History. rev. ed. LC 80-81364. 1969. reprint ed. 65.00 (*0-527-69101-1*) Periodicals Srv.

Paetow, Louis J., ed. Crusades & Other Historical Essays, Presented to Dana C. Munro by His Former Students. LC 68-14902. (Essay Index Reprint Ser.). 1977. 23.95 (*0-8369-0354-4*) Ayer.

Paetro, Maxine. How to Put Your Book Together & Get a Job in Advertising. (Illus.). 254p. 1998. pap. 24.95 (*1-887229-01-9*, Pub. by Copy Wrkshp) Natl Bk Netwk.

Paetzel, Hans W., ed. Complete Multilingual Dictionary of Advertising, Marketing & Communications. (ENG, FRE & GER., Illus.). 608p. 1994. pap. 49.95 (*0-8442-9111-0*, Natl Textbk Co) NTC Contemp Pub Co.

Paetzel, Mary. Spirit of the Siskiyous: The Journals of a Mountain Naturalist. Webb, Lee & Elliott, Jackie, eds. LC 98-36704. (Illus.). 192p. 1998. pap. 21.95 (*0-87071-449-X*) Oreg St U Pr.

Paetznick, Ryan, ed. see Miller, Byron & West, Richard.

Paevsky, L. Basis for the Veneration of Saints. 1993. pap. 0.25 (*0-89981-143-4*) Eastern Orthodox.

Paez, Jorge L. Donas Herlinda y Su Hijo y Otros Hijos (Dona Herlinda & Her Son, & Other Sons) (SPA.). 323p. 1993. pap. 8.99 (*968-16-4101-9*, Pub. by Fondo) Continental Bk.

— Mi Hermano Carlos (My Brother Carlos) (SPA.). 224p. 1965. 11.99 (*968-16-4475-1*, Pub. by Fondo) Continental Bk.

Paez, Ramon T., tr. see Hislop, Alexander.

Pafel, Jurgen, jt. ed. see Lutz, Uli.

Paff, Joseph. The Tibetans. (Illus.). 160p. 1999. 19.95 (*0-8478-2175-7*) Rizzoli Intl.

Paffe, E. Claire, ed. & illus. see John, Jesse W.

Paffen, K. A. Deutsch-Russisches Satzlexikon: German-Russian Syntax Lexicon, 2 vols., Set. (GER & RUS.). 1680p. 1980. 110.00 (*0-8288-1240-3*, F19660) Fr & Eur.

***Paffenbarger, John.** Electric Power Technology: Opportunities & Challenges of Competition. 60p. 1999. pap. 40.00 (*92-64-17133-9*, 61 1999 22 1 P, Pub. by Org for Econ) OECD.

Paffenbarger, John. Oil in Power Generation. LC 99-172828. 96p. 1997. pap. 27.00 (*92-64-15451-5*, 61-97-04-1, Pub. by Org for Econ) OECD.

Paffenbarger, Ralph S. & Olsen, Eric. LifeFit: An Effective Exercise Program for Optimal Health & a Longer Life. LC 95-49235. 440p. (Orig.). 1996. pap. 16.95 (*0-87322-429-9*, PPAF0429) Human Kinetics.

Paffenholz, Thania, jt. ed. see Reychler, Luc.

Paffenroth, Kim. The Story of Jesus According to Luke. LC 97-205809. (JSNT Supplement Ser.: No. 147). 200p. 1997. 57.50 (*1-85075-675-9*, Pub. by Sheffield Acad) CUP Services.

Pafford, J. H., ed. see Shakespeare, William.

Pafford, John. John Clavell, 1601 43: Highwayman, Author, Lawyer, Doctor. 309p. 1993. 22.00 (*0-904920-28-3*, Pub. by Leopards Head Pr) David Brown.

Pafford, Ward. Obligations. 100p. (Orig.). 1994. pap., per. 10.00 (*1-883199-03-4*) St U W Georgia.

— The Unforgettable. (Illus.). 144p. 1998. per. 12.00 (*1-883199-09-3*) St U W Georgia.

Paffrath, Christine, ed. see Paffrath, James D.

Paffrath, Christine, ed. see Paffrath, Jim & Cangialosi, Karen.

Paffrath, James D. How Do You Think Japan? Photographs of a Foreign Resident. Paffrath, Christine, ed. LC 82-90777. (Illus.). 96p. (Orig.). 1982. pap. 8.95 (*0-910703-01-9*) JP Pubns CA.

Paffrath, Jim & Cangialosi, Karen. L.I.S.T. A Listing of International Schools Today. Gilbride, Colleen & Paffrath, Christine, eds. (Orig.). 1984. pap. 3.95 (*0-910703-09-4*) JP Pubns CA.

Pafik, Marie-Reine A., jt. auth. see Guiheen, Anna M.

Pagan, A. R., jt. auth. see Preston, A. J.

Pagan, Adrian & Ullah, Aman. Nonparametric Econometrics. LC 98-37218. (Themes in Modern Econometrics Ser.). (Illus.). 440p. (C). 1999. 74.95 (*0-521-35564-8*) Cambridge U Pr.

***Pagan, Adrian & Ullah, Aman.** Nonparametric Econometrics. LC 98-37218. (Themes in Modern Econometrics Ser.). (Illus.). 424p. (C). 1999. pap. 29.95 (*0-521-58611-9*) Cambridge U Pr.

***Pagan, Angelique.** Demon Lover. 2000. 40.00 (*0-9662702-0-7*) Belladonna Unltd.

Pagan, Barbara, jt. auth. see Lamplugh, Diana.

Pagan, Ernesto Vega, see Vega Pagan, Ernesto.

Pagan, Frank G. A Practical Guide to Algol 68. LC 75-6925. (Wiley Series in Computing). 223p. reprint ed. pap. 69.20 (*0-7837-4388-2*, 204412800012) Bks Demand.

Pagan, Jill C. Taxation Aspects of Currency Fluctuations. 2nd ed. 1991. 150.00 (*0-406-50886-0*, U.K., MICHIE) LEXIS Pub.

***Pagan, Joe D., ed.** Advances in Equine Nutrition. 566p. 1999. 200.00 (*1-897676-83-2*, Pub. by Nottingham Univ Pr) St Mut.

Pagan, Juan A. Lorca en la Lirica Puertorriquena. LC 80-17628. (Coleccion Mente y Palabra). (Illus.). 359p. 1981. 12.00 (*0-8477-0574-9*); pap. 9.60 (*0-8477-0575-7*) U of PR Pr.

Pagan, Luis N. Rivera, see Rivera Pagan, Luis N.

Pagan, Margarita, tr. see Mozeleski, Peter A.

Pagan, Nicholas. Rethinking Literary Biography: A Postmodern Approach to Tennessee Williams. LC 92-55117. 150p. 1993. 29.50 (*0-8386-3516-4*) Fairleigh Dickinson.

Pagan, Nicholas O., jt. ed. see Haney, William S., II.

Pagan, Samuel. Esdras, Nehemias, Ester. (Serie Comentario Biblico Hispanoamericano). (SPA.). 303p. 1992. 19.99 (*0-89922-380-X*, C850-380X) Caribe Betania.

Pagan, Samuel. El Tiempo Esta Cerca (The Time Is at Hand) (What You Need to Know about ... in 12 Lessons Ser.). (SPA.). 142p. 7.99 (*0-89922-497-0*) Caribe Betania.

Pagan, Samuel. La Vision de Isaias. (SPA.). 1997. 7.99 (*0-89922-287-0*, C086-2870) Caribe Betania.

Pagan, Sylvette. Face-Painting & Fancy Dress. (Crafty Hands Collection). (Illus.). 48p. 1995. pap. text 9.95 (*1-85410-331-8*) Aurum Pr.

Pagana, Kathleen D. Mosbys Diagnostic & Laboratory Test, 1900-2000. 4th ed. LC 98-27246. 1998. 27.95 (*0-323-00288-9*) Mosby Inc.

Pagana, Kathleen D. & Pagana, Timothy. Mosby's Manual of Diagnostic & Laboratory Tests. LC 97-40589. (Illus.). 960p. (C). (gr. 13). 1998. pap. text 29.95 (*0-8151-5586-7*, 29626) Mosby Inc.

Pagana, Kathleen D. & Pagana, Timothy J. Diagnostic Testing & Nursing Implications: A Case Study Approach. 5th ed. LC 98-34086. (Illus.). 640p. 1998. text. write for info. (*0-323-00289-7*) Mosby Inc.

***Pagana, Kathleen D. & Pagana, Timothy J.** Mosby's Rapid Reference to Diagnostic & Laboratory Tests. 350p. 1999. text 17.95 (*1-55664-515-5*) Mosby Inc.

Pagana, Timothy, jt. auth. see Pagana, Kathleen D.

Pagana, Timothy J., jt. auth. see Pagana, Kathleen D.

Paganelli, C. V. & Farhi, Leon E., eds. Physiological Function in Special Environments. (Illus.). 240p. 1989. 141.00 (*0-387-96833-4*) Spr-Verlag.

Paganelli, Carlo. Rinaldo Olivieri: Set & City/La Scena e la Citta, 1. 1999. pap. text 25.00 (*88-7838-048-2*) L'Arca It.

Paganetti, JoAn, ed. The Best in Sale Ads, Vol. I. (Illus.). 300p. 1984. 19.95 (*0-934590-13-3*) Visual Refer.

Pagani, et al. The Sea Around Us. 146p. (C). 1997. spiral bd. 26.95 (*0-7872-4674-3*) Kendall-Hunt.

Pagani, Dalia. Mercy Road. LC 97-40249. 336p. 1998. 21.95 (*0-385-32016-7*) Delacorte.

— Mercy Road. 352p. 1999. pap. 11.95 (*0-385-32356-5*, Delta Trade) Dell.

Pagani, Linda, jt. ed. see Pinard, Georges-Franck.

Pagani, Mark, et al. The Sea Around Us: Laboratory Manual. 152p. (C). 1996. pap. text, spiral bd. 24.95 (*0-7872-2001-9*) Kendall-Hunt.

Pagani-Tousignant, Celina. Breaking the Rules: Counseling Ethnic Minorities. 40p. 1992. pap. 5.95 (*1-56246-031-5*, 3274, HazeldenJohnson Inst) Hazelden.

Paganini, Emil P., ed. Acute Continuous Renal Replacement Therapy. (Developments in Nephrology Ser.). (C). 1986. text 120.50 (*0-89838-793-0*) Kluwer Academic.

Paganini, F., jt. auth. see Dullerud, G. E.

***Paganini, Loretta.** My Bologna. LC 00-24272. (Illus.). 256p. 2000. text 23.95 (*0-312-26208-6*) St Martin.

Paganini, M. Paganini: Caprice No. 24 for Electric Classical Guitar. 32p. 1993. pap. 17.95 (*0-7935-2335-4*, 00699381) H Leonard.

Paganini, Maria. Reading Proust: In Search of the Wolf-Fish. Litherland, Caren, tr. from FRE. LC 93-27830. (Theory & History of Literature Ser.: Vol. 84).Tr. of A la Peche au Poisson-Loup. 1994. pap. 19.95 (*0-8166-2040-7*); text 49.95 (*0-8166-2039-3*) U of Minn Pr.

Paganini, Nicolo. La Campanella. Stang, Aaron, ed. 16p. (Orig.). (C). 1985. pap. text 5.95 (*0-7692-1333-2*, K04180) Wrner Bros.

— Caprice No. 24 for Electric Classical Guitar. 1993. pap. 14.95 incl. audio (*0-614-96401-6*) H Leonard.

— Moto Perpetuo for Violin & Piano, Op. 11. Mittell, P., ed. (Carl Fischer Music Library: No. 88). 1968. pap. 6.00 (*0-8258-0014-5*, L88) Fischer Inc NY.

— Six Grand Etudes: Piano. 60p. 1986. pap. 8.95 (*0-7935-4533-1*) H Leonard.

Paganini, Nicolo & Wieniawski, Henryk. Caprices & Etudes for Solo Violin. 128p. pap. text 9.95 (*0-486-27883-2*) Dover.

Pagano. I.S.M. Principles of Biostatistics. 2nd ed. (Statistics Ser.). 1998. pap. write for info. (*0-534-22903-4*) Brooks-Cole.

— Principles of Biostatistics. (Statistics Ser.). 1993. pap., teacher ed. 26.25 (*0-534-14066-1*) Brooks-Cole.

— Understanding Statistics in the Behavioral Sciences. 5th ed. (Psychology Ser.). 1998. pap., student ed. 12.00 (*0-534-35393-2*) Brooks-Cole.

— Understanding Statistics in the Behaviorial Sciences. 6th ed. (Psychology Ser.). 2000. text 59.00 (*0-534-57771-7*) Wadsworth Pub.

Pagano, Alfonse, jt. auth. see Mastalia, Francesco.

Pagano, Anthony. Melrose. (Images of America Ser.). (Illus.). 128p. 1998. pap. 16.99 (*0-7524-0485-7*) Arcadia Publng.

— Melrose II. LC 98-87779. (Images of America Ser.). 1998. write for info. (*0-7524-1393-7*) Arcadia Publng.

Pagano, Anthony & Verdin, JoAnn. The External Environment of Business: Political, Economic, Social & Regulatory. 516p. (C). 1997. pap. text 34.95 (*0-87563-682-9*) Stipes.

Pagano, Carmen. Recipes for a Sensual Bath. iv, 42p. (Orig.). 1997. pap. write for info. (*0-9657518-8-0*) Carmen.

***Pagano, Carmen F. P.** Golddiggers True Stories of Love, Lust & Lies. Boss, Shirley, ed. 254p. 1999. pap. 19.95 (*0-9657518-9-9*) Carmen.

Pagano, Christian, jt. auth. see Fages, Jean-Baptiste.

Pagano, Claudia & Goulding, Mary M. Lupus - What's It All About? xi, 210p. 1997. pap. 14.95 (*0-9661036-3-7*) Abiding Health.

Pagano, Concettina N. M. Psychological Research with Human Subjects. (C). lab manual ed. 20.00 (*0-9678220-0-9*) Luce Tech.

Pagano de Divitiis, Gigliola. English Merchants in Seventeenth-Century Italy. Parkin, Stephen, tr. (Studies in Italian History & Culture). 220p. (C). 1998. text 59.95 (*0-521-58031-5*) Cambridge U Pr.

Pagano, Frank N., ed. & intro. see Burke, Edmund.

Pagano, Jo Anne. Exiles & Communities: Teaching in the Patriarchal Wilderness. LC 89-29352. (SUNY Series, Feminist Theory in Education). 165p. (C). 1990. text 64.50 (*0-7914-0273-8*); pap. text 21.95 (*0-7914-0274-6*) State U NY Pr.

— Golden Wedding. LC 74-17941. (Italian American Experience Ser.). 308p. 1975. reprint ed. 21.95 (*0-405-06412-8*) Ayer.

Pagano, Joanne. Adolescent Culture, Knowledge & Gender in Contemporary Film & Music. Kincheloe, Joe & Steinberg, Shirley R., eds. (Critical Education Practice Ser.). 200p. Date not set. text 30.00 (*0-8153-1885-5*) Garland.

Pagano, John O. Healing Psoriasis: The Natural Alternative. (Illus.). (Orig.). 1991. pap. 24.95 (*0-9628847-0-7*) Pagano Organization.

Pagano, Jules, jt. auth. see Hoffman, Hy.

Pagano, M., ed. Cell Cycle Control. LC 98-10581. (Results & Problems in Cell Differentiation Ser.: Vol. 22). (Illus.). 300p. 1998. 129.00 (*3-540-64031-2*) Spr-Verlag.

Pagano, Marcello & Gauvreau, Kimberlee. Principles of Biostatistics. LC 92-32841. 524p. 1993. text 52.95 (*0-534-14064-5*) Wadsworth Pub.

Pagano, Marian, jt. auth. see Coughlin, Mary Ann.

Pagano, Michael A. & Bowman, Ann O. Cityscapes & Capital: The Politics of Urban Development. (Illus.). 224p. 1995. text 32.50 (*0-8018-5034-7*) Johns Hopkins.

— Cityscapes & Capital: The Politics of Urban Development. LC 94-40582. 208p. 1997. reprint ed. pap. text 15.95 (*0-8018 5767-8*) Johns Hopkins.

Pagano, Michael P. Communicating Effectively in Medical Records: A Guide for Physician-Authors. 128p. (C). 1992. 34.00 (*0-8039-4316-4*); pap. 15.95 (*0-8039-4317-2*) Sage.

Pagano, Michael P. & Jacocks, M. Alex. Communicating Effectively in Medical Records: A Guide for Physicians. LC 91-42004. 134p. 1992. reprint ed. pap. 41.60 (*0-608-07675-9*, 206776500010) Bks Demand.

Pagano, Michael P. & Ragan, Sandra L. Communication Skills for Professional Nurses. 160p. (C). 1992. 34.00 (*0-8039-4556-6*); pap. 15.95 (*0-8039-4557-4*) Sage.

Pagano, Michael P., et al. Communication Skills for Professional Nurses. LC 92-7628. 160p. 1992. pap. 49.60 (*0-608-05178-0*, 205259900001) Bks Demand.

Pagano, Michele. Cell Cycle: Materials & Methods. 300p. 1995. 97.95 (*0-387-58066-2*) Spr-Verlag.

Pagano, Michele, ed. Cell Cycle: Materials & Methods. LC 95-3810. (Laboratory Ser.). 1995. 79.00 (*3-540-58066-2*) Spr-Verlag.

Pagano, Nicholas J. Elasticity: Tensor, Dyadic, & Engineering Aproaches. (Illus.). xiv, 290p. 1992. pap. 10.95 (*0-486-66958-0*) Dover.

Pagano, Nicholas J., ed. Interlaminar Response of Composite Materials. (Composite Materials Ser.: No. 5). 260p. 1989. 166.25 (*0-444-87285-X*) Elsevier.

***Pagano, Ricki S.** For the Record: A Personal Facts & Document Organizer. 2nd rev. ed. Caputo, Salvatoro, ed. 61p. 1999. ring bd. 26.95 (*0-9670226-1-4*, Pub. by Pagano Pr) Five Star AZ.

Pagano, Robert R. Principles of Biostatistics with Disk. (Statistics Ser.). 1994. mass mkt. 55.50 (*0-534-14069-6*) Wadsworth Pub.

An Asterisk (*) at the beginning of an entry indicates that the title is appearing for the first time.

Understanding Statistics. 4th ed. Date not set. pap. text, teacher ed. write for info. (*0-314-03371-8*) West Pub.
— Understanding Statistics. 4th ed. 1994. mass mkt., student ed. 18.50 (*0-314-03707-1*) West Pub.
— Understanding Statistics in the Behavioral Sciences. 4th ed. Perlee, Clyde, ed. LC 93-41157. 550p. (C). 1994. mass mkt. 52.50 (*0-314-02691-6*) West Pub.
Pagano, Robert R. Understanding Statistics in the Behavioral Sciences. 5th ed. 1997. pap. 17.50 (*0-534-35392-4*) Brooks-Cole.
Pagano, Robert R. Understanding Stats in the Behavioral Sciences. 5th ed. LC 97-40018. (Psychology). 249p. 1998. pap. 82.95 (*0-534-35390-8*) Brooks-Cole.
Pagano, Robert R., et al. Principles of Biostatistics. 2nd ed. (Statistics Ser.). 525p. (C). 2000. pap. 77.95 (*0-534-22902-6*) Wadsworth Pub.
***Pagano, Roseanne, ed.** The Alaska Almanac, Facts about Alaska. 24th ed. (Illus.). 2000. pap. 11.95 (*0-88240-531-4*) Gr Arts Ctr Pub.
Pagano, Tullio. Experimental Fictions: From Emile Zola's Naturalism to Giovanni Verga's Verism. LC 97-50389. 189p. 1999. write for info. (*0-8386-3756-6*) Fairleigh Dickinson.
Pagano, Ugo & Rowthorn, Robert, eds. Democracy & Efficiency in the Economic Enterprise. LC 95-24559. (Studies in Business Organization & Networks Ser.: Vol. 1). 352p. (C). 1996. 85.00 (*0-415-12586-3*) Routledge.
Paganuzzi, P. N. Visoko-Dechanskaja Lavra Na Kosovje Polje (V Serbii)Tr. of Visoko-Dechansky Monastery at Kosova Polija (in Serbia). 1976. pap. 1.00 (*0-317-30331-7*) Holy Trinity.
Pagden, Anthony. European Encounter with the New World: From Renaissance to Romanticism. LC 92-21947. (Illus.). 256p. (C). 1993. 35.00 (*0-300-05285-5*); pap. 15.00 (*0-300-05950-7*) Yale U Pr.
— Lords of All the World: Ideologies of Empire in Spain, Britain, & France, 1492-1830. 256p. 1998. pap. 18.00 (*0-300-07449-2*) Yale U Pr.
— Spanish Imperialism & the Political Imagination. (Illus.). 196p. 1990. pap. 18.00 (*0-300-07660-6*) Yale U Pr.
***Pagden, Anthony, ed.** Facing Each Other: The World's Perception of Europe & Europe's Perception of the World, 2 vols. (Expanding World Ser.: Vol. 31). 848p. 2000. text 240.95 (*0-86078-526-2*, Pub. by Ashgate Pub) Ashgate Pub Co.
— The Idea of Europe: From Antiquity to the European Union. (Woodrow Wilson Center Press Ser.). 325p. (C). 2000. text Price not set. (*0-521-79171-5*); pap. text Price not set. (*0-521-79552-4*) Cambridge U Pr.
Pagden, Anthony, jt. ed. see Canny, Nicholas.
Pagden, Anthony, ed. see Vitoria, Francisco.
Pagden, Anthony, ed. & tr. see Cortes, Hernan.
Pagdin, Christopher. Assessing Tourism Impacts in the Third World: A Nepal Case Study. 88p. 1995. pap. text 105.75 (*0-08-042670-0*) Elsevier.
***Page.** Dog on a Broomstick. (J). 2000. pap. 6.95 (*0-552-54538-4*, Pub. by Transworld Publishers Ltd) Trafalgar.
Page. The Kings African Rifles. (Illus.). 1997. 35.00 (*0-85052-538-1*) Leo Cooper.
— Physiology of Human Placenta. 192p. 1993. 75.00 (*1-85728-065-2*, Pub. by UCL Pr Ltd); pap. 29.50 (*1-85728-066-0*, Pub. by UCL Pr Ltd) Taylor & Francis.
— Pre-Calculus. (Mathematics Ser.). 2002. mass mkt. 64.95 (*0-534-34137-3*) Brooks-Cole.
— Rediscovering Midwifery. (C). 1998. pap. text. write for info. (*0-443-05572-6*) Church.
— Spanish Made Easy, Custom Pub. (C). 1992. pap. text 9.74 (*0-07-048135-0*) McGraw.
***Page.** Transport & Tourism. 360p. (C). 1998. pap. 34.60 (*0-582-32025-9*) Longman.
Page, jt. auth. see Greenberg.
Page, Christopher I. Boogie Woogie Stomp: Albert Ammons & His Music. LC 98-222086. 1997. write for info. (*1-885066-32-5*) Four-G Pubs.
Page, William R. Economics at Work. LC 68-121687. xiii, 162 p. 1968. write for info. (*0-304-92356-7*) Continuum.
Page, A. C. & Ferguson, R. B. Investor Protection. (Law in Context Ser.). 384p. (C). 1994. pap. text 37.95 (*0-297-82132-6*) Northwestern U Pr.
— Investor Protection. (Law in Context Ser.). xiv, 351p. (C). 1992. 75.00 (*0-297-82131-8*) W S Hein.
***Page, A. D.** Disney Days, 1. 1999. 11.99 (*0-8362-1908-2*) Andrews & McMeel.
***Page, A. Day.** Daily Horoscope Leo. 1999. pap. 8.95 (*0-7611-1584-6*) Workman Pub.
— 365 Dogs. 1998. pap. 10.95 (*0-7611-1154-9*) Workman Pub.
Page, A. L., et al, eds. Land Application of Sludge. (Illus.). 168p. 1987. 105.00 (*0-87371-083-5*, S657, CRC Reprint) Franklin.
Page, A. L., ed. see Huang, P. M.
Page, Alan, jt. auth. see Daintith, Terence.
Page, Alex, tr. see Buber, Martin.
Page, Alexis. Three-Guy Weekend. (Love Stories Ser.). 192p. (YA). (gr. 7-12). 1996. mass mkt. 3.99 (*0-553-57044-7*) Bantam.
***Page, Alison & Shepard, Tristram.** Getting IT Right Skills Book 1 Levels 3-4. (Getting IT Right Ser.). (Illus.). 205p. (YA). (gr. 9-11). 2000. pap. 22.50 (*0-7487-4421-5*, Pub. by S Thornes Pubs) Trans-Atl Phila.
— Getting IT Right Skills Book 3 Levels 5 Plus. (Getting IT Right Ser.). (Illus.). 205p. (YA). (gr. 9-11). 2000. pap. 22.50 (*0-7487-4530-0*, Pub. by S Thornes Pubs) Trans-Atl Phila.
— Getting IT Right Skills Book 2 Levels 4-5. (Getting IT Right Ser.). (Illus.). 205p. (YA). (gr. 9-11). 2000. pap. 22.50 (*0-7487-4423-1*, Pub. by S Thornes Pubs) Trans-Atl Phila.
— Getting IT Right Teacher Support Packs 1 Levels 3-4. (Getting IT Right Ser.). (Illus.). 188p. (YA). (gr. 9-11). 2000. pap. 120.00 (*0-7487-4422-3*, Pub. by S Thornes Pubs) Trans-Atl Phila.
— Getting IT Right Teacher Support Packs 1 Levels 3-4 (CD-Rom) (Getting IT Right Ser.). (Illus.). (YA). (gr. 9-11). 2000. audio compact disk 210.00 (*0-7487-5172-6*, Pub. by S Thornes Pubs) Trans-Atl Phila.
— Getting IT Right Teacher Support Packs 2 Levels 4-5. (Getting IT Right Ser.). (Illus.). 188p. (YA). (gr. 9-11). 2000. pap. 120.00 (*0-7487-4424-X*, Pub. by S Thornes Pubs) Trans-Atl Phila.
— Getting IT Right Teacher Support Packs 2 Levels 4-5 (CD-Rom) (Getting IT Right Ser.). (Illus.). 2000. audio compact disk 210.00 (*0-7487-5173-4*, Pub. by S Thornes Pubs) Trans-Atl Phila.
— Getting IT Right Teacher Support Packs 3 Levels 5 Plus. (Getting IT Right Ser.). (Illus.). 188p. (YA). (gr. 9-11). 2000. pap. 120.00 (*0-7487-4531-9*, Pub. by S Thornes Pubs) Trans-Atl Phila.
— Getting IT Right Teacher Support Packs 3 Levels 5 Plus (CD-Rom) (Getting IT Right Ser.). (Illus.). (YA). 2000. audio compact disk 210.00 (*0-7487-5174-2*, Pub. by S Thornes Pubs) Trans-Atl Phila.
***Page, Andre.** Babies' Names A-Z. 3rd ed. (Illus.). 192p. 2001. pap. 8.95 (*0-7160-2083-1*, Pub. by Elliot RW Bks) Midpt Trade.
Page, Andre. Photographic Interpretation. (Illus.). 128p. 1973. 12.00 (*0-7207-0633-5*) Transatl Arts.
Page, Anita. Mohegan Fun & Learn Book. (Illus.). 16p. (Orig.). (J). 1997. pap. 5.00 (*0-9656933-1-7*) Lttle People.
Page, Anna Laura & Shafferman, Jean A. Kids' Kreations: Teacher's Handbook. 1997. pap. 49.95 incl. audio compact disk (*0-88284-843-7*) Alfred Pub.
— Kids' Kreations: Teachers Handbook, Bk. 2. 60p. 1998. pap. 24.95 (*0-88284-928-X*, 18037) Alfred Pub.
Page, Anna Laura & Shafferman, Jean Anne. Carriers of the Light, Director's Score. 36p. 1997. pap. 19.95 (*0-7390-0867-6*, 16077) Alfred Pub.
Page, Anna Laura, et al. Kids' Kreations: Teacher's Handbook, Bk. 2. 1998. pap., teacher ed. 49.95 incl. audio compact disk (*0-88284-930-1*, 18039) Alfred Pub.
Page, Anne. Pie in the Sky. (Illus.). 40p. (Orig.). (J). (ps-3). 1985. pap. 4.95 (*0-9613925-2-5*) Joane Pubns.
Page, Anne, jt. auth. see Page, John.
Page, Anthea. Ancient Egyptian Figured Ostraca. (Petrie Collection). 1983. pap. 36.95 (*0-85668-216-0*, Pub. by Aris & Phillips) David Brown.
Page, B. Encyclopedia of Defensive Basketball Drills. LC 86-2507. 288p. (C). 1986. text 27.95 (*0-13-275777-X*) P-H.
Page, B. M., ed. see Zonenshain, L. P., et al.
***Page, Barbara.** Rock of Ages Sands of Time. 1999. 45.00 (*0-226-64479-0*) U Ch Pr.
Page, Benjamin B., ed. Marxism & Spirituality: An International Anthology. LC 92-18499. 248p. 1993. 57.95 (*0-89789-291-7*, H291, Bergin & Garvey) Greenwood.
Page, Benjamin I. Choices & Echoes in Presidential Elections. LC 78-4997. (Rational Man & Electoral Democracy Ser.). (Illus.). xvi, 336p. 1978. lib. bdg. 25.00 (*0-226-64470-7*) U Ch Pr.
— Choices & Echoes in Presidential Elections: Rational Man & Electoral Democracy. LC 78-4997. 1979. pap. text 12.00 (*0-226-64471-5*, P858) U Ch Pr.
— Who Deliberates? Mass Media in Modern Democracy. (Illus.). 136p. 1996. pap. text 11.00 (*0-226-64473-1*) U Ch Pr.
— Who Deliberates? Mass Media in Modern Democracy. (Illus.). 136p. 1997. lib. bdg. 29.00 (*0-226-64472-3*) U Ch Pr.
— Who Gets What from Government. LC 82-13454. 264p. 1983. pap. 16.95 (*0-520-04703-6*, Pub. by U CA Pr) Cal Prin Full Svc.
Page, Benjamin I. & Shapiro, Robert Y. The Rational Public: Fifty Years of Trends in Americans' Policy Preferences. (Illus.). 506p. 1992. pap. text 22.00 (*0-226-64478-2*) U Ch Pr.
— The Rational Public: Fifty Years of Trends in Americans' Policy Preferences. (Illus.). 488p. 1994. lib. bdg. 59.95 (*0-226-64477-4*) U Ch Pr.
Page, Benjamin I., jt. auth. see Greenberg, Edward S.
Page, Benjamin M., tr. see Zonenshain, L. P., et al.
Page, Bernd, jt. ed. see Guariso, Giorgio.
Page, Bette. Mynarski's Lanc. LC 90-112140. (Illus.). 192p. 1996. 32.00 (*1-55046-006-4*, Pub. by Boston Mills) Genl Dist Srvs.
Page, Beverly. Cartoon Art: An Adventure in Creativity. Smith, Linda H., ed. (Triad Series Prototype). 1980. pap. 7.95 (*0-936386-10-X*) Creative Learning.
Page, Bishpham. Tea at Miss Jean's. LC 91-65465. (Illus.). 28p. (Orig.). (J). (gr. 2 up). 1991. pap. 8.95 (*0-9628129-1-9*) Roberts Rinehart.
Page-Blanchard, Marjorie. Home Gardener's Month-by-Month Cookbook. LC 85-4507. (Illus.). 208p. 1985. reprint ed. pap. 9.95 (*0-88266-013-6*) Storey Bks.
Page, Bob. Crystal Stemware: Identification Guide. 1998. pap. text 18.95 (*1-57432-031-9*, 5021) Collector Bks.
Page, Bob & Frederiksen, Dale. A Collection of American Crystal: A Stemware Identification Guide. (Illus.). 124p. 1994. 24.95 (*1-889977-01-2*) Replacements.
— Seneca Glass Company, 1891-1983: A Stemware Identification Guide. (Illus.). 104p. 1995. 24.95 (*1-889977-02-0*) Replacements.
— Tiffin Is Forever: A Stemware Identification Guide. (Illus.). 169p. 1994. 29.95 (*1-889977-00-4*) Replacements.
Page, Brian T. Assessment Center Handbook. 125p. 1995. pap. 21.95 (*0-87526-429-8*) Gould.
— Getting Ready for That Assessment Center. (Illus.). 120p. (Orig.). 1983. pap. 8.95 (*0-9611284-0-2*) Sweets Corners.
Page, Bruce & Holm, Diana. Web Publishing with Adobe Acrobat & PDF. LC 96-18035. 363p. 1996. pap. text 39.95 incl. cd-rom (*0-471-14948-9*) Wiley.
Page, Burdys. Learning to Color with Rhymes: A Workbook. (Illus.). 32p. (Orig.). (J). 1990. pap. 6.95 (*0-86534-146-X*) Sunstone Pr.
Page, C. E. How to Feed the Baby to Make It Healthy & Happy. 1991. lib. bdg. 66.95 (*0-8490-4521-5*) Gordon Pr.
— How to Feed the Baby to Make It Healthy & Happy. 162p. 1996. reprint ed. spiral bd. 15.00 (*0-7873-0650-9*) Hlth Research.
Page, C. H., jt. auth. see Stacey, T. R.
Page, C. N. Ferns of Britain & Ireland. 2nd ed. LC 96-38838. (Illus.). 560p. (C). 1997. text 130.00 (*0-521-58380-2*); pap. text 64.95 (*0-521-58658-5*) Cambridge U Pr.
Page, C. P., et al, eds. Pharmacology of Asthma. (Handbook of Experimental Pharmacology Ser.: No. 98). (Illus.). 352p. 1991. 276.95 (*0-387-52839-3*) Spr-Verlag.
Page, C. P. & Gardiner, P. J. Airways Hyperresponsiveness. (Illus.). 352p. 1993. 145.00 (*0-632-03061-5*) Blackwell Sci.
***Page, C. P., et al.** Cellular Mechanisms in Airways Inflammation. LC 00-37848. (Progress in Inflammation Research Ser.). 2000. write for info. (*3-7643-5852-1*) Birkhauser.
Page, Calvin A. Air Medal. 400p. 1998. 24.95 (*0-9664917-0-X*) DuPont Bk Co.
Page, Camille. American Knives & Weapons: Coutellerie d'Amerique l'Origine a 1900: Fabrication Ancienne & Moderne. 60p. 1900. 25.00 (*0-87556-951-X*) Saifer.
Page, Camille. American Knives & Weapons to 1900. (FRE., Illus.). 60p. 1993. reprint ed. pap. 25.00 (*0-87556-181-0*) Saifer.
Page, Carey P. & Hardin, Thomas C. Nutritional Assessment & Support: A Primer. 2nd ed. (Illus.). 256p. (Orig.). 1994. pap. 19.00 (*0-683-06705-2*) Lppncott W & W.
Page, Carl. Philosophical Historicism & the Betrayal of First Philosophy. 256p. 1995. 38.50 (*0-271-01330-3*) Pa St U Pr.
***Page, Carol G.** A Family to Cherish. (Love Inspired Ser.: No. 88). 2000. per. 4.50 (*0-373-87094-9*, 1-87094-8, Harlequin) Harlequin Bks.
Page, Carole G. Carrie. (SpringSong Bks.). 192p. (YA). 1994. mass mkt. 4.99 (*1-55661-523-X*) Bethany Hse.
— Decidedly Married. (Love Inspired Ser.). 1998. per. 4.50 (*0-373-87022-1*, Steeple Hill) Harlequin Bks.
— The Hope of Herrick House. (Heartland Memories Ser.: Vol. 3). 252p. 1996. pap. 11.99 (*0-8407-6780-3*) Nelson.
— Kara. (Springsong Bks.). 192p. (Orig.). (J). (gr. 7-10). 1994. mass mkt. 4.99 (*1-55661-448-9*) Bethany Hse.
— Rachel's Hope. (Love Inspired Ser.: Vol. 40). 1998. per. 4.50 (*0-373-87040-X*, 1-87040-1) Harlequin Bks.
— A Rose for Jenny. No. 5. LC 99-229241. (Heartland Memories Ser.: No. 5). 276p. 1999. pap. 10.99 (*0-7852-7672-6*) Nelson.
— Storms over Willowbrook: A Novel. LC 98-5803. (Heartland Memories Ser.: Vol. 4). 252p. 1998. pap. 11.99 (*0-7852-7671-8*) Nelson.
Page, Carole Gift. In Search of Her Own. (Love Inspired Ser.). 1997. per. 4.50 (*0-373-87005-1*, 1-87005-4, Steeple Hill) Harlequin Bks.
***Page, Carole Gift.** Locket for Maggie. (Heartland Memories Ser.: Vol. 6). 2000. pap. write for info. (*0-7852-7673-4*) Nelson.
— Misty: A Motherus Journey Through Sorrow to Healing. 160p. 2000. mass mkt. 6.99 (*0-8007-8688-2*, Spire) Revell.
Page, Caroline. U. S. Official Propaganda During the Vietnam War, 1965-1973: The Limits of Persuasion. LC 95-41263. 1996. pap. 19.95 (*0-7185-1999-X*) Bks Intl VA.
— U. S. Official Propaganda During the Vietnam War, 1965-1973: The Limits of Persuasion. LC 95-41263. 240p. 1996. pap. 18.95 (*0-7185-1376-2*, Pub. by Cassell) LPC InBook.
Page, Carolyn. Troy Corner Poems. Zarucchi, Roy, ed. & illus. by. (Chapbook Ser.). 24p. (Orig.). 1994. pap. 5.00 (*1-879205-46-7*) Nightshade Pr.
Page, Carolyn, ed. see Chute, Robert M.
Page, Carolyn, ed. see Coulehan, Jack.
Page, Carolyn, jt. ed. see Holmes, Edward M.
Page, Carolyn, jt. ed. see Moose, Ruth.
Page, Carolyn, ed. see Silano, Martha.
Page, Carolyn, ed. see Tiger, Madeline.
Page, Carolyn, jt. ed. see Zarucchi, Roy.
Page, Carolyn, ed. & illus. see Abrons, Richard.
Page, Carolyn, ed. & illus. see Pies, Ronald M.
***Page, Carolyn W., ed.** Potato Eyes. (Illus.). 120p. 1999. pap. 9.95 (*1-879205-82-3*) Nightshade Pr.
Page, Charles H. Fifty Years in the Sociological Enterprise: A Lucky Journey. LC 82-7046. 288p. 1985. pap. 17.95 (*0-87023-490-0*) U of Mass Pr.
Page, Charles R., III. Jesus & the Land. LC 95-7415. 224p. (Orig.). 1995. pap. text 16.95 (*0-687-00544-2*) Abingdon.
Page, Charles R. & Volz, Carl. The Land & the Book: An Introduction to the World of the Bible. LC 92-43245. 288p. (Orig.). 1993. pap. 16.95 (*0-687-46289-4*) Abingdon.
Page, Cheryl A., jt. auth. see Cook, Sybilla A.
Page, Christina, ed. The Smart Girl's Guide to College: A Serious Book Written by Women in College to Help You Make the Perfect College Choice. LC 97-12833. 256p. 1997. pap. 12.00 (*0-374-52514-5*, Noonday) FS&G.
***Page, Christine R.** Beyond the Obvious: Bringing Intuition into Our Awakening Consciousness. 1998. pap. 21.95 (*0-85207-322-4*) C W Daniel.
Page, Christine R. Frontiers of Health: From Healing to Wholeness. 105p. 1992. pap. 19.95 (*0-85207-256-2*, Pub. by C W Daniel) Natl Bk Netwk.
***Page, Christine R.** Frontiers of Health: From Healing to Wholeness. 2000. reprint ed. pap. 29.95 (*0-85207-340-2*, Pub. by C W Daniel) Natl Bk Netwk.
Page, Christine R. Frontiers of Health from Healing to Wholeness. 256p. (Orig.). pap. 29.95 (*0-8464-4180-2*) Beekman Pubs.
— The Mirror of Existence: Stepping into Wholeness. (Illus.). 144p. 1996. pap. 14.50 (*0-85207-294-5*, Pub. by C W Daniel) Natl Bk Netwk.
***Page, Christine R. & Hagenbach, Keith.** Divine Healing of Mind & Body. 2000. pap., wbk. ed. 27.95 (*0-85207-333-X*) C W Daniel.
Page, Christopher. Command in the Royal Naval Division: A Military Biography of Brigadier General A. M. Asquith, DS. 224p. 1997. write for info. (*1-86227-048-1*, Pub. by Spellmnt Pubs) St Mut.
Page, Christopher. Discarding Images: Reflections on Music & Culture in Medieval France. LC 97-12911. (Illus.). 246p. 1997. pap. text 28.00 (*0-19-816679-6*) OUP.
— Music & Instruments of the Middle Ages: Studies on Text & Performance. LC 97-2605. (Variorum Collected Studies Ser.: Vol. 562). 352p. 1997. text 98.95 (*0-86078-623-4*, Pub. by Variorum) Ashgate Pub Co.
Page, Christopher, ed. Summa Musice: A Thirteenth-Century Manual for Singers. (Musical Texts & Monographs). (Illus.). 293p. (C). 1991. text 80.00 (*0-521-40420-7*) Cambridge U Pr.
Page, Clarence. Showing My Color: Impolite Essays on Race in America. 320p. 1997. pap. 14.00 (*0-06-092801-8*, Perennial) HarperTrade.
Page, Clarence, jt. auth. see McClain, Leanita.
Page, Clarence, ed. see McClain, Leanita.
***Page, Claudia & Ruiz, Susan.** The Guide to Medi-Cal Programs: A Description of Medi-Cal Programs, Aid Codes, & Eligibility Groups. unabridged ed. (Illus.). 42p. 1999. spiral bd. write for info. (*1-929008-17-1*) CA HlthCare Fnd.
Page, Clint & Cuff, Penelope. Negotiating for Amenities: Zoning & Management Tools That Build Livable Cities, Pt. II: Models & Resources. (Illus.). 80p. (Orig.). 1982. pap. 12.50 (*0-941182-06-1*) Partners Livable.
— The Public Sector Designs. LC 83-82147. (Illus.). 64p. (Orig.). 1984. pap. 12.00 (*0-941182-12-6*) Partners Livable.
Page, Clint, ed. see McNulty, Robert H., et al.
Page, Clive & Black, Judith, eds. Airways & Vascular Remodelling in Asthma & Cardiovascular Disease: Implications for Therapeutic Intervention. (Illus.). 189p. 1994. text 87.00 (*0-12-543540-1*) Acad Pr.
Page, Clive P. & Metzger, W. James, eds. Drugs & the Lung. LC 93-42148. (Advances in Clinical Pharmacology Ser.). (Illus.). 621p. 1994. reprint ed. pap. 192.60 (*0-608-07214-1*, 206743900009) Bks Demand.
Page, Clive P., et al. Integrated Pharmacology. 606p. 1997. pap. 49.95 (*0-7234-2556-6*, Pub. by Wolfe Pub) Mosby Inc.
Page, Collin F. & Kitching, John. Technical Aids to Teaching Higher Education. 3rd ed. 92p. 1981. pap. 32.00 (*0-900868-49-X*) OpUniv Pr.
Page, Curtis H. British Poets of the Nineteenth Century. 1027p. 1977. 46.95 (*0-8369-8246-0*) Ayer.
Page, Curtis W. & Selden, Charles J. Asking "Just Right" Business Questions: A Proven Process for Developing Leaders & Organizations. rev. ed. LC 94-76163. 200p. 1994. 21.95 (*1-885207-00-X*); pap. 14.95 (*1-885207-01-8*) MPOWER Pr.
Page, Curtis W., jt. auth. see Ends, Earl J.
Page, D., jt. ed. see Hirsch, J. G.
Page, D. E., ed. Observations of the Outer Heliosphere: Proceedings of the Symposium D2 of the COSPAR 29th Plenary Meeting Held in Washington, D. C., U. S. A., 28 August-5 September, 1992. (Advances in Space Research Ser.: Vol. 13). 312p. 1993. pap. 190.25 (*0-08-042208-X*, Pergamon Pr) Elsevier.
Page, D. E. & Marsden, R. G. The Heliosphere As Solar Minimum & Beyond. (Advances in Space Research Ser.: Vol. 19/6). 160p. 1997. pap. 110.00 (*0-08-043107-0*) Elsevier.
Page, D. E., jt. ed. see Antonucci, E.
Page, D. E., ed. see ESLAB-ESRIN Symposium Staff.
Page, D. E., jt. ed. see Grzedzielski, S.
***Page, D. L. & Anderson, T. J.** Diagnostic Histopathology of the Breast - 2. (Illus.). 400p. 1998. text. write for info. (*0-443-04758-8*) Church.
Page, Dave. Ship vs. Shore: Civil War Engagements Between Land & Sea. LC 94-15005. (Illus.). 320p. 1994. 22.95 (*1-55853-267-6*) Rutledge Hill Pr.
Page, Dave & Koblas, John J. F. Scott Fitzgerald in Minnesota: Toward the Summit. LC 96-34806. 1996. pap. 14.95 (*0-87839-107-X*) North Star.
Page, David. Prelude to Partition: The Indian Muslims & the Imperia; System of Control, 1920-32. 1982. 29.95 (*0-19-561303-1*) OUP.
Page, David, ed. Inductive Logic Programming: Proceedings of the 8th International Conference, ILP-98, Madison, Wisconsin, U. S. A., July 22-24, 1998. LC 98-27947. (Lecture Notes in Artificial Intelligence Ser.: Vol. 1446). viii, 301p. 1998. pap. 55.00 (*3-540-64738-4*) Spr-Verlag.
Page, David, jt. auth. see Shinn, Barbara.
Page, David, jt. auth. see Wilson, Keith.
Page, David A. & Chval, Kathryn. Maneuvers with Number Patterns. (Maneuvers with Math Ser.). (Illus.). 118p. (Orig.). 1994. teacher ed. 15.95 (*0-86651-935-1*) Seymour Pubns.

An Asterisk (*) at the beginning of an entry indicates that the title is appearing for the first time.

— Maneuvers with Number Patterns. (Maneuvers with Math Ser.). (Illus.). 116p. (Orig.). (J). (gr. 5-8). 1994. student ed. 5.50 (*0-86651-934-3*) Seymour Pubns.

Page, David L. & Anderson, Thomas J. Diagnostic Histopathology of the Breast. (Illus.). 362p. 1988. text 159.00 (*0-443-02240-2*) Church.

Page, David P. Theory & Practice of Teaching. LC 77-89216. (American Education: Its Men, Institutions, & Ideas. Series 1). 1970. reprint ed. 18.95 (*0-405-01455-4*) Ayer.

Page, David W. Body Trauma: A Writer's Guide to Wounds & Injuries. (Howdunit Ser.). (Illus.). 240p. 1996. pap. 16.99 (*0-89879-741-1*, Wrtrs Digest Bks) F & W Pubns Inc.

Page, Deanna, ed. see Lemons, Terry.

Page, Debra. Orcas Around Me: My Alaskan Summer. LC 95-52647. (Illus.). 40p. (J). (gr. 1-4). 1997. lib. bdg. 15.95 (*0-8075-6137-1*) A Whitman.

Page, Denys, ed. Medea. 258p. 1976. pap. text 24.00 (*0-19-872092-0*) OUP.

Page, Denys L. Folktales in Homer's Odyssey. LC 73-75056. (Carl Newell Jackson Lectures: 1972). 152p. reprint ed. pap. 47.20 (*0-608-10784-0*, 201768400007) Bks Demand.

— The Homeric Odyssey, 1954. LC 76-39798. (Mary Flexner Lectures Ser., 1954). 186p. 1982. reprint ed. lib. bdg. 71.50 (*0-8371-9308-7*, PAHO, Greenwood Pr) Greenwood.

— Sappho & Alcaeus. 350p. 1979. reprint ed. pap. text 36.00 (*0-19-814375-3*) OUP.

Page, Denys L., ed. Epigrammata Graeca: From the Beginning to the Garland of Phillip. (Oxford Classical Texts Ser.). 388p. 1976. text 42.00 (*0-19-814581-0*) OUP.

— Lyrica Graece Selecta. (Oxford Classical Texts Ser.). 276p. 1968. text 24.95 (*0-19-814567-5*) OUP.

Page, Denys L., ed. see Aeschylus.

***Page, Diamond Dallas.** Positively Page: The Diamond Dallas Page Journey. 2000. 28.95 (*0-9679922-0-6*) Pos Pubns MD.

Page, Diamond Dallas & Genta, Larry. Postively Page: The Diamond Dallas Page Journey. (Illus.). 480p. 27.95 (*1-880325-28-4*) Borderlnds NH.

***Page, Dianne.** Food Processors Properly Explained: With Recipes. 160p. 2000. pap. 6.95 (*0-7160-2063-7*, Pub. by Elliot RW Bks) Midpt Trade.

— Slow Cooking Properly Explained. 240p. 2000. pap. 6.95 (*0-7160-2047-5*, Pub. by Elliot RW Bks) Midpt Trade.

Page, Donald, jt. ed. see Hillmer, Norman.

Page, Dorothy. The National Council of Women: A Centennial History. (Illus.). 252p. 1997. pap. 29.95 (*1-86940-154-9*, Pub. by Auckland Univ) Paul & Co Pubs.

Page, Dorothy & Wiedman, Katie. Building Profitable Nutrition Practices. (Illus.). 350p. 1992. text 55.95 (*0-442-00914-3*, VNR) Wiley.

Page, E. S. & Wilson, Leslie B. Information Representation & Manipulation Using Pascal. LC 82-4505. (Cambridge Computer Science Texts Ser.: No. 15). (Illus.). 284p. 1983. pap. text 24.95 (*0-521-27096-0*) Cambridge U Pr.

Page, Earle C. Looking at Type. 3rd ed. LC 83-2028. (Illus.). 40p. 1997. pap. 5.75 (*0-935652-09-4*) Ctr Applications Psych.

— Una Mirada a los Tipos Psicologicos: Una Descripcion de las Preferencias Dadas Por el Indicador de Tipos Psicologicos Myers-Briggs (MBTI) Moody, Raymond A., tr. from ENG. LC 93-40958. (SPA., Illus.). 41p. 1993. pap. 5.75 (*0-935652-18-3*) Ctr Applications Psych.

Page, Edward. One Hundred One Timex-Sinclair 1000 ZX-81 Programming Tips & Tricks. 128p. (Orig.). (gr. 7-12). 1982. pap. 7.95 (*0-86668-020-9*) ARCsoft.

— Practical Timex-Sinclair Computer Programs for Beginners. 96p. 1983. 7.95 (*0-86668-027-6*) ARCsoft.

— Thirty-Seven Timex-Sinclair 1000 ZX-81 Computer Programs for Home, School & Office. (Illus.). 96p. (Orig.). 1982. pap. 8.95 (*0-86668-021-7*) ARCsoft.

— Timex-Sinclair Computer Games Programs. 96p. 1983. 7.95 (*0-86668-026-8*) ARCsoft.

Page, Edward & Van Treese, James B. Political Authority & Bureaucratic Power: A Comparative Analysis. LC 84-21895. 202p. 1985. pap. 62.70 (*0-608-05190-X*, 206572700001) Bks Demand.

Page, Edward C. Localism & Centralism in Europe: The Political & Legal Bases of Local Self-Government. (Comparative Politics Ser.). 200p. 1992. 59.00 (*0-19-827727-X*) OUP.

— People Who Run Europe. LC 96-32409. (Illus.). 188p. (C). 1997. text 60.00 (*0-19-828079-3*) OUP.

Page, Edward C. & Goldsmith, Michael J., eds. Central & Local Government Relations: A Comparative Analysis of West European Unitary States. (Modern Politics Ser.: Vol. 13). 184p. (C). 1987. text 45.00 (*0-8039-8071-X*) Sage.

***Page, Edward C. & Wright, Vincent, eds.** Bureaucratic Elites in Western European States: A Comparative Analysis of Top Officials. LC 99-36966. 304p. 2000. 65.00 (*0-19-829447-6*); write for info. (*0-19-829446-8*) OUP.

Page, Edward C., jt. ed. see Hayward, Jack.

Page, Elizabeth. The Tree of Liberty. 1000p. 1990. reprint ed. lib. bdg. 57.95 (*0-89966-658-2*) Buccaneer Bks.

Page, Elwin L. George Washington in New Hampshire. (Portsmouth Marine Society Ser.). (Illus.). 95p. 1990. reprint ed. 25.00 (*0-915819-15-5*, 16) Portsmouth Marine Soc.

Page, Emma. Every Second Thursday. large type ed. (Mystery Ser.). 304p. 1983. 27.99 (*0-7089-0922-1*) Ulverscroft.

— Final Moments. large type ed. 368p. 1988. 27.99 (*0-7089-1805-0*) Ulverscroft.

— In the Event of My Death. large type ed. 410p. 1996. 11.50 (*0-7505-0878-7*, Pub. by Mgna Lrg Print) Ulverscroft.

***Page, Emma.** Intent to Kill. large type ed. 352p. 1999. pap. 20.99 (*1-85389-931-3*, Dales) Ulverscroft.

Page, Emma. Murder Comes Calling. large type ed. (Magna Large Print Ser.). 363p. 1997. 27.99 (*0-7505-1081-1*) Ulverscroft.

— Scent of Death. large type ed. (Mystery Ser.). 352p. 1987. 27.99 (*0-7089-1579-5*) Ulverscroft.

— Scent of Death. 224p. 1989. reprint ed. mass mkt. 3.50 (*0-373-26012-1*) Harlequin Bks.

Page, Eugene R. George Colman, the Elder. LC 74-181965. reprint ed. 29.50 (*0-404-04857-9*) AMS Pr.

Page, Evelyn & Page, Tim. Party Punches. LC 86-202652. (Illus.). 190p. (Orig.). 1986. pap. 14.95 (*0-942557-00-X*) Page Pr & Assocs.

Page, Frank, jt. auth. see Smith, Billy K.

Page, Frederick, ed. see Byron, George Gordon.

Page, Frederick, ed. see Trollope, Anthony.

Page, G. F., et al, eds. Application of Neural Networks to Modelling & Control. LC 93-14878. 144p. 1993. mass mkt. 50.95 (*0-412-54760-0*) Chapman & Hall.

Page, G. William. Contaminated Sites & Environmental Cleanup: International Approaches to Prevention, Remediation, & Reuse. LC 96-29220. (Illus.). 212p. 1997. text 59.95 (*0-12-543580-0*) Morgan Kaufmann.

Page, G. William & Patton, Carl V. Quick Answers to Quantitative Problems: A Pocket Primer. (Illus.). 277p. (C). 1991. pap. text 39.95 (*0-12-543570-3*) Acad Pr.

Page, Gary S. Being the Parent You Want to Be: 12 Communication Skills for Effective Parenting. LC 98-45965. (Illus.). 368p. 1999. pap. 19.95 (*1-892334-07-0*, BK0668) Perf Lrn Systs.

***Page, Gary Screaton.** Being a Parent You Want to Be Facilitator Guide: 12 Communication Skills for Effective Parenting. 2000. write for info. (*1-892334-08-9*) Perf Lrn Systs.

Page, Geoff. Winter Vision. 200p. (Orig.). 1989. pap. 14.95 (*0-7022-2239-9*, Pub. by Univ Queensland Pr) Intl Spec Bk.

Page, Geoffrey. Shot Down in Flames: A World War II Fighter Pilot's Remarkable Tale of Survival. (Illus.). 224p. 1999. pap. 17.95 (*1-902304-10-1*, Pub. by Grub St) Seven Hills Bk.

Page, George. The Humble Poet. 1997. pap. write for info. (*1-57553-675-7*) Watermrk Pr.

Page, George. Inside the Animal Mind: A Groundbreaking Exploration of Animal Intelligence. LC 99-32431. 304p. 1999. 24.95 (*0-385-49291-X*) Doubleday.

***Page, George.** Inside the Animal Mind: A Groundbreaking Exploration of Animal Intelligence. 2000. reprint ed. pap. 14.00 (*0-7679-0559-8*) Broadway BDD.

Page, Geraldine. Midi: Music Technology Access for VIPs. large type ed. (Ulverscroft Large Print Ser.). 95p. 1996. pap. 27.50 (*0-7089-4999-1*) Ulverscroft.

Page, Gillian, et al. Journal Publishing. 419p. (C). 1997. text 59.95 (*0-521-44137-4*) Cambridge U Pr.

Page, Glen B. A Book of Hard Criticisms: Watching the America Show (versus) A Revisioning for an Alternative America in the Twenty-First Century. LC 90-85738. 368p. 1991. 22.00 (*0-9628845-0-2*) Canopus Pub.

Page, Gordon T. Deals on Wheels: How to Buy, Care for & Sell a Car: Complete Buyer's Guide & Expose of the Automotive Jungle. (Illus.). 304p. (Orig.). 1984. pap. 9.95 (*0-9607804-0-8*) Page Pub FL.

Page, Gregory A. The Diary of Judas Iscariot of the Gospel According to Judas. 246p. 1997. reprint ed. pap. 24.95 (*0-7661-0050-2*) Kessinger Pub.

Page, H. A. Thoreau: His Life & Aims. 1972. 59.95 (*0-8490-1205-8*) Gordon Pr.

— Thoreau: His Life & Aims. LC 72-3653. (American Literature Ser.: No. 49). 1972. reprint ed. lib. bdg. 75.00 (*0-8383-1585-2*) M S G Haskell Hse.

Page, Helen C. Stanford University Healthy Heart Cookbook & Life Plan: Over 200 Delicious Low-Fat Recipes. 1997. pap. 17.95 (*0-8118-1750-4*) Chronicle Bks.

Page, Hilary. Color Right from the Start: Progressive Lessons in Seeing & Understanding Color. LC 93-48927. (Illus.). 144p. 1994. 29.95 (*0-8230-0751-0*) Watsn-Guptill.

— Hilary Page's Guide to Watercolor Paints: A Completely Up-to-Date Guide to More Than 1000... LC 96-49038. (Illus.). 160p. 1996. pap. text 24.95 (*0-8230-2261-7*) Watsn-Guptill.

— Watercolor Right from the Start. LC 92-17440. (Illus.). 144p. 1992. 29.95 (*0-8230-5688-0*) Watsn-Guptill.

Page, Hugh R., Jr. Exploring New Paradigms in Biblical & Cognate Studies. LC 95-25242. (Mellen Biblical Press Ser.: No. 48). 116p. 1996. write for info. (*0-7734-2407-5*, Mellen Biblical Pr) E Mellen.

— Waves, Clouds, & Flames: Impressions from Journeys Past & Present. 31p. 1997. pap. 14.95 (*0-9650283-0-5*) Quiet Fire.

Page, Hugh Rowland, Jr. The Myth of Cosmic Rebellion: A Study of Its Reflexes in Ugaritic & Biblical Literature. (Vetus Testamentum, Supplements Ser.: Vol. 65). (Illus.). Xvi, 232p. 1996. text 100.00 (*90-04-10563-8*) Brill Academic Pubs.

Page, J. A. A Guide to the Qutb. Delhi. 1986. reprint ed. 85.00 (*81-85046-33-6*, Pub. by Scientific) St Mut.

— Moments of Delhi Vols. 1-4: Lasting Splendour of the Great Mughals & Others, 4 vols. 1997. 1725.00 (*81-7305-114-3*, Pub. by Print Hse) St Mut.

Page, J. K. Advances in European Solar Radiation Climatology. (C). 1986. 100.00 (*0-7855-4201-9*, Pub. by Interntl Solar Energy Soc) St Mut.

Page, J. K., ed. Prediction of Solar Radiation on Inclined Surfaces. 1986. text 209.50 (*90-277-2260-9*) Kluwer Academic.

Page, Jack. Checkpoints. 3rd ed. LC 97-11799. 300p. (C). 1997. pap. text 52.00 (*0-321-01214-3*) Addson-Wesley Educ.

***Page, Jack.** Checkpoints: Developing College English Skills. 4th ed. 368p. 2000. pap. 42.00 (*0-321-08014-9*) Longman.

Page, Jack. Checkpoints with Reading. LC 96-748. 360p. (C). 1997. pap. text 52.00 (*0-673-98153-3*) Addson-Wesley Educ.

***Page, Jake.** Cavern: A Novel. LC 99-50965. 2000. 24.95 (*0-8263-2226-3*) U of NM Pr.

Page, Jake. A Certain Malice. 1998. mass mkt. 6.99 (*0-345-40539-0*) Ballantine Pub Grp.

— The Smithsonian Guide to Natural America: The Southwest. (Illus.). 304p. 1995. pap. 19.95 (*0-679-76154-3*) Random.

— Smithsonian's New Zoo. LC 89-29626. (Illus.). 208p. 1990. 29.95 (*0-87474-734-1*) Smithsonian.

— Songs to Birds. (Illus.). 160p. 1993. pap. 12.95 (*1-56792-042-X*) Godine.

— Songs to Birds. (Illus.). 160p. 1993. 18.95 (*0-87923-957-3*) Godine.

— Zoo: The Modern Ark. (Illus.). 192p. 1990. 35.00 (*0-8160-2345-X*) Facts on File.

Page, Jake & Dale, Bruce. The American Southwest: Land of Challenge & Promise. LC 98-5493. 1998. 12.95 (*0-7922-7063-0*); write for info. (*0-7922-7067-3*) Natl Geog.

Page, Jake & Officer, Charles B. Tales of the Earth. LC 92-28320. (Illus.). 240p. 1993. text 30.00 (*0-19-507785-7*) OUP.

— Tales of the Earth: Paroxysms & Perturbations of the Blue Planet. (Illus.). 240p. 1994. reprint ed. pap. text 14.95 (*0-19-509048-9*) OUP.

Page, Jake & Page, Susanne. Field Guide to Southwest Indian Arts & Crafts. LC 97-39490. 1998. pap. 18.00 (*0-679-77027-5*) Random.

Page, Jake, jt. auth. see Leeming, David.

Page, Jake, jt. auth. see Officer, Charles.

Page, Jake, jt. auth. see Page, Susanne.

Page, James. Effective Company Command for Company Officers in the Professional Fire Service. 1996. pap. 10.00 (*0-87505-121-9*) Borden.

Page, James A. Foundations of College Math. 1994. teacher ed. 68.93 (*0-256-14945-3*, Irwn McGrw-H) McGrw-H Hghr Educ.

Page, James D., jt. auth. see Landis, Carney.

Page, James H. Foundations of College Math. LC 94-208955. 688p. (C). 1994. text 23.90 (*0-256-14567-9*, Irwn McGrw-H) McGrw-H Hghr Educ.

Page, James L. Love Spells for More Fulfilling & Intimate Relationships. 144p. (Orig.). 1992. pap. 14.95 (*0-572-01621-2*, Pub. by W Foulsham) Trans-Atl Phila.

Page, James O. The Magic of Three A. M. Griffiths, Keith, ed. LC 86-82551. 177p. 1986. text 14.95 (*0-936174-02-1*) Jems Comm.

Page, Jane A., jt. ed. see Pool, Harbison.

***Page, Jane M.** Reframing the Early Childhood Curriculum: Educational Imperatives for the Future. LC 00-36625. (Futures & Education Ser.). 2000. pap. write for info. (*0-415-19118-1*) Routledge.

***Page, Jason.** Athletics, Field: Pole Vault, Long Jump, Hammer, Javelin & Lots, Lots More. (Zeke's Olympic Pocket Guide Ser.). (Illus.). 32p. (YA). 2000. pap. 3.95 (*0-8225-5053-9*, Lerner Publctns) Lerner Pub.

— Athletics, Tracks: 100 Meters, 200 Meters, Relays, Hurdles & Lots, Lots More. (Zeke's Olympic Pocket Guide Ser.). (Illus.). 32p. (YA). (gr. 3 up). 2000. pap. 3.95 (*0-8225-5054-7*) Lerner Pub.

— Atlas. (Interfact Reference Ser.). (Illus.). (J). (gr. 2-7). 2000. spiral bd. 14.95 (*1-58728-471-5*) Two Can Pub.

— Ball Games: Soccer, Table Tennis, Handball, Hockey, Badmington & Lots, Lots More. (Zeke's Olympic Pocket Guide Ser.). (Illus.). 32p. (YA). 2000. pap. 3.95 (*0-8225-5057-1*, Lerner Publctns) Lerner Pub.

— Combat: Fencing, Judo, Wrestling, Boxing, Taekwondo & Lots, Lots More. (Zeke's Olympic Pocket Guide Ser.). (Illus.). 32p. (YA). 2000. pap. 3.95 (*0-8225-5055-5*, LernerSports) Lerner Pub.

— Gymnastics: The Balance Beam, Floor, Rings, Team Events & Lots, Lots More. (Zeke's Olympic Pocket Guide Ser.). (Illus.). 32p. (YA). 2000. pap. 3.95 (*0-8225-5052-0*, LernerSports) Lerner Pub.

— On the Water: Rowing, Yachting, Canoeing & Lots, Lots More. (Zeke's Olympic Pocket Guide Ser.). (Illus.). 32p. (YA). 2000. pap. 3.95 (*0-8225-5051-2*, LernerSports) Lerner Pub.

— Power & Precision: Cycling, Equestrian, Shooting & Lots, Lots More. (Zeke's Olympic Pocket Guide Ser.). (Illus.). 32p. (YA). (gr. 3 up). 2000. 3.95 (*0-8225-5050-4*, LernerSports) Lerner Pub.

— The Secret Side of You: A Fun Guide to Your Star Signs, Dreams, Lucky Numbers & More! (Illus.). 128p. (J). 1999. pap. 5.95 (*1-902618-21-1*, Pub. by Element Childrns) Penguin Putnam.

— Swimming: Sprints, Medleys, Diving, Water-Polo & Lots, Lots More. (Zeke's Olympic Pocket Guide Ser.). (Illus.). 32p. (YA). 2000. pap. 3.95 (*0-8225-5056-3*, LernerSports) Lerner Pub.

Page, Jason & Mitchell, Rob. Earth. (Interfact Reference Ser.). (Illus.). 48p. (J). (gr. 2-8). 1999. write for info. incl. cd-rom (*0-7166-9911-7*) World Bk.

***Page, Jason & Mitchell, Rob.** Space. (Interfact Reference Ser.). (Illus.). 48p. (J). (gr. 2-8). 1999. write for info. incl. cd-rom (*0-7166-9912-5*) World Bk.

Page, Jeanette, ed. A Country Diary. (Illus.). 160p. 1995. 22.95 (*1-85702-254-8*) Fourth Estate.

***Page, Jeanne M.** Hammered Dulcimer Chords. 64p. 1998. pap. 12.95 (*0-7866-2892-8*, 96675) Mel Bay.

***Page, Jennifer.** Enter Hermees. Caye, Leslie, ed. (Illus.). 36p. 2000. pap. write for info. (*0-9658996-5-9*) Positive Pr MA.

***Page, Jenson.** Soccer. rev. ed. (Sports Club Ser.). (Illus.). (J). 2000. 9.95 (*1-58728-001-9*); pap. 4.95 (*1-58728-003-5*) Two Can Pub.

Page, Jesse. The Black Bishop: Samuel Adjai Crowther. LC 79-100. (Illus.). 440p. 1979. reprint ed. lib. bdg. 69.50 (*0-8371-4610-0*, PBB&) Greenwood.

— David Brainerd, Vol. 2. 1979. pap. 7.99 (*0-88019-015-9*) Schmul Pub Co.

Page, Jim, et al, eds. The Best of JEMS: Timeless Essays from the First 15 Years. LC 96-75305. 1996. write for info. (*0-8151-7342-3*) Jems Comm.

Page, Jo A. Index to the Cherokee Freedmen Enrollment Cards of the Dawes Commission 1901-1906. LC 96-210325. (Orig.). 1996. pap. 21.00 (*0-7884-0495-4*, P021) Heritage Bk.

***Page, JoAnn Curls.** Extract of the Rejected Applications of the Guida Mille Rok of the Eastern Cherokee. 418p. 1999. pap. 60.00 (*0-7884-1315-5*, P022) Heritage Bk.

Page, Joanne. The River & the Lake. (Illus.). 88p. 1993. pap. 12.95 (*1-55082-090-7*, Pub. by Quarry Pr) LPC InBook.

Page, John. Cost Estimating Man-Hour Manual for Pipelines & Marine Structures. LC 76-40868. 336p. 1977. 75.00 (*0-87201-157-7*, 1157) Gulf Pub.

Page, John & Page, Anne. The Bunny System. 36p. (Orig.). (J). (ps-4). 1985. pap. 5.95 (*0-9613925-1-7*) Joane Pubns.

Page, John R. What Will Dr. Newman Do? John Henry Newman & Papal Infallibility, 1865-1875. LC 94-5538. (John Henry Newman & Papal Infallibility Ser.). 464p. 1994. pap. 24.95 (*0-8146-5027-9*, M Glazier) Liturgical Pr.

Page, John R., jt. auth. see Stillman, Richard J.

Page, John S. Conceptual Cost Estimating Manual. LC 83-22601. (Illus.). 352p. reprint ed. pap. 109.20 (*0-608-07940-5*, 206791300012) Bks Demand.

— Conceptual Cost Estimating Manual. 2nd ed. LC 95-52313. 352p. 1996. pap. 75.00 (*0-88415-267-7*, 5267) Gulf Pub.

— Estimator's Electrical Man-Hour Manual. 3rd ed. LC 99-18584. 448p. 1999. pap. 75.00 (*0-88415-228-6*) Gulf Pub.

— Estimator's Equipment Installation Man-Hour Manual. 3rd ed. LC 99-18582. 200p. 1999. pap. 75.00 (*0-88415-287-1*) Gulf Pub.

— Estimator's General Construction Man-Hour Manual. 2nd ed. LC 60-1386. (Estimator's Man-Hour Library). 274p. 1977. 75.00 (*0-87201-320-0*) Gulf Pub.

— Estimator's Man-Hour Manual on Heating, Air Conditioning, Ventilating & Plumbing. 2nd ed. LC 61-10176. (Estimator's Man-Hour Library). 218p. 1978. 75.00 (*0-87201-364-2*) Gulf Pub.

— Estimator's Piping Man-Hour Manual. 5th ed. LC 99-18583. 256p. 1999. pap. 75.00 (*0-88415-259-6*) Gulf Pub.

Page-Jones. Practical Guide to Object-Oriented Systems Development. (C). 1999. pap. text 53.33 (*0-13-619966-6*, Prentice Hall) P-H.

***Page-Jones, Meilir.** Fundamentals of Object-Oriented Design in UML. LC 99-45825. (Object Technology Ser.). 352p. 1999. pap. 39.95 (*0-201-69946-X*) Addison-Wesley.

Page-Jones, Meilir. Practical Guide to Structured Systems Design. 2nd ed. (Illus.). 384p. 1988. pap. 75.00 (*0-13-690769-5*) P-H.

— Practical Project Management: Restoring Quality to DP Projects & Systems. LC 85-71101. (Illus.). 248p. (Orig.). 1985. pap. 34.95 (*0-932633-00-5*) Dorset Hse Pub Co.

— What Every Programmer Should Know About Object-Oriented Design. LC 95-22067. (Illus.). 392p. 1995. text 44.95 (*0-932633-31-5*) Dorset Hse Pub Co.

Page, Joseph A. The Brazilians. LC 94-45812. 560p. 1995. 26.50 (*0-201-40913-5*) Addison-Wesley.

— The Brazilians. 560p. 1996. pap. 17.50 (*0-201-44191-8*) Addison-Wesley.

Page, Joseph A. & Elder, David A. The Law of Premises Liability. 2nd ed. 413p. 1988. 78.50 (*0-87084-684-1*) Anderson Pub Co.

Page, Joshua A. July Sunrise. LC 98-75535. 80p. 1999. 10.95 (*0-9668534-0-7*) Lighthse Memories.

Page, Judith W. Wordsworth & the Cultivation of Women. LC 93-34121. (C). 1994. 45.00 (*0-520-08493-4*, Pub. by U CA Pr) Cal Prin Full Svc.

Page, Julia V. Intelligence Officer in the Peninsula: Letters & Diaries of Major the Hon. Edward Charles Cocks 1786-1812. 256p. (C). 1991. 95.00 (*0-946771-71-5*, Pub. by Spellmnt Pubs) St Mut.

Page, Julie A., jt. ed. see Drewes, Jeanne M.

Page, Karen, jt. auth. see Dornenburg, Andrew.

Page, Kate & Gotkin, Janet, eds. Health Inform's Resource Guide to Alternative Health: An Annual Directory of Information Sources on Alternative & Complementary Therapies. 325p. 1997. pap. 79.95 (*0-9659104-0-7*) Infolink New York.

***Page, Katherine H.** Bon Voyage, Christie & Company. 1998. 14.00 (*0-380-97398-7*) HarpC.

***Page, Katherine Hall.** The Body in the Basement. large type ed. LC 99-20970. (Mystery Ser.). 1999. 24.95 (*1-57490-206-7*, Beeler LP Bks) T T Beeler.

Page, Katherine Hall. The Body in the Basement. (Faith Fairchild Mystery Ser.). 304p. 1995. reprint ed. mass mkt. 5.99 (*0-380-72339-5*, Avon Bks) Morrow Avon.

***Page, Katherine Hall.** The Body in the Belfry. 2000. 24.95 (*1-57490-277-6*) T T Beeler.

Page, Katherine Hall. The Body in the Belfry. 256p. 1991. reprint ed. mass mkt. 5.99 (*0-380-71328-4*, Avon Bks) Morrow Avon.

Page, Katherine Hall. The Body in the Big Apple. LC 99-33511. 256p. 1999. 22.00 (*0-688-15748-3*, Wm Morrow) Morrow Avon.

Page, Katherine Hall. The Body in the Bog. 272p. 1997. mass mkt. 5.99 (*0-380-72712-9*, Avon Bks) Morrow Avon.

— The Body in the Bog. large type ed. LC 97-22950. 1997. lib. bdg. 23.95 (*1-57490-087-0*, Beeler LP Bks) T T Beeler.

— The Body in the Bookcase. LC 98-36708. 272p. 1998. 22.00 (*0-688-15747-5*, Wm Morrow) Morrow Avon.

***Page, Katherine Hall.** The Body in the Bookcase. LC 98-36708. 272p. 1999. mass mkt. 6.50 (*0-380-73237-8*, Avon Bks) Morrow Avon.

Page, Katherine Hall. The Body in the Bouillon. 224p. 1992. mass mkt. 5.99 (*0-380-71896-0*, Avon Bks) Morrow Avon.

— The Body in the Cast. 272p. 1994. mass mkt. 5.99 (*0-380-72338-7*, Avon Bks) Morrow Avon.

***Page, Katherine Hall.** The Body in the Cast. large type ed. LC 99-51851. (Beeler Large Print Mystery Ser.). 1999. 24.95 (*1-57490-239-3*) T T Beeler.

Page, Katherine Hall. The Body in the Fjord. LC 97-24377. 272p. 1997. 22.00 (*0-688-14574-4*, Wm Morrow) Morrow Avon.

— The Body in the Fjord. 304p. 1998. mass mkt. 5.99 (*0-380-73129-0*, Avon Bks) Morrow Avon.

— The Body in the Fjord. large type ed. LC 98-6711. 1998. pap. 23.95 (*1-56895-562-6*, Wheeler) Wheeler Pub.

— The Body in the Kelp. 1992. mass mkt. 5.99 (*0-380-71329-2*, Avon Bks) Morrow Avon.

— The Body in the Kelp. large type ed. LC 98-44380. 246p. 1998. 24.95 (*1-57490-188-5*, Beeler LP Bks) T T Beeler.

— The Body in the Vestibule. 224p. 1993. mass mkt. 5.99 (*0-380-72079-5*, Avon Bks) Morrow Avon.

— Bon Voyage, Christie & Company. 160p. (J). (gr. 3-7). 1999. mass mkt. 3.99 (*0-380-78035-6*, Avon Bks) Morrow Avon.

— Christie & Company. 160p. (J). (gr. 3-7). 1997. pap. 3.99 (*0-380-78032-1*, Avon Bks) Morrow Avon.

Page, Katherine Hall. Christie & Company. 1997. 9.09 (*0-606-11205-7*, Pub. by Turtleback) Demco.

Page, Katherine Hall. Christie & Company down East. LC 96-31431. 160p. (J). 1997. mass mkt. 14.00 (*0-380-97396-0*, Avon Bks) Morrow Avon.

— Christie & Company down East. (Christie & Company Ser.). 1998. 9.09 (*0-606-13271-6*, Pub. by Turtleback) Demco.

— Christie & Company down East. 160p. (J). (gr. 3-7). 1998. reprint ed. pap. 3.99 (*0-380-78033-X*, Avon Bks) Morrow Avon.

— The Ghost of Winthrop: A Mystery Jigsaw Puzzle. (BePuzzled Ser.). (Orig.). (C). 1993. 20.00 (*0-922242-55-0*) Bepuzzled.

— In the Year of the Dragon. (Christie & Company Ser.). 160p. 1998. pap. 3.99 (*0-380-78034-8*, Avon Bks) Morrow Avon.

Page, Ken. The Way It Works. 104p. 1997. pap. 5.95 (*0-9649703-6-8*) Clr Light Arts.

Page, Ken & Hemingway, Simon P. The Traveler & the End of Time: The Secret Life of Ken Page. Page, Mary D., ed. (The Traveler Ser.). 195p. (Orig.). 1996. pap. text 11.95 (*0-9649703-1-7*) Clr Light Arts.

Page, Kirby, jt. auth. see Eddy, George S.

Page, Lafern. Menopause & Emotions: Making Sense of Your Feelings When Your Feelings Make No Sense. Vol. 1. 256p. 1996. pap. 19.95 (*0-9697874-0-5*) Primavera.

Page, Lawrence M. The Genera & Subgenera of Darters: (Percidae, Etheostomatini) (Occasional Papers: No. 90). 69p. 1981. 1.00 (*0-317-04830-9*) U KS Nat Hist Mus.

— Redescription of Etheostoma Australe & a Key for the Identification of Mexican Etheostoma (Percidae) (Occasional Papers: No. 89). 10p. 1981. 1.00 (*0-317-04828-7*) U KS Nat Hist Mus.

Page, Lawrence M. & Braasch, Marvin E. Systematic Studies of Darters of the Subgenus Catonotus (Percidae), with the Description of a New Species from the Lower Cumberland & Tennessee River Systems. (Occasional Papers: No. 60). 18p. 1976. pap. 1.00 (*0-686-79828-7*) U KS Nat Hist Mus.

— Systematic Studies of Darters of the Subgenus Catonotus with the Description of a New Species from the Duck River System. (Occasional Papers: No. 63). 18p. 1977. pap. 1.00 (*0-686-79827-9*) U KS Nat Hist Mus.

Page, Lawrence M. & Burr, Brooks M. Three New Species of Darters (Percidae, Etheostoma) of the Subgenus Nanostoma from Kentucky & Tennessee. (Occasional Papers: No. 101). (Illus.). 20p. 1982. 1.00 (*0-317-04835-X*) U KS Nat Hist Mus.

Page, Lawrence M., jt. auth. see Braasch, Marvin E.

Page, Lawrence M., jt. ed. see Lingquist, David G.

Page, Leigh. The Emission Theory of Electromagnetism. (Connecticut Academy of Arts & Sciences Ser., Trans.: Vol. 26). 1924. pap. 79.50 (*0-685-22821-5*) Elliots Bks.

— The Principle of General Relativity & Einstein's Theory of Gravitation. (Connecticut Academy of Arts & Sciences Ser., Trans.: Vol. 23). 1920. pap. 49.50 (*0-685-22830-4*) Elliots Bks.

Page, Lesley, ed. Effective Group Practice in Midwifery. (Illus.). 224p. 1994. pap. 24.95 (*0-632-03825-X*, Pub. by Blckwll Scitfc UK) Blackwell Sci.

Page, Levon B., jt. auth. see Paur, Sandra O.

Page, Lincoln R. Contributions to the Stratigraphy of New England. LC 76-9220. (Geological Society of America Ser.: Vol. 148). (Illus.). 465p. 1976. reprint ed. pap. 144.20 (*0-608-07705-4*, 206779500001) Bks Demand.

— Contributions to the Stratigraphy of New England: Supplement. LC 76-9220. (Geological Society of America Ser.: Vol. 148). (Illus.). 212p. 1976. reprint ed. pap. 65.80 (*0-608-07706-2*, 206779500002) Bks Demand.

Page, Linda. Detoxification: All You Need to Know to Recharge, Renew & Rejuvenate Your Body, Mind & Spirit. (Illus.). 264p. 1999. pap. 21.95 (*1-884334-54-7*) Hlthy Healing.

***Page, Linda.** Healthy Healing: A Guide to Self-Healing for Everyone. 11th ed. (Illus.). 576p. 2000. pap. 32.95 (*1-884334-89-X*, Pub. by Hlthy Healing) Words Distrib.

— Healthy Healing: A Guide to Self-Healing for Everyone. 11th rev. ed. (Illus.). 576p. 2000. spiral bd. 35.95 (*1-884334-88-1*) Hlthy Healing.

— Quiet Moments for Busy Moms. 200p. 2000. pap. write for info. (*1-56955-196-0*) Servant.

Page, Linda. Stress & Energy: Reduce Stress-Increase Energy. 1999. pap. text 9.95 (*1-884334-67-9*) Hlthy Healing.

Page, Linda G. & Smith, Hilton, eds. The Foxfire Book of Appalachian Toys & Games. LC 93-9660. (Illus.). xx, 204p. 1993. reprint ed. pap. 17.95 (*0-8078-4425-X*) U of NC Pr.

Page, Linda G. & Wigginton, Eliot, eds. Aunt Arie: A Foxfire Portrait. LC 91-50882. (Illus.). xxxii, 196p. (C). 1992. reprint ed. 15.95 (*0-8078-4377-6*) U of NC Pr.

— The Foxfire Book of Appalachian Cookery. LC 92-53627. xxii, 330p. 1992. reprint ed. pap. 19.95 (*0-8078-4395-4*) U of NC Pr.

Page, Linda M. Quiet Moments for Teachers. LC 98-17019. 220p. 1998. pap. 9.99 (*1-56955-063-8*, Vine Bks) Servant.

Page, Linda M. & Johnsey, Betty Z., eds. Frantic Elegance: Recipes from Clock Conscious Cooks. (Illus.). 283p. (Orig.). 1989. pap. 13.50 (*0-9623309-0-6*) Arendell Parrott.

Page, Linda R. Boosting Immunity with Power Plants. 2nd rev. ed. (Healthy Healing Library: Vol. 9). (Illus.). 32p. (Orig.). 1996. pap. 3.50 (*1-884334-34-2*) Hlthy Healing.

***Page, Linda R.** Cancer: Can Alternative Therapies Really Help? 2nd rev. ed. (Dr. Linda Page's Guides: Vol. 12). 96p. 1998. per. 8.95 (*1-884334-36-9*) Hlthy Healing.

Page, Linda R. Colds, Flu & You: Building Optimum Immunity. 3rd rev. ed. (Healthy Healing Library). (Illus.). 32p. 1996. pap. 3.50 (*1-884334-47-4*) Hlthy Healing.

— Cooking for Healthy Healing: Diets Programs & Recipes for Alternative Healing. 2nd ed. (Illus.). 720p. 1996. reprint ed. pap. 29.95 (*1-884334-56-3*) Hlthy Healing.

— Fatigue Syndromes & Immune Disorders: Fibromyalgia, Candida Albicans & More. expanded ed. (Healthy Healing Library: Vol. 15). (Illus.). 48p. 1997. pap. 3.95 (*1-884334-14-8*) Hlthy Healing.

— Healthy Healing: A Guide to Self-Healing for Everyone. 10th rev. ed. (Illus.). 480p. 1997. pap. 28.95 (*1-884334-85-7*) Hlthy Healing.

— How to Be Your Own Herbal Pharmacist: Herbal Traditions, Expert Formulations. 2nd rev. ed. (Illus.). 264p. 1998. pap. 18.95 (*1-884334-78-4*) Hlthy Healing.

— Menopause & Osteoporosis: Taking Control of Your Life Change. 6th rev. ed. (Dr. Linda Page's Guides: Vol. 2). (Illus.). 64p. 1997. per. 5.95 (*1-884334-90-3*) Hlthy Healing.

— Renewing Female Balance: PMS, Breast, Uterine Fibroids, Ovarian Cysts, Endometriosis, Yeast Infections & More. 4th expanded ed. (Library Ser.). (Illus.). 48p. 1997. per. 4.50 (*1-884334-64-4*) Hlthy Healing.

— Renewing Male Health & Energy with Herbs. 2nd rev. ed. (Healthy Healing Library). (Illus.). 32p. 1995. pap. 3.50 (*1-884334-30-X*) Hlthy Healing.

— Revealing the Secrets of Anti-Aging: Ageless Vitality. (Healthy Healing Library: Vol. 13). (Illus.). 32p. (Orig.). 1996. pap. 3.50 (*1-884334-13-X*) Hlthy Healing.

— Sexuality: Enhancing Your Body Chemistry. (Dr. Linda Page's Guides: Vol. 16). (Illus.). 96p. 1998. pap. 8.95 (*1-884334-15-6*) Hlthy Healing.

Page, Lorna. Doctor's Prescription. large type ed. (Linford Romance Library). 288p. 1996. pap. 16.99 (*0-7089-7922-X*) Ulverscroft.

***Page, Lorna.** Nurse in Conflict. large type ed. 336p. 1999. pap. 20.99 (*1-85389-940-2*, Dales) Ulverscroft.

— The Nurse Investigates. large type ed. 288p. 2000. pap. 20.99 (*1-85389-994-1*, Dales) Ulverscroft.

Page, Lot B., jt. ed. see Horan, Michael J.

Page, Louise. Diplomatic Wives. (Methuen Modern Plays Ser.). 90p. (Orig.). (C). 1989. pap. write for info. (*0-413-61430-1*, A0388, Methuen Drama) Methn.

— Page: Plays One. (Methuen World Dramatists Ser.). 324p. (Orig.). (C). 1990. pap. 13.95 (*0-413-64500-2*, A0498, Methuen Drama) Methn.

— Real Estate. (Methuen New Theatrescripts Ser.). 39p. (Orig.). (C). 1988. pap. write for info. (*0-413-57950-6*, A0233, Methuen Drama) Methn.

— Salonika. (Methuen New Theatrescripts Ser.). 35p. (C). 1988. pap. write for info. (*0-413-52180-X*, A0252, Methuen Drama) Methn.

Page, Lucius R. The History of Hardwick, Mass., with a Genealogical Register. 555p. 1989. reprint ed. lib. bdg. 57.50 (*0-8328-0830-X*, MA0187) Higginson Bk Co.

Page, Luke J. Page: Genealogical Registers of Ancestors & Descendants of Lemuel Page & Polly Paige, Peter Joslin & Sarah Kidder, with Brief Accounts of Them & Their Ancestors. (Illus.). 155p. 1994. reprint ed. pap. 25.00 (*0-685-75322-0*); reprint ed. lib. bdg. 35.00 (*0-685-75321-2*) Higginson Bk Co.

Page, Lynda. Evie. large type ed. 1995. 27.99 (*0-7505-0720-9*, Pub. by Mgna Lrg Print) Ulverscroft.

— Just by Chance. large type ed. (Magna Large Print Ser.). 589p. 1998. 29.99 (*0-7505-1150-8*, Pub. by Mgna Lrg Print) Ulverscroft.

Page, M. I., ed. The Chemistry of Enzyme Action. (New Comprehensive Biochemistry Ser.: Vol. 6). 568p. 1984. 167.50 (*0-444-80504-4*, I-017-84) Elsevier.

Page, Malcolm. File on Frayn. 96p. 1994. pap. 13.95 (*0-413-65310-2*, A0700, Methuen Drama) Methn.

— File on Pinter. (Methuen Writer-Files Ser.). 110p. (C). 1993. pap. 14.95 (*0-413-53620-3*, A0677, Methuen Drama) Methn.

Page, Malcolm, compiled by. Arden on File. (Methuen Writer-Files Ser.). 96p. (C). 1988. pap. write for info. (*0-413-56280-8*, A0011, Methuen Drama) Methn.

Page, Malcolm & Morgan, Margery, eds. File on Shaw. (Methuen Writer-Files Ser.). 124p. (Orig.). (C). 1989. pap. write for info. (*0-413-15280-4*, A0102, Methuen Drama) Methn.

Page, Malcolm & Trussler, Simon. File on Hare. (Methuen Writer-Files Ser.). 87p. (C). 1988. pap. write for info. (*0-413-15620-6*, A0095, Methuen Drama) Methn.

Page, Malcolm & Trussler, Simon, eds. File on Osborne. (Methuen Writer-Files Ser.). 96p. (C). 1988. pap. 9.95 (*0-413-14460-7*, A0098, Methuen Drama) Methn.

Page, Malcolm, jt. ed. see Trussler, Simon.

Page, Margot. Just Horses: Living with Horses in America. LC 98-30022. (Just Ser.). (Illus.). 144p. 1998. 35.00 (*1-57223-137-8*, 1378) Willow Creek Pr.

***Page, Margot.** Just Horses: Living with Horses in America. LC 99-16540. (Half-Pint Ser.). (Illus.). 96p. 1999. 12.95 (*1-57223-285-4*, 2854) Willow Creek Pr.

Page, Margot. Little Rivers: Tales of a Woman Angler. (Illus.). 144p. 1995. 16.95 (*1-55821-367-8*) Lyons Pr.

***Page, Margot & Fersen, Paul.** The Art of Fly Fishing. 2000. 19.98 (*0-7624-0846-4*, Courage) Running Pr.

Page, Margot, jt. auth. see Bort, Mary H.

Page, Marilyn L., jt. auth. see Marlowe, Bruce A.

***Page, Marion.** Dirty Mary No More. large type ed. LC 97-69264. 176p. (J). (gr. 5-7). 1999. pap. 10.95 (*0-943864-96-8*) Davenport.

Page, Marion R. & Symonds, David. Ancestors of Charles A. Stymus & His Wife Ella C. Smith: Orleans County New York, Back to New York, New Jersey, New England, 1620-1989. LC 89-61922. (Illus.). 104p. 1989. 20.00 (*0-9623355-0-9*) M R Page.

Page, Martin. The Gardener's Guide to Growing Peonies. LC 97-13756. (Gardener's Guide Ser.). (Illus.). 160p. 1997. 29.95 (*0-88192-408-3*) Timber.

Page, Mary, jt. ed. see Guthrie, Peter.

Page, Mary D., jt. auth. see Rogers, Daniel L.

Page, Mary D., ed. see Page, Ken & Hemingway, Simon P.

***Page, Mary S. & Metzger, Larry.** Voices & Masks: The Experience of Nineteenth Century Mill Girls & Enslaved Women from Primary Sources. 223p. (YA). (gr. 10-12). 2000. 12.67 (*1-877653-67-5*) Wayside Pub.

Page, Max. Creative Destruction Manhattan. 1997. pap. 18.95 (*0-226-64469-3*) U Ch Pr.

— The Creative Destruction of Manhattan, 1900-1940. LC 99-22544. (Historical Studies of Urban America). 304p. 2000. 27.50 (*0-226-64468-5*) U Ch Pr.

Page, Melvin E. Chiwaya War: Malawians in World War I. 296p. 1999. pap. 65.00 (*0-8133-0735-X*) Westview.

— Your Body Is Your Best Doctor. Orig. Title: Health Versus Disease. 236p. 1991. reprint ed. pap. 5.95 (*0-87983-540-0*, Keats Publng) NTC Contemp Pub Co.

Page, Melvin E., jt. auth. see Woods, Anthony.

Page, Michael. The Power of Ch'i: An Introduction to Chinese Mysticism & Philosophy. (Illus.). 128p. (Orig.). 1988. pap. 10.00 (*0-85030-764-3*, Pub. by Aqrn Pr) Harper SF.

Page, Michael, jt. auth. see Ingpen, Robert.

Page, Michael J. & Scheinman, Andrew. The Romancing of Rome. LC 94-75890. xiii, 34p. 1994. pap. write for info. (*1-883015-03-0*) Krannert Art.

Page, Michael V. Prisons, Peace, & Terrorism: Penal Policy in the Reduction of Political Violence in Northern Ireland, Italy, & the Spanish Basque Country, 1968-1997. LC 98-23859. 1998. text 65.00 (*0-312-21655-6*) St Martin.

Page, Micheal I. Bio Organic Mechanisms P. (C). 1996. pap. 44.06 (*0-582-07484-3*, Pub. by Addison-Wesley) Longman.

Page, Monte M., ed. see Nebraska Symposium on Motivation Staff.

Page, Myra. Daughter of the Hills: A Woman's Part in the Coal Miners' Struggles. LC 86-9866. (Novels of the Thirties Ser.). 304p. 1983. reprint ed. pap. 8.95 (*0-935312-59-5*) Feminist Pr.

— Moscow Yankee. LC 95-2992. (Radical Novel Reconsidered Ser.). 320p. 1995. 15.95 (*0-252-06499-2*) U of Ill Pr.

Page, Neil, intro. Dynamic Loading in Manufacturing & Service. (National Conference Publication Ser.: No. 93-1). (Illus.). 254p. (Orig.). 1993. pap. 96.00 (*0-85825-571-5*, Pub. by Inst Engrs Aust-EA Bks) Accents Pubns.

***Page, Nick.** Keep It Simple. 1999. pap. 7.95 (*0-00-274023-0*, Pub. by HarpC) Trafalgar.

Page, Nick. Music As a Way of Knowing. (Strategies for Teaching & Learning Ser.). 80p. (C). 1996. reprint ed. pap. text 15.00 (*1-57110-052-0*) Stenhse Pubs.

— Sing & Shine On! The Classroom Teacher's Guide to Multicultural Song Leading. LC 95-12279. (Illus.). 177p. 1995. pap. text 21.00 (*0-435-08673-1*, 08673) Heinemann.

***Page, Nick.** The Tabloid Bible. LC 99-27165. 160p. 1999. pap. 15.95 (*0-664-25843-3*) Westminster John Knox.

— Tabloid Shakespeare: The Bard. 1999. pap. 17.95 (*0-00-274053-2*, Pub. by HarpC) Trafalgar.

Page, Norman. Auden & Isherwood: The Berlin Years. LC 97-35010. 232p. 1998. text 29.95 (*0-312-21173-2*) St Martin.

***Page, Norman.** Auden & Isherwood: The Berlin Years. 232p. 2000. pap. 16.95 (*0-312-22712-4*) St Martin.

Page, Norman. Bleak House: A Novel of Connections. Lecker, Robert, ed. (Twayne's Masterwork Studies: No. 42). 1990. 23.95 (*0-8057-8082-3*, 455, Twyne); per. 13.95 (*0-8057-8128-5*, Twyne) Mac Lib Ref.

— A Byron Chronology. 144p. 1988. 40.00 (*0-8161-8952-8*, Hall Reference) Macmillan.

— A Dickens Chronology. 144p. 1988. 40.00 (*0-8161-8949-8*, Hall Reference) Macmillan.

— A Dr. Johnson Chronology. 140p. 1990. 40.00 (*0-8161-9091-7*, Hall Reference) Macmillan.

— E. M. Forster. (Modern Novelists Ser.). 143p. 1993. text 12.95 (*0-333-40695-8*, Pub. by Macmillan) St Martin.

— An Evelyn Waugh Chronology. LC 96-53540. x, 210 p. 1997. text 49.95 (*0-312-17417-9*) St Martin.

— The Language of Jane Austen, Vol. 13. LC 74-190473. (Language & Style Series, Fourteen Ser.). viii, 208p. 1972. write for info. (*0-631-08280-8*) Blackwell Pubs.

— An Oscar Wilde Chronology. (Author Chronologies Ser.). 128p. 1991. 40.00 (*0-8161-7298-6*, Hall Reference) Macmillan.

Page, Norman. Speech in the English Novel. LC 74-166355. x, 172 p. 1973. write for info. (*0-582-55036-X*) Longman.

Page, Norman. Speech in the English Novel. rev. ed. LC 87-19718. 208p. (C). 1988. pap. 17.50 (*0-391-03563-0*) Humanities.

— Tennyson: An Illustrated Life. (Illus.). 192p. 1993. 30.00 (*1-56131-060-3*, NAB) I R Dee.

***Page, Norman, ed.** Charles Dickens Family History, 5 vols., set. (Illus.). 1500p. (C). 2000. text 745.00 (*0-415-22233-8*) Routledge.

Page, Norman, ed. Dr. Johnson: Interviews & Recollections. LC 86-3472. 256p. 1986. 53.00 (*0-389-20628-8*, N8186) B&N Imports.

— Nabokov: The Critical Heritage. (Critical Heritage Ser.). 400p. 1982. 69.50 (*0-7100-9223-7*, Routledge Thoemms) Routledge.

***Page, Norman, ed.** Oxford Reader's Companion to Hardy. (Illus.). 448p. 2000. 49.95 (*0-19-860074-7*) OUP.

Page, Norman, ed. Tennyson: Interviews & Recollections. (Interviews & Recollections Ser.). 218p. 1983. 44.00 (*0-389-20066-2*, N6836) B&N Imports.

— Vladimir Nabokov. (Critical Heritage Ser.). 264p. (C). 1997. 125.00 (*0-415-15916-4*) Routledge.

— Wilkie Collins: The Critical Heritage. (Critical Heritage Ser.). 1974. 69.50 (*0-7100-7843-9*, Routledge Thoemms) Routledge.

Page, Norman, jt. auth. see Hardy, Thomas.

Page, Norman, ed. see Braddon, Mary Elizabeth.

Page, Norman, ed. see Brown, Richard.

Page, Norman, ed. see Collins, Wilkie.

Page, Norman, ed. see Dickens, Charles.

Page, Norman, ed. see Hardy, Thomas.

Page, Norman, ed. see Tennyson, Alfred Lord.

Page, Norman, ed. see Wilde, Oscar.

Page, Norman, ed. & intro. see Collins, Wilkie.

Page, Norman, ed. & intro. see Thomas, Julian.

Page, O. J. History of Massac County, Ill. with Life Sketches & Portraits. (Illus.). 383p. 1997. reprint ed. lib. bdg. 44.50 (*0-8328-5767-X*) Higginson Bk Co.

Page, P., ed. Organosulphur Chemistry: Synthetic Aspects. (Illus.). 277p. 1995. text 87.00 (*0-12-543560-6*) Acad Pr.

***Page, P. C. B., et al, eds.** Organosulfur Chemistry I. (Topics in Current Chemistry Ser.: Vol. 204). (Illus.). 210p. 1999. 135.00 (*3-540-65787-8*) Spr-Verlag.

— Organosulfur Chemistry II. (Topics in Current Chemistry Ser.: Vol. 205). (Illus.). 200p. 1999. 149.00 (*3-540-65729-0*) Spr-Verlag.

Page, P. K. The Hidden Room: Collected Poems. LC 98-113870. 224p. 1997. pap. write for info. (*0-88984-190-X*) Porcup Quill.

— The Hidden Room: Collected Poems, Vol. 2. LC 98-113870. 224p. 1997. pap. write for info. (*0-88984-193-4*) Porcup Quill.

— Hologram: A Book of Glosas. LC 94-225152. 72p. 1994. pap. 11.95 (*0-919626-72-6*, Pub. by Brick Bks) Genl Dist Srvs.

— Hologram: A Book of Glosas. large type ed. 72p. 1995. pap. 14.00 (*0-919626-80-7*, Pub. by Brick Bks) Genl Dist Srvs.

— The Travelling Musicians. unabridged ed. (Illus.). 32p. (J). (gr. k-2). 1991. 12.95 (*1-55074-039-3*, Pub. by Kids Can Pr) Genl Dist Srvs.

Page, Parker. Getting Along: A Fun-Filled Set of Stories, Songs & Activities to Help Kids Work & Play Together. LC 88-71899. (Illus.). 64p. (J). (ps-5). 1989. 18.95 incl. audio (*0-929831-00-4*) Childrens TV Resource.

Page, Parker, et al. Getting along Complete Kit. (J). (gr. k-4). 1991. 120.95 (*0-88671-407-9*, 4670) Am Guidance.

— Getting along Teachers Guide. (Orig.). 1991. pap. 11.95 (*0-88671-408-7*, 4671) Am Guidance.

Page, Pat. Cowbells & Courage. Johnson, Joy, ed. (Illus.). 24p. 1993. pap. 3.25 (*1-56123-067-7*) Centering Corp.

Page, Patrick & Goshman, Albert. Magic by Gosh: The Life Times of Albert Goshman. Diamond, Kathy, ed. LC 85-90956. (Illus.). 160p. 1985. 49.95 (*0-318-19317-5*) Magic By Gosh.

Page, Patty, jt. auth. see Campbell, Caroline.

Page, Paul. Mantras for the Season. 1998. pap. 16.95 (*0-937690-44-9*, 7194) Wrld Lib Pubns.

Page, Penny B. Children of Alcoholics: A Sourcebook. LC 91-19611. 270p. 1991. text 15.00 (*0-8240-3045-1*, 461) Garland.

Page, Philip. Dangerous Freedom: Fusion & Fragmentation in Toni Morrison's Novels. LC 95-44261. 256p. 1996. 45.00 (*0-87805-860-5*); pap. 17.50 (*0-87805-861-3*) U Pr of Miss.

— Reclaiming Community in Contemporary African-American Fiction. LC 98-39517. 256p. 1999. pap. 18.00 (*1-57806-123-7*) U Pr of Miss.

— Reclaiming Community in Contemporary African-American Fiction. LC 98-39517. 256p. 1999. 45.00 (*1-57806-122-9*) U Pr of Miss.

P

An Asterisk (*) at the beginning of an entry indicates that the title is appearing for the first time.

Page, Philip, ed. Organosulfur Chemistry Vol. 2: Synthetic & Stereochemical Aspects. (Organosulfur Chemistry Ser.: Vol. 2). (Illus.). 328p. 1997. text 135.00 (*0-12-543562-2*) Morgan Kaufmann.

Page, Priscilla. A Mallorcan Affair. large type ed. (Linford Romance Library). 256p. 1993. pap. 16.99 (*0-7089-7472-4*, Linford) Ulverscroft.

***Page, Priscilla.** The Surgeon's Daughter. large type ed. 256p. 1999. pap. 20.99 (*1-85389-939-9*, Dales) Ulverscroft.

Page, R. Good News for Landlords & Tenants. (Illus.). 184p. (Orig.). 1982. pap. 12.95 (*0-9609672-0-6*) Jeanies Classics.

— Man & Machines. 1975. pap. 3.55 (*0-08-016889-2*, Pergamon Pr) Elsevier.

Page, R. C. & Schroeder, H. E. Periodontitis in Man & Other Animals. (Illus.). x, 330p. 1982. 129.75 (*3-8055-2479-X*) S Karger.

Page, R. I. Chronicles of the Vikings: Records, Memorials & Myths. 240p. 1996. text 50.00 (*0-8020-0803-8*); pap. text 17.95 (*0-8020-7165-1*) U of Toronto Pr.

***Page, R. I.** An Introduction to English Runes. 2nd ed. LC 99-40062. (Illus.). 256p. 2000. 55.00 (*0-85115-768-8*, Suffolk Records Soc) Boydell & Brewer.

Page, R. I. Matthew Parker & His Books: Sandars Lectures in Bibliography Delivered on 14, 16, & 18 May 1990 at the University of Cambridge. LC 93-1097. (Illus.). (C). 1990. boxed set 40.00 (*1-879288-20-6*) Medieval Inst.

— Norse Myths. (Legendary Past Ser.). (Illus.). 80p. 1991. pap. 12.95 (*0-292-75546-5*) U of Tex Pr.

— Runes. (Reading the Past Ser.: Vol. 4). 64p. 1987. pap. 13.95 (*0-520-06114-4*, Pub. by U CA Pr) Cal Prin Full Svc.

— Runes & Runic Inscriptions: Collected Essays on Anglo-Saxon & Viking Runes. LC 98-150013. (Illus.). 360p. 1999. pap. 45.00 (*0-85115-599-5*, Boydell Pr) Boydell & Brewer.

— Runes & Runic Inscriptions: Collected Essays on Anglo-Saxon & Viking Runes. (Illus.). 360p. 1998. reprint ed. 90.00 (*0-85115-387-9*, Boydell Pr) Boydell & Brewer.

Page, Ralph. An Elegant Collection of Contras & Squares. LC 84-10687. (Orig.). 1984. pap. 5.00 (*0-915213-00-1*) L Shaw Found.

— Heritage Dances of Early America. 64p. 1976. pap. 6.00 (*0-915213-02-8*) L Shaw Found.

Page, Ralph, jt. auth. see Senese, Guy.

Page, Randy & Page, Tana. Fostering Emotional Well-Being in the Classroom. (Health Science Ser.). 304p. (C). 1993. pap. text 38.75 (*0-86720-753-1*) Jones & Bartlett.

Page, Randy, et al. Basic Epidemilgcl Method & Biostat. (Life Science Ser.). 448p. (C). 1995. pap. text 45.00 (*0-86720-869-4*) Jones & Bartlett.

— Comprehensive School Health Education: Totally Awesome Strategies for Teaching Health. 2nd ed. Turpie, Ann & DeVillers, Julie, eds. (Illus.). 835p. (C). 1995. pap. text 55.00 (*1-886693-09-9*) Everyday Learn.

— Drugs, Alcohol, & Tobacco: Totally Awesome Teaching Strategies. 2nd rev. ed. Baker, Mary & Turpie, Ann, eds. LC 94-76120. (Illus.). 594p. (Orig.). (C). 1994. pap. text 55.00 (*0-9630009-5-0*) Everyday Learn.

— Violence Prevention: Awesome Me & Violence-Free. DeVillers, Julie, ed. LC 95-95035. (Illus.). 157p. (J). (gr. 6-8). 1995. pap. text 15.00 (*0-9630009-7-7*) Everyday Learn.

— Violence Prevention: Special Me & Violence-Free. DeVillers, Julie, ed. LC 95-95033. (Illus.). 80p. (Orig.). (J). (gr. k-2). 1995. pap. 12.00 (*0-9630009-9-3*) Everyday Learn.

— Violence Prevention: Super Cool & Violence-Free. DeVillers, Julie, ed. LC 95-95034. (Illus.). 80p. (Orig.). (J). (gr. 3-5). 1995. pap. 14.00 (*0-9630009-8-5*) Everyday Learn.

***Page, Randy M. & Page, Tana S.** Fostering Emotional Well-Being in the Classroom. 2nd ed. LC 99-42856. 336p. 2000. write for info. (*0-7637-1264-7*) Jones & Bartlett.

Page, Reba. Lower-Track Classrooms: A Curricular & Cultural Perspective. 288p. (C). 1991. text 48.00 (*0-8077-3092-0*); pap. text 22.95 (*0-8077-3093-9*) Tchrs Coll.

Page, Reba & Valli, Linda, eds. Curriculum Differentiation: Interpretive Studies in U. S. Secondary Schools. LC 90-31585. (SUNY Series, Frontiers in Education). 261p. (C). 1990. pap. text 21.95 (*0-7914-0470-6*) State U NY Pr.

— Curriculum Differentiation: Interpretive Studies in U. S. Secondary Schools. LC 90-31585. (SUNY Series, Frontiers in Education). 261p. (C). 1990. text 64.50 (*0-7914-0469-2*) State U NY Pr.

Page, Reba N. Lower-Track Classrooms: A Curricular & Cultural Perspective. LC 91-3141. 287p. reprint ed. pap. 89.00 (*0-608-20002-6*, 207127900010) Bks Demand.

Page, Rex L., et al. FORTRAN 77 for Humans. 3rd ed. LC 85-20318. (Illus.). 462p. (C). 1986. pap. text 49.25 (*0-314-93404-9*) West Pub.

Page, Rex L., jt. auth. see Mueller, Robert A.

Page, Richard C. Page: Genealogy of the Page Family in Virginia, Also a Condensed Account of the Nelson, Walker, Pendleton & Randolph Families with References to Other Distinguished Families in Virginia. 2nd ed. (Illus.). 275p. 1993. reprint ed. pap. 45.00 (*0-8328-3093-3*); reprint ed. lib. bdg. 55.00 (*0-8328-3092-5*) Higginson Bk Co.

Page, Richard C. & Berkow, Daniel N. Creating Contact, Choosing Relationship: The Dynamics of Unstructured Group Therapy. LC 93-48625. (Social & Behavioral Science Ser.). 333p. 1994. 38.95 (*1-55542-654-9*) Jossey-Bass.

Page, Rick. Hope is Not a Strategy: Keys to the Complex Sale. (Illus.). 176p. 1999. write for info. (*0-9669102-4-9*) Nautilus.

Page, Robert. Altruism & the British Welfate State. LC 96-84030. 192p. 1996. text 64.95 (*1-85628-077-2*, Pub. by Avebry) Ashgate Pub Co.

Page, Robert, jt. auth. see Deakin, Nicholas.

Page, Robert, jt. auth. see Jordanoff, Christine.

Page, Robert, jt. ed. see Ferris, John.

Page, Robert E., III. Page, Carolina Pages: A Compilation of Genealogical Information on Page Families in the Carolinas Beginning in 1521 to Present Time. (Illus.). 293p. 1992. pap. 45.00 (*0-8328-2701-0*); lib. bdg. 55.00 (*0-8328-2700-2*) Higginson Bk Co.

Page, Robert E., Jr., jt. auth. see Laidlaw, Harry H., Jr.

Page, Robert G., ed. see Conference on the Optimal Preparation for the Stud.

Page, Robert M. The Origin of Radar. LC 78-25844. (Illus.). 196p. 1979. reprint ed. lib. bdg. 38.50 (*0-313-20781-X*, PAOR, Greenwood Pr) Greenwood.

***Page, Robert R.** Cultural Landscape Reports: Process & Techniques; Landscape Lines. 16 Bks. (364p. 1999. per. 28.00 (*0-16-061687-5*) USGPO.

Page, Roberta & Makinson, Robert. Horace Morris: International Edition. 2nd rev. ed. (Illus.). 36p. (J). (ps-6). 1992. pap. 9.00 (*0-9654228-3-6*) R Makinson.

Page-Roberts, James. Wines from a Small Garden: From Planting to Bottling. (Illus.). 128p. 1995. 24.95 (*0-7892-0076-7*) Abbeville Pr.

Page, Robin. Working with Your Foreign Language Assistant. (Handbooks for Language Teachers Ser.: Vol. 9). 42p. (Orig.). 1997. pap. 23.50 (*0-7487-3031-1*, Pub. by S Thornes Pubs) Trans-Atl Phila.

Page, Roderic D. & Holmes, Edward C. Molecular Evolution: A Phylogenic Approach. LC 98-4696. (Illus.). 346p. 1998. pap. 51.95 (*0-86542-889-1*) Blackwell Sci.

Page, Roland. How to Be Prepared for Any Crisis. 69p. 1974. pap. 3.95 (*0-89036-033-2*) Liahona Pub Trust.

Page, Rosewell. Hanover County, Virginia, Its History & Legends. (Illus.). 153p. 1997. reprint ed. pap. 19.50 (*0-8328-7182-6*); reprint ed. lib. bdg. 27.50 (*0-8328-7181-8*) Higginson Bk Co.

— Thomas Nelson Page: A Memoir of a Virginia Gentleman, by His Brother. (BCL1-PS American Literature Ser.). 210p. 1992. reprint ed. lib. bdg. 79.00 (*0-7812-6916-4*) Rprt Serv.

Page, Ruth. God & the Web of Creation. 1997. pap. 26.00 (*0-334-02653-9*) TPI PA.

Page, S. G. Mathematics: A Second Start. (Mathematics & Its Applications Ser.). 409p. 1986. pap. text 29.95 (*0-470-20752-3*) P-H.

***Page, Schubert M.** Badger a Legend in His Own Time. (Illus.). iv, 52p. 2000. 24.00 (*0-944619-60-6*) Gregath Pub Co.

Page, Sheila. How Developing Countries Trade: The Institutional Constraints. 288p. (Orig.). (C). 1995. pap. 29.99 (*0-415-11718-X*, B4576) Routledge.

***Page, Sheila.** Regionalism among Developing Countries. LC 99-33860. 2000. text 69.95 (*0-312-22660-8*) St Martin.

Page, Sheila. Trade, Finance & Developing Countries: Strategies & Constraints in the 1990s. 426p. (C). 1989. lib. bdg. 76.50 (*0-389-20890-6*, N 8446) B&N Imports.

***Page, Sheila, ed.** Regions & Development: Politics, Security & Economics. LC 99-41946. (EADI Book Ser.: No. 23). 288p. 2000. 64.50 (*0-7146-5023-4*, Pub. by F Cass Pubs); pap. 29.50 (*0-7146-4465-X*, Pub. by F Cass Pubs) Intl Spec Bk.

***Page, Simon R. & Hall, George M.** Diabetes: Emergency & Hospital Management. (Illus.). 246p. 1999. pap. 45.00 (*0-7279-1229-1*) BMJ Pub.

Page, Stanley. 10 Minute Guide to Buying & Selling Your Home. 144p. 1996. 10.95 (*0-02-861286-8*) Macmillan.

Page, Stanley W. The Geopolitics of Leninism. (East European Monographs: No. 97). 238p. 1982. text 52.50 (*0-914710-91-5*, Pub. by East Eur Monographs) Col U Pr.

— Lenin: Dedicated Marxist or Revolutionary Pragmatist. LC 77-76608. (Problems in Civilization Ser.). 1977. pap. text 7.95 (*0-88273-402-4*) Forum Pr IL.

Page, Stephanie, et al. Trying Drug Cases in Massachusetts. LC 92-62586. 610p. 1992. ring bd. 75.00 (*0-944490-43-3*) Mass CLE.

— Trying Drug Cases in Massachusetts, 1996 Supplement. LC 92-62586. 278p. 1996. ring bd., suppl. ed. 39.50 (*1-57589-028-3*, 96-06.23-SP) Mass CLE.

— Trying Sex Offense Cases in Massachusetts. LC 96-80040. 976p. 1997. ring bd. 75.00 (*1-57589-052-6*, 97-06.11-BK) Mass CLE.

Page, Stephen. Introductory Marketing. 256p. (C). 1995. pap. 42.50 (*0-7487-1783-8*, Pub. by S Thornes Pubs) Trans-Atl Phila.

— The Soviet Union & the Yemens. LC 84-512. 254p. 1985. 59.95 (*0-275-90153-X*, C0153, Praeger Pubs) Greenwood.

— The Timbre of Sand. LC 98-94183. iii, 50p. 1998. pap. 8.95 (*0-9668353-0-1*) Gorion Pr.

Page, Stephen, jt. auth. see Getz, Don.

Page, Stephen, jt. auth. see Hall, C. Michael.

Page, Stephen, jt. auth. see Knitzer, Jane.

Page, Stephen, jt. auth. see Ryan, Chris.

***Page, Stephen B.** Achieving 100Compliance of Policies & Procedures. xxviii, 337p. 2000. per. 42.10 (*1-929065-49-3*) Process Improvement.

Page, Stephen B. Establishing a System of Policies & Procedures. (Illus.). 168p. 1998. pap. 25.95 (*1-929065-00-0*) Process Improvement.

Page, Stephen J. Transport for Tourism. LC 93-39536. (Topics in Tourism Ser.). 224p. (Orig.). (C). 1994. pap. 17.99 (*0-415-10238-3*, B4436) Thomson Learn.

— Urban Tourism. LC 94-28174. (Topics in Tourism Ser.). 224p. (C). 1995. pap. 17.99 (*0-415-11218-4*, B4858) Thomson Learn.

Page, Stephen J. & Wood, Roy, eds. The Leisure Workbook. (Tourism & Hospitality Management Ser.). 304p. 1995. 59.00 (*0-415-09963-3*); pap. 22.95 (*0-415-09964-1*) Routledge.

Page, Stephen J., jt. auth. see Hall, Colin M.

Page, Stephen J., jt. ed. see Hall, C. Michael.

Page, Steve. Putting Secrets: Weekend Golfer. 2nd ed. LC 96-36558. (Illus.). 144p. 1997. pap. 11.95 (*0-312-15197-7*) St Martin.

— Shadow & the Counsellor. LC 98-45952. 1999. 80.00 (*0-415-13144-8*); pap. 25.99 (*0-415-13145-6*) Routledge.

Page, Steve & Wosket, Val. Supervising the Counsellor: A Cyclical Model. LC 94-8492. (Illus.). 256p. (C). 1994. 80.00 (*0-415-10213-8*, B4078) Routledge.

Page, Sue E. Hearts & Hands & Voices: Growing in Faith Through Choral Music. 216p. (C). 1995. 34.95 (*0-9646552-0-9*); pap. 27.95 (*0-9646552-1-7*) F Bock Music.

Page, Susan. The 8 Essential Traits of Couples Who Thrive. 1997. pap. write for info. (*0-614-20464-X*, Delta Trade) Dell.

— Eight Essential Traits of Couples Who Thrive. 320p. 1997. pap. 11.95 (*0-440-50782-0*) Dell.

— How One of You Can Bring the Two of You Together. 320p. 1998. pap. 14.00 (*0-7679-0042-1*) Broadway BDD.

— If Im So Wonderful Why Am I Still Single? 288p. 1989. mass mkt. 6.50 (*0-553-28299-9*) Bantam.

— The Shortest Distance Between You & Published Book: Everything You Need to Know in the Order You Need to Know It. LC 96-29710. 288p. 1997. pap. 14.00 (*0-553-06177-1*) Broadway BDD.

Page, Susanne & Page, Jake. Hopi. LC 94-4489. (Illus.). 240p. 1994. reprint ed. pap. 29.98 (*0-8109-8127-0*, Pub. by Abrams) Time Warner.

Page, Susanne, jt. auth. see Page, Jake.

Page, Sydney H. T. The Powers of Evil: A Biblical Study of Satan & Demons. LC 95-18467. 296p. 1994. pap. 19.99 (*0-8010-7137-2*) Baker Bks.

Page, Talbot. Conservation & Economic Efficiency: An Approach to Materials Policy. LC 76-22846. 266p. 1977. pap. 14.95 (*0-8018-1951-2*) Resources Future.

Page, Tana, jt. auth. see Page, Randy.

Page, Tana S., jt. auth. see Page, Randy M.

Page, Terry. Air Jammin' (Illus.). 24p. (J). (gr. 2-6). 1996. pap. text 4.00 (*1-887864-55-5*); lib. bdg. 7.00 (*1-887864-10-5*) Boo Bks.

— Air Jammin' Coloring Book. (Illus.). 32p. (J). (ps-5). 1996. pap. 3.00 (*1-887864-11-3*) Boo Bks.

— The Bad Little Seed. (Illus.). 26p. (J). (gr. 2-6). 1996. pap. text 4.00 (*1-887864-57-1*); lib. bdg. 7.00 (*1-887864-14-8*) Boo Bks.

— The Bad Little Seed Coloring Book. (Illus.). 32p. (J). (ps-5). 1996. pap. 3.00 (*1-887864-15-6*) Boo Bks.

— A Brand New Foot. (Illus.). 24p. (J). (gr. 2-6). 1997. pap. text 4.00 (*1-887864-65-2*); lib. bdg. 7.00 (*1-887864-30-X*) Boo Bks.

— A Brand New Foot Coloring Book. (Illus.). 32p. (J). (ps-5). 1997. pap. 3.00 (*1-887864-31-8*) Boo Bks.

— The Captain's Coins. (Illus.). 24p. (J). (gr. 2-6). 1995. pap. text 4.00 (*1-887864-50-4*); lib. bdg. 7.00 (*1-887864-00-8*) Boo Bks.

— The Captain's Coins Coloring Book. (Illus.). 32p. (J). (ps-5). 1995. pap. 3.00 (*1-887864-01-6*) Boo Bks.

— The Case of the Missing Blue. (Illus.). 24p. (J). (gr. 2-6). 1995. pap. text 4.00 (*1-887864-53-9*); lib. bdg. 7.00 (*1-887864-06-7*) Boo Bks.

— The Case of the Missing Blue Coloring Book. (Illus.). 32p. (J). (ps-5). 1995. pap. 3.00 (*1-887864-07-5*) Boo Bks.

— Cool Cat. (Illus.). 24p. (J). (gr. 2-6). 1996. pap. text 4.00 (*1-887864-59-8*); lib. bdg. 7.00 (*1-887864-18-0*) Boo Bks.

— Cool Cat Coloring Book. (Illus.). 32p. (J). (ps-5). 1996. pap. 3.00 (*1-887864-19-9*) Boo Bks.

— The Fathers of the Friendly Forest. (Illus.). 24p. (J). (gr. 2-6). 1996. pap. text 4.00 (*1-887864-69-5*); lib. bdg. 7.00 (*1-887864-38-5*) Boo Bks.

— The Fathers of the Friendly Forest Coloring Book. (Illus.). 32p. (J). (ps-5). pap. 3.00 (*1-887864-39-3*) Boo Bks.

— Fraidy Cat. (Illus.). 24p. (J). (gr. 2-6). 1996. pap. text 4.00 (*1-887864-58-X*); lib. bdg. 7.00 (*1-887864-16-4*) Boo Bks.

— Fraidy Cat Coloring Book. (Illus.). 32p. (J). (ps-5). 1996. pap. 3.00 (*1-887864-17-2*) Boo Bks.

— Horse-N-Around. (Illus.). 24p. (J). (gr. 2-6). 1995. pap. text 4.00 (*1-887864-51-2*); lib. bdg. 7.00 (*1-887864-02-4*) Boo Bks.

— Horse-N-Around Coloring Book. (Illus.). 32p. (J). (ps-5). 1995. pap. 3.00 (*1-887864-03-2*) Boo Bks.

— My Wings. (Illus.). 24p. (J). (gr. 2-6). 1995. pap. text 4.00 (*1-887864-52-0*); lib. bdg. 7.00 (*1-887864-04-0*) Boo Bks.

— My Wings Coloring Book. (Illus.). 32p. (J). (ps-5). 1995. pap. 3.00 (*1-887864-05-9*) Boo Bks.

— Octopooh Saves the Day. (Illus.). 24p. (J). (gr. 2-6). 1995. pap. text 4.00 (*1-887864-54-7*); lib. bdg. 7.00 (*1-887864-08-3*) Boo Bks.

— Octopooh Saves the Day Coloring Book. (Illus.). 32p. (J). (ps-5). 1995. pap. 3.00 (*1-887864-09-1*) Boo Bks.

— One-on-One. (Illus.). 24p. (J). (gr. 2-6). 1996. pap. text 4.00 (*1-887864-56-3*); lib. bdg. 7.00 (*1-887864-12-1*) Boo Bks.

— One-on-One Coloring Book. (Illus.). 32p. (J). (ps-5). 1996. pap. 3.00 (*1-887864-13-X*) Boo Bks.

— The Saddest Centaur. (Illus.). 24p. (J). (gr. 2-6). pap. text 4.00 (*1-887864-68-7*); lib. bdg. 7.00 (*1-887864-36-9*) Boo Bks.

— The Saddest Centaur Coloring Book. (Illus.). 32p. (J). (ps-5). pap. 3.00 (*1-887864-37-7*) Boo Bks.

— The Secret of the Silver Shell. (Illus.). 24p. (J). (gr. 2-6). 1997. pap. text 4.00 (*1-887864-64-4*); lib. bdg. 7.00 (*1-887864-28-8*) Boo Bks.

— The Secret of the Silver Shell Coloring Book. (Illus.). 32p. (J). (ps-5). 1997. pap. 3.00 (*1-887864-29-6*) Boo Bks.

— Sweet Dreams My King. (Illus.). 24p. (J). (gr. 2-6). 1996. pap. text 4.00 (*1-887864-61-X*); lib. bdg. 7.00 (*1-887864-22-9*) Boo Bks.

— Sweet Dreams My King Coloring Book. (Illus.). 32p. (J). (ps-5). 1996. pap. 3.00 (*1-887864-23-7*) Boo Bks.

— There Was a High Horse. (Illus.). 24p. (J). (gr. 2-6). 1997. pap. text 4.00 (*1-887864-66-0*); lib. bdg. 7.00 (*1-887864-32-6*) Boo Bks.

— There Was a High Horse Coloring Book. (Illus.). 32p. (J). (ps-5). 1997. pap. 3.00 (*1-887864-33-4*) Boo Bks.

— The Time Machine: Duck for Hire. (Illus.). 24p. (J). (gr. 2-6). 1997. pap. text 4.00 (*1-887864-67-9*); lib. bdg. 7.00 (*1-887864-34-2*) Boo Bks.

— The Time Machine Coloring Book: Duck for Hire. (Illus.). 32p. (J). (ps-5). 1997. pap. 3.00 (*1-887864-35-0*) Boo Bks.

— The Tin Tuba. (Illus.). 24p. (J). (gr. 2-6). 1977. pap. text 4.00 (*1-887864-63-6*) Boo Bks.

— The Tin Tuba. (Illus.). 24p. (J). (gr. 2-6). 1997. lib. bdg. 7.00 (*1-887864-26-1*) Boo Bks.

— The Tin Tuba Coloring Book. (Illus.). 32p. (J). (ps-5). 1997. pap. 3.00 (*1-887864-27-X*) Boo Bks.

— When I Become King. (Illus.). 24p. (J). (gr. 2-6). 1977. pap. text 4.00 (*1-887864-62-8*) Boo Bks.

— When I Become King. (Illus.). 24p. (J). (gr. 2-6). 1997. lib. bdg. 7.00 (*1-887864-24-5*) Boo Bks.

— When I Become King Coloring Book. (Illus.). 32p. (J). (ps-5). 1997. pap. 3.00 (*1-887864-25-3*) Boo Bks.

— Where's My Web. (Illus.). 24p. (J). (gr. 2-6). 1996. pap. text 4.00 (*1-887864-60-1*); lib. bdg. 7.00 (*1-887864-20-2*) Boo Bks.

— Where's My Web Coloring Book. (Illus.). 32p. (J). (ps-5). 1996. pap. 3.00 (*1-887864-21-0*) Boo Bks.

Page, Terry, ed. Business & Technology. 154p. (C). 1987. 75.00 (*1-85184-027-3*) St Mut.

Page, Terry & Love, Bob. The Bob (Butterbean) Love Story. 24p. (J). (gr. 2-6). 1996. pap. 4.00 (*0-614-97099-7*); lib. bdg. 7.00 (*0-614-97096-2*) Boo Bks.

Page, Thomas N. Among the Camps. (J). 1996. 17.99 (*0-87377-173-7*) GAM Pubns.

— Among the Camps. (Notable American Authors Ser.). 1999. reprint ed. lib. bdg. 125.00 (*0-7812-4690-3*) Rprt Serv.

— Bred in the Bone. LC 77-86151. (Short Story Index Reprint Ser.). 1977. 20.95 (*0-8369-3057-6*) Ayer.

— Bred in the Bone. (Notable American Authors Ser.). 1999. reprint ed. lib. bdg. 125.00 (*0-7812-4701-2*) Rprt Serv.

— The Burial of the Guns. 1972. reprint ed. 27.25 (*0-8422-8103-7*) Irvington.

— Burial of the Guns. (C). 1986. reprint ed. pap. text 7.95 (*0-8290-1905-7*) Irvington.

— The Burieal of the Guns. (Notable American Authors Ser.). 1999. reprint ed. lib. bdg. 125.00 (*0-7812-4694-6*) Rprt Serv.

— A Captured Santa Claus. (Notable American Authors Ser.). 1999. reprint ed. lib. bdg. 125.00 (*0-7812-4699-7*) Rprt Serv.

— The Coast of Bohemia. (Notable American Authors Ser.). 1999. reprint ed. lib. bdg. 125.00 (*0-7812-4709-8*) Rprt Serv.

— Dante & His Influence. (Notable American Authors Ser.). 1999. reprint ed. lib. bdg. 125.00 (*0-7812-4715-2*) Rprt Serv.

— Elsket, & Other Stories. LC 73-85693. (Short Story Index Reprint Ser.). 1977. 19.95 (*0-8369-3036-3*) Ayer.

— Elsket & Other Stories. (Notable American Authors Ser.). 1999. reprint ed. lib. bdg. 125.00 (*0-7812-4692-X*) Rprt Serv.

— Fiction - In Ole Virginia, Marse Chan, & Other Stories. (Notable American Authors Ser.). 1999 reprint ed. lib. bdg. 125.00 (*0-7812-4688-1*) Rprt Serv.

— Gordon Keith. (Notable American Authors Ser.). 1999. reprint ed. lib. bdg. 125.00 (*0-7812-4700-4*) Rprt Serv.

— In Ole Virginia: Or, Marse Chan & Other Stories. LC 68-23723. (Americans in Fiction Ser.). 230p. reprint ed. lib. bdg. 19.00 (*0-8398-1550-6*) Irvington.

— In Ole Virginia: Or, Marse Chan & Other Stories. (Americans in Fiction Ser.). 230p. (C). 1986. reprint ed. pap. text 7.95 (*0-8290-1864-6*) Irvington.

— In Ole Virginia: Or, Marse Chan & Other Stories. LC 92-62891. (Southern Classics Ser.). 250p. (C). 1993. reprint ed. pap. 10.95 (*1-879941-04-X*) J S Sanders.

— In Ole Virginia: Or, Marse Chan & Other Stories. (BCL1-PS American Literature Ser.). 230p. 1992. reprint ed. lib. bdg. 79.00 (*0-7812-6822-2*) Rprt Serv.

— Italy & the World War. (Notable American Authors Ser.). 1999. reprint ed. lib. bdg. 125.00 (*0-7812-4714-4*) Rprt Serv.

— John Marvel, Assistant. (Notable American Authors Ser.). 1999. reprint ed. lib. bdg. 125.00 (*0-7812-4703-9*) Rprt Serv.

— The Land of the Spirit. (Notable American Authors Ser.). 1999. reprint ed. lib. bdg. 125.00 (*0-7812-4713-6*) Rprt Serv.

— The Negro - The Southerner's Problem. (Notable American Authors Ser.). 1999. reprint ed. lib. bdg. 125.00 (*0-7812-4708-X*) Rprt Serv.

— Non-Fiction - Befo de War (Verse, with Armistead Churchill Gordon) (Notable American Authors Ser.). 1999. reprint ed. lib. bdg. 125.00 (*0-7812-4705-5*) Rprt Serv.

— The Novels, Stories, Sketches & Poems of Thomas

P

Nelson Page. 18 vols., Set. (BCL1-PS American Literature Ser.). 1992. reprint ed. pap. text 990.00 (*0-685-51403-X*); reprint ed. lib. bdg. 1350.00 (*0-7812-6821-4*) Rprt Serv.

— The Old Dominion - Her Making & Her Manners. (Notable American Authors Ser.). 1999. reprint ed. lib. bdg. 125.00 (*0-7812-4711-X*) Rprt Serv.

— The Old Gentleman of the Black Stock. (Notable American Authors Ser.). 1999. reprint ed. lib. bdg. 125.00 (*0-7812-4695-4*) Rprt Serv.

— The Old South: Essays Social & Historical. (Notable American Authors Ser.). 1999. reprint ed. lib. bdg. 125.00 (*0-7812-4706-3*) Rprt Serv.

— Old South: Essays Social & Political. LC 69-14026. (Illus.). 269p. 1970. reprint ed. lib. bdg. 38.50 (*0-8371-1977-4*, PAO&) Greenwood.

— Old South: Essays Social & Political. LC 68-24992. (American History & Americana Ser.: No. 47). 1969. reprint ed. lib. bdg. 75.00 (*0-8383-0226-2*) M S G Haskell Hse.

— The Old South: Essays Social & Political. (BCL1 - United States Local History Ser.). 344p. 1991. reprint ed. text 89.00 (*0-7812-6284-4*) Rprt Serv.

— On Newfound River. LC 78-110427. reprint ed. 39.50 (*0-404-04858-7*) AMS Pr.

— On Newfound River. (BCL1-PS American Literature Ser.). 240p. 1992. reprint ed. lib. bdg. 79.00 (*0-7812-6823-0*) Rprt Serv.

— On Newfound River. (Notable American Authors Ser.). 1999. reprint ed. lib. bdg. 125.00 (*0-7812-4691-1*) Rprt Serv.

— Pastime Stories. LC 76-75784. (Short Story Index Reprint Ser.). (Illus.). 1977. 19.95 (*0-8369-3009-6*) Ayer.

— Pastime Stories. (Notable American Authors Ser.). 1999. reprint ed. lib. bdg. 125.00 (*0-7812-4693-8*) Rprt Serv.

— The Red Riders (Completed by Rosewell Page) (Notable American Authors Ser.). 1999. reprint ed. lib. bdg. 125.00 (*0-7812-4704-7*) Rprt Serv.

— Red Rock. Carpenter, Lucas, ed. 1991. 16.95 (*0-8084-0439-3*) NCUP.

— Red Rock. (Notable American Authors Ser.). 1999. reprint ed. lib. bdg. 125.00 (*0-7812-4697-0*) Rprt Serv.

— Red Rock, a Chronicle of Reconstruction. LC 67-29275. (Americans in Fiction Ser.). (Illus.). 599p. reprint ed. lib. bdg. 22.00 (*0-8398-1551-4*) Irvington.

— Red Rock, a Chronicle of Reconstruction. (Americans in Fiction Ser.). (Illus.). 599p. 1986. reprint ed. pap. text 9.95 (*0-8290-1920-0*) Irvington.

— Robert E. Lee: Man & Soldier. (Notable American Authors Ser.). 1999. reprint ed. lib. bdg. 125.00 (*0-7812-4712-8*) Rprt Serv.

— Robert E. Lee: The Southerner. (Notable American Authors Ser.). 1999. reprint ed. lib. bdg. 125.00 (*0-7812-4710-1*) Rprt Serv.

— Santa Claus' Partner. (Notable American Authors Ser.). 1999. reprint ed. lib. bdg. 125.00 (*0-7812-4698-9*) Rprt Serv.

— Social Life in Old Virginia. (Notable American Authors Ser.). 1999. reprint ed. lib. bdg. 125.00 (*0-7812-4707-1*) Rprt Serv.

— Social Life in Old Virginia Before the War. (Illus.). 80p. 1994. pap. 9.95 (*0-939218-02-X*) Chapman Billies.

— Social Life in Old Virginia Before the War. LC 73-130560. (Select Bibliographies Reprint Ser.). (Illus.). 1977. reprint ed. 13.95 (*0-8369-5533-1*) Ayer.

— Two Little Confederates. (J). 1996. 17.99 (*0-87377-174-5*) GAM Pubns.

— Two Little Confederates. (Notable American Authors Ser.). 1999. reprint ed. lib. bdg. 125.00 (*0-7812-4689-X*) Rprt Serv.

— Two Prisoners. (Notable American Authors Ser.). 1999. reprint ed. lib. bdg. 125.00 (*0-7812-4696-2*) Rprt Serv.

— Under the Crust. (Notable American Authors Ser.). 1999. reprint ed. lib. bdg. 125.00 (*0-7812-4702-0*) Rprt Serv.

Page, Thomas N., et al. Stories of the South. LC 74-110217. (Short Story Index Reprint Ser.). 1977. 24.95 (*0-8369-3369-9*) Ayer.

Page, Thomas N., jt. auth. see Gordon, A. C.

Page, Thomas W. Making Tariff in the United States. (Brookings Institution Reprint Ser.). reprint ed. lib. bdg. 40.50 (*0-685-70237-5*) Irvington.

Page, Tim. Dawn Powell: A Biography. LC 98-19907. (Illus.). 352p. 1998. 30.00 (*0-8050-5068-X*) H Holt & Co.

— Dawn Powell: A Biography. 384p. 1999. pap. text 16.00 (*0-8050-6301-3*, Owl) H Holt & Co.

— Derailed in Uncle Ho's Victory. 1999. 191.76 (*0-671-71926-2*) S&S Trade.

— Mid-Term Report. LC 94-60653. (Illus.). 112p. 1995. pap. 29.95 (*0-500-27795-8*, Pub. by Thames Hudson) Norton.

***Page, Tim.** Selected Letters of Dawn Powell, 1913-1965. 400p. 2000. pap. 16.00 (*0-8050-6505-9*, Owl) H Holt & Co.

Page, Tim, ed. Glenn Gould Reader. LC 90-50141. 496p. 1990. pap. 17.00 (*0-679-73135-0*) Vin Bks.

Page, Tim, jt. auth. see Page, Evelyn.

Page, Tim, jt. ed. see Faas, Horst.

Page, Tim, ed. see Powell, Dawn.

Page, Tim, ed. & intro. see Powell, Dawn.

Page, Tom. Hong Kong Blues. 250p. mass mkt. 4.99 (*1-55197-115-1*) Picasso Publ.

***Page, Tony.** Diary of a Change Agent. 296p. 1998. pap. 39.95 (*0-566-08093-1*) Ashgate Pub Co.

Page, Tony. Diary of a Change Agent. 296p. 1996. 65.95 (*0-566-07779-5*, Pub. by Gower) Ashgate Pub Co.

— Vivisection Unveiled: An Expose of the Medical Futility of Animal Experimentation. 160p. 1998. pap. 14.95 (*1-897766-31-9*, Pub. by Jon Carpenter) Paul & Co Pubs.

Page, Vicki. The Lottery of Love. large type ed. (Lythway Ser.). 208p. 1991. 19.95 (*0-7451-1276-5*, G K Hall Lrg Type) Mac Lib Ref.

***Page, Vicki.** Miranda. large type ed. LC 98-33778. 162p. 1999. write for info. (*0-7540-3532-8*) Chivers N Amer.

Page, Vicki. Miranda. large type ed. LC 98-33778. 1999. 30.00 (*0-7838-0359-1*, G K Hall Lrg Type) Mac Lib Ref.

— Winter of the Heart. large type ed. LC 98-23161. (Romance Ser.). 183p. 1998. pap. write for info. (*0-7540-3419-4*) Chivers N Amer.

— Winter of the Heart. large type ed. LC 98-23161. (Hall Nightingale Ser.). 1998. pap. 18.95 (*0-7838-0248-X*, G K Hall & Co) Mac Lib Ref.

Page, Victor W. Chevy Six, the Early Years: Construction, Operation, Service for the Restorer. LC 76-26324. (Illus.). 912p. 1979. reprint ed. 28.95 (*0-911160-40-X*) Post Group.

Page, Victoria Le, see Le Page, Victoria.

Page, Virginia, jt. auth. see Garnsey, Wayne.

Page, Virginia, jt. auth. see Garnsey, Wayne H.

Page, W. R. Government & Politics at Work in Britain. LC 73-92007. (Illus.). 219p. reprint ed. pap. 62.50 (*0-608-09942-2*, 2010164) Bks Demand.

Page, Walter H. The Rebuilding of Old Commonwealths. LC 79-125175. reprint ed. 34.50 (*0-404-04859-5*) AMS Pr.

— The Rebuilding of Old Commonwealths: Being Essays Towards the Training of the Forgotten Man in the Southern States. (BCL1 - United States Local History Ser.). 153p. 1991. reprint ed. text 69.00 (*0-7812-6293-3*) Rprt Serv.

Page, Warren. The Accurate Rifle. 276p. 1997. 24.95 (*1-886681-04-X*); pap. 17.95 (*1-886681-06-6*) Claymore Pub.

— Calculus. 768p. (C). 1998. write for info. (*0-02-390325-2*, Macmillan Coll) P-H.

— Topological Uniform Structures. 416p. 1989. pap. 9.95 (*0-486-65808-2*) Dover.

Page, Wayne E. Ten Steps Dynamic Presentation. 276p. (C). 1995. pap. 21.95 (*0-7872-1544-9*) Kendall-Hunt.

Page, Wayne E., jt. auth. see Levin, Alan M.

Page, William. Play Is Work. 40p. (Orig.). 1992. pap. text 6.00 (*0-935493-94-8*) Modern Learn Pr.

Page, William, ed. Commerce & Industry: A Historical View of the Economic Conditions of the British Empire 1815-1914, 2 Vols in One. LC 67-19709. (Reprints of Economic Classics Ser.). 1968. reprint ed. 75.00 (*0-678-00404-8*) Kelley.

Page, William, ed. see Round, John H.

Page, William F., jt. auth. see Institute of Medicine Staff.

Page, William F., ed. see Institute of Medicine Staff.

Page, Willie F. The Dutch Triangle: The Netherlands & the Atlantic Trade, 1621-1664. rev. ed. LC 97-2203. (Studies in African American History & Culture). (Illus.). 304p. 1997. text 66.00 (*0-8153-2881-8*) Garland.

***Page, Willie F.** Encyclopedia of African History & Culture Set. (Illus.). 2000. 225.00 (*0-8160-4472-4*) Facts on File.

Page, Winni R. Panning for Pleasure: An Alaska Cookbook. Andrews, Betsy et al, eds. (Illus.). 262p. 1991. reprint ed. write for info. (*0-9621777-0-9*) W R Page.

Pageant Limited Staff. The Electronic Commerce Handbook 1996. 320p. 1996. pap. 290.95 (*1-85554-670-1*) Blackwell Pubs.

Pagedas, C., jt. ed. see Otte, Thomas G.

***Pagedas, Constantine A.** Anglo-American Strategic Relations & the French Problem, 1960-1963: A Troubled Partnership. LC 99-38921. 308p. 2000. 59.50 (*0-7146-5002-1*, Pub. by F Cass Pubs) Intl Spec Bk.

Pagel, B. G. & Thomson, W. T. Insecticide, Herbicide, Fungicide Quick Guide: 2000 Edition. rev. ed. 200p. 2000. pap. 19.95 (*0-913702-49-8*) Thomson Pubns.

Pagel, Bernard E. Nucleosynthesis & Chemical Evolution of Galaxies. (Illus.). 392p. (C). 1997. text 74.95 (*0-521-55061-0*); pap. text 30.95 (*0-521-55958-8*) Cambridge U Pr.

***Pagel, Daniels.** Basics of Proofreading a Programmed Approach. 4th ed. (C). 2000. pap. 19.00 (*0-538-72374-2*) Sth-Wstrn College.

Pagel, Danita, jt. auth. see Thomas, John E.

Pagel, David. Fifteen: A Fifteen-Year Survey of Jim Isermann's Work. (Illus.). 52p. 1998. pap. 15.00 (*0-9664020-0-6*) Inst Visl Arts.

— Los Angeles: Not Paintings? 18p. (Orig.). 1993. 15.00 (*0-318-71699-2*) San Barb CAF.

Pagel, David, et al, contrib. by. Plane/Structures. (Illus.). 64p. 1994. pap. 18.00 (*0-911291-23-7*, Pub. by Fellows Cont Art) RAM Publications.

***Pagel, David & Coffin, E. B.** Irene Hardwicke Olivieri: Paintings. (Illus.). 60p. 2000. pap. 35.00 (*0-9701690-0-0*) H Olivieri.

Pagel, David, et al. Postmark: An Abstract Effect. LC 99-60968. (Illus.). 56p. 1999. pap. write for info. (*0-9650583-6-0*) Site Santa Fe.

Pagel, Horst, et al, eds. Pathophysiology & Pharmacology of Erythropoietin. LC 92-2312. (Illus.). xv, 328p. 1992. 100.00 (*0-387-54777-0*) Spr-Verlag.

***Pagel, J.** Biographisches Lexicon des Neunzehnten Jahrhunderts. (Illus.). 1003p. 2000. 110.00 (*1-57898-165-4*) Martino Pubng.

Pagel, J. L. Biographisches Lexikon hervorragender Aerzte des 19. Jahrhunderts: Mit einer historischen Einleitung. (Illus.). xxxii, 998p. 1990. reprint ed. 254.00 (*3-8055-4817-6*) S Karger.

Pagel, Mark D., jt. auth. see Harvey, Paul H.

Pagel, Mary E. Computer Tutor 1.0: Your Complete Guide to Self Computer Training. (Illus.). 106p. (Orig.). (C). 1989. teacher ed. write for info. (*0-318-64482-7*); pap. text 14.95 (*0-9621823-0-3*) Comput Tutor.

***Pagel, Maurice, et al, eds.** Cathodoluminescence in Geosciences. LC 99-12504. (Illus.). 430p. 2000. 135.00 (*3-540-65987-0*) Spr-Verlag.

Pagel, Maurice & Leroy, Jacques L., eds. Source, Transport & Deposition of Metals: Proceedings of the 25 Years SGA Anniversary Meeting, Nancy, 30 August-3 September 1991. (Illus.). 850p. 1991. text 181.00 (*90-5410-020-6*, Pub. by A A Balkema) Ashgate Pub Co.

Pagel-Paden, Elaine. Exercises in Phonetic Transcription: A Programmed Workbook. 2nd ed. 40p. 1989. pap. text, wbk. ed. 25.00 (*0-7506-9681-8*) Buttrwrth-Heinemann.

Pagel, Scott B., ed. The Legal Bibliography: Tradition, Transitions, & Trends. (Legal Reference Services Quarterly Ser.: Vol. 9, Nos. 1-2). 183p. 1989. 39.95 (*0-86656-932-4*) Haworth Pr.

Pagel, Stephen, jt. ed. see Griffith, Nicola.

Pagel, Ulrich. The Bodhisattvapitaka: Its Doctrines Practices & Their Position in Mahayana Literature. LC 95-194227. (C). 1995. 68.00 (*0-9515424-4-3*, Pub. by Inst Buddhist Stud) S Asia.

Pagel, Ulrich, jt. ed. see Skorupski.

Pagel, W. New Light on William Harvey. (Illus.). 200p. 1975. 78.50 (*3-8055-2209-6*) S Karger.

— Paracelsus. 2nd ed. (Illus.). xii, 400p. 1982. 121.00 (*3-8055-3518-X*) S Karger.

— The Smiling Spleen. (Illus.). x, 214p. 1984. 133.25 (*3-8055-3707-7*) S Karger.

Pagel, Walter. Religion & Neoplatonism in Renaissance Medicine. Winder, Marianne, ed. (Collected Studies: No. CS226). (Illus.). 346p. (C). 1985. reprint ed. text 115.95 (*0-86078-174-7*, Pub. by Variorum) Ashgate Pub Co.

Pagel, Walter, jt. ed. see Needham, Joseph.

Pageler, Elaine. The Ecology Kidds, 5 bks., Set. Kratoville, Betty Lou, ed. (Illus.). 48p. (Orig.). (J). (gr. 4-10). 1995. pap. text 17.00 (*1-57128-007-3*, 007-3) Acad Therapy.

— Near Star Planets, 5 vols. Kratoville, Betty Lou, ed. (Illus.). 48p. (Orig.). 1998. pap. 17.00 (*1-57128-092-8*, 8092-8) High Noon Bks.

— Numero Uno Gang Mysteries, 5 novels, Set. (Illus.). 240p. (Orig.). (J). (gr. 3-9). 1988. pap. 17.00 (*0-87879-550-2*) High Noon Bks.

— Riddle Street, 5 vols., Set 2. Kratoville, Betty Lou, ed. (Illus.). 48p. (Orig.). (YA). (gr. 5 up). 1997. pap. 17.00 (*1-57128-061-8*, 8061-8) Acad Therapy.

— The Riddle Street Mystery Series: Wrong Robber Mystery, Market Stake-Out Mystery, Haunted Apartment House Mystery, Book Party Mystery, Radio Station Mystery, 5 bks. Kratoville, Betty Lou, ed. (Illus.). 48p. (J). (gr. 1 up). 1994. pap. text 17.00 (*0-87879-983-4*) High Noon Bks.

— Runaway Magic. Kratoville, Betty Lou, ed. (Meridian Bks.). (Illus.). 64p. (J). (gr. 3-9). 1989. lib. bdg. 4.95 (*0-87879-652-5*) High Noon Bks.

***Pagell, Ruth A., ed.** International Business Information: How to Find It, How to Use It. 450p. 1998. pap. text 100.00 (*1-57958-093-9*) Fitzroy Dearborn.

***Pagell, Ruth A. & Halperin, Michael.** International Business Information: How to Find It, How to Use It. 450p. 2000. pap. 65.00 (*0-8144-0577-0*) AMACOM.

— International Business Information: How to Find It, How to Use It. 450p. 2000. pap. 65.00 (*1-888998-83-0*, 98-83-0) Glenlake Pub.

Pagell, Ruth A. & Halperin, Michael. International Business Information: How to Find It, How to Use It. 2nd rev. ed. LC 97-31548. (Illus.). 432p. 1997. boxed set 84.50 (*1-57356-050-2*) Oryx Pr.

***Pagell, Ruth A. & Halperin, Michael.** International Business Information: How to Find It, How to Use It. 3rd ed. 464p. 2001. text, boxed set 84.50 (*1-57356-353-6*) Oryx Pr.

***Pagello, E., et al, eds.** Intelligent Autonomous Systems 6. 1100p. 2000. 126.00 (*1-58603-078-7*) IOS Press.

Pagelow, Mildred D. Family Violence. LC 84-8244. 592p. 1984. 75.00 (*0-275-91239-6*, C1239, Praeger Pubs); pap. 27.95 (*0-275-91623-5*, B1623, Praeger Pubs) Greenwood.

Pagels. Master Classes 7. 176p. 1997. 20.00 (*0-465-04518-9*, Pub. by Basic) HarpC.

Pagels, Douglas. Chasing Away the Clouds: Words of Encouragement That Will Help You Through Any Hard Times & Bring More Happiness to Your Life. LC 97-36606. 32p. 1998. pap. 8.95 (*0-88396-454-6*) Blue Mtn Art.

***Pagels, Douglas.** These Are the Gifts I'd Like to Give to You: A Sourcebook of Joy & Encouragement. LC 99-16855. (Illus.). 96p. 2000. 16.95 (*0-88396-524-0*) Blue Mtn Art.

— To the One Person I Consider to Be My Soul Mate. (Illus.). 64p. 2000. pap. 8.95 (*1-58786-003-1*, Blue Mtn Pr Bks) SPS Studios.

Pagels, Douglas, ed. It's Great to Have a Brother Like You: A Collection. LC 98-50185. (Language of...Ser.). (Illus.). 48p. 1999. 14.95 (*0-88396-492-9*, L4929) Blue Mtn Art.

— The Language of Courage & Inner Strength: A Wonderful Gift of Inspiring Thoughts. LC 99-18692. (Language of...Ser.). (Illus.). 48p. 1999. 14.95 (*0-88396-508-9*, L5089) Blue Mtn Art.

— Thoughts to Share with a Wonderful Son: A Collection. LC 98-46833. (Language of...Ser.). (Illus.). 48p. 1999. 14.95 (*0-88396-489-9*, L4899) Blue Mtn Art.

Pagels, Elaine. Adam, Eve & the Serpent. 1989. pap. 12.00 (*0-679-72232-7*) Vin Bks.

Pagels, Elaine H. The Gnostic Gospels. LC 89-40159. 224p. 1989. pap. 11.00 (*0-679-72453-2*) Vin Bks.

— The Gnostic Paul: Gnostic Exegesis of the Pauline Letters. LC 92-7932. 192p. 1992. pap. 16.00 (*1-56338-039-0*) TPI PA.

— The Origin of Satan: The New Testament Origins of Christianity's Demonization of Jews, Pagans & Heretics. Date not set. 23.00 (*0-614-32354-1*) Random.

— The Origin of Satan: The New Testament Origins of Christianity's Demonization of Jews, Pagans & Heretics. 1996. pap. 12.00 (*0-679-73118-0*) Random.

— The Origins of Satan. 1996. pap. 12.00 (*0-614-97751-7*) Vin Bks.

Pagen, Dennis. Hang Gliding Training Manual: Learning Hang Gliding Skills for Beginner to Intermediate Pilots. (Illus.). 370p. 1995. pap. 29.95 (*0-936310-12-X*, Sport Aviation Pubns) Black Mntn.

— Paragliding Flight: Walking on Air. (Illus.). 200p. 1990. pap. 19.95 (*0-936310-09-X*, Sport Aviation Pubns) Black Mntn.

— Performance Flying: Hang Gliding Techniques for Intermediate & Advanced Pilots. (Illus.). 342p. (Orig.). 1993. pap. 29.95 (*0-936310-11-1*, Sport Aviation Pubns) Black Mntn.

— Powered Ultralight Flying. (Illus.). 190p. (Orig.). 1983. pap. 11.95 (*0-936310-06-5*, Sport Aviation Pubns) Black Mntn.

— Powered Ultralight Training Course. rev. ed. (Illus.). 112p. 1991. pap. 9.95 (*0-936310-04-9*, Sport Aviation Pubns) Black Mntn.

— Towing Aloft: Learning to Surface-Tow & Aerotow Hang Gliders, Paragliders & Ultralight Sailplanes. (Illus.). 364p. (Orig.). 1998. pap. 29.95 (*0-936310-13-8*) Black Mntn.

— Understanding the Sky. (Illus.). 290p. 1992. pap. 19.95 (*0-936310-10-3*, Sport Aviation Pubns) Black Mntn.

Pagenkopf, Gordon K. Introduction to Natural Water Chemistry. LC 78-16089. (Environmental Science & Technology Ser.: No. 3). 286p. reprint ed. pap. 88.70 (*0-7837-0105-5*, 204038300016) Bks Demand.

Pager, Sean. Hawaii: Off the Beaten Path: A Guide to Unique Places. 4th ed. LC 99-52157. (Illus.). 340p. 1999. pap. text 14.95 (*0-7627-0532-9*) Globe Pequot.

Pages, Alain, jt. ed. see Thomson, Clive.

Pages, Alain, ed. see Zola, Emile.

Pages, Beatriz. Can Cuba Survive? An Interview with Fidel Castro. 105p. 1993. pap. 9.95 (*1-875284-58-3*) Ocean Pr NJ.

Pages, Erik R. Responding to Defense Dependence: Policy Ideas & the American Defense Industrial Base. LC 95-11275. 208p. 1996. 57.95 (*0-275-95313-0*, Praeger Pubs) Greenwood.

Pages Europa Staff, ed. French Directory 1998: The Complete Guide to Learning French in France. 1998. pap. text 12.95 (*1-84024-015-6*, Pub. by Summers) Howell Pr VA.

Pages in a Snap, Inc. Staff, ed. see Wannamaker, Catherine A.

Pages in a Snap Staff, ed. see Wannamaker, Catherine A.

Pages, Xiomara J. Mi Cruz Llena de Rosas: Cartas a Sandra, mi Hija Enferma. rev. ed. LC 95-83639. (Coleccion Felix Varela: 6). (SPA., Illus.). 80p. (Orig.). 1998. pap. 12.00 (*0-89729-885-3*) Ediciones.

***Pages, Xiomara J.** Una Pizca de Sal, Vol. 1. LC 99-60997. (Coleccion Felix Varela: Vol. 7). (SPA., Illus.). 112p. 1999. pap. 12.00 (*0-89729-888-8*) Ediciones.

— Una Pizca de Sal, Vol. II. (Coleccion Felix Varela: Vol. 7). (SPA.). 111p. pap. 12.00 (*0-89729-903-5*) Ediciones.

Paget. No Other Way to Tell It: Dramadoc/Docudrama on Television. LC 98-164426. 256p. 1998. 69.95 (*0-7190-4532-0*, Pub. by Manchester Univ Pr); pap. 19.95 (*0-7190-4533-9*, Pub. by Manchester Univ Pr) St Martin.

Paget, Becky. The Belle of Nauvoo. LC 94-204508. 1994. pap. 9.95 (*1-55503-690-2*, 01111698) Covenant Comms.

Paget, F., ed. see Hooker, Richard & Walton, Isaac.

Paget, Francis E. St. Antholin's: or Old Churches & New: A Tale for the Times, 1841. Wolff, Robert L., ed. LC 75-469. (Victorian Fiction Ser.). 1975. lib. bdg. 73.00 (*0-8240-1547-9*) Garland.

Paget, James C. The Epistle of Barnabas: Outlook & Background. LC 95-101962. (WissUNT Zum Neuen Testament Ser.). 340p. (Orig.). 1994. pap. text 72.50 (*3-16-146161-4*, Pub. by JCB Mohr) Coronet Bks.

Paget, John. An Answer to the Unjust Complaints of W. Best: Also an Answer to Mr. John Davenport. LC 76-57403. (English Experience Ser.: No. 819). 1977. reprint ed. lib. bdg. 20.00 (*90-221-0819-8*) Walter J Johnson.

— Hungary & Transylvania: With Remarks on Their Social, Political & Economical Condition. LC 79-135827. (Eastern Europe Collection). 1971. reprint ed. 65.95 (*0-405-02769-9*) Ayer.

— Judicial Puzzles: Gathered from the State Trials. (Legal Recreations Ser.: Vol. 3). 155p. 1979. reprint ed. 35.00 (*0-8377-1003-0*, Rothman) W S Hein.

— Paradoxes & Puzzles, Historical, Judicial & Literary. LC 75-30035. reprint ed. 57.50 (*0-404-14037-8*) AMS Pr.

***Paget, Julian.** Battlefield Napoleonic: Hougoumont. 2000. pap. 16.95 (*0-85052-716-3*, Pub. by Pen & Sword) Combined Pub.

Paget, Julian. Discovering London Ceremonial & Traditions. 1989. pap. 25.00 (*0-85263-994-5*, Pub. by Shire Pubns) St Mut.

— Wellington's Peninsular War: Battles & Battlefields. (Illus.). 285p. 1996. 29.95 (*0-85052-603-5*, Pub. by Leo Cooper) Trans-Atl Phila.

Paget, Lou. How to Be a Great Lover: Girlfriend-to-Girlfriend Totally Explicit Techniques That Will Blow His Mind. LC 98-41537. (Illus.). 235p. 1999. 20.00 (*0-7679-0287-4*) Broadway BDD.

***Paget, Lou.** How to Give Her Absolute Pleasure: The Totally Explicit Techniques That Every Woman Wants Her Man to Know. 256p. 2000. 20.00 (*0-7679-0452-4*) Broadway BDD.

Paget, Marianne A. A Complex Sorrow: Reflections on Cancer & an Abbreviated Life. DeVault, Marjorie L., ed. LC 92-49403. (Illus.). 176p. 1993. 39.95 (*1-56639-041-9*) Temple U Pr.

P

— A Complex Sorrow: Reflections on Cancer & an Abbreviated Life. DeVault, Marjorie L., ed. LC 92-49403. (Illus.). 176p. (C). 1993. pap. 19.95 (*1-56639-192-X*) Temple U Pr.

— The Unity of Mistakes: A Phenomenological Interpretation of Medical Work. LC 87-26716. 224p. (C). 1988. 34.95 (*0-87722-533-8*) Temple U Pr.

Paget, R. L. Cap & Gown: Third Series. LC 78-74825. (Granger Poetry Library). 1979. reprint ed. 30.00 (*0-89609-144-9*) Roth Pub Inc.

Paget, Richard. Beyond Death's Door. LC 78-14485. 1979. 22.95 (*0-87949-113-2*) Ashley Bks.

Paget, Richard A. Human Speech: Some Observations, Experiments, & Conclusions As to the Origin, Purpose, & Possible Improvement of Human Speech. LC 75-41208. reprint ed. 34.50 (*0-404-14692-9*) AMS Pr.

Paget, Stephen. I Have Reason to Believe. LC 68-16964. (Essay Index Reprint Ser.). 1977. reprint ed. 233.10 (*0-8369-0763-9*) Ayer.

— I Sometimes Think. LC 67-26769. (Essay Index Reprint Ser.). 1977. 18.95 (*0-8369-0764-7*) Ayer.

— I Wonder: Essays for the Young People. LC 68-54365. (Essay Index Reprint Ser.). (YA). (gr. 7 up). 1977. reprint ed. 17.95 (*0-8369-0765-5*) Ayer.

*__Paget, Stephen A.__ Manual of Rheumatology & Outpatient Orthopaedic Disorders: Diagnosis & Therapy. 4th ed. LC 99-45307. 568p. 2000. 36.95 (*0-7817-2442-2*) Lppncott W & W.

Paget, Stephen A., et al. Manual of Rheumatology & Outpatient Orthopaedic Disorders: Diagnosis & Therapy. 4th ed. 512p. spiral bd. 34.95 (*0-7817-1576-8*) Lppncott W & W.

Paget-Thomlinson, Edward. The Illustrated History of Canal & River Navigations. (Illus.). 450p. 1993. 60.00 (*1-85075-276-1*, Pub. by Sheffield Acad); pap. 27.50 (*1-85075-277-X*, Pub. by Sheffield Acad) CUP Services.

Paget-Tomlinson, Edward. The Railway Carriers. 192p. (C). 1989. 60.00 (*0-86138-082-7*, Pub. by T Dalton) St Mut.

Paget, Violet. Baldwin: Being Dialogues on Views & Aspirations. LC 72-291. (Essay Index Reprint Ser.). 1977. reprint ed. 23.95 (*0-8369-2817-2*) Ayer.

— For Maurice: Five Unlikely Stories. Reginald, R. & Menville, Douglas A., eds. LC 75-1462. 1976. reprint ed. lib. bdg. 23.95 (*0-405-08423-4*) Ayer.

— Hauntings: Fantastic Stories. LC 75-37280. (Short Story Index Reprint Ser.). 1977. reprint ed. 19.95 (*0-8369-4093-8*) Ayer.

Paget-Wilkes, M. Poverty, Revolution & the Church. 142p. (Orig.). 1982. pap. text 13.50 (*0-85364-285-0*) Attic Pr.

Pagett, jt. auth. see Swannell.

Pagiola, Stefano. The Global Environmental Benefits of Land Degradation Control on Agricultural Land: Global Overlays Program. LC 98-53728. (World Bank Environmental Paper Ser.: No. 16). 60p. 1999. pap. 22.00 (*0-8213-4421-8*, 14421) World Bank.

Pagiola, Stefano, et al. Mainstreaming Biodiversity in Agricultural Development: Toward Good Practice. LC 97-994. (Environment Papers: No. 15). 50p. 1997. pap. 22.00 (*0-8213-3884-6*, 13884) World Bank.

Pagis, Dan. Last Poems, Volume #67. Keller, tr. (QRL Poetry Bks.: Vol. XXXI). 1992. 20.00 (*0-614-06444-9*) Quarterly Rev.

— The Selected Poetry of Dan Pagis. Mitchell, Stephen, tr. from HEB. LC 96-14395. (Literature of the Middle East Ser.: Vol. 7). 160p. (C). 1996. pap. 15.95 (*0-520-20539-1*, Pub. by U CA Pr) Cal Prin Full Svc.

Paglia, Camille. The Birds. LC 98-215540. (Film Classics Ser.). (Illus.). 80p. 1998. pap. 10.95 (*0-85170-651-7*) Ind U Pr.

— Sex, Art, & American Culture. LC 91-50933. 1992. pap. 14.00 (*0-679-74101-1*) Vin Bks.

— Sexual Personae: Art & Decadence from Nefertiti to Emily Dickinson. LC 91-50024. 736p. 1991. pap. 17.00 (*0-679-73579-8*) Vin Bks.

— Sexual Personae: Art & Decadence from Nefertiti to Emily Dickinson. LC 89-31659. 712p. (C). 1990. 45.00 (*0-300-04396-1*) Yale U Pr.

— Vamps & Tramps: New Essays. LC 94-12191. (Illus.). 352p. 1994. pap. 15.00 (*0-679-75120-3*) Vin Bks.

*__Paglia, Michael, et al.__ Denver: The Modern City. 96p. 1999. pap. 9.95 (*0-914248-23-5*) Hist Denver.

Pagliano, Paul. Multisensory Environments. 1999. pap. text 28.95 (*1-85346-553-4*) Taylor & Francis.

Pagliari, Robert. Fourteen Steps to Dynamic Preaching. LC 93-78616. 96p. (Orig.). 1993. pap. 9.95 (*0-89243-525-9*); pap. text, wbk. ed. 4.95 (*0-89243-626-3*) Liguori Pubns.

Pagliaro, Ann M. & Pagliaro, Louis A. Substance Abuse among Children & Adolescents: Its Nature, Extent & Effects from Conception to Adulthood. LC 95-25496. 416p. 1996. 85.00 (*0-471-58042-2*) Wiley.

*__Pagliaro, Ann M. & Pagliaro, Louis A.__ Substance Use among Women: A Reference & Resource Guide. LC 99-41873. 1999. write for info. (*1-58391-035-2*) Brunner-Mazel.

Pagliaro, Ann M., jt. auth. see Pagliaro, Louis A.

Pagliaro, Ann Marie, jt. ed. see Pagliaro, Louis A.

Pagliaro, Harold. Selfhood & Redemption in Blakes's Songs. LC 86-43162. (Illus.). 176p. 1987. 27.50 (*0-271-00603-X*) Pa St U Pr.

Pagliaro, Harold E. Henry Fielding: A Literary Life. LC 97-18186. (Literary Lives Ser.). 224p. 1998. text 35.00 (*0-312-21032-9*) St Martin.

— Naked Heart: A Soldier's Journey to the Front. LC D811.P2678 1996. (Illus.). 238p. (C). 1996. pap. 12.00 (*0-943549-41-8*) Truman St Univ.

*__Pagliaro, John Anthony, Jr.__ The Story Behind the Rock: The World's Most Creative Directory of Romantic & Surprising. vi, 108p. 1999. mass mkt. 9.95 (*0-9675151-0-6*) Pagliaro.

*__Pagliaro, Louis A.__ Pndr, Psychologists' Neuropsychotropic Drug Reference. LC 98-32463. 1999. 54.95 (*0-87630-956-2*) Brunner-Mazel.

Pagliaro, Louis A. Psychologist's Psychotropic Desk Reference. LC 98-26775. 1998. 59.95 (*0-87630-964-3*) Brunner-Mazel.

Pagliaro, Louis A. & Pagliaro, Ann M. The Pharmacologic Basis of Psychotherapeutics: An Introduction for Psychologists. LC 97-19994. 1997. pap. write for info. (*1-56032-678-6*); boxed set. write for info. (*1-56032-677-8*) Hemisp Pub.

Pagliaro, Louis A. & Pagliaro, Ann Marie, eds. Problems in Pediatric Drug Therapy. 3rd rev. ed. LC 94-37762. 1145p. 1995. pap. 60.00 (*0-914768-53-0*, T168) Am Pharm Assn.

*__Pagliaro, Louis A. & Pagliaro, Ann Marie, eds.__ Problems in Pediatric Drug Therapy. 4th rev. ed. 600p. 2000. 80.00 (*1-58212-001-3*) Am Pharm Assn.

Pagliaro, Louis A., jt. auth. see Pagliaro, Ann M.

Pagliaro, Michael J. Everything You Should Know about Musical Instruments. (Illus.). 133p. (Orig.). (C). 1992. reprint ed. pap. text 17.95 (*0-945864-49-3*) Columbia Pacific U Pr.

— The Violin. (How Musical Instruments Work Ser.: Vol. I). (Illus.). 60p. (J). (gr. 4-8). 1993. student ed. 6.95 (*1-884417-00-0*) Ardsley Pr.

*__Pagliaro, Michael J.__ The Violin: How it Works. (Illus.). 46p. (YA). (gr. 9-12). 2000. pap. 7.95 (*1-884417-01-9*) Ardsley Pr.

Pagliaro, Penny, ed. I Like Poems & Poems Like Me. LC 76-50343. (Illus.). (J). (gr. 1-6). 1977. lib. bdg. 8.95 (*0-916630-03-X*) Pr Pacifica.

Pagliarulo. Introduction to Physical Therapy. (Illus.). 320p. (gr. 13). 1995. pap. text 31.95 (*0-8151-6714-8*, 24738) Mosby Inc.

Pagliarulo, Michael A. Introduction to Physical Therapy. (Illus.). 1996. teacher ed. write for info. (*0-8151-4323-0*) Mosby Inc.

Paglin, Max D., ed. A Legislative History of the Communications Act of 1934. (Illus.). 1008p. 1990. text 125.00 (*0-19-504915-2*) OUP.

Paglin, Morton. Poverty & Transfers In-Kind: A Re-Evaluation of Poverty in the United States. LC 79-88586. (Publication Ser.: No. 219). 108p. 1980. pap. 2.78 (*0-8179-7192-0*) Hoover Inst Pr.

Paglino, Joseph, jt. auth. see Corvasce, Mauro.

Paglino, Joseph R., jt. auth. see Corvasce, Mauro V.

Pagliore, Virginia. Oracles of Light. LC 84-61992. 96p. 1986. pap. 8.00 (*0-918618-26-6*) Pella Pub.

Pagliuca, William, ed. Perspectives on Grammaricalization. LC 94-14551. (Current Issues in Linguistic Theory Ser.: No. 109). xx, 306p. 1994. lib. bdg. 79.00 (*1-55619-563-X*) J Benjamins Pubng Co.

Pagliughi, Debbie. Collard Greens, Watermelons & "Miss" Charlotte's Pie. 381p. 1993. 19.95 (*0-9652935-0-5*) Swansboro UMW.

Pagna, Tom. Petals from a Rose. (Illus.). 250p. 1998. 24.95 (*0-89651-556-7*) Hardwood Pr.

Pagna, Tom & Best, Bob. Notre Dame's Era of Ara. LC 94-16378. (Illus.). 310p. 1994. reprint ed. pap. 14.95 (*0-912083-74-3*) Diamond Communications.

Pagni, Carlo A., jt. auth. see Cassinari, Valentino.

Pagni, Patrick J. & Grant, Cecile E., eds. Fire Safety Science: Proceedings of the August International Symposium. 1226p. 1986. 260.00 (*0-89116-456-1*) Hemisp Pub.

Pagni, Patrick J., jt. auth. see Levine, Robert S.

Pagnol. Le Chateau de Ma Mere. text 8.95 (*0-88436-045-8*) EMC-Paradigm.

— Jean de Florette: C Level. 8.95 (*0-8219-1851-6*) EMC-Paradigm.

Pagnol, Marcel. Angele. pap. 9.95 (*0-685-23894-6*, F117230) Fr & Eur.

— Angele. (FRE.). 216p. 1976. pap. 10.95 (*0-8288-9889-8*, F117420) Fr & Eur.

— Cesar. 1956. 11.50 (*0-685-23892-X*) Fr & Eur.

— Cesar. (FRE.). 292p. 1976. 13.95 (*0-8288-9890-1*, F117430) Fr & Eur.

— Le Chateau de Ma Mere. (FRE.). 280p. 13.95 (*0-8288-9897-9*, F117481) Fr & Eur.

— Cigalon. 180p. 1978. 9.95 (*0-686-54820-5*) Fr & Eur.

— Confidences. (FRE.). 1990. pap. 13.95 (*0-7859-3329-8*, 2877060691) Fr & Eur.

— Critique des Critiques. (Coll. Litterature). (FRE.). 168p. 1987. pap. 19.95 (*0-7859-1548-6*, 2826308173) Fr & Eur.

— Discours sous la Coupole. (FRE.). 76p. 1961. pap. 10.95 (*0-7859-5389-2*) Fr & Eur.

— L' Eau des Collines, 2 tomes. Incl. Tome I. Jean de Florette. 19.95 Tome II. Manon des Sources. 19.95 write for info. (*0-318-51988-7*) Fr & Eur.

— Fabien: Theatre. (FRE.). 331p. 1976. 27.95 (*0-7859-5559-3*) Fr & Eur.

— Fanny. (FRE.). 283p. 1970. 13.95 (*0-8288-9891-X*, F117440) Fr & Eur.

— La Femme du Boulanger. (FRE.). 279p. 1974. 13.95 (*0-8288-9892-8*, F117450); pap. 4.95 (*0-685-23893-8*) Fr & Eur.

— La Fille du Puisatier. pap. 9.95 (*0-685-37002-X*) Fr & Eur.

— La Fille du Puisatier. (FRE., Illus.). 304p. 1975. pap. 13.95 (*0 7859-0112-4*, M3832) Fr & Eur.

— La Gloire de Mon Pere. (FRE.). 13.95 (*0-8288 9896-0*, F117480) Fr & Eur.

— Jazz. (FRE., Illus.). 296p. 1976. 10.95 (*0-7859-0113-2*, M3834) Fr & Eur.

— Jazz: Comedie Dramatique en 4 Actes. pap. 4.95 (*0-685-37003-8*) Fr & Eur.

— Jean de Florette. (FRE.). 320p. 1976. 13.95 (*0-8288-9893-6*, F117460) Fr & Eur.

— Jean de Florette. (FRE.). 318p. 1988. pap. 13.95 (*0-7859-1668-7*, 2877060543) Fr & Eur.

— Jofroi. (FRE.). 160p. 1990. pap. 13.95 (*0-7859-1562-1*, 2877060675) Fr & Eur.

— Judas. (FRE., Illus.). 258p. 1975. pap. 11.95 (*0-7859-0114-0*, M3836) Fr & Eur.

— Manon des Sources. (FRE.). 320p. 1976. 13.95 (*0-8288-9894-4*, F117461) Fr & Eur.

— Manon des Sources. (FRE.). 318p. 1988. pap. 13.95 (*0-7859-1657-1*, 2877060551) Fr & Eur.

— Marius. (FRE., Illus.). 297p. 1973. 13.95 (*0-8288-9895-2*, F117470) Fr & Eur.

— Le Masque de Fer. pap. 9.50 (*0-685-37005-4*) Fr & Eur.

— Les Merchands de Gloire: Piece en Cinq Actes. (FRE.). 291p. 1976. write for info. (*0-7859-4879-1*) Fr & Eur.

— Merlusse-Cigalon. (FRE.). 1974. 19.95 (*0-7859-0115-9*, M3838) Fr & Eur.

— My Father's Glory & My Mother's Castle: Marcel Pagnol's Memories of Childhood. Barisse, Rita, tr. LC 86-60989. 342p. 1986. pap. 13.00 (*0-86547-257-2*) N Point Pr.

— Nais: Theatre. (FRE.). 160p. 1990. pap. 13.95 (*0-7859-1561-3*, 2877060659) Fr & Eur.

— Notes sur le Rire. (FRE.). 127p. 1987. pap. 13.95 (*0-7859-1549-4*, 2826308203) Fr & Eur.

— Oeuvres Completes, Tome III. pap. 9.95 (*0-685-35902-6*) Fr & Eur.

— La Petite Fille aux Yeux Sombres. (FRE.). 1991. pap. 13.95 (*0-7859-3330-1*, 2877060713) Fr & Eur.

— Pirouettes. pap. 9.95 (*0-685-37007-0*) Fr & Eur.

— Pirouettes. (FRE.). 1991. pap. 13.95 (*0-7859-3440-5*) Fr & Eur.

— Priere aux Etoiles. (FRE.). 386p. 1978. 39.95 (*0-7859-4775-2*) Fr & Eur.

— Regain. (FRE.). 254p. 1973. 11.95 (*0-8288-9750-6*, 2877060632) Fr & Eur.

— Le Schpountz. pap. 9.95 (*0-685-37008-9*) Fr & Eur.

— Le Schprountz. (FRE., Illus.). 288p. 1976. 10.95 (*0-7859-0119-1*, M3842) Fr & Eur.

— Le Secret du Masque de Fer. (FRE., Illus.). 416p. 1978. 27.95 (*0-7859-4880-5*) Fr & Eur.

— Les Sermons de Marcel Pagnol. Calmels, ed. 12.50 (*0-685-37009-7*) Fr & Eur.

— Souvenirs D'Enfance, 3 tomes. Incl. Tome I. Gloire de Mon Pere. 14.95 Tome II. Chateau de Ma Mere. 15.50 Tome III. Temps des Secrets. 15.95 write for info. (*0-318-52267-5*) Fr & Eur.

— Souvenirs d'Enfance: Le Temps des Amours, Vol. 4. (FRE.). 290p. 1979. 21.95 (*0-7859-4730-2*) Fr & Eur.

— Le Temps de Amours. (Souvenirs d'Enfance Ser.: No. 4). (FRE.). 1988. pap. 13.95 (*0-7859-3334-4*, 2877060535) Fr & Eur.

— Le Temps des Secrets. (Souvenirs d'Enfance Ser.: No. 3). (FRE.). 1988. pap. 13.95 (*0-7859-3327-1*, 2877060527) Fr & Eur.

— Topaze. (FRE.). 1988. pap. 13.95 (*0-7859-3328-X*, 2877060594) Fr & Eur.

— Topaze: Comedie en 4 Actes. pap. 9.95 (*0-685-37013-5*) Fr & Eur.

Pagnoni, A. Project Engineering: Computer-Oriented Planning & Operational Decision Making. 256p. 1990. 42.95 (*0-387-52475-4*) Spr-Verlag.

Pagnoni, Mario & Robinson, Gerald. Softball: Fast & Slow Pitch. (Spalding Sports Library). (Illus.). 256p. (Orig.). 1995. pap. 12.95 (*1-57028-025-8*, 80258H, Mstrs Pr) NTC Contemp Pub Co.

Pagnucci, Franco. Ancient Moves. (Illus.). 60p. 1998. pap. 6.99 (*0-929326-14-8*) Bur Oak Pr Inc.

— I Never Had a Pet. Pagnucci, Gian, ed. (Illus.). 32p. (Orig.). (J). (gr. 1-5). 1992. pap. 5.99 (*0-929326-09-1*) Bur Oak Pr Inc.

Pagnucci, Franco & Pagnucci, Susan. Hansel & Gretel & Grimm & More: With Big Flannel Board Patterns. (Illus.). 64p. (J). (ps-3). 1996. pap. 8.99 (*0-929326-13-X*) Bur Oak Pr Inc.

*__Pagnucci, Franco & Pagnucci, Susan.__ Jonah & the Whale & Other Old Testament Stories. (Illus.). 64p. (J). (ps-3). 2000. pap. 8.99 (*0-929326-15-6*) Bur Oak Pr Inc.

Pagnucci, Franco & Pagnucci, Susan. Paul Revere & Other Story Hours. (Illus.). 72p. (Orig.). (J). (gr. k-6). 1988. pap. 8.99 (*0-929326-00-8*) Bur Oak Pr Inc.

— Story - Start Dinosaurs. 1991. 7.99 (*0-86653-998-0*) Fearon Teacher Aids.

— Story - Start Monsters. 1991. 7.99 (*0-86653-999-9*) Fearon Teacher Aids.

— Story Start Animals. (J). (gr. 2-5). 1990. pap. 7.99 (*0-8224-6398-9*) Fearon Teacher Aids.

— Story-Start Set, 3 bks., Set. (J). (gr. 2-5). 20.99 (*1-56417-736-X*, FE0012) Fearon Teacher Aids.

Pagnucci, Franco, jt. auth. see Pagnucci, Susan.

*__Pagnucci, Gian.__ Don't Count Your Chickens: Stories for Kids to Tell. (Illus.). 64p. (J). (gr. k-3). 2000. pap. 8.99 (*0-929326-17-2*) Bur Oak Pr Inc.

Pagnucci, Gian, ed. see Pagnucci, Franco.

Pagnucci, Gianfranco. Out Harmsen's Way. 62p. (Orig.). 1991. pap. 7.00 (*1-878660-10-1*) Fireweed WI.

Pagnucci, Gianfranco, ed. Face the Poem. (Illus.). 32p. (Orig.). (J). (gr. 2-8). 1979. pap. 3.99 (*0-929326-02-4*) Bur Oak Pr Inc.

Pagnucci, Susan. Games to Cut. (Illus.). 20p. (Orig.). (J). (gr. k-3). 1978. 4.99 (*0-929326-03-2*) Bur Oak Pr Inc.

— Number Chomp. (Illus.). 48p. (Orig.). (J). (gr. 1-2). 1984. pap. 4.50 (*0-929326-04-0*) Bur Oak Pr Inc.

— Shortcuts for Librarians & Teachers. (Illus.). 64p. (Orig.). 1993. pap. 8.99 (*0-929326-05-9*) Bur Oak Pr Inc.

— Storytelling Patterns. (Illus.). 32p. (Orig.). (J). (ps-3). 1991. pap. 4.99 (*0-929326-06-7*) Bur Oak Pr Inc.

Pagnucci, Susan & Pagnucci, Franco. Do Me! Stories. (Illus.). 64p. (Orig.). (J). (ps-3). 1993. pap. 8.99 (*0-929326-07-5*) Bur Oak Pr Inc.

— I Can! Folktales: Stories from Around the World for Young Children. (Illus.). 64p. (Orig.). (J). (ps-3). 1995. pap. 8.99 (*0-929326-10-5*) Bur Oak Pr Inc.

— Storytelling Magic. (Illus.). 32p. (Orig.). (J). (ps-3). 1997. pap. 4.99 (*0-929326-08-3*) Bur Oak Pr Inc.

— The 3 Bears: And Other Great Stories with Hats. (Illus.). 64p. (Orig.). (J). (ps-3). 1995. pap. 8.99 (*0-929326-12-1*) Bur Oak Pr Inc.

— The 3 Little Pigs: And Other Great Stories with Masks. (Illus.). 64p. (Orig.). (J). (ps-3). 1994. pap. 8.99 (*0-929326-11-3*) Bur Oak Pr Inc.

Pagnucci, Susan, jt. auth. see Pagnucci, Franco.

Pagnucco, Maurice, ed. see Artificial Intelligence Conference Staff.

Pagnucco, Rino. There Isn't Enough Toilet Paper in the World. LC 96-90029. (Orig.). 1996. pap. 10.95 (*0-533-11789-5*) Vantage.

Pagoan, Gianni. Break-Up. LC 90-46156. 28p. (J). 1989. 11.99 (*0-85953-310-7*) Childs Play.

Pagoldh, Susanne. Nordic Knitting. LC 91-28263. 120p. 1991. write for info. (*0-7136-3525-8*) A & C Blk.

Pagoldh, Susanne. Nordic Knitting. Rhoades, Carol, tr. from SWE. LC 91-28263. (Illus.). 120p. 1991. 21.95 (*0-934026-68-8*) Interweave.

Pagolu, Augustine. The Religion of the Patriarchs. LC 99-158573. (JSOTS Ser.: Vol. 277). 290p. 1998. 85.00 (*1-85075-935-9*, Pub. by Sheffield Acad) CUP Services.

Pagone, Tony, jt. auth. see Wallace, Jude.

Pagonis, Constantine, jt. ed. see Butterfield, Jeremy.

Pagonis, William G. Moving Mountains: Lessons in Leadership & Logistics from the Gulf War. 300p. 1992. 29.95 (*0-07-103388-2*) McGraw.

Pagonis, William G. & Cruikshank, Jeffrey L. Moving Mountains: Lessons in Leadership & Logistics from the Gulf War. LC 92-15641. 272p. 1992. 29.95 (*0-87584-360-3*) Harvard Busn.

— Moving Mountains: Lessons in Leadership & Logistics from the Gulf War. 1994. pap. 16.95 (*0-87584-508-8*) Harvard Busn.

Pagoota, Terry. The Angel Drank Diet Soda: Eleven Plays & Sketches for Performance & Praise. 1989. 8.99 (*0-8341-9049-4*, MP-654) Lillenas.

Pagoulaton, Regina, ed. see Livaditakis, Petros.

Pagoulatos, Angelos. Major Determinants Affecting the Demand & Supply of Energy Resources: An Analysis of the Petroleum Market. Bruchey, Stuart, ed. LC 78-22704. (Energy in the American Economy Ser.). (Illus.). 1979. lib. bdg. 23.95 (*0-405-12006-0*) Ayer.

Pagoulatos, Menelaos. O Navmachos: A Play in Three Acts. LC 88-62480. (GRE.). 71p. (Orig.). 1988. pap. text 5.00 (*0-918618-38-X*) Pella Pub.

Pagoulatou, Regina. The Ambassadors. LC 85-73011. (GRE.). 126p. 1985. pap. 8.00 (*0-918618-31-2*) Pella Pub.

— The Angels. Athanasakis, Apostolos, tr. from GRE.Tr. of E Angeli. (Illus.). 77p. (Orig.). 1988. pap. text 15.00 (*0-918618-33-9*) Pella Pub.

*__Pagoulatou, Regina.__ Exile: A Chronicle, 1948-1950. (Illus.). 175p. 1999. pap. 15.00i (*0-918618-75-4*) Pella Pub.

Pagoulatou, Regina. From the U. S. A. LC 84-72488. (GRE.). 151p. 1984. pap. 8.00 (*0-317-39603-X*, Anthe Pubns) Pella Pub.

— The Magic World & Ninety-One Other Stories. LC 83-72497. (GRE.). 275p. 1983. 10.00 (*0-317-39604-8*, Anthe Pubns) Pella Pub.

— Motherhood. LC 85-62595. 87p. 1985. pap. 8.00 (*0-918618-25-8*) Pella Pub.

— The Nepenthes. Pilitsis, George, tr. from GRE. LC 95-68182.Tr. of Ta Nipenthi. (ENG & GRE.). 63p. (Orig.). 1995. pap. text 10.00 (*0-614-28600-X*) Pella Pub.

— Pyrrhichios. Athanassakis, Apostolos N., tr. from GRE. LC 78-62044.Tr. of Pyrrichios. (ENG & GRE., Illus.). 111p. 1978. pap. text 5.00 (*0-918618-15-0*) Pella Pub.

Pagram, Beverly. Folk Wisdom for a Natural Home. (Illus.). 144p. 1997. 22.95 (*1-57076-078-0*, Trafalgar Sq Pub) Trafalgar.

Pagram, Beverly. Heaven & Hearth. 1997. pap. 15.95 (*0-7043-4540-4*, Pub. by Womens Press) Trafalgar.

Pagram, Beverly. Home & Heart: Simple, Beautiful Ways to Create Spirit, Harmony, & Warmth in Every Room. LC 97-44909. (Illus.). 160p. 1998. text 19.95 (*0-87596-522-9*) Rodale Pr Inc.

Pagter, Carl R., jt. auth. see Dundes, Alan.

Paguio, Ligaya, et al. Observational Guide for Child Study. (Illus.). 64p. (Orig.). (C). 1990. pap. text 7.95 (*0-918772-20-6*) Daye Pr.

Pagurek, Joyce. Writing Workshop: Paragraph & Sentence Practice. (YA). 1994. mass mkt. 21.95 (*0-8384-2998-X*, Newbury) Heinle & Heinle.

Pahari, S. Physical Chemistry, Vol. I. (C). 1989. 150.00 (*0-89771-408-3*, Pub. by Current Dist) St Mut.

Pahariya, N. C., jt. auth. see Panagariya, B. L.

Paher, Stanley, ed. see Fey, Marshall.

Paher, Stanley W. Colorado River Ghost Towns. (Illus.). 80p. 1976. pap. 14.95 (*0-913814-08-3*) Nevada Pubns.

— Death Valley Ghost Towns. LC 72-97900. (Illus.). 48p. 1973. 14.95 (*0-913814-03-2*) Nevada Pubns.

— Death Valley Ghost Towns, Vol. 1. LC 82-97900. (Illus.). 32p. 1981. pap. 5.95 (*0-913814-35-0*) Nevada Pubns.

— Death Valley Ghost Towns, Vol. 2. (Illus.). 32p. 1982. pap. 5.95 (*0-913814-36-9*) Nevada Pubns.

— Death Valley's Scotty's Castle: The Story Behind the Scenery. LC 82-84292. (Illus.). 48p. (Orig.). 1985. pap. 7.95 (*0-916122-87-5*) KC Pubns.

— Destination-Lake Tahoe: The Story Behind the Scenery. LC 94-78129. (Illus.). 48p. (Orig.). 1994. pap. 7.95 (*0-88714-088-2*) KC Pubns.

P

An Asterisk (*) at the beginning of an entry indicates that the title is appearing for the first time.

— Early Mining Days - California Gold Country: The Story Behind the Scenery. LC 96-75337. (Illus.). 48p. (Orig.). 1996. pap. 7.95 (*0-88714-111-0*) KC Pubns.
— The Eternal Covenant: God's Invitation to Faith & Life. 176p. 1997. pap. 9.95 (*0-913814-96-2*) Nevada Pubns.
— The Eternal Covenant of Peace. (Illus.). 286p. (Orig.). 1996. pap. 14.95 (*0-913814-54-7*) Nevada Pubns.
— Goldfield: Boom Town of Nevada. (Illus.). 17p. 1977. 4.95 (*0-913814-14-8*) Nevada Pubns.
— The Identity of Babylon & the Dating of the Book of Revelation. 2nd rev. ed. (Illus.). 176p. 1997. pap. 9.95 (*0-913814-94-6*) Nevada Pubns.
— If Thou Hadst Known. rev. ed. Orig. Title: If Thou Hadst Known. (Illus.). 128p. 1978. 12.95 (*0-913814-21-0*) Nevada Pubns.
— Las Vegas, As It Began, As It Grew. LC 70-175144. (Illus.). 1971. 29.95 (*0-913814-01-6*); pap. 19.95 (*0-913814-74-1*) Nevada Pubns.
— Matthew 24: First Century Fulfillment or End-Time Expectation. (Illus.). 192p. (Orig.). 1996. pap. 10.95 (*0-913814-40-7*) Nevada Pubns.
— Natural Law: Universal in Scope, Moral in Design. 72p. 1996. pap. 4.95 (*0-913814-93-8*) Nevada Pubns.
— Nevada: An Annotated Bibliography. (Illus.). 585p. 1980. 95.00 (*0-913814-26-1*) Nevada Pubns.
— Nevada Ghost Towns & Mining Camps. (Illus.). 500p. 1970. 49.95 (*0-913814-04-0*) Nevada Pubns.
— Nevada Ghost Towns & Mining Camps: An Illustrated Atlas, 2 vols., Set. (Illus.). 208p. 1993. 29.95 (*0-913814-11-3*) Nevada Pubns.
— Nevada Ghost Towns & Mining Camps: An Illustrated Atlas, Vol. 1. (Illus.). 104p. 1993. pap. 14.95 (*0-913814-09-1*) Nevada Pubns.
— Nevada Ghost Towns & Mining Camps: An Illustrated Atlas, Vol. 2. (Illus.). 104p. 1993. pap. 14.95 (*0-913814-10-5*) Nevada Pubns.
— Ponderosa Country: A Scenic & Historic Guide to Reno & Vicinity. LC 72-87135. (Illus.). 1972. 14.95 (*0-913814-02-4*) Nevada Pubns.
— Tonopah Nevada Silver Camp. (Illus.). 17p. 1978. pap. 4.95 (*0-913814-18-0*) Nevada Pubns.
— Western Arizona Ghost Towns. (Illus.). 64p. 1991. 7.95 (*0-913814-89-X*) Nevada Pubns.
Paher, Stanley W., ed. Chloride Mines & Murals. (Illus.). 1972. pap. 4.95 (*0-913814-15-6*) Nevada Pubns.
— Fort Churchill: Nevada Military Outpost of the 1860s. (Illus.). 48p. 1981. pap. 5.95 (*0-913814-38-5*) Nevada Pubns.
— Nevada Towns & Tales: North, Vol. 1. (Illus.). 224p. 1981. 19.95 (*0-913814-41-5*) Nevada Pubns.
— Nevada Towns & Tales: South, Vol. 2. (Illus.). 224p. 1982. 19.95 (*0-913814-45-8*) Nevada Pubns.
Paher, Stanley W., jt. auth. see Gamett, James.
Paher, Stanley W., jt. auth. see Spude, Robert L.
Paher, Stanley W., ed. see Curran, Harold.
Pahkinen, Erkki J., jt. auth. see Lehtonen, Risto.
Pahl & Werner. Computing in Civil & Building Engineering, Vol. 1. 750p. 1995. 129.00 (*90-5410-557-7*) Ashgate Pub Co.
— Computing in Civil & Building Engineering, Vol. 2. 750p. 1995. 129.00 (*90-5410-558-5*) Ashgate Pub Co.
Pahl, David. West Point. 1987. 7.98 (*0-671-08917-X*) S&S Trade.
Pahl, Ellen. Best All-Time Tips for Quilters Vol. 7: Rodale's Successful Quilting Library. 1999. text 19.95 (*0-87596-822-8*) Rodale Pr Inc.
— The Quilter's Ultimate Visual Guide: From A to Z--Hundreds of Tips & Techniques for Successful Quiltmaking. LC 96-27757. (Illus.). 288p. 1997. 29.95 (*0-87596-710-8*) Rodale Pr Inc.
Pahl, Ellen, ed. Quilter's Ultimate Visual Guide. (Illus.). 288p. 1998. pap. 19.95 (*0-87596-987-9*) Rodale Pr Inc.
Pahl, Gary W., ed. Periphery of the Southeastern Classic Maya Realm. LC 86-7502. (Latin American Indians Ser.). 304p. (Orig.). 1986. pap. 48.50 (*0-87903-061-5*) UCLA Lat Am Ctr.
Pahl, Gerald & Beitz, Wolfgang. Engineering Design: A Systematic Approach. 2nd enl. rev. ed. Blessing, Lucienne et al, trs. from GER. LC 95-10248. (Illus.). 544p. 1996. pap. 49.50 (*3-540-19917-9*) Spr-Verlag.
***Pahl, Greg.** The Complete Idiot's Guide to Saving the Environment. 2000. pap. 16.95 (*0-02-863982-0*, Alpha Ref) Macmillan Gen Ref.
Pahl, Jan, ed. Private Violence & Public Policy: The Needs of Battered Women & the Response of the Public. 208p. (Orig.). 1985. pap. 13.95 (*0-7100-9992-4*, Routledge Thoemms) Routledge.
Pahl, Jan, jt. auth. see Bramley, Peter.
Pahl, John. Ghost Towns & Ghosts. (Illus.). 40p. 1992. pap. 6.00 (*0-9626408-5-9*) Priscilla Pr.
***Pahl, John.** Youth Ministry in Modern America: 1930-Present. Alexander, Patrick H., ed. 200p. (C). 2000. pap. 16.95 (*1-56563-467-5*) Hendrickson MA.
Pahl, Jon. Hopes & Dreams of All: The International Walther League. 360p. 1993. write for info. (*0-9636446-0-2*); pap. 15.00 (*0-9636446-1-0*) Wheat Rdge Minist.
— Paradox Lost: Free Will & Political Liberty in American Culture, 1637-1760. (New Studies in American Intellectual & Cultural History). 224p. 1992. text 42.50 (*0-8018-4334-0*) Johns Hopkins.
Pahl, Kate. Transformations: Meaning Making in Nursery Education. (Illus.). 140p. 1998. pap. 19.95 (*1-85856-098-5*, Trentham Bks) Stylus Pub VA.
Pahl, Paul D., tr. see Luther, Martin.
Pahl, Peter J., jt. ed. see Werner, Heinrich.
***Pahl, Ray.** On Friendship. 2000. 56.95 (*0-7456-2280-1*, Pub. by Polity Pr); pap. 21.95 (*0-7456-2281-X*, Pub. by Polity Pr) Blackwell Pubs.
Pahl, Raymond E. After Success: "Fin-de-Siecle" Anxiety & Identity. 232p. (C). 1996. text 55.95 (*0-7456-1333-0*); pap. text 24.95 (*0-7456-1334-9*) Blackwell Pubs.
Pahl, Raymond E., et al. Structures & Processes of Urban Life. 2nd ed. LC 82-13093. (Aspects of Modern Sociology: the Social Structure of Modern Britain Ser.). 170p. reprint ed. pap. 52.70 (*0-7837-1581-1*, 204187300024) Bks Demand.
***Pahl, Ron H.** Creative Ways to Teach World History, 2 vols. Incl. Enlightenment-20th Century. (Illus.). 280p. 2000. pap., teacher ed. 39.95 (*0-8108-3760-9*); Prehistory-Renaissance. (Illus.). 300p. 2000. pap., teacher ed. 39.95 (*0-8108-3759-5*); (Illus.). 2000. Set pap., teacher ed. 69.95 (*0-8108-3761-7*) Scarecrow.
Pahl-Wostl, Claudia. The Dynamic Nature of Ecosystems: Chaos & Order Entwined. 280p. 1995. 250.00 (*0-471-95570-1*) Wiley.
Pahlavan, Kaveh & Levesque, Allen H. Wireless Information Networks. LC 94-22900. (Telecommunications & Signal Processing Ser.). 592p. 1995. 105.00 (*0-471-10607-0*) Wiley.
Pahlavan, Kaveh, jt. auth. see Ganesh, Rajamani.
Pahlavi, Asaraf. Time for Truth. Keitlen, Tomi, ed. LC 95-76051. (Illus.). 224p. 1995. pap. 14.85 (*1-886966-00-1*) In Print.
Pahler. Advanced Accounting. 7th ed. (C). 1999. text 107.00 (*0-03-026386-7*); pap. text, student ed. 29.50 (*0-03-026396-4*) Harcourt.
Pahler, Arnold J. Advanced Accounting. 5th ed. (C). 1994. 288.00 (*0-03-003602-X*, Pub. by Harcourt Coll Pubs) Harcourt.
— Oht T/a Advanced Accounting, 6e. 6th ed. (C). 1997. text 246.00 (*0-03-018617-X*) Harcourt Coll Pubs.
— Study Guide to Accompany Advanced Accounting: Concepts & Practice. 6th ed. (C). 1997. pap. text, student ed. 29.50 (*0-03-018613-7*) Harcourt.
— Working Papers to Accompany Advanced Accounting. 6th ed. (C). 1997. teacher ed. 18.00 (*0-03-018618-8*) Harcourt Coll Pubs.
Pahler, Arnold J. & Mori, Joseph E. Advance Accounting: Concepts & Practice. 6th ed. LC 96-85081. 1204p. (C). 1996. text 99.00 (*0-03-018612-9*) Dryden Pr.
— Advanced Accounting: Concepts & Practice. 5th ed. LC 93-71908. 1325p. (C). 1993. text 83.00 (*0-03-098697-4*) Dryden Pr.
— Advanced Accounting: Concepts & Practices: Instructor's Resource Manual & Testbook to Accompany. 5th ed. 500p. (C). 1994. pap. text 49.75 (*0-03-003589-9*) Dryden Pr.
Pahlitzsch, G. Dictionary of Production Engineering: Electroerosive & Electrochemical Removal, Vol. 9. (ENG, FRE & GER.). 170p. 1984. 75.00 (*0-8288-0606-3*, M 4000) Fr & Eur.
Pahlka, William H. Saint Augustine's Meter & George Herbert's Will. fac. ed. LC 87-4252. 263p. 1987. pap. 81.60 (*0-7837-7629-2*, 204738100007) Bks Demand.
Pahlow, Mannfried. The Healing Plants. (Illus.). 224p. 1993. pap. 18.95 (*0-8120-1498-7*) Barron.
***Pahlsson, Christer.** Decision-Making & Limited Resources: Studies in Interlanguage Vocabulary Space of Learners of English for Special Purpose. LC 99-58531. (Scandinavian University Studies : Vol. 20). 486p. 1999. pap. text 63.95 (*0-8204-4721-8*) P Lang Pubng.
— Decision-Making & Limited Resources: Studies in Interlanguage Vocabulary Space of Learners of English for Special Purposes. (Scandinavian University Studies). (Illus.). 486p. 1999. pap. 63.95 (*3-631-35632-3*) P Lang Pubng.
Pahmeier, Gailmarie. The House on Breakaheart Road: Poems. LC 97-32319. (Western Literature Ser.). 80p. 1998. pap. 10.00 (*0-87417-313-2*) U of Nev Pr.
Pahnke, Vickey. K. I. S. S. Gospel Guidelines for Better Relationships. LC 98-73149. 1998. pap. 10.95 (*1-57008-539-0*) Bookcraft Inc.
Pahnos, Markella. Creative Teaching Strategies for Comprehensive Elementary Health Education. (C). 1999. pap. text 42.67 (*0-205-27476-5*, Macmillan Coll) P-H.
Pahor, Boris. Pilgrim among the Shadows. Biggins, Michael, tr. from SLV. LC 94-20605. 1995. 20.00 (*0-15-171958-6*) Harcourt.
Pahr, Art. Invincible Fidelity: A History of the Kiel Municipal Band. Fried, Carmen V., ed. LC 98-90544. (Illus.). xiii, 263p. 1998. pap. 21.95 (*0-9667200-0-8*) Windridge Prodns.
Pahre, Robert. Leading Questions: How Hegemony Affects the International Political Economy. LC 98-40162. (Studies in International Political Economy). 266p. 1999. text 49.50 (*0-472-10970-7*, 10970) U of Mich Pr.
Pahud, P., jt. auth. see Del Pedro, M.
Pai. Chromosomal Syndromes. text. write for info. (*0-471-37217-X*) Wiley.
***Pai, Chhu-i & Watson, Burton.** Po Chhu-i: Selected Poems. LC 99-24284. (Translations from the Asian Classics Ser.). 2000. 14.50 (*0-231-11839-2*) Col U Pr.
Pai, E., jt. auth. see Farkas-Janke, M.
Pai, Hsien Y. Taipei People: Bilangual Edition. (Illus.). 480p. (C). pap. text 23.00 (*962-201-859-9*, Pub. by Chinese Univ) U of Mich Pr.
Pai, Hyung. Nationalism & the Construction of Korean Identity. LC 98-37408. 1999. pap. 18.00 (*1-55729-062-8*) IEAS.
***Pai, Hyung, Il.** Constructing "Korean" Origins: A Critical Review of Archaeology, Historiography & Racial Myth in Korean State-Formation Theories, 187. LC 99-56872. (East Asian Monographs). (Illus.). 2000. write for info. (*0-674-00244-X*) HUP.
Pai, K. M., tr. see Dubinin, G. N.
Pai, K. M., tr. see Samsonov, G. V., ed.
Pai, M. A. Energy Function Analysis for Power System Stability. (C). 1989. text 137.00 (*0-7923-9035-0*) Kluwer Academic.
***Pai, Man Sill.** Traditional Korean Furniture. (Illus.). 2000. 65.00 (*4-7700-2538-6*) Kodansha.
Pai, Margaret K. The Dreams of Two Yi-Min. LC 88-29539. (Illus.). 216p. 1989. 19.95 (*0-8248-1179-8*, Kolowalu Bk) UH Pr.
***Pai, Miao & Elsworth, Derek.** Coupled Processes in Subsurface Deformation, Flow & Transport. LC 00-24569. 360p. 2000. 59.00 (*0-7844-0460-7*) Am Soc Civil Eng.
Pai, Narendra M. Stop Heart Disease Now! Atherolysis: My Program for the Prevention & Reversal of Heart Disease. LC 98-92140. (Dr. Pai Publications). (Illus.). 134p. 1999. pap. 23.98 (*0-9667295-0-1*, 001, Left Front) Dr Pai Pubns.
***Pai Panandiker, V. A. & Nandy, Ashis.** Contemporary India. LC 99-936627. 1999. write for info. (*0-07-463335-X*) McGrw-H Hghr Educ.
Pai, R., jt. auth. see Govil-Pai, S.
Pai, S. T. & Zhang, Qi. Introduction to High Power Pulse Technology. (Series in Electrical & Computer Engineering). 500p. 1995. text 90.00 (*981-02-1714-5*) World Scientific Pub.
Pai Shih-I. Magnetogasdynamics & Plasma Dynamics. (Illus.). 1962. 39.95 (*0-387-80608-3*) Spr-Verlag.
Pai, Sudha. Uttar Pradesh Agrarian Change & Electoral Politics. (Illus.). 183p. 1993. 18.00 (*81-85402-21-3*, Pub. by Shipra Pubns) Nataraj Bks.
Pai, Young & Adler, Susan A. Cultural Foundations of Education. 2nd ed. LC 96-4176. (Illus.). 1996. pap. text 41.00 (*0-13-396979-7*, Merrill Pub Co) Macmillan.
Pai, Young, jt. auth. see Morris, Van Cleave.
Paic, Guy, ed. Ionizing Radiation: Protection & Dosimetry. (Health Physicists Ser.). 272p. 1988. lib. bdg. 210.00 (*0-8493-6713-1*, QC795) CRC Pr.
Paice, Chris, jt. ed. see McEnery, Tony.
Paice, Derek A. Power Electronic Converter Harmonics: Multipulse Methods for Clean Power. LC 95-33342. 224p. 1995. 69.95 (*0-7803-1137-X*, PC5604) Inst Electrical.
Paice, Edward. Bradt Guide to Eritrea. 2nd ed. LC 96-11674. (Bradt Guides Ser.). (Illus.). 192p. (Orig.). 1996. pap. 16.95 (*1-56440-951-1*, Pub. by Bradt Pubns) Globe Pequot.
Paice, Kimberly. Winifred Lutz: Place of Nature, Nature of Place. (Illus.). 13p. 1997. pap. 5.00 (*1-58442-031-6*) Galleries at Moore.
Paice, Mary M. Longanimity: A Disposition to Bear Injuries Patiently. 2nd ed. 103p. 1998. reprint ed. pap. 12.00 (*0-9666321-0-9*) Tucker Thompson.
Paice, Michael G., jt. ed. see Lewis, Norman G.
Paidar, Meridith. Merchandising Mathematics: High Margin Returns for Retailers & Vendors. LC 93-25984. 405p. (C). 1994. pap. 37.50 (*0-8273-5703-6*) Delmar.
— Merchandising Mathematics: High Margin Returns for Retailers & Vendors. 71p. 1994. teacher ed. 15.75 (*0-8273-5704-4*) Delmar.
Paidar, Parvin. Women & the Political Process in Twentieth-Century Iran. (Middle East Studies: No. 1). 417p. (C). 1995. text 69.95 (*0-521-47340-3*) Cambridge U Pr.
— Women & the Political Process in Twentieth-Century Iran. (Illus.). 424p. 1997. pap. text 24.95 (*0-521-59572-X*) Cambridge U Pr.
Paidar, Vaclav, jt. ed. see Lejcek, Pavel.
Paidoussi, Eleni. The Other Kind: A Cultural Conversion. 200p. 1995. pap. 12.95 (*1-885778-03-1*) Seaburn.
Paidoussis, M. P., et al, eds. 1997 International Mechanical Engineering Congress & Exposition, Dallas, Texas, November 16-21, 1997 Vol. 1: Fluid-Structure Interaction, Aeroelasticity, Flow-Induced Vibration & Noise. (AD Ser.: Vol. 53-1). 480p. 1997. 160.00 (*0-7918-1821-7*, H1102A) ASME Pr.
— Third International Symposium on Flow-Induced Vibration & Noise, Vol. 1: FSI - FIV in Cylinder Arrays in Cross-Flow. (HTD Series, Vol. 230: NE: Vol. 9). 284p. 1992. 62.50 (*0-7918-1078-X*, G00722) ASME.
— Third International Symposium on Flow-Induced Vibration & Noise, Vol. 2: Cross-Flow Induced Vibration of Cylinder Arrays. (PVP Ser.: Vol. 242). 356p. 1992. 65.00 (*0-7918-1079-8*, G00723) ASME.
— Third International Symposium on Flow-Induced Vibration & Noise, Vol. 6: Bluff-Body - Fluid & Hydraulic Machine Interactions. (FED Ser.: Vol. 138). 264p. 1992. 62.50 (*0-7918-1083-6*, G00727) ASME.
— Third International Symposium on Flow-Induced Vibration & Noise, Vol. 7: Fundamental Aspects of Fluid-Structure Interactions. (AMD Series, Vol. 151: PVP: Vol. 247). 232p. 1992. 57.50 (*0-7918-1084-4*, G00728) ASME.
Paidoussis, M. P. & Au-Yang, M. K., eds. Third International Symposium on Flow-Induced Vibration & Noise, Vol. 5: Axial & Annular Flow-Induced Vibrations & Instabilities. (PVP Ser.: Vol. 244). 232p. 1992. 57.50 (*0-7918-1082-8*, G00726) ASME.
Paidoussis, M. P. & Namachchivaya, N. S., eds. Third International Symposium on Flow-Induced Vibration & Noise, Vol. 8: Stability & Control of Pipes Conveying Fluid. (AMD Ser.: Vol. 152). 140p. 1992. 45.00 (*0-7918-1085-2*, G00729) ASME.
Paidoussis, M. P. & Sandifer, J. B., eds. Third International Symposium on Flow-Induced Vibration & Noise, Vol. 4: Acoustical Effects in FSI. (PVP Ser.: Vol. 243). 164p. 1992. 45.00 (*0-7918-1081-X*, G00725) ASME.
Paidoussis, M. P., jt. ed. see Farabee, T. M.
Paidoussis, Michael P. Fluid-Structure Interactions: Slender Structures & Axial Flow. LC 98-86469. 572p. (C). 1998. text 145.00 (*0-12-544360-9*) Acad Pr.
Paietta, Ann & Kauppila, Jean. Health Professionals on Screen. LC 99-11137. 448p. 1999. 55.00 (*0-8108-3636-X*) Scarecrow.
Paietta, Ann C. Access Services: A Handbook. LC 90-53601. (Illus.). 220p. Date not set. reprint ed. pap. 68.20 (*0-608-20721-7*, 207181900002) Bks Demand.
Paietta, Ann C. & Kauppila, Jean L. Animals on Screen & Radio: An Annotated Sourcebook. LC 94-29182. 397p. 1994. 47.50 (*0-8108-2939-8*) Scarecrow.
Paiewonsky, Michael. Conquest of Eden, 1493-1515: Other Voyages of Columbus. (Illus.). 176p. 1990. 28.50 (*0-926330-03-9*) Mapes Monde.
— Conquest of Eden, 1493-1515: 1493-1515 Other Voyages of Columbus. (Illus.). 176p. 1993. reprint ed. pap. 20.95 (*0-926330-04-7*) Mapes Monde.
Paige, Andrew. Emerging from Depression. LC 96-78832. 96p. (Orig.). 1997. pap. 5.95 (*0-7648-0064-7*) Liguori Pubns.
Paige, D. D., tr. see Pavese, Cesare.
Paige, David. A Day in the Life of a Marine Biologist. LC 80-54097. (Illus.). 32p. (J). (gr. 4-8). 1997. pap. 3.95 (*0-89375-447-1*) Troll Communs.
Paige, David H., ed. see Lustig & Brown Staff.
Paige, David M. & Bayless, Theodore M., eds. Lactose Digestion: Clinical & Nutritional Implications. LC 81-1537. (Illus.). 300p. 1981. reprint ed. pap. 93.00 (*0-608-04011-8*, 206474700011) Bks Demand.
Paige, E. G., jt. auth. see Ash, E. A.
Paige, Edward St., see St. Paige, Edward.
Paige, Emeline K., ed. see Bland, Shirley T., et al.
Paige, Frances. Blood Ties. 288p. 1996. 24.00 (*0-7278-4836-4*) Severn Hse.
— Blood Ties. large type ed. (Magna Large Print Ser.). 404p. 1997. 27.99 (*0-7505-1035-8*) Ulverscroft.
— Confetti Bed. 288p. 1996. 22.00 (*0-7278-4956-5*) Severn Hse.
— The Confetti Bed. large type ed. (Magna Large Print Ser.). 408p. 1998. 29.99 (*0-7505-1158-3*, Pub. by Mgna Lrg Print) Ulverscroft.
Paige, Frances. Love Is a Stranger. 192p. 25.00 (*0-7278-5525-5*) Severn Hse.
— Passions of the Mind. 1999. 25.00 (*0-7278-5444-5*, Pub. by Severn Hse) Chivers N Amer.
Paige, Frances. The Swimming Pool. 224p. 1999. 25.00 (*0-7278-2271-3*, Pub. by Severn Hse) Chivers N Amer.
***Paige, Frances.** The Swimming Pool. large type ed. 336p. 2000. 31.99 (*0-7505-1487-6*, Pub. by Mgna Lrg Print) Ulverscroft.
Paige, Glenn D. & Gilliatt, Sarah, eds. Nonviolence in Hawaii's Spiritual Traditions. LC 91-36117. 103p. 1991. pap. 5.00 (*1-880309-00-9*) S M Matsunaga.
Paige, Glenn D. & Haaheo, Lou A., eds. Hawai'i Journeys in Nonviolence: Autobiographical Reflections. LC 95-33132. 1995. pap. 5.00 (*1-880309-10-6*) S M Matsunaga.
Paige, Glenn D., jt. auth. see Snyder, Richard C.
Paige, Glenn D., ed. see Governor's Conference on the Year 2000.
Paige, Harry W. Songs of the Teton Sioux. lib. bdg. 20.95 (*0-8488-1902-0*) Amereon Ltd.
Paige, Howard. Aspects of African American Foodways Pt. 1: Some Glimpse of its Beginning in 16-18th Century West Africa, in the West Indies, & Early Colonial America, Up to & Including the Civil War, 2 vols. (Aspects of African American Foodways Ser.: Pt. 2). (Illus.). 260p. 1999. lib. bdg. 27.95 (*0-9618780-1-0*) Aspects Publishing Co.
Paige, Irene E. Antiques: A Buyers' Guide to London. rev. ed. (Illus.). 160p. 1987. pap. 6.95 (*0-938699-01-6*) Paige Pubns.
Paige, Irene E., ed. Antiques: A Buyer's Guide to London. 3rd ed. (Illus.). 160p. 1989. pap. 7.95 (*0-938699-03-2*) Paige Pubns.
Paige, J. & Dale, B. National Geographic Destinations: American Southwest. 200p. 1999. per. 15.00 (*0-7922-7452-0*, Pub. by Natl Geog) S&S Trade.
Paige, Jeffery M. Coffee & Power: Revolution & the Rise of Democracy in Central America. LC 96-3469. (Illus.). 432p. 1997. 48.00 (*0-674-13648-9*) HUP.
— Coffee & Power: Revolution & the Rise of Democracy in Central America. (Illus.). 448p. 1998. pap. text 18.95 (*0-674-13649-7*) HUP.
***Paige, Jeffrey S.** The Shaker Kitchen: Over 100 Recipes from Canterbury Shaker Village. rev. exp. ed. (Illus.). 205p. 2000. pap. 16.00 (*0-9678095-0-9*) J S Paige.
Paige, Jessica, jt. auth. see Paige, Michele.
Paige, Laurie. The Baby Pursuit. 256p. 1999. per. 4.50 (*0-373-65031-0*) Silhouette.
— Caleb's Son. (Romance Ser.). 1994. per. 2.75 (*0-373-08994-5*, 5-08994-1) Silhouette.
— Cara's Beloved. (Romance Ser.). 1993. pap. 2.69 (*0-373-08917-1*, 5-08917-2) Silhouette.
***Paige, Laurie.** Cheyenne Bride. 256p. 2000. pap. 4.50 (*0-373-65047-7*, 1-65047-2, Harlequin) Harlequin Bks.
Paige, Laurie. Christmas Kisses for a Dollar. 1995. per. 3.50 (*0-373-52009-3*, 1-52009-7) Silhouette.
— A Family Homecoming: Montana Mavericks: Return to White Horn. Vol. 1292. 249p. 2000. mass mkt. 4.25 (*0-373-24292-1*, 1-24292-4) Silhouette.
— Father - To - Be: That's My Baby! (Special Edition Ser.: No. 1201). 1998. per. 4.25 (*0-373-24201-8*, 1-24201-5) Harlequin Bks.
— Father Found. (Montana Mavericks Ser.). 1995. per. 3.99 (*0-373-50173-0*, 1-50173-1) Harlequin Bks.
— Guardian de Corazones: Guardian's Hearts. (Harlequin Bianca Ser.).Tr. of Guardian's Heart. (SPA.). 156p. 1999. per. 3.50 (*0-373-33506-7*, 1-33506-6) Harlequin Bks.
— The Guardian's Bride. (Romance Ser.). 1998. per. 3.50 (*0-373-19318-1*, 1-19318-4) Silhouette.
— A Hero's Homecoming. 1998. per. 4.25 (*0-373-24178-X*, 1-24178-5) Silhouette.
— Home for a Wild Heart. (Special Edition Ser.). 1993. mass mkt. 3.50 (*0-373-09828-6*, 5-09828-0) Silhouette.

P

An Asterisk (*) at the beginning of an entry indicates that the title is appearing for the first time.

— Husband: Bought & Paid For. 1997. per. 3.99 (*0-373-24139-9*, 1-24139-7) Silhouette.
— Live-In Mom. 1997. per. 3.99 (*0-373-24077-5*, 1-24077-9) Silhouette.
***Paige, Laurie.** Live In Mum. large type ed. (Silhouette Romance Ser.). 1999. 21.95 (*0-373-59599-9*) Harlequin Bks.
— Man from the North Country. 2000. mass mkt. 4.50 (*0-373-82221-9*, 1-82221-2) Harlequin Bks.
Paige, Laurie. Molly Darling. 1996. per. 3.99 (*0-373-24021-X*, 1-24021-7) Silhouette.
— Molly Darling. large type ed. 1998. 21.95 (*0-373-59927-7*) Silhouette.
— The Once & Future Wife. 1994. per. 3.99 (*0-373-50168-4*, 1-50168-3) Harlequin Bks.
— Only One Groom Allowed. (Yours Truly Ser.). 1997. per. 3.50 (*0-373-52046-8*, 1-52046-9) Silhouette.
— A Place for Eagles. (Wild River Trilogy Ser.). 1993. per. 3.50 (*0-373-09839-1*, 5-09839-7) Silhouette.
— The Ready-Made Family. 1997. per. 3.99 (*0-373-24114-3*, 1-24114-0) Silhouette.
— A River to Cross. (Special Edition Ser.). 1994. per. 3.50 (*0-373-09910-X*, 1-09910-0) Harlequin Bks.
— A Rogue's Heart. (Silhouette Romance Ser.). 1994. per. 2.75 (*0-373-19013-1*, 5-19013-7) Harlequin Bks.
— A Rougue's Heart. 1997. per. 14.00 (*0-373-91013-4*, 5-91013-8) Harlequin Bks.
— Sally's Beau. large type ed. LC 93-21001. 1993. pap. 13.95 (*0-7862-0059-6*) Thorndike Pr.
— A Season for Butterflies. (Men at Work Ser.: Vol. 23). 1998. mass mkt. 4.50 (*0-373-81035-0*, 1-81035-7) Harlequin Bks.
— An Unexpected Delivery. (Romance Ser.). 1996. per. 3.25 (*0-373-19151-0*, 1-19151-9) Silhouette.
— Victoria's Conquest. (Romance Ser.). 1993. pap. 2.69 (*0-373-08933-3*, 5-08933-9) Silhouette.
— Wanted: One Son. 1997. per. 3.25 (*0-373-19246-0*, 1-19246-7) Silhouette.
— Warrior's Woman. (Special Edition Ser.). 1998. per. 4.25 (*0-373-24193-3*, 1-24193-4) Silhouette.
— The Way of a Man: Wild River Trilogy. (Special Edition Ser.). 1993. per. 3.50 (*0-373-09849-9*, 5-09849-6) Silhouette.
— Wild Is the Wind. 1994. per. 3.50 (*0-373-09887-1*) Silhouette.
Paige, Laurie & Knoll, Patricia. The Cowboy Next Door. (Duets Ser.: No. 3). 1999. per. 5.99 (*0-373-44069-3*, 1-44069-2, Harlequin) Harlequin Bks.
Paige, LeRoy S. Maybe I'll Pitch Forever. LC 92-35221. xiv, 298p. 1993. text 45.00 (*0-8032-3702-2*) U of Nebr Pr.
— Maybe I'll Pitch Forever. LC 92-35221. (Illus.). xiv, 299p. 1993. pap. 12.95 (*0-8032-8732-1*, Bison Books) U of Nebr Pr.
Paige, Leroy S. Pitchin' Man. (American Autobiography Ser.). 96p. 1995. reprint ed. lib. bdg. 69.00 (*0-7812-8606-9*) Rprt Serv.
— Pitchin' Man: Satchel Paige's Own Story. (Baseball & American Society Ser.: No. 20). (Illus.). 130p. 1992. lib. bdg. 29.50 (*0-88736-836-0*) Mecklermedia.
Paige, Leslie Z. The Identification & Treatment of School Phobia. 1993. pap. text 19.00 (*0-932955-08-8*) Natl Assn Schl Psych.
Paige, Lori A. Passion's Legacy. 256p. (Orig.). 1991. pap. 8.95 (*0-941483-81-9*) Naiad Pr.
Paige, Lucius R. History of Cambridge, Massachusetts, 1630-1877. 732p. 1986. reprint ed. 50.00 (*1-55613-011-2*) Heritage Bk.
— History of Hardwick MA: With a Genealogical Register. 571p. (Orig.). 1994. pap. text 35.00 (*0-7884-0021-5*) Heritage Bk.
— List of Freemen of Massachusetts, 1630-1691. LC 78-50979. 60p. 1998. reprint ed. pap. 10.95 (*0-8063-0806-0*) Clearfield Co.
Paige, Marvin, jt. auth. see Logan, Tom.
Paige, Mary, jt. auth. see Guthrie, Peter.
Paige, Michele & Paige, Jessica. Blues Busters: Suggestions for Beating the Blues. 200p. (Orig.). 1996. pap. 8.95 (*1-880336-10-3*) Turtle CT.
Paige, Michele A. After the SATs: An Insider's Guide to Freshman Year. 240p. 1991. pap. 9.95 (*0-8120-4477-0*) Barron.
Paige, Michelle L. Practicing Racial Reconciliation in Your Church. 20p. 1998. pap. 1.95 (*1-56212-345-9*, 1930-0322) CRC Pubns.
Paige, Morton L. Things Your Family Should Know. 88p. 1993. student ed. 14.95 (*0-9635236-0-0*) Paige Pub CA.
***Paige, Nicholas D.** Being Interior: Autobiography & the Contradictions of Modernity in 17th Century France. LC 00-41802. (New Cultural Studies). (Illus.). 2001. write for info. (*0-8122-3577-0*) U of Pa Pr.
Paige, Nigel, jt. auth. see George, Susan.
Paige, R. Michael, ed. Cross Cultural Orientation: New Conceptualizations & Applications. LC 86-15999. (Orig.). (C). 1986. pap. 31.00 (*0-8191-5608-6*) U Pr of Amer.
— Education for the Intercultural Experience. LC 93-31313. 344p. (Orig.). 1993. pap. text 27.95 (*1-877864-25-0*) Intercult Pr.
Paige, Richard. The Door to December. 1990. pap. 4.95 (*0-451 16667-1*) NAL.
Paige, Richard E. The Science of Creating Ideas for Industry. 113p. (Orig.). 1980. pap. text. write for info. (*1-877782-12-2*) MGM & Assocs.
Paige, Robert A. Formal Differentiation: A Program Synthesis Technique. Stone, Harold, ed. LC 81-7632. (Computer Science: Artificial Intelligence Ser.: No. 6). 289p. 1981. reprint ed. pap. 89.60 (*0-8357-1213-3*, 207004500063) Bks Demand.
Paige, Robin. Death at Bishop's Keep. 272p. (Orig.). 1994. mass mkt. 4.99 (*0-380-77498-4*, Avon Bks) Morrow Avon.
— Death at Bishop's Keep: A Victorian Mystery. 1998. mass mkt. 5.99 (*0-425-16435-7*, Prime Crime) Berkley Pub.
— Death at Daisy's Folly. 1997. mass mkt. 5.99 (*0-425-15671-0*, Prime Crime) Berkley Pub.
— Death at Devil's Bridge. 1998. mass mkt. 5.99 (*0-425-16195-1*, Prime Crime) Berkley Pub.
***Paige, Robin.** Death at Epsom Downs. LC 00-31146. 2001. write for info. (*0-425-17807-2*, Prime Crime) Berkley Pub.
Paige, Robin. Death at Gallows Green. 1998. mass mkt. 5.99 (*0-425-16399-7*) Berkley Pub.
— Death at Gallows Green. (Victorian Mystery Ser.). 272p. 1995. mass mkt. 4.99 (*0-380-77499-2*, Avon Bks) Morrow Avon.
— Death at Rottingdean. (A Victorian Mystery Ser.). 304p. 1999. mass mkt. 5.99 (*0-425-16782-8*, Prime Crime) Berkley Pub.
***Paige, Robin.** Death at Whitechapel. (Victorian Mystery Ser.: Vol. 6). 276p. 2000. mass mkt. 5.99 (*0-425-17341-0*, Prime Crime) Berkley Pub.
Paige, Roger. Dealing with Divorce. 1979. pap. 1.00 (*0-8309-0240-6*) Herald Pub Hse.
Paige, Terence, jt. ed. see Wilkins, Michael J.
Paigen, Jennifer. The Sea Kayaker's Guide to Mt. Desert Island. LC 97-6534. (Illus.). 176p. (Orig.). 1997. pap. 14.95 (*0-89272-380-7*) Down East.
Paigen, Rebecca. Mr. Popper's Penguins. (Literature Units Ser.). 48p. (J). (gr. 3-5). 1997. pap. 7.95 (*1-55734-549-X*) Tchr Create Mat.
Paijmans, Theo. Free Energy Pioneer: John Worrell Keely. LC 98-12457. (Illus.). 472p. 1998. pap. 19.95 (*1-881532-15-1*) IllumiNet Pr.
Paik, et al. From Pusan to Panmunjom. (Association of the U. S. Army Book Ser.). (Illus.). 288p. 1992. 26.95 (*0-02-881002-3*, 4048M) Brasseys.
Paik, C. M. Quantitative Methods for Managerial Decisions. LC 72-7093. xiii, 403p. 1973. write for info. (*0-07-048086-9*) McGraw.
Paik, Hae J., jt. auth. see Comstock, George.
Paik, Helen C. Local Government Finances since Proposition 13: An Historical Primer. 32p. 1995. pap. write for info. (*1-58703-042-X*, CRB-95-007) CA St Libry.
Paik, Keun-Wook. Gas & Oil in North-East Asia: Policies, Projects & Prospects. 274p. (C). 1995. pap. 19.95 (*0-905031-94-6*) Brookings.
***Paik, Keun-Wook.** Gas for Power in Northeast Asia. 1999. pap. 29.95 (*1-86203-034-0*) Royal Inst Intl Affairs.
Paik, Nam J. Nam June Paik: Baraoque Laser. 1996. pap. 14.95 (*3-89322-295-2*, Pub. by Edition Cantz) Dist Art Pubs.
Paik, Woon K. & Kim, Sangduk, eds. Protein Methylation. 432p. 1989. lib. bdg. 254.00 (*0-8493-6818-9*, QP551) CRC Pr.
Paikeday, Thomas M. The Native Speaker Is Dead! An Informal Discussion of a Linguistic Myth. 120p. (C). 1985. pap. 16.00 (*0-920865-00-3*) Lexicography.
Paikoff, Roberta L., ed. Shared Views in the Family During Adolescence. LC 85-644581. (New Directions for Child Development Ser.: No. CD 51). 1991. 25.00 (*1-55542-787-1*) Jossey-Bass.
Pailet, Joshua M. The World's Fair, New Orleans. LC 85-81259. (Illus.). 120p. 1987. 39.95 (*0-9615647-0-9*) Gallery Fine.
Pailin, David A. The Anthropological Character of Theology: Conditioning Theological Understanding. 301p. (C). 1990. text 75.00 (*0-521-39069-9*) Cambridge U Pr.
Pailin, David A., jt. ed. see Coakley, Sarah.
Paillard, Bernard. Notes on the Plague Years: AIDS in Marseilles. Frank, Berkeley, tr. from FRE. LC 98-28154. (Social Problems & Social Issues Ser.). 313p. 1998. pap. text 24.95 (*0-202-30555-4*); lib. bdg. 51.95 (*0-202-30554-6*) Aldine de Gruyter.
Paillard, Jacques, ed. Brain & Space. (Illus.). 520p. 1991. 95.00 (*0-19-854284-4*) OUP.
Paillard, Philippe. Dictionnaire des Communes Savoyardes. (FRE.). 450p. 1981. 150.00 (*0-7859-7949-2*, 2717102299) Fr & Eur.
Paillat, P. M. & Bunch, M. E., eds. Age, Work & Automation. (Interdisciplinary Topics in Gerontology Ser.: Vol. 6). 1970. 26.25 (*3-8055-0507-8*) S Karger.
Paillere, A. M. Application of Admixtures in Concrete. (Rilem Proceedings Ser.: No. 10). (Illus.). 144p. (C). 1994. 90.00 (*0-419-19960-8*, E & FN Spon) Routledge.
Paillet, Frederick & Cheng, C. H., eds. Acoustic Waves in Boreholes. (Illus.). 176p. 1991. lib. bdg. 119.00 (*0-8493-8890-2*, TN871) CRC Pr.
Paillet, Frederick L. & Saunders, Wayne R., eds. Geophysical Applications for Geotechnical Investigations. LC 90-40924. (Special Technical Publication (STP) Ser.: STP 1101). (Illus.). 118p. 1990. text 40.00 (*0-8031-1403-6*, STP1101) ASTM.
Paillet, Jean-Pierre & Dugas, Andre. Approaches to Syntax. (Lingvisticae Investigationes Supplementa Ser.: 5). viii, 282p. 1982. 71.00 (*90-272-3115-X*) J Benjamins Pubng Co.
Paillet, Jean-Pierre, tr. see Foran, Max.
Pailliotet, Ann W., jt. ed. see Semali, Ladislaus.
Paillon, Pierre. Secrets of Good French Cooking. (Illus.). 192p. 1996. 55.00 (*0-471-16062-8*) Wiley.
Paillotin, G., ed. see Institut National de la Recherche Agronomique.
Paillotin, Guy, ed. The Living Cell in Four Dimensions. LC 91-55209. (AIP Conference Proceedings Ser.: No. 226). 608p. 1991. 105.00 (*0-88318-794-9*) Am Inst Physics.
Pailloux, Jean-Pierre, jt. auth. see Denoux, Jean-Marie.
Pailthorpe. Chichester: A Contemporary View. 172p. 1994. text 32.00 (*0-471-95033-5*) Wiley.
Pain. Physics of Vibrations & Waves. 5th ed. LC 98-36212. 576p. (C). 1999. 140.00 (*0-471-98542-2*) Wiley.
***Pain.** Physics of Vibrations & Waves. 5th ed. LC 98-36212. 576p. 1999. pap. 69.95 (*0-471-98543-0*) Wiley.
Pain, Andrew J. Adverse Possession: A Conveyancer's Guide. 224p. 1992. 125.00 (*1-85190-183-3*, Pub. by Tolley Pubng) St Mut.
Pain, Andrew J., jt. auth. see Convey, Stephen R.
Pain, Andrew J., jt. auth. see Coveney, Stephen R.
Pain, Barry E. Humorous Stories. LC 79-37281. (Short Story Index Reprint Ser.). 1977. reprint ed. 39.95 (*0-8369-4091-1*) Ayer.
Pain, Bedabrata & Lomheim, Terrence S., eds. Infrared Readout Electronics IV. LC 98-226779. (Proceedings of SPIE Ser.: Vol. 3360). 150p. 1998. 59.00 (*0-8194-2809-4*) SPIE.
Pain, Colin, jt. auth. see Ollier, Cliff.
Pain, F. The Practical Woodturner. 1990. pap. 12.95 (*0-8273-5384-7*) Delmar.
Pain, Herbert J. The Physics of Vibrations & Waves. 3rd ed. LC 86-1597. (Illus.). 432p. reprint ed. pap. 134.00 (*0-7837-1876-4*, 204207700001) Bks Demand.
Pain, Kenneth W. Licensing Practice & Procedure. 202p. 1986. 125.00 (*1-85190-009-8*, Pub. by Fourmat Pub) St Mut.
— Licensing Practice & Procedure. 250p. 1990. 69.00 (*1-85190-102-7*, Pub. by Tolley Pubng) St Mut.
— Licensing Practice & Procedure. 3rd ed. 228p. (C). 1988. 90.00 (*1-85190-059-4*, Pub. by Fourmat Pub) St Mut.
— Minors - The Law & Practice: The Juvenile Courts - The Offences - The Role of the Local Authorities. 293p. 1987. 136.00 (*1-85190-030-6*, Pub. by Fourmat Pub) St Mut.
Pain, Kenneth W., ed. Licensing Practice & Procedure. 5th ed. 295p. 1994. 90.00 (*0-85459-890-1*, Pub. by Tolley Pubng) St Mut.
Pain, Kenneth W. & Whale, Stephen J. Emergency Applications to Magistrates. 179p. 1986. 104.00 (*1-85190-001-2*, Pub. by Fourmat Pub) St Mut.
Pain, Nigel, jt. ed. see Barrell, Ray.
Pain, Robin. Practical Electronic Fault Finding & Troubleshooting. LC 95-18106. (Illus.). 240p. 1996. pap. text 39.95 (*0-7506-2461-2*) Buttrwrth-Heinemann.
Pain, Roger H., ed. Mechanisms of Protein Folding. LC 93-47574. (Illus.). 284p. (C). 1994. pap. text 55.00 (*0-19-963397-5*) OUP.
Pain, Roger H., jt. ed. see Smith, B. J.
Pain, Stephen, ed. Animal Poems. 1999. mass mkt. 3.50 (*0-460-87992-8*) Tuttle Pubng.
Pain, Stephen, et al. Find a Space! A Primary Teacher's Guide to Physical Education & Health Related Exercise. LC 97-132131. (Roehampton Teaching Studies). 112p. 1996. pap. 24.95 (*1-85346-452-X*, Pub. by David Fulton) Taylor & Francis.
***Pain, Thomas J.** Common Sense Too. LC 00-90230. 2000. 8.95 (*0-533-13494-3*) Vantage.
Paine. Fortune's Gun. 1999. 20.00 (*0-7862-1003-6*) Mac Lib Ref.
— Murder Without Motive. LC 98-48527. Date not set. 30.00 (*0-7838-0443-1*, G K Hall Lrg Type) Mac Lib Ref.
Paine, jt. auth. see Hirsch.
Paine, ed. see Bingham & Stryker, Sandy.
Paine, Albert. The Hollow Tree & Deep Woods Book. 272p. 1993. 22.95 (*1-56723-082-2*) Yestermorrow.
Paine, Albert B. The Arkansas Bear: A Tale of Fanciful Adventure Told in Song & Story. 22.95 (*0-89190-367-4*) Amereon Ltd.
— Great White Way. lib. bdg. 24.95 (*0-8488-2011-8*) Amereon Ltd.
— The Great White Way: An Unusual Voyage of Discovery, & Some Romantic Love Affairs Amid Strange Surroundings. LC 74-16514. (Science Fiction Ser.). (Illus.). 330p. 1975. reprint ed. 26.95 (*0-405-06309-1*) Ayer.
— The Hollow Tree & Deep Woods Book. 272p. 1993. 20.95 (*0-89190-368-2*) Amereon Ltd.
— The Hollow Tree Nights & Days. 1998. lib. bdg. 20.95 (*1-56723-084-9*) Yestermorrow.
— The Hollow Tree Snowed in Book. 1998. lib. bdg. 23.95 (*1-56723-083-0*) Yestermorrow.
— Mark Twain: A Biography, 3 vols. Aaron, Daniel, ed. LC 96-51552. (American Men & Women of Letters Ser.). 600p. 1997. 134.95 (*0-7910-4539-0*) Chelsea Hse.
— Mark Twain, a Biography, 3 vols. 1992. reprint ed. lib. bdg. 225.00 (*0-7812-5072-2*) Rprt Serv.
— The Mystery of Evelin Delorme: A Hypnotic Story. Reginald, R. & Menville, Douglas A., eds. LC 75-46299. (Supernatural & Occult Fiction Ser.). 1976. reprint ed. lib. bdg. 17.95 (*0-405-08159-6*) Ayer.
— Side Steps: A Communicative Course for Learners of English. LC 96-51583. (YA). 1997. pap. write for info. (*0-13-619891-0*) P-H.
— Tent Dwellers. (Illus.). 280p. 1993. reprint ed. pap. 8.95 (*1-55109-047-3*) Nimbus Publ.
— Thomas Nast: His Period & His Pictures. LC 78-177504. (Illus.). 1972. reprint ed. 30.95 (*0-405-08831-0*) Ayer.
Paine, Albert W. New Philosophy (1884) 174p. 1998. reprint ed. pap. 17.95 (*0-7661-0570-9*) Kessinger Pub.
Paine, Charles. The Art of Railroading. 143p. 1987. pap. 6.95 (*0-933905-03-3*) Claycomb Pr.
— The Resistant Writer: Rhetoric As Immunity, 1850 to the Present. LC 98-27341. (SUNY Series, Literacy, Culture, & Learning). 288p. (C). 1999. text 65.50 (*0-7914-4049-4*); pap. text 21.95 (*0-7914-4050-8*) State U NY Pr.
Paine, Crispin. Godly Things: Museums, Objects & Religion. LC 98-49731. 1999. 78.95 (*0-7185-0153-5*) Bks Intl VA.
Paine, Crispin, jt. auth. see Ambrose, Tim.
Paine, D. C., jt. ed. see Bravman, J. C.
Paine, David P. Aerial Photography & Image Interpretation for Resource Management. LC 81-4287. 584p. 1981. text 99.95 (*0-471-01857-0*) Wiley.
Paine, Debby. There is Hope: Poems from the Heart for the Heart. (Illus.). 80p. 1998. pap. 12.95 (*0-9668961-0-6*) Rhyme In Time.
Paine, Ed J. Poetry of Our World. 320p. 2000. pap. 17.00 (*0-06-095193-1*, Perennial) HarperTrade.
Paine, Francis F. Diego Rivera. LC 74-169310. (Museum of Modern Art Publications in Reprint). (Illus.). 128p. 1979. reprint ed. 25.95 (*0-405-01569-0*) Ayer.
Paine, Frank A. The Packaging User's Handbook. 1991. text 139.95 (*0-442-30283-5*) Chapman & Hall.
Paine, Fred K. & Paine, Nancy E. Magazines: A Bibliography for Their Analysis with Annotations & Study Guide. LC 86-29825. 698p. 1987. 66.00 (*0-8108-1975-9*) Scarecrow.
Paine-Gernee, Karen & Hunt, Terry. Emotional Healing: A Program for Emotional Sobriety. 2nd rev. ed. 340p. 1997. reprint ed. pap. 12.95 (*0-9656788-0-6*) Havenhurst.
Paine-Gernee, Karen & Rothstein, Larry. Secrets to Tell, Secrets to Keep. Hunt, Terry, ed. LC 94-12754. 270p. (Orig.). 1994. mass mkt. 10.99 (*0-446-39479-3*, Pub. by Warner Bks) Little.
Paine, Gordon. The Choral Journal: An Index to Volumes 1-18. (Monograph Ser.: No. 3). 170p. 1978. 7.50 (*0-614-05590-3*) Am Choral Dirs.
— The Choral Journal: An Index to Volumes 1-18. (Monographs: No. 3). 170p. (C). 1978. pap. 7.50 (*1-882648-02-1*) Am Choral Dirs.
Paine, Gordon, ed. Five Centuries of Choral Music: Essays in Honor of Howard Swan. LC 87-32816. (Festschrift Ser.: No. 6). 250p. 1989. lib. bdg. 52.00 (*0-918728-84-3*) Pendragon NY.
Paine, Gordon, tr. see Rilling, Helmuth.
Paine, Gregory L. Southern Prose Writers: Representative Selections. (BCL1-PS American Literature Ser.). 392p. 1993. reprint ed. lib. bdg. 89.00 (*0-7812-6930-X*) Rprt Serv.
Paine, Gregory L., ed. Southern Prose Writers. LC 79-101832. (Biography Index Reprint Ser.). 1977. 39.95 (*0-8369-8006-9*) Ayer.
Paine, H. O., ed. Paine Family Records: A Journal of Genealogical & Biographical Information Respecting the American Family of Payne, Paine, Payn, Etc., 2 vols. in 1. (Illus.). 522p. 1989. reprint ed. pap. 78.00 (*0-8328-0929-2*); reprint ed. lib. bdg. 86.00 (*0-8328-0928-4*) Higginson Bk Co.
Paine, J. G. Shallow-Seismic Evidence for Playa Basin Development by Dissolution-Induced Subsidence on the Southern High Plains, Texas. (Reports of Investigations: No. 233). (Illus.). 47p. (Orig.). 1995. pap. 7.00 (*0-614-11611-2*) Bur Econ Geology.
Paine, J. G. & Morton, R. A. Shoreline & Vegetation-Line Movement, Texas Gulf Coast, 1974 to 1982. (Geological Circular Ser.: GC 89-1). (Illus.). 50p. 1989. pap. 3.00 (*0-317-03108-2*) Bur Econ Geology.
Paine, J. H., jt. ed. see Dale, Corrine H.
Paine, J. R. Smart Homeseller's Sale by Owner Kit. 1986. 19.95 (*0-8187-0065-3*) Harlo Press.
Paine, James R., ed. IUCN Directory of Protected Areas in Oceania. 472p. 1991. 40.00 (*2-8317-0069-8*, B710, Pub. by IUCN) Island Pr.
Paine, Jeffery M. The Simplication of American Life: Hollywood's Films of the 1930's. 1977. 29.95 (*0-405-09893-6*, 11489) Ayer.
Paine, Jeffrey. Father India: A Western Adventure. LC 98-12590. 336p. 1998. 25.00 (*0-06-017303-3*) HarpC.
— Father India: Westerners Under the Spell of an Ancient Culture. LC 98-12590. (Illus.). 336p. 1999. pap. 14.00 (*0-06-093101-9*) HarpC.
Paine, Jeffrey, ed. The Poetry of Our World: An International Anthology of Contemporary Poetry. LC 99-34921. 528p. 2000. 35.00 (*0-06-055369-3*) HarpC.
Paine, Jocelyn. The Logic Programming Tutor. 320p. 1992. text 95.00 (*0-7923-1448-4*) Kluwer Academic.
Paine, Joclyn. The Logic Programming Tutor. 366p. 1992. pap. text 37.95 (*1-871516-09-9*, Pub. by Intellect) Cromland.
Paine, John K. Complete Piano Music. LC 83-18890. (Earlier American Music Ser.: No. 27). 100p. 1984. reprint ed. lib. bdg. 25.00 (*0-306-77323 6*) Da Capo.
— The History of Music to the Death of Schubert. LC 78-127280. (Music Ser.). (Illus.). 1971. reprint ed. lib. bdg. 37.50 (*0-306-70038-7*) Da Capo.
— John Knowles Paine: 3 Chamber Works for Piano & Strings. Schmidt, John C., ed. (Recent Researches in American Music Ser.). (Illus.). 89, xxvp. 1991. pap. 40.00 (*0-89579-261-3*) A-R Eds.
— Symphony No. 1: Opus 23. LC 73-171077. (Earlier American Music Ser.: No. 1). 180p. 1972. reprint ed. lib. bdg. 32.50 (*0-306-77301-5*) Da Capo.
***Paine, John Knowles.** John Knowles Paine: Vocal Chamber Music. Schmidt, John C., ed. (Recent Researches in American Music Ser.: Vol. A35). (Illus.). xiv, 76p. 1999. pap. 40.00 (*0-89579-447-0*) A-R Eds.
Paine, L. Hospitals & the Health Care Revolution. 118p. 1988. 20.00 (*92-4-156116-5*) World Health.
***Paine, Lauran.** Apache Trail. large type ed. LC 99-54980. 2000. pap. 23.95 (*0-7838-8928-3*, G K Hall & Co) Mac Lib Ref.
Paine, Lauran. Bags & Saddles. large type ed. LC 99-30783. 1999. 20.95 (*1-57490-198-2*, Sagebrush LP West) T T Beeler.
***Paine, Lauran.** The Bandoleros. large type ed. LC 00-40273. 2000. write for info. (*1-57490-287-3*, Sagebrush LP West) T T Beeler.
Paine, Lauran. Buckskin Buccaneer. large type ed. LC 97-39298. (Sagebrush Large Print Westerns Ser.). 1998. 18.95 (*1-57490-121-4*, Sagebrush LP West) T T Beeler.
— Cache Cadnon. LC 98-43048. (Thorndike Large Print Western Ser.). 304 p. 1999. write for info. (*0-7540-3666-9*) Chivers N Amer.

P

An Asterisk (*) at the beginning of an entry indicates that the title is appearing for the first time.

[illegible] Canon. 208p. 2000. mass mkt. 3.99 [illegible], Leisure Bks) Dorchester Pub Co.

[illegible] Cache Canon. LC 97-38422. 1998. 18.95 [illegible]989-5) Mac Lib Ref.

[illegible]non: A Western Story. large type ed. LC [illegible]048. 1999. 30.00 (*0-7862-1028-1*) Thorndike Pr.

[illegible]alifornios. large type ed. (Sagebrush Large Print [illegible]esterns Ser.). 1996. lib. bdg. 18.95 (*1-57490-053-6*, Sagebrush LP West) T T Beeler.

— The Cloverleaf Cattle Company. large type ed. (Linford Western Library). 288p. 1997. pap. 16.99 (*0-7089-5050-7*) Ulverscroft.

***Paine, Lauran.** Death of a Millionaire. LC 99-42646. 2000. 30.00 (*0-7838-8756-6*, G K Hall Lrg Type) Mac Lib Ref.

Paine, Lauran. The Devil on Horseback. 224p. 1995. 19.95 (*0-8027-4148-7*) Walker & Co.

— The General Custer Story. large type ed. LC 96-20237. 1996. 19.95 (*0-7838-1852-1*, G K Hall Lrg Type) Mac Lib Ref.

— The Grand Ones of San Ildefonso. LC 97-9307. 238p. 1997. lib. bdg. 17.95 (*0-7862-0744-2*) Five Star.

— The Grand Ones of San Ildefonso. LC 98-24416. 311 p. 1998. write for info. (*0-7540-3458-5*) Mac Lib Ref.

— Greed at Gold River. large type ed. LC 94-11176. (Western Ser.). 175p. 1994. lib. bdg. 18.95 (*0-7862-0257-2*) Thorndike Pr.

— The Gunman's Legacy. large type ed. (Dales Large Print Ser.). (Illus.). 229p. 1996. pap. 18.99 (*1-85389-615-2*) Ulverscroft.

***Paine, Lauran.** The Guns of Summer. 2000. 20.95 (*1-57490-270-9*, Sagebrush LP West) T T Beeler.

Paine, Lauran. Guns of the Law. large type ed. LC 98-48131. 1999. 19.95 (*1-57490-173-7*, Sagebrush LP West) T T Beeler.

***Paine, Lauran, Jr.** High Ridge Range. large type ed. LC 99-45560. (G. K. Hall Paperback Ser.). 1999. pap. 21.95 (*0-7838-8792-2*, G K Hall Lrg Type) Mac Lib Ref.

Paine, Lauran. The Homesteaders. 192p. 1987. pap. 2.75 (*0-380-70185-5*, Avon Bks) Morrow Avon.

Paine, Lauran, Jr. If Airplanes Could Talk: The Pilots Book of Wit & Wisdom. rev. ed. (Illus.). 70p. 1999. pap. 7.95 (*0-9657607-1-5*) Cascade Publng.

Paine, Lauran. The Killer Gun. large type ed. LC 99-36341. 1999. 20.00 (*0-7838-8427-3*, G K Hall & Co) Mac Lib Ref.

— The Killer Gun. large type ed. LC 98-28227. 1998. 18.95 (*0-7862-1371-X*) Thorndike Pr.

— Lockwood. large type ed. 1999. 20.00 (*0-7838-1669-3*, G K Hall Lrg Type) Mac Lib Ref.

— Lockwood: A Western Story. LC 96-6300. 230p. 1996. 16.95 (*0-7862-0658-6*) Five Star.

— Lockwood: A Western Story. large type ed. LC 97-18661. 299p. 1997. 18.95 (*0-7862-1121-0*) Thorndike Pr.

***Paine, Lauran.** Man from Butte City. large type ed. (Paperback Ser.). 2000. pap. 23.95 (*0-7838-8927-5*, G K Hall Lrg Type) Mac Lib Ref.

— The Man from Coyanosa. large type ed. 224p. 1999. pap. 20.99 (*1-85389-938-0*, Dales) Ulverscroft.

Paine, Lauran, Jr. Man Things: Equal Time for Men. LC 97-67125. 160p. (Orig.). 1997. 12.95 (*0-9657607-3-1*) Cascade Publng.

Paine, Lauran. The Manhunter. large type ed. LC 94-45644. 214p. 1995. 18.95 (*0-7862-0397-8*) Thorndike Pr.

— The Marshal. 154p. 1985. 14.95 (*0-8027-4053-7*) Walker & Co.

— The Marshall. 176p. 1987. pap. 2.50 (*0-380-70187-1*, Avon Bks) Morrow Avon.

Paine, Lauran. The Misplaced Psyche LC 96-30932. 1997. write for info. (*0-7451-6955-4*) Chivers N Amer.

***Paine, Lauran, Jr.** Murder In Paradise. large type ed. LC 99-52855. 2000. 30.00 (*0-7838-8799-X*, G K Hall Lrg Type) Mac Lib Ref.

***Paine, Lauran.** Murder Without Motive. LC 98-48527. 212p. 1999. write for info. (*0-7540-3646-4*) Chivers N Amer.

Paine, Lauran. The Mustangers. LC 99-35274. (Westerns Ser.). 250p. 1999. 19.95 (*0-7862-1577-1*) Five Star.

— The Mustangers. large type ed. 275p. 2000. 30.00 (*0-7862-1586-0*) Thorndike Pr.

Paine, Lauran. Nightrider's Moon. 160p. 1988. 16.95 (*0-8027-4083-9*) Walker & Co.

Paine, Lauran. The Old Ones of San Ildefonso. large type ed. LC 98-24416. 1999. 18.95 (*0-7862-0767-1*) Thorndike Pr.

— The Open Range Men. 206p. 1990. 19.95 (*0-8027-4105-3*) Walker & Co.

— The Open Range Men. large type ed. LC 90-40665. 304p. 1990. reprint ed. lib. bdg. 16.95 (*1-56054-041-9*) Thorndike Pr.

— The Past Won't End. large type ed. (Sagebrush Large Print Westerns Ser.). 192p. 1995. lib. bdg. 18.95 (*1-57490-010-2*) T T Beeler.

— The Prairieton Raid. 192p. 1994. 19.95 (*0-8027-4139-8*) Walker & Co.

— The Prairieton Raid. large type ed. LC 94-32216. 245p. 1995. 19.95 (*0-7862-0328-5*) Thorndike Pr.

— The Rawhiders. large type ed. LC 96-19309. (Sagebrush Large Print Westerns Ser.). 272p. 1996. lib. bdg. 18.95 (*1-57490-021-8*) T T Beeler.

— The Renegade. large type ed. LC 94-45643. 219p. 1995. lib. bdg. 19.95 (*0-7862-0396-X*) Thorndike Pr.

— Riders of the Trojan Horse. 192p. 1991. 19.95 (*0-8027-4116-9*) Walker & Co.

— Riders of the Trojan Horse. large type ed. 302p. 1991. reprint ed. lib. bdg. 17.95 (*1-56054-241-1*) Thorndike Pr.

— Six-Gun Atonement. large type ed. LC 98-8375. 1998. 18.95 (*1-57490-148-6*, Sagebrush LP West) T T Beeler.

— Skye. 192p. 1987. pap. 2.75 (*0-380-70186-3*, Avon Bks) Morrow Avon.

— The Taurus Gun. 192p. 1989. 18.95 (*0-8027-4086-3*) Walker & Co.

— Tears of the Heart. large type ed. LC 95-31058. 1996. write for info. (*0-7838-1410-0*, G K Hall Lrg Type) Mac Lib Ref.

— Tears of the Heart. large type ed. (Western Ser.). 286p. 1996. 18.95 (*0-7862-0806-6*) Thorndike Pr.

— Tears of the Heart: A Western Story. (Five-Star Western Ser.). 176p. 1995. 16.95 (*0-7862-0511-3*) Thorndike Pr.

— Thunder Valley. large type ed. LC 93-1385. 294p. 1993. lib. bdg. 18.95 (*1-56054-720-0*) Thorndike Pr.

— Timberline. large type ed. LC 94-45642. (Western Ser.). 177p. 1995. 17.95 (*0-7862-0398-6*) Thorndike Pr.

***Paine, Lauran.** Trail of the Freighters. large type ed. LC 99-12627. 235p. 1999. pap. write for info. (*0-7540-3770-3*) Chivers N Amer.

— Trail of the Freighters. large type ed. LC 99-12627. 1999. 21.95 (*0-7862-1880-0*) Mac Lib Ref.

Paine, Lauran. Trail to Trouble. large type ed. (Linford Western Library). 272p. 1996. pap. 16.99 (*0-7089-7950-5*, Linford) Ulverscroft.

— Valor in the Land. large type ed. LC 96-53913. 1997. lib. bdg. 18.95 (*1-57490-059-5*, Sagebrush LP West) T T Beeler.

***Paine, Lauran.** The White Bird. 192p. 2000. pap. 4.50 (*0-8439-4675-X*, Leisure Bks) Dorchester Pub Co.

Paine, Lauran. The White Bird. large type ed. LC 96-43958. (Five Star Ser.). 219p. 1997. 17.95 (*0-7862-0735-3*) Five Star.

— The White Bird. large type ed. LC 97-44874. 1998. 18.95 (*0-7862-0758-2*) Thorndike Pr.

***Paine, Lauran.** Wilderness Road. large type ed. 224p. 2000. 22.95 (*0-7862-2578-5*) Mac Lib Ref.

Paine, Lauran, jt. auth. see Dana, Richard.

***Paine, Lincoln P.** Ships of Discovery & Exploration. (Ships of the World Ser.). (Illus.). 160p. 2000. pap. 17.00 (*0-395-98415-7*, Mariner Bks) HM.

Paine, Lincoln P. Ships of the World: An Historical Encyclopedia. LC 97-12872. (Illus.). 704p. 1997. 50.00 (*0-395-71556-3*) HM.

***Paine, Lincoln P.** Warships of the World to 1900. (Ships of the World Ser.). (Illus.). 256p. 2000. pap. 17.00 (*0-395-98414-9*, Mariner Bks) HM.

Paine, Lynn S. Cases in Leadership, Ethics & Organizational Integrity: A Strategic Perspective. 320p. (C). 1996. text 23.00 (*0-256-19790-3*, Irwn McGrw-H) McGrw-H Hghr Educ.

Paine, Mabel H., compiled by. Divine Art of Living. 4th ed. 174p. 1986. reprint ed. pap. 9.95 (*0-87743-194-9*) Bahai.

Paine McBrien, Judith. Chicago Neighborhoods: Design & Diversity. Pomaranc, Joan C., ed. (Skyline: Pt. V). (Illus.). 1998. lib. bdg. 6.95 (*1-880005-08-5*) Perspectvs Intl.

Paine, Melanie. Curtains & Shades: A Step-by-Step Guide to Creative Window Treatments. Reader's Digest Editors, ed. LC 97-22202. (Practical Home Decorating Ser.). 1997. 24.95 (*0-89577-979-X*, Pub. by RD Assn) Penguin Putnam.

— Fabric Magic. LC 87-43004. 216p. 1989. pap. 24.00 (*0-679-72598-9*) McKay.

— The New Fabric Magic. (Illus.). 216p. 1995. pap. 25.00 (*0-679-75840-2*) Pantheon.

Paine, Melanie, jt. auth. see Clifton-Mogg, Caroline.

Paine, Michael. Harrap's Spanish Commercial Correspondence. 1994. pap. 12.00 (*0-671-89991-0*) P-H.

Paine, Milton J. English Toy Spaniel: AKC Rank #119. (Rare Breed Ser.). (Illus.). 96p. 1997. 19.95 (*0-7938-0765-4*, RX-115) TFH Pubns.

Paine, Nancy E., jt. auth. see Paine, Fred K.

***Paine, Nigel & Galbraith, Jackie.** Distance Learning in Schools. 192p. 2000. 59.95 (*0-7494-3090-7*, Kogan Pg Educ); pap. 29.95 (*0-7494-3089-3*, Kogan Pg Educ) Stylus Pub VA.

Paine, Orphelia. Look & See the Town: Historic Sites of Nashville & Davidson County. 68p. 1989. pap. write for info. (*0-9630176-0-8*) Metro Hist Comm.

Paine, Penelope C. Molly's Magic. (Key Concepts in Personal Development Ser.). (Illus.). 32p. (J). (gr. 1-4). 1995. 16.95 (*1-55942-068-5*, 7660) Marsh Media.

— Time for Horatio. Stryker, Sandy, ed. LC 89-18304. (Illus.). 48p. (J). (ps up). 1990. 14.95 (*0-911655-33-6*) Advocacy Pr.

Paine, Penelope C. & Bingham, Mindy. My Way Sally. LC 88-2653. (Illus.). 48p. (J). (ps up). 1988. 14.95 (*0-911655-27-1*) Advocacy Pr.

Paine, Penelope C., ed. see Bingham, Mindy & Stryker, Sandy.

Paine, Penelope C., ed. & tr. see Rosenthiel, Agnes & Rosenthiel, Agnes.

Paine, R. W. Recollections of a Pacific Entomologist, 1925-1966. 120p. 1994. pap. 120.00 (*1-86320-106-8*, Pub. by ACIAR) St Mut.

Paine, Ralph D. The Book of Pirate Treasures: Being a True History of the Gold, Jewels, & Plate of Pirates, Galleons, Etc., Which Are Sought for to This Day. (Illus.). 472p. 1992. pap. 15.00 (*0-87380-177-6*) Popular E Commerce.

— Joshua Barney: A Forgotten Hero of Blue Water. LC 79-124249. (Select Bibliographies Reprint Ser.). 1977. reprint ed. 29.95 (*0-8369-5437-8*) Ayer.

***Paine, Randall.** The Universe & Mr. Chesterton. iii, 164p. 1999. pap. 12.95 (*0-89385-511-1*) Sugden.

Paine, Rhiannon. Too Late for the Festival: An American Salary Woman in Japan. LC 99-11637. 200p. 1999. 22.50 (*0-89733-471-X*) Academy Chi Pubs.

Paine, Richard R., ed. Integrating Archaeological Demography: Multidisciplinary Approaches to Prehistoric Population. LC 96-83230. (Center for Archaeological Investigations Occasional Paper Ser.: No. 24). (Illus.). xvi, 395p. (C). 1997. pap. 40.00 (*0-88104-081-9*) Center Archaeol.

Paine, Richmond S., jt. auth. see Crothers, Bronson.

Paine, Robert. Herds of the Tundra: A Portrait of Saami Reindeer Pastoralism. LC 93-38390. (Series in Ethnographic Inquiry). (Illus.). 272p. (C). 1994. text 59.00 (*1-56098-271-3*) Smithsonian.

Paine, Robert, et al. Generation & Interpretation of the Electrocardiogram. LC 87-25996. 291p. (Orig.). reprint ed. pap. 90.30 (*0-7837-2736-4*, 204311600006) Bks Demand.

Paine, Robert T., Jr. The Works in Verse & Prose of the Late Robert Treat Paine, Jr. (Notable American Authors Ser.). 1999. reprint ed. lib. bdg. 125.00 (*0-7812-4716-0*) Rprt Serv.

Paine, Robert T., jt. auth. see Soper, Alexander C.

Paine, Ruth B. Thematic Analysis of Francois Mauriac's "Genitrix, le Desert de L'amour, & le Noeud de Viperes" LC 76-8024. (Romance Monographs: No. 20). 1976. 26.00 (*84-399-4950-2*) Romance.

Paine, S. C. Imperial Rivals: China, Russia, & Their Disputed Frontier, 1858-1924. LC 96-10750. 440p. (gr. 13). 1996. pap. text 31.95 (*1-56324-724-0*) M E Sharpe.

— Imperial Rivals: China, Russian & Their Disputed Frontier, 1858-1924. LC 96-10750. 440p. (C). (gr. 13-13). 1996. text 78.95 (*1-56324-723-2*) M E Sharpe.

— Paine Ancestry: The Family of Robert Treat Paine, Signer of the Declaration of Independence, Including Maternal Lines. Pope, Charles H., ed. 336p. 1989. reprint ed. pap. 50.50 (*0-8328-0927-6*); reprint ed. lib. bdg. 58.50 (*0-8328-0926-8*) Higginson Bk Co.

***Paine, Sheila.** Artists Emerging: Sustaining Expression Through Drawing. LC 00-25721. (Illus.). 2000. write for info. (*0-7546-0200-1*) Ashgate Pub.

Paine, Sheila. Chikan Embroidery: The Floral Whitework of India. (Ethnography Ser.: No. 12). (Illus.). 60p. 1989. pap. 10.50 (*0-7478-0009-X*, Pub. by Shire Pubns) Parkwest Pubns.

— Embroidered Textiles. LC 97-60234. (Illus.). 192p. 1997. pap. 22.50 (*0-500-27823-7*, Pub. by Thames Hudson) Norton.

Paine, Sheperd. How to Build Dioramas. 2nd ed. 1999. pap. text 24.95 (*0-89024-195-3*) Kalmbach.

Paine, Sidney B. The Romans Built Aqua Ducks Everywhere & Other Student Perceptions. LC 99-159125. 1998. write for info. (*0-939241-39-0*) Faith Print.

***Paine, Sidney B.** Thomas Paine Wrote Common Scents, & Other Student Interpretations. LC 99-206702. (Illus.). 1998. write for info. (*0-939241-43-9*) Faith Print.

Paine, Stan C., et al. Structuring Your Classroom for Academic Success. LC 83-61812. (Illus.). 188p. 1983. pap. text 14.95 (*0-87822-228-6*, 2286) Res Press.

Paine, Stefani H. The World of the Arctic Whales: Belugas, Bowheads & Narwhals. (Illus.). 128p. 1997. pap. 18.00 (*0-87156-957-4*, Pub. by Sierra) Random.

Paine, Stefani H., jt. auth. see Naito, Hiromi.

Paine, Stephen W. Beginning Greek: A Functional Approach. 348p. (YA). (gr. 9 up). 1961. text 34.95 (*0-19-501013-2*) OUP.

Paine, Stephen W., ed. see James, Henry.

Paine, Thomas. The Age of Reason. 20.95 (*0-8488-0604-2*) Amereon Ltd.

— The Age of Reason. 192p. 1995. pap. 9.95 (*0-8065-0549-4*, Citadel Pr) Carol Pub Group.

— The Age of Reason. LC 84-62825. (Great Books in Philosophy). 190p. 1984. pap. 13.95 (*0-87975-273-4*) Prometheus Bks.

— The Age of Reason. 1986. reprint ed. lib. bdg. 18.95 (*0-89966-543-8*) Buccaneer Bks.

— The Age of Reason. 194p. 1996. reprint ed. spiral bd. 14.00 (*0-7873-0651-7*) Hlth Research.

— The Age of Reason. (Notable American Authors Ser.). 1999. reprint ed. lib. bdg. 125.00 (*0-7812-4723-3*) Rprt Serv.

— Age of Reason: Special Two Hundredth Anniversary Edition. LC 92-64310. 155p. 1992. reprint ed. pap. 5.00 (*0-9632612-2-3*) Wet Water.

— The Age of Reason Pt. 3: Examination of the Prophecies. Zindler, Frank, ed. LC 92-45546. 95p. 1993. pap. 12.00 (*0-910309-70-1*, 5575) Am Atheist.

— Agrarian Justice. (Notable American Authors Ser.). 1999. reprint ed. lib. bdg. 125.00 (*0-7812-4725-X*) Rprt Serv.

— The Case of the Officers of Excise. (Notable American Authors Ser.). 1999. reprint ed. lib. bdg. 125.00 (*0-7812-4717-9*) Rprt Serv.

— Collected Writings: Common Sense; The Crisis; Rights of Man; The Age of Reason. Foner, Eric, ed. LC 94-25756. 906p. 1995. text 35.00 (*1-883011-03-5*, Pub. by Library of America) Penguin Putnam.

— Common Sense. Kramnick, Isaac, ed. & intro. by. (American Library). 128p. (C). 1982. pap. 7.95 (*0-14-039016-2*) Addson-Wesley Educ.

— Common Sense. 17.95 (*0-8488-1088-0*) Amereon Ltd.

***Paine, Thomas.** Common Sense. 2001. mass mkt. 7.50 (*0-553-21465-9*) Bantam.

Paine, Thomas. Common Sense. LC 94-22773. (Great Books in Philosophy). 67p. (C). 1995. pap. 6.95 (*0-87975-918-6*) Prometheus Bks.

— Common Sense. 1986. reprint ed. lib. bdg. 18.95 (*0-89966-542-X*) Buccaneer Bks.

— Common Sense. LC 96-47115. (Thrift Editions Ser.). 64p. 1997. reprint ed. pap. text 1.00 (*0-486-29602-4*) Dover.

— Common Sense. (Notable American Authors Ser.). 1999. reprint ed. lib. bdg. 125.00 (*0-7812-4718-7*) Rprt Serv.

— Common Sense, the Rights of Man, & Other Essential Writings of Thomas Paine. 288p. 1984. pap. 10.95 (*0-452-00921-9*, Mer) NAL.

— The Crisis. (Notable American Authors Ser.). 1999. reprint ed. lib. bdg. 125.00 (*0-7812-4719-5*) Rprt Serv.

— The Crisis Essays. Norman, Charles J., ed. 1991. 12.95 (*0-8084-0434-2*) NCUP.

— Dissertations on Government, the Affairs of the Bank, & Paper Money. (Notable American Authors Ser.). 1999. reprint ed. lib. bdg. 125.00 (*0-7812-4721-7*) Rprt Serv.

— Letter to George Washington. (Notable American Authors Ser.). 1999. reprint ed. lib. bdg. 125.00 (*0-7812-4724-1*) Rprt Serv.

***Paine, Thomas.** Paine: Political Writings. 2nd ed. Kuklick, Bruce, ed. (Cambridge Studies in Comparative Politics). 300p. (C). 2000. text 47.95 (*0-521-66088-2*); pap. text 14.95 (*0-521-66799-2*) Cambridge U Pr.

Paine, Thomas. Public Good. 41p. 1989. reprint ed. 5.00 (*0-935680-24-1*) Kentucke Imprints.

— Public Good. (Notable American Authors Ser.). 1999. reprint ed. lib. bdg. 125.00 (*0-7812-4720-9*) Rprt Serv.

— The Rights of Man. 19.95 (*0-8488-1443-6*) Amereon Ltd.

— The Rights of Man. 1976. pap. 9.95 (*0-8065-0548-6*, Citadel Pr) Carol Pub Group.

— The Rights of Man. LC 99-48658. (Dover Thrift Editions Ser.). 256p. 1999. pap. text 2.00 (*0-486-40893-0*) Dover.

— The Rights of Man. LC 92-20305. 226p. (C). 1992. pap. text 6.95 (*0-87220-147-3*); lib. bdg. 27.95 (*0-87220-148-1*) Hackett Pub.

— The Rights of Man. LC 86-64007. (Great Books in Philosophy). 188p. 1987. pap. 7.95 (*0-87975-379-X*) Prometheus Bks.

— The Rights of Man. 288p. 1993. pap. 6.95 (*0-460-87140-4*, Everyman's Classic Lib) Tuttle Pubng.

— The Rights of Man. (Pelican Classics Ser.). 288p. 1984. pap. 9.95 (*0-14-039015-4*, Penguin Classics) Viking Penguin.

— The Rights of Man. (Classics of World Literature Ser.). 1997. pap. 5.95 (*1-85326-467-9*, 4679WW, Pub. by Wrdsworth Edits) NTC Contemp Pub Co.

— The Rights of Man. 1989. reprint ed. lib. bdg. 18.95 (*0-89966-626-4*) Buccaneer Bks.

— The Rights of Man. (Notable American Authors Ser.). 1999. reprint ed. lib. bdg. 125.00 (*0-7812-4722-5*) Rprt Serv.

***Paine, Thomas.** Rights of Man. 158p. 1998. reprint ed. pap. 16.95 (*0-7661-0441-9*) Kessinger Pub.

Paine, Thomas. The Rights of Man & Common Sense. 352p. 1994. 17.00 (*0-679-43314-7*) Random.

— Rights of Man, Common Sense, & Other Political Writings. Philp, Mark, ed. & intro. by. (Oxford World's Classics Ser.). 542p. 1998. pap. 9.95 (*0-19-283557-2*) OUP.

— The Rights of Man, 1791, Pt. I. LC 92-25538. 174p. 1992. reprint ed. 48.00 (*1-85477-109-4*) Continuum.

— Common Sense. (C). 1997. pap. text. write for info. (*0-321-02609-8*) Addson-Wesley Educ.

— The Thomas Paine Reader. Kramnick, Isaac & Foot, Michael, eds. 544p. 1987. pap. 13.95 (*0-14-044496-3*, Penguin Classics) Viking Penguin.

— The Writings of Thomas Paine: The Standard Edition, 4 vols. Conway, Moncure D., ed. LC 78-181966. reprint ed. 175.00 (*0-404-04870-6*) AMS Pr.

Paine, Thomas, jt. auth. see Burke, Edmund.

Paine, Thomas O., ed. Leaving the Cradle: Human Exploration of Space in the 21st Century, 28th Goddard Memorial Symposium, Mar. 14-16, 1990, Washington, D.C. LC 57-43769. (Science & Technology Ser.: Vol. 78). (Illus.). 348p. 1991. 70.00 (*0-87703-336-6*, Am Astronaut Soc); pap. 55.00 (*0-87703-337-4*, Am Astronaut Soc) Univelt Inc.

***PAINE, TIM.** The Complete Guide to Sports Massage. 192p. 2000. pap. 14.95 (*0-7136-5007-9*, Pub. by A & C Blk) Midpt Trade.

Paine, Tom. Scar Vegas: And Other Stories. LC 99-16416. 256p. 2000. 22.00 (*0-15-100489-7*, Harvest Bks) Harcourt.

***Paine, Tom.** Scar Vegas: And Other Stories. 228p. 2000. pap. 13.00 (*0-15-601420-3*) Harcourt.

Paine, Tommis. Books, Bottles Bum Raps. 304p. 1996. mass mkt. 4.99 (*1-55197-159-3*) Picasso Publ.

Paine, Whiton S., ed. Job Stress & Burnout: Research, Theory & Intervention Series. LC 82-7339. (Sage Focus Editions Ser.: Vol. 54). 296p. 1982. reprint ed. pap. 91.80 (*0-608-02986-6*, 205962600006) Bks Demand.

Paine, Wingate. Tilling the Soul. 215p. 1984. pap. 10.95 (*0-935358-20-5*) Aurora Press.

***Painell, Chrissie.** Home Spa: Pamper Yourself from Head to Toe. (Illus.). 144p. 2000. 24.95 (*1-85868-872-8*, Pub. by Carlton Bks Ltd) Natl Bk Netwk.

— Over 150 Astonishing Beauty Tips. (Illus.). 128p. 2000. 9.95 (*1-85868-978-3*, Pub. by Carlton Bks Ltd) Natl Bk Netwk.

Paino, Frankie. Out of Eden. LC 97-65398. (Poetry Ser.: Vol. LIV). 90p. (Orig.). 1997. pap. 12.00 (*1-880834-33-2*) Cleveland St Univ Poetry Ctr.

— The Rapture of Matter. (Cleveland Poets Ser.: No. 47). 61p. (Orig.). 1991. pap. 8.00 (*0-914946-91-9*) Cleveland St Univ Poetry Ctr.

Paino, John & Messinger, Lisa. The Tofu Book: The New American Cuisine. LC 91-46079. (Illus.). 184p. (Orig.). pap. 12.95 (*0-89529-409-5*, Avery) Penguin Putnam.

Paino, Paul E. Is the Holy Spirit Real? 80p. 1992. pap. 7.95 (*1-882357-01-9*) P E Paino Minist.

— The Ministry: What's Right? What's Wrong? 48p. 1992. pap. 4.95 (*1-882357-02-7*) P E Paino Minist.

— The Missing Element in Church Development. 224p. 1992. pap. 12.95 (*1-882357-03-5*) P E Paino Minist.

— Our Father's Promises . . . to Us! 64p. 1992. pap. 6.95 (*1-882357-00-0*) P E Paino Minist.

Painter. Close Corp, 2 vols., 1. 3rd ed. 1991. 175.00 (*0-316-68874-6*, Aspen Law & Bus) Aspen Pub.

— Close Corp, 2 vols., 2. 3rd ed. 1991. 175.00 (*0-316-68879-7*, Aspen Law & Bus) Aspen Pub.

— Early Language Development. 1992. text 49.00 (*0-86187-463-3*, Pub. by P P Pubs) Cassell & Continuum.

An Asterisk (*) at the beginning of an entry indicates that the title is appearing for the first time.

— Employment Rights: A Reference Handbook. LC 93-15994. 450p. (C). 75.00 (*0-7453-0584-9*, Pub. by Pluto GBR); pap. 30.00 (*0-7453-0589-X*, Pub. by Pluto GBR) Stylus Pub VA.

Painter, Ann F., ed. Reader in Classification & Descriptive Cataloging. LC 72-78204. 320p. 1983. lib. bdg. 59.95 (*0-313-24035-3*, ZRC/, Praeger Pubs) Greenwood.

Painter, Anthony A. Butterworths Law of Food & Drugs. 265p. 1992. pap. 80.00 (*0-406-00642-3*, UK, MICHIE) LEXIS Pub.

Painter, Anthony A. & Harvey, Brian W., eds. Butterworths Law of Food & Drugs. ring bd. write for info. (*0-406-99647-4*, BLFDASET, MICHIE) LEXIS Pub.

— O'Keefe: The Law of Weights & Measures. 2nd ed. ring bd. write for info. (*0-406-99896-5*, OWMASET, MICHIE) LEXIS Pub.

— O'Keefe: The Law of Weights & Measures, 2 vols., Set. 2nd ed. ring bd. 390.00 (*0-406-32645-2*, U.K., MICHIE) LEXIS Pub.

Painter, Carol. Friends Helping Friends: A Manual for Peer Counselors. Sorenson, Don L., ed. 224p. (Orig.). (YA). (gr. 9-12). 1989. pap. text 9.95 (*0-932796-28-1*) Ed Media Corp.

— Leading a Friends Helping Friends Program. Sorenson, Don L., ed. 160p. (Orig.). (YA). (gr. 9-12). 1989. pap. text 9.95 (*0-932796-29-X*) Ed Media Corp.

— Workshop Winners: Developing Creative & Dynamic Workshops. LC 93-70535. 184p. (Orig.). (C). 1993. pap. text 12.95 (*0-932796-57-5*) Ed Media Corp.

Painter, Charles C. The Condition of Affairs in Indian Territory & California. LC 74-15121. reprint ed. 29.50 (*0-404-11981-6*) AMS Pr.

Painter, Charlotte. Conjuring Tibet. LC 96-42526. 224p. 1996. pap. 14.95 (*1-56279-095-1*) Mercury Hse Inc.

— Gifts of Age: Portraits & Essays of 32 Remarkable Women. LC 85-13627. 150p. 1985. pap. 16.95 (*0-87701-368-3*) Chronicle Bks.

— Who Made the Lamb? LC 88-72025. 224p. (Orig.). 1988. reprint ed. pap. 8.95 (*0-88739-063-3*) Creat Arts Bk.

Painter, Charlotte, jt. ed. see Moffat, Mary J.

Painter, Clare. Learning the Mother Tongue. 2nd ed. 93p. (C). 1995. pap. 34.00 (*0-7300-1249-2*, ECS805, Pub. by Deakin Univ) St Mut.

— Learning Through Language in Early Childhood. LC 98-2895. (Open Linguistics Ser.). 1998. 82.95 (*0-304-70056-8*) Continuum.

***Painter, Colin.** At Home with Art. 2000. 24.95 (*1-85332-200-8*) U CA Pr.

Painter, Colin. Gonja: A Phonological & Grammatical Study. LC 71-626566. (African Ser.: Vol. 1). (Illus.). 1970. pap. text 20.00 (*0-87750-139-4*) Res Inst Inner Asian Studies.

Painter, David S. Allied Relations in Iran, 1941-1945. (Pew Case Studies in International Affairs). 50p. (C). 1986. pap. text 3.50 (*1-56927-425-8*) Geo U Inst Dplmcy.

— The Baruch Plan & the International Control of Atomic Energy. (Pew Case Studies in International Affairs). 50p. (C). 1990. pap. text 3.50 (*1-56927-324-3*) Geo U Inst Dplmcy.

— The Cold War: An Interdisciplinary History. LC 98-49205. (Making of the Contemporary World Ser.). 1999. pap. 14.99 (*0-415-15316-6*) Routledge.

***Painter, David S.** The Cold War: An Interdisciplinary History. LC 98-49205. (Making of the Contemporary World Ser.). 1999. write for info. (*0-415-19446-6*) Routledge.

Painter, David S. Deciding Germany's Future, 1943-1945. (Pew Case Studies in International Affairs). 50p. (C). 1996. pap. text 3.50 (*1-56927-323-5*) Geo U Inst Dplmcy.

— The German Question & the Cold War. (Pew Case Studies in International Affairs). 50p. (C). 1995. pap. text 3.50 (*1-56927-415-0*) Geo U Inst Dplmcy.

— The United States, Great Britain & Mossadegh. (Pew Case Studies in International Affairs). 50p. (C). 1993. pap. text 3.50 (*1-56927-332-4*) Geo U Inst Dplmcy.

Painter, David S., jt. auth. see Fain, William T.

Painter, David S., jt. auth. see Howard, James R.

Painter, David S., jt. auth. see Irvine, Sally G.

Painter, David S., jt. ed. see Leffler, Melvyn P.

Painter, Derrick, tr. see Henry, Georges.

Painter, Derrick, tr. see Mari, Jean Luc.

Painter, Desmond, et al. Religion. Yapp, Malcolm et al, eds. (World History Program Ser.). (Illus.). 32p. (YA). (gr. 6-11). 1980. reprint ed. pap. text 5.90 (*0-89908-120-7*) Greenhaven.

Painter, Doug. The Field & Stream Firearms Safety Handbook. LC 99-13206. (Field & Stream Fishing & Hunting Library). 1999. pap. 9.95 (*1-55821-912-9*) Lyons Pr.

Painter, Ellen, jt. auth. see Weisel, Deborah L.

Painter, Floyd, jt. auth. see Hranicky, W. Jack.

Painter, Francis O., jt. ed. see Gherman, Paul M.

Painter, Franklin V. History of Education. enl. rev. ed. LC 73-137265. reprint ed. 29.50 (*0-404-04866-8*) AMS Pr.

— Poets of the South. LC 68-57064. (Granger Index Reprint Ser.). 1977. 17.95 (*0-8369-6037-8*) Ayer.

Painter, Franklin V., ed. Great Pedagogical Essays: Plato to Spencer. LC 77-137266. reprint ed. 47.50 (*0-404-04865-X*) AMS Pr.

Painter, Genevieve, et al, eds. Alfred Adler: As We Remember Him. 2nd ed. (Illus.). 122p. 1998. reprint ed. pap. write for info. (*0-926164-00-7*) N Am Soc Adlerian.

Painter, George D. Marcel Proust: A Biography, 2 vols. 1978. pap. 4.95 (*0-685-04271-5*) Vin Bks.

Painter, Gwenda. A Different River: River Trade & Development along the Murray Valley Network. LC 94-102598. 112p. 1993. write for info. (*1-875657-26-6*, Pub. by Hyland Hse) Seven Hills Bk.

Painter, Hal. The Captain Nemo Cookbook Papers: Everyone's Guide to Zen & the Art of Boat in Hard Times Illustrated. 2nd ed. 135p. 1999. pap. 15.00 (*1-892590-52-2*) Out Your Bk.

— The Cross Country Ski, Cook, Look & Pleasure Book... And Welcome to the Alice in Snowpeople Land. 2nd ed. (Illus.). 154p. 1999. pap. 15.00 (*1-892590-51-4*) Out Your Bk.

Painter, Jack W. Deep Bodywork & Personal Development: Harmonizing Our Bodies, Emotions, & Thoughts. 1987. 19.00 (*0-938405-01-2*) Bodymind Bks.

— Technical Manual of Deep Wholistic Bodywork: Postural Integration. 203p. 1987. pap. 22.00 (*0-938405-05-5*) Bodymind Bks.

Painter, Jacqueline B. The German Invasion of Western North Carolina. 1998. pap. text 17.95 (*1-57072-074-6*) Overmountain Pr.

— The German Invasion of Western North Carolina: A Pictorial History. LC 92-93524. (Illus.). 128p. (YA). (gr. 8 up). 1992. 28.00 (*0-9634256-0-9*) J B Painter.

— The Season of Dorland-Bell: History of an Appalachian Mission School. LC 87-62800. (Illus.). 304p. 1987. reprint ed. 23.95 (*0-614-09745-2*); reprint ed. pap. 17.95 (*0-614-09746-0*) Appalach Consortium.

Painter, James. Guatemala: False Hope, False Freedom. rev. ed. (Illus.). 160p. 1989. pap. 12.00 (*0-85345-732-8*, Pub. by Lat Am Bur) Monthly Rev.

— Guatemala: False Hope, False Freedom. 2nd rev. ed. (Illus.). 160p. 1989. 22.00 (*0-85345-748-4*, Pub. by Lat Am Bur) Monthly Rev.

Painter, James & CIIR & Latin America Bureau, eds. Guatemala: False Hope, False Freedom. 144p. (C). 1987. 90.00 (*0-7855-6041-6*); pap. 40.00 (*0-7855-3788-0*) St Mut.

Painter, Jeff. Laser Locator: Reference Manual & Workbook. Blinn, William, ed. 1992. 50.00 (*1-880933-01-2*) Mgmt Comp Srvs.

Painter, Jerry. Great Trails for Family Hiking: The Tetons. LC 95-3519. (Illus.). 201p. 1995. pap. 17.50 (*0-87108-857-6*) Pruett.

Painter, Jerry, jt. auth. see Fuller, Margaret C.

Painter, Joe. Geography & Politics: Contemporary Approaches. (Arnold Publications). 216p. 1995. pap. text 35.00 (*0-340-56735-X*) OUP.

— Politics, Geography, & "Political Geography" A Critical Approach. 1995. text. write for info. (*0-340-63215-1*, Pub. by E A) Routldge.

***Painter, John.** Just James: The Brother of Jesus in History & Tradition. 1999. pap. text 22.00 (*0-8006-3169-2*) Augsburg Fortress.

Painter, John. Just James: The Brother of Jesus in History & Tradition. LC 97-21237. 320p. 1997. 34.95 (*1-57003-174-6*) U of SC Pr.

— Letters of John. (Sacra Pagina Ser.). Date not set. write for info. (*0-8146-5812-1*, M Glazier) Liturgical Pr.

— Mark's Gospel. LC 96-9727. (New Testament Readings Ser.). 272p. (C). 1997. 65.00 (*0-415-11364-4*); pap. 24.99 (*0-415-11365-2*) Routledge.

— The Quest for the Messiah: The History, Literature & Theology of the Johannine. 424p. 1991. text 49.95 (*0-567-09592-4*, Pub. by T & T Clark) Bks Intl VA.

— The Quest for the Messiah: The History, Literature & Theology of the Johannine Community. LC 93-31675. 466p. (C). 1994. pap. text 24.95 (*0-687-35153-7*) Abingdon.

Painter, John. The Quest for the Messiah: The History, Literature & Theology of the Johannine Community. 2nd ed. 512p. pap. 39.95 (*0-567-29246-0*, Pub. by T & T Clark) Bks Intl VA.

Painter, John. Theology As Hermeneutics: Rudolf Bultmann's Interpretation of the History of Jesus. (Historic Texts & Interpreters Ser.: Vol. 265). 265p. 18.95 (*1-85075-051-3*) CUP Services.

***Painter, Kate & Tilley, Nick, eds.** Surveillance of Public Space: CCTV, Street Lighting & Crime. (Crime Prevention Studies: Vol. 10). (Illus.). 273p. 1999. 47.50 (*1-881798-18-6*, Pub. by Willow Tree NY); pap. text 37.50 (*1-881798-22-4*, Pub. by Willow Tree NY) Lib Res.

Painter, Kenneth, jt. ed. see Newby, Martine.

Painter, Lee J. Each Day Is a Gift: That's Why It's Called the Present. LC 95-82233. (Illus.). 57p. 1996. pap. 8.95 (*1-56352-295-0*) Longstreet.

— If Forever Came Tomorrow: These Are the Things I'd Like to Do Today. LC 93-79665. (Illus.). 64p. 1993. 8.95 (*1-56352-108-3*) Longstreet.

Painter, Louis W. Israel Is Real. LC 94-71504. 1996. 21.95 (*0-8158-0502-0*) Chris Mass.

Painter, Mark & Hopkins, Cathy, eds. The Complete RBRVS (RBRC) rev. ed. 500p. 1998. pap. 109.95 (*1-56329-501-6*) St Anthony Pub.

Painter, Mark, et al. Complete RBRVS (RBRC) Print. 400p. Date not set. 89.95 (*1-56329-331-5*) St Anthony Pub.

***Painter, Mark N. & Sturgeon, Stacy Louck, eds.** Relative Value Studies: Includes RBRVS, 1999 (ASCII) 1999. 189.95 incl. disk (*1-929061-01-3*) Relative Val.

— Relative Value Studies, Inc.'s Complete RBRVS, 1999. 560p. 1999. pap. 99.95 (*1-929061-00-5*) Relative Val.

Painter, Mark N., jt. ed. see Sturgeon, Stacy Louck.

Painter, Mark P. & Looker, James M. Ohio Driving under the Influence Law, 1996-97. 3rd ed. 581p. 1996. pap. text 60.00 (*0-8322-0665-2*) Banks-Baldwin.

Painter, Mark S. Mercer County Archives Vol. 1: Deeds. 130p. 1995. per. 12.00 (*1-55856-211-7*, 065) Closson Pr.

— Mercer County Archives Vol. 2: Naturalizations. 258p. 1996. per. 19.95 (*1-55856-221-4*, 066) Closson Pr.

— Mercer County, PA Archives, Vol. 4. LC 96-83436. 266p. 1996. per. 24.95 (*1-55856-228-1*, 068) Closson Pr.

— Shenango Valley Cemetery Bk. 1: 1882-1913. LC 98-70652. 1998. per. 21.00 (*1-55856-269-9*, 186) Closson Pr.

Painter, Martin. Collaborative Federalism: Economic Reform in Australia in the 1990s. LC 98-13520. (Reshaping Australian Institutions Ser.). (Illus.). 217p. (C). 1998. text 64.95 (*0-521-59071-X*) Cambridge U Pr.

Painter, Martin, jt. auth. see Considine, Mark.

Painter, Michael & Durham, William H., eds. The Social Causes of Environmental Destruction in Latin America. (Linking Levels of Analysis Ser.). (Illus.). 288p. 1995. pap. text 24.95 (*0-472-06560-2*, 06560) U of Mich Pr.

Painter, Mike. Satellite Fever. Balkwill, Fran, ed. (Making Sense of Science Ser.). (Illus.). 32p. (J). 1997. pap. 12.00 (*1-85578-091-7*, Pub. by Portland Pr Ltd) Ashgate Pub Co.

Painter, Mirra, ed. see Gilbert-Rolfe, Jeremy, et al.

Painter, Muriel T. With Good Heart: Yaqui Beliefs & Ceremonies in Pascua, Village. Spicer, Edward H. & Kaemlein, Wilma, eds. LC 86-893. (Illus.). 533p. 1986. 50.95 (*0-8165-0875-5*) U of Ariz Pr.

— A Yaqui Easter. LC 74-153706. 40p. 1971. pap. 8.50 (*0-8165-0168-8*) U of Ariz Pr.

Painter, Nell I. Exodusters: Black Migration to Kansas After Reconstruction. (Illus.). 1992. reprint ed. pap. 12.95 (*0-393-00951-3*) Norton.

— The Narrative of Hosea Hudson. (Illus.). 424p. 1993. pap. 12.95 (*0-393-31015-9*) Norton.

— The Narrative of Hosea Hudson: His Life As a Negro Communist in the South. LC 79-4589. 416p. reprint ed. pap. 129.00 (*0-7837-2308-3*, 205739600004) Bks Demand.

— Sojourner Truth: A Life, A Symbol. LC 95-47595. 370p. 1996. 28.00 (*0-393-02739-2*) Norton.

— Sojourner Truth: A Life, A Symbol. 384p. 1997. pap. 14.95 (*0-393-31708-0*) Norton.

— Soul Murder & Slavery. unabridged ed. LC 95-78744. (Charles Edmondson Historical Lectures). 38p. (Orig.). 1995. pap. 5.95 (*0-918954-62-2*) Baylor Univ Pr.

— Standing at Armageddon: The United States, 1877-1919. LC 86-33111. 1989. pap. 17.95 (*0-393-30588-0*) Norton.

Painter, Nell I., ed. see Anderson, Karen.

Painter, Nell I., ed. see Harris, Robert L., Jr.

Painter, Nell I., ed. see Hune, Shirley.

Painter, Nell I., ed. see Okihiro, Gary Y.

Painter, Nell I., ed. see Reimers, David M.

Painter, Nell I., ed. see Sanchez Korrol, Virginia.

Painter, Nell I., ed. see Wilson, Terry P.

Painter, Pamela. The Long & Short of It. LC 98-71950. (Series in Short Fiction). 202p. 1999. pap. 15.95 (*0-88748-286-4*, Pub. by Carnegie-Mellon) Cornell U Pr.

Painter, Pamela, jt. auth. see Bernays, Anne.

Painter, Patricia S. Henry Ford Hospital: The First 75 Years. 1997. 20.00 (*0-9659494-0-0*) H F Hlth Syst.

Painter, Paul C. & Coleman, Michael M. Fundamentals of Polymer Science: An Introductory Text. 2nd ed. LC 97-60515. 494p. 1997. text 99.95 (*1-56676-559-5*) Technomic.

— Fundamentos de Ciencia de Polimeros: Un Texto Introductorio. Fernandez-Berridi, M. J. & Iruin, J. J., trs. LC 96-60554. 496p. 1996. pap. 29.95 (*1-56676-430-0*) Technomic.

Painter, Pennell C., contrib. by. Laboratory Design: Proposed Guideline (1994) 1994. 85.00 (*1-56238-246-2*, GP18-P) NCCLS.

***Painter, Richard.** Employment Rights. 2nd ed. 456p. 1998. 89.95 (*0-7453-1319-1*, Pub. by Pluto GBR) Stylus Pub VA.

Painter, Richard W., et al. Cases & Materials on Employment Law, Vol. 1. 3rd ed. 891p. 1995. pap. 54.00 (*1-85431-197-2*, Pub. by Blackstone Pr) Gaunt.

Painter, Richard W., jt. auth. see Noonan, John T., Jr.

Painter, Robert. Auto Theft: Let the Truth Be Known! (Illus.). 210p. 1998. ring bd. 69.95 (*0-9664635-0-1*) Shdw Pubns WI.

— The Native American Indian Artist Directory. LC 98-96874. 300p. 1999. pap. 19.95 (*0-9668806-0-9*) First Nations Art.

Painter, Robert B., jt. auth. see Gatti, Richard A.

Painter, Robert B., jt. ed. see Gatti, Richard A.

Painter, Robert W., jt. auth. see Holmes, Ann E.

***Painter, Robin.** A Signal Honour: With the Chindits & the XIV Army in Burma. (Illus.). 2000. 36.95 (*0-85052-707-4*, Pub. by Leo Cooper) Combined Pub.

***Painter, Sally.** Shadows of Love. Schulte, Colleen, ed. 288p. 2000. mass mkt. 6.50 (*1-929613-27-X*) Avid MI.

Painter, Sandra J. Orthopaedic Patient Education Resource Manual. LC 94-1342. ring bd. 189.00 (*0-8342-0545-9*, S126) Aspen Pub.

Painter, Sandra J., ed. see Aspen Reference Group Staff.

Painter, Sandra J., ed. see Aspen Reference Group Staff & Di Lima, Sara N.

Painter, Sandra J., jt. ed. see Lawrence, Kenneth E.

Painter, Sidney. French Chivalry: Chivalric Ideas & Practices in Medieval France. 188p. 1957. pap. text 10.95 (*0-8014-9061-8*) Cornell U Pr.

— Mediaeval Society. 107p. 1951. pap. text 8.95 (*0-8014-9850-3*) Cornell U Pr.

— Medieval Society: Everyday Life in the Middle Ages. rev. ed. (Illus.). 64p. (C). 1991. pap. text 2.25 (*1-877891-06-1*) Paperbook Pr Inc.

— The Reign of King John. 1979. 33.95 (*0-405-10619-X*) Ayer.

— The Rise of the Feudal Monarchies. 147p. 1951. pap. text 9.95 (*0-8014-9851-1*) Cornell U Pr.

— Studies in the History of the English Feudal Barony. LC 78-64191. (Johns Hopkins University. Studies in the Social Sciences. Thirtieth Ser. 1912: 3). reprint ed. 37.50 (*0-404-61298-9*) AMS Pr.

— William Marshal: Knight-Errant, Baron & Regent of England. (Medieval Academy Reprints for Teaching Ser.: No. 13). 318p. 1982. reprint ed. pap. text 14.95 (*0-8020-6498-1*) U of Toronto Pr.

Painter, Sidney, jt. auth. see Tierney, Brian.

Painter, Sigrid D. Aussprache des Fruehneuhochdeutschen nach Lesemeistern des 16. Jahrhunderts. (Berkeley Insights in Linguistics & Semiotics Ser.: Vol. 1). XVI, 202p. 1989. text 39.95 (*0-8204-0498-5*) P Lang Pubng.

Painter, Susan. Edgar the Playwright. 1996. pap. 19.95 (*0-413-69960-9*, Methuen Drama) Methn.

Painter, Suzanne, et al. Microsoft Works 4.0 for the Macintosh: A Workbook for Educators. rev. ed. (Illus.). 274p. 1996. spiral bd., wbk. ed. 26.95 (*1-56484-126-X*) Intl Society Tech Educ.

Painter, W. H. Close Corp, 2 vols., Set. 3rd ed. 1248p. 1997. ring bd. 295.00 (*0-316-68880-0*, Aspen Law & Bus) Aspen Pub.

Painter, William H. Business Planning, Teacher's Manual to Accompany. 3rd ed. (American Casebook Ser.). 137p. 1994. pap. text. write for info. (*0-314-04066-8*) West Pub.

— Corporate & Tax Aspects of Closely Held Corporations. 2nd ed. 670p. 1981. suppl. ed. 80.00 (*0-316-68854-1*, Aspen Law & Bus) Aspen Pub.

— Problems & Materials in Business Planning. 3rd ed. LC 94-5570. (American Casebook Ser.). 1127p. 1994. 65.00 (*0-314-03451-X*) West Pub.

Painter, William M. Palace of Pleasure, 4 vols. Miles, Hamish, ed. LC 30-20341. reprint ed. 240.00 (*0-404-04880-3*) AMS Pr.

Paioff, Mitch. Accounting Software Guide: A Directory of Microcomputer Accounting Software Products for Specific Industries. Scott, Jan, ed. 170p. (Orig.). 1989. pap. 29.95 (*1-877683-05-1*) Anderson Laser.

— Tax Preparer's Marketing Guide: More New Clients Every Year. 2nd rev. ed. (Illus.). 92p. 1996. pap. 29.98 (*0-614-14933-9*) Anderson Laser.

Pair, Iola. Ashlee's Smile Quilt Coloring Book. (Illus.). 32p. (J). (gr. 1-8). 1997. pap. 7.00 (*0-9651775-1-3*) I Pair.

— A Humming Bird Named Friendly Vol. 1: World's Smallest Bird. LC 96-92286. (Illus.). ix, 56p. (Orig.). (J). (gr. 3 up). 1996. pap. 12.00 (*0-9651775-0-5*, 96-598) I Pair.

— The Moore Kids: A Look Back. 152p. (YA). (gr. 3 up). 1997. pap. 12.95 (*0-9651775-2-1*) I Pair.

Pair, Joyce, ed. Women & the Constitution: Symposium Papers Collection. 169p. (C). 1990. pap. text 14.95 (*1-879413-01-9*) Emory U Carter Ctr.

Paira, Audrey. Guinea Pigs in Your Life. LC 97-31105. 1997. 6.95 (*0-87605-440-8*) Howell Bks.

***Pairbizkovba, Jana & Hills, Andrew P.** Childhood Obesity: Prevention & Treatment. LC 00-31171. (Series in Modern Nutrition). 2000. write for info. (*0-8493-8736-1*) CRC Pr.

Pairis, Gunther Von, see Von Pairis, Gunther.

Pairo, Preston. Winner's Cut. 256p. 1988. pap. 3.95 (*0-373-97069-2*) Harlequin Bks.

Pairo, Preston A., III. Angel's Crime. 1998. mass mkt. 6.50 (*0-451-40710-5*, Onyx) NAL.

— The Captain Drowns. (Ocean City Mysteries Ser.). 177p. (Orig.). 1986. pap. 2.95 (*0-9616584-0-1*) Maryland Locale.

Pais, Abraham. Einstein Lived Here: Essays for the Layman. LC 93-32095. (Illus.). 298p. 1994. 25.00 (*0-19-853994-0*, Clarendon Pr) OUP.

***Pais, Abraham.** The Genius of Science: A Portrait of 20th-Century Physicists. LC Q141.P29 2000. (Illus.). 368p. 2000. 30.00 (*0-19-850614-7*) OUP.

Pais, Abraham. Inward Bound: Of Matter & Forces in the Physical World. 688p. 1988. pap. 22.50 (*0-19-851997-4*) OUP.

— Niels Bohr's Times: In Physics, Philosophy, & Polity. (Illus.). 582p. 1991. 35.00 (*0-19-852049-2*) OUP.

— Niels Bohr's Times: In Physics, Philosophy, & Polity. (Illus.). 582p. 1994. reprint ed. pap. 19.95 (*0-19-852048-4*) OUP.

— Subtle Is the Lord: The Science & Life of Albert Einstein. LC 82-2273. (Illus.). 568p. 1983. pap. 17.95 (*0-19-520438-7*) OUP.

— A Tale of Two Continents: The Life of a Physicist in a Turbulent World. LC 96-39313. 520p. 1997. 35.00 (*0-691-01243-1*, Pub. by Princeton U Pr) Cal Prin Full Svc.

P

Pais, Abraham, et al. Paul Dirac: The Man & His Work. LC 97-22443. (Illus.). 140p. (C). 1998. 19.95 (*0-521-58382-9*) Cambridge U Pr.

Pais, Ettore. Ancient Legends of Roman History. Cosenza, Mario E., tr. LC 74-179532. (Select Bibliographies Reprint Ser.). 1977. reprint ed. 35.95 (*0-8369-6661-9*) Ayer.

Pais, Istavan & Jones, J. B., Jr. The Handbook of Trace Elements. LC 97-157041. 250p. 1997. lib. bdg. 75.00 (*1-884015-34-4*) St Lucie Pr.

Pais, Janet. Suffer the Children. 1991. pap. 9.95 (*0-8091-3226-5*) Paulist Pr.

Paisey, David, compiled by. Catalogue of Books Printed in the German-Speaking Countries & of German Books Printed in Other Countries from 1601 to 1700 Now in the British Library, 5 vols., Set. (Catalogues of the British Library Collections). 3024p. 1994. 590.00 (*0-7123-0351-0*, Pub. by B23tish Library) U of Toronto Pr.

Paish, Frank W. Long-Term & Short-Term Interest Rates in the United Kingdom. LC 67-4633. vii, 56p. 1967. 15.00 (*0-678-06764-3*) Kelley.

Paish, Wilf. The Complete Manual of Sports Science. 224p. 1998. pap. 24.95 (*0-7136-4854-6*, Pub. by A & C Blk) Midpt Trade.

— Introduction to Athletics. (Illus.). 1974. 9.50 (*0-571-10191-7*) Transatl Arts.

— Nutrition for Sport. (Illus.). 128p. 1991. pap. 22.95 (*1-85223-380-X*, Pub. by Crolwood) Trafalgar.

... Registrum Monasterii de Passelet. ...N., ed. LC 75-174311. (Maitland Club, ...Publications: No. 17). reprint ed. 67.50 (...2954-2) AMS Pr.

...**ton.** From Cotton to Quail: An Agricultural ...icle of Leon County, Florida, 1860-1967. LC ...708. (Illus.). xi, 162p. 1981. reprint ed. pap. 18.95 (0-8130-0718-6) U Press Fla.

— The Red Hills of Florida, 1528-1865. LC 88-5767. (Illus.). 306p. 1989. pap. 94.90 (0-608-05137-3, 206569800005) Bks Demand.

Paisley, Clyde A. Wouldn't You Rather Be Rich? How to Achieve Financial Independence Soundly & Surely. Selph, Alexa M., ed. LC 88-9188. 320p. 1990. pap. 13.95 (0-87797-163-3) Cherokee.

Paisley College Staff. Market Planning. (Marketing for Manufacturing Managers Ser.). 1989. 105.00 (0-08-037127-2) Elsevier.

— Market Research & Sales Forecast. (Marketing for Manufacturing Managers Ser.). 1989. pap. text 84.00 (0-08-040466-9, Pergamon Pr) Elsevier.

— Marketing for Manufacturing Managers. Incl. Marketing for Manufacturing Managers., 6 vols. 1989. pap. text 435.00 (0-08-040476-6, Pergamon Pr); 1. Introduction to Marketing. 1989. pap. text 84.00 (0-08-040464-2, Pergamon Pr); 3. Product Development. 1989. pap. text 84.00 (0-08-040468-5, Pergamon Pr); 4. Pricing for Profit. 1989. pap. text 84.00 (0-08-040470-7, Pergamon Pr); 5. Market Planning. 1989. pap. text 84.00 (0-08-040472-3, Pergamon Pr); 6. Strategic Marketing. 1989. pap. 84.00 (0-08-040474-X, Pergamon Pr); 1989. 22.00 (0-08-040475-8, Pergamon Pr) Elsevier.

— Pricing for Profit. (Marketing for Manufacturing Managers Ser.). 1989. 105.00 (0-08-037126-4) Elsevier.

— Product Development. (Marketing For Manufacturing Managers Ser.). 1989. 105.00 (0-08-037125-6) Elsevier.

— Strategic Marketing. (Marketing for Manufacturing Managers Ser.). 1989. 105.00 (0-08-037128-0) Elsevier.

Paisley, Dennis, ed. Selected Papers on Scientific & Engineering High-Speed Photography: Technology, Systems, & Applications. LC 95-1595. (Milestone Ser.: Vol. MS 109). 1995. text 50.00 (0-8194-1854-4) SPIE.

Paisley, Dennis L., ed. 22nd International Congress on High-Speed Photography & Photonics, Vol. 2869. 1140p. 1997. 174.00 (0-8194-2266-5) SPIE.

Paisley, Harold S. This Daniel. 190p. (Orig.). 1991. pap. text 10.95 (0-9631200-1-8) OlivePr CT.

— This Ruth. (Illus.). 175p. 1996. 14.99 (0-9631200-2-6) OlivePr CT.

Paisley, Ian. Exposition of the Epistle to the Romans. 1997. pap. text 9.99 (1-898787-71-9) Emerald House Group Inc.

***Paisley, Ian.** Grow Old Along with Me. 130p. 2000. pap. 9.99 (1-84030-070-1, Ambassador-Emerald) Emerald House Group Inc.

Paisley, Ian. Sermons with Startling Titles. 197p. (Orig.). 1999. pap. 9.99 (1-84030-048-5) Ambassador Prodns Ltd.

— Text a Day Keeps the Devil Away. 1998. pap. text 9.99 (1-898787-86-7) Ambassador Prodns Ltd.

Paisley, Ian R. Into the Millennium: 20th Century Messager for 21st Century Living. 110p. 1998. pap. 9.99 (1-84030-025-6) Emerald House Group Inc.

— My Plea for the Old Sword. 111p. (Orig.). 1997. pap. text 8.99 (1-84030-015-9) Ambassador Prodns Ltd.

— Rent Veils at Calvary. 93p. 1997. pap. 9.99 (1-898787-34-4) Emerald House Group Inc.

— Sermons on Special Occasions. 158p. 1996. pap. 9.99 (1-898787-73-5) Emerald House Group Inc.

Paisley, Joanna. A Model of Building Society Interest Setting. LC 95-3185. (Bank of England, Economics Division. Working Paper Ser.: No. 22). (Illus.). 40p. reprint ed. pap. 30.00 (0-608-20162-6, 207142600011) Bks Demand.

***Paisley, Joe & Paisley, Page.** Western Scroll Saw & Inlay Patterns. (Illus.). 100p. (Orig.). 2000. pap. 14.95 (1-56523-118-X, Pub. by Fox Chapel Pub) IPG Chicago.

Paisley, Melvyn & Paisley, Vicki. Ace! Autobiography of a Fighter Pilot World War II. Caso, Adolph, ed. (Illus.). 320p. 1998. pap. 19.95 (0-8283-2034-9) Branden Bks.

Paisley, Page, jt. auth. see Paisley, Joe.

Paisley, Pam, ed. see Petersen, Phil.

Paisley, Pamela O. & Hubbard, Glenda T. Developmental School Counseling Programs: From Theory to Practice. LC 94-850. 221p. 1994. 29.95 (1-55620-139-7, 72582) Am Coun Assn.

Paisley, R. K. Christian Foundation. 1997. pap. 9.99 (1-898787-70-0) Emerald House Group Inc.

— Expository Sermons. 1997. pap. 9.99 (1-898787-74-3) Emerald House Group Inc.

— Garments of Christ. 1997. pap. 9.99 (1-898787-72-7) Emerald House Group Inc.

Paisley, Rebecca. The Barefoot Bride. 400p. 1990. pap. 3.95 (0-380-76019-3, Avon Bks) Morrow Avon.

— Diamonds & Dreams. 432p. (Orig.). 1991. mass mkt. 4.50 (0-380-76564-0, Avon Bks) Morrow Avon.

— Midnight & Magnolias. 416p. (Orig.). 1992. mass mkt. 4.50 (0-380-76566-7, Avon Bks) Morrow Avon.

— Moonlight & Magic. 1990. pap. 3.95 (0-380-76020-7, Avon Bks) Morrow Avon.

— Rainbows & Rapture. 400p. (Orig.). 1992. mass mkt. 4.50 (0-380-76565-9, Avon Bks) Morrow Avon.

— Yonder Lies Heaven. 1997. mass mkt. 5.99 (0-440-22158-7) Dell.

Paisley, Rebecca, et al. Love Potion. 272p. (Orig.). 1995. mass mkt. 4.99 (0-515-11549-5, Jove) Berkley Pub.

Paisley, Rhonda. My Power Diary. 1998. pap. 11.99 (1-84030-028-0) Ambassador Prodns Ltd.

***Paisley, Rhonda.** My Power Words File: Big Bible Words Made Small. 192p. (J). (gr. 1-6). 1998. pap. 9.99 (1-84030-027-2) Ambassador Prodns Ltd.

Paisley, Tim. To Catch a Carp. (Illus.). 192p. 1998. 40.00 (1-86126-081-4, Pub. by Crolwood) Trafalgar.

Paisley, Vicki, jt. auth. see Paisley, Melvyn.

Paisley, William, jt. ed. see Butler, Matilda.

Paisley, William J., jt. ed. see Chen, Milton.

Paisley, William J., jt. ed. see Rice, Ronald E.

***Paisner, Daniel.** The Ball: Mark McGwire's 70th Home Run Ball & the Marketing of the American Dream. LC 99-26135. 224p. 1999. 22.95 (0-670-88776-5) Viking Penguin.

Paisner, Daniel. Horizontal Hold: The Making & Breaking of a Network Pilot. (Illus.). 256p. 1992. 18.95 (1-55972-148-0, Birch Ln Pr) Carol Pub Group.

Paisner, Daniel, jt. auth. see Jones, Star.

Paisner, Daniel, jt. auth. see Koch, Edward Irving.

Paisner, Daniel, jt. auth. see Paisner, Emme.

Paisner, Daniel, jt. auth. see Pataki, George.

Paisner, Daniel, jt. auth. see Quinn, Anthony.

Paisner, Emme & Paisner, Daniel. True Beauty: Positive Attitudes & Practical Tips from the World's Leading Plus-Size Model. 272p. 1998. pap. 14.00 (0-399-52383-9, Perigee Bks) Berkley Pub.

Paisner, Marshall B. Sustaining the Family Business: An Insider's Guide to Managing Across Generations. LC 99-61218. (Illus.). 240p. 1999. text 26.00 (0-7382-0114-6, Pub. by Perseus Pubng) HarpC.

***Paisner, Marshall B.** Sustaining the Family Business: An Insider's Guide to Managing Across Generations. 2000. pap. 16.00 (0-7382-0320-3) Perseus Pubng.

Paison, Jean, jt. auth. see Sprenger, Nancy L.

Paithanakar, Yeshwaint. Transmission Network Protection: Theory & Practice. LC 97-36224. (Power Engineering Ser.: Vol. 2). (Illus.). 400p. 1997. text 159.75 (0-8247-9911-9) Dekker.

Paitnaik, Prabhat. Economics & Egalitarianism. (Oxford India Paperbacks Ser.). 46p. (C). 1991. 5.95 (0-19-562496-3) OUP.

Paitson, Hupi. Maui Booklet. (Illus.). 1970. pap. 0.50 (0-941200-00-0) Aquarius.

Paitson, Hupi & Paitson, Lloyd. Maui: Notes from a Private Guidebook. (Illus.). (Orig.). 1970. pap. 1.50 (0-941200-01-9) Aquarius.

Paitson, Lloyd, jt. auth. see Paitson, Hupi.

Paiuk & Weisz. Low Cost Automation. LC 96-223480. (IFAC Postprint Ser.). 432p. 1995. pap. 82.25 (0-08-042239-X, Pergamon Pr) Elsevier.

Paiva, Bob. The Program Director's Handbook. (Illus.). 168p. (Orig.). 1983. pap. 16.95 (0-8306-1363-3, 1363) McGraw-Hill Prof.

Paiva, Bonnie S. My Best to You: A Collection of Choice Recipes for the New Cook. (Orig.). 1994. pap. 12.50 (0-9639227-1-8) B S Paiva.

Paiva, Judith L., jt. auth. see O'Donnell, Teresa D.

Paiva, Manuel, ed. see Chang, H. K.

Paiva, Marcelo R. Happy Old Year. George, David, tr. from POR. LC 90-26921. (Discoveries Ser.). 238p. 1991. pap. 15.95 (0-935480-53-6) Lat Am Lit Rev Pr.

Paiva, Ricardo M. & Tolman, Jon M. Travessia Manual de Laboratorio. (Travessia, Portuguese Language Textbook Program Ser.). 248p. (Orig.). (C). 1991. pap., student ed. 15.95 (0-87840-235-7) Georgetown U Pr.

Paivanen, J., jt. auth. see Paavilainen, E.

Paivarinta, L. J. & Somersalo, E., eds. Inverse Problems in Mathematical Physics: Proceedings of the Lapland Conference on Inverse Problems Held at Saariselka, Finland, 14-20 June 1992. LC 93-29276. (Lecture Notes in Physics Ser.: Vol. 422). 256p. 1993. 76.95 (0-387-57195-7) Spr-Verlag.

Paivio, Allan. Imagery & Verbal Processes. LC 73-150787. 608p. 1971. text 99.95 (0-89859-069-8) L Erlbaum Assocs.

— Mental Representations: A Dual Coding Approach. (Oxford Psychology Ser.: No. 9). (Illus.). 336p. 1990. reprint ed. pap. text 40.00 (0-19-506666-9) OUP.

Paivio, Sandra C., jt. auth. see Greenberg, Leslie S.

Paixao, F., et al. Electronic Structure of Atoms, Molecules & Solids: Proceedings of 2nd Brazilian Sch. 180p. 1990. text 92.00 (981-02-0119-2) World Scientific Pub.

Paiz. Polish Taxation. 1993. pap. text 53.50 (90-6544-737-7) Kluwer Academic.

Paizis, George. Love & the Novel: The Poetics & Politics of Romantic Fiction. LC 98-13758. 256p. 1998. text 65.00 (0-312-21547-9) St Martin.

Paizis, George, jt. auth. see Leak, Andrew N.

Paizis, Suzanne. Getting Her Elected: A Political Woman's Handbook. 1977. pap. 5.95 (0-917982-03-7, Cougar Books) Capitol Enquiry.

Pajackowska, Claire, tr. see Aumont, Jacques.

Pajaczkowska, Claire, tr. see Bleandonu, Gerard.

***Pajak, Edward.** Approaches to Clinical Supervision: Alternatives for Improving Instruction. 2nd ed. LC 99-66237. 352p. 1999. 52.95 (1-929024-00-2) CG Pubs Inc.

— Handbook of Research on School Supervision. 1998. 118.75 (0-02-864662-2) Macmillan Gen Ref.

Pajares, C. Multiparticle Dynamics, 1992: Twenty-Second International Symposium. 700p. 1993. text 178.00 (981-02-1239-9) World Scientific Pub.

Pajares, J. A. & Tascon, J. M. Coal Science: Proceedings of the Eighth International Conference on Coal Science, Oviedo, Spain, Held September 10-15, 1995, 2 vols., Vols. 1-2. 2074p. 1995. text 621.75 (0-444-82227-5) Elsevier.

Pajares, J. M., et al, eds. Helicobacter Pylori & Gastroduodenal Pathology. LC 92-30270. 1993. 217.00 (0-387-55432-7) Spr-Verlag.

Pajares, Maria T., jt. ed. see Callejo, Alfonso.

Pajari, George. Writing Unix Device Drivers. (C). 1993. pap. text. write for info. (0-201-59462-5) Addison-Wesley.

Pajarola, G. F., jt. auth. see Sailer, H. F.

Pajarola, Gion F., jt. auth. see Sailer, Hermann F.

Pajeau, Tammy S., jt. auth. see Bennett, Charles L.

Pajeon, Kala & Pajeon, Ketz. The Candle Magick Workbook. LC 98-198199. (Illus.). 250p. 1991. pap. 12.00 (0-8065-1268-7, Citadel Pr) Carol Pub Group.

— The Talisman Magick Workbook: Master Your Destiny Through the Use of Talismans. LC 92-28896. (Illus.). 254p. 1992. pap. 9.95 (0-8065-1366-7, Citadel Pr) Carol Pub Group.

Pajeon, Ketz, jt. auth. see Pajeon, Kala.

Pajer, Beverly A., jt. auth. see Milstead, Jessica L.

Pajewski, Thomas. Anesthesia Pocket Guide. LC 97-20505. 300p. 1997. pap. text 29.95 (0-7817-0141-4) Lppncott W & W.

***Pajot, J. G.** Dancing with Shadows: A Raven's Winter Tale. LC 99-91286. 1999. 25.00 (0-7388-0736-2); pap. 18.00 (0-7388-0737-0) Xlibris Corp.

Pajot-Smith, Jean. Li'l Tuffy & His ABC's. (Ebony Jr. Bks.). (Illus.). 64p. (J). (ps-4). pap. 5.00 (0-87485-063-0) Johnson Chicago.

— Li'l Tuffy & His Friends. (ENG & SPA.). 47p. (J). 1976. 5.00 (0-87485-077-0) Johnson Chicago.

Pajou, Augustin, jt. auth. see Draper, James D.

Pajpai, U. S. & Viswam, S., eds. UNESCO: In Retrospect & Prospect. 197p. 1986. 25.00 (81-7062-000-7, Pub. by Lancer India) S Asia.

***Pajunen, O'Dell.** The Butterfly Customer. 384p. 2000. pap. 16.95 (0-471-64518-4) Wiley.

Pajunen, Petri. Modern Fur Flies. (Illus.). 48p. 1998. pap. 16.95 (952-5254-00-3) F Amato Pubns.

Pak, Charles Y., ed. Pharmacological Treatment of Endocrinopathies. (Progress in Basic & Clinical Pharmacology Ser.: Vol. 5). (Illus.). x, 142p. 1991. 126.25 (3-8055-5214-9) S Karger.

— Renal Stone Disease: Pathogenesis, Prevention, & Treatment. (Topics in Renal Medicine Ser.). (C). 1987. text 162.50 (0-89838-886-4) Kluwer Academic.

Pak, Charles Y., jt. auth. see Resnick, Donald.

Pak, Charles Y., jt. ed. see Adams, Perrie M.

Pak, Chi Young. The Korean Straits. (International Straits of the World Ser.: No. 10). 184p. 1988. lib. bdg. 100.50 (90-247-3724-9) Kluwer Academic.

***Pak, Choi-yfong.** Korea & the United Nations. LC 00-37551. (Nijhoff Law Specials Ser.). 2000. pap. write for info. (90-411-1382-7) Kluwer Law Intl.

Pak, Gary. A Ricepaper Airplane. LC 97-50407. (Intersections Ser.). 264p. 1998. pap. 18.95 (0-8248-1301-4) UH Pr.

— The Watcher of Waipuna & Other Stories. LC 92-426. (Bamboo Ridge Ser.: Nos. 55-56). 179p. 1992. pap. 8.00 (0-910043-28-0) Bamboo Ridge Pr.

***Pak, Hfui-gwfon.** The Law of the Sea & Northeast Asia: A Challenge for Cooperation. LC 00-42836. (Publications on Ocean Development). 2000. write for info. (90-411-1407-6) Kluwer Law Intl.

Pak, James Y. Paul As Missionary: A Comparative Study of Missionary Discourse in Paul's Epistles & Selected Contemporary Jewish Texts. (European University Studies: Theology: Ser. 23, Vol. 410). V, 208p. 1990. pap. 52.00 (3-631-43459-6) P Lang Pubng.

Pak, Mog-wol. Selected Poems of Pak Mogwol. Kim, Uchang, tr. & intro. by. LC 90-39264. 214p. reprint ed. pap. 66.40 (0-7837-5212-1, 204494300005) Bks Demand.

Pak, Pyong-ho. Modernization & Its Impact upon Korean Law. LC 80-84987. (California University Center for Korean Studies.-Korea Research Monograph: No. 3). 163p. pap. 50.60 (0-608-18567-1, 201946900011) Bks Demand.

***Pak, Ronald Y. S., et al.** Soil Dynamics & Liquefaction 2000: Proceedings of Sessions of Geo-Denver 2000: August 5-8, 2000, Denver, Colorado. LC 00-42133. (Geotechnical Special Publications). 2000. write for info. (0-7844-0520-4) Am Soc Civil Eng.

***Pak, Soyung.** Dear Juno. LC 98-43408. (Illus.). (J). (ps-2). 1999. 15.99 (0-670-88252-6) Viking Penguin.

Pak, Tong-won, jt. auth. see Mun, Myong-dae.

Pak, Ty. An Axiomatic Theory of Language with Applications to English. LC 80-12010. (Edward Sapir Monographs in Language, Culture & Cognition: No. 6). vi, 129p. (Orig.). (C). 1979. pap. 20.00 (0-933104-08-1) Jupiter Pr.

— Cry, Korea, Cry. LC 98-94006. 531p. 1999. pap. 12.00 (0-9667458-0-9) Woodhouse.

— Guilt Payment. LC 83-71242. (Bamboo Ridge Ser.: No. 18). 196p. (Orig.). 1983. pap. 8.00 (0-910043-01-9) Bamboo Ridge Pr.

— Moonbay: Short Stories by Ty Pak. LC 98-94005. 214p. 1999. pap. 12.00 (0-9667458-1-7) Woodhouse.

Pakaluk, Michael, ed. Other Selves: Philosophers on Friendship. 288p. (C). 1991. pap. text 12.95 (0-87220-113-9); lib. bdg. 32.95 (0-87220-114-7) Hackett Pub.

Pakaluk, Michael, tr. & comment see Aristotle.

Pakarinan, U., jt. auth. see Hukki, P.

Pake, George E., jt. auth. see Feenberg, Eugene.

Pakenham, ed. see Adam.

Pakenham, ed. see Nouveau.

Pakenham, Kenneth J. Expectations: Language & Reading Skills for Students of ESL. (Illus.). 336p. (C). 1986. pap. text 21.40 (0-13-294414-6) P-H.

— Making Connections: An Interactive Approach to Academic Reading. 384p. (C). 1994. pap. text 21.95 (0-521-65762-8) Cambridge U Pr.

— Making Connections: An Interactive Approach to Academic Reading: Instructor's Manual. 96p. (C). 1994. pap., teacher ed. 6.00 (0-521-65716-4) Cambridge U Pr.

Pakenham, Thomas. Boer War. 784p. 1992. reprint ed. pap. 20.00 (0-380-72001-9, Avon Bks) Morrow Avon.

— Meetings with Remarkable Trees. 192p. 1998. pap. 24.95 (0-375-75268-4) Random.

— Scramble for Africa... LC 91-52681. 800p. 1992. reprint ed. pap. 17.50 (0-380-71999-1, Avon Bks) Morrow Avon.

— The Year of Liberty. abr. ed. LC 98-34453. (Illus.). 120p. 1998. 35.00 (0-8129-3088-6, Times Bks) Crown Pub Group.

Pakenham, Thomas & Pakenham, Valerie. Dublin: A Traveller's Companion. 1988. write for info. (0-318-62730-2) Macmillan.

Pakenham, Thomas C., jt. auth. see Abdullah, Achmed.

Pakenham, Valerie, jt. auth. see Pakenham, Thomas.

Pakenham, W. T. Naval Command & Control. (Sea Power: Naval Vessels Weapon Systems & Technology Ser.: No. 8). 147p. (Orig.). 1989. 40.00 (0-08-034750-9, Pub. by Brasseys); 25.00 (0-08-036254-0, Pub. by Brasseys) Brasseys.

Paker, Joseph. Christ's Finished Work, Vol. 3. rev. ed. LC 98-84823. 1998. pap. 14.99 (0-89957-240-5) AMG Pubs.

Paker, Josephine. Music from Strings. LC 92-5162. (Millbrook Arts Library). (Illus.). 48p. (J). (gr. 2-6). 1992. lib. bdg. 22.90 (1-56294-283-2) Millbrook Pr.

Paker, Saliha, tr. see Tekin, Latife.

Paker, Yacup. Minicomputers: A Reference Book for Engineers, Scientists & Managers. (Abacus Bks.). 506p. 1981. text 249.00 (0-85626-188-2) Gordon & Breach.

Paker, Yacup, et al, eds. Distributing Operating System. (NATO Asi Series F: Vol. 28). x, 379p. 1987. 100.95 (0-387-17699-3) Spr-Verlag.

Paker, Yakup & Wilbur, Sylvia B., eds. Image Processing for Broadcast & Video Production: Proceedings of the European Workshop on Combined Real & Synthetic Image Processing for Broadcast & Video Production, Hamburg, 23-24 November 1994. LC 94-49416. (Workshops in Computing Ser.). 1995. 79.00 (3-540-19947-0) Spr-Verlag.

Pakes, Anthony G. & Maller, R. A. Mathematical Ecology of Plant Species Competition. (Cambridge Studies in Mathematical Biology). (Illus.). 207p. (C). 1990. text 69.95 (0-521-37388-3) Cambridge U Pr.

Pakesch, G., jt. ed. see Lenz, G.

Pakhmutova, A. Concerto for Trumpet & Orchestra. 40p. 1985. pap. 6.95 (0-7935-3341-4, 00121840) H Leonard.

Pakin, Sandra & Computer Innovations Staff. APL: A Short Course. (Illus.). 176p. 1973. pap. text 25.00 (0-13-038877-7) P-H.

Pakin, Sandra, & Associates, Inc. Staff. Documentation Development Methodology: Techniques for Improved Communications. LC 82-90102. (Illus.). 230p. (C). 1986. pap. write for info. (0-9608178-1-6); ring bd. 95.00 incl. disk (0-9608178-0-8) Pakin Assocs.

Pakis, Vic. Immigrant Soldier: From the Baltics to Vietnam. LC 99-48351. 240p. 2000. pap. text 15.95 (1-55571-512-5) PSI Resch.

Pakiser, L. C. & Mooney, W. D., eds. Geophysical Framework of the Continental United States. (Memoir Ser.: No. 172). (Illus.). 840p. 1990. 45.00 (0-8137-1172-X) Geol Soc.

Pakistan - Indian People's Forum for Peace & Democ, compiled by. Other Voices from Pakistan: Collection of Essays, News Reports, & Literary Writing. (C). 1995. pap. 14.00 (81-224-0735-8) S Asia.

Pakistani. English-Urdu Dictionary. (ENG & URD.). 1989. 65.00 (0-935782-96-6) Kazi Pubns.

Pakizer, Debi & Sears, Mary A. Vaulting: The Art of Gymnastics on Horseback. Anderson, Julia & Barnette, Jackie, eds. (Illus.). 24p. (Orig.). (J). (gr. k-6). pap. 5.00 (0-9639785-6-X) M A Sears.

Pakkala, Alaine. Taking Every Thought Captive. 112p. 1994. write for info. (1-886461-32-5) Lydia Press.

Pakrashi, S. C. & Phondke, G. P. Science Tech & Industrial Development in India. 1995. write for info. (81-7236-101-7, Pub. by Wiley Estrn) Franklin.

Pakrasi, Himadri, jt. ed. see Ho, Tuan-Hua D.

Pakravan, Saideh. The Arrest of Hoveyda: Stories of the Iranian Revolution. 144p. 1998. 17.95 (1-56859-100-4, Blind Owl Pr) Mazda Pubs.

***Pakroo, Peri.** Open Your California Business in 24 Hours: The Complete Start-Up Kit. 2nd ed. LC 00-40210. 2000. write for info. (0-87337-603-X) Nolo com.

Pakroo, Peri, ed. see Smith, Robin.

Pakroo, Peri H. Open Your California Business in 24 Hours: The Complete Start-Up Kit. LC 97-37388. (Illus.). 250p. 1998. pap. 24.95 incl. cd-rom (0-87337-410-X) Nolo com.

Paksoy, H. B., ed. Central Asia Reader: The Rediscovery of History. LC 93-31045. 216p. (C). (gr. 13). 1994. text 85.95 (1-56324-201-X); pap. text 35.95 (1-56324-202-8) M E Sharpe.

Paktor, Vera. Federal Regulations & the Freight Forwarder. Taylor, Scott Warren, ed. (Illus.). 90p. 1992. 39.95 (1-893495-00-0, PN 5501, Boskage Commerce) Boskage Pr.

Pakula, Dennis. New Story, New God. 251p. 1998. pap. 11.95 (1-891929-05-4) Four Seasons.

Pakula, Hannah. An Uncommon Woman: Empress Frederick, Daughter of Queen Victoria, Wife of the Crown Prince of Prussia, Mother of Kaiser Wilhelm. LC 95-36848. (Illus.). 710p. 1995. 34.50 (0-684-80818-8) Simon & Schuster.

— An Uncommon Woman: The Empress Frederick, Daughter of Queen Victoria, Wife of the Crown Prince of Prussia, Mother of Kaiser Wilhelm. 704p. 1997. per. 17.00 (0-684-84216-5) S&S Trade.

***Pakulak, Eric.** At the Side of David: A Multiple-Ending Bible Adventure. LC 00-8969. (Illus.). (J). 2000. pap. write for info. (0-8198-0768-0) Pauline Bks.

Pakulski, Jan & Waters, Malcolm. The Death of Class. 176p. 1995. 69.95 (0-8039-7838-3); pap. 25.95 (0-8039-7839-1) Sage.

P

Pakvasa, S. & Tuan, S. F., eds. Hawaii Topical Conferences in Particle Physics: Selected Lectures, 2 vols., 1. 1006p. 1983. text. write for info. (9971-950-16-2); pap. text. write for info. (9971-950-17-0) World Scientific Pub.
— Hawaii Topical Conferences in Particle Physics: Selected Lectures, 2 vols., 2. 1006p. 1983. text 130.00 (9971-950-36-7); pap. text 63.00 (9971-950-37-5) World Scientific Pub.

***Pal, S. K. & Skowron, A., eds.** Rough-Fuzzy Hybridization: A New Trend in Decision Making. LC 98-36664. 490p. 1999. 49.95 (981-4021-00-8) Spr-Verlag.

Pal, Aswwini. Wheat Revolution in India: Constraints & Prospects. 1990. 58.00 (81-7099-198-6, Pub. by Mittal Pubs Dist) S Asia.

Pal, Gaspal. Changes & Challenges: Economic Transformation in East Central Europe. 1995. pap. 75.00 (963-05-6987-6, Pub. by Akade Kiado) St Mut.

Pal, H. Bhisham. Handicrafts of Rajasthan. (Illus.). 71p. 1984. 14.95 (0-318-36263-5) Asia Bk Corp.
— The Plunder of Art. (C). 1992. 72.00 (81-7017-285-3, Pub. by Abhinav) S Asia.

Pal, Ila. Beyond the Canvas: An Unfinished Portrait of M. F. Husain. (C). 1994. 34.00 (81-7223-107-5, Pub. by Indus Pub) S Asia.

Pal, Izzud-Din. Pakistan, Islam & Economics: Failure of Modernity. LC 99-921971. 220p. 1999. text 19.95 (0-19-579068-5) OUP.

Pal, J. C., ed. Current Trends in Surgery, Vol. I. (C). 1989. 75.00 (0-89771-368-0, Pub. by Current Dist) St Mut.
— Current Trends in Surgery, Vol. II. (C). 1989. 175.00 (0-89771-369-9, Pub. by Current Dist) St Mut.

Pal, J. K., jt. ed. see Tzafestas, Spyros G.

Pal, Jaladhar. The Moral Philosophy of Gandhi. 345p. 1998. 30.00 (81-212-0524-7, Pub. by Gyan Publishing Hse) Nataraj Bks.

Pal, L., jt. auth. see Donner, R. O.

***Pal, Leslie A.** How Ottawa Spends, 2000-2001: Redefining the Federal Role. rev. ed. 392p. 2000. pap. 24.95 (0-19-541539-6) OUP.

Pal, Leslie A. Interests of State: The Politics of Language, Multiculturalism & Feminism in Canada. 352p. 1993. 65.00 (0-7735-0974-7, Pub. by McG-Queens Univ Pr) CUP Services.
— Interests of State: The Politics of Language, Multiculturalism & Feminism in Canada. 344p. (C). 1995. pap. text 24.95 (0-7735-1327-2, Pub. by McG-Queens Univ Pr) CUP Services.
— State, Class & Bureaucracy: Canadian Unemployment Insurance & Public Policy. 224p. 1988. 65.00 (0-7735-0623-3, Pub. by McG-Queens Univ Pr) CUP Services.

Pal, M. K., et al. Medium & High Energy Nuclear Physics: Proceedings of the Conference. 240p. 1992. text 95.00 (981-02-1095-7) World Scientific Pub.

Pal, Mahesh. Population & Rural Poor in India. (C). 1991. 21.00 (0-8364-2762-9, Pub. by Chugh Pubns) S Asia.

Pal, N. L. Malaria - That Remains a Killer. 1994. pap. 100.00 (0-7855-2755-9, Pub. by Scientific Pubs) St Mut.

Pal, Palash B., jt. auth. see Mohapatra, R. N.

Pal, Palash B., jt. auth. see Mohapatra, Rabindra N.

Pal, Pratapaditya. Art of Tibet: A Catalogue of the Los Angeles County Museum of Art Collection. (Illus.). 328p. 1990. 60.00 (0-8109-1899-4, Pub. by Abrams) Time Warner.
— Court Paintings of India. (Illus.). 344p. 1983. 140.00 (0-9611400-0-3) N Kumar.
— Divine Images, Human Visions. (Illus.). 160p. 1998. pap. text 29.95 (1-896209-05-X, Pub. by Bayeux Arts) Assoc Pubs Grp.
— Hindu Religion & Iconology According to the Tantrasara. LC 81-52893. (Tantric Tradition Ser.). Orig. Title: Tantrasara. (Illus.). 172p. 1982. pap. 10.95 (0-941582-00-0) Vichitra Pr.
— The Ideal Image: The Gupta Sculptural Tradition & Its Influence. LC 78-14901. (Illus.). 1978. 19.95 (0-87848-052-8) Asia Soc.
— Indian Painting: A Catalogue of the Los Angeles County Museum of Art Collection, Vol. I. LC 93-317. (Illus.). 384p. 1993. 65.00 (0-8109-3465-5, Pub. by Abrams) Time Warner.
— The Sacred & Secular in Indian Art. (Illus.). 54p. 1974. pap. 3.00 (0-942006-57-7) U of CA Art.

Pal, Pratapaditya, ed. Ganesh, the Benevolent. LC 95-901568. (C). 1995. 98.50 (81-85026-31-9, Pub. by Marg Publns) Art Media Resources.
— On the Path to Void: Buddhist Art of the Tibetan Realm. LC 96-900302. (C). 1996. 95.00 (81-85026-33-5, Pub. by Marg Publns) Art Media Resources.

Pal, Pratapaditya & Dehejia, Vidya. From Merchants to Emperors: British Artist in India, 1757-1930. LC 85-48273. (Illus.). 264p. 1986. 80.00 (0-8014-1907-7); pap. text 37.50 (0-8014-9386-2) Cornell U Pr.

Pal, Pratapaditya & Little, Stephen. A Collecting Odyssey: Indian, Himalayan, & Southeast Asian Art from the James & Marilynn Alsdorf Collection. LC 97-60325. (Illus.). 360p. 1997. 70.00 (0-500-97454-3, Pub. by Thames Hudson) Norton.

Pal, Pratapaditya & Meech-Pekarik, Julia. Buddhist Book Illuminations. LC 87-92183. (Illus.). 339p. 1988. lib. bdg. 225.00 (0-87817-328-5) Hacker.

Pal, Pratapaditya & Reynolds, Valrae. Art of the Himalayas: Treasures from Nepal & Tibet. LC 91-71551. (Illus.). 208p. 1991. 50.00 (1-55595-066-3) Hudson Hills.

Pal, Pratapaditya, et al. Pleasure Gardens of the Mind: Indian Paintings from the Jane Greenough Green Collection. (Illus.). 160p. 1993. 50.00 (81-85822-15-8, Pub. by Mapin Pubng) Antique Collect.

Pal, R., jt. auth. see Brown, A. W.

***Pal, R. K.** Sentinels of the Sky: Glimpses of the Indian Air Force. 180p. 2000. 180.00 (1-86227-097-X, Pub. by Spellmnt Pubs) St Mut.

***Pal, R. M. & Bhargava, G. S.** Human Rights of Dalits: Societal Violation. LC 99-940156. 1999. 34.00 (81-212-0648-0, Pub. by Gyan Publishing Hse) S Asia.

Pal, Rick. Mastering SQL Server 7. 1008p. 1998. pap. text 59.99 (0-7821-2209-4) Sybex.

Pal Ruhela, Satya. My Life with Sri Shirdi Sai Baba: Thrilling Memories of Shivamma Thayee. (Thrilling Memories of Shivamma Thayee Ser.). 78p. 1996. pap. 50.00 (81-7533-003-1, Pub. by Print Hse) St Mut.

Pal, S. B., ed. Handbook of Laboratory Health & Safety Measurement. 2nd rev. ed. 600p. 1991. text 267.50 (0-7462-0077-3) Kluwer Academic.
— Handbook of Laboratory Health & Safety Measures. 1985. text 296.00 (0-85200-766-3) Kluwer Academic.
— Immunoassay Technology, Vol. 2. (Illus.). x, 247p. 1986. pap. 119.25 (3-11-010948-4) De Gruyter.
— Immunossay Technology, Vol. 1. viii, 192p. 1985. pap. 106.95 (3-11-010062-2) De Gruyter.
— Reviews of Immunoassay, 2 vols. 1988. lib. bdg. write for info. (0-318-63139-3) Routledge.
— Reviews of Immunoassay, 2 vols., Vol. 1. 200p. 1988. lib. bdg. 89.95 (0-412-01841-1) Routledge.
— Reviews of Immunoassay, 2 vols., Vol. 2. 208p. 1988. lib. bdg. 89.95 (0-412-01851-9) Routledge.

Pal, S. B., jt. auth. see Pulcino, Paola.

Pal, S. B., jt. ed. see Fotherby, K.

***Pal, S. K., et al, eds.** Soft Computing for Image Processing. (Studies in Fuzziness & Soft Computing: Vol. 42). (Illus.). xviii, 588p. 2000. 139.00 (3-7908-1268-4, Pub. by Physica-Verlag) Spr-Verlag.

Pal, Sankar K. Neuro-Fuzzy Pattern Recognition: Methods in Soft Computing. LC 99-24974. 378p. 1999. 89.95 (0-471-34844-9) Wiley.

Pal, Sankar K. & Wang, Paul P., eds. Genetic Algorithms for Pattern Recognition. LC 95-46195. 336p. 1996. boxed set 104.95 (0-8493-9467-8) CRC Pr.

***Pal, Sankar K., et al.** Soft Computing in Case Based Reasoning. LC 00-32973. 2000. write for info. (1-85233-262-X) Spr-Verlag.

Pal, Yash, ed. Space & Development: Proceedings of Vikram Sarabhi Symposium of the Twenty-Second Plenary Meeting of the Committee on Space Research, Bangalore, India, 29 May -9 June 1979. LC 79-41358. (Illus.). 100p. 1980. 25.00 (0-08-024441-6, Pergamon Pr) Elsevier.

Pal, Yash, et al, eds. Science & Society: Some Perspectives. (C). 32.00 (81-212-0458-5, Pub. by Gian Publng Hse) S Asia.

Pala, Achola O., ed. Connecting Across Cultures & Continents: Black Women Speak Out on Identity, Race & Development. 89p. (Orig.). 1995. pap. 9.95 (0-912917-35-0) UNIFEM

Palac, Lisa. The Edge of the Bed: How Dirty Pictures Changed My Life. LC 97-45118. 224p. (gr. 8). 1998. 22.95 (0-316-68849-5) Little.

Palac-McMiken, Evanor D. Rescheduling Creditworthiness & Market Prices. 274p. 1995. 77.95 (1-85628-879-X, Pub. by Avebry) Ashgate Pub Co.

Palacas, James G., ed. Petroleum Geochemistry & Source Rock Potential of Carbonate Rocks. LC 84-45746. (AAPG Studies in Geology: Vol. 18). 216p. 1984. reprint ed. pap. 67.00 (0-608-03019-8, 206346900006) Bks Demand.

Palacci, Patrick. Optional Implant Positioning & Soft Tissue Management for the Branemark System. LC 95-15503. (Illus.). 83p. 1995. text 68.00 (0-86715-308-3) Quint Pub Co.

Palace. Kumbha Mela: The World's Largest Act of Faith. 1991. pap. 15.95 (0-945475-02-0, Pub. by Mandala Pub Grp) Words Distrib.

Palace Home Inspections, Inc, Staff. Palace Home Inspections, Inc. Vol. 1: Home Inspection Reporting System. large type ed. (Illus.). i, 45p. 1997. spiral bd. 29.95 (0-9661124-0-7, 001) Palace Home.

Palace, Jon, ed. see Kibel, Harvey R.

Palache, John. Four Novelists of the Old Regime: Crebillon, Laclos, Diderot, Restif de la Bretonne. LC 73-132443. (Studies in French Literature: No. 45). 1970. reprint ed. lib. bdg. 75.00 (0-8383-1193-8) M S G Haskell Hse.

Palachos, Argentina, tr. see Myers, Bernice.

Palaci, jt. auth. see Payne.

Palacio, David, jt. ed. see Ashcroft, Kate.

***Palacio, Jaimes.** Stuck in the Middle. 52p. 2000. 4.95 (1-929250-17-7) FarStarFire Pr.

Palacio Valdes, Armando. La Aldea Perdida. Ruiz de la Pena, Alvaro, ed. (Nueva Austral Ser.: Vol. 180). (SPA.). 1991. pap. text 24.95 (84-239-1980-3) Elliots Bks.

***Palacios, Argentina.** Adventures of Don Quixote. LC 99-28847. (Children's Thrift Classics Ser.). (Illus.). 80p. (J). 1999. pap. text 1.00 (0-486-40791-8) Dover.

Palacios, Argentina. A Christmas Surprise for Chabelita. LC 93-22336. (Illus.). 32p. (J). (gr. k-4). 1996. pap. 3.95 (0-8167-3132-2, Troll Medallion) Troll Communs.

Palacios, Argentina. Christmas Surprise for Chabelita. LC 93-22336. 1993. 9.15 (0-606-06278-5, Pub. by Turtleback) Demco.

Palacios, Argentina. The Hummingbird King: A Guatemalan Legend. LC 92-21437. (Legends of the World Ser.). (Illus.). 32p. (J). (gr. 2-5). 1993. pap. 4.95 (0-8167-3052-0) Troll Communs.
— The Hummingbird King: A Guatemalan Legend. LC 92-21437. (Legends of the World Ser.). (Illus.). 32p. (J). (gr. 2-5). 1997. lib. bdg. 18.60 (0-8167-3051-2) Troll Communs.
— Hummingbird King: A Guatemalan Legend. (Legends of the World Ser.). (J). 1993. 10.15 (0-606-05364-6, Pub. by Turtleback) Demco.
— Llama's Secret: A Peruvian Legend. LC 92-21436. (Legends of the World Ser.). (Illus.). 32p. (J). (gr. 2-5). 1996. pap. 4.95 (0-8167-3050-4) Troll Communs.
— Llama's Secret: A Peruvian Legend. LC 92-21436. (Legends of the World Ser.). (Illus.). 32p. (J). (gr. 2-5). 1997. lib. bdg. 18.60 (0-8167-3049-0) Troll Communs.
— Llama's Secret: A Peruvian Legend. (Legends of the World Ser.). 1993. 9.15 (0-606-05438-3, Pub. by Turtleback) Demco.
— Peanut Butter, Apple Butter, Cinnamon Toast: Food Riddles for You to Guess. (Ready-Set-Read Ser.). (Illus.). 32p. (J). (ps-3). 1990. lib. bdg. 21.40 (0-8172-3584-1) Raintree Steck-V.
— Peanut Butter, Apple Butter, Cinnamon Toast: Food Riddles for You to Guess. 28p. (J). (ps-3). 1995. pap. text 4.95 (0-8114-6745-7) Raintree Steck-V.
— El Rey Colibri: Un Leyenda Guatemalteca. (Leyendas del Mundo Ser.). (SPA.). 1993. 9.15 (0-606-05258-5, Pub. by Turtleback) Demco.
— El Rey Colibri (The Hummingbird King) Una Leyenda Guatemalteca. LC 92-21437. (J). (gr. 4-7). 1993. lib. bdg. 18.60 (0-8167-3122-5) Troll Communs.
— El Rey Colibri (The Hummingbird King) Una Leyenda Guatemalteca. LC 92-21437. (SPA.). (J). (gr. 4-7). 1996. pap. 4.95 (0-8167-3071-7) Troll Communs.
— El Secreto de la Llama: Una Leyenda Peruana. (Leyendas del Mundo Ser.). (SPA.). (J). 1993. 10.15 (0-606-05260-7, Pub. by Turtleback) Demco.
— El Secreto de la Llama - the Llama's Secret: Una Leyenda Peruana. LC 93-21436. (SPA.). (J). (gr. 2-5). 1997. pap. 4.95 (0-8167-3072-5) Troll Communs.
— Sorpresa De Navidad Para Chabelita. 1993. 9.15 (0-606-06754-X, Pub. by Turtleback) Demco.
— Sorpresa de Navidad para Chabilita. (SPA., Illus.). 32p. (J). (gr. k-4). 1996. pap. 3.95 (0-8167-3541-7, Troll Medallion) Troll Communs.
— Standing Tall: The Stories of Ten Hispanic Americans. LC 95-112761. 192p. (J). (gr. 4-7). 1994. pap. 3.50 (0-590-47140-6) Scholastic Inc.

Palacios, Argentina. Standing Tall: The Stories of Ten Hispanic Americans. 1994. 8.60 (0-606-07095-8, Pub. by Turtleback) Demco.

Palacios, Argentina. Viva Mexico! The Story of Benito Juarez & Cinco de Mayo. Haley, Alex, ed. LC 92-18071. (Stories of America Ser.). (Illus.). 32p. (J). (gr. 4-7). 1993. pap. 4.95 (0-8114-8054-2) Raintree Steck-V.
— Viva Mexico! The Story of Benito Juarez & Cinco de Mayo. Haley, Alex, ed. LC 92-18071. (Stories of America Ser.). (Illus.). 32p. (J). (gr. 2-5). 1992. lib. bdg. 22.83 (0-8114-7214-0) Raintree Steck-V.

Palacios, Argentina, tr. see Bridwell, Norman.

Palacios, Argentina, tr. see Bright, Robert.

Palacios, Argentina, tr. see Cleary, Beverly.

Palacios, Argentina, tr. see Goring, Ruth.

Palacios, Argentina, tr. see Hazen, Barbara Shook.

Palacios, Argentina, tr. see Lester, Helen.

Palacios, Argentina, tr. see Lindsay, Jeanne W.

Palacios, Argentina, tr. see Lindsay, Jeanne W. & Brunelli, Jean.

Palacios, Argentina, tr. see Miller, Pam.

Palacios, Argentina, tr. see Myers, Bernice.

Palacios, Argentina, tr. see Nayer, Judy.

Palacios, Argentina, tr. see Noonan, Joe.

Palacios, Argentina, tr. see O'Brien, Anne S.

Palacios, Argentina, tr. see Pape, Donna L.

Palacios, Argentina, tr. see Pico, Fernando.

Palacios, Argentina, tr. see Selsam, Millicent E.

Palacios, Carl, ed. English-Spanish Cross-World Puzzles: Bilingual Crossword Puzzles, No. 1. (ENG & SPA.). 96p. 1982. pap. 3.95 (0-940038-00-5) Andante Pub.

Palacios, Diego Garcia De, see Garcia De Palacios, Diego.

Palacios, E., et al. Magnetic Resonance of the Temporomandibular Joint. (Illus.). 135p. 1990. text 85.00 (0-86577-363-7) Thieme Med Pubs.

Palacios, Esteban J. Yo Vengo de los Arabos. LC 86 82605. (Coleccion Caniqui). 131p. (Orig.). 1987. pap. 9.95 (0-89729-420-3) Ediciones.

Palacios, Fernando A., ed. see Sanchez, Francisco.

Palacios, Rafael. New Horizons in Nitrogen Fixation: Proceedings of the 9th International Congress on Nitrogen Fixation, Cancun, Mexico, December 6-12, 1992. (Current Plant Science & Biotechnology in Agriculture Ser.). 808p. (C). 1993. text 289.50 (0-7923-2207-X) Kluwer Academic.

Palacios, Rafael, jt. auth. see Asimov, Isaac.

Palacios, S., jt. ed. see Gomez, F. Gonzalez.

Palacios, Vicente. Fascinating Origami: 101 Models by Adolfo Cerceda. unabridged ed. LC 96-47582. (Illus.). 208p. reprint ed. pap. 9.95 (0-486-29351-3) Dover.
— Origami for Beginners. LC 98-42549. (Illus.). 96p. 1999. pap. 4.95 (0-486-40284-3) Dover.

Palade, George E., et al, eds. Annual Review of Cell & Developmental Biology, Vol. 5. 1989. 41.00 (0-8243-3105-2) Annual Reviews.
— Annual Review of Cell Biology, Vol. 1. (Illus.). (C). 1985. text 41.00 (0-8243-3101-X) Annual Reviews.
— Annual Review of Cell Biology, Vol. 2. (Illus.). 1986. text 41.00 (0-8243-3102-8) Annual Reviews.
— Annual Review of Cell Biology, Vol. 4. (Illus.). 1988. text 41.00 (0-8243-3104-4) Annual Reviews.
— Annual Review of Cell Biology, Vol. 6. 1990. text 41.00 (0-8243-3106-0) Annual Reviews.
— Annual Review of Cell Biology, Vol. 7. 1991. text 41.00 (0-8243-3107-9) Annual Reviews.
— Annual Review of Cell Biology, Vol. 8. 1992. text 46.00 (0-8243-3108-7) Annual Reviews.
— Annual Review of Cell Biology, Vol. 9. (Illus.). 1993. text 46.00 (0-8243-3109-5) Annual Reviews.

Paladin, David C. Painting the Dream: The Visio Navajo Painter David Chethlahe Paladin. LC (Illus.). 96p. (Orig.). 1992. pap. 24.95 (0-89281 Park St Pr) Inner Tradit.

Paladin, Giovanni, jt. ed. see Vulpiani, Angelo.

Paladin Press. How to Make a Silencer for a Mini-14. 97-140193. (Illus.). 48p. 1997. pap. 14.00 (0-87364-913-3) Paladin Pr.

Paladin, Vivian, jt. auth. see Baucus, Jean.

Paladino, Catherine. One Good Apple: Growing Our Food for the Sake of the Earth. LC 97-45866. (Illus.). 32p. (YA). (gr. 4 up). 1999. 15.00 (0-395-85009-6) HM.

Paladino, Enzo. Novo Dicionario Tecnico de Informatica Ingles - Portuguese. (ENG & POR.). 1986. pap. 75.00 (0-8288-3965-4, F119705) Fr & Eur.

Paladino, Larry, jt. auth. see Canham, Donald B.

Palady, Paul. Design Development & Process Planning. Campbell, Robert & Itabashi-Campbell, Rachel R., eds. (Illus.). 507p. Date not set. 65.00 (0-9663160-1-0) Pract Applns.
— Failure Modes & Effects Analysis. LC 95-36603. 329p. 1995. 39.95 (0-945456-17-4) PT Pubns.
— Failure Modes & Effects Analysis: Author's Edition. (Illus.). 300p. 1997. 57.95 (0-9663160-0-2) Pract Applns.
— Fundamentals of Manufacturing. Campbell, Robert S. & Itabashi-Campbell, Rachel R., eds. (Illus.). 184p. 1999. text 65.00 (0-9663160-2-9) Pract Applns.
— Red Light: The Universal System. Campbell, Robert & Itabashi-Campbell, Rachel, eds. (Illus.). 180p. Date not set. 57.95 (0-9663160-7-X) Pract Applns.
— Twelve Tools for Project Management. Campbell, Robert & Itabashi-Campbell, Rachel, eds. Date not set. 57.95 (0-9663160-3-7) Pract Applns.

Palady, Paul & Campbell, Robert. Taps: A Total Approach to Problem Solving. Itabashi-Campbell, Rachel, ed. (Illus.). 200p. Date not set. 65.00 (0-9663160-4-5) Pract Applns.

Palaephatus. On Unbelievable Tales: Palaephatus Peri Apiston. Stern, Jacob, ed. & intro. by. LC 96-17173. (ENG & GEC.). 1996. 40.00 (0-86516-310-3); pap. 20.00 (0-86516-320-0) Bolchazy-Carducci.

Palaez Casablanca, Manuel. Cuadernos de Trabajo No. 7: Presencia de la Antropologia en los Estudios Sobre Alimenticion. (SPA.). 81p. 1997. pap. 7.00 (968-36-6238-2, UN56, Pub. by Instit de Invest) UPLAAP.

Palafox, Francisco. La Diferencia. 1997. pap. text 6.99 (0-88113-452-X) Caribe Betania.
— Lo Primero.Tr. of First One. (SPA.). 64p. 1995. 6.99 (0-88113-345-0, B088-3450) Caribe Betania.

Palagachev, Dian K., jt. auth. see Popivanov, Peter R.

Palagia, Olga. The Pediments of the Parthenon. (Monumenta Graeca et Romana Ser.: Vol. 7). (Illus.). viii, 168p. 1998. reprint ed. 57.00 (90-04-11198-0) Brill Academic Pubs.

Palagia, Olga & Coulson, William, eds. Regional Schools in Hellenistic Sculpture. (Oxbow Monographs: Vol. 90). (Illus.). 291p. 1998. 98.00 (1-900188-45-7, Pub. by Oxbow Bks) David Brown.

Palagia, Olga & Pollitt, J. J., eds. Personal Styles in Greek Sculpture. (Yale Classical Studies. No. 30). (Illus.). 247p. (C). 1999. pap. text 22.95 (0-521-65738-5) Cambridge U Pr.

Palagia, Olga, ed. see Harrison, Evelyn B., et al.

Palahniuk, Chuck. Fight Club. LC 97-20023. 208p. 1997. pap. 12.00 (0-8050-5437-5) H Holt & Co.
— Fight Club. LC 97-20023. 208p. 1999. pap. 13.00 (0-8050-6297-1) H Holt & Co.
— Fight Club. LC 95-47591. 192p. 1996. 21.00 (0-393-03976-5) Norton.
— Invisible Monsters: A Novel. LC 99-25107. 224p. 1999. pap. 13.00 (0-393-31929-6) Norton.

***Palahniuk, Chuck.** Survivor: A Novel. 2000. pap. 13.00 (0-385-49872-1, Anchor NY) Doubleday.

Palahniuk, Chuck. Survivor. A Novel. LC 98-28874. 288p. 1999. 23.95 (0-393-04702-4) Norton.

***Palahunk, Sam.** God's Little Secret. LC 99-55289. (Illus.). 30p. 1999. pap. 19.50 (1-892343-07-X) Oak Tree Pub.

Palaia, Franc. Great Walls of China. (CHI & ENG., Illus.). 72p. (Orig.). 1984. pap. 14.95 (0-89860-125-8) Eastview.

***Palaima, Thomas G., et al.** Unlocking the Secrets of Ancient Writing: The Parallel Lives of Michael Ventris & Linda Schele & the Decipherment of Mycenaean & Mayan Writing. (Illus.). 40p. 2000. pap. text. write for info. (0-9649410-4-X) UnivTex Dept Classics.

Palairet, Michael. The Balkan Economies, C. 1800-1914: Evolution Without Development. LC 96-48210. (Studies in Modern Economic History: Vol. 6). (Illus.). 432p. (C). 1998. text 69.95 (0-521-58051-X) Cambridge U Pr.

Palairet, Michael, tr. see Emmerich, Anne C.

Palais, James B. Confucian Statecraft & Korean: Yu Hyongwon & the Late Choson Dynasty. LC 94-35259. 1248p. 1996. 65.00 (0-295-97455-9) U of Wash Pr.

Palais, James B. Politics & Policy in Traditional Korea. (East Asian Monographs: No. 159). (Illus.). 390p. (C). 1992. pap. text 16.00 (0-674-68771-X) HUP.
— Politics & Policy in Traditional Korea, 1864-1876. (East Asian Monographs). 288p. 1990. 24.50 (0-674-19058-0) HUP.

Palais, Joseph C. Fiber Optic Communications. 1997. 59.00 (0-614-18450-9, B25003) Info Gatekeepers.
— Fiber Optic Communications. 4th ed. LC 98-9634. 342p. (C). 1998. 81.00 (0-13-895442-9, Prentice Hall) P-H.

Palais, Richard S. The Classification of G-Spaces. LC 52-42839. (American Mathematical Society Ser.: No. 36). 78p. 1960. reprint ed. pap. 30.00 (0-608-02657-3, 205255200004) Bks Demand.
— The Classification of G-Spaces. 4th ed. LC 52-42839. (Memoirs Ser.: No. 1/36). 72p. 1987. reprint ed. pap. 17.00 (0-8218-1236-X, MEMO/1/36) Am Math.

P

An Asterisk (*) at the beginning of an entry indicates that the title is appearing for the first time.

...y of ... (Memoirs Ser.: ... 17.00 ... Math.

... e Atiyah-Singer Index ... ls of Mathematics ... 5. reprint ed. pap. 116.60 ... 900001) Bks Demand.

... **Eleanora, eds.** Light upon the ... of Wisdom for the Future ... ative Hawaiians. 125p. reprint ed. pap. ... 635173-0-9) Mahina Prods.

... **nie.** Thundersea. LC 99-20. 360p. 1999. pap. ... 55212-251-4, Trade Winds) Trafford Pub.

... **Gregory.** The Decalogue. 1988. pap. 0.50 ... 9981-202-3) Eastern Orthodox.

... **as, Keostees.** The Twelve Words of the Gypsy. Will, Frederic, tr. & intro. by. LC 64-17223. 229p. reprint ed. pap. 71.00 (*0-7837-6175-9*, 204589700009) Bks Demand.

Palamidese, Patrizia, ed. Scientific Visualization: Advanced Software Techniques. LC 93-19127. (Ellis Horwood Workshop Ser.). 1993. text 39.95 (*0-13-710337-9*, Pub. by Tavistock-E Horwood) Routldge.

Palamidessi, C., et al, eds. PLILP/ALP'98: Proceedings of the 10th International Symposium, PLILP '98: Held Jointly with the 6th International Conference, ALP '98, Pisa, Italy, September, 1998. LC 98-41640. (Lecture Notes in Computer Science Ser.: Vol. 1490). xi, 497p. 1998. pap. 75.00 (*3-540-65012-1*) Spr-Verlag.

Palamodov, V. P. Linear Differential Operators with Constant Coefficients. Brown, A. A., tr. LC 79-104712. (Grundlehren der Mathematischen Wissenschaften Ser.: Vol. 168). 1970. 97.95 (*0-387-04838-3*) Spr-Verlag.

Palan, Ronan & Abbott, Jason. State Strategies in the Global Political Economy. 256p. 1996. 79.50 (*1-85567-342-8*) Bks Intl VA.

***Palan, Ronen P.** Global Political Economy: Contemporary Theories. LC 00-20054. (Ripe Studies in Global Political Economy). 2000. pap. write for info. (*0-415-20489-5*) Routledge.

— State Strategies in the Global Political Economy. 2000. pap. 24.95 (*1-85567-638-9*) Continuum.

Palanca, Clinton. Landscapes. 182p. 1998. pap. text 18.00 (*971-542-130-X*) UH Pr.

Palance, Jack. The Forest of Love. LC 96-42025. 96p. 1996. 22.00 (*1-887714-07-3*) Summerhse Pr.

— The Forest of Love: A Love Story in Free Verse. 1999. pap. text 10.00 (*1-887714-35-9*) Summerhse Pr.

***Palande, P. S.** Coping with Liberalisation: The Industry's Response to New Competition. LC 00-24739. 2000. write for info. (*0-7619-9434-3*) Sage.

Palandri, Angela J., ed. Modern Verse from Taiwan. LC 79-161994. 225p. reprint ed. pap. 69.80 (*0-608-15828-3*, 203131100074) Bks Demand.

Palandri, Enrico. Way Back. (Masks Ser.). 176p. 1994. pap. 14.99 (*1-85242-246-7*) Serpents Tail.

Palangi, Paula. Last Straw. LC 91-44346. 32p. (J). (ps-3). 1992. pap. 9.99 (*0-7814-0562-9*, Chariot Bks) Chariot Victor.

Palango, Paul. Above the Law: The Crooks, the Politicians, the Mounties, & Rod Stamler. 320p. 1995. reprint ed. pap. text 19.99 (*0-7710-6905-7*) McCland & Stewart.

***Palango, Paul.** The Last Guardians: The Crisis in the RCMP - And in Canada. 320p. 2000. pap. 19.99 (*0-7710-6908-1*) McClland & Stewart.

Palango, Paul. The Last Guardians: The Crisis in the RCMP. . . And in Canada. LC 99-172856. 316p. 1999. text 19.99 (*0-7710-6906-5*) McCland & Stewart.

Palani, Satya. Ominous Evenings: Memories of Madness by Satya Palani. LC 94-67019. 72p. 1994. pap. 7.00 (*0-9641928-0-2*) Ominous Whispers.

Palaniappan, S. P. Agricultural Inputs & Environment. 446p. 1995. pap. 120.00 (*81-7233-122-3*, Pub. by Scientific Pubs) St Mut.

Palaniswami, Marimthu, et al, eds. Computational Intelligence: A Dynamic System Perspective. 340p. 1995. pap. 69.95 (*0-7803-1182-5*, PP5376) Inst Electrical.

P

Palanithurai, G. Dynamics of Tamil Nadu Politics in Sri Lankan Ethnicity. 1993. 14.00 (*81-7211-040-5*) S Asia.

— Management of Ethnic Conflict in India & Canada: A Comparative Analysis. (C). 1993. 16.00 (*81-85475-74-1*, Pub. by Kanishka) S Asia.

Palanithurai, G., ed. Perspectives on Indian Regionalism. (C). 1992. 16.00 (*81-85475-58-X*, Pub. by Kanishka) S Asia.

Palanithural, G. Polyethnicity in India & Canada: Possibilities for Exploration. LC 97-906773. 120p. 1997. pap. 90.00 (*81-7533-039-2*, Pub. by Print Hse) St Mut.

Palanithural, Ghandi, ed. Perception of Grass Root Democracy & Political Performance. LC 98-903584. 205p. 1998. pap. 108.00 (*81-7533-068-6*, Pub. by Print Hse) St Mut.

Palanque, Philippe, ed. Formal Methods in Human-Computer Interaction. LC 97-27729. (Formal Approaches to Computing & Information Technology Ser.). (Illus.). 376p. (C). 1997. pap. 54.95 (*3-540-76158-6*) Spr-Verlag.

Palanque, Philippe, jt. ed. see Bastide, Francois-Regis.

Palanque, Philippe, jt. ed. see Benyon, David.

Palant, C. E., jt. ed. see Yanagawa, N.

Palao, George. The Guns & Towers of Gibraltar. (C). 1988. text 25.00 (*0-948466-01-4*, Pub. by Gibraltar Bks) St Mut.

***Palardy, Debra J.** Sweetie, Here's the Best Reason on the Planet to Say No to Your Boyfriend: Even If You've Already Said Yes. 34p. (YA). 2000. pap. 8.00 (*0-8059-4875-9*) Dorrance.

Palardy, Jean, jt. auth. see Wilson, P. Roy.

Palardy, Michael J. Modern Elementary School Programs & Practices, Custom Pub. (C). 1992. text. write for info. (*0-07-048133-4*) McGraw.

Palardy, Michael J. & Rogers, Mary S. Phonics for Teachers. (C). 1996. pap. text 14.25 (*0-07-048227-6*) McGraw.

Palassis, Neketas S. The Life of Our Father among the Saints: Moses the Ethiopian. (Illus.). 1992. pap. 3.00 (*0-913026-30-1*) St Nectarios.

Palassis, Neketas S., ed. A Lenten Cookbook for Orthodox Christians. 260p. 1982. pap. 9.00 (*0-913026-13-1*) St Nectarios.

— St. Nectarios Orthodox Conference, 1980. LC 80-53258. 176p. (Orig.). 1981. pap. 15.00 (*0-913026-14-X*) St Nectarios.

Palastanga. Anatomy & Human Movement. 3rd ed. LC 98-228749. 880p. 1998. pap. text 80.00 (*0-7506-3268-2*) Buttrwrth-Heinemann.

Palastanga, Nigel, et al. Anatomy & Human Movement: Structure & Function. 2nd ed. LC 94-24695. (Illus.). 896p. 1994. pap. text 61.50 (*0-7506-0970-2*) Buttrwrth-Heinemann.

Palastanga, Nigel, jt. ed. see Boyling, Jeffrey D.

Palat, Ravi A., ed. Pacific-Asia & the Future of the World-System, 142. LC 92-18384. (Contributions in Economics & Economic History Ser.: No. 142). 224p. 1993. 65.00 (*0-313-28401-6*, PPG, Greenwood Pr) Greenwood.

***Palatine Historical Society Staff.** Palatine. (Images of America Ser.). 128p. 1999. pap. 18.99 (*0-7385-0149-2*) Arcadia Publng.

Palatini. Zoom Broom. 32p. (J). 1998. lib. bdg. 15.49 (*0-7868-5094-9*, Pub. by Disney Pr) Little.

***Palatini, Margie.** Bedhead. LC 98-31660. (Illus.). (J). (gr. k-3). 2000. 16.00 (*0-689-82397-5*) S&S Bks Yung.

— Broom Mates. 32p. (J). 2000. lib. bdg. 16.49 (*0-7868-2365-8*, Pub. by Disney Pr) Little.

— Broom Mates. (J). 2000. 15.99 (*0-7868-0418-1*, Pub. by Hyprn Child); lib. bdg. 16.49 (*0-7868-2371-2*) Hyprn Child.

Palatini, Margie. Ding Dong Ding Dong. LC 98-39548. (Illus.). 32p. (J). (ps-3). 1999. 15.99 (*0-7868-0420-3*, Pub. by Disney Pr) Time Warner.

— Ding Dong Ding Dong. LC 98-39548. (Illus.). 32p. (J). (ps-3). 1999. lib. bdg. 16.49 (*0-7868-2367-4*, Pub. by Hyperion) Little.

— Elf Help: http://www.falala.com. LC 96-53314. (Illus.). 32p. (J). (ps-2). 1997. 14.95 (*0-7868-0359-2*, Pub. by Hyprn Child); lib. bdg. 14.89 (*0-7868-2304-6*, Pub. by Hyprn Child) Little.

***Palatini, Margie.** Goldie 2. 32p. (J). 2000. lib. bdg. 15.49 (*0-7868-2490-5*, Pub. by Disney Pr) Time Warner.

Palatini, Margie. Goldie 2. 32p. (J). 2000. 14.99 (*0-7868-0565-X*) Little.

— Good As Goldie. LC 99-19643. (Illus.). 32p. (J). 2000. lib. bdg. 15.49 (*0-7868-2435-2*, Pub. by Hyprn Child) Time Warner.

— Good As Goldie. LC 99-19643. (Illus.). 32p. (J). (ps-k). 2000. 14.99 (*0-7868-0502-1*, Pub. by Hyprn Child) Time Warner.

***Palatini, Margie.** Lab Coat Girl: Full of Baloney. LC 99-41497. 32p. (J). 2000. lib. bdg. 14.49 (*0-7868-2441-7*, Pub. by Hyperion) Little.

— Lab Coat Girl #3: The Story of a Prima Swanerina. (Illus.). 96p. (J). 2000. lib. bdg. write for info. (*0-7868-2442-5*) Hyprn Ppbks.

Palatini, Margie. Lab Coat Girl & the Amazing Benjamin Bone. LC 98-55226. 32p. 1999. lib. bdg. 13.49 (*0-7868-2440-9*, Pub. by Disney Pr) Little.

— Lab Coat Girl & the Amazing Benjamin Bone, Bk. 1. LC PZ7.P1755Laf 1999. 32p. (J). (gr. 2-6). 1999. pap. 3.99 (*0-7868-1346-6*, Pub. by Hyprn Ppbks) Little.

***Palatini, Margie.** Lab Coat Girl in Cool Fuel Trudie, Bk. 2. LC 99-41497. (Illus.). 96p. (J). (gr. 3-7). 2000. pap. 3.99 (*0-7868-1347-4*, Pub. by Hyperion) Time Warner.

— Mary Had A Little Ham. 32p. (J). 2005. 15.99 (*0-7868-0566-8*, Pub. by Hyperion) Little.

— Mooseltoe. LC 99-86322. (Illus.). 32p. (J). (gr. k-4). 2000. 16.49 (*0-7868-2492-1*) Hyprn Child.

Palatini, Margie. Moosetache. LC 96-26256. (Illus.). 32p. (J). (ps-2). 1997. 15.95 (*0-7868-0306-1*, Pub. by Hyprn Child); lib. bdg. 15.89 (*0-7868-2246-5*, Pub. by Hyprn Child) Little.

— Moosetache. (Illus.). 32p. (J). (ps-2). 1999. pap. 5.99 (*0-7868-1170-6*, Pub. by Hyprn Child) Time Warner.

— Moostletoe. LC 99-86322. (Illus.). 32p. (J). (gr. k-4). 2000. 15.99 (*0-7868-0567-6*) Little.

— Piggie Pie! LC 94-19726. (Illus.). 32p. (J). (ps-3). 1995. 15.00 (*0-395-71691-8*) HM.

— Piggie Pie! (Illus.). 32p. (J). (ps-3). 1997. pap. 5.95 (*0-395-86618-9*, Clarion Bks) HM.

— Piggie Pie! (J). 1997. 11.15 (*0-606-12792-5*, Pub. by Turtleback) Demco.

***Palatini, Margie.** Piggie Pie. (Illus.). (J). (ps-3). 1998. 9.95 incl. audio (*0-395-90063-8*, Clarion Bks) HM.

Palatini, Margie. Trudie, Vol. 3. 32p. 2000. pap. 4.99 (*0-7868-1348-2*, Pub. by Hyprn Ppbks) Little.

***Palatini, Margie.** The Web Files. LC 99-58747. 32p. (J). Date not set. 16.99 (*0-7868-0419-X*, Pub. by Disney Pr) Little.

— The Web Files. LC 99-58747. (Illus.). 32p. (J). Date not set. lib. bdg. 16.49 (*0-7868-2366-6*, Pub. by Disney Pr) Little.

Palatini, Margie. The Wonder Worm Wars. LC 96-50920. 196p. (gr. 3-7). 1999. pap. 4.99 (*0-7868-1352-0*, Pub. by Hyperion) Time Warner.

— The Wonder Worm Wars. LC 96-50920. (Illus.). 176p. (J). (gr. 3-7). 1997. 14.95 (*0-7868-0321-5*, Pub. by Hyprn Child); lib. bdg. 14.89 (*0-7868-2295-3*, Pub. by Hyprn Child) Little.

— Zak's Lunch. LC 97-18799. (Illus.). 32p. (J). (gr. k-3). 1998. 15.00 (*0-395-81674-2*, Clarion Bks) HM.

***Palatini, Margie.** Zoom Broom. 32p. (J). 2000. pap. 5.99 (*0-7868-1467-5*, Pub. by Disney Pr) Time Warner.

— Zoom Broom. LC 97-32205. (Illus.). 32p. (J). (ps-3). 1998. 14.45 (*0-7868-0322-3*, Pub. by Hyperion) Time Warner.

***Palatini, Margie & Koelsch, Michael.** Tub Boo Boo. LC 99-39434. (J). 2001. write for info. (*0-689-82394-0*) S&S Childrens.

Palatnik, Lori. Friday Night & Beyond. 1998. 30.00 (*0-7657-6067-3*) Aronson.

— Friday Night & Beyond: The Shabbat Experience - Step-by-Step. LC 93-26264. 200p. 1994. pap. 25.00 (*1-56821-035-3*) Aronson.

— Friday Night & Beyond: The Shabbat Experience - Step-by-Step. LC 93-26264. 200p. 1997. pap. 25.00 (*1-56821-999-7*) Aronson.

— Remember My Soul: A Guided Journey Through Shiva & the Thirty Days of Mourning for a Loved One. LC 99-218295. 1998. pap. 17.00 (*1-881927-16-4*) Leviathan OH.

Palatnik, Sam & Alburt, Lev. Chess Tactics for the Tournament Player: From Tournament Player to Expert. 2nd ed. Parr, Larry, ed. LC 95-72089. (Comprehensive Chess Course Ser.: Vol. 3). (Illus.). 256p. (Orig.). 1996. pap. 19.95 (*1-889323-02-0*) L Alburt.

— The King in Jeopardy: The Best Techniques for Attack & Defense. 2nd rev. ed. Parr, Larry, ed. (Illus.). 256p. 1998. pap. 19.95 (*1-889323-13-6*) L Alburt.

Palatnik, Sam, jt. auth. see Alburt, Lev.

Palau. Corazon para Dios.Tr. of Heart for God. (SPA.). 126p. 1996. pap. write for info. (*0-614-27020-0*) Editorial Unilit.

— Decisiones Equivocadas: Caida Sin Retorno? (Serie Cruzada Palau Org. - Crusade Palau).Tr. of Wrong Decisions: Falling Off Without Return. (SPA.). 1993. pap. write for info. (*0-614-27028-6*) Editorial Unilit.

Palau, Gabriel. The Active Catholic. LC 84-50405. 224p. 1984. reprint ed. pap. 7.00 (*0-89555-238-8*) TAN Bks Pubs.

Palau i Fabre, Josep. Picasso: The Early Years, 1881-1907. (Illus.). 560p. 1985. boxed set 225.00 (*1-55660-166-2*) A Wofsy Fine Arts.

Palau, Joseph, ed. Europe at Peace: VIII Convention for European Nuclear Disarmament. (Orig.). 1990. 75.00 (*0-85124-518-8*, Pub. by Spkesman); pap. 25.00 (*0-85124-519-6*, Pub. by Spkesman) Dufour.

Palau, Luis. A Su Manera: El Camino de Dios Hacia la Cumbre - Vida Cristiana.Tr. of Scheamer & the Dreamer. (SPA.). 162p. 1987. pap. 4.50 (*0-8423-6483-8*, 498022) Editorial Unilit.

— Amor y Pasion. (Serie Cruzada - Crusade Ser.).Tr. of Love & Passion. (SPA.). 28p. 1992. pap. 1.99 (*1-56063-180-5*, 498014) Editorial Unilit.

— Armagedon: El Climax de la Historia.Tr. of Armageddon: The Climax of History. (SPA.). 3.99 (*0-8423-6476-5*, 498020) Editorial Unilit.

— Armagedon: El Climax de la Historia - The Climax of History. (Escatologia - Escatology Ser.). (SPA.). 90p. 1986. write for info. (*1-56063-314-X*) Editorial Unilit.

— Com. Bib. Continente Nuevo (New Continent Com) Juan (John), Vol. I. (SPA.). pap. 8.99 (*0-685-74915-0*, 498632) Editorial Unilit.

— Com. Bib. Continente Nuevo (New Continent Com) Juan (John), Vol. II. (SPA.). pap. 8.99 (*0-685-74916-9*, 498634) Editorial Unilit.

— Comentario Biblico Continente Nuevo: Juan, Vol. 1.Tr. of New Continent Bible Commentary: John. (SPA.). 260p. 1991. pap. 5.99 (*1-56063-089-2*, 498631) Editorial Unilit.

— Comentario Biblico Continente Nuevo: Juan, Vol. 2.Tr. of New Continent Bible Commentary: John. (SPA.). 260p. 1991. pap. 5.99 (*1-56063-115-5*, 498634) Editorial Unilit.

— Comentario Biblico del Continente Nuevo: Juan 1.Tr. of New Continent Bible Commentary: John 1. (SPA.). 1991. write for info. (*0-614-27003-0*) Editorial Unilit.

— Comentario Biblico del Continente Nuevo: Juan 2.Tr. of New Continent Bible Commentary: John 2. (SPA.). 1991. write for info. (*0-614-27006-5*) Editorial Unilit.

— Con Quien Me Casare?Tr. of Whom Shall I Marry?. (SPA.). 1976. 4.29 (*0-8423-6451-X*, 498017) Editorial Unilit.

— Con Quien Me Casare?Tr. of Whom Shall I Marry?. (SPA.). 122p. 1986. pap. write for info. (*0-614-27015-4*) Editorial Unilit.

— Una Conciencia Transparente. (Serie Cruzada - Crusade Ser.).Tr. of Clear Conscience. (SPA.). 1986. 1.99 (*0-8423-6338-6*, 498004); pap. write for info. (*0-614-27019-7*) Editorial Unilit.

***Palau, Luis.** Construyamos Hogares Felices. 1998. pap. text 12.99 (*0-88113-473-2*) Caribe Betania.

Palau, Luis. Corazon para Dios.Tr. of Heart for God. (SPA.). 4.99 (*0-7899-0141-2*, 498628) Editorial Unilit.

— Corazon para Dios - Heart for God. (SPA.). 126p. 1996. write for info. (*0-614-24356-4*) Editorial Unilit.

— Crecimiento Dinamico. (Serie Cruzada - Crusade Ser.).Tr. of Three Stages of the Christian Life. (SPA.). 1991. pap. 1.99 (*1-56063-007-8*, 498009) Editorial Unilit.

— Cristo a las Naciones: La Historia de Luis Palau y Su Equipo.Tr. of Christ to the Nations. (SPA.). 258p. 1988. pap. 5.99 (*0-945792-22-0*, 498023) Editorial Unilit.

— Cuando la Soledad Duele.Tr. of When Loneliness Hurts. (SPA.). 1993. pap. 3.99 (*0-88113-119-9*) Caribe Betania.

— De la Mano de Jesus: Pasos Hacia la Madurez Cristiana.Tr. of So You Want to Grow: Steps along the Way. (SPA.). 158p. 1989. pap. 4.99 (*1-56063-006-X*, 498024) Editorial Unilit.

— Decisiones a la Sombra de la Cruz. (Serie Cruzada - Crusade Ser.).Tr. of Decisions in the Shadow of the Cross. (SPA.). 36p. 1987. 1.99 (*0-8423-6477-3*, 498005) Editorial Unilit.

— Decisiones Equivocadas: Caida Sin Retorno? (Serie Cruzada - Crusade Ser.).Tr. of Wrong Decisions: Falling off Without Return?. (SPA.). 1993. 1.99 (*1-56063-540-1*, 498027) Editorial Unilit.

Palau, Luis. Dios Esta a Mi Lado.Tr. of God Is at My Side. (SPA.). 1993. pap. 3.99 (*0-88113-113-X*) Caribe Betania.

Palau, Luis. Disciplinas Libertadoras.Tr. of Liberating Disciplines. (SPA.). 76p. 1987. pap. 2.99 (*0-8423-6484-6*, 498021) Editorial Unilit.

— Eres Cristiano Si o No? (Serie Cruzada - Crusade Ser.).Tr. of Are You Christian Yes or No?. (SPA.). 34p. 1986. pap. 1.99 (*0-8423-6336-X*, 498003) Editorial Unilit.

— A Favor o en Contra de Dios? (Serie Cruzada - Crusade Ser.).Tr. of For or Against God?. (SPA.). 34p. 1987. pap. 1.99 (*0-8423-6519-2*, 498008) Editorial Unilit.

— God Is Relevant. pap. 7.99 (*0-8297-2152-5*) Vida Pubs.

— God Is Relevant: Finding Strength & Peace in Today's World. 240p. 1998. pap. 10.00 (*0-385-48679-0*) Doubleday.

— Grito de Victoria! A Moment to Shout! Calcada, Leticia, tr. from ENG. (SPA.). 144p. 1986. pap. 6.50 (*0-311-46106-9*) Casa Bautista.

— Healthy Habits for Spiritual Growth: Fifty-Two Principles for Personal Change. LC 94-8633. 144p. 1994. pap. 9.99 (*0-929239-87-3*) Discovery Hse Pubs.

— A Man after God's Heart. LC 97-51672. Orig. Title: Heart after God. 160p. 1998. pap. 12.99 (*1-57293-030-6*) Discovery Hse Pubs.

— Me Quiere Mucho un Poquito Nada. (Serie Cruzada - Crusade Ser.).Tr. of You Love Me a Lot a Little, Not at All. (SPA.). 20p. 1993. pap. 1.99 (*1-56063-541-X*, 498028) Editorial Unilit.

— Mi Respuesta.Tr. of My Response. (SPA.). 112p. 1987. pap. 3.79 (*0-8423-6485-4*, 498018) Editorial Unilit.

— The Moment to Shout: God's Way to Face Walls. LC 98-48824. 224p. 1999. pap. 9.99 (*1-57293-049-7*) Discovery Hse Pubs.

— No Te Dejare Hasta Que Seas Perfecto.Tr. of Peter Promise. (SPA.). 1997. pap. 7.99 (*0-88113-453-8*) Caribe Betania.

— Ocultismo y Brujeria Frente a Dios. (Serie Cruzada - Crusade Ser.).Tr. of Witchcraft & Occult Before God. (SPA.). 1987. 1.99 (*0-8423-6518-4*, 498007); pap. write for info. (*0-614-27088-X*) Editorial Unilit.

— The Peter Promise: Powerful Principles from the Life of Peter. LC 96-10501. Orig. Title: Walk on Water, Pete!. 128p. 1996. reprint ed. pap. 9.99 (*1-57293-011-X*) Discovery Hse Pubs.

— Por la Senda del Perdon. (Serie Cruzada - Crusade Ser.).Tr. of Walk of Forgiveness. (SPA.). 33p. 1991. pap. 1.99 (*1-56063-117-1*, 498011) Editorial Unilit.

— Predicacion: Manos a la Obra.Tr. of Preaching: Hands at Work. (SPA.). 142p. 1995. 7.99 (*0-7899-0106-4*, 498629) Editorial Unilit.

— Promesas Personales de la Biblia. (Serie Guia de Bolsillo - Pocket Guides Ser.).Tr. of Personal Promises of the Bible. (SPA.). 2.79 (*0-945792-29-8*, 490208) Editorial Unilit.

— Que Quieres Que Haga Por Ti? (Serie Cruzada - Crusade Ser.).Tr. of What Do You Want Me to Do?. (SPA.). 1986. 1.99 (*0-8423-6337-8*, 498002); pap. write for info. (*0-614-27126-6*) Editorial Unilit.

— Quien Ganara Esta Guerra?Tr. of Say Yes! How to Renew Your Spiritual Passion. (SPA.). 142p. 1992. pap. 1.50 (*1-56063-179-1*, 498499) Editorial Unilit.

— Quieres un Hogar Feliz? (Serie Cruzada - Crusade Ser.).Tr. of Do You Want a Happy Home?. (SPA.). 45p. 1989. pap. 1.99 (*1-56063-322-0*, 498001) Editorial Unilit.

— Renovacion Interior: Moda Pasajera. (Serie Cruzada - Crusade Ser.).Tr. of Interior Renewal: Transient Fashion. (SPA.). 26p. 1991. pap. 1.99 (*1-56063-116-3*, 498012) Editorial Unilit.

— Renovacion Interior (Interior Renewal) Moda Pasajera (Transient Fashion) (SPA.). 1.79 (*0-685-74979-7*, 498012) Editorial Unilit.

— Say Yes! How to Renew Your Spiritual Passion. LC 95-23200. 176p. (Orig.). 1995. pap. 10.99 (*0-929239-96-2*) Discovery Hse Pubs.

— The Schemer & the Dreamer: God's Way to the Top. LC 98-48899. 192p. 1998. pap. 9.99 (*1-57293-048-9*) Discovery Hse Pubs.

— Sexo y Juventud.Tr. of Sex & Youth. (SPA.). 1987. 3.99 (*0-8423-6522-2*, 498019); pap. write for info. (*0-614-27140-1*) Editorial Unilit.

— Suena Grande Suenos. (Serie Cruzada - Crusade Ser.).Tr. of Dream Great Dreams. (SPA.). 36p. 1987. pap. 1.99 (*0-8423-6479-X*, 498006) Editorial Unilit.

— Tengo Todo . . . Casi Todo. (Serie Cruzada - Crusade Ser.).Tr. of I Have It All...Almost All. (SPA.). 26p. 1991. pap. write for info. (*0-614-27143-6*) Editorial Unilit.

— Tengo Todo... Casi Todo. (Serie Cruzada - Crusade Ser.).Tr. of I Have It All... Almost All. (SPA.). 1991. 1.99 (*1-56063-118-X*, 498013) Editorial Unilit.

***Palau, Luis.** Where Is God When Bad Things Happen? 240p. 2000. pap. 10.95 (*0-385-49264-2*) Doubleday.

Palau, Luis. Your New Life in Christ. LC 95-45413. 1996. pap. 8.99 (*0-89107-871-1*) Crossway Bks.

Palau, Luis & Dobson, James C. Una Mirada Biblica a la Familia. (Serie Enfoque a la Familia - Focus on the Family Ser.).Tr. of Biblical Look at the Family. (SPA.). 20p. 1992. pap. 1.99 (*1-56063-348-4*, 497440) Editorial Unilit.

***Palau, Luis & Halliday, Steve.** Where Is God When Bad Things Happen? Finding Solace in Times of Trouble. large type ed. LC 99-33090. 1999. 26.95 (*0-7838-8679-9*, G K Hall Lrg Type) Mac Lib Ref.

An Asterisk (*) at the beginning of an entry indicates that the title is appearing for the first time.

Palau, Luis & Sanford, David. Luis Palau: Calling America & the Nations to Christ. LC 94-21741. 1994. pap. text 8.99 (*0-7852-7984-9*) Nelson.

Palau, Luis & Umlandt, Mike. The Only Hope for America: The Transforming Power of the Gospel of Jesus Christ. LC 95-44520. 192p. 1996. pap. 10.99 (*0-89107-882-7*) Crossway Bks.

Palau, Luis P. Papa, Mama Quiero Ir Al Cielo. (Serie Cruzada - Crusade Ser.).Tr. of Mom, Dad, I Want to Go to Heaven. (SPA.). 27p. 1992. pap. 1.99 (*1-56063-181-3*, 498015) Editorial Unilit.

Palau, Silvio M. Made in U. S. A. Estudio en Naturalezas Muertas. (SPA.). 167p. 1985. pap. 9.50 (*0-910061-27-0*, 1116) Ediciones Norte.

Palau, Susan M., jt. auth. see Meltzer, Marilyn.

Palay. Ophthalmology for the Primary Care Practitioner. (Illus.). 331p. (C). (gr. 13). 1997. pap. text 59.95 (*0-8151-8898-6*, 30318) Mosby Inc.

Palay & Krachmer, Palay. Cornea Color Atlas. (Illus.). 336p. (C). (gr. 13). 1995. text 174.00 (*0-8151-5147-0*, 24920) Mosby Inc.

Palay, Andrew J. Searching with Probabilities. (Research Notes in Artificial Intelligence Ser.). 1998. pap. text 30.95 (*0-273-08664-2*) Morgan Kaufmann.

Palay, Simin. Dictionnaire du Bearnais et du Gascon Modernes. (FRE.). 1072p. 1991. 95.00 (*0-8288-6022-X*, M6645) Fr & Eur.

Palay, Thomas, jt. auth. see Galanter, Marc.

Palaz, I. & Sengupta, S., eds. Automated Pattern Analysis in Petroleum Exploration. (Illus.). 304p. 1991. 145.00 (*0-387-97468-7*) Spr-Verlag.

Palaz, Ibrahim & Marfurt, K. J., eds. Carbonate Seismology. (Geophysical Developments Ser.: Vol. 6). 443p. 1996. text 125.00 (*1-56080-038-0*, 126A) Soc Expl Geophys.

Palazchenko, Pavel & Oberdorfer, Don. My Years with Gorbachev & Shevardnadze: The Memoir of a Soviet Interpreter. LC 96-25686. 1997. 35.00 (*0-271-01603-5*) Pa St U Pr.

Palazchenko, Pavel, tr. see Appel, Wendy S., et al.

***Palazeti, Toulla.** My Name Is Neofytos. Wise, Noreen, ed. (Book-a-Day Collection). (Illus.). 32p. (YA). (ps up). 2000. pap. 5.95 (*1-58584-387-3*) Huckleberry CT.

***Palazetti, Toulla.** The Nick & Pete Stories. Wise, Noreen, ed. (Book-a-Day Collection). (Illus.). 48p. (J). (ps up). 2000. pap. 6.95 (*1-58584-417-9*) Huckleberry CT.

Palazotto, Anthony N. & Dennis, Scott T. Nonlinear Analysis of Shell Structures. (Educ Ser.). 245p. (C). 1992. text 61.95 (*1-56347-033-0*, 33-0) AIAA.

Palazuelos, Susanna. Mexican Favorites. Wertz, Laurie, ed. LC 93-28229. (Williams-Sonoma Kitchen Library). (Illus.). 108p. 1994. lib. bdg. write for info. (*0-7835-0271-0*) Time-Life.

Palazuelos, Susanna, et al. Mexico: The Beautiful Cookbook. (Beautiful Cookbook Ser.). (Illus.). 256p. 1991. 50.00 (*0-00-215949-X*) Collins SF.

Palazzeschi, Aldo. Man of Smoke. Perella, Nicholas J. & Stefanini, Ruggero, trs. from ITA. LC 92-1240. 272p. (Orig.). 1992. pap. 14.95 (*0-934977-26-7*) Italica Pr.

Palazzi, F. New Dictionary of the Italian Language: Novissimo Dizionario della Lingua Italiana. Folena, G., ed. (ITA.). 1624p. 1981. 150.00 (*0-8288-4673-1*, M9363) Fr & Eur.

Palazzi, Tonya, ed. see Brylske, Alex.

Palazzi, Tonya, ed. see Brylske, Alex, et al.

Palazzo, Albert. Seeking Victory on the Western Front: The British Army & Chemical Warfare in World War I. LC 99-42637. 288p. 2000. text 50.00 (*0-8032-3725-1*) U of Nebr Pr.

Palazzo-Craig, Janet. Bobo's Magic Wishes: A Story from Puerto Rico. (First-Start Legends Ser.). (Illus.). 32p. (Orig.). (J). (gr. k-2). 1996. pap. 4.95 (*0-8167-3986-7*) Troll Communs.

— Bobo's Magic Wishes: A Story from Puerto Rico. (Orig.). 1999. pap. text 18.95 (*0-8167-3987-0*) Troll Communs.

— Emerald Tree: A Story from Africa. (First-Start Legends Ser.). (Illus.). 32p. (Orig.). (J). (gr. k-2). 1996. pap. 4.95 (*0-8167-3988-9*) Troll Communs.

— Emerald Tree; A Story from Africa: First-Start Legends: First-Start Legends. enl. ed. 1999. pap. text 18,95 (*0-8167-3989-7*) Troll Communs.

— Gloden Flower: A Story from Egypt. enl. ed. 1999. pap. text 18.95 (*0-8167-3991-9*) Troll Communs.

— The Golden Flower: A Story from Egypt. LC 96-131042. (First-Start Legends Ser.). (Illus.). 32p. (Orig.). (J). (gr. k-2). 1997. pap. 4.95 (*0-8167-3990-0*) Troll Communs.

— How Llama Saved the Day: A Story from Peru. LC 96-131089. (First-Start Legends Ser.). (Illus.). 32p. (Orig.). (J). (gr. k-2). 1996. pap. 4.95 (*0-8167-3992-7*) Troll Communs.

— How Llams Saved the Day: A Story from Peru. enl. ed. (J). 1999. pap. text 19.95 (*0-8167-3993-5*) Troll Communs.

— How Night Came to Be: A Story from Brazil. (First-Start Legends Ser.). (Illus.). 32p. (Orig.). (J). (gr. k-2). 1996. pap. 4.95 (*0-8167-3994-3*) Troll Communs.

— I Can Read about Manatees. (I Can Read about Ser.). (Illus.). 48p. (J). (ps-3). 1998. pap. 4.95 (*0-8167-4718-0*) Troll Communs.

— The Magic Peach: A Story from Japan. LC 96-131603. (First-Start Legends Ser.). (Illus.). 32p. (Orig.). (J). (gr. k-2). 1996. pap. 4.95 (*0-8167-3996-X*) Troll Communs.

— Magic Peach: A Story from Japan. enl. ed. 1999. pap. text 18.95 (*0-8167-3997-8*) Troll Communs.

— Mancrow's Feather: A Story from Jamaica. (First-Start Legends Ser.). (Illus.). 32p. (Orig.). (J). (gr. k-2). 1996. pap. 4.95 (*0-8167-3998-6*) Troll Communs.

— Mancrow's Feather: A Story from Jamaica. enl. ed. (Orig.). 1999. pap. text 18.95 (*0-8167-3999-4*) Troll Communs.

— Tam's Slipper: A Story from Vietnam. (First-Start Legends Ser.). (Illus.). 32p. (Orig.). (J). (gr. k-2). 1997. pap. 4.95 (*0-8167-4000-3*) Troll Communs.

— Tam's Slipper: A Story from Vietnam. enl. ed. (Orig.). 1999. pap. text 18.95 (*0-8167-4001-1*) Troll Communs.

— When Sun Ruled the Land: A Story from Cuba. (First-Start Legends Ser.). (Illus.). 32p. (Orig.). (J). (gr. k-2). 1997. pap. 4.95 (*0-8167-4002-X*) Troll Communs.

— When Sun Ruled the Land: A Story from Cuba. enl. ed. (Orig.). 1999. pap. text 18.95 (*0-8167-4003-8*) Troll Communs.

— Why Opossum Is Gray: A Story from Mexico. LC 96-131022. (First-Start Legends Ser.). (Illus.). 32p. (J). (gr. k-2). 1997. pap. 4.95 (*0-8167-4004-6*) Troll Communs.

— Why Oppossum Is Gray: A Story from Mexico, Big Book Edition. 1999. pap. text 9.95 (*0-8167-4005-4*) Troll Communs.

— Why Owl Comes Out at Night: A Story from Haiti. (First-Start Legends Ser.). (Illus.). 32p. (Orig.). (J). (gr. k-2). 1997. pap. 4.95 (*0-8167-4006-2*) Troll Communs.

— Why Owl Comes Out at Night: A Story from Haiti. (Orig.). 1999. pap. text 18.95 (*0-8167-4007-0*) Troll Communs.

— Why Spider Spins Tales: A Story from Africa. (First-Start Legends Ser.). (Illus.). 32p. (Orig.). (J). (gr. k-2). 1997. pap. 4.95 (*0-8167-4008-9*) Troll Communs.

— Why Spider Spins Tales: A Story from Africa, Big Book Edition. 1999. pap. text 18.95 (*0-8167-4009-7*) Troll Communs.

Palazzo Crassi Metropolitan Museum of Art. The Maya: The Most Comprehensive Illustrated Survey of Mayan Culture. (Illus.). 695p. 2000. 85.00 (*0-8478-2129-3*, Pub. by Rizzoli Intl) St Martin.

Palazzo, Eric. A History of Books from the Beginning to the Thirteenth Century. Beaumont, Madeleine M., tr. LC 97-52988. xxx, 258 p. 1998. pap. 32.95 (*0-8146-6167-X*) Liturgical Pr.

Palazzo, Janet. Our Friend the Sun. LC 81-11460. (Now I Know Ser.). (Illus.). 32p. (J). (gr. k-2). 1997. pap. 3.50 (*0-89375-651-2*) Troll Communs.

— Rainy Day Fun. LC 87-10842. (Illus.). 32p. (J). (gr. k-2). 1988. lib. bdg. 17.25 (*0-8167-1095-3*) Troll Communs.

— Rainy Day Fun. LC 87-10842. (Illus.). 32p. (J). (gr. k-2). 1997. pap. 3.95 (*0-8167-1096-1*) Troll Communs.

— What Makes the Weather. LC 81-11383. (Now I Know Ser.). (Illus.). 32p. (J). (gr. k-2). 1982. pap. 3.50 (*0-89375-655-5*) Troll Communs.

***Palazzo, Robert E. & Schatten, Gerald P., eds.** Current Topics in Developmental Biology. (Current Topics in Developmental Biology Ser.: Vol. 49). 500p. 2000. 109.95 (*0-12-153149-X*) Acad Pr.

Palazzo, Tony. The Biggest & the Littlest Animals. LC 77-112374. (Illus.). 40p. (J). (gr. k-3). 1985. lib. bdg. 13.95 (*0-87460-225-4*) Lion Bks.

— Magic Crayon. (Illus.). (J). (gr. k-7). 1967. lib. bdg. 12.95 (*0-87460-089-8*) Lion Bks.

Palazzoli, Mara S., et al. Family Games. Kleiber, Veronica, tr. 1989. 27.95 (*0-393-70070-4*) Norton.

— The Hidden Games of Organizations. LC 86-5079. 212p. 1990. text 29.95 (*0-87630-619-9*) Brunner-Mazel.

— Paradox & Counterparadox. Burt, Elisabeth V., tr. from ITA. LC 84-45862. 208p. 1990. reprint ed. 45.00 (*0-87668-764-8*) Aronson.

Palazzolo, Daniel J. Done Deal? The Politics of the 1997 Budget Agreement. LC 99-6031. (Illus.). 256p. (C). 1999. pap. text 24.95 (*1-889119-20-2*, Chatham House Pub) Seven Bridges.

Palazzolo, Laurie. The Spider Trampoline: A Storybook for Children & Families. LC 97-69738. (Illus.). 40p. (J). (ps-3). 1997. 14.95 (*1-882792-53-X*) Proctor Pubns.

Palberg, T., et al, eds. Optical Methods & Physics of Colloidal Dispersions. (Progress in Colloid & Polymer Science Ser.: No. 104). viii, 204p. 1997. text 79.95 (*3-7985-1085-7*) Spr-Verlag.

***Palbykin, Donald J.** Palbykin: My Life as a Doll. (Illus.). ix, 436p. 2000. 29.95 (*0-9679577-0-2*); pap. 17.95 (*0-9679577-1-0*) Pal Pubng.

Palca, Julia. Employment Law Checklists, 1993. (Blackstone's Employment Law Library). 1992. pap. 58.00 (*1-85431-212-X*, Pub. by Blackstone Pr) Gaunt.

Palca, Julia & Taylor, Catherine. Employment Law Checklists. 2nd ed. (Employment Law Library). 161p. 1997. pap. 44.00 (*1-85431-637-0*, Pub. by Blackstone Pr) Gaunt.

Palchik, Mark Y., jt. auth. see Fradkin, E. S.

Palchikov, V. G. & Shevelko, V. P. Reference Data on Multicharged Ions. LC 94-29200. (Series on Atoms & Plasmas: Vol. 16). 1994. 152.95 (*0-387-58259-2*) Spr-Verlag.

Palciauskas, Victor, jt. auth. see Gueguen, Yves.

Palcich, C. W. & Palcich, W. J. The Teachers' Phrasebook: Describing & Reporting Student Character & Achievement. 172p. 1996. pap. 14.95 (*0-9659238-5-1*) Proconsul Pr.

Palcich, W. J., jt. auth. see Palcich, C. W.

Palda, K. Filip. Here the People Rule: A Toolbook for Reforming Democracy. LC 96-48220. 1997. 15.95 (*1-885118-04-X*) Prof World Peace.

— How Much Is Your Vote Worth? LC 93-42715. 1993. pap. 19.95 (*1-55815-284-9*) ICS Pr.

Paldam, Martin. Economic Development in Greenland. 228p. 1996. pap. 27.00 (*87-7288-544-0*, Pub. by Aarhus Univ Pr) David Brown.

Paldan, Leena, jt. ed. see Hanninen, Sakari.

Palden, Yeshe, jt. auth. see Zi, Lao.

Palder, Edward L. The Catalog of Catalogs VI: The Complete Mail-Order Directory. 6th ed. LC 98-55354. Vol. 6. 567p. 1999. pap. 24.95 (*1-890627-08-9*) Woodbine House.

Paldiel, Mordecai. The Path of the Righteous: Gentile Rescuers of Jews During the Holocaust. 35.00 (*0-88125-376-6*) Ktav.

***Paldiel, Mordecai.** Saving the Jews: Amazing Stories of Men & Women Who Defied the 'Final Solution' 2000. pap. 24.95 (*1-887563-55-5*) Schreiber Pub.

Paldiel, Mordecai. Sheltering the Jews: Stories of Holocaust Rescuers. 200p. 1995. pap. 19.00 (*0-8006-2897-7*) Augsburg Fortress.

Paldy, Lester G. For an Okay Free Woman. LC 92-80282. 58p. 1992. pap. 9.95 (*0-9632277-0-X*) Night Heron.

— Wildflowers at Babi Yar. LC 94-67429. 40p. (Orig.). 1994. pap. 6.95 (*0-9632277-1-8*) Night Heron.

***Paleczny, Barbara & Canadian Corporation for Studies in Religion Staff.** Clothed in Integrity: Weaving Just Cultural Relations & the Garment Industry. LC 99-932722. (Studies in Women & Religion: Vol. 6). 424p. (C). 2000. pap. 29.95 (*0-88920-340-7*) Wilfrid Laurier.

Palefsky, Cliff, jt. auth. see Quackenbush, Willaim C.

***Palefsky, Jay.** Alphamorphabet. (Illus.). 52p. 1999. 16.00 (*0-9656782-1-0*) Kutzkies Artwrks.

Palefsky, Jay. Metamorphimals. (Illus.). 38p. 1996. 16.00 (*0-9656782-0-2*) Kutzkies Artwrks.

***Paleg, Kim.** Ten Things Every Parent Needs to Know. 160p. 2000. 6.98 (*1-56731-395-7*, MJF Bks) Fine Comms.

Paleg, Kim. The Ten Things Every Parent Needs to Know: A Guide for New Parents & Everyone Else Who Cares about Children. LC 96-71154. 168p. (Orig.). 1997. pap. 12.95 (*1-57224-065-2*) New Harbinger.

Paleg, Kim & Klein, Mona. Kids Today, Parents Tomorrow. LC 98-66710. 150p. (YA). (gr. 10-12). 1999. pap. text 9.95 (*1-57224-154-3*) New Harbinger.

— Kids Today, Parents Tomorrow: Teacher's Guide. (Illus.). 1999. pap., teacher ed. 18.95 (*1-57224-180-2*, Pub. by New Harbinger) Publishers Group.

Paleg, Kim, jt. auth. see Jongsma, Arthur E., Jr.

Paleg, Kim, jt. ed. see McKay, Matthew.

***Palehan, Israel.** Hebrew-English, English-Hebrew Dictionary & Phrasebook. (HEB & ENG.). 180p. 2000. pap. 11.95 (*0-7818-0811-1*) Hippocrene Bks.

Palen, Debbie, jt. auth. see Cerf, Bennett.

***Palen, J. John.** Social Problems for the Twenty-First Century. LC 00-22122. 2001. write for info. (*0-07-048141-5*) McGraw.

Palen, J. John. Suburbs. 208p. (C). 1994. 28.75 (*0-07-048128-8*) McGraw.

— The Urban World. 5th ed. LC 96-5369. 544p. (C). 1996. 59.38 (*0-07-048168-7*) McGraw.

Palen, J. John & London, Bruce, eds. Gentrification, Displacement & Neighborhood Revitalization. LC 83-5038. (SUNY Series in Urban Public Policy). 271p. (C). 1985. text 64.50 (*0-87395-784-9*); pap. text 21.95 (*0-87395-785-7*) State U NY Pr.

Palen, Jerry. Stampede, the First Really Big Book. (Illus.). 54p. (Orig.). 1986. pap. 6.95 (*0-941803-00-7*) Stampede Cartoons.

Palen, John. Staying Intact. 24p. 1997. pap. 6.00 (*0-932412-11-4*) Mayapple Pr.

Palen, Margaret K. Genealogical Guide to Tracing Ancestors in Germany. (Illus.). 159p. 1995. pap. 17.50 (*0-7884-0280-3*) Heritage Bk.

— German Settlers of Iowa: Their Descendants & European Ancestors. 360p. (Orig.). 1994. pap. text 29.50 (*1-55613-981-0*) Heritage Bk.

Palencia, E. Sanchez, jt. auth. see Hubert, J. Sanchez.

***Palencia, Elaine.** Brier Country: Stories from Blue Valley. LC 99-58478. 215p. 2000. pap. 17.95 (*0-8262-1279-4*) U of Mo Pr.

Palencia, Elaine F. Small Caucasian Woman. 176p. (C). 1993. pap. 17.95 (*0-8262-0943-2*) U of Mo Pr.

— Taking the Train. limited ed. O'Dell, Mary E., ed. (Chapbook Ser.). (Illus.). 30p. 1997. pap. 6.00 (*0-9623666-7-6*) Green Rvr Writers.

— Thigmotropism. 1998. pap. text 6.50 (*0-9623666-9-2*) Green Rvr Writers.

Palencia-Roth, Michael, jt. auth. see Neuman, Isaac.

Palenik, Charles John, jt. auth. see Miller, Chris H.

Palenque, ed. see Rueda, Salvador.

Palenski, Joseph E. Community Police: Product or Process. 125p. (Orig.). 1996. pap. 20.00 (*0-9654008-0-8*) St Bertram Bks.

Palenski, Ronald J. ADAPSO Sales & Use Tax Survey. rev. ed. write for info. (*0-318-62080-4*) ITAA.

Palenzuela, Fernando. Amuletos del Sueno. (SPA.). 1971. pap. 9.00 (*0-89729-003-8*) Ediciones.

Paleo, Lyn, jt. ed. see Garber, Eric.

Paleologue, Maurice. Cavour. Morrow, Ian F. & Morrow, Muriel M., trs. LC 77-130561. (Select Bibliographies Reprint Ser.). 1977. reprint ed. 23.95 (*0-8369-5534-X*) Ayer.

Paleontological Research Insitution, Ithaca NY, Staff, jt. auth. see Sorauf, James E.

Paleos, Constantinos M. Polymerization in Organized Media. 376p. 1992. text 161.00 (*2-88124-538-2*) Gordon & Breach.

Paleos, Kalliopy. Are There Animals Hiding Inside You? (Illus.). 32p. 1991. pap. 8.00 (*0-925062-04-9*) Writers Ink Pr.

— Girl in the Yellow Caboose: Remembering Writers. (Illus.). 32p. (Orig.). 1992. pap. 8.00 (*0-9631128-0-5*) Karma Dog.

Palepu & Healy. Spanish Translation-Business Analysis & Valuation. (SWC-Accounting). (SPA.). (C). 1999. pap. 60.95 (*0-324-00277-7*) Thomson Learn.

Palepu, et al. Business Analysis. 1996. 36.75 (*0-538-86620-9*) Thomson Learn.

Palepu, Krishna, et al. Business Analysis & Valuation Using Financial Statements. 273p. 1996. mass mkt. 28.95 (*0-538-86619-5*) S-W Pub.

Palepu, Krishna G. Business Analysis & Valuati Financial Statements: Text & Cases. 2nd ed. L 99-58727. (SWC-Accounting). 1999. pap. 114. (*0-324-01565-8*) Sth-Wstrn College.

***Palepu, Krishna G.** Business Analysis & Valuation: Financial Statements: Text & Cases. 2nd ed. LC 99-58727. 1999. pap. text 69.95 (*0-324-02002-3*) Sth-Wstrn College.

Palepu, Krishna G., et al. Business Analysis & Valuation: Using Financial Statements: Text & Cases. LC 95-24971. 896p. (C). 1995. pap. 86.95 (*0-538-84332-2*) S-W Pub.

Palepu, Krishna G., et al. Step-By-Step Business Analysis & Valuation: Using Financial Statements to Value Any Business. (SWC-Accounting Ser.). (Illus.). 208p. 1999. pap. 24.95 (*0-324-01504-6*) Thomson Learn.

***Palerm.** Anthropology Marxism & Mesoamerican. 2000. 45.00 (*0-8133-3795-X*, Pub. by Westview); pap. 19.00 (*0-8133-3796-8*, Pub. by Westview) HarpC.

Palerm, Angel, jt. auth. see Kelly, Isabel T.

Palerm, Juan-Vicente. Chicano & Mexican Communities in Rural California. (Conflict & Social Change Ser.). 180p. (C). 2000. pap. 29.95 (*0-8133-8399-4*) Westview.

Palermo, Blinky. Palermo. Greenidge, Delano & Maas, Erich, eds. LC 88-51594. (ENG & GER.). 160p. 1989. 60.00 (*0-929445-01-5*) D Greenidge Editions.

Palermo, D. S., jt. ed. see Hoffman, R. R.

Palermo, David S., ed. Coping with Uncertainty: Behavioral & Developmental Perspectives. (Penn State Series on Child & Adolescent Development). 224p. 1989. 45.00 (*0-8058-0157-X*) L Erlbaum Assocs.

Palermo, David S., jt. ed. see Hoffman, R. R.

Palermo, David S., jt. ed. see Overton, Willis F.

Palermo, David S., jt. ed. see Weimer, Walter B.

Palermo, George B. The Faces of Violence. LC 94-31664. (American Series in Behavioral Science & Law). 300p. (C). 1994. pap. 46.95 (*0-398-05952-7*) C C Thomas.

Palermo, George B. The Faces of Violence. LC 94-31664. (American Series in Behavioral Science & Law). (Illus.). 300p. (C). 1994. text 72.95 (*0-398-05934-9*) C C Thomas.

***Palermo, George B. & Del Re, Michele C.** Satanism: Psychiatric & Legal Views. LC 99-41451. (American Series in Behavioral Science & Law: Vol. 1099). 224p. 1999. text 42.95 (*0-398-07007-5*); pap. text 29.95 (*0-398-07008-3*) C C Thomas.

Palermo, George B. & Scott, Edward M. The Paranoid: In & out of Prison. LC 96-44157. (American Series in Behavioral Science & Law: No. 1093). 208p. 1997. text 49.95 (*0-398-06727-9*); pap. text 37.95 (*0-398-06728-7*) C C Thomas.

Palermo, George B. & White, Maxine A. Letters from Prison: A Cry for Justice. LC 97-51866. (American Series in Behavioral Science & Law: Vol. 1095). 276p. 1998. text 55.95 (*0-398-06851-8*); pap. text 41.95 (*0-398-06852-6*) C C Thomas.

***Palermo, Nita J.** Saying Goodbye with a Enlogy. 56p. 2000. 14.95 (*0-9701945-0-1*) Mamas Daughter.

Palermo, Richard C., ed. see Xerox Quality Services Staff.

Palerne, Guillaume De, see De Palerne, Guillaume.

Palerno, Tony. Sex Advisor: 100 of the Most Frequently Asked Questions about Gay Sex. LC 99-188013. 225p. 1999. pap. 11.95 (*1-55583-485-X*) Alyson Pubns.

Pales Matos, Luis. Obras: Luis Pales Matos, Nineteen Fourteen to Nineteen Fifty-Nine, 2 vols., Set. Arce de Vazquez, Margot, ed. LC 79-16469. (SPA.). 609p. 1984. 25.00 (*0-8477-3219-3*) U of PR Pr.

— Obras: Luis Pales Matos, Nineteen Fourteen to Nineteen Fifty-Nine, 2 vols., Vol. I: Poetry. Arce de Vazquez, Margot, ed. LC 79-16469. (SPA.). 609p. 1984. 15.00 (*0-8477-3220-7*) U of PR Pr.

— Obras: Luis Pales Matos, Nineteen Fourteen to Nineteen Fifty-Nine, 2 vols., Vol. II: Prose. Arce de Vazquez, Margot, ed. LC 79-16469. (SPA.). 609p. 1984. 10.00 (*0-8477-3221-5*) U of PR Pr.

— Poesia, 1915-1956. 5th rev. ed. (SPA.). 304p. 1974. 5.00 (*0-88473-212-6*) U of PR Pr.

***Pales Matos, Luis.** Selected Poems - Poesia Selecta. 224p. 2000. pap. 12.95 (*1-55885-303-0*) Arte Publico.

Pales Matos, Luis. Tuntun de Pasa y Grifería. (Coleccion Puertorriquena Ser.). (SPA.). 226p. 1994. 11.50 (*0-8477-0217-0*); pap. 9.50 (*0-8477-0178-6*) U of PR Pr.

Pales Matos, Luis & Lopez-Baralt, Mercedes. La Poesia de Pales Matos. (SPA.). 800p. 1995. 34.95 (*0-8477-0193-X*) U of PR Pr.

Palescandolo, Frank, tr. see Di Giacomo, Salvatore.

Palese, Peter. Genetics of Influenza Viruses. (Illus.). 340p. 1983. 112.00 (*0-387-81743-3*) Spr-Verlag.

Palestine Economic Society Bulletin Staff. Palestine Economic Society Bulletin: Proceedings of the Bulletin of the Palestine Economic Society, Tel Aviv, Aug. 21 - Feb., 1934, 6 vols. in 5. reprint ed. write for info. (*0-404-56240-X*) AMS Pr.

Palestine Pilgrims' Text Society Staff. The Library of the Palestine Pilgrims' Text Society: Circa 1480-1483 A.D., 11 vols., Set. Stewart, Aubrey et al, trs. Incl. Vol. 12, 1895-1897., 3 pts. reprint ed. 37.50 (*0-404-04902-8*); Vol. 4, 1893-1897., 3 pts. reprint ed. 37.50 (*0-404-04894-3*); 1887-1891., 5 pts. reprint ed. 37.50 (*0-404-04891-9*); 1890-1897., 4 pts. reprint ed. 37.50 (*0-404-04892-7*); 1893-1897., 4 pts. reprint ed. 37.50 (*0-404-04893-5*); 1896-1897., 5 pts. reprint ed. 37.50 (*0-404-04895-1*); 1894-1897., 4 pts. reprint ed. 37.50 (*0-404-04896-X*); 1892-1897., 4 pts. in 2 vols reprint ed. 49.00: 1892-1897., 4 pts. in 2 vols. reprint ed. (*0-404-04897-8*); Set. 1892-1897., 4 pts. in 2 vols reprint ed. 98.00: 1895-1897., 2 pts. reprint ed. 37.50 (*0-404-04901-X*); 1897. reprint ed. 37.50 (*0-404 04903-6*); LC 74-141802. (Palestine Pilgrim's Text Society Ser.: Nos. 7-10). reprint ed. 742.50 (*0-404-04890-0*) AMS Pr.

P

An Asterisk (*) at the beginning of an entry indicates that the title is appearing for the first time.

ration: Leading 38 p. 1998.

Leadership: A 6. 105p. 1998. pap. ecrow.

rence on Mathematics eds. Proceedings of the national Conference on & An-Najah University, Nablus, 19-23, 1998. LC 00-20881. 2000. 81-02-4220-4) World Scientific Pub.

Have You Ever Had a Hunch? Getting Critics Out of the Way. Westheimer, Mary, .). 192p. (Orig.). (C). 1994. pap. 12.95 0001-01-0) Via Press.

ant, Ellen & Miller, Lisa, eds. Remembering Dolores: An Experiment in Collaborative Conversation. 100p. (Orig.). 1997. pap. write for info. (*0-9657557-0-3*) Phoenix Coll.

Palestrina, G. Missa Breva: A Capella. (LAT.). 32p. 1986. pap. 3.95 (*0-7935-4904-3*, 50324020) H Leonard.

Palestrina, Giovanni P. Ten Four-Part Motets for the Church's Year. Harman, Alec, tr. (ENG & LAT.). 112p. 1985. 18.95 (*0-19-353332-4*) OUP.

Palestrina, Giovanni P. Da, see Da Palestrina, Giovanni P.

Palestrina, Pierluigi D., et al. Two Settings of Palestrina's Missa Papae Marcelli. Busch, Hermann J., ed. (Recent Researches in Music of the Baroque Era Ser.: Vol. RRB16). 106p. 1973. pap. 35.00 (*0-89579-048-3*) A-R Eds.

Palestrini, Giovanni P. Pope Marcellus Mass. rev. ed. Lockwood, Lewis C., ed. (Critical Scores Ser.). (C). 1975. pap. text 15.50 (*0-393-09242-9*) Norton.

Palestro, Christopher J. Radionuclide Diagnosis of Infectious Disease. 220p. 1998. text 135.00 (*0-397-51638-X*) Lppncott W & W.

Palethorpe, Jan, ed. Bush Tucker Magic. 1997. 14.95 (*1-86368-186-8*, Pub. by Fremantle Arts) Intl Spec Bk.

Paletta, Michael S. The New Marine Aquarium: Step-by-Step Setup & Stocking Guide. Lawrence, James, ed. LC 98-34407. (Illus.). 144p. 1999. pap. 19.95 (*1-890087-52-1*) Microcosm Ltd.

Paletti, John T. & Radke, Gary M. Art in Renaissance Italy. LC 96-18459. (Illus.). 480p. 1997. 60.00 (*0-8109-1978-8*, Pub. by Abrams) Time Warner.

Paletz. Media & Politics. 416p. (C). 1998. text. write for info. (*0-321-04496-7*) Addison-Wesley.

Paletz, ed. Media Am Pol. (C). 1999. text 25.50 (*0-06-501031-0*) Addison-Wesley.

***Paletz, David L.** The Media in American Politics. LC 98-35082. 352p. (C). 1998. pap. 45.00 (*0-321-02991-7*) Addson-Wesley Educ.

Paletz, David L., ed. Political Communication in Action: States, Institutions, Movements, Audiences. LC 95-36519. (Communication Series). 352p. (C). 1995. text 72.50 (*1-57273-000-5*); pap. text 26.50 (*1-57273-001-3*) Hampton Pr NJ.

Paletz, David L. & Entman, Robert M. Media Power Politics. 304p. 1981. pap. 13.95 (*0-685-03271-X*) Macmillan.

Paletz, David L. & Schmid, Alex P., eds. Terrorism & the Media. (Illus.). 320p. (C). 1992. 44.00 (*0-8039-4482-9*); pap. 19.50 (*0-8039-4483-7*) Sage.

Paletz, David L., et al. Glasnost & After: Media & Change in Central & Eastern Europe. LC 94-46168. (Communication Series). lp. 1995. text 55.00 (*1-881303-86-1*); pap. text 23.95 (*1-881303-87-X*) Hampton Pr NJ.

Paletz, David L., jt. ed. see Bennett, W. Lance.

Paletz, David L., ed. see Kedrowski, Karen M.

Paletz, David L., ed. see Kepplinger, Hans M., et al.

Paletz, David L., ed. see Schoenbach, Klaus & Semetko, Holli.

Paletz, David L., ed. see Schoenbach, Klaus & Semetko, Holli A.

Palev, T. D., jt. ed. see Doebner, H. D.

Paleveda, Carl A. Is the U. S. Constitution Unconstitutional? (Illus.). 136p. (C). 1991. text 7.95 (*0-9626760-1-2*) Paleveda Pres.

P

Paleveda, Gloria S. The Best of Times. (Illus.). 139p. 1986. pap. 8.95 (*0-936676-83-3*) Inst Achieve Human Pot.

***Palevsky, Mary.** Atomic Fragments: A Daughter's Questions. LC 99-87422. (Illus.). 272p. 2000. 24.95 (*0-520-22055-2*, Pub. by U CA Pr) Cal Prin Full Svc.

Palevsky, Nicholas, jt. auth. see Kinoshita, June.

Paley. Ilizarov Technique. 1993. write for info. (*0-397-51086-1*) Lppncott W & W.

Paley, Aaron, ed. see Fringe Festival-Los Angeles Staff & Community Arts Resources, Inc. Staff.

Paley, Albert. The Metalwork of Albert Paley. (Illus.). 60p. 1980. pap. 8.50 (*0-932718-06-X*) Kohler Arts.

Paley, Bruce. Jack the Ripper: The Simple Truth. (Illus.). 288p. 1997. pap. 13.95 (*0-7472-5218-1*, Pub. by Headline Bk Pub) Trafalgar.

Paley, F. A., comment. Euripides, 3 vols. 2nd rev. ed. (ENG & GER.). cxxxiv, 1829p. write for info. (*0-318-70528-1*) G Olms Pubs.

***Paley, Grace.** Begin Again: Collected Poems. LC 99-46996. 208p. 2000. text 23.00 (*0-374-12642-9*) FS&G.

— Begin Again: Collected Poems. 192p. 2001. pap. 13.00 (*0-374-52724-5*) FS&G.

Paley, Grace. The Collected Stories. LC 93-42230. 386p. 1994. 27.50 (*0-374-12636-4*) FS&G.

— The Collected Stories. 386p. 1995. pap. 15.00 (*0-374-52431-9*, Noonday) FS&G.

— The Collected Stories. limited ed. 464p. 1994. 100.00 (*0-374-12638-0*) FS&G.

— Enormous Changes at the Last Minute. 200p. 1985. pap. 12.00 (*0-374-51524-7*) FS&G.

— Enormous Changes at the Last Minute. 198p. 1980. 5.99 (*0-86068-108-4*) Random.

— Just As I Thought. LC 97-37630. 332p. 1998. 24.00 (*0-374-18060-1*) FS&G.

***Paley, Grace.** Just As I Thought. 352p. 1999. pap. text 13.00 (*0-374-52585-4*) FS&G.

Paley, Grace. The Little Disturbances of Man. LC 84-18951. (Fiction Ser.). 192p. 1985. pap. 16.99 (*0-14-007557-7*, Penguin Bks) Viking Penguin.

— Long Walks & Intimate Talks. LC 90-27844. (Illus.). 80p. 1991. 29.95 (*1-55861-043-X*); pap. 12.95 (*1-55861-044-8*) Feminist Pr.

Paley, Grace, pref. The Shalom Seders: Three Passover Haggadahs. LC 83-25857. (Illus.). 104p. 1984. pap. 12.95 (*0-915361-03-5*, 09747-1) Lambda Pubs.

Paley, Grace, et al. Conversations with Grace Paley. LC 96-47449. (Literary Conversations Ser.). 1997. 42.00 (*0-87805-961-X*); pap. 17.00 (*0-87805-962-8*) U Pr of Miss.

— Ergo! The Bumbershoot Literary Magazine, Vol. 7, No. 1. 144p. 1992. pap. 8.00 (*0-929696-04-2*) Bumbershoot.

Paley, Gregory S., ed. International Recognition & Enforcement of Money Judgments. LC 94-233146. 600p. 1994. 125.00 (*1-56789-015-6*, 141) Busn Laws Inc.

***Paley, Julia.** Marketing Democracy: Power & Social Movements in Post-Dictatorship Chile. LC 00-37405. 2001. pap. write for info. (*0-520-22768-9*) U CA Pr.

***Paley, Karen Surman.** I-Writing: The Politics & Practice of Teaching First-Person Writing. LC 00-39505. 2001. pap. write for info. (*0-8093-2351-6*) S Ill U Pr.

***Paley, Maggie.** The Book of the Penis. LC 99-20348. (Illus.). 272p. 1999. 20.00 (*0-8021-1648-5*, Grove) Grove-Atltic.

— The Book of the Penis. 2000. pap. 12.00 (*0-8021-3693-1*, Pub. by Grove-Atltic) Publishers Group.

Paley, Morton D. Apocalypse & Millennium in English Romantic Poetry. LC 99-15283. (Illus.). 336p. 1999. text 72.00 (*0-19-818500-6*) OUP.

— The Apocalyptic Sublime. LC 86-1706. 208p. 1986. 47.00 (*0-300-03674-4*) Yale U Pr.

— Coleridge's Later Poetry. (Illus.). 160p. (C). 1996. text 45.00 (*0-19-818372-0*) OUP.

— Coleridge's Later Poetry. (Illus.). 160p. 2000. pap. text 19.95 (*0-19-818685-1*) OUP.

— Portraits of Coleridge. LC 98-49200. (Illus.). 190p. 1999. text 55.00 (*0-19-818469-7*) OUP.

Paley, Morton D., ed. see Blake, William, et al.

Paley, Morton D., jt. ed. see Fulford, Tim.

Paley, Morton D., ed. & intro. see Shelley, Mary Wollstonecraft.

Paley, Nicholas. Finding Art's Place: Experiments in Contemporary Education & Culture. (Illus.). 224p. (C). (gr. 13). 1995. 70.00 (*0-415-90606-7*, A7344); pap. 23.99 (*0-415-90607-5*, A7348) Routledge.

***Paley, Nicholas & Jipson, Janice.** Questions of You & the Struggle of Collaborative Life. LC 98-30630. (Counterpoints: Vol. 104). 190p. 2000. pap. text 29.95 (*0-8204-4251-8*) P Lang Pubng.

Paley, Nicholas & Jipson, Janice, eds. Daredevil Research: Re-Creating Analytic Practice. LC 95-22935. (Counterpoints Studies in the Postmodern Theory of Education Ser.: Vol. 21). (Illus.). XIII, 233p. (C). 1997. pap. 32.95 (*0-8204-2776-4*) P Lang Pubng.

Paley, Nina. Nina's Adventures. (Illus.). 96p. 1993. pap. 7.95 (*0-9637283-1-8*) Pentshack Pr.

Paley, Nina. Inside-Out Feelings. LC 93-8953. (Contemporary Health Ser.). (J). 1993. 3.00 (*1-56071-315-1*) ETR Assocs.

— What about Me? LC 93-8955. (Contemporary Health Ser.). (J). 1993. 3.00 (*1-56071-314-3*) ETR Assocs.

Paley, Norton. The Manager's Guide to Competitive Marketing Strategies 2nd ed. LC 98-51466. 1999. 49.95 (*1-57444-234-1*) St Lucie Pr.

Paley, Norton, jt. auth. see Elam, Houston G.

Paley, Raymond & Wiener, Norbert. Fourier Transforms in the Complex Domain. LC 35-3273. (Colloquium Publications: Vol. 19). 183p. 1934. reprint ed. pap. 45.00 (*0-8218-1019-7*, COLL/19) Am Math.

Paley, Russ. Network Your Way to Millions: The Definitive Step by Step Guide to Wealth in Network Marketing. Kleine, Walt, ed. (Illus.). 280p. Date not set. pap. 14.95 (*0-9672238-0-6*) Wealth Network.

***Paley, Russell.** Russ Paley's Ultimate Guide to Network Marketing: Your Step-by-Step Guide to Wealth. LC 00-37899. 256p. 2000. pap. 14.99 (*1-56414-478-X*) Career Pr Inc.

Paley, S. M. Robotics Illustrated Dictionary: French-English-German-Russian. (ENG, FRE, GER & RUS., Illus.). 347p. 1993. 85.00 (*0-7859-8827-0*) Fr & Eur.

— Robotics Illustrated Dictionary, French-English-German-Russian. (ENG, FRE, GER & RUS., Illus.). 1993. 98.00 (*0-7859-9410-6*) Fr & Eur.

Paley, Vivian G. Bad Guys Don't Have Birthdays: Fantasy Play at Four. LC 87-21748. x, 128p. 1991. pap. 12.00 (*0-226-64496-0*) U Ch Pr.

— Bad Guys Don't Have Birthdays: Fantasy Play at Four. 128p. 1992. 12.95 (*0-226-64495-2*) U Ch Pr.

— The Boy Who Would Be a Helicopter. 76p. 1990. 29.95 (*0-674-08030-0*) HUP.

— The Boy Who Would Be a Helicopter. 176p. 1990. pap. text 10.95 (*0-674-08031-9*) HUP.

— Boys & Girls: Superheroes in the Doll Corner. LC 84-93. xii, 128p. (C). 1986. pap. 8.95 (*0-226-64492-8*) U Ch Pr.

— Boys & Girls: Superheroes in the Doll Corner. LC 84-93. xii, 116p. (C). 1992. 15.95 (*0-226-64490-1*) U Ch Pr.

— The Girl with the Brown Crayon. LC 96-34708. 112p. 1997. 18.95 (*0-674-35439-7*) HUP.

— The Girl with the Brown Crayon. 112p. 1998. pap. 10.95 (*0-674-35442-7*) HUP.

— Kwanzaa & Me: A Teacher's Story. LC 94-25002. 152p. 1995. text 18.95 (*0-674-50585-9*, PALKWA) HUP.

— Kwanzaa & Me: A Teacher's Story. 152p. 1996. pap. 12.95 (*0-674-50586-7*) HUP.

— Mollie Is Three: Growing up in School. xvi, 160p. 1988. pap. 9.95 (*0-226-64494-4*) U Ch Pr.

— Molly Is Three: Growing up in School. LC 85-24589. xvi, 144p. (C). 1995. 19.50 (*0-226-64493-6*) U Ch Pr.

— Wally's Stories: Conversations in the Kindergarten. LC 80-21882. 223p. 1981. pap. text 14.50 (*0-674-94593-X*) HUP.

Paley, Vivian Gussin. The Kindness of Children. LC 98-37322. 129p. 1999. 18.95 (*0-674-50358-9*) HUP.

***Paley, Vivian Gussin.** Kindness of Children. 144p. 2000. pap. 12.95 (*0-674-00390-X*) HUP.

— White Teacher. LC 99-58993. 2000. pap. 12.95 (*0-674-00273-3*) HUP.

Paley, Vivian Gussin. White Teacher. 156p. 1979. reprint ed. pap. text 12.50 (*0-674-95186-7*) HUP.

— You Can't Say You Can't Play. (Illus.). 144p. 1992. 19.95 (*0-674-96589-2*) HUP.

— You Can't Say You Can't Play. (Illus.). 144p. 1993. pap. text 10.95 (*0-674-96590-6*) HUP.

Paley, William. Natural Theology. 1986. reprint ed. pap. 33.95 (*0-935005-62-5*); reprint ed. lib. bdg. 50.95 (*0-935005-61-7*) Lincoln-Rembrandt.

— The Works of William Paley, 1830 Edition, 6 vols. (Major Work Ser.). 1998. 875.00 (*1-85506-576-2*) Thoemmes Pr.

Paley, William & Loyd, J. H. Treatise on the Law of Principal & Agent, Chiefly with Reference to Mercantile Transactions. 2nd ed. xvi, 202p. 1982. reprint ed. 36.50 (*0-8377-1010-3*, Rothman) W S Hein.

Palfai & Jankiewic. Drugs & Human Behavior. 2nd ed. 1996. teacher ed. 19.68 (*0-697-12714-1*) McGraw.

Palfai, Tibor & Jankiewicz, Henry. Drugs & Human Behavior. 2nd ed. LC 96-83185. 560p. (C). 1996. text. write for info. (*0-697-12713-3*) Brown & Benchmark.

Palfey, Colin. The Scottish Trip. 1986. 30.00 (*0-86243-041-0*, Pub. by Y Lolfa) St Mut.

Palframan, Diane, et al. European Logistics Integration: Challenge of the Alps LC 99-161344. (Report Ser). 31 p. 1995. write for info. (*0-8237-0584-6*) Conference Bd.

— Recovery in Europe: The Work Force Dimension : A Council Report. LC 98-209994. (Report). 29 p. 1995. write for info. (*0-8237-0567-6*) Conference Bd.

Palfreeman, A. AIDS Therapeutics in HIV Disease. 2nd ed. LC 97-43724. 124p. 1998. pap. 38.95 (*0-471-97063-8*) Wiley.

Palfreeman, Anthony C., jt. auth. see Mediansky, Fedor.

***Palfreman, Andrew.** Fish Business Management: Stragegy, Marketing, Development. LC 98-33448. 1999. 56.95 (*0-85238-255-3*) Blackwell Corp.

Palfreman, Jon & Swade, Doron. The Dream Machine: Exploring the Computer Age. (Illus.). 1993. pap. 24.95 (*0-563-36992-2*, BBC-Parkwest) Parkwest Pubns.

Palfreman, Jon, jt. auth. see Langston, J. William.

Palfrey, Colin, et al. Policy Evaluation in the Public Sector: Approaches & Methods. 182p. 1992. 72.95 (*1-85628-393-3*, Pub. by Avebry) Ashgate Pub Co.

Palfrey, Colin, jt. auth. see Harding, Nancy H.

Palfrey, Evelyn. Dangerous Dilemmas. LC 98-92147. 355p. 1999. pap. 14.95 (*0-9654190-2-9*) Moon Child.

— The Price of Passion. LC 97-93486. 350p. 1997. pap. 14.95 (*0-9654190-1-0*) Moon Child.

***Palfrey, Evelyn.** The Price of Passion. 384p. 2000. pap. 12.95 (*0-671-04220-3*, PB Trade Paper) PB.

Palfrey, Evelyn. Three Perfect Men. LC 96-94883. 310p. (Orig.). 1997. pap. 10.95 (*0-9654190-0-2*) Moon Child.

Palfrey, Francis W. The Antietam & Fredericksburg. LC 95-45863. (Campaigns of the Civil War Ser.). (Illus.). 244p. 1996. reprint ed. pap. 13.95 (*0-306-80691-6*) Da Capo.

Palfrey, John G. History of New England, 5 vols. LC 01-7587. reprint ed. 345.00 (*0-404-04910-9*) AMS Pr.

Palfrey, Judith, et al. The Disney Encyclopedia of Baby & Child Care, 2 vols. Subak-Sharpe, Genell, ed. (Illus.). 672p. (J). 1999. pap. 19.45 (*0-7868-8297-2*, Pub. by Hyperion) Time Warner.

Palfrey, Judith S. Community Child Health: An Action Plan for Today. LC 94-8641. 328p. 1994. 59.95 (*0-275-94696-7*, Praeger Pubs) Greenwood.

— Community Child Health: An Action Plan for Today. LC 94-8641. 328p. 1995. pap. 22.95 (*0-275-95472-2*, Praeger Pubs) Greenwood.

Palfrey, Judith S., jt. ed. see Green, Morris.

Palfrey, Simon. Late Shakespeare: A New World of Words. LC 97-10036. (Oxford English Monographs). 310p. (C). 1997. text 85.00 (*0-19-818619-3*) OUP.

***Palfrey, Simon.** Late Shakespeare: A New World of Words. (Oxford English Monographs). 312p. 2000. pap. text 21.00 (*0-19-818689-4*) OUP.

Palfrey, Stephen M., ed. Clinical Applications of Capillary Electrophoresis. (Methods in Molecular Medicine Ser.: Vol. 27). 208p. 1999. 79.50 (*0-89603-639-1*) Humana.

Palfrey, Thomas R. Panorama Litteraire de l'Europe, 1833-1834. LC 73-128990. (Northwestern Humanities Ser.: No. 22). (FRE.). reprint ed. 29.50 (*0-404-50722-0*) AMS Pr.

Palfrey, Thomas R. & Kinder, Donald R., eds. Experimental Foundations of Political Science. (Michigan Studies in Political Analysis). (Illus.). 512p. (C). 1993. text 64.50 (*0-472-10273-7*, 10273); pap. text 25.95 (*0-472-08181-0*, 08181) U of Mich Pr.

Palfrey, Thomas R. & Srivastava, Sanjay. Bayesian Implementation. Postlewaite, A., ed. LC 92-32494. (Fundamentals of Pure & Applied Economics Ser.: Vol. 53). 116p. 1993. pap. text 29.00 (*3-7186-5314-1*) Gordon & Breach.

Palfrey, Thomas R. & Will, Samuel F., eds. Petite Anthologie: Poesies Francaises. (FRE.). (Orig.). 1961. pap. text 7.95 (*0-89197-337-0*) Irvington.

***Palfreyman, David & Tapper, Ted.** Collegiality & Mass Higher Education. 256p. 1999. 45.50 (*0-7130-0212-3*); pap. 22.50 (*0-7130-4033-5*) Intl Spec Bk.

Palfreyman, David, jt. ed. see Warner, David.

Palfreyman, John W., jt. ed. see Bruce, Alan.

Palfreyman, Michael G., et al, eds. Direct & Allosteric Control of Glutamate Receptors. LC 94-7075. (Series on Pharmacology & Toxicology). 192p. 1994. lib. bdg. 149.00 (*0-8493-8307-2*, 8307) CRC Pr.

Palgrave, Derek A., ed. Fluid Fertilizer Science & Technology. (Fertilizer Science & Technology Ser.: Vol. 7). (Illus.). 648p. 1991. text 255.00 (*0-8247-7703-4*) Dekker.

Palgrave, F. M., ed. A List of Words & Phrases in Every-Day Use by the Natives of Hetton-Le-Hole. (English Dialect Society Publications: No. 74). 1969. reprint ed. pap. 25.00 (*0-8115-0492-1*) Periodicals Srv.

Palgrave, Frances. Astrology & Alchemy. 1994. pap. 7.95 (*1-55818-295-0*) Holmes Pub.

Palgrave, Francis. The History of Normandy & England, 4 vols. LC 80-2218. reprint ed. 345.00 (*0-404-18770-6*) AMS Pr.

Palgrave, Francis T. Francis Turner Palgrave: His Journals & Memories of His Life. Palgrave, Gwenllian F., ed. LC 73-148283. reprint ed. 45.00 (*0-404-04867-6*) AMS Pr.

— The Golden Treasury. 483p. 1990. reprint ed. lib. bdg. 27.95 (*0-89966-721-X*) Buccaneer Bks.

Palgrave, Francis T., ed. The Golden Treasury of English Songs & Lyrics. rev. ed. 496p. 1991. pap. 9.95 (*0-460-87029-7*, Everyman's Classic Lib) Tuttle Pubng.

Palgrave, Francis T. & Press, John, eds. The Golden Treasury of the Best Songs & Lyrical Poems in the English Language. 6th ed. 714p. 1995. (*0-19-210012-2*) OUP.

Palgrave, Gwenllian F., ed. see Palgrave, Francis T.

Palgrave, William G. Central & Eastern Arabia. 448p. 1985. 370.00 (*1-85077-039-5*, Pub. by Darf Pubs Ltd) St Mut.

— Narrative of a Year's Journey Through Central & Eastern Arabia, 1862-63, 2 vols. (Illus.). xii, 864p. reprint ed. write for info. (*0-318-71549-X*) G Olms Pubs.

— Reise in Arabien, 2 vols. in 1. xii, 646p. reprint ed. write for info. (*0-318-71548-1*) G Olms Pubs.

Palia, Kyamas A., et al. Grand Corporate Strategy & Critical Functions: Interactive Effects of Organizational Dimensions. LC 82-430. 214p. 1982. 55.00 (*0-275-90876-3*, C0876, Praeger Pubs) Greenwood.

Palich, E. Hungarian-Serbocroatian Concise Dictionary. 3rd ed. (HUN & SER.). 944p. 1982. 49.95 (*0-8288-1669-7*, M8579) Fr & Eur.

Palicia, Joan. Flexible Flyers & Other Great Sleds for Collectors. (Schiffer Book for Collectors Ser.). (Illus.). 160p. 1997. pap. 29.95 (*0-7643-0103-9*) Schiffer.

Palics, E. Hungarian-Serbo Croatian Concise Dictionary. 944p. 1988. 36.00 (*963-205-217-X*, Pub. by Akade Kiado) St Mut.

Paliferro, Ben. Mor-Ling: Catalyst for Survival. (Illus.). 192p. 1997. pap. 14.00 (*0-8059-4098-7*) Dorrance.

Palihawadana, Mahinda, jt. ed. see Carter, John.

Palihawadana, Mahinda, jt. tr. see Carter, John R.

Palik. Handbook of Optical Constants of Solids, Vol. 3. 900p. 1997. 259.95 (*0-12-544423-0*) Acad Pr.

Palik, Edward D. Handbook of Optical Constants of Solids & Index Kit, Vol. III. (Illus.). 1997. 250.00 (*0-12-544425-7*) Acad Pr.

Palik, Edward D., ed. Handbook of Optical Constants of Solids. LC 97-33341. (C). 1985. text 250.00 (*0-12-544420-6*) Acad Pr.

— Handbook of Optical Constants of Solids II. 1096p. (C). 1991. text 250.00 (*0-12-544422-2*) Acad Pr.

***Palik, Edward D. & Ghosh, Gorachand.** Electronic Handbook of Optical Constants & Thermo-Optic Coefficients. 110p. 1999. audio compact disk 2495.00 (*0-12-544455-9*) Acad Pr.

— Electronic Handbook Of Optical Constants of Solids. 1999. 2920.00 incl. audio compact disk (*0-12-544458-3*) Acad Pr.

Palik, Edward D. & Ghosh, Gorachand, eds. Handbook of Optical Constants of Solids, 5 vols. (Illus.). 3400p. 1997. 850.00 (*0-12-544415-X*) Acad Pr.

Palika, Liz. The Australian Shepherd: An Owner's Guide to a Happy, Healthy Pet. LC 96-37577. 160p. 1997. 12.95 (*0-87605-503-X*) Howell Bks.

— The Australian Shepherd: Champion of Versatility. LC 95-3753. (Illus.). 240p. 1995. 32.95 (*0-87605-039-9*) Howell Bks.

***Palika, Liz.** Australian Shepherds. 1999. pap. 14.95 (*1-58245-150-8*) Howell Bks.

Palika, Liz. The Complete Idiot's Guide to Reptiles & Amphibians. LC 98-15972. 352p. 1998. pap. 16.95 (*0-87605-145-X*) Macmillan Gen Ref.

— The Complete Idiot's Guide to Turtles & Tortoises. LC 97-35928. (Illus.). 270p. 1997. 16.95 (*0-87605-143-3*) Macmillan Gen Ref.

— Consumer's Guide to Cat Food. LC 96-37358. 1997. 9.95 (*0-87605-722-9*) Howell Bks.

— A Consumer's Guide to Dog Food: Everything You Want & Need to Know to Feed Your Dog Right. LC 96-11579. (Consumers Guide Ser.). (Illus.). 160p. (Orig.). 1996. 9.95 (*0-87605-467-X*) Howell Bks.

— The Consumer's Guide to Feeding Birds: What Bird Owners Need to Know about What's Good - & What's Not - For Their Pets & Why. LC 97-1167. 144p. 1997. 9.95 (*0-87605-641-9*) Howell Bks.

— The Consumer's Guide to Feeding Reptiles. LC 96-49678. 144p. 1997. pap. 9.95 (*0-87605-681-8*) Howell Bks.

— The German Shepherd Dog: An Owner's Guide to a

An Asterisk (*) at the beginning of an entry indicates that the title is appearing for the first time.

Happy, Healthy Pet. (Owner's Guide to a Happy, Healthy Pet Ser.). (Illus.). 160p. 1995. 12.95 (0-87605-382-7) Howell Bks.

Palika, Liz. How to Train Your Cocker Spaniel. (How to Train Ser.). (Illus.). 96p. 9.95 (0-7938-3655-7) TFH Pubns.

— How to Train Your Dalmatian. (How to Train Ser.). (Illus.). 96p. 9.95 (0-7938-3657-3) TFH Pubns.

— How to Train Your Doberman Pinscher. (How to Train Ser.). (Illus.). 96p. 9.95 (0-7938-3656-5) TFH Pubns.

— How to Train Your German Shepherd. LC 99-484127. (How to Train Ser.). (Illus.). 96p. 1999. 9.95 (0-7938-3651-4) TFH Pubns.

— How to Train Your Golden Retriever. LC 99-205966. (How to Train Ser.). (Illus.). 96p. 1998. 9.95 (0-7938-3650-6) TFH Pubns.

— How to Train Your Labrador Retriever. (How to Train Ser.). (Illus.). 96p. 9.95 (0-7938-3652-2) TFH Pubns.

— How to Train Your Rottweiler. (How to Train Ser.). (Illus.). 96p. 9.95 (0-7938-3653-0) TFH Pubns.

— How to Train Your Siberian Husky. (How to Train Ser.). (Illus.). 96p. 9.95 (0-7938-3654-9) TFH Pubns.

Palika, Liz. Love on a Leash: Giving Joy to Others Through Pet Therapy. Ohala, Catherine, ed. LC 94-3877. (Illus.). 176p. 1996. pap. 14.95 (0-931866-76-6) Alpine Pubns.

— Raising a Puppy. (Complete Idiot's Guides (Lifestyle) Ser.). 1998. pap. write for info. (1-58245-040-4) Macmillan Gen Ref.

— Save That Dog! LC 97-6183. (Illus.). 128p. 1997. 9.95 (0-87605-407-6) Howell Bks.

***Palika, Liz.** What Your Bird Needs. LC 00-8257. (What Your Pet Needs Ser.). 2000. 4.95 (0-7894-6310-5) DK Pub Inc.

— What Your Cat Needs. LC 00-8260. (What Your Pet Needs Ser.). (Illus.). 64p. 2000. 4.95 (0-7894-6308-3) DK Pub Inc.

— What Your Dog Needs. LC 00-8259. (What Your Pet Needs Ser.). 2000. 4.95 (0-7894-6307-5) DK Pub Inc.

— Your Bearded Dragon's Life. 8th ed. 288p. 2000. pap. 14.99 (0-7615-2771-0) Prima Pub.

— Your Boxer's Life: Your Complete Guide to Raising Your Pet from Puppy to Companion. 2000. pap. 14.99 (0-7615-2048-1) Prima Pub.

— Your Iguana's Life. 4th ed. 288p. 2000. pap. 14.99 (0-7615-2623-4) Prima Pub.

Palika, Liz, jt. auth. see Paull, Richard C.

Palim & Power. Jamboree: Communication Activities for Children. (J). 1992. pap. text. write for info. (0-17-555895-7) Addison-Wesley.

Palin, David. Groundwork of Philosophy of Religion. 1986. pap. text 18.95 (0-7162-0418-5) Epworth Pr.

Palin, Michael. Around the World in Eighty Days. LC 94-41914. (Illus.). 262p. 1995. pap. 17.95 (0-912333-39-1) BB&T Inc.

— Around the World in Eighty Days. (Illus.). 256p. 1992. pap. 24.95 (0-563-36213-8, BBC-Parkwest) Parkwest Pubns.

— Around the World in Eighty Days. large type ed. 1991. 27.99 (0-7089-8573-4, Charnwood) Ulverscroft.

— Full Circle. LC 97-14664. 1997. text 29.95 (0-312-16960-4) St Martin.

— Full Circle. 320p. 1999. pap. 16.95 (0-312-19455-2) St Martin.

— Hemingway's Chair. LC 99-174895. 288p. 1998. text 23.95 (0-312-18593-6) St Martin.

— Hemingway's Chair. 2nd ed. 288p. 1999. pap. 12.95 (0-312-20550-3) St Martin.

— Michael Palin's Hemingway Adventure. (Illus.). 255p. 2000. 29.95 (0-312-24399-5, Thomas Dunne) St Martin.

— Pole to Pole: North to South by Camel, River Raft, & Balloon. LC 95-6608. (Illus.). 326p. 1995. pap. 18.95 (0-912333-41-3) BB&T Inc.

— Pole to Pole: With Michael Palin. (Illus.). 320p. 1993. 29.95 (0-563-36283-9, BBC-Parkwest) Parkwest Pubns.

— Ripping Yarns. 1991. pap. 17.95 (0-413-63980-0) Routledge.

Palin, Michael, intro. Happy Holidays: The Golden Age of Railway Posters. (Illus.). 96p. 1998. pap. 19.95 (1-86205-189-5, Pub. by Pavilion Bks Ltd) Trafalgar.

Palin, Michael, jt. auth. see Jones, Terry.

***Palin, Philip J. & Sandhaas, Kari.** Architect for Learning: Utilizing the Internet as an Effective Educational Environment. (Illus.). 126p. 2000. pap. 29.95 (0-9679608-0-0) St Thomas Didymus.

Palin, Poppy. Season of Sorcery: On Becoming a Wise Woman. (Orig.). 1997. pap. 23.95 (1-898307-96-2, Pub. by Capall Bann Pubng) Holmes Pub.

Palin, Roger H. Multinational Military Forces: Problems & Prospects: A European Perspective. LC 95-221020. (Adelphi Papers). 88p. 1995. pap. text 23.00 (0-19-828025-4) OUP.

***Palin, Steve.** The Songs of Birds: Stories & Poems from Many Cultures. 80p. (YA). (gr. 3 up). 2000. 19.95 (1-84148-045-2) Barefoot Bks NY.

Paling, Dennis. Jurisprudence & Legal Theory Sourcebook. 278p. 1992. pap. 100.00 (0-7510-0234-8, Pub. by HLT Pubns) St Mut.

Paling, John. Up to Your Armpits in Alligators? How to Sort Out What Risks Are Worth Worrying About! 2nd rev. ed. LC 97-163011. (Illus.). 176p. 1997. pap., per. 22.50 (0-9642236-6-X) J Paling & Co.

Paling, John & Paling, Sean. Up to Your Armpits in Alligators? How to Sort Out What Risks Are Worth Worrying About! (Illus.). 155p. 1994. pap. 15.00 (0-9642236-0-0) J Paling & Co.

Paling, Sean, jt. auth. see Paling, John.

Paling, Stephen. A Hardware & Software Primer for Librarians: What Your Vendor Forgot to Tell You. LC 98-38884. (Illus.). 216p. 1999. 35.00 (0-8108-3572-X) Scarecrow.

Palingenius, Marcellus. The Zodiake of Life. Googe, Barnabe, tr. LC 48-275. 368p. 1977. reprint ed. 60.00 (0-8201-1214-3) Schol Facsimiles.

Palinski, John A. Oracle Database Construction Kit. LC 97-68697. 1997. 49.99 incl. cd-rom (0-7897-1419-1) Que.

Palis, J. Hyperbolicity & Sensitive Chaotic Dynamics at Homoclinic Bifurcations: Fractal Dimensions & Infinitely Many Attractors in Dynamics. 244p. 1995. pap. text 32.95 (0-521-47572-4) Cambridge U Pr.

Palis, Jacob, Jr., ed. Geometric Dynamics. (Lecture Notes in Mathematics Ser.: Vol. 1007). 827p. 1983. 72.95 (0-387-12336-9) Spr-Verlag.

Palisca, Claude V. Baroque Music. 2nd ed. (History of Music Ser.). (Illus.). 1981. text 19.95 (0-13-055954-7) P-H.

— Baroque Music. 3rd ed. 368p. 1990. pap. 48.00 (0-13-058496-7, 650102) P-H.

— Studies in the History of Italian Music & Music Theory. (Illus.). 534p. 1994. text 59.00 (0-19-816167-0) OUP.

Palisca, Claude V., ed. Musica Enchiriadis: And Scolica Enchiriadis. Erickson, Raymond, tr. from LAT. & intro. by. LC 94-34601. (Music Theory Translation Ser.). 106p. 1995. 35.00 (0-300-05818-7) Yale U Pr.

— The Norton Anthology of Western Music Vol. I: Ancient to Baroque, Vol. 1. 3rd ed. 600p. (C). 1996. pap. 40.50 (0-393-96906-1, Norton Paperbks) Norton.

— The Norton Anthology of Western Music Vol. II: Classic to Modern, Vol. 2. 3rd ed. 800p. (C). 1996. pap. text 40.50 (0-393-96907-X, Norton Paperbks) Norton.

Palisca, Claude V., jt. auth. see Grout, Donald J.

Palisca, Claude V., ed. see Burmeister, Joachim.

Palisca, Claude V., ed. see Gaffurius, Franchinus.

Palisca, Claude V., jt. ed. see Holoman, D. Kern.

Palisca, Claude V., ed. see Vincentino, Nicola.

Palisca, Claude V., tr. see Zarlino, Gioseffo.

Palisono, Robert, ed. see Campbell, Suzann K.

***Palit, Chittabrata.** Tensions in Begal Rural Society: Landlords, Planters & Colonial Rule 1830-1860. 1998. 28.00 (81-250-0684-2, Pub. by Orient Longman Ltd) S Asia.

Palit, D. K. War in High Himalaya: The Indian Army in Crisis, 1962. (C). 1991. 30.00 (81-7062-138-0, Pub. by Lancer International) S Asia.

Palitz, Wendy, jt. ed. see Robbins, Michael.

Paliwal, Bhudatt & Herbert, Donald, eds. Volume & Kinetics in Tumor Control & Normal Tissue Complications No. 10: AAPM Proceedings of the 5th International Conference on Dose, Time, & Fractionation in Radiation Oncology. LC 98-66138. 500p. 1998. pap. write for info. (1-888340-11-8) AAPM.

Paliwal, Bhudatt R. Therapy Physics Review Pt. 1: Basic Physics Examination & Study Guide. 65p. (Orig.). 1996. spiral bd. 24.95 (0-944838-67-7) Med Physics Pub.

Paliwal, Bhudatt R., et al, eds. Biological, Physical & Clinical Aspects of Hyperthermia: Proceedings of the 1987 AAPM - NAHG Hyperthermia School Held at the Sheraton University Center, Durham, North Carolina, April 27-May 1, 1987. (American Association of Physicists in Medicine Symposium Ser.: No. 16). 483p. 1988. 75.00 (0-88318-558-X, Pub. by Am Inst Physics) Med Physics Pub.

— Optimization of Cancer Radiotherapy: Proceedings of the 2nd International Conference on Dose, Time Fractionation in Radiation Oncology Held at the University of Wisconsin, Madison, Wisconsin, September 12-14, 1984. (American Association of Physicists in Medicine Symposium Ser.: No. 5). 560p. 1985. 45.00 (0-88318-483-4, Pub. by Am Inst Physics) Med Physics Pub.

— Prediction of Response in Radiation Therapy, Pts. 1 & 2: Proceedings of the Third International Conference on Dose, Time & Fractionation Held at the University of Wisconsin, Madison, Wisconsin, September 14-17, 1988, Pt. 1. (American Association of Physicists in Medicine Symposium Ser.: No. 7). 770p. 1989. 60.00 (0-685-72476-X, Pub. by Am Inst Physics) Med Physics Pub.

— Prediction of Response in Radiation Therapy, Pts. 1 & 2: Proceedings of the Third International Conference on Dose, Time & Fractionation Held at the University of Wisconsin, Madison, Wisconsin, September 14-17, 1988, Pt. 2. 770p. 1989. text. write for info. (0-318-68430-6, Pub. by Am Inst Physics) Med Physics Pub.

Paliwal, C. D., tr. see Stutterheim, Willem.

Paliwal, G. S. The Vegetational Wealth of Himalaya. (C). 1988. 40.00 (0-7855-2255-7, Pub. by Scientific) St Mut.

Paliwal, K. K., jt. ed. see Kleijn, W. B.

Paliwal, K. V., ed. Pesticidal Pollution of Environment & Control: An Annotated Bibliography. 594p. 1994. pap. 375.00 (81-85880-23-9, Pub. by Print Hse) St Mut.

Paliwal, M. R. Social Change & Education. 1985. 30.00 (0-8364-1255-9, Pub. by Uppal Pub Hse) S Asia.

Paliwal, Rajesh K. Janata Phase in Indian Politics. 200p. 1986. 31.00 (81-7032-026-7, Pub. by Manohar) S Asia.

Paliwala, A. H., jt. auth. see Chalmers, Dalzell R.

Paliwala, Abdul, jt. ed. see Adelman, Sammy.

Paliwoda & Thomas. International Marketing. 768p. Date not set. pap. text 34.95 (0-7506-2241-5) Buttrwrth-Heinemann.

Paliwoda, Stan, ed. see EMC Staff.

Paliwoda, Stanley J., ed. New Perspectives on International Marketing. 272p. (C). (gr. 13). 1991. pap. 75.95 (0-415-05344-7, A5117) Thomson Learn.

Paliwoda, Stanley J. & Ryans, John K., Jr., eds. International Marketing Reader. LC 94-43146. 288p. (C). 1995. pap. 20.99 (0-415-10039-9, C0481) Thomson Learn.

— International Marketing Reader. LC 94-43146. 288p. (C). (gr. 13). 1995. pap. 86.95 (0-415-11400-4, C0417) Thomson Learn.

Paliwoda, Stanley J., jt. ed. see Turnbull, Peter W.

Paliyenko, Adrianna M. Mis-Reading the Creative Impulse: The Poetic Subject in Rimbaud & Claudel, Restaged. LC 96-35091. 1997. 34.95 (0-8093-2122-X) S Ill U Pr.

Palk, N. Iron Age Bridle Bits from Britain. (Illus.). 109p. 1984. pap. 16.00 (0-614-21827-6) David Brown.

Palka, B. P. An Introduction to Complex Function Theory. rev. ed. Ewing, J. H. 117 et al et al, eds. (Undergraduate Texts in Mathematics Ser.). (Illus.). 559p. 1995. 42.95 (0-387-97427-X) Spr-Verlag.

***Palka, Eugene J.** Valued Landscapes of the Far North: A Geographic Journey Through Denali National Park. LC 99-49769. 160p. 2000. pap. 24.95 (0-8476-9823-8); text 65.00 (0-8476-9822-X) Rowman.

***Palka, Joel W.** Historical Dictionary of Mesoamerica. LC 99-87307. (Historical Dictionaries of Ancient Civilizations & Historical Eras Ser.: No. 2). (Illus.). 296p. 2000. 59.50 (0-8108-3715-3) Scarecrow.

Palkhivala, B. A. Tax Audit Manual. 2nd ed. (C). 1989. 460.00 (0-7855-4726-6) St Mut.

Palkhivala, Nani A. We, the Nation: The Lost Decades. (C). 1994. 9.50 (81-85944-90-3, Pub. by UBS Pubs Dist) S Asia.

Palkhivala, Nani A. We, the Nation: The Lost Decades. 1994. reprint ed. 20.00 (81-86112-00-6, Pub. by UBS Pubs) S Asia.

Palko, Hilda, jt. auth. see Palko, Tom.

Palko, Tom & Palko, Hilda. Glencoe Medical Laboratory Procedures. LC 97-46117. (Allied Health Ser.). 1997. pap. 14.00 (0-02-802015-4) Glencoe.

— Glencoe Medical Laboratory Procedures. 2nd ed. LC 97-46117. (Allied Health Ser.). 1997. 30.00 (0-02-802014-6) Glencoe.

— Laboratory Procedures for the Medical Office. LC 94-22538. (Illus.). 1995. 34.87 (0-02-800065-X) Glencoe.

Palkovic & Cauthen. Index to Cd Record Reviews, 1987-1997. 1998. 300.00 (0-7838-8191-6) Mac Lib Ref.

Palkovic, Cauthen. Index to CD & Record Reviews 1987-1997 , Vol. 3. 1999. 150.00 (0-7838-8487-7) Mac Lib Ref.

Palkovic, Mark, ed. & tr. see Zingel, Hans J.

Palkovich, Ann M. Pueblo Population & Society: The Arroyo Hondo Skeletal & Mortuary Remains. LC 80-51310. (Arroyo Hondo Archaeological Ser.: Vol. 3). (Illus.). 194p. 1981. pap. 14.95 (0-933452-03-9) Schol Am Res.

Palkovits, M. Topographical Anatomy of Neuropeptides in the Rat Brain. 1992. write for info. (0-8493-6270-9, CRC Reprint) Franklin.

Palkovits, M., jt. auth. see Mitro, A.

Palkovits, Miklos & Brownstein. Maps & Guide to Microdissection of the Rat Brain. (Illus.). 262p. (C). 1987. pap. text 70.00 (0-8385-6159-4, A6159-6, Apple Lange Med) McGraw.

Palkovitz, Robin J. & Sussman, Marvin B., eds. Transitions to Parenthood. LC 88-853. (Marriage & Family Review Ser.: Vol. 12, Nos. 3-4). (Illus.). 396p. 1989. text 49.95 (0-86656-787-9) Haworth Pr.

Palkus, Vitalij, jt. auth. see Bochorishvili, Natalia.

Pall, Ellen. Among the Ginzburgs: A Novel. LC 95-43972. 256p. 1996. 22.95 (0-944072-61-5) Zoland Bks.

Pall, Gabriel A. Process-Centered Enterprise: The Power of Commitments. LC 99-48848. 325p. 1999. boxed set 29.95 (1-57444-239-2) St Lucie Pr.

Palla, L., jt. ed. see Horvath, Z.

Palla, Marco. Mussolini & Fascism. LC 99-44263. (Illustrated Histories Ser.). (Illus.). 160p. 2000. pap. 15.00 (1-56656-340-2) Interlink Pub.

Palladin, Aleksandr V., et al. Protein Metabolism of the Brain. Haigh, Basill, tr. from RUS. LC 77-2307. (Studies in Soviet Science). (Illus.). 347p. 1977. reprint ed. pap. 107.60 (0-608-05495-X, 206596400006) Bks Demand.

Palladino. Annual Editions: Abnormal Psychology. 256p. (C). 1995. per. write for info. (1-56134-440-0) Brown & Benchmark.

Palladino, Anita, ed. Diary of a Yankee Engineer: The Civil War Story of John Henry Westervelt. LC 96-42521. (North's Civil War Ser.: No. 1). (Illus.). xxiv, 265p. 1996. 27.00 (0-8232-1724-8) Fordham.

Palladino, Connie. Developing Self-Esteem: A Guide for Positive Success. rev. ed. Crisp, Michael, ed. LC 93-74054. (Fifty-Minute Ser.). (Illus.). 114p. (Orig.). 1994. pap. 10.95 (1-56052-261-5) Crisp Pubns.

— Developing Self-Esteem for Students: A Guide for Personal Success. Crisp, Michael, ed. LC 93-74716. (Fifty-Minute Ser.). (Illus.). 96p. (Orig.). 1994. pap. 10.95 (1-56052-289-5) Crisp Pubns.

Palladino, Grace. Another Civil War: Labor, Capital, & the State in Anthracite Regions of Pennsylvania, 1840 to 1868. (Working Class in American History Ser.). 216p. 1990. text 26.50 (0-252-01671-8) U of Ill Pr.

Palladino, Grace, jt. ed. see Albert, Peter J.

Palladino, Joseph J. Abnormal Psychology, '98/'99. 3rd ed. (Annual Ser.). (Illus.). 240p. 1998. pap. text 12.25 (0-697-39126-4, Dshkn McG-Hill) McGrw-H Hghr Educ.

— Abnormal Psychology 97/98. 2nd ed. (Annual Ser.). 256p. (C). 1997. pap. text 11.75 (0-697-37196-4, Dshkn McG-Hill) McGrw-H Hghr Educ.

Palladino, Joseph J., jt. auth. see Davis, Stephen F.

Palladino, Judith & Jeffries, Ruth. The Occupational Therapy Fieldwork Manual for Assessing Professional Skills. 80p. 2000. pap. text 24.95 (0-8036-0556-0) Davis Co.

***Palladino, Lawrence.** The Coeur d'Alen Reservation: Our Friends the Coeur d'Aleine Indians. 51p. 2000. reprint ed. pap. 8.95 (0-87770-711-1) Ye Galleon.

Palladino, Leo & Hunt, June. The Nail File. (Illus.). 154p. 1992. pap. text 22.95 (0-333-52584-1) Scholium Intl.

Palladino, Lucy J. Dreamers, Discoverers & D[...] 336p. 1999. pap. 14.00 (0-345-40573-0) Bal[...] Grp.

— The Edison Trait: Eight Steps for Raising Succes[...] Dreamers,Discovers & Dynamos. LC 96-37660[...] 1997. 24.00 (0-8129-2737-0) Random.

Palladino, Paulo. Entomology, Ecology & Agriculture:[...] Making of Scientific Careers in North America, 1885-1985. 208p. 1996. text 35.00 (3-7186-5907-7, Harwood Acad Pubs) Gordon & Breach.

Palladio, Andrea. The Four Books of Architecture. Taverno[...] Robert & Scholfield, Richard, trs. from ITA. LC 96-36406. (Illus.). 472p. 1997. 55.00 (0-262-16162-1) MIT Pr.

— The Four Books of Architecture. 1990. 29.00 (0-8446-5464-7) Peter Smith.

— Four Books of Architecture. Ware, Isaac, ed. 110p. 1965. pap. text 15.95 (0-486-21308-0) Dover.

— I'Quattro Libri dell'Architettura. (Illus.). iv, 312p. 1979. reprint ed. write for info. (3-487-06824-9) G Olms Pubs.

Palladius. The Lausiac History. (Ancient Christian Writers Ser.: No. 34). 1985. 34.95 (0-8091-0083-5) Paulist Pr.

— Life of St. Moses the Black. 1990. pap. 1.00 (0-89981-113-2) Eastern Orthodox.

— Spiritual Struggles of the Early Ascetics. 1991. pap. 2.95 (0-89981-115-9) Eastern Orthodox.

Palladius, Rutilius T. Palladius on Husbondrie. Lodge, Barton & Herrtage, S. J., eds. (EETS, OS Ser.: No. 52, 72). 1974. reprint ed. 63.00 (0-527-00047-7) Periodicals Srv.

Pallady, Stephen. Irony in the Poetry of Jose de Espronceda, 1834-1842. LC 90-44200. (Hispanic Literature Ser.: Vol. 8). 184p. 1991. lib. bdg. 79.95 (0-88946-227-5) E Mellen.

Pallain, Georges M. The Correspondence of Prince Tallyrand & King Louis XVIII During the Congress of Vienna. LC 70-126616. (Europe 1815-1945 Ser.). 654p. 1973. reprint ed. lib. bdg. 69.50 (0-306-70047-6) Da Capo.

Pallais, Don, et al. Guide to Auditor's Reports, 2 vols. Incl. Vol. 1. 1997. ring bd. 156.00 (0-7646-0339-6); Vol. 2. 1997. ring bd. 156.00 (0-7646-0340-X); 150.00 (0-7646-0055-9) Prctnrs Pub Co.

Pallais, Don, et al. Guide to Auditor's Reports, 2 vols. Incl. Vol. 1. 1997. ring bd. 156.00 (0-7646-0339-6); Vol. 2. 1997. ring bd. 156.00 (0-7646-0340-X); 150.00 (0-7646-0338-8) Prctnrs Pub Co.

Pallais, Don, et al. Guide to Forecasts & Projections, 3 vols. Incl. Vol. 1. 1997. ring bd. (0-7646-0164-4); Vol. 2. 1997. ring bd. (0-7646-0165-2); Vol. 3. 1997. ring bd. (0-7646-0166-0); 156.00 (0-7646-0163-6) Prctnrs Pub Co.

— Guide To Forecasts & Projections, 3 vols. Incl. Vol. 1. 1998. ring bd. 164.00 (0-7646-0407-4); Vol. 2. 1998. ring bd. 164.00 (0-7646-0408-2); Vol. 3. 1998. ring bd. 164.00 (0-7646-0409-0); 164.00 (0-7646-0406-6) Prctnrs Pub Co.

***Pallais, Don, et al.** PPC's Practitioners Update, Vol. 1. 1998. ring bd. 135.00 (0-7646-0601-8) Prctnrs Pub Co.

Pallais, Don M., et al. Guide to Non-Traditional Engagements, 3 vols. Incl. Vol. 1. 1997. ring bd. (0-7646-0086-9); Vol. 2. 1997. ring bd. (0-7646-0087-7); Vol. 3. 1997. ring bd. (0-7646-0088-5); 150.00 (0-7646-0085-0) Prctnrs Pub Co.

***Pallais, Don M., et al.** Guide to Nontraditional Engagements, 3 vols. 1999. ring bd. 164.00i (0-7646-0911-4) Prctnrs Pub Co.

— Guide to Nontraditional Engagements, Vol. 1. 1999. ring bd. write for info. (0-7646-0912-2) Prctnrs Pub Co.

— Guide to Nontraditional Engagements, Vol. 2. 1999. ring bd. write for info. (0-7646-0913-0) Prctnrs Pub Co.

— Guide to Nontraditional Engagements, Vol. 3. 1999. ring bd. write for info. (0-7646-0945-9) Prctnrs Pub Co.

Pallak, Michael S. & Perloff, Robert, eds. Psychology & Work: Productivity, Change, & Employment. LC 86-7952. (Master Lectures: Vol. 5). 220p. (Orig.). 1986. pap. 24.95 (0-912704-48-9) Am Psychol.

Pallak, Michael S. & Perloff, Robert O., eds. Psychology & Work: Productivity, Change, & Employment. LC 86-7952. (Master Lectures). (Illus.). 224p. (Orig.). reprint ed. pap. 69.50 (0-608-09011-5, 206964600005) Bks Demand.

Pallamary, Matthew J. Land Without Evil. unabridged ed. LC 99-33503. 352p. 2000. 24.95 (0-912880-09-0) Charles Pub.

— The Small Dark Room of the Soul: And Other Stories. LC 94-67377. 150p. (Orig.). 1994. pap. 14.95 (1-885516-00-2) SD Writs Mnthly.

Pallandt, Nicolas Van, see Abrams, Michael D.

Pallant, N. Brighton to Portsmouth Line. (C). 1985. 39.00 (0-85361-279-X) St Mut.

— Gravesend West Branch. (C). 1985. 39.00 (0-85361-307-9) St Mut.

Pallanti, Giuseppe. La Maremma Senese Nella Crisi Del Seicento. Bruchey, Stuart, ed. LC 80-2820. (Dissertations in European Economic History Ser.).Tr. of Sienese Maremma in the Crisis of the Seventeenth Century. (Illus.). 1981. lib. bdg. 23.95 (0-405-14004-5) Ayer.

Pallardi, Stephen G., jt. auth. see Kozlowski, Theodore T.

Pallardy, Stephen G., jt. ed. see Kozlowski, Theodore T.

Pallares, Eduardo. Diccionario de Derecho Procesal Civil. (SPA.). 877p. 37.50 (0-7859-0710-6, S-12340) Fr & Eur.

— Diccionario Teorico y Practico del Juicio de Amparo. (SPA.). 321p. 24.95 (0-7859-0717-3, S-21916) Fr & Eur.

Pallares, Jose C. A Poor Man Called Jesus: Reflections on the Gospel of Mark. Barr, Robert R., tr. from SPA. LC 85-15339. 144p. reprint ed. pap. 44.70 (0-7837-6974-1, 204678500004) Bks Demand.

Pallaro, Patrizia, ed. see Whitehouse, Mary, et al.

... of Education &

... nalog Signal
... 105.00
... Wiley.
... ol. 1. 2nd ed. 480p. (C).
... Wiley.
... nsors & Signal Conditioning.
... 98.95 (*0-471-54565-1*) Wiley.
... ier. LC 95-76651. 32p. (J). (ps-1).
... *403-23-X*) Good Growing Bks.
... ulator Puzzles, Tricks & Games. 81st ed.
... ap. 3.95 (*0-486-26670-2*) Dover.
... Codes & Ciphers. LC 94-12569. (Illus.).
...). (gr. 4-7). 1994. pap. text 3.95 (*0-486-28209-0*)
... er.

..., P. S. Travels Through the Southern Provinces of the Russian Empire Performed in the Years 1793 & 1794, 2 vols., 1. LC 72-115573. (Russia Observed, Series I). 1970. reprint ed. 35.95 (*0-405-03238-2*) Ayer.

— Travels Through the Southern Provinces of the Russian Empire Performed in the Years 1793 & 1794, 2 vols., Set. LC 72-115573. (Russia Observed, Series I). 1971. reprint ed. 66.95 (*0-405-03055-X*) Ayer.

— Travels Through the Southern Provinces of the Russian Empire Performed in the Years 1793 & 1794, 2 vols., Vol. 2. LC 72-115573. (Russia Observed, Series I). 1970. reprint ed. 35.95 (*0-405-03239-0*) Ayer.

Pallasama, Juhani. The Melnikhov House, Moscow, 1927 - 1929. 81p. 1996. pap. 25.00 (*1-85490-413-2*, Pub. by Wiley) Wiley.

Pallasch, Thomas J. & Oksas, Richard M. Synopsis of Pharmacology for Students in Dentistry. LC 74-8951. 152p. reprint ed. 47.20 (*0-8357-9422-9*, 201457100093) Bks Demand.

Pallaschke, D., jt. ed. see Neumann, K.

Pallaschke, D., jt. ed. see Oettli, W.

Pallaschke, Diethard & Rolewicz, Stefan. Foundations of Mathematical Optimization: Convex Analysis Without Linearity. LC 96-52453. (Mathematics & Its Applications Ser.). 1997. text 264.50 (*0-7923-4424-3*) Kluwer Academic.

Pallasmaa, Juhani. The Eyes of the Skin. LC 96-210446. (New Polemics Ser.). 59p. 1996. pap. 15.95 (*1-85490-439-6*) Academy Ed UK.

Pallavicini, R., ed. Hot Thin Plasmas in Astrophysics. (C). 1988. text 218.00 (*90-277-2812-7*) Kluwer Academic.

Pallavicini, Roberto & Dupree, Andrea K., eds. Cool Stars, Stellar Systems, & the Sun Vol. 109: 9th Cambridge Workshop. (ASP Conference Series Proceedings). 832p. 1996. 34.00 (*1-886733-29-5*) Astron Soc Pacific.

Pallavicino, Ferrante. Whore's Rhetoric. 1961. 10.95 (*0-8392-1132-5*) Astor-Honor.

Pallay, Steven G., compiled by. Cross Index Title Guide to Classical Music, 12. LC 86-25723. (Music Reference Collection: No. 12). 215p. 1987. lib. bdg. 65.00 (*0-313-25531-8*, PCR/, Greenwood Pr) Greenwood.

Pallay, Steven G., ed. Cross Index Title Guide to Opera & Operetta, 19. LC 89-2131. (Music Reference Collection: No. 19). 222p. 1989. lib. bdg. 55.00 (*0-313-25622-5*, PCX, Greenwood Pr) Greenwood.

Pallen, Conde B. Meaning of the Idylls of the King. LC 65-26453. (Studies in Tennyson: No. 27). (C). 1969. reprint ed. lib. bdg. 75.00 (*0-8383-0607-1*) M S G Haskell Hse.

Pallen, Conde B., tr. see Salvany, Feliz S.

Pallen, Conte B. Crucible Island. 1972. 59.95 (*0-87968-971-4*) Gordon Pr.

Pallen, Mark, ed. Guide to the Internet. 2nd ed. (Illus.). 15p. 1998. pap. text 9.00 (*0-7279-1255-0*, Pub. by BMJ Pub) Login Brothers Bk Co.

Pallen, Thomas A., tr. see Vasari, Giorgio.

Palleros, Daniel. Experimental Organic Chemistry. (C). 1998. text, lab manual ed. write for info. (*0-8053-0560-2*) Addison-Wesley.

Palleros, Daniel R. Experimental Organic Chemistry. LC 99-35417. 864p. 2000. text 92.95 (*0-471-28250-2*) Wiley.

Pallet. Aircraft Instruments. 2nd ed. 1988. pap. text. write for info. (*0-582-01898-6*, Pub. by Addison-Wesley) Longman.

***Pallett-Chiarolli, Maria.** Someone You Know: A Friend's Farewell. 240p. 2000. pap. 14.95 (*1-86254-271-6*, Pub. by Wakefield Pr) BHB Intl.

Pallett, E. H. Aircraft Electrical Systems. 3rd ed. (C). 1987. pap. 82.95 (*0-582-98819-5*, Pub. by Addison-Wesley) Longman.

— Automatic Flight Control. 4th ed. LC 93-25282. 320p. 1993. pap. 49.95 (*0-632-03495-5*) Blackwell Sci.

Pallett, Simon, jt. auth. see Lewis, Dave.

Pallette, Earla. Down the Lonely Heartbreak Road. 272p. 1999. pap. 14.95 (*0-7392-0262-6*) Morris Pubng.

Palley, Howard A. & Oktay, Julianne S., eds. The Chronically Limited Elderly: The Case for a National Policy for In-Home & Supportive Community-Based Services. LC 83-10686. (Home Health Care Services Quarterly Ser.: Vol. 4, No. 2). 142p. 1983. text 39.95 (*0-86656-236-2*) Haworth Pr.

Palley, Julian. Bestiary. (Illus.). 53p. 1987. pap. write for info. (*0-9624205-7-3*) Inevitable Pr.

— Family Portraits: Poems, 1989-1993. 80p. 1994. pap. write for info. (*0-9624205-6-5*) Inevitable Pr.

— Pictures at an Exhibition: Poems. 88p. (Orig.). 1989. pap. 6.00 (*0-9624205-0-6*) Inevitable Pr.

Palley, Julian, ed. Best New Chicano Literature 1986. 84p. 1986. pap. 9.00 (*0-916950-66-2*) Biling Rev-Pr.

— Best New Chicano Literature, 1989. 126p. 1989. pap. 11.00 (*0-927534-01-0*) Biling Rev-Pr.

Palley, Julian, tr. see Castellanos, Rosario.

Palley, Marian L., jt. auth. see Gelb, Joyce.

Palley, Marian L., jt. ed. see Galb, Joyce.

Palley, Marian L., jt. ed. see Preston, Michael.

Palley, Reese. There Be No Dragons: How to Cross a Big Ocean in a Small Sailboat. (Illus.). 224p. 1996. 24.95 (*1-57409-010-0*) Sheridan.

— Unlikely Passages. LC 97-52028. (Illus.). 192p. 1998. pap. 14.95 (*1-57409-051-8*) Sheridan.

— Unlikely People. LC 98-39617. 224p. (Orig.). 1998. pap. 16.50 (*1-57409-057-7*) Sheridan.

Palley, Thomas I. Plenty of Nothing: The Downsizing of the American Dream & the Case for Structural Keynesianism. LC 97-34907. 227p. 1998. 27.95 (*0-691-04847-9*, Pub. by Princeton U Pr) Cal Prin Full Svc.

***Palley, Thomas I.** Plenty of Nothing: The Downsizing of the American Dream & the Case for Structural Keynesianism. (Illus.). 240p. 2000. pap. 16.95 (*0-691-05031-7*) Princeton U Pr.

Palliakarakis, N., ed. Information Exchange of Medical Devices. LC 95-8174. (Studies in Health Technology & Informatics: Vol. 28). 200p. (YA). (gr. 12). 1996. 95.00 (*90-5199-249-1*, 249-1) IOS Press.

Palliere, Aime. The Unknown Sanctuary. Wise, Louise W., tr. LC 79-150294. 243p. 1985. pap. 9.95 (*0-8197-0498-9*) Bloch.

Pallikaris, Ioannis & Siganos, Dimitrios. Lasik. LC 97-37263. (Illus.). 384p. 1997. text 149.00 (*1-55642-323-3*, 63233) SLACK Inc.

Pallikaris, Ioannis, jt. auth. see Agarwal, Sunita.

Pallin, Paddy. Never Truly Lost: A Bushwalker's Life. 224p. 1996. reprint ed. pap. 19.95 (*0-86840-194-3*, Pub. by New South Wales Univ Pr) Intl Spec Bk.

Palling, Bruce. India: A Literary Companion. (Illus.). 272p. 1993. pap. 24.95 (*0-7195-5183-8*, Pub. by John Murray) Trafalgar.

Pallingston, Jessica. Lipstick. LC 98-27749. (Illus.). 228p. 1998. text 17.95 (*0-312-19914-7*) St Martin.

***Pallis.** The Big Book of Air & Space Flight. 1999. 14.95 (*0-07-134820-4*) McGraw.

Pallis, M., tr. see Schuon, Frithjof.

Pallis, Marco. A Buddhist Spectrum. 175p. 1980. 23.95 (*0-04-294116-4*, Pub. by SRI Lanka) S Perennis.

— Peaks & Lamas. 1975. lib. bdg. 300.00 (*0-87968-327-9*) Gordon Pr.

— Way & the Mountain. 226p. 1991. pap. 22.00 (*0-7206-0841-4*) Dufour.

Pallis, Michael, tr. see Ghassemlou, A. R., et al.

Pallis, Svend A. The Antiquity of Iraq. LC 78-72755. (Ancient Mesopotamian Texts & Studies). reprint ed. 37.50 (*0-404-18199-6*) AMS Pr.

— The Babylonian Akitu Festival. LC 78-72756. (Ancient Mesopotamian Texts & Studies). reprint ed. 42.50 (*0-404-18203-8*) AMS Pr.

Palliser, Bury. History of Lace. enl. rev. ed. (Illus.). 672p. 1984. reprint ed. pap. 19.95 (*0-486-24742-2*) Dover.

Palliser, Charles. The Quincunx. 800p. 1991. reprint ed. pap. 16.00 (*0-345-37113-5*) Ballantine Pub Grp.

***Palliser, Charles.** The Unburied. LC 99-14740. 400p. 1999. 24.00 (*0-374-28035-5*) FS&G.

— The Unburied. large type ed. LC 00-23381. (Basic Ser.). 2000. 29.95 (*0-7862-2543-2*) Thorndike Pr.

— The Unburied. 416p. 2000. reprint ed. 13.95 (*0-7434-1051-3*) PB.

***Palliser, D. M., ed.** The Cambridge Urban History of Britain Vol. 1: c. 600 - c. 1540. (Illus.). 822p. 2000. 125.00 (*0-521-44461-6*) Cambridge U Pr.

Palliser, David. York Company of Merchant Adventurers. (C). 1990. 30.00 (*0-7855-5099-2*, Pub. by W Sessions) St Mut.

Palliser, David & Palliser, Mary. York As They Saw It. 1999. pap. 21.00 (*0-900657-45-6*, Pub. by W Sessions) St Mut.

Palliser, David, jt. auth. see Rees, Yvonne.

Palliser, David M. Age Elizabeth 1547 1603. 2nd ed. 516p. (C). 1995. pap. 44.00 (*0-582-01322-4*, 79279) Addison-Wesley.

Palliser, Margaret A. Christ, Our Mother of Mercy: Divine Mercy & Compassion in the Theology of the Shewings of Julian of Norwich. LC 92-24301. xiv, 262p. (C). 1992. lib. bdg. 129.25 (*3-11-013558-2*) De Gruyter.

Palliser, Mary, jt. auth. see Palliser, David.

Palliser Palliser & Co Staff. American Victorian Cottage Homes. 112p. 1990. pap. 8.95 (*0-486-26506-4*) Dover.

Pallister, C. & Dunn, C., eds. Progress in Haematology No. 2. (Illus.). 208p. 1999. pap. text 45.00 (*1-900151-79-0*) OUP.

***Pallister, Chris.** Haematology. LC 99-13003. 262p. 1999. pap. text 40.00 (*0-7506-2457-4*) Buttrwrth-Heinemann.

Pallister, Chris, et al, eds. Introduction to Medical Laboratory Technology. 7th ed. LC 97-48992. (Illus.). 456p. 2000. pap. text 75.00 (*0-7506-2190-7*) Buttrwrth-Heinemann.

Pallister, Christopher J. Blood: Physiology & Pathophysiology. LC 95-103064. 384p. 1994. text 53.00 (*0-7506-0581-2*) Buttrwrth-Heinemann.

Pallister, Jan. Confrontations. Westburg, John E., ed. LC 76-29602. (Illus.). 1976. pap. 6.00 (*0-87423-022-5*) Westburg.

Pallister, Janis L. The Cinema of Quebec: Masters in Their Own House. LC 94-43507. (Illus.). 608p. 1995. 59.50 (*0-8386-3562-8*) Fairleigh Dickinson.

— French-Speaking Women Film Directors: A Guide. LC 97-8224. (Illus.). 256p. 1997. 40.00 (*0-8386-3736-1*) Fairleigh Dickinson.

Pallister, Janis L., tr. see Pare, Ambroise.

Pallister, John C. In the Steps of the Great American Entomologist, Frank Eugene Lutz. Forbes, John R., ed. (In the Steps of the Great American Naturalists Ser.). (Illus.). 127p. 1976. reprint ed. 3.95 (*0-916544-10-9*) Natural Sci Youth.

***Pallister, Kay, ed.** Vanessa Beecroft: VB 43. (Illus.). 75p. 2000. write for info. (*1-880154-39-0*) Gagosian Gallery.

Pallister, Kay, ed. see Joselit, David.

Pallman, David. Programming Bots, Spiders & Intelligent Agents in Microsoft Visual C++ LC 99-10774. 500p. 1999. pap. 49.99 (*0-7356-0565-3*) Microsoft.

Palloff, Rena M. & Pratt, Keith. Building Learning Communities in Cyberspace: Effective Strategies for the Online Classroom. LC 98-58077. (Higher & Adult Education Ser.). 1999. pap. 29.95 (*0-7879-4460-2*) Jossey-Bass.

Pallone, Nathaniel, ed. Altruism, Narcissism, Comity: Research Perspectives from Current Psychology. LC 98-33870. 200p. 1999. pap. 24.95 (*0-7658-0467-0*) Transaction Pubs.

Pallone, Nathaniel, jt. auth. see Hennessy, James.

Pallone, Nathaniel J. Mental Disorder among Prisoners: Toward an Epidemiologic Inventory. 186p. (C). 1990. 39.95 (*0-88738-383-1*) Transaction Pubs.

— On the Social Utility of Psychopathology: A Deviant Majority & Its Keepers. 110p. 1985. 34.95 (*0-88738-048-4*) Transaction Pubs.

— Rehabilitating Criminal Sexual Psychopaths: Legislative Mandates, Clinical Quandries. 140p. 1990. 34.95 (*0-88738-340-8*) Transaction Pubs.

***Pallone, Nathaniel J., ed.** Race, Ethnicity, Sexual Orientation, Violent Crime: The Realities & the Myths. LC 99-87451. 181p. (C). 1999. 49.95 (*0-7890-0968-4*); pap. text 29.95 (*0-7890-0986-2*) Haworth Pr.

Pallone, Nathaniel J., ed. Young Victims, Young Offenders. LC 94-31967. (Journal of Offender Rehabilitation). (Illus.). 252p. 1994. lib. bdg. 49.95 (*1-56024-703-7*) Haworth Pr.

Pallone, Nathaniel J. & Hennessy, James J. Criminal Behavior: A Process Psychology Analysis. 436p. (C). 1992. 34.95 (*1-56000-044-9*) Transaction Pubs.

— Criminal Behavior: A Process Psychology Analysis. 436p. (C). 1994. pap. 29.95 (*1-56000-729-X*) Transaction Pubs.

Pallone, Nathaniel J. & Hennessy, James J., eds. Fraud & Fallible Judgment: Deception in the Social & Behavioral Sciences. LC 94-46395. 150p. 1995. pap. 21.95 (*1-56000-813-X*) Transaction Pubs.

Pallone, Nathaniel J., jt. ed. see Chaneles, Sol.

Pallone, Nathaniel J., jt. ed. see Hillbrand, Marc.

Pallot, James, ed. The Motion Picture Guide 1995 Annual: The Films of 1994. 600p. 1997. 99.50 (*0-933997-35-3*) CineBks.

— The Motion Picture Guide, 1993 Annual: The Films of 1992. 635p. 1993. 99.50 (*0-918432-95-2*) CineBks.

— The Motion Picture Guide 1992 Annual: The Films of 1991. (Illus.). 593p. 1992. 99.50 (*0-918432-93-6*) CineBks.

***Pallot, Judith.** Land Reform in Russia, 1906-1917: Peasant Responses to Stolypin's Project of Rural Transformation. LC 98-33244. (Illus.). 272p. 1999. text 75.00 (*0-19-820656-9*) OUP.

Pallot, Judith. Transforming Peasants: Society, State & the Peasantry, 1861-1930: Selected Papers from the 5th World Congress of Central & East European Studies. LC 97-49890. 278p. 1998. text 69.95 (*0-312-21349-2*) St Martin.

Pallot, Judith & Shaw, Denis J. Landscape & Settlement in Romanov Russia, 1613 to 1917. (Illus.). 336p. 1990. text 75.00 (*0-19-823246-2*) OUP.

Pallot, Marc & Sandoval, Victor. Concurrent Enterprising: Toward the Concurrent Enterprise in the Era of the Internet & Electronic Commerce, Vol. 449. LC 98-23430. (Kluwer International Series in Engineering & Computer Science). 1998. 135.00 (*0-7923-8172-6*) Kluwer Academic.

Pallot, William, jt. auth. see Callard, Lloyd.

Pallotta, Jerry. Airplane Alphabet Book. (Illus.). (J). 1997. 12.40 (*0-606-18020-6*) Turtleback.

— The Big Engine: Counting on the Big Engine. large type ed. (The Big Engine: 1). 12p. (J). (ps). 2000. 7.99 (*0-9700383-0-5*) Great Trn Stores.

Pallotta, Jerry. The Bird Alphabet Book. LC 89-60423. (Jerry Pallotta's Alphabet Bks.). (Illus.). 32p. (J). (ps-3). 1989. 15.95 (*0-88106-457-2*); pap. 6.95 (*0-88106-451-3*) Charlesbridge Pub.

— The Boat Alphabet Book. LC 97-39442. (Illus.). (J). 1998. 15.95 (*0-88106-910-8*) Charlesbridge Pub.

— Cuenta los Insectos (The Icky Bug Counting Book) LC 93-70041. (SPA., Illus.). 32p. (J). (ps-3). 1993. pap. 6.95 (*0-88106-419-X*); lib. bdg. 15.88 (*0-88106-639-7*) Charlesbridge Pub.

— The Desert Alphabet Book. LC 93-42651. (Illus.). 32p. (Orig.). (J). (ps-3). 1994. 15.95 (*0-88106-473-4*); pap. 6.95 (*0-88106-472-6*) Charlesbridge Pub.

Pallotta, Jerry. Desert Alphabet Book. LC 93-1512. 1994. 12.15 (*0-606-06319-6*, Pub. by Turtleback) Demco.

Pallotta, Jerry. The Dinosaur Alphabet Book. LC 90-83114. (Jerry Pallotta's Alphabet Bks.). (Illus.). 32p. (Orig.). (J). (ps-3). 1990. 15.95 (*0-88106-467-X*); pap. 6.95 (*0-88106-466-1*) Charlesbridge Pub.

— Dory Story. LC 98-37756. (Illus.). 32p. (ps-3). 2000. 15.95 (*0-88106-075-5*, Talewinds) Charlesbridge Pub.

— The Extinct Alphabet Book. LC 93-1512. (Jerry Pallotta's Alphabet Bks.). (Illus.). (J). (ps-3). 1993. 15.95 (*0-88106-471-8*); pap. 6.95 (*0-88106-470-X*) Charlesbridge Pub.

— Extinct Alphabet Book. (J). 1993. 12.15 (*0-606-05827-3*, Pub. by Turtleback) Demco.

— The Flower Alphabet Book. LC 89-60422. (Jerry Pallotta's Alphabet Bks.). (Illus.). 32p. (J). (ps-3). 1989. 15.95 (*0-88106-459-9*); pap. 6.95 (*0-88106-453-X*) Charlesbridge Pub.

— Flower Alphabet Book. (J). 1988. 12.15 (*0-606-01111-0*, Pub. by Turtleback) Demco.

— The Freshwater Alphabet Book. LC 95-20138. (Illus.). 32p. (J). (ps-3). 1996. 15.95 (*0-88106-901-9*); pap. 6.95 (*0-88106-900-0*) Charlesbridge Pub.

— Freshwater Alphabet Book. LC 95-20138. 1996. 12.15 (*0-606-09299-4*, Pub. by Turtleback) Demco.

— The Frog Alphabet Book. LC 90-80288. (Jerry Pallotta's Alphabet Bks.). (Illus.). 32p. (Orig.). (J). (ps-3). 1990. 15.95 (*0-88106-463-7*); pap. 6.95 (*0-88106-462-9*) Charlesbridge Pub.

— The Furry Animal Alphabet Book. LC 90-80287. (Jerry Pallotta's Alphabet Bks.). (Illus.). 32p. (Orig.). (J). (ps-3). 1990. 15.95 (*0-88106-465-3*); pap. 6.95 (*0-88106-464-5*) Charlesbridge Pub.

— Going Lobstering. (Illus.). 32p. (J). 1990. 16.95 (*0-88106-475-0*) Charlesbridge Pub.

— Going Lobstering. LC 90-80286. (Illus.). 32p. (J). (ps-3). 1990. pap. 7.95 (*0-88106-474-2*) Charlesbridge Pub.

***Pallotta, Jerry.** Hershey's Milk Chocolate Bar Fractions Book. (Illus.). (J). 1999. 10.40 (*0-606-18559-3*) Turtleback.

— Hershey's Milk Chocolate Bar Fractions Book, Vol. 1. (Illus.). 32p. (J). (gr. 1-4). 1999. pap. 5.95 (*0-439-13519-2*) Scholastic Inc.

Pallotta, Jerry. The Icky Bug Alphabet Book. LC 89-60421. (Jerry Pallotta's Alphabet Bks.). (Illus.). 32p. (J). (ps-3). 1989. 15.95 (*0-88106-456-4*); pap. 6.95 (*0-88106-450-5*) Charlesbridge Pub.

***Pallotta, Jerry.** The Icky Bug Alphabet Book. (Illus.). 30p. (J). (ps-k). 2000. bds. 6.95 (*1-57091-439-7*) Charlesbridge Pub.

Pallotta, Jerry. Icky Bug Alphabet Book. (J). 1986. 12.15 (*0-606-01150-8*, Pub. by Turtleback) Demco.

— The Icky Bug Counting Book. LC 91-73360. (Illus.). 32p. (J). (ps-3). 1991. 15.95 (*0-88106-497-1*); pap. 6.95 (*0-88106-496-3*) Charlesbridge Pub.

— Jet Alphabet Book. LC 98-46034. (Illus.). 32p. (J). (ps-3). 1999. 15.95 (*0-88106-916-7*) Charlesbridge Pub.

— The Ocean Alphabet Book. LC 89-60424. (Jerry Pallotta's Alphabet Bks.). (Illus.). 32p. (J). (ps-3). 1989. 15.95 (*0-88106-458-0*); pap. 6.95 (*0-88106-452-1*) Charlesbridge Pub.

— Ocean Alphabet Book. (J). 1986. 12.15 (*0-606-03878-7*, Pub. by Turtleback) Demco.

— The Ocean Counting Book. LC 98-46035. (Illus.). (J). Date not set. 15.95 (*0-88106-151-4*); pap. 6.95 (*0-88106-150-6*) Charlesbridge Pub.

***Pallotta, Jerry.** Reese's Pieces: Count by Fives. LC 99-43785. (Illus.). 32p. (J). (ps-3). 2000. pap. 5.95 (*0-439-13520-6*, Cartwheel) Scholastic Inc.

Pallotta, Jerry. Reese's Pieces Peanut Butter Counting Board Book, 1. 1998. 4.95 (*0-9662445-1-6*) Corp Board.

— The Spice Alphabet Book: Herbs, Spices, & Other Natural Flavors. LC 94-5178. (Jerry Pallotta Alphabet Bks.). (Illus.). 32p. (Orig.). (J). (ps-3). 1994. 15.95 (*0-88106-898-5*); pap. 6.95 (*0-88106-897-7*) Charlesbridge Pub.

— The Underwater Alphabet Book. LC 91-70015. (Jerry Pallotta's Alphabet Bks.). (Illus.). 32p. (J). (ps-3). 1991. 15.95 (*0-88106-461-0*); pap. 6.95 (*0-88106-455-6*) Charlesbridge Pub.

— Yucky Reptile Alphabet Book. LC 89-60425. (Jerry Pallotta Alphabet Bks.). (Illus.). 32p. (J). (ps-3). 1990. 16.95 (*0-88106-460-2*); pap. 6.95 (*0-88106-454-8*) Charlesbridge Pub.

— Yucky Reptile Alphabet Book. (J). 1989. 12.15 (*0-606-04433-7*, Pub. by Turtleback) Demco.

Pallotta, Jerry & Ryan, Pam. The Crayon Counting Board Book. LC 97-65410. (Illus.). 10p. (J). (ps-k). 1997. bds. 4.95 (*0-88106-945-0*) Charlesbridge Pub.

Pallotta, Jerry & Stillwell, Fred. The Airplane Alphabet Book. LC 96-11360. (Illus.). 32p. (J). 1997. 15.95 (*0-88106-907-8*) Charlesbridge Pub.

— The Airplane Alphabet Book. LC 96-11360. (Illus.). 32p. (J). 1999. pap. 6.95 (*0-88106-906-X*) Charlesbridge Pub.

Pallotta, Jerry & Thomson, Bob. The Victory Garden Vegetable Alphabet Book. LC 92-71580. (Alphabet Book Ser.). (Illus.). 32p. (J). (ps-3). 1992. 16.95 (*0-88106-469-6*); pap. 6.95 (*0-88106-468-8*) Charlesbridge Pub.

Pallotta, Jerry, jt. auth. see Cassie, Brian.

Pallotta, Jerry, jt. auth. see Ryan, Pam Munoz.

Pallotta, Joseph. Union Station Remembered. 2nd ed. (Illus.). 173p. 1985. pap. 19.95 (*0-9616091-0-9*) J & C Bks.

Pallottino, Massimo. A History of Earliest Italy. Ryle, Martin & Soper, Kate, trs. 224p. (C). 1991. reprint ed. text 44.50 (*0-472-10097-1*, 10097) U of Mich Pr.

Pallud, Jean-Paul. Ardennes 1944: Peiper & Skorzeny. (Elite Ser.: No. 11). (Illus.). 64p. pap. 12.95 (*0-85045-740-8*, 9410, Pub. by Ospry) Stackpole.

Palluth, William. Composition Made Easy. (How to Draw & Paint Ser.). (Illus.). 32p. (Orig.). 1989. pap. 6.95 (*0-929261-43-7*, HT194) W Foster Pub.

— Painting in Four Mediums: Oil, Watercolor, Acrylic, Pastel. (How to Draw & Paint Ser.). (Illus.). 32p. (Orig.). 1990. pap. 6.95 (*1-56010-055-9*, HT226) W Foster Pub.

— Painting in Oils. (Artist's Library). (Illus.). 64p. (Orig.). 1989. pap. 7.95 (*0-929261-01-1*, AL01) W Foster Pub.

Pally, Marcia. Sex & Sensibility: The Vanity of Bonfires. LC 93-40142. 1994. pap. 11.00 (*0-88001-364-8*) HarpC.

Palm. Systems Dynamics. 1998. text 47.96 (*0-256-11449-8*, Irwn McGrw-H) McGrw-H Hghr Educ.

***Palm, Carl Magnus.** From Abba to Mama Mia! The Official Book. (Illus.). 256p. 2000. 39.95 (*0-8230-8317-9*) Watsn-Guptill.

Palm, Charles G. & Reed, Dale, compiled by. Guide to the Hoover Institution Archives. (Bibliography Ser.: No. 59). 430p. 1980. 50.00 (*0-8179-2591-0*) Hoover Inst Pr.

P

An Asterisk (*) at the beginning of an entry indicates that the title is appearing for the first time.

Palm, Daniel C. Homosexuality & Health: Some Public Health Facts That America's Children Are Not Getting. 16p. (C). 1994. pap. text 2.50 (*0-930783-22-0*) Claremont Inst.

Palm, Daniel C., ed. On Faith & Free Government. LC 97-18641. 215p. 1997. 60.50 (*0-8476-8602-7*); pap. 24.95 (*0-8476-8603-5*) Rowman.

Palm, E., ed. see Ophthalmic Microsurgery Study Group Staff.

Palm, Franklin C. Calvinism & the Religious Wars. LC 83-45628. reprint ed. 32.50 (*0-404-19880-5*) AMS Pr.

Palm, G., jt. ed. see Shaw, G.

Palm, Gordon F. Advances in Phosphate Fertilizer Technology. Atwood, Wes et al, eds. LC 93-12275. (Symposium Ser.: No. 292, Vol. 89). 175p. 1993. 35.00 (*0-8169-0593-2*) Am Inst Chem Eng.

Palm, James E. & Poethig, Eunice B. Acting in Faith: A Study Guide on the Philippines. 48p. (Orig.). 1989. pap. 4.95 (*0-377-00193-7*) Friendship Pr.

Palm, L. C., ed. The Collected Letters of Antoni van Leeuwenhoek Pt. XIV: 1701-1704. (Illus.). 522p. 1996. 233.00 (*90-265-1450-6*) Swets.

***Palm, L. C., ed.** The Collected Letters of Antoni van Leeuwenhoek, 1704-1707, Pt. XV. (Illus.). 442p. 1999. 210.00 (*90-265-1548-0*) Swets.

Palm, L. C., ed. see Leeuwenhoek, Antoni Van.

Palm, Mary E., et al, eds. Mycologia Index, 1967-1988, Vols. 59-80. LC 57-51730. 496p. 1991. lib. bdg. 82.00 (*0-89327-357-0*) NY Botanical.

Palm, Mary E. & Chapela, Ignacio H., eds. Mycology in Sustainable Development: Expanding Concepts & Vanishing Borders. LC 96-3693. 150p. (C). 1997. 40.00 (*1-887905-01-4*) Pkway Pubs.

Palm, Miriam, et al, eds. If We Build It - Scholarly Communications & Networking Technologies: Proceedings of the North American Serials Interest Group, Inc., 7th Annual Conference, June 18-21, 1992, the University of Illinois at Chicago. LC 93-19928. (Serials Librarian Ser.: Vol. 23, Nos. 3-4). (Illus.). 326p. 1993. lib. bdg. 49.95 (*1-56024-450-X*) Haworth Pr.

Palm, R., jt. ed. see Driankov, D.

Palm, Rainer, et al. Model-Based Fuzzy Control: Fuzzy Gain Schedulers & Sliding Mode Fuzzy Control. LC 96-47571. 184p. 1997. 44.95 (*3-540-61471-0*) Spr-Verlag.

Palm, Richard L., jt. auth. see Toma, J. Douglas.

Palm, Risa. Natural Hazards: An Integrative Framework for Research & Planning. LC 89-45490. 200p. reprint ed. pap. 62.00 (*0-608-08799-8*, 206943800004) Bks Demand.

Palm, Risa & Carroll, John. Illusions of Safety: Culture & Earthquake Hazard Response in the California & Japan. LC 97-53186. (C). 1998. pap. 55.00 (*0-8133-3452-7*, Pub. by Westview) HarpC.

Palm, Risa I. Real Estate Agents & Special Studies Zones Disclosure: The Response of California Home Buyers to Earthquake Hazards Information. (Program on Environment & Behavior Monograph Ser.: No. 32). 147p. (Orig.). (C). 1981. pap. 20.00 (*0-685-28106-X*) Natural Hazards.

Palm, Risa I. & Hodgson, Michael E. After a California Earthquake: Attitude & Behavior Change. LC 91-857. (Illus.). 146p. 1992. pap. text 17.50 (*0-226-64499-5*) U Ch Pr.

— Earthquake & Hurricane Hazard in Puerto Rico: A Survey of Attitudes & Behavior. LC 92-44744. (Program on Environment & Behavior Monograph Ser.: No. 55). 1993. 20.00 (*1-877943-09-6*) Natural Hazards.

Palm, Risa I., et al. Home Mortgage Lenders, Real Property Appraisers & Earthquake Hazards. (Program on Environment & Behavior Monograph Ser.: No. 38). 157p. (Orig.). (C). 1984. pap. 20.00 (*0-685-28112-4*) Natural Hazards.

— Women & the Social Costs of Economic Development: Two Colorado Case Studies. (Illus.). 225p. 1981. text 48.50 (*0-89158-594-X*) Westview.

Palm, William J. Control Systems Engineering. LC 85-26590. 720p. (C). 1986. text 106.95 (*0-471-81086-X*) Wiley.

— Introduction to Matlab for Engineers. LC 97-44444. 336p. 1998. pap. 35.63 (*0-07-047328-5*) McGraw.

— MATLAB for Engineering Applications. LC 98-40456. 552p. 1998. pap. 40.94 (*0-07-047330-7*) McGraw.

— Modeling, Analysis & Control of Dynamic Systems. 370p. (C). 1983. pap. text, suppl. ed. 25.00 (*0-471-88581-9*) Wiley.

Palma, Andre De, see Anderson, Simon P.

Palma, Andre De, see Anderson, Simon P. & De Palma, Andre.

***Palma, Anthony D.** Baptism in the Holy Spirit. 79p. 1999. pap. 4.99 (*0-88243-323-7*, 02-0323) Gospel Pub.

Palma, Anthony D. Truth-Antidote for Error. LC 76-52177. (Radiant Life Ser.). 128p. 1977. pap. 3.95 (*0-88243-904-9*, 02-0904); pap., teacher ed. 5.50 (*0-88243-174-9*, 32-0174) Gospel Pub.

Palma, Bruce. Pig Soup. unabridged ed. LC 99-231478. xiv, 90p. 1998. pap. 10.00 (*0-9662452-0-2*) Pisix Pr.

Palma, Clemente. Malignant Tales. Castillo-Feliu, Guillermo I., tr. from SPA. LC 87-35997. (C). 1988. lib. bdg. 25.50 (*0-8191-6879-3*) U Pr of Amer.

Palma, Delores P. & Hyett, Doyle G. Business Clustering: How to Leverage Sales. (Publications Ser.). (Illus.). 40p. 1993. pap. 30.00 (*1-893312-03-8*) HyettPalma Pubns.

— Business Retention & Expansion. (Publications Ser.). i, 47p. 1992. pap. 30.00 (*1-893312-00-3*) HyettPalma Pubns.

— Downtown Safety: Addressing the Myths & the Realities. (Publications Ser.). ii, 40p. 1994. pap. 24.00 (*1-893312-05-4*) HyettPalma Pubns.

— Downtowns & Utilities in Partnership. (Publications Ser.). ii, 28p. 1996. pap. 24.00 (*1-893312-08-9*) HyettPalma Pubns.

— Focus Groups for Downtown. (Publications Ser.). i, 28p. Date not set. pap. 25.00 (*1-893312-02-X*) HyettPalma Pubns.

— Funding Your Downtown Organization. (Publications Ser.). i, 39p. 1999. pap. 25.00 (*1-893312-09-7*) HyettPalma Pubns.

— Maintaining Downtown's Curb Appeal. (Publications Ser.). (Illus.). ii, 36p. 1995. pap. 21.00 (*1-893312-07-0*) HyettPalma Pubns.

— Successful Retail Recruitment Strategies. (Publications Ser.). i, 44p. 1995. pap. 30.00 (*1-893312-01-1*) HyettPalma Pubns.

Palma, Delores P., jt. auth. see Hyett, Doyle G.

Palma, Dolores P. & Hyett, Doyle G. Parking for Downtown's Spenders. (Publications Ser.). (Illus.). ii, 32p. 1995. pap. 21.00 (*1-893312-06-2*) HyettPalma Pubns.

Palma, Gabriel, jt. ed. see Arestis, Philip.

Palma-Gamiz, J. L., jt. ed. see Heusch, G.

Palma, Gloria M., see Palma, Marigloria, pseud.

***Palma, J. M., et al, eds.** Vector & Parallel Processing-VECPAR'98: 3rd International Conference, Porto, Portugal, June 21-23, 1998, Selected Papers & Invited Talks. LC 99-36440. (Lecture Notes in Computer Science Ser.: Vol. 1573). xvi, 706p. 1999. pap. 102.00 (*3-540-66228-6*) Spr-Verlag.

Palma, Jose M.L.M. Rence on Vector & Parallel Proc & Dongarra, J. J. Vector & Parallel Processing-Vecpar, 96: Second International Conference on Vector & Parallel Processing-Systems & Applications, Porto, Portugal, September 1996: Selected Papers, Vol. 121. LC 97-8372. (Lecture Notes in Computer Science Ser.). 1997. write for info. (*3-540-62828-2*) Spr-Verlag.

Palma, L. Dalla. Syllabus. 5th Radiological Refresher Course: Chest, Musculoskeleton, G.I. & Abdomen, Urinary Tract. 200p. 1996. pap. 79.50 (*3-540-75019-3*) Spr-Verlag.

Palma, Marigloria, pseud. Cuentos De la Abeja Encinta. LC 76-6153. (UPREX, Ficcion Ser.: No. 48). (SPA.). (Orig.). 1976. pap. 1.50 (*0-8477-0048-8*) U of PR Pr.

— Versos de Cada Dia: Estampas Numeradas. LC 79-10463. (UPREX, Poesia Ser.: No. 58). 228p. (Orig.). 1980. pap. 1.50 (*0-8477-0058-5*) U of PR Pr.

Palma, Michael, jt. ed. see Gioia, Dana.

Palma, Michael, tr. see Herder, Johann G.

Palma, Ray Di, see Di Palma, Ray.

Palma, Ricardo. Tradiciones Peruanas. (Coleccion Archivos de Ediciones Criticas). (SPA.). 30.99 (*84-88344-00-7*, Pub. by Fondo) Continental Bk.

— Tradiciones Peruanas. (SPA.). pap. 8.95 (*968-432-572-X*, Pub. by Porrua) Continental Bk.

Palma, Robert J. Karl Barth's Theology of Culture. LC 83-2371. (Pittsburgh Theological Monographs, New Ser.: No 2). 122p. 1983. pap. 10.00 (*0-915138-54-9*) Pickwick.

Palma, Robert J., Sr. & Espenscheid, Mark. The Complete Guide to Household Chemicals. LC 94-21778. 325p. 1995. 25.95 (*0-87975-983-6*) Prometheus Bks.

Palma, Ronald M., jt. auth. see Madsen, David A.

Palma, Russell. Physics 115. (C). 1995. pap. text 15.37 (*1-56870-196-9*) RonJon Pub.

Palmadesco, Peter J. & Papadopoulos, K., eds. Wave Instabilities in Space Plasmas. (Astrophysics & Space Science Library: No. 74). 1979. lib. bdg. 104.50 (*90-277-1028-7*) Kluwer Academic.

Palmaitis, Letas, jt. auth. see Gudjedjiani, Chato.

Palmanteer & Rogers. Man Spirit. 1979. 4.00 (*0-912678-38-0*, Greenfld Rev Pr) Greenfld Rev Lit.

Palmarini, Terra, jt. auth. see Baldwin, Rahima.

Palmason, G., ed. Continental & Oceanic Rifts. (Geodynamics Ser.: Vol. 8). 309p. 1982. 26.00 (*0-87590-504-8*) Am Geophysical.

Palmatier, George E. & Shull, Joseph E. The Marketing Edge: The New Leadership Role of Sales & Marketing in Manufacturing. LC 88-51917. 183p. 1988. 40.00 (*0-939246-08-2*) Wiley.

Palmatier, George E. & Shull, Joseph S. The Marketing Edge: The New Leadership Role of Sales & Marketing in Manufacturing. 208p. 1995. 42.50 (*0-471-13270-5*) Wiley.

***Palmatier, Robert A.** Food: A Dictionary of Literal & Nonliteral Terms. LC 99-88203. 488p. 2000. lib. bdg. 89.50 (*0-313-31436-5*, GR1436, Greenwood Pr) Greenwood.

Palmatier, Robert A. Speaking of Animals: A Dictionary of Animal Metaphors. LC 94-29273. 496p. 1995. lib. bdg. 75.00 (*0-313-29490-9*, Greenwood Pr) Greenwood.

Palmatier, Robert A. & Ray, Harold L. Sports Talk: A Dictionary of Sports Metaphors. LC 88-24646. 245p. 1989. lib. bdg. 45.00 (*0-313-26426-0*, PSK, Greenwood Pr) Greenwood.

Palmatier, Susan M., jt. auth. see Bremer, Suzanne W.

Palmberg, Mai, ed. AIDS i Afrika. (Afrikabiblioteket Ser.: Nr. 4). 236p. 1993. write for info. (*91-7106-322-6*, Pub. by Nordic Africa) Transaction Pubs.

Palmberg, Mai & Strand, Per. Sydafrika - En Regnbagsnation Fods. (Afrikabiblioteket Ser.: Nr. 5). 243p. 1995. write for info. (*91-7106-372-2*, Pub. by Nordic Africa) Transaction Pubs.

Palmberg, Mai, jt. auth. see Dunton, Chris.

Palmberg, Mai, jt. ed. see Hallencreutz, Carl F.

Palmberg, Mal, ed. Problems of Socialist Orientation in Africa. (Seminar Proceedings Ser.: No. 12). 243p. 1978. write for info. (*91-7106-141-X*, Pub. by Nordic Africa) Transaction Pubs.

Palmblad, Harry V. Strindberg's Conception of History. 1972. 250.00 (*0-8490-1144-2*) Gordon Pr.

Palme, Cole, ed. see Dee, Denise.

Palme, Joakim. Pension Rights in Welfare Capitalism: The Development of Old-Age Pensions in 18 OECD Countries 1930-1985. (Swedish Institute for Social Research Ser.: No. 14). 196p. (Orig.). 1990. pap. 69.50 (*91-7604-039-9*) Coronet Bks.

Palme, Klaus, ed. Signals & Signal Transduction Pathways in Plants. LC 94-48295. 452p. (C). 1995. text 184.00 (*0-7923-3364-0*) Kluwer Academic.

Palmedo, Philip. Voices in Bronze. (Illus.). 138p. 1999. 34.95 (*1-58244-034-4*) Rutledge Bks.

Palmegiani, Francesco. Matta Battistini: Il Re Dei Baritoni. Farkas, Andrew, ed. LC 76-29960. (Opera Biographies Ser.).Tr. of Mattia Battistini: the Kind of Baritones. (ITA., Illus.). 1977. reprint ed. lib. bdg. 23.95 (*0-405-09700-X*) Ayer.

Palmegiano, E. M., compiled by. Crime in Victorian Britain: An Annotated Bibliography from Nineteenth-Century British Magazines, 31. LC 92-44640. (Bibliographies & Indexes in World History Ser.: No. 31). 192p. 1993. lib. bdg. 69.50 (*0-313-26523-2*, PCM, Greenwood Pr) Greenwood.

Palmeirim, Jorge M. Bats of Portugal: Zoogeography & Systematics. (Miscellaneous Publications: No. 82). (Illus.). 53p. (C). 1990. pap. text 3.25 (*0-89338-034-2*) U KS Nat Hist Mus.

***Palmen, Connie.** The Friendship. Rilke, Ina, tr. (DUT.). 2000. pap. 18.00 (*1-86046-560-9*, Pub. by Harvill Press) FS&G.

Palmen-Goemans, Marlene, tr. see Smulders, Jacintha.

Palmen, Pauline K., jt. auth. see Giordano, Albert G.

Palmen, Ralph H. Principles & Success Strategies for Everyday Living. (Orig.). 1986. pap. 6.95 (*0-9617213-0-8*) Palmen Inst.

Palmer. Art Loans, Vol. IBAS. LC 97-202778. 1997. 350.00 (*90-411-0667-7*) Kluwer Law Intl.

— Collective Agreement Arbitration in Canada. 3rd ed. 904p. 1991. boxed set 148.00 (*0-409-89647-0*, MICHIE) LEXIS Pub.

— Command at Sea. 1997. 24.95 (*0-02-923665-7*) Free Pr.

— Command at Sea. 1997. 24.95 (*0-684-82805-7*) Free Pr.

Palmer. Constitutional Rights of Prisoners. 5th ed. pap., suppl. ed. 5.00 (*0-87084-331-1*) Anderson Pub Co.

Palmer. Evolutionary Psychology. (C). 2000. 62.00 (*0-205-27868-X*, Macmillan Coll) P-H.

***Palmer.** Hands-On Microsoft Window NT 4.0 Workstation with Project for Server & Network Adiminstration. (Networking Ser.). (C). 1999. text 41.95 (*0-619-01546-2*) Course Tech.

— Hands-on Networking Essentials with Projects. (Networking Ser.). (C). 1999. pap. 39.95 incl. cd-rom (*0-619-01628-0*) Course Tech.

Palmer. Hap Palmer Favorites. 1981. pap. text 19.95 (*0-88284-189-0*) Alfred Pub.

***Palmer.** Helping People with Eating Disorders: A Clinical Guide to Assessment & Treatment. LC 99-89738. 272p. 2000. pap. text 55.00 (*0-471-98647-X*) Wiley.

— Introducing Windows 2000 Server. (Networking Ser.). (C). 2000. pap. 24.00 (*0-619-01564-0*) Course Tech.

Palmer. Latin American Politics. 2000. pap. text. write for info. (*0-312-17853-0*) St Martin.

***Palmer.** Managing People & Self-Part of Team Leader Development. 256p. 1998. pap. text 28.95 (*0-7506-3861-3*) Buttrwrth-Heinemann.

Palmer. Manual of Neurosurgery. 1995. pap. text 58.00 (*0-443-05391-X*, W B Saunders Co) Harcrt Hlth Sci Grp.

***Palmer.** MCSE Guide to MS Windows 2000 Server. (Networking Ser.). (C). 2000. pap. 60.95 (*0-619-01517-9*) Course Tech.

— Ohio Courtroom Evidence, Issue 3. 100p. 1999. ring bd. write for info. (*0-327-01304-4*, 8220215) LEXIS Pub.

Palmer. Palmer D'Amico Accounting for Canadian Colleges. 1997. text. write for info. (*0-201-34634-6*) Addison-Wesley.

— Passageways. (C). 1993. pap. text 20.00 (*0-15-501292-4*) Harcourt Coll Pubs.

— Passageways, Vol. 1. LC 97-74864. (C). 1998. pap. text 25.00 (*0-15-502482-5*, Pub. by Harcourt Coll Pubs) Harcourt.

— Passageways, Vol. 2. LC 97-74864. (C). 1998. pap. text 25.00 (*0-15-502483-3*, Pub. by Harcourt Coll Pubs) Harcourt.

— Passageways: A History of Black America. (C). 1997. pap. text 18.75 (*0-03-055139-0*) Harcourt Coll Pubs.

Palmer. People & Self Management. 128p. pap. text. write for info. (*0-7506-4865-1*) Buttrwrth-Heinemann.

Palmer. Principles of Marketing. 2nd ed. (SB - Marketing Education Ser.). 1990. 5.95 (*0-538-60439-5*); mass mkt. 38.95 (*0-538-60437-9*) S-W Pub.

— Real Estate Principles & Practices. 4th ed. 456p. (C). 1996. pap. text 30.60 (*0-13-777335-8*) P-H.

— Rest, Vol. 1. 1995. 38.75 (*0-316-69028-7*) Little.

— Rest, Vol. 2. 1995. 38.75 (*0-316-69027-9*) Little.

— Rest, Vol. 3. 1995. 38.75 (*0-316-69026-0*) Little.

— Rest, Vol. 4. 1995. 38.75 (*0-316-69025-2*) Little.

— The Trained Eye: Introduction to Astronomy. 2nd ed. (C). 2001. pap. text 12.00 (*0-03-001367-4*) Harcourt Coll Pubs.

— Wise up, Custom Pub. 2nd ed. (C). 1993. pap. text 9.25 (*0-07-048453-8*) McGraw.

Palmer & Cheesman. Play & Playwork. 1993. pap. text. write for info. (*0-582-09370-8*, Pub. by Addison-Wesley) Longman.

Palmer & Powell, eds. Treaty of Bayonne with Preliminary Treaties of Trancoso. (Exeter Hispanic Text Ser.: No. 47). 92p. Date not set. pap. text 17.95 (*0-85989-316-2*, Pub. by Univ Exeter Pr) Northwestern U Pr.

Palmer & Ray, Charles M. Office Automation: A Systems Approach. 2nd ed. (KK - Legal Secretary Studies). (C). pap. 43.75 (*0-538-70036-X*) S-W Pub.

Palmer & Short. Health Care & Public Policy: A Australian Analysis. 2nd ed. 350p. 1994. 69.9 (*0-7329-2008-6*, Pub. by Macmill Educ); pap. (*0-7329-2007-8*, Pub. by Macmill Educ) Paul & Pubs.

***Palmer & Sinclair.** Guide to Designing & Implement. Local & Wide Area Networks. (C). 1999. 60.95 (*0-7600-1093-5*) Thomson Learn.

Palmer, jt. auth. see Cooper.

Palmer, jt. auth. see Evans.

Palmer, jt. auth. see Lee.

***Palmer, A.** Encyclopedia of Napolean's Europe. 1998. text 45.00 (*0-09-478700-X*, Pub. by Constable & Co) Trafalgar.

Palmer, A. R., jt. ed. see Bally, A. W.

Palmer, A. R., ed. see International Symposium on Hearing Staff.

Palmer, A. Smythe. The Samson Saga & Its Place in Comparative Religion. 1977. lib. bdg. 59.95 (*0-8490-2565-6*) Gordon Pr.

Palmer, Abram S. Folk-Etymology: A Dictionary of Verbal Corruptions or Words Perverted in Form. LC 68-26365. (Studies in Language: No. 41). 1969. reprint ed. lib. bdg. 75.00 (*0-8383-0279-3*) M S G Haskell Hse.

— Folk-Etymology, a Dictionary of Verbal Corruptions or Words Perverted in Form or Meaning, by False Derivation or Mistaken Analogy. LC 68-57636. (Illus.). 664p. 1970. reprint ed. lib. bdg. 85.00 (*0-8371-1153-6*, PAFE) Greenwood.

— Samson-Saga & Its Place in Comparative Religion. Dorson, Richard M., ed. LC 77-70613. (International Folklore Ser.). 1977. reprint ed. lib. bdg. 25.95 (*0-405-10112-0*) Ayer.

Palmer, Adele R. & Larson, Eric V. Cost Factors in the Army: Vol. 2, Factors Methods & Models. LC 92-15576. 1992. pap. text 15.00 (*0-8330-1241-X*, R-4078/2-PA&E) Rand Corp.

Palmer, Adele R., jt. auth. see Larson, Eric V.

Palmer, Adell. Butterfly Children. 1974. pap. 3.95 (*0-89036-050-2*) Liahona Pub Trust.

Palmer, Adrian. Principles of Services Marketing. LC 94-4289. 1994. 18.95 (*0-07-707746-6*) McGraw.

Palmer, Adrian & Cole, Catherine. Services Marketing: Principles & Practice. LC 94-36242. 480p. (C). 1995. 90.67 (*0-02-390563-8*, Macmillan Coll) P-H.

Palmer, Adrian & Hartley, Bob. The Business & Marketing Environment. 2nd ed. LC 96-1955. 1996. pap. write for info. (*0-07-709262-7*) McGraw.

Palmer, Adrian, jt. auth. see Bachman, Lyle.

Palmer, Adrian S., et al. Back & Forth: Pair Activities for Language Development. (Illus.). viii, 110p. 1985. pap. text 16.95 (*1-882483-73-1*) Alta Bk Ctr.

Palmer, Agnes M. To God Be All Glory. (Illus.). (Orig.). 1988. write for info. (*0-318-68750-X*) Forest Hills.

— To God Be All Glory: Mini-Biography (Authentic Excerpts) (Illus.). 149p. (Orig.). 1987. 12.00 (*0-9617983-1-9*) Forest Hills.

***Palmer, Alan.** The East End: Four Centuries of London Life. LC 99-54335. (Illus.). 200p. 2000. pap. 20.00 (*0-8135-2826-7*) Rutgers U Pr.

— Napoleon & Marie-Louise: The Emperor's Second Wife. (Illus.). 288p. 2000. 26.00 (*0-7867-0804-2*, Pub. by Carroll & Graf) Publishers Group.

— Victory 1918. LC 99-45459. 384p. 2000. 27.00 (*0-87113-803-4*, Pub. by Grove-Atltic) Publishers Group.

Palmer, Alan J. Who's Minding Main Street? A Political Primer for Future Leaders of America's Hometowns. LC 97-13506. (Illus.). 160p. 1997. pap. 12.95 (*1-880090-48-1*) Galde Pr.

Palmer, Alan R. The Decline & Fall of the Ottoman Empire. LC 93-24525. 320p. 1993. 22.50 (*0-87131-754-0*) M Evans.

— Dictionary of the British Empire & Commonwealth. LC 96-197535. 395p. 1997. pap. 22.95 (*0-7195-5657-0*, Pub. by John Murray) Trafalgar.

Palmer, Alan R. Penguin Dictionary of 20th Century History. 5th ed. (Illus.). 448p. pap. 15.95 (*0-14-051404-X*, Pub. by Pngnin Bks Ltd) Trafalgar.

Palmer, Alan R. Twilight of the Habsburgs: The Life & Times of Emperor Francis Joseph. 400p. 1997. reprint ed. pap. 14.00 (*0-87113-665-1*, Atlntc Mnthly) Grove-Atltic.

— Who's Who in World Politics: From 1860 to the Present Day. LC 95-53055. 376p. 1996. pap. 24.99 (*0-415-13162-6*) Routledge.

— Who's Who in World Politics: From 1860 to the Present Day. LC 95-53055. 376p. (C). 1996. 75.00 (*0-415-13161-8*) Routledge.

Palmer, Alan R. & Palmer, Veronica. Who's Who in Shakespeare's England. (Illus.). 350p. 1981. text 32.50 (*0-312-87096-5*) St Martin.

Palmer, Alan W. Dictionary of the British Empire & Commonwealth. LC 96-197535. 395p. 1996. 39.95 (*0-7195-5650-3*, Pub. by John Murray) Trafalgar.

Palmer, Alan W. & Palmer, Veronica. The Chronology of British History LC 93-144999. 569 p. 1992. write for info. (*0-7126-5616-2*) CEN3.

Palmer, Alan Warwick, jt. auth. see Palmer, Veronica.

Palmer, Albert W. The Mountain Trail & Its Message. 2nd expanded ed. Fisk, Charles P., ed. & photos by by. LC 97-66260. (Illus.). 96p. 1997. pap. 12.00 (*0-9641404-7-0*) Sixth St Pr.

Palmer, Alice F. Chicago Child. (Illus.). 276p. text. write for info. (*0-9638309-0-2*) A E Palmer.

Palmer, Alix. Name Your Pet. 1996. mass mkt. 4.99 (*1-85782-041-X*, Pub. by Blake Publng) Seven Hills Bk.

Palmer, Amanda. Schooling Comprehensive Kids: Pupil Responses to Education. LC 97-77643. (Illus.). 227p. 1998. text 59.95 (*1-85628-889-7*, Pub. by Ashgate Pub) Ashgate Pub Co.

P

…venth Century …23. …2p. (Orig.). …Pub. by Liverpool …

…on the Tigris Frontier. …ental Publications). (Illus.). …(0-521-36026-9) Cambridge …

… **see McGeorge, W. D.**

… Mexico. 48p. 1978. pap. 3.50 … SB-044) Sun Pub.

… **auth. see Morton-Cooper, Alison.**

… **Marie.** Prudentius on the Martyrs. (Oxford …l Monographs). 336p. 1989. text 69.00 (…-814721-X) OUP.

…, Anthony. Concept & Object: The Unity of the Proposition in Logic & Psychology. (Studies in Philosophical Psychology). 176p. 1988. text 32.50 (*0-415-00172-2*) Routledge.

Palmer, Anthony, jt. ed. see Monk, Ray.

Palmer, Anthony M., et al, eds. Reflective Practice in Nursing: The Growth of the Professional Practitioner. LC 93-38307. (Illus.). 193p. 1994. pap. 28.95 (*0-632-03597-8*) Blackwell Sci.

Palmer, Arlene. Glass in Early America: Selections from the Henry Francis du Pont Winterthur Museum. rev. ed. LC 93-32489. (Illus.). 435p. 1993. reprint ed. 85.00 (*0-393-03660-X*) Winterthur.

Palmer, Arlene C. New Britain. (Images of America Ser.). 1995. pap. 16.99 (*0-7524-0209-9*) Arcadia Publng.

— New Britain, Vol. II. (Images of America Ser.). 1996. pap. 16.99 (*0-7524-0414-8*) Arcadia Publng.

***Palmer, Arlene C.** New Britain, Vol. III. (Images of America Ser.). 1999. pap. 16.99 (*0-7385-0025-9*) Arcadia Publng.

Palmer, Arnold. A Golfer's Life. LC 98-51681. (Illus.). 408p. 1999. 26.95 (*0-345-41481-0*) Ballantine Pub Grp.

Palmer, Arnold. Play Great Golf. (Illus.). 1996. 14.99 (*0-88365-942-5*) Galahad Bks.

Palmer, Arnold. Play Great Golf: Mastering the Fundabmentals of Your Game. 1998. pap. text 14.95 (*0-88486-191-0*, Bristol Park Bks) Arrowood Pr.

Palmer, Arnold & Dodson, James. Arnold Palmer: A Golfer's Life. large type ed. LC 98-33139. 1999. pap. 25.00 (*0-375-70574-0*) Random.

***Palmer, Arnold & Dodson, James.** A Golfer's Life. (Illus.). 432p. 2000. pap. 15.00 (*0-345-41482-9*) Ballantine Pub Grp.

Palmer, Arnold & Guest, Larry. Arnie: Inside the Legend. 1993. 19.99 (*0-941263-92-4*) NTC Contemp Pub Co.

Palmer, Arthur N. A Geological Guide to Mammoth Cave National Park. LC 79-5041. (Illus.). 210p. (Orig.). 1981. pap. 6.95 (*0-914264-28-1*) Cave Bks MO.

Palmer, Arthur N., et al, eds. Karst Modeling: Proceedings of the Symposium Held February 24 Through 27, 1999, Charlottesville, Virginia. LC 99-60215. (Special Publication Ser.: Vol. 5). (Illus.). 300p. 1999. pap. 38.00 (*0-9640258-4-1*) Karst Waters.

Palmer, Arthur N., jt. ed. see Palmer, Margaret V.

Palmer, B. J., jt. auth. see Barge, Fredrick H.

Palmer, B. M. The Broken Home: Lessons in Sorrow. Duncan, J. Ligon, III, ed. 112p. (C). 1995. reprint ed. pap. text 6.95 (*1-884416-07-1*) A Press.

— Theology of Prayer. 1992. 24.99 (*0-87377-956-8*) GAM Pubns.

Palmer, B. M. & Alexander, J. W. The Family. 1992. 28.99 (*0-87377-933-9*) GAM Pubns.

Palmer-Ball, Brainard L., Jr. The Kentucky Breeding Bird Atlas. LC 96-807. (Illus.). 384p. 1996. 29.95 (*0-8131-1965-0*) U Pr of Ky.

Palmer, Barbara. Early Art of the West Riding of Yorkshire: A Subject List of Extant & Lost Art Including Items Relevant to Early Drama. (Early Drama, Art & Music Monograph: No. 6). 1990. pap. 17.95 (*0-918720-33-8*); boxed set 37.95 (*0-918720-32-X*) Medieval Inst.

— Establishing Your Roots as a Planted Tree of the Lord. LC 99-72369. 115p. 1999. pap. 8.00 (*0-9653700-3-8*) B L Pubng.

— Oklahoma: Off the Beaten Path: A Guide to Unique Places. 2nd ed. LC 98-36932. (Off the Beaten Path Ser.). (Illus.). 288p. (Orig.). 1998. pap. 12.95 (*0-7627-0274-5*) Globe Pequot.

***Palmer, Barbara.** Oklahoma: The Spirit of America, State by State. Landau, Diana, ed. LC 98-43098. (Art of the State Ser.). (Illus.). 96p. 1999. 12.95 (*0-8109-5563-6*, Pub. by Abrams) Time Warner.

Palmer, Barbara C., et al. Developing Cultural Literacy Through the Writing Process: Empowering Learners across all Grades. LC 93-23699. 512p. (C). 1994. pap. text 38.00 (*0-205-13989-2*, Longwood Div) Allyn.

Palmer, Barbara C., jt. auth. see Simmons, John S.

***Palmer, Barbara H.** Growing in Faith & Knowledge. LC 99-54181. (Foundations in Children's Ministry Ser.). 2000. write for info. (*1-57895-087-2*) Bridge Resources.

***Palmer, Barbara Jean.** Black Conservatives. LC 99-88808. 1999. write for info. (*0-86663-087-2*) Ide Hse.

Palmer Barnes, Fiona. Complaints & Grievances in Psychotherapy: A Handbook of Ethical Practice. LC 98-18079. 208p. (C). 1998. 75.00 (*0-415-15250-X*); pap. 24.99 (*0-415-15251-8*) Routledge.

Palmer, Barry, jt. auth. see McCaughan, Nano.

Palmer, Barton, ed. The Cinematic Text: Methods & Approaches. LC 87-45796. (Georgia State Literary Studies: No. 3). 1988. 55.00 (*0-404-63203-3*) AMS Pr.

Palmer, Benjamin M. Life & Letters of James Henry Thornwell. LC 78-83432. (Religion in America, Ser. 1). 1970. reprint ed. 43.95 (*0-405-00257-2*) Ayer.

Palmer-Bermudez, Neyssa A. Las Mujeres en Los Cuentos de Rene Marquez. LC 85-26384. 103p. 1988. pap. 7.50 (*0-8477-3803-5*) U of PR Pr.

Palmer, Bernard. Men of Habit: The Franciscan Ideal in Action. 198p. 1995. pap. 21.95 (*1-85311-092-2*, 850, Pub. by Canterbury Press Norwich) Morehouse Pub.

Palmer, Bernard, ed. Medicine & the Bible. 272p. 1992. reprint ed. pap. 17.95 (*0-85364-423-3*, Pub. by Paternoster Pub) OM Literature.

Palmer, Bernard & Palmer, Marjorie. Light a Small Candle. LC 82-84439. 1982. pap. 8.95 (*7-100-07672-2*) Free Church Pubns.

Palmer, Bernard, jt. auth. see Dunn, Jerry G.

Palmer, Bernard, jt. auth. see Palmer, Marjorie.

Palmer, Betty. Travelling the Miracle Road. LC 88-90635. (Orig.). 1988. pap. 5.95 (*0-910487-16-2*) Royalty Pub.

— Travelling the Miracle Road. Scoggan, Nita, ed. LC 88-90635. (Illus.). 224p. (Orig.). 1988. 10.00 (*0-910487-17-0*) Royalty Pub.

Palmer, Beverly W. The Selected Letters of Charles Sumner, Set, Vols. 1 & 2. (Illus.). 1504p. 1990. text 200.00 (*1-55553-078-8*) NE U Pr.

Palmer, Beverly W. & Ochoa, Holly B., eds. The Papers of Thaddeus Stevens, Vol. I. LC 96-53675. 692p. 1997. text 37.50 (*0-8229-3972-X*) U of Pittsburgh Pr.

— The Papers of Thaddeus Stevens Vol. 2: April 1865-August 1868. LC 96-53675. 547p. 1998. text 37.50 (*0-8229-4052-3*) U of Pittsburgh Pr.

— The Thaddeus Stevens Papers: Guide & Index to the Microfilm Edition. LC 94-2585. 184p. 1994. pap. 40.00 (*0-8420-4146-X*) Scholarly Res Inc.

Palmer, Bill & Hughes, Bill. Palmer-Hughes Accordion Course Lesson Book 2. 48p. 1952. pap. 7.50 (*0-7390-0366-6*, 204) Alfred Pub.

— Palmer-Hughes Prep Accordian Course, Bk. 1A. 32p. 1952. 5.95 (*0-7390-0566-9*, 215) Alfred Pub.

Palmer, Bill, et al. The Encyclopedia of Martial Arts Movies. (Illus.). 492p. 1995. 75.00 (*0-8108-3027-2*) Scarecrow.

Palmer, Bill, tr. see Lesley, Ted.

Palmer, Bruce, III. How to Restore Your Harley-Davidson Motorcycle. LC 91-10058. (Illus.). 640p. 1994. pap. 39.95 (*0-87938-934-6*) MBI Pubg.

Palmer, Bruce, Jr. Intervention in the Caribbean: The Dominican Crises of 1965. LC 89-16761. 256p. 1989. 29.95 (*0-8131-1691-0*) U Pr of Ky.

Palmer, Bruce. Man over Money: The Southern Populist Critique of American Capitalism. LC 79-24698. (Fred W. Morrison Series in Southern Studies). 329p. reprint ed. pap. 102.00 (*0-608-06000-3*, 206632800008) Bks Demand.

Palmer, Bruce, Jr. The Twenty-Five-Year War: America's Military Role in Vietnam. LC 84-5091. (Illus.). 248p. 1984. 32.00 (*0-8131-1513-2*) U Pr of Ky.

— The Twenty-Five Year War: America's Military Role in Vietnam. (Quality Paperbacks Ser.). (Illus.). 264p. 1990. pap. 13.95 (*0-306-80383-6*) Da Capo.

Palmer, Bruce. Wine-Making at Home. 2nd ed. 1975. pap. 3.95 (*0-911104-58-5*) Workman Pub.

Palmer, Bruce R., ed. see Western Regional Conference on Gold, Silver, Urani.

Palmer, Bryan D. A Culture in Conflict: Skilled Workers & Industrial Capitalism in Hamilton, Ontario 1860-1914. LC 80-481234. 361p. reprint ed. pap. 112.00 (*0-7837-1024-0*, 204133500020) Bks Demand.

Palmer, Bryan D. Cultures of Darkness: Night Travels in the Histories of Transgression. text 55.00 (*1-58367-026-2*); pap. text 24.00 (*1-58367-027-0*) Monthly Rev.

Palmer, Bryan D. Descent into Discourse. (Critical Perspectives on the Past Ser.). 312p. 1990. pap. 22.95 (*0-87722-720-9*) Temple U Pr.

— E. P. Thompson: Objections & Oppositions. 256p. (C). (gr. 13). 1994. pap. 19.00 (*1-85984-070-1*, B4545, Pub. by Verso) Norton.

— Goodyear Invades the Backcountry: The Corporate Takeover of a Rural Town. (Illus.). 176p. (C). 1994. text 38.00 (*0-85345-909-6*, Pub. by Monthly Rev); pap. text 18.00 (*0-85345-910-X*, Pub. by Monthly Rev) NYU Pr.

Palmer, C. Everard. A Dog Called Houdini.Tr. of Houdini, le Chien. (FRE.). (J). pap. 5.99 (*0-590-73092-4*) Scholastic Inc.

Palmer, Carl. Chemistry of Ground Water. (Illus.). 300p. Date not set. 69.95 (*0-87371-077-0*, L077) Lewis Pubs.

Palmer, Carleton H. Report of the Ellis Island Committee. LC 78-145478. (American Immigration Library). 149p. 1971. reprint ed. lib. bdg. 22.95 (*0-89198-021-0*) Ozer.

***Palmer, Carol.** Real Food from Just One Pan. (Illus.). 128p. 2000. pap. 9.95 (*0-572-02500-9*) Foulsham UK.

Palmer, Carol. Stir-Fry Cookbook. (Quick & Easy Ser.). 1998. pap. 9.95 (*0-572-02382-0*, Pub. by W Foulsham) Trans-Atl Phila.

Palmer, Carole, et al. Nutrition, Diet & Dental Health: Concepts & Methods. 78p. 1981. 32.00 (*0-318-17799-4*) Am Dental Hygienists.

Palmer, Carole, jt. auth. see Arvetis, Chris.

Palmer, Carole L., jt. auth. see McCombs, Judith.

Palmer, Caroline. Cuttings. 184p. 1998. pap. 26.95 (*0-8464-4616-2*) Beekman Pubs.

Palmer, Caroline, ed. Arthurian Bibliography III: (1978-1992) Author Listing & Subject Index. (Arthurian Studies: Vol. 31). 792p. (C). 1998. 210.00 (*0-85991-399-6*) Boydell & Brewer.

Palmer, Caroline, tr. see Pinet, Helene.

Palmer, Carolyn J. Violent Crimes & Other Forms of Victimization in Residence Halls. LC 93-18795. (Higher Education Administration Ser.). 128p. 1994. pap. 18.95 (*0-912557-15-X*) Coll Admin Pubns.

Palmer, Carolyn J. & Gehring, Donald D., eds. A Handbook for Complying with the Program & Review Requirements of the 1989 Amendments to the Drug-Free Schools & Communities Act. LC 92-23726. 224p. 1994. pap. 25.95 (*0-912557-14-1*) Coll Admin Pubns.

Palmer, Catherine. Finders Keepers. LC 99-29831. (HeartQuest Ser.). 1999. pap. text 9.99 (*0-8423-1164-5*) Tyndale Hse.

— For the Love of a Child. (Intimate Moments Ser.). 1994. per. 3.50 (*0-373-07551-0*, 5-07551-0) Silhouette.

— His Best Friend's Wife. (Intimate Moments Ser.). 1995. per. 3.75 (*0-373-07627-4*, 1-07627-2) Silhouette.

— Prairie Rose. LC 97-23018. (Town Called Hope Ser.: Vol. 1). 272p. 1997. pap. 10.99 (*0-8423-7056-0*) Tyndale Hse.

— Prairie Storm, Vol. 3. LC 98-31508. 300p. 1999. pap. text 9.99 (*0-8423-7058-7*) Tyndale Hse.

Palmer, Catherine. Sometimes Forever. 336p. 1996. mass mkt. 5.99 (*0-515-11922-9*, Jove) Berkley Pub.

— A Town Called Hope No. 2: Prairie Fire. LC 98-19977. (Town Called Hope Ser.). 270p. 1998. pap. 9.99 (*0-8423-7057-9*) Tyndale Hse.

Palmer, Catherine. The Treasure of Timbuktu. LC 96-32139. (HeartQuest Ser.: No. 1). 1997. pap. 10.99 (*0-8423-5775-0*) Tyndale Hse.

— A Victorian Christmas Tea. LC 97-23054. 1997. pap. 9.99 (*0-8423-7775-1*) Tyndale Hse.

— A Victorian Christmas Tea. large type ed. LC 98-8443. 1998. 23.95 (*0-7862-1541-0*) Thorndike Pr.

***Palmer, Catherine, et al.** Prairie Christmas. LC 00-37783. (Illus.). (J). 2000. pap. write for info. (*0-8423-3562-5*) Tyndale Hse.

— A Victorian Christmas Cottage. LC 99-34158. (Heart Quest Ser.). 1999. pap. 9.99 (*0-8423-1905-0*) Tyndale Hse.

Palmer, Catherine, et al. A Victorian Christmas Quilt. LC 98-20563. 375p. 1998. pap. 9.99 (*0-8423-7773-5*) Tyndale Hse.

Palmer, Cecil, jt. ed. see Saintsbury, Harry A.

Palmer, Charles & Schenk, Lucile, eds. History of Delaware County, 2 vols., Set. (Illus.). 452p. 1995. reprint ed. lib. bdg. 52.00 (*0-8328-5107-8*) Higginson Bk Co.

Palmer, Charles F. Inebriety: Its Source, Prevention, & Cure. Grob, Gerald N., ed. LC 80-1242. (Addiction in America Ser.). 1981. reprint ed. lib. bdg. 15.95 (*0-405-13612-9*) Ayer.

Palmer, Charles H. & Hurry, Edmund A. Hurry. Memorial of the Family of Hurry of Gt. Yarmouth & of New York, with Additions. (Illus.). 132p. 1997. reprint ed. pap. 21.50 (*0-8328-9287-4*); reprint ed. lib. bdg. 31.50 (*0-8328-9286-6*) Higginson Bk Co.

Palmer, Charles J. & Palmer, Jacqueline. Of Sunlight & Shadows. LC 97-69556. (Illus.). 260p. 1997. 54.95 (*1-881808-35-1*) Creat Arts & Sci.

— Our Captured Moments. LC 96-86077. (Illus.). 250p. 1996. 49.95 (*1-881808-29-7*) Creat Arts & Sci.

Palmer, Charles J. & Palmer, Jacwueline. Reaching Other Worlds. LC 98-92294. (Illus.). 250p. 1998. 49.95 (*1-881808-43-2*) Creat Arts & Sci.

Palmer, Charles J., ed. see Manship, Henry.

***Palmer, Charlie.** Charlie Palmer's Casual Cooking: A Four Star Chef Cooks for Family & Friends. LC 00-41882. (Illus.). 2001. write for info. (*0-688-17873-1*) Morrow Avon.

Palmer, Charlie & Choate, Judith. Great American Food. LC 97-153297. (Illus.). 224p. 1996. 55.00 (*0-679-43794-0*) McKay.

Palmer, Chelese Guthrie, ed. see Henslin, Earl R.

Palmer, Chelese Guthrie, ed. see Seiden, Jerry.

Palmer, Chris. Dynamics of Natal Astrology. LC 83-71153. 152p. 1984. 19.00 (*0-86690-244-9*, P2297-014) Am Fed Astrologers.

Palmer, Christopher. The Composer in Hollywood. 1992. pap. 19.95 (*0-7145-2950-8*) M Boyars Pubs.

Palmer, Christopher, jt. auth. see Herzog, Brad.

Palmer, Christopher, ed. see Prokofiev, Sergei.

Palmer, Christopher A., jt. ed. see McKinney, Wayne R.

Palmer, Christopher M. Principles of Contaminant Hydrogeology. LC 96-4967. 256p. 1996. reprint ed. lib. bdg. 75.00 (*1-56670-169-4*, L1169) Lewis Pubs.

Palmer, Christopher M., et al. Principles of Contaminant Hydrogeology. 232p. 1991. lib. bdg. 59.95 (*0-87371-280-3*, L280) Lewis Pubs.

Palmer, Clara. You Can Be Healed. 187p. 1937. 3.48 (*0-87159-181-2*) Unity Bks.

Palmer, Clare. Environmental Ethics: A Reference Handbook. LC 97-25966. (Contemporary Ethical Issues Ser.). 192p. 1998. lib. bdg. 55.00 (*0-87436-840-5*, FN-1647) ABC-CLIO.

— Environmental Ethics & Process Thinking. (Oxford Theological Monographs). 256p. 1998. text 69.00 (*0-19-826952-8*) OUP.

Palmer, Clare, jt. auth. see Lidstone, Ken.

Palmer, Claude I. & Mrachek, L. A. Practical Mathematics. 7th ed. 560p. 1985. text 68.50 (*0-07-048254-3*) McGraw.

Palmer, Colin A. Human Cargoes: The British Slave Trade in Spanish America, 1700-1739. LC 81-3326. (Blacks in the New World Ser.). (Illus.). 212p. 1981. pap. text 10.95 (*0-252-00917-7*) U of Ill Pr.

— Human Cargoes: The British Slave Trade to Spanish America, 1700-1739. LC 81-3326. (Blacks in the New World Ser.). 200p. 1981. reprint ed. pap. 62.00 (*0-7837-8082-6*, 204783500008) Bks Demand.

— Passageways: An Interpretive History of Black America, 2 vols. 1998. pap. text 50.00 (*0-15-510257-5*) Harcourt.

— Slaves of the White God: Blacks in Mexico, 1570-1650. LC 75-34054. 246p. reprint ed. pap. 76.30 (*0-8357-8324-3*, 203393800087) Bks Demand.

Palmer, Colin A., ed. The Worlds of Unfree Labour: From Indentured Servitude to Slavery. LC 98-74000. (Expanding World Ser.: Vol. 16). 5p. 1999. text 130.95 (*0-86078-515-7*, Pub. by Ashgate Pub) Ashgate Pub Co.

Palmer, Colin A., jt. ed. see Knight, Franklin W.

Palmer, Craig T., jt. auth. see Thornhill, Randy.

Palmer, Cynthia, jt. ed. see Horowitz, Michael.

Palmer, Cynthia, ed. see Huxley, Aldous.

Palmer, D. & Helbig, K. Refraction Seismics Vol. 13: Lateral Resolution Structure & Seismic Velocity. (Handbook of Geophysical Exploration Ser.). 1986. 129.00 (*0-946631-13-1*, Pub. by Pergamon Repr) Franklin.

Palmer, D. D. The Chiropractor. 115p. 1996. reprint ed. pap. 13.00 (*0-7873-0652-5*) Hlth Research.

— The Chiropractor (1914) 117p. 1996. reprint ed. pap. 12.95 (*1-56459-775-X*) Kessinger Pub.

Palmer, D. G., jt. auth. see Weston, W. J.

Palmer, D. J. Shakespeare: Twelfth Night. LC 73-150101. (Casebook Ser.). 253p. 1972. write for info. (*0-333-12168-6*) Macmillan.

Palmer, Darwin, et al. The Infection Control Book. 400p. (C). 1996. ring bd. 99.95 (*1-56930-051-8*) Skidmore Roth Pub.

Palmer, Daryl W. Hospitable Performances: Dramatic Genre & Cultural Practices in Early Modern England. LC 91-16223. 232p. 1992. 32.95 (*1-55753-014-9*) Purdue U Pr.

Palmer, Dave R. Summons of the Trumpet: U. S.-Vietnam in Perspective. LC 77-28339. (Illus.). 348p. 1995. pap. 14.95 (*0-89141-550-5*) Presidio Pr.

— The Way of the Fox: American Strategy in the War for America, 1775-1783, 8. LC 74-5992. (Contributions to Military History Ser.: No. 8). 229p. 1975. 37.50 (*0-8371-7531-3*, PAF/, Greenwood Pr) Greenwood.

Palmer, David. Light & Sound. (Tell Me about Ser.). (Illus.). (J). 9.95 (*0-563-39625-3*, BBC-Parkwest) Parkwest Pubns.

— Organizing the Shipyards: Union Strategy in Three Northeast Ports, 1933-1945. LC 98-26635. (Illus.). 272p. 1998. 39.95 (*0-8014-2734-7*, ILR Press) Cornell U Pr.

Palmer, David, jt. auth. see Casler, Ken.

Palmer, David, jt. ed. see Bradbury, Malcolm.

Palmer, David A. Handbook of Applied Thermodynamics. 2nd ed. 1994. 207.00 (*0-8493-4484-0*, TJ265) CRC Pr.

— In Search of Cumorah: New Evidences for the Book of Mormon from Ancient Mexico. LC 80-83866. (Illus.). 300p. 1981. 18.98 (*0-88290-169-9*, 1063) Horizon Utah.

Palmer, David A., ed. Handbook of Applied Thermodynamics. 288p. 1987. boxed set 239.00 (*0-8493-3271-0*, TJ265) CRC Pr.

Palmer, David J., jt. ed. see Chaker, Victor.

Palmer, David R., jt. auth. see Hassel, Patricia L.

Palmer, David R., jt. auth. see Weinstein, Claire E.

Palmer, David S. Peru: The Authoritarian Tradition. LC 80-12176. 134p. 1980. 29.95 (*0-275-90531-4*, C0531, Praeger Pubs) Greenwood.

— Shining Path of Peru. 2nd ed. 287p. 1994. pap. 26.95 (*0-312-10619-X*) St Martin.

Palmer de Dueno, Rosa M. Sentido, Forma y Estilo de "Redentores" de Manuel Zeno Gandia. (UPREX, Estudios Literarios Ser.: No. 34). 124p. (C). 1974. pap. 1.50 (*0-8477-0034-8*) U of PR Pr.

Palmer, Derek. Surrey Rambles. 64p. 1987. 35.00 (*0-905392-77-9*) St Mut.

***Palmer, Diana.** After the Music. 2000. per. 3.99 (*1-55166-565-4*, Mira Bks) Harlequin Bks.

— After the Music. LC 00-39611. 2001. write for info. (*0-7838-9054-0*, G K Hall & Co) Mac Lib Ref.

Palmer, Diana. Amelia. (Orig.). 1996. pap. 2.99 (*0-8041-9705-9*) Ivy Books.

— Un Asunto de Familia: Man of Ice. (Deseo Ser.) (SPA.). 1996. per. 3.50 (*0-373-35166-6*, 1-35166-7) Harlequin Bks.

— The Australian. 1993. per. 4.50 (*0-373-48269-8*, 5-48269-0) Silhouette.

— Beloved: Man of the Month/Anniversary/Long Tall Texans. 1998. per. 3.75 (*0-373-76189-9*, 1-76189-9, Mira Bks) Harlequin Bks.

— Betrayed by Love. LC 95-13582. (Western Lovers Ser.). 250p. 1995. mass mkt. 3.99 (*0-373-88501-6*, 1-88501-1) Harlequin Bks.

— Blind Promises. (Love Inspired Ser.: Bk. 61). 1999. per. 4.50 (*0-373-87061-2*, 1-87061-7, Harlequin) Harlequin Bks.

— Bound by a Promise-Passion Flower. (Diana Palmer Duets Ser.: No. 5). 1990. mass mkt. 3.25 (*0-373-48226-4*) Harlequin Bks.

— Brianna et le Roi. (Azur Ser.). (FRE.). 1994. pap. 3.50 (*0-373-34436-8*, 1-34436-5) Harlequin Bks.

— The Bride's Choice. abr. ed. 1999. 21.95 (*0-373-59564-6*) Harlequin Bks.

— By Request: Long Tall Texans II. 1995. per. 5.50 (*0-373-20112-5*) Harlequin Bks.

— Calamity Mom. (To Mother with Love Ser.). 1993. mass mkt. 4.99 (*0-373-48254-X*, 5-48254-2) Silhouette.

— Callaghan's Bride (Virgin Bride) (Silhouette Romance Ser.: No. 1355). 1999. per. 3.50 (*0-373-19355-6*, 1-19355-6) Harlequin Bks.

— The Case of the Confirmed. (Desire Ser.: No. 715). 1992. pap. 2.89 (*0-373-05715-6*, 5-05715-3) Harlequin Bks.

— The Case of the Mesmerising Boss. 1999. per. 4.50 (*0-373-65103-1*) Harlequin Bks.

— The Case of the Mesmerizing Boss. (And the Winner Is...Ser.). 1997. mass mkt. 3.99 (*0-373-48343-0*, 1-48343-7) Harlequin Bks.

— The Case of the Missing Secretary. (Desire Ser.). 1992. per. 2.89 (*0-373-05733-4*, 5-05733-6) Silhouette.

— Cattleman's Choice. 1995. per. 4.99 (*1-55166-056-3*, Mira Bks) Harlequin Bks.

***Palmer, Diana.** Cattleman's Choice. 2000. per. 3.99 (*1-55166-566-2*, Mira Bks) Harlequin Bks.

Palmer, Diana. Champagne Girl. 1997. per. 5.50 (*1-55166-292-2*, 1-66292-3, Mira Bks) Harlequin Bks.

***Palmer, Diana.** Circle of Gold. 2000. mass mkt. write for info. (*0-373-15330-9*, 1-15330-3) Harlequin Bks.

— Coltrain's Proposal. large type ed. (Romance Ser.). 2000. 22.95 (*0-373-59732-0*) Silhouette.

An Asterisk (*) at the beginning of an entry indicates that the title is appearing for the first time.

— In Pictures Sequoia & Kings Canyon: The Continuing Story. Marapodi, Carlos, tr. (SPA., Illus.). 48p. (Orig.). 1990. pap. 8.95 (*0-88714-756-9*) KC Pubns.
— In Pictures Sequoia & Kings Canyon: The Continuing Story. Le Bras, Yvon, tr. (FRE., Illus.). 48p. (Orig.). 1991. pap. 8.95 (*0-88714-754-2*) KC Pubns.
— In Pictures Sequoia & Kings Canyon: The Continuing Story. Petzinger, Saori, tr. (JPN., Illus.). 48p. (Orig.). 1991. pap. 8.95 (*0-88714-755-0*) KC Pubns.
Palmer, John J. & Flanagan, Stephen. Comparative Negligence Manual. LC 85-21297. 1986. ring bd. 135.00 (*0-685-59925-6*) West Group.
Palmer, John L. Studies in the Contemporary Theatre. LC 70-97716. (Essay Index Reprint Ser.). 1977. 20.95 (*0-8369-1369-8*) Ayer.
Palmer, John L., ed. Creating Jobs: Public Employment Programs & Wage Subsidies. LC 78-12241. (Studies in Social Economics). 379p. 1978. pap. 16.95 (*0-8157-6891-5*) Brookings.
Palmer, John L. & Pechman, Joseph A., eds. Welfare in Rural Areas: The North Carolina-Iowa Income Maintenance Experiment. LC 77-91826. (Studies in Social Economics). 273p. 1978. 34.95 (*0-8157-6896-6*); pap. 14.95 (*0-8157-6895-8*) Brookings.
Palmer, John L., jt. ed. see Haveman, Robert H.
Palmer, John M. America in Arms. Kohn, Richard H., ed. LC 78-22392. (American Military Experience Ser.). 1980. reprint ed. lib. bdg. 18.95 (*0-405-11868-6*) Ayer.
— Anatomy for Speech & Hearing. 4th ed. (Illus.). 304p. 1993. pap. 31.00 (*0-683-06737-0*) Lppncott W & W.
— Survey of Communication Disorders. (Illus.). 288p. 1990. 39.00 (*0-683-06743-5*) Lppncott W & W.
Palmer, John T. Career Education For Physically Disabled Students: Development As A Lifetime Activity. LC 80-82642. 64p. 1980. 2.00 (*0-686-38799-6*) Human Res Ctr.
Palmer, John W. Constitutional Rights of Prisoners. 5th ed. LC 96-85365. 804p. (C). 1996. pap. text 48.95 (*0-87084-694-9*) Anderson Pub Co.
— Ohio Courtroom Evidence. 1994. ring bd., suppl. ed. 37.00 (*0-614-03765-4*, MICHIE) LEXIS Pub.
— Ohio Courtroom Evidence. 2nd ed. 500p. 1988. spiral bd. 115.00 (*1-55943-132-6*, MICHIE) LEXIS Pub.
Palmer, John W. Ohio Courtroom Evidence. 3rd ed. 115.00 (*0-327-12477-6*) LEXIS Pub.
Palmer, John W. Pioneer Days in San Francisco. Jones, William R., ed. (Illus.). 24p. 1977. reprint ed. pap. 2.95 (*0-89646-015-0*) Vistabooks.
***Palmer, John W. & Palmer, Stephen E.** Constitutional Rights of Prisoners. 6th ed. LC 99-13292. xiii, 823p. 1999. pap. 52.95 (*0-87084-227-7*) Anderson Pub Co.
Palmer, Jon. Wineries of the Mid-Atlantic. 220p. (Orig.). (C). 1988. text 35.00 (*0-8135-1346-4*) Rutgers U Pr.
Palmer, Joy. Environmental Education in the 21st Century: Theory, Practice, Progress & Promise. LC 97-15814. 304p. (C). 1998. 85.00 (*0-415-13196-0*) Routledge.
— Theory of Environmental Education. 304p. (C). 1998. pap. 25.99 (*0-415-13197-9*) Routledge.
Palmer, Joy, jt. auth. see Cooper, David E.
Palmer, Joy A. Deserts. (First Starts Ser.). 32p. (J). (gr. 1-4). 1993. pap. 4.95 (*0-8114-4912-2*) Raintree Steck-V.
— Oceans. 32p. (J). (gr. 1-4). 1993. pap. 4.95 (*0-8114-4915-7*) Raintree Steck-V.
— Rain. LC 92-38554. (What About...? Ser.). (Illus.). 32p. (J). (gr. 1-5). 1992. lib. bdg. 5.00 (*0-8114-3413-3*) Raintree Steck-V.
— Rain. 32p. (J). (gr. 1-4). 1994. pap. 4.95 (*0-8114-7774-6*) Raintree Steck-V.
— Rain Forests. 32p. (J). (gr. 1-4). 1993. pap. 4.95 (*0-8114-4911-4*) Raintree Steck-V.
— Snow & Ice. 32p. (J). (gr. 1-4). 1994. pap. 4.95 (*0-8114-7775-4*) Raintree Steck-V.
— Sunshine. (J). (ps-3). 1994. pap. 4.95 (*0-8114-6440-7*) Raintree Steck-V.
Palmer, Joy A. & Cooper, David E. Just Environments: Intergenerational, International, & Inter-Species Issues. LC 94-23953. 208p. (C). 1995. pap. 24.99 (*0-415-10336-3*, C0017) Routledge.
Palmer, Joy A., jt. ed. see Cooper, David E.
Palmer, Juan S., tr. see Arnold, Johann C.
Palmer, Julia, jt. auth. see Moriarity, Cay.
Palmer, Julia, jt. ed. see Hart, Anita.
Palmer, Julia, jt. ed. see Moriarity, Cay.
Palmer, Julia R. Read for Your Life: 2 Successful Efforts to Help People Read & an Annotated List of Books That Made Them Want To. LC 73-14695. 508p. 1974. 39.50 (*0-8108-0654-1*) Scarecrow.
Palmer, Julia R., ed. see Endahl, Carol F. & Britt, Greg.
Palmer, Julie G., jt. auth. see Walters, LeRoy.
Palmer, K. A. Local Government Law in New Zealand. 2nd ed. 1993. write for info. (*0-455-21180-9*, Pub. by LawBk Co); pap. write for info. (*0-455-21181-7*, Pub. by LawBk Co) Gaunt.
Palmer, K. J., jt. auth. see Kirchgraber, Urs.
Palmer, K. T. Notes for the MRCGP. 2nd ed. (Illus.). 336p. 1992. pap. 42.95 (*0-632-02909-9*) Blackwell Sci.
— Notes for the MRCGP. 3rd ed. LC 97-46538. 1998. 39.95 (*0-86542-777-1*) Blackwell Sci.
Palmer, Karen. All Saints. LC 97-16736. 272p. 1997. 24.00 (*1-56947-105-3*) Soho Press.
— All Saints. LC 97-16736. 272p. 1999. pap. 13.00 (*1-56947-138-X*) Soho Press.
***Palmer, Kari Gilliam.** One Tiny Hope. 240p. 1999. write for info. (*0-9674656-5-6*) Wheeler Holland.
Palmer, Kate S. A Gracious Plenty. (Illus.). 32p. (J). (gr. 1-4). 1998. reprint ed. pap. 7.95 (*0-9667114-0-8*) Warbranch Pr Inc.
Palmer, Katherine V. The Unpublished Velins of Lamarck, 1802 to 1809: Illustrations of Fossils of the Paris Basin Eocene. (Illus.). 67p. 1977. 21.00 (*0-87710-373-9*) Paleo Res.
Palmer, Katheryn Ann. Butterfly Dust. LC 96-36877. (Values for Young Women Ser.). 185p. (YA). 1996. pap. 7.95 (*1-56236-452-9*, Pub. by Aspen Bks) Origin Bk Sales.
Palmer, Kathleen, ed. see Basler, Lucille.
Palmer, Kenneth. Ceremonial Barges on the River Thames: A History of the Barges of the City of London Livery Company. 1999. 81.00 (*0-906290-17-1*) Unicorn Pr Lon.
Palmer, Kenneth, ed. see Shakespeare, William.
***Palmer, Kenneth J.** Shadowing in Dynamical Systems: Theory & Applications. LC 00-21743. (Mathematics & Its Applications Ser.). 2000. write for info. (*0-7923-6179-2*) Kluwer Academic.
Palmer, Kenneth J., jt. ed. see Kloeden, Peter E.
Palmer, Kenneth T., et al. Maine Politics & Government. LC 92-6080. (Politics & Governments of the American States Ser.). (Illus.). xxviii, 240p. 1992. pap. text 22.00 (*0-8032-8718-6*) U of Nebr Pr.
— Maine Politics & Government. LC 92-6080. (Politics & Governments of the American States Ser.). (Illus.). xxviii, 240p. 1992. text 45.00 (*0-8032-3680-8*) U of Nebr Pr.
Palmer, King. Piano & Keyboards. LC 97-76229. (Teach Yourself Ser.). (Illus.). 192p. 1998. pap. 10.95 (*0-8442-0040-9*, 00409, Teach Yrslf) NTC Contemp Pub Co.
— Piano & Keyboards. (Teach Yourself Ser.). 192p. 1999. pap. 17.95 incl. audio (*0-8442-1082-X*, 1082X, Teach Yrslf) NTC Contemp Pub Co.
Palmer, King C. Teach Yourself Music. (Illus.). 256p. 1995. pap. 9.95 (*0-8442-3934-8*, Teach Yrslf) NTC Contemp Pub Co.
— Teach Yourself Piano. (Illus.). 152p. 1995. pap. 7.95 (*0-8442-3936-4*, Teach Yrslf) NTC Contemp Pub Co.
— Teach Yourself Piano Audio Pack. 152p. 1995. pap. 17.95 incl. audio (*0-8442-3973-9*, Teach Yrslf) NTC Contemp Pub Co.
Palmer, Kris E. The Constitutional Amendments, 1789-1996. LC 99-33754. 716p. 1999. 95.00 (*0-7876-0782-7*, GML00198-109969) Gale.
Palmer, Kristine C. The Transition to Parenthood: Understanding & Adjusting to the Changes Couples Face. (Illus.). 150p. (Orig.). 1996. pap. 12.95 (*0-9654639-0-7*) Bright Fame.
Palmer, L. M., ed. see Croce, Benedetto.
Palmer, L. M., tr. & intro. see Vico, Giambattista.
Palmer, L. P., tr. see Zeller, Eduard.
Palmer, L. Pearl. Historical Review of the Town of Lysander. 173p. 1997. reprint ed. pap. 21.50 (*0-8328-6168-5*) Higginson Bk Co.
Palmer, Larry. Harpsichord in America: A Twentieth-Century Revival. LC 88-45446. (Illus.). 218p. 1989. 27.50 (*0-253-32710-5*) Ind U Pr.
— Harpsichord in America: A Twentieth-Century Revival. LC 88-45446. (Illus.). 218p. 1993. pap. 14.95 (*0-253-20840-8*) Ind U Pr.
***Palmer, Larry I.** Endings & Beginnings: Law, Medicine & Society in Assisted Life & Death. LC 99-54876. 160p. 2000. 39.95 (*0-275-96681-X*, Praeger Pubs) Greenwood.
Palmer, Laura. Shrapnel in the Heart: Letters & Remembrances from the Vietnam Veterans Memorial. 1988. pap. 13.00 (*0-394-75988-5*) Vin Bks.
Palmer, Laura & Willison, Marilyn. Touched by Magic. 238p. (Orig.). 1992. pap. 19.95 (*0-9631899-0-5*) Angel Ink.
Palmer, Laura K. Osgood & Anthony Perkins: A Comprehensive History of Their Work in Theatre, Film & Other Media, with Credits & an Annotated Bibliography. LC 90-53518. (Illus.). 423p. 1991. lib. bdg. 49.95 (*0-89950-577-5*) McFarland & Co.
Palmer, Leon. The Trained Eye: An Introduction to Astronomical Observing. (Illus.). 274p. (C). 1991. pap. text 15.00 (*0-03-047363-2*, Pub. by SCP) Harcourt.
Palmer, Leonard. The Sherman Letter. 200p. 1995. 18.95 (*1-885173-08-3*) Write Way.
Palmer, Leonard R. The Greek Language. LC 95-44855. (Illus.). 370p. 1996. pap. 21.95 (*0-8061-2844-5*) U of Okla Pr.
— The Latin Language. LC 87-40564. 384p. 1988. pap. 21.95 (*0-8061-2136-X*) U of Okla Pr.
— Mycenaeans & Minoans: Aegean Prehistory in the Light of the Linear B Tablets. 2nd ed. LC 79-22315. (Illus.). 368p. 1980. reprint ed. lib. bdg. 37.50 (*0-313-22160-X*, PAMY, Greenwood Pr) Greenwood.
Palmer, Les. Bowling. (Illus.). 54p. 1981. pap. text 8.95 (*0-89641-063-3*) American Pr.
— Fastpitch Softball. (Illus.). 100p. (C). 1998. pap. text 12.95 (*0-89641-300-4*) American Pr.
Palmer, Les & Johnson, Dewayne J. Softball. (Illus.). 54p. 1980. pap. text 9.95 (*0-89641-044-7*) American Pr.
Palmer, Leslie. Lena Horne: Entertainer. Huggins, Nathan I., ed. (Black Americans of Achievement Ser.). (Illus.). 124p. (YA). (gr. 5 up). 1989. lib. bdg. 19.95 (*1-55546-594-3*) Chelsea Hse.
Palmer, Leslie A., jt. auth. see Harris, David P.
Palmer, Lisa McNair, see Adkison, Danny M. & Palmer, Lisa McNair.
Palmer, Lisa McNair, jt. auth. see Adkison, Danny M.
Palmer, Lloyd. Steam Towards the Sunset: The Railroads of Lincoln County. LC 82-84454. (Lincoln County Historical Society Ser.: No. 23). (Illus.). 192p. (Orig.). 1982. pap. 19.95 (*0-911443-00-2*) Lincoln Coun Hist.
Palmer, Louis. Adventures in Afghanistan. 239p. 1990. 30.00 (*0-86304-053-5*, Pub. by Octagon Pr); pap. 15.00 (*0-86304-057-8*, Pub. by Octagon Pr) ISHK.
Palmer, Louis, jt. auth. see Cleckley, Franklin.
Palmer, Louis J., Jr. The Death Penalty: An American Citizen's Guide for Understanding Federal & State Laws. LC 98-27178. (Illus.). 295p. 1998. lib. bdg. 39.95 (*0-7864-0444-2*) McFarland & Co.
— Organ Transplants from Executed Prisoners: An Argument for the Creation of Death Sentence Organ Removal Statutes. LC 99-15655. 166p. 1999. lib. bdg. 35.00 (*0-7864-0673-9*) McFarland & Co.
Palmer, Lyman L. A Genealogical Record of the Descendants of John & Mary Palmer of Concord, Chester (Now Delaware County), Pennsylvania, Especially Through Their Son, John, Jr. & Sons-in-Law, William & James Trimble. (Illus.). 474p. 1989. reprint ed. pap. 74.00 (*0-8328-0931-4*); reprint ed. lib. bdg. 84.00 (*0-8328-0930-6*) Higginson Bk Co.
— History of Napa & Lake Counties: Comprising Their Geography, Geology, Topography...Also Extended Sketches of the Milling, Mining, Pisciculture & Wine Interests. With Biographical Sketches. (Illus.). 891p. 1995. reprint ed. lib. bdg. 92.50 (*0-8328-4978-2*) Higginson Bk Co.
— Palmer (& Trimble) Genealogical Record of the Descendants of John & Mary Palmer of Concord, PA. Also Includes Surnames Almond, Arment, Baker, & Others. (Illus.). 725p. 1990. reprint ed. pap. 107.00 (*0-8328-1527-6*); reprint ed. lib. bdg. 115.00 (*0-8328-1526-8*) Higginson Bk Co.
— Trimble (& Palmer) A Genealogical Record of Descendants of William & Ann Trimble of Concord Co., PA & James & Mary Trimble of Chester Co., PA & Others. (Illus.). 398p. 1990. reprint ed. pap. 59.50 (*0-8328-1529-2*); reprint ed. lib. bdg. 67.50 (*0-8328-1528-4*) Higginson Bk Co.
***Palmer, Lynn.** Are You Compatible with Your Boss, Partner, Coworker, Clients, Employees? 360p. 2000. pap. 20.00 (*0-9652296-9-6*) Star Bright.
— Beginners Guide to Angels. (Guides for Beginners Ser.). (Illus.). 96p. 1999. mass mkt. 11.95 (*0-340-73771-9*, Pub. by Headway) Trafalgar.
Palmer, Lynn M. & Toms, Janice E. Manual for Functional Training. 3rd ed. LC 91-34541. (Illus.). 351p. 1992. pap. text 29.95 (*0-8036-6759-0*) Davis Co.
Palmer, Lynne. ABC Basic Chart Reading. 76p. 1974. 13.00 (*0-86690-136-1*, P1363-014) Am Fed Astrologers.
— ABC Chart Erection. 224p. 1971. 14.00 (*0-86690-137-X*, P1364-014) Am Fed Astrologers.
— Astro-Guide to Nutrition. 1993. 14.00 (*0-86690-438-7*) Am Fed Astrologers.
— Astrological Almanac for 1999. 266p. (YA). (gr. 7-12). 1998. pap. 20.00 (*0-9652296-5-3*) Star Bright.
***Palmer, Lynne.** Astrological Almanac for 2000. 226p. (YA). (gr. 7-12). 1999. pap. 20.00 (*0-9652296-1-0*, Pub. by Star Bright) New Leaf Dist.
— Astrological Almanac for 2001. 248p. (YA). (gr. 8-12). 2000. pap. 20.00 (*0-9652296-6-1*, Pub. by Star Bright) New Leaf Dist.
Palmer, Lynne. Astrological Compatibility. LC 76-25674. 352p. 1976. 19.50 (*0-86690-139-6*, P1366-014) Am Fed Astrologers.
— Do-It-Yourself Publicity Directory. LC 84-70907. 184p. 1984. 20.00 (*0-86690-274-0*, P2532-014) Am Fed Astrologers.
— Gambling to Win. 118p. 1994. 14.95 (*0-86690-444-1*, P3503-014) Am Fed Astrologers.
***Palmer, Lynne.** Is Your Name Lucky for You? 170p. 1999. pap. 18.00 (*0-9652296-7-X*, Pub. by Star Bright) New Leaf Dist.
Palmer, Lynne. Lynne Palmer's Astrological Almanac for 1998. 286p. 1997. pap. 19.95 (*0-9652296-3-7*) Star Bright.
— Money Magic. 2nd rev. ed. LC 96-68440. (Illus.). 124p. (Orig.). 1996. pap. 11.00 (*0-9652296-0-2*) Star Bright.
— Nixon's Horoscope. 176p. 1975. 10.00 (*0-86690-140-X*, P1367-014) Am Fed Astrologers.
— Pluto Ephemeris, 1900-2000. LC 74-181511. 316p. 1974. 15.00 (*0-86690-200-7*, P1680-004) Am Fed Astrologers.
— Your Lucky Days & Numbers. LC 98-90169. (Illus.). 80p. 1998. pap. 8.95 (*0-9652296-8-8*) Star Bright.
Palmer, M. D. Henry VIII. 2nd ed. LC 82-23980. (Seminar Studies in History). (Illus.). 144p. (C). 1989. pap. text 15.00 (*0-582-35437-4*, 72225) Longman.
Palmer, M. Dale. True Esoteric Traditions: A Search for Western Cultural Values. LC 94-66752. (Illus.). 350p. (C). 1994. 29.00 (*0-9642633-0-0*) Noetics Inst.
Palmer, M. Lynn & Epler, Marcia. Fundamentals of Musculoskeletal Assessment Techniques. 2nd ed. LC 97-48521. 400p. 1998. spiral bd. 47.95 (*0-7817-1007-3*) Lppncott W & W.
Palmer, Margaret V., ed. Cave Research Foundation Annual Report, 1980. (Illus.). 51p. (Orig.). 1981. pap. 5.00 (*0-939748-03-7*) Cave Bks MO.
Palmer, Margaret V. & Palmer, Arthur N., eds. Cave Research Foundation Annual Report, 1982. (Illus.). 45p. (Orig.). 1983. pap. 5.00 (*0-939748-06-1*) Cave Bks MO.
Palmer, Marilyn. Framework Knitting. (Album Ser.: No. 119). (Illus.). 32p. 1989. pap. 6.95 (*0-85263-668-7*, Pub. by Shire Pubns) Parkwest Pubns.
Palmer, Marilyn & Neaverson, Peter. Industrial Archaeology: Principles & Practice. LC 97-25430. (Illus.). 200p. (C). 1998. 110.00 (*0-415-16626-8*); pap. 39.99 (*0-415-16769-8*) Routledge.
Palmer, Marilyn, jt. auth. see Evans, A. J.
Palmer, Marjorie & Palmer, Bernard. While the Sun Is High. LC 83-83388. (Heritage Ser.: Vol. 7). 1984. 10.95 (*0-911802-60-6*) Free Church Pubns.
Palmer, Marjorie, jt. auth. see Palmer, Bernard.
Palmer, Mark, jt. ed. see Collinge, John.
Palmer, Mark T., ed. see Barnett, George.
Palmer, Marlene. Expert Systems & Related Topics: A Selected Bibliography & Guide to Information Sources. LC 89-81134. 156p. 1990. 32.95 (*1-878289-03-9*) Idea Group Pub.
Palmer, Martha. Advanced Multiplication & Division. Hoffman, Joan, ed. (I Know It! Book Ser.). (Illus.). 32p. (J). (ps-3). 1980. student ed. 2.49 (*0-938256-36-X*, 02036) Sch Zone Pub Co.
— Beginning Addition & Subtraction. Hoffman, Joan, ed. (I Know It! Book Ser.). (Illus.). 32p. (J). (ps-3). 1980. student ed. 2.49 (*0-938256-29-7*, 02029) Sch Zone Pub Co.
— Beginning Multiplication & Division. Hoffman, Joan, ed. (I Know It! Book Ser.). (Illus.). 32p. (J). (ps-3). 1980. student ed. 2.49 (*0-938256-34-3*, 02034) Sch Zone Pub Co.
— Fractions. Hoffman, Joan, ed. (I Know It! Book Ser.). (Illus.). 32p. (J). (gr. 5-6). 1981. student ed. 2.49 (*0-938256-43-2*, 02043) Sch Zone Pub Co.
— Transition Math. Hoffman, Joan, ed. (I Know It! Book Ser.). (Illus.). 32p. (J). (gr. 4-7). 1979. student ed. 2.49 (*0-938256-27-0*, 02027) Sch Zone Pub Co.
Palmer, Martha S. Semantic Processing for Finite Domains. (Studies in Natural Language Processing). 209p. (C). 1990. text 69.95 (*0-521-36226-1*) Cambridge U Pr.
***Palmer, Martin.** Chinese Face & Hand Reading. (Illus.). 144p. (Orig.). 2000. pap. 9.95 (*0-7499-1929-9*, Pub. by Piatkus Bks) London Brdge.
Palmer, Martin. Element Classics: Tao Te Ching. LC 96-49587. (Element Classics of World Spirituality Ser.). 144p. 1997. pap. 16.95 (*1-85230-916-4*, Pub. by Element MA) Penguin Putnam.
— Elements of Taoism. (Illus.). 144p. 1997. pap. 9.95 (*1-86204-040-0*, Pub. by Element MA) Penguin Putnam.
— The Onset of Industrialisation. (C). 1976. text 45.00 (*0-7855-3204-8*, Pub. by Univ Nottingham) St Mut.
— Sacred Britain: A Guide to the Sacred Sites & Pilgrim Routes of England, Scotland & Wales. 1999. pap. 24.95 (*0-7499-1976-0*) Piatkus Bks.
— Yin & Yang: Understanding the Chinese Philosophy of Opposites & How to Apply It to Your Life. 1998. pap. text 14.95 (*0-7499-1628-1*, Pub. by Piatkus Bks) London Brdge.
Palmer, Martin & Breuilly, Elizabeth, trs. The Book of Chuang Tzu. 464p. 1996. pap. 13.95 (*0-14-019488-6*, Penguin Bks) Viking Penguin.
Palmer, Martin & O'Brien, Joanne, eds. The Book of Reincarnation & the Afterlife. 144p. (Orig.). 1997. pap. text 12.95 (*0-7499-1602-8*, Pub. by Piatkus Bks) London Brdge.
***Palmer, Martin & Palmer, Nigel.** The Spiritual Traveler: England, Scotland, Wales. 320p. 2000. pap. 18.00 (*1-58768-002-5*, 002-5) HiddenSprg.
Palmer, Martin, et al. Kuan Yin: Myths & Revelations of the Chinese Goddess of Compassion. (Illus.). 160p. 1995. 18.00 (*1-85538-417-5*) Thorsons PA.
— Religions of the World: The Illustrated Guide to Origins, Beliefs, Traditions & Festivals. Marty, Martin E., ed. LC 97-22829. (Illus.). 160p. (YA). (gr. 7 up). 1997. 29.95 (*0-8160-3723-X*) Facts on File.
Palmer, Martin, jt. auth. see Xiaomin, Zhao.
Palmer, Martin, jt. tr. see Ramsay, Jay.
Palmer, Martin E. Living Christianity. 1993. pap. 11.95 (*1-85230-327-1*, Pub. by Element MA) Penguin Putnam.
Palmer, Martin E., tr. from LAT. On Giving the Spiritual Exercises: The Early Jesuit Manuscript Directories & the Official Directory of 1599. LC 95-81839. (Jesuit Primary Sources in English Translation Ser.: Series I, Vol. 14). viii, 363p. (Orig.). 1996. 42.95 (*1-880810-17-4*); pap. 34.95 (*1-880810-18-2*) Inst Jesuit.
Palmer, Martin E., et al. Religion for a Change: An Integrated Course in Religious & Personal Education, 3 vols., Set. (Illus.). 272p. (Orig.). (J). (gr. 7-10). 1991. pap. 42.50 (*0-7487-0473-6*, Pub. by S Thornes Pubs) Trans-Atl Phila.
Palmer, Martin E., tr. see Favre, Pierre.
Palmer, Mary. Big Rivers & Whitewater of the World. 1998. pap. text 19.95 (*0-934007-37-3*) Paws Four Pub.
— The Complete Moose. Weinberger, Jane, ed. (Illus.). 40p. (Orig.). (J). (ps-5). 1997. pap. 10.00 (*1-883650-40-2*) Windswept Hse.
— Denali Curriculum: Climbing America's Highest Peak. LC 96-67596. 160p. (J). (gr. 3-6). 1996. spiral bd. 19.95 (*0-934007-27-6*) Paws Four Pub.
— Urinary Continence: Assessment & Promotion. 256p. 1996. 35.00 (*0-8342-0747-8*, 20747) Aspen Pub.
Palmer, Mary, et al, eds. Promising Practices: High School General Music. (Promising Practices Ser.). (Illus.). 112p. (C). 1989. pap. text 20.00 (*0-940796-65-1*, 1499) MENC.
Palmer, Mary & Sims, Wendy L., eds. Music in Prekindergarten: Planning & Teaching. (Illus.). 80p. (C). 1993. pap. text 20.00 (*1-56545-017-5*, 1031) MENC.
Palmer, Mary, jt. ed. see Paterson, David.
Palmer, Mary, ed. see Stevens, C. A.
Palmer, Mary A. Cucina di Calabria: Treasured Recipes & Family Traditions from Southern Italy. (Illus.). 280p. 1997. 32.95 (*0-571-19918-6*) Faber & Faber.
Palmer, Mary E. A Rating Scale to Be Used As a Guide in Grade Determination for Clinical Practice in the Medical & Surgical Nursing Course of a Specific Basic Collegiate Program. LC 60-12193. 99p. reprint ed. pap. 30.70 (*0-608-14440-1*, 205186000011) Bks Demand.
Palmer, Mary R. As Clean As a Whistle. LC 90-70148. 48p. (J). (ps-4). 1990. pap. 4.00 (*0-932433-66-9*) Windswept Hse.
— Poems Downeast. Whitaker, Kate, ed. LC 93-61629. (Illus.). 96p. 1994. pap. 8.95 (*1-883650-10-0*) Windswept Hse.
— Sharing Secrets. LC 91-65294. (Illus.). 60p. (J). (ps-4). 1991. pap. 4.00 (*0-932433-82-0*) Windswept Hse.
Palmer, Mary S. & Coffman, Elizabeth T. MemoraMOBILEia: Alabama Gulf Coast Potpourri. 195p. pap. 11.95 (*0-9639773-0-X*) Mobile & Bayside.
Palmer, Matthew, jt. auth. see Palmer, Geoffrey.
Palmer, Melba P. Are You Ready? 81p. (Orig.). 1984. pap. 7.95 (*0-942494-88-1*) Coleman Pub.

Palmer Memorial Episcopal Churchwomen, Houston, Te. Not by Bread Alone: Recipes of the Women of Palmer Church. Roberts, Michele S., ed. (Illus.). 288p. (Orig.). pap. text 12.95 (0-318-20648-X) D Armstrong.

Palmer, Michael. At Passages. LC 94-43613. 128p. (Orig.). 1995. pap. 12.95 (0-8112-1294-7, NDP803, Pub. by New Directions) Norton.
— Critical Judgment. large type ed. 1996. 25.95 (0-7838-1940-4, G K Hall Lrg Type) Mac Lib Ref.
— Critical Judgment. 480p. 1998. reprint ed. mass mkt. 7.50 (0-553-57408-6) Bantam.

***Palmer, Michael.** The Danish Notebook. 51p. 1999. pap. 9.95 (1-880713-18-7, Pub. by AVEC Bks) SPD-Small Pr Dist.

Palmer, Michael. Extreme Measures. 448p. 1992. mass mkt. 7.50 (0-553-29577-2) Bantam.
— Flashback. 416p. (Orig.). 1995. mass mkt. 7.50 (0-553-27329-9) Bantam.
— The Lion Bridge: Selected Poems, 1972-1995. LC 97-47579. 260p. 1998. pap. 18.95 (0-8112-1383-8, NDP863, Pub. by New Directions) Norton.
— Love of Glory & the Common Good: Aspects of the Political Thought of Thucydides. 188p. (C). 1992. text 54.50 (0-8476-7731-1); pap. text 22.95 (0-8476-7732-X) Rowman.
— Miracle Cure. LC 98-4884. 496p. 1999. reprint ed. mass mkt. 7.50 (0-553-57662-3) Bantam.
— Miracle Cure: A Novel. large type ed. LC 98-24433. 1998. 26.95 (1-56895-612-6) Wheeler Pub.
— Moral Problems in Medicine: A Practical Coursebook. LC 99-206718. 224p. 1999. text 19.95 (0-8020-8257-2) U of Toronto Pr.
— Natural Causes. 496p. 1994. mass mkt. 7.50 (0-553-56876-0) Bantam.

***Palmer, Michael.** The Patient. large type ed. LC 99-87235. 2000. 24.95 (0-375-40977-7) Random Hse Lrg Prnt.
— The Patient: A Novel. LC 99-57838. 336p. 2000. 24.95 (0-553-10983-9) Bantam.
— The Promises of Glass. LC 99-88019. 128p. 2000. 21.95 (0-8112-1443-5, Pub. by New Directions) SPD-Small Pr Dist.

Palmer, Michael. Side Effects. 368p. 1995. mass mkt. 7.50 (0-553-27618-2) Bantam.

***Palmer, Michael.** Side Effects. large type ed. 450p. 2000. lib. bdg. 26.95 (1-58547-028-7) Ctr Point Pubg.

Palmer, Michael. Silent Treatment. large type ed. LC 95-19989. 632p. 1995. 26.95 (0-7838-1406-2, G K Hall Lrg Type) Mac Lib Ref.
— Silent Treatment. large type ed. LC 95-19989. (Core Collection). 632p. 1996. 23.95 (0-7838-1405-4, G K Hall Lrg Type) Mac Lib Ref.
— Silent Treatment. 480p. 1996. reprint ed. mass mkt. 7.50 (0-553-57221-0) Bantam.
— The Sisterhood. 368p. 1994. mass mkt. 7.50 (0-553-27570-4) Bantam.
— The Sisterhood. large type ed. (Niagara Large Print Ser.). 390p. 1996. 29.50 (0-7089-5820-6) Ulverscroft.
— Three Complete Novels. 784p. 1996. 13.99 (0-517-14959-1) Wings Bks.
— Tratamiento Criminal. 1999. pap. text 11.95 (84-08-02189-3) Planeta.

Palmer, Michael & Pangle, Thomas L., eds. Political Philosophy & the Human Soul: Essays in Memory of Allan Bloom. LC 95-9024. 320p. (C). 1995. 34.95 (0-8476-8059-2) Rowman.

Palmer, Michael, et al. Avec Sampler #2. Chadwick, Cydney, ed. 162p. 1998. pap. 12.95 (1-880713-15-2, Pub. by AVEC Bks) SPD-Small Pr Dist.

Palmer, Michael, jt. auth. see Roberts, Simon.

Palmer, Michael, ed. see Tillich, Paul Johannes.

Palmer, Michael, tr. see Berger, John & Tanner, Alain.

Palmer, Michael, tr. see Bonvicino, Regis.

Palmer, Michael, tr. see Hocquard, Emmanuel.

Palmer, Michael, tr. see Parshchikov, Alexei.

Palmer, Michael A. General Robert E. Lee on the Offensive. LC 97-18182. 189p. 1998. 24.95 (0-471-16401-1) Wiley.
— Guardians of the Gulf: A History of America's Expanding Role in the Persian Gulf, 1833-1992. 1992. 29.95 (0-02-923843-9) Free Pr.
— Lee Moves North: Robert E. Lee on the Offensive. 189p. 1999. pap. 14.95 (0-471-35059-1) Wiley.
— On Course: Strategies for Creating Success in College in Life: A Guided Journal Appproach. (Contributions to Naval History Ser.: No. 5). (Illus.). 201p. (Orig.). (C). 1992. pap. 11.00 (0-945274-08-4) Naval Hist Ctr.
— On Course to Desert Storm: The U. S. Navy & the Persian Gulf. (Illus.). 201p. (Orig.). (C). 1993. pap. text 35.00 (1-56806-556-6) DIANE Pub.
— On Course to Desert Storm: The U. S. Navy & the Persian Gulf. 213p. (Orig.). 1992. per. 14.00 (0-16-035946-5) USGPO.
— Origins of the Maritime Strategy: American Naval Strategy in the First Postwar Decade. (Contributions to Naval History Ser.: No. 1). (Illus.). 129p. (C). 1988. pap. 7.50 (0-945274-01-7) Naval Hist Ctr.
— Origins of the Maritime Strategy: The Development of American Naval Strategy, 1945-1955. LC 90-30117. (Illus.). 192p. 1990. 24.95 (0-87021-667-8) Naval Inst Pr.

***Palmer, Michael A.** Stoddert's War: Naval Operations During the Quasi-War with France, 1798-1801. LC 99-50203. 1999. 34.95 (1-55750-664-7) Naval Inst Pr.

Palmer, Michael A. The War That Never Was. (Illus.). 368p. 1994. 19.95 (0-918339-28-6) Vandamere.

Palmer, Michael D. Names, Reference & Correctness in Platos Cratylus. (American University Studies: Philosophy: Ser. 5, Vol. 55). XX, 207p. 1988. 34.40 (0-8204-0708-9) P Lang Pubng.

Palmer, Michael D. & Horton, Stanley M. Elements of a Christian Worldview. LC 98-19264. 576p. 1998. 39.95 (0-88243-489-6) Gospel Pub.

Palmer, Michael F. Freud & Jung on Religion. LC 96-51720. (Illus.). 256p. (C). 1997. 80.00 (0-415-14746-8) Routledge.
— Freud & Jung on Religion. LC 96-51720. (Illus.). 256p. (C). 1997. pap. 24.99 (0-415-14747-6) Routledge.
— Paul Tillich's Philosophy of Art. LC 83-15056. (Theologische Bibliothek Toepelmann Ser.: Vol. 41). xxii, 217p. 1983. 76.15 (3-11-009681-1) De Gruyter.

Palmer, Michael J. Advanced Networking Concepts. 264p. (C). 1996. pap. 42.95 (0-7895-0195-3) Course Tech.
— A Guide to Microsoft NT Server 4.0. 612p. (C). 1998. pap. 60.95 (0-7600-5875-X) Course Tech.
— A Guide to Microsoft NT Server 4.0 in the Enterprise. 612p. (C). 1998. pap. 45.00 (0-7600-5876-8) Course Tech.
— Hands-On Microsoft Windows NT 4.0 Server with Projects. 320p. (C). 1997. pap. 24.00 (0-7600-5008-2) Course Tech.
— Hands-on Microsoft Windows NT 4.0 Server with Projects. 320p. (C). 1997. teacher ed. 49.95 (0-7600-5009-0) Course Tech.
— Hands-on Microsoft Windows NT 4.0 Server with Projects. 10th ed. 320p. (C). 1997. 3.5 hd. write for info. (0-7600-5052-X) Course Tech.
— MCSE NT Server 4. LC 98-4254. (Exam Prep Ser.). (Illus.). 640p. 1998. pap. text 49.99 (1-57610-252-1) Coriolis Grp.
— Network Administrator: Microsoft Windows NT 4.0. 800p. 1997. pap. write for info. (0-7600-5010-4) Course Tech.

Palmer, Michael J. & Sinclair, Robert B. Advanced Networking Concepts. 264p. (C). 1997. teacher ed. 49.95 (0-7895-0594-0) Course Tech.

Palmer, Michael J., jt. auth. see Rains, Alvin L.

Palmer, Michael W. Levels of Constituent Structure in New Testament Greek. LC 93-30457. (Studies in Biblical Greek: Vol. 4). X, 143p. (C). 1995. pap. text 24.95 (0-8204-2115-4) P Lang Pubng.

Palmer, Michele. Zoup Soup. LC 78-66342. (Illus.). (J). (ps-1). 1978. pap. 1.95 (0-932306-00-4) Rocking Horse.

Palmer, Michele, ed. A Mother Goose Feast: Rhymes & Recipes. LC 79-65819. (Illus.). (J). (ps-12). 1979. pap. 1.95 (0-932306-01-2) Rocking Horse.
— Rainy Day Rhymes: A Collection of Chants, Forecasts & Tales. LC 84-60412. (Illus.). 24p. (Orig.). (J). (gr. k up). 1984. pap. 2.95 (0-932306-02-0) Rocking Horse.

Palmer, Mick, jt. ed. see Etter, Barbara.

Palmer, Mike. Systematic Golf: A Complete Golf Instruction Course. LC 92-38184. (Illus.). 160p. 1993. pap. 16.95 (0-8069-0329-5) Sterling.

Palmer, Mike, jt. auth. see Dickinson, Gill.

Palmer, Monte. Comparative Politics: Political Economy, Political Culture & Political Interdependency. LC 96-70030. (Illus.). 700p. (C). 1997. boxed set 50.00 (0-87581-407-7, CPOL) F E Peacock Pubs.
— Political Development: Dilemmas & Challenges. LC 96-70031. Orig. Title: Dilemmas of Political Development. (Illus.). 400p. (C). 1997. pap. text 35.00 (0-87581-406-9, PD) F E Peacock Pubs.
— Survey Research in the Arab World. (C). 1980. pap. text 43.50 (0-906559-09-X) Westview.

Palmer, Monte, et al. The Egyptian Bureaucracy. 200p. 1988. 34.95 (0-8156-2455-7) Syracuse U Pr.

Palmer, Myles. Small Talk, Big Names: Forty Years of Rock Quotes 1953-1993. 192p. 1994. pap. 13.95 (1-85158-573-7, Pub. by Mainstream Pubng) Trafalgar.

Palmer, Nancy, ed. see Palmer, Joe E.

Palmer, Nancy S., et al. The Family Puzzle: Putting the Pieces Together: A Guide to Parenting the Blended Family. LC 96-6006. 185p. (Orig.). 1996. pap. 12.00 (0-89109-949-2) Pinon Press.

Palmer, Nellie M., ed. see Palmer, Horace W.

Palmer, Nettie. Nettie Palmer. Smith, Vivian, ed. LC 88-17606. (UQP Australian Authors Ser.). 548p. (Orig.). 1989. pap. text 16.95 (0-7022-2130-9, Pub. by Univ Queensland Pr) Intl Spec Bk.

Palmer, Niall A. The New Hampshire Primary & the American Electoral Process. LC 96-50322. 216p. 1997. 55.00 (0-275-95569-9, Praeger Pubs) Greenwood.

***Palmer, Niall A.** The New Hampshire Primary & the American Electoral Process. LC 96-50322. 195p. 2000. reprint ed. 22.00 (0-8133-3777-1) Westview.

Palmer, Nigel, jt. auth. see Palmer, Martin.

Palmer, Nina, ed. see Moore Educational Publishers Staff.

Palmer, Noel. Daily Notes to God. 112p. 1991. 7.00 (0-9631717-0-4) N Palmer.

Palmer, Norma E. Central Coast (California) Miller, Kristine, ed. 356p. (Orig.). 1995. pap. 11.95 (1-56413-309-5) Auto Club.

Palmer, Norman, ed. The Recovery of Stolen Art. LC 99-159693. 262p. 1998. 100.00 (90-411-9658-7) Kluwer Law Intl.

Palmer, Norman & McKendrick, Ewan. Product Liability in the Construction Industry. 326p. 1993. 100.00 (1-85044-530-3) LLP.

Palmer, Norman & McKendrick, Ewan, eds. Interest in Goods. (Lloyd's Commercial Law Library). 670p. 1993. 190.00 (1-85044-445-5) LLP.

Palmer, Norman, jt. auth. see Moore, Margaret.

Palmer, Norman D. Elections & Political Development: The South Asian Experience. LC 75-4032. 350p. reprint ed. pap. 108.50 (0-608-15058-4, 202621200048) Bks Demand.
— The United States & India: The Dimensions of Influence. LC 84-8272. (Studies of Influence in International Relations). 302p. 1984. 55.00 (0-275-91240-X, C1240, Praeger Pubs); pap. 21.95 (0-275-91624-3, B1624, Praeger Pubs) Greenwood.

Palmer, P. E. Manual of Darkroom Technique: WHO Basic Radiological System. (CHI, FRE & SPA.). 25p. 1985. pap. text 8.00 (92-4-154178-4, 1150238) World Health.

Palmer, P. E., ed. Manual of Diagnostic Ultrasound. (FRE & SPA., Illus.). 334p. (C). 1995. pap. 65.00 (92-4-154461-9, 1150393) World Health.

Palmer, P. L. Stability of Collisionless Stellar Systems: Mechanisms for the Dynamical Structure of Galaxies. LC 94-32551. (Astrophysics & Space Science Library: Vol. 185). 360p. (C). 1994. lib. bdg. 151.50 (0-7923-2455-2) Kluwer Academic.

***Palmer, Pam.** Tatting, 323. (Shire Album Ser.). 1999. pap. text 6.25 (0-7478-0312-9) Shire Pubns.

Palmer, Pam & Podlin, Sharon. Hands-On Visual Basic 5. LC 97-66157. 480p. 1997. per. 40.00 (0-7615-1046-X) Prima Pub.

***Palmer, Pamela.** Teach Yourself Word 2000 Automation in 24 Hours. (Teach Yourself . . . Ser.). 528p. 1999. pap. 19.99 (0-672-31652-8) Sams.

Palmer, Pamela. Using VBA for Office 2000. (Special Edition Using... Que Ser.). 800p. 2000. pap. text 29.99 (0-7897-1953-3) Que.

Palmer, Pamela, jt. auth. see Cassel, Paul.

Palmer, Pamela, jt. auth. see Dameron, J. Lasley.

Palmer, Parker J. The Active Life: A Spirituality of Work, Creativity, & Caring. LC 99-20274. 176p. 1999. pap. 16.00 (0-7879-4934-5) Jossey-Bass.
— The Active Life: Wisdom for Work, Creativity, & Caring. LC 91-55088. 160p. 1991. reprint ed. pap. 13.00 (0-06-066458-4, Pub. by Harper SF) HarpC.
— The Company of Strangers: Christians & the Renewal of America's Public Life. 169p. 1983. reprint ed. pap. 14.95 (0-8245-0601-4) Crossroad NY.
— In the Belly of a Paradox: The Thought of Thomas Merton. LC 78-71769. 1979. pap. 4.00 (0-87574-224-6) Pendle Hill.
— Let Your Life Speak: Listening for the Voice of Vocation. LC 99-6467. 112p. 1999. 18.00 (0-7879-4735-0) Jossey-Bass.
— A Place Called Community. LC 77-75909. (Orig.). 1977. pap. 4.00 (0-87574-212-2) Pendle Hill.
— To Know as We Are Known: A Spirituality of Education. LC 92-54712. 160p. 1993. reprint ed. pap. 13.00 (0-06-066451-7, Pub. by Harper SF) HarpC.

Palmer, Parker J., et al, eds. Caring for the Commonweal: Education for Religious & Public Life. LC 89-78103. 272p. (C). 1990. text 30.00 (0-86554-358-5, MUP-H286) Mercer Univ Pr.

Palmer, Pat. I Wish I Could Hold Your Hand: A Child's Guide to Grief & Loss. LC 94-25611. (Illus.). 32p. (J). (ps-6). 1994. pap. 8.95 (0-915166-82-8, Little Imp Books) Impact Pubs CA.

***Palmer, Pat & Froehner, Melissa A.** Teen Esteem: A Self-Direction Manual for Young Adults. 2nd rev. ed. (Illus.). 112p. 2000. pap. 9.95 (1-886230-14-5, Little Imp Books) Impact Pubs CA.

***Palmer, Pat, et al.** The Medical Bill Survival Guide: What You Need to Know Before You Pay a Dime. 2000. mass mkt. 6.99 (0-446-60862-9) Warner Bks.

Palmer, Pati. Restitution, 4 vols., 1. 1978. 165.00 (0-316-69000-7, Aspen Law & Bus) Aspen Pub.
— Restitution, 4 vols., 2. 1978. 165.00 (0-316-69001-5, Aspen Law & Bus) Aspen Pub.
— Restitution, 4 vols., 3. 1978. 165.00 (0-316-69002-3, Aspen Law & Bus) Aspen Pub.

Palmer, Pati & Alto, Marta. Fit for Real People: Sew Great Clothes Using Any Pattern. Gosch, Ann P., ed. LC 98-139894. (Illus.). 208p. (Orig.). 1998. pap. 24.95 (0-935278-43-5) Palmer-Pletsch.

Palmer, Pati & Pletsch, Susan. Easy, Easier, Easiest Tailoring. rev. ed. LC 83-61672. (Illus.). 128p. 1983. pap. 8.95 (0-935278-09-5) Palmer-Pletsch.
— Mother Pletsch's Painless Sewing. rev. ed. (Illus.). 128p. 1996. pap. 8.95 (0-935278-44-3) Palmer-Pletsch.
— Pants for Any Body. rev. ed. LC 82-61290. (Illus.). 128p. (Orig.). 1982. pap. 8.95 (0-935278-08-7) Palmer-Pletsch.

Palmer, Pati, et al. Creative Serging, Vol. II. (Illus.). 128p. 1995. pap. 8.95 (0-935278-12-5) Palmer-Pletsch.
— The New Creative Serging Illustrated: The Complete Guide to Decorative Overlock Sewing. rev. ed. LC 93-38107. (Creative Machine Arts Ser.). (Illus.). 176p. 1993. pap. 18.95 (0-8019-8382-7) Krause Pubns.

Palmer, Pati, ed. see Black, Lynnette R.

Palmer, Pati, ed. see Cherry, Winky.

Palmer, Pati, ed. & intro. see Cherry, Winky.

Palmer, Patricia, jt. auth. see Baskerville, Patricia E.

Palmer, Patricia G. & Gerbeth-Jones, Susan. A Scanning Electron Microscope Survey of the Epidermis of East African Grasses, Vol. 4. LC 80-19201. (Smithsonian Contributions to Botany Ser.: No. 62). 124p. reprint ed. pap. 38.50 (0-608-15311-7, 202955100061) Bks Demand.

Palmer, Patricia G., et al. A Scanning Electron Microscope Survey of the Epidermis of East African Grasses, Pt. 3. LC 80-19201. (Smithsonian Contributions to Botany Ser.: No. 55). 142p. reprint ed. pap. 44.10 (0-608-14946-2, 202568400045) Bks Demand.

Palmer, Patti, jt. auth. see Miller, Marcy.

Palmer, Paul, jt. auth. see Wellman, Frank.

Palmer, Paul C., jt. auth. see O'Neil, A. W.

Palmer, Paul M. One Hundred Twenty-One Real Estate T. I. P. S. Techniques & Ideas on Purchasing & Selling. Lipstein, Sherman & Cockhill, Pat B., eds. (Illus.). 272p. (Orig.). 1985. pap. 12.95 (0-935679-01-4) Commercial Choice.

Palmer, Paulina. Lesbian Gothic: Transgressive Fictions. LC 99-12385. 160p. 1999. 49.95 (0-304-70153-X); pap. 19.95 (0-304-70154-8) Continuum.

Palmer, Pauline. Contemporary Lesbian Writing: Dreams, Desire, Difference. LC 93-2467. (Gender in Writing Ser.). 160p. 1994. pap. 31.95 (0-335-09038-9) OpUniv Pr.

Palmer, Pete, jt. auth. see Clifton, Merritt.

Palmer, Peter. The Complete Orienteering Manual. (Illus.). 192p. 1998. pap. 29.95 (1-86126-095-4, Pub. by Crolwood) Trafalgar.

Palmer, Peter, tr. see Brinkmann, Reinhold.

Palmer, Peter, tr. see Kropfinger, Klaus.

Palmer, Peter L. The Web Server Handbook. LC 96-220301. 496p. (C). 1996. pap. text 39.95 (0-13-239930-X) P-H.

Palmer, Peter S. History of Lake Champlain: From Its First Exploration by the French in 1609 to the Close of the Year 1814. 4th ed. LC 92-15003. (Illus.). 250p. 1996. reprint ed. pap. 14.50 (0-935796-31-2) Purple Mnt Pr.
— History of Lake Champlain, from Its First Exploration by the French in 1609, to the Close of the Year 1814. (Illus.). 276p. 1997. reprint ed. lib. bdg. 35.00 (0-8328-6084-0) Higginson Bk Co.

Palmer, Phil. Michigan Portraits. (Illus.). (C). text. write for info. (0-472-10433-0) U of Mich Pr.

***Palmer, Philip E. & Reeder, Maurice M.** The Imaging of Tropical Diseases Vol. 2: Epidemiological, Pathological & Clinical Correlation. 2nd ed. LC 99-39417. (Illus.). xxiv, 776p. 2000. 350.00 (3-540-62471-6) Spr-Verlag.

***Palmer, Philip E. S. & Reeder, Maurice M.** The Imaging of Tropical Diseases: Epidemiological, Pathological & Clinical Correlation, 2 vols. 2nd ed. LC 99-39417. (Illus.). 2000p. 2000. 589.00 (3-540-66219-7) Spr-Verlag.
— The Imaging of Tropical Diseases: Epidemiological, Pathological & Clinical Correlation. 2nd rev. ed. LC 99-39417. (Illus.). xxiv, 776p. 2000. 350.00 (3-540-56028-9) Spr-Verlag.

Palmer, Philip M. & More, Robert P. Sources of the Faust Tradition. LC 65-29231. (Studies in Comparative Literature: No. 35). 1969. reprint ed. lib. bdg. 75.00 (0-8383-0608-X) M S G Haskell Hse.

Palmer, Phobe. Full Salvation. 1979. pap. 5.99 (0-88019-028-0) Schmul Pub Co.

Palmer, Phoebe. Entire Devotion to God. 1979. 5.99 (0-88019-385-9) Schmul Pub Co.
— Faith & Its Effects: How to Receive the Blessing of a Sanctified Life. 224p. 1999. pap. 11.99 (0-88019-392-1) Schmul Pub Co.
— The Promise of the Father. pap. 19.99 (0-88019-099-X) Schmul Pub Co.

Palmer, Phoebe. The Way of Holiness. 1988. pap. 10.99 (0-88019-233-X) Schmul Pub Co.

Palmer, Phyllis. Domesticity & Dirt: Housewives & Domestic Servants in the United States, 1920-1945. (Women in the Political Economy Ser.). 248p. 1991. pap. 19.95 (0-87722-901-5) Temple U Pr.

Palmer Preservation Society Staff, ed. see Blocker, Francis A.

Palmer, Prudence T. & Palmer, T. J. St. Clements: The Chronicle of a Connecticut River Castle. (Illus.). 208p. (Orig.). 1992. pap. 25.00 (0-9634150-0-X) Paper Rock Pub.

Palmer, Prudence Taylor & Palmer, Theodore J. Letters to Harry, 1872-1874: A Man of Letters. (Illus.). 208p. 1999. pap. write for info. (0-9634150-1-8) Paper Rock Pub.

Palmer Publications Staff, ed. see Faythines.

Palmer, R. Brain Train. 2nd ed. (Illus.). 352p. (C). 1996. pap. 22.99 (0-419-19830-X) Routledge.

Palmer, R. A., jt. auth. see Ladd, M. F.

Palmer, R. A., jt. ed. see Ladd, M. F.

Palmer, R. B., ed. Chaucer's French Contemporaries: The Poetry - Poetics of Self & Tradition. LC 91-58148. (Georgia State Literary Studies: No. 10). xxxi, 360p. 1992. 55.00 (0-404-63210-6) AMS Pr.

Palmer, R. Barton. Hollywood's Dark Cinema: The American Film Noir. (Twayne's Filmmakers Ser.). (Illus.). 200p. 1994. pap. 20.00 (0-8057-9335-6, Twayne) Mac Lib Ref.
— Perspectives on Film Noir. 1996. 55.00 (0-8161-1601-6, G K Hall & Co) Mac Lib Ref.

Palmer, R. Barton, ed. Guillaume de Machaut: Fonteinne Amoureuse. LC 93-1095. (Library of Medieval Literature). 360p. 1993. text 20.00 (0-8240-8781-X) Garland.

Palmer, R. Barton, ed. from FRE. Guillaume de Machaut: Le Confort D'ami (Comfort for a Friend) LC 91-39839. (Library of Medieval Literature: Vol. 67A). 314p. 1992. text 21.00 (0-8240-4032-5) Garland.

Palmer, R. Barton, tr. see Leech-Wilkinson, Daniel & Wilhelm, James J., eds.

Palmer, R. Dale. Knowing . . . What You Want: A Seeker's Handbook to Desire. 150p. 1997. pap. 9.45 (0-9661343-0-3) WORDsync.

Palmer, R. E., jt. ed. see Beecroft, K. A.

Palmer, R. E., ed. see Library Association, Conference Staff.

Palmer, R. L. Anorexia Nervosa: A Guide for Sufferers & Their Families. 144p. 1989. pap. 11.95 (0-14-010034-2, Penguin Bks) Viking Penguin.

Palmer, R. R., ed. & tr. see De Tocqueville, Herve.

Palmer, R. R., tr. see Say, Jean-Baptiste.

Palmer, Raenette. Santa Quits. LC 97-69129. (Illus.). 32p. (J). (gr. k-5). 1998. 15.95 (1-890394-08-4, Sage Creek) Rhodes & Easton.

Palmer, Ralph & Richer, Elaine. Maine Real Estate. 4th ed. LC 97-22040. 363p. (C). 1997. pap. text 35.40 (0-13-899642-3) P-H.

Palmer, Ralph A. & Bailey, Joanne. Maryland Real Estate Principles. 456p. (C). 1995. pap. text 32.67 (0-13-777624-1) P-H.

Palmer, Ralph A. & Frank, Gregory J. Oregon Real Estate Practices, Finance, Law. 468p. (C). 1996. pap. text 33.60 (0-13-777681-0) P-H.

Palmer, Ralph A. & Fraser, Marge. Michigan Real Estate: Principles & Practices. 2nd ed. LC 97-31189. 464p. (C). 1997. pap. text 38.00 (0-13-899659-8) P-H.

P

An Asterisk (*) at the beginning of an entry indicates that the title is appearing for the first time.

Palmer, Ralph A. & Lusht, Kenneth M. Pennsylvania Real Estate Fundamentals & Practices. 478p. (C). 1997. pap. text 19.20 (*0-13-777384-6*) P-H.

Palmer, Ralph A., jt. auth. see Keck, Nancy F.

Palmer, Ralph S. Handbook of North American Birds: Condors & Raptors, Vol. 4, Pt. 1. LC 62-8259. Vol. 1. 448p. (C). 1988. 50.00 (*0-300-04059-8*) Yale U Pr.

— Handbook of North American Birds: Condors & Raptors, Vol. 5, Pt. 2. LC 62-8259. Vol. 2. (C). 1988. 50.00 (*0-300-04060-1*) Yale U Pr.

***Palmer, Randy.** Herschell Gordon Lewis, Godfather of Gore: The Films. LC 99-88929. (Illus.). 203p. 2000. 32.50 (*0-7864-0808-1*) McFarland & Co.

Palmer, Randy. Paul Blaisdell, Monster Maker: A Biography of the B Movie Makeup & Special Effects Artist. LC 96-45718. (Illus.). 304p. 1997. lib. bdg. 45.00 (*0-7864-0270-9*) McFarland & Co.

Palmer, Ransford W. Caribbean Dependence on the United States Economy. LC 78-19770. (Praeger Special Studies). 173p. 1979. 38.95 (*0-275-90406-7*, C0406, Praeger Pubs) Greenwood.

— Contemporary Caribbean Migration to the U. S. LC 94-36254. (Immigrant Heritage of America Ser.). 1995. pap. 20.00 (*0-8057-4546-7*, Twyne) Mac Lib Ref.

— Contemporary Caribbean Migration to the U. S. The Economics of West Indian Migration to America. LC 94-36254. (Immigrant Heritage of America Ser.). 1995. 33.00 (*0-8057-8431-4*, Twyne) Mac Lib Ref.

Palmer, Ransford W., ed. In Search of a Better Life: Perspectives on Migration from the Caribbean. LC 89-29658. (Illus.). 208p. 1990. 52.95 (*0-275-93409-8*, C3409, Greenwood Pr) Greenwood.

— The Repositioning of U. S. Caribbean Relations in the New World Order. LC 97-5591. 232p. 1997. 62.95 (*0-275-95858-2*, Praeger Pubs) Greenwood.

— U. S.-Caribbean Relations: Their Impact on Peoples & Culture. LC 96-53610. 176p. 1998. 49.95 (*0-275-95859-0*, Praeger Pubs) Greenwood.

Palmer, Ray, jt. auth. see Arnold, Kenneth.

Palmer, Richard. The Cutting Edge: The Music of Sonny Rollins. (East Note - Hull Studies in Jazz). 230p. 1998. pap. 19.95 (*0-85958-667-7*, Pub. by Univ of Hull Pr) Paul & Co Pubs.

Palmer, Richard & Pope, Chris. Brain Train: Studying for Success. 230p. 1984. pap. 12.95 (*0-419-13110-8*, NO. 9185, E & FN Spon) Routledge.

***Palmer, Richard D.** Maintenance Planning & Scheduling Manual. 1999. 79.95 (*0-07-048264-0*) McGraw.

Palmer, Richard E. Hermeneutics: Interpretation Theory in Schleiermacher, Dilthey, Heidegger, & Gadamer. LC 68-54885. (Studies in Phenomenology & Existential Philosophy). 283p. 1969. pap. 15.95 (*0-8101-0459-8*) Northwestern U Pr.

Palmer, Richard E., jt. ed. see Michelfelder, Diane P.

Palmer, Richard E., ed. & tr. see Husserl, Edmund, et al.

Palmer, Richard F. & Roehl, Harvey N. Railroads in Early Postcards Vol. 1: Upstate New York. LC 89-70721. (Illus.). 112p. (Orig.). 1990. pap. 11.95 (*0-911572-87-2*, Vestal Pr) Madison Bks UPA.

Palmer, Richard H. The Contemporary British History Play, 81. LC 97-38985. (Contributions in Drama & Theatre Studies: Vol. 81). 272p. 1998. 65.00 (*0-313-30497-1*, Greenwood Pr) Greenwood.

— The Critics' Canon: Standards of Theatrical Reviewing in America, 26. LC 88-5671. (Contributions in Drama & Theatre Studies: No. 26). 195p. 1988. 55.00 (*0-313-26211-X*, PAO/, Greenwood Pr) Greenwood.

— The Lighting Art: The Aesthetics of Stage Lighting Design. 2nd ed. LC 93-225. 251p. 1993. 79.00 (*0-13-501081-0*) P-H.

— Tragedy & Tragic Theory: An Analytical Guide. LC 91-46861. 252p. 1992. lib. bdg. 65.00 (*0-313-28203-X*, PTT, Greenwood Pr) Greenwood.

Palmer, Richard P. Case Studies in Library Computer Systems. LC 73-17008. (Bowker Series in Problem-Centered Approaches to Librianship). 230p. reprint ed. pap. 71.30 (*0-608-15141-6*, 202305200031) Bks Demand.

Palmer, Richard P. & Varnet, Harvey. How to Manage Information: A Systems Approach. LC 89-27690. (Illus.). 152p. 1990. pap. 29.50 (*0-89774-603-1*) Oryx Pr.

Palmer, Rob. Baha Mar: The Shallow Seas: An Underwater Guide to the Bahamas. (Illus.). 208p. (C). 1995. 90.00 (*0-907151-82-5*, Pub. by IMMEL Pubng) St Mut.

— Deep into Blue Holes. 2nd ed. (Illus.). 192p. 1997. pap. 17.95 (*0-9643786-6-3*) Media Pubng.

— Undersea Britain. 160p. (C). 1995. 36.00 (*0-907151-52-3*, Pub. by IMMEL Pubng) St Mut.

Palmer, Robert. Deep Blues. 320p. 1982. pap. 13.95 (*0-14-006223-8*, Penguin Bks) Viking Penguin.

— History of the Modern World. 9th ed. 2001. 54.00 (*0-07-231655-1*) McGraw.

— A Tale of Two Cities: Memphis Rock, New Orleans Roll. (I.S.A.M. Monographs: No. 12). (Illus.). 38p. 1979. pap. 10.00 (*0-914678-12-4*) Inst Am Music.

— Which Father Are You Following? 64p. 1987. pap. text 1.95 (*0-937580-11-2*) Sumrall Pubng.

Palmer, Robert, ed. Underwater Expeditions. (C). 1990. 30.00 (*0-907649-31-9*, Pub. by Expedit Advisory Ctr) St Mut.

Palmer, Robert, ed. see Smith, Clyde L.

Palmer, Robert B., tr. & rev. see Strecker, Karl.

Palmer, Robert C. The County Courts of Medieval England, 1150-1350. LC 81-47939. 379p. reprint ed. pap. 117.50 (*0-7837-0094-6*, 204037100016) Bks Demand.

— The Whilton Dispute, 1264-1380: A Social-Legal Study of Dispute Settlement in Medieval England. LC 83-13858. 318p. reprint ed. pap. 98.60 (*0-8357-7073-7*, 203337700085) Bks Demand.

Palmer, Robert E. Roman Religion & Roman Empire: Five Essays. LC 73-89279. (Haney Foundation Ser.: No. 15). 303p. reprint ed. 94.00 (*0-608-16119-5*, 205528100012) Bks Demand.

— Studies of the Northern Campus Martius in Ancient Rome. LC 90-55217. (Transactions Ser.: Vol. 80, Pt. 2). (Illus.). 64p. (C). 1990. pap. 12.00 (*0-87169-802-1*, T802-PAR) Am Philos.

Palmer, Robert G. & Troeh, Frederick R. Introductory Soil Science: Laboratory Manual. 3rd ed. (Illus.). 128p. (C). 1995. pap. text 29.95 (*0-19-509436-0*) OUP.

Palmer, Robert P., ed. see Guenther, John J., et al.

Palmer, Robert R. History of the Modern World. 8th ed. 1995. 75.00 (*0-679-43253-1*) Knopf.

— The Improvement of Humanity: Education & the French Revolution. LC 84-15048. 356p. 1985. reprint ed. pap. 110.40 (*0-7837-9411-8*, 206015600004) Bks Demand.

— Twelve Who Ruled. 432p. 1941. pap. text 19.95 (*0-691-00761-6*, Pub. by Princeton U Pr) Cal Prin Full Svc.

Palmer, Robert R., ed. Historical Atlas of the World. 48p. (C). 1991. pap. 10.00 (*0-528-83081-3*) Rand McNally.

Palmer, Robert R., ed. From Jacobin to Liberal: Marc-Antoine Jullien, 1775-1848. LC 92-46872. 272p. 1993. text 45.00 (*0-691-03299-8*, Pub. by Princeton U Pr) Cal Prin Full Svc.

Palmer, Robert R., tr. The School of the French Revolution: A Documentary History of the College of Louis-le-Grand & Its Director, Jean-Francois Champagne, 1762-1814. LC 74-25625. 311p. 1975. reprint ed. pap. 96.50 (*0-7837-9412-6*, 206015700004) Bks Demand.

Palmer, Robert R., tr. see Bergeron, Louis.

Palmer, Robert R., tr. see Lefebvre, Georges.

Palmer, Robin. Contested Land in Eastern & Southern Africa: A Literature Survey. (Working Papers). 306p. 1997. pap. 19.95 (*0-85598-391-4*, Pub. by Oxfam Pub) Stylus Pub VA.

— Dictionary of Mythical Places. 17.95 (*0-8488-1122-4*) Amereon Ltd.

Palmer, Robin & Birch, Isobel. Zimbabwe: A Land Divided. (Country Profiles Ser.). (Illus.). 64p. (C). 1992. pap. 9.95 (*0-85598-178-4*, Pub. by Oxfam Pub) Stylus Pub VA.

Palmer, Rodney, jt. auth. see Belford, Ros.

Palmer, Roger C. The Bar Code Book: Reading, Printing, & Specification of Bar Code Symbols. 253p. 1990. pap. 24.95 (*0-685-45327-8*) Helmers Pub.

— The Bar Code Book: Reading, Printing, & Specification of Bar Code Symbols. 2nd ed. (Illus.). 320p. 1991. pap. 29.95 (*0-911261-06-0*) Helmers Pub.

— The Bar Code Book: Reading, Printing, Specification & Application of Bar Code & Other Machine Readable Symbols. 3rd ed. (Illus.). 400p. 1995. pap. text. write for info. (*0-911261-09-5*) Helmers Pub.

Palmer, Roger F., ed. see Clinical Pharmacology Symposium Staff.

Palmer, Ron, jt. ed. see Jain, Vijay.

Palmer, Ronald D. & Reckford, Thomas J. Building ASEAN: Twenty Years of Southeast Asian Cooperation, 127. LC 87-14609. (Washington Papers: No. 127). 160p. 1987. 45.00 (*0-275-92815-2*, C2815, Praeger Pubs); pap. 14.95 (*0-275-92816-0*, B2816, Praeger Pubs) Greenwood.

Palmer, Ruby T. Chopin - An Introduction to His Piano Works. 64p. 1971. pap. 8.95 (*0-7390-0092-6*, 635) Alfred Pub.

Palmer, Ruby T. J. S. Bach - 18 Short Preludes. Palmer, Willard, ed. 48p. 1971. pap. 6.95 (*0-7390-0041-1*, 601) Alfred Pub.

Palmer, Ruby T. Schumann - Scenes from Childhood, Op 15. 32p. 1971. pap. 6.95 (*0-7390-0069-1*, 632) Alfred Pub.

Palmer, Ruby T., ed. Bach - Two-Part Inventions. (Alfred Masterwork Edition Ser.). 64p. 1973. pap. 7.95 (*0-7390-0759-9*, 604) Alfred Pub.

Palmer, Ruby T., ed. Clementi - Six Sonatinas, Op. 36. 64p. 1968. pap. 8.50 (*0-7390-0070-5*, 609) Alfred Pub.

— Czerny the Young Pianist, Op. 823. (Alfred Masterworks Ser.). 80p. 1986. pap. 8.95 (*0-7390-0312-7*, 590) Alfred Pub.

Palmer, Ruby T., ed. Schumann - Album for the Young. 80p. 1969. pap. 8.95 (*0-7390-0734-3*, 620) Alfred Pub.

Palmer, Russell. World Religions Study Guide. 2nd ed. 100p. (C). 1999. spiral bd. 16.95 (*0-7872-5748-6*, 41574801) Kendall-Hunt.

Palmer, S. & Humphrey, J. A. Deviant Behavior: Patterns, Sources, & Control. LC 88-23264. (Illus.). 312p. (C). 1990. 54.50 (*0-306-43285-4*, Plenum Trade) Perseus Pubng.

Palmer, S. B., jt. auth. see Rogalski, M. S.

Palmer, Sally. Information Management. LC 98-228857. 192p. 1998. pap. text 27.95 (*0-7506-3862-1*) Buttrwrth-Heinemann.

— Supervisory Skills. 450p. 1996. pap. 120.00 (*0-85297-407-8*, Pub. by Chartered Bank) St Mut.

Palmer, Sally, jt. auth. see Jones, Steve.

Palmer, Sally E. Maintaining Family Ties: Inclusive Practice in Foster Care. LC 95-185858. 1995. pap. 9.95 (*0-87868-599-5*) Child Welfare.

***Palmer, Sara, et al.** Spinal Cord Injury: A Guide for Living. LC 99-52572. 304p. 2000. 42.50 (*0-8018-6352-X*); pap. 15.95 (*0-8018-6353-8*) Johns Hopkins.

Palmer, Sarah. Blue Whales. (Whale Discovery Library). (Illus.). 24p. (J). (gr. k-5). 1988. lib. bdg. 14.60 (*0-86592-480-5*) Rourke Enter.

— Delfines. (Mamifero Marino Ser.).Tr. of Dolphins. 24p. (J). (gr. k-4). 1991. lib. bdg. 14.60 (*0-86592-849-5*) Rourke Enter.

— Dolphins. (Sea Mammal Discovery Library). (Illus.). (J). (gr. k-5). 1989. 8.95 (*0-685-58619-7*) Rourke Corp.

— Dolphins. (Sea Mammal Discovery Library). (Illus.). 24p. (J). (gr. k-4). 1989. lib. bdg. 14.60 (*0-86592-363-9*) Rourke Enter.

— Fin Whales. (Whale Discovery Library). (Illus.). 24p. (J). (gr. k-5). 1988. 8.95 (*0-685-58331-7*) Rourke Corp.

— Fin Whales. (Whale Discovery Library). (Illus.). 24p. (J). (gr. k-5). 1988. lib. bdg. 14.60 (*0-86592-479-1*) Rourke Enter.

— Grandes Tiburones Blancos. (Tiburones Ser.).Tr. of Great White Sharks. 24p. (J). (gr. k-4). 1994. lib. bdg. 10.95 (*0-86593-202-6*) Rourke Corp.

— Gray Whales. (Whale Discovery Library). (Illus.). 24p. (J). (gr. k-5). 1988. lib. bdg. 14.60 (*0-86592-477-5*) Rourke Enter.

— Great White Sharks. (Shark Discovery Library). (Illus.). 24p. (J). (gr. k-4). 1988. lib. bdg. 14.60 (*0-86592-462-7*) Rourke Enter.

— Hammerhead Sharks. (Shark Discovery Library). (Illus.). 24p. (J). (gr. k-4). 1988. lib. bdg. 14.60 (*0-86592-461-9*) Rourke Enter.

— Humpback Whales. (Whale Discovery Library). (Illus.). 24p. (J). (gr. k-5). 1988. lib. bdg. 8.95 (*0-685-58329-5*) Rourke Corp.

— Humpback Whales. (Whale Discovery Library). (Illus.). 24p. (J). (gr. k-5). 1988. lib. bdg. 14.60 (*0-86592-478-3*) Rourke Enter.

— Killer Whales. (Whale Discovery Library). (Illus.). 24p. (J). (gr. k-5). 1988. lib. bdg. 14.60 (*0-685-58330-9*) Rourke Corp.

— Killer Whales. (Whale Discovery Library). (Illus.). 24p. (J). (gr. k-5). 1988. lib. bdg. 14.60 (*0-86592-481-3*) Rourke Enter.

— Leones Marinos. (Mamifero Marino Ser.).Tr. of Sea Lions. 24p. (J). (gr. k-4). 1991. lib. bdg. 14.60 (*0-86592-674-3*) Rourke Enter.

— Manatees. (Sea Mammal Discovery Library). (Illus.). 24p. (J). (gr. k-5). 1989. 8.95 (*0-685-58620-0*) Rourke Corp.

— Manatees. (Sea Mammal Discovery Library). (Illus.). 24p. (J). (gr. k-4). 1989. lib. bdg. 14.60 (*0-86592-359-0*) Rourke Enter.

— Manaties. (Mamifero Marino Ser.).Tr. of Manatees. 24p. (J). (gr. k-4). 1991. lib. bdg. 14.60 (*0-86592-672-7*) Rourke Enter.

— Morsas. (Mamifero Marino Ser.).Tr. of Walruses. 24p. (J). (gr. k-4). 1991. lib. bdg. 14.60 (*0-86592-689-1*) Rourke Enter.

— Narwhals. (Whale Discovery Library). (Illus.). 24p. (J). (gr. k-5). 1988. 8.95 (*0-685-58328-7*) Rourke Corp.

— Narwhals. (Whale Discovery Library). (Illus.). 24p. (J). (gr. k-5). 1988. lib. bdg. 14.60 (*0-86592-476-7*) Rourke Enter.

— Nurse Sharks. (Shark Discovery Library). (Illus.). 24p. (J). (gr. k-5). 1988. 8.95 (*0-685-58311-2*) Rourke Corp.

— Nurse Sharks. (Shark Discovery Library). (Illus.). 24p. (J). (gr. k-4). 1988. lib. bdg. 14.60 (*0-86592-459-7*) Rourke Enter.

— Nutrias de Mar. (Mamifero Marino Ser.).Tr. of Sea Otters 24p. (J). (gr. k-4). 1991. lib. bdg. 14.60 (*0-86592-681-6*) Rourke Enter.

— Osos Polares. (Mamifero Marino Ser.).Tr. of Polar Bears. 24p. (J). (gr. k-4). 1991. lib. bdg. 14.60 (*0-86592-673-5*) Rourke Enter.

— Polar Bears. (Sea Mammal Discovery Library). (Illus.). 24p. (J). (gr. k-4). 1989. lib. bdg. 14.60 (*0-86592-360-4*) Rourke Enter.

— Sea Lions. (Sea Mammal Discovery Library). (Illus.). 24p. (J). (gr. k-5). 1989. lib. bdg. 8.95 (*0-685-58622-7*) Rourke Corp.

— Sea Lions. (Sea Mammal Discovery Library). (Illus.). 24p. (J). (gr. k-4). 1989. lib. bdg. 14.60 (*0-86592-362-0*) Rourke Enter.

— Sea Mammal Discovery Library, 6 bks., Reading Level 2. (Illus.). 144p. (J). (gr. k-5). 1989. lib. bdg. 53.70 (*0-685-58759-2*) Rourke Corp.

— Sea Mammal Discovery Library, 6 bks., Set, Reading Level 2. (Illus.). 144p. (J). (gr. k-5). 1989. lib. bdg. 87.60 (*0-86592-357-4*) Rourke Enter.

— Sea Otters. (Sea Mammal Discovery Library). (Illus.). 24p. (J). (gr. k-4). 1989. lib. bdg. 14.60 (*0-86592-361-2*) Rourke Enter.

— Spanish Language Books Set 4: Mamifero Marino (Sea Mammals), 6 bks. (J). 1991. 87.60 (*0-86592-835-5*) Rourke Enter.

— Thresher Sharks. (Shark Discovery Library). (Illus.). 24p. (J). (gr. k-5). 1988. lib. bdg. 8.95 (*0-685-58313-9*) Rourke Corp.

— Thresher Sharks. (Shark Discovery Library). (Illus.). 24p. (J). (gr. k-4). 1988. lib. bdg. 14.60 (*0-86592-460-0*) Rourke Enter.

— Tiburones Ballenas. (Tiburones Ser.).Tr. of Whale Sharks. 24p. (J). (gr. k-4). 1994. lib. bdg. 17.97 (*0-86593-204-2*) Rourke Corp.

— Tiburones Makos. (Tiburones Ser.).Tr. of Mako Sharks. 24p. (J). (gr. k-4). 1994. lib. bdg. 17.97 (*0-86593-203-4*) Rourke Corp.

— Tiburones Martillos. (Tiburones Ser.).Tr. of Hammerhead Sharks. (SPA.). 24p. (J). (gr. k-4). 1994. lib. bdg. 17.97 (*0-86593-201-8*) Rourke Corp.

— Tiburones Nodrizas. (Tiburones Ser.).Tr. of Nurse Sharks. (SPA., Illus.). 24p. (J). (gr. k-4). 1994. lib. bdg. 10.95 (*0-86593-205-0*) Rourke Corp.

— Tiburones Trilladors. (Tiburones Ser.).Tr. of Thresher Sharks. 24p. (J). (gr. k-4). 1994. lib. bdg. 17.97 (*0-86593-206-9*) Rourke Corp.

— Walruses. (Sea Mammal Discovery Library). (Illus.). 24p. (J). (gr. k-5). 1989. lib. bdg. 8.95 (*0-685-58621-9*) Rourke Corp.

— Walruses. (Sea Mammal Discovery Library). (Illus.). 24p. (J). (gr. k-4). 1989. lib. bdg. 14.60 (*0-86592-358-2*) Rourke Enter.

— Whale Sharks. (Shark Discovery Library). (Illus.). 24p. (J). (gr. k-5). 1988. lib. bdg. 8.95 (*0-685-58309-0*) Rourke Corp.

— Whale Sharks. (Shark Discovery Library). (Illus.). 24p. (J). (gr. k-4). 1988. lib. bdg. 14.60 (*0-86592-463-5*) Rourke Enter.

***Palmer, Scott.** Access 2000 Intermediate. Freeman, Holly & Pronk, Ron, eds. (Illus.). 194p. 2000. pap. 20.00 (*1-58264-106-4*) ActiveEd.

Palmer, Scott. British Film Actors' Credits, 1895-1987. LC 87-31098. 935p. 1988. lib. bdg. 95.00 (*0-89950-316-0*) McFarland & Co.

Palmer, Scott. Build Your Own Pc Game in Seven Easy Steps: Using Visual Basic. 528p. 1995. pap. 36.95 (*0-201-48911-2*) Addison-Wesley.

Palmer, Scott. Jack the Ripper: A Reference Guide. LC 95-1498. (Illus.). 160p. 1995. 34.50 (*0-8108-2996-7*) Scarecrow.

— A Who's Who of Australian & New Zealand Film Actors: The Sound Era. LC 87-32215. 179p. 1988. 25.00 (*0-8108-2090-0*) Scarecrow.

— Wing Beat, 1996-97: The Sportsmen's Directory Devoted to Upland Game Bird Hunting & Related Business. (Illus.). 28p. (Orig.). 1996. pap. 5.95 (*0-9654342-0-6*) Palmer Mktg.

Palmer, Scott D. Access 2 for Dummies. LC 94-75648. (For Dummies Ser.). 350p. 1994. pap. 19.95 (*1-56884-090-X*) IDG Bks.

— dBASE for DOS for Dummies. LC 94-76886. (For Dummies Ser.). 384p. 1994. pap. 19.95 (*1-56884-188-4*) IDG Bks.

— dBASE for Windows for Dummies. LC 94-76888. (For Dummies Ser.). 360p. 1994. pap. 19.95 (*1-56884-179-5*) IDG Bks.

Palmer, Spencer J. Confucian Rituals in Korea. LC 84-256844. (Religions of Asia Ser.: No. 3). 274p. pap. 85.00 (*0-8357-4423-X*, 203725300008) Bks Demand.

— Religions of the World: A Latter-Day Saint View. 2nd ed. LC 97-33721. 294p. 1997. pap. text 19.95 (*0-8425-2350-2*, Friends of the Library) Brigham.

Palmer, Stanley & Reinhartz, Dennis, eds. Essays on the History of North American Discovery & Exploration. LC 87-10166. (Walter Prescott Webb Memorial Lectures: No. 21). (Illus.). 160p. 1988. 18.95 (*0-89096-373-8*) Tex A&M Univ Pr.

Palmer, Stanley, jt. ed. see Wolfskill, George.

Palmer, Stephen. Human Ontology & Rationality. (Avebury Series in Philosophy). 236p. 1992. 77.95 (*1-85628-235-X*, Pub. by Avebry) Ashgate Pub Co.

Palmer, Stephen, et al, eds. Counseling: The BAC Counselling Reader. (Illus.). 512p. 1996. 79.95 (*0-8039-7476-0*); pap. 32.50 (*0-8039-7477-9*) Sage.

Palmer, Stephen & Dryden, Windy, eds. Stress Management & Counselling: Theory, Practice, Research & Methodology. LC 96-5302. (Stress Counselling Ser.). (Illus.). 160p. 1996. pap. 29.95 (*0-304-33565-7*); text 90.00 (*0-304-33564-9*) Continuum.

***Palmer, Stephen & Laungani, Pittu, eds.** Counselling in a Multicultural Society. LC 98-75103. 214 p. 1998. write for info. (*0-7619-5065-6*) Sage.

Palmer, Stephen & McMahon, Gladeana, eds. Client Assessment. (Professional Skills for Counselors Ser.). 160p. (C). 1997. 39.95 (*0-8039-7502-3*, 75023); pap. 18.95 (*0-8039-7503-1*, 75031) Sage.

Palmer, Stephen & Varma, Ved, eds. The Future of Counselling & Psychotherapy. LC 97-65038. 240p. 1997. 65.00 (*0-7619-5106-7*); pap. 24.95 (*0-7619-5107-5*) Sage.

Palmer, Stephen & Wilkinson, Theon, eds. Pensions - Involving the Members: A Review & Assessment of Current Practice. (C). 1983. 45.00 (*0-85292-324-4*) St Mut.

Palmer, Stephen, jt. auth. see Dryden, Windy.

Palmer, Stephen, jt. auth. see Milner, Patricia.

Palmer, Stephen, jt. auth. see Scott, Michael.

Palmer, Stephen E. Vision Science: Photons to Phenomenology. LC 99-11785. (Illus.). 800p. 1999. 70.00 (*0-262-16183-4*) MIT Pr.

Palmer, Stephen E., Jr. & King, Robert. Yugoslav Communism & the Macedonian Question. 247p. 1971. 69.50 (*0-208-00821-7*) Elliots Bks.

Palmer, Stephen E., jt. auth. see Palmer, John W.

Palmer, Stephen P. & Lingley, William S., Jr. An Assessment of the Oil & Gas Potential of the Washington Outer Continental Shelf. (Washington State & Offshore Oil & Gas Ser.). (Illus.). 88p. (Orig.). 1989. pap. 45.00 (*0-934539-09-X*, WSG89-2) Wash Sea Grant.

Palmer, Stephen R., et al, eds. Zoonoses: Biology, Clinical Practice & Public Health Control. LC 97-30387. (Illus.). 968p. 1998. text 198.50 (*0-19-262380-X*) OUP.

Palmer, Steve. The Heyday of Blackpool's Trams. 28.95 (*0-7110-2459-6*) Spec Mkting Intl.

Palmer, Steve & Birkett, Ken, eds. The Change Agent: Pay's New Role. 150p. (C). 1989. 65.00 (*0-85292-416-X*) St Mut.

Palmer, Steve, jt. auth. see Evans, Alastair.

Palmer, Stuart. Deviance & Conformity. 1969. 21.95 (*0-317-18409-1*) NCUP.

— Murder on the Blackboard. LC 92-70420. 186p. 1992. reprint ed. pap. 5.95 (*1-55882-124-4*, Lib Crime Classics) Intl Polygonics.

— Murder on Wheels. 307p. 1992. pap. 6.95 (*1-55882-113-9*) Intl Polygonics.

— The Penguin Pool Murder. LC 90-84274. 182p. 1990. reprint ed. pap. 7.95 (*1-55882-076-0*) Intl Polygonics.

— Understanding Other People. 208p. 1977. pap. 1.75 (*0-449-30815-4*, Prem) Fawcett.

P

An Asterisk (*) at the beginning of an entry indicates that the title is appearing for the first time.

— The Violent Society. 1972. pap. 21.95 (*0-8084-0353-2*) NCUP.

Palmer, Stuart B. & Rogalski, M. S. Advanced University Physics. 876p. 1995. text 137.00 (*2-88449-065-5*) Gordon & Breach.

— Advanced University Physics. 876p. 1995. pap. text 43.00 (*2-88449-066-3*) Gordon & Breach.

Palmer, Stuart B., jt. auth. see Rogalski, Mircea S.

Palmer, Stuart H. The Universities Today: Scholarship, Self-Interest, & Politics. LC 97-49928. 208p. (C). 1998. 37.00 (*0-7618-1006-4*) U Pr of Amer.

Palmer, Susan. The Tabernacle Bar: A Novel. LC 97-28907. 184p. 1997. pap. 17.95 (*1-56085-096-5*) Signature Bks.

Palmer, Susan J. AIDS & the Apocalyptic Metaphor in North America: The New Religions Respond to a Plague. 176p. 1996. text 45.00 (*0-8020-0662-0*); pap. text 17.95 (*0-8020-7616-5*) U of Toronto Pr.

— Moon Sisters, Krishna Mothers, Rajneesh Lovers: Women's Roles in New Religions. LC 94-17364. (Women & Gender in North American Religion Ser.). (Illus.). 208p. 1994. 45.00 (*0-8156-0297-9*) Syracuse U Pr.

— Moon Sisters, Krishna Mothers, Rajneesh Lovers: Women's Roles in New Religions. (Women & Gender in North American Religions Ser.). (Illus.). 264p. (C). 1996. pap. 19.95 (*0-8156-0382-7*, PAMSP) Syracuse U Pr.

— Rajneesh Papers: Studies in a New Religious Movement. (C). 1993. text 24.00 (*81-208-1080-5*, Pub. by Motilal Bnarsidass) S Asia.

Palmer, Susan J. & Hardman, Charlotte E., eds. Children in New Religions. LC 98-30474. (Illus.). 272p. (C). 1999. pap. 22.00 (*0-8135-2620-5*); text 52.00 (*0-8135-2619-1*) Rutgers U Pr.

Palmer, Susan J., jt. ed. see Robbins, Thomas.

Palmer, Susan L., jt. auth. see Clarke, Simon.

Palmer, T. J., jt. auth. see Palmer, Prudence T.

Palmer, T. Norman, ed. Alcoholism: A Molecular Perspective. (NATO ASI Ser.: Vol. 206). (Illus.). 376p. (C). 1991. text 138.00 (*0-306-43926-3*, Kluwer Plenum) Kluwer Academic.

Palmer, T. S. Biographies of Members of the American Ornithologist's Union. 630p. 1998. reprint ed. 75.00 (*1-57898-108-5*) Martino Pubng.

— Chronology of the Death Valley Region in California, 1849-1949, & Place Names of the Death Valley Region in California & Nevada, 1845-1947. LC 88-34098. (West Coast Studies: No. 3). 102p. (C). 1989. reprint ed. pap. 17.00 (*0-89370-937-9*) Millefleurs.

— Index Generum Mammalium: A List of the Genera & Families of Mammals. 1968. reprint ed. 160.00 (*3-7682-0535-5*) Lubrecht & Cramer.

Palmer, Ted. Individualized Intervention with Young Multiple Offenders: The California Community Treatment Project, Issues & Perspectives. McShane, Marilyn D. & Williams, Frank P., eds. (Current Issues in Criminal Justice Ser.). 1000p. 1997. text 150.00 (*0-8153-2122-8*) Garland.

— A Profile of Correctional Effectiveness & New Directions for Research. LC 93-24925. (New Directions in Crime & Justice Studies). 339p. (C). 1994. pap. text 21.95 (*0-7914-1910-X*) State U NY Pr.

— A Profile of Correctional Effectiveness & New Directions for Research. LC 93-24925. (SUNY Series in New Directions in Crime & Justice Studies). 339p. (C). 1994. text 64.50 (*0-7914-1909-6*) State U NY Pr.

— The Re-Emergence of Correctional Intervention: Developments Through the 1980s & Prospects for the Future. 200p. (C). 1992. 48.00 (*0-8039-4537-X*); pap. 21.00 (*0-8039-4538-8*) Sage.

***Palmer, Ted & D'Amico, Vic.** Accounting for Canadian Colleges. 3rd ed. 528p. 2000. text. write for info. (*0-201-70306-8*) Addison-Wesley.

— Accounting for Canadian Colleges: Working Papers. 3rd ed. 400p. 2000. pap. 35.93 (*0-201-70866-3*) Addison-Wesley.

***Palmer, Thelma.** High White Moon - Poems From Three Islands: Guemes, Fidalgo & Honshu. LC 00-37038. 2000. pap. write for info. (*0-9615580-9-1*) Island Pubs WA.

Palmer, Thelma. The Sacred Round. LC 85-18006. (Illus.). 68p. (Orig.). 1985. pap. 7.95 (*0-9615580-0-8*) Island Pubs WA.

— The Sacred Round. 2nd ed. (Illus.). 68p. (Orig.). 1988. pap. 7.95 (*0-9615580-3-2*) Island Pubs WA.

Palmer, Thelma, jt. auth. see Tursi, John.

Palmer, Theodore J., jt. auth. see Palmer, Prudence Taylor.

Palmer, Theodore W. Banach Albegras & the General Theory of Algebras. Algebras & Banach Algebras, Vol. 1. (Encyclopedia of Mathematics & Its Applications Ser.: No. 49). 808p. (C). 1994. text 105.00 (*0-521-36637-2*) Cambridge U Pr.

***Palmer, Theodore W.** Banach Algebras & the General Theory of *-Algebras, Vol. 2. (Encyclopedia of Mathematics & Its Applications Ser.: No. 79). 550p. (C). 2000. 80.00 (*0-521-36638-0*) Cambridge U Pr.

Palmer, Thomas. An Essay of the Meanes How to Make Our Travailes More Profitable. LC 72-6020. (English Experience Ser.: No. 546). 140p. 1973. reprint ed. 30.00 (*90-221-0546-6*) Walter J Johnson.

Palmer, Tim. America by Rivers. 272p. 1998. pap. 16.95 (*1-55963-264-X*) Island Pr.

— America by Rivers. (Illus.). 272p. (C). 1998. text 29.95 (*1-55963-263-1*) Island Pr.

— The Columbia: Sustaining a Modern Resource. LC 97-12007. (Illus.). 144p. 1997. pap. 24.95 (*0-89886-474-7*) Mountaineers.

— Endangered Rivers & the Conservation Movement. 1986. pap. 16.95 (*0-520-05715-5*, Pub. by U CA Pr) Cal Prin Full Svc.

— Heart of America: Our Landscape, Our Future. LC 99-33646. (Illus.). 350p. 1999. 24.95 (*1-55963-436-7*, Shearwater Bks) Island Pr.

— Lifelines: The Case for River Conservation. LC 94-8951. 200p. 1994. pap. 19.95 (*1-55963-220-8*) Island Pr.

— The Snake River: Window to the West. LC 91-8585. (Illus.). 320p. (Orig.). 1991. 40.00 (*0-933280-59-9*) Island Pr.

— Stanislaus, the Struggle for a River. LC 81-43692. (Illus.). 311p. reprint ed. pap. 96.50 (*0-7837-4696-2*, 204444300003) Bks Demand.

— The Wild & Scenic Rivers of America. LC 92-32660. (Illus.). 339p. 1993. pap. 27.50 (*1-55963-144-9*); text 50.00 (*1-55963-145-7*) Island Pr.

— Youghiogheny: Appalachian River. LC 84-2301. (Illus.). 350p. 1984. pap. 19.95 (*0-8229-5361-7*); text 35.00 (*0-8229-3495-7*) U of Pittsburgh Pr.

Palmer, Tod. Shadowless Flight. 38p. 1997. pap. 8.95 (*0-941363-43-0*) Lake Shore Pub.

Palmer, Tom. Dream Science. 352p. 1990. 19.45 (*0-89919-858-9*, Pub. by Ticknor & Fields) HM.

Palmer, Tom. La Grande Compaignie de Colonisation: Documents of a New Plan. 10.00 (*0-914206-20-6*) Clark U Pr.

Palmer, Tom G. & Cato Institute Staff. Learning about Liberty: The Cato University Study Guide. LC 97-48820. 1997. 10.00 (*1-882577-66-3*) Cato Inst.

Palmer, Trevor. Controversy-Catastrophism & Evolution: The Ongoing Debate. LC 98-34256. (Illus.). 470p. (C). 1999. text 85.00 (*0-306-45751-2*, Kluwer Plenum) Kluwer Academic.

Palmer, Vernon V. The Paths to Privity: The History of Third Party Beneficiary Contracts at English Law. LC 92-29490. 250p. 1993. 64.95 (*1-880921-16-2*); pap. 44.95 (*1-880921-15-4*) Austin & Winfield.

***Palmer, Vernon Valentine.** Louisiana: Microcosm of a Mixed Jurisdiction. LC 99-67316. 336p. 1999. 39.95 (*0-89089-892-8*) Carolina Acad Pr.

***Palmer, Veronica & Palmer, Alan Warwick.** Who's Who in Shakespeare's England. LC 99-10938. (Illus.). 306p. 2000. pap. 17.95 (*0-312-22086-3*, Pub. by Tor Bks) St Martin.

Palmer, Veronica, jt. auth. see Palmer, Alan R.

Palmer, Veronica, jt. auth. see Palmer, Alan W.

Palmer, Virginia A., jt. auth. see Buck, Diane M.

Palmer, W. Ross & Schlichter, Carol L. Thinking Smart: A Primer of the Talents Unlimited Model. 1993. pap. 23.95 (*0-936386-64-9*) Creative Learning.

Palmer, W. S., tr. see Bergson, Henri.

Palmer, Walter L., ed. Gastric Irradiation in Peptic Ulcer. LC 73-87306. 173p. reprint ed. pap. 53.70 (*0-608-30211-2*, 201998100015) Bks Demand.

Palmer, Will, ed. see Eagle, Rich.

Palmer, Willard, et al. Alfred Basic Adult Christmas Book, Level One. (Alfred's Basic Adult Piano Course Ser.). 32p. 1984. pap. 6.95 (*0-7390-0382-8*, 2466) Alfred Pub.

Palmer, Willard, et al. Alfred's Basic Piano Lesson Book Level 4: Italian Edition. (Alfred's Basic Piano Library Ser.). (ITA.). Date not set. pap. write for info. (*0-7390-0098-5*, 14597) Alfred Pub.

— Alfred's Basic Piano Theory Book, Level 4. (Alfred's Basic Piano Library Ser.). (ITA.). Date not set. pap. write for info. (*0-7390-0101-9*, 14824) Alfred Pub.

Palmer, Willard, et al. The Complete Book of Scales, Chords, Arpeggios & Cadences. (Basic Piano Library). 88p. 1994. pap. 8.50 (*0-7390-0368-2*, 5743) Alfred Pub.

— Hymn Book, Complete Levels 2 & 3. (Alfred's Basic Piano Library). 48p. 1995. pap. 6.95 (*0-7390-0406-9*, 6485) Alfred Pub.

Palmer, Willard, ed. see Palmer, Ruby T.

***Palmer, Willard A.** Bach - 2-Part Inventions. (Exploring Piano Masterworks). 16p. 1999. 4.95 (*0-7390-0278-3*, 16722) Alfred Pub.

Palmer, Willard A. Bach/ Well Tempered Clavier, Bk. 1. (Alfred Masterwork Edition Ser.). 1994. spiral bd. 24.95 (*0-88284-831-3*) Alfred Pub.

Palmer, Willard A. Beethoven - Sonata Pathetique, Theme from 2nd Movement. (Simply Classics Ser.). 4p. 1995. pap. 2.50 (*0-7390-0791-2*, 14301) Alfred Pub.

— Beethoven/Moonlight Sonata, Opus 27, No. 2. (Masterwork Edition Ser.). 24p. 1986. pap. 4.95 (*0-7390-0526-X*, 2502) Alfred Pub.

— Brahms - Hungarian Dance No. 5. (Simply Classics Ser.). 4p. 1996. pap. 2.50 (*0-7390-0775-0*, 16701) Alfred Pub.

— Burgmueller/25 Progressive Pieces, Opus 100. (Masterwork Edition Ser.). 48p. 1968. pap. 7.95 (*0-7390-0614-2*, 608) Alfred Pub.

— Chopin/Waltzes. (Exploring Piano Masterworks Ser.). 16p. 1999. 4.95 (*0-7390-0279-1*, 16723) Alfred Pub.

Palmer, Willard A. Essential Keyboard Repertoire, Vol. 7. 1995. spiral bd. 14.95 (*0-88284-784-8*) Alfred Pub.

Palmer, Willard A. Mozart - 21 of His Most Popular Piano Pieces. (Alfred Masterwork Edition Ser.). 64p. 1976. pap. 8.50 (*0-7390-0442-5*, 391) Alfred Pub.

Palmer, Willard A., ed. Bach - Inventions & Sinfonias. (Alfred Masterwork Editions Ser.). 116p. (C). 1993. pap. text 13.95 (*0-88284-626-4*, 606C) Alfred Pub.

Palmer, Willard A., ed. Bach - Partita No. 1 in B-Flat Major. 32p. 1971. pap. 5.95 (*0-7390-0832-3*, 634) Alfred Pub.

— Bartok/Evening in the Country: For the Piano. (Masterwork Edition Ser.). 4p. 1987. pap. 2.50 (*0-7390-0524-3*, 3294) Alfred Pub.

— Beethoven - The First Book for Pianists. (Alfred Masterwork Edition Ser.). 24p. 1977. pap. 5.95 (*0-7390-0776-9*, 490) Alfred Pub.

— Brahms - Three Intermezzi, Opus 117. (Alfred Masterwork Edition Ser.). 16p. 1985. pap. 4.95 (*0-7390-0777-7*, 2417) Alfred Pub.

— Chopin - Fantastic Impromptu for the Piano. (Alfred Masterwork Edition Ser.). 12p. 1985. pap. 3.50 (*0-7390-0826-9*, 2546) Alfred Pub.

— Chopin - 24 Preludes for the Piano. (Alfred Masterwork Edition Ser.). 80p. 1968. pap. 8.95 (*0-7390-0441-7*, 610) Alfred Pub.

— Chopin/Nocturnes for the Piano - Complete. (Masterwork Edition Ser.). 128p. 1994. pap. 15.95 (*0-7390-0902-8*, 2482C) Alfred Pub.

— Clementi - Sonatina in C, Opus 36, No. 1. 8p. 1982. pap. 2.95 (*0-7390-0843-9*, 2159) Alfred Pub.

— Clementi/Six Sonatinas, Opus 4. (Masterwork Edition Ser.). 64p. 1984. pap. 8.95 (*0-7390-0662-2*, 2421) Alfred Pub.

— Czerny - 30 New Studies in Technics, Opus 849. (Alfred Masterwork Edition Ser.). 64p. 1986. pap. 8.50 (*0-7390-0852-8*, 591) Alfred Pub.

— Ellmenreich - Spinning Song, Opus 14, Vol. 4. (Alfred Masterwork Edition Ser.). 4p. 1986. pap. 2.95 (*0-7390-0821-8*, 874) Alfred Pub.

— Haydn - Six Sonatinas for the Piano. 48p. 1970. pap. 7.95 (*0-7390-0855-2*, 618) Alfred Pub.

Palmer, Willard A., ed. J. S. Bach - An Introduction to His Keyboard Music. (Alfred Masterwork Editions Ser.). 64p. 1973. pap. text 8.95 (*0-88284-253-6*, 638) Alfred Pub.

— J. S. Bach - Selections from Anna Magdalena's Notebook. (Alfred Masterwork Editions Ser.). 48p. 1969. pap. text 6.50 (*0-88284-262-5*, 605) Alfred Pub.

— J. S. Bach - The Well-Tempered Clavier, Book 1. (Alfred Masterwork Editions Ser.). 224p. 1994. pap. text 22.00 (*0-88284-120-3*, 2098C) Alfred Pub.

Palmer, Willard A., ed. Mendelssohn - Six Christmas Pieces. (Alfred Masterwork Edition Ser.). 16p. 1980. 4.95 (*0-7390-0590-1*, 1958) Alfred Pub.

— Mendelssohn/Songs Without Words: Selected Favorites for the Piano. (Masterwork Edition Ser.). 64p. 1978. pap. 8.95 (*0-7390-0365-8*, 468) Alfred Pub.

— Mendelssohn/Songs Without Words: Selected Favorites for the Piano. (Exploring Piano Masterworks Ser.). 16p. 1999. 4.95 (*0-7390-0280-5*, 16724) Alfred Pub.

Palmer, Willard A., ed. Mozart - An Introduction to His Keyboard Works. (Alfred Masterwork Editions Ser.). 64p. 1974. pap. text 7.95 (*0-88284-254-4*, 664) Alfred Pub.

Palmer, Willard A., ed. Mozart - Rondo Alla Turca. (Simply Classics Ser.). 4p. 1995. pap. 2.50 (*0-7390-0823-4*, 14315) Alfred Pub.

— Mozart - Sonata in C Major, K.545. 16p. 1985. pap. 4.95 (*0-7390-0854-4*, 2543) Alfred Pub.

— Schmitt - Preparatory Exercises, Opus 16. 40p. 1978. pap. 5.95 (*0-7390-0853-6*, 1709) Alfred Pub.

— Streabbog/12 Melodious Pieces, Opus 63. (Masterwork Edition Ser.). 24p. 1968. pap. 5.95 (*0-7390-0615-0*, 621) Alfred Pub.

Palmer, Willard A. & Manus, Morton. Alfred's Basic Adult Christmas Book: Level 2. (Alfred's Basic Adult Piano Course Ser.). 32p. 1984. pap. 6.95 (*0-7390-0757-2*, 2467) Alfred Pub.

Palmer, Willard A., et al. Alfred's Basic Adult All-in-One, Bk. 1. (Alfred's Basic Adult Piano Library). 1994. pap. 14.95 (*0-88284-818-6*) Alfred Pub.

Palmer, Willard A., et al. Alfred's Basic Adult All-in-One Course Level 1: Lesson - Theory - Technic. (Alfred's Basic Adult Piano Course Ser.). 1995. 14.95 (*0-7390-0556-1*, 5725) Alfred Pub.

Palmer, Willard A., et al. Alfred's Basic Adult Lesson Book, Level 1. (Alfred's Basic Adult Piano Course Ser.). 1995. pap. 19.95 incl. audio compact disk (*0-88284-832-1*) Alfred Pub.

— Alfred's Basic Adult Lesson Book, Level 1. (Alfred's Basic Adult Piano Course Ser.). 1995. pap. 17.90 incl. audio (*0-88284-833-X*) Alfred Pub.

Palmer, Willard A., et al. Alfred's Basic Adult Piano Lesson Book 1: French Edition. (Basic Piano Library).Tr. of Cours de Base Alfred pour le Piano pour les Adultes Livre de Lecons, 1. (FRE.). 96p. 1987. pap. 9.95 (*0-7390-0746-7*, 2237) Alfred Pub.

Palmer, Willard A., et al. Alfred's Basic All-in-One Course Vol. 1: Italian Edition. (Alfred's Basic Piano Library). (ITA.). 1997. pap. 6.50 (*0-88284-769-4*) Alfred Pub.

— Alfred's Basic All-in-One Course Vol. 2: Italian Edition. (Alfred's Basic Piano Library). (ITA.). 1997. pap. 5.95 (*0-88284-770-8*) Alfred Pub.

Palmer, Willard A., et al. Alfred's Basic Choral Approach Technic Book, Level 1. (Alfred's Basic Piano Library). 32p. 1987. pap. 6.95 (*0-7390-0437-9*, 2654) Alfred Pub.

— Alfred's Basic Chord Approach, Christmas Book Level 1: A Piano Method for the Later Beginner. (Basic Piano Library). 16p. 1987. pap. 5.50 (*0-7390-0728-9*, 2652) Alfred Pub.

— Alfred's Basic Chord Approach to Electronic Keyboards: Lesson Book 3. (Alfred's Basic Piano Library). 48p. 1989. pap. 8.95 (*0-7390-0820-X*, 3111) Alfred Pub.

Palmer, Willard A., et al. Alfred's Basic Piano All-in-One, Level 1. (Alfred's Basic Piano Library). 1994. pap. 6.50 (*0-88284-787-2*) Alfred Pub.

— Alfred's Basic Piano Complete Lesson Book, Level 1. (Alfred's Basic Piano Library). 1983. pap. 8.50 (*0-88284-817-8*) Alfred Pub.

Palmer, Willard A., et al. Alfred's Basic Piano Duet Book, Level 1. (Alfred's Basic Piano Library). 32p. 1987. pap. 6.50 (*0-7390-0338-0*, 2648) Alfred Pub.

— Alfred's Basic Piano Fun Book, Level 2. (Alfred's Basic Piano Library). 32p. 1986. pap. 5.95 (*0-7390-0789-0*, 2392) Alfred Pub.

— Alfred's Basic Piano Hymn Book, Level 2. (Basic Piano Library). 32p. 1985. pap. 5.95 (*0-7390-0557-X*, 2523) Alfred Pub.

Palmer, Willard A., et al. Alfred's Basic Piano Lesson Book, Level 13, (Alfred's Basic Piano Library). 1982. pap. 6.50 (*0-88284-815-1*) Alfred Pub.

— Alfred's Basic Piano Lesson Book, Level A. (Alfred's Basic Piano Library). 1988. pap. 5.95 (*0-88284-816-X*) Alfred Pub.

— Alfred's Basic Piano Lesson Book, Level 1. (Alfred's Basic Piano Library). 96p. 1983. pap. text 8.95 (*0-88284-616-7*, 2236) Alfred Pub.

— Alfred's Basic Piano Lesson Book, Level 1A. (Alfred's Basic Piano Library). 1981. pap. 6.95 (*0-88284-788-0*) Alfred Pub.

Palmer, Willard A., et al. Alfred's Basic Piano Lesson Book, Level 1A: (Universal Edition) (Basic Piano Library). 64p. 1993. pap. 6.50 (*0-7390-0717-3*, 6489) Alfred Pub.

Palmer, Willard A., et al. Alfred's Basic Piano Lesson Book, Level 1B. (Alfred's Basic Piano Library). 1981. pap. 6.50 (*0-88284-789-9*) Alfred Pub.

Palmer, Willard A., et al. Alfred's Basic Piano Lesson Book, Level 1B: (French Edition) (Basic Piano Library).Tr. of Cours de Base Alfred Livre de Lecons Niveau 1B. (FRE.). 48p. 1987. pap. 6.50 (*0-7390-0540-5*, 2105) Alfred Pub.

— Alfred's Basic Piano Lesson Book, Level 1B: Universal Edition. (Basic Piano Library). 48p. 1993. pap. 5.50 (*0-7390-0664-9*, 6490) Alfred Pub.

Palmer, Willard A., et al. Alfred's Basic Piano Lesson Book, Level 2. (Alfred's Basic Piano Library). 1981. pap. 6.50 (*0-88284-812-7*) Alfred Pub.

Palmer, Willard A., et al. Alfred's Basic Piano Lesson Book, Level 5. (Basic Piano Library). 48p. 1983. pap. 6.50 (*0-7390-0544-8*, 2111) Alfred Pub.

Palmer, Willard A., et al. Alfred's Basic Piano Library: Prep Theory, Bk. B. 1988. pap. 5.95 (*0-88284-829-1*) Alfred Pub.

Palmer, Willard A., et al. Alfred's Basic Piano Recital Book, Level 3. (Alfred's Basic Piano Library). 32p. 1982. pap. 5.95 (*0-7390-0856-0*, 2115) Alfred Pub.

— Alfred's Basic Piano Recital Book, Level 4. (Alfred's Basic Piano Library). 32p. 1982. pap. 5.95 (*0-7390-0822-6*, 2116) Alfred Pub.

— Alfred's Basic Piano Technic Book, Complete Level 1. (Alfred's Basic Piano Library). 32p. 1984. pap. 6.95 (*0-7390-0785-8*, 2459) Alfred Pub.

— Alfred's Basic Piano Theory Book, Level 4. (Basic Piano Library). 32p. 1983. pap. 6.50 (*0-7390-0744-0*, 2124) Alfred Pub.

Palmer, Willard A., et al. Alfred's Basic Piano Theory, Level 1A. (Alfred's Basic Piano Library). 1981. pap. 6.50 (*0-88284-813-5*) Alfred Pub.

Palmer, Willard A., et al. Alfred's Basic Prep Solo Book, Level E. (Alfred's Basic Piano Library). 32p. 1992. pap. 5.50 (*0-7390-0439-5*, 6295) Alfred Pub.

— Alfred's Basic Prep Teacher's Guide, Lesson Book, Level A. (Alfred's Basic Piano Library). 48p. 1988. pap. write for info. (*0-7390-0814-5*, 8889) Alfred Pub.

— Alfred's Basic Prep Technic Book, Level C. (Alfred's Basic Piano Library). 24p. 1993. pap. 5.95 (*0-7390-0438-7*, 6438) Alfred Pub.

— Alfred's Basic Prep Technic Book, Level D. (Basic Piano Library). 24p. 1993. pap. 5.50 (*0-7390-0606-1*, 6400) Alfred Pub.

— All-in-One Course, Level 4. (Basic Piano Library). 48p. 1995. pap. 5.95 (*0-7390-0883-8*, 14512) Alfred Pub.

Palmer, Willard A., et al. All-in-One Course Vol. 3: Italian Edition. (Alfred's Basic Piano Library). (ITA.). 1997. pap. 5.95 (*0-88284-771-6*) Alfred Pub.

— Basix Electronic Keyboard Method, Bk. 1. 1996. pap. 7.95 (*0-88284-701-5*); pap. 9.95 incl. audio compact disk (*0-88284-702-3*) Alfred Pub.

— Basix Scales & Arpeggios for the Keyboard. 1997. pap. 8.95 (*0-88284-740-6*); pap. 10.95 incl. audio compact disk (*0-88284-741-4*) Alfred Pub.

Palmer, Willard A., et al. Boogie Woogie Band. (Alfred's Basic Piano Library). 4p. 1986. pap. 2.50 (*0-7390-0859-5*, 2384) Alfred Pub.

— Christmas Joy: Level A. (Alfred's Basic Piano Library). 16p. 1992. pap. 5.50 (*0-7390-0380-1*, 6476) Alfred Pub.

— Christmas Joy: Level C. (Alfred's Basic Piano Library). 16p. 1993. pap. 5.50 (*0-7390-0339-9*, 6478) Alfred Pub.

— Christmas Joy, Level E. (Alfred's Basic Piano Library). 16p. 1994. pap. 4.95 (*0-7390-0782-3*, 6480) Alfred Pub.

Palmer, Willard A., et al. Complete Lesson Book: Level 2 & 3. (Alfred's Basic Piano Library). 1992. pap. 8.50 (*0-88284-830-5*) Alfred Pub.

Palmer, Willard A., et al. Complete Theory, Levels 2 & 3. 48p. 1992. pap. 6.95 (*0-7390-0866-8*, 6235) Alfred Pub.

Palmer, Willard A., et al. Complete Theory: Level 1. (Alfred's Basic Piano Library). 1983. pap. 7.50 (*0-88284-827-5*) Alfred Pub.

Palmer, Willard A., et al. Electronic Keyboard Course. (Alfred's Basic Piano Library). 96p. 1986. pap. 10.95 (*0-7390-0790-4*, 2238) Alfred Pub.

Palmer, Willard A., et al. Lesson Book: Level C, (Alfred's Basic Piano Library). 1990. pap. 5.95 (*0-88284-828-3*) Alfred Pub.

Palmer, Willard A., et al. Lesson Book Level 1B: Teacher's Guide. (Basic Piano Library). 48p. 1986. pap. write for info. (*0-7390-0864-1*, 8650) Alfred Pub.

— Lesson Book Level 2: Teacher's Guide. (Basic Piano Library). 48p. 1986. pap., teacher ed. write for info. (*0-7390-0865-X*, 9180) Alfred Pub.

— Merry Christmas, Level 3. (Alfred's Basic Piano Library). 16p. 1982. 5.50 (*0-7390-0568-5*, 2213) Alfred Pub.

— Merry Christmas, Level 4. (Alfred's Basic Piano Library). 16p. Date not set. 5.50 (*0-7390-0574-X*, 2233) Alfred Pub.

— Merry Christmas, Complete, Levels 2 & 3. (Basic Piano Library). 24p. 1995. pap. 5.95 (*0-7390-0882-X*, 6486) Alfred Pub.

P

An Asterisk (*) at the beginning of an entry indicates that the title is appearing for the first time.

— Recital Book, Level 5. (Basic Piano Library). 32p. 1984. pap. 5.95 (*0-7390-0894-3*, 2117) Alfred Pub.

Palmer, Willard A., et al. Recital Book: Level 1B. (Alfred's Basic Piano Library). 1981. pap. 5.95 (*0-88284-825-9*) Alfred Pub.

— Recital Book: Level 2, (Alfred's Basic Piano Library). 1982. pap. 5.95 (*0-88284-826-7*) Alfred Pub.

Palmer, Willard A., et al. Solo Book, Level C. (Basic Piano Library). 24p. 1990. pap. 5.50 (*0-7390-0900-1*, 3137) Alfred Pub.

Palmer, Willard A., et al. Teach Yourself to Play Electric Keyboard. 1987. pap. 10.95 (*0-88284-680-9*) Alfred Pub.

— Teach Yourself to Play Piano. (Teach Yourself Ser.). 1991. pap. 12.95 (*0-88284-670-1*) Alfred Pub.

— Teach Yourself to Play Piano. 1994. pap. 19.95 incl. audio compact disk (*0-88284-674-4*) Alfred Pub.

Palmer, Willard A., et al. Technic Book, Level 3. 32p. 1985. pap. 5.95 (*0-7390-0901-X*, 2518) Alfred Pub.

Palmer, Willard A., et al. Theory: Level 1B. (Alfred's Basic Piano Library). 1981. pap. 6.50 (*0-88284-820-8*) Alfred Pub.

— Theory: Level 2. (Alfred's Basic Piano Library). 1982. pap. 6.50 (*0-88284-819-4*) Alfred Pub.

Palmer, Willard A., et al. The Thing That Has No Name! (Alfred's Basic Piano Library). 4p. 1982. pap. 2.50 (*0-7390-0844-7*, 2289) Alfred Pub.

Palmer, Willard A., ed. see Bach, Johann Sebastian.

***Palmer, William.** Audubon Guide to the National Wildlife Refuges Southern Midwest: South Central. (Illus.). 256p. 2000. pap. 19.95 (*0-312-24487-8*) St Martin.

Palmer, William. The Pardon of St. Anne. 256p. 1997. pap. 17.95 (*0-224-04311-0*, Pub. by Jonathan Cape) Trafalgar.

— The Political Career of Oliver St. John, 1637-1649. LC 91-51138. 160p. (C). 1992. 32.50 (*0-87413-453-6*) U Delaware Pr.

— The Problem of Ireland in Tudor Foreign Policy, 1485-1603. 171p. (C). 1995. 60.00 (*0-85115-562-6*) Boydell & Brewer.

Palmer, William E. MRI of Musculoskeletal System. 1994. vdisk 700.00 (*1-56815-021-0*) Mosby Inc.

Palmer, William G. Experimental Inorganic Chemistry. 612p. reprint ed. pap. 174.50 (*0-608-13047-8*, 2024514) Bks Demand.

— Experimental Physical Chemistry. 2nd ed. LC 42-10734. 333p. reprint ed. pap. 95.00 (*0-608-10098-6*, 2050760) Bks Demand.

Palmer, William J. Dickens & New Historicism. LC 97-16019. 224p. 1997. text 39.95 (*0-312-17427-6*) St Martin.

— The Films of the Eighties: A Social History. LC 92-33720. 335p. 1995. pap. 20.95 (*0-8093-2029-0*) S Ill U Pr.

— The Hoydens & Mr. Dickens. LC 96-31892. 256p. 1996. 21.95 (*0-312-15145-4*) St Martin.

***Palmer, William J.** Strange Case of the Oxford Christmas Plot. 2000. 23.95 (*0-312-26576-X*) St Martin.

Palmer, William J. & Selvin, Paul P. The Development of Law in California. 1983. write for info. (*0-318-58310-0*) West Pub.

Palmer, William J., 3rd, et al. Construction Insurance, Bonding, & Risk Management. LC 96-14592. (Construction Ser.). (Illus.). 384p. 1996. 79.95 (*0-07-048594-1*) McGraw.

Palmer, William M. Cambridge Castle. rev. ed. (Cambridge Town, Gown & County Ser.: Vol. 5). (Illus.). 1976. pap. 5.95 (*0-902675-67-2*) Oleander Pr.

Palmer, William M. & Braswell, Alvin L. Reptiles of North Carolina. LC 94-5711. (Illus.). 1995. 59.95 (*0-8078-2158-6*) U of NC Pr.

Palmer, William R. Why the North Star Stands Still. LC 57-11627. (Illus.). 118p. 1978. pap. 6.95 (*0-915630-12-5*) Zion.

Palmer, Wilson. Reminiscences of Candia. (Illus.). 345p. 1997. reprint ed. lib. bdg. 39.50 (*0-8328-5980-X*) Higginson Bk Co.

Palmeri, Frank. Critical Essays on Jonathan Swift. (Critical Essays on British Literature Ser.). 200p. 1993. lib. bdg. 40.00 (*0-685-60864-6*, Twyne) Mac Lib Ref.

— Satire in Narrative: Petronius, Swift, Gibbon, Melville, & Pynchon. 195p. 1990. text 30.00 (*0-292-77631-4*) U of Tex Pr.

Palmeri, Frank, ed. Critical Essays on Jonathan Swift. LC 92-42993. (Critical Essays on British Literature Ser.). 288p. 1993. 48.00 (*0-7838-0003-7*, G K Hall & Co) Mac Lib Ref.

Palmeri, Joseph & Milligan, E. E. French for Reading Knowledge. 2nd ed. 310p. (C). 1997. reprint ed. text 45.00 (*0-9661843-6-X*) Higby Fam Trust.

Palmerini, Luca & Mistretta, Gaetano. Spaghetti Nightmares: Italian Fantasy-Horror as Seen Through the Eyes of Their Protagonists. Winick, Margot, ed. LC 95-61740. (Illus.). 192p. 1996. pap. 25.95 (*0-9634982-7-4*) Fantasma Bks.

Palmerio, Giovanni. Perspectives on Economic Thought. (Luiss Ser.). 222p. 1991. 66.95 (*1-85521-189-0*, Pub. by Dartmth Pub) Ashgate Pub Co.

Palmerson, James N. Population - Control, Density, Dynamics, Growth, & Surveillance: Index of New Information with Authors, Subjects & Bibliography. rev. ed. LC 94-34027. 136p. 1994. 47.50 (*0-7883-0382-1*); pap. 44.50 (*0-7883-0383-X*) ABBE Pubs Assn.

Palmerston, Henry T. The Palmerston Papers, Gladstone & Palmerston. Guedalla, Philip, ed. LC 73-151351. (Select Bibliographies Reprint Ser.). 1977. reprint ed. 28.95 (*0-8369-5812-8*) Ayer.

Palmes, James, tr. see Breton, Genevieve.

Palmes, James C. Architectural Drawing in the R. I. B. A. pap. 7.95 (*0-685-20562-2*) Transatl Arts.

Palmes, James C., tr. see Burckhardt, Jacob.

Palmeter, Erin T. Recovering the Soul: A Season of Change. (Illus.). 32p. (Orig.). 1995. 14.95 (*0-9650744-7-1*, RTS-101) Palmeter Grp.

Palmeter, N. David & Mavroidis, Petros C. Dispute Settlement in the World Trade Organization: Practice & Procedure. LC 98-49974. 1999. 78.00 (*90-411-0634-0*) Kluwer Law Intl.

Palmetto Cabinet Staff. A Taste of South Carolina. LC 85-14573. (Illus.). 345p. 1985. reprint ed. spiral bd. 16.95 (*0-87844-064-X*) Sandlapper Pub Co.

Palmgen, V. & Hartmann, E. Svensk-Dansk Ordbog: Swedish-Danish Dictionary. (DAN & SWE.). 251p. 1978. 39.95 (*0-8288-5273-1*, M1287) Fr & Eur.

Palmgren, Charlie. Chicken Conspiracy: Breaking The Cycle of Personal Stress & Organizational Mediocrity. 1999. pap. text 13.95 (*1-891874-02-0*) Recover Comns.

Palmgren, Karin, tr. see Williams, Henrick, et al, eds.

Palmie, Stephan, ed. Slave Cultures & the Cultures of Slavery. LC 95-4374. 336p. 1996. text 35.00 (*0-87049-903-3*) U of Tenn Pr.

Palmier, J. Hegel. (Breviarios Ser.). (SPA.). pap. 6.99 (*968-16-2375-4*, Pub. by Fondo) Continental Bk.

Palmier, L. H. Social Status & Power in Java. (London School of Economics Monographs on Social Anthropology: No. 20). 174p. (C). 1969. pap. 16.95 (*0-485-19620-4*, Pub. by Athlone Pr) Humanities.

Palmier, Leslie. The Control of Bureaucratic Corruption: Case Studies in Asia. 292p. 1985. 29.95 (*0-317-38650-6*, Pub. by Allied Pubs) Asia Bk Corp.

Palmier, Leslie, ed. State & Law in Eastern Asia. LC 96-21350. 166p. 1996. text 82.95 (*1-85521-781-3*, Pub. by Dartmth Pub) Ashgate Pub Co.

Palmieri, Anthony F. Elmer Rice: A Playwright's Vision of America. LC 78-75182. 248p. 1970. 33.50 (*0-8386-2333-6*) Fairleigh Dickinson.

Palmieri, Deborah A., ed. Russia & the NIS in the World Economy: East-West Investment, Financing & Trade. LC 93-48213. 200p. 1994. 59.95 (*0-275-94531-6*, Praeger Pubs) Greenwood.

— The U. S. S. R. & the World Economy: Challenges for the Global Integration of Soviet Markets under Perestroika. LC 91-44452. 208p. 1992. 57.95 (*0-275-94015-2*, C4015, Praeger Pubs) Greenwood.

Palmieri, Deborah A., jt. auth. see Adelman, Jonathan R.

Palmieri, Dennis. Counselor. LC 93-87613. 416p. (Orig.). 1994. pap. 28.00 (*0-9646354-1-0*) Callon Pr Inc.

Palmieri, Ferdinando, et al, eds. Thirty Years of Progress in Mitochondrial Bioenergetics & Molecular Biology, 5. (Progress in Cell Research Ser.: Vol. 5). 278p. 1995. 217.50 (*0-444-82235-6*) Elsevier.

Palmieri, James. Sky Adventures. Palmieri, Maggie, ed. (Illus.). 260p. (Orig.). 1996. pap. 14.99 (*1-57502-268-0*, P0955) Morris Pubng.

Palmieri, Jim & Palmieri, Maggie. Sky Adventures: Stories of Our Heritage. LC 98-90599. (Illus.). 490p. 1998. pap. 24.95 (*1-57502-882-4*, P02401) Morris Pubng.

Palmieri, John, et al. Pennsylvania Juvenile Delinquency & Deprivation. 340p. 1997. text 59.50 (*1-887024-56-5*) Bisel Co.

Palmieri, Maggie, jt. auth. see Palmieri, Jim.

Palmieri, Maggie, ed. see Palmieri, James.

***Palmieri, Marco, ed.** The Lives of Dax. (Star Trek Ser.). 1999. per. 14.00 (*0-7434-0081-X*, Star Trek); per. 14.00 (*0-671-02840-5*, Star Trek) PB.

Palmieri, Patricia A. In Adamless Eden: The Community of Women Faculty at Wellesley. LC 94-31662. 400p. 1995. 45.00 (*0-300-05529-3*) Yale U Pr.

— In Adamless Eden: The Community of Women Faculty at Wellesley. (Illus.). 400p. 1997. pap. 18.00 (*0-300-06388-1*) Yale U Pr.

Palmieri, Robert. Encyclopedia of the Piano. LC 93-4742. (Illus.). 536p. 1996. pap. text 27.95 (*0-8153-2582-7*) Garland.

Palmieri, Robert, ed. Encyclopedia of Keyboard Instruments Vol. I: The Piano. LC 93-4742. 536p. 1993. text 100.00 (*0-8240-5685-X*, H1131) Garland.

Pal'mina, N. P., jt. ed. see Kurganov, Boris I.

Palmiotto, Michael J. Community Policing: A Policing Strategy for the 21st Century. LC 99-14791. 1999. write for info. (*0-8342-1087-8*) Aspen Pub.

***Palmiotto, Michael J.** Criminal Investigations. 2nd ed. LC 98-20486. (Illus.). 574p. 1998. pap. 29.95 (*1-57292-115-3*) Austin & Winfield.

Palmiotto, Michael J. Policing: Concepts, Strategies, & Current Issues in American Police Forces. LC 97-13942. 386p. (C). 1997. pap. 28.00 (*0-89089-867-7*) Carolina Acad Pr.

Palmiotto, Michael J., jt. auth. see Chang, Dae H.

Palmisano, Anna C. & Barlaz, Morton A., eds. Microbiology of Solid Waste. LC 96-18240. (Microbiology of Extreme & Unusual Environments Ser.). 240p. 1996. boxed set 89.95 (*0-8493-8361-7*) CRC Pr.

Palmisano, Donald J. & Mang, Herbert J., Jr. Informed Consent: A Survival Guide. 47p. (C). 1987. 15.00 (*0-940019-00-9*); 15.00 (*0-940019-01-9*) Invictus LA.

Palmisano, Giuseppe, et al. CMOS Current Amplifiers. LC 99-12052. (International Series In Engineering & Computer Science). xiv, 159 p. 1999. write for info. (*0-7923 8469-5*) Kluwer Academic.

Palmisano, Joanna. The Vermont Wedding Resource Guide, 1999 Edition. (Illus.). 288p. 1998. pap. 9.95 (*0-9657890-2-0*) Happy Hollow.

***Palmisano, Joanna.** The Vermont Wedding Resource Guide, 2000 Edition. 320p. 2000. pap. 9.95 (*0-9657890-0-4*) Happy Hollow.

Palmisano, Joseph M., jt. ed. see Morgan, Bradley J.

Palmisano, Louis, tr. see Bruno, Emmy.

Palmisano, Tony. Restoration to Fellowship. 32p. 1988. pap. 0.75 (*0-88144-126-0*) Christian Pub.

Palmiter, Alan R. Securities Regulations: Examples & Explanations. LC 97-36852. 440p. 1998. pap. text. write for info. (*1-56706-637-2*) Panel Pubs.

Palmiter, Alan R., jt. auth. see Solomon, Lewis D.

Palmiter, Larry & Wheeling, Terry. SUNCODE Documentation & User's Manual. 235p. 1981. ring bd. 35.00 (*0-934478-29-5*) Ecotope.

Palmiter, Larry, ed. see Straub, Davis.

Palmo, Artis, ed. Career Development: Contemporary Readings. LC 77-2721. (Illus.). 367p. (C). 1977. text 39.50 (*0-8422-5270-3*) Irvington.

Palmo, Artis J., jt. auth. see Weikel, William J.

Palmon, Dan, jt. auth. see Kleinman, Gary.

Palmore, Angela. Marje: The Guilt & the Gingerbread. large type ed. 24.95 (*1-85695-121-9*, Pub. by ISIS Lrg Prnt) Transaction Pubs.

Palmore, Erdman B. Ageism: Negative & Positive. 2nd ed. LC 99-22800. (Illus.). 280p. 1999. pap. text 29.95 (*0-8261-7002-1*) Springer Pub.

***Palmore, Erdman B.** Ageism: Negative & Positive. 2nd ed. LC 99-22800. (Illus.). 280p. 1999. text 44.95 (*0-8261-7001-3*) Springer Pub.

Palmore, Erdman B. The Facts on Aging Quiz. 2nd ed. LC 98-20243. 192p. 1998. 41.95 (*0-8261-5771-8*); pap. 28.95 (*0-8261-5772-6*) Springer Pub.

— Normal Aging 2: Reports from the Duke Longitudinal Study, 1970-1973. LC 74-132028. xix, 316p. 1974. text 49.95 (*0-8223-0311-6*) Duke.

Palmore, Erdman B., ed. Developments & Research on Aging. LC 92-25737. 456p. 1993. lib. bdg. 89.50 (*0-313-27785-0*, PDV, Greenwood Pr) Greenwood.

— Handbook on the Aged in the United States. LC 84-4463. (Illus.). 458p. 1984. lib. bdg. 105.00 (*0-313-23721-2*, PHA/, Greenwood Pr) Greenwood.

— International Handbook on Aging: Contemporary Developments & Research. LC 78-73802. (Illus.). 529p. 1980. lib. bdg. 59.95 (*0-313-20890-5*, PIH/, Greenwood Pr) Greenwood.

— Normal Aging 1: Reports from the Duke Longitudinal Study, 1955-1969. LC 74-132028. xxiv, 431p. 1970. text 49.95 (*0-8223-0238-1*) Duke.

Palmore, James A. & Gardner, Robert W. Measuring Mortality, Fertility, & Natural Increase: A Self-Teaching Guide to Elementary Measures. rev. ed. 1994. pap. 15.00 (*0-86638-165-1*) EW Ctr HI.

Palmour, Hayne, III, et al, eds. Sintering '85. 442p. 1987. 105.00 (*0-306-42541-6*, Plenum Trade) Perseus Pubng.

— The Windows of St. Michael's: Lift High the Cross. LC 97-69048. (Illus.). 68p. (Orig.). 1997. pap. 15.95 (*0-943335-09-4*) Marblehead Pub.

Palmour, Hayne, III, jt. ed. see Kriegel, W. W., III.

Palmour, Hayne, ed. see Research Conference on Structure & Property of Engineering Materials Staff.

Palmour, Vernon E., et al, compiled by. A Study of the Characteristics, Costs & Magnitude of Interlibrary Loans in Academic Libraries. LC 70-39344. 127p. 1972. 47.95 (*0-8371-6340-4*, PIL/); pap. 8.50 (*0-685-02011-8*) Greenwood.

Palmov, V. Vibrations of Elasto-Plastic Bodies. Belyaev, A., tr. from RUS. LC 98-16285. (Foundations of Engineering Mechanics Ser.). iv, 311p. 1998. 98.00 (*3-540-63724-9*) Spr-Verlag.

Palmowski, Jan. A Dictionary of Twentieth-Century World History. (Oxford Paperback Reference Ser.). (Illus.). 692p. 1997. pap. 15.95 (*0-19-280016-7*) OUP.

— Urban Liberalism in Imperial Germany: Frankfurt-Am-Main, 1866-1914. LC 98-42428. (Oxford Historical Monographs). (Illus.). 408p. 1999. text 85.00 (*0-19-820750-6*) OUP.

Palmquist, jt. auth. see Zimmerman.

***Palmquist, Bonnie Beatson.** Voices of Minnesota History, 1836-1946. LC 99-45484. (Illus.). 168p. 2000. pap. 12.95 (*1-880090 88 0*) Galde Pr.

***Palmquist, J. Phil.** Signs & Wonders. LC 99-93642. 2000. pap. 10.95 (*0-533-13102-2*) Vantage.

Palmquist, Joe, ed. see Odell, Michael E.

Palmquist, John C., ed. Wisconsin's Door Peninsula: A Natural History. (Illus.). 196p. (Orig.). 1989. pap. 10.95 (*0-929682-00-9*) Perin Pr.

Palmquist, Judy, jt. auth. see Bennett, Mary K.

Palmquist, M. K., tr. see Maffesoli, Michel.

Palmquist, P., et al. Journal of California & Great Basin Anthropology. fac. ed. (Malki Museum, Journal of California & Great Basin Anthropology Ser.: Vol. 5:1&2). (Illus.). 292p. (C). 1983. reprint ed. pap. text 30.63 (*1-55567-771-1*) Coyote Press.

***Palmquist, Peter.** Dassonville: William E. Dassonville, California Photographer (1879-1957) Hertzmann, Paul & Herzig, Susan, eds. (Illus.). 112p. 1999. 65.00 (*1-887694-16-1*, Pub. by C Mautz Pubng); pap. 35.00 (*1-887694-15-3*, Pub. by C Mautz Pubng) Stackpole.

Palmquist, Peter, ed. The Daguerreian Annual, 1992. 264p. 1992. pap. 45.00 (*1-881186-92-X*) Daguerreian.

— Photography in the West II. (Illus.). 132p. 1989. pap. 15.00 (*0-89745-084-1*) Sunflower U Pr.

Palmquist, Peter, et al. Silver Shadows: A Directory & History of Early Photography in Chico & the Twelve Counties of Northern California. LC 92-73662. 84p. 1993. pap. 24.95 (*0-9634512-0-0*) Chico Mus Assn.

Palmquist, Peter, ed. see Dornin, George D.

Palmquist, Peter, ed. see Kibbey, Mead.

Palmquist, Peter E., ed. Camera Fiends & Kodak Girls I - Fifty Selections by & about Women in Photography 1840-1930. LC 89-61496. (Illus.). 272p. (Orig.). 1989. pap. text 14.90 (*1-877675-00-8*) Midmarch Arts.

— Camera Fiends & Kodak Girls II - Sixty Selections by & about Women in Photography 1855-1965. LC 93-81153. 362p. (Orig.). 1995. pap. 18.00 (*1-877675-15-6*) Midmarch Arts.

— The Daguerreian Annual, 1991. 264p. 1991. pap. 45.00 (*1-881186-91-1*) Daguerreian.

— The Daguerreian Annual, 1993. (Illus.). 288p. (Orig.). 1993. pap. 45.00 (*1-881186-93-8*) Daguerreian.

— The Daguerreian Annual, 1990. 202p. 1990. pap. 45.00 (*1-881186-90-3*) Daguerreian.

— Photography in the West. (Illus.). 116p. 1987. pap. 15.00 (*0-89745-102-3*) Sunflower U Pr.

***Palmquist, Peter E. & Kailbourn, Thomas R.** Pioneer Photographers of the Far West: A Biographical Dictionary, 1840-1865. LC 00-40009. 2000. write for info. (*0-8047-3883-1*) Stanford U Pr.

Palmquist, Roland E. Electrical Course for Apprentices & Journeymen. 3rd ed. 480p. 1988. 24.95 (*0-02-594550-5*, Aude IN) IDG Bks.

Palmquist, Stephen R. Kant's System of Perspectives & Architectonic Interpretation of the Critical Philosophy. LC 92-33937. 490p. (C). 1992. lib. bdg. 65.00 (*0-8191-8927-8*) U Pr of Amer.

Palmqvist, Lennart. Opuscula Atheniensia XV. (Acta Instituti Atheniensis Regni Sueciae Ser.: Vol. XXXI). (Illus.). 200p. 1984. pap. 87.50 (*91-85086-59-2*, Pub. by P Astroms) Coronet Bks.

Palmqvist, Lennart, ed. Opuscula Romana XIV. (Acta Instituti Romani Regni Sueciae, Series in 4 Degrees: Vol. XXXIX). (Illus.). 102p. 1983. pap. 67.50 (*91-7042-085-8*, Pub. by P Astroms) Coronet Bks.

Palms, Roger. Celebrate Life after 50. 180p. 1995. pap. 9.99 (*1-56476-453-2*, 6-3453, Victor Bks) Chariot Victor.

— Enjoying the Closeness of God: Know the Pleasure of Being His Friend. 272p. 1998. reprint ed. pap. 9.95 (*1-886158-14-2*) Macalester.

***Palms, Roger C.** Effective Magazine Writing: Let Your Words Reach the World. LC 00-37383. 2000. pap. write for info. (*0-87788-211-8*, H Shaw Pubs) Waterbrook Pr.

Palms, Roger C. Let God Help You Choose: Learning to Make Decisions That Honor God. 163p. 1998. reprint ed. pap. 10.99 (*0-89367-231-9*) Light & Life Comm.

— An Unexpected Hope: Finding Satisfaction When Life Disappoints. LC 97-40401. 176p. 1998. pap. 9.99 (*0-89107-978-5*) Crossway Bks.

Palnitkar, Samir. Verilog HDL. 448p. (C). 1996. 76.00 (*0-13-451675-3*) P-H.

Palo Alto Historical Association Staff & Winslow, Ward. Palo Alto: A Centennial History. LC 93-85698. (Illus.). 352p. 1993. write for info. (*0-9638098-3-0*) Palo Alto Hist.

Palo Alto Pre-School Staff, jt. auth. see Jackins, Tim.

Palo, Matti & Uusivuori, Jussi. World Forests, Society, & Environment. LC 99-10165. (World Forests Ser.). 1999. write for info. (*0-7923-5594-6*) Kluwer Academic.

— World Forests, Society & Environment LC 99-10165. 1999. write for info. (*0-7923-5301-3*) Kluwer Academic.

Palo, Matti, ed. see Mery, Gerardo.

Palo, R. Thomas & Robbins, Charles T. Plant Defenses Against Mammalian Herbivory. 192p. 1991. lib. bdg. 139.00 (*0-8493-6550-3*, SB292) CRC Pr.

Paloczi-Horvath, George. From Monitor to Missile Boat: Coast Defence Ships & Coastal Defence since 1860. (Illus.). 256p. 1996. 59.95 (*1-55750-270-6*) Naval Inst Pr.

Paloczi, Katalin. Clinical Applications of Immunophenotypic Analysis. LC 94-32881. (Medical Intelligence Unit Ser.). 1994. 99.00 (*1-57059-194-6*) Landes Bioscience.

***Palokangas, Tapio.** Labour Unions, Public Policy & Economic Growth. 256p. (C). 2000. 64.95 (*0-521-66323-7*) Cambridge U Pr.

Palomar, Joyce D. Title Insurance Law. LC 93-50657. (Real Property-Zoning Ser.). 1994. ring bd. 135.00 (*0-87632-989-X*) West Group.

Palomares, Susanna. All about Me: Reproducible Activity Sheets to Develop Self-Esteem in Your Students. Schilling, Dianne, ed. (Illus.). 64p. (J). (gr. 3-6). 1991. pap., teacher ed. 14.95 (*0-9625486-9-3*, IP4869) Innerchoice Pub.

— The Inside Story: A Journal of Self-Discovery. Schilling, Dianne, ed. & illus. by. 96p. (J). (gr. 4-8). 1994. teacher ed., spiral bd. 18.95 (*1-56499-018-4*, IP9018) Innerchoice Pub.

— Smiling Inside, Smiling Outside: Learning to Care for Myself, My Family, My World. Schilling, Dianne, ed. (Illus.). 96p. (J). (gr. k-3). 1993. pap., teacher ed. 14.95 (*1-56499-014-1*) Innerchoice Pub.

Palomares, Susanna. Social Skill Activities for the Elementary Grades. (Illus.). 96p. (J). (gr. k-6). 1997. pap. text 19.95 (*1-56499-036-2*, Pub. by Innerchoice Pub) Jalmar Pr.

Palomares, Susanna & Akins, Terri. Managing Conflict. Schilling, Dianne, ed. (Orig.). (J). (gr. k-6). 1995. spiral bd. 19.95 (*1-56499-028-1*, IP9028) Innerchoice Pub.

***Palomares, Susanna & Cowan, David.** Working with Kids. (Illus.). 144p. (J). (gr. 3-9). 1999. pap. text 18.95 (*1-56499-038-9*, Pub. by Innerchoice Pub) Jalmar Pr.

Palomares, Susanna & Schilling, Dianne. Helping Teens Reach Their Dreams. (Illus.). 152p. (YA). (gr. 7-12). 1993. pap., teacher ed. 19.95 (*1-56499-013-3*, IP901Z) Innerchoice Pub.

— Life Skills for Teens. (Illus.). 91p. (Orig.). (YA). (gr. 7-12). 1994. pap. text 26.95 (*1-56499-024-9*, IP9024) Innerchoice Pub.

Palomares, Susanna, et al. The Sharing Circle Handbook: Topics for Teaching Self-Awareness, Communication, & Social Skills. Schilling, Dianne, ed. 181p. (Orig.). 1992. pap. text 16.95 (*1-56499-007-9*, IP9007) Innerchoice Pub.

Palomares, Susanna, jt. auth. see Schilling, Dianne.

Palomba, Cathrine A. & Banta, Trudy W. Assessment Essentials: Planning, Implementing, Improving. (Education Ser.). 1999. 32.95 (*0-7879-4180-8*) Jossey-Bass.

Palomba, Rossella, jt. ed. see Moors, Hein.

Palomba, Rossella, jt. ed. see Morrs, Hein.

Palombi, Fabrizio, ed. see Rota, Gian-Carlo.

P

An Asterisk (*) at the beginning of an entry indicates that the title is appearing for the first time.

Palombo, Bernadette J. Academic Professionalism in Law Enforcement. LC 94-47477. (Current Issues in Criminal Justice Ser.: Vol. 11). 296p. 1995. text 54.00 (*0-8153-1863-4*, SS998) Garland.

Palombo, Fulvio, jt. auth. see Lucchesi, Tony.

Palombo, Philip J., jt. auth. see Hausman, Carl.

Palombo, Ruth D., ed. see Massachusetts General Hospital Department of Nursing Staff.

Palombo, Stanley R. The Emergent Ego: Complexity & Coevolution in the Psychoanalytic Process. LC 98-22827. 395p. 1999. 65.00 (*0-8236-1666-5*, 01666) Intl Univs Pr.

***Palome, Edgar C., et al.** Miscellanea Indo-Europea. (Journal of Indo-European Studies Monographs: Vol. 33). 314p. (C). 1999. pap. text 48.00 (*0-941694-71-2*) Inst Study Man.

Palomino, Rafael. Low-Fat Latin Cooking. 2001. write for info. (*0-688-16725-X*, Hearst) Hearst Commns.

Palomino, Rafael & Moskin, Julia. Bistro Latino: Home Cooking Fired Up With The Flavors Of Latin America. Hoenig, Pam, ed. LC 97-49353. (Illus.). 288p. 1998. 25.00 (*0-688-15503-0*, Wm Morrow) Morrow Avon.

Palomo, Adolfo M. Las Amibas, Enemigos Invisibles. (Ciencia para Todos Ser.). (SPA.). pap. 6.99 (*968-16-2713-X*, Pub. by Fondo) Continental Bk.

Palomo, Jose. Recollection of Olden Days. (Educational Ser.: No. 13). (Illus.). 175p. (C). 1992. 9.95 (*1-878453-11-4*) Univ Guam MAR Ctr.

Palonen, Kari, jt. ed. see Ahonen, Perti.

Palonsky, Stuart B. Nine Hundred Shows a Year. 288p. (C). 1985. pap. 32.19 (*0-07-554645-0*) McGraw.

Palos, Monika, tr. see Lendvai, Erno.

Paloscia, S., jt. ed. see Pampaloni, P.

Palotta, Joseph L. The Robot Psychiatrist. 603p. 1981. pap. 29.95 (*0-9604852-0-1*) Revelation Hse.

— Success over Stress. 184p. 1990. pap. 6.95 (*0-9604852-3-6*) Revelation Hse.

— That Your Joy Might Be Full. 247p. 1981. pap. 6.95 (*0-9604852-1-X*) Revelation Hse.

— True Riches. 319p. (Orig.). 1985. pap. 8.95 (*0-9604852-2-8*) Revelation Hse.

— Winning over the Mind. LC 98-121153. 187p. 1998. pap. 6.95 (*0-9604852-5-2*) Revelation Hse.

Palou, Francisco. Historical Memoirs of New California, 4 vols., Set. (BCL1 - United States Local History Ser.). 1991. reprint ed. lib. bdg. 300.00 (*0-7812-6340-9*) Rprt Serv.

— Life & Apostolic Labors of the Venerable Father Junipero Serra, Founder of the Franciscan Missions of California. 1992. reprint ed. lib. bdg. 75.00 (*0-7812-5073-0*) Rprt Serv.

Palou, Pedro A., tr. see Watt, Donley.

Palous, J., et al, eds. Evolution of Interstellar Matter & Dynamics of Galaxies. (Illus.). 438p. (C). 1992. text 80.00 (*0-521-41984-0*) Cambridge U Pr.

Paloutzian, Raymond F. Invitation to the Psychology of Religion. 2nd ed. LC 95-36563. 400p. 1996. pap. text 41.00 (*0-205-14840-9*) Allyn.

***Paloutzian, Raymond F., ed.** Religious Orientation & Authoritarianism in Cross-Cultural Perspective. 80p. 1999. pap. 20.00 (*0-8058-9769-0*) L Erlbaum Assocs.

— Spiritual Intelligence: A Special Issue of The International Journal for the Psychology of Religion. 68p. 2000. pap. write for info. (*0-8058-9760-7*) L Erlbaum Assocs.

Palovak, Jewel, jt. auth. see Treadwell, Timothy.

Palow, jt. auth. see Jordan.

Palow, Sally. Robotix Teacher's Guide: The Science of Robotics. (Illus.). 188p. 1997. ring bd. 69.00 (*1-890647-25-X*) Lrning Curve.

Palow, William P., jt. auth. see Jordan, Bill E.

Palowski, Franciszek. The Making of Schindler's List: Behind the Scenes of an Epic Film. LC 97-41443. (Illus.). 196p. 1998. 21.95 (*1-55972-445-5*) Carol Pub Group.

Palrewala, Rajni, jt. ed. see Dube, Leela.

Palriwala, Rajni & Risseeuw, Carla, eds. Shifting Circles of Support: Contextualising Kinship & Gender in South Asia & Sub-Saharan Africa. LC 95-30053. (Illus.). 343p. 1996. 44.95 (*0-8039-9275-0*) Sage.

Pals. Early in Morning Big Book. 16p. 1995. pap. 23.30 (*0-201-85303-5*) S&S Trade.

Pals. Early in the Morning Little Book. 16p. (J). 1995. ring bd. 4.78 (*0-201-85310-8*) Addison-Wesley.

— The Electronic Library. (SPA.). 1995. 144.03 (*0-201-83255-0*) Addison-Wesley.

— The Electronic Library A. (SPA.). 1995. 144.03 (*0-201-83257-7*) Addison-Wesley.

— The Electronic Library B. (SPA.). 1995. 144.03 (*0-201-83259-3*) Addison-Wesley.

— Little Ant Little Book Level B, Level B. 16p. (J). 1995. ring bd. 4.78 (*0-201-85357-4*) Addison-Wesley.

— Only a Nickel Big Bks. 1995. pap. 23.30 (*0-201-85350-7*) S&S Trade.

— Only a Nickel Little Book Level B. (J). 1995. ring bd. 4.78 (*0-201-85358-2*) Addison-Wesley.

— Run, Run, Run, Little Book. 16p. (J). 1995. ring bd. 4.78 (*0-201-85311-6*) Addison-Wesley.

Pals. Why Coqui Sings Big Book. 16p. 1995. pap. 23.30 (*0-201-85351-5*) S&S Trade.

Pals. Why the Coqui Sings Little Book Level B, Level B. 16p. (J). 1995. ring bd. 4.78 (*0-201-85359-0*) Addison-Wesley.

Pals, Daniel L. Seven Theories of Religion. 304p. 1996. 30.00 (*0-19-508724-0*) OUP.

— Seven Theories of Religion. 304p. (C). 1996. reprint ed. pap. text 22.95 (*0-19-508725-9*) OUP.

Pals, Ellen. Create a Celebration. (Illus.). 368p. pap. 22.95 (*0-9627721-0-0*) Aladdin CO.

— Create a Celebration: Ideas & Resources for Theme Parties, Holidays, & Special Occasions - Activities for All Ages. LC 96-12612. (Fulcrum Resources Bks.). (Illus.). 256p. (Orig.). 1996. reprint ed. pap. 19.95 (*1-55591-949-9*) Fulcrum Pub.

Pals Frandsen, H. Legal Dictionary English-Danish. (DAN & ENG.). 208p. 1994. 68.00 (*87-12-02026-5*, Pub. by GAD) IBD Ltd.

Pals, Nikolaus V. Gilse Van Der, see Gilse Van Der Pals, Nikolaus V.

Palsberg, Jens & Schwartzbach, Michael J. Object Oriented Type Systems. 192p. 1994. 95.00 (*0-471-94128-X*) Wiley.

Palsberg, Jens, jt. auth. see International Static Analysis Symposium Staff.

Palshaugen, Oyvind. The End of Organization Theory? Language as a Tool in Action Research & Organizational Development. LC 98-25042. (Dialogues on Work & Innovation Ser.: No. 5). vi, 149p. 1999. 39.95 (*1-55619-828-0*) J Benjamins Pubng Co.

Palsson, Bernhard, jt. auth. see Masters, John R. W.

Palsson, Erik K. Niels Stensen: Scientist & Saint. 75p. (Orig.). 1989. pap. 30.00 (*0-7855-6979-0*, Pub. by Veritas Pubns) St Mut.

Palsson, Gisli. The Textual Life of the Savants. (Studies in Anthropology & History). 240p. 1995. pap. text 27.00 (*3-7186-5722-8*, Harwood Acad Pubs) Gordon & Breach.

— The Textual Life of the Savants, Vol. 18. (Studies in Anthropology & History). 240p. 1995. text 60.00 (*3-7186-5721-X*, Harwood Acad Pubs) Gordon & Breach.

Palsson, Gisli, ed. From Water to World-Making: African Models & Arid Lands. 202p. 1990. 23.95 (*91-7106-313-7*, Pub. by Nordic Africa) Transaction Pubs.

Palsson, Gisli, et al, eds. Beyond Boundaries: Understanding, Translation & Anthropological Discourse. LC 92-10102. (Explorations in Anthropology Ser.). (Illus.). 272p. 1994. 49.50 (*0-85496-813-X*, Pub. by Berg Pubs) NYU Pr.

Palsson, Gisli & Durrenberger, E. Paul, eds. Images of Contemporary Iceland: Everyday Lives & Global Contexts. LC 95-35078. (Illus.). 285p. 1995. text 29.95 (*0-87745-528-7*) U of Iowa Pr.

Palsson, Gisli & Gledhill, John, eds. Beyond Boundaries: Understanding, Translation & Anthropological Discourse. (Illus.). 272p. 1994. pap. 19.50 (*1-85973-021-3*, Pub. by Berg Pubs) NYU Pr.

Palsson, Gisli, jt. ed. see Descola, Philippe.

Palsson, Gisli, jt. ed. see Durrenberger, E. Paul.

Palsson, Herman. Seven Viking Romances. (Classics Ser.). 304p. 1986. pap. 12.95 (*0-14-044474-2*, Penguin Classics) Viking Penguin.

P'alsson, Herman & Edwards, Paul. Knytlinga Saga: History of the Kings of Denmark. 198p. (Orig.). 1986. pap. text 37.50 (*91-7492-571-7*) Coronet Bks.

Palsson, Hermann. Eyrbyggja Saga. Edwards, Paul, tr. LC 72-97525. (Unesco Collection of Representative Works, Series of Translations from the Literature of the Union of Soviet Socialist Republics). (Illus.). 198p. reprint ed. pap. 61.40 (*0-8357-8128-3*, 203405500088) Bks Demand.

— Gautrek's Saga & Other Medieval Tales. LC 68-16829. 156p. reprint ed. pap. 48.40 (*0-608-30840-4*, 205024600058) Bks Demand.

— Gongu-Hrolfs Saga. LC PT7287.G7E5. (UNESCO Collection of Representative Works. Icelandic Ser.). 128p. reprint ed. pap. 39.70 (*0-8357-6364-1*, 203571800069) Bks Demand.

— Hrafnkel's Saga. (Classics Ser.). 144p. 1971. pap. 11.95 (*0-14-044238-3*, Penguin Classics) Viking Penguin.

— Hrolf Gautreksson, a Viking Romance. LC 73-185728. 149p. reprint ed. pap. 46.20 (*0-8357-4163-X*, 203693700007) Bks Demand.

— Orkneyinga Saga: The History of the Earls of Orkney. (Classics Ser.). 250p. 1981. pap. 13.95 (*0-14-044383-5*, Penguin Classics) Viking Penguin.

Palsson, Hermann, ed. Eyrbyggja Saga. Edwards, Paul, tr. 192p. 1989. pap. 12.95 (*0-14-044530-7*, Penguin Classics) Viking Penguin.

Palsson, Hermann, jt. tr. see Fox, Denton.

Palsson, Hermann, jt. tr. see Magnusson, Magnus.

Palsson, Hermann, tr. see Sturluson, Snorri.

Palsson, S. H., jt. ed. see Edwards, Paul.

Palsule, Sanjay. Aerospace Polymers & Composites: Fundamentals & Applications. LC 95-39623. (Wiley-Praxis Series in Space Science & Technology). 1995. write for info. (*0-471-96016-0*) Wiley.

Paltauf, F., jt. ed. see Ceve, G.

Palter, Robert. Whitehead's Philosophy of Science. LC 60-7241. (Illus.). 248p. reprint ed. pap. 76.90 (*0-608-09565-6*, 205436700005) Bks Demand.

Palter, Robert, jt. auth. see Basalla, George.

Palti, Yoram, jt. ed. see Rosen, Michael R.

Paltian, Wolfgang, jt. auth. see Iserhardt, Louis.

Paltis, Jacqueline L. The Sugar Control Bible & Cookbook: The Complete Nutrition Guide to Revitalizing Your Health. 220p. (Orig.). 1998. pap. 29.95 (*1-892241-02-1*) New Energy.

Paltridge, Brian. Genre, Frames & Writing in Research Settings. LC 97-8793. (Pragmatics & Beyond New Ser.: Vol. 45). x, 192p. 1997. lib. bdg. 49.00 (*1-55619-807-8*) J Benjamins Pubng Co.

Paltro, Piera. Learning My Prayers, 8 bks. Daughters of St. Paul Staff, tr. Incl. Angel of God. (Illus.). 16p. (J). (gr. k-3). 1981. pap. 2.95 (*0-8198-0739-7*, CH0031P); Eternal Rest: A Prayer for People Who Have Died. (Illus.). 15p. (Orig.). (J). (gr. k-3). 1992. pap. 2.50 (*0-8198-2332-5*); Glory to the Father. (Illus.). 21p. (Orig.). (J). (ps up). 1987. pap. 2.50 (*0-8198-3043-7*, CH0227); Hail, Holy Queen. (Illus.). 15p. (Orig.). (J). (gr. k-3). 1992. pap. 2.50 (*0-8198-3365-7*); Hail Mary. (Illus.). 22p. (J). (gr. k-3). 1992. pap. 2.50 (*0-8198-3316-9*); I Believe: The Profession of Faith or Creed. (Illus.). 29p. (Orig.). (J). (gr. k-3). 1992. pap. 2.50 (*0-8198-3664-8*); My Mass. (Illus.). 32p. (J). (gr. k-3). 1992. pap. 2.50 (*0-8198-4765-8*); Our Father. (Illus.). 23p. (Orig.). (J). (ps-1). 1991. pap. 2.95 (*0-8198-5416-6*, CH0416P); Set pap. 18.80 (*0-8198-4483-7*) Pauline Bks.

Paltrowitz, Donna, jt. auth. see Paltrowitz, Stuart.

Paltrowitz, Stuart & Paltrowitz, Donna. Content Area Reading Skills-Competency Canada: Main Idea. (Illus.). (J). (gr. 4). 1987. pap. text 3.25 (*0-89525-853-6*) Ed Activities.

— Content Area Reading Skills-Competency Mexico: Locating Details. (Illus.). (J). (gr. 4). 1987. pap. text 3.25 (*0-89525-854-4*) Ed Activities.

— Content Area Reading Skills-Competency U. S. History: Detecting Sequence. (Illus.). (J). (gr. 4). 1987. pap. text 3.25 (*0-89525-856-0*) Ed Activities.

— Content Area Reading Skills U. S. Geography: Cause & Effect. (Illus.). (J). (gr. 4). 1987. pap. text 3.25 (*0-89525-855-2*) Ed Activities.

Paltsits, Victor H., ed. Minutes of the Commissioners for Detecting & Defeating Conspiracies in the State of New York, 3 vols. in 2, Set. LC 72-8752. (American Revolutionary Ser.). 1972. reprint ed. lib. bdg. 110.00 (*0-8398-1574-3*) Irvington.

— Washington's Farewell Address. LC 74-137706. (New York Public Library Publications in Reprint). (Illus.). 1971. reprint ed. 31.95 (*0-405-01742-1*) Ayer.

Paltsits, Victor H., ed. see Melville, Herman.

Paltsits, Victor H., ed. & intro. see Miller, John.

Paltz, Johannes von. Werke, Vol. 2. (Illus.). 504p. 1983. 176.95 (*3-11-004955-4*) De Gruyter.

Palubiak, R. Craig. Business Growth Strategies. (Business Person's Handbook Ser.: Vol. 1). 20p. (Orig.). 1998. pap. 8.95 (*1-893308-00-6*) Optim Consult Grp.

— The Business Person's Handbook: Selling Your Company, Vol. 12. 20p. 1999. pap. 8.95 (*1-893308-11-1*) Optim Consult Grp.

— Company Profile: The Business Resume. (Business Person's Handbook Ser.: Vol. 2). 28p. (Orig.). 1998. pap. 8.95 (*1-893308-01-4*) Optim Consult Grp.

— Corporate Mission: Think Mission Before Commission. (Business Person's Handbook Ser.: Vol. 4). 24p. (Orig.). 1998. pap. 8.95 (*1-893308-03-0*) Optim Consult Grp.

— Customerization: Targeting Optimal Customers. (Business Person's Handbook Ser.: Vol. 5). 20p. (Orig.). 1998. pap. 8.95 (*1-893308-04-9*) Optim Consult Grp.

— Employee Feedback: Measuring Corporate Performance. (Business Person's Handbook Ser.: Vol. 6). 16p. (Orig.). 1998. pap. 8.95 (*1-893308-05-7*) Optim Consult Grp.

— Employee Partnership: The Internal Customer. (Business Person's Handbook Ser.: Vol. 7). 20p. (Orig.). 1998. pap. 8.95 (*1-893308-06-5*) Optim Consult Grp.

— Goal Setting: Corporate Versus Personal. (Business Person's Handbook Ser.: Vol. 8). 18p. (Orig.). 1998. pap. 8.95 (*1-893308-07-3*) Optim Consult Grp.

— The Height of Ingratitude: Will Customers Ever Be Satisfied? (Business Person's Handbook Ser.: Vol. 9). 20p. (Orig.). 1998. pap. 8.95 (*1-893308-08-1*) Optim Consult Grp.

— Learn to Read the Need: Identifying Customer Desires. Kochelek, Jeffrey, ed. (Business Person's Handbook Ser.: Vol. 10). 16p. (Orig.). 1998. pap. 8.95 (*1-893308-09-X*) Optim Consult Grp.

— Product Offering: The Right Mix. (Business Person's Handbook Ser.: Vol. 11). 20p. (Orig.). 1998. pap. 8.95 (*1-893308-10-3*) Optim Consult Grp.

Palubniak, Nancy, jt. auth. see Gross, Gay M.

Paluch, Jim. Five Important Things: A Motivational Novel for Every Individual Family or Team Pursuing a Dream. 137p. 1996. reprint ed. pap. 10.00 (*0-937539-21-X*) Executive Bks.

***Paluch, Jim.** Leaving a Legacy: An Inspirational Guide to Taking Action & Making a Difference. LC 98-83119. 1999. pap. text 11.95 (*0-937539-32-5*) Executive Bks.

Paluch, Jim & JP Horizons, Inc. Staff. Five Important Things: A Motivational Novel. 152p. 1996. pap. text, per. 14.95 (*0-7872-2077-9*) Kendall-Hunt.

Paluch, Mark, ed. see Duncan Peterson Publishing Ltd. Staff.

Palucki, Michael. Chicago Bicycle Guidebook: Great Bicycle Riding Through Chicago's Lakefront Neighborhoods. LC 92-85158. (Illus.). (Orig.). 1993. pap. 9.95 (*0-9634829-7-1*) Pastime.

Paludan, Ann. The Chinese Spirit Road: The Classical Tradition of Stone Tomb Statuary. LC 90-2359. (Illus.). 303p. 1991. reprint ed. pap. 94.00 (*0-608-07843-3*, 205401900011) Bks Demand.

— Chronicle of the Chinese Emperors: A Reign-by-Reign Record of the Rulers of Imperial China. LC 98-60041. (Illus.). 224p. 1998. 29.95 (*0-500-05090-2*, Pub. by Thames Hudson) Norton.

— The Ming Tombs. (Images of Asia Ser.). (Illus.). 94p. (C). 1991. 15.95 (*0-19-585003-3*) OUP.

Paludan, Eva. The Romance Writer's Pink Pages, 1996-1997. 336p. 1995. pap. text 14.95 (*0-7615-0168-1*) Prima Pub.

Paludan, Eve. The Romance Writer's Pink Pages: The Insider's Guide to Getting Your Romance Novel Published. 272p. (Orig.). 1993. pap. 12.95 (*1-55958-349-5*) Prima Pub.

— The Romance Writer's Pink Pages, 1955-1996: The Insider's Guide to Getting Your Romance Novel. 272p. 1994. pap. 12.95 (*1-55958-581-1*) Prima Pub.

Paludan, Jacob. Jorgen Stein. Malmberg, Carl, tr. from DAN. LC 66-22852. (Nordic Translation Ser.). 744p. 1966. reprint ed. pap. 200.00 (*0-608-01945-3*, 206260000003) Bks Demand.

Paludan, Lis. Crochet: History & Technique. Olsen, Jean & Fredricksson, Kristine, trs. from DAN. (Illus.). 320p. 1995. 35.00 (*1-883010-09-8*) Interweave.

Paludan-Mueller, Frederik. Adam Homo. Klass, Stephen, tr. from DAN. LC 81-58568. (Illus.). 543p. (Orig.). (C). 1981. pap. 26.95 (*0-936726-02-4*) Twickenham Pr.

Paludan-Muller, Carsten, jt. ed. see Kristiansen, Kristian.

Paludan, Phillip S. A Covenant with Death: The Constitution, Law, & Equality in the Civil War Era. LC 74-34324. 323p. 1975. text 29.95 (*0-252-00261-X*) U of Ill Pr.

— A Covenant with Death: The Constitution, Law, & Equality in the Civil War Era. LC 74-34324. 325p. 1975. reprint ed. pap. 100.80 (*0-7837-8083-4*, 204783600008) Bks Demand.

— A People's Contest: The Union & Civil War, 1861-1865. 2nd ed. LC 96-21303. (Modern War Studies). (Illus.). 524p. 1996. pap. 16.95 (*0-7006-0812-5*) U Pr of KS.

— The Presidency of Abraham Lincoln. LC 93-46830. (American Presidency Ser.). 408p. (Orig.). (C). 1994. 29.95 (*0-7006-0671-8*) U Pr of KS.

— The Presidency of Abraham Lincoln. LC 93-46830. 388p. (Orig.). (C). 1995. pap. 15.95 (*0-7006-0745-5*) U Pr of KS.

— Victims: A True Story of the Civil War. LC 81-2578. 160p. 1981. 26.00 (*0-87049-316-7*); pap. 13.00 (*0-87049-442-2*) U of Tenn Pr.

Paludi, Michele A. Exploring/Teaching the Psychology of Women: A Manual of Resources. 2nd ed. LC 95-8028. (SUNY Series, the Psychology of Women). 131p. (C). 1996. text 59.50 (*0-7914-2771-4*); pap. text 19.95 (*0-7914-2772-2*) State U NY Pr.

Paludi, Michele A. The Psychology of Women. 416p. (C). 1992. text. write for info. (*0-697-11499-6*) Brown & Benchmark.

Paludi, Michele A. The Psychology of Women. LC 97-41464. 406p. (C). 1998. pap. text 42.00 (*0-13-955840-3*) P-H.

Paludi, Michele A., ed. Sexual Harassment on College Campuses: Abusing the Ivory Power. LC 95-15813. (SUNY Series, the Psychology of Women). 311p. (C). 1996. text 59.50 (*0-7914-2801-X*); pap. text 19.95 (*0-7914-2802-8*) State U NY Pr.

Paludi, Michele A. & Barickman, Richard B. Academic & Workplace Sexual Harassment: A Resource Manual. LC 90-24364. (SUNY Series in the Psychology of Women). 235p. (C). 1991. text 21.50 (*0-7914-0829-9*) State U NY Pr.

— Sexual Harassment, Work, & Education: A Resource Manual for Prevention. 2nd ed. LC 97-49416. (Series, the Psychology of Women). 192p. (C). 1998. text 59.50 (*0-7914-3891-0*); pap. text 19.95 (*0-7914-3892-9*) State U NY Pr.

Paludi, Michele A. & Steuernagel, Gertrude A., eds. Foundations for a Feminist Restructuring of the Academic Disciplines. LC 89-15529. (Haworth Series on Women: No. 3). 276p. 1990. text 49.95 (*0-86656-878-6*) Haworth Pr.

— Foundations for a Feminist Restructuring of the Academic Disciplines. 266p. 1994. pap. 24.95 (*0-918393-64-7*, Harrington Park) Haworth Pr.

Paludi, Michele A., jt. auth. see Doyle, James A.

Paludi, Michele A., jt. auth. see Tedisco, James N.

Paludi, Michele A., jt. ed. see Denmark, Florence L.

Paludi, Michele Antoinette, ed. The Psychology of Sexual Victimization: A Handbook. LC 98-14239. 272p. 1999. lib. bdg. 69.50 (*0-313-30248-0*, Greenwood Pr) Greenwood.

Paluiak, R. Craig. Competitive Intelligence: Let Competition Drive - Not Guide. (Business Person's Handbook Ser.: Vol. 3). 22p. (Orig.). 1998. pap. 8.95 (*1-893308-02-2*) Optim Consult Grp.

Palumbi, Stephen R., jt. auth. see Ferraris, Joan D.

Palumbi, Stephen R., jt. ed. see Ferraris, Joan D.

Palumbo, Anne V. The Stay-at-Home Mom's Survival Guide. Boucke, Laurie, ed. LC 97-10761. (Illus.). 232p. (Orig.). 1997. pap. 15.00 (*1-888580-05-4*) White-Boucke.

***Palumbo, Dennis.** Writing From the Inside Out: Transforming Your Psychological Blocks to Release the Writers Within. LC 00-24252. 256p. 2000. pap. 15.95 (*0-471-38266-3*) Wiley.

Palumbo, Dennis, ed. Evaluating & Optimizing Public Policy. (C). 1980. pap. 15.00 (*0-918592-38-0*) Pol Studies.

Palumbo, Dennis & Calista, Donald, eds. Implementation: What We Have Learned & Still Need to Know. (Orig.). 1987. pap. 15.00 (*0-918592-96-8*) Pol Studies.

Palumbo, Dennis G. The Essence of Hakkoryo Jujutsu: Techniques of Sandan Gi. (Illus.). 120p. 1995. pap. 25.00 (*0-87364-860-9*) Paladin Pr.

— Secret Nidan Techniques of Hakkoryu Jujutsu. (Illus.). 136p. 1988. pap. 14.00 (*0-87364-455-7*) Paladin Pr.

— The Secrets of Hakkoryu Jujutsu: Shodan Tactics. (Illus.). 144p. 1987. pap. 17.50 (*0-87364-422-0*) Paladin Pr.

Palumbo, Dennis J. Public Policy in America. 2nd ed. LC 94-75332. (C). 1994. text 56.00 (*0-15-500383-6*, Pub. by Harcourt Coll Pubs) Harcourt.

Palumbo, Dennis J., ed. The Politics of Program Evaluation. 304p. (C). 1987. text 44.00 (*0-8039-2736-3*); pap. text 21.95 (*0-8039-2737-1*) Sage.

— The Politics of Program Evaluation. LC 86-13899. (Sage Yearbooks in Politics & Public Policy Ser.: No. 15). 309p. 1987. reprint ed. pap. 95.80 (*0-608-01501-6*, 205954500001) Bks Demand.

Palumbo, Dennis J. & Calista, Donald J., eds. Implementation & the Policy Process: Opening up the Black Box, 252. LC 89-23640. (Contributions in Political Science Ser.: No. 252). 298p. 1990. 49.95 (*0-313-27283-2*, PIP/, Greenwood Pr) Greenwood.

Palumbo, Dennis J., jt. auth. see Hallett, Michael A.

An Asterisk (*) at the beginning of an entry indicates that the title is appearing for the first time.

***Palumbo-DeSimone, Christine.** Sharing Secrets: Nineteenth-Century Women's Relations in the Short Story. LC 99-53350. 176p. 2000. 34.50 (*0-8386-3840-6*) Fairleigh Dickinson.

Palumbo, Donald, ed. Eros in the Mind's Eye: Sexuality & the Fantastic in Art & Film, 21. LC 85-24777. (Contributions to the Study of Science Fiction & Fantasy Ser.: No. 21). (Illus.). 318p. 1986. 65.00 (*0-313-24102-3*, PER/) Greenwood.

— Erotic Universe: Sexuality & Fantastic Literature, 18. LC 85-14696. (Contributions to the Study of Science Fiction & Fantasy Ser.: No. 18). 323p. 1986. 55.00 (*0-313-24101-5*, PAE/, Greenwood Pr) Greenwood.

— Spectrum of the Fantastic: Selected Essays from the Sixth International Conference on the Fantastic in the Arts, 31. LC 87-25216. (Contributions to the Study of Science Fiction & Fantasy Ser.: No. 31). (Illus.). 285p. 1988. 65.00 (*0-313-25502-4*, PPF/) Greenwood.

***Palumbo, Eugene.** Mother Teresa: God's Slumlord. 80p. 2000. pap. 5.95 (*1-878718-59-2*, Resurrection Pr) Catholic Bk Pub.

Palumbo, Eugene, tr. see Lopez Vigil, Maria.

Palumbo, Frank A. Major General George Henry Thomas: The Dependable General. LC 83-17261. (Illus.). 465p. 1983. 35.00 (*0-89029-311-2*) Morningside Bkshop.

Palumbo, Giorgio G. Catalogue of Radial Velocities of Galaxies. xvi, 576p. 1983. text 335.00 (*0-677-06090-4*) Gordon & Breach.

Palumbo, Linda J. & Gaik, Frank J. Vocabulary for a New World. (Orig.). (C). 1991. pap., teacher ed. 6.00 (*0-02-390568-9*, U5301-9) Allyn.

Palumbo, Linda J., jt. auth. see Otte, George.

Palumbo-Liu, David. Asian/American: Historical Crossings of a Racial Frontier. LC 98-48250. 1999. pap. text 24.95 (*0-8047-3445-3*) Stanford U Pr.

***Palumbo-Liu, David.** Asian/American: Historical Crossings of a Racial Frontier. LC 98-48250. 1999. 65.00 (*0-8047-3444-5*) Stanford U Pr.

Palumbo-Liu, David. The Ethnic Canon: Histories, Institutions, & Interventions. 1995. pap. 19.95 (*0-8166-2557-3*); text 49.95 (*0-8166-2556-5*) U of Minn Pr.

— The Poetics of Appropriation: The Literary Theory & Practice of Huang Tingjian. LC 92-22990. 280p. 1993. 39.50 (*0-8047-2126-2*) Stanford U Pr.

Palumbo-Liu, David & Gumbrecht, Hans U., eds. Streams of Cultural Capital. LC 97-67436. (Illus.). 250p. 1997. 45.00 (*0-8047-3036-9*); pap. 17.95 (*0-8047-3037-7*) Stanford U Pr.

*** Palumbo, Maria Luisa.** New Wombs: Electronic Bodies & Architectural Disorder. (Illus.). 96p. 2000. pap. 12.50 (*3-7643-6294-4*, Pub. by Birkhauser) Princeton Arch.

Palumbo, Michael. Human Rights: Meaning & History. Snyder, Louis L., ed. LC 81 18592. (Anvil Ser.). 208p. (Orig.). (C). 1982. pap. text 11.50 (*0-89874-259 5*) Krieger.

— The Palestinian Catastrophe. 1990. pap. 11.95 (*0-7043-0099-0*, Pub. by Quartet) Interlink Pub.

Palumbo, Michael & Shanahan, William O., eds. Nationalism: Essays in Honor of Louis L. Snyder, 65. LC 81-6501. (Contributions in Political Science Ser.: No. 65). 219p. 1981. 57.95 (*0-313-23176-1*, PNA/, Greenwood Pr) Greenwood.

Palumbo, Nancy. A Birthday Present for Ree-Ree: Un Cadeau d'Anniversaire Pour Ree-Ree. (Illus.). 32p. (J). (ps-6). 1989. student ed. 0.95 (*0-927024-15-2*) Crayons Pubns.

— A Birthday Present for Ree-Ree: Un Regalo Cumpleanos Para Ree-Ree. (Illus.). 32p. (J). (gr. k-6). 1989. student ed. 0.95 (*0-927024-14-4*) Crayons Pubns.

— Early Learning Shape Book: El Libro de Figuras Geometricas. (Illus.). 32p. (J). (gr. k-6). 1989. student ed. 0.45 (*0-927024-06-3*) Crayons Pubns.

— Early Learning Shape Book: Le Livre Des Formes. (Illus.). 32p. (J). (gr. k-6). 1989. student ed. 0.95 (*0-927024-07-1*) Crayons Pubns.

— J. J. Goes to School (J. J. Va a la Escuela) (Illus.). 32p. (J). (gr. k-6). 1989. student ed. 0.95 (*0-927024-12-8*) Crayons Pubns.

— J. J. Goes to School (J. J. Va a L'Ecole) (Illus.). 32p. (J). (gr. k-6). 1989. student ed. 0.95 (*0-927024-13-6*) Crayons Pubns.

— Lets Color & Count: Colorions et Comptons. (Illus.). 32p. (J). (gr. k-6). 1989. student ed. 0.45 (*0-927024-09-8*) Crayons Pubns.

— Meet Penelope P'Nutt: Conoza Penelope P'Nutt. (Illus.). 32p. (J). (gr. k-6). 1989. student ed. 0.45 (*0-927024-04-7*) Crayons Pubns.

— Meet Penelope P'Nutt: Viens Recontrer Penelope P'Nutt. (Illus.). 32p. (J). (gr. k-6). 1989. student ed. 0.45 (*0-927024-05-5*) Crayons Pubns.

— Penelope P'Nutt & the Spirit of Christmas: Penelope P'Nutt et l'Ambiance de Noel. (Illus.). 16p. (J). (gr. k-6). 1989. student ed. 0.45 (*0-927024-03-9*) Crayons Pubns.

— Penelope P'Nutt & the Spirit of Christmas: Penelope P'Nutt y el Espiritu de la Navidad. (Illus.). 16p. (J). (gr. k-6). 1989. student ed. 0.45 (*0-927024-02-0*) Crayons Pubns.

— Penelope P'Nutt at Play: Los Juegos de Penelope P'Nutt. (Illus.). 32p. (J). (gr. k-6). 1989. student ed. 0.95 (*0-927024-16-0*) Crayons Pubns.

— Penelope P'Nutt at Play: Penelope P'Nutt au Jeu. (Illus.). 32p. (J). (gr. k-6). 1989. student ed. 0.95 (*0-927024-17-9*) Crayons Pubns.

— Rainy Days Are for Baking: Les Recettes Preferee de Penelope P'Nutt. (Illus.). 32p. (J). (gr. k-6). 1989. student ed. 0.45 (*0-927024-01-2*) Crayons Pubns.

— Rainy Days Are for Baking: Penelope P'Nutt los Dias Lluviosos Son Para Cocinar. (Illus.). 1988. 0.45 (*0-927024-00-4*) Crayons Pubns.

Palumbo, P. J. & Margic, Joyce D. The All-in-One Diabetic Cookbook. 1989. pap. 14.95 (*0-452-26467-7*, Plume) Dutton Plume.

Palumbo, Paul. Interactive Publishers Handbook. 320p. 1996. pap. 24.95 (*1-885452-07-1*) Carronade Grp.

***Palumbo, Ron & Furmanek, Robert.** Abbott & Costello's Buck Privates Vol. 2: Original Shooting Script for the Abbott & Costello Comedy Classic. Conforti, John, ed. (Universal Filmscript Series: Vol. 2). (Illus.). 192p. 2000. pap. 19.95 (*1-882127-40-4*) Magicimage Filmbooks.

Palumbo, Terri L., ed. see Hoff, Adele R.

Palumbo, Terrie L., ed. see Hoff, Adele R.

Palumbo, Thomas J. Beverly Cleary in the Classroom. 176p. teacher ed. 14.99 (*0-86653-610-8*, GA1329) Good Apple.

— Integrating the Literature of John Bellairs in the Classroom. (Illus.). 176p. (J). (gr. 3-7). 1994. 14.99 (*0-86653-808-9*, GA1500) Good Apple.

— Language Arts Thinking Motivators. 96p. (J). (gr. 2-7). 1988. student ed. 11.99 (*0-86653-432-6*, GA1050) Good Apple.

— Maurice Sendak in the Classroom. 176p. teacher ed. 14.99 (*0-86653-713-9*, GA1430) Good Apple.

— Roald Dahl in the Classroom. 176p. teacher ed. 14.99 (*0-86653-744-9*, GA1459) Good Apple.

Palumbo, Tom. Integrating the Literature of Chris Van Allsburg in the Classroom. (Illus.). 176p. 1992. 13.99 (*0-86653-658-2*, GA1390) Good Apple.

— Integrating the Literature of Judy Blume in the Classroom. 176p. 1990. 14.99 (*0-86653-558-6*, GA1152) Good Apple.

— Measurement Motivators. 96p. (J). (gr. 3-7). 1989. 11.99 (*0-86653-500-4*, GA1095) Good Apple.

Palus, Charles J. & Drath, Wilfred H. Evolving Leaders: A Model for Promoting Leadership Development in Programs. LC 95-36809. 44p. (Orig.). 1995. pap. 15.00 (*1-882197-11-9*, 165) Ctr Creat Leader.

Palus, Charles J., et al. Understanding Executive Performance: A Life-Story Perspective. (Reports: No. 148G). 48p. pap. 10.00 (*0-912879-45-9*, 148) Ctr Creat Leader.

Palus, Charles J., jt. auth. see Drath, Wilfred H.

Palusamy, S. S., ed. see Pressure Vessels & Piping Conference Staff.

Paluszek, John L. Business & Society: 1976-2000. LC 75-44485. (AMA Survey Report Ser.). 46p. reprint ed. pap. 30.00 (*0-8357-7485-6*, 205019800078) Bks Demand.

Palvia, Prashant, et al, eds. The Global Issues of Information Technology Management. LC 90-82964. 688p. (C). 1992. text 84.95 (*1-878289-10-1*) Idea Group Pub.

Palwick, Susan. Flying in Place. 224p. 1993. mass mkt. 4.99 (*0-8125-1334-7*, Pub. by Tor Bks) St Martin.

Paly, M., jt. auth. see Goldstein, E.

Palyers Club Staff. The Pocket Idiot's Guide to Bartending. (Pocket Idiot's Guides Ser.). 1998. pap. 9.95 (*0-02-862700-8*) Macmillan Gen Ref.

***Palyi, Gyula, et al.** Advances in Biochirality. 416p. 1999. 175.00 (*0-08-043404-5*) Elsevier.

Palyi, Melchior. The Chicago Credit Market: Organization & Institutional Structure. LC 75-2659. (Wall Street & the Security Market Ser.). 1975. reprint ed. 40.95 (*0-405-06983-9*) Ayer.

— Hauptprobleme der Soziologie: Erinnerungsgabe Fuer Max Weber: Major Problems in Socology, 2 vols. LC 74-25773. (European Sociology Ser.). 741p. 1975. reprint ed. 53.95 (*0-405-06527-2*) Ayer.

— Managed Money at the Crossroads: The European Experience. LC 57-11375. 206p. reprint ed. pap. 63.90 (*0-608-15040-1*, 202594500047) Bks Demand.

Palz, Wolfgang. Photovoltaic Power Generation. 1982. text 171.00 (*90-277-1386-3*) Kluwer Academic.

— Solar Energy to Dwellings. 1982. text 176.50 (*90-277-1491-6*) Kluwer Academic.

— Third E. C. Photovoltaic Solar Energy Conference. 1981. text 381.00 (*90-277-1230-1*) Kluwer Academic.

Palz, Wolfgang, ed. Photovoltaic Power Generation. 1984. text 141.50 (*90-277-1725-7*) Kluwer Academic.

— Solar Energy Data. 1983. text 148.50 (*90-277-1566-1*) Kluwer Academic.

— Solar Radiation Data. 1982. text 85.50 (*90-277-1387-1*) Kluwer Academic.

Palz, Wolfgang, et al, eds. Medium-Size Photovoltaic Power Plants. 1981. text 124.00 (*90-277-1279-4*) Kluwer Academic.

— Solar Collectors in Architecture: Integration of Photovoltaic & Thermal Collectors in New & Old Building Structures. 320p. 1984. text 147.50 (*90-277-1784-2*) Kluwer Academic.

Palz, Wolfgang & Fittipaldi, F., eds. Photovoltaic Solar Energy Conference, 5th E. C. 1984. text 426.00 (*90-277-1724-9*) Kluwer Academic.

Palz, Wolfgang & Pirrwitz, D. Energy from Biomass. 1983. text 206.50 (*90-277-1700-1*) Kluwer Academic.

Palz, Wolfgang & Schnell, W. Wind Energy. 1983. text 106.00 (*90-277-1603-X*) Kluwer Academic.

Palz, Wolfgang & Steemers, Theo C., eds. Solar Energy Applications to Dwellings. 1982. text 106.00 (*90-277-1372-3*) Kluwer Academic.

Palz, Wolfgang & Treble, F. C., eds. 6th E. C. Photovoltaic Solar Energy Conference. 1985. text 403.00 (*90-277-2104-1*) Kluwer Academic.

Palz, Wolfgang, et al. Renewable Energy, 2000. (Illus.). 145p. 1993. write for info. (*3-540-56882-4*) Spr-Verlag.

Palz, Wolfgang, jt. auth. see Schmid, J.

Palz, Wolfgang, jt. auth. see Starr, Michael R.

Palz, Wolfgang, jt. ed. see Chartier, Philippe.

Palz, Wolfgang, jt. ed. see Grassi, G.

Palz, Wolfgang, jt. ed. see Greif, J.

Palz, Wolfgang, jt. ed. see Hall, D. O.

Palz, Wolfgang, jt. ed. see Luque, Antonio.

Palz, Wolfgang, jt. ed. see Steemers, Theo C.

Palz, Wolfgang, jt. ed. see Van OverStraeten, R. J.

Palzer, Bob & Palzer, Jody. Whitewater, Quietwater: A Guide to the Rivers of Wisconsin, Upper Michigan & Northeast Minnesota. LC 83-80899. (Illus.). 160p. 1983. pap. 14.95 (*0-89732-086-7*) Menasha Ridge.

— Whitewater, Quietwater: A Guide to the Rivers of Wisconsin, Upper Michigan, & Northeast Minnesota. 176p. 1998. pap. 17.95 (*0-89732-199-5*) Menasha Ridge.

— Whitewater; Quietwater: A Guide to the Wild Rivers of Wisconsin, Upper Michigan, & Northeast Minnesota. 5th ed. LC 83-80899. (Illus.). 160p. 1983. pap. 9.95 (*0-916166-04-X*) Evergreen WI.

— Whitewater; Quietwater: A Guide to the Wild Rivers of Wisconsin, Upper Michigan, & Northeast Minnesota. 5th ed. (Illus.). 160p. 1985. suppl. ed. write for info. (*0-318-51868-6*) Evergreen WI.

Palzer, Jody, jt. auth. see Palzer, Bob.

Pam, Alvin & Pearson, Judith. Splitting Up: Enmeshment & Estrangement in the Process of Divorce. LC 98-22648. 448p. 1998. lib. bdg. 42.00 (*1-57230-367-0*) Guilford Pubns.

***Pam Bono Designs Staff.** Quilt It for Kids: 11 Quilt Projects. Aneloski, Liz & Aune, Carolyn, eds. LC 99-6826. (Illus.). 112p. 2000. pap. 24.95 (*1-57120-090-8*, 10207, Pub. by C & T Pub) Watsn-Guptill.

Pam, Martin D. & Meisel, Jurgen M., eds. Linear Order & Generative Theory. (Current Issues in Linguistic Theory Ser.: No. 7). ix, 512p. 1979. 94.00 (*90-272-0908-1*) J Benjamins Pubng Co.

Pam, Max. Indian Ocean Journals. 1998. 34.95 (*3-88243-573-9*, Pub. by Steidl) Dist Art Pubs.

Pama, R. P., et al, eds. Low Income Housing: Technology & Policy: Proceedings of the International Conference, Bangkok, June 1977, 3 vols. 1978. 674.00 (*0-08-023241-8*, Pub. by Pergamon Repr) Franklin.

Pama, R. P., jt. auth. see Cusens, Anthony R.

Pamadi, Bandu N. Performance, Stability, Dynamics, & Control of Airplanes. LC 98-34737. (AIAA Education Ser.). 766p. 1998. write for info. (*1-56347-222-8*) AIAA.

Paman, Jose G. & Goodwin, Rod. Comprehensive Self-Defense. LC 93-70988. (Illus.). (Orig.). 1993. pap. 14.00 (*0-9636286-8-2*) Eghty-Three Brixton.

***Pambianchi, Daniel.** Techniques in Home Winemaking: A Practical Guide to Chateau-Style Wines. (Illus.). 276p. 1999. pap. 17.95 (*1-55065-127-7*) Vehicule Pr.

Pamborides, G. P. International Shipping Law: Legislation & Enforcement. LC 99-22827. 1999. 81.00 (*90-411-1193-X*) Kluwer Law Intl.

Pamei, Ramkhun. Zwliangrong Nagas: A Study of Tribal Christianity. xvi, 152p. 1996. 21.00 (*81-85565-68-6*, Pub. by Uppal Pub Hse) S Asia.

Pamel, Gregory J., jt. ed. see Arca, Emil.

Pamensky, Robin. Avi's Adventures in the Mitzvah Car. (J). 1995. text 12.95 (*965-229-138-2*, Pub. by Gefen Pub Hse) Gefen Bks.

Pamental, George L. Ethics in the Business Curriculum: A Preliminary Survey of Undergraduate Business Programs. LC 87-37193. 210p. (Orig.). (C). 1988. pap. text 22.50 (*0-8191-6871-8*) U Pr of Amer.

Pamepinto, Sharon. Can States Stop Corporate Takeovers? 51p. 1987. pap. 25.00 (*0-931035-20-1*) IRRC Inc DC.

Pamer, Nan. I Will Not Bow: Manifesting Holiness in an Unholy World. LC 97-9330. 48p. 1997. 3.99 (*1-56722-203-X*) Word Aflame.

Pamer, Nan M. Modesty. LC 90-30491. (Illus.). 50p. (Orig.). (YA). 1990. pap. 3.99 (*0-932581-62-5*) Word Aflame.

Pami, Louise T., jt. auth. see Tchana, Katrin H.

Pamies, Alberto N., jt. auth. see Fernandez de la Vega, Oscar.

Pamilo, Pekka, jt. auth. see Croxier, Ross H.

Pamilo, Pekka, jt. auth. see Crozier, Ross H.

Pamin, J. Gradient-Dependent Plasticity in Numerical Simulation of Localization Phenomena. 142p. 1994. pap. 57.50 (*90-407-1042-2*, Pub. by Delft U Pr) Coronet Bks.

Pamm, Anthony. Honours & Rewards in the British Empire & Commonwealth, 2 Vols., Set. 1657p. 1995. 499.95 (*0-85967-911-X*, Pub. by Scolar Pr) Ashgate Pub Co.

— Honours & Rewards in the British Empire & Commonwealth, Vol. 1. 1995. 341.95 (*0-85967-984-5*) Ashgate Pub Co.

— Honours & Rewards in the British Empire & Commonwealth, Vol. 2. 1995. 288.95 (*0-85967-985-3*) Ashgate Pub Co.

Pammel, L. H. A Manual of Poisonous Plants: Chiefly of Eastern North America, with Brief Notes on Economic & Medicinal Plants. (Illus.). 977p. 1992. reprint ed. lib. bdg. 75.00 (*0-945345-43-7*) Lubrecht & Cramer.

Pammer, William J., Jr. Managing Fiscal Strain in Major American Cities: Understanding Retrenchment in the Public Sector, 247. LC 89-17073. (Contributions in Political Science Ser.: No. 247). 151p. 1990. 49.95 (*0-313-26656-5*, PMF/, Greenwood Pr) Greenwood.

Pampaloni, P. Microwave Radiometry & Remote Sensing Applications. (Illus.). 167p. 1989. 135.00 (*90-6764-108-1*, Pub. by VSP) Coronet Bks.

Pampaloni, P., ed. Passive Microwave Remote Sensing of Land-Atmosphere Interactions. 680p. 1994. 225.00 (*90-6764-186-3*, Pub. by VSP); pap. 85.00 (*90-6764-188-X*, Pub. by VSP) Coronet Bks.

***Pampaloni, P. & Paloscia, S., eds.** Microwave Radiometry & Remote Sensing of the Earth's Surface & Atmosphere. (Illus.). 566p. 1999. 247.50 (*90-6764-318-1*, Pub. by Uppsala Universitet) Coronet Bks.

Pampana, Emilio. Textbook of Malaria Eradication. 2nd ed. 1970. 24.00 (*0-19-264212-X*) OUP.

Pampanini, Andrea H. Cities from the Arabian Desert: The Building of Jubail & Yanbu in Saudi Arabia. LC 96-24218. 256p. 1997. 59.95 (*0-275-95594-X*, Praeger Pubs) Greenwood.

Pampel, Bert, jt. ed. see Haase, Norbert.

Pampel, Fred C. Aging, Social Inequality, & Public Policy. LC 97-45279. (Sociology for a New Century Ser.). (Illus.). 168p. (C). 1998. pap. text 19.95 (*0-8039-9095-2*) Pine Forge.

Pampel, Fred C. An Introduction to Sociology. write for info. (*1-57259-858-1*) Worth.

— Logistic Regression: A Primer. LC 00-8060. (Quantitative Applications in the Social Sciences Ser.). 2000. pap. write for info. (*0-7619-2010-2*) Sage.

— Sociological Lives & Ideas. write for info. (*1-57259-859-X*) Worth.

Pampel, Fred C. & Williamson, John B. Age, Class, Politics, & the Welfare State. (ASA Rose Monographs). (Illus.). 217p. (C). 1992. pap. text 19.95 (*0-521-43791-1*) Cambridge U Pr.

Pampel, Fred C., jt. auth. see Williamson, John B.

Pampel, Fred C., jt. ed. see Tracy, Martin B.

Pampero Foundation Staff, ed. see De Valencia, Ruby & Volsky, Jeannine S.

Pamphili, Eusebius. Ecclesiastical History, Bks. 6-10. Deferrari, Ray J., tr. LC 65-27501. (Fathers of the Church Ser.: Vol. 29). 325p. 1955. 39.95 (*0-8132-0029-6*) Cath U Pr.

Pamphill, Eusebius. Ecclesiastical History, Bks. 1-5. Deferrari, Ray J., tr. LC 65-27501. (Fathers of the Church Ser.: Vol. 19). 347p. 1953. 20.95 (*0-8132-0019-9*) Cath U Pr.

Pamphilon, Derwood H., ed. Modern Transfusion Medicine: A Practical Approach. 288p. 1995. boxed set 144.95 (*0-8493-8922-4*) CRC Pr.

Pamphilon, Derwood H., jt. auth. see Murphy, Michael F.

Pamphilus, Eusebius. Eusebius' Ecclesiastical History: A Third Century Historian Looks at the Early Church. 478p. 1998. 24.95 (*1-56563-371-7*) Hendrickson MA.

Pampillo, C. A., ed. see American Society for Metals Staff.

Pampillo, C. A., ed. see Symposium Aluminum Transformation Technology & Its.

Pamplin, Brian R. Crystal Growth. 2nd ed. 1980. 267.00 (*0-08-026489-1*, Pub. by Pergamon Repr) Franklin.

— Crystal Growth. 2nd ed. LC 79-42662. (International Series of Monographs on the Strength & Fracture of Materials & Structures: Vol. 16). 1980. 267.00 (*0-08-025043-2*, Pub. by Pergamon Repr) Franklin.

— Molecular Beam Epitaxy. (Illus.). 178p. 1980. 48.00 (*0-08-025050-5*, Pergamon Pr) Elsevier.

Pamplin, Brian R., ed. Inorganic Biological Crystal Growth. (Illus.). 284p. 1981. 73.00 (*0-08-028420-5*, C999, H210, H999, Pergamon Pr) Elsevier.

— Progress in Crystal Growth, Vol. 2, Complete. (Illus.). 404p. 1981. 140.00 (*0-08-026040-3*, Pergamon Pr) Elsevier.

— Progress in Crystal Growth & Characterization, Pt. 2. 1978. pap. 28.00 (*0 08-023050-4*, Pub. by Pergamon Repr) Franklin.

— Progress in Crystal Growth & Characterization, Pt. 3. 1978. pap. 28.00 (*0-08-023051-2*, Pub. by Pergamon Repr) Franklin.

— Progress in Crystal Growth & Characterization, Pt. 4. 1979. pap. 21.00 (*0-08-023083-0*, Pub. by Pergamon Repr) Franklin.

— Progress in Crystal Growth & Characterization, Vol. 1. (Illus.). 248p. 1980. 140.00 (*0-08-026013-6*, Pergamon Pr) Elsevier.

— Progress in Crystal Growth & Characterization, Vol. 3, No. 2-3. (Illus.). 166p. 1981. pap. 72.00 (*0-08-027149-9*, Pergamon Pr) Elsevier.

— Progress in Crystal Growth & Characterization, Vol. 4. (Illus.). 345p. 1982. 160.00 (*0-08-029681-5*, Pergamon Pr) Elsevier.

— Progress in Crystal Growth & Characterization, Vol. 5. (Illus.). 425p. 1983. 155.00 (*0-08-031011-7*, Pergamon Pr) Elsevier.

— Progress in Crystal Growth & Characterization, Vol. 6. (Illus.). 424p. 1984. 155.00 (*0-08-030997-6*, Pergamon Pr) Elsevier.

— Progress in Crystal Growth & Characterization, Vol. 8. (Illus.). 475p. 1985. 180.00 (*0-08-032736-2*, Pub. by PPL) Elsevier.

— Progress in Crystal Growth & Characterization, Vol. 9. (Illus.). 385p. 1985. 180.00 (*0-08-032737-0*, Pub. by PPL) Elsevier.

Pamplin, Brian R., et al, eds. Progress in Crystal Growth & Characterization Vol. 10: Proceedings of the 6th International Conference on Ternary & Multinary Compounds, Car acas, Venezuela, 15-17 August 1984. (Illus.). 430p. 1985. 180.00 (*0-08-032344-8*, Pergamon Pr) Elsevier.

***Pamplin, Jean.** Memories of Don Meredith & Hometown Mount Vernon. Johnson, Ray Loyd, ed. (Illus.). 92p. 1999. pap. 12.95 (*0-9642481-5-8*) NE Texas Pub.

Pamplin, Jean, jt. auth. see Ellis, John M.

Pamplin, Jean, jt. ed. see Thompson, Larry.

Pamplin, Laurel J. Masquerade on the Western Trail. Roberts, M., ed. (Illus.). 112p. (J). (gr. 6-7). 1991. 9.95 (*0-89015-755-3*) Sunbelt Media.

Pamplin, Robert B., Jr. Heritage: The Making of an American Family. 1995. pap. text 12.95 (*0-942691-96-2*) Beta Bks.

Pamplin, Robert B., Jr. & Eisler, Gary K. American Heroes. large type ed. 342p. 1995. 22.95 (*0-7862-0541-5*) Thorndike Pr.

P

Pamplona, Marco A. Riots, Republicanism, & Citizenship: New York City & Rio de Janeiro City During the Consolidation of the Republican Order. rev. ed. LC 95-39434. (Studies in African American History & Culture). (Illus.). 224p. 1996. text 20.00 (*0-8153-2364-6*) Garland.

Pampreen, Ronald C. Compressor Surge & Stall. LC 92-70348. (Illus.). 505p. 1993. text 130.00 (*0-933283-05-9*) Concepts ETI.

Pampuch, R. Constitution & Properties of Ceramic Materials. (Materials Science Monographs: No. 58). 456p. 1991. 221.75 (*0-444-98794-0*) Elsevier.

***Pamuk, E., ed.** Health, United States, 1998: With Socioeconomic Status & Health Chart Book. (Illus.). 460p. 1999. pap. text 50.00 (*0-7881-7895-4*) DIANE Pub.

Pamuk, Orhan. The Black Book. Gun, Guneli, tr. LC 94-4791. 356p. 1994. text 25.00 (*0-374-11394-7*) FS&G.

— The Black Book. Gun, Guneli, tr. 416p. 1996. pap. 16.00 (*0-15-600329-5*) Harcourt.

— Call Me Crimson. write for info. (*0-375-40695-6*) Knopf.

— The New Life. Gun, Guneli, tr. LC 96-45722. 296p. 1997. 24.00 (*0-374-22129-4*) FS&G.

— The New Life. Gun, Guneli, tr. LC 97-35622. 1998. pap. 13.00 (*0-375-70171-0*) Vin Bks.

— The White Castle. Holbrook, Victoria, tr. from TUR. 162p. 1991. 17.50 (*0-8076-1264-2*) Braziller.

— The White Castle. Holbrook, Victoria, tr. from TUR. LC 97-35630. 1998. pap. 12.00 (*0-375-70161-3*) Vin Bks.

***Pamuk, Sevket.** A Monetary History of the Ottoman Empire. LC 98-43861. (Cambridge Studies in Islamic Civilization). (Illus.). 336p. (C). 2000. 69.95 (*0-521-44197-8*) Cambridge U Pr.

***Pamuk, Sevket & Williamson, Jeffrey G.** The Mediterranean Response to Globalization Before 1950. LC 99-53473. 376p. 2000. 115.00 (*0-415-22425-X*) Routledge.

Pamuk, Sevket, jt. auth. see Owen, Edward R.

Pamuk, Svket, jt. auth. see Owen, Edward R.

Pamukcu, Sibel. Second International Symposium on Environmental Geotechnology (May 15-18, 1989), Vol. 2: Proceedings: 15-18, 1989. Hsai-Yang Fang, ed. LC 89-80286. 375p. 1991. pap. 55.00 (*0-932871-18-6*) Envo Pub Co.

Pamukcu, Sibel, jt. ed. see Hsai-Yang Fang.

Pamukhina, L. G. Russian-English Phrase Book on Foreign Economic Relations. (ENG & RUS.). 700p. 1993. 95.00 (*0-7859-9098-4*) Fr & Eur.

Pamukhina, L. G., et al. Russian-English Phrase Book on Foreign Economic Relations. unabridged ed. (ENG & RUS.). 654p. (C). 1993. 27.95 (*0-8285-5094-8*) Firebird NY.

Pan-Am Editors. Artists of the Southwest. (Illus.). 105p. 1988. pap. 14.95 (*0-932906-22-2*) Pan-Am Publishing Co.

Pan-Am Editors, ed. Artists of New Mexico. LC 86-8172. (Illus.). 105p. (Orig.). 1986. pap. 14.95 (*0-932906-15-X*) Pan-Am Publishing Co.

***Pan American Health Organization Staff.** Health in the Americas: 1998 Edition. (Scientific Publications: Vol. 569). 544p. 1998. pap. 60.00 (*92-75-11569-9*) PAHO.

— Health Statistics from the Americas: 1998 Edition. (Scientific Publication Ser.: Vol. 567). 476p. (C). 1999. pap. 34.00 (*92-75-11567-2*) PAHO.

Pan American Union Staff, ed. Mexico. 1976. lib. bdg. 34.95 (*0-8490-0622-8*) Gordon Pr.

Pan American University Press, ed. see Green, Shirley B.

Pan, B. W., tr. see Rusthoi, Ralph W.

Pan, C. H., jt. ed. see Ling, Frederick F.

Pan Chongbiao, jt. auth. see Pan Chongdong.

Pan Chongdong & Pan Chongbiao. Goldbach Conjecture. rev. ed. 240p. 1996. suppl. ed. 59.95 (*7-03-002626-8*, Pub. by Sci Pr) Lubrecht & Cramer.

***Pan, David.** Primitive Renaissance: Rethinking German Expressionism. (Modern German Culture & Literature Ser.). 2001. text 49.95 (*0-8032-3727-8*) U of Nebr Pr.

Pan, Don Le, see Le Pan, Don.

Pan, Erica Y. The Impact of the 1906 Earthquake on San Francisco's Chinatown, Vol. 173. LC 94-25600. (American University Studies: Series IV). (Illus.). VIII, 158p. (C). 1995. text 33.95 (*0-8204-2607-5*) P Lang Pubng.

Pan, Fung-Shine, jt. ed. see Major, John B.

***Pan, Goucheng & Harris, Deverle P.** Information Synthesis for Mineral Exploration. (Spatial Information Systems Ser.). (Illus.). 416p. 2000. text 95.00 (*0-19-511848-0*) OUP.

Pan, Haihua. Constraints on Reflexivization in Mandarin Chinese. rev. ed. LC 96-53126. (Outstanding Dissertations in Linguistics Ser.). (Illus.). 280p. 1997. text 76.00 (*0-8153-2851-6*) Garland.

Pan, Heng. SNMP-Based ATM Network Management: Telecommunications & Network Management. LC 98-28217. 1998. 89.00 (*0-89006-983-2*) Artech Hse.

Pan Instytut Geografii Staff, ed. Narodowy Atlas Polski. (POL., Illus.). 60p. 1978. 220.00 (*0-614-25056-0*) Szwede Slavic.

Pan Instytut Geografii Staff, jt. contrib. by see Piotrowski, Remigiusz.

***Pan, Jian-Xin & Fang, Koai-Toai.** Growth Curve Models & Statistical Diagnostics. LC 00-41910. (Series in Statistics). 2000. write for info. (*0-387-95053-2*) Spr-Verlag.

Pan, Julia, jt. ed. see Hayhoe, Ruth.

Pan, Laura Y. Novell's Bordermanager Administrator's Handbook. LC 99-15720. 350p. 1999. pap. 34.99 (*0-7645-4565-5*) IDG Bks.

Pan, Lawrence S., ed. Diamond: Electronic Properties & Applications. (International Series in Engineering & Computer Science, Natural Language Processing & Machine Translation). 488p. (C). 1994. text 204.50 (*0-7923-9524-7*) Kluwer Academic.

Pan-Ling, Chen. Chen Pan-Ling's Original Tai Chi Chuan Textbook (Tai Chi Chuan Chiao Tsai) Carruthers, Ann et al, eds. Chang, Y. W., tr. from CHI. (Illus.). 1998. 44.99 (*0-9660240-3-6*); pap. text 29.99 (*0-9660240-5-2*) Blitz Design.

Pan, Loretta. Character Text for Speak Chinese. 1964. 16.95 (*0-88710-009-0*) Yale Far Eastern Pubns.

Pan, Lynn. Alcohol in Colonial Africa. (Finnish Foundation for Alcohol Studies: Vol. 22). 1975. 6.50 (*951-9191-20-8*) Rutgers Ctr Alcohol.

***Pan, Lynn.** Mao Memorabilia: The Man & the Myth. (Illus.). 130p. 1999. pap. 38.00 (*962-7283-20-7*, Pub. by FormAsia) Weatherhill.

Pan, Lynn. Shanghai: The Paris of the Orient. 2nd ed. (Illus.). 144p. 1994. pap. 14.95 (*0-8442-9686-4*) NTC Contemp Pub Co.

— Sons of the Yellow Emperor: A History of the Chinese Diaspora. De Angelis, Paul, ed. LC 94-14938. (Illus.). 432p. 1994. pap. 16.00 (*1-56836-032-0*) Kodansha.

— Tracing It Home: A Chinese Journey. 240p. 1995. reprint ed. pap. 14.00 (*1-56836-043-6*) Kodansha.

— True to Form: A Celebration of the Art of the Chinese Craftsman. (Illus.). 148p. 1998. 50.00 (*962-7283-16-9*, Pub. by FormAsia) Weatherhill.

***Pan, Lynn.** TrueToForm: A Celebration of the Art of the Chinese Craftsman. (Illus.). 148p. 1998. 51.00 (*962-7283-15-0*, Pub. by FormAsia) Weatherhill.

Pan, Lynn & Chinese Heritage Center Staff. The Encyclopedia of the Chinese Overseas. LC 98-35466. 416p. 1999. 59.95 (*0-674-25210-1*) HUP.

Pan, Lynn & Hunt, Jill. Shanghai. 5th ed. LC 98-53868. (Odyssey Passport Ser.). (Illus.). 174p. 1999. pap. 19.95 (*962-217-605-4*) Norton.

Pan, Lynn & Wiltshire, Trea. Saturday's Child: Hong Kong in the Sixties. (Illus.). 88p. 1995. 40.00 (*962-7283-10-X*, Pub. by FormAsia) Weatherhill.

Pan, Lynn, et al. Shanghai: The Paris of the Orient. 3rd ed. (Illus.). 168p. 1995. pap. 16.95 (*0-8442-9704-6*, Passprt Bks) NTC Contemp Pub Co.

Pan, Lynn, jt. auth. see Holledge, Simon.

Pan, M. R. L., jt. auth. see Hancock, B. A.

Pan, Robert. Homeowner's Income Tax Benefits. LC 96-90373. (Illus.). 187p. (Orig.). 1996. pap. 14.95 (*0-9653156-0-6*) Taxinfo Pub.

Pan, Tianmin, et al, eds. Unsteady Aerodynamics & Aeroelasticity of Turbomachines & Propellers: Proceedings of the Fifth International Symposium, Beijing, China, 18-21 September, 1989. (International Academic Publishers Ser.). 528p. 1990. 135.00 (*0-08-040187-2*, Pub. by IAP) Elsevier.

Pan, Victor, jt. auth. see Bini, Dario.

Pan, Winston, jt. auth. see Min Chen.

Pan, Xing-Wang & Feng, Da H. Contemporary Nuclear Shell Models: Proceedings of an International Workshop Held in Philadelphia, Pa, U. S. A., 29-30 April 1996, Vol. 482. LC 97-662. (Lecture Notes in Physics Ser.). 1997. 73.00 (*3-540-62551-8*) Spr-Verlag.

Pan, Yeng, ed. see Reynolds, Terry.

Pan, Yihong. Son of Heaven & Heavenly Qaghan: Si-Tang China & Its Neighbors. LC 97-29484. (Studies on East Asia: Vol. 20). xii, 442p. 1997. pap. 35.00 (*0-914584-20-0*) WWUCEAS.

Pan, Yong. The Alternate Fate: The Discovery of Hereditary Pattern of Human Innate Intelligence & Its Implications. (Illus.). 341p. 1998. pap. 19.95 (*0-9663158-0-4*) Pan Pacific.

Pana, Irina G., jt. tr. see Sorkin, Adam J.

Panabiere, Louis. Ciudad Aguila, Villa Serpiente (Eagle City, Serpent Village) (SPA.). 165p. 1996. pap. 15.99 (*968-16-4805-6*, Pub. by Fondo) Continental Bk.

Panaccione, Carol, ed. see Johnson, Allen A.

Panagariya, Arvind. Regionalism in Trade Policy: Essays on Preferential Trading. LC 99-45509. 226p. 1999. 60.00 (*981-02-3841-X*) World Scientific Pub.

***Panagariya, Arvind.** Regionalism in Trade Policy: Essays on Preferential Trading. LC 99-45509. 230p. 1999. pap. 24.00 (*981-02-3842-8*) World Scientific Pub.

Panagariya, Arvind, et al, eds. The Global Trading System & Developing Asia. (An Asian Development Bank Bk.). (Illus.). 588p. 1998. text 85.00 (*0-19-590502-4*) OUP.

Panagariya, Arvind & Bhagwati, Jagdish N. Lectures on International Trade. 2nd ed. 1998. pap. text 22.50 (*0-262-52247-0*) MIT Pr.

Panagariya, Arvind, jt. auth. see De Melo, Jaime.

Panagariya, Arvind, jt. ed. see De Melo, Jaime.

Panagariya, Arvind, ed. see Oates, Wallace E.

Panagariya, B. L. & Pahariya, N. C. Rajasthan: Polity, Economy & Society. 1996. 36.00 (*0-614-25279-2*, Pub. by Rawat Pubns) S Asia.

Panaggio, Edna. Into the Spirit. 24p. 1998. pap. 9.95 (*1-885206-58-5*) Cader Pubng.

Panaggio, Leonard J. Portrait of Newport II. (Illus.). 160p. (Orig.). 1994. pap. text 9.95 (*0-9642783-0-8*) Bank of Newport.

Panagiotaki, Maria. The Central Palace Sanctuary at Knossos. (BSA Supplementary Volumes Ser.: Vol. 31). (Illus.). 300p. 1999. lib. bdg. 120.00 (*0-904887-30-8*, Pub. by Brit Sch Athens) David Brown.

***Panagiotopoulos, Melanie.** Greece. 464p. 2000. pap. 4.97 (*1-57748-642-0*) Barbour Pub.

Panagiotopoulos, P. D. Hemivariational Inequalities: Applications in Mechanics & Engineering. (Illus.). 465p. 1993. write for info. (*3-540-54963-3*); 149.95 (*0-387-54963-3*) Spr-Verlag.

Panagiotopoulos, P. D., jt. auth. see Antes, H.

Panagiotopoulos, P. D., jt. auth. see Naniewicz, Z.

Panagiotopoulos, P. D., jt. ed. see Moreau, J. J.

Panagiotou, G. N. & Michalakopoulos, T. N., eds. Information Technologies in the Minerals Industry: Proceedings of the 1st International Conference on Information Technologies in the Minerals Industry Via the Internet, 1-12 December 1997. (Illus.). 200p. 1998. 95.00 incl. cd-rom (*90-5410-932-7*, Pub. by A A Balkema) Ashgate Pub Co.

Panagiotou, G. N. & Sturgul, J. R. Mine Simulation: Proceedings of the First International Symposium on Mine Simulation Via the Internet, 2-13 December 1996. (Illus.). 200p. (C). 1997. text 110.00 incl. cd-rom (*90-5410-863-0*, Pub. by A A Balkema) Ashgate Pub Co.

Panagopoulos, Beata M. Cistercian & Mendicant Monasteries in Medieval Greece. LC 78-10769. (Illus.). 214p. reprint ed. pap. 66.40 (*0-608-09491-9*, 205429200005) Bks Demand.

Panagopoulos, Epaminodes P. New Smyrna: An Eighteenth Century Greek Odyssey. 2nd ed. LC 77-16303. (Illus.). 207p. 1978. reprint ed. 14.95 (*0-916586-13-8*, Pub. by Holy Cross Orthodox) BookWorld.

Panagopoulos, Janie L. Erie Trail West: A Dream-Quest Adventure. 184p. (J). (gr. 3-7). 1997. pap. 7.95 (*0-938682-43-1*) River Rd Pubns.

— Journey Back to Lumberjack Camp: A Dream-Quest Adventure. 176p. (J). (gr. 3-7). 1995. pap. 7.95 (*0-938682-36-9*, 682-36-9) River Rd Pubns.

— Little Ship under Full Sail. LC 97-9604. 146p. (J). 1997. 15.95 (*0-938682-46-6*) River Rd Pubns.

— North to Iron Country. (Dream-Quest Adventure Ser.). 224p. (J). (gr. 3-7). 1998. pap. 7.95 (*0-938682-48-2*, 682-48-2) River Rd Pubns.

— North to Iron Country: A Dream-Quest Adventure. LC 96-157418. 224p. (J). 1996. 14.95 (*0-938682-40-7*, 682-40-7) River Rd Pubns.

— Traders in Time: A Dream-Quest Adventure. 200p. (J). (gr. 3-6). 1993. 14.95 (*0-938682-24-5*) River Rd Pubns.

— Traders in Time: A Dream-Quest Adventure. (J). (gr. 3-6). 1994. pap. 7.95 (*0-938682-27-X*) River Rd Pubns.

— Train to Midnight: A Dream-Quest Adventure. 208p. (J). (gr. 3-8). 1999. 15.95 (*0-938682-53-9*) River Rd Pubns.

***Panagopoulos, Janie Lynn.** Train to Midnight: A Dream-Quest Adventure. 180p. (J). (gr. 3-7). 1999. pap. 7.95 (*0-938682-57-1*) River Rd Pubns.

Panagopoulos, Nic. The Fiction of Joseph Conrad: The Influence of Schopenhauer & Nietzsche. Ahrens, Rudiger & Cope, Kevin, eds. (Anglo-American Studies: Vol. 12). 209p. 1998. 37.95 (*3-631-33759-0*) P Lang Pubng.

— The Fiction of Joseph Conrad: The Influence of Schopenhauer & Nietzsche. LC 98-46377. (Anglo-American Studies: Vol. 12). 209p. (C). 1998. pap. text 37.95 (*0-8204-3623-2*) P Lang Pubng.

Panagrosso, David. MCSD TestPrep: Visual Basic 6 Exam 70-175. LC 98-88002. (TestPrep (New Riders') Ser.). (Illus.). 450p. 1999. pap. 29.99 (*0-7357-0032-X*) New Riders Pub.

— Visual Basic 6; Exam 70-176. (MCSD TestPrep Ser.). 1999. pap. text 19.99 (*0-7357-0037-0*) New Riders Pub.

Panah, Kambiz Y., ed. see Obolensky, Serge, et al.

Panahi, K. K., et al, eds. Advances in Vibration Issues, Active & Passive Vibration Mitigation, Damping & Seismic Isolation. LC 95-77602. (Proceedings of the 1995 ASME/JSME Pressure Vessels & Piping Conference Ser.: PVP-Vol. 309). 152p. 1995. 90.00 (*0-7918-1340-1*, H00972) ASME.

Panahi, K. Karim, ed. Advances in Analytical, Experimental & Computational Technologies in Fluids, Structures, Transients & Natural Hazards: Proceedings, ASME Pressure Vessels & Piping Conference (1997, Orlando, FL) LC 97-73602. (PVP Ser.: Vol. 355). 341p. 1997. pap. 130.00 (*0-7918-1572-2*) ASME.

Panahi, Patricia. The Well-Woman Cookbook. LC 98-33851. (Illus.). 175p. (Orig.). 1998. pap. 14.95 (*1-56072-343-2*, Nova Kroshka Bks) Nova Sci Pubs.

Panaiotopoulos. Benign Childhood Partial Seizures & Related Epileptic Syndromes. 416p. 105.00 (*0-86196-577-9*, Pub. by J Libbey Med) Bks Intl VA.

***Panaite, Viorel.** The Ottoman Law of War & Peace. 240p. 2000. text 30.00 (*0-88033-461-4*) Col U Pr.

Panakul, Thanyarat, jt. ed. see Warotamasikkhadit, Udom.

Panalos, P. M. & Du Dingzhu. Network Design: Connectivity & Facilities Location: DIMACS Workshop, April 28-30, 1997. LC 97-45788. (DIMACS Series in Discrete Mathematics & Theoretical Computer Science). 461p. 1998. text 79.00 (*0-8218-0834-6*) Am Math.

Panamanian Business Law Staff. Panamanian Business Law. LC KZ0132.. 308p. reprint ed. pap. 95.50 (*0-7837-2409-8*, 204009400006) Bks Demand.

Panandiker, D. H. Pollution Control in Indian Industry. (C). 1991. 14.50 (*81-7018-633-1*, Pub. by BR Pub) S Asia.

***Panandiker, V. A., ed.** Fifty Years of Swaraj: Highlights & Shadows. LC 98-908368. 1998. 34.00 (*81-220-0519-5*, Pub. by Konark Pubs Pvt Ltd) S Asia.

Panandiker, Vapai A. & Mehra, Ajay K. People's Participation in Family Planning. 1987. 29.00 (*81-85024-10-3*, Pub. by Uppal Pub Hse) S Asia.

***Panandiker, W. A.** Problems of Governance in South Asia. 2000. 36.00 (*81-220-0559-4*, Pub. by Konark Pubs Pvt Ltd) S Asia.

Panara, Robert, jt. auth. see Moore, Matthew S.

Panara, Robert F. On His Deafness & Other Melodies Unheard. LC 97-33126. 90p. 1997. pap. 12.95 (*0-9634016-5-3*, Deaf Life Pr) MSM Prods.

Panarella, Alfredo. The Maastricht Treaty & the Economic & Monetary Union. (Law Ser.: Vol. 2). 83p. (Orig.). 1995. pap. 34.00 (*90-6186-689-8*, Pub. by Leuven Univ) Coronet Bks.

Panarella, E. Current Trends in International Fusion Research: Based on the Proceedings of the First International Symposium Held in Washington, D. C., November 14-18, 1994. LC 97-11196. (Illus.). 612p. (C). 1997. text 191.00 (*0-306-45513-7*, Kluwer Plenum) Kluwer Academic.

Panarella, Merriann. Moving for Injunctive Relief. LC 94-73530. 1995. pap. text 59.00 (*0-944490-80-8*) Mass CLE.

Panarese, William C., jt. auth. see Kosmatka, Steven H.

Panaro, Gerard P. Employment Law Manual No. 2195: Recruitment, Selection, Termination. 608p. 1990. suppl. ed. 60.00 (*0-685-56161-5*); boxed set 126.00 (*0-7913-0375-6*) Warren Gorham & Lamont.

— Pregnancy & Childcare Issues in the Workplace. 1987. pap. 39.95 (*0-88057-775-4*) Exec Ent Pubns.

Panaro, Gerard P., ed. Personnel Practice Ideas. 125.00 (*0-685-69668-5*, PPI) Warren Gorham & Lamont.

Panas, Epaminondas E. Almost Homogeneous Functions: A Theoretical & Empirical Analysis with Special Emphasis on Labour Input-The Case of Swedish Manufacturing Industries. (Studia Oeconomica Upsaliensia: No. 11). 130p. 1987. pap. text 39.50 (*91-554-1972-0*, Pub. by Uppsala Univ Acta Univ Uppsaliensis) Coronet Bks.

Panas, Jerold. Boardroom Verities. LC 91-66145. 238p. 1991. 40.00 (*0-944496-26-1*) Precept Pr.

— Born to Raise: What Makes a Great Fundraiser, What Makes a Fundraiser Great. LC 88-61232. 228p. 1988. 40.00 (*0-944496-02-4*) Precept Pr.

— Finders Keepers: Lessons I've Learned About Dynamic Fundraising. (Illus.). 268p. 1999. 39.95 (*1-56625-119-2*) Bonus Books.

— Mega Gifts: Who Gives Them, Who Gets Them. LC 83-62498. 231p. 1984. 40.00 (*0-931028-39-6*) Precept Pr.

— Official Fundraising Almanac. LC 89-61428. 424p. 1989. pap. 50.00 (*0-944496-07-5*) Precept Pr.

Panas, John, Jr. Aircraft Mishap Photography: Documenting the Evidence. LC 96-11965. (Illus.). 192p. 1996. pap. text 34.95 (*0-8138-2622-5*) Iowa St U Pr.

***Panas, Peter.** I Can Draw. (J). 2000. pap. 1.99 (*0-375-80491-9*, Pub. by Random Bks Yng Read) Random.

Panas, Peter. The Shalom Sesame Players Present: The Story of Passover. (Sharing Passover Ser.). 32p. (J). 1994. pap. 5.95 (*1-884857-02-7*) Sisu Home Enter.

Panasenko, G., jt. auth. see Bakhvalov, N.

Panasiuk, V. A., jt. auth. see Schroeter, A. L.

Panassie, Hughes. Hot Jazz: The Guide to Swing Music. LC 74-135606. 363p. 1970. reprint ed. lib. bdg. 35.00 (*0-8371-5181-3*, PAJ&) Greenwood.

— The Real Jazz. LC 73-13328. 284p. 1973. reprint ed. lib. bdg. 65.00 (*0-8371-7123-7*, PARJ, Greenwood Pr) Greenwood.

Panassie, Hughes & Gautier, Madeleine. Dictionnaire du Jazz. rev. ed. (FRE.). 384p. 1987. pap. 49.95 (*0-8288-2170-4*, M6648) Fr & Eur.

Panassie, Hugues. Louis Armstrong. LC 79-20828. (Roots of Jazz Ser.). (Illus.). 148p. 1979. reprint ed. pap. 7.95 (*0-306-80116-7*); reprint ed. lib. bdg. 25.00 (*0-306-79611-2*) Da Capo.

Panasyuk, V. V. Limiting Equilibrium of Brittle Solids with Fractures. LC 75-135093. 325p. 1969. 39.00 (*0-403-04527-4*) Scholarly.

Panasyuk, V. V., ed. Advances in Fracture Resistance & Structural Integrity: Selected Papers from the Eighth International Conference on Fractures (ICF8), Kyiv, Ukraine, 8-14 June 1993. LC 94-34031. (International Series on the Strength & Fracture of Materials & Structure). 780p. 1994. 215.00 (*0-08-042256-X*, Pergamon Pr) Elsevier.

Panat, P. V., jt. ed. see Clark, John W.

Panati, Charles. The Browser's Book of Beginnings: Origins of Everything Under & Including the Sun. LC 99-187147. 428p. 1998. pap. 15.95 (*0-14-027694-7*) Viking Penguin.

***Panati, Charles.** The Browser's Book of Endings: The End of Practically Everything & Everybody. (Illus.). 496p. 1999. pap. 15.95 (*0-14-028690-X*, Penguin Bks) Viking Penguin.

Panati, Charles. Extraordinary Origins of Everyday Things. LC 89-45180. 480p. 1989. pap. 16.00 (*0-06-096419-7*, Perennial) HarperTrade.

— Sacred Origins of Profound Things. LC 96-14594. (Illus.). 608p. 1996. pap. 15.95 (*0-14-019533-5*) Viking Penguin.

— Sexy Origins & Intimate Things: The Rites & Rituals of Straights, Gays, Bi's, Drags, Trans, Virgins, & Others. LC 97-30701. 432p. 1998. pap. 15.95 (*0-14-027144-9*) Viking Penguin.

— Words to Live By: The Origins of Conventional Wisdom & Commonsense Advice. LC 98-44967. (Illus.). 403p. 1999. pap. 15.95 (*0-14-028156-8*) Viking Penguin.

Panati, Charles & Hudson, Michael. The Silent Intruder: Surviving the Radiation Age. 224p. 1981. 9.95 (*0-685-02309-5*) HM.

***Panavu Staff.** 50 State Commemorative Quarters Coins on Map Folder. (Illus.). 2000. write for info. (*0-9700051-3-X*) PANAVU.

— 50 State Commemorative Quarters Album. (Illus.). 2000. write for info. (*0-9700051-0-5*) PANAVU.

— 50 State Commemorative Quarters Folder. (Illus.). 2000. write for info. (*0-9700051-1-3*) PANAVU.

— 50 State Commemorative Quarters Map Folder. (Illus.). 2000. write for info. (*0-9700051-2-1*) PANAVU.

— Sacagawea Folder. (Illus.). 2000. write for info. (*0-9700051-4-8*) PANAVU.

Panayi. Impact Of Immigrat In Post-war. 1999. pap. 22.95 (*0-7190-4685-8*) St Martin.

— Impact of Immigrat in Post-War. 212p. 1999. text 59.95 (*0-7190-4684-X*) St Martin.

An Asterisk (*) at the beginning of an entry indicates that the title is appearing for the first time.

Panayi, G. S., ed. Immunology of Connective Tissue Diseases. LC 93-39860. (Immunology & Medicine Ser.: Vol. 22). 416p. (C). 1994. text 191.50 (*0-7923-8988-3*) Kluwer Academic.

Panayi, Panikos. The Enemy in Our Midst: Germans in Britain During the First World War. LC 89-18464. 324p. 1991. 39.50 (*0-85496-308-1*) Berg Pubs.

***Panayi, Panikos.** An Ethnic History of Europe since 1945: Nations, States & Minorities. 274p. (C). 1999. pap. 27.53 (*0-582-38134-7*) Longman.

— An Ethnic History of Europe Since 1945: Nations, States & Minorities. 350p. (C). 1999. 79.95 (*0-582-38135-5*) Longman.

Panayi, Panikos. German Immigrants in Britain During the Nineteenth Century, 1815-1914. LC 94-49025. 301p. 1995. 55.00 (*1-85973-092-2*) Berg Pubs.

— Immigration, Ethnicity, & Racism in Britain, 1815-1945. LC 93-49041. (New Frontiers in History Ser.). 1994. text 27.95 (*0-7190-3698-4*, Pub. by Manchester Univ Pr) St Martin.

— Outsiders: A History of European Minorities. LC 98-35351. 1998. 35.00 (*1-85285-179-1*) Hambledon Press.

Panayi, Panikos, ed. Germans in Britain since 1500. LC 95-49120. 1996. 55.00 (*1-85285-126-0*) Hambledon Press.

— A History of Racial Violence in Britain. 2nd rev. ed. LC 95-23847. 212p. 1996. pap. 24.95 (*0-7185-2408-X*) Bks Intl VA.

— Minorities in Wartime: National & Racial Groupings in Europe, North America, & Australia During the Two World Wars. LC 92-15669. 280p. 1993. 39.50 (*0-85496-339-1*) Berg Pubs.

— Racial Violence in Britain, 1840-1950. LC 92-36259. 256p. 1993. 59.00 (*0-7185-1397-5*) St Martin.

Panayi, Panikos, jt. ed. see Larres, Klaus.

Panayiotis, jt. auth. see Nellas.

Panayiotopoulos, Prodromos. Small Enterprises in the Third World. 63.95 (*1-85972-553-8*) Ashgate Pub Co.

***Panayiotopoulos, Prodromos & Capps, Gavin.** World Development: An Introduction. 196p. 2000. 69.95 (*0-7453-1407-4*, Pub. by Pluto GBR); pap. 22.50 (*0-7453-1402-3*, Pub. by Pluto GBR) Stylus Pub VA.

Panayotakis, Costas. Theatrum Arbitri: Theatrical Elements in the Satyrica of Petronius. LC 94-40910. (Mnemosyne, Bibliotheca Classica Batava). 1995. 74.50 (*90-04-10229-9*) Brill Academic Pubs.

Panayotou, Theodore & Ashton, Peter S. Not by Timber Alone: Economics & Ecology for Sustaining Tropical Forests. LC 92-10222. 280p. 1992. text 45.00 (*1-55963-195-3*); pap. text 27.00 (*1-55963-196-1*) Island Pr.

Panayotou, Theodore, et al. The Economics of Catfish Farming in Central Thailand. (ICLARM Technical Reports: No. 4). (Illus.). 60p. (Orig.). 1983. pap. 10.00 (*971-02-0338-X*, Pub. by ICLARM) Intl Spec Bk.

Panayotova, Dora. Bulgarian Mural Paintings of the 14th Century. Alexieva, Marguerite & Athanassova, Theodora, trs. (Illus.). 40.50 (*0-8057-5003-7*) Irvington.

Panbe, Rambon & Arrom, Josbe Juan. An Account of the Antiquities of the Indians: Chronicles of the New World Encounter. LC 99-19365. (Latin America in Translation/en Traduccibon/en Tradupcdao Ser.). 1999. 12.95 (*0-8223-2347-8*) Duke.

Panbratz, Roger, jt. ed. see Houston, W. Robert.

Panc, V. Theories of Elastic Plates. (Mechanics of Surface Structures Ser.: No. 2). 736p. 1975. text 288.00 (*90-286-0104-X*) Kluwer Academic.

Pancak, Katharine A. Modern Real Estate Practice, Connecticut Supplement. 7th ed. LC 96-39572. 1997. pap. 16.95 (*0-7931-2267-8*, 15102707, Real Estate Ed) Dearborn.

Pancak, Katherine A. Connecticut Real Estate: Practice & Law. 8th ed. LC 99-10263. 215p. 1999. pap. 17.95 (*0-7931-3197-9*) Dearborn.

Pancake, Breece D'J. The Stories of Breece D'J Pancake. LC 83-22530. 192p. 1995. pap. 9.95 (*0-8050-0720-2*, Owl) H Holt & Co.

Pancake, John S. 1777: The Year of the Hangman. LC 76-30797. 280p. 1977. pap. text 19.95 (*0-8173-0687-0*) U of Ala Pr.

Pancaratra, Narada-Pancaratra. Sri Narada Pancharatnam, the Jnanamrita Sara Samhita. Swami Vijnanananda, tr. LC 73-3816. (Sacred Books of the Hindus: No. 23). reprint ed. 32.50 (*0-404-57823-3*) AMS Pr.

Pancel, Laslo, ed. Tropical Forestry Handbook, 2 vols. LC 93-34006. (Illus.). 1900p. 1993. 558.95 (*0-387-56420-9*) Spr-Verlag.

Pancero, Jim. Leading Your Sales Team. 241p. 1995. 31.50 (*0-85013-200-2*) Dartnell Corp.

Panchadasi, Swami. Astral World. reprint ed. pap. 3.00 (*0-911662-36-7*) Yoga.

— Clairvoyance & Occult Powers. reprint ed. 15.00 (*0-911662-35-9*) Yoga.

— A Course of Advanced Lessons in Clairvoyance & Occult Powers. 319p. 1996. reprint ed. spiral bd. 18.50 (*0-7873-0653-3*) Hlth Research.

— A Course of Advanced Lessons in Clairvoyance & Occult Powers, 1916. 319p. 1996. reprint ed. pap. 18.00 (*1-56459-786-5*) Kessinger Pub.

— Human Aura. reprint ed. pap. 3.00 (*0-911662-37-5*) Yoga.

Panchal, Boverdhan. Theaters of Bharata & Some Aspects of Sanskrit Play-Production. (C). 1996. 40.00 (*81-215-0661-1*, Pub. by M Manoharial) Coronet Bks.

Panchal, Chandra J., ed. Yeast Strain Selection. LC 96-1294. (Bioprocess Technology Ser.: Vol. 8). (Illus.). 368p. 1990. text 199.00 (*0-8247-8276-3*) Dekker.

Pancham Sinh, tr. see Svatmarama, S.

Panchanathan, Sethuraman, et al, eds. Multimedia Hardware Architectures, 1998, Vol. 3311. LC 98-191001. 150p. 1998. 59.00 (*0-8194-2751-9*) SPIE.

***Panchanathan, Sethuraman, et al, eds.** Multimedia Storage & Archiving Systems IV. 492p. 1999. pap. text 92.00 (*0-8194-3439-6*) SPIE.

Panchanathan, Sethuraman & Sijstermans, Frans, eds. Multimedia Hardware Architectures, 1997, Vol. 3021. LC 97-200941. 320p. 1997. 69.00 (*0-8194-2432-3*) SPIE.

Panchani, C. S. The Himalayan Tribes. 1994. pap. 75.00 (*0-7855-0412-5*, Pub. by Ratna Pustak Bhandar) St Mut.

Panchani, Chander S. Arunachal Pradesh: Religion, Culture & Society. vi, 347p. 1989. text 35.00 (*0-685-32870-8*, Pub. by Konark Pubs Pvt Ltd) Advent Bks Div.

Panchapakesan, S. & Balakrishnan, N. Advances in Statistical Decision Theory & Applications. LC 97-26991. (Statistics for Industry & Technology Ser.). (Illus.). 532p. 1997. text. write for info. (*0-8176-3965-9*) Birkhauser.

— Advances in Statistical Decision Theory & Applications. LC 97-26991. (Statistics for Industry & Technology Ser.). (Illus.). xlix, 448p. 1997. write for info. (*3-7643-3965-9*) Birkhauser.

Panchen, Alec L. Batrachosauria (Anthrosauria) (Encyclopedia of Paleoherpetology Ser.: Pt. 5-A). (Illus.). 1970. pap. text 46.80 (*3-437-30111-X*) Lubrecht & Cramer.

— Evolution. LC 93-18377. (Mind Matters Ser.). 182p. 1993. text 24.95 (*0-312-09697-6*) St Martin.

Panchen, Ngari. Perfect Conduct: Ascertaining the Three Vows. 192p. 1996. pap. 18.00 (*0-86171-083-5*) Wisdom MA.

***Panchenko, Vladislav Y. & Golubev, Vladimir S., eds.** Industrial Lasers & Laser Applications '98. 536p. 1999. pap. text 103.00 (*0-8194-3162-1*) SPIE.

Pancheri, Francesco S. The Universal Primacy of Christ. Carol, Juniper B., tr. from ITA. Orig. Title: Il Primato universale de Christo. 144p. (Orig.). (C). 1984. pap. 6.95 (*0-931888-16-6*) Christendom Pr.

Pancheri, G., et al, eds. Multiparticle Production: Proceedings of the Perugia Workshop. 496p. (C). 1989. text 138.00 (*9971-5-0884-2*) World Scientific Pub.

Panchev, S. Dynamic Meteorology. 1985. text 247.50 (*90-277-1744-3*) Kluwer Academic.

Panchillia, Susan V., jt. auth. see Ponchillia, Paul E.

Panchishkin, A. A., et al. Non-Archimedean L-Functions: Of Siegel & Hilbert Modular Forms. Dold, A. et al, eds. (Lecture Notes in Mathematics Ser.: Vol. 1471). vii, 157p. 1991. 28.95 (*0-387-54137-3*) Spr-Verlag.

Pancho, Eric, ed. see Davis, Theresa M.

Panchyk, Richard. Birth Index for Buda Jewry: Covering the Years 1820-49 for Neolog Jews in Buda (Budapest), Hungary. 56p. (Orig.). 1993. pap. text 3.75 (*0-9622473-6-7*) No Ink.

— Streetlamps & Distant Stars: A Collection of Poems (1986-89) 36p. (Orig.). 1989. pap. 2.25 (*0-9622473-0-8*) No Ink.

Panchyk, Richard, ed. Obuda Jewish Census of 1850: Original Census with Alphabetical Index. 100p. (Orig.). 1996. pap. 11.50 (*0-9622473-1-6*) No Ink.

Panchyk, Richard, jt. auth. see Levy, Matthys.

Panciera, Matthew, tr. see Starks, John H., Jr., et al, eds.

***Pancioli, Diana.** Extruded Ceramics: Techniques, Projects, Inspirations. Truscott, Danielle, ed. LC 99-27802. (Illus.). 144p. 2000. 27.95 (*1-57990-130-1*) Lark Books.

***Pancoast, Chalmers L.** Modern Templar. 200p. 1999. reprint ed. pap. 14.95 (*0-7661-0771-X*) Kessinger Pub.

Pancoast, Chalmers L. Templar Tales (1935) 170p. 1998. reprint ed. pap. 16.95 (*0-7661-0160-6*) Kessinger Pub.

— Trail Blazers of Advertising: Stories of the Romance & Adventure of the Old-Time Advertising Game. LC 75-39264. (Getting & Spending: The Consumer's Dilemma Ser.). (Illus.). 1976. reprint ed. 26.95 (*0-405-08037-9*) Ayer.

Pancoast, Diane L., et al, eds. Rediscovering Self-Help: Its Role in Social Care. LC 83 3126. (Social Service Delivery Systems Ser.: No. 6). 295p. reprint ed. pap. 91.50 (*0-8357-8503-3*, 203478200091) Bks Demand.

Pancoast, Diane L., jt. auth. see Collins, Alice H.

***Pancoast, Douglas & Architectural League of New York Staff.** Young Architects--Scale. LC 99-53588. (Illus.). 112p. 2000. pap. 24.95 (*1-56898-219-4*) Princeton Arch.

Pancoast, Henry S., ed. Standard English Poems. LC 72-149107. (Granger Index Reprint Ser.). 1977. 42.95 (*0-8369-6232-X*) Ayer.

— Vista of English Verse. LC 76-149108. (Granger Index Reprint Ser.). 1977. 40.95 (*0-8369-6233-8*) Ayer.

Pancoast, S. The Kabbala: or True Science of Light: An Introduction to the Philosophy & Theosophy of the Ancient Sages Together with a Chapter on Light in the Vegetable Kingdom. 312p. 1992. reprint ed. pap. 24.95 (*1-56459-167-0*) Kessinger Pub.

Pancoast, Scott R. & White, Lance M. Business Grammar Handbook. LC 85-20248. (Illus.). 210p. 1992. pap. 9.95 (*0-87131-709-5*) M Evans.

Pancoast, William T. Crashing. 187p. 1983. 7.95 (*0-9610562-0-7*) Blazing Flowers.

Pancoe, Joan. Openings: A Guide to Psychic Living in the Real World. LC 95-3846. 352p. (Orig.). 1995. pap. 18.95 (*0-9644936-0-8*) Modern Myst.

Panconcelli-Calzia, Giulio. Geschichtszahlen der Phonetik: Quellenatlas der Phonetic. LC 93-37819. (Studies in the History of the Language Sciences: No. 16). xxxviii, 88p. 1994. reprint ed. 65.00 (*90-272-0957-X*) J Benjamins Pubng Co.

Pancrazi, Pierrette. My Private Spider Webs. 1998. pap. write for info. (*1-57553-932-2*) Watermrk Pr.

Pancsofar, Ernest. Positive Profiles: Building Community Together. LC 98-34028. (Illus.). 86p. (Orig.). 1998. pap. 25.00 (*1-883302-26-9*) Trning Res.

Pancsofar, Ernest & Blackwell, Robert, eds. A User's Guide to Community Entry for the Severely Handicapped. LC 84-24139. (SUNY Series in Special Education). 182p. (C). 1985. pap. text 21.95 (*0-88706-035-8*) State U NY Pr.

Pancza-Graham, Arlene, ed. see Turner, C. M.

Panczenko, Russell, ed. Patrick Ireland: Labyrinths, Language, Pyramids, & Related Acts. (Illus.). 112p. 1994. pap. 24.95 (*0-932900-33-X*) Elvejhem Mus.

Panczenko, Russell, jt. auth. see Golay, Jean-Pierre.

Panczenko, Russell, jt. auth. see Wolff, Theodore F.

Panczner, Bill, jt. auth. see Panczner, Sharon.

Panczner, Sharon & Panczner, Bill. Arizona Traveler: Gems & Minerals of Arizona - A Guide to Native Gemstones. (American Traveler Ser.: Vol. 45). (Illus.). 48p. 1988. pap. 4.95 (*1-55838-097-3*) R H Pub.

Panczner, William D. Rocky Mountain Traveler: A Travelers Guide to Tracking Dinosaurs in the Western U. S. LC 96-104011. (American Traveler Ser.: Vol. 31). 1995. pap. 5.95 (*1-55838-149-X*) R H Pub.

Panczyk, Krzysztof. Archangel & New Archangel. 2000. pap. text 18.95 (*1-85744-260-1*) Cadgn Bks.

Panda, Preeti R., et al. Memory Issues in Embedded Systems-on-Chip: Optimizations & Exploration. LC 98-44229. xvii, 188 p. 1999. write for info. (*0-7923-8362-1*) Kluwer Academic.

Panda, B. N. & Tewari, A. D. Teacher Education. LC 97-905925. (Illus.). xxxviii, 471p. 1997. 59.00 (*81-7024-904-X*, Pub. by APH Pubng) Nataraj Bks.

Panda, Chitta. The Decline of the Bengal Zamindars: Midnapore 1870-1920. LC 96-906244. (Oxford University South Asian Studies). (Illus.). 242p. 1997. text 24.95 (*0-19-563295-8*) OUP.

***Panda, Dhabaleswar K. & Shiratori, Norio, eds.** Parallel Processing: Proceedings International Conference Aizu-Wakamatsu City, Japan, 1999. 561p. 1999. 145.00 (*0-7695-0350-0*) IEEE Comp Soc.

Panda, Dhabaleswar K. & Stunkel, Craig B. Communication & Architectural Support for Network-Based Parallel Computing: First International Workshop, CANPC '97, San Antonio, Texas, U. S. A., February 1997: Proceedings. LC 97-877. (Lecture Notes in Computer Science Ser.: Vol. 119). 1997. pap. 49.00 (*3-540-62573-9*) Spr-Verlag.

— Communication, Architecture, & Applications for Network-Based Parallel Computing: Proceedings of the Second International Workshop, Canpc '98, Las Vegas, U. S. A., January 31-February 1, 1998, Vol. 136. LC 98-2802. (Lecture Notes in Computer Science Ser.: Vol. 1362). x, 247p. 1998. pap. 449.00 (*3-540-64140-8*) Spr-Verlag.

***Panda, Dhabaleswar K. & Takizawa, Makoto, eds.** Parallel Processing: Proceedings International Workshops Aizu-Wakamaatsu City, Japan, 1999. LC 99-64614. 644p. 1999. 155.00 (*0-7695-0353-5*) IEEE Comp Soc.

Panda, Jaganath. Development Banking in India. (C). 1991. 21.00 (*81-7141-144-4*) S Asia.

Panda, K. C. Education of Exceptional Children. 1994. pap. 225.00 (*81-259-0247-3*, Pub. by Print Hse) St Mut.

Panda, N. C. Maya in Physics: 6 Meanings Other Than Illusion. (C). 1991. 32.00 (*81-208-0698-0*, Pub. by Motilal Bnarsidass) S Asia.

— Mind & Supermind. 1996. 88.00 (*81-246-0053-8*, Pub. by DK Pubs Ind) S Asia.

— Principles of Host-Plant Resistance to Insect Pests. LC 78-59169. (Illus.). 406p. 1980. text 59.00 (*0-916672-93-X*) Rowman.

— Vibrating Universe. (C). 1995. 18.00 (*81-208-1291-3*, Pub. by Motilal Bnarsidass) S Asia.

Panda, R. K. Industrial Sickness: A Study of Small Scale Industries. (C). 1992. 18.00 (*81-7024-452-8*, Pub. by Ashish Pub Hse) S Asia.

Panda, Rabindra K. Research in Indology: A New Perspective. LC 98-907624. xix, 147p. 1998. write for info. (*81-86050-22-1*, Pub. by B K Prakashan) S Asia.

Panda, Rajaram. Japan & the Third World: Political & Economic Inter-actions, 1980's-1990's. LC 94-905347. (C). 1995. 28.00 (*81-7095-046-5*, Pub. by Lancer India) S Asia.

Panda, S. P., jt. auth. see Murty, B. S.

Panda, Snehalata. Gender, Environment & Participation in Politics. LC 94-906349. 160p. 1995. pap. 140.00 (*81-85880-55-7*, Pub. by Print Hse) St Mut.

— Women & Social Change in India. (C). 1991. 17.50 (*81-7024-423-4*, Pub. by Ashish Pub Hse) S Asia.

— Women & Social Change in India. viii, 124p. 1992. 12.95 (*1-881338-14-2*) Nataraj Bks.

***Pandak, Carol A.** Rebuilding Civil Society. (Studies in Pedagogy, Andragogy & Gerontagogy). xi, 214p. 1999. 39.95 (*3-631-34470-8*) P Lang Pubng.

Pandak, Carol A. Rebuilding Civil Society: Nonformal Adult Education & Voluntary Organizations - the Hungarian Experience. (Studien zur Padagogik, Andragogik und Gerontagogik: Vol. 44). xi, 214p. 1999. pap. text 39.95 (*0-8204-4301-8*) P Lang Pubng.

Panday, Daulat. The Tales of India, Vol. 1. 114p. (J). (gr. 3-8). 1985. pap. 5.95 (*0-89071-330-8*, Pub. by SAA) Acrpls Bks CO.

— The Tales of India, Vol. 1. (Illus.). 114p. 1998. pap. 3.50 (*81-7058-234-2*, Pub. by SAA) E-W Cultural Ctr.

— The Tales of India, Vol. 2. 126p. (J). (gr. 3-8). 1985. pap. 5.95 (*0-89071-331-6*, Pub. by SAA) Acrpls Bks CO.

***Panday, Daulat.** The Tales of India, Vol. 2. 110p. 1999. pap. 3.50 (*81-7058-212-1*, Pub. by SAA) E-W Cultural Ctr.

— The Tales of India, Vol. 3. 126p. 1995. pap. 3.50 (*81-7058-235-0*, Pub. by SAA) E-W Cultural Ctr.

Panday, J. P., ed. Immunogenetic Risk Assessment in Human Disease Vol. 12, No. 3: Experimental & Clinical Immunogenetics, 1995. (Journal: Experimental & Clinical Immunogenetics Ser.: Vol. 12, No. 3, 1995). (Illus.). 108p. 1995. pap. 50.50 (*3-8055-6215-2*) S Karger.

Panday, R. K. Nepalese Cartoons (Himalayan Humour) 1997. pap. 26.00 (*0-7855-7446-8*, Pub. by Ratna Pustak Bhandar) St Mut.

***Panday, Ram Kumar.** Mountain Dimensions: An Altitude Geographic Analysis of the Environment & Development of the Himalayas. 1999. pap. 94.00 (*0-7855-7610-X*) St Mut.

Pande, A. Handbook of Moisture Determination & Control: Principles, Techniques, Applications, 4 vols., Vol. 1. LC 73-86820. (Illus.). 280p. reprint ed. pap. 86.80 (*0-7837-0654-5*, 204099300001) Bks Demand.

— Handbook of Moisture Determination & Control: Principles, Techniques, Applications, 4 vols., Vol. 2. LC 73-86820. (Illus.). 335p. reprint ed. pap. 103.90 (*0-7837-0655-3*, 204099300002) Bks Demand.

— Handbook of Moisture Determination & Control: Principles, Techniques, Applications, 4 vols., Vol. 3. LC 73-86820. (Illus.). 302p. reprint ed. pap. 93.70 (*0-7837-0656-1*, 204099300003) Bks Demand.

— Handbook of Moisture Determination & Control: Principles, Techniques, Applications, 4 vols., Vol. 4. LC 73-86820. (Illus.). 327p. reprint ed. pap. 101.40 (*0-7837-0657-X*, 204099300004) Bks Demand.

Pande, Alaka & Rao, V. G. A Compendium of Fungi on Legumes from India. LC 98-908790. 1998. pap. 90.00 (*81-7233-181-9*, Pub. by Scientifc Pubs) St Mut.

Pande, Alka. Musical Instruments of the Punjab, 1. 1999. 27.50 (*1-890206-15-6*) Grantha.

***Pande, B. D. & Karki, U.** Primary School Student Achievement in Environmental Education. 1998. pap. 25.00 (*0-7855-7619-3*) St Mut.

Pande, B. M., jt. auth. see Sarkar, H.

Pande, B. N., ed. Centenary History of the Indian National Congress, 1885-1919, Vol. 1. 1985. 28.00 (*0-8364-5665-3*) S Asia.

— Centenary History of the Indian National Congress, 1947-1964, Vol. 4. 1985. 28.00 (*0-8364-5679-3*) S Asia.

Pande, C. S., jt. auth. see Polak, T. A.

Pande, C. S., ed. see American Society for Metals Staff.

Pande, C. S., jt. ed. see Ankem, S.

Pande, D. C., ed. Managing Agriculture for a Better Tomorrow: The Indian Experience. LC 98-901504. 468p. 1998. pap. 250.00 (*81-7533-067-8*, Pub. by Print Hse) St Mut.

Pande, G., et al. Computer Methods in Structural Masonry-4: Proceedings of the Fourth International Symposium on Computer Methods in Structural Masonry, 3-5 September 1997, Florence, Italy. LC 98-29365. 1998. 135.00 (*0-419-23540-X*, E & FN Spon) Routledge.

Pande, G. C. Foundations of Indian Culture Vol. 1: Spiritual Vision & Symbolic Forms in Ancient India. 1990. 44.00 (*81-208-0710-3*, Pub. by Motilal Bnarsidass) S Asia.

— Foundations of Indian Culture Vol. II: Dimensions of Ancient Indian Social History. 1990. 47.50 (*81-208-0711-1*, Pub. by Motilal Bnarsidass) S Asia.

— Indian Tribes: Habitat, Society, Economy & Change. (C). 1991. 46.00 (*0-685-59771-7*, Pub. by Anmol) S Asia.

Pande, G. N. Numerical Models in Geomechanics, Vol. 1. 1992. 116.00 (*90-5410-089-3*) Ashgate Pub Co.

***Pande, G. N., et al, eds.** Numerical Models in Geomechanics: Proceedings of the 7th International Symposium, NUMOG VII, Graz, Austria, 1-3 September 1999. (Illus.). 690p. (C). 1999. text 115.00 (*90-5809-095-7*) A A Balkema.

Pande, G. N. & Middleton, J., eds. Numerical Techniques for Engineering Analysis & Design, Set. (C). 1987. lib. bdg. 156.50 (*90-247-3597-1*) Kluwer Academic.

— Numerical Techniques for Engineering Analysis & Design, Vol. 1. (C). 1987. text 316.50 (*90-247-3565-3*) Kluwer Academic.

— Numerical Techniques for Engineering Analysis & Design, Vol. 1: Engineering. (C). 1987. text 294.00 (*90-247-3564-5*) Kluwer Academic.

Pande, G. N. & Pietruszczak, S., eds. Numerical Models in Geomechanics: Proceedings of the Fourth International Symposium - NUMOG IV - Swansea, U. K. 24-27 August 1992, 2 vols., Set. (Illus.). 1032p. (C). 1992. text 239.00 (*90-5410-088-5*, Pub. by A A Balkema) Ashgate Pub Co.

— Numerical Models in Geomechanics NUMOG V: Proceedings of the Fifth International Symposium on Numerical Models in Geomechanics-Numog V, Davos, Switzerland, 6-8 September 1995. (Illus.). 720p. (C). 1995. text 194.00 (*90-5410-568-2*, Pub. by A A Balkema) Ashgate Pub Co.

Pande, G. N. & Zienkiewicz, O. C., eds. Soil Mechanics, Transient & Cyclic Loads: Constitutive Relations & Numerical Treatment. LC 81-16485. (Wiley Series in Numerical Methods in Engineering). (Illus.). 639p. reprint ed. pap. 198.10 (*0-608-15940-9*, 203305300083) Bks Demand.

— Soils under Cyclic & Transient Loading: Proceedings from the International Symposium, Swansea, 7-11th January 1980, 2 vols., Set. 894p. (C). 1980. text 311.00 (*90-6191-076-5*, Pub. by A A Balkema) Ashgate Pub Co.

Pande, G. N., jt. ed. see Middleton, J.

Pande, G. N., jt. ed. see Pietruszczak, S.

Pande, Govind C. Studies in the Origins of Buddhism. (C). 1995. 31.00 (*81-208-1016-3*, Pub. by Motilal Bnarsidass) S Asia.

Pande, P. K. & Gangopadhyay, S. R. Health Education for School Children. 1994. pap. 150.00 (*81-7216-018-6*, Pub. by Print Hse) St Mut.

Pande, P. N. Self-Employment Programme in India. (C). 1988. 17.50 (*81-7024-213-4*, Pub. by Ashish Pub Hse) S Asia.

Pande, P. N., ed. Wage Equality among Sexes - A Study of Equal Remuneration Act. 275p. (C). 1992. 150.00 (*81-85009-39-2*, Pub. by Print Hse) St Mut.

Pande, P. N., jt. auth. see Mishra, G. P.

***Pande, Peter S.** Six Sigma Way: How GE, Motorola & Other Top Companies Are Honing Their Performance. 448p. 2000. 29.95 (*0-07-135806-4*) McGraw.

Pande, Rameshwar S. Fodder & Pasture Development in Nepal. 1997. pap. 114.00 (*0-7855-7399-2*, Pub. by Ratna Pustak Bhandar) St Mut.

Pande, Rekha. Succession in the Dehli Sultante. 1990. 29.00 (*81-7169-069-6*, Commonwealth) S Asia.

Pande, Savita. Pakistan's Nuclear Policy. (C). 1991. 14.00 (*81-7018-657-9*, Pub. by BR Pub) S Asia.

Pande, Sunanda. Trends of Occupational Mobility among Migrants. 232p. (C). 1986. 31.00 (*81-7033-023-8*, Pub. by Rawat Pubns) S Asia.

Pandeez. Pre-Historic Archaelogy of Madhya Pradesh. (C). 1987. 62.50 (*81-85067-04-X*, Pub. by Sundeep Prak) S Asia.

Pandell, Karen. I Love You, Sun I Love You, Moon. LC 93-86837. (Illus.). 18p. (J). (ps). 1994. bds. 6.99 (*0-399-22628-1*, G P Putnam) Peng Put Young Read.

***Pandell, Karen.** Journey Through the Northern Rainforest. LC 99-31646. (Illus.). (J). (gr. 3-5). 1999. 17.99 (*0-525-45804-2*, Dutton Child) Peng Put Young Read.

Pandell, Karen & Stall, Chris. Animal Tracks of the Pacific Northwest. LC 81-2041. (Illus.). 120p. (Orig.). 1981. pap. 6.95 (*0-89886-012-1*) Mountaineers.

Pander Brothers Staff. Triple-X International. (Illus.). 340p. 24.95 (*1-56971-218-2*) Dark Horse Comics.

Pandey. Elements of Physiological Psychology. 1995. pap. text, student ed. write for info. (*0-07-055570-2*) McGraw.

Pandey & Arya. Liberalization & Development in Nepal. 1997. pap. 30.00 (*0-7855-7426-3*, Pub. by Ratna Pustak Bhandar) St Mut.

Pandey, jt. auth. see Borre.

Pandey, A. K. Kinship & Tribal Polity. (C). 1989. 37.50 (*81-7033-077-7*, Pub. by Rawat Pubns) S Asia.

***Pandey, Anup Chandra.** Governance in Ancient India: From the Rgvedic Period to C. AD 650. xv, 224p. 2000. 20.00 (*81-246-0135-6*, Pub. by D K Printwrld) Nataraj Bks.

Pandey, B. N. Role of Science & Technology in Rural & Economic Development in India. 220p. 1983. 27.95 (*0-318-37334-3*) Asia Bk Corp.

Pandey, B. N., ed. Centenary History of the Indian National Congress, 1885-1985, 4 vols. 1995. 98.00 (*0-7069-6470-5*, Pub. by Vikas) S Asia.

Pandey, B. N., ed. Role of Science & Technology in Rural & Economic Development in India. 1983. text 26.50 (*0-685-14096-2*) Coronet Bks.

Pandey, B. P. Gandhi Sarvodaya & Organizations. (C). 1988. 26.00 (*81-85076-55-3*, Pub. by Chugh Pubns) S Asia.

Pandey, B. P., ed. Gandhi & Economic Development. 233p. 1991. text 35.00 (*0-685-40677-6*, Pub. by Radiant Pubs) S Asia.

Pandey, Chandra B. Risis in Ancient India. 265p. 1987. 26.00 (*0-8364-2022-5*, Pub. by Sundeep Prak) S Asia.

Pandey, D. & Wadhawan, V. K., eds. Modulated Structures, Polytypes & Quasicrystals: Proceedings of the International Conference in India, December 1988: A Special Issue of the Journal Phase Transitions. xii, 636p. 1989. pap. text 1396.00 (*0-677-25810-0*) Gordon & Breach.

Pandey, D. P. & Sharma, V. P. Collins Gem English-Hindi Dictionary. (ENG & HIN.). 755p. 1993. write for info. (*0-7859-7416-4*, 0004589645) Fr & Eur.

Pandey, D. P., jt. auth. see Murthy, N. A.

Pandey, G. P., jt. ed. see SIngh, J. L.

Pandey, Gaya, jt. auth. see Saran, A. B.

Pandey, Gaya, jt. auth. see Upadhyay, V. S.

Pandey, Geetanjali. Between Two Worlds an Intellectual Biography of Premchand. (C). 1989. 25.00 (*81-85054-59-2*, Pub. by Manohar) S Asia.

Pandey, Gyanendra. Medicinal Flowers: Puspayurveda Medicinal Flowers of India & Adjacent Regions. (Indian Medical Science Ser.: No. 14). (C). 1992. 18.00 (*81-7030-351-6*) S Asia.

— Medicinal Plants of Himalaya. (C). 1995. 44.00 (*81-7030-464-4*, Pub. by Sri Satguru Pubns) S Asia.

— Some Lesser Known Herbal Drugs in Ayurveda. (C). 1996. 22.00 (*81-7030-512-8*, Pub. by Sri Satguru Pubns) S Asia.

— Uncommon Plant Drugs of Ayurveda. LC 94-904592. (C). 1995. 34.00 (*81-7030-404-0*, Pub. by Sri Satguru Pubns) S Asia.

Pandey, Gyanendra, ed. The Indian Nation in Nineteen Forty-Two. (C). 1988. 22.50 (*81-7074-024-X*) S Asia.

Pandey, Gyanendra, jt. ed. see Chatterjee, Partha.

Pandey, I. C. Tectonic & Metamorphic Investigations of Kumaon-Garhwal Himachal Lesser Himalaya. Saklani, P. S., ed. (Current Trends in Geology Ser.: Vol. 13). (Illus.). 179p. 1991. 65.00 (*1-55528-240-7*) Scholarly Pubns.

Pandey, Indu P. Romantic Feminism in Hindi Novels Written by Women. 1989. 21.50 (*81-85313-00-8*, Pub. by Usha) S Asia.

Pandey, J. N. The Hilbert Transform of Schwartz Distributions & Applications. LC 95-18944. (Pure & Applied Mathematics: A Wiley-Interscience Series of Texts, Monographs & Tracts). 262p. 1995. 94.95 (*0-471-03373-1*, Wiley-Interscience) Wiley.

***Pandey, J. N., ed.** Respiratory Medicine in the Tropics. (Illus.). 500p. 2000. pap. text 39.95 (*0-19-565202-9*) OUP.

***Pandey, Janak.** Psychology in India Revisited: Developments in the Discipline. LC 00-22300. 2000. pap. write for info. (*0-7619-9442-4*) Sage.

Pandey, Janak, ed. Psychology in India Vol. 1: The State-of-the-Art: Personality & Mental Process, Vol. 1. 336p. (C). 1989. text 35.00 (*0-8039-9552-0*) Sage.

— Psychology in India Vol. 2: The State-of-the-Art: Basic & Applied Social Psychology, Vol. 2. 356p. (C). 1989. text 35.00 (*0-8039-9553-9*) Sage.

— Psychology in India Vol. 3: The State-of-the-Art: Organizational Behavior & Mental Health, Vol. 3. 342p. (C). 1989. text 35.00 (*0-8039-9554-7*) Sage.

Pandey, Janak, et al. Asian Contributions to Cross-Cultural Psychology. 328p. 1995. 38.00 (*0-8039-9244-0*); pap. 16.95 (*0-8039-9245-9*) Sage.

Pandey, Janardan. Gandhi & Voluntary Organizations. LC 98-901475. 172p. 1998. pap. 100.00 (*81-7533-069-4*, Pub. by Print Hse) St Mut.

Pandey, Jitendra. Civil Liberty under Indian Constitution. (C). 1992. 28.00 (*81-7100-383-4*, Pub. by Deep & Deep Pubns) S Asia.

Pandey, K. & Shukla, J. P. Elements of Toxicology. (C). 1991. 24.00 (*81-85484-26-0*, Pub. by Classical Pubng) S Asia.

Pandey, K. C. An Outline of History of Saiva Philosophy. Dwivedi, R. C., ed. 278p. 1986. 14.95 (*0-317-60575-5*, Pub. by Motilal Bnarsidass) S Asia.

Pandey, K. K. Jara Juri Going to the Roots of Grassroots Environmentalists in Nepal. 1997. pap. 100.00 (*0-7855-7604-5*) St Mut.

Pandey, Kanti C. An Outline of History of Saiva Philosophy. Dwivedi, R. C., ed. 300p. 1986. reprint ed. 20.00 (*81-208-0091-5*, Pub. by Motilal Bnarsidass) S Asia.

Pandey, Lalta P. History of Ancient Indian Science: Botanical Science & Economic Growth. 1996. 30.00 (*81-215-0693-X*, Pub. by M Manoharial) Coronet Bks.

Pandey, Manaj & Kedia, Onkar. Fundamentals of Indian Constitution. (C). 1995. 16.00 (*0-7069-8380-7*, Pub. by Vikas) S Asia.

Pandey, Manoj, jt. auth. see Gusain, P. P.

Pandey, Manoj K., jt. auth. see Kashiwagi, Dean T.

Pandey, N. P. Geography of Transportation: A Case Study of Western Madhya Pradesh. 1990. 48.50 (*81-210-0252-4*, Pub. by Inter-India Pubns) S Asia.

Pandey, Pradyumana, ed. Modern Geographical Trends Felicitation: Volume in Honour of Professor Enayat Ahmad. xxxvi, 616p. 1984. 89.00 (*1-55528-068-4*, Pub. by Today Tomorrow) Scholarly Pubns.

Pandey, R., ed. Biotechnology & Comparative Medicine. (Progress in Veterinary Microbiology & Immunology Ser.: Vol. 3). (Illus.). xvi, 268p. 1987. 182.75 (*3-8055-4399-9*) S Karger.

— Infection & Immunity in Farm Animals. (Progress in Veterinary Microbiology & Immunology Ser.: Vol. 1). (Illus.). xiv, 258p. 1984. 142.75 (*3-8055-3925-8*) S Karger.

— Moving Frontiers in Veterinary Immunology. (Progress in Veterinary Microbiology & Immunology Ser.: Vol. 4). (Illus.). xii, 252p. 1987. 182.75 (*3-8055-4632-7*) S Karger.

— Nononcogenic Avian Viruses. (Progress in Veterinary Microbiology & Immunology Ser.: Vol. 5). (Illus.). viii, 136p. 1989. 100.00 (*3-8055-4827-3*) S Karger.

— Veterinary Microbiology. (Progress in Veterinary Microbiology & Immunology Ser.: Vol. 2). (Illus.). x, 222p. 1985. 128.75 (*3-8055-4067-1*) S Karger.

Pandey, R., et al, eds. Veterinary Vaccines. (Progress in Vaccinology Ser.: Vol. 4). (Illus.). 376p. 1992. 240.00 (*0-387-97819-4*) Spr-Verlag.

Pandey, R. C. & Bhatt, S. R., eds. Knowledge Culture & Value: Papers Presented at the World Conference New Delhi at the Time of Golden Jubilee Session of the Indian Philosophical Congress 1975-76. 215p. 1977. 19.00 (*0-88065-175-X*) Scholarly Pubns.

Pandey, R. K., et al, eds. Handbook of Semiconductor Electrodesposition. (Applied Physics Ser.: Vol. 5). (Illus.). 304p. 1996. text 150.00 (*0-8247-9701-9*) Dekker.

— Integrated Thin Films & Applications. (Ceramic Transactions Ser.: Vol. 86). (Illus.). 274p. 1998. 95.00 (*1-57498-032-7*, CT086) Am Ceramic.

Pandey, R. K. & Guo, Ruyan, eds. Crystal Growth of Novel Electronic Materials. (Ceramic Transactions Ser.: Vol. 60). 361p. 1995. 95.00 (*1-57498-003-3*, CT060) Am Ceramic.

Pandey, R. N. Commercial Banks & Rural Development. (C). 1989. 250.00 (*0-7855-6123-4*) St Mut.

Pandey, R. P., jt. auth. see Shetty, B. V.

***Pandey, R. R.** Rupamati: A Novel Translated from the Nepali. 1999. pap. 34.00 (*0-7855-7633-9*) St Mut.

Pandey, Rajbali. Hindu Samskaras: Socio-Religious Study of the Hindu Sacraments. (C). 1987. 22.00 (*81-208-0396-5*, Pub. by Motilal Bnarsidass); pap. 15.50 (*81-208-0434-1*, Pub. by Motilal Bnarsidass) S Asia.

Pandey, Rajendra. Breast Feeding & the Working Women of India. 1990. 40.00 (*81-85076-92-8*, Pub. by Chugh Pubns) S Asia.

— Minorities in India: Protection & Welfare. 288p. (C). 1997. 42.00 (*81-7024-873-6*, Pub. by APH Pubng) Nataraj Bks.

— Social Problems of Contemporary India. (Illus.). vi, 373p. 1994. 43.00 (*81-7024-604-0*, Pub. by Ashish Pub Hse) Nataraj Bks.

— Street Children of India. (C). 1991. 42.50 (*81-85613-37-0*, Pub. by Chugh Pubns) S Asia.

Pandey, Rajyashree. Writing & Renunciation in Medieval Japan: The Works of the Poet-Priest Kamo no Chomei. LC 98-12208. (Michigan Monograph Series in Japanese Studies: No. 21). 197p. 1998. 32.95 (*0-939512-86-6*) U MI Japan.

Pandey, Ram N. Making of Modern Nepal: A Study of History, Art & Culture of the Principalities of Western Nepal. 1997. pap. 106.00 (*0-7855-7436-0*, Pub. by Ratna Pustak Bhandar) St Mut.

Pandey, Rehka & Upadnyay, Neelam U. Women in India Past & Present. (C). 1991. pap. 11.00 (*0-685-49090-4*, Pub. by Chugh Pubns) S Asia.

Pandey, Rekha. Women from Subjection to Liberation. (C). 1989. 34.00 (*81-7099-085-8*, Pub. by Mittal Pubs Dist) S Asia.

Pandey, S. K. Indian Rock Art. (C). 1993. 82.00 (*81-7305-032-5*, Pub. by Aryan Bks Intl) S Asia.

Pandey, S. N., jt. auth. see Tripathi, A. K.

Pandey, Sachchidanand. Naxal Violence. 1985. 18.00 (*81-7001-003-9*, Pub. by Chanakya) S Asia.

Pandey, Shashi. Community Action for Social Justice: Grassroots Organizations in India. 258p. 1991. text 32.00 (*0-8039-9674-8*) Sage.

Pandey, Sheojee. Sri Aurobindo & Vedanta Philosophy. (C). 1987. 21.00 (*81-7100-028-2*, Pub. by Deep & Deep Pubns) S Asia.

Pandey, Suchakar, ed. Contemporary Indian Drama. 120p. 1990. text 15.95 (*0-685-56101-1*, Pub. by Prestige) Advent Bks Div.

Pandey, Sudhakar, ed. George Bernard Shaw - A Critical Response. 150p. 1991. text 22.95 (*81-85218-36-6*) Advent Bks Div.

— Glimpses of Ancient Indian Poetics: (From Bharata to Jagannatha) (Sri Garib Dass Oriental Ser.: No. 166). (C). 1993. 21.00 (*81-7030-360-5*) S Asia.

Pandey, Sumana. Women in Politics. 1990. 26.50 (*81-7033-088-2*, Pub. by Rawat Pubns) S Asia.

Pandey, Surya N. Writing in a Post-Colonial Space. LC 99-932977. xvii, 174 p. 1999. write for info. (*81-7156-823-8*, Pub. by Atlantic Pubs) S Asia.

Pandey, V. N. Textbook of Labour & Industrial Laws. 416p. 1980. 90.00 (*0-7855-1353-1*) St Mut.

***Pandeya, Avinash C.** The Art of Kathakali. (Illus.). 240p. 1999. 36.50 (*81-215-0898-3*, Pub. by M Manoharial) Coronet Bks.

Pandeya, R. C., ed. Pramanavarttika of Dharmakirti (with Dharmakirti's Own Commentary on the Third Chapter & Manorathanandin's Commentary on the Entire Text. (C). 1989. 42.00 (*81-208-0546-1*, Pub. by Motilal Bnarsidass) S Asia.

Pandeya, Raghunath. The Madhyamakasastram of Nagarjuna, Vol. 1. (C). 1988. 58.00 (*81-208-0554-2*, Pub. by Motilal Bnarsidass) S Asia.

Pandeya, Raghunath, ed. The Madhyamakasastram of Nagarjuna, Vol. 2. (C). 1989. 48.50 (*81-208-0555-0*, Pub. by Motilal Bnarsidass) S Asia.

Pandeya, Ram C. Nagarjuna's Philosophy of No-Identity: With Philosophical Translations of the Madhyamaka-Karika, Sunyata-Saptati & Vigrahavyavartani. (C). 1991. 20.00 (*0-685-63332-2*, Pub. by Eastern Bk Linkers) S Asia.

Pandeya, Ram C. & Manju. Nagarjuna's Philosophy of No-Identity: With Philosophical Translations of the Madhyamaka-Karika, Sunyata-Saptati & Vigrahavyavartani. xxvi, 165p. 1991. 18.00 (*0-685-62634-2*, Pub. by Eastern Bk Linkers) Nataraj Bks.

Pandeya, Ramchandra. Indian Studies in Philosophy. 1977. 15.50 (*0-89684-224-X*, Pub. by Motilal Bnarsidass) S Asia.

Pandeya, S. C. & Lieth, Helmut, eds. Ecology of Cenchrus Grass Complex: Environmental Conditions & Population Differences in Western India. LC 92-18658. (Tasks for Vegetation Science Ser.: Vol. 23). 248p. (C). 1993. text 223.00 (*0-7923-0768-2*) Kluwer Academic.

Pandharipande, Rajeshwari. Marathi. LC 96-38089. (Descriptive Grammars Ser.). 680p. (C). 1997. 190.00 (*0-415-00319-9*) Routledge.

Pandharipande, Rajeshwari V. Eternal Self & the Cycle of Samsars: An Introduction to Asian Mythology & Religion. 3rd ed. 210p. (C). 1996. pap. 31.80 (*0-536-59296-9*) Pearson Custom.

Pandian, Jacob. Anthropology & the Western Tradition: Toward an Authentic Anthropology. 135p. 1985. pap. text 10.50 (*0-88133-127-9*) Waveland Pr.

— Culture, Religion & the Sacred Self: A Critical Introduction to the Anthropological Study of Religion. 352p. (C). 1990. pap. text 26.80 (*0-13-194226-3*) P-H.

— The Making of India & Indian Traditions. LC 94-16912. 304p. 1994. pap. text 34.40 (*0-13-124421-3*) P-H.

— Nationalism & Ethnicity: An Interpretation of Tamil Cultural History & Social Order. 1987. 27.00 (*0-86132-136-7*, Pub. by Popular Prakashan) S Asia.

Pandian, M. S. The Image Trap: M. G. Ramachandran in Film & Politics. (Illus.). 164p. (C). 1992. text 28.00 (*0-8039-9403-6*) Sage.

— The Political Economy of Agrarian Change: Nanchilnadu, 1880-1939. (Illus.). 196p. (C). 1990. 25.00 (*0-8039-9642-X*) Sage.

Pandian, Natasa & Sanders, Stephen P. Textbook of Echocardiography. 750p. 1994. write for info. (*0-683-06744-3*) Lppncott W & W.

Pandian, Natesa G., jt. ed. see Roelandt, Jos R.

Pandiit, M. P. How Do I Begin? 52p. 1980. pap. 2.50 (*0-941524-48-5*) Lotus Pr.

Pandikattu, Kuruvila. Religious Dialogue as Hermeneutics: Bede Griffith's Advaitic Approach. LC 99-36006. (Cultural Heritage & Contemporary Change Ser.). pap. write for info. (*1-56518-138-7*) Coun Res Values.

Pandimakil, Peter G., tr. see Mooren, Thomas.

Pandiri, Ananda M., compiled by. A Comprehensive, Annotated Bibliography on Mahatma Gandhi Vol. 1: Biographies, Works by Gandhi, & Bibliographical Sources, 42. LC 95-18659. (Bibliographies & Indexes in World History Ser.: No. 42). 424p. 1995. lib. bdg. 105.00 (*0-313-25337-4*, Greenwood Pr) Greenwood.

Pandis, Spyros N., jt. auth. see Seinfeld, John H.

Pandit, A. K. Freshwater Ecosystems of the Himalaya. LC 96-47924. (Illus.). 208p. 1998. text 75.00 (*1-85070-782-0*) Prthnon Pub.

Pandit, B. N. Mirror of Self-Supremacy or Svatantrya-Darpana. (C). 12.50 (*81-215-0559-3*, Pub. by M Manoharial) Coronet Bks.

Pandit, B. N., tr. Essence of the Exact Reality or Parmathasara of Abhinavagupta. (C). 1991. 10.00 (*0-685-54511-3*, Pub. by M Manoharial) S Asia.

Pandit, Bansi. Hindu Dharma. (Illus.). 136p. (Orig.). 1996. pap. 9.00 (*0-9634798-3-0*) B&V Ent.

— Hindu Mind: Fundamentals of Hindu Religion & Philosophy for All Ages. 3rd ed. 448p. 1998. 24.00 (*0-9634798-2-2*) B&V Ent.

— The Hindu Mind: Fundamentals of Hindu Religion & Philosophy for All Ages. 3rd ed. 448p. 1998. pap. 16.00 (*0-9634798-4-9*) B&V Ent.

Pandit, G. L. Methodological Variance: Essays in Epistemological Ontology & the Methodology of Science. (Boston Studies in the Philosophy of Science). 440p. (C). 1991. lib. bdg. 215.00 (*0-7923-1263-5*, Pub. by Kluwer Academic) Kluwer Academic.

Pandit, H. N. Fragments of History: India's Freedom Movement & After. 299p. 1982. 19.95 (*0-940500-55-8*, Pub. by Sterling) Asia Bk Corp.

Pandit, Kavita & Withers, Suzanne D., eds. Migration & Restructuring in the United States: A Geographic Perspective. LC 99-10342. 352p. 1999. pap. 34.95 (*0-8476-9393-7*) Rowman.

***Pandit, Kavita & Withers, Suzanne D., eds.** Migration & Restructuring in the United States: A Geographic Perspective. LC 99-10342. 352p. 1999. text 69.00 (*0-8476-9392-9*) Rowman.

Pandit, Lalita, jt. ed. see Hogan, Patrick C.

Pandit, M. D. Mathematics As Known to the Vedic Samhitas. (Sri Garib Dass Oriental Ser.: No. 169). (C). 1993. text 22.00 (*81-7030-368-0*) S Asia.

Pandit, M. P. Demands of Sadhana. 480p. 1982. pap. 19.50 (*0-941524-47-7*) Lotus Pr.

— Dhyana. 60p. 1990. reprint ed. pap. 1.95 (*0-941524-03-5*) Lotus Pr.

— Dhyana (Meditation) 3rd ed. 60p. 1990. pap. text 1.95 (*81-7509-015-4*, Pub. by DIPTI Pubns) E-W Cultural Ctr.

— How Do I Begin? A Primer of Affirmative Spirituality. 61p. 1996. pap. 2.50 (*81-7509-030-8*, Pub. by DIPTI Pubns) E-W Cultural Ctr.

— How Do I Proceed? 60p. 1982. pap. 3.00 (*0-941524-49-3*) Lotus Pr.

— How Do I Proceed: Key to Sadhana. 60p. 1998. pap. text 3.00 (*81-7509-026-X*, Pub. by DIPTI Pubns) E-W Cultural Ctr.

— Kundalini Yoga: A Brief Study of Sir John Woodroffe's "The Serpent Power" 2nd ed. LC 79-88734. 74p. 1993. pap. 4.95 (*0-941524-50-7*) Lotus Pr.

— Legends in the Life Divine. 284p. 1988. 16.00 (*0-941524-34-5*) Lotus Pr.

— Occult Lines Behind Life. 100p. (Orig.). 1992. reprint ed. pap. 7.95 (*0-941524-35-3*) Lotus Pr.

— Sri Aurobindo & His Yoga. LC 87-80572. 200p. (Orig.). 1987. pap. 9.95 (*0-941524-25-6*) Lotus Pr.

— Upanishads: Gateways of Knowledge. LC 88-83077. 259p. (Orig.). 1988. pap. 9.95 (*0-941524-44-2*) Lotus Pr.

— Vedic Deities. LC 89-84765. 129p. (Orig.). 1989. pap. 7.95 (*0-941524-45-0*) Lotus Pr.

— Wisdom of the Gita: First Series. 128p. 1992. pap. 9.95 (*0-941524-72-8*) Lotus Pr.

— Wisdom of the Veda. LC 89-84764. 102p. (Orig.). 1990. pap. 7.95 (*0-941524-55-8*) Lotus Pr.

— Yoga for the Modern Man. 236p. 1979. 5.95 (*0-941524-13-2*) Lotus Pr.

— The Yoga of Knowledge: Talks at Centre, Vol. II. LC 86-80692. 280p. (Orig.). 1986. pap. 7.95 (*0-941524-23-X*) Lotus Pr.

— The Yoga of Love. LC 81-86373. (Talks at Center Ser.: Vol. III). 104p. (Orig.). 1982. pap. 3.95 (*0-941524-16-7*) Lotus Pr.

— Yoga of Self-Perfection. LC 83-81299. (Talks at Center Ser.: Vol. IV). 308p. (Orig.). 1983. pap. 7.95 (*0-941524-20-5*) Lotus Pr.

— The Yoga of Transformation. 134p. 1995. pap. text 9.95 (*81-7509-010-3*, Pub. by DIPTI Pubns) E-W Cultural Ctr.

— The Yoga of Works: Talks at Centre I. LC 85-50695. 186p. (C). 1985. pap. 7.95 (*0-941524-21-3*) Lotus Pr.

Pandit, M. P., compiled by. Gems from Sri Aurobindo, 4 vols., Set. 633p. 1998. pap. 35.00 (*0-941524-94-9*) Lotus Pr.

Pandit, M. P., ed. see Aurobindo, Sri.

Pandit, M. P., tr. see Parasurama.

Pandit, Madhav Pundalik. Sri Aurobindo & His Yoga. LC 98-906378. (Builders of Indian Philosophy Ser.). x, 118 p. 1998. write for info. (*81-215-0789-8*, Pub. by M Manoharial) Coronet Bks.

Pandit, Maneesha S. It's I Can Do Anything Day! LC 96-92918. (Illus.). 20p. (Orig.). (J). (gr. k-6). 1997. spiral bd. 12.95 (*0-9655776-0-0*) Shivam Pub.

***Pandit, Moti Lal.** Transcendence & Negation: A Study of Buddhist Compassion & Christian Love. LC 99-938041. 208p. 1999. 29.50 (*81-215-0907-6*, Pub. by Munshiram) S Asia.

Pandit, P. N. The Novels of Graham Greene: Impact of Childhood on Adult Life. 208p. 1990. text 27.50 (*81-85218-17-X*, Pub. by Prestige) Advent Bks Div.

Pandit, Ranjit S., tr. Kahlanas' Rajatarangini: The Saga of the Kings of Kashmir. (C). 1991. 25.00 (*0-8364-2629-0*, Pub. by National Sahitya Akademi) S Asia.

Pandit, S. A. From Making to Music: The History of Thorn Emi. 16p. 1996. text 40.00 (*0-340-68045-8*, Pub. by Hodder & Stought Ltd) Trafalgar.

Pandit, Sri M. Japa. 47p. 1991. reprint ed. 2.50 (*0-941524-09-4*) Lotus Pr.

Pandit, U. K. & Alderweireldt, F. C., eds. Bioorganic Chemistry in Healthcare & Technology. (NATO ASI Ser.: Vol. 207). (Illus.). 326p. (C). 1991. text 138.00 (*0-306-44007-5*, Kluwer Plenum) Kluwer Academic.

P

An Asterisk (*) at the beginning of an entry indicates that the title is appearing for the first time.

Pandit, V., ed. Coastal Fishery Projects: Construction, Maintenance & Development. Tankha, Brij, tr. from JPN. LC 99-227585. (ENG., Illus.). 520p. (C). 1994. text 123.00 (*90-5410-229-2*, Pub. by A A Balkema) Ashgate Pub Co.

Pandit, Yeshwant S. India's Balance of Indebtedness: Eighteen Ninety-Eight to Nineteen Thirteen. Wilkins, Mira, ed. LC 78-3944. (International Finance Ser.). 1979. reprint ed. lib. bdg. 21.95 (*0-405-11244-0*) Ayer.

*__Pandita, Sakya.__ Ordinary Wisdom: Sakya Pandita's Treasury of Good Advice. Davenport, John T., tr. 384p. 2000. pap. 21.95 (*0-86171-161-0*) Wisdom MA.

Pandita, Sayadaw U. In This Very Life: The Liberation Teachings of the Buddha. LC 92-42813. 300p. 1992. pap. 16.00 (*0-86171-094-0*) Wisdom MA.

Pandley, B. N., ed. see De Silva, Chandra R.

Pando, Francisco, jt. auth. see Lado, Carlos.

Pando, Magdalen M. Cuba's Freedom Fighter, Antonio Maceo: Eighteen Forty-Five to Eighteen Ninety-Six. LC 79-93001. (Illus.). 144p. (Orig.). (gr. 10-12). 1980. pap. 9.95 (*0-9603846-0-X*) Felicity.

Pando, Miguel, ed. see Huidobro, Matias M., et al.

Pando y Villaroya, Jose L. Diccionario de Marina. 2nd ed. (SPA.). 252p. 1985. pap. 39.95 (*0-7859-6031-7*, 8439847068) Fr & Eur.

Pandolf, Kent B. Exercise & Sports Sciences Review, Vol. 18. (Illus.). 480p. 1990. 46.95 (*0-683-00047-0*) Lppncott W & W.

Pandolf, Kent B., ed. Exercise & Sports Sciences Review, Vol. 17. (American College of Sports Medicine Ser.). (Illus.). 584p. 1989. pap. 46.95 (*0-683-00046-2*) Lppncott W & W.

Pandolfini. Bobby Fischer's Outrageous Chess Moves. 1993. per. write for info. (*0-671-87955-3*, Fireside) S&S Trade Pap.

Pandolfini, Bruce. The ABCs of Chess. 208p. 1986. per. 11.00 (*0-671-61982-9*) S&S Trade.

— Beginning Chess: Over Three Hundred Elementary Problems for Players New to the Game. LC 93-9693. (Illus.). 272p. 1993. pap. 12.00 (*0-671-79501-5*, Fireside) S&S Trade Pap.

— Bobby Fischer's Outrageous Chess Moves: A Study of 101 Outrageous Moves by the Greatest Chess Champion of All Time. 144p. 1993. per. 10.00 (*0-671-87432-2*, Fireside) S&S Trade Pap.

— Chess Doctor: Sure Fire Cures for What Ails Your Game. LC 95-36679. (Illus.). 288p. 1995. pap. 14.00 (*0-684-80121-3*, Fireside) S&S Trade Pap.

— Chess Openings: Traps & Zaps. 256p. 1989. pap. 12.00 (*0-671-65690-2*, Fireside) S&S Trade Pap.

— Chess Thinking: The Visual Dictionary of Chess Moves, Rules, Strategies, & Concepts. (Illus.). 320p. 1995. per. 15.00 (*0-671-79502-3*, Fireside) S&S Trade Pap.

— Chessercizes: New Winning Techniques for Players of All Levels. (Illus.). 224p. (Orig.). 1991. pap. 10.00 (*0-671-70184-3*, Fireside) S&S Trade Pap.

— Kasparov & Deep Blue. LC 97-30448. 1997. pap. 11.00 (*0-684-84852-X*) S&S Trade.

— More Chess Openings: Traps & Zaps 2. 256p. 1993. per. 11.00 (*0-671-79499-X*) S&S Trade Pap.

— More Chessercizes: Checkmate: Three Hundred Strategies for Players of All Levels. (Illus.). 208p. 1991. per. 11.00 (*0-671-70185-1*) S&S Trade Pap.

— Pandolfini's Chess Complete: The Most Comprehensive Guide to the Game, from History to Strategy. LC 92-16152. 352p. 1992. pap. 15.00 (*0-671-70186-X*, Fireside) S&S Trade Pap.

— Pandolfini's Endgame Course. (Illus.). 320p. 1988. pap. 11.00 (*0-671-65688-0*, Fireside) S&S Trade Pap.

— Power Mates. 1996. pap. 14.00 (*0-684-80120-5*) S&S Trade.

— Square One: A Chess Drill Book for Beginners. LC 94-17956. 256p. 1994. pap. 12.00 (*0-671-88424-7*, Fireside) S&S Trade Pap.

— Weapons of Chess: An Omnibus of Chess Strategy. 288p. 1989. per. 12.00 (*0-671-65972-3*, Fireside) S&S Trade Pap.

— The Winning Way: The How What & Why of Opening Strategems. LC 98-12164. 224p. 1998. per. 12.00 (*0-684-83949-0*, Fireside) S&S Trade Pap.

Pandolfo, Stefania. Impasse of the Angels: Scenes from a Moroccan Space of Memory. LC 97-5473. 336p. 1997. pap. text 22.50 (*0-226-64532-0*) U Ch Pr.

— Impasse of the Angels: Scenes from a Moroccan Space of Memory. LC 97-5473. 336p. 1997. lib. bdg. 60.00 (*0-226-64531-2*) U Ch Pr.

Pandolph, Robyn. Radiant Earth: Caress'd by Sun & Dew of Morn, Radiant Is This Earth Adorn'd. (Illus.). 28p. 1998. pap. 10.00 (*1-888237-14-7*) Baxter Pr.

*__Pandolph, Robyn.__ Stitched with Love: A Mother's Quilting Legacy. (Illus.). 96p. 2000. pap. 24.95 incl. cd-rom (*1-893824-06-3*, Pub. by Electric Quilt) Watsn-Guptill.

Pandora, Katherine. Rebels Within the Ranks: Psychologists' Critique of Scientific Authority & Democratic Realities in New Deal America. (Studies in the History of Psychology). 272p. (C). 1997. text 59.95 (*0-521-58358-6*) Cambridge U Pr.

Pandosy, Marie C. Grammar & Dictionary of the Yakama Language. LC 10-30204. (Library of American Linguistics: Vol. 6). reprint ed. 42.75 (*0-404-50986-X*) AMS Pr.

Pandozzi, Frank W. Medigap Insurance: A License to Steal. 61p. (Orig.). 1990. pap. 9.95 (*0-9628734-0-3*) Aa Zz Pub.

Pandratz, Ronald, jt. auth. see Preston, Seaton T., Jr.

*__Pandrea, Teodor, ed.__ Cel Ce Sfarama Lanturile Robiei. Iacob, Iulian, tr. from ENG. Orig. Title: The Bondage Breaker. (RUM.). 2000. pap. 10.00 (*1-930529-00-7*) Up Room Fellow Min.

Pandrich, Bruce, jt. ed. see Spear, Hilda D.

Pandurang, Mala. Post-Colonial African Fiction: The Crisis of Consciousness. 141st rev. ed. LC 97-900873. 251p. 1997. write for info. (*81-85753-14-8*, Pub. by Pencraft International) Advent Bks Div.

Pandy, A. K. Local Level Planning & Rural Development: An Analytical Study. 1990. 21.50 (*81-7099-189-7*, Pub. by Mittal Pubs Dist) S Asia.

Pandya, Abhijit S. ATM Technology for Broadband Telecommunications Network. LC 98-34477. 304p. 1998. boxed set 74.95 (*0-8493-3139-0*) CRC Pr.

Pandya, Abhijit S. & Macy, Robert B. Pattern Recognition with Neural Networks in C Plus Plus. 432p. 1995. pap. 94.95 (*0-8493-9462-7*, 9462) CRC Pr.

Pandya, Basudev. Indian Bureaucracy. 213p. 1978. 19.95 (*0-318-36585-5*) Asia Bk Corp.

Pandya, C. G. Hazards in Chemical Units. 1988. 20.00 (*81-204-0242-1*, Pub. by Oxford IBH) S Asia.

Pandya, H., jt. auth. see Khan, A.

Pandya, Haribhai, ed. Issues in Veda & Astrology. LC 95-910032. (C). 1995. 16.00 (*81-7081-332-8*, Pub. by Nag Pubs) S Asia.

Pandya, J. F., et al, eds. Energy: A Classified Bibliography, (1970-1985) (C). 1991. 28.00 (*81-85119-99-6*, Pub. by Northern Bk Ctr) S Asia.

Pandya, Meenal. Here Comes Diwali. (Illus.). 16p. (J). (ps up). 1994. pap. text 6.95 (*0-9635539-1-7*) Meera Pubns.

Pandya, Meenal A. & Bhanot, Rashmee P. Pick a Pretty Indian Name for Your Baby. (Illus.). 256p. 1991. 19.95 (*0-9635539-0-9*) Meera Pubns.

Pandya, Michael. Indian Microwave Cookery. 230p. 1998. pap. 15.95 (*1-85375-255-X*) Prion.

— Indian Vegetarian Cooking. 192p. 1989. pap. 12.95 (*0-89281-342-3*) Inner Tradit.

*__Pandya, Raj.__ Flowers in Flame. 300p. 2001. pap. 14.95 (*1-57532-227-7*) Press-Tige Pub.

— Mobile & Personal Communication Services & Systems. LC 99-31330. (Series on Digial & Mobile Communications). 1999. 59.95 (*0-7803-4708-0*) IEEE Standards.

*__Pandya, Sachin, et al, eds.__ Premiere Generation Ink: Winter 2000. 46p. 2000. pap. 4.00 (*1-930254-04-0*) Premiere Gen.

Pandya, Vishwajit. Above the Forest: A Study of Andamanese Ethnoanemology, Cosmology & the Power of Ritual. (Illus.). 356p. (C). 1993. text 26.00 (*0-19-562971-X*) OUP.

Pandyan, David. Dr. B. N. Ambedkar & the Dynamics of Neo-Buddhism. 1996. 30.00 (*0-614-25273-3*, Pub. by Gian Publng Hse) S Asia.

Pandyan, K. David. Dr. B. R. Ambedkar & the Dynamics of Neo-Buddhism. xi, 231p. (C). 1996. 25.00 (*81-212-0508-5*, Pub. by Gyan Publishing Hse) Nataraj Bks.

Pandzic, Bazilije. Zivotopis Fra Dominika Mandica. Ziral Staff & Lasic, Vinko D., eds. (Sabrana Djela Dr. O. Dominika Mandica, Sv. 12 Ser.). (Illus.). 236p. 1994. 25.00 (*1-880829-04-5*) Z I R A L.

Pane, Armijn. Shackles: A Novel. McGlynn, John H., tr. LC 84-18930. (Monographs in International Studies, Southeast Asia Ser.: No. 67). 136p. reprint ed. pap. 42.20 (*0 7837-6478-2*, 204648300001) Bks Demand.

Pane, Fray Ramon. An Account of the Antiquities of the Indians: Chronicles of the New World Encounter. Arrom, Jose Juan, ed. Griswold, Susan C., tr. (Illus.). 128p. Date not set. 39.95 (*0-8223-2325-7*) Duke.

Pane, Remigio U., ed. Italian Americans in the Professions. 1979. 9.95 (*0-934675-12-0*) Am Italian.

Panek, Dennis. Catastrophe Cat: Story & Pictures. LC 77-90951. 34p. 1978. 7.95 (*0-87888-130-1*, Bradbury S&S) S&S Childrens.

— Detective Whoo. Vol. 1. 1981. 9.95 (*0-87888-183-2*, Bradbury S&S) S&S Childrens.

Panek, Julian R., ed. Building Seals & Sealants-STP 606. 356p. 1990. 36.00 (*0-8031-0608-4*, STP606) ASTM.

Panek, Julian R. & Cook, John P. Construction Sealants & Adhesives. 3rd ed. LC 91-23362. (Series of Practical Construction Guides: No. 1344). 400p. 1991. 120.00 (*0-471-53474-9*) Wiley.

Panek, LeRoy L. An Introduction to the Detective Story. LC 87-70502. 214p. 1987. 23.95 (*0-87972-377-7*); pap. 12.95 (*0-87972-378-5*) Bowling Green Univ Popular Press.

*__Panek, Leroy L.__ New Hard-Boiled Writers, 1970s-1990s. LC 00-37889. 2000. pap. 25.95 (*0-87972-820-5*) Bowling Green Univ Popular Press.

Panek, LeRoy L. New Hard-Boiled Writers, 1970s-1990s. 51.95 (*0-87972-819-1*) Bowling Green Univ Popular Press.

Panek, LeRoy L. Probable Cause: Crime Fiction in America. LC 89-81987. 167p. (C). 1990. 34.95 (*0-87972-485-4*); pap. 16.95 (*0-87972-486-2*) Bowling Green Univ Popular Press.

Panek, Leroy L. The Special Branch: The Spy Novel from 1890 to 1980. LC 81-80214. 288p. 1981. 22.95 (*0-87972-178-2*) Bowling Green Univ Popular Press.

— Watteau's Shepherds: The Detective Novel in Britain 1914-1940. LC 79-83887. 232p. 1979. 14.95 (*0-87972-131-6*); pap. 7.95 (*0-87972-132-4*) Bowling Green Univ Popular Press.

Panek, Paul E. The Use of Projective Techniques with Persons with Mental Retardation: A Guide for Assessment Instrument Selection. LC 96-53508. (Illus.). 188p. 1997. text 45.95 (*0 398-06756-2*); pap. text 33.95 (*0-398-06757-0*) C C Thomas.

Panek, Richard. Seeing & Believing: How the Telescope Opened Our Eyes & Minds to the Heavens. LC 98-18766. 192p. 1998. 21.95 (*0-670-87628-3*) Viking Penguin.

*__Panek, Richard.__ Seeing & Believing: How the Telescope Opened Our Eyes & Minds to the Heavens. 208p. 1999. pap. 11.95 (*0-14-028061-8*, Penguin Bks) Viking Penguin.

Panek, Richard. Waterloo Diamonds. 304p. 1995. 22.95 (*0-312-13209-3*) St Martin.

Panel of Bioethical Concerns of the National Counc. Genetic Engineering. 5.95 (*0-685-16485-3*, CS1011) General Board.

Panel on Child Care Policy, National Research Coun, et al. Who Cares for America's Children? Hayes, Cheryl D. et al, eds. 388p. 1990. 29.95 (*0-309-04032-9*) Natl Acad Pr.

Panel on Foreign Trade Statistics Staff & National Research Council Staff. Behind the Numbers: U. S. Trade in the World Economy. Kester, Anne Y., ed. 312p. 1992. 29.95 (*0-309-04590-8*) Natl Acad Pr.

Panel on Global Climate Change Sciences in China, et al. China & Global Change: Opportunities for Collaboration. LC 92-62952. (Illus.). 240p. (Orig.). (C). 1992. pap. text 27.00 (*0-309-04841-9*) Natl Acad Pr.

Panel on Microlivestock, National Research Council, ed. Microlivestock: Little-Known Small Animals with a Promising Economic Future. 472p. 1991. pap. text 29.95 (*0-309-04295-X*) Natl Acad Pr.

Panel on Reactor-Related Options for Dispositioin, jt. auth. see National Research Council Staff.

Panel on Reproductive Health, National Research Co. Reproductive Health in Developing Countries: Expanding Dimensions, Building Solutions. Tsui, Amy O. et al, eds. LC 97-4867. 420p. (C). 1997. text 44.95 (*0-309-05644-6*, Joseph Henry Pr) Natl Acad Pr.

Panel on the Assessment of Wind Engineering Issues, et al. Wind & the Built Environment: U. S. Needs in Wind Engineering & Hazard Mitigation. 144p. (Orig.). (C). 1993. pap. text 35.00 (*0-309-04449-9*) Natl Acad Pr.

Panel on the Future Design & Implementation of U., et al. Finding Common Ground: U. S. Export Controls in a Changed Global Environment. 412p. 1991. 34.95 (*0-309-04392-1*) Natl Acad Pr.

Panel on the Government Role in Civilian Technolog, et al. The Government Role in Civilian Technology: Building a New Alliance. 240p. 1992. pap. text 22.95 (*0-309-04630-0*) Natl Acad Pr.

Panel Publishers, Inc. Staff. Multistate Corporate Tax Almanac, 2 Vol. Set, 1. write for info. (*1-878375-05-9*) Panel Pubs.

— Multistate Corporate Tax Almanac, 2 Vol. Set, 2. write for info. (*1-878375-06-7*) Panel Pubs.

— Multistate Corporate Tax Almanac, 2 Vol. Set, Set. pap. 185.00 (*1-878375-23-7*) Panel Pubs.

Panel to Study Gender Differences in Career Outcom. The Gender Gap in Science & Engineering: Illuminating the Differences in Career Outcomes of Ph.D.s. Long, J. Scott et al, eds. 450p. (Orig.). 1998. text 49.95 (*0-309-05580-6*) Natl Acad Pr.

Panella, Deborah S. Basics of Law Librarianship. (Haworth Series in Special Librarianship). 118p. (C). 1990. pap. text 14.95 (*0-86656-990-1*) Haworth Pr.

— Basics of Law Librarianship. (Haworth Series in Special Librarianship). 118p. (C). 1991. text 39.95 (*0-86656-989-8*) Haworth Pr.

*__Panella, Vincent.__ Cutler's Island: Caesar in Captivity. 192p. 2000. 23.00 (*0-89733-484-1*) Academy Chi Pubs.

Panem, Sandra. The Interferon Crusade. LC 84-17629. 109p. 1984. 26.95 (*0-8157-6900-8*); pap. 9.95 (*0-8157-6899-0*) Brookings.

Panem, Sandra, ed. Biotechnology: Implications for Public Policy. LC 85-48176. (Dialogues on Public Policy Ser.). 99p. 1986. pap. 10.95 (*0-8157-6903-2*) Brookings.

— Public Policy, Science, & Environmental Risk. LC 83-73029. 65p. 1983. pap. 10.95 (*0-8157-6901-6*) Brookings.

Panem, Sandra & Thier, Samuel O. The AIDS Bureaucracy. LC 87-22972. 208p. 1988. pap. text 11.95 (*0-674-01271-2*) HUP.

— The AIDS Bureaucracy: Why Society Failed to Meet the AIDS Crisis & How We Might Impove Our Response. LC 87-22972. (Illus.). 208p. 1988. 37.95 (*0-674-01270-4*) HUP.

Panepinto, Roshlind. Monarch Notes: Isak Dinesen's Out of Africa. 128p. 1988. pap. 4.50 (*0-671-67127-8*, Arco) Macmillan Gen Ref.

Panero, Jose L. Systematics of Pappobolus (Asteraceae-Heliantheae) Anderson, Christiane, ed. (Systematic Botany Monographs: Vol. 36). (Illus.). 195p. 1993. pap. 25.00 (*0-912861-36-3*) Am Soc Plant.

Panero, Julius & Zelnik, Martin. Human Dimension & Interior Space. (Illus.). 352p. 1979. 39.95 (*0-8230-7271-1*, Whitney Lib) Watsn-Guptill.

Panet, J. P., et al. Honduras & the Bay Islands: New Authorized Edition. 4th ed. (Central America Ser.). (Illus.). 288p. (Orig.). 1997. pap. 15.95 (*0-930016-23-8*) Pass Pr Trvl Line.

*__Panet, Jean-Pierre.__ Honduras & Bay Islands Guide. 5th ed. 336p. 1999. pap. 16.95 (*1-892975-00-9*) Open Rd Pub.

Panet, Peter G. Non-Profit Housing Development in Hawaii. 167p. (Orig.). (C). 1995. pap. text 30.00 (*0-7881-2517-6*) DIANE Pub.

Paneth, Nigel, et al. Brain Damage in the Preterm Infant. (Clinics in Developmental Medicine Ser.: No. 131). (Illus.). 300p. (C). 1995. 69.95 (*0-521-68300-9*) Cambridge U Pr.

*__Panetta, Clayann Gilliam, ed.__ Contrastive Rhetoric Revisited & Redefined. 224p. 2000. write for info. (*0-8058-3634-9*); pap. write for info. (*0 8058-3635-7*) L Erlbaum Assocs.

Panetta, P. V., jt. ed. see Angelopoulos, V.

Panfili, Natalie, jt. auth. see Kucera, Dennis C.

Panfilov, Alexander & Holden, Arun V., eds. Computational Biology of the Heart. LC 97-139642. 428p. 1997. 220.00 (*0-471-96020-9*) Wiley.

Panfilov, M., jt. ed. see Dmitrievsky, A.

*__Panfilov, Mikhail.__ Macroscale Models of Flow Through Highly Heterogeneous Porous Media. LC 99-86779. (Theory & Applications of Transport in Porous Media Ser.). 2000. write for info. (*0-7923-6176-8*) Kluwer Academic.

Panfilov, V. Z. Grammar & Logic. LC 68-15535. (Janua Linguarum, Ser. Minor: No. 63). (Orig.). 1968. pap. text 21.55 (*90-279-0591-6*) Mouton.

Pang, Alex, jt. ed. see Erbacher, Robert F.

Pang, Calvin C., jt. ed. see Lam, Stephen T.

Pang, Chia S. & Hock, Goh E. T'ai Chi: Ten Minutes to Health. LC 85-22388. (Illus.). 132p. (Orig.). 1986. pap. 16.95 (*0-916360-30-X*) CRCS Pubns CA.

Pang, Chien-Kuo. The State & Economic Transformation: The Taiwan Case. LC 91-41620. (Developing Economies of the Third World Ser.). 336p. 1992. text 10.00 (*0-8153-0635-0*) Garland.

Pang, Ching-Lin. Negotiating Identity in Contemporary Japan: The Case of the Kikokushijo. (Japanese Studies Ser.). 220p. 1999. 110.00 (*0-7103-0651-2*, Pub. by Kegan Paul Intl) Col U Pr.

Pang, Dachling, ed. Disorders of the Pediatric Spine. LC 94-9398. 694p. 1994. text 200.00 (*0-7817-0158-9*) Lppncott W & W.

Pang, Eul-Soo. Bahia in the First Brazilian Republic: Coronelismo & Oligarchies, 1889-1934. LC 78-2682. (Latin American Monographs: Ser. 2, No. 23). (Illus.). 294p. reprint ed. pap. 91.20 (*0-7837-4942-2*, 204460800004) Bks Demand.

— In Pursuit of Honor & Power: Noblemen of the Southern Cross in Nineteenth Century in Brazil. LC 86-7081. (Illus.). 355p. reprint ed. pap. 110.10 (*0-608-09239-8*, 205274300005) Bks Demand.

Pang, G. K. & McFarlane, A. G. An Expert Systems Approach to Computer-Aided Design of Multivariable Systems. (Lecture Notes in Control & Information Sciences: Vol. 89). (Illus.). xiii, 325p. 1988. 45.95 (*0-387-17356-0*) Spr-Verlag.

Pang, Hilda D. Pre-Columbian Art: Investigations & Insights. LC 91-23661. (Illus.). 330p. 1992. 70.00 (*0-8061-2379-6*) U of Okla Pr.

Pang Jeng Lo, Benjamin, et al. The Essence of T'ai Chi Ch'uan: The Literary Tradition. Inn, Martin et al, eds. (Illus.). 104p. 1979. pap. 11.95 (*0-913028-63-0*) North Atlantic.

Pang Jeng Lo, Benjamin, tr. see Chen Wei-Ming.

Pang, Jong-Shi, jt. auth. see Mangasarian, Olvi L.

Pang, Jong-Shi, jt. ed. see Ferris, Michael C.

Pang, Keum-Young C. Korean Elderly Women in America: Everyday Life, Health & Illness. (Immigrant Communities & Ethnic Minorities in the U. S. & Canada Ser.: No. 69). 1991. 59.50 (*0-404-19479-6*) AMS Pr.

*__Pang, Keum Young Chung.__ Virtuous Transcendence: Holistic Self-Cultivation & Self-Healing in Elderly Korean Immigrants. LC 99-55442. 258p. 2000. pap. text 29.95 (*0-7890-0929-3*) Haworth Pr.

— Virtuous Transcendence: Holistic Self-Cultivation & Self-Healing in Elderly Korean Immigrants. LC 99-55442. 258p. (C). 2000. lib. bdg. 49.95 (*0-7890-0928-5*) Haworth Pr.

*__Pang-Kwong, Li.__ Hong Kong from Britain to China: Political Cleavages, Electoral Dynamics & Institutional Changes. (Social & Political Studies from Hong Kong). 292p. 2000. text 74.95 (*0-7546-1122-1*, Pub. by Ashgate Pub) Ashgate Pub Co.

Pang-Kwong, Li, ed. Political Order & Power Transition in Hong Kong. 280p. 1998. pap. text 27.50 (*962-201-783-5*, Pub. by Chinese Univ) U of Mich Pr.

Pang, Peter K., ed. see Epple, A.

Pang, Peter Y., jt. auth. see Agarwal, Ravi P.

Pang, S. F., ed. Annual Physiology Symposium: Symposium Hong Kong, April 1998 - Symposium Tainan, October 1997. (Biological Signals & Receptors, Vol. 7, No. 5 (1998) Ser.: Vol. 7 No. 5). (Illus.). 58p. 1998. pap. 27.00 (*3-8055-6778-2*) S Karger.

Pang, S. F., et al, eds. Putative Melatonin Receptors in Peripheral Tissues. (Journal: Biological Signals: Vol. 2, No. 4, 1993). (Illus.). 64p. 1994. pap. 28.75 (*3-8055-5947-X*) S Karger.

*__Pang, S. F. & Shiu, S.Y.W.__ Receptor & Non-Receptor Mediated Acgtions of Melatonin: International Symposium held in Hong Kong, China, November 1999: Selected Papers. (Biological Signals & Receptors Ser.: 9). (Illus.). 82p. 2000. pap. 34.00 (*3-8055-7125-9*) S Karger.

Pang, S. F. & Tang, F., eds. Special Neuroendocrine Systems: Journal: Neuroendocrinology, Vol. 53, Suppl. 1, 1991. (Illus.). iv, 84p. 1991. pap. 54.00 (*3-8055-5357-9*) S Karger.

Pang, Stella W., et al, eds. Diagnostic Techniques for Semiconductor Materials Processing II: Materials Research Society Symposium Proceedings. (MRS Symposium Proceedings Ser.: Vol. 406). 585p. 1996. 67.00 (*1-55899-309-6*) Materials Res.

Pang, Stella W. & Chang, Shih-Chia, eds. Micromachining & Microfabrication Process Technology II, Vol. 2879. 376p. 1996. 76.00 (*0-8194-2277-0*) SPIE.

Pang, Stella W., jt. ed. see Chang, Shih-Chia.

Pang, T. Typhoid Fever: Strategies for the '90s. 300p. 1992. text 95.00 (*981-02-0953-3*) World Scientific Pub.

Pang, T. Y. On Tai Chi Chuan. (Illus.). 325p. (Orig.). 1988. pap. 25.00 (*0-9612070-1-9*) Tai Chi Schl Philos.

Pang, Tao. An Introduction to Computational Physics. LC 96-45574. (Illus.). 393p. (C). 1997. text 85.00 (*0-521-48143-0*); pap. text 42.95 (*0-521-48592-4*) Cambridge U Pr.

Pang, Trude & Shinoki, Amy. Keyboarding with Computer Applications. 176p. 1992. pap. text 29.95 (*0-89863-145-9*) Star Pub CA.

P

An Asterisk (*) at the beginning of an entry indicates that the title is appearing for the first time.

Pang, Valerie O. & Cheng, Li-Rong L., eds. Struggling to Be Heard: The Unmet Needs of Asian Pacific American Children. LC 97-47482. (SUNY Series, the Social Context of Education). 334p. (C). 1998. text 65.50 (*0-7914-3839-2*); pap. text 21.95 (*0-7914-3840-6*) State U NY Pr.

*__Pang, Valerie Ooka.__ Multicultural Education: A Caring-Centered, Reflective Approach. LC 00-36433. 2001. pap. write for info. (*0-07-236953-1*) McGraw.

Pang, Yang, jt. ed. see Hai-Cang Ren.

Pang-Yuan, Chi, et al. An Anthology of Contemporary Chinese Literature, 2 vols., Set. 1976. 50.00 (*0-295-95504-X*) U of Wash Pr.

Pang-Yuan, Chi, tr. see Hai-yin, Lin.

Pangaea Press Staff, ed. see Wing, Ralph.

Pangalis, Celia S., jt. auth. see Galaydh, Ali K.

Pangalis, Gerassimos A., ed. Malignant Lymphomas: Biology & Treatment, Vol. VIII. LC 95-33049. (ESO Monographs). (Illus.). 189p. 1995. 137.00 (*3-540-60122-8*) Spr-Verlag.

Pangalis, Gerassimos A. & Polliack, Aaron, eds. Benign & Malignant Lymphadenopathies: A Guide to Clinical & Laboratory Diagnosis. LC 92-49470. 338p. 1993. text 128.00 (*3-7186-5232-3*) Gordon & Breach.

Pangallo, Karen L. George Eliot: A Reference Guide, 1972-1987. (Reference Guides to Literature Ser.). 335p. 1989. 50.00 (*0-8161-8973-0*, Hall Reference) Macmillan.

Pangallo, Karen L., ed. The Critical Response to George Eliot, 11. LC 93-41224. (Critical Responses in Arts & Letters Ser.: No. 11). 256p. 1994. lib. bdg. 62.95 (*0-313-28773-2*, Greenwood Pr) Greenwood.

Panganiban, J. Villar. Concise English - Taglog Dictionary. 170p. 1994. pap. 14.95 (*0-8048-1962-9*) Tuttle Pubng.

Pangarazi, Robert P. Teaching Elementary Physical Education. LC 96-24587. 212p. (C). 1996. pap. text 29.00 (*0-205-19362-5*) P-H.

Pangborn, Brenda J., ed. Culinary Counterpoint: Detroit Symphony Orchestra Cookbook. LC 83-71434. (Illus.). 432p. (Orig.). 1983. pap. 12.00 (*0-9611348-0-1*) Detroit Symphony.

Pangborn, Cyrus R. Zoroastrianism. 178p. 1982. text 25.00 (*0-89891-006-4*) Advent Bks Div.

Pangborn, Edgar. A Mirror for Observers. 1993. reprint ed. lib. bdg. 18.95 (*0-89968-358-4*, Lghtyr Pr) Buccaneer Bks.

Pangborn, Georgia W. The Wind at Midnight. 1989. lib. bdg. 25.00 (*0-910489-19-X*) Scream Pr.

*__Pangborn, Georgia Wood.__ The Wind at Midnight. Salmonson, Jessica Amanda, ed. xx, 184p. 1999. 39.50 (*1-899562-76-1*) Ash-Tree.

Pangborn, M. & Almeida, J. Cardiolipin Antigens. (WHO Monograph Ser.: No. 6). 63p. 1951. 5.00 (*92-4-140006-4*) World Health.

Pangburn, Robert P. No Better Place: Than in the Center of His Presence. 308p. 1993. pap. write for info. (*0-9638693-0-2*) Pearl Pubng.

Panger, Daniel. The Dance of the Wild Mouse. LC 79-51409. 240p. (C). 1979. 9.95 (*0-9601428-4-3*); pap. 7.95 (*0-9601428-5-1*) Entwhistle Bks.

— Soldier Boys. LC 87-62533. 240p. (Orig.). (C). 1988. pap. 16.95 (*0-89390-102-4*) Resource Pubns.

Panger, Janet S., ed. see Frye, Nora.

Pangestu, Mari, jt. auth. see Bora, Bijit.

Pangestu, Mari, jt. ed. see Soesastro, Hadi.

Pangis, Elly, tr. see Joy, Janet L.

Pangle, Lorraine S. & Pangle, Thomas L. The Learning of Liberty: The Educational Ideas of the American Founders. LC 92-29956. (American Political Thought Ser.). 370p. (Orig.). (C). 1995. pap. 19.95 (*0-7006-0746-3*) U Pr of KS.

Pangle, Mary A., jt. auth. see Forte, Imogene.

Pangle, Sarag F. Faubion: The Faubions. (Illus.). 82p. 1997. reprint ed. pap. 16.00 (*0-8328-8538-X*); reprint ed. lib. bdg. 26.00 (*0-8328-8537-1*) Higginson Bk Co.

Pangle, Thomas L. The Ennobling of Democracy: The Challenge of the Postmodern Age. (Series in Constitutional Thought). 288p. 1993. reprint ed. pap. 14.95 (*0-8018-4635-8*) Johns Hopkins.

— Montesquieu's Philosophy of Liberalism: A Commentary on "The Spirit of the Laws" 1994. lib. bdg. 25.00 (*0-226-64543-6*) U Ch Pr.

— Montesquieu's Philosophy of Liberalism: A Commentary on the Spirit of the Laws. LC 73-77139. (Illus.). x, 346p. 1989. pap. text 18.00 (*0-226-64545-2*) U Ch Pr.

— The Spirit of Modern Republicanism: The Moral Vision of the American Founders & the Philosophy of Locke. 352p. 1994. 24.95 (*0-226-64540-1*) U Ch Pr.

Pangle, Thomas L., ed. The Roots of Political Philosophy: Ten Forgotten Socratic Dialogues. LC 87-47550. 424p. (C). 1987. text 49.95 (*0-8014-1986-7*) Cornell U Pr.

Pangle, Thomas L. & Ahrensdorf, Peter J. Justice among Nations: On the Moral Basis of Power & Peace. LC 98-33168. 400p. 1999. 45.00 (*0-7006-0959-8*) U Pr of KS.

Pangle, Thomas L., jt. auth. see Pangle, Lorraine S.

Pangle, Thomas L., jt. ed. see Palmer, Michael.

Pangle, Thomas L., ed. see Plato.

Pangle, Thomas L., ed. see Strauss, Leo, et al.

Pangle, Thomas L., tr. & notes see Plato.

Pangman, Julie K. Guide to Environmental Issues, 1995. (Illus.). 84p. 1997. reprint ed. pap. text 30.00 (*0-7881-3960-6*) DIANE Pub.

Pangman, Julie K., ed. Guide to Environmental Issues. (Illus.). 84p. (Orig.). (C). 1994. pap. text 25.00 (*0-7881-1415-8*) DIANE Pub.

Pangonis, William J. Tables of Light Scattering Functions for Spherical Particles. LC 56-12604. 123p. reprint ed. pap. 38.20 (*0-7837-3790-4*, 204361000010) Bks Demand.

Pangonis, William J. & Heller, Wilfried. Angular Scattering Functions for Spherical Particles. LC 60-8930. 227p. reprint ed. pap. 70.40 (*0-7837-3828-5*, 204364900010) Bks Demand.

Pangotra, Prem, jt. ed. see Huddleston, Jack.

Pangrazi, Robert B., jt. auth. see Corbin, Charles B.

Pangrazi, Robert P. Dynamic Physical Education for Elementary School Children. 12th ed. 725p. 1997. 70.00 (*0-205-26905-2*) P-H.

Pangrazi, Robert P. Dynamic Physical Education for Elementary School Children: Examination Copy. 12th ed. 752p. (C). 1997. text. write for info. (*0-205-27654-7*, T7654-1) Allyn.

— Elementary Physical Education Activities. LC 96-46299. 91p. (J). (gr. 5-6). 1996. pap. 17.00 (*0-205-19365-X*) P-H.

— Lesson Plans for Classroom Teachers: Kindergarten Through 2nd Grade. LC 96-46298. 87p. (C). 1996. pap. text 17.00 (*0-205-19363-3*) Allyn.

*__Pangrazi, Robert P.__ Lesson Plans for Dynamic Physical Education for Elementary School Children. 4th ed. 291p. 2000. pap. 21.33 (*0-205-32631-5*) Allyn.

— Lessons Plans for Classroom Teachers: Third & Fourth Grades. LC 96-46651. 88p. (C). 1996. pap. text 17.00 (*0-205-19364-1*) Allyn.

Pangrazi, Robert P. & Darst, Paul W. Dynamic Physical Education for Secondary School Students. 3rd ed. LC 96-13396. 458p. 1996. 79.00 (*0-205-19982-8*) Allyn.

Pangrazi, Robert P. & Hastad, Douglas N. Physical Fitness in the Elementary School. 110p. (Orig.). 1989. pap. 8.00 (*0-88314-426-3*, A4263) AAHPERD.

Pangrazi, Robert P., et al. Racquetball. (Sport for Life Ser.). (C). 1997. pap. text 12.66 (*0-673-18313-0*, Scott Frsmn) Addson-Wesley Educ.

Pangrazzi, Arnaldo. Your Words in Prayer in Time of Illness. 72p. (Orig.). 1982. pap. 1.95 (*0-8189-0417-8*) Alba.

*__Pangritz, Andreas.__ Karl Barth in the Theology of Dietrich Bonhoeffer. 168p. 2000. pap. 20.00 (*0-8028-4281-X*) Eerdmans.

Pangstey, Y. P. High Altitudes of the Himalaya: Biogeography, Ecology & Conservation. 1994. pap. 232.50 (*0-7855-0449-4*, Pub. by Ratna Pustak Bhandar) St Mut.

Pangtay, Susana C. Petroquimica y Sociedad. (Ciencia para Todos Ser.). (SPA.). pap. 6.99 (*968-16-2669-9*, Pub. by Fondo) Continental Bk.

Panholzer, Rudolf, ed. Proceedings of the Fourth International Symposium on Integrated Ferroelectrics. (Illus.). (Orig.). (C). 1992. pap. 55.00 (*0-9634605-0-1*) ISOI Ferroelect.

Panhorst, Don. How Ordinary People Can Become Extraordinary Leaders: Empowerment Principles for Leadership Success. LC 92-75737. 213p. 1993. 24.95 (*0-9634723-4-8*) Baton Pub.

Panhuis, Dirk G. The Communicative Perspective in the Sentence: A Study of Latin Word Order. (Studies in Language Companion: No. 11). viii, 172p. 1982. 52.00 (*90-272-3010-2*) J Benjamins Pubng Co.

Panhuys. Yearbook of the AAA, 1974. (Association of Attenders & Alumni of the Hague Academy of International Law Ser: No. 44). 1977. pap. text 75.50 (*90-247-1945-3*) Kluwer Academic.

Pani, A. Hygiene in Mexico. 1976. lib. bdg. 59.95 (*0-8490-2029-8*) Gordon Pr.

Pani, Binita. Indian Scriptures & the Life Divine. (C). 1993. 32.00 (*81-7024-592-3*, Pub. by Ashish Pub Hse) S Asia.

Pani, Jiwan. Sonal Mansingh: Contribution to Odissi Dance. (C). 1992. 5.00 (*81-7304-002-8*, Pub. by Manohar) S Asia.

Pani, Narendar. Redefining Conservatism: An Essay on the Bias of India's Economic Reform. LC 93-48277. 1994. 28.50 (*0-8039-9164-9*) Sage.

Pani, R. N. Integral Education: Thought & Practice. xxii, 670p. 1997. 67.00 (*81-7024-903-1*, Pub. by APH Pubng) Nataraj Bks.

Paniagua, Freddy A. Assessing & Treating Culturally Diverse Clients: A Practical Guide. LC 94-17662. (Multicultural Aspects of Counseling Ser.: Vol. 4). 136p. 1994. pap. 18.95 (*0-8039-5496-4*) Sage.

— Assessing & Treating Culturally Diverse Clients: A Practical Guide. 2nd ed. LC 97-45260. (Multicultural Aspects of Counseling Ser.: Vol. 4). 161p. 1998. 48.50 (*0-7619-1049-2*); pap. write for info. (*0-7619-1050-6*) Sage.

— Assessing & Treating Culturally Diverse Clients: A Practical Guide, No. 4. LC 94-17662. (Multicultural Aspects of Counseling Ser.: Vol. 4). 136p. 1994. 42.00 (*0-8039-5495-6*) Sage.

Paniaqua Soto, Jose R. Vocabulario Basico de la Arquitectura: Basic Architecture Vocabulary. 5th ed. (SPA.). 408p. 1987. pap. 24.00 (*0-7859-5059-1*) Fr & Eur.

Panic, W. H., ed. see International Union of Pure & Applied Chemistry.

*__Paniccia, Patti.__ Work Smarts for Women: The Essential Sex Discrimination Survival Guide. LC 99-41292. 480p. 2000. pap. 14.00 (*0-345-42261-9*) Ballantine Pub Grp.

Paniccia, Renato, jt. ed. see Cornia, Giovanni Andrea.

Panicelli, Ida, et al. Fellini, Costumes & Fashion: Costumes & Fashion. (Illus.). 200p. 1996. pap. text 35.00 (*88-86158-82-3*, Pub. by Charta) Dist Art Pubs.

Panich, Catherine. Sanctuary? Remembering postwar immigration / LC 91-174319. 1988. write for info. (*0-04-330386-2*) Routledge.

Panichas, G., ed. Simone Weil Reader. 1994. pap. 9.95 (*0-679-50673-X*) McKay.

Panichas, George A. The Burden of Vision: Dostoevsky's Spiritual Art. LC 84-25925. 216p. 1985. pap. 8.95 (*0-89526-821-3*) Regnery Pub.

— The Courage of Judgment: Essays in Criticism, Culture, & Society with a Forward by Austin Warren. LC 81-4050. 319p. 1982. pap. 98.90 (*0-608-05196-9*, 206573300001) Bks Demand.

— The Critic As Conservator: Essays in Literature, Society, & Culture. LC 91-32217. 262p. 1992. text 49.95 (*0-8132-0762-2*) Cath U Pr.

— The Critical Legacy of Irving Babbitt. LC 98-73010. 170p. 1998. 24.95 (*1-882926-22-6*) ISI Books.

— Growing Wings to Overcome Gravity: Criticism As the Pursuit of Virtue. LC 98-33378. 360p. 1999. text 35.00 (*0-86554-606-1*, H457); pap. text 20.00 (*0-86554-618-5*, P177) Mercer Univ Pr.

— The Reverent Discipline: Essays in Literary Criticism & Culture. LC 73-15749. 488p. 1974. reprint ed. pap. 151.30 (*0-7837-9507-6*, 206025700005) Bks Demand.

Panichas, George A., ed. In Continuity: The Last Essays of Austin Warren. 192p. 1996. text 32.00 (*0-86554-501-4*, MUP/H393) Mercer Univ Pr.

— Modern Age: The First Twenty-Five Years: a Selection. LC 88-8600. 914p. (C). 1988. text 17.50 (*0-86597-061-0*) Liberty Fund.

— Modern Age: The First Twenty-Five Years: A Selection. LC 88-8600. 914p. (C). 1988. pap. 8.50 (*0-86597-062-9*) Liberty Fund.

Panichas, George A. & Ryn, Claes G., eds. Irving Babbitt in Our Time. LC 85-21260. 256p. 1986. 27.95 (*0-8132-0625-1*) Cath U Pr.

Panichas, George A., ed. see Babbitt, Irving.

Panichas, George A., ed. see Weil, Simone.

Panichas, George E. Larry Fink: Fish & Wine, Larry Fink's Photographs of Portugal. (Illus.). 24p. 1997. pap. 8.50 (*0-9660322-0-9*) Lafayette Coll.

Panichas, George E., jt. ed. see Gruen, Lori.

Panichello, Joseph J. X-Ray Repair: A Comprehensive Guide to the Installation & Servicing of Radiographic Equipment. LC 97-28600. (Illus.). 284p. 1998. text 59.95 (*0-398-06815-1*) C C Thomas.

Panichi, Louisa, tr. see Del Conde, Teresa, ed.

Panici, William F., ed. Three French Short Verse Satirists: Marot, Magny, & Du Bellay. LC 90-3800. (Studies in Comparative Literature). 152p. 1990. reprint ed. 15.00 (*0-8240-0010-2*) Garland.

*__Panico, Alfonso E.__ The Italians of America. (Illus.). 120p. 1999. pap. 20.00 (*0-9666075-5-4*) A E Panico.

Panico, Alfonso E. The Italians of the New New Haven. LC 98-91672. (Illus.). 60p. 1998. pap. 12.95 (*0-9666075-0-3*) A E Panico.

Panico, Ambrose P. Discipline & the Classroom Community: Recapturing Control of Our Schools. (Illus.). 200p. 1998. pap. 29.95 (*1-878016-18-0*) Stylex Pub.

Panico, Carlo & Salvadori, Neri, eds. Post-Keynesian Theory of Growth & Distribution. (International Library of Critical Writings in Economics: Vol. 21). 484p. 1993. 210.00 (*1-85278-613-2*) E Elgar.

Panico, Carlo, jt. ed. see Musella, Marco.

Panico, Marie J., jt. auth. see Bejel, Emilio.

Panico, R., ed. see International Union of Pure & Applied Chemistry.

Panidis, John P., ed. Cardiac Ultrasound. (Practical Cardiac Diagnosis Ser.). (Illus.). 354p. 1995. pap. 59.95 (*0-86542-275-3*) Blackwell Sci.

Panigrahi, Lalita. British Social Policy & Female Infanticide in India. 1972. 16.00 (*0-8364-2617-7*, Pub. by M Manoharial) S Asia.

Panigrahi, P. K. Political Elite in Tribal Society. LC 98-901418. 1998. 30.00 (*81-7169-496-9*, Pub. by Commonwealth) S Asia.

Panigrahi, S. & Ting, K. C. Artificial Intelligence for Biology & Agriculture. LC 98-21022. 1998. 105.00 (*0-7923-5098-7*) Kluwer Academic.

Panigrahi, Sarat C. Testing, Evaluation & Measurements in Metal Casting. 304p. (C). 1987. 15.00 (*81-204-0171-9*, Pub. by Oxford IBH) S Asia.

Panigrahy, Dibakar. New Dimensions in Modern Management. 130p. (C). 1994. pap. 75.00 (*81-85880-24-7*, Pub. by Print Hse) St Mut.

Panik, Michael J. Fundamentals of Convex Analysis: Duality, Separation, Representation, & Resolution. LC 93-17082. (Theory & Decision Library, Series B, Mathematical & Statistical Methods: Vol. 24). 320p. (C). 1993. text 192.50 (*0-7923-2279-7*) Kluwer Academic.

— Linear Programming: Mathematics, Theory & Algorithms. (Applied Optimization Ser.: Vol. 2). 508p. (C). 1996. text 217.50 (*0-7923-3782-4*) Kluwer Academic.

Panik, Michele, jt. auth. see Paz, Jaime.

Panik, Sharon, jt. auth. see Parke, Marilyn.

Panikar, K. A., ed. Malayalam Short Stories. 152p. 1981. 16.95 (*0-318-36917-6*) Asia Bk Corp.

Paniker, Ayyappa, ed. Making of Indian Literature: A Consolidated Report of Workshops on Literary Translation, 1986-88. (C). 1991. 17.50 (*81-7201-115-6*, Pub. by Indian Pubs) S Asia.

Paniker, K. A. International Cooperation in the Higher Education of Science & Technology. (C). 1985. 32.50 (*81-204-0067-4*, Pub. by Oxford IBH) S Asia.

*__Paniker, K. Ayyappa, ed.__ Medieval Indian Literature. 1999. 38.00 (*81-260-0648-X*, Pub. by Rabindra Bhawn) S Asia.

Paniker, K. Ayyappa, ed. Indian English Literature since Independence. 220p. 1991. text 25.00 (*81-85218-34-X*, Pub. by Prestige) Advent Bks Div.

Panikkar, K. Madhu. Revolution in Africa. LC 74-27428. 202p. 1975. reprint ed. lib. bdg. 59.50 (*0-8371-7901-7*, PARA, Greenwood Pr) Greenwood.

Panikkar, Kavalam N. Against Lord & State: Religion & Peasant Uprisings in Malabar (1836-1921) (Illus.). 248p. 1989. 29.95 (*0-19-562139-5*) OUP.

— Communalism in India: History, Politics & Culture. (C). 1991. 21.50 (*81-85425-51-5*, Pub. by Manohar) S Asia.

— Culture, Ideology, Hegemony: Intellectuals & Social Consciousness in Colonial India. (C). 1995. 22.00 (*81-85229-02-3*, Pub. by Manohar) S Asia.

— Karimkutty & the Lone Tusker. (C). 1992. pap. text 5.00 (*81-7046-092-1*, Pub. by Seagull Bks) S Asia.

— Right to Rule & the Domain of the Sun. (C). 1989. pap. 10.00 (*81-7046-071-9*, Pub. by Seagull Bks) S Asia.

Panikkar, M. V., jt. auth. see Usha, Devi K.

Panikkar, Raimon. The Cosmotheandric Experience: Emerging Religious Consciousness. LC 92-46195. 150p. 1993. 27.00 (*0-88344-862-9*) Orbis Bks.

— Cultural Disarmament: The Way to Peace. Barr, Robert, tr. LC 95-18715. 144p. (Orig.). 1995. pap. 22.95 (*0-664-25549-3*) Westminster John Knox.

— Invisible Harmony: Essays on Contemplation & Responsibility. Cargas, Harry J., ed. LC 95-10456. 208p. 1995. pap. 20.00 (*0-8006-2609-5*, 1-2609, Fortress Pr) Augsburg Fortress.

Panikkar, Raimundo. The Trinity & the Religious Experience of Man: Icon, Person, Mystery. LC 73-77329. 98p. reprint ed. pap. 30.40 (*0-608-12662-4*, 202512200042) Bks Demand.

— Worship & Secular Man: An Essay on the Liturgical Nature of Man. LC 72-93339. 119p. reprint ed. pap. 36.90 (*0-608-12664-0*, 202512300042) Bks Demand.

Panikkar, Raimundo, et al. Blessed Simplicity: The Monk As Universal Archetype. 224p. (Orig.). 1984. 17.95 (*0-8164-0531-X*) Harper SF.

Panikkar, Ramon. The Intrareligious Dialogue. rev. ed. LC 98-49313. 192p. 1999. pap. 19.95 (*0-8091-3763-1*) Paulist Pr.

Panikkar, Shivaji. Sapta Matrka: Worship & Sculptures. LC 96-912033. (C). 1997. 120.00 (*81-246-0074-0*, Pub. by DK Pubs Ind) S Asia.

Panikkar, T. K. Malabar & Its Folk. 288p. 1986. reprint ed. 12.00 (*0-8364-1730-5*, Pub. by Manohar) S Asia.

Panimolle, Salvatore A. Like the Deer That Yearns. 128p. (C). 1996. pap. 39.95 (*0-85439-319-6*, Pub. by St Paul Pubns) St Mut.

Panimolle, Salvatore A., ed. Like the Deer That Yearns: Listening to the Word & Prayer. LC 95-44297. 1998. pap. 12.95 (*1-879007-16-9*) St Bedes Pubns.

Panin, George, ed. see Zetlin, Mikhail O.

Panin, V. E., ed. Physical Mesomechanics of Heterogeneous Media & Computer-Aided Design of Materials. 450p. 1995. boxed set 130.00 (*1-898326-19-3*, Pub. by CISP) Balogh.

Panin, V. E., et al. Design of New Materials & Strengthening Technologies. 140p. 1995. pap. 65.00 (*1-898326-20-7*, Pub. by CISP) Balogh.

Panini. Astadhyayi of Panini: In Roman Transliteration by Sumitra M. Katre. LC 86-19338. (Texas Linguistics Ser.). 1396p. reprint ed. pap. 200.00 (*0-608-08704-1*, 206922700003) Bks Demand.

Panini, M. N. From the Female Eye: Account of Women Field Workers Studying Their Own Communities. (C). 1991. 12.50 (*81-7075-020-2*, Pub. by Hindustan) S Asia.

Panis, Constantijn W. A., jt. auth. see Bikson, Tora K.

Panis, Patrice. Essential Cuisine Vol. I: A New Respect for Food, a New Respect for You! Amodéo, Corine A., ed. (Illus.). 264p. 1997. spiral bd. 19.95 (*0-9659375-5-0*, Eq 500) Equiforme.

*__Panisch, Leonard S.__ A Difficult Trade: The Baseball Mystery. 212p. 2000. 24.95 (*1-885003-63-3*, Pub. by R D Reed Pubs) Midpt Trade.

Panish, Jon. The Color of Jazz: Race & Representation in Postwar American Culture. LC 97-11364. 190p. 1997. 45.00 (*1-57806-035-4*); pap. 18.00 (*1-57806-033-8*) U Pr of Miss.

Panish, M. B. & Temkin, H. Gas Source Molecular Beam Epitaxu: Growth & Properties of Phosphorus Containing III-V Heterostructures. (Materials Science Ser.: Vol. 26). (Illus.). 450p. 1993. write for info. (*3-540-56540-X*) Spr-Verlag.

— Gas Source Molecular Beam Epitaxy: Growth & Properties Containing III-Vheterostructures. LC 93-7842. (Materials Science Ser.: Vol. 26). 1993. 75.95 (*0-387-56540-X*) Spr-Verlag.

Panisha. The New Astrology. 1990. pap. 30.95 (*0-86690-346-1*, 2813-014) Am Fed Astrologers.

Panisset, Maurice, jt. auth. see Sonea, Sorin.

*__Panisset, Ulysses B.__ International Health Statecraft: Foreign Policy & Public Health in Peru's Cholera Epidemic. LC 99-59182. 288p. 2000. 47.50 (*0-7618-1601-1*) U Pr of Amer.

Panitch, Leo. The Communist Manifesto Now: The Socialist Register, 1998. 1998. pap. text 18.00 (*0-85345-935-5*, Pub. by Monthly Rev) NYU Pr.

— Global Capitalism Versus Democracy: Socialist Register 1999. 1999. pap. text 23.00 (*0-85345-948-7*, Pub. by Monthly Rev) NYU Pr.

Panitch, Leo, ed. Are There Alternatives? Socialist Register 1996. 342p. 1997. pap. 18.00 (*0-85345-984-3*, Pub. by Lat Am Bur) Monthly Rev.

— The Canadian State: Political Economy & Political Power. 1977. pap. text 18.95 (*0-8020-6322-5*) U of Toronto Pr.

— Ruthless Criticism of All That Exists: Socialist Register, 1997. 342p. 1998. pap. 18.00 (*0-85345-995-9*, Pub. by Monthly Rev) NYU Pr.

Panitch, Leo & Leys, Colin, eds. Necessary & Unnecessary Utopias: Socialist Register 2000. LC 99-40304. 300p. 1999. pap. 23.00 (*1-58367-021-1*, Pub. by Monthly Rev) NYU Pr.

*__Panitch, Leo & Leys, Colin, eds.__ Socialist Register, 1999: Global Capitalism Versus Democracy. 250p. 1999. 55.00 (*0-85036-481-7*, Pub. by MRLN); pap. 25.00 (*0-85036-480-9*, Pub. by MRLN) Paul & Co Pubs.

Panitch, Leo & Wood, Ellen M., eds. The Socialist Register, 1995: Why Not Capitalism. 304p. (Orig.). (C). 1995. pap. text 18.00 (*0-85345-964-9*, Pub. by Merlin) Monthly Rev.

P

An Asterisk (*) at the beginning of an entry indicates that the title is appearing for the first time.

Panitch, Leo, jt. ed. see Miliband, Ralph.

Panitz, Esther L. Simon Wolf: Private Conscience & Public Image. LC 86-45378. (Illus.). 224p. 1987. 35.00 (*0-8386-3293-9*) Lubrecht & Cramer.

Paniz, Neela. Bombay Cafe Cookbook. LC 97-52728. (Illus.). 224p. 1998. pap. 17.95 (*0-89815-935-0*) Ten Speed Pr.

***Panizza, Letizia, ed.** Women in Italian Renaissance Culture & Society. (Legenda Ser.). 540p. (C). 2000. pap. 69.50 (*1-900755-09-2*, Pub. by E H R C) David Brown.

Panizza, M. Environmental Geomorphology. LC 96-27525. (Developments in Earth Surface Processes Ser.: Vol. 4). 284p. 1996. text 218.75 (*0-444-89830-1*) Elsevier.

Panizzi, Antonio R., jt. auth. see Schaefer, Carl W.

Panizzon, R. G., jt. auth. see Goldschmidt, H. L.

***Panja.** Many Indias, Many Literatures: New Critical Essays. 1999. 20.00 (*81-86423-34-6*, Pub. by Gyan Publishing Hse) S Asia.

Panjabi, Camellia. The Essential Curry Kit. 1998. pap. 34.95 (*0-8048-3161-0*) Tuttle Pubng.

— The Great Curries of India. LC 94-44460. 192p. 1995. 30.00 (*0-684-80383-6*) S&S Trade.

Panjabi, M. M. & White, Augusta A. Biomechanics in the Musculoskeletal System. (Illus.). 255p. write for info. (*0-443-06585-3*, W B Saunders Co) Harcrt Hlth Sci Grp.

Panjabi, Ranee K. The Earth Summit at Rio: Politics, Economics, & the Environment. LC 97-11423. 432p. 1997. text 55.00 (*1-55553-283-7*) NE U Pr.

Panjani, Shakuntala. Pancadasi: A Critical Study. 1985. 29.95 (*0-318-37028-X*) Asia Bk Corp.

Panje, William R. & Moran, William J. Free Flap Reconstruction of the Head & Neck. (American Academy of Facial Plastic & Reconstructive Surgery Monograph). (Illus.). 112p. 1989. text 72.00 (*0-86577-303-3*) Thieme Med Pubs.

Panje, William R., et al. Musculocutaneous Flap Reconstruction of the Head & Neck. LC 89-3746. 256p. 1989. reprint ed. pap. 79.40 (*0-608-04678-7*, 2065399000004) Bks Demand.

Panje, William R., jt. ed. see Anand, Vijay K.

(Proceedings of Symposia in Applied Mathematics. LC 86-3306. (Proceedings of Symposia in Applied Mathematics Ser.: Vol. 35). 127p. 1986. reprint ed. pap. 29.00 (*0-8218-0096-5*, PSAPM/35) Am Math.

Panjer, Harry H., ed. see Boyle, Phelim P., et al.

Panjwani, H. Ergonomics: Practical Guide. (Engineering Ser.). 1992. text. write for info. (*0-442-00742-6*, VNR) Wiley.

Pank, Rachel. Delilah Digs for Treasure. (Blue Bananas Ser.). (Illus.). 1997. pap. 4.99 (*0-7497-2632-6*) London Brdge.

— Sonia & Barnie & the Noise in the Night. (J). 1991. pap. 13.95 (*0-590-44657-6*) Scholastic Inc.

Pankake, Anita M. Implementation: Making Things Happen. LC 97-48822. (School Leadership Library). 160p. 1998. 29.95 (*1-883001-53-6*) Eye On Educ.

Pankake, Anita M., Jr. & Burnett, I. Emett. The Effective Elementary School Principal. (Effective School Administration Ser.: No. 3). (Illus.). 128p. 1990. 21.95 (*0-88280-094-9*) ETC Pubns.

Pankau, Ed. The Investigator's Guidebook: The Ultimate Resource for Background Checks, Asset Searches & People Locates. 1997. pap. 35.00 (*1-891247-09-3*) Thomas Investigative.

Pankau, Edmund J. Check It Out! rev. ed. LC 98-17088. 160p. 1998. pap. 14.95 (*0-8092-2900-5*, 290050, Contemporary Bks) NTC Contemp Pub Co.

— Check It Out: A Top Investigator Tells You How to Use Publicly Available Sources. 160p. 1992. pap. 12.95 (*0-8092-3945-0*) NTC Contemp Pub Co.

— Check It Out: Everyone's Guide to Investigation. 146p. (Orig.). 1991. pap. 19.95 (*0-89896-444-X*) Larksdale.

— Hide Your Assets & Disappear: A Step-by-Step Guide to Vanishing Without a Trace. LC 98-50354. 224p. 1999. 22.00 (*0-06-018394-2*) HarpC.

***Pankau, Edmund J.** Hide Your Assets & Disappear: A Step-by-Step Guide to Vanishing Without a Trace. LC 98-50354. 240p. 2000. pap. 14.00 (*0-06-098750-2*, ReganBks) HarperTrade.

Pankau, Edmund J. How to Make One Hundred Thousand Dollars a Year as a Private Investigator. (Illus.). 128p. 1993. pap. 21.95 (*0-87364-720-3*) Paladin Pr.

Panken, Shirley. The Joy of Suffering: The Psychoanalytic Theory & Therapy of Masochism. LC 73-96532. 256p. 1973. 35.00 (*0-87668-065-1*) Aronson.

— The Joy of Suffering: The Psychoanalytic Theory & Therapy of Masochism. LC 83-15841. 264p. 1993. 40.00 (*1-56821-120-1*) Aronson.

— Virginia Woolf & the "Lust of Creation" A Psychoanalytic Exploration. LC 86-29991. 336p. (C). 1987. text 64.50 (*0-88706-200-8*); pap. text 24.95 (*0-88706-201-6*) State U NY Pr.

Pankey, Eric. Cenotaph: Poems. LC 99-31088. 88p. 2000. 22.00 (*0-375-40764-2*) Knopf.

— Heartwood: Poems. LC 98-18689. 72p. 1998. reprint ed. pap. 12.95 (*0-914061-78-X*) Orchises Pr.

— The Late Romances: Poems. LC 96-36676. 88p. 1997. 2.99 (*0-679-45454-3*) Knopf.

— The Late Romances: Poems. 1999. pap. 13.00 (*0-679-76605-7*) Knopf.

***Pankey, George A.** Sheffield Dawson Guide to Urinary Tract Infections. 70p. 2000. pap. 23.95 (*0-9668202-5-8*) S Dawson Pubs.

Pankey, Lindsey D. & Davis, William J. A Philosophy of the Practice of Dentistry. Sanitate, Veronica, ed. (Illus.). 323p. 1987. text 69.50 (*0-944742-01-7*); audio 127.50 (*0-944742-02-5*) Med Coll of OH Pr.

Pankey, Robert. To Fall from Athletics Gracefully. 156p. 1993. per. 12.95 (*0-8403-8962-0*) Kendall-Hunt.

Pankhurst. William Thompson. 71.95 (*0-7453-0401-X*); 25.95 (*0-7453-0517-2*) Pluto GBR.

Pankhurst, C., et al, eds. Biological Indicators of Soil Health. LC 97-13061. 464p. 1997. text 110.00 (*0-85199-158-0*) OUP.

Pankhurst, Emmeline. My Own Story. LC 85-952. (Illus.). 364p. 1985. reprint ed. lib. bdg. 59.75 (*0-313-24926-1*, PMOS, Greenwood Pr) Greenwood.

Pankhurst, F. C., jt. auth. see Ower, Ernest.

Pankhurst, Helen. Gender, Development & Identity: An Ethiopian Study. LC 92-35076. 192p. (C). 1992. text 65.00 (*1-85649-157-9*, Pub. by Zed Books); text 25.00 (*1-85649-158-7*, Pub. by Zed Books) St Martin.

Pankhurst, James, et al, eds. Learnability & Second Languages: A Book of Readings. vi, 208p. 1989. pap. 46.15 (*90-6765-389-6*) Mouton.

Pankhurst, Jerry G. & Sacks, Michael P., eds. Contemporary Soviet Society: Sociological Perspectives. LC 80-22324. 272p. 1980. 49.95 (*0-275-90532-2*, C0532, Praeger Pubs) Greenwood.

Pankhurst, Jerry G., jt. auth. see Houseknecht, Sharon K.

Pankhurst, Jerry G., jt. ed. see Sacks, Michael P.

Pankhurst, Richard. The Ethiopian Borderlands: Essays in Regional History from Ancient Times to the End of the 18th Century. LC 97-10205. 1997. write for info. (*0-932415-18-0*) Red Sea Pr.

— The Ethiopians. LC 98-9224. (Peoples of Africa Ser.). (Illus.). 320p. 1998. 59.95 (*0-631-18468-6*) Blackwell Pubs.

***Pankhurst, Richard.** The Ethiopians. 2000. pap. 27.95 (*0-631-22493-9*) Blackwell Pubs.

Pankhurst, Richard. History of the Ethiopian Borderlands. LC 97-10205. 1995. pap. 18.95 (*0-932415-19-9*) Red Sea Pr.

— An Introduction to the Medical History of Ethiopia. LC 90-50990. 340p. (C). 1990. 45.00 (*0-932415-44-X*); pap. 14.95 (*0-932415-45-8*) Red Sea Pr.

— A Social History of Ethiopia. LC 92-14746. (Illus.). 385p. 1992. 49.95 (*0-932415-85-7*); pap. 16.95 (*0-932415-86-5*) Red Sea Pr.

Pankhurst, Richard & Gerard, Denis. Ethiopia Photographed: Original Photographs from 1860 to 1936. LC 96-36344. (Illus.). 1997. 127.50 (*0-7103-0504-4*, Pub. by Kegan Paul Intl) Col U Pr.

Pankhurst, Richard J. Practical Taxonomic Computering. (Illus.). 160p. 1991. 45.00 (*0-340-55149-6*, A5557, Pub. by E A) Routledge.

Pankhurst, Richard K. The Ethiopian Royal Chronicles: Extracts. LC 68-81028. (Illus.). 240p. reprint ed. pap. 74.40 (*0-608-11625-4*, 200231400012) Bks Demand.

Pankhurst, Richard K. & Ingrams, Leila. Ethiopia Engraved. (Illus.). 140p. 1987. lib. bdg. 59.95 (*0-7103-0241-X*) Routledge.

Pankhurst, Richard K., ed. see Huntingford, George W.

***Pankiewicz, Flavia.** American Eclipse. Carravetta, Peter, tr. from ITA. LC 99-28928. (Crossings Ser.: Vol. 4). 70p. 1999. 9.00 (*1-884419-23-2*) Bordighera.

Pankin, Boris. The Last Hundred Days of the Soviet Union. 356p. 1996. 29.95 (*0-614-19282-X*) St Martin.

***Pankin, Boris.** The Last Hundred Days of the Soviet Union. 282p. 1999. reprint ed. text 30.00 (*0-7881-6588-7*) DIANE Pub.

Pankin, Boris. Last 100 Days of the Soviet Union. 256p. 1996. 29.95 (*1-85043-878-1*, Pub. by I B T) St Martin.

Pankin, Robert M., ed. Social Approaches to Sport. LC 81-65466. (Illus.). 360p. 1982. 39.50 (*0-8386-3015-4*) Fairleigh Dickinson.

Panko, Bill & Greenup, Louis. Bouncing Back from Bad Decisions. 400p. (Orig.). 1996. pap. 19.95 (*1-885342-05-5*) Creative Ways.

Panko, Bill & Panko, Margaret. Beyond the Blue Flambeau. 125p. (Orig.). Date not set. pap. 14.95 (*1-885342-13-6*) Creative Ways.

— The Dual Embodiment of Christ & Satan: A Character Study of Judas Iscariot. 100p. (Orig.). Date not set. pap. 9.95 (*1-885342-10-1*) Creative Ways.

— For God's Sake Surrender. 100p. (Orig.). Date not set. pap. 9.95 (*1-885342-22-5*) Creative Ways.

— Glorious Global Revival, Pt. 1. 150p. (Orig.). Date not set. pap. 14.95 (*1-885342-23-3*) Creative Ways.

— Glorious Global Revival, Pt. 2. 150p. (Orig.). Date not set. pap. 14.95 (*1-885342-24-1*) Creative Ways.

— Groaning for Miracles: An Expository Analysis of the Resurrection of Lazarus. 300p. (Orig.). 1996. pap. 19.95 (*1-885342-02-0*) Creative Ways.

— Mantles of Glory. 250p. (Orig.). Date not set. pap. 19.95 (*1-885342-20-9*) Creative Ways.

— Mastering Death! 175p. (Orig.). Date not set. pap. 14.95 (*1-885342-09-8*) Creative Ways.

— The Miracle of Marriage. 48p. 1994. pap. 4.95 (*1-885342-00-4*) Creative Ways.

— Miracles, the Glory of God. 250p. (Orig.). Date not set. pap. 19.95 (*1-885342-17-9*) Creative Ways.

— Miracles, the Prelude to Glory. 250p. (Orig.). Date not set. pap. 19.95 (*1-885342-16-0*) Creative Ways.

— Miracles, the Speaking of Glory. 250p. (Orig.). Date not set. pap. 19.95 (*1-885342-19-5*) Creative Ways.

— Miracles, the Working of Glory. 250p. (Orig.). Date not set. pap. 19.95 (*1-885342-18-7*) Creative Ways.

— A Most Vehement Flame. 300p. (Orig.). Date not set. pap. 19.95 (*1-885342-12-8*) Creative Ways.

— Nevertheless. 100p. (Orig.). Date not set. pap. 9.95 (*1-885342-21-7*) Creative Ways.

— The Overwhelming, Overpowering, Overshadowing. (Illus.). 100p. (Orig.). Date not set. pap. 9.95 (*1-885342-11-X*) Creative Ways.

— Prophetic Commands. 150p. (Orig.). Date not set. pap. 14.95 (*1-885342-25-X*) Creative Ways.

— A Quickening Spirit. 150p. (Orig.). Date not set. pap. 14.95 (*1-885342-08-X*) Creative Ways.

— Razing the Ded! The Biblical Administrations for Resurrection. 300p. (Orig.). 1996. pap. 19.95 (*1-885342-04-7*) Creative Ways.

— Supernatural Provision. 150p. (Orig.). Date not set. pap. 14.95 (*1-885342-27-6*) Creative Ways.

— The Supernatural Weapon of Love. 112p. 1995. per. 7.95 (*1-885342-01-2*) Creative Ways.

— Treasures in the Wind. 200p. (Orig.). Date not set. pap. 14.95 (*1-885342-14-4*) Creative Ways.

— Votary in the Face of God. 100p. (Orig.). Date not set. pap. 9.95 (*1-885342-26-8*) Creative Ways.

— The Working of Miracles. 125p. (Orig.). Date not set. pap. 11.95 (*1-885342-15-2*) Creative Ways.

Panko, Margaret, jt. auth. see Panko, Bill.

***Panko, Raymond R.** Business Data Communications & Networking. 3rd ed. 464p. 2000. 82.67 (*0-13-088262-3*) P-H.

Panko, Raymond R. Business Data Communications & Networking: A Modular Approach. 2nd ed. LC 98-19428. 464p. 1998. 83.00 (*0-13-082182-9*) P-H.

Pankoch, Leanne, ed. see Fanning, Larry A.

Pankoke-Babatz, Uta, ed. Computer Based Group Communication: The Amigo Activity Model. 1989. text 74.95 (*0-470-21461-9*) P-H.

Pankov, A. A. Bounded & Almost Periodic Solutions of Nonlinear Operator Differential Equations. (C). 1990. text 175.00 (*0-7923-0585-X*) Kluwer Academic.

— G-Convergence & Homogenization of Nonlinear Partial Differential Operators. LC 97-26711. (Mathematics & Its Applications Ser.). 264p. 1997. text 140.50 (*0-7923-4720-X*) Kluwer Academic.

Pankove, Jacques & Moustakas, Theodore D., eds. Semiconductors & Semimetals Vol. 57: Gallium-Nitride (GaN) II. (Illus.). 489p. (C). 1998. boxed set 155.00 (*0-12-752166-6*) Acad Pr.

Pankove, Jacques I. Optical Processes in Semiconductors. 2nd ed. LC 75-16756. (Illus.). 428p. 1976. reprint ed. pap. text 13.95 (*0-486-60275-3*) Dover.

Pankove, Jacques I., ed. Display Devices. (Topics in Applied Physics Ser.: Vol. 40). (Illus.). 300p. 1980. 66.95 (*0-387-09868-2*) Spr-Verlag.

Pankove, Jacques I. & Moustakas, T. D., eds. Semiconductors & Semimetals Vol. 50: Gallium Nitride (GaN) (Illus.). 537p. 1997. text 135.00 (*0-12-752158-5*) Acad Pr.

***Pankove, Jacques I.** Gallium Nitride, Vol. 2. 1005p. 1999. pap. 129.95 (*0-12-544055-3*) Acad Pr.

Pankovich, Arsen. I Died in Rio: A Story of a Man Who Fought for Human Dignity When the World Had a Date with Death. 520p. 1999. write for info. (*0-9672101-0-0*); pap. 15.00 (*0-9672101-1-9*) A Pankovich.

Pankow, David. Tempting the Palette: A Survey of Color Printing Processes. (Illus.). 58p. 1997. pap. 29.95 (*1-890543-01-2*) Digital Pub.

Pankow, H., et al. Die Algenflora der Schirmacheroase (Ostantarktika) (Nova Hedwigia, Beihefte/Supplementary Issues Ser.: Beih 103). (GER., Illus.). 198p. 1991. 95.00 (*3-443-51025-6*, Pub. by Gebruder Borntraeger) Balogh.

Pankow, James F. Aquatic Chemistry Concepts. 702p. 1991. lib. bdg. 85.00 (*0-87371-150-5*, L150) Lewis Pubs.

— Aquatic Chemistry Problems. (Illus.). 500p. (Orig.). 1992. pap. 34.95 (*0-9627452-5-3*) Titan Pr OR.

— Introduction to the Chemistry Organic Compounds in Natural Waters. Date not set. 59.95 (*0-87371-594-2*) CRC Pr.

Pankow, James F. & Cherry, Lohr A., eds. Dense Chlorinated Solvents & Other DNAPLs in Groundwater: History, Fate, & Remediation. 522p. 1995. 95.00 (*0-9648014-1-8*) Waterloo Pr.

Pankow, James F., tr. see Schwille, Friedrich.

Pankowski, Joseph M., jt. auth. see Koehler, Jerry W.

Pankowski, Marian, et al. Rudolf. LC 96-9840. (Writings from an Unbound Europe). 128p. 1996. 39.95 (*0-8101-1417-8*); pap. 14.95 (*0-8101-1418-6*) Northwestern U Pr.

Pankowsky, Hanna D. East of the Storm: Outrunning the Holocaust in Russia. LC 98-35211. (Illus.). 218p. 1998. 28.95 (*0-89672-408-5*) Tex Tech Univ Pr.

Pankratz, Alan. Forecasting with Dynamic Regression Models. LC 90-12484. (Probability & Mathematical Statistics: Applied Probability & Statistics Section Ser.: No. 1346). 400p. 1991. 129.95 (*0-471-61528-5*) Wiley.

— Forecasting with Univariate Box-Jenkins Models: Concepts & Cases. (Probability & Mathematical Statistics: Applied Probability & Statistics Section Ser.). 576p. 1983. 199.95 (*0-471-09023-9*, 1-346, Wiley-Interscience) Wiley.

Pankratz, Carol, jt. ed. see Mayers, Marlene G.

Pankratz, David B. Multiculturalism & Public Arts Policy. LC 93-25008. 248p. 1993. 57.95 (*0-89789-361-1*, H361, Bergin & Garvey) Greenwood.

Pankratz, David B. & Morris, Valerie B., eds. The Future of the Arts: Public Policy & Arts Research. LC 90-32098. 344p. 1990. 49.95 (*0-275-93377-6*, C3377, Greenwood Pr) Greenwood.

Pankratz, David B. & Mulcahy, Kevin V., eds. The Challenge to Reform Arts Education: What Role Can Research Play? LC 88-34274. (ACA Arts Research Seminar Ser.). 98p. (Orig.). 1989. pap. 12.95 (*0-915400-73-1*, ACA Bks) Am for the Arts.

Pankratz, Elsie P. Through the Years: Memoirs of Elsie Penner Pankratz. LC 93-61427. (Illus.). xiv, 149p. (Orig.). 1993. pap. 12.00 (*0-945530-10-2*) Wordsworth KS.

Pankratz, Loren. Patients Who Deceive: Assessment & Management of Risk in Providing Health Care & Financial Benefits. LC 98-12041. (American Series in Behavioral Science & Law). 274p. 1998. text 55.95 (*0-398-06866-6*); pap. text 41.95 (*0-398-06867-4*) C C Thomas.

***Pankratz, Roger S.** All Children Can Learn: Lessons from the Kentucky Reform Experience. 2000. pap. 25.00 (*0-7879-5523-X*) Jossey-Bass.

Pankratz, Ronald, jt. auth. see Preston, Seaton T.

Pankratz, Ronald E., jt. auth. see Preston, Seaton T.

Pankratz, Tom M. Concise Dictionary of Environmental Engineering. LC 96-16853. 416p. 1996. per. 29.95 (*1-56670-212-7*) CRC Pr.

— Dictionary of Water & Wastewater Treatment Trademarks & Brand Names. 160p. 1991. boxed set 75.00 (*0-87371-673-6*, L673) Lewis Pubs.

— Screening Equipment Handbook. 2nd ed. LC 94-62045. 300p. 1995. text 99.95 (*1-56676-256-1*) Technomic.

Panksepp, Jaak. Affective Neuroscience: The Foundations of Human & Animal Emotions. (Series in Affective Science). (Illus.). 480p. 1998. text 75.00 (*0-19-509673-8*) OUP.

Panksepp, Jaak, ed. Advances in Biological Psychiatry, Vol. 1. 312p. 1991. 128.50 (*0-7623-0026-4*) Jai Pr.

— Advances in Biological Psychiatry, Vol. 2, 1996. (Illus.). 258p. 1996. 128.50 (*0-7623-0170-8*) Jai Pr.

— Advances in Biological Psychiatry, Vol. 3. Date not set. 128.50 (*0-7623-0404-9*) Jai Pr.

Panksepp, Jaak, jt. ed. see Clynes, Manfred.

Panksepp, Jaak, jt. ed. see Morgane, Peter J.

***PanLener, Robin.** Handbook to Minnesota State Government. (Illus.). 60p. 2000. pap. write for info. (*0-9647451-8-6*) MN Bkstore.

***Panlilio, F.** Vector Algebra: An Introduction. LC 99-83982. 1999. pap. 9.95 (*0-533-13207-X*) Vantage.

Panlwala, H. A. Study of the Concept of Transfer & Closure under Industrial Disputes Act, 1947. (C). 1990. 45.00 (*0-89771-306-0*) St Mut.

Panman, Richard & Panman, Sandra. Short Stories: Reading, Thinking, Writing. 2nd rev. ed. Gluck, Linda, ed. (Illus.). 192p. (YA). 1995. pap. text 11.95 (*0-912813-23-7*) Active Lrn.

Panman, Richard, jt. auth. see Panman, Sandra.

Panman, Sandra & Panman, Richard. The Active Reader for Writers. (Illus.). 288p. (Orig.). (YA). (gr. 9 up). 1991. pap. text 15.95 (*0-912813-16-4*) Active Lrn.

— Essays - Letters - Reports. rev. ed. Gluck, Linda, ed. (Illus.). 128p. (YA). (gr. 7-12). 1995. pap. text 9.95 (*0-912813-22-9*) Active Lrn.

— Student Management Forms for Writing Guides. 2nd ed. 1990. 2.50 (*0-912813-11-3*) Active Lrn.

— Writing Basics. rev. ed. Gluck, Linda, ed. (Illus.). 128p. (YA). (gr. 6-12). 1996. pap. text 9.95 (*0-912813-24-5*) Active Lrn.

— Writing Guides. 3rd ed. (YA). (gr. 6-12). 1996. pap. text 16.95 (*0-912813-25-3*) Active Lrn.

Panman, Sandra, jt. auth. see Panman, Richard.

Pannabecker, James H., jt. auth. see Clontz, Ralph C., Jr.

Pannain, Guido. Modern Composers. LC 76-99644. (Essay Index Reprint Ser.). 1977. 23.95 (*0-8369-1715-4*) Ayer.

Pannam, C. L. The Horse & the Law. 2nd ed. xv, 327p. 1986. 48.50 (*0-455-20646-5*, Pub. by LawBk Co) Gaunt.

Pannbacker, Mary & Middleton, Grace. Introduction to Clinical Research in Communication Disorders. (Illus.). 302p. (Orig.). (C). 1994. pap. text 34.95 (*1-56593-219-6*, 0579) Thomson Learn.

Pannbacker, Mary, jt. auth. see Middleton, Grace F.

Pannbacker, Mary H., et al. Ethical Practices in Speech-Language Pathology & Audiology: Case Studies. LC 95-34209. 214p. 1995. pap. 39.95 (*1-56593-280-3*, 1246) Thomson Learn.

Pannekoek, A. History of Astronomy. (Illus.). 521p. 1989. pap. 12.95 (*0-486-65994-1*) Dover.

Pannekoek, A. & Croone, E., eds. Principal Works of Simon Stevin Vol. 3: Astronomy & Navigation. v, 632p. 1961. text 211.00 (*90-265-0073-4*) Swets.

Pannell, Alistair D., tr. see Beller, Ilex.

Pannell-Allen, Myra. The Honey Dipper's Legacy. LC 98-204412. 307p. 1998. pap. 14.95 (*1-885478-28-3*, Pub. by Genesis Press) BookWorld.

Pannell, C. M. Taxonomic Monograph of the Genus Aglaia Lour: Meliaceae. (Kew Bulletin Additional Ser.: Vol. XVI). (Illus.). viii, 379p. 1992. pap. 120.00 (*0-11-250067-6*, HM00676, Pub. by Royal Botnic Grdns) Balogh.

Pannell, Clifton W. Tai-chung, Taiwan: Structure & Function. LC 72-91223. (University of Chicago, Department of Geography, Research Paper Ser.: No. 144). 214p. 1973. reprint ed. pap. 66.40 (*0-608-02269-1*, 206291000004) Bks Demand.

Pannell, Clifton W., ed. East Asia, Geographical & Historical Approaches to Foreign Area Studies. LC 82-83653. (National Council for Geographic Education, Pacesetter Ser.). (Illus.). 267p. 1983. reprint ed. pap. 82.80 (*0-7837-9723-0*, 206045400005) Bks Demand.

Pannell, David J. Introduction to Practical Linear Programming. LC 96-6185. 332p. 1996. 84.95 (*0-471-51789-5*) Wiley.

Pannell, Gerard. MMXXVI - The Vision. LC 93-84363. (Illus.). 12p. (Orig.). (YA). 1993. pap. 9.50 (*1-883588-00-6*) PAAS Pr.

Pannell, Henry C. The Preparation & Work of Alabama High School Teachers. LC 77-177142. (Columbia University. Teachers College. Contributions to Education Ser.: No. 551). reprint ed. 37.50 (*0-404-55551-9*) AMS Pr.

Pannell, Ian. Shoot Pool. 1989. 12.98 (*1-55521-413-4*) Bk Sales Inc.

***Pannell, Maggie.** The Allergy-free Cookbook. (Healthy Eating Library). 1999. pap. 12.95 (*0-7548-0182-9*, Lorenz Bks) Anness Pub.

Pannell, Maggie. Calorie Counter. (Select Pocket Library). 96p. 1997. 4.98 (*0-7858-0450-1*) Bk Sales Inc.

— Dairy-Free Cookbook, 1. (Healthy Eating Library Series). 1999. pap. text 12.95 (*1-85967-882-3*, Lorenz Bks) Anness Pub.

— The Vegan Cookbook. (Healthy Eating Library). 1999. pap. 12.95 (*0-7548-0185-3*, Lorenz Bks) Anness Pub.

Pannell, Marjorie, ed. see Kelly, Robert E.

P

An Asterisk (*) at the beginning of an entry indicates that the title is appearing for the first time.

Jr.
, Jr.
al
ks

...en Light a ... 1997. pap. write ...k Pr.

...ogy in Theological ...hew J., tr. 552p. 1999. pap. ...T Clark Pubs.

...ropology of Theological ....95 (*0-567-09368-9*) Bks Intl VA.

...tion & History. 118p. 1994. pap. ...*519-4*) St Mut.

... Election, & History. LC 77-22026. 116p. ...pap. 36.00 (*0-7837-2628-7*, 2042978000006) ...and.

...ion to Systematic Theology. 82p. (Orig.). 1998. ...17.95 (*0-567-29195-2*, Pub. by T & T Clark) Bks ...l VA.

...etaphysics & the Idea of God. 184p. 1998. 37.95 (*0-567-09570-3*, Pub. by T & T Clark) Bks Intl VA.

— Systematic Theology, Vol. 1. Bromiley, Geoffrey W., tr. from GER. xiv, 460p. (C). 1991. 45.00 (*0-8028-3656-9*) Eerdmans.

— Systematic Theology, Vol. 2. Bromiley, Geoffrey W., tr. 515p. (C). 1994. text 45.00 (*0-8028-3707-7*) Eerdmans.

— Systematic Theology, Vol. 3. 729p. 1997. 49.00 (*0-8028-3708-5*) Eerdmans.

Pannenborg, Charles O. A New International Health Order. 476p. 1980. lib. bdg. 72.00 (*90-286-0239-9*) Kluwer Academic.

Pannes, Ernestine D. Waters of the Lonely Way: A Chronicle of Weston, Vermont from 1761-1978. LC 82-13314. (Illus.). 352p. 1982. 22.00 (*0-914016-89-X*) Phoenix Pub.

Pannese, Ennio. Neurocytology: Fine Structure of Neurons, Nerve Processes, & Neuroglial Cells. LC 93-18191. 1994. 99.00 (*0-86577-456-0*) Thieme Med Pubs.

— The Satellite Cells of the Sensory Ganglia. (Advances in Anatomy, Embryology & Cell Biology Ser.: Vol. 65). (Illus.). 98p. 1981. 48.95 (*0-387-10219-1*) Spr-Verlag.

Pannet, Robert, et al. Dictionnaire Marial. (FRE.). 1991. write for info. (*0-7859-8092-X*, 2-85443-217-7) Fr & Eur.

Pannett. Principle Hotel Catering Law. (C). 1984. pap. write for info. (*0-03-910481-8*) Harcourt Coll Pubs.

Pannett, Alan. Managing the Law Firm: Legal Practice Handbook. 2nd ed. 194p. 1995. pap. 26.00 (*1-85431-457-2*, Pub. by Blackstone Pr) Gaunt.

— Principles of Hotel & Catering Law. 3rd ed. LC 92-34125. 384p. 1992. text 100.00 (*0-304-32609-7*) Continuum.

— Recruitment & Training in the Solicitors' Practice. 164p. 1989. pap. 62.00 (*0-406-12750-6*, U.K., MICHIE) LEXIS Pub.

Pannett, Alan & Boella, Michael. Principles of Hospitality Law. 400p. 1996. pap. 37.95 (*0-304-33575-4*); text 90.00 (*0-304-33574-6*) Continuum.

Pannett, Alan, jt. auth. see Boella, Michael.

Pannett, Alan, jt. auth. see Johnson, Nick.

Pannick, David. Advocates. 318p. 1993. reprint ed. pap. 13.95 (*0-19-285289-2*) OUP.

— Sex Discrimination Law. 288p. 1986. 69.00 (*0-19-825481-4*) OUP.

Pannier, Dominique, ed. Corporate Governance of Public Enterprises in Transitional Economies. LC 96-14997. (World Bank Technical Papers: No. 323). 168p. 1996. pap. 22.00 (*0-8213-3636-3*, 13636) World Bank.

Panniker, Raimundo. The Vedic Experience. 937p. 1983. 36.00 (*0-89744-011-0*) Auromere.

***Pannikkar, Raimon.** The Cosmotheandric Experience: Emerging Religious Consciousness. Eastham, Scott, ed. 160p. 1998. pap. 125.00 (*81-208-1340-5*, Pub. by Motilal Bnarsidass) St Mut.

Pannikodu, Kuriakose. BCC Patent Review, No. TAP-16: Batteries. LC 98-120809. 248p. 1993. 1000.00 (*1-56965-300-3*) BCC.

Panning, Anne. The Price of Eggs. LC 92-817. 160p. (Orig.). 1992. pap. 11.95 (*0-918273-95-1*) Coffee Hse.

Panning, Armin J. Galatians - Ephesians. LC 97-67252. (People's Bible Ser.). 222p. 1997. pap. 10.99 (*0-8100-0704-5*, 15N0579) Northwest Pub.

***Panning, Armin J.** Romans. (People's Bible Ser.). 258p. 1999. pap. 11.99 (*0-8100-0932-3*) Northwest Pub.

Pannonius, Ionnas S. Grammatica Hungaro-Latina. LC 68-65313. (Uralic & Altaic Ser.: Vol. 55). 78p. 1968. pap. text 8.00 (*0-87750-019-3*) Res Inst Inner Asian Studies.

Pannor, Reuben, jt. auth. see Baran, Annette.

Pano, Nicholas C. Albania. (Marxist Regimes Ser.). 220p. 1989. 47.50 (*0-86187-392-0*); pap. 17.50 (*0-86187-393-9*) St Martin.

— The People's Republic of Albania. LC 68-27736. (Integration & Community Building in Eastern Europe Ser.). 203p. 1968. reprint ed. pap. 63.00 (*0-608-04018-5*, 206475400011) Bks Demand.

Panoff, M., jt. auth. see Godelier, M.

Panofsky, Erwin. Codex Huygens & Leonardo Da Vinci's Art Theory. LC 79-109814. (Illus.). 1971. reprint ed. lib. bdg. 26.00 (*0-8371-4306-3*, PACH, Greenwood Pr) Greenwood.

— Life & Art of Albrecht Durer. (Illus.). 500p. 1955. pap. text 35.00 (*0-691-00303-3*, Pub. by Princeton U Pr) Cal Prin Full Svc.

— Meaning in the Visual Arts. LC 82-13600. (Right Brain - Whole Brain Learning Ser.). (Illus.). xx, 384p. (C). 1983. pap. text 18.95 (*0-226-64551-7*) U Ch Pr.

— Perspective As Symbolic Form. Wood, Christopher S., tr. from GER. LC 91-10716. (Illus.). 196p. 1991. 26.00 (*0-942299-52-3*) Zone Bks.

— Perspective As Symbolic Form. Wood, Christopher S., tr. from GER. LC 91-10716. (Illus.). 196p. 1997. pap. 15.00 (*0-942299-53-1*) Zone Bks.

Panofsky, Erwin. Rena West Art. (Icon Editions Ser.). (Illus.). 380p. 1972. pap. 32.00 (*0-06-430026-9*, IN-26, Icon Edns) HarpC.

— Studies in Iconology. (Icon Editions Ser.). (Illus.). 306p. 1972. reprint ed. pap. 30.00 (*0-06-430025-0*, IN-25, Icon Edns) HarpC.

Panofsky, Erwin. Studies in Iconology: Humanistic Themes in the Art of the Renaissance. 1992. 39.50 (*0-8446-6619-X*) Peter Smith.

— Three Essays on Style. Lavin, Irving, ed. (Illus.). 256p. 1995. 30.00 (*0-262-16151-6*) MIT Pr.

— Three Essays on Style. (Illus.). 256p. 1997. reprint ed. pap. text 16.50 (*0-262-66103-9*) MIT Pr.

— Tomb Sculpture: Its Changing Aspects from Ancient Egypt to Bernini. (Illus.). 320p. 1992. 75.00 (*0-8109-3870-7*) Abrams.

Panofsky, Erwin & Panofsky-Soergel, Gerda, eds. Abbot Suger on the Abbey Church of St. Denis & Its Art Treasures. LC 55-11598. 315p. 1979. pap. text 19.95 (*0-691-00314-9*, Pub. by Princeton U Pr) Cal Prin Full Svc.

Panofsky, Hans E. A Bibliography of Africana, 11. LC 72-823. (Contributions in Librarianship & Information Science Ser.: No. 11). 350p. 1975. 59.95 (*0-8371-6391-9*, PAA/, Greenwood Pr) Greenwood.

Panofsky, Margaret. Bass Viol Technique. (Educational Ser.: No. 1). (Illus.). xiv, 336p. (Orig.). 1991. pap. text 40.00 (*1-56571-042-8*) PRB Prods.

Panofsky, Ruth. Adele Wiseman: An Annotated Bibliography. 150p. (C). 1992. text 30.00 (*1-55022-103-5*, Pub. by ECW) Genl Dist Srvs.

Panofsky, Ruth, ed. see Laurence, Margaret.

Panofsky-Soergel, Gerda, jt. ed. see Panofsky, Erwin.

Panofsky, Wolfgang K. Particles & Policy. LC 93-14011. (Masters of Modern Physics Ser.: Vol. 8). 232p. 1994. 34.95 (*1-56396-060-5*) Spr-Verlag.

Panogopoulos, Andreas. Captives & Hostages in the Peloponnesian War. 296p. 1989. pap. 60.00 (*90-256-0935-X*, Pub. by AM Hakkert) BookLink Distributors.

***Panontin, T. L. & Sheppard, S. D., eds.** Fatigue & Fracture Mechanics, Vol. 29. (STP Ser.: No. 1332). (Illus.). 920p. 1999. 117.00 (*0-8031-2486-4*, STP1332) ASTM.

Panopolitanus, Nonnus. Dionysiaca, Vol. I. Keydell, Rudolf, ed. lxxxiv, 500p. 1959. write for info. (*3-296-14701-2*) G Olms Pubs.

— Dionysiaca, Vol. II. Keydell, Rudolf, ed. iv, 555p. 1959. write for info. (*3-296-14702-0*) G Olms Pubs.

Panopolos, Gersten G. Religion with Medical, Psychological & Philosophical Aspects: Index of New Information & Bible of Progress. 160p. 1996. 47.50 (*0-7883-0226-4*); pap. 44.50 (*0-7883-0227-2*) ABBE Pubs Assn.

Panopoulos, Nickolas J. Genetic Engineering in the Plant Sciences. LC 81-10564. 271p. 1981. 65.00 (*0-275-90698-1*, C0698, Praeger Pubs) Greenwood.

Panos, Chris. God's Spy. 284p. 1977. reprint ed. pap. 8.95 (*0-88270-214-9*) Bridge-Logos.

Panos, Ingo Sanchez & Cano, Elena. Harrap's Vocabulario Ingles. 1995. per. 5.00 (*0-671-52080-6*) S&S Trade.

Panos, Maesimund B. & Himlich, Jane. Homeopathic Medicine at Home. LC 79-63802. 288p. 1981. pap. 12.95 (*0-87477-195-1*, Tarcher Putnam) Putnam Pub Group.

Panos, Nancy. Hazard Communication Training Program. Zmich, Jeanne, ed. 133p. 1994. pap. 8.00 (*0-940394-79-4*) Labelmaster.

— Trucker's Pocketbook to Hazardous Materials Regulations. 650p. 2000. pap. 2.80 (*0-940394-84-7*) Labelmaster.

***Panos, Nancy, ed.** Biller's Guide to Hazardous Material, 2000 Edition: A 49CFR Reference Tool for Proper Completion of Shipping Papers. 2nd ed. 150p. 2000. pap. 9.95 (*0-940394-89-8*) Labelmaster.

— Biller's Guide to Hazardous Materials Transportation. 200p. 1998. pap. 9.95 (*0-940394-77-4*) Labelmaster.

— Early 49CFR. rev. ed. 1250p. 1999. pap. 39.95 (*0-940394-75-8*) Labelmaster.

— HAZ - All Reference Book: A Hazardous Materials & Waste Reference Book, 2000 Edition. 2000. pap. 49.00 (*0-940394-88-X*) Labelmaster.

— Trucker's Guide to Hazardous Materials. 650p. 1999. pap. 9.00 (*0-940394-78-2*) Labelmaster.

Panosenko, O. Physicochemical Aspects of Medicine Reviews Vol. 3, Pt. 3: Peroxidation of Blood Lipoproteins & the Development of Atherosclerosis, Vol. 3. (Soviet Medical Reviews Ser.: Section B). 76p. 1992. pap. text 92.00 (*3-7186-5290-0*, Harwood Acad Pubs) Gordon & Breach.

Panosian, Edward, et al. The Providence of God in History. 48p. 1996. pap. 3.25 (*0-89084-865-3*, 093286) Bob Jones Univ.

Panourgia, Neni. Fragments of Death, Fables of Identity: An Athenian Anthropography. LC 95-6196. (New Directions in Anthropological Writing Ser.). 268p. 1995. 55.00 (*0-299-14560-3*); pap. 19.95 (*0-299-14564-6*) U of Wis Pr.

Panov, E. N. Physiology & General Biology Reviews Pt. 2: Bird Comparitive Ethology, Vol. 12. 2nd ed. (Soviet Scientific Reviews Ser.). 125p. 1997. pap. text 48.00 (*90-5702-234-6*, Harwood Acad Pubs) Gordon & Breach.

— Population Ethology, Vol. 3. iv, 104p. 1989. text 75.00 (*3-7186-4881-4*) Gordon & Breach.

Panov, V. N., jt. auth. see Estrin, Yakov B.

Panova, Sneschka. Die Juden Zwischen Toleranz und Volkerrecht Im Osmanischen Reich: Die Wirtschaftstatigkeit der Juden Im Osmanischen Reich (die Sudosteuropalander) Vom 15. Bis Zum 18. Jahrundert. (Europaische Hochschulschriften Ser.: Reihe 3, Bd. 752). (GER.). 218p. 1997. 44.95 (*3-631-30754-3*) P Lang Pubng.

Panova, Vera. Seryozha: Several Stories from the Life of a Very Small Boy. 7th ed. Bierkoff, Nicholas, tr. (Illus.). 110p. 1999. 25.00 (*0-939074-10-9*) Harvest Pubns.

Panovski, Naum. Directing Poiesis. LC 92-43331. (American University Studies: Fine Arts: Ser. XX, Vol. 18). XIV, 236p. (C). 1993. text 49.95 (*0-8204-2074-3*) P Lang Pubng.

Panozzo, David A. Awakening from Oz: A Path to Enlightenment in a Paradoxical Universe. LC 97-91553. 128p. 1997. pap. 10.00 (*0-9656556-5-2*) Obodoni Pr.

Panozzo, Joseph G. An American in Jeopardy. LC 85-90478. 215p. (Orig.). 1986. text 14.95 (*0-9615974-0-2*); pap. text 9.95 (*0-9615974-1-0*) J G Panozzo.

Panozzo, Michael E., jt. auth. see Mizerak, Steve.

Panozzo, Patricia. Breakfast at Panozzo's: A Cookbook by Patricia Panozzo. (Illus.). 192p. 1989. per. 9.95 (*0-9623704-1-X*) Panozzo.

— A Need to Feed: With a Mix & Match Salad Section: User Friendly. (Illus.). 121p. 1999. spiral bd. 17.95 (*0-9623704-0-1*) Panozzo.

Panruk, Eva. Aklut Atutuk'ngaput.Tr. of Clothes We Wear. (ESK., Illus.). 16p. (J). (gr. k-3). 1998. pap. text 6.00 (*1-58084-027-2*) Lower Kuskokwim.

Panse, Ujjwala. Some Issues in Nyaya, Mimamasa & Dharmasastra. (C). 1996. pap. 18.00 (*81-7030-477-6*, Pub. by Sri Satguru Pubns) S Asia.

Panshin, A. J. & De Zeeuw, Carl. Textbook of Wood Technology, Vol. 1. 4th ed. 736p. (C). 1980. 100.31 (*0-07-048441-4*) McGraw.

Panshin, Alexei. Heinlein in Dimension. rev. ed. LC 68-2797. 214p. 1968. reprint ed. 17.00 (*0-911682-01-5*) Advent.

— Heinlein in Dimension. rev. ed. LC 68-2797. 214p. 1969. reprint ed. pap. 10.00 (*0-911682-12-0*) Advent.

Panshin, Alexei & Panshin, Cory. SF in Dimension: A Book of Explorations. 2nd ed. LC 80-68572. 430p. 1980. pap. 12.00 (*0-911682-24-4*) Advent.

Panshin, Cory, jt. auth. see Panshin, Alexei.

Pansini & Fairmont Press, Staff. Engineering Economic Analysis Guidebook. 196p. (C). 1995. 72.00 (*0-13-389421-5*) P-H.

Pansini, A. Median Longitudinal Cervical Somatotomy. (Illus.). 158p. 1986. text 71.00 (*88-299-0382-5*, Pub. by Piccin Nuova) Gordon & Breach.

Pansini, A. & Conti, P. Median Longitudinal Cervical Somatotomy. 158p. 1986. text 64.0[illegible] Piccin Nuova.

— Spinal Meningiomas. LC 96-3703[illegible] (Illus.). 260p. 1996. 279.00 (*3-540-75030-4*) Spr-Verlag.

Pansini, A. J. & Smalling, Kenneth D. Guide to Electric Power Generation. 223p. 1994. 95.00 (*0-87814-637-7*) PennWell Bks.

Pansini, Anna, ed. Best Jokes & Riddles. LC 89-20324. (Illus.). 48p. (J). (gr. 2-6). 1990. lib. bdg. 8.95 (*0-8167-1917-9*) Troll Communs.

— I Wonder Why. LC 90-44455. (Illus.). 48p. (J). (gr. k-2). 1991. pap. text 2.95 (*0-8167-2305-2*); lib. bdg. 11.50 (*0-8167-2304-4*) Troll Communs.

Pansini, Anthony J. Basics of Electric Motors. 2nd ed. 1996. 49.95 (*0-87814-673-3*) PennWell Bks.

— Electrical Distribution Engineering. 2nd ed. 1992. 74.95 (*0-87814-633-4*) PennWell Bks.

— Electrical Transformers & Power Equipment. 3rd ed. LC 98-31729. 390p. 1998. 86.00 (*0-88173-311-3*) Fairmont Pr.

***Pansini, Anthony J.** Electrical Transformers & Power Equipment. 3rd ed. 401p. 1999. 86.00 (*0-13-012967-4*) P-H.

Pansini, Anthony J. Engineering Economic Analysis Guidebook. 187p. 1995. 79.00 (*0-88173-216-8*) Fairmont Pr.

— The Federalist, Continued. unabridged ed. 154p. (Orig.). 1995. pap. 15.00 (*0-911876-06-5*) Greenvale.

— Guide to Electrical Power Distribution Systems. 5th ed. 1996. 49.95 (*0-87814-639-3*) PennWell Bks.

— Il Duce's Dilemma: An Analysis of the Tragic Events Associated with Italy's Part in WWII. LC 97-39170. 500p. (Orig.). 1997. pap. 30.00 (*0-614-29902-0*) Greenvale.

— Machiavelli & the United States: 500th Anniversary Edition, 6 vols. in 1. LC 70-108252. 1371p. 1969. 20.00 (*0-911876-02-2*) Greenvale.

— Maximizing Management Effectiveness. LC 77-85653. (Illus.). 1977. pap. 15.00 (*0-911876-04-9*, 0-911976-04) Greenvale.

Pansini, Anthony J. Power Systems Stability Handbook. 1991. 25.00 (*0-87814-647-4*) PennWell Bks.

Pansini, Anthony J., ed. from ITA. Common Manual of Our Revolutionary History: History of the War of Independence of the United States of America, 2 vols. unabridged ed. LC 76-53356. lxxii, 841p. 1999. pap. 35.00 (*0-911876-08-1*) Greenvale.

***Pansini, Anthony J. & Smalling, Kenneth D.** Guide to Electric Load Managment. LC 98-46938. 196p. 1998. 74.95 (*0-87814-729-2*) PennWell Bks.

— Guide to Electric Power Transmission. LC 99-188031. vii, 263p. 1999. 69.95 (*0-87814-732-2*) PennWell Bks.

— High Voltage Power Equipment Engineering. LC 94-27238. 1994. 69.95 (*0-87814-642-3*) PennWell Bks.

Pansini, Anthony J. & Smalling, Kenneth D. Underground Electric Lines. 1993. 74.00 (*0-87814-677-6*) PennWell Bks.

Pansini, Anthony J., ed. & comment see Levi-Malvano, E.

Pansius, David K., jt. auth. see Nanda, Ved P.

Pansky, Ben, et al. Review of Neuroscience. 2nd ed. 576p. 1991. text 39.00 (*0-07-105304-2*) McGraw-Hill HPD.

Pansy. Tip Lewis & His Lamp. 208p. (YA). (gr. 11). 1987. 8.50 (*0-7399-0144-3*, 2434) Rod & Staff.

Pansy & Pearl, Betty. Betty & Pansy's Severe Queer Review of San Francisco, No. 3. 3rd ed. (Illus.). 153p. (Orig.). 1993. pap. 9.95 (*0-9633048-1-X*) Bedpan Prods.

Pansy, jt. auth. see Betty.

Pansy, jt. auth. see Pearl, Betty.

Pansy, Michael D. A Guide to Planning Your Wedding Reception. (Illus.). 1978. ring bd. 6.95 (*0-9602460-1-0*) P D Michael.

Panszczyk, Linda. 1998 U. S. Master Employee Benefits Guide. 3rd ed. 655p. 1997. pap. 59.00 (*0-8080-0151-5*) CCH INC.

***Panszczyk, Linda.** U. S. Master Employee Benefits Guide, 2000. 760p. 1999. pap. text 49.00 (*0-8080-0392-5*) CCH INC.

Pant, B. Trade & Development: Nepal's Experiences. 1994. pap. 60.00 (*0-7855-0488-5*, Pub. by Ratna Pustak Bhandar) St Mut.

Pant, G. B. Selected Works of G. B. Pant, Vol. 11. Nanda, B. R., ed. 464p. 1999. text 27.00 (*0-19-564437-9*) OUP.

Pant, G. B. & Kumar, Rupa K. Climates of South Asia. LC 96-32858. (Belhaven Studies in Climatology). 344p. 1997. 180.00 (*0-471-94948-5*) Wiley.

Pant, G. N. Indian Archery. (C). 1993. reprint ed. 110.00 (*0-8364-2873-0*, Pub. by Agam) S Asia.

— Mughal Weapons in the Babur Nama. (C). 1989. 125.00 (*0-8364-2473-5*, Pub. by Agam) S Asia.

Pant, Girish. Foreign Aid, Economic Growth & Social Cost-Benefit Analysis: Some Experiences from Nepal. 427p. 1991. text 101.95 (*1-85628-222-8*, Pub. by Avebry) Ashgate Pub Co.

Pant, Govind B. Selected Works of Govind Ballabh Pant, Vol. I. Nanda, B. R., ed. LC 93-908793. (Illus.). 362p. 1994. 27.00 (*0-19-563150-1*) OUP.

— Selected Works of Govind Ballabh Pant, Vol. 4. Nanda, B. R., ed. (Illus.). 464p. 1995. 24.95 (*0-19-563674-0*) OUP.

— Selected Works of Govind Ballabh Pant, Vol. 5. Nanda, B. R., ed. (Illus.). 546p. (C). 1996. 22.00 (*0-19-563675-9*) OUP.

— Selected Works of Govind Ballabh Pant, Vol. 6. Nanda, B. R., ed. (Illus.). 440p. 1997. text 25.00 (*0-19-563952-9*) OUP.

— Selected Works of Govind Ballabh Pant, Vol. [illegible] R., ed. (Illus.). 510p. (C). 1997. te[illegible] (*0-19-563954-5*) OUP.

— Selected Works of Govind Ballabh Pant, Vol. 9. Nanda, B. R., ed. (Illus.). 502p. (C). 199[illegible] 22.95 (*0-19-564117-[illegible]*) OUP.

Pant, Govind Ballabh. Selected Works of Govind Ballabh Pant, Vol. 13. Nanda, B. R., ed. 532p. 1999. text 27.95 (*0-19-564729-7*) OUP.

— Selected Works of Govind Ballabh Pant, Vol. 14. Nanda, B. R., ed. (Illus.). 480p. 2000. text 27.95 (*0-19-564961-3*) OUP.

***Pant, Govind Ballabh.** Selected Works of Govind Ballabh Pant Volume 10. Nanda, B. R., ed. (Illus.). 532p. 1999. text 21.95 (*0-19-564118-3*) OUP.

— Selected Works of Govind Ballabh Pant Volume 15. Nanda, B. R., ed. (Illus.). 480p. 2000. text 22.95 (*0-19-565120-0*) OUP.

Pant, Kusum. The Kashmiri Pandit: Story of a Community in Exile in the 19th & 20th Centuries. 1987. 17.50 (*0-8364-2279-1*, Pub. by Allied Pubs) S Asia.

Pant, M. M. & Goel, M. P. Systems Analysis, Data Processing & Quantitive Techniques. 416p. 1997. pap. 195.00 (*81-209-1008-7*, Pub. by Pitambar Pub) St Mut.

***Pant, Mahes Raj.** Jatarupa's Commentary on Amarkakosa, 2 Pts. 468, 512p. 1999. pap. 648.00 (*81-208-1690-0*, Pub. by Motilal Bnarsidass) St Mut.

Pant, Niranjan. New Trend in Indian Irrigation: Commercialisation of Ground Water. (C). 1992. 14.50 (*81-7024-467-6*, Pub. by Ashish Pub Hse) S Asia.

— Status of Girl Child & Women in India. LC 95-906914. (Illus.). xxxiii, 175p. 1995. 22.00 (*81-7024-708-X*, Pub. by Ashish Pub Hse) Nataraj Bks.

Pant, Niranjan & Rai, R. P. Community Tubewell & Agricultural Development. 1985. 15.00 (*0-8364-1380-6*, Pub. by Ashish Pub Hse) S Asia.

***Pant, Pushpesh.** Buddhism. LC 97-913835. 1999. 19.95 (*81-7437-089-7*) Heian Intl.

Pant, S. D. Social Economy of the Himalayas. (C). 1988. 31.50 (*0-8364-2431-X*, Pub. by Mittal Pubs Dist) S Asia.

Pant, Shastra D. District Administration in Nepal. 1997. pap. 87.00 (*0-7855-7383-6*, Pub. by Ratna Pustak Bhandar) St Mut.

Pant, Somendra, jt. auth. see Hsu, Cheng.

***Pant, V. K. & Bisht, B. S., eds.** Backward Communities: Identity Development & Transformation. LC 99-931889. 1999. 36.00 (*81-212-0625-1*, Pub. by Gyan Publishing Hse) S Asia.

Pant, Y. P. Trade & Cooperation in South Asia: A Nepalese Perspective. (C). 1992. 15.95 (*0-7069-5694-X*, Pub. by Vikas) S Asia.

Pantaeva, Irina. Siberian Dream. 320p. (YA). (gr. 8 up). 1999. pap. 12.50 (*0-380-79371-7*, Avon Bks) Morrow Avon.

— Siberian Dream: A Memoir. LC 98-23799. 320p. 1998. mass mkt. 23.00 (*0-380-97554-8*, Avon Bks) Morrow Avon.

Pantaleo, G., jt. ed. see Fauci, Anthony S.

***Pantaleo, Giuseppe & Walker, Bruce D., eds.** Retroviral Immunology. 425p. 2000. 125.00 (*0-89603-675-8*) Humana.

***Pantaleo, Jack.** Mother Julian & the Gentle Vampire. (New Voices in American Fiction Ser.). 230p. 2000. pap. 14.95 (*1-883938-66-X*) Dry Bones Pr.

Pantaleoni, Hewitt. On the Nature of Music. LC 85-50599. (Illus.). 464p. (C). 1985. 36.00 (*0-9614873-0-5*) Welkin Bks.

Pantaleoni, Hewitt, ed. see Serwadda, W. Moses.

Pantaleoni, Maffeo. Pure Economics. iii, 315p. 1957. reprint ed. 39.50 (*0-678-00674-1*) Kelley.

Pantano, Eugene. The Voyage of Tonquin. LC 97-90981. 1998. pap. 12.95 (*0-533-12527-8*) Vantage.

Pantano, Garlo G., jt. ed. see Chen, E. J.

P

An Asterisk (*) at the beginning of an entry indicates that the title is appearing for the first time.

***Pantas, Lee.** The Ultimate Guide to Asheville & Hendersonville Including the Great Smoky Mountains National Park: Your Complete Guide to the Western North Carolina Region. 440p. 2000. pap. 14.99 (*1-57090-105-8*, Pub. by Alexander Dist) Midpt Trade.

Pantas, Lee J. The Ultimate Guide to Asheville & Hendersonville: Including the Great Smoky Mountains National Park & the Blue Ridge Mountains of North Carolina. LC 98-10465. (Illus.). 400p. 1998. pap. 14.95 (*1-56664-129-2*) WorldComm.

Pantazis, Andreas. Epsilon of Aurigae: Selected Excerpts. 18p. 1990. pap. 9.95 (*0-948259-87-6*) Dufour.

Pantazis, Christina, jt. ed. see Gordon, David.

Pantazis, Panayotis, et al. The Camptothecins: From Discovery to the Patient. LC 96-39276. (Annals of the New York Academy of Sciences Ser.). 1996. 100.00 (*1-57331-056-5*); pap. 100.00 (*1-57331-057-3*) NY Acad Sci.

Pantazopol, D. French-Rumanian Dictionary of Aeronautics: Dictionar de Aeronautica Francez-Roman. (FRE & RUM.). 1984. write for info. (*0-8288-1171-7*, M15834) Fr & Eur.

Pantazopoulos, N. J. Church & Law in the Balkan Peninsula during the Ottoman Rule. (Illus.). 125p. 1983. reprint ed. pap. text 29.50 (*90-256-0800-0*, Pub. by AM Hakkert) Coronet Bks.

Pantazzi, Michael, et al. Corot. (Illus.). 540p. 1996. 75.00 (*0-8109-6501-1*, Pub. by Abrams) Time Warner.

— Corot. LC 96-6768. (Illus.). Date not set. 60.00 (*0-87099-769-6*) Metro Mus Art.

— Corot. LC 96-6768. (Illus.). 1996. pap. 45.00 (*0-87099-771-8*) Metro Mus Art.

Pantazzi, Michael, jt. auth. see Loyrette, Henri.

***Pantel, Gerda.** Canadian Bed & Breakfast 98/99. 14th ed. 432p. 1998. pap. 14.95 (*0-14-027493-6*) Viking Penguin.

Pantel, Pauline S., jt. auth. see Orrieux, Claude.

Pantel, Pauline S., jt. auth. see Zaidman, Louise B.

Pantel, Pauline S., jt. ed. see Duby, Georges.

Pantelakis, jt. auth. see Nakou.

Panteli, Marija & Nazor, Anica, comments. Brevarium Novi II. fac. ed. (Codices Selecti B Ser.: Vol. LXI). (ENG & GER., Illus.). 1000p. 1977. lthr. 355.00 (*3-201-01029-4*, Pub. by Akademische Druck-und) Balogh.

Panteli, Stavros. Historical Dictionary of Cyprus. LC 94-18869. (European Historical Dictionaries Ser.: No. 6). (Illus.). 258p. 1995. 52.00 (*0-8108-2912-6*) Scarecrow.

Panteliadis, C. P. & Darras, B. T., eds. Pediatric Neurology: Theory & Praxis. (Illus.). x, 684p. 1995. 170.50 (*3-8055-6287-X*) S Karger.

***Pantelides, S. T., et al, eds.** Molecular Electronics Vol. 582: Materials Research Society Symposium Proceedings. 2000. text 90.00 (*1-55899-490-4*) Materials Res.

Pantelides, Sokrates T. Deep Centers in Semiconductors: A State-of-the-Art Approach. xii, 778p. 1986. text 290.00 (*2-88124-109-3*) Gordon & Breach.

Pantelides, Sokrates T., ed. Deep Centers in Semiconductors: A State of the Art Approach. 2nd ed. LC 92-18744. 928p. 1992. text 205.00 (*2-88124-562-5*) Gordon & Breach.

Pantelidis, Veronica S. The Arab World: Libraries & Librarianship 1960-1976; a Bibliography. 116p. 1979. pap. 100.00 (*0-7201-0821-7*) Continuum.

— Robotics in Education: An Information Guide. LC 91-24541. 449p. 1991. 50.00 (*0-8108-2466-3*) Scarecrow.

Pantelis, Christos, et al. Schizophrenia: A Neuropsychological Perspective. LC 96-25494. 484p. 1997. 185.00 (*0-471-96644-4*) Wiley.

Pantell. Take Care of Youself. 4th ed. 1994. pap. write for info. (*0-201-40782-5*) Addison-Wesley.

— Taking Care of Your Child. 5th ed. LC 98-89110. 544p. 1999. pap. text 18.00 (*0-7382-0060-3*) Perseus Pubng.

Pantell, Richard H. Techniques of Environmental Systems Analysis. LC 76-98. (Illus.). 201p. 1976. reprint ed. pap. 62.40 (*0-7837-3524-3*, 205785900008) Bks Demand.

Pantell, Robert. Rudolph's Pediatrics: A Study Guide. 2nd ed. 256p. 1992. pap. text 29.95 (*0-8385-8489-6*, A8489-5) Appleton & Lange.

Pantell, Robert H. Take Care of Your Child. (C). 1992. pap. text. write for info. (*0-201-55617-0*) Addison-Wesley.

— Take Care of Your Child: U. S. Benefits. 1996. pap. write for info. (*0-201-15451-X*) Addison-Wesley.

Pantell, Robert H., et al. Taking Care of Your Child. rev. ed. 1990. pap. 15.95 (*0-201-08278-0*) Addison-Wesley.

— Taking Care of Your Child. 5th ed. 480p. 1998. pap. 25.00 (*0-201-32815-1*) Addison-Wesley.

— Taking Care of Your Child: A Parent's Guide to Complete Medical Care. 4th ed. (Illus.). 608p. 1993. pap. 17.95 (*0-201-63293-4*) Addison-Wesley.

Panter, Barry & Virshup, Bernard, eds. Creativity & Madness: Psychological Studies of Art & Artists. 2nd ed. 220p. 1996. 29.95 (*0-9641185-2-1*) AIMED.

Panter, Barry, et al. Creativity & Madness: Psychological Studies of Art & Artists, Vol. I. LC 94-94521. (Illus.). 320p. 1994. 24.95 (*0-9641185-1-3*) AIMED.

Panter-Brick, C., ed. Biosocial Perspectives on Children. LC 97-27946. (Biosocial Society Symposium Ser.: Vol. 10). (Illus.). 142p. (C). 1998. 54.95 (*0-521-57297-5*); pap. text 19.95 (*0-521-57595-8*) Cambridge U Pr.

Panter-Brick, C. & Worthman, C. M., eds. Hormones, Health & Behavior: A Socio-Ecological & Lifespan Perspective. LC 98-15373. (Illus.). 300p. (C). 1999. text 69.95 (*0-521-57332-7*) Cambridge U Pr.

***Panter-Brick, Catherine & Smith, Malcolm, eds.** Abandoned Children. LC HV875.A26 2000. (Illus.). 272p. (C). 2000. 59.95 (*0-521-77276-1*); pap. 19.95 (*0-521-77555-8*) Cambridge U Pr.

Panter-Brick, Keith, ed. Soldiers & Oil: The Transformation of Nigeria. (Studies in Commonwealth Politics & History: No. 5). 375p. 1978. 47.50 (*0-7146-3098-5*, Pub. by F Cass Pubs) Intl Spec Bk.

Panter, Gary, jt. auth. see Burns, Charles.

Panter, Nicole, ed. Unnatural Disasters: Recent Writings from the Golden State. LC 97-130528. 250p. (Orig.). 1996. pap. 15.00 (*1-884615-16-3*) Incommcdo San Diego.

Pantev, C., et al. Oscillatory Event-Related Brain Dynamics. LC 94-48769. (NATO ASI Ser.: Vol. 271). (Illus.). 478p. (C). 1995. text 130.00 (*0-306-44894-7*, Kluwer Plenum) Kluwer Academic.

Pantfoeder, Dorman. A New Owner's Guide to Dog Training. LC 99-205928. (New Owner's Guide to Ser.). (Illus.). 160p. 1997. 12.95 (*0-7938-2766-3*, JG-117) TFH Pubns.

Panth, Sanjaya. Technological Innovation, Industrial Evolution, & Economic Growth. LC 97-22274. (Studies on Industrial Productivity). 1997. 39.00 (*0-614-31310-4*) Garland.

— Technological Innovations, Industrial Evolution, & Economic Growth. LC 97-22274. (Studies on Industrial Productivity). 136p. 1997. text 43.00 (*0-8153-2784-6*) Garland.

***Pantham, Satyaraj.** Pure JFC Swing: The Swing Toolkit. LC 98-87276. (Illus.). 806p. 1999. pap. 19.99 (*0-672-31423-1*) Sams.

— Pure JFC 2D Graphics & Imaging. (Pure... Ser.). 1999. pap. 24.99 (*0-672-31669-2*) Sams.

Pantham, Thomas. Political Theories & Social Reconstruction: A Critical Survey of the Literature on India. LC 94-45237. 200p. 1995. 24.00 (*0-8039-9216-5*) Sage.

Panthel, Hans W., tr. see Dewran, Hasan.

Pantheon Photo Library Staff. American Photographers of the Depression. Incl. Eugene Atget. 1985. 1985. 1985. Set pap. 7.95 (*0-394-74086-6*) Pantheon.

— Henri Cartier-Bresson. 1985. write for info. (*0-318-59516-8*) Pantheon.

— Robert Frank. 1985. write for info. (*0-318-59517-6*) Pantheon.

Panther, Abraham. A Very Surprising Narrative of a Young Woman Discovered in a Rocky Cave after Having Been Taken by the Savage Indians of the Wilderness in the Year 1777. 1972. reprint ed. pap. 5.95 (*0-87770-095-8*) Ye Galleon.

Panthey, Saroj. Iconography of Siva in Pahari Paintings. (C). 1987. 78.00 (*81-7099-016-5*, Pub. by Motilal Bnarsidass) S Asia.

Pantic, Vladimir, jt. ed. see McKerns, Kenneth W.

Pantin, William A. The English Church in the Fourteenth Century. (Medieval Academy Reprints for Teaching Ser.). 1980. reprint ed. pap. text 7.50 (*0-8020-6411-6*) U of Toronto Pr.

Panting, Gerald E., jt. auth. see Sager, Eric W.

Panting, Gerard, jt. auth. see Lawrence, Clifford M.

***Panting-Lauri, Elizabeth.** Suenos y Esperanzas de Mi Gente (Hopes & Dreams of My People) Latin Immigration in the 90's. Sealy, Karen, ed. LC 00-102384. (SPA., Illus.). 108p. 2000. pap. 9.95 (*0-9678832-4-5*) Highbridge Pr.

Pantke, Mechthild. Der Arabische Bahram-Roman: Untersuchungen zur Quellen - und Stoffgeschichte. (Studien zur Sprache, Geschichte und Kultur des Islamischen Orients: Vol. 6). 230p. (C). 1973. 115.40 (*3-11-003990-7*) De Gruyter.

***Pantley, Elizabeth.** Hidden Messages: What Our Words & Actions Are Really Telling Our Children. LC 00-26128. 256p. 2000. pap. 14.95 (*0-8092-9770-1*, Contemporary Bks) NTC Contemp Pub Co.

Pantley, Elizabeth. Kid Cooperation: How to Stop Yelling, Nagging, & Pleading & Get Kids to Cooperate. LC 95-72223. 208p. 1996. pap. 13.95 (*1-57224-040-7*) New Harbinger.

— Perfect Parenting. LC 98-17024. 368p. 1998. pap. 14.95 (*0-8092-2847-5*, 284750, Contemporary Bks) NTC Contemp Pub Co.

Pantoja, Enrique R. Building Wealth on a Shoestring. 288p. 1996. 30.00 (*0-614-17417-1*) Perusa Pub.

Pantoja-Hidalgo, Cristina. I Remember...Travel Essays. 122p. (Orig.). 1993. pap. 8.75 (*971-10-0522-0*, Pub. by New Day Pub) Cellar.

Pantoja, Segundo, jt. ed. see Stevens-Arroyo, Anthony M.

Pantojas-Garcia, Emilio. Development Strategies As Ideology. LC 90-33397. 205p. 1990. 18.50 (*0-8477-0175-1*) U of PR Pr.

— Development Strategies As Ideology: Puerto Rico's Export-Led Industrialization Experience. LC 90-33397. 208p. 1990. lib. bdg. 38.00 (*1-55587-198-4*) L Rienner.

Panton, G. A., jt. ed. see Donaldson, D.

Panton, Kenneth J. & Cowlard, Keith A. Historical Dictionary of the United Kingdom, 2 vols. Incl. Historical Dictionary of the United Kingdom. LC 96-23996. 704p. 1997. 79.00 (*0-8108-3150-3*); Historical Dictionary of the United Kingdom Vol. 2: Scotland, Wales & Northern Ireland. LC 96-23996. (Illus.). 465p. 1998. 60.00 (*0-8108-3441-3*); 115.00 (*0-8108-3442-1*) Scarecrow.

Panton, R. L., ed. Self-Sustaining Mechanisms of Wall Turbulence. LC 97-66138. (Advances in Fluid Mechanics Ser.: Vol. 15). 440p. 1997. 134.00 (*1-85312-453-2*, 4532) Computational Mech MA.

Panton, Ronald L. Incompressible Flow. 2nd ed. LC 95-10084. 864p. 1995. 130.00 (*0-471-59358-3*, Wiley-Interscience) Wiley.

***Pantry, Sheila.** Building Community Information Networks: Strategies & Experiences. 196p. 1999. 70.00 (*1-85604-337-1*, LAP3371, Pub. by Library Association) Bernan Associates.

Pantry, Sheila & Griffiths, Peter. Becoming a Successful Entrepreneur: A Practical Guide to Creating an Innovative Information Service. (Successful LIS Professional Ser.). (Illus.). 98p. 1998. pap. 30.00 (*1-85604-292-8*, LAP2928, Pub. by Library Association) Bernan Associates.

— Your Successful LIS Career: Planning Your Career, CVS, Interviews & Self-Promotion. (Successful LIS Professional Ser.: Vol. 45004000). 127p. 1999. pap. 30.00 (*1-85604-329-0*, LAP3290, Pub. by Library Association) Bernan Associates.

Pantry, Stuart, ed. Occupational Health. 304p. 1995. 39.95 (*1-56593-415-6*, 1081) Singular Publishing.

***Pantsov, Alexander.** The Bolsheviks & the Chinese Revolution, 1919-1927. LC 99-49835. (Chinese Worlds Ser.). 320p. 2000. text 45.00 (*0-8248-2319-2*) UH Pr.

Panttaja, Dawn. Play Guide 1: Building Adventures. (Illus.). 1989. teacher ed. 10.00 (*1-879616-00-9*, 34891) Brio Scanditoy.

Panttaja, Dean. Theater: Practical Approach. 352p. (C). 1999. per. 44.95 (*0-7872-5709-5*, 41570901) Kendall-Hunt.

Panttaja, Jim. Microsoft SQL Server Survival Guide. LC 96-14607. 432p. 1996. pap. 44.99 (*0-471-12743-4*) Wiley.

— The Sybase SQL Server Survival Guide. LC 96-10798. 359p. 1996. pap. 36.95 (*0-471-12745-0*) Wiley.

Pantulu, G. R. Folk-Lore of the Telugus. (C). 1991. text 14.00 (*81-206-0691-4*, Pub. by Asian Educ Servs) S Asia.

Pantumsinchai, Pricha, et al. BASIC Programs for Production & Operations Management. (Illus.). 448p. (C). 1983. pap. 23.33 (*0-685-55652-2*) P-H.

Pantuso, John C., ed. see Graham, Robert A. & Lichten, Joseph L.

Pantziarka, P. Games of Deceit. (Crime & Passion Ser.). mass mkt. 5.95 (*0-7535-0119-8*, Pub. by Virgin Bks) London Brdge.

***Pantziarka, Pan.** House of Pain. 192p. (Orig.). 2000. pap. 13.95 (*1-84068-052-0*, Pub. by Creation Bks) Subterranean Co.

Pantziarka, Pan. House of Pain. (Velvet Ser.: Vol. 6). 192p. (Orig.). 1995. pap. 12.95 (*1-871592-57-7*) Creation Books.

***Pantziarka, Pan.** Lone Wolf: True Stories of Spree Killers. (Illus.). 304p. 2000. mass mkt. 7.95 (*0-7535-0437-5*, Pub. by Virgin Bks) London Brdge.

Pantziarka, Pan. A Moment of Madness. (Crime & Passion Ser.). 256p. (Orig.). 1997. mass mkt. 5.95 (*0-7535-0024-8*, Pub. by Virgin Bks) London Brdge.

— A Tangled Web. (Crime & Passion Ser.). (Orig.). 1997. mass mkt. 5.95 (*0-7535-0156-2*, Pub. by Virgin Bks) London Brdge.

Panum, Hortense. The Stringed Instruments of the Middle Ages. LC 73-127279. (Music Ser.). (Illus.). 1971. reprint ed. lib. bdg. 55.00 (*0-306-70039-5*) Da Capo.

Panunzio, Constantine M. Deportation Cases of Nineteen-Nineteen to Nineteen-Twenty. LC 77-109547. (Civil Liberties in American History Ser.). 1970. reprint ed. lib. bdg. 18.50 (*0-306-71901-0*) Da Capo.

— Immigration Crossroads. LC 79-145489. (American Immigration Library). xii, 309p. 1971. reprint ed. lib. bdg. 36.95 (*0-89198-022-9*) Ozer.

— Soul of an Immigrant. LC 69-18787. (American Immigration Collection. Series 1). 1969. reprint ed. 16.95 (*0-405-00535-0*) Ayer.

Panush. Let's Chat. 1995. 28.00 (*0-7616-3218-2*) Commun Skill.

— Rheumatology, Arthritis & Musculoskeletal Disease Two Thousand. (Illus.). 400p. 2000. text 84.95 (*0-8151-2926-2*, 31667) Mosby Inc.

***Panush, Richard S., ed.** Year Book of Rheumatology, Arthritis & Musculoskeletal Disease, 2001. (Illus.). 385p. 2001. write for info. (*0-323-01519-0*) Mosby Inc.

— Year Book of Rheumatology, Arthritis & Musculoskeletal Disease, 2002. (Illus.). 385p. 2002. write for info. (*0-323-01520-4*) Mosby Inc.

— Year Book of Rheumatology, Arthritis & Musculoskeletal Disease, 2003. (Illus.). 385p. Date not set. write for info. (*0-323-01521-2*) Mosby Inc.

— Year Book of Rheumatology, Arthritis & Musculoskeletal Disease, 2005. (Illus.). 385p. Date not set. write for info. (*0-323-01523-9*) Harcrt Hlth Sci Grp.

Panuthos, Claudia. Transformation Through Birth: A Woman's Guide. LC 83-15559. (Illus.). 213p. 1984. pap. 18.95 (*0-89789-038-8*, Bergin & Garvey) Greenwood.

Panuthos, Claudia & Romeo, Catherine. Ended Beginnings: Healing Childbearing Losses. LC 84-12284. (Illus.). 236p. 1984. 29.95 (*0-89789-053-1*, Bergin & Garvey); pap. 14.95 (*0-89789-054-X*, Bergin & Garvey) Greenwood.

Panvini, R. S., ed. Particle Searches & Discoveries: Proceedings, International Conference, Vanderbilt University, 1-3 March 1976. LC 76-19949. (AIP Conference Proceedings Ser.: No. 30). 1976. 18.50 (*0-88318-129-0*) Am Inst Physics.

Panvini, R. S., et al, eds. Novel Results in Particle Physics. LC 82-73954. (AIP Conference Proceedings Ser.: No. 93). 384p. 1982. lib. bdg. 35.00 (*0-88318-192-4*) Am Inst Physics.

Panvini, R. S. & Csorna, S. E., eds. High Energy E Plus E Minus Interactions Vanderbilt 1980. LC 80-53377. (AIP Conference Proceedings Ser.: No. 62). 405p. 1980. lib. bdg. 23.00 (*0-88318-161-4*) Am Inst Physics.

— New Results in High Energy Physics, 1978: Proceedings of the 3rd International Conference, Vanderbilt Univ., Mar. 1978. LC 78-67196. (AIP Conference Proceedings Ser.: No. 45). (Illus.). 1978. lib. bdg. 20.25 (*0-88318-144-4*) Am Inst Physics.

Panvini, R. S. & Weiler, T., eds. Quarks, Strings, Dark Matter & All the Rest: Proceedings of the Vanderbilt High Energy Physics Conference, 7th, Nashville, Tennessee, May 15-17, 1987. 344p. 1987. pap. 40.00 (*9971-5-0278-X*); text 110.00 (*9971-5-0272-0*) World Scientific Pub.

Panvini, R. S. & Word, G. B., eds. High Energy & Interactions: Vanderbilt 1984. LC 84-72632. (AIP Conference Proceedings Ser.: No. 121). 429p. 1984. lib. bdg. 43.75 (*0-88318-320-X*) Am Inst Physics.

Panvini, R. S., ed. see American Institute of Physics.

Panvini, Robert S. & Weiler, Thomas J., eds. Fundamental Particles & Interactions: Frontiers in Contemporary Physics - An International Lecture & Workshop Series at Vanderbilt University. LC 98-70005. (AIP Conference Proceedings Ser.: Vol. 423). (Illus.). 272p. 1998. 95.00 (*1-56396-725-1*) Am Inst Physics.

Panwar, J. S. Marketing in the New Era: Combating Competition in a Globalizing Economy. LC 97-10585. 1997. pap. write for info. (*0-8039-9383-8*) Sage.

— Marketing in the New Era: Combating Competition in a Globalizing Economy. LC 97-10585. 272p. 1997. 36.00 (*0-8039-9382-X*) Sage.

***Panwar, Purabi.** Indian in the Works of Kipling, Forster & Naipaul. 2000. 30.00 (*81-85753-32-6*, Pub. by Pencraft International) S Asia.

Pany, Beth K., photos by. The People of Clarksville & Its Cemetery: El Dorado County, California. (Illus.). 75p. 1999. pap. 12.00 (*0-9672409-0-5*) CA Genealogical.

Pany, Kurt & Whittington, Ray O. Auditing (Canadian) LC 95-80681. 800p. (C). 1995. text 62.95 (*0-256-20502-7*, Irwn McGrw-H) McGrw-H Hghr Educ.

Pany, Kurt, jt. auth. see Whittington, O. Ray.

Pany, Kurt J. & Whittington, O. Ray. Principles of Auditing. 11th ed. 216p. (C). 1994. text, student ed. 28.12 (*0-256-13371-9*, Irwn McGrw-H) McGrw-H Hghr Educ.

Pany, Kurt J., et al. Principles of Auditing: With Audit Practice Case. 11th ed. 752p. (C). 1996. text 97.20 (*0-256-24127-9*, Irwn McGrw-H) McGrw-H Hghr Educ.

Panyan, Marion V. How to Teach Social Skills. 2nd ed. LC 97-43061. (How to Manage Behavior Ser.). 1998. pap. text 8.00 (*0-89079-761-7*, 8673) PRO-ED.

— How to Use Shaping. (How to Teach Ser.). 30p. 1980. pap. 8.00 (*0-89079-050-7*, 1006) PRO-ED.

Panych. 7 Stories. (NFS Canada Ser.). 104p. 1990. pap. 11.95 (*0-88922-281-9*, Pub. by Talonbks) Genl Dist Srvs.

Panych, Morris. The Ends of the Earth. 144p. 1994. pap. 12.95 (*0-88922-334-3*, Pub. by Talonbks) Genl Dist Srvs.

— Other Schools of Thought: Three Dramatic Pieces. LC 94-234169. (Illus.). 140p. 1994. pap. 12.95 (*0-88922-346-7*, Pub. by Talonbks) Genl Dist Srvs.

— Vigil. 80p. 1997. pap. 10.95 (*0-88922-365-3*) LPC InBook.

***Panza, G. F., et al, eds.** Seismic Hazard of the Circum-Pannonian Region. (PAGEOPH Topical Volumes Ser.). 260p. 2000. pap. 44.95 (*3-7643-6263-4*) Birkhauser.

***Panza, Greg.** J. D. Edwards One World: An Administrator's Guide. 608p. 2000. pap. text 60.00 (*0-07-212462-8*) Osborne-McGraw.

***Panza, Julio A. & Cannon, Richard O., eds.** Endothelium, Nitrix Oxide, & Atherosclerosis: From Basic Mechanisms to Clinical Implications. LC 99-15251. (Illus.). 320p. 1999. 75.00 (*0-87993-436-0*) Futura Pub.

Panzano, Phyllis, jt. auth. see Campbell, Paul B.

***Panzardi, Anthony.** Auriga: Between Yellow Night & Refractive Sea. 64p. 1999. per. 8.00 (*1-881901-17-3*) LEGAS.

Panzardi, Anthony. Pyxis: Among Lost Children & Grizzled Dogs. LC 93-13585. 64p. 1993. pap. 14.95 (*0-7734-2774-0*, Mellen Poetry Pr) E Mellen.

***Panzarine, Susan.** A Parent's Guide to the Teen Years: Raising Your 11- to 14-Year-Old in the Age of Chat Rooms & Naval Rings. LC HQ777.15.P36 2000. 256p. 2000. 24.95 (*0-8160-4032-X*, Checkmark); pap. 14.95 (*0-8160-4033-8*, Checkmark) Facts on File.

Panzarino, Connie. The Me in the Mirror. LC 93-41623. 272p. (Orig.). 1994. pap. 12.95 (*1-878067-45-1*) Seal Pr WA.

Panzenhagen, Tom, ed. Michigan: The Wolverines Championship Season. (Illus.). 112p. 1998. pap. 12.95 (*0-937247-25-1*) Detroit Pr.

Panzer, B. I., jt. auth. see Grove, David J.

***Panzer, Baldur.** Die Slavischen Sprachen in Gegenwart und Geschichte: Sprachstrukturen und Verwandtschaft 3, Durchgesehene Auflage. 3rd ed. (GER., Illus.). XIV, 464p. 1999. 57.00 (*3-631-34311-6*) P Lang Pubng.

Panzer, Georg W. Annalen der Alteren Deutschen Literatur, 3 vols., Set. 1961. reprint ed. write for info. (*0-318-71851-0*) G Olms Pubs.

— Annales Typographici, 11 vols., Set. 1964. reprint ed. write for info. (*0-318-71852-9*) G Olms Pubs.

Panzer, Joel S. The Popes & Slavery. LC 96-22753. 137p. (Orig.). 1996. pap. 7.95 (*0-8189-0764-9*) Alba.

Panzer, Martin. How to Develop a Winning Personality. 1975. pap. 10.00 (*0-87980-057-7*) Wilshire.

Panzer, Mary. In My Studio: Rudolf Eickemeyer, Jr., & the Art of the Camera, 1885-1930. (Illus.). 112p. (Orig.). (C). 1987. pap. 26.95 (*0-87474-739-2*) Smithsonian.

— In My Studio: Rudolf Eickemeyer, Jr. & the Art of the Camera, 1885-1930. LC 87-401421. (Illus.). 106p. (Orig.). 1986. pap. 9.50 (*0-943651-01-8*) Hudson Riv.

Panzer, Mary, et al. Mathew Brady & the Image of History. LC 97-9493. 232p. 1997. 39.95 (*1-56098-793-6*) Smithsonian.

***Panzer, Nora.** Celebrate America. 96p. (J). 1999. pap. 12.99 (*0-7868-1423-3*, Pub. by Disney Pr) Little.

P

An Asterisk (*) at the beginning of an entry indicates that the title is appearing for the first time.

Panzer, Nora, ed. Celebrate America: In Poetry & Art. LC 93-32336. (Illus.). 96p. (YA). (gr. 5 up). 1994. 18.95 (*1-56282-664-6*, Pub. by Hyprn Child) Time Warner.
Panzer, Richard. Relationship Intelligence: Why Your RQ is More Important to Your Success & Happiness Than Your IQ. 1998. pap. text 11.95 (*1-888933-11-9*) Ctr Educ Media.
Panzer, Richard, jt. auth. see Ayad, Grace.
Panzer, Richard, jt. auth. see Ayad, Graciela.
Panzer, Richard A. Angel's Bar & Grill. (Illus.). 28p. (Orig.). 1995. pap. text. write for info. incl. audio (*1-888933-01-1*) Ctr Educ Media.
— Condom Nation: Blind Faith, Bad Science. LC 96-84281. (Illus.). 160p. 1997. pap. text 12.00 (*1-888933-02-X*) Ctr Educ Media.
— Free Teens Relationship Training Student Journal: Adventures in Character & Relationships. (Illus.). 176p. (YA). (gr. 9-12). 1999. pap. 17.95 (*1-888933-13-5*) Ctr Educ Media.
— Preventing Violence: Why Families Are Important, What They Can Do. (Illus.). 88p. 1999. pap. 7.95 (*1-888933-12-7*) Ctr Educ Media.
Panzer, Rober J. Diagnostic Strategies for Common Medical Problems. 2nd ed. LC 98-34279. 674p. 1999. 45.00 (*0-943126-74-6*) Amer Coll Phys.
***Panzer, Ronald.** The Hospice Patients Alliance Family Guide to Hospice Care: (What No Hospice Will Tell You!) large type ed. LC 99-68080. xiv, 241p. 1999. 20.00 (*0-9677045-0-2*) Hospice Pat Allian.
Panzer, Ursula, ed. see Husserl, Edmund.
Panzera, Lisa & Stewart, Patricia. Harry Anderson - Finders Keepers: Collections/Installations/Illuminations. (Illus.). 48p. 1996. pap. 20.00 (*1-58442-001-4*) Galleries at Moore.
Panzieri, Peter. Little Big Horn, 1876. (Campaign Ser.). (Illus.). 96p. 1995. pap. 14.95 (*1-85532-458-X*, 9535, Pub. by Ospry) Stackpole.
Pao, Angela C. The Orient of the Boulevards: Exoticism, Empire, & Nineteenth-Century French Theater. LC 97-29126. (New Cultural Studies). (Illus.). 256p. (C). 1997. 39.95 (*0-8122-3425-1*) U of Pa Pr.
Pao, C. V. Nonlinear Parabolic & Elliptic Equations. LC 92-30342. (Illus.). 794p. (C). 1993. 155.00 (*0-306-44343-0*, Plenum Trade) Perseus Pubng.
Pao, John, ed. The CRM Study Bible: New Testament. (CHI.). 848p. 1992. 20.00 (*1-56582-000-2*, Christ Renew Min.
— The CRM Study Bible: Old & New Testament. deluxe ed. (CHI.). 2452p. 1996. lthr. 68.00 (*1-56582-113-0*) Christ Renew Min.
Pao-min Chang. Beijing, Hanoi & the Overseas Chinese. LC 82-2641. (China Research Monographs: No. 24). 1982. pap. 7.00 (*0-912966-50-5*) IEAS.
Pao-Min, Chang. Kampuchea Between China & Vietnam. 204p. 1985. pap. 26.50 (*9971-69-089-6*, Pub. by Sngapore Univ Pr) Coronet Bks.
Pao, Ping-Nie. Schizophrenic Disorders: Theory & Treatment from a Psychodynamic Point of View. LC 77-92180. 456p. 1979. 70.00 (*0-8236-5990-9*) Intl Univs Pr.
Pao, Y. C. & Foltz, Michael E. Engineering Drafting & Solid Modeling with SilverScreen. 224p. 1992. lib. bdg. 69.95 (*0-8493-4471-9*, T353) CRC Pr.
Pao, Y. H. & LeClair, S. R. Artificial Intelligence in Real Time Control. LC 99-54558. (Illus.). 279p. 1999. pap. write for info. (*0-08-043227-1*, Pergamon Pr) Elsevier.
Pao, Yen-Ching. Engine Analysis: Interactive Methods & Programs. LC 98-36518. 384p. 1998. boxed set 84.95 (*0-8493-2016-X*) CRC Pr.
Pao, Yi-Hsin, jt. auth. see Lau, John H.
Pao, Yih-Ho & Goldburg, Arnold, eds. Clear Air Turbulence & Its Detection: Proceedings of a Symposium. LC 73-76507. 556p. reprint ed. pap. 172.40 (*0-608-16536-0*, 202629000049) Bks Demand.
Paogucci, Henry, ed. see Bigongiari, Dino.
Paola, Angelo S. Under the Fig Leaf: A Comprehensive Guide to the Care & Maintenance of the Penis, Prostate & Related Organs. LC 98-39340. (Illus.). 320p. 1998. pap. 14.95 (*1-885987-15-3*, ME090); pap. 14.95 (*1-885489-15-3*, ME090) Practice Mgmt Info.
Paola, C., jt. ed. see Kleinspehn, K.
Paola, Fredi, ed. Volcanic Geomorphology: Proceedings of the 4th International Conference on Geomorphology Bologna, 1997, Vol. I. (Zeitschrift fur Geomorphologie Supplement Ser.: Vol. 114). (Illus.). xii, 112p. 1999. 44.00 (*3-443-21114-3*, Pub. by Gebruder Borntraeger) Balogh.
Paola, Roberta J., et al. South Africa. LC 98-35199. (Handbook for the Admission of International Students to Elementary & Secondary Schools in the United States Ser.). 24p. (C). 1998. ring bd. 22.00 (*0-929851-86-2*, 1263) Am Assn Coll Registrars.
Paola, Suzanne. Bardo. LC 98-23341. 112p. 1998. 18.95 (*0-299-16010-6*); pap. 11.95 (*0-299-16014-9*) U of Wis Pr.
— Petitioner. (Poetry Ser.). 46p. (Orig.). 1985. pap. 12.00 (*0-937669-17-2*) Owl Creek Pr.
Paola, Tomie De, see De Paola, Tomie.
Paolantonio, S. A. Frank Rizzo: The Last Big Man in Big City America. LC 93-12076. (Illus.). 412p. 1993. 22.00 (*0-940159-18-X*) Camino Bks.
— Frank Rizzo: The Last Big Man in Big City America. LC 93-12076. (Illus.). 420p. 1993. reprint ed. pap. 12.00 (*0-940159-27-9*) Camino Bks.
Paolella, G., jt. auth. see De Simone, R.
Paolella, Michael A. Auditing Health Care Benefits: How to Manage Costs & Minimize Risk. LC 95-12461. 288p. 1995. 125.00 (*0-471-11918-0*) Wiley.
— Auditing Health Care Benefits: How to Manage Costs & Minimize Risks - 1997 Supplement. 144p. 1996. pap. 55.00 (*0-471-16778-9*) Wiley.
Paolella, Peter. Introduction to Molecular Genetics. LC 96-83781. 352p. (C). 1997. text. write for info. (*0-697-20939-3*, WCB McGr Hill) McGrw-H Hghr Educ.
Paolenti, Rodolfo, et al, eds. Phagocytes: Biology, Physiology, Pathology, & Pharmacotherapeutics. LC 97-43318. (Annals of the New York Academy of Sciences Ser.: No. 832). 450p. 1997. 110.00 (*1-57331-102-2*); pap. 110.00 (*1-57331-103-0*) NY Acad Sci.
Paoletta, Toni, jt. auth. see Tulloch, Mitch.
Paoletti, A. & Tucciarone, A., eds. The Physics of Diamonds. (International School of Physics Enrico Fermi Ser.: Vol. 135). 630p. 1997. write for info. (*90-5199-352-8*) IOS Press.
Paoletti, Franco, jt. ed. see Bernabei, Stefano.
Paoletti, Isabella. Bring an Older Woman: A Study in the Social Construction of Identity. LC 97-23945. 130p. 1997. text. write for info. (*0-8058-2120-1*); pap. text. write for info. (*0-8058-2121-X*) L Erlbaum Assocs.
Paoletti, John T. The Critical Eye, I. LC 83-51290. (Illus.). 87p. 1984. 12.95 (*0-930606-46-9*) Yale Ctr Brit Art.
Paoletti, John T. & Radke, Gary M. Art in Renaissance Italy. 480p. (C). 1996. pap. text 57.33 (*0-13-596925-5*) P-H.
Paoletti, John T., jt. auth. see Rychlik, Otmar.
Paoletti, Lawrence C. & McInnes, Pamela M. Vaccines, from Concept to Clinic: A Guide to the Development & Clinical Testing of Vaccines for Human Use. LC 98-21739. 224p. 1998. boxed set 109.95 (*0-8493-1168-3*) CRC Pr.
Paoletti, M. G. & Pimentel, D. Biotic Diversity in Agroecosystems. 356p. 1992. 150.75 (*0-444-89390-3*) Elsevier.
Paoletti, P., et al, eds. Neuro-Oncology. (Developments in Oncology Ser.). (C). 1991. text 243.00 (*0-7923-1215-5*) Kluwer Academic.
Paoletti, R., et al, eds. Women's Health in Menopause: Risk reduction Strategies. LC 97-23945. (Medical Science Symposia Ser.: No. 11). 356p. 1997. text 115.00 (*0-7923-4697-1*) Kluwer Academic.
***Paoletti, Rodolfo, et al, eds.** Vitamin C: The State of the Art of Disease Prevention Sixty Years after the Nobel Prize. LC 98-24805. (Illus.). 160p. 1998. pap. 105.00 (*88-470-0027-0*) Spr-Verlag.
Paoletti, Rodolfo & Gotto, Antonio M., Jr., eds. Atherosclerosis Reviews, Vol. 5. LC 76-640124. 274p. 1979. reprint ed. pap. 85.00 (*0-608-00265-8*, 204712500005) Bks Demand.
Paoletti, Rodolfo, jt. auth. see Gotto, Antonio M., Jr.
Paoletti, Rodolfo, ed. see Atherosclerosis Reviews Staff.
Paoletti, Rodolfo, jt. ed. see Gotto, Antonio M.
Paoletti, Rodolfo, jt. ed. see Gotto, Antonio M., Jr.
Paoletti, Rodolfo, ed. see International Congress for Fat Research Staff.
Paoletti, Rodolfo, ed. see International Symposium on Atherosclerosis Staff.
Paoletti, Rodolfo, jt. ed. see Samuelsson, Bengt.
Paoletti, Rodolfo, jt. ed. see Vanhoutte, Paul M.
Paoletti, Rudolfo, ed. see Atherosclerosis Reviews Staff.
Paoli, Arturo. Meditations on Saint Luke. McWilliams, Bernard F., tr. LC 76-58539. 204p. reprint ed. pap. 63.30 (*0-8357-8949-7*, 203351400086) Bks Demand.
Paoli, Carlo De, see De Paoli, Carlo.
Paoli, Erika, tr. see Baumbusch, Brigitte.
Paoli, Erika, tr. see Rossi, Renzo.
Paoli, Francisco M. Bajo el Signo del Amor. (Aqui y Ahora Ser.). 118p. 1997. pap. 6.95 (*0-8477-0279-0*) U of PR Pr.
— La Locura de la Cruz. (SPA.). 108p. 1997. lib. bdg. 8.00 (*1-881708-16-0*) Edcnes Mairena.
Paoli, Francisco Matos, see Matos Paoli, Francisco.
Paoli, Geri De, see Gelburd, Gail & De Paoli, Geri.
Paoli, Geri De, see De Paoli, Geri.
Paoli, Shirley B. Poetry - A Legacy of Love: Featuring an Era of Poetry Then & Now. 55p. (Orig.). 1989. pap. 5.95 (*0-685-44869-X*) S B Paoli.
Paoli, U. Rome: Its People, Life & Customs. 1996. pap. 26.95 (*1-85399-121-X*, Pub. by Brist Class Pr) Focus Pub-R Pullins.
***Paolicelli, Paul.** Dances with Luigi: A Grandson's Determined Quest to Comprehend Italy & the Italians. LC 99-98196. 320p. 2000. text 24.95 (*0-312-25188-2*) St Martin.
Paolieri, Annarita. Paolo Uccello, Domenico Veneziano, Andrea del Castagno. Pelletti, Lisa C., tr. from ITA. (Library of Great Masters). (Illus.). 80p. (Orig.). 1991. pap. 12.99 (*1-878351-20-6*) Riverside NY.
***Paolilli, Paul, et al.** Silver Seeds: A Book of Nature Poems. LC 00-9469. (Illus.). (YA). 2001. write for info. (*0-670-88941-5*) Viking Penguin.
Paolini, Albert J. Navigating Modernity: Postcolonialism, Identity & International Relations. Elliott, Anthony & Moran, Anthony, eds. LC 99-19297. (Critical Perspectives on World Politics Ser.). 240p. 1999. 52.00 (*1-55587-875-X*) L Rienner.
Paolini, Claire J., ed. La CHISPA '97: Selected Proceedings. (SPA.). 488p. 1997. pap. 70.00 (*0-9607798-7-6*) Tulane U Conf Hispanic Lit.
Paolini, Claire J. & Paolini, Gilbert, eds. La CHISPA '95: Selected Proceedings. (POR & SPA.). 416p. 1995. pap. 60.00 (*0-9607798-6-8*) Tulane U Conf Hispanic Lit.
Paolini, Gilbert, ed. LA CHISPA, '85: Selected Proceedings. LC 85-51632. 400p. 1985. pap. 30.00 (*0-9607798-2-5*) Tulane U Conf Hispanic Lit.
— LA CHISPA, '81: Selected Proceedings. LC 81-52692. (POR & SPA.). 360p. 1981. pap. 30.00 (*0-9607798-0-9*) Tulane U Conf Hispanic Lit.
— LA CHISPA, '87: Selected Proceedings. LC 87-51270. 352p. 1987. pap. 30.00 (*0-9607798-3-3*) Tulane U Conf Hispanic Lit.
— LA CHISPA, '83: Selected Proceedings. LC 83-81630. 336p. (Orig.). 1983. pap. 30.00 (*0-9607798-1-7*) Tulane U Conf Hispanic Lit.
— LA CHISPA, '93: Selected Proceedings. (SPA.). 334p. 1993. pap. 50.00 (*0-9607798-5-X*) Tulane U Conf Hispanic Lit.
Paolini, Gilbert, intro. LA CHISPA, '89: Selected Proceedings. LC 89-51388. (ENG & SPA.). 424p. (Orig.). 1989. pap. 50.00 (*0-9607798-4-1*) Tulane U Conf Hispanic Lit.
Paolini, Gilbert, jt. ed. see Paolini, Claire J.
Paolini, Kenneth, jt. auth. see Paolini, Talita.
***Paolini, Marco & Vacis, Gabriele.** The Story of Vajont. Nasi, Franco & Simpson, Thomas, eds. (Crossings Ser.: No. 9). (Illus.). 136p. (C). 2000. pap. 13.00 (*1-884419-41-0*) Bordighera.
Paolini, Mary. Moments with You God. 1986. 8.95 (*0-88271-028-1*) Regina Pr.
***Paolini, Nicole.** Swamp Gas. LC 00-24866. 304p. 2000. 23.95 (*0-312-26235-3*) St Martin.
Paolini, Shirley J. Creativity, Culture, & Values: Comparative Essays in Literary Aesthetics. LC 90-5873. (New Studies in Aesthetics: Vol. 5). (Illus.). XVII, 239p. (C). 1991. text 47.95 (*0-8204-1341-0*) P Lang Pubng.
***Paolini, Talita & Paolini, Kenneth.** Play & Learn with Cereal O's: Simple, Effective Activities to Help You Educate Your Preschool Child. LC 00-102400. (Illus.). 108p. 2000. pap. 9.95 (*0-9666213-2-8*) Paolini Intl.
Paolino, Adele. Agoraphobia: Fear of Fear. 256p. 1985. pap. text 8.95 (*0-9611448-1-5*) A Paolino.
— Agoraphobia: How I Overcame This Crippling Disease. 80p. 1983. pap. 5.95 (*0-9611448-0-7*) A Paolino.
Paolino, Andrea R., ed. see Krill, Mary A.
Paolino, Thomas J., Jr., jt. auth. see Nichols, Michael P.
Paolo, C., et al, eds. Coordination: Languages & Models. LC 99-23414. (Lecture Notes in Computer Science Ser.: Vol. 1594). ix, 419p. 1999. pap. 69.00 (*3-540-65836-X*) Spr-Verlag.
Paoloni, G., jt. auth. see Battimelli, G.
***Paolozzi, Eduardo.** Eduardo Paolozzi: Writings & Interviews. Spencer, Robin, ed. (Illus.). 400p. 2000. text 74.00 (*0-19-817412-8*) OUP.
— Machines, 68. 254p. 1999. pap. 12.95 (*1-885490-19-4*, Pub. by Grnd St Pr) Dist Art Pubs.
Paolozzi, Gabriel & Sedwick, Frank. Conversation in Italian: Points of Departure. 3rd ed. 120p. (C). 1985. mass mkt. 32.95 (*0-8384-1276-9*) Heinle & Heinle.
Paolucci, Anne. The Armenian Literary Legacy: A Bridge among the Nations. 1985. pap. 2.95 (*0-918680-30-1*) Griffon House.
Paolucci, Anne. Cipango: New Short Version. 132p. 1987. pap. 4.95 (*0-918680-34-4*) Griffon House.
— From Tension to Tonic: The Plays of Edward Albee. 2nd ed. 160p. 2000. pap. 19.95 (*0-918680-84-0*) Griffon House.
Paolucci, Anne. Gorbachev in Concert (& Other Poems) 60p. 1991. 12.00 (*0-918680-47-6*) Griffon House.
***Paolucci, Anne.** In the Greeen Room: A Play by Anne Paolucci. LC 99-41307. 67p. 1999. pap. 19.95 (*0-918680-82-4*) Griffon House.
Paolucci, Anne. Minions of the Race. 1978. pap. 2.95 (*0-918680-09-3*) Griffon House.
— Pirandello's Theater: The Recovery of the Modern Stage for Dramatic Art. Moore, Harry T., ed. LC 73-20324. (Crosscurrents-Modern Critiques Ser.). 159p. 1974. 12.00 (*0-8093-0594-1*) Griffon House.
— Queensboro Bridge: And Other Poems. (Petites Major Ser.). 64p. 1995. pap. 6.95 (*1-884754-27-9*) Potpourri Pubns.
— Terminal Degrees: A Novella. 128p. 1997. pap. 12.00 (*1-884754-28-7*) Potpourri Pubns.
— Three Short Plays: Minions of the Race, Incident at the Great Wall, The Actor in Search of His Mask. (Illus.). 176p. 1994. pap. 6.95 (*0-918680-36-0*) Griffon House.
Paolucci, Anne, ed. Comparative Literary Theory: New Perspectives. (Review of National Literatures Ser.: Vol. 15). 148p. 1989. pap. 6.95 (*0-918680-24-7*) Griffon House.
Paolucci, Anne, ed. Dante's Influence on American Writers, 1776-1976: Proceedings of the Bicentennial Meeting of the Dante Society of America. 1976. pap. 4.95 (*0-918680-02-6*) Griffon House.
— Eight Short Stories. 1977. pap. 6.95 (*0-918680-04-2*) Griffon House.
— Machiavelli '500. LC 77-126039. (Review of National Literatures Ser.: Vol. 1, No. 1). 1970. 6.95 (*0-918680-56-5*) Griffon House.
— Poems Written for Sbek's Mummies, Marie Menken & Other Important Persons, Places & Things. 1977. pap. 6.95 (*0-918680-03-4*) Griffon House.
Paolucci, Anne, et al. Cultures of the Aztecs, Mayas, & Incas. Paolucci, Henry, ed. (Review of National Literatures Ser.: Vol. 20). (Illus.). 216p. 1996. pap. 14.95 (*0-918680-50-6*) Griffon House.
— Early Spanish, French, & English Encounters with the American Indians. Paolucci, Henry, ed. (Review of National Literatures Ser.: Vol. 21). (Illus.). 192p. 1997. pap. 14.95 (*0-918680-54-9*) Griffon House.
— Multicultural Perspectives: New Approaches. (CNL/World Report Ser.: Vol. VI). 128p. 1993. pap. 4.95 (*0-918680-52-2*) Griffon House.
Paolucci, Anne, jt. auth. see Paolucci, Henry.
Paolucci, Anne, ed. see Paolucci, Henry.
Paolucci, Anne A. The Actor in Search of His Mask: A One-Act Play. 1987. pap. 6.95 (*0-918680-26-3*) Griffon House.
Paolucci, Anne A. CIPANGO! A One Act Play in Three Scenes about Christopher Columbus. LC 85-14731. 1985. pap. 4.95 (*0-918680-29-8*) Griffon House.
— Riding the Mast Where It Swings. 2nd ed. LC 80-68090. 1981. pap. 6.95 (*0-918680-10-7*) Griffon House.
Paolucci, Anne A., ed. The Doctor of Arts Degree: Assessing Teaching & Research Priorities. (CNL/World Report Ser.: Vol. III). 108p. 1989. pap. 4.95 (*0-918680-42-5*) Griffon House.
— Problems in National Literary Identity & the Writer As Social Critic: Selected Papers of the Fourth Annual NDEA Seminar on Foreign Area Studies, February, 1980. LC 80-83126. (CNL/World Report Ser.). 72p. 1980. pap. 4.95 (*0-918680-11-5*) Griffon House.
Paolucci, Anne A., intro. Columbus: Selected Papers on Columbus & His Time. (CNL/World Report Ser.: Vol. IV). 80p. 1989. pap. 4.95 (*0-918680-40-9*) Griffon House.
— Comparative Literature & International Studies. (CNL/World Report Ser.: Vol. II). 64p. 1987. pap. 4.95 (*0-918680-39-5*) Griffon House.
Paolucci, Anne A., ed. see Hegel, Georg Wilhelm Friedrich.
Paolucci, Anne A., jt. ed. see Paolucci, Henry.
Paolucci, Anne A., jt. ed. see Warwick, Ronald.
Paolucci, Anne A., ed. see Winsor, Justin.
Paolucci, Anne A., tr. see Machiavelli, Niccolo.
Paolucci, Antonio. Luca Signorelli. Pelletti, Lisa C., tr. from ITA. (Library of Great Masters). (Illus.). 80p. (Orig.). 1990. pap. 12.99 (*1-878351-12-5*) Riverside NY.
— Luca Signorelli. (Grandes Maestros del Arte Ser.). (SPA., Illus.). 80p. (Orig.). 1993. pap. 12.99 (*1-878351-31-1*) Riverside NY.
***Paolucci, Antonio.** Michelangelo: The Pietas. 208p. 2000. 65.00 (*88-8118-318-8*, Pub. by Skira IT) Abbeville Pr.
Paolucci, Antonio. The Origins of Renaissance Art: The Baptistery Doors, Florence. Chiarini, Francoise Pouncey, tr. LC 96-28403. (Illus.). 176p. 1996. 60.00 (*0-8076-1413-0*) Braziller.
Paolucci, Antonio, et al. Michelangelo: The Medici Chapel. 2nd ed. LC 94-60290. (Illus.). 216p. 2000. reprint ed. 75.00 (*0-500-23690-9*, Pub. by Thames Hudson) Norton.
Paolucci, Antonio, jt. auth. see Hodson, Rupert.
Paolucci, Beatrice, et al. Personal Perspectives. 2nd ed. (Illus.). (gr. 9-12). 1978. text 32.80 (*0-07-048438-4*) McGraw.
— Personal Perspectives: A Guide to Decision Making. LC 72-8842. 466 p. 1973. write for info. (*0-07-048437-6*) McGraw.
Paolucci, Henry. A Brief History of Political Thought & Statecraft. LC 78-62295. 1979. 6.95 (*0-918680-08-5*) Griffon House.
***Paolucci, Henry.** Henry Paolucci: Selected Writings on Literature & the Arts, Science, Astronomy, Law, Government, Political Philosophy. Paolucci, Anne, ed. LC 99-38479. 314p. 1999. 45.00 (*0-918680-79-4*); pap. 18.00 (*0-918680-81-6*) Griffon House.
Paolucci, Henry. Iran, Israel, & the United States: An American Foreign Policy Background Study. xii, 404p. 1991. 14.95 (*0-918680-44-1*); pap. 9.95 (*0-918680-76-X*) Griffon House.
— Kissinger's War, 1957-1980. LC 80-83056. 1980. pap. 4.95 (*0-918680-14-X*) Griffon House.
— Mandragola: Machiavelli. 80p. (C). 1957. pap. text 8.20 (*0-02-391350-9*, Macmillan Coll) P-H.
— The Political Thought of G. W. F. Hegel. LC 78-62416. 1978. pap. 2.50 (*0-918680-06-9*) Griffon House.
— A Separate & Equal Station: Hegel, America & the Nation-State System. LC 78-62415. 1978. pap. 2.50 (*0-918680-05-0*) Griffon House.
— The South & the Presidency: From Reconstruction to Carter. LC 78-62417. 1978. pap. 2.50 (*0-918680-07-7*) Griffon House.
— War, Peace & the Presidency. LC 68-8774. 1968. 9.95 (*0-918680-71-9*) Griffon House.
— Who Is Kissinger? LC 80-83057. 1980. pap. 2.50 (*0-918680-13-1*) Griffon House.
— Zionism, the Superpowers, & the P. L. O. LC 82-15728. 80p. 1982. pap. 6.95 (*0-918680-18-2*, GHGP 708) Griffon House.
Paolucci, Henry, et al, eds. Australia. (Review of National Literatures Ser.: Vol. 11). 256p. 1980. pap. 6.95 (*0-918680-16-6*) Griffon House.
Paolucci, Henry & Paolucci, Anne. Dante & the "Quest for Eloquence" in India's Vernacular Languages. 78p. 1984. pap. 4.95 (*0-918680-28-X*) Griffon House.
Paolucci, Henry & Paolucci, Anne A., eds. Columbus: Modern Views on Columbus & His Time. annuals (CNL/World Reports: Vol. 2). (Illus.). 112p. 1990. pap. 4.95 (*0-918680-46-8*) Griffon House.
— Columbus, America, & the World. (Review of National Literatures Ser.: Vol. 16). 1991. pap. 14.95 (*0-918680-33-6*) Griffon House.
***Paolucci, Henry, et al.** APSA Meeting Papers - 1998: Morale in the Military in War & Peace & Gender, Public Policy & the State. 112p. 1999. pap. 8.95 (*0-918680-83-2*) Griffon House.
Paolucci, Henry, ed. see Augustine, Saint.
Paolucci, Henry, ed. see Hegel, Georg Wilhelm Friedrich.
Paolucci, Henry, ed. see Paolucci, Anne, et al.
Paolucci, Henry, ed. see Winsor, Justin.
Paolucci, Henry, tr. see Beccaria, Cesare.
Paolucci, Henry, tr. see Machiavelli, Niccolo.
Paolucci, Nishan. Grandma, Pray for Me. 68p. 1990. pap. 6.95 (*0-918680-43-3*) Griffon House.
Paolucci, Robert, tr. see Forte, Bruno.
Paolucci, V. & Schaeff, B., eds. Gasless Laparoscopy in General Surgery & Gynecology: Diagnostic-Operative Procedures. LC 96-4646. (Illus.). 176p. 1996. pap. text 89.00 (*0-86577-604-0*) Thieme Med Pubs.
Paon, Michelle, ed. see Careless, Dolores A.
Paone, Donald V. To Be or Not to Be: Reflections on Modern Bioethical Choices. 116p. 1999. pap. 9.95 (*0-9667222-0-5*) Blue Skies.

An Asterisk (*) at the beginning of an entry indicates that the title is appearing for the first time.

Paone, Rocco M. Strategic Nonfuel Minerals & Western Security. 242p. (C). 1992. lib. bdg. 47.50 (*0-8191-8469-1*) U Pr of Amer.

Paonessa, Pamela N. Public & Social Policy: Subject Analysis with Reference Bibliography. rev. ed. LC 94-3138. 1994. 47.50 (*0-7883-0346-5*) ABBE Pubs Assn.

Paonessa, Pamella N. Public & Social Policy: Subject Analysis with Reference Bibliography. rev. ed. LC 94-31238. 1994. pap. 44.50 (*0-7883-0347-3*) ABBE Pubs Assn.

Paoni, Frank. Becoming a Teacher. 256p. (C). 1995. pap. text, per. 39.95 (*0-7872-1505-8*) Kendall-Hunt.

— On Becoming a Teacher. 2nd ed. 272p. (C). 1997. per. 40.62 (*0-7872-4196-2*) Kendall-Hunt.

Paoni, Frank. On Becoming a Teacher: Some Important Things You'll Need to Know & Use. 2nd ed. 238p. (C). per. 50.95 (*0-7872-6434-2*) Kendall-Hunt.

Paoni, Frank. Strategies & Techniques for Successful Teaching. 2nd ed. 160p. (C). 1997. per. 48.95 (*0-7872-4440-6*, 41444001) Kendall-Hunt.

— Strategies & Techniques for Successful Teaching Classroom Techniques. 148p. (C). 1994. per. 26.95 (*0-8403-9276-1*) Kendall-Hunt.

Paor, De, see De Paor.

Paor, Liam De, see De Paor, Liam.

Paor, Louis de, see de Paor, Louis, ed.

Paorici, C., jt. ed. see Baldereschi, A.

Paorici, C., jt. ed. see Fornari, R.

Paorici, C., jt. ed. see Rodriguez-Clemente, R.

Paozols, Alex. All the Women in Florida. 2nd rev. ed. 100p. 1998. pap. 8.00 (*1-891051-09-1*) Back Cover Pr.

Pap, Arthur, jt. ed. see Edwards, Paul.

Pap, Endre. Complex Analysis Through Examples & Exercises. LC 99-15360. (Texts in the Mathematical Sciences Ser.). 1999. write for info. (*0-7923-5787-6*) Kluwer Academic.

— Null-Additive Set Functions. (Mathematics & Its Applications Ser.: Vol. 337). 324p. (C). 1995. text 154.50 (*0-7923-3658-5*) Kluwer Academic.

Pap, Endre, et al. Partial Differential Equations Through Examples & Exercises. LC 97-18393. (Texts in Mathematical Sciences Ser.). 416p. 1997. text 214.00 (*0-7923-4724-2*) Kluwer Academic.

Pap, Judit M., ed. The Sea As a Variable Star - Solar & Stellar Irradiance Variations: Proceedings of the 143rd Colloquim of the International Astronomical Union Held in Clarion Harvest House, Boulder, California, June 20-25, 1993. 328p. (C). 1994. text 186.50 (*0-7923-3040-4*) Kluwer Academic.

Pap, Judit M., et al, eds. The Sun As a Variable Star: Solar & Stellar Irradiance Variations, Proceedings of the 143rd IAU Colloquium, Boulder, CO, 1993. 312p. 1994. 132.00 (*0-614-32146-8*) Kluwer Academic.

Pap, Judith M., et al. Solar Electromagnetic Radiation Study for Solar Cycle 22. LC 98-11762. 517p. 1998. write for info. (*0-7923-4999-7*) Kluwer Academic.

Pap, Leo. The Portuguese in the United States: A Bibliography. LC 76-9270. (Bibliographies & Documentation Ser.). 100p. 1976. pap. 9.95 (*0-913256-21-8*) CMS.

Papa. Familiar British & American Songs. Date not set. pap. text. write for info. (*0-582-79088-3*, Pub. by Addison-Wesley) Longman.

— Turning Points High School Teacher Edition System - Texas. 1995. 0.00 (*0-201-51889-9*) Addison-Wesley.

— Turning Points Middle School Teacher Edition System - Texas. 1989. 0.00 (*0-201-51888-0*) Addison-Wesley.

Papa, Albert R., jt. auth. see Wooley, Peter J.

Papa, Anthony J., jt. ed. see Kuryla, William C.

Papa, Carrie. The Carousel Keepers: An Oral History of American Carousels. LC 96-48713. (Illus.). 264p. 1998. pap. 16.95 (*0-939923-67-X*) M & W Pub Co.

Papa-Grimaldi, Alba. Time & Reality. LC 97-78426. (Avebury Series in Philosophy). 229p. 1998. text 63.95 (*1-84014-334-7*, Pub. by Ashgate Pub) Ashgate Pub Co.

Papa, Iantorno. Turning Points 4. (Turning Points Ser.). 128p. (YA). (gr. 7-12). 1989. pap. text 12.48 (*0-201-06324-7*) Addison-Wesley.

Papa Jim, pseud. Book of Shadows: Personal Use. Ayala, Leticia M., ed. (Illus.). 60p. 1990. pap. 3.95 (*1-878575-05-8*) El Rey Pub.

— Papa Jim Magical Herb Book: How to Use Herbs for Magical Purposes. Ayala, Leticia M., ed. (Papa Jim Bks.: No. 1). (Illus.). 63p. 1985. pap. 3.95 (*1-878575-00-7*) El Rey Pub.

— Papa Jim Magical Oil Book: How to Use Oils for Magical Purposes. Ayala, Leticia M., ed. (Papa Jim Bks.: No. 2). (Illus.). 55p. 1989. pap. 3.95 (*1-878575-01-5*) El Rey Pub.

— Papa Jim Medicinal Herbs: Commonly Used Herbs. Ayala, Leticia M., ed. (Papa Jim Bks.: No. 4). (Illus.). 106p. 1990. pap. 3.95 (*1-878575-03-1*) El Rey Pub.

— Papa Jim's Herbs for Illnesses: Herbs & Herbal Combinations. Ayala, Leticia M., ed. (Papa Jim Bks.: No. 5). (Illus.). 78p. 1990. pap. 3.95 (*1-878575-02-3*) El Rey Pub.

— Papa Jim's Spell Book: Rituals & Spells for Voodoo. Ayala, Leticia M., ed. (Papa Jim Bks.: No. 3). (Illus.). 69p. 1989. pap. 3.95 (*1-878575-04-X*) El Rey Pub.

Papa, John & Shepker, Matthew. Microsoft SQL Server 7 Programming Unleashed. 2nd ed. (Sams Unleashed Series). (Illus.). 946p. 1999. pap. 49.99 (*0-672-31293-X*) Sams.

Papa, Kondaveeti. Women in Rural Areas. (C). 1992. 16.00 (*81-85613-60-5*, Pub. by Chugh Pubns) S Asia.

Papa, Mario. Papa! Turning Points, Level 3. 1989. pap. text, wbk. ed. 8.00 (*0-201-06322-0*) Addison-Wesley.

— Papa! Turning Points, Level 4. 1989. pap. text, wbk. ed. 8.00 (*0-201-06325-5*) Addison-Wesley.

— Placmnt Tsts Turn Points. 2nd ed. 80p. 1995. pap. text 39.73 (*0-201-53804-0*) Addison-Wesley.

— Turning Points, Bk. 1B. 2nd ed. 1994. pap. text, student ed. 7.01 (*0-201-76520-9*) Addison-Wesley.

— Turning Points, Bk. 3A. (C). 1988. ring bd., wbk. ed. 4.11 (*0-201-19026-5*) Addison-Wesley.

— Turning Points, Level 1. 1989. pap. text, wbk. ed. 8.00 (*0-201-06316-6*) Addison-Wesley.

— Turning Points, Vol. 1A. (C). 1988. ring bd., wbk. ed. 3.99 (*0-201-19022-2*) Addison-Wesley.

— Turning Points, Vol. 3A. (C). 1988. pap. text 6.57 (*0-201-19016-8*) Addison-Wesley.

— Turning Points, Vol. 3B. (C). 1988. ring bd., wbk. ed. 3.89 (*0-201-19027-3*) Addison-Wesley.

— Turning Points, Vol. 4A. (C). 1988. ring bd., wbk. ed. 3.89 (*0-201-19028-1*) Addison-Wesley.

— Turning Points, Vol. 4B. (C). 1988. pap. text 6.57 (*0-201-19019-2*) Addison-Wesley.

— Turning Points: Puerto Rico. (SPA.). 1992. text 14.50 (*0-201-50087-6*) Addison-Wesley.

— Turning Points 1B. 2nd ed. 64p. 1994. ring bd., wbk. ed. 4.67 (*0-201-76522-5*) Addison-Wesley.

— Turning Points 2, Bk. 2. 2nd ed. 1994. ring bd., wbk. ed. 9.26 (*0-201-53819-9*) Addison-Wesley.

— Turning Points 1A. 2nd ed. 64p. 1994. ring bd., wbk. ed. 4.67 (*0-201-76521-7*) Addison-Wesley.

— Turning Points 1A, No. 1A. 1988. pap. text 6.96 (*0-201-19012-5*) Addison-Wesley.

— Turning Points 2A, Bk. 2A. 1988. ring bd., wbk. ed. 4.11 (*0-201-19024-9*) Addison-Wesley.

— Turning Points 2A, Bk. 2A. 2nd ed. 1994. ring bd., wbk. ed. 4.67 (*0-201-76525-X*) Addison-Wesley.

— Turning Points 2A, Bk. 2A. 2nd ed. 1994. pap. text, student ed. 7.01 (*0-201-76523-3*) Addison-Wesley.

— Turning Points 2B, Bk. 2B. 1988. ring bd., wbk. ed. 4.11 (*0-201-19025-7*) Addison-Wesley.

— Turning Points 2B, Bk. 2B. 2nd ed. 1994. pap. text, student ed. 7.01 (*0-201-76524-1*); ring bd., wbk. ed. 4.67 (*0-201-76526-8*) Addison-Wesley.

— Turning Points 2B, No. 2B. 1988. pap. text 6.96 (*0-201-19015-X*) Addison-Wesley.

— Turning Points 3, Bk. 3. 2nd ed. 112p. 1994. ring bd., wbk. ed. 9.27 (*0-201-53823-7*) Addison-Wesley.

— Turning Points 3, No. 3. 2nd ed. 144p. 1994. pap. text, student ed. 14.03 (*0-201-53822-9*) Addison-Wesley.

— Turning Points 3A, Bk. 3A. 2nd ed. 1994. pap. text, student ed. 7.01 (*0-201-76527 6*) Addison-Wesley.

— Turning Points 3A, Bk. 3A. 2nd ed. 1994. ring bd., wbk. ed. 4.67 (*0-201-76529-2*) Addison-Wesley.

— Turning Points 3B, Bk. 3B. 2nd ed. 1994. pap. text, student ed. 7.01 (*0-201-76528-4*) Addison-Wesley.

— Turning Points 3B, Bk. 3B. 2nd ed. 1994. ring bd., wbk. ed. 4.67 (*0-201-76530-6*) Addison-Wesley.

— Turning Points 4, Bk. 4. rev. ed. 1992. ring bd., wbk. ed. 7.83 (*0-201-52680-8*) Addison-Wesley.

— Turning Points 4, Bk. 4. 2nd ed. 1994. ring bd., wbk. ed. 9.26 (*0-201-53827-X*) Addison-Wesley.

— Turning Points 4, No. 4. 2nd ed. 144p. 1994. pap. text, student ed. 14.03 (*0-201-53826-1*) Addison-Wesley.

— Turning Points 4A, Bk. 4A. 2nd ed. 1994. ring bd., wbk. ed. 4.67 (*0-201-76533-0*) Addison-Wesley Educ.

Papa, Mario & Iantorno, Giuliano. Turning Points, Bk. 1. 2nd ed. (ESL Ser.). (Illus.). 144p. (C). 1994. pap. text, student ed. 14.03 (*0-201-53814-8*); ring bd., wbk. ed. 9.26 (*0-201-53815-6*) Addison-Wesley.

Papa, Michael J. Good Communication: A Lost Art. LC 97-51496. 96p. 1998. 9.95 (*1-56825-070-3*) Rainbow Books.

Papa, Mike, Jr. The Papa Gambit vs. the French Defense: Beating the French. (Illus.). 50p. (Orig.). 1991. pap. text 10.00 (*0-9628959-0-3*) Mich Pubns.

Papa, O. A., jt. auth. see Boelhouwer, P.

Papa, Robert D. The Dissolved Face of God, Vol. 1. large type ed. 110p. 1999. pap. 4.95 (*0-9638855-1-0*) Prisoners Web.

— Let the Seasons Change: Four Introspections on God's Providence. 100p. (Orig.). 1993. pap. 5.95 (*0-9638855-0-2*) Prisoners Web.

Papa, S., et al, eds. Frontiers of Cellular Bioenergetics: Molecular Biology, Biochemistry & Physiopathology. LC 98-49078. (Illus.). xxx, 801p. (C). 1999. text. write for info. (*0-306-45851-9*, Kluwer Plenum) Kluwer Academic.

Papa, S. & Tager, J. M., eds. Biochemistry of Cell Membranes: A Compendium of Selected Topics. (Molecular & Cell Biology Updates Ser.). 376p. 1995. 149.00 (*3-7643-5056-3*) Birkhauser.

Papa, Sergio, et al, eds. Cytochrome Systems: Molecular Biology & Bioenergetics. LC 87-25766. 822p. 1988. 135.00 (*0-306-42693-5*, Plenum Trade) Perseus Pubng.

Papa, Sergio, jt. ed. see Tager, J. M.

Papa, Stephen. The Last Man Jailed for Blasphemy. LC 97-91370. 92p. 1998. pap. 10.00 (*0-9660325-1-9*) Trillium Bks.

Papa, Wendy. Public Speaking Workbook. 252p. (C). 1996. pap. text, per. 26.95 (*0-7872-2353-0*) Kendall-Hunt.

— Survival Tips for Public Speaking. 168p. (C). 1998. per. 33.95 (*0-7872-5136-4*, 41513601) Kendall-Hunt.

Papachristopoulou, Ioannis, jt. ed. see Dietz, Soren.

***Papachristos, Katherine.** L'Inscription de l'Oral et de l'Ecrit Dans le Theatre de Tristan Tzara. (Currents in Comparative Romance Languages & Literatures Ser.: Vol. 69). xi, 226p. (C). 1999. text 51.00 (*0-8204-3956-8*) P Lang Pubng.

Papaconstantinou, Helen. Free Trade & Competition in the EEC: Law, Policy & Practice. 256p. 1988. lib. bdg. 57.50 (*0-415-00110-2*) Routledge.

— Free Trade & Competition in the EEC: Law, Policy & Practice. LC 89-117115. 234p. reprint ed. pap. 72.60 (*0-608-20368-8*, 207162100002) Bks Demand.

Papacosma, S. Victor. The Military in Greek Politics: The 1909 Coup D'Etat. LC 77-22391. 266p. reprint ed. pap. 82.50 (*0-7837-0505-0*, 204082900018) Bks Demand.

Papacosma, S. Victor & Heiss, Mary A., eds. NATO in the Post-Cold War Era: Does It Have a Future? (Illus.). 384p. 1995. text 55.00 (*0-312-12130-X*) St Martin.

Papacosma, S. Victor & Laurent, Pierre H., eds. NATO & the European Union: Confronting the Challenges of European Security & Enlargement. pap. 12.50 (*1-882160-04-5*) Kent St U L L Lemnitzer.

Papacosma, S. Victor, ed. see Gazdag, Ferenc, et al.

Papacosma, S. Victor, ed. see Hurwitz, Leon.

Papacosma, S. Victor, ed. see Khadiagala, Gilbert M.

Papacosma, S. Victor, jt. ed. see Rubin, Mark R.

Papacostas, C. S., ed. Energy Systems for the Twenty-First Century. LC 86-25916. 112p. 1986. 16.00 (*0-87262-571-0*) Am Soc Civil Eng.

Papacostas, C. S. & Prevedouros, P. D. Transportation Engineering & Planning. 2nd ed. 642p. (C). 1992. 105.00 (*0-13-958075-1*) P-H.

***Papacostas, C. S. & Prevedouros, Panos D.** Transportation Engineering & Planning. 3rd ed. 750p. 2000. 105.00 (*0-13-081419-9*, Prentice Hall) P-H.

Papadakis, A., et al, eds. Deconstruction Omnibus. 1p. 1989. 85.00 (*0-85670-996-4*, Pub. by Academy Ed UK) Wiley.

Papadakis, Andreas. Architecture of Today. 1997. pap. 27.50 (*2-87939-134-2*) St Martin.

— Theory & Experimentation, Vol. 1. 1993. 95.00 (*0-312-08935-X*) St Martin.

Papadakis, Andreas, ed. Contemporary Architecture. (Architectural Design Ser.: No. 74). (Illus.). 96p. 1988. pap. 21.95 (*0-85670-953-0*) Academy Ed UK.

— Deconstruction, No. III. (Academy Editions Ser.). (Illus.). 96p. (Orig.). 1991. pap. 21.95 (*0-312-06127-7*) St Martin.

***Papadakis, Andreas C.** The End of Innovation in Architecture, Vol. 2. (New Architecture Ser.). 144p. 1998. pap. text 27.50 (*1-901092-09-7*) Andreas Papadakis.

Papadakis, Angie, jt. auth. see Shafer, Harry P.

Papadakis, Aristeides. The Christian East & the Rise of the Papacy: The Church 1071-1453 A.D. LC 94-16429. 434p. 1994. 29.95 (*0-88141-058-6*); pap. 17.95 (*0-88141-057-8*) St Vladimirs.

— Crisis in Byzantium: The Filioque Controversy in the Patriarchate of Gregory II of Cyprus (1283-1289) LC 97-33514. 1997. pap. 17.95 (*0-88141-176-0*) St Vladimirs.

Papadakis, Brenda M. Dear Jane: The Two Hundred Twenty-Five Patterns from the 1863 Jane Stickle Quilt. (Illus.). 160p. (Orig.). 1996. pap. 25.95 (*1-881588-15-7*, 882670199) EZ Quilting.

Papadakis, C. M., jt. ed. see Webb, D.

Papadakis, C. N., ed. see American Society of Mechanical Engineers Staff.

Papadakis, Constantine & Scarton, Henry, eds. Fluid Transients & Acoustics in the Power Industry: Presented at the Winter Annual Meeting of the American Society of Mechanical Engineers, San Francisco, California, December 10-15, 1978. LC 78-60044. (Illus.). 366p. reprint ed. pap. 113.50 (*0-608-11712-9*, 201387500087) Bks Demand.

Papadakis, Elim. Environmental Politics & Institutional Change. (Reshaping Australian Institutions Ser.: No. 4). (Illus.). 256p. (C). 1997. text 69.95 (*0-521-55407-1*) Cambridge U Pr.

— Historical Dictionary of the Green Movement. LC 98-7912. (Historical Dictionaries of Religions, Philosophies, & Movements Ser.: No. 20). 256p. 1998. 62.00 (*0-8108-3502-9*) Scarecrow.

— Politics & the Environment. 240p. (Orig.). 1993. pap. text 22.95 (*1-86373-363-9*, Pub. by Allen & Unwin Pty) Paul & Co Pubs.

***Papadakis, Emmanuel P.** Ultrasonic Instruments & Devices. (Illus.). 850p. 2000. pap. text 99.95 (*0-12-531951-7*) Acad Pr.

***Papadakis, M. P., ed.** Civil Trial Practice: Winning Techniques of Successful Trial Attorneys. 900p. 2000. 149.00 (*0-913875-89-9*, 5899-N) Lawyers & Judges.

Papadakis, M. P., jt. auth. see McCormick, Barnes W.

Papadakis, Myron P., jt. auth. see McCormick, Barnes W.

Papadakis, Nikos & Glassner, Martin I., eds. International Law of the Sea & Marine Affairs: A Bibliography-A Supplement to the 1980 Edition. 1984. lib. bdg. 228.50 (*90-247-2815-0*) Kluwer Academic.

Papadakis, Vassilis & Barwise, Patrick, eds. Strategic Decisions. LC 97-26546. 328p. 1997. 126.50 (*0-7923-9987-0*) Kluwer Academic.

Papadatos, Androa, tr. see Darsinos, Spiros.

Papadatos, Costa & Papadatou, Danai, eds. Children & Death. (Death Education, Aging & Health Care Ser.). 280p. 1991. 72.95 (*1-56032-043-5*) Hemisp Pub.

Papadatou, Danai, jt. ed. see Papadatos, Costa.

Papademetr. Generalized Functions. 250p. 1998. write for info. (*0-12-544955-0*) Acad Pr.

***Papademetriou, Demetrios G.** Balancing Acts: Toward a Fair Bargain on Seasonal Agricultural Workers. 1999. pap. 10.95 (*0-87003-175-9*) Carnegie Endow.

Papademetriou, Demetrios G. & DiMarzio, Nicholas. Undocumented Aliens in the New York Metropolitan Area. LC 85-23385. 292p. (C). 1986. pap. 14.95 (*0-913256-99-4*) CMS.

Papademetriou, Demetrios G. & Hamilton, Kimberly. Converging Paths to Restriction: French, Italian, & British Responses to Immigration. (International Migration Policy Issues Ser.). 80p. 1995. pap. 9.95 (*0-87003-073-6*) Carnegie Endow.

— Managing Uncertainty: Regulating Immigration Flows in Advanced Industrial Countries. (International Migration Policy Issues Ser.). 42p. 1995. pap. 8.95 (*0-87003-069-8*) Carnegie Endow.

Papademetriou, Demetrios G. & Larkin, Mary A. The Border & Beyond: Cooperation & Conflict on Migration Issues in U. S. - Mexico Relations. (International Migration Policy Ser.). 80p. 1999. pap. 9.95 (*0-87003-085-X*) Carnegie Endow.

Papademetriou, Demetrios G. & Yale-Loehr, Stephen. Balancing Interests: Rethinking the U. S. Selection of Skilled Immigrants. (International Migration Policy Ser.). 214p. 1996. pap. 14.95 (*0-87003-107-4*) Carnegie Endow.

Papademetriou, Demetrios G., et al. Reorganizing the Immigration Function: Toward a New Framework for Accountability. LC 98-73642. (International Migration Policy Issues Ser.: Vol. 7). 56p. 1998. pap. 9.95 (*0-87003-138-4*) Carnegie Endow.

Papademetriou, Demetrios G., jt. ed. see Lowell, Lindsay.

Papademetriou, Demetrious G. & Martin, Philip L., eds. The Unsettled Relationship: Labor Migration & Economic Development, 33. LC 90-45603. (Contributions in Labor Studies: No. 33). 336p. 1991. 69.50 (*0-313-25463-X*, PDA, Greenwood Pr) Greenwood.

Papademetriou, George C. The Cults. 20p. 1985. pap. 1.00 (*0-917651-20-0*) Holy Cross Orthodox.

— Essays on Orthodox Christian-Jewish Relations. LC 90-50392. 135p. (C). 1990. text 32.00 (*1-55605-165-4*); pap. text 16.00 (*1-55605-164-6*) Wyndham Hall.

***Papademetriou, George C.** The History of Philosophy: A Concise Guide for Students. 125p. 2000. pap. text 28.00 (*1-55605-301-0*) Wyndham Hall.

Papademetriou, George C. An Introduction to Orthodox Spirituality. 24p. (Orig.). 1988. pap. 1.50 (*0-917651-53-7*) Holy Cross Orthodox.

— Maimonides & Palamas on God. LC 93-50531. 127p. (Orig.). (C). 1994. pap. text 9.95 (*0-916586-68-5*, Pub. by Holy Cross Orthodox) BookWorld.

Papademetriou, Lisa. Lucky Me! (Illus.). 48p. (J). 1999. 17.90 (*0-7613-2071-7*, Copper Beech Bks) Millbrook Pr.

***Papademetriou, Lisa.** Lucky Me! (Real Kids Readers Ser.). (Illus.). 48p. (J). (gr. 1-3). 1999. pap. write for info. (*0-7613-2096-2*, Copper Beech Bks) Millbrook Pr.

Papademetriou, Lisa. My Pen Pal, Pat. LC 98-16596. (Real Kids Readers Ser.). (Illus.). 48p. (J). (gr. 1-3). 1998. pap. 3.99 (*0-7613-2048-2*, Copper Beech Bks); lib. bdg. 17.90 (*0-7613-2023-7*, Copper Beech Bks) Millbrook Pr.

— Really? LC 99-12778. 48p. (J). (gr. 1-3). 1999. 17.90 (*0-7613-2072-5*, Copper Beech Bks) Millbrook Pr.

***Papademetriou, Lisa.** Really? LC 99-12778. (Real Kids Readers Ser.). (Illus.). 48p. (J). (gr. 1-3). 1999. pap. 3.99 (*0-7613-2097-0*, Copper Beech Bks) Millbrook Pr.

Papademetriou, Lisa. You're in Big Trouble, Brad! LC 98-11026. (Real Kids Readers Ser.). (Illus.). 48p. (J). (gr. 1-3). 1998. pap. 3.99 (*0-7613-2047-4*); lib. bdg. 17.90 (*0-7613-2022-9*) Millbrook Pr.

Papademetriou, Theresa. A Comparative Survey of the Laws on Abortion of Selected Countries. 181p. (Orig.). (C). 1993. pap. text 30.00 (*1-56806-214-1*) DIANE Pub.

Papadiamantis, Alexandros. The Murderess. Levi, Peter, tr. from GRE. 127p. 1983. 13.95 (*0-904613-94-1*); pap. 5.95 (*0-906495-72-5*) Writers & Readers.

— Tales from a Greek Island. 200p. (C). 1994. reprint ed. pap. text 12.95 (*0-8018-4846-6*) Johns Hopkins.

Papadimitrakopoulos, Elias. Toothpaste with Chlorophyll & Maritime Hot Baths. Taylor, John, tr. from GRE. & intro. by. LC 91-76941. (Illus.). 104p. (Orig.). 1992. 17.95 (*1-878580-42-6*); pap. 8.95 (*1-878580-43-4*) Asylum Arts.

Papadimitriou. Modernizing Financial Systems. LC 99-15311. 1999. text 79.95 (*0-312-22255-6*) St Martin.

Papadimitriou, Christos, jt. auth. see Lewis, Harry.

Papadimitriou, Christos H. Computational Complexity. (Illus.). 500p. (C). 1993. 42.67 (*0-201-53082-1*) Addison-Wesley.

— Computational Complexity. LC 93-5662. 1993. write for info. (*0-02-015308-2*) Macmillan.

— The Theory of Database Concurrency Control. (Principles of Computer Science Ser.). (C). 1986. text 36.80 (*0-7167-8055-0*, Computer Sci Pr) W H Freeman.

Papadimitriou, Christos H. & Steiglitz, Kenneth. Combinatorial Optimization: Algorithms & Complexity. unabridged ed. LC 98-21476. 496p. 1998. pap. 14.95 (*0-486-40258-4*) Dover.

***Papadimitriou, Dimitri B.** Full Employment Has Not Been Achieved. (Public Policy Brief Highlights Ser.: Vol. 53A). 6p. 1999. pap. write for info. (*0-941276-74-0*) J Levy.

— Full Employment Has Not Been Achieved: Full Employment Policy: Theory & Practice. (Public Policy Brief Ser.: Vol. 53). 32p. 1999. pap. write for info. (*0-941276-73-2*) J Levy.

Papadimitriou, Dimitri B., ed. Aspects of Distribution of Wealth & Income. LC 93-40402. 1994. text 69.95 (*0-312-12101-6*) St Martin.

***Papadimitriou, Dimitri B. & Wray, L. Randall.** Does Social Security Need Savings? Providing for Retirees Throughout the Twenty-First Century. 48p. 1999. pap. write for info. (*0-941276-77-5*) J Levy.

Papadimitriou, Dimitri B. & Wray, L. Randall. Monetary Policy Uncovered: Flying Blind: The Federal Reserve's Experiment with Unobservables. (Public Policy Brief Ser.: Vol. 15). (Illus.). 60p. (Orig.). 1994. pap. write for info. (*0-941276-03-1*) J Levy.

— Targeting Inflation: The Effects of Monetary Policy on the CPI & Its Housing Component. (Public Policy Brief Ser.: Vol. 27). (Illus.). 54p. (Orig.). 1996. pap. 3.00 (*0-941276-18-X*) J Levy.

*Papadimitriou, Dimitri B. & Wray, Randall. Does Social Security Need Saving? (Public Policy Brief Highlights Ser.: Vol. 55A). 6p. 1999. pap. write for info. (0-941276-78-3) J Levy.

Papadimitriou, Dimitri B., et al. An Alternative in Small Business Finance: Community-Based Factoring Companies & Small Business Lending. (Public Policy Brief Ser.: No. 12). (Illus.). 48p. (Orig.). 1994. pap. write for info. (0-941276-00-7) J Levy.

Papadimitriou, Dimitri B., jt. ed. see Fazzari, Steven.

Papadopolos, Gerasimos. Reflections: Christian Faith. 1995. pap. 9.95 (1-885652-37-2, Pub. by Holy Cross Orthodox) BookWorld.

Papadopoullos, Theodore H. Greek Church & People under Turkish Domination. 2nd ed. 580p. 1990. text 114.95 (0-86078-278-6, Pub. by Variorum) Ashgate Pub Co.

— Studies & Documents Relating to the History of the Greek Church & People Under Turkish Domination. LC 78-38759. reprint ed. 39.50 (0-404-56314-7) AMS Pr.

Papadopoulos, Alex G. Urban Regimes & Strategies: Building Europe's Central Executive District in Brussels. (Illus.). 288p. 1996. pap. text 23.00 (0-226-64559-2) U Ch Pr.

Papadopoulos, Apostolos G., jt. ed. see Kasimis, Charalambos.

Papadopoulos, Athanase. Multilateral Diplomacy Within the Commonwealth. 1982. lib. bdg. 96.00 (90-247-2568-2) Kluwer Academic.

Papadopoulos, Athanase, jt. auth. see Coornaert, Michel.

Papadopoulos, Athanasios. Excavations at Aigion, 1970. (Studies in Mediterranean Archaeology: Vol. XLVI). (Illus.). 165p. (Orig.). 1976. pap. 67.95 (91-85058-68-8) P Astroms.

Papadopoulos, Athanasios J. Mycenaean Achaea Pts. 1 & 2: Text & Figures. (Studies in Mediterranean Archaeology: Vol. LV:1-2). (Illus.). 573p. (Orig.). 1979. pap. 165.00 (91-85058-83-1) P Astroms.

Papadopoulos, C. True Visual Magnitude Photographic Star Atlas: Southern Stars & Equatorial Stars. 1979. 865.00 (0-08-021622-6, Pergamon Pr) Elsevier.

Papadopoulos, Chris. Sexual Aspects of Cardiovascular Disease, 10. LC 89-3973. (Sexual Medicine Ser.: No. 10). 120p. 1989. 55.00 (0-275-92523-4, C2523, Praeger Pubs) Greenwood.

Papadopoulos, Christos. Clean Combustion Technologies Pt. B: Proceedings of the Second International Conference. Da Graca Carvalho, Maria et al, eds. (Energy, Combustion & the Environment Ser.: Vol. 2). 572p. 1999. text 120.00 (90-5699-621-5, ECU154, Harwood Acad Pubs) Gordon & Breach.

*Papadopoulos, George. Breaking Time's Barriers. (Illus.). 210p. (Orig.). 1999. pap. 13.95 (0-9668015-1-2) OceanTides Pubg.

— The Last Dynasty of the Angels. Moore, Charles, tr. LC 98-68080. (Illus.). 338p. (Orig.). 1998. pap. 14.95 (0-9668015-0-4) OceanTides Pubg.

Papadopoulos, George A. Fracture Mechanics: The Experimental Method of Caustics & the Det. - Criterion of Fracture. LC 92-27308. 1996. 305.00 (0-387-19768-0) Spr-Verlag.

Papadopoulos, George S. Die Entwicklung des Bildungswesens von 1960 bis 1990: Der Beitrag der OECD. (Bildungsforschung Internationaler Organisationen Ser.: Bd. 13). (GER.). 239p. 1996. pap. 31.95 (3-631-31171-0) P Lang Pubng.

Papadopoulos, Gerasimos. At the End of Time: The Eshatological Expectations of the Church. Chamberos, Peter, tr. LC 97-49366. 1997. pap. 5.95 (1-885652-06-2, Pub. by Holy Cross Orthodox) BookWorld.

Papadopoulos, Gerasimos & Chamberas, Peter A. Agape & Diakonia: Essays in Memory of Bishop Gerasimos of Abydos. LC 98-3082. 1998. write for info. (1-885652-16-X, Pub. by Holy Cross Orthodox) BookWorld.

Papadopoulos, Gerasimos, et al. Bishop Gerasimos of Abydos: The Spiritual Elder of America. Chamberas, Peter, ed. & tr. by. LC 97-43838. 137p. 1997. pap. 7.95 (1-885652-04-6, Pub. by Holy Cross Orthodox) BookWorld.

P

Papadopoulos, Gregory M. Implementation of a General Purpose Dataflow Multiprocessor. (Pitman Ser.). 175p. 1991. pap. text 27.95 (0-262-66069-5) MIT Pr.

Papadopoulos, K., jt. ed. see Palmadesco, Peter J.

Papadopoulos, Nicolas & Heslop, Louise A. Product-Country Images: Impact & Role in International Marketing. LC 91-35947. (Illus.). 480p. 1993. lib. bdg. 79.95 (1-56024-236-1) Haworth Pr.

Papadopoulos, Nicolas & Heslop, Louise A., eds. Product-Country Images: Impact & Role in International Marketing. 477p. 1993. pap. 29.95 (1-56024-237-X) Haworth Pr.

Papadopoulos, Renos, ed. Carl Gustav Jung: Critical Assessments, 4 vols., Set. LC 92-1044. 1875p. (C). 1992. 660.00 (0-415-04830-3, A7769) Routledge.

Papadopoulou, T. Elementary Particle Physics: Proceedings of the First Hellenic School held in Corfu, Greece, Sept. 12-30, 1982. 700p. (C). 1984. 108.00 (9971-950-99-5) World Scientific Pub.

Papadopulos, Leo, jt. auth. see Holy Apostles Convent Staff.

Papadopulos, Leonidas J. & Lizardos, Georgia, trs. from GRE. The Life & Sufferings of Saint Catherine the Great Martyr. (Illus.). 1986. pap. 2.00 (0-913026-63-8) St Nectarios.

Papadopulos, V. & Gordon, A. Non-Timber Tree Products: A Partial Inventory of Products Available in the Mount Cameroon Area. 1977. pap. 60.00 (0-85954-465-6, Pub. by Nat Res Inst) St Mut.

Papadoupoulos, Renos K. & Byng-Hall, John. Multiple Voices: Narrative in Systemic Family Psychotherapy. LC 97-44057. 304p. (C). 1998. pap. 24.99 (0-415-92085-X) Routledge.

— Multiple Voices: Narrative in Systemic Family Psychotherapy. LC 97-44057. 304p. (C). 1998. 75.00 (0-415-92084-1) Routledge.

Papadrakakis, M., ed. Innovative Computational Mechanics for Structural Mechanics. 300p. 1997. 240.00 (1-874672-05-9, Pub. by Civil-Comp) St Mut.

Papadrakakis, M. & Topping, B. H. V. Advances in Computational Mechanics with High Performance Computing. 375p. 1994. pap. (0-948749-28-8, Pub. by Civil-Comp) St Mut.

— Advances in Finite Element Techniques. 235p. 1994. pap. (0-948749-24-5, Pub. by Civil-Comp) St Mut.

— Advances in Post & Preprocessing for Finite Element Technology. 220p. 1994. pap. (0-948749-23-7, Pub. by Civil-Comp) St Mut.

— Advances in Simulation & Interaction Techniques. 243p. 1994. pap. (0-948749-25-3, Pub. by Civil-Comp) St Mut.

— Computional Structural Engineering for Practice. 289p. 1994. pap. 245.00 (0-948749-30-X, Pub. by Civil-Comp) St Mut.

Papadrakakis, M., jt. auth. see Topping, B. H. V.

Papadrakakis, Manolis, ed. Parallel Solution Methods in Computational Mechanics. 520p. 1997. 230.00 (0-471-95696-1) Wiley.

Papadrakakis, Manolis, ed. Solving Large-Scale Problems in Mechanics: The Development & Application of Computational Solution Methods. 488p. 1993. 215.00 (0-471-93809-2) Wiley.

Papaevangelou, G. & Hennessen, W., eds. Viral Hepatitis: Standardization in Immunoprophylaxis of Infections by Hepatitis Viruses. (Developments in Biological Standardization Ser.: Vol. 54). (Illus.). xviii, 590p. 1983. pap. 61.00 (3-8055-3826-X) S Karger.

Papafava, Francesco. Vatican. (Illus.). 191p. 1993. 75.00 (88-86921-03-9); pap. 55.00 (88-86921-02-0) Treasures Inc.

Papagapitos, Karen. Gemini Code II. Kleinman, Estelle & Nicholson, David, eds. (JB Ser.). (Illus.). 96p. (Orig.). (J). (gr. 5-8). 1996. 7.95 (0-9637328-2-X) Kapa Hse Pr.

— Jose's Basket. 2nd ed. Kleinman, Estelle, ed. (JB Ser.). (Illus.). 32p. (J). (gr. 1-3). 1993. 6.95 (0-9637328-1-1) Kapa Hse Pr.

— Socorro, Daughter of the Desert. Kleinman, Estelle, ed. (JB Ser.). (Illus.). 64p. (J). (gr. 3-6). 1993. 6.95 (0-9637328-0-3) Kapa Hse Pr.

*Papagaroufalis, C., et al, eds. New Challenges in Surfactant Research: Proceedings of the 15th International Workshop on Surfactant Replacement, Kos, June 2000. (Biology of the Neonate Ser.: Vol. 77, Suppl. 1 (2000)). (Illus.). iv, 30p. 2000. pap. 25.25 (3-8055-7094-5) S Karger.

Papageorge & Fellmeth. California White Collar Crime, Issue 3. 251p. 1998. ring bd. write for info. (0-327-00528-9, 8026612) LEXIS Pub.

Papageorge, Thoams A. & Fellmeth, Robert C. California White Collar Crime: Civil Remedies & Criminal Sanctions. 800p. 1995. reprint ed. 115.00 (0-614-10362-2, MICHIE) LEXIS Pub.

*Papageorge, Thomas A. & Fellmeth, Robert C. California White Collar Crime, Issue 4. 100p. 1999. ring bd. write for info. (0-327-01683-3, 8026613) LEXIS Pub.

*Papageorges, Marc. Understanding & Using Telemedicine: How to Harness the Telecomunication Revolution. (Illus.). 213p. 2000. 115.00 (0-615-11257-9) V D I C Pubng.

Papageorgiadou-Banis, Ch., jt. ed. see Sheedy, K. A.

Papageorgiou, jt. auth. see Korhonen.

Papageorgiou, Fouli T., jt. ed. see Ewbank, Alison J.

Papageorgiou, G. C., et al, eds. Ion Interactions in Energy Transfer Biomembranes. LC 85-31707. 344p. 1986. 79.50 (0-306-42220-4, Plenum Trade) Perseus Pubng.

Papageorgiou, M., ed. Concise Encyclopedia of Traffic & Transportation Systems. (Advances in Systems Control & Information Engineering Ser.: No. 6). (Illus.). 676p. 1991. 387.25 (0-08-036203-6, Pergamon Pr) Elsevier.

Papageorgiou, M., et al. Transportation Systems, 1997: A Proceedings Volume from the 8th IFAC, IFIP, IFORS Symposium, Chania, Greece, 16-18 June, 1997. LC 97-44027. 1997. 309.00 (0-08-042931-9) Elsevier.

Papageorgiou, Nikolaos S., jt. auth. see Hu, Shouchuan.

Papageorgiou, Vasilis. Euripides' Medea & Cosmetics. 112p. (Orig.). 1986. pap. text 37.50 (91-22-00797-0) Coronet Bks.

Papageorgiou, Yorgos Y. The Isolated City State: An Economic Geography of Urban Spatial Structure. LC 89-6180. (Illus.). 488p. reprint ed. pap. 151.30 (0-608-20369-6, 207162200005) Bks Demand.

Papageorgiou, Yorgos Y. & Pines, David. An Essay on Urban Economic Theory LC 98-44115. (Advances in Urban & Regional Economics Ser.). 12p. 1998. 129.95 (0-7923-8343-5) Kluwer Academic.

Papagiannakis, A. T. & Schwartz, C. W. Application of Geotechnical Principles in Pavement Engineering. LC 98-38900. (Geotechnical Special Publication Ser.). 88p. 1998. 25.00 (0-7844-0392-9) Am Soc Civil Eng.

Papagiannis, George J., jt. auth. see Bock, John C.

Papagiannis, George J., jt. ed. see Bock, John C.

Papagiannis, Michael. Strategies Search. (Astrophysics & Space Science Library). 1980. pap. text 70.50 (90-277-1226-3); lib. bdg. 100.50 (90-277-1181-X) Kluwer Academic.

Papagiannis, Michael, ed. The Search for Extraterrestrial Life: Recent Developments. 1985. lib. bdg. 182.50 (90-277-2113-0) Kluwer Academic.

Papagiannis, Michael D. Space Physics & Space Astronomy. LC 72-179021. (Illus.). xiv, 294p. (C). 1972. text 218.00 (0-677-04000-8) Gordon & Breach.

Papagiannopoulou, Angelia G. The Influence of Middle Minoan Pottery on the Cyclades. (Studies in Mediterranean Archaeology & Literature: No. 96). (Illus.). 497p. (Orig.). 1991. pap. 115.00 (91-7081-016-8, Pub. by P Astroms) Coronet Bks.

Papahadjopoulos, Demetrios, jt. auth. see Lasic, D. D.

Papahristodoulou, Christos. Inventions, Innovations, & Economic Growth in Sweden: An Appraisal of the Schumpeterian Theory. (Studia Oeconomica Upsaliensia: No. 12). 152p. (Orig.). 1987. pap. 37.50 (91-554-1983-6) Coronet Bks.

Papai, Franki B. Cat Lover's Cookbook. 1993. pap. 6.95 (0-312-08904-X) St Martin.

Papailiou, K. D., et al. Computational Fluid Dynamics '98, Vol. 1. LC 98-38689. 1388p. 1998. 680.00 (0-471-98579-1) Wiley.

— Computational Fluid Dynamics '98, Vol. 2. LC 98-38689. 888p. 1998. 680.00 (0-471-98580-5) Wiley.

Papaioannou, G. From Mars Hill to Manhattan: History of Greek Orthodox Church in U. S. 1976. pap. 10.95 (0-937032-08-5) Light&Life Pub Co MN.

Papaioannou, George, ed. see Rouvelas, Marilyn.

Papaioannou, George J., jt. ed. see Fischer, Klaus P.

Papaioannou, Michael & Tsetsekos, George. Emerging Market Portfolios: Diversification & Hedging Strategies. 408p. 1996. 85.00 (0-7863-0337-9, Irwn Prfssnl) McGraw-Hill Prof.

Papaioannou, William. The Adhesion of Porphyromonas Gingivalis & Periodontitis. (Acta Biomedica Lovaniensia Ser.). (Illus.). 128p. 1998. pap. 42.50 (90-6186-896-3, Pub. by Leuven Univ) Coronet Bks.

Papajohn, Dean. Toward Speaking Excellence: The Michigan Guide to Maximizing Your Performance on the TSE Test & SPEAK Test. LC 98-229054. 144p. 1998. pap. text 17.95 (0-472-08524-7, 08524) U of Mich Pr.

Papajohn, John & Spiegel, John. Transactions in Families. LC 74-6740. (Jossey-Bass Behavioral Science Ser.). 335p. reprint ed. pap. 103.90 (0-608-16929-3, 202776400056) Bks Demand.

— Transactions in Families: Resolving Cultural & Generational Conflicts. LC 95-4759. (Master Works). 336p. 1995. reprint ed. pap. 45.00 (1-56821-575-4) Aronson.

Papajohn, John C. The Hyphenated American: The Hidden Injuries of Culture, 38. LC 99-14837. (Contributions in Psychology Ser.: No. 38). 168p. 1999. 55.00 (0-313-30930-2, GM0930, Greenwood Pr) Greenwood.

*Papalambros, Panos Y. & Wilde, Douglass J. Principles of Optimal Design: Modeling & Computation. (Illus.). 475p. 2000. pap. write for info. (0-521-62727-3) Cambridge U Pr.

— Principles of Optimal Design: Modeling & Computation. 2nd ed. LC 99-47982. 2000. write for info. (0-521-62215-8) Cambridge U Pr.

Papalas, Anthony. Ancient Icaria. (Illus.). 216p. 1991. 39.00 (0-86516-243-3); pap. 24.00 (0-86516-244-1) Bolchazy-Carducci.

Papalia. Child Development. 2001. 57.74 (0-07-231639-X); pap., student ed. 19.00 (0-07-231646-2) McGraw.

— Human Development. 7th ed. 784p. 1997. pap. 21.88 (0-07-049414-2) McGraw.

— Human Development. 8th ed. 2000. 55.25 (0-07-232139-3); pap., student ed. 21.88 (0-07-232189-X) McGraw.

— Human Development W. Readings. 6th ed. 1996. 14.50 (0-07-048782-0) McGraw.

Papalia, Anthony S. An Inside Look at Outplacement Counseling: The Relocation of Smith Carona to Mexico. LC 96-109228. 92p. (Orig.). (C). 1995. pap. text 10.00 (0-9647244-1-3) Cortland NY.

Papalia, Diane E. A Child's World. 8th ed. 312p. 1998. pap., student ed. 23.75 (0-07-290157-8) McGraw.

Papalia, Diane E. & Olds, Sally W. A Child's World: Infancy Through Adolescence. 7th ed. LC 95-10671. (C). 1995. text 57.00 (0-07-048765-0) McGraw.

— Human Development. 6th ed. LC 94-7636. 1994. text 61.87 (0-07-048760-X) McGraw.

Papalia, Diane E., et al. Adult Development & Aging. LC 95-39802. 609p. (C). 1995. 63.75 (0-07-048756-1) McGraw.

— A Child's World: Infancy Through Adolescence. 8th ed. LC 98-5943. 1998. 68.06 (0-07-048785-5); write for info. (0-07-115828-6) McGraw.

Papaloizos, Theodore C. A Grammar of Modern Greek in English. 76p. (Orig.). student ed. 2.50 (0-932416-05-5, 05); pap. 3.50 (0-932416-04-7, 04) Papaloizos.

— Modern Greek for Adults, Pt. I. (Illus.). 173p. 1978. pap. 5.00 (0-932416-01-2, 01) Papaloizos.

— Modern Greek for Adults, Pt. II. (Illus.). 300p. 1978. student ed. 3.00 (0-932416-03-9, 03); pap. 6.00 (0-932416-02-0, 02) Papaloizos.

— Workbook for My Greek Reader. (GRE., Illus.). 88p. (Orig.). 1986. pap. 4.50 (0-932416-47-0) Papaloizos.

Papamichael, N., et al, eds. Computational Methods & Function Theory, 1997: Proceedings of the 3rd CMFT Conference Nicosia, Cyprus, 13-17 October 1997. LC 99-14411. (Series in Approximations & Decompositions). 530p. 1999. 86.00 (981-02-3626-3) World Scientific Pub.

Papamichalis, Panos & Kerwin, Robert, eds. Digital Signal Processing Technology: Proceedings of a Conference Held 17-18 April, 1995, Orlando, Florida. LC 95-131. (Critical Reviews of Optical Science & Technology Ser.: Vol. 57). 1995. pap. 66.00 (0-8194-1847-1) SPIE.

*Papananous, Yannis E. Radio-Frequency Microelectronic Circuits for Telecommunication Applications. LC 99-46250. 1999. text 120.00 (0-7923-8641-8) Kluwer Academic.

Papanastasiou, Tasos & Alexandrou, Andreas N. Viscous Fluid Flow. LC 99-42163. 440p. 1999. boxed set 89.95 (0-8493-1606-5) CRC Pr.

Papanastassiou, Marina, jt. auth. see Peace, Robert.

Papanastassiou, Marina, jt. auth. see Pearce, Robert D.

Papandreou, Andreas A. Externality & Institutions. 320p. 1998. reprint ed. pap. 29.95 (0-19-829307-0) OUP.

Papandreou, Andreas G. Paternalistic Capitalism. LC 79-187169. 200p. 1972. reprint ed. pap. 62.00 (0-7837-2929-4, 205752500006) Bks Demand.

Papandreou, Nicholas. A Crowded Heart. LC 98-10789. 192p. 1998. text 21.00 (0-312-18685-1) St Martin.

— A Crowded Heart. 192p. 1999. text 12.00 (0-312-20400-0, Picador USA) St Martin.

Papanek, Ernest. The Austrian School Reform: Its Bases, Principles & Development--The Twenty Years Between the Two World Wars. LC 78-866. 130p. 1978. reprint ed. lib. bdg. 49.50 (0-313-20292-3, PAAS, Greenwood Pr) Greenwood.

Papanek, Gustav F. A Plan for Planning: The Need for a Better Method of Assisting Underdeveloped Countries on Their Economic Policies. LC 78-38759. (Harvard University. Center for International Affairs. Occasional Papers in International Affairs: No. 1). reprint ed. 27.50 (0-404-54601-3) AMS Pr.

Papanek, Gustav F., ed. The Indonesian Economy. LC 80-18752. 438p. 1981. 75.00 (0-275-90699-X, C0699, Praeger Pubs) Greenwood.

Papanek, Gustav F., jt. ed. see Falcon, Walter P.

Papanek, Victor. Design for the Real World: Human Ecology & Social Change. 2nd rev. ed. (Illus.). 394p. (C). 1982. reprint ed. pap. 17.00 (0-89733-153-2) Academy Chi Pubs.

— The Green Imperative: Natural Design for the Real World. LC 95-60281. (Illus.). 256p. (Orig.). 1995. pap. 19.95 (0-500-27846-6, Pub. by Thames Hudson) Norton.

Papanicolaou, A. C. Emotion: A Reconsideration of the Somatic Theory. xiv, 142p. 1988. text 62.00 (2-88124-274-X); pap. text 35.00 (2-88124-283-9) Gordon & Breach.

— Fundamentals of Functional Brain Imaging: A Guide to the Methods & Their Applications to Psychology & Behavioral Neuroscience. LC 98-30131. (Studies on Neuropsychology, Development, & Cognition Ser.: Vol. 1). (Illus.). 156p. 1998. 72.00 (90-265-1528-6) Swets.

Papanicolaou, Andrew C. & Gunter, Pete A., eds. Bergson & Modern Thought Towards a Unified Science, 3. (Models of Scientific Thought Ser.: Vol. 3). xxii, 394p. 1987. text 141.00 (3-7186-0380-2) Gordon & Breach.

Papanicolaou, G., ed. Hydrodynamic Behavior & Interacting Particle System. (IMA Ser.: Vol. 9). 215p. 1987. 54.95 (0-387-96584-X) Spr-Verlag.

Papanicolaou, George C., ed. Advances in Multiphase Flow & Related Problems. LC 87-60050. (Proceedings in Applied Mathematics Ser.: No. 26). (Illus.). x, 295p. 1987. text 32.00 (0-89871-212-2) Soc Indus-Appl Math.

Papanicolaou, George C., jt. ed. see Caflisch, Russell E.

Papanicolaou, N. I., et al. Handbook of Calculated Electron Momentum Distributions, Compton Profiles, & X-Ray Form Factors of Elemental Solids. (Illus.). 152p. 1991. boxed set 119.00 (0-8493-0538-1, QC176) CRC Pr.

Papanicolas, C. N., et al, eds. Electron Scattering in Nuclear & Particle Science. LC 87-72403. (AIP Conference Proceedings Ser.: No. 161). 256p. 1987. lib. bdg. 60.00 (0-88318-361-7) Am Inst Physics.

Papanicolau, G., et al, eds. Wave Propagation in Complex Media. LC 97-26382. (IMA Volumes in Mathematics & Its Applications Ser.: No. 96). (Illus.). 307p. 1997. 59.95 (0-387-98309-0) Spr-Verlag.

Papanier Wells, MaryAnn & Bradley, Mary. Surgical Instruments: A Pocket Guide. 2nd ed. Connor, Maura, ed. LC 98-5488. (Illus.). 480p. (C). 1998. pap. text 32.00 (0-7216-7801-7, W B Saunders Co) Harcrt Hlth Sci Grp.

Papanikolas, Helen. The Apple Falls from the Apple Tree: Stories. LC 96-13264. 250p. 1996. pap. 14.95 (0-8040-0994-5); text 27.95 (0-8040-0993-7) Swallow.

— Small Bird, Tell Me: Stories of Greek Immigrants. LC 93-8426. 208p. 1994. reprint ed. pap. 15.95 (0-8040-0982-1) Swallow.

— The Time of the Little Black Bird. LC 98-50080. 256p. 1999. 28.95 (0-8040-1016-1); pap. 16.95 (0-8040-1017-X) Swallow.

Papanikolas, Helen Z. Aimilia-Georgios - Emily-George. LC 86-28266. (Utah Centennial Ser.: No. 3). (ENG & GRE.). 341p. 1987. pap. 105.80 (0-7837-8552-6, 204936700011) Bks Demand.

— A Greek Odyssey in the American West. LC 97-19099. (Illus.). viii, 327p. 1997. pap. 17.95 (0-8032-8747-X) U of Nebr Pr.

Papanikolas, Zeese. Buried Unsung: Louis Tikas & the Ludlow Massacre. LC 82-13475. (University of Utah Publications in the American West: No. 14). (Illus.). 351p. reprint ed. pap. 108.90 (0-8357-8821-0, 203335800085) Bks Demand.

— Trickster in Land of Dreams. LC 94-36924. x, 186p. (C). 1995. text 30.00 (0-8032-3703-0) U of Nebr Pr.

— Trickster in the Land of Dreams. 196p. 1998. pap. 10.00 (0-8032-8754-2, PAPTRX) U of Nebr Pr.

Papanikolau. Technical Greek-English & English-Greek Dictionary. (ENG & GRE.). 684p. 1990. 150.00 (0-7859-9052-6) Fr & Eur.

Papannareddy, R. Introduction to Lightwave Communication Systems. LC 97-1921. (Optoelectronics Engineering Ser.). 294p. 1997. 87.00 (0-89006-572-1) Artech Hse.

Papano, Marilyn. Passion. 1996. pap. 5.99 (0-614-98106-9) Warner Bks.

Papantchev, George D. Colloquial Bulgarian. LC 93-26730. 27p. (C). (gr. 13). 1994. audio 27.99 (0-415-07964-0) Routledge.

— Colloquial Bulgarian. LC 93-26730. (Illus.). 288p. (gr. 13). 1994. pap. 18.99 (0-415-07963-2) Routledge.

— Colloquial Bulgarian. LC 93-26730. 272p. (C). (gr. 13). 1994. pap. 39.99 incl. audio (0-415-07965-9) Routledge.

An Asterisk (*) at the beginning of an entry indicates that the title is appearing for the first time.

Papantoni-Kazakos, P. & Kazakos, Dimitri, eds. Nonparametric Methods in Communications. LC 77-14049. (Electrical Engineering & Electronics Ser.: No. 2). 303p. reprint ed. pap. 94.00 (*0-7837-3317-X*, 204330500008) Bks Demand.

Papantonio, Mike. Clarence Darrow, the Journeyman: Lessons for the Modern Lawyer. unabridged ed. (Illus.). 260p. 1997. mass mkt. 24.95 (*0-9649711-1-9*, Seville Sq) Seville Pubng.

— In Search of Atticus Finch: A Motivational Book for Lawyers. 2nd ed. Fitch, D., ed. LC 97-106845. (Illus.). 257p. 1996. mass mkt. 24.95 (*0-9649711-0-0*, Seville Sq) Seville Pubng.

***Papantonio, Mike.** Resurrecting Aesop: Fables Lawyers Should Remember. (Illus.). 250p. 2000. 24.95 (*0-9649711-2-7*) Seville Pubng.

Papantoniou, D. The Greek Children. (GRE., Illus.). (J). (gr. 2-3). text 4.00 (*0-686-79628-4*) Divry.

— Greek Letters. (GRE.). 158p. (J). (gr. 4-5). 4.00 (*0-686-79634-9*) Divry.

— Greek Stories. (GRE.). (J). (gr. 3-4). 4.00 (*0-686-79633-0*) Divry.

Papantoniou, Pando C. Marketing the Complete Awakening. (C). 1990. 85.00 (*1-872684-30-0*, Pub. by P A S S Pubns); pap. 60.00 (*1-872684-18-1*, Pub. by P A S S Pubns) St Mut.

Papapetrou, A. Lectures on General Relativity. LC 74-81943. 203p. 1974. pap. text 88.00 (*90-277-0540-2*); lib. bdg. 104.50 (*90-277-0514-3*) Kluwer Academic.

Papapoulos, S., jt. auth. see World Congress on Osteoporosis Staff.

Paparella. 1999 Yearbook of Otolaryngology-Head & Neck Surgery. 2nd ed. (Illus.). 350p. 1999. text 79.00 (*0-8151-9719-5*, 25006) Mosby Inc.

— 1998 Year Book of Otolaryngology - Head & Neck Surgery. (Illus.). 368p. 1998. text 76.00 (*0-8151-9718-7*, 25005) Mosby Inc.

Paparella, Emanuel L. Hermeneutics in the Philosophy of Giambattista Vico: A Revolutionary Humanistic Vision for the New Age. LC 93-13091. 220p. 1993. pap. 29.95 (*0-7734-1939-X*) E Mellen.

Paparella, Michael M. & Shumrick, Donald A. Otolaryngology, 4 vols., 1. 3rd ed. Meyerhoff, William L., ed. LC 77-25566. (Illus.). 3536p. 1990. text 195.00 (*0-7216-1505-8*, W B Saunders Co) Harcrt Hlth Sci Grp.

— Otolaryngology, 4 vols., 2. 3rd ed. Meyerhoff, William L., ed. LC 77-25566. (Illus.). 3536p. 1990. text 195.00 (*0-7216-1506-6*, W B Saunders Co) Harcrt Hlth Sci Grp.

— Otolaryngology, 4 vols., 3. 3rd ed. Meyerhoff, William L., ed. LC 77-25566. (Illus.). 3536p. 1990. text 195.00 (*0-7216-1507-4*, W B Saunders Co) Harcrt Hlth Sci Grp.

— Otolaryngology, 4 vols., 4. 3rd ed. Meyerhoff, William L., ed. LC 77-25566. (Illus.). 3536p. 1990. text 195.00 (*0-7216-3446-X*, W B Saunders Co) Harcrt Hlth Sci Grp.

— Otolaryngology, 4 vols., Set. 3rd ed. Meyerhoff, William L., ed. LC 77-25566. (Illus.). 3536p. 1990. text 625.00 (*0-7216-1504-X*, W B Saunders Co) Harcrt Hlth Sci Grp.

Paparian, Michael, ed. California Energy Directory: A Guide to Organizations & Information Resources. LC 78-78313. (California Information Guides Ser.). (Illus.). 98p. (Orig.). 1980. pap. 16.50 (*0-912102-51-9*) Cal Inst Public.

Paparis, Steve Y. Food Analysis - Contents & Toxicology: Index of New Information. 160p. 1997. 47.50 (*0-7883-1712-1*); pap. 44.50 (*0-7883-1713-X*) ABBE Pubs Assn.

Paparone, Pamela. Who Built the Ark? LC 93-31383. (Illus.). 40p. (J). (ps-1). 1994. 15.00 (*0-671-87129-3*) S&S Bks Yung.

Paparone, Pamela. Cinq Petits Canards.Tr. of Five Little Ducks. (FRE.). (J). (ps-1). pap. 15.95 (*3-314-20938-X*, Pub. by North-South Bks NYC) Chronicle Bks.

Paparone, Pamela. Five Little Ducks: An Old Rhyme. LC 95-13136. 32p. (J). (ps-1). 1995. 15.95 (*1-55858-473-0*, Pub. by North-South Bks NYC); lib. bdg. 15.88 (*1-55858-474-9*, Pub. by North-South Bks NYC) Chronicle Bks.

— Five Little Ducks: An Old Rhyme. LC 95-13136. 32p. (J). (ps-1). 1997. pap. 6.95 (*1-55858-700-4*, Pub. by North-South Bks NYC) Chronicle Bks.

Papas, jt. auth. see Nizel, Abraham E.

Papas, A., jt. auth. see Raizis, M. Byron.

Papas, Al, Jr. Gopher Sketch Book: Drawing Sketches & Thumbnail Sketches from the "U" of Minnesota's Earliest Football Days to Now. (Illus.). 1990. 0.99 (*0-931714-41-9*, Pub. by Nodin Pr) Bookmen Inc.

Papas, Andreas M. Antioxidants in Nutrition & Health. LC 98-22208. (Contemporary Food Science Ser.). 672p. 1998. boxed set 94.95 (*0-8493-8009-X*) CRC Pr.

— The Vitamin E Factor: The Miraculous Anti-Oxidant for the Prevention & Treatment of Heart Disease, Cancer & Aging. LC 99-22840. 416p. 1999. pap. 12.95 (*0-06-098443-0*) HarpC.

Papas, Anthony A. Greece. LC 92-44131. (European Financial Reporting Ser.). 272p. (C). (gr. 13). 1993. pap. 114.95 (*0-415-06196-2*, A9717) Thomson Learn.

Papas, Bill, jt. auth. see Papas, Tessa.

Papas, Charles H. Theory of Electromagnetic Wave Propagation. xiii, 244p. 1988. reprint ed. pap. 6.95 (*0-486-65678-0*) Dover.

Papas, Diana L., jt. auth. see Natural.

Papas, Meryl, jt. auth. see Vyse, Maureen.

Papas, Tessa. Papas' Greece. (Illus.). 96p. 1997. 49.95 (*0-9644651-1-6*) Chetwynd Stapylton.

Papas, Tessa & Papas, Bill. Papas' Portland. (Illus.). 96p. (Orig.). 1994. pap. 24.95 (*0-9644651-0-8*) Chetwynd Stapylton.

***Papas, William.** Papas' Instant Greek: How to Communicate in Greek as Quickly as You Can Twist Your Wrist! 12th ed. (GRE & ENG.). 1999. pap. text 12.95 (*0-9644651-2-4*) Chetwynd Stapylton.

Papasaki, Andreas. Theory & Experimentation: An Intellectual Extravaganza. 408p. 1992. 95.00 (*1-85490-157-5*, Pub. by Wiley) Wiley.

Papasogli, Benedetta. Wisdom of the Heart. LC 93-78050. 1993. pap. 11.95 (*0-910984-57-3*) Montfort Pubns.

Papastavridis, John G. Tensors & Their Applications to Analytical Dynamics. LC 98-29656. (Engineering Mathematics Ser.). 448p. 1998. boxed set 74.95 (*0-8493-8514-8*) CRC Pr.

Papastavridis, Stavros G., jt. ed. see Godole, Anant P.

***Papastavrou, Vasili.** Whale. (Eyewitness Books). (Illus.). (J). (gr. 4-7). 2000. 19.99 (*0-7894-6595-7*) DK Pub Inc.

— Whale. (Eyewitness Books). (J). (gr. 4-7). 2000. 15.95 (*0-7894-5870-5*) DK Pub Inc.

Papastephanou. From a Transcendental-Semiotic. LC 99-213548. 247p. 2000. pap. 24.95 (*0-7190-5538-5*, Pub. by Manchester Univ Pr) St Martin.

***Papastephanou.** From a Transcendental-Semiotic Point of View. LC 99-213548. 224p. 2000. text 74.95 (*0-7190-5384-6*, Pub. by Manchester Univ Pr) St Martin.

Papastergi, Nikos. Dialogues in the Diaspora. LC 98-211634. 1997. 50.00 (*1-85489-094-8*, Pub. by Rivers Oram) NYU Pr.

***Papastergiadis, Nikos.** Dialogues in the Diasporas: Essays & Conversations on Cultural Identity LC 98-211634. xi, 228p. 1998. 18.50 (*1-85489-095-6*, Pub. by Rivers Oram) NYU Pr.

Papastergiadis, Nikos. The Turbulence of Migration: Globalization, Deterritorialization & Hybridity. LC 99-27521. 304p. (C). 2000. text 59.95 (*0-7456-1430-2*, Pub. by Polity Pr); pap. text 27.95 (*0-7456-1431-0*, Pub. by Polity Pr) Blackwell Pubs.

Papastergiadis, Nikos & Turney, Laura, eds. Jimmie Durham on Becoming Authentic. (Pamphlets Ser.: No. 10). 60p. 1996. pap. text 5.00 (*1-891754-09-2*) Prickly Pear Pmphlts NA.

Papastergiadis, Nikos, jt. ed. see Grimshaw, Anna.

Papatassos, jt. auth. see Winterer, Mary.

Papataxiarchis, Evthymios, jt. ed. see Loizos, Peter.

***Papathansiou, Ilias.** Acquired Neurogenic Communication Disorders: A Clinical Perspective. 1999. pap. 34.95 (*1-86156-111-3*) Whurr Pub.

Papatheofanis, Frank J. Bioelectromagnetics: Biophysical Principles in Medicine & Biology. (Experimental Biology & Medicine Ser.: Vol. 12). (Illus.). x, 98p. 1987. 85.25 (*3-8055-4587-8*) S Karger.

Papatheofanis, Frank J., jt. auth. see Shaw, Leslee.

Papathomas, Thomas V., et al, eds. Early Vision & Beyond. LC 94-3117. 284p. 1995. 65.00 (*0-262-16146-X*, Bradford Bks) MIT Pr.

Papathomopoulos, Manolis. Apollonius Rhodius - Appollonii Rhodii Argonauticorum Concordantia. 410p. 1996. write for info. (*3-487-10237-4*) G Olms Pubs.

— Nicandrus - Nicandri Theriacorum et Alexipharmacorum Concordantia. 431p. 1996. write for info. (*3-487-10206-4*) G Olms Pubs.

— Oppianus - Oppiani Apamensis Cynegeticorum Concordantia. 471p. 1997. write for info. (*3-487-10224-2*) G Olms Pubs.

Papatola, Kathleen J. Balancing Your Work/Family Responsibilities: A Guide for Employees. 1993. pap. 4.50 (*1-56246-083-8*, 3294, HazeldenJohnson Inst) Hazelden.

— How to Help Your Employees Balance Work & Family Responsibilities: A Guide for Managers. 56p. 1993. pap. 9.95 (*1-56246-082-X*, 3295, HazeldenJohnson Inst) Hazelden.

— The Therapy Answer Book: Getting the Most Out of Counseling. LC 97-30506. 224p. 1997. pap. 12.95 (*1-57749-048-7*) Fairview Press.

Papatsonis, Takis. Ursa Minor & Other Poems. Friar, Kimon & Myrsiades, Kostas, trs. (Modern Greek History & Culture Ser.). 103p. 1988. 25.00 (*0-932963-05-6*) Nostos Bks.

Papavero, N. The World Oestridae (Diptera), Mammals & Continental Drift. (Series Entomologica: No. 14). 1977. text 141.50 (*90-6193-124-X*) Kluwer Academic.

Papavizas, George C., ed. Biological Control in Crop Production. LC 81-65017. (Beltsville Symposia in Agricultural Research Ser.: No. 5). 474p. 1982. text 64.50 (*0-86598-037-3*) Rowman.

Papay, J. A., ed. see Jolly, Randy.

Papayani, John, jt. auth. see Mourdoukoutas, Panos.

Papayanis, Nicholas. Coachmen of Nineteenth-Century Paris: Service Workers & Class Consciousness. LC 93-834. 269p. (C). 1993. text 45.00 (*0-8071-1814-1*) La State U Pr.

— Horse-Drawn Cabs & Omnibuses in Paris: The Idea of Circulation & the Business of Public Transit. LC 95-26129. (Illus.). 304p. (C). 1996. text 49.50 (*0-8071-2043-X*) La State U Pr.

Papayoanou, Paul. Power Ties: Economic Interdependence, Balancing & War. LC 98-40093. 216p. 1999. text 44.50 (*0-472-10960-X*, 10960) U of Mich Pr.

Papazian, Charlie. The Complete Joy of Home Brewing. (Illus.). 352p. (Orig.). 1984. pap. 8.95 (*0-380-88369-4*, Avon Bks) Morrow Avon.

— Home Brewer's Gold: Prize-Winning Recipes from the 1996 World Beer Cup Competition. LC 97-23662. (Illus.). 448p. 1997. pap. 12.00 (*0-380-79192-7*, Avon Bks) Morrow Avon.

— Homebrewer's Companion. LC 94-1647. 320p. 1994. pap. 12.50 (*0-380-77287-6*, Avon Bks) Morrow Avon.

— New Compl. Joy Home Brew. 2nd ed. 416p. 1991. pap. 12.50 (*0-380-76366-4*, Avon Bks) Morrow Avon.

Papazian, Charlie, jt. auth. see Gayre, Robert.

Papazian, Charlie, ed. see American Homebrewers Association Staff.

Papazian, Ed. Magazine Dimensions, '98. 366p. 1997. pap. 205.00 (*0-9621947-8-6*) Media Dynamics.

— Magazine Dimensions '99. 390p. 1998. pap. 225.00 (*1-892605-02-3*) Media Dynamics.

— Magazine Dimensions, '97. 364p. 1996. pap. 185.00 (*0-9621947-6-X*) Media Dynamics.

— The People Book, '95: A Marketer's Guide to Consumer Demographics. 78p. 1995. pap. 75.00 (*0-9621947-5-1*) Media Dynamics.

— TV Dimensions, '98. 492p. 1998. pap. 260.00 (*0-9621947-9-4*) Media Dynamics.

— TV Dimensions, '97. 484p. 1997. pap. 245.00 (*0-9621947-7-8*) Media Dynamics.

— TV Dimensions '99. 492p. 1999. pap. 285.00 (*1-892605-01-5*) Media Dynamics.

Papazian, K. S. Merchants from Ararat. Manuelian, P. M., ed. LC 79-63061. 1979. pap. 3.50 (*0-933706-04-9*) Ararat Pr.

Papazian, Sandy. Growing up with Joey: A Mother's Story of Her Son's Disability & Her Family's Triumph. LC 96-18076. (Illus.). 272p. 1997. 24.95 (*1-56474-184-2*) Fithian Pr.

Papazoglou, Ioannis A., jt. auth. see Cacciabue, Pietro C.

Papazoglou, J. P., jt. ed. see Schemel, J. H.

Papazoglou, M. P. & Schlageter, G., eds. Cooperative Information Systems: Trends & Directions. (Illus.). 384p. 1997. pap. text 69.95 (*0-12-544910-0*) Morgan Kaufmann.

Papazoglou-Margari, Theano. Two Worlds: Short Stories. LC 93-86372.Tr. of Dio Kosmi. (GRE.). 184p. (Orig.). 1993. pap. text 10.00 (*0-918618-59-2*) Pella Pub.

Papazoglou, Michael P., ed. OOER '95: Object-Oriented & Entity-Relationship Modelling: Proceedings, 14th International Conference, Gold Coast, Australia, December 13-15, 1995. LC 95-49513. (Lecture Notes in Computer Science Ser.: No. 1021). 451p. 1995. pap. 75.00 (*3-540-60672-6*) Spr-Verlag.

***Papazoglou, Michael P., et al, eds.** Advances in Object-Oriented Data Modeling. LC 99-45287. (Cooperative Information Systems Ser.). (Illus.). 399p. 2000. 45.00 (*0-262-16189-3*) MIT Pr.

Papazoglou, Orania, pseud. Charisma. 384p. 1993. mass mkt. 5.99 (*0-8217-4119-5*, Zebra Kensgtn) Kensgtn Pub Corp.

***Papazoglou, Orania, pseud.** Wicked, Loving Murder: A Patience McKenna Mystery. 182p. 2000. pap. 7.95 (*1-55882-034-5*, Pub. by Intl Polygonics) IPG Chicago.

Papazoglu, Fanula. The Central Balkan Tribes in Pre-Roman Times: Triballi, Autariatae, Dardanians, Scordisci, & Moesians. Stansfield-Popovic, Mary, tr. xii, 664p. 1978. pap. 208.00 (*90-256-0793-4*, Pub. by AM Hakkert) BookLink Distributors.

Papcak, Gregory K. The Exceptional Seven Percent: The Nine Secrets of the World's Happiest Couples. LC 99-14066. 192p. 1999. 19.95 (*1-55972-505-2*, Birch Ln Pr) Carol Pub Group.

Papconstantopoulos, D. A. Handbook of the Band Structure of Elemental Solids. LC 86-22667. (Illus.). 422p. (C). 1986. text 144.00 (*0-306-42338-3*, Kluwer Plenum) Kluwer Academic.

Papcun, Ron. A Scentimental Journey: Reflections on Life. 128p. (Orig.). 1994. pap. 7.95 (*0-9641644-0-X*) Regenerat Concepts.

Papdemetriou, Demetrios G. Coming Together or Pulling Apart? The European Union's Struggle with Immigration & Asylum. LC 96-25598. (International Migration Policy Issues Ser.). 133p. 1996. pap. 9.95 (*0-87003-116-3*) Carnegie Endow.

Pape. British Social Welfare 20th Century. LC 98-46442. 1999. text 59.95 (*0-312-22114-2*) St Martin.

Pape, et al. Oddo Sound Series, 1968, 1974, 1978. 10 vols., Set. (Illus.). (J). (gr. 2-5). 1978. lib. bdg. 109.50 (*0-87783-165-3*) Oddo.

Pape, Craig, ed. see Berry, Jeff & Kaye, Annene.

Pape, D. L. Three Thinkers of Thay-Lee. LC 68-56828. (Sound Ser.). (Illus.). 48p. (J). (gr. 2-5). 1968. lib. bdg. 10.95 (*0-87783-040-1*) Oddo.

Pape, Dan. Astrology Test. (Illus.). 32p. (Orig.). (C). 1993. pap. text. write for info. (*1-882330-17-X*) Magni Co.

— The Cambridge Love & Relationships Test. 33p. (Orig.). (C). 1995. write for info. (*1-882330-41-2*) Magni Co.

— Childrens Self Scoring I. Q. Test. (Illus.). 40p. (Orig.). (C). pap. text. write for info. (*1-882330-14-5*) Magni Co.

— Personality Test: See Yourself As Others See You. (Illus.). 32p. (Orig.). (C). 1993. pap. write for info. (*1-882330-16-1*) Magni Co.

— Self Scoring I. Q. Test. (Illus.). 32p. (Orig.). (C). 1993. pap. text. write for info. (*1-882330-13-7*) Magni Co.

Pape, David S., ed. The Story Hour: A Collection for Young Readers, Vol. 1. (Illus.). 166p. (J). (gr. 3-8). 1994. 11.95 (*0-922613-64-8*) Hachai Pubng.

— The Story Hour: A Collection for Young Readers, Vol. 2. LC 94-230830. (Illus.). 160p. (J). (gr. 3-9). 1995. 11.95 (*0-922613-65-6*) Hachai Pubng.

— The Three Gifts & Other Stories. LC 97-73200. (Illus.). (J). (gr. 3-9). 1997. 13.95 (*0-922613-68-0*) Hachai Pubng.

— The Wise Little Judge. LC 96-76783. (Illus.). 175p. (J). (gr. 3-9). 1996. 13.95 (*0-922613-66-4*) Hachai Pubng.

Pape, David S., ed. see Rosenfeld, Dina.

Pape, Dennis R., ed. Advances in Optical Information Processing VIII. (Proceedings of SPIE Ser.: Vol. 3388). 276p. 1998. 80.00 (*0-8194-2837-X*) SPIE.

Pape, Donna L. La Casita del Pajarito. Palacios, Argentina, tr. (Spanish Whole Language Big Bks.).Tr. of Little Bird's House. (SPA., Illus.). 16p. (Orig.). (J). (ps-2). 1994. pap. 16.95 (*1-56784-099-X*) Newbridge Educ.

— King Robert, the Resting Ruler. LC 68-56823. (Sound Ser.). (Illus.). 48p. (J). (gr. 2-5). 1968. lib. bdg. 10.95 (*0-87783-021-5*) Oddo.

— Little Bird's House. (Whole-Language Big Bks.). (Illus.). 16p. (Orig.). (J). (ps-2). 1994. pap. 16.95 (*1-56784-072-8*) Newbridge Educ.

— Liz Dearly's Silly Glasses. LC 68-56824. (Sound Ser.). (Illus.). 48p. (J). (gr. 2-5). 1968. lib. bdg. 10.95 (*0-87783-023-1*) Oddo.

— Professor Fred & the Fid Fuddlephone. LC 68-56825. (Sound Ser.). (Illus.). 48p. (J). (gr. 2-5). 1968. lib. bdg. 10.95 (*0-87783-032-0*) Oddo.

— Scientist Sam. LC 68-56826. (Sound Ser.). (Illus.). 48p. (J). (gr. 2-5). 1968. lib. bdg. 10.95 (*0-87783-034-7*) Oddo.

Pape, Donna L., et al. Florida Puzzle Book. LC 96-23271. (Illus.). 144p. (Orig.). 1996. pap. 4.95 (*1-56164-107-3*) Pineapple Pr.

Pape, Garry R. & Campbell, John M. North American XB-70 Valkyrie: A Photo Chronicle. LC 94-66966. (Illus.). 288p. (YA). (gr. 10-13). 1995. pap. 9.95 (*0-88740-906-7*) Schiffer.

— Northrop Flying Wings: A History of Jack Northrop's Visionary Aircraft. (Illus.). 288p. 1994. 49.95 (*0-88740-689-0*) Schiffer.

Pape, Garry R. & Harrison, Ronald C. Queen of the Midnight Skies: The Story of America's Air Force Night Fighters. LC 92-60359. (Illus.). 320p. 1992. text 45.00 (*0-88740-415-4*) Schiffer.

Pape, Garry R., et al. Northrop P-61 Black Widow: The Complete History & Combat Record. LC 90-64611. (Illus.). 144p. 1995. pap. 24.95 (*0-88740-738-2*) Schiffer.

Pape, Greg. Storm Pattern. LC 91-50873. (Poetry Ser.). 96p. 1992. pap. 10.95 (*0-8229-5472-9*); text 19.95 (*0-8229-3708-5*) U of Pittsburgh Pr.

— Sunflower Facing the Sun. LC 92-5881. (Edwin Ford Piper Poetry Award Ser.). 96p. (Orig.). 1992. pap. 11.95 (*0-87745-382-9*) U of Iowa Pr.

Pape, H. D., et al, eds. Carcinoma of the Oral Cavity & Oropharynx, No. 134. LC 93-30355. (Recent Results in Cancer Research Ser.: Vol. 134). 1994. 98.00 (*0-387-56819-0*) Spr-Verlag.

Pape, Hansgeorg. Development of a Geochemical Mapping Method for the Prospecting of Deposits, Environmental Research & Regional Planning on the Basis of Multi-Element Investigations of Plant Ashes. Allard, K., tr. (Monograph Series on Mineral Deposits: No. 19). (Illus.). viii, 65p. 1981. 33.00 (*3-443-12019-9*, Pub. by Gebruder Borntraeger) Balogh.

Pape, John. Hill Country Chronicles: Sophisticated Tales of Life in the Texas Hill Country. LC 92-16978. (Illus.). 1992. pap. text 10.95 (*1-877740-18-7*) Nel-Mar Pub.

Pape, Larry, ed. see Stuckey, M. M.

Pape, Marieanna. Composition Companion. 2nd ed. 80p. (Orig.). 1993. pap. text 15.95 (*0-940139-28-6*) Consortium RI.

Pape, Mark, jt. auth. see Brockett, Oscar G.

Pape, Moritz E. The Indian Trader & the Navajo Rug. LC 97-90315. 1998. pap. 11.95 (*0-533-12363-1*) Vantage.

— The Lost Gospel Also Depth of Soul & Quest of Man. (Illus.). 24p. 1992. lib. bdg. 2.50 (*0-9630599-0-4*) Ltd Ex Pr.

— Poetic Variables & Other Thoughts. (Illus.). 50p. (Orig.). 1990. text 4.50 (*0-9630599-1-2*, TXU432-733) Ltd Ex Pr.

Pape, Ralph. Beyond Your Command. 1988. pap. 5.25 (*0-8222-0113-5*) Dramatists Play.

— Girls We Have Known & Other One Act Plays. 1983. pap. 5.25 (*0-8222-0449-5*) Dramatists Play.

— Hearts Beating Faster. 1997. pap. 5.25 (*0-8222-1584-5*) Dramatists Play.

— Say Goodnight, Gracie. 1979. pap. 5.25 (*0-8222-0993-4*) Dramatists Play.

Pape, Robert A. Bombing to Win: Air Power & Coercion in War. (Studies in Security Affairs). (Illus.). 408p. 1996. text 49.95 (*0-8014-3134-4*); pap. text 19.95 (*0-8014-8311-5*) Cornell U Pr.

Pape, Sharon. The Portal. 1994. per. 3.50 (*0-373-27033-X*, 5-27033-5) Harlequin Bks.

Pape, Thomas. Catalogue of the Sarcophagidae of the World (Insecta: Diptera) Gupta, Virendra K., ed. LC 96-26554. (Memoirs on Entomology, International Ser.: Vol. 8). 560p. (C). 1996. 75.00 (*1-56665-063-1*) Assoc Pubs FL.

— The Sarcophagidae (Diptera) of Fennoscandia & Denmark. (Fauna Entomologica Scandinavica Ser.: No. 19). (Illus.). 203p. 1987. text 51.00 (*90-04-08184-4*) Lubrecht & Cramer.

Pape, Walter. Joachim Ringelnatz: Parodie und Selbstparodie in Leben und Werk. LC 73-88303. (Quellen und Forschungen zur Sprach und Kulturgeschichte der Germanischen Voelker: NF 62). (GER.). 457p. (C). 1974. 106.95 (*3-11-004483-8*) De Gruyter.

Pape, Walter, ed. German Unifications & the Change of Literary Discourse, 1870-71 - 1989-1990: European Cultures - Studies in Literature & the Arts. LC 93-35566. (European Cultures Ser.: Vol. 1). vi, 382p. 1993. lib. bdg. 49.95 (*3-11-013878-6*) De Gruyter.

Pape, Walter & Burwick, Frederick, eds. Reflecting Senses: Perception & Appearance in Literature, Culture & the Arts. LC 94-37129. 375p. (C). 1995. lib. bdg. 190.00 (*3-11-014580-4*) De Gruyter.

Pape, Walter, jt. ed. see Burwick, Frederick.

Pape, William. The Lordship of Jesus Christ. 145p. 1995. pap. 8.00 (*1-882840-06-2*) Comm Christian.

Pape, William J. History of Waterbury & the Naugatuck Valley, Connecticut. 1668p. 1997. reprint ed. lib. bdg. 173.00 (*0-8328-5693-2*) Higginson Bk Co.

Pape, William J. & Scott, William W., eds. The News' History of Passaic, from the Earliest Settlement to the Present Day, Embracing a Descriptive History of Its

Municipal, Religious, Social & Commerical Institutions, with Biographical Sketches. (Illus.). 320p. 1996. reprint ed. lib. bdg. 39.00 (0-8328-5068-3) Higginson Bk Co.

***Pape, Wolfgang.** East Asia By Year 2000 & Beyond: Shaping Factors - A Study for the European Commission. LC 98-16503. Vol. 1. 220p. 1998. text 59.95 (0-312-21528-2) St Martin.

Papegaaij, Bart C. Word Expert Semantics: An Interlingual Knowledge-Based Approach. (Distributed Language Translation Ser.). x, 254p. 1986. 73.85 (3-11-013331-8); pap. 65.40 (90-6765-261-X) Mouton.

***Papel, Ira D., et al.** Facial Plastic & Reconstructive Surgery. 2nd ed. (Illus.). 608p. 2000. 149.00 (0-86577-918-X) Thieme Med Pubs.

Papell, Ben, jt. ed. see Lowe, James L.

Papell, Catherine P. & Rothman, Beulah, eds. Co-Leadership in Social Work with Groups. LC 80-28698. (Social Work with Groups Ser.: Vol. 3, No. 4). 81p. (Orig.). 1981. pap. text 2.95 (0-917724-90-9) Haworth Pr.

Papell, David, jt. auth. see Rudin, Jeremy R.

Papell, Helen. Talking with Eve Leah Hagar Miriam. iv, 71p. (Orig.). 1996. pap. 6.00 (1-879742-24-1) Jewish Wom Rsce.

Papen, Franz Von, see Von Papen, Franz.

Papen, Uta, jt. ed. see Mauch, Werner.

Papendick, R. I., et al. Alternative Agriculture: An Introduction & Overview: Symposium Proceedings. 49p. 1984. pap. 6.00 (1-893182-01-0) H A Wallace Inst.

Papendieck, Henner. Britische Managing Agencies in Indischen Kohlenbergrau, 1893-1918. Bruchey, Stuart, ed. LC 80-2822. (Dissertations in European Economic History Ser.).Tr. of British Managing Agencies in the Indian Coal Mining Industry 1893-1918. (Illus.). 1981. lib. bdg. 42.95 (0-405-14006-1) Ayer.

***Papenfus, S. G.** Soul on Fire: The Journey Beyond Anxiety. (Illus.). 320p. (C). 1998. pap. 26.95 (1-85327-103-9, Pub. by Prism Pr) Assoc Pubs Grp.

Papenfuse, Edward C. Doing Good to Posterity The Move of the Capital of Maryland from St. Mary's City to Anne Arunde. 1995. pap. text 10.00 (0-942370-40-6) MD St Archives.

— In Pursuit of Profit: The Annapolis Merchants in the Era of the American Revolution, 1763-1805. LC 74-6835. (Maryland Bicentennial Studies). (Illus.). 320p. 1975. 49.95 (0-8018-1573-8) Johns Hopkins.

Papenfuse, Edward C., et al. Maryland: A New Guide to the Old Line State. LC 76-17224. (Illus.). 488p. 1976. 29.50 (0-8018-1874-5) Johns Hopkins.

Papenfuse, Eric R. The Evils of Necessity: Robert Goodloe Harper & the Moral Dilemma of Slavery. LC 96-84055. (Transactions Ser.: Vol. 87, Pt. 1). (Illus.). 110p. (Orig.). 1997. pap. 18.00 (0-87169-871-4, T871-pae) Am Philos.

Paper. B-OE-LSY-Recovery Ver NT Blk. 1997. pap. text 15.00 (1-57593-907-X) Living Stream Ministry.

— B-OE-LSY-Recovery Ver NT Bur. (Orig.). 1997. pap. text 15.00 (1-57593-394-2) Living Stream Ministry.

Paper Bag Players Staff, jt. auth. see Martin, Judith.

Paper, Herbert H., ed. Language & Texts: The Nature of Linguistic Evidence. LC 75-36885. 204p. 1975. pap. 10.00 (0-89824-425-0) Trillium Pr.

Paper, Herbert H. & Jazayery, Mohammad A. English for Iranians. (English for Foreigners Ser.). (ENG & PER.). xiv, 318p. 1980. pap., student ed. 20.00 (0-87950-304-1) Spoken Lang Serv.

Paper, Herbert H. & Jazayery, Mohammad A. English for Iranians. (Spoken English As a Foreign Language Ser.). (ENG & PER.). 1980. audio 90.00 (0-87950-618-0) Spoken Lang Serv.

Paper, Herbert H. & Jazayery, Mohammad A. English for Iranians. (Spoken English As a Foreign Language Ser.). (ENG & PER.). xiv, 318p. 1980. reprint ed. pap. 110.00 incl. audio (0-87950-619-9) Spoken Lang Serv.

— The Writing System of Modern Persian. LC 76-40543. 40p. (C). 1976. reprint ed. pap. 5.00 (0-87950-284-3) Spoken Lang Serv.

Paper, Herbert H., ed. & tr. see Rastorgueva, V. S.

Paper, Jordan. Offering Smoke: The Sacred Pipe & Native American Religion. LC 88-28378. (Illus.). 181p. 1989. pap. 22.95 (0-89301-126-6) U of Idaho Pr.

— Through the Earth Darkly: Female Spirituality in Comparative Perspective. LC 97-23307. 320p. (C). 1997. pap. 24.95 (0-8264-1050-2) Continuum.

Paper, Jordan & Thompson, Laurence G. The Chinese Way in Religion. 2nd ed. LC 97-12647. 255p. (C). 1997. 35.95 (0-534-53735-9) Wadsworth Pub.

Paper Machine Dynamic - Foundation Design Comt. St. Paper Machine Dynamic - Foundation Design. 82p. 1994. 45.00 (0-89852-284-6, 0101R239) TAPPI.

Paper Tiger Television Collective Staff. The Paper Tiger Guide to TV Repair. 32p. (Orig.). 1992. pap. 5.00 (0-930495-19-5) San Fran Art Inst.

— Roar! The Paper Tiger Television Guide to Media Activism. Marcus, Daniel, ed. (Illus.). 67p. (Orig.). (C). 1991. pap. 10.00 (0-9630999-3-0) Paper Tiger TV.

Papera, Susan, jt. auth. see Lichtman, Ronnie.

Paperblank Book Co. Bars: Amish Quilts. 1995. 12.95 (1-55156-022-4) Paperblank.

***Paperblank Book Company Staff.** Aristotle: Ethics. (Illuminated Manuscripts Unlined Ser.). (Illus.). 160p. 1999. 14.95 (1-55156-030-5) Paperblank.

Paperblank Book Company Staff. Celestial Planisphere: Wired Maps. 1999. 10.95 (1-55156-120-4) Paperblank.

— Century of Memories: Two Women. 1999. 9.95 (1-55156-125-5) Pprblnk.

— Diamond in the Square: Amish Quilts. 1995. pap. 12.95 (1-55156-021-6) Paperblank.

— Double Hemisphere: Wired Maps. 1999. 10.95 (1-55156-123-9) Paperblank.

— Double Nine-Patch: Amish Quilts. 160p. 1999. 12.95 (1-55156-023-2) Paperblank.

***Paperblank Book Company Staff.** Egypt 2500 B.C. 128p. 2000. 19.95 (1-55156-173-5) Paperblank.

— Indus Valley 2500 B.C. 128p. 2000. 19.95 (1-55156-170-0) Paperblank.

— Lady Slipper. (Wildflowers Ser.). 160p. 1999. 14.95 (1-55156-017-8) Paperblank.

— Mesoamerica 250 B.C. 128p. 2000. 19.95 (1-55156-172-7) Paperblank.

— Sumeria 3200 A.D. 128p. 2000. 19.95 (1-55156-171-9) Paperblank.

— Terrestrial Planisphere: Wired Maps. 1999. 10.95 (1-55156-121-2) Paperblank.

Paperblank Book Company Staff. Tiger. (Japanese Screens & Scrolls Lined Ser.). 160p. 1999. 14.95 (1-55156-012-7) Paperblank.

***Paperblank Book Company Staff.** Tiger Lilly. (Wildflowers Ser.). 160p. 1999. 14.95 (1-55156-018-6) Paperblank.

— Wildflower Bouquet. (Wildflowers Ser.). (Illus.). 1995. 14.95 (1-55156-019-4) Paperblank.

Paperblank Book Staff. Century of Memories: Beach Boy. 1999. 9.95 (1-55156-126-3) Pprblnk.

***Paperblank Book Staff.** Double Hemisphere: Map of the New World. (Early Cartography Ser.). 160p. 1999. 12.95 (1-55156-003-8, Pub. by Paperblank) Andrews & McMeel.

— Western Hemisphere. 1999. 10.95 (1-55156-122-0) Paperblank.

***Paperblank Books Staff.** Wired Cat: Hnizdovsky's Animals. (Hnizdovsky's Wired Animals Ser.). 160p. 1998. 9.95 (1-55156-060-7, Pub. by Paperblank) Andrews & McMeel.

— Wired Ibex: Hnizdovsky's Animals. (Hnizdovsky's Wired Animals Ser.). 160p. 1998. 9.95 (1-55156-061-5, Pub. by Paperblank) Andrews & McMeel.

Paperblank Books Staff. Wired Sheep Unlined. 160p. 1997. pap. text 9.95 (1-55156-062-3, Pub. by Paperblank) Andrews & McMeel.

— Wired Zebra Unlined: Hnizdovsky's Animals. 160p. 1997. pap. text 9.95 (1-55156-063-1, Pub. by Paperblank) Andrews & McMeel.

***Paperblank Books Staff, ed.** Bird. (Wired Morris Ser.). 160p. 2000. 10.95 (1-55156-146-8) Paperblank.

***Paperblanks Books Staff.** Celestial Planisphere: Map of the Heavens. (Early Cartography Lined Ser.). 160p. 1999. 12.95 (1-55156-000-3, Pub. by Paperblank) Andrews & McMeel.

***Paperblanks Books Staff, ed.** Honeysuckle. (Wired Morris Ser.). 160p. 2000. 10.95 (1-55156-148-4) Paperblank.

— Iris. (Wired Morris Ser.). 160p. 2000. 10.95 (1-55156-147-6) Paperblank.

— Windrush. (Wired Morris Ser.). 160p. 2000. 10.95 (1-55156-149-2) Paperblank.

Paperna, Ilan. Parasites, Infections & Diseases of Fishes in Africa: An Update. (CIFA Technical Papers: No. 31). (Illus.). 230p. 1996. pap. 27.00 (92-5-103772-8, F37728, Pub. by FAO) Bernan Associates.

Paperno, Dmitry I. Notes of a Moscow Pianist. LC 97-21882. (Illus.). 238p. 1998. 27.95 (1-57467-034-4, Amadeus Pr) Timber.

Paperno, Irina. Chernyshevsky & the Age of Realism: A Study in the Semiotics of Behavior. LC 88-2311. (Illus.). 320p. 1988. 39.50 (0-8047-1453-3) Stanford U Pr.

— Suicide As a Cultural Institution in Dostoevsky's Russia. LC 97-22593. 288p. 1997. text 42.50 (0-8014-3397-5) Cornell U Pr.

— Suicide As a Cultural Institution in Dostoevsky's Russia. LC 97-22593. 288p. 1997. pap. 16.95 (0-8014-8425-1) Cornell U Pr.

Paperno, Irina & Grossman, Joan D., eds. Creating Life: The Aesthetic Utopia of Russian Modernism. LC 93-27948. xii, 288p. 1994. 39.50 (0-8047-2288-9) Stanford U Pr.

Paperno, Irina, jt. ed. see Hughes, Robert P.

Paperno, Lora. Getting Around Town in Russian: Situational Dialogs. Sylvester, Richard D., tr. (Illus.). 123p. (Orig.). (C). 1987. pap. text 11.95 (0-89357-171-7) Slavica.

Paperno, Lora, ed. see Baranskaya, Natalya.

Paperno, Slava, et al. Intermediate Russian: The Twelve Chairs. (Illus.). 326p. (Orig.). (C). 1985. pap. text 21.95 (0-89357-144-X) Slavica.

Paperno, Slava, jt. auth. see Iordanskaja, Lidija.

Paperno, Slava, jt. auth. see Leed, Richard L.

Paperno, Slava, ed. see Zoshchenko, Mikhail.

Papernow, Patricia L. Becoming a Stepfamily: Patterns of Development in Remarried Families. (Gestalt Institute of Cleveland Book Ser.). 448p. 1998. reprint ed. 37.50 (0-88163-309-7) Analytic Pr.

Papers of T. Jefferson Staff. Jefferson Legal Papers. 0.00 (0-691-04721-9) Princeton U Pr.

Papert, Seymour A. Connected Family: Bridging the Digital Generation Gap. LC 96-76500. 208p. 1996. 22.95 incl. cd-rom (1-56352-335-3) Longstreet.

— Mindstorms: Children, Computers & Powerful Ideas. 2nd ed. LC 92-53249. 230p. 1999. pap. 14.00 (0-465-04674-6, Pub. by Basic) HarpC.

Papert, Seymour A., jt. auth. see Minsky, Marvin L.

Papert, Seymour A., jt. auth. see Taylor, James G.

Papert, Seymour A., jt. ed. see Harel, Idit.

Papesca, John P. Fetch. 32p. 1994. pap. 5.95 (0-9643082-0-7) White Knuckle.

Papgapitos, Karen. Gemini Code II. Kleinman, Estelle & Nicholson, David, eds. (JB Ser.). (Illus.). 96p. (Orig.). (J). (gr. 5-9). 1994. pap. 4.95 (0-9637328-3-8) Kapa Hse Pr.

Papi, Luca, jt. auth. see Monticelli, Carlo.

Papi, Stefano & Rhodes, Alexandra. Famous Jewelry Collectors. LC 99-18038. 208p. 1999. 49.50 (0-8109-3341-1, Pub. by Abrams) Time Warner.

Papia, Dan, jt. auth. see Kawakami, Kenji.

Papia, Dan, tr. see Kawakami, Kenji.

Papich, Stephen. Saunders Handbook Veterinary Disease. 2000. pap. text Price not set. (0-7216-7387-2, W B Saunders Co) Harcrt Hlth Sci Grp.

Papierski, Betty P. Flat Tires & Coffe Fires: Being Tales from the TIL Ranch. (Illus.). 160p. 1993. 22.50 (0-914224-25-5) Tales Mojave Rd.

***Papiha, Surinder Singh, et al.** Genomic Diversity: Applications in Human Population Genetics. LC 99-43453. 246p. 1999. write for info. (0-306-46295-8) Kluwer Academic.

***Papike, J. J.** Planetary Materials. LC 99-474392. (Reviews in Mineralogy Ser.: Vol. 36). (Illus.). 1056p. 1998. pap. 40.00 (0-939950-46-4) Mineralogical Soc.

Papillion, Marie. A Million & One Love Strategies. 1995. mass mkt. 5.99 (0-312-95466-2) St Martin.

Papillon, J. B. Traite Historique et Pratique de la Gravure en Bois, 2 vols. (FRE.). 1125p. 1985. pap. text 213.00 (2-903928-30-4) Gordon & Breach.

Papillon, Lucy. When Hope Can Kill: Reclaiming Your Soul in a Romantic Relationship. LC 98-18434. 317p. 1998. 16.95 (1-58029-100-7, Everywhere) Hambleton-Hill.

Papillon, Marie. A Million & One Love Strategies: How to Be Irresistible to the Opposite Sex! 343p. 1998. pap. text 15.00 (0-7881-5628-4) DIANE Pub.

Papillon, Nick. Radio Controlled Helicopters: The Guide to Building & Flying R/C Helicopters. (Illus.). 170p. (Orig.). 1996. pap. 22.50 (1-85486-137-9) Nexus Special Interests.

Papillon, Terry. Rhetorical Studies in the Aristocratea of Demosthenes. (Lang Classical Studies: Vol. 11). XI, 157p. (C). 1998. text 40.95 (0-8204-3986-X) P Lang Pubng.

Papin, Liliane. L' Autre Scene: Le Theatre de Marguerite Duras. (Stanford French & Italian Studies: No. 54). (FRE.). 176p. 1988. pap. 56.50 (0-915838-70-2) Anma Libri.

Papineau, Andre. Breaking up, down & Through: Discovering Spiritual & Psychological Opportunities in Your Transitions. LC 97-15032. 144p. (Orig.). 1997. pap. 9.95 (0-8091-3715-1, 3751-1) Paulist Pr.

— Breakthrough: Stories of Conversion. (Illus.). 152p. (C). 1988. pap. 7.95 (0-89390-128-8) Resource Pubns.

— Sermons for Sermon Haters. LC 91-48019. 184p. (Orig.). 1992. pap. 10.95 (0-89390-229-2) Resource Pubns.

***Papineau, David.** Introducing Consciousness. (Illus.). 176p. 2000. pap. 10.95 (1-84046-115-2) Totem Bks.

Papineau, David, ed. The Philosophy of Science. (Readings in Philosophy Ser.). 346p. 1996. pap. text 17.95 (0-19-875165-6) OUP.

— The Philosophy of Science. (Readings in Philosophy Ser.). 352p. 1996. text 55.00 (0-19-875164-8) OUP.

Papineau, Lucie. Casse-Noisette. (Best-Sellers Ser.).Tr. of Nutcracker. (FRE., Illus.). (J). (ps-2). 2000. pap. 9.95 incl. audio (2-921997-40-1) Coffragants.

***Papineau, Lucie, et al.** Baby Vampire, Gulp! LC 99-900630. (Monster Country Ser.). (Illus.). (J). 1999. pap. 7.95 (1-894363-21-3) Dom1 & Friends.

— Baby Witch, Yuck! LC 99-900629. (Monster Country Ser.). (Illus.). (J). 1999. pap. 7.95 (1-894363-22-1) Dom1 & Friends.

Papini. Adolescent Psychology. 3rd ed. 1994. text, teacher ed. 40.00 (0-07-060545-9) McGraw.

Papini, Giovanni. The Failure. Pope, Virginia, tr. from ITA. LC 76-137070. 326p. 1972. reprint ed. lib. bdg. 35.00 (0-8371-5533-9, PAFA, Greenwood Pr) Greenwood.

— Four & Twenty Minds. LC 78-121496. (Essay Index Reprint Ser.). 1977. 21.95 (0-8369-1770-7) Ayer.

— Four & Twenty Minds. LC 76-174357. 324p. 1972. reprint ed. 26.95 (0-405-08832-9, Pub. by Blom Pubns) Ayer.

Papini, Roberto. The Christian Democrat International. LC 96-25434. 312p. 1996. 68.00 (0-8476-8299-4); pap. 28.95 (0-8476-8300-1) Rowman.

Papini, Roberto, et al. Living in the Global Society. 304p. 1997. text 74.95 (1-85972-575-9, Pub. by Ashgate Pub) Ashgate Pub Co.

***Papirer, Eugene.** Adsorption on Silica Surfaces. LC 00-28050. (Surfactant Science Ser.). 2000. write for info. (0-8247-0003-1) Dekker.

Papirmeister, Bruno, et al. Medical Defense Against Mustard Gas: Toxic Mechanisms & Pharmacological Implications. (Illus.). 360p. 1991. lib. bdg. 139.00 (0-8493-4257-0, RA1247) CRC Pr.

Papirno, Ralph, et al, eds. Factors That Affect the Precision of Mechanical Tests. LC 89-34779. (Special Technical Publication Ser.: No. STP 1025). (Illus.). 250p. 1989. text 59.00 (0-8031-1251-3, STP1025) ASTM.

Papirno, Ralph, jt. ed. see Richard, Chait.

Papka, Raymond E., ed. Anatomy: Embryology, Gross Anatomy, Neuroanatomy, Microanatomy. LC 94-45449. (Oklahoma Notes Ser.). 231p. 1995. 17.95 (0-387-94395-1) Spr-Verlag.

Papke, David R. Framing the Criminal: Crime, Cultural Work & the Loss of Critical Perspective, 1830-1900. LC 86-26475. (Illus.). xviii, 255p. (C). 1987. lib. bdg. 35.00 (0-208-02127-2, Archon Bks) Shoe String.

— Heretics in the Temple: Americans Who Reject the Nation's Legal Faith. LC 98-15987. (Critical America Ser.). 240p. 1998. text 35.00 (0-8147-6632-3) NYU Pr.

— The Pullman Case: The Clash of Labor & Capital in Industrial American. LC 98-50880. (Landmark Law Cases & American Society Ser.). 152p. 1999. 25.00 (0-7006-0953-9); pap. 12.95 (0-7006-0954-7) U Pr of KS.

Papke, Mary E. Susan Glaspell: A Research & Production Sourcebook, 4. LC 92-42696. (Modern Dramatists Research & Production Sourcebooks Ser.: No. 4). 320p. 1993. lib. bdg. 79.50 (0-313-27383-9, PSA, Greenwood Pr) Greenwood.

— Verging on the Abyss: The Social Fiction of Kate Chopin & Edith Wharton, 119. LC 90-38412. (Contributions in Women's Studies: No. 119). 208p. 1990. 49.95 (0-313-26877-0, PAJ, Greenwood Pr) Greenwood.

Papke, Max, jt. auth. see Deutschen Akademie der Wissenschaften Staff.

Papke, William L. The Living Trust: A Private Will That Does Not Have to Be Probated. (Illus.). 144p. (Orig.). 1987. pap. 14.95 (0-9619568-0-1) Wm L Papke.

Papkoff, Lee. Anza-Borrego Desert Natural History Association: The Golden Years: 1971-1980. Cone, Ollie, ed. (Illus.). 83p. (Orig.). 1996. pap., spiral bd. 10.00 (0-910805-07-5) Anza-Borrego.

Papmehl. Freedom of Expression. 1971. lib. bdg. 55.00 (90-247-1111-8, Pub. by M Nijhoff) Kluwer Academic.

Papo, Eliezer. The Essential Pele Yoetz: An Encyclopedia of Ethical Jewish Living. Angel, Marc D., tr. & intro. by. 320p. 1991. 24.95 (0-87203-137-3) Hermon.

***Papola, T. S., et al.** Gender & Employment in India. LC 99-931902. 439p. 1999. write for info. (81-259-0700-9) S Asia.

Papolas, Janince. Virgin Homeowner: The Essential Guide to Owning, Maintaining & Surviving 1st Home. (Illus.). 448p. 1999. pap. 14.95 (0-14-027476-6) Viking Penguin.

Papolos, Demitri. Overcoming Depression. 3rd ed. 1998. 4.62 (0-06-093177-9) HarpC.

***Papolos, Demitri & Papolos, Janice.** The Bipolar Child: The Definitive & Reassuring Guide to Childhood's Most Misunderstood Disorder. LC 99-23764. 398p. 2000. 25.00 (0-7679-0316-1) Broadway BDD.

Papolos, Janice. Overcoming Depression. 3rd ed. LC 96-33534. (Illus.). 432p. 1997. reprint ed. pap. 15.00 (0-06-092782-8, Perennial) HarperTrade.

Papolos, Janice. The Virgin Homeowner: The Essential Guide to Owning, Maintaining, & Surviving Your First Home. LC 96-31304. (Illus.). 288p. 1997. 27.50 (0-393-04035-6) Norton.

Papolos, Janice, jt. auth. see Papolos, Demitri.

Papon, R. Donald. Homeopathy Made Simple: A Quick Reference Guide. LC 98-71592. 264p. 1998. pap. 11.95 (1-57174-110-0) Hampton Roads Pub Co.

Papoulias, Christos. Hypertopos: Two Architectural Projects. (Illus.). 168p. 1999. pap. 16.95 (3-89322-350-9, Pub. by Edition Cantz) Dist Art Pubs.

Papoulias, F., jt. ed. see Falzarano, J. M.

Papoulis, Athanasios. The Fourier Integral & Its Applications. (Classic Textbook Reissue Ser.). 320p. (C). 1962. 99.38 (0-07-048447-3) McGraw.

— Probability & Statistics. 512p. 1989. boxed set 46.00 (0-685-27164-1) P-H.

— Probability & Statistics. (C). 1989. text 54.00 (0-13-711698-5) P-H.

— Probability, Random Variances & Stochastic Processes. 3rd ed. 624p. (C). 1991. 96.88 (0-07-048477-5) McGraw.

— Signal Analysis. (C). 1977. text 82.50 (0-07-048460-0) McGraw.

— Systems & Transforms with Applications in Optics. LC 81-5995. 484p. (C). 1981. reprint ed. lib. bdg. 51.50 (0-89874-358-3) Krieger.

Papousek, H., et al, eds. Nonverbal Vocal Communication: Comparative & Developmental Approaches. (Studies in Emotion & Social Interaction). (Illus.). 319p. (C). 1992. text 59.95 (0-521-41265-X) Cambridge U Pr.

Papoutsakis, E. Terry, jt. auth. see Lee, Sang Yup.

Papows, Jeff. Enterprise.Com: An Insider's Guide to the IT Revolution. 256p. 1999. pap. text 15.00 (0-7382-0226-6, Pub. by Perseus Pubng) HarpC.

Papp. Quality Managment in the Imaging Sciences. LC 97-46903. (Illus.). 320p. (gr. 13). 1998. text 38.00 (0-8151-2968-8, 31848) Mosby Inc.

— Secret Heritage. 1994. 22.95 (0-02-923845-5) S&S Trade.

Papp, A., et al. M4 Badenien (Moravien, Wielicien, Kosovien), Band VI. (Chronostratigraphie und Neostratotypen Ser.). (DUT.). 594p. 1978. 44.00 (3-510-60006-1, Pub. by E Schweizerbartsche) Balogh.

Papp Carrington, Ildiko De, see De Papp Carrington, Ildiko.

Papp, Daniel S. Contemporary International Relations: Frameworks for Understanding. 5th ed. LC 96-26041. 582p. (C). 1996. pap. text 59.00 (0-205-26521-9) Allyn.

Papp, Daniel S. & Diehl, John, eds. The United Nations: Issues of Peace & Conflict, 1989: The Study & Background Guide, Set. LC 89-64408. 1990. 60.00 (0-935082-15-8) Southern Ctr Intl Stud.

Papp, Daniel S. & McIntyre, John R., eds. International Space Policy: Legal, Economic, & Strategic Options for the Twentieth Century & Beyond. LC 87-2519. 341p. 1987. 85.00 (0-89930-215-7, PPS/, Quorum Bks) Greenwood.

Papp, Daniel, S., jt. ed. see McIntyre, John R.

Papp, E. Derivation of Q-Analogs for the Radial Schrodinger Equation in N Space-Dimension. 202p. (C). 1997. lib. bdg. 95.00 (1-56072-443-9) Nova Sci Pubs.

Papp E, Illan. The Israel Palestine Question. LC 98-36351. (Rewriting Histories Ser.). 2p. 1999. write for info. (0-415-16947-X); pap. write for info. (0-415-16948-8) Routledge.

Papp, Ferenc. Contrastive Studies. 168p. 1984. 35.00 (0-569-08800-3, Pub. by Collets) St Mut.

— Mathematical Linguistics in the Soviet Union. (Janua Linguarum, Ser. Minor: No. 40). (Orig.). 1966. pap. text 20.80 (0-686-22446-9) Mouton.

Papp, Ferenc & Szepe, Gyorgy, eds. Papers in Computational Linguistics. (Janua Linguarum, Ser. Major: No. 91). 585p. 1977. text 147.70 (90-279-3285-9) Mouton.

Papp, I. Finnish-Hungarian Concise Dictionary. 1120p. (C). 1993. 54.00 (963-05-6498-X, Pub. by Akade Kiado) St Mut.

Papp, I. & Jakab, L. Hungarian-Finnish Concise Dictionary. 855p. (C). 1993. 54.00 (963-05-6594-3, Pub. by Akade Kiado) St Mut.

P

— Hungarian-Finnish Dictionary: Magyar-Finn Szotar. (FIN & HUN.). 855p. 1985. 49.95 (*0-8288-1657-3*, M4580) Fr & Eur.

Papp, I. & Rug, W. Arbeit mit Texten: Textbuch. (GER.). 128p. (C). 1976. pap. text 28.00 (*3-12-558100-1*, Pub. by Klett Edition) Intl Bk Import.

Papp, J. Gy. Cardiovascular Pharmacology 1987. 649p. (C). 1986. 204.00 (*963-05-4651-5*, Pub. by Akade Kiado) St Mut.

***Papp, Jeffrey.** Lecture Notes on Radiographic Equipment, Exposure & Radiation Protection. 3rd ed. (Illus.). 286p. (C). 1999. pap. text 20.40 (*0-87563-857-0*) Stipes.

— Quality Management in the Imaging Sciences. (Illus.). 320p. 1998. teacher ed. write for info. (*1-55664-474-4*) Mosby Inc.

Papp, John P., ed. Endoscopic Control of Gastrointestinal Hemorrhage. 200p. 1981. 119.00 (*0-8493-6295-4*, RC802, CRC Reprint) Franklin.

Papp, Joseph. Shakespeare Alive! 1988. 11.09 (*0-606-03652-0*, Pub. by Turtleback) Demco.

Papp, Joseph & Kirkland, Elizabeth, eds. Shakespeare Alive! 224p. 1988. mass mkt. 6.50 (*0-553-27081-8*) Bantam.

Papp, Julius Gy. & Szekeres, Laszlo, eds. Pharmacology of Smooth Muscle. LC 94-17635. (Handbook of Experimental Pharmacology Ser.: Vol. 111). 1994. 465.95 (*0-387-57888-9*) Spr-Verlag.

Papp, Laszlo. EMEFESZ, az Amerikai Magyar Egyetemistak Mozgalma az 1956 os Forradalom Utan (Hungarian Student Movement in the U. S. A. after the 1956 Revolution) LC 87-92053. (Tanuk Korukrol Ser.). (Illus.). 96p. 1988. pap. 7.00 (*0-910539-04-9*) Hungarian Alumni.

Papp, Laszlo & Soos, Arpad. Dolichopodidae-Platypezidae. (Catalogue of Palaearctic Diptera Ser.: Vol. 7). 292p. 1991. 272.00 (*0-444-98731-2*, COP 7) Elsevier.

Papp, Laszlo, jt. auth. see Soos, Arpad.

Papp, M., ed. European Pancreatic Club EPC, 20th Meeting, Budapest, August 1988, Abstracts. (Journal: Digestion: Vol. 40, No. 2, 1988). 68p. 1988. pap. 50.50 (*3-8055-4902-4*) S Karger.

Papp, Peggy. Family Therapy: Full Length Case Studies. LC 77-16641. 1977. pap. text 24.95 (*0-89876-019-4*) Gardner Pr.

— The Process of Change. LC 83-12814. (Guilford Family Therapy Ser.). 248p. 1983. lib. bdg. 39.95 (*0-89862-052-X*) Guilford Pubns.

— The Process of Change. LC 83-12814. 248p. 1994. pap. text 22.00 (*0-89862-501-7*) Guilford Pubns.

***Papp, Peggy, ed.** Couples on the Fault Line: New Directions for Therapists. LC 99-86313. 344p. 2000. pap. 35.00 (*1-57230-536-3*, CO536) Guilford Pubns.

Papp, R. B., jt. auth. see Taylor, L. R.

Papp, Richard. Bear Flag Country: Legacy of the Revolt. (Illus.). 224p. (Orig.). 1996. 45.95 (*0-9652136-0-9*); pap. 34.95 (*0-9652136-1-7*) ANALECTA.

Papp, Thunde, jt. auth. see Kecskbes, Istvban.

Papp, Zoltan & Lindenbaum, Richard H. Obstetric Genetics. 627p. (C). 1990. 207.00 (*963-05-5689-8*, Pub. by Akade Kiado) St Mut.

Pappacena, Flavia, ed. see Albano, Roberta, et al.

Pappadakis, John & Pappadakis, Micki. Aphrodite's Food for the Gods. 2nd ed. 83p. 1998. spiral bd. 15.95 (*1-888217-00-6*) Jomic Prods.

Pappadakis, Micki, jt. auth. see Pappadakis, John.

***Pappadopoulos, George.** Blackjack's Hidden Secrets: Win Without Counting. rev. expanded ed. De Dan, Francine G., ed. 28p. 2000. pap. 11.95 (*0-9673795-1-2*) ME n U.

— Blackjack's Hidden Secrets, Win Without Counting. De Dan, Francine G. & De Dan, Rose, eds. 20p. 1999. pap. 19.95 (*0-9673795-0-4*) ME n U.

Pappageotes, George. Say It in Modern Greek. 1956. pap. 3.50 (*0 486-20813-3*) Dover.

Pappageotes, George C. Vest Pocket Modern Greek. 1999. pap. 5.95 (*0-8489-5106-9*) Inst Lang Study.

Pappageotes, George C., tr. see Kazantzakis, Nikos.

Pappalardo, Carlos, jt. auth. see Monafo, William W.

Pappalardo, Ed. Tales of Terror for the Pleasure Boater. LC 94-96101. 235p. (Orig.). 1994. pap. 16.95 (*0-9641978-0-4*) Hickory NY.

Pappani, Debra A. Just Look into My Eyes. (Illus.). 106p. (Orig.). 1981. pap. 4.95 (*0-9606062-0-3*) Pappani.

Pappanikou, A. J. & Paul, James L., eds. Mainstreaming Emotionally Disturbed Children. (Special Education & Rehabilitation Monograph Ser.: No. 10). (C). 1981. pap. 18.95 (*0-8156-2246-5*) Syracuse U Pr.

Pappano, Laura. Connection Gap. 2000. 25.00 (*0-465-01391-0*) HarpC.

Pappano, Marilyn. L' Amour Hors-la-Loi. (Amours d'Aujourd'Hui Ser.: No. 301). (FRE.). 1998. pap. 4.99 (*0-373-38301-0*, 1-38301-7) Harlequin Bks.

***Pappano, Marilyn.** Big Sky Lawman. (Montana Mavericks Ser.: Bk. 5). 2000. mass mkt. 4.50 (*0-373-65050-7*, 1-65050-6, Harlequin) Harlequin Bks.

Pappano, Marilyn. Cattleman's Promise: The Cowboy Code. (Intimate Moments Ser.: No. 925). 1999. mass mkt. 4.25 (*0-373-07925-7*, 1-07925-0) Silhouette.

— Convincing Jamey. 1997. per. 3.99 (*0-373-07812-9*, 1-07812-0) Silhouette.

— Discovered: Daddy. 1996. per. 3.99 (*0-373-07746-7*, 1-07746-0) Silhouette.

— Father to Be. 384p. 1999. mass mkt. 5.99 (*0-553-57985-1*) Bantam.

— Finally a Father: (Romantic Traditions) (Intimate Moments Ser.). 1994. per. 3.50 (*0-373-07542-1*, 5-07542-9) Silhouette.

***Pappano, Marilyn.** First Kiss. 384p. 2000. mass mkt. 5.99 (*0-553-58231-3*) Bantam.

— Un Homme en Colere. (Rouge Passion Ser.: No. 532). (FRE.). 1999. mass mkt. 3.99 (*0-373-37532-8*, 1-37532-8, Harlequin French) Harlequin Bks.

Pappano, Marilyn. The Horseman's Bride: Heartbreak Canyon. (Intimate Moments Ser.: No. 957). 1999. per. 4.25 (*0-373-07957-5*, 1-07957-3) Silhouette.

— Knight Errant: Southern Knights. (Intimate Moments Ser.). 1998. per. 4.25 (*0-373-07836-6*, 1-07836-9) Silhouette.

— The Lights of Home. (Family Continuity Program Ser.: No. 17). 1999. per. 4.50 (*0-373-82165-4*, 1-82165-1) Harlequin Bks.

— A Man Like Smith: (Southern Knights) (Intimate Moments Ser.). 1995. per. 3.75 (*0-373-07626-6*, 1-07626-4) Silhouette.

— Memories of Laura. (Intimate Moments Ser.). 1993. per. 3.39 (*0-373-07486-7*, 5-07486-9) Silhouette.

— Michael's Gift: (American Hero, New Orleans Knights) (Intimate Moments Ser.). 1994. per. 3.50 (*0-373-07583-9*, 1-07583-7) Harlequin Bks.

— Murphy's Law: Men in Blue. (Silhouette Intimate Moments Ser.: Vol. 901). 1998. per. 4.25 (*0-373-07901-X*, 1-07901-1, Mira Bks) Harlequin Bks.

— Older, Wiser . . . Pregnant. (Special Edition Ser.). 1998. per. 4.25 (*0-373-24200-X*, 1-24200-7) Silhouette.

— Operation Homefront. (Intimate Moments Ser.: No. 424). 1992. per. 3.39 (*0-373-07424-7*, 5-07424-0) Harlequin Bks.

— The Overnight Alibi. 1998. per. 4.25 (*0-373-07848-X*, 1-07848-4) Silhouette.

— Passion. 416p. (Orig.). 1996. mass mkt. 5.99 (*0-446-60117-9*, Pub. by Warner Bks) Little.

— Regarding Remy: Southern Knights. (Intimate Moments Ser.). 1994. per. 3.50 (*0-373-07609-6*, 1-07609-0) Silhouette.

***Pappano, Marilyn.** Rogue's Reform. Vol. 1003. 250p. 2000. mass mkt. 4.50 (*0-373-27073-9*) Harlequin Bks.

— Safe Haven. 2000. mass mkt. 4.50 (*0-373-82208-1*, 1-82208-9) Harlequin Bks.

Pappano, Marilyn. A Season for Miracles. 416p. (Orig.). 1997. mass mkt. 6.99 (*0-446-60356-2*, Pub. by Warner Bks) Little.

— Some Enchanted Seasons. 384p. 1998. mass mkt. 5.99 (*0-553-57982-7*) Bantam.

— Survive the Night (Heartbreakers) (Intimate Moments Ser.). 1996. per. 3.99 (*0-373-07703-3*, 1-07703-1) Silhouette.

— Suspicion. 416p. 1997. mass mkt. 6.50 (*0-446-60355-4*, Pub. by Warner Bks) Little.

— Sweet Annie's Pass. (Intimate Moments Ser.). 1993. per. 3.50 (*0-373-07512-X*, 5-07512-2) Silhouette.

— The Taming of Reid Donovan: Southern Knights. (Intimate Moments Ser.: No. 824). 1997. per. 3.99 (*0-373-07824-2*, 1-07824-5) Harlequin Bks.

— Within Reach. (Men Made in America Ser.). 1995. per. 3.59 (*0-373-45181-4*, 1-45181-4) Silhouette.

— You Must Remember This. (Thirty-Six Hours Ser.). 1998. per. 4.50 (*0-373-65017-5*, 1-65017-5) Harlequin Bks.

Pappano, Marilyn & Palmer, Diana. Christmas Memories: Room at the Inn; Woman Hater. (Harlequin Reprint Ser.). 1994. mass mkt. 4.99 (*0-373-15186-1*, 1-15186-9) Harlequin Bks.

Pappano, Marilyn, jt. auth. see Shayne, Maggie.

Papparella, Michael, ed. see Allen, Jane I.

Pappas. Atlas of Laperascopic Surgery. 2nd ed. LC 99-24984. 300p. 1999. 125.00 (*0-8385-0408-6*, Apple Lange Med) McGraw.

— An Intergrated Language Perspective in the Elementary School: Theory Into Action. 3rd ed. LC 98-28989. 384p. (C). 1998. pap. text 45.00 (*0-8013-3055-6*) Longman.

Pappas, jt. auth. see Murray.

Pappas, Alceste T. Reengineering Your Nonprofit Organization: A Guide to Strategic Transformation. LC 95-400. (Nonprofit Law, Finance, & Management Ser.). 224p. 1995. 34.95 (*0-471-11807-9*) Wiley.

Pappas, Anthony. Money, Motivation, & Mission in the Small Church. Walrath, Douglas A., ed. (Small Church in Action Ser.). 128p. (Orig.). 1989. pap. 12.00 (*0-8170-1146-3*) Judson.

Pappas, Anthony & Planting, Scott. Mission: The Small Church Reaches Out. LC 93-1337. (Small Church in Action Ser.). 128p. 1993. pap. 12.00 (*0-8170-1174-9*) Judson.

Pappas, Anthony G. Entering the World of the Small Church: A Guide for Leaders. LC 88-71623. 97p. (Orig.). 1989. pap. 10.25 (*1-56699-030-0*, AL109) Alban Inst.

— Pastoral Stress: Sources of Tension - Resources for Transformation. LC 95-75682. 156p. 1995. pap. 15.25 (*1-56699-150-1*, AL160) Alban Inst.

Pappas, Arthur M., et al, eds. Upper Extremity Injuries in the Athlete. LC 94-33757. (Illus.). 514p. 1994. text 170.00 (*0-443-08836-5*) Church.

Pappas, Barbara. Are You Saved? The Orthodox Christian Process of Salvation. 4th ed. LC 95-79640. (Illus.). 63p. 1997. reprint ed. 4.00 (*0-9623721-4-5*) Amnos Pubns.

— The Christian Life in the Early Church & Today: According to St. Paul's First Epistle to the Corinthians. LC 89-38262. xvi, 172p. (Orig.). 1989. pap. 7.95 (*0-9623721-3-7*) Amnos Pubns.

— The Christian Life in the Early Church & Today: According to St. Paul's Second Epistle to the Corinthians. LC 96-18301. 254p. 1998. pap. 8.95 (*0-9623721-5-3*) Amnos Pubns.

***Pappas, Barbara & Boutzarelos, Irene.** God's Bubbly, Gurgly, Overwhelming, Overflowing Love. LC 99-52809. (Illus.). 2000. write for info. (*0-9623721-6-1*) Amnos Pubns.

Pappas, Benjamin C., jt. auth. see Ludlow, Nicholas H.

Pappas, Charles. Momentary Regards. 80p. 1995. pap. 9.95 (*0-916147-16-9*) Regent Pr.

***Pappas, Charles.** Saving the Tiger, P. S. Tibet. 52p. 1999. pap. 6.00 (*1-889059-75-7*) Regent Pr.

Pappas, Charles N. The Life & Times of G. V. Black. (Illus.). 128p. (Orig.). 1983. pap. text 38.00 (*0-931386-55-1*) Quint Pub Co.

Pappas, Chris & Murray, William. Visual C++ 6: The Complete Reference. 2nd ed. LC 98-228429. (Complete Reference Ser.). 1015p. 1998. pap. 39.99 (*0-07-882510-5*) Osborne-McGraw.

Pappas, Chris, jt. auth. see Murray, William.

***Pappas, Chris H.** Debugging C++ Troubleshooting for Programmers. (Debugging Ser.). 2000. pap. 39.99 (*0-07-212519-5*) Osborne-McGraw.

Pappas, Chris H. Digital Design. (West Engineering Ser.). 1994. pap., student ed. 8.75 (*0-534-93840-X*) PWS Pubs.

— Guide How Computers Can Manage Your Spec. (Culinary Arts Ser.). 1997. pap. 19.95 (*0-442-02562-9*, VNR) Wiley.

— Guide How Computers Can Save Your Business. (Culinary Arts Ser.). 1997. pap. 19.95 (*0-442-02563-7*, VNR) Wiley.

— Guide How Computers Can Save Your Food. (Culinary Arts Ser.). 1997. pap. 19.95 (*0-442-02561-0*, VNR) Wiley.

— Guide How Computers Can Save Your Restaurant. (Culinary Arts Ser.). 1997. pap. 19.95 (*0-442-02564-5*, VNR) Wiley.

— Guide Software Vendors Foodservice Industry. (Culinary Arts Ser.). 1997. pap. 19.95 (*0-442-02565-3*, VNR) Wiley.

— The Visual C++ Handbook. 982p. 1994. pap. text 34.95 (*0-07-882056-1*) Osborne-McGraw.

Pappas, Chris H., jt. auth. see Murray, William H., III.

Pappas, Chris H., jt. auth. see Murray, William H.

Pappas, Chris H., jt. auth. see Murray, William H., 3rd.

Pappas, Chris H., jt. auth. see Murray, William H., III.

Pappas, Chris H., jt. auth. see Murray, William H.

***Pappas, Christine C. & Zecker, Lilliana Barro.** Teacher Inquiries in Literacy Teaching-Learning: Learning to Collaborate in Elementary Urban Classrooms. LC 00-25451. 2000. write for info. (*0-8058-2400-6*) L Erlbaum Assocs.

— Transforming Literacy Curriculum Genres: Working with Teacher Researchers in Urban Classrooms. LC 00-26730. 2000. write for info. (*0-8058-2401-4*) L Erlbaum Assocs.

Pappas, Christine C., et al. An Integrated Language Perspective in the Elementary School. 384p. (C). 1990. pap. text 38.95 (*0-8013-0175-0*, 75834) Longman.

Pappas, Debra S., ed. see Goudeaux, Phillip G.

Pappas, Debra S., ed. see Larson, Verna.

Pappas, Dennis G. Diagnosis & Treatment of Hearing Loss in Children. 2nd ed. LC 98-5580. (Illus.). 279p. 1998. pap. 65.95 (*1-56593-865-8*, 1690) Thomson Learn.

Pappas, Dina. Quick Watercolor Quilts: The Fuse, Fold & Stitch Method. LC 99-15970. (Illus.). 96p. 1999. pap. 26.95 (*1-56477-270-5*, B393) Martingale & Co.

Pappas, Edward H. & Steiger, Jon R. Michigan Business Torts. LC 91-73439. 332p. 1991. 115.00 (*0-685-51910-4*, 91-009) U MI Law CLE.

Pappas, Edward J., jt. auth. see Linkugel, Wil A.

Pappas, Elizabeth. Eddie's Shopping Surprise: A Lift-the-Flap Book. (Fisher-Price Mini Lift the Flap Bks.: No. 1). (Illus.). 18p. (J). (gr. k-3). 1998. bds. 3.99 (*1-57584-198-3*, Pub. by Rdrs Digest) Random.

— Sonya's Special Secret: A Lift-the-Flap Book. (Fisher Price Mini-Flap Playbks.: No. 3). (Illus.). 18p. (J). (gr. k-3). 1998. bds. 3.99 (*1-57584-201-7*, Pub. by Rdrs Digest) Random.

***Pappas, George Charles.** Synpan: Inside the Wellness Universe: A Poetic Guide. Parrish-Harra, Carol E., ed. LC 99-72820. (Illus.). 366p. 1999. pap. 19.95 (*0-945027-18-4*, Pub. by Sparrow Hawk Pr) Distributors.

***Pappas, George S.** Berkeley's Thought. LC 99-88432. 288p. 2000. 39.95 (*0-8014-3700-8*) Cornell U Pr.

Pappas, George S. Laboratory Manual of Histology. 2nd ed. 176p. (C). 1993. text, lab manual ed. write for info. (*0-697-12244-1*, WCB McGr Hill) McGrw-H Hghr Educ.

— To the Point: The United States Military Academy, 1802-1902. LC 92-36632. 528p. 1993. 65.00 (*0-275-94329-1*, C4329, Praeger Pubs) Greenwood.

Pappas, George S., ed. Justification & Knowledge: New Studies in Epistemology. (Philosophical Studies in Philosophy: No. 17). 233p. 1979. pap. text 59.00 (*90-277-1024-4*, D Reidel); lib. bdg. 80.00 (*90-277-1023-6*, D Reidel) Kluwer Academic.

Pappas, Gregory. The Magic City: Unemployment in a Working-Class Community. LC 88-47935. (Anthropology of Contemporary Issues Ser.). (Illus.). 232p. 1989. 39.95 (*0-8014-2277-9*) Cornell U Pr.

— The Magic City: Unemployment in a Working-Class Community. LC 88-47935. (Anthropology of Contemporary Issues Ser.). (Illus.). 224p. reprint ed. pap. 69.50 (*0-608-20094-8*, 207136600011) Bks Demand.

Pappas, Ioannis A. & Tatsiopoulos, Ilias P., eds. Advances in Production Management Systems: Proceedings of the IFIP TC5 - WG5.7 Fifth International Conference on Advances in Production Management Systems, APMS '93, Athens, Greece, 28-30 September 1993. LC 93-27019. (IFIP Transactions B: Applications in Technology Ser.: Vol. B-13). 646p. 1993. 177.25 (*0-444-81598-8*, North Holland) Elsevier.

Pappas, Irene, ed. see Quinby, Marge M.

***Pappas, James, adapted by.** New Amplified Pilgrim's Progress: From This World to That Which Is to Come. (Illus.). 348p. 1999. pap. 24.95 (*0-9671269-0-8*) Orions Gate.

Pappas, James G., jt. auth. see Lulat, Y. G.

Pappas, James L., jt. auth. see Brigham, Eugene F.

Pappas, James L., jt. auth. see Hirschey, Mark.

Pappas, John J., intro. Annual Review of Communications: National Engineering Consortium, Vol. XXXXVI. (Illus.). 1108p. 1992. 139.00 (*0-933217-08-0*) Prof Educ Intl.

***Pappas, Joseph & Hunter, Diana, eds.** Before You Hire a Contractor: A Construction Guidebook for Consumers. LC 94-37497. 184p. 1999. pap. 12.95 (*1-891264-65-6*) Consumer Press.

Pappas, Joseph, ed. see Gonzalez, Steve.

Pappas, Joseph, ed. see Hunter, Diana.

Pappas, Lou S. Classic Dishes of Decades Past: The Cookbook of Nostalgic House Favorites. (Illus.). 144p. 1999. per. 14.95 (*1-55867-235-4*) Bristol Pub Ent CA.

— Cooking with Fresh Herbs. 176 p. 1998. pap. 8.95 (*1-55867-192-7*, Nitty Gritty Ckbks) Bristol Pub Ent CA.

— Extra-Special Crockery Pot Recipes. rev. ed. (Illus.). 160p. 1995. pap. 8.95 (*1-55867-107-2*, Nitty Gritty Ckbks) Bristol Pub Ent CA.

— Favorite Soup Recipes. 62p. 1997. 4.95 (*1-55867-172-2*, Magnetic Bks) Bristol Pub Ent CA.

— Unbeatable Chicken Recipes. LC 98-125201. (Illus.). 176p. 1997. pap. 8.95 (*1-55867-189-7*, Nitty Gritty Ckbks) Bristol Pub Ent CA.

***Pappas, Lou Seibert.** Favorite Cookie Recipes. 144p. 2000. pap. 14.95 (*1-55867-237-0*) Bristol Pub Ent CA.

Pappas, Lou Seibert. Omelettes, Souffles & Frittatas. LC 98-30315. (Illus.). 96p. 1999. pap. 14.95 (*0-8118-2120-X*) Chronicle Bks.

— The Vegetarian Table: Japan. LC 97-34414. (Illus.). 132p. 1998. 24.95 (*0-8118-1565-X*) Chronicle Bks.

— The Vegetarian Table: Mexico. LC 94-870. (Vegetarian Table Ser.: Vol. 2). (Illus.). 156p. 1995. 22.95 (*0-8118-0475-5*) Chronicle Bks.

Pappas, Lou Seibert & Hoffman, Susanna. The Well-Filled Microwave Cookbook. LC 95-32830. (Illus.). 448p. 1996. pap. 14.95 (*1-56305-177-X*, 3177) Workman Pub.

— The Well-Filled Tortilla Cookbook. LC 89-40730. (Illus.). 304p. 1990. pap. 9.95 (*0-89480-364-6*, 1364) Workman Pub.

***Pappas, Marjorie, et al.** Searching Electronic Resources. 2nd ed. LC 98-54104. 105p. 1999. 34.95 (*0-938865-67-6*) Linworth Pub.

Pappas, Michael G. The Biotech Business Handbook. 2nd ed. 1999. 125.00 (*0-89603-503-4*) Humana.

— The Biotech Business Handbook: How to Organize & Operate a Biotechnology Business, Including the Most Promising Applications for the 1990s. (Illus.). 461p. 1994. ring bd. 189.50 (*0-89603-320-1*) Humana.

— The Biotech Entrepreneur's Glossary: Including Terms in Accounting, Biotechnology, Business, Computers, Fund Acquisition, Human Resources... abr. ed. 182p. 1998. pap. 39.00 (*0-9665558-2-1*, 100) M G Pappas.

***Pappas, Michael G.** Small Business Innovation Research Grants, 1998: Including Fast-Track SBIRs. unabridged ed. (C). 1998. ring bd. 179.00 (*0-9665558-0-5*, 101) M G Pappas.

Pappas, Mike J. Computer Software & Hardware for the Foodservice Industry. LC 96-17744. 360p. 1997. pap. 49.95 (*0-442-02269-7*, VNR) Wiley.

Pappas, Mike J. Eat Food, Not Profits! How Computers Can Save Your Restaurant. 446p. 1996. pap. 59.95 (*0-471-28764-4*, VNR) Wiley.

Pappas, Milt, et al. Out at Home: Triumph & Tragedy in the Life of Milt Pappas. 350p. 2000. 28.00 (*0-939995-30-1*) Angel Pr WI.

Pappas, Nickolas. Plato & the Republic. LC 94-33894. (Philosophy Guidebooks Ser.). 256p. (C). (gr. 13). 1995. pap. 12.99 (*0-415-09532-8*, C0410) Routledge.

— Plato & the Republic. LC 94-33894. (Philosophy Guidebooks Ser.). 256p. (C). (gr. 13). 1995. 60.00 (*0-415-09531-X*, C0409) Routledge.

***Pappas, Norman A.** Passing the Bucks: Protecting Your Wealth from One Generation to the Next. (Illus.). 250p. 1999. 29.95 (*0-9674518-0-9*) Enter Group.

Pappas, Paul. The United States & the Greek War for Independence, 1821-1828. 1985. text 48.50 (*0-88033-065-1*, 173, Pub. by East Eur Monographs) Col U Pr.

Pappas, Paul C. Jesus' Tomb in India: The Debate on His Death & Resurrection. LC 91-19080. (Illus.). 214p. (Orig.). 1991. reprint ed. pap. 66.40 (*0-608-01772-8*, 206243000003) Bks Demand.

Pappas, Peter, ed. see Pavlenkov, Victor.

Pappas, Peter, tr. see Vasilikos, Vasilis.

Pappas, Peter G., jt. auth. see Cooper, J. Allen D.

Pappas, Richard J., ed. Strategic Marketing for Presidents. LC 94-228032. 72p. 1994. pap. 15.00 (*0-87117-273-9*, 1364) Comm Coll Pr Am Assn Comm Coll.

***Pappas, Rita.** Barbra Streisand: Entertainer. (Women of Achievement Ser.). (Illus.). 112p. (YA). (gr. 4-7). 2000. write for info. (*0-7910-5285-0*) Chelsea Hse.

Pappas, S. Chris. Fulminant Hepatic Failure. 250p. 1999. text. write for info. (*0-7817-0018-3*) Lppncott W & W.

Pappas, S. P. Radiation Curing: Science & Technology. (Topics in Applied Chemistry Ser.). (Illus.). 464p. (C). 1992. text 110.00 (*0-306-43999-9*, Kluwer Plenum) Kluwer Academic.

Pappas, S. Peter, ed. UV Curing: Science & Technology. LC 78-56293. (Illus.). 1978. per. 95.00 (*0-936840-04-8*) Tech Marketing.

— UV Curing Vol. 2: Science & Technology. 360p. 1985. text 99.00 (*0-936840-08-0*) Tech Marketing.

Pappas, S. Peter & Winslow, F. H., eds. Photodegradation & Photostabilization of Coatings. LC 81-467. (ACS Symposium Ser.: No. 151). 1981. 43.95 (*0-8412-0611-2*) Am Chemical.

— Photodegradation & Photostabilization of Coatings: Based on a Symposium. LC 81-467. (ACS Symposium Ser.: Vol. 151). 317p. 1981. reprint ed. pap. 98.30 (*0-608-03037-6*, 206349000007) Bks Demand.

P

Pappas, Steven. Managing Mobile Home Parks. (IREM Monographs). (Illus.). 194p. (Orig.). (C). 1991. pap. text 44.95 (*0-944298-57-5*) Inst Real Estate.

Pappas, Theodore. Plagiarism & the Culture War: The Writings of Martin Luther King, Jr. & Other Prominent American's. LC 98-72137. 256p. 1998. pap. 16.95 (*0-87319-045-9*) Hallberg Pub Corp.

Pappas, Theodore N., et al, eds. Atlas of Laparoscopic Surgery. (Illus.). 328p. 1996. text 149.00 (*1-878132-20-2*) Current Med.

Pappas, Theodore N., et al. The Duke Atlas of Laparoscopic Surgery. 2nd ed. LC 99-24984. 1999. write for info. (*1-57340-130-7*) Current Med.

Pappas, Theoni. The Adventures of Penrose - The Mathematical Cat. LC 97-41182. (Illus.). 132p. (Orig.). (J). (gr. 3-8). 1997. pap. 10.95 (*1-884550-14-2*) Wide World-Tetra.

— Fractals, Googols & Other Mathematical Tales. LC 92-41343. (Illus.). 72p. (Orig.). (J). (gr. 4 up). 1993. pap. 9.95 (*0-933174-89-6*) Wide World-Tetra.

— The Joy of Mathematics. 2nd rev. ed. (Illus.). 256p. (Orig.). 1989. pap. 10.95 (*0-933174-65-9*) Wide World-Tetra.

— Let's Dance: The Greek Way. (Illus.). 1977. pap. 2.95 (*0-933174-07-1*) Wide World-Tetra.

— Magic of Mathematics: Discovering the Spell of Mathematics. LC 94-11653. 224p. 1994. pap. 10.95 (*0-933174-99-3*) Wide World-Tetra.

— Math-a-Day: A Book of Days for Your Mathematical Year. LC 99-88313. (Illus.). 288p. 1999. pap. 12.95 (*1-884550-20-7*) Wide World-Tetra.

— Math for Kids - And Other People Too. LC 97-43091. (Illus.). 132p. (YA). (gr. 2 up). 1997. pap. 10.95 (*1-884550-13-4*) Wide World-Tetra.

— Math Talk. LC 90-25380. (Illus.). 72p. (Orig.). 1991. pap. 8.95 (*0-933174-74-8*) Wide World-Tetra.

— Mathematical Footprints: Discovering Mathematical Impressions All Around Us. LC 99-58173. (Illus.). 224p. 1999. pap. 10.95 (*1-884550-21-5*) Wide World-Tetra.

— Mathematical Scandals. LC 97-12297. (Illus.). 192p. 1997. pap. 10.95 (*1-884550-10-X*) Wide World-Tetra.

— Mathematics Appreciation. 154p. 1987. pap. 10.95 (*0-933174-28-4*) Wide World-Tetra.

— More Joy of Mathematics. LC 91-11295. (Illus.). 304p. (Orig.). 1991. pap. 10.95 (*0-933174-73-X*) Wide World-Tetra.

— The Music of Reason: Experience the Beauty of Mathematics Through Quotations. LC 95-38362. (Illus.). 128p. (Orig.). 1995. pap. 9.95 (*1-884550-04-5*) Wide World-Tetra.

— What Do You See? An Optical Illusion Slide Show. rev. ed. 32p. 1988. pap. 29.95 incl. sl. (*0-933174-78-0*) Wide World-Tetra.

Pappas, Theoni & Monroe, Elvira. Greek Cooking for Everyone. 2nd ed. 167p. (Orig.). 1989. pap. 8.95 (*0-933174-61-6*) Wide World-Tetra.

Pappas, Thrasyvoulos N., jt. ed. see Rogowitz, Bernice E.

Pappas, Tom, jt. auth. see Scott, David.

Pappaz, Michel, ed. see International Conference on Modeling of Casting &.

Pappe, Ilan. The Making of the Arab-Israeli Conflict, 1947-1951. 320p. 1992. text 69.50 (*1-85043-357-7*, Pub. by I B T) St Martin.

— The Making of the Arab-Israeli Conflict, 1947-1951. 336p. 1994. text 24.95 (*1-85043-819-6*, Pub. by I B T) St Martin.

Pappe, Ilan, jt. ed. see Maoz, Moshe.

Pappe, Ilan, jt. ed. see Nevo, Joseph.

Pappenheim, Dick. Going Dutch: An Easy Guide to Dutch Business Culture for Expatriates. LC 97-183979. (Illus.). 96p. (Orig.). 1997. pap. 12.95 (*90-5727-003-X*, Pub. by Uitgeverij Arkel) LPC InBook.

Papper, Joanne. Easier Said Than Done: Elimating Judgments & Changing Our Attitudes. (Illus.). 160p. (Orig.). 1998. pap. 7.95 (*0-9667929-0-4*) Missouri Pubg Co.

Papper, E. M. Romance, Poetry & Surgical Sleep: Literature Influences Medicine, 42. LC 94-24189. (Contributions in Medical Studies: Vol. 42). 176p. 1995. 57.95 (*0-313-29405-4*, Greenwood Pr) Greenwood.

Papper, Robert A. Broadcast News Writing. LC 94-25081. 272p. 1994. pap. text 37.00 (*0-205-14693-7*) Allyn.

Papper, Solomon. Doing Right: Everyday Medical Ethics. 148p. 1983. 30.95 (*0-316-69044-9*, Little Brwn Med Div) Lppncott W & W.

— Sodium: Its Biological Significance. (CRC Uniscience Ser. on Cations of Biological Significance). 304p. 1981. 113.95 (*0-8493-5873-6*, RC632) CRC Pr.

Papper, Solomon, et al. Manual of Medical Care of the Surgical Patient. 3rd ed. 304p. 1985. 24.50 (*0-316-69058-9*, Little Brwn Med Div) Lppncott W & W.

Papper, Solomon, jt. auth. see Kaufman, Christian E., Jr.

Pappert, Eric J., jt. auth. see Goetz, Christopher G.

Pappetti, F. & Succi, S. An Introduction to Parallel Computational Fluid Dynamics. (Illus.). 237p. (C). 1996. lib. bdg. 115.00 (*1-56072-354-8*) Nova Sci Pubs.

Pappin, Joseph, III. The Metaphysics of Edmund Burke. LC 92-41383. xx, 188p. 1993. 30.00 (*0-8232-1365-X*); pap. 19.95 (*0-8232-1366-8*) Fordham.

Pappo, Harry A. Simulations for Skills Training: Design & Development. LC 97-33505. (Illus.). 208p. 1998. 42.95 (*0-87778-299-7*) Educ Tech Pubns.

Pappo, M., jt. ed. see Marty, M.

Pappoutsakis, James, ed. see Brooke, A.

Pappu, S. S., ed. Dimension of Karma. (C). 1994. 44.00 (*81-7001-101-9*, Pub. by Chanakya) S Asia.

— New Essays in the Philosophy of Sarvepalli Radhakrishnan. LC 95-911089. (C). 1995. 64.00 (*81-7030-461-X*, Pub. by Sri Satguru Pubns) S Asia.

Pappu, S. S. & Rao, R., eds. The Dimensions of Karma. 450p. (C). 1987. 42.95 (*0-685-43948-8*) Asia Bk Corp.

Pappus, Lou S. Pesto. 1994. 99.50 (*0-8118-9175-5*) Chronicle Bks.

***Paprocki, Joe.** God's Library: Introducing Catholics to the Bible. 117p. 1999. pap. 9.95 (*0-89622-970-X*) Twenty-Third.

— Renewing Your Ministry: Walking with Jesus in All That You Do. LC 00-8463. 128p. 2000. pap. 9.95 (*0-87793-941-1*) Ave Maria.

Paprocki, Joe. Tools for Teaching: Classroom Tips for Catechists. LC 97-60103. 96p. 1997. pap. 7.95 (*0-89622-726-X*) Twenty-Third.

Paprocki, Joe, jt. auth. see Costello, Gwen.

Paprocki, Joseph. In the Beginning. Sawyer, Kieran, ed. (Developing Faith Ser.). 136p. (YA). (gr. 9-12). 1996. pap. text, teacher ed. 16.95 (*0-87793-586-6*); pap. text, student ed. 5.95 (*0-87793-585-8*) Ave Maria.

— Jesus, Should I Follow You? Sawyer, Kieran, ed. (Developing Faith Ser.). (Illus.). 80p. (YA). (gr. 9-12). 1999. pap. text, student ed. 6.95 (*0-87793-557-2*) Ave Maria.

— Jesus, Should I Follow You? Director Manual. Sawyer, Kieran, ed. (Developing Faith Ser.). (Illus.). 128p. (YA). (gr. 9-12). 1996. pap. text, teacher ed. 16.95 (*0-87793-556-4*) Ave Maria.

— You Give Them Something to Eat: Ministering When You Think You Can't. LC 98-19807. 112p. 1998. pap. 6.95 (*0-87793-655-2*) Ave Maria.

***Paprocki, Sherry.** Michelle Kwan. LC 00-29041. 2000. 17.95 (*0-7910-5792-5*) Chelsea Hse.

***Paprocki, Sherry Beck.** Katie Couric. (Women of Achievement Ser.). 2000. 19.95 (*0-7910-5881-6*) Chelsea Hse.

— Katie Couric. (Women of Achievement Ser.). (Illus.). 2001. pap. 9.95 (*0-7910-5882-4*) Chelsea Hse.

— Michelle Kwan. (Women Who Win Ser.). (Illus.). 2000. pap. 7.95 (*0-7910-6152-3*) Chelsea Hse.

Paprocki, Steve. What Color Is Your Proposal? A Guide to Corporate Grantmaking for Recial/Ethnic Populations, 3 vols. (Corporate Grant Making to Racial/Ethnic Populations Ser.). 400p. 1997. pap. write for info. (*1-891465-08-2*) Natl Comm Philan.

Paprocki, Steve, jt. auth. see Bothwell, Robert O.

Paprocki, Steve L. & Bothwell, Robert O. Answering the Call? The Telecommunication Industry's Grant Making for Racial/Ethnic Communities. (Corporate Grant Making to Racial/Ethnic Populations Ser.: 2 vol.). Date not set. spiral bd. 25.00 (*1-891465-09-0*) Natl Comm Philan.

Paprocki, Steven, jt. auth. see Henry, Jennifer.

Paprocki, Steven L. & Bothwell, Robert O. Corporate Grantmaking: Giving to Racial - Ethnic Populations. LC 94-20702. (Illus.). 544p. (C). 1994. reprint ed. pap. text 55.00 (*0-8191-9573-1*) U Pr of Amer.

Paprotte, Wolf, jt. auth. see Alain, Dumort.

Papson, Stephen. In a World Not of His Own Making. 195p. (Orig.). 1993. pap. 7.95 (*0-9635722-0-2*) Blue Canary.

Papson, Stephen, jt. auth. see Goldman, Robert.

Papson, Thomas C. & Young, Charlotte D. Business Uses of the Freedom of Information Act, No. 14. 2nd ed. (Corporate Practice Ser.). 1991. ring bd. 95.00 (*1-55871-231-3*) BNA.

Papstein, Robert. Eritrea: A Tourist Guide. (Illus.). 128p. 1995. pap. 9.95 (*1-56902-011-6*) Red Sea Pr.

— Eritrea: Revolution at Dusk: A Pictorial Rendering. LC 90-81661. (Illus.). 200p. (C). 1991. 49.95 (*0-932415-63-6*); pap. 18.95 (*0-932415-64-4*) Red Sea Pr.

PAPTAC Bleaching Committee. Glossary of Bleaching Terms. 42p. 1996. 18.36 (*1-895288-90-8*) Pulp & Paper.

PAPTAC Energy Committee. Energy Conservation Opportunities, 1981-1992 (Possibilites d'Economie d'Energie 1981-1992) (ENG & FRE.). 1992. 17.00 (*1-895288-34-7*) Pulp & Paper.

— Energy Conservaiton Opportunities 1994 (Possibilites d'Economie d'Energie 1994) 24p. 1994. 6.80 (*1-895288-54-1*) Pulp & Paper.

— Energy Conservation Opportunities 1993 (Possibilites d'Economie d'Energie 1993) (ENG & FRE.). 31p. 1993. 6.80 (*1-895288-72-X*) Pulp & Paper.

Papthanasiou, T. D. & Guell, D. C., eds. Flow Induced Alignment in Composite Materials. 384p. 1997. 170.00 (*1-85573-254-8*, Pub. by Woodhead Pubng) Am Educ Systs.

Papunen, Heikki, ed. Mineral Deposits: Research & Exploration - Where Do They Meet? Proceedings of the 4th Biennial SGA Meeting, Turku, Finland, 11-13 August 1997. (Illus.). 1008p. (C). 1997. text 162.00 (*90-5410-889-4*, Pub. by A A Balkema) Ashgate Pub Co.

Papurt, M. L., jt. auth. see Redding, Richard W.

Papurt, David M. Inside the Object Model: The Sensible Use of C++ (Advances in Object Technology Ser.: No. 4). 544p. (Orig.). 1995. pap. text 44.95 (*0-13-207366-8*) Cambridge U Pr.

***Papurt, M. L.** Compatible Canines: Keeping the Peace among Your Pets. LC 98-44323. (Illus.). 144p. 1999. pap. 9.95 (*0-7641-0724-0*) Barron.

— Hand-Raising Orphaned Kitten. LC 98-48069. (Illus.). 96p. 1999. pap. 8.95 (*0-7641-0727-5*) Barron.

***Papus, Gerard E.** What Is Occultism? A Philosophical & Critical Study. 104p. 1999. reprint ed. pap. 17.95 (*0-7661-0764-7*) Kessinger Pub.

Papus, pseud. Astrology for Initiates: Astrological Secrets of the Western Mystery Tradition. Lehman, J. Lee, tr. LC 96-28287. 160p. 1996. pap. 15.95 (*0-87728-894-1*) Weiser.

***Papus, pseud.** The Qabalah: Secret Tradition of the West. (Illus.). 384p. 2000. pap. (*1-57863-936-0*); pap. 19.95 (*0-87728-936-0*) Weiser.

Papus, pseud. Reincarnation. Vallior, Marguerite, tr. (Illus.). 132p. (Orig.). 1991. reprint ed. pap. 6.95 (*0-922802-10-6*) Kessinger Pub.

— Tarot of the Bohemians. 385p. 1978. pap. 10.00 (*0-87980-158-1*) Wilshire.

— What Is Occultism? 104p. 1981. pap. 10.00 (*0-89540-073-1*, SB-073) Sun Pub.

Papus, pseud & Vallior, Marguerite, trs. Reincarnation: Physical, Astral & Spiritual Evolution. 142p. 1996. reprint ed. spiral bd. 14.00 (*0-7873-0654-1*) Hlth Research.

***Papworth, Carolyn.** Out to Eat: Melbourne. (Out to Eat Guides). (Illus.). 248p. 1999. pap. 12.95 (*1-86450-040-9*) Lonely Planet.

Papworth, John. Small Is Powerful: The Future As if People Really Mattered. LC 95-22714. (Praeger Studies on the 21st Century). 248p. 1995. 65.00 (*0-275-95424-2*, Praeger Pubs); pap. 20.95 (*0-275-95425-0*, Praeger Pubs) Greenwood.

Papy, C. I., ed. see Papy, Frank M.

Papy, Frank M. Cruising Guide to the Florida Keys. 8th ed. Gregg, R. L., ed. (Illus.). 260p. 1992. pap. 18.95 (*0-9619838-2-5*) F Papy Cruising Guide.

— Cruising Guide to the Florida Keys, No. 10. 10th ed. LC 81-176805. (Illus.). 256p. Date not set. pap. 19.95 (*0-9619838-4-1*) F Papy Cruising Guide.

— Cruisins Guide to the Florida Keys. 7th ed. Papy, C. I., ed. (Illus.). 256p. 1989. pap. 16.95 (*0-9619838-1-7*) F Papy Cruising Guide.

Papyk, Bob. How to Increase Your Kitchen & Bath Business by 25...Starting Next Week! (Illus.). 109p. (Orig.). 1996. pap. text 30.00 (*1-887127-33-X*, 5305) Natl Kit Bath.

Papzzoni, Marco, jt. auth. see Righini, Fernando.

***Paque, Karl-Heinz.** Real Wage Rigidity & Structural Unemployment in Germany. 2000. 95.00 (*3-16-147269-1*) JCB Mohr.

Paquet, jt. auth. see Carr.

Paquet, Alfons. The Prophecies. Waidson, H. M., tr. & intro. by. LC 82-84465. (GERM Ser.: Vol. 10). (Illus.). xxii, 130p. 1983. 35.00 (*0-938100-08-4*) Camden Hse.

Paquet, Gilles, jt. auth. see De La Mothe, John.

Paquet, Gilles, jt. ed. see Bazoge, Benoit.

Paquet, Gilles, ed. see De la Mothe, John.

Paquet, H. & Clauer, N., eds. Soils & Sediments: Mineralogy & Geochemistry. LC 97-8044. (Illus.). 260p. 1997. 115.00 (*3-540-61599-7*) Spr-Verlag.

Paquet, K. J. & Kozuschek, W. A., eds. Pankreas: Diagnostik, Therapie. (Illus.). 584p. 1991. 178.50 (*3-8055-5545-8*) S Karger.

Paquet, K. J. & Schoelmerich, J., eds. Pfortaderhochdruck. (GER., Illus.). x, 702p. 1994. 181.75 (*3-8055-5659-4*) S Karger.

Paquet, K. J., et al. Portale Hypertension. Denck, H. & Berchtold, R., eds. x, 282p. 1982. pap. 56.75 (*3-8055-3480-9*) S Karger.

Paquet, K. J., jt. ed. see Nilius, R.

***Paquet, Laura.** Lord Langdon's Tutor. (Regency Romance Ser.). 224p. 2000. mass mkt. 4.99 (*0-8217-6675-9*, Zebra Kensgtn) Kensgtn Pub Corp.

Paquet, Marcel. Magritte, 11 vols. (Thunder Bay Artists Ser.). (Illus.). 96p. 1997. pap. text 4.99 (*1-57145-126-9*, Thunder Bay) Advantage Pubs.

— Magritte. (SPA.). 1996. pap. 9.99 (*3-8228-0684-6*) Taschen Amer.

Paquet, Paul C., jt. ed. see Harrington, Fred H.

***Paquet, Peter.** Helldunkel, Raum und Form Georges Seurat als Zeichner: Mit einem Anhang Seurats schriftliche Selbstzeugnisse und annotierter Bibliographie. 2000. 63.95 (*3-631-35934-9*) P Lang Pubng.

Paquette. Reactions, Vol. 53. 672p. 1998. 95.00 (*0-471-32609-7*) Wiley.

Paquette, G. C., tr. see Mori, Hazime & Kuramoto, Yoshiki.

Paquette, Gerard A. Structured COBOL. 2nd ed. 848p. (C). 1990. text 59.08 (*0-697-07763-2*) Bus & Educ Tech.

Paquette, Gerard A. Structured COBOL. 3rd ed. 864p. (C). 1994. text 59.08 (*0-697-12394-4*) Bus & Educ Tech.

Paquette, Gerard A. Structured COBOL with Compiler. 2nd ed. 848p. (C). 1991. pap. text 69.60 incl. 3.5 ld (*0-697-14305-8*, Irwn McGrw-H) McGrw-H Hghr Educ.

Paquette, Gerard A., et al. Advanced Structured COBOL. 2nd ed. 608p. (C). 1990. per. 62.35 (*0-697-07771-3*) Bus & Educ Tech.

— Structured COBOL/Wolff's RM COBOL-85. 3rd ed. 864p. (C). 1994. pap. text 69.60 incl. disk (*0-697-25984-6*, Irwn McGrw-H) McGrw-H Hghr Educ.

Paquette, Jerry. Social Purpose & Schooling: Alternatives, Agendas & Issues. 204p. 1991. pap. 34.95 (*1-85000-921-X*, Falmer Pr) Taylor & Francis.

Paquette, Lee A. Only More So: The History of East Hartford, 1783-1976. LC 92-61362. 372p. 1992. reprint ed. 30.00 (*0-89725-076-1*, 1410) Picton Pr.

***Paquette, Leo.** Organic Reactions, Vol. 55. 654p. 1999. 95.00 (*0-471-37614-0*) Wiley.

Paquette, Leo & Bittman, Robert. Organic Reactions, Vol. 54. 442p. 1999. 89.95 (*0-471-34888-0*) Wiley.

Paquette, Leo A. Organic Reactions, Vol. 39. 608p. 1990. 120.00 (*0-471-52632-0*) Wiley.

— Organic Reactions, Vol. 41. 672p. 1992. 99.95 (*0-471-54409-4*) Wiley.

— Organic Reactions, Vol. 42. 696p. 1992. 99.95 (*0-471-54410-8*) Wiley.

— Organic Reactions, Vol. 43. 832p. 1993. 105.00 (*0-471-58479-7*) Wiley.

— Organic Reactions, Vol. 45. 688p. 1994. 105.00 (*0-471-03615-5*) Wiley.

Paquette, Leo A. Organic Reactions, Vol. 49. LC 42-20265. (Organic Reactions Ser.). 700p. 1996. 98.95 (*0-471-15655-8*) Wiley.

Paquette, Leo A. Organic Reactions, Vol. 51. LC 42-20265. (Organic Reactions Ser.). 502p. 1997. 98.95 (*0-471-18394-6*) Wiley.

— Organic Syntheses, Vol. 69. 328p. 1991. 78.95 (*0-471-54560-0*) Wiley.

— The Renaissance in Cyclooctatetraene Chemistry. Barton et al, eds. 1976. pap. 15.50 (*0-08-020479-1*, Pergamon Pr) Elsevier.

Paquette, Leo A., ed. Encyclopedia of Reagents for Organic Synthesis, 8 vols. 6234p. 1995. 3950.00 (*0-471-93623-5*) Wiley.

— Organic Reactions, Vol. 38. 832p. 1990. 125.00 (*0-471-51594-9*) Wiley.

— Organic Reactions, Vol. 40. 528p. 1991. 110.00 (*0-471-53841-8*) Wiley.

— Organic Reactions, Vol. 44. 624p. 1993. 105.00 (*0-471-30302-X*) Wiley.

— Organic Reactions, Vol. 50. LC 42-20265. (Organic Reactions Ser.). 704p. 1997. 105.00 (*0-471-15657-4*) Wiley.

— Organic Reactions, Vol. 52. 600p. 1998. 95.00 (*0-471-18395-4*) Wiley.

Paquette, Leo A., et al, eds. Organic Reactions, Vol. 46. 416p. 1994. 105.00 (*0-471-08619-3*) Wiley.

— Organic Reactions, Vol. 47. LC 42-20265. 592p. 1995. 99.95 (*0-471-11737-4*) Wiley.

— Organic Reactions, Vol. 48. LC 42-20265. 880p. 1996. 105.00 (*0-471-14699-4*) Wiley.

Paquette, Leo A. & Doherty, A. M. Polyquinane Chemistry Synthesis & Reactions. (Reactivity & Structure Ser.: Vol. 26). (Illus.). 250p. 1987. 142.95 (*0-387-17703-5*) Spr-Verlag.

Paquette, Leo A., et al. Encyclopedia of Nuclear Magnetic Resonance, 8 Vol. Set, 8 vols. LC 95-23825. 5590p. 1996. 4950.00 (*0-471-93871-8*) Wiley.

Paquette, Mari L., ed. see Brandt, Beverly F.

Paquette, Mary & Rodemich, Christine. Psychiatric Nursing Diagnosis Care Plans DSM IV. 4th ed. LC 96-45656. (Nursing Ser.). 224p. 1997. pap. 41.25 (*0-7637-0255-2*) Jones & Bartlett.

Paquette, Mary F. Psychiatric Nursing Diagnosis Care Plans. 1991. pap. text 40.00 (*0-86720-310-2*) Jones & Bartlett.

Paquette, Mary G. Basques to Bakersfield. (Illus.). 138p. 1982. 15.00 (*0-943500-00-1*) Kern Historical.

— Then Came the French: The History of the French in Tuolumne County, California. LC 96-60553. (Illus.). ix, 160p. (Orig.). 1996. pap. 17.50 (*0-9652608-0-1*) Tuolumne Cnty.

Paquette, Mary G., ed. & tr. see De Rutte, Theophile.

Paquette, Penny. Parenting a Child with a Behavior Problem. 2nd ed. LC 99-43084. 216p. 1999. pap. 16.95 (*0-7373-0256-9*, 02569W) NTC Contemp Pub Co.

Paquette, Penny & Tuttle, Cheryl G. Parenting a Child with a Behavior Problem. 216p. 1996. pap. 16.00 (*1-56565-477-3*) Lowell Hse.

Paquette, Penny, jt. auth. see Tuttle, Cheryl.

Paquette, Penny, jt. auth. see Tuttle, Cheryl G.

Paquette, Randor J., jt. auth. see Wright, Paul H.

Paquette, Robert L. Sugar is Made with Blood: The Conspiracy of La Escalera & the Conflict Between Empires Over Slavery in Cuba. LC 87-34503. (Illus.). 389p. Date not set. reprint ed. pap. 120.60 (*0-608-20687-3*, 207179500002) Bks Demand.

Paquette, Robert L. & Engerman, Stanley L., eds. The Lesser Antilles in the Age of European Expansion. LC 95-45478. (Illus.). 432p. (C). 1996. 49.95 (*0-8130-1428-X*) U Press Fla.

***Paquette, Robert Louis & Ferieger, Louis A., eds.** Slavery, Secession & Southern History. LC 99-49449. 256p. 2000. 49.50 (*0-8139-1951-7*) U Pr of Va.

***Paquette, Robert Louis & Ferleger, Lou, eds.** Slavery, Secession & Southern History. LC 99-49449. 256p. 2000. pap. 18.50 (*0-8139-1952-5*) U Pr of Va.

Paquette Suarez, Marie-Helene, jt. auth. see Fox, Debbie.

Paquette, Yanick, jt. auth. see Lacombe, Michael.

Paquin, J. R. & Crowley, R. E. Die Design Fundamentals. 2nd ed. LC 86-19132. (Illus.). 256p. 1987. 29.95 (*0-8311-1172-0*) Indus Pr.

Paquin, Laurent. English - French Vocabulary of Road Transport Vehicles. (ENG & FRE.). 167p. 1991. pap. 49.95 (*0-8288-9416-7*) Fr & Eur.

Paquot, Annette, jt. ed. see Maniet, Albert.

Paquot, Annette, ed. see Plautus.

Par, Sandra. God Inspired. 90p. (Orig.). 1999. pap. write for info. (*1-889732-22-2*) Word-For-Word.

PAR Staff. Apptitude Test Form B. 2nd ed. (C). 1992. text 54.30 (*0-256-11862-0*, Irwn McGrw-H) McGrw-H Hghr Educ.

P.A.R. Staff. Business. 64p. (C). 1988. 10.55 (*0-89702-078-2*, Irwn McGrw-H) McGrw-H Hghr Educ.

— Career Math. 2nd ed. 176p. (C). 1989. 15.25 (*0-89702-089-8*, Irwn McGrw-H) McGrw-H Hghr Educ.

— Career Reading. 2nd ed. 280p. (C). 1989. 21.95 (*0-89702-088-X*, Irwn McGrw-H) McGrw-H Hghr Educ.

— Hospitality & Travel. 64p. (C). 1988. 10.55 (*0-89702-079-0*, Irwn McGrw-H) McGrw-H Hghr Educ.

— Power Reading 1: Reading for Power. (C). 1983. pap. text, suppl. ed. 9.90 (*0-256-10595-2*, Irwn McGrw-H) McGrw-H Hghr Educ.

— Technical. 64p. (C). 1988. 10.55 (*0-89702-080-4*, Irwn McGrw-H) McGrw-H Hghr Educ.

P.A.R. Staff & Smith, Barry. Power Reading. 2nd ed. 64p. (C). 1986. per. 9.90 (*0-256-10551-0*, Irwn McGrw-H) McGrw-H Hghr Educ.

P.A.R. Staff, jt. auth. see Smith, Barry.

Para, Gladys C., ed. see Gotchy, Joe.

Para, Marco A. De La, see De La Para, Marco A.

Para Research Staff. World Ephemeris for the 20th Century, Midnight Edition. LC 83-60063. 624p. 1992. pap. 29.95 (*0-914918-60-5*, Whitford) Schiffer.

P

An Asterisk (*) at the beginning of an entry indicates that the title is appearing for the first time.

***Parasuraman, Raja, ed.** The Attentive Brain. (Illus.). 604p. (C). 2000. reprint ed. pap. 39.95 (*0-262-66112-8*, Bradford Bks) MIT Pr.

Parasuraman, Raja & Mouloua, Mustapha, eds. Automation & Human Performance: Theory & Applications. (Human Factors in Transportation Ser.). 536p. 1996. text 89.95 (*0-8058-1616-X*) L Erlbaum Assocs.

Parasuraman, S., jt. ed. see Unnikrishnan, P. V.

Parasuraman, Saroj H. & Greenhaus, Jeffrey, eds. Integrating Work & Family: Challenges & Choices for a Changing World. LC 96-43932. 272p. 1997. 65.00 (*1-56720-038-9*, Quorum Bks) Greenwood.

— Integrating Work & Family: Challenges & Choices for a Changing World. 272p. 1999. pap. 24.95 (*0-275-96805-7*) Greenwood.

Parati, Graziella. Mediterranean Crossroads: Migration Literature in Italy. LC 99-19418. 224p. 1999. 37.50 (*0-8386-3813-9*) Fairleigh Dickinson.

— Public History, Private Stories: Italian Women's Autobiography. LC 95-39547. 1996. pap. 17.95 (*0-8166-2607-3*); text 44.95 (*0-8166-2606-5*) U of Minn Pr.

Paratore, Coleen M. Remembering. (Books Worth Writing). 128p. 1992. 24.95 (*0-9630250-0-7*) Bks Worth Writing.

Paratore, Jeanne R. & McCormick, Rachael L., eds. Peer Talk in the Classroom: Learning from Research. LC 97-27908. 250p. 1997. pap. text 28.95 (*0-87207-181-2*, 181) Intl Reading.

Paratore, Jeanne R., et al. What Should We Expect of Family Literacy? Experiences of Latino Children Whose Parents Participate in an Intergenerational Literacy Project. LC 98-53892. (Literacy Studies Ser.). 15p. 1999. pap. 27.75 (*0-87207-246-0*, 246) Intl Reading.

Paratore, Virginia M. Cookbook, USS Columbus Veterans Association. LC 97-61801. 1997. write for info. (*0-918744-02-4*) Solo Pubs.

Paratte, Henri-Dominique, tr. see Fry, Macon & Posner, Julie.

***Paravicini, Werner.** Europaische Reiseberichte des Spaten Mittelalters: Eine Analytische Bibliographie Teil 2: Franzosische Reiseberichte Bearbeitet von Jorg Wettlaufer in Zusammenarbeit Mit Jacques Paviot. (Kieler Werkstucke, Reihe D Ser.). 270p. 1999. 42.95 (*3-631-47685-X*) P Lang Pubng.

***Paravicini Bagliani, Agostino.** The Pope's Body. LC 99-36181. (Illus.). 352p. 2000. 28.00 (*0-226-03437-2*) U Ch Pr.

Paravisini-Gebert, Lizabeth. Jamaica Kincaid: A Critical Companion. LC 98-55341. (Critical Companions to Popular Contemporary Writers Ser.). 200p. 1999. 29.95 (*0-313-30295-2*) Greenwood.

— Phyllis Shand Allfrey: A Caribbean Life. LC 95-33061. (Illus.). 300p. (C). 1996. text 50.00 (*0-8135-2264-1*); pap. text 18.95 (*0-8135-2265-X*) Rutgers U Pr.

Paravisini-Gebert, Lizabeth & Esteves, Carmen C., eds. Green Cane & Juicy Flotsam: Short Stories by Caribbean Women. 220p. (C). 1991. pap. 13.95 (*0-8135-1738-9*); text 40.00 (*0-8135-1737-0*) Rutgers U Pr.

Paravisini-Gebert, Lizabeth, jt. ed. see Fernandez-Olmos, Margarite.

Paravisini-Gebert, Lizabeth, jt. ed. see Olmos, Margarite Fernandez.

Paravisini-Gerbe. Women at Sea. LC 99-37439. 1999. text 49.95 (*0-312-21996-2*) St Martin.

***Paray-Clarke, Geeta.** La Feerie Erotique: Crebillon et ses Lecteurs. (Age of Revolution & Romanticism: Vol. 24). (FRE.). 176p. (C). 1999. text 45.95 (*0-8204-3993-2*) P Lang Pubng.

Parayil, Govindan. Conceptualizing Technological Change: Theoretical & Empirical Explorations. LC 99-20491. 224p. 1999. 57.00 (*0-8476-9520-4*) Rowman.

***Parayil, Govindan.** Kerala's Development Experience: Reflections on Sustainability & Replicability. LC 99-51632. 2000. pap. write for info. (*1-85649-727-5*, Pub. by Zed Books) St Martin.

Parazette, Joan. A Child's Health Journal: A Record of the First Ten Years. 160p. 1996. spiral bd. 15.95 (*1-55670-514-X*) Stewart Tabori & Chang.

Parbe, Anthony, jt. auth. see Dias, Patrick.

Parberry, Ian. Circuit Complexity & Neural Networks. (Foundations of Contemporary Interpretation Ser.). (Illus.). 304p. 1994. 40.00 (*0-262-16148-6*) MIT Pr.

***Parberry, Ian.** Learn Computer Game Programming with DirectX 7.0. (Illus.). 500p. 2000. pap. 49.95 (*1-55622-741-8*) Wordware Pub.

— Problems on Algorithms. LC 94-48519. 192p. (C). 1995. pap. 18.40 (*0-13-433558-9*) P-H.

Parbetsi, Ghazar. Patmuwt'iwn Hayots: History of the Armenians. Kouymjian, Dickran, ed. LC 85-11340. 276p. 1987. reprint ed. 50.00 (*0-88206-031-7*) Caravan Bks.

Parbhoo, Santilal, jt. ed. see Stoll, Basil A.

Parboni, Ricardo. The Dollar & Its Rivals: Recession, Inflation & International Finance. Rothschild, Jon, tr. from ITA. 207p. 1985. pap. text 15.95 (*0-86091-744-4*) Routledge.

Parbury, Kathleen. Women of Grace: A Biographical Dictionary of British Women Saints, Martyrs & Reformers. 224p. 1984. 25.00 (*0-85362-213-2*) Routledge.

Parce, Mead. Railroad Through the Back of Beyond: The Murphy Branch Also Known As the Great Smoky Mountains Railroad. Lawson, Alice, ed. LC 98-129583. (Illus.). 128p. (Orig.). 1997. pap. 8.95 (*0-9657461-1-9*) Harmon Den.

— Twice-Told Tales of the Blue Ridge & Great Smokies, Vol. 1. Lawson, Alice, ed. (Illus.). 114p. 1995. reprint ed. pap. 7.95 (*0-9657461-0-0*) Harmon Den.

Parcel, John & Moorman, Robert B. Analysis of Statically Indeterminate Structures. LC 55-6908. 597p. reprint ed. pap. 185.10 (*0-8357-5432-4*, 205594600040) Bks Demand.

Parcel, Toby L. & Menaghan, Elizabeth G. Parents' Jobs & Children's Lives. (Sociology & Economics Ser.). 228p. 1994. pap. text 21.95 (*0-202-30484-1*); lib. bdg. 43.95 (*0-202-30483-3*) Aldine de Gruyter.

Parcell, Lillian. Horn of the Unicorn. (Destiny Ser). 7.50 (*0-686-00947-9*) Wagon & Star.

Parcell, Stephen, jt. auth. see Perez-Gomez, Alberto.

Parcell, Stephen, jt. ed. see Perez-Gomez, Alberto.

***Parcells, Bill.** The Final Season: My Last Year as Head Coach in the NFL. (Illus.). 256p. 2000. 25.00 (*0-688-17491-4*) HarpC.

Parcells, Bill & Coplon, Jeff. Finding a Way to Win: The Principles of Leadership, Teamwork, & Motivation. 230p. 1998. 23.00 (*0-7881-5707-8*) DIANE Pub.

***Parchemin, Richard.** Life & History of North America's Indian Reservations. 192p. 1998. write for info. (*1-57215-255-9*) World Pubns.

Parcher, James V. The Immortal Regi Gressen. LC 98-87121. 192p. 1999. pap. 11.95 (*1-56315-170-7*) SterlingHse.

Parcher, Jean, ed. see Bianchi, Susan & Butler, Jan.

Parcher, Jon F. & Chester, Tom L. Unified Chromatography. LC 99-47736. (ACS Symposium Ser.). (Illus.). 250p. 1999. text 110.00 (*0-8412-3638-0*, Pub. by Am Chemical) OUP.

Parcher, Michael J. Wastewater Collection System Maintenance. LC 97-61510. 375p. 1997. pap. text 59.95 (*1-56676-569-2*) Technomic.

Parchment, S. R. Ancient Operative Masonry. 209p. 1996. reprint ed. spiral bd. 17.00 (*0-7873-1114-6*) Hlth Research.

— Ancient Operative Masonry & the Mysteries of Antiquity. 210p. 1996. reprint ed. pap. 16.95 (*1-56459-791-1*) Kessinger Pub.

— Astrology: Mundane & Spiritual, 2 vols., Set. 1996. reprint ed. pap. 72.00 (*0-7873-0657-6*) Hlth Research.

— Astrology, Mundane & Spiritual (1933) 900p. 1998. reprint ed. pap. 49.95 (*0-7661-0144-4*) Kessinger Pub.

— The Just Law of Compensation. 126p. 1996. reprint ed. spiral bd. 10.00 (*0-7873-0656-8*) Hlth Research.

— The Just Law of Compensation. 126p. 1996. reprint ed. pap. 9.95 (*1-56459-679-6*) Kessinger Pub.

— The Middle Path - The Safest: The Religion of "Head & Heart" 119p. 1996. reprint ed. spiral bd. 11.00 (*0-7873-0655-X*) Hlth Research.

— The Middle Path - The Safest: The Religion of "Head & Heart" 120p. 1996. reprint ed. pap. 9.95 (*1-56459-790-3*) Kessinger Pub.

— Steps to Self-Mastery. 223p. 1996. reprint ed. pap. 15.95 (*1-56459-627-3*) Kessinger Pub.

— Steps to Self-Mastery. 3rd ed. 242p. 1996. reprint ed. spiral bd. 16.50 (*0-7873-1095-6*) Hlth Research.

Parchomenko, Walter. Soviet Images of Dissidents & Nonconformists. LC 86-3178. 268p. 1986. 49.95 (*0-275-92021-6*, C2021, Praeger Pubs) Greenwood.

Parchon, Nerys. The Handbook of Natural Healing: The Complete Home-Reference Guide. (Illus.). 432p. 1998. pap. 19.95 (*1-86448-645-7*) IPG Chicago.

Parchure, R. Theory of International Values. 1994. write for info. (*81-224-0664-5*, Pub. by Wiley Estrn) Franklin.

Parco, Vincent. Researching Public Records: How to Get Anything on Anybody. LC 93-44224. 1994. 8.95 (*0-8065-1522-8*, Citadel Pr) Carol Pub Group.

***Parco, Vincent.** Researching Public Records: How to Get Anything on Anybody. 146p. 1999. 25.00 (*0-7351-0109-4*) Replica Bks.

Parczyk, K., jt. auth. see Humphrey.

Pardailhe-Galabrun, Annik. The Birth of Intimacy: Privacy & Domestic Life in Early Modern Paris. Phelps, Jocelyn, tr. from FRE. LC 91-50607. 256p. (C). 1992. text 42.50 (*0-8122-3124-4*) U of Pa Pr.

Pardalos, P. M., et al, eds. Parallel Processing of Discrete Problems. LC 98-46021. (IMA Volumes in Mathematics & Its Applications Ser.: Vol. 106). (Illus.). 249p. 1999. 69.95 (*0-387-98664-2*) Spr-Verlag.

Pardalos, P. M. & Rajasekaran, Sanguthevar. Advances in Randomized Parallel Computing. LC 99-24910. 1999. write for info. (*0-7923-5714-0*) Kluwer Academic.

Pardalos, P. M., jt. auth. see Floudas, Christodoulos A.

***Pardalos, Panos M.** Approximation & Complexity in Numerical Optimization: Continuous & Discrete Problems. 594p. 2000. 255.00 (*0-7923-6275-6*, Kluwer Plenum) Kluwer Academic.

Pardalos, Panos M. Complexity in Numerical Optimization. LC 93-4827. 400p. 1993. text 121.00 (*981-02-1415-4*) World Scientific Pub.

— Minimax & Applications. LC 95-30189. (Nonconvex Optimization & Its Applications Ser.: Vol. 4). 308p. (C). 1995. text 154.50 (*0-7923-3615-1*) Kluwer Academic.

Pardalos, Panos M., et al, eds. Advances in Multicriteria Analysis, Vol. 5. LC 95-34337. (Nonconvex Optimization & Its Applications Ser.). 276p. (C). 1995. lib. bdg. 136.00 (*0-7923-3671-2*) Kluwer Academic.

— Parallel Processing of Discrete Optimization Problems: DIMACS Workshop, April 28-29, 1994. LC 95-10880. (DIMACS Series in Discrete Mathematics & Theoretical Computer Science: Vol. 22). 374p. 1995. text 89.00 (*0-8218-0240-2*, DIMACS/22) Am Math.

— Randomization Methods in Algorithm Design: DIMACS Workshop, December 12-14, 1997. LC 98-34537. (DIMACS: Series in Discrete Mathematics & Theoretical Computer Science: Vol. 43). 318p. 1998. 69.00 (*0-8218-0916-4*) Am Math.

Pardalos, Panos M. & Wolkowicz, Henry. Topics in Semidefinite & Interior-Point Methods. LC 97-43573. (Fields Institute Communications Ser.). 250p. 1998. text 69.00 (*0-8218-0825-7*) Am Math.

Pardalos, Panos M. & Wolkowicz, Henry, eds. Quadratic Assignment & Related Problems. LC 94-20393. (DIMACS Series in Discrete Mathematics & Theoretical Computer Science: Vol. 16). 364p. 1994. 73.00 (*0-8218-6607-9*, DIMACS/16C) Am Math.

Pardalos, Panos M., et al. Network Optimization, Vol. 450. LC 97-642. (Lecture Notes in Economics & Mathematical Systems Ser.). 1997. pap. write for info. (*3-540-62541-0*) Spr-Verlag.

Pardalos, Panos M., jt. auth. see Du, D. Z.

Pardalos, Panos M., jt. auth. see Du Dingzhu.

Pardalos, Panos M., jt. auth. see Floudas, Christodoulos A.

Pardalos, Panos M., jt. auth. see Hager, William W.

Pardalos, Panos M., jt. ed. see Ferreira, Alfonso.

Pardalos, Panos M., jt. ed. see Floudas, Christodoulos A.

Pardalos, Panos M., jt. ed. see Horst, Reiner.

Parde, Duane. Less-Taxation & More Democracy, the Amendment 6 Prescription for Prosperity Looking at the Pros & Cons. 16p. 1988. pap. text 8.00 (*1-57655-115-6*) Independ Inst.

Pardech, John T., ed. Child Abuse & Neglect: Theory, Research & Practice. x, 194p. 1989. text 69.00 (*0-677-25860-7*) Gordon & Breach.

Pardech, John T., jt. ed. see Murphy, J. W.

Pardeck, Jean A. & Pardeck, John T. Young People with Problems: A Guide to Bibliotherapy. LC 83-18601. 176p. 1984. lib. bdg. 47.95 (*0-313-23836-7*, PYP/, Greenwood Pr) Greenwood.

Pardeck, Jean A., jt. auth. see Pardeck, John T.

Pardeck, Jean A., ed. see Pardeck, John T.

Pardeck, Jean A., jt. ed. see Pardeck, John T.

Pardeck, John & Markward, Martha, eds. Reassessing Social Work Practice with Children. (Special Aspects of Education Ser.: Vol. 17). 210p. 1997. text 44.00 (*90-5699-546-4*, ECU57) Gordon & Breach.

Pardeck, John T. Bibliotherapy: A Guide to Using Books in Clinical Practice. Pardeck, Jean A., ed. LC 92-49235. 168p. 1992. pap. text 59.95 (*0-7734-1954-3*) E Mellen.

— The Forgotten Children: A Study of the Stability & Continuity of Foster Care. LC 82-20007. (Illus.). 116p. (Orig.). (C). 1983. pap. text 18.00 (*0-8191-2845-7*) U Pr of Amer.

— Social Work after the Americans with Disabilities Act: New Challenges & Opportunities for Social Service Professionals. LC 97-50078. 152p. 1998. 49.95 (*0-86569-265-3*, Auburn Hse); pap. 17.95 (*0-86569-277-7*, Auburn Hse) Greenwood.

— Social Work Practice: An Ecological Approach. LC 95-40691. 184p. 1996. 52.95 (*0-86569-236-X*, Auburn Hse) Greenwood.

— Using Bibliotherapy in Clinical Practice: A Guide to Self-Help Books, 22. LC 93-20499. (Contributions in Psychology Ser.: No. 22). 160p. 1993. 57.95 (*0-313-27991-8*, PUB/, Greenwood Pr) Greenwood.

— Using Books in Clinical Social Work Practice: A Guide to Bibliotherapy. LC 97-30713. 157p. (C). 1997. 29.95 (*0-7890-0120-9*); pap. 19.95 (*0-7890-0430-5*) Haworth Pr.

Pardeck, John T., ed. Books for Early Childhood: A Developmental Perspective, 3. LC 86-14989. (Bibliographies & Indexes in Psychology Ser.: No. 3). 182p. 1986. lib. bdg. 49.95 (*0-313-24576-2*, PBK/, Greenwood Pr) Greenwood.

— Technology & Human Service Delivery: Challenges & a Critical Perspective. LC 88-2794. (Computers in Human Services Ser.: Vol. 3, Nos. 1-2). (Illus.). 161p. 1988. text 39.95 (*0-86656-731-3*) Haworth Pr.

Pardeck, John T. & Pardeck, Jean A. Children in Foster Care & Adoption: A Guide to Bibliotherapy. LC 98-15323. 120p. 1998. lib. bdg. 55.00 (*0-313-30775-X*, Greenwood Pr) Greenwood.

Pardeck, John T. & Pardeck, Jean A., eds. Bibliotherapy: A Clinical Approach for Helping Children. LC 92-49528. (Special Aspects of Education Ser.: Vol. 16). 149p. 1993. pap. text 32.00 (*3-7186-5347-8*) Gordon & Breach.

Pardeck, John T. & Yuen, Francis K. O., eds. Family Health: A Holistic Approach to Social Work Practice. LC 98-47756. 208p. 1999. 55.00 (*0-86569-268-8*, Auburn Hse) Greenwood.

Pardeck, John T., jt. auth. see Murphy, John W.

Pardeck, John T., jt. auth. see Pardeck, Jean A.

Pardeck, John T., ed. see Langino, Charles F., Jr. & Murphy, John W.

Pardeck, John T., jt. ed. see Murphy, John W.

Pardee, Arthur B. & Liang, Peng, eds. Differential Display Methods & Protocols. (Methods in Molecular Biology Ser.: Vol. 85). (Illus.). 320p. 1997. 79.50 (*0-89603-405-4*) Humana.

Pardee, Arthur B., ed. see McClelland, Michael.

Pardee, Arthur B., jt. ed. see McClelland, Michael.

Pardee, Bettie B. Great Entertaining: 1001 Party Tips & Timesavers. LC 90-41753. 128p. 1990. pap. 11.95 (*1-56145-001-4*) Peachtree Pubs.

— Great Weekend Entertaining: An Essential Companion for Fun-Loving Hosts & Guests. LC 90-28261. 128p. 1991. pap. 9.95 (*1-56145-022-7*) Peachtree Pubs.

Pardee, Caroline J., jt. auth. see Jones, Robert H.

Pardee, Deborah. Find Your Own Path: A Workbook for Adolescents Recovering from Chemical Dependency. (Illus.). xii, 180p. 1997. pap. 24.95 (*1-57931-100-8*, 100) ToucanEd Pubns.

— A Voice of Hope: A Workbook for Adults Recovering from Chemical Dependency. (Illus.). xii, 164p. 1997. pap., wbk. ed. 24.95 (*1-57931-101-6*, 101) ToucanEd Pubns.

Pardee, Michael, jt. auth. see Waite, Mitchell.

Pardee, Peter W. Scales & Arpeggios for Five String Banjo. 2nd ed. (Illus.). 180p. (Orig.). 1985. pap. 25.00 (*0-933611-00-5*) Harbinger Pubns.

***Pardee, Thomas, et al.** Karmapa the Sacred Prophecy. (Illus.). 128p. 1999. 60.00 (*0-9674184-0-2*) K T Choling.

Pardee, W. D., jt. ed. see McDonald, M. B., Jr.

Pardee, William J. To Satisfy & Delight Your Customer: How to Manage for Customer Value. LC 96-22181. (Illus.). 340p. 1996. 39.95 (*0-932633-35-8*) Dorset Hse Pub Co.

Pardeiro, Nancy, ed. see Finley, Ernestine & Finley, Mark.

Pardeiro, Nancy, ed. see Thompson, Walter C.

Pardella, Edward. The Judy Garland Collector's Guide: An Unauthorized Reference & Price Guide. (Illus.). 155p. 1999. pap. 29.95 (*0-7643-0764-9*) Schiffer.

Pardella, Edward R. Shirley Temple Dolls & Fashions: A Collector's Guide to the World's Darling. LC 92-60624. (Illus.). 176p. 1992. pap. 29.95 (*0-88740-420-0*) Schiffer.

— Shirley Temple Dolls & Fashions: A Collector's Guide to the World's Darling. 2nd rev. ed. (Illus.). 176p. 1999. pap. 29.95 (*0-7643-0855-6*) Schiffer.

Pardes, Herbert, jt. ed. see Pincus, Harold A.

***Pardes, Ilana.** The Biography of Ancient Israel. LC 99-27865. (Contraversion Ser.). 220p. 2000. 24.95 (*0-520-21110-3*, Pub. by U CA Pr) Cal Prin Full Svc.

Pardes, Ilana. Countertraditions in the Bible: A Feminist Approach. (Illus.). 240p. 1992. 34.95 (*0-674-17542-5*) HUP.

— Countertraditions in the Bible: A Feminist Approach. (Illus.). 208p. 1993. pap. 16.00 (*0-674-17545-X*) HUP.

— The Shulamite's Song: A Feminist Approach to the Bible. LC 98-45848. (Illus.). 240p. (C). 1992. text 29.95 (*0-674-80733-2*) HUP.

Pardey, Andreas. Vegetationsentwicklung Kleinflaechiger Sekundaergewaesser. (Dissertationes Botanicae Ser.: Band 195). (Illus.). 178p. 1992. pap. 65.00 (*3-443-64107-5*, Pub. by Gebruder Borntraeger) Balogh.

***Pardey, Larry.** Details of Classic Boat Construction: The Hull. 2nd rev. ed. Pardey, Lin, ed. LC 90-30677. (Illus.). 520p. 1999. 49.95 (*0-9646036-8-3*) Pardey Bks.

Pardey, Larry & Pardey, Lin. The Self-Sufficient Sailor. rev. ed. (Illus.). 320p. 1997. 30.00 (*0-9646036-7-5*, Pub. by Pardey Bks) Paradise Cay Pubns.

Pardey, Larry, jt. auth. see Pardey, Lin.

Pardey, Larry, ed. see Pardey, Lin.

Pardey, Lin. The Care & Feeding of Sailing Crew. 2nd rev. ed. Pardey, Larry, ed. (Illus.). 388p. 1996. 29.95 (*0-9646036-0-8*, Pub. by Pardey Bks) Paradise Cay Pubns.

— Storm Tactics Handbook: Modern Methods of Heaving-To for Survival in Extreme Conditions. (Orig.). 1996. pap. text 19.95 (*1-85310-787-5*) Airlife Publishing.

Pardey, Lin & Pardey, Larry. The Capable Cruiser. (Illus.). 385p. 1995. 32.00 (*0-9646036-2-4*, Pub. by Pardey Bks) Paradise Cay Pubns.

— The Care & Feeding of Sailing Crew. 2nd ed. 1996. text 35.00 (*0-07-048602-6*) McGraw.

— Cost Conscious Cruiser: Champagne Cruising on a Beer Budget. LC 98-65766. (Illus.). 362p. 1998. 29.95 (*0-9646036-5-9*, Pub. by Pardey Bks) Paradise Cay Pubns.

— Cruising in Seraffyn. (Illus.). 192p. 1992. pap. 14.95 (*0-924486-36-8*) Sheridan.

— Seraffyn's European Adventure. 3rd rev. ed. LC 78-32032. (Illus.). 318p. 1999. pap. 16.95 (*0-9646036-4-0*, Pub. by Pardey Bks) Paradise Cay Pubns.

— Seraffyn's Mediterranean Adventure. (Illus.). 256p. 1991. pap. 14.95 (*0-924486-15-5*) Sheridan.

— Seraffyn's Oriental Adventure. 2nd ed. LC 82-14289. (Illus.). 252p. 1996. reprint ed. pap. 16.95 (*0-9646036-3-2*, Pub. by Pardey Bks) Paradise Cay Pubns.

— Storm Tactics Handbook: Modern Methods of Heaving-To for Survival in Extreme Conditions. (Illus.). 192p. (Orig.). 1995. pap. 19.95 (*0-9646036-6-7*, Pub. by Pardey Bks) Paradise Cay Pubns.

Pardey, Lin, jt. auth. see Pardey, Larry.

Pardey, Lin, ed. see Pardey, Larry.

Pardey, Philip G. & Roseboom, Johannes, eds. ISNAR Agricultural Research Indicator Series: A Global Database on National Agricultural Research Systems. (Illus.). 560p. (C). 1989. text 100.00 (*0-521-37368-9*) Cambridge U Pr.

Pardey, Philip G., jt. auth. see Alston, Julian M.

***Pardi, William J.** XML in Action. LC 98-52991. 400p. 1999. pap. 39.99 (*0-7356-0562-9*) Microsoft.

Pardi, William J. & Schurman, Eric M. Dynamic HTML in Action. 2nd ed. LC 98-51581. (In Action Ser.). (Illus.). 497p. 1999. pap. 39.99 (*0-7356-0563-7*) Microsoft.

***Pardie, Lynn & Luchetta, Tracy.** The Construction of Attitudes Toward Lesbians & Gay Men. 1999. pap. 14.95 (*1-56023-942-5*, Harrington Park) Haworth Pr.

Pardieu, Charles-Henri De, see De Pardieu, Charles-Henri.

Pardillo, Ozzie. Obvious Letters: The Associative Alphabet Every Child Will Remember. 34p. (J). (ps-1). 1998. pap. 10.95 (*0-9664217-0-1*) Educ-Easy.

Pardina, Martin R., jt. auth. see Green, Richard.

Pardington, George P. The Crisis of the Deeper Life. LC 91-70910. 176p. 1991. pap. 9.99 (*0-87509-454-6*) Chr Pubns.

— Outline Studies in Christian Doctrine. 370p. 1926. pap. 11.99 (*0-87509-116-4*) Chr Pubns.

Pardington, John H. Dear Sarah: Letters Home from a Soldier of the Iron Brigade. Lassen, Coralou P., ed. LC 98-56077. 1999. 24.95 (*0-253-33560-4*) Ind U Pr.

Pardini, Alan & Lerner, Deborah. Health Promotion for Older Persons: A Selected Annotated Bibliography. 41p. 1986. write for info. (*0-318-61575-4*) US HHS.

P

Pardini, Alan & Mahoney, Connie. A Resource Guide for Fitness Programs for Older Persons. 115p. 1986. write for info. (0-318-61580-0) US HHS.

Pardini, Albert L. The Legendary Norden Bombsight. LC 98-87635. (Illus.). 352p. 1999. 29.95 (0-7643-0723-1) Schiffer.

Pardini, Priscilla, et al. Barriers & Breakthroughs - Technology in Urban Schools. (Illus.). 55p. 1999. pap. 10.00 (0-943445-08-6) Education Writers Association.

Pardo, Michael Jerome. You Are One Too! A Book for All Children. 32p. (J). (gr. 1-8). 1998. 15.00 (0-9666633-3-0, 9807001) Universal Way.

Pardo, Michael Jerome, et al. Il Progetto Universale: A Proposal Towards Love, Peace, & Freedom in the Universe! 4th ed. 320p. 1998. reprint ed. 35.00 (0-9666633-0-6, 9603001) Universal Way.

Pardo, Angel. Neomambi. LC 89-83445. (Coleccion Espejo de Paciencia). (SPA., Illus.). 94p. (Orig.). 1989. pap. 9.95 (0-89729-530-7) Ediciones.

Pardo, Bazan E. Los Pazos de Ulloa. (SPA.). 1989. 9.95 (0-8288-2571-8) Fr & Eur.

Pardo Bazan, Emilia. El Encaje Roto y Otros Cuentos. Tolliver, Joyce, ed. (MLA Texts & Translations Ser.: Vol. 5a). (SPA.). xxxiv, 132p. (Orig.). 1996. pap. 7.95 (0-87352-783-6, P005P) Modern Lang.

— Insolacion. (Nueva Austral Ser.: Vol. 25). (SPA.). 1991. pap. text 24.95 (84-239-1825-4) Elliots Bks.

— Los Pazos de Ulloa. (SPA.). 317p. 1984. 10.00 (0-8288-8586-9) Fr & Eur.

— Torn Lace: And Other Stories. Urruela, Maria C., tr. from SPA. LC 96-41223. (MLA Texts & Translations Ser.: Vol. 5b). xxxiv, 141p. (Orig.). 1996. pap. 7.95 (0-87352-784-4, Q005P) Modern Lang.

Pardo Bazan, Emilia, adapted by. Los Pazos de Ulloa, Level 6. (Leer en Espanol Ser.). (SPA.). (C). 1998. pap. 6.95 (84-294-3615-4) Santillana.

Pardo, Bonnye G. Intimate Encounters: Creating Healthy Relationships. 107p. (Orig.). 1991. pap. 10.00 (0-9645437-2-9) B G Pardo.

Pardo, Italo. Managing Existence in Naples: Morality, Action & Structure. (Cambridge Studies in Social & Cultural Anthropology: No. 104). 248p. (C). 1996. text 64.95 (0-521-56227-9); pap. text 25.95 (0-521-56665-7) Cambridge U Pr.

Pardo, J. Joaquin. Catalogo de los Manuscritos Existentes en la Coleccion Latino Americana de la Biblioteca de la Universidad de Texas Relativos a la History de Centro America. (SPA.). 45p. 1988. reprint ed. pap. 6.00 (0-913129-19-4) La Tienda.

Pardo, Jesus, tr. see Andrews, V. C.

Pardo, Jose C. & Schneider, Friedrich, eds. Current Issues in Public Choice. LC 95-16698. (Illus.). 304p. 1996. 95.00 (1-85898-134-4) E Elgar.

Pardo, Marcel, tr. see Comstock, Esther J.

Pardo, Mary. Mexican American Women Activists: Identity & Resistance in Two Los Angeles Communities. LC 97-13960. 256p. 1998. 59.95 (1-56639-572-0) Temple U Pr.

Pardo-Maurer, R. The Contras, 1980-1989: A Special Kind of Politics, 147. LC 90-44608. (Washington Papers: No. 147). 288p. 1990. 55.00 (0-275-93817-4, B3818, Praeger Pubs); pap. 17.95 (0-275-93818-2, C3817, Praeger Pubs) Greenwood.

Pardo, Robert. Design, Testing, & Optimization of Trading Systems. LC 92-372. (Traders Library). 176p. 1992. 49.95 (0-471-55446-4) Wiley.

Pardoe, Alan. Practical Guide for Employer & Employee to the Industrial Relations Act 1971. xx, 319p. 1972. pap. 6.50 (0-85308-024-0); pap. 6.50 (0-8377-1022-7, Rothman) W S Hein.

Pardoe, Blaine. Cubicle Warfare: Self-Defense Tactics for Today's Hypercompetitive Workplace. LC 97-20427. 256p. 1997. per. 16.00 (0-7615-1066-4) Prima Pub.

— Star Trek Generations: Official PC Game Strategy Guide. 216p. 1997. 19.99 (1-56686-589-1) Brady Pub.

Pardoe, Blaine L. Exodus Road: Twilight of the Clans. (Battletech Ser.: No. 33). 1997. mass mkt. 5.99 (0-451-45612-2, ROC) NAL.

— Future for Space Technology. 1992. text 47.50 (0-86187-462-5) St Martin.

— Impetus. (Battletech Ser.: No. 30). 1996. mass mkt. 5.99 (0-451-45529-0, ROC) NAL.

***Pardoe, Blaine Lee.** Measure of a Hero. (Battletech Ser.: Vol. 48). 2000. mass mkt. 5.99 (0-451-45794-3, ROC) NAL.

Pardoe, Blaine Lee. Roar of Honor. 1999. mass mkt. 5.99 (0-451-45761-7, ROC) NAL.

Pardoe, Geoffrey K., ed. Remote Sensing: Proceedings of an EARSEL-ESA Symposium, Guildford, U. K., April 8-11. (Illus.). 64p. 1985. pap. 39.00 (0-08-032538-6, Pub. by PPL) Elsevier.

— Space Industry International. 353p. 1987. 155.00 (0-582-00314-8, 071053-99584) Longman.

Pardoe, Jenifer. How Many Times Can You Say Goodbye? Living with Bereavement. 112p. (Orig.). 1992. pap. 6.95 (0-8146-2109-0) Liturgical Pr.

Pardoe, Julia. The City of the Sultan: And Domestic Manners of the Turks in 1836, 2 vols., Set. LC 77-87633. reprint ed. 67.50 (0-404-16540-0) AMS Pr.

Pardoe, T. Earl. Pantomimes for Stage & Study. LC 73-173118. 404p. 1972. reprint ed. 29.95 (0-405-08833-7, Pub. by Blom Pubns) Ayer.

Pardoen, Gerald C., ed. Recent Advances in Structural Dynamics. (Sessions Proceedings Ser.). 53p. 1986. 3.00 (0-87262-530-3) Am Soc Civil Eng.

Pardon, William. Local Surgery & the Exact Sequence of a Localization for Wall Groups. LC 77-11963. (Memoirs Ser.: No. 12/196). 171p. 1977. pap. 22.00 (0-8218-2196-2, MEMO/12/196) Am Math.

Pardoux, E., jt. ed. see Metivier, Michel.

Pardridge, William M. Peptide Drug Delivery to the Brain. LC 91-7861. (Illus.). 367p. 1991. reprint ed. pap. 113.80 (0-608-07215-X, 206744000009) Bks Demand.

Pardridge, William M., ed. The Blood-Brain Barrier: Cellular & Molecular Biology. LC 92-48543. 496p. 1993. text 100.00 (0-7817-0015-9) Lppncott W & W.

— Introduction to the Blood-Brain Barrier: Methodology, Biology & Pathology. LC 97-26483. (Illus.). 500p. (C). 1998. text 135.00 (0-521-58124-9) Cambridge U Pr.

Parducci, Allen. Happiness, Pleasure, & Judgment: The Contextual Theory & Its Applications. 232p. 1995. text 45.00 (0-8058-1891-X) L Erlbaum Assocs.

Parducci, Allen, jt. ed. see Sarris, Viktor.

Pardue, Diana. Chispas! Cultural Warriors of New Mexico, February 15, 1992-April 25, 1993: Eppie Archuleta, Teresa Archuleta-Sagel, Charles Carrillo, Marie Romero Cash, Juanita Jaramillo-Lavadie, Felix Lopez et al. Brennan, Mary, ed. (Illus.). 34p. (Orig.). 1992. pap. 6.95 (0-934351-34-1) Heard Mus.

Pardue, Harry L., jt. auth. see Bodner, George M.

Pardue, Lisa D. Let's Take a Wingwalk. (Illus.). 48p. (Orig.). (J). (gr. 2 up). 1994. pap. 8.99 (1-877633-25-9) Luthers.

Pardue, Tommie, jt. ed. see Hilley, Martha F.

Pardun, Robert. The Steel Fabricator's Handbook. (Illus.). 99p. (Orig.). 1991. student ed., spiral bd. 9.50 (0-9630780-0-3) Pardun Pub.

Pardy, Wayne. Safety Incentives & Recognition: Creating an Achievement - Baseo Culture. 276p. 1998. pap. 59.95 (1-890966-53-3) Moran Assocs.

Pare. Descriptive Geometry: Worksheet B. 9th ed. 1996. pap. text 30.00 (0-02-391344-4) Macmillan.

Pare, jt. auth. see Makkai.

Pare, Ambroise. An Explanation of the Fashion & Use of Instruments of Chirurgery. Crooke, H., tr. LC 75-26045. (English Experience Ser.: No. 141). 64p. 1969. reprint ed. 35.00 (90-221-0141-X) Walter J Johnson.

— Life & Time of Ambroise Pare, 1510-1590. Packard, Francis R., ed. LC 79-160607. (Illus.). 1972. reprint ed. 23.95 (0-405-08834-5, Pub. by Blom Pubns) Ayer.

— On Monsters & Marvels. Pallister, Janis L., tr. from FRE. LC 81-16297. (Illus.). xxxii, 224p. (C). 1983. pap. text 23.00 (0-226-64563-0) U Ch Pr.

Pare, Bill, jt. auth. see Kistler, Vivian.

Pare, C. F. Wagons & Wagon-Graves of the Early Iron Age in Central Europe. (Illus.). 1992. 135.00 (0-947816-35-6, Pub. by Oxford Univ Comm Arch) David Brown.

Pare, E. G., ed. Descriptive Geometry. 9th ed. 455p. (C). 1996. 88.00 (0-02-391341-X, Macmillan Coll) P-H.

Pare, Eugene G. & Shook, Micheal. Computer Graphics Project for Design & Descriptive Geometry. 149p. (C). 1986. pap. 33.09 (0-02-390980-3, Macmillan Coll) P-H.

Pare, Eugene G., et al. Descriptive Geometry. 8th ed. 1991. write for info. (0-318-68104-8); write for info. (0-318-68105-6) Macmillan.

Pare, Francois. Exiguity: Reflections on the Margins of Literature. Burman, Lin, tr. from FRE. LC 97-221986.Tr. of Les Litteratures de l'Exquite. vi, 183p. 1997. pap. 24.95 (0-88920-265-6) W Laurier U Pr.

Pare, J. A. & Fraser, Robert G. Synopsis of Diseases of the Chest. 2nd rev. ed. LC 93-25873. (Illus.). 732p. 1993. reprint ed. text 105.00 (0-7216-3669-1, W B Saunders Co) Harcrt Hlth Sci Grp.

Pare, J. A., jt. auth. see Fraser, Robert G.

Pare, J. R. & Belanger, J. M. Instrumental Methods in Food Analysis. LC 97-7256. (Techniques & Instrumentation in Analytical Chemistry Ser.: No. 18). 506p. 1997. 287.50 (0-444-81868-5) Elsevier.

Pare, J. R., jt. ed. see Belanger, J. M.

Pare, Jean. Baking Delights. 80p. 1995. pap. 4.99 (1-895455-38-3) Companys Coming.

— Beef Today! 1996. pap. 15.99 (1-896891-00-4) Companys Coming.

— Beverages, 1. (Illus.). 80p. 1997. pap. 4.99 (1-895455-31-6) Companys Coming.

***Pare, Jean.** Biscuits, Muffins & Loaves. (Greatest Hits Ser.). 1999. pap. 12.99 (1-896891-05-5) RF Inc.

Pare, Jean. Breads. (Illus.). 156p. pap. 10.95 (1-895455-09-X) Peguis Pubs Ltd.

— Breakfasts & Brunches. 160p. 1998. pap. 10.99 (1-895455-33-2) Companys Coming.

— Buffets. (Company's Coming Pint Size Bks.). 80p. 1995. pap. 4.99 (1-895455-28-6) Companys Coming.

— Chocolate. (Company's Coming Pint Size Bks.). (Illus.). 80p. 1995. pap. 4.99 (1-895455-07-3) Companys Coming.

— Company's Coming for Christmas. (Illus.). 192p. text 19.99 (1-895455-19-7) Peguis Pubs Ltd.

— Company's Coming for Kids: Lunches. 142p. (gr. 5-12). 1998. pap. 12.99 (1-896891-36-5) Companys Coming.

— Cooking for Two. LC 97-18570. (Illus.). 160p. 1997. pap. 10.99 (1-895455-27-8) Companys Coming.

— Desserts. 160p. pap. 10.95 (0-9690695-5-3) CCL.

***Pare, Jean.** Dips, Spreads & Dressings. 1999. pap. 12.99 (1-896891-03-9) Companys Coming.

Pare, Jean. Easy Entertaining: Flair Without Fuss. 1998. text 19.99 (1-896891-40-3) Companys Coming.

— Ground Beef. 1997. pap. 7.99 (1-896891-04-7) CCL.

— Kid's Cooking. (Illus.). 126p. 1995. pap. 10.95 (1-895455-48-0) Companys Coming.

— Make-Ahead Salads. 80p. 1998. pap. 7.99 (1-896891-22-5) Companys Coming.

— No-Bake Desserts. 80p. 1998. pap. 7.99 (1-896891-24-1) Companys Coming.

***Pare, Jean.** One Dish Meals. 1999. pap. 10.99 (1-895455-54-5) Companys Coming.

— 150 Delicious Squares. 160p. 1989. pap. 10.99 (0-9690695-0-2) Companys Coming.

Pare, Jean. Party Planning. (Company's Coming Pint Size Bks.). 80p. 1995. pap. 4.99 (1-895455-26-X) Companys Coming.

***Pare, Jean.** Pizza! 1999. pap. 10.99 (1-895455-52-9) Companys Coming.

— Slow Cooker Recipes. 1998. pap. 10.99 (1-895455-37-5) Companys Coming.

— Starters. 160p. 1999. pap. 10.99 (1-895455-60-X) Companys Coming.

Pare, Jean. 30-Minute Meals. 80p. 1998. pap. 7.99 (1-896891-20-9) Companys Coming.

Pare, Michael A. Certification & Accreditation Programs Directory. 620p. 1995. 99.00 (0-7876-0463-1) Gale.

Pare, Michael A. Sports Stars, 2 vols., Series 2. LC 96-10646. 574p. (J). 1996. text 55.00 (0-7876-0867-X, GML00597-110132, UXL) Gale.

Pare, Michael A. Sports Stars, Series 3. LC 97-622. 342p. (J). (gr. 4 up). 1997. text 55.00 (0-7876-1749-0, UXL) Gale.

— Sports Stars, Vol. 1. LC 94-21835. 1994. write for info. (0-8103-9860-5, UXL) Gale.

Pare, Michael A. Sports Stars, 2 vols., vol. 1. LC 94-21835. 622p. (J). 1994. text 55.00 (0-8103-9859-1, GML00597-107533, UXL) Gale.

Pare, Michael A. Sports Stars, Vol. 2. LC 94-21835. 1994. write for info. (0-8103-9861-3, UXL) Gale.

— Sports Stars II, Vol. 1, A-K. LC 96-10646. (J). 1996. write for info. (0-7876-0868-8, UXL) Gale.

— Sports Stars II, Vol. 2, L-Z. LC 96-10646. (J). 1996. write for info. (0-7876-0869-6, UXL) Gale.

— Sports Stars Series: Series 4, Vol. 4. LC 98-5008. (Illus.). 350p. (J). 1998. 39.00 (0-7876-2784-4, GML00198-111321) Visible Ink Pr.

***Pare, Michael A.** Sports Stars Series 5, Ser. 5. 300p. 1999. text 39.00 (0-7876-3683-5, GML00299-113311, UXL) Gale.

Pare, Paul, jt. auth. see Kasenow, Michael.

Pare, R. A Friend Like You. (Illus.). 24p. (J). (ps-8). 1984. 12.95 (0-920303-04-8, Pub. by Annick) Firefly Bks Ltd.

Pare, Richard. Photography & Architecture: Eighteen Thirty-Nine to Nineteen Thirty-Nine. (Illus.). 282p. 1985. reprint ed. 80.00 (0-262-16101-X) MIT Pr.

***Pare, Richard.** Tadae Ando: The Colors of Light. (Illus.). 2000. 19.95 (0-7148-3999-X) Phaidon Pr.

Pare, Richard. Tadao Ando: The Colors of Light. LC 96-155045. (Illus.). 272p. 1996. 95.00 (0-7148-3374-6, Pub. by Phaidon Press) Phaidon Pr.

— Tadao Ando: The Colors of Light. limited ed. (Illus.). 272p. 1996. 450.00 (0-7148-3541-2, Pub. by Phaidon Press) Phaidon Pr.

Pare, Richard, pref. Roger Fenton. (Masters of Photography Ser.: Vol. 4). (Illus.). 96p. 1988. 34.95 (0-89381-270-6); pap. 23.95 (0-89381-271-4) Aperture.

Pare, Roger. L' Alphabet. (Gout de Savoir Ser.). (FRE., Illus.). 24p. (J). (ps up). 1994. pap. 6.95 (2-89021-224-6, Pub. by La Courte Ech) Firefly Bks Ltd.

— L' Alphabet. (FRE & ENG., Illus.). 40p. (J). 1990. 7.95 (0-8442-1395-0, 13950, Passprt Bks) NTC Contemp Pub Co.

— Animal Capers. (Illus.). 24p. (J). 1992. pap. 4.95 (1-55037-244-0, Pub. by Annick); text 14.95 (1-55037-243-2, Pub. by Annick) Firefly Bks Ltd.

— The Annick ABC. (Annikins Press Ser.: Vol. 6). (Illus.). 24p. (J). (ps-2). 1989. pap. 0.99 (0-920303-78-1, Pub. by Annick) Firefly Bks Ltd.

— Les Chiffres. (Gout de Savoir Ser.). (FRE., Illus.). 24p. (J). (ps up). 1994. pap. 6.95 (2-89021-223-8, Pub. by La Courte Ech) Firefly Bks Ltd.

— Circus Days. (Illus.). 24p. (J). (ps-8). 1988. pap. 4.95 (1-55037-020-0, Pub. by Annick); text 15.95 (1-55037-021-9, Pub. by Annick) Firefly Bks Ltd.

— Les Contraires. (FRE., Illus.). 24p. pap. write for info. (2-89021-272-6, Pub. by La Courte Ech) Firefly Bks Ltd.

— Les Couleurs. 24p. (2-89021-304-8) La Courte Ech.

— A Friend Like You. (Illus.). 24p. (J). (ps-8). 1984. pap. 4.95 (0-920303-05-6, Pub. by Annick) Firefly Bks Ltd.

— A Friend Like You. (Annikins Ser.: Vol. 6). (Illus.). 24p. (J). (ps-2). 1989. pap. 0.99 (0-920303-80-3, Pub. by Annick) Firefly Bks Ltd.

— On the Go. (Illus.). 24p. (J). 1996. pap. 4.95 (1-55037-476-1, Pub. by Annick); text 15.95 (1-55037-409-5, Pub. by Annick); lib. bdg. 15.95 (1-55037-477-X, Pub. by Annick) Firefly Bks Ltd.

— On The Go. (FRE & ENG., Illus.). 24p. (J). 1996. pap. 4.95 (1-55037-408-7, Pub. by Annick) Firefly Bks Ltd.

— Plaisirs D'Aimer. (Plaisirs Ser.). (FRE., Illus.). 24p. (J). (ps up). 1988. pap. 6.95 (2-89021-087-1, Pub. by La Courte Ech) Firefly Bks Ltd.

— Plaisirs D'Animaux. (Plaisirs Ser.). (FRE., Illus.). 24p. (J). (ps up). 1990. pap. 6.95 (2-89021-140-1, Pub. by La Courte Ech) Firefly Bks Ltd.

— Plaisirs de Chats. (Plaisirs Ser.). (FRE., Illus.). 24p. (J). (ps up). 1983. pap. 6.95 (2-89021-044-8, Pub. by La Courte Ech) Firefly Bks Ltd.

— Plaisirs de Cirque. (Plaisirs Ser.). (FRE., Illus.). 24p. (J). (ps up). 1988. pap. 6.95 (2-89021-086-3, Pub. by La Courte Ech) Firefly Bks Ltd.

— Plaisirs de Vacances. (Plaisirs Ser.). (FRE., Illus.). 24p. (J). (ps up). 1995. pap. 6.95 (2-89021-253-X, Pub. by La Courte Ech) Firefly Bks Ltd.

— Plaisirs D'Ete. (Plaisirs Ser.). (FRE., Illus.). 24p. (J). (ps up). 1988. pap. 6.95 (2-89021-088-X, Pub. by La Courte Ech) Firefly Bks Ltd.

— Plaisirs d'Hiver. (Plaisirs Ser.). (FRE., Illus.). 24p. (J). (ps up). 1990. pap. 6.95 (2-89021-141-X, Pub. by La Courte Ech) Firefly Bks Ltd.

— Play Time. (Illus.). 24p. (J). (ps-8). 1988. text 12.95 (1-55037-087-1, Pub. by Annick) Firefly Bks Ltd.

— Play Time. (Illus.). 24p. (J). (ps-8). 1988. pap. 4.95 (1-55037-086-3, Pub. by Annick) Firefly Bks Ltd.

— Summer Days. (Illus.). 24p. (J). (ps-8). 1988. pap. 4.95 (1-55037-044-8, Pub. by Annick); text 14.95 (1-55037-043-X, Pub. by Annick) Firefly Bks Ltd.

— Winter Games. (Illus.). 24p. (J). 1991. pap. 4.95 (1-55037-184-3, Pub. by Annick); lib. bdg. 14.95 (1-55037-187-8, Pub. by Annick) Firefly Bks Ltd.

Pare, William. Co-Operative Agriculture. LC 76-47884. reprint ed. 29.00 (0-404-60087-5) AMS Pr.

Paredaens, J. & Tenenbaum, L., eds. Advances in Database Systems. LC 95-161695. (CISM International Centre for Mechanical Sciences Ser.: Vol. 347). 377p. 1994. 93.95 (3-211-82614-9) Spr-Verlag.

Paredes, Alfonso, et al, eds. Cocaine: Physiological & Physiopathological Effects. LC 92-19390. (Journal of Addictive Diseases: Vol. 11, No. 4). (Illus.). 120p. 1993. 39.95 (1-56024-311-2) Haworth Pr.

Paredes, Alfonso & Gorlick, David A., eds. Cocaine: Physiological & Physiopathological Effects. 130p. 1992. pap. 10.95 (1-56024-385-6) Haworth Pr.

Paredes, Americo. Folklore & Culture on the Texas-Mexican Border. Bauman, Richard, ed. 288p. 1993. 34.95 (0-292-72472-1) U of Tex Pr.

— Folklore & Culture on the Texas-Mexican Border. Bauman, Richard, ed. (Illus.). 317p. 1995. pap. 18.95 (0-292-76564-9) U of Tex Pr.

— George Washington Gomez. LC 89-48145. 302p. (Orig.). 1990. pap. 12.95 (1-55885-012-0) Arte Publico.

— The Hammon & the Beans & Other Stories. LC 93-45644. 230p. 1994. pap. 11.95 (1-55885-071-6) Arte Publico.

— Mexican-American Authors. Adams, William, ed. (Multi-Ethnic Literature Ser.). (YA). (gr. 9-12). 1976. teacher ed. 8.24 (0-685-02295-1) HM.

— The Shadow. LC 98-10313. 114 p. 1998. pap. 9.95 (1-55885-230-1) Arte Publico.

— A Texas-Mexican Cancionero: Folksongs of the Lower Border. (SPA., Illus.). 218p. 1995. pap. 10.95 (0-292-76558-4) U of Tex Pr.

— With His Pistol in His Hand: A Border Ballad & Its Hero. (Illus.). 275p. 1958. pap. 11.95 (0-292-70128-4) U of Tex Pr.

Paredes, Americo, ed. Folktales of Mexico. LC 79-107225. (Folktales of the World Ser.). 1974. pap. text 11.95 (0-226-64573-8, FW9) U Ch Pr.

— Humanidad: Essays in Memory of George I. Sanchez. (Monographs: No. 6). 144p. 1977. pap. 15.00 (0-89551-007-3) UCLA Chicano Studies.

Paredes, Blanca L. Unidades Habitacionales en Tula, Hidalgo. 248p. 1990. pap. 10.00 (968-6487-39-5, IN015) UPLAAP.

Paredes, Carlos & Sachs, Jeffrey D., eds. Peru's Path to Recovery: A Plan for Economic Stabilization & Growth. 336p. 1991. 44.95 (0-8157-6914-8); pap. 19.95 (0-8157-6913-X) Brookings.

Paredes, Ellen S. De, see De Paredes, Ellen S.

Paredes, J. Anthony, ed. Indians of the Southeastern United States in the Late Twentieth Century. LC 91-15048. 256p. (C). 1992. pap. text 22.95 (0-8173-0534-3) U of Ala Pr.

Paredes, J. Anthony, jt. ed. see Higgins, Patricia J.

Paredes, J. M., jt. ed. see Taylor, A. R.

Paredes, Joseph. Mary & the Kingdom of God: A Synthesis of Mariology. 282p. (C). 1996. pap. 39.95 (0-85439-379-X, Pub. by St Paul Pubns) St Mut.

Paredes-Lopez, Octavio, ed. Amaranth: Biology, Chemistry, & Technology. LC 93-36812. 234p. 1994. lib. bdg. 189.00 (0-8493-5374-2) CRC Pr.

— Molecular Biotechnology for Plant Food Production. LC 98-89342. 650p. 1999. text 178.95 (1-56676-685-0) Technomic.

Paredes, Raymund, jt. ed. see Romo, Ricardo.

Paredes, Ricardo & Riveros, Luis A., eds. Human Resources & the Adjustment Process. (Inter-American Development Bank Ser.). 215p. 1994. 18.50 (0-940602-90-3) IADB.

Paredes, Ruby R., ed. Philippine Colonial Democracy. LC 87-51575. (Monographs: No. 32). (Illus.). 166p. 1989. pap. 15.00 (0-938692-34-8) Yale U SE Asia.

Paredi, Angela. St. Ambrose: His Life & Times. LC 63-19325. 495p. reprint ed. pap. 153.50 (0-608-12331-5, 202437200037) Bks Demand.

Pareek, Udai. Training Questionnaires & Surveys for Human Resource Development: Reproducible Instruments for Working with Teams, Individuals, & Organizations. 400p. 1998. ring bd. 149.95 (0-07-913723-7) McGraw.

Pareek, Udai, jt. auth. see Lynton, Rolf P.

Pareek, Udai, jt. ed. see Lynton, Rolf P.

Pareek, Udai Narain, jt. auth. see Lynton, Rolf P.

***Pareige, P.** Influence of Long Term Thermal Aging on the Microstructural Evolution of Nuclear Reactor Pressure Vessel Materials: Atom Probe Study. 30p. 1998. pap. 2.75 (0-16-062899-7) USGPO.

Parejko, Ken. Remember Me Dancing. 1996. pap. 14.95 (1-878569-36-8) Badger Bks Inc.

Parek, Naru, ed. Financial Engineer. 450p. 1995. pap. 765.00 (1-85564-239-5, Pub. by Euromoney) Am Educ Systs.

Parekh, B. C., jt. ed. see King, Preston T.

Parekh, B. K. & Groppo, J. G., eds. Processing of Utilization of High-Sulfur Coals, Vol. 5. (Coal Science & Technology Ser.: Vol. 21). 644p. 1993. 471.75 (0-444-81476-0) Elsevier.

Parekh, B. K. & Miller, J. D. Advances in Flotation Technology. LC 99-12355. 500p. 1999. pap. 99.00 (0-87335-184-3, 184-3) SMM&E Inc.

Parekh, Bhikhu. Colonialism, Tradition & Reform: An Analysis of Gandhi's Political Discourse. 288p. (C). 1989. text 24.00 (0-8039-9605-5) Sage.

— Gandhi. (Past Masters Ser.). 120p. 1997. pap. text 9.95 (0-19-287692-9) OUP.

— Gandhi's Political Philosophy: A Critical Examination. 1995. 28.00 (81-202-0439-5, Pub. by Ajanta) S Asia.

Parekh, Bhikhu, ed. Jeremy Bentham: Critical Assessments, 4 vols., Set. LC 92-21151. (Critical Assessments of Leading Political Philosophers Ser.). (Illus.). 400p. (C). (gr. 13). 1993. text, boxed set 820.00 (*0-415-04654-8*, B2382) Routledge.

Parekh, Bhikhu, jt. auth. see Baxi Upendra.

Parekh, Bhikhu, jt. ed. see Pieterse, Jan.

***Parekh, Bhikhu C.** Colonialism, Tradition & Reform: An Analysis of Gandhi's Political Discourse. rev. ed. LC 99-46952. 1999. pap. write for info. (*0-7619-9383-5*) Pine Forge.

Parekh, Bhikhu C. Marx's Theory of Ideology. LC 81-13743. 255p. reprint ed. pap. 79.10 (*0-608-06180-8*, 206651200008) Bks Demand.

***Parekh, Bhikhu C.** Rethinking Multiculturalism: Political Theory & Cultural Diversity. LC 00-36975. 432p. 2000. write for info. (*0-674-00436-1*) HUP.

Parekh, Bhikhu C., ed. Jeremy Bentham: Ten Critical Essays. 204p. 1974. 32.00 (*0-7146-2959-6*, Pub. by F Cass Pubs) Intl Spec Bk.

Parekh, Bipin S. Reverse Osmosis Technology: Applications of High-Purity-Water Production. (Chemical Industries Ser.: Vol. 35). (Illus.). 536p. 1988. text 210.00 (*0-8247-7985-1*) Dekker.

Parekh, D. E., ed. Turbulence Control. LC 94-71667. (Fluid Engineering Division Conference Ser.: Vol. 193). 63p. 1994. pap. 25.00 (*0-7918-1376-2*) ASME.

Parekh, D. E. & Morris, M. J., eds. Turbulent Mixing, 1993. LC 93-73259. 77p. pap. 35.00 (*0-7918-1023-2*) ASME.

Parekh, M. P., et al, eds. Nehru & India's Labour Movement. (C). 1991. text 16.00 (*81-204-0581-1*, Pub. by Oxford IBH) S Asia.

Parekh, N. Derivatives: Practitioner's Guide. 479p. 1996. 170.00 (*1-85564-248-4*, Pub. by Euromoney) Am Educ Systs.

Parekh, Pushpa N. Response to Failure: Poetry of Gerard Manley Hopkins, Francis Thompson, Lionel Johnson, & Dylan Thomas. LC 93-18360. (American University Studies IV: Vol. 169). 200p. (C). 1998. text 41.95 (*0-8204-2152-9*) P Lang Pubng.

Parekh, Pushpa N., ed. Post-Colonial African Writers. 1998. lib. bdg. 85.00 (*1-57958-053-X*) Fitzroy Dearborn.

Parekh, Pushpa N. & Jagne, Siga F. Postcolonial African Writers: A Bio-Bibliographical Critical Sourcebook. LC 97-5856. 560p. 1998. lib. bdg. 85.00 (*0-313-29056-3*, Greenwood Pr) Greenwood.

Parekh, R., jt. auth. see Fowler, M.

Parekh, S. I., jt. auth. see Barton, Derek H.

Parel, Anthony J. The Machiavellian Cosmos. 216p. (C). 1992. 37.50 (*0-300-05169-7*) Yale U Pr.

***Parel, Anthony J., ed.** Gandhi, Freedom & Self-Rule. 176p. 2000. 70.00 (*0-7391-0136-6*); pap. 23.95 (*0-7391-0137-4*) Lxngtn Bks.

Parel, Anthony J., ed. Hind Swaraj & Other Writings. (Cambridge Texts in Modern Politics Ser.). 284p. (C). 1997. text 54.95 (*0-521-57405-6*); pap. text 17.95 (*0-521-57431-5*) Cambridge U Pr.

— The Political Calculus: Essays on Machiavelli's Philosophy. LC 77-185729. 232p. reprint ed. pap. 72.00 (*0-608-30272-4*, 201433000093) Bks Demand.

Parel, J., ed. Ophthalmic Technologies II. 1992. 20.00 (*0-8194-0790-9*, 1644) SPIE.

Parel, Jean-Marie, et al. Proceedings of Ophthalmic Technologies III: 16-18 January 1992, Los Angeles, California. LC 93-83345. xii, 374 p. 1993. write for info. (*0-8194-1104-3*) SPIE.

Pareles, Jon, et al, eds. The New Rolling Stone Encyclopedia of Rock & Roll. rev. ed. LC 95-35045. (Illus.). 1136p. 1995. per. 25.00 (*0-684-81044-1*, Fireside) S&S Trade Pap.

Parella, Elizabeth, ed. see Diamond, Wendy.

Parella, Frederick J., jt. ed. see Bulman, Raymond F.

Parella, Robert E. & Miller, Joel E. Modern Trust Forms & Checklists. 1990. 185.00 (*0-88262-275-7*) Warren Gorham & Lamont.

— Modern Trust Forms & Checklists, No. 1. 1992. suppl. ed. 93.00 (*0-7913-1182-1*) Warren Gorham & Lamont.

— Modern Trust Forms & Checklists, No. 2. 1992. suppl. ed. 97.00 (*0-685-32294-7*) Warren Gorham & Lamont.

Parelli, Pat & Kadash, Kathy. Natural Horse-Man-Ship. (Illus.). 223p. (Orig.). 1993. pap. 14.95 (*0-911647-27-9*) Western Horseman.

Parelli, Robert J. An Analysis of the Automatic Exposure Device System. (Illus.). 28p. (Orig.). 1997. pap., wbk. ed. 10.00 (*1-880359-11-1*) Par Rad.

— An Analysis of the California Syllabus on Radiation Protection: Radiology Student Workbook. (Illus.). 179p. (Orig.). (C). 1996. pap., wbk. ed. 35.00 (*1-880359-09-X*) Par Rad.

— Basic Principles of Fluoroscopic Image Intensifier & Television Systems, Set, Vols. I & II. 175p. 1993. pap. text 35.00 (*1-880359-07-3*) Par Rad.

— Measuring & Evaluating the Radiography Student's Educational Achievement. 28p. (Orig.). 1997. pap., wbk. ed. 10.00 (*1-880359-10-3*) Par Rad.

— Medicolegal Issues for Radiographers. 115p. (C). 1991. pap. text 23.95 (*0-9628440-2-0*) Bellwether-Cross.

— Medicolegal Issues for Radiographers. 3rd ed. 200p. 1996. lib. bdg. 39.95 (*1-57444-081-0*) St Lucie Pr.

— Medicolegal Issues for Radiographers. 4th ed. 184p. 1998. spiral bd. 80.00 (*1-880359-15-4*) Par Rad.

— Principles of Fluoroscopic Image Intensification & Television Systems: Workbook & Laboratory Manual. (Illus.). 240p. 1996. lib. bdg. 39.95 (*1-57444-082-9*) St Lucie Pr.

— Principles of Magnetic Resonance Imaging. (Illus.). 28p. (Orig.). 1997. pap., wbk. ed. 15.00 (*1-880359-12-X*) Par Rad.

— Radiation Technology Clinical Manual. (Illus.). 300p. 1997. lib. bdg. 39.95 (*1-57444-147-7*) St Lucie Pr.

***Parelli, Robert J.** Radiographic Technique: Laboratory Manual. 4th rev. ed. 92p. (C). 1999. pap. text 26.00 (*1-880359-18-9*) Par Rad.

— Radiology Physics/Electronics: Student Workbook. 4th rev. ed. (Illus.). 118p. (C). 1998. pap. text 28.00 (*1-880359-19-7*) Par Rad.

Parelli, Robert J. Venipuncture Technique for Contrast Media Administration. (Illus.). 136p. 1998. 80.00 (*1-880359-16-2*) Par Rad.

Parelli, Robert J., jt. auth. see Ross, Lynn.

Parello, Anthony. The Ultimate Guide to Scales. 2nd ed. LC 92-93279. 96p. (Orig.). 1992. 14.95 (*0-9632995-0-6*); pap. 9.95 (*0-9632995-3-0*); text 12.95 (*0-9632995-2-2*); pap. text 10.95 (*0-9632995-4-9*); lib. bdg. 13.95 (*0-9632995-1-4*) Theory Guides.

Parelskin, Debra M., jt. auth. see Silber, Kathleen.

***Parens, Erik, ed.** Enhancing Human Traits: Ethical & Social Implications. LC 98-16197. (Hastings Center Studies in Ethics). 272p. 2000. reprint ed. pap. 17.95 (*0-87840-780-4*) Georgetown U Pr.

Parens, Erik, et al, eds. Enhancing Human Traits: Ethical & Social Implications. LC 98-16197. (Hastings Center Studies in Ethics). 288p. 1998. 49.95 (*0-87840-703-0*) Georgetown U Pr.

***Parens, Erik & Asch, Adrienne, eds.** Prenatal Testing & Disability Rights. LC 00-26361. (Hastings Center Studies in Ethics). 352p. 2000. pap. 23.95 (*0-87840-804-5*); text 65.00 (*0-87840-803-7*) Georgetown U Pr.

Parens, Henri. Aggression in Our Children: Coping with It Constructively. LC 87-19547. 180p. 1987. 30.00 (*0-87668-979-9*) Aronson.

— The Development of Aggression in Early Childhood. LC 94-41957. 426p. 1995. pap. 60.00 (*1-56821-441-3*) Aronson.

Parens, Henri & Kramer, Selma, eds. Prevention in Mental Health. LC 93-19429. 232p. 1993. pap. 27.50 (*1-56821-027-2*) Aronson.

Parens, Henri, jt. ed. see Akhtar, Salman.

Parens, Joshua. Metaphysics As Rhetoric: Alfarabi's Summary of Plato's "Laws" LC 94-49027. (SUNY Series in Middle Eastern Studies). 195p. (C). 1995. text 54.50 (*0-7914-2573-8*); pap. text 17.95 (*0-7914-2574-6*) State U NY Pr.

— Metaphysics As Rhetoric: Alfarabi's Summary of Plato's Laws. 195p. 1996. pap. 17.95 (*0-614-21233-2*, 1489) Kazi Pubns.

Parent. Orange You Glad? (Captain Kangaroo Ser.). 32p. (J). (gr. k-1). 2000. pap. 3.99 (*0-06-107157-9*, HarpEntertain) Morrow Avon.

— Treasure House. (Captain Kangaroo Ser.). 32p. (J). (gr. k-1). 2000. pap. 3.99 (*0-06-107158-7*, HarpEntertain) Morrow Avon.

Parent, Andre. Comparative Biology of the Normal Lung, Vol. 1. 848p. 1992. boxed set 195.00 (*0-8493-8839-2*, RC732) CRC Pr.

— Human Neuroanatomy. 9th ed. LC 94-40506. (Illus.). 976p. 1996. 79.00 (*0-683-06752-4*) Lppncott W & W.

Parent-Child Nursing Department. Empty Arms & Aching Hearts. Laprise, Susan et al, eds. (Illus.). 16p. (Orig.). 1987. reprint ed. pap. 2.50 (*0-9615491-6-5*) Loma Linda U.

Parent, Claude, jt. auth. see Virilio, Paul.

Parent, D. P. Exercises in Number Theory. Cole, M., tr. from FRE. (Problem Books in Mathematics). x, 542p. 1984. 69.95 (*0-387-96063-5*) Spr-Verlag.

Parent, Dale G. & Wentworth, Dan. Responding to Probation & Parole Violations. 65p. (Orig.). (C). 1995. pap. text 20.00 (*0-7881-2380-7*) DIANE Pub.

Parent, David J., ed. & tr. see Landmann, Michael.

Parent, David J., tr. see Landauer, Gustav.

Parent, David J., tr. see Landmann, Michael.

Parent, David J., tr. see Neumayr, Anton.

Parent, David J., tr. see Schutz, Alfred & Luckmann, Thomas.

Parent, David J., tr. see Waldenfels, Bernhard.

Parent, Derek A. La Mosquita: A Guide to the Land of Savannas, Rain Forests & Turtle Hunters. (Illus.). 74p. (Orig.). 1995. pap. 14.95 (*1-896677-00-2*) Intrepid Travel.

Parent-Duchatelet, Alexandre J. Prostitution in Paris, Considered Morally, Politically, & Medically: Prepared for Philanthropists & Legislators from Statistical Documents. LC 72-9671. reprint ed. 37.50 (*0-404-57488-2*) AMS Pr.

Parent, Edward A., jt. auth. see Gaunt, Larene.

Parent, Frederick, jt. auth. see Rundquist, Thomas J.

Parent, Gail, et al. What's Stopped Happening to Me? 1990. 12.00 (*0-8184-0522-8*, L Stuart) Carol Pub Group.

Parent, Gail, jt. auth. see Cowan, Connell.

Parent, Joseph D. Storage of Natural Gas As Hydrate. (Research Bulletin Ser.: No. 1). iv, 40p. 1948. pap. 25.00 (*1-58222-046-8*) Inst Gas Tech.

— A Survey of United States & Total World Production, Proved Reserves, & Remaining Recoverable Resources of Fossil Fuels & Uranium, as of December 31, 1982. xviii, 250p. 1984. pap. 30.00 (*0-910091-52-8*) Inst Gas Tech.

Parent, Laurence. Hiking New Mexico. rev. ed. (Illus.). 240p. 1998. pap. 14.95 (*1-56044-676-5*) Falcon Pub Inc.

— Scenic Driving North Carolina. LC 98-16610. (Illus.). 220p. 1998. pap. 15.95 (*1-56044-622-6*) Falcon Pub Inc.

Parent, Laurence. Texas Hill Country: A Postcard Book. (Illus.). 1993. pap. text. write for info. (*0-9634758-0-0*) L Parent Photo.

Parent, Laurence E. Big Bend of the Rio Grande. (Illus.). 48p. (Orig.). 1993. pap. 5.95 (*0-912001-19-4*) Big Bend.

— Big Thicket National Preserve. Priehs, T. J. & Foreman, Ronald J., eds. LC 92-62154. 16p. (Orig.). 1993. pap. 3.95 (*1-877856-21-5*) SW Pks Mnmts.

— Capulin Volcano National Monument. Priehs, T. J. & Jorgen, Randolph, eds. LC 91-60463. (Illus.). 16p. (Orig.). 1991. pap. 3.95 (*0-911408-94-0*) SW Pks Mnmts.

— Chickasaw National Recreation Area. Foreman, Ronald J. & Scott, Sandra, eds. LC 92-62474. (Illus.). 16p. (Orig.). 1993. pap. 3.95 (*1-877856-28-2*) SW Pks Mnmts.

— Chiricahua National Monument. Scott, Sandra & Priehs, T. J., eds. LC 93-86935. (Illus.). 16p. (Orig.). 1994. pap. 3.95 (*1-877856-41-X*) SW Pks Mnmts.

— Gila Cliff Dwellings National Monument. Jorgen, Randolph & Foreman, Ronald J., eds. LC 91-60461. (Illus.). 16p. (Orig.). 1992. pap. 3.95 (*0-911408-96-7*) SW Pks Mnmts.

— The Hill Country. (Texas Sights & Scenes Ser.). 64p. 1995. 7.95 (*0-88719-262-9*, 9262) Gulf Pub.

— Lake Meredith National Recreation Area. Foreman, Ronald J. & Scott, Sandra, eds. LC 92-62160. (Illus.). 16p. (Orig.). 1993. pap. 3.95 (*1-877856-16-9*) SW Pks Mnmts.

— Official Guide to Texas State Parks. Zappler, George, ed. LC 96-22956. (Illus.). 216p. 1997. pap. 19.95 (*0-292-76575-4*, Pub. by TX Prks & Wldlife) U of Tex Pr.

— Santa Fe. LC 96-5215. (New Mexico Sights & Scenes Ser.). (Illus.). 64p. 1996. pap. 7.95 (*0-88415-839-X*, 5839) Gulf Pub.

— Scenic Driving New Mexico. LC 96-19634. Orig. Title: New Mexico Scenic Drives. (Illus.). 160p. 1997. reprint ed. pap. 14.95 (*1-56044-453-3*) Falcon Pub Inc.

— Scenic Driving Texas. (Illus.). 178p. 1996. pap. 15.95 (*1-56044-462-2*) Falcon Pub Inc.

— Scenic Driving Wyoming. LC 97-10042. (Illus.). 200p. (Orig.). 1997. pap. 12.95 (*1-56044-536-X*) Falcon Pub Inc.

Parent, Laurence E., photos by. Austin. LC 94-43909. (Texas Sights & Scenes Ser.). (Illus.). 64p. 1995. pap. 7.95 (*0-87719-260-X*, 9260) Gulf Pub.

— The Hill Country. LC 94-43862. (Texas Sights & Scenes Ser.). (Illus.). 64p. 1995. pap. 7.95 (*0-87719-262-6*, 9262) Gulf Pub.

Parent, Laurence E. & Kelton, Elmer. Texas. (Illus.). 142p. 1995. 39.95 (*1-55868-202-3*) Gr Arts Ctr Pub.

Parent, Lawrence. Hiking Texas. (Illus.). 184p. 1996. pap. 12.95 (*1-56044-383-9*) Falcon Pub Inc.

Parent, Len, jt. auth. see Williams, Anna F.

Parent, Lucia E. Beagles: Everything about Purchase, Care, Nutrition, Breeding, Behavior, & Training. 2nd ed. Vriends, Matthew M., ed. LC 95-305. (Complete Pet Owner's Manual Ser.). (Illus.). 88 p. 1995. pap. 6.95 (*0-8120-9017-9*) Barron.

Parent, Marc. Believing It All. 2000. write for info. (*0-316-69015-5*) Little.

***Parent, Marc.** Stella. (Illus.). 192p. 2000. 44.95 (*1-893263-14-2*) Ipso Facto.

Parent, Marc. Turning Stones: My Days & Nights with Children at Risk. LC 97-97004. 384p. 1998. pap. 13.95 (*0-449-91235-3*) Fawcett.

— Turning Stones: My Days & Nights with Children at Risk. 366p. 1996. 25.00 (*0-15-100204-5*) Harcourt.

Parent, Mark. Spiritscapes: Mapping the Spiritual & Scientific Terrain at the Turn of the Century. LC 98-198977. 224p. 1998. pap. 15.95 (*1-896836-11-9*) NStone Publ.

Parent, Michael & Olivier, Julien. Of Kings & Fools: Stories from the French Tradition in North America. LC 96-24379. 208p. 1996. pap. text 12.95 (*0-87483-481-3*) August Hse.

Parent, Michel & Laurgeau, Claude. Robot Technology: Logic & Programming, Vol. 5. (Illus.). 192p. (C). 1985. text 66.00 (*0-13-782178-6*) P-H.

***Parent, Nancy.** Friends Forever! A Witzy's World Storybook. LC 00-105054. (Illus.). (J). (ps-1). 2001. 5.95 (*1-58668-058-7*) Lyrick Studios.

Parent, Nancy. Let's Go Riding. (Barbie Glittery Window Bks.). (Illus.). 12p. (J). (gr. k-3). 2000. bds. 4.99 (*1-57584-409-5*, RD Childrens) Rdrs Digest.

***Parent, Nancy.** My Favorite Things. (Barbie Scented Flap Bk.). 10p. (J). (ps-k). 2001. 6.99 (*1-57584-731-0*, Pub. by Rdrs Digest) S&S Trade.

— Putt-Putt Lost in Time! LC 00-105017. (Humongous Ser.). (Illus.). 24p. (J). (ps-1). 2001. 3.99 (*1-58668-060-9*) Lyrick Studios.

— Shapes Everywhere. (Illus.). 12p. (J). (ps-1). 2000. bds. 5.99 (*1-57584-455-5*, Pub. by Rdrs Digest) S&S Trade.

— What Time Is It? (Barbie Clock Bk.). (Illus.). 10p. (J). 2001. 6.99 (*1-57584-730-2*, Pub. by Rdrs Digest) S&S Trade.

— Witzy to the Rescue! A Witzy's World Storybook. LC 00-105053. (Illus.). (J). (ps-1). 2001. 5.95 (*1-58668-059-5*) Lyrick Studios.

Parent, Nancy, ed. see Disney Press Staff.

Parent, Neil A., ed. Serving Life & Faith: Adult Religious Education & the American Catholic Community. 72p. 1986. pap. 9.95 (*1-55586-982-3*) US Catholic.

Parent, Phil, frwd. Public Works Guide to Automated Mapping & Facilities Management. (Special Reports: No. 64). (Illus.). 167p. (Orig.). 1992. pap. text 75.00 (*0-917084-40-3*) Am Public Works.

Parent-Pomerleau, Celine, tr. see Gawain, Shakti.

Parent, Raymond, ed. see Edmund, Norman W.

Parent, Remi. Life to the Limits: From Everyday Losses to New Possibilities. Heinegg, Peter, tr. from FRE. LC 97-53211. 112p. 1998. reprint ed. pap. 9.00 (*0-7648-0185-6*, Liguori Triumph) Liguori Pubns.

Parent, Richard. In Heavenly Places Now. LC 93-61524. 64p. 1993. per. 5.95 (*0-945383-48-7*) Teach Servs.

Parent, Shaun. North of Superior Orient Bay Ice Climber's Guide. Hynek, Don, ed. (Illus.). 104p. (Orig.). 1993. pap. write for info. (*0-9619571-3-1*) Granite WI.

Parent, Sylvain. Dictionnaire des Science de l'Environnement Terminologie. (ENG & FRE.). 748p. 1991. 95.00 (*0-7859-7911-5*, 2700211065) Fr & Eur.

Parent Teacher Guide of Sacred Heart Elementary School Staff. The Heart of Pittsburgh. LC 98-61264. 238p. 1999. 17.95 (*0-9667438-0-6*) Sacred Heart.

Parent, Tom & Lindstrom, Paul D. The Safety Net Plan: Developing a Christian Worldview Through Family Devotions. 45p. (C). 1994. pap. 1.95 (*1-930367-43-0*, CLP 89940) Christian Liberty.

Parent, Wayne S. & Perry, Huey L. Blacks & the American Political System. LC 95-5917. (Illus.). 312p. 1995. 49.95 (*0-8130-1372-0*) U Press Fla.

Parent, Wayne S., jt. ed. see Perry, Huey L.

Parent, Wendy, et al. Employee Satisfaction in Supported Employment Services: A Resource Tool for Evaluation. unabridged ed. LC 98-15292. 68p. 1998. ring bd. 89.00 (*1-883302-25-0*) Trning Res.

Parent, Wendy S., et al. Vocational Integration Index. 112p. 1992. pap. 48.00 (*0-9626521-9-9*) PRO-ED.

— Vocational Integration Index: Measuring Integration of Workers with Disabilities. LC 94-40055. 1995. 64.00 (*0-89079-659-9*) PRO-ED.

Parent, William A., jt. ed. see Meyer, Michael J.

Parent, William A., ed. see Thomson, Judith J.

Parente. Advertising. (C). 2000. text. write for info. (*0-03-026776-5*) Harcourt.

— Advertising Camp Strategy. 2nd ed. (C). 1999. text 66.50 (*0-03-021114-X*, Pub. by Harcourt Coll Pubs) Harcourt.

— Advertising Campaign Strategy. LC 97-124262. (C). 1996. text 66.50 (*0-03-012898-6*, Pub. by Harcourt Coll Pubs) Harcourt.

Parente, Audrey. Pulp Man's Odyssey: The Hugh B. Cave Story. LC 87-26706. (Starmont Popular Culture Studies: Vol. 6). xiv, 146p. 1988. pap. 19.00 (*1-55742-038-6*) Millefleurs.

— Pulpmaster: The Theodore Roscoe Story. LC 93-202524. (Starmont Popular Culture Studies: No. 13). xvi, 173p. 1992. pap. 21.00 (*1-55742-169-2*) Millefleurs.

Parente Cunha, Helena. Woman Between Mirrors. Ellison, Fred P. & Lindstrom, Naomi, trs. from POR. LC 89-14613. (Texas Pan American Ser.). 144p. 1989. pap. 11.95 (*0-292-79052-X*) U of Tex Pr.

Parente, Diane & Petersen, Stephanie. Mastering Your Professional Image: Dressing to Enhance Your Credibility. Johnson, Karen, ed. LC 95-77376. (Illus.). 130p. (Orig.). 1995. pap. 19.95 (*0-9646688-0-7*) Image Dev & Mgt.

Parente, Fausto, ed. see Smith, Morton.

Parente, James A. & Schade, Richard E., eds. Studies in German & Scandinavian Literature after 1500: A Festschrift in Honor of George C. Schoolfield. (GERM Ser.). xiv, 322p. 1993. 65.00 (*1-879751-23-2*) Camden Hse.

Parente, James A., Jr., et al. Literary Culture in the Holy Roman Empire, 1555-1720. LC 90-12891. (Germanic Languages & Literatures Ser.: No. 113). (Illus.). xiv, 292p. (C). 1991. 45.00 (*0-8078-8113-9*) U of NC Pr.

Parente, Pascal P. The Angels: The Catholic Teaching on the Angels. LC 94-61948. Orig. Title: Beyond Space: A Book about the Angels. 159p. 1994. reprint ed. pap. 9.00 (*0-89555-515-8*, 1264) TAN Bks Pubs.

— City on a Mountain - Padre Pio. Orig. Title: Padre Pio. 154p. 1995. pap. 6.95 (*0-911988-35-1*, 42003) AMI Pr.

***Parente Randolph Orlando Carey & Associates Staff.** The Pennsylvania Business Handbook. Pennsylvania Chamber of Business & Industry Educational Foundation Staff, ed. 151p. 1998. pap. 70.00 (*1-929744-01-3*) Penn Chamber of Bus.

Parente, Rick & Anderson-Parente, Janet K. Retraining Memory Techniques & Applications. (Illus.). (C). 1991. 49.95 (*0-945541-02-3*) CSY Pub Inc.

Parente, Rick & Herrmann, Douglas. Retraining Cognition: Techniques & Applications. LC 96-12260. 304p. 1996. 54.00 (*0-8342-0764-8*) Aspen Pub.

***Parente, Stephen L. & Prescott, Edward C.** Barriers to Riches. LC 00-25414. (Walras-Pareto Lecture Ser.: Vol. 3). (Illus.). 141p. 2000. 29.95 (*0-262-16193-1*) MIT Pr.

Parenteau & Bolger. Approaches to Ecosystem. 96.95 (*0-7546-2037-9*) Ashgate Pub Co.

Parenteau, John. Prisoner for Peace: Aang San Suu Kyi & Burma's Struggle for Democracy. LC 94-4100. (Champions of Freedom Ser.). (Illus.). 152p. (YA). (gr. 5 up). 1994. lib. bdg. 18.95 (*1-883846-05-6*) M Reynolds.

Parenteau, Mary, ed. see Patterson, Don.

Parenteau, Rene. Habitat et Environnement Urbain au Viet Nam. (FRE.). 1997. pap. 28.00 (*0-88936-825-2*, Pub. by IDRC Bks) Stylus Pub VA.

Parenteral Drug Association Incorporated Staff. PDA International Conference on Liquid Borne Particle Inspection & Metrology: Conference Proceedings. Feldman, Marcy, ed. (Illus.). 662p. 1987. pap. text 95.00 (*0-939459-12-4*) PDA.

Parenti. Democracy for the Few. 7th ed. pap. text. write for info. (*0-312-15449-6*) St Martin.

Parenti. Democracy for the Few. 7th ed. 2000. 47.00 (*1-57259-724-0*) St Martin.

Parenti-Castelli, Vincenzo. Recent Advances in Robot Kinematics. Lenarcic, Jadran, ed. LC 96-22088. (Diverse Ser.). 468p. (C). 1996. text 235.50 (*0-7923-4124-4*) Kluwer Academic.

***Parenti, Christian.** Lockdown America: Police & Prisons in the Age of Crisis. LC 99-37182. 256p. 1999. 25.00 (*1-85984-718-8*, Pub. by Verso) Norton.

— Lockdown America: Police & Prisons in the Age of Crisis. 320p. 2000. pap. 15.00 (*1-85984-303-4*, Pub. by Verso) Norton.

Parenti, Francesco, et al. Antibiotics: A Multidisciplinary Approach. LC 95-11625. (Illus.). 288p. (C). 1995. text 69.50 (*0-306-44924-2*, Kluwer Plenum) Kluwer Academic.

P

Parenti, Francesco, jt. auth. see Lancini, Giancarlo L.

***Parenti, Jessica G.** Teacher for Hire. Carter, Angela M., ed. 62p. 2000. 29.95 (*1-58532-090-0*) Basic Ed Materials.

Parenti, Lynne R., jt. auth. see Humphries, Christopher J.

Parenti, Marino, jt. auth. see Frati, Carlo.

Parenti, Michael. Against Empire. 256p. (Orig.). 1995. pap. text 12.95 (*0-87286-298-4*) City Lights.

— America Besieged. LC 98-9487. 210p. 1998. pap. 9.95 (*0-87286-338-7*) City Lights.

— Blackshirts & Reds: Rational Fascism & the Overthrow of Communism. 208p. (Orig.). 1997. 24.95 (*0-87286-330-1*); per. 12.95 (*0-87286-329-8*) City Lights.

— Dirty Truths. 232p. 1996. 21.95 (*0-87286-318-2*); pap. 14.95 (*0-87286-317-4*) City Lights.

— History As Mystery. LC 99-34698. 296p. 1999. pap. 14.95 (*0-87286-357-3*, Pub. by City Lights) Subterranean Co.

***Parenti, Michael.** History as Mystery. LC 99-34698. 296p. 1999. 26.95 (*0-87286-364-6*, Pub. by City Lights) Subterranean Co.

— To Kill a Nation: The Attack on Yugoslavia. 160p. 2000. 22.00 (*1-85984-776-5*, Pub. by Verso) Norton.

Parenti, Michael J. Democracy for the Few. 6th ed. 368p. (Orig.). 1994. pap. text 32.95 (*0-312-05233-2*) St Martin.

— Ethnic & Political Attitudes. LC 74-17942. (Italian American Experience Ser.). 354p. 1979. 30.95 (*0-405-06413-6*) Ayer.

— Inventing Reality: The Politics of News Media. 2nd ed. 274p. 1992. pap. text 25.95 (*0-312-02013-9*) St Martin.

— Land of Idols: Political Mythology in America. 208p. 1993. pap. text 25.95 (*0-312-09497-3*) St Martin.

— Make-Believe Media: The Politics of Entertainment. 4th ed. LC 90-63541. 241p. (Orig.). (C). 1991. pap. text 24.95 (*0-312-05603-6*) St Martin.

— Power & Pluralism: A View from the Bottom. (Reprint Series in Social Sciences). (C). 1993. reprint ed. pap. text 5.00 (*0-8290-3569-9*, PS-528) Irvington.

— The Sword & the Dollar. 240p. 1988. text 16.95 (*0-312-02295-6*) St Martin.

Parenti, Richard L. The Spiritual Drunkard: Secrets to Healing Stress. (Illus.). 99p. 1998. pap. 12.95 (*0-9664007-0-4*) Stress Mgmt Tech.

Parenti, Umberto. Diccionario de Zoologia. 3rd ed. (SPA.). 244p. 1982. 29.95 (*0-8288-2390-1*, S50257) Fr & Eur.

Parenting Magazine Editors & Krueger, Anne. Parenting Guide to Your Baby's First Year. LC 98-21987. 384p. 2000. pap. 16.00 (*0-345-41180-3*, Ballantine) Ballantine Pub Grp.

Parenting Magazine Staff, ed. see Spencer, Paula.

Parentini, Lynn. The Joy of Healthy Skin: A Lifetime Guide to Beautiful, Problem-Free Skin. LC 95-37691. 38468p. 1995. text 24.95 (*0-13-127267-5*) P-H.

Parentini, Lynn J. The Joy of Healthy Skin: A Lifetime Guide to Beautiful, Problem-Free Skin. (Illus.). 366p. 1999. reprint ed. text 25.00 (*0-7881-6286-1*) DIANE Pub.

Parents & Families of Natural Communication, Inc., Staff. We Can Hear & Speak! The Power of Auditory-Verbal Communication for Children Who Are Deaf or Hard of Hearing. LC 98-72815. 171p. 1998. write for info. (*0-88200-209-0*) Alexander Graham.

Parents Anonymous of Connecticut, Inc. Staff. Family Album Cookbook. 1991. pap. 10.00 (*0-87197-311-1*) Favorite Recipes.

***Parents Magazine Editors.** I Can Do It: Physical Milestones for One Year Olds. 1999. 9.95 (*1-58238-042-2*, Whitman Coin) St Martin.

— I Can Do It: Physical Milestones for the First Twelve Months, Bk. 1. unabridged ed. (Illus.). 1999. 9.95 (*1-58238-010-4*, Whitman Coin) St Martin.

— I Can Do It: Physical Milestones for Two Year Olds. 1999. 9.95 (*1-58238-043-0*, Whitman Coin) St Martin.

— The Parents Answer Book. (Illus.). 896p. 2000. pap. 21.95 (*0-312-26372-4*, St Martin Griffin) St Martin.

Parents Magazine Editors. The Parents Party Book. LC 99-13235. 2000. pap. 12.95 (*1-58238-039-2*, Whitman Coin) St Martin.

***Parents Magazine Staff.** Parents Book of Lists. 192p. 2000. pap. 12.95 (*0-312-26373-2*) St Martin.

Parents Magazine Staff. Play & Learn. 1999. pap. write for info. (*0-312-24559-9*) St Martin.

***Parents Magazine Staff, ed.** Physical Milestones for One-Year-Old. (I Can Do It Ser.). (Illus.). 24p. (J). 2000. pap. 9.95 (*0-312-25360-5*, St Martin Griffin) St Martin.

— Physical Milestones for the First 12 Months. (I Can Do It Ser.). (Illus.). 24p. 2000. pap. 9.95 (*0-312-25359-1*) St Martin.

— Physical Milestones for Three & Four-Year-Old. (I Can Do It Ser.). (Illus.). 24p. (J). 2000. pap. 9.95 (*0-312-25363-X*, St Martin Griffin) St Martin.

— Physical Milestones for Two-Year-Old. (I Can Do It Ser.). (Illus.). 24p. (J). 2000. pap. 9.95 (*0-312-25362-1*, St Martin Griffin) St Martin.

— Your One-Year-Old: As They Grow. 160p. 2000. pap. 12.95 (*0-312-25370-2*, St Martin Griffin) St Martin.

— Your Two-Year-Old: As They Grow. 160p. 2000. pap. 12.95 (*0-312-25371-0*, St Martin Griffin) St Martin.

Parents Magazine Staff, ed. see Murphy, Ann P.

***Parents Magazine's Staff.** Your Three-& Four-Year-Old as They Gro. 2000. pap. 12.95 (*0-312-26419-4*, St Martin Griffin) St Martin.

Parents of the Sabot School, ed. see Sabot School Staff.

Parer. Handbook of Fetal Heart Rate Monitoring. 2nd ed. (C). 1998. pap. text. write for info. (*0-8089-2102-9*, Grune & Strat) Harcrt Hlth Sci Grp.

Parer, Julian T. Handbook of Fetal Heart Rate Monitoring. 2nd ed. Schmitt, William, ed. LC 96-37238. 304p. 1997. pap. text 33.00 (*0-7216-3639-X*, W B Saunders Co) Harcrt Hlth Sci Grp.

Pareras, Luis G. Medicine & the Internet. 704p. 1996. pap. text 39.95 (*0-316-69059-7*) Lppncott W & W.

Pares, Bernard. The Fall of the Russian Monarchy: A Study of Evidence. LC 83-45831. reprint ed. 47.50 (*0-404-20196-2*) AMS Pr.

— A History of Russia. LC 77-78308. (Illus.). 688p. reprint ed. write for info. (*0-404-15122-1*) AMS Pr.

— My Russian Memoirs. LC 78-96471. reprint ed. write for info. (*0-404-04878-1*) AMS Pr.

Pares, Richard. Colonial Blockade & Neutral Rights 1739-1763. LC 75-25796. (Perspectives in European History Ser.: No. 10). vii, 323p. 1975. reprint ed. lib. bdg. 39.50 (*0-87991-616-8*) Porcupine Pr.

Pares, Richard & Taylor, Alan J., eds. Essays Presented to Sir Lewis Namier. LC 70-134124. (Essay Index Reprint Ser.). 1977. 36.95 (*0-8369-2010-4*) Ayer.

Pares, Susan, jt. auth. see Hoare, James.

Paresce, Francesco, ed. Science with the VLT Interferometer: Proceedings of the ESO Workshop Held at Garching, Germany, 18-21 June 1996. LC 97-27286. (ESO Astrophysics Symposia Ser.). xxii, 404p. 29.95 (*3-540-63264-6*) Spr-Verlag.

Pareschi, R., jt. ed. see Borghoff, Uwe.

Pareschi, Remo & Fronhhofer, B. Dynamic Worlds: From the Frame Problems to Knowledge Management. LC 98-51452. 19p. 1999. write for info. (*0-7923-5535-0*) Kluwer Academic.

Pareschi, Remo, jt. ed. see Tokor, Mario.

Paret, B. First Harp Book. 40p. 1987. pap. 7.95 (*0-7935-5523-X*, 50327750) H Leonard.

Paret, Dominique. The I2C Bus: From Theory to Practice. LC 96-49615. 314p. 1997. 145.00 (*0-471-96268-6*) Wiley.

Paret, P. Lautrec: Women. (Rhythm & Color Two Ser.). 1970. 9.95 (*0-8288-9520-1*) Fr & Eur.

Paret, Peter. Art As History: Episodes in the Culture & Politics of Nineteenth-Century Germany. LC 88-22623. (Illus.). 237p. reprint ed. pap. 73.50 (*0-608-20152-9*, 207142400011) Bks Demand.

— The Berlin Secession: Modernism & Its Enemies in Imperial Germany. (Illus.). 279p. 1989. pap. text 17.50 (*0-674-06774-6*) Belknap Pr.

— Clausewitz & the State: The Man, His Theories, & His Times. LC 85-6570. 480p. 1985. pap. text 19.95 (*0-691-00806-X*, Pub. by Princeton U Pr) Cal Prin Full Svc.

— Imagined Battles: Reflections of War in European Art. LC 96-52518. (Illus.). 144p. (gr. 13). 1997. 34.95 (*0-8078-2356-2*) U of NC Pr.

— On Clausewitz & the History of War: Essays. 224p. 1992. text 39.50 (*0-691-03199-1*, Pub. by Princeton U Pr) Cal Prin Full Svc.

Paret, Peter, et al, eds. Makers of Modern Strategy from Machiavelli to the Nuclear Age. LC 85-17029. (Illus.). 944p. 1986. pap. text 24.95 (*0-691-02764-1*, Pub. by Princeton U Pr) Cal Prin Full Svc.

Paret, Peter & Moran, Daniel, eds. Carl Von Clausewitz: Historical & Political Writings. (Illus.). 422p. 1992. text 47.50 (*0-691-03192-4*, Pub. by Princeton U Pr) Cal Prin Full Svc.

Paret, Peter, et al. Persuasive Images: Posters of War & Revolution from the Archives of the Hoover Institution. (Illus.). 280p. 1992. 57.50 (*0-691-03204-1*, Pub. by Princeton U Pr) Cal Prin Full Svc.

Paret, Peter, ed. see Von Clausewitz, Carl.

Paret, Peter, ed. & tr. see Von Clausewitz, Carl.

Paret, Peter, tr. & intro. see Ritter, Gerhard A.

Pareto, Vilfredo. Compendium of General Sociology: Abridged in Italian with Approval of the Author by Giulio Farina from Pareto's Trattato di Sociologia Generale. Abbott, Elisabeth, ed. LC 79-24899. 517p. reprint ed. pap. 160.30 (*0-7837-2928-6*, 205752600006) Bks Demand.

— Manuel d'Economie Politique. Bonnet, Alfred, tr. LC 79-108770. reprint ed. 55.00 (*0-404-04879-X*) AMS Pr.

— The Mind & Society, 4 vols., Set. Livingston, Arthur, ed. Bongiorno, Andrew, tr. LC 78-63704. (Studies in Fascism: Ideology & Practice). reprint ed. 300.00 (*0-404-16990-2*) AMS Pr.

— The Rise & Fall of Elites: An Application of Theoretical Sociology. 120p. (C). 1991. pap. 21.95 (*0-88738-872-8*) Transaction Pubs.

— The Rise & Fall of the Elites: An Application of Theoretical Sociology. Coser, Lewis A. & Powell, Walter W., eds. LC 79-7011. (Perennial Works in Sociology). 1980. reprint ed. lib. bdg. 19.95 (*0-405-12110-5*) Ayer.

— The Ruling Class in Italy Before 1900. LC 73-20130. 143p. 1975. reprint ed. 30.00 (*0-86527-176-3*) Fertig.

— The Transformation of Democracy. Powers, Charles, ed. Girola, Renata, tr. from ITA. 128p. (Orig.). 1984. pap. 18.95 (*0-87855-949-3*) Transaction Pubs.

Paretsky, Sara. Bitter Medicine. 272p. 1988. mass mkt. 6.99 (*0-345-34722-6*) Ballantine Pub Grp.

— Bitter Medicine. 352p. 1999. 5.25 hd 6.99 (*0-440-23476-X*) Dell.

— Blood Shot. 384p. 1989. mass mkt. 6.99 (*0-440-20420-8*) Dell.

— Burn Marks. 368p. 1991. mass mkt. 6.99 (*0-440-20845-9*) Dell.

— Deadlock. 272p. 1992. mass mkt. 6.99 (*0-440-21332-0*) Dell.

— Ghost Country. 416p. 1999. pap. 13.95 (*0-385-33336-6*, Delta Trade) Dell.

— Ghost Country. LC 98-44855. 1998. 26.95 (*1-56895-682-7*) Wheeler Pub.

— Guardian Angel. 432p. 1993. mass mkt. 6.99 (*0-440-21399-1*) Dell.

***Paretsky, Sara.** Hard Time. (V. I. Warshawski Novels Ser.). 512p. 2000. mass mkt. 6.99 (*0-440-22470-5*, Delta Trade) Dell.

— Hard Time. large type ed. 2000. pap. 13.95 (*0-375-70780-8*) Random.

— Hard Time: A V. I. Warshawski Mystery. large type ed. LC 99-28426. 1999. 24.95 (*0-375-40853-3*) Wheeler Pub.

Paretsky, Sara. Hard Time: A V. I. Warshawski Novel. LC 99-22214. 400p. 1999. 24.95 (*0-385-31363-2*) Delacorte.

— Indemnity Only. 256p. 1991. mass mkt. 6.99 (*0-440-21069-0*) Dell.

— Indemnity Only. large type ed. (General Ser.). 381p. 1992. 18.95 (*0-8161-5456-2*, G K Hall Lrg Type); lib. bdg. 20.95 (*0-8161-5455-4*, G K Hall Lrg Type) Mac Lib Ref.

— Killing Orders. 352p. 1993. mass mkt. 6.99 (*0-440-21528-5*, Dell Trade Pbks) Dell.

— Killing Orders. large type ed. LC 93-13221. 370p. 1993. lib. bdg. 22.95 (*0-8161-5598-4*) Thorndike Pr.

— Tunnel Vision: A V. I. Warshawski Novel. 480p. 1995. mass mkt. 6.99 (*0-440-21752-0*) Dell.

— Windy City Blues. 1996. pap. 6.99 (*0-440-29546-7*) Doubleday.

— Windy City Blues: V. I. Warshawski Stories. large type ed. LC 95-36362. 336p. 1996. 24.95 (*0-7838-1561-1*, G K Hall Lrg Type) Mac Lib Ref.

— Windy City Blues: V.I. Warshawski Stories. 352p. 1996. mass mkt. 6.99 (*0-440-21873-X*) Dell.

— Windy City Blues: V.I. Warshawski Stories. large type ed. LC 95-36362. 1996. pap. 22.95 (*0-7838-1562-X*, G K Hall Lrg Type) Mac Lib Ref.

— Women on the Case. 464p. 1997. mass mkt. 6.99 (*0-440-22325-3*) Dell.

Paretsky, Sara, intro. A Woman's Eye. large type ed. (General Ser.). 569p. 1992. lib. bdg. 21.95 (*0-8161-5457-0*, G K Hall Lrg Type) Mac Lib Ref.

— A Woman's Eye. 464p. 1992. reprint ed. mass mkt. 6.99 (*0-440-21335-5*) Dell.

Paretsky, T. Reservoirs of Faith: The Yeshiva Through the Ages. 1996. 21.95 (*0-87306-779-7*) Feldheim.

Paretta, Joseph, ed. see Vollaro, Joseph.

Parette, Howard P. & Judge, Sharon L., eds. Assistive Technology for Children: A Guide for Providing Family-Centered Services. LC 98-39363. 288p. 1998. pap. 24.95 (*1-57129-051-6*) Brookline Bks.

Paretti, Sandra. The Magic Ship. Hein, Ruth, tr. from GER. LC 98-46493. Tr. of Das Zauberschiff. 320p. 1999. reprint ed. pap. 16.95 (*0-89272-463-3*) Down East.

Paretzke, Herwig. Health Impacts of Large Releases of Radionuclides - Symposium No. 203. LC 97-294. 256p. 1997. 140.00 (*0-471-96510-3*) Wiley.

Paretzky, Yvonne R. Guide to the London Insurance Market. LC 88-7344. 246p. reprint ed. pap. 76.30 (*0-7837-4594-X*, 204431300002) Bks Demand.

***Paretzky, Zev.** The Chida: His Life & Contentious Times. 300p. 1999. 18.95 (*1-56871-198-0*, Pub. by Targum Pr) Feldheim.

Parezo, Nancy. Hidden Scholars: Women Anthropologists & the Native American Southwest. LC 93-9994. 429p. 1993. 24.95 (*0-8263-1428-7*) U of NM Pr.

Parfaict, Claude, jt. auth. see Parfaict, Francois.

Parfaict, Francois & Parfaict, Claude. Histoire de l'Ancien Theatre Italien: Depuis son Origine en France Jusqu'a sa Suppression en l'Annee 1697. LC 76-43932. (Music & Theatre in France in the 17th & 18th Centuries Ser.). reprint ed. 62.50 (*0-404-60178-2*) AMS Pr.

— Memoires pour Servir a l'Histoire des Spectacles de la Foire, 2 vols., 1 bk. LC 76-43933. (Music & Theatre in France in the 17th & 18th Centuries Ser.). reprint ed. 72.50 (*0-404-60179-0*) AMS Pr.

Parfect, Michael, jt. auth. see Power, Gordon.

Parfenov, Alexandr T. & Price, Joseph G., eds. Russian Essays on Shakespeare & His Contemporaries. LC 97-18597. (International Studies in Shakespeare & His Contemporaries). 208p. (C). 1998. 36.50 (*0-87413-619-9*) U Delaware Pr.

Parfield, Fiona M., ed. Perspectives on Company Law, Vol. 2. 352p. 1997. 140.00 (*90-411-0678-2*) Kluwer Academic.

Parfionovitch, Yuri. Tibetan Medical Paintings: Illustrations of the Blue Beryl Treatise of Sangye Gyamtso (1653-1705), Vols. I - II. Meyer, Fernand et al, eds. (Illus.). 340p. (gr. 13). 1992. 195.00 (*0-8109-3861-8*) Mosby Inc.

Parfit, Derek. Reasons & Persons. (Illus.). 560p. 1986. pap. text 29.95 (*0-19-824908-X*) OUP.

Parfit, Michael. South Light. large type ed. 400p. 1992. 27.99 (*0-7089-8627-7*) Ulverscroft.

Parfitt. Context & Legacy. 2001. pap. text. write for info. (*0-312-20157-5*) St Martin.

Parfitt & Nini. Israel & Ishmael: Studies in Muslim-Jewish Relations. 1999. text 65.00 (*0-312-22228-9*) St Martin.

Parfitt, Barbara A. Working Across Cultures: A Study of Expatriate Nurses Working in Developing Countries in Primary Health Care. (Developments in Nursing & Health Care Ser.). (Illus.). 212p. 1998. text 63.95 (*1-85972-251-2*, Pub. by Ashgate Pub) Ashgate Pub Co.

Parfitt, Ben. Forest Follies: Adventures & Misadventures in the Great Canadian Forest. 220p. 1998. pap. 16.95 (*1-55017-192-5*) Harbor Bks.

Parfitt, Clara M. In Love to Him: Reaching out in Love to Them. 149p. 1985. pap. 4.95 (*0-88144-050-7*) Christian Pub.

Parfitt, Geoffrey D. & Rochester, Colin H., eds. Absorption from Solution at the Solid Liquid Interface. 1983. text 209.00 (*0-12-544980-1*) Acad Pr.

Parfitt, Geoffrey D., jt. auth. see Jaycock, M. J.

Parfitt, George. English Poetry of the First World War: Context & Themes. 192p. 1990. 69.00 (*0-389-20940-6*) B&N Imports.

Parfitt, George & Houlbrooke, Ralph, eds. The Courtship Narrative of Leonard Wheatcroft: Derbyshire Yeoman. 96p. 1986. 23.00 (*0-7049-0111-0*, WK2) Pegasus Pr.

Parfitt, George & Shepherd, Simon, eds. Thomas of Woodstock: An English History Play of Shakespeare's Time. (C). 1989. 35.00 (*0-907839-36-3*, Pub. by Brynmill Pr Ltd) St Mut.

Parfitt, George, ed. see Jonson, Ben.

***Parfitt, Kathleen.** Martindale: The Complete Drug Reference. 32nd ed. 1999. 299.00 (*0-85369-429-X*, Pub. by Pharmaceutical Pr) Rittenhouse.

Parfitt, Patti. Laughing All over the World: My Life Married to Status Quo. 256p. 1998. pap. 14.95 (*1-85782-198-X*, Pub. by Blake Publng) Seven Hills Bk.

Parfitt, R. T., jt. auth. see Casy, A. F.

Parfitt, Trevor & Riley, Stephen. The African Debt Crisis. 256p. 1989. 49.95 (*0-415-00441-1*) Routledge.

Parfitt, Tudor. The Jews in Palestine, 1800-1882. (Royal Historical Society: Studies in History). 1987. 75.00 (*0-86193-209-9*) Boydell & Brewer.

***Parfitt, Tudor.** Journey to the Vanished City: The Search for a Lost Tribe of Israel. LC 99-89015. (Departures Ser.). (Illus.). 384p. 2000. pap. text 14.00 (*0-375-72454-0*) Vin Bks.

Parfitt, Tudor. The Road to Redemption: The Jews of the Yemen, 1900-1950. (Series in Jewish Studies: Vol. 17). 1996. 105.00 (*90-04-10544-1*) Brill Academic Pubs.

Parfitt, Tudor & Nini, Yehuda, eds. Israel & Ishmael: Studies in Muslim-Jewish Relations. 288p. 1998. 75.00 (*0-7007-1091-4*, Pub. by Curzon Pr Ltd) Paul & Co Pubs.

Parfitt, Tudor & Semi, Emanuela T. The Beta Israel in Ethiopia & Israel: Studies on the Ethiopian Jews. LC 99-202734. 288p. 1998. 75.00 (*0-7007-1092-2*, Pub. by Curzon Pr Ltd) Paul & Co Pubs.

Parfitt, Tudor, jt. ed. see Abramson, Glenda.

Parfitt, Tudor, tr. see Amichai, Yehuda.

Parfitt, Will. Elements of Psychosynthesis. (Elements of Ser.). 1993. pap. 9.95 (*1-85230-156-2*, Pub. by Element MA) Penguin Putnam.

— Elements of Qabalah. LC 97-177312. (Elements of...Ser.). 1997. pap. 9.95 (*1-86204-072-9*, Pub. by Element MA) Penguin Putnam.

— New Living Qabalah. 1995. pap. 19.95 (*1-85230-682-3*, Pub. by Element MA) Penguin Putnam.

— Walking Through Walls: Practical Esoteric Psychology. 1993. pap. 14.95 (*1-85230-115-5*, Pub. by Element MA) Penguin Putnam.

Parfrey, Adam. Apocalypse Culture. 2nd rev. ed. (Illus.). 360p. (Orig.). 1990. pap. 14.95 (*0-922915-05-9*) Feral Hse.

Parfrey, Adam, ed. Apocalypse Culture II. (Illus.). 320p. 1999. pap. 16.95 (*0-922915-57-1*, Pub. by Feral Hse) Publishers Group.

Parfrey, Adam, ed. see Stafford, Harvey.

Parfrey, P. S. & Cramer, B. C. X-Ray Interpretation for the MRCP. (Illus.). 240p. 1983. pap. write for info. (*0-443-02594-0*) Church.

Parfrey, Patrick, jt. ed. see Brown, Edwina.

Parfrey, Patrick S. & Harnett, John D., eds. Cardiac Dysfunction in Chronic Uremia. (Topics in Renal Medicine Ser.). (C). 1991. text 237.00 (*0-7923-1351-8*) Kluwer Academic.

Pargament, Kenneth I. The Psychology of Religion & Coping: Theory, Research, Practice. LC 97-9599. 548p. 1997. lib. bdg. 55.00 (*1-57230-214-3*, 0214) Guilford Pubns.

Pargament, Kenneth I., et al. Religion & Prevention in Mental Health: Research, Vision & Action. LC 92-5887. (Prevention in Human Services Ser.: Vol. 9, No.2). (Illus.). 232p. 1992. text 59.95 (*1-56024-225-6*); pap. text 24.95 (*1-56024-226-4*) Haworth Pr.

Pargeter, Edith. Afterglow & Nightfall: The Brothers of Gwynedd IV. 342p. 1991. mass mkt. 10.95 (*0-7472-3030-7*, Pub. by Headline Bk Pub) Trafalgar.

— A Bloody Field by Shrewsbury. LC 73-162828. 412p. 1972. write for info. (*0-333-13748-5*) Macmillan.

— The Brothers of Gwynedd Quartet. 822p. 1990. mass mkt. 16.95 (*0-7472-3267-9*, Pub. by Headline Bk Pub) Trafalgar.

— By Firelight. 310p. 1996. mass mkt. 11.95 (*0-7472-4561-4*, Pub. by Headline Bk Pub) Trafalgar.

— The Heaven Tree Trilogy. 912p. 1993. 24.95 (*0-446-51708-9*, Pub. by Warner Bks) Little.

— The Hounds of Sunset: The Brothers of Gwynedd III. 340p. 1991. mass mkt. 11.95 (*0-7472-3029-3*, Pub. by Headline Bk Pub) Trafalgar.

— The Marriage of Meggotta. large type ed. 1995. 27.99 (*0-7505-0713-6*, Pub. by Mgna Lrg Print) Ulverscroft.

— A Means of Grace. 311p. 1996. mass mkt. 11.95 (*0-7472-4679-3*, Pub. by Headline Bk Pub) Trafalgar.

— A Means of Grace. large type ed. LC 96-3375. 1996. pap. 20.95 (*0-7862-0684-5*) Thorndike Pr.

— Reluctant Odyssey. 295p. 1991. pap. 13.95 (*0-7472-3336-5*, Pub. by Headline Bk Pub) Trafalgar.

— She Goes to War. 313p. 1991. pap. 9.95 (*0-7472-3277-6*, Pub. by Headline Bk Pub) Trafalgar.

— Warfare Accomplished. 362p. 1991. pap. 13.95 (*0-7472-3399-3*, Pub. by Headline Bk Pub) Trafalgar.

Pargeter, Edith & Peters, Ellis. The Lily Hand & Other Stories. 281p. 1996. pap. 13.95 (*0-7472-4697-1*, Pub. by Headline Bk Pub) Trafalgar.

Pargeter, Edith, tr. see Hrabal, Bohumil.

Pargeter, Edith, tr. see Neruda, Jan.

Pargeter, Margaret. Misconception. (Scarlet Ser.). 1997. mass mkt. 3.99 (*1-85487-997-9*, Pub. by Scarlet Bks) London Brdge.

Pargeter, R. J., ed. Quantifying Weldability. (Illus.). 80p. (Orig.). (C). 1988. pap. 49.95 (*0-85300-222-3*, Pub. by Woodhead Pubng) Am Educ Systs.

An Asterisk (*) at the beginning of an entry indicates that the title is appearing for the first time.

Pargeter, William. Observations on Maniacal Disorders. Jackson, Stanley W., ed. & intro. by. LC 88-18630. (Tavistock Classics in the History of Psychiatry Ser.). 188p. reprint ed. pap. 58.30 (*0-608-20349-1*, 207160200002) Bks Demand.

— Observations on Maniacal Disorders: (1792) Jackson, Stanley, ed. (Tavistock Classic Reprints in the History of Psychiatry Ser.). 208p. 1989. 37.50 (*0-415-00638-4*) Routledge.

Pargetter, Robert, jt. auth. see Bigelow, John.

Pargh, Andy. Gadget Guru's Guide to the Best. 1997. mass mkt. 87.92 (*0-446-16539-5*) Warner Bks.

Pargh, Andy & Biracree, Tom. The Gadget Guru's Guide to the Best. LC 97-24331. 304p. (Orig.). 1997. reprint ed. mass mkt. 10.99 (*0-446-67323-4*, Pub. by Warner Bks) Little.

Pargh, Andy & Buracree, Tom. The Gadget Guru's Make-It-Easy Guide to Home Repair. LC 97-13223. 272p. (Orig.). 1997. mass mkt. 9.99 (*0-446-67293-9*, Pub. by Warner Bks) Little.

***Pargh, Andy & Kelley, John.** The Gadget Guru's Guide to the Kitchen. LC 98-24373. (Illus.). 224p. 1998. mass mkt. 11.99 (*0-446-67431-1*, Pub. by Warner Bks) Little.

Pargman, David. Stress & Motor Performance: Understanding & Coping. (Illus.). 204p. 1986. pap. 15.95 (*0-685-17375-5*) Mouvement Pubns.

— Understanding Sport Behavior. LC 97-36536. 318p. (C). 1997. pap. text 49.00 (*0-13-149196-2*) P-H.

Pargman, David, ed. Psychological Bases of Sport Injuries. LC 92-73668. 315p. (C). 1993. 38.00 (*0-9627926-3-2*) Fit Info Tech.

***Pargman, David, ed.** Psychological Bases of Sport Injuries. 2nd rev. ed. 376p. (C). 1999. text 39.00 (*1-885693-18-4*) Fit Info Tech.

Pargment, Lila. Beginner's Russian Reader. 224p. 1985. pap. 26.50 (*0-8442-4227-6*) NTC Contemp Pub Co.

Parham, et al. The HLA Factsbook. 424p. 1998. 49.95 (*0-12-545025-7*) Acad Pr.

Parham, A. Philip. Letting God: Christian Meditations for Recovering Persons. LC 86-45835. (Illus.). 384p. 1987. pap. 14.00 (*0-06-250669-2*, Pub. by Harper SF) HarpC.

Parham, David M., ed. Pediatric Neoplasia: Morphology & Biology. LC 95-42517. 576p. 1996. text 187.00 (*0-7817-0273-9*) Lppncott W & W.

Parham, Deborah, ed. see Kilpatrick, Towonda.

Parham, Ellen. Baby. 150p. (Orig.). 1992. pap. 12.95 (*0-9630835-1-1*) Whitefield Bks.

Parham, H. B. Fiji Native Plants, with Their Medicinal & Other Uses. LC 75-35146. reprint ed. 32.50 (*0-404-14162-5*) AMS Pr.

Parham, H. J. & Belfield, E. M. Unarmed into Battle: The Story of the Air Observation Post. 1987. reprint ed. 91.00 (*0-7855-2174-7*, Pub. by Picton) St Mut.

Parham, Iris A., ed. Gerontological Social Work: An Annotated Bibliography, 19. LC 92-21543. (Bibliographies & Indexes in Gerontology Ser.: No. 19). 224p. 1993. lib. bdg. 59.95 (*0-313-28538-1*, PHG, Greenwood Pr) Greenwood.

Parham, Iris A., jt. compiled by see Teitelman, Jodi L.

Parham, Jim. Off the Beaten Track Vol. II: A Guide to Mountain Biking in Western North Carolina - Pisgah. 2nd rev. ed. (Off the Beaten Track Mountain Bike Guide Ser.). (Illus.). 88p. 1999. pap. 12.95 (*0-9631861-6-7*) Milestone NC.

***Parham, Jim.** Off the Beaten Track Vol. III: A Guide to Mountain Biking in North Georgia. 2nd rev. ed. (Illus.). 144p. 1999. pap. 12.95 (*1-889596-07-8*) Milestone NC.

Parham, Jim. Off the Beaten Track Vol. IV: A Guide to Mountain Biking in East Tennessee. rev. ed. (Illus.). 96p. (Orig.). 1998. pap. 12.95 (*1-889596-03-5*) Milestone NC.

— Off the Beaten Track Vol. V: A Guide to Mountain Biking in Northern Virginia. (Off the Beaten Track Mountain Bike Guide Ser.). (Illus.). 71p. (Orig.). 1995. pap. 12.95 (*0-9631861-7-5*) Milestone NC.

— Off the Beaten Track Vol. VI: A Guide to Mountain Biking in West Virginia - Northern Highlands. (Off the Beaten Track Mountain Bike Guide Ser.). (Illus.). 73p. (Orig.). 1995. pap. 12.95 (*0-9631861-8-3*) Milestone NC.

***Parham, Jim.** Off the Beaten Trade Vol. 1: A Guide to Mountain Biking in Western North Carolina - The Smokies. 3rd rev. ed. (Off the Beaten Track Mountain Bike Guide Ser.: Vol. I). (Illus.). 96p. 2000. pap. 12.95 (*1-889596-08-6*) Milestone NC.

Parham, Jim. Road Bike North Georgia: 25 Great Rides in the Mountains & Valleys of North Georgia. LC 98-10276. (Illus.). 136p. 1998. pap. 11.95 (*1-889596-04-3*) Milestone NC.

— Road Bike the Smokies: 16 Great Rides in North Carolina's Great Smoky Mountains. LC 97-18741. (Illus.). 96p. (Orig.). 1997. pap. 9.95 (*1-889596-02-7*) Milestone NC.

Parham, Jim & Hammond, Mary Ellen. Natural Adventures in the Mountains of Western North Carolina. LC 99-13487. (Illus.). 144p. 1999. pap. 12.95 (*1-889596-06-X*) Milestone NC.

Parham, Jim, jt. auth. see Hammond, Mary Ellen.

Parham, L. Diane, ed. Play in Pediatric Occupational Therapy. (Illus.). 288p. (C). (gr. 13). 1996. text 47.00 (*0-8016-7838-2*, 07838) Mosby Inc.

Parham, Maggie, tr. see Vanier, Jean.

Parham, Marisa. African American Student's Guide to College, 1999. LC 99-216576. (Princeton Review Ser.). 352p. 1998. pap. 17.95 (*0-679-77878-0*) Random.

Parham, Peter, jt. auth. see Cassell, Julian.

***Parham, R. E., 3rd.** Firearms Instructor's Manual: Simplified Course Outlines. LC 99-18794. (Illus.). 122p. 1999. spiral bd. 19.95 (*0-398-06960-3*) C C Thomas.

***Parham, Richard E.** Poems from the Southend of the Rink. LC 99-94707. viii, 103p. 1999. 9.95 (*0-9670748-0-0*) Black Duck.

Parham, Robert. Loving Neighbors Across Time: A Christian's Guide to Protecting the Earth. Nelson, Becky, ed. (Illus.). 114p. 1991. pap. text 6.95 (*1-56309-042-2*, N924106, New Hope) Womans Mission Union.

Parham, Russell A. & Gray, Richard L. The Practical Identification of Wood Pulp Fibers. LC 82-50114. 220p. 1982. 118.00 (*0-89852-400-8*, 0101R100) TAPPI.

— The Practical Identification of Wood Pulp Fibers. LC 82-50114. reprint ed. pap. 55.00 (*0-608-12028-6*, 2022820) Bks Demand.

Parham, Sandra, jt. auth. see Jordan, Barbara.

Parham, Sydney F., Jr. Title Examination in Virginia. 207p. 1965. 17.50 (*0-614-05983-6*, MICHIE) LEXIS Pub.

Parham, Thomas. Psychological Storms. rev. ed. (Illus.). 91p. 1993. pap. 6.95 (*0-913543-34-9*) African Am Imag.

Parham, Thomas A., jt. auth. see White, Joseph L.

Parham, Vanessa R. The African-American Child's Heritage Cookbook. Rolle-Whatley, R., ed. LC 92-60006. (Illus.). 296p. (Orig.). (J). 1992. pap. 19.95 (*0-9627756-2-2*) Sandcastle Pub.

Parham, Vistara. What's Wrong with Eating Meat? LC 79-52319. (Illus.). (Orig.). (J). 1979. pap. 3.50 (*0-88476-009-X*) Ananda Marga.

Parham, Walter E. Improving Degraded Lands: Promising Experiences from South China. (Bishop Museum Bulletin in Botany Ser.: Vol. 3). (Illus.). 243p. (C). 1993. pap. 15.95 (*0-930897-84-6*) Bishop Mus.

Parham, Will E. Blount County, Tennessee, Marriages, 1795-1865. iv, 422p. 1982. 25.00 (*0-89308-240-6*, TN 52) Southern Hist Pr.

Parhami, Behrooz. Computer Arithmetic: Algorithms & Hardware Designs. LC 98-44899. (Illus.). 512p. (C). 1999. text 85.00 (*0-19-512583-5*) OUP.

— Introduction to Parallel Processing: Algorithms & Architectures. LC 98-45719. (Computer Science : 1). (Illus.). 556p. (C). 1999. 88.00 (*0-306-45970-1*, Kluwer Plenum) Kluwer Academic.

Parhar, Madhu, jt. auth. see Mukhopadhyay, Marmar.

Parhi, Keshab. VLSI Digital Signal Processing Systems: Design & Implementation. LC 98-36462. 808p. 1998. 115.00 (*0-471-24186-5*) Wiley.

***Parhi, Keshab K. & Nishitani, Takao, eds.** Digital Signal Processing for Multimedia Systems. LC 99-17276. (Signal Processing for Multimedia Systems Ser.: Vol. 1). (Illus.). 880p. 1999. text 195.00 (*0-8247-1924-7*) Dekker.

Parhi, Keshab K., jt. auth. see Chung, Jin-Gyun.

Parhi, Keshab K., jt. auth. see Hartley, Richard J.

Parhi, Keshab K., jt. auth. see Shanbhag, Naresh R.

Pari, Caroline, jt. auth. see Shor, Ira.

Pari, Caroline, jt. ed. see Shor, Ira.

Pari, Susanne. The Fortune Catcher. 480p. 1999. mass mkt. 6.99 (*0-446-60631-6*, Pub. by Warner Bks) Little.

Pariaux, Olivier. Micro-Optical Technologies for Measurement Sensors & Mircosystems II & Optical Fiber Sensor Technologies & Applications. LC 98-125243. 418p. 1997. pap. 89.00 (*0-8194-2519-2*) SPIE.

Paribeni, Roberto. Optimus Princeps: Saggio Sulla Storia & Sui Tempi Dell' Imperatore Traiano. LC 75-7334. (Roman History Ser.). (ITA., Illus.). 1975. reprint ed. 58.95 (*0-405-07051-9*) Ayer.

Paricio, Miguel A. Gaspar. Spanish Dictionary of Environmental Technology/Diccionario Ingles de Tecnologia Medioambiental: Spanishenglish/ Englishspanish. LC 98-227268. (Routledge Bilingual Specialist Dictionaries Ser.). (ENG & SPA.). 288p. (C). 1998. 140.00 (*0-415-15265-8*) Routledge.

***Parida, Gunanidhi.** Ecology & Development in Conflicts: A Gandhian Approach. 2000. 38.00 (*81-7648-162-9*, Pub. by Ashish Pub Hse) S Asia.

Paridario, Maria R., jt. auth. see Therivel, Riki.

Paridis, Lenora F., ed. Stress & Burnout among Providers Caring for the Terminally Ill & Their Families. LC 87-25949. (Hospice Journal: Vol. 3, Nos. 2-3). 276p. 1988. text 39.95 (*0-86656-674-0*) Haworth Pr.

Pariente, Vita, jt. ed. see Rowe, Gilbert T.

Paries, Jeff. The Animation: Master Handbook. 2nd ed. (Illus.). 564p. 1998. pap. 49.95 incl. cd-rom (*1-886801-82-7*) Chrles River Media.

***Paries, Jeff.** The Animation: Master 2000 Handbook. 3rd rev. ed. (Illus.). 550p. 2000. pap. write for info. (*1-58450-042-5*) Chrles River Media.

Paries, Jeff. Hash Animation Master Power Guide. 1997. pap. text 44.99 incl. cd-rom (*1-56205-777-4*) New Riders Pub.

Parietti, G. Dictionary Francais-Foufoulde. (FRE.). 1998. 120.00 (*0-320-00233-0*) Fr & Eur.

Parietti, Jeff. Book of Truly Stupid Sports Quotes. LC 95-46840. 224p. 1996. pap. 12.00 (*0-06-273408-3*, Perennial) HarperTrade.

— More Truly Stupid Sports Quotes. LC 98-51521. (Illus.). 208p. 1999. pap. 10.95 (*0-06-273647-7*) HarpC.

Parigi, Sam F. A Case Study of Latin American Unionization in Austin, Texas. Cortes, Carlos E., ed. LC 76-1265. (Chicano Heritage Ser.). 1977. 28.95 (*0-405-09518-X*) Ayer.

Parik, Carol, jt. auth. see Melone, Mary A.

Parikh, Ajay M. Magnetic Resonance Image Techniques. (Illus.). 349p. (C). 1991. pap. text 65.00 (*0-8385-6084-9*, A6084-6, Apple Lange Med) McGraw.

Parikh, Annop. Ikea Book of Home Design: Using IKEA Home Furnishings. (Illus.). 208p. 1995. pap. 27.50 (*0-06-273405-9*) HarpC.

Parikh, Anoof. Making the Most of Small Spaces. 80p. 1994. 19.95 (*0-8478-1801-2*, Pub. by Rizzoli Intl) St Martin.

Parikh, Anoop. Decorator's Fact File. LC 99-17167. (Fact File Ser.). (Illus.). 176p. 1999. spiral bd. 25.00 (*1-57959-041-1*, SOMA) BB&T Inc.

Parikh, Bharati A. Feminine Sensibility: A Study of Black American & Indian Women Novelists. 200p. 1993. text 35.00 (*81-85218-37-4*, Pub. by Prestige) Advent Bks Div.

Parikh, C. K., ed. Handbook of Pharmaceutical Granulation Technology. LC 97-11743. (Drugs & the Pharmaceutical Science Ser.: Vol. 81). (Illus.). 536p. 1997. text 189.00 (*0-8247-9882-1*) Dekker.

Parikh, Girish. How to Measure Programmer Productivity. LC 81-9046. (Illus.). 95p. 1981. pap. 20.00 (*0-685-04593-5*) Shetal Ent.

— How to Measure Programmer Productivity LC 81-9046. 95p. 1981. write for info. (*0-932888-02-X*) Shetal Ent.

— The One Minute Organizing Secret: Finding Electronic Files, Papers, Books & Almost Everything Fast! LC 85-62926. 64p. (Orig.). 1985. pap. 11.00 (*0-932888-37-2*, POT) Shetal Ent.

— Techniques of Program System Maintenance. 2nd ed. LC 87-36023. 483p. reprint ed. pap. 149.80 (*0-7837-4065-4*, 204401500011) Bks Demand.

— There Is a Fortune to Be Made in Software Maintenance: Opportunities in the 30 Billion Dollar Software AfterMarket. LC 84-51942. (Illus.). 402p. (Orig.). 1985. pap. 500.00 (*0-932888-00-3*; TFSM) Shetal Ent.

Parikh, Indira J. Women Weavers. (C). 1991. 12.50 (*81-204-0597-8*, Pub. by Oxford IBH) S Asia.

Parikh, Indira J. & Garg, Pulin K. Indian Women: An Inner Dialogue. 224p. (C). 1989. text 25.00 (*0-8039-9597-0*); pap. text 12.50 (*0-8039-9598-9*) Sage.

Parikh, Indira J., jt. auth. see Garg, Pulin K.

***Parikh, J. P.** Metamorphosis: Change Your Mind, Change Your Body. LC 99-64521. (Illus.). 248p. 2000. pap. 18.95 (*1-58501-012-X*, Pub. by CeShore Pubg) Natl Bk Netwk.

Parikh, Jagdish. Managing Relationships: How to Make a Life While Making a Living. 106p. 1999. 14.95 (*1-900961-18-0*) Capstone Pub NH.

— Managing Your Self: Management by Detached Involvement. (Developmental Management Ser.). 1994. pap. 30.95 (*0-631-19307-3*) Blackwell Pubs.

Parikh, Jagdish, et al. Intuition: The New Frontier of Management. (Developmental Management Ser.). (Illus.). 320p. 1994. 47.95 (*0-631-19225-5*) Blackwell Pubs.

Parikh, Jyoti K. Energy Systems & Development: Constraints, Demand & Supply for Developing Countries. (Illus.). 1981. 17.95 (*0-19-561193-4*) OUP.

— Superconductors in Power Systems. (C). 1990. text 21.00 (*81-7023-295-3*, Pub. by Allied Pubs) S Asia.

Parikh, Jyoti K., ed. Sustainable Development of Agriculture. (C). 1988. lib. bdg. 218.00 (*90-247-3642-0*) Kluwer Academic.

Parikh, Kirit S. Towards Free Trade in Agriculture. (C). 1988. lib. bdg. 140.50 (*90-247-3632-3*) Kluwer Academic.

***Parikh, Kirit S., ed.** India Development Report, 1999-2000. (Illus.). 316p. 2000. pap. 19.95 (*0-19-565121-9*) OUP.

— India Development Report 1997. LC 97-903518. (Illus.). 284p. 1998. pap. 16.95 (*0-19-564207-4*) OUP.

Parikh, Narahari D., ed. see Desai, Mahadev.

Parikh, Narahari D., ed. see Gandhi, Mohandas Karamchand.

Parikh, Navinchandra T. Parikh Normal (Error) & Log-Normal (Error) Distributions Versus Incorrect First Discovery of Normal Law by De Moivre 1733, Laplace (1777), & Gauss (1816) 140p. (C). 1996. pap. text 100.00 (*0-9651959-0-2*, SNPN-001) S N Publng.

Parikh, R., ed. Logics of Programs. (Lecture Notes in Computer Science Ser.: Vol. 193). vi, 424p. 1985. 42.00 (*0-387-15648-8*) Spr-Verlag.

Parikh, R., ed. see Logic Symposium Staff.

Parikh, R. D. The Press & Society. 154p. 1965. 9.95 (*0-318-37280-0*) Asia Bk Corp.

Parikh, Rachel, jt. auth. see Lanzer, Harriette.

Parikh, Rohit, ed. Theoretical Aspects of Reasoning about Knowledge: Proceedings of the 3rd Conference, Tark 1990. (C). 1998. pap. text 39.95 (*1-55860-105-8*) Morgan Kaufmann.

Parikh, Sunita. The Politics of Preference: Democratic Institutions & Affirmative Action in the United States & India. LC 96-25176. 248p. (C). 1997. text 42.50 (*0-472-10745-3*, 10745) U of Mich Pr.

Parilis, E. S., et al. Atomic Collisions on Solid Surfaces. 678p. 1993. 337.25 (*0-444-89105-6*, North Holland) Elsevier.

Parilla, Catherine A. A Theory for Reading Dramatic Texts: Selected Plays by Pirandello & Garcia Lorca. (Currents in Comparative Romance Languages & Literatures Ser.: Vol. 24). IX, 186p. (C). 1995. text 44.95 (*0-8204-2368-8*) P Lang Pubng.

Parillo, John. John Parillo's Fifty Workout Secrets. Greenwood-Robinson, Maggie, ed. (Illus.). 192p. (Orig.). 1994. pap. 16.00 (*0-399-51862-2*, Perigee Bks) Berkley Pub.

Parillo, Joseph E., ed. see Year Book of Critical Care Medicine Staff.

Parillo, Tony. Michelangelo's Surprise. LC 97-37244. 32p. (YA). (ps-3). 1998. 16.00 (*0-374-34961-4*) FS&G.

Parilov & Ushakov, S. Testing & Servicing of Steam Boilers. 1990. 154.00 (*1-56032-094-X*) Hemisp Pub.

Parim D'Aulaire, Edgar, jt. auth. see Parim D'Aulaire, Ingri.

Parim D'Aulaire, Ingri. Buffalo Bill. LC 97-78369. 41p. (J). (gr. k-6). 1998. reprint ed. pap. 11.95 (*0-9643803-7-4*) Beautiful Feet.

Parim D'Aulaire, Ingri & Parim D'Aulaire, Edgar. Pocahontas. LC 97-78469. (Illus.). 45p. (J). (gr. k-6). 1998. reprint ed. pap. 11.95 (*0-9643803-6-6*) Beautiful Feet.

Parimoo, B. N. The Ascent of Self. 1978. 13.95 (*0-89684-047-6*, Pub. by Motilal Bnarsidass) S Asia.

— The Ascent of Self: A Reinterpretation of the Mystical Poetry of Lalla-Ded. 2nd rev. ed. (C). 1987. 15.00 (*81-208-0305-1*, Pub. by Motilal Bnarsidass) S Asia.

Parimoo, Ratan, et al, eds. Ellora Caves: Sculptures & Architecture. (C). 1988. 95.00 (*81-85016-23-2*, Pub. by Bks & Bks) S Asia.

Parimoo, Ratan & Sharma, Indramohan, eds. Creative Arts in Modern India, 2 vols., Set. (C). 1995. 240.00 (*81-85016-46-1*, Pub. by Bks & Bks) S Asia.

Parimoo, Ratan, et al. The Art of Ajanta: New Perspectives Papers Presented on the Occasion of an International Seminar. 608p. 1991. pap. 1146.00 (*81-85016-32-1*, Pub. by Print Hse) St Mut.

Parin, Paul, et al. Fear Thy Neighbor As Thyself: Psychoanalysis & Society Among the Anyi of West Africa. Klamerth, Patricia, tr. from GER. LC 79-24360. 424p. 1997. lib. bdg. 37.50 (*0-226-64583-5*) U Ch Pr.

— Fear Thy Neighbor As Thyself: Psychoanalysis & Society among the Anyi of West Africa. Klamerth, Patricia, tr. LC 79-24360. (Illus.). 440p. reprint ed. pap. 136.40 (*0-608-09030-1*, 206966500005) Bks Demand.

Parinder, Patrick, ed. see Gissing, George R.

Parinello, Anthony. The Power of Will: Key Strategies to Unlock Your Inner Strengths & Enjoy Success in All Aspects of Life. LC 97-77505. 228p. 1998. 15.95 (*1-886284-09-1*, Pub. by Chandler Hse) Natl Bk Netwk.

***Parinello, Anthony.** Selling to VITO: The Very Important Top Officer. 2nd ed. LC 99-15771. 240p. 1999. pap. 12.95 (*1-58062-224-0*) Adams Media.

Paringer, William A. John Dewey & the Paradox of Liberal Reform. LC 89-77669. (SUNY Series, Global Conflict & Peace Education). 215p. (C). 1990. text 64.50 (*0-7914-0253-3*); pap. text 21.95 (*0-7914-0254-1*) State U NY Pr.

***Parini, Jay.** American Writers Supplement, Vol. 5. 2000. 125.00 (*0-684-80625-8*, Free Press) Free Pr.

— American Writers Supplement, Vol. 6. 2000. 125.00 (*0-684-80623-1*) Gale.

— American Writers Supplement, Vol. 7. 2000. 125.00 (*0-684-80624-X*) Gale.

Parini, Jay. Benjamin's Crossing. LC 96-31959. 309p. 1995. 23.00 (*0-8050-3180-4*) H Holt & Co.

— Benjamin's Crossing. 320p. 1998. pap. 15.00 (*0-8050-5824-9*, Owl) H Holt & Co.

— House of Days. LC 97-28897. 1998. 23.00 (*0-8050-5713-7*); pap. 13.00 (*0-8050-5714-5*) H Holt & Co.

— An Invitation to Poetry. 416p. (C). 1986. pap. text 32.20 (*0-13-505546-6*) P-H.

— John Steinbeck: A Biography. 1995. 30.00 (*0-8050-1673-2*) H Holt & Co.

— John Steinbeck: A Biography. (Illus.). 560p. 1996. pap. 14.95 (*0-8050-4700-X*, Owl) H Holt & Co.

— The Last Station: A Novel of Tolstoy's Last Year. 304p. 1998. pap. 14.00 (*0-8050-5823-0*, Owl) H Holt & Co.

— The Love Run. (Orig.). 1989. mass mkt. 4.95 (*0-929654-22-6*, 66) Blue Moon Bks.

— The Patch Boys. LC 86-4823. 1995. pap. 8.95 (*0-8050-0770-9*, Owl) H Holt & Co.

— Robert Frost: A Life. LC 98-26690. (Illus.). 640p. 1999. 35.00 (*0-8050-3181-2*) H Holt & Co.

***Parini, Jay.** Robert Frost: A Life. 2000. pap. 16.00 (*0-8050-6341-2*, Owl) H Holt & Co.

— Some Necessary Angels: Essays on Writing & Politics. LC 97-25379. 288p. 1997. 26.50 (*0-231-11070-7*) Col U Pr.

***Parini, Jay.** Some Necessary Angels: Essays on Writing & Politics. 2000. pap. text 15.00 (*0-231-11071-5*) Col U Pr.

Parini, Jay, ed. The Columbia Anthology of American Poetry. LC 94-32423. 648p. 1995. 35.00 (*0-231-08122-7*) Col U Pr.

— Columbia History of American Poetry: From the Puritans to Our Time. 928p. 1998. 12.98 (*1-56731-276-4*, MJF Bks) Fine Comms.

Parini, Jay, ed. Gore Vidal: Writer Against the Grain. 389p. (C). 1992. text 40.50 (*0-231-07208-2*) Col U Pr.

— Gore Vidal: Writer Against the Grain. 389p. (C). 1994. pap. 20.00 (*0-231-07209-0*) Col U Pr.

***Parini, Jay, ed.** The Norton Book of American Autobiography. LC 98-43398. 704p. 1999. 32.50 (*0-393-04677-X*) Norton.

Parini, Jay & Miller, Brett C., eds. The Columbia History of American Poetry. LC 92-29399. 894p. 1993. 72.00 (*0-231-07836-6*) Col U Pr.

Parini, Jay, jt. ed. see Ciongoli, A. Kenneth.

Parini, Jay, jt. ed. see Pack, Robert.

Parins, James W. John Rollin Ridge: His Life & Works. LC 90-40464. (American Indian Lives Ser.). (Illus.). x, 260p. 1991. text 45.00 (*0-8032-3683-2*) U of Nebr Pr.

Parins, James W., jt. auth. see Littlefield, Daniel F., Jr.

Parins, James W., ed. see La Flesche, Francis.

Parins, James W., jt. ed. see Littlefield, Daniel F., Jr.

Parins, Marylyn. Malory. (Critical Heritage Ser.). 420p. 1988. text 75.00 (*0-415-00223-0*) Routledge.

Parins, Marylyn, ed. Sir Thomas Malory. 424p. (C). 1996. 140.00 (*0-415-13400-5*) Routledge.

Paris. Textbook of Acute Pain Management. (Illus.). 800p. 1999. pap. text. write for info. (*0-7216-6644-2*, W B Saunders Co) Harcrt Hlth Sci Grp.

Paris, Alain. Dictionnaire General de la Technique Industrielle: Francais - Allemand. 3rd ed. (FRE & GER.). 1110p. 1990. pap. 49.95 (*0-7859-4740-X*) Fr & Eur.

Paris, Alan. Jerusalem, 3000: Kids Discover the City of Gold. (Illus.). 47p. (J). (gr. 4-8). 1995. 16.95 (*0-943706-59-9*) Pitspopany.

Paris, Alexander. A Complete Guide to Trading Profits. (Illus.). 196p. 1999. pap. 19.95 (*0-934380-58-9*, 38) Traders Pr.

P

An Asterisk (*) at the beginning of an entry indicates that the title is appearing for the first time.

Paris Assemblee Electorale Staff. Assemblee Electorale de Paris, 18 Novembre 1790-15, Juin 1791: Collection de Documents Relatifs a l'Histoire de Paris Pendant la Revolution Francaise. LC 79-173488. reprint ed. 135.00 (*0-404-52614-4*) AMS Pr.
— Assemblee Electorale de Paris, 2 Septembre 1792. LC 75-38036. reprint ed. 135.00 (*0-404-52616-0*) AMS Pr.
— Assemblee Electorale de Paris, 26 Aout 1791-12 Aout 1792: Collection de Documents Relatifs a l'Histoire de Paris Pendant la Revolution Francaise. LC 71-38035. reprint ed. 135.00 (*0-404-52615-2*) AMS Pr.
***Paris, Barry.** Louise Brooks: A Biography. 2000. reprint ed. pap. 19.95 (*0-8166-3781-4*) U of Minn Pr.
Paris, Barry. Song of Haiti: The Lives of Dr. Larimer & Gwen Mellon at the Albert Schweitzer Hospital of Deschapelles. LC 99-46266. (Illus.). 368p. 2000. text 27.50 (*1-891620-13-4*, Pub. by PublicAffairs NY) HarpC.
Paris, Barry, ed. & pref. see Adler, Stella.
Paris, Beltran. Beltran. Basque Sheepman of the American West. LC 79-20311. (Basque Ser.). (Illus.). 203p. 1979. reprint ed. pap. 63.00 (*0-608-02955-6*, 206342000006) Bks Demand.
Paris, Bernard J. Character As a Subversive Force in Shakespeare: The History & Roman Plays. LC 90-55839. 224p. 1991. 39.50 (*0-8386-3429-X*) Fairleigh Dickinson.
— Experiments in Life: George Eliot's Quest for Values. LC 65-13719. 296p. reprint ed. pap. 91.80 (*0-7837-3613-4*, 204347900009) Bks Demand.
— Imagined Human Beings. LC 97-4879. 1997. text 55.00 (*0-8147-6655-2*); pap. text 20.00 (*0-8147-6656-0*) NYU Pr.
— Karen Horney: A Psychoanalyst's Search for Self-Understanding. LC 94-14935. (Illus.). 288p. 1994. 37.50 (*0-300-05956-6*) Yale U Pr.
— Karen Horney: A Psychoanalyst's Search for Self-Understanding. (Illus.). 288p. 1996. pap. 18.00 (*0-300-06860-3*) Yale U Pr.
***Paris, Bernard J.** The Unknown Karen Horney: Essays on Gender, Culture & Psychoanalysis. LC 99-39715. 384p. 2000. 35.00 (*0-300-08042-5*) Yale U Pr.
Paris, Bernard J., ed. Third Force Psychology & the Study of Literature. LC 85-47629. 344p. 1986. 45.00 (*0-8386-3263-7*) Fairleigh Dickinson.
Paris, Bernard J., jt. auth. see Horney, Karen.
Paris, Bernard J., ed. see Holland, Norman N.
Paris, Betty B. Coca-Cola Trivia. unabridged ed. 160p. 1995. pap. 14.95 (*0-9668683-0-7*, 0001) B B Paris.
Paris, Betty B., jt. auth. see Murray-Slutsky, Carolyn.
Paris. Bibliotheque Nationale Staff. Cinquantenaire du symbolisme: Exposition de manuscrits autographes, estamps, peintures, sculptures, editions rares, portraits, objets d'art. LC 77-11471. (Symbolists Ser.). (FRE., Illus.). reprint ed. 54.00 (*0-404-16333-5*) AMS Pr.
Paris, Bob. Flawless: The Ten-Week, Total-Image Method for Transforming Your Physique. (Illus.). 304p. (Orig.). 1993. mass mkt. 15.99 (*0-446-39406-8*, Pub. by Warner Bks) Little.
Paris, Bob. Generation Queer: A Gay Man's Quest for Hope, Love & Justice. 197p. 1999. mass mkt. 13.99 (*0-446-67535-0*, Pub. by Warner Bks) Little.
— Gorilla Suit: My Adventures in Body Building. 288p. 1998. pap. 14.95 (*0-312-19458-7*, Pub. by Tor Bks) St Martin.
— Natural Fitness. 288p. (Orig.). 1996. mass mkt. 14.99 (*0-446-67029-4*, Pub. by Warner Bks) Little.
Paris, C., ed. Critical Readings in Planning Theory. (Urban & Regional Planning Ser.: Vol. 27). (Illus.). 260p. 1982. text 151.00 (*0-08-024681-8*, Pub. by Pergamon Repr) Franklin.
Paris, Carmi Z., jt. auth. see Paris, Jay.
Paris, Catherine & Batouka, Niaz. Dictionnaire Abkhaz. (FRE.). 1992. write for info. (*0-7859-8185-3*, 2-87723-044-9) Fr & Eur.
Paris, Cecile L. User Modeling in Text Generation. (Communication in Artificial Intelligence Ser.). 240p. 1993. text 79.00 (*0-86187-809-4*) St Martin.
Paris, Cecile L., et al, eds. Natural Language Generation in Artificial Intelligence & Computational Linguistics. (C). 1990. text 147.50 (*0-7923-9098-9*) Kluwer Academic.
Paris Commune, 1789-1794 Staff. Actes de la Commune de Paris Pendant la Revolution, 9 vols. LC 73-15863. (Second Ser.). reprint ed. 1215.00 (*0-404-52630-6*) AMS Pr.
— Actes de la Commune de Paris Pendant la Revolution, 10 vols. LC 72-173489. (First Ser.). 1994. reprint ed. 1350.00 (*0-404-52620-9*) AMS Pr.
Paris, Cynthia L. Teacher Agency & Curriculum Making in the Classroom. LC 92-34554. 176p. (C). 1993. pap. text 18.95 (*0-8077-3225-7*) Tchrs Coll.
Paris, Dan. Regaining Wholeness Through the Subtle Dimensions. 1998. pap. 15.95 (*1-884246-13-3*) Liv from Vis.
Paris, Darlene. Healthy & Natural Living in Chicago: The Best Alternative Resources in the City & Suburbs. LC 98-7682. 136p. 1998. pap. 11.95 (*1-55652-295-9*) Chicago Review.
***Paris, Domonic.** The Sleepless. 174p. 2000. pap. 18.00 (*0-7388-2142-X*) Xlibris Corp.
Paris, Don. Regaining Wholeness Through the Subtle Dimensions: Where Science Meets Magic. (Illus.). 160p. (Orig.). 1993. pap. 12.95 (*1-884246-00-1*) Liv from Vis.
Paris, Edmond. The Secret History of the Jesuits. rev. ed. 208p. 1982. reprint ed. pap. 7.50 (*0-937958-10-7*) Chick Pubns.
Paris, Eileen, jt. auth. see Paris, Thomas.
Paris, Erna. The End of Days: A Story of Tolerance, Tyranny & the Expulsion of the Jews from Spain. LC 95-24016. (Illus.). 327p. 1995. 28.95 (*1-57392-017-7*) Prometheus Bks.
— The Garden & the Gun. 292p. 1991. 24.95 (*1-879601-00-1*); pap. 16.95 (*1-879601-01-X*) Semaphore Bks.
Paris, Federico & Canas, Jose. Boundary Element Method: Fundamentals & Applications. (Illus.). 408p. 1997. text 140.00 (*0-19-856537-2*); pap. text 65.00 (*0-19-856543-7*) OUP.
Paris, Gaston B. Francois Villon. LC 70-178550. reprint ed. 37.50 (*0-404-56657-X*) AMS Pr.
— La Litterature Francaise au Moyen Age (Eleventh to Fourteenth Centuries) LC 73-178583. reprint ed. 62.50 (*0-404-56658-8*) AMS Pr.
— Mediaeval French Literature. LC 78-154160. (Select Bibliographies Reprint Ser.). 1977. reprint ed. 19.95 (*0-8369-5776-8*) Ayer.
Paris, Ginette. Pagan Grace: Dionysos, Hermes & Goddess Memory in Daily Life. Mott, Joanna, tr. from FRE. LC 89-26330. 152p. (Orig.). 1990. pap. 16.00 (*0-88214-342-5*) Spring Pubns.
— Pagan Meditations: Aphrodite, Hestia, Artemis. Moore, Gwendolyn, tr. from FRE. LC 86-6675. 204p. (Orig.). (C). 1986. pap. 19.00 (*0-88214-330-1*) Spring Pubns.
Paris, Henry G., jt. ed. see Kim, D. K.
Paris, Henry G., ed. see Minerals, Metals & Materials Society Staff.
Paris, Howard. Clip-Art Activity Features for Children. (Repro Bks.). (Illus.). 112p. (Orig.). (gr. 11). 1992. pap. 5.99 (*0-8010-7119-4*) Baker Bks.
Paris, I. Mark, tr. The Splendor of Ethnic Jewelry: From the Colette & Jean-Pierre Ghysels Collection. LC 94-8417. (Illus.). 256p. 1994. 75.00 (*0-8109-4453-7*, Pub. by Abrams) Time Warner.
Paris, I. Mark, tr. see Chabout, Rene.
Paris, I. Mark, tr. see Loyrette, Henri.
Paris, I. Mark, tr. see Maury, Jean-Pierre.
Paris, I. Mark, tr. see Thuan, Trinh X.
Paris, I. Mark, tr. see Van Zuylen, Gabrielle.
Paris, J. B. The Uncertain Reasoner's Companion: A Mathematical Perspective. (Tracts in Theoretical Computer Science Ser.: No. 39). 222p. (C). 1995. text 47.95 (*0-521-46089-1*) Cambridge U Pr.
Paris, James. Money Management for Those Who Don't Have Any. LC 96-48957. 224p. (Orig.). 1997. pap. 9.99 (*1-56507-532-3*) Harvest Hse.
Paris, James L. Absolutely Amazing Ways to Save Money on Everything. LC 98-42238. 249p. 1999. pap. 9.99 (*1-56507-917-5*) Harvest Hse.
***Paris, James L.** The Christian Financial Crisis: Why Christians Are Broke, Make Bad Investments, & Are over Their Heads in Debt. LC 98-83253. 160p. 1999. 17.95 (*0-9669821-1-8*) Avatar Pub.
Paris, James L., jt. auth. see Dicks, J. W.
Paris, James R. Classic Foreign Films: From Nineteen Sixty to Today. (Illus.). 256p. 1993. pap. 17.95 (*0-8065-1442-6*, Citadel Pr) Carol Pub Group.
— The Great French Films. (Illus.). 288p. 1983. 18.95 (*0-8065-0806-X*, Citadel Pr) Carol Pub Group.
Paris, Janelle A. Planning Bulletin Boards for Church & Synagogue Libraries. LC 83-7331. (Guide Ser.: No. 11). 48p. (Orig.). 1984. pap. 8.25 (*0-915324-20-2*) CSLA.
Paris, Janis, ed. see Davis, Margaret R. & Weckler, David A.
Paris, Janis, ed. see Jaffe, Dennis & Scott, Cynthia D.
Paris, Janis, ed. see Kravitz, S. Michael.
Paris, Janis, ed. see Layton, Sarah, et al.
Paris, Janis, ed. see Maddux, Robert B.
Paris, Janis, ed. see Manzo, Jean Q.
Paris, Janis, ed. see Northington, Marshall.
Paris, Janis, ed. see Patterson, James G.
Paris, Janis, ed. see Potter, Beverly A.
Paris, Janis, ed. see Van Daele, Carrie A.
Paris, Jay & Paris, Carmi Z. 100 Best All-Inclusive Resorts in the World. LC 99-33143. (Illus.). 320p. 1999. pap. text 16.95 (*0-7627-0415-2*) Globe Pequot.
***Paris, Jennell Williams & Eyring, Margot Owen.** Urban Disciples: A Beginner's Guide to Serving God in the City. 112p. (YA). 2000. pap. 14.00 (*0-8170-1367-9*) Judson.
Paris, Joel. Borderline Personality Disorder: A Multidimensional Approach. 288p. 1994. text 34.00 (*0-88048-655-4*, 8655) Am Psychiatric.
***Paris, Joel.** Myths of Childhood. LC 00-21546. 272p. 2000. 34.95 (*0-87630-966-X*) Brunner-Mazel.
Paris, Joel. Nature & Nurture in Psychiatry: A Predisposition-Stress Model of Mental Disorders. 1999. 49.50 (*0-88048-781-X*, 8781) Am Psychiatric.
— Social Factors in the Personality Disorders: A Biopsychosocial Approach to Etiology & Treatment. (Studies in Social & Community Psychiatry). (Illus.). 254p. (C). 1996. text 64.95 (*0-521-47224-5*) Cambridge U Pr.
— Working with Traits: Psychotherapy of Personality Disorders. LC 97-18482. 272p. 1998. text 50.00 (*0-7657-0096-4*) Aronson.
Paris, Joel, ed. Borderline Personality Disorder: Etiology & Treatment. 420p. 1992. text 52.00 (*0-88048-408-X*, 8408) Am Psychiatric.
Paris, John D. How to Successfully Sell Your Home-Yourself! 66p. (Orig.). 1997. pap. 7.95 (*0-9654973-0-5*) Sterling Pr WA.
— The Spirit of Democracy in America. 102p. (J). (gr. 5-8). 1997. pap. 14.95 (*0-9654973-1-3*) Sterling Pr WA.
Paris, Lance K. Crisis Response & Emergency Action Plan. Drummond, Inez B., ed. (Illus.). 65p. 1995. ring bd. 99.00 (*1-891621-03-3*, CREAP1) Safety Pubns.
— Safety Compliance & Management Program: California SB198, 2 vols. Drummond, Inez B., ed. (Illus.). 105p. 1992. ring bd. 198.00 (*1-891621-00-9*, SCAMP/CA1) Safety Pubns.
— Safety Compliance & Management Program: Federal Edition, 2 vols. Drummond, Inez B., ed. (Illus.). 105p. 1992. ring bd. 198.00 (*1-891621-02-5*, SCAMP/FED1) Safety Pubns.
— Safety Compliance & Management Program: Nevada NRS 618.383, 2 vols. Drummond, Inez B., ed. (Illus.). 105p. 1992. ring bd. 198.00 (*1-891621-01-7*, SCAMP/NV1) Safety Pubns.
— Safety Trainings for Everyone. Drummond, Inez B., ed. 60p. 1997. ring bd. 79.00 (*1-891621-04-1*, TRAIN 1) Safety Pubns.
***Paris, M.** Great Unfrocked: Two Thousand Years of Church Scandal. 266p. 1999. text 29.95 (*1-86105-129-8*) Robson.
Paris, Maine Historical Society Staff. Paris, Maine: The Second Hundred Years, 1893-1993. LC 94-66187. (Illus.). 1216p. 1994. 60.00 (*0-89725-165-2*, 1512, Penobscot Pr) Picton Pr.
Paris, Margaret L., jt. auth. see Taslitz, Andrew E.
Paris, Marion. Library School Closings: Four Case Studies. LC 88-7276. 176p. 1988. 25.00 (*0-8108-2130-3*) Scarecrow.
Paris, Matthew. English History, from the Year Twelve Hundred Thirty-Five to Twelve Hundred Seventy-Three, 3 vols. Giles, J. A., tr. LC 68-55554. (Bohn's Antiquarian Library). reprint ed. 150.00 (*0-404-50050-1*) AMS Pr.
— Life of St. Edmund by Matthew Paris. 1997. pap. text 21.95 (*0-7509-1129-8*, Pub. by Sutton Pub Ltd) Intl Pubs Mktg.
Paris, Michael. From the Wright Brothers to Top Gun: Aviation & Popular Cinema. LC 94-29774. 1995. text 27.95 (*0-7190-4074-4*, Pub. by Manchester Univ Pr); text 79.95 (*0-7190-4073-6*, Pub. by Manchester Univ Pr) St Martin.
— The Novels of World War II: An Annotated Bibliography of World War Two Fiction. LC 90-176799. 196p. 1990. reprint ed. pap. 60.80 (*0-7837-9271-9*, 206000900004) Bks Demand.
— Silvertown, 1917. 1993. pap. 8.00 (*0-86025-401-1*, Pub. by I Henry Pubns) Empire Pub Srvs.
***Paris, Michael, ed.** The First World War & Popular Cinema: 1914 to the Present. LC 99-55762. (Illus.). 240p. 2000. pap. 20.00 (*0-8135-2825-9*); text 52.00 (*0-8135-2824-0*) Rutgers U Pr.
Paris, Mike & Comber, Chris. Jimmie the Kid: The Life of Jimmie Rodgers. LC 80-29198. (Quality Paperbacks Ser.). (Illus.). 211p. 1981. reprint ed. pap. 8.95 (*0-306-80133-7*) Da Capo.
***Paris Musees Staff.** Paris 3D. (Illus.). 288p. 2000. 75.00 (*1-86154-162-7*, Pub. by Booth-Clibborn) Dist Art Pubs.
Paris, P. C., ed. Fracture Mechanics: 12th Conference - STP 700. 587p. 1980. 53.25 (*0-8031-0363-8*, STP700) ASTM.
Paris, Pam, et al. Responsible Steps Toward Violence Prevention: A Family Intervention Strategy. LC 99-60706. (Illus.). 194p. 1999. spiral bd. 29.95 (*0-932796-91-5*) Ed Media Corp.
Paris, Pat. Christmas at the Zoo Pop Up. 10p. (J). (ps-3). 1990. pap. 3.95 (*0-8167-2185-8*) Troll Communs.
— The First Noel: A Holiday Pop-Up Book. (Illus.). 10p. (J). 1998. 16.95 (*0-8054-1793-1*) Broadman.
— Old MacDonald Had a Farm. (Illus.). 12p. (J). (ps-1). 1989. text 11.95 (*0-8120-6107-1*) Barron.
— On a Rainy Day: A Playtime Pop-Up. (Illus.). 10p. (J). (ps). 1992. pap., boxed set 4.95 (*0-671-74175-6*) Litle Simon.
— On a Windy Day: A Playtime Pop-Up. (Illus.). 10p. (J). (ps). 1992. pap., boxed set 4.95 (*0-671-74174-8*) Litle Simon.
— On Christmas Day. (Illus.). 10p. (J). (ps). 1991. pap., boxed set 4.95 (*0-671-74173-X*) Litle Simon.
Paris, Paul C., jt. ed. see Jerina, Kenneth L.
Paris, Paul M. & Roth, Ronald N., eds. Prehospital Medicine: The Art of on-Line Medical Command. (Illus.). 288p. (C). (gr. 13). 1996. pap. text 50.95 (*0-8151-6849-7*, 24810) Mosby Inc.
Paris, Paul M., jt. auth. see Dunmire, Susan M.
Paris, Paul M., jt. auth. see Wolfson, Allan B.
***Paris Peace Conference Staff.** Violation of the Laws & Customs of War: Reports of Majority & Dissenting Reports of American & Japanese Members of the Commission of Responsibilities, Conference of Paris, 1919. LC 99-48869. 2000. write for info. (*1-57588-607-3*) W S Hein.
Paris, Peter J. Black Religious Leaders: Conflict in Unity: Insights from Martin Luther King, Jr., Malcolm X, Joseph H. Jackson, & Adam Clayton Powell, Jr. (Illus.). 272p. (Orig.). 1991. pap. 22.95 (*0-664-25145-5*) Westminster John Knox.
— The Social Teaching of the Black Churches. LC 84-47930. 162p. 1985. pap. 16.00 (*0-8006-1805-X*, 1-1805, Fortress Pr) Augsburg Fortress.
— The Spirituality of African Peoples: The Search for a Common Moral Discourse. LC 94-32866. 176p. 1995. pap. 17.00 (*0-8006-2854-3*, 1-2854, Fortress Pr) Augsburg Fortress.
Paris, Pierre. Manual of Ancient Sculpture. Harrison, Jane E., ed. (Illus.). xvi, 369p. 1984. lib. bdg. 55.00 (*0-89241-373-5*) Caratzas.
Paris, Quirino. An Economic Interpretation of Linear Programming. LC 90-31285. (Illus.). 352p. (C). 1991. text 52.95 (*0-8138-0469-8*) Iowa St U Pr.
***Paris, Raina M.** The Mother-to-Be's Dream Book: Understanding the Dreams of Pregnancy. LC 99-49032. 304p. 2000. mass mkt. 12.95 (*0-446-67524-5*) Warner Bks.
Paris Review Staff. Beat Writers at Work. LC 98-7985. 1999. pap. 13.95 (*0-375-75215-3*) Modern Lib NY.
— Paris Review, 143. 1997. pap. 10.00 (*0-679-77847-0*) Random.
— Paris Review, No. 14. Vol. 144. 304p. 1998. pap. 10.00 (*0-375-75049-5*) Random.
— Paris Review, No. 146. 1998. pap. 10.00 (*0-375-75178-5*) Random Ref & Info.
— Paris Review, No. 147. 1998. pap. 10.00 (*0-375-75177-7*) Random.
— Paris Review, Vol. 145. 1998. pap. 10.00 (*0-375-75110-6*) Random.
***Paris Review Staff.** Playwrights at Work. LC 99-44064. (Illus.). 320p. 2000. pap. 15.95 (*0-679-64021-5*) Modern Lib NY.
Paris, Scott G. Propositional Logical Thinking & Comprehension of Language Connectives: A Developmental Analysis. LC 74-75824. (Janua Linguarum, Series Minor: No. 216). (Illus.). 101p. 1975. pap. text 23.10 (*90-279-3197-6*) Mouton.
Paris, Scott G., et al, eds. Learning & Motivation in the Classroom. LC 83-8962. 347p. reprint ed. pap. 107.60 (*0-7837-2424-1*, 204257100005) Bks Demand.
Paris, Scott G. & Ayres, Linda R. Becoming Reflective Students & Teachers with Portfolios & Authentic Assessment. LC 94-12481. (Psychology in the Classroom Ser.). (Illus.). 177p. 1994. pap. text 17.95 (*1-55798-252-X*) Am Psychol.
Paris, Susan. Mommy & Daddy Are Fighting: A Book for Children about Family Violence. LC 85-22193. (New Leaf Ser.). (Illus.). 24p. (Orig.). (J). (ps-4). 1986. pap. 8.95 (*0-931188-33-4*) Seal Pr WA.
Paris, Thomas & Paris, Eileen. I'll Never Do to My Kids What My Parents Did to Me! 176p. 1994. pap. 8.99 (*0-446-39546-3*) Warner Bks.
— I'll Never Do to My Kids What My Parents Did to Me! A Guide to Conscious Parenting. 168p. 1993. pap. 9.95 (*1-56565-031-X*) Lowell Hse.
Paris, Twila. Celebrate the Gift of Jesus Every Day: Song Lyrics & Devotionals. 96p. 10.95 (*0-87162-667-5*) Warner Pr.
— Twila Paris-Twenty Favorites. 136p. 1997. otabind 14.95 (*0-7935-7857-4*) H Leonard.
Paris, William F. Personalities in American Art. LC 72-107731. (Essay Index Reprint Ser.). 1977. 17.95 (*0-8369-1582-8*) Ayer.
Paris, Yvette. Dying to be Marilyn. (Illus.). 331p. 1996. 29.95 (*1-878117-08-4*) Lagumo Corp.
Parise, Charles J., ed. Science & Technology of Glazing Systems. LC 89-28496. (Special Technical Publication Ser.: No. 1054). (Illus.). 150p. 1990. text 29.00 (*0-8031-1286-6*, STP1054) ASTM.
Parise, Frank, jt. auth. see Marum, Andrew.
Parise, George & Haynes, John H. The Haynes Fuel Injection Diagnostic Manual: The Haynes Automotive Repair Manual for Maintaining, Troubleshooting & Repairing Fuel Injection Systems. LC 97-74145. 1997. write for info. (*1-56392-275-4*) Haynes Manuals.
Parise, Goffredo. Abecedary. Marcus, James, tr. from ITA. LC 90-60881. 147p. 1990. pap. 10.95 (*0-910395-61-6*) Marlboro Pr.
— Abecedary. Marcus, James, tr. from ITA. LC 90-60881. 147p. 1990. 29.95 (*0-910395-60-8*) Marlboro Pr.
— Abecedary. Marcus, James, tr. LC 98-36566. 160p. 1998. pap. 14.95 (*0-8101-6060-9*, Marlboro) Northwestern U Pr.
— Solitudes. Quigly, Isabel, tr. LC 98-36565. 180p. 1998. pap. 14.95 (*0-8101-6059-5*, Marlboro) Northwestern U Pr.
Parise, Michael & Berger, Mary J. Jesus Is Forever. 347p. spiral bd. 18.95 (*0-8198-3947-7*) Pauline Bks.
Parise, Michael & Flanagan, Anne J., texts. Jesus Is Forever. 235p. pap. 8.95 (*0-8198-3945-0*) Pauline Bks.
Pariseau, Earl J., ed. Handbook of Latin American Studies, Vol. 24: 1962. LC 36-32633. 1962. 49.95 (*0-8130-0178-1*) U Press Fla.
Pariseau, Earl J. & Adams, Henry E., eds. Handbook of Latin American Studies, Vol. 28: Humanities 1962-64. LC 36-32633. 1966. 49.95 (*0-8130-0181-1*) U Press Fla.
Pariser, David M., jt. auth. see Eaglstein, William H.
Pariser, Harry S. Adventure Guide to Costa Rica. 3rd ed. (Adventure Guide Ser.). (Illus.). 530p. (Orig.). 1996. pap. 16.95 (*1-55650-722-4*) Hunter NJ.
— Adventure Guide to Puerto Rico. 3rd ed. (Adventure Guide Ser.). (Illus.). 288p. (Orig.). 1996. pap. 15.95 (*1-55650-749-6*) Hunter NJ.
***Pariser, Harry S.** Explore Barbados. 338p. 2000. pap. 18.95 (*1-893643-51-4*, Pub. by Manatee Pr) SCB Distributors.
Pariser, Harry S. Explore Belize. 4th rev. ed. Orig. Title: Adventure Guide to Belize. (Illus.). 320p. 1997. pap. 16.95 (*1-55650-785-2*) Hunter NJ.
***Pariser, Harry S.** Explore Costa Rica. 432p. 1999. pap. 19.95 (*1-893643-50-6*) Manatee Pr.
Pariser, Harry S. Explore the Dominican Republic. 3rd ed. (Adventure Guide). 1998. pap. text 15.95 (*1-55650-814-X*) Hunter NJ.
Pariser, Michael. Elie Wiesel: Bearing Witness. LC 93-37126. (Gateway Biography Ser.). (Illus.). 48p. (J). (gr. 2-4). 1994. lib. bdg. 21.90 (*1-56294-419-3*) Millbrook Pr.
Pariser, Stephen F. & Levine, Stephen B., eds. Clinical Sexuality. LC 83-2096. (Reproductive Medicine Ser.: No. 3). (Illus.). 232p. reprint ed. pap. 72.00 (*0-7837-0936-6*, 204124100019) Bks Demand.
Parish. Spectroscopic Methods in Organic Chemistry. text. write for info. (*0-471-48928-X*); pap. text. write for info. (*0-471-48929-8*) Wiley.
Parish, Anthony, ed. World Electronics Development, 1998. (Illus.). 88p. (C). 1998. pap. text 60.00 (*0-7881-4985-7*) DIANE Pub.
Parish, Bobbi. Create Your Own Personal Sacred Text. LC 99-24026. 288p. 1999. pap. 15.00 (*0-7679-0368-4*) Bantam.

P

An Asterisk (*) at the beginning of an entry indicates that the title is appearing for the first time.

Parish, Charles. Tristram Shandy Notes. (Cliffs Notes Ser.). 128p. 1968. pap. 4.95 (*0-8220-1311-8*, Cliff) IDG Bks.

Parish, D. H. Possibilities for the Improvement of Nitrogen Fertilizer Efficiency in Rice Production. (Papers: No. P-1). 1980. pap. text 4.00 (*0-88090-061-X*) Intl Fertilizer.

Parish, D. H., et al. Research on Modified Fertilizer Materials for Use in Developing-Country Agriculture. (Papers: No. P-2). 1980. pap. text 4.00 (*0-88090-062-8*) Intl Fertilizer.

Parish, David. Successful Rifle Shooting. (Illus.). 128p. 1997. 35.00 (*1-86126-019-9*, Pub. by Crolwood) Trafalgar.

Parish, Dennis H. Agricultural Productivity, Sustainability, & Fertilizer Use. LC 93-16931. (Papers: No. P-18). (Illus.). 21p. (Orig.). 1993. pap. text 4.00 (*0-88090-102-0*) Intl Fertilizer.

Parish, Edward J. & Nes, W. David. Biochemistry & Function of Sterols. LC 96-28235. 288p. 1997. boxed set 179.95 (*0-8493-7674-2*) CRC Pr.

Parish, Elijah, jt. auth. see M'Clure, David.

Parish, Fawn. The Power of Honor: What Love Looks Like. LC 99-25908. 224p. 1999. pap. 9.99 (*0-8307-2381-1*) Gospel Lght.

Parish, Helen R. Bartolome de las Casas: The Only Way. Sullivan, Francis P., tr. LC 91-32835. (Sources of American Spirituality Ser.). 288p. 1992. 22.95 (*0-8091-0367-2*) Paulist Pr.

Parish, Helen-Rand & Weidman, Harold E. Las Casas en Mexico (Bartolome de las Casas in Mexico) (SPA.). 409p. 1992. 20.99 (*968-16-3731-3*, Pub. by Fondo) Continental Bk.

***Parish, Herman.** Bravo, Amelia Bedelia! (Amelia Bedelia Ser.). (J). (gr. k-2). 1999. write for info. (*0-613-17657-X*) Econo-Clad Bks.

Parish, Herman. Bravo, Amelia Bedelia. LC 96-9589. (Amelia Bedelia Ser.). (Illus.). 40p. (J). (gr. 1-4). 1997. 11.95 (*0-688-15154-X*, Grenwillow Bks) HarpC Child Bks.

Parish, Herman. Bravo, Amelia Bedelia. LC 96-9589. (Amelia Bedelia Ser.). (Illus.). 40p. (J). (gr. 1-4). 1997. 11.89 (*0-688-15155-8*, Grenwillow Bks) HarpC Child Bks.

— Bravo, Amelia Bedelia. (Amelia Bedelia Ser.). (Illus.). 48p. (J). (gr. k-2). 1999. mass mkt. 3.99 (*0-380-73215-7*, Avon Bks) Morrow Avon.

***Parish, Herman.** Good Driving, Amelia Bedelia. (Amelia Bedelia Ser.). (J). (gr. k-2). 1999. write for info. (*0-613-06649-9*) Econo-Clad Bks.

Parish, Herman. Good Driving, Amelia Bedelia. LC 94-4112. (Amelia Bedelia Ser.). (Illus.). 40p. (J). (gr. 1-4). 1995. 15.00 (*0-688-13358-4*, Grenwillow Bks) HarpC Child Bks.

Parish, Herman. Good Driving, Amelia Bedelia. LC 94-4112. (Amelia Bedelia Ser.). (Illus.). 40p. (J). (gr. 1-4). 1995. 15.89 (*0-688-13359-2*, Grenwillow Bks) HarpC Child Bks.

Parish, Herman. Good Driving, Amelia Bedelia. (Amelia Bedelia Ser.). (Illus.). 48p. (J). (gr. k-2). 1996. mass mkt. 3.99 (*0-380-72510-X*, Avon Bks) Morrow Avon.

Parish, Herman. Good Driving, Amelia Bedelia. LC 94-4112. (Amelia Bedelia Ser.). (J). (gr. k-2). 1996. 9.19 (*0-606-09341-9*, Pub. by Turtleback) Demco.

***Parish, Herman S.** Amelia Bedelia 4 Mayor. LC 98-46158. (Amelia Bedelia Ser.). (Illus.). 48p. (J). (gr. 1-4). 1999. 14.95 (*0-688-16721-7*, Grenwillow Bks); lib. bdg. 14.89 (*0-688-16722-5*, Grenwillow Bks) HarpC Child Bks.

— Amelia Bedelia 4 Mayor. (Amelia Bedelia Ser.). (J). (gr. k-2). 2001. pap. write for info. (*0-380-73216-5*) Morrow Avon.

Parish, J. Gary, ed. see Mollison, David.

Parish, James R. Film Actors Guide: Western Europe. LC 77-22485. 621p. 1977. 47.50 (*0-8108-1044-1*) Scarecrow.

— Gays & Lesbians in Mainstream Cinema: Plots, Critiques, Casts & Credits for 272 Theatrical & Made-for-Television Hollywood Releases. LC 92-56678. (Illus.). 520p. 1993. lib. bdg. 65.00 (*0-89950-791-3*) McFarland & Co.

— Ghosts & Angels in Hollywood Films: Plots, Critiques, Casts & Credits for 264 Theatrical & Made-for-Television Releases. LC 93-41192. (Illus.). 431p. 1994. lib. bdg. 55.00 (*0-89950-676-3*) McFarland & Co.

— The Great Combat Pictures: Twentieth-Century Warfare on the Screen. LC 90-8457. (Illus.). 486p. 1990. 52.00 (*0-8108-2315-2*) Scarecrow.

— The Great Cop Pictures. LC 90-39259. (Illus.). 693p. 1990. 69.50 (*0-8108-2316-0*) Scarecrow.

— Pirates & Seafaring Swashbucklers on the Hollywood Screen: Plots, Critiques, Casts & Credits for 137 Theatrical & Made-for-Television Releases. LC 94-24197. 240p. 1995. lib. bdg. 43.50 (*0-89950-935-5*) McFarland & Co.

— Prison Pictures from Hollywood: Plots, Critiques, Casts & Credits for 293 Theatrical & Made-for-Television Releases. LC 90-53519. (Illus.). 544p. 1991. lib. bdg. 62.50 (*0-89950-563-5*) McFarland & Co.

— Prostitution in Hollywood Films: Plots, Critiques, Casts & Credits for 389 Theatrical & Made-for-Television Releases. LC 91-51213. (Illus.). 616p. 1992. lib. bdg. 65.00 (*0-89950-677-1*) McFarland & Co.

— Rosie: Rosie O'Donnell's Biography. LC 96-6561. (Illus.). 288p. 1997. 23.00 (*0-7867-0410-1*) Carroll & Graf.

— Today's Black Hollywood. LC 95-133256. 465p. 1995. mass mkt. 4.99 (*0-7860-0104-6*, Pinncle Kensgtn) Kensgtn Pub Corp.

— The Unofficial Murder, She Wrote Casebook. LC 97-204872. (Illus.). 384p. 1997. pap. 15.00 (*1-57566-210-8*, Knsington) Kensgtn Pub Corp.

— Whoopi Goldberg: Her Journey from Poverty to Mega-Stardom. LC 97-27808. (Illus.). 320p. 1997. 22.50 (*1-55972-431-5*, Birch Ln Pr) Carol Pub Group.

— Whoopi Goldberg: Her Journey from Poverty to Mega-Stardom. 400p. 1999. reprint ed. 37.95 (*0-7351-0078-0*) Replica Bks.

Parish, James R. & Hill, George H. Black Action Films: Plots, Critiques, Cast & Credits for 235 Theatrical & Made-for-TV Releases. LC 89-42871. (Illus.). 399p. 1989. lib. bdg. 55.00 (*0-89950-456-6*) McFarland & Co.

Parish, James R. & Pitts, Michael R. The Great Detective Pictures. LC 90-8551. (Illus.). 630p. 1990. 65.00 (*0-8108-2286-5*) Scarecrow.

— Great Gangster Pictures II. LC 86-28002. (Illus.). 407p. 1987. 45.00 (*0-8108-1961-9*) Scarecrow.

— The Great Hollywood Musical Pictures. LC 92-7483. (Illus.). 816p. 1992. 92.00 (*0-8108-2529-5*) Scarecrow.

— The Great Science Fiction Pictures II. 2nd ed. LC 89-24058. (Illus.). 499p. 1990. 52.00 (*0-8108-2247-4*) Scarecrow.

— The Great Spy Pictures II. LC 86-11900. (Illus.). 444p. 1986. 48.00 (*0-8108-1913-9*) Scarecrow.

— The Great Western Pictures. LC 76-28224. (Illus.). 477p. 1976. 49.50 (*0-8108-0980-X*) Scarecrow.

— The Great Western Pictures II. LC 88-6528. (Illus.). 438p. 1988. 52.00 (*0-8108-2106-0*) Scarecrow.

— Hollywood Songsters: A Biographical Dictionary. LC 90-41110. (Illus.). 840p. 1990. text 30.00 (*0-8240-3444-9*, H1164) Garland.

Parish, James R. & Stanke, Don E. The All-Americans. (Illus.). 1978. pap. 12.95 (*0-89508-011-7*) Rainbow Bks.

— Hollywood Baby Boomers: A Biographical Dictionary. LC 91-38768. (Illus.). 686p. 1992. text 25.00 (*0-8240-6104-7*, H1295) Garland.

Parish, James R. & Terrace, Vincent. The Complete Actors' Television Credits, 1948- 1988 Vol. 1: Actors. 2nd ed. LC 89-10607. (Illus.). 560p. 1989. 70.00 (*0-8108-2204-0*) Scarecrow.

— Complete Actors' Television Credits, 1948-1988 Vol. 2: Actresses. 2nd ed. LC 89-10607. (Illus.). 447p. 1990. 60.00 (*0-8108-2258-X*) Scarecrow.

Parish, James R., et al. Film Directors Guide: Western Europe. LC 76-1891. (Illus.). 300p. 1976. 34.50 (*0-8108-0908-7*) Scarecrow.

***Parish, James Robert.** Jason Biggs. (Illus.). 160p. 2000. mass mkt. 4.99 (*0-312-97622-4*, St Martins Paperbacks) St Martin.

Parish, James Robert. Rosie: The Rosie O'Donnell Story. (Illus.). 288p. 1998. pap. 11.95 (*0-7867-0542-6*) Carroll & Graf.

— Whoopi Goldberg: Her Journey from Poverty to Mega-Stardom. rev. ed. LC 99-38430. 1999. pap. text 15.95 (*0-8065-2142-2*) Carol Pub Group.

Parish, John C. Persistence of the Westward Movement & Other Essays. LC 68-14909. (Essay Index Reprint Ser.). 1977. 19.95 (*0-8369-0767-1*) Ayer.

Parish, Lawrence C., et al, eds. Cutaneous Infestations of Man & Animal. LC 82-18946. 392p. 1983. 79.50 (*0-275-91407-0*, C1407, Praeger Pubs) Greenwood.

— The Decubitus Ulcer in Clinical Practice, Vol. XII. LC 96-31691. (Illus.). 241p. 1997. 110.00 (*3-540-61526-1*) Spr-Verlag.

— Textbook of Pediatric Dermatology. (Illus.). 880p. 1989. text 255.00 (*0-8089-1863-X*, 793249, Grune & Strat) Harcrt Hlth Sci Grp.

Parish, Lawrence C. & Millikan, Larry E., eds. Global Dermatology: Diagnosis & Management According to Geography, Climate, & Culture. LC 93-26905. 1994. 199.00 (*0-387-94140-1*) Spr-Verlag.

Parish, Lawrence C., et al. Color Atlas of Cutaneous Infections. (Illus.). 200p. 1995. 99.95 (*0-86542-435-7*) Blackwell Sci.

— Color Atlas of Difficult Diagnoses in Dermatology. LC 92-1573. (Illus.). 184p. 1993. 135.00 (*0-89640-226-6*) Igaku-Shoin.

Parish, Lawrence C., jt. auth. see Crissey, John T.

Parish, Lawrence C., jt. ed. see Gashnait, F.

***Parish, Lawrence Charles & Brenner, Sara, eds.** Women's Dermatology: From Infancy to Maturity. (Illus.). 600p. 2000. 98.00 (*1-85070-086-9*) Prthnon Pub.

***Parish, N.** Christians Can Possess Demons but Cannot Be Possessed. 1999. pap. 5.95 (*0-89228-140-5*) Impact Christian.

Parish of St. Mary Labeth Staff, jt. auth. see London County Council Staff.

Parish of St. Mary Labeth Staff, jt. auth. see Louisiana Historical Society Staff.

Parish, Pat, jt. auth. see Pierce, Jan.

***Parish, Peggy.** Amelia Bedelia. (I Can Read Bks.). (J). (gr. 1-3). 1999. write for info. (*0-88103-916-0*); write for info. (*0-613-09959-1*) Econo-Clad Bks.

Parish, Peggy. Amelia Bedelia, 5 bks. (Illus.). (J). (gr. k-3). 1988. pap. 17.50 (*0-06-444123-7*, HarpTrophy) HarpC Child Bks.

— Amelia Bedelia. LC 91-10163. (I Can Read Bks.). (Illus.). 64p. (J). (ps-3). 1992. 15.95 (*0-06-020186-X*); pap. 3.95 (*0-06-444155-5*, HarpTrophy); lib. bdg. 15.89 (*0-06-020187-8*) HarpC Child Bks.

— Amelia Bedelia. Canetti, Yanitzia, tr. LC 95-23469. (I Can Read Bks.). (SPA., Illus.). 64p. (J). (gr. 1-3). 1996. 15.95 (*0-06-026247-8*, HpArco Iris); pap. 4.95 (*0-06-444200-4*, HpArco Iris) HarpC Child Bks.

***Parish, Peggy.** Amelia Bedelia. LC 98-31782. (I Can Read Bks.). (Illus.). 64p. (J). (ps-3). 1999. 12.95 (*0-694-01296-3*) HarpC Child Bks.

Parish, Peggy. Amelia Bedelia. LC 91-10163. (I Can Read Bks.). (Illus.). 64p. (J). (ps-3). 1993. 8.95 incl. audio (*1-55994-782-9*) HarperAudio.

***Parish, Peggy.** Amelia Bedelia. (J). (gr. 1-3). 1999. 9.95 (*1-56137-023-1*) Novel Units.

Parish, Peggy. Amelia Bedelia. (I Can Read Bks.). (J). (gr. 1-3). 1963. 8.95 (*0-606-01041-6*, Pub. by Turtleback) Demco.

— Amelia Bedelia. (I Can Read Bks.). (J). (gr. 1-3). 1996. 10.15 (*0-606-10377-5*, Pub. by Turtleback) Demco.

Parish, Peggy. Amelia Bedelia & Baby. LC 80-22263. (Amelia Bedelia Ser.). (Illus.). 64p. (J). (gr. 1-4). 1981. lib. bdg. 15.89 (*0-688-00321-4*, Grenwillow Bks) HarpC Child Bks.

— Amelia Bedelia & the Baby. (Amelia Bedelia Ser.). (J). (gr. k-2). 1999. write for info. (*0-88103-914-4*) Econo-Clad Bks.

Parish, Peggy. Amelia Bedelia & the Baby. LC 80-22263. (Amelia Bedelia Ser.). (Illus.). 64p. (J). (gr. 1-4). 1981. 16.00 (*0-688-00316-8*, Grenwillow Bks) HarpC Child Bks.

— Amelia Bedelia & the Baby. (Amelia Bedelia Ser.). (Illus.). 64p. (J). (gr. k-2). 1982. pap. 3.99 (*0-380-57067-X*, Avon Bks) Morrow Avon.

— Amelia Bedelia & the Baby. LC 80-22263. (Amelia Bedelia Ser.). (Illus.). 64p. (J). (gr. k-3). 1996. pap. 3.99 (*0-380-72795-1*, Avon Bks) Morrow Avon.

Parish, Peggy. Amelia Bedelia & the Baby. (Amelia Bedelia Ser.). (J). (gr. k-2). 1996. 9.19 (*0-606-00368-1*, Pub. by Turtleback) Demco.

— Amelia Bedelia & the Surprise Shower. (I Can Read Bks.). (J). (gr. 1-3). 1999. write for info. (*0-88103-911-X*) Econo-Clad Bks.

Parish, Peggy. Amelia Bedelia & the Surprise Shower. LC 66-18655. (I Can Read Bks.). (Illus.). 64p. (J). (ps-3). 1966. 15.95 (*0-06-024642-1*); lib. bdg. 15.89 (*0-06-024643-X*) HarpC Child Bks.

— Amelia Bedelia & the Surprise Shower. LC 93-24263. (I Can Read Bks.). (Illus.). 64p. (J). (gr. 1-3). 1979. pap. 3.95 (*0-06-444019-2*, HarpTrophy) HarpC Child Bks.

Parish, Peggy. Amelia Bedelia & the Surprise Shower. (I Can Read Bks.). (J). (gr. 1-3). 1994. 8.70 (*0-606-02009-8*, Pub. by Turtleback) Demco.

Parish, Peggy. Amelia Bedelia & the Surprise Shower. unabridged ed. (I Can Read Bks.). (Illus.). 64p. (J). (gr. 1-3). 1990. pap. 8.95 incl. audio (*1-55994-216-9*, Caedmon) HarperAudio.

— Amelia Bedelia Goes Camping. LC 84-7979. (Amelia Bedelia Ser.). (Illus.). 56p. (J). (gr. 1-4). 1985. 16.00 (*0-688-04057-8*, Grenwillow Bks) HarpC Child Bks.

Parish, Peggy. Amelia Bedelia Goes Camping. LC 84-7979. (Amelia Bedelia Ser.). (Illus.). 56p. (J). (gr. 1-4). 1985. lib. bdg. 15.89 (*0-688-04058-6*, Grenwillow Bks) HarpC Child Bks.

Parish, Peggy. Amelia Bedelia Goes Camping. (Amelia Bedelia Ser.). (Illus.). 48p. (J). (gr. k-3). 1986. pap. 3.99 (*0-380-70067-0*, Avon Bks) Morrow Avon.

— Amelia Bedelia Goes Camping. (Amelia Bedelia Ser.). (Illus.). 60p. (J). (gr. k-2). 1997. mass mkt. 3.99 (*0-380-72917-2*, Avon Bks) Morrow Avon.

Parish, Peggy. Amelia Bedelia Goes Camping. (Amelia Bedelia Ser.). (J). (gr. k-2). 1985. 9.19 (*0-606-01980-4*, Pub. by Turtleback) Demco.

— Amelia Bedelia Helps Out. (Amelia Bedelia Ser.). (J). (gr. k-2). 1999. write for info. (*0-88103-917-9*) Econo-Clad Bks.

Parish, Peggy. Amelia Bedelia Helps Out. LC 79-11729. (Amelia Bedelia Ser.). (Illus.). 64p. (J). (gr. 1-4). 1979. 16.00 (*0-688-80231-1*, Grenwillow Bks) HarpC Child Bks.

Parish, Peggy. Amelia Bedelia Helps Out. LC 79-11729. (Amelia Bedelia Ser.: Vol. 1). (Illus.). 64p. (J). (gr. 1-4). 1979. 15.93 (*0-688-84231-3*, Grenwillow Bks) HarpC Child Bks.

Parish, Peggy. Amelia Bedelia Helps Out. (Amelia Bedelia Ser.). (Illus.). 64p. (J). (gr. k-2). 1981. pap. 3.99 (*0-380-53405-3*, Avon Bks) Morrow Avon.

— Amelia Bedelia Helps Out. LC 79-11729. (Amelia Bedelia Ser.). (Illus.). 64p. (J). (gr. k-3). 1997. mass mkt. 3.99 (*0-380-72796-X*, Avon Bks) Morrow Avon.

Parish, Peggy. Amelia Bedelia Helps Out. (Amelia Bedelia Ser.). (J). (gr. k-2). 1997. 9.19 (*0-606-02010-1*, Pub. by Turtleback) Demco.

Parish, Peggy. Amelia Bedelia's Family Album. (Amelia Bedelia Ser.). 48p. (J). (gr. k-2). 1989. mass mkt. 3.99 (*0-380-70760-8*, Avon Bks) Morrow Avon.

— Amelia Bedelia's Family Album. (Amelia Bedelia Ser.). (Illus.). 48p. (J). (gr. k-2). 1991. pap. 3.99 (*0-380-71698-4*, Avon Bks) Morrow Avon.

— Amelia Bedelia's Family Album. (Amelia Bedelia Ser.). (J). (gr. k-2). 1997. mass mkt. 3.99 (*0-380-72860-5*, Avon Bks) Morrow Avon.

Parish, Peggy. Amelia Bedelia's Family Album. (Amelia Bedelia Ser.). (J). (gr. k-2). 1988. 9.19 (*0-606-04154-0*, Pub. by Turtleback) Demco.

Parish, Peggy. Be Ready at Eight. LC 87-1040. (Ready-to-Read Ser.: Level 2). (Illus.). 64p. (J). (gr. k-4). 1996. pap. 3.99 (*0-689-80791-0*) S&S Bks Yung.

— Be Ready at Eight. (Ready-to-Read Ser.). (Illus.). 64p. (J). (gr. k-4). 1996. mass mkt. 14.00 (*0-689-80792-9*) S&S Childrens.

Parish, Peggy. Be Ready at Eight. (Ready-to-Read Ser.). 1996. 9.19 (*0-606-09059-2*, Pub. by Turtleback) Demco.

Parish, Peggy. The Cats' Burglar. LC 82-11751. (Greenwillow Read-Alone Bks.). (Illus.). 64p. (J). (gr. 1-3). 1983. lib. bdg. 15.93 (*0-688-01826-2*, Grenwillow Bks) HarpC Child Bks.

— The Cats' Burglar. (J). 1998. 9.19 (*0-606-13258-9*, Pub. by Turtleback) Demco.

— The Cats' Burglar. LC 82-11751. (Illus.). 64p. (J). (gr. k-3). 1998. reprint ed. mass mkt. 3.99 (*0-380-72973-3*, Avon Bks) Morrow Avon.

— Clues in the Woods. 160p. (J). (gr. k-6). 1980. pap. 3.99 (*0-440-41461-X*, YB BDD) BDD Bks Young Read.

Parish, Peggy. Clues in the Woods. (J). 1968. 9.09 (*0-606-02328-3*, Pub. by Turtleback) Demco.

— Come Back, Amelia Bedelia. (I Can Read Bks.). (J). (gr. 1-3). 1999. write for info. (*0-88103-918-7*) Econo-Clad Bks.

Parish, Peggy. Come Back, Amelia Bedelia. (I Can Read Bks.). (Illus.). 64p. (J). (gr. 1-3). 1995. pap. 3.95 (*0-06-444204-7*, HarpTrophy) HarpC Child Bks.

— Come Back, Amelia Bedelia. (I Can Read Bks.). (Illus.). 64p. (J). (gr. 1-3). 1995. lib. bdg. 15.89 (*0-06-026691-0*) HarpC Child Bks.

— Come Back, Amelia Bedelia. (I Can Read Bks.). (J). (gr. 1-3). 1995. 8.95 (*0-606-02068-3*, Pub. by Turtleback) Demco.

— Come Back, Amelia Bedelia. unabridged ed. LC 94-29904. (I Can Read Bks.). (Illus.). 64p. (J). (ps-3). 1990. pap. 8.95 incl. audio (*1-55994-225-8*, Caedmon) HarperAudio.

— Come Back, Amelia Bedelia. 2nd ed. (I Can Read Bks.). (Illus.). 64p. (J). (gr. 1-3). 1995. 15.95 (*0-06-026688-0*) HarpC Child Bks.

— Dinosaur Time. (I Can Read Bks.). (Illus.). 32p. (J). (ps-1). 1974. 14.95 (*0-06-024653-7*); lib. bdg. 15.89 (*0-06-024654-5*) HarpC Child Bks.

— Dinosaur Time. (I Can Read Bks.). (Illus.). 32p. (J). (ps-1). 1983. pap. 3.95 (*0-06-444037-0*, HarpTrophy) HarpC Child Bks.

Parish, Peggy. Dinosaur Time. (I Can Read Bks.). (J). (ps-1). 1983. 8.95 (*0-606-03201-0*, Pub. by Turtleback) Demco.

Parish, Peggy. Family Album Amelia Bedelia. LC 87-15641. (Amelia Bedelia Ser.). (Illus.). 48p. (J). (gr. 1-4). 1988. 15.95 (*0-688-07676-9*, Grenwillow Bks) HarpC Child Bks.

Parish, Peggy. Family Album Amelia Bedelia. LC 87-15641. (Amelia Bedelia Ser.). (Illus.). 48p. (J). (gr. 1 up). 1988. 15.89 (*0-688-07677-7*, Grenwillow Bks) HarpC Child Bks.

Parish, Peggy. Good Hunting, Blue Sky. (I Can Read Bks.). (Illus.). 64p. (J). (gr. 1-3). 1988. 14.00 (*0-06-024661-8*) HarpC Child Bks.

— Good Hunting, Blue Sky. LC 84-43143. (I Can Read Bks.). (Illus.). 32p. (J). (ps-3). 1988. lib. bdg. 15.89 (*0-06-024662-6*) HarpC Child Bks.

— Good Hunting, Blue Sky. LC 84-43143. (I Can Read Bks.). (Illus.). 64p. (J). (ps-3). 1991. pap. 3.95 (*0-06-444148-2*, HarpTrophy) HarpC Child Bks.

***Parish, Peggy.** Good Work, Amelia Bedelia. (Amelia Bedelia Ser.). (J). (gr. k-2). 1999. write for info. (*0-88103-915-2*) Econo-Clad Bks.

Parish, Peggy. Good Work, Amelia Bedelia. LC 75-20360. (Amelia Bedelia Ser.: Vol. 1). (Illus.). 56p. (J). (gr. 1-4). 1976. 15.95 (*0-688-80022-X*, Grenwillow Bks) HarpC Child Bks.

Parish, Peggy. Good Work, Amelia Bedelia. LC 75-20360. (Amelia Bedelia Ser.: Vol. 1). (Illus.). 56p. (J). (gr. 1-4). 1976. 15.93 (*0-688-84022-1*, Grenwillow Bks) HarpC Child Bks.

Parish, Peggy. Good Work, Amelia Bedelia. (Amelia Bedelia Ser.). (Illus.). 164p. (J). (gr. k-2). 1980. pap. 3.99 (*0-380-49171-0*, Avon Bks) Morrow Avon.

— Good Work, Amelia Bedelia. (Amelia Bedelia Ser.). (Illus.). 52p. (J). (gr. k-2). 1996. mass mkt. 3.99 (*0-380-72831-1*, Avon Bks) Morrow Avon.

Parish, Peggy. Good Work, Amelia Bedelia. (Amelia Bedelia Ser.). (J). (gr. k-2). 1996. 9.19 (*0-606-02124-8*, Pub. by Turtleback) Demco.

Parish, Peggy. Granny & the Desperadoes. LC 96-163144. (Ready-to-Read Ser.: Level 2). (Illus.). 40p. (J). (gr. k-4). 1996. pap. 3.99 (*0-689-80877-1*) Aladdin.

— Granny & the Desperadoes. LC 74-117959. (Ready-to-Read Ser.: Level 2). (Illus.). 40p. (J). (gr. k-4). 1996. mass mkt. 14.00 (*0-689-80878-X*) S&S Bks Yung.

— Granny & the Desperadoes. LC 74-117959. (Ready-to-Read Ser.). (J). 1996. 9.19 (*0-606-09351-6*, Pub. by Turtleback) Demco.

— Haunted House. 160p. (J). (gr. k-6). 1981. pap. 3.99 (*0-440-43459-9*, YB BDD) BDD Bks Young Read.

— Haunted House. (J). (gr. 4-6). 1991. 18.50 (*0-8446-6391-3*) Peter Smith.

— Haunted House. (J). 1971. 9.09 (*0-606-02272-4*, Pub. by Turtleback) Demco.

— Key to the Treasure. 160p. (J). (gr. k-6). 1980. pap. 4.50 (*0-440-44438-1*, YB BDD) BDD Bks Young Read.

Parish, Peggy. Key to the Treasure. 154p. pap. 4.50 (*0-8072-1398-5*) Listening Lib.

Parish, Peggy. Key to the Treasure. (J). 1966. 9.09 (*0-606-02349-6*, Pub. by Turtleback) Demco.

***Parish, Peggy.** Merry Christmas, Amelia Bedelia. (Amelia Bedelia Ser.). (J). (gr. k-2). 1999. write for info. (*0-8335-0739-7*) Econo-Clad Bks.

— Merry Christmas, Amelia Bedelia. LC 85-24919. (Amelia Bedelia Ser.: Vol. 1). (Illus.). 64p. (J). (gr. 1-4). 1986. 15.89 (*0-688-06102-8*, Grenwillow Bks) HarpC Child Bks.

Parish, Peggy. Merry Christmas, Amelia Bedelia. LC 85-24919. (Amelia Bedelia Ser.). (J). (gr. 5-7). 1996. mass mkt. 3.99 (*0-380-72797-8*, Avon Bks) Morrow Avon.

Parish, Peggy. Merry Christmas, Amelia Bedelia. (Amelia Bedelia Ser.). (J). (gr. k-2). 1996. 9.19 (*0-606-03615-6*, Pub. by Turtleback) Demco.

Parish, Peggy. Merry Christmas, Amelia Bedelia. (Amelia Bedelia Ser.). (Illus.). 64p. (J). (gr. k-2). 1987. reprint ed. pap. 3.99 (*0-380-70325-4*, Avon Bks) Morrow Avon.

Parish, Peggy. Mind Your Manners! LC 93-11732. 1994. 10.15 (*0-606-06572-5*, Pub. by Turtleback) Demco.

Parish, Peggy. Mind Your Manners. LC 93-11732. (Illus.). 56p. (J). (gr. 1-4). 1994. reprint ed. mass mkt. 5.95 (*0-688-13109-3*, Wm Morrow) Morrow Avon.

— No More Monsters for Me! LC 81-47111. (I Can Read Bks.). (Illus.). 64p. (J). (gr. k-3). 1981. lib. bdg. 15.89 (*0-06-024658-8*) HarpC Child Bks.

— No More Monsters for Me! (I Can Read Bks.). (Illus.). 64p. (J). (ps-1). 1981. 14.00 (*0-06-024657-X*) HarpC Child Bks.

P

— No More Monsters for Me! LC 81-47111. (I Can Read Bks.). (Illus.). 64p. (J). (ps-3). 1987. pap. 3.95 (*0-06-444109-1*, HarpTrophy) HarpC Child Bks.

Parish, Peggy. No More Monsters for Me! (I Can Read Bks.). (J). (ps-1). 1987. 8.95 (*0-606-03049-2*, Pub. by Turtleback) Demco.

— No More Monsters for Me! abr. ed. LC 81-47111. (I Can Read Bks.). 64p. (J). (ps-3). 1991. audio 8.95 (*1-55994-353-X*, TBC 353X) HarperAudio.

— Play Ball, Amelia Bedelia. (I Can Read Bks.). (J). (gr. 1-3). 1999. write for info. (*0-88103-913-6*) Econo-Clad Bks.

Parish, Peggy. Play Ball, Amelia Bedelia. LC PZ7.P219Pl 1996. (I Can Read Bks.). (Illus.). 64p. (J). (gr. 1-3). 1972. 14.95 (*0-06-024655-3*); lib. bdg. 14.89 (*0-06-024656-1*) HarpC Child Bks.

— Play Ball, Amelia Bedelia. (I Can Read Bks.). (Illus.). 64p. (J). (gr. 1-3). 1986. pap. 2.50 (*0-590-06203-4*) Scholastic Inc.

Parish, Peggy. Play Ball, Amelia Bedelia. (I Can Read Bks.). (J). (gr. 1-3). 1978. 8.70 (*0-606-01549-3*, Pub. by Turtleback) Demco.

Parish, Peggy. Play Ball, Amelia Bedelia. rev. ed. (I Can Read Bks.). (Illus.). 64p. (J). (gr. 1-3). 1995. pap. 3.95 (*0-06-444205-5*, HarpTrophy) HarpC Child Bks.

— Play Ball, Amelia Bedelia. rev. ed. (I Can Read Bks.). (Illus.). 64p. (J). (gr. 1-3). 1996. lib. bdg. 15.89 (*0-06-026701-1*) HarpC Child Bks.

— Play Ball, Amelia Bedelia. rev. ed. LC 94-27141. (I Can Read Bks.). (Illus.). 64p. (J). (ps-3). 1996. 15.95 (*0-06-026700-3*) HarpC Child Bks.

— Play Ball, Amelia Bedelia. unabridged ed. LC 71-85028. (I Can Read Bks.). (Illus.). 64p. (J). (ps-3). 1990. pap. 8.95 incl. audio (*1-55994-241-X*) HarperAudio.

— Scruffy. LC 87-45564. (I Can Read Bks.). (Illus.). 64p. (J). (gr. k-3). 1988. lib. bdg. 15.89 (*0-06-024660-X*) HarpC Child Bks.

— Scruffy. (I Can Read Bks.). (Illus.). 64p. (J). (gr. 1-3). 1988. 14.00 (*0-06-024659-6*) HarpC Child Bks.

— Scruffy. LC 87-45564. (I Can Read Bks.). (Illus.). 64p. (J). (ps-3). 1990. pap. 3.95 (*0-06-444137-7*, HarpTrophy) HarpC Child Bks.

Parish, Peggy. Scruffy. (I Can Read Bks.). (J). (gr. 1-3). 1988. 8.95 (*0-606-02344-5*, Pub. by Turtleback) Demco.

— Teach Us, Amelia Bedelia. (Amelia Bedelia Ser.). (J). (gr. k-2). 1999. write for info. (*0-88103-912-8*) Econo-Clad Bks.

Parish, Peggy. Teach Us, Amelia Bedelia. LC 76-22663. (Amelia Bedelia Ser.: Vol. 1). (Illus.). 56p. (J). (gr. 1-4). 1977. 16.00 (*0-688-80069-6*, Grenwillow Bks) HarpC Child Bks.

Parish, Peggy. Teach Us, Amelia Bedelia. LC 76-22663. (Amelia Bedelia Ser.: Vol. 1). (Illus.). 56p. (J). (gr. 1-4). 1977. lib. bdg. 15.89 (*0-688-84069-8*, Grenwillow Bks) HarpC Child Bks.

Parish, Peggy. Teach Us, Amelia Bedelia. (Hello Reader! Ser.). (Illus.). 64p. (J). (gr. k-2). 1987. pap. 2.95 (*0-590-43345-8*) Scholastic Inc.

— Teach Us, Amelia Bedelia. LC 00-3633. (Hello Reader! Ser.). (Illus.). 56p. (J). (gr. 2-3). 1995. pap. 3.99 (*0-590-53773-3*, Cartwheel) Scholastic Inc.

Parish, Peggy. Teach Us, Amelia Bedelia. (Hello, Reader! Ser.). (J). (gr. k-2). 1977. 9.19 (*0-606-08272-7*, Pub. by Turtleback) Demco.

— Thank You, Amelia Bedelia. (I Can Read Bks.). (J). (gr. 1-3). 1999. write for info. (*0-88103-910-1*) Econo-Clad Bks.

Parish, Peggy. Thank You, Amelia Bedelia. (I Can Read Bks.). (Illus.). 64p. (J). (gr. 1-3). 1993. pap. 3.95 (*0-06-444171-7*, HarpTrophy) HarpC Child Bks.

— Thank You, Amelia Bedelia. LC 92-5746. (I Can Read Bks.). (Illus.). 64p. (J). (ps-3). 1993. 15.95 (*0-06-022979-9*); lib. bdg. 15.89 (*0-06-022980-2*) HarpC Child Bks.

Parish, Peggy. Thank You, Amelia Bedelia. (I Can Read Bks.). (J). (gr. 1-3). 1993. 8.95 (*0-606-06053-7*, Pub. by Turtleback) Demco.

Parish, Peggy. Thank You, Amelia Bedelia. unabridged ed. LC 92-5746. (I Can Read Bks.). (Illus.). 64p. (J). (ps-3). 1995. pap. 8.95 incl. audio (*0-694-70002-9*) HarperAudio.

— Too Many Rabbits. 48p. (J). (ps-3). 1992. pap. 3.99 (*0-440-40591-2*) Dell.

— Too Many Rabbits. 1974. 9.19 (*0-606-00954-X*, Pub. by Turtleback) Demco.

***Parish, Peggy & Brookes, Diane.** Amelia Bedelia & the Surprise Shower Novel Study. 1998. pap. text, teacher ed. 7.95 (*0-9683234-4-8*) RRP.

Parish, Peggy & Lobel, Arnold. Dinosaur Time. (I Can Read Bks.). 32p. (J). (ps-1). 1990. pap. 8.95 incl. audio (*1-55994-262-2*) HarperAudio.

Parish, Penny E., jt. auth. see Grattarola, Gina C.

Parish, Peter J. The American Civil War. LC 74-84660. 728p. 1975. reprint ed. 55.00 (*0-8419-0176-7*) Holmes & Meier.

Parish, Peter J. Slavery. LC 88-45541. 208p. 1990. pap. 22.00 (*0-06-430182-6*, Icon Edns) HarpC.

Parish, Peter J., ed. Reader's Guide to American History. LC 98-101338. 880p. 1997. lib. bdg. 135.00 (*1-884964-22-2*) Fitzroy Dearborn.

Parish, R., ed. Racine: Phedre. (French Texts Ser.). (FRE.). 144p. 1996. pap. 18.95 (*1-85399-459-6*, Pub. by Brist Class Pr) Focus Pub-R Pullins.

Parish, Richard. Pascal's Lettres Provinciales: A Study in Polemic. (Illus.). 224p. 1989. text 55.00 (*0-19-815155-1*) OUP.

Parish, Rick. Art Gecko & the Chromatones: The Journey Begins. LC 98-93320. (Illus.). 32p. (J). (gr. k-12). 1998. pap. 17.95 (*0-9665260-0-7*) Blk Diamond Prod.

Parish, Robert. Alaska Where Only the Tough Survive. (Illus.). 1987. 6.95 (*0-9607358-7-9*) Fathom Pub.

***Parish, Roberta, et al.** Plants of Southern Interior British Columbia & the Inland Northwest. Orig. Title: Plants of Southern Interior British Columbia. (Illus.). 454p. 1999. pap. 19.95 (*1-55105-219-9*) Lone Pine.

Parish, Roberta, jt. auth. see Coupe, Ray.

Parish, Roger, tr. see Neruda, Pablo.

Parish, Ruth A. Your Baby's First Year: Spiritual Reflections on Infant Development. LC 96-50943. 172p. 1997. pap. 11.99 (*0-87788-560-5*, H Shaw Pubs) Waterbrook Pr.

Parish, Ruth Ann. Your Child's Toddler Years: Spiritual Reflections on Development Months 13-36. LC 99-35178. 172p. 1999. pap. 11.99 (*0-87788-924-4*, H Shaw Pubs) Waterbrook Pr.

Parish, Scott. BOCA Code Manual: A Compliance Guide for Architects, Builders, & Design Professionals. LC 98-4861. 352p. 1998. 64.95 incl. cd-rom (*0-07-048613-1*) McGraw-Hill Prof.

— Uniform Building Code Compliance Manual : 1997 Uniform Building Code. LC 98-20269. 352p. 1998. 64.95 (*0-07-048615-1*) McGraw.

Parish, Scott B. Southern Building Code Conference: International Compliance Manual. 352p. 1999. 64.95 incl. cd-rom (*0-07-048614-X*, 639785308751) McGraw.

Parish, Steven M. Hierachy & Its Discontents: Culture & the Politics of Consciousness in Caste Society. 1977. pap. 96.00 (*0-7855-7415-8*, Pub. by Ratna Pustak Bhandar) St Mut.

— Hierarchy & Its Discontents: Culture & the Politics of Consciousness in Caste Society. (Illus.). 264p. 1996. text 39.95 (*0-8122-3313-1*); pap. text 17.95 (*0-8122-1551-6*) U of Pa Pr.

— Moral Knowing in a Hindu Sacred City: An Exploration of Mind, Emotion, & Self. LC 94-366. 1994. pap. 22.00 (*0-231-08439-0*) Col U Pr.

— Moral Knowing in a Hindu Sacred City: An Exploration of Mind, Emotion, & Self. LC 94-366. 1994. 57.50 (*0-231-08438-2*) Col U Pr.

Parish, Tanya & Stoker, Neil G. Mycobacteria Protocols. LC 98-22177. (Methods in Molecular Biology Ser.: Vol. 101). (Illus.). 488p. 1998. 89.50 (*0-89603-471-2*) Humana.

Parish, Theodore A., et al. Safety Issues Associated with Plutonium Involvement in the Nuclear Fuel Cycle. LC 99-10169. 23p. 1999. write for info. (*0-7923-5592-X*) Kluwer Academic.

Parish, W. Alton & Kindsfather, William. Essentials of Business Mathematics. 4th ed. 368p. (C). 1988. pap. text 32.95 (*0-89863-120-3*) Star Pub CA.

Parish, W. D. & Shaw, W. F. A Dictionary of the Kentish Dialect & Provicialisms in Use in the County of Kent. (English Dialect Society Publications: No. 54). 1972. reprint ed. pap. 25.00 (*0-8115-0476-X*) Periodicals Srv.

Parish, William J. Charles Ilfeld Company: A Study in the Rise & Decline of Mercantile Capitalism in New Mexico. LC 61-9687. (Studies in Business History: No. 20). (Illus.). 452p. 1961. 29.95 (*0-674-11075-7*) HUP.

Parish, William L. Chinese Rural Development: The Great Transformation. LC 84-22193. 286p. (gr. 13). 1985. pap. text 42.95 (*0-87332-344-0*, East Gate Bk) M E Sharpe.

Parish, William L., ed. Chinese Rural Development: The Great Transformation. LC 84-22193. (East Gate Bks.). (Illus.). 286p. 1985. reprint ed. pap. 88.70 (*0-7837-9990-X*, 206071700006) Bks Demand.

Parish, William L. & Whyte, Martin K. Village & Family in Contemporary China. LC 78-3411. (Illus.). 1978. lib. bdg. 30.00 (*0-226-64590-8*) U Ch Pr.

— Village & Family in Contemporary China. LC 78-3411. (Illus.). 440p. 1980. pap. text 19.50 (*0-226-64591-6*, P899) U Ch Pr.

Parish, William L., jt. auth. see Tang, Wenfang.

Parish, William L., jt. auth. see Whyte, Martin K.

Parisher, Roy A. & Rhea, Robert A. Pipe Drafting & Design: Using Manual, AutoCAD, & PRO-PIPE Applications. LC 95-13984. (Illus.). 288p. 1996. text 39.95 (*0-88415-657-5*, 5657) Gulf Pub.

— Pipe Drafting & Design: Using Manual, AutoCAD, & PRO-PIPE Applications. (Illus.). 56p. 1996. pap. text, teacher ed. 20.00 (*0-88415-659-1*, 5659); pap. text, wbk. ed. 16.00 (*0-88415-658-3*, 5658) Gulf Pub.

Parisi. Civilization & Its Discontents. LC 98-47742. 1999. write for info. (*0-8057-7934-5*, Twyne); per. write for info. (*0-8057-7933-7*, Twyne) Mac Lib Ref.

Parisi, Barbara & Pasternack, Barbara. Empowerment Through Communication. 336p. (C). 1996. pap., per. 29.95 (*0-7872-1295-4*) Kendall-Hunt.

***Parisi, Barbara & Singer, Robert.** The History of Brooklyn's Three Major Performing Arts Institutions. (Illus.). 2000. write for info. (*0-8108-3765-X*) Scarecrow.

Parisi, Dan. The Legend of Doll Fin. LC 96-95274. (Illus.). 32p. (Orig.). (J). (ps-3). 1997. pap. 5.95 (*0-9655066-0-6*, 1) A&D Publishing.

Parisi, Francesco. Liability for Negligence & Judicial Discretion. 2nd ed. LC 92-13434. (Research Ser.: No. 82). 1992. pap. text 18.50 (*0-87725-702-7*) U of Cal IAS.

Parisi, Francesco, jt. ed. see Posner, Richard A.

Parisi, Giorgio. Field Theory, Disorder & Simulations. 512p. 1993. text 86.00 (*981-02-0964-9*) World Scientific Pub.

— Field Theory, Disorder & Stimulations. (Lecture Notes in Physics Ser.). 512p. 1993. pap. text 46.00 (*981-02-1356-5*) World Scientific Pub.

— Statistical Field Theory. (Frontiers in Physics Ser.: No. 66). 608p. (C). 1988. 54.95 (*0-201-05985-1*) Addison-Wesley.

— Statistical Field Theory. (C). 1988. text 48.50 (*0-317-69757-9*) Addison-Wesley.

— Statistical Field Theory. LC 98-88187. (Advanced Book Classics Ser.). 368p. 1998. pap. text 35.00 (*0-7382-0051-4*) Perseus Pubng.

Parisi, Helen. Introduction to Telecommunications. Doyle, Maureen et al, eds. (Illus.). 196p. (Orig.). (C). 1990. reprint ed. pap. 32.00 (*0-9625818-0-1*, 103-1) A G Comns Systs.

— Telecommunications Applications: An Introduction to Designing Solutions to Meet Telecommunication Needs. Doyle, Maureen et al, eds. (Illus.). 182p. (Orig.). (C). 1989. pap. text 32.00 (*0-9625818-1-X*, 105-1) A G Comns Systs.

***Parisi, Hope.** The Narrative Learner: Writing, Reading & Analysis for the New College Student. 152p. (C). 1999. per. 38.95 (*0-7872-6486-5*, 41648601) Kendall-Hunt.

Parisi, J., et al, eds. A Perspective Look at Nonlinear Media: From Physics to Biology & Social Sciences. (Lecture Notes in Physics). viii, 372p. 1998. 86.00 (*3-540-63995-0*) Spr-Verlag.

Parisi, J. Urgen, et al. Nonlinear Physics of Complex Systems: Current Status & Future Trends. LC 96-41822. (Lecture Notes in Physics Ser.: Vol. 476). xiii, 388p. 1996. 92.00 (*3-540-61734-5*) Spr-Verlag.

Parisi, J. Urgen, jt. ed. see Kapusta, F.

Parisi, Janie. I Broke for Pansies. (Illus.). 54p. 1997. 9.95 (*1-57377-017-5*) Easl Pubns.

Parisi, Joseph. Poets in Person: A Listener's Guide. 2nd ed. LC 99-208341. (Illus.). 1997. pap. 11.95 (*1-881505-08-1*) Modern Poetry.

Parisi, Joseph, ed. Marianne Moore: The Art of a Modernist. LC 89-20476. (Studies in Modern Literature: No. 109). 202p. (C). reprint ed. 62.70 (*0-8357-2031-4*, 207066500016) Bks Demand.

Parisi, Joseph, jt. ed. see Hine, Daryl.

Parisi, Laura. Granda. LC 96-2639. 144p. (Orig.). 1996. pap. 9.95 (*0-9642874-1-2*) Liebling Press.

Parisi, Lynn S. The World: Lands & Peoples: Copy Masters. (Illus.). 236p. 1992. 125.00 (*0-87746-361-1*) Graphic Learning.

Parisi, Lynn S., ed. Hot Rods: Storage of Spent Nuclear Fuel. 2nd ed. (Creative Role-Playing Exercises in Science & Technology Ser.). 60p. 1989. pap. 9.95 (*0-89994-343-8*) Soc Sci Ed.

Parisi, Lynn S., et al. Tokugawa Japan: The Great Peace & the Development of Urban Culture. (Humanities Approach to Japanese History Ser.). (Illus.). 146p. (Orig.). (YA). (gr. 9-12). 1995. pap. 37.95 (*0-89994-380-2*) Soc Sci Ed.

Parisi, Paula. Titanic & the Making of James Cameron: The Inside Story of the Three-Year Adventure That Rewrote Motion Picture History. LC 98-6445. 256p. 1998. 24.95 (*1-55704-364-7*, Pub. by Newmarket); pap. 14.95 (*1-55704-365-5*, Pub. by Newmarket) Norton.

Parisi-Presicce, F., ed. Recent Trends in Algebraic Development Techniques: Selected Papers of the 12th International Workshop, WADT '97, Tarquinia, Italy, June 3-7, 1997. LC 98-6358. (Lecture Notes in Computer Science: Vol. 1376). viii, 435p. 1998. pap. 67.00 (*3-540-64299-4*) Spr-Verlag.

Parisien. Current Techniques in Arthroscopy. 3rd ed. 139.95 (*0-86577-738-1*) Thieme Med Pubs.

Parisien, J. Serge. Current Techniques in Arthroscopy. (Illus.). 256p. 1994. text 149.95 (*1-878132-04-0*) Current Med.

— Techniques in Therapeutic Arthroscopy. 392p. 1993. text 160.00 (*0-7817-0054-X*) Lppncott W & W.

— Techniques in Therapeutic Arthroscopy. 392p. 1994. sl. 500.00 (*0-7817-0055-8*) Lppncott W & W.

Parisotto, G. Learning Portuguese Without a Teacher. 60p. 1991. write for info. incl. audio (*0-9629515-9-5*); pap. write for info. (*0-9629515-3-6*) Sunrising Pub.

Parissakis, George, ed. Science Policy & Research Management in the Balkan Countries: Proceedings of the NATO Advanced Research Workshop, Athens, Greece, November 23-25, 1994. (NATO ASI - Partnership Sub-Series 4). 248p. (C). 1995. lib. bdg. 161.50 (*0-7923-3599-6*) Kluwer Academic.

Parisse, Rita, jt. auth. see Joseph, Oreste.

Parisse, Rita, jt. auth. see Joseph, Oreste R.

Parisse, Rita, ed. see Joseph, Oreste.

Parisse, Rita, ed. see Joseph, Oreste R.

Parisse, Rita, ed. see Joseph, Oroste.

Parisse, Rita, ed. & tr. see Joseph, Oreste R.

Parissianos, George P. Chloramines: Index of New Information & Research Reference Book. 150p. 1996. 47.50 (*0-7883-1142-5*); pap. 44.50 (*0-7883-1143-3*) ABBE Pubs Assn.

Parissien, Steven. Adam Style. (Illus.). 240p. 1995. pap. 35.00 (*0-7148-3453-X*, Pub. by Phaidon Press) Phaidon Pr.

— Adam Style. (Illus.). 240p. 1997. 59.95 (*0-7148-2727-4*, Pub. by Phaidon Press) Phaidon Pr.

— Adam Style. (Illus.). 240p. 1992. 60.00 (*0-89133-197-2*) Wiley.

— The Georgian House in Britain & America. LC 95-1233. (Illus.). 240p. 1995. 60.00 (*0-8478-1911-6*, Pub. by Rizzoli Intl) St Martin.

***Parissien, Steven.** Palladian Style. (Illus.). 2000. pap. 29.95 (*0-7148-4026-2*) Phaidon Pr.

Parissien, Steven. Palladian Style. LC 95-128883. (Illus.). 240p. (C). 1994. text 55.00 (*0-7148-2921-8*, Pub. by Phaidon Press) Phaidon Pr.

— Pennsylvania Station: New York, 1905-10, McKim, Mead & White. (Architecture in Detail Ser.). 60p. (Orig.). 1996. pap. 29.95 (*0-7148-3466-1*, Pub. by Phaidon Press) Phaidon Pr.

— Regency Style. (Illus.). 240p. 1995. pap. 35.00 (*0-7148-3454-8*, Pub. by Phaidon Press) Phaidon Pr.

— Regency Style. (Illus.). 240p. 1992. 60.00 (*0-89133-172-7*) Wiley.

— Station to Station. (Illus.). 240p. 1997. 59.95 (*0-7148-3467-X*, Pub. by Phaidon Press) Phaidon Pr.

Paritsis, N. C. & Stewart, D. J. A Cybernetic Approach to Colour Perception, Vol.2. LC 81-1624. (Studies in Cybernetics: Vol. 2). (Illus.). xiv, 168p. 1983. text 82.00 (*0-677-05620-6*) Gordon & Breach.

Paritzky-Joshua, Karin, tr. see Hirsch, Sampson R.

Paritzky, Karen, tr. see Ehrmann, Naftali H.

Paritzky, Karen, tr. see Hirsch, Samson R.

Parium, Marmor. Chronicum Parium. Jacoby, F., ed. 219p. 1980. pap. 20.00 (*0-89005-362-6*) Ares.

Parivaraj, P. Shiva & Arun. 160p. 1998. pap. 12.95 (*0-85449-265-8*, Pub. by Gay Mens Pr) LPC InBook.

Parizeau, Alice & Szabo, Denis. Le Traitement de la Criminalite au Canada. LC 77-479632. (FRE.). 435p. reprint ed. pap. 134.90 (*0-7837-6948-2*, 204677700003) Bks Demand.

Parizeau, M. Vocabulaire - Mots de la Bioethique. (FRE.). 375p. 1993. 140.00 (*0-320-00667-0*) Fr & Eur.

Parizkova, Jana. Body Fat & Physical Fitness. Osancova, K., tr. from CZE. (Illus.). 280p. 1977. 193.00 (*90-247-1925-9*, Pub. by Kluwer Academic) Kluwer Academic.

— Nutrition, Physical Activity, & Health in Early Life: Studies in Preschool Children. LC 95-41134. (Nutrition in Exercise & Sport Ser.). 320p. 1996. boxed set 94.95 (*0-8493-7919-9*) CRC Pr.

Parizkova, Jana & Hills, Andrew, eds. Physical Fitness & Nutrition During Growth: Studies in Children & Youth in Different Environments. LC 98-25054. (Medicine & Sport Science Ser.: Vol. 43, 1998). (Illus.). viii, 1672p. 1998. 169.75 (*3-8055-6679-4*) S Karger.

Parizkova, Jane, jt. ed. see Shephard, Roy J.

Park. Complementary Notions: A Critical Study of Berkeley's Theory of Concepts. 174p. 1972. pap. text 65.00 (*90-247-1338-2*, Pub. by M Nijhoff) Kluwer Academic.

— Contemporary Engineering Economics A Canadian Perspective 2nd ed. 944p. 2000. text. write for info. (*0-201-61390-5*) Addison-Wesley.

— Environment: Principles & Applications. LC 97-208961. (Illus.). 640p. (C). 1997. 100.00 (*0-415-12199-X*) Routledge.

— Hand of Prophecy Reader's Guide. 1998. write for info. (*0-380-97257-3*, Avon Bks) Morrow Avon.

— Rethnk Security Post Cold. LC 97-39093. (C). 1998. pap. text 22.50 (*0-582-30376-1*, Pub. by Addison-Wesley) Longman.

Park, jt. auth. see Crull.

Park, Yoon-Soo & Ramaswamy, Ramu V., eds. Optoelectronic Integrated Circuits, Vol. 3006. LC 97-200943. 498p. 1997. 89.00 (*0-8194-2417-X*) SPIE.

***Park, Alice Crandall.** Park/e/s & Bunch on the Trail West. rev. fac. ed. LC 74-16831. 487p. 2000. 84.50 (*0-7404-0025-8*); pap. 74.50 (*0-7404-0026-6*) Higginson Bk Co.

Park, Andrew S. Racial Conflict & Healing: An Asian-American Theological Perspective. LC 97-100852. 176p. (Orig.). 1996. pap. 18.00 (*1-57075-078-5*) Orbis Bks.

— The Wounded Heart of God. 224p. (Orig.). 1993. pap. 17.95 (*0-687-38536-9*) Abingdon.

Park, Andy, jt. ed. see Roper, Charles S.

Park, Barbara. Almost Starring Skinnybones. (J). 1988. 9.09 (*0-606-04152-4*, Pub. by Turtleback) Demco.

Park, Barbara. Beanpole. 160p. (J). (gr. 5 up). 1984. pap. 2.95 (*0-380-69840-4*, Avon Bks) Morrow Avon.

— Buddies. (YA). (gr. 7 up). 1986. pap. 2.95 (*0-380-69992-3*, Avon Bks) Morrow Avon.

— Dear God, Help! Love, Earl. LC 92-20909. 108p. (J). (gr. 3-7). 1994. pap. 3.99 (*0-679-85395-2*, Pub. by Random Bks Yng Read) Random.

— Don't Make Me Smile. LC 81-4880. 128p. (J). (gr. 4-7). 1981. lib. bdg. 10.99 (*0-394-94978-1*) Knopf Bks Yng Read.

— Don't Make Me Smile. 132p. (J). (gr. 4-7). 1983. pap. 2.95 (*0-380-61994-6*, Avon Bks) Morrow Avon.

Park, Barbara. Don't Make Me Smile. 1981. 9.60 (*0-606-03233-9*, Pub. by Turtleback) Demco.

Park, Barbara. Don't Make Me Smile. LC 81-4880. 128p. (J). (gr. 3-7). 1990. reprint ed. pap. 4.50 (*0-394-84745-8*, Pub. by Random Bks Yng Read) Random.

***Park, Barbara.** The Graduation of Jake Moon. LC 99-87475. (Illus.). (J). 2000. 15.00 (*0-689-83912-X*) Atheneum Yung Read.

Park, Barbara. Junie B. Jones & a Little Monkey Business. LC 92-56706. (First Stepping Stone Bks.). (Illus.). 80p. (J). (gr. 1-4). 1993. pap. 3.99 (*0-679-83886-4*, Pub. by Random Bks Yng Read) Random.

— Junie B. Jones & a Little Monkey Business. LC 92-56706. (Junie B. Jones Ser.: No. 2). (Illus.). (J). (gr. 1-4). 1993. 9.19 (*0-606-09498-9*, Pub. by Turtleback) Demco.

— Junie B. Jones & Her Big Fat Mouth. LC 92-50957. (Junie B. Jones Ser.: No. 3). (Illus.). 80p. (J). (gr. 1-4). 1993. pap. 3.99 (*0-679-84407-4*, Pub. by Random Bks Yng Read) Random.

— Junie B. Jones & Her Big Fat Mouth. LC 92-50957. (First Stepping Stone Bks.). (Illus.). 80p. (J). (gr. 1-4). 1993. lib. bdg. 11.99 (*0-679-94407-9*, Pub. by Random Bks Yng Read) Random.

— Junie B. Jones & Her Big Fat Mouth. (Junie B. Jones Ser.: No. 3). (Illus.). (J). (gr. 1-3). 1993. 9.19 (*0-606-05896-6*, Pub. by Turtleback) Demco.

Park, Barbara. Junie B. Jones & Some Sneaky Peeky Spying. LC 93-5557. (Junie B. Jones Ser.: No. 4). (Illus.). 66p. (J). (gr. 1-4). 1994. pap. 3.99 (*0-679-85101-1*, Pub. by Random Bks Yng Read) Random.

Park, Barbara. Junie B. Jones & Some Sneaky Peeky Spying. LC 93-5557. (First Stepping Stone Bks.). (Illus.). 80p. (J). (gr. 1-4). 1994. lib. bdg. 11.99 (*0-679-95101-6*, Pub. by Random Bks Yng Read) Random.

P

An Asterisk (*) at the beginning of an entry indicates that the title is appearing for the first time.

Park, Barbara. Junie B. Jones & Some Sneaky Peeky Spying. (Junie B. Jones Ser.: No. 4). (Illus.). (J). (gr. 1-4). 1994. 9.19 (0-606-07018-4, Pub. by Turtleback) Demco.

Park, Barbara. Junie B. Jones & That Meanie Jim's Birthday. LC 95-35513. (Junie B. Jones Ser.: No. 6). (Illus.). 85p. (J). (gr. 1-4). 1996. pap. 3.99 (0-679-86695-7) Random.

— Junie B. Jones & That Meanie Jim's Birthday. LC 95-35513. (Junie B. Jones Ser.: No. 6). (Illus.). 80p. (J). (gr. 1-4). 1996. lib. bdg. 11.99 (0-679-96695-1) Random.

— Junie B. Jones & That Meanie Jim's Birthday. LC 95-35513. (Junie B. Jones Ser.: No. 6). (Illus.). (J). (gr. 1-4). 1996. 9.09 (0-606-09499-7, Pub. by Turtleback) Demco.

— Junie B. Jones & the Mushy Gushy Valentine. LC 99-40615. (Junie B. Jones Ser.: No. 14). (Illus.). 80p. (J). (gr. 1-4). 1999. pap. 3.99 (0-375-80039-5) Random.

— Junie B. Jones & the Mushy Gushy Valentine, No. 14. LC 99-40615. (Junie B. Jones Ser.: No. 14). (Illus.). (J). (gr. 1-4). 1999. lib. bdg. 11.99 (0-375-90039-X, Pub. by Random Bks Yng Read) Random.

***Park, Barbara.** Junie B. Jones & the Stupid Smelly Bus. (Junie B. Jones Ser.: No. 1). (Illus.). (J). (gr. 1-4). 1999. pap. 1.99 (0-375-80599-0) Random.

Park, Barbara. Junie B. Jones & the Stupid Smelly Bus. LC 91-51104. (Junie B. Jones Ser.: No. 1). (Illus.). 80p. (J). (gr. 1-4). 1992. pap. 3.99 (0-679-82642-4, Pub. by Random Bks Yng Read) Random.

— Junie B. Jones & the Stupid Smelly Bus. LC 91-51104. (Junie B. Jones Ser.: No. 14). (Illus.). 80p. (J). (gr. 1-4). 1992. lib. bdg. 11.99 (0-679-92642-9, Pub. by Random Bks Yng Read) Random.

— Junie B. Jones & the Stupid Smelly Bus. (Junie B. Jones Ser.: No. 1). (Illus.). (J). (gr. 1-4). 1992. 9.19 (0-606-02321-6, Pub. by Turtleback) Demco.

— Junie B. Jones & the Yucky Blucky Fruitcake. LC 94-40891. (Junie B. Jones Ser.: No. 5). (Illus.). 71p. (J). (gr. 1-4). 1995. pap. 3.99 (0-679-86694-9, Pub. by Random Bks Yng Read) Random.

— Junie B. Jones & the Yucky Blucky Fruitcake. LC 94-40891. (Junie B. Jones Ser.: No. 5). (Illus.). (J). (gr. 1-4). 1995. lib. bdg. 11.99 (0-679-96694-3, Pub. by Random Bks Yng Read) Random.

— Junie B. Jones & the Yucky Blucky Fruitcake. (Junie B. Jones Ser.: No. 5). (Illus.). (J). (gr. 1-4). 1995. 9.19 (0-606-08557-2, Pub. by Turtleback) Demco.

Park, Barbara. Junie B. Jones Has a Monster under Her Bed. LC 96-42561. (Junie B. Jones Ser.: No. 8). (Illus.). (J). (gr. 1-4). 1997. 9.44 (0-606-11529-3) Turtleback.

— Junie B. Jones Has a Peep in Her Pocket. LC 00-29067. (Junie B. Jones Ser.: No. 15). (Illus.). 80p. (J). (gr. k-3). 2000. pap. 3.99 (0-375-80040-9, Pub. by Random Bks Yng Read); pap. 11.99 (0-375-90040-3, Pub. by Random Bks Yng Read) Random.

— Junie B. Jones Has a Peep in Her Pocket. (Illus.). (J). 2000. 9.44 (0-606-18499-6) Turtleback.

Park, Barbara. Junie B. Jones Is a Beauty Shop Guy. LC 97-49197. (Illus.). (J). (gr. 1-4). 1998. lib. bdg. 11.99 (0-679-98931-5, Pub. by Random Bks Yng Read) Random.

— Junie B. Jones Is a Beauty Shop Guy. LC 97-49197. (Junie B. Jones Ser.: No. 11). (Illus.). 80p. (J). (gr. 1-4). 1998. pap. 3.99 (0-679-88931-0, Pub. by Random Bks Yng Read) Random.

— Junie B. Jones Is a Beauty Shop Guy. (Junie B. Jones Ser.: No. 11). (Illus.). (J). (gr. 1-4). 1998. 9.09 (0-606-13963-X, Pub. by Turtleback) Demco.

— Junie B. Jones Is a Party Animal. LC 96-42561. (J). 1997. pap. 3.99 (0-679-86697-3) Random.

— Junie B. Jones Is a Party Animal. (Junie B. Jones Ser.: No. 10). (Illus.). (J). (gr. 1-4). 1997. pap. 3.99 (0-614-28936-X) Random Bks Yng Read.

— Junie B. Jones Is a Party Animal. LC 97-17320. (Junie B. Jones Ser.: No. 10). (Illus.). 80p. (J). (gr. 1-4). 1997. pap. 3.99 (0-679-88663-X, Pub. by Random Bks Yng Read) Random.

Park, Barbara. Junie B. Jones Is a Party Animal. (Junie B. Jones Ser.: No. 10). (Illus.). (J). (gr. 1-4). 1997. 9.19 (0-606-12747-X, Pub. by Turtleback) Demco.

Park, Barbara. Junie B. Jones Is a Party Animal, No. 8. LC 96-42561. (Junie B. Jones Ser.: No. 10). (Illus.). (J). (gr. 1-4). 1997. lib. bdg. 11.99 (0-679-96697-8) Random.

— Junie B. Jones Is a Party Animal, No. 10. LC 97-17320. (Junie B. Jones Ser.: No. 10). (Illus.). (J). (gr. 1-4). 1997. lib. bdg. 11.99 (0-679-98663-4, Pub. by Random Bks Yng Read) Random.

— Junie B. Jones Is (Almost) a Flower Girl. LC 99-17611. (Junie B. Jones Ser.: No. 13). (Illus.). (J). (gr. 1-4). 1999. pap. 3.99 (0-375-80038-7) Random.

— Junie B. Jones Is (Almost) a Flower Girl. LC 99-17611. (Junie B. Jones Ser.: No. 13). (Illus.). (J). (gr. 1-4). 1999. lib. bdg. 11.99 (0-375-90038-1) Random.

***Park, Barbara.** Junie B. Jones Is Captain Field Day. (Junie B. Jones Ser.: No. 16). (Illus.). (J). (gr. 1-4). 2000. 11.99 (0-375-90291-0) Random Bks Yng Read.

— Junie B. Jones Is Captain Field Day. 16th ed. (Junie B. Jones Ser.: No. 16). (J). (gr. 1-4). 2000. pap. 3.99 (0-375-80291-6, Pub. by Random Bks Yng Read) Random.

Park, Barbara. Junie B. Jones Is Not a Crook. (Junie B. Jones Ser.: No. 9). (Illus.). (J). (gr. 1-4). 1997. lib. bdg. 11.99 (0-679-98342-2) Random.

— Junie B. Jones Is Not a Crook. (Junie B. Jones Ser.: No. 9). (Illus.). (J). (gr. 1-4). 1997. pap. 3.99 (0-614-28937-8) Random Bks Yng Read.

— Junie B. Jones Is Not a Crook. (Junie B. Jones Ser.: No. 9). (Illus.). (J). (gr. 1-4). 1997. pap. 3.99 (0-679-88342-8, Pub. by Random Bks Yng Read) Random.

— Junie B. Jones Is Not a Crook. LC 96-42542. (Junie B. Jones Ser.: No. 9). (Illus.). (J). (gr. 1-4). 1997. 9.19 (0-606-11530-7, Pub. by Turtleback) Demco.

— Junie B. Jones Loves Handsome Warren. LC 96-1440. (Junie B. Jones Ser.: No. 7). (Illus.). 71p. (J). (gr. 1-4). 1996. pap. 3.99 (0-679-86696-5) Random.

— Junie B. Jones Loves Handsome Warren. LC 96-1440. (Illus.). (J). (gr. 1-4). 1996. lib. bdg. 11.99 (0-679-96696-X) Random.

— Junie B. Jones Loves Handsome Warren. (Junie B. Jones Ser.: No. 7). (Illus.). (J). (gr. 1-4). 1996. 9.19 (0-606-10855-6, Pub. by Turtleback) Demco.

— Junie B. Jones Smells Something Fishy. LC 98-28176. (Junie B. Jones Ser.: No. 12). (Illus.). (J). (gr. 1-4). 1998. pap. 3.99 (0-679-89130-7) Random.

— Junie B. Jones Smells Something Fishy. LC 98-28176. (Junie B. Jones Ser.: No. 12). (Illus.). (J). (gr. 1-4). 1998. lib. bdg. 11.99 (0-679-99130-1, Pub. by Random Bks Yng Read) Random.

— The Kid in the Red Jacket. (J). (gr. 5). 1995. 9.32 (0-395-73330-8) HM.

— The Kid in the Red Jacket. LC 86-20113. 96p. (J). (gr. 3-6). 1987. lib. bdg. 18.99 (0-394-98189-8, Pub. by Knopf Bks Yng Read) Random.

— The Kid in the Red Jacket. (J). 1987. 9.09 (0-606-04093-5, Pub. by Turtleback) Demco.

— The Kid in the Red Jacket. large type ed. 134p. (J). (gr. 5). 33.50 (0-614-20602-2, L-38194-00 APHB) Am Printing Hse.

— The Kid in the Red Jacket. LC 86-20113. 128p. (J). (gr. 3-7). 1988. reprint ed. pap. 3.99 (0-394-80571-2, Pub. by Knopf Bks Yng Read) Random.

Park, Barbara. Maxie, Rosie & the Earl Partners in Crime. 1991. 10.09 (0-606-04974-6, Pub. by Turtleback) Demco.

Park, Barbara. Mick Harte Was Here. LC 94-27272. (J). (gr. 3-6). 1995. 15.00 (0-679-87088-1) Knopf.

Park, Barbara. Mick Harte Was Here. 88p. (J). (gr. 4-6). pap. 4.99 (0-8072-1502-3) Listening Lib.

Park, Barbara. Mick Harte Was Here. 89p. (J). (gr. 3-6). 1996. pap. 4.99 (0-679-88203-0, Pub. by Random Bks Yng Read) Random.

— Mick Harte Was Here. (J). 1996. 9.84 (0-606-10991-9, Pub. by Turtleback) Demco.

— Operation: Dump the Chump. 112p. (J). (gr. 3-7). 1983. pap. 2.75 (0-380-63974-2, Avon Bks) Morrow Avon.

Park, Barbara. Operation: Dump the Chump. (J). 1995. 9.60 (0-606-08583-1, Pub. by Turtleback) Demco.

Park, Barbara. Operation: Dump the Chump. LC 81-8147. 128p. (J). (gr. 3-9). 1989. reprint ed. pap. 4.99 (0-394-82592-6, Pub. by Knopf Bks Yng Read) Random.

— Psst! It's Me The Bogeyman. LC 97-10123. (Illus.). 40p. (J). (ps-4). 1998. 16.00 (0-689-81667-7) Atheneum Yung Read.

— Rosie Swanson: Fourth-Grade Geek for President. (J). 1992. 10.09 (0-606-01563-9, Pub. by Turtleback) Demco.

— Skinnybones. LC 81-20791. 128p. (J). (gr. 7 up). 1982. lib. bdg. 13.99 (0-394-94988-9, Pub. by Knopf Bks Yng Read) Random.

***Park, Barbara.** Skinnybones. (Illus.). 112p. (J). (gr. 4-7). 2000. mass mkt. 2.99 (0-375-80672-5) Random.

Park, Barbara. Skinnybones. LC 97-65624. 120p. (J). (gr. 3-7). 1997. pap. 3.99 (0-679-88792-X, Pub. by Random Bks Yng Read) Random.

— Skinnybones. (J). 1995. 8.84 (0-606-04326-8, Pub. by Turtleback) Demco.

— Skinnybones. large type ed. (J). 1993. 30.50 (0-614-09855-6, L-34135-00) Am Printing Hse.

***Park, Barbara & Lubotsky, Dana.** Mick Harte Was Here. unabridged ed. (J). 1998. pap. 16.98 incl. audio (0-8072-7796-7, 395059, Pub. by Listening Lib) Lndmrk Audiobks.

Park, Bert E. Ailing, Aging, & Addicted Leaders: Studies of Compromised Leadership. LC 93-19550. 288p. 1993. 32.00 (0-8131-1853-0) U Pr of Ky.

— Catastrophic Illness & the Family. LC 91-70967. 1992. 19.95 (0-8158-0471-7) Chris Mass.

— The Impact of Illness on World Leaders. LC 86-16136. 396p. 1986. 38.95 (0-8122-8005-9) U of Pa Pr.

Park, Beth. The Bedside Table. LC 96-85555. (Illus.). 32p. (Orig.). 1996. pap. 10.00 (0-9653314-0-7) Dream Press.

Park, Betsy, jt. auth. see Martin, Murray S.

***Park, Bok Nam.** Fundamentals of Pa Kua Chang. (Illus.). 224p. 1998. pap. 19.95 (0-86568-172-4) Unique Pubns.

— Fundamentals of Pa Kua Chang, Vol. 2. (Illus.). 212p. 1999. pap. 24.95 (0-86568-173-2) Unique Pubns.

Park, Byong-Chul. Phenomenological Aspects of Wittgenstein's Philosophy. LC 97-34899. (Synthese Library). 249p. 1997. text 120.50 (0-7923-4813-3) Kluwer Academic.

Park, Byung H. & Good, Robert A. Principles of Modern Immunobiology: Basic & Clinical. LC 73-13831. (Illus.). 627p. reprint ed. 194.40 (0-8357-9416-4, 201457300093) Bks Demand.

Park, C. Taxonomy of Polygonum Section Echinocaulon (Polygonaceae) LC 88-5361. (Memoirs Ser.: Vol. 47). (Illus.). 82p. (C). 1988. pap. text 19.00 (0-89327-329-5) NY Botanical.

Park, C., jt. ed. see Lanzerotti, L. J.

Park, C. H. Computer-Aided Numerical Determination of Hofer, Lewis, Niemann & Colbourne Points, (Nineteen Ninety-Four Fall Technical Meeting Ser.: Vol. 94FTMS1). (Illus.). 17p. 1994. pap. text 30.00 (1-55589-642-1) AGMA.

Park, C. H., ed. The Law of the Sea in the 1980's, 14th Annual Conference Proceeding. 636p. 1983. 18.00 (0-911189-05-X) Law Sea Inst.

Park, C. H., jt. ed. see Nordquist, M.

Park, C. Whan & Smith, Daniel, eds. AMA Winter Educators' Conference, 1994 Vol. 5: Marketing Theory & Applications. 394p. 1994. pap. 50.00 (0-87757-248-8) Am Mktg.

Park, Chan-eung, ed. see Curry, Lindy S.

Park, Chan S. Contemporary Engineering Economics. (Illus.). 850p. (C). 1992. text 68.33 incl. disk (0-201-14508-1) Addison-Wesley.

— Contemporary Engineering Economics. 2nd ed. LC 96-46611. 840p. (C). 1996. 99.00 (0-201-83598-3) Addison-Wesley.

— Fundamentals of Engineering Economics. (C). 2000. text. write for info. (0-201-32685-X) Addison-Wesley.

— Interactive Microcomputer Graphics. 1985. text 54.95 (0-201-05541-4) Addison-Wesley.

Park, Chan S. & Sharp-Bette, Gunther. Advanced Engineering Economics. LC 89-24851. 768p. 1990. text 105.95 (0-471-79989-0) Wiley.

Park, Charles F., Jr. & Freeman, Margaret C. Earthbound: Minerals, Energy & Man's Future (With Prologue) LC 73-87688. (Illus.). 1975. pap. text 35.00 (0-87735-318-2) Jones & Bartlett.

Park, Charles F., jt. auth. see Guilbert, John M.

Park, Charles S. Conflict at the Border: True Tales of a U. S. Customs Border Officer. LC 89-1923. (Illus.). 160p. (Orig.). 1989. pap. 5.00 (0-914846-41-8) Golden West Pub.

Park, Choon-ho & Park, Jae Kyu, eds. The Law of the Sea: Problems from the East Asian Perspective. (Law of the Sea Workshop Ser.: No. 8). 620p. 1987. 42.00 (0-911189-14-9) Law Sea Inst.

Park, Choon-Ho, et al. Korean International Law. (Korea Research Monographs: No. 4). 53p. 1982. pap. 8.00 (0-912966-40-8) IEAS.

Park, Chris. Environment: Principles Applications. 160p. (C). 1998. pap., teacher ed. 50.00 (0-415-16663-2) Routledge.

Park, Chris C. Acid Rain: Rhetoric & Reality. LC 87-20398. 1989. pap. 25.00 (0-416-92200-7) Routledge.

— Acid Rain: Rhetoric & Reality. (Illus.). 272p. 1990. pap. 25.00 (0-685-26313-4) Routledge.

— Chernobyl: The Long Shadow. 192p. 1989. 39.95 (0-415-03553-8, A3394) Routledge.

— Environment: Principles & Applications. LC 97-208961. 598p. (C). 1997. pap. 27.95 (0-415-12200-7) Routledge.

— Sacred Worlds: An Introduction to Geography & Religion. LC 93-36709. (Illus.). 336p. (C). 1994. pap. 27.99 (0-415-09013-X, A9828) Routledge.

— Tropical Rainforests. LC 92-5659. (Illus.). 208p. (C). 1992. pap. 20.99 (0-415-06239-X, A7416) Routledge.

Park, Chris C., ed. Environmental Policies: An International Review. LC 85-22370. 336p. 1985. 45.00 (0-7099-2062-8, Pub. by C Helm) Routldge.

Park, Chris C., ed. see Jones, G. E.

Park, Chung I. Advertisement Digest: Library & Information Services, 1978. 89p. 1979. pap. 5.00 (0-939670-06-2) Info Digest.

— Best Books by Consensus, 1983-1984. (Orig.). 1984. pap. 3.25 (0-939670-05-4) Info Digest.

— Best Books by Consensus, 1984-1985. LC 84-648497. 48p. 1985. pap. 4.25 (0-939670-08-9) Info Digest.

— Best Sellers & Best Choices, 1980. x, 95p. 1981. pap. 4.00 (0-939670-00-3) Info Digest.

— Best Sellers & Best Choices, 1981. LC 81-640911. x, 112p. (Orig.). 1982. pap. 4.00 (0-939670-01-1) Info Digest.

— Best Sellers & Best Choices, 1982. LC 81-640911. 146p. (Orig.). pap. 4.95 (0-939670-02-X) Info Digest.

Park, Chung I., ed. Best Books by Consensus, 1985-1986. 50p. (Orig.). 1986. pap. 4.25 (0-939670-14-3) Info Digest.

— Best Books by Consensus, 1986-87. 1987. pap. 4.25 (0-939670-19-4) Info Digest.

— Best Books by Consensus, 1987-1988. 1988. pap. 4.25 (0-939670-21-6) Info Digest.

— Communications & Information Handling Equipment & Services, 1979. 244p. 1979. pap. 5.00 (0-939670-07-0) Info Digest.

Park City Education Foundation Staff. Park City - A Taste of Past & Present. 224p. 1996. 19.95 (1-883004-02-0) Game of Work.

Park, Clara C. The Siege: A Family's Journey into the World of an Autistic Child. (Illus.). 330p. 1982. pap. 15.95 (0-316-69069-4, Back Bay) Little.

Park, Clara C. & Chi, Marilyn Mei-Ying, eds. Asian-American Education: Prospects & Challenges. LC 98-55902. 320p. 1999. 65.00 (0-89789-602-5, Bergin & Garvey); pap. 22.95 (0-89789-603-3, Bergin & Garvey) Greenwood.

Park, Clara C. & Shapiro, Leon N. You Are Not Alone: Understanding & Dealing with Mental Illness. 1979. 17.50 (0-316-69073-2, Little Brwn Med Div) Lppncott W & W.

Park, Clara Claiborne. Exiting Nirvana: My Daughter's Life with Autism. (Illus.). 208p. 2001. 23.95 (0-316-69117-8) Little.

Park, Colin. Management Training: Starting up Training & Development Programs in Medium-Sized Corporations. (Illus.). 180p. pap. 15.00 (0-318-13279-6, PAMPB) Am Soc Train & Devel.

Park, D. A. Classical Dynamics & Its Quantum Analogues. 2nd enl. ed. (Illus.). 352p. 1990. reprint ed. 54.95 (0-387-51398-1) Spr-Verlag.

Park, Dabney G., Jr. Planejamento Estrategico e Conselho Diretor Na Organizacao Sem Fins Lucrativos.Tr. of Strategic Planning & the Nonprofit Board. (POR.). 12p. (Orig.). 1996. pap. write for info. (0-925299-69-3) Natl Ctr Nonprofit.

Park, Dave, jt. auth. see Anderson, Neil.

Park, Dave, jt. auth. see Anderson, Neil T.

Park, David. The Fire Within the Eye. 1999. pap. 16.95 (0-691-05051-1, Pub. by Princeton U Pr) Cal Prin Full Svc.

— The How & the Why: An Essay on the Origins & Development of Physical Theory. (Illus.). 488p. (C). 1988. pap. text 24.95 (0-691-02508-8, Pub. by Princeton U Pr) Cal Prin Full Svc.

Park, David, jt. ed. see Davis, Philip J.

Park, David A. The Fire within the Eye: A Historical Essay on the Nature Essay on the Nature & Meaning of Light. LC 96-45573. 400p. 1997. 29.95 (0-691-04332-9, Pub. by Princeton U Pr) Cal Prin Full Svc.

— Introduction to the Quantum Theory. 3rd ed. 1992. text. write for info. (0-07-048554-2) McGraw.

Park-Davis & Company Staff. Medical Word Building. 125p. 1970. pap. 19.95 (0-87489-043-8) Practice Mgmt Info.

***Park, Denise C.** Aging & Cognition. LC 99-43572. 256p. 1999. pap. text 29.95 (0-86377-692-2) L Erlbaum Assocs.

Park, Denise C., et al, eds. Processing of Medical Information in Aging Patients: Cognitive & Human Factors Perspectives. LC 98-30256. 344p. 1999. 69.95 (0-8058-2889-3) L Erlbaum Assocs.

***Park, Deuk-Hoon.** Christian Praxis & Economic Justice. LC 99-41837. (European University Studies: Vol. 675, Series 23). 250p. (C). 1999. pap. 36.95 (0-8204-4604-1) P Lang Pubng.

***Park, Deuk-Hoon, contrib. by.** Christian Praxis & Economic Justice. LC 99-41837. (European University Studies: No. 23). 250p. 1999. pap. 36.95 (3-906763-05-6, Pub. by P Lang) P Lang Pubng.

Park, Dorcas D., jt. auth. see Park, Maurice E.

Park, E. K., ed. Computer Applications in Design, Simulation & Analysis: Proceedings of ISMM Symposium, New Orleans, U. S. A., March 5-7, 1990. 323p. 1990. 95.00 (0-88986-140-4) Acta Pr.

Park, E. K. & Chae, K., eds. Computer Communications & Networks (IC3N-92) June 8-10, 1992, San Diego, CA. (Conference Proceedings Ser.). 327p. 1992. write for info. (1-880843-01-3) Int Soc Comp App.

Park, E. K., jt. ed. see Hudson, D.

Park, E. K., jt. ed. see Suda, T.

Park, Ed, jt. auth. see Park, Lue.

Park, Edwards. Angels Twenty: A Young American Flier a Long Way from Home. LC 96-44279. 224p. 1997. 22.95 (0-07-582125-7) McGraw.

— Treasures of the Smithsonian. LC 83-40203. (Illus.). 496p. 1983. 42.96 (0-89599-012-1) Smithsonian Bks.

Park, Edwards & Carlhian, Jean Paul. A New View from the Castle: The Smithsonian's Museum & Garden Complex on the National Mall. LC 87-42555. (Illus.). 160p. (C). 1987. pap. 15.95 (0-87474-749-X) Smithsonian.

Park, Eue-Choon. Fontanes Zeitromane: Zur Kritik der Grunderzeit. (Europaische Hochschulschriften Ser.: Reihe 1, Bd. 1641). 205p. 1997. 42.95 (3-631-32538-X) P Lang Pubng.

Park, Eui H. Human Interaction with Complex Systems: Conceptual Principles & Design Practice. Ntuen, Celestine A., ed. LC 96-32854. (Kluwer International Series in Engineering & Computer Science). 448p. (C). 1996. text 157.50 (0-7923-9779-7) Kluwer Academic.

***Park, Eung Won.** The Kite Fighters. LC 99-36936. 144p. (J). (gr. 4-8). 2000. 15.00 (0-395-94041-9, Clarion Bks) HM.

Park, Frances. Hotline Heaven. LC 97-4369. 160p. 1998. 22.00 (1-57962-011-6) Permanent Pr.

***Park, Frances.** When My Sister Was Cleopatra Moon. LC 99-54524. 224p. 2000. 22.95 (0-7868-6647-0, Pub. by Hyperion) Time Warner.

Park, Frances & Park, Ginger. My Freedom Trip: A Child's Escape to South Korea. LC 97-77911. (Illus.). 32p. (J). (gr. k-3). 1998. 15.95 (1-56397-468-1) Boyds Mills Pr.

Park, Frances & Park, Ginger. The Royal Bee. LC 98-88234. (Illus.). 32p. 2000. 15.95 (1-56397-614-5) Boyds Mills Pr.

***Park, Frances & Park, Ginger.** The Royal Bee. LC 98-88234. (Illus.). 32p. (J). (gr. 1-4). 2000. pap. 8.95 (1-56397-867-9) Boyds Mills Pr.

Park, Francis Y. Speaking Korean, Bk. I. rev. ed. LC 84-80023. (ENG & KOR.). 1994. audio 125.00 (0-930878-77-9) Hollym Intl.

— Speaking Korean, Bk. 1. rev. ed. LC 84-80023. (ENG & KOR.). 484p. 1995. pap. text 38.50 (1-56591-101-6) Hollym Intl.

— Speaking Korean, Bk. 2. rev. ed. LC 84-80023. (KOR.). 493p. 1994. pap. text 38.50 (1-56591-103-2) Hollym Intl.

— Speaking Korean: A Guide to Chinese Characters, Bk. III. LC 89-83652. 401p. 1995. pap. text 38.50 (0-930878-81-7) Hollym Intl.

Park, Frank, jt. auth. see Park, Libbie.

Park, G. & Ryan, D. W. Color Atlas of Critical & Intensive Care: Diagnosis & Investigation. 1995. 64.95 (0-7234-1956-6) Mosby Inc.

Park, G. N., jt. ed. see Kelly, G. C.

Park, G. R., ed. Fluid Balance & Volume Resuscitation Made Easy: A Practical Guide. (Greenwich Medical Media Ser.). (Illus.). 150p. 1999. pap. text 24.50 (1-900151-54-5) OUP.

Park, G. R. & Pinsky, M. R., eds. Critical Care Management - Case Studies: Tricks & Traps. (Illus.). 375p. 1997. pap. text 63.00 (0-7020-1909-7, Pub. by W B Saunders) Saunders.

Park, G. R., et al. Sedation & Analgesia in the Critically Ill. (Illus.). 250p. 1995. 89.95 (0-86542-905-7) Blackwell Sci.

P

Park Genealogical Books Staff. Minnesota's World War II Combat Connected Naval Casualties: Navy, Marine Corps, Coast Guard. Bakeman, Mary H., ed. LC 96-31751. 1996. pap. 12.50 (*0-915709-27-9*) Pk Geneal Bk.

Park, George S., et al. The Class of 2014: Preserving Access to California Higher Education. LC 98-7045. (Illus.). 64p. 1998. pap. 15.00 (*0-8330-2614-3*, MR-971-EDU) Rand Corp.

***Park, Gilbert, et al.** The Management of Acute Pain. 2nd ed. (Illus.). 208p. 2000. pap. text 44.95 (*0-19-262467-9*) OUP.

Park, Gilbert R. & Kang, Yoogoo. Anesthesia & Intensive Care for the Patients with Liver Disease. LC 94-11812. 340p. 1994. text 97.50 (*0-7506-9554-4*) Buttrwrth-Heinemann.

Park, Ginger, jt. auth. see Park, Frances.

Park, Glen. Art of Changing: A New Approach to the Alexander Technique. 7th ed. 1997. pap. text 18.95 (*1-85398-001-3*, Pub. by Ashgrove Pr) Words Distrib.

— A New Approach to the Alexander Technique: Moving Toward a More Balanced Expression of the Whole Self. rev. ed. LC 98-5016. (Illus.). 304p. 1998. pap. 18.95 (*0-89594-918-0*) Crossing Pr.

Park, H. C., jt. ed. see Lee, H. B.

Park, Hae Ok, jt. auth. see Park, Mary J.

Park, Han S. Human Needs & Political Development: Dissent to Utopian Solutions. 280p. 1984. 29.95 (*0-87073-997-2*); pap. 22.95 (*0-87073-998-0*) Schenkman Bks Inc.

Park, Harold, jt. auth. see Park, Miriam.

Park, Heon-Joo. Housing Land in Government Intervention: With Special Reference to Land Readjustment in Seoul, Korea, & Municipal Site-Leasehold in Stockholm. (University of Stockholm Human Geography Ser.: No. B76). 306p. (Orig.). 1991. pap. 109.00 (*91-7146-924-9*) Coronet Bks.

Park, Hongsuk H. American Politics & Foreign Economic Challenge. LC 90-41583. (Foreign Economic Policy of the United States Ser.). 283p. 1990. reprint ed. text 10.00 (*0-8240-7434-3*) Garland.

Park, Hyo S., jt. auth. see Adeli, Hojjat.

Park, Innwon. Regional Integration among the Asian Nations: A Computable General Equilibrium Model Study. LC 94-37884. 176p. 1995. 59.95 (*0-275-94981-8*, Praeger Pubs) Greenwood.

Park, Irene. Heaven Rejoices. Orig. Title: Witch That Switched. 95p. 1996. mass mkt. 5.99 (*0-88368-434-9*) Whitaker Hse.

Park, J. B. Biomaterials Science & Engineering. LC 84-16016. (Illus.). 474p. (C). 1984. text 65.00 (*0-306-41689-1*, Kluwer Plenum) Kluwer Academic.

Park, J. B. & Lakes, R. S. Biomaterials: An Introduction. 2nd ed. (Illus.). 408p. (C). 1992. text 59.50 (*0-306-43992-1*, Kluwer Plenum) Kluwer Academic.

Park, J. F. & Pelroy, R. A., eds. Multilevel Health Effects Research: From Molecules to Man. LC 89-18083. (Proceedings of the 27th Hanford Symposium on Health & the Environment (Oct. 1988) Ser.). 492p. 1990. pap. text 57.50 (*0-935470-55-7*) Battelle.

Park, J. R., ed. Environmental Management in Agriculture: European Perspectives. (Belhaven Press Bk.). (Illus.). 224p. 1992. 67.95 (*1-85293-036-5*, Pub. by P P Pubs) CRC Pr.

Park, Jack. MVP-FORTH Expert System Toolkit. Haydon, Glen B., ed. (MVP-Forth Bks.: Vol. 4). 80p. (Orig.). 1984. pap. 22.00 (*0-317-56526-5*) Mntn View Pr.

Park, Jack L. Ohio State Football . . . The Great Tradition. Stephenson, Dave, ed. LC 92-90355. (Illus.). 248p. 1992. 19.95 (*1-881462-45-5*) Lexington OH.

— Ohio State Football Encyclopedia. (Illus.). 1999. 39.95 (*1-58261-006-1*) Sprts Pubng.

Park, Jacqueline. The Secret Book of Grazia Dei Rossi. LC 97-3218. 576p. 1997. 25.50 (*0-684-81603-2*) S&S Trade.

— The Secret Book of Grazia Dei Rossi. 576p. 1998. pap. 13.00 (*0-684-84840-6*, Scribner Pap Fic) S&S Trade Pap.

Park, Jacquelyn H. A Stone Gone Mad. 2nd ed. LC 91-52674. 320p. 1996. reprint ed. pap. text 9.95 (*1-55583-364-0*) Alyson Pubns.

Park, Jae Hyung, jt. auth. see Han, Man Chung.

Park, Jae Kyu, jt. ed. see Park, Choon-ho.

***Park, Jae Won.** Surimi & Surimi Seafood. LC 00-28052. (Food Science & Technology Ser.). (Illus.). 2000. write for info. (*0-8247-0372-3*) Dekker.

Park, James. Romans: An Existential Interpretation. 2nd ed. LC 83-8852. 96p. 1991. pap. text 10.50 (*0-89231-200-9*) Existential Bks.

Park, James L. Becoming More Authentic: The Positive Side of Existentialism. 4th rev. ed. LC B105.A8P37 1999. 96p. (C). 1999. pap. text 15.00 (*0-89231-104-5*) Existential Bks.

— Existential Anxiety: Angst. rev. ed. LC BF575.A6P37 1996. 1996. pap. 9.00 (*0-89231-906-2*) Existential Bks.

— An Existential Understanding of Death: A Phenomenology of Ontological Anxiety. rev. ed. LC BD444.P37 1995. 1995. pap. 10.50 (*0-89231-909-7*) Existential Bks.

— From Romantic Illusions to Authentic Loving. rev. ed. LC BF575.L8 P37 1996. (Love among Authentic Persons Ser.: No. 1). Orig. Title: Authentic Love: An Existential Vision. 1995. pap. 3.75 (*0-89231-501-6*) Existential Bks.

***Park, James L.** In Quest of Fulfillment: Money, Achievement, Marriage, Children, Pleasure & Religion. LC BJ1481.P37. 40p. 1999. pap. 6.00 (*0-89231-920-8*) Existential Bks.

Park, James L. Love Without Marrying. LC HQ728.P37 1996. (Love among Authentic Persons Ser.: No. 6). 1995. pap. 3.75 (*0-89231-506-7*) Existential Bks.

— Loving Freely Without Needing. rev. ed. LC BD436.P37 1996. (Love among Authentic Persons Ser.: No. 2). Orig. Title: Love among Authentic Persons Ser.: No. 2). Orig. Title: Authentic Love: An Existential Vision. 1995. pap. 3.75 (*0-89231-502-4*) Existential Bks.

— Multiple Loving Without Jealousy. rev. ed. LC BF575.J4P37 1996. (Love among Authentic Persons Ser.: Vol. 3). 1995. pap. 3.75 (*0-89231-503-2*) Existential Bks.

— Our Existential Predicament: Loneliness, Depression, Anxiety, & Death. rev. ed. LC B819.P37 1995. 308p. (Orig.). 1996. pap. text 50.00 (*0-89231-900-3*) Existential Bks.

— Sex & Gender. rev. ed. LC HQ21.P37 1996. (Love among Authentic Persons Ser.: No. 4). 1995. pap. 3.75 (*0-89231-504-0*) Existential Bks.

— Spirituality for Humanists: Six Capacities of Our Human Spirits. 2nd ed. LC B778.P37 1995. Orig. Title: Capacities of the Human Spirit: Spirituality for Humanists. 1995. pap. 3.00 (*0-89231-022-7*) Existential Bks.

— Why Have (More) Children? rev. ed. LC HQ7558.P37 1996. (Love among Authentic Persons Ser.: No. 5). 1995. pap. 3.75 (*0-89231-505-9*) Existential Bks.

***Park, James Leonard.** New Ways of Loving: How Authenticity Transforms Relationships. 4th rev. ed. 264p. 2000. pap. 45.00 (*0-89231-520-2*) Existential Bks.

Park, James Leonard. Opening to Grace: Transcending Our Spiritual Malaise. LC BT761.2.P37. 64p. 1999. pap. 9.00 (*0-89231-921-6*) Existential Bks.

Park, James W. Latin American Underdevelopment: A History of Perspectives in the United States, 1870-1965. LC 94-37209. (Illus.). 312p. 1995. text 42.50 (*0-8071-1969-5*) La State U Pr.

Park, Jane & Muller, Kathryn. Just the Facts: What Science Has Found Out about Teenage Sexuality & Pregnancy in the U. S. 2nd rev. ed. Card, Josephina T. & Gibson, Anjalique C., eds. (Illus.). vii, 133p. (YA). (gr. 6-12). 1998. pap. write for info. (*0-9666901-0-9*) Sociometrics Corp.

Park, Jason. Helping LDS Men Resolve Their Homosexual Problems: A Guide for Family, Friends, & Church Leaders. LC 97-67740. 256p. (Orig.). 1997. pap. 14.95 (*0-941846-07-5*) Centry Pub.

— Resolving Homosexual Problems: A Guide for LDS Men. LC 97-67741. 296p. (Orig.). 1997. pap. 15.95 (*0-941846-06-7*) Centry Pub.

— Understanding Male Homosexual Problems: An Introduction for Latter-Day Saints. LC 98-133357. 48p. (Orig.). 1997. pap. 2.95 (*0-941846-08-3*) Centry Pub.

Park, Jeff, jt. auth. see Powell, Betty B.

Park, Jennifer, et al. Creative Aerobic Fitness. 2nd ed. 128p. 1995. pap. text, per. 19.95 (*0-8403-9884-0*, 40988401) Kendall-Hunt.

Park, Jihang. Profit-Sharing & Industrial Co-Partnership in British Industry, 1880-1920: Class Conflict or Class Collaboration. (Modern European History Ser.). 512p. 1987. text 15.00 (*0-8240-7827-6*) Garland.

***Park, Jonathon.** Y2K - The Danger Is Real: A Washington Insider's Report. 1999. pap. 19.95 (*0-9676728-0-5*) Mantford.

Park, Jong C. Paul Tillich's Categories for the Interpretation of History: An Application to the Encounter of Eastern & Western Cultures. LC 93-11395. (American University Studies: Vol. 165). 1994. write for info. (*0-8204-2281-9*) P Lang Pubng.

Park, Jong-Chun. Crawl with God, Dance in the Spirit! A Creative Formulation of Korean Theology of the Spirit. LC 98-28388. 1998. pap. 9.95 (*0-687-05689-6*) Abingdon.

Park, Joseph H. British Prime Ministers of the Nineteenth Century. LC 76-111855. (Essay Index Reprint Ser.). 1977. 28.95 (*0-8369-1892-4*) Ayer.

— British Prime Ministers of the Nineteenth Century: Policies & Speeches. (Essay Index Reprint Ser.). 390p. 1982. reprint ed. lib. bdg. 25.00 (*0-8290-0788-1*) Irvington.

— English Reform Bill of Eighteen Sixty-Seven. LC 76-78002. (Columbia University. Studies in the Social Sciences: No.210). reprint ed. 29.50 (*0-404-51210-0*) AMS Pr.

Park, Joseph S. AS-400 Security in a Client/Server Environment. LC 95-4052. (Technical Communication Library). 290p. 1995. pap. 49.99 incl. disk (*0-471-11683-1*) Wiley.

Park, Julian, ed. & tr. see Balmain, Aleksandr.

Park, Julie. My First Alphabet Book. 36p. (J). 1995. (*0-19-910332-1*) OUP.

Park, June. The Bingo Queens of Paradise. LC 98-54267. 288p. 1999. 24.00 (*0-06-019312-3*) HarpC.

— The Bingo Queens of Paradise. 288p. 2000. pap. 13.00 (*0-06-093128-0*) HarpC.

Park, Jung-Dong. The Special Economic Zones of China & Their Impact on Its Economic Development. LC 96-26875. 240p. 1997. 65.00 (*0-275-95613-X*, Praeger Pubs) Greenwood.

Park, Jung S. Contractarian Liberal Ethics & the Theory of Rational Choice. LC 91-18282. (American University Studies: Philosophy: Ser. V, Vol. 122). XIV, 291p. (C). 1992. text 49.95 (*0-8204-1566-9*) P Lang Pubng.

Park, K. C., ed. see American Society of Mechanical Engineers Staff.

Park, Katharine. Doctors & Medicine in Early Renaissance Florence. LC 84-42898. 311p. 1985. reprint ed. pap. 96.50 (*0-608-03353-7*, 206406500008) Bks Demand.

Park, Katharine, jt. auth. see Daston, Lorraine.

Park, Kathryn E. Five Steps to an SAP Career: Your Guide to Getting into SAP. Park, Robert S., ed. 104p. 1999. pap. 19.95 (*0-9656621-3-6*) Bobkat Pr.

— SAP Documentation & Training Development Guide: A Straight Forward Approach to Planning & Developing Documentation & Training for Your SAP Project. Park, Robert S., ed. (Illus.). ix, 182p. (Orig.). 1997. pap. 44.95 (*0-9656621-2-8*) Bobkat Pr.

Park, Keith, jt. auth. see Grove, Nicola.

Park, Keith K. & Van Agtmael, Antoine W., eds. The World's Emerging Stock Markets: Structure, Development, Regulations & Opportunities. (Guide to World Markets Ser.). 375p. 1992. text 70.00 (*1-55738-240-9*, Irwn Prfssnl) McGraw-Hill Prof.

Park, Keith K., jt. ed. see Lederman, Jess.

Park, Kenneth G., jt. auth. see Thompson, Alastair M.

Park, Kihong & Willinger, Walter. Self-Similar Network Traffic & Performance Evaluation. LC 99-15962. 544p. 2000. text 89.95 (*0-471-31974-0*, Wiley-Interscience) Wiley.

Park-Kim, Sunnie. Science Kids: General Science Workbook, Vol. I. Kim, Peter, ed. (Illus.). (J). (gr. 2-6). 1997. pap., wbk. ed. 4.50 (*1-891418-00-9*) Science Kids.

Park, Kinam, ed. Controlled Drug Delivery: Challenges & Strategies. LC 96-51016. (ACS Professional Reference Bk.). (Illus.). 720p. 1997. text 150.00 (*0-8412-3418-3*, Pub. by Am Chemical) OUP.

Park, Kinam & Mrsny, Randall J., eds. Controlled Drug Delivery: Designing Technologies for the Future. LC 99-58688. (ACS Symposium : Vol. 752). (Illus.). 448p. 2000. text 150.00 (*0-8412-3625-9*, Pub. by Am Chemical) OUP.

Park, Kinam, et al. Biodegradable Hydrogels for Drug Delivery. LC 93-60193. 250p. 1993. text 104.95 (*1-56676-004-6*) Technomic.

Park, Kun I. Personal & Wireless Communications: Digital Technology & Standards. LC 96-16696. (International Series in Engineering & Computer Science, Natural Language Processing & Machine Translation). 240p. (C). 1996. text 115.00 (*0-7923-9727-4*) Kluwer Academic.

Park, Kwan-Hwa, ed. see Choi, Yang-Do.

Park, Kwangsoo. The Won Buddhism (Wonbulgyo) of Sot'aesan: A Twentieth-Century Religious Movement in Korea. 407p. 1997. 74.95 (*1-57309-178-2*, Cath Scholar Pr); pap. 54.95 (*1-57309-177-4*, Cath Scholar Pr) Intl Scholars.

Park, Kyeyoung. The Korean American Dream: Immigrants & Small Business in New York City. LC 97-3083. (Anthropology of Contemporary Issues Ser.). (Illus.). 224p. 1996. text 37.50 (*0-8014-3343-6*); pap. text 14.95 (*0-8014-8391-3*) Cornell U Pr.

Park, Kyung-Sun. Die Variabilitat des Realen Wechselkurses & Ihr Okonomischen Auswirkungen: Eine Untersuchung Am Beispiel Korea. (GER., Illus.). 174p. 1996. 42.95 (*3-631-49454-8*) P Lang Pubng.

Park, Leslie D., jt. ed. see Warms, Dorothy.

Park, Libbie & Park, Frank. Anatomy of Big Business. 271p. 1973. 30.00 (*0-88862-039-X*, Pub. by J Lorimer); pap. 14.95 (*0-88862-040-3*, Pub. by J Lorimer) Formac Dist Ltd.

***Park, Linda Sue.** Seesaw Girl. 2001. pap. 4.50 (*0-440-41672-8*) BDD Bks Young Read.

— Seesaw Girl. LC 98-31654. (Illus.). 96p. (J). (gr. 3-7). 1999. 15.00 (*0-395-91514-7*, Clarion Bks) HM.

Park, Lue & Park, Ed. The Smoked-Foods Cookbook: How to Flavor, Cure, & Prepare Savory Meats, Game, Fish, Nuts, & Cheese. LC 92-7047. 224p. 1992. 18.95 (*0-8117-0116-6*) Stackpole.

Park, M., jt. auth. see Anderson, N.

Park, M. E. & Maxey, M. Two Studies on the Roman Lower Classes: An Original Anthology. LC 75-7347. (Roman History Ser.). 1977. reprint ed. 33.95 (*0-405-07069-1*) Ayer.

Park, M. K. Chemiemission Model & Fracto Emission. Park, Myungkark, ed. 100p. (Orig.). 1990. pap. write for info. (*1-877974-05-6*) Prompter Pubns.

— Computational Physics. Park, Myungkark, ed. (Illus.). 200p. (C). Date not set. pap. write for info. (*1-877974-03-X*) Prompter Pubns.

— A Foundation of Prompter Physics III. Park, Myungkark, ed. (Illus.). 130p. 1992. pap. write for info. (*1-877974-72-2*) Prompter Pubns.

— Mechanism of Fracto Emission. (Illus.). 100p. (Orig.). 1989. pap. write for info. (*1-877974-04-8*) Prompter Pubns.

— Physics of the Blue Sack. Park, Myungkark, ed. 100p. (C). 1989. pap. write for info. (*1-877974-00-5*) Prompter Pubns.

— Physics of the Green-Back Dollar. 100p. (Orig.). (C). 1990. pap. write for info. (*1-877974-01-3*) Prompter Pubns.

— Physics of the Seoul Guy. (Illus.). 100p. (Orig.). 1990. pap. write for info. (*1-877974-02-1*) Prompter Pubns.

Park, M. K., ed. see Park, Myungkark.

Park, Margaret. Crab-Bags & Other Bean-Beings. (Illus.). (J). (gr. 5 up). 1979. pap. 2.95 (*0-915556-05-7*) Great Ocean.

Park, Marian F. A Season of Pause. (Illus.). 44p. (Orig.). 1994. 5.95 (*1-878116-46-0*) JVC Bks.

Park, Marion Ford. New Tales of Robin's Wood. unabridged ed. 20p. 1995. spiral bd. 5.00 (*1-929326-44-0*) Hal Bar Pubg.

— Tales of Robin's Wood. 20p. 1995. spiral bd. 5.00 (*1-929326-42-4*) Hal Bar Pubg.

Park, Marlene & Markowitz, Gerald E. New Deal for Art: The Government Art Projects of the 1930s with Examples from New York City & State. (Illus.). 172p. 1977. 30.00 (*0-934483-00-0*) Gal Assn NY.

Park, Mary J. Conscious Living: A Practical Guide to Living the Life You Want. 140p. 1999. pap. 12.00 (*0-9672495-1-1*) Hot Pot Pubg.

Park, Mary J. & Olson, Keith R. Grandma's Homestyle Recipes: Doris Olson's Cookbook. 124p. 1999. pap. 12.00 (*0-9672495-0-3*) Hot Pot Pubg.

***Park, Mary J. & Park, Hae Ok.** Everyday Korean Cooking. 133p. 1999. pap. 12.00 (*0-9672495-2-X*) Hot Pot Pubg.

Park, Mary W. InfoThink: Practical Strategies for Using Information in Business. LC 97-42346. (Illus.). 280p. 1998. 29.50 (*0-8108-3424-3*) Scarecrow.

Park, Maurice E. & Park, Dorcas D. Real Estate Law, with Forms: 85 Pocket Parts, 2 vols. 2nd ed. LC 80-54847. (Massachusetts Practice Ser.). 1981. 106.00 (*0-685-42577-0*) West Pub.

Park, Maxwell G. Training in Objective Educational Measurements for Elementary School Teachers. LC 70-177143. (Columbia University. Teachers College. Contributions to Education Ser.: No. 520). (C). reprint ed. 37.50 (*0-404-55520-9*) AMS Pr.

Park, Merri L. Menopause Time for a Change: The Menopause Handbook for Safe & Effective, Natural Self-Care Approaches. 4th ed. LC 97-91907. 304p. 1997. pap. 16.95 (*0-920470-33-5*) Alive Bks.

Park, Mia, ed. see Brady, Michael K.

Park, Michael A. Biological Anthropology. 2nd ed. LC 98-4068. xviii, 412p. 1998. pap. text 47.95 (*0-7674-0512-9*, 0512-9) Mayfield Pub.

Park, Michael A., jt. auth. see Feder, Kenneth L.

***Park, Michael Alan.** Biological Anthropology: An Introductory Reader. 2nd ed. LC 99-53183. xv, 230p. 2000. pap. text 24.95 (*0-7674-1188-9*, 1188-9) Mayfield Pub.

Park, Miriam & Park, Harold. Fannettsburg Presbyterian Records, 1851-1970. LC 96-163063. 446p. 1995. per. 39.95 (*1-55856-206-0*, 023) Closson Pr.

***Park, Mungo.** Travels in the Interior Districts of Africa: Performed Under the Direction of the African Association in the Years 1795, 1796 1797. Marsters, Kate Ferguson, ed. LC 00-21534. (Illus.). 408p. 2000. lib. bdg. 59.95 (*0-8223-2502-0*) Duke.

Park, Mungo & Rennell, James. Travels in the Interior Districts of Africa. 1977. 18.95 (*0-405-18974-5*, 16889) Ayer.

***Park, Mungo, et al.** Travels in the Interior Districts of Africa: Performed under the Direction of the African Association in the Years 1795, 1796, 1797. LC 00-21534. (Illus.). 408p. 2000. pap. 19.95 (*0-8223-2537-3*) Duke.

Park, Myosik. Jungsoon. LC 84-90581. (Illus.). 304p. 1984. 21.95 (*0-932187-00-5*) M P Pubns.

Park, Myung-Jin, jt. ed. see Curran, James.

Park, Myung K. Pediatric Cardiology for Practitioners. 3rd ed. (Illus.). 560p. (C). (gr. 13). 1995. text 69.95 (*0-8151-6632-X*, 24218) Mosby Inc.

— The Pediatric Cardiology Handbook. 2nd ed. (Illus.). 368p. (C). (gr. 13). 1996. pap. text 29.95 (*0-8151-9005-0*, 29094) Mosby Inc.

Park, Myung K. & Guntheroth, Warren G. How to Read Pediatric ECGS. 3rd ed. (Illus.). 264p. (C). (gr. 13). 1992. pap. text 47.95 (*0-8016-6834-4*, 06834) Mosby Inc.

Park, Myungkark. Does He Open up on a Shoe String? (Illus.). 100p. 1997. pap. write for info. (*1-877974-31-5*) Prompter Pubns.

— Does Winter Come Earlier in the Basement? (Orig.). 1995. pap. write for info. (*1-877974-27-7*) Prompter Pubns.

— A Foundation of Prompter Physics V. Park, M. K., ed. 95p. 1993. pap. write for info. (*1-877974-74-9*) Prompter Pubns.

— A Foundation of Prompter Physics IV. (Illus.). 136p. 1992. pap. write for info. (*1-877974-73-0*) Prompter Pubns.

— A Foundation of Prompter Physics II. Park, M. K., ed. (Illus.). 110p. 1992. pap. write for info. (*1-877974-71-4*) Prompter Pubns.

— A Foundation of Prompter Physics VI. Park, M. K., ed. 122p. 1994. pap. write for info. (*1-877974-75-7*) Prompter Pubns.

— A Foundation of Prompter Physics VII. Park, M. K., ed. 100p. 1994. pap. write for info. (*1-877974-76-5*) Prompter Pubns.

— Here We Go... (Illus.). 92p. 1998. pap. write for info. (*1-877974-32-3*) Prompter Pubns.

— It's a Good Start . . . M. K.! (Illus.). 100p. (Orig.). 1989. pap. write for info. (*1-877974-06-4*) Prompter Pubns.

— Lotus. LC 91-67959. (Illus.). 130p. (Orig.). 1992. pap. write for info. (*1-877974-22-6*) Prompter Pubns.

— New Horizon . . . (Illus.). 100p. (Orig.). 1991. pap. write for info. (*1-877974-19-6*) Prompter Pubns.

— November Rain. (Illus.). 100p. 1997. pap. write for info. (*1-877974-30-7*) Prompter Pubns.

***Park, Myungkark.** One More, This Time... (Illus.). 100p. 1999. pap. write for info. (*1-877974-37-4*) Prompter Pubns.

Park, Myungkark. Physics Family. (Illus.). 100p. (Orig.). 1991. pap. write for info. (*1-877974-21-8*) Prompter Pubns.

— Prompter Is a Royal Publisher. 100p. 1996. pap. write for info. (*1-877974-28-5*) Prompter Pubns.

— RR of '90s I. (Illus.). 100p. 1994. pap. write for info. (*1-877974-24-2*) Prompter Pubns.

— RR of '90s II. 100p. 1994. pap. write for info. (*1-877974-25-0*) Prompter Pubns.

— Sounds All Right! (Illus.). 100p. 1998. pap. write for info. (*1-877974-33-1*) Prompter Pubns.

— Stars in Heaven & Stars on Earth. 1995. pap. write for info. (*1-877974-26-9*) Prompter Pubns.

— Streak of Fire Balls. 100p. 1996. pap. write for info. (*1-877974-29-3*) Prompter Pubns.

***Park, Myungkark.** This, This, This & That. (Illus.). 98p. 1999. pap. write for info. (*1-877974-34-X*) Prompter Pubns.

Park, Myungkark. Two Dimensional Heaven & Earth. 100p. (Orig.). 1993. pap. write for info. (*1-877974-23-4*) Prompter Pubns.

***Park, Myungkark.** Where Is the Stack Pointer? (Illus.). 100p. 1999. pap. write for info. (*1-877974-36-6*) Prompter Pubns.

An Asterisk (*) at the beginning of an entry indicates that the title is appearing for the first time.

Park, Myungkark. Wow, Prompter Did It Again . . . (Illus.). 100p. (Orig.). 1991. pap. write for info. (*1-877974-15-3*) Prompter Pubns.

***Park, Myungkark.** You're Right on Time, Pluto... 1999. write for info. (*1-877974-35-8*) Prompter Pubns.

Park, Myungkark, ed. see Park, M. K.

Park, N. J., tr. see Baehr, H. D. & Stephan, K.

Park, Namgi, jt. auth. see Weidman, John.

Park, Nick. Wallace & Gromit: A Close Shave. LC 97-113328. (J). 1996. pap. 7.99 (*0-385-32321-2*, DD Bks Yng Read) BDD Bks Young Read.

Park, O. Pselaphidae of Oceania, with Special Reference to the Fiji Islands. (BMB Ser.). 1974. reprint ed. pap. 25.00 (*0-527-02315-9*) Periodicals Srv.

***Park, O'Hyun.** An Invitation to Dialouge Between East & West: A Critique of the Modern & the Postmodern Thought. (Asian Thought & Culture Ser.: Vol. 29). 160p. 1999. pap. text 27.95 (*0-8204-4944-X*) P Lang Pubng.

Park, O'Hyun, tr. see Xishan.

Park, P., ed. Prevention & Social Medicine. 12th ed. (C). 1989. 110.00 (*0-7855-4677-4*, Pub. by Current Dist) St Mut.

Park, Patricia D., et al. Environmental Education & Training. 140p. 1997. text 51.95 (*1-85972-443-4*, Pub. by Ashgate Pub Co) Ashgate Pub Co.

Park, Paul. Celestis. 1997. pap. 13.95 (*0-312-86285-7*) St Martin.

— Coelestis: Man into Beast. 288p. 1995. 21.95 (*0-312-85899-X*, Pub. by Tor Bks) St Martin.

— The Cult of Loving Kindness. 320p. 1992. mass mkt. 4.50 (*0-380-71819-7*, Avon Bks) Morrow Avon.

— The Gospel of Corax. 1997. pap. write for info. (*0-15-600506-9*); pap. 13.00 (*0-15-600517-4*) Harcourt.

— Soldiers of Paradise. 288p. 1990. pap. 3.95 (*0-380-70581-8*, Avon Bks) Morrow Avon.

— Sugar Rain. 384p. 1990. reprint ed. pap. 3.95 (*0-380-71179-6*, Avon Bks) Morrow Avon.

Park, Peter. Growth Management & Environmental Quality. (Publications in Architecture & Urban Planning Ser.: Vol. R94-11). 82p. 1994. pap. 12.00 (*1-886437-03-3*) U of Wis Ctr Arch-Urban.

Park, Peter. Sociology Tomorrow: An Evaluation of Sociological Theories in Terms of Science. LC 68-27989. 1968. reprint ed. pap. 12.95 (*0-672-63596-8*) Irvington.

Park, Peter, et al, eds. Voices of Change: Participatory Research in the United States & Canada. LC 92-42898. 232p. 1993. 55.00 (*0-89789-334-4*, H334, Bergin & Garvey) Greenwood.

Park, Peter, jt. auth. see Moses, James.

Park, Polly, ed. To Save Their Heathen Souls: Voyage to & Life in Foochow, China, Based on Wentworth Diaries & Letters, 1854-1858. LC 84-4247. (Pittsburgh Theological Monographs, New Ser.: No. 9). (Illus.). (Orig.). 1984. pap. 6.00 (*0-915138-66-2*) Pickwick.

Park, R. E. Sketch of Twelfth Alabama Infantry. 26.95 (*0-8488-0218-7*, J M C & Co) Amereon Ltd.

Park, R. G. Geological Structures & Moving Plates. 350p. (gr. 13). 1988. mass mkt. 56.95 (*0-412-01631-1*, Chap & Hall NY) Chapman & Hall.

Park, R. W., jt. auth. see Harrigan, W. F.

Park, Rebecca, tr. see Mamonova, Tatyana, ed.

Park, Richard J. Value Engineering: A Plan for Invention. LC 98-36770. 352p. 1998. boxed set 54.95 (*1-57444-235-X*) St Lucie Pr.

Park, Richard L. & Lambert, Richard D., eds. The American Revolution Abroad. LC 76-19935. (Annals Ser.: No. 428). 200p. 1976. 28.00 (*0-87761-206-4*); pap. 18.00 (*0-87761-207-2*) Am Acad Pol Soc Sci.

Park, Richard L., ed. see Newell, Richard S.

Park, Richard W., jt. auth. see Koff, Theodore H.

***Park, Robert.** Voodoo Science: The Road from Foolishness to Fraud. LC 99-40911. 256p. 2000. 25.00 (*0-19-513515-6*) OUP.

Park, Robert & Paulay, Thomas. Reinforced Concrete Structures. 800p. 1975. 165.00 (*0-471-65917-7*, Wiley-Interscience) Wiley.

Park, Robert, ed. see Smith, Ronald H.

Park, Robert Ezra. The Crowd & the Public: And Other Essays. Elsner, Henry, Jr., ed. Elsner, Charlotte, tr. from GER. LC 78-189361. (Heritage of Sociology Ser.). 184p. (C). 1994. lib. bdg. 15.00 (*0-226-64609-2*) U Ch Pr.

— The Crowd & the Public & Other Essays. Elsner, Henry, Jr., ed. Elsner, Charlotte, tr. from GER. LC 78-189361. (Heritage of Sociology Ser.). xxxii, 146p. (C). 1992. pap. text 2.25 (*0-226-64610-6*, P459) U Ch Pr.

— Immigrant Press & Its Control. LC 77-145223. (Illus.). 1971. reprint ed. 15.00 (*0-403-01140-X*) Scholarly.

Park, Robert Ezra & Burgess, Ernest W. Introduction to the Science of Sociology. 3rd ed. Janowitz, Morris, ed. LC 69-15366. (Heritage of Sociology Ser.). 1996. lib. bdg. 48.00 (*0-226-64604-1*) U Ch Pr.

Park, Robert Ezra & Miller, Herbert A. Old World Traits Transplanted. LC 69-18788. (American Immigration Collection. Series 1). (Illus.). 1969. reprint ed. 16.95 (*0-405-00536-9*) Ayer.

Park, Robert Ezra, et al. The City. LC 66-23694. (Heritage of Sociology Ser.). 250p. 1984. reprint ed. pap. text 16.00 (*0-226-64611-4*) U Ch Pr.

Park, Robert S., ed. see Park, Kathryn E.

Park, Roberta J. & Eckert, Helen M., eds. New Possibilities, New Paradigms? LC 90-23215. (American Academy of Physical Education Papers). 176p. 1991. pap. text 15.00 (*0-87322-313-6*, BPAR0313) Human Kinetics.

Park, Roberta J. & Mangan, James A., eds. From "Fair Sex" to Feminism: Sport & the Socialization of Women in the Industrial & Post-Industrial Eras. LC 86-17529. 224p. 1986. 47.50 (*0-7146-3288-0*, Pub. by F Cass Pubs) Intl Spec Bk.

Park, Roberta J., jt. ed. see Berryman, Jack W.

Park, Roberta J., jt. ed. see Harris, Janet C.

Park, Roger C. & McFarland, Douglas D. Computer-Aided Exercises on Civil Procedure. 4th ed. LC 95-16454. 239p. (C). 1995. pap. 25.50 (*0-314-06194-0*) West Pub.

Park, Roger C. & Waltz, Jon R. 1998 Supplement to Cases & Materials on Evidence. 8th ed. (University Casebook Ser.). 119p. (C). 1998. pap. text 7.95 (*1-56662-670-6*) Foundation Pr.

Park, Roger C., et al. Evidence Law: A Student's Guide to the Law of Evidence As Applied to American Trials (Hornbook Series) LC 98-26831. (Paralegal). 500p. 1998. pap. text 28.50 (*0-314-21475-5*) West Pub.

— Minnesota Evidentiary Foundations. LC 96-75722. 1996. 80.00 (*1-55834-353-9*, 66836-10, MICHIE) LEXIS Pub.

— Minnesota Evidentiary Foundations: 1998 Cumulative Supplement. 32p. 1998. pap. 80.00 (*0-327-00572-6*, 6683711) LEXIS Pub.

Park, Roger C., jt. auth. see Waltz, Jon R.

Park, Rolla E. Incremental Costs & Efficient Prices with Lumpy Capacity: The Two Product Case. LC 94-9620. 1994. pap. text 13.00 (*0-8330-1523-0*, MR-427-ICTF) Rand Corp.

Park, Rolla E., et al. The Search for Equity in School Finance. LC 79-12408. (Report Ser.). ix, 29 p. 1979. pap. 10.00 (*0-8330-0120-5*) Rand Corp.

Park, Rolla E., jt. auth. see Heilbrunn, Joanna Z.

Park, Rosemarie, et al. Reading: Skill Enhancement. 200p. 1994. teacher ed. 8.00 (*0-318-70382-3*) Paradigm MN.

— Reading: Skill Enhancement, Text. LC 93-5465. 200p. 1994. pap. text 10.95 (*1-56118-204-4*) Paradigm MN.

— Reading for Workplace Success. 351p. (C). 1991. pap. text 17.95 (*1-56118-200-1*); pap. text, teacher ed. 8.00 (*1-56118-201-X*) Paradigm MN.

Park, Ruth. My Sister Sif. 1997. 10.50 (*0-606-11657-5*, Pub. by Turtleback) Demco.

— Things in Corners. 1999. pap. 3.99 (*0-14-036331-9*, Viking) Viking Penguin.

Park, Sam O. & LeHeron, Richard, eds. The Asian Pacific Rim & Globalization. LC 95-75576. 208p. 1995. 68.95 (*1-85628-894-3*, Pub. by Avebry) Ashgate Pub Co.

Park, Se-Hark & Labys, Walter C. Industrial Development & Environmental Degradation: A Source Book on the Origins of Global Pollution. LC 98-5815. 208p. 1998. 80.00 (*1-85898-883-7*) E Elgar.

Park, Semin. The Duty of Disclosure in Insurance Contract Law. LC 96-44638. (Illus.). 304p. 1996. 89.95 (*1-85521-923-9*, Pub. by Dartmth Pub) Ashgate Pub Co.

Park, Seok Jae, jt. auth. see Vishniac, Ethan T.

Park, Seung-Chan. Die Rezeption der Sprachphilosophie in der Theologie Des Thomas Von Aquin: Mit Besonderer Berucksichtigung der Analogie. LC 98-56174. (Studien und Texte zur Geistesgeschichte des Mittelalters Ser.: No. 65). 528p. 1999. 153.00 (*90-04-11272-3*) Brill Academic Pubs.

***Park, Severna.** The Annunciate. LC 99-31434. 304p. 1999. 23.00 (*0-380-97737-0*, Avon Bks) Morrow Avon.

Park, Severna. Hand of Prophecy. LC 97-27459. 320p. 1998. mass mkt. 14.00 (*0-380-97639-0*, Avon Bks) Morrow Avon.

— Hand of Prophecy. LC 97-27459. 320p. 1999. mass mkt. 5.99 (*0-380-79158-7*, Eos) Morrow Avon.

— Speaking Dreams. LC 96-95167. 256p. 1997. mass mkt. 5.99 (*0-380-72924-5*, Avon Bks); mass mkt. 5.99 (*0-614-27711-6*, Avon Bks) Morrow Avon.

Park, Sharon C. Appropriate Methods for Reducing Lead Paint Hazards in Historic Housing. 16p. 1995. pap. 1.75 (*0-16-061668-9*) USGPO.

— Heating, Ventilating & Cooling Historic Buildings: Problems & Recommended Approaches. 14p. 1991. pap. 1.00 (*0-16-061650-6*) USGPO.

— Holding the Line: Controlling Unwanted Moisture in Historic Buildings. 16p. 1996. pap. 1.50 (*0-16-061678-6*) USGPO.

— Mothballing Historic Buildings. 14p. 1993. pap. 1.50 (*0-16-061659-X*) USGPO.

Park, Soon-Ung, jt. auth. see Bashkin, V. N.

Park, Soon Won. Colonial Industrialization & Labor in Korea: The Onoda Cement Factory. LC 99-24359. (Harvard-Hallym Series on Korean Studies). 325p. 1999. 42.50 (*0-674-14240-3*) HUP.

Park, Stephen K., ed. Visual Information Processing VI. 41p. 1997. pap. 80.00 (*0-8194-2489-7*) SPIE.

***Park, Stephen K. & Juday, Richard D., eds.** Visual Information Processing VIII. 270p. 1999. pap. text 84.00 (*0-8194-3190-7*) SPIE.

Park, Stephen K. & Juday, Richard D., eds. Visual Information Processing VII. adapted ed. (Proceedings of SPIE Ser.: Vol. 3387). 412p. 1998. 89.00 (*0-8194-2836-1*) SPIE.

Park Street Press Staff, ed. The Return of the Tribal Body Adornment Kit. (Illus.). 64p. 1998. pap. 25.00 (*0-89281-792-5*) Inner Tradit.

Park, Sun-Kwang. Geschlecht und Klasse: Die Frauenfrage in Den Proletarischen Selbstdarstellungen der Frugen Deutschen und Koreanischen Arbeiterliteratur. (GER.). 190p. 1997. 42.95 (*3-631-31644-5*) P Lang Pubng.

Park, Sung-Bong. An Aesthetics of the Popular Arts. (Aesthetica Upsaliensia Ser.: No. 5). 188p. (Orig.). 1993. pap. 47.50 (*91-554-3047-3*, Pub. by Uppsala Universitet) Coronet Bks.

Park, Sung H. Bridge Inspection & Structural Analysis: Handbook of Bridge Inspection. LC 80-81421. (Illus.). 312p. (Orig.). 1980. pap. text 20.00 (*0-9604440-0-9*) S H Park.

— Bridge Rehabilitation & Replacement (Bridge Repair Practice) LC 82-90094. (Illus.). 818p. (C). 1984. text 70.00 (*0-9604440-1-7*) S H Park.

***Park, Sung H. & Vining, G. Geoffrey, eds.** Statistical Process Monitoring & Optimization. LC 99-38518. (Statistics, Textbooks & Monographs: Vol. 160). (Illus.). 489p. 1999. text 175.00 (*0-8247-6007-7*) Dekker.

Park, Susan, jt. ed. see Starr, Mildred.

Park, Taeun, jt. auth. see Buchanan, Relva C.

Park, Taisoo, ed. Taxonomy & Distribution of the Marine Calanoid Copepod Family Euchaetidae. LC 94-28941. 1995. pap. text 26.00 (*0-520-09802-1*, Pub. by U CA Pr) Cal Prin Full Svc.

Park, Tarjei, ed. The English Mystics: An Anthology. LC 99-218566. 144p. 1998. pap. text 15.95 (*0-281-05110-0*) Intl Pubs Mktg.

***Park, Ted.** Israel. LC 99-58639. (Taking Your Camera to Ser.). (Illus.). 32p. (J). 2000. lib. bdg. 22.83 (*0-7398-1801-5*) Raintree Steck-V.

***Park, Ted, contrib. by.** Brazil. LC 99-58641. (Taking Your Camera to Ser.). 32p. (J). 2000. lib. bdg. 22.83 (*0-7398-1802-3*) Raintree Steck-V.

— Canada. LC 99-57515. (Taking Your Camera to Ser.). 32p. 2000. lib. bdg. 22.83 (*0-7398-1803-1*) Raintree Steck-V.

— Mexico. LC 99-58643. (Taking Your Camera to Ser.). 32p. (J). 2000. lib. bdg. 22.83 (*0-7398-1804-X*) Raintree Steck-V.

— Taking Your Camera to Japan. LC 99-58640. (Taking Your Camera to Ser.). 32p. (J). 2000. lib. bdg. 22.83 (*0-7398-1805-8*) Raintree Steck-V.

Park, Thelma. The House of Neh. (Illus.). 178p. (Orig.). 1986. pap. 9.95 (*1-55630-023-9*) Brentwood Comm.

Park, Therese. A Gift of the Emperor. LC 97-25489. 360p. 1997. pap. 10.95 (*1-883523-21-4*) Spinsters Ink.

Park, Thomas, ed. Harleian Miscellany, 10 vols. LC 02-21219. reprint ed. 950.00 (*0-404-03140-4*) AMS Pr.

Park, Thomas, ed. see Harington, John.

Park, Thomas K. Historical Dictionary of Morocco. LC 96-7300. (African Historical Dictionaries Ser.: No. 74). 544p. 1996. 69.50 (*0-8108-3168-6*) Scarecrow.

Park, Thomas K., ed. Risk & Tenure in Arid Lands: The Political Ecology of Development in the Senegal River Basin. LC 93-9691. (Monographs on Arid Lands Development). 383p. 1993. 35.00 (*0-8165-1374-0*) U of Ariz Pr.

Park, Thomas K., et al. Conflicts over Land & the Crisis of Nationalism in Mauritania. (LTC Papers: No. 142). 55p. 1991. pap. 7.00 (*0-934519-59-5*, LTC 142) U of Wis Land.

— Les Conflits Fonciers et la Crise du Nationalisme en Mauritanie. (LTC Papers: Vól. 142-F).Tr. of Conflicts over Land & the Crisis of Nationalism in Mauritania. (FRE.). xi, 51p. (C). 1991. pap. 7.00 (*0-934519-60-9*, LTC142-F) U of Wis Land.

Park, Tom. Runamok: A Novel about the Realties of Small Business. (Pacesetter Bks.). 256p. 1996. text 19.95 (*1-56079-662-6*, Petersons Pacesetter) Petersons.

Park, Tong Whan. The U. S. & the Two Koreas: A New Triangle. LC 98-11346. 325p. 1998. 55.00 (*1-55587-807-5*) L Rienner.

Park, Vicki. The Complete Live Don't Diet! LC 98-29455. viii, 521 p. 1998. write for info. (*1-58173-146-9*) Sweetwater Pr.

— Exceed the Feed Limit! Out of the Fat Lane into a Healthier Life Without Diets or Deprivation. LC 96-71399. 256p. (Orig.). 1997. pap. 16.95 (*0-9642733-1-4*) Pepper Tree Pr.

— Instant Willpower: Mind over Platter in a Flash! A Portable Pocket-Size Willpower Coach. LC 98-91196. 128p. 1998. pap. 6.95 (*0-9642733-3-0*) Pepper Tree Pr.

— Live, Don't Diet! The Low-Fat Cookbook That Can Change Your Life! LC 95-35775. 252p. 1996. mass mkt. 16.99 (*0-446-67229-7*, Pub. by Warner Bks) Little.

Park, W. H. & Enos, J. L. The Adoption & Diffusion of Imported Technology: The Case of Korea. 224p. 1985. 55.00 (*0-7099-2030-X*, Pub. by C Helm) Routldge.

Park, W. W. & Corkhill, J. W. The Histology of Borderline Cancer. LC 79-26151. (Illus.). 480p. 1980. 93.00 (*3-540-09792-9*) Spr-Verlag.

Park, Wan-suh. A Sketch of the Fading Sun. Sallee, Hyun-jae Yee, ed. & tr. by. from KOR. (Terra Incognito Ser.: Vol. 4). 200p. 1999. pap. 15.00 (*1-877727-93-8*, Pub. by White Pine) SPD-Small Pr Dist.

Park, William. The Idea of Rococo. LC 90-51017. (Illus.). 144p. (C). 1993. 55.00 (*0-87413-434-X*) U Delaware Pr.

Park, William D., jt. auth. see Cromie, Stephen.

Park, William R. & Chapin-Park, Sue. How to Succeed in Your Own Business. LC 77-28955. (Wiley-Interscience Publications). 362p. reprint ed. pap. 112.30 (*0-608-12432-X*, 202517900042) Bks Demand.

Park, William R. & Chapin, Wayne B., Jr. Construction Bidding: Strategic Pricing for Profit. 2nd ed. LC 92-4460. (Practical Construction Guides Ser.). 328p. 1992. 110.00 (*0-471-54763-8*) Wiley.

Park, William W. International Forum Selection. LC 94-47495. 1995. 124.50 (*90-6544-883-7*) Kluwer Law Intl.

Park, Won C., ed. see International Congress on Applied Mineralogy in th.

Park, Won C., ed. see Metallurgical Society of AIME Staff.

Park, Y. H. Taekwondo Dinosaurs: How Dinosaurs Train to Get Their Black Belts. (Illus.). 32p. (J). 1994. pap. 5.95 (*0-9637151-4-3*) YH Pk Taekwondo.

— Taekwondo for Children. (Illus.). 128p. 1994. pap. text 9.95 (*0-9637151-5-1*) YH Pk Taekwondo.

Park, Y. H. & Leibowitz, Jeff. Taekwondo for Children: The Ultimate Reference Guide for Children Interested in the World's Most Popular Martial Art. (Illus.). 128p. (Orig.). (J). (gr. 4-8). 1994. pap. 9.95 (*0-9637151-0-0*) YH Pk Taekwondo.

***Park, Y. J.** Finite Element Analyses for Seismic Shear Wall International Standard Problem. 281p. 1998. per. 23.00 (*0-16-062912-8*) USGPO.

— Vibration Tests of Main Steam & Feedwater Piping Systems With Conventional & Energy-Absorbing Supports: Evaluation of Test Results & Post Test Analysis. 480p. 1998. per. 38.00 (*0-16-062951-9*) USGPO.

Park, Y. S., jt. ed. see Woo, J. C.

Park, Yeon H. & Seabourne, Thomas D. Taekwondo Techniques & Tactics. LC 96-37724. (Martial Arts Ser.). (Illus.). 192p. (Orig.). 1997. pap. 15.95 (*0-88011-644-7*, PPAR0644) Human Kinetics.

Park, Yoon S., ed. Semiconductors & Semimetals: Sic Material & Devices, Vol. 52. (Illus.). 420p. (C). 1998. boxed set 130.00 (*0-12-752160-7*) Acad Pr.

Park, Yoon S., jt. auth. see Buljevich, Esteban C.

Park, Yoon S., jt. ed. see Wang, Shih-Yuan.

***Park, You-me & Sunder Rajan, Rajeswari.** Austen in the World: Postcolonial Mappings. LC 00-22540. (Research in Postcolonial Literatures Ser.). 2000. write for info. (*0-415-23290-2*) Routledge.

***Park, Youngwon.** Milton & Isaiah: A Journey Through the Drama of Salvation in "Paradise Lost" LC 99-46192. (Seventeenth-Century Texts & Studies: Vol. 5). 160p. (C). 2000. text 47.95 (*0-8204-4288-7*) P Lang Pubng.

Park, Yung C., jt. auth. see Cole, David C.

Park, Yung C., jt. ed. see Patrick, Hugh T.

Park, Yung H. Bureaucrats & Ministers in Contemporary Japanese Government. LC 85-82273. (Japan Research Monographs: No. 8). 192p. 1986. pap. 15.00 (*0-912966-84-X*) IEAS.

Parkany, M., ed. Quality Assurance & TQM for Analytical Laboratories. 288p. 1995. 76.00 (*0-85404-760-3*) CRC Pr.

Parkany, M., jt. ed. see Fajgelj, A.

Parkanyi, Cyril. Theoretical Organic Chemistry, Vol. 5. LC 97-41024. (Theoretical & Computational Chemistry Ser.). 622p. 1997. 330.50 (*0-444-82660-2*) Elsevier.

Parkash, I. Desert Ecology. (C). 1988. text 125.00 (*81-85046-75-1*, Pub. by Scientific Pubs) St Mut.

Parkash, Ram. Advances in Forestry Research in India, Set, Vols. 1-10. 1993. pap. 495.00 (*0-7855-2744-3*, Pub. by Intl Bk Distr) St Mut.

— Advances in Forestry Research in India, Vols. 1-6. 265p. 1990. 148.00 (*0-7855-6541-8*, Pub. by Intl Bk Distr) St Mut.

— Advances in Forestry Research in India, Vols. 1-10. 265p. 1993. 210.00 (*81-7089-901-X*, Pub. by Intl Bk Distr) St Mut.

— Forest Management. 256p. 1986. 140.00 (*81-7089-082-9*, Pub. by Intl Bk Distr); pap. 175.00 (*0-7855-2743-5*, Pub. by Intl Bk Distr) St Mut.

— Forest Management. 256p. (C). 1986. 295.00 (*0-7855-6876-X*, Pub. by Intl Bk Distr); text 150.00 (*0-7855-6584-1*, Pub. by Intl Bk Distr) St Mut.

— Forest Surveying. 371p. (C). 1982. pap. 175.00 (*81-7089-001-2*, Pub. by Intl Bk Distr) St Mut.

— Propagation & Practice of Important Indian Trees. 460p. (C). 1991. pap. 250.00 (*81-7089-112-4*, Pub. by Intl Bk Distr) St Mut.

— Silviculture & Propagation of Indian Forest Trees. 400p. 1990. 210.00 (*81-7089-113-2*, Pub. by Intl Bk Distr) St Mut.

— Some Favorite Trees for Fuel & Fodder. 187p. (C). 1986. pap. 125.00 (*81-7089-039-X*, Pub. by Intl Bk Distr) St Mut.

— Theory & Practice of Silvicultural Systems. 256p. (C). 1983. text 150.00 (*0-7855-6585-X*, Pub. by Intl Bk Distr) St Mut.

— Theory & Practice of Silvicultural Systems. 256p. 1991. 195.00 (*81-7089-062-4*, Pub. by Intl Bk Distr); pap. 175.00 (*0-7855-2742-7*, Pub. by Intl Bk Distr) St Mut.

— Theory & Practice of Silvicultural Systems. 256p. (C). 1991. 260.00 (*0-7855-6875-1*, Pub. by Intl Bk Distr) St Mut.

— Theory & Practice of Silvicultural Systems. 300p. 1991. pap. 88.00 (*81-7089-148-5*, Pub. by Intl Bks & Periodicals) St Mut.

Parkay, Forrest W. & Hardcastle, Beverly. Becoming a Teacher. 4th annot. ed. 576p. (C). 1997. text, teacher ed. write for info. (*0-205-27992-9*, T7992-5) Allyn.

— Becoming a Teacher: Accepting the Challenge of a Profession. 560p. 1990. text 47.00 (*0-205-11910-7*, H19102) Allyn.

— Becoming a Teacher: Examination Copy. 4th ed. 608p. (C). 1997. text, teacher ed. write for info. (*0-205-27417-X*, T7417-3) Allyn.

Parkay, Forrest W. & Stanford, Beverly H. Becoming a Teacher. 4th ed. LC 97-11802. 584p. 1997. 73.00 (*0-205-26861-7*) P-H.

Parke, Barbara. Catch a Classic: Fun with Victorian Fiction. (Illus.). 44p. 1996. pap. 9.95 (*0-9644061-1-X*) Angell Pubns.

— Toni Morrison: A Guide to Her Novels. 2nd rev. ed. 32p. (Orig.). 1999. pap. text 9.95 (*0-9644061-3-6*) Angell Pubns.

— Virginia Woolf: A Reader's Guide. (Illus.). 40p. 1998. pap. 9.95 (*0-9644061-2-8*) Angell Pubns.

Parke, Brenda. A Pond. Curry, Don, ed. (Guided Reading Ser.). 8p. (J). (gr. k). 1997. pap. text 2.75 (*1-56784-920-2*) Newbridge Educ.

Parke, Caroline, ed. see Lodo, Venerable L.

Parke, Catherine N. Biography. LC 96-24584. 1996. 33.00 (*0-8057-0965-7*) Macmillan.

— Other People's Lives. LC 93-48034. 64p. (Orig.). 1994. pap. 9.00 (*0-933532-97-0*) BkMk.

— Samuel Johnson & Biographical Thinking. 200p. 1991. text 34.95 (*0-8262-0789-8*) U of Mo Pr.

Parke, Catherine N., ed. In the Shadow of Parnassus: Zoe Akin's Essays on American Poetry. LC 94-6472. 1994. 42.50 (*0-945636-60-1*) Susquehanna U Pr.

Parke, Charles R. Dreams to Dust: A Diary of the California Gold Rush, 1849-1850. Davis, James E., ed. LC 88-27763. 314p. 1989. reprint ed. pap. 97.40 (*0-608-03475-4*, 206418500008) Bks Demand.
Parke County Historical Society Staff, jt. auth. see Turner Publishing Company Staff.
Parke, D. V. The Biochemistry of Foreign Compounds. 1968. 129.00 (*0-08-012202-7*, Pub. by Pergamon Repr) Franklin.
Parke, David. The Epic of Unitarianism: Original Writings from the History of Liberal Religion. 1994. pap. 16.00 (*1-55896-246-8*, Skinner Hse Bks) Unitarian Univ.
***Parke, Elaine.** Join the Golden Rule Revolution: Practice One Habit Each Month of the Year. Patric, Darlene, ed. (Illus.). 288p. 2000. pap. 19.95 (*0-9677460-0-0*) Caring Media Intl.
Parke, Frederic I. & Waters, Keith. Computer Facial Animation. LC 96-25110. (Illus.). 384p. (C). 1996. text 66.00 (*1-56881-014-8*) AK Peters.
Parke, G. A. & Howard, C. M., eds. Space Structures, No. 4. 102p. 1993. 31.00 (*0-7277-1968-8*) Am Soc Civil Eng.
Parke, H. W. Festivals of the Athenians. LC 76-12819. (Aspects of Greek & Roman Life Ser.). (Illus.). 208p. 1977. pap. text 15.95 (*0-8014-9440-0*) Cornell U Pr.
— Greek Mercenary Soldiers. 250p. 1981. pap. 20.00 (*0-89005-386-3*) Ares.
— Sibyls & Sibylline Prophecy in Classical Antiquity. McGing, Brian C., ed. 256p. 1988. lib. bdg. 42.50 (*0-415-00343-1*) Routledge.
— Sibyls & Sibylline Prophecy in Classical Antiquity. LC 91-43625. 256p. (C). 1992. pap. 18.95 (*0-415-07638-2*, Pub. by Tavistock) Routldge.
***Parke, Hilary.** Ski & Snowboard Scotland. (Illus.). 124p. 1999. pap. 9.95 (*0-946487-35-9*, Pub. by Luath Pr Ltd) Midpt Trade.
Parke, J. P. & Ward, T. Lloyd: Genealogical Notes Relating to the Families of Lloyd, Pemberton, Hutchinson, Hudson & Parke. Glenn, T. A., ed. 89p. 1992. reprint ed. pap. 18.00 (*0-8328-2679-0*); reprint ed. lib. bdg. 28.00 (*0-8328-2678-2*) Higginson Bk Co.
Parke, Janet E., jt. auth. see Floyd, Patricia A.
Parke, Lawrence. Acting Truths & Fictions. LC 95-75729. 448p. (Orig.). 1995. pap. 22.50 (*0-9615288-7-7*) Acting World Bks.
— The Film Actor's Complete Career Guide. LC 91-73555. (Illus.). 394p. (Orig.). 1992. pap. 24.95 (*0-9615288-9-3*) Acting World Bks.
— How to Start Acting in Film & Television Wherever You Are in America. LC 93-70044. (Illus.). 144p. (Orig.). 1993. pap. 19.95 (*0-9615288-4-2*) Acting World Bks.
— Since Stanislavski & Vakhtangov: The Method As a System for Today's Actor. 272p. (Orig.). 1986. pap. 12.95 (*0-9615288-8-5*) Acting World Bks.
Parke, Margaret. A Garden for Cutting: Gardening for Flower Arrangements. LC 93-10806. (Illus.). 224p. 1993. 35.00 (*1-55670-250-7*) Stewart Tabori & Chang.
Parke, Marilyn & Panik, Sharon. A Quetzalcoatl Tale of Corn. (SPA.). 1992. pap. 8.99 (*0-86653-964-6*) Fearon Teacher Aids.
— A Quetzalcoatl Tale of the Ball Game - Teachers Guide. 1992. pap. 8.99 (*0-86653-960-3*) Fearon Teacher Aids.
Parke, N. Grier, II. Ackley. Ancestry of Lorenzo Ackley & His Wife Emma Arabella Bosworth. Jacobus, Donald L., ed. (Illus.). 325p. 1997. reprint ed. pap. 49.00 (*0-8328-7207-5*); reprint ed. lib. bdg. 59.00 (*0-8328-7206-7*) Higginson Bk Co.
Parke, N. Grier, II, jt. auth. see Camp, John F., Jr.
Parke, Peter S., compiled by. Satellite Imagery Interpretation for Forecasters, 3 vols., Set. (Monograph Ser.: No. 2-86). (C). 1993. reprint ed. pap. text 51.00 (*1-883563-04-6*) Natl Weather.
— Satellite Imagery Interpretation for Forecasters, Vol. 1. (Monograph Ser.: No. 2-86). 240p. (C). 1993. reprint ed. pap. text 20.00 (*1-883563-01-1*) Natl Weather.
— Satellite Imagery Interpretation for Forecasters, Vol. 2. (Monograph Ser.: No. 2-86). 248p. (C). 1993. reprint ed. pap. text 20.00 (*1-883563-02-X*) Natl Weather.
— Satellite Imagery Interpretation for Forecasters, Vol. 3. (Monograph Ser.: No. 2-86). (C). 1993. reprint ed. pap. text 20.00 (*1-883563-03-8*) Natl Weather.
Parke, Preston G. Biorhythms, Biological Clocks & Periodicity: Index of New Information with Authors & Subjects. 180p. 1993. 47.50 (*1-55914-900-0*); pap. 44.50 (*1-55914-901-9*) ABBE Pubs Assn.
Parke, Robert B., jt. auth. see Searles, Robert A.
Parke, Ross D. Fatherhood. (Developing Child Ser.). 304p. 1996. 32.50 (*0-674-29517-X*); pap. 12.95 (*0-674-29518-8*) HUP.
— Fathers. LC 80-29079. (Developing Child Ser.). (Illus.). 144p. (C). 1981. pap. text 6.95 (*0-674-29516-1*) HUP.
Parke, Ross D., ed. Review of Child Development Research, Vol. 7. LC 64-20472. (Review of Child Development Research Ser.). x, 480p. 1999. lib. bdg. 36.00 (*0-226-64666-1*) U Ch Pr.
Parke, Ross D., et al, eds. A Century of Developmental Psychology. LC 94-4484. 684p. 1994. pap. text 34.95 (*1-55798-238-4*, 431-6411) Am Psychol.
Parke, Ross D. & Brott, Armin A. Throwaway Dads: The Myths & Barriers That Keep Men from Being the Fathers They Want to Be. LC 98-39656. 272p. 1999. 24.00 (*0-395-86041-5*) HM.
Parke, Ross D. & Kellam, Sheppard G., eds. Exploring Family Relationships with Other Social Contexts. (Advances in Family Research Ser.). 248p. 1994. text 59.95 (*0-8058-1073-0*) L Erlbaum Assocs.
Parke, Ross D. & Ladd, Gary W., eds. Family-Peer Relationships: Modes of Linkage. 424p. 1992. pap. 49.95 (*0-8058-0601-6*); text 89.95 (*0-8058-0600-8*) L Erlbaum Assocs.
Parke, Ross D., jt. auth. see Hetherington, E. Mavis.
Parke, Sara. No Fair Peeking. LC 90-85436. (Minnie 'n Me Ser.). (Illus.). 32p. (J). (gr. k-3). 1991. 5.95 (*1-56282-037-0*) Disney Pr.
Parke, Simon. Desert Ascent: or A Brief History of Eternity. 128p. 1997. pap. 10.95 (*0-340-69397-5*, Pub. by Hodder & Stought Ltd) Trafalgar.
— Desert Child: or Just How Amusing Can a Nightmare Be? 176p. 1998. pap. 10.95 (*0-340-69412-2*, Pub. by Hodder & Stought Ltd) Trafalgar.
Parke, Solitaire. Beyond the Astral Planes. (Larger World Trilogy Ser.). (Illus.). 245p. (C). 1994. text 21.95 (*1-885431-00-7*) Gray Wolf Prods.
***Parke-Taylor, Geoffrey H.** The Formation of the Book of Jeremiah: Doublets & Recurring Phrases. LC 00-27497. 2000. write for info. (*0-88414-003-2*) Soc Biblical Lit.
Parkel, Paula. Raven Cloud's Poems to Her Father: A Healing Journey. Rhiannon, Thea, ed. 26p. (Orig.). 1991. pap. text 5.95 (*0-9629349-0-9*) Raven Cloud.
Parkenham, Bette M. Sexology Encyclopedia Vol. 14: Menstruation Disorders: Index & Reference Books of New Information. Bartone, John C., ed. (Illus.). 150p. 1996. 49.95 (*0-7883-0876-9*); pap. 39.95 (*0-7883-0877-7*) ABBE Pubs Assn.
Parkening, Virtuoso. Virtuoso Parkening Plays Bach. 24p. 1997. 9.95 (*0-7935-8526-0*) H Leonard.
Parker. Favorite Sticker Album. (Little Activity Bks.). (Illus.). (J). 1991. pap. 1.00 (*0-486-26627-3*) Dover.
Parker. Handbook of Project Management. 1999. pap. 35.00 (*0-7494-2843-0*) Kogan Page Ltd.
Parker. Hip Fracture Management. 1994. pap. 230.00 (*0-8151-6051-8*) Mosby Inc.
Parker. I Love Spiders. (J). (ps-2). 1989. 19.95 (*0-590-50153-4*) Scholastic Inc.
***Parker.** Intro to Plant Science Lab Manual. 160p. 1999. lab manual ed. 25.00 (*0-7668-1542-0*) Delmar.
— Intro to Plant Science Lab Manual, IML. 48p. 1999. teacher ed., lab manual ed. 16.00 (*0-7668-1543-9*) Delmar.
Parker. Introduction to Food Science. (C). 2000. pap. 37.50 (*0-7668-1314-2*) Delmar.
***Parker.** An Introduction to Philosophy. 128p. (C). 2001. 40.00 (*0-02-391701-6*, Macmillan Coll) P-H.
Parker. Introduction to Tax 84: Update. Date not set. pap. text. write for info. (*0-314-88556-0*) West Pub.
— Management Information Systems. 2nd ed. 1993. teacher ed. 50.00 (*0-07-048574-7*) McGraw.
— Methods & Materials of Dental Hygiene. pap. write for info. (*0-7216-6014-2*, W B Saunders Co); pap. text, lab manual ed. write for info. (*0-7216-6015-0*, W B Saunders Co) Harcrt Hlth Sci Grp.
— Mfc Application Programming. 2000. 32.00 (*0-13-244971-4*) P-H.
***Parker.** More Innocent Times. 2000. pap. 10.95 (*0-552-14498-3*, Pub. by Transworld Publishers Ltd) Trafalgar.
Parker. New Cold Molded Boat Building. 1989. 29.95 (*0-07-157179-5*) McGraw.
— Psychology & Society: Radical Theory & Practice. 384p. 1996. pap. 21.95 (*0-7453-0879-1*, Pub. by Pluto GBR) Stylus Pub VA.
— The Reader's Companion to the Twentieth-Century Novel. write for info. (*1-85702-209-2*) OUP.
— Resignation or Revolt: The Political Economy of the Peace Process in Gaza, Vol. 1. 256p. 1999. text 59.50 (*1-86064-335-3*, Pub. by I B T) St Martin.
— Russia Reborn? The Labor Pains of the New Russia. 1996. 25.00 (*0-02-874078-5*) Free Pr.
— Science Navigator. 4th ed. 1998. 195.00 (*0-07-913762-8*) McGraw-Hill Prof.
***Parker.** Training the Racehorse. 2000. 29.95 (*0-85131-586-0*, Pub. by J A Allen) Trafalgar.
Parker. Volpone or The Fox. rev. ed. (Illus.). 250p. 1999. pap. 19.95 (*0-7190-3093-5*) St Martin.
Parker & Crist. Apollo vs. Dionysus: A Philosophy to Increase College Success. LC 97-186325. 208p. (C). 1997. per. 28.95 (*0-7872-3722-1*) Kendall-Hunt.
Parker & Derwent. Justice, Law & Society, Bk. 1. Date not set. pap. text. write for info. (*0-582-87002-X*, Pub. by Addison-Wesley) Longman.
— Justice, Law & Society, Bk. 2. Date not set. pap. text. write for info. (*0-582-87175-1*, Pub. by Addison-Wesley) Longman.
Parker & McIntyre. Women's Rights. 1996. mass mkt. 8.95 (*0-340-65589-5*, Pub. by Hodder & Stought Ltd) Trafalgar.
Parker & Wyatt. Practical Design Compiler. (C). 2001. pap. text 42.67 (*0-13-246117-X*) P-H.
Parker, jt. auth. see Derwent.
Parker, jt. auth. see Murphy.
Parker, jt. auth. see Roddenberry, Gene.
Parker & Parker Staff, jt. auth. see Parker, Wilbur A.
***Parker & Riley, ed.** Linguistics for Non-Linguistics: A Primer with Exercises. 3rd ed. LC 99-36109. 341p. (C). 1999. pap. text 41.00 (*0-205-29930-X*) Allyn.
Parker, A. Parker in America, Sixteen Thirty to Nineteen Ten, Genealogy, Biography, & History. (Illus.). 608p. 1989. reprint ed. pap. 91.00 (*0-8328-0937-3*); reprint ed. lib. bdg. 99.00 (*0-8328-0936-5*) Higginson Bk Co.
— Sediment Diagenesis. 1983. lib. bdg. 165.00 (*90-277-1677-3*) Kluwer Academic.
Parker, A. & Rae, J. E., eds. Environmental Interactions of Clays: Clays & the Environment. LC 97-46101. (Illus.). 210p. 1998. 84.95 (*3-540-58738-1*) Spr-Verlag.
Parker, A. & Sellwood, Bruce W., eds. Sediment Diagenesis. 1983. pap. text 84.00 (*90-277-1874-1*) Kluwer Academic.
Parker, A. C. Archeological History of New York, 2 vols., Set. 1993. reprint ed. lib. bdg. 180.00 (*0-7812-5163-X*) Rprt Serv.
— Constitution of the Five Nations. 158p. 1993. reprint ed. lib. bdg. 69.00 (*0-7812-5161-3*) Rprt Serv.
— Seneca Myths & Folk Tales. 465p. 1993. reprint ed. lib. bdg. 99.00 (*0-7812-5162-1*) Rprt Serv.
Parker, A. H., tr. see Steiner, Rudolf.
Parker, A. J., et al, eds. Mafic Dykes & Emplacement Mechanisms: Proceedings of the Second International Conference, Adelaide, South Australia, 12 - 15 September 1990. (Illus.). 560p. (C). 1990. text 123.00 (*90-6191-158-3*, Pub. by A A Balkema) Ashgate Pub Co.
Parker, A. Rani, et al. Gender Relations Analysis: A Guide for Trainers. 142p. 1995. pap. 19.95 (*1-888393-00-9*) Save the Children.
***Parker, Adam D.** African Americans in California. (California Cultures Ser.). (Illus.). 64p. 2000. pap. 14.95 (*1-884925-93-6*) Toucan Valley.
— Mountain Men in California. (California Biography Ser.). (Illus.). 64p. (J). (gr. 4-8). 1999. pap. text 14.95 (*1-884925-80-4*) Toucan Valley.
— People of the California Gold Rush. (California Biography Ser.). (Illus.). 64p. (J). (gr. 4-8). 1999. pap. text 14.95 (*1-884925-82-0*) Toucan Valley.
Parker, Addison. Breaking the Bank: Your Insider's Guide to Obtaining Business Loans. LC 94-32763. 148p. 1995. 17.95 (*0-945456-14-X*) PT Pubns.
— How to Obtain Business Loans: An Insider's Guide. LC 94-32763. 341p. 1995. pap. 17.95 (*0-945456-16-6*) PT Pubns.
Parker, Adrian. Images in Ochre: The Art & Craft of the Kunwinjku. 1998. pap. 18.95 (*0-86417-892-1*, Pub. by Kangaroo Pr) Seven Hills Bk.
***Parker, Al.** Murder in Detroit. LC 99-65321. 192p. 2000. pap. 11.95 (*1-56315-260-6*, Pub. by SterlingHse) Natl Bk Netwk.
Parker, Alan J. Algorithms & Data Structures in C ++ 272p. 1993. boxed set 68.95 (*0-8493-7171-6*, QA) CRC Pr.
Parker, Alan M. Days Like Prose. (Series of Poetry & Translation). 48p. (Orig.). 1997. pap. 12.00 (*1-882509-04-8*) Alef Bks.
— The Vandals. LC 98-76203. (American Poets Continuum Ser.: Vol. 53). 96p. 1999. pap. 12.50 (*1-880238-74-8*, Pub. by BOA Edns) Consort Bk Sales.
Parker, Alan M. & Willhardt, Mark, eds. The Routledge Anthology of Cross-Gendered Verse. LC 95-18991. 240p. (gr. 13). 1996. pap. 25.99 (*0-415-11291-5*) Routledge.
— The Routledge Anthology of Cross-Gendered Verse. 240p. (C). 1996. 85.00 (*0-415-11290-7*) Routledge.
Parker, Alan M., jt. auth. see Willhardt, Mark.
Parker, Alastair, ed. Winston Churchill: Studies in Statesmanship. (Illus.). 282p. (C). 1995. 24.95 (*1-85753-151-5*, Pub. by Brasseys) Brasseys.
Parker, Albert. Survey Methodology & Uses. Bryant, Laurie J., ed. 15p. (Orig.). 1979. pap. 9.00 (*0-317-04922-4*) Natl Coun Econ Dev.
Parker, Alice. Adolescent Chemical Workbook. rev. ed. 394p. 1995. pap. 11.95 (*1-55691-139-4*, 394) Learning Pubns.
— Creative Hymn Singing. 2nd ed. 74p. 1976. pap. 4.95 (*0-937276-03-0*, HMB103) Hinshaw Mus.
— The Get along Gang & the Christmas Thief. (J). 1986. 5.95 (*0-590-33372-0*) Scholastic Inc.
— Melodious Accord: Good Singing in Church. (Illus.). 100p. (Orig.). 1991. pap. 5.95 (*0-929650-43-3*, ACCORD) Liturgy Tr Pubns.
***Parker, Alice.** Sweet Manna, 1. 1999. 15.95 (*5-550-07300-5*) Nairi.
Parker, Alice A. Liminal Visions of Nicole Brossard. LC 96-38657. (Francophone Cultures & Literatures Ser.: Vol. 16). X, 287p. (C). 1998. text 53.95 (*0-8204-3065-X*) P Lang Pubng.
— Understand Your Dreams: 1500 Basic Dream Images & How to Interpret Them. 2nd ed. Carleton, Nancy, ed. LC 94-36260. 228p. 1995. pap. 12.00 (*0-915811-59-6*) H J Kramer Inc.
Parker, Alice A. & Meese, Elizabeth A., eds. Feminist Critical Negotiations. LC 91-46958. (Critical Theory Ser.: No. 9). xiv, 188p. 1992. 56.00 (*1-55619-175-8*); pap. 27.95 (*1-55619-176-6*) J Benjamins Pubng Co.
Parker, Alice A., jt. ed. see Meese, Elizabeth A.
Parker, Alice Anne. The Last of the Dream People. LC 97-37454. 228p. 1998. pap. 12.95 (*0-915811-79-0*) H J Kramer Inc.
Parker, Alice C. The Exploration of the Secret Smile: The Language of Art & of Homosexuality in Frank O'Hara's Poetry. (American University Studies: American Literature: Ser. XXIV, Vol. 25). 164p. (C). 1990. text 38.95 (*0-8204-0958-8*) P Lang Pubng.
— Global Communication - Thinking in English Bks. 1 & 2: Teachers Guide. Takahashi, Yoko, tr. (Illus.). 112p. 1998. pap., teacher ed. 15.95 (*1-892463-03-2*) JAB Prodns Inc.
— Global Communication Thinking in English, Vol. 1. Takahashi, Yoko, tr. (Illus.). 143p. 1998. pap. text 19.95 (*1-892463-00-8*) JAB Prodns Inc.
— Global Communication Thinking in English, Vol. 2. Takahashi, Yoko, tr. (Illus.). 100p. 1998. pap. text 19.95 (*1-892463-01-6*) JAB Prodns Inc.
— Global Communication-Toeic Skills Development. Takahashi, Yoko, tr. (Illus.). 212p. 1998. pap. text 39.95 (*1-892463-02-4*) JAB Prodns Inc.
Parker, Alison M. Purifying America: Women, Cultural Reform & Pro-Censorship Activism, 1873-1933. LC 96-45897. 304p. 1997. pap. text 16.95 (*0-252-06625-1*) U of Ill Pr.
***Parker, Alison M. & Cole, Stephanie.** Women & the Unstable State in Nineteenth-Century America. LC 99-54871. (Walter Prescott Webb Memorial Lectures Ser.: Vol. 33). 192p. 2000. 24.95 (*0-89096-930-2*) Tex A&M Univ Pr.
Parker, Allene, jt. auth. see Mansell, John.
Parker, Amasa J. Landmarks of Albany County, New York Pt. II: Biography. (Illus.). 1992. reprint ed. lib. bdg. 58.50 (*0-8328-2891-2*) Higginson Bk Co.
Parker, Amasa J., ed. Landmarks of Albany County, New York Pt. I: History. (Illus.). 1992. reprint ed. lib. bdg. 58.50 (*0-8328-2890-4*) Higginson Bk Co.
Parker, Amos A. Trip to the West & Texas: Far Western Frontier. LC 72-9463. (Illus.). 1973. reprint ed. 28.95 (*0-405-04991-9*) Ayer.
Parker, Andrew. The Internet Business Information Desk Reference. 1999. pap. 24.95 (*0-07-048621-2*) McGraw.
— Painfully Clear: The Parables of Jesus. (Biblical Seminar Ser.: No. 37). 166p. 1996. pap. 19.95 (*1-85075-771-2*, Pub. by Sheffield Acad) CUP Services.
Parker, Andrew, et al, eds. Nationalisms & Sexualities. (Illus.). 384p. (C). (gr. 13). 1991. pap. 23.99 (*0-415-90433-1*, A5731) Routledge.
Parker, Andrew & Sellwood, Bruce W., eds. Quantitative Diagenesis: Recent Developments & Applications to Reservoir Geology. LC 94-39299. (NATO ASI Series, Series C, Mathematical & Physical Sciences: Vol. 453). 1995. text 132.50 (*0-7923-3261-X*) Kluwer Academic.
***Parker, Andrew & Stamford, Jane.** Basic Skills - An Early Language Programme, Bk. 1. (J). (gr. k-3). 1999. pap. 20.00 (*0-7217-0608-8*, Pub. by Schofield) St Mut.
— Basic Skills - An Early Language Programme, Bk. 2. (J). (gr. k-3). 1999. pap. 20.00 (*0-7217-0609-6*, Pub. by Schofield) St Mut.
— Basic Skills - An Early Language Programme, Bk. 3. (J). (gr. k-3). 1999. pap. 20.00 (*0-7217-0610-X*, Pub. by Schofield) St Mut.
— Basic Skills - An Early Language Programme, Bk. 4. (J). (gr. k-3). 1999. pap. 20.00 (*0-7217-0611-8*, Pub. by Schofield) St Mut.
— Basic Skills - An Early Language Programme, Bk. 5. (J). (gr. k-3). 1999. pap. 20.00 (*0-7217-0612-6*, Pub. by Schofield) St Mut.
— English Practice: Year 3. (J). (gr. 2-7). 1999. pap. 45.00 (*0-7217-0661-4*, Pub. by Schofield) St Mut.
— English Practice: Year 4. (J). (gr. 2-7). 1999. pap. 45.00 (*0-7217-0662-2*, Pub. by Schofield) St Mut.
— English Practice: Year 5. (J). (gr. 2-7). 1999. pap. 45.00 (*0-7217-0663-0*, Pub. by Schofield) St Mut.
— English Practice: Year 6. (J). (gr. 2-7). 1999. pap. 45.00 (*0-7217-0664-9*, Pub. by Schofield) St Mut.
— Key Maths, Bk. 1. (J). (gr. k-2). 1999. pap., wbk. ed. 15.00 (*0-7217-2454-X*, Pub. by Schofield) St Mut.
— Key Maths, Bk. 2. (J). (gr. k-2). 1999. pap., wbk. ed. 15.00 (*0-7217-2455-8*, Pub. by Schofield) St Mut.
— Key Maths, Bk. 3. (J). (gr. k-2). 1999. pap., wbk. ed. 15.00 (*0-7217-2456-6*, Pub. by Schofield) St Mut.
— Key Maths, Bk. 4. (J). (gr. k-2). 1999. pap., wbk. ed. 15.00 (*0-7217-2457-4*, Pub. by Schofield) St Mut.
— Key Maths, Bk. 5. (J). (gr. k-2). 1999. pap., wbk. ed. 15.00 (*0-7217-2458-2*, Pub. by Schofield) St Mut.
— Number Books, Bk. 1. (J). (ps-2). 1999. pap., wbk. ed. 15.00 (*0-7217-2341-1*, Pub. by Schofield) St Mut.
— Number Books, Bk. 2. (J). (gr. 1-3). 1999. pap., wbk. ed. 15.00 (*0-7217-2342-X*, Pub. by Schofield) St Mut.
— Number Books, Bk. 3. (J). (ps-2). 1999. pap., wbk. ed. 15.00 (*0-7217-2343-8*, Pub. by Schofield) St Mut.
— Number Books, Bk. 4. (J). (ps-2). 1999. pap., wbk. ed. 15.00 (*0-7217-2344-6*, Pub. by Schofield) St Mut.
— Number Books, Bk. 5. (J). (ps-2). 1999. pap., wbk. ed. 15.00 (*0-7217-2345-4*, Pub. by Schofield) St Mut.
— Sound Practice, Bk. 1. (J). (gr. 1-3). 1999. pap. 20.00 (*0-7217-0392-5*, Pub. by Schofield) St Mut.
— Sound Practice, Bk. 2. (J). (gr. 1-3). 1999. pap. 20.00 (*0-7217-0393-3*, Pub. by Schofield) St Mut.
— Sound Practice, Bk. 3. (J). (gr. 1-3). 1999. pap. 20.00 (*0-7217-0394-1*, Pub. by Schofield) St Mut.
— Sound Practice, Bk. 4. (J). (gr. 1-3). 1999. pap. 20.00 (*0-7217-0395-X*, Pub. by Schofield) St Mut.
— Sound Practice, Bk. 5. (J). (gr. 1-3). 1999. pap. 20.00 (*0-7217-0396-8*, Pub. by Schofield) St Mut.
— Starting Science Bk. 1: Materials. (J). (gr. 1-3). 1999. pap., wbk. ed. 24.00 (*0-7217-3606-8*, Pub. by Schofield) St Mut.
— Starting Science Bk. 2: Living Things. (J). (gr. 1-3). 1999. pap., wbk. ed. 24.00 (*0-7217-3607-6*, Pub. by Schofield) St Mut.
— Starting Science Bk. 3: Light, Sound, Movement & Electricity. (J). (gr. 1-3). 1999. pap., wbk. ed. 24.00 (*0-7217-3608-4*, Pub. by Schofield) St Mut.
Parker, Andrew, jt. ed. see Sedgwick, Eve K.
Parker, Andrew D. Keeping the Promise: A Guide for Mentors. 48p. 1994. pap., student ed. 7.95 (*0-8192-4113-X*) Morehouse Pub.
Parker, Ann, photos by. Hajj Paintings: Folk Art of the Great Pilgrimage. LC 95-14994. (Illus.). 176p. 1995. 26.95 (*1-56098-546-1*) Smithsonian.
Parker, Anne, jt. auth. see Ball, Jody.
Parker, Anne M., jt. auth. see Friedman, Dana E.
Parker, Ant. Colors. (Touch & Feel Ser.). (Illus.). 12p. (J). 1999. pap. 4.95 (*0-7373-0288-7*, 02887W, Pub. by Lowell Hse) NTC Contemp Pub Co.
— Counting. (Touch & Feel Ser.). (Illus.). 12p. (J). 1999. pap. 4.95 (*0-7373-0292-5*, 02925W, Pub. by Lowell Hse) NTC Contemp Pub Co.
***Parker, Ant.** Ginger. (Illus.). 32p. (J). (gr. 8-11). 2000. pap. 5.95 (*1-57255-429-0*) Mondo Pubng.
— Ginger. 1999. pap. write for info. (*0-09-926564-8*, Pub. by Random) Random House.
Parker, Ant. It's Snacktime. LC 95-82378. (Illus.). 10p. (J). 1996. pap. 4.95 (*0-15-201370-9*) Harcourt.
— Opposites. (Touch & Feel Ser.). (Illus.). 12p. (J). 1999. pap. 4.95 (*0-7373-0294-1*, 02941W, Pub. by Lowell Hse) NTC Contemp Pub Co.
— Shapes. (Touch & Feel Ser.). 12p. (J). 1999. pap. 4.95 (*0-7373-0290-9*, 02909W, Pub. by Lowell Hse) NTC Contemp Pub Co.
***Parker, Ant.** Wake Up, Ginger. 1999. pap. write for info. (*0-09-926565-6*, Pub. by Random) Random House.

P

An Asterisk (*) at the beginning of an entry indicates that the title is appearing for the first time.

*Parker, Ant & Mitton, Tony. Terrific Trains. LC 97-39703. (J). 1998. 8.95 (*0-7534-5102-6*, Kingfisher) LKC.

Parker, Ant, jt. auth. see Emmett, Jonathan.

Parker, Anthony W. Scottish Highlanders in Colonial Georgia: The Recruitment, Emigration, & Settlement at Darien, 1735-1748. LC 97-15730. 192p. 1997. text 35.00 (*0-8203-1915-5*) U of Ga Pr.

Parker, Arliene. Forever & Always: A Love Story. 200p. 1998. pap. 9.95 (*1-57636-064-4*) SunRise Pbl.

Parker, Arlita D. History of Pemaquid Maine, with Sketches of Monhegan, Popham & Castine. (Illus.). 226p. 1997. reprint ed. lib. bdg. 29.50 (*0-8328-7108-7*) Higginson Bk Co.

Parker, Arthur C. The Archaeological History of New York, 2 vols. in 1. LC 76-43800. (New York State Museum Bulletin Ser.: Nos. 235, 236, 237, 238). reprint ed. 53.50 (*0-404-15656-8*) AMS Pr.

— The Indian How Book. LC 74-18592. (Illus.). 335p. 1975. reprint ed. pap. 7.95 (*0-486-21767-1*) Dover.

— The Life of General Ely S. Parker: Last Grand Sachem of the Iroquois & General Grant's Military Secretary. LC 83-19752. (Buffalo Historical Society, Publication Ser.: 23). (Illus.). 408p. reprint ed. 52.50 (*0-404-15658-4*) AMS Pr.

— Manual for History Museums. LC 36-985. reprint ed. 20.00 (*0-404-04887-0*) AMS Pr.

— The Monongahela: River of Dreams, River of Sweat. LC 99-14652. (Illus.). 200p. 1999. 35.00 (*0-271-01875-5*) Pa St U Pr.

— Parker on the Iroquois: Iroquois Uses of Maize & Other Food Plants. Fenton, William N., ed. LC 68-31036. (Illus.). 478p. 1981. pap. 16.95 (*0-8156-0115-8*) Syracuse U Pr.

— Red Jacket: Seneca Chief. LC 98-24221. (Illus.). 228p. 1998. pap. 10.00 (*0-8032-8755-0*, PARREX) U of Nebr Pr.

— Seneca Myths & Folk Tales. LC 89-4869. (Illus.). xxxiv, 485p. 1989. pap. 15.00 (*0-8032-8723-2*, Bison Books) U of Nebr Pr.

— Seneca Myths & Folk Tales. LC 76-43803. (Buffalo Historical Society, Publications Ser.: Vol. 27). reprint ed. 74.50 (*0-404-15659-2*) AMS Pr.

— Skunny Wundy: Seneca Indian Tales. (Iroquois & Their Neighbors Ser.). (Illus.). 224p. (C). 1994. reprint ed. pap. 17.95 (*0-8156-0292-8*) Syracuse U Pr.

Parker, B. Computer Literacy. 1996. pap. text 11.45 (*1-56870-245-0*) RonJon Pub.

— Creation: The Story of the Origin & Evolution of the Universe. LC 88-17893. (Illus.). 312p. (C). 1988. 22.95 (*0-306-42952-7*, Plenum Trade) Perseus Pubng.

— Einstein's Dream: The Search for a Unified Theory of the Universe. LC 86-15139. (Illus.). 298p. (C). 1988. 24.95 (*0-306-42343-X*, Plenum Trade) Perseus Pubng.

— Stairway to the Stars: The Story of the World's Largest Observatory. LC 94-21016. (Illus.). 360p. (C). 1994. 27.95 (*0-306-44763-0*, Plenum Trade) Perseus Pubng.

Parker, B., ed. Terrestrial Biology 3, 9 papers, Paper 5. (Antarctic Research Ser.: Vol. 30). (Illus.). 155p. 1979. write for info. (*0-87590-148-4*) Am Geophysical.

— Terrestrial Biology 3, 9 papers, Set 30-9. (Antarctic Research Ser.: Vol. 30). (Illus.). 155p. 1979. write for info. (*0-87590-146-8*); write for info. (*0-87590-147-6*); write for info. (*0-87590-145-X*) Am Geophysical.

— Terrestrial Biology III: Feeding Chases in the Adelie Penguin; the Mummified Seals of Southern Victoria Land, 9 papers, Set 30-9. (Antarctic Research Ser.: Vol. 30). (Illus.). 155p. 1979. 42.00 (*0-87590-175-1*) Am Geophysical.

— Terrestrial Biology II. (Antarctic Research Ser.: Vol. 37). 170p. 1983. 37.00 (*0-87590-185-9*) Am Geophysical.

Parker, B. & Hankins, J. Computer Science Lab Manual Using C++ 1996. pap. text 21.68 (*1-56870-246-9*) RonJon Pub.

Parker, B. F. History of Wolfeboro. (Illus.). 557p. 1989. reprint ed. lib. bdg. 57.50 (*0-8328-0569-6*) Higginson Bk Co.

Parker, B. F., ed. Solar Energy in Agriculture, Vol. 4. (Energy in World Agriculture Ser.). 448p. 1991. 275.50 (*0-444-88622-2*) Elsevier.

Parker, Barbara. Blood Relations. 448p. 1997. mass mkt. 6.99 (*0-451-18473-4*, Sig) NAL.

— Criminal Justice. large type ed. LC 97-34585. 1997. 25.95 (*1-56895-498-0*) Wheeler Pub.

— Globalization & Business Practice: Managing Across Boundaries. LC 98-60535. 655 p. 1998. write for info. (*0-7619-5693-X*) Sage.

***Parker, Barbara.** Suspicion of Betrayal. 432p. 2000. mass mkt. 6.99 (*0-451-19838-7*, Sig) NAL.

Parker, Barbara. Suspicion of Betrayal. LC 98-52080. 352p. 1999. 23.95 (*0-525-94468-0*, Dutton Studio) Studio Bks.

— Suspicion of Betrayal. LC 99-26443. 1999. 28.95 (*0-7862-2000-7*) Thorndike Pr.

— Suspicion of Deceit. 417p. 1999. reprint ed. mass mkt. 6.99 (*0-451-19549-3*, Sig) NAL.

— Suspicion of Guilt. 432p. 1996. mass mkt. 6.99 (*0-451-17703-7*, Sig) NAL.

— Suspicion of Guilt. large type ed. LC 95-16352. 1995. 25.95 (*1-56895-232-5*) Wheeler Pub.

— Suspicion of Innocence. 1994. 20.95 (*0-525-93747-1*, Dutt) Dutton Plume.

— Suspicion of Innocence. 432p. 1994. mass mkt. 6.99 (*0-451-17340-6*, Sig) NAL.

— Suspicion of Innocence. large type ed. LC 94-6064. 602p. 1994. reprint ed. lib. bdg. 22.95 (*0-7862-0212-2*) Thorndike Pr.

***Parker, Barbara.** Suspicion of Malice: A Gail Connor & Anthony Quintana Novel. 352p. 2000. 22.95 (*0-525-94542-3*) NAL.

— Suspicion of Malice: A Gail Connor & Anthony Quintana Novel. LC 00-30297. 2000. write for info. (*0-7862-2655-2*) Thorndike Pr.

Parker, Barbara., jt. auth. see George, Ted.

Parker, Barbara J., jt. auth. see Creasia, Joan L.

Parker, Barbara J., jt. auth. see McFarlane, Judith.

Parker, Barbara J., jt. ed. see Creasia, Joan L.

Parker, Barbara Keevil. North American Wolves. LC 97-41572. (J). (gr. 2-5). 1997. 19.93 (*1-57505-095-1*, Carolrhoda) Lerner Pub.

Parker, Barbara Keevil. Susan B. Anthony: Daring to Vote. LC 97-26310. (Gateway Biographies Ser.). (Illus.). 48p. (J). (gr. 5 up). 1998. lib. bdg. 20.90 (*0-7613-0358-8*) Millbrook Pr.

***Parker, Barbara Keevil.** Susan B. Anthony: Daring to Vote. (Gateway Biography Ser.). (Illus.). 48p. (J). (gr. 2-4). 2000. pap. text 8.95 (*0-7613-1378-8*, Copper Beech Bks) Millbrook Pr.

Parker, Barbara N., jt. ed. see Phillips, John M.

***Parker, Barry.** Einstein's Brainchild: Relativity Made Relatively Easy! 300p. 2000. 28.00 (*1-57392-857-7*) Prometheus Bks.

Parker, Barry. For the People: The Commitment Continues. 160p. 1993. 25.00 (*0-9637427-0-1*) Univ Hosp GA.

— The Tennesseans: A People Revisited. LC 97-91850. (Illus.). 160p. 1997. 45.00 (*0-9645704-2-4*) Parker Hood Pr.

Parker, Barry M. The Folger Shakespeare Filmography: A Directory of Feature Films Based on the Works of Shakespeare. LC 79-3141. (Folger Guides to the Age of Shakespeare Ser.). 1979. pap. 7.95 (*0-918016-19-3*) Folger Bks.

***Parker, Barry R.** Alien Life: The Search for Extraterrestrials & Beyond. LC 98-4552. (Illus.). 264p. (C). 1998. 27.95 (*0-306-45795-4*, Plenum Trade) Perseus Pubng.

Parker, Barry R. Chaos in the Cosmos: The Stunning Complexity of the Universe. (Illus.). 316p. (C). 1996. 28.95 (*0-306-45261-8*, Plenum Trade) Perseus Pubng.

— Cosmic Time Travel: A Scientific Odyssey. (Illus.). 320p. (C). 1991. 24.50 (*0-306-43966-2*, Plenum Trade) Perseus Pubng.

Parker, Bart. A Close Brush with Reality: Photographs & Writings, 1970-1981. LC 81-51478. (Artists' Books Ser.). (Illus.). 56p. (Orig.). 1981. pap. 12.95 (*0-89822-018-1*) Visual Studies.

Parker, Ben. Ethiopia: Breaking New Ground. (Country Profiles Ser.). (Illus.). 64p. (C). 1995. pap. 9.95 (*0-85598-270-5*, Pub. by Oxfam Pub) Stylus Pub VA.

Parker, Ben H., Jr. Colorado Placers & Placering. Carson, Mary, ed. (Illus.). 112p. 1994. reprint ed. pap. 10.95 (*0-941620-61-1*) Carson Ent.

— Gold Panning & Placering in Colorado: How & Where. (Information Ser.: No. 33). (Illus.). 83p. (Orig.). 1992. pap. 12.00 (*1-884216-23-4*) Colo Geol Survey.

Parker, Bess. The Herbalist Guide to Supersex. write for info. (*0-318-58992-3*) World Pr Ltd.

Parker, Beth. Thomas Knew There Were Pirates Living in the Bathroom. (Illus.). 28p. (J). (ps-3). 1990. 12.95 (*0-88753-224-1*); pap. 4.95 (*0-88753-201-2*) Black Moss.

Parker, Betty. Color New Canaan: A Coloring & Activity Book for Children of All Ages. (Illus.). 32p. (Orig.). (J). (ps-6). 1995. pap. 5.95 (*0-9648031-0-0*) Bound Two.

Parker, Betty, jt. auth. see Parker, Franklin.

Parker, Betty J. Women's Education, 2 vols., Set. 1981. lib. bdg. 125.00 (*0-313-23205-9*, PEV/, Greenwood Pr) Greenwood.

Parker, Betty J., ed. Women's Education, A World View: Annotated Bibliography of Doctoral Dissertations, Vol. 1. LC 78-73791. 470p. 1979. lib. bdg. 75.00 (*0-313-20891-3*, PEW/, Greenwood Pr) Greenwood.

Parker, Betty J & Parker, Franklin. American Dissertations on Foreign Education - A Bibliography with Abstracts Vol. 10: A Bibliography with Abstracts: Central America. LC 73-155724. (American Dissertations on Foreign Education Ser.). 1979. 38.50 (*0-87875-133-5*) Whitston Pub.

Parker, Betty J., jt. auth. see Parker, Francis.

Parker, Betty J., jt. auth. see Parker, Franklin.

Parker, Betty J., jt. ed. see Parker, Franklin.

Parker, Beulah. The Evolution of a Psychiatrist: Memoirs of a Woman Doctor. LC 86-28069. 237p. reprint ed. pap. 73.50 (*0-7837-4531-1*, 208021200003) Bks Demand.

Parker, Bill. The International Guide to Building a Classical Music Library. 4th ed. 320p. 1997. pap. 14.95 (*1-878427-59-8*, XC5501) B Parker.

***Parker, Bill & Simon, Joe.** Shazam! Archives, Vol. 2. (Illus.). 232p. 1999. 49.95 (*1-56389-521-8*, Pub. by DC Comics) Time Warner.

Parker, Blanford. The Triumph of Augustan Poetica: English Literary Culture from Butler to Johnson. LC 96-51679. (Studies in Eighteenth-Century English Literature & Thought: Vol. 36). 264p. (C). 1998. 59.95 (*0-521-59088-4*) Cambridge U Pr.

Parker, Bob. The Complete & Unauthorized Book of Hot Wheels. 3rd ed. LC 98-38893. 1999. pap. 29.95 (*0-7643-0704-5*) Schiffer.

— The Complete & Unauthorized Book of Hot Wheels. 3rd rev. ed. 160p. 1998. pap. 29.95 (*0-7643-0612-X*) Schiffer.

— Hot Wheels: A Collector's Guide. rev. ed. (Illus.). 160p. 1996. pap. 19.95 (*0-7643-0000-8*) Schiffer.

— Hot Wheels: A Collector's Guide. 3rd rev. ed. LC 99-60785. (Illus.). 176p. 1999. pap. 19.95 (*0-7643-0662-6*) Schiffer.

Parker, Bobbi. The Soybean Family Tree: Tasty Thrifty Vegan Food. LC 97-188047. (Illus.). viii, 72p. 1998. pap. 12.95 (*0-9663878-0-5*) Just Be Pubns.

Parker, Brad. Oh Boy! Sex Comics by Brad Parker. (Illus.). 96p. (Orig.). 1988. pap. 10.95 (*0-943595-11-8*) Leyland Pubns.

Parker, Bradley, jt. auth. see Neddermeyer, Dorothy M.

Parker, Brenda. Arresting Love. large type ed. (Linford Romance Library). 1991. pap. 16.99 (*0-7089-7063-X*, Linford) Ulverscroft.

— Safe Harbour. large type ed. (Linford Romance Library). 288p. 1993. pap. 16.99 (*0-7089-7321-3*, Linford) Ulverscroft.

Parker, Brenda C., et al. Computer Science I: Using C++ 206p. (C). 1995. mass mkt., lab manual ed. 30.95 (*0-314-06945-3*) West Pub.

Parker, Brian. Handbook of Project Management. (Business & Management Ser.). 1996. 50.00 (*0-7494-1953-9*) Kogan Page Ltd.

Parker, Brian, ed. see Shakespeare, William.

Parker, Brook S. To Soar Without Leaving the Ground: Poems & Narratives. (Illus.). 103p. (Orig.). 1996. pap. 12.00 (*0-9654415-0-4*) To Soar Pub.

***Parker, Bruce & Robbins, Robert.** Experiences in Biology: Biology 1020 Laboratory Manual. 88p. (C). 1999. spiral bd. 11.95 (*0-7872-5815-6*, 41581501) Kendall-Hunt.

Parker, Bruce B., ed. Tidal Hydrodynamics. LC 91-16603. 912p. 1991. 200.00 (*0-471-51498-5*) Wiley.

Parker, Bruce L., et al, eds. Thrips Biology & Management: Proceedings of a NATO ARW on Thysanoptera: Toward Understanding Thrips Management, Held at the University of Vermont, Burlington, September 28-30, 1993, Vol. 276A. LC 95-16545. (NATO ASI Ser.: Vol. 276). (Illus.). 652p. (C). 1995. text 165.00 (*0-306-45013-5*, Kluwer Plenum) Kluwer Academic.

Parker, Burliss E., Jr. Tablets of Inspiration: A Personal Journal. 224p. 1997. pap. 13.95 (*0-9647028-5-1*) Sowers Press.

Parker, C. & Riches, C. Parasitic Weeds of the World. (Illus.). 304p. 1993. text 105.00 (*0-85198-873-3*) OUP.

Parker, C. A., et al, eds. Ecology & Management of Soilborne Plant Pathogens. 358p. 1985. text 43.00 (*0-89054-066-7*) Am Phytopathol Soc.

Parker, C. M. Boron Engineering Steels. (Technical Papers: Vol. P249.05). (Illus.). 5p. 1951. pap. text 30.00 (*1-55589-347-3*) AGMA.

Parker, Calvin. The Complete PalmPilot Guide. LC 97-38723. 480p. 1997. pap. 29.95 (*1-55828-586-5*, MIS Pr) IDG Bks.

Parker, Cam. Camp Off-the-Wall. 128p. (J). (gr. 3-7). 1987. pap. 2.50 (*0-380-75196-8*, Avon Bks) Morrow Avon.

— A Horse in New York. 144p. (Orig.). (J). (gr. 5 up). 1989. pap. 2.75 (*0-380-75704-4*, Avon Bks) Morrow Avon.

Parker, Carol. Bumpity, Bumpity, Bump. (Illus.). 12p. (Orig.). (J). (gr. k-1). 1997. pap. 3.75 (*1-880612-56-9*) Seedling Pubns.

— Why Do You Call Me Chocolate Boy? LC 93-79098. (Illus.). 28p. (Orig.). (J). (gr. 2-6). 1993. pap. 7.95 (*0-9637267-0-6*) Gull Crest.

Parker, Carolyn. The Friends in Action Manual: A Model for Establishing a Volunteer Program to Build Caring & Supportive Relationships with Poor & Homeless Families. (Illus.). 200p. (Orig.). (C). 1993. pap. text 30.00 (*0-9631995-0-1*) Comm Minist Mont Cty.

Parker, Carolyn, photos by. Poetry of Roses. LC 94-42121. (Illus.). 64p. 1995. 19.95 (*0-8109-3736-0*, Pub. by Abrams) Time Warner.

Parker, Carolyn & Arnold, Stephen, eds. When the Drumbeat Changes. 293p. (Orig.). 1981. 22.00 (*0-89410-262-1*); pap. 14.00 (*0-89410-263-X*) Cornell AS&RC.

Parker, Celia. Passion Flowers. (Black Lace Ser.). 300p. 1996. mass mkt. 5.95 (*0-352-33118-6*, Pub. by Virgin Bks) London Brdge.

Parker, Chan. My Life in E-Flat. LC 98-19682. (Illus.). 256p. 1999. pap. 16.95 (*1-57003-245-9*) U of SC Pr.

Parker, Charles H. The Reformation of Community: Social Welfare & Calvinist Charity in Holland, 1572-1620. LC 98-3782. (Cambridge Studies in Early Modern History). (Illus.). 200p. (C). 1998. text 59.95 (*0-521-62305-7*) Cambridge U Pr.

Parker, Charles H., jt. ed. see Critchlow, Donald T.

Parker, Charles R. & Wiggins, Glenn B. Revision of the Caddisfly Genus Psilotreta: Trichoptera, Odontoceridae. (Illus.). 55p. pap. 13.71 (*0-88854-332-8*) Brill Academic Pubs.

Parker, Charles S. A Beginner's Guide to BASIC. (C). 1994. pap. write for info. (*0-15-555416-6*) Harcourt Coll Pubs.

— Beginner's Guide to QBA. (C). 1995. pap. text, teacher ed. 33.50 (*0-03-018252-2*) Harcourt Coll Pubs.

— A Beginner's Guide to QBasic. (C). 1995. pap. text, lab manual ed. 21.00 (*0-03-017653-0*, Pub. by Harcourt Coll Pubs) Harcourt.

— Beginners Guide to QBasic. (C). 1996. pap. write for info. (*0-15-504923-2*) Harcourt Coll Pubs.

— Database Management with DBASE IV: Productivity Software Guide Module. 4th ed. 95p. (C). 1993. pap. text 9.75 (*0-03-097120-9*) Dryden Pr.

— Disk Operating System - DOS Module from Productivity Software Guide. 4th ed. 64p. (C). 1993. pap. text 9.75 (*0-03-097121-7*) Dryden Pr.

— Kit Understanding. 6th ed. (C). 1996. pap. 56.00 (*0-03-018558-0*) Harcourt Coll Pubs.

— Management Information Systems. 2nd ed. 888p. (C). 1993. text 81.75 (*0-07-048573-9*) McGraw.

— Spreadsheets with Lotus 1-2-3: Productivity Software Guide Module. 4th ed. 96p. (C). 1993. pap. text 9.75 (*0-03-097122-5*) Dryden Pr.

— Spreadsheets with Lotus 1-2-3 & Joe Spreadsheet. 80p. (C). 1991. pap. text 9.50 (*0-03-072287-X*) Dryden Pr.

— Understanding Computer & Information Processing. 6th ed. LC 95-70004. (C). 1995. pap. text 58.00 (*0-03-013827-2*, Pub. by Harcourt Coll Pubs) Harcourt.

— Understanding Computer & Information Processing. 6th ed. (C). 1996. pap. text, teacher ed. 33.75 (*0-03-016433-8*) Harcourt Coll Pubs.

— Understanding Computers. 6th ed. (C). 199
student ed. 25.00 (*0-03-016742-6*) Harcou

— Understanding Computers. 7th ed. (C). 1997.
teacher ed. 29.50 (*0-03-024657-1*, Pub. by H
Pubs) Harcourt.

— Understanding Computers & Information Process
Today & Tomorrow with Basic. 5th ed. 650p. (C
text 44.00 (*0-03-097905-6*) Dryden Pr.

— Understanding Computers, 1998. 7th ed. (C). 1997.
text, teacher ed. 26.75 (*0-03-024658-X*) Harcourt Co
Pubs.

— Understanding Computers, 1998. 7th ed. LC 97-69297. (C). 1997. pap. text 59.00 (*0-03-024481-1*, Pub. by Harcourt Coll Pubs) Harcourt.

— Understanding Networking & the Internet. 158p. (C). 1997. pap. text 18.00 (*0-03-024578-8*) Dryden Pr.

— Word Processing with WordPerfect 5.1: Productivity Software Guide Module. 4th ed. 72p. (C). 1993. pap. text 12.50 (*0-03-097123-3*) Dryden Pr.

Parker, Charles S. & Martin, Edward G. MAST TODAY S SWR-LOTUS 1-2-3 (2. 2nd ed. 231p. (C). 1994. pap. text 22.50 (*0-03-098590-0*) Dryden Pr.

Parker, Charles S., jt. auth. see Martin, Edward G.

Parker, Charley. Argon Zark! (Illus.). 64p. 1997. pap. 6.95 (*0-9660532-0-6*) Arclight Pub.

Parker, Charlotte. Beauty for Young Women. 156p. 1999. pap. 7.95 (*1-58169-025-8*) Genesis Comm Inc.

***Parker, Cheryl V.** Valentine's Numstrology 2 Lucky Pet Numbers Booklet. (Illus.). 16p. 1999. pap. 6.00 (*0-8059-4448-6*) Dorrance.

Parker, Chris, et al. 153 "Fold & Say" Artic Stories: S, R, L, D, CH, SH, TH, F, G, K, T, V, S, R, L Blends. 185p. (J). (gr. k-5). 1997. spiral bd., wbk. ed. 34.95 (*1-58650-062-7*, BK-259) Super Duper.

***Parker, Christine.** Just Lawyers: Regulation & Access to Justice. LC 99-37268. 280p. 2000. 74.00 (*0-19-826841-6*) OUP.

— Patient's Notes: A 30-Day Calendar on the Path to Wellness. 64p. 1999. pap. 15.00 (*0-9669179-3-6*) Fifth Wrld.

***Parker, Christopher.** The English Idea of History from Coleridge to Collingwood. LC 99-52630. 256p. 2000. text 78.95 (*1-84014-254-5*, Pub. by Ashgate Pub) Ashgate Pub Co.

Parker, Christopher, ed. The English Historical Tradition since Eighteen Fifty. 260p. (C). 1989. text 75.00 (*0-7855-6985-5*, Pub. by J Donald) St Mut.

— Gender Roles & Sexuality in Victorian Literature. LC 94-42738. 208p. 1995. 67.95 (*1-85928-146-X*, Pub. by Scolar Pr) Ashgate Pub Co.

Parker, Christopher, jt. auth. see Kakabadse, Andrew.

Parker, Clayton A. My Will Be Done. 201p. 1982. pap. 3.00 (*0-686-86578-2*, 0-9606438) C A Parker Pubns.

***Parker, Clifton Blue.** Fouled Away: The Baseball Tragedy of Hack Wilson. (Illus.). 232p. 2000. per. 29.50 (*0-7864-0864-2*) McFarland & Co.

Parker, Constance-Anne. A Picture of the Royal Academy. 80p. (C). 1989. 110.00 (*0-903696-33-9*, Pub. by Hurtwood Pr Ltd); pap. 70.00 (*0-903696-34-7*, Pub. by Hurtwood Pr Ltd) St Mut.

Parker, Cordell, jt. auth. see Hamilton, Cheryl.

***Parker, Cornelia S.** Cornelia Parker. 80p. 2000. pap. 29.95 (*0-910663-57-2*, Pub. by ICA Inc) Dist Art Pubs.

Parker, Craig H. Timeless Wisdom of the Egyptians. (Timeless Wisdom Ser.). (Illus.). 112p. 1998. mass mkt. 11.95 (*0-340-70482-9*, Pub. by Hodder & Stought Ltd) Trafalgar.

— Timeless Wisdom of the Tibetans. (Timeless Wisdom Ser.). (Illus.). 112p. 1998. mass mkt. 11.95 (*0-340-70483-7*, Pub. by Hodder & Stought Ltd) Trafalgar.

Parker, Cristian. Popular Religion & Modernization in Latin America: A Different Logic. Barr, Robert R., tr. from SPA. LC 96-11398. 325p. 1996. 45.00 (*1-57075-067-X*) Orbis Bks.

Parker, Cynthia, jt. auth. see Lavin, Paul.

Parker, D. & Turk, J. L., eds. Contact Hypersensitivity in Experimental Animals. (Monographs in Allergy: Vol. 8). (Illus.). 182p. 1974. 73.25 (*3-8055-1666-5*) S Karger.

Parker, D., ed. see Collegium Internationale Allergologicum Staff.

Parker, D., jt. ed. see Creese, A.

Parker, D. C. Codex Bezae: An Early Christian Manuscript & Its Text. 373p. (C). 1992. text 105.00 (*0-521-40037-6*) Cambridge U Pr.

— The Living Text of the Gospels. 240p. (C). 1997. text 59.95 (*0-521-59062-0*); pap. text 18.95 (*0-521-59951-2*) Cambridge U Pr.

— Some Aspects of Gipsy Music. 61p. 1991. reprint ed. 59.00 (*0-7812-9317-0*) Rprt Serv.

Parker, D. C., tr. & intro. see Melanchthon, Philip.

Parker, D. F., ed. IUTAM Symposium on Anisotropy, Inhomogeneity & Nonlinearity in Solid Mechanics: Proceedings of the IUTAM-ISIMM Symposium Held in Nottingham, U. K. 30 August - 3 September 1994. (Solid Mechanics & Its Applications Ser.). 536p. (C). 1995. text 239.50 (*0-7923-3594-5*) Kluwer Academic.

Parker, D. M., jt. ed. see Crawford, J. R.

Parker, D. S. The Idea of the Middle Class: White-Collar Workers & Peruvian Society. LC 97-16294. 266p. 1998. 49.50 (*0-271-01743-0*); pap. 19.95 (*0-271-01744-9*) Pa St U Pr.

Parker, D. W. Calendar of Papers in Washington Archives Relating to the Territories of the United States, to 1873. (Carnegie Institute Ser.: Vol. 4). 1911. 40.00 (*0-527-00684-X*) Periodicals Srv.

— Guide to the Materials for United States History in Canadian Archives. (Carnegie Institute Ser.: Vol. 9). 1913. 40.00 (*0-527-00689-0*) Periodicals Srv.

Parker, D. Young, ed. see Pavela, Gary.

P

An Asterisk (*) at the beginning of an entry indicates that the title is appearing for the first time.

Wisdom of the ...0.00

... Complete ... (Illus.). 256p. ...) Info Today

... United States & ... Sailing Ships. Harris, ...s.). 72p. 1994. pap. 9.50 ... Trails.

...-50564. (Countdown Ser.: No. ... up). 1999. per. 3.99 ... Aladdin.

...0015. (Countdown Ser.: No. 8). 128p. ... up). 1999. mass mkt. 3.99 (*0-689-81826-2*)

...er. LC 99-46893. (Countdown Ser.: No. 12). 128p. ... 1999. per. 3.99 (*0-689-81830-0*) Aladdin.

...bruary. LC 98-45811. (Countdown Ser.: No. 2). 128p. (YA). (gr. 7-12). 1999. mass mkt. 3.99 (*0-689-81820-3*) Aladdin.

— January. LC 98-7692. (Countdown Ser.: No. 1). 208p. (YA). (gr. 7-12). 1998. per. 1.99 (*0-689-81819-X*) Aladdin.

— July. LC 99-25318. (Countdown Ser.: No. 7). 128p. (YA). (gr. 5 up). 1999. mass mkt. 3.99 (*0-689-81825-4*, 076714003996) Aladdin.

— June. LC 99-13407. (Countdown Ser.: No. 6). 128p. (YA). (gr. 5 up). 1999. per. 3.99 (*0-689-81824-6*, 076714003996) Aladdin.

— March. LC 98-46984. (Countdown Ser.: No. 3). 128p. (YA). (gr. 7-12). 1999. per. 3.99 (*0-689-81821-1*) Aladdin.

— May. LC 99-14012. (Countdown Ser.: No. 5). 128p. (YA). (gr. 7-12). 1999. per. 3.99 (*0-689-81823-8*) Aladdin.

— November. (Countdown Ser.: No. 11). 128p. (YA). (gr. 7-12). 1999. mass mkt. 3.99 (*0-689-81829-7*) Aladdin.

— October. LC 99-16429. (Countdown Ser.: No. 10). 128p. (YA). (gr. 5 up). 1999. mass mkt. 3.99 (*0-689-81828-9*) Aladdin.

— September. LC 99-34683. (Countdown Ser.: No. 9). 128p. (YA). (gr. 5 up). 1999. mass mkt. 3.99 (*0-689-81827-0*) Aladdin.

***Parker, Daniel.** Sweet Sixteen: Trent, No. 4. LC 99-66684. (Sweet Sixteen Ser.: No. 4). 240p. (YA). (gr. 7-12). 2000. pap. 5.95 (*0-06-440812-4*, HarpTrophy) HarpC Child Bks.

***Parker, Danny S.** Battle of the Bulge: Hitler's Ardennes Offensive, 1944-45. 1999. pap. 24.95 (*1-58097-023-0*, 970230) Combined Pub.

Parker, Danny S. Battle of the Bulge: The View of the German High Command. LC 98-47036. 1p. 1999. 34.95 (*1-85367-354-4*) Stackpole.

— Hitler's Ardennes Offensive: The German View of the Battle of the Bulge. LC 96-49841. (Illus.). 256p. 1997. write for info. (*1-85367-272-6*) Stackpole.

— To Win the Winter Sky: The Air War Over the Ardennes 1944-1945. 1998. pap. 21.95 (*1-58097-006-0*, 970060) Combined Pub.

Parker, David. Broken Images: The Figured Landscape of Nazca. 1993. pap. text 29.95 (*0-948797-86-X*, Pub. by Cmerhse) Dist Art Pubs.

— Class & State in Early Modern France: The Road to Modernity. LC 95-31902. 368p. (C). 1997. 75.00 (*0-415-13647-4*) Routledge.

— Ethics, Theory, & the Novel. LC 93-43929. 228p. (C). 1995. text 59.95 (*0-521-45283-X*) Cambridge U Pr.

— Privatisation in the European Union: Theory & Policy Perspectives. LC 97-30751. 256p. (C). 1998. 85.00 (*0-415-15469-3*) Routledge.

***Parker, David.** Revolutions: The Revolutionary Tradition in the West, 1560-1991. LC 00-20197. 2000. pap. write for info. (*0-415-17295-0*) Routledge.

Parker, David. The Strategic Finance Workout: Test & Build Your Financial Performance. (Illus.). 250p. (Orig.). 1996. pap. text 25.00 (*0-273-62565-9*) F T P-H.

Parker, David, ed. Innovations in GIS III. 272p. 1996. 99.95 (*0-7484-0458-9*); pap. 49.95 (*0-7484-0459-7*) Taylor & Francis.

— Macrocyle Synthesis: A Practical Approach. (Practical Approach in chemistry Ser.). (Illus.). 266p. 1996. text 90.00 (*0-19-855841-4*); spiral bd. 45.00 (*0-19-855840-6*) OUP.

— Through Different Eyes: The Cultural Identity of Young Chinese in Britain. (Research in Ethnic Relations Ser.). 285p. 1995. 77.95 (*1-85628-923-0*, Pub. by Avebury) Ashgate Pub Co.

Parker, David, intro. Nicholas Nickleby. 416p. 1994. 5.95 (*0-460-87480-2*, Everyman's Classic Lib) Tuttle Pubng.

Parker, David & Stacey, Ralph. Chaos, Management & Economics: The Implications of Non-Linear Thinking. (IEA Hobart Paper Ser.: No. 125). 112p. 1994. pap. 26.50 (*0-255-36333-8*, Pub. by Inst Economic Affairs) Coronet Bks.

Parker, David, jt. auth. see Clark, Charles.

Parker, David, jt. auth. see Cowen, Tyler.

Parker, David, jt. auth. see Martin, Stephen.

Parker, David, jt. auth. see Oldcorn, Roger.

Parker, David A. & De Cecco, John P., eds. Sex, Cells, & Same-Sex Desire: The Biology of Sexual Preference. LC 95-6140. 1995. 49.95 (*1-56024-700-2*) Haworth Pr.

Parker, David B., jt. auth. see Patton, Randall L.

Parker, David E., jt. auth. see Luxon, James T.

Parker, David F. Marketing: New Homes. LC 98-52745. 1999. write for info. (*0-86718-447-7*) Home Builder.

Parker, David L., et al. Stolen Dreams: Portraits of Working Children. LC 97-4939. (Illus.). 112p. (J). (gr. 5-9). 1997. lib. bdg. 14.95 (*0-8225-2960-2*) Lerner Pub.

Parker, David R. The Commonplace Book in Tudor London: An Examination of BL MSS Egerton 1995, Harley 2252, Lansdowne 762, & Oxford Balliol College, MS 354. LC 98-33809. 188p. 1998. 42.00 (*0-7618-1242-3*) U Pr of Amer.

Parker, De Witt. The Analysis of Art. LC 75-3304. reprint ed. 39.50 (*0-404-59289-9*) AMS Pr.

— Human Values: An Interpretation of Ethics Based on a Study of Values. LC 75-3305. reprint ed. 55.00 (*0-404-59290-2*) AMS Pr.

— The Self & Nature. LC 75-3306. reprint ed. 32.50 (*0-404-59291-0*) AMS Pr.

***Parker, DeAnsin & Bressler, Karen W.** Yoga Baby: Exercises to Help You Bond with Your Baby Physically, Emotionally & Spiritually. (Illus.). 208p. 2000. pap. 16.00 (*0-7679-0405-2*) Broadway BDD.

***Parker, Deborah.** Bronzing: Renaissance Painter as Poet. LC 99-87658. (Illus.). 224p. (C). 2000. Price not set. (*0-521-78166-3*) Cambridge U Pr.

Parker, Deborah. Commentary & Ideology: Dante in the Renaissance. LC 92-12651. (Illus.). 264p. 1993. text 37.95 (*0-8223-1281-6*) Duke.

Parker, Dee, jt. auth. see Parker, Weldon.

Parker, Dennis. Parrots As a Hobby. (Illus.). 96p. 1994. pap. 8.95 (*0-7938-0094-3*, TT037) TFH Pubns.

Parker, Dennis, et al. Urban Flood Protection Benefits: A Project Appraisal Guide. Orig. Title: The Indirect Benefits of Urban Flood Alleviation. 1987. text 152.95 (*0-291-39707-7*, Pub. by Avebury Technical) Ashgate Pub Co.

***Parker, Derek.** KISS Guide to Astrology. LC 00-8797. (Illus.). 352p. (J). 2000. pap. 18.95 (*0-7894-6044-0*) DK Pub Inc.

— Nell Gwyn. (Illus.). 224p. 2000. 29.95 (*0-7509-1992-2*) Sutton Publng.

Parker, Derek. The Power of Magic: Ancient Secrets & Modern Mysteries. 1999. pap. text 17.95 (*1-84000-222-0*) Millers Pubns.

— Writing Erotic Fiction. 115p. (Orig.). 1996. pap. 10.95 (*1-56924-833-8*) Marlowe & Co.

Parker, Derek & Parker, Julia. Aquarius. LC 92-52794. (Sun & Moon Signs Library). (Illus.). 58p. 1992. 8.95 (*1-56458-094-6*) DK Pub Inc.

— Aquarius. (Parker's Love Signs Ser.). 1996. 8.95 (*0-614-20700-2*) DK Pub Inc.

— Aries. LC 92-52784. (Sun & Moon Signs Library). (Illus.). 58p. (Orig.). 1992. 8.95 (*1-56458-084-9*) DK Pub Inc.

— Cancer. LC 92-52787. (Sun & Moon Signs Library). (Illus.). 58p. 1992. 8.95 (*1-56458-087-3*) DK Pub Inc.

— Capricorn. LC 92-52793. (Sun & Moon Signs Library). (Illus.). 58p. 1992. 8.95 (*1-56458-093-8*) DK Pub Inc.

— Dreaming. 224p. 1989. per. 17.00 (*0-671-76630-9*, Fireside) S&S Trade Pap.

— Gemini. LC 92-52786. (Sun & Moon Signs Library). (Illus.). 58p. 1992. 8.95 (*1-56458-086-5*) DK Pub Inc.

— Leo. LC 92-52788. (Sun & Moon Signs Library). (Illus.). 58p. 1992. 8.95 (*1-56458-088-1*) DK Pub Inc.

— Libra. LC 92-52790. (Sun & Moon Signs Library). (Illus.). 58p. 1993. 8.95 (*1-56458-090-3*) DK Pub Inc.

— Parkers' Astrology. LC 91-60388. (Illus.). 416p. 1994. pap. 24.95 (*1-56458-710-X*) DK Pub Inc.

— Pisces. LC 92-52795. (Sun & Moon Signs Library). (Illus.). 58p. 1992. 8.95 (*1-56458-095-4*) DK Pub Inc.

— The Power of Magic: Ancient Secrets & Modern Mysteries. LC 92-12175. 224p. 1993. 20.00 (*0-671-76921-9*) S&S Trade.

— Sagittarius. LC 92-52792. (Sun & Moon Signs Library). (Illus.). 58p. 1992. 8.95 (*1-56458-092-X*) DK Pub Inc.

— Scorpio. LC 92-52791. (Sun & Moon Signs Library). (Illus.). 58p. 1992. 8.95 (*1-56458-091-1*) DK Pub Inc.

— Taurus. LC 92-52785. (Sun & Moon Signs Library). (Illus.). 58p. 1992. 8.95 (*1-56458-085-7*) DK Pub Inc.

— Virgo. LC 92-52789. (Sun & Moon Signs Library). (Illus.). 58p. 1992. 8.95 (*1-56458-089-X*) DK Pub Inc.

Parker, Derek, jt. auth. see Parker, Julia.

Parker, Diane. Jamie: A Literacy Story. LC 96-53586. (Illus.). 128p. (Orig.). (C). 1997. pap. text 14.00 (*1-57110-058-X*) Stenhse Pubs.

Parker, Diane, ed. see Flemming, Gerhard.

Parker, Diane, ed. see Smith, Donald M.

Parker Directory Staff, ed. Parker Directory of California Attorneys: The Comprehensive Guide to the California Legal Community. 1700p. 1999. 54.95 (*1-56160-430-5*) Martindale-Hubbell.

Parker, Don. Officer Needs Assistance . . . Again! 256p. 1990. 15.95 (*0-9620073-2-3*) Caroldon Bks.

— Using Biblical Hebrew in Ministry: A Practical Guide for Pastors, Seminarians, & Bible Students. 278p. (Orig.). (C). 1995. pap. text 26.50 (*0-7618-0124-3*) U Pr of Amer.

— You're under Arrest, I'm Not Kidding: The Trials & Tribulations of a Reluctant Cop. 243p. 1990. reprint ed. pap. 9.95 (*0-9620073-1-5*) Caroldon Bks.

Parker, Don & Bennett, Matthew. Maternal Journal: Your Personal Pregnancy Guide. (Illus.). 27p. 1992. 10.00 (*0-671-76031-9*) S&S Trade.

Parker, Don, jt. auth. see Alexander, Tom.

Parker, Don H., et al. The Metric System: Syllabus. 1974. pap. text 19.95 (*0-89420-052-6*, 280222); audio 18.15 (*0-89420-163-8*, 280000) Natl Book.

Parker, Donald, jt. auth. see Burkett, Kathryn Lewis.

Parker, Donald D. Bewley & Related Families. (Illus.). 135p. 1997. reprint ed. pap. 21.00 (*0-8328-7513-9*); reprint ed. lib. bdg. 31.00 (*0-8328-7512-0*) Higginson Bk Co.

— Local History: How to Gather It, Write It, & Publish It. LC 78-11873. 186p. 1979. reprint ed. lib. bdg. 59.50 (*0-313-21100-0*, PLAH, Greenwood Pr) Greenwood.

— Local History: How to Gather It, Write It, & Publish It. (History - United States Ser.). 186p. 1993. reprint ed. lib. bdg. 69.00 (*0-7812-4842-6*) Rprt Serv.

Parker, Donald E. Management Application of Value Engineering: For Business & Government. LC 94-76015. (Illus.). 204p. (C). 1994. text 44.95 (*0-9641052-0-9*) L D Miles.

Parker, Donald E. & Dell'Isola, Alphonse. Project Budgeting for Buildings. (Illus.). 256p. (gr. 13). 1991. text 57.95 (*0-442-00483-4*) Chapman & Hall.

Parker, Donn. Fighting Computer Crime: A New Framework for Protecting Information. LC 98-28151. 528p. 1998. pap. 39.99 (*0-471-16378-3*) Wiley.

Parker, Donn B. & Anderson, James, eds. Information Systems Security (Journal of) 149.00 (*0-685-69693-6*, ZISS) Warren Gorham & Lamont.

Parker, Doraetta H. How to Kill Cockroaches & Never Again Be Reinfested & Other Good News. (Illus.). 80p. (Orig.). 1986. 14.95 (*0-937305-00-6*); pap. 12.95 (*0-937305-01-4*); audio 19.00 (*0-937305-02-2*) Gramies Ultd.

Parker, Doris. A Poetry Collection: A Compilation of Original Verse. LC 96-92399. 70p. (Orig.). 1996. pap. 3.00 (*1-57502-243-5*) Morris Pubng.

Parker, Dorothy. Complete Poems. LC 98-47392. 408p. 1999. pap. 13.95 (*0-14-118022-6*) Penguin Putnam.

— Cooking with Potatoes. 1990. pap. 2.95 (*0-88266-601-0*, Garden Way Pub) Storey Bks.

***Parker, Dorothy.** Dorothy Parker Stories: Booth,&Shirley. abr. ed. 1998. audio 12.00 (*1-55994-006-9*, CPN 1136) HarperAudio.

— Here We Are, a Telephone Call. (Short Stories Ser.). 22p. 2000. pap. 3.95 (*1-86092-017-9*, Pub. by Travelman Pub) IPG Chicago.

Parker, Dorothy. Not Much Fun: The Lost Poems of Dorothy Parker. Silverstein, Stuart, ed. 256p. 1996. 21.50 (*0-684-81855-8*) S&S Trade.

Parker, Dorothy & Evans, Ross. The Coast of Illyria: A Play in Three Acts. LC 89-20251. (Illus.). 232p. 1990. pap. 16.95 (*0-87745-288-1*) U of Iowa Pr.

Parker, Dorothy D. Parker: Collected Stories. 1999. pap. 22.95 (*0-670-86442-0*) Viking Penguin.

Parker, Dorothy Mills, ed. see Lee, Cazenove Gardner.

Parker, Dorothy R. Collected Stories. Breese, Mikki, ed. LC 95-15524. 352p. (Orig.). 1995. pap. 13.95 (*0-14-018939-4*, Penguin Classics) Viking Penguin.

— Dorothy Parker at Her Best. 26.95 (*0-8488-0177-2*) Amereon Ltd.

— Dorothy Parker's Favorites. 18.95 (*0-8488-0095-8*) Amereon Ltd.

— Phoenix Indian School: The Second Half-Century. LC 96-31381. 96p. 1996. 14.95 (*0-8165-1679-0*) U of Ariz Pr.

— Poetry & Short Stories of Dorothy Parker. (Illus.). 504p. 1994. 16.50 (*0-679-60132-5*) Modern Lib NY.

— The Portable Dorothy Parker. rev. ed. (Portable Library: No. 74). 640p. 1976. pap. 14.95 (*0-14-015074-9*, Penguin Bks) Viking Penguin.

— Singing an Indian Song: A Biography of D'Arcy McNickle. LC 92-7616. (American Indian Lives Ser.). (Illus.). x, 317p. 1992. pap. 13.00 (*0-8032-8730-5*, Bison Books) U of Nebr Pr.

Parker, Dorothy R., ed. Modern American Drama: Williams, Miller, Albee, & Shepard. 1987. pap. 17.95 (*0-8020-3434-9*) U of Toronto Pr.

Parker, Douglas, ed. see Roye, William.

Parker, Douglas C. George Bizet: His Life & Works. 278p. 1990. reprint ed. lib. bdg. 69.00 (*0-7812-9050-3*) Rprt Serv.

— Georges Bizet, His Life & Works. LC 73-94280. (Select Bibliographies Reprint Ser.). 1977. 23.95 (*0-8369-5054-2*) Ayer.

Parker, Douglas H. Praier & Complaynte of the Ploweman into Christe. LC 98-116769. 256p. 1997. text 60.00 (*0-8020-4268-6*) U of Toronto Pr.

Parker, Douglas H., ed. see Barlowe, Jerome & Roye, William.

Parker, Douglass, ed. & tr. see Aristophanes.

Parker, Douglass, tr. see Plautus & Terence.

Parker, E. Astrology & Its Practical Application (1927) Goedhart, Coba, tr. 210p. 1996. reprint ed. pap. 14.95 (*1-56459-830-6*) Kessinger Pub.

Parker, E. & Goedhart, Coba, trs. Astrology & Its Practical Application. 202p. 1996. reprint ed. spiral bd. 15.50 (*0-7873-0658-4*) Hlth Research.

Parker, E. H., jt. ed. see Dowsett, M. G.

Parker, E. J. The Doctor's Guide to Partnership Accounts. 76p. 1984. 40.00 (*0-7212-0698-0*, Pub. by Regency Pr GBR) St Mut.

Parker, E. W. Enjoying Poetry, Bk. 4. Date not set. pap. text. write for info. (*0-582-34112-4*, Pub. by Addison-Wesley) Longman.

Parker, E. W. Into Battle, 1914-1918: A Seventeen-Year-Old Joins Kitchener's Army. 98p. 1994. reprint ed. 16.95 (*0-85052-428-8*, Pub. by Leo Cooper) Trans-Atl Phila.

Parker, Earl R. & Colombo, Umberto, eds. The Science of Materials Used in Advanced Technology. LC 73-1065. 572p. reprint ed. pap. 177.40 (*0-608-30775-0*, 201517300092) Bks Demand.

Parker, Earle W. Kangaroos, Characters & Bunyips. 88p. 1994. pap. 7.95 (*1-57087-088-8*) Prof Pr NC.

Parker, Ed. Jack & the Beanstalk. LC 78-18072. 32p. (J). (gr. k-4). 1996. pap. 3.95 (*0-89375-103-0*) Troll Communs.

— Three Billy Goats Gruff. LC 78-18068. 32p. (J). (gr. k-3). 1979. lib. bdg. 15.85 (*0-89375-121-9*); audio 9.95 (*0-685-04953-1*) Troll Communs.

— Three Billy Goats Gruff. LC 78-18068. 32p. (J). (gr. k-3). 1997. pap. 3.95 (*0-89375-099-9*) Troll Communs.

***Parker, Edward.** Central America. LC 98-45554. (Illus.). (J). (gr. 4-8). 1999. 24.26 (*0-8172-5406-4*) Raintree Steck-V.

Parker, Edward. Ecuador, Peru & Bolivia. LC 97-40241. (Country Fact Files Ser.). 1998. 24.26 (*0-8172-5403-X*) Raintree Steck-V.

— Forests for the Future. LC 97-17983. (Protecting Our Planet Ser.). (Illus.). 48p. (J). (gr. 4-7). 1998. 25.69 (*0-8172-4934-6*) Raintree Steck-V.

— Fuels for the Future. LC 97-17983. (Protecting Our Planet Ser.). (Illus.). 48p. (J). 1998. lib. bdg. 25.69 (*0-8172-4937-0*) Raintree Steck-V.

***Parker, Edward, photos by.** Ancient Trees: Trees That Live for 1,000 Years. (Illus.). 192p. 1999. 35.00 (*1-85585-704-9*, Pub. by Collins & Br) Sterling.

Parker, Edward, jt. auth. see Lewington, Anna.

Parker, Edward A. Mexico. LC 96-52702. (Country Insights Ser.). (J). 1998. lib. bdg. 25.69 (*0-8172-4791-2*) Raintree Steck-V.

— Peru. LC 96-18331. (Economically Developing Countries Ser.). (J). 1997. lib. bdg. 24.26 (*0-8172-4525-1*) Raintree Steck-V.

Parker, Edward A., tr. see Declareuil, Joseph.

Parker, Edward E. History of Brookline, New Hampshire, Formerly Raby, with Tables of Family Records & Genealogies. (Illus.). 664p. 1988. reprint ed. lib. bdg. 71.00 (*0-8328-0043-0*, NH0051) Higginson Bk Co.

Parker, Edward G. Reminiscences of Rufus Choate, the Great American Advocate. Mersky, Roy M. & Jacobstein, J. Myron, eds. (Classics in Legal History Reprint Ser.: Vol. 16). 524p. 1972. reprint ed. lib. bdg. 45.00 (*0-89941-015-4*, 301130) W S Hein.

Parker, Edward L. History of Londonderry, New Hampshire, Comprising the Towns of Derry & Londonderry. (Illus.). 418p. 1988. reprint ed. lib. bdg. 43.00 (*0-8328-0062-7*, NH0054) Higginson Bk Co.

Parker, Edward L., ed. Index to the History of Londonderry, N.H. 19p. (Orig.). 1992. pap. ... (*0-929539-93-1*, 1387) Picton Pr.

Parker, Edwin B., et al. Electr... Byways: State Policies for Rural Developm... Through Telecommunications. 2nd ed. LC 9...-47. 1995. pap. 10.00 (*0-89843-178-6*) Th... Aspen Inst.

— Rural America in the Information Age: Telecommunications Policy for Rural Development. 186p. (Orig.). (C). 1989. pap. text 19.50 (*0-8191-7494-7*); lib. bdg. 38.50 (*0-8191-7493-9*) U Pr of Amer.

Parker, Eleanor. Dad's Doodle-Bug. (Stories We Tell Ser.). 27p. 1993. pap. 4.00 (*1-884983-05-7*) Homegrown Bks.

Parker, Eleanor, ed. see Brummell, George B.

Parker, Elinor, ed. One Hundred More Story Poems. LC 60-11543. (Illus.). (J). (gr. 5 up). 1960. 15.95 (*0-690-59690-1*) HarpC Child Bks.

***Parker, Elisabeth.** The Little Web Cam Book. 250p. 1999. pap. text 18.99 (*0-201-35420-9*, Pub. by Peachpit Pr) Addison-Wesley.

Parker, Elisabeth A. Complete Idiot's Guide to Microsoft FrontPage 2000. LC 98-88241. (Complete Idiot's Guides (Computers) Ser.). (Illus.). 376p. 1999. pap. 16.99 (*0-7897-1806-5*) Que.

— Netscape Navigator: Jumpstart Tutorial. (Illus.). 350p. (Orig.). 1996. pap. 20.95 (*1-886801-64-9*) Thomson Learn.

— Netscape Navigator 2.0 Jumpstart Tutorial. (Illus.). 317p. 1996. pap. 19.95 (*1-886801-46-0*) Thomson Learn.

Parker, Elizabeth. Gilded Splendor. 400p. (Orig.). 1993. mass mkt. 4.99 (*0-505-51914-3*, Love Spell) Dorchester Pub Co.

***Parker, Elizabeth.** Managing Your Organization's Records. (Successful LIS Professional Ser.). 181p. 1999. 30.00 (*1-85604-335-5*, Pub. by Library Association) Bernan Associates.

Parker, Elizabeth. The Seven Ages of Women. Breck, Evelyn, ed. LC 60-8739. 621p. reprint ed. pap. 192.60 (*0-608-30511-1*, 201485300093) Bks Demand.

Parker, Elizabeth, jt. auth. see O'Connor, Marylou.

Parker, Elizabeth A. Microsoft Internet Explorer Three Point O: A Jumpstart Tutorial. (Illus.). 300p. (Orig.). 1996. pap. 19.95 (*1-886801-05-3*) Thomson Learn.

— Netscape Navigator Two Point O: A Jumpstart Tutorial. (Illus.). 317p. (Orig.). 1996. pap. 19.95 (*1-886801-16-9*) Thomson Learn.

Parker, Elizabeth C. The Cloisters Cross: Its Art & Meaning. (Illus.). 352p. 1994. text. write for info. (*1-872501-90-7*) Gordon & Breach.

— A Natural History of Camden & Rockport. LC 99-491482. (Illus.). 152p. (J). (gr. k-12). 1984. reprint ed. pap. 16.00 (*0-9669907-0-6*) E C Parker.

Parker, Elizabeth C. & Little, Charles T. The Cloisters Cross: Its Art & Meaning. LC 93-8585. (Illus.). 336p. 1993. 50.00 (*0-87099-682-7*, 0-8109-6434-1) Metro Mus Art.

Parker, Elizabeth L., ed. Cobb County, Georgia Cemeteries, Vol. II. LC 81-45599. (Illus.). 756p. 1991. lib. bdg. 65.00 (*1-879768-00-3*) Cobb Cnty Geneal.

Parker, Elizabeth S., jt. ed. see Weingartner, Herbert.

Parker, Ellen M. Laboratory Experiences in Group Theory. LC 96-77787. (Classroom Resource Materials Ser.). (Illus.). 112p. (Orig.). 1996. pap. text, suppl. ed. 26.50 (*0-88385-705-7*, LABE) Math Assn.

Parker, Elmer O., jt. auth. see Holcomb, Brent H.

Parker, Elsa. Astrology & Its Practical Application. (Arcana Ser.). 1977. pap. 5.95 (*0-87877-039-9*) Newcastle Pub.

***Parker, Emily King.** Closing Sales & Winning the Customer's Heart. Young, George, ed. LC 99-75057. 98p. 1999. pap. 11.95 (*1-56052-565-7*) Crisp Pubns.

Parker, Emma & Cowan, Nell B. True Story of Bonnie & Clyde. Date not set. lib. bdg. 18.95 (*0-8488-2154-8*) Amereon Ltd.

P

An Asterisk (*) at the beginning of an entry indicates that the title is appearing for the first time.

Parker, Emmett. Albert Camus: The Artist in the Arena. LC 65-13502. 261p. reprint ed. pap. 81.00 (*0-608-20466-8*, 207171800002) Bks Demand.

Parker, Errol. A Flat Tire on My Ass: The Autobiography of Errol Parker. (Illus.). 160p. (Orig.). 1995. pap. 17.00 (*1-881993-27-2*) Cadence Jazz.

Parker, Eugene N. Interplanetary Dynamical Processes. LC 63-13630. (Interscience Monographs & Texts in Physics & Astronomy: No. 8). (Illus.). 279p. reprint ed. pap. 86.50 (*0-7837-3461-1*, 205778900008) Bks Demand.

— Spontaneous Current Sheets in Magnetic Fields: With Applications to Stellar X-Rays. (International Series in Astronomy & Astrophysics). (Illus.). 440p. 1994. text 80.00 (*0-19-507371-1*) OUP.

Parker, Eve. The Preschool Church: Church School Lesson for Three to Five Year Olds. LC 96-6866. (Orig.). 1996. pap. 10.95 (*0-7880-0848-X*) CSS OH.

Parker, Everett L. Beyond Moosehead: A History of the Great North Woods of Maine. (Illus.). 197p. (Orig.). 1996. pap. 12.95 (*0-9646054-5-7*) Moosehead Communs.

— Moosehead Reflections. (Illus.). 94p. (Orig.). 1996. pap. 8.95 (*0-9646054-4-9*) Moosehead Communs.

Parker, Everett L., ed. see Gagnon, Lana.

Parker, F. Calvin. Precious Mother, Precious Crown: The Life & Mission of Elizabeth Taylor Watkins. 336p. 1997. pap. 16.95 (*1-57087-343-7*) Prof Pr NC.

— The Southern Baptist Mission in Japan, 1889-1989. (Illus.). 362p. (Orig.). (C). 1991. pap. text 34.50 (*0-8191-8108-0*); lib. bdg. 54.50 (*0-8191-8107-2*) U Pr of Amer.

Parker, F. Charles, IV. Vietnam: Strategy for a Stalemate. LC 88-25482. 268p. 1988. text 19.95 (*0-88702-041-0*) Washington Inst Pr.

Parker, F. M. The Assassins. large type ed. (General Ser.). 350p. 1990. lib. bdg. 18.95 (*0-8161-4999-2*, G K Hall Lrg Type) Mac Lib Ref.

***Parker, F. M.** Blood & Dust. 384p. 2000. mass mkt. 5.99 (*0-7860-1152-1*, Pinncle Kensgtn) Kensgtn Pub Corp.

— Blood Debt. 2000. mass mkt. 5.99 (*0-7860-1093-2*, Pinncle Kensgtn) Kensgtn Pub Corp.

Parker, F. M. Distant Thunder. 384p. 1999. mass mkt. 5.99 (*0-7860-0647-1*) Pinnacle Books.

***Parker, F. M.** Score to Settle,A. 1999. 4.99 (*0-7860-1016-9*, Pinncle Kensgtn) Kensgtn Pub Corp.

Parker, F. M. The Seekers. 304p. 1998. pap. 4.99 (*0-7860-0493-2*, Pinncle Kensgtn) Kensgtn Pub Corp.

— Shadow of the Wolf. 192p. 1988. pap. 2.75 (*0-317-66101-9*, Sig) NAL.

— Winter Woman. 304p. 1996. mass mkt. 4.99 (*0-7860-0347-2*, Pinncle Kensgtn) Kensgtn Pub Corp.

Parker-Fairbanks, Dixie. Essential Passions Fairbanks-Salmenhaara Letters 1959-1987. LC 00-272593. (Illus.). 208p. 1999. pap. text 29.95 (*0-295-97832-5*) U of Wash Pr.

Parker-Fairbanks, Dixie, et al. Richard Fairbanks, 1929-1989: A Retrospective. Nix, Neeleke, ed. Goebel, Robert & Alport, Rita, trs. from FIN. (Illus.). 50p. 1995. pap. 8.95 (*1-881067-05 X*) N Nelleke Studio.

Parker, Fan. Lewis Carroll in Russia: Translations of Alice in Wonderland 1879-1989. 89p. 1994. pap. text 15.00 (*0-9644886-0-4*) Russian Hse.

Parker, Fan & Parker, Stephen J. Russia on Canvas: Ilya Repin. LC 79-20577. (Illus.). 196p. 1980. 35.00 (*0-271-00252-2*) Pa St U Pr.

Parker, Farris, jt. auth. see Miller, Judy.

Parker-Fisher, Stacy. AD/HD: What It Is. What It Isn't. What to Do. 56p. (Orig.). 1997. pap. text 7.95 (*0-7842-0835-2*) Agency Instr Tech.

Parker, Florence E. & Stewart, Estelle M. Care of the Aged Persons in the United States. LC 75-17235. (Social Problems & Social Policy Ser.). 1976. reprint ed. 25.95 (*0-405-07504-9*) Ayer.

Parker, Florence R. How to Avoid Student Loan Defaults - Even If You Never Attended College. Glidden, Kathy, ed. LC 96-29685. 299p. (Orig.). 1997. pap. 21.95 (*0-9654700-0-8*) F R Parker.

Parker, Fran. Listen. 50p. 1983. pap. 8.00 (*0-686-40982-5*) TarPar.

— Mushrooms, Turnip Greens & Pickled Eggs. 2nd ed. 288p. 1975. 5.25 (*0-686-11664-X*) TarPar.

— Ponderings. 50p. 1976. pap. 3.50 (*0-686-40981-7*) TarPar.

Parker, Fran, jt. auth. see Tartan, Beth.

Parker, Francis & Parker, Betty J. American Dissertations on Foreign Education Vol. 13: A Bibliography with Abstracts: Israel. LC 73-155724. 464p. 1980. 32.00 (*0-87875-152-1*) Whitston Pub.

Parker, Francis, jt. auth. see Simons, Richard S.

Parker, Francis H. Reason & Faith Revisited. LC 79-154285. (Aquinas Lectures). 1971. 15.00 (*0-87462-136-4*) Marquette.

— The Story of Western Philosophy. LC 67-13033. 352p. reprint ed. pap. 109.20 (*0-608-10066-8*, 205008700058) Bks Demand.

Parker, Francis J. Civil War Infantry, the Story of the 32nd Massachusetts Infantry, Whence It Came, Where It Went, What It Saw & What It Did. (Illus.). 260p. 1995. reprint ed. lib. bdg. 35.00 (*0-8328-4632-5*) Higginson Bk Co.

— Genealogy of Ainsworth Families in America. 212p. 1988. reprint ed. pap. 32.00 (*0-8328-0095-3*); reprint ed. lib. bdg. 40.00 (*0-8328-0094-5*) Higginson Bk Co.

Parker, Francis W. Talks on Pedagogics: An Outline of the Theory of Concentration. LC 70-89217. (American Education: Its Men, Institutions, & Ideas. Series 1). 1978. reprint ed. 23.95 (*0-405-01456-2*) Ayer.

Parker, Frank. Togo. (World Bibliographical Ser.). 224p. 1995. lib. bdg. 57.00 (*1-85109-160-2*) ABC-CLIO.

Parker, Frank & Riley, Kathryn. Writing for Academic Publication: A Guide to Getting Started. 160p. 1995. pap. text 21.95 (*0-9644636-1-X*) Parlay Enter.

Parker, Frank, jt. auth. see Riley, Kathryn L.

Parker, Frank J. Caryl Chessman: The Red Light Bandit. LC 75-8760. (Illus.). 243p. 1975. text 32.95 (*0-88229-188-2*) Burnham Inc.

— The Law & the Poor. LC 72-97696. 230p. reprint ed. pap. 71.30 (*0-8357-8937-3*, 203351200086) Bks Demand.

Parker, Frank R. Black Votes Count: Political Empowerment in Mississippi after 1965. LC 89-39074. (Illus.). xviii, 254p. (C). 1990. pap. text 18.95 (*0-8078-4274-5*) U of NC Pr.

Parker, Frank S. Applications of Infrared, Raman, & Resonance Raman Spectroscopy in Biochemistry. 516p. 1983. 120.00 (*0-306-41206-3*, Plenum Trade) Perseus Pubng.

Parker, Franklin. Education in Puerto Rico: Abstracts of American Doctoral Dissertations. LC 77-87895. 1977. 27.00 (*0-913480-36-3*) Inter Am U Pr.

— George Peabody: A Biography. rev. ed. LC 94-24306. (Illus.). 264p. (C). 1994. 29.95 (*0-8265-1255-0*); pap. 16.95 (*0-8265-1256-9*) Vanderbilt U Pr.

Parker, Franklin & Parker, Betty. Education in England & Wales: An Annotated Bibliography. LC 90-25455. (Reference Books in International Education: Vol. 19). 624p. 1991. text 85.00 (*0-8240-5943-3*, SS581) Garland.

Parker, Franklin & Parker, Betty J. American Dissertations on Foreign Education: A Bibliography with Abstracts: India, Vol. 2. LC 73-155724. 241p. 1972. 11.00 (*0-87875-018-5*) Whitston Pub.

— American Dissertations on Foreign Education Vol. 1: A Bibliography with Abstracts: Canada. LC 73-155724. 175p. 1971. 9.50 (*0-87875-013-4*) Whitston Pub.

— American Dissertations on Foreign Education Vol. 3: A Bibliography with Abstracts: Essential Japan. LC 73-155724. 173p. 1972. 9.50 (*0-87875-035-5*) Whitston Pub.

— American Dissertations on Foreign Education Vol. 4: A Bibliography with Abstracts: Africa. LC 73-155724. 508p. 1973. 18.00 (*0-87875-043-6*) Whitston Pub.

— American Dissertations on Foreign Education Vol. 5: A Bibliography with Abstracts: Scandinavia. LC 73-155724. 249p. 1974. 12.50 (*0-87875-051-7*) Whitston Pub.

— American Dissertations on Foreign Education Vol. 6: A Bibliography with Abstracts: China, 2 pts. LC 73-155724. 969p. 1974. 40.00 (*0-87875-052-5*) Whitston Pub.

— American Dissertations on Foreign Education - A Bibliography with Abstracts Vol. 9: South America. LC 73-155724. 1977. 30.00 (*0-87875-101-7*) Whitston Pub.

— Education in the People's Republic of China Past & Present: A Bibliography. LC 84-48394. (Books in International Education). 904p. 1986. text 127.00 (*0-8240-8797-6*) Garland.

Parker, Franklin & Parker, Betty J., eds. American Dissertations on Foreign Education: A Bibliography with Abstracts: Philippines, 2 vols., Vol. 18. LC 73-155724. xxv, 1062p. 1986. 80.00 (*0-87875-333-8*) Whitston Pub.

— American Dissertations on Foreign Education Vol. 8: A Bibliography with Abstracts: Mexico. LC 73-155724. xiv, 456p. 1976. 16.00 (*0-87875-086 X*) Whitston Pub.

— American Dissertations on Foreign Education Vol. 20: A Bibliography with Abstracts: Britain. LC 73-155724. 460p. 1990. 55.00 (*0-87875-368-0*) Whitston Pub.

— American Dissertations on Foreign Education - A Bibliography with Abstracts: Vol. 17: A Bibliography with Abstracts: Pacific. LC 73-155724. xiii, 208p. 1986. 25.00 (*0-87875-327-3*) Whitston Pub.

— Women's Education, A World View Vol. 2: Annotated Bibliography of Books, Vol. 2. LC 78-73791. 689p. 1981. lib. bdg. 85.00 (*0-313-23206-7*, PEY/, Greenwood Pr) Greenwood.

Parker, Franklin, jt. auth. see Parker, Betty J.

Parker, Franklin D. The Central American Republics. LC 81-2572. (Illus.). 348p. 1981. reprint ed. lib. bdg. 65.00 (*0-313-22991-0*, PACA, Greenwood Pr) Greenwood.

— Troubled Earth Acquires Lunar Perspective: A World History, 1961-1970. LC 82-45052. 922p. (Orig.). (C). 1982. pap. text 64.00 (*0-8191-2478-8*) U Pr of Amer.

***Parker, Freddie L.** Fugitive Slaves: An International Phenomenon. 250p. 2000. 38.00 (*0-8153-2300-X*) Garland.

Parker, Freddie L. Running for Freedom: Slave Runaways in North Carolina, 1775 to 1840. LC 92-38603. (Studies in African American History & Culture). 264p. 1993. text 20.00 (*0-8153-1005-6*) Garland.

Parker, G. A., ed. River Meandering. (Water Resources Monograph Ser.: Vol. 12). 496p. 1989. pap. 26.00 (*0-87590-316-9*) Am Geophysical.

Parker, G. F. Johnson's Shakespeare. 226p. 1991. reprint ed. pap. text 16.95 (*0-19-811271-8*, 10971) OUP.

Parker, Gail R. The Bed 'N Breakfast Directory, 1984-1985. 3rd ed. 56p. 1984. pap. 3.95 (*0-910115-01-X*) PS Pubns.

— Holidays for One: Vacations for the Solo Traveler. (Illus.). 64p. (Orig.). 1981. pap. 5.50 (*0-910115-00-1*) PS Pubns.

— Recipes & Rendezvous. (Illus.). 108p. (Orig.). 1984. pap. 5.95 (*0-910115-02-8*) PS Pubns.

Parker, Gail T. Mind Cure in New England: From the Civil War to World War I. LC 72-92704. 209p. reprint ed. pap. 64.80 (*0-608-15383-4*, 202925400059) Bks Demand.

Parker, Gail U. Relax with Me. LC 97-91927. 130p. 1997. pap. write for info. (*1-57502-509-4*, P01512) Morris Pubng.

Parker, Garda. Bartered Bridegroom. 1995. pap. 4.99 (*0-8217-5169-7*) NAL.

— Wild Hearts. 1997. mass mkt. 4.99 (*0-8217-5645-1*) Kensgtn Pub Corp.

Parker, Garland G. Syria. (Pelham Guides Ser.). 45p. (C). 1996. write for info. (*0-929851-99-4*) Am Assn Coll Registrars.

Parker, Gary. Dry Bones & Other Fossils. LC 79-51174. (Illus.). 80p. (J). (gr. 1-7). 1995. boxed set 12.95 (*0-89051-203-5*, DBROO2) Master Bks.

— OL/Last Gift: A Christmas Story about Family Forgiveness. LC 99-27375. 1999. 12.99 (*1-56476-779-5*) SP Pubns.

— Skeletons in Your Closet: A Sequel to Dry Bones. LC 97-75949. 79p. 1998. boxed set 13.95 (*0-89051-230-2*) Master Bks.

Parker, Gary & Tennet, Les. Desert Water. 312p. 1995. pap. 10.99 (*1-56476-450-8*, 6-3450, Victor Bks) Chariot Victor.

Parker, Gary, jt. auth. see Morris, Henry M.

Parker, Gary E. A Capital Offense: One Woman, One Gamble, One Chance. LC 97-46995. 271p. 1998. pap. 10.99 (*0-7852-7786-2*, J Thoma Bks) Nelson.

— Creation: Facts of Life. LC 94-96175. 216p. 1994. pap. 10.95 (*0-89051-200-0*, CRFALI) Master Bks.

— Dark Road to Daylight. LC 96-42229. 1997. pap. 12.99 (*0-7852-7785-4*) Nelson.

***Parker, Gary E.** Ephesus Fragment. LC 99-6479. 352p. 1999. 10.99 (*0-7642-2256-2*) Bethany Hse.

Parker, Gary E. Life Before Birth. LC 87-70955. 88p. (J). (gr. 5-7). 1997. boxed set 12.95 (*0-89051-164-0*, LIBEBI) Master Bks.

***Parker, Gary E.** Rumors of Peace. 352p. 2000. pap. 10.99 (*0-7642-2257-0*) Bethany Hse.

Parker, Genevieve. The Afterglow. LC 93-86984. 248p. 1994. 22.95 (*0-9638987-0-1*) Parker Homestead.

Parker, Geoffrey. Army of Flanders & the Spanish Road: 1567-1659. LC 76-180021. (Cambridge Studies in Early Modern History). (Illus.). 309p. 1975. pap. text 24.95 (*0-521-09907-2*) Cambridge U Pr.

— The Geopolitics of Domination. LC 88-4410. (Illus.). 192p. reprint ed. pap. 59.60 (*0-608-20370-X*, 207162300002) Bks Demand.

— The Geopolitics of Domination: Territorial Supremacy in Europe & the Mediterranean from the Ottoman Empire to the Soviet Union. 240p. 1988. lib. bdg. 55.00 (*0-415-00483-7*) Routledge.

— The Grand Strategy of Philip II. LC 98-7352. (Illus.). 472p. 1998. 40.00 (*0-300-07540-5*) Yale U Pr.

***Parker, Geoffrey.** The Grand Strategy of Philip II. (Illus.). 472p. 2000. pap. 17.95 (*0-300-08273-8*) Yale U Pr.

Parker, Geoffrey. The Military Revolution: Military Innovation & the Rise of the West, 1500-1800. 2nd ed. (Illus.). 284p. (C). 1996. pap. 22.95 (*0-521-47958-4*) Cambridge U Pr.

— Philip II. 3rd ed. 264p. 1995. pap. 16.95 (*0-8126-9279-9*) Open Court.

— Random House Compact Atlas of World History. 1999. pap. 16.95 (*0-375-70505-8*) Random Ref & Info.

— The Thirty Years War. (Illus.). 320p. 1985. 47.50 (*0-7100-9788-3*, Routledge Thoemms) Routledge.

Parker, Geoffrey, ed. The Cambridge Illustrated History of Warfare. (Illustrated Histories Ser.). (Illus.). 416p. (C). 1995. 39.95 (*0-521-44073-4*) Cambridge U Pr.

***Parker, Geoffrey, ed.** The Cambridge Illustrated History of Warfare. (Cambridge Illustrated Histories Ser.). (Illus.). 416p. 2000. pap. 29.95 (*0-521-79431-5*) Cambridge U Pr.

Parker, Geoffrey, ed. The Thirty Years' War. 384p. (C). 1988. pap. text 15.95 (*0-7102-1181-3*, Routledge Thoemms) Routledge.

— Thirty Years' War. 2nd ed. LC 97-143765. 384p. (C). 1994. pap. 24.99 (*0-415-12883-8*) Routledge.

Parker, Geoffrey & Smith, Lesley M. The General Crisis of the Seventeenth Century. 2nd ed. LC 96-45505. 320p. (C). 1997. 85.00 (*0-415-16518-0*); pap. 22.99 (*0-415-12882-X*) Routledge.

Parker, Geoffrey, jt. auth. see Martin, Colin.

Parker, Geoffrey, jt. ed. see Kagan, Richard L.

Parker, Geoffrey A., jt. auth. see Mock, Douglas W.

Parker, George. Estudios sobre Romanos.Tr. of Studies on Romans. (SPA.). 256p. 1996. pap. 8.99 (*0-8254-1558-6*, Edit Portavoz) Kregel.

— Lexico-Concordancia Del Nuevo Testamento en Griego y Espanol: Greek-Spanish Lexicon Concord. of the N.T. (SPA.). 1000p. 1991. pap. 35.50 (*0-311-42065-6*) Casa Bautista.

— Medical Malpractice Lawsuit: A Case Study. 198p. 2000. lib. bdg. 45.00 (*1-56072-470-6*) Nova Sci Pubs.

— Medical Malpractice Lawsuit: A Case Study. (Illus.). 198p. 2000. pap. 17.95 (*1-56072-340-8*, Nova Kroshka Bks) Nova Sci Pubs.

— NCSU Physics 205 & 208 Text Pack, 1996-1997. 2nd ed. 150p. (C). 1996. pap. text, ring bd. 9.95 (*0-7872-2658-0*) Kendall-Hunt.

— Ncsu Physics 205 & 208 Test Pack: 1998/1999. 4th ed. 128p. (C). 1998. spiral bd. 13.95 (*0-7872-5469-X*, 41546901) Kendall-Hunt.

Parker, George D., jt. auth. see Millman, R. S.

Parker, George D., jt. auth. see Millman, Richard S.

Parker, George F. Recollections of Grover Cleveland. LC 70-165649. (Select Bibliographies Reprint Ser.). 1977. reprint ed. 36.95 (*0-8369-5958-2*) Ayer.

Parker, George G. The Standard Bank Game Version 11: Commercial Manual. (Principles of Management Ser.). 1995. pap. 26.50 (*0-7895-0094-9*) Course Tech.

— The Stanford Bank Game Version 11: International Commercial Manual. (GC - Principles of Management Ser.). 1995. pap. 26.50 (*0-7895-0095-7*) Course Tech.

Parker, George G. & Beaver, William. Risk Management: Challenges & Solutions. 400p. (C). 1995. 37.19 (*0-07-048588-7*) McGraw.

Parker, George L. The Beginnings of the Book Trade in Canada. 376p. 1985. text 50.00 (*0-8020-2547-1*) U of Toronto Pr.

Parker, George W. Children of the Sun. 31p. 1981. reprint ed. pap. 2.00 (*0-933121-10-5*) Black Classic.

Parker, Gerald. How to Play: The Theatre of James Reaney. 260p. (C). 1991. pap. text 25.00 (*1-55022-119-1*, Pub. by ECW) Genl Dist Srvs.

Parker, Gerry. Eastern Coyote: The Story of Its Success. LC QL737. (Illus.). 254p. 1995. pap. 18.95 (*1-55109-111-9*) Nimbus Publ.

Parker, Gertrude M. Little Drops of Water Little Grains of Sand. 32p. (Orig.). 1983. pap. write for info. (*0-89279-055-5*) G M Parker.

Parker, Gilbert. Adventurer of the North. LC 74-98589. (Short Story Index Reprint Ser.). 1977. 19.95 (*0-8369-3163-7*) Ayer.

— Battle of the Strong. 1976. lib. bdg. 18.50 (*0-89968-078-X*, Lghtyr Pr) Buccaneer Bks.

— Battle of the Strong: A Romance of Two Kingdoms. (Jersey Heritage Editions Ser.). 1991. 40.00 (*0-86120-020-9*, Pub. by Aris & Phillips) David Brown.

— Born with a Golden Spoon. 1976. lib. bdg. 13.85 (*0-89968-081-X*, Lghtyr Pr) Buccaneer Bks.

— The Hill of Pains. 1976. lib. bdg. 9.95 (*0-89968-082-8*, Lghtyr Pr) Buccaneer Bks.

— The Judgement House. 1976. lib. bdg. 19.50 (*0-89968-080-1*, Lghtyr Pr) Buccaneer Bks.

— Pierre & His People. LC 74-101287. (Short Story Index Reprint Ser.). 1977. 21.95 (*0-8369-3224-2*) Ayer.

— The Right of Way. 1976. lib. bdg. 16.25 (*0-89968-079-8*, Lghtyr Pr) Buccaneer Bks.

— Romany of the Snows. LC 79-94741. (Short Story Index Reprint Ser.). 1977. 19.95 (*0-8369-3121-1*) Ayer.

— Seats of the Mighty. 1976. lib. bdg. 16.75 (*0-89968-077-1*, Lghtyr Pr) Buccaneer Bks.

— The Trespasser. 1976. lib. bdg. 13.85 (*0-89968-083-6*, Lghtyr Pr) Buccaneer Bks.

Parker, Gilbert & Bryan, Claude G. Old Quebec, the Fortress of New France. (Illus.). 486p. 1992. reprint ed. pap. 30.00 (*1-55613-594-7*) Heritage Bk.

Parker, Gillian. Getting & Spending: Credit & Debt in Britain. 246p. 1990. text 82.95 (*1-85628-053-5*, Pub. by Avebry) Ashgate Pub Co.

Parker, Gillian. With This Body: Caring & Disability in Marriage. LC 92-18284. 160p. 1993. 123.00 (*0-335-09947-5*); pap. 34.95 (*0-335-09946-7*) OpUniv Pr.

Parker, Gillian & Lawton, Dot. Different Types of Care, Different Types of Carer: Evidence from General Households. 121p. 1994. pap. 25.00 (*0-11-701783-3*, HM17833, Pub. by Statnry Office) Bernan Associates.

Parker, Gillian, jt. ed. see Walker, Robert, Jr.

Parker, Glenn. Cross-Functional Teams: Tool Kit. 192p. 1997. 119.00 (*0-7879-0856-8*) Jossey-Bass.

Parker, Glenn A., jt. auth. see Smith, Phillip H.

Parker, Glenn M. Cross-Functional Teams: Working with Allies, Enemies, & Other Strangers. LC 93-48674. (Business-Management Ser.). 254p. 1994. mass mkt. 26.00 (*1-55542-609-3*) Jossey-Bass.

— Handbook of Best Practices for Teams, Vol. 1. 1996. pap. text 59.95 (*0-87425-336-5*) HRD Press.

— Team Players & Teamwork: The New Competitive Business Strategy. (The Management Ser.). 210p. 1996. mass mkt. 16.50 (*0-7879-0185-7*) Jossey-Bass.

Parker, Glenn M. & Kropp, Richard P., Jr. Fifty Activities for Self-Directed Teams. 250p. 1994. ring bd. 139.95 (*0-87425-969-X*) HRD Press.

***Parker, Glenn M., et al.** Rewarding Teams: Lessons from the Trenches. LC 99-50601. (Illus.). 240p. 2000. 27.00 (*0-7879-4809-8*, Pfffr & Co) Jossey-Bass.

Parker, Glenn M., jt. auth. see Thiagarajan, Sivasailam.

Parker, Glenn R. Congress & the Rent-Seeking Society. LC 95-42912. 184p. (C). 1996. text 44.50 (*0-472-10662-7*, 10662) U of Mich Pr.

— Institutional Change, Discretion, & the Making of Modern Congress: An Economic Interpretation. 128p. (C). 1992. text 39.50 (*0-472-10329-6*, 10329) U of Mich Pr.

Parker, Glenn R., ed. Studies of Congress. LC 84-16993. (Illus.). 586p. reprint ed. pap. 181.70 (*0-8357-8536-X*, 203483900091) Bks Demand.

Parker, Glenn R. & Parker, Suzanne L. Factions in House Committees. LC 85 3150. (Illus.). 335p. 1985. pap. 103.90 (*0-608-05193-4*, 206573000001) Bks Demand.

Parker, Gordon & Hadzi-Pavlovic, Dusan, eds. Melancholia: A Disorder of Movement & Mood: A Phenomenological & Neurobiological Review. (Illus.). 350p. (C). 1996. text 80.00 (*0-521-47275-X*) Cambridge U Pr.

***Parker, Graham.** Carp Fishing on Valium. LC 00-27855. 256p. 2000. 22.95 (*0-312-26485-2*) St Martin.

— The FPSO Design & Construction Guidance Manual. LC 99-67553. 121p. 1999. pap. text 365.00 (*0-9676640-0-4*) Reserve Tech Inst.

Parker, Graham W. Achieving Cost-Efficient Quality: A PARSEC Guide. 118p. 1995. pap. 78.95 (*0-566-07582-2*, Pub. by Gower) Ashgate Pub Co.

— Internal Auditing of Management Systems. LC 95-1063. (PRASEC Guide Ser.). 145p. 1995. pap. 78.95 (*0-566-07584-9*, Pub. by Gower) Ashgate Pub Co.

Parker, Grant. Mayday: The History of a Village Holocaust. 260p. 1992. reprint ed. pap. 8.95 (*0-9604958-0-0*) Parker Pr MI.

Parker, Grant, tr. & comment see Capitein, Jacobus E.

Parker Guidry, Virginia, jt. auth. see Campbell Thorton, Kim.

Parker, Gwendolyn M. Trespassing: My Sojourn in the Halls of Privilege. LC 97-19951. 208p. 1997. 23.00 (*0-395-82297-1*) HM.

— Trespassing: My Sojourn in the Halls of Privilege. 224p. 1999. pap. 11.00 (*0-395-92620-3*) HM.

Parker, H. Ancient Ceylon. (Illus.). 696p. 1986. reprint ed. 32.00 (*0-8364-1742-9*, Pub. by Manohar) S Asia.

***Parker, H.** Ancient Ceylon. 4th ed. 1999. reprint ed. 48.50 (*81-206-0208-0*, Pub. by Asian Educ Servs) S Asia.

P

Parker, H. & Pitt, G. D. Pollution Control Instrumentation for Oil & Effluents. 272p. (C). 1987. reprint ed. lib. bdg. 163.00 (*0-86010-368-4*, Pub. by Graham & Trotman) Kluwer Academic.

Parker, H. Dennison, ed. GIS Applications in Natural Resources 2. (Illus.). 540p. 1996. pap. text 39.95 (*1-882610-17-2*) GIS World Bks.

Parker, H. M. The Roman Legions. 286p. 1980. reprint ed. pap. 20.00 (*0-89005-356-1*) Ares.

Parker, Hankins. Memory Loss - Changing Tracks - Growing Older: Don't Act Your Age. (Illus.). (Orig.). 1994. pap. 5.00 (*0-85132-200-X*) Park Hurst Pubs.

— Micajah's White Horse & Red Wagon. (Illus.). 189p. (Orig.). 1995. pap. 12.50 (*1-885132-02-6*) Park Hurst Pubs.

Parker Hanni Law Corporation Staff. Industrial Pneumatic Technology. Schrader, Lawrence F, Jr., ed. (Illus.). 150p. (Orig.). 1980. teacher ed. 34.25 (*1-55769-016-2*, 0275-B2) Parker Hannifin.

— Industrial Pneumatic Technology. Schrader, Lawrence F, Jr., ed. (Illus.). 150p. (Orig.). 1980. pap. text 22.90 (*1-55769-015-4*, 0275-B1) Parker Hannifin.

Parker Hannifin Corporation Staff. Design Engineers Handbook. Schrader, Lawrence F., Jr., ed. (Illus.). 304p. (Orig.). (C). 1979. pap. text 25.45 (*1-55769-018-9*, 0224-B1) Parker Hannifin.

— Design of Electrohydraulic Systems for Industrial Motion Control. 2nd ed. Johnson, Jack L., ed. (Illus.). 386p. 1995. 112.95 (*1-55769-032-4*, Bul. 0246-B1) Parker Hannifin.

— Filtration Technology. Riedel, Raymond T., ed. (Illus.). 304p. 1995. 65.85 (*1-55769-033-2*, Bul. 0250-B1); pap. 38.45 (*1-55769-030-8*, Bul. 0241-B1) Parker Hannifin.

— Fluid Power Basics. Schrader, Lawrence F., Jr., ed. (Illus.). 176p. 1993. pap. 22.90 (*1-55769-029-4*, Bul. 0239-B1) Parker Hannifin.

— Hydraulic Maintenance Technology. Cohn, Joseph, Jr., ed. (Illus.). 148p. (Orig.). 1989. teacher ed. 76.70 (*1-55769-024-3*, 0240-B2); pap. text 22.90 (*1-55769-019-7*, 0240-B1) Parker Hannifin.

— Hydraulic Pumps & Controls. Schrader, Lawrence F., Jr., ed. LC 95-232534. (Illus.). 204p. 1995. pap. 35.65 (*1-55769-031-6*, Bul. 0238-B1) Parker Hannifin.

— Industrial Hydraulic Technology. 2nd ed. Schrader, Lawrence F., ed. (Illus.). 331p. (Orig.). 1991. pap. text 39.55 (*1-55769-025-1*, BUL. 0232-B1) Parker Hannifin.

Parker, Harold M., Jr. The United Synod: The Southern New School Presbyterian Church, 20. LC 87-37564. (Contributions to the Study of Religion Ser.: No. 20). 363p. 1988. 59.95 (*0-313-26289-6*, PSY/, Greenwood Pr) Greenwood.

Parker, Harold M., Jr., compiled by. Bibliography of Published Articles on American Presbyterianism, 1901-1980, 4. LC 85-7987. (Bibliographies & Indexes in Religious Studies: No. 4). 261p. 1985. lib. bdg. 59.95 (*0-313-24544-4*, PBP/, Greenwood Pr) Greenwood.

Parker, Harold T. An Administrative Bureau During the Old Regime: The Bureau of Commerce & Its Relations to French Industry from May 1781 to November 1783. LC 92-50634. 160p. 1993. 29.50 (*0-87413-467-6*) U Delaware Pr.

— Three Napoleonic Battles. LC 82-21082. (Illus.). xxiii, 235p. 1983. reprint ed. pap. text 17.95 (*0-8223-0547-X*) Duke.

Parker, Harold T. & Herr, Richard, eds. Ideas in History: Essays Presented to Louis Gottschalk by His Former Students. LC 65-14546. 400p. reprint ed. 124.00 (*0-8357-9107-6*, 201791800010) Bks Demand.

Parker, Harold T., jt. ed. see Iggers, Georg G.

Parker, Harriet F., jt. auth. see Marsh, Lucius B.

Parker, Harrison. Hawley, Massachusetts: The First Fifty Years: 1770-1820. LC 92-28144. 1992. pap. 35.00 (*0-9633340-1-8*) Sara Pub MA.

Parker, Harry. Simplified Mechanics & Strength of Materials. 5th ed. LC 91-42711. (Parker Simplified Design Guides Ser.: No. 1879). 408p. 1992. 79.00 (*0-471-54170-2*) Wiley.

Parker, Harry & Ambrose, James. Simplified Design of Wood Structures. 5th ed. LC 93-35635. 351p. 1994. 79.00 (*0-471-30366-6*) Wiley.

Parker, Harry & Ambrose, James E. Simplified Design of Wood Structures. 5th ed. LC 93-35635. 351p. 1997. pap. 59.95 (*0-471-17989-2*) Wiley.

Parker, Harry & MacGuire, John W. Simplified Site Engineering. 2nd ed. 192p. 1997. pap. 59.95 (*0-471-17987-6*) Wiley.

Parker, Harry, jt. auth. see Ambrose, James E.

***Parker, Harry J. & Reisch, Joan S.** A Study of Remington's Smoot Patent & Number Four Revolvers. (Antique Arms Enthusiast Ser.: Vol. 1). (Illus.). 96p. 2000. pap. 11.95 (*1-882824-21-0*) Graphic Pubs.

Parker, Harry L. Clinical Studies in Neurology. 384p. 1969. 55.95 (*0-398-01449-3*); pap. 40.95 (*0-398-06313-3*) C C Thomas.

Parker, Harry W. Iron John Reflections No. 1: Choose - One Precious Thing. (Orig.). 1992. pap. 5.95 (*0-89672-311-9*) Tex Tech Univ Pr.

Parker, Harvey C. Adapt: Attention Deficit Accommodation Plan for Teaching. (Illus.). 16p. 1992. pap. 8.00 (*1-886941-09-2*, 0900B); pap., student ed., wbk. ed. 16.00 (*1-886941-05-X*, 0900C) Spec Pr FL.

— The ADD Hyperactivity Handbook for Schools: Effective Strategies for Identifying & Teaching ADD Students in Elementary & Secondary Schools. (Illus.). 330p. (Orig.). 1992. pap. 29.00 (*0-9621629-2-2*) Spec Pr FL.

— The ADD Hyperactivity Workbook for Parents, Teachers & Kids. rev. ed. LC 96-127644. (Illus.). 108p. 1994. pap. 17.00 (*0-9621629-6-5*) Spec Pr FL.

— Behavior Management at Home: A Token Economy Program for Children & Teens. 24p. 1995. pap. 15.00 (*0-9621629-3-0*, 0965) Spec Pr FL.

— Cuaderno do Trabajo para Padres, Maestros y Ninos sobre el Trasterno de Bajo Nivel de Atencion (ADD) o Hiperactividad. (Illus.). 142p. 1994. pap., student ed. 17.00 (*0-9621629-5-7*) Spec Pr FL.

— The Goal Card Program: A Home-School Based Behavioral Management Program for Training Children with Attention Deficit Disorders. 12p. 1991. pap. 16.00 (*1-886941-13-0*, 0953) Spec Pr FL.

— The Good Behavior Chart: A Program for Managing Young Children's Behavior. LC 96-33818. (Illus.). 20p. (J). 1996. pap. 16.00 (*1-886941-08-4*) Spec Pr FL.

— Listen Look & Think: A Self-Regulation Program for Children. 8p. (Orig.). 1992. pap., teacher ed. 22.00 (*1-886941-12-2*, 0955) Spec Pr FL.

***Parker, Harvey C.** Problem Solver Guide for Students with ADHD: Ready-to-Use Interventions for Elementary & Secondary Students. 125p. (Orig.). 2000. pap. 15.00 (*1-886941-39-4*, 0982, Pub. by Spec Pr FL) IPG Chicago.

Parker, Harvey C. & Goodstat, Alan. Put Yourself in Their Shoes: Understanding Teenagers with Attention-Deficit Hyperactivity Disorder. LC 98-43908. 249p. 1999. pap. 19.00 (*1-886941-19-X*, 0950) Spec Pr FL.

Parker, Harvey C., jt. auth. see Parker, Roberta N.

Parker, Heather. Fantastic Animal Features. 1999. pap. 5.95 (*0-7398-1479-6*) Raintree Steck-V.

Parker, Hedy, tr. see Boas, Franz.

Parker, Helen, ed. see Hawthorne, Linden.

Parker, Helen N. Biological Themes in Modern Science Fiction. LC 84-8768. (Studies in Speculative Fiction: No. 6). 115p. reprint ed. pap. 35.70 (*0-8357-1577-9*, 207051600097) Bks Demand.

Parker, Helene C. & Virtue, Doreen L. If This Is Love, Why Am I So Lonely? 224p. 1996. 19.95 (*0-925190-82-9*) Fairview Press.

Parker, Henry. The Case of Shipmony Briefly Discoursed, According to the Grounds of Law, Policy & Conscience. LC 76-57404. (English Experience Ser.: No. 820). 1977. reprint ed. lib. bdg. 15.00 (*90-221-0820-1*) Walter J Johnson.

— The Rich & the Poor. LC 77-7419. (English Experience Ser.: No. 882). 1977. reprint ed. lib. bdg. 75.00 (*90-221-0882-1*) Walter J Johnson.

— Village Folk-Tales of Ceylon, 3 vols., Set. Dorson, Richard M., ed. LC 77-70614. (International Folklore Ser.). 1977. reprint ed. lib. bdg. 108.95 (*0-405-10113-9*) Ayer.

— Village Folk-Tales of Ceylon, 3 vols., Vol. 1. Dorson, Richard M., ed. LC 77-70614. (International Folklore Ser.). 1977. reprint ed. lib. bdg. 36.95 (*0-405-10114-7*) Ayer.

— Village Folk-Tales of Ceylon, 3 vols., Vol. 2. Dorson, Richard M., ed. LC 77-70614. (International Folklore Ser.). 1977. reprint ed. lib. bdg. 36.95 (*0-405-10115-5*) Ayer.

— Village Folk-Tales of Ceylon, 3 vols., Vol. 3. Dorson, Richard M., ed. LC 77-70614. (International Folklore Ser.). 1977. reprint ed. lib. bdg. 36.95 (*0-405-10116-3*) Ayer.

Parker, Henry H. & Crist, Marilyn I. Teaching Minorities to Play the Corporate Language Game. 51p. (Orig.). 1996. pap. 20.00 (*1-889271-20-9*) Nat Res Ctr.

Parker, Henry T. Eighth Notes: Voices & Figures of Music & the Dance. LC 68-29236. (Essay Index Reprint Ser.). 1977. 19.95 (*0-8369-0768-X*) Ayer.

Parker, Herbert M. The Squares of the Natural Numbers in Radiation Protection. LC 77-81781. (Taylor Lectures: No. 1). 1977. pap. 20.00 (*0-913392-39-1*) NCRP Pubns.

Parker, Hermione. Taxes, Benefits & Family Life: The Seven Deadly Traps. (Research Monographs: No. 50). 149p. 1995. pap. 34.50 (*0-255-36370-2*, Pub. by Inst Economic Affairs) Coronet Bks.

Parker, Hermione, ed. see Williams, Brandon R.

Parker, Hershel. Flawed Texts & Verbal Icons: Literary Authority in American Fiction. LC 84-613439. 249p. 1984. pap. 14.95 (*0-8101-0667-1*) Northwestern U Pr.

— Herman Melville Vol. 1: A Biography, 1819-1851. LC 96-18984. (Illus.). 928p. 1996. 39.95 (*0-8018-5428-8*) Johns Hopkins.

— Life of Herman Melville, 1. Date not set. write for info. (*0-393-03842-4*) Norton.

— Reading Billy Budd. 190p. (Orig.). 1990. pap. 14.95 (*0-8101-0962-X*) Northwestern U Pr.

Parker, Hershel & Hayes, Kevin J., eds. Checklist of Melville Reviews. 157p. 1992. 39.95 (*0-8101-1028-8*) Northwestern U Pr.

Parker, Hershel, jt. ed. see Higgins, Brian.

Parker, Hershel, ed. see Melville, Herman.

Parker, Hilary. Flight to Enchantment. large type ed. (Linford Romance Library). 1989. pap. 16.99 (*0-7089-6788-4*) Ulverscroft.

Parker, Hohn & Bryan, Peter. Landscape Management & Maintenance: A Guide to Its Costing & Organization. (Illus.). 176p. 1989. text 69.95 (*0-566-09018-X*) Ashgate Pub Co.

Parker, Homer W., Sr. Evolution of Man Since the Earth Was Created: Mankind's Roots. LC 89-91069. 144p. (Orig.). 1989. pap. 12.95 (*0-922958-06-8*) H W Parker.

Parker, Homer W., Sr., ed. Software Handbook for DOS for IBM PC, XT, AT, PS2 & Compatibles. LC 88-92322. 240p. (Orig.). 1989. pap. 12.95 (*0-922958-00-9*) H W Parker.

Parker, Horatio. Hora Novissima (Opus 30) LC 75-169652. (Earlier American Music Ser.: No. 2). 167p. 1972. reprint ed. lib. bdg. 32.50 (*0-306-77302-3*) Da Capo.

Parker, Horatio W., ed. Music & Public Entertainment. LC 74-24180. (Illus.). reprint ed. 49.50 (*0-404-13082-8*) AMS Pr.

Parker, Howard. View from the Boys: Sociology of Down-Town Adolescents. (Modern Revivals in Sociology Ser.). 238p. 1992. 51.95 (*0-7512-0046-8*, Pub. by Gregg Revivals) Ashgate Pub Co.

Parker, Howard & Jarvis, Graham. Unmasking the Magistrates: The "Custody-or-Not" Decision in Sentencing Young Offenders. 176p. 1989. 113.00 (*0-335-09936-X*); pap. 34.95 (*0-335-09935-1*) OpUniv Pr.

Parker, Howard, et al. Living with Heroin: The Impact of a Drugs "Epidemic" on an English Community. 192p. 1988. 113.00 (*0-335-15565-0*); pap. 36.95 (*0-335-15564-2*) OpUniv Pr.

Parker, Howard J., et al. Illegal Leisure: The Normalization of Adolescent Recreational Drug Use. LC 98-10388. (Adolescence & Society Ser.). (Illus.). 160p. (C). 1998. 75.00 (*0-415-15809-5*); pap. 24.99 (*0-415-15810-9*) Routledge.

Parker, Hugh C. Greek Gods in Italy in Ovid's "Fasti" A Greater Greece. LC 97-27242. (Studies in Classics: Vol. 5). 192p. 1997. text 79.95 (*0-7734-8589-9*) E Mellen.

Parker, Huw, jt. auth. see Matthews, Sarah.

Parker, Huw, ed. see Swift, Jonathan.

Parker, Ian. Complete Rollei TLF User's Manual. (Illus.). 180p. 1996. pap. text 19.95 (*1-874031-96-7*, Pub. by Hove Foto) Watsn-Guptill.

— Complete Rollei TLR Collector's Guide. (Illus.). 180p. 1996. pap. text 19.95 (*1-874031-95-9*, Pub. by Hove Foto) Watsn-Guptill.

— The Crisis in Modern Social Psychology: How to End It. 176p. 1989. 45.00 (*0-685-26090-9*, A1668); pap. 12.95 (*0-415-01494-8*, A3373) Routledge.

— Psychoanalytic Culture: Psychoanalytic Discourse in Western Society. 304p. 1997. 45.00 (*0-7619-5642-5*); pap. 14.99 (*0-7619-5643-3*) Sage.

— Rollei 6000 Series User's Manual: SLX Through to 6008. (Illus.). 180p. 1997. pap. 29.95 (*1-874657-02-5*, Pub. by Jersey Photographic) Watsn-Guptill.

— Rollei TLR: The History. 1996. 19.95 (*1-874657-01-7*, Pub. by Hove Foto) Watsn-Guptill.

— Rollei TLR: The History. (Illus.). 192p. 1996. 19.95 (*1-874657-00-9*, Pub. by Jersey Photographic) Watsn-Guptill.

— Social Constructionism, Discourse, & Realism LC 98-60145. xii, 159p. 1998. write for info. (*0-7619-5377-9*) Sage.

Parker, Ian & Bolton Discourse Network Staff. Critical Textwork: An Introduction to Varieties of Discourse & Analysis. LC 98-39283. 1999. 85.00 (*0-335-20205-5*); pap. 26.95 (*0-335-20204-7*) OpUniv Pr.

Parker, Ian, et al. Deconstructing Psychopathology. 176p. 1996. 65.00 (*0-8039-7480-9*); pap. 24.95 (*0-8039-7481-7*) Sage.

Parker, Ian, jt. ed. see Gordo-Lopez, Angel J.

Parker, Idella. Idella Parker: From Reddick To Cross Creek. LC 99-31361. 1999. 19.95 (*0-8130-1706-8*) U Press Fla.

Parker, Idella & Keating, Mary. Idella: Marjorie Rawlings' "Perfect Maid" (Illus.). 156p. 1992. 24.95 (*0-8130-1143-4*); pap. 13.95 (*0-8130-1144-2*) U Press Fla.

***Parker, Imogen.** These Foolish Things. 1999. 26.00 (*0-7278-5451-8*, Pub. by Severn Hse) Chivers N Amer.

***Parker, J.** Inside the Foreign Legion: A Sensational Story of the World's Toughest Army. 1999. 28.95 (*0-7499-1856-X*) Piatkus Bks.

Parker, J. Anthony. Image Reconstruction in Radiology. 536p. 1990. boxed set 198.95 (*0-8493-0150-5*, RC78) CRC Pr.

Parker, J. Anthony, jt. auth. see Holman, B. Leonard.

Parker, J. B., jt. auth. see Dunigan, Mike.

Parker, J. C., et al, eds. Nanophase & Nanocomposite Materials II. LC 97-6975. (Materials Research Society Symposium Proceedings Ser.: No. 457). 558p. 1997. text 72.00 (*1-55899-361-4*) Materials Res.

Parker, J. Carlyle. City, County, Town & Township Index to the 1850 Federal Census Schedules. (Gale Genealogy & Local History Ser.: Vol. 6). 215p. 1990. reprint ed. fiche 9.95 (*0-934153-06-X*, OCLC 27863673) Marietta Pub.

— City, County, Town & Township Index to the 1850 Federal Census Schedules. LC 96-129394. (Gale Genealogy & Local History Ser.). 215p. 1994. reprint ed. 29.95 (*0-934153-13-2*, OCLC 30992699) Marietta Pub.

— Going to Salt Lake City to Do Family History Research. 3rd expanded rev. ed. LC 95-25948. (Illus.). 262p. (Orig.). 1996. pap. 15.95 (*0-934153-14-0*, OCLC 33361524) Marietta Pub.

— Pennsylvania & Middle Atlantic States Genealogical Manuscripts: A User's Guide to the Manuscript Collections of the Genealogical Society of Pennsylvania as Indexed in Its Manuscript Materials Index. LC 86-2504. 45p. 1986. pap. 14.95 (*0-934153-01-9*, OCLC 13214741) Marietta Pub.

Parker, J. Carlyle, compiled by. An Index to the Biographies in 19th Century California County Histories, Vol. 7. (Gale Genealogy & Local History Ser.). 279p. 1994. reprint ed. fiche 14.95 (*0-934153-12-4*, OCLC 37778663) Marietta Pub.

— Rhode Island Biographical & Genealogical Sketch Index. LC 90-25871. 272p. 1991. 29.95 (*0-934153-08-6*, OCLC 22859101) Marietta Pub.

Parker, J. Carlyle & Parker, Janet G. Nevada Biographical & Genealogical Sketch Index. LC 86-12556. 96p. 1986. 23.95 (*0-934153-02-7*, OCLC 13642809) Marietta Pub.

Parker, J. D., ed. The Sheet-Forming Process. LC 72-75337. 104p. 1972. pap. 33.00 (*0-685-45540-8*, 0102BS09) TAPPI.

Parker, J. D., et al. An Introduction to Fluid Mechanics & Heat Transfer. (Engineering Ser.). (C). 1969. text. write for info. (*0-201-05710-7*) Addison-Wesley.

Parker, J. Harold, ed. Environmental Handbook for Fertilizer & Agrichemical Dealers. 300p. (Orig.). (C). 1994. pap. text 75.00 (*0-7881-1223-6*) DIANE Pub.

Parker, J. Harold, ed. see Nelson, Lewis B.

***Parker, J. I.** Concise Theology: A Guide to Historic Christian Beliefs - Chinese Edition. Chang, Paul, tr. (CHI.). 226p. 1999. 12.00 (*1-56582-135-1*) Christ Renew Min.

Parker, J. M., jt. ed. see Cable, M.

Parker, J. R. Practical Computer Vision Using C. LC 93-549. 1993. 32.00 (*0-471-59411-3*); pap. 74.99 incl. disk (*0-471-59262-5*) Wiley.

Parker, J. R., ed. Petroleum Geology of Northwest Europe: Proceedings of the 4th Conference. (Illus.). 1600p. (C). 1993. 250.00 (*0-903317-85-0*, 294, Pub. by Geol Soc Pub Hse) AAPG.

Parker, J. S. Asking the Right Questions: Case Studies in Library Development Consultancy. 248p. 1988. text 130.00 (*0-7201-1898-0*) Continuum.

Parker, J. S., ed. Information Consultants in Action. 272p. 1986. text 120.00 (*0-7201-1753-4*) Continuum.

Parker, Jack. You Want It When?! 128p. 39.00 (*0-614-25581-3*, 00GM44678) Print Indus Am.

Parker, Jack H. Gil Vicente. LC 67-25183. (Twayne's World Authors Ser.). 1967. lib. bdg. 20.95 (*0-8057-2956-9*) Irvington.

***Parker, James.** Turned On: A Biography of Henry Rollins. (Illus.). 2000. pap. 17.95 (*0-8154-1050-6*) Cooper Sq.

Parker, James & Peck, Amelia. Period Rooms in the Metropolitan Museum of Art. (Illus.). 256p. 1996. 60.00 (*0-8109-3744-1*, Pub. by Abrams) Time Warner.

Parker, James, jt. auth. see Endler, Norman.

Parker, James, ed. see Miller, Byron E.

Parker, James D. A., jt. auth. see Bar-On, Reuven.

Parker, James E., Jr. Codename Mule: Fighting the Secret War in Laos for the C.I.A. LC 94-48538. (Naval Institute Special Warfare Ser.). (Illus.). 232p. 1995. 32.95 (*1-55750-668-X*) Naval Inst Pr.

— Covert OPS: The CIA's Secret War in Laos. 1997. mass mkt. 5.99 (*0-312-96340-8*) St Martin.

— Last Man Out. 240p. 1997. pap. text 14.95 (*1-887269-33-9*) J Culler & Sons.

***Parker, James E., Jr.** Last Man Out: A Personal Account of the Vietnam War. 256p. 2000. mass mkt. 6.99 (*0-8041-1941-4*) Ivy Books.

Parker, James E., Jr. Last Man Out: A Personal Account of the Vietnam War. (Illus.). 240p. 1997. 23.95 (*1-887269-22-3*) J Culler & Sons.

Parker, James G. Lord Curzon, 1859-1925: A Bibliography, 5. LC 91-9473. (Bibliographies of British Statesmen Ser.: No. 5). 136p. 1991. lib. bdg. 59.95 (*0-313-28122-X*, PLZ, Greenwood Pr) Greenwood.

Parker, James H. Health Care & Freedom: An American Dilemma. 88p. (Orig.). (C). 1993. pap. text 16.50 (*0-8191-9303-8*); lib. bdg. 39.00 (*0-8191-9302-X*) U Pr of Amer.

— Logics: A Sociobiological Approach to Social & Other Logics, No. 2. LC 92-23596. 104p. (Orig.). (C). 1993. pap. text 17.50 (*0-8191-8882-4*); lib. bdg. 38.50 (*0-8191-8881-6*) U Pr of Amer.

— The New England Book of the Dead. LC 95-4058. (Illus.). 110p. (C). 1995. pap. text 28.50 (*0-8191-9903-6*); lib. bdg. 43.00 (*0-8191-9902-8*) U Pr of Amer.

— Social History & the Dynamics of Belief. LC 94-9254. (Illus.). 130p. (Orig.). (C). 1994. pap. text 24.50 (*0-8191-9518-9*) U Pr of Amer.

Parker, James R. Algorithms for Image Processing & Computer Vision. LC 96-15598. 432p. 1996. pap., pap. text 59.99 incl. cd-rom (*0-471-14056-2*) Wiley.

— Practical Computer Vision Using C. 476p. 1993. pap. 37.95 (*0-471-59259-5*) Wiley.

Parker, James W. & Dublin, Wayne. First Aid to Dating. 1989. write for info. (*0-9625950-0-4*) Entrprse NY.

Parker, Jan L. & Guest, Diana. The Clinician's Guide to 12-Step Programs: How, When & Why to Refer a Client. LC 99-10064. 168p. 1999. 49.95 (*0-86569-278-5*, T278, Auburn Hse) Greenwood.

Parker, Jane. Fantastic Book of Horses. LC 96-48289. (Fantastic Book of...Ser.). (Illus.). 46p. (J). (gr. 2-6). 1997. lib. bdg. 22.40 (*0-7613-0566-1*, Copper Beech Bks) Millbrook Pr.

— Fantastic Book of Horses. LC 96-48289. (Fantastic Book of...Ser.). (Illus.). 32p. (J). (gr. 4-6). 1997. 10.95 (*0-7613-0580-7*, Copper Beech Bks) Millbrook Pr.

***Parker, Jane.** Oceans. LC 99-35801. 1999. 21.90 (*0-7613-3259-6*) Millbrook Pr.

Parker, Jane. Pyramids & Temples. LC 96-4769. (Superstructures Ser.). (Illus.). 48p. (J). (gr. 4-8). 1997. lib. bdg. 24.26 (*0-8172-4330-5*) Raintree Steck-V.

— Rainforests. LC 99-31618. 1999. 21.90 (*0-7613-3258-8*) Millbrook Pr.

Parker, Jane & Parker, Steve. Rivers. LC 97-30406. (Take 5 Geography Ser.). 32p. (J). 1998. 19.00 (*0-531-14458-5*) Watts.

— Seas & Oceans. LC 97-29104. (Take 5 Geography Ser.). 32p. (J). 1998. 19.00 (*0-531-14459-3*) Watts.

Parker, Jane, jt. auth. see Parker, Steve.

Parker, Jane, jt. text see Parker, Steve.

***Parker, Janet & Gribble, Mary.** Poetically Yours. LC 99-61337. 76p. 1999. pap. 6.00 (*1-886467-49-8*) WJM Press.

Parker, Janet & Ostrum, Gus, eds. Contemporary Nephrology Nursing. (Illus.). 800p. 1998. 95.00 (*0-9653379-0-1*) Am Nephrology.

Parker, Janet, jt. auth. see Gribble, Mary.

Parker, Janet, jt. auth. see Nicholson, Peter.

Parker, Janet G., jt. auth. see Parker, J. Carlyle.

Parker, Janet R. Suncatchers. LC 97-60554. (Illus.). 52p. (Orig.). 1997. pap. 5.00 (*1-886467-17-X*) WJM Press.

***Parker, Janice.** California. (American States Ser.). (Illus.). 32p. (J). (gr. 3-7). 2000. write for info. (*1-930954-45-X*) Weigl Pubs.

P

Parker, Janice. Cockroaches, Cocoons, & Honeycombs: The Science of Insects. LC 98-50029. (Science at Work Ser.). 48p. 1999. lib. bdg. 25.69 (*0-7398-0135-X*) Raintree Steck-V.

***Parker, Janice.** Engines, Elevators & X-Rays. LC 99-41594. (Science at Work Ser.). (J). (gr. 4-7). 2000. lib. bdg. 25.69 (*0-7398-0142-2*) Raintree Steck-V.

Parker, Janice. Grizzly Bears. LC 96-2834. (Untamed World Ser.). (Illus.). 64p. (J). (gr. 5-9). 1997. lib. bdg. 27.12 (*0-8172-4563-4*) Raintree Steck-V.

***Parker, Janice.** Messengers, Morse Code & Modems: The Science of Communication. LC 99-40872. (Science at Work Ser.). (gr. 4-7). 2000. lib. bdg. 25.69 (*0-7398-0138-4*) Raintree Steck-V.

Parker, Janice. Sunburns, Twisters, & Thunderclaps. LC 98-50030. (Science at Work Ser.). 48p. 1999. lib. bdg. 25.69 (*0-7398-0131-7*) Raintree Steck-V.

***Parker, Janice.** Texas. (American States Ser.). (Illus.). 32p. (J). (gr. 3-7). 2000. write for info. (*1-930954-40-9*) Weigl Pubs.

***Parker, Janice, contrib. by.** Forgeries, Fingerprints, & Forensics: The Science of Crime. LC 98-55476. 48p. 1999. lib. bdg. 25.69 (*0-7398-0133-3*) Raintree Steck-V.

Parker, Janna S., jt. auth. see Stone, Joshua D.

Parker, Janna Shelley, jt. auth. see Stone, Joshua David.

Parker, Jay, jt. auth. see Wooden, Wayne S.

Parker, Jeffery G., jt. ed. see Gottman, John M.

Parker-Jenkins, Marie. Children of Islam. 180p. 1995. pap. 20.00 (*1-85856-034-9*, Trentham Bks) Stylus Pub VA.

Parker, Jennifer. An Artist's Resource Book. 197p. (Orig.). (C). 1993. pap. text 12.00 (*0-9644338-0-X*) Go Far Press.

Parker, Jennifer. Love from Grandma Gift Book. 96p. 1998. 12.99 (*1-58375-422-9*) Garborgs.

Parker, Jenny M. Rochester: A Story Historical. (Illus.). 412p. 1997. reprint ed. lib. bdg. 44.50 (*0-8328-6214-2*) Higginson Bk Co.

Parker, Jerald D., jt. auth. see McQuiston, Faye C.

Parker, Jerry. Eureka! The Story of the California Gold Rush. LC 97-37471. 1998. 22.98 (*1-56799-559-4*) M Friedman Pub Grp Inc.

Parker, Jim. AIDS: Ending an Epidemic. rev. ed. 2000. pap. 0.50 (*0-89230-166-X*) Do It Now.

— All about Downers: A Special Report for Young People. rev. ed. 1999. pap. 0.50 (*0-89230-202-X*) Do It Now.

— All about Sniffing: A Special Report for Young People. rev. ed. 1999. pap. 0.50 (*0-89230-218-6*) Do It Now.

— All about Speed: A Special Report for Young People. rev. ed. 1999. pap. 0.50 (*0-89230-127-9*) Do It Now.

— Booze: A Guide for Young People. rev. ed. 1999. pap. 0.50 (*0-89230-139-2*) Do It Now.

— Brown Ale: History, Brewing Techniques, Recipes. LC 98-30008. (Classic Beer Style Ser.). (Illus.). 144p. 1998. pap. 14.95 (*0-937381-60-8*) Brewers Pubns.

— Club Drugs: Destination X. rev. ed. 2000. pap. 0.50 (*0-89230-248-8*) Do It Now.

— Crystal, Crank, Speedy Stuff: A Guide to Stimulant Drugs. rev. ed. 2000. pap. 0.50 (*0-89230-120-1*) Do It Now.

— Darvon & Other Prescription Narcotics. rev. ed. 1999. pap. 0.50 (*0-89230-147-3*) Do It Now.

— Downers: New Facts about Depressant Drugs. rev. ed. 1999. pap. 0.50 (*0-89230-140-6*) Do It Now.

— Drug Crisis Response. 52p. 2000. 3.50 (*0-89230-234-8*) Do It Now.

— DrugWise: A Handbook for Young People. rev. ed. (YA). 1999. pap. 3.50 (*0-89230-229-1*) Do It Now.

— Everyday Detox: A Guide to Living Without Chemicals. rev. ed. 1999. pap. 0.50 (*0-89230-200-3*) Do It Now.

— Fast Facts: Alcohol. rev. ed. 2000. pap. 0.25 (*0-89230-253-4*) Do It Now.

— Fast Facts: Cocaine. rev. ed. 2000. pap. 0.25 (*0-89230-255-0*) Do It Now.

— Fast Facts: Crystal. rev. ed. 2000. pap. 0.25 (*0-89230-257-7*) Do It Now.

— Fast Facts: Downers. rev. ed. 2000. pap. 0.25 (*0-89230-258-5*) Do It Now.

— Fast Facts: Heroin. rev. ed. 2000. pap. 0.25 (*0-89230-256-9*) Do It Now.

— Fast Facts: Inhalants. rev. ed. 2000. pap. 0.25 (*0-89230-259-3*) Do It Now.

— Fast Facts: LSD. rev. ed. 2000. pap. 0.25 (*0-89230-260-7*) Do It Now.

— Fast Facts: Marijuana. rev. ed. 2000. pap. 0.25 (*0-89230-252-6*) Do It Now.

— Fast Facts: Methcathinone. rev. ed. 2000. pap. 0.25 (*0-89230-263-1*) Do It Now.

— Fast Facts: Smokeless Tobacco. rev. ed. 2000. pap. 0.25 (*0-89230-264-X*) Do It Now.

— Fast Facts: Smoking. rev. ed. 2000. pap. 0.25 (*0-89230-261-5*) Do It Now.

— Fast Facts: Steroids. rev. ed. 2000. pap. 0.25 (*0-89230-262-3*) Do It Now.

— Heroin: The Junk Equation. rev. ed. 2000. pap. 0.50 (*0-89230-164-3*) Do It Now.

— Marijuana: Medical Uses. 1999. pap. 0.50 (*0-89230-159-7*) Do It Now.

— Pot: New Facts, Old Fictions. rev. ed. 1999. pap. 0.50 (*0-89230-162-7*) Do It Now.

— Prozac: Pros & Cons. rev. ed. 1998. pap. 0.50 (*0-89230-245-3*) Do It Now.

— Street Gangs: Bringing Back the Home Boys. rev. ed. 2000. pap. 0.50 (*0-89230-249-6*) Do It Now.

— Total Recovery: Lifestyle Management in Recovery from Drugs & Alcohol. 1999. pap. 3.50 (*0-89230-231-3*) Do It Now.

— Tranx: Minor Tranquilizers, Major Problems. rev. ed. (Illus.). 2000. pap. 3.50 (*0-89230-180-5*) Do It Now.

— Valium, Librium & the Benzodiazepine Blues. rev. ed. 2000. pap. 0.50 (*0-89230-163-5*) Do It Now.

Parker, Jo A. The Author's Inheritance: Henry Fielding, Jane Austen, & the Establishment of the Novel. LC 98-12957. 255p. 1998. 36.00 (*0-87580-239-7*) N Ill U Pr.

***Parker, Joe, ed.** International Who's Who of Professional Management, 2 vols. 5th ed. (Illus.). 2000. lib. bdg. write for info. (*1-882952-21-9*) Gibraltar Pub.

Parker, Joe, jt. ed. see Gillard, Carrie.

Parker, John. At the Heart of Darkness: Witchcraft, Black Magic & Satanism Today. (Illus.). 344p. 1993. pap. 12.95 (*0-8065-1428-0*, Citadel Pr) Carol Pub Group.

— Bruce Willis: The Unauthorised Biography. (Illus.). 224p. 1997. text 22.95 (*1-85227-652-5*, Pub. by Virgin Bks) London Brdge.

— Bruce Willis: The Unauthorized Biography. 1998. mass mkt. 7.95 (*0-7535-0275-5*, Pub. by Virgin Bks) London Brdge.

— The Coming Russian Boom. 400p. 1996. 27.00 (*0-684-82743-3*) Free Pr.

— Cross Numbers: A Collection of 32 Mathematical Puzzles. (J). (gr. 5-7). pap. 8.50 (*0-906212-95-2*, Pub. by Tarquin Pubns) Parkwest Pubns.

— De Niro. (Illus.). 288p. 1998. 29.95 (*0-575-05876-5*, Pub. by V Gollancz); pap. 9.95 (*0-575-60026-8*, Pub. by V Gollancz) Trafalgar.

— Five for Hollywood: Their Friendship, Their Fame, Their Tragedies. 1991. 19.95 (*0-8184-0539-2*) Carol Pub Group.

— A Formal & Historical Sociology of Western Picture-Making with Special Reference to J. M. W. Turner: Power, Space & Light. LC 98-2585. (Illus.). 476p. 1998. text 109.95 (*0-7734-8483-3*) E Mellen.

***Parker, John.** The Gurkhas: The Inside Story of the World's Most Feared Soldiers. 2000. pap. 15.95 (*0-7472-6243-8*, Pub. by Headline Bk Pub) Trafalgar.

— The Gurkhas: The Inside Story of the World's Most Feared Soldiers. 2000. 40.00 (*0-7472-7577-7*, Pub. by Headline Bk Pub) Trafalgar.

Parker, John. His Promised Land: The Autobiography of John P. Parker, Former Slave & Conductor on the Underground Railroad. 96p. 1996. 20.00 (*0-393-03941-2*) Norton.

— Hymn Readings for Christian Worship. 1997. pap. text 19.95 (*0-7673-3012-9*, Genevox Mus) LifeWay Christian.

***Parker, John.** Inside the Foreign Legion. (Illus.). 320p. 2000. pap. 12.95 (*0-7499-1992-2*) Piatkus Bks.

Parker, John. Kremlin in Transition: From Brezhnev to Gorbachev, 1978-1989, Vol.1. 480p. (C). 1990. text 75.00 (*0-685-46016-9*) Routledge.

***Parker, John.** Making the Town: Ga State & Society in Early Colonial Accra. LC 00-25969. 325p. 2000. 25.00 (*0-325-00190-1*, E00190); write for info. (*0-325-00191-X*) Greenwood.

Parker, John. Polanski. (Illus.). 288p. 1995. 29.95 (*0-575-05615-0*, Pub. by V Gollancz) Trafalgar.

— Prince Philip. large type ed. (Non-Fiction Ser.). 528p. 1992. 27.99 (*0-7089-8642-0*) Ulverscroft.

— The Queen: The New Biography. large type ed. (Charnwood Library). (Illus.). 736p. 1993. 27.99 (*0-7089-8713-3*) Ulverscroft.

— Run down Fired up & Teed Off. 80p. 1993. 6.95 (*0-915297-11-6*) Cedarwinds.

— SBS - The Inside Story of the Special Boat Service. (Illus.). 320p. 1998. text 35.00 (*0-7472-1976-1*, Pub. by Headline Bk Pub) Trafalgar.

***Parker, John.** Structuration. LC 00-37513. (Concepts in the Social Sciences Ser.). 2000. pap. write for info. (*0-335-20394-9*) Taylor & Francis.

Parker, John. The Twelfth Man. (Illus.). 208p. 1992. 23.95 (*0-233-98769-X*, Pub. by Andre Deutsch) Trafalgar.

— Windows into China: The Jesuits & Their Books, 1580-1730. 1978. 3.00 (*0-89073-050-4*, 192) Boston Public Lib.

— The World for a Marketplace: Episodes in the History of European Expansion. LC 78-71068. (Illus.). 1978. 15.00 (*0-9601798-0-1*) Assocs James Bell.

Parker, John & Urness, Carol, eds. The American Revolution: A Heritage of Change. LC 75-24503. 1975. 15.00 (*0-685-00552-6*) Assocs James Bell.

— The American Revolution: A Heritage of Change. 1975. 10.00 (*0-87018-078-9*) Ross.

Parker, John, ed. see Carver, Jonathan.

Parker, John, jt. ed. see De Vorsey, Louis, Jr.

Parker, John, ed. & tr. see Raleigh, Walter.

Parker, John, tr. see Torres, Antonio.

Parker, John A., jt. ed. see D'Alelio, Gaetano F.

Parker, John C., jt. auth. see Agre, Peter.

Parker, John E. The Economics of Innovation: The National & Multinational Enterprise in Technological Change. 2nd ed. LC 77-14535. 406p. reprint ed. pap. 125.90 (*0-7837-1606-0*, 204189800024) Bks Demand.

Parker, John F. The Independent Writer. 782p. (C). 1986. pap. text 22.75 (*0-15-541340-6*); pap. text, teacher ed. 3.50 (*0-15-541341-4*) Harcourt Coll Pubs.

— The Independent Writer. (C). 1995. pap. text 39.00 (*0-15-503449-9*) Harcourt Coll Pubs.

— Twenty-Minute Workshops. rev. ed. (Illus.). (Orig.). 1992. pap. 150.00 incl. disk (*0-9694762-1-3*); disk. write for info. (*0-9694762-2-1*) JFP Prodns.

— Workshops for Active Learning. (Illus.). 194p. (Orig.). 1990. pap., student ed. 19.95 (*0-9694762-0-5*) JFP Prodns.

Parker, John H. A Concise Glossary of Architectural Terms. (Illus.). 335p. (C). 1998. reprint ed. pap. text 15.00 (*0-7881-5188-6*) DIANE Pub.

— We Remember Cuba. Gianelloni, Giles S., ed. (Illus.). 233p. (Orig.). 1993. pap. 21.95 (*0-9635705-0-1*) Gldn Quill FL.

Parker, John L. Heart Monitor Training for the Complete Idiot. 2nd ed. 1998. pap. 14.95 (*0-915297-25-6*) Cedarwinds.

— Living off the Country: For Fun & Profit. Lever, B., ed. (Fun & Profit Ser.). (Illus.). 1978. 7.95 (*0-916302-23-7*); pap. 4.95 (*0-916302-24-5*) Bookworm Pub.

Parker, John L., Jr. Once a Runner. rev. ed. LC 78-59993. 194p. (Orig.). 1990. pap. 12.95 (*0-915297-01-9*, OAR) Cedarwinds.

— Runners & Other Dreamers. 211p. (Orig.). 1988. pap. 12.95 (*0-915297-24-8*) Cedarwinds.

Parker, John L. & Carter, Robert G. History of the 22nd Massachusetts Infantry, the Second Co. Sharpshooters, & the 3rd Light Battery: Henry Wilson's Regiment. (Army of the Potomac Ser.). (Illus.). 693p. (C). 1997. reprint ed. 45.00 (*0-935523-65-0*) Butternut & Blue.

Parker, John L., jt. ed. see Gunn, Robert.

Parker, John L., Jr., ed. see Shapiro, James E., et al.

Parker, John M., tr. see Dourado, Autran.

Parker, John M., tr. & intro. see Garrett, Almeida.

Parker, John R. Burp: A Journal about Food & How to Enjoy It. (Illus.). 190p. (Orig.). 1986. pap. 8.95 (*0-912095-01-6*) Johmax Bks Inc.

— How to Sink a Sub: A Substitute Teacher's Rather Strange Appraisal of the American Educational System. (Illus.). 175p. (Orig.). 1990. pap. 8.95 (*0-912095-02-4*) Johmax Bks Inc.

— No Butts about It: How to Want to Stop Smoking. 3rd ed. (Illus.). 88p. (Orig.). 1989. pap. 6.95 (*0-912095-00-8*) Johmax Bks Inc.

Parker, John R., ed. The Euterpeiad or Musical Intelligencer, 3 vols. LC 65-23389. (Music Ser.). 1977. reprint ed. lib. bdg. 110.00 (*0-306-70920-1*) Da Capo.

Parker, John W. Kremlin in Transition: From Brezhnev to Chernenko, 1978-1985, Vol. 1. 480p. (C). 1990. 100.00 (*0-04-445889-4*) Routledge.

Parker, John W., ed. see International Leucocyte Culture Conference, 15th:.

Parker, Jonathan. Manhattan Ocean Club Seafood Cookbook. LC 99-23463. 1999. 30.00 (*1-56799-798-8*, Friedman-Fairfax) M Friedman Pub Grp Inc.

Parker, Jonathan & Penhale, Bridget. Forgotten People: Positive Approaches to Dementia Care. LC 97-49445. 150p. 1998. text 63.95 (*1-85742-414-X*, Pub. by Ashgate Pub) Ashgate Pub Co.

Parker, Jonathan, jt. auth. see Randall, Peter.

Parker, Joni M. & Maurer, Ruth A. An Economic Feasibility Study for a Geothermal-Coal Hybrid Power Plant in Chaffee County, Colorado. Raese, Jon W. & Goldberg, J. H., eds. LC 83-1922. (Colorado School of Mines Quarterly Ser.: Vol. 78, No. 1). (Illus.). 34p. 1983. pap. 12.00 (*0-686-45174-0*) Colo Sch Mines.

Parker, Jorge. Estudios Sobre Los Hechos. (SPA.). 304p. 1995. pap. 9.99 (*0-8254-1557-8*, Edit Portavoz) Kregel.

Parker, Joseph. The Inner Life of Christ. rev. ed. LC 98-70070. 1998. pap. 14.99 (*0-89957-242-1*) AMG Pubs.

— The Paraclete: An Essay on the Personality & Ministry of the Holy Ghost. 402p. 1997. pap. 32.00 (*1-57910-083-X*) Wipf & Stock.

— Prayers & Sermons from the City Pulpit. (Bible Sermon Ser.: Pulpit Legends Colletions). 1996. 19.99 (*0-89957-208-1*) AMG Pubs.

— Preaching Through the Bible, 14. 11300p. 1978. reprint ed. 295.00 (*0-8010-7032-5*) Baker Bks.

— Servant of All, Vol. 3. rev. ed. LC 98-70692. 1998. pap. 14.99 (*0-89957-241-3*) AMG Pubs.

Parker, Joseph B. Morrison Era: Reform Politics in New Orleans. LC 74-7142. 172p. 1974. pap. 25.00 (*1-56554-550-8*) Pelican.

Parker, Joseph D. Zen Buddhist Landscape Arts of Early Muromachi Japan (1336-1573) LC 97-52581. (SUNY Series in Buddhist Studies). (Illus.). 302p. (C). 1999. pap. text 24.95 (*0-7914-3910-0*) State U NY Pr.

— Zen Buddhist Landscape Arts of Early Muromachi Japan (1336-1573) LC 97-52581. (Series in Buddhist Studies). (Illus.). 320p. (C). 1999. text 74.50 (*0-7914-3909-7*) State U NY Pr.

Parker, Joy. Scarlet Christmas: Abortion: The Grandparent Connection. 32p. (Orig.). 1991. pap. 2.95 (*0-9628088-1-4*) Laser Pr Pubs.

Parker, Joy, jt. auth. see Avila, Elena.

Parker, Judith R. The House Sitter. 320p. 1994. mass mkt. 4.50 (*0-8217-4594-8*, Zebra Kensgtn) Kensgtn Pub Corp.

Parker, Julia. The Astrologer's Handbook. (Illus.). 256p. (Orig.). 1995. pap. 12.00 (*0-916360-59-8*) CRCS Pubns CA.

— Sagittarius. (Love Signs Library). 64p. 1996. 8.95 (*0-7894-1097-4*) DK Pub Inc.

***Parker, Julia.** Sun & Moon Signs. LC 99-49270. (Illus.). 2000. write for info. (*0-7894-5122-0*, D K Ink) DK Pub Inc.

Parker, Julia. Sun & Moon Signs: An Indispensable Illustrated Guide to Astrological Characteristics. LC 97-13320. (Illus.). 619p. 2000. 29.95 (*0-7894-0367-6*, D K Ink) DK Pub Inc.

***Parker, Julia.** Sun & Moon Signs Aquarius Gift Set. 64p. 1999. 12.95 (*0-7894-5448-3*, D K Ink) DK Pub Inc.

— Sun & Moon Signs Aries Gift Set. 64p. 1999. 12.95 (*0-7894-5438-6*, D K Ink) DK Pub Inc.

— Sun & Moon Signs Cancer Gift Set. 64p. 1999. 12.95 (*0-7894-5441-6*, D K Ink) DK Pub Inc.

— Sun & Moon Signs Capricorn Gift Set. 64p. 1999. 12.95 (*0-7894-5447-5*, D K Ink) DK Pub Inc.

— Sun & Moon Signs Gemini Gift Set. 64p. 1999. 12.95 (*0-7894-5440-8*, D K Ink) DK Pub Inc.

— Sun & Moon Signs Leo Gift Set. 64p. 1999. 12.95 (*0-7894-5442-4*, D K Ink) DK Pub Inc.

— Sun & Moon Signs Libra Gift Set. 64p. 1999. 12.95 (*0-7894-5444-0*, D K Ink) DK Pub Inc.

— Sun & Moon Signs Pisces Gift Set. 64p. 1999. 12.95 (*0-7894-5449-1*, D K Ink) DK Pub Inc.

— Sun & Moon Signs Sagittarius Gift Set. 64p. 1999. 12.95 (*0-7894-5446-7*, D K Ink) DK Pub Inc.

— Sun & Moon Signs Scorpio Gift Set. 64p. 1999. 12.95 (*0-7894-5445-9*, D K Ink) DK Pub Inc.

— Sun & Moon Signs Taurus Gift Set. 64p. 1999. 12.95 (*0-7894-5439-4*, D K Ink) DK Pub Inc.

— Sun & Moon Signs Virgo Gift Set. 64p. 1999. 12.95 (*0-7894-5443-2*, D K Ink) DK Pub Inc.

Parker, Julia. The Zodiac Family. 1989. 18.95 (*0-87951-374-8*, Pub. by Overlook Pr) Penguin Putnam.

— The Zodiac Family: How Astrology Can Help You Understand & Raise Your Child. (Illus.). 1992. pap. 10.95 (*0-87951-378-0*, Pub. by Overlook Pr) Penguin Putnam.

Parker, Julia & Parker, Derek. Aquarius. (Love Signs Library). 64p. 1996. 8.95 (*0-7894-1087-7*) DK Pub Inc.

— Aries. (Love Signs Library). 64p. 1996. 8.95 (*0-7894-1089-3*) DK Pub Inc.

— Cancer. (Love Signs Library). 64p. 1996. 8.95 (*0-7894-1092-3*) DK Pub Inc.

— Capricorn. (Love Signs Library). 64p. 1996. 8.95 (*0-7894-1086-9*) DK Pub Inc.

— Gemini. (Little Love Signs Library). 64p. 1996. 8.95 (*0-7894-1091-5*) DK Pub Inc.

— Leo. (Love Signs Library). 64p. 1996. 8.95 (*0-7894-1093-1*) DK Pub Inc.

— Libra. (Love Signs Library). 64p. 1996. 8.95 (*0-7894-1095-8*) DK Pub Inc.

***Parker, Julia & Parker, Derek.** Millennium Parkers' Prediction Pack. LC 99-30470. 80p. 1999. pap. 29.95 (*0-7894-4611-1*) DK Pub Inc.

Parker, Julia & Parker, Derek. Parker's Astrology Pack. (Illus.). 96p. 1997. 29.95 incl. audio compact disk (*0-7894-1441-4*) DK Pub Inc.

— Parkers' Complete Book of Dreams. LC 94-27918. (Illus.). 208p. 1995. 24.95 (*1-56458-855-6*) DK Pub Inc.

— Pisces. (Love Signs Library). 64p. 1996. 8.95 (*0-7894-1088-5*) DK Pub Inc.

— Scorpio. (Love Signs Library). 64p. 1996. 8.95 (*0-7894-1096-6*) DK Pub Inc.

— The Secret World of Your Dreams. 240p. 1991. reprint ed. pap. 11.00 (*0-399-51700-6*, Perigee Bks) Berkley Pub.

— Taurus. (Love Signs Library). 64p. 1996. 8.95 (*0-7894-1090-7*) DK Pub Inc.

— Virgo. (Love Signs Library). 64p. 1996. 8.95 (*0-7894-1094-X*) DK Pub Inc.

Parker, Julia, jt. auth. see Parker, Derek.

Parker, Julie. All about Silk: A Fabric Dictionary & Swatchbook. LC 93-117999. (Fabric Reference Ser.: Vol. 1). 92p. 1992. pap. 35.00 (*0-9637612-0-X*) Rain City.

— All about Wool: A Fabric Dictionary & Swatchbook. LC 96-92209. (Fabric Reference Ser.: Vol. 3). (Illus.). 144p. (Orig.). 1996. pap. 45.00 (*0-9637612-2-6*) Rain City.

Parker, Julie. All about Cotton: A Fabric Dictionary & Swatchbook. rev. ed. (Fabric Reference Ser.). 120p. 1998. pap. 40.00 (*0-9637612-3-4*) Rain City.

Parker, Julie F. Everything You Need to Know about Decision-Making, 8 vols. LC 95-14904. (Need to Know Library). (Illus.). 64p. (YA). (gr. 7-12). 1996. lib. bdg. 17.95 (*0-8239-2055-0*) Rosen Group.

— Everything You Need to Know about Decision-Making. rev. ed. (Need to Know Library). (Illus.). 64p. (YA). (gr. 7 up). 1998. lib. bdg. 17.95 (*0-8239-2746-6*) Rosen Group.

— Everything You Need to Know about Living in a Shelter. LC 94-21280. (Need to Know Library). (Illus.). 64p. (YA). (gr. 7-12). 1995. lib. bdg. 17.95 (*0-8239-1874-2*) Rosen Group.

— High Performance Through Leadership, 10 vols. LC 96-2609. (Learning-a-Living Library). (Illus.). 64p. (YA). (gr. 7-12). 1996. lib. bdg. 16.95 (*0-8239-2205-7*) Rosen Group.

Parker, Julius. Grab Life & Hang On: Insights into the Art of Everyday Living. 249p. 1990. 21.95 (*0-9627915-0-4*) Harvest Hill Pr.

Parker, K. Langloh, compiled by. Wise Women of the Dreamtime: Aboriginal Tales of the Ancestral Powers. LC 93-377. (Illus.). 160p. (Orig.). 1993. pap. 12.95 (*0-89281-477-2*) Inner Tradit.

Parker, K. R., ed. Applied Electrostatic Precipitation. (Illus.). 544p. 1997. write for info. (*0-7514-0266-4*) Kluwer Academic.

Parker, Karen, jt. auth. see Fishlow, Albert.

Parker, Kathleen M. Athletic Scholarships: A Complete Guide. 2nd ed. (Illus.). 584p. 1996. pap. 22.00 (*1-884669-14-X*) Conway Greene.

Parker, Kathleen M., jt. intro. see Green, John.

***Parker, Kathleene.** The Colorado Plateau: The Land & the Indians. Compton, K. C., ed. Orig. Title: The Only True People. (Illus.). 88p. 1999. pap. 14.95 (*0-9625717-1-7*) Thunder Mesa.

Parker, Kathryn E. Talking with Your Child about Feelings. LC 90-33014. (Growing Together Ser.). (Orig.). 1990. pap. 2.25 (*0-8298-0861-2*) Pilgrim OH.

Parker, Kathryn E., ed. see Ebbers, Bert C.

Parker, Kathy, ed. Breaking into the Trade Game: A Small Business Guide to Exporting. (Illus.). 322p. 1997. reprint ed. pap. text 40.00 (*0-7881-4474-X*) DIANE Pub.

Parker, Kathy G. Cumulative Trauma Disorders: Current Issues & Ergonomic. 160p. 1992. lib. bdg. 89.95 (*0-87371-322-2*, L322) Lewis Pubs.

Parker, KayLee. Mom, Help! It's the Holidays: Holiday Planning Book. rev. ed. (Illus.). 68p. 1995. pap. 4.95 (*1-883924-12-X*, 430) Your Moms Organizers.

— Mom, How Do You Get a Meal on the Table? rev. ed. (Illus.). 106p. 1995. pap. 8.95 (*1-883924-04-9*, 200) Your Moms Organizers.

P

An Asterisk (*) at the beginning of an entry indicates that the title is appearing for the first time.

— Mom, How Do You Get Organized? rev. ed. (Illus.). 110p. 1995. pap. 8.95 (1-883924-02-2, 400) Your Moms Organizers.
— Mom, How Do You Plan a Camping Trip? rev. ed. (Illus.). 114p. 1995. pap. 8.95 (1-883924-11-1, 330) Your Moms Organizers.
— Mom's Packing Lists. rev. ed. (Illus.). 52p. 1995. pap. 4.95 (1-883924-10-3, 310) Your Moms Organizers.
— Permanent Menu Planning List: Mom's Meal Planners. rev. ed. (Illus.). 52p. 1995. pap. 3.95 (1-883924-06-5, 250) Your Moms Organizers.
— Weekly Menu Planning List: Mom's Meal Planners. rev. ed. 52p. 1995. pap. 3.95 (1-883924-05-7, 240) Your Moms Organizers.
Parker, Kelly A. The Continuity of Peirce's Thought. LC 97-21191. (Library of American Philosophy). 320p. (C). 1998. 39.95 (0-8265-1296-8) Vanderbilt U Pr.
*Parker, Ken. Buying & Running a Small Hotel: The Complete Guide to Setting up & Managing Your Own Hotel, Guest House of B & B. 3rd ed. 144p. 2000. pap. 14.95 (1-85703-617-4, Pub. by How To Bks) Midpt Trade.
Parker, Ken. No Longer Lonely. 21p. 1982. 0.50 (0-89814-056-0) Grace Publns.
— Purposeful Prayer. 20p. 1980. 0.50 (0-89814-051-X) Grace Publns.
— What Happens When a Christian Sins? 18p. 1980. 0.50 (0-89814-050-1) Grace Publns.
Parker, Ken, et al, eds. Test Conference, 25th Anniversary Compendium International (ITC 1970-1994) LC 94-77462. 816p. 1994. 50.00 (0-8186-6617-X, BP06617) IEEE Comp Soc.
Parker, Kenneth. Antony & Cleopatra. Armstrong, Isobel & Loughrey, Bryan, eds. (Writers & Their Work Ser.). 1997. pap. 15.00 (0-7463-0825-6, Pub. by Northcote House) U Pr of Miss.
— Early Modern Tales of Orient: Critical Anthology. LC 98-54316. 1999. text. write for info. (0-415-14756-5) Routledge.
— Early Modern Tales of Orient: Critical Anthology. LC 98-54316. (Illus.). 304p. 1999. pap. 27.99 (0-415-14757-3) Routledge.
Parker, Kenneth, ed. The South African Novel in English: Essays in Criticism & Society. LC 78-18343. 202p. 1979. 39.50 (0-8419-0425-1, Africana) Holmes & Meier.
Parker, Kenneth L. & Carlson, Eric J. Practical Divinity: The Works & Life of Reverend Richard Greenham. LC 97-38530. (St. Andrews Studies in Reformation History). 250p. 1998. 105.95 (1-84014-200-6, BX9339.G74P37, Pub. by Ashgate Pub) Ashgate Pub Co.
Parker, Kenneth P. The Boundary-Scan Handbook. 3rd ed. LC 92-27976. 288p. (C). 1992. reprint ed. text 139.50 (0-7923-9270-1) Kluwer Academic.
— The Boundary-Scan Handbook: Analog & Digital. 2nd ed. LC 98-37891. 1998. 125.00 (0-7923-8277-3) Kluwer Academic.
Parker, Kim I. Wisdom & Law in the Reign of Solomon. LC 92-45201. (Biblical Press Ser.: Vol. 6). 136p. 1993. text 69.95 (0-7734-2356-7) E Mellen.
Parker, Kim I., ed. Liberal Democracy & the Bible. LC 92-23478. 196p. 1992. text 79.95 (0-7734-9154-6) E Mellen.
Parker, L. Craig, Jr. Parole & the Community-Based Treatment of Offenders in Japan & the United States. LC 86-50431. (Illus.). 200p. (Orig.). 1986. pap. text 8.95 (0-936285-03-6) U New Haven Pr.
Parker, L. F. History of Poweshiek County: Record of Settlement, Organization, Progress & Achievement, 2 vols. (Illus.). 1151p. 1997. reprint ed. lib. bdg. 117.50 (0-8328-6701-2) Higginson Bk Co.
Parker, L. N. History & Genealogy of the Ancestors & Descendants of Captain Israel Jones Who Removed from Enfield to Barkhamstead, Conn. in 1759. (Illus.). 303p. reprint ed. pap. 45.50 (0-8328-0722-2); reprint ed. lib. bdg. 53.50 (0-8328-0721-4) Higginson Bk Co.
Parker, L. P. The Songs of Aristophones. 604p. (C). 1997. text 150.00 (0-19-814944-1) OUP.
Parker, L. Stevenson, jt. auth. see Rosenbaum, Robert D.
Parker, Lara. Dark Shadows: Angelique's Descent. 528p. 1998. pap. 6.99 (0-06-105751-7, HarperFlamingo) HarpC.
Parker, Larry. Principles of Electronic Devices & Circuits - Ross & LaLond: Flashcards. 128p. 1994. 19.95 (0-8273-6420-2) Delmar.
Parker, Larry M., ed. Research in Accounting Regulation: Supplement 1, Tenth Anniversary Special International Edition. 417p. 1997. 78.50 (0-7623-0338-7) Jai Pr.
Parker, Laura. Found: One Marriage. (Intimate Moments Ser.). 1996. per. 3.99 (0-373-07731-9, 1-07731-2) Silhouette.
— The Gamble. 416p. 1998. pap. 5.99 (0-8217-5863-2, Zebra Kensgtn) Kensgtn Pub Corp.
— Indiscreet. LC 95-15774. (Intrigue Ser.). 249p. 1995. per. 3.50 (0-373-22327-7, 1-22327-0) Harlequin Bks.
— Stranger in Town. (Intimate Moments Ser.). 1994. per. 3.50 (0-373-07562-6, 5-07562-7) Silhouette.
— Tempest. 416p. 1997. mass mkt. 4.99 (0-8217-5550-1, Zebra Kensgtn) Kensgtn Pub Corp.
— Tiger in the Rain: Rogue's Gallery. 1995. per. 3.75 (0-373-07663-0) Harlequin Bks.
— Together Again. 1995. per. 3.75 (0-373-07682-7, 1-07682-7) Silhouette.
Parker, Laura & Major, Ann. Too Hot to Handle. (Silhouette Romance Ser.). 1995. per. 4.99 (0-373-48287-6, 1-48287-6) Harlequin Bks.
Parker, Laurence, et al, eds. Race Is... Race Isn't: Critical Race Theory & Qualitative Studies in Education. LC 99-11946. 320p. 1999. 60.00 (0-8133-9069-9, Pub. by Westview) HarpC.
Parker, Laurie. All over Alabama. LC 97-25384. (Illus.). 32p. 1997. 15.95 (0-937552-89-5, 001) Quail Ridge.
— Everywhere in Mississippi. LC 96-8538. 32p. 1996. 15.95 (0-937552-71-2) Quail Ridge.
— Mississippi Alphabet. LC 98-23274. 1998. 5.95 (0-937552-92-5) Quail Ridge.
*Parker, Laurie. Texas Alphabet. LC 00-35291. (Illus.). 32p. (ps-3). 2000. write for info. (1-893062-17-1) Quail Ridge.
Parker, Lea. Environmental Communication: Messages, Media & Methods. 248p. 1996. per. 38.95 (0-7872-3251-3, 41325101) Kendall-Hunt.
Parker, Lea J. Environmental Communication: Messages, Media & Methods. 164p. 1995. ring bd. 24.95 (0-7872-0613-X) Kendall-Hunt.
Parker, Lena. Y2K Crisis: The Possibilities. 117p. 1999. pap. 13.95 (0-9669874-0-3, 001) Maple Leaf.
Parker, Leonard & Christensen, Steven M. Math Tensor: A System for Doing Tensor Analysis by Computer. 1994. write for info. (0-318-72530-4) Addison-Wesley.
— MathTensor: A System for Doing Tensor Analysis by Computer. 400p. (C). 1999. 54.95 (0-201-56990-6) Addison-Wesley.
Parker, Lesley H., jt. auth. see Sate.
Parker, Lewis C. What Squashes Your Spirit? 1992. pap. 7.95 (1-55673-493-X, 7943) CSS OH.
Parker, Lewis K. Australia, Set I. LC 94-4249. (Dropping in On Ser.). 32p. (J). (gr. 2-5). 1994. lib. bdg. 21.27 (1-55916-007-1) Rourke Bk Co.
— Canada, LC 93-42778. (Dropping in On Ser.). 32p. (J). (gr. 2-5). 1994. lib. bdg. 21.27 (1-55916-002-0) Rourke Bk Co.
— Egypt, LC 93-47098. (Dropping in On Ser.). 32p. (J). (gr. 2-5). 1994. lib. bdg. 21.27 (1-55916-004-7) Rourke Bk Co.
— England, Set I. LC 94-5471. (Dropping in On Ser.). 32p. (J). (gr. 2-5). 1994. lib. bdg. 21.27 (1-55916-006-3) Rourke Bk Co.
— India, Set I. LC 94-614. (Dropping in On Ser.). 32p. (J). (gr. 2-5). 1994. lib. bdg. 21.27 (1-55916-005-5) Rourke Bk Co.
— Japan, LC 93-47097. (Dropping in On Ser.). 32p. (J). (gr. 2-5). 1994. lib. bdg. 21.27 (1-55916-003-9) Rourke Bk Co.
— Mexico, LC 93-42777. (Dropping in On Ser.). 32p. (J). (gr. 2-5). 1994. lib. bdg. 21.27 (1-55916-001-2) Rourke Bk Co.
— Vietnam, Set I. LC 94-7558. (Droppin in On Ser.). 32p. (J). (gr. 2-5). 1994. lib. bdg. 21.27 (1-55916-008-X) Rourke Bk Co.
Parker, Linda S. Native American Estate: The Struggle over Indian & Hawaiian Lands. LC 89-4892. 256p. 1996. pap. text 16.00 (0-8248-1807-5) UH Pr.
Parker, Lisa A. Larry the Lobster: Everyday Songs from Everywhere. Bennett, Michael D., ed. 40p. (Orig.). 1993. pap. 10.95 (0-934017-19-0) Memphis Musicraft.
Parker, Lisa T. Too Many Puppies. LC 93-73620. (Look-Look Bks.). (Illus.). 24p. (J). (ps-3). 1996. pap. text 3.29 (0-307-12840-7) Gldn Bks Pub Co.
Parker, Liz, ed. see Bankier, William.
Parker, Liz, ed. see Bricker, Sandra D.
Parker, Liz, ed. see Brin, Susannah.
Parker, Liz, ed. see Buchanan, Paul.
Parker, Liz, ed. see Cruise, Robin.
Parker, Liz, ed. see Horton, Randy.
Parker, Liz, ed. see Kim, Kenneth H.
Parker, Liz, ed. see Press, Skip.
Parker, Liz, ed. see Schraff, Anne.
Parker, Liz, ed. see Steel, Richard.
Parker, Liz, ed. see Welch, Irene.
Parker, Liz, ed. see Wells, Colin.
Parker, Liz, ed. see Woodson, Frank.
Parker, Lois & McConnell, David. A Little Peoples' Beginning on Michigan. (Illus.). 32p. (Orig.). (J). (gr. 1-2). 1981. pap. 5.50 (0-910726-06-X) Hillsdale Educ.
Parker, Lois J. Mythopoesis & the Crisis of Postmodernism: Toward Integrating Image & Story. 220p. 1998. pap. text 25.00 (0-913412-79-1) Brandon Hse.
Parker, Lorne A. & Monson, Mavis K. Teletechniques: An Instructional Model for Interactive Teleconferencing. Langdon, Danny G., ed. LC 79-24442. (Instructional Design Library). 108p. 1980. 27.95 (0-87778-158-3) Educ Tech Pubns.
Parker, Lorraine, jt. auth. see Webster, Helen L.
Parker, Lorraine T. Success over Stress. (Illus.). 68p. 1997. pap. 29.95 (1-888343-10-9) Hartman Pub.
Parker, Lowell. Chemistry - Molecules, Matter, & Change: Instructor's Resource Manual. 3rd ed. 1997. teacher ed. 40.00 (0-7167-2761-7) W H Freeman.
Parker, Lucile. Southern Wildflowers. LC 98-21866. 144p. 1999. pap. 14.95 (1-56554-419-6) Pelican.
— Wildflower Postcard Book. (Illus.). 30p. 1999. pap. 9.95 (1-56554-420-X) Pelican.
Parker, Lucy V. How to Start a Home-Based Writing Business. 2nd rev. ed. LC 97-17530. (How to Start a Home-Based Business Ser.). (Illus.). 288p. 1997. pap. 17.95 (1-56440-998-8) Globe Pequot.
*Parker, Lucy V. How to Start a Home-Based Writing Business. 3rd ed. (Home-Based Business Ser.). (Illus.). 336p. 2000. pap. 18.95 (0-7627-0660-0) Globe Pequot.
Parker, Lula J. Parker's History of Bedford County, Virginia. rev. ed. Viemeister, Peter, ed. & pref. by. LC 88-82103. (Indexed Edition Ser.). 160p. 1988. reprint ed. pap. 17.95 (0-9608598-4-5) Hamiltons.
Parker, Lynn, jt. auth. see Horton, Rozila.
Parker, Lynn, jt. auth. see Olkowski, Thomas T.
Parker, Lynn M. & LePla, F. Joseph. Integrated Branding: Becoming Brand-Driven Through Companywide Action. LC 99-10385. 320p. 1999. 69.50 (1-56720-238-1, Quorum Bks) Greenwood.
Parker, M. Socrates & Athens. (Inside the Ancient World Ser.). 88p. 1986. reprint ed. pap. 16.95 (0-86292-185-6, Pub. by Brist Class Pr) Focus Pub-R Pullins.
Parker, M., ed. Growth Regulation by Nuclear Hormone Receptors. (Cancer Surveys Ser.: Vol. 14). (Illus.). 256p. (C). 1992. text 49.00 (0-87969-371-1) Cold Spring Harbor.
Parker, M. A. & Pickup, F. Engineering Drawing with Worked Examples, Bk. 1. 226p. (C). 1997. pap. 27.00 (0-7487-0311-X, Pub. by S Thornes Pubs) Trans-Atl Phila.
Parker, M. T. Hospital-Acquired Infections: Guidelines to Laboratory Methods. (WHO Regional Publications, European Ser.: No. 4). 63p. 1978. 8.00 (92-9020-104-5, 1310004) World Health.
— Topley & Wilson's Principles of Bacteriology, Virology & Immunity, 5 vols., Set. 8th ed. 2742p. text. write for info. (0-7131-4594-3, Pub. by E A) Routldge.
Parker, Malcolm G., ed. Nuclear Hormone Receptors: Molecular Mechanisms, Cellular Functions Clinical Abnormalities. 404p. 1991. text 125.00 (0-12-545072-9) Acad Pr.
— Steroid Hormone Action. LC 93-1165. 230p. 1993. 68.00 (0-19-963393-2) OUP.
— Steroid Hormone Action. LC 93-1165. (Illus.). 226p. 1993. pap. text 45.00 (0-19-963392-4) OUP.
Parker, Margaret. The Didactic Structure & Content of el Libro de Calila e Digna. LC 76-51194. (Coleccion de Estudios Hispanicos - Hispanic Studies Collection). 1978. pap. 12.00 (0-89729-188-3) Ediciones.
Parker, Margaret R. The Story of a Story Across Cultures: The Case of the "Doncella Teodor" (Monografias A Ser.: Vol. 161). 166p. (C). 1996. 63.00 (1-85566-038-5, Pub. by Tamesis Bks Ltd) Boydell & Brewer.
Parker, Margot. What Is Martin Luther King, Jr. Day? LC 89-29254. (Understanding Holidays Ser.). (Illus.). 48p. (J). (gr. 1-3). 1990. pap. 4.95 (0-516-43784-4) Childrens.
— What Is Thanksgiving Day? LC 88-11112. (Understanding Holidays Ser.). (Illus.). 48p. (J). (gr. 1-3). 1988. pap. 4.95 (0-516-43783-6) Childrens.
Parker, Maria G., jt. auth. see Imber, Brenda P.
Parker, Marie. Anything Goes! 144p. (Orig.). 1995. pap. 9.95 (0-925854-15-8) Defiant Pr.
Parker, Marilyn E. Nursing Theories & Nursing Practice. (Illus.). 512p. 2000. pap. text 36.95 (0-8036-0604-4) Davis Co.
Parker, Marilyn E., ed. Nursing Theories in Practice. 320p. 1991. 24.95 (0-88737-497-2) Natl League Nurse.
— Patterns of Nursing Theories in Practice. LC 93-3402. 1993. 25.95 (0-88737-600-2, 15-2548) Natl League Nurse.
Parker, Marilyn M. Information Economics: Linking Business Performance to Information Technology. (C). 1988. text 66.80 (0-13-464595-2) P-H.
— Information Strategy & Economics. 528p. 1989. pap. text 63.80 (0-13-464901-X) P-H.
— Strategic Transformation & Information Technology: Paradigms for Performing While Transforming. LC 95-18153. (William R. King Series in Information Management). 606p. 1995. 74.20 (0-13-190794-8) P-H.
Parker, Marjorie. Bread from My Oven. (Quiet Time Books for Women). 128p. pap. 4.99 (0-8024-0910-5, 408) Moody.
Parker, Marjorie H. Jellyfish Can't Swim, & Other Secrets from the Animal World. LC 91-3236. 64p. (J). (gr. 4-7). 1991. pap. 5.99 (1-55513-393-2, Chariot Bks) Chariot Victor.
*Parker, Mark. X-Calibre: The Absurd Legend of Cantiger the Wizard. 320p. 2000. pap. 11.95 (0-7867-0802-6, Pub. by Carroll & Graf) Publishers Group.
Parker, Mark & McKnew, Ed. Powerboat Guide: 2000 Edition. (Illus.). 1650p. 1999. pap. 89.95 (0-9622134-1-1, Pub. by Amer Marine Pub) R Hale & Co.
Parker, Mark, et al. Songs of the Season. (SoundForth Ser.). (Illus.). 80p. (Orig.). (YA). 1991. pap. 8.95 (0-89084-555-7, 051532) Bob Jones Univ.
Parker, Mark, jt. auth. see McKnew, Ed.
Parker, Mark M. Fat Free Jokes for Fun-Loving Folks: Lighten up America. LC 94-96644. (Illus.). 155p. (Orig.). 1994. pap. 7.95 (0-9644629-0-7) Laugh Out Loud.
Parker, Marla, ed. She Does Math! Real-Life Problems from Women on the Job. LC 95-76294. (Classroom Resource Materials Ser.). 272p. 1995. pap. text 30.95 (0-88385-702-2) Math Assn.
Parker, Marshall E. & Peattie, Edward G. Pipeline Corrosion & Cathodic Protection. 3rd ed. LC 83-22630. 166p. 1984. 39.00 (0-87201-149-6, 1149) Gulf Pub.
Parker, Martha. Mother Goose: Designs for Applique & Embroidery Based on Traditional Nursery Rhymes. (Illus.). 48p. (Orig.). 1983. pap. 8.00 (0-932946-10-0) Burdett CA.
Parker, Martha. Test Preparation Guide for AAPA 313. (Associate, Annuity Products & Administration Program Ser.). (C). pap. 24.00 (1-57974-047-2, Pub. by Life Office) PBD Inc.
Parker, Martha, jt. auth. see Gilley, Sean S.
Parker, Martha, jt. auth. see Noles, Gwendolyn.
Parker, Martha B. Kin-i-wak, Kenewick, the Kennewick. 414p. 1987. 22.95 (0-87770-397-3) Ye Galleon.
— Tales of Richland, White Bluffs & Hanford, 1805-1943. (Illus.). 407p. 1987. 22.95 (0-87770-223-3) Ye Galleon.
— Washington & Oregon, a Map History of the Oregon Country. 1988. 25.00 (0-685-19905-3) Ye Galleon.
Parker, Martin, jt. auth. see Hassard, John.
Parker, Martyn, et al. Handbook of Hip Fracture Management. LC 96-40887. 160p. 1997. pap. text 57.50 (0-7506-2179-6) Buttrwrth-Heinemann.
Parker, Martyn J. & Pryor, Glyn. Hip Fracture Management. LC 92-49128. 304p. 1993. 150.00 (0-632-03263-4) Blackwell Sci.
Parker, Mary. Santas, Reinas, Martires y Cortesanas: El Tratamiento de la Mujer en Diamante. (SPA.). 200p. 69.95 (1-882528-17-4) Scripta.
— Sashiko: Easy & Elegant Designs for Decorative Machine Stitching. Cusick, Dawn, ed. LC 99-16235. (Illus.). 144p. 1999. 24.95 (1-57990-132-8, Pub. by Lark Books) Random.
Parker, Mary, ed. Spanish Dramatists of the Golden Age: A Bio-Bibliographical Sourcebook. LC 97-21976. 296p. 1998. lib. bdg. 89.50 (0-313-28893-3, Greenwood Pr) Greenwood.
Parker, Mary A. Eighteenth-Century Music in Theory & Practice: Essays in Honor of Alfred Mann. LC 94-34216. (Festschrift Ser.: No. 13). 1994. 54.00 (0-945193-11-4) Pendragon NY.
Parker, Mary C. Kids T. A. L. K! (Teach Articulation & Language to Kids) A Communication Development Program for K-6th Grades Regular-Special-Bilingual Education. (Illus.). 535p. 1988. 195.00 (0-9621178-0-3) Kids TALK.
Parker, Mary E. The Sex Girl. (William Blake Prize Poets Ser.: No. 2). 64p. 1999. pap. 12.00 (0-9648305-3-1) Urthona Pr.
*Parker, Matthew. Celaine. 1999. pap. 10.95 (1-84002-111-X, Pub. by Theatre Comm) Consort Bk Sales.
Parker, Matthew, jt. ed. see Carter, Novella.
Parker, Matthew, ed. see Institute for the Black Family Staff.
Parker, Matthew, jt. ed. see June, Lee.
Parker, Mattie. North Carolina Charters & Constitutions, 1578-1698. (Colonial Records of North Carolina Ser.: Vol. 1). xxii, 247p. 1963. 15.00 (0-86526-022-2) NC Archives.
Parker, Mattie, ed. North Carolina Charters & Constitutions, 1578-1698. deluxe ed. (Colonial Records of North Carolina Ser.). xxii, 247p. 1963. lthr. 20.00 (0-86526-021-4) NC Archives.
— North Carolina Higher-Court Records, 1697-1701. (Colonial Records of North Carolina Ser.: Vol. 3). (Illus.). lxviii, 620p. 1971. 15.00 (0-86526-024-9) NC Archives.
Parker, Maurice. Manual of British Standards in Engineering Drawing & Design. 226p. (C). 1999. pap. 75.00 (0-7487-1031-0, Pub. by S Thornes Pubs) Trans-Atl Phila.
Parker, Michael. The Amouous Ambassador: An American Farce LC 99-213837. 104p. 1990. write for info. (0-573-67040-4) French.
Parker, Michael. Ethics & Community in the Health Care Profession. LC 98-35439. (Professional Ethics Ser.). 1999. write for info. (0-415-15027-2); pap. write for info. (0-415-15028-0) Routledge.
— The Geographical Cure: Novellas & Stories. LC 93-40188. 288p. 1994. 20.00 (0-684-19682-4, Scribners Ref) Mac Lib Ref.
— The Growth of Understanding: Beyond Individuals & Communities. 160p. 1995. 66.95 (1-85972-268-7, Pub. by Avebry) Ashgate Pub Co.
— Hello down There. large type ed. LC 92-47099. (General Ser.). 432p. 1993. reprint ed. lib. bdg. 18.95 (1-56054-671-9) Thorndike Pr.
— The Hurt World. LC 95-182513. 376p. 1995. pap. 24.95 (0-85640-557-4, Pub. by Blackstaff Pr) Dufour.
— The Kingdom of Character: The Student Volunteer Movement for Foreign Missions, 1886-1926. LC 97-46435. 264p. (C). 1998. 57.00 (0-7618-1012-9); pap. 32.50 (0-7618-1013-7) U Pr of Amer.
— Priest of the World's Destiny: John Paul the Second. Faith Publishing Company Staff, ed. LC 95-60847. 192p. 1995. pap. 9.00 (1-880033-19-4) Queenship Pub.
*Parker, Michael. Thatcherism & the Fall of Coal: Politics & Economics of Uk Coal, 1979-2000. 180p. 2000. text 65.00 (0-19-730025-1) OUP.
Parker, Michael & Starkey, Roger, eds. Postcolonial Literatures: Achebe, Ngugi, Desai, Walcott. LC 95-9734. (New Casebooks Ser.). 1995. text 45.00 (0-312-12664-6) St Martin.
Parker, Michael, jt. auth. see Harte, Liam.
Parker, Michael A. War of Tomorrow: Arctic Strike, A Visual Novel of Michael A. Parker. (Illustrated History of Near Future Warfare Ser.: No. 2). (Illus.). 224p. (Orig.). 1991. mass mkt. 6.95 (0-380-75844-X, Avon Bks) Morrow Avon.
Parker, Michael A., jt. ed. see Pirich, Andrew R.
Parker, Michael W. Protein Toxin Structure. LC 96-21770. (Molecular Biology Intelligence Unit Ser.). 200p. 1996. 99.00 (1-57059-368-X) Landes Bioscience.
— Seamus Heaney: The Making of the Poet. LC 92-61949. (Illus.). 306p. 1993. text 27.95 (0-87745-398-5) U of Iowa Pr.
Parker, Michael W., jt. auth. see Schmidt, Jan A.
Parker, Mike. Inside the Circle: A Union Guide to Quality of Work Life. LC 85-50600. (Illus.). 153p. 1985. pap. 15.00 (0-89608-302-0) Labor Notes.
— Irish Scene. 1996. pap. 10.95 (0-85449-234-8, Pub. by Gay Mens Pr) LPC InBook.
— Prospects for Hard Coal in Europe. 75p. (C). pap. 14.95 (0-905031-79-2) Brookings.
— Rivers of Yesterday: A New Brunswick Hunting & Fishing Journal. LC 98-119296. (Illus.). 192p. 1998. pap. text 17.95 (1-55109-225-5) Nimbus Publ.
— Scottish Scene. (Illus.). 200p. (Orig.). 1997. pap. 12.95 (0-85449-248-8, Pub. by Gay Mens Pr) LPC InBook.
Parker, Mike & Slaughter, Jane. Working Smart: A Union Guide to Participation Programs & Reeingineering. LC 94-73182. (Illus.). 317p. (Orig.). 1994. pap. 20.00 (0-914093-08-8) Labor Notes.

Parker, Mike & Whitfield, Paul. Wales. 2nd ed. (Rough Guides Ser.). 464p. 1997. pap. 17.95 (*1-85828-245-4*) Viking Penguin.

Parker, Mike, jt. auth. see Gruelle, Martha.

Parker, Monique, jt. auth. see Cahen, Michel.

***Parker, Monroe.** A Virtuous Woman. 14p. 1999. pap. write for info. (*0-87398-877-9*) Sword of the Lord.

Parker, Morris B. Mules, Mines & Me in Mexico, 1895-1932. Day, James M, ed. LC 79-15206. (Illus.). 248p. 1979. reprint ed. pap. 76.90 (*0-7837-9235-2*, 204998600004) Bks Demand.

Parker, Muriel M. Illuminated Letter Designs in the Historiated Style of the 13th to 15th Centuries. (International Design Library). (Illus.). 48p. 1986. pap. 5.95 (*0-88045-082-7*) Stemmer Hse.

Parker, N. C., et al. Fish-Marking Techniques. LC 90-84827. (Symposium Ser.: No. 7). 879p. (C). 1990. text 89.00 (*0-913235-59-8*, 540.07) Am Fisheries Soc.

***Parker, Nancy.** Double Helix: A Novel. Cope, Judith, ed. (Illus.). 512p. 2000. pap. 15.00 (*0-9642272-1-5*) Ashland Hills.

Parker, Nancy. The Omega Transmissions. LC 94-94606. 404p. 1994. pap. 12.95 (*0-9642272-0-7*) Ashland Hills.

***Parker, Nancy & Kalish, Nancy.** Beautiful Brows: The Ultimate Guide to Styling, Shaping & Maintaining Your Eyebrows. LC 00-30219. (Illus.). 112p. 2000. pap. 9.00 (*0-609-80670-X*, Three Riv Pr) Crown Pub Group.

Parker, Nancy, ed. see Crew, Randolph E.

Parker, Nancy, ed. see Dunkins, Betty M. & Gray, Joy.

Parker, Nancy Winslow. Bugs. (Reading Rainbow Bks.). (J). 1988. 10.15 (*0-606-04178-8*, Pub. by Turtleback) Demco.

Parker, Nancy Winslow. Frogs, Toads, Lizards & Salamanders. 1996. 11.15 (*0-606-08747-8*, Pub. by Turtleback) Demco.

Parker, Nancy Winslow. Land Ho! From Columbus to Cabrillo & How They Managed to Make So Many Mistakes & Still End up Being So Famous. LC 99-23006. (Illus.). 32p. (J). (gr. 1-5). 2001. lib. bdg. 15.89 (*0-06-027760-2*) HarpC Child Bks.

***Parker, Nancy Winslow.** Land Ho! From Columbus to Cabrillo & How They Managed to Make So Many Mistakes & Still End up Being So Famous. LC 99-23006. (Illus.). 32p. (J). (gr. 1-5). 2001. 15.95 (*0-06-027759-9*) HarpC Child Bks.

Parker, Nancy Winslow. Locks, Crocs, & Skeeters: The Story of the Panama Canal. (Illus.). 32p. (J). (gr. 3 up). 1996. 16.00 (*0-688-12241-8*, Grenwillow Bks) HarpC Child Bks.

— Money, Money, Money: The Meaning of the Art & Symbols on United States Paper Currency. LC 93-43534. (Illus.). 32p. (J). (gr. 2-7). 1995. 16.95 (*0-06-023411-3*); lib. bdg. 16.89 (*0-06-023412-1*) HarpC Child Bks.

— The President's Cabinet & How It Grew. LC 89-70851. (Illus.). 40p. (J). (gr. 3-5). 1991. 14.95 (*0-06-021617-4*) HarpC Child Bks.

— The President's Car. LC 79-7898. (Illus.). 64p. (J). (gr. 3-5). 1981. 11.95 (*0-690-03963-8*); lib. bdg. 11.89 (*0-690-03964-6*) HarpC Child Bks.

Parker, Nancy Winslow, jt. auth. see Wright, Joan R.

Parker, Nathan H. The Minnesota Handbook for 1856-1857. LC 75-114. (Mid-American Frontier Ser.). 1975. reprint ed. 16.95 (*0-405-06880-8*) Ayer.

Parker, Noel. Portrayals of Revolution: Images, Debates, & Patterns of Thought on the French Revolution. LC 89-26365. (Illus.). 256p. (C). 1990. 31.95 (*0-8093-1684-6*) S Ill U Pr.

— Revolutions & History: An Essay in Interpretation. LC 99-10927. 240p. 1999. text 59.95 (*0-7456-1135-4*, Pub. by Polity Pr); pap. text 26.95 (*0-7456-1136-2*, Pub. by Polity Pr) Blackwell Pubs.

***Parker, Noel & Armstrong, Bill.** Margins in European Integration. LC 99-59898. 2000. 65.00 (*0-312-22958-5*) St Martin.

***Parker, Norman.** In the Company of Killers: True Life Stories From a Two Time Murderer. 2000. mass mkt. 6.99 (*1-85782-303-6*) Blake Publng.

Parker, Norman S. Parkhurst Tales 2. (Illus.). 314p. 1999. pap. 7.95 (*1-85782-317-6*, Pub. by Blake Publng) Seven Hills Bk.

Parker, Norton S. Audiovisual Script Writing. 1974. reprint ed. pap. 15.00 (*0-8135-0797-9*) Rutgers U Pr.

Parker, Oliver. Fabricate Your Own Boat Covers or Start Your Own Marine Canvas Business at Home. (Illus.). 1982. pap. 24.95 (*0-937155-00-4*) O Parker Pub.

Parker, Ophelia S. Forgive Me My Debts: Credit Repair Guide. LC 93-91060. 528p. (Orig.). 1994. ring bd. 64.95 (*0-937895-03-2*) By Faith Direct.

— In the Black Plus...Call Us. 324p. 1990. pap. 40.00 (*0-937895-02-4*) By Faith Direct.

— Thoughts - Shackles of the Mind. (Illus.). (Orig.). 1986. 14.95 (*0-937895-01-6*); pap. 12.95 (*0-937895-00-8*) By Faith Direct.

Parker, Owen. Tack Now, Skipper. 1979. 29.95 (*0-8464-0065-0*) Beekman Pubs.

Parker, P. & Cooper, A., eds. Geology & Seismic Stratigraphy of the Antarctic Margin 2. (Antarctic Research Ser.: Vol. 71). 187p. 1997. 60.00 (*0-87590-897-7*) Am Geophysical.

Parker, P. & Pawson, T., eds. Cell Signalling. LC 96-226674. (Cancer Surveys Ser.: Vol. 27). (Illus.). 450p. (C). 1996. text 90.00 (*0-87969-484-X*) Cold Spring Harbor.

***Parker, P. G. & Burley, N. T., eds.** Avian Reproductive Tactics: Female & Male Perspectives. (Ornithological Monographs: Vol. 49). 1998. 20.00 (*0-935868-95-X*) Am Ornithologists.

Parker, Pat. Jonestown & Other Madness. LC 85-1679. 80p. 1985. pap. 9.95 (*0-932379-00-1*); lib. bdg. 20.95 (*0-932379-01-X*) Firebrand Bks.

— Movement in Black. LC 98-55775. 1999. 26.95 (*1-56341-109-1*); pap. 16.95 (*1-56341-108-3*) Firebrand Bks.

Parker, Patricia. Literary Fat Ladies: Rhetoric, Gender, Property. 320p. 1988. text 47.50 (*0-416-91600-7*); pap. text 15.95 (*0-416-91610-4*) Routledge.

— One Hundred Years of History in the California Desert No. 13: An Overview of Historical Resources at Joshua Tree National Monument. (National Park Service Ser.). (Illus.). 160p. 1980. reprint ed. pap. text 17.50 (*1-55567-422-4*) Coyote Press.

— Shakespeare from the Margins: Language, Culture, Context. LC 95-36472. 352p. 1996. pap. text 19.95 (*0-226-64585-1*) U Ch Pr.

— Shakespeare from the Margins: Language, Culture, Context. LC 95-36472. 392p. 1997. lib. bdg. 52.00 (*0-226-64584-3*) U Ch Pr.

Parker, Patricia & Hartman, Geoffrey H., eds. Shakespeare & the Question of Theory. 300p. 1986. 27.00 (*0-416-36920-0*, 9479); pap. 19.95 (*0-416-36930-8*, 9480) Routledge.

— Shakespeare & the Question of Theory. 352p. (C). 1986. pap. 29.99 (*0-415-05113-4*) Routledge.

Parker, Patricia & Quint, David, eds. Literary Theory - Renaissance Texts. LC 85-23799. 408p. 1986. reprint ed. pap. 126.50 (*0-608-03741-9*, 206456600009) Bks Demand.

Parker, Patricia, jt. ed. see Hendricks, Margo.

Parker, Patricia A. Inescapable Romance: Studies in the Poetics of a Mode. LC 78-70312. 300p. reprint ed. pap. 93.00 (*0-8357-3693-8*, 203641700003) Bks Demand.

Parker, Patricia L., jt. auth. see King, Thomas F.

Parker, Patty, jt. ed. see Fara, Frank.

Parker, Patty E. For My Boys. (Illus.). 192p. 1997. 14.95 (*0-9659989-0-8*) Cerf Kitchen.

Parker, Paul. Free-Heel Skiing: Telemark & Parallel Techniques for All Conditions. 2nd ed. LC 95-12628. (Illus.). 192p. 1995. pap. 19.95 (*0-89886-412-7*) Mountaineers.

Parker, Paul O. Industry & Health Affairs: Index of Modern Authors & Subjects with Guide for Rapid Research. LC 90-56270. 200p. 1991. 47.50 (*1-55914-308-8*); pap. 44.50 (*1-55914-309-6*) ABBE Pubs Assn.

— Peripheral Nerve Injuries: Medical Subject Analysis with Reference Bibliography. LC 85-48078. 1987. 44.50 (*0-88164-426-9*); pap. 39.50 (*0-88164-427-7*) ABBE Pubs Assn.

Parker, Penny L., ed. see State Bar of Texas Real Estate Forms Manual Committee.

Parker, Peter. Ackerley: The Life of J. R. Ackerley. (Illus.). 288p. 1991. pap. 15.00 (*0-374-52279-0*) FS&G.

Parker, Peter & Kermode, Frank, eds. A Reader's Guide to Twentieth-Century Writers. Orig. Title: The Reader's Companion to Twentieth-Century Writers. 846p. (C). 1996. 45.00 (*0-19-521215-0*) OUP.

Parker, Peter & Mokhesi-Parker, Joyce. In the Shadow of Sharpeville: Apartheid & Criminal Justice. LC 97-34297. 400p. 1998. text 50.00 (*0-8147-6659-5*) NYU Pr.

Parker, Peter D., ed. Chloride Electrometallurgy: Proceedings of a Symposium. LC 82 63095. (Conference Proceedings Ser.). (Illus.). 243p. reprint ed. pap. 75.40 (*0-608-17834-9*, 203259300080) Bks Demand.

Parker, Peter J. & Dekker. Protein Kinase C. LC 96-50979. (Molecular Biology Intelligence Unit Ser.). 219p. 1997. 99.00 (*1-57059-424-4*) Landes Bioscience.

Parker, Petey. Corporate Kitty Litter. 152p. 1995. pap. text, per. 16.95 (*0-7872-1842-1*) Kendall-Hunt.

Parker, Phil. Kiss Yourself Hello! 200p. 1999. 19.95 (*1-890412-69-4*) Glden Eight Intl.

***Parker, Philip.** The Art & Science of Screenwriting. 2nd ed. LC 99-495100. 224p. 1999. pap. 24.95 (*1-84150-000-3*, Pub. by Intellect) Cromland.

Parker, Philip. Global Cities. LC 94-22445. (Project Eco-City Ser.). (Illus.). 48p. (J). (gr. 2-7). 1995. lib. bdg. 7.95 (*1-56847-286-2*) Raintree Steck-V.

***Parker, Philip.** Physioeconomics: The Basis for Long-Run Economic Growth. LC 00-21973. (Illus.). 252p. 2000. 29.95 (*0-262-16194-X*) MIT Pr.

Parker, Philip M. Climatic Effects on Individual, Social & Economic Behavior: A Physioeconomic Review of Research Across Disciplines, 2. LC 94-41521. (Bibliographies & Indexes in Geography Ser.: Vol. 2). 304p. 1995. lib. bdg. 85.00 (*0-313-29400-3*, Greenwood Pr) Greenwood.

— Ethnic Cultures of the World: A Statistical Reference. LC 96-43832. (Cross-Cultural Statistical Encyclopedia of the World: Vol. 3). 424p. 1997. lib. bdg. 95.00 (*0-313-29767-3*, Greenwood Pr) Greenwood.

— Linguistic Cultures of the World: A Statistical Reference. LC 96-36681. (Cross-Cultural Statistical Encyclopedia of the World: Vol. 2). 448p. 1997. lib. bdg. 95.00 (*0-313-29769-X*, Greenwood Pr) Greenwood.

— National Cultures of the World: A Statistical Reference. LC 96-41974. (Cross-Cultural Statistical Encyclopedia of the World: Vol. 4). 264p. 1997. lib. bdg. 79.50 (*0-313-29770-3*, Greenwood Pr) Greenwood.

— Religious Cultures of the World: A Statistical Reference. LC 96-43833. (Cross-Cultural Statistical Encyclopedia of the World: Vol. 1). 160p. 1997. lib. bdg. 69.50 (*0-313-29768-1*, Greenwood Pr) Greenwood.

Parker, Phillip E., jt. auth. see Dodson, C. T.

Parker, Phyllis R. Brazil & the Quiet Intervention, 1964. LC 78-25856. (Texas Pan American Ser.). 161p. reprint ed. pap. 50.00 (*0-608-20107-3*, 207137900011) Bks Demand.

Parker-Pope, Tara. Cigarettes. 208p. 2001. pap. 24.95 (*1-56584-503-X*, Pub. by New Press NY) Norton.

Parker, R. Roger Parker's Guide to Web Content & Design. 1997. 39.95 (*0-8052-8553-9*, M&T Bks) IDG Bks.

Parker, R. A. Chamberlain & Appeasement: British Policy & the Coming of the Second World War. 384p. 1993. pap. text 30.95 (*0-312-09969-X*) St Martin.

— The Second World War: A Short History. 2nd rev. ed. LC 97-10038. (Illus.). 342p. 1997. pap. 14.95 (*0-19-289285-1*) OUP.

Parker, R. A., jt. auth. see Neugebauer, O.

Parker, R. B. & Zitner, Sheldon P., eds. Elizabethan Theater: Essays in Honor of S. Schoenbaum. LC 95-41887. (Illus.). 328p. 1996. 45.00 (*0-87413-587-7*) U Delaware Pr.

Parker, R. B., ed. see Shakespeare, William.

Parker, R. Charles. Going for Growth: Technological Innovation in Manufacturing Industries. LC 84-21902. 273p. reprint ed. pap. 84.70 (*0-8357-6943-7*, 203900200009) Bks Demand.

— The Management of Innovation. LC 82-2737. (Illus.). 239p. reprint ed. pap. 74.10 (*0-8357-4321-7*, 203712000007) Bks Demand.

Parker, R. E. Introductory Statistics for Biology. 2nd ed. (Studies in Biology: No. 43). 129p. 1991. pap. text 16.95 (*0-521-42778-9*) Cambridge U Pr.

Parker, R. E., ed. The Middle English Stanzaic Versions of the Life of Saint Anne. (EETS, OS Ser.: No. 174). 1974. reprint ed. 40.00 (*0-527-00171-6*) Periodicals Srv.

Parker, R. Gary. Deterministic Scheduling Theory. LC 95-15181. 296p. (C). (gr. 13). 1996. ring bd. 69.95 (*0-412-99681-2*, Chap & Hall CRC) CRC Pr.

— Deterministic Scheduling Theory. 320p. 1995. write for info. (*0-412-05051-X*) Chapman & Hall.

Parker, R. Gary & Rardin, Ronald L., eds. Discrete Optimization. (Computer Science & Scientific Computing Ser.). 472p. 1988. text 116.00 (*0-12-545075-3*) Acad Pr.

Parker, R. H. Bibliographies for Accounting Historians. Brief, Richard P., ed. LC 80-1462. (Dimensions of Accounting Theory & Practice Ser.). 1980. lib. bdg. 37.95 (*0-405-13484-3*) Ayer.

— British Accountants: A Biographical Sourcebook. Brief, Richard P., ed. LC 80-1463. (Dimensions of Accounting Theory & Practice Ser.). 1980. lib. bdg. 31.95 (*0-405-13485-1*) Ayer.

— The Development of the Accountancy Profession in Britain to the Early Twentieth Century. (Monograph Series of the Academy of Accounting Historians; Monograph 5). 74p. 1986. pap. 10.00 (*1-879750-03-1*) Acad Acct Hist.

— An Introduction to Chemical Metallurgy: In SI-Metric Units. 2nd ed. 1978. 162.00 (*0-08-022125-4*, Pub. by Pergamon Repr) Franklin.

Parker, R. H. Understanding Financial Statements. 1994. pap. 17.95 (*0-14-017378-1*, Pub. by Pnguin Bks Ltd) Trafalgar.

Parker, R. H., et al, eds. Readings in True & Fair. LC 95-52020. (New Works in Accounting History). 344p. 1996. reprint ed. text 77.00 (*0-8153-2273-9*) Garland.

Parker, R. H. & Nobes, C. W., eds. An International View of True & Fair Accounting. LC 94-6174. (International Accounting Ser.). (Illus.). 128p. (C). (gr. 13). 1994. pap. 45.00 (*0-415-11463-2*, B4184) Thomson Learn.

Parker, R. H. & Yamey, Basil S., eds. Accounting History: Some British Contributions. (Illus.). 670p. 1994. text 85.00 (*0-19-828886-7*) OUP.

Parker, R. H. & Zeff, Stephen A., compiled by. Milestones in the British Accounting Literature. LC 95-52263. (New Works in Accounting History). 472p. 1996. reprint ed. text 109.00 (*0-8153-2272-0*) Garland.

Parker, R. H., jt. auth. see Nobes, Christopher.

Parker, R. H., jt. ed. see Lemarchand, Yannick.

Parker, R. K., jt. ed. see Fliflet, A. W.

Parker, R. N. Forest Flora for the Punjab with Hazara & Delhi. 577p. (C). 1973. reprint ed. 250.00 (*0-7855-3125-4*, Pub. by Intl Bk Distr) St Mut.

Parker, R. N., ed. Forest Flora for the Punjab with Hazara & Delhi. 591p. (C). 1984. text 375.00 (*0-89771-618-3*, Pub. by Intl Bk Distr) St Mut.

Parker, R. S. Traumatic Brain Injury & Neuropsychological Impairment. xii, 452p. 1990. 105.00 (*0-387 97239-0*) Spr-Verlag.

Parker, R. Tommy. Is God Really Still in Control? Questions of A Lifetime Believer. LC 99-168788. 119 p. 1998. write for info. (*0-7880-0985-0*, Fairway Pr) CSS OH.

Parker, R. Wayne. The Computer Buyer's Handbook: How to Select & Buy Personal Computers for Your Home or Business. LC 90-83233. (Illus.). 240p. (Orig.). 1991. pap. 16.95 (*0-9627370-6-2*) Fast Forward Pub.

Parker, Rachel, jt. auth. see Parker, William.

Parker, Ralph, tr. see Solzhenitsyn, Aleksandr.

Parker, Randall M. & Szymanski, Edna. Rehabilitation Counseling: Basics & Beyond. 3rd ed. LC 97-10241. (Orig.). 1997. pap. 39.00 (*0-89079-723-4*) PRO-ED.

Parker, Randall M., jt. ed. see Szymanski, Edna M.

Parker, Randall M., jt. ed. see Szymanski, Edna.

Parker, Randy S. & McElmurry, Beverly J. Annual Review of Women's Health. Vol. III. 400p. 1996. pap. 37.95 (*0-88737-672-X*) Natl League Nurse.

Parker, Rani. Another Point of View: A Gender Analysis Training Manual for Grassroots Workers. 106p. (Orig.). 1993. pap. 15.95 (*0-912917-41-5*) UNIFEM.

Parker, Ray, Jr. RV Having Fun Yet? Comic Adventures on the Road. LC 94-65905. (Illus.). 151p. (Orig.). 1995. 12.95 (*0-9640924-0-9*) Oldfield Pub.

Parker, Reese, jt. auth. see McFarland, Thomas D.

Parker, Reeve. Coleridge's Meditative Art. LC 74-25367. 270p. 1975. 39.50 (*0-8290-0340-1*) Irvington.

Parker, Rembert N. Airwaves: An Adventure Resource for Over the Edge. (Over the Edge Ser.). 16p. 1993. pap. 4.95 (*1-887801-04-9*, Atlas Games) Trident MN.

***Parker, Rene Denise.** Reflections of Courage. 2000. pap. 9.00 (*0-8059-4968-2*) Dorrance.

***Parker, Rennie.** The Georgian Poets: Abercrombie, Brooke, Drinkwater, Gibson, Thomas. (Writers & Their Works Ser.). 112p. 1999. pap. text 21.00 (*0-7463-0899-X*, Pub. by Northcote House) U Pr of Miss.

Parker, Reuel B. The New Cold-Molded Boatbuilding: From Lofting to Launching. (Illus.). 336p. 1992. pap. 23.95 (*0-87742-358-X*) Intl Marine.

— The New Cold-Molded Boatbuilding: From Lofting to Launching. 336p. 1992. pap. 23.95 (*0-07-048578-X*) McGraw.

— The Sharpie Book. 1993. pap. text 19.95 (*0-87742-304-0*) Intl Marine.

— The Sharpie Book. 179p. 1993. pap. 19.95 (*0-07-158013-1*) McGraw.

Parker-Rhodes, A. F. The Theory of Indistinguishables: A Search for Explanatory Principles Below the Level of Physics. 230p. 1981. text 126.50 (*90-277-1214-X*, D Reidel) Kluwer Academic.

Parker-Rhodes, Frederick. Wholesight. LC 77-95406. 30p. (Orig.). 1978. pap. 4.00 (*0-87574-217-3*) Pendle Hill.

Parker, Richard. Maple for Algebra. LC 96-44278. (Trade/Tech Math Ser.). 320p. (C). 1996. text, mass mkt. 20.95 incl. disk (*0-8273-7407-0*) Delmar.

— Maple for Basic Calculus. LC 97-4462. (Trade/Tech Math Ser.). 352p. (C). 1997. 19.95 incl. disk (*0-8273-7408-9*) Delmar.

— Maple for Trigonometry. LC 97-159703. (Trade/Tech Math Ser.). (C). 1997. pap. 20.95 (*0-8273-7409-7*) Thomson Learn.

— Mixed Signals: The Prospects for Global Television News. LC 95-19651. 105p. (C). 1995. pap. 7.95 (*0-87078-374-2*) Century Foundation.

— The Old Powder Line. (J). (gr. 4-7). 1990. 20.25 (*0-8446-6432-4*) Peter Smith.

— A Reader on Culture, Society & Sexuality. 1998. 79.95 (*1-85728-810-6*) UCL Pr Ltd.

***Parker, Richard.** A Reader on Culture, Society & Sexuality. 1998. 26.95 (*1-85728-811-4*) UCL Pr Ltd.

Parker, Richard. Troubleshooting DC & AC Circuits with Electronics Workbench. 52p. (C). 1994. mass mkt. 27.50 (*0-8273-6721-X*) Delmar.

— Wildflowers. LC 81-51068. (Illus.). 128p. (Orig.). 1986. pap. 7.95 (*0-89317-034-8*) Windward Pub.

Parker, Richard, et al, eds. Framing the Sexual Subject: The Politics of Gender, Sexuality, & Power. LC 99-38466. 281p. 2000. pap. 18.95 (*0-520-21838-8*, Pub. by U CA Pr) Cal Prin Full Svc.

— Framing the Sexual Subject: The Politics of Gender, Sexuality, & Power. LC 99-38466. 281p. 2000. 50.00 (*0-520-21836-1*, Pub. by U CA Pr) Cal Prin Full Svc.

Parker, Richard & Aggleton, Peter, eds. Culture, Society & Sexuality: A Reader. (Social Aspects of AIDS Ser.). 320p. 1997. 79.95 (*0-7484-0532-1*, Pub. by Tay Francis Ltd); pap. 24.95 (*0-7484-0533-X*, Pub. by Tay Francis Ltd) Taylor & Francis.

Parker, Richard & Daniel, Herbert. Sexuality, Politics & AIDS in Brazil: In Another World? (Social Aspects of AIDS Ser.). 196p. 1993. 85.00 (*0-7507-0135-8*, Falmer Pr); pap. 29.95 (*0-7507-0136-6*, Falmer Pr) Taylor & Francis.

Parker, Richard & Young, Kasey. Troubleshooting DC/AC Circuits with Electronic Workbench - Meade Version. 43.95 (*0-7608-1132-8*, Pub. by Delmar) Thomson Learn.

Parker, Richard, jt. auth. see Cordesman, Anthony H.

Parker, Richard, jt. auth. see Ensminger, M. E.

Parker, Richard, jt. auth. see Moore, Brooke N.

Parker, Richard, jt. auth. see Moore, Brooke Noel.

Parker, Richard A. Demotic Mathematical Papyri. LC 77-177501. (Brown Egyptological Studies: No. 7). 142p. reprint ed. pap. 44.10 (*0-8357-5549-5*, 203516800093) Bks Demand.

— Troubleshooting Electronic Devices with Electronics Workbench. 57p. (C). 1994. mass mkt. 27.50 (*0-8273-6760-0*) Delmar.

Parker, Richard A., ed. A Vienna Demotic Papyrus on Eclipes & Lunar-Omina. LC QB0019.P3. (Brown Egyptological Studies: No. 2). 76p. reprint ed. pap. 30.00 (*0-608-30071-3*, 202239800026) Bks Demand.

Parker, Richard A., jt. auth. see Rea, Louis M.

Parker, Richard B. North Africa: Regional Tensions & Strategic Concerns. LC 87-6954. 226p. 1987. 57.95 (*0-275-92773-3*, C2773, Praeger Pubs); pap. 16.95 (*0-275-92774-1*, B2774, Praeger Pubs) Greenwood.

— The Politics of Miscalculation in the Middle East. LC 92-23947. (Indiana Series in Arab & Islamic). 320p. (C). 1993. 46.95 (*0-253-34298-8*); pap. 18.95 (*0-253-20781-9*, MB-781) Ind U Pr.

Parker, Richard B., ed. The Six-Day War: A Retrospective. LC 95-43804. (Illus.). 400p. 1996. 49.95 (*0-8130-1383-6*) U Press Fla.

Parker, Richard B., et al. Islamic Monuments in Cairo: A Practical Guide. 4th ed. (Illus.). 352p. (C). 1993. 35.00 (*977-424-290-4*, Pub. by Am Univ Cairo Pr) Col U Pr.

Parker, Richard D. Here, the People Rule: A Constitutional Populist Manifesto. LC 94-2387. 144p. 1994. text 29.95 (*0-674-38925-5*, PARHER); pap. text 16.00 (*0-674-38926-3*, PARHEX) HUP.

Parker, Richard G. Beneath the Equator. LC 98-17428. (Illus.). 256p. (C). 1998. 75.00 (*0-415-91619-4*) Routledge.

— Beneath the Equator. LC 98-17428. (Illus.). 276p. (C). 1999. pap. 19.99 (*0-415-91620-8*) Routledge.

Parker, Richard G. & Gagnon, John H., eds. Conceiving Sexuality: Approaches to Sex Research in a Postmodern World. LC 94-17761. 320p. (C). 1994. pap. 23.99 (*0-415-90928-7*, B3848) Routledge.

Parker, Richard O. Mastering the THINK Class Library: Using Symantec C++ & Visual Architect. LC 95-218. 496p. (C). 1995. pap. text 29.95 (*0-201-48356-4*) Addison-Wesley.

P

An Asterisk (*) at the beginning of an entry indicates that the title is appearing for the first time.

Parker, Richard W. New Jersey in the Colonial Wars. Cutler, Timothy G., ed. (New Jersey in the French & Indian Wars Ser.: Vol. 1). 84p. 1997. 7.95 (*1-58057-020-8*, NJCW003B) Digital Antiq.

Parker, Rick. Aquaculture. (Agriculture Ser.). 1995. 12.75 (*0-8273-6455-5*) Delmar.

— Aquaculture Science. LC 94-34435. 672p. 1995. mass mkt. 58.95 (*0-8273-6454-7*) Delmar.

— Aquaculture Science CTB. 1995. teacher ed. 12.75 (*0-8273-7080-6*); lab manual ed. 17.00 (*0-8273-7079-2*) Delmar.

— Aquaculture Science CTB. (Agriculture Ser.). 1995. 105.95 (*0-8273-7078-4*) Delmar.

— Equine Science. (Agriculture Ser.). (C). 1997. pap. text, teacher ed., lab manual ed. 13.95 (*0-8273-8098-4*); pap. text, lab manual ed. 18.95 (*0-8273-8097-6*) Delmar.

— Equine Science. LC 96-35298. 1997. mass mkt. 55.95 (*0-8273-7136-5*) Delmar.

— Equine Science. (Agriculture Ser.). 1997. teacher ed. 13.95 (*0-8273-7137-3*, VNR) Wiley.

— Introduction to Plant Science. (Agriculture Ser.). 1997. teacher ed. 12.00 (*0-8273-7308-2*) Delmar.

— Introduction to Plant Science. LC 98-2707. (Agriculture Ser.). 720p. 1998. text 50.95 (*0-8273-7307-4*) Delmar.

Parker, Robert. Athenian Religion: A History. (Illus.). 396p. 1998. reprint ed. pap. text 26.00 (*0-19-815240-X*) OUP.

— Miasma: Pollution & Purification in Early Greek Religion. 432p. (C). 1996. reprint ed. pap. text 45.00 (*0-19-814742-2*) OUP.

Parker, Robert, ed. Adam Rener, Collected Works. (Gesamtausgaben - Collected Works: Vol. II, Pt. 2). 160p. 1975. lib. bdg. 7.00 (*0-912024-43-7*) Inst Mediaeval Mus.

Parker, Robert, et al. Weeds of the West. 5th ed. (Illus.). 630p. (C). 1998. pap. text 60.00 (*0-7881-4926-1*) DIANE Pub.

Parker, Robert A. A Yankee Saint: John Humphrey Noyes & the Oneida Community. 322p. 1993. reprint ed. lib. bdg. 89.00 (*0-7812-5314-4*) Rprt Serv.

Parker, Robert A. The Woman Who Fell from the Sky: The Iroquois Story of Creation. LC 92-5591. 32p. (J). (gr. k up). 1993. lib. bdg. 14.93 (*0-688-10681-1*, Wm Morrow) Morrow Avon.

***Parker, Robert Andrew.** The People with Five Fingers: A Native Californian Creation Tale. LC 99-28795. 32p. (J). (gr. k-3). 2000. 15.95 (*0-7614-5058-0*, Cav Child Bks) Marshall Cavendish.

Parker, Robert B. All Our Yesterdays. 480p. 1995. mass mkt. 6.99 (*0-440-22146-3*) Dell.

— A Catskill Eagle. 384p. 1986. mass mkt. 6.99 (*0-440-11132-3*) Dell.

— Ceremony. 224p. 1987. mass mkt. 6.99 (*0-440-10993-0*) Dell.

— Chance. 1997. mass mkt. 6.99 (*0-614-27721-3*) Berkley Pub.

— Chance. 336p. 1997. reprint ed. mass mkt. 6.99 (*0-425-15747-4*) Berkley Pub.

Parker, Robert B. Crimson Joy. 304p. 1989. mass mkt. 6.99 (*0-440-20343-0*) Dell.

Parker, Robert B. Double Deuce. 256p. 1993. mass mkt. 6.99 (*0-425-13793-7*) Berkley Pub.

— Early Autumn. 224p. 1992. mass mkt. 6.99 (*0-440-12214-7*) Dell.

— Early Autumn. large type ed. LC 91-37915. 285p. 1992. reprint ed. lib. bdg. 20.95 (*1-56054-286-1*) Thorndike Pr.

— Family Honor. LC 99-27488. 322p. 1999. 22.95 (*0-399-14566-4*, G P Putnam) Peng Put Young Read.

***Parker, Robert B.** Family Honor. large type ed. LC 99-52174. 1999. 26.95 (*1-56895-788-2*) Wheeler Pub.

Parker, Robert B. God Save the Child. 208p. 1987. mass mkt. 6.99 (*0-440-12899-4*) Dell.

— The Godwulf Manuscript. 208p. 1987. mass mkt. 6.99 (*0-440-12961-3*) Dell.

— The Godwulf Manuscript. 192p. 1994. reprint ed. lib. bdg. 29.95 (*1-56849-317-7*) Buccaneer Bks.

***Parker, Robert B.** Hugger Mugger. large type ed. LC 00-25380. 2000. 26.95 (*1-56895-865-X*) Wheeler Pub.

— Hugger Mugger: A Spenser Novel. LC 99-56105. 320p. 2000. 23.95 (*0-399-14587-7*) Putnam Pub Group.

— Hush Money. 336p. 2000. mass mkt. 7.50 (*0-425-17401-8*) Berkley Pub.

Parker, Robert B. Hush Money. LC 98-37344. 336p. 1999. 22.95 (*0-399-14458-7*) Putnam Pub Group.

***Parker, Robert B.** Hush Money. LC 99-15869. 1999. write for info. (*1-56895-739-4*) Wheeler Pub.

Parker, Robert B. The Judas Goat. 20.95 (*0-89190-371-2*) Amereon Ltd.

— The Judas Goat. 208p. 1992. mass mkt. 6.99 (*0-440-14196-6*) Dell.

— Looking for Rachel Wallace. 224p. 1987. mass mkt. 6.99 (*0-440-15316-6*) Dell.

— Love & Glory. 224p. 1984. mass mkt. 6.99 (*0-440-14629-1*) Dell.

— Mature Advertising: A Handbook of Effectiveness in Print. 1981. 19.95 (*0-201-05714-X*) Addison-Wesley.

— Mortal Stakes. 336p. 1987. mass mkt. 6.99 (*0-440-15758-7*) Dell.

— Mortal Stakes. LC 95-15248. 1995. Not sold separately (*0-614-32323-1*) Random.

— Mortal Stakes. large type ed. LC 92-23911. 290p. 1992. reprint ed. lib. bdg. 20.95 (*1-56054-314-0*) Thorndike Pr.

— Mortal Stakes. 1994. reprint ed. lib. bdg. 32.95 (*1-56849-316-9*) Buccaneer Bks.

— Night Passage. large type ed. LC 97-47199. (Compass Press Large Print Book Ser.). 1998. 26.95 (*1-56895-530-8*) Wheeler Pub.

— Night Passage. 336p. 1998. reprint ed. mass mkt. 6.99 (*0-515-12349-8*, Jove) Berkley Pub.

Parker, Robert B. Pale Kings & Princes. abr. ed. 1988. 14.95 incl. audio (*0-671-66073-X*) S&S Audio.

Parker, Robert B. Pale Kings & Princes. 320p. 1988. reprint ed. mass mkt. 6.99 (*0-440-20004-0*) Dell.

— Paper Doll. 288p. 1994. mass mkt. 6.99 (*0-425-14155-1*) Berkley Pub.

— Paper Doll. large type ed. LC 93-22854. 309p. 1993. lib. bdg. 22.95 (*0-7862-0003-0*) Thorndike Pr.

— Paper Doll. large type ed. LC 93-22854. 309p. 1994. lib. bdg. 14.95 (*0-7862-0004-9*) Thorndike Pr.

— Parker on Writing. 50p. 1985. 50.00 (*0-935716-34-3*) Lord John.

— Pastime. large type ed. (General Ser.). 269p. 1992. pap. 16.95 (*0-8161-5348-5*, G K Hall Lrg Type) Mac Lib Ref.

— Pastime. 1992. reprint ed. mass mkt. 6.99 (*0-425-13293-5*) Berkley Pub.

— Perchance to Dream. 288p. 1993. mass mkt. 6.99 (*0-425-13131-9*) Berkley Pub.

— Perchance to Dream: Robert B. Parker's sequel to Raymond Chandler's The big sleep. large type ed. LC 91-3776. 304p. 1991. reprint ed. lib. bdg. 21.95 (*1-56054-186-5*) Thorndike Pr.

— Perchance to Dream: Robert B. Parker's sequel to Raymond Chandler's The big sleep. large type ed. LC 91-3776. 304p. 1992. reprint ed. lib. bdg. 13.95 (*1-56054-977-7*) Thorndike Pr.

***Parker, Robert B.** Perish Twice. 320p. 2000. 23.95 (*0-399-14668-7*) Putnam Pub Group.

Parker, Robert B. Playmates. 1990. mass mkt. 6.99 (*0-425-12001-5*) Berkley Pub.

— Playmates. large type ed. LC 89-20218. 268p. 1990. lib. bdg. 11.95 (*0-89621-947-X*) Thorndike Pr.

— Promised Land. 224p. 1983. mass mkt. 6.99 (*0-440-17197-0*) Dell.

— A Savage Place. 192p. 1982. mass mkt. 6.99 (*0-440-18095-3*) Dell.

— A Savage Place: A Spenser Novel. LC 80-29370. 1981. 6.99 (*0-440-08094-0*) Dell.

— Small Vices. 338p. 1998. mass mkt. 6.99 (*0-425-16248-6*) Berkley Pub.

— Small Vices. LC 96-9827. (Spenser Thriller Ser.). 320p. (J). 1997. 21.95 (*0-399-14244-4*, G P Putnam) Peng Put Young Read.

— Small Vices. large type ed. LC 97-23289. (Wheeler Large Print Book Ser.). 1997. 25.95 (*1-56895-466-2*) Wheeler Pub.

— Sports Illustrated Training with Weights. (Orig.). 1990. pap. 11.95 (*1-56800-032-4*, Pub. by Sports Illus Bks) Natl Bk Netwk.

— Stardust. 1991. mass mkt. 6.99 (*0-425-12723-0*) Berkley Pub.

— Stardust. large type ed. LC 90-11276. 306p. 1991. lib. bdg. 13.95 (*1-56054-996-3*) Thorndike Pr.

— Sudden Mischief. LC 98-24005. 1998. 26.95 (*1-56895-569-3*) Wheeler Pub.

— Taming a Seahorse. 320p. 1987. mass mkt. 6.99 (*0-440-18841-5*) Dell.

— Thin Air. large type ed. LC 95-15712. 1995. 26.95 (*1-56895-212-0*) Wheeler Pub.

— Thin Air. 304p. 1996. reprint ed. mass mkt. 6.99 (*0-425-15290-1*) Berkley Pub.

— Three Complete Novels. pap. (*0-517-12435-1*) Random.

— Three Complete Novels, 3 vols. Incl. God Save the Child. LC 95-15248. 1995. Not sold separately Godwulf Manuscript. LC 95-15248. 1995. Not sold separately LC 95-15248. 560p. 1995. 13.99 (*0-517-14802-1*) Random.

— Trouble in Paradise. LC 98-7354. 336p. 1998. 22.95 (*0-399-14433-1*, G P Putnam) Peng Put Young Read.

***Parker, Robert B.** Trouble in Paradise. large type ed. 304p. 2000. write for info. (*0-7089-9137-8*) Ulverscroft.

Parker, Robert B. Trouble in Paradise. large type ed. LC 98-44848. 1998. 26.95 (*1-56895-681-9*) Wheeler Pub.

***Parker, Robert B.** Trouble in Paradise. 1999. reprint ed. mass mkt. 6.99 (*0-515-12649-7*, Jove) Berkley Pub.

Parker, Robert B. Valediction. 288p. 1987. mass mkt. 6.99 (*0-440-19246-3*) Dell.

— Walking Shadow. 304p. 1995. mass mkt. 6.99 (*0-425-14774-6*) Berkley Pub.

— Walking Shadow. large type ed. LC 94-19124. 1994. 25.95 (*1-56895-106-X*) Wheeler Pub.

— The Widening Gyre. 192p. 1992. mass mkt. 6.99 (*0-440-19535-7*) Dell.

— Wilderness. 256p. 1980. mass mkt. 6.99 (*0-440-19328-1*) Dell.

Parker, Robert B. & Cohen, Stan. Sudden Mischief. 306p. 1999. reprint ed. mass mkt. 6.99 (*0-425-16828-X*) Berkley Pub.

Parker, Robert B. & Penzler, Otto, eds. The Best American Mystery Stories, 1997. 357p. 1997. pap. 13.00 (*0-395-83583-6*) HM.

Parker, Robert B. & Vermette, Chuck. Boston: History in the Making. LC 99-19132. (Urban Tapestry Ser.). (Illus.). 1999. 49.95 (*1-881096-66-1*) Towery Pub.

Parker, Robert B., et al. Military Memoirs of Marlborough's Campaigns, 1702-1712. LC 98-19844. (Illus.). 276p. 1998. 34.95 (*1-85367-330-7*, Pub. by Greenhill Bks) Stackpole.

Parker, Robert B., jt. auth. see Chandler, Raymond.

Parker, Robert C., jt. auth. see Carlisle, John A.

Parker, Robert C., jt. auth. see Wang, Wallace.

Parker, Robert D. Absalom, Absalom! The Questioning of Fictions. (Twayne's Masterwork Studies: No. 76). 184p. (C). 1991. 25.95 (*0-8057-8071-8*, Twayne) Mac Lib Ref.

— Faulkner & the Novelistic Imagination. LC 84-2519. 176p. 1985. text 19.95 (*0-252-01155-4*) U of Ill Pr.

— The Unbeliever: The Poetry of Elizabeth Bishop. LC 87-34285. 184p. 1988. text 24.95 (*0-252-01509-6*) U of Ill Pr.

Parker, Robert E. Flesh Peddlers & Warm Bodies: The Temporary Help Industry & Its Workers. LC 93-24222. (Arnold & Caroline Rose Monograph Series of the American Sociological Association). 187p. (C). 1994. text 40.00 (*0-8135-2036-3*); pap. text 16.00 (*0-8135-2089-4*) Rutgers U Pr.

Parker, Robert H. Wines of Burgundy. 1990. 45.00 (*0-671-63378-3*) S&S Trade.

Parker, Robert H. & Harcourt, G. C., eds. Readings in the Concept & Measurement of Income. LC 75-87137. 410p. reprint ed. pap. 116.90 (*0-608-13045-1*, 2024513) Bks Demand.

Parker, Robert H., jt. auth. see Cooke, Terence E.

Parker, Robert H., jt. ed. see Carnegie, Garry D.

Parker, Robert H., ed. see Haverstock, Henry W.

Parker, Robert L. Carlos Chavez: A Guide to Research. Marco, Guy A., ed. LC 98-12202. (Composer Resource Manuals Ser.: Vol. 46). 180p. 1998. 46.00 (*0-8153-2087-6*) Garland.

— Geophysical Inverse Theory. LC 93-44915. 400p. 1994. text 45.00 (*0-691-03634-9*, Pub. by Princeton U Pr) Cal Prin Full Svc.

Parker, Robert L., ed. see American Gas Association Operating Section Compres.

Parker, Robert L., tr. see Niggli, Paul.

Parker, Robert M., Jr. Bordeaux. 3rd rev. ed. LC 98-28778. (Illus.). 1440p. 1998. 50.00 (*0-684-80015-2*) S&S Trade.

— Bordeaux: A Comprehensive Guide to the Wines Produced from 1961-1990. rev. ed. (Illus.). 700p. 1991. 40.00 (*0-671-67460-9*) S&S Trade.

— Parkers Wine Buyers Guide: Complete Easy to Use Reference on Recent Vintages Prices & Ratings for More. 5th ed. LC 99-47380. 1704p. 1999. 60.00 (*0-684-84184-3*); per. 30.00 (*0-684-80014-4*) S&S Trade.

— Parker's Wine Buyer's Guide: Third Edition. 3rd ed. Orig. Title: Wine Buyer's Guide. (Illus.). 1168p. 1995. 45.00 (*0-684-80282-1*, Fireside) S&S Trade Pap.

— Parker's Wine Buyer's Guide: Third Edition. 3rd rev. ed. Orig. Title: Wine Buyer's Guide. (Illus.). 960p. 1993. pap. 21.00 (*0-671-79914-2*, Fireside) S&S Trade Pap.

— Parker's Wine Buyer's Guide: Third Edition. 4th ed. LC 95-23983. Orig. Title: Wine Buyer's Guide. (Illus.). 1216p. 1995. per. 25.00 (*0-684-80283-X*) S&S Trade Pap.

— Wines of the Rhone Valley & Provence: The Definitive Guide. 2nd rev. ed. LC 97-5507. 1997. 40.00 (*0-684-80013-6*) S&S Trade.

Parker, Robert M. SoHo Guide, 1996-1997. 3rd ed. 186p. 1996. 15.00 (*1-886016-04-6*) SoHo Prtnship.

Parker, Robert P. Shih Tzu. (Illus.). 1997. pap. 9.95 (*0-7938-2326-9*, KW-084S) TFH Pubns.

Parker, Robert P. & Davis, Frances A., eds. Developing Literacy: Young Children's Use of Language. LC 82-20329. 195p. reprint ed. pap. 60.50 (*0-8357-8650-1*, 203509400092) Bks Demand.

Parker, Robert P. & Goodkin, Vera. The Consequences of Writing: Enhancing Learning in the Disciplines. LC 86-14712. 183p. (Orig.). (C). 1986. pap. text 21.00 (*0-86709-117-7*, 0117, Pub. by Boynton Cook Pubs) Heinemann.

Parker, Robert P., jt. auth. see Lash, William H., 3rd.

Parker, Roberta N. Slam Dunk: A Young Boy's Struggle with Attention Defecit Disorder. (Illus.). 55p. (Orig.). (J). (gr. 3-8). 1993. pap. 11.00 (*0-9621629-4-9*) Spec Pr FL.

Parker, Roberta N. & Parker, Harvey C. Como Pasar de Grado: La Lucha de un Adolescente Con ADD. (Illus.). 48p. (Orig.). (J). (gr. 4-11). 1994. pap. 11.00 (*0-9621629-7-3*) Spec Pr FL.

— Making the Grade: An Adolescent's Struggle with ADD. DiMatteo, Richard, tr. (Illus.). 48p. (Orig.). (J). (gr. 5-10). 1992. pap. 11.00 (*0-9621629-1-4*) Spec Pr FL.

Parker, Rodger D. Wellsprings of a Nation: America Before 1801. LC 77-72082. (Illus.). 1977. pap. 10.00 (*0-912296-13-5*) Am Antiquarian.

Parker, Roger. Freelance Graphics 96 for Windows 95 for Dummies. 352p. 1996. pap. 19.99 (*1-56884-236-8*) IDG Bks.

— Leonora's Last Act: Essays in Verdian Discourse. LC 97-5487. 208p. 1997. text 32.50 (*0-691-01557-0*, Pub. by Princeton U Pr) Cal Prin Full Svc.

— Mastering the Power of Persuasion. 300p. 1990. pap. 28.00 (*1-55623-243-8*, Irwn Prfssnl) McGraw-Hill Prof.

— Roger Parker's One Minute Designer. (Illus.). 288p. (Orig.). 1993. 24.95 (*1-56529-216-2*) Que.

Parker, Roger, ed. The Oxford History of Opera. (Illus.). 400p. 1996. reprint ed. pap. 15.95 (*0-19-284028-2*) OUP.

— The Oxford Illustrated History of Opera. (Illus.). 556p. 1995. 49.95 (*0-19-816282-0*) OUP.

Parker, Roger, jt. auth. see Wang, Wallace.

Parker, Roger, jt. ed. see Abbate, Carolyn.

Parker, Roger, jt. ed. see Groos, Arthur.

Parker, Roger, ed. see Verdi, Giuseppe.

Parker, Roger, tr. see Petrobelli, Pierluigi.

Parker, Roger C. Desktop Publishing & Design for Dummies. (For Dummies Ser.). 384p. 1995. pap. 19.99 (*1-56884-234-1*) IDG Bks.

— Harvard Graphics 2 for Windows for Dummies. LC 94-75651. 350p. 1994. pap. 19.95 (*1-56884-092-6*) IDG Bks.

***Parker, Roger C.** Looking Good in Print. 3rd ed. 400p. 2000. pap. text 34.99 (*1-57610-616-0*) Coriolis Grp.

Parker, Roger C. Mastering the Printed Page: Electronic Publishing with Quark XPress. (Illus.). 224p. 1988. 29.95 (*0-8306-0223-2*, 3023); pap. 19.95 (*0-8306-9323-8*) McGraw-Hill Prof.

Parker, Roger C. Microsoft Office for Windows 95 for Dummies. 362p. 1995. pap. 19.99 (*1-56884-917-6*) IDG Bks.

Parker, Roger C. Microsoft Office X for Dummies Quick Reference. 224p. 1996. spiral bd. 12.99 (*1-56884-978-8*) IDG Bks.

— Parker's One Minute Designer. LC 97-37145. 304p. 1997. pap. 24.95 (*1-55828-593-8*, MIS Pr) IDG Bks.

***Parker, Roger C.** Publisher 2000 Professional Results. (Illus.). 448p. 2000. pap. 29.99 (*0-07-212298-6*) McGrw-H Intl.

Parker, Roger C. Roger C. Parker's Guide to Web Content & Design. LC 97-42048. (Illus.). 272p. 1997. pap. 39.95 (*1-55828-553-9*, MIS Pr) IDG Bks.

— Roger C. Parker's One Minute Web. (Illus.). 1998. 29.95 (*1-55828-602-0*, MIS Pr) IDG Bks.

***Parker, Roger C.** Streetwise Relationship Marketing on the Internet. 352p. 2000. pap. 17.95 (*1-58062-255-0*) Adams Media.

Parker, Roger C. Using Microsoft Publisher 2000. 1999. pap. text 39.99 (*0-7897-1970-3*) Que.

— Web Design & Desktop Publishing for Dummies. 2nd ed. LC 97-70742. 400p. 1997. pap. 19.99 (*0-7645-0139-9*) IDG Bks.

Parker, Roger C. & Holzgang, David A. WordPerfect 6 Secrets. 650p. 1993. pap. 39.95 (*1-56884-040-3*) IDG Bks.

Parker, Roger C., jt. auth. see Tyson, Eric.

Parker, Rolland S. Effective Decisions & Emotional Fulfillment. LC 76-54652. 308p. 1977. text 36.95 (*0-88229-303-6*) Burnham Inc.

Parker, Rollin J. Advances in Permanent Magnetism. LC 89-16461. 352p. 1990. 179.00 (*0-471-82293-0*) Wiley.

Parker, Ron. Under the Influence: A Drama about Co-Dependency. (Illus.). 42p. 1993. pap. 4.25 (*0-88680-378-0*) I E Clark.

Parker, Ronald, et al. Administrative Law. (Illus.). 245p. 1990. pap. 35.00 (*0-685-14620-0*) NJ Inst CLE.

Parker, Ronald B., jt. auth. see Ensminger, M. E.

Parker, Ronald E. Do I Belong in Seminary? LC 98-72483. 1998. pap. 10.95 (*1-56699-201-X*, AL192) Alban Inst.

Parker, Ronald L., et al. Small Enterprises Adjusting to Liberalization in Five African Contries. LC 95-191. (Discussion Papers: Africa Technical Department Ser.: Vol. 271). 106p. 1995. pap. 22.00 (*0-8213-3154-X*, 13154) World Bank.

Parker, Rosika. The Subversive Stitch: Embroidery & the Making of the Feminine. 247p. (C). 1989. pap. 19.99 (*0-415-90206-1*, A3787) Routledge.

Parker, Rowland. The Common Stream: Two Thousand Years of the English Village. LC 93-34738. 252p. 1994. reprint ed. pap. 12.00 (*0-89733-391-8*) Academy Chi Pubs.

Parker, Rowland & Rubinstein, Michael. Malta's Ancient Temples & Ruts. (Institute for Cultural Research Monograph: No. 26). (Illus.). 70p. (Orig.). 1988. pap. 10.00 (*0-904674-14-2*, Pub. by Octagon Pr) ISHK.

Parker, Roy, Jr. Cumberland County: A Brief History. (Illus.). xi, 158p. (Orig.). 1990. pap. 10.00 (*0-86526-243-8*) NC Archives.

Parker, Roy. Safeguarding Standards. (C). 1990. 45.00 (*0-7855-0066-9*, Pub. by Natl Inst Soc Work); pap. 30.00 (*0-902789-68-6*, Pub. by Natl Inst Soc Work) St Mut.

Parker, Roy H. The Final Four. LC 81-69265. 259p. 1981. 14.95 (*0-941974-00-6*) Baranski Pub Co.

— The Final Four. rev. ed. 1988. pap. 3.95 (*0-944003-00-1*) Faction Pub.

Parker, Rozsika & Pollack, Griselda, eds. Framing Feminism: Art & the Women's Movement, 1970-1985. (Illus.). 360p. 1987. pap. text 21.50 (*0-86358-179-X*) NYU Pr.

Parker, Rozsika & Pollock, Griselda. Old Mistresses: Women, Art & Ideology. 1981. pap. 19.50 (*0-86358-185-4*, Pub. by Rivers Oram) NYU Pr.

Parker, Ruth E. Mathematical Power: Lessons from a Classroom. LC 92-46283. 48p. 1993. pap. text 19.00 (*0-435-08339-2*, 08339) Heinemann.

Parker, S. McGraw-Hill Dictionary of Scientific & Technical Terms. 5th ed. (Illus.). 2200p. 1994. 150.00 (*0-07-042333-4*) McGraw.

— Reflective Teach Postmodern World: A Manifesto for Education in Postmodernity. LC 96-28699. 1997. pap. 31.95 (*0-335-19585-7*) OpUniv Pr.

Parker, Salina, tr. see Tekin, Latife & Christie, Ruth.

Parker, Sally, jt. auth. see Mason, Patience.

Parker, Samanthe. Star Vision. (Illus.). 64p. (Orig.). 1992. pap. 4.95 (*0-910241-00-7*) ShaunTar Ent.

Parker, Sammy, jt. auth. see Morris, Libby V.

Parker, Samuel. A Free & Impartial Censure of the Platonick Philosophie: Being a Letter Written to His Much Honoured Friend Mr. N. B. rev. ed. LC 83-46032. (Scientific Awakening in the Restoration Ser.: No. 3). 144p. 1985. reprint ed. 45.00 (*0-404-63303-X*) AMS Pr.

— Journal of Exploring Tour Etc. To Oregon in 1835, '36 & '37. 1976. reprint ed. 15.00 (*0-87018-046-0*) Ross.

***Parker, Sandra.** After the Western Reserve: The Ohio Fiction of Jessie Brown Pounds. LC 98-48224. 1999. 49.95 (*0-87972-787-X*) Bowling Green Univ Popular Press.

Parker, Sandra. Home Material: Ohio's Nineteenth-Century Regional Women's Fiction. LC 98-11977. 240p. 1998. 49.95 (*0-87972-765-9*); pap. 24.95 (*0-87972-766-7*) Bowling Green Univ Popular Press.

Parker, Sandra D. & Will, Carol. Activities for the Elderly, Vol. 2: A Guide to Working with Residents with Significant Physical & Cognitive Disabilities. (Activities Ser.). 170p. 1993. pap. 30.00 (*1-882883-01-2*, 171) Idyll Arbor.

Parker, Sandra D., et al. Activities for the Elderly, Vol. 1: A Guide to Quality Programming. (Activities Ser.). 171p. 1993. reprint ed. pap. 30.00 (*1-882883-00-4*, 170) Idyll Arbor.

Parker, Sandra V. Richmond's Civil War Prisons. (Virginia Civil War Battles & Leaders Ser.). (Illus.). 101p. 1990. 19.95 (*0-930919-97-1*) H E Howard.

Parker, Sara, jt. auth. see Smith, Jewell.

P

An Asterisk (*) at the beginning of an entry indicates that the title is appearing for the first time.

Parker School of Foreign & Comparative Law, Columb. International Commercial Arbitration & the Courts: A Source Guide. 472p. (C). 1989. lib. bdg. 150.00 (1-57823-016-0) Juris Pubng.

Parker School of Foreign & Comparative Law, Columb, ed. Guides to International Arbitration & Arbitrators, 1992, 7 vols. 1992. lib. bdg. 125.00 (1-57823-010-1) Juris Pubng.

Parker, Sharon & Wall, Toby D. Job & Work Design: Organizing Work to Promote Well-Being & Effectiveness. LC 98-8932. (Advanced Topics in Organizational Behavior Ser.). 1998. 38.00 (0-7619-0419-0); pap. write for info. (0-7619-0420-4) Sage.

***Parker, Shonda.** Mommy Diagnostics: The Naturally Healthy Family's Guide to Herbs & Whole Foods for Health. (Illus.). 298p. 2000. pap. 14.99 (1-929125-11-9, Pub. by Loyal Pubng) BookWorld.

Parker, Shonda. The Naturally Healthy Pregnancy: An Essential Guide of Nutritional & Botanical Medicine for the Childbearing Years. LC 98-96432. 323 p. 1998. write for info. (1-892513-10-2) Naturally Healthy.

***Parker, Shonda.** The Naturally Healthy Pregnancy: The Essential Guide to Nutritional & Botanical Medicine for the Child Bearing Years. (Illus.). 323p. 2000. pap. 14.99 (1-929125-12-7, Pub. by Loyal Pubng) BookWorld.

Parker, Siglinda, jt. auth. see Scoglietti, Constance.

Parker, Simon, jt. ed. see Gundle, Stephen.

Parker, Simon B. Stories in Scripture & Inscriptions: Comparative Studies on Narratives in Northwest Semitic Inscriptions & the Hebrew Bible. LC 96-52802. 208p. (C). 1997. text 42.00 (0-19-511620-8) OUP.

***Parker, Stamford.** The Words That Reshaped America: FDR. 256p. 2000. pap. 13.00 (0-380-80070-5) Morrow Avon.

Parker, Stan, jt. auth. see Aungles, Stan.

Parker, Star. Keep Your Hard Earned Money. LC 99-187459. 1998. per. 14.00 (0-671-01530-3, PB Trade Paper) PB.

Parker, Star & Benet, Lorenzo. Pimps, Whores & Welfare Brats. 1998. per. 14.00 (0-671-53466-1, PB Trade Paper) PB.

Parker, Stephen. The Craft of Writing. 245p. 1993. pap. 29.00 (1-85396-200-7, Pub. by P Chapman) Taylor & Francis.

***Parker, Stephen.** Fantastic Facts -the Body. 64p. (J). 2000. pap. 6.95 (1-84215-084-7) Anness Pub.

Parker, Stephen. Peter Huchel: A Literary Life in 20th-Century Germany. (British & Irish Studies in German Language & Literature: Vol. 15). 617p. 1998. 63.95 (3-906760-55-3) P Lang.

— Peter Huchel: A Literary Life in 20th-Century Germany. LC 98-22312. (British & Irish Studies in German Language & Literature: No. 15). 617p. 1998. pap. text 63.95 (0-8204-4202-X) P Lang Pubng.

Parker, Stephen & Sampford, Charles, eds. Legal Ethics & Legal Practice: Contemporary Issues. 278p. 1996. text 69.00 (0-19-825945-X) OUP.

Parker, Stephen, et al. Australian Family Law in Context: Commentary & Materials. 938p. 1994. pap. 95.00 (0-455-21222-8, Pub. by LawBk Co) Gaunt.

Parker, Stephen, jt. auth. see Bottomley, Stephen.

Parker, Stephen, jt. ed. see Hayhoe, Mike.

Parker, Stephen E. Led by the Spirit: Toward a Practical Theology of Pentecostal Discernment & Decision Making. LC 96-159687. (JPT Supplement Ser.: No. 7). 227p. 1996. pap. 21.95 (1-85075-746-1, Pub. by Sheffield Acad) CUP Services.

Parker, Stephen J. The Achievements of Vladimir Nabokov: Essays, Studies, Reminiscences & Stories. Gibian, George, ed. 256p. (Orig.). (C). 1984. pap. text 6.95 (0-86731-079-0) Cornell CIS RDC.

Parker, Stephen J., jt. auth. see Parker, Fan.

Parker, Steve. Airplanes. (What If...Ser.). (Illus.). 32p. (J). (gr. 4-6). 1995. pap. 5.95 (1-56294-946-2, Copper Beech Bks); lib. bdg. 19.90 (1-56294-911-X, Copper Beech Bks) Millbrook Pr.

— Airplanes. LC 95-23981. (What If--Ser.). 1995. 11.15 (0-606-10045-8, Pub. by Turtleback) Demco.

— Alarming Animals. (Illus.). 32p. (J). (gr. 4-7). 1995. pap. text 5.95 (0-8114-6332-X) Raintree Steck-V.

— Animals Can Think? LC 94-19405. (How Do We Know? Ser.). (Illus.). 48p. (J). (gr. 4-8). 1995. lib. bdg. 24.26 (0-8114-3882-1) Raintree Steck-V.

***Parker, Steve.** Astronomy. (Factfinders Ser.). (Illus.). 256p. (gr. 4-7). 1999. 9.98 (0-7651-1034-2) Smithmark.

Parker, Steve. Beginner's Guide to Animal Autopsy: A Hands-In Approach to Zoology. LC 97-10032. (Illus.). 48p. (YA). (gr. 5 up). 1997. pap. 8.95 (0-7613-0627-7, Copper Beech Bks); lib. bdg. 23.90 (0-7613-0702-8, Copper Beech Bks) Millbrook Pr.

— Blood. LC 97-1254. (Look at Your Body! Ser.). (Illus.). 31p. (J). (gr. 3-6). 1997. lib. bdg. 20.90 (0-7613-0611-0, Copper Beech Bks) Millbrook Pr.

— The Body Atlas. LC 92-54307. (Illus.). 64p. (J). (gr. 4-7). 1993. 19.95 (1-56458-224-8) DK Pub Inc.

— Brain & Nerves. LC 97-31925. (Look at Your Body Ser.). (Illus.). 32p. (J). (gr. 4-6). 1998. 20.90 (0-7613-0812-1, Copper Beech Bks) Millbrook Pr.

— The Brain & the Nervous System. LC 96-36804. (Human Body Ser.). 1997. write for info. (0-08-172480-2) Elsevier.

— The Brain & the Nervous System. LC 96-36804. (Human Body Ser.). (Illus.). 48p. (J). (gr. 5-10). 1997. lib. bdg. 25.69 (0-8172-4802-1) Raintree Steck-V.

— Camcorder. (Collins Pocket Reference Ser.). 1996. pap. 14.00 (0-00-412779-X) Collins.

— Computers. LC 96-31189. (20th Century Inventions Ser.). (Illus.). 48p. (J). (gr. 4-9). 1997. lib. bdg. 24.26 (0-8172-4811-0) Raintree Steck-V.

— Deserts. LC 97-20772. (Take 5 Geography Ser.). 32p. (J). 1998. 19.00 (0-531-14460-7) Watts.

— Digestion. LC 97-10097. (Look at Your Body Ser.). (Illus.). 32p. (J). (gr. 4-6). 1997. lib. bdg. 20.90 (0-7613-0603-X, Copper Beech Bks) Millbrook Pr.

— Dinosaurs & How They Lived. LC 91-60143. (See & Explore Library). (Illus.). 64p. (J). (gr. 3 up). 1991. 12.95 (1-879431-13-0) DK Pub Inc.

— The Earth. (What If...Ser.). (Illus.). 32p. (J). (gr. 4-6). 1995. pap. 5.95 (1-56294-948-9, Copper Beech Bks); lib. bdg. 19.90 (1-56294-913-6, Copper Beech Bks) Millbrook Pr.

— Earth. LC 95-12138. (What If--Ser.). 1995. 11.15 (0-606-10049-0, Pub. by Turtleback) Demco.

— The Earth & How It Works. LC 92-54317. (See & Explore Library). (Illus.). 64p. (YA). (gr. 3 up). 1993. 12.95 (1-56458-235-3) DK Pub Inc.

***Parker, Steve.** Earth's Resources. (Illus.). (J). 2000. 27.12 (0-7398-1009-X) Raintree Steck-V.

Parker, Steve. Electricity. LC 92-6926. (Eyewitness Books). (Illus.). 64p. (J). (gr. 4-7). 1992. 15.95 (1-879431-82-3) DK Pub Inc.

***Parker, Steve.** Electricty & Magnetism. (Illus.). (J). 2000. 27.12 (0-7398-1010-3) Raintree Steck-V.

Parker, Steve. 53 1/2 Things that Changed the World & Some that Didn't. 1995. 13.15 (0-606-08960-8, Pub. by Turtleback) Demco.

***Parker, Steve.** Fish. (Eyewitness Books). (Illus.). (J). (gr. 4-7). 2000. 19.99 (0-7894-6569-8) DK Pub Inc.

— Fish. (Eyewitness Books). (J). (gr. 4-7). 2000. 15.95 (0-7894-5810-1) DK Pub Inc.

Parker, Steve. Flight & Flying Machines. LC 92-54316. (See & Explore Library). (Illus.). 64p. (J). (gr. 3-7). 1993. 12.95 (1-56458-236-1) DK Pub Inc.

— Frankenstein. (In the Footsteps of...Ser.). (Illus.). 40p. (J). (gr. 4-6). 1995. lib. bdg. 21.90 (1-56294-647-1, Copper Beech Bks) Millbrook Pr.

— Frankenstein. LC 95-11523. 1995. 12.15 (0-606-09461-X, Pub. by Turtleback) Demco.

— Giraffes. LC 95-40838. (What If...Ser.). (Illus.). 32p. (J). (gr. 4-6). 1996. lib. bdg. 19.90 (0-7613-0457-6, Copper Beech Bks) Millbrook Pr.

— Giraffes. LC 95-50313. (What If--Ser.). 1996. 11.15 (0-606-10046-6, Pub. by Turtleback) Demco.

— High in the Sky. LC 96-34408. (Supersmarts ser.). (Illus.). 24p. (J). (gr. 2-5). 1998. pap. text 4.99 (0-7636-0631-6) Candlewick Pr.

— High in the Sky: Flying Machines. LC 96-34408. (SuperSmarts Ser.). (Illus.). 24p. (J). (gr. 2-5). 1997. 11.99 (0-7636-0128-4) Candlewick Pr.

— How the Body Works: 100 Ways Parents & Kids Can Share the Miracle of the Human Body. LC 93-31689. (Illus.). 192p. 1994. 24.00 (0-89577-575-1, Pub. by RD Assn) Penguin Putnam.

— The Human Body. (What If...Ser.). (Illus.). 32p. (J). (gr. 4-6). 1995. pap. 5.95 (1-56294-949-7, Copper Beech Bks); lib. bdg. 19.90 (1-56294-914-4, Copper Beech Bks) Millbrook Pr.

— The Human Body. LC 95-53787. (Nature Company Discoveries Library). (Illus.). 64p. (J). (gr. 4-7). 1999. 16.00 (0-7835-4802-8) Time-Life.

— Human Body. LC 93-31076. (Eyewitness Explorers Ser.). (Illus.). 64p. (J). (gr. 4-7). 1994. 9.95 (1-56458-322-8) DK Pub Inc.

— Human Body. LC 95-12139. (What If--Ser.). 1995. 11.15 (0-606-10050-4, Pub. by Turtleback) Demco.

***Parker, Steve.** I Can Experiment: Fun-to-Do Simple Science Projects for Young Children. (Show Me How Ser.). 1999. write for info. (1-84038-281-3) Hermes Hse.

Parker, Steve. I Wonder Why Tunnels Are Round: And Other Questions about Building. LC 94-45113. (I Wonder Why Ser.). (Illus.). (J). (gr. k-4). 1995. 11.95 (1-85697-580-0) LKC.

— Identifying Dinosaurs. 80p. 1997. 7.98 (0-7858-0775-6) Bk Sales Inc.

— It's a Frog's Life: My Story of Life in a Pond. LC 98-38271. (Snappy Fun Bks.: Vol. 8). (Illus.). 32p. (J). (gr. 4-6). 1999. 9.99 (1-57584-250-5, Pub. by Rdrs Digest) Random.

***Parker, Steve.** Light & Sound. (Illus.). (J). 2000. 27.12 (0-7398-1011-1) Raintree Steck-V.

Parker, Steve. Lungs. LC 96-7961. (Look at Your Body Ser.). (Illus.). 32p. (J). (gr. 4-6). 1996. lib. bdg. 20.90 (0-7613-0530-0, Copper Beech Bks) Millbrook Pr.

— The Lungs & Respiratory System. LC 96-43516. (Human Body Ser.). (Illus.). 48p. (J). (gr. 5-10). 1997. lib. bdg. 25.68 (0-8172-4803-X) Raintree Steck-V.

— Magnets. (Learn about Ser.). (Illus.). 64p. (J). (gr. 3-7). 1997. 7.95 (1-85967-179-9, Lorenz Bks) Anness Pub.

— Making Tracks. LC 96-38759. (Supersmarts Ser.). (Illus.). 24p. (J). (gr. 2-5). 1998. pap. text 4.99 (0-7636-0628-6) Candlewick Pr.

— Making Tracks: Land Machines. LC 96-38759. (SuperSmarts Ser.). 24p. (J). (gr. 2-5). 1997. 11.99 (0-7636-0129-2) Candlewick Pr.

— Mamiferos. (SPA.). Date not set. 14.95 (84-372-3714-9) Santillana.

***Parker, Steve.** Mammal. (Eyewitness Books). (Illus.). (J). (gr. 4-7). 2000. 19.99 (0-7894-6560-4) DK Pub Inc.

— Mammal. (Eyewitness Books). (J). (gr. 4-7). 2000. 15.95 (0-7894-5818-7) DK Pub Inc.

Parker, Steve. Marie Curie & Radium. LC 92-3616. (Science Discoveries Ser.). (Illus.). 32p. (J). (gr. 3-7). 1992. pap. 5.95 (0-06-446143-2, HarpTrophy) HarpC Child Bks.

— Medical Advances. LC 97-17985. (20th Century Inventions Ser.). 1998. lib. bdg. 24.26 (0-8172-4896-X) Raintree Steck-V.

— Medicine. LC 94-34860. (Eyewitness Books). (Illus.). 64p. (J). (gr. 4-7). 1995. 15.95 (1-56458-882-3) DK Pub Inc.

***Parker, Steve.** Medicine. (Eyewitness Books). 64p. (J). (gr. 4-7). 2000. 15.95 (0-7894-5580-3, D K Ink) DK Pub Inc.

Parker, Steve. Muscles. LC 97-8023. (Look at Your Body! Ser.). (Illus.). 32p. (J). (gr. 4-6). 1997. lib. bdg. 20.90 (0-7613-0612-9, Copper Beech Bks) Millbrook Pr.

— Ocean Life. 1995. 7.98 (0-7858-0418-8) Bk Sales Inc.

— Los Peces. 1995. 18.95 (84-372-3729-7) Santillana.

***Parker, Steve.** Pond & River. (Eyewitness Books). (Illus.). (J). (gr. 4-7). 2000. 19.99 (0-7894-6555-8) DK Pub Inc.

— Pond & River. (Eyewitness Books). (J). (gr. 4-7). 2000. 15.95 (0-7894-5838-1) DK Pub Inc.

Parker, Steve. Practical Paleontologist. Bernor, Raymond L., ed. (Illus.). 160p. 1991. per. 15.00 (0-671-69307-7, Fireside) S&S Trade Pap.

— Prehistoric Life. LC 92-54452. (See & Explore Library). (Illus.). 64p. (J). (gr. 3-7). 1993. 12.95 (1-56458-238-8) DK Pub Inc.

— Professor Protein's Book of F. H. H. A. R. T. (Illus.). 48p. 1996. pap. 6.95 (0-7613-0500-9, Copper Beech Bks) Millbrook Pr.

— Professor Protein's Fitness, Health, Hygiene & Relaxation Tonic. (Illus.). 48p. (YA). (gr. 5 up). 1996. lib. bdg. 23.90 (0-7613-0494-0, Copper Beech Bks) Millbrook Pr.

— Reproduction & Growth. LC 97-43128. (Look at Your Body Ser.). (Illus.). 32p. (J). (gr. 4-6). 1998. lib. bdg. 20.90 (0-7613-0813-X, Copper Beech Bks) Millbrook Pr.

— Satellites. LC 96-27730. (20th Century Inventions Ser.). (Illus.). 48p. (J). (gr. 4-9). 1997. lib. bdg. 24.26 (0-8172-4810-2) Raintree Steck-V.

— Satellites. LC 98-2730. (Future Tech Ser.). (J). 1998. 17.95 (0-382-39957-9); pap. 8.95 (0-382-39958-7) Silver Burdett Pr.

— Science Discoveries, 12 bks. Incl. Albert Einstein & the Laws of Relativity. LC 94-43924. (Illus.). 32p. (J). (gr. 3 up). 1995. lib. bdg. 15.95 (0-7910-3003-2); Alexander Graham Bell & the Telephone. LC 94-8263. (Illus.). 32p. (J). (gr. 3 up). 1995. lib. bdg. 15.95 (0-7910-3004-0); Aristotle & Scientific Thought. (Illus.). 32p. (J). (gr. 3 up). 1995. lib. bdg. 15.95 (0-7910-3005-9); Benjamin Franklin & Electricity. LC 94-25255. (Illus.). 32p. (J). (gr. 3 up). 1995. lib. bdg. 15.95 (0-7910-3006-7); Charles Darwin & Evolution. LC 94-20656. (Illus.). 32p. (J). (gr. 3 up). 1995. lib. bdg. 15.95 (0-7910-3007-5); Galileo & the Universe. LC 94-20659. (Illus.). 32p. (J). (gr. 3 up). 1995. lib. bdg. 15.95 (0-7910-3008-3); Guglielmo Marconi & Radio. LC 94-8253. (Illus.). 32p. (J). (gr. 3 up). 1995. lib. bdg. 15.95 (0-7910-3009-1); Isaac Newton & Gravity. LC 94-8260. (Illus.). 32p. (J). (gr. 3 up). 1995. lib. bdg. 15.95 (0-7910-3010-5); Louis Pasteur & Germs. LC 94-8262. (Illus.). 32p. (J). (gr. 3 up). 1995. lib. bdg. 15.95 (0-7910-3002-4); Marie Curie & Radium. LC 94-20657. (Illus.). 32p. (J). (gr. 3 up). 1995. lib. bdg. 15.95 (0-7910-3011-3); Thomas Edison & Electricity. LC 94-20658. (Illus.). 32p. (J). (gr. 3 up). 1995. lib. bdg. 15.95 (0-7910-3012-1); Wright Brothers & Aviation. LC 94-25254. (Illus.). 32p. (J). (gr. 3 up). 1995. lib. bdg. 15.95 (0-7910-3013-X); 1995. Set pap. text 179.40 (0-7910-3001-6) Chelsea Hse.

— Science Works!, 4 bks. Incl. Energy. Roberts, Steve & Spong, Clive. LC 97-10475. 48p. (J). (gr. 4 up). 1997. lib. bdg. 22.60 (0-8368-1962-4); Light. Lyons, Chris. LC 97-10476. 48p. (J). (gr. 4 up). 1997. lib. bdg. 22.60 (0-8368-1963-2); Numbers. LC 97-10477. 48p. (J). (gr. 4 up). 1997. lib. bdg. 22.60 (0-8368-1964-0); Sound. LC 97-11525. 48p. (J). (gr. 4 up). 1997. lib. bdg. 22.60 (0-8368-1965-9); (J). Set lib. bdg. 85.07 (0-8368-1961-6) Gareth Stevens Inc.

***Parker, Steve.** Seashore. (Eyewitness Books). (Illus.). (J). (gr. 4-7). 2000. 19.99 (0-7894-6564-7) DK Pub Inc.

— Seashore. (Eyewitness Books). (J). (gr. 4-7). 2000. 15.95 (0-7894-5826-8) DK Pub Inc.

Parker, Steve. Seashore. LC 88-27173. (Eyewitness Books). (Illus.). 64p. (J). (gr. 5 up). 1989. lib. bdg. 18.99 (0-394-92254-9, Pub. by Knopf Bks Yng Read) Random.

— Seashore: A Fact Finder Book. (Illus.). 48p. (J). (gr. 7-9). 1992. pap. 8.95 (0-563-34411-3, BBC-Parkwest) Parkwest Pubns.

— Senses. LC 97-10080. (Look at Your Body Ser.). (Illus.). 32p. (J). (gr. 4-6). 1997. lib. bdg. 20.90 (0-7613-0602-1, Copper Beech Bks) Millbrook Pr.

— The Shark. (Illus.). 192p. 1997. 19.98 (0-7858-0819-1) Bk Sales Inc.

— Sharks. (What If...Ser.). (Illus.). 32p. (J). (gr. 4-6). 1996. pap. 6.95 (0-7613-0471-1, Copper Beech Bks); lib. bdg. 19.90 (0-7613-0456-8, Copper Beech Bks) Millbrook Pr.

— Sharks. LC 95-50311. (What If--Ser.). 1996. 11.15 (0-606-10047-4, Pub. by Turtleback) Demco.

— Shocking, Slimy, Stinky, Shiny Science Experiments. LC 99-162341. (Illus.). 96p. (J). (gr. 3-7). 1998. 19.95 (0-8069-6295-X) Sterling.

***Parker, Steve.** Skeleton. (Eyewitness Books). (Illus.). (J). (gr. 4-7). 2000. 19.99 (0-7894-6552-3) DK Pub Inc.

— Skeleton. (Eyewitness Books). (J). (gr. 4-7). 2000. 15.95 (0-7894-5834-9) DK Pub Inc.

Parker, Steve. Skeleton. LC 87-26314. (Eyewitness Books). (Illus.). 64p. (J). (gr. 5 up). 1988. lib. bdg. 20.99 (0-394-99620-8, Pub. by Knopf Bks Yng Read) Random.

— The Skeleton. LC 96-7962. (Look at Your Body Ser.). (Illus.). 32p. (J). (gr. 4-6). 1996. lib. bdg. 20.90 (0-7613-0529-7, Copper Beech Bks) Millbrook Pr.

— Space. LC 95-23980. (What If...Ser.). (Illus.). 32p. (J). (gr. 4-6). 1995. pap. 6.95 (1-56294-947-0, Copper Beech Bks); lib. bdg. 19.90 (1-56294-912-8, Copper Beech Bks) Millbrook Pr.

— Space. LC 95-23980. 1995. 12.15 (0-606-10048-2, Pub. by Turtleback) Demco.

— The Story of Dinosaurs. LC 91-39007. (Story of Ser.). (Illus.). 32p. (J). (gr. 1-4). 1997. pap. 4.95 (0-8167-2708-2) Troll Communs.

— The Story of Dinosaurs. LC 91-39007. (Story of Ser.). (Illus.). 32p. (J). (gr. 1-4). 1997. lib. bdg. 18.60 (0-8167-2707-4) Troll Communs.

— Thomas Edison & Electricity. LC 92-6805. (Science Discoveries Ser.). (Illus.). 32p. (J). (gr. 3-7). 1992. 14.00 (0-06-020859-7); pap. 5.95 (0-06-446144-0, HarpTrophy) HarpC Child Bks.

— Waste, Recycling & Re-Use. LC 97-29907. (Protecting Our Planet Ser.). (Illus.). 48p. (J). (gr. 4-7). 1998. 25.69 (0-8172-4940-0) Raintree Steck-V.

— Whales & Dolphins. LC 93-38518. (Look into Nature Ser.). (Illus.). 60p. (J). (gr. 3-6). 1994. 16.95 (0-87156-465-3, Pub. by Sierra Club Childrens) Little.

— What's Inside Airplanes? LC 94-48544. (What's Inside? Ser.). (Illus.). 44p. (YA). (gr. 3 up). 1995. lib. bdg. 17.95 (0-87226-394-0, P Bedrick Books) NTC Contemp Pub Co.

— What's Inside Buildings? LC 94-48543. (What's Inside? Ser.). (Illus.). 44p. (YA). (gr. 3 up). 1995. lib. bdg. 17.95 (0-87226-395-9, P Bedrick Books) NTC Contemp Pub Co.

Parker, Steve, ed. Eyewitness Natural World. LC 94-18467. (Illus.). 192p. (YA). (gr. 7 up). 1994. 29.95 (1-56458-719-3) DK Pub Inc.

Parker, Steve & Dewan, Ted. Inside Dinosaurs & Other Prehistoric Creatures. (Illus.). (J). 18.95 (0-590-74839-4) Scholastic Inc.

— Inside the Whale & Other Animals. (Illus.). (J). 18.95 (0-590-73869-0) Scholastic Inc.

Parker, Steve & Industrial Art Studio Staff. Communications. LC 98-37969. (Future Tech Ser.). (J). 1998. 12.00 (0-382-39955-2, Dillon Silver Burdett) Silver Burdett Pr.

— Computers. LC 98-37966. (Future Tech Ser.). (J). 1998. 21.00 (0-382-39951-X, Dillon Silver Burdett) Silver Burdett Pr.

— Lasers: Now & into the Future. LC 98-17950. (Future Tech Ser.). (J). 1998. 21.00 (0-382-39953-6, Dillon Silver Burdett); pap. 12.00 (0-382-39954-4, Dillon Silver Burdett) Silver Burdett Pr.

Parker, Steve & Parker, Jane. The Encyclopedia of Sharks. (Illus.). 192p. 1999. text 24.95 (1-55209-324-7) Firefly Bks Ltd.

***Parker, Steve & Parker, Jane.** I Can Experiment: Fun to Do Simple Science Projects for Young Children. (Show Me How Ser.). (Illus.). 40p. (J). 2000. pap. 7.95 (0-7548-0098-9, Lorenz Bks) Anness Pub.

— Nature Works. (Show Me How Ser.). (Illus.). 40p. (J). 2000. pap. 7.95 (0-7548-0099-7, Lorenz Bks) Anness Pub.

Parker, Steve & Parker, Jane, texts. Deserts & Drylands, 6 vols. unabridged ed. LC 96-10644. (Changing World Ser.). (Illus.). 80p. (J). (gr. 3-7). 1996. 12.95 (1-57145-123-4, Silver Dolph) Advantage Pubs.

— Mountains & Valleys, 6 vols. unabridged ed. LC 96-5010. (Changing World Ser.). (Illus.). 80p. (J). (gr. 3-7). 1996. 12.95 (1-57145-026-2, Silver Dolph) Advantage Pubs.

Parker, Steve & West, David. Brain Surgery for Beginners & Other Major Operations for Minors. (Illus.). 64p. (J). (gr. 4-12). 1995. lib. bdg. 21.90 (1-56294-604-8) Millbrook Pr.

— Brain Surgery for Beginners & Other Major Operations for Minors. (Illus.). 64p. (gr. 4-12). 1995. pap. 7.95 (1-56294-895-4) Millbrook Pr.

— Fifty Three & a Half Things That Changed the World & Some That Didn't. LC 94-36649. (Illus.). 64p. (J). (gr. 4-12). 1995. pap. 8.95 (1-56294-894-6); lib. bdg. 21.90 (1-56294-603-X) Millbrook Pr.

***Parker, Steve, et al.** Civilizations. LC 98-61393. (Factfinders Ser.). (Illus.). 256p. (gr. 4-7). 1999. 9.98 (0-7651-1036-9) Smithmark.

Parker, Steve, et al. Ultimate Atlas of Almost Everything. LC 99-39413. 117p. (J). (gr. 4-6). 1999. 24.95 (0-8069-7759-0) Sterling.

Parker, Steve, jt. auth. see Parker, Jane.

Parker, Steve, tr. see Nusom, Lynn.

***Parker, Steven.** How the Body Works: 100 Ways Parents & Kids Can Share the Miracles of the Human Body. (Illus.). 192p. (YA). (gr. 3-9). 1999. pap. text 16.95 (0-7621-0236-5, Pub. by RD Assn) Penguin Putnam.

Parker, Steven & Zuckerman, Barry S. Behavioral & Developmental Pediatrics: A Handbook for Primary Care. 2nd ed. 496p. pap. text 49.95 (0-7817-1683-7) Lppncott W & W.

Parker, Steven & Zuckerman, Barry S., eds. Behavioral & Developmental Pediatrics: A Handbook for Primary Care. LC 94-17875. 480p. 1995. pap. text 42.00 (0-316-69090-2) Lppncott W & W.

Parker, Steven, jt. auth. see Spock, Benjamin.

Parker, Steven C., jt. auth. see Iverson, Patricia L.

Parker, Steven H. & Jobe, William E., eds. Percutaneous Breast Biopsy. LC 93-14055. 192p. 1993. text 92.00 (0-7817-0010-8) Lppncott W & W.

Parker, Steven J., jt. auth. see Spock, Benjamin.

Parker, Stewart. Catchpenny Twist: A Charade in Two Acts. 72p. 1980. pap. 12.95 (0-904011-13-5, Pub. by Gallery Pr) Dufour.

***Parker, Stewart.** Stewart Parker Plays: Includes Spokesong, Catchpenny Twist, Nightshade & Pratt's Fall. (Contemporary Dramatists Ser.). 2000. pap. 14.95 (0-413-74340-3, Methuen Drama) Methn.

Parker, Stewart. Three Plays for Ireland. (Oberon Bks.). 208p. 1997. pap. 18.95 (1-870259-17-3) Theatre Comm.

Parker, Sue. Sounding the Silence: or Why People Sing in the Shower Workbook. 76p. 1995. wbk. ed. 12.95 (0-9641407-1-3) RNIX.

P

Parker, Sue & Nix, Rebekah. Sounding the Silence: or Why People Sing in the Shower. LC 94-219605. (Illus.). 172p. (Orig.). 1994. pap. 12.99 (*0-9641407-0-5*) RNIX.

*__Parker, Sue H., ed.__ God's Treasure: Baby's First Seven Years. (Illus.). 32p. 2000. 19.50 (*0-937739-46-4*) Roman IL.

— God's Treasure: Baby's First Seven Years - Catholic Edition. (Illus.). 32p. 2000. 19.50 (*0-937739-47-2*) Roman IL.

Parker, Sue H., ed. see Petrusic, Anthony A.

Parker, Sue T., et al, eds. The Mentalities of Gorillas & Orangutans: Comparative Perspectives. (Illus.). 560p. (C). 1999. text 85.00 (*0-521-58027-7*) Cambridge U Pr.

— Self-Awareness in Animals & Humans: Developmental Perspectives. (Illus.). 464p. (C). 1994. text 69.95 (*0-521-44108-0*) Cambridge U Pr.

Parker, Sue T. & Gibson, Kathleen R., eds. Language & Intelligence in Monkeys & Apes: Comparative Developmental Perspectives. (Illus.). 608p. (C). 1994. pap. text 27.95 (*0-521-45969-9*) Cambridge U Pr.

Parker, Sue T. & McKinney, Michael L. Origins of Intelligence: The Evolution of Cognitive Development in Monkeys, Apes & Humans. LC 98-37428. (Illus.). 404p. 1999. 55.00 (*0-8018-6012-1*) Johns Hopkins.

Parker, Sue T., jt. auth. see Meikle, W. Eric.

*__Parker, Sue Taylor, et al, eds.__ Biology, Brains & Behavior: The Evolution of Human Development. (Advanced Seminar Ser.). 2000. text 60.00 (*0-933452-63-2*); pap. text 24.95 (*0-933452-64-0*) Schol Am Res.

Parker, Susan. Computers for Municipal Government. (Illus.). 65p. (Orig.). (C). 1996. pap. text 20.00 (*0-7881-3059-5*) DIANE Pub.

Parker, Susan, jt. auth. see Gooden, Selvyn.

Parker, Susan J. Napa Valley Mustard Celebration Cookbook. 152p. 1995. pap. text 11.95 (*1-887534-02-4*) NVMC.

Parker, Suzanne L., jt. auth. see Parker, Glenn R.

Parker, Sybil P. Computer Science Source Book. (Science Reference Ser.). (Illus.). 250p. 1989. 64.95 (*0-07-045507-4*) McGraw.

— McGraw-Hill Concise Encyclopedia of Science & Technology. 4th ed. LC 98-3875. (Illus.). 2450p. 1998. 150.00 (*0-07-052659-1*) McGraw.

— McGraw-Hill Encyclopedia of Environmental Science & Engineering. 3rd ed. 1993. 105.00 (*0-07-051396-1*) McGraw.

— Physical Chemistry Source Book. (Science Reference Ser.). (Illus.). 416p. 1988. 49.50 (*0-07-045504-X*) McGraw.

Parker, Sybil P., ed. Diccionario McGraw-Hill de Fisica. (SPA.). 1992. text 32.95 (*0-07-104157-5*) McGraw.

— McGraw-Hill Encyclopedia of Science & Technology, 20 vols. 8th ed. (Illus.). 15108p. 1997. 125.00 (*0-07-052418-1*) McGraw.

Parker, Sybil P. & Pasachoff, Jay M., eds. McGraw-Hill Encyclopedia of Astronomy. 2nd ed. LC 92-40523. 544p. 1993. 85.00 (*0-07-045314-4*) McGraw.

Parker, T., jt. auth. see Haynes, J. H.

Parker, T. Donald. International Pharmaceutical Services: The Drug Industry & Pharmacy Practice in Twenty-Three Major Countries of the World. Spivey, Richard N. et al, eds. LC 91-6794. 675p. 1996. pap. 39.95 (*0-7890-0078-4*) Haworth Pr.

Parker, T. Donald & Griffinhagen, George. International Pharmaceutical Services: The Drug Industry & Pharmacy Practice in Twenty-Three Major Countries of the World. Spivey, Richard N. et al, eds. LC 91-6794. (Illus.). 675p. 1992. 89.95 (*0-86656-906-5*) Haworth Pr.

Parker, T. H. Calvin: An Introduction to His Thought. LC 95-1055. 160p. (Orig.). 1995. pap. 19.95 (*0-664-25602-3*) Westminster John Knox.

— Calvin's New Testament Commentaries. 2nd ed. 272p. 1998. pap. 29.95 (*0-567-29241-X*, Pub. by T & T Clark) Bks Intl VA.

— Calvin's Old Testament Commentaries. 248p. 1986. 39.95 (*0-567-09365-4*, Pub. by T & T Clark) Bks Intl VA.

— Calvin's Old Testament Commentaries. 256p. 1998. pap. 29.95 (*0-567-29242-8*, Pub. by T & T Clark) Bks Intl VA.

— Calvin's Preaching. 240p. 1998. pap. 27.95 (*0-567-29211-8*, Pub. by T & T Clark) Bks Intl VA.

— Commentaries on Romans Fifteen Thirty-Two to Fifteen Forty-Two. 240p. 1986. 37.95 (*0-567-09366-2*, Pub. by T & T Clark) Bks Intl VA.

— Commentaries on Romans, 1532-1542. 240p. 1996. pap. 27.95 (*0-567-08536-8*, Pub. by T & T Clark) Bks Intl VA.

Parker, T. Jefferson. The Blue Hour. LC 98-43135. 359p. 1999. 23.95 (*0-7868-6288-2*, Pub. by Hyperion) Time Warner.

— The Blue Hour. 464p. 2000. mass mkt. 7.99 (*0-7868-8969-1*, Pub. by Hyperion) Time Warner.

— The Blue Hour. aut. limited ed. 384p. 1999. 23.95 (*0-7868-6559-8*, Pub. by Disney Pr) Time Warner.

*__Parker, T. Jefferson.__ The Blue Hour. large type ed. LC 99-36547. 623p. 1999. 28.95 (*0-7862-2164-X*, G K Hall Lrg Type) Mac Lib Ref.

Parker, T. Jefferson. Laguna Heat-MTV. 1993. mass mkt. 4.99 (*0-312-95205-8*) St Martin.

*__Parker, T. Jefferson.__ Red Light. LC 99-47293. 384p. 2000. 23.95 (*0-7868-6600-4*, Pub. by Hyperion) Time Warner.

Parker, T. Jefferson. The Triggerman's Dance. 352p. 1996. 21.45 (*0-7868-6142-8*, Pub. by Hyperion) Time Warner.

— The Triggerman's Dance. 512p. 1998. mass mkt. 6.99 (*0-7868-8917-9*, Pub. by Hyperion) Time Warner.

— The Triggerman's Dance. large type ed. LC 96-42242. (Cloak & Dagger Ser.). 674p. 1996. 23.95 (*0-7862-0897-X*) Thorndike Pr.

— Where Serpents Lie. 1999. mass mkt. 6.99 (*0-7868-8949-7*, Pub. by Hyperion) Little.

— Where Serpents Lie. 562p. 1999. mass mkt. 6.99 (*0-7868-8944-6*, Pub. by Hyperion) Time Warner.

— Where Serpents Lie. large type ed. LC 98-7892. 1998. write for info. (*0-7862-1526-7*) Thorndike Pr.

Parker, T. S. & Chua, L. O. Practical Numerical Algorithms for Chaotic Systems. (Illus.). xiv, 348p. 1991. reprint ed. 60.95 (*0-387-96689-7*) Spr-Verlag.

Parker, Terrence C. Country Cop. 138p. (Orig.). 1989. pap. 8.95 (*0-685-30391-8*) Tihtiyas Pub.

Parker, Terry. Golden Hours: The Paintings of Arthur J. Elsley, 1860-1952. (Illus.). 160p. 1998. 60.00 (*0-903685-57-4*, Pub. by R Dennis) Antique Collect.

Parker, Theodore. Boston Kidnapping: A Discourse to Commemorate the Rendition of Thomas Simms. LC 70-82208. (Anti-Slavery Crusade in America Ser.). 1969. reprint ed. 7.50 (*0-405-00646-2*) Ayer.

— A Discourse of Matters Pertaining to Religion. LC 72-4968. (Romantic Tradition in American Literature Ser.). 510p. 1972. reprint ed. 38.95 (*0-405-04639-1*) Ayer.

— A Letter to the People of the U. S. Touching the Matter of Slavery. LC 76-92450. 120p. 1972. reprint ed. 13.00 (*0-403-00180-3*) Scholarly.

— Letter to the People of the United States: Touching the Matter of Slavery. LC 76-154086. (Black Heritage Library Collection). 1977. 17.95 (*0-8369-8797-7*) Ayer.

— A Letter to the People of the United States Touching the Matter of Slavery. rev. ed. 122p. 1991. pap. text 34.95 (*0-9627882-5-2*) Bradley Mann.

— The Nebraska Question: Some Thoughts on the New Assault upon Freedom in America & the General State of the Country in Relation Thereunto. 1977. 12.95 (*0-8369-9191-5*, 9060) Ayer.

— Slave Power. LC 74-82209. (Anti-Slavery Crusade in America Ser.). 1970. reprint ed. 27.95 (*0-405-00647-0*) Ayer.

— Theodore Parker's Works, 14 vols. (Notable American Authors Ser.). 1999. reprint ed. lib. bdg. 1750.00 (*0-7812-4726-8*) Rprt Serv.

— The Trial of Theodore Parker: For the Misdemeanor of a Speech in Fanenil Hall Against Kidnapping. LC 70-154087. (Black Heritage Library Collection). 1977. 28.95 (*0-8369-8798-5*) Ayer.

— The Trial of Theodore Parker, with the Defence by Theodore Parker. (American Biography Ser.). 221p. 1991. reprint ed. lib. bdg. 69.00 (*0-7812-8306-X*) Rprt Serv.

— Works: Centenary Edition, 15 vols., Set. LC 75-3307. reprint ed. 595.00 (*0-404-59300-3*) AMS Pr.

Parker, Theodore, contrib. by. The Trial of Theodore Parker for the "Misdemeanor" of a Speech in Faneuil Hall Against Kidnapping Before the Circuit Court of the United States at Boston, April 3, 1855. xx, 221p. 1999. reprint ed. 75.00 (*1-56169-490-8*) Gaunt.

Parker, Theodore A. Ecological Database Neotropical Birds. 1996. lib. bdg. 14.95 (*0-226-64676-9*) U Ch Pr.

Parker, Theodore A., 3rd & Bailey, Brent, eds. A Biological Assessment of the Alto Madidi Region & Adjacent Areas of Northwest Bolivia, May 18 - June 15, 1990. LC 91-78133. 108p. 1995. pap. 7.00 (*1-881173-05-4*, Pub. by Conser Intl) U Ch Pr.

Parker, Theodore A., 3rd & Carr, John L., eds. Status of Forest Remnants in the Cordillera de la Costa & Adjacent Areas of Southwestern Ecuador. LC 92-73741. 172p. 1995. pap. 10.00 (*1-881173-04-6*, Pub. by Conser Intl) U Ch Pr.

Parker, Theodore A., 3rd, et al. A Biological Assessment of the Columbia River Forest Reserve, Toledo District, Belize. LC 93-71145. 81p. 1993. pap. 7.00 (*1-881173-03-8*) Conser Intl.

— The Lowland Dry Forests of Santa Cruz, Bolivia: A Global Conservation Priority. LC 93-72263. 104p. 1995. pap. 7.00 (*1-881173-02-X*, Pub. by Conser Intl) U Ch Pr.

Parker, Theresa, jt. auth. see Vickers, Robert.

Parker, Thomas. The Road to Camp David: U. S. Negotiating Strategy Towards the Arab-Israeli Conflict. (American University Studies: Political Science: Ser. X, Vol. 9). X, 175p. (C). 1988. text 39.00 (*0-8204-0495-0*) P Lang Pubng.

Parker, Thomas & Nelson, Douglas. Day by Day: The Sixties, 2 vols., Set. 1136p. 1983. 195.00 (*0-87196-648-4*) Facts on File.

Parker, Thomas F. America's Foreign Policy, Nineteen Forty-Five to Nineteen Seventy-Six: Its Creators & Critics. LC 80-21192. 272p. reprint ed. pap. 84.40 (*0-8357-4249-0*, 203703800007) Bks Demand.

Parker, Thomas R. Flying in Northern California. 106p. (Orig.). 1987. pap. 65.00 (*0-9618154-0-X*) T R Parker.

Parker, Thomas W. The Knights Templars in England. LC 63-11983. 207p. reprint ed. pap. 64.20 (*0-608-10056-0*, 205537000017) Bks Demand.

Parker, Tim. GURPS Diabolic Constructions. pap. 19.95 (*1-55634-410-4*, Pub. by S Jackson Games) BookWorld.

Parker, Tim. Linux Unleashed. 3rd ed. LC 98-85650. 1998. pap. 39.99 (*0-672-31372-3*) Sams.

*__Parker, Tim.__ TCP/IP to Go. (Illus.). 320p. 2000. pap. 34.99 (*0-13-025877-6*) P-H.

*__Parker, Timothy.__ Linux System Administrator's Survival Guide. 2nd ed. (Illus.). 1999. pap. 49.99 (*0-672-31793-1*) Sams.

— Linux Unleashed. 4th ed. (Unleashed Ser.). (Illus.). 1999. pap. 49.99 (*0-672-31688-9*) Sams.

Parker, Timothy. SCO System Administration. (C). 2001. 29.95 (*0-13-443664-4*) P-H.

— SCO UNIX System Administration. 1996. 29.95 (*0-614-14495-7*); 29.95 (*0-614-14496-5*) P-H.

— TCP/IP Unleashed. 880p. 1996. 55.00 (*0-672-30603-4*) Sams.

— TCP/IP Unleashed: MCSE Edition. 850p. 1999. 59.99 (*0-672-31185-2*) Sams.

— Teach Yourself TCP/IP in 14 Days. 464p. 1994. 29.99 (*0-672-30549-6*) Sams.

— Teach Yourself TCP/IP in 14 Days. 2nd ed. 512p. 1996. 39.99 (*0-672-30885-1*) Sams.

Parker, Timothy, et al. Microsoft TCP/IP Unleashed. 2nd ed. 900p. 1999. 49.99 (*0-672-31112-7*) Sams.

*__Parker, Todd C.__ Sexing the Text: The Rhetoric of Sexual Difference in British Literature, 1700-1750. LC 99-56707. (C). 2000. text 54.50 (*0-7914-4485-6*); pap. text 17.95 (*0-7914-4486-4*) State U NY Pr.

Parker, Tom. Topley & Wilson's Principles of Bacteriology, Virology & Immunity. 8th ed. 724p. text. write for info. (*0-7131-4590-0*, Pub. by E A) Routldge.

Parker, Tom, jt. auth. see Kurtzig, Sandra L.

Parker, Tom, jt. auth. see Winfield, Dave.

Parker, Tom W. Proportional Form in the Sonnets of the Sidney Circle: Loving in Truth. (Oxford English Monographs). (Illus.). 268p. 1998. text 75.00 (*0-19-818443-3*) OUP.

Parker, Toni Trent, jt. auth. see Rand, Donna.

Parker, Tony. Bird, Kansas. 352p. 1990. pap. 8.95 (*0-380-71137-0*, Avon Bks) Morrow Avon.

*__Parker, Tony.__ Criminal Conversations: An Anthology of the Work of Tony Parker. 1999. 85.00 (*0-415-19739-2*); pap. 27.99 (*0-415-19740-6*) Routledge.

Parker, Tony. May the Lord in His Mercy Be Kind to Belfast. LC 93-40754. 1995. 25.00 (*0-8050-3053-0*); pap. 13.95 (*0-8050-3806-X*, Owl) H Holt & Co.

— Studs Terkel: A Life in Words. 89p. 1995. 27.50 (*0-8050-3483-8*) H Holt & Co.

*__Parker, Tony.__ Studsterkel: A Life in Words. 237p. 1999. reprint ed. text 27.00 (*0-7881-6642-5*) DIANE Pub.

Parker, Tony. The Violence of Our Lives. 384p. 1995. 22.50 (*0-8050-3058-1*) H Holt & Co.

Parker, Torrance R. 20,000 Jobs under the Sea: A History of Diving & Underwater Engineering. Walsh, Don, ed. LC 97-92206. (Illus.). 368p. 1997. reprint ed. 87.00 (*0-9657823-3-6*) Sub Sea.

The real story of the men & jobs that helped build America's ports, harbors, dams & other underwater structures. The author was a commercial diver for nearly half a century & can tell this story from the inside out. Jim Bladh, Director of Ocean Engineering, Supervisor of Salvage, U. S. Navy says... "An excellent reference, well illustrated & indexed. Immersed: The International Technical Diving Magazine wrote... "If there is one book on commercial diving that is suitable for inclusion in a time capsule, this is that book." From Kenneth Downey of Morse Diving Equipment Company... "What a great book. I use it as a source of information." Winner Historical Diving Society 1998 Dr. Art Bachrach Literary Award. Available through Ingram, Baker & Taylor, Quality Books, or the publisher. ***Publisher Paid Annotation.***

Parker, Trillis. Horses Talk: It Pays to Listen. rev. ed. LC 88-93037. (Illus.). 205p. 1989. pap. 19.95 (*0-915700-07-7*) Jacada Pubns.

Parker, Trudy A. Aunt Sarah Woman of the Dawnland. 2nd rev. ed. lxii, 275p. 1994. reprint ed. per. 24.95 (*0-9662523-8-1*) Dawnland Pubns.

— Big Snow, Little Snow: Log Driving in the Connecticut River Valley. (Illus.). 208p. 1998. 22.95 (*0-9662523-2-2*) Dawnland Pubns.

Parker, Una-Mary. A Dangerous Desire. 320p. 1997. 27.00 (*0-7472-1543-X*, Pub. by Headline Bk Pub) Trafalgar.

*__Parker, Una-Mary.__ Dark Passions. large type unabridged ed. 321p. 1999. 26.95 (*0-7531-5921-X*, 15921X, Pub. by ISIS Lrg Prnt) ISIS Pub.

Parker, Una-Mary. Taking Control. 314p. 1997. pap. 11.95 (*0-7472-5139-8*, Pub. by Headline Bk Pub) Trafalgar.

Parker, V. Ballet. (Illus.). mass mkt. 8.95 (*0-340-71519-7*, Pub. by Hodder & Stought Ltd) Trafalgar.

Parker, V. D., jt. auth. see Hammerich, O.

Parker, Vaughn. Aquaculture Science. 2nd abr. rev. ed. 384p. 1995. text 89.95 (*0-8273-6976-X*) Delmar.

Parker, Vic. Bearobics. (J). (ps-2). 1999. pap. 5.99 (*0-14-056494-2*, PuffinBks) Peng Put Young Read.

— Bearobics: A Hip-Hop Counting Story. LC 96-60042. (Illus.). 32p. (J). 1997. 14.99 (*0-670-87034-X*) Viking Penguin.

*__Parker, Victoria.__ Birth of Jesus. (Discovering the Bible Ser.). (Illus.). (J). 2000. 12.95 (*0-7548-0484-4*, Lorenz Bks) Anness Pub.

— David & Goliath: And Other Old Testament Stories. (Discovering the Bible Ser.). (Illus.). (J). 2000. 12.95 (*0-7548-0458-5*, Lorenz Bks) Anness Pub.

— Jesus in Galilee: And Other New Testament Stories. (Discovering the Bible Ser.). (Illus.). (J). 2000. 12.95 (*0-7548-0477-1*, Lorenz Bks) Anness Pub.

— Jonah & the Whale. (Discovering the Bible Ser.). (Illus.). (J). 2000. 12.95 (*0-7548-0456-9*, Lorenz Bks) Anness Pub.

Parker, Victoria. Noah's Ark & Other First Bible Stories. (Discovering the Bible Ser.). (Illus.). 64p. (J). 1999. 12.95 (*0-7548-0205-1*, Lorenz Bks) Anness Pub.

*__Parker, Victoria.__ Samson, Delilah & Other Old Testament Stories. (Discovering the Bible Ser.). (Illus.). 64p. (J). 2000. 12.95 (*0-7548-0206-X*, Lorenz Bks) Anness Pub.

Parker, Victoria. Test Your Punctuation. (Test Yourself Ser.). (Illus.). 32p. (J). (gr. 5-9). 1995. pap. 5.95 (*0-7460-1749-9*, Usborne) EDC.

— Test Your Punctuation. (Test Yourself Ser.). (Illus.). 32p. (YA). (gr. 5 up). 1999. lib. bdg. 13.95 (*0-88110-766-2*, Usborne) EDC.

— Test Your Spelling. (Test Your self Ser.). (Illus.). 32p. (J). (gr. 5 up). 1995. pap. 5.95 (*0-7460-1735-9*, Usborne) EDC.

— Test Your Spelling. (Test Your Self Ser.). (Illus.). 32p. (J). (gr. 5 up). 1999. lib. bdg. 13.95 (*0-88110-754-9*, Usborne) EDC.

Parker, Violette & Mammen, Lori. TAAS Quick Review Reading, Grade 4. (Illus.). 96p. 1992. pap. text 12.95 (*0-944459-36-6*) ECS Lrn Systs.

Parker, Virginia C. Indian Summers: A Memoir of Fort Duchesne, 1925-1935. LC 98-72415. (Illus.). 300p. 1998. pap. 17.00 (*1-888106-44-1*) Agreka Bks.

— Rabbits! LC 98-24683. (Fun & Care Bks.). (Illus.). 112p. 1998. pap. 16.95 (*1-889540-08-0*) Bowtie Press.

Parker, W., ed. Alicyclic Chemistry, Vols. 2-6. Incl. 1972 Literature. LC 72-83459. 1974. 47.00 (*0-85186-522-4*); Vol. 3. 1973 Literature. LC 72-82047. 1973. 61.00 (*0-85186-552-6*); 1974 Literature. LC 72-83459. 1976. 70.00 (*0-85186-582-8*); 1975 Literature. LC 72-83459. 1977. 72.00 (*0-85186-612-3*); 1976 Literature. LC 72-23822. 1978. 73.00 (*0-85186-632-8*); LC 72-82047. write for info. (*0-318-50459-6*) Am Chemical.

Parker, W. B. Through Unexplored Texas. LC 84-80800. 242p. 1990. reprint ed. 21.95 (*0-87611-064-2*); reprint ed. pap. 12.95 (*0-87611-065-0*) Tex St Hist Assn.

Parker, W. H. Health & Disease in Farm Animals. 3rd ed. 1980. text 86.00 (*0-08-025900-6*, Pergamon Pr); pap. text 21.00 (*0-08-025899-9*, Pergamon Pr) Elsevier.

Parker, W. H., tr. Priapea: Poems for a Phallic God. 240p. 1988. 27.00 (*0-7099-4099-8*, Pub. by C Helm) Routldge.

Parker, W. J. The Great Coal Schooners of New England, 1870-1909. LC 49-3820. (Marine Historical Association Publication: Vol. 2, No. 6). 139p. reprint ed. pap. 43.10 (*0-8357-2789-0*, 203991500014) Bks Demand.

Parker, W. M., ed. see Scott, Sir Walter.

Parker, W. Oren. Sceno-Graphic Techniques. 3rd ed. LC 86-17859. (Illus.). 158p. (C). 1987. pap. 19.95 (*0-8093-1350-2*) S Ill U Pr.

Parker, W. Oren & Wolf, R. Craig. Scene Design & Stage Lighting. 7th ed. 690p. (C). 1996. text 60.50 (*0-15-501620-2*, Pub. by Harcourt Coll Pubs) Harcourt.

Parker, Wallace. Humor & Wisdom: Thoughts to Brighten & Enlighten Your Way. pap. 9.95 (*0-9671468-0-1*) ONeil Pubg.

*__Parker, Walter.__ Social Studies in Elementary Education. 11th ed. LC 00-28366. 2001. write for info. (*0-13-021337-3*) Prntice Hall Bks.

Parker, Walter & Jarolimek, John. Citizenship & the Critical Role of the Social Studies. LC 84-60983. (Bulletin Ser.: No. 72). 58p. (Orig.). 1984. pap. text 7.95 (*0-89994-287-3*, 498-15316) Nat Coun Soc Studies.

Parker, Walter C., ed. Educating the Democratic Mind. LC 94-49551. (SUNY Series, Democracy & Education). 381p. (C). 1995. text 62.50 (*0-7914-2707-2*); pap. text 23.95 (*0-7914-2708-0*) State U NY Pr.

Parker, Walter C. & Jarolimek, John. Social Studies in Elementary Education. 10th ed. LC 96-3433. (Illus.). 416p. (C). 1996. text 68.00 (*0-13-470015-5*, Merrill Pub Co) Macmillan.

Parker, Watson. Deadwood: The Golden Years. LC 80-24100. (Illus.). xiv, 334p. 1981. pap. 14.95 (*0-8032-8702-X*, Bison Books) U of Nebr Pr.

Parker, Watson & Lambert, Hugh K. Black Hills Ghost Towns. (Illus.). 215p. 1993. reprint ed. pap. 24.95 (*0-8040-0638-5*) Swallow.

Parker, Wayne, tr. see Baumann, Bommi.

Parker, Weldon & Parker, Dee. Down the Magical Mississippi. (Illus.). (Orig.). 1985. pap. 6.95 (*0-9614662-0-0*) Sun Seeker Bks.

Parker, Wilbur & Goodwin, Ruby P. On the USS Colorado. (Illus.). 345p. pap. 12.95 (*0-934482-03-9*) Hathor House Bks.

Parker, Wilbur A. Wilbur's Book, 1876-1984. Goodwin, Ruby P., ed. & compiled by by. (Illus.). 128p. reprint ed. pap. 9.95 (*0-934482-02-0*) Hathor House Bks.

Parker, Wilbur A. & Parker & Parker Staff. Wilbur's Last Book. Goodwin, Ruby P., ed. & compiled by by. (Illus.). 130p. pap. 9.95 (*0-934482-04-7*) Hathor House Bks.

Parker, William. Homosexuality Bibliography: Second Supplement, 1976-1982. LC 84-20299. 401p. 1985. 37.00 (*0-8108-1753-5*) Scarecrow.

— Paris Bourse & French Finance with Reference to Organized Speculation in New York. LC 20-18734. (Columbia University. Studies in the Social Sciences: No. 204). reprint ed. 20.00 (*0-404-51204-6*) AMS Pr.

Parker, William & Parker, Rachel. A Gynecologist's Second Opinion: The Questions & Answers You Need to Take Charge of Your Health. 2nd ed. 432p. 1996. pap. 13.95 (*0-452-27674-8*, Plume) Dutton Plume.

Parker, William A. Alderman. The Aldermans in America. (Illus.). 714p. 1996. reprint ed. pap. 99.50 (*0-8328-5396-8*) Higginson Bk Co.

— Alderman. The Aldermans in America. (Illus.). 714p. 1996. reprint ed. lib. bdg. 109.50 (*0-8328-5395-X*) Higginson Bk Co.

Parker, William C., ed. The Fabric of Friendship. LC 74-22705. (Illus.). 224p. 1975. pap. 5.95 (*0-915102-00-5*) Eastham Edns.

Parker, William D. A Concise History of the United States Marine Corps, 1775 to 1969. LC 80-29554. (Illus.). 143p. 1981. reprint ed. lib. bdg. 35.00 (*0-313-22854-X*, PACO, Greenwood Pr) Greenwood.

Parker, William E., intro. Roger L. Crossgrove Three Decades: Works on Paper & Photographs. LC 65-15853. (Illus.). 15p. Date not set. 4.50 (*0-614-10429-7*) W Benton Mus.

Parker, William E., ed. see Schwarz, Heinrich.

P

An Asterisk (*) at the beginning of an entry indicates that the title is appearing for the first time.

*Parkinson-Bailey, John J. Manchester: An Architectural History. LC 99-55329. (Illus.). 352p. 2000. 39.95 (0-7190-5606-3) Manchester Univ Pr.

Parkinson, Barbara. Any Change for the Jugglers: And Other Poems. LC 96-102388. 64p. 1995. pap. 12.95 (1-897648-31-6, Pub. by Poolbeg Pr) Dufour.

Parkinson, Benson Y. The MTC: Set Apart. LC 95-25066. 302p. 1995. pap. 9.95 (1-56236-310-7) Aspen Bks.

Parkinson, Bradford W. & Spilker, James J., Jr., eds. The Global Positioning System: Theory & Application, 2 vols., Vol. 1. LC 94-44737. 1995. 89.95 (1-56347-106-X, V-163) AIAA.

— The Global Positioning System: Theory & Application, 2 vols., Vol. 2. LC 94-44737. 1995. 89.95 (1-56347-107-8, V-164) AIAA.

Parkinson, Brian. Ideas & Realities of Emotion. LC 95-1096. (International Library of Philosophy). 352p. (C). 1995. pap. 27.99 (0-415-02859-0) Routledge.

Parkinson, Brian & Colman, Andrew M., eds. Emotion Motivation. LC 95-18115. (Essential Psychology Ser.). 107p. (C). 1995. pap. 17.86 (0-582-27808-2) Addison-Wesley.

Parkinson, C. Devil to Pay. 278p. 1973. text. write for info. (0-7195-2838-0, Pub. by John Murray) Trafalgar.

Parkinson, C. F. A Forest Flora of the Andaman Islands. 326p. (C). 1984. pap. 125.00 (81-7089-012-8, Pub. by Intl Bk Distr) St Mut.

Parkinson, C. Northcote. Dead Reckoning. LC 79-303758. 276p. (J). 1978. write for info. (0-7195-3484-4, Pub. by John Murray) Trafalgar.

Parkinson, C. Northcote. East & West. LC 81-1195. (Illus.). 330p. 1981. reprint ed. lib. bdg. 65.00 (0-313-22955-4, PAEW, Greenwood Pr) Greenwood.

Parkinson, C. Northcote. The Fireship. LC 76-352471. 187p. (J). 1975. write for info. (0-7195-3175-6, Pub. by John Murray) Trafalgar.

Parkinson, C. Northcote. In-Laws & Outlaws. 1993. reprint ed. lib. bdg. 18.95 (1-56849-102-6) Buccaneer Bks.

— The Law & the Profits. 1993. reprint ed. lib. bdg. 18.95 (1-56849-101-8) Buccaneer Bks.

Parkinson, C. Northcote. The Life & Times of Horatio Hornblower. LC 74-590381. 304p. (J). 1970. write for info. (0-7181-0787-X, M Joseph) Viking Penguin.

Parkinson, C. Northcote. The Life & Times of Horatio Hornblower. 1994. reprint ed. lib. bdg. 32.95 (1-56849-318-5) Buccaneer Bks.

— The Life & Times of Horatio Hornblower: A Fictional Biography of Horatio Hornblower. 1998. pap. 10.95 (0-7509-2109-9) Bks Intl VA.

— Parkinson's Law. 1993. reprint ed. lib. bdg. 25.95 (1-56849-015-1) Buccaneer Bks.

— Portsmouth Point: British Navy in Fiction, 1793-1815. 1979. 20.00 (0-87556-509-3) Saifer.

Parkinson, C. Northcote. Touch & Go. LC 77-373026. 230p. (J). 1977. 0.00 (0-7195-3371-6, Pub. by John Murray) Trafalgar.

Parkinson, C. Northcote. Trade in the Eastern Seas, 1793-1813. (Illus.). 437p. 1966. 35.00 (0-7146-1348-7, Pub. by F Cass Pubs) Intl Spec Bk.

Parkinson, Can. Timecop: The Scavenger, Vol.. 2. 1998. mass mkt. 5.99 (0-345-42196-5, Del Rey) Ballantine Pub Grp.

Parkinson, Carolyn S. Mommy's in the Hospital Again. (Illus.). 40p. (Orig.). (J). (gr. k-4). 1996. pap. 14.95 (0-9630287-1-5) Solace Pub.

— My Mommy Has Cancer. (Illus.). 20p. (J). (ps-4). 1991. pap. 8.95 (0-9630287-0-7) Solace Pub.

Parkinson, Christopher, ed. The Timing of Toxicological Studies to Support Clinical Trials: Proceedings: C. M. R. Discussion Meeting on the Timing of Toxicological Studies (1994: Nutfield, U. K.) 150p. 1995. text 92.50 (0-7923-8872-0) Kluwer Academic.

Parkinson, Claire L. Earth from Above: Using Color-Coded Satellite Images to Examine the Global Environment. LC 97-7657. 192p. 1997. pap. text 38.00 (0-935702-41-5) Univ Sci Bks.

— Gospel Cryptograms. (Quiz & Puzzle Bks.). (Illus.). 96p. (gr. 10). 1994. pap. 5.99 (0-8010-7127-5) Baker Bks.

Parkinson, Claire L., jt. auth. see Washington, Warren M.

Parkinson, Clayton. Understanding Pathophysiology. 368p. (C). (gr. 13). 1995. pap. text, student ed. 19.95 (0-8151-7299-0, 28196) Mosby Inc.

*Parkinson, Connie. Old World Charm. (Illus.). 52p. 1999. 10.95 (1-57377-068-X, 19884-2282) Easl Pubns.

Parkinson, Connie. Perfectly English, Vol. 1. (Illus.). 46p. 1997. write for info. (1-57377-030-2) Easl Pubns.

Parkinson, Connie, jt. ed. see Foster, Kim.

Parkinson, Connie, ed. see Hopley, Claire.

Parkinson, Connie, ed. see Karoff, Barbara.

Parkinson, Connie, ed. see Lilie, Tish.

Parkinson, Connie, ed. see Peddie, Mary, et al.

Parkinson, Connie, ed. see Siegler, Madeleine H.

Parkinson, Cornelia M. Alex Livingston, the Tomato Man. (Illus.). 20p. (J). (gr. 4 up). 1985. pap. 3.00 (0-938404-05-9, AWL) Hist Tales.

— Connell Hardware, a Family Tradition: One Hundred Twenty-Five Years. (Illus.). 66p. (Orig.). 1997. pap. 4.00 (0-938404-10-5) Hist Tales.

— More Historical Tales of Old Reynoldsburg, Vol. II. (Illus.). 168p. (Orig.). 1985. pap. 5.00 (0-938404-04-0, MORE HT) Hist Tales.

Parkinson, Curtis. Mr. Reez's Sneezes. (Illus.). 24p. (J). (ps-2). 1999. pap. 5.95 (1-55037-556-3, Pub. by Annick Pr); text 15.95 (1-55037-557-1, Pub. by Annick Pr) Firefly Bks Ltd.

Parkinson, D. Blood Arrow. 1989. pap. 3.50 (0-8217-3027-4) NAL.

— Thunderland. 1989. pap. 3.95 (0-8217-3031-2) NAL.

Parkinson, D. N., jt. ed. see Hesselbo, S. P.

Parkinson, D. R., ed. see European School of Oncology Staff.

Parkinson, Dan. Drifter's Luck. 288p. 1991. mass mkt. 3.95 (0-8217-3396-6, Zebra Kensgtn) Kensgtn Pub Corp.

— Dust on the Wind. 1992. mass mkt. 3.99 (0-8217-3635-3, Zebra Kensgtn) Kensgtn Pub Corp.

— Faces of Infinity. (The Gates of Time Ser.: Bk. 2). 1999. mass mkt. 6.50 (0-345-41381-4, Del Rey) Ballantine Pub Grp.

— The Fox & the Faith. 1989. mass mkt. 3.95 (1-55817-204-1, Pinncle Kensgtn) Kensgtn Pub Corp.

— The Fox & the Faith. 352p. 1998. pap. 4.99 (0-7860-0555-6, Pinncle Kensgtn) Kensgtn Pub Corp.

— The Fox & the Faith. (Illus.). 352p. 1999. 25.00 (0-7278-2284-5, Pub. by Severn Hse) Chivers N Amer.

*Parkinson, Dan. The Fox & the Faith. large type ed. 408p. 2000. 31.99 (0-7089-4185-0) Ulverscroft.

Parkinson, Dan. The Fox & the Flag. 1990. mass mkt. 3.95 (1-55817-349-8, Pinncle Kensgtn) Kensgtn Pub Corp.

Parkinson, Dan. The Fox & the Flag. 352p. 26.00 (0-7278-5547-6) Severn Hse.

Parkinson, Dan. Fox & the Flag. 352p. 1999. mass mkt. 4.99 (0-7860-0648-X) Pinnacle Books.

— The Fox & the Fortune. 1992. mass mkt. 3.99 (1-55817-600-4, Pinncle Kensgtn) Kensgtn Pub Corp.

— Fox & the Fortune. 256p. 1999. mass mkt. 4.99 (0-7860-1010-X) Kensgtn Pub Corp.

— The Fox & the Fury. 1989. mass mkt. 3.95 (1-55817-291-2, Pinncle Kensgtn) Kensgtn Pub Corp.

— Fox & the Fury. 352p. 1999. mass mkt. 4.99 (0-7860-0612-9) Kensgtn Pub Corp.

— Fox & The Fury. 1999. 26.00 (0-7278-5472-0, Pub. by Severn Hse) Chivers N Amer.

— The Gates of Thorbardin. LC 89-51892. (DragonLance Heroes II Trilogy: Vol. 2). (Illus.). 320p. (Orig.). 1990. pap. 5.99 (0-88038-912-5, Pub. by TSR Inc) Random.

— The Gully Dwarves. (DragonLance Lost Histories Ser.: Vol. 5). 1996. pap. 5.99 (0-7869-0497-6, Pub. by TSR Inc) Random.

— The Guns of No Man's Land. 320p. 1992. mass mkt. 3.99 (0-8217-3960-3, Zebra Kensgtn) Kensgtn Pub Corp.

— Jubilation Gap. 1987. mass mkt. 3.95 (0-8217-2209-3, Zebra Kensgtn) Kensgtn Pub Corp.

— Ride the Devil's Trail. 1990. mass mkt. 3.95 (0-8217-2894-6, Zebra Kensgtn) Kensgtn Pub Corp.

— Summer Land. 352p. 1989. mass mkt. 3.95 (0-8217-2683-8, Zebra Kensgtn) Kensgtn Pub Corp.

— Thunderland. 368p. 1987. mass mkt. 3.50 (0-8217-1991-2, Zebra Kensgtn) Kensgtn Pub Corp.

— Timecop: Blood Ties, Vol.. 3. 1999. mass mkt. 5.99 (0-345-42197-3, Del Rey) Ballantine Pub Grp.

— The Way to Wyoming. 432p. 1988. mass mkt. 3.95 (0-8217-2411-8, Zebra Kensgtn) Kensgtn Pub Corp.

— The Westering. 352p. 1989. mass mkt. 3.95 (0-8217-2559-9, Zebra Kensgtn) Kensgtn Pub Corp.

Parkinson, Dan & Hicks, David. Gunpowder Wind. 400p. 1988. mass mkt. 3.95 (0-8217-2456-8, Zebra Kensgtn) Kensgtn Pub Corp.

— Texians. 1990. mass mkt. 3.95 (0-8217-3097-5, Zebra Kensgtn) Kensgtn Pub Corp.

Parkinson, Dan, jt. auth. see Hicks, David L.

Parkinson, David. The History of Film. LC 94-60287. (World of Art Ser.). (Illus.). 264p. 1996. pap. 14.95 (0-500-20277-X, Pub. by Thames Hudson) Norton.

— The Young Oxford Book of the Movies. LC 96-4684. (Illus.). 162p. (YA). (gr. 5 up). 1997. 25.00 (0-19-521244-4) OUP.

Parkinson, David, ed. The Graham Greene Film Reader: Reviews, Essays, Interviews & Film Stories. LC 94-33547. 766p. 1999. 35.00 (1-55783-188-2); pap. 23.95 (1-55783-249-8) Applause Theatre Bk Pubs.

Parkinson, David, ed. see Douglas, Gavin.

Parkinson, David H. & Mulhall, Brian E. The Generation of High Magnetic Fields. LC 67-13568. (International Cryogenics Monograph). 179p. reprint ed. pap. 55.50 (0-608-13250-0, 205578900038) Bks Demand.

Parkinson, Dilworth B. Constructing the Social Context of Communication: Terms of Address in Egyptian Arabic. (Contributions to the Sociology of Language Ser.: Vol. 41). x, 239p. 1985. 75.40 (0-89925-148-X) Mouton.

Parkinson, Dilworth B., jt. ed. see Eid, Mushira.

Parkinson, Dilworth B., jt. ed. see Rammuny, Raji M.

Parkinson, Eric. Clixi Technology. Stillman, Meg, ed. (Illus.). 25p. (J). (gr. 3-9). 1994. 9.99 (1-884461-10-7) NES Arnold.

— Teaching Techniques. rev. ed. Doyle, Connie, ed. (Design & Make Ser.). (Illus.). 45p. (J). (gr. 3-6). 1994. reprint ed. 9.99 (1-884461-05-0) NES Arnold.

Parkinson, Eric, jt. auth. see Carlton, Kevin.

Parkinson, F. Conquering the Past: Austrian Nazism Yesterday & Today. LC 88-31328. 346p. 1989. 39.95 (0-8143-2054-6) Wayne St U Pr.

Parkinson, F., ed. Conquering the Past: Austrian Nazism Yesterday & Today. LC 88-31328. (Illus.). 347p. reprint ed. pap. 107.60 (0-608-10544-9, 2071164) Bks Demand.

Parkinson, Frank. Listening & Helping in the Workplace: A Guide for Mangers, Supervisors & Colleagues Who... 272p. 1996. pap. text 14.95 (0-285-63242-6, Pub. by Souvenir Pr Ltd) IPG Chicago.

— Post-Trauma Stress. LC 93-35868. 192p. (Orig.). 1993. pap. 12.95 (1-55561-058-7) Fisher Bks.

*Parkinson, Frank. Post-Trauma Stress: Recovery from Hidden Emotional Damage Caused by Violence & Disaster. 192p. 2000. pap. 14.00 (1-55561-249-0) Fisher Bks.

Parkinson, G. & Shaw, G. Masonry. LC 96-136374. 162p. 1996. 57.00 (0-7277-2055-4) Am Soc Civil Eng.

*Parkinson, G. H. R., ed. Spinoza: Ethics. LC 99-57765. (Oxford Philosophical Texts). 300p. (C). 2000. pap. 11.95 (0-19-875214-8) OUP.

Parkinson, George. Guide to Coal Mining Collections in the United States. 182p. 1978. pap. 12.00 (0-937058-41-6) West Va U Pr.

Parkinson, George H. Spinoza's Theory of Knowledge. (Modern Revivals in Philosophy Ser.). 208p. 1993. 61.95 (0-7512-0159-6, Pub. by Gregg Pub) Ashgate Pub Co.

Parkinson, George H., ed. Routledge History of Philosophy Vol. 4: The Renaissance & Seventeenth Century Rationalism, Vol. 4. LC 92-37350. 448p. (C). (gr. 13). 1993. 90.00 (0-415-05378-1, B0731) Routledge.

Parkinson, George H. & Spinoza, Baruch. Ethics. 260p. 1993. pap. 8.95 (0-460-87317-4, Everyman's Classic Lib) Tuttle Pubng.

Parkinson, George H., ed. see Leibniz, Gottfried Wilhelm.

Parkinson, George H., tr. see Leibniz, Gottfried Wilhelm.

Parkinson, Glenn. First Tracks: Stories from Maine's Skiing Heritage. (Illus.). 60p. (Orig.). 1995. pap. 15.95 (0-9647517-0-4) Maine Skiing.

Parkinson, Henry J. How Things Got Better: Speech, Writing, Printing & Cultural Change. LC 94-38492. 192p. 1995. 55.00 (0-89789-431-6, Bergin & Garvey) Greenwood.

Parkinson, J. E., ed. see Dugdale, A. M. & Stanton, K. M.

Parkinson, J. Elizabeth. Corporate Power & Responsibility: Issues in the Theory of Company Law. 502p. 1995. pap. text 35.00 (0-19-825989-1) OUP.

Parkinson, J. F., jt. ed. see Lancaster, Jack R.

Parkinson, J. R. How to Get People to Do Things Your Way. 224p. 1998. pap. 6.95 (0-8092-2876-9, 287690, Contemporary Bks) NTC Contemp Pub Co.

Parkinson, J. Robert. How to Get People to Do Things Your Way. LC 96-52870. 240p. 1997. pap. 12.95 (0-8092-3062-3, Jamestwn Pub) NTC Contemp Pub Co.

— How to Get People to Do Things Your Way. 2nd ed. (Illus.). 232p. 1995. 12.95 (0-8442-4488-0, Natl Textbk Co) NTC Contemp Pub Co.

— How to Take Charge of Your Child's Early Education. (Illus.). 160p. 1995. pap. 9.95 (0-8442-4394-9, VGM Career) NTC Contemp Pub Co.

— Planning Your Young Child's Education. 1986. pap. 6.95 (0-8442-6683-3, Passprt Bks) NTC Contemp Pub Co.

Parkinson, James. Organic Remains of a Former World, 3 vols. Albritton, Claude C., Jr., ed. LC 77-6534. (History of Geology Ser.). (Illus.). 1978. lib. bdg. 108.95 (0-405-10454-5) Ayer.

Parkinson, James W. Focus on Your Language. LC 75-17952. 279p. 1976. teacher ed. 6.67 (0-672-61363-8, Bobbs); pap. 9.50 (0-672-61358-1, Bobbs) Macmillan.

Parkinson, Jane P., ed. see Hargrave, Harriet.

Parkinson, Jerry, jt. auth. see Rossow, Lawrence.

Parkinson, Jerry, jt. auth. see Rossow, Lawrence F.

Parkinson, John. The Diplomatic Sailor. 1981. 30.00 (0-7223-1360-8, Pub. by A H S Ltd) St Mut.

— Paradisi in Sole, Paradisus Terrestris, or a Garden of All Sorts of Pleasant Flowers Which Our English Ayre Will Permit. LC 74-28880. (English Experience Ser.: No. 758). 1975. reprint ed. 145.00 (90-221-0758-2) Walter J Johnson.

Parkinson, John, jt. auth. see Ernst & Young LLP Staff.

Parkinson, John, jt. ed. see Horsley, David.

Parkinson, Joy E. A Manual of English for the Overseas Doctor. 4th ed. (Illus.). 286p. 1991. pap. text 32.00 (0-443-04188-1) Church.

— A Manual of English for the Overseas Doctor. 5th ed. LC 98-31755. 1998. write for info. (0-443-06136-X) Church.

*PARKINSON, JUDY. Edward & Sophie: A Royal Wedding, 1. LC 99-31500. (Illus.). 128p. 1999. 23.95 (0-8092-2428-3, 242830) NTC Contemp Pub Co.

Parkinson, Kathy. The Enormous Turnip. LC 85-14432. (Illus.). 32p. (J). (gr. k-3). 1987. lib. bdg. 14.95 (0-8075-2062-4) A Whitman.

*Parkinson, Kenneth L. Cash Flow Forecasting. (Management Ser.). 150p. 2000. pap. write for info. (0-9633680-4-4) Treasury Info.

— Cash Management in Business. (Management Ser.). 150p. 2000. pap. write for info. (0-9633680-5-2) Treasury Info.

— Preparing for Cash Management Certification: A Self-Study Guide. 200p. 2000. pap. 75.00 (0-9633680-3-6) Treasury Info.

*Parkinson, Kenneth L. & Epstein, Lee. Short-Term Borrowing & Investing. (Management Ser.). 150p. 2000. pap. write for info. (0-9633680-7-9) Treasury Info.

Parkinson, Kenneth L. & Kallberg, Jarl G. Working Capital Management: Theory & Practice. 400p. (C). Date not set. pap. text. write for info. (0-9633680-6-0) Treasury Info.

*Parkinson, Kenneth L. & Ruzek, Raymond P. How to Prepare an RFP for Treasury Services. 3rd ed. (Management Ser.). 140p. 1999. pap. 45.00 (0-9633680-2-8) Treasury Info.

Parkinson, Kenneth L., jt. auth. see Kallberg, Jarl G.

Parkinson, Marie & Zervas, Naoni. The Total Drill Team Dimension: A Textbook for Student & Adult Leaders. (Illus.). 541p. (C). 1985. pap. text 29.95 (0-89641-153-2) American Pr.

Parkinson, Mark. How to Master Psychometric Tests: Winning Strategies for Test Takers. 1998. pap. text 14.95 (0-7494-2254-8) Kogan Page Ltd.

*Parkinson, Mark. Using Psychology in Business: A Practical Guide for Managers. LC 99-34481. 256p. 1999. 69.95 (0-566-08129-6, Pub. by Ashgate Pub) Ashgate Pub Co.

*Parkinson, Mary Jane. And Ride Away Singing. (Illus.). 384p. (C). 1998. 75.00 (1-930140-00-2) Arabian Horse Trust.

Parkinson, Michael, ed. Reshaping Local Government, Vol. III. (Reshaping the Public Sector Ser.). 256p. 1988. 34.95 (0-946967-19-9); pap. 21.95 (0-946967-31-8) Transaction Pubs.

Parkinson, Michael, jt. ed. see Judd, Dennis.

Parkinson, Norman & Ackerley, Lisa. Your Food. (C). 1989. 30.00 (0-86242-099-7, Pub. by Age Concern Eng) St Mut.

Parkinson, P. G., jt. auth. see Chapman, Valentine J.

Parkinson, Patrick. Tradition & Change in Australian Law. 280p. 1995. pap. 39.00 (0-455-21292-9, Pub. by LawBk Co) Gaunt.

Parkinson, Patrick, ed. The Principles of Equity. LC 97-146623. 1000p. 1996. pap. 100.00 (0-455-21395-X, Pub. by LawBk Co) Gaunt.

Parkinson, R. B. Voices from Ancient Egypt: An Anthology of Middle Kingdom Writings. LC 91-7250. (Oklahoma Series in Classical Culture: Vol. 9). (Illus.). 160p. 1991. pap. 22.95 (0-8061-2362-1) U of Okla Pr.

Parkinson, R. B., tr. from EGY. The Tale of Sinuhe: And Other Ancient Egyptian Poems, 1940-1640 B.C. LC 98-32140. (Oxford World's Classics Ser.). (Illus.). 332p. 1999. pap. 13.95 (0-19-283966-7) OUP.

Parkinson, Richard. Cracking Codes: The Rosetta Stone & Decipherment. LC 99-490359. 224p. 1999. 50.00 (0-520-22306-3, Pub. by U CA Pr) Cal Prin Full Svc.

*Parkinson, Richard. Cracking Codes: The Rosetta Stone & Decipherment. LC 99-490359. 224p. 1999. pap. 27.50 (0-520-22248-2, Pub. by U CA Pr) Cal Prin Full Svc.

Parkinson, Richard. Thirty Years in The South Seas. Dennison, John, tr. (Illus.). 700p. 2000. text 75.00 (0-8248-2245-5) UH Pr.

— A Tour in America in Seventeen Ninety-Eight, Seventeen Ninety-Nine, & 1800..., 2 vols. (BCL1 - U. S. History Ser.). 1991. reprint ed. lib. bdg. 150.00 (0-7812-6014-0) Rprt Serv.

Parkinson, Richard & Quirke, Stephen. Papyrus. (Egyptian Bookshelf Ser.). (Illus.). 100p. (Orig.). 1995. pap. 19.95 (0-292-76563-0) U of Tex Pr.

Parkinson, Richard N. Edward Gibbon. LC 72-13382. (Twayne's English Authors Ser.). 158p. (C). 1973. lib. bdg. 18.95 (0-8057-1218-6) Irvington.

Parkinson, Roger. Clausewitz. lib. bdg. 25.95 (0-8488-1903-9) Amereon Ltd.

— Clausewitz. LC 79-150602. (Illus.). 1979. reprint ed. pap. 12.95 (0-8128-6021-7, Scrbrough Hse) Madison Bks UPA.

*Parkinson, Roger. The Peninsular War. (Illus.). 2000. pap. 12.99 (1-84022-228-X, Pub. by Wrdsworth Edits) Combined Pub.

Parkinson, Ronald. British Watercolours at the Victoria & Albert Museum. 1998. 50.00 (1-85177-251-0, Pub. by V&A Ent) Antique Collect.

— John Constable: The Man & His Art. LC 99-491082. (Illus.). 144p. 1998. 50.00 (1-85177-243-X, Pub. by V&A Ent) Antique Collect.

Parkinson, Ronald, jt. auth. see Casteras, Susan P.

*Parkinson, Rosemary, ed. The Caribbean. (Culinaria Ser.). (Illus.). 460p. 1999. 29.95 (3-89508-902-8, 520381) Konemann.

Parkinson, Siobhan. Amelia. 208p. (YA). 1997. pap. 6.95 (0-86278-352-6, Pub. by OBrien Pr) Irish Amer Bk.

— Four Kids, Three Cats, Two Cows, One Witch (Maybe) 144p. (YA). 1998. pap. 7.95 (0-86278-515-4, Pub. by OBrien Pr) Irish Amer Bk.

*Parkinson, Siobhan. The Leprechaun Who Wished He Wasn't. (Illus.). 80p. (J). 2000. pap. 6.95 (0-86278-334-8, Pub. by OBrien Pr) IPG Chicago.

Parkinson, Siobhan. No Peace for Amelia. 224p. (YA). 1997. pap. 7.95 (0-86278-378-X, Pub. by OBrien Pr) Irish Amer Bk.

— Sisters...No Way! 224p. (YA). 1997. pap. 7.95 (0-86278-495-6, Pub. by OBrien Pr) Irish Amer Bk.

Parkinson, Siobhan, ed. Home: An Anthology of New Irish Writing. LC 96-231167. 217p. 1996. pap. 15.95 (1-899047-24-7, Pub. by A A Farmar) Irish Bks Media.

— A Part of Ourselves: Lament for Lives That Ended Too Soon. LC 98-120095. 188p. 1998. pap. 15.95 (1-899047-34-4, Pub. by A A Farmar) Irish Bks Media.

Parkinson, Stanley, jt. auth. see Levine, Gustav.

*Parkinson, Stephen, ed. Cobras e Son: Papers on the Text, Music & Manuscripts of the 'Cantigas de Santa Maria' (Legenda Ser.). 200p. (C). 2000. pap. 49.50 (1-900755-12-2, Pub. by E H R C) David Brown.

Parkinson, Susan, et al. The Real Taste of the Pacific. (Illus.). 112p. (Orig.). 1996. pap. 17.95 (1-895629-66-7) Warwick Publ.

Parkinson, Susan, et al. Taste of the Pacific. (Illus.). 112p. 1995. pap. 16.95 (0-8248-1791-5) UH Pr.

Parkinson, T. J., jt. ed. see Raw, Mary-Elizabeth.

Parkinson, T. L. Written in Water. 1999. pap. 20.00 (0-525-93642-4) NAL.

Parkinson, Thomas. Thanatos: Earth Poems. 1976. pap. 2.00 (0-685-79271-4) Oyez.

— Yorkshire Legends & Traditions. Dorson, Richard M., ed. LC 77-70615. (International Folklore Ser.). 1977. reprint ed. lib. bdg. 21.95 (0-405-10117-1) Ayer.

Parkinson, Thomas, ed. see Yeats, William Butler.

Parkinson, Thomas F. Hart Crane & Yvor Winters: Their Literary Correspondence. LC 77-80475. 198p. reprint ed. pap. 61.40 (0-608-17970-1, 202905500058) Bks Demand.

— Poems: New & Selected. 140p. 1988. pap. 14.95 (0-915032-96-1) Natl Poet Foun.

— W. B. Yeats, Self-Critic: A Study of His Early Verse, & the Later Poetry, 2 vols. in one. LC 75-160480. 484p. reprint ed. pap. 150.10 (0-608-18294-X, 203154400075) Bks Demand.

Parkinson, Wenda. This Gilded African: Toussaint L'Ouverture. 12.95 (0-7043-2187-4, Pub. by Quartet) Charles River Bks.

Parkinson, William A., jt. ed. see Galaty, Michael L.

Parkinson, William L. The Remnant Wars: Vanishing Brethren. LC 96-92674. 242p. (Orig.). 1996. pap. 7.95 (0-9655478-0-9) Parkinson Pub.

P

An Asterisk (*) at the beginning of an entry indicates that the title is appearing for the first time.

Parkison, Jami. Amazing Mallika. Talley, Carol, ed. LC 96-9571. (Key Concepts in Personal Development Ser.). (Illus.). 32p. (J). (gr. k-4). 1996. 16.95 (*1-55942-087-1*) Marsh Media.

— Inger's Promise. LC 95-34472. (Key Concepts in Personal Development Ser.). (Illus.). 32p. (J). (gr. 1-5). 1995. 16.95 (*1-55942-080-4*) Marsh Media.

— Path to Glory: A Pictorial Celebration of the Santa Fe Trail. LC 96-77350. (Illus.). 132p. 1996. 29.95 (*1-888903-01-5*) Highwater Edits.

— Pequena the Burro. LC 93-30377. (Key Concepts in Personal Development Ser.). (Illus.). 32p. (J). (gr. k-4). 1994. teacher ed. 79.95 incl. VHS (*1-55942-058-8*, 9376) Marsh Media.

— Pequena the Burro. LC 93-30377. (Key Concepts in Personal Development Ser.). (Illus.). 32p. (J). (gr. 1-4). 1994. 16.95 (*1-55942-055-3*, 7657) Marsh Media.

Parkison, Jami, ed. see Beaty, Sandy & Wilkerson, J. L.

Parkison, Ralph F. Big Red & the Fence Post. Withrow, Marion O., ed. (Illus.). 53p. (Orig.). (J). (gr. 2-8). 1988. pap. write for info. (*0-318-63993-9*) Little Wood Bks.

— Days. Withrow, Marion O., ed. (Illus.). 60p. (Orig.). (J). (gr. 2-8). 1988. pap. write for info. (*0-318-64003-1*) Little Wood Bks.

— Eovl. Withrow, Marion O., ed. (Illus.). 36p. (Orig.). (J). (gr. 2-8). 1988. pap. write for info. (*0-318-63994-7*) Little Wood Bks.

— In the Middle of the Corn Patch. Withrow, Marion O., ed. (Illus.). 55p. (Orig.). (J). (gr. 2-8). 1988. pap. write for info. (*0-318-64002-3*) Little Wood Bks.

— The Little Flea. Withrow, Marion O., ed. (Illus.). 21p. (Orig.). (J). (gr. 2-8). 1988. pap. write for info. (*0-318-63995-5*) Little Wood Bks.

— The Little Girl & the Inchworm. Withrow, Marion O., ed. (Illus.). 75p. (Orig.). (J). (gr. 2-8). 1988. pap. write for info. (*0-318-63996-3*) Little Wood Bks.

— The Little Girl, the Lillipop, & the Green Bird, Bk. 1. Withrow, Marion O., ed. (Illus.). 31p. (Orig.). (J). (gr. 2-6). 1988. pap. 4.25 (*0-929949-00-5*) Little Wood Bks.

— The Old Goat. Withrow, Marion O., ed. (Illus.). 112p. (Orig.). (J). (gr. 2-8). 1988. pap. write for info. (*0-318-64004-X*) Little Wood Bks.

— The Pea in the Pod, Bk. 3. Withrow, Marion O., ed. (Illus.). 10p. (Orig.). (J). (gr. 2-6). 1988. pap. text 3.00 (*0-929949-02-1*) Little Wood Bks.

— The Pencil. Withrow, Marion O., ed. (Illus.). 47p. (Orig.). (J). (gr. 2-8). 1988. pap. write for info. (*0-318-64000-7*) Little Wood Bks.

— Santa's Wheat Kernels. Withrow, Marion O., ed. (Illus.). 60p. (Orig.). (J). (gr. 2-8). 1988. pap. write for info. (*0-318-64005-8*) Little Wood Bks.

— Seeds & Seeds. Withrow, Marion O., ed. (Illus.). 65p. (Orig.). (J). (gr. 2-8). 1988. pap. write for info. (*0-318-64001-5*) Little Wood Bks.

— The Soda Pop Can & the Road Sign, Bk. 4. Withrow, Marion O., ed. (Illus.). 13p. (Orig.). (J). (gr. 2-6). 1988. pap. text 3.73 (*0-929949-03-X*) Little Wood Bks.

— The Spot on the Ground. Withrow, Marion O., ed. (Illus.). 83p. (Orig.). (J). (gr. 2-8). 1988. pap. write for info. (*0-318-63997-1*) Little Wood Bks.

— A This or a That. Withrow, Marion O., ed. (Illus.). 53p. (Orig.). (J). (gr. 2-8). 1988. pap. write for info. (*0-318-63999-8*) Little Wood Bks.

— The Twig & the Mouse, Bk. 2. Withrow, Marion O., ed. (Illus.). 17p. (Orig.). (J). (gr. 2-6). 1988. pap. 4.25 (*0-929949-01-3*) Little Wood Bks.

— Yodeling. Withrow, Marion O., ed. (Illus.). 71p. (Orig.). (J). (gr. 2-8). 1988. pap. write for info. (*0-318-63998-X*) Little Wood Bks.

Parkka, Daniel J. Equation Directory for the Reconstructionist. 2nd rev. ed. LC 97-171095. 210p. 1996. pap. text 34.95 (*1-884566-24-3*) Inst Police Tech.

***Parkman, Allen M.** Good Intentions Gone Awry: No-fault Divorce & the American Family. LC 99-45669. 256p. 2000. pap. 22.95 (*0-8476-9869-6*); text 60.00 (*0-8476-9868-8*) Rowman.

Parkman, Anna W., jt. auth. see Surkin, Howard B.

Parkman, Aubrey L. David Jayne Hill & the Problem of World Peace. LC 72-3530. 293p. 1975. 39.50 (*0-8387-1259-2*) Bucknell U Pr.

P

Parkman, E. B., et al. Papers on California Prehistory, Vol. 41, Pt. 4. Breschini, G. S. & Haversat, Trudy, eds. (Archives of California Prehistory Ser.: Vol. 41). (Illus.). 136p. (Orig.). (C). 1995. pap. text 15.00 (*1-55567-109-8*) Coyote Press.

Parkman, Elmerina L. & Leone, Norma L. From Nonnie's Italian Kitchen: The Recipes of Mary Baldini Leonardi. LC 88-13414. 160p. (Orig.). 1988. pap. 8.95 (*0-936635-25-8*) Lion Pr & Vid.

***Parkman, Francis.** The Book of Roses. (Notable American Authors Ser.). 1999. reprint ed. lib. bdg. 125.00 (*0-7812-4731-4*) Rprt Serv.

— The California & Oregon Trail. (Notable American Authors Ser.). 1999. reprint ed. lib. bdg. 125.00 (*0-7812-4727-6*) Rprt Serv.

Parkman, Francis. The Conspiracy of Pontiac & the Indian War after the Conquest of Canada: From the Spring of 1763 to the Death of Pontiac, Vol. 2. LC 94-20956. (Illus.). x, 384p. 1994. pap. 12.50 (*0-8032-8737-2*, Bison Books) U of Nebr Pr.

— The Conspiracy of Pontiac & the Indian War after the Conquest of Canada: To the Massacre at Michillimackinac, Vol. 1. LC 94-20956. (Illus.). xxxv, 367p. 1994. pap. 12.50 (*0-8032-8733-X*, Bison Books) U of Nebr Pr.

***Parkman, Francis.** Count Frontenac & New France under Louis XIV. (Notable American Authors Ser.). 1999. reprint ed. lib. bdg. 125.00 (*0-7812-4735-7*) Rprt Serv.

— The Discovery of the Great West. (Notable American Authors Ser.). 1999. reprint ed. lib. bdg. 125.00 (*0-7812-4733-0*) Rprt Serv.

Parkman, Francis. France & England in North America Vol. I: Pioneers of France; The Jesuits in North America; LaSalle & the Discovery of the Great West; The Old Regime in Canada. Levin, David, ed. LC 82-18658. (Library of America Ser.). 1504p. 1983. 40.00 (*0-940450-10-0*, Pub. by Library of America) Penguin Putnam.

— France & England in North America Vol. 2: Count Frontenac & New France under Louis XIV; A Half Century of Conflict; Montcalm & Wolfe. Levin, David, ed. LC 82-18658. (Library of America Ser.). 1620p. 1983. 45.00 (*0-940450-11-9*, Pub. by Library of America) Penguin Putnam.

— The Francis Parkman Reader. Morison, Samuel Eliot, ed. LC 97-42967. Orig. Title: The Parkman Reader. (Illus.). 533p. 1998. reprint ed. pap. 17.95 (*0-306-80823-4*) Da Capo.

***Parkman, Francis.** A Half Century of Conflict. (Notable American Authors Ser.). 1999. reprint ed. lib. bdg. 125.00 (*0-7812-4737-3*) Rprt Serv.

Parkman, Francis. A Half Century of Conflict, 2 vols., Set. 1993. reprint ed. lib. bdg. 180.00 (*0-7812-5194-X*) Rprt Serv.

***Parkman, Francis.** History of the Conspiracy of Pontiac & the Indian War of Conquest. (Notable American Authors Ser.). 1999. reprint ed. lib. bdg. 125.00 (*0-7812-4728-4*) Rprt Serv.

— The Jesuits in North America in the 17th Century. (Notable American Authors Ser.). 1999. reprint ed. lib. bdg. 125.00 (*0-7812-4732-2*) Rprt Serv.

Parkman, Francis. The Jesuits in North America in the Seventeenth Century. LC 97-30487. (Illus.). xxxi, 587p. 1997. pap. 25.00 (*0-8032-8746-1*, Bison Books) U of Nebr Pr.

***Parkman, Francis.** La Salle & the Discovery of the Great West. Krakauer, Jon, ed. LC 99-41401. (Modern Library Exploration Ser.). 352p. 1999. pap. 14.95 (*0-375-75475-X*) Modern Lib NY.

Parkman, Francis. La Salle & the Discovery of the Great West. 1993. reprint ed. lib. bdg. 75.00 (*0-7812-5892-8*) Rprt Serv.

— Lasalle & the Discovery of the Great Northwest. 560p. 1968. reprint ed. 38.95 (*0-87928-004-2*) Corner Hse.

— LaSalle & the Discovery of the Great West. 1990. pap. 9.50 (*0-679-72615-2*) Vin Bks.

— LaSalle & the Discovery of the Great West. Taylor, William R., ed. LC 86-22763. 377p. 1986. reprint ed. lib. bdg. 89.50 (*0-313-24223-2*, PDGW, Greenwood Pr) Greenwood.

— Letters of Francis Parkman, 2 Vols, 1. Jacobs, Wilbur R., ed. LC 60-8754. (Illus.). 284p. 1960. reprint ed. pap. 88.10 (*0-8357-9730-9*, 201010000068) Bks Demand.

— Letters of Francis Parkman, 2 Vols, 2. Jacobs, Wilbur R., ed. LC 60-8754. (Illus.). 342p. 1960. reprint ed. pap. 106.10 (*0-608-08255-4*, 201010000069) Bks Demand.

— Montcalm & Wolfe. Carr, Caleb, ed. LC 98-48972. (Modern Library War Ser.). 522p. 1999. pap. 16.95 (*0-375-75420-2*) Modern Lib NY.

***Parkman, Francis.** Montcalm & Wolfe. (Notable American Authors Ser.). 1999. reprint ed. lib. bdg. 125.00 (*0-7812-4736-5*) Rprt Serv.

Parkman, Francis. Montcalm & Wolfe: The French & Indian War. (Illus.). 674p. 1995. reprint ed. pap. 18.95 (*0-306-80621-5*) Da Capo.

***Parkman, Francis.** The Old Regime in Canada. (Notable American Authors Ser.). 1999. reprint ed. lib. bdg. 125.00 (*0-7812-4734-9*) Rprt Serv.

— The Oregon Trail. Rosenthal, Bernard, ed. (Oxford World's Classics Ser.). (Illus.). 384p. 2000. pap. 10.95 (*0-19-283912-8*) OUP.

Parkman, Francis. The Oregon Trail. Feltskog, E. N., ed. LC 94-19303. (Illus.). xviii, 758p. 1994. pap. 25.00 (*0-8032-8739-9*, Bison Books) U of Nebr Pr.

— The Oregon Trail. Levin, David, ed. & intro. by. (American Library). 500p. 1982. pap. 11.95 (*0-14-039042-1*, Penguin Classics) Viking Penguin.

— The Oregon Trail. Feltskog, E. N., ed. LC 68-9017. 854p. reprint ed. pap. 200.00 (*0-608-15032-0*, 202594800047) Bks Demand.

— The Oregon Trail: Sketches of Prairie & Rocky Mountain Life. 1996. reprint ed. lib. bdg. 26.95 (*0-8488-1768-0*) Amereon Ltd.

— Oregon Trail: The Sketches of Prairie & Rocky - Mountain Life. 479p. 1980. reprint ed. 34.95 (*0-87928-103-0*) Corner Hse.

— The Oregon Trail & the Conspiracy of Pontiac. Taylor, William R., ed. 951p. 1991. 35.00 (*0-940450-54-2*, Pub. by Library of America) Penguin Putnam.

— Pioneers of France in the New World. LC 96-17586. (Illus.). xxxiv, 473p. 1996. pap. 20.00 (*0-8032-8744-5*, Bison Books) U of Nebr Pr.

***Parkman, Francis.** Pioneers of France in the New World. (Notable American Authors Ser.). 1999. reprint ed. lib. bdg. 125.00 (*0-7812-4730-6*) Rprt Serv.

Parkman, Francis. Representative Selections. (BCL1-PS American Literature Ser.). 1993. reprint ed. lib. bdg. write for info. (*0-7812-6997-0*) Rprt Serv.

***Parkman, Francis.** Vassall Morton (Novel) (Notable American Authors Ser.). 1999. reprint ed. lib. bdg. 125.00 (*0-7812-4729-2*) Rprt Serv.

Parkman, Francis. Works, 20 vols. LC 69-19160. (Illus.). reprint ed. 1395.00 (*0-404-04920-6*) AMS Pr.

— Works, 12 vols., Set. (BCL1 - History - Canada Ser.). 1991. reprint ed. lib. bdg. 1060.00 (*0-7812-6353-0*) Rprt Serv.

Parkman, Francis, intro. Historical Account of Bouquet's Expedition Against the Ohio Indians in 1764. (Illus.). 162p. 1993. reprint ed. lib. bdg. 25.00 (*0-8328-3000-3*) Higginson Bk Co.

Parkman, Mary R. Fighters for Peace. LC 73-167399. (Essay Index Reprint Ser.). 1977. reprint ed. 23.95 (*0-8369-2439-8*) Ayer.

— Heroines of Service. LC 68-58808. (Essay Index Reprint Ser.). 1977. 23.95 (*0-8369-1152-0*) Ayer.

— High Adventurers. LC 67-26770. (Essay Index Reprint Ser.). 1977. 20.95 (*0-8369-0770-1*) Ayer.

Parkman, Patricia. Insurrectionary Civil Strikes in Latin America: 1931-1961. (Monograph Ser.). 55p. 1990. 3.00 (*1-880813-00-9*) A Einstein Inst.

— Nonviolent Insurrection in El Salvador: The Fall of Maximiliano Hernandez Martinez. LC 88-9432. 168p. 1988. 33.50 (*0-8165-1062-8*) U of Ariz Pr.

Parkoff, Eliezer. Fine Lines of Faith. LC 93-48518. 1994. 20.95 (*0-87306-669-3*) Feldheim.

Parks. Aging & Mental Health. 160p. 1996. pap. text, per. 14.95 (*0-7872-2233-X*) Kendall-Hunt.

***Parks.** Big Questions, Worthy Dreams: Mentoring Young Adults In Their Search for Meaning, Purpose & Faith. 240p. 2000. write for info. (*0-7879-4171-9*) Jossey-Bass.

Parks. Cheating an Appointment with Death. 1995. pap. 6.00 (*0-927936-42-9*) Vincom Pubng Co.

— Math Life. 1996. pap. text, student ed. 29.33 (*0-13-259417-X*) P-H.

— Structuring Paragraphs. 5th ed. Date not set. pap. text. write for info. (*0-312-19558-3*) St Martin.

Parks. Superconductivity, Vol. 1. (Illus.). 1969. text 370.00 (*0-8247-1520-9*) Dekker.

Parks & Gamble. Reinforced Concrete Slabs. 2nd ed. LC 99-28984. 736p. 1999. 110.00 (*0-471-34850-3*) Wiley.

Parks, et al. Structuring Paragraphs. 4th ed. 1995. pap. text, teacher ed. 24.00 (*0-312-11514-8*); pap. text, teacher ed. 5.00 (*0-312-11516-4*) St Martin.

— Structuring Paragraphs: A Guide to Effective Writing. 272p. 1995. pap. text 36.95 (*0-312-11513-X*) St Martin.

Parks & History Association Staff. Frederick Douglass at Home: The Frederick Douglass National Historic Site. (Illus.). 40p. (Orig.). 1995. pap. 3.50 (*1-887878-03-3*) Pks & Hist.

Parks, A. Marine Insurance & Average: The Law & Practice, 2 vols. (C). 1988. 1145.00 (*0-7855-6044-0*, Pub. by Witherby & Co) St Mut.

Parks, A. Franklin, et al. Structuring Paragraphs: A Guide to Effective Writing. 200p. (C). 1981. pap. text 8.76 (*0-312-76865-6*) St Martin.

— Structuring Paragraphs: A Guide to Effective Writing. 3rd ed. LC 89-63925. 256p. (C). 1991. pap. text, teacher ed. 0.40 (*0-312-05586-2*) St Martin.

***Parks, Adele.** Playing Away. 336p. 2000. 23.95 (*0-671-77543-X*, PB Hardcover) PB.

Parks, Aileen W. Davy Crockett: Young Rifleman. LC 86-10781. (Childhood of Famous Americans Ser.). (Illus.). 192p. (J). (gr. 3-7). 1986. reprint ed. mass mkt. 4.95 (*0-02-041840-X*) Macmillan.

— Davy Crockett, Young Rifleman. (Childhood of Famous Americans Ser.). (J). 1986. 10.05 (*0-606-03191-X*, Pub. by Turtleback) Demco.

Parks, Alex L. The Law & Practice of Marine Insurance & Average, 2 vols. LC 87-13667. 1652p. 1987. text 190.00 (*0-87033-368-2*) Cornell Maritime.

Parks, Alex L. & Cattell, Edward V., Jr. The Law of Tug, Tow & Pilotage. 3rd ed. LC 93-49862. 1410p. 1994. text 175.00 (*0-87033-448-4*) Cornell Maritime.

***Parks, Alexia.** American GULAG: Secret P. O. W. Camps for Teens. 2000. pap. 19.95 (*1-930418-01-9*) Educ Exchg.

— An American GULAG: Secret P.O.W. Camps for Teens. LC 00-90030. xii, 278p. (Orig.). 2000. pap. 19.95 (*1-930418-03-5*) Educ Exchg.

Parks, Arnold G. Black Elderly in Rural America: A Comprehensive Study. LC 88-40246. (Illus.). 345p. (C). 1988. pap. text 28.00 (*1-55605-054-2*) Wyndham Hall.

Parks, Arva M. Harry Truman & the Little White House in Key West. LC 93-144349. (Illus.). 63p. 1991. pap. 4.95 (*0-9629402-0-8*) Centennial Pr.

— Miami: The Magic City. 2nd ed. LC 91-75436. (Illus.). 256p. 1991. 39.95 (*0-9629402-2-4*) Centennial Pr.

— Miami: Then & Now. LC 92-85502. (Illus.). 64p. 1992. pap. 4.95 (*0-9629402-1-6*) Centennial Pr.

Parks, Barbara. Barbara Parks Series. (Illus.). 1994. 24.98 (*0-679-87019-9*) Random.

Parks, Barbara, jt. auth. see Catron, Carol.

Parks, Barbara A., jt. auth. see Johnson, Dewayne J.

***Parks, C. V.** Assessment & Recommendations for Fissile-Material Packaging Exemptions & General Licenses Within 10 CFR PT. 71. 112p. 1998. per. 9.00 (*0-16-062942-X*) USGPO.

— Review & Prioritization of Technical Issues Related to Burnup Credit for LWR Fuel. 70p. 2000. pap. 7.00 (*0-16-059114-7*) USGPO.

Parks Canada Staff, jt. auth. see Kalff, Sarah A.

Parks, Carol. Complete Book of Window Treatments & Curtains: Traditional & Innovative Ways to Dress up Your Windows. (Illus.). 144p. 1995. pap. 14.95 (*0-8069-0613-8*) Sterling.

— Great Sewing Accessories, to Sew. LC 96-48136. (Illus.). 112p. 1997. 24.95 (*0-8069-9566-1*) Sterling.

— Great Sewing Accessories to Sew. (Illus.). 112p. 1998. 14.95 (*0-8069-9569-6*) Sterling.

— Make Your Own Great Vests: 90 Ways to Jazz up Your Wardrobe. (Illus.). 160p. 1996. pap. 14.95 (*0-8069-0973-0*) Sterling.

— Making Handbags & Purses: 50 Patterns & Designs from Casual to Corporate. LC 97-31147. (Illus.). 128p. 1997. 24.95 (*1-57990-012-7*, Pub. by Lark Books) Random.

***Parks, Carol.** Making Handbags & Purses: 50 Patterns & Designs from Casual to Corporate. (Illus.). 2000. pap. 16.95 (*1-57990-149-2*) Lark Books.

Parks, Carol. Patterns: Sewing for a New Class. Date not set. 3.75 (*0-8069-5966-5*) Sterling.

— Sewing the New Classics: Clothes with Easy Style. (Illus.). 144p. 1996. pap. 14.95 (*0-8069-3194-9*) Sterling.

— Simple Upholstery & Slipcovers: Great New Looks for Every Room. (Illus.). 144p. 1997. pap. text 14.95 (*0-8069-8159-8*) Sterling.

— Terrific Totes & Carryalls: 40 Bags to Sew for Shopping, Working, Hiking, Biking, & More. LC 97-46563. 128p. 1998. 24.95 (*1-57990-019-4*, Pub. by Lark Books) Random.

Parks, Carol, ed. see Bennett, D. J.

Parks, Carol, ed. see Haberstich, Kurt.

Parks, Carol, ed. see Rankin, Chris.

Parks, Catherine G. & Schmitt, Craig L. Wild Edible Mushrooms in the Blue Mountains: Resource & Issues. (Illus.). 32p. 1998. reprint ed. 11.00 (*0-89904-775-0*, Cascade Geog Soc); reprint ed. pap. 6.00 (*0-89904-776-9*, Cascade Geog Soc) Crumb Elbow Pub.

Parks, Catherine G., et al. Field Guide for the Identification of Snags & Logs in the Interior Columbia River Basin. (Illus.). 50p. 1998. 15.00 (*0-89904-936-2*, Cascade Geog Soc); spiral bd. 10.00 (*0-89904-937-0*, Cascade Geog Soc) Crumb Elbow Pub.

— Field Guide for the Identification of Snags & Logs in the Interior Columbia River Basin. (Illus.). 50p. 1998. 5.00 (*0-89904-870-6*, Cascade Geog Soc) Crumb Elbow Pub.

Parks, Clark K. Traveling I-80 with Otto: Travel Guide. 3rd ed. 384p. 1993. pap. text 12.95 (*1-878959-01-8*) Trav Guide Pubns.

***Parks Company Staff.** Greetings from Grand Canyon Arizona. (Illus.). 20p. 2000. pap. 8.95 (*0-87905-960-5*) Gibbs Smith Pub.

— Greetings from Yosemite National Park. (Illus.). 20p. 1999. pap. 8.95 (*0-87905-961-3*) Gibbs Smith Pub.

Parks, Craig D. Group Performance & Interaction. LC 98-27911. 296p. (C). 1998. text 69.00 (*0-8133-3319-9*, Pub. by Westview); pap. text 24.00 (*0-8133-3320-2*, Pub. by Westview) HarpC.

Parks, David. GI Diary. (Howard University Press Library of Contemporary Literature). 133p. 1984. pap. 12.95 (*0-88258-113-9*) Howard U Pr.

Parks, David C. Environmental Management for Real Estate Professionals. LC 91-45631. (Illus.). 225p. 1992. text 62.95 (*0-944298-69-9*, 763) Inst Real Estate.

Parks, Deborah. Climb Away: Chasing the Dream. LC 95-8684. (YA). (gr. 7 up). 1995. lib. bdg. 13.95 (*0-382-39093-8*) Silver Burdett Pr.

Parks, Deborah. Climb Away: Chasing the Dream. LC 95-8684. 112p. (YA). (gr. 7 up). 1995. pap. 4.95 (*0-382-39094-6*) Silver Burdett Pr.

***Parks, Deborah A.** Jane Addams: Freedom's Innovator. Hobson, Bonnie H., ed. LC 99-46876. (History Makers Ser.: Vol. 4). (Illus.). 128p. (YA). 2000. 16.95 (*0-7835-5445-1*) Time-Life.

Parks, Deborah A., jt. auth. see Time-Life Books Editors.

Parks, Dennis. A Potter's Guide to Raw Glazing & Oil Firing LC 79-17357. 112p. 1980. write for info. (*0-684-16392-6*) Scribner.

Parks, Don & Dyer, William. Jo. 1964. pap. 5.25 (*0-8222-0592-0*) Dramatists Play.

Parks, Douglas R. Traditional Narratives of the Arikara Indians, 2 vols. LC 90-12889. (Studies in the Anthropology of North American Indians). 1991. audio 20.00 (*0-8032-3697-2*) U of Nebr Pr.

— Traditional Narratives of the Arikara Indians, 2 vols., Vol. 2: Stories of Other Narrators. LC 90-12889. (Studies in the Anthropology of North American Indians). xiv, 659p. 1991. text 95.00 (*0-8032-3692-1*) U of Nebr Pr.

— Traditional Narratives of the Arikara Indians: Interlinear Translations, 2 vols., Vol. 1: Stories of Alfred Morsette. LC 90-12889. (Studies in the Anthropology of North American Indians). xxiv, 684p. 1991. text 95.00 (*0-8032-3691-3*) U of Nebr Pr.

— Traditional Narratives of the Arikara Indians, English Translations, 2 vols., Vol. 4: Stories of Other Narrators. LC 90-12889. (Studies in Anthropology of North American Indians). (Illus.). xvii, 431p. 1992. text 70.00 (*0-8032-3695-6*) U of Nebr Pr.

— Traditional Narratives of the Arikara Indians, English Translations: Stories of Alfred Morsette, 2 vols., Vol. 3: Stories of Alfred Morsette. LC 90-12889. (Studies in Anthropology of North American Indians). xxvi, 468p. 1992. text 70.00 (*0-8032-3694-8*) U of Nebr Pr.

Parks, Douglas R., compiled by. Myths & Traditions of the Arikara Indians. LC 95-43855. (Sources of American Indian Oral Literature Ser.). (Illus.). xix, 406p. 1996. pap. 17.95 (*0-8032-8742-9*, Bison Books) U of Nebr Pr.

Parks, Douglas R., jt. ed. see DeMallie, Raymond J.

Parks, Douglas R., ed. see Murie, James R.

Parks-Doyle, Jodi, jt. ed. see Bayles, Patricia.

Parks, E. Taylor. Colombia & the United States. LC 77-111728. (American Imperialism: Viewpoints of United States Foreign Policy, 1898-1941 Ser.). 1970. reprint ed. 34.95 (*0-405-02043-0*) Ayer.

— Colombia & the United States, 1765-1934. (History - United States Ser.). 554p. 1993. reprint ed. lib. bdg. 99.00 (*0-7812-4865-5*) Rprt Serv.

Parks, E. Taylor, ed. see Anderson, Richard C.

Parks, Edd W. Teddy Roosevelt: Young Rough Rider. LC 89-37819. (Childhood of Famous Americans Ser.). (Illus.). 192p. (J). (gr. 3-7). 1989. reprint ed. mass mkt. 4.95 (*0-689-71349-5*) Aladdin.

— Teddy Roosevelt, Young Rough Rider. (Childhood of Famous Americans Ser.). (J). 1961. 10.05 (*0-606-04343-8*, Pub. by Turtleback) Demco.

Parks, Edilbert P. The Roman Rhetorical Schools As Preparation for the Courts Under the Early Empire. LC 78-64198. (Johns Hopkins University. Studies in the Social Sciences. Thirtieth Ser. 1912: 2). reprint ed. 32.50 (*0-404-61304-7*) AMS Pr.

Parks, Edward. The Apartment Hunter's Guide: Boston: How to Find Your Perfect Apartment for No Money. LC 95-60224. (Illus.). 96p. (Orig.). 1995. pap. 7.95 (*0-9645575-0-9*) Tri Light Pub Grp.

Parks, F. Newton. Happiness Is Shooting Your Age. 1994. pap. 11.95 (*0-89876-213-8*) Gardner Pr.

Parks, F. S. Genealogy of the Parke Family of Connecticut: Including Robert of New London, Edward of Guilford & Others; Also a List of Parke, Park, Parks, Etc. Who Fought in the Revolution. (Illus.). 333p. 1989. reprint ed. pap. 50.00 (*0-8328-0933-0*); reprint ed. lib. bdg. 58.00 (*0-8328-0932-2*) Higginson Bk Co.

***Parks, Fanny.** Wanderings of a Pilgrim: In Search of the Picturesque, During Four & Twenty Years in the East; with Revelations of Life in the Zenana, 2 vols. (Illus.). 1115p. 1999. 115.00 (*81-215-0909-2*, Pub. by M Manoharial) Coronet Bks.

Parks-Flack, Carla. Tarot 2000: Lifting the Veil of Illusion, Incls. 72 cards. (Illus.). 201p. 1995. text 24.95 (*1-885499-52-3*) Angelight.

Parks, Fred. Fred Parks Guide to Gaming & Fun. 127p. (Orig.). 1988. pap. 9.95 (*0-9620980-0-0*) Parks Pub.

Parks, Frederick J. The Celebrated Oyster House Cookbook. LC 85-221680. (Illus.). 65p. 1985. pap. 9.95 (*0-911403-28-0*) Seven Hills Bk.

Parks, Gabe. Nebraska Trivia. LC 98-17242. 192p. 1998. pap. 6.95 (*1-55853-605-1*) Rutledge Hill Pr.

Parks, Gary W. Index to the 1820 Census of Maryland & Washington, D. C. 274p. 1999. pap. 27.50 (*0-8063-1148-7*) Clearfield Co.

Parks, George. Physics of Space Plasmas: An Introduction. (C). 1991. pap. 65.00 (*0-201-48987-2*) Addison-Wesley.

Parks, George B., ed. see Thomas, William.

Parks, Gerald, tr. see Natali, Carlo.

Parks, Gleen H. Medical Analysis & Reviews of Human Immunodeficiency Virus (HIV) Index of Synthesis of New Information by Research Scientists. 161p. 1998. 47.50 (*0-7883-1892-6*); pap. 44.50 (*0-7883-1893-4*) ABBE Pubs Assn.

Parks, Glenn H. Medical Analysis & Reviews of Human Immunodeficiency Virus: Index of Syntheses of New Information by Research Scientists. 150p. 1996. pap. 44.50 (*0-7883-0817-3*) ABBE Pubs Assn.

— Medical Analysis & Reviews of Human Immunodeficiency Virus: Index of Syntheses of New Information by Research Scientists. 150p. 1996. 47.50 (*0-7883-0816-5*) ABBE Pubs Assn.

Parks, Gordon, Jr. Arias in Silence. LC 93-47352. (Illus.). 128p. 1994. 40.00 (*0-8212-2120-5*, Pub. by Bulfinch Pr) Little.

— A Choice of Weapons. LC 86-17993. xii, 274p. 1986. reprint ed. pap. 14.95 (*0-87351-202-2*, Borealis Book) Minn Hist.

— Glimpses Toward Infinity. LC 95-42377. (Illus.). 112p. (gr. 8). 1996. 45.00 (*0-8212-2297-X*) Little.

— Half Past Autumn: A Retrospective. LC 97-19797. (Illus.). 360p. 1997. 65.00 (*0-8212-2298-8*, Pub. by Bulfinch Pr) Little.

— Half Past Autumn: A Retrospective, Vol. 1. (Illus.). 360p. 1998. pap. 40.00 (*0-8212-2551-0*) Little.

— The Learning Tree. 1987. mass mkt. 5.99 (*0-449-21504-0*, Crest) Fawcett.

Parks, Gordon, Jr. Learning Tree. 1983. 11.09 (*0-606-00946-9*, Pub. by Turtleback) Demco.

***Parks, Gordon.** A Star for Noon: An Homage to Women in Images, Poetry & Music. LC 99-86225. (Illus.). 112p. 2000. 50.00 incl. audio compact disk (*0-8212-2685-1*) Bulfinch Pr.

Parks, Gordon, Jr., et al. Half Past Autumn: A Retrospective. LC 97-19797. 1997. pap. 40.00 (*0-8212-2503-0*, Pub. by Bulfinch Pr) Little.

Parks, Grace E. 20th Century Memoirs of Kirtland, Ohio. LC 97-68829. 198p. 1997. 24.95 (*1-880047-52-7*); pap. 14.95 (*1-880047-53-5*) Creative Des.

Parks, Graham, tr. see Berthier, Francois.

Parks, Greg. Freedom, Justice, & Equality: The Teachings of the Nation of Islam. 48p. (Orig.). 1992. pap. 4.95 (*1-56411-023-0*) Untd Bros & Sis.

Parks, H. R., jt. auth. see Krantz, S. G.

***Parks, Harold B.** Mathematics in Life, Society & the World. 2nd ed. LC 99-43379. 814p. 1999. 86.00 (*0-13-011690-4*) P-H.

Parks, Harold R. Explicit Determination of Area Minimizing Hypersurfaces, II. LC 86-1039. (Memoirs of the AMS Ser.: No. 60/342). 90p. 1986. pap. 18.00 (*0-8218-2339-6*, MEMO/60/342) Am Math.

Parks, Harold R., jt. auth. see Krantz, Steven George.

Parks, J. E., jt. ed. see Miller, C.

Parks, J. S., jt. ed. see Laron, Z.

Parks, James D. Robert S. Duncanson: Nineteenth Century Black Romantic Painter. (YA). 1990. 12.95 (*0-87498-011-9*) Assoc Pubs DC.

Parks, James E. & Winograd, Nicholas, eds. Resonance Ionization Spectroscopy, 1996: 8th International Symposium. (AIP Conference Proceedings Ser.: Vol. 388). 500p. 1997. text 130.00 (*1-56396-611-5*) Am Inst Physics.

Parks, Janet. New York on the Rise. (Illus.). 80p. 1999. 24.95 (*0-85331-763-1*) Antique Collect.

Parks, Janet B., et al, eds. Contemporary Sport Management. 2nd ed. LC 97-35194. (Illus.). 360p. 1998. text 45.00 (*0-87322-836-7*, BPAR0836) Human Kinetics.

Parks, Joe E. Christmas Around the World. 36p. 1981. 5.99 (*0-8341-9558-5*, MC-45) Lillenas.

Parks, John. Breeding Better Beagles. (Illus.). 96p. 1990. pap. 6.95 (*0-936369-49-3*) Son Rise Pubns.

Parks, Joseph H. General Edmund Kirby Smith, C.S.A. (Southern Biography Ser.). (Illus.). 537p. 1992. pap. 16.95 (*0-8071-1800-1*) La State U Pr.

— General Leonidas Polk, C.S.A. The Fighting Bishop. LC 62-15028. (Southern Biography Ser.). (Illus.). 408p. 1992. pap. 16.95 (*0-8071-1801-X*) La State U Pr.

Parks, Joyce. Single, but Not Sorry. rev. ed. 235p. 1985. pap. 8.25 (*0-89084-307-4*, 003632) Bob Jones Univ.

Parks, Julie A. Storytellers: A Novel of Supernatural Terror. 256p. 1998. pap. 15.95 (*1-891946-04-8*) Design Image.

Parks, K. S. Human Reliability: Analysis, Prediction, & Prevention of Human Errors. (Advances in Human Factors-Ergonomics Ser.: No. 7). 340p. 1987. 191.50 (*0-444-42727-9*) Elsevier.

Parks, Karen J., jt. ed. see Lagerborg, Mary Beth.

Parks, Kathy, ed. see Klawitter, Pamela A. & Schwartz, Linda.

Parks, Lawrence C., jt. auth. see Atlas, Ronald M.

Parks, Lloyd C., tr. see Stendhal, pseud.

Parks, Lois F., ed. see Chivers, Thomas Holley.

Parks, Lori, ed. see Breschini, Gary S., et al.

Parks, Lori, ed. see Brigandi, Phil.

Parks, Lori, ed. see Burns, John F.

Parks, Lori, ed. see Dymond, Lura.

Parks, Lori, ed. see Fracchia, Charles A.

Parks, Lori, ed. see Gardner, Mark L.

Parks, Lori, ed. see Grabowski, John & Grabowski, Diane E.

Parks, Lori, ed. see Harris, Bill.

Parks, Lori, ed. see Kent, Bill, et al.

Parks, Lori, ed. see Lavoie, Steven.

Parks, Lori, ed. see Luckingham, Brad & Luckingham, Barbara.

Parks, Lori, ed. see Marsh, Diann.

Parks, Lori, ed. see McRae, Norman.

Parks, Lori, ed. see Murphy, Victoria.

Parks, Lori, ed. see Noel, Thomas J.

Parks, Lori, ed. see Noel, Thomas J. & Corson, Dan W.

Parks, Lori, ed. see Olislagers, Robert P.

Parks, Lori, ed. see Orton, Charles W. & Marsh, Diann.

Parks, Lori, ed. see Rehart, Catherine M.

Parks, Lori, ed. see Roth, Darlene.

Parks, Lori, ed. see Rovanpera, Brad.

Parks, Lori, ed. see Sherman, Lola.

Parks, Lori, ed. see Showley, Roger.

Parks, Lori, ed. see Showley, Roger M.

Parks, Lori, jt. ed. see Sorenson, John.

Parks, Lori M., ed. see Marsh, Diann.

Parks, Lori M., ed. see Noel, Thomas Jacob.

Parks, Lori M., ed. see Showley, Roger M.

Parks, Louise, ed. see Ard, Linda & Pitts, Mabel.

Parks, Lynn A. Capitalism in Early American Literature: Texts & Contexts. LC 95-39533. (Studies on Themes & Motifs in Literature: Vol. 27). 183p. (C). 1997. 44.95 (*0-8204-2895-7*) P Lang Pubng.

Parks, M. G., ed. see Howe, Joseph.

Parks, Marjorie M., jt. ed. see Harvey, John H.

Parks, Marty. Because He Lives. 1997. pap. 2.50 (*0-8341-9739-1*) Lillenas.

Parks, Marty. Spirit of Christmas: A Musical for Senior Choir & Congregation. 1998. pap. 5.99 (*0-8341-9685-9*) Lillenas.

Parks, Marty, jt. auth. see Bolton, Martha.

Parks, Mary A. The Circle Leads Home. LC 97-48793. (Women's West Ser.). 224p. 1998. 22.50 (*0-87081-488-5*) Univ Pr Colo.

Parks, Michael E. The Art Teacher's Desktop Reference. LC 93-8104. 272p. 1994. pap. text 62.67 (*0-13-052234-1*) P-H.

Parks, Nancy. Si Si Knows You Need to Feel Safe! A Guide for Parents - Caregiver - Professionals. Corfman, Ann & Davis, Ken, eds. (Illus.). 8p. (Orig.). 1996. pap., wbk. ed. 1.50 (*1-888282-02-9*) Little Otter.

— Si Si Knows You Need to Feel Safe: A Guide for Young People. Corfman, Ann & Davis, Ken, eds. (Illus.). 19p. (Orig.). (J). (gr. 2-4). 1996. pap., student ed. 3.25 (*1-888282-01-0*) Little Otter.

Parks, Pat. The Railroad That Died at Sea - the Florida East Coast's Key West Extension. LC 68-54448. (Illus.). 48p. Date not set. reprint ed. pap. 7.95 (*0-911607-05-6*) Langley Pr Inc.

Parks, Paula L. Uno: A Collection of One-Paragraph Essays & Writing Assignments for the Emerging College Writer. 2nd large type ed. (Illus.). 153p. (C). 1998. pap. text. write for info. (*0-9667779-0-5*); pap. text, teacher ed. write for info. (*0-9667779-1-3*) Wordsmith CA.

***Parks, Paula L.** Uno: A Collection of One-Paragraph Essays & Writing Assignments for the Emerging College Writer. 3rd ed. (Illus.). 213p. (C). 1999. pap. text 16.90 (*0-9667779-2-1*); pap. text, teacher ed. 17.25 (*0-9667779-3-X*) Wordsmith CA.

Parks, Peggy, jt. auth. see Ford, Gerald.

Parks, Penny. Rescuing the "Inner Child" Therapy for Adults Sexually Abused As Children. 194p. 21.95 (*0-285-65084-X*, Pub. by Souvenir Pr Ltd) IPG Chicago.

— Rescuing the "Inner Child" Therapy for Adults Sexually Abused As Children. 194p. 1995. pap. 12.95 (*0-285-65089-0*, Pub. by Souvenir Pr Ltd) IPG Chicago.

Parks, R. D., ed. Superconductivity, Vol. 2. (Illus.). 1456p. 1969. text 185.00 (*0-8247-1521-7*) Dekker.

Parks, Randolph W., et al, eds. Fundamentals of Neural Network Modeling: Neuropsychology & Cognitive Neuroscience. LC 97-34792. (Computational Neuroscience Ser.). (Illus.). 442p. 1998. 60.00 (*0-262-16175-3*, Bradford Bks) MIT Pr.

— Neuropsychology of Alzheimer's Disease & Other Dementias. LC 92-49274. (Illus.). 698p. 1993. text 79.00 (*0-19-506612-X*) OUP.

Parks, Richard. Fishing Yellowstone National Park. LC 98-7741. (Illus.). 208p. 1998. pap. 14.95 (*1-56044-625-0*) Falcon Pub Inc.

Parks, Richard M., ed. Manual on the Use of Thermocouples in Temperature Measurement. LC 92-47237. (Manual Ser.: No. MNL 12). (Illus.). 311p. 1993. text 49.00 (*0-8031-1466-4*, MNL12) ASTM.

Parks, Richard S. The Music of Claude Debussy. 360p. (C). 1990. 50.00 (*0-300-04439-9*) Yale U Pr.

Parks, Rick, contrib. by. Organ Praises. 52p. 1983. 10.99 (*0-8341-9360-4*, MB-524) Lillenas.

Parks, Rita. The Western Hero in Film & Television: Mass Media Mythology. LC 81-21826. (Studies in Cinema: No. 10). 198p. reprint ed. pap. 56.50 (*0-8357-1287-7*, 2070675) Bks Demand.

Parks, Robert, et al. From Jackson to Lincoln: Democracy & Dissent. LC 95-589. (Orig.). 1995. write for info. (*0-87598-113-5*) Pierpont Morgan.

— From Jackson to Lincoln: Democracy & Dissent. (Illus.). 80p. (Orig.). 1995. pap. text 25.95 (*0-8122-1577-X*) U of Pa Pr.

Parks, Robert E., ed. Proceedings from ASPE Spring Conference on Sub-Surface Damage in Glass. 237p. 1989. pap. write for info. (*1-887706-03-8*) Am Soc Prec Engr.

Parks, Robert E., ed. see OSA Standards Committee.

Parks, Robert E., jt. ed. see Xin, Qiming.

Parks, Robert H. Unlocking the Secrets of Wall Street: A Noted Expert Guides You Through Today's Financial Market. LC 98-20698. 355p. 1998. pap. text 16.95 (*1-57392-231-5*) Prometheus Bks.

Parks, Robert J. European Origins of the Economic Ideas of Alexander Hamilton. Bruchey, Stuart, ed. LC 76-39838. (Nineteen Seventy-Seven Dissertations Ser.). 1977. lib. bdg. 23.95 (*0-405-09918-5*) Ayer.

Parks, Rosa. Dear Mrs. Parks: A Dialogue with Today's Youth. LC 96-33845. (Illus.). 112p. (J). (gr. 2 up). 1996. 16.95 (*1-880000-45-8*) Lee & Low Bks.

— Dear Mrs. Parks, a Dialogue with Today's Youth. 1997. 14.05 (*0-606-12674-0*, Pub. by Turtleback) Demco.

***Parks, Rosa.** I Am Rosa Parks. (Illus.). (J). 2000. 9.34 (*0-606-18410-4*) Turtleback.

— Quiet Strength. (Illus.). 2000. pap. 9.99 (*0-310-23587-1*) Zondervan.

Parks, Rosa. Rosa Parks: My Story. LC 89-1124. (Illus.). 200p. (YA). (gr. 5-9). 1992. 17.00 (*0-8037-0673-1*, Dial Yng Read) Peng Put Young Read.

Parks, Rosa & Haskins, Jim. I Am Rosa Parks. (J). (gr. 4-8). 1997. 12.99 (*0-614-25382-9*, Dial Yng Read) Peng Put Young Read.

Parks, Rosa & Reed, Gregory J. Dear Mrs. Parks: A Dialogue with Today's Youth. (Illus.). 112p. (J). (gr. 3 up). 1997. reprint ed. pap. 8.95 (*1-880000-61-X*) Lee & Low Bks.

Parks, Roy, jt. auth. see Wireman, Terry.

Parks, Ruth M. Treacle on the Tongue. Egan, Roger E., Sr., ed. (Illus.). 80p. (Orig.). 1994. pap. 12.00 (*0-9632687-3-2*) PenRose Pub.

Parks, S., et al. On Track: Activity Book. (Illus.). 62p. 1990. pap. text 8.95 (*0-19-458496-8*) OUP.

Parks, Sandra & Black, Howard. Building Thinking Skills Bk 1. 2nd ed. (Illus.). 327p. (J). (gr. 2-4). 1997. pap., student ed. 24.95 (*0-89455-250-3*) Crit Think Bks.

— Building Thinking Skills Bk 1: Lesson Plans & Teacher's Manual. 2nd ed. 277p. (Orig.). (J). 1997. pap., teacher ed. 18.95 (*0-89455-320-8*) Crit Think Bks.

— Building Thinking Skills Bk 2. 2nd ed. 365p. (YA). (gr. 4 up). 1998. pap., student ed. 25.95 (*0-89455-252-X*) Crit Think Bks.

— Building Thinking Skills Bk 2: Lesson Plans & Teacher's Manual. 2nd ed. 291p. (Orig.). (YA). 1998. pap., teacher ed. 18.95 (*0-89455-321-6*) Crit Think Bks.

— Building Thinking Skills Bk 3-Figural. 259p. (Orig.). (YA). (gr. 6 up). 1985. pap., student ed. 23.95 (*0-89455-291-0*) Crit Think Bks.

— Building Thinking Skills Bk 3-Figural: Lesson Plans & Teacher's Manual. 207p. (Orig.). (YA). 1987. pap., teacher ed. 18.95 (*0-89455-322-4*) Crit Think Bks.

— Building Thinking Skills Bk 3-Verbal. 350p. (YA). (gr. 6 up). 1985. pap., student ed. 24.95 (*0-89455-300-3*) Crit Think Bks.

— Building Thinking Skills Bk 3-Verbal: Lesson Plans & Teacher's Manual. 327p. (Orig.). (YA). 1988. pap., teacher ed. 18.95 (*0-89455-301-1*) Crit Think Bks.

Parks, Sandra & Black, Howard. Organizing My Learning: Daily Student Planner Using Graphic Organizers. 108p. (J). (gr. 5-9). 1999. pap. 12.95 (*0-89455-678-9*, MP6501) Crit Think Bks.

Parks, Sandra & Black, Howard. Organizing Thinking Book 1: Graphic Organizers. 307p. (Orig.). (J). (gr. 2-5). 1992. pap. 34.95 (*0-89455-354-2*) Crit Think Bks.

— Organizing Thinking Book 2: Graphic Organizers. 342p. (Orig.). (J). (gr. 4-8). 1990. pap. 34.95 (*0-89455-355-0*) Crit Think Bks.

Parks, Sandra, jt. auth. see Swartz, Robert J.

Parks, Sandy, jt. auth. see Miller, Ruth.

Parks, Sarah T. & Kalman, Bob. A+ Certification Success Guide for Computer Technicians. 2nd expanded rev. ed. 325p. 1998. pap. 29.99 (*0-07-048618-2*) McGraw.

***Parks, Sharon.** The Critical Years. 245p. 1999. 23.00 (*1-57910-268-9*) Wipf & Stock.

***Parks, Stephen.** Class Politics: The Movement for the Student's Right to Their Own Language. LC 99-56418. 372p. 2000. 28.95 (*0-8141-0678-1*) NCTE.

Parks, Stephen. The Elizabethan Club of Yale University & Its Library. LC 86-7789. Vol. 8. 280p. 1986. 50.00 (*0-300-03669-8*) Yale U Pr.

Parks, Stephen M. Jim Wagner, Taos: An American Artist. LC 93-5732. (Illus.). 264p. 1993. 87.50 (*0-9636890-0-2*) Rancho Milagro.

Parks, Susan H., jt. auth. see Pilisuk, Marc.

Parks, Suzan-Lori. The America Play. 1995. pap. 5.25 (*0-8222-1423-7*) Dramatists Play.

— The American Play & Other Works. 224p. 1995. pap. 14.95 (*1-55936-092-5*) Theatre Comm.

Parks, Suzan-Lori. In the Blood. Date not set. pap. 5.95 (*0-8222-1756-2*) Dramatists Play.

— Red a Plays. 224p. 2000. pap. 14.95 (*1-55936-195-6*) Theatre Comm.

Parks, Suzan-Lori. Venus. 1998. pap. 5.25 (*0-8222-1567-5*) Dramatists Play.

— Venus. LC 97-5739. 96p. 1997. pap. 10.95 (*1-55936-135-2*) Theatre Comm.

***Parks, Theodore E.** Looking at Looking: An Introduction to the Intelligence of Vision. LC 00-9062. 2000. pap. write for info. (*0-7619-2204-0*) Sage.

***Parks, Thomas.** A Distant Crossing. 525p. 1999. pap. 8.95 (*0-9676031-0-2*) P S S Pubng.

Parks, Thomas W., jt. auth. see Burrus, C. S.

Parks, Tim. Adultery: And Other Diversions. LC 98-43657. 192p. 1999. 23.95 (*1-55970-470-5*, Pub. by Arcade Pub Inc) Time Warner.

***Parks, Tim.** Adultery & Other Diversions. 2000. pap. text 12.95 (*1-55970-518-3*, Pub. by Arcade Pub Inc) Time Warner.

— Destiny. 256p. 2000. 24.95 (*1-55970-517-5*, Pub. by Arcade Pub Inc) Time Warner.

Parks, Tim. Europa. 272p. 1999. pap. 12.95 (*1-55970-506-X*, Pub. by Arcade Pub Inc) Time Warner.

— Europa: A Novel. LC 98-24718. 272p. 1998. 23.95 (*1-55970-444-6*, Pub. by Arcade Pub Inc) Time Warner.

— Family Planning. LC 89-7610. 288p. 1991. pap. 11.95 (*0-8021-3243-X*, Grove) Grove-Atltic.

— Goodness: A Novel. LC 91-21937. 352p. 1993. pap. 9.95 (*0-8021-3304-5*, Grove) Grove-Atltic.

— Italian Education. LC 95-1699. 352p. 1996. pap. 12.50 (*0-380-72760-9*, Avon Bks) Morrow Avon.

— Italian Neighbors: or a Lapsed Anglo-Saxon in Verona. 288p. 1993. pap. 10.00 (*0-449-90818-6*, Columbine) Fawcett.

***Parks, Tim.** Juggling the Stars. 2001. pap. 12.95 (*1-55970-551-5*, Pub. by Arcade Pub Inc) Time Warner.

— Mimi's Ghost. (Illus.). 2001. 24.95 (*1-55970-556-6*, Pub. by Arcade Pub Inc) Time Warner.

Parks, Tim. Shear. LC 94-7058. 224p. 1995. pap. 11.00 (*0-8021-3360-6*, Grove) Grove-Atltic.

Parks, Tim. Translating Style: The English Modernists & Their Italian Translations. LC 97-3591. 256p. 1997. 29.95 (*0-304-70098-3*) Continuum.

***Parks, Tim.** Translating Style: The English Modernists & Their Italian Translations. (Illus.). 2000. pap. 24.95 (*0-304-70354-0*) Continuum.

Parks, Tim, tr. see Calasso, Roberto.

Parks, Tim, tr. see Jaeggy, Fleur.

Parks, Tim, tr. see Tabucchi, Antonio.

Parks, Tom. You Don't Say! The Ten Worst Mistakes You Can Make in Speech & Writing. 128p. (Orig.). 1998. mass mkt. 5.99 (*0-446-60428-3*, Pub. by Warner Bks) Little.

Parks, Van Dyke. Jump on Over. LC 89-7417. (Illus.). 48p. (J). 1998. pap. 8.00 (*0-15-201707-0*, Harcourt Child Bks) Harcourt.

Parks, Virginia. Pensacola: Spaniards to Space Age. (Illus.). 128p. 1986. 9.95 (*0-939566-04-4*) Pensacola Hist.

Parks, Virginia & Vickers, Elizabeth. Naval Live Oak Reservation. (Illus.). 1995. 3.00 (*0-939566-08-7*) Pensacola Hist.

Parks, W. Crime & the Law. 1994. pap. 42.00 (*0-409-30518-9*, Austral, MICHIE) LEXIS Pub.

Parks, Walter P. The Famous Fliers' Wall of the Mission Inn. (Illus.). 266p. 1986. text 28.00 (*0-9637655-1-5*) Coulter Pr.

— The Miracle of Mata Ortiz: Juan Quezada & the Potters of Northern Chihuahua. 142p. 1994. pap. 19.95 (*0-9637655-0-7*) Coulter Pr.

Parks, William C., et al, eds. Matrix Metalloproteinases. LC 98-133584. (Biology of Extracellular Matrix Ser.). (Illus.). 362p. 1998. text 89.95 (*0-12-545090-7*) Morgan Kaufmann.

Parks Williams, Shannon. Catmania: A Celebration of Kentucky Basketball Mania. 1999. 34.95 (*1-57243-346-9*) Triumph Bks.

Parkside Publication Inc. Staff. Quick 'n Easy Country Cookin' Best of 1992-1993. Schrag, Pam, ed. 106p. 1994. pap. 6.95 (*0-9618379-7-7*) Parkside Pubns.

Parkstone, P. Avant-Garde Art in Russia, 1920-1930. 1997. pap. 7.95 (*1-85995-435-9*) Parkstone Pr.

Parkstone Press Limited Staff. Renaissance Engravers. (Temporis Ser.). (Illus.). 208p. 1996. 55.00 (*1-85995-278-X*) Parkstone Pr.

— Saint Petersburg. (Great Cities Ser.). (Illus.). 96p. 1996. 20.00 (*1-85995-178-3*) Parkstone Pr.

Parkstone Press Staff. Russian Landscapes: Levitan & Shishkin. (Illus.). 1997. pap. text 7.95 (*1-85995-430-8*) Parkstone Pr.

***Parkstone Press Staff, ed.** Dix. (Reveries Ser.). 2000. 14.95 (*1-85995-760-9*) Parkstone Pr.

Parkstone Press Staff, ed. Peoples of the Great North. (Blank Book Ser.). (Illus.). 115p. 2000. 15.95 (*1-85995-154-6*) Parkstone Pr.

Parkus, H. Thermoelasticity. 2nd enl. rev. ed. 1976. 42.95 (*0-387-81375-6*) Spr-Verlag.

Parkus, H., ed. Electromagnetic Interactions in Elastic Solids. (CISM Courses & Lectures: Vol. 257). (Illus.). 425p. 1979. 56.95 (*0-387-81509-0*) Spr-Verlag.

Parkus, H., ed. see CISM (International Center for Mechanical Sciences.

Parkway, Christopher. Pedal for Your Life: By Bicycle from the Baltic to the Black Sea. LC 96-196828. (Illus.). 202p. 1997. 28.95 (*0-7188-2946-8*, Lutterworth-Parkwest) Parkwest Pubns.

Parkyn, Herbert A. Auto-Suggestion. 190p. 1993. pap. 15.00 (*0-89540-199-1*, SB-199) Sun Pub.

Parkyns, Mansfield. Life in Abyssinia: Being Notes Collected During Three Years' Residence & Travels in That Country. (Illus.). 446p. 1966. 55.00 (*0-7146-1844-6*, Pub. by F Cass Pubs) Intl Spec Bk.

Parl, Fritz F. Estrogens, Estrogen Receptor & Breast Cancer. (Biomedical & Health Research Ser.: Vol. 36). 1999. 115.00 (*0-9673355-4-X*) IOS Press.

P

An Asterisk (*) at the beginning of an entry indicates that the title is appearing for the first time.

*__Parla, Paul & Mitchell, Charles P.__ Screen Sirens Scream! Interviews with 20 Actresses from Science Fiction, Horror, Film Noir & Mystery Movies, 1930s to 1960s. LC 99-55379. (Illus.). 256p. 2000. boxed set 36.50 (*0-7864-0701-8*) McFarland & Co.

Parlagreco, C. Dizionario Portoghese-Italiano, Italiano-Portoghese: Portuguese-Italian, Italian-Portuguese Dictionary. (ITA & POR.). 1138p. 1979. 49.95 (*0-8288-4736-3*, M9183) Fr & Eur.

Parlak, Rosemary. Pittsburgh Walking Map & Guide: Rivers Edition. rev. ed. 1994. pap. 3.50 (*0-944101-19-4*) New Pittsburgh.

*__Parlakian, Nishan & Cowe, S. Peter, eds.__ Modern Armenian Drama: An Anthology. 480p. 2000. text 35.00 (*0-231-11630-6*) Col U Pr.

Parlakian, Nishan, tr. see Asadour, Zabel.

Parlakian, Nishan, tr. see Shirvanzadeh, pseud.

Parlakian, Nishan, tr. & intro. see Babayan, Aramashot.

Parlamis, Franklin, jt. auth. see Weber, Eric.

Parland, Oscar. The Enchanted Way. Tate, Joan, tr. from SWE. 202p. 1991. 30.00 (*0-7206-0829-5*, Pub. by P Owen Ltd) Dufour.

Parland, Oscar. From Bolshevism to Nationalism. 69.95 (*1-85521-877-1*) Ashgate Pub Co.

Parland, Oscar. The Year of the Bull. Tate, Joan, ed. 198p. 1991. 29.00 (*0-7206-0807-4*, Pub. by P Owen Ltd) Dufour.

Parlange, Marc B. & Hopmans, Jan W. Vadose Zone Hydrology: Cutting Across Disciplines. LC 98-3468. (Illus.). 480p. 1999. text 50.00 (*0-19-510990-2*) OUP.

Parlapiano, Ellen H. & Cobe, Patricia. Mompreneurs: A Mother's Step-by-Step Guide to Work-at-Home Success. LC 96-3661. 288p. 1996. pap. 13.00 (*0-399-52233-6*, Perigee Bks) Berkley Pub.

Parlar, H., jt. auth. see Scheunert, I.

Parlar, Harun. Environmental Chemistry of Toxaphene. Date not set. 169.95 (*0-8493-4874-9*) CRC Pr.

*__Parlar, Mahmut.__ Interactive Operations Research with Maple: Methods & Models. (Illus.). 2000. 54.95 (*0-8176-4165-3*) Birkhauser.

— Interactive Operations Research with Maple: Methods & Models. LC 00-31232. (Illus.). 2000. write for info. (*3-7643-4165-3*) Birkhauser.

Parlato, Salvatore. America from A to Z. Freifeld, Art, ed. (Illus.). 161p. (C). 1989. pap. text, student ed. 16.95 (*0-916177-67-X*) Am Eng Pubns.

Parlatore, Anselm. The Circa Poems. 1975. pap. 5.00 (*0-685-56281-6*) Stone-Marrow Pr.

— Hybrid Inoculum. LC 75-302485. 66p. 1974. 3.45 (*0-87886-049-5*, Greenfld Rev Pr) Greenfld Rev Lit.

Parle, G. J. Two Were Prisoners. 493p. 1986. 35.00 (*0-7223-1941-X*, Pub. by A H S Ltd) St Mut.

Parlebas, P. Jeux, Sports, Societes, Lexique Praxeologie Motrice. (FRE.). 1998. 95.00 (*0-320-00155-5*) Fr & Eur.

Parlej, Piotr. Romantic Theory of the Novel: Genre & Reflection in Cervantes, Melville, Flaubert, Joyce, & Kafka. LC 97-9301. (Horizons in Theory & American Culture Ser.). 344p. 1997. text 50.00 (*0-8071-2141-X*) La State U Pr.

Parlett, Beresford. The Symmetric Eigenvalue Problem. LC 97-40623. (Classics in Applied Mathematics Ser.: Vol. 20). (Illus.). xxiv, 398p. 1997. reprint ed. pap. text 51.50 (*0-89871-402-8*, CL20) Soc Indus-Appl Math.

Parlett, David. Card Games for One. (Illus.). 160p. 1995. pap. 8.95 (*0-8442-3686-1*, Teach Yrslf) NTC Contemp Pub Co.

— A Dictionary of Card Games. (Oxford Paperback Reference). (Illus.). 358p. 1992. pap. 13.95 (*0-19-869173-4*) OUP.

— The Oxford Book of Board Games. LC 99-229056. (Illus.). 400p. 1999. 45.00 (*0-19-212998-8*) OUP.

*__Parlett, David.__ Teach Yourself Card Games 2/e. (Teach Yourself Ser.). 288p. 2000. pap. 9.95 (*0-658-00085-3*, 000853, Teach Yrslf) NTC Contemp Pub Co.

Parlett, David, tr. see Bachmann, MArie L.

Parlett, David F., ed. see Weaver, Russell L. & Strachan, Kristine.

Parlett, Graham. A Catalogue of the Works of Sir Arnold Bax. LC 98-7972. (Illus.). 428p. 1999. text 105.00 (*0-19-816586-2*) OUP.

Parlette, Snowden, 3rd. The Brain Workout Book. LC 96-51056. (Illus.). 240p. (Orig.). 1997. pap. 14.95 (*0-87131-813-X*) M Evans.

Parlevliet, J. E., jt. ed. see Jacobs, Thomas.

Parley, Louis I., jt. auth. see Hodgson, Beverly J.

Parley, Louis I., jt. auth. see Lindey, Alexander.

Parley, Peter, pseud. Recollections of a Lifetime: or Men & Things I Have Seen, 2 vols., Set. (American Biography Ser.). 1991. reprint ed. lib. bdg. 148.00 (*0-7812-8149-0*) Rprt Serv.

Parliamentary Debates, Great Britain Staff. Report from the Select Committee on the High Price of Gold Bullion. Wilkins, Mira, ed. LC 78-3915. (International Finance Ser.). 1979. reprint ed. lib. bdg. 33.95 (*0-405-11219-X*) Ayer.

Parliamentary Office of Science and Technology, jt. auth. see Kass, Gary.

Parlier, Cap. Phoenix Seduction. 1997. mass mkt. 4.99 (*1-55197-238-7*) Picasso Publ.

Parlier, Cap, jt. auth. see Ready, Kevin E.

Parlier, Jaki. Poking Holes in the Darkness. 192p. 1994. pap. 8.95 (*0-939497-34-4*) Promise Pub.

*__Parliment, Thomas H., et al, eds.__ Caffeinated Beverages. LC 99-58369. (ACS Symposium Ser.). (Illus.). 416p. 2000. text 150.00 (*0-8412-3654-2*, Pub. by Am Chemical) OUP.

Parliment, Thomas H., et al, eds. Thermally Generated Flavors: Maillard, Microwave, & Extrusion Processes. LC 93-36609. (ACS Symposium Ser.: No. 543). (Illus.). 494p. 1994. text 120.00 (*0-8412-2742-X*, Pub. by Am Chemical) OUP.

Parliment, Thomas H. & Croteau, Rodney, eds. Biogeneration of Aromas. LC 86-3534. (ACS Symposium Ser.: No. 317). (Illus.). ix, 399p. 1986. 87.95 (*0-8412-0987-1*, Pub. by Am Chemical) OUP.

— Biogeneration of Aromas. LC 86-17334. (ACS Symposium Ser.: Vol. 317). 408p. 1986. reprint ed. pap. 126.50 (*0-608-03521-1*, 206424000008) Bks Demand.

Parlin, Andrew, jt. auth. see Harper, John.

Parlin, John. Amelia Earhart. (Illus.). 80p. (J). 1991. pap. 3.99 (*0-440-40117-8*) Dell.

Parloff, Morris B., ed. see Conference on Research in Psychotherapy Staff.

Parloff, Roger. Triple Jeopardy: How Determined Lawyers Fought to Save One Man's Life. LC 95-53721. 1996. write for info. (*0-614-95867-9*) Little.

Parlor, Karen W. Heir Jordan: How's Your Hang Time? unabridged ed. 23p. 1997. pap. 10.00 (*0-9637561-2-5*) Com Sense Christian.

Parlor, Randy E. And Build Your Church with Me: Your Guide to Spiritual & Financial Empowerment. unabridged ed. 45p. 1998. pap. 10.00 (*0-9637561-3-3*) Com Sense Christian.

— Common Sense: Receiving God's Financial Promises. LC 93-90574. 120p. (Orig.). 1993. student ed. 10.00 (*0-9637561-1-7*); pap. 10.00 (*0-9637561-0-9*) Com Sense Christian.

Parlour, Margaret. Vermont Kitchens Revisited. 288p. (Orig.). 1990. pap. 14.95 (*0-9627253-0-7*) VT Kitchen.

Parlow, E., ed. Progress in Environmental Remote Sensing Research & Application: Proceedings of the 15th EARSEL Symposium Basel, 1995. (Illus.). 670p. (C). 1996. text 155.00 (*90-5410-598-4*, Pub. by A A Balkema) Ashgate Pub Co.

Parma, Art. Biennial Flight Review. LC 99-209315. (Illus.). 48p. (Orig.). 1994. pap. 8.95 (*0-9631973-0-4*) Flight Time.

— Instrument Flight Review. LC 99-209432. (Flight Bag Ser.). (Illus.). 64p. (Orig.). 1995. pap. 8.95 (*0-9631973-1-2*) Flight Time.

— Pocket Pilot Handbook: Flight Calculations, Weather Decoder, Aviation Acronyms, Charts & Checklists Pilot Memory Aids. LC 99-209328. (Illus.). 53p. 1998. pap. 6.95 (*0-9631973-8-X*) Flight Time.

— Student Pilot Handbook. (Illus.). 84p. (Orig.). 1992. reprint ed. pap. 12.95 (*0-9631973-3-9*) Flight Time.

Parma, Art & Lecorre, Emille. Pilot's Rules of Thumb: Easy Aviation Math, Handy Formulas, Quick Tips. LC 99-209325. (Illus.). 48p. 1998. pap. 6.95 (*0-9631973-4-7*) Flight Time.

Parma, S., jt. auth. see Gulati, Ramesh D.

Parma, Terra. Christmas Traditions in Glass. (Illus.). 52p. 1994. pap. 12.95 (*0-936459-25-5*) Stained Glass.

*__Parma, Terra.__ Garden Delights. (Illus.). 48p. 1999. pap. 12.95 (*0-936459-43-3*) Stained Glass.

Parma, Terra. Holiday Images. (Illus.). 52p. 1993. pap. 12.95 (*0-936459-19-0*) Stained Glass.

— Homespun Country Images. (Illus.). 52p. 1998. pap. 12.95 (*0-936459-39-5*) Stained Glass.

— New Dimensions. (Illus.). 52p. 1996. pap. 12.95 (*0-936459-32-8*) Stained Glass.

— Plumes 'n' Blooms. (Illus.). 52p. 1997. pap. 12.95 (*0-936459-37-9*) Stained Glass.

— Potpourri in Glass. Stained Glass Images Inc. Staff, ed. (Illus.). 52p. 1991. pap. 12.95 (*0-936459-16-6*) Stained Glass.

— Seasons in Stained Glass. (Illus.). 52p. 1996. pap. 12.95 (*0-936459-36-0*) Stained Glass.

— Ultimate Images. (Illus.). 52p. 1995. pap. 12.95 (*0-936459-28-X*) Stained Glass.

— Victorian Impressions. (Illus.). 52p. 1997. pap. 12.95 (*0-936459-38-7*) Stained Glass.

— Walk on the Wild Side. (Illus.). 52p. 1998. pap. 12.95 (*0-936459-41-7*) Stained Glass.

*__Parma, Terra.__ Walk on the Wildside, Bk. II. (Illus.). 48p. 1999. pap. 12.95 (*0-936459-46-8*) Stained Glass.

Parma, Terra, et al. Image Is Everything! (Illus.). 80p. 1996. pap. 12.95 (*0-936459-33-6*) Stained Glass.

Parmadale Christmas Committee. Beyond the Village Gate: Cookbook. (Illus.). 320p. 1985. 11.95 (*0-9615123-0-X*) Parmadale.

Parmahans, Yogeshwaranand. First Steps to Higher Yoga: An Exposition of First Five Constituents of Yoga. Brahmachari, Bala & Shastri, Ram P., trs. xxxiv, 384p. 1985. 20.00 (*0-614-06350-7*, Pub. by Yoga Niketan) Nataraj Bks.

— Himalaya Ka Yogi, 2 vols., Set. 1991. 35.00 (*0-614-06356-6*, Pub. by Yoga Niketan) Nataraj Bks.

— Science of Divine Lights: A Latest Research on Self & God-Realization of the 154 Divine Lights. Kapoor, Devendra K., tr. xviii, 262p. 1991. 15.00 (*0-614-06355-8*, Pub. by Yoga Niketan) Nataraj Bks.

— Science of Divinity, Vol. 4. 480p. 1992. 25.00 (*0-614-06351-5*, Pub. by Yoga Niketan) Nataraj Bks.

*__Parmal, Pamela A.__ Samplers from A to Z. LC 99-69945. (Illus.). 64p. 2000. pap. 17.95 (*0-87846-481-6*) Mus Fine Arts Boston.

Parmalee, Paul W. Amphibians of Illinois. (Story of Illinois Ser.: No. 10). (Illus.). 38p. 1954. pap. 1.00 (*0-89792-011-2*) Ill St Museum.

Parmalee, Paul W. & Bogan, Arthur E. The Freshwater Mussels of Tennessee. LC 97-45371. (Illus.). 344p. (C). 1998. text 50.00 (*1-57233-013-9*) U of Tenn Pr.

Parmalee, Paul W. & Oesch, Ronald D. Pleistocene & Recent Faunas from the Brynjulfson Caves, Missouri. (Reports of Investigations: No. 25). (Illus.). 52p. 1972. pap. 2.00 (*0-89792-049-X*) Ill St Museum.

Parmalee, Paul W., et al. Animals Utilized by Woodland Peoples Occupying the Apple Creek Site, Illinois. (Reports of Investigations: No. 23). (Illus.). 62p. 1972. pap. 3.00 (*0-89792-048-1*) Ill St Museum.

— Pleistocene & Recent Vertebrate Faunas from Crankshaft Cave, Missouri. (Reports of Investigations: No.14). (Illus.). 37p. 1969. pap. 1.00 (*0-89792-036-8*) Ill St Museum.

Parmalee, Paul W., jt. auth. see Paul, John R.

Parmaliana, A. Natural Gas Conversion V: Proceedings of the 5th International Natural Gas Conversion Symposium, Giardini Naxos-Taormina, Italy, September 20-25, 1998. LC 98-42600. (Studies in Surface Science & Catalysis). 1998. write for info. (*0-444-82967-9*) Elsevier.

Parman, Donald L. Indians & the American West in the Twentieth Century. LC 93-48060. (American West in the Twentieth Century Ser.). 256p. 1994. 35.00 (*0-253-34289-9*); pap. 13.95 (*0-253-20892-0*) Ind U Pr.

Parman, Donald L., ed. Window to a Changed World: The Personal Memoirs of William Graham. LC 98-6513. (Illus.). xxix, 289p. 1998. 29.95 (*0-87195-127-4*) Ind Hist Soc.

Parman, Ray, Jr. & Brown, Donald N. Rare & Unusual Artifacts of the First Americans. (Illus.). 296p. (Orig.). 1989. pap. 24.95 (*0-9623868-0-4*) F Pruett.

Parman, Susan. Dream & Culture: An Anthropological Study of the Western Intellectual Tradition. LC 90-7459. 144p. 1990. 45.00 (*0-275-93230-3*, C3230, Praeger Pubs) Greenwood.

Parman, Susan, ed. Europe in the Anthropological Imagination. LC 97-13591. (Exploring Cultures Ser.). 274p. 1997. pap. text, suppl. ed. 33.40 (*0-13-337460-2*) P-H.

Parmanand, jt. auth. see Piyasena, S.

Parmann, Georg, jt. ed. see Bergesen, Helge O.

Parmann, Georg, jt. ed. see Bergessen, Helge O.

Parmar, H. A., jt. auth. see Taylor, S. E.

Parmar, Inderjeet. Special Interests, the State & the Anglo-American Alliance, 1939-1945. LC 95-14432. 200p. (C). 1995. 52.50 (*0-7146-4569-9*, Pub. by F Cass Pubs); pap. 22.50 (*0-7146-4226-6*, Pub. by F Cass Pubs) Intl Spec Bk.

Parmar, Leena. Society, Culture & Military System. (C). 1995. 22.00 (*81-7033-264-8*, Pub. by Rawat Pubns) S Asia.

Parmar, Mahesh K. & Machin, David. Survival Analysis: A Practical Approach. LC 95-32240. 268p. 1995. 99.95 (*0-471-93640-5*) Wiley.

Parmar, Pramila. Mithai: Collection of Traditional Indian Sweets. 1999. reprint ed. 16.00 (*81-85944-88-1*, Pub. by UBS Pubs) S Asia.

Parmar, Pratibha, jt. auth. see O'Sullivan, Sue.

Parmar, Pratibha, jt. auth. see Walker, Alice.

Parmar, Shyam. Folklore of Madhya Pradesh. 204p. 1972. 8.95 (*0-318-36318-6*) Asia Bk Corp.

Parmasto, Erast & Parmasto, Ilmi. Variation of Basidiospores in the Hymenomycetes & Its Significance to Their Taxonomy. (Bibliotheca Mycologica: Vol. 115). (GER., Illus.). 168p. 1987. 48.00 (*3-443-59016-0*, Pub. by Gebruder Borntraeger) Balogh.

Parmasto, Ilmi, jt. auth. see Parmasto, Erast.

Parme, Douglas, tr. see Zola, Emile.

Parmee, D., ed. see Baudelaire, Charles.

Parmee, Douglas, ed. see Laclos, Choderlos de.

Parmee, Douglas, tr. see Fontane, Theodor.

Parmee, Douglas, tr. see Maupassant, Guy de.

Parmee, Douglas, tr. & intro. see Zola, Emile.

Parmee, I. C., jt. auth. see ACDM '00 Staff.

Parmee, Ian. Adaptive Computing in Design & Manufacture: The Integration of Evolutionary & Adaptive Computing Technologies with Product System Design & Realisation. LC 98-6382. 1998. 119.00 (*3-540-76254-X*) Spr-Verlag.

Parmeggiani, Lougi, ed. Encyclopedia of Occupational Health & Safety, 1983, 2 vols., Set. 3rd rev. ed. 1991. 270.00 (*92-2-103289-2*) Intl Labour Office.

Parmeggiani, P. L., jt. auth. see Lugaresi, E.

Parmelee, Alice. Guide to the New Testament. LC 79-87617. (Illus.). 144p. 1980. pap. 4.00 (*0-8192-1255-5*) Morehouse Pub.

Parmelee, Cullen W. & Harman, Cameron G. Ceramic Glazes. 3rd ed. LC 70-183371. (Illus.). 624p. (C). 1993. reprint ed. text 133.00 (*1-878907-05-0*, RAN) TechBooks.

Parmelee, David. Preparing the Marketing Plan. (AMA Marketing Toolbox Ser.). (Illus.). 160p. 1995. pap. 19.95 (*0-8442-3579-2*) NTC Contemp Pub Co.

Parmelee, David F. Antarctic Birds: An Ecological & Behavioral Approach (Exploration of Palmer Archipelago by an Artist-Ornithologist. (Illus.). 221p. (C). 1992. 39.95 (*0-8166-2000-8*) U of Minn Pr.

Parmelee, Dean X., ed. Child & Adolescent Psychiatry. LC 95-52516. (Access Ser.). (Illus.). 360p. (C). (gr. 13). 1996. text 66.95 (*0-8151-6809-8*, 25198) Mosby Inc.

Parmelee, Deolece, jt. auth. see Henson, Margaret S.

Parmelee, John, jt. auth. see Godin, Seth.

Parmelee, Kara, ed. see Toohil, Barbara & Toohil, Peter.

Parmelee, Lisa F. Good Newes from Fraunce: French Anti-League Propaganda in Late Elizabethan England. LC 95-53091. (Illus.). 216p. (C). 1996. 50.00 (*1-878822-65-9*) Univ Rochester Pr.

Parmelee, Maurice. Principles of Anthropology & Sociology in Their Relations to Criminal Procedure. viii, 410p. 1980. reprint ed. 45.00 (*0-8377-1004-9*, Rothman) W S Hein.

Parmelee, Robert D. Chicago's Railroads & Parmelee's Transfer Company: A Century of Travel. (Illus.). 165p. 2000. pap. 21.95 (*1-889029-03-3*) Golden Hl Pr NY.

— Chicago's Railroads & Parmelee's Transfer Company: A Century of Travel. limited ed. (Illus.). 165p. 2000. 49.95 (*1-889029-01-7*) Golden Hl Pr NY.

Parmelee, Robert L. Mullins Red Cap Utility Trailer: History & Handbook. Get-A-Long Graphics Staff, ed. & illus. by. LC 98-91614. 184p. 1998. 34.95 (*0-9665217-1-4*, 98-300) Milcap Pubg.

Parmenides of Elea. Parmenides of Elea: Fragments: A Text & Translation with an Introduction. Gallop, David, ed. (Phoenix Supplementary Volumes Ser.: Vol. XVIII; Pre-Socratics I). 160p. 1991. pap. text 17.95 (*0-8020-6908-8*) U of Toronto Pr.

Parmenius, Stephanus, et al. The New Found Land of Stephen Parmenius: The Life & Writings of a Hungarian Poet, Drowned on a Voyage from Newfoundland, 1583. LC 78-151386. xii, 250 p. 1972. write for info. (*0-8020-0027-4*) U of Toronto Pr.

Parmenter, Barbara M. Giving Voice to Stones: Place & Identity in Palestinian Literature. LC 94-8643. (Illus.). 128p. (C). 1994. pap. 9.95 (*0-292-76555-X*); text 25.00 (*0-292-72751-8*) U of Tex Pr.

Parmenter, Barbara M., tr. see Abouzeid, Lelia.

Parmenter, Barbara M., tr. see Al-Amir, Daisy.

Parmenter, Bruce. Christians Caught in the Divorce Trap: Helping Families Recover from Divorce. LC 95-18758. 1995. pap. 8.99 (*0-89900-738-4*) College Pr Pub.

Parmenter, C. O. History of Pelham, MA, from Seventeen Thirty-Eight to Eighteen Ninety-Eight, Including the Early History of Prescott. (Illus.). 531p. 1990. reprint ed. lib. bdg. 54.00 (*0-8328-1638-8*) Higginson Bk Co.

Parmenter, Fisher & Mallette Staff. Fisher: The Life of George Fisher (1795-1873) & the History of the Fisher Family in Mississippi. (Illus.). 299p. 1991. reprint ed. pap. 47.00 (*0-8328-1906-9*); reprint ed. lib. bdg. 57.00 (*0-8328-1905-0*) Higginson Bk Co.

Parmenter, Michael M. Theory of Interest & Life Contingencies with Pension Applications: A Problem-Solving Approach. 3rd ed. (Illus.). 308p. (C). 1999. pap. text 55.00 (*1-56698-333-9*) Actex Pubns.

Parmenter, Michael M., jt. auth. see Goodaire, Edgar G.

Parmenter, Ross. D. H. Lawrence in Oaxaca: A Quest for the Novelist in Mexico. (Illus.). 384p. 1984. 22.95 (*0-318-35420-9*) Hawkshead Bk.

— Explorer, Linguist & Ethnologist: A Descriptive Bibliography of the Published Works of Alphonse Louis Pinart, with Notes on His Life. LC 66-24190. (Frederick Webb Hodge Publications: No. 9). (Illus.). 1966. 12.50 (*0-916561-20-8*) Southwest Mus.

— Four Lienzos of the Coixtlahuaca Valley. LC 82-4967. (Studies in Pre-Columbian Art & Archaeology: No. 26). (Illus.). 88p. 1983. pap. 15.00 (*0-88402-109-2*) Dumbarton Oaks.

— A House for Buddha: A Memoir with Drawings. (Illus.). 529p. Date not set. 35.00 (*1-885241-00-3*) Woodstock Pr.

— The Lienzo of Tulancingo: An Introductory Study of a Ninth Painted Sheet from the Coixtlahuaca Valley. LC 93-73287. (Transactions Ser.: Vol. 83, Pt. 7). (Illus.). 86p. (C). 1994. pap. 15.00 (*0-87169-837-4*, T827-PAR) Am Philos.

Parmenter, Ross, jt. ed. see Smith, Mary E.

Parmentier, L., jt. ed. see Bidez, J.

Parmentier, Michel, tr. see Breton, Andre.

Parmentier, Richard J. The Sacred Remains: Myth, History, & Polity in Belau. LC 87-6051. (Illus.). 368p. (Orig.). 1987. lib. bdg. 60.00 (*0-226-64695-5*) U Ch Pr.

— The Sacred Remains: Myth, History, & Polity in Belau. LC 87-6051. (Illus.). 368p. (Orig.). 1998. pap. text 19.50 (*0-226-64696-3*) U Ch Pr.

— Signs in Society: Studies in Semiotic Anthropology. LC 93-27758. 252p. 1994. 35.00 (*0-253-32757-1*) Ind U Pr.

Parmer, J. Norman. Colonial Labor Policy & Administration 1910-1941. 15.00 (*0-685-71735-6*) J J Augustin.

Parmer, Leticia. An Astrological Guide to Your Child: A Handbook for Parents. LC 97-17003. 224p. 1997. pap. 10.95 (*0-8065-1912-6*) Carol Pub Group.

— An Astrological Guide to Your Child: A Handbook for Parents. (Illus.). 242p. 1999. reprint ed. 27.95 (*0-7351-0115-9*) Replica Bks.

Parmer, Lynette. Collecting Occupied Japan. LC 95-25821. (Illus.). 112p. 1996. pap. 19.95 (*0-88740-968-7*) Schiffer.

Parmer, Paul. Overcoming that "After-Camp Spiritual Dive" 10p. (YA). (gr. 3 up). Date not set. pap. write for info. (*1-884838-17-0*) Walterick Pubs.

*__Parmerlee, David.__ Analyzing the Market: AMA Marketing Toolbox. LC 99-56227. (American Marketing Association Marketing Toolbox Ser.). 240p. 2000. pap. 24.95 (*0-658-00133-7*, 001337, NTC Business Bks) NTC Contemp Pub Co.

Parmerlee, David. Developing Successful Marketing Strategies. (AMA Marketing Toolbox Ser.). (Illus.). 192p. 1994. pap. 19.95 (*0-8442-3580-6*, NTC Business Bks) NTC Contemp Pub Co.

— Evaluating Marketing Strengths & Weaknesses. (AMA Marketing Toolbox Ser.). (Illus.). 256p. 1995. pap. 24.95 (*0-8442-3578-4*) NTC Contemp Pub Co.

— Identifying the Right Markets. (AMA Marketing Toolbox Ser.). (Illus.). 176p. 1994. pap. 24.95 (*0-8442-3576-8*, NTC Business Bks) NTC Contemp Pub Co.

*__Parmerlee, David.__ Preparing the Marketing Plan: AMA Marketing Toolbox. LC 99-52068. (American Marketing Association Marketing Toolbox Ser.). 176p. 2000. pap. 24.95 (*0-658-00134-5*, 001345, NTC Business Bks) NTC Contemp Pub Co.

*__Parmerlee, David & American Marketing Association Staff.__ Developing Successful Marketing Strategies: AMA Marketing Toolbox. LC 99-55445. (Marketing Toolbox Ser.). 224p. 2000. pap. 24.95 (*0-658-00132-9*, 001329) NTC Contemp Pub Co.

*__Parmesani, Loredana.__ A Century of Art: Movements, Theories, Schools & Trends, 1900-2000. (Illus.). 192p. 2000. pap. 16.95 (*88-8118-652-7*, Pub. by Skira IT) Abbeville Pr.

P

An Asterisk (*) at the beginning of an entry indicates that the title is appearing for the first time.

***Parmesani, Loredana, text.** Century of Art: Movements, Theories, Schools & Trends, 1900-2000. (Illus.). 192p. 2000. 24.95 (*88-8118-688-8*, Pub. by Skira IT) Abbeville Pr.

Parmeswaran, Uma, ed. Quilting a New Canon: Stitching Women's Words. LC 97-200383. 424p. 1996. write for info. (*1-896705-06-5*) Sister Vis Pr.

Parmet, Herbert S. Eisenhauer & the American Crusades. LC 98-5460. (American Presidents Ser.). 660p. 1998. pap. text 29.95 (*0-7658-0437-9*) Transaction Pubs.

Parmet, Herbert S. George Bush: The Life of a Lone Star Yankee. LC 97-33616. (Illus.). 554p. 1997. 32.00 (*0-684-19452-X*) S&S Trade.

***Parmet, Herbert S.** George Bush: The Life of a Lone Star Yankee. 585p. 2000. pap. 24.95 (*0-7658-0730-0*) Transaction Pubs.

Parmet, Robert D. Labor & Immigration in Industrial America. LC 86-15193. 268p. (C). 1987. reprint ed. pap. text 16.50 (*0-89874-968-9*) Krieger.

Parmett, Doris. Risk. 336p. (Orig.). 1994. mass mkt. 4.99 (*0-515-11333-6*, Jove) Berkley Pub.

Parmiani, Floria. Classic Italian Tales/Novelline Italiane. (Illus.). 32p. (Orig.). 1982. pap. 5.00 (*0-9653783-3-0*) Floria Publns.

— Imagery & Reality. LC 97-90627. 103p. (Orig.). 1998. pap. 14.00 (*0-9653783-1-4*) Floria Publns.

— Images of Our Lives: A Collection of Essays. LC 98-94870. 185p. (Orig.). 1999. pap. 16.95 (*0-9653783-4-9*) Floria Publns.

— San Francisco in Colors. (Illus.). 32p. (Orig.). 1984. pap. 5.00 (*0-9653783-2-2*) Floria Publns.

— Vegitalian: Italian Vegetarian Cooking. LC 96-96908. (Illus.). 153p. (Orig.). 1996. pap. 14.00 (*0-9653783-0-6*) Floria Publns.

Parmigiani, Stefano & Von Saal, Frederick S., eds. Infanticide & Parental Care. LC 93-41749. (Ettore Majorana International Life Sciences Ser.: Vol. 13). 512p. 1994. text 105.00 (*3-7186-5505-5*) Gordon & Breach.

Parmigiani, Stefano, ed. see Robertson, Bengt D.

Parmiter, Karen B. Fulfilling the Prophecies: The Journey of Education. 261p. 1999. pap. 15.95 (*0-7414-0055-3*) Buy Books.

Parmley. Field Engineer's Manual. 3rd ed. 2001. 54.95 (*0-07-135624-X*) McGraw.

— Hydraulics Field Manual. 2nd ed. 2000. 64.95 (*0-07-134832-8*) McGraw.

Parmley, Mary T. Road Maps for Retirement from NCOA: Making Your Dollars Work Harder. Stewart, Lisa B. & Joyce, Elizabeth, eds. LC 97-39501. (Road Maps for Retirement Ser.). (Illus.). 22p. 1997. pap. 6.95 (*0-910883-90-4*, R-03) Natl Coun Aging.

— Road Maps for Retirement from NCOA: Negotiating the Elder Care Maze. Stewart, Lisa B. & Joyce, Elizabeth, eds. LC 97-31715. (Road Maps for Retirement Ser.). (Illus.). 1997. pap. 6.95 (*0-910883-92-0*, R-06) Natl Coun Aging.

— Road Maps for Retirement from NCOA: Restoring Quality to Your Life. Steward, Lisa B. & Joyce, Elizabeth, eds. LC 97-39502. (Road Maps for Retirement Ser.). (Illus.). 26p. 1997. pap. 6.95 (*0-910883-89-0*, R-02) Natl Coun Aging.

— Road Maps for Retirement from NCOA: Retirement Curve Ahead! Stewart, Lisa B. & Joyce, Elizabeth, eds. (Road Maps for Retirement Ser.). (Illus.). 26p. 1997. pap. 6.95 (*0-910883-88-2*, R-01) Natl Coun Aging.

— Road Maps for Retirement from NCOA: You Can't Take It with You! Stewart, Lisa B. & Joyce, Elizabeth, eds. (Road Maps for Retirement Ser.). (Illus.). 18p. 1997. pap. 6.95 (*0-910883-87-4*, R-05) Natl Coun Aging.

— Road Maps to Retirement from NCOA: New Work Styles for Your Retirement Career. Stewart, Lisa B. & Joyce, Elizabeth, eds. LC 97-38265. (Road Maps to Retirement Ser.). (Illus.). 18p. 1997. pap. 6.95 (*0-910883-91-2*, R-04) Natl Coun Aging.

Parmley, Robert O. Field Engineer's Manual. 2nd ed. 730p. 1994. 49.95 (*0-07-048579-8*) McGraw.

— HVAC Design Data Sourcebook. 489p. 1994. 49.50 (*0-07-048572-0*) McGraw.

— Hydraulics Field Manual. LC 92-12036. 334p. 1992. pap. 44.50 (*0-07-048556-9*) McGraw.

***Parmley, Robert O.** Illustrated Sourcebook of Mechanical Components. (Illus.). 1200p. 2000. 125.00 (*0-07-048617-4*) McGraw-Hill Prof.

Parmley, Robert O., ed. Standard Handbook of Fastening & Joining. 3rd ed. LC 96-27689. (Illus.). 1032p. 1996. 105.00 (*0-07-048589-5*) McGraw.

Parnall, Peter. Gato Salvaje (Marsh Cat) Villegas, Paloma, tr. (SPA., Illus.). (YA). 1994. pap. 6.99 (*968-16-4464-6*, Pub. by Fondo) Continental Bk.

— Spaces. LC 92-1712. (Illus.). 32p. (J). (gr. k-3). 1993. lib. bdg. 21.90 (*1-56294-336-7*) Millbrook Pr.

***Parnas, Richard S.** Liquid Composite Molding. LC 00-31931. 2000. write for info. (*1-56990-287-9*) Hanser-Gardner.

Parnaso. Diccionario Sopena de Literatura, 3 vols., Set. (SPA.). 1820p. 150.00 (*0-7859-0886-2*, S-50140) Fr & Eur.

Parnass, Barbara, ed. see Caldwell, Mark.

Parnau, Jeffery R. Desktop Publishing: The Awful Truth. Lefevre, Ken, ed. 128p. 1989. pap. 19.95 (*0-9623020-0-7*) Parnau Graphics.

Parncutt, R. Harmony: A Psychoacoustical Approach. (Information Sciences Ser.: Vol. 19). (Illus.). 225p. 1989. 75.95 (*0-387-51279-9*) Spr-Verlag.

Parnell. Building High-Speed Networks. LC 99-192938. 1999. pap. 44.99 (*0-07-211858-X*) McGraw.

— Party Bag. 1997. pap. 8.99 (*1-85792-286-7*, Pub. by Christian Focus) Spring Arbor Dist.

Parnell & Schaeffer. Introduction to Manufacturing & Construction Lab Manual MC 151. 3rd ed. 68p. (C). 1997. spiral bd. 9.95 (*0-7872-4495-3*) Kendall-Hunt.

Parnell, Allan M., jt. auth. see Kasarda, John D.

Parnell, Andrea. Small Town Secrets. 320p. 1993. mass mkt. 4.50 (*0-8217-4264-7*, Zebra Kensgtn) Kensgtn Pub Corp.

— Wild Glory. 352p. (Orig.). 1990. mass mkt. 4.95 (*0-445-21007-9*, Pub. by Warner Bks) Little.

Parnell, Anthony D. In Search of Soul: A Collection of Poems. LC 94-74124. 57p. (Orig.). 1995. pap. 7.95 (*0-9644205-0-3*) Dreams & Visions.

— Mind Games. LC 96-84121. 88p. 1997. pap. 12.95 (*0-9644205-1-1*) Dreams & Visions.

Parnell, Ben. Carpetbaggers: America's Secret War in Europe. rev. ed. Roberts, Melissa, ed. (Illus.). 304p. 1993. 24.95 (*0-89015-592-5*) Sunbelt Media.

Parnell, Christina & Heyder, Carolin. Russische Prosaautorinnen, 1975-1995. 212p. 1997. pap. 42.95 (*3-631-30917-1*) P Lang Pubng.

Parnell, Dale. Dateline 2000: The New Higher Education Agenda. 286p. 1990. pap. 33.00 (*0-87117-198-8*, 1310) Comm Coll Pr Am Assn Comm Coll.

— The Neglected Majority. 1985. pap. 33.00 (*0-87117-154-6*, 1068) Comm Coll Pr Am Assn Comm Coll.

Parnell, Dale, ed. Associate Degree Preferred. LC LB2328.A87. 88p. (Orig.). reprint ed. pap. 30.00 (*0-7837-2484-5*, 204264100005) Bks Demand.

Parnell, Dale P. Why Do I Have to Learn This? Teaching the Way People Learn Best. Leary, Margaret M., ed. LC 95-70034. 144p. 1995. 16.00 (*1-55502-704-0*) CORD Commns.

Parnell, Frances B. & Wooten, Joyce H. Skills for Living. rev. ed. LC 95-44581. 622p. 1997. 46.60 (*1-56637-287-9*) Goodheart.

Parnell, Geoffrey. The Tower of London: Past & Present. LC 99-188229. (Illus.). 128p. 1998. pap. 19.95 (*0-7509-1763-6*, Pub. by Sutton Pub Ltd) Intl Pubs Mktg.

***Parnell, Geoffrey.** Tower of London: The Official Illustrated History. 2000. pap. text 17.95 (*1-85894-106-7*) Merrell Holberton.

Parnell, Helga. Cooking the German Way. (Easy Menu Ethnic Cookbooks Ser.). (Illus.). 48p. (J). (gr. 5 up). 1988. lib. bdg. 19.93 (*0-8225-0918-0*, Lerner Publctns) Lerner Pub.

— Cooking the South American Way. (Easy Menu Ethnic Cookbooks Ser.). (Illus.). 48p. (J). (gr. 5 up). 1991. lib. bdg. 19.93 (*0-8225-0925-3*, Lerner Publctns) Lerner Pub.

Parnell, J., ed. Basins on the Atlantic Seaboard: Petroleum Geology, Sedimentology & Basin Evolution. (Geological Society Special Publications: No. 62). (Illus.). x, 470p. (C). 1992. 120.00 (*0-903317-76-1*, 275, Pub. by Geol Soc Pub Hse) AAPG.

— Geofluids: Origin, Migration & Evolution of Fluids in Sedimentary Basins. (Geological Society Special Publication Ser.: No. 78). (Illus.). 374p. 1994. 108.00 (*1-897799-05-5*, 296, Pub. by Geol Soc Pub Hse) AAPG.

Parnell, J., et al. Bitumens in Ore Deposits. LC 92-36492. (Society for Geology Applied to Mineral Deposits Special Publication Ser.: No. 9). 1993. 219.95 (*3-540-55621-4*) Spr-Verlag.

Parnell, J. T., jt. ed. see Downie, J. A.

Parnell, James F., jt. auth. see Biggs, Walter C., Jr.

Parnell, James F., jt. auth. see Lee, David S.

Parnell, Joan W. & Kendrick, Kevin D. Study Skills for Nursing: A Practical Guide. LC 94-26096. 1994. pap. text 15.95 (*0-443-04686-7*) Church.

Parnell, John. Original Mini Coop: The Restorer's Guide to 997 & 998 Cooper & 970, 1071 & 1275 Cooper S. (Bayview Ser.). (Illus.). 120p. 1993. 34.95 (*1-870979-32-X*) MBI Pubg.

Parnell, Laurel. EMDR in the Treatment of Adults Abused as Children. LC 99-21288. 224p. 1999. text 30.00 (*0-393-70298-7*) Norton.

— Transforming Trauma: EMDR. 288p. 1998. pap. 13.95 (*0-393-31757-9*) Norton.

— Transforming Trauma - EDMR: The Revolutionary New Therapy for Freeing the Mind, Clearing the Body, & Opening the Mind. LC 96-44478. 208p. (C). 1997. 21.00 (*0-393-04053-4*) Norton.

Parnell, Margaret. The Blue Peter Book of Things to Make. (Illus.). 48p. (J). (ps-3). 1996. pap. 6.95 (*0-563-40386-1*, Pub. by BBC) Parkwest Pubns.

Parnell, Martha A. Bye-Bye Poverty! Ole Mexico! LC 90-91761. 192p. (Orig.). 1990. 8.95 (*0-9626982-0-2*) M A Parnell.

— Easy Spanish Conjugations. 2p. (C). 1993. 3.00 (*0-9626982-2-9*) M A Parnell.

Parnell, Martin F. The German Tradition of Organized Capitalism: Self-Government in the Coal Industry. (Government-Industry Relations Ser.: No. 7). 272p. 1994. text 65.00 (*0-19-827761-X*) OUP.

Parnell, Mary D. Block Salt & Candles: A Rhondda Childhood. (Illus.). 192p. 1991. 29.95 (*1-85411-056-X*, Pub. by Seren Bks) Dufour.

— Block Salt & Candles: A Rhondda Childhood. (Illus.). 200p. 1994. pap. 16.95 (*1-85411-103-5*, Pub. by Seren Bks) Dufour.

— Plateaux, Gateaux, Chateaux. LC 98-140836. 214p. 1998. 25.95 (*1-85411-207-4*, Pub. by Seren Bks) Dufour.

Parnell, Michael. Laughter from the Dark: A Life of Gwyn Thomas. (Illus.). 242p. 1997. pap. 22.95 (*1-85411-146-9*, Pub. by Seren Bks) Dufour.

Parnell, Michael, ed. see Thomas, Gwyn.

Parnell, Peter. The Cider House Rules: Part One: Here at St. Clouds & Part Two: In Other Parts of the World. 5.95 (*0-8222-1725-2*); pap. 5.95 (*0-8222-1726-0*) Dramatists Play.

Parnell, Peter. Flaubert's Latest. 1993. pap. 5.25 (*0-8222-1328-1*) Dramatists Play.

— Hyde in Hollywood. 1991. pap. 5.95 (*0-88145-090-1*) Broadway Play.

— An Imaginary Life. 1994. pap. 5.25 (*0-8222-1394-X*) Dramatists Play.

— The Rise & Rise of Daniel Rocket. 1984. pap. 5.25 (*0-8222-0956-X*) Dramatists Play.

— Scooter Thomas Makes It to the Top of the World. 1982. pap. 3.25 (*0-8222-1000-2*) Dramatists Play.

Parnell, Philip C. Escalating Disputes: Social Participation & Change in the Oaxacan Highlands. LC 88-17114. (PROFMEX Ser.). 175p. 1988. 31.95 (*0-8165-1053-9*) U of Ariz Pr.

Parnell, Robyn. Supplicants: An Advent Drama. 1999. pap. 2.50 (*1-57514-344-5*, 3117) Encore Perform Pub.

Parnell, T. W. Postal Exam Complete Study Program: Test Battery 470 & R$ural Cqrrier Exam 460 - Money BackGuarantee for Score of 95-100, Audio Tapes & Text/Work Book. rev. ed. 130p. 1997. pap. 39.95 incl. audio (*0-940182-06-8*) Pathfinder Dist.

— Postal Exam Text/Work Book: Data Conversion Operator Exam 710. rev. ed. 120p. 1995. pap. 19.95 (*0-940182-04-1*) Pathfinder Dist.

— Postal Exam Text/Work Book: Test Battery 470 & Rural Carrier Exam 460 - Money Back Guarantee for Score of 95-100. rev. ed. 107p. 1997. pap. 19.95 (*0-940182-05-X*) Pathfinder Dist.

***Parnell, T. W.** Postal Exam Training Guide: Free Live Support & Guaranteed Score of 95-1005th rev. ed. (Illus.). 380p. 2000. pap. 19.95 (*0-940182-11-4*) Pathfinder Dist.

Parnell, Tere. Guide to Building High-Speed Networks, Special Edition. LC 99-187496. 104p. 1998. pap. 5.50 (*0-07-211957-8*) McGraw.

— LAN Times Guide to Building High-Speed Networks. (LAN Times Ser.). 512p. 1996. pap. text 29.95 (*0-07-882200-9*) Osborne-McGraw.

— Network Administrator's Reference. 1999. pap. text 49.99 (*0-07-882588-1*) Osborne-McGraw.

Parnell, Tere, jt. auth. see Bestpitch, Barry G.

Parnell, Teresa F. & Day, Deborah O., eds. Munchausen by Proxy Syndrome: Misunderstood Child Abuse. LC 97-4838. 240p. 1997. text 52.00 (*0-8039-5811-0*); pap. text 24.95 (*0-8039-5812-9*) Sage.

Parnell, Thomas. Poetical Works. LC 70-39664. (Select Bibliographies Reprint Ser.). 1977. reprint ed. 19.95 (*0-8369-9942-8*) Ayer.

— The Poetical Works. Mitford, John, ed. (Anglistica & Americana Ser.: No. 158). xxxii, 185p. 1976. reprint ed. 37.70 (*3-487-05844-8*) G Olms Pubs.

Parnell, Thomas A., jt. ed. see Ramsey, Brian D.

Parnell, Tyrone. Standing in the Doorway of Life. 80p. 1995. pap. 12.00 (*0-9645299-0-4*) Inspired Images.

Parnell, Tyrone J. Words from the Well. 70p. 1997. write for info. (*0-9645299-1-2*) Inspired Images.

Parnell, Veronica, jt. auth. see Crutchley, Zoe.

Parnes, Beatrice, jt. auth. see Potter, Tom.

Parnes, Herbert S. Developing Human Capital. 46p. 1986. 5.50 (*0-318-22075-X*, IN 306) Ctr Educ Trng Employ.

— Policy Issues in Work & Retirement. LC 83-4950. 288p. 1983. pap. text 14.00 (*0-88099-010-4*) W E Upjohn.

Parnes, Marvin, ed. Innovations in Social Group Work: Feedback from Practice to Theory. LC 85-30222. (Social Work with Groups Supplement Ser.: No. 1). 203p. 1986. 39.95 (*0-86656-564-7*) Haworth Pr.

Parnes, Robert. Canoeing the Jersey Pine Barrens: Paddling Adventures along the Batso River, Toms River, Rancocas Creek, Great Egg Harbor River & Mullica River. 5th ed. LC 99-25247. (Illus.). 256p. 1999. pap. 11.95 (*0-7627-0222-2*) Globe Pequot.

Parnes, Robert. Fertile Soil: A Grower's Guide to Organic & Inorganic Fertilizers. 1990. pap. 39.95 (*0-914330-59-4*, Pub. by Ag Access) Fertile Ground Bks.

Parnes, Robert. Fertile Soil: A Grower's Guide to Organic & Inorganic Fertilizers. 190p. (C). 1990. pap. text 39.95 (*0-932857-03-5*) Ag Access.

— Organic & Inorganic Fertilizers. 167p. (Orig.). 1996. pap. text 39.95 (*0-9603554-3-X*) Woods End.

Parnes, S. E. The Personnel Manager's Handbook of Performance Evaluation Programs. rev. ed. 85p. 1981. per. 27.95 (*1-55645-117-2*, 404) Busn Legal Reports.

Parnes, Sidney J. Visionizing. 1992. reprint ed. 24.95 (*0-930222-88-1*) Creat Educ Found.

Parnes, Sidney J., ed. Source Book for Creative Problem Solving: A Fifty Year Digest of Proven Innovation Processes. (Orig.). 1992. pap. 37.95 (*0-930222-92-X*) Creat Educ Found.

Parnes, Sidney J., et al. Optimize the Magic of Your Mind. LC 98-138866. 196p. 1997. pap. 18.95 (*0-943456-41-X*) Bearly Ltd.

Parnes, Stephan. The Art of the Passover. 119p. 1997. 35.00 (*0-88363-494-5*) H L Levin.

Parnes, Steven. Productivity & the Quality of Working Life. (Studies in Productivity: Highlights of the Literature Ser.: Vol. 2). 43p. 1978. pap. 55.00 (*0-89361-014-3*) Work in Amer.

***Parness, Jeffrey A.** Advanced Civil Procedure: Civil Claim Settlements. LC 99-53918. 600p. 2000. boxed set 75.00 (*0-89089-898-7*) Carolina Acad Pr.

Parness, Jeffrey A. Illinois Civil Procedure. LC 98-86941. 519p. 1998. 105.00 (*0-327-00304-9*, 6007610) LEXIS Pub.

***Parness, Jeffrey A.** Illinois Civil Procedure, 1999 Supplement Pocketpart. 50p. 1999. suppl. ed. write for info. (*0-327-01719-8*, 6007510) LEXIS Pub.

Parness, Jeffrey M. The Complete Guide to Washington Internships, Vol. 1. LC 88-83185. 144p. (Orig.). (C). 1989. pap. text 16.95 (*0-9621953-0-8*) JMP Enter.

Parnet, Claire, jt. auth. see Deleuze, Gilles.

Parnham, David. Sir Henry Vane, Theologian: A Study in Seventeenth-Century Religious & Political Discourse. LC 95-9478. 368p. 1997. 46.50 (*0-8386-3681-0*) Fairleigh Dickinson.

Parnham, M. J., jt. ed. see Nijkamp, F. P.

Parnham, Michael J. Advantages & Problems with Non-Opioids in Pain Management: Vancouver, Canada, August 19th, 1996. LC 97-511. (Illus.). 20p. 1997. pap. write for info. (*0-8176-5678-2*); pap. write for info. (*3-7643-5678-2*) Birkhauser.

— Are the Medical Needs for the Treatment of Acute Pain Fulfilled? Istanbul, Turkey, October 5, 1996. LC 97-512. 1997. pap. write for info. (*0-8176-5679-0*) Birkhauser.

— Are the Medical Needs for the Treatment of Acute Pain Fulfilled? Istanbul, Turkey, October 5th, 1996. LC 97-512. 1997. pap. write for info. (*3-7643-5679-0*) Birkhauser.

— Cologne Atherosclerosis Conference No. 2: Lipids. (Agents & Actions Supplements Ser.: No. 16). 1984. 68.00 (*0-8176-1645-4*) Birkhauser.

— Non-Opioid Analgesics in the Treatment of Acute Pain: Johannesbergs Slott, Sweden, March 14th, 1996. LC 97-513. 1997. write for info. (*0-8176-5680-4*); write for info. (*3-7643-5680-4*) Birkhauser.

— Non-Opioids in Pain Management: Vancouver, August 19, 1996. LC 97-10915. 1997. write for info. (*0-8176-5700-2*); write for info. (*3-7643-5700-2*) Birkhauser.

Parnham, Michael J., ed. Ethical Issues in Drug Research: Through a Glass Darkly. LC 96-77455. 200p. (gr. 12). 1996. 70.00 (*90-5199-279-3*, 279-3) IOS Press.

Parnham, Michael J. & Prop, G., eds. Cologne Atherosclerosis Conference Three: Platelets. (Agents & Actions Supplements Ser.: No. 20). 278p. 1986. 77.00 (*0-8176-1805-8*) Birkhauser.

Parnham, Michael J., jt. auth. see Nijkamp, Franciscus P.

Parnham, Michael J., jt. ed. see Van Den Berg, W. B.

***Parnham, P. & Rispin, C.** Residential Property Appraisal. 136p. 2000. pap. 49.99 (*0-419-22570-6*, E & FN Spon) Routledge.

Parnham, Phil, ed. Prevention of Premature Staining of New Buildings. (Illus.). 72p. (C). 1996. pap. 45.00 (*0-419-17130-4*, E & FN Spon) Routledge.

Parnwell, E. C. The New Oxford Picture Dictionary. LC 87-23950. (MUL., Illus.). 124p. 1988. pap. 9.95 (*0-19-434199-2*) OUP.

— The New Oxford Picture Dictionary. (ENG & JPN., Illus.). 150p. 1990. pap. text 9.95 (*0-19-434356-1*) OUP.

— The New Oxford Picture Dictionary: Beginner's Workbook. (Illus.). 1988. pap. text, wbk. ed. 7.95 (*0-19-434326-X*) OUP.

— New Oxford Picture Dictionary: Chinese - English. (ENG & CHI., Illus.). 128p. 1989. pap. text 9.95 (*0-19-434357-X*) OUP.

— The New Oxford Picture Dictionary: English-Navajo Edition. (Illus.). 148p. 1990. pap. text 9.95 (*0-19-434362-6*) OUP.

— The New Oxford Picture Dictionary: Intermediate Workbook. (Illus.). 144p. 1988. pap. text, wbk. ed. 7.95 (*0-19-434325-1*) OUP.

— The New Oxford Picture Dictionary: Overhead Transparencies (100) 1993. 199.95 (*0-19-434532-7*) OUP.

— New Oxford Picture Dictionary: Russian - English. (RUS & ENG., Illus.). 1994. pap. text 9.95 (*0-19-434651-X*) OUP.

— Oxford Picture Dictionary of American English. (Illus.). 1988. pap. write for info. (*0-318-54877-1*) OUP.

Parnwell, E. C., ed. New Oxford Picture Dictionary: American English - Spanish. (Illus.). 148p. 1989. pap. text 9.95 (*0-19-434355-3*) OUP.

Parnwell, Michael J., ed. Uneven Development in Thailand. 368p. 1996. 87.95 (*1-85972-085-4*, Pub. by Avebry) Ashgate Pub Co.

Parnwell, Michael J., jt. ed. see Bryant, Raymond L.

Parnwell, Michael J., jt. ed. see King, Victor J.

Parnwell, Mike. Population Movements & the Third World. LC 92-13687. (Introductions to Development Ser.). (Illus.). 160p. (C). 1993. pap. 17.99 (*0-415-06953-X*, A4477) Routledge.

Parod, Ted W. 1996/1997 Auctioneers Association of Arizona Directory. 1996. pap. 9.95 (*0-9627432-1-6*) Echo Lake Pr.

— Oh, Oh . . . Daddy's Cooking! LC 91-75372. (Illus.). 128p. 1994. spiral bd. 9.95 (*0-9627432-4-0*) Echo Lake Pr.

— Old Indian Recipes (Not Really) A Father's Method of Feeding His "Tribe" (Illus.). 118p. 1990. spiral bd. 9.95 (*0-9627432-3-2*) Echo Lake Pr.

***Parodi, Jorge.** To Be a Worker: Identity & Politics in Peru. LC 99-49579. (Latin America in Translation/en Traduccion/em Traducao Series). 208p. 2000. pap. 17.95 (*0-8078-4860-3*); lib. bdg. 39.95 (*0-8078-2548-4*) U of NC Pr.

Parodi, Juan C., et al. Endovascular Grafting Techniques. (Illus.). 300p. 1998. write for info. (*0-683-06769-9*) Lppncott W & W.

Parodi, Juan Carlos, et al. Endovascular Grafting Techniques. LC 98-28509. 155p. 1998. 125.00 (*0-683-30209-4*) Lppncott W & W.

Parodi, Luis M. La Educacion Especial y Sus Servicios. (SPA.). 478p. pap. write for info. (*0-929441-45-1*) Pubns Puertorriquenas.

— La Filosofia y el Ser Humano. (SPA.). 490p. 1996. pap. write for info. (*0-929441-76-1*) Pubns Puertorriquenas.

— La Sexualidad Humana. (SPA.). 592p. 1993. pap. write for info. (*0-929441-33-8*) Pubns Puertorriquenas.

Parodi, R., ed. Computer Communications: Towards a New World. 750p. 1992. 140.00 (*90-5199-110-X*, Pub. by IOS Pr) IOS Press.

P

An Asterisk (*) at the beginning of an entry indicates that the title is appearing for the first time.

Paroissien, David. The Companion to Oliver Twist. (Illus.). 400p. 1992. text 85.00 (0-7486-0272-0, Pub. by Edinburgh U Pr) Col U Pr.
***Paroissien, David.** Oliver Twist. LC 99-24649. 1999. write for info. (0-404-62471-5) AMS Pr.
Parola, Rene. Optical Art: Theory & Practice. LC 95-45369. (Illus.). 144p. 1998. reprint ed. pap. 13.95 (0-486-29054-9) Dover.
***Parola, Shirley Tong & Gaynier, Lisa Parola.** Remembering Diamond Head, Remembering Hawaii: A Cookbook Memoir of Hawaii & Its Foods. LC 99-96015. (Illus.). 320p. 1999. pap. 15.95 (0-9666457-0-7) Diamond Hawaii Pr.
Parole Commission, Commonwealth of Pennsylvania. The Report of the Pennsylvania State Parole Commission to the Legislature, 1927 Part I, & Part Ii. LC 74-3849. (Criminal Justice in America Ser.). 1974. reprint ed. 28.95 (0-405-06163-3) Ayer.
***Parolini.** The Value Net. LC 99-25241. 264p. 1999. 55.00 (0-471-98719-0) Wiley.
Parolini, Cindy, ed. Group's Best Junior High Meetings, Vol. 1. 323p. (Orig.). 1987. pap. 19.99 (0-931529-58-1) Group Pub.
Parolini, Stephen. Celebrating Christ with Youth-Led Worship: Teenagers Will Present Creative Worship Segments about the Life of Jesus. Warden, Michael, ed. (Projects with a Purpose for Youth Ministry Ser.). 37p. (YA). 1994. pap. 11.99 (1-55945-410-5, 4105) Group Pub.
— Controversial Discussion Starters for Youth Ministry: Topics Include Abortion, Euthanasia, Premarital Sex, New Age Movement. 108p. 1992. pap. 14.99 (1-55945-156-4, Group Bks) Group Pub.
— Sharing Your Faith Without Fear: Teenagers Will Learn How to Talk about Their Faith with Friends. Warden, Michael, ed. (Projects with a Purpose for Youth Ministry Ser.). 44p. (YA). 1994. pap. 11.99 (1-55945-409-1) Group Pub.
— You-Choose-the-Ending Skits for Youth Ministry: For Great Discussions. LC 96-37023. (YA). (gr. 7-12). 1997. pap. 14.99 (1-55945-627-2) Group Pub.
Parolini, Stephen & Lauffer, Lisa B. Fun Bible-Learning Projects for Young Teenagers: Over 100 Meaningful Games, Crafts & Activities. LC 95-7800. 112p. 1995. 14.99 (1-55945-796-1) Group Pub.
Parolini, Stephen, ed. see Roehlkepartain, Jolene L.
Parolini, Stephen, ed. see Rydberg, Denny.
Parolly, Gerald. Die Steinschuttfluren (Heldreichietea) Des Westlichen und Mittleren Taurus (Tuerkei) Pflanzensoziologisahe, Floristische und Oekologische Untersuchungen. (Dissertationes Botanicae Ser.: Band 247). (Illus.). x, 374p. 1995. pap. 100.00 (3-443-64159-8, Pub. by Gebruder Borntraeger) Balogh.
Paros, Ben J., jt. auth. see Paros, Lawrence.
***Paros, Lawrence.** A Word with You America, Vol. I. (Illus.). 128p. 1999. pap. 11.95 (0-9672005-0-4) Kvetch Pr.
— A Word with You America, Vol. II. (Illus.). 128p. 1999. pap. 11.95 (0-9672005-1-2) Kvetch Pr.
Paros, Lawrence & Paros, Ben J. Smash Caps: The Official Milk-Cap Manual. (Illus.). 55p. (Orig.). (J). (gr. 3-6). 1995. pap. 7.99 (0-380-78459-9, Avon Bks) Morrow Avon.
Parot, Joseph J. Polish Catholics in Chicago, 1850-1920: A Religious History. LC 81-11297. 298p. 1982. 18.00 (0-87580-081-5) N Ill U Pr.
Parotti, Phillip. The Trojan Generals Talk: Memoirs of the Greek War - Stories. LC 87-34282. (Illinois Short Fiction Ser.). 184p. 1988. 14.95 (0-252-01510-X) U of Ill Pr.
Paroubkova, J. Czech-English, English-Czech Medical Dictionary. (CZE & ENG.). 1991. 95.00 (0-8288-7198-1, F26310) Fr & Eur.
***Paroun, Robert.** How to Build with Steel. Orig. Title: Steel Fabricator's Handbook. (Illus.). 96p. 1999. pap. 10.00 (0-918828-19-8) Shire Pr.
Parouty, Michel. Mozart: From Child Prodigy to Tragic Hero. Skrine, Celia, tr. (Discoveries Ser.). (Illus.). 192p. 1993. pap. 12.95 (0-8109-2846-9, Pub. by Abrams) Time Warner.
Parparov, L. F. German-Russian Dictionary of Military Abbreviations: Deutsch-Russisches Woerterbuch der Militaerischen Abkuerzungen. (GER & RUS.). 320p. 1983. 29.95 (0-8288-1165-2, M15317) Fr & Eur.
Parpart, Jane, jt. ed. see Zalewski, Marysia.
Parpart, Jane L., ed. Women & Development in Africa: Comparative Perspectives. LC 88-36271. (Dalhousie African Studies: No. 7). (Illus.). 354p. (Orig.). (C). 1989. pap. text 35.50 (0-8191-7379-7, Pub. by Dalhousie Univ Pr); lib. bdg. 57.00 (0-8191-7378-9, Pub. by Dalhousie Univ Pr) U Pr of Amer.
***Parpart, Jane L., et al, eds.** Theoretical Perspectives on Gender & Development. 250p. 2000. pap. 22.00 (0-88936-910-0, Pub. by IDRC Bks) Stylus Pub VA.
Parpart, Jane L., jt. auth. see Bastian, Misty L.
Parpart, Jane L., jt. auth. see Bastian, Misty L.
Parpart, Jane L., jt. ed. see Marchand, marianne H.
Parpart, Jane L., jt. ed. see Marchand, Marianne H.
Parpart, Paulette K. Index to the Death & Burial Records of Missoula County, Montana, Vol. 1: Burials: Missoula City Cemetery. 212p. (Orig.). 1989. pap. 17.00 (0-9624566-1-6) Western MT Geneal.
— Index to the Death & Burial Records of Missoula County, Montana, Vol. 2: Burials: Carlton, Fort Missoula, Frenchtown, St. Mary's, St. Mary's Annex, Sunset Memorial Park, Sunset Crematorium Records, & Other Small Private Cemeteries or Burials. LC 89-51676. 142p. (Orig.). 1989. write for info. (0-9624566-0-8); pap. 13.00 (0-9624566-2-4) Western MT Geneal.
Parpola, Asko. Deciphering the Indus Script. LC 92-37773. (Illus.). 396p. (C). 1994. text 109.95 (0-521-43079-8) Cambridge U Pr.
Parpola, S. & Whiting, R. M., eds. Assyria, 1995: Proceedings of the 10th Anniversary Symposium of the Neo-Assyrian Text Corpus Project Helsinki, September 7-11, 1995. (State Archives of Assyria Studies). (Illus.). 389p. 1997. pap. text 50.00 (951-45-7703-5, Pub. by Neo-Assyrian Text) Eisenbrauns.
Parpola, Simo. Assyrian Prophecies. Reade, Julian, ed. (State Archives of Assyria Studies: Vol. 9). (Illus.). cxxi, 84p. 1997. pap. 32.00 (951-570-166-X, Pub. by Neo-Assyrian Text); text 43.00 (951-570-167-8, Pub. by Neo-Assyrian Text) Eisenbrauns.
Parpola, Simo. Collations to Neo-Assyrian Legal Texts from Nineveh. LC 82-151156. (Assur Ser.: Vol. 2, Pt. 5). 89p. 1979. pap. 19.00 (0-89003-004-9) Undena Pubns.
— The Standard Babylonian Epic of Gilgamesh. (State Archives of Assyria Studies). xxviii, 165p. 1997. pap. text 25.00 (951-45-7760-4, Pub. by Neo-Assyrian Text) Eisenbrauns.
Parpworth, Neil, jt. auth. see Hawke, Neil.
Parque, Richard. Hellbound. 1985. mass mkt. 3.50 (0-8217-1591-7, Zebra Kensgtn) Kensgtn Pub Corp.
— Sweet Vietnam. 288p. 1984. mass mkt. 3.50 (0-8217-1423-6, Zebra Kensgtn) Kensgtn Pub Corp.
Parr & Rudnitsky. The Superstar Workout. 1999. per. 2.25 (0-671-89675-X) PB.
Parr, A. C. National Measurement System for Radiometry, Photometry, & Pyrometry Based Upon Absolute Detectors. 36p. 1996. pap. 5.00 (0-16-053383-X) USGPO.
Parr, A. L. The Mysterious Cave: Includes Audio Cassette, Coloring Pad & Crayons. (Illus.). 16p. (J). (gr. k-4). 1998. pap. 12.50 incl. audio (0-9662994-1-8) Adven Meadow.
Parr, Andrew. Hydraulics & Pneumatics: A Technician's & Engineer's Guide. (Illus.). 240p. 1992. pap. text 49.95 (0-7506-0793-9) Buttrwrth-Heinemann.
— Logic Designer's Handbook: Circuits & Systems. 2nd ed. LC 92-31023. (Illus.). 488p. 1993. pap. text 69.95 (0-7506-0535-9) Buttrwrth-Heinemann.
— Programmable Controllers: An Engineer's Guide. LC 92-30189. (Illus.). 256p. 1993. text 69.95 (0-7506-0498-0) Buttrwrth-Heinemann.
***Parr, Ann.** Low Riders. (Illus.). 2000. 16.95 (0-7910-5849-2) Chelsea Hse.
— Low Riders. (Illus.). 2001. pap. 5.95 (0-7910-5850-6) Chelsea Hse.
***Parr, Anthony.** The Staple of News by Ben Jonson: Back in Print. 292p. 2000. pap. 19.95 (0-7190-5906-2, Pub. by Manchester Univ Pr) St Martin.
— Three Renaissance Travel Plays: New in Paperback. 330p. 2000. pap. 29.95 (0-7190-5800-7, Pub. by Manchester Univ Pr) St Martin.
Parr, Anthony, ed. see Dekker, Thomas.
Parr, Barry. Guangzhou - Canton: Where China Meets the 21st Century. (Illus.). 160p. 1995. pap. 14.95 (0-8442-9954-5, Passprt Bks) NTC Contemp Pub Co.
— Hiking the Sierra Nevada. LC 99-22343. (Illus.). 304p. 1999. pap. 15.95 (1-56044-724-9) Falcon Pub Inc.
— San Francisco & the Bay Area. Castleman, Deke, ed. (Discover America Ser.). (Illus.). 396p. 1992. pap. 12.95 (1-878867-00-8, Compass Amrcn) Fodors Travel.
Parr, Barry, ed. see Castleman, Deke.
Parr, Barry, ed. see Cheek, Lawrence W.
Parr, Benard F. Sports: Index of Modern Developments for Prompt Applications. LC 90-56308. 160p. 1991. 47.50 (1-55914-390-8); pap. 44.50 (1-55914-391-6) ABBE Pubs Assn.
Parr, Catharine. Prayers or Meditations, Where the Mind Is Stirred Patiently to Suffer All Afflictions Here. LC 76-57370. (English Experience Ser.: No. 788). 1977. reprint ed. lib. bdg. 20.00 (90-221-0788-4) Walter J Johnson.
Parr, Charles H. Preliminary List of Early Alaska Imprints, Eighteen Sixty-Nine Through Nineteen Thirteen. LC 76-623405. (Elmer E. Rasmuson Library Occasional Papers: No. 3). 66p. 1974. pap. 2.00 (0-937592-04-8) U Alaska Rasmuson Lib.
Parr, Charles M. So Noble a Captain: The Life & Times of Ferdinand Magellan. LC 75-31439. (Illus.). 423p. 1975. reprint ed. lib. bdg. 49.75 (0-8371-8521-1, PASN, Greenwood Pr) Greenwood.
Parr, Delia. By Fate's Design. 1996. mass mkt. 5.99 (0-614-20522-0, St Martins Paperbacks) St Martin.
— Evergreen, Vol. 1. 1995. mass mkt. 4.99 (0-312-95376-3) St Martin.
— Fire in Autumn. 1996. mass mkt. 5.50 (0-312-95690-8, Pub. by Tor Bks) St Martin.
— The Ivory Duchess. 1997. mass mkt. 5.99 (0-312-96213-4); mass mkt. 5.99 (0-614-27779-5) St Martin.
— Lavender & Lace. 1996. mass mkt. 5.99 (0-312-95926-5) St Martin.
— The Minister's Wife. 320p. 1998. mass mkt. 5.99 (0-312-96650-4) St Martin.
***Parr, Delia.** The Promise of Flowers. 272p. 2000. mass mkt. 5.99 (0-312-97505-8) St Martin.
Parr, Delia. Sunrise. 1999. mass mkt. 5.99 (0-312-97091-9, St Martins Paperbacks) St Martin.
***Parr, E .A.** Hydraulics & Pneumatics. 2nd ed. 244p. 2000. pap. text 49.95 (0-7506-4419-2) Buttrwrth-Heinemann.
Parr, E. A. Hydraulics & Pneumatics: A Technician's & Engineer's Guide. 2nd ed. LC 98-22010. 244p. 1998. 66.95 (0-7506-3937-7) Buttrwrth-Heinemann.
— Industrial Control Engineering. (Illus.). 416p. 1996. pap. text 59.95 (0-7506-2407-8) Buttrwrth-Heinemann.
— Industrial Control Handbook. 3rd ed. LC 99-166317. (Illus.). 832p. 1998. text 155.00 (0-7506-3934-2, Newnes) Buttrwrth-Heinemann.
— Industrial Control Handbook. 3rd ed. 1999. 59.95 (0-8311-3085-7) Industrial Products Corp.
Parr, E. A. Industrial Control Handbook Vol. 3: Theory & Applications. (Illus.). 412p. 1989. 34.95 (0-8311-1179-8) Indus Pr.
Parr, E. A. Industrial Control Handbook, Vol. 1: Tranducers. LC 87-3675. (Illus.). 304p. 1987. 34.95 (0-8311-1175-5) Indus Pr.
— Newnes Electronics Pocket Book. 1988. 22.00 (0-434-91519-X) CRC Pr.
Parr, Ed. The Last American Whale-Oil Company: A History of Nye Lubricants, Inc., 1844-1994. (Illus.). iii, 99p. 1996. write for info. (0-9653026-0-1); pap. write for info. (0-9653026-1-X) Nye Lubricants.
Parr, Elizabeth. I'm Glad You're Not Dead: A Liver Transplant Story. unabridged ed. LC 96-94745. 172p. 1996. pap. 9.95 (0-9654728-0-9) Jrny Pub TX.
***Parr, Elizabeth.** I'm Glad You're Not Dead: A Liver Transplant Story. 2nd unabridged ed. LC 00-90041. (Illus.). 2000. pap. 12.95 (0-9654728-1-7) Jrny Pub TX.
Parr, Elizabeth, jt. auth. see Poole, Catherine.
Parr, Frederique, ed. see Waggoner, Carmen.
Parr, Hector C. Time, Science & Philosophy. 160p. 1998. pap. 14.95 (0-7188-2964-6, Lutterworth-Parkwest) Parkwest Pubns.
Parr, Hester, jt. ed. see Butler, Ruth.
Parr, J. F., et al, eds. Water Potential Relations in Soil Microbiology. (Special Publications: No. 9). 151p. 1981. pap. 4.40 (0-89118-767-7) Soil Sci Soc Am.
Parr, J. Gordon, jt. auth. see Beddoes, Jonathan.
Parr, Jack E., jt. ed. see Horowitz, Emanual.
Parr, James A. On Cervantes: Essays for L. A. Murillo. (Documentacion Cervantina Ser.: Vol. 11). 305p. 1991. 22.00 (0-936388-49-8) Juan de la Cuesta.
Parr, James A., ed. see De Cervantes Saavedra, Miguel.
Parr, James A., ed. see De Molina, Tirso.
Parr, James G. & Hanson, Albert. An Introduction to Stainless Steel. LC 65-27458. 157p. reprint ed. pap. 48.70 (0-608-30901-X, 205098500069) Bks Demand.
Parr, James Gordon. Man, Metals, & Modern Magic. LC 77-25186. 238p. 1978. reprint ed. lib. bdg. 65.00 (0-313-20122-6, PAMM, Greenwood Pr) Greenwood.
Parr, Jan. Amelia Earhart: First Lady of Flight. LC 97-8156. (Book Report Biography Ser.). (J). 1997. 22.00 (0-531-11407-4) Watts.
— The Young Vegetarian's Companion. 144p. (J). 1996. pap. 9.00 (0-531-15789-X) Watts.
— The Young Vegetarian's Companion. LC 96-13303. 144p. (YA). (gr. 7-12). 1996. lib. bdg. 24.00 (0-531-11277-2) Watts.
Parr, John. Introduction to Ophthalmology. (Illus.). 244p. 1996. pap. 65.00 (0-908569-48-3, Pub. by Univ Otago Pr) Intl Spec Bk.
Parr, John, jt. ed. see Adams, Bruce.
Parr, Joy. The Gender of Breadwinners: Women, Men & Change in Two Industrial Towns, 1880-1950. 320p. 1990. text 45.00 (0-8020-5853-1); pap. text 21.95 (0-8020-6760-3) U of Toronto Pr.
— Labouring Children: British Immigrant Apprentices to Canada, 1869-1924. LC 95-104383. (Reprints in Canadian History Ser.). 224p. 1993. pap. text 19.95 (0-8020-7443-X) U of Toronto Pr.
Parr, Joy, ed. A Diversity of Women: Women in Ontario since 1945. (Illus.). 392p. 1995. text 65.00 (0-8020-2615-X); pap. text 21.95 (0-8020-7695-5) U of Toronto Pr.
Parr, Joy & Rosenfeld, Mark, eds. Gender & History in Canada. 1996. write for info. (0-7730-5541-X) Addison-Wesley.
Parr, Judith D. I Talk with the Trees. Rome, Dorothy, ed. (Illus.). 21p. 1991. pap. 3.50 (0-941971-09-0) Peacock CO.
— Many Avenues of Healing. Rome, Dorothy, ed. (Illus.). 169p. 1989. pap. 11.00 (0-941971-06-6) Peacock CO.
— Meditations from My Garden. Gay, Marie, ed. (Illus.). 126p. 1987. spiral bd. 9.00 (0-941971-00-7) Peacock CO.
— The Upward Climb: An Epic Poem. 55p. 1994. pap. 4.50 (0-941971-10-4) Peacock CO.
— Wise Woman: Whisperings of the Angels. Rome, Dorothy, ed. (Illus.). 52p. 1990. write for info. incl. audio (0-941971-08-2); pap. 15.95 incl. audio (0-941971-07-4) Peacock CO.
***Parr, Lance A.** Report Writing Essentials. LC 91-70495. 73p. 2000. pap. 11.95 (0-942728-99-8) Copperhouse.
Parr, Larry. Viktors Pupols, American Master. Long, Robert B., ed. (Illus.). 78p. (Orig.). 1983. pap. 6.50 (0-938650-31-9) Thinkers Pr.
Parr, Larry, jt. auth. see Albert, Lev.
Parr, Larry, jt. auth. see Denker, Arnold.
Parr, Larry, ed. see Palatnik, Sam & Albert, Lev.
Parr, Leland W. Introduction to the Anthropology of the Near East in Ancient & Recent Times, with a Chapter on Near Eastern Bloodgroups. 1980. lib. bdg. 59.95 (0-8490-3164-8) Gordon Pr.
Parr, Leslie G. A Will of Her Own: Sarah Towles Reed & the Pursuit of Democracy in Southern Public Education. LC 97-33400. 248p. 1998. text 40.00 (0-8203-1932-5) U of Ga Pr.
Parr, Letitia. When Sea & Sky Are Blue. LC 78-151272. (Illus.). 32p. (J). (ps-3). 13.95 (0-87592-059-4) Scroll Pr.
Parr, Lona. Aerobics: Lab Manual. 1998. text, lab manual ed. 11.53 (1-56870-322-8) RonJon Pub.
— Self Paced Weight Training. 1998. text 14.52 (1-56870-323-6) RonJon Pub.
— Traditional Weight Training. 1998. text 12.53 (1-56870-321-X) RonJon Pub.

Parr, Marilyn K., ed. The Presidents of the United States: The First Twenty Years. LC 92-18145. 1992. 5.50 (0-8444-0698-8) Lib Congress.
***Parr, Martin.** Autoportrait. 2000. 29.95 (1-899235-72-8) Dewi Lewis.
— Boring Postcards U: S. A. (Illus.). 2000. 24.95 (0-7148-4000-9) Phaidon Pr.
Parr, Martin. Martin Parr: Common Sense. (Illus.). 160p. 1999. 50.00 (1-899235-07-8, Pub. by Dewi Lewis) Dist Art Pubs.
***Parr, Martin.** Think of England. 2000. 39.95 (0-7148-3991-4) Phaidon Pr.
Parr, Martin, photos by. Last Resort. (Illus.). 88p. 1998. 45.00 (1-899235-16-7, 810322, Pub. by Dewi Lewis) Dist Art Pubs.
Parr, Martin, jt. auth. see Davies, John.
Parr, Michael, jt. auth. see Juniper, Tony.
Parr, Mike, jt. auth. see Bell, Douglas.
Parr, Peggy. Mountain High, Mountain Rescue. LC 86-25773. 202p. 1986. 15.95 (1-55591-005-X) Fulcrum Pub.
Parr, Rob & Rubnitsky, David. Rob Parr's Post-Pregnancy Workout. LC 97-108483. 208p. 1997. pap. 13.00 (0-425-15607-9) Berkley Pub.
Parr, Robert. The Dillonwood Grove Site (CA-TUL-1985) Tulane County, California. (California Department of Forestry & Fire Protection Ser.). (Illus.). 58p. (C). 1997. pap. text 6.25 (1-55567-841-6) Coyote Press.
Parr, Robert, tr. see Son, Pham, ed.
Parr, Robert G. & Weitao, Yang. Density-Functional Theory of Atoms & Molecules. (International Series of Monographs on Chemistry: Vol. 16). (Illus.). 352p. 1994. reprint ed. pap. text 55.00 (0-19-509276-7) OUP.
Parr, Robert G., ed. see International Congress of Quantum Chemistry Staff.
Parr, Roger P. Matthieu de Vendome, ars Versificatoria. Robb, James, ed. LC 80-84768. 1981. pap. 15.00 (0-87462-222-0) Marquette.
Parr, Roger P., tr. Geoffery of Vinsauf: Instruction in the Method & Art of Speaking & Versifying. (Medieval Philosophical Texts in Translation Ser.). 1968. pap. 15.00 (0-87462-217-4) Marquette.
Parr, Royse, jt. auth. see Burke, Bob.
***Parr, Russell L.** Intellectual Property Infringement Damages: A Litigation Support Handbook. 2nd ed. (Intellectual Property Ser.). 320p. 1999. text 145.00 (0-471-32015-3) Wiley.
— Intellectual Property Infringement Damages: A Litigation Support Handbook, April 2000 Supplement. 2nd ed. 96p. 2000. pap. 60.00 (0-471-36141-0) Wiley.
Parr, Russell L. & Sullivan, Patrick H., eds. Technology Licensing Strategies. LC 95-53195. (Intellectual Property Library Ser.). 320p. 1996. 82.95 (0-471-13081-8) Wiley.
Parr, Russell L., jt. auth. see Smith, Gordan V.
Parr, Russell L., jt. auth. see Smith, Gordon V.
Parr, Samuel, ed. Metaphysical Tracts by English Philosophers of the 18th Century. 351p. reprint ed. lib. bdg. 63.70 (3-487-05311-X) G Olms Pubs.
Parr, Scott & Guinness, Rupert. Tales from the Toolbox: Inside a Pro Cycling Team. LC 97-26360. (Illus.). 224p. 1997. pap. 14.95 (1-884737-39-0) VeloPress.
Parr, Susan R. The Moral of the Story: Literature, Values & American Education. 236p. (C). 1982. pap. text 17.95 (0-8077-2716-4) Tchrs Coll.
Parr, Susan R. & Savery, Pancho, eds. Approaches to Teaching Ellison's Invisible Man. LC 88-13786. (Approaches to Teaching World Literature Ser.: No. 24). xi, 154p. 1989. pap. 18.00 (0-87352-506-X, AP24P); lib. bdg. 37.50 (0-87352-505-1, AP24C) Modern Lang.
Parr, Susie, et al. Talking about Aphasia: Living with Loss of Language after Stroke. LC 97-15402. 1997. 94.00 (0-335-19937-2); pap. 27.95 (0-335-19936-4) OpUniv Pr.
Parr, Terence. Language Translation Using PCCTS & C++ A Referenced Guide. Date not set. 34.95 (0-9627488-5-4) Automata Pub.
Parr, Timothy P., jt. ed. see Kuo, Kenneth K.
***Parr, Todd.** The Best Friend's Book. LC 98-46961. 24p. (YA). 2000. 5.95 (0-316-69201-8) Little.
— Big & Little. (J). 2001. bds. 4.95 (0-316-69291-3, Pub. by Little) Time Warner.
— Black & White. (J). 2001. bds. 4.95 (0-316-69225-5, Pub. by Little) Time Warner.
Parr, Todd. Do's & Don'ts. LC 98-3284. (Illus.). 24p. (J). (gr. k-3). 1999. 5.95 (0-316-69213-1) Little.
***Parr, Todd.** Dos' & Don'ts at the Zoo. LC 98-49137. 24p. (YA). 2000. 5.95 (0-316-69212-3) Little.
— The Feelings Book. LC 99-42775. (Illus.). 24p. (J). (ps up). 2000. 5.95 (0-316-69131-3) Little.
Parr, Todd. My Really Cool Baby Book. (J). 2000. 13.95 (0-316-69241-7) Little.
— The Okay Book. LC 98-3283. (Illus.). 24p. (J). (gr. k-3). 1999. 5.95 (0-316-69220-4) Little.
— Things That Make You Feel Good, Things That Make You Feel Bad. LC 98-13081. (Illus.). 24p. (J). (gr. k-3). 1999. 5.95 (0-316-69270-0) Little.
— This Is My Hair. LC 98-13080. (Illus.). 24p. (J). (gr. k-3). 1999. 5.95 (0-316-69236-0) Little.
***Parr, Todd.** Underwear Do's & Don'ts. LC 99-52647. (Illus.). 24p. (J). (ps up). 2000. 5.95 (0-316-69151-8) Little.
Parra, Ale, tr. see McCrea, Steve.
Parra, Dann. Model Mystique Unraveled. 96p. 1996. pap. 29.95 (0-9643162-7-7) Dancyn Pubng.

An Asterisk (*) at the beginning of an entry indicates that the title is appearing for the first time.

Parra, Eduardo. Spanish/English Advertising Dictionary. (ENG & SPA.). 345p. 1994. pap. 69.95 (*0-7859-9648-6*) Fr & Eur.

Parra-Elliott, Ligia, jt. ed. see Ramirez, Bernardo.

Parra, Fernando. Dictionary of Ecology & the Environment: Diccionario de Ecologia, Ecologismo y Medio Ambiente. (ENG & SPA.). 288p. 1984. pap. 19.95 (*0-8288-1404-X*, S60012) Fr & Eur.

***Parra Luna, Francisco.** The Performance of Social Systems: Perspectives & Problems. LC 99-54947. 2000. write for info. (*0-306-46309-1*, Kluwer Plenum) Kluwer Academic.

Parra, Margaret. Family Cooking. (Illus.). 109p. 1972. pap. 5.00 (*1-888947-08-X*) Sudbury Valley.

Parra, Mario & Canterbury, Gloria. Ghostown of White Oaks, N. M. Stearns, Johnson & Leslie, Robert, eds. (Illus.). 176p. 1998. pap., per. 15.95 (*1-888711-01-9*) Bravo Pr.

Parra, Mario & Canterbury, Gloria. Trails to Ruidoso: (A History of New Mexico) 360p. 1996. pap., per. 25.00 (*1-888711-00-0*, 11-19:RAK) Bravo Pr.

Parra Murga, Eduardo. Diccionario de Publicidad y Marketing. (SPA.). 238p. 1990. 75.00 (*0-7859-6348-0*, 8485783069) Fr & Eur.

Parra, Nicanor. Antipoems: New & Selected. Unger, David, ed. Ferlinghetti, Lawrence et al, trs. from SPA. LC 85-11507. 224p. 1985. pap. 8.95 (*0-8112-0960-1*, NDP603, Pub. by New Directions) Norton.

— Antipoems: New & Selected. Unger, David, ed. Ferlinghetti, Lawrence et al, trs. from SPA. LC 85-11507. 224p. 1985. 19.95 (*0-8112-0959-8*, Pub. by New Directions) Norton.

— Poemas para Combatir la Calvicie (Poetry Against Hairloss) (SPA.). 382p. 1993. pap. 25.99 (*968-16-3931-6*, Pub. by Fondo) Continental Bk.

— Sermons & Homilies of the Christ of Elqui by Nicanor Parra. Reyes, Sandra, tr. LC 84-2187. 120p. 1984. text 19.95 (*0-8262-0451-1*) U of Mo Pr.

Parra, Nicanor, jt. auth. see Neruda, Pablo.

Parramon Ediciones Team Staff. The Basics of Oil Painting. LC 95-12037. (Complete Course on Painting & Drawing Ser.). Orig. Title: Bases de la Pintura Al Oleo. (Illus.). 128p. 1995. pap. 16.95 (*0-8120-9403-4*) Barron.

Parramon Ediciones Team Staff, ed. Drawing Basic Subjects. LC 95-2347. (Easy Painting & Drawing Ser.). Orig. Title: Temas Basicos de Dibujo. (Illus.). 64p. 1995. pap. 13.95 (*0-8120-9290-2*) Barron.

— Painting Flowers with Watercolors. Barron's Educational Editors, tr. LC 94-46433.Tr. of Fores a la Acuarela. (ENG & SPA., Illus.). 64p. 1995. 12.95 (*0-8120-9292-9*) Barron.

— Painting Landscapes in Oil. LC 94-49011. (Easy Painting & Drawing Ser.). (Illus.). 64p. 1995. 12.95 (*0-8120-9291-0*) Barron.

Parramon Editorial Staff. All about Techniques in Pastel. LC 98-20374. (All About Techniques Ser.). (Illus.). 145p. 1998. 24.95 (*0-7641-5105-3*) Barron.

Parramon Editorial Team Staff. All about Techniques in Oil. LC 97-23436. (Illus.). 144p. 1997. 24.95 (*0-7641-5045-6*) Barron.

— All about Techniques in Watercolor. LC 97-21750. (Illus.). 144p. 1997. 24.95 (*0-7641-5046-4*) Barron.

— Animals. LC 97-12302. (We Imagine, We Draw Ser.). (Illus.). 48p. (J). (gr. 4). 1997. 12.95 (*0-7641-5044-8*) Barron.

— Complementary Themes for Painting Techniques. LC 97-72658. (Complete Course on Painting & Drawing Ser.). (Illus.). 128p. 1997. pap. text 16.95 (*0-7641-0266-4*) Barron.

— Fascinating World of Primates. (Illus.). 32p. (J). (gr. 4-7). 1996. pap. text 6.95 (*0-8120-9755-6*) Barron.

— Figures. LC 96-86677. (Art Handbooks). (Illus.). 96p. 1997. 9.95 (*0-7641-5008-1*) Barron.

— Landscapes. LC 97-17667. (We Imagine, We Draw Ser.). (Illus.). 48p. (J). (gr. 4). 1997. 12.95 (*0-7641-5041-3*) Barron.

— Objects. LC 97-21413. (Illus.). 48p. (J). (gr. 4). 1997. 12.95 (*0-7641-5042-1*) Barron.

Parramon Editorial Team Staff, ed. Fascinating World of Birds of Prey. (Illus.). 32p. (gr. 3-7). 1996. pap. 6.95 (*0-8120-9424-7*) Barron.

Parramon Editorial Team Staff. Drawing. LC 96-86671. (Art Handbooks). 96p. 1997. 9.95 (*0-7641-5007-3*) Barron.

Parramon Editorial Team Staff & Marcel Socias Studio Staff. The Fascinating World of Beetles. LC 95-7404. (Fascinating World of... Ser.). (Illus.). 32p. (J). (gr. 3-7). 1995. pap. 6.95 (*0-8120-9423-9*) Barron.

Parramon, J. M. Los Arboles Frutales. (SPA., Illus.). 32p. (J). (ps-3). 1991. pap. 6.95 (*0-8120-4714-1*) Barron.

— El Bosque. (SPA., Illus.). 32p. (J). (ps-3). 1991. pap. 6.95 (*0-8120-4712-5*) Barron.

— The Fascinating World of Ants. (Fascinating World of...Ser.). (Illus.). 32p. (J). (gr. 3-7). 1991. pap. 7.95 (*0-8120-4721-4*) Barron.

— The Fascinating World of Bees. (Fascinating World of...Ser.). (Illus.). 32p. (J). (gr. 3-7). 1991. pap. 7.95 (*0-8120-4720-6*) Barron.

— The Fascinating World of Butterflies. (Fascinating World of...Ser.). (Illus.). 32p. (J). (gr. 3-7). 1991. pap. 7.95 (*0-8120-4722-2*) Barron.

— El Huerto. (SPA., Illus.). 32p. (J). (ps-3). 1991. pap. 6.95 (*0-8120-4716-8*) Barron.

— El Jardin. (SPA., Illus.). 32p. (J). (ps-3). 1991. pap. 6.95 (*0-8120-4713-3*) Barron.

— Mi Primera Visita a la Granja. (SPA., Illus.). 32p. (J). 1990. pap. 6.95 (*0-8120-4400-2*) Barron.

— Mi Primera Visita al Aviario. (SPA., Illus.). 32p. (J). 1990. pap. 5.95 (*0-8120-4403-7*) Barron.

— Mi Primera Visita al Zoo. (SPA., Illus.). 32p. (J). 1990. pap. 6.95 (*0-8120-4402-9*) Barron.

— Mi Primeros Colores. (SPA., Illus.). 32p. (J). (ps-3). 1991. pap. 6.95 (*0-8120-4726-5*) Barron.

— Mi Primeros Formas. (SPA., Illus.). 32p. (J). (ps-3). 1991. pap. 6.95 (*0-8120-4728-1*) Barron.

— Mi Primeros Numeros. (SPA., Illus.). 32p. (J). (ps-3). 1991. pap. 6.95 (*0-8120-4727-3*) Barron.

— My First Visit to a Farm. (Illus.). 32p. (J). 1990. pap. 5.95 (*0-8120-4305-7*) Barron.

— My First Visit to the Aviary. (My First Visit Ser.). (Illus.). 32p. (J). (ps). 1990. pap. 4.95 (*0-8120-4303-0*) Barron.

— My First Visit to the Zoo. (My First Visit Ser.). (Illus.). 32p. (J). (ps). 1990. pap. 6.95 (*0-8120-4302-2*) Barron.

— Plants & Trees, 4 vols. (Illus.). 32p. (J). (ps-3). 1991. pap., boxed set 23.95 (*0-8120-7771-7*) Barron.

— Taste. (Five Senses Ser.). (J). 1985. 12.15 (*0-606-01130-7*, Pub. by Turtleback) Demco.

Parramon, J. M. & Puig, J. J. Hearing. (Child's Guide to the Five Senses Ser.). (Illus.). 32p. (Orig.). (J). (ps-1). 1985. pap. 6.95 (*0-8120-3563-1*); pap. 6.95 (*0-8120-3606-9*) Barron.

— Sight. (Five Senses Ser.). (Illus.). 32p. (Orig.). (J). (ps). 1985. pap. 6.95 (*0-8120-3564-X*); pap. 6.95 (*0-8120-3605-0*) Barron.

— Smell. (Five Senses Ser.). (Illus.). 32p. (J). (ps). 1985. pap. 6.95 (*0-8120-3565-8*); pap. 6.95 (*0-8120-3607-7*) Barron.

— Taste. (Five Senses Ser.). (Illus.). 32p. (J). (ps). 1985. pap. 6.95 (*0-8120-3566-6*); pap. 6.95 (*0-8120-3608-5*) Barron.

— Touch. (Five Senses Ser.). (Illus.). 32p. (Orig.). (J). (ps). 1985. pap. 6.95 (*0-8120-3567-4*); pap. 6.95 (*0-8120-3609-3*) Barron.

Parramon, J. M. & Rius, Maria. Life in the Sea. (Habitats Ser.).Tr. of La Vida en el Mar. (Illus.). 32p. (J). (gr. 3-5). 1987. pap. 6.95 (*0-8120-3865-7*) Barron.

— Life on the Land. (Habitats Ser.).Tr. of La Vida Sobre la Tierra. (Illus.). 32p. (J). (gr. 3-5). 1987. pap. 6.95 (*0-8120-3864-9*) Barron.

— Life Underground. (Habitats Ser.).Tr. of La Vida Bajo la Tierra. (Illus.). 32p. (J). (gr. 3-5). 1987. pap. 6.95 (*0-8120-3862-2*) Barron.

— La Vida Bajo la Tierra. (Habitats Ser.).Tr. of La Vida Bajo la Tierra. (SPA., Illus.). 32p. (J). (gr. 3-5). 1987. pap. 6.95 (*0-8120-3866-5*) Barron.

— La Vida en el Aire. (Habitats Ser.).Tr. of La Vida en el Aire. (SPA., Illus.). 32p. (J). (gr. 3-5). 1987. pap. 6.95 (*0-8120-3867-3*) Barron.

— La Vida en el Mar. (Habitats Ser.).Tr. of La Vida en el Mar. (SPA., Illus.). 32p. (J). (gr. 3-5). 1987. pap. 6.95 (*0-8120-3869-X*) Barron.

— La Vida Sobre la Tierra. (Habitats Ser.).Tr. of La Vida Sobre la Tierra. (SPA., Illus.). 32p. (J). (gr. 3-5). 1987. pap. 6.95 (*0-8120-3868-1*) Barron.

Parramon, J. M., et al. El Agua. (Four Elements Ser.). (SPA., Illus.). 32p. (J). (ps). 1985. pap. 6.95 (*0-8120-3621-2*) Barron.

— Air. (Four Elements Ser.). (Illus.). 32p. (J). (ps). 1985. pap. 6.95 (*0-8120-3597-6*) Barron.

— El Aire. (Four Elements Ser.). (SPA., Illus.). 32p. (J). (ps). 1985. pap. 6.95 (*0-8120-3620-4*) Barron.

— Children. (Barron's Family Ser.). (Illus.). 32p. (J). (gr. 3-5). 1987. pap. 6.95 (*0-8120-3850-9*) Barron.

— Children. (Barron's Family Ser.). (SPA., Illus.). 32p. (J). (gr. 3-5). 1987. pap. 6.95 (*0-8120-3854-1*) Barron.

— Earth. (Four Elements Ser.). (Illus.). 32p. (J). (ps). 1985. pap. 6.95 (*0-8120-3596-8*) Barron.

— Earth. (Four Elements Ser.). (J). 1986. 6.95 (*0-8120-5742-2*) Barron.

— Five Senses, 5 bks. (Illus.). 32p. (J). (ps). 1985. boxed set 34.95 (*0-8120-7365-7*) Barron.

— El Fuego. LC 85-9062. (Four Elements Ser.). (SPA., Illus.). 32p. (J). (ps-k). 1985. pap. 6.95 (*0-8120-3619-0*) Barron.

— Grandparents. (Barron's Family Ser.). (Illus.). 32p. (J). (gr. 3-5). 1987. pap. 6.95 (*0-8120-3853-3*) Barron.

— Invierno. (Four Seasons Ser.). (SPA., Illus.). 32p. (J). (ps). 1985. pap. 6.95 (*0-8120-3645-X*) Barron.

— El Otono. (Four Seasons Ser.). (SPA., Illus.). 32p. 1985. pap. 6.95 (*0-8120-3646-8*) Barron.

— Parents.Tr. of Los Padres. (Illus.). 32p. (J). (gr. 3-5). 1987. pap. 6.95 (*0-8120-3852-5*) Barron.

— Parents.Tr. of Los Padres. (SPA., Illus.). 32p. (J). (gr. 3-5). 1987. pap. 6.95 (*0-8120-3856-8*) Barron.

— La Primavera. (Four Seasons Ser.). (SPA., Illus.). 32p. (J). (ps). 1986. pap. 6.95 (*0-8120-3648-4*) Barron.

— Teenagers. (Barron's Family Ser.).Tr. of Los Jovenes. (Illus.). 32p. (J). (gr. 3-5). 1987. pap. 3.95 (*0-8120-3851-7*) Barron.

— Teenagers. (Barron's Family Ser.).Tr. of Los Jovenes. (SPA., Illus.). 32p. (J). (gr. 3-5). 1987. pap. 6.95 (*0-8120-3855-X*) Barron.

— El Verano. (Four Seasons Ser.). (SPA., Illus.). 32p. (J). 1985. pap. 6.95 (*0-8120-3647-6*) Barron.

— Water. (Four Elements Ser.). (Illus.). 32p. (J). (ps). 1985. pap. 6.95 (*0-8120-3599-2*) Barron.

Parramon, J. M., jt. auth. see Rius, Maria.

Parramon, Jose M. The Basics of Artistic Drawing. (Complete Course on Painting & Drawing Ser.). (Illus.). 128p. 1994. pap. 18.95 (*0-8120-1929-6*) Barron.

— The Basics of Artistic Painting. (Complete Course on Painting & Drawing Ser.). (Illus.). 128p. 1994. pap. 16.95 (*0-8120-1928-8*) Barron.

— The Big Book of Oil Painting. (Illus.). 192p. 1990. pap. 32.50 (*0-8230-0498-8*) Watsn-Guptill.

— The Big Book of Watercolor. (Illus.). 192p. 1984. 32.50 (*0-8230-0496-1*) Watsn-Guptill.

— Color Theory. (Artist's Library). (Illus.). 112p. 1989. pap. 14.95 (*0-8230-0755-3*) Watsn-Guptill.

— Drawing with Crayons, Pastels, Sanguine & Chalks. (Complete Course on Painting & Drawing Ser.). (Illus.). 128p. 1994. pap. 16.95 (*0-8120-1931-8*) Barron.

***Parramon, Jose M.** Exotic Animals. (Workbooks for Painting Ser.). (Illus.). 32p. 1999. pap. 5.95 (*0-7641-1211-2*) Barron.

— Garden Flowers. (Workbooks for Painting Ser.). (Illus.). 32p. 1999. pap. 5.95 (*0-7641-1209-0*) Barron.

Parramon, Jose M. How to Draw Heads & Portraits. (Artist's Library). (Illus.). 112p. 1989. pap. 14.95 (*0-8230-2357-5*) Watsn-Guptill.

— How to Draw the Human Figure. (Artist's Library). (Illus.). 112p. 1990. pap. 14.95 (*0-8230-2358-3*) Watsn-Guptill.

— Landscape & Seasons. (Workbooks for Painting). (Illus.). 32p. 1999. pap. 5.95 (*0-7641-1213-9*) Barron.

***Parramon, Jose M.** Landscapes Painting Book. 1999. pap. text 26.00 (*84-95323-11-7*) LEMA.

— Mixed Media. 95p. 1999. pap. 18.95 (*84-89730-95-4*) LEMA.

— Nudes. (Workbooks for Painting Ser.). (Illus.). 32p. 1999. pap. 5.95 (*0-7641-1210-4*) Barron.

Parramon, Jose M. Painting Figures & Portraits in Watercolor: Basic Techniques & Exercise Series. LC 98-38267. (Basic Techniques & Exercises). (Illus.). 96p. 1999. pap. 18.95 (*0-8230-5130-7*) Watsn-Guptill.

— Painting in Watercolors, Markers, Acrylics, & Gouache. LC 93-6203. (Complete Course on Painting & Drawing Ser.). (Illus.). 128p. 1994. pap. 16.95 (*0-8120-1926-1*) Barron.

— Painting Landscapes & Still Lifes in Watercolor: Basic Techniques & Exercises Series. LC 98-30026. 96p. 1999. pap. 18.95 (*0-8230-5129-3*) Watsn-Guptill.

***Parramon, Jose M.** Pastel Painting. 95p. 1999. pap. 18.95 (*84-89730-96-2*) LEMA.

Parramon, Jose M. & Ferron, Miguel. The Big Book of Airbrush. (Illus.). 144p. 1990. pap. 24.95 (*0-8230-0164-4*) Watsn-Guptill.

***Parramon, Jose Maria.** Acrylic Painting. (Illus.). 96p. 2000. pap. 18.95 (*84-95323-33-8*) Lema Pubns.

— Airbrush. LC 98-42872. (Learning to Paint Ser.). (ENG & SPA., Illus.). 64p. 1999. pap. 13.95 (*0-7641-0888-3*) Barron.

— Color Mixing. (Illus.). 96p. 2000. pap. 18.95 (*84-95323-32-X*) Lema Pubns.

— Composition & Interpretation. (Illus.). 96p. 2000. pap. 16.95 (*84-89730-87-3*) Lema Pubns.

Parramon, Jose Maria. Drawing in Pencil: Basic Techniques & Exercises Series. LC 98-30027. 96p. 1999. pap. 18.95 (*0-8230-5128-5*) Watsn-Guptill.

***Parramon, Jose Maria.** Figures & Portraits. (Illus.). 24p. 2000. pap. 6.95 (*84-95323-04-4*) Lema Pubns.

— Human Anatomy. (Illus.). 24p. 2000. pap. 6.95 (*84-95323-07-9*) Lema Pubns.

Parramon, Jose Maria. Landscapes & Seasons. (Workbooks for Painting Ser.). 32p. 1999. pap. text 6.95 (*0-7641-1212-0*) Barron.

***Parramon, Jose Maria.** Landscapes Techniques. (Illus.). 96p. 2000. pap. 16.95 (*84-89730-88-1*) Lema Pubns.

— Oil Painting. (Illus.). 96p. 2000. pap. 18.95 (*84-95323-31-1*) Lema Pubns.

— Painting Landscapes & Atmsphere. (Illus.). 64p. 2000. pap. 11.95 (*84-95323-34-6*) Lema Pubns.

— Painting Nightscapes with Artificial Light. (Illus.). 64p. 2000. pap. 11.95 (*84-95323-36-2*) Lema Pubns.

— Painting Texture & Volume. (Illus.). 64p. 2000. pap. 11.95 (*84-95323-35-4*) Lema Pubns.

— Seascapes. (Illus.). 24p. 2000. pap. 6.95 (*84-95323-05-2*) Lema Pubns.

— Urban Landscapes. (Illus.). 24p. 2000. pap. 6.95 (*84-95323-06-0*) Lema Pubns.

Parramon, Josep M., jt. auth. see Rius, Maria.

Parramon, Merce. The Digestive System. (Invisible World Ser.). (Illus.). 32p. (J). (gr. 4 up). 1994. lib. bdg. 15.95 (*0-7910-2126-2*) Chelsea Hse.

— How Our Blood Circulates. (Invisible World Ser.). (Illus.). 32p. (J). (gr. 4 up). 1994. lib. bdg. 15.95 (*0-7910-2127-0*) Chelsea Hse.

— The Miracle of Life. (Invisible World Ser.). (Illus.). 32p. (J). (gr. 4 up). 1994. lib. bdg. 15.95 (*0-7910-2130-0*) Chelsea Hse.

Parramon Studios Staff. Atlas of Anatomy. LC 96-79470. 1997. 19.95 (*0-7641-5000-6*) Barron.

***Parramon Studios Staff.** Cabinet Making. (Woodworking Class Ser.). (Illus.). 64p. 2000. 12.95 (*0-7641-5242-4*) Barron.

— Marquetry. (Woodworking Class Ser.). (Illus.). 64p. 2000. 12.95 (*0-7641-5244-0*) Barron.

— Restoration. (Woodworking Class Ser.). (Illus.). 64p. 2000. 12.95 (*0-7641-5246-7*) Barron.

— Upholstery. (Woodworking Class Ser.). (Illus.). 64p. 2000. 12.95 (*0-7641-5243-2*) Barron

— Wood Turning. (Woodworking Class Ser.). (Illus.). 64p. 2000. 12.95 (*0-7641-5245-9*) Barron.

Parramon Studios Staff & Arnau, Eduard. The Human Body. LC 98-17944. (Illus.). 96p. 1998. 19.95 (*0-7641-5078-2*) Barron.

Parramon Studios Staff, jt. auth. see Cuevas, David S.

Parramona, Joan B. New Dictionary of the Catalan Dictionary: Nou Diccionari de la Llengua Catalana. 11th ed. (CAT.). 832p. 1990. 26.95 (*0-7859-4961-5*) Fr & Eur.

Parramon's Editorial Staff, ed. Baroque Painting. LC 98-72293. (Art Handbooks). (Illus.). 96p. 1998. 9.95 (*0-7641-5086-3*) Barron.

— Mixing Colors: Oil, Vol. 2. (Art Handbooks). (Illus.). 96p. 1998. 9.95 (*0-7641-5087-1*) Barron.

— Modern Painting: The Impressions & the Avant Garde of the Twentieth Century. LC 98-72513. (Art Handbooks). (Illus.). 400p. 1998. 15.00 (*0-7641-5119-3*) Barron.

Parramon's Editorial Team. Acrylics. LC 97-42797. (Learn to Paint Ser.). (Illus.). 64p. 1998. pap. text 13.95 (*0-7641-0549-3*) Barron.

***Parramon's Editorial Team.** All about Techniques in Color. (Illus.). 144p. 2000. write for info. (*0-7641-5229-7*, Pub. by Barron) Prodn Assocs.

Parramon's Editorial Team. All about Techniques in Drawing. LC 99-14655. 144p. 1999. 24.95 (*0-7641-5163-0*) Barron.

— Drawing Figures. LC 97-9417. (Easy Painting & Drawing Ser.). (Illus.). 64p. 1997. pap. text 13.95 (*0-7641-0105-6*) Barron.

— Learning to Draw. LC 97-42798. (Learn to Paint Ser.). (Illus.). 64p. 1998. pap. 13.95 (*0-7641-0550-7*) Barron.

— Mixing Watercolors. LC 97-42795. (Learn to Paint Ser.). (Illus.). 64p. 1998. pap. 13.95 (*0-7641-0551-5*) Barron.

***Parramon's Editorial Team.** Pastels. LC 98-72917. (Art Handbooks). (Illus.). 96p. 1999. 9.95 (*0-7641-5106-1*) Barron.

Parramon's Editorial Team. Perspective & Composition. LC 98-74346. (Barron's Handbook Collection). (Illus.). 96p. 1999. 9.95 (*0-7641-5104-5*) Barron.

***Parramon's Editorial Team.** Portraits. LC 98-74719. (Art Handbooks). (Illus.). 96p. 1999. 9.95 (*0-7641-5108-8*) Barron.

Parramon's Editorial Team. The Renaissance. LC 99-216016. (Art Handbooks). (Illus.). 96p. 1999. 9.95 (*0-7641-5103-7*) Barron.

Parramon's Editorial Team Staff. Airbrush. (Art Handbooks). (Illus.). 96p. 1999. 9.95 (*0-7641-5161-4*) Barron.

— Learning to Paint in Oil. LC 97-9415. (Art Guides Ser.). (Illus.). 64p. 1997. pap. text 13.95 (*0-7641-0239-7*) Barron.

— Learning to Paint in Pastel. LC 97-9414. (Art Guides Ser.). (Illus.). 64p. 1997. pap. text 13.95 (*0-7641-0241-9*) Barron.

— Learning to Paint in Watercolor. LC 97-9413. (Art Guides Ser.). (Illus.). 64p. 1997. pap. text 13.95 (*0-7641-0240-0*) Barron.

***Parramon's Editorial Team Staff.** Light & Shade. (Art Handbooks). (Illus.). 96p. 2000. pap. 9.95 (*0-7641-5228-9*) Barron.

— Mixing Colors: Oil. LC 99-20235. (Learning to Paint Ser.). (Illus.). 64p. 1999. pap. 13.95 (*0-7641-0889-1*) Barron.

— Mixing Colors 3: Dry Techniques. (Art Handbooks). (Illus.). 96p. 2000. pap. 9.95 (*0-7641-5227-0*) Barron.

— Romanticism. (Art Handbooks). (Illus.). 96p. 2000. pap. 9.95 (*0-7641-5291-2*) Barron.

Parramon's Editorial Team Staff. Trees in Oil. LC 97-9416. (Easy Painting & Drawing Ser.). (Illus.). 64p. 1997. pap. text 13.95 (*0-7641-0106-4*) Barron.

***Parramon's Editorial Team Staff.** Water Effects. (Art Handbooks). (Illus.). 96p. 1999. 9.95 (*0-7641-5162-2*) Barron.

Parramont Puig Staff. El Olfato. 1986. 12.15 (*0-606-13365-8*, Pub. by Turtleback) Demco.

Parramore, Barbara & Hopke, William E. Career Exploration Activities Booklet: 25 Activities to Help Explore Occupations. 48p. (Orig.). (J). (gr. 6 up). 1989. pap. text 17.75 (*0-685-31414-6*) Careers Inc.

Parramore, Barbara, et al. Early Occupational Awareness Program for Kindergarten & Grades One & Two 2nd ed. LC 99-17386. 1999. 19.95 (*0-89434-279-7*) Ferguson.

Parramore, Barbara, jt. auth. see Parramore, Tom.

Parramore, Barbara M. & Butler, Jane M. Children's Dictionary of Occupations Activities Grades 3-4. rev. ed. Sears, Twila et al, eds. (Illus.). 29p. (J). (gr. 2-6). 1998. pap. 15.95 (*1-56191-587-4*, 3055) Meridian Educ.

— Children's Dictionary of Occupations Activities Grades 5-6. rev. ed. Sears, Twila et al, eds. (Illus.). 29p. (J). (gr. 2-6). 1998. pap. 15.95 (*1-56191-588-2*, 3056) Meridian Educ.

Parramore, Barbara M., et al. Children's Dictionary of Occupations: Corporation. rev. ed. Sears, Twila et al, eds. LC 99-461816. (Illus.). 126p. (J). (gr. 2-6). 1998. wbk. ed. 15.95 (*1-56191-586-6*, 3054) Meridian Educ.

Parramore, Keith, jt. auth. see Watsham, Terry J.

Parramore, Thomas C. Carolina Quest. (gr. 7-8). 1978. text 22.80 (*0-13-114900-8*) P-H.

— Triumph at Kitty Hawk: The Wright Brothers & Powered Flight. (Illus.). ix, 123p. (YA). (gr. 8-12). 1999. reprint ed. pap. 10.00 (*0-86526-259-4*) NC Archives.

Parramore, Thomas C., et al. Norfolk: The First Four Centuries. LC 94-9457. 480p. (C). 1994. 29.95 (*0-8139-1557-0*) U Pr of Va.

***Parramore, Thomas C., et al.** Norfolk: The First Four Centuries. 2000. 17.95 (*0-8139-1988-6*) U Pr of Va.

Parramore, Tom & Parramore, Barbara. Looking for the "Lost Colony" (Illus.). 32p. 1984. pap. 3.00 (*0-318-03650-9*) Tanglewood Press.

Parratore, Phil. Hands-On Science: For the Active Learning Classroom. LC 97-62544. 232p. 1998. pap. 29.95 (*1-57517-079-5*, 1591) SkyLght.

Parratore, Phil M. Wacky Science: A Cookbook for Elementary Teachers. 152p. 1995. per. 24.90 (*0-8403-9013-0*) Kendall-Hunt.

Parratt, David. Radioimmunoassay of Antibody & Its Clinical Applications. LC 81-12939. 174p. reprint ed. pap. 54.00 (*0-608-15667-1*, 203194000077) Bks Demand.

Parratt, James R., ed. Control & Manipulation of Calcium Movement: A Biological Council Symposium. fac. ed. LC 84-42718. (Illus.). 408p. pap. 126.50 (*0-7837-7219-X*, 204707900005) Bks Demand.

Parratt, James R., jt. auth. see Wainwright, Cherry L.

Parratt, John. Reinventing Christianity: African Theology Today. 227p. 1996. 45.95 (*0-86543-522-7*); pap. 14.95 (*0-86543-523-5*) Africa World.

Parratt, Margaret E., jt. auth. see Parratt, Mark W.

P

An Asterisk (*) at the beginning of an entry indicates that the title is appearing for the first time.

Parratt, Mark W. & Parratt, Margaret E. A Spaceship Called Earth: Our Living Environment. LC 82-82532. xv, 368 p. 1982. write for info. (0-8403-2741-2) Kendall-Hunt.

Parratt, Smitty & Welker, Doug. Place Names of the Isle Royale. (Illus.). 96p. 1999. pap. 7.95 (0-935289-10-0) Isle Royale Hist.

Parravano, John, ed. see Lynch, Michael & Edgar, William.

Parravicini, G. Pastori, jt. auth. see Bassani, F.

Parrella, Deborah. Project Seasons: Hands-On Activities for Discovering the Wonders of the World. 2nd ed. (Illus.). 336p. 1999. pap. 24.95 (0-9642163-0-2, Pub. by Shelburne Farms) Chelsea Green Pub.

Parrella, Frederick J., ed. Paul Tillich's Theological Legacy: Spirit & Community: International Paul Tillich Conference, New Harmony, June 17-20, 1993. LC 95-40723. (Theologishce Bibliothek Toepelmann Ser.: Vol. 73). xxiii, 185p. (C). 1995. lib. bdg. 106.15 (3-11-014667-3) De Gruyter.

Parren, M. P. & De Graaf, N. R. Quest for Natural Forest Management in Ghana, Cote d'Ivoire & Liberia. (Tropenbos Technical Ser.: No. 13). (Illus.). 200p. 1995. pap. 80.00 (90-5113-025-2, Pub. by Backhuys Pubs) Balogh.

Parrent, George B., jt. auth. see Beran, Mark J.

Parrent, Joanne. Once More with Feeling: You'll Never Make Love in This Town Again, Again, 2 cass. abr. ed. 1996. audio. write for info. (0-7871-1036-1, Dove Audio) NewStar Media.

Parret, Herman. The Aesthetics of Communication: Pramatics & Beyond. (Library of Rhetorics). 184p. (C). 1993. text 120.50 (0-7923-2198-7) Kluwer Academic.

— Contexts of Understanding, Vol 1. (Pragmatics & Beyond Ser.: Vol. 1:6). viii, 109p. 1980. pap. 29.00 (90-272-2509-5) J Benjamins Pubng Co.

— Discussing Language: Dialogues with N. Chomsky, A. J. Greimas, M. A. K. Holiday, et al. 1974. pap. text 50.00 (90-279-2705-7) Mouton.

— Language & Discourse. LC 73-170002. (Janua Linguarum, Ser. Minor: No. 119). (Illus.). 292p. (Orig.). 1971. pap. text 49.25 (90-279-1854-6) Mouton.

— Semiotics & Pragmatics: An Evaluative Comparison of Conceptual Frameworks. (Pragmatics & Beyond Ser.: Vol. IV:7). xii, 136p. 1983. pap. 44.00 (90-272-2532-X) J Benjamins Pubng Co.

— Le Sublime du Quotidien. (Actes Semiotiques Ser.: Vol. 6). (FRE.). 286p. 1988. pap. 65.00 (90-272-2266-5) J Benjamins Pubng Co.

Parret, Herman, ed. History of Linguistic Thought & Contemporary Linguistics: Foundations of Communication. 816p. (C). 1975. 188.50 (3-11-005818-9) De Gruyter.

— Kants Aesthetick/Kant's Aesthetics/l'Esthetique de Kant. (GER.). 830p. (C). 1997. lib. bdg. 260.00 (3-11-012930-2) De Gruyter.

— Peirce & Value Theory: On Peircian Ethics & Aesthetics. LC 93-39339. (Semiotic Crossroads (SC) Ser.: No. 6). xiii, 381p. 1994. 95.00 (1-55619-340-8) J Benjamins Pubng Co.

— Pretending to Communicate. LC 93-46021. 1993. 136.95 (3-11-011832-7) De Gruyter.

— Pretending to Communicate. (Foundations of Communication & Cognition Ser.). xv, 304p. (C). 1993. lib. bdg. 118.70 (3-11-011732-0) Mouton.

Parret, Herman, et al, eds. Possibilities & Limitations of Pragmatics: Proceedings of the Conference on Pragmatics, Urbino, Italy, July 8-14, 1979. (Studies in Language Companion Ser.: No. 7). x, 854p. 1981. 177.00 (90-272-3006-4) J Benjamins Pubng Co.

Parret, Herman & Ruprecht, H., eds. Aims & Prospects of Semiotics: To Honor A. J. Greimas, 2 Vols., 1. LC 85-11049. lxxxv, 550p. 1985. write for info. (90-272-2020-4) J Benjamins Pubng Co.

— Aims & Prospects of Semiotics: To Honor A. J. Greimas, 2 Vols., 2. LC 85-11049. lxxxv, 550p. 1985. write for info. (90-272-2021-2) J Benjamins Pubng Co.

Parret, Herman & Ruprecht, H. G., eds. Aims & Prospects of Semiotics: Essays in Honor of A. J. Greimas, 2 Vols., Set. LC 85-11049. 1066p. 1985. 260.00 (90-272-2019-0) J Benjamins Pubng Co.

Parret, Herman, et al. Le Langage en Contexte: Etudes Philosophiques et Linguistiques de Pragmatique. (Linguisticae Investigationes Supplementa Ser.: Vol. 3). iv, 790p. 1980. 143.00 (90-272-3112-5, 3) J Benjamins Pubng Co.

Parret, Herman H., ed. On Believing - De La Croyance: Epistemological & Semetic Approaches. LC 83-15232. (Foundations of Communication & Cognition Ser.).Tr. of Approches Epistemologiques et Semiotiques. viii, 359p. 1983. 113.10 (3-11-008884-3) De Gruyter.

Parret, Herman H., jt. ed. see Bouveresse, Jacques.

Parrett, Bryan. PzKpfw IV. (New Vanguard Ser.: Vol. 28). (Illus.). 48p. 1999. pap. 12.95 (1-85532-843-7, Pub. by Ospry) Stackpole.

***Parrett, Dan.** Alaska Seafood Industry Room & Board Job Guide: One Stop Guide to Alaska Seafood Job Opportunities. LC 00-90920. 70p. 2000. pap. 19.95 (0-9667753-1-7) Malezi Pub.

Parrett, Joan L., et al. How Am I Teaching? Forms & Activities for Acquiring Instructional Input. rev. ed. 100p. 1988. student ed. 24.95 (0-912150-06-8) Atwood Pub LLC.

Parrett, Richard. DC - AC Circuits: Concepts & Applications. 480p. (C). 1992. pap. text 17.20 (0-13-042615-6) P-H.

Parrett, Sherii & Browne, Sylvia. Slippy Cleans Up. (Tub Tales of Slippy Jr. Ser.). (Illus.). 24p. (Orig.). (J). (ps-6). 1992. pap. 2.99 (1-56722-002-9) Word Aflame.

Parrett, William, jt. auth. see Barr, Robert D.

Parrett, William H., jt. auth. see Barr, Robert D.

Parrick, Jerry. Touched by a Miracle. 2nd rev. ed. LC 97-73693. Orig. Title: The Twentieth Century Miracle. 188p. 1997. reprint ed. pap. 9.99 (0-88270-746-9, Logos NJ) Bridge-Logos.

Parrill, Abby L. & Reddy, M. Rami, eds. Rational Drug Design: Novel Methodology & Practical Applications. LC 98-32087. (ACS Symposium Ser.: No. 719). (Illus.). 400p. 1999. text 130.00 (0-8412-3603-8) OUP.

Parrill, William. The Long Haul: Conversations with Southern Novelists. 194p. (Orig.). (C). pap. text 22.50 (0-8191-9078-0); lib. bdg. 47.50 (0-8191-9077-2) U Pr of Amer.

Parrillo. 1998 Year Book of Critical Care Medicine. (Illus.). 432p. (C). (gr. 13). 1998. text 78.00 (0-8151-9605-9, 24944) Mosby Inc.

***Parrillo.** Strangers to These Shores: Race & Ethnic Relations in the United States. 6th ed. LC 99-26303. 634p. 1999. 66.00 (0-205-29332-8) Allyn.

Parrillo, John & Greenwood-Robinson, Maggie. High-Performance Bodybuilding. LC 92-15571. (Illus.). 192p. (Orig.). 1993. pap. 16.95 (0-399-51771-5, Perigee Bks) Berkley Pub.

***Parrillo, Joseph, ed.** 2000 Year Book of Critical Care Medicine. (Illus.). 400p. 2000. 84.00 (0-323-01500-X) Mosby Inc.

Parrillo, Joseph E. Current Therapy in Critical Care Medicine. 3rd ed. (Illus.). 448p. (C). (gr. 13). 1996. text 89.95 (0-8151-7327-X, 27780) Mosby Inc.

***Parrillo, Joseph E., ed.** Year Book of Critical Care, 2002. (Illus.). 380p. 2002. write for info. (0-323-01518-2) Mosby Inc.

— Year Book of Critical Care, 2001. (Illus.). 380p. 2001. write for info. (0-323-01517-4) Mosby Inc.

Parrillo, Joseph E., ed. see Year Book of Critical Care Medicine Staff.

Parrillo, Norman K. Biology of Stains & Staining: Index of New Information & Research Reference Book. 169p. 1997. 47.50 (0-7883-1546-3); pap. 44.50 (0-7883-1547-1) ABBE Pubs Assn.

Parrillo, Rosemary. Welcome to Exit Four: Enter at Own Risk. LC 93-72527. 224p. (Orig.). 1994. pap. 12.00 (0-9635720-1-6) August Pr.

***Parrillo, Vincent.** Ridgewood. (Images of America Ser.). 128p. 1999. pap. 18.99 (0-7385-0189-1) Arcadia Publng.

Parrillo, Vincent J., jt. auth. see Macionis, John J.

Parrillo, Vincent N. Diversity in America. LC 95-16608. 1995. pap. 19.95 (0-8039-9049-9) Pine Forge.

Parrillo, Vincent N., ed. Rethinking Today's Minorities, 93. LC 90-40733. (Contributions in Sociology Ser.: No. 93). 224p. 1991. 55.00 (0-313-27537-8, PRT, Greenwood Pr) Greenwood.

Parrillo, Vincent N., et al. Contemporary Social Problems. 4th ed. LC 98-17398. 510p. 1998. pap. text 57.00 (0-205-28553-8) Allyn.

— Contemporary Social Problems: Examination Copy. 3rd ed. (C). 1995. write for info. (0-205-18654-8, H8654-9) Allyn.

Parrillo, Vincent N., jt. auth. see Macionis, John J.

Parrinder. Georgia Real Estate Forms, 4 disks, Set. 1994. disk 95.00 (0-614-03608-9, MICHIE) LEXIS Pub.

Parrinder, Edward G. West African Psychology. LC 74-15076. reprint ed. 37.50 (0-404-12125-X) AMS Pr.

Parrinder, Geoffrey. Avatar & Incarnation: The Divine in Human Form in the World's Religions. LC 97-164983. 1997. pap. 22.95 (1-85168-130-2, Pub. by Onewrld Pubns) Penguin Putnam.

— The Bhagavad Gita: In Day-to-Day Life. 120p. (Orig.). 1996. pap. 10.95 (1-85168-117-5, Pub. by Onewrld Pubns) Penguin Putnam.

— Christianity. 288p. 1998. pap. text 14.95 (1-85168-174-4, Pub. by Onewrld Pubns) Penguin Putnam.

— Comparative Religion. LC 73-19116. 130p. 1975. reprint ed. lib. bdg. 59.50 (0-8371-7301-9, PACR, Greenwood Pr) Greenwood.

— Jesus in the Qur'an. 190p. 1996. pap. 13.95 (0-614-21670-2, 1458) Kazi Pubns.

— Jesus in the Qur'an. 190p. 1995. pap. 14.95 (1-85168-094-2, Pub. by Onewrld Pubns) Penguin Putnam.

— Mysticism in the World's Religions. 220p. 1995. pap. 14.95 (1-85168-101-9, Pub. by Onewrld Pubns) Penguin Putnam.

— Religion in an African City. LC 74-142921. (Illus.). 211p. 1973. reprint ed. lib. bdg. 49.50 (0-8371-5947-4, PAC&) Greenwood.

— Sexual Morality in the World's Religions. 290p. 1995. pap. 14.95 (1-85168-108-6, Pub. by Onewrld Pubns) Penguin Putnam.

— Son of Joseph: The Parentage of Jesus. 132p. 1992. pap. text 19.95 (0-567-29213-4, Pub. by T & T Clark) Bks Intl VA.

***Parrinder, Geoffrey.** Wisdom of Jesus. 2000. 15.95 (1-85168-225-2, Pub. by Onewrld Pubns) Penguin Putnam.

Parrinder, Geoffrey, ed. The Saying Of The Buddha. LC 98-4311. 64p. 1998. reprint ed. pap. 5.95 (0-88001-638-8) HarpC.

— World Religions: From Ancient History to the Present. (Illus.). 528p. 1984. 40.00 (0-87196-129-6) Facts on File.

— World Religions: From Ancient History to the Present. (Illus.). 528p. 1985. pap. 17.95 (0-8160-1289-X) Facts on File.

Parrinder, Patrick. Authors & Authenticity. 400p. 1991. text 99.00 (0-231-07646-0); pap. text 31.00 (0-231-07647-9) Col U Pr.

— Shadows of the Future: H. G. Wells, Science Fiction, & Prophecy. LC 95-21827. (Utopianism & Communitarianism Ser.). (C). 1996. pap. 19.95 (0-8156-0332-0, PASFP); text 39.95 (0-8156-2691-6, PASF) Syracuse U Pr.

Parrinder, Patrick, ed. H. G. Wells: The Critical Heritage. (Critical Heritage Ser.). 1972. 69.50 (0-7100-7387-9, Routledge Thoemms) Routledge.

— Later Nineteenth & Early Twentieth Century English & European Novelists: H. G. Wells. (Critical Heritage Ser.). 368p. (C). 1997. 125.00 (0-415-15910-5) Routledge.

— Learning from Other Worlds: Estrangement, Cognition & the Politics of Science Fiction & Utopia. (Liverpool Science Fiction Texts & Studies: 17). 288p. 1999. 49.95 (0-85323-574-0, Pub. by Liverpool Univ Pr); pap. 24.95 (0-85323-534-1, Pub. by Liverpool Univ Pr) U of Pa Pr.

— Science Fiction: A Critical Guide. LC 78-40686. 252p. reprint ed. pap. 78.20 (0-8357-3528-1, 203447600090) Bks Demand.

Parrinder, Patrick & Rolfe, Christopher, eds. H. G. Wells under Revision: Proceedings of the International H. G. Wells Symposium, London, July 1986. LC 88-43425. 264p. 1990. 40.00 (0-945636-05-9) Susquehanna U Pr.

Parrinder, Patrick, et al. H. G. Wells: Reality & Beyond. LC 86-62053. (Illus.). 91p. 1986. pap. 5.00 (0-9617184-0-4) Champaign Pub Lib.

Parrington, Norman & Roper, Mac. Understanding Software Testing. 1989. text 39.95 (0-470-21462-7) P-H.

Parrington, S. Whillan's Tax Tables, 1995-96. 49th ed. 1995. pap. write for info. (0-406-04457-0, MICHIE) LEXIS Pub.

Parrington, Sheila. Whillans's Tax Tables, 1996-1997. 51st ed. 100p. 1996. pap. 7.00 (0-406-06448-2, MICHIE) LEXIS Pub.

Parrington, Sheila, ed. Whillan's Tax Tables, 1994-95. 47th ed. 1994. pap. 3.50 (0-406-03644-6, UK, MICHIE) LEXIS Pub.

— Whillans's Tax Tables, 1994-1995. 48th ed. 1994. pap. write for info. (0-406-04979-3, MICHIE) LEXIS Pub.

— Whillans's Tax Tables 1997-98. 1997. pap. write for info. (0-406-99932-5, WTT1997, MICHIE) LEXIS Pub.

Parrington, Vernon L. Colonial Mind. 442p. 28.95 (0-8488-2572-1) Amereon Ltd.

— Main Currents in American Thought, 3 vols., Set. 1993. reprint ed. lib. bdg. 225.00 (0-7812-5283-0) Rprt Serv.

— Main Currents in American Thought, Vol. II. LC 87-6028. 516p. 1987. pap. 21.95 (0-8061-2081-9) U of Okla Pr.

— Sinclair Lewis: Our Own Diogenes. LC 73-11205. (American Literature Ser.: No. 49). 1974. lib. bdg. 75.00 (0-8383-1720-0) M S G Haskell Hse.

Parrini, Paolo. Knowledge & Reality: An Essay in Positive Philosophy. Baracchi, Paolo, tr. from ITA. LC 97-49905. (Western Ontario Series in Philosophy of Science). 218p. 1998. write for info. (0-7923-4939-3) Kluwer Academic.

Parrini, Paolo, ed. Kant & Contemporary Epistemology. LC 93-48849. (University of Western Ontario Series in Philosophy of Science). 384p. (C). 1994. lib. bdg. 178.50 (0-7923-2681-4, Pub. by Kluwer Academic) Kluwer Academic.

Parrino, Janice. Welcome to Good Cooking. LC 87-90514. (Illus.). (Orig.). pap. write for info. (0-9618347-0-6) N A & J Parrino.

Parrino, Maria, jt. ed. see Albright, Carol B.

Parriott, Donald, ed. A Practical Guide to HPLC Detection. LC 92-13082. (Illus.). 293p. 1992. text 71.00 (0-12-545680-8) Acad Pr.

Parris, Alyssia J. & Adams, Howard G., contrib. by. Your Internship Is As Good As You Make It. (C). 1994. 5.00 (1-887284-00-1) Natl Consortium.

Parris, B. S. Noteworthy Species of Grammitidaceae from South-East Asia. (Illus.). 129p. 1990. pap. 20.00 (0-9504876-8-6, Pub. by Royal Botnic Grdns) Balogh.

Parris, B. S., et al. The Plants of Mount Kinabalu Vol. 1: Ferns. viii, 165p. 1992. pap. 30.00 (0-947643-38-9, Pub. by Royal Botnic Grdns) Balogh.

Parris, B. S., jt. auth. see Grimes, J. W.

Parris, C. Mastering Executive Arts & Skills. 1985. 14.95 (0-13-560086-3, Parker Publishing Co) P-H.

Parris, Ed. The Boy in the Bushes: Poems. LC 96-11661. 64p. 1996. pap. 14.95 (0-7734-2688-4, Mellen Poetry Pr) E Mellen.

***Parris, Joyce J.** Family History of Western North Carolina. LC 99-199879. 316p. 1998. reprint ed. pap. 27.50 (0-8063-4825-9) Clearfield Co.

Parris, Judith H. The Convention Problem: Issues in Reform of Presidential Nominating Procedures. LC 72-143. (Brookings Institution Studies in Presidential Selection). 208p. reprint ed. pap. 64.50 (0-608-12464-8, 202539900043) Bks Demand.

Parris, Judith H., jt. auth. see Bain, Richard C.

Parris, Judy. Moonlight Run Till Daylight Catch It. 1998. pap. 10.95 (1-874509-56-5) X Pr.

Parris, L. Eileen, jt. ed. see Williams, Gregory L.

Parris, Leslie, ed. The Pre-Raphaelites. (Illus.). 312p. 1995. pap. 60.00 (1-85437-144-4) U of Wash Pr.

Parris, Leslie & Williams, Ian-Fleming. Constable. (Illus.). 544p. 1993. 125.00 (1-55859-636-4) Abbeville Pr.

Parris, Leslie, jt. auth. see Shields, Conal.

Parris, Lorri A., tr. see Lispector, Clarice.

Parris, Matthew. Great Parliamentary Scandals. 3rd ed. (Illus.). 376p. 1997. pap. 17.95 (1-86105-152-2, Robson-Parkwest) Parkwest Pubns.

— Great Parliamentary Scandals: Four Centuries of Calumny, Smear & Innuendo. LC 97-69431. (Illus.). 1996. 26.95 (0-86051-957-0, Robson-Parkwest) Parkwest Pubns.

— I Couldn't Possibly Comment . . . Sketches & Follies from the Commons Again. LC 97-69433. (Illus.). 260p. 1997. 25.95 (1-86105-095-X, Pub. by Robson Bks) Parkwest Pubns.

— Inca-Kola: A Traveller's Tale of Peru. large type ed. (Non-Fiction Ser.). (Illus.). 576p. 1992. 11.50 (0-7089-2630-4) Ulverscroft.

Parris, Matthew & Mason, Phil. Read My Lips: A Treasury of Things Politicians Wish They Hadn't Said. LC 97-66434. (Illus.). 230p. 1997. 25.95 (1-86105-043-7, Pub. by Robson Bks) Parkwest Pubns.

***Parris, Michael.** Fords of the Fifties. (Illus.). 168p. 2000. pap. 24.95 (1-55561-182-6, 130728AE) Fisher Bks.

Parris, Nicholas, et al, eds. Macromolecular Interactions in Food Technology. LC 96-36455. (ACS Symposium Ser.: No. 650). (Illus.). 322p. 1996. text 105.00 (0-8412-3466-3, Pub. by Am Chemical) OUP.

Parris, Peter. Act Like a Man: Daily Readings for Men. 385p. 1995. text 14.95 (0-9648902-0-8) P Parris.

Parris, Ronald G. Hausa. (Heritage Library of African Peoples: Set 2). (Illus.). 64p. (YA). (gr. 7-12). 1996. lib. bdg. 16.95 (0-8239-1983-8) Rosen Group.

— Rendille. LC 94-7246. (Heritage Library of African Peoples: Set 1). (Illus.). 64p. (YA). (gr. 7-12). 1994. lib. bdg. 16.95 (0-8239-1763-0) Rosen Group.

Parris, Sonia L. & Burney, Cindy. The Ultimate Miracle: You! 208p. 1999. pap. 12.95 (0-9665906-0-0) Infinite Horiz.

Parris, Winston C. Cancer Pain Management: Principles & Practice. LC 96-28928. 596p. 1996. text 133.00 (0-7506-9491-2) Buttrwrth-Heinemann.

Parris, Winston C., ed. Contemporary Issues in Chronic Pain Management. (Current Management of Pain Ser.). 311p. (C). 1991. text 188.00 (0-7923-1182-5) Kluwer Academic.

Parrish. Charlie Oscar. 1995. mass mkt. write for info. (0-312-95379-8) St Martin.

— Patchwork Patterns. 1998. 9.95 (1-56570-045-7) Meridian MI.

Parrish, Ada, et al. Central Brevard County. LC 98-88260. (Images of America Ser.). (Illus.). 128p. 1998. 18.99 (0-7385-0044-5) Arcadia Publng.

Parrish, Alfredo. Know Your Rights: A Guide Through Iowa's Criminal Justice System. (Illus.). (Orig.). 1995. pap. 12.00 (0-9645860-0-2) A Parrish.

Parrish, Alton & Crull, Anna. Commercial Amino Acids. LC 97-144963. 181p. 1997. 2850.00 (1-56965-361-5, C-056U) BCC.

Parrish, Angela & Griffith, R. Riggs. Managing Retirement Assets: An Approach to Administering Investments for Qualified Plans. (Building Blocks Ser.: Vol. 23). (Illus.). 24p. (Orig.). 1995. pap. 24.95 (1-57963-026-X, A043) Am Compensation.

Parrish, Anita, et al, eds. The Heritage of Franklin County, Alabama. (Heritage of Alabama Ser.: No. 30). (Illus.). 316p. 1998. 55.00 (1-891647-14-8) Herit Pub Consult.

Parrish, Anne. All Kneeling. 1976. lib. bdg. 13.95 (0-89968-154-9, Lghtyr Pr) Buccaneer Bks.

— The Perennial Bachelor. 1976. lib. bdg. 13.95 (0-89968-153-0, Lghtyr Pr) Buccaneer Bks.

Parrish, Archie, jt. auth. see Sproul, R. C.

***Parrish, C.** Treasury of Early Music: Masterworks of the Middle Ages, the Renaissance & the Baroque Era. 2000. pap. 12.95 (0-486-41088-9) Dover.

Parrish, Carl. The Notation of Medieval Music. LC 78-11831. 230p. 1978. lib. bdg. 30.00 (0-918728-08-8) Pendragon NY.

Parrish, Clarence R. Expressions of Faith. (Illus.). 15.00 (0-9638379-1-5) P & P Pubng.

— Images of Democracy: (I Can't Go Home) 10.00 (0-9638379-0-7) P & P Pubng.

Parrish, Crystal. Faith Tabernacle Publications Inc. (Illus.). 40p. 1997. 10.00 (1-892712-00-8); pap. 10.00 (1-892712-01-6); pap. 12.00 (1-892712-02-4) Faith Taber.

Parrish, Darrell. Lease Cars: How to Get One. 3rd ed. (Illus.). 250p. 1997. reprint ed. pap. 9.95 (1-890308-00-5) Bk Express.

Parrish, Dee A. How to Break the Vicious Circles in Your Relationships: A Guide for Couples. LC 93-4794. 128p. 1993. 8.95 (0-88268-144-3) Station Hill Pr.

Parrish, Dee Anna. Abused: A Guide to Recovery for Adult Survivors of Emotional/Physical Child Abuse. rev. expanded ed. 208p. 1998. pap. 14.95 (1-58177-019-7, P2091, Pub. by Barrytown Ltd) Consort Bk Sales.

Parrish, Dorothy B. Planning & Directing a Wedding: Guidelines for a Bride, Mother & Director. unabridged ed. LC 86-641927. (Illus.). 65p. 1996. reprint ed. pap. 9.95 (0-9656331-0-1) D Parrish.

Parrish, Duane. A Postcard to Heaven. LC 93-84140. 150p. (Orig.). 1994. pap. 9.95 (0-89221-235-7) New Leaf.

Parrish, Frank. Snare in the Dark. large type ed. (Mystery Ser.). 320p. 1983. 27.99 (0-7089-1007-6) Ulverscroft.

— Sparks from His Heart. 110p. 1992. pap. text 9.00 (1-881068-00-5) Oaktree Bks.

Parrish, Fred. Photojournalism: An Introduction. 420p. 2000. pap. 43.25 (0-314-04564-3) West Pub.

Parrish, Fred L. A Yank in the British YMCA. 183p. 1975. pap. text 27.00 (0-89126-009-9) MA-AH Pub.

Parrish, Frederick, Jr. Animal Science, Introductory Meats. 1996. spiral bd. 31.90 (0-88252-205-1) Paladin Hse.

Parrish, G. & Harper, G. S. Production Gas Carburizing. (Materials Engineering Practice Ser.). (Illus.). 250p. 1985. 142.00 (0-08-027312-2, Pub. by Pergamon Repr) Franklin.

***Parrish, Geoffrey.** Carburizing: Microstructures & Properties. 300p. 1999. 135.00 (0-87170-666-0) ASM.

Parrish, Geoffrey. The Influence of Microstructure on the Properties of Case-Carburized Components. LC 80-10679. (Illus.). 248p. reprint ed. pap. 76.90 (0-8357-6156-8, 203430900089) Bks Demand.

***Parrish, Geoffrey.** The Other Side of Twilight: A Story of Intrigue & Betrayal. LC 99-91800. 2000. 25.00 (0-7388-1278-1); pap. 18.00 (0-7388-1279-X) Xlibris Corp.

***Parrish, George I., Jr.** Instant Losers. LC 00-190579. 2000. 25.00 (0-7388-1566-7); pap. 18.00 (0-7388-1567-5) Xlibris Corp.

An Asterisk (*) at the beginning of an entry indicates that the title is appearing for the first time.

Parrish-Harra, Carol E. Adventure in Meditation: Spirituality for the 21st Century, Vol. 2. LC 95-71835. 1996. 17.95 (*0-945027-14-1*) Sparrow Hawk Pr.
— Adventure in Meditation Vol. I: Spirituality for the 21st Century, Vol. I. Marvin, Mary B., ed. LC 95-71835. (Illus.). 240p. (Orig.). 1995. pap. 17.95 (*0-945027-13-3*) Sparrow Hawk Pr.
— Adventure in Meditation Vol. II: Spirituality for the 21st Century. Marvin, Mary B. & Hallstrom, Norma, eds. (Illus.). (Orig.). 1996. pap. 9.95 (*0-614-14038-2*) Sparrow Hawk Pr.
— Adventure in Meditation Vol. III: Spirituality for the 21st Century. Marvin, Mary B., ed. LC 95-71835. (Orig.). 1997. pap. 17.95 (*0-945027-15-X*) Sparrow Hawk Pr.
— The Book of Rituals: Personal & Planetary Transformation. 280p. 1990. 23.95 (*0-945027-10-9*) Sparrow Hawk Pr.
— The New Age Handbook on Death & Dying. LC 89-864. 196p. 1982. 10.95 (*0-945027-09-5*) Sparrow Hawk Pr.
— The New Dictionary of Spiritual Thought. Marvin, Mary B. & Hallstrom, Norma, eds. LC 93-87756. (Illus.). 213p. (Orig.). 1994. pap. 14.95 (*0-945027-11-7*) Sparrow Hawk Pr.
— Reflections. Marvin, Mary B., ed. LC 97-62035. 146p. 1997. pap. 10.95 (*0-945027-16-8*) Sparrow Hawk Pr.
Parrish-Harra, Carol E., jt. auth. see Gray, Mary.
Parrish-Harra, Carol E., ed. see Brown, Sarah Leigh.
Parrish-Harra, Carol E., ed. see Pappas, George Charles.
Parrish-Harra, Carol W. The Aquarian Rosary: Reviving the Art of Mantra Yoga. LC 87-63437. (Illus.). 136p. 1988. pap. 9.95 (*0-945027-01-X*) Sparrow Hawk Pr.
Parrish, I. S. Military Veterans PTSD Reference Manual. 244p. 1999. pap. 19.95 (*0-7414-0077-4*) Buy Books.
Parrish, J. Totman, jt. ed. see McCabe, Peter J.
Parrish, James R. Today's Black Hollywood. 480p. 1995. mass mkt. 4.99 (*0-8217-0104-5*, Zebra Kensgtn) Kensgtn Pub Corp.
Parrish, Jenni, ed. Abortion Law in the United States. LC 95-30126. (Controversies in Constitutional Law Ser.). 1996. write for info. (*0-8153-2185-6*) Garland.
Parrish, Jenni, ed. see Deaf Action Committee Staff.
Parrish, Joan & Arrington, Kenna. Great Games, Vol. 1. (Illus.). 32p. 1997. pap., teacher ed. 6.95 (*0-9656478-2-X*) Finger Works.
Parrish, Joan, jt. auth. see Arrington, Kenna.
Parrish, John A., et al, eds. Photoimmunology. LC 83-4216. 320p. 1983. 85.00 (*0-306-41280-2*, Plenum Trade) Perseus Pubng.
Parrish, John A., et al. UV-A: Biological Effects of Ultraviolet Radiation with Emphasis on Human Responses to Longwave Ultraviolet. LC 78-14968. 272p. reprint ed. pap. 84.40 (*0-608-12365-X*, 205207600033) Bks Demand.
Parrish, Joseph. Alcoholic Inebriety from a Medical Standpoint. Grob, Gerald N., ed. LC 80-1243. (Addiction in America Ser.). 1981. reprint ed. lib. bdg. 18.95 (*0-405-13613-7*) Ayer.
Parrish, Judith T. Interpreting Pre-Quaternary Climate from the Geologic Record. LC 98-6659. (Perspectives in Paleobiology Ser.). (Illus.). 544p. 1998. 65.00 (*0-231-10206-2*) Col U Pr.
Parrish, Julia K. & Hamner, William M., eds. Animal Groups in Three Dimensions: How Species Aggregate. LC 97-25867. (Illus.). 384p. (C). 1997. text 90.00 (*0-521-46024-7*) Cambridge U Pr.
***Parrish, Karen, ed.** Digital Parcel Mapping Handbook: Standards & Stratagies for New Jersey Parcel Mapping Communities. (Illus.). 220p. 1999. pap. 55.00 (*0-916848-12-4*) Urban & Regional Information Systems.
Parrish, Karen, jt. ed. see Katz, Bill.
Parrish Kvaltine & Associates, Inc. Staff. Lightning Protection Manual for Rural Electric Systems. 1993. pap. text. write for info. (*0-917599-12-8*) Natl Rural.
***Parrish, Laura, pseud.** Love's Quiet Corner. large type ed. (Paperback Ser.). 2000. pap. 23.95 (*0-7838-8981-X*, G K Hall Lrg Type) Mac Lib Ref.
Parrish, Lydia A. Slave Songs of the Georgia Sea Islands. 256p. reprint ed. lib. bdg. 39.00 (*0-685-43693-4*) Rprt Serv.
Parrish, M. L. Victorian Lady Novelists. (Illus.). 173p. 1995. reprint ed. 90.00 (*1-888262-57-5*) Martino Pubng.
Parrish, Maxfield. Maxfield Parrish: Postcard Book. (Illus.). 1992. pap. text 9.95 (*0-87654-942-3*) Pomegranate Calif.
Parrish, Maxfield. Slave Songs of Georgia. text. write for info. (*0-374-26579-8*) FS&G.
***Parrish, Maxfield & Harburg, E. Y.** Over the Rainbow. LC 00-27015. (Illus.). 32p. 2000. 17.95 (*0-941807-38-X*) Welcome Enterprises.
Parrish, Michael. Careers in Business & the Public Sector: An Annotated Bibliography. 34p. 1986. pap. text 8.00 (*0-9617990-0-5*) Ars Biblio.
— The Lesser Terror: Soviet State Security, 1939-1953. LC 94-38565. 456p. 1996. 69.50 (*0-275-95113-8*, Praeger Pubs) Greenwood.
— Sacrifice of the Generals: Soviet Senior Officer Losses, January 1939-December 1953. LC 98-55340. 544p. 2000. lib. bdg. 105.00 (*0-313-31070-X*) Greenwood.
— Soviet Security & Intelligence Organizations 1917-1990: A Biographical Dictionary & Review of Literature in English. LC 91-34996. 704p. 1992. lib. bdg. 85.00 (*0-313-28305-2*, PSV/, Greenwood Pr) Greenwood.
Parrish, Michael, et al. Introduction to Entrepreneurship: Building the Dream, 2 vols. 381p. 1998. pap. text, teacher ed. write for info. (*1-58313-062-4*) Univ Access.
— Introduction to Entrepreneurship: Building the Dream, 2 vols. 269p. (C). 1998. pap. text, student ed., per. 25.00 (*1-58313-061-6*) Univ Access.
Parrish, Michael, jt. ed. see Hopkins, Jack.
Parrish, Michael E. Anxious Decades: America in Prosperity & Depression 1920-1941. 1994. pap. 15.95 (*0-393-31134-1*) Norton.
***Parrish, Michael E.** The Hughes Court: Justices, Rulings, & Legacy. 2002. lib. bdg. 55.00 (*1-57607-197-9*) ABC-CLIO.
Parrish, Michael E. Securities Regulation & the New Deal. LC 70-118735. (Yale Historical Publications: No. 93). 282p. reprint ed. pap. 87.50 (*0-608-30095-0*, 202202700024) Bks Demand.
***Parrish, Michael T.** General P.T.G. Beauregard. 2000. 35.00 (*0-679-43165-9*) Random Hse Value.
***Parrish, Nancy C.** Lee Smith, Annie Dillard & the Hollins Group: A Genesis of Writers. LC 88-27632. (Southern Literary Studies). (Illus.). 256p. 1999. reprint ed. pap. text 16.95 (*0-8071-2434-6*) La State U Pr.
Parrish, Noel F. Behind the Sheltering Bomb. Kohn, Richard H., ed. LC 78-22415. (American Military Experience Ser.). 1980. lib. bdg. 24.95 (*0-405-11889-9*) Ayer.
Parrish, P. J. Dark of the Moon. (Illus.). 384p. 1999. 23.00 (*1-57566-394-5*) Kensgtn Pub Corp.
***Parrish, P. J.** Dark of the Moon. 2000. mass mkt. 6.99 (*0-7860-1054-1*, Pinncle Kensgtn) Kensgtn Pub Corp.
***Parrish, Patt.** Escape the Past. LC 99-27126. 1999. 18.95 (*0-7862-2028-7*) Thorndike Pr.
Parrish, Phyllis W. & Parrish, Stephen R. House Management: A Guide for Greek Chapter Houses: How to Successfully Operate a Fraternity or Sorority House, Vol. 1. (Illus.). 496p. 1989. pap. 35.00 (*0-9623776-0-0*) P Parrish.
Parrish, Preston. The Lions' Den: Facing Yours. 88p. 1992. pap. text 4.95 (*0-9633470-8-X*) Awakenings.
Parrish, Randall. Bob Hampton of Placer. 1976. lib. bdg. 16.70 (*0-89968-084-4*, Lghtyr Pr) Buccaneer Bks.
— Contraband, A Romance of the North Atlantic. 1976. lib. bdg. 18.25 (*0-89968-085-2*, Lghtyr Pr) Buccaneer Bks.
— Last Voyage of the Donna Isabel. 369p. 26.95 (*0-8488-2658-2*) Amereon Ltd.
— My Lady of the North. 1976. lib. bdg. 16.30 (*0-89968-086-0*, Lghtyr Pr) Buccaneer Bks.
— My Lady of the South. 1976. lib. bdg. 16.30 (*0-89968-087-9*, Lghtyr Pr) Buccaneer Bks.
Parrish, Richard. Abandoned Heart. 1995. 23.95 (*0-614-96281-1*, Dutt) Dutton Plume.
— Defending Truth. 1998. mass mkt. 6.50 (*0-451-40833-0*, Onyx) NAL.
— Our Choice of Gods. Richardson, Stewart, ed. 464p. 1989. 19.95 (*1-55972-002-6*, Birch Ln Pr) Carol Pub Group.
— Wind & Lies. 1999. pap. 22.95 (*0-525-93871-0*) NAL.
***Parrish, Richard K., II.** Bascom Palmer Eye Institute's Atlas of Opthalmology. LC 99-14084. 500p. 1999. text 195.00 (*0-7506-7075-4*) Buttrwrth-Heinemann.
Parrish, Ritah. Pink Menace. 36p. 1998. 3.00 (*0-9653194-9-0*) Future Tense.
Parrish, Robert. Great Tricks Revisited: New Approaches, Applications, Routines & Patter for Classic Magic Tricks. Willmarth, Phil, ed. & pref. by. (Illus.). 136p. 1995. 25.00 (*0-916638-80-4*, D M Magic Bks) Meyerbooks.
— Growing up in Hollywood. (Illus.). 236p. 1988. 17.95 (*0-316-69256-5*); pap. 9.95 (*0-316-69257-3*) Little.
— Hollywood Doesn't Live Here Anymore. (Illus.). 240p. 1989. reprint ed. pap. 9.95 (*0-316-69258-1*) Little.
— Words about Wizards: Recollections of Magicians & Their Magic, 1930-1950. (Illus.). 72p. 1994. 25.00 (*0-916638-79-0*, D M Magic Bks) Meyerbooks.
Parrish, Ruth G. Eugenics: Index to Modern Information with Bibliography. 193p. 1997. 47.50 (*0-7883-1639-7*); pap. 44.50 (*0-7883-1640-0*) ABBE Pubs Assn.
***Parrish, Shelley Berlin.** Sharing Grandma's Gift. LC 99-64040. (Illus.). 40p. 2000. 18.00 (*0-89716-936-0*, Peanut Btr Pubng) Elton-Wolf Pub.
Parrish, Stephen E. God & Necessity: A Defense of Classical Theism. LC 96-53209. 332p. 1997. 47.50 (*0-7618-0693-8*) U Pr of Amer.
Parrish, Stephen E., jt. auth. see Beckwith, Francis J.
Parrish, Stephen M., ed. see Austen, Jane.
Parrish, Stephen M., ed. see Coleridge, Samuel Taylor.
Parrish, Stephen M., ed. see La Fontaine, Jean de.
Parrish, Stephen M., ed. see Wordsworth, William.
Parrish, Stephen M., ed. see Yeats, William Butler.
Parrish, Stephen R., jt. auth. see Parrish, Phyllis W.
Parrish, T. Michael. Richard Taylor: Soldier Prince of Dixie. LC 91-46467. (Illus.). xvi, 554p. (C). 1992. 45.00 (*0-8078-2032-6*) U of NC Pr.
Parrish, T. Michael & Willingham, Robert M. Confederate Imprints: A Bibliography of Southern Publications from Secession to Surrender. (Illus.). 1133p. 1987. 95.00 (*0-318-37956-2*, PA-999-2) Jenkins.
Parrish, T. Michael, jt. ed. see Cutrer, Thomas W.
Parrish, Thomas. Berlin in the Balance, 1945-1949: The Blockade, the Airlift, the First Major Battle of the Cold War, 1 vol. 400p. 1999. pap. text 16.00 (*0-7382-0149-9*, Pub. by Perseus Pubng) HarpC.
— Berlin In The Balance, 1945-1949: The Blockade, the Airlift, the First Major Battle of the Cold War. LC 97-52968. 400p. 1998. 27.50 (*0-201-25832-3*) Addison-Wesley.
— The Cold War Encyclopedia. 88p. 1995. 60.00 (*0-8050-2778-5*) H Holt & Co.
— The Cold War Encyclopedia: The Complete Guide to the Most Important Conflict of Our Time. (Illus.). 490p. 1998. text 50.00 (*0-7881-5786-8*) DIANE Pub.
Parrish, Thomas B., et al, eds. Funding Special Education. (Yearbook of the American Education Finance Association Ser.: Vol. 19). (Illus.). 296p. 1999. lib. bdg. 54.95 (*0-8039-6624-5*, 81389) Corwin Pr.
Parrish, Thomas B., et al. Inequalities in Public School District Revenues. LC 98-186088. (Education Department Publication NCES 98 Ser.: Vol. 210). (Illus.). 268p. 1998. pap. 19.00 (*0-16-049652-7*) USGPO.
***Parrish, Timothy A.** Red Stick Men: Stories. LC 99-87871. 228p. 2000. 22.00 (*1-57806-263-2*) U Pr of Miss.
Parrish, Timothy A., jt. auth. see Crews, Edward R.
Parrish, Vernon. Earning Megabucks the Video Way in the 90's. LC 91-91353. 179p. (Orig.). 1992. pap. 19.95 (*0-9615774-1-X*) V Parrish.
Parrish, W. D. A Dictionary of the Sussex Dialect & Collection of Provincialisms in Use in the County of Sussex. (English Dialect Society Publications: No. 6). 1972. reprint ed. pap. 25.00 (*0-8115-0440-9*) Periodicals Srv.
Parrish, W. R. & Lewis, E. A. Handbook of Calorimetry. Date not set. write for info. (*0-8247-9529-6*) Dekker.
Parrish, Wayland M. & Hochmuth, Marie, eds. American Speeches. LC 69-14028. 518p. 1969. reprint ed. lib. bdg. 35.00 (*0-8371-1962-6*, PAAM, Greenwood Pr) Greenwood.
Parrish, William E. Frank Blair: Lincoln's Conservative. LC 97-32334. (Missouri Biography Ser.). (Illus.). 336p. 1998. 29.95 (*0-8262-1156-9*) U of Mo Pr.
— A History of Missouri, Volume III: 1860 to 1875. LC 76-155844. (Missouri Sesquicentennial History Ser.). (Illus.). 344p. 1973. text 29.95 (*0-8262-0148-2*) U of Mo Pr.
Parrish, William E., et al. Missouri: The Heart of the Nation. 2nd ed. (Illus.). 423p. 1992. pap. text 24.95 (*0-88295-887-9*) Harlan Davidson.
***Parrish, William Earl, et al.** A History of Missouri: Volume II, 1820 to 1860. LC 99-57213. 336p. 2000. 18.95 (*0-8262-1286-7*) U of Mo Pr.
Parrot. Feliz a Pesar de Todo.Tr. of How to Change a Negative Attitude. (SPA.). 212p. pap. write for info. (*958-9269-23-0*) Editorial Unilit.
— How to Write Psychology Papers. 2nd ed. (C). 1999. pap. text 12.00 (*0-321-03111-3*) Addson-Wesley Educ.
Parrot, Andre. The Temple of Jerusalem. Hooke, Beatrice E., tr. from FRE. LC 85-8037. (Studies in Biblical Archaeology: No. 5).Tr. of Le/Temple de Jerusalem. (Illus.). 112p. 1985. reprint ed. lib. bdg. 38.50 (*0-313-24224-0*, PATJ, Greenwood Pr) Greenwood.
Parrot, Andrea & Bechhofer, Laurie, eds. Acquaintance Rape: The Hidden Crime. LC 90-38127. (Personality Processes Ser.). 401p. 1991. 89.95 (*0-471-51023-8*) Wiley.
Parrot, Andrea, et al. Rape 101: Sexual Assault Prevention for College Athletes. LC 95-141527. 1994. pap. 21.95 (*1-55691-099-1*, 991) Learning Pubns.
Parrot, Andrea, jt. ed. see Feldman, Harold.
Parrot, Cecil, tr. & intro. see Hasek, Jaroslav.
Parrot, Edward, ed. see Borelli, Antonio A., et al.
Parrot, Edward, ed. see De Oliveira, Plinio C.
Parrot, Friedrich. Journey to Ararat. LC 73-115576. (Russia Observed, Series I). 1970. reprint ed. 23.95 (*0-405-03057-6*) Ayer.
Parrot, J. Edward, ed. I Am the Lady of the Rosary. (Illus.). 18p. pap. write for info. (*1-877905-31-3*) Am Soc Defense TFP.
Parrot, J. Edward, ed. see Marin, Antonio R.
Parrot, Jasper, jt. auth. see Ashkenazi, Vladimir.
Parrot, Les. Understanding Psychological Science. 2nd ed. (C). 1999. pap. text. write for info. (*0-8013-3127-7*) Longman.
Parrot, Les & Parrott, Leslie. The Career Counselor. 1995. pap. text 14.99 (*0-8499-3677-2*) Word Pub.
Parrot, Leslie, jt. auth. see Parrott, Les.
Parrot, Roxanne L., jt. auth. see Maibach, Edward.
Parrott. Counsel & Psychotherapy. 1996. wbk. ed. 57.00 (*0-07-913273-1*) McGraw.
— Drugs. 250p. 2000. pap. 29.95 (*0-471-98640-2*) Wiley.
— Extraordinary Love. Date not set. 19.99 (*0-310-20748-7*) Zondervan.
— When Bad Things Happen to Good People. 2000. 19.99 (*0-310-22459-4*) Zondervan.
***Parrott, A. C., ed.** MDMA - Methylenedioxymethamphetamine. (Neuropsychobiology Ser.: Vol. 42). (Illus.). 50p. 2000. pap. 25.25 (*3-8055-7110-0*) S Karger.
Parrott, Allen, jt. auth. see Flude, Ray.
***Parrott, Andrew.** The Essential Bach Choir. LC 99-87035. 150p. 2000. pap. 24.95 (*0-85115-786-6*) Boydell & Brewer.
Parrott, Andrew, ed. see Keyte, Hugh.
***Parrott, Bob W.** Albert C. Outler: The Gifted Dilettante. 504p. 1999. 29.95 (*1-885224-28-1*) Bristol Hse.
Parrott, Bob W., ed. Albert Outler: The Churchman. 496p. 1995. 19.95 (*1-885224-02-8*) Bristol Hse.
— Albert Outler: The Preacher. 280p. 1995. 19.95 (*1-885224-01-X*) Bristol Hse.
— Albert Outler: University Professor. 480p. 1995. 19.95 (*1-885224-03-6*) Bristol Hse.
Parrott, Bruce, ed. The Dynamics of Soviet Defense Policy. 400p. 1992. text 25.25 (*0-943875-25-0*) W Wilson Ctr Pr.
— Trade, Technology & Soviet-American Relations. LC 84-48549. (CSIS Publication Series on the Soviet Union in the 1980's; Midland Bks.). (Illus.). 414p. 1985. 35.00 (*0-253-36025-0*); pap. 18.95 (*0-253-20351-1*, MB 351) Ind U Pr.
Parrott, Bruce, jt. auth. see Dawisha, Karen.
Parrott, Bruce, jt. ed. see Dawisha, Karen.
Parrott, Cecil, tr. see Hasek, Jaroslav.
Parrott, David. The Deception of the Thrush. 1986. 50.00 (*0-7223-2049-3*, Pub. by A H S Ltd) St Mut.
Parrott, Douglas M., ed. Nag Hammadi: Codices III, 3-4 & V, 1: Eugnostos & the Sophia of Jesus Christ. LC 91-19243. (Nag Hammadi Studies: Vol. 27). xxii, 216p. 1991. 108.00 (*90-04-08366-9*) Brill Academic Pubs.
Parrott, E. O., compiled by. The Penguin Book of Limericks. (Illus.). 304p. 1985. pap. 19.99 (*0-14-007669-7*, Penguin Bks) Viking Penguin.
Parrott, E. O., ed. How to Be Well-Versed in Poetry. 288p. 1992. pap. 15.99 (*0-14-011275-8*, Penguin Bks) Viking Penguin.
Parrott, Ian. The Crying Curlew: Peter Warlock, Family & Influences. 116p. 1998. pap. 28.95 (*0-8464-4669-3*) Beekman Pubs.
— The Spiritual Pilgrims. fac. ed. LC 72-466773. (Illus.). 228p. 1969. pap. 70.70 (*0-7837-7302-1*, AU0045100007) Bks Demand.
Parrott, Ian & Peter Warlock Society Staff. The Crying Curlew: Peter Warlock-Family & Influences Centenary 1994. LC 95-207013. 116p. 1994. pap. 30.00 (*1-85902-121-2*, Pub. by Gomer Pr) St Mut.
Parrott, Jo. Template-Free Stars. (Illus.). 64p. 1993. pap. text 7.95 (*0-486-29473-0*) Dover.
— Two for Your Money. (Illus.). 104p. (Orig.). 1996. pap. text 8.95 (*0-486-29474-9*) Dover.
Parrott, Kenard J. The Son. 216p. 1997. 5.00 (*0-9659232-0-7*) K J Parrott.
Parrott, L. E. Saving Your Marriage Before Star. pap. 12.99 (*0-310-21932-9*, Zondervan Gifts) Zondervan.
***Parrott, Les.** The Control Freak. LC 00-22191. 2000. pap. write for info. (*0-8423-3793-8*) Tyndale Hse.
— Control Freak: Coping With Those Around You. 2000. 19.99 (*0-8423-3792-X*) Tyndale Hse.
Parrott, Les, III. Counseling & Psychotherapy. LC 96-27915. 448p. (C). 1996. 60.94 (*0-07-048581-X*) McGraw.
***Parrott, Les.** Helping the Struggling Adolescent: A Guide to Thirty Common Problems for Parents, Counselors, Pastors & Youth Workers. 2000. 29.99 (*0-310-23407-7*) Zondervan.
Parrott, Les. High-Maintenance Relationships. 1997. pap. 10.99 (*0-8423-1466-0*) Tyndale Hse.
***Parrott, Les.** How to Write Psychology Papers. 2nd ed. LC 98-27536. 144p. (C). 1998. pap. text 17.00 (*0-321-04466-5*) Allyn.
Parrott, Les. Manual Del Ujier.Tr. of Usher's Manual. (SPA.). 68p. 1992. pap. 4.99 (*0-8297-0329-2*) Vida Pubs.
***Parrott, Les.** Meditations on Proverbs for Couples. 2000. 12.99 (*0-310-23446-8*) Zondervan.
Parrott, Les, III. Once upon a Family. 36p. 1996. pap., teacher ed. 4.99 (*0-8341-1593-X*) Nazarene.
— Once upon a Family: Building a Healthy Home When Your Family Isn't a Fairy Tale. LC 96-44598. 112p. (Orig.). 1997. pap. 9.99 (*0-8341-1597-2*) Beacon Hill.
— 7 Secrets of a Healthy Dating Relationship. 112p. (YA). 1995. pap. 9.99 (*0-8341-1554-9*) Beacon Hill.
Parrott, Les & Parrot, Leslie. Love Is: Meditations for Couples on I Corinthians 13. LC 98-44037. 1999. 12.99 (*0-310-21666-4*) Zondervan.
Parrott, Les, III & Parrott, Leslie. Becoming Soul Mates: Cultivating Spiritual Intimacy in the Early Years of Marriage. 160p. 1995. 15.99 (*0-310-20014-8*) Zondervan.
Parrott, Les & Parrott, Leslie. Becoming Soul Mates: Cultivating Spiritual Intimacy in the Early Years of Marriage. 240p. 1997. pap. 12.99 (*0-310-21926-4*) Zondervan.
— Relationships 101. 1998. pap. 6.99 (*1-56292-450-8*) Honor Bks OK.
Parrott, Les, III & Parrott, Leslie. Saving Your Marriage Before It Starts: Seven Questions to Ask Before & after You Marry. 48p. 1995. teacher ed. write for info. (*0-310-20448-8*) Zondervan.
Parrott, Les & Parrott, Leslie C. Relationships: An Open & Honest Guide to Making Bad Relationships Better & Good Relationships Great. 80p. 1998. pap., wbk. ed. 8.99 (*0-310-22438-1*) Zondervan.
Parrott, Les & Parrott, Leslie L. Getting Ready for the Wedding: All You Need to Know Before You Say I Do. LC 97-30560. 160p. 1997. pap. 9.99 (*0-310-21148-4*) Zondervan.
— A Good Friend: 10 Traits for Enduring Ties. LC 98-14299. 130p. 1998. 6.97 (*1-56955-058-1*, Vine Bks) Servant.
— Like a Kiss on the Lips: Devotions from Proverbs for Couples. LC 97-3352. 1997. 12.99 (*0-310-21623-0*) Zondervan.
***Parrott, Les & Parrott, Leslie L.** Relationships: An Open & Honest Guide to Making Bad Relationships Better & Good Relationships Great. LC 97-50106. 208p. 1998. 16.99 (*0-310-20755-X*) Zondervan.
Parrott, Leslie. Battle for Your Mind: Understanding the Sanctified Personality. 199p. 1985. pap. 9.99 (*0-8341-1124-1*) Beacon Hill.
— The Bible Speaks to Me about My Church. 112p. (Orig.). 1987. pap. 8.99 (*0-8341-1213-2*) Beacon Hill.
Parrott, Leslie, III. Counseling & Psychotherapy. Exercises for Effective Counseling & Psychotherapy. (C). 1996. pap., student ed. 27.19 (*0-07-048582-8*) McGraw.
Parrott, Leslie. Future Church: How Congregations Choose Their Character & Destiny. 180p. 1988. kivar 10.99 (*0-8341-1261-2*) Beacon Hill.
Parrott, Leslie, Jr. The Greeter's Manual: A Guide to Warm-Hearted Churches. 48p. 1993. pap. 6.99 (*0-310-37481-2*) Zondervan.
Parrott, Leslie, III. Helping the Struggling Adolescent: A Guide for Parents, Counselors & Youth Workers. 272p. 1993. pap. 14.99 (*0-310-57821-3*) Zondervan.
— How to Write Psychology. LC 93-3171. 144p. (C). 1997. pap. 14.00 (*0-06-501798-6*) Addson-Wesley Educ.
Parrott, Leslie. Introducing the Nazarenes. 52p. 1969. pap. 3.99 (*0-8341-0222-6*) Nazarene.

P

— Keeping Love in the Family. 192p. 1987. kivar 10.99 (*0-8341-1195-0*) Beacon Hill.

— The Marriage Mentor Manual: Couples Encouraging Couples in the First Year of Marriage. 80p. 1995. pap. 5.99 (*0-310-50131-8*) Zondervan.

— Motivating Volunteers in the Local Church. 144p. 1991. pap. 9.99 (*0-8341-1415-1*) Beacon Hill.

— Questions Couples Ask: Answers to the Top 100 Marital Questions. 320p. 1996. pap. 12.99 (*0-310-20754-1*) Zondervan.

— Relationships Leader's Guide: An Open & Honest Guide to Making Bad Relationships Better & Good Relationships Great. 1999. pap. text 19.99 (*0-310-22473-X*) Zondervan.

— Relationships Participant's Guide: An Open & Honest Guide to Making Bad Relationships Better & Good Relationships Great. 1999. pap. 7.99 (*0-310-22585-X*) HarpC.

— Seven Secrets of a Healthy Dating Relationship Leader Guide. 78p. 1995. pap. text 8.99 (*0-8341-1571-9*) Beacon Hill.

— Softly & Tenderly: The Altar: A Place to Encounter God. 228p. 1989. 15.99 (*0-8341-1304-X*) Beacon Hill.

Parrott, Leslie, III. The Usher's Manual. 48p. 1970. mass mkt. 6.99 (*0-310-30651-5*, 10513P) Zondervan.

Parrott, Leslie. What Is Sanctification? Understanding the Meaning of Entire Sanctification. 48p. 1979. pap. 3.99 (*0-8341-0077-0*) Beacon Hill.

— Why Millions Believe. 20p. 1976. pap. 1.50 (*0-8341-0976-X*) Nazarene.

— Why Millions Tithe. 28p. 1981. pap. 1.50 (*0-8341-1032-6*) Nazarene.

Parrott, Leslie, jt. auth. see Parrot, Les.

Parrott, Leslie, jt. auth. see Parrott, Les, III.

Parrott, Leslie, jt. auth. see Parrott, Les.

Parrott, Leslie C., jt. auth. see Parrott, Les.

Parrott, Leslie L., jt. auth. see Parrott, Les.

Parrott, Linda J., jt. ed. see Reese, Hayne W.

Parrott, Lora L. The Original Sunday Dinner: Meals from Family Kitchens. 304p. 1979. kivar 18.99 (*0-8341-0594-2*) Beacon Hill.

Parrott, M. R. To Lie Within the Moment. LC 98-96006. 1998. 24.95 (*0-9662635-4-5*) rimric pr.

Parrott, Martin. Tasks for Language Teachers: A Resource Book for Training & Development. LC 92-34467. (Teacher Training & Development Ser.). 335p. (C). 1993. text 64.95 (*0-521-41648-5*); pap. text 29.95 (*0-521-42666-9*) Cambridge U Pr.

Parrott, Mary Ann. Hymns & Songs of the Bible. LC 98-22517. (Covenant Bible Studies). 1998. 5.95 (*0-87178-014-3*) Brethren.

Parrott, Ray J., Jr. & Rakova, Alfia A. Schaum's Outline of Russian Vocabulary. LC 98-53368. (ENG & RUS., Illus.). 240p. 1999. pap., student ed. 14.95 (*0-07-038211-5*) McGraw.

Parrott, Robert H. & Rathlev, Mary. Access to Primary Health Care for Children with HIV: A Guide for Pediatricians, Family Physicians & Nurse Practitioners. 1993. pap. 9.95 (*0-9634295-1-5*) Childs Hosp.

Parrott, Roxanne, jt. auth. see Pfau, Michael.

Parrott, Roxanne L. & Condit, Celeste M., eds. Communicating Women's Health Messages: A Resource Book. 445p. 1996. 75.00 (*0-7619-0056-X*); pap. 35.00 (*0-7619-0057-8*) Sage.

Parrott, S. Relativistic Electrodynamics & Differential Geometry. (Illus.). 320p. 1986. 89.95 (*0-387-96435-5*) Spr-Verlag.

Parrott, Sarah B., ed. see Gwaltney, Jack M., Jr.

Parrott, Thomas M. A Companion to Victorian Literature. 1988. reprint ed. lib. bdg. 59.00 (*0-7812-0070-9*) Rprt Serv.

— Studies of a Booklover. LC 67-28763. (Essay Index Reprint Ser.). 1977. 20.95 (*0-8369-0771-X*) Ayer.

Parrott, Thomas M. & Long, Augustus W. English Poems from Chaucer to Kipling. LC 75-108587. (Granger Index Reprint Ser.). 1977. 20.95 (*0-8369-6115-3*) Ayer.

Parrott, Thomas M. & Robert, Martin. A Companion to Victorian Literature. 1981. reprint ed. lib. bdg. 59.00 (*0-403-01495-6*) Scholarly.

Parrott, Thomas M. & Thorp, Willard, eds. Poetry of the Transition, 1850-1914. LC 72-5594. (Granger Index Reprint Ser.). 1977. reprint ed. 44.95 (*0-8369-6384-9*) Ayer.

Parrott, Thomas M., ed. see Shakespeare, William.

Parrott, Tonya M., jt. ed. see Steckenrider, Janie S.

Parrott, W. Gerrod, jt. auth. see Harre, Rom.

Parrott, Wanda S., jt. auth. see Dashiell, Jackie.

Parrott, Wanda S., jt. auth. see Recana, Mel R.

Parrotte, Timothy, ed. see Zimmerman, Tracy & Shapiro, Lawrence E.

Parrow, Joachim, jt. auth. see Jonsson, Bengt.

Parrow, Kathleen. From Defense to Resistance: Justification of Violence During the French Wars of Religion. LC 93-72130. (Transactions Ser.: Vol. 83, Pt. 6). 80p. 1993. pap. 15.00 (*0-87169-836-6*, T836-PAK) Am Philos.

Parry, jt. auth. see Heintz.

Parry, jt. auth. see Heintz, James A.

Parry, jt. auth. see Morcom.

Parry, A., jt. auth. see Parry, L.

Parry, Abbot, tr. The Rule of Saint Benedict. 144p. 1991. pap. 9.95 (*0-85244-168-1*, 960, Pub. by Gra1cewing) Morehouse Pub.

Parry, Adam M. The Language of Achilles & Other Papers. (Illus.). 352p. 1989. 98.00 (*0-19-814892-5*) OUP.

— Logos & Ergon in Thucydides. rev. ed. Connor, W. R., ed. LC 80-2660. (Monographs in Classical Studies). 223p. 1981. lib. bdg. 29.95 (*0-405-14045-2*) Ayer.

Parry, Adam M. & Dorson, Richard M., eds. The Making of Homeric Verse: The Collected Papers of Milman Parry. LC 80-747. (Folklore of the World Ser.). (Illus.). 1981. reprint ed. lib. bdg. 63.95 (*0-405-13321-9*) Ayer.

Parry, Adam M., ed. see Parry, Milman.

***Parry, Alan.** Progress of the Pilgrim Mouse: An Adaption of the Pilgrim's Progress. (J). 2000. pap. 9.99 (*0-8024-2930-0*) Moody.

Parry, Alan & Doan, Robert E. Story Re-Visions: Narrative Therapy in the Postmodern World. LC 94-18296. 216p. 1994. pap. text 21.00 (*0-89862-570-X*); lib. bdg. 42.00 (*0-89862-213-1*, 2213) Guilford Pubns.

Parry, Alan & Parry, Linda. Bedtime Prayers. LC 94-3642. (Little Prayers Ser.). (Illus.). 12p. (J). (ps-k). 1995. 3.99 (*0-8499-1148-6*) Tommy Nelson.

— Best-Loved Prayers No. 4, Vol. 4. LC 97-66279. (Time to Pray Ser.). (Illus.). 12p. (J). (ps). 1997. 4.99 (*0-8499-1469-8*) Tommy Nelson.

— The Bible Made Easy: A Pop-Up, Pull-Out, Interactive Bible Adventure, 1. (Illus.). 24p. (J). (ps-2). 1999. 16.99 (*0-8499-5902-0*) Tommy Nelson.

— Classic Children's Prayers. LC 94-28656. (Little Prayers Ser.). (Illus.). 12p. (J). (ps-5). 1995. 3.99 (*0-8499-1160-5*) Tommy Nelson.

— Go with Christian: A Child's Version of Pilgrim's Progress. LC 95-42211. (Illus.). 12p. (J). (gr. 2-7). 1996. 14.99 (*0-8499-1305-5*) Tommy Nelson.

— God's Littlest Angel. LC 97-222456. 1997. 12.99 (*0-8423-1177-7*) Tyndale Hse.

— The Herald Angels. 16p. (J). (ps-2). 1996. pap. 12.99 (*0-8499-1306-3*) Tommy Nelson.

— Mealtime Prayers. LC 94-5435. (Little Prayers Ser.). (Illus.). 12p. (J). (ps-k). 1995. 3.99 (*0-8499-1149-4*) Tommy Nelson.

— Prayers for Bedtime, No. 2. LC 97-66276. (Time to Pray Ser.). (Illus.). 12p. (J). (ps). 1997. 4.99 (*0-8499-1466-3*) Tommy Nelson.

— Prayers for My Family, No. 1. LC 97-66278. (Time to Pray Ser.). (Illus.). 12p. (J). (ps). 1997. 4.99 (*0-8499-1465-5*) Tommy Nelson.

— Prayers from the Bible, No. 3. LC 97-66277. (Time to Pray Ser.). (Illus.). 12p. (J). (ps). 1997. 4.99 (*0-8499-1467-1*) Tommy Nelson.

— Prayers of Praise. LC 94-3641. (Little Prayers Ser.). (Illus.). 12p. (J). (ps-k). 1995. 3.99 (*0-8499-1159-1*) Tommy Nelson.

Parry, Alan, jt. auth. see Robertson, Jenny.

Parry, Albert W. America Learns Russian: A History of the Teaching of the Russian Language in the United States. LC 67-27162. 217p. reprint ed. pap. 67.30 (*0-8357-5351-4*, 202739900055) Bks Demand.

— Education in England in the Middle Ages. LC 77-178584. reprint ed. 35.00 (*0-404-56659-6*) AMS Pr.

— Terrorism. 1980. 24.50 (*0-8149-0746-6*) Random.

Parry, Ann. The Poetry of Rudyard Kipling: Rousing the Nation. 160p. 1992. 113.00 (*0-335-09495-3*); pap. 36.95 (*0-335-09494-5*) OpUniv Pr.

Parry, Anne. Physiotherapy Assessment. 2nd ed. LC 85-4615. 168p. (Orig.). 1985. pap. 17.95 (*0-7099-4009-2*, Pub. by C Helm) Routldge.

Parry, Anne, et al. Choosing Nonviolence: The Rainbow House Handbook to a Violence-Free Future for Young Children. LC 90-62582. (Illus.). (Orig.). 1990. pap. 25.45 (*0-9627528-9-4*) Rainbow Hse.

Parry, Benita. Delusions & Discoveries: India in the British Imagination, 1880-1930. 240p. 1998. pap. 20.00 (*1-85984-128-7*, Pub. by Verso) Norton.

Parry, Benita, et al. Cultural Readings of Imperialism: Edward Said & the Gravity of History. LC 97-18542. 256p. 1998. pap. 19.95 (*0-312-17642-2*); text 55.00 (*0-312-17641-4*) St Martin.

Parry, Benita, jt. ed. see Chrisman, Laura.

Parry, Betty. Shake the Parrot Cage. 112p. 1994. 10.00 (*0-932616-47-X*) Brick Hse Bks.

Parry, Betty, ed. The Unicorn & the Garden. LC 78-64531. (Illus.). 1978. per. 15.00 (*0-915380-04-8*) Word Works.

Parry, Bob & Perkins, Chris, eds. World Mapping Today. 2nd ed. 750p. Date not set. 250.00 (*1-85739-035-0*) Bowker-Saur.

Parry, C. Hubert, jt. auth. see Benoliel, Bernard.

Parry, Caroline. Let's Celebrate! Canada's Special Days. (Illus.). 256p. (J). 1987. pap. 18.95 (*0-921103-40-9*) Kids Can Pr.

Parry, Charles H. The Evolution of the Music. 483p. 1990. reprint ed. lib. bdg. 89.00 (*0-7812-9024-4*) Rprt Serv.

— Johann Sebastian Bach. LC 73-109818. 584p. 1970. reprint ed. lib. bdg. 65.00 (*0-8371-4309-8*, PAJB, Greenwood Pr) Greenwood.

— Johann Sebastian Bach: The Story of the Development of a Great Personality. 1988. reprint ed. lib. bdg. 59.00 (*0-7812-0778-9*) Rprt Serv.

— Style in Musical Art. lib. bdg. 25.00 (*0-403-01752-1*) Scholarly.

— Style in Musical Art. 438p. 1990. reprint ed. lib. bdg. 89.00 (*0-7812-9128-3*) Rprt Serv.

Parry, Christopher. English Through Drama: A Way of Teaching. LC 72-184902. 243p. reprint ed. pap. 69.30 (*0-608-18375-X*, 2026352) Bks Demand.

***Parry, Christopher.** Lending & Securities: A Practical Guide to the Principles of Good Lending. 208p. 1999. pap. 80.00 (*0-85297-510-4*, Pub. by Chartered Bank) St Mut.

Parry, Cindy. Activities That Build Young Women, Vol. 2. 48p. (YA). 1993. pap. 7.98 (*0-88290-457-4*) Horizon Utah.

— Activities That Inspire Young Women, Vol. 1. 48p. 1994. 7.98 (*0-88290-489-2*, 2063) Horizon Utah.

— Activities That Inspire Young Women, Vol. 2. 48p. (YA). 1994. pap. 7.98 (*0-88290-490-6*, 2064) Horizon Utah.

— Young Women Activities: Activities That Build Young Women, Set Vols. 1 & 2. 1994. pap. 14.98 (*0-88290-472-8*) Horizon Utah.

— Young Women Inspirational Activities: Activities That Inspire Young Women, Set, Vols. 1 & 2. 1994. pap. 14.98 (*0-88290-510-4*) Horizon Utah.

Parry, Clarie, jt. ed. see Lano, Kevin.

Parry, Clive M. The Sources & Evidences of International Law. LC 65-17525. (Melland Schill Lectures). 130p. reprint ed. pap. 40.30 (*0-608-14444-4*, 205186800012) Bks Demand.

Parry, Clive M., ed. Consolidated Treaty Series, 1648-1920: Including 12 Index Volumes, 243 vols., Set. annot. ed. LC 70-76750. 1969. text 11595.00 (*0-379-13000-9*) Oceana.

Parry, Clive M. & Hopkins, John A., eds. Commonwealth International Law Cases, 19 vols., Set. LC 73-20151. 1974. lib. bdg. 1425.00 (*0-379-00950-1*) Oceana.

Parry, Colin & Parry, Wendy. Tim: An Ordinary Boy. (Illus.). 240p. 1995. 29.95 (*0-340-61789-6*, Pub. by Hodder & Stought Ltd) Trafalgar.

Parry, Colleen. Bearing All Seasons. (Illus.). 36p. 1996. 8.99 (*1-58050-072-2*, 40-6083) Provo Craft.

— Bearing All Seasons & Some Bunny Too. (Illus.). 32p. 1998. 9.99 (*1-58050-048-X*, 40-6175) Provo Craft.

— Patchwork Pals. (Illus.). 44p. 1997. 9.99 (*1-58050-011-0*, 40-6133) Provo Craft.

***Parry, Colleen.** Say It with a Lil' Something Special. (Illus.). 44p. 2000. write for info. (*1-58050-092-7*, 40-6213) Provo Craft.

Parry, Danaan. The Essene Book of Days, 2000. 1999. pap. 15.95 (*0-9653808-5-8*) Erthstewards.

***Parry, Danaan.** Essene Book of Days, 2001. 19th ed. (Illus.). 412p. 2000. pap. 15.95 (*0-9653808-6-6*) Erthstewards.

— Essene Book of Days 2002: 20th Anniversary Edition. (Illus.). 414p. 2001. pap. 16.95 (*0-9653808-8-2*) Erthstewards.

Parry, Danaan. Essene Book of Meditations & Blessings. rev. ed. (Illus.). 128p. (Orig.). 1996. pap. 6.95 (*0-913319-17-1*) Erthstewards.

***Parry, Danaan.** Essene Book of Meditations & Blessings. 2nd rev. ed. (Illus.). 144p. (Orig.). 2000. pap. 6.95 (*0-9653808-7-4*) Erthstewards.

Parry, Danaan. Warriors of the Heart. LC 90-70815. (Illus.). 224p. (Orig.). 1991. pap. 9.95 (*0-913319-09-0*) Erthstewards.

— Warriors of the Heart: A Handbook for Conflict Resolution. (Illus.). 190p. (Orig.). Date not set. reprint ed. pap. 12.95 (*0-9653808-2-3*) Erthstewards.

Parry, Danaan & Forest, Lila. Earthsteward's Handbook. rev. ed. LC 88-134579. (Illus.). 160p. (Orig.). 1991. pap. 6.95 (*0-913319-19-8*) Erthstewards.

Parry, David, jt. auth. see Harrison, Bob.

Parry, David A. & Steinert, Peter M. Intermediate Filament Structure. (Molecular Biology Intelligence Unit Ser.). 140p. 1995. text 79.00 (*1-57059-120-2*, LN9120) Landes Bioscience.

Parry, David H. Sancity of Contracts in English Law. (Legal Reprint Ser.). viii, 72p. 1986. reprint ed. 30.00 (*0-8377-2509-7*, Rothman); reprint ed. 20.00 (*0-421-37600-7*) W S Hein.

Parry, David M. Hegel's Phenomonology of the "We" (American University Studies: Philosophy: Ser. V, Vol. 57). X, 272p. (C). 1988. text 39.80 (*0-8204-0733-X*) P Lang Pubng.

— Scarlet Empire. LC 77-154456. (Utopian Literature Ser.). (Illus.). 1976. reprint ed. 33.95 (*0-405-03538-1*) Ayer.

Parry, Deborah L., et al, eds. Butterworths Trading & Consumer Law. ring bd. write for info. (*0-406-99655-5*, BTCLASET, MICHIE) LEXIS Pub.

Parry, Deborah L., jt. auth. see Harvey, Brian W.

Parry, Donald & Parry, Jay. Understanding the Book of Revelation. LC 98-30965. 1998. 19.95 (*1-57345-438-9*) Deseret Bk.

Parry, Donald & Ulrich, Eugene C. The Provo International Conference on the Dead Sea Scrolls: Technological Innovations, New Texts, & Reformulated Issues. LC 98-44346. (Studies on the Texts of the Desert of Judah). 1998. 184.00 (*90-04-11155-7*) Brill Academic Pubs.

Parry, Donald A., jt. ed. see Hinde, Robert A.

Parry, Donald W., ed. Temples of the Ancient World: Ritual & Symbolism. LC 93-36629. xxiv, 805p. 1994. 29.95 (*0-87579-811-X*) Deseret Bk.

***Parry, Donald W. & Parry, Jay A.** Understanding the Signs of the Times. LC 99-43431. 1999. write for info. (*1-57345-588-1*) Deseret Bk.

Parry, Donald W & Qimron, Elisha, eds. The Great Isaiah Scroll: A New Edition. (Studies on the Texts of the Desert of Judah: Ser. 32). 124p. 1998. write for info. (*90-04-11277-4*) Brill Academic Pubs.

Parry, Donald W. & Ricks, Stephen D. A Bibliography on Temples of the Ancient Near East & Mediterranean World: Arranged by Subject & by Author. Welch, John W., ed. LC 91-516. (Ancient Near Eastern Texts & Studies: Vol. 9). 324p. 1991. lib. bdg. 99.95 (*0-7734-9775-7*) E Mellen.

Parry, Donald W. & Ricks, Stephen D., eds. Current Research & Technological Developments on the Dead Sea Scrolls: Conference on the Texts from the Judean Desert, Jerusalem, 30 April 1995. LC 96-26931. (Studies on the Texts of the Desert of Judah: Vol. 20). (Illus.). 287p. 1996. 98.00 (*90-04-10662-6*) Brill Academic Pubs.

***Parry, Donald W. & Ricks, Stephen David.** The Dead Sea Scrolls: Questions & Responses for Latter-Day Saints. LC 00-21497. 2000. pap. write for info. (*0-934893-51-9*, F A R M S) Brigham.

Parry, Donald W. & Welch, John W. Isaiah in the Book of Mormon. LC 97-39238. 1997. write for info. (*0-934893-29-2*, F A R M S) Brigham.

Parry, Donald W., et al. Understanding Isaiah. LC 98-15654. vii, 659 p. 1998. write for info. (*1-57345-361-7*) Deseret Bk.

Parry, Donald W., jt. auth. see Martinez, F. Garcia.

Parry, E. H., ed. Principles of Medicine in Africa. 2nd ed. (Illus.). 1985. 115.00 (*0-19-261337-5*) OUP.

Parry, E. J. Encyclopedia of Perfumery, 2 vols., Set. 1992. lib. bdg. 1500.75 (*0-8490-5418-4*) Gordon Pr.

Parry, Edward. The Bloody Assize. 301p. 1998. reprint ed. 95.00 (*1-56169-423-1*) Gaunt.

Parry, Edward. Drama of the Law. 317p. 1996. 75.00 (*1-56169-223-9*) Gaunt.

Parry, Edward A. The Overbury Mystery: A Chronicle of Fact & Drama of the Law. LC 71-174850. 1972. reprint ed. 22.95 (*0-405-08835-3*) Ayer.

— Seven Lamps of Advocacy. LC 68-16965. (Essay Index Reprint Ser.). 1977. reprint ed. 17.95 (*0-8369-0773-6*) Ayer.

— Vagabonds All. LC 73-93370. (Essay Index Reprint Ser.). 1977. 23.95 (*0-8369-1425-2*) Ayer.

— What the Judge Thought. LC 68-29237. (Essay Index Reprint Ser.). 1977. 20.95 (*0-8369-0772-8*) Ayer.

Parry, Ellwood C., III. The Art of Thomas Cole: Ambition & Imagination. LC 85-40511. (Illus.). 424p. 1989. 95.00 (*0-87413-214-2*) U Delaware Pr.

Parry, Ellwood C. Friedrich Schiller in America. 1976. lib. bdg. 59.95 (*0-8490-1866-8*) Gordon Pr.

Parry, Eugenia. Crime Album Stories. (Illus.). 319p. 2000. 45.00 (*3-908247-18-7*, Pub. by Scalo Pubs) Dist Art Pubs.

Parry, Evelyn P. On the Yaquina & Big Elk. (Illus.). (Orig.). 1985. pap. text 9.95 (*0-911443-07-X*) Lincoln Coun Hist.

— Pictorial Toledo, Oregon: Then & Now. LC 83-81298. (Illus.). 97p. (Orig.). 1983. pap. 9.95 (*0-911443-01-0*) Lincoln Coun Hist.

Parry, G. Trilingual Cotton Terminologie: Terminologie Cotonniere Trilingue. (ENG, FRE & SPA.). 87p. 1986. pap. 34.95 (*0-8288-0039-1*, M15818) Fr & Eur.

Parry, Gareth J. Guillain-Barre Syndrome. LC 92-49287. 208p. 1992. 62.00 (*0-86577-444-7*) Thieme Med Pubs.

Parry, Geraint. Political Elites. (Studies in Political Science). 1969. pap. text 15.95 (*0-04-320059-1*) Routledge.

Parry, Geraint, ed. Politics in an Interdependent World: Essays Presented to Ghita Ionescu. LC 93-42473. 208p. 1994. text 90.00 (*1-85278-737-6*) E Elgar.

Parry, Geraint & Moran, Michael, eds. Democracy & Democratization. LC 93-725. 256p. (C). 1994. pap. 27.99 (*0-415-09050-4*, B2441) Routledge.

Parry, Geraint, et al. Freedom & Trade. LC 97-28941. 328p. (C). 1998. 85.00 (*0-415-15525-8*) Routledge.

Parry, Glyn. Scooter Boy. 1998. pap. 12.95 (*0-7022-2990-3*, Pub. by Univ Queensland Pr) Intl Spec Bk.

Parry, Graham. The Seventeenth Century, the Intellectual & Cultural Context of English Literature, 1603-1700. (Literature in English Ser.). 286p. (Orig.). (C). 1989. pap. 41.40 (*0-582-49376-5*, 73590) Longman.

— The Trophies of Time: English Antiquarians of the Seventeenth Century. (Illus.). 394p. 1996. text 85.00 (*0-19-812962-9*) OUP.

Parry, Gwyn. Crossings. 96p. 1998. pap. 15.95 (*1-897648-35-9*, Pub. by Salmon Poetry) Dufour.

Parry, Herbert B. Scrapie Disease in Sheep: Historical, Clinical, Epidemiological, Pathological & Practical Aspects of the Natural Disease. 1984. text 104.00 (*0-12-545750-2*) Acad Pr.

Parry, Hildegarde W., tr. see Leipp, Emile.

Parry, J. H. The Age of Reconnaissance: Discovery, Exploration, & Settlement, 1450-1650. LC 81-51175. (Illus.). 400p. 1982. pap. 16.95 (*0-520-04235-2*, Pub. by U CA Pr) Cal Prin Full Svc.

— The Audiencia of New Galicia in the Sixteenth Century: A Study in Spanish Colonial Government. LC 85-10039. (Illus.). 205p. 1985. reprint ed. lib. bdg. 59.75 (*0-313-24957-1*, PANG, Greenwood Pr) Greenwood.

— Europa y la Expansion Del Mundo. (Breviarios Ser.). (SPA.). pap. 8.99 (*968-16-0716-3*, Pub. by Fondo) Continental Bk.

— Offences Against Property. (Criminal Law Library: Vol. 7). 464p. 1989. 100.00 (*0-08-033070-3*) Macmillan.

— The Spanish Seaborne Empire. 417p. 1990. pap. 16.95 (*0-520-07140-9*, Pub. by U CA Pr) Cal Prin Full Svc.

Parry, J. H., et al, eds. Geomagnetism & Palaeomagnetism. (C). 1988. text 206.50 (*0-7923-0084-X*) Kluwer Academic.

Parry, J. T., jt. ed. see Eden, M. J.

Parry, James N. Parry: Legal Aid in Criminal Proceedings. 1996. pap. write for info. (*0-406-04605-0*, CPPG, MICHIE) LEXIS Pub.

Parry, Jay, jt. auth. see Hanks, Kurt.

Parry, Jay, jt. auth. see Parry, Donald.

Parry, Jay A. Soldiers, Statesman & Heroes: America's Founding Presidents. LC 88-21146. (Illus.). 250p. 1990. 15.95 (*0-88080-027-5*) Natl Ctr Constit.

— Traveling with Kids - 101 Tips for a Great Trip. (Illus.). 193p. 1989. pap. text 9.95 (*0-944803-69-5*) Brite Music.

Parry, Jay A. & Allison, Andrew M. The Real George Washington. LC 90-5607. (American Classic Ser.). (Illus.). 928p. 1990. 24.95 (*0-88080-013-5*); pap. 19.95 (*0-88080-014-3*) Natl Ctr Constit.

Parry, Jay A., jt. auth. see Lewis, C. S.

Parry, Jay A., jt. auth. see Parry, Donald W.

Parry, Jay A., jt. auth. see Price, Alvin H.

Parry, Jo-Ann & Hornsby, David. Write On: A Conference Approach to Writing. LC 87-22929. 92p. (Orig.). (C). 1988. pap. text 18.50 (*0-435-08460-7*, 08460) Heinemann.

Parry, Joan & Freudenberg, Marie. Creativity Doesn't Die. Costa, Gwen, ed. LC 91-33875. 1990. pap. 13.95 (*0-87949-337-2*) Ashley Bks.

An Asterisk (*) at the beginning of an entry indicates that the title is appearing for the first time.

***Parry, Joan K.** Social Work Theory & Practice with the Terminally Ill. 2nd ed. LC 00-38318. 278p. (C). 2000. 49.95 (*0-7890-1082-8*); pap. text 24.95 (*0-7890-1083-6*) Haworth Pr.

Parry, Joan K., ed. From Prevention to Wellness Through Group Work. LC 96-48820. 180p. 1997. 49.95 (*0-7890-0164-0*) Haworth Pr.

— Social Work Theory & Practice with the Terminally Ill. LC 88-29623. (Social Work Practice Ser.: No. 3). (Illus.). 130p. 1989. 39.95 (*0-86656-750-X*) Haworth Pr.

— Social Work Theory & Practice with the Terminally Ill. LC 88-29623. 130p. 1996. pap. 14.95 (*0-7890-0084-9*) Haworth Pr.

Parry, Joan K. & Ryan, Angela S., eds. A Cross-Cultural Look at Death, Dying, & Religion. LC 94-42941. (Nelson-Hall Series in Social Work). 251p. 1995. pap. text 37.95 (*0-8304-1333-2*) Thomson Learn.

Parry, John. The Americans with Disabilities Act Manual State & Local Government Services, Employment, & Public Accommodations. 111p. (Orig.). (C). 1992. pap. 13.95 (*0-89707-801-2*) ABA Prof Educ Pubns.

Parry, John & Keith, Robert G., eds. New Iberian World: A Documentary History of the Discovery & Settlement of Latin America to the Early 17th. Century, 5 vols., Set. LC 82-19664. (New Iberian World Ser.). 2912p. 1988. text 250.00 (*0-8240-4839-3*) Garland.

Parry, John, et al. National Benchbook on Psychiatric & Psychological Evidence & Testimony. LC 99-185195. 1998. write for info. (*1-57073-581-6*) Amer Bar Assn.

Parry, John T., jt. ed. see Eden, Michael J.

Parry, John W., ed. Mental Disabilities & the Americans with Disabilities Act. 2nd ed. LC 97-207758. 144p. 1997. pap. 40.00 (*1-57073-462-3*, 441-0080) Amer Bar Assn.

Parry, John W., ed. see Owens, Sabra.

Parry, Jonathan. Rise & Fall of Liberal Government in Victorian Britain. 1996. pap. text 20.00 (*0-300-06718-6*) Yale U Pr.

Parry, Jonathan. The Rise Fall of Liberal Government in Victorian Britain. LC 93-5937. 392p. 1994. 50.00 (*0-300-05779-2*) Yale U Pr.

Parry, Jonathan P. Death in Banaras. LC 93-31990. (Lewis Henry Morgan Lectures: No. 1990). (Illus.). 340p. (C). 1995. pap. text 26.95 (*0-521-46625-3*) Cambridge U Pr.

***Parry, Jonathan P., et al.** The Worlds of Indian Industrial Labour. LC 99-46951. (Contributions to Indian Sociology Ser.). 1999. write for info. (*0-7619-9395-9*) Sage.

Parry, Jonathan P., jt. ed. see Bloch, Maruice.

Parry, Jonathan P., jt. ed. see Bloch, Maurice.

Parry, Jonathan P., jt. ed. see Guha, Ramachandra.

Parry-Jones, D. Welsh Legends & Folklore. 1972. 59.95 (*0-8490-1282-1*) Gordon Pr.

Parry-Jones, Jemima. Amazing Birds of Prey. LC 92-909. (Eyewitness Juniors Ser.: No. 24). (Illus.). 32p. (J). (ps-3). 1992. pap. 9.99 (*0-679-82771-4*, Pub. by Knopf Bks Yng Read); lib. bdg. 11.99 (*0-679-92771-9*, Pub. by Knopf Bks Yng Read) Random.

***Parry-Jones, Jemima.** Eagle & Birds of Prey. (Eyewitness Books). (Illus.). (J). (gr. 4-7). 2000. 19.99 (*0-7894-6618-X*) DK Pub Inc.

— Really Useful Owl Guide. (Illus.). 1999. 6.95 (*1-85279-125-X*) TFH Pubns.

Parry-Jones, Jemima. Understanding Owls. (Illus.). 120p. 1998. 29.95 (*0-7153-0643-X*) Sterling.

Parry, Julie. Induction: Library Training Guide. 64p. 1993. pap. 35.00 (*1-85604-078-X*, LAP078X, Pub. by Library Association) Bernan Associates.

***Parry, Karima.** Antiquing on the Internet. (Illus.). 128p. 2000. pap. 12.95 (*1-57432-169-2*) Collector Bks.

— Bakelite Bangle Price & Identification Guide. LC 99-60505. (Illus.). 144p. 1999. pap. 24.95 (*0-87341-809-3*) Krause Pubns.

Parry, Ken. The American Winemakers Cookbook. (Illus.). 200p. (Orig.). 1995. pap. 13.95 (*1-886026-03-3*) Wine Grape.

Parry, Ken, ed. The California Winemaker's Cook Book. 180p. 1994. pap. text 13.95 (*1-886026-00-9*) Wine Grape.

— The Italian Winemaker's Cook Book. 180p. 1996. pap. text 13.95 (*1-886026-02-5*) Wine Grape.

— The Winemaker's Cook Book. 125p. 1993. pap. text 9.95 (*1-886026-01-7*) Wine Grape.

Parry, Kenneth. Depicting the Word: Byzantine Iconophile Thought of the Eighth & Ninth Centuries. LC 96-27351. (Medieval Mediterranean Ser.). x, 216p. 1996. 93.00 (*90-04-10502-6*) Brill Academic Pubs.

Parry, L. Jesus Hace Amigos.Tr. of Jesus Makes Friends. (SPA.). (J). 1.99 (*0-7899-0537-X*, 495666) Editorial Unilit.

— Jesus Llama a Sus Discipulos.Tr. of Jesus Calls His Disciples. (SPA.). (J). 1.99 (*0-7899-0538-8*, 495665) Editorial Unilit.

Parry, L. The Victoria & Albert Museum's Textile Collection Vol. 4: British Textiles from 1850 to 1900. (Illus.). 1993. pap. 36.00 (*1-85177-127-1*, Pub. by V&A Ent) Antique Collect.

Parry, L. & Parry, A. Maravilloso Jesus!Tr. of Wonderful Jesus!. (SPA.). 5p. (J). 1995. 9.99 (*1-56063-719-6*, 498749) Editorial Unilit.

— Siguiendo la Estrella Actividades.Tr. of Follow the Star Activity Book. (SPA.). (J). 9.99 (*1-56063-834-6*, 497746) Editorial Unilit.

Parry, Leonard A. History of Torture in England: With Intro. & Index Added. LC 74-172590. (Criminology, Law Enforcement, & Social Problems Ser.: No. 180). 1975. 30.00 (*0-87585-180-0*) Patterson Smith.

— Some Famous Medical Trials. LC 74-95631. x, 326p. 1976. reprint ed. 45.00 (*0-678-03754-X*) Kelley.

Parry, Leonard A., ed. Trial of Dr. Smethurst, No. 1. (Notable British Trials Ser.). xiii, 259p. 1995. reprint ed. 82.00 (*1-56169-136-4*) Gaunt.

***Parry, Linda.** The Beatitudes. LC 99-74438. (Prayers with Bears Ser.). (Illus.). 16p. (J). (ps). 1999. bds. 3.99 (*0-8499-5977-2*) Tommy Nelson.

Parry, Linda. Bible Brainteasers NT. (J). 1996. 3.50 (*1-56476-574-1*, 6-3574) Chariot Victor.

— Bible Brainteasers OT. (J). 1996. 3.50 (*1-56476-573-3*, 6-3573) Chariot Victor.

— Blossom's Prize. (Honey-Bear Farm Ser.). (Illus.). 28p. (J). 1998. pap. 4.99 (*0-8054-1790-7*) Broadman.

— Bramble Forgets. (Honey-Bear Farm Ser.). (Illus.). 28p. (J). 1998. pap. 4.99 (*0-8054-1791-5*) Broadman.

— Christmas Countdown. (Illus.). 16p. 1999. pap. 6.99 (*0-8054-1896-2*) Broadman.

***Parry, Linda.** First Corinthians 13. LC 99-74437. (Prayers with Bears Ser.). (Illus.). 16p. (J). (ps). 1999. bds. 3.99 (*0-8499-5976-4*) Tommy Nelson.

Parry, Linda. Jesus Calls His Disciples. (Illus.). 12p. (J). 1998. pap. text 2.99 (*0-8054-1786-9*) Broadman.

— Jesus Makes Friends. (Illus.). 12p. (J). 1998. pap. text 2.99 (*0-8054-1787-7*) Broadman.

***Parry, Linda.** The Lord's Prayer. LC 99-74439. (Prayers with Bears Ser.). (Illus.). 16p. (J). (ps). 1999. 3.99 (*0-8499-5970-5*) Tommy Nelson.

Parry, Linda. Mary's Story. LC 98-215204. (Illus.). 24p. (J). (ps-2). 1998. 12.99 (*0-8010-4359-X*) Baker Bks.

— My First Little Bible Story Book. LC 95-48118. (Illus.). 200p. (J). 1996. 3.00 (*1-57312-035-9*) Smyth & Helwys.

— The Picnic. (Honey-Bear Farm Ser.). 28p. 1998. pap. 4.99 (*0-8054-1789-3*) Broadman.

— Textiles of the Arts & Crafts Movement. LC 87-51290. (Illus.). 200p. 1988. pap. 22.50 (*0-500-27497-5*, Pub. by Thames Hudson) Norton.

***Parry, Linda.** The 23rd Psalm. LC 99-74440. (Prayers with Bears Ser.). (Illus.). 16p. (J). (ps). 1999. bds. 3.99 (*0-8499-5978-0*) Tommy Nelson.

Parry, Linda. Where's Pipkin? (Honey-Bear Farm Ser.). (Illus.). 28p. (J). 1998. pap. 4.99 (*0-8054-1788-5*) Broadman.

Parry, Linda, ed. William Morris. LC 95-51845. (Illus.). 394p. 1996. 60.00 (*0-8109-4282-8*, Pub. by Abrams) Time Warner.

— William Morris: Art & Kelmscott. (Occasional Papers: Vol. 18). (Illus.). 164p. 1996. pap. 29.95 (*0-85115-670-3*, Boydell Pr) Boydell & Brewer.

Parry, Linda, jt. auth. see Parry, Alan.

Parry, M. L., et al. The Impact of Climatic Variations on Agriculture, Vol. 1: Assessments in Cool Temperate & Cold Regions. (C). 1988. lib. bdg. 197.00 (*90-277-2700-7*) Kluwer Academic.

— The Impact of Climatic Variations on Agriculture, Vol. 2: Assessments in Semi-Arid Regions. (C). 1988. lib. bdg. 180.50 (*90-277-2719-8*) Kluwer Academic.

Parry, M. M., et al, eds. The Changing Voices of Europe: Social & Political Changes & Their Linguistic Repercussions, Past, Present & Future. xviii, 335p. 1994. write for info. (*0-7083-1259-4*, Pub. by Univ Wales Pr) Paul & Co Pubs.

Parry, Mair, jt. ed. see Maiden, Martin.

Parry, Marian. City Mouse - Country Mouse & Two More Mouse Tales from Aesop: Big Book. (J). (gr. 2-3). 1989. 28.67 (*0-590-65228-1*) Scholastic Inc.

Parry, Martin. Climate Change World Economy. 1999. 24.95 (*1-85383-109-3*, Pub. by Escan Pubns) Island Pr.

Parry, Martin & Carter, Timothy. Climate Impact & Adaptation Assessment: The IPCC Method. 192p. 1997. 70.00 (*1-85383-271-5*, Pub. by Escan Pubns); pap. 30.00 (*1-85383-266-9*, Pub. by Escan Pubns) Island Pr.

Parry, Martin & Duncan, R. Economic Implications Climate Change Brit. 1995. 30.00 (*1-85383-240-5*, Pub. by Escan Pubns) Island Pr.

Parry, Melanie, ed. Chambers Biographical Dictionary. 2016p. 1997. 55.00 (*0-550-16060-4*) LKC.

— Larousse Dictionary of Women. (Illus.). 608p. 1996. 40.00 (*0-7523-0015-6*, Larousse LKC) LKC.

Parry, Michael. Harrap's Arabic Phrase Book. 1993. pap. 4.00 (*0-671-84765-1*, Harraps IN) Macmillan Gen Ref.

Parry, Millman. Serbocroation Heroic Songs Vol. III: Wedding of Smailagic Meho. Lord, Albert B. & Bynum, David E., eds. & trs. by. Vol. 1. 338p. 1974. 22.50 (*0-674-80163-6*) HUP.

Parry, Milman. The Making of Homeric Verse: The Collected Papers of Milman Parry. Parry, Adam M., ed. (Illus.). 552p. 1987. pap. text 35.00 (*0-19-520560-X*) OUP.

— Serbo-Croatian Heroic Songs: Bihacka Krajina: Epics from Bihac, Cazin, & Kulen Vakuf, Vol. 4. Bynum, David E., ed. (Milman Parry Collection, Texts & Translation Ser.). (Illus.). 529p. (C). 1980. 22.50 (*0-674-80165-2*) HUP.

***Parry, Nigel.** Sharp. 2000. 50.00 (*1-57687-088-X*) pwerHse Cultrl.

Parry, Owen. Faded Coat of Blue. LC 99-25523. 352p. 1999. 23.00 (*0-380-97642-0*, Avon Bks) Morrow Avon.

***Parry, Owen.** Faded Coat of Blue. 368p. 2000. mass mkt. 6.99 (*0-380-79739-9*) Morrow Avon.

— Shadows of Glory. 320p. 2000. 24.00 (*0-380-97643-9*, Wm Morrow) Morrow Avon.

***Parry, Pam.** Bottom Line: How to Build a Business Case for ISO 14001. LC 99-40302. 216p. 1999. per. 39.95 (*1-57444-249-X*) St Lucie Pr.

— Citizens of Two Kingdoms: Lessons for Youth in Baptist History & Religious Liberty. 48p. 1996. pap. 5.00 (*1-57312-151-7*) Smyth & Helwys.

Parry, Pam. On Guard for Religious Liberty: Six Decades of the Baptist Joint Committee. LC 96-31881. (Illus.). 96p. 1996. pap. 9.00 (*1-57312-090-1*) Smyth & Helwys.

Parry, Pamela J., compiled by. Contemporary Art & Artists: An Index to Reproductions. LC 78-57763. 327p. 1978. lib. bdg. 65.00 (*0-313-20544-2*, PCO/, Greenwood Pr) Greenwood.

— Photography Index: A Guide to Reproductions. LC 78-26897. 372p. 1979. lib. bdg. 42.95 (*0-313-20700-3*, PPI/, Greenwood Pr) Greenwood.

Parry, Pamela J. & Chipman, Kathe, compiled by. Print Index: A Guide to Reproductions, 4. LC 83-12824. (Art Reference Collection Ser.: No. 4). 310p. 1983. lib. bdg. 65.00 (*0-313-22063-8*, PPR/, Greenwood Pr) Greenwood.

Parry, Philip, jt. auth. see Bloy, Duncan.

Parry, R. B. & Perkins, C. R. Mapping the U. K. 448p. 1996. 210.00 (*1-85739-030-X*) Bowker-Saur.

Parry, R. B., jt. ed. see Perkins, C. R.

Parry, R. H., ed. The English Civil War & After, 1642-1658. LC 74-111423. (C). 1970. pap. 15.95 (*0-520-01783-8*, Pub. by U CA Pr) Cal Prin Full Svc.

Parry, R. H., jt. auth. see Fookes, P. G.

Parry, R. H. G. MOHR Circles, Stress Paths & Geotechnics. LC 95-143362. (Illus.). 256p. (C). 1995. 110.00 (*0-419-19290-5*, E & FN Spon) Routledge.

***Parry, Richard.** That Fateful Lightning. 368p. 2000. 24.95 (*0-345-42728-9*) Ballantine Pub Grp.

Parry, Richard. The Winter Wolf: Wyatt Earp in Alaska. 1998. pap. text 6.99 (*0-8125-4946-5*, Pub. by Forge NYC) St Martin.

— The Winter Wolf: Wyatt Earp in Alaska. LC 96-18269. 384p. 1996. text 24.95 (*0-312-86017-X*) St Martin.

— The Wolf's Cub. 1999. mass mkt. 6.99 (*0-8125-4947-3*, Pub. by Forge NYC) St Martin.

— The Wolf's Cub. LC 97-13268. 384p. 1997. text 23.95 (*0-312-86018-8*) St Martin.

— The Wolf's Pack. LC 98-23448. 336p. 1998. 24.95 (*0-312-86020-X*, Pub. by Forge NYC) St Martin.

Parry, Richard, ed. Privatisation. (Research Highlights in Social Work Ser.: Vol. 18). 128p. 1990. 37.95 (*1-85302-015-X*, Pub. by Jessica Kingsley) Taylor & Francis.

Parry, Richard, jt. auth. see Deakin, Nicholas.

Parry, Richard, jt. ed. see Brown, Alice.

Parry, Richard D. Plato's Craft of Justice. LC 95-3471. (SUNY Series in Ancient Greek Philosophy). 268p. (C). 1995. text 57.50 (*0-7914-2731-5*); pap. text 18.95 (*0-7914-2732-3*) State U NY Pr.

***Parry, Richard LLoyd.** Japan-3 Cities: Tokyo, Kyoto & Ancient Nara: 3 Cities: Tokyo, Kyoto & Ancient Nara. 2nd ed. (Cadogan Guides Ser.). 512p. 1999. pap. text 22.95 (*1-86011-917-4*) Cadgn Bks.

Parry, Robert. In Defense of Astrology: Astrology's Answers to Its Critics. LC 91-16850. (Illus.). 224p. 1999. reprint ed. pap. 9.95 (*0-87542-596-8*) Llewellyn Pubns.

— Lost History: Contras, Cocaine, the Press & 'Project Truth' unabridged ed. 300p. 1999. pap. 19.95 (*1-893517-00-4*) Media Consort.

— Tai Chi Made Easy: Step-By-Step Guide to Health & Relaxation. LC 96-37162. (Illus.). 144p. 1997. 16.95 (*1-882606-25-6*) Peoples Med Soc.

— Trick or Treason: The October Surprise Mystery. 380p. 1993. 24.95 (*1-879823-08-X*) Sheridan Sq Pr.

Parry, Robert W., Jr., jt. auth. see Heintz, James A.

Parry, Scott B. Evaluating the Impact of Training: A Collection of Tools & Techniques. LC 97-74234. viii, 216p. 1997. write for info. (*1-56286-063-1*) Am Soc Train & Devel.

— From Managing to Empowering: An Action Guide to Developing Winning Facilitation Skills. LC 93-47184. (Illus.). 184p. 1994. pap. 22.50 (*0-527-76232-6*) Productivity Inc.

***Parry, Scott B.** Training for Results: Key Tools & Techniques to Sharpen Trainer's Skills. LC 99-68258. 298p. 2000. pap. 45.95 (*1-56286-132-8*) Am Soc Train & Devel.

Parry, Steve, jt. auth. see Foley, Eugene.

Parry, Susan J. Activation Spectrometry in Chemical Analysis. LC 91-12496. (Chemical Analysis: A Series of Monographs on Analytical Chemistry & Its Applications: No. 1075). 264p. 1991. 129.00 (*0-471-63844-7*) Wiley.

Parry, Terrence & Gregory, Gayle. Designing Brain-Compatible Learning. LC 98-60720. 288p. 1998. pap. 45.00 (*1-57517-042-6*, 1595) SkyLght.

Parry, Thomas G. The Multinational Enterprise: International Investment & Host-Country Impacts. Altman, Edward I. & Walter, Ingo I., eds. LC 77-24394. (Contemporary Studies in Economic & Financial Analysis: Vol. 20). 225p. 1980. 78.50 (*0-89232-092-3*) Jai Pr.

Parry, Virginia, ed. see Ford, Raymond W.

Parry, Vivienne. The Antenatal Testing Handbook: The Complete Guide to Testing in Pregnancy. 232p. 1998. pap. text 12.00 (*0-7881-5808-2*) DIANE Pub.

Parry, W. E., ed. Essays in Theoretical Physics: In Honor of Dirk ter Haar. (Illus.). 352p. 1984. 151.00 (*0-08-026523-5*, Pub. by Pergamon Repr) Franklin.

Parry, Wendy, jt. auth. see Parry, Colin.

***Parry, William D.** Understanding & Controlling Stuttering Vol. 2: A Comprehensive New Approach Based on the Valsalva Hypothesis. 2nd rev. ed. (Illus.). 166p. 2000. pap. write for info. (*1-929773-01-3*) Natl Stutter.

Parry, William E. Journal of Voyage of Discovery to Arctic Regions. (Shorey Historical Ser.). 118p. reprint ed. pap. 10.00 (*0-8466-0046-3*, S46) Shoreys Bkstore.

Parry, William J. Chipped Stone Tools in Formative Oaxaca, Mexico: Their Procurement, Production & Use. (Memoirs Series, Prehistory & Human Ecology of the Valley of Oaxaca: No. 20, Vol. 8). (Illus.). xvi, 178p. (Orig.). 1987. pap. 18.00 (*0-915703-10-6*) U Mich Mus Anthro.

Parry, William J. & Christenson, Andrew L. Prehistoric Stone Technology on Northern Black Mesa, Arizona. LC 87-72676. (Center for Archaeological Investigations Occasional Paper Ser.: No. 12). (Illus.). xx, 312p. (Orig.). 1988. pap. 23.00 (*0-88104-052-5*) Center Archaeol.

Parry, William J. & Speth, John D. The Garnsey Spring Campsite: Late Prehistoric Occupation in Southeastern New Mexico. (Technical Reports Ser.: No. 15). (Illus.). 228p. (Orig.). 1984. pap. text 8.00 (*0-932206-99-9*) U Mich Mus Anthro.

Parry, William J., jt. auth. see Speth, John D.

Parry, William J., jt. ed. see Christenson, Andrew L.

***Parry, William T., ed.** ASME International Steam Tables for Industrial Use. 286p. 2000. 75.00 (*0-7918-0154-3*) ASME.

Parry, William T., jt. auth. see Wilson, Paula N.

Parry-Wingfield, Maurice, jt. auth. see Davey, Nigel.

Parrya. Where Is Jesus. 1998. 9.99 (*0-8423-8024-8*, 859994) Tyndale Hse.

Pars, L. A. Introduction to Dynamics. LC 54-354. 523p. reprint ed. pap. 149.10 (*0-608-30893-5*, 2051462) Bks Demand.

— A Treatise on Analytical Dynamics. LC 79-87498. 1979. reprint ed. 95.00 (*0-918024-07-2*) Ox Bow.

***Parsa, Ali A.** Global Hypocrisy & the Dawning of Neo-Slavery: The Unprecedented Assault of Hypocrisy & Moral Famine on Education & Democracy LC 98-91358. 144p. 1998. write for info. (*0-9663361-1-9*) A A Parsa.

Parsa, Misagh. Social Origins of the Iranian Revolution. LC 88-31285. (Social Foundations of the Policy Process Ser.). 256p. (C). 1989. pap. text 17.95 (*0-8135-1412-6*) Rutgers U Pr.

***Parsa, Misagh.** States, Ideologies, & Social Revolutions: A Comparative Analysis of Iran, Nicaragua, & the Philippines. LC 99-87457. (Illus.). 327p. 2000. write for info. (*0-521-77337-7*); pap. write for info. (*0-521-77430-6*) Cambridge U Pr.

Parsa-Stay, Flora. The Complete Book of Dental Remedies: A Guide to Safe & Effective Relief to the Most Common Dental Problems Using Homemopathy, Nutritional Supplements, Herbs, & Conventional Dental Care. LC 95-9682. (Illus.). 220p. pap. 15.95 (*0-89529-657-8*, Avery) Penguin Putnam.

Parsa, Zohreh, ed. Beam Stability & Nonlinear Dynamics: Proceedings on the Conference Held in Santa Barbara, 1996. LC 97-74676. (Conference Proceedings Ser.: Vol. 405). (Illus.). 240p. 1997. 80.00 (*1-56396-731-6*) Am Inst Physics.

— Future High Energy Colliders. LC 97-73333. (AIP Conference Proceedings Ser.: Vol. 397). (Illus.). ix, 368p. 1997. 110.00 (*1-56396-729-4*) Am Inst Physics.

— New Modes of Particle Acceleration - Techniques & Sources: Proceedings of a Conference Held in Santa Barbara, CA, 1996. LC 97-72977. (AIP Conference Proceedings Ser.: Vol. 396). (Illus.). 201p. 1997. 70.00 (*1-56396-728-6*) Am Inst Physics.

Parsaei, Hamid R. & Jamshidi, Mohammad, eds. Design & Implementation of Intelligent Manufacturing Systems: From Expert Systems, Neural Networks, to Fuzzy Logic. LC 95-4068. (Environmental & Intelligent Manufacturing Systems Ser.). (C). 1995. text 75.00 (*0-13-192030-8*) P-H.

Parsaei, Hamid R., jt. ed. see Sarkis, Joseph.

Parsan, Elizabeth. South-South Trade in Global Development. 193p. 1993. 72.95 (*1-85628-432-8*, Pub. by Avebury Technical) Ashgate Pub Co.

— South-South Trade Options & Development. 1991. text 59.00 (*0-86187-163-4*) St Martin.

Parsaye, Kamran & Chignell, Marc. Expert Systems for Experts. 462p. 1988. pap. 29.95 (*0-471-60721-5*) Wiley.

Parsaye, Kamran & Chignell, Mark. Intelligent Database Tools & Applications: Hyperinformation Access, Data Quality, Visualization, Automatic Discovery. LC 92-33080. 560p. 1993. 74.99 (*0-471-57065-6*); pap. 34.95 (*0-471-57066-4*) Wiley.

Parsaye, Kamran, et al. Intelligent Databases: Object Oriented, Deductive Hypermedia Technologies. LC 88-33948. 496p. 1989. pap. 39.95 (*0-471-50345-2*) Wiley.

Parscoe, G. & Foster-Lynam, Craig. Sand - Small Book. 8p. (J). 1987. 3.95 (*0-88679-554-0*) Educ Insights.

— Sand - Tall Book. 8p. (J). 1987. 19.95 (*0-88679-553-2*) Educ Insights.

Parscoe, G., jt. auth. see Kenneth, David.

Parse, Rosemarie R. Hope: An International Human Becoming Perspective. LC 98-43151. (National League for Nursing Ser.). 303p. 1998. 39.95 (*0-7637-0958-1*) Jones & Bartlett.

— The Human Becoming School of Thought. LC 98-8893. 130p. 1998. 51.00 (*0-7619-0582-0*); pap. 24.50 (*0-7619-0583-9*) Sage.

— Nursing Science: Major Paradigms, Theories & Critiques. (Illus.). 224p. 1987. text 48.00 (*0-7216-1803-0*, W B Saunders Co) Harcrt Hlth Sci Grp.

Parse, Rosemarie R., ed. Illuminations: The Human Becoming Theory in Practice & Research. 1995. 35.95 (*0-88737-637-1*) Natl League Nurse.

***Parse, Rosemarie Rizzo & NLN Staff.** Hope: An International Human Becoming Perspective. (Illus.). 256p. (C). 1999. pap. text 32.50 (*0-7637-0976-X*) JB Pubns.

— Illuminations: A Human Becoming Theory. (Illus.). 424p. (C). 1999. pap. text 32.50 (*0-7637-1110-1*) JB Pubns.

Parsekian, Penny, jt. ed. see Kushigian, Julia A.

Parsell, Cheryl. Best of the Best: An Astrology Primer. LC 98-41381. (Illus.). 440p. Date not set. pap. 19.95 (*1-57733-020-X*) B Dolphin Pub.

Parsell, David B. Louis Auchincloss. (United States Authors Ser.: No. 534). 152p. 1988. 21.95 (*0-8057-7516-1*, Twyne) Mac Lib Ref.

P

An Asterisk (*) at the beginning of an entry indicates that the title is appearing for the first time.

— Michel de Ghelderode. (Twayne's World Authors Ser.). 128p. 1993. 24.95 (*0-8057-4303-0*, Twyne) Mac Lib Ref.

— Romain Gary. 1996. 24.95 (*0-8057-4532-7*, Twayne) Mac Lib Ref.

Parsell, Roger, jt. auth. see Breuer, Hans-Peter.

***Parselle, Matt.** Basketball. (Sports Club Ser.). (Illus.). (J). 2000. pap. 4.95 (*1-58728-002-7*) Two Can Pub.

— Basketball. rev. ed. (Sports Club Ser.). (Illus.). (J). 2000. 9.95 (*1-58728-000-0*) Two Can Pub.

Parsenow, Gunter. Swedish & German Economics & Law Dictionary: Fachwoerterbuch Fuer Recht und Wirtschaft. 2nd ed. (GER & SWE.). 520p. 1985. 195.00 (*0-8288-0825-2*, M7399) Fr & Eur.

Parsey, J. M., Jr., ed. see International Conference on Defects in Semiconduct.

Parshall, Brian J., jt. ed. see Haboush, William J.

Parshall, Craig & Parshall, Janet. Tough Faith: Trusting God in Trouble Times. LC 99-21977. 275p. 1999. pap. 10.99 (*1-56507-997-3*) Harvest Hse.

Parshall, Craig, jt. auth. see Parshall, Janet.

Parshall, G. W. Inorganic Syntheses, 15. 298p. 1978. 35.00 (*0-89874-386-9*) Krieger.

Parshall, George W. Homogeneous Catalysis: The Applications & Chemistry of Catalysis by Soluble Transition Metal Complexes. LC 79-27696. (Wiley-Interscience Publications). 254p. reprint ed. pap. 78.80 (*0-7837-2370-9*, 204005600006) Bks Demand.

Parshall, George W. & Ittel, Steven D. Homogeneous Catalysis: The Applications & Chemistry of Catalysis by Soluble Transition Metal Complexes. LC 92-5108. 360p. 1992. 87.95 (*0-471-53829-9*) Wiley.

Parshall, Horace F. Parshall Family, a.d. 870-1913: A Collection of Historical Records & Notes to Accompany of the Parshall Pedigree. (Illus.). 186p. 1996. reprint ed. pap. 29.00 (*0-8328-5418-2*); reprint ed. lib. bdg. 39.00 (*0-8328-5417-4*) Higginson Bk Co.

Parshall, J. C. The History of the Parshall Family from 1066 to the Close of the Nineteenth Century. (Illus.). 309p. 1989. reprint ed. pap. 46.50 (*0-8328-0939-X*); reprint ed. lib. bdg. 54.50 (*0-8328-0938-1*) Higginson Bk Co.

Parshall, James C. Barker Genealogy, Giving the Names & Descendants of Several Ancestors Who Settled in the U. S. Previous to the Declaration of Independence, A. D. 1776. (Illus.). 36p. 1997. reprint ed. pap. 7.00 (*0-8328-7377-2*); reprint ed. lib. bdg. 17.00 (*0-8328-7376-4*) Higginson Bk Co.

***Parshall, Janet & Parshall, Craig.** The Light in the City: Why Christians Must Advance. 264p. 2000. pap. 12.99 (*0-7852-6890-1*) Nelson.

Parshall, Janet, jt. auth. see Parshall, Craig.

***Parshall, Jim & Lamb, Larry.** Applying S88: Batch Control from a User's Perspective. LC 99-42402. (Illus.). 155p. 1999. pap. 50.00 (*1-55617-703-8*) ISA.

Parshall, Karen H. James Joseph Sylvester: Life & Work in Letters. LC 99-176066. (Illus.). 338p. 1998. text 98.00 (*0-19-850391-1*) OUP.

Parshall, Karen H. & Rowe, David E. The Emergence of the American Mathematical Research Community, 1876 to 1900. LC 94-2218. (History of Mathematics Ser.: Vol. 8). 500p. 1994. pap. 39.00 (*0-8218-0907-5*) Am Math.

— The Emergence of the American Mathematical Research Community, 1876-1900: J. J. Sylvester, Felix Klein, & E. H. Moore. LC 94-2218. (History of Mathematics Ser.: Vol. 8). 500p. 1994. 39.00 (*0-8218-9004-2*, HMATH/8) Am Math.

Parshall, Linda B., jt. auth. see Parshall, Peter W.

Parshall, Peter W. & Parshall, Linda B. Art & the Reformation: An Annotated Bibliography. (Reference Books-Reference Publications in Art History). 320p. 1986. 55.00 (*0-8161-8602-2*, G K Hall & Co) Mac Lib Ref.

Parshall, Phil. Inside the Community: Understanding Muslims Through Their Traditions. LC 94-2526. 256p. 1994. pap. 13.99 (*0-8010-7132-1*) Baker Bks.

Parshchikov, Alexei. Blue Vitriol. Chadwick, Cydney, ed. Palmer, Michael et al, trs. from RUS. 64p. 1994. pap. text 9.50 (*1-880713-02-0*) AVEC Bks.

Parshin, A. M. Structure, Strength & Radiation Damage of Corrosion-Resistant Steels & Alloys. LC 96-36371. (Russian Materials Monographs). 388p. 1996. 45.00 (*0-89448-563-6*) Am Nuclear Soc.

Parshin, A. N., et al, eds. Number Theory I: Fundamental Problems, Ideas & Theories. LC 94-46819. (Encyclopaedia of Mathematical Sciences Ser.: Vol. 49).Tr. of Teoriia Chisel 1. (Illus.). 344p. 1995. 107.95 (*0-387-53384-2*) Spr-Verlag.

— Number Theory IV: Transcendental Numbers. Nesterenko, Yu V., tr. from RUS. & contrib. by by. (Encyclopaedia of Mathematical Sciences Ser.: No. 44). (Illus.). 345p. 1997. 95.00 (*3-540-61467-2*) Spr-Verlag.

Parshin, A. N. & Shafarevich, I. R., eds. Algebra Seven: Combinatorial Group Theory. Applications to Geometry. LC 92-13652. (Encyclopedia of Mathematical Sciences Ser.: Vol. 58). 1993. 118.95 (*0-387-54700-2*) Spr-Verlag.

— Algebraic Geometry IV: Linear Algebraic Groups, Invariant Theory. LC 93-13928. (Encyclopedia of Mathematical Sciences Ser.: Vol. 55).Tr. of Algebraicheskaia Geometriia IV. (Illus.). 291p. 1994. 118.95 (*0-387-54682-0*) Spr-Verlag.

— Algebraic Geometry III: Complex Algebraic Varieties. Algebraic Curves & Their Jacobians. (Encyclopaedia of Mathematical Sciences Ser.: Vol. 36). v, 270p. 1998. text 99.95 (*3-540-54681-2*) Spr-Verlag.

— Number Theory I: Fundamental Problems, Ideas & Theories. (Encyclopedia of Mathematical Sciences Ser.: Vol. 49).Tr. of Teoriia Chisel 1. 308p. 1996. 98.00 (*3-540-53384-2*) Spr-Verlag.

Parshin, A. N., ed. see Koch, H.

Parsigian, Elise. The Dynamics of Media Writing. (Communication Textbook Journalism Ser.). 376p. (C). 1992. pap. 39.95 (*0-8058-1131-1*); text 79.95 (*0-8058-1130-3*) L Erlbaum Assocs.

Parsigian, Elise K. Proposal Savvy: A Guide for Journalists, Public Relations, & Advertising Writers. LC 95-41789. 240p. 1996. 45.00 (*0-7619-0026-8*); pap. 21.95 (*0-7619-0027-6*) Sage.

Parsinejad, Iraj. Akhundzadeh As a Modern Literary Critic. (Middle Eastern Ser.: No. 17). (Illus.). 125p. (Orig.). 1986. pap. 9.00 (*0-936665-03-3*) Jahan Bk Co.

Parsippany Historical Society Staff. Parsippany Troy Hills. (Images of America Ser.). 1997. pap. 16.99 (*0-7524-0479-2*) Arcadia Publng.

Parsipur, Shahrnush. Women Without Men: A Novella. Talattof, Kamran & Sharlet, Jocelyn, trs. from PER. LC 98-33981. 150p. 1998. 22.95 (*0-8156-0552-8*) Syracuse U Pr.

Parsky, Larry M. Reading Your Newspaper. 1991. pap. text 13.82 (*0-87694-367-9*) Ed Design Inc.

Parsley, Bonnie M. The Choice Is Yours: A Teenager's Guide to Self-Discovery, Relationships, Values, & Spiritual Growth. 144p. (Orig.). (YA). 1992. pap. 10.00 (*0-671-75046-1*, Fireside) S&S Trade Pap.

— Intelligent Living. (Illus.). 83p. (J). (gr. 5-7). 1995. pap., student ed., wbk. ed. 11.25 (*0-9650838-0-2*) StarBright Pubs.

— Intelligent Living. 78p. 1995. pap., teacher ed. 24.95 (*0-9650838-1-0*) StarBright Pubs.

— Intelligent Living: Activity Book. (Illus.). 97p. (J). 1998. 39.95 (*0-9650838-2-9*) StarBright Pubs.

— Intelligent Living: Parent/Child Program, Parent Manual. 50p. 1998. pap. text 39.95 (*0-9650838-3-7*) StarBright Pubs.

Parsley, Jamie. Cloud. LC 97-32325. 182p. 1997. pap. 14.95 (*0-7734-2823-2*) E Mellen.

— The Loneliness of Blizzards: Poems. LC 94-13799. 64p. 1995. pap. 14.95 (*0-7734-0011-7*, Mellen Poetry Pr) E Mellen.

Parsley, Jamie A. Paper Doves, Falling: Poems. Smith, James C., Jr., ed. LC 91-38890. 48p. (Orig.). 1992. pap. 6.95 (*0-86534-172-9*) Sunstone Pr.

Parsley, Karen & Corrigan, Philomena. A Practical Approach to Quality Improvement. LC 93-36305. 1993. write for info. (*0-412-48360-2*) Chapman & Hall.

— A Practical Approach to Quality Improvement. LC 93-36305. 176p. 1993. pap. 54.25 (*1-56593-236-6*, 0556) Singular Publishing.

— Quality Improvement in Health Care: Putting Evidence into Practice. 2nd ed. (Illus.). 448p. 1999. pap. 37.50 (*0-7487-3355-8*) Standard Pub.

Parsley, R. L. Bulletins of American Paleontology Vol. 58, Issue 259: Revision of the North American Pleurocystitidae (Rhombifera-Cystoidea) 82p. 1970. 4.00 (*0-87710-198-1*) Paleo Res.

— Bulletins of American Paleontology Vol. 100, No. 336: Review of Selected North American Mitrate Stylophorans (Homalozoa: Echinodermata) 57p. 1991. 23.00 (*0-87710-418-2*) Paleo Res.

Parsley, Reed. Meadow Boy. (Illus.). 40p. (J). 1997. 18.00 (*0-9660288-0-5*) Penultimate.

Parsley, Rod. The Answer. 48p. (Orig.). Date not set. 1.00 (*0-614-10666-4*) Wrld Harvest Church.

— The Backside of Calvary: Where Healing Stained the Cross. 107p. 1991. pap. 5.99 (*1-880244-01-2*) Wrld Harvest Church.

— The Best of Both Worlds. 32p. (Orig.). 1986. pap. 0.75 (*0-88144-083-3*) Christian Pub.

— Breakthrough: Power-Packed Quotes from One of the World's Most Dynamic Preachers. LC 97-178851. 160p. 1996. pap. 6.99 (*1-57778-015-9*, AP-015, Pub. by Albury Pub) Appalach Bk Dist.

— Bridge Builders' Bible. 1555p. 1995. pap. text 50.00 (*1-880244-22-5*) Wrld Harvest Church.

— By His Stripes. 48p. (Orig.). Date not set. 1.00 (*0-614-10665-6*) Wrld Harvest Church.

— The Commanded Blessing: Overtaken by God's Provision for a Life Without Lack, Acts 4:34. 212p. (Orig.). 1994. pap. 8.99 (*1-880244-17-9*) Wrld Harvest Church.

— Daily Breakthrough: Daily Devotions to Take You into God's Promise. LC 98-70643. 318p. 1998. 14.99 (*0-88419-522-8*) Creation House.

— The Day Before Eternity: The End of the Age May Be Closer Than You Think. LC 98-45970. 208p. 1998. 17.99 (*0-88419-574-0*) Creation House.

— Financial Abundance: What God Opens No Man Can Close. 32p. (Orig.). 1992. pap. 1.00 (*1-880244-05-5*) Wrld Harvest Church.

— Free at Last. 144p. (Orig.). 1994. pap. 7.99 (*1-880244-18-7*) Wrld Harvest Church.

— God's Answer to Insufficient Funds. 96p. (Orig.). 1992. pap. 5.99 (*0-89274-626-2*, HH-626) Harrison Hse.

— God's Answer to Insufficient Funds. 94p. (Orig.). 1992. pap. 5.99 (*1-880244-06-3*) Wrld Harvest Church.

— Holiness: Living Leaven Free. 288p. (Orig.). 1993. 11.99 (*0-89274-681-5*, HH-681) Harrison Hse.

— Holiness: Living Leaven Free. 273p. (Orig.). 1993. pap. 11.99 (*1-880244-11-X*) Wrld Harvest Church.

— I See an Underground Church. 61p. (Orig.). 1986. pap. 4.00 (*0-88144-067-1*) Christian Pub.

— If God Hadn't Wanted to Heal You, He Shouldn't Have! 48p. (Orig.). 1992. pap. 1.00 (*1-880244-04-7*) Wrld Harvest Church.

— I'm Glad You Asked: Biblical Answers to Some of Life's Toughest Questions. 114p. (Orig.). 1993. pap. text 10.00 (*1-880244-12-8*) Wrld Harvest Church.

— My Promise Is the Palace: So What Am I Doing in the Pit? 155p. (Orig.). 1993. pap. 8.99 (*1-880244-14-4*) Wrld Harvest Church.

— New Direction. 41p. (Orig.). 1994. pap. 1.00 (*1-880244-16-0*) Wrld Harvest Church.

— No Dry Season: Raising High God's Standard of Living for this Final Generation. 1997. 10.99 (*0-88419-456-6*) Creation House.

— No Dry Season: Raising High God's Standard of Living for This Final Generation. 1997. pap. 11.99 (*0-88419-464-7*) Creation House.

— No More Crumbs. LC 97-36037. 1997. 14.99 (*0-88419-521-X*); pap. 11.99 (*0-88419-510-4*) Creation House.

***Parsley, Rod.** On the Brink: Breaking Through Every Obstacle into the Glory of God. 192p. 2000. 16.99 (*0-7852-6808-1*) Nelson.

Parsley, Rod. A Power from Above: The Gift of the Holy Spirit to the Body of Christ. 48p. (Orig.). Date not set. 1.00 (*0-614-10667-2*) Wrld Harvest Church.

— Praise & Worship. 128p. 1993. pap. 6.99 (*0-89274-637-8*, HH-637) Harrison Hse.

— Refiner's Fire: Living Holy in a World of Compromise. 78p. (Orig.). 1992. pap. 5.95 (*0-89274-903-2*) Christian Pub.

— Renamed & Redeemed: Operating in the Name of Jesus. 69p. (Orig.). 1991. pap. text 10.00 (*1-880244-02-0*) Wrld Harvest Church.

— Repairers of the Breach. 320p. 1993. pap. 12.99 (*0-89274-636-X*, HH-636) Harrison Hse.

— Repairers of the Breach: There Is Much to Be Gained by a Return to the Discarded Values of the Past. 410p. (Orig.). 1992. pap. 11.99 (*1-880244-09-8*) Wrld Harvest Church.

— Serious Survival Strategies: For Victory. 229p. (Orig.). 1992. pap. 9.99 (*1-880244-08-X*) Wrld Harvest Church.

— The Someday Syndrome. 37p. 1986. pap. 2.95 (*0-88144-069-8*) Christian Pub.

— Strengthening the Roots of Your Family Tree: A Teaching Syllabus. 110p. (Orig.). 1991. pap. 10.00 (*1-880244-03-9*) Wrld Harvest Church.

— Ten Golden Keys to Your Abundance. 190p. (Orig.). 1995. pap. 9.99 (*1-880244-20-9*) Wrld Harvest Church.

— Worshipping the Unknown God. 31p. 1986. pap. 2.75 (*0-88144-070-1*) Christian Pub.

Parsley, Rod, ed. Ten Golden Keys to Your Abundance Study Guide. 57p. 1995. pap. 10.00 (*1-880244-19-5*) Wrld Harvest Church.

Parsley, Rod & Brown, Clint. Praise, the Ultimate Experience: Worship, The Ultimate Relationship. 124p. (Orig.). 1992. pap. 7.99 (*1-880244-10-1*) Wrld Harvest Church.

***Parsloe & Allen.** Learning for Earning. 96p. 2000. pap. 17.95 (*0-8464-5104-2*) Beekman Pubs.

***Parsloe & Wright.** Businesslike Budgeting. 48p. 2000. pap. 17.95 (*0-8464-5009-7*) Beekman Pubs.

Parsloe, C. J. Allocation of Design Responsibilities: Example Drawings. 1977. pap. 100.00 (*0-86022-475-9*, Pub. by Build Servs Info Assn) St Mut.

— Allocation of Design Responsibilities for Building Engineering Services a Code of Conduct to Avoid Conflict. 1997. pap. 100.00 (*0-86022-474-0*, Pub. by Build Servs Info Assn) St Mut.

Parsloe, C. J. The Commissioning of Air Systems in Buildings. 1989. 120.00 (*0-86022-231-4*, Pub. by Build Servs Info Assn) St Mut.

***Parsloe, C. J.** The Commissioning of Air Systems in Buildings. 1998. pap. 100.00 (*0-86022-478-3*, Pub. by Build Servs Info Assn) St Mut.

Parsloe, C. J. The Commissioning of Water Systems in Building. 1992. 180.00 (*0-86022-230-6*, Pub. by Build Servs Info Assn) St Mut.

***Parsloe, C. J.** The Commissioning of Water Systems in Building. 68p. 1998. pap. 100.00 (*0-86022-507-0*, Pub. by Build Servs Info Assn) St Mut.

Parsloe, C. J. Design Briefing Manual. 1990. pap. 60.00 (*0-86022-266-7*, Pub. by Build Servs Info Assn) St Mut.

— Design for Maintainability. (C). 1992. pap. 80.00 (*0-86022-308-6*, Pub. by Build Servs Info Assn) St Mut.

— Design Responsibilities. (C). 1994. pap. 50.00 (*0-86022-371-X*, Pub. by Build Servs Info Assn) St Mut.

— European Commissioning Procedures. 1990. pap. 100.00 (*0-86022-249-7*, Pub. by Build Servs Info Assn) St Mut.

— Pre-Commission Cleaning of Water Systems. 1991. pap. 100.00 (*0-86022-291-8*, Pub. by Build Servs Info Assn) St Mut.

Parsloe, C. J. & Spencer, A. W. Commisioning of Pipework Systems Design Considerations. 1996. pap. 100.00 (*0-86022-422-8*, Pub. by Build Servs Info Assn) St Mut.

***Parsloe, C. J. & Wild, L. J., eds.** Project Management Handbook for Building Services. 220p. 1998. pap. 120.00 (*0-86022-502-X*, Pub. by Build Servs Info Assn) St Mut.

Parsloe, C. J., jt. auth. see BSRIA Staff.

Parsloe, C. J., jt. auth. see Hejab, M.

***Parsloe, Eric.** Coaching & Mentoring. 160p. 2000. pap. 25.00 (*0-7494-3118-0*, Kogan Pg Educ) Stylus Pub VA.

— Manager as Coach & Mentor. 96p. 2000. pap. 17.95 (*0-8464-5109-3*) Beekman Pubs.

Parsloe, Phyllida, jt. ed. see Cnaan, Ram A.

Parslow, Christopher C. Rediscovering Antiquity: Karl Weber & the Excavation of Herculaneum, Pompeii & Stabiae. LC 99-162504. (Illus.). 416p. (C). 1998. pap. 27.95 (*0-521-64664-2*) Cambridge U Pr.

Parslow, Percy. Hamsters. (Illus.). 128p. 1989. 9.95 (*0-86622-831-4*, KW-015) TFH Pubns.

Parslow, R. D. & Green, R. Elliot, eds. Advanced Computer Graphics, Economics, Techniques, & Applications. LC 71-137740. (Illus.). 1244p. 1971. reprint ed. pap. 200.00 (*0-608-05492-5*, 206596100006) Bks Demand.

Parslow, Robert D. Information Technology for the Eighties: BCS '81: Proceedings of the British Computer Society Conference, London, 1-3 July, 1981. LC 84-36784. (Illus.). 784p. reprint ed. pap. 200.00 (*0-608-18454-3*, 203267400080) Bks Demand.

Parson. Computer Concepts. (Illus.). (C). 1998. pap. 12.95 incl. cd-rom (*0-7600-5488-6*) Course Tech.

Parson & Oja. New Perspectives on Excel 97: Expert Supplement. (C). 1997. 10.50 (*0-7600-7211-6*) Thomson Learn.

Parson, jt. auth. see Fenwick.

Parson, Alice A. Bikini Diary: Proud to Be Chosen. (Illus.). 190p. 1999. pap. 19.95 (*0-9652928-1-9*) A A Parson.

— The Final Curtain: A Biography of Dan Parson. (Illus.). 235p. (Orig.). 1996. pap. 19.95 (*0-9652928-0-0*) A A Parson.

Parson, Ann B., jt. auth. see Shiff, Isaac.

***Parson, Donna.** The Days of Miss Julie. 225p. 1998. pap. 9.95 (*0-935931-96-1*, DOMJ) Iberian Pub.

Parson, E. R., jt. auth. see Brende, J. O.

Parson, Florence M. She Incomparable Siddons. 1977. 30.95 (*0-8369-5193-X*) Ayer.

Parson, Harry, ed. see Johnson, Dawn M.

Parson, Jack, ed. Succession to High Office on Botswana: Three Case Studies. LC 90-30851. (Monographs in International Studies, Africa: No. 54). 455p. 1990. pap. 20.00 (*0-89680-157-8*) Ohio U Pr.

Parson, L. M., et al, eds. Hydrothermal Vents & Processes. (Geological Society Special Publication Ser.: No. 87). (Illus.). 416p. 1995. 108.00 (*1-897799-25-X*, 300, Pub. by Geol Soc Pub Hse) AAPG.

— Ophiolites & Their Modern Oceanic Analogues. (Geological Society Special Publications: No. 60). (Illus.). vi, 330p. (C). 1992. 92.00 (*0-903317-69-9*, 262, Pub. by Geol Soc Pub Hse) AAPG.

Parson, Lynn H. John Quincy Adams. LC 97-34987. (American Profiles Ser.). xviii, 284p. 1998. text 29.95 (*0-945612-54-0*) Madison Hse.

***Parson, Lynn Hudson.** John Quincy Adams. (American Profiles Ser.). 1999. pap. 29.95 (*0-945612-59-1*) Madison Hse.

Parson, Maria. Up-Lot Reveries: A Sense of Place. 24.95 (*0-8488-0186-5*) Amereon Ltd.

— Up-Lot Reveries: An Oral History of the North Fork. 22.95 (*0-8488-0122-9*) Amereon Ltd.

Parson, Mary J. An Executive's Coaching Handbook. LC 85-20524. 297p. reprint ed. pap. 92.10 (*0-8357-4251-2*, 203704100007) Bks Demand.

— The Single Solution: A Taxpayer's Guide to Sheltering More of the 20,000, 50,000, or 100,000 Dollars You Make As a Single Person. LC 86-13561. (Illus.). 192p. reprint ed. pap. 59.60 (*0-8357-4253-9*, 203704200007) Bks Demand.

Parson, Nels A. The Compleat Journal of London Vickers: A Memoir of the Days Leading to American Independence. (Illus.). 250p. 1996. pap. 9.95 (*0-935931-90-2*, CJLV) Iberian Pub.

— Missiles & the Revolution in Warfare. LC 62-19221. (Illus.). 255p. reprint ed. pap. 79.10 (*0-608-30818-8*, 200282500014) Bks Demand.

Parson-Nesbitt, Julie. Finders. 72p. (Orig.). 1996. pap. 8.95 (*0-931122-83-X*) West End.

Parson, Robert. Vignettes of a Small Town. LC 97-204767. 320p. 1997. pap. 15.95 (*1-895387-82-5*) Creative Bk Pub.

Parson, Steve R. Transforming Schools into Community Learning Centers. LC 98-35987. 190p. 1999. pap. 29.95 (*1-883001-61-7*) Eye On Educ.

Parsonage, M. J., jt. auth. see Kerr, James A.

Parsonage, Maurice, ed. see Epilepsy International Symposium Staff.

Parsonage, N. G., jt. auth. see Nicholson, D.

Parsonnet, Julie, ed. Microbes & Malignancy: Infection as a Cause of Human Cancers. LC 98-22168. (Illus.). 480p. 1999. text 79.95 (*0-19-510401-3*) OUP.

Parsonnet, Mia. What's in Our Food? Fact & Fiction about Fat & Fiber, Vitamins & Minerals, Nutrients & Contaminants. 145p. 1996. pap. 14.95 (*1-56833-049-9*) Madison Bks UPA.

Parsons. Biology of Microorganisms. (C). 1994. pap. text 36.74 (*0-07-045666-6*) McGraw.

— Canadian Mining Taxation. 2nd ed. 272p. 1990. 84.00 (*0-409-89384-6*, MICHIE) LEXIS Pub.

— Cd-np On The Practical Pc. (NEW PERSPECTIVES). (C). 1999. cd-rom 25.00 (*0-7600-7067-9*) Course Tech.

— Computer Concepts. 2nd ed. (Illus.). (C). 1998. pap. 32.95 incl. cd-rom (*0-7600-5491-6*) Course Tech.

***Parsons.** Courtship. 2000. 23.50 (*0-684-87357-5*) S&S Trade.

— Letter Does Not Blush. 1985. write for info. (*0-907675-21-2*) Random House.

Parsons. New Perspectives on the Practical PC. (New Perspectives Ser.). (C). 1999. pap. 40.95 (*0-7600-7066-0*) Course Tech.

— 1998 AIDS & STDS. 9. 46p. 1998. pap. text, student ed. 3.00 (*0-536-01166-4*) Pearson Custom.

***Parsons.** NP on Advanced VBA. (New Perspectives Ser.). (C). 2000. pap. 48.95 (*0-619-01936-0*) Course Tech.

— NP on Publisher 2000. (New Perspectives Ser.). (C). 2000. pap. 31.95 (*0-619-01932-8*) Course Tech.

— Searching for Healing Through Reincarnation. (Orig.). 1995. pap. 12.95 (*0-7459-3127-8*, Pub. by Lion Pubng) Trafalgar.

— Thomas Hare & Political Representation in Victoria. 74.95 (*1-85928-332-2*) Ashgate Pub Co.

***Parsons & Oja.** Computer Concepts. 4th ed. (New Perspectives Ser.). (C). 2000. text 52.95 (*0-7600-6499-7*) Course Tech.

— Microsoft Windows 95 Comprehensive. (C). 2000. pap. 33.50 (*0-619-01990-5*) Course Tech.

— New Perspectives on Computer Concepts. 4th ed. (New Perspectives Ser.). (C). 1999. text 32.95 (*0-7600-6490-3*) Course Tech.

Parsons, et al. Educational Psychology. (Education Ser.). 2000. pap. text, student ed. 14.00 (*0-534-55702-3*) Wadsworth Pub.

— New Perspectives on Computer Concepts: Introductory with Microsoft Office Professional for Windows 3.1 - Illustrated Enhanced Edition. 10th ed. (New Perspectives Ser.). (Illus.). 944p. (C). 1996. pap. 39.80 (*0-7600-4647-6*) Course Tech.

— New Perspectives on MS Window 98-Comprehensive. 10th ed. (New Perspectives Ser.). (C). 1998. pap. 44.95 (*0-7600-5448-7*) Course Tech.

***Parsons, et al.** NP on MS Win 98. (C). 1998. per. 21.95 (*0-7600-5447-9*) Course Tech.

Parsons, jt. auth. see Carey.

Parsons, Adam. Five Days of a Grand Prix: A Photographic Perspective of the 1998 Formula One. (Illus.). 192p. 1999. 37.50 (*0-333-74700-3*) Trans-Atl Phila.

Parsons, Agnes. Abdu'l-Baha in America: Agnes Parsons' Diary. Hollinger, Richard V., ed. (Illus.). 1996. pap. 19.95 (*0-933770-91-X*, Pub. by Kalimat) Pubs Services.

Parsons, Albert R. Parsifal: The Finding of Christ Through Art. 2nd ed. 113p. 1996. reprint ed. spiral bd. 11.00 (*0-7873-0659-2*) Hlth Research.

— Parsifal: The Finding of Christ Through Art or Richard Wagner As Theologian. 113p. 1993. reprint ed. pap. 9.95 (*1-56459-368-1*) Kessinger Pub.

— Parsifal & the Finding of Christ Through Art: Richard Wagner As Theologian. 1991. lib. bdg. 79.95 (*0-8490-4934-2*) Gordon Pr.

Parsons, Alexandra. Amazing Birds. (Eyewitness Juniors Ser.: No. 1). (Illus.). (J). (ps-3). 1990. pap. 9.99 (*0-679-80223-1*, Pub. by Knopf Bks Yng Read) Random.

— Amazing Birds. (Eyewitness Juniors Ser.: No. 1). (J). (ps-3). 1990. 15.19 (*0-606-03010-7*, Pub. by Turtleback) Demco.

— Amazing Cats. LC 90-31885. (Eyewitness Juniors Ser.: No. 5). (Illus.). 32p. (J). (ps-3). 1990. pap. 9.99 (*0-679-80690-3*, Pub. by Knopf Bks Yng Read) Random.

— Amazing Cats. (Eyewitness Juniors Ser.: No. 5). (J). (ps-3). 1990. 15.19 (*0-606-04601-1*, Pub. by Turtleback) Demco.

— Amazing Mammals. LC 89-38831. (Eyewitness Juniors Ser.: No. 2). (Illus.). 32p. (J). (ps-3). 1990. pap. 9.99 (*0-679-80224-X*, Pub. by Knopf Bks Yng Read) Random.

— Amazing Mammals. LC 89-38831. (Eyewitness Juniors Ser.: No. 2). (Illus.). 32p. (J). (ps-3). 1990. lib. bdg. 11.99 (*0-679-90224-4*, Pub. by Knopf Bks Yng Read) Random.

— Amazing Mammals. (Eyewitness Juniors Ser.: No. 2). (J). (ps-3). 1990. 13.19 (*0-606-03011-5*, Pub. by Turtleback) Demco.

— Amazing Poisonous Animals. LC 90-31883. (Eyewitness Juniors Ser.: No. 8). (Illus.). 32p. (J). (ps-3). 1990. pap. 9.99 (*0-679-80699-7*, Pub. by Knopf Bks Yng Read) Random.

— Amazing Poisonous Animals. LC 90-31883. (Eyewitness Juniors Ser.: No. 8). (Illus.). 32p. (J). (ps-3). 1991. lib. bdg. 11.99 (*0-679-90699-1*, Pub. by Knopf Bks Yng Read) Random.

— Amazing Poisonous Animals. (Eyewitness Juniors Ser.: No. 8). (J). (ps-3). 1990. 15.19 (*0-606-04604-6*, Pub. by Turtleback) Demco.

— Amazing Snakes. LC 89-38944. (Eyewitness Juniors Ser.: No. 3). (Illus.). 32p. (J). (ps-3). 1990. pap. 9.99 (*0-679-80225-8*, Pub. by Knopf Bks Yng Read) Random.

— Amazing Snakes. LC 89-38944. (Eyewitness Juniors Ser.: No. 3). (Illus.). 32p. (J). (ps-3). 1990. lib. bdg. 11.99 (*0-679-90225-2*, Pub. by Knopf Bks Yng Read) Random.

— Amazing Spiders. LC 89-38833. (Eyewitness Juniors Ser.: No. 4). (Illus.). 32p. (J). (ps-3). 1990. pap. 9.99 (*0-679-80226-6*, Pub. by Knopf Bks Yng Read) Random.

— Amazing Spiders. LC 89-38833. (Eyewitness Juniors Ser.: No. 4). (Illus.). 32p. (J). (ps-3). 1990. lib. bdg. 11.99 (*0-679-90226-0*, Pub. by Knopf Bks Yng Read) Random.

Parsons, Alexandra. Amazing Spiders. (Eyewitness Juniors Ser.: No. 4). (J). (ps-3). 1990. 15.19 (*0-606-03012-3*, Pub. by Turtleback) Demco.

— Ancient Egypt. (Make It Work! History Ser.). (Illus.). (J). (gr. 4-7). 2000. pap. 6.95 (*1-58728-300-X*) Two Can Pub.

Parsons, Alexandra. Being Me. LC 95-37522. (Life Education Ser.). (Illus.). 32p. (J). (gr. 5-8). 1996. lib. bdg. 19.00 (*0-531-14381-3*) Watts.

— Facts & Phalluses: A Collection of Bizarre & Intriguing Truths, Legends, & Measurements. 80p. (Orig.). 1990. pap. 7.95 (*0-312-04670-7*) St Martin.

— Fit for Life. LC 95-20922. (Life Education Ser.). (Illus.). 32p. (J). (gr. 5-8). 1996. lib. bdg. 19.00 (*0-531-14372-4*) Watts.

— I Am Special. LC 96-2136. (Life Education Ser.). (J). (gr. 5-8). 1997. lib. bdg. 19.00 (*0-531-14421-6*) Watts.

— I'm Happy, I'm Heathy. LC 95-46359. (Life Education Ser.). (J). (gr. 5-8). 1997. lib. bdg. 19.00 (*0-531-14410-0*) Watts.

— Living in the World. LC 96-11877. (Life Education Ser.). 1997. lib. bdg. 19.00 (*0-531-14430-5*) Watts.

— Look Good, Feel Good. LC 96-11727. (Life Education Ser.). (J). 1997. lib. bdg. 19.00 (*0-531-14428-3*) Watts.

— Me & My World. LC 95-37521. (Life Education Ser.). (Illus.). 32p. (J). (gr. 5-8). 1996. lib. bdg. 19.00 (*0-531-14375-9*) Watts.

***Parsons, Alexandra.** North American Indians. (Make It Work! History Ser.). (Illus.). (J). (gr. 4-7). 2000. pap. 6.95 (*1-58728-301-8*) Two Can Pub.

— Plants. (Make It Work! Science Ser.). (Illus.). (J). (gr. 4-7). 2000. pap. 6.95 (*1-58728-359-X*) Two Can Pub.

Parsons, Alexandra. You're Special, Too. LC 96-16323. (Life Education Ser.). (J). 1997. lib. bdg. 19.00 (*0-531-14422-4*) Watts.

Parsons, Alexandra & Barnes, Jon. Electricity. (Make It Work! Ser.). (Illus.). 48p. (J). 1997. pap. 7.95 (*0-590-24404-3*) Scholastic Inc.

— Plants. (Make It Work! Ser.). (Illus.). 48p. (J). pap. 7.95 (*0-590-24403-5*) Scholastic Inc.

Parsons, Alice B. Woman's Dilemma. LC 74-3966. (Women in America Ser.). 320p. 1974. reprint ed. 28.95 (*0-405-06115-3*) Ayer.

Parsons, Andrew W., jt. auth. see Andrews, David W.

***Parsons, Anthea.** Beyond the Horizon. 1998. pap. 6.99 (*0-340-70989-8*, Pub. by Hodder & Stought Ltd) Trafalgar.

Parsons, Anthea. On Being a Jewish Christian. 1998. 10.99 (*0-340-71377-1*, Pub. by Hodder & Stought Ltd) Trafalgar.

Parsons, Anthony. The Design Supplement: A Practical Approach to Studying Design. (Illus.). 128p. 1999. pap., suppl. ed. 19.95 (*0-7506-2389-6*) Buttrwrth-Heinemann.

Parsons, Anthony, ed. Antarctica: The Next Decade. (Studies in Polar Research). (Illus.). 176p. 1987. text 64.95 (*0-521-33181-1*) Cambridge U Pr.

Parsons, Arthur, jt. auth. see Parsons, Particia.

Parsons, Arthur, jt. auth. see Parsons, Patricia.

Parsons, Benny. Inside Track: A Photo Documentary of Nascar Stock Car Racing. LC 96-9468. (Illus.). 144p. 1996. 24.95 (*1-885183-59-3*) Artisan.

***Parsons, Betty.** The Expectant Father. 2nd ed. (Illus.). 128p. 2001. pap. 6.95 (*0-7160-2017-3*, Pub. by Elliot RW Bks) Midpt Trade.

Parsons, Betty. Preparing for Childbirth: Relaxing for Labor, Learning for Life. LC 97-7177. (Illus.). 144p. 1997. pap. 9.95 (*1-55561-128-1*) Fisher Bks.

Parsons, Bill. Electronic Prepress: A Hands-On Introduction. 192p. (C). 1995. pap. 29.50 (*0-8273-6449-0*) Delmar.

— Graphic Design with Pagemaker 6.5: MAC - Windows. LC 97-18395. 640p. (C). 1997. 56.95 (*0-7668-0070-9*) Delmar.

— PageMaker: Graphic Design with Pagemaker Macintosh Version 5.0. LC 93-37661. 337p. 1993. pap. 31.95 (*0-8273-5751-6*) Delmar.

Parsons, Bob, ed. Design Guide for Cool Thermal Storage. LC 96-113694. (Illus.). 1993. pap. 72.00 (*1-883413-07-9*) Am Heat Ref & Air Eng.

Parsons, Bob & Reilly, Kurt. RVing in Alaska Vol. 3: Campgrounds & Services. 3rd rev. ed. LC 98-160209. 226p. 1998. pap. 19.95 (*0-9629325-5-8*) Billiken Pr.

Parsons, Bonnie & Mazik, James M. Touring Jacob's Ladder Trail by Bicycle or Car. 126p. 1994. pap. 10.00 (*0-9643910-0-7*) Pioneer Valley.

Parsons, Brian, ed. see Time-Life Books Editors.

Parsons, Brinckerhoff, et al. Consequences of the Interstate Highway System for Transit: Summary of Findings. LC 98-61203. (Transit Cooperative Research Program Report Ser.). 64 p. 1998. write for info. (*0-309-06309-4*) Natl Acad Pr.

Parsons, Brinckerhoff, Quade & Douglas, Inc. Staff. Bridge Inspection & Rehabilitation: A Practical Guide. LC 94-4225. 312p. 1992. 125.00 (*0-471-53262-2*) Wiley.

Parsons, Burke A. British Trade Cycles & American Bank Credit: Some Aspects of Economic Fluctuations in the United States, 1815-1840. Bruchey, Stuart, ed. LC 76-39839. (Nineteen Seventy-Seven Dissertations Ser.). (Illus.). 1977. lib. bdg. 37.95 (*0-405-09919-3*) Ayer.

Parsons, C. G. Inside View of Slavery: Or a Tour Among the Planters. 1969. reprint ed. 20.00 (*0-87266-025-7*) Argosy.

Parsons, Carl. Excluded Children. LC 98-35361. 1999. 75.00 (*0-415-17496-1*); pap. 24.99 (*0-415-17497-X*) Routledge.

Parsons, Carl, ed. Quality Improvement in Education: Case Studies in Schools, Colleges & Universities. 160p. 1994. pap. 27.00 (*1-85346-327-2*, Pub. by David Fulton) Taylor & Francis.

Parsons, Charles. Mathematics in Philosophy: Selected Essays. LC 83-45153. 368p. 1983. text 55.00 (*0-8014-1471-7*) Cornell U Pr.

— Montauk Point, Long Island: An 1871 Visit. (Illus.). 15p. (Orig.). 1990. reprint ed. pap. 2.95 (*0-89646-082-7*) Vistabooks.

Parsons, Charles D. History & Records of the Oakland United Mehodist Church, Faulkner Co., Arkansas. (Illus.). 126p. 1993. 24.95 (*1-56869-012-6*); pap. 18.95 (*1-56869-013-4*) Oldbuck Pr.

Parsons, Charles G. Inside View of Slavery or a Tour among the Planters. LC 73-92436. 1970. reprint ed. 9.00 (*0-403-00181-1*) Scholarly.

Parsons, Charles H. Opera Premiere Reviews & Re-Assessments: A Listing. LC 97-29099. (Mellen Opera Reference Index Ser.: Vol. 19). 139p. 1997. 149.95 (*0-88946-172-4*) E Mellen.

Parsons, Charles H., compiled by. Miscellanea Opera, Vol. 24. 1987. write for info. (*0-88946-421-9*) E Mellen.

— Opera & the Librarian, Vol. 25. 1987. write for info. (*0-88946-422-7*) E Mellen.

— Opera Bibliography, Vol. 17. LC 95-1400. (Mellen Opera Reference Index Ser.). 1987. write for info. (*0-88946-416-2*) E Mellen.

— Opera Bibliography, Vol. 18. LC 95-1400. (Mellen Opera Reference Index Ser.). 400p. 1996. text 149.95 (*0-88946-417-0*) E Mellen.

— Opera Composers & Their Works A-D, 22 vols. LC 86-7252. (Mellen Opera Reference Index Ser.: Vol. 1). 534p. 1986. lib. bdg. 149.95 (*0-88946-401-4*) E Mellen.

— Opera Composers & Their Works E-K, Vol. 1. LC 86-7252. (Mellen Opera Reference Index Ser.: Vol. 2). 496p. 1986. lib. bdg. 149.95 (*0-88946-402-2*) E Mellen.

— Opera Composers & Their Works L-Q. LC 86-7252. (Mellen Opera Reference Index Ser.: Vol. 3). 480p. 1986. lib. bdg. 149.95 (*0-88946-403-0*) E Mellen.

— Opera Composers & Their Works R-Z. LC 86-7252. (Mellen Opera Reference Index Ser.: Vol. 4). 512p. 1986. lib. bdg. 149.95 (*0-88946-404-9*) E Mellen.

— Opera Discography - Composers A-O, Vol. 10. LC 89-13814. 360p. 1989. lib. bdg. 149.95 (*0-88946-410-3*) E Mellen.

— Opera Discography - Composers P-Z, Vol. 11. LC 89-13814. 376p. 1989. lib. bdg. 149.95 (*0-88946-411-1*) E Mellen.

— Opera Discography - Performers, Vol. 12. LC 89-13814. 568p. 1989. lib. bdg. 149.95 (*0-88946-497-9*) E Mellen.

— Opera Librettists & Their Works A-L, Vol. 5. (Opera Reference Index Ser.). 1987. write for info. (*0-88946-405-7*) E Mellen.

— Opera Librettists & Their Works M-Z, Vol. 6. (Opera Reference Index Ser.). 1987. 149.95 (*0-88946-406-5*) E Mellen.

— Opera Premieres: Reviews, 22 vols., Vols. 15. LC 87-24680. 1987. write for info. (*0-88946-400-6*) E Mellen.

— Opera Premieres - Geographical Index A-H. LC 88-12902. (Opera Reference Index Ser.: Vol. 7). 460p. (C). 1988. lib. bdg. 149.95 (*0-88946-407-3*) E Mellen.

— Opera Premieres - Geographical Index I-Z. LC 88-12902. (Opera Reference Index Ser.: Vol. 8). 450p. (C). 1988. lib. bdg. 149.95 (*0-88946-408-1*) E Mellen.

— Opera Premieres/Cast Index A-L. LC 92-9245. (Mellen Opera Reference Index Ser.: Vol. 13). 690p. 1992. lib. bdg. 149.95 (*0-88946-412-X*) E Mellen.

— Opera Premieres/Cast Index M-Z. (Mellen Opera Reference Index Ser.: Vol. 14). 686p. 1992. lib. bdg. 149.95 (*0-88946-413-8*) E Mellen.

— Opera Subjects, 22 vols., Vol. 9. 1989. 149.95 (*0-88946-409-X*) E Mellen.

— Opera That Is Not Opera, 22 vols., Vol. 23. 1987. write for info. (*0-88946-420-0*) E Mellen.

— An Opera Videography. LC 97-51913. (Mellen Opera Reference Index Ser.: Vol. 20). 368p. 1997. text 199.95 (*0-88946-641-6*) E Mellen.

— Printed Opera Scores in American Libraries, Bk. 1. LC 98-36427. (Opera Reference Index Ser.: Vol. 21A). 558p. 1987. text 139.95 (*0-88946-418-9*) E Mellen.

— Printed Opera Scores in American Libraries, Bk. 2. LC 98-36427. (Opera Reference Index Ser.: Vol. 21B). 1998. text 199.95 (*0-88946-419-7*) E Mellen.

— Printed Opera Scores in American Libraries, Bk. 3. LC 98-36427. (Opera Reference Index Ser.: Vol. 21C). 1998. text 199.95 (*0-88946-695-5*) E Mellen.

Parsons, Charles H., ed. A Benjamin Britten Discography. LC 90-6219. (Studies in History & Interpretation of Music: Vol. 31). 260p. 1990. lib. bdg. 89.95 (*0-88946-486-3*) E Mellen.

— Opera Premieres - Performers A-J. LC 93-4741. (Mellen Opera Reference Index Ser.: Vol. 15). 1993. write for info. (*0-88946-414-6*) E Mellen.

— Opera Premieres - Performers K-Z, Vol. 15. LC 93-4741. (Mellen Opera Reference Index Ser.: Vol. 16). 1993. write for info. (*0-88946-415-4*) E Mellen.

Parsons, Christina. Dangerous Marine Animals of the Pacific Coast. LC 85-81586. (Illus.). 96p. 1986. pap. 4.95 (*0-936940-03-4*) Helm Pub.

Parsons, Christine. Decorating with Marble, Stone & Granite. 1990. 16.98 (*1-55521-576-9*) Bk Sales Inc.

***Parsons, Chuck.** Captain L.H. McNelly - Texas Ranger: The Life & Times of a Fighting Man. LC 00-44545. 2000. pap. write for info. (*1-880510-74-X*) State House Pr.

Parsons, Chuck. James Madison Brown: Texas Sheriff, Texas Turfman. (Illus.). xiv, 167p. 1993. 39.95 (*0-318-72629-7*) Hartmann Heritage.

Parsons, Chuck & Fitterer, Gary P. Captain C. B. McKinney: The Law in South Texas. (Illus.). 160p. 1993. 39.95 (*0-9614936-0-7*) Hartmann Heritage.

Parsons, Chuck & Parsons, Marjorie. Bowen & Hardin. LC 91-24946. (Illus.). 112p. 1991. 21.95 (*0-932702-91-0*) Creative Texas.

Parsons, Claire D. Healing Practices in the South Pacific. LC 85-14191. (Illus.). 266p. (C). 1995. reprint ed. pap. 19.00 (*0-939154-56-0*) Inst Polynesian.

Parsons, Claude. Flowers: Basic Skills. (How to Draw & Paint Ser.). (Illus.). 32p. (Orig.). 1989. pap. 6.95 (*0-929261-17-8*, HT75) W Foster Pub.

Parsons, Coleman O., ed. The Scottish Enlightenment: An AMS Press Reprint Series. reprint ed. write for info. (*0-404-17120-6*) AMS Pr.

Parsons, Colin. Encounters with the Unknown: True Accounts of Modern Paranormal Experiences. large type ed. 248p. 1991. 21.95 (*1-85089-545-7*, Pub. by ISIS Lrg Prnt) Transaction Pubs.

Parsons, Cynthia. The Co-Op Bridge: Cooperative Education - Thoroughly Integrating Study & Work. LC 90-15482. 128p. (Orig.). 1991. pap. 7.95 (*0-88007-185-9*) Woodbridge Pr.

***Parsons, Cynthia.** The Discoverer, Mary Baker Eddy. (Illus.). 160p. (J). (gr. 4-8). 2000. 20.00 (*1-892286-00-9*, Pub. by VT Schoolhse Pr) Enfield Pubs NH.

Parsons, Cynthia. George Bird Grinnell: A Biographical Sketch. 2nd ed. (Illus.). 205p. 1993. reprint ed. 19.95 (*0-9635190-0-X*) Grinnell & Lawton.

— "I Never Found a Kindlier People" The Early History of Christian Science in Vermont. LC 96-61405. (Illus.). 200p. 1996. 12.00 (*0-9617872-8-7*) VT Schoolhse Pr.

— The Purple Hills. 200p. (Orig.). 1990. pap. 5.00 (*0-9617872-6-0*) VT Schoolhse Pr.

— Seeds: Some Good Ways to Improve Our Schools. LC 84-29160. 224p. (Orig.). 1992. pap. 12.95 (*0-88007-200-8*) Woodbridge Pr.

— Serving to Learn, Learning to Serve: Civics & Service from A-Z. LC 95-21434. (Illus.). 112p. 1995. 43.95 (*0-8039-6364-5*); pap. 18.95 (*0-8039-6365-3*) Corwin Pr.

Parsons, Cynthia, compiled by. Spinach & Zwieback: Writings of Newell Martin. LC 93-73174. (Illus.). 512p. 1993. 29.95 (*0-9635190-1-8*) Grinnell & Lawton.

Parsons, Cynthia, ed. What'll You Have: Fifty Plus Non-Alcoholic Drinks for Brunch, Lunch & Dinner. 52p. (Orig.). 1986. pap. 5.00 (*0-9617872-0-1*) VT Schoolhse Pr.

Parsons, Cynthia, ed. see Webb, Susan H.

Parsons, Cynthia M. Impressions: Men's Summer Soccer '96. (Illus.). 48p. (J). (gr. k up). 1996. pap. 24.95 (*1-890229-00-8*) ArtSouth Ent.

Parsons, D. Object Oriented Programming. 328p. 1994. pap. 59.95 (*1-85805-089-8*, Pub. by DP Publns) St Mut.

Parsons, Dave, tr. see Basov, N. G., ed.

Parsons, Dave, tr. see Skobel'tsyn, D. V., ed.

Parsons, David, tr. see Isaev, P. S.

Parsons, David K. Bugles Echo Across the Valley: Oswego County, New York & the Civil War. rev. ed. (Illus.). 250p. 1995. pap. 17.50 (*1-886303-09-6*) Write to Print.

— Bugles Echo Across the Valley Vol. 2: Civil War Muster Rolls for 24th, 81st,110th,184th, Inf., 24th Cav. (Illus.). 130p. (Orig.). 1995. pap. 12.50 (*1-886303-10-X*) Write to Print.

— The Muster Roll: Men from Oswego County Who Served in Other Regiments. (Bugles Echo Across the Valley Ser.: Vol. 3). (Illus.). 165p. (Orig.). (J). (gr. 6). 1996. pap. 18.00 (*1-886303-11-8*) Write to Print.

— The Saddlebag Patriot: Service of Lt. Underfoot in the War for Independence. 106p. 1992. pap. 10.00 (*1-886303-00-2*) Write to Print.

***Parsons, David M.** Editing Sky. LC 99-36188. 72p. 1999. 20.00 (*1-881515-23-0*); pap. 12.00 (*1-881515-24-9*) TX Review Pr.

***Parsons, Deborah Todaro.** I Live Next Door to My Neighbor. LC 99-68798. (Illus.). 120p. 2000. 10.95 (*0-9678049-0-6*) Burdock.

Parsons, Donald O. Poverty & the Minimum Wage. LC 80-24407. (AEI Studies: No. 300). (Illus.). 72p. reprint ed. pap. 30.00 (*0-8357-4525-2*, 203738700008) Bks Demand.

Parsons, Douglas. Dynamic Living in Difficult Days. 125p. (Orig.). 1989. pap. 4.95 (*0-940999-40-4*, C-2152) Star Bible.

***Parsons, Dwayne.** Flying over Rainbows: A Lifetime of Fishing, Flying & Fly Fishing. (Illus.). 128p. 1999. 24.95 (*1-879628-19-8*) Keokee ID.

Parsons, E. M. The Easy Gun. 128p. 1979. mass mkt. 1.50 (*0-449-14293-0*, GM) Fawcett.

Parsons, E. W. Folk-Lore from the Cape Verde Islands. LC 24-4017. (American Folklore Society Memoirs Ser.: Vol. 15). 1972. reprint ed. 62.00 (*0-527-01067-7*) Periodicals Srv.

Parsons, Edward B. Wilsonian Diplomacy. LC 77-80967. 1978. text 12.95 (*0-88273-006-1*) Forum Pr IL.

Parsons, Edward E. Humboldt Homegrown: The Golden Age. LC 85-81069. 604p. 1985. 15.00 (*0-9615730-0-7*) Egret Pub Co.

Parsons, Edwin C. I Flew with the Lafayette Escadrille. LC 74-169432. (Literature & History of Aviation Ser.). 1972. reprint ed. 34.95 (*0-405-03775-9*) Ayer.

Parsons, Eleanor. Rockport: The Making of a Tourist Treasure. (Illus.). 216p. 1998. pap. 15.95 (*1-885435-03-7*) Twin Lights.

Parsons, Elsie C. Fear & Conventionality. LC 97-1996. 1997. pap. text 14.95 (*0-226-64746-3*) U Ch Pr.

— Isleta Paintings. (Bureau of American Ethnology Bulletins Ser.). 299p. 1995. lib. bdg. write for info. (*0-7812-4181-2*) Rprt Serv.

— Isleta Paintings. 1988. reprint ed. lib. bdg. 99.00 (*0-7812-0927-7*) Rprt Serv.

— Isleta Paintings. reprint ed. 59.00 (*0-403-03619-4*) Scholarly.

— Journal of a Feminist. Roberts, Marie M., ed. (Subversive Women Ser.). (Illus.). 144p. 1994. pap. 19.95 (*1-85506-250-X*) Bks Intl VA.

— Notes on Zuni, 2 pts., Pt. I. (American Anthropological Association Memoirs Ser.: No. 20). 1917. 15.00 (*0-527-00518-5*) Periodicals Srv.

— Notes on Zuni, 2 pts., Pt. II. (American Anthropological Association Memoirs Ser.: No. 20). 1917. 25.00 (*0-527-00519-3*) Periodicals Srv.

— The Old-Fashioned Woman: Primitive Fancies about the Sex. LC 72-2618. (American Women Ser.: Images & Realities). 378p. 1974. reprint ed. 26.95 (*0-405-04471-2*) Ayer.

— Pueblo Indian Religion, Vol. 1. LC 95-47046. (Illus.). xl, 577p. 1996. pap. 25.00 (*0-8032-8735-6*, Bison Books) U of Nebr Pr.

— Pueblo Indian Religion, Vol. 2. LC 95-47046. (Illus.). xix, 760p. 1996. pap. 25.00 (*0-8032-8736-4*, Bison Books) U of Nebr Pr.

— Pueblo Mothers & Children: Essays by Elsie Clews Parsons, 1915-1924. Babcock, Barbara, ed. LC 89-82082. (Illus.). 140p. 1991. 29.95 (*0-941270-66-1*); pap. 17.95 (*0-941270-65-3*) Ancient City Pr.

— Scalp Ceremonial of Zuni. LC 25-1663. (American Anthropological Association Memoirs Ser.). 1924. pap. 25.00 (*0-527-00530-4*) Periodicals Srv.

— Social Organization of the Tewa of New Mexico. LC 30-5855. (American Anthropological Association Memoirs Ser.). 1929. 35.00 (*0-527-00535-5*) Periodicals Srv.

— Taos Tales. unabridged ed. LC 95-45565. 192p. 1996. reprint ed. pap. text 7.95 (*0-486-28974-5*) Dover.

— Tewa Tales. 304p. 1994. reprint ed. pap. 18.95 (*0-8165-1452-6*) U of Ariz Pr.

— Winter & Summer Dance Series in Zuni in 1918. fac. ed.

P

(University of California Publications in American Archaeology & Ethnology: Vol. 17: 3). 45p. (C). 1922. reprint ed. pap. text 5.00 (*1-55567-229-9*) Coyote Press.

Parsons, Elsie C., ed. American Indian Life: New Edition. LC 91-16847. (Illus.). xvi, 467p. 1991. reprint ed. pap. 12.95 (*0-8032-8728-3*, Bison Books) U of Nebr Pr.

— North American Indian Life: Customs & Traditions of 23 Tribes. unabridged ed. LC 92-22904. Orig. Title: American Indian Life by Several of Its Students. (Illus.). 1993. reprint ed. pap. text 10.95 (*0-486-27377-6*) Dover.

Parsons, Elsie C., ed. see Stephen, Alexander M.

Parsons, Elsie W. Educational Legislation & Administration of the Colonial Governments. LC 79-165741. (American Education Ser., No. 2). 1975. reprint ed. 38.95 (*0-405-03612-4*) Ayer.

— Folk Tales of Andros Island, Bahamas. LC 19-4413. (American Folklore Society Memoirs Ser.: Vol. 13). 1969. reprint ed. 45.00 (*0-527-01065-0*) Periodicals Srv.

— The Pueblo of Jemez. LC 76-43805. (Phillips Academy: No. 3). reprint ed. 67.50 (*0-404-15661-4*) AMS Pr.

— Religious Chastity: An Ethnological Study, by John Main (Pseud.) LC 72-9672. reprint ed. 54.00 (*0-404-57489-0*) AMS Pr.

Parsons, Elsie W., ed. Folk-Lore of the Antilles, French & English, 3 Vols, Set. LC 34-20249. (AFS Memoirs Ser.: Vol. 26, Pt. 1-3). (ENG & FRE.). 1972. reprint ed. 150.00 (*0-527-01078-2*) Periodicals Srv.

— Folk-Lore of the Sea Islands, South Carolina. LC 23-12312. (AFS Memoirs Ser.: Vol. 16). 1972. reprint ed. 25.00 (*0-527-01068-5*) Periodicals Srv.

Parsons, Elsie Worthington, see Worthington Parsons, Elsie.

Parsons, Eugene, jt. compiled by see La Moille, T. G.

Parsons, Florence M. Garrick & His Circle. LC 78-82837. (Illus.). 441p. 1972. 35.95 (*0-405-08836-1*, Pub. by Blom Pubns) Ayer.

— The Incomparable Siddons. LC 77-84847. (Illus.). 320p. 1972. 30.95 (*0-405-08837-X*, Pub. by Blom Pubns) Ayer.

— The Incomparable Siddons. LC 74-107824. (Illus.). 298p. reprint ed. lib. bdg. 24.00 (*0-8290-0514-5*) Irvington.

Parsons, Frances D. Solomon Shilling - Come to Court. 538p. 1944. reprint ed. pap. 12.00 (*0-87012-492-7*) McClain.
This true romantic story of the late 1800s takes place in Saint George, West Virginia, the first county seat of Tucker County. Although the rape victim & those who protected her & her child are fictitious, it is now known that the families involved included Hebbs, Bowmans, Minears, Bonners & Deitz (Deets). Reprinted, 1991. *Publisher Paid Annotation.*

Parsons, Frances M. & Stewart, Larry G. American Sign Language: Shattering the Myth. Bertling, Tom, ed. 112p. (C). 1998. pap. 19.95 (*0-9637813-5-9*) Kodiak Media.

Parsons, Francis. Six Men of Yale. LC 72-156702. (Essay Index Reprint Ser.). 1977. reprint ed. 20.95 (*0-8369-2329-4*) Ayer.

Parsons, Frank. Legal Doctrine & Social Progress. 219p. 1982. reprint ed. 37.00 (*0-8377-1014-6*, Rothman) W S Hein.

***Parsons, Frank.** A Treatise on the Law of Banks & Banking, 2 vols. 4th ed. cv, 1490p. 2000. 320.00 (*1-56169-614-5*) Gaunt.

Parsons, Frank W. Understanding Salvation Faith in Christ. LC 97-61155. 272p. 1997. 24.99 (*1-57921-042-2*) WinePress Pub.

Parsons, Friedmann & Central, Inc. Staff. The Official Guidebook to Boston & Its Neighborhoods, 97-98. (ENG, FRE, GER, ITA & JPN., Illus.). 120p. (Orig.). 1997. pap. 4.95 (*1-887819-00-2*) P F & C Inc.

***Parsons, G.** Nelsonian Reminiscences; A Dramatic Eye-Witness Account of the War at Sea 1795-1810. 1999. pap. text 21.95 (*1-86176-083-3*, Chatham Pubg) G Duckworth.

Parsons, G., et al, eds. Flat-Panel Display Materials, 1998 Vol. 508: Proceedings Materials Research Society Symposium. LC 98-34675. 342p. 1998. text 84.00 (*1-55899-414-9*) Materials Res.

Parsons, Gary A., et al. California Lithic Studies, No. 11, Pt. 1. Breschini, Gary S. & Haversat, Trudy, eds. (Archives of California Prehistory Ser.: No. 11). (Illus.). 100p. (Orig.). 1987. pap. 11.25 (*1-55567-044-X*) Coyote Press.

Parsons, Gary L., jt. auth. see Gitisetan, Darrin D.

Parsons, Geoffrey. The Land of Fair Play. (Illus.). 180p. (YA). (gr. 7-12). 1994. pap. text 8.00 (*1-930092-98-9*, CLP79995) Christian Liberty.

— The Land of Fair Play: Answer Key. 2nd ed. 180p. 1994. 3.00 (*1-930092-99-7*, CLP79995) Christian Liberty.

Parsons, George D. & Leas, Speed B. Understanding Your Congregation As a System: The Manual. LC 93-73158. 154p. (Orig.). 1994. pap. 19.25 (*1-56699-118-8*, AL147) Alban Inst.

Parsons, George W. Put the Vermonters Ahead: The First Vermont Brigade in the Civil War. LC 96-2060. (Illus.). 216p. 1996. 24.95 (*0-942597-97-4*) White Mane Pub.

***Parsons, George W.** Put the Vermonters Ahead: The First Vermont Brigade in the Civil War. 228p. 2000. pap. 12.95 (*1-57249-193-0*, Burd St Pr) White Mane Pub.

Parsons, Gerald. The Growth of Religious Diversity: Britain from 1945, 1. LC 94-44326. (Illus.). 304p. (C). 1994. pap. 24.99 (*0-415-08326-5*, B3941) Routledge.

— The Growth of Religious Diversity: Britain from 1945, 2. LC 94-44326. (Illus.). 304p. (C). 1994. pap. 24.99 (*0-415-08328-1*, B3945) Routledge.

Parsons, Gerald, ed. Religion in Victorian Britain Vol. II: Controversies. LC 88-12359. (Illus.). 256p. 1989. text 24.95 (*0-7190-2513-3*, Pub. by Manchester Univ Pr) St Martin.

— Religion in Victorian Britain Vol. IV: Interpretations. 208p. 1989. text 89.95 (*0-7190-2945-7*, Pub. by Manchester Univ Pr) St Martin.

— Religion in Victorian Britain Vol. IV: Interpretations, Vol. 4. 208p. 1989. text 18.95 (*0-7190-2946-5*) Manchester Univ Pr.

Parsons, H. E., ed. see Parsons, S. D.

Parsons, Henry M. Man-Machine System Experiments. LC 71-166483. (Illus.). 648p. reprint ed. pap. 200.00 (*0-608-06181-6*, 206651300008) Bks Demand.

Parsons, Howard L. Christianity Today in the U. S. S. R. LC 86-27320. 211p. (Orig.). reprint ed. pap. 65.50 (*0-7837-0582-4*, 204092600019) Bks Demand.

— Self, Global Issues, & Ethics. 209p. 1980. pap. 27.00 (*90-6032-178-2*, Pub. by B R Gruner) Humanities.

Parsons, Howard L., jt. auth. see Somerville, John.

Parsons, Howard L., ed. see Marx, Karl & Engels, Friedrich.

Parsons, Ian, ed. Feldspars & Their Reactions: Proceedings of the NATO Advanced Study Institute, Edinburgh, United Kingdom, June 29-July 10, 1993. LC 94-2625. (NATO Advanced Study Institutes Series C, Mathematical & Physical Sciences: Vol. 421). 650p. (C). 1994. text 332.00 (*0-7923-2722-5*) Kluwer Academic.

Parsons, Irene. Doria. LC 98-6623. 160p. 1998. pap. 12.95 (*1-880090-73-2*) Galde Pr.

Parsons, Israel. Centennial History of the Town of Marcellus. (Illus.). 108p. 1997. reprint ed. pap. 15.00 (*0-8328-6172-3*) Higginson Bk Co.

Parsons, J. D. Mobile Communication Systems. 292p. 1989. text 115.00 (*0-470-21213-6*) Halsted Pr.

— The Mobile Radio Propagation Channel. 328p. 1996. 180.00 (*0-471-96415-8*) Wiley.

***Parsons, J. D.** The Mobile Radio Propagation Channel. 2nd ed. LC 00-32482. 2000. write for info. (*0-471-98857-X*) Wiley.

Parsons, J. E., ed. see Emerson, Ralph Waldo.

Parsons, Jack. Human Population Competition: A Study of the Pursuit of Power Through Numbers, Vol. 1. LC 98-13666. (Symposium Ser.: Vol. 46A). 372p. 1998. text 109.95 (*0-7734-8372-1*) E Mellen.

— Human Population Competition As Biological Warfare: The Pursuit of Power Through Numbers, Vol. 2. LC 98-13666. (Symposium Ser.: Vol. 46B). 1998. text 109.95 (*0-7734-8374-8*) E Mellen.

Parsons, Jack, jt. auth. see Padilla, Carmella.

Parsons, Jack W. Freedom Is a Two Edged Sword. Beta, Hymenaeus, ed. LC 89-81555. (Oriflamme Ser.). 100p. (Orig.). 1990. pap. 12.95 (*1-56184-116-1*) New Falcon Pubns.

Parsons, James. The Art Fever: Passages Through the Western Art Trade. Fox, Steve & Schlede, Nancy, eds. LC 81-83141. (Illus.). 111p. 1981. 29.95 (*0-9610550-0-6*) Gallery West.

— The Art Fever: Passages Through the Western Art Trade. deluxe ed. Fox, Steve & Schlede, Nancy, eds. LC 81-83141. (Illus.). 111p. 1981. 300.00 (*0-9610550-1-4*) Gallery West.

Parsons, James, tr. see Marias, Julian.

Parsons, James B. The Peasant Rebellions of the Late Ming Dynasty. LC 68-9341. (Monographs: No. 26). xv, 292p. 1993. reprint ed. 23.00 (*0-8165-0155-6*) Assn Asian Studies.

Parsons, James J. Antioqueno Colonization in Western Colombia. 2nd rev. ed. LC 68-58002. (University of California Publications in Social Welfare: No. 32). (Illus.). 260p. reprint ed. pap. 80.60 (*0-8357-5635-1*, 202995900066) Bks Demand.

Parsons, James J., jt. ed. see Davidson, William V.

Parsons, James M. Northampton. LC 97-112794. (Images of America Ser.). 1996. pap. 16.99 (*0-7524-0425-3*) Arcadia Publng.

Parsons, Jeffrey R. Prehistoric Settlement Patterns in the Texcoco Region, Mexico. (Memoirs Ser.: No. 3). (Illus.). 1971. pap. 4.00 (*0-932206-65-4*) U Mich Mus Anthro.

Parsons, Jeffrey R. & Parsons, Mary H. Maguey Utilization in Highland Central Mexico: An Archaeological Ethnography. LC 90-34597. (Anthropological Papers Ser.: No. 82). (Illus.). xvi, 388p. (Orig.). 1990. pap. 22.00 (*0-915703-20-3*) U Mich Mus Anthro.

Parsons, Jeffrey R., et al. Archaeological Settlement Pattern Data from the Chalco, Xochimilco, Ixtapalapa, Texcoco, & Zumpango Regions, Mexico. LC 84-21935. (Technical Reports Ser.: No. 14). (Illus.). 222p. 1983. pap. 8.00 (*0-932206-98-0*) U Mich Mus Anthro.

***Parsons, Jeffrey R., et al.** Pre-Hispanic Settlement Patterns in the Upper Mantaro & Tarma Drainages, Junbin, Peru. LC 00-30886. (Memoirs of the Museum of Anthropology, University of Michigan Ser.). 2000. write for info. (*0-915703-49-1*) U Mich Mus Anthro.

Parsons, Jeffrey R., et al. Prehistoric Settlement Patterns in the Southern Valley of Mexico: The Chalco-Xochimilco Region. (Memoirs Ser.: No. 14). (Orig.). 1982. pap. 16.00 (*0-932206-88-3*) U Mich Mus Anthro.

Parsons, Jim & Beauchamp, Larry. Stories of Teaching. 1993. pap. 12.95 (*0-590-73607-8*) Scholastic Inc.

Parsons, John. Away Beyond the Virgin Rocks: A Tribute to John Cabot. LC 98-114173. 256p. 1997. pap. 11.95 (*1-895387-86-8*) Creative Bk Pub.

Parsons, John. Deceiving Trout. (Illus.). 176p. (Orig.). 1989. pap. 14.95 (*0-88317-141-4*) Stoeger Pub Co.

***Parsons, John.** The Official Wimbledon Annual, 1999. (Illus.). 160p. 2000. 39.95 (*1-56554-714-4*) Pelican.

Parsons, John. The Official Wimbledon Championships 1998. (Illus.). 160p. 1998. 35.00 (*1-56554-411-0*) Pelican.

— Ultimate Encyclopedia of Tennis. (Ultimate Encyclopedias Ser.). 1999. 29.95 (*1-85868-539-7*, Pub. by Carlton Bks Ltd) Natl Bk Netwk.

Parsons, John & Janes, Burton K. The King of Baffin Land: The Story of William Ralph Parsons, Last Fur Trade Commissioner of the Hudson's Bay Company. 256p. 1996. pap. 11.95 (*1-895387-65-5*) Creative Bk Pub.

Parsons, John A., ed. Endocrinology of Calcium Metabolism. LC 82-7590. (Comprehensive Endocrinology Ser.). (Illus.). 566p. 1982. reprint ed. pap. 175.50 (*0-608-00599-1*, 206118600007) Bks Demand.

Parsons, John C. Court & Household of Eleanor. pap. text 25.14 (*0-88844-037-5*) Brill Academic Pubs.

— Eleanor of Castile: Queen & Society in Thirteenth Century England. (Illus.). 384p. 1995. text 55.00 (*0-312-08649-0*) St Martin.

— Eleanor of Castile: Queen & Society in Thirteenth Century England. 1997. pap. 17.95 (*0-312-17297-4*) St Martin.

— Medieval Queenship. 272p. 1997. pap. 17.95 (*0-312-17298-2*) St Martin.

Parsons, John C., ed. Medieval Queenship. LC 93-10879. 272p. 1993. text 55.00 (*0-312-05217-0*) St Martin.

Parsons, John C. & Wheeler, Bonnie, eds. Medieval Mothering. (New Middle Ages Ser.: Vol. 3). (Illus.). 400p. 1996. text 72.00 (*0-8153-2341-7*) Garland.

Parsons, John F.C., jt. auth. see Garrigan, Richard T.

Parsons, John P., tr. see Amerio, Romano.

Parsons, Johnson, Ruble & Frieze Staff. Women & Sex Roles. 2nd ed. pap. text, teacher ed. 0.00 (*0-393-95425-0*) Norton.

Parsons, Joy. Days Out in Dorset. (C). 1988. text 40.00 (*0-7855-6064-5*, Pub. by Thornhill Pr) St Mut.

***Parsons, Julie.** The Courtship Gift: A Novel. 320p. 2000. 23.50 (*0-684-86982-9*) Simon & Schuster.

Parsons, Julie. Mary, Mary LC 99-175779. viii, 376p. 1998. write for info. (*1-86059-080-2*, Pub. by Town Hse) Roberts Rinehart.

— Mary, Mary: A Novel. LC 98-33753. 304p. 1999. 22.50 (*0-684-85324-8*) S&S Trade.

***Parsons, Julie & Simon & Schuster Staff.** Mary, Mary. 448p. 2000. mass mkt. 6.99 (*0-06-103049-X*) HarpC.

Parsons, June. Computer Concepts. 1997. pap. text 24.99 (*0-7600-5618-8*) Course Tech.

— New Perspectives on Computers, Technology & Society. 2nd ed. 1998. pap. text 48.95 (*0-7600-7022-9*) Course Tech.

— New Perspectives on Microsoft Windows NT Workstation 4.0 Comprehensive. 1997. pap. text 39.99 (*0-7600-5611-0*) Course Tech.

***Parsons, June & Oja, Dan.** Computer Concepts Illustrated. 2nd ed. (C). 1998. pap. 21.50 (*0-7600-5972-1*) Thomson Learn.

— E-course Microsoft Windows 98. 104p. pap. 21.95 incl. cd-rom (*0-7600-7276-0*, Pub. by Course Tech) Thomson Learn.

Parsons, June & Oja, Dan. New Perspectives on Computer Concepts: Brief. 3rd ed. (New Perspectives Ser.). 304p. (C). 1997. pap. text, mass mkt. 29.95 incl. cd-rom (*0-7600-5796-6*) Course Tech.

— New Perspectives on Computer Concepts: Comprehensive. 3rd ed. (New Perspectives Ser.). 648p. (C). 1998. pap. text, mass mkt. 36.00 incl. cd-rom (*0-7600-5500-9*) Course Tech.

— New Perspectives on Computer Concepts: Introductory. 3rd ed. (New Perspectives Ser.). 424p. (C). 1997. pap. text, mass mkt. 41.95 incl. cd-rom (*0-7600-5449-5*) Course Tech.

***Parsons, June, et al.** New Perspectives on Computer. 3rd ed. 1998. pap. 8.95 (*0-7600-7331-7*) Course Tech.

Parsons, June, et al. New Perspectives on Office: 1997 Edition. (New Perspectives Ser.). (Illus.). 300p. 1998. pap. 53.95 (*0-7600-5798-2*) Course Tech.

Parsons, June, jt. auth. see Oja, Dan.

Parsons, June J. A Guide to Microsoft Windows 3.1, Incl. instr. resource kit, test bank, transparency. (Windows for Business Ser.). (Illus.). 336p. (C). 1993. text. write for info. (*1-56527-070-3*) Course Tech.

— New Perspectives on Microsoft Excel. 1997. pap. text 46.95 (*0-7600-7261-2*) Course Tech.

— New Perspectives on Microsoft Excel 2000 Comprehensive Edition. 1999. pap. text 44.95 (*0-7600-7087-3*) Course Tech.

Parsons, June J. & Halvorson, Michael. Brief Microsoft Windows 3.1 & DOS 5/6, Incl. instr. resource kit, test bank, transparency. 144p. (C). 1994. pap. 7.50 (*1-56527-238-2*) Course Tech.

Parsons, June J. & Oja, Dan. Computer Concepts. (Illustrated Ser.). (Illus.). 192p. 1996. pap. 20.00 (*0-7600-3728-0*) Course Tech.

— Computer Concepts: Brief Edition. (Illustrated Ser.). (Illus.). 88p. 1996. pap. 8.50 (*0-7600-3835-X*) Course Tech.

— Computer Concepts: Brief Edition, Incl. instr. manual, test manager, labs. 2nd ed. (New Perspectives Ser.). (Illus.). 376p. (C). 1996. pap. 26.50 (*0-7600-3439-7*) Course Tech.

Parsons, June J. & Oja, Dan. Computer Concepts - Illustrated Complete. (Illus.). 376p. per. 37.95 (*0-7600-6144-0*, Pub. by Course Tech) Thomson Learn.

Parsons, June J. & Oja, Dan. E-Course Microsoft Internet Explorer 4. 10th ed. 144p. (C). 1998. pap. text 21.95 incl. cd-rom (*0-7600-7278-7*) Course Tech.

Parsons, June J. & Oja, Dan. E-Course Microsoft Internet Explorer 4 Extra on Web Page Development. 19.95 (*0-7600-7033-4*, Pub. by Course Tech) Thomson Learn.

Parsons, June J. & Oja, Dan. Microsoft Excel 5 for Windows - New Perspectives Introductory, Incl. instr. resource kit, test bank, transparency. (New Perspectives Ser.). (Illus.). 304p. (C). 1994. text 20.25 (*1-56527-154-8*) Course Tech.

— Microsoft Excel 7 for Windows 95 - Introductory, Incl. instr. resource kit, test mgr., labs, files. (New Perspectives Ser.). (Illus.). 624p. 1995. text, mass mkt. 30.95 incl. 3.5 ld (*0-7600-3541-5*) Course Tech.

— Microsoft Windows 95 - Brief, Incl. instr. resource kit, online comp., test mgr. rev. ed. (New Perspectives Ser.). (Illus.). 64p. 1995. pap. 8.00 (*1-56527-287-0*) Course Tech.

— Microsoft Windows 95 - Comprehensive, Incl. instr. resource kit, online comp., test mgr. (New Perspectives Ser.). (Illus.). 504p. 1996. pap. 44.95 (*1-56527-998-0*) Course Tech.

— Microsoft Windows 95 - Introductory, Incl. instr. resource kit, online comp., test mgr. expanded rev. ed. (New Perspectives Ser.). (Illus.). 176p. 1996. pap. 21.95 (*0-7600-3489-3*) Course Tech.

— New Perspectives on Computer Concepts. 2nd ed. (New Perspectives Ser.). 256p. 1996. pap. 19.75 (*0-7600-4312-4*) Course Tech.

Parsons, June J. & Oja, Dan. New Perspectives on Computer Concepts: Complete, Incl. instr. manual, test manager, labs. 2nd ed. (New Perspectives Ser.). (Illus.). 840p. (C). 1996. pap. 33.50 (*0-7600-3440-0*) Course Tech.

Parsons, June J. & Oja, Dan. New Perspectives on Computers, Technology & Society. (New Perspectives Ser.). 560p. 1997. pap. 35.50 (*0-7600-4604-2*) Course Tech.

Parsons, June J., et al. Computer Concepts - Illustrated with Microsoft Works 4 for Windows 95 - Illustrated, Incl. instr. resource kit, labs, test mgr. (Illus.). 376p. 1996. text, student ed. write for info. (*0-7600-3747-7*) Course Tech.

— Computer Concepts Brief Second Edition & Microsoft Works 4 for Windows 95, Incl. instr. resource kit, labs, test mgr., files. (New Perspectives Ser.). (Illus.). 792p. 1996. text. write for info. (*0-7600-3582-2*) Course Tech.

— Computer Concepts Brief Second Edition & Microsoft Works 4 for Windows 95 - Illustrated, Incl. instr. manual, test mgr., labs, files. (New Perspectives Ser.). (Illus.). 576p. 1996. text. write for info. (*0-7600-3746-9*) Course Tech.

— Computer Concepts Second Edition Brief & Microsoft Office Professional for Windows 95 Integrated - Introductory, Incl. instr. resource kit, test mgr., labs, files. (New Perspectives Ser.). (Illus.). 1996. text. write for info. (*0-7600-3580-6*) Course Tech.

— Computer Concepts with Microsoft Office 95, Professional Edition: A First Course, Incl. instr. resource kit, test mgr., labs, files. (Illustrated Ser.). (Illus.). 688p. 1996. pap. 57.95 (*0-7600-3744-2*) Course Tech.

Parsons, June J., et al. E-Course Microsoft Excel 97 Extra. 19.95 (*0-7600-7027-X*, Pub. by Course Tech) Thomson Learn.

— E-Course MS Office 97: Windows 95-Certified. (C). 1997. pap. 52.95 (*0-7600-7224-8*) Thomson Learn.

— E-Course Netscape Communicator Extra on Web Page Development. (C). 19.95 (*0-7600-7031-8*, Pub. by Course Tech) Thomson Learn.

Parsons, June J., et al. Four in One: Brief Windows/DOS, WordPerfect 6.0, Quatro Pro 5.0, Paradox 1.0/4.5. (New Perspectives Ser.). 1032p. pap. write for info. (*1-56527-226-9*) Course Tech.

— Microsoft Excel 5 for Windows - New Perspectives Comprehensive, Incl. instr. resource kit, test bank, transparency. (New Perspectives Ser.). (Illus.). 600p. (C). 1994. pap. 28.50 (*1-56527-324-9*) Course Tech.

— Microsoft Excel 5.0 for Windows: Comprehensive. 10th ed. (New Perspectives Ser.). 600p. (C). 1997. pap. 42.95 (*0-7600-4578-X*) Course Tech.

— Microsoft Excel 7 for Windows 95 - Comprehensive, Incl. instr. resource kit, test mgr., labs, files. (New Perspectives Ser.). (Illus.). 328p. 1996. text 42.95 (*0-7600-3535-0*) Course Tech.

— Microsoft Office Professional - New Perspectives, Incl. instr. resource kit, test bank, transparency. (New Perspectives Ser.). (Illus.). 982p. 1995. pap. 41.50 (*0-7600-3465-6*) Course Tech.

— Microsoft Office Professional (Win 3.1) 988p. 1995. write for info. (*0-7600-3467-2*) Course Tech.

— Microsoft Office Professional (Win 3.1) 10th ed. (New Perspectives Ser.). 988p. (C). 1996. pap. 63.95 (*0-7600-4664-6*) Course Tech.

— New Perspectives on Microsoft Excel 7 for Windows 95: Introduction & Comprehensive. 624p. 1996. teacher ed. 18.50 (*0-7600-3974-7*) Course Tech.

— New Perspectives on Microsoft Excel 97: Brief Edition. (New Perspectives Ser.). 160p. 1997. pap. 21.95 (*0-7600-4553-4*) Course Tech.

— New Perspectives on Microsoft Excel 97: Comprehensive Edition. 10th ed. (New Perspectives Ser.). 552p. (C). 1997. pap. 33.50 (*0-7600-5261-1*) Course Tech.

— New Perspectives on Microsoft Excel 97: Introductory Edition. 10th ed. (New Perspectives Ser.). 304p. (C). 1997. pap. 31.95 (*0-7600-5260-3*) Course Tech.

— New Perspectives on Microsoft Office 2000. (New Perspectives Ser.). (Illus.). 856p. 1999. pap. 58.95 (*0-7600-6961-1*) Course Tech.

— New Perspectives on Microsoft Windows NT Workstation 4.0: Comprehensive. 10th ed. (New Perspectives Ser.). 504p. (C). 1997. pap. 44.95 (*0-7600-5221-2*) Course Tech.

— New Perspectives on Microsoft Windows NT Workstation 4.0: Introductory. (New Perspectives Ser.). 152p. (C). 1996. pap. 13.00 (*0-7600-5218-2*) Course Tech.

— New Perspectives on Microsoft Windows NT Workstation 4.0: Introductory & Comprehensive. 656p. (C). 1997. teacher ed. 18.50 (*0-7600-5223-9*) Course Tech.

Parsons, June J., et al. New Perspectives on Microsoft Windows 98 Brief. 80p. per. 11.95 (*0-7600-5446-0*, Pub. by Course Tech) Thomson Learn.

Parsons, June J., jt. auth. see Oja, Dan.

P

An Asterisk (*) at the beginning of an entry indicates that the title is appearing for the first time.

Parsons, June Jamrich & Oja, Dan. New Perspectives on Computer Concepts -- Introductory. 4th ed. 472p. per. 42.95 (*0-7600-6491-1*, Pub. by Course Tech) Thomson Learn.

— New Perspectives on Office 2000 - Second Course. 1016p. per. 62.95 (*0-7600-6433-4*, Pub. by Course Tech) Thomson Learn.

Parsons, June Jamrich, et al. New Perspectives on Computers, Technology & Society - Brief. 2nd ed. 168p. per. 21.95 (*0-7600-7107-1*, Pub. by Course Tech) Thomson Learn.

— New Perspectives on Microsoft Excel 2000 - Brief. 184p. per. 21.95 (*0-7600-7085-7*, Pub. by Course Tech) Thomson Learn.

— New Perspectives on Microsoft Excel 2000 - Introductory. 432p. per. 31.95 (*0-7600-7086-5*, Pub. by Course Tech) Thomson Learn.

— New Perspectives on Microsoft Windows 2000 Professional - Comprehensive. 512p. per. 44.95 (*0-7600-7094-6*, Pub. by Course Tech) Thomson Learn.

Parsons, K. F. & Fitzpatrick, J. M. Practical Urology in Spinal Cord Injury. (Clinical Practice in Urology Ser.). (Illus.). xii, 145p. 1991. 126.00 (*0-387-19676-5*) Spr-Verlag.

Parsons, Kathy. CLIXI for the Intermediate Classroom. rev. ed. 1996. teacher ed. 9.99 (*1-884461-22-0*) NES Arnold.

***Parsons, Kathy.** Spanish for Cruisers: Boat Repairs & Maintenance Phrase Book. LC 99-67832. (Illus.). 224p. 2000. pap. 24.95 (*0-9675905-0-7*) Aventuras Pubng Co.

Parsons, Kathy. Piano Collection. (New Voices Ser.). 57p. 1999. 14.95 (*0-9671341-0-2*) Solo Piano Pubns.

Parsons, Kathy A., jt. auth. see Poague, Leland.

Parsons, Keith M. God & the Burden of Proof. LC 89-35013. 156p. (C). 1989. 40.95 (*0-87975-551-2*) Prometheus Bks.

Parsons, Kenneth C. Human Thermal Environments. LC 93-20570. 450p. 1993. 99.00 (*0-7484-0040-0*, Pub. by Tay Francis Ltd); pap. 49.50 (*0-7484-0041-9*, Pub. by Tay Francis Ltd) Taylor & Francis.

Parsons, Kermit C., jt. auth. see Stein, Clarence S.

Parsons, Kitty. Gloucester Sea Ballads. 2nd rev. ed. (Illus.). 64p. 1981. reprint ed. pap. 4.95 (*0-939792-00-1*) Fermata.

Parsons, L. S. Management of Marine Fisheries in Canada. 784p. 1993. 87.50 (*0-660-15002-6*) NRC Res Pr.

Parsons, L. S. & Lear, W. H., eds. Perspectives on Canadian Marine Fisheries Management. 486p. 1994. 68.95 (*0-660-15003-4*) NRC Res Pr.

***Parsons, Laila.** The Druze Between Palestine & Israel, 1947-49. LC 99-54117. 2000. 65.00 (*0-312-23107-5*) St Martin.

Parsons, Langdon & Sommers, Sheldon C. Gynecology. 2 vols. 2nd ed. LC 75-8184. (Illus.). 1660p. 1978. text 180.00 (*0-7216-7081-4*, W B Saunders Co) Harcrt Hlth Sci Grp.

Parsons, Langdon B. History of the Town of Rye, New Hampshire, from Its Discovery & Settlement to December 31, 1903. (Illus.). viii, 675p. 1992. reprint ed. pap. 38.50 (*1-55613-668-4*) Heritage Bk.

— History of the Town of Rye, New Hampshire, 1623-1903. (Illus.). 675p. 1988. reprint ed. lib. bdg. 68.00 (*0-8328-0071-6*, NH0018) Higginson Bk Co.

Parsons, Laurie & Freed, Jeffrey. Right-Brained Children in a Left-Brained World: Unlocking the Potential of Your ADD Child. LC 97-39515. 256p. 1997. 22.50 (*0-684-84271-8*) Simon & Schuster.

Parsons, Laurie, jt. auth. see Freed, Jeffery.

Parsons, Lee A. Origins of Maya Art: Monumental Stone Sculpture of Kaminaljuyu, Guatemala, & the Southern Pacific Coast. LC 85-31148. (Studies in Pre-Columbian Art & Archaeology: No. 28). (Illus.). 224p. (Orig.). 1986. pap. text 30.00 (*0-88402-148-3*, PAORP) Dumbarton Oaks.

Parsons, Lee A., et al, eds. The Face of Ancient America: The Wally & Brenda Zollman Collection of Precolumbian Art. LC 88-81793. (Illus.). 238p. 1988. pap. 37.50 (*0-936260-24-6*) Ind Mus Art.

Parsons, Lee A., et al. The Face of Ancient America: The Wally & Brenda Zollman Collection of Precolumbian Art. LC 88-81793. (Illus.). 238p. 1988. 57.50 (*0-936260-23-8*) Ind Mus Art.

Parsons, Lee A., jt. auth. see Cahalan, Margaret W.

Parsons, Leonard J., jt. auth. see Dalrymple, Douglas J.

Parsons, Les. Expanding Response Journals: In All Subject Area. LC 93-47193. 96p. (C). 1994. pap. text 17.50 (*0-435-08813-0*, 08813) Heinemann.

— Poetry, Themes, & Activities: Exploring the Fun & Fantasy of Language. 112p. (C). 1992. pap. text 16.50 (*0-435-08730-4*, 08730) Heinemann.

— Response Journals. LC 90-117341. 90p. (Orig.). (C). 1989. pap. text 17.50 (*0-435-08517-4*, 08517) Heinemann.

— Writing in the Real Classroom. LC 90-28694. 112p. (C). 1991. pap. text 16.50 (*0-435-08587-5*, 08587) Heinemann.

Parsons, Linda. Home Fires. 80p. (Orig.). 1997. 22.00 (*1-885912-14-5*); pap. 12.00 (*1-885912-12-9*) Sows Ear Pr.

***Parsons, Lucy.** Lucy Parson Speaks. 208p. 2000. 28.00 (*0-88286-247-2*) C H Kerr.

Parsons, Lucy, ed. Famous Speeches of the Eight Chicago Anarchists in Court. LC 77-90187. (Mass Violence in America Ser.). 1974. reprint ed. 12.95 (*0-405-01330-2*) Ayer.

Parsons, Luke, jt. auth. see Steel, David.

Parsons, Lynn H., compiled by. John Quincy Adams: A Bibliography, 6. LC 92-33703. (Bibliographies of the Presidents of the United States Ser.: No. 6). 240p. 1993. lib. bdg. 65.00 (*0-313-28164-5*, AP06, Greenwood Pr) Greenwood.

Parsons, Lynn H., jt. ed. see O'Brien, Kenneth P.

Parsons, M. J., et al. Current Names of Wild Plants in New Zealand. 206p. 1998. pap. 42.50 (*0-478-09319-5*) Balogh.

Parsons, Malcolm L. Color Atlas of Clinical Neurology. 2nd ed. (Illus.). 320p. (C). (gr. 13). 1993. text 113.00 (*0-8151-6613-3*, 22762) Mosby Inc.

***Parsons, Maria.** Mental Health & Professional Procedure. 256p. 2000. pap. 35.00 (*0-7506-3844-3*) Buttrwrth-Heinemann.

Parsons, Marilyn, jt. ed. see Smith, Deborah F.

Parsons, Marjorie, jt. auth. see Parsons, Chuck.

Parsons, Mark H. The Drummer's Studio Survival Guide: How to Get the Best Possible Drum tracks on Any Recording Project. Van Horn, Rick, ed. 96p. 1996. per. 12.95 (*0-7935-7222-3*) H Leonard.

Parsons, Marnie. Touch Monkeys: Nonsense Strategies for Reading Twentieth-Century Poetry. LC 93-94817. (Theory - Culture Ser.). 262p. 1993. text 50.00 (*0-8020-2983-3*) U of Toronto Pr.

Parsons, Marsha B., jt. auth. see Reid, Dennis H.

Parsons, Mary E. The Wild Flowers of California. 1992. reprint ed. lib. bdg. 75.00 (*0-7812-5074-9*) Rprt Serv.

Parsons, Mary H., jt. auth. see Parsons, Jeffrey R.

Parsons, Michael. The Butterflies of Papua New Guinea: Their Systematics & Biology. (Illus.). 800p. (C). 1998. boxed set 275.00 (*0-12-545555-0*) Morgan Kaufmann.

— Butterflies of the Bulolo-Wau Valley. 1992. 24.95 (*0-930897-61-7*) Bishop Mus.

***Parsons, Michael.** The Dove That Returns. LC 99-46205. (New Library of Psychoanalysis Ser.). 2000. pap. write for info. (*0-415-21182-4*) Routledge.

— The Falklands War. 128p. 2000. pap. 9.95 (*0-7509-2354-7*) Sutton Publng.

Parsons, Michael, ed. see Balint, Enid.

Parsons, Michael D. Power & Politics: Federal Higher Education Policymaking in the 1990s. LC 96-43399. 254p. (C). 1997. text 59.50 (*0-7914-3423-0*); pap. text 19.95 (*0-7914-3424-9*) State U NY Pr.

Parsons, Michael H. Part-Time Occupational Faculty: A Contribution to Excellence. 40p. 1985. 5.50 (*0-317-01306-8*) Ctr Educ Trng Employ.

Parsons, Michael J. & Blocker, H. Gene. Aesthetics & Education. LC 92-21377. (Disciplines in Art Education Ser.). 208p. 1993. text 34.95 (*0-252-01988-1*); pap. text 14.95 (*0-252-06293-0*) U of Ill Pr.

Parsons, Michael L. Global Warming: The Truth Behind the Myth. (Illus.). 288p. (C). 1995. 27.95 (*0-306-45083-6*, Plenum Trade) Perseus Pubng.

Parsons, Michael L., jt. auth. see Wolff, Diane D.

Parsons, Mickey L. Patient Centered Care: A Model for Restructuring. 7p. 1994. 89.00 (*0-8342-0573-4*, 20573) Aspen Pub.

Parsons, Mickey L. & Murdaugh, Carolyn L. Patient Centered Care: A Model for Restructuring. 646p. 1994. pap. 39.00 (*0-8342-0983-7*, 20983) Aspen Pub.

Parsons, Mickey L., et al. Guide to Clinical Resource Management: Strategies for Improving Patient Care. 256p. 1996. 49.00 (*0-8342-0849-0*, 20849) Aspen Pub.

— Interdisciplinary Case Studies in Health Care Redesign. LC 97-21500. (Strategies for Improving Patient Care Ser.). 384p. 1997. pap. 49.00 (*0-8342-0970-5*, 20970) Aspen Pub.

Parsons, Mikeal C. The Departure of Jesus in Luke-Acts: Ascension Narratives in Context. (JSNTS Ser.: Vol. 21). 301p. 1988. pap. 28.50 (*1-85075-076-9*, Pub. by Sheffield Acad) CUP Services.

Parsons, Mikeal C., jt. ed. see Sloan, Robert B.

Parsons, N., tr. see Stanyukovich, Konstantin.

***Parsons, Nancy & Amsterdam, Dick.** Morsels from the Better Mousetrap: Tips, Tricks & Tales about Corporate Communications for Small Businesses. LC 00-190419. 227p. 2000. 25.00 (*0-7388-1673-6*); pap. 18.00 (*0-7388-1674-4*) Xlibris Corp.

Parsons, Nancy S., ed. Stockton Springs Vital Records, 1859-1891. LC 79-55454. (Orig.). 1979. pap. 19.95 (*0-918768-02-0*) Cay-Bel.

Parsons, Neil. King Khama, Emperor Joe, & the Great White Queen: Victorian Britain Through African Eyes. LC 97-37111. (Illus.). 296p. 1997. pap. 18.95 (*0-226-64745-5*) U Ch Pr.

— King Khama, Emperor Joe, & the Great White Queen: Victorian Britain Through African Eyes. LC 97-37111. 296p. 1997. lib. bdg. 50.00 (*0-226-64744-7*) U Ch Pr.

Parsons, Neil, ed. see Rey, Charles.

***Parsons, Nicholas.** Austria. 4th ed. (Blue Guide Ser.). (Illus.). 448p. 2000. pap. 23.95 (*0-393-32017-0*) Norton.

Parsons, Nicholas. Prague. (Illustrated Travel Guides from Thomas Cook Ser.). (Illus.). 192p. 1994. pap. 12.95 (*0-8442-9065-3*, Passprt Bks) NTC Contemp Pub Co.

Parsons, Nicholas T. Hungary Insider's Guide: A Traveller's Guide. (Illus.). 366p. (Orig.). 1991. pap. 16.95 (*0-87052-976-5*) Hippocrene Bks.

— Thailand: Reopening the Rewards of Growth. (Illus.). 200p. 1996. 170.00 (*1-85564-409-6*, Pub. by Euromoney) Am Educ Systs.

— Vienna. (Blue Guide Ser.). (Illus.). 224p. (Orig.). 1997. pap. 18.95 (*0-393-31423-5*) Norton.

Parsons, Nicholas T., tr. see Werkner, Patrick.

Parsons, Nick. Dead Heart: The Screenplay. 1997. pap. 17.95 (*0-86819-459-X*, Pub. by Currency Pr) Accents Pubns.

— Employee Participation in Europe: A Case Study in the British & French Gas Industries. (Illus.). 200p. 1997. text 59.95 (*1-85972-522-8*, Pub. by Avebry) Ashgate Pub Co.

Parsons, Noel R., ed. N-C Machinability Data Systems. LC 74-153852. (Society of Manufacturing Engineers Numerical Control Ser.). 219p. reprint ed. pap. 67.90 (*0-608-30083-7*, 201599900097) Bks Demand.

***Parsons, Oja.** Microsoft Windows 2000: Brief. (New Perspectives Ser.). (C). 2000. text 11.95 (*0-7600-6548-9*) Course Tech.

— NP on Microsoft Window NT 4.0 Workstation. (New Perspectives Ser.). (C). 1999. spiral bd. 14.00 (*0-619-01912-3*) Course Tech.

— NP On Office 97 "Millenium Edition" ed. (C). 1999. pap. 58.95 (*0-7600-6505-5*) Thomson Learn.

— Practical Office Procedures. (New Perspectives Ser.). (C). 2000. text 40.95 (*0-619-01919-0*) Course Tech.

Parsons, Oscar A., et al, eds. Neuropsychology of Alcoholism: Implications for Diagnosis & Treatment. LC 86-29583. 414p. 1987. lib. bdg. 55.00 (*0-89862-696-X*) Guilford Pubns.

Parsons, P., jt. auth. see Sato, Sadakatsu.

Parsons, Particia & Parsons, Arthur. Hippocrates Now! Is Your Doctor Ethical? 240p. 1995. text 35.00 (*0-8020-0526-8*) U of Toronto Pr.

***Parsons, Patriee A.** Tales of Folly. LC 99-96131. 275p. 1999. pap. 27.50 (*0-9674412-1-8*) Parsons Printwrks.

***Parsons, Patrice A. & Parsons, Patricia A.** Parenting Smart: (Everything You Need to Know to Do It Right!) LC 99-96130. (Illus.). 120p. 1999. pap. 20.00 (*0-9674412-0-X*) Parsons Printwrks.

Parsons, Patricia. Patient Power! The Smart Patient's Guide to Health Care. LC 97-139173. (Illus.). 240p. 1997. pap. 14.95 (*0-8020-7186-4*) U of Toronto Pr.

Parsons, Patricia & Parsons, Arthur. Hippocrates Now! Is Your Doctor Ethical? 220p. 1995. pap. 14.95 (*0-8020-6963-0*) U of Toronto Pr.

Parsons, Patricia A., jt. auth. see Parsons, Patrice A.

Parsons, Patrick & Frieden, Rob. The Cable & Satellite Television Industry. LC 97-27532. 384p. 1997. pap. 34.67 (*0-205-20013-3*) Allyn.

Parsons, Patrick R., jt. auth. see Knowlton, Steven R.

Parsons, Patrick R., jt. ed. see Knowlton, Steven R.

Parsons, Paul. Getting Published: The Acquisition Process at University Presses. LC 89-31711. 256p. 1989. pap. 16.95 (*0-87049-612-3*) U of Tenn Pr.

Parsons, Paul F. Inside America's Christian Schools. LC 87-24709. 176p. 1988. pap. text 12.95 (*0-86554-303-8*, P054) Mercer Univ Pr.

Parsons, Penny, et al. The Bluegrass Music Cookbook. LC 97-7346. (Illus.). (Orig.). 1997. pap. 16.95 (*0-89587-162-9*) Blair.

Parsons, Peter A. The Evolutionary Biology of Colonizing Species. LC 82-19763. (Illus.). 272p. 1983. text 57.95 (*0-521-25247-4*) Cambridge U Pr.

Parsons, Peter A., jt. auth. see Hoffmann, Ary A.

Parsons, Philip, ed. A Companion to Theatre in Australia. (Illus.). 704p. (C). 1995. text 80.00 (*0-521-34528-6*) Cambridge U Pr.

Parsons, Philip & Chance, Victoria. The Concise Companion to Theatre on Australia. 352p. (Orig.). 1997. pap. 29.95 (*0-86819-499-9*, Pub. by Currency Pr) Accents Pubns.

Parsons, Philip A. Responsibility for Crime: An Investigation of the Nature & Causes of Crime & a Means of Its Prevention. LC 75-76683. (Columbia University. Studies in the Social Sciences: No. 91). reprint ed. 29.50 (*0-404-51091-4*) AMS Pr.

Parsons, Polly E. & Heffner, John E., eds. Pulmonary/Respiratory Therapy Secrets. LC 96-47624. (Secrets Ser.). (Illus.). 350p. (Orig.). 1996. pap. text 38.00 (*1-56053-163-0*) Hanley & Belfus.

Parsons, Polly E. & Wiener-Kronish, Jeanine P. Critical Care Secrets: Questions You Will be Asked on Rounds, in the ICU, OR & ER & on Oral Exams. 2nd ed. LC 98-21153. 1998. 39.00 (*1-56053-274-2*) Hanley & Belfus.

Parsons, R., jt. ed. see Kalvoda, Robert.

Parsons, Ramon M. La Moral en la Educacion. LC 83-10594. (SPA.). 90p. 1983. 6.00 (*0-8477-2746-7*) U of PR Pr.

Parsons, Reg. Woodcarving: A Manual of Techniques. (Illus.). 192p. 1994. pap. 29.95 (*1-85223-770-8*, Pub. by Crolwood) Trafalgar.

Parsons, Richard & Brooks, Neal A. Baltimore County Panorama. Phillips, Nancy O., ed. LC 88-22953. (Baltimore County Heritage Publications). (Illus.). 375p. 1988. text 29.95 (*0-937076-03-1*) Baltimore Co Pub Lib.

Parsons, Richard D. Action Research. (C). 2000. pap. text. write for info. (*0-321-03775-8*) Addson-Wesley Educ.

— Action Research: Increasing the Validity & Utility of Theory & Practice. (C). 2000. pap. text. write for info. (*0-321-03774-X*) Addison-Wesley.

***Parsons, Richard D.** The Ethics of Professional Practice. LC 00-41629 2000. write for info. (*0-205-30878-3*) Allyn.

— The Skilled Consultant. 352p. 1995. 79.00 (*0-205-16119-7*) Allyn.

Parsons, Richard D. The Skilled Consultant: A Systematic Approach to the Theory & Practice of Consultation. (C). 1995. teacher ed. write for info. (*0-205-18701-3*, H8701-8) Allyn.

— The Skills of Helping. LC 94-6038. 224p. 1994. pap. text 44.00 (*0-205-14713-5*) Allyn.

Parsons, Richard D. & Meyers, Joel. Developing Consultation Skills: A Guide to Training, Development, & Assessment for Human Services Professionals. LC 84-5744. (Social & Behavioral Science Ser.). 279p. 1984. 53.00 (*0-87589-605-7*) Jossey-Bass.

Parsons, Richard D. & Wicks, Robert J. Counseling Strategies & Intervention. 4th ed. LC 93-1560. 213p. 1993. pap. text 52.00 (*0-205-14791-7*) Allyn.

Parsons, Richard D., jt. ed. see Wicks, Robert J.

Parsons, Richard E. Sir Edwyn Hoskyns As a Biblical Theologian. LC 85-25038. 152p. 1986. text 29.95 (*0-312-72647-3*) St Martin.

Parsons, Rob. Almost Everything I Need to Know about God I Learned in Sunday School. LC 98-54237. 180p. 1999. pap. 10.99 (*0-7852-7032-9*) Nelson.

— The Sixty Minute Father. LC 96-1357. 112p. 1996. pap. 7.99 (*0-8054-6289-9*, 4262-89) Broadman.

— The Sixty Minute Marriage Builder. LC 97-42260. 1998. pap. 7.99 (*0-8054-0178-4*) Broadman.

— The Sixty Second Father: Ideas for Making Lifelong Memories with Your Child. LC 97-6305. 128p. 1997. pap. 5.99 (*0-8054-6353-4*) Broadman.

Parsons, Robert. Conference About the Next Succession to the Crown of England. LC 70-38217. (English Experience Ser.: No. 481). 1972. reprint ed. 50.00 (*90-221-0481-8*) Walter J Johnson.

— Handbook of Refrigeration. (Illus.). 1015p. 1998. text 134.00 (*1-883413-54-0*, 81981-S1) Am Heat Ref & Air Eng.

— Lost at Sea, Vol. 1. 128p. 1991. reprint ed. pap. 9.95 (*0-920021-96-4*) Creative Bk Pub.

— Lost at Sea, Vol. 2. 192p. 1995. reprint ed. pap. 9.95 (*1-895387-09-4*) Creative Bk Pub.

***Parsons, Robert.** Survive the Savage Sea: Tales from our Ocean Heritage. LC 99-208819. 350p. 1999. pap. 15.95 (*1-895387-96-5*) Creative Bk Pub.

Parsons, Robert. Wake of the Schooners. 286p. 1995. reprint ed. pap. 11.95 (*1-895387-24-8*) Creative Bk Pub.

— The Warn-Word to Sir Francis Hastinges Wast-Word, 1602 LC 76-375995. (English Recusant Literature, 1558-1640 Ser.). 131p. 1976. write for info. (*0-85967-309-X*) Scolar Pr.

Parsons, Robert, ed. Handbook of Fundaments. 900p. 1997. text 134.00 (*1-883413-45-1*, 81971) Am Heat Ref & Air Eng.

— Handbook of Refrigeration. (ASHRAE Handbook Ser.). (Illus.). 1001p. 1998. text 134.00 (*1-883413-53-2*, 81980-1P) Am Heat Ref & Air Eng.

***Parsons, Robert, ed.** 1999 HVAC Systems & Equipment. 1999. 134.00 (*1-883413-71-0*) Am Heat Ref & Air Eng.

Parsons, Robert, ed. 1996 HVAC Systems & Equipment. rev. ed. (ASHRAE Handbook Ser.). (Illus.). 1500p. 1996. 134.00 (*1-883413-35-4*); 134.00 (*1-883413-34-6*) Am Heat Ref & Air Eng.

Parsons, Robert & Costello, William T. The Judgment of a Catholicke English-Man Living in Banishment for His Religion. LC 57-9033. 160p. 1978. reprint ed. 50.00 (*0-8201-1240-2*) Schol Facsimiles.

Parsons, Robert, ed. see Sauer, H., et al.

Parsons, Robert, ed. see Saures, H., et al.

***Parsons, Robert C.** Committed to the Deep: Stories & Memoirs. 288p. 1999. pap. 12.95 (*1-894294-09-2*, Pub. by Creative Bk Pub) Genl Dist Srvs.

Parsons, Robert C. Toll of the Sea: Stories from the Forgotten Coast. (Illus.). 224p. 1996. reprint ed. pap. 11.95 (*1-895387-51-5*) Creative Bk Pub.

Parsons, Roger, tr. see Damaskin, Boris B., et al.

Parsons, Rosamond H. Anglo-Norman Books of Courtesy & Nurture. (English Literature Ser.: No. 33). 1970. reprint ed. pap. 39.95 (*0-8383-0059-6*) M S G Haskell Hse.

Parsons, Ruth, jt. auth. see Gutierrez, Lorraine.

Parsons, S. D. Putting Profit into Ranching: The Livestock Owner's Guide to Success! Parsons, H. E., ed. (Illus.). 150p. (Orig.). 1988. pap. write for info. (*0-318-63364-7*) Ranch Pubns.

***Parsons, Sara Mitchell.** From Southern Wrongs to Civil Rights: The Memoir of a White Civil Rights Activist. 192p. 2000. 24.95 (*0-8173-1026-6*) U of Ala Pr.

Parsons, Simon. Qualitative Methods for Reasoning under Uncertainty. LC 96-44044. (A. I. Ser.). (Illus.). 404p. Date not set. 45.00 (*0-262-16168-0*) MIT Pr.

Parsons, Simon, ed. see Hunter, Anthony.

***Parsons Staff.** American Greetings Spiritual Expressions 2. 2nd ed. (Illus.). 1999. pap. 34.99 (*0-7630-3462-2*) Softkey Inc MA.

Parsons, Stanley B. The Populist Context: Rural Versus Urban Power on a Great Plains Frontier. 22. LC 72-824. (Contributions in American History Ser.: No. 22). (Illus.). 205p. 1973. 57.95 (*0-8371-6392-7*, PAC/, Greenwood Pr) Greenwood.

Parsons, Stanley B., et al. U. S. Congressional Districts & Data, 1843-1883. LC 85-67582. (Illus.). 254p. 1986. lib. bdg. 85.00 (*0-313-22045-X*, PUN/, Greenwood Pr) Greenwood.

— United States Congressional Districts, 1883-1913. LC 89-675315. 464p. 1990. lib. bdg. 115.00 (*0-313-26482-1*, PUC/, Greenwood Pr) Greenwood.

— United States Congressional Districts, 1788-1841. LC 77-83897. (Illus.). 416p. 1978. lib. bdg. 115.00 (*0-8371-9828-3*, PUS/, Greenwood Pr) Greenwood.

***Parsons, Stephen P.** Interviewing & Investigating. LC 99-56931. 2000. pap. text 35.95 (*0-7355-1251-5*) Panel Pubs.

Parsons, Steven L., ed. see Nabokov, Vladimir.

Parsons, Susan F. Feminism & Christian Ethics. (New Studies in Christian Ethics: No. 8). 298p. (C). 1996. text 64.95 (*0-521-46281-9*) Cambridge U Pr.

— Feminism & Christian Ethics. (New Studies in Christian Ethics: No. 8). 297p. (C). 1996. pap. text 19.95 (*0-521-46820-5*) Cambridge U Pr.

Parsons, T. Voice & Speech Processing. (Electrical Engineering Ser.). 448p. (C). 1986. text 80.00 (*0-07-048541-0*) McGraw.

Parsons, Talcott. Age & Sex in the Social Structure of the United States. (Reprint Series in Social Sciences). (C). 1993. reprint ed. pap. text 5.00 (*0-8290-3751-9*, S-217) Irvington.

— The Early Essays. LC 90-19213. (Heritage of Sociology Ser.). 361p. 1991. pap. text 24.00 (*0-226-09237-2*); lib. bdg. 54.00 (*0-226-09236-4*) U Ch Pr.

— Social Structure & Personality. LC 64-11218. 1964. 24.95 (*0-02-924850-7*) Free Pr.

P

— The Social System. 1964. pap. 22.95 (*0-02-924190-1*) Free Pr.
— Structure of Social Action, 1. 2nd ed. LC 49-49353. 1967. pap. 14.95 (*0-02-924240-1*) Free Pr.
— Structure of Social Action, 2. 2nd ed. LC 49-49353. 1967. pap. 21.95 (*0-02-924250-9*) Free Pr.
— Talcott Parsons on Institutions & Social Evolution: Selected Writings. Mayhew, Leon H., ed. LC 82-4911. (Heritage of Sociology Ser.). 368p. 1985. pap. text 18.00 (*0-226-64749-8*) U Ch Pr.
— Talcott Parsons on Institutions & Social Evolution: Selected Writings. Mayhew, Leon H., ed. LC 82-4911. (Heritage of Sociology Ser.). 304p. 1992. lib. bdg. 30.00 (*0-226-64747-1*) U Ch Pr.
***Parsons, Talcott.** The Talcott Parsons Reader. Turner, Bryan S., ed. LC 99-25740. (Reader Ser.). 384p. (C). 1999. 64.95 (*1-55786-543-4*); pap. 29.95 (*1-55786-544-2*) Blackwell Pubs.
Parsons, Talcott, ed. Theories of Society, Vol. 1. LC 61-9171. 1965. 60.00 (*0-02-924450-1*) Free Pr.
Parsons, Talcott & Platt, Gerald M. The American University. LC 73-77470. 477p. reprint ed. pap. 147.90 (*0-7837-1524-2*, 204180100024) Bks Demand.
Parsons, Talcott & Shils, Edward, eds. Toward a General Theory of Action. LC 51-14629. 518p. reprint ed. pap. 160.60 (*0-608-30125-6*, 201768200007) Bks Demand.
Parsons, Talcott, et al. Socialization & Schools. LC 68-59278. (Reprint Ser.: No. 1). 90p. 1968. pap. 6.95 (*0-916690-00-8*) Harvard Educ Rev.
Parsons, Talcott, et al. Working Papers in the Theory of Action. LC 80-24475. 269p. 1981. reprint ed. lib. bdg. 35.00 (*0-313-22468-4*, PAWP, Greenwood Pr) Greenwood.
Parsons, Talcott, tr. see Weber, Max.
Parsons, Talcott, tr. see Weber, Max M.
***Parsons Technology Staff.** Clickart Christian Publishing Suite III. 1999. 69.99 (*1-57264-317-X*) Parsons Tech.
— Complete Book of Zingers. 1997. 19.00 (*1-57264-221-1*) Parsons Tech.
— Membership Plus 6, 8 vols. 1999. 269.99 (*1-57264-322-6*) Parsons Tech.
***Parsons Technology Staff, ed.** QuickVerse 6 Essentials. (Illus.). 2000. 59.99 (*0-7630-5327-9*) Softkey Inc MA.
Parsons, Terence. Events in the Semantics of English: A Study in Subatomic Semantics. (Illus.). 352p. 1994. pap. text 23.00 (*0-262-66093-8*) MIT Pr.
***Parsons, Terence.** Indeterminate Identity: Metaphysics & Semantics. (Illus.). 210p. 2000. text 49.95 (*0-19-825044-4*) OUP.
Parsons, Terence. Nonexistent Objects. LC 79-21682. 280p. 1980. 50.00 (*0-300-02404-5*) Yale U Pr.
Parsons, Terry D. Iowa Legal Forms: Family Law, 1984-1993. 160p. ring bd. 85.00 incl. disk (*0-685-49477-2*, MICHIE) LEXIS Pub.
— Iowa Legal Forms: Family Law, 1984-1993. 160p. 1993. ring bd. 60.00 incl. disk (*0-86678-171-4*, 81013-10, MICHIE) LEXIS Pub.
— Iowa Legal Forms: Family Law, 1984-1993. (Illus.). 160p. 1993. suppl. ed. 30.00 (*0-614-03180-X*, MICHIE) LEXIS Pub.
***Parsons, Theophilus.** Laws of Business for All the States of the Union & the Dominion of Canada: With Forms & Directions for All Transactions & Abstracts of the Laws of All the States on Various Topics. LC 99-58129. 822p. 2000. 85.00 (*1-57588-613-8*) W S Hein.
Parsons, Theophilus. Memoir of Theophilus Parsons. LC 71-118032. (American Constitutional & Legal History Ser). 1970. reprint ed. lib. bdg. 55.00 (*0-306-71939-8*) Da Capo.
— Personal & Property Rights of a Citizen of the United States: How to Exercise & How to Preserve Them. xvi, 744p. 1993. reprint ed. 70.00 (*0-8377-2519-4*, Rothman) W S Hein.
***Parsons, Thomas & Gale, Iain.** Post-Impressionism: The Rise of Modern Art, 1880-1920. (Illus.). 424p. 2000. 94.95 (*0-9684749-6-9*, Pub. by NDE Pub) IPG Chicago.
Parsons, Thomas E. Introduction to Algorithms in Pascal. 444p. 1994. text 70.95 (*0-471-30594-4*) Wiley.
— Introduction to Compiler Construction. 359p. (C). 1992. pap. text 60.95 (*0-7167-8261-8*) W H Freeman.
— Introduction to Compiler Construction. 1992. pap. text, student ed. 17.95 (*0-7167-8262-6*) W H Freeman.
Parsons, Thomas S., jt. auth. see Gans, Carl.
Parsons, Timothy. Britain's Imperial Century, 1815-1914: Imperialism from the Perspective of World History. LC 99-11765. (Critical Issues in History Ser.). 128p. 1998. 53.00 (*0-8476-8824-0*) Rowman.
— The British Imperial Century, 1815-1914: Imperialism from the Perspective of World History. LC 99-11765. (Critical Issues in History Ser.). 128p. 1999. pap. 11.95 (*0-8476-8825-9*) Rowman.
Parsons, Timothy H. The African Rank & File: Social Implications of Colonial Military Service in the King's African Rifles, 1902-1964. LC 99-25009. 328p. 1999. 25.95 (*0-325-00140-5*); 60.00 (*0-325-00141-3*, E00141) Greenwood.
Parsons, Timothy Richard, jt. auth. see Harrison, Paul J.
Parsons, Tom. Auguste Rodin: French Sculptor. (Reveries Ser.). 120p. 1999. 14.95 (*1-85995-481-2*) Parkstone Pr.
— Insider Travel Secrets. 2nd rev. ed. LC 97-71857. (Illus.). 416p. (Orig.). 1998. pap. 19.95 (*0-9650960-1-7*) Best Fares USA.
— Pierre Auguste Renoir. LC 96-25747. (Art for Young People Ser.). (Illus.). 32p. (J). 1996. 14.95 (*0-8069-6162-7*) Sterling.
***Parsons, Tony.** As It Is: The Open Secret to Living an Awakened Life. 160p. 2000. pap. 14.95 (*1-878019-10-4*) Inner Drctns.
Parsons, Vicki. Developing & Managing a Nursing Home Volunteer Program. (C). 1987. 16.50 (*1-877735-32-9*, 2179pp) Prof Prnting & Pub.
— Simple Expressions: Creative & Therapeutic Arts for the Elderly in Long-Term Care Facilities. LC 98-84476. (Illus.). xvi, 167p. 1998. pap. 19.95 (*0-910251-97-5*, SMP102) Venture Pub PA.
— Year of Holidays: A Planning & Idea Book for Holiday Activities in Nursing Homes. (Illus.). 177p. (C). 1993. 19.50 (*1-877735-41-8*, 2225PP) Prof Prnting & Pub.
Parsons, Virginia. Pinocchio Series. Incl. Pinocchio & Geppetto. 1979. (*0-07-048531-3*); Pinocchio Goes on Stage. 1979. 4.95 (*0-07-048532-1*); Pinocchio Plays Truant. 1979. 4.95 (*0-07-048530-5*); (J). (gr. k-3). 1979. write for info. (*0-318-54173-4*) McGraw.
Parsons, W. J. Improving Marketing Performance. 200p. 1987. text 55.95 (*0-566-02595-7*, Pub. by Gower) Ashgate Pub Co.
Parsons, Ward C., jt. auth. see Wentz, Gini.
Parsons, Wayne. Keynes & the Quest for a Moral Science: A Study of Economics & Alchemy. LC 96-49722. 240p. 1997. 85.00 (*1-85898-373-8*) E Elgar.
— The Power of the Financial Press: Journalism & Economic Opinion in Britain & America. 272p. 1989. 95.00 (*1-85278-039-8*) E Elgar.
— The Power of the Financial Press: Journalism & Economic Opinion in Britain & America. LC 89-43066. 300p. 1990. text 24.95 (*0-8135-1497-5*) Rutgers U Pr.
— Public Policy: An Introduction to the Theory & Practice of Policy Analysis. LC 95-10756. 704p. 1996. 100.00 (*1-85278-553-5*); pap. text 35.00 (*1-85278-554-3*) E Elgar.
Parsons, Wilfrid. Mexican Martyrdom: Firsthand Experiences of the Religious Persecution in Mexico, 1926-1935. LC 87-51412. 295p. 1994. reprint ed. pap. 10.00 (*0-89555-330-9*) TAN Bks Pubs.
— Which Way, Democracy? LC 72-5747. (Essay Index Reprint Ser.). 1977. reprint ed. 21.95 (*0-8369-7296-1*) Ayer.
Parsons, Wilfrid, tr. see Augustine, Saint.
Parsons, William. Lifetime & Testamentary Estate Planning. 9th ed. 228p. 1983. 27.00 (*0-8318-0431-9*, B431) Am Law Inst.
Parsons, William, jt. auth. see Tweed, Harrison.
Parsons, William B., Jr. Cholesterol Control Without Diet! The Niacin Solution. LC 98-65160. (Illus.). 228p. 1998. 19.95 (*0-9662568-6-7*) Lilac Pr.
Parsons, William B. The Enigma of the Oceanic Feeling: Revisioning the Psychoanalytic Theory of Mysticism. 264p. 1999. text 45.00 (*0-19-511508-2*) OUP.
— Graphic Design with PageMaker 6.0, Mac & Windows. 2nd ed. LC 95-50836. 576p. (C). 1996. mass mkt. 49.95 (*0-8273-7814-9*) Delmar.
Parsons, William S. Everyone's Not Here: Families of the Armenian Genocide, a Study Guide. (Illus.). 88p. (YA). (gr. 7-12). 1989. spiral bd. 10.00 (*0-925428-04-3*) Armenian Assembly.
Parsons, William S., jt. auth. see Strom, Margot S.
Parsons, William T., ed. Arms Control & Strategic Stability: Challenges for the Future. 184p. (Orig.). (C). 1986. pap. text 20.00 (*0-8191-5475-X*) U Pr of Amer.
Parsons, William W., jt. auth. see Houston, James G.
Parsons, Y., et al. A Manual of Chemical & Biological Methods for Seawater Analysis. (Illus.). 144p. 1984. text 51.00 (*0-08-030288-2*, Pergamon Pr); pap. text 35.25 (*0-08-030287-4*, Pergamon Pr) Elsevier.
Parsonson, Ian. The Australian Ark: A History of Domesticated Animals in Australia. (Illus.). 304p. 59.95 (*0-643-06384-6*, Pub. by CSIRO) Accents Pubns.
Parsonson, Jack. A Time to Remember. Frisque, Tom, ed. (Illus.). 127p. (Orig.). 1994. pap. 17.95 (*0-9623080-4-8*) Aviation Usk.
Parsont, Meg. Bulldozer. LC 98-87653. (Go Bks.). (Illus.). 12p. (J). 1999. bds. 5.95 (*0-7892-0543-2*, Abbeville Kids) Abbeville Pr.
— Helicopter. LC 98-87654. (Go Bks.). (Illus.). 12p. (J). 1999. bds. 5.95 (*0-7892-0544-0*, Abbeville Kids) Abbeville Pr.
— Race Car. LC 98-87655. (Go Bks.). (Illus.). 12p. (J). 1999. bds. 5.95 (*0-7892-0545-9*, Abbeville Kids) Abbeville Pr.
— Seaplane. LC 98-87656. (Go Bks.). (Illus.). 12p. (J). 1999. bds. 5.95 (*0-7892-0546-7*, Abbeville Kids) Abbeville Pr.
Parsowith, B. Scott. Fundamentals of Quality Auditing. 144p. 1995. pap. 35.00 (*0-87389-240-2*, H0794) ASQ Qual Pr.
— Transparency Masters to Accompany Fundamentals of Quality Auditing. 197p. 1995. pap. 18.00 (*0-87389-342-5*, H0794A) ASQ Qual Pr.
Parssinen, Diane, jt. auth. see Rubin, Charles.
Parssinen, Terry, jt. auth. see Meyer, Kathryn.
Parsson, Jens O. Dying of Money: Lessons of the Great German & American Inflations. LC 73-92727. 372p. 1974. 19.95 (*0-914688-01-4*) Wellspring Pr.
Part of the 3rd Symposium Staff. Microtunnel Construction: Proceedings: International Symposium on Microtunnel Construction (3d: 1995: Munich, Germany) (Illus.). 166p. (C). 1995. 91.00 (*90-5410-542-9*, Pub. by A A Balkema) Ashgate Pub Co.
Partain, C. Leon, et al. Magnetic Resonance (NMR) Imaging, 2 vols., 1. 2nd ed. (Illus.). 1988. text 250.00 (*0-7216-2516-9*, W B Saunders Co) Harcrt Hlth Sci Grp.
— Magnetic Resonance (NMR) Imaging, 2 vols., 2. 2nd ed. (Illus.). 1988. text 315.00 (*0-7216-2517-7*, W B Saunders Co) Harcrt Hlth Sci Grp.
— Magnetic Resonance (NMR) Imaging, 2 vols., Set. 2nd ed. (Illus.). 1988. text 555.00 (*0-7216-1340-3*, W B Saunders Co) Harcrt Hlth Sci Grp.
Partain, Calvin T. Trusted Steward: Moving Toward Total Stewardship. Edwards, Judith, ed. LC 96-164499. 96p. (Orig.). 1996. pap. text 7.95 (*1-56309-162-3*, W963101) Womans Mission Union.
Partain, Katherine. Honey Delights: Cooking with Whole Wheat Flour & Honey. Thomson, Thomas, ed. (Illus.). 150p. (Orig.). 1989. pap. 19.95 (*0-912495-02-2*) San Diego Pub Co.
Partain, Larry D., ed. Solar Cells & Their Applications. LC 94-29987. 600p. 1995. 180.00 (*0-471-57420-1*) Wiley.
Partan, Daniel G. International Law Process. LC 91-76016. 886p. 1992. boxed set 70.00 (*0-89089-465-5*) Carolina Acad Pr.
Partan, Daniel G., jt. auth. see Baram, Michael S.
Partanen, J. Sociability & Intoxication: Alcohol & Drinking in Kenya, Africa & the Modern World. (Finnish Foundation for Alcohol Studies: Vol. 39). 1991. pap. 35.00 (*951-9192-48-4*) Rutgers Ctr Alcohol.
Partanen, J. & Montonen, M. Alcohol & the Mass Media. (Euro Reports & Studies Ser.: No. 108). 73p. 1988. pap. text 8.00 (*92-890-1274-9*) World Health.
Partanen, J., et al. Inheritance of Drinking Behavior. (Finnish Foundation for Alcohol Studies: Vol. 14). 1966. 5.50 (*951-9192-05-0*) Rutgers Ctr Alcohol.
Partch, George E. Patch. Supplement to Qinoton Patch of Connecticut, & His Descendants. 48p. 1996. reprint ed. pap. 10.00 (*0-8328-5420-4*); reprint ed. lib. bdg. 20.00 (*0-8328-5419-0*) Higginson Bk Co.
Partch, Harry. Bitter Music: Collected Journals, Essays, Introductions & Librettos. McGeary, Thomas, ed. (Music in American Life Ser.). (Illus.). 520p. 1991. text 44.95 (*0-252-01660-2*) U of Ill Pr.
***Partch, Harry.** Bitter Music: Collected Journals, Essays, Introductions, & Librettos. McGeary, Thomas, ed. & intro. by. (Music in American Life Ser.). 520p. 2000. reprint ed. pap. 24.95 (*0-252-06913-7*) U of Ill Pr.
Partch, Harry. Genesis of a Music. 2nd ed. LC 76-87373. (Music Reprint Ser.). 1974. lib. bdg. 49.50 (*0-306-71597-X*) Da Capo.
— Genesis of a Music. 2nd ed. LC 76-87373. (Music Reprint Ser.). (Illus.). 518p. 1998. reprint ed. pap. 17.95 (*0-306-80106-X*) Da Capo.
— Genesis of a Music: Music Book Index. 362p. 1993. reprint ed. lib. bdg. 89.00 (*0-7812-9645-5*) Rprt Serv.
Partch, Harry, jt. auth. see Blackburn, Philip.
Partch, Peter, jt. auth. see Weygers, Alexander.
Partee, Barbara H. & Sgall, Petr, eds. Discourse & Meaning: Papers in Honor of Eva Hajicova. LC 95-46465. xiv, 430p. 1996. lib. bdg. 100.00 (*1-55619-499-4*) J Benjamins Pubng Co.
Partee, Barbara H., et al. Mathematical Methods in Linguistics. 684p. (C). 1990. pap. text 35.00 (*90-277-2245-5*, D Reidel); lib. bdg. 185.00 (*90-277-2244-7*, D Reidel) Kluwer Academic.
Partee, Glenda. Ensuring All Students Access to STW Opportunity Systems in the States. 5th ed. 20p. 1995. pap. write for info. (*1-884037-15-1*) Coun Chief St Schl Offs.
— Youth Work, Youth Development & the Transition from Schooling to Employment in England: Impressions from a Study Mission. 72p. 1996. pap. text. write for info. (*1-887031-56-1*) Am Youth Policy.
Partee, JoAnn. How I See, What I See, When I See: A Collection of Poetry. (Voices of Great Poetry Ser.). 36p. 1997. pap. 5.00 (*0-9652316-4-X*) Griot Publns.
Partee, Linda. Attribute Pattern Boards. (Illus.). 80p. 1982. 10.95 (*0-9607366-4-6*, KP114) Kino Pubns.
Partee, Morriss H. Plato's Poetics: The Authority of Beauty. LC 81-3332. 238p. reprint ed. pap. 73.80 (*0-8357-6846-5*, 203554100095) Bks Demand.
Partee, Phillip E. The Layman's Guide to Fasting & Losing Weight: Introduced by Dick Gregory. Levy, H. M., Jr., ed. LC 78-64863. (Illus.). (Orig.). (J). (gr. 10-12). 1979. pap. text 4.95 (*0-685-94383-6*) United Pr.
Partelpoeg, E. H., ed. see Materials, Metals & Materials Society Staff.
***Parten, Marjorie N.** Bible Prophecy, Unleavened & Unveiled. 334p. 1999. pap. 12.50 (*0-7392-0383-5*, PO3603) Morris Pubng.
Partenheimer, David, tr. see Nick, Dagmar.
Partenheimer, Maren, tr. see Nick, Dagmar.
Parthamanathan, I. Managing Health Systems Research. (Health System Research Training Ser.: Vol. 4). 1992. pap. 17.50 (*0-88936-588-1*, Pub. by IDRC Bks) Stylus Pub VA.
Parthasarasthi, G. & Chattopadhyaya, Debiprasad, eds. Radhakrishnan: The Centenary Volume. (Illus.). 362p. 1990. text 28.00 (*0-19-562439-4*) OUP.
Parthasarathi, G., ed. see Nehru, Jawaharlal.
Parthasarathy, K. R. An Introduction to Quantum Stochastic Calculus. (Monographs in Mathematics: Vol. 85). 304p. 1992. 137.00 (*0-8176-2697-2*) Birkhauser.
Parthasarathy, R. Rough Passage. (New Poetry in India: a Three Crowns Book). 1978. pap. 4.95 (*0-19-560690-6*) OUP.
Parthasarathy, Rangaswami. God Who Walked on Earth: Life & Times of Shirdi Sai Baba. (C). 1996. pap. write for info. (*81-207-1809-7*) Sterling Pubs.
— Journalism in India: From the Earliest Times to the Present Day. (C). 1995. reprint ed. pap. write for info. (*81-207-1807-0*) Sterling Pubs.
— Memoirs of a News Editor: Thirty Years with the Hindu. 1983. 17.50 (*0-8364-0930-2*, Pub. by Naya Prokash) S Asia.
Parthasarathy, T., et al, eds. Game Theoretical Applications to Economics & Operations Research. LC 97-33652. (Theory & Decision Library). 316p. 1997. 159.50 (*0-7923-4712-9*) Kluwer Academic.
Parthe, E. Cristallochamie De Structures Tetraedriques. (FRE.). xvi, 350p. (C). 1972. text 494.00 (*0-677-50280-X*) Gordon & Breach.
Parthe, Erwin. Crystal Chemistry of Tetrahedral Structures. xii, 176p. 1964. text 274.00 (*0-677-00700-0*) Gordon & Breach.
Parthe, Erwin, ed. Modern Perspectives in Inorganic Crystal Chemistry. LC 92-26740. 292p. (C). 1992. text 171.00 (*0-7923-1954-0*) Kluwer Academic.
Parthe, Kathleen F. Russian Village Prose: The Radiant Past. 216p. 1992. text 37.50 (*0-691-06889-5*, Pub. by Princeton U Pr); pap. text 14.95 (*0-691-01534-1*, Pub. by Princeton U Pr) Cal Prin Full Svc.
Parthemore, E. W. Genealogy of the Ludwig Bretz Family, 1750-1890. 149p. 1988. reprint ed. pap. 30.00 (*0-8328-0313-8*); reprint ed. lib. bdg. 38.00 (*0-8328-0312-X*) Higginson Bk Co.
Parthenius. Erotika Pathemata: The Love Stories of Parthenius. Stern, Jacob, tr. from GRE. LC 91-43279. (Library of World Literature in Translation: Vol. 28). (GEC.). 100p. 1992. text 32.00 (*0-8240-0441-8*) Garland.
Parthier, B. & Boulter, D., eds. Nucleic Acids & Proteins in Plants II: Structure, Biochemistry & Physiology of Nucleic Acids. (Encyclopedia of Plant Physiology Ser.: Vol. 14 B). (Illus.). 774p. 1982. 336.95 (*0-387-11140-9*) Spr-Verlag.
Partian, Debbie. Caddie Woodlawn. (Literature Unit Ser.). (Illus.). 48p. 1995. pap., teacher ed. 7.95 (*1-55734-445-0*) Tchr Create Mat.
Particle Size Analysis Conference Staff. Particle Size Analysis, 1981: Proceedings of the Fourth Particle Size Analysis Conference, Loughborough University of Technology, 21-24 September 1981. Stanley-Wood, N. G. & Allen, T., eds. LC TR0418.. 471p. reprint ed. pap. 146.10 (*0-608-14539-4*, 204280500038) Bks Demand.
— Particle Size Analysis, 1988: Proceedings of the Sixth Particle Size Analysis Conference, University of Surrey, Guildford, U. K., 19-20th April, 1988 Organized by the Analytical Division of the Royal Society of Chemistry. fac. ed. Lloyd, Peter John, ed. LC 88-5633. (Illus.). 371p. 1987. pap. 115.10 (*0-7837-7654-3*, 204740700007) Bks Demand.
***Partidario, Maria do Rosario.** Perspectives on Strategic Environmental Assessment. LC 99-44581. 287p. 1999. 59.95 (*1-56670-360-3*) Lewis Pubs.
Partidge, Norman. Slippin' into Darkness. 304p. 1996. mass mkt. 4.99 (*1-57566-004-0*) Kensgtn Pub Corp.
Partin, Beth. Microgravity: A Novel. unabridged ed. LC 98-65281. 124p. 1998. pap. 9.95 (*0-942979-49-4*); lib. bdg. 19.95 (*0-942979-50-8*) Livingston U Pr.
Partin, Charlotte C. Daydreams & Sunbeams: An Album of Framable Word Pictures. (Illus.). 18p. (Orig.). (YA). (gr. 7 up). 1987. pap. 4.00 (*0-9619816-0-1*) C C Partin.
Partin, Earl. And This Is How It Is. LC 77-81768. 1977. 10.00 (*0-8187-0028-9*) Harlo Press.
Partin, Harry, jt. auth. see Ellwood, Robert S., Jr.
Partin, James G., et al. Nacogdoches, the History of Texas' Oldest City. 308p. 25.00 (*1-878096-39-7*, Epigram Pr) Best E TX Pubs.
Partin, Malcolm O. Waldeck-Rousseau, Combes, & the Church: The Politics of Anticlericalism, 1899-1905. LC 74-76167. 311p. reprint ed. pap. 96.50 (*0-608-11978-4*, 202343200033) Bks Demand.
Partin, Marjorie, jt. auth. see Forquer, Nancy.
Partin, Nell, ed. see St. Ann's Altar Society Staff.
***Partin, Ronald L.** Classroom Teacher's Survival Guide: Practical Strategies, Management Techniques & Reproducible. LC 95-18036. (Illus.). 289p. 1999. pap. 27.50 (*0-13-084474-8*) P-H.
Partin, Ronald L. Classroom Teacher's Survival Guide: Practical Strategies, Management Techniques, & Reproducibles for New & Experienced Teachers. LC 95-18036. 289p. 1995. pap. text 27.95 (*0-87628-909-X*) Ctr Appl Res.
— Prentice Hall Directory of On-Line Social Studies Resources: 1,000 of the Most Valuable Social Studies Web Sites, Electronic Mailing Lists & Newsgroups. LC 97-30121. 249p. (C). 1997. pap. text 32.95 (*0-13-679887-X*) P-H.
— The Social Studies Teacher's Book of Lists. (Illus.). 304p. (C). 1991. spiral bd. 29.95 (*0-13-824970-9*) P-H.
— The Social Studies Teacher's Book of Lists: With Ready-to-Use Teaching Ideas & Activities. 304p. (C). 1998. pap. 29.50 (*0-13-095812-3*, Parker Publishing Co) P-H.
Partington, Alan. Patterns & Meanings: Using Corpora for English Language Research & Teaching. LC 98-36312. (Studies in Corpus Linguistics: Vol. 2). x, 158p. 1998. pap. 24.95 (*1-55619-396-3*) J Benjamins Pubng Co.
— Patterns & Meanings: Using Corpora for English Language Research & Teaching. LC 98-36312. (Studies in Corpus Linguistics: Vol. 2). x, 158p. 1998. 50.00 (*1-55619-343-2*) J Benjamins Pubng Co.
Partington, Angela, ed. The Concise Oxford Dictionary of Quotations. 2nd rev. ed. LC 97-15232. (Oxford Paperback Reference Ser.). 606p. 1998. pap. 11.95 (*0-19-280070-1*) OUP.
Partington, Angela, ed. The Oxford Dictionary of Quotations. 4th deluxe ed. 1078p. 1993. 90.00 (*0-19-866202-5*) OUP.
Partington, Angela, ed. The Oxford Dictionary of Quotations. 4th rev. ed. 1104p. 1996. 45.00 (*0-19-860058-5*) OUP.
Partington, Geoffrey. The Australian Nation: Its British & Irish Roots. LC 96-17938. 360p. 1996. text 44.95 (*1-56000-295-6*) Transaction Pubs.
***Partington, Geoffrey.** Teacher Education in England & Wales. (Studies in Education: Vol. 8). 164p. 1999. pap. 28.50 (*0-255-36476-8*, Pub. by Inst Economic Affairs) Coronet Bks.
Partington, I. Applied Economics in Banking & Finance. 4th ed. (Illus.). 536p. 1990. 55.00 (*0-19-828329-6*) OUP.
Partington, I., jt. auth. see Carter, H. C.
***Partington, J. A.** Governing Independent Schools. LC 98-185997. 1998. pap. text 28.95 (*1-85346-507-0*) David Fulton.

An Asterisk (*) at the beginning of an entry indicates that the title is appearing for the first time.

Partington, James R. An Advanced Treatise on Physical Chemistry, 4 vols. Incl. Vol. 1. Fundamental Principles-The Properties of Gases. LC 49-50157. 985p. 1949. pap. 200.00 (0-8357-5134-1, 200589000056); Vol. 2. Properties of Liquid. LC 49-50157. 492p. 1949. pap. 152.60 (0-8357-5135-X, 200589000057); Vol. 3. Properties of Solids. LC 49-50157. 699p. 1949. pap. 200.00 (0-8357-5136-8, 200589000058); Vol. 5. Molecular Spectra & Structure Dielectrics & Dipole Moments. LC 49-50157. 575p. 1949. pap. 178.30 (0-608-16080-6, 200589000059); LC 49-50157. reprint ed. pap. write for info. (0-608-18686-4, 2005890) Bks Demand.

— A History of Greek Fire & Gunpowder. LC 98-11738. (Illus.). 393p. 1998. reprint ed. pap. text 19.95 (0-8018-5954-9) Johns Hopkins.

— Origins & Development of Applied Chemistry. LC 74-26284. (History, Philosophy & Sociology of Science Ser.). 1975. reprint ed. 50.95 (0-405-06611-2) Ayer.

— A Short History of Chemistry. 428p. 1989. pap. 11.95 (0-486-65977-1) Dover.

Partington, James R. & McKie, Douglas. Historical Studies on the Phlogiston Theory. Cohen, I. Bernard, ed. LC 80-2140. (Development of Science Ser.). (Illus.). 1981. lib. bdg. 15.95 (0-405-13895-4) Ayer.

Partington, Jonathan R. Interpolation, Identification & Sampling. LC 97-13157. (London Mathematical Society Monographs: No. 17). (Illus.). 280p. 1997. text 115.00 (0-19-850024-6) OUP.

***Partington, Martin & Harris, Michael, eds.** Administrative Justice in the 21st Century. 512p. 1999. 80.00 (1-901362-66-3, Pub. by Hart Pub) Intl Spec Bk.

Partington, Michael & Werner, Raymond E. QR/Harvard Graphics for Windows for Dummies. LC 94-79836. 224p. 1994. spiral bd. 9.99 (1-56884-962-1) IDG Bks.

Partington, Paul G. The Moon Illustrated Weekly: Black America's First Weekly Magazine. 1986. pap. 10.00 (0-9602538-2-3) P G Partington.

— W. E. B. Du Bois: A Bibliography of His Published Writings. 3rd ed. 1985. lib. bdg. 35.00 (0-9602538-3-1) P G Partington.

— W. E. B. Du Bois: A Bibliography of His Published Writings, Supplement. 1984. pap. 10.00 (0-685-08855-3) P G Partington.

— Who's Who on the Postage Stamps of the World, 1840-1984: A Master Index. 1989. lib. bdg. 45.00 (0-685-26477-7) P G Partington.

Partington, Paul G. & McDonnell, Robert W. W. E. B. Du Bois: A Bibliography of Writings about Him. rev. ed. 1989. lib. bdg. 30.00 (0-9602538-8-2) P G Partington.

***Partington, Peter.** Learn to Draw Wildlife. (Learn to Draw Ser.). (Illus.). 64p. 1999. pap. 14.95 (0-00-413362-5, Pub. by HarpC) Trafalgar.

Partington, Peter, et al. Drawing for Beginners: A Step-by-Step Guide to Drawing Success. (Illus.). 192p. 1998. 24.95 (0-00-413330-7, Pub. by HarpC) Trafalgar.

Partington, T. B. Women & the Chinese Poets. 1972. 59.95 (0-8490-1320-8) Gordon Pr.

***Partis, Joanne.** Stripe. LC 99-39108. (Picture Bks.). (Illus.). 32p. (J). (ps-3). 2000. 15.95 (1-57505-450-7, Carolrhoda) Lerner Pub.

Partisan Review Staff. Fifty-Year Cumulative Index, 1934-1983, Vol. 1-50. LC 84-22228. (Studies in Modern Literature: No. 15). 1984. 67.50 (0-404-61585-6) AMS Pr.

Partise, David A., ed. see Dar Systems International Staff.

Partlett, David F., jt. auth. see Nurcombe, Barry.

Partlow, Francis. Training of Children in the New Thought. 88p. 1997. pap. 7.00 (0-89540-273-4, SB-273) Sun Pub.

Partlow, Robert B., Jr. & Moore, Harry T., eds. D. H. Lawrence, The Man Who Lived. Papers. LC 80-15262. 320p. 1980. 18.95 (0-8093-0981-5) S Ill U Pr.

***Partlow, Thomas E.** DeKalb County, Tennessee, 1838-1869, Land Deed Genealogy Of. 349p. 1999. 35.00 (0-89308-722-X) Southern Hist Pr.

Partlow, Thomas E. The People of Wilson County, Tennessee, 1800-1899. 158p. 1983. 22.00 (0-89308-308-9) Southern Hist Pr.

***Partlow, Thomas E.** Rutherford Co., Tennessee, 1845-1867 Chancery Court Records. 117p. 1999. 25.00 (0-89308-723-8) Southern Hist Pr.

Partlow, Thomas E. Wilson County, Tennessee, Circuit Court Records, 1810-1855. 144p. 1988. pap. 24.50 (0-89308-635-5, TN 109) Southern Hist Pr.

— Wilson County, Tennessee, Deed Books C-M, 1793-1829. 248p. 1984. 25.00 (0-89308-540-5) Southern Hist Pr.

— Wilson County, Tennessee, Deed Books N-Z, 1829-1853. 464p. 1984. 35.00 (0-89308-541-3) Southern Hist Pr.

— Wilson County, Tennessee, Deeds, Marriages & Wills, 1800-1902. 244p. 1987. pap. 32.50 (0-89308-605-3, TN 101) Southern Hist Pr.

Partlow, Thomas E. Wilson County, Tennessee, Genealogical Resource Material, 1827-1869. LC 98-105111. 1997. 35.00 (0-89308-524-3) Southern Hist Pr.

Partlow, Thomas E. Wilson County, Tennessee, Miscellaneous Records, 1800-1875. 270p. 1982. 25.00 (0-89308-283-X, TN 60) Southern Hist Pr.

Partlow, Thomas E. Wilson County, Tennessee, Trust Deeds, 1828-1868. LC 98-105104. 1997. 38.50 (0-89308-320-8) Southern Hist Pr.

***Partner, Daniel.** Devotional Classics. LC 99-42243. (Quiknotes Ser.). 2000. pap. 6.99 (0-8423-3333-9) Tyndale Hse.

— Disorders First Diagnosed in Childhood. LC 99-30847. (Encyclopedia of Psychological Disorders Ser.). (Illus.). 144p. 1999. 24.95 (0-7910-5312-1) Chelsea Hse.

— Go for the Goal: Motivational Stories about Men of Achievement. 40p. 2000. 1.99 (1-57748-710-9) Barbour Pub.

— Great Women of Faith. (Illus.). 2000. pap. 6.99 (0-8423-3332-0) Tyndale Hse.

— Sounds of the Season: The Stories Behind Your Favorite Carols. 2000. 9.97 (1-57748-796-6) Barbour Pub.

***Partner, Daniel, ed.** The Story of Jesus: A Portrait of Christ from the Gospels. (Inspirational Library Ser.). 320p. 2000. 4.97 (1-57748-732-X) Barbour Pub.

Partner, Daniel, jt. auth. see Partner, Margaret.

Partner, Daniel, jt. auth. see Partner, Margret.

***Partner, Margaret & Partner, Daniel.** A Cloud of Witnesses: Fifty Readings on Women of Faith. 128p. 2000. pap. 9.99 (0-8007-5734-3) Chosen Bks.

***Partner, Margret & Partner, Daniel.** Women of Sacred Song: Meditations on Hymns by Women. LC 99-16336. 112p. (C). (gr. 13). 1999. pap. 9.99 (0-8007-5700-9) Revell.

Partner, Nancy F. Serious Entertainments: The Writing of History in Twelfth-Century England. LC 77-4402. 1994. lib. bdg. 20.00 (0-226-64763-3) U Ch Pr.

Partner, Nancy F., ed. Studying Medieval Women: Sex, Gender, Feminism. (Speculum Book). (Illus.). vii, 197p. 1993. pap. 15.00 (0-915651-06-8) Medieval Acad.

Partner, Peter. God of Battles: Holy Wars of Christianity & Islam. LC 98-28813. 364p. 1998. pap. 16.95 (0-691-00235-5, Pub. by Princeton U Pr) Cal Prin Full Svc.

— The Knights Templar & Their Myth. rev. ed. 230p. 1990. pap. 12.95 (0-89281-273-7) Inner Tradit.

— The Lands of St. Peter: The Papal State in the Middle Ages & the Early Renaissance. LC 73-182793. (Illus.). 495p. reprint ed. pap. 153.50 (0-608-17985-X, 202905600058) Bks Demand.

— Papal State under Martin V. 264p. 1958. 45.00 (0-614-21816-0, Pub. by British Schl Rome) David Brown.

— The Pope's Men: The Papal Civil Service in the Renaissance. 288p. 1990. text 75.00 (0-19-821995-4) OUP.

— Renaissance Rome: A Portrait of a Society, 1500-1559. 1976. pap. 15.95 (0-520-03945-9, Pub. by U CA Pr) Cal Prin Full Svc.

— Renaissance Rome: A Portrait of a Society, 1500-1559. LC 75-13154. (Illus.). 285p. reprint ed. pap. 88.40 (0-608-18038-6, 202905700058) Bks Demand.

***Partner, Peter.** Two Thousand Years - The First Millennium: The Birth of Christianity to the Crusades. (Illus.). 192p. 2000. 29.95 (0-233-99665-6, Pub. by Andre Deutsch) Trafalgar.

— Two Thousand Years - The Second Millennium: From Medieval Christendom to Global Christianity. (Illus.). 192p. 2000. 29.95 (0-233-99666-4, Pub. by Andre Deutsch) Trafalgar.

***Partner, Simon.** Assembled in Japan: Electrical Goods & the Making of the Japanese Consumer LC 98-37375. 334p. 1999. 55.00 (0-520-21792-6, Pub. by U CA Pr); pap. 19.95 (0-520-21939-2, Pub. by U CA Pr) Cal Prin Full Svc.

Partners. Multicultural Art Activities. 1997. pap. text 10.95 (1-55734-617-8) Tchr Create Mat.

***Partners for Livable Communities.** The Livable City: Revitilizing Urban Communities. LC 00-35164. (Illus.). 224p. 2000. pap. text 49.95 (0-07-135913-3) McGraw-Hill Prof.

Partnership, Derek L. & Bartlett, Roger. Spon's Landscape Handbook. 4th rev. ed. (Illus.). 496p. (C). (gr. 13). 1998. 80.00 (0-419-20490-3, B9088, E & FN Spon) Routledge.

Partnership for Environmental Technology Education. Site Characterization: Sampling & Analysis. 316p. 1997. pap. 49.95 (0-471-29270-2, VNR) Wiley.

Partnow, Elaine. The New Quotable Woman. rev. ed. 736p. 1992. 40.00 (0-8160-2134-1) Facts on File.

***Partnow, Elaine.** The Quotable Woman: The 1st 4,000 Years. LC 00-37660. 736p. 2001. pap. 55.00 (0-8160-4012-5) Facts on File.

Partnow, Elaine & Alexander, Claudia B., eds. The Quotable Woman: From Eve to 1799. LC 82-15511. 549p. 1985. reprint ed. pap. 170.20 (0-608-02842-8, 206390900007) Bks Demand.

Partnow, Elaine & Hyatt, Lesley. The Female Dramatists: Profiles of Women Playwrights from the Middle Ages to the Contemporary Times. LC 97-26501. (Illus.). 304p. 1998. 45.00 (0-8160-3015-4) Facts on File.

Partnoy, Alicia. The Little School: Tales of Disappearance & Survival 2nd Edition. 2nd ed. Athey, Lois et al, trs. (Illus.). 200p. (Orig.). (C). 1998. reprint ed. pap. 14.95 (1-57344-029-9) Cleis Pr.

— Revenge of the Apple: Venganza de la Manzana. (Orig.). 1999. pap. text 12.95 (1-885214-19-7) Azul Edits.

Partnoy, Frank. F. I. A. S. C. O. Blood in the Water on Wall Street. LC 97-22845. 252p. 1997. text 25.00 (0-393-04622-2) Norton.

— Fiasco: The Inside Story of a Wall Street Trader. 256p. 1999. pap. 13.95 (0-14-027879-6) Viking Penguin.

Partohardjono, S., jt. ed. see Grubben, G. J.

Parton, Anthony. Applied Mechanics Vol. 1: Stability & Analytical Mechanics. (Soviet Reviews Ser.). 1990. 245.00 (0-89116-720-X) Hemisp Pub.

— Mikhail Larionov & the Russian Avant-Garde. 280p. 1993. pap. text 31.95 (0-691-02620-3, Pub. by Princeton U Pr) Cal Prin Full Svc.

— Mikhail Larionov & the Russian Avant-Garde. LC 92-20814. (Illus.). 216p. (C). 1993. text 80.00 (0-691-03603-9, Pub. by Princeton U Pr) Cal Prin Full Svc.

Parton, Craig. Richard Whately: A Man for All Seasons. 167p. 1997. pap. 10.00 (1-896363-07-5) CN Inst for Law.

Parton, Dolly. Coat of Many Colors. LC 93-3886. (Trophy Picture Bk.). (Illus.). 32p. (J). (gr. 2 up). 1996. pap. 4.95 (0-06-443447-8, HarpTrophy) HarpC Child Bks.

Parton, Dolly. Coat of Many Colors. LC 93-3866. 1994. 10.15 (0-606-09155-6, Pub. by Turtleback) Demco.

Parton, Dolly. Dolly: My Life & Other Unfinished Business. large type ed. LC 94-39240. 468p. 1995. pap. 19.95 (0-7862-0364-1) Thorndike Pr.

Parton, James. Captains of Industry: Or, Men of Business Who Did Something Besides Making Money; a Book for Young Americans. LC 72-2660. (Essay Index Reprint Ser.). 1977. reprint ed. 27.95 (0-8369-2853-9) Ayer.

— Humorous Poetry of the English Language. LC 70-149109. (Granger Index Reprint Ser.). 1977. 41.95 (0-8369-6234-6) Ayer.

— Life of Horace Greeley. LC 70-125711. (American Journalists Ser.). 442p. 1977. reprint ed. 35.95 (0-405-01692-1) Ayer.

Parton, James, ed. Impact: Taking the War to the Foe: The Army Air Forces' Confidential Picture History of World War II. (Illus.). 200p. 1997. reprint ed. pap. text 30.00 (0-7881-5019-7) DIANE Pub.

Parton, James, et al. Eminent Women of the Age: Being Narratives of the Lives & Deeds of the Most Prominent Women of the Present Generation. LC 74-3968. (Women in America Ser.). 656p. 1974. reprint ed. 50.95 (0-405-06116-1) Ayer.

***Parton, Jim.** The Millennium Experience. 2000. pap. 24.95 (0-00-220169-0, Pub. by HarpC) Trafalgar.

Parton, Nigel. Child Protection & Family Support: Tensions, Contradictions, & Possibilities. LC 96-21373. 272p. (C). 1997. 85.00 (0-415-14224-5); pap. 25.99 (0-415-14225-3) Routledge.

***Parton, Nigel.** Child Sexual Abuse. LC 99-12585. 256p. 1999. pap. 34.00 (0-471-98334-9) Wiley.

Parton, Nigel, ed. Social Theory, Social Change & Social Work. LC 95-31962. (State of Welfare Ser.). 256p. (C). 1996. pap. 25.99 (0-415-12698-3) Routledge.

Parton, Roger, jt. ed. see Wardlaw, Alastair C.

Parton, Sara P. Fern Leaves from Fanny's Port-folio. (American Biography Ser.). 400p. 1991. reprint ed. lib. bdg. 79.00 (0-7812-8307-8) Rprt Serv.

— Fern Leaves from Fannys Port-Folio, Second Series. LC 77-164572. (American Fiction Reprint Ser.). 1977. reprint ed. 35.95 (0-8369-7049-7) Ayer.

Parton, V. Z. Fracture Mechanics: From Theory to Practice. 208p. 1992. text 235.00 (2-88124-780-6) Gordon & Breach.

Parton, V. Z. & Boriskovsky, V. G. Dynamic Fracture Mechanics Vol. 1: Stationary Cracks. Hetnarski, Richard B., ed. Wadwha, Ram S., tr. from RUS. 260p. 1989. 185.00 (0-89116-550-9) Hemisp Pub.

— Dynamic Fracture Mechanics Vol. 2: Propagating Cracks. Hetnarski, Richard B., ed. LC 66-55120. 1989. 215.00 (0-89116-605-X) Hemisp Pub.

Parton, V. Z. & Kudryavtsev, B. A. Electromagnetoelasticity: Piezoelectrics & Electrically Conductive Solids. xx, 504p. 1988. text 555.00 (2-88124-671-0) Gordon & Breach.

Parton, V. Z., et al. Engineering Composite Materials. 750p. 1991. 115.00 (0-89116-965-2) CRC Pr.

Parton, V. Z., jt. auth. see Mikhailov, G. K.

Parton, W. Julian. The Death of a Great Company: Reflections on the Decline & Fall of the Lehigh Coal & Navigation Company. 2nd ed. LC 98-17707. 123p. 1998. pap. 15.95 (0-930973-18-6) H M Historical.

— The Story of the General Crushed Stone Company. (Illus.). 100p. 1992. text 11.95 (0-930973-13-5) H M Historical.

Parton, Willadeene. All-Day Singing & Dinner on the Ground: Recipes from the Parton Family Kitchen. LC 97-11449. (Illus.). 256p. 1997. pap. 14.95 (1-55853-483-0) Rutledge Hill Pr.

— Smoky Mountain Memories: Stories from the Hearts of the Parton Family. LC 96-13776. 229p. 1996. pap. text 14.95 (1-55853-404-0) Rutledge Hill Pr.

Parton, William W. Wingshooter's Guide to Arizona. LC 96-60842. (Illus.). 320p. (Orig.). 1996. pap. 26.95 (1-885106-41-6) Wild Adven Pr.

Partonen, T. & Ekberg, eds. Improving the Quality of Life for the European Citizen: Technology for Inclusive Design & Equality. (Assistive Technology Research Ser.: Vol. 4). Date not set. 113.00 (90-5199-406-0, Pub. by IOS Pr) IOS Press.

Partos, Gabriel. The World That Came in from the Cold. 303p. (C). 1994. pap. 15.95 (0-905031-58-X) Brookings.

Partovi, Zahra, tr. see Rumi, Jalal Al-Din.

Partow, Cameron & Partow, Donna. Families That Play Together Stay Together: Fun Healthy T. V. Free Ideas. 24p. 1996. pap. 8.99 (1-55661-711-9) Bethany Hse.

— How to Work with the One You Love--& Live to Tell About It. LC 95-20784. 224p. 1995. pap. 9.99 (1-55661-532-9) Bethany Hse.

Partow, Donna. Becoming a Vessel God Can Use. 24p. (Orig.). 1996. pap. 9.99 (1-55661-663-5) Bethany Hse.

— Homemade Business: A Woman's Step-by-Step Guide to Earning Money at Home. (Renewing the Heart Ser.). 276p. 1999. mass mkt. 5.99 (1-56179-713-8) Focus Family.

***Partow, Donna.** A Ten-Week Journey to Living in Absolute Freedom. 256p. 2000. pap. 10.99 (0-7642-2292-9) Bethany Hse.

Partow, Donna. Walking in Total God-Confidence. LC 99-6379. 256p. 1999. pap. text 10.99 (0-7642-2185-X) Bethany Hse.

Partow, Donna, jt. auth. see Partow, Cameron.

Partrick, Theodore H. Traditional Egyptian Christianity: A History of the Coptic Orthodox Church. LC 96-84373. 256p. (Orig.). 1996. pap. 14.95 (0-9652396-0-8) Fisher Park.

Partridge. Dictionary of the Underworld. (Reference Library). 1998. pap. 6.95 (1-85326-361-3, 3613WW, Pub. by Wrdsworth Edits) NTC Contemp Pub Co.

— Italian Politics Today. LC 98-7197. 240p. 1998. text 64.95 (0-7190-4943-1 Pub. by Manchester Univ Pr); text 19.95 (0-7190-4944-X, Pub. by Manchester Univ Pr) St Martin.

Partridge, A., et al. Punishments Imposed on Federal Offenders, 2 vols., Set. LC 86-81506. v, 1336p. 1986. reprint ed. lib. bdg. 150.00 (0-89941-469-9, 304270) W S Hein.

Partridge, A. E. Astrology in a Nutshell. 72p. 1969. 4.75 (0-86690-018-7, P2262-034) Am Fed Astrologers.

Partridge, Ashley C. Art of Renaissance Rome. (C). 1996. pap. text 16.40 (0-13-570185-6) P-H.

Partridge, Astley C. Substantive Grammar of Shakespeare's Nondramatic Texts. LC 75-44106. 246p. 1976. reprint ed. pap. 76.30 (0-608-05666-9, 206618200006) Bks Demand.

Partridge, C. H., tr. see Farmer, H. H., ed.

Partridge, Christopher H. H. H. Farmer's Theological Interpretation of Religion: Towards a Personalist Theology of Religions. LC 98-17654. (Toronto Studies in Theology: Vol. 76). 416p. 1998. text 109.95 (0-7734-8394-2) E Mellen.

Partridge, Colin. Senso - Visconti's Film & Boito's Novella: A Case Study in the Relation Between Literature & Film. LC 91-38740. 124p. 1992. lib. bdg. 59.95 (0-7734-9746-3) E Mellen.

— Tristana: Bunuel's Film & Galdos' Novel: A Case Study in the Relation Between Literature & Film. LC 94-39161. 244p. 1995. text 89.95 (0-7734-9089-2) E Mellen.

— Yuri Trifonov's The Moscow Cycle: A Critical Study. LC 89-12941. (Studies in Slavic Language & Literature: Vol. 3). 208p. 1990. lib. bdg. 89.95 (0-88946-293-3) E Mellen.

Partridge, Colin, jt. ed. see Coustillas, Pierre.

Partridge, Craig. Gigabit Networking. 416p. (C). 1993. 52.95 (0-201-56333-9) Addison-Wesley.

Partridge, Craig, ed. Innovations in Internetworking. LC 88-26314. (Artech House Telecommunications Library). 544p. reprint ed. pap. 168.70 (0-7837-0414-3, 204073600018) Bks Demand.

Partridge, D. & Hussain, K. M. Knowledge-Based Information Systems. LC 94-20437. 1994. 29.95 (0-07-707624-9) McGraw.

***Partridge, Derek.** Artificial Intelligence & Software Engineering. 375p. 1999. lib. bdg. 55.00 (1-57958-062-9) Fitzroy Dearborn.

Partridge, Derek. Artificial Intelligence: Applications in the Future of Software Engineering. LC 86-7171. (Artificial Intelligence Ser.). 241p. 1986. text 49.95 (0-470-20315-3) P-H.

— Artificial Intelligence & Software Engineering. 375p. 1998. 55.00 (1-57958-064-5) Fitzroy Dearborn.

Partridge, Derek. Artificial Intelligence & Software Engineering: Understanding the Promise of the Future. 240p. 1998. 55.00 (0-8144-0441-3) AMACOM.

***Partridge, Derek.** Artificial Intelligence & Software Engineering: Understanding the Promise of the Future. 368p. 1999. 55.00 (1-888998-36-9, 98-36-9) Glenlake Pub.

Partridge, Derek & Rowe, Jon. Computers & Creativity. 224p. (Orig.). 1994. pap. text 22.95 (1-871516-51-X, Pub. by Intellect) Cromland.

Partridge, Derek & Wilks, Yorick, eds. The Foundations of Artificial Intelligence: A Sourcebook. (Illus.). 512p. (C). 1990. pap. text 30.95 (0-521-35944-9) Cambridge U Pr.

Partridge, Dixie. Deer in the Haystacks. 2nd ed. Boyer, Dale, ed. LC 83-73659. (Ahsahta Press Modern & Contemporary Poets of the West Ser.). 60p. 1984. pap. 6.95 (0-916272-23-0) Ahsahta Pr.

— Watermark. LC 91-16235. (Eileen W. Barnes Award Ser.). (Illus.). 80p. (Orig.). 1991. pap. 7.00 (0-938158-11-2) Saturday Pr.

Partridge, Edward, ed. see Jonson, Ben.

Partridge, Edward B. The Broken Compass: A Study of the Major Comedies of Ben Jonson. LC 75-38386. 254p. 1976. reprint ed. lib. bdg. 59.75 (0-8371-8662-5, PABC, Greenwood Pr) Greenwood.

Partridge, Edward B., ed. see Jonson, Ben.

Partridge, Elizabeth. Children of the Changing World. 1998. lib. bdg. write for info. (0-517-70922-8) Random.

— Children of the Changing World. 1998. write for info. (0-517-70921-X) Random.

— Clara & the Hoodoo Man. (J). 1998. 10.09 (0-606-13278-3, Pub. by Turtleback) Demco.

***Partridge, Elizabeth.** Oranges on Golden Mountain. LC 99-462287. (Illus.). (J). 2000. write for info. (0-525-46453-0, Dutton Child) Peng Put Young Read.

— Pig's Eggs. (Family Storytime Ser.). (Illus.). 32p. (J). 2000. 9.95 (0-307-10232-7) Gldn Bks Pub Co.

Partridge, Elizabeth. Restless Spirit: The Life & Work of Dorothea Lange. LC 98-9807. (Illus.). 96p. (YA). (gr. 4-7). 1998. 19.99 (0-670-87888-X, Viking) Viking Penguin.

Partridge, Elizabeth, ed. Dorothea Lange: A Visual Life. LC 94-25869. (Illus.). 176p. 1994. pap. 34.95 (1-56098-455-4) Smithsonian.

— Dorothea Lange: A Visual Life. LC 94-25869. (Illus.). 176p. 1994. 55.00 (1-56098-350-7) Smithsonian.

Partridge, Eric. Adventuring among Words. LC 76-39202. (Select Bibliographies Reprint Ser.). 1977. reprint ed. 12.95 (0-8369-6804-2) Ayer.

— A Charm of Words: Essays & Papers on Language. LC 73-167400. (Essay Index Reprint Ser.). 1977. reprint ed. 18.95 (0-8369-2707-9) Ayer.

— Concise Usage & Abusage: A Modern Guide to Good English. LC 73-94615. 219p. 1969. reprint ed. lib. bdg. 59.50 (0-8371-2466-2, PAUA, Greenwood Pr) Greenwood.

— A Covey of Partridge: An Anthology. LC 71-117898. (Select Bibliographies Reprint Ser.). 1977. reprint ed. 26.95 (0-8369-5351-7) Ayer.

— Critical Medley. LC 73-148894. (Select Bibliographies Reprint Ser.). 1977. reprint ed. 21.95 (0-8369-5680-X) Ayer.

— A Dictionary of Catch Phrases: American & British, from

P

the Sixteenth Century to the Present Day. rev. ed. Beale, Paul, ed. LC 85-40997. 408p. 1977. 24.95 (*0-8128-3101-2*, Scrbrough Hse) Madison Bks UPA.

— A Dictionary of Catch Phrases: American & British, from the Sixteenth Century to the Present Day. rev. ed. Beale, Paul, ed. LC 85-40997. 408p. 1992. pap. 12.95 (*0-8128-8536-8*, Scrbrough Hse) Madison Bks UPA.

— A Dictionary of Cliches. 5th ed. 272p. (C). 1978. pap. 16.99 (*0-415-06555-0*) Routledge.

— A Dictionary of Cliches. 5th ed. 1978. reprint ed. pap. 13.95 (*0-7100-0049-9*, Routledge Thoemms) Routledge.

— A Dictionary of Slang & Unconventional English. 8th ed. 1408p. 1985. 75.00 (*0-02-594980-2*) Macmillan.

— Eighteenth Century English Romantic Poetry. LC 75-117900. (Select Bibliographies Reprint Ser.). 1977. reprint ed. 24.95 (*0-8369-5353-3*) Ayer.

— English: A Course for Human Beings. 4th ed. LC 79-117901. (Select Bibliographies Reprint Ser.). 1977. reprint ed. 31.95 (*0-8369-5354-1*) Ayer.

— The French Romantics' Knowledge of English Literature: 1820-1848. LC 72-117902. (Select Bibliographies Reprint Ser.). 1977. reprint ed. 30.95 (*0-8369-5355-X*) Ayer.

— From Sanskrit to Brazil. LC 77-94281. (Select Bibliographies Reprint Ser.). 1977. 20.95 (*0-8369-5055-0*) Ayer.

— Glimpses. LC 70-150194. (Select Bibliographies Reprint Ser.). 1977. 21.95 (*0-8369-5707-5*) Ayer.

— Here, There & Everywhere. LC 75-86775. (Essay Index Reprint Ser.). 1977. 19.95 (*0-8369-1187-3*) Ayer.

— Journey to the Edge of Morning. LC 77-84331. (Essay Index Reprint Ser.). 1977. 16.95 (*0-8369-1101-6*) Ayer.

— Literary Sessions. LC 70-117904. (Select Bibliographies Reprint Ser.). 1977. reprint ed. 21.95 (*0-8369-5357-6*) Ayer.

— Name into Word. 2nd ed. LC 77-117906. (Select Bibliographies Reprint Ser.). 1977. reprint ed. 44.95 (*0-8369-5361-4*) Ayer.

— A New Testament Word Book: A Glossary. LC 70-117907. (Select Bibliographies Reprint Ser.). 1977. reprint ed. 21.95 (*0-8369-5359-2*) Ayer.

— Robert Eyres Landor: A Biographical & Critical Sketch, 2 Vols. LC 78-117909. (Select Bibliographies Reprint Ser.). 1977. reprint ed. 26.95 (*0-8369-5362-2*) Ayer.

— The Shaggy Dog Story. LC 72-117910. (Select Bibliographies Reprint Ser.). (Illus.). 1977. reprint ed. 18.95 (*0-8369-5363-0*) Ayer.

— Shakespeare's Bawdy. 3rd ed. 240p. (C). (gr. 13). 1990. pap. 19.99 (*0-415-05076-6*, A4700) Routledge.

— Smaller Slang Dictionary. 1976. reprint ed. pap. 13.95 (*0-7100-8331-9*, Routledge Thoemms) Routledge.

— Usage & Abusage: A Guide to Good English. 400p. 1997. pap. 13.95 (*0-393-31709-9*) Norton.

— Usage & Abusage: How to Pick the Right Words & Avoid the Wrong Ones in Speech & Writing. 400p. 1995. 27.50 (*0-393-03761-4*) Norton.

— Words at War, Words at Peace: Essays on Language in General & Particular Words. LC 76-117911. (Select Bibliographies Reprint Ser.). 1977. reprint ed. 20.95 (*0-8369-5364-9*) Ayer.

— Words, Words, Words! LC 70-117912. (Select Bibliographies Reprint Ser.). 1977. reprint ed. 23.95 (*0-8369-5365-7*) Ayer.

— The World of Words: An Introduction to Language in General & to English & American in Particular. 3rd ed. LC 73-117913. (Select Bibliographies Reprint Ser.). 1977. reprint ed. 24.95 (*0-8369-5366-5*) Ayer.

Partridge, Eric, ed. A Book of English Prose: Seventeen Hundred to Nineteen Fourteen. LC 73-119942. (Select Bibliographies Reprint Ser.). 1977. reprint ed. 21.95 (*0-8369-5385-1*) Ayer.

— Ixion in Heaven & Endymion: Disraeli's Skit & Aytoun's Burlesque. LC 76-117903. (Select Bibliographies Reprint Ser.). 1977. 17.95 (*0-8369-5356-8*) Ayer.

— Poems of Cuthbert Shaw & Thomas Russell. LC 74-117908. (Select Bibliographies Reprint Ser.). 1977. 19.95 (*0-8369-5360-6*) Ayer.

— The Three Wartons. LC 71-128881. (Select Bibliographies Reprint Ser.). 1977. reprint ed. 19.95 (*0-8369-5501-3*) Ayer.

Partridge, Eric, et al, eds. A Dictionary of Forces' Slang: 1939-1945. LC 75-117899. (Select Bibliographies Reprint Ser.). 1977. reprint ed. 21.95 (*0-8369-5352-5*) Ayer.

— Martial Medley. LC 73-117905. (Select Bibliographies Reprint Ser.). 1977. 29.95 (*0-8369-5358-4*) Ayer.

Partridge, Eric & Beale, Paul. Shorter Slang Dictionary. Fergusson, Rosalind, ed. 224p. (C). (gr. 13). 1993. pap. 17.99 (*0-415-08866-6*, B0566) Routledge.

Partridge, Eric & Clark, John W. British & American English since Nineteen Hundred. LC 68-9711. (Illus.). 341p. 1968. reprint ed. lib. bdg. 69.50 (*0-8371-0189-1*, PABA, Greenwood Pr) Greenwood.

Partridge, Eric, jt. auth. see Brophy, John.

Partridge, Eric, ed. see Grose, Francis.

Partridge, Frances, tr. see Asturias, Miguel Angel.

***Partridge, Francis.** Life Regained: Diaries, 1970-1972. 1999. pap. 15.95 (*0-7538-0754-8*) Phoenix Hse.

Partridge, G., jt. ed. see Bedford, M.

Partridge, G. E. Studies in the Psychology of Intemperance. Grob, Gerald N., ed. LC 80-1244. (Addiction in America Ser.). 1981. reprint ed. lib. bdg. 27.95 (*0-405-13614-5*) Ayer.

***Partridge, Gerald N., et al.** Courtroom Survival: Making the Traffic Officer a Powerful Witness, 1999 Edition. (Criminal & Traffic Law Ser.). 115p. 1999. pap. 25.00 (*0-327-04950-2*, 3758010) LEXIS Pub.

Partridge, Henry V., jt. auth. see Goddard, M. E.

Partridge, J. Arthur. The Making of the American Nation: or The Rise & Decline of Oligarchy in the West. 1977. 27.95 (*0-8369-9192-3*, 9061) Ayer.

Partridge, James. Changing Faces: The Challenge of Facial Disfigurement. 1990. pap. 11.95 (*0-14-011597-8*) Phoenix Soc.

Partridge, John. Micropanastron: or An Astrological Vade Mecum. large type ed. Wiggers, Carol A., ed. Lehman, J. Lee, tr. (Illus.). 352p. (C). 1995. pap. text 30.00 (*1-878935-12-7*) JustUs & Assocs.

Partridge, Karen E., jt. auth. see Partridge, Michael S.

Partridge, Kathleen. Book of Tranquil Moments. (Kathleen Partridge's Book of...Ser.). (Illus.). 28p. 1997. 4.95 (*0-7117-0904-1*, Pub. by JARR UK) Seven Hills Bk.

— Kathleen Partridge's Book of Faith. (Kathleen Partridge's Book of...Ser.). 1998. 4.95 (*0-7117-0970-X*, Pub. by JARR UK) Seven Hills Bk.

— Kathleen Partridge's Book of Flowers. (Kathleen Partridge's Book of...Ser.). (Illus.). 28p. 1997. 4.95 (*0-7117-0901-7*, Pub. by JARR UK) Seven Hills Bk.

— Kathleen Partridge's Book of Golden Thoughts. (Kathleen Partridge's Book of...Ser.). (Illus.). 28p. 1997. 4.95 (*0-7117-0903-3*, Pub. by JARR UK) Seven Hills Bk.

— Kathleen Partridge's Book of Happiness. (Kathleen Partridge's Book of...Ser.). 1998. 4.95 (*0-7117-0971-8*, Pub. by JARR UK) Seven Hills Bk.

— Kathleen Partridge's Book of Hope. (Kathleen Partridge's Book of...Ser.). 1998. 4.95 (*0-7117-0972-6*) JARR UK.

— Kathleen Partridge's Book of Seasons. (Kathleen Partridge's Book of...Ser.). 1998. 4.95 (*0-7117-0969-6*, Pub. by JARR UK) Seven Hills Bk.

Partridge, Kathleen & Watkins, Jane. Kathleen Partridge's Book of Friendship. (Kathleen Partridge's Book of...Ser.). (Illus.). 28p. 1997. 4.95 (*0-7117-0902-5*, Pub. by JARR UK) Seven Hills Bk.

Partridge, L. Donald, jt. auth. see Partridge, Lloyd D.

***Partridge, Larry.** Flying Tigers Over Cambodia: An American Pilot's Memoir of the 1975 Phnom Penh Airlift. (Illus.). 200p. 2000. per. 28.50 (*0-7864-0768-9*) McFarland & Co.

Partridge, Linda, jt. ed. see Harvey, Paul H.

Partridge, Lloyd D. & Partridge, L. Donald. The Nervous System: Its Function & Its Interaction with the World. (Illus.). 593p. 1992. 75.00 (*0-262-16134-6*, Bradford Bks); pap. text 39.00 (*0-262-66079-2*, Bradford Bks) MIT Pr.

Partridge, Loren. The Art of Renaissance Rome: 1400-1600. LC 96-6048. (The Perspectives Ser.). (Illus.). 184p. 1996. 16.95 (*0-8109-2718-7*, Pub. by Abrams) Time Warner.

— Michelangelo: The Sistine Chapel Ceiling, Rome. LC 96-31543. (Great Fescoes of the Italian Renaissance Ser.). (Illus.). 128p. 1996. 25.00 (*0-8076-1315-0*) Braziller.

Partridge, Loren W., et al. Michelangelo--The Last Judgment: A Glorious Restoration. LC 97-16157. (Illus.). 208p. 1997. 65.00 (*0-8109-1549-9*, Pub. by Abrams) Time Warner.

Partridge, M. & Perren, L. The Strategic Accountant. (Financial Times Management Briefings Ser.). 1997. pap. 94.50 (*0-273-63263-9*, Pub. by F T P-H) Trans-Atl Phila.

Partridge, Michael. History of the Royal Naval College: Osborne, 1903-23. 2000. 36.00 (*0-7509-1969-8*) Sutton Pub Ltd.

Partridge, Michael S. The Duke of Wellington: A Bibliography, 10. LC 90-6574. (Bibliographies of British Statesmen Ser.: No. 10). 248p. 1990. lib. bdg. 65.00 (*0-313-28075-4*, PDB/, Greenwood Pr) Greenwood.

— Military Planning for Defense of the United Kingdom, 1814-1870, 91. LC 88-20637. (Contributions in Military Studies Ser.: No. 91). 248p. 1989. 65.00 (*0-313-26871-1*, PMY/, Greenwood Pr) Greenwood.

Partridge, Michael S. & Partridge, Karen E. Lord Palmerston, 1784-1865: A Bibliography, 16. LC 93-43710. (Bibliographies of British Statesmen Ser.: No. 16). 328p. 1994. lib. bdg. 95.00 (*0-313-28292-7*, Greenwood Pr) Greenwood.

***Partridge, Norman.** The Crow: Wicked Prayer. 256p. 2000. pap. 13.00 (*0-06-107349-0*) HARP Ent.

Partridge, Norman. Saguaro Riptide. 256p. 1997. mass mkt. 5.99 (*0-425-15699-0*, Prime Crime) Berkley Pub.

— Slipping into Darkness. 304p. 1996. pap. 4.99 (*0-8217-5189-1*) NAL.

— Ten Ounce Siesta. 1998. mass mkt. 5.99 (*0-425-16143-9*, Prime Crime) Berkley Pub.

— Wildest Dreams: A Horror Novel. (Short Novel Ser.: Vol. 1). (Illus.). 200p. 1998. 40.00 (*1-892284-00-6*) Subtrrnean Pr.

Partridge, Norman & Greenberg, Martin H., eds. It Came from the Drive-In. 320p. 1996. mass mkt. 5.50 (*0-88677-680-5*, Pub. by DAW Bks) Penguin Putnam.

Partridge, P. W. Transport Analysis Using Boundary Elements. 1993. 506.00 (*1-85312-194-0*) Computational Mech MA.

Partridge, P. W., ed. Computer Modelling of Seas & Coastal Regions. LC 91-77632. (Coastal Ser.: Vol. 1). 534p. 1992. 210.00 (*1-56252-092-X*, 1649) Computational Mech MA.

Partridge, P. W., et al. The Dual Reciprocity Boundary Element Method. 300p. 1991. 137.00 (*1-85312-098-7*) Computational Mech MA.

Partridge, P. W., et al. The Dual Reciprocity Boundary Element Method. LC 91-70442. (Computational Engineering Ser.). 300p. 1991. text 188.00 incl. disk (*0-945824-82-3*, 0987) Computational Mech MA.

Partridge, P. W., jt. ed. see Brebbia, C. A.

Partridge, P. W., jt. ed. see Brebbia, Carlos A.

Partridge, Penny M. How to Buy & Apply Cosmetics. Bourassa, Hester, ed. (Illus.). 48p. (Orig.). 1988. pap. write for info. (*0-929164-24-5*) Alco Pub.

Partridge, R. B. 3K: The Cosmic Microwave Background Radiation. (Cambridge Astrophysics Ser.: No. 25). (Illus.). 393p. (C). 1995. text. write for info. (*0-521-35254-1*) Cambridge U Pr.

Partridge, R. T. Operation Skua. 160p. (C). 1990. pap. 35.00 (*0-902633-86-4*, Pub. by Picton) St Mut.

Partridge, Ralph. Broadmoor: A History of Criminal Lunacy & Its Problems. LC 75-31440. (Illus.). 278p. 1976. reprint ed. lib. bdg. 22.50 (*0-8371-8520-3*, PABRO, Greenwood Pr) Greenwood.

Partridge, Richard, jt. auth. see Oliver, Michael.

Partridge, Robert B. Faces of the Pharaohs. (Illus.). 256p. 1996. reprint ed. pap. 29.95 (*0-948695-32-3*, Pub. by Rubicon Pr) David Brown.

— Transport in Ancient Egypt. (Illus.). 160p. 1996. 34.95 (*0-948695-42-0*, Pub. by Rubicon Pr); pap. 25.95 (*0-948695-43-9*, Pub. by Rubicon Pr) David Brown.

Partridge, Roy. Sailing the Mirror. (C). 1990. text 59.00 (*0-906754-01-1*, Pub. by Fernhurst Bks) St Mut.

Partridge, Stephen. Manuscript Glosses to the Canterbury Tales. (Chaucer Studies). 352p. 2000. 110.00 (*0-85991-533-6*) Boydell & Brewer.

***Partridge, Stephen.** This Is a Sentence: Electric Art 5. 1999. pap. 22.00 (*1-899858-84-9*, Pub. by Ellipsis) Norton.

Partridge, Susan. AIMS: Developmental Indicators of Emotional Health. 1991. write for info. (*0-939561-10-7*) Univ South ME.

Partridge, Sylvia, ed. see Phillips, Marjorie.

Partridge, T. R. The Sand Dune & Beach Vegetation Inventory of NZ: North Island, Vol. I. 1992. 50.00 (*0-477-02610-9*, Pub. by Manaaki Whenua) Balogh.

***Partridge, Timothy C. & Maud, Rodney R., eds.** The Cenozoic of Southern Africa. LC 99-42440. (Oxford Monographs on Geology & Geophysics). 416p. 2000. text 80.00 (*0-19-512530-4*) OUP.

Partridge, Tom. The Castle. (Illus.). (J). 1994. text 19.95 (*0-312-11156-8*) St Martin.

Partridge, Virginia P. & Watkins, Susan F. Transcript of the 1800, 1810 & 1820 Federal Census of Schoharie County, New York. LC 94-140420. 251p. 1992. lib. bdg. 49.95 (*1-56012-112-2*, 114) Kinship Rhinebeck.

— Transcript of the 1830 & 1840 Federal Census of Schoharie County, New York. 350p. 1991. lib. bdg. 69.95 (*1-56012-113-0*, 106) Kinship Rhinebeck.

Partridge, William L., jt. auth. see Kimball, Solon T.

Parts, C. Estonian-English Dictionary for Schools. 2nd rev. ed. (ENG & EST.). 336p. 1984. 29.95 (*0-7859-1090-5*, 4602020000) Fr & Eur.

Partsch-Bergsohn, Isa. Modern Dance in Germany & the United States: Crosscurrents & Influences. (Choreography & Dance Studies: Vol. 5). 176p. 1995. text 30.00 (*3-7186-5557-8*, ECU30, Harwood Acad Pubs) Gordon & Breach.

— Modern Dance in Germany & the United States: Crosscurrents & Influences, Vol. 5. (Choreography & Dance Studies). 176p. 1995. pap. text 15.00 (*3-7186-5558-6*, Harwood Acad Pubs) Gordon & Breach.

— Modern Dance in Germany & the United States: Crosscurrents & Influences, NTSC Video Cassette. (Choreography & Dance Studies: Vol. 5). 167p. 1995. VHS 15.00 (*3-7186-5736-8*, ECU12, Harwood Acad Pubs) Gordon & Breach.

— Modern Dance in Germany & the United States: Crosscurrents & Influences, PAL Video Cassette. (Choreography & Dance Studies: Vol. 5). 1995. VHS 15.00 (*3-7186-5737-6*, ECU12, Harwood Acad Pubs) Gordon & Breach.

Partsch, S. Marc. 1994. pap. 9.99 (*3-8228-0544-0*) Taschen Amer.

Partsch, Susanna. Klee. 1994. pap. 9.99 (*3-8228-0299-9*) Taschen Amer.

— Klee. 1995. 8.99 (*3-8228-9773-6*) Taschen Amer.

— Klee. (SPA.). 1996. pap. 9.99 (*3-8228-0227-1*) Taschen Amer.

***Partsch, Susanna.** Klimt. anniversary ed. LC 99-217989. (Pegasus Library). (Illus.). 120p. 1999. 14.95 (*3-7913-2007-6*, Pub. by Prestel) te Neues.

— Marc. 1996. pap. 12.99 (*3-8228-0673-0*) Benedikt Taschen.

Partsch, Susanna, et al. Gustav Klimt: Painter of Women. (Pegasus Library). (Illus.). 120p. 1994. 25.00 (*3-7913-1428-9*, Pub. by Prestel) te Neues.

Parturier, ed. see Merimee, Prosper.

Party, Boston T. Boston on Guns & Courage: Proven Tools for Chronic Problems. Royce, Kenneth W., ed. LC 98-65085. (Illus.). 192p. 1998. pap. 16.95 (*1-888766-04-2*) Javelin Pr.

— Boston on Surviving Y2K: And Other Lovely Disasters. Royce, Kenneth W., ed. LC 98-75298. 352p. 1998. pap. 22.00 (*1-888766-05-0*) Javelin Pr.

— Bulletproof Privacy: How to Live Hidden, Happy, & Free! Royce, Kenneth W., ed. 160p. (Orig.). 1997. pap. 15.95 (*1-888766-02-6*) Javelin Pr.

— Good-Bye April 15th! Royce, Kenneth W., ed. (Illus.). 392p. (Orig.). 1992. pap. 40.00 (*1-888766-00-X*) Javelin Pr.

— You & the Police! Royce, Kenneth W., ed. (Illus.). 128p. (Orig.). 1996. pap. 14.95 (*1-888766-01-8*) Javelin Pr.

Paruccini, M., ed. Applying Multiple Criteria Aid for Decision to Environmental Management: Based on the Papers Presented at the 38th Meeting of the European Working Group 'Multicriteria Aid for Decision,' Held at the Joint Research Centre, Ispra, Italy, October 7-8, 1993. LC 94-12573. (Eurocourses: Environmental Management Ser.: Vol. 3). 374p. (C). 1994. text 200.00 (*0-7923-2922-8*) Kluwer Academic.

Paruit, Bernard H., ed. Illustrated Glossary of Process Equipment-Glossaire Illustre des Equipements de Procede. fac. ed. LC 81-18257. (ENG.). 352p. pap. 109.20 (*0-7837-7420-6*, 204721500006) Bks Demand.

— Illustrated Glossary of Process Equipment-Glossaire Illustre des Equipements de Procede-Glosario Ilustrado de Equipos de Proceso. fac. ed. LC 81-18257. (ENG.). 352p. pap. 109.20 (*0-7837-7427-3*, 204722200006) Bks Demand.

Paruk, Jim. Sierra Nevada Tree Identifier. (Illus.). 96p. 1997. pap. 9.95 (*0-939666-83-9*) Yosemite Assn.

Parulis. Network, Level 5. (College ESL Ser.). (J). 1998. mass mkt. write for info. (*0-8384-6972-8*); mass mkt., teacher ed. write for info. (*0-8384-6974-4*) Heinle & Heinle.

— Network, Level 6. (College ESL Ser.). (J). 1998. mass mkt. write for info. (*0-8384-6936-1*); mass mkt., teacher ed. write for info. (*0-8384-6938-8*) Heinle & Heinle.

Parulski, George R., Jr. Sword of the Samurai: The Classical Art of Japanese Swordsmanship. (Illus.). 144p. 1985. 39.95 (*0-87364-332-1*) Paladin Pr.

Parums, Dinah V. Essential Clinical Pathology. LC 41-50522. (Essentials Ser.). 707p. 1996. pap. 64.95 (*0-632-03088-7*) Blackwell Sci.

Parunak, Van Dyke H. Linguistic Density Plots in Ezekiel: The Computer Bible, Vol. 27, A & B. Baird, Arthur J. & Freedman, David, eds. 528p. 1984. pap. 89.95 (*0-935106-22-7*) E Mellen.

***Paruszkiewicz, Gary F.** Aging Is Inevitable, Misery Is Optional: A Practical Guide to Stress Management. unabridged ed. (Illus.). 48p. 2000. text 10.00 (*0-9669249-1-6*) Stress Mgmt.

Paruszkiewkz, Gary F. Tai Chi for Wellness - A Student Wookbook: Tai Chi for Stress Management. 2nd rev. ed. (Illus.). v, 97p. 1998. text 15.00 (*0-9669249-0-8*) Stress Mgmt.

Paruthi, S. N. Library Techniques & Technologies Vols. 1-3: Perspectives in Multimedia Library Development, 3 vols. 1997. 725.00 (*81-7391-172-X*, Pub. by Print Hse) St Mut.

Parv, Valerie. Amor en Exclusiva: Baby Wishes & Bachelor Kisses. (Bianca Ser.: No. 176).Tr. of Exclusive Love. (SPA.). 1999. per. 3.50 (*0-373-33526-1*, 1-33526-4) Harlequin Bks.

— Art of Romance Writing: How to Create, Write & Sell Your Contemporary Romance Novel. 160p. 1993. pap. 11.95 (*1-86373-424-4*, Pub. by Allen & Unwin Pty) IPG Chicago.

— Baby Wishes & Bachelor Kisses. (Romance Ser.). 1998. per. 3.50 (*0-373-19313-0*, 1-19313-5) Silhouette.

— The Billionaire's Baby Chase: Fabulous Fathers. (Romance Ser.: No. 1270). 1998. per. 3.25 (*0-373-19270-3*, 1-19270-7) Silhouette.

— Centrefold. large type ed. 1995. 27.99 (*0-7505-0781-0*, Pub. by Mgna Lrg Print) Ulverscroft.

— The Idea Factory: A Guide to More Creative Thinking & Writing. 240p. (Orig.). 1996. pap. 12.95 (*1-86373-918-1*, Pub. by Allen & Unwin Pty) IPG Chicago.

— La Isla de la Fantasias (Island of Dreams) (Harlequin Bianca - Harlequin Presents Ser.: Vol. 362).Tr. of Island of Dreams. (ENG & SPA.). 1996. per. 3.50 (*0-373-33362-5*) Harlequin Bks.

— Island of Dreams. large type ed. 1992. reprint ed. 18.95 (*0-263-13092-4*) Mac Lib Ref.

— Kissed by a Stranger. (Romance Ser.: No. 406). 1998. pap. 3.50 (*0-373-17406-3*, 1-17406-9) Harlequin Bks.

— Love Like Gold. large type ed. 1993. 19.95 (*0-263-13319-2*) Thorndike Pr.

— Man Shy. large type ed. 232p. 1990. 19.95 (*0-7451-1167-X*, G K Hall Lrg Type) Mac Lib Ref.

***Parv, Valerie.** The Monarch's Son. (Romance Ser.: Bk. 1459). 2000. mass mkt. 3.50 (*0-373-19459-5*, 1-19459-6) Silhouette.

Parv, Valerie. P. S. I Love You. LC 95-6885. (Romance Ser.). 189p. 1995. per. 2.99 (*0-373-03366-4*, 1-03366-1) Harlequin Bks.

— P. S. I Love You. large type ed. (Harlequin Romance Ser.). 1995. 19.95 (*0-263-14239-6*) Thorndike Pr.

— Pour le Bonheur d'Un Enfant. (Horizon Ser.: No. 482). (FRE.). 1998. mass mkt. 3.50 (*0-373-39482-9*, 1-39482-4) Harlequin Bks.

***Parv, Valerie.** The Prince's Bride-to-Be. (Romance Ser.). 2000. mass mkt. 3.50 (*0-373-19465-X*, 1-19465-3) Silhouette.

Parv, Valerie. The Princess & the Playboy. (Romance Ser.: No. 416). 1999. mass mkt. 3.50 (*0-373-17416-0*, 1-17416-8) Harlequin Bks.

***Parv, Valerie.** The Princess's Proposal. (Silhouette Romance Ser.: Vol. 1471). 2000. mass mkt. 3.50 (*0-373-19471-4*, 1-19471-1) Harlequin Bks.

Parv, Valerie. A Reluctant Attraction. large type ed. 1995. 23.99 (*0-263-14359-7*, Pub. by Mills & Boon) Ulverscroft.

— Venganza Apasionada. (SPA.). 1997. per. 3.50 (*0-373-33407-9*, 1-33407-7) Harlequin Bks.

Parvan, Vasile. Dacia: An Outline of the Early Civilizations of the Carpatho-Danubian Countries. Evans, I. L. & Charlesworth, Martin P., trs. LC 78-26364. (Illus.). 1979. reprint ed. lib. bdg. 45.00 (*0-313-20798-4*, PADA, Greenwood Pr) Greenwood.

Parvatham, R., jt. auth. see Gnanam, A.

Parvathamma, C. Scheduled Castes & Tribes: A Socio-Economic Survey. 1985. 37.50 (*0-8364-1253-2*, Pub. by Ashish Pub Hse) S Asia.

— Scheduled Castes at the Crossroads. (C). 1989. 24.00 (*81-7024-257-6*, Pub. by Ashish Pub Hse) S Asia.

Parvathamma, C. & Satyanarayana, G. Housing Rural Poor & Their Living Condition. 114p. 1987. 7.00 (*81-212-0088-1*, Pub. by Gian Publng Hse) S Asia.

An Asterisk (*) at the beginning of an entry indicates that the title is appearing for the first time.

Parvathy & Kuzmic, Nada. Heavenly Father Speaks Vol. 1: Second Arrival. (Illus.). 175p. 1997. pap. 14.00 (*0-9662466-0-8*) Maitreya Pub.

Parvati Baker, Jeannine. Prenatal Yoga & Natural Birth. rev. ed. (Illus.). 64p. 1986. reprint ed. pap. 9.95 (*0-938190-89-X*) North Atlantic.

Parvati, Jeannine. Hygieia: A Woman's Herbal. LC 78-67918. (Illus.). 52p. 1979. pap. 15.00 (*0-913512-54-0*) Freestone Pub Co.

Parveen, Walji, jt. auth. see Monsted, Mette.

Parvensky, Catherine A. Teaching EMS: An Educator's Guide to Improved Instruction. LC 95-4793. (Illus.). 384p. (gr. 13). 1995. pap. text 36.95 (*0-8151-6611-7*, 26240) Mosby Inc.

Parvev, Ivan. Habsburgs & Ottomans Between Vienna & Belgrade: 1683-1789. 300p. 1996. 42.00 (*0-88033-328-6*, 431, Pub. by East Eur Monographs) Col U Pr.

Parveva-Kern, Elka. Deutsche Lehnworter In der Bulgarischen Sprache: Phonetisch-Phonologische und Morphologische Besonderheiten. 390p. 1999. 67.95 (*3-631-33421-4*) P Lang Pubng.

Parvey, Karen G. A Katie Dog Day on Nantucket. LC 95-94818. (Illus.). 34p. (J). (ps-3). 1995. 15.95 (*0-9648685-5-5*) Isl Dog Pr.

Parvez, H., et al, eds. Capillary Electrophoresis in Biotechnology & Environmental Analysis. (Progress in HPLC-HPCE Ser.: Vol. 5). (Illus.). 490p. 1996. 173.00 (*90-6764-213-4*, Pub. by VSP) Coronet Bks.

— Progress in Alcohol Research Vol. 2: Alcohol & Behaviour: Basic & Clinical Aspects. 285p. 1990. 160.00 (*90-6764-124-3*, Pub. by VSP) Coronet Bks.

— Progress in Neuroendocrinology Vol. 1: Neuroendricrinology of Hormone-Transmitter Interactions. 315p. 1985. lib. bdg. 127.50 (*90-6764-049-2*, Pub. by VSP) Coronet Bks.

Parvez, S. H., et al, eds. Progress in Alcohol Research Vol. 1: Alcohol Nutrition & the Nervous System. 340p. 1985. lib. bdg. 135.00 (*90-6764-050-6*, Pub. by VSP) Coronet Bks.

— Progress in HPLC Vol. 2: Electromechanical Detection in Medicine & Chemistry. 480p. 1987. lib. bdg. 190.00 (*90-6764-062-X*, Pub. by VSP) Coronet Bks.

Parvez, S. H., jt. ed. see Naoi, M.

Parvez, Z. Immunoassays in Coagulation Testing. (Illus.). xvi, 173p. 1984. 67.00 (*0-387-90932-X*) Spr-Verlag.

Parvez, Z. & Moncada, Rogelio. Contrast Media Biological Effects & Clinical Application, Vol. 3. LC 86-11697. 1987. reprint ed. 104.00 (*0-8493-4503-0*, CRC Reprint) Franklin.

Parvez, Zaheer, et al. Contrast Media: Biologic Effects & Clinical Application, 3 vols., Set. 688p. 1987. 147.00 (*0-8493-4500-6*, RS341) CRC Pr.

Parviainen, P., jt. auth. see Gadsden, M.

***Parvikko, Tuija.** The Responsibility of the Pariah. 229p. 1999. pap. 22.95 (*951-34-0795-0*, Pub. by SoPhi Academic) Intl Spec Bk.

***Parvin, Brian.** Dead Wood. large type ed. 304p. 1999. pap. 18.99 (*0-7089-5464-2*, Linford) Ulverscroft.

Parvin, Brian. Death in the Past. large type ed. (Dales Large Print Ser.). 262p. 1997. pap. 18.99 (*1-85389-741-8*) Ulverscroft.

— Then There Was Murder. large type ed. (Dales Large Print Ser.). 227p. 1996. pap. 18.99 (*1-85389-671-3*, Dales) Ulverscroft.

***Parvin, Brian.** Wreath for a Ragman. large type ed. 280p. 1999. pap. 18.99 (*0-7089-5608-4*, Linford) Ulverscroft.

Parvin, Manoucher. Avicenna & I: The Journey of Spirits. 389p. 1996. text 26.95 (*1-56859-040-7*, Blind Owl Pr) Mazda Pubs.

Parvin, Rose A. Answer to Humanity: Reclaiming Individual Power & Dignity, Bk. 2. LC 95-5196. 288p. 1995. lib. bdg. 15.00 (*1-885917-01-5*) Univrsl Pubng.

— Beyond Patterns: The Psychology of Health & Excellence, Bk. 7. 288p. 1995. lib. bdg. 15.00 (*1-885917-06-6*) Univrsl Pubng.

— Humanity Held Hostage: The Day America Cried, Bk. 5. 288p. 1995. lib. bdg. 15.00 (*1-885917-04-X*) Univrsl Pubng.

— Pattern Change Programing: Creating Your Own Destiny, Bk. 1. Brooks, Marlo, ed. LC 94-23106. 768p. 1995. lib. bdg. 40.00 (*1-885917-00-7*) Univrsl Pubng.

— Pattern Changes: Universal Laws of Success & Spiritual Excellence, Bk. 9. LC 95-130. 288p. 1995. lib. bdg. 15.00 (*1-885917-08-2*) Univrsl Pubng.

— Power Balance Therapy & Pattern Change Programing, Bk. 3. 288p. 1995. lib. bdg. 15.00 (*1-885917-02-3*) Univrsl Pubng.

— Preventive Family Therapy: Patterns of Change in the Family, Bk. 6. LC 95-35697. 288p. 1995. write for info. (*1-885917-05-8*) Univrsl Pubng.

— Programing Excellence: Self Power Balance: The Revolution of Psychology, Bk. 4. LC 95-35695. 288p. 1995. write for info. (*1-885917-03-1*) Univrsl Pubng.

— Self Programer: The Psychology of Destiny Making: An Evo-Revolution in Psychology of Being, Bk. 8. LC 95-35694. 288p. 1995. write for info. (*1-885917-07-4*) Univrsl Pubng.

***Parvin, Roy.** In the Snow Forest: Three Novellas. 176p. 2000. 23.95 (*0-393-04977-9*) Norton.

Parvin, Roy. The Loneliest Road in America: Stories. LC 96-41761. 192p. 1997. pap. 11.95 (*0-8118-1435-1*) Chronicle Bks.

Parvin, Samuel. The Catacomb Project: Hope for 2000 & Beyond. 24p. 1999. pap. 3.95 (*0-687-07491-6*) Abingdon.

— Revelation: Unlocking the Mysteries with Youth. 96p. 1999. pap. 9.95 (*0-687-08698-1*) Abingdon.

***Parvin, Samuel & Byrum, C. Stephen.** Unlocking the Mysteries: 100 FAQ's about Revelation & the End of the World. LC 99-20319. 112p. 1999. pap. 6.95 (*0-687-08708-2*) Abingdon.

Parvini, R. S. & Brau, J. Colliders Physics: Current Status & Future Prospects: Proceedings of the 8th Vanderbilt High Energy Physics Conference, Nashville, Tennesse, U. S. A. 508p. (C). 1988. pap. 52.00 (*9971-5-0544-4*); text 110.00 (*9971-5-0543-6*) World Scientific Pub.

Parvis, Sheila & Kachur, Karen, eds. The Complete Guide to Part B Billing & Compliance (BCP) 400p. (C). 1999. pap. 279.00 (*1-56329-604-7*) Thomson Learn.

Parvis, Sheila R., jt. ed. see Hart, Anita.

Parvu, Sorin. The Romanian Novel. 320p. 1994. text 49.00 (*0-88033-226-3*, Pub. by East Eur Monographs) Col U Pr.

Paryjczak, Tadeusz. Gas Chromatography in Adsorption & Catalysis. 1987. text 129.00 (*0-470-20131-2*) P-H.

Parzen, Benjamin. Design of Crystal & Other Harmonic Oscillators. LC 82-13620. (Wiley-Interscience Publications). 474p. reprint ed. pap. 147.00 (*0-7837-2405-5*, 204009000006) Bks Demand.

Parzen, Emanuel. Modern Probability Theory & Its Applications. LC 91-42308. (Classics Library: No. 1826). 480p. 1992. pap. 115.00 (*0-471-57278-0*) Wiley.

— Stochastic Processes. LC 62-9243. (Illus.). 1962. pap. 26.95 (*0-8162-6664-6*) Holden-Day.

***Parzen, Emanuel.** Stochastic Processes. LC 99-27282. (Classics in Applied Mathematics : Vol. 24). xix, 324p. 1999. pap. 37.00 (*0-89871-441-9*, CL24) Soc Indus-Appl Math.

Parzen, Emanuel, ed. see Kitagawa, G. & Akaike, Hirotsugu.

Parzen, Jeremy, tr. see Marinetti, Filippo Tommaso.

Parzen, Julia A. & Kieschnick, Michael H. Credit Where It's Due: Development Banking for Communities. 288p. (C). 1992. 69.95 (*0-87722-811-6*) Temple U Pr.

— Credit Where It's Due: Development Banking for Communities. 288p. (C). 1993. pap. 24.95 (*1-56639-185-7*) Temple U Pr.

***Parzer, I.** RELAP5 Assessment Against Pactel Experimental Data: Revision 1. 100p. 1998. per. 8.00 (*0-16-063230-7*) USGPO.

***Parzych, Cynthia & Turner, John.** Pol Roger. (Illus.). 168p. 2000. 45.00 (*0-9702611-0-1*) C Parzych.

Parzych, Kenneth. Test Yourself Principles of Macroeconomics. (Test Yourself Ser.). (Illus.). 104p. (Orig.). 1996. pap. 9.95 (*0-8442-2371-9*, NTC Learningworks) NTC Contemp Pub Co.

— Test Yourself Principles of Microeconomics. (Test Yourself Ser.). (Illus.). 104p. (Orig.). 1996. pap. 9.95 (*0-8442-2372-7*, NTC Learningworks) NTC Contemp Pub Co.

Parzych, Kenneth M. Public Policy & the Regulatory Environment. LC 92-42156. 1993. 57.50 (*0-8191-9024-1*); pap. 32.00 (*0-8191-9025-X*) U Pr of Amer.

Parzyck. Basics of Resume Writing & Interviewing. 2000. pap. text 25.95 (*0-538-69028-3*) Brooks-Cole.

Pas, Harold, jt. auth. see Denise, J. Paul.

Pas, Julian F. Historical Dictionary of Taoism. Woronoff, Jon, ed. LC 97-25780. (Historical Dictionaries of Religions, Philosophies & Movements Ser.: No. 18). (Illus.). 400p. 1998. 64.00 (*0-8108-3369-7*) Scarecrow.

— Visions of Sukhavati: Shan-tao's Commentary on the Kuan Wu-liang-shou-Fo Ching. LC 94-31689. (SUNY Series in Buddhist Studies). 452p. (C). 1995. text 74.50 (*0-7914-2519-3*); pap. text 24.95 (*0-7914-2520-7*) State U NY Pr.

***Pas, Julian F.** Wisdom of the Tao. 2000. 15.95 (*1-85168-232-5*, Pub. by Onewrld Pubns) Penguin Putnam.

Pas, Julian F., tr. from DUT. The Recorded Sayings of Ma-Tsu. annot. ed. LC 87-18536. (Studies in Asian Thought & Religion: Vol. 6). 140p. 1987. lib. bdg. 99.95 (*0-88946-058-2*) E Mellen.

Pas, Julian F., tr. see Robinet, Isabelle.

Pas, Marianne Van de, see Van der Wolf, Willem-Jan & Van de Pas, Marianne.

Pas, Sixto. The Invitation. LC 97-61871. 250p. 1999. pap. 17.95 (*1-887472-29-0*) Sunstar Pubng.

Pasacheff. Astronomy: From the Earth to the Universe. 5th ed. 312p. 1998. pap., teacher ed. write for info. (*0-03-024464-1*) SCP.

Pasacho. Astronomy: Earth to Universe, '98. 5th ed. 1998. 232.00 (*0-03-024461-7*); pap. text 31.00 (*0-03-024463-3*) Harcourt Coll Pubs.

— Astronomy Earth Universe. 3rd ed. 1987. teacher ed. 13.00 (*0-03-008117-3*) H Holt & Co.

Pasachoff. Astronomy: From Earth to the Universe. 5th ed. LC 97-68077. (Illus.). 643p. (C). 1997. pap. text 79.50 (*0-03-024347-5*, Pub. by SCP) Harcourt.

— Contemporary Astronomy. 5th ed. (C). 2002. pap. text 57.00 (*0-03-072459-7*) Harcourt Coll Pubs.

Pasachoff, Jay M. Astronomy: Earth to You. 95th ed. (C). 1995. pap. text, teacher ed., lab manual ed. 28.00 (*0-03-005907-0*) Harcourt Coll Pubs.

— Astronomy: Earth/Universe, Testbank. 4th ed. (C). 1991. pap. text, teacher ed., suppl. ed. 40.50 (*0-03-054667-2*, Pub. by Harcourt Coll Pubs) Harcourt.

***Pasachoff, Jay M.** Astronomy: From the Earth to the Universe with 1999 Updates. 5th ed. (Golden Sunburst Ser.). (Illus.). 1998. pap. text 79.50 (*0-03-030722-8*) SCP.

Pasachoff, Jay M. A Brief View of Astronomy. 336p. (C). 1986. pap. text 55.50 (*0-03-058422-1*) SCP.

— Contemporary Astronomy. 4th ed. (C). 1989. pap. text, teacher ed. 34.00 (*0-03-023353-4*) Harcourt Coll Pubs.

— Contemporary Astronomy. 4th ed. (Illus.). 579p. (C). 1989. pap. text 60.50 (*0-03-023247-3*) SCP.

***Pasachoff, Jay M.** A Field Guide to the Stars & Planets. 4th ed. LC 99-27354. (Peterson Field Guides Ser.). (Illus.). 512p. 1999. 30.00 (*0-395-93432-X*); pap. 19.00 (*0-395-93431-1*) HM.

— A First Guide to the Solar System. (Peterson First Guide Ser.). (Illus.). 1999. pap. 5.95 (*0-395-97194-2*) HM.

Pasachoff, Jay M. Journey Through the Universe. LC 93-34229. (C). 1993. pap. text 60.50 (*0-03-097283-3*, Pub. by SCP) Harcourt.

— Journey Through the Universe. 3rd ed. (C). 1992. pap. text, teacher ed. 34.00 (*0-03-075038-5*) Harcourt Coll Pubs.

Pasachoff, Jay M., ed. Proceedings of the 1991 Undergraduate Symposium on Research in Astronomy. 120p. (C). 1992. pap. text. write for info. (*1-882334-01-9*) Keck NE Astron.

Pasachoff, Jay M. & Covington, Michael A. The Cambridge Eclipse Photography Guide: How & Where to Observe & Photograph Solar & Lunar Eclipses. (Illus.). 143p. (C). 1993. pap. 18.95 (*0-521-45651-7*) Cambridge U Pr.

Pasachoff, Jay M. & Filippenko, Alex. The CosmosAstronomy at the New Milleunium. 2nd ed. (C). 1999. pap. text 49.00 (*0-03-005218-1*, Pub. by Harcourt Coll Pubs) Harcourt.

Pasachoff, Jay M., et al. The Farthest Things in the Universe. (Illus.). 114p. (C). 1995. pap. 21.95 (*0-521-46931-7*); text 39.95 (*0-521-45170-1*) Cambridge U Pr.

Pasachoff, Jay M., jt. auth. see Golub, Leon.

Pasachoff, Jay M., jt. auth. see Olson, Roberta J.

Pasachoff, Jay M., jt. ed. see Parker, Sybil P.

Pasachoff, Naomi. Alexander Graham Bell: Making Connections. (Portraits in Science Ser.). (Illus.). 144p. (YA). (gr. 7 up). 1996. 22.00 (*0-19-509908-7*) OUP.

— Alexander Graham Bell: Making Connections. Gingerich, Owen, ed. (Oxford Portraits in Science Ser.). (Illus.). 144p. (J). 1998. reprint ed. pap. 11.95 (*0-19-512321-2*) OUP.

— Basic Judaism Vol. 1: Israel. 1987. pap., teacher ed. 14.95 (*0-87441-441-5*) Behrman.

— Basic Judaism for Young People Vol. 1: Israel. 150p. (J). (gr. 4-5). 1987. pap. text 9.95 (*0-87441-423-7*) Behrman.

— Basic Judaism for Young People Vol. 1: Israel, Vol. 1. 90p. (J). (gr. 4-5). 1987. pap., wbk. ed. 5.25 (*0-87441-440-7*) Behrman.

— Basic Judaism for Young People Vol. 2: Torah. 150p. (J). (gr. 5-6). 1986. pap. 9.95 (*0-87441-424-5*) Behrman.

— Basic Judaism for Young People Vol. 2: Torah, Vol. 2. 92p. (J). (gr. 5-6). 1986. pap., wbk. ed. 5.25 (*0-87441-442-3*) Behrman.

— Basic Judaism for Young People Vol. 3: God. pap., teacher ed. 14.95 (*0-87441-472-5*) Behrman.

— Basic Judaism for Young People Vol. 3: God. (Basic Judaism Ser.). (J). (gr. 6-7). pap. 9.95 (*0-87441-425-3*); pap., wbk. ed. 5.25 (*0-87441-473-3*) Behrman.

— Frances Perkins: Champion of the New Deal. LC 99-27292. (Oxford Portraits Ser.). (Illus.). 160p. (YA). (gr. 6 up). 2000. lib. bdg. 22.00 (*0-19-512222-4*) OUP.

— Great Jewish Thinkers: Their Lives & Work. LC 92-30148. 1992. pap. 14.95 (*0-87441-529-2*) Behrman.

— Great Jewish Thinkers: Their Lives & Work. 1995. pap., teacher ed. 6.95 (*0-87441-550-0*) Behrman.

— Links in the Chain: Shapers of the Jewish Tradition. (Oxford Profiles Ser.). (Illus.). 240p. (YA). (gr. 5 up). 1997. 35.00 (*0-19-509939-7*) OUP.

— Marie Curie: And the Science of Radioactivity. (Oxford Portraits in Science Ser.). (Illus.). 112p. (YA). (gr. 7 up). 1997. reprint ed. pap. 11.95 (*0-19-512011-6*) OUP.

— Marie Curie & the Science of Radioactivity: And the Science of Radioactivity. (Oxford Scientists Ser.). (Illus.). 112p. (YA). (gr. 7 up). 1996. 22.00 (*0-19-509214-7*) OUP.

— A Topical Bible: Bible Answers to Modern Questions. Feldman, Sarah & Cutter, William, eds. LC 96-48039. (Illus.). 96p. (Orig.). (J). (gr. 4-6). 1996. pap. text 6.50 (*0-87441-618-3*) Behrman.

Pasachoff, Naomi & Littman, Robert J. Jewish History in One Hundred Nutshells. LC 94-6114. 368p. 1995. 30.00 (*1-56821-179-1*) Aronson.

— Jewish History in One Hundred Nutshells. LC 94-6114. 368p. 1997. pap. 30.00 (*1-56821-886-9*) Aronson.

Pasadena Art Alliance Staff. Canvassing L.A., an Artful Guide to Galleries, Museums, & Restaurants. (Illus.). 80p. 1988. pap. text 12.95 (*0-937042-07-2*) Pasadena Art.

***Pasahow, Edward.** Electronics Pocket Reference. 3rd ed. LC 99-32008. (Pocket References Ser.). (Illus.). 544p. 1999. pap. 29.95 (*0-07-134700-3*) McGraw.

Pasahow, Edward, ed. 1998 Information Systems Spending: Technology Trends Planner: Budget Trends Analysis: Technology Trends Planner Update, Vols. 1-3. 550p. 1998. ring bd. 1995.00 (*0-945052-34-0*) Computer Econ.

— 1997 Information Systems Spending Vol. 1-3: Technology Trends Planner/Budget Trends Analysis/Technology Trends Planner Update, 3 vols. LC 98-171673. 450p. 1997. ring bd. 595.00 (*0-945052-32-4*) Computer Econ.

Pasahow, edward J. Electronics Pocket Reference. 2nd ed. LC 93-5244. (Illus.). 496p. 1993. pap. 24.95 (*0-07-048737-5*) McGraw.

Pasahow, Edward J. Mathematics for Electronics. (Electronics Technology Ser.). 1984. text 52.95 (*0-8273-3929-8*) Delmar.

Pasahow, Lynn H., jt. auth. see American Bar Association. Section of Antitrust Law.

Pasahow, Lynn H., jt. auth. see Schwarzer, William W.

Pasakarnis, Ernest. Business Dictionary, English-German/German-English. (ENG & GER.). 1995. 175.00 (*0-7859-9929-9*) Fr & Eur.

Pasamanick, Benjamin, et al. Schizophrenics in the Community: An Experimental Study in the Prevention of Hospitalization. LC 66-25455. (Illus.). 1967. 32.50 (*0-89197-390-7*) Irvington.

Pasamanick, Benjamin, jt. auth. see Knobloch, Hilda.

Pasamanik, Luisa. The Exiled Angel. Hirschman, Jack, tr. from SPA. 1973. 2.00 (*0-88031-009-X*) Invisible-Red Hill.

Pasamehmetoglu, A. G., et al, eds. Assessment & Prevention of Failure Phenomena in Rock Engineering: Proceedings, Istanbul, April 1993. (Illus.). 800p. (C). 1993. text 194.00 (*90-5410-309-4*, Pub. by A A Balkema) Ashgate Pub Co.

— Mining Planning & Equipment Selection, 1994: Proceedings of the 3rd International Symposium, Istanbul, Turkey, 18-20 October 1994. (Illus.). 964p. (C). 1994. text 162.00 (*90-5410-327-2*, Pub. by A A Balkema) Ashgate Pub Co.

***Pasamehnetglu, A. G. & Ozgenoglu, A., eds.** Environmental Issues & Waste Management in Energy & Mineral Production: Proceedings of the 5th International Symposium SWEMP'98, Ankara, Turkey, 18-20, 1998. (Illus.). 900p. (C). 1998. text 116.00 (*90-5410-956-4*, Pub. by A A Balkema) Ashgate Pub Co.

Pasamontes, Carlos M. Diccionario de Pintores. (SPA.). 1987. pap. 250.00 (*0-7859-5910-6*, 8433310216) Fr & Eur.

***Pasanella, Marco.** Living in Style Without Losing Your Mind. LC 00-21408. (Illus.). 200p. 2000. 30.00 (*0-684-85047-8*) S&S Trade.

Pasanen, M. Russian-Finnish Trade - Business Dictionary: Venalais-Suomalainen Kaupan Sanakirja. (FIN & RUS.). 341p. 1985. 250.00 (*0-8288-0834-1*, F17170) Fr & Eur.

Pasannante, Frances, ed. A Guide to Florida State Programs. 10th ed. (Illus.). (C). 1996. pap. 80.00 (*0-614-15884-2*) FL Fund Pubns.

Pasapane. CPI Reading Lab Manual: Rea 008 L College Prep Reading. 124p. (YA). 1997. pap. text 15.95 (*0-7872-3954-2*, 41395401) Kendall-Hunt.

Pasarell, Emilio J. Origenes y Desarrollo de la Aficion Teatral en Puerto Rico. Incl. Bk. 2. Siglo XX. pap. 3.50 (*0-8477-3144-8*); (Illus.). (C). Set pap. 6.00 (*0-8477-3142-1*) U of PR Pr.

Pasarro, John, ed. see Hartinger, James V.

Pasathosm. First Guide to Astronomy. 128p. 1998. pap. 5.95 (*0-395-93542-3*) HM.

Pasau-Buck, Shirlee & Jones, Edward M. Male Ordered Health Care: The Inequities of Women. LC 94-65426. 184p. 1994. pap. 9.95 (*0-9627246-2-9*) Power NY.

Pasava, Jan, ed. see Kribek, Bohdan & Zak, Karel.

Pasay, Marcelle H., ed. see Hill, Edwin A.

Pasbach, E. F. Perspectives: Poems. LC 95-92762. 148p. (Orig.). 1995. pap. 9.95 (*0-9649797-0-5*) E F Pasbach.

Pasca, Sue-Rhee. Your First Canary. (YF Ser.). (Illus.). 32p. (Orig.). (YA). 1991. pap. 2.29 (*0-86622-059-3*, YF-103) TFH Pubns.

Pascal. Industrial Electronics. 2001. 68.00 (*0-13-238858-8*) P-H.

Pascal & Naps, Thomas L. Algorithm. Date not set. pap. text, teacher ed., lab manual ed. write for info. (*0-314-06908-9*) West Pub.

Pascal, Alana. DHEA...the Fountain of Youth Discovered? Exploring the Link Between Youth & Aging. Maurier, Anina, ed. LC 96-60057. (Illus.). 128p. (Orig.). 1996. pap. 12.95 (*0-9645352-1-1*) Van der Kar Pr.

Pascal, Alana & VanderKar, Lynne. Kombucha: How to & What It's All About. Maurier, Anina, ed. LC 95-90065. (Illus.). 128p. (Orig.). 1995. pap. text 12.95 (*0-9645352-0-3*) Van der Kar Pr.

Pascal, Anthony H. A Guide to Installing Equitble Beneficiary-Based Finance in Local Government. LC 84-13366. 1994. pap. text 4.00 (*0-8330-0582-0*, R-31240HHS/SP/F) Rand Corp.

Pascal, Blaise. A Concordance to Pascal's "Pensees" Davidson, Hugh M. & Dube, Pierre H., eds. LC 75-16808. (Cornell Concordances Ser.). 1488p. 1975. text 105.00 (*0-8014-0972-1*) Cornell U Pr.

— Daily Readings with Blaise Pascal. Van De Weyer, Robert, ed. LC 95-60057. 96p. 1995. pap. 4.95 (*0-87243-212-2*) Templegate.

— Extraits des Traites de l'Equilibre des Liqueurs et de la Pesanteur de la Masse de l'A Ir. (FRE.). 64p. 1963. 9.95 (*0-686-54846-9*) Fr & Eur.

— Maximes et Pensees. (FRE.). 9.95 (*0-686-54848-5*) Fr & Eur.

— The Mind on Fire: A Christian's Character Before God. (Classics of Faith & Devotion Ser.: No. 3). 32p. 1997. pap. 9.99 (*1-55661-831-X*) Bethany Hse.

— Oeuvres Completes, deluxe ed. Chevalier, ed. (Pleiade Ser.). (FRE.). 1936. 73.95 (*2-07-010432-X*) Schoenhof.

— Pascal's Letters: Reasoning & Morals of the Jesuits. 319p. 1997. reprint ed. pap. text 25.00 (*0-87556-836-X*) Saifer.

— Pensees, 2 vols. 4.50 (*0-685-73318-1*); pap. 5.95 (*0-685-34246-8*) Fr & Eur.

— Pensees. Desgranges, ed. (Coll. Prestige). 29.95 (*0-685-34245-X*) Fr & Eur.

— Pensees, 2 vols. 1977. pap. 10.95 (*0-7859-4079-0*); pap. 11.95 (*0-7859-4080-4*) Fr & Eur.

— Pensees. Desgranges, ed. (FRE.). 657p. 1991. pap. 55.00 (*0-7859-4650-0*) Fr & Eur.

— Pensees. rev. ed. Krailsheimer, Alban J., tr. from FRE. 368p. 1995. pap. 9.95 (*0-14-044645-1*, Penguin Classics) Viking Penguin.

— Pensees - Lettres a un Provincial. unabridged ed. (FRE.). pap. 8.95 (*2-87714-297-3*, Pub. by Bookking Intl) Distribks Inc.

— Pensees & Other Writings. Levi, Honor & Levi, Anthony, trs. (Oxford World's Classics Ser.). 312p. 1999. pap. 8.95 (*0-19-283655-2*) OUP.

Pascal, Blaise. The Provincial Letters. 210p. 1997. pap. 18.00 (*1-57910-096-1*) Wipf & Stock.

P

Pascal, Blaise. Les Provinciales. (FRE.). 1966. 10.95 (*0-8288-9947-9*, F40580) Fr & Eur.
— Selections from the Thoughts. Beattie, Arthur H., ed. & tr. by. (Crofts Classics). 144p. 1965. pap. text 4.95 (*0-88295-065-7*) Harlan Davidson.
— The Thoughts of Blaise Pascal. LC 78-12814. 320p. 1978. reprint ed. lib. bdg. 65.00 (*0-313-20530-2*, PATH, Greenwood Pr) Greenwood.
Pascal, Blaise & Brunschvicg, Leon. Oeuvres, 14 vols., Set. (FRE.). 895.00 (*0-686-54849-3*) Fr & Eur.
Pascal, Blaise & Gobry, Ivan. Pages sur Crist. (FRE.). 128p. 1963. pap. 10.95 (*0-7859-5390-6*) Fr & Eur.
Pascal, Blaise & Lafuma, Louis. Deux Pieces Imparfaites sur la Grace et le Concile de Trente, Extraites du M. S. de l'Abbe Perier. (FRE.). 76p. 1947. pap. 13.95 (*0-686-54845-0*, 2711605930) Fr & Eur.
Pascal, Christine & Ribbens, Peter. Understanding Primary Headteachers. 240p. 1998. pap. 24.95 (*0-304-70269-2*) Continuum.
— Understanding Primary Headteachers. 240p. 1998. 79.95 (*0-304-70268-4*) Continuum.
Pascal, Dominque. Grand Dictionnaire des Motos Francaises. (FRE.). 127p. 1988. 59.95 (*0-7859-7926-3*, 2707201340) Fr & Eur.
Pascal, Eugene. Jung to Live By. 288p. (Orig.). 1992. mass mkt. 13.99 (*0-446-39294-4*, Pub. by Warner Bks) Little.
***Pascal, Fabian.** Practical Issues in Database Management: A Reference for the Thinking Practitioner. LC 00-22984. 304p. 2000. pap. 39.95 (*0-201-48555-9*) Addison-Wesley.
Pascal, Fabian. Understanding Relational Databases: With Examples in SQL-92. LC 93-7595. 304p. 1993. pap. 39.99 (*0-471-58538-6*) Wiley.
Pascal, Francine. Andy & the Alien. (Sweet Valley Kids Ser.: No. 29). 80p. (J). (gr. 1-3). 1992. pap. 2.99 (*0-553-15925-9*) Bantam.
— Best Friends. (Sweet Valley Twins Ser.: No. 1). (Illus.). (J). (gr. 3-7). 1986. pap. 6.95 (*0-553-16655-7*) BDD Bks Young Read.
— Best Friends. (Sweet Valley Twins Ser.: No. 1). 112p. (J). (gr. 3-7). 1986. pap. 3.99 (*0-553-15655-1*, Skylark BDD) BDD Bks Young Read.
***Pascal, Francine.** Blood. (Fearless Ser.: No. 9). 224p. (YA). (gr. 7-12). 2000. per. 5.99 (*0-671-03949-0*, Pocket Pulse) PB.
Pascal, Francine. Elizabeth & the Tattletale. (Sweet Valley Kids Ser.: No. 47). 80p. (J). 1994. pap. 3.50 (*0-553-48110-X*) Bantam.
— Fearless. (Fearless Ser.: No. 1). (YA). (gr. 7-12). 1999. per. 5.99 (*0-671-03941-5*) S&S Trade.
***Pascal, Francine.** Heat. (Fearless Ser.: No. 8). 240p. (YA). (gr. 7-12). 2000. per. 5.99 (*0-671-03948-2*, Pocket Pulse) PB.
Pascal, Francine. Jessica's Blind Date. (Sweet Valley Kids Ser.: No. 79). 144p. (J). 1994. pap. 3.50 (*0-553-48108-8*) Bantam.
***Pascal, Francine.** Killer. (Fearless Ser.: No. 12). 240p. (YA). (gr. 7-12). 2000. mass mkt. 5.99 (*0-671-03953-9*, Pocket Pulse) PB.
— Kiss. (Fearless Ser.: No. 5). 240p. (YA). (gr. 7-12). 2000. per. 5.99 (*0-671-03945-8*, Pocket Pulse) PB.
— Liar. (Fearless Ser.: No. 10). 240p. (YA). (gr. 7-12). 2000. per. 5.99 (*0-671-03951-2*, Pocket Pulse) PB.
Pascal, Francine. My First Love & Other Disasters. 176p. (J). (gr. 7 up). 1986. mass mkt. 2.95 (*0-440-95447-9*, LLL BDD) BDD Bks Young Read.
***Pascal, Francine.** Payback. (Fearless Ser.: No. 6). 240p. (YA). (gr. 7-12). 2000. per. 5.99 (*0-671-03946-6*, Pocket Pulse) PB.
— Rebel. (Fearless Ser.: No. 7). 240p. (YA). (gr. 7-12). 2000. per. 5.99 (*0-671-03947-4*, Pocket Pulse) PB.
— Run! (Fearless Ser.: No. 3). (YA). (gr. 7-12). 1999. per. 5.99 (*0-671-03943-1*, Pocket Books) PB.
— Sam. (Fearless Ser.: No. 2). (YA). (gr. 7-12). 1999. per. 5.99 (*0-671-03942-3*, Pocket Books) PB.
— Secret Love Diaries: Chloe. (Sweet Valley University Ser.: No. 63). (YA). 2000. mass mkt. 4.50 (*0-553-49352-3*, Sweet Valley) BDD Bks Young Read.
— Secret Love Diaries: Elizabeth. (Sweet Valley University Ser.: No. 60). 240p. (YA). (gr. 8-12). 2000. mass mkt. 4.50 (*0-553-49349-3*, Sweet Valley) BDD Bks Young Read.
— Secret Love Diaries: Jessica. (Sweet Valley University Ser.: No. 61). (YA). (gr. 7 up). 2000. mass mkt. 4.50 (*0-553-49350-7*, Sweet Valley) BDD Bks Young Read.
— Secret Love Diaries: Sam. (Sweet Valley University Ser.: No. 62). (YA). 2000. mass mkt. 4.50 (*0-553-49351-5*, Sweet Valley) BDD Bks Young Read.
Pascal, Francine. Sweet Valley High. 1995. 8.98 (*1-57042-243-5*) Warner Bks.
— Sweet Valley High. 1995. 8.98 (*1-57042-244-3*) Warner Bks.
***Pascal, Francine.** Trust. (Fearless Ser.: No. 11). 240p. (YA). (gr. 7-12). 2000. mass mkt. 5.99 (*0-671-03952-0*, Pocket Pulse) PB.
Pascal, Francine. Twisted. (Fearless Ser.: No. 4). 224p. (YA). (gr. 7-12). 2000. per. 5.99 (*0-671-03944-X*, Pocket Pulse) PB.
***Pascal, Francine, creator.** All about Love. (Sweet Valley High Senior Year Ser.: No. 13). 192p. (YA). (gr. 7 up). 2000. pap. 4.50 (*0-553-49312-4*) BDD Bks Young Read.
Pascal, Francine, creator. All Night Long. (Sweet Valley High Ser.: No. 5). 128p. (YA). (gr. 7 up). 1984. mass mkt. 3.99 (*0-553-27568-2*) Bantam.
— Almost Married. (Sweet Valley High Ser.: No. 102). 208p. (YA). (gr. 7 up). 1994. mass mkt. 3.99 (*0-553-29859-3*) Bantam.
— The Amazing Jessica. (Sweet Valley Kids Ser.: No. 60). 96p. (J). (gr. 1-3). 1995. pap. 3.50 (*0-553-48212-2*) Bantam.
— Amy Moves In. (Sweet Valley Twins Ser.: No. 44). 144p. (J). (gr. 3-7). 1990. pap. 3.50 (*0-553-15837-6*) Bantam.
— Amy's Secret Sister. (Sweet Valley Twins Ser.: No. 83). 144p. (J). (gr. 3-7). 1994. pap. 3.50 (*0-553-48101-0*) Bantam.
— Amy's Secret Sister. (Sweet Valley Twins Ser.: No. 83). (J). (gr. 3-7). 1994. 8.60 (*0-606-07110-5*, Pub. by Turtleback) Demco.
— Anything for Love. (Sweet Valley University Ser.: No. 4). 240p. (YA). (gr. 7 up). 1994. mass mkt. 4.50 (*0-553-56311-4*) Bantam.
— The Arrest. (Sweet Valley High Ser.: No. 96). 224p. (YA). (gr. 7 up). 1993. mass mkt. 3.99 (*0-553-29853-4*) Bantam.
***Pascal, Francine, creator.** As if I Care. (Sweet Valley High Senior Year Ser.: No. 18). 192p. (YA). (gr. 7-12). 2000. mass mkt. 4.50 (*0-553-49317-5*, Sweet Valley) BDD Bks Young Read.
— Backstabber. (Sweet Valley High Senior Year Ser.: No. 17). (Illus.). 192p. (YA). (gr. 7-12). 2000. mass mkt. 4.50 (*0-553-49316-7*, Sweet Valley) BDD Bks Young Read.
— Bad Girl. (Sweet Valley High Senior Year Ser.: No. 12). 192p. (YA). (gr. 7 up). 1999. mass mkt. 4.50 (*0-553-49284-5*) Bantam.
Pascal, Francine, creator. Battle of the Cheerleaders. LC PZ7.S96915Bat 1996. (Sweet Valley Twins Ser.: No. 95). 144p. (J). (gr. 3-7). 1996. pap. 3.50 (*0-553-48199-1*) Bantam.
— The Beast is Watching You. (Sweet Valley Twins Ser.: No. 98). 144p. (J). (gr. 3-7). 1996. pap. 3.50 (*0-553-48203-3*, Sweet Valley) BDD Bks Young Read.
— The Beast Must Die. (Sweet Valley Twins Ser.: No. 99). 144p. (J). (gr. 3-7). 1996. pap. 3.50 (*0-553-48204-1*, Sweet Valley) BDD Bks Young Read.
— Beauty & the Beach. (Sweet Valley University Ser.: No. 30). 240p. (YA). (gr. 7 up). 1997. mass mkt. 3.99 (*0-553-57054-4*, Sweet Valley) BDD Bks Young Read.
— Behind Closed Doors. (Sweet Valley University Ser.: No. 15). 240p. (YA). (gr. 7 up). 1995. mass mkt. 3.99 (*0-553-56695-4*) BDD Bks Young Read.
— Beware the Babysitter. (Sweet Valley High Ser.: No. 99). 224p. (YA). (gr. 7 up). 1993. mass mkt. 3.50 (*0-553-29856-9*) Bantam.
— Beware the Wolfman. (Sweet Valley High Ser.: No. 106). (YA). (gr. 7 up). 1994. mass mkt. 4.99 (*0-553-54188-9*) BDD Bks Young Read.
— Beware the Wolfman. (Sweet Valley High Ser.: No. 106). 240p. (YA). (gr. 7 up). 1994. mass mkt. 3.99 (*0-553-56234-7*) Bantam.
— Big Brother's in Love. (Sweet Valley Twins Ser.: No. 57). 144p. (J). (gr. 3-7). 1992. pap. 3.50 (*0-553-15943-7*) Bantam.
— Big Brother's in Love Again. (Sweet Valley Twins Ser.: No. 104). 144p. (J). (gr. 3-7). 1997. pap. 3.50 (*0-553-48435-4*, Sweet Valley) BDD Bks Young Read.
— The Big Night. (Sweet Valley High Ser.: No. 142). 208p. (YA). (gr. 7 up). 1998. mass mkt. 3.99 (*0-553-49232-2*, Sweet Valley) BDD Bks Young Read.
— Boy. Friend. (Sweet Valley Junior High Ser.: No. 5). 160p. (J). (gr. 3-7). 1999. pap. 4.50 (*0-553-48664-0*) BDD Bks Young Read.
— Boy Meets Girl. (Sweet Valley High Senior Year Ser.: No. 7). 192p. (YA). (gr. 7 up). 1999. mass mkt. 3.99 (*0-553-48613-6*) Bantam.
— The Boyfriend Game. (Sweet Valley Twins Ser.: No. 113). 144p. (J). (gr. 3-7). 1998. pap. 3.50 (*0-553-48597-0*, Sweet Valley) BDD Bks Young Read.
— The Boyfriend Mess. (Sweet Valley Twins Ser.: No. 114). 144p. (J). (gr. 3-7). 1998. pap. 3.50 (*0-553-48598-9*, Sweet Valley) BDD Bks Young Read.
— Boys Against Girls. (Sweet Valley Twins Ser.: No. 17). 112p. (J). (gr. 3-7). 1988. pap. 2.50 (*0-318-33018-0*) Bantam.
— The Boys of Summer. (Sweet Valley University Ser.: No. 32). 240p. (YA). (gr. 7 up). 1997. mass mkt. 3.99 (*0-553-57056-0*, Sweet Valley) BDD Bks Young Read.
— Breakfast of Enemies. (Sweet Valley Twins Ser.: No. 106). 144p. (J). (gr. 3-7). 1997. pap. 3.50 (*0-553-48437-0*, Sweet Valley) BDD Bks Young Read.
— Breaking Away. (Sweet Valley University Ser.: No. 37). 240p. (YA). (gr. 7 up). 1998. mass mkt. 3.99 (*0-553-49221-7*, Sweet Valley) BDD Bks Young Read.
— Broken Angel. (Sweet Valley High Senior Year Ser.: No. 10). 192p. (YA). (gr. 7 up). 1999. mass mkt. 4.50 (*0-553-49282-9*) Bantam.
— Broken Promises, Shattered Dreams. (Sweet Valley University Ser.: No. 19). 240p. (YA). (gr. 7 up). 1996. mass mkt. 3.99 (*0-553-56701-2*) Bantam.
— The Bully. (Sweet Valley Twins Ser.: No. 19). (J). (gr. 3-7). 1988. pap. 3.25 (*0-553-16827-4*) Bantam.
— Busted! (Sweet Valley University Ser.: No. 25). 240p. (YA). (gr. 7 up). 1996. mass mkt. 3.99 (*0-553-57006-4*) Bantam.
— California Love. (Sweet Valley High (TV) Ser.: No. 1). (YA). (gr. 7 up). 1995. 9.60 (*0-606-08228-X*, Pub. by Turtleback) Demco.
— Cammi's Crush. (Sweet Valley Twins Ser.: No. 108). 144p. (J). (gr. 3-7). 1997. pap. 3.50 (*0-553-48439-7*, Sweet Valley) BDD Bks Young Read.
— Cammi's Crush. (Sweet Valley Twins Ser.: No. 108). (J). (gr. 3-7). 1997. 8.60 (*0-606-11957-4*, Pub. by Turtleback) Demco.
— Can't Stay Away. (Sweet Valley High Senior Year Ser.: No. 1). 192p. (YA). (gr. 7 up). 1999. mass mkt. 4.50 (*0-553-49234-9*) BDD Bks Young Read.
— Caroline's Halloween Spell. (Sweet Valley Kids Ser.: No. 33). 80p. (J). (gr. 1-3). 1992. pap. 2.99 (*0-553-48006-5*) Bantam.
— Center of Attention. (Sweet Valley Twins Ser.: No. 18). (J). (gr. 3-7). 1988. pap. 3.25 (*0-553-16823-1*) Bantam.
— Channel X. (Sweet Valley University Thriller Edition Ser.: No. 10). 288p. (Orig.). (YA). (gr. 7 up). 1997. mass mkt. 4.50 (*0-553-57062-5*) BDD Bks Young Read.
— Cheating on Anna. (Sweet Valley Junior High Ser.: No. 8). 160p. (J). (gr. 3-7). 1999. pap. 3.99 (*0-553-48666-7*) Bantam.
— Choosing Sides. (Sweet Valley Twins Ser.: No. 4). 112p. (J). (gr. 3-7). 1986. pap. 3.50 (*0-553-15658-6*) Bantam.
— The Christmas Ghost. (Sweet Valley Twins Super Chiller Ser.: No. 1). 192p. (J). (gr. 3-7). 1989. pap. 3.99 (*0-553-15767-1*) Bantam.
— The Christmas Ghost. (Sweet Valley Twins Super Chiller Ser.: No. 1). (J). (gr. 3-7). 1990. pap. write for info. (*0-318-66852-1*) Bantam.
— A Christmas Without Elizabeth. (Sweet Valley Twins Magna Edition Ser.: No. 2). 256p. (J). (gr. 3-7). 1993. pap. 3.99 (*0-553-15947-X*) Bantam.
— Class Picture Day! (Sweet Valley Kids Ser.: No. 69). 96p. (J). (gr. 1-3). 1997. pap. 3.50 (*0-553-48335-8*, Sweet Valley) BDD Bks Young Read.
— Class Picture Day! (Sweet Valley Kids Ser.: No. 69). (J). (gr. 1-3). 1997. 8.60 (*0-606-11949-3*, Pub. by Turtleback) Demco.
***Pascal, Francine, creator.** Clueless. (Sweet Valley Junior High Ser.: No. 24). (Illus.). (J). (gr. 3-7). 2000. pap. 4.50 (*0-553-48726-4*, Sweet Valley) BDD Bks Young Read.
Pascal, Francine, creator. College Cruise. (Sweet Valley University Ser.: No. 12). 240p. (YA). (gr. 7 up). 1995. mass mkt. 4.50 (*0-553-56657-1*) Bantam.
— College Girls. (Sweet Valley University Ser.: No. 1). 240p. (YA). (gr. 7 up). 1993. mass mkt. 4.50 (*0-553-56308-4*) Bantam.
— College Weekend. LC 00-3653. (Sweet Valley High Ser.: No. 118). 208p. (YA). (gr. 7 up). 1995. mass mkt. 3.99 (*0-553-56636-9*, Sweet Valley) BDD Bks Young Read.
— The Cool Crowd. (Sweet Valley Junior High Ser.: No. 4). 160p. (J). (gr. 3-7). 1999. pap. 3.99 (*0-553-48663-2*) BDD Bks Young Read.
— The Cousin War. (Sweet Valley Twins Ser.: No. 90). (J). (gr. 3-7). 1995. pap. 4.75 (*0-553-54215-X*) BDD Bks Young Read.
— The Cousin War. (Sweet Valley Twins Ser.: No. 90). 144p. (J). (gr. 3-7). 1995. pap. 3.50 (*0-553-48192-4*, Sweet Valley) BDD Bks Young Read.
— Cover Girls. (Sweet Valley High Ser.: No. 129). 224p. (YA). (gr. 7 up). 1997. mass mkt. 3.99 (*0-553-57063-3*, Sweet Valley) BDD Bks Young Read.
— The Curse of the Golden Heart. (Sweet Valley Twins Super Chiller Ser.: No. 6). 192p. (J). (gr. 3-7). 1994. pap. 3.99 (*0-553-56403-X*) Bantam.
— The Curse of the Ruby Necklace. (Sweet Valley Twins Super Chiller Ser.: No. 5). 192p. (J). (gr. 3-7). 1993. pap. 3.99 (*0-553-15949-6*) Bantam.
— A Curse on Elizabeth: A Hair Raiser Super Special. (Sweet Valley Kids Super Special Ser.: No. 3). 112p. (J). (gr. 1-3). 1995. pap. 3.50 (*0-553-48284-X*) Bantam.
— Cyberstalker: The Return of William White Part 1. (Sweet Valley University Thriller Edition Ser.: No. 13). 288p. (YA). (gr. 7 up). 1998. mass mkt. 4.50 (*0-553-49227-6*) BDD Bks Young Read.
— Dance of Death. LC 49-122330. (Sweet Valley High Ser.: No. 127). 208p. (YA). (gr. 7 up). 1996. mass mkt. 3.99 (*0-553-56765-9*, Sweet Valley) BDD Bks Young Read.
— A Date with a Werewolf. (Sweet Valley High Ser.: No. 105). 208p. (YA). (gr. 7 up). 1994. mass mkt. 3.99 (*0-553-56228-2*) Bantam.
— Dead Before Dawn. (Sweet Valley University Thriller Edition Ser.: No. 8). 288p. (YA). (gr. 7 up). 1997. mass mkt. 4.50 (*0-553-57060-9*, Sweet Valley) BDD Bks Young Read.
— Deadly Attraction. (Sweet Valley University Ser.: No. 17). 240p. (YA). (gr. 7 up). 1995. mass mkt. 3.99 (*0-553-56698-9*, Sweet Valley) BDD Bks Young Read.
— Deadly Christmas. (Sweet Valley High Ser.: No. 111). (YA). (gr. 7 up). 1994. mass mkt. 4.99 (*0-553-54171-4*) BDD Bks Young Read.
— Deadly Christmas. (Sweet Valley High Ser.: No. 111). 240p. (YA). (gr. 7 up). 1994. mass mkt. 4.50 (*0-553-56629-6*) Bantam.
— Deadly Terror: The Return of William White Part 2. (Sweet Valley University Thriller Edition Ser.: No. 14). 288p. (YA). (gr. 7 up). 1999. mass mkt. 4.50 (*0-553-49262-4*) BDD Bks Young Read.
— Deadly Voyage. (Sweet Valley Twins Ser.: No. 91). 144p. (J). (gr. 3-7). 1995. pap. 3.50 (*0-553-48193-2*, Sweet Valley) BDD Bks Young Read.
— Dear Sister. (Sweet Valley High Ser.: No. 7). 160p. (YA). (gr. 7 up). 1984. mass mkt. 3.99 (*0-553-27672-7*) Bantam.
— Don't Answer the Phone. (Sweet Valley University Thriller Edition Ser.: No. 12). 288p. (YA). (gr. 7 up). 1998. mass mkt. 4.50 (*0-553-49226-8*) BDD Bks Young Read.
— Don't Go in the Basement. (Sweet Valley Twins Ser.: No. 109). 144p. (J). (gr. 3-7). 1997. pap. 3.50 (*0-553-48440-0*, Sweet Valley) BDD Bks Young Read.
— Don't Go in the Basement. (Sweet Valley Twins Ser.: No. 109). (J). (gr. 3-7). 1997. 8.60 (*0-606-11958-2*, Pub. by Turtleback) Demco.
— Don't Let Go. (Sweet Valley University Ser.: No. 45). (YA). (gr. 7 up). 1999. mass mkt. 3.99 (*0-553-49265-9*) BDD Bks Young Read.
— Don't Talk to Brian. (Sweet Valley Twins Ser.: No. 94). 144p. (J). (gr. 3-7). 1996. pap. 3.50 (*0-553-48197-5*) Bantam.
— Double Jeopardy. (Sweet Valley High Super Thriller Ser.). (YA). (gr. 7 up). 1987. mass mkt. 2.95 (*0-553-16801-0*) BDD Bks Young Read.
— Double Love. (Sweet Valley High Ser.: No. 1). 192p. (YA). (gr. 7 up). 1984. mass mkt. 3.99 (*0-553-27567-4*) Bantam.
— Down with Queen Janet! (Sweet Valley Twins Ser.: No. 117). 144p. (J). (gr. 3-7). 1998. pap. 3.50 (*0-553-48601-2*, Skylark BDD) BDD Bks Young Read.
***Pascal, Francine, creator.** The Dreaded Ex. (Sweet Valley University Ser.: No. 58). 240p. (YA). (gr. 9-12). 2000. mass mkt. 4.50 (*0-553-49310-8*, Sweet Valley) BDD Bks Young Read.
— Dropping Out. (Sweet Valley University Ser.: No. 56). (YA). (gr. 7 up). 2000. pap. 4.50 (*0-553-49308-6*, Sweet Valley) BDD Bks Young Read.
Pascal, Francine, creator. Earthquake. (Sweet Valley High Super Edition Ser.). 227p. (YA). (gr. 7-12). 1998. mass mkt. 4.50 (*0-553-57024-2*) BDD Bks Young Read.
— Elizabeth: Next Stop Jr. High. (Sweet Valley Twins Diary Ser.). 192p. (J). (gr. 3-7). 1998. pap. 4.50 (*0-553-49237-3*) BDD Bks Young Read.
— Elizabeth & Jessica Run Away. (Sweet Valley Kids Ser.: No. 31). 80p. (J). (gr. 1-3). 1992. pap. 3.50 (*0-553-48004-9*) Bantam.
— Elizabeth & Todd Forever. (Sweet Valley University Ser.: No. 27). 240p. (YA). (gr. 7 up). 1997. mass mkt. 3.99 (*0-553-57051-X*, Sweet Valley) BDD Bks Young Read.
— Elizabeth Hatches an Egg. (Sweet Valley Kids Super Special Ser.: No. 5). 224p. (J). (gr. 1-3). 1996. pap. 3.99 (*0-553-48340-4*) Bantam.
***Pascal, Francine, creator.** Elizabeth in Love. (Sweet Valley University Ser.: No. 59). (YA). (gr. 7 up). 2000. pap. 4.50 (*0-553-49347-7*, Sweet Valley) BDD Bks Young Read.
Pascal, Francine, creator. Elizabeth Is Mine. (Sweet Valley High Ser.: No. 139). 240p. (YA). (gr. 7-12). 1998. mass mkt. 3.99 (*0-553-49229-2*, Sweet Valley) BDD Bks Young Read.
— Elizabeth Loves New York. (Sweet Valley University Ser.: No. 39). 240p. (YA). (gr. 7 up). 1998. mass mkt. 3.99 (*0-553-49223-3*) BDD Bks Young Read.
— Elizabeth Solves It All. (Sweet Valley Twins Ser.: No. 103). 144p. (J). (gr. 3-7). 1996. pap. 3.50 (*0-553-48434-6*, Sweet Valley) BDD Bks Young Read.
— Elizabeth the Seventh Grader. (Sweet Valley Twins Ser.: No. 85). 144p. (J). (gr. 3-7). 1995. pap. 3.50 (*0-553-48109-6*) Bantam.
— Elizabeth the Spy. (Sweet Valley Twins Ser.: No. 96). 144p. (J). (gr. 3-7). 1996. pap. 3.50 (*0-553-48200-9*) Bantam.
— Elizabeth's Broken Arm. (Sweet Valley Kids Ser.: No. 35). 80p. (J). (gr. 1-3). 1992. pap. 3.50 (*0-553-48009-X*) Bantam.
— Elizabeth's First Kiss. (Sweet Valley Twins Ser.: No. 43). 144p. (J). (gr. 3-7). 1990. pap. 3.50 (*0-553-15835-X*) Bantam.
— Elizabeth's Heartbreak. (Sweet Valley University Ser.: No. 28). 256p. (YA). (gr. 7 up). 1997. mass mkt. 3.99 (*0-553-57052-8*, Sweet Valley) BDD Bks Young Read.
— Elizabeth's Piano Lessons. (Sweet Valley Kids Ser.: No. 45). 80p. (J). (gr. 1-3). 1993. pap. 3.50 (*0-553-48102-9*) Bantam.
— Elizabeth's Rival. (Sweet Valley High Ser.: No. 123). 208p. (YA). (gr. 4-7). 1996. mass mkt. 3.99 (*0-553-56759-4*) Bantam.
Pascal, Francine, creator. Elizabeth's Secret Diary, Vol. 1. (Sweet Valley High Secret Diary Ser.). 336p. (YA). (gr. 7 up). 1994. mass mkt. 4.50 (*0-553-56658-X*) Bantam.
Pascal, Francine, creator. Elizabeth's Secret Diary, Vol. 3. (Sweet Valley High Secret Diary Ser.). 336p. (YA). (gr. 7 up). 1997. mass mkt. 4.50 (*0-553-49215-2*, Sweet Valley) BDD Bks Young Read.
— Elizabeth's Summer Love. (Sweet Valley University Ser.: No. 22). 240p. (YA). (gr. 7 up). 1996. mass mkt. 3.99 (*0-553-56705-5*, Sweet Valley) BDD Bks Young Read.
— Elizabeth's Video Fever. (Sweet Valley Kids Ser.: No. 36). 80p. (J). (gr. 1-3). 1993. pap. 3.50 (*0-553-48010-3*) Bantam.
— Escape to New York. (Sweet Valley University Ser.: No. 41). 240p. (YA). (gr. 7 up). 1998. mass mkt. 3.99 (*0-553-57029-3*, Sweet Valley) BDD Bks Young Read.
— Evil Elizabeth. (Sweet Valley Twins Super Chiller Ser.: No. 9). 192p. (J). (gr. 3-7). 1995. pap. 3.99 (*0-553-48283-1*, Sweet Valley) BDD Bks Young Read.
— The Evil Twin. (Sweet Valley High Ser.: No. 100). 352p. (YA). (gr. 7 up). 1993. mass mkt. 4.50 (*0-553-29857-7*) Bantam.
***Pascal, Francine, creator.** Face It. (Sweet Valley University Thriller Edition Ser.: No. 18). 288p. (YA). (gr. 7 up). 2000. pap. 4.99 (*0-553-49348-5*, Sweet Valley) BDD Bks Young Read.
— Falling Apart. (Sweet Valley High Senior Year Ser.: No. 23). (YA). (gr. 7 up). 2000. mass mkt. 4.50 (*0-553-49339-6*, Sweet Valley) BDD Bks Young Read.
Pascal, Francine, creator. Falling for Lucas. (Sweet Valley High Super Edition Ser.: Vol. 22). 240p. (YA). (gr. 7 up). 1996. mass mkt. 4.50 (*0-553-57022-6*) Bantam.
— Fashion Victim. (Sweet Valley High Ser.: No. 131). 208p. (YA). (gr. 7-12). 1997. mass mkt. 3.99 (*0-553-57065-X*, Sweet Valley) BDD Bks Young Read.
— Fight Fire with Fire. (Sweet Valley High Ser.: No. 137). 208p. (Orig.). (YA). (gr. 7-12). 1997. mass mkt. 3.99 (*0-553-57071-4*) BDD Bks Young Read.
***Pascal, Francine, creator.** The First Time. (Sweet Valley University Ser.: No. 55). (YA). (gr. 7 up). 2000. pap. 4.50 (*0-553-49307-8*, Sweet Valley) BDD Bks Young Read.
Pascal, Francine, creator. Fooling Around. (Sweet Valley University Ser.: No. 52). 240p. (YA). (gr. 7 up). 1999. mass mkt. 4.50 (*0-553-49272-1*) Bantam.
— For the Love of Ryan. (Sweet Valley University Ser.: No. 21). 240p. (YA). (gr. 7 up). 1996. mass mkt. 3.99 (*0-553-56704-7*, Sweet Valley) BDD Bks Young Read.
— The Fowlers of Sweet Valley. (Sweet Valley Saga). 336p. (YA). (gr. 7 up). 1996. mass mkt. 4.50 (*0-553-57003-X*) Bantam.

An Asterisk (*) at the beginning of an entry indicates that the title is appearing for the first time.

— Get Real. (Sweet Valley Junior High Ser.: No. 1). 160p. (J). (gr. 3-7). 1999. pap. 4.50 (*0-553-48603-9*) BDD Bks Young Read.

— Get the Teacher! (Sweet Valley Kids Ser.: No. 46). 80p. (J). (gr. 1-3). 1994. pap. 3.50 (*0-553-48106-1*) Bantam.

— Good-Bye, Elizabeth. (Sweet Valley University Ser.: No. 38). 240p. (YA). (gr. 7 up). 1998. mass mkt. 3.99 (*0-553-49222-5*, Sweet Valley) BDD Bks Young Read.

— Good-Bye, Middle School! (Sweet Valley Twins Super Edition Ser.: No. 12). 192p. (J). (gr. 3-7). 1998. pap. 3.99 (*0-553-48606-3*, Sweet Valley) BDD Bks Young Read.

— Good-Bye, Mrs. Otis. (Sweet Valley Kids Ser.: No. 70). 96p. (J). (gr. 1-3). 1997. pap. 3.50 (*0-553-48336-6*, Sweet Valley) BDD Bks Young Read.

— Good-Bye to Love. (Sweet Valley University Ser.: No. 7). 240p. (YA). (gr. 7 up). 1994. mass mkt. 4.50 (*0-553-56652-0*) Bantam.

— Got A Problem? (Sweet Valley Junior High Ser.: No. 11). 160p. (J). (gr. 3-7). 1999. pap. 4.50 (*0-553-48669-1*) Bantam.

— The Great Boyfriend Switch. (Sweet Valley Twins Ser.: No. 66). 144p. (J). (gr. 3-7). 1993. pap. 3.50 (*0-553-48053-7*) Bantam.

***Pascal, Francine, creator.** Hands Off! (Sweet Valley Junior High Ser.: No. 15). (J). (gr. 3-7). 2000. pap. 4.50 (*0-553-48703-5*, Sweet Valley) BDD Bks Young Read.

Pascal, Francine, creator. Happily Ever After. (Sweet Valley High Ser.: No. 134). 208p. (YA). (gr. 7 up). 1997. mass mkt. 3.99 (*0-553-57068-4*, Sweet Valley) BDD Bks Young Read.

— Happy Mother's Day, Lila. (Sweet Valley Twins Ser.: No. 115). 144p. (J). (gr. 3-7). 1998. pap. 3.50 (*0-553-48599-7*, Sweet Valley) BDD Bks Young Read.

— The Haunted Burial Ground. (Sweet Valley Twins Super Chiller Ser.: No. 7). (J). (gr. 3-7). 1994. pap. 3.95 (*0-553-54146-3*) BDD Bks Young Read.

— The Haunted Burial Ground. (Sweet Valley Twins Super Chiller Ser.: No. 7). 192p. (J). (gr. 3-7). 1994. pap. 3.99 (*0-553-56404-8*) Bantam.

— The Haunted House. (Sweet Valley Twins Ser.: No. 3). 112p. (J). (gr. 3-7). 1986. pap. 3.99 (*0-553-15657-8*) Bantam.

— Have You Heard about Elizabeth? (Sweet Valley University Ser.: No. 36). 240p. (YA). (gr. 7 up). 1998. mass mkt. 3.99 (*0-553-49220-9*, Sweet Valley) BDD Bks Young Read.

— Heartbreaker. (Sweet Valley High Ser.: No. 8). 144p. (YA). (gr. 7 up). 1984. mass mkt. 3.99 (*0-553-27569-0*) Bantam.

— Here Comes the Bride. (Sweet Valley University Ser.: No. 20). 240p. (YA). (gr. 7 up). 1996. mass mkt. 4.50 (*0-553-56702-0*) Bantam.

— He's Watching You. (Sweet Valley University Thriller Edition Ser.: No. 2). 288p. (YA). (gr. 7 up). 1995. mass mkt. 4.50 (*0-553-56689-X*) Bantam.

— The High School War. (Sweet Valley High Ser.: No. 121). 176p. (YA). (gr. 7 up). 1996. mass mkt. 3.99 (*0-553-56639-3*) Bantam.

— His Secret Past. (Sweet Valley University Ser.: No. 24). 240p. (YA). (gr. 7 up). 1996. mass mkt. 3.99 (*0-553-56708-X*, Sweet Valley) BDD Bks Young Read.

— Holiday Mischief. (Sweet Valley Twins Super Edition Ser.: No. 2). (Illus.). (J). (gr. 3-7). 1988. pap. 3.95 (*0-553-16871-1*) BDD Bks Young Read.

— Home for Christmas. (Sweet Valley University Ser.: No. 8). 240p. (YA). (gr. 7 up). 1994. mass mkt. 4.50 (*0-553-56653-9*) Bantam.

— The House of Death. (Sweet Valley University Thriller Edition Ser.: No. 4). 288p. (YA). (gr. 7 up). 1995. mass mkt. 4.50 (*0-553-57008-0*, Sweet Valley) BDD Bks Young Read.

— How to Ruin a Friendship. (Sweet Valley Junior High Ser.: No. 7). 160p. (J). (gr. 3-7). 1999. pap. 3.99 (*0-553-48619-5*) BDD Bks Young Read.

— If I Die Before I Wake. (Sweet Valley Twins Ser.: No. 100). 256p. (J). (gr. 3-7). 1996. pap. 4.50 (*0-553-48344-7*) BDD Bks Young Read.

— If Looks Could Kill. (Sweet Valley Twins Ser.: No. 112). 144p. (Orig.). (J). (gr. 3-7). 1997. pap. 3.50 (*0-553-48443-5*) BDD Bks Young Read.

— If You Only Knew. (Sweet Valley High Senior Year Ser.: No. 5). 176p. (YA). (gr. 7 up). 1999. mass mkt. 3.99 (*0-553-49279-9*) BDD Bks Young Read.

— I'll Never Love Again. (Sweet Valley University Ser.: No. 46). (YA). (gr. 7 up). 1999. mass mkt. 3.99 (*0-553-49266-7*) BDD Bks Young Read.

***Pascal, Francine, creator.** I'm So Outta Here. (Sweet Valley Junior High Ser.: No. 21). (Illus.). 160p. (J). (gr. 4-7). 2000. pap. 4.50 (*0-553-48723-X*, Sweet Valley) BDD Bks Young Read.

Pascal, Francine, creator. In Love with the Enemy. (Sweet Valley High Ser.: No. 120). 208p. (YA). (gr. 7 up). 1995. mass mkt. 3.99 (*0-553-56638-5*, Sweet Valley) BDD Bks Young Read.

— The Incredible Madame Jessica. (Sweet Valley Twins Ser.: No. 93). 144p. (J). (gr. 3-7). 1995. pap. 3.50 (*0-553-48196-7*, Sweet Valley) BDD Bks Young Read.

***Pascal, Francine, creator.** Invisible Me. (Sweet Valley Junior High Ser.: No. 23). (Illus.). (J). (gr. 3-7). 2000. pap. 4.50 (*0-553-48725-6*, Sweet Valley) BDD Bks Young Read.

Pascal, Francine, creator. It Can't Happen Here. (Sweet Valley Twins Ser.: No. 86). 144p. (J). (gr. 3-7). 1995. pap. 3.50 (*0-553-48113-4*) Bantam.

***Pascal, Francine, creator.** It Guy. (Sweet Valley High Senior Year Ser.: No. 21). 192p. (YA). (gr. 8-12). 2000. mass mkt. 4.50 (*0-553-49337-X*, Sweet Valley) BDD Bks Young Read.

— It's My Life. (Sweet Valley High Senior Year Ser.: No. 19). (YA). (gr. 7 up). 2000. pap. 4.50 (*0-553-49335-3*, Sweet Valley) BDD Bks Young Read.

Pascal, Francine, creator. I've Got a Secret. (Sweet Valley High Senior Year Ser.: No. 4). 192p. (YA). (gr. 7-12). 1999. mass mkt. 3.99 (*0-553-49278-0*) BDD Bks Young Read.

— Jessica: Next Stop, Jr. High. (Sweet Valley Twins Diary Ser.). 192p. (J). (gr. 3-7). 1998. pap. 4.50 (*0-553-48607-1*) BDD Bks Young Read.

— Jessica Goes for the Gold. (Sweet Valley Team Ser.: No. 1). 144p. (J). (gr. 3-7). 1996. pap. 3.50 (*0-553-57025-0*, Sweet Valley) BDD Bks Young Read.

— Jessica + Jessica = Trouble. (Sweet Valley Kids Ser.: No. 59). 96p. (J). (gr. 1-3). 1995. pap. 3.50 (*0-553-48211-4*) Bantam.

— Jessica Quits the Squad. (Sweet Valley High Ser.: No. 112). 208p. (YA). (gr. 7 up). 1994. mass mkt. 3.99 (*0-553-56630-X*) Bantam.

— Jessica Takes Charge. (Sweet Valley Twins Ser.: No. 116). 144p. (YA). (gr. 3-7). 1998. pap. 3.50 (*0-553-48600-4*) BDD Bks Young Read.

— Jessica the Baby-Sitter. (Sweet Valley Kids Ser.: No. 14). 80p. (J). (gr. 1-3). 1990. pap. 3.50 (*0-553-15838-4*) Bantam.

— Jessica the Genius. LC 00-3652. (Sweet Valley High Ser.: No. 117). 208p. (YA). (gr. 7 up). 1995. mass mkt. 3.99 (*0-553-56635-0*, Sweet Valley) BDD Bks Young Read.

— Jessica the TV Star. (Sweet Valley Kids Ser.: No. 16). 80p. (J). (gr. 1-3). 1991. pap. 3.50 (*0-553-15850-3*) Bantam.

— Jessica's Cookie Disaster. (Sweet Valley Twins Ser.: No. 89). 144p. (J). (gr. 3-7). 1995. pap. 3.50 (*0-553-48191-6*) Bantam.

— Jessica's First Kiss. (Sweet Valley Twins Super Edition Ser.: No. 8). 192p. (J). (gr. 3-7). 1997. pap. 3.99 (*0-553-48392-7*, Sweet Valley) BDD Bks Young Read.

— Jessica's First Kiss. (Sweet Valley Twins Super Edition Ser.: No. 8). 192p. (J). (gr. 3-7). 1997. pap. 3.99 (*0-553-54290-7*, Sweet Valley) BDD Bks Young Read.

— Jessica's Lucky Millions. (Sweet Valley Twins Ser.: No. 105). 144p. (J). (gr. 3-7). 1997. pap. 3.50 (*0-553-48436-2*, Sweet Valley) BDD Bks Young Read.

— Jessica's Lucky Millions. (Sweet Valley Twins Ser.: No. 105). (J). (gr. 3-7). 1997. 8.60 (*0-606-11954-X*, Pub. by Turtleback) Demco.

— Jessica's Mermaid. (Sweet Valley Kids Ser.: No. 49). 80p. (J). (gr. 1-3). 1994. pap. 3.50 (*0-553-48118-5*) Bantam.

— Jessica's Monster Nightmare. (Sweet Valley Kids Ser.: No. 42). 80p. (J). (gr. 1-3). 1993. pap. 3.50 (*0-553-48008-1*) Bantam.

— Jessica's No Angel. (Sweet Valley Twins Super Edition Ser.: No. 11). 192p. (J). (gr. 3-7). 1998. pap. 3.99 (*0-553-48350-1*, Sweet Valley) BDD Bks Young Read.

— Jessica's Older Guy. (Sweet Valley High Ser.: No. 119). 208p. (YA). (gr. 7 up). 1995. mass mkt. 3.99 (*0-553-56637-7*, Sweet Valley) BDD Bks Young Read.

— Jessica's Secret Diary, Vol. 1. (Sweet Valley High Secret Diary Ser.). 336p. (YA). (gr. 7 up). 1994. mass mkt. 4.50 (*0-553-56659-8*) Bantam.

— Jessica's Secret Diary, Vol. 2. (Sweet Valley High Secret Diary Ser.). 336p. (YA). (gr. 7 up). 1996. mass mkt. 4.99 (*0-553-57004-8*, Sweet Valley) BDD Bks Young Read.

— Jessica's Secret Diary, Vol. 3. (Sweet Valley High Secret Diary Ser.). 336p. (YA). (gr. 7 up). 1997. mass mkt. 4.50 (*0-553-49216-0*, Sweet Valley) BDD Bks Young Read.

— Jessica's Secret Friend. (Sweet Valley Kids Ser.: No. 71). 96p. (J). (gr. 1-3). 1997. pap. 3.50 (*0-553-48338-2*, Sweet Valley) BDD Bks Young Read.

— Jessica's Secret Friend. (Sweet Valley Kids Ser.: No. 71). (J). (gr. 1-3). 1997. 8.60 (*0-606-11951-5*, Pub. by Turtleback) Demco.

— Jessica's Secret Love. (Sweet Valley High Ser.: No. 107). 208p. (YA). (gr. 7 up). 1994. mass mkt. 3.50 (*0-553-56229-0*) Bantam.

— Julie the Karate Kid. (Sweet Valley Kids Ser.: No. 52). 80p. (J). (gr. 1-3). 1994. pap. 3.50 (*0-553-48103-7*) Bantam.

***Pascal, Francine, creator.** Keepin' It Real. (Sweet Valley Junior High Ser.: No. 16). (J). (gr. 3-7). 2000. pap. 4.50 (*0-553-48704-3*, Sweet Valley) BDD Bks Young Read.

Pascal, Francine, creator. Keeping Secrets. (Sweet Valley Twins Ser.: No. 12). 96p. (J). (gr. 3-7). 1987. pap. 3.50 (*0-553-15702-7*, Skylark BDD) BDD Bks Young Read.

— Kidnapped! (Sweet Valley High Ser.: No. 13). (Orig.). (YA). (gr. 7 up). 1991. mass mkt. 3.95 (*0-553-54041-6*) BDD Bks Young Read.

— Killer at Sea. (Sweet Valley University Thriller Edition Ser.: No. 9). 288p. (YA). (gr. 7 up). 1997. mass mkt. 4.50 (*0-553-57061-7*, Sweet Valley) BDD Bks Young Read.

— A Killer on Board. (Sweet Valley High Super Thriller Ser.). 240p. (YA). (gr. 7 up). 1995. mass mkt. 4.50 (*0-553-56714-4*) Bantam.

— Killer Party. (Sweet Valley University Thriller Edition Ser.: No. 16). 288p. (YA). (gr. 7 up). 1999. mass mkt. 4.99 (*0-553-49264-0*) Bantam.

— A Kiss Before Dying. LC 00-4840. (Sweet Valley High Ser.: No. 122). 208p. (YA). (gr. 7 up). 1996. mass mkt. 3.99 (*0-553-56640-7*) Bantam.

— Kiss of a Killer. LC 49-117620. (Sweet Valley High Ser.: No. 128). 208p. (YA). (gr. 7 up). 1996. mass mkt. 3.99 (*0-553-57049-8*) Bantam.

— Kiss of the Vampire. (Sweet Valley University Thriller Edition Ser.: No. 3). 288p. (YA). (gr. 7 up). 1995. mass mkt. 4.50 (*0-553-56690-3*, Sweet Valley) BDD Bks Young Read.

— Kiss of the Vampire. (Sweet Valley University Thriller Edition Ser.: No. 3). (YA). (gr. 7 up). 1995. mass mkt. 5.99 (*0-553-54233-8*) BDD Bks Young Read.

— Lacey's Crush. (Sweet Valley Junior High Ser.: No. 6). 160p. (J). (gr. 3-7). 1999. pap. 3.99 (*0-553-48665-9*) Bantam.

— Last Wish. (Sweet Valley High Super Edition Ser.). 240p. (YA). (gr. 7 up). 1998. mass mkt. 4.99 (*0-553-49235-7*, Sweet Valley) BDD Bks Young Read.

— Left-Out Elizabeth. (Sweet Valley Kids Ser.: No. 25). 80p. (J). (gr. 1-3). 1991. pap. 2.99 (*0-553-15921-6*) Bantam.

— Lila's Birthday Bash. (Sweet Valley Kids Ser.: No. 58). 96p. (J). (gr. 1-3). 1995. pap. 3.50 (*0-553-48209-2*) Bantam.

— Lila's Haunted House Party. (Sweet Valley Kids Ser.: No. 23). 80p. (J). (gr 1-3). 1991. pap. 3.50 (*0-553-15919-4*) Bantam.

— Lila's New Flame. (Sweet Valley High Ser.: No. 135). 208p. (Orig.). (YA). (gr. 7-12). 1997. mass mkt. 3.99 (*0-553-57069-2*) BDD Bks Young Read.

— Lila's Secret. (Sweet Valley Kids Ser.: No. 6). (J). (gr. 1-3). 1994. pap. 4.99 (*0-553-54182-X*) BDD Bks Young Read.

***Pascal, Francine, creator.** Living Together. (Sweet Valley University Ser.: No. 51). 240p. (YA). (gr. 7 up). 1999. mass mkt. 4.50 (*0-553-49271-3*) Bantam.

Pascal, Francine, creator. Lois & the Sleepover. (Sweet Valley Kids Ser.: No. 51). 80p. (J). (gr. 1-3). 1994. pap. 3.50 (*0-553-48099-5*) Bantam.

— Love & Death in London. (Sweet Valley High Ser.: No. 104) 224p. (YA). (gr. 7 up). 1994. mass mkt. 3.50 (*0-553-56227-4*) Bantam.

— Love & Murder. (Sweet Valley University Thriller Edition Ser.: No. 11). 288p. (YA). (gr. 7 up). 1998. mass mkt. 4.50 (*0-553-49225-X*, Sweet Valley) BDD Bks Young Read.

— Love, Lies, & Jessica Wakefield. (Sweet Valley University Ser.: No. 2). 240p. (YA). (gr. 7 up). 1993. mass mkt. 4.50 (*0-553-56306-8*) Bantam.

— Love Me Always. (Sweet Valley University Ser.: No. 44). 240p. (YA). (gr. 7 up). 1998. mass mkt. 3.99 (*0-553-57032-3*) BDD Bks Young Read.

— The Love Potion. (Sweet Valley Twins Ser.: No. 72). 144p. (J). (gr. 3-7). 1993. pap. 3.50 (*0-553-48058-8*) Bantam.

— Loving the Enemy. (Sweet Valley University Thriller Edition Ser.: No. 15). 272p. (YA). (gr. 7 up). 1999. mass mkt. 4.50 (*0-553-49263-2*) BDD Bks Young Read.

— The Macaroni Mess. (Sweet Valley Kids Ser.: No. 72). 96p. (J). (gr. 1-3). 1997. pap. 3.50 (*0-553-48339-0*, Sweet Valley) BDD Bks Young Read.

— The Macaroni Mess. (Sweet Valley Kids Ser.: No. 72). (J). (gr. 1-3). 1997. 8.60 (*0-606-11952-3*, Pub. by Turtleback) Demco.

— The Magic Christmas. (Sweet Valley Twins Magna Edition Ser.: No. 1). 256p. (J). (gr. 3-7). 1992. pap. 3.99 (*0-553-48051-0*) Bantam.

— Mandy Miller Fights Back. (Sweet Valley Twins Ser.: No. 48). 144p. (J). (gr. 3-7). 1991. pap. 3.50 (*0-553-15880-5*) Bantam.

— Maria Who? (Sweet Valley High Senior Year Ser.: No. 8). 175p. (YA). (gr. 7-12). 1999. mass mkt. 3.99 (*0-553-49280-2*) Bantam.

— A Married Woman. (Sweet Valley University Ser.: No. 5). 240p. (YA). (gr. 7 up). 1994. mass mkt. 4.50 (*0-553-56309-2*) Bantam.

— Meet Me at Midnight. (Sweet Valley High Ser.: No. 124). 208p. (YA). (gr. 7 up). 1996. mass mkt. 3.99 (*0-553-56761-6*, Sweet Valley) BDD Bks Young Read.

— Model Flirt. (Sweet Valley High Ser.: No. 130). 208p. (YA). (gr. 7 up). 1997. mass mkt. 3.99 (*0-553-57064-1*, Sweet Valley) BDD Bks Young Read.

— The Morning After. (Sweet Valley High Ser.: No. 95). 224p. (YA). (gr. 7-12). 1993. mass mkt. 3.50 (*0-553-29852-6*) Bantam.

— The Mother-Daughter Switch. (Sweet Valley Twins Ser.: No. 87). 144p. (J). (gr. 3-7). 1995. pap. 3.50 (*0-553-48117-7*) Bantam.

— Murder in Paradise. (Sweet Valley High Super Thriller Ser.). 240p. (YA). (gr. 7 up). 1995. mass mkt. 3.99 (*0-553-56710-1*) Bantam.

— Murder on the Line. (Sweet Valley High Super Thriller Ser.). 224p. (YA). (gr. 7 up). 1992. mass mkt. 3.50 (*0-553-29308-7*) Bantam.

***Pascal, Francine, creator.** My Perfect Guy. (Sweet Valley Junior High Ser.: No. 14). (J). (gr. 3-7). 2000. pap. 4.50 (*0-553-48702-7*, Sweet Valley) BDD Bks Young Read.

Pascal, Francine, creator. The Mysterious Dr. Q. (Sweet Valley Twins Ser.: No. 102). 144p. (J). (gr. 3-7). 1996. pap. 3.50 (*0-553-48433-8*) Bantam.

— Mystery Date. (Sweet Valley High Super Edition Ser.). 240p. (YA). (gr. 7 up). 1998. mass mkt. 4.50 (*0-553-57073-0*, Sweet Valley) BDD Bks Young Read.

***Pascal, Francine, creator.** Never Let Go. (Sweet Valley High Senior Year Ser.: No. 24). (YA). (gr. 7 up). 2000. mass mkt. 4.50 (*0-553-49340-X*, Sweet Valley) BDD Bks Young Read.

Pascal, Francine, creator. Nightmare in Death Valley. (Sweet Valley High Ser.: No. 116). 208p. (YA). (gr. 7-12). 1995. mass mkt. 3.99 (*0-553-56634-2*) Bantam.

— No Escape! (Sweet Valley Twins Ser.: No. 118). 144p. (J). (gr. 3-7). 1998. pap. 3.50 (*0-553-48602-0*) BDD Bks Young Read.

— No Girls Allowed. (Sweet Valley Kids Ser.: No. 57). 96p. (J). (gr. 1-3). 1995. pap. 3.50 (*0-553-48208-4*) Bantam.

— No Means No. (Sweet Valley University Ser.: No. 10). 240p. (YA). (gr. 7 up). 1995. mass mkt. 4.50 (*0-553-56655-5*) Bantam.

— No Rules. (Sweet Valley University Ser.: No. 48). (YA). (gr. 7 up). 1999. mass mkt. 3.99 (*0-553-49268-3*) BDD Bks Young Read.

***Pascal, Francine, creator.** Nothing Is Forever. (Sweet Valley High Senior Year Ser.: No. 20). 192p. (YA). (gr. 7 up). 2000. pap. 4.50 (*0-553-49336-1*, Sweet Valley) BDD Bks Young Read.

Pascal, Francine, creator. The Older Boy. (Sweet Valley Twins Ser.: No. 15). (J). (gr. 3-7). 1987. pap. 4.95 (*0-553-16788-X*) BDD Bks Young Read.

***Pascal, Francine, creator.** On My Own. (Sweet Valley High Senior Year Ser.: No. 15). (YA). (gr. 7 up). 2000. pap. 4.50 (*0-553-49314-0*, SweetDreams) BDD Bks Young Read.

Pascal, Francine, creator. Once upon a Time. (Sweet Valley High Ser.: No. 132). 208p. (YA). (gr. 7 up). 1997. mass mkt. 3.99 (*0-553-57066-8*, Sweet Valley) BDD Bks Young Read.

— One Last Kiss. (Sweet Valley University Ser.: No. 29). 240p. (YA). (gr. 7 up). 1997. mass mkt. 3.99 (*0-553-57053-6*, Sweet Valley) BDD Bks Young Read.

— One of the Gang. (Sweet Valley Twins Ser.: No. 10). 112p. (J). (gr. 3-7). 1987. pap. 3.50 (*0-553-15677-2*) Bantam.

***Pascal, Francine, creator.** The One that Got Away. (Sweet Valley High Senior Year Ser.: No. 9). 192p. (YA). (gr. 7 up). 1999. mass mkt. 4.50 (*0-553-49281-0*) Bantam.

Pascal, Francine, creator. One 2 Many. (Sweet Valley Junior High Ser.: No. 2). 144p. (J). (gr. 3-7). 1999. pap. 4.50 (*0-553-48604-7*) BDD Bks Young Read.

— The Other Woman. (Sweet Valley University Ser.: No. 16). 240p. (YA). (gr. 7 up). 1995. mass mkt. 3.99 (*0-553-56696-2*, Sweet Valley) BDD Bks Young Read.

— Out of the Picture. (Sweet Valley University Ser.: No. 33). 240p. (Orig.). (YA). (gr. 7 up). 1997. mass mkt. 3.99 (*0-553-57057-9*) BDD Bks Young Read.

— Outcast. (Sweet Valley High Ser.: No. 41). (YA). (gr. 7 up). 1987. mass mkt. 3.95 (*0-553-16797-9*) BDD Bks Young Read.

— Party Weekend! (Sweet Valley High Ser.: No. 143). 208p. (YA). (gr. 7-12). 1998. mass mkt. 3.99 (*0-553-49233-0*, Sweet Valley) BDD Bks Young Read.

— The Patmans of Sweet Valley. (Sweet Valley Saga). 352p. (YA). (gr. 8 up). 1996. mass mkt. 4.50 (*0-553-57023-4*) Bantam.

— A Picture-Perfect Prom? (Sweet Valley High Ser.: No. 141). 208p. (YA). (gr. 7-12). 1998. mass mkt. 3.99 (*0-553-49231-4*, Sweet Valley) BDD Bks Young Read.

— Playing with Fire. (Sweet Valley High Ser.: No. 3). 160p. (YA). (gr. 7 up). 1984. mass mkt. 3.99 (*0-553-27669-7*) Bantam.

— Please Forgive Me. (Sweet Valley High Ser.: No. 140). 208p. (YA). (gr. 7 up). 1998. mass mkt. 3.99 (*0-553-49230-6*, Sweet Valley) BDD Bks Young Read.

— The Pom-Pom Wars. (Sweet Valley High Ser.: No. 113). 208p. (YA). (gr. 7 up). 1995. mass mkt. 3.99 (*0-553-56631-8*) Bantam.

— Power Play. (Sweet Valley High Ser.: No. 4). 176p. (YA). (gr. 7 up). 1984. mass mkt. 3.99 (*0-553-27493-7*) Bantam.

— The Price of Love. (Sweet Valley University Ser.: No. 43). 240p. (YA). (gr. 7 up). 1998. mass mkt. 3.99 (*0-553-57031-5*) BDD Bks Young Read.

— Private Jessica. (Sweet Valley University Ser.: No. 40). 240p. (YA). (gr. 7 up). 1998. mass mkt. 3.99 (*0-553-49224-1*) BDD Bks Young Read.

— Promises. (Sweet Valley High Ser.: No. 15). 160p. (YA). (gr. 7 up). 1984. mass mkt. 3.99 (*0-553-27940-8*) Bantam.

— Psychic Sisters. (Sweet Valley Twins Ser.: No. 70). 144p. (J). (gr. 3-7). 1993. pap. 3.50 (*0-553-48057-X*) Bantam.

— Pumpkin Fever. (Sweet Valley Twins Ser.: No. 110). 144p. (Orig.). (J). (gr. 3-7). 1997. pap. 3.50 (*0-553-48441-9*) BDD Bks Young Read.

— R for Revenge. (Sweet Valley High Super Thriller Ser.: Vol. 24). 231p. (Orig.). (YA). (gr. 7-12). 1997. mass mkt. 4.50 (*0-553-57072-2*) BDD Bks Young Read.

— Racing Hearts. (Sweet Valley High Ser.: No. 9). 160p. (YA). (gr. 7 up). 1984. mass mkt. 3.99 (*0-553-27878-9*) Bantam.

— Return of the Evil Twin. (Sweet Valley High Magna Edition Ser.). (YA). (gr. 7 up). 1995. pap. 5.99 (*0-553-54216-8*) BDD Bks Young Read.

— Return of the Evil Twin. (Sweet Valley High Magna Edition Ser.). 352p. (YA). (gr. 7 up). 1995. mass mkt. 4.50 (*0-553-57002-1*) Bantam.

— Robbery at the Mall. (Sweet Valley Twins Ser.: No. 81). 144p. (J). (gr. 3-7). 1994. pap. 3.50 (*0-553-48116-9*) Bantam.

— A Roller Coaster for the Twins! (Sweet Valley Kids Ser.: No. 68). 96p. (J). (gr. 1-3). 1996. pap. 3.50 (*0-553-48334-X*) Bantam.

— Romeo & 2 Juliets. (Sweet Valley Twins Ser.: No. 112). (J). (gr. 3-7). 1994. pap. 4.50 (*0-553-54180-3*) BDD Bks Young Read.

— Romeo & 2 Juliets. (Sweet Valley Twins Ser.: No. 84). 144p. (J). (gr. 3-7). 1994. pap. 3.50 (*0-553-48105-3*) Bantam.

— The Roommate. (Sweet Valley University Thriller Edition Ser.: No. 6). 288p. (YA). (gr. 7 up). 1996. mass mkt. 4.50 (*0-553-57010-2*, Sweet Valley) BDD Bks Young Read.

— Runaway Hamster. (Sweet Valley Kids Ser.: No. 2). 80p. (J). (gr. 1-3). 1989. pap. 3.50 (*0-553-15759-0*, Skylark BDD) BDD Bks Young Read.

— Running for Her Life. (Sweet Valley University Thriller Edition Ser.: No. 5). 288p. (YA). (gr. 7 up). 1996. mass mkt. 4.99 (*0-553-57009-9*) Bantam.

***Pascal, Francine, creator.** Rush Week. (Sweet Valley University Ser.: No. 54). 240p. (YA). (gr. 7 up). 2000. pap. 4.50 (*0-553-49306-X*, Sweet Valley) BDD Bks Young Read.

Pascal, Francine, creator. S. S. Heartbreak. (Sweet Valley University Ser.: No. 13). 240p. (YA). (gr. 7 up). 1995. mass mkt. 4.50 (0-553-56692-X) Bantam.

— Say It to My Face. (Sweet Valley High Senior Year Ser.: No. 2). 176p. (YA). (gr. 7-12). 1999. mass mkt. 4.50 (0-553-57027-7) BDD Bks Young Read.

— Second Best. (Sweet Valley Twins Ser.: No. 16). (J). (gr. 3-7). 1987. pap. 3.95 (0-553-16802-9) BDD Bks Young Read.

— Secret Admirer. (Sweet Valley High Ser.: No. 39). (Illus.). (YA). (gr. 7 up). 1987. mass mkt. 3.95 (0-553-16777-4) BDD Bks Young Read.

— The Secret of the Magic Pen. (Sweet Valley Twins Super Chiller Ser.: No. 8). 192p. (J). (gr. 3-7). 1995. pap. 3.99 (0-553-48282-3) Bantam.

— Secrets. (Sweet Valley High Ser.: No. 2). 128p. (YA). (gr. 7 up). 1984. mass mkt. 3.99 (0-553-27578-X) Bantam.

***Pascal, Francine, creator.** She Loves Me... Not. (Sweet Valley Junior High Ser.: No. 19). (J). (gr. 3-7). 2000. pap. 4.50 (0-553-48721-3, Sweet Valley) BDD Bks Young Read.

Pascal, Francine, creator. Shipboard Wedding. (Sweet Valley University Ser.: No. 14). 240p. (YA). (gr. 7 up). 1995. mass mkt. 4.50 (0-553-56693-8) Bantam.

— Sisters at War. (Sweet Valley Twins Ser.: No. 111). 144p. (Orig.). (J). (gr. 3-7). 1997. pap. 3.50 (0-553-48442-7) BDD Bks Young Read.

— Sneaking In. (Sweet Valley University Ser.: No. 42). 240p. (YA). (gr. 7 up). 1998. mass mkt. 3.99 (0-553-57030-7) BDD Bks Young Read.

— Sneaking Out. (Sweet Valley Twins Ser.: No. 5). 112p. (J). (gr. 3-7). 1986. pap. 3.50 (0-553-15659-4) Bantam.

— So Cool. (Sweet Valley High Senior Year Ser.: No. 3). 192p. (YA). (gr. 7 up). 1999. mass mkt. 4.50 (0-553-57028-5) BDD Bks Young Read.

***Pascal, Francine, creator.** So Not Me. (Sweet Valley High Senior Year Ser.: No. 22). (YA). (gr. 7 up). 2000. mass mkt. 4.50 (0-553-49338-8, Sweet Valley) BDD Bks Young Read.

Pascal, Francine, creator. Sorority Scandal. (Sweet Valley University Ser.: No. 9). 240p. (YA). (gr. 7 up). 1995. mass mkt. 3.99 (0-553-56654-7) Bantam.

— Soulmates. (Sweet Valley Junior High Ser.: No. 3). 160p. (J). (gr. 3-7). 1999. pap. 3.99 (0-553-48605-5) BDD Bks Young Read.

***Pascal, Francine, creator.** Split Decision. (Sweet Valley High Senior Year Ser.: No. 14). (YA). (gr. 7 up). 2000. pap. 4.50 (0-553-49313-2, Sweet Valley) BDD Bks Young Read.

Pascal, Francine, creator. Spring Break. (Sweet Valley High Super Edition Ser.). (YA). (gr. 7 up). 1986. 8.60 (0-606-01738-0, Pub. by Turtleback) Demco.

— Spy Girl. (Sweet Valley University Ser.: No. 34). 240p. (Orig.). (YA). (gr. 7 up). 1997. mass mkt. 3.99 (0-553-57058-7) BDD Bks Young Read.

— Standing Out. (Sweet Valley Twins Ser.: No. 25). (J). (gr. 3-7). 1988. pap. 4.95 (0-553-16872-X) BDD Bks Young Read.

— Steven Gets Even. (Sweet Valley Twins Ser.: No. 88). 144p. (J). (gr. 3-7). 1995. pap. 3.50 (0-553-48189-4) Bantam.

— Steven the Zombie. (Sweet Valley Twins Ser.: No. 78). 144p. (J). (gr. 3-7). 1994. pap. 3.50 (0-553-48104-5) Bantam.

— Steven's Bride. large type ed. LC 93-1350. (Sweet Valley High Ser.: No. 83). (YA). (gr. 7 up). 1993. pap. 15.95 (1-56054-756-1) Thorndike Pr.

— Steven's Enemy. (Sweet Valley Twins Ser.: No. 82). (J). (gr. 3-7). 1994. pap. 4.50 (0-553-54151-X) BDD Bks Young Read.

— Steven's Enemy. (Sweet Valley Twins Ser.: No. 82). 144p. (J). (gr. 3-7). 1994. pap. 3.50 (0-553-48097-9) Bantam.

— Steven's Twin. (Sweet Valley Kids Ser.: No. 50). 80p. (J). (gr. 1-3). 1994. pap. 2.99 (0-553-48095-2) Bantam.

— Stranded. (Sweet Valley University Ser.: No. 49). 240p. (YA). (gr. 7 up). 1999. mass mkt. 3.99 (0-553-49269-1) BDD Bks Young Read.

— A Stranger in the House. (Sweet Valley High Super Thriller Ser.). 224p. (YA). (gr. 7 up). 1995. mass mkt. 4.50 (0-553-56711-X) Bantam.

— Summer of Love. (Sweet Valley University Ser.: No. 50). 240p. (YA). (gr. 7 up). 1999. mass mkt. 3.99 (0-553-49270-5) BDD Bks Young Read.

— Surprise! Surprise! (Sweet Valley Kids Ser.: No. 1). 80p. (J). (gr. 1-3). 1989. pap. 3.99 (0-553-15758-2, Skylark BDD) BDD Bks Young Read.

— Sweet Valley Blizzard! (Sweet Valley Kids Ser.: No. 74). (Illus.). 96p. (Orig.). (J). (gr. 1-3). 1997. pap. 3.50 (0-553-48343-9) BDD Bks Young Read.

— Sweet Valley Clean-Up Team. (Sweet Valley Kids Ser.: No. 27). 80p. (J). (gr. 1-3). 1992. pap. 2.99 (0-553-15923-2) Bantam.

Pascal, Francine, creator. Sweet Valley High Super Edition Boxed Set # 1: Perfect Summer; Special Christmas; Spring Break; Malibu Summer. (Sweet Valley High Super Edition Ser.). (YA). (gr. 7 up). 1991. mass mkt. 14.00 (0-553-61820-2) Bantam.

Pascal, Francine, creator. Take Back the Night. (Sweet Valley University Ser.: No. 11). 240p. (YA). (gr. 7 up). 1995. mass mkt. 3.99 (0-553-56656-3) Bantam.

— Take Me On. (Sweet Valley High Senior Year Ser.: No. 11). 192p. (YA). (gr. 7 up). 1999. mass mkt. 4.50 (0-553-49283-7) Bantam.

— Teacher's Pet. (Sweet Valley Twins Ser.: No. 2). (Illus.). (J). (gr. 3-7). 1986. pap. 7.95 (0-553-16654-9) BDD Bks Young Read.

— Teacher's Pet. (Sweet Valley Twins Ser.: No. 2). 112p. (J). (gr. 3-7). 1986. pap. 3.99 (0-553-15656-X) Bantam.

— Teamwork. (Sweet Valley Twins Ser.: No. 27). (J). (gr. 3-7). 1989. pap. 3.25 (0-553-16889-4) BDD Bks Young Read.

***Pascal, Francine, creator.** Third Wheel. (Sweet Valley Junior High Ser.: No. 12). 160p. (J). (gr. 3-7). 1999. pap. 4.50 (0-553-48670-5) Bantam.

— Three Days, Two Nights. (Sweet Valley Junior High Ser.: No. 13). 176p. (J). (gr. 3-7). 2000. pap. 4.50 (0-553-48701-9, Sweet Valley) BDD Bks Young Read.

— Three Girls & a Guy. (Sweet Valley High Senior Year Ser.: No. 16). (YA). (gr. 7 up). 2000. mass mkt. 4.50 (0-553-49315-9, Sweet Valley) BDD Bks Young Read.

Pascal, Francine, creator. To Catch a Thief. (Sweet Valley High Ser.: No. 133). 208p. (YA). (gr. 7-12). 1997. mass mkt. 3.99 (0-553-57067-6, Sweet Valley) BDD Bks Young Read.

— Todd Runs Away. (Sweet Valley Twins Ser.: No. 77). 144p. (J). (gr. 3-7). 1994. pap. 3.50 (0-553-48100-2) Bantam.

— Too Hot to Handle. (Sweet Valley High Ser.: No. 136). 208p. (Orig.). (YA). (gr. 7 up). 1997. mass mkt. 3.99 (0-553-57070-6) BDD Bks Young Read.

— Too Popular. (Sweet Valley Junior High Ser.: No. 9). 160p. (J). (gr. 3-7). 1999. pap. 4.50 (0-553-48667-5) Bantam.

— Too Scared to Sleep. (Sweet Valley Twins Ser.: No. 97). 144p. (J). (gr. 3-7). 1996. pap. 3.50 (0-553-48201-7, Sweet Valley) BDD Bks Young Read.

— Trapped in Toyland. (Sweet Valley Kids Super Special Ser.: No. 1). 112p. (J). (gr. 1-3). 1994. pap. 3.99 (0-553-48251-3) Bantam.

— The Treasure of Death Valley. (Sweet Valley High Ser.: No. 115). 208p. (YA). (gr. 7 up). 1995. mass mkt. 3.99 (0-553-56633-4) Bantam.

— The Trial of Jessica Wakefield. (Sweet Valley University Ser.: No. 26). 240p. (YA). (gr. 7 up). 1996. mass mkt. 3.99 (0-553-57007-2) Bantam.

***Pascal, Francine, creator.** True Blue. (Sweet Valley Junior High Ser.: No. 18). (Illus.). 160p. (J). (gr. 3-7). 2000. pap. 4.50 (0-553-48706-X, Sweet Valley) BDD Bks Young Read.

Pascal, Francine, creator. The Truth about Ryan. (Sweet Valley University Ser.: No. 31). 240p. (YA). (gr. 7 up). 1997. mass mkt. 3.99 (0-553-57055-2, Sweet Valley) BDD Bks Young Read.

— Truth Or Dare. (Sweet Valley University Ser.: No. 53). 240p. (YA). (gr. 7 up). 1999. mass mkt. 4.50 (0-553-49273-X) Bantam.

— Tug of War. (Sweet Valley Twins Ser.: No. 14). (J). (gr. 3-7). 1987. pap. 2.50 (0-553-16799-5) BDD Bks Young Read.

— Tug of War. (Sweet Valley Twins Ser.: No. 14). 112p. (J). (gr. 3-7). 1988. pap. 2.75 (0-685-18297-5, Skylark BDD) BDD Bks Young Read.

— Twin Hearts. (Sweet Valley High (TV) Ser.: No. 2). 144p. (YA). (gr. 7 up). 1995. mass mkt. 4.50 (0-553-57012-9, Sweet Valley) BDD Bks Young Read.

— Twin Hearts. (Sweet Valley High (TV) Ser.: No. 2). (YA). (gr. 7 up). 1996. 9.60 (0-606-08629-3, Pub. by Turtleback) Demco.

***Pascal, Francine, creator.** Twin Switch. (Sweet Valley Junior High Ser.: No. 10). 160p. (J). (gr. 3-7). 1999. pap. 4.50 (0-553-48668-3) Bantam.

Pascal, Francine, creator. The Twins & the Wild West. (Sweet Valley Kids Ser.: No. 10). 80p. (J). (gr. 1-3). 1990. pap. 3.50 (0-553-15811-2) Bantam.

— The Twins Get Caught. (Sweet Valley Twins Ser.: No. 41). 144p. (J). (gr. 3-7). 1990. pap. 3.50 (0-553-15810-4) Bantam.

— The Twins Go to College. (Sweet Valley Twins Super Edition Ser.: No. 9). 192p. (J). (gr. 3-7). 1997. pap. 3.99 (0-553-48347-1, Sweet Valley) BDD Bks Young Read.

— The Twins Hit Hollywood. LC 49-254470. (Sweet Valley Twins Ser.: No. 107). 144p. (J). (gr. 3-7). 1997. pap. 3.50 (0-553-48438-9, Sweet Valley) BDD Bks Young Read.

— Twins in Love. (Sweet Valley Twins Ser.: No. 101). 144p. (J). (gr. 3-7). 1996. pap. 3.50 (0-553-48346-3) BDD Bks Young Read.

— The Twin's Mystery Teacher. (Sweet Valley Kids Ser.: No. 3). 80p. (J). (gr. 1-3). 1989. pap. 3.50 (0-553-15760-4, Skylark BDD) BDD Bks Young Read.

— The Twins Take Paris. (Sweet Valley Twins Super Edition Ser.: No. 6). 192p. (J). (gr. 3-7). 1996. pap. 3.99 (0-553-48390-0) Bantam.

— Undercover Angels. (Sweet Valley University Ser.: No. 35). 240p. (Orig.). (YA). (gr. 7 up). 1997. mass mkt. 3.99 (0-553-57059-5) BDD Bks Young Read.

— The Unicorns Go Hawaiian. (Sweet Valley Twins Super Edition Ser.: No. 4). 192p. (J). (gr. 3-7). 1991. pap. 3.99 (0-553-15948-8) Bantam.

— The Verdict. LC 94-102829. (Sweet Valley High Ser.: No. 97). 224p. (YA). (gr. 7 up). 1993. mass mkt. 3.50 (0-553-29854-2) Bantam.

***Pascal, Francine, creator.** Very Bad Things. (Sweet Valley University Thriller Edition Ser.: No. 17). 288p. (YA). (gr. 7 up). 2000. pap. 4.99 (0-553-49311-6, Sweet Valley) BDD Bks Young Read.

Pascal, Francine, creator. The Wakefield Legacy: The Untold Story. (Sweet Valley Saga: Vol. 2). 352p. (YA). (gr. 7 up). 1992. mass mkt. 4.50 (0-553-29794-5, Starfire BDD) BDD Bks Young Read.

— The Wakefields of Sweet Valley. (Sweet Valley Saga: Vol. 1). 352p. (YA). (gr. 7-12). 1991. mass mkt. 4.50 (0-553-29278-1) Bantam.

— Wanted for Murder. (Sweet Valley University Thriller Edition Ser.: No. 1). 288p. (YA). (gr. 7 up). 1994. mass mkt. 4.50 (0-553-56688-1) Bantam.

— The War Between the Twins. (Sweet Valley Twins Ser.: No. 37). 144p. (J). (gr. 3-7). 1990. pap. 3.50 (0-553-15779-5) Bantam.

— What Jessica Wants . . . (Sweet Valley High Ser.: No. 138). 208p. (YA). (gr. 7-12). 1998. mass mkt. 3.99 (0-553-49228-4, Sweet Valley) BDD Bks Young Read.

— What Winston Saw. (Sweet Valley University Thriller Edition Ser.: No. 7). 288p. (YA). (gr. 7 up). 1996. mass mkt. 4.50 (0-553-57050-1) Bantam.

***Pascal, Francine, creator.** What You Don't Know. (Sweet Valley Junior High Ser.: No. 22). (Illus.). (J). (gr. 3-7). 2000. pap. 4.50 (0-553-48724-8, Sweet Valley) BDD Bks Young Read.

Pascal, Francine, creator. What Your Parents Don't Know... (Sweet Valley University Ser.: No. 3). 240p. (YA). (gr. 9 up). 1994. mass mkt. 4.50 (0-553-56307-6) Bantam.

***Pascal, Francine, creator.** Whatever. (Sweet Valley Junior High Ser.: No. 17). (Illus.). 160p. (J). (gr. 3-7). 2000. pap. 4.50 (0-553-48705-1, Sweet Valley) BDD Bks Young Read.

Pascal, Francine, creator. White Lies. (Sweet Valley High Ser.: No. 52). (YA). (gr. 7 up). 1988. mass mkt. 3.95 (0-553-16878-9) BDD Bks Young Read.

***Pascal, Francine, creator.** Who Knew? (Sweet Valley University Ser.: No. 57). (Illus.). 240p. (YA). (gr. 9-12). 2000. mass mkt. 4.50 (0-553-49309-4, Sweet Valley) BDD Bks Young Read.

— Wild Child. (Sweet Valley Junior High Ser.: No. 20). 160p. (J). (gr. 3-7). 2000. pap. 4.50 (0-553-48722-1, Sweet Valley) BDD Bks Young Read.

Pascal, Francine, creator. The Witch in the Pumpkin Patch. (Sweet Valley Kids Ser.: No. 73). 96p. (J). (gr. 1-3). 1997. pap. 3.50 (0-553-48342-0) BDD Bks Young Read.

— Won't Someone Help Anna? (Sweet Valley Twins Ser.: No. 69). 144p. (J). (gr. 3-7). 1993. pap. 3.50 (0-553-48056-1) Bantam.

— The Year Without Christmas. (Sweet Valley Twins Super Edition Ser.: No. 10). 192p. (Orig.). (J). (gr. 3-7). 1997. pap. 3.99 (0-553-48348-X) BDD Bks Young Read.

— Your Basic Nightmare. (Sweet Valley High Senior Year Ser.: No. 6). 192p. (YA). (gr. 7-12). 1999. mass mkt. 3.99 (0-553-48612-8) BDD Bks Young Read.

— You're Not My Sister. (Sweet Valley University Ser.: No. 47). 240p. (YA). (gr. 7 up). 1999. mass mkt. 3.99 (0-553-49267-5) BDD Bks Young Read.

— Yours for a Day. (Sweet Valley Twins Ser.: No. 76). 144p. (J). (gr. 3-7). 1994. pap. 3.50 (0-553-48096-0) Bantam.

Pascal, Janet B. Arthur Conan Doyle: Beyond Baker Street. LC 99-36643. (Oxford Portraits Ser.). (Illus.). 160p. (YA). 2000. text 22.00 (0-19-512262-3) OUP.

Pascal, Jean M. The Political Ideas of James Wilson, 1742-1798. LC 91-10728. (Political Theory & Political Philosophy Ser.). 368p. 1991. text 10.00 (0-8153-0139-1) Garland.

Pascal, Jean-Noel. Les Successeurs de la Fontaine au Siecle des Lumieres (1715-1815) (Eighteenth Century French Intellectual History Ser.: Vol. 3). (FRE.). XVII, 264p. (C). 1995. text 57.95 (0-8204-2534-6) P Lang Pubng.

***Pascal, Julia.** Holocaust Trilogy. (Oberon Bks.). 2000. pap. 20.95 (1-84002-094-6) Theatre Comm.

Pascal, Julia, ed. Women in Theatre, Vol. 2, Part 3. (Contemporary Theatre Review Ser). 130p. 1995. pap. text 16.00 (3-7186-5598-5, Harwood Acad Pubs) Gordon & Breach.

Pascal, Lawrence. Virginia Workers Compensation: Law & Practice 1986, 1991 Supplement. 1986. text 40.00 (0-87473-238-7, 65780-10, MICHIE) LEXIS Pub.

— Virginia Workers Compensation: 1989 Cumulative Supplement. 1989. write for info. (0-87473-489-4, 65782-10, MICHIE) LEXIS Pub.

Pascal, Lawrence J. Virginia Workers' Compensation: Law & Practice. 1986. 55.00 (0-87473-256-5, MICHIE) LEXIS Pub.

— Virginia Workers' Compensation: Law & Practice, 1998 Cumulative Supplement. 140p. 1998. pap. write for info. (0-327-00624-2, 6578915) LEXIS Pub.

— Virginia Workers' Compensation Law & Practice, 1993. 2nd ed. 378p. 1993. text 75.00 (1-55834-027-0, 65785-10, MICHIE) LEXIS Pub.

Pascal, Nanette R. & Rojas, Maria P. Relaciones Comerciales. (SPA.). 352p. (C). 1995. pap. text 35.16 (0-669-32579-1) HM Trade Div.

— Relaciones Comericales. (SPA.). (C). 1996. text, teacher ed. 2.66 (0-669-41783-1) HM Trade Div.

Pascal, Paul. Concilium Romarici Montis. (Latin Commentaries Ser.). 28p. (Orig.). (C). 1993. pap. text 5.00 (0-929524-77-2) Bryn Mawr Commentaries.

— Hrotsvitha Dulcitius & Paphnutius. (Latin Commentaries Ser.). 83p. (Orig.). (C). 1985. pap. text 6.00 (0-929524-41-1) Bryn Mawr Commentaries.

Pascal, Pierre. The Religion of the Russian People. LC 76-24462. 130p. 1976. pap. 8.95 (0-913836-30-3) St Vladimirs.

Pascal, Roy. German Literature in the Sixteenth & Seventeenth Centuries: Renaissance-Reformation-Baroque, Volume II. LC 79-9993. 274p. 1979. reprint ed. lib. bdg. 65.00 (0-313-21461-1, PAGL, Greenwood Pr) Greenwood.

— The German Novel: Studies. LC 57-3904. (Canadian University Paperbooks Ser.: No. 24). 354p. reprint ed. pap. 109.80 (0-8357-4164-8, 203693800007) Bks Demand.

Pascal, Sevran. Dictionary of the French Chanson(song) Dictionnaire de la Chanson Francaise. (ENG & FRE.). 384p. 1986. 32.50 (0-8288-2173-9, M2355) Fr & Eur.

***Pascale, A. J.** Are You a Superficial Man or Are You Dating One? (Illus.). 64p. (C). 1999. pap. 9.95 (0-9675137-0-7) Big Prodn.

Pascale, Celine-Marie. The Blue Corn Cookbook. (Border Bks.). 103p. (Orig.). 1990. pap. 7.95 (0-685-66859-2) Out West Pub.

— The Blue Corn Cookbook. (Chile Pepper Cookbook Ser.). (Illus.). 125p. (Orig.). 1992. pap. 7.95 (0-9623865-1-0) Out West Pub.

Pascale, J. & Olson, R. E. Theoretical Methods for Atomic & Molecular Collisions: WS Lecture Notes in Physics, Vol. 14. 450p. (C). 1993. text 77.00 (9971-5-0424-3); pap. text 37.00 (9971-5-0425-1) World Scientific Pub.

Pascale, Richard T. Managing on the Edge: How the Smartest Companies Use Conflict to Stay Ahead. (Illus.). 352p. 1991. pap. 12.00 (0-671-73285-4, Touchstone) S&S Trade Pap.

Pascali, D. & Sburlan, S. Nonlinear Mappings of Monotone Type. 351p. 1979. lib. bdg. 115.50 (90-286-0118-X) Kluwer Academic.

Pascalis, Andrea De, see De Pascalis, Andrea.

Pascalis, William K., jt. auth. see Ferguson, S. W.

Pascall, Gillian. Social Policy: A Feminist Analysis. 250p. 1986. text 47.50 (0-422-78660-8, 1026, Pub. by Tavistock) Routldge.

Pascall, Gillian. Social Policy: A Feminist Analysis. 250p. 1986. pap. text 15.95 (0-422-78670-5, 1043, Pub. by Tavistock) Routldge.

Pascall, Gillian. Social Policy: A New Feminist Analysis. 2nd ed. LC 96-21372. 288p. (C). 1996. 85.00 (0-415-09927-7); pap. 25.99 (0-415-09928-5) Routledge.

Pascall, Gillian & Cox, Roger. Women Returning to Higher Education. LC 93-13275. 169p. 1994. pap. 39.95 (0-335-19055-3) OpUniv Pr.

Pascall, Glenn. The Trillion Dollar Budget: How to Stop the Bankrupting of America. LC 84-40665. (Illus.). 328p. 1985. pap. 14.95 (0-295-96237-2) U of Wash Pr.

Pascall, Stephan C. Commercial Satellite Communications. 512p. 1997. text 130.00 (0-7506-1235-5) Buttrwrth-Heinemann.

Pascarella, Ernest T., ed. Studying Student Attrition. LC 81-48576. (New Directions for Institutional Research Ser.: No. IR 36). 1982. pap. 22.00 (0-87589-906-4) Jossey-Bass.

Pascarella, Ernest T. & Terenzini, Patrick T. How College Affects Students: Findings & Insights from Twenty Years of Research. LC 90-46068. (Higher & Adult Education Ser.). 920p. 1991. pap. text 48.00 (1-55542-338-8) Jossey-Bass.

Pascarella, Perry, jt. auth. see Nagle, Bernard A.

Pascarelli, Emil & Quilter, Deborah. Repetitive Strain Injury: A Computer User's Guide. 240p. 1994. pap. 17.95 (0-471-59533-0) Wiley.

Pascarelli, Peter. The Toughest Job in Baseball: What Managers Do, How They Do It & Why It Gives Them Ulcers. LC 93-16572. 288p. 1993. 21.00 (0-671-79331-4) S&S Trade.

***Pascavage, Barbara A.** Oracle8 DBA: Network Administration Exam Cram. LC 99-52992. (Exam Cram Ser.). (Illus.). 2000. pap. 29.99 (1-57610-578-4) Coriolis Grp.

Pascenkova, N. A., et al. Czech-Russian Dictionary of Geology. (CZE & RUS.). 248p. 1960. 39.95 (0-8288-6833-6, M-9067) Fr & Eur.

Pasch, Brian & Polk, Jacqueline K. The Readability Machine: Radio Shack, TRS-80 Model 4 (Software & Documentation) 48p. 1986. 84.95 (0-13-753609-7) P-H.

— The Readability Machine: The Readability Machine for Apple II; Apple IIe, Apple IIc, & Apple-Compatible Microcomputers. 48p. 1986. 84.95 (0-13-753617-8) P-H.

***Pasch, Grete & Norsworthy, Kent, eds.** Using Internet Primary Sources to Teach Critical Thinking in World Languages. (Greenwood Professional Guides in School Librarianship). 170p. 2000. 40.00 (0-313-31259-1, Greenwood Pr) Greenwood.

Pasch, H. & Trathnigg, B. HPLC of Polymers. LC 99-20246. (Desktop Editions in Chemistry Ser.). 240p. 1999. pap. 54.95 (3-540-65551-4) Spr-Verlag.

Pasch, Harald & Trathnigg, Bernd. HPLC of Polymers. LC 97-29893. (Laboratory Ser.). (Illus.). 220p. 1997. 84.95 (3-540-61689-6) Spr-Verlag.

Pasch, Marvin. Teaching As Decision Making. 3rd ed. (C). 1998. text. write for info. (0-8013-1864-5) Addison-Wesley.

Pasch, Robert A. Wisconsin Collection Law. LC 79-91165. 1993. 125.00 (0-317-05728-6) West Group.

Pascha, Werner, jt. ed. see Metzger-Court, Sarah.

Paschal, Andrew G., ed. see Du Bois, W. E. B.

***Paschal, David.** Words on Papers. 1999. pap. write for info. (1-58235-196-1) Watermrk Pr.

Paschal, Eric & Buckingham, Bruce. Rhythm Guitar The Complete Guide. 144p. 1997. student ed., otabind 16.95 (0-7935-8184-2) H Leonard.

***Paschal, Eric & Trovato, Steve.** Contemporary Acoustic Guitar. 48p. 2000. pap. 14.95 (0-7935-9589-4) H Leonard.

Paschal, G. W. History of North Carolina Baptists. 1990. reprint ed. 54.00 (0-685-34316-2) Stevens Bk Pr.

Paschal, Hugh. A Formalistic Approach to Freshman Composition, Course II. 5th ed. 182p. (C). 1998. per. 33.95 (0-7872-2138-4, 41213801) Kendall-Hunt.

— A Formalistic Approach to Freshman Composition, Course 1. 5th ed. 378p. (C). 1998. per. 52.95 (0-7872-5179-8, 41517901) Kendall-Hunt.

***Paschal, Hugh.** A Formalistic Approach to Freshman Computer Course I. 6th ed. 356p. (C). 2000. per. 52.95 (0-7872-7218-3) Kendall-Hunt.

— A Formalistic Approach to Freshman Computer Course II. 6th ed. 144p. (C). 2000. per. 36.95 (0-7872-7219-1) Kendall-Hunt.

Paschal, Hugh H. A Formalistic Approach to Freshman Composition, Course 1. 356p. (C). 1996. pap. text, per. 34.95 (0-7872-2170-8) Kendall-Hunt.

— A Formalistic Approach to Freshman Composition, Course 2. 184p. 1996. pap. text, per. 20.95 (0-7872-2171-6) Kendall-Hunt.

Paschal, Huston. Michael Timpson. LC 91-66802. (Illus.). 24p. (Orig.). 1991. pap. 7.95 (0-88259-964-X) NCMA.

Paschal, Huston, intro. Tom Phillips: Words & Texts. (Illus.). 1993. pap. 34.95 (0-500-97402-0, Pub. by Thames Hudson) Norton.

***Paschal, Janet.** Songs for a Lifetime. 88p. 2000. otabind 14.95 (0-634-01228-2) H Leonard.

P

***Paschal, John.** EC&M's Electrical Calculations Handbook. (Illus.). 420p. 2000. 54.95 (*0-07-136095-6*) McGraw.

Paschal, John & Dorman, John. Paschal's Principles of Weight Training. (Illus.). 1979. pap. 2.95 (*0-89826-003-5*) Natl Paperback.

Paschal, Mary. The Structure of the Roman de Thebes. LC 80-66540. 96p. 1980. pap. 12.95 (*0-89729-261-8*) Ediciones.

Paschal, R. Wade, Jr. Serving with Christ: A Study of Jesus' Farewell Commission to His Disciples. LC 94-72242. 104p. 1994. pap. 8.95 (*0-88177-137-6*, DR137) Discipleship Res.

— Vital Adult Learning: Choices to Fit Your Church. LC 93-28212. (Choices to Fit Your Church Ser.). 144p. (Orig.). 1994. pap. 7.77 (*0-687-00773-9*) Abingdon.

Paschalis, Michael. Virgil's Aeneid: Semantic Relations & Proper Names. 454p. (C). 1998. text 115.00 (*0-19-814688-4*) OUP.

Paschall, Dorothy M. Vocabulary of Mental Aberration in Roman Comedy & Petronius. (Language Dissertations Ser.: No. 27). 1939. pap. 25.00 (*0-527-00773-0*) Periodicals Srv.

Paschall, Douglas & Swanson, Alice, eds. Homewords: A Book of Tennessee Writers. LC 85-26394. 408p. (Orig.). (C). 1986. 35.00 (*0-87049-494-5*) U of Tenn Pr.

Paschall, H. Franklin. Teacher's Bible Commentary. Hobbs, Hershel H., ed. LC 75-189505. 1972. 49.99 (*0-8054-1116-X*, 4211-16) Broadman.

Paschall, Jenny & Lyon, Ron. Hatches, Matches & Dispatches. 122p. 1998. pap. 8.95 (*0-00-638815-9*, Pub. by HarpC) Trafalgar.

Paschall, Jenny, jt. auth. see Lyon, Ron.

Paschall, Michael A., jt. auth. see Hawkins, George B.

Paschall, Rod. Critical Incident Management. (Illus.). 104p. (Orig.). 1992. pap. 7.95 (*0-942511-54-9*) OICJ.

— The Defeat of Imperial Germany, 1917-1918. LC 94-11169. Orig. Title: Major Battles & Campaigns, Vol. 1. (Illus.). 288p. 1994. reprint ed. pap. 13.95 (*0-306-80585-5*) Da Capo.

— Witness to War: Korea. LC 94-39653. (Illus.). 256p. 1995. pap. 12.00 (*0-399-51934-3*, Perigee Bks) Berkley Pub.

Paschel, Ulrike. No Mean City? The Image of Dublin in the Novels of Dermot Bolger, Roddy Doyle & Val Mulkerns. LC 98-30126. (Aachen British & American Studies: Vol. 10). X, 170p. 1998. pap. text 37.95 (*0-8204-3611-9*) P Lang Pubng.

Pascheles, Wolf, ed. Sippurim, 5 pts. in 2, Set. (Volkskundliche Quellen Ser.: No. IV). 1976. reprint ed. write for info. (*3-487-06035-3*) G Olms Pubs.

Paschen, Elise. Infidelities. LC 96-42457. (Nicholas Ruerich Poetry Prize Winner Ser.). 72p. 1996. 20.00 (*1-885266-32-4*) Story Line.

— Infidelities: Poems. LC 96-42457. (Nicholas Ruerich Poetry Prize Winner Ser.). 88p. 1996. pap. 10.95 (*1-885266-28-6*) Story Line.

Paschen, Elise, et al, eds. Poetry in Motion: 100 Poems from the Subways & Buses. 128p. 1996. 18.95 (*0-393-03977-3*) Norton.

Paschen, Herbert, jt. ed. see Vig, Norman J.

Paschen, Stephen H. Molding a Legacy: A Centennial History of the Akron Porcelain & Plastics Company. (Illus.). 73p. (Orig.). 1989. pap. 6.95 (*0-9621895-3-7*) Summit Cty Hist Soc.

— Speaking of Summit: An Oral History Handbook. 55p. 1989. pap. 6.95 (*0-9621895-2-9*) Summit Cty Hist Soc.

Paschen, Stephen H., ed. What We Wore: An Exhibit Catalogue Celebrating 150 Years of Summit County Costume. (Illus.). 31p. (Orig.). 1990. pap. 9.50 (*0-9621895-4-5*) Summit Cty Hist Soc.

Pascher, A. Suesswasserflora von Mitteleuropa Band 2\2: Bacillariophyceae: Bacillariaceae, Epithemiaceae, Surirellaceae. Krammer, K. & Lange-Bertalot, H., eds. (Illus.). 611p. 1997. reprint ed. lib. bdg. 130.00 (*3-437-35388-8*) Balogh.

— Suesswasserflora von Mitteleuropa Band 10: Chlorophyta II: Tetrasporales, Chlorococcales, Gloeodendrales. rev. ed. Ettl, H. & Gaertner, G., eds. (GER., Illus.). 436p. 1988. lib. bdg. 103.00 (*3-437-30409-7*, Pub. by Gustav Fischer) Balogh.

— Suesswasserflora von Mitteleuropa Band 20: Schizomycetes-Bakterien. Ettl, H. & Gerloff, J., eds. (GER., Illus.). 588p. 1982. lib. bdg. 96.50 (*3-437-30344-9*, Pub. by Gustav Fischer) Balogh.

— Suesswasserflora von Mitteleuropa Vol. 2, Pt. 2: Bacillariophyceae: Bacillariaceae, Epithemiaceae. rev. ed. Krammer, K. & Lange-Bertalot, H., eds. (GER., Illus.). 596p. 1988. lib. bdg. 109.50 (*3-437-30508-5*, Pub. by Gustav Fischer) Balogh.

— Suesswasserflora von Suedeuropa Band 24: Pteridophyta und Antophyta 2: Saururaceae bis Asteraceae. Ettl, H. et al, eds. (Illus.). 540p. 1981. lib. bdg. 89.95 (*3-437-30341-4*, Pub. by Gustav Fischer) Balogh.

Pascher, A., ed. Suesswasserflora von Mitteleuropa Band 1: Chrysophyceae und Haptophyceae. (Chrysophyceae und Haptophyceae Ser.: Band 1). (Illus.). 515p. 1985. lib. bdg. 89.95 (*3-437-30402-X*, Pub. by Gustav Fischer) Balogh.

Pascher, A., ed. see Casper, S. J. & Krausch, H. D.

Pascher, A., ed. see Ettl, H.

Pascher, A., ed. see Kadlubowska, J. Z.

Pascher, A., ed. see Krammer, Kurt.

Pascher, A., ed. see Lange-Bertalot, H. & Krammer, Kurt.

Pascher, A., ed. see Mrozinska, T.

Pascher, A., ed. see Rieth, A.

Paschich, Ed & Hendricks, Paula. The Timber Reduced Energy Efficient Home: A Guidebook. Smith, James C., Jr., ed. LC 93-35704. (Illus.). 128p. (Orig.). 1993. pap. 17.95 (*0-86534-208-3*) Sunstone Pr.

— The Tire House: A Guide to Building Homes from Tires. LC 95-1012. (Illus.). 96p. (Orig.). 1995. pap. 14.95 (*0-86534-215-6*) Sunstone Pr.

Paschke, Barbara, ed. see Dalton, Roque.

Paschke, Barbara, jt. ed. see Murguia, Alejandro.

Paschke, Barbara, jt. ed. see Volpendesta, David.

Paschke, Barbara, tr. see Zamora, Daisy.

***Paschke, Chris A.** Creative Mounting, Wrapping & Laminating. (Illus.). 176p. 1999. pap. 19.95 (*0-9657625-1-3*) Designs Ink.

Paschke, Chris A. The Mounting & Laminating Handbook. LC 97-91792. (Illus.). xx, 160p. 1997. pap. 19.95 (*0-9657625-0-5*) Designs Ink.

***Paschke, Ed, et al.** Photography's Multiple Roles: Art, Document, Market, Science. Neff, Terry A., ed. LC 98-26380. (Illus.). 256p. 1998. pap. 40.00 (*0-9658887-2-X*) Mus Contemp Photo.

Paschkis, Julie. Play All Day. LC 96-14234. (Illus.). 32p. (J). (gr. k-4). 1998. 14.95 (*0-316-69043-0*) Little.

— So Happy/So Sad. LC 94-41654. 89p. (J). (ps-1). 1995. 12.95 (*0-8050-3862-0*) H Holt & Co.

— So Sleepy/Wide Awake. (J). 1995. write for info. (*0-8050-3174-X*) H Holt & Co.

Paschkis, Julie. Happy Adoption Day! 32p. (J). (gr. k-3). 1996. 15.95 (*0-316-55455-3*) Little.

Paschkis, Julie, jt. auth. see Fairchild, Dennis.

Paschkoff, A. G., tr. see Lyeskov, Nicolai.

Paschmann, Monika & Teichmann, Dirk-Holger. Duden-Bildworterb. F. Kinder. 72p. 1991. 20.50 (*3-411-04581-7*, Pub. by Bibliogr Inst Brockhaus) Langenscheidt.

Paschos, E. A., jt. ed. see Kleinknecht, K.

Paschos, Emmanuel A. & Sotiroudis, Panagiotis. The Schemata of the Stars: Byzantine Astronomy from 1300 A. D. LC 98-40050. (Illus.). 210p. 1998. 38.00 (*981-02-3489-9*) World Scientific Pub.

Paschos, Jacqueline & Destang, Francoise. Come to School. (Rejoice Ser.). (J). (ps). 1986. pap. 0.35 (*0-8091-6505-8*) Paulist Pr.

Pasco, Allan. Novel Configurations: A Study of French Fiction. 2nd ed. LC 86-63079. 1994. pap. 24.95 (*1-883479-00-2*) Summa Pubns.

Pasco, Allan H. Allusion: A Literary Craft. (Theory - Culture Ser.). 272p. (C). 1994. text 55.00 (*0-8020-0449-0*) U of Toronto Pr.

— Balzacian Montage: Configuring La Comedie Humaine. (Romance Ser.: No. 65). 192p. 1991. text 45.00 (*0-8020-2776-8*) U of Toronto Pr.

— Sick Heroes: French Society & Literature in the Romantic Age, 1750-1850. LC 98-150513. (Illus.). 272p. 1998. pap. text 24.95 (*0-85989-550-5*, Pub. by Univ Exeter Pr); pap. text 24.95 (*0-85989-549-1*, Pub. by Univ Exeter Pr) Northwestern U Pr.

Pasco, Allan H., jt. auth. see Booker, John T.

Pasco, Britt. Hellfire Town. large type ed. (Linford Western Library). 272p. 1994. pap. 16.99 (*0-7089-7586-0*) Ulverscroft.

Pasco, Dennis. Tested. (Illus.). 208p. 1999. 29.95 (*1-902304-35-7*, Pub. by Grub St) Seven Hills Bk.

Pasco, Elizabeth, ed. see Charles, Rodney.

Pasco, Elizabeth, ed. see Charles, Rodney & Jordan, Anna.

Pasco, Elizabeth, ed. see Clute, Sylvia.

Pasco, Elizabeth, ed. see Friedman, Gil.

Pasco, Elizabeth, ed. see Gallo, Anna M.

Pasco, Elizabeth, ed. see Hovin, Carol.

Pasco, Elizabeth, ed. see Kohl, Chrystelle.

Pasco, Elizabeth, ed. see Mayhew, Ed & Mayhew, Mary.

Pasco, Elizabeth, ed. see Murphy, Andy & Murphy, Teri.

Pasco, Elizabeth, ed. see Norsic, Donald.

Pasco, Elizabeth, ed. see Raymondo, Chris.

Pasco, Elizabeth, ed. see Sarath, E. Noah.

Pasco, Elizabeth, ed. see Scott, Gary.

Pasco, Elizabeth, ed. see Sylvest, Vernon M.

Pasco, Elizabeth, ed. see Tarabilda, Ed & Grimes, Doug.

Pasco, Elizabeth, ed. see Theriault, George.

Pasco, Elizabeth, ed. see Thomas, Edith.

Pasco, Elizabeth, ed. see Weldon, James.

Pasco, Elizabeth, ed. see Yellin, Jerry.

Pasco, Rowanne. Catechism: One Hundred Questions & Answers. 136p. 1995. pap. 8.95 (*0-8146-2397-2*) Liturgical Pr.

Pasco, Rowanne & Redford, John, eds. Faith Alive: A New Presentation of Catholic Belief & Practice. LC 89-51904. 324p. (Orig.). 1990. pap. 12.95 (*0-89622-408-2*) Twenty-Third.

Pascoe. Equine Dermatology Handbook. (Illus.). 255p. (C). 1998. text 45.00 (*0-7020-1968-2*, W B Saunders Co) Harcrt Hlth Sci Grp.

— Introduction to Properties of Engineering Materials. 3rd ed. 1978. pap. 27.95 (*0-442-30233-9*) Chapman & Hall.

Pascoe, Ann. Story of St. Ives. (C). 1990. pap. 24.95 (*0-85025-303-9*, Pub. by Tor Mark Pr) St Mut.

Pascoe, Charles E. Wild Horse - Musical. 1993. pap. 5.50 (*0-87129-272-6*, W08) Dramatic Pub.

Pascoe, Charles E., ed. The Dramatic List: A Record of the Principal Performances of Living Actors & Actresses on the British Stage with Criticisms from Contemporary Journals. LC 74-145225. 358p. 1879. reprint ed. 39.00 (*0-403-00781-X*) Scholarly.

— Our Actors & Actresses: The Dramatic List. 2nd enl. rev. ed. LC 70-91911. 1972. 30.95 (*0-405-08838-8*) Ayer.

Pascoe, David. Peter Greenaway: Museums & Moving Images. (Essays in Art & Culture Ser.). (Illus.). 248p. 1997. pap. 24.95 (*1-86189-005-2*, Pub. by Reaktion Bks) Consort Bk Sales.

Pascoe, David, ed. & notes see Dickens, Charles.

Pascoe, David P. Hearing Aids - Who Needs Them? What They Can Do for You, Where to Buy Them, How to Use Them. Pascoe, Muriel S., ed. LC 90-86318. (Illus.). 176p. (Orig.). 1991. pap. 10.50 (*0-9628963-0-6*) Muriel S Pascoe.

Pascoe, Elaine. America's Courts on Trial. LC 97-1091. (Issue & Debate Ser.). (Illus.). 112p. (YA). (gr. 7 up). 1997. lib. bdg. 23.90 (*0-7613-0104-6*) Millbrook Pr.

— Animal Intelligence: Why Is This Dolphin Smiling? LC 96-42983. (New Explorers Ser.). 48p. (YA). (gr. 5 up). 1997. lib. bdg. 17.95 (*1-56711-226-9*) Blackbirch.

— Ants. LC 97-43571. (Nature Close-Up Ser.). (Illus.). 48p. (YA). (gr. 5-7). 1998. lib. bdg. 17.95 (*1-56711-183-1*) Blackbirch.

***Pascoe, Elaine.** Beetles. LC 99-53770. (Nature Close-Up Ser.). (Illus.). 48p. (J). (gr. 4-7). 2000. lib. bdg. 17.95 (*1-56711-175-0*) Blackbirch.

— The Brooklyn Bridge. LC 98-46096. (Building America Ser.). (Illus.). 48p. (J). (gr. 4-6). 1999. lib. bdg. 17.95 (*1-56711-173-4*) Blackbirch.

Pascoe, Elaine. Butterflies & Moths. Bowman, Nicole, ed. LC 95-42704. (Nature Close-up Ser.). (Illus.). 48p. (J). (gr. 4-7). 1996. lib. bdg. 18.95 (*1-56711-180-7*) Blackbirch.

— Crickets & Grasshoppers. LC 97-43572. (Nature Close-up Ser.). (Illus.). 48p. (J). (gr. 4-7). 1998. lib. bdg. 18.95 (*1-56711-176-9*) Blackbirch.

— Earthworms. Bowman, Nicole, ed. LC 95-25177. (Nature Close Up Ser.). (Illus.). 48p. (J). (gr. 4-7). 1996. lib. bdg. 18.95 (*1-56711-177-7*) Blackbirch.

— First Facts about the Presidents. Glassman, Bruce, ed. LC 95-22705. (First Facts Ser.). (Illus.). 112p. (J). (gr. 5 up). 1996. lib. bdg. 25.45 (*1-56711-167-X*) Blackbirch.

***Pascoe, Elaine.** Flies. LC 99-53769. (Nature Close-Up Ser.). (Illus.). 48p. (J). (gr. 4-7). 2000. lib. bdg. 17.95 (*1-56711-149-1*) Blackbirch.

Pascoe, Elaine. Freedom of Expression: The Right to Speak Out in America. LC 92-7150. (Issue & Debate Ser.). (Illus.). 128p. (YA). (gr. 7 up). 1992. lib. bdg. 23.90 (*1-56294-255-7*) Millbrook Pr.

***Pascoe, Elaine.** How & Why Animals Are Poisonous. Kupperstein, Joel, ed. (How & Why Ser.: Vol. 2973). (Illus.). 16p. (J). 2000. pap. 2.99 (*1-57471-666-2*) Creat Teach Pr.

— How & Why Animals Grow New Parts. Kupperstein, Joel, ed. (How & Why Ser.: Vol. 2970). 16p. (J). 2000. pap. 2.99 (*1-57471-663-8*) Creat Teach Pr.

— How & Why Animals Hatch from Eggs. Kupperstein, Joel, ed. (How & Why Ser.: Vol. 2967). (Illus.). 16p. (J). 2000. pap. 2.99 (*1-57471-660-3*) Creat Teach Pr.

— How & Why Animals Hide. Kupperstein, Joel, ed. (How & Why Ser.: Vol. 2969). 16p. (J). 2000. pap. 2.99 (*1-57471-662-X*) Creat Teach Pr.

— How & Why Animals Prepare for Winter. Kupperstein, Joel, ed. (How & Why Ser.: Vol. 2971). (Illus.). 16p. (J). 2000. pap. 2.99 (*1-57471-664-6*) Creat Teach Pr.

— How & Why Birds Build Nests. Kupperstein, Joel, ed. (How & Why Ser.: Vol. 2963). (Illus.). 16p. (J). 2000. pap., teacher ed. 2.99 (*1-57471-656-5*) Creat Teach Pr.

— How & Why Birds Use Their Bills. Kupperstein, Joel, ed. (How & Why Ser.: Vol. 2966). (Illus.). 16p. (J). 2000. pap. 2.99 (*1-57471-659-X*) Creat Teach Pr.

— How & Why Insects Grow & Change. Kupperstein, Joel, ed. (How & Why Ser.: Vol. 2972). (Illus.). 16p. (J). 2000. pap. 2.99 (*1-57471-665-4*) Creat Teach Pr.

— How & Why Insects Visit Flowers. Kupperstein, Joel, ed. (How & Why Ser.: Vol. 2964). (Illus.). 16p. (J). (gr. 1-3). 2000. pap. 2.99 (*1-57471-657-3*) Creat Teach Pr.

— How & Why Plants Eat Insects. Kupperstein, Joel, ed. (How & Why Ser.: Vol. 2974). (Illus.). 16p. (J). 2000. pap. 2.99 (*1-57471-667-0*) Creat Teach Pr.

— How & Why Seeds Travel. Kupperstein, Joel, ed. (How & Why Ser.: Vol. 2965). 16p. (J). 2000. pap. 2.99 (*1-57471-658-1*) Creat Teach Pr.

— How & Why Spiders Spin Silk. Kupperstein, Joel, ed. (How & Why Ser.: Vol. 2968). (Illus.). 16p. (J). 2000. pap. 2.99 (*1-57471-661-1*) Creat Teach Pr.

Pascoe, Elaine. Mysteries of the Rainforest: 20th Century Medicine Man. LC 96-47736. (New Explorers Ser.). (Illus.). 48p. (YA). (gr. 5 up). 1997. lib. bdg. 17.95 (*1-56711-229-3*) Blackbirch.

— New Dinosaurs: Skeletons in the Sand. LC 96-43530. (New Explorers Ser.). (Illus.). 48p. (YA). (gr. 5 up). 1997. lib. bdg. 17.95 (*1-56711-231-5*) Blackbirch.

***Pascoe, Elaine.** Pacific Rim. LC 98-28556. 128p. (YA). (gr. 7 up). 1999. 24.90 (*0-7613-3015-1*) TFC Bks NY.

Pascoe, Elaine. Racial Prejudice: Why Can't We Overcome? LC 96-36913. (Impact Bks.). 1997. lib. bdg. 24.00 (*0-531-11402-3*) Watts.

— The Right to Vote. LC 96-21965. (Land of the Free Ser.). (Illus.). 48p. (J). (gr. 2-4). 1997. lib. bdg. 19.90 (*0-7613-0066-X*) Millbrook Pr.

— Seeds & Seedlings. Bowman, Nicole, ed. LC 95-25178. (Nature Close Up Ser.). (Illus.). 48p. (J). (gr. 4-7). 1996. lib. bdg. 18.95 (*1-56711-178-5*) Blackbirch.

— Slime, Molds & Fungi. LC 97-36751. (Nature Close-up Ser.). (Illus.). 48p. (YA). (gr. 4-7). 1998. lib. bdg. 18.95 (*1-56711-182-3*) Blackbirch.

— Snails & Slugs. LC 97-29159. (Nature Close-up Ser.). (Illus.). 48p. (J). (gr. 5-8). 1998. lib. bdg. 16.95 (*1-56711-181-5*) Blackbirch.

— Tadpoles. Bowman, Nicole, ed. LC 95-40848. (Nature Close-up Ser.). (Illus.). 48p. (J). (gr. 4-7). 1996. lib. bdg. 18.95 (*1-56711-179-3*) Blackbirch.

— Virtual Reality: Beyond the Looking Glass. LC 96-42984. (New Explorers Ser.). 48p. (YA). (gr. 5 up). 1997. lib. bdg. 17.95 (*1-56711-228-5*) Blackbirch.

***Pascoe, Elaine.** A World in Focus: North America. (Illus.). 80p. 2000. pap. 11.95 (*1-56711-345-1*) Blackbirch.

Pascoe, Elaine & Kops, Deborah. Scholastic Kid's Almanac for the 21st Century: Hundreds of Full-Color Graphics, Tables & Charts Provide Kids with a Stimulating & Comprehensive Reference for the New Millennium. LC 98-48739. (Illus.). 352p. (YA). (gr. 3-7). 1999. pap. 12.95 (*0-590-30724-X*, Pub. by Scholastic Inc) Penguin Putnam.

Pascoe, Elaine, jt. auth. see Kops, Deborah.

Pascoe, Elaine, ed. see Schwartz, David M.

Pascoe, Gwen. The Sea Where I Swim. LC 93-6647. (Illus.). (J). 1994. write for info. (*0-383-03712-3*) SRA McGraw.

Pascoe, Jed. The Complete Wimp's Guide to Sex. Carle, Cliff, ed. 1994. pap. 4.99 (*0-918259-66-5*) CCC Pubns.

— The Total Bastard's Guide to Golf. Carle, Cliff, ed. 1996. pap. 5.95 (*1-57644-028-1*) CCC Pubns.

Pascoe, Jim, jt. auth. see Fassbender, Tom.

Pascoe, Judith. Romantic Theatricality: Gender, Poetry, & Spectatorship. LC 96-34905. (Illus.). 272p. 1996. text 39.95 (*0-8014-3304-5*) Cornell U Pr.

Pascoe, Judith, ed. see Robinson, Mary.

Pascoe, K. J. Properties of Materials for Electrical Engineers. LC 72-8612. (Illus.). 336p. reprint ed. pap. 104.20 (*0-7837-1877-2*, 204207800001) Bks Demand.

Pascoe, L. C. Teach Yourself Mathematics. (Illus.). 240p. 1995. pap. 12.95 (*0-8442-3931-3*, Teach Yrslf) NTC Contemp Pub Co.

***Pascoe, Louis B., et al.** Reform & Renewal in the Middle Ages & the Renaissance: Studies in Honor of Louis Pascoe. LC 00-20674. (Studies in the History of Christian Thought). 2000. write for info. (*90-04-11399-1*) Brill Academic Pubs.

Pascoe, Monte, jt. auth. see Swalm, Paul.

Pascoe, Muriel S., ed. see Pascoe, David P.

Pascoe, Natalie T. Caribbean Spice: A Traveler's Guide to Cultural Festivals & Events. LC 97-92454. (Illus.). 196p. 1998. pap. 34.95 (*0-9660101-2-4*) DePas Publ.

Pascoe, Peggy. Relations of Rescue: The Search for Female Moral Authority in the American West, 1874-1939. (Illus.). 328p. 1993. reprint ed. pap. text 19.95 (*0-19-508430-6*) OUP.

Pascoe Publ. Pty. Ltd. Staff, ed. The Largest Island Study Guide-Ridgeway et Al Pascoe Publishing Pty. Ltd. 88p. (C). 1990. 33.00 (*0-7855-6620-1*, Pub. by Pascoe Pub) St Mut.

Pascoe, Reg R., jt. auth. see Knottenbelt, Derek C.

Pascoe, Robin. Culture Shock! A Parent's Guide. LC 98-86356. 1999. pap. text 12.95 (*1-55868-425-5*) Gr Arts Ctr Pub.

Pascoe, W. H. Teudar: A King of Cornwall. (C). 1989. 40.00 (*1-85022-001-8*, Pub. by Dyllansow Truran) St Mut.

Pascoe, William E., ed. Catalysis of Organic Reactions. (Chemical Industries Ser.: Vol. 47). (Illus.). 408p. 1991. text 225.00 (*0-8247-8573-8*) Dekker.

Pascolait, Connie & Fimbrez, Louie. The American Citizenship Handbook: A Powerful Step-by-Step Bilingual Study Guide to Becoming an American Citizen. 2nd rev. ed. Pascolait, Steve, ed. Winicker, Susanne, tr. from ENG. (SPA., Illus.). pap. text 39.95 (*1-56813-113-5*) Madera Cinevideo.

Pascolait, Steve, ed. see Pascolait, Connie & Fimbrez, Louie.

Pascolati, Connie. The American Citizenship Handbook: A Step-by-Step Guide to Help You Become an American Citizen. Pascolati, Steve et al, eds. (Illus.). 84p. Date not set. pap. 39.95 (*1-56813-169-0*) Madera Cinevideo.

Pascolati, Steve, ed. see Pascolati, Connie.

Pascolini. Pan XIII - Particles & Nuclei: Procedings of the Thirteenth International Conference. 864p. 1994. text 162.00 (*981-02-1799-4*) World Scientific Pub.

Pascolini, Alessandro, jt. ed. see Schroeer, Dietrich.

Pascolo, P. & Brebbia, C. A., eds. GIS Technologies & Their Environmental Applications. (Illus.). 368p. 1998. 155.00 (*1-85312-595-4*, 5954, Pub. by WIT Pr) Computational Mech MA.

Pascolo, P. & Brebbia, Carlos A., eds. Management Information Systems. (Management Information Systems Ser.). 516p. 2000. 248.00 (*1-85312-815-5*, 8155, Pub. by WIT Pr) Computational Mech MA.

Pascon, Paul. Capitalism & Agriculture in the Haouz of Marrakesh. Hall, John R., ed. Vaughan, C. Edwin & Ingham, Veronique, trs. 300p. 1986. 59.95 (*0-7103-0189-8*, 01898) Routledge.

***Pascouau, Brian J.** NAFCU's Auto Lending Program for Credit Unions: Strategies for Auto Lending Success. LC 99-186950. 1998. write for info. (*1-55827-273-9*) Sheshunoff.

Pascu, Stefan. A History of Transylvania. Ladd, D. Robert, tr. LC 82-8669. (Illus.). 345p. reprint ed. pap. 107.00 (*0-608-16067-9*, 203319900084) Bks Demand.

Pascual, Benjamin M. Selmo Comes Home & Other Stories. 138p. (Orig.). (C). 1989. pap. 10.75 (*971-10-0351-1*, Pub. by New Day Pub) Cellar.

***Pascual i Miro, Eva, et al.** Restoring Wood. (Illus.). 160p. 2000. 29.95 (*0-7641-5223-8*) Barron.

Pascual, J. A., jt. auth. see Corominas i Vigneaux, Joan.

Pascual, J. A., jt. auth. see Corominas, J.

Pascual, J. F. & Calcagno, P. L., eds. Nephrologic Problems of the Newborn. (Contributions to Nephrology Ser.: Vol. 15). (Illus.). 1979. pap. 29.75 (*3-8055-2947-3*) S Karger.

— Recent Advances in Pediatric Nephrology. (Contributions to Nephrology Ser.: Vol. 27). (Illus.). vi, 98p. 1981. pap. 29.75 (*3-8055-1851-X*) S Karger.

Pascual-Leone, J., tr. see Kong, Shiu L. & Samuda, Ronald J.

Pascual, Lope, tr. see Galvez, Alfonso.

Pascual, Luis D. What Goes Around Comes Around: The Feedback Loop. LC 94-90701. (Illus.). 99p. (Orig.). 1994. pap. 12.95 (*0-9644398-3-2*) WGACA.

Pascual, Maria, ed. see Sotillos, Eugenio.

Pascual, P., jt. auth. see Galindo, A.

Pascual, R., jt. auth. see Fernandez, E.

Pascual Recuero, Pascual. Diccionario Basico Ladino Espanol. (LAD & SPA.). 182p. 1977. pap. 29.95 (*0-7859-3362-X*, 8472130886) Fr & Eur.

Pascual-Sanz, Fabriciano. Historia de Cristobal Colon. (SPA., Illus.). 522p. 1986. 19.95 (*84-599-1657-X*, Pub. by Tecnograf) Ediciones.

P

An Asterisk (*) at the beginning of an entry indicates that the title is appearing for the first time.

Pascual, Suazo. Ortografia Practica. 5th ed. (SPA.). 195p. 1996. pap. 14.00 (*84-7640-553-7*, Pub. by Edaf Edit) IBD Ltd.

Pascualy, Ralph A. & Soest, Sally W. Snoring & Sleep Apnea: Personal & Family Guide to Diagnosis & Treatment. 2nd ed. LC 95-46517. (Illus.). 256p. 1995. pap. 24.95 (*0-939957-82-5*) Demos Medical.

***Pascualy, Ralph A. & Soest, Sally Warren.** Snoring & Sleep Apnea: Sleep Well, Feel Better. 3rd rev. ed. 256p. 2000. pap. 24.95 (*1-888799-29-3*, Pub. by Demos Medical) SCB Distributors.

Pascucci, John & Stauth, Cameron. The Manhunter: The Astounding True Story of the U. S. Marshal Who Tracked down the World's Most Evil Criminals. 384p. 1996. 23.00 (*0-671-88518-9*) PB.

— The Manhunter: The Astounding True Story of the U. S. Marshal Who Tracked down the World's Most Evil Criminals. 367p. 1997. per. 6.50 (*0-671-88517-0*, Pocket Star Bks) PB.

***Pasculli, Joseph.** Eden's Fall. 307p. 1999. mass mkt. 6.99 (*0-9669139-0-6*) Victory Bks IN.

Pascuzzi, Edward, jt. auth. see Harrington, Philip S.

Pasda, Patricia J. & DiEdwardo, Maryann P. Writing. (Illus.). 145p. (J). (gr. k-12). 1999. pap. text 49.95 (*0-9641468-4-3*) M DiEdwardo Pubng.

Pasda, Patricia J. & DiEdwardo, Mary A. The Animal Sketch Book. 50p. 1995. 6.95 (*0-9641468-2-7*) M DiEdwardo Pubng.

— Write a Book of Haiku. (Illus.). 40p. (J). (gr. 2 up). 1994. student ed. write for info. (*0-9641468-1-9*) M DiEdwardo Pubng.

Pasda, Patricia J. & DiEdwards, Mary A. The Integrated Creative Curriculum Log Book. 100p. 1994. spiral bd. 9.95 (*0-9641468-0-0*) M DiEdwardo Pubng.

Pasda, Patricia J., jt. auth. see DiEdwardo, Mary Ann P.

***PASDC Staff.** Municipal Population in Pennsylvania 1960 to 1998. 188p. 1999. pap. 40.00 (*1-58036-136-6*) Penn State Data Ctr.

PASDC Staff. 1998 PA Abstract. Shultz, Jennifer, ed. (Illus.). 310p. 1998. pap. 50.00 (*1-58036-059-9*) Penn State Data Ctr.

— 1990 Geographic Codes Book, Pennsylvania. (Pennsylvania State Data Center Ser.). 72p. 1994. pap. 20.00 (*1-885925-00-X*) Penn State Data Ctr.

***PASDC Staff.** 1999 Pennsylvania Abstract. Shultz, Jennifer, ed. (Illus.). 303p. 1999. pap. 50.00 (*1-58036-134-X*) Penn State Data Ctr.

Pasdermadjian, Hrant. The Department Store: Its Origins Evolution & Economics. LC 75-39265. (Getting & Spending: The Consumer's Dilemma Ser.). 1976. reprint ed. 20.95 (*0-405-08038-7*) Ayer.

Pasechnik, Gennady, tr. see Eidelman, S. D. & Zhitarashu, N. V.

Pasek, Jan Chryzostom. Memoirs of the Polish Baroque: The Writings of Jan Chryzostom Pasek, a Squire of the Commonwealth of Poland & Lithuania. Leach, Catherine S., ed. LC 74-77731. 415p. reprint ed. pap. 128.70 (*0-608-17277-4*, 202959000061) Bks Demand.

Pasemann, F. & Doebner, H. D., eds. Neurodynamics. (Series in Neural Networks: Vol. 1). 240p. (C). 1991. text 83.00 (*981-02-0811-1*) World Scientific Pub.

Paseo Pantera Project Staff. Central America: A Natural & Cultural History. Coates, Anthony G., ed. LC 97-11105. (Illus.). 296p. 1997. 40.00 (*0-300-06829-8*) Yale U Pr.

Pasero, Christine. Acute Pain Management. 152p. 1994. spiral bd. 95.00 (*1-879575-44-2*) Acad Med Sys.

Pasero, Christine, jt. auth. see McCaffery, Margo.

***Paseta, Senia.** Before the Revolution: Nationalism, Social Change & Ireland's Catholic Elite, 1879-1922. LC 99-197968. 240p. 2000. 55.00 (*1-85918-226-7*, Pub. by Cork Univ); pap. 22.50 (*1-85918-227-5*, Pub. by Cork Univ) Stylus Pub VA.

Pasetti, Mario, ed. Los Escritos y las Ensenanzas del Bienaventurado Jose Marello. LC 93-78554. (SPA.). 292p. (Orig.). 1993. pap. 14.95 (*1-883839-03-3*) Guard Redeemer.

Pasewark. Applications for Computers: Generic Course. (DF - Computer Applications Ser.). 1997. mass mkt. 32.95 (*0-538-71767-X*) S-W Pub.

***Pasewark.** Electronic Calculators: Display/Print. 3rd ed. 1998. pap. 21.95 (*0-538-68247-7*) Thomson Learn.

Pasewark. Electronic Office Machines. 6th ed. (Office Machines Ser.). 1986. teacher ed. 27.50 (*0-538-28088-3*) S-W Pub.

Pasewark. Machine Transcription for Document Processing. 3rd ed. (C). 1994. 400.00 (*0-538-71075-6*) Thomson Learn.

Pasewark. Machine Transcription Word Processing. 2nd ed. (Office Machines Ser.). 1986. teacher ed. 16.50 (*0-538-27237-6*) S-W Pub.

— Microsoft Access 2000: Complete Tutorial. LC 99-23423. (Computer Applications Ser.). 1999. pap. 36.95 (*0-538-68841-6*); pap., wbk. ed. 12.95 (*0-538-68843-2*) S-W Pub.

— Microsoft Excel 2000: Complete Tutorial. (Computer Applications Ser.). 1999. pap. 36.95 (*0-538-68836-X*); pap., wbk. ed. 12.95 (*0-538-68838-6*) S-W Pub.

***Pasewark.** Microsoft Office 2000: An Introduction. (Computer Applications Ser.). 1999. 6.90 (*0-538-50904-X*); 20.00 (*0-538-50905-8*); 9.50 (*0-538-50906-6*); 4.50 (*0-538-50907-4*) Sth-Wstrn College.

— Microsoft Office 2000: An Introduction. (Computer Applications Ser.). (C). 1999. text 4.50 (*0-538-50903-1*); text 18.50 (*0-538-50902-3*) Sth-Wstrn College.

Pasewark. Microsoft Office 2000: Introductory Course. LC 99-23219. (Computer Applications Ser.). 1999. pap. 52.95 (*0-538-68824-6*); pap., wbk. ed. 12.95 (*0-538-68826-2*) S-W Pub.

— Microsoft Word 2000: Complete Tutorial. (Computer Applications Ser.). 1999. pap. 12.95 (*0-538-68834-3*) S-W Pub.

Pasewark. Microsoft Works 2.0 & 3.0 DOS Application. 1995. pap. 24.50 (*0-538-64380-3*) Thomson Learn.

Pasewark. Tests, Tenkey Skill Builder. (Office Machines Ser.). 1991. 0.75 (*0-538-61411-0*) S-W Pub.

— Understanding Corporate Annual Reports. 3rd ed. 1997. text 25.31 (*0-07-290132-2*) McGraw.

***Pasewark & Skintik.** MS Powerpoint 2000. (C). 2000. pap. text 12.95 (*0-538-72443-9*); spiral bd. 36.95 (*0-538-72441-2*) Sth-Wstrn College.

Pasewark, Kyle A. & Paul, Garrett E. The Emphatic Christian Center: Reforming American Political Practice. LC 99-15043. 1999. 29.00 (*0-687-00225-7*) Abingdon.

Pasewark, Pasewark. Microsoft Office for Windows 3.1: Tutorial & Applications, Vol. 4. 1996. 46.50 (*0-538-71718-1*) Sth-Wstrn College.

— Microsoft Office 97 for Windows: Tutorial & Applications. (Computer Applications Ser.). 1997. pap. 28.25 (*0-538-71921-4*) Sth-Wstrn College.

— Microsoft Works 2000 Basics. (C). 2000. pap., student ed. 43.95 (*0-538-72340-8*) Thomson Learn.

Pasewark, S. R. Microcomputer Survey. (C). pap. text 14.00 (*0-685-65257-2*) P-H.

Pasewark, Sr. Quicktorial: Pagemaker 6.0 F/wndws & Mac. 1996. pap. 22.95 (*0-538-71639-8*) Thomson Learn.

Pasewark, William. Microsoft Word 2000: Complete Tutorial. LC 99-23416. (Computer Applications Ser.). 1999. pap. 52.95 (*0-538-68832-7*) S-W Pub.

***Pasewark, William.** Microsoft Works 4.5 for Windows: Tutorial & Applications. (C). 1998. pap. 43.95 (*0-538-72158-8*) Sth-Wstrn College.

***Pasewark, William & Cable, Sandra.** Microsoft Excel 2000: Complete Tutorial. LC 99-23439. 432p. 1999. pap. 40.95 (*0-538-68837-8*) Sth-Wstrn College.

***Pasewark, William & Morrison, Connie.** Microsoft Word 2000: Complete Tutorial. LC 99-23416. (Tutorial Ser.). 752p. 1999. pap. 54.95 (*0-538-68833-5*) Sth-Wstrn College.

Pasewark, William, jt. auth. see Cable, Sandra.

***Pasewark, William P.** Microsoft Office 2000: Introductory Course. LC 99-23219. (Tutorial Ser.). 688p. 1999. pap. 54.95 (*0-538-68825-4*) Sth-Wstrn College.

Pasewark, William R. Calculating Machines Simulation. 4th ed. (Office Machines Ser.). 1990. 14.50 (*0-538-60204-X*) S-W Pub.

— Calculator Math for Job & People. 1992. pap. 9.95 (*0-7854-1410-X*) Am Guidance.

— Calculator Math for Job & Personal Use. (YA - Adult Education Ser.). 1992. pap. 9.95 (*0-538-70481-0*) S-W Pub.

— ClarisWorks 4.0 for Mac: Tutorial & Applications. (DF - Computer Applications Ser.). 1996. mass mkt. 33.95 (*0-538-71501-4*) S-W Pub.

— ClarisWorks 4.0 for Mac: Tutorial & Applications. (DF - Computer Applications Ser.). 1996. mass mkt., student ed. 37.95 (*0-538-71502-2*) S-W Pub.

— Electronic Calculators: Display/Print. 2nd ed. (KH - Office Machines Ser.). 1991. mass mkt. 15.50 (*0-538-60200-7*) S-W Pub.

— Electronic Display Calculator. 2nd ed. (KH - Office Machines Ser.). 1984. mass mkt. 15.00 (*0-538-13650-2*) S-W Pub.

— Electronic Office Machines. 7th ed. LC 94-5040. 1995. mass mkt. 14.25 (*0-538-62762-X*) S-W Pub.

— Electronic Office Machines - Pretest. 6th ed. (KH - Office Machines Ser.). 1986. 1.75 (*0-538-13813-0*) S-W Pub.

— Electronic Printing Calculators. 3rd ed. (KH - Office Machines Ser.). 1989. mass mkt. 14.75 (*0-538-60150-7*) S-W Pub.

— Fractions/Decimals/Percentages using a Calculator: Calculator Math for the Job & Personal Use. (YA - Adult Education Ser.). 1993. pap., wbk. ed. 5.95 (*0-538-70769-0*) S-W Pub.

— Machine Transcription & Word Processing. 2nd ed. (KH - Office Machines Ser.). 1986. mass mkt. 15.50 (*0-538-23250-1*) S-W Pub.

— Machine Transcription, Dictation & Proofreading. (KH - Office Machines Ser.). 1987. mass mkt. 11.00 (*0-538-23350-8*) S-W Pub.

— Machine Transcription for Document Processing. 3rd ed. LC 94-15008. (C). 1994. mass mkt. 18.00 (*0-538-71074-8*) S-W Pub.

— Microsoft Office for Windows 95: Tutorial & Applications. (DF - Computer Applications Ser.). (C). 1996. mass mkt. 43.95 (*0-538-71490-5*) S-W Pub.

Pasewark, William R., Sr. Microsoft Office for Windows 95 Reproduction Study Exercise Set: Tutorial & Applications. (DF - Computer Applications Ser.). 1996. mass mkt. 37.95 (*0-538-71491-3*) S-W Pub.

Pasewark, William R. Microsoft Office 4.3 for Windows 3.1: Tutorial & Applications. LC 96-3087. 1996. mass mkt. 41.95 (*0-538-71715-7*) S-W Pub.

— Microsoft Office 97 for Windows. (Tutorial & Applications Ser.). 1997. pap. text 33.95 (*0-538-71958-3*) S-W Pub.

Pasewark, William R., Sr. Microsoft Works for Windows. (DF - Computer Applications Ser.). (C). 1994. mass mkt., wbk. ed. 43.95 (*0-538-70940-5*) S-W Pub.

— Microsoft Works for Windows: Tutorial & Applications. (DF - Computer Applications Ser.). 1994. mass mkt. 30.95 (*0-538-62281-4*) S-W Pub.

Pasewark, William R. Microsoft Works 4.0 for Mac: Tutorial & Applications. (DF - Computer Applications Ser.). 1995. mass mkt. 35.95 (*0-538-64727-2*) S-W Pub.

— Microsoft Works 4.0 for Windows 95. (Quicktorial Ser.). 1996. mass mkt. 21.95 (*0-538-71547-2*) S-W Pub.

Pasewark, William R., Sr. Microsoft Works 4.0 for Windows 95: Quick Course. (DF - Computer Applications Ser.). 1996. mass mkt. 22.95 (*0-538-71475-1*) S-W Pub.

— Microsoft Works 4.0 for Windows 95: Tutorial & Applications. LC 95-47943. (DF - Computer Applications Ser.). (C). 1996. mass mkt. 40.95 (*0-538-71497-2*) S-W Pub.

— Microsoft Works 4.0 for Windows 95: Tutorial & Applications. (DF - Computer Applications Ser.). 1996. mass mkt., student ed. 37.95 (*0-538-71498-0*) S-W Pub.

Pasewark, William R. Microsoft Works 4.0 MAC Quick Course. (DF - Computer Applications Ser.). 1995. mass mkt., wbk. ed. 18.95 (*0-538-64073-1*) S-W Pub.

— Microsoft Works, 3.0 DOS: Tutorial & Applications Text. LC 93-86135. (DT-Fortran Ser.). 1995. mass mkt. 35.95 (*0-538-63435-9*) S-W Pub.

— Microsoft Works 3.0 for Windows, Quick Course. (DF - Computer Applications Ser.). 1995. mass mkt. 15.95 (*0-538-64389-7*) S-W Pub.

— Microsoft Works 3.0 for Windows: Tutorial & Applications. (DF - Computer Applications Ser.). 1994. mass mkt. 35.95 (*0-538-64068-5*) S-W Pub.

— Microsoft Works 3.0 Mac Version: Tutorial & Applications. LC 93-84939. (DF - Computer Appications Ser.). 1994. mass mkt. 30.95 (*0-538-63360-3*) S-W Pub.

— Microsoft Works 3.0 - 4.0 Mac: Applications for Reinforcement. (DF - Computer Applications Ser.). 1996. mass mkt. 31.95 (*0-538-65197-0*) S-W Pub.

— Microsoft Works 2.0 - 3.0 for Windows: Applications for Reinforcement. LC 95-69606. (DF - Computer Applications Ser.). 1995. mass mkt. 31.95 (*0-538-65194-6*) S-W Pub.

— MS Office 97 for Windows: Tutorial & Applications. (Df - Computer Applications Ser.). 1997. mass mkt. 41.95 (*0-538-71919-2*) S-W Pub.

— PageMaker 5.0 for Windows & Macintosh: Quick Course. (Quicktorial Ser.). 1996. mass mkt. 22.95 (*0-538-71505-7*) S-W Pub.

— PageMaker 6 for Windows & Macintosh Quicktorial. (DF - Computer Applications Ser.). 1996. pap. text, mass mkt. 21.95 incl. disk (*0-538-71640-1*) S-W Pub.

— Procedures for the Modern Office, Tests. 7th ed. (KM - Office Procedures Ser.). 1983. 2.95 (*0-538-11393-6*) S-W Pub.

— Reprographics. 3rd ed. (KH - Office Machines Ser.). 1984. pap. 16.95 (*0-538-11910-1*) S-W Pub.

— Ten-Key Skill Builder. (KH - Office Machines Ser.). 1991. mass mkt. 8.75 (*0-538-61410-2*) S-W Pub.

— Ten-Key Skill Builder for Computers. (Office Procedures Ser.). 1996. pap. 75.75 (*0-538-62920-7*) S-W Pub.

— Understanding Corporate Annual Reports: A Practice Set for Financial Accounting. 2nd ed. 64p. (C). 1995. text 20.75 (*0-256-19075-5*, Irwn McGrw-H) McGrw-H Hghr Educ.

— Ventura Desktop Publishing for the PC. (DF - Computer Applications Ser.). 1993. pap. 21.95 (*0-87835-694-0*) Course Tech.

Pasewark, William R. & Knowlton, Todd. Ten-Key Skill Builder for Computers. (J). 1995. pap. 10.50 (*0-538-62919-3*) S-W Pub.

Pasewark, William R., Jr., et al. Microsoft Works: Tutorial & Applications: IBM Version. large type ed. 1991. 124.00 (*0-614-09876-9*, L-83972-00) Am Printing Hse.

***Pasewark, William Robert.** Microsoft Works 2000 Basics. LC 00-37417. (Illus.). 2000. ring bd. write for info. (*0-538-72411-0*) S-W Pub.

***Pasewark, William Robert & Skintik, Catherine H.** Microsoft Powerpoint 2000 Complete Tutorial. LC 00-37416. (Illus.). 2000. ring bd. write for info. (*0-538-72442-0*) S-W Pub.

Pasewark, Williuam R. Microsoft Works 3.0 DOS: Quick Course. (DF - Computer Applications Ser.). 1995. mass mkt. 18.95 (*0-538-64103-7*) S-W Pub.

Pash, Mark. E=mCf: Theory of Economic Relativity. Barnard, Jack, ed. (Illus.). 131p. 1999. 15.00 (*0-9669653-0-2*) Global Comm.

***Pasha.** Otolaryngology: Head & Neck Surgery. 2000. pap. 59.95 (*0-7693-0053-7*) Singular Publishing.

Pasha, A., jt. ed. see Wyn-Davies, M.

***Pasha, A. K.** India, Iran & the GCC States. 2000. 38.00 (*81-7049-110-X*, Pub. by Manas Pubns) S Asia.

Pasha, Cemal. Memoirs of a Turkish Statesman, 1913-1919. LC 73-6295. (Middle East Ser.). 1973. reprint ed. 25.95 (*0-405-05328-2*) Ayer.

Pasha, Johnson. Mahmud Shabistari The Secret Garden. 1999. 17.00 (*0-86304-019-5*) Octagon Pr.

Pasha, Johnson, tr. The Secret Garden of Mahumud Shabistari. 86p. 1969. 18.00 (*0-900860-38-3*, Pub. by Octagon Pr) ISHK.

Pasha, Mustapha K. Colonial Political Economy: Recruitment & Underdevelopment in the Punjab. LC 98-206645. (Illus.). 326p. 1998. 42.00 (*0-19-577762-X*) OUP.

— South Asia: Civil Society, State, & Politics. (Comparative Political Economy Ser.). 288p. 1999. 69.00 (*0-8133-2874-8*); pap. 25.00 (*0-8133-2875-6*) Westview.

Pasha, Mustapha K., jt. auth. see Mittelman, James H.

Pashaev, O. K., jt. ed. see Makhankov, Vladimir G.

Pashard, jt. auth. see Nichols.

Pashayan, Hermione, jt. auth. see Feingold, Murray.

Pashi, Lumana & Turnbull, Alan. Lingala-English Dictionary. LC 94-71163. 256p. 1994. text 54.00 (*0-931745-86-1*) Dunwoody Pr.

Pashigian. Price Theory Applications Sg. 2nd ed. 1997. pap. 23.44 (*0-07-048781-2*) McGraw.

Pashigian, B. Peter. Price Theory & Applications. 2nd ed. LC 97-1282. 784p. 1997. 83.44 (*0-07-048778-2*) McGraw.

Pashigian, Peter B. Price Theory & Applications. (C). 1994. text 87.25 (*0-07-048741-3*) McGraw.

Pashin, Jack C. & Ettensohn, Frank R. Reevaluation of the Bedford-Berea Sequence in Ohio & Adjacent States: Forced Regression in a Foreland Basin. LC 95-3060. (Special Papers: Vol. 298). 1995. pap. 30.00 (*0-8137-2298-5*) Geol Soc.

Pashinin, P. P., ed. Formation & Control of Optical Wavefronts. (Proceedings of the Institute of General Physics of the Academy of Sciences of the U. S. S. R. Ser.: Vol. 7). 207p. 1990. text 165.00 (*0-941743-29-2*) Nova Sci Pubs.

— Laser-Induced Raman Spectroscopy in Crystals & Gases. (Proceedings of the Institute of General Physics of the Academy of Sciences of the U. S. S. R. Ser.: Vol. 2). 215p. (C). 1988. text 165.00 (*0-941743-13-6*) Nova Sci Pubs.

Pashkeuch, Olga, jt. auth. see King, Yvonne.

Pashkevich, Nicolas. Nicolas Pashkevich. LC 94-77354. (Illus.). 168p. 1996. 35.00 (*0-9617756-8-8*) Galerija.

Pashkov, P. Orders & Badges of the White Armies in the Civil War. limited ed. (Illus.). 31p. 1983. pap. 10.00 (*0-317-06616-1*) Quaker.

— The White Armies' Orders & Badges in the Civil War, 1917-1922. Budzilovich, G. N. & Zander, R., trs. from RUS. (Illus.). vi, 31p. (Orig.). 1983. pap. 8.50 (*0-912671-04-1*) Russian Numis.

Pashkow, Frederic & Libov, Charlotte. The Woman's Heart Book: A Vital Resourse for Women's Health from One of the Nation's Top Cardiologists. (Illus.). 352p. 2001. pap. 14.00 (*0-7868-8428-2*, Pub. by Hyperion) Time Warner.

Pashkow, Fredric J. & DaFoe, William A., eds. Clinical Cardiac Rehabilitation: A Cardiologist's Guide. 2nd ed. LC 98-15106. 565p. 1998. 89.95 (*0-683-30224-8*) Lppncott W & W.

Pashkow, Peggy, et al. Successful Cardiac Rehabilitation: The Complete Guide for Building Cardiac Rehab Programs. 1988. 39.95 (*0-9619796-0-7*) HeartWatchers Pr.

Pashkow, Sidney A. & Jackson, Victoria A. Focusing on Foreclosures: A Step by Step Primer in the Art of Acquiring Foreclosure Properties. 2nd ed. 53p. 1994. reprint ed. pap. 24.95 (*0-9670891-0-7*) Foreclosure News.

Pashler, Harold E. The Psychology of Attention. LC 96-29300. 510p. 1997. 49.50 (*0-262-16165-6*, Bradford Bks) MIT Pr.

— The Psychology of Attention. (Illus.). 512p. 1999. reprint ed. pap. 24.50 (*0-262-66156-X*, Bradford Bks) MIT Pr.

Pashley, David H., jt. auth. see Nakabayashi, Nobuo.

Pashley, Don W., ed. Imperial College Inaugural Lectures in Materials Science & Engineering. 150p. 1998. 24.00 (*1-86094-106-0*, Pub. by Imperial College) World Scientific Pub.

Pashley, H. N. Notes on the Birds of Cley Norfolk. 127p. (C). 1992. pap. text 95.00 (*0-9512263-3-9*, Pub. by Enchanted Abiary) St Mut.

Pashley, H. N., ed. & tr. see Beauvoir, Simone de.

Pashley, M. D., jt. ed. see Salemink, H. W.

Pashman, Susan. The Speed of Light. LC 96-3048. 1997. 24.00 (*1-877946-86-9*) Permanent Pr.

Pashukanis, Evgeny B. Law & Marxism. 196p. (C). pap. 16.95 (*0-86104-740-0*, Pub. by Pluto GBR) Stylus Pub VA.

Pasi, Gabriella, jt. ed. see Crestani, Fabio.

Pasi, K. John, jt. ed. see Perry, David J.

Pasi, Mario. Bellini. (Portraits of Greatness Ser.). (Illus.). 80p. 1989. text 17.50 (*0-918367-33-6*); pap. text 12.50 (*0-918367-32-8*) Elite.

— Mascagni. (Portraits of Greatness Ser.). (Illus.). 48p. 1989. 17.50 (*0-918367-30-1*); pap. text 12.50 (*0-918367-31-X*) Elite.

Pasic, N., et al, eds. Workers' Management in Yugoslavia: Recent Developments & Trends. x, 198p. 1982. 31.50 (*92-2-103034-2*); pap. 22.50 (*92-2-103035-0*) Intl Labour Office.

Pasich, Kirk A. Casualty & Liability Insurance. Vol. IN2. text 82.00 (*0-8205-2417-4*) Bender.

***Pasich, Kirk A., et al.** The Year 2000 & Beyond: Liability & Insurance for Computer Code Problems. 552p. 1999. ring bd. 389.00 (*0-8080-0382-8*) CCH INC.

Pasich, Kriss R. Facial Attraction. (Illus.). 98p. 1998. pap. write for info. (*1-57502-715-1*, PO2011) Morris Pubng.

Pasichnyk, Richard, jt. auth. see Johnson, Robert.

Pasiciel, Sara. A Change in the Wind. 1996. pap. 8.99 (*0-8341-9496-1*, MP-771) Nazarene.

Pasiciel, Sara. Sunshine Valley A Two-Act Play about the Importance of Family. 1999. pap. text 8.99 (*0-8341-9978-5*) Lillenas.

Pasick, Patricia. Almost Grown: Launching Your Child from High School to College. 2nd ed. LC 97-37065. 224p. 1998. pap. 14.95 (*0-393-31710-2*) Norton.

Pasick, Patrick. Almost Grown: Launching Your Child from High School to College. 224p. Date not set. 25.00 (*0-393-04616-8*) Norton.

***Pasick, Robert.** Conversations with My Old Dog. (Illus.). iv, 39p. 1999. 10.95 (*0-9675375-0-9*) Adpar Pr.

Pasierbska, Halina. Dolls' House Furntiure. (Illus.). 40p. 1999. pap. text 8.50 (*0-7478-0382-X*, Pub. by Shire Pubns) Parkwest Pubns.

— Doll's Houses. (Shire Album Ser.: No. 271). (Illus.). 32p. 1991. pap. text 5.25 (*0-7478-0135-5*, Pub. by Shire Pubns) Lubrecht & Cramer.

***Pasil, Alessandro.** Beetle Mania. (Illus.). 144p. 2000. 24.95 (*0-312-26524-7*, Thomas Dunne) St Martin.

Pasik-Duncan, B., jt. ed. see Duncan, T. E.

Pasik, P., ed. & tr. see Cajal, S. R.

Pasik, T., ed. & tr. see Cajal, S. R.

Pasika, Wallace M., ed. Carbon-13 NMR in Polymer Science. LC 79-13384. (ACS Symposium Ser.: No. 103). 344p. 1979. 38.95 (*0-8412-0505-1*) Am Chemical.

An Asterisk (*) at the beginning of an entry indicates that the title is appearing for the first time.

— Carbon-13 NMR in Polymer Science. LC 79-13384. (ACS Symposium Ser.: Vol. 103). 343p. 1979. reprint ed. pap. 106.40 (0-608-03091-0, 206354300007) Bks Demand.

Pasin, Paul, jt. auth. see Pasini, Roberto.

Pasinetti, Luigi, ed. Italian Economic Papers, Vol. 3. 392p. 1998. text 85.00 (0-19-829034-9) OUP.

Pasinetti, Luigi L. Structural Economic Dynamics: A Theory of the Economic Consequences of Human Learning. LC 92-13438. (Illus.). 206p. (C). 1993. text 57.95 (0-521-43282-0) Cambridge U Pr.

Pasinetti, Luigi L., ed. Italian Economic Papers. (Illus.). 320p. 1993. 55.00 (0-19-828769-0) OUP.

— Italian Economic Papers, Vol. 2. 288p. 1995. 55.00 (0-19-828930-8) OUP.

Pasinetti, Luigi L., et al. The Impact of Keynes on Economics in the 20th Century. LC 98-34329. 272p. 1999. 95.00 (1-85898-861-6) E Elgar.

Pasinetti, P. M. & Spacks, Patricia M. Teaching with the Norton Anthology of World Masterpieces. 6th expanded ed. (C). 1995. pap. text, teacher ed. write for info. (0-393-96364-0) Norton.

Pasinetti, P. M., et al. The Norton Anthology of World Masterpieces, Vol. 2. 6th expanded ed. LC 94-42732. Vol. 2. 2p. (C). 1995. pap. 53.50 (0-393-96348-9) Norton.

Pasini, A. Diagram Geometrics. (Mathematical Monographs). 496p. 1994. text 95.00 (0-19-853497-3) OUP.

***Pasini, Paolo & Zannoni, Claudio.** Advances in the Computer Simulations of Liquid Crystals. 440p. 1999. pap. 69.00 (0-7923-6099-0) Kluwer Academic.

— Advances in the Computer Simulations of Liquid Crystals. LC 99-54205. (NATO Science Ser.). (Illus.). 1999. write for info. (0-7923-6098-2) Kluwer Academic.

Pasini, Roberto. The Verona Arena: The Largest Opera House in the World. (Illus.). 220p. 1995. 45.00 (88-7743-154-7, Pub. by Arsenale Editrice) Antique Collect.

***Pasini, Roberto & Pasin, Paul.** My Little Red Wagon: Radio Flyer Memories, 1. LC 99-31516. 1999. pap. 18.95 (0-7407-0044-8) Andrews & McMeel.

Pasiuk, Joan P. Adventures in Careering: A Twin Cities Field Guide. 187p. 1991. pap. 12.95 (0-9631399-0-8) Basswood Pr.

Pask, Joseph A. & Evans, A. G., eds. Ceramic Microstructures '86: Role of Interfaces. LC 87-22758. (Materials Science Research Ser.: Vol. 21). 1002p. 1987. 175.00 (0-306-42681-1, Plenum Trade) Perseus Pubng.

Pask, Joseph A. & Evans, Anthony, eds. Surfaces & Interfaces in Ceramic & Ceramic-Metal Systems. LC 81-5878. (Materials Science Research Ser.: Vol. 14). 768p. 1981. 125.00 (0-306-40726-4, Plenum Trade) Perseus Pubng.

Pask, Judith M. User Education for Online Systems in Libraries: A Selective Bibliography, 1970-1988. LC 90-9102. 220p. 1990. 28.50 (0-8108-2378-0) Scarecrow.

Pask, Kevin. The Emergence of the English Author: Scripting the Life of the Poet in Early Modern England. LC 96-37731. (Cambridge Studies in Renaissance Literature & Culture: No. 12). (Illus.). 228p. (C). 1996. text 54.95 (0-521-48155-4) Cambridge U Pr.

Paska, Jocelyn, tr. see Munoz, Silverio.

Paskaleva, K. Bulgarian Icons Through the Centuries. (Illus.). 332p. (C). 1987. text 350.00 (0-7855-5809-8, Pub. by Collets) St Mut.

— Icons from Bulgaria. (Illus.). 222p. (C). 1987. text 400.00 (0-7855-5808-X, Pub. by Collets) St Mut.

Paskaleva, Krassimira, et al. Bulgaria in Transition. (Studies in Green Research). (Illus.). 278p. 1998. text 67.95 (1-85972-619-4, Pub. by Ashgate Pub) Ashgate Pub Co.

Paskauskas, R. Andrew, ed. The Complete Correspondence of Sigmund Freud & Ernest Jones, 1908-1939. LC 92-23913. (Illus.). 888p. 1993. 48.00 (0-674-15423-1) Belknap Pr.

— The Complete Correspondence of Sigmund Freud & Ernest Jones, 1908-1939. 896p. (Orig.). (C). 1995. pap. text 24.95 (0-674-15424-X) Belknap Pr.

Paskavitz, Michael R. Y2k Survival Guide: A Step-By-Step Workbook for Physicians. 32p. pap. text 43.95 (0-7817-2271-3) Lppncott W & W.

Paske, Bradley A. Te, see Te Paske, Bradley A.

Paske, Janet V., jt. auth. see Van Amber, Rita.

Paske, Janet V., jt. auth. see Van Amber, Rita C.

Paske-Smith, Montague, ed. Japanese Traditions of Christianity: Being Some Old Translations from the Japanese, with British Consular Reports of the Persecutions of 1868-1872. LC 79-65365. (Studies in Japanese History & Civilization). 142p. 1979. reprint ed. lib. bdg. 62.50 (0-313-26983-1, U6983) Greenwood.

Paskett, Parley J. Wild Mustangs. LC 86-13165. (Western Experience Ser.). 151p. 1986. reprint ed. pap. 46.90 (0-7837-9256-5, 204999600004) Bks Demand.

Paskevicius, Mykolas. Mykolas Paskevicius. Lapkus, Danas, ed. & intro. by. LC 94-77355. (LIT., Illus.). 168p. 1995. 35.00 (0-9617756-9-6) Galerija.

Paskevska, Anna. Both Sides of the Mirror: The Science & Art of Ballet. 2nd ed. LC 79-51362. (Illus.). 224p. 1992. pap. 18.95 (0-87127-180-X) Princeton Bk Co.

— Getting Started in Ballet: A Parent's Guide to Dance Education. LC 97-18849. (Illus.). 176p. 1997. pap. 11.95 (0-19-511717-4); text 29.95 (0-19-511716-6) OUP.

Paskiet, Clare Ann, ed. see Griffith, J. A.

Paskiewicz, Steve & Schroedel, Roger. Scrimshaw: A Complete Illustrated Manual. 60p. 1999. pap. 14.95 (1-56523-095-7) Fox Chapel Pub.

***Paskin, Barbra.** Dudley Moore: The Authorized Biography. (Illus.). 2000. 24.95 (1-893224-17-1) New Millenn Enter.

Paskin, Sylvia, jt. ed. see Lyndon, Sonja.

Paskins, Barrie, ed. Ethics & European Security. LC 86-3580. 199p. 1986. 49.95 (0-86569-146-0, Auburn Hse) Greenwood.

Pasko, Marvin. The Superman Story, Vol. 1. 160p. 1995. 3.99 (0-8125-7742-6, Pub. by Tor Bks) St Martin.

***Pasko, Mary T. & Komorowski-Swiatek, Denise.** Ambulatory Care Clinical Skills Program: Anticoagulation Management Module. 250p. 2000. pap. text. write for info. (1-58528-015-1) Am Soc Hlth-Syst.

Paskoff, L. & Kelletat, D., eds. Geomorphology & Geoecology: Coastal Dynamics & Environments. (Annals of Geomorphology Ser.: Suppl. 81). (Illus.). 199p. 1991. pap. text 82.50 (3-443-21081-3) Lubrecht & Cramer.

Paskoff, Paul F., ed. The Iron & Steel Industry in the Nineteenth Century. (Encyclopedia of American Business History & Biography Ser.). (Illus.). 432p. 1988. 99.00 (0-8160-1890-1) Facts on File.

Paskoff, Paul F. & Wilson, Daniel J., eds. The Cause of the South: Selections from De Bow's Review, 1846-1867. LC 81-23680. (Library of Southern Civilization). xii, 306p. (C). 1982. pap. text 19.95 (0-8071-1039-6) La State U Pr.

Paskov, Victor. A Ballad for Georg Henig. Sturm, R., tr. 144p. 1990. 29.95 (0-7206-0796-5, Pub. by P Owen Ltd) Dufour.

Paskow, Irwin, jt. auth. see Paskow, Joan.

Paskow, Joan & Paskow, Irwin. VIP Investments: How to Make Big Money from Real Estate's Sleeping Giants. 1977. 69.50 (0-13-942128-9) Exec Reports.

Paskowitz, Karen, jt. auth. see McColl, Nancy.

Paskuly, Steven, ed. see Hoss, Rudolf.

Paskuly, Steven, ed. see Hoss, Rudolph.

***Paslack, Rainer & Stolte, Hilmar.** Gene, Klone und Organe: Neue Perspektiven der Biomedizin. (Medizin, Technik und Gesellschaft Ser.). 219p. 1999. 37.95 (3-631-33606-3) P Lang Pubng.

Pasle-green, Jeanne & Haynes, Jim, eds. Hello, I Love You! Voices from Within the Sexual Revolution. LC 77-77389. 175p. (Orig.). 1977. pap. 7.95 (0-87810-032-6) Times Change.

Pasler, Friedrich A. Dental Radiology. Hassell, Thomas M. & Hefti, Arthur F., trs. LC 92-49748. (Color Atlas of Dental Medicine Ser.). 1992. 159.00 (0-86577-460-9) Thieme Med Pubs.

Pasler, Margaret C., jt. auth. see Pasler, Rudolph J.

Pasler, Rudolph J. & Pasler, Margaret C. The New Jersey Federalists. LC 73-22570. 256p. 1975. 36.50 (0-8386-1525-2) Fairleigh Dickinson.

Pasley, Fred. Al Capone: The Biography of a Self-Made Man. LC 78-150196. (Select Bibliographies Reprint Ser.). 1977. reprint ed. 37.95 (0-8369-5709-1) Ayer.

Pasley, James N. Review Questions for Human Physiology. (Review Questions Ser.). (Illus.). 142p. 1998. pap. 19.95 (1-85070-601-8) Prthnon Pub.

Pasley, James W., jt. auth. see Gupta, Kapil.

Pasley, Jane S. Let Me Be Your Friend . . . (Illus.). 52p. (Orig.). 1989. pap. text 6.95 (0-685-29398-X) J S Pasley.

Pasley, Kay & Ihinger-Tallman, Marilyn, eds. Remarriage & Stepparenting: Current Research & Theory. LC 87-17718. (Perspectives on Marriage & the Family Ser.). 323p. 1987. pap. text 22.95 (0-89862-922-5) Guilford Pubns.

— Stepparenting: Issues in Theory, Research, & Practice. LC 93-25073. (Contributions in Sociology Ser.: 108). 304p. 1995. pap. 24.95 (0-275-95381-5, Greenwood Pr) Greenwood.

— Stepparenting: Issues in Theory, Research, & Practice, 108. LC 93-25073. (Contributions in Sociology Ser.: No. 108). 304p. 1994. 65.00 (0-313-28502-0, PSO/, Greenwood Pr) Greenwood.

Pasley, Malcolm. Germany: A Companion to German Studies. 2nd ed. 700p. 1982. pap. 23.50 (0-416-33660-4, 3698) Routledge.

— Die Schrift ist Unveraenderlich: Essays zu Kafka. (GER.). 224p. 1995. pap. 18.00 (3-596-12251-1, Pub. by Fischer Tasch) Intl Bk Import.

Pasley, Malcolm, ed. see Kafka, Franz.

Pasley, Malcolm, ed. & tr. see Kafka, Franz.

Pasley, Malcolm, tr. see Kafka, Franz.

Pasley, Sally. The Tao of Cooking. LC 98-16918. 240p. 1998. pap. 15.95 (0-253-21237-5) Ind U Pr.

Pasley, Sally, jt. auth. see Williams, Dorothy.

Pasley, Virginia & Green, Jane. You Can Do Anything with Crepes LC 85-2108. 174 p. 1985. 5.95 (0-671-60198-9) Simon & Schuster.

Paslick, Robert H., tr. & intro. see Gadamer, Hans-Georg.

Paslow, R. D., ed. see Computer Graphics 70 International Symposium Staff.

Pasmanik, G. A., jt. auth. see Bespalov, V. I.

Pasmantier, Jeanne, jt. auth. see Resnick, Seymour.

Pasmore, William, jt. auth. see Woodman, Richard.

Pasmore, William A. Creative Strategic Change: Designing the Flexible, High-performing Organization. 304p. 1994. 39.95 (0-471-59729-5) Wiley.

Pasmore, William A., jt. ed. see Woodman, Richard W.

Pasnak, R., jt. ed. see Howe, M. L.

Pasnak, William. Exit Stage Left. (Degrassi Book Ser.). 187p. (J). (gr. 5-9). 1995. mass mkt. 4.95 (1-55028-015-5) Formac Dist Ltd.

— Mimi & the Ginger Princess. (Blue Kite Adventure Ser.). (Illus.). 117p. (J). (gr. 3-6). bds. 16.95 (1-55028-107-0) Formac Dist Ltd.

— Sink or Swim. 89p. (J). (gr. 3-8). 1995. bds. 16.95 (1-55028-481-9) Formac Dist Ltd.

— Sink or Swim. 89p. (J). (gr. 3-8). 1999. pap. 5.50 (1-55028-480-0) Formac Dist Ltd.

Pasnau, Robert. Theories of Cognition in the Later Middle Ages. 341p. (C). 1997. text 59.95 (0-521-58368-3) Cambridge U Pr.

Pasnau, Robert, tr. see Aquinas, Thomas, Saint.

Pasniczek, Jacek. The Logic of Intentional Objects: A Meinongian Version of Classical Logic. LC 97-32487. (Synthese Library Ser.). 220p. 1998. text 124.00 (0-7923-4880-X) Kluwer Academic.

Paso, Fernando Del. Linda 67: Historia De Un Crimen. 2nd ed. 1996. pap. 26.95 (968-11-0163-4) Plaza.

Paso, Alfonso. Blue Heaven. 1962. pap. 5.25 (0-8222-0128-3) Dramatists Play.

— Oh, Mama! No Papa! adapted ed.Tr. of Cosas de Papa y Mama'. 1962. pap. 5.25 (0-8222-0839-3) Dramatists Play.

— Recipe for a Crime. adapted ed.Tr. of Receta para un Crimen. 1962. pap. 5.25 (0-8222-0936-5) Dramatists Play.

Pasold, E. W. Ladybird, Ladybird: A Story of Private Enterprise. 1977. 36.00 (0-7855-2817-2, Pub. by Textile Inst) St Mut.

Pasolini, Pier Paolo. Roman Poems. Ferlinghetti, Lawrence & Valente, Francesca, trs. (Pocket Poets Ser.: No. 41). (ENG & ITA., Illus.). 96p. (Orig.). 1986. pap. 7.95 (0-87286-187-2) City Lights.

— The Savage Father. Verdicchio, Pasquale, tr. 64p. 1999. pap. 8.00 (1-55071-081-8) Guernica Editions.

Pasotti, Ezekiel. The Neocatechumenal Way According to Paul VI & John Paul II. 220p. 1996. pap. 39.95 (0-85439-520-2, Pub. by St Paul Pubns) St Mut.

Pasotti, Robert, et al. Vulcan's Forge. LC 98-150434. (Star Trek Ser.). 1997. 23.00 (0-671-00926-5) PB.

Pasotti, Robert N. Interpretation of Dreams & Other Works. (YA). (gr. 7-12). 1977. 4.50 (0-671-00986-9, Arco) Macmillan Gen Ref.

Pasour, Ernest C., Jr. Agriculture & the State: Market Processes & Bureaucracy. (Independent Studies in Political Economy). 279p. (Orig.). (C). 1993. reprint ed. pap. 19.95 (0-945999-29-1) Independent Inst.

Pasqariello, Ron. Almanac of Quotable Quotes from 1990. 300p. 1991. 29.95 (0-685-38168-4, Busn); pap. 9.95 (0-685-38169-2, Busn) P-H.

Pasqua, Sandra, ed. see Anderson, Ed.

Pasqua, Sandra, ed. see Evans, Gwendolyn L.

***Pasqua, Sandra M.** The Navajo Nation. LC 99-52187. (Native Peoples Ser.). (Illus.). 24p. (J). (ps-3). 2000. lib. bdg. 15.93 (0-7368-0499-4, Bridgestone Bks) Capstone Pr.

Pasquale, Bruno, Jr. The Great Chicago-Style Pizza Cookbook. (Illus.). 148p. 1983. pap. 95.40 (0-8092-5508-1) NTC Contemp Pub Co.

Pasquale, Emanuel P. Di, see Di Pasquale, Emanuel P.

Pasquale, Frank. Basic Drafting. LC 79-730980. 1980. student ed. 7.00 (0-8064-0283-0, 720) Bergwall.

— Basic Drafting II. LC 80-730729. 1981. student ed. 7.00 (0-8064-0285-7, 721) Bergwall.

Pasquale, Giuseppe Di, see Di Pasquale, Giuseppe, ed.

Pasquale, Jennifer. Memories & Milestones: Stepping Forward by Looking Back. Lopez, Luis, tr. 185p. (Orig.). 1997. pap. 10.00 (0-9658095-4-4) J Pasquale.

Pasquale, Robert C., Jr. The Car Club Directory. 2nd ed. 1991. 12.95 (0-9631114-0-X) Genesis CA.

Pasqualetti, Martin J., ed. The Evolving Landscape: Homer Aschmann's Geography. LC 96-27473. (Illus.). 464p. 1997. text 49.95 (0-8018-5310-9) Johns Hopkins.

Pasquali, ed. Procli Diadochi. (GER & GRE.). 1994. reprint ed. 35.00 (3-8154-1731-7, T1731, Pub. by B G Teubner) U of Mich Pr.

***Pasquali, Georgius, ed.** Epistulae. (Gregorii Nysseni Opera Ser.: Vol. 2). (GRE., Illus.). xci, 192p. 1998. text 78.00 (90-04-11182-4) Brill Academic Pubs.

Pasqualin, A. & Da Pian, R., eds. New Trends in Management of Cerebro-Vascular Malformation: Proceedings of the International Conference, Verona, Italy, June 8-12, 1992. LC 94-7680. 1994. 280.00 (0-387-82528-2) Spr-Verlag.

Pasqualin, A. & DaPian, R., eds. New Trends in Management of Cerebro-Vascular Malformation: Proceedings of the International Conference, Verona, Italy, June 8-12, 1992. LC 94-7680. 1994. write for info. (3-211-82528-2) Spr-Verlag.

Pasqualini, Jean. Prisonnier de Mao, 2 vols., 1. 1976. pap. 10.95 (0-7859-4062-6) Fr & Eur.

— Prisonnier de Mao, 2 vols., 2. 1976. pap. 10.95 (0-7859-4063-4) Fr & Eur.

Pasqualini, Jorge R., ed. Recent Advances in Steroid Biochemistry, Vol. 2. LC 75-4332. 312p. 1975. pap. 67.00 (0-08-019709-4, Pub. by Pergamon Repr) Franklin.

— Receptors & Mechanism of Action of Steroid Hormones, 2 pts., Pt. 1. LC 76-40597. (Modern Pharmacology-Toxicology Ser.: No. 8). (Illus.). 325p. reprint ed. pap. 100.80 (0-7837-0679-0, 204101300001) Bks Demand.

— Receptors & Mechanism of Action of Steroid Hormones, 2 pts., Pt. 2. LC 76-40597. (Modern Pharmacology-Toxicology Ser.: No. 8). (Illus.). 439p. reprint ed. pap. 136.10 (0-7837-0680-4, 204101300002) Bks Demand.

***Pasqualino, Fortunato.** The Little Jesus of Sicily. Rozier, Louise, tr. from ITA. LC 99-38364. (Illus.). 96p. 1999. 22.00 (1-55728-572-1); pap. 14.00 (1-55728-573-X) U of Ark Pr.

***Pasquarelli, John.** Pauline Hanson Story. 1999. pap. text 16.95 (1-86436-341-X) New Holland.

***Pasquarelli, Len.** Jamal Anderson: Running up the Mountain. (SuperStar Series: Vol. 2). 96p. (J). 2000. pap. 4.95 (1-58261-161-0, Pub. by Sprts Pubng) Partners-West.

Pasquarelli, N., jt. auth. see Ibarrola, J.

Pasquarelli, Timothy L. & Woid-Black, Frankie K. Emergency Preparedness Planning: A Primer. LC TP155.5.P32 1999. (Illus.). 126p. (C). 1999. text 29.95 (0-8412-3579-1, Pub. by Am Chemical) OUP.

Pasquarello, Tony J. The Altar Boy Chronicles. LC 99-19323. (Orig.). 1999. pap. 16.00 (1-57884-953-5, 5583) Gustav Broukal.

Pasquarette, Chris. Pac-Rim Sourcebook. (Illus.). 160p. 1994. 12.00 (0-937279-46-3, CP3311) Talsorian.

Pasquariella, Susan K., ed. Union List of Population-Family Planning Periodicals. 135p. 1978. 25.00 (0-318-03477-8, LC-78-60528); 10.00 (0-318-03478-6) Assn Pop Lib.

Pasquariello, Anthony M., ed. see Lopez-Rubio, Jose.

Pasquariello, Nicholas. Sounds of Movies: Interviews with Creators of Feature Sound Tracks. LC 96-92394. 240p. (Orig.). 1996. pap. 19.95 (0-9653114-7-3) Port Bridge.

Pasquariello, Patrick S., Jr., et al. Primary Care Pediatric Otolaryngology. 244p. 1995. text 35.00 (1-887064-00-1) J M Ryan.

Pasquariello, Patrick S., ed. see Children's Hospital of Philadelphia Staff, et al.

Pasquariello, Ron. Almanac of Quotable Quotes from 1990. 1991. pap. 9.95 (0-685-47732-0) P-H.

Pasquariello, Ronald. Tax Justice: Social & Moral Aspects of American Tax Policy. LC 85-3250. (Illus.). 132p. (Orig.). 1985. pap. text 14.00 (0-8191-4607-2); lib. bdg. 41.00 (0-8191-4606-4) U Pr of Amer.

Pasquariello, Ronald D. Jesus & the Message of Love. LC 97-49427. 191p. (Orig.). 1998. pap. 12.95 (0-9620507-7-6) Cosmic Concepts Pr.

Pasquella. Comfort of Dreams: Photographs. 1995. per. 19.95 (0-85449-140-6, Pub. by Gay Mens Pr) LPC InBook.

Pasquerella, Lynn G., et al, eds. Ethical Dilemmas in Public Administration. LC 95-37644. 200p. 1996. 59.95 (0-275-95040-9, Praeger Pubs) Greenwood.

Pasquero, Fedele. I Will Follow You: Meditations on Jesus. Lane, Edmund C., tr. LC 92-3174. 200p. (Orig.). 1992. pap. 9.95 (0-8189-0647-2) Alba.

Pasquet, Iris. Dreaming Hawaii: An Island Story. (Illus.). 64p. (Orig.). 1996. pap. 8.95 (0-930492-37-4) Hawaiian Serv.

Pasquier, Alain. The Louvre: Greek, Etruscan & Roman Antiquities. (Illus.). 96p. 1991. 30.00 (1-870248-79-1) Scala Books.

Pasquier, Binnie. Elemental. (Illus.). (C). 1996. pap. text 5.00 (1-878173-39-1) Birnham Wood.

Pasquier, C., et al, eds. Oxidative Stress, Cell Activation & Viral Infection. LC 93-44396. (Molecular & Cell Biology Updates Ser.). (Illus.). 376p. 1993. 99.00 (0-8176-2941-6) Birkhauser.

Pasquier, C., jt. ed. see Montagnier, Luc.

Pasquier, Jacqueline du. Les Arts Decoratifs Bordelais: Mobiliers et Objets Domestiques (1714-1895) (FRE.). 208p. 1993. lib. bdg. 195.00 (0-7859-3647-5, 2859171142) Fr & Eur.

Pasquier, M. & Foucher, P. An Analytical Method for the Calculation of the Efficiency of Planetary Gears. (Nineteen Ninety-Four Fall Technical Meeting Ser.: Vol. 94FTM2). (Illus.). 6p. 1994. pap. text 30.00 (1-55589-636-7) AGMA.

Pasquier, Roger F., ed. Conservation of New World Parrots: Proceedings of the ICBP Parrot Working Group Meeting, St. Lucia, 1980. 486p. 1983. pap. text 22.50 (0-87474-745-7, PANPP) Smithsonian.

Pasquier, Roger F. & Farrand, John, Jr. Masterpieces of Bird Art: 700 Years of Ornithological Illustration. (Illus.). 256p. 1991. 75.00 (1-55859-134-6) Abbeville Pr.

Pasquill, F. & Smith, F. B. Atmospheric Diffusion: Study of the Dispersion of Windborne Material from Industrial & Other Sources. 3rd ed. LC 83-219. (Environmental Sciences Ser.). 437p. 1983. text 86.95 (0-470-27404-2) P-H.

***Pasquini, John J.** Atheism & Salvation: Atheism from the Perspective of Anonymous Christianity in the Thought of the Revolutionary Mystic & Theologian Karl Rahner. LC 99-58652. 120p. 2000. 47.00 (0-7618-1602-X); pap. 24.50 (0-7618-1603-8) U Pr of Amer.

Pasquini, Katie. Design & Make Your Own Contemporary Sampler Quilt. LC 94-22078. (Needlework Ser.). (Illus.). 64p. 1994. pap. text 5.95 (0-486-28197-3) Dover.

— Mandala Quilt Designs. LC 94-40103. (Needlework Ser.). (Illus.). 112p. 1995. pap. text 8.95 (0-486-28491-3) Dover.

— Three-Dimensional Design. Loft, Randi, ed. LC 88-70657. (Illus.). 80p. (Orig.). 1988. pap. text 16.95 (0-914881-19-1, 10024) C & T Pub.

Pasquini, Mark T., jt. auth. see Minkema, Douglas D.

Pasquini, Philip L. Indentured Immigrants: A Jewish Family Odyssey from Madeira to the Sandwich Islands. LC 99-90012. (Illus.). xi, 144p. 1999. pap. 19.95 (0-9670016-0-9, 654070) Flypaper.

Pasquino, Gianfranco, jt. ed. see Hellman, Stephen M.

Pasquino, Gianfranco, jt. ed. see Hellman, Stephen.

***Pasquinucci, Marinella & Trement, Frederic, eds.** Non-Destructive Techniques Applied to Landscape Archaeology. (Archaeology of the Mediterranean Landscape, Populus Monograph: Vol. 4). 250p. 2000. 81.95 (1-900188-74-0, Pub. by Oxbow Bks) David Brown.

Pasrici, C., jt. ed. see Leccabue, F.

Pass, Anastas F. Systemic Ocular Assessment. (Illus.). 256p. Date not set. text 50.00 (0-7506-9566-8) Buttrwrth-Heinemann.

Pass, Christopher. Collins Dictionary of Business. 2nd ed. 1995. pap. 20.00 (0-00-470803-2) Collins.

Pass, Christopher L. Business & Microeconomics: An Introduction to the Market Environment. LC 93-39826. (Elements of Business Ser.). 320p. (C). 1994. pap. 26.95 (0-415-06846-0, B0184) Thomson Learn.

Pass, Christopher L., et al. Business & Economics. 1995. pap. 18.99 (1-86152-207-X, Pub. by ITBP) Thomson Learn.

Pass, Christopher L., et al. Business & Macroeconomics. LC 94-42204. (Elements of Business Ser.). 304p. (C). 1995. pap. 24.95 (0-415-12400-X) Thomson Learn.

Pass, Claudia W., ed. Carolina Blessings. (Illus.). 288p. 1995. 17.95 (0-9643051-0-0) Chldrns Home Soc.

P

Pass, Destin. Scenes of Beautiful Japan: Memories of a U. S. Airman's 1969 Tour of Duty. LC 90-45924. (Illus.). 80p. (Orig.). 1990. pap. 9.95 (*0-912526-50-5*) Lib Res.

Pass, Dorie F. Everybody's Doing It...and Here's How to Quit. (Orig.). 1990. pap. 12.95 (*0-9625992-3-9*) Golden One Pub.

Pass, Erica. New York Nightmare! (Secret World of Alex Mack Ser.: No. 31). (J). (gr. 3-6). 1998. pap. 3.99 (*0-671-01957-0*) PB.

Pass, Gail. Surviving Sisters. 252p. 1989. reprint ed. pap. 8.95 (*0-941483-16-9*) Naiad Pr.

Pass, Geoff & LaBossiere, Mike. Protect & Serve. (Cyberpunk Ser.). (Illus.). 96p. (Orig.). 1992. pap. 10.00 (*0-937279-25-0*, CP3171) Talsorian.

***Pass, Harvey I.** Lung Cancer: Principles & Practice. LC 99-51908. (Illus.). 2000. 159.00 (*0-7817-1791-4*) Lppncott W & W.

Pass, Harvey I., et al. Lung Cancer: Principles & Practice. 982p. 1995. text 151.00 (*0-397-51361-5*) Lppncott W & W.

Pass, Joe. Joe Pass Chord Solos: For Guitar, Vibes, & All Keyboard Instruments. 20p. 1987. pap. 5.95 (*0-7390-0745-9*, 3320) Alfred Pub.

Pass, Joe. Joe Pass Guitar Chords. 24p. 1986. pap. 6.95 (*0-87166-615-4*, 94108) Mel Bay.

— Joe Pass Guitar Style. 1986. pap. 9.95 (*1-56222-005-5*, 94106) Mel Bay.

Pass, Joe. Joe Pass Improvising Ideas. Hibler, Jude, ed. 64p. 1994. pap. 9.95 (*0-7866-0030-6*, 95201) Mel Bay.

***Pass, John.** Water Stair. (Orig.). 1999. pap. 15.95 (*0-88982-179-8*, Pub. by Oolichan Bks) Genl Dist Srvs.

Pass, Linda D. Accepting the Readiness Idea. 40p. (Orig.). 1992. pap. text 6.00 (*0-935493-84-0*) Modern Learn Pr.

Pass, Lowes. Dictionary of Economics. 2nd ed. 1993. pap. 19.95 (*0-00-470372-3*, Pub. by HarpC) Trafalgar.

Pass, Ray, jt. auth. see Cody, Ron.

Pass the Plate, Inc. Staff. Pass the Plate. Underhill, Alice & Stewart, Bobbie, eds. 520p. 1981. pap. 13.95 (*0-939114-13-5*) Pass the Plate.

Passafiume, John F. & Michta, Andrew A. Selected Developments in Soviet Airborne Computer Technology, 1958-1977. 76p. (Orig.). 1986. pap. text 100.00 (*1-55831-065-7*) Delphic Associates.

Passafiume, Joseph. TEC Course - Interconnections: Bridges & Routers. 1992. ring bd. write for info. (*0-201-41887-8*) Addison-Wesley.

Passage, Charles E., tr. see Goethe, Johann Wolfgang Von.

***Passage, David.** The United States & Columbia: Untying the Gordian Knot. (Illus.). 36p. 2000. pap. write for info. (*1-58487-019-2*) SSI US Army.

***Passaglia, Elio.** Unique Institution: The National Bureau of Standards, 1950-1969. 836p. 1999. per. 63.00 (*0-16-058904-5*) USGPO.

Passalacqua, Carlos M. Antologia Poetica. LC 84-7594. (SPA., Illus.). 143p. 1985. pap. 5.00 (*0-8477-3234-7*) U of PR Pr.

— Noche, Fuente: Poesia. 2nd ed. LC 79-23317. (Illus.). 98p. 1981. 6.00 (*0-8477-3226-6*) U of PR Pr.

Passalacqua, Francesca, jt. ed. see Newton, Jeremiah.

Passalacqua, John L. De, see Silva-Ruiz, Pedro F. & De Passalacqua, John L.

Passalacqua, Juan Garcia, see Garcia Passalacqua, Juan.

Passalacqua, Juan M. Dignidad y Jaiberia: Temer y Ser. 1993. pap. write for info. (*1-56758-023-8*) Edit Cultl.

Passalacqua, Rose, tr. see Caulfield, Carlota, et al, eds.

Passalacque, Francesca, jt. ed. see Newton, Jeremiah.

Passali, D. Pediatric Otorhinolaryngology: An Update. (Illus.). x, 432p. 1998. 137.00 (*90-6299-158-0*) Kugler Pubns.

Passamaneck, Marge. People Are Different, People Are the Same. 1983. pap. 3.25 (*0-89536-615-0*, 1629) CSS OH.

Passamaneck, Stephen M., ed. Jewish Law & Jewish Life, 8 bks. in 4 vols. Incl. Bk. 1. Lawyers, Judges & Legal Ethics. Passamaneck, Stephen M., tr. 1978. pap. 5.00 (*0-8074-0034-3*, 180210); Bks. 2-4. Jewish Law & Jewish Life: Credit, Law Enforcement, Taxation. Bazak, Jacob. 57p. 1998. pap. 5.00 (*0-8074-0035-1*, 180211); Bks. 5-6. Credit, Law Enforcement, Taxation. Bazak, Jacob, ed. Passamaneck, Stephen M., tr. & anno. by. 1978. pap. 5.00 (*0-8074-0036-X*, 180212); Bks. 7-8. Criminal & Domestic Relations. Bazak, Jacob, ed. Passamaneck, Stephen M., tr. & anno. by. 1978. pap. 5.00 (*0-8074-0037-8*, 180213); 1978. Set pap. 12.50 (*0-8074-0038-6*, 180218) UAHC.

Passamaneck, Stephen M., tr. & anno. see Karo, Joseph E.

Passamante, Frances S., ed. Florida State Grant Programs, 1997-98. 11th ed. (Illus.). 270p. (Orig.). 1997. pap., per. 80.00 (*1-879543-18-4*) FL Fund Pubns.

Passamonte, Jane A. Pills, Pearls & Potions. 2nd ed. 114p. (Orig.). 1997. pap. 11.95 (*1-884441-02-5*) Tyler Pr.

***Passanante, Joy.** Sinning in Italy. 40p. 1999. pap. 15.00 (*0-931659-56-6*) Limberlost Pr.

— Sinning in Italy. limited ed. 40p. 1999. 50.00 (*0-931659-57-4*) Limberlost Pr.

Passannante, Frances S., ed. Florida State Grant Programs, 1998-99 Directory. 12th ed. 1998. pap. 80.00 (*1-879543-21-4*) FL Fund Pubns.

— A Guide to Florida State Programs: 1996-1997. 10th ed. 350p. (Orig.). 1996. pap. 80.00 (*1-879543-16-8*) FL Fund Pubns.

Passannante, Frances S., ed. see Adams, John L.

Passano, Eleanor P. An Index of the Source Records of Maryland: Genealogical, Biographical, Historical. LC 67-17943. 478p. 1994. reprint ed. 21.00 (*0-8063-0271-2*, 4400) Genealog Pub.

Passante, Jeff. Housatonic River: Fly Fishing Guide. LC 99-484159. (Illus.). 55p. 1998. pap. 14.95 (*1-57188-151-4*) F Amato Pubns.

***Passantino, Erika D. & Scott, David W., eds.** The Eye of Duncan Phillips: A Collection in the Making. LC 99-15182. (Illus.). 832p. 1999. 100.00 (*0-300-08090-5*) Yale U Pr.

Passantino, Erika D., ed. see Phillips Collection Staff.

Passantino, Gretchen. Satanism. (Guide to Cults & Religious Movements Ser.). 64p. 1995. 5.99 (*0-310-70451-0*) Zondervan.

Passar, Patricia R., ed. Caribbean Circuits: New Directions in the Study of Caribbean Migration. LC 96-36181. 231p. (C). 1997. pap. 19.95 (*0-934733-94-5*) CMS.

Passarella, J. G. Wither. LC 99-11214. 320p. 1999. 23.00 (*0-671-02480-9*) PB.

***Passarella, J. G.** Wither. 448p. 2000. reprint ed. mass mkt. 6.99 (*0-671-02481-7*) PB.

***Passarella, John.** Ghoul Trouble. (Buffy the Vampire Slayer Ser.: Vol. 18). 192p. (YA). (gr. 7 up). 2000. 5.99 (*0-7434-0042-9*, Pocket Pulse) PB.

Passarella, Lee. Asrael. 25p. 1995. pap. 4.50 (*0-9647127-1-7*) Coreopsis Bks.

— Working from Memory. 20p. 1992. pap. 4.00 (*0-9647127-0-9*) Coreopsis Bks.

***Passarge, Eberhard.** Color Atlas of Genetics. 2nd ed.Tr. of Taschenatlas der Genetik. (Illus.). 370p. 2000. pap. 32.00 (*0-86577-958-9*) Thieme Med Pubs.

Passarge, Harro. Pflanzengesellschaften Nordostdeutschlands Vol. I: Hydro- und Therophytosa. (Botanical Bks.). (GER., Illus.). xiv, 298p. 1996. text 29.00 (*3-443-50020-X*, Pub. by Gebruder Borntraeger) Balogh.

Passariello, R., jt. auth. see Pavone, P.

Passarino, Giampiero, jt. auth. see Bardin, Dima.

Passaro, Edward, jt. auth. see Stamos, Michael J.

Passaro, Joanne. The Unequal Homeless: Men on the Streets, Women in Their Place. LC 95-47036. 136p. (C). 1996. 75.00 (*0-415-90902-3*) Routledge.

— The Unequal Homeless: Men on the Streets, Women in Their Place. 2nd ed. LC 95-47036. 136p. (C). 1996. pap. 18.99 (*0-415-90903-1*) Routledge.

***Passaro, John.** Colin Powell. LC 99-19250. (Journey to Freedom Ser.). (Illus.). 32p. (YA). (gr. 4 up). 1999. lib. bdg. 24.21 (*1-56766-619-1*) Childs World.

— Frederick Douglass. LC 99-19252. (Journey to Freedom Ser.). (Illus.). 32p. (YA). (gr. 4 up). 1999. lib. bdg. 24.21 (*1-56766-621-3*) Childs World.

Passaro, John. The Story of Disney. LC 98-48719. (Spirit of Success Ser.). (Illus.). 48p. (YA). (gr. 5 up). 1999. lib. bdg. 23.95 (*1-58340-002-8*) Smart Apple.

— The Story of Harley-Davidson. LC 98-47571. (Spirit of Success Ser.). (Illus.). 48p. (YA). (gr. 5 up). 1999. lib. bdg. 23.95 (*1-58340-003-6*) Smart Apple.

Passaro, John, ed. see Jennings, Robert W.

Passaro, Maria P., tr. see Tasso, Torquato.

Passas, Nikos. Subsidizing Fraud: The Nature & Control of Subsidy Frauds in the EC. 250p. (C). Date not set. pap. 45.00 (*0-8133-8636-5*) Westview.

Passas, Nikos, ed. Organized Crime. (International Library of Criminology & Criminal Justice). 612p. 1995. 199.95 (*1-85521-437-7*, Pub. by Dartmth Pub) Ashgate Pub Co.

— Transnational Crime. LC 98-46598. (International Library of Criminology, Criminal Justice & Penology). 550p. 1999. text 184.95 (*1-84014-000-3*, Pub. by Ashgate Pub) Ashgate Pub Co.

Passas, Nikos & Agnew, Robert, eds. The Future of Anomie Theory. LC 97-15769. 320p. 1997. text 50.00 (*1-55553-321-3*) NE U Pr.

Passath, A. & Hoefler, H. Thyrotropin: Ultrasensitive TSH Measurement in Clinical Research & Diagnostics. Leb, G. et al, eds. (Illus.). x, 361p. (C). 1987. 113.85 (*0-89925-209-5*) De Gruyter.

Passatore, Mary Anne, jt. auth. see Sivak, Patricia.

Passauer, L. K., jt. auth. see Christian, N. L.

Passchier, C. W. & Trouw, R. A. Microtectonics, Vol. X. LC 98-41286. (Illus.). 289p. 1995. 44.95 (*3-540-58713-6*) Spr-Verlag.

Passchier, C. W., et al. Field Geology of High-Grade Gneiss Terrains. (Illus.). 160p. 1990. 29.95 (*0-387-53053-3*) Spr-Verlag.

Passchier, D. M., jt. auth. see Tummers, M. J.

Passchier, Maja. Abracadabra Cello: Way to Learn. 64p. (J). (gr. k-3). 1998. pap. 8.95 (*0-7136-5637-9*, Pub. by A & C Blk) Midpt Trade.

Passcuant, P., ed. see International Congress of Pharmacology Staff.

Passe. Elementary Curriculum. 1994. teacher ed. 7.81 (*0-697-20610-6*, WCB McGr Hill) McGrw-H Hghr Educ.

Passe, Derrel B. De, see De Passe, Derrel B., ed.

Passe, Jeff. Elementary School Curriculum. 432p. (C). 1994. text. write for info. (*0-697-20107-4*) Brown & Benchmark.

— Elementary School Curriculum. 2nd ed. LC 98-30206. 336p. 1998. pap. 46.25 (*0-697-29883-3*) McGraw.

— When Students Choose Content: A Guide to Increasing Motivation, Autonomy, & Achievement. LC 96-18455. (Illus.). 112p. 1996. 43.95 (*0-8039-6448-X*); pap. 18.95 (*0-8039-6449-8*) Corwin Pr.

Passe-Smith, John T., jt. auth. see Williams, Edward J.

Passe-Smith, John T., jt. ed. see Seligson, Mitchell A.

Passek, Jean-Loup. Dictionary of the French Cinema: Dictionnaire du Cinema Francais. (ENG & FRE.). 867p. 1987. 28.95 (*0-8288-2602-1*, F11830) Fr & Eur.

— Dictionnaire du Cinema. (FRE.). 1998. 175.00 (*0-320-00199-7*) Fr & Eur.

— Larousse Dictionnaire du Cinema. (FRE.). 800p. 1991. 175.00 (*0-8288-9476-0*) Fr & Eur.

Passek, Lynn. The Thinnest Thread. 48p. (Orig.). Date not set. pap. 12.00 (*0-614-16391-9*) Em Pr.

Passekov, Vladimir P., jt. auth. see Svirezhev, Yuri M.

Passel, Anne. Your Words: Public & Private. 2nd ed. LC 81-40773. (Illus.). 248p. 1982. pap. text 22.00 (*0-8191-1867-2*) U Pr of Amer.

Passel, Charles F. Ice: The Antarctic Diary of Charles F. Passel. Baughman, T. H., ed. & intro. by. (Illus.). 448p. 1995. 29.95 (*0-89672-347-X*) Tex Tech Univ Pr.

Passel, Jeffrey S., jt. ed. see Edmonston, Barry.

Passelecq, Georges & Suchecky, Bernard. The Hidden Encyclical of Pius XI. 330p. 1998. pap. 14.00 (*0-15-600631-6*, Harvest Bks) Harcourt.

— The Hidden Encyclical of Pope Pius XI. Rendell, Stephen, tr. from FRE. LC 97-7227. 352p. 1997. 25.00 (*0-15-100244-4*) Harcourt.

Passell, Peter. Essays in the Economics of Nineteenth Century American Land Policy. LC 75-2590. (Dissertations in American Economic History Ser.). (Illus.). 1975. 19.95 (*0-405-07212-0*) Ayer.

— How to Read the Financial Pages. 1989. mass mkt. 4.99 (*0-446-35914-9*, Pub. by Warner Bks) Little.

— How to Read the Financial Pages. 1998. mass mkt. 6.50 (*0-446-60670-7*, Pub. by Warner Bks) Little.

— How to Read the Financial Pages. rev. ed. 176p. 1993. mass mkt. 5.99 (*0-446-36504-1*, Pub. by Warner Bks) Little.

Passell, Peter, jt. auth. see Cloverdale Press Staff.

***Passen, Lisa.** Incredible Shrinking Teacher. 2001. text 15.95 (*0-8050-6452-4*) H Holt & Co.

Passer, Harold C. The Electrical Manufacturers, 1875-1900: A Study in Competition, Entrepreneurship, Technical Change, & Economic Growth. LC 72-5066. (Technology & Society Ser.). (Illus.). 436p. 1979. reprint ed. 40.95 (*0-405-04717-7*) Ayer.

Passerello, C. E., jt. auth. see Huston, R. L.

***Passerin d'Entraeves, Maurizio & Vogel, Ursula.** Public & Private: Legal, Political & Philosophical Perspectives. LC 00-28413. 2000. pap. write for info. (*0-415-16684-5*) Routledge.

Passerini, Luisa. Autobiography of a Generation: Italy, 1968. Erdberg, Lisa, tr. from ITA. LC 96-15984. 182p. 1996. 25.00 (*0-8195-5286-0*, Wesleyan Univ Pr) U Pr of New Eng.

— Europe in Love, Love in Europe: Imagination & Politics Between the Wars. LC 98-55135. 1999. 38.50 (*0-8147-6673-0*) NYU Pr.

***Passerini, Luisa.** Europe in Love, Love in Europe: Imagination & Politics Between the Wars LC 98-55135. viii, 358 p. 1999. text 38.50 (*0-8147-6698-6*) NYU Pr.

Passerini, Luisa, et al, eds. International Yearbook of Oral History & Life Stories Vol. 1: Memory & Totalitarianism. 224p. 1993. 59.00 (*0-19-820248-2*) OUP.

Passerini, Luisa, jt. ed. see Leydesorff, Selma.

Passero, Virginia A. The Mature Gravida. Damus, Karla et al, eds. LC 95-33586. 1995. write for info. (*0-86525-067-7*) March of Dimes.

Passeron, Jean-Claude, jt. auth. see Bourdieu, Pierre.

Passeron, Rene. Lexikon des Surrealismus. (GER.). 1975. 45.00 (*0-8288-5923-X*, M7220) Fr & Eur.

Passeron, Rene, jt. auth. see Biro, Adam.

Passeron, Roger. Cathelin Lithographs, 1957-89 with Two Original Lithographs, 2 vols. (Illus.). 1990. 375.00 (*1-55660-212-X*) A Wofsy Fine Arts.

Passeron, Roger & Josselin, Jean F. Cassigneuls's Graphic Work, 1965-1988: Catalogue Raisonne, 2 vols. (ENG & FRE., Illus.). 408p. 1997. 275.00 (*1-55660-091-7*) A Wofsy Fine Arts.

Passes, Alan, jt. auth. see Overing, Joanna.

Passet, Joanne, jt. auth. see Maack, Mary N.

Passet, Joanne E. Cultural Crusaders: Women Librarians in the American West, 1900-1917. LC 93-46764. 227p. 1994. 40.00 (*0-8263-1530-5*) U of NM Pr.

Passett, Barry A. Leadership Development for Public Service. LC 70-149755. 149p. reprint ed. pap. 46.20 (*0-608-18159-5*, 203285500081) Bks Demand.

Passfield, Sidney J. The History of Trade Unionism. LC 75-173495. reprint ed. 74.50 (*0-404-06885-5*) AMS Pr.

Passfield, Sidney J. & Webb, Beatrice Potter. Industrial Democracy. LC 79-173496. reprint ed. 35.00 (*0-404-06886-3*) AMS Pr.

— Methods of Social Study. LC 67-30866. vii, 263p. 1968. reprint ed. 39.50 (*0-678-00351-3*) Kelley.

Passi, Delia & Biza, Ted. A Couple's Guide to Keeping the Relationship Alive. 1994. pap. write for info. (*0-9641081-2-7*) Tedel Pubns.

— Your Guide to Finding the Right One & Being the Right One, Book 1. (Illus.). 70p. 1994. 8.95 (*0-9641081-0-0*); pap. 5.95 (*0-9641081-1-9*) Tedel Pubns.

Passi, Lois E. A Guide to Creative Group Programming in the Psychiatric Day Hospital. LC 43-9237. (Illus.). 244p. 1998. lib. bdg. 39.95 (*0-7890-0406-2*) Haworth Pr.

Passic, Jon T., ed. see Rolfe, Jack W.

Passicot, Monique. Favorite Fairy Tales Told in Spain. LC 94-1499. 96p. (J). (gr. 2 up). 1995. reprint ed. pap. 4.95 (*0-688-12605-7*, Wm Morrow) Morrow Avon.

Passie, Torsten. Psycholytic & Psychedelic Therapy Research, 1931-1995: A Complete International Bibliography LC 97-195979. (Kleine Bibliographische Reihe Ser.). 102p. 1997. write for info. (*0-393-61483-2*) Norton.

Passikoff, Barbara & Witt, Verla. Fitness Workbook: A Step-by-Step Guide to Individualized Fitness. 2nd ed. 80p. (C). 1994. pap. text, spiral bd. 17.95 (*0-8403-9264-8*) Kendall-Hunt.

Passiment. Clinical Laboratory Education. 220p. 1996. pap. text, per. 37.95 (*0-7872-2601-7*) Kendall-Hunt.

Passin, Herbert. Japanese Education: A Bibliography of Materials in the English Language. LC 74-93507. (Columbia University Publications of the Center for Education in Industrial Nations Ser.). 149p. reprint ed. pap. 46.20 (*0-608-13814-2*, 201776600008) Bks Demand.

Passin, Herbert, et al. Japan in the 1980s, Vol. II. LC 83-61309. (Papers on International Issues: No. 6). (Illus.). 73p. (Orig.). (C). 1983. pap. text 5.00 (*0-935082-05-0*) Southern Ctr Intl Stud.

Passingham, Bernard & Harmer, Caroline. Law & Practice in Matrimonial Causes. 4th ed. 1985. pap. 60.00 (*0-406-63707-5*, U.K., MICHIE) LEXIS Pub.

Passingham, Ian. Pillars of Fire: The Battle of Messines Ridge 1917. LC 99-193844. 1999. 39.99 (*0-7509-1704-0*) Bks Intl VA.

Passingham, R. E. The Frontal Lobes & Voluntary Action. (Oxford Psychology Ser.: Vol. 21). (Illus.). 322p. 1995. reprint ed. pap. text 35.00 (*0-19-852364-5*) OUP.

Passingham, W. J. Romance of London's Underground. LC 72-80705. (Illus.). 1972. reprint ed. 36.95 (*0-405-08839-6*) Ayer.

Passino, Kevin M. Fuzzy Control: Theory & Applications. LC 97-14003. 450p. (C). 1997. 100.00 (*0-201-18074-X*, Prentice Hall) P-H.

***Passino, Kevin M. & Burgess, Kevin L.** Stability Analysis of Discrete Event Systems. LC 97-26396. (Adaptive & Learning Systems for Signal Processing, Communications & Control Ser.). 202p. 1998. 71.50 (*0-471-24185-7*, Wiley-Interscience) Wiley.

Passino, Kevin M., jt. ed. see Antsaklis, Panos J.

Passino, Roberto, jt. ed. see Patterson, James W.

Passler, David L. Time, Form & Style in Boswell's Life of Johnson. LC 70-151585. (Yale Studies in English: No. 155). 180p. reprint ed. 55.80 (*0-8357-9591-8*, 201338400087) Bks Demand.

Passman & Kaplan P. C. Staff. Federal Employees Legal Survival Guide: How to Protect & Enforce Your Job Rights. LC 99-30896. 520p. 1999. pap. 39.95 (*0-9656000-1-7*, Pub. by Nat Employee) Wash Bk Distrib.

***Passman, Don.** The Visionary. 432p. 2000. mass mkt. 7.99 (*0-446-60831-9*) Warner Bks.

Passman, Donald S. The Algebraic Structure of Group Rings. LC 84-15403. 750p. (C). 1985. reprint ed. lib. bdg. 76.50 (*0-89874-789-9*) Krieger.

— All You Need to Know about the Music Business, Vol. B. LC 96-6610. (Illus.). 416p. 1997. 27.50 (*0-684-83600-9*) S&S Trade.

***Passman, Donald S.** All You Need to Know about the Music Business: Revised & Updated for the 21st Century. 2000. write for info. (*0-684-87064-9*) S&S Trade.

Passman, Donald S. A Course in Ring Theory. (C). 1991. pap. 79.00 (*0-534-13776-8*) Thomson Learn.

— Group Rings, Crossed Products & Galois Theory. LC 86-1177. (CBMS Regional Conference Series in Mathematics: No. 64). 71p. 1986. pap. 18.00 (*0-8218-0714-5*, CBMS/64) Am Math.

— Infinite Group Rings. LC 72-163311. (Pure & Applied Mathematics Ser.: No. 6). 159p. reprint ed. pap. 49.30 (*0-7837-2638-4*, 204299100006) Bks Demand.

***Passman, Donald S.** Mirage. 336p. 2000. 25.95 (*0-446-52724-6*) Warner Bks.

Passman, Donald S. The Visionary. LC 98-34907. 448p. 1999. 25.00 (*0-446-52159-0*, Pub. by Warner Bks) Little.

Passman, Ellen, ed. see Lillis, James.

Passman, S. L., jt. auth. see Drew, D. A.

Passmore, Colin. Privilege. LC 98-183521. 288p. 1998. 134.50 (*1-85811-078-5*, Pub. by CLT Prof) Gaunt.

Passmore, Debbie. Tales of Girliegate: A Poetic Satire of the White House Scandal. Du Toit, Johan, ed. & illus. by. 132p. 1999. pap. 16.95 (*1-883707-39-0*) Protea Publng GA.

Passmore, Gregory, jt. ed. see Mundy, Wanda M.

Passmore, J. A. Moore: Ancestors & Descendants of Andrew Moore, 1612-1897. (Illus.). 1599p. 1991. reprint ed. pap. 179.00 (*0-8328-1800-3*); reprint ed. lib. bdg. 189.00 (*0-8328-1799-6*) Higginson Bk Co.

Passmore, Jacki. China: The Beautiful Cookbook. LC 16-4. (Beautiful Cookbook Ser.). (Illus.). 256p. 1992. 50.00 (*0-00-255115-2*) Collins SF.

— Complete Chinese Cookbook. 1998. 39.95 (*0-8048-3163-7*) Tuttle Pubng.

— Complete Spanish Cookbook. 416p. 1993. 34.95 (*0-8048-1823-1*) Tuttle Pubng.

— Fire & Spice: 200 Hot & Spicy Recipes from the Far East. (Illus.). 298p. 1998. text 25.00 (*0-7881-5424-9*) DIANE Pub.

— The Vegetarian Table: Thailand. LC 96-51123. 1997. 24.95 (*0-8118-1214-6*) Chronicle Bks.

Passmore, Jacki & Reid, Daniel. The Complete Chinese Cookbook. (Illus.). 304p. 1998. 39.95 (*0-8048-3158-0*) Tuttle Pubng.

***Passmore, James.** Beyond the Stars. (Science Comic Bks.). (J). (gr. 4-7). 1998. pap. text 8.95 (*957-8741-81-2*) Large Nature.

Passmore, James. World of Dinosaurs. (Science Comic Bks.). (YA). (gr. 4-7). 1998. pap. text 8.95 (*957-8741-83-9*) Large Nature.

Passmore, John. Memoirs of a Semidetached Australian. LC 98-109991. (Illus.). 288p. 1998. 39.95 (*0-522-84766-8*, Pub. by Melbourne Univ Pr) Paul & Co Pubs.

— Perfectability of Man. LC 77-129625. 1978. 25.00 (*0-684-15521-4*) S&S Trade.

***Passmore, John.** The Perfectibility of Man. 2nd ed. LC 99-87606. 546p. 2000. 25.00 (*0-86597-257-5*); pap. 14.00 (*0-86597-258-3*) Liberty Fund.

Passmore, John. Serious Art. 304p. (C). 1991. 49.95 (*0-8126-9181-4*) Open Court.

***Passmore, Jon.** Stakeholder Housing: A Third Way. 1999. pap. 25.00 (*0-7453-1500-3*) Pluto GBR.

***Passmore, Jon & Brown, Tim.** Stakeholder Housing: A Third Way LC 99-35171. 1999. write for info. (*0-7453-1505-4*, Pub. by Pluto GBR) Stylus Pub VA.

An Asterisk (*) at the beginning of an entry indicates that the title is appearing for the first time.

Passmore, Kevin. From Liberalism to Fascism: The Right in a French Province, 1928-1939. 351p. (C). 1997. text 59.95 (*0-521-58018-8*) Cambridge U Pr.

Passmore, Matthew, ed. see Schorr, Daniel.

Passmore, N. I. & Carruthers, V. C. South African Frogs: A Complete Guide. 320p. 1999. 37.95 (*1-86812-517-3*) Menasha Ridge.

Passmore, Nancy, ed. The Lunar Calendar: Dedicated to the Goddess in Her Many Guises. 32p. Date not set. 20.00 (*1-877920-10-X*) Luna Pr MA.

Passmore, Reginald, et al, eds. William Cullen & the 18th Century Medical World. (Illus.). 256p. 1993. text 51.00 (*0-7486-0302-6*, Pub. by Edinburgh U Pr) Col U Pr.

***Passno, Diane.** Feminist Mistake: Sorting Through the Rhetoric to Find God's Plan for Women. 250p. 2000. 15.99 (*1-56179-790-1*) Focus Family.

Passoff, Michelle. Lighten Up! Free Yourself from Clutter. LC 97-45040. 208p. 1998. pap. 13.00 (*0-06-095265-2*) HarpC.

Passoli, Robert. Book on the Open Theatre. LC 78-81296. 1970. 7.50 (*0-672-50775-7*, Bobbs) Macmillan.

Passons, W. Gestalt Approaches in Counseling. LC 74-22223. (C). 1975. pap. text 33.25 (*0-03-089421-2*) Harcourt Coll Pubs.

Passos, John Dos, see Dos Passos, John.

***Passot, Thierry & Sulem, P. L., eds.** Nonlinear MHD Waves & Turbulence: Proceedings of the Workshop Held in Nice, France, 1-4 December 1998. LC 99-57894. (Lecture Notes in Physics Ser.: Vol. 536). x, 385p. 1999. 89.90 (*3-540-66697-4*) Spr-Verlag.

Passow. For All Practical Purposes, Vol. 1. 4th ed. (C). 1996. 23.20 (*0-7167-2766-8*) St Martin.

Passow, ed. Educating the Gifted & Talented. (C). 1999. text. write for info. (*0-673-98270-X*) Addson-Wesley Educ.

Passow, A. Harry, jt. ed. see Flaxman, Erwin.

Passow, David. The Prime of Yiddish. LC 96-1786. 128 1p. 1995. 16.95 (*965-229-152-8*, Pub. by Gefen Pub Hse) Gefen Bks.

Passow, Eli. Schaum's Outline of Core Concepts of Calculus: A Friendly Approach. 215p. (C). 1996. pap. 15.95 (*0-07-048738-3*) McGraw.

Passow, Harry A., ed. Developing Programs for the Educationally Disadvantaged. LC 67-19026. 382p. 1968. reprint ed. pap. 118.50 (*0-608-08160-4*, 201694600004) Bks Demand.

Passow, Harry A., ed. see Work Conference on Curriculum & Teaching in Depres.

Passow, Harry A., ed. see Work Conference on Urban Education Staff.

Passow, Heidi. But I Can't Eat That: Kitchen Tested Recipes for People with Multiple Allergies. LC 93-90578. (Illus.). 240p. 1993. pap. 19.99 (*0-9637260-9-9*) Dragon Express.

Passow, Hermann, jt. ed. see Bamberg, Ernst.

Passport Books Editorial Staff, jt. compiled by see LEXUS Staff.

Passport Books Editors. Andalucia. (Illus.). 120p. 1993. pap. 17.95 (*0-8442-9970-7*, Passprt Bks) NTC Contemp Pub Co.

Passport Books Editors. Aprendamos Ingles Diccionario Ilustrado. (Let's Learn...Picture Ser.). (SPA., Illus.). 80p. (J). (gr. 4-7). 1995. 11.95 (*0-8442-7489-5*, 74895, Passprt Bks) NTC Contemp Pub Co.

Passport Books Editors. Italian Lakes. (Illus.). 120p. 1994. pap. 17.95 (*0-8442-9972-3*, 99723, Passprt Bks) NTC Contemp Pub Co.

— Provence & the Cote D'Azur. (Illus.). 120p. 1994. pap. 17.95 (*0-8442-9968-5*, Passprt Bks) NTC Contemp Pub Co.

— Tuscany & Umbria. (Illus.). 120p. 1994. pap. 17.95 (*0-8442-9971-5*, 99715, Passprt Bks) NTC Contemp Pub Co.

Passport Books Editors & Lye, Keith. Getting to Know United States. 2nd ed. LC 94-66260. (Getting to Know Ser.). (Illus.). 48p. (J). (gr. 4-7). 1994. pap. 9.95 (*0-8442-0724-1*, 07241, Passprt Bks) NTC Contemp Pub Co.

Passport Books Editors, ed. see Urban, Mike.

Passport Books Publishing Staff. My First Spanish & English Dictionary. (ENG & SPA.). (J). 1992. 12.15 (*0-606-02341-0*, Pub. by Turtleback) Demco.

Passport Books Staff. Aprendamos Espanol Diccionario Ilustrado. LC 97-44568. (SPA., Illus.). 72p. (J). (gr. 4-7). 1995. 11.95 (*0-8442-7499-2*, 74992, Natl Textbk Co) NTC Contemp Pub Co.

Passport Books Staff. Complete Multilingual Dictionary of Aviation & Aeronautical Terminology. (SPA, FRE & ENG., Illus.). 672p. 1994. pap. 49.95 (*0-8442-9109-9*) NTC Contemp Pub Co.

— Cuba. (Passport Essential Guide Ser.). (Illus.). 128p. 1998. pap. 8.95 (*0-8442-0087-5*, 00875, Passprt Bks) NTC Contemp Pub Co.

— Diccionario Practico de la Lengua Espanola del Nuevo Mundo.Tr. of Practical Dictionary of the Spanish of the New World. (SPA., Illus.). 274p. 1994. 10.95 (*0-8442-7968-4*, 79684, Passprt Bks) NTC Contemp Pub Co.

— Egypt: A Complete Guide. 1993. pap. 12.95 (*0-8442-9700-3*, Passprt Bks) NTC Contemp Pub Co.

— Essential Amsterdam. 2nd ed. (Essential Travel Guides Ser.). (Illus.). 128p. 1997. pap. text 7.95 (*0-8442-4799-5*, 47995, Passprt Bks) NTC Contemp Pub Co.

— Essential Bulgaria. 2nd ed. (Essential Travel Guides Ser.). (Illus.). 128p. 1997. pap. text 7.95 (*0-8442-4802-9*, 48029, Passprt Bks) NTC Contemp Pub Co.

— Essential Egypt. 2nd ed. (Essential Travel Guides Ser.). (Illus.). 128p. 1996. pap. text 7.95 (*0-8442-4803-7*, Passprt Bks) NTC Contemp Pub Co.

— Essential Florida. (Essential Travel Guides Ser.). (Illus.). 128p. 1998. pap. 8.95 (*0-8442-4936-X*, 4936X, Passprt Bks) NTC Contemp Pub Co.

— Essential Paris. (Essential Travel Guides Ser.). (Illus.). 94p. 1994. pap. 7.95 (*0-8442-8927-2*, Passprt Bks) NTC Contemp Pub Co.

— Essential Provence. (Essential Travel Guides Ser.). (Illus.). 128p. 1994. pap. 7.95 (*0-8442-8929-9*, Passprt Bks) NTC Contemp Pub Co.

— Essential Rome. (Essential Travel Guides Ser.). (Illus.). 128p. 1994. pap. 7.95 (*0-8442-8930-2*, Passprt Bks) NTC Contemp Pub Co.

— Essential Scotland. (Essential Travel Guides Ser.). 128p. 1994. pap. 7.95 (*0-8442-8932-9*, Passprt Bks) NTC Contemp Pub Co.

— Essential Thailand. (Essential Travel Guides Ser.). (Illus.). 128p. 1994. pap. 7.95 (*0-8442-8935-3*, 89353, Passprt Bks) NTC Contemp Pub Co.

— Essential Toronto. (Essential Travel Guides Ser.). 128p. 1995. pap. 7.95 (*0-8442-8936-1*, Passprt Bks) NTC Contemp Pub Co.

— Everyday Indonesian. (IND & ENG.). 224p. 1994. pap. 14.95 (*0-8442-9913-8*, 99138, Passprt Bks) NTC Contemp Pub Co.

— French for Beginners: Passport's Language Guides. (Language for Beginners Ser.). 48p. (J). 1999. pap. 12.95 incl. audio (*0-8442-1624-0*, 16240, Passprt Bks) NTC Contemp Pub Co.

— Handbook for Multilingual Business Writing. (ENG, FRE, GER, ITA & SPA., Illus.). 360p. 1993. 24.95 (*0-8442-9121-8*, NTC Business Bks) NTC Contemp Pub Co.

— Handbook for Multilingual Business Writing. 2nd ed. (ENG, FRE, GER, ITA & SPA., Illus.). 360p. 1994. pap. 17.95 (*0-8442-9122-6*, NTC Business Bks) NTC Contemp Pub Co.

— Indonesia: The All-in-One Travel & Language Guide. LC 97-40712. (Get Around in . . . Ser.). (IND., Illus.). 128p. 1998. pap. 8.95 (*0-8442-0168-5*, 01685) NTC Contemp Pub Co.

— Just Enough Hungarian: How to Get by & Be Easily Understood. (Phrase Bks.). (HUN., Illus.). 144p. 1994. pap. 4.95 (*0-8442-9519-1*, 95191, Passprt Bks) NTC Contemp Pub Co.

— Koh Samui: Thailand's Tropical Haven. (Illus.). 172p. 1994. pap. 14.95 (*0-8442-9698-8*, Passprt Bks) NTC Contemp Pub Co.

— Let's Learn: Spanish Word Book. (SPA., Illus.). 16p. (J). 1996. pap. 7.95 (*0-8442-7885-8*, 78858) NTC Contemp Pub Co.

— Malaysia: A Complete Guide. 1992. pap. 12.95 (*0-8442-9719-4*, Passprt Bks) NTC Contemp Pub Co.

— Map of Italy. 1991. pap. 9.95 (*0-8442-9594-9*) NTC Contemp Pub Co.

— My First Spanish & English Dictionary. LC 99-86167. (SPA & ENG., Illus.). 64p. (J). (gr. 4-7). 2000. pap. 6.95 (*0-8442-0055-7*, 00557, Natl Textbk Co) NTC Contemp Pub Co.

— New Zealand: A Complete Guide. 1991. pap. 12.95 (*0-8442-9722-4*, Passprt Bks) NTC Contemp Pub Co.

— NTC's Compact Swedish & English Dictionary. LC 97-2621. (ENG & SWE., Illus.). 800p. 1997. 24.95 (*0-8442-4959-9*, 49599, Natl Textbk Co) NTC Contemp Pub Co.

— Passport Road Atlas: Europe. 2nd ed. LC 93-86310. 162p. 1995. pap. 16.95 (*0-8442-9474-8*, Passprt Bks) NTC Contemp Pub Co.

— Resumes for Business Management Careers. LC 91-15449. (VGM Professional Resumes Ser.). (Illus.). vii, 151p. 1994. pap. 9.95 (*0-8442-8544-7*, 85447, VGM Career) NTC Contemp Pub Co.

— Resumes for College Students & Other Recent Graduates. 160p. 1994. pap. 9.95 (*0-8442-4150-4*, VGM Career) NTC Contemp Pub Co.

— Singapore: A Complete Guide. 1992. pap. 10.95 (*0-8442-9720-8*, Passprt Bks) NTC Contemp Pub Co.

Passport Books Staff, contrib. by. Portugal. LC 97-40727. (Get Around in . . . Ser.). (POR., Illus.). 128p. 1998. pap. 8.95 (*0-8442-0158-8*, 01588) NTC Contemp Pub Co.

— Spanish. LC 97-38600. (Get Around in . . . Ser.). (SPA., Illus.). 128p. 1998. pap. 8.95 (*0-8442-0153-7*, 01537) NTC Contemp Pub Co.

Passport Books Staff, ed. British English Picture Dictionary. (Let's Learn...Picture Dictionary Ser.). (Illus.). 72p. (J). (gr. 4-7). 1995. 9.95 (*0-8442-9114-5*, 91145) NTC Contemp Pub Co.

— Italian Picture Dictionary. (Let's Learn...Picture Dictionary Ser.). (ITA., Illus.). 72p. (J). 1990. 9.95 (*0-8442-8065-8*, 80658, Natl Textbk Co) NTC Contemp Pub Co.

— Let's Learn American English. LC 97-44570. (Let's Learn...Picture Dictionary Ser.). (Illus.). 72p. (J). 1995. 9.95 (*0-8442-5453-3*, 54533, Passprt Bks) NTC Contemp Pub Co.

— Let's Learn French. (Let's Learn...Picture Ser.). (FRE., Illus.). 72p. (J). 1995. 9.95 (*0-8442-1392-6*, 13926, Natl Textbk Co) NTC Contemp Pub Co.

— Let's Learn German. (Let's Learn...Picture Ser.). (GER., Illus.). 72p. (J). 1995. 9.95 (*0-8442-2167-8*, 21678, Passprt Bks) NTC Contemp Pub Co.

— Let's Learn Hebrew. LC 97-38801. (Let's Learn...Picture Dictionary Ser.). (HEB., Illus.). 72p. (J). (gr. 4-7). 1995. 11.95 (*0-8442-8490-4*, 84904, Passprt Bks) NTC Contemp Pub Co.

— Let's Learn Japanese Picture Dictionary: Elementary Through Junior High. LC 97-38795. (Let's Learn...Picture Dictionary Ser.). (JPN., Illus.). 80p. (J). (gr. 4-7). 1992. 11.95 (*0-8442-8494-7*, 84947, Natl Textbk Co) NTC Contemp Pub Co.

— Let's Learn Portuguese. LC 97-41121. (Let's Learn...Picture Dictionary Ser.). (POR., Illus.). 72p. (J). (gr. 4-7). 1995. 11.95 (*0-8442-4699-9*, 46999, Passprt Bks) NTC Contemp Pub Co.

— Spanish Picture Dictionary. LC 97-44567. (Let's Learn...Picture Dictionary Ser.). (SPA., Illus.). 72p. (J). (gr. 4-7). 1997. 9.95 (*0-8442-7558-1*, 75581, Natl Textbk Co) NTC Contemp Pub Co.

Passport Books Staff, jt. auth. see Bonavia, Judy.

Passport Books Staff, jt. auth. see Hunt, Lindsay.

Passport Publications Staff & Cimperman, Wayne. Passport to Palm Springs. 120p. 1994. 9.95 (*0-9645114-0-1*) Passprt Publ.

Passty, Jeanette N. Eros & Androgyny: The Legacy of Rose Macaulay. LC 85-46027. 1988. 34.50 (*0-8386-3284-X*) Fairleigh Dickinson.

Passuth, Krisztina. Moholy-Nagy. Heribert, Theirry. tr. from HUN. (GER., Illus.). 466p. (C). 1987. 118.00 (*3-8170-2005-8*, Pub. by Knstvrlag Weingrtn) Intl Bk Import.

— Moholy-Nagy. LC 83-50107. (Illus.). 300p. 1987. pap. 24.95 (*0-500-27449-5*, Pub. by Thames Hudson) Norton.

Passwater, Richard. All about Selenium: Frequently Asked Questions. (FAQs All about Health Ser.). 96p. 1999. mass mkt. 2.99 (*0-89529-967-4*, Avery) Penguin Putnam.

Passwater, Richard & South, James. 5 Htp: The Real Serotonin Story. (Good Health Guides Ser.). 48p. 1998. pap. 3.95 (*0-87983-939-2*, 39392K, Keats Publng) NTC Contemp Pub Co.

Passwater, Richard A. The Antioxidants. (Good Health Guide Ser.). 30p. 1985. pap. 3.50 (*0-87983-404-8*, Keats Publng) NTC Contemp Pub Co.

— The Antioxidants. (Good Health Guides Ser.). 48p. 1997. pap. 3.95 (*0-87983-787-X*, 3787XK, Keats Publng) NTC Contemp Pub Co.

— Beta-Carotene. Mindell, Earl S., ed. (Good Health Guide Ser.). 32p. 1984. pap. 2.95 (*0-87983-363-7*, Keats Publng) NTC Contemp Pub Co.

— Beta-Carotene & Other Carotenoids. (Good Health Guides Ser.). 48p. 1996. pap. 3.95 (*0-87983-705-5*, 37055K, Keats Publng) NTC Contemp Pub Co.

— Cancer Prevention & Nutritional Therapies. rev. ed. LC 78-57646. 250p. 1993. pap. 16.95 (*0-87983-607-5*, Keats Publng) NTC Contemp Pub Co.

— Chromium Picolinate. 48p. 1992. pap. 3.95 (*0-87983-588-5*, 35885K, Keats Publng) NTC Contemp Pub Co.

— Creatine. (Good Health Guides Ser.). 48p. 1997. pap. 3.95 (*0-87983-868-X*, 3868XK, Keats Publng) NTC Contemp Pub Co.

— Evening Primrose Oil. (Good Health Guide Ser.). 30p. 1982. pap. 3.95 (*0-87983-263-0*, 32630K, Keats Publng) NTC Contemp Pub Co.

— Fish Oils Update. (Good Health Guide Ser.). 31p. 1987. pap. 3.55 (*0-87983-432-3*, 34323K, Keats Publng) NTC Contemp Pub Co.

— Frequently Asked Questions All about Antioxidants. (FAQs All about Health Ser.). 96p. 1998. mass mkt. 2.99 (*0-89529-895-3*, Avery) Penguin Putnam.

— Frequently Asked Questions All about Pycnogenol. (FAQs All about Health Ser.). 1998. mass mkt. 2.99 (*0-89529-906-2*, Avery) Penguin Putnam.

— Glutathione. (Good Health Guides Ser.). Date not set. pap. 3.95 (*0-87983-887-6*, 38876K, Keats Publng) NTC Contemp Pub Co.

— GTF-Chromium. (Good Health Guide Ser.). 31p. 1982. pap. 2.95 (*0-87983-272-X*, Keats Publng) NTC Contemp Pub Co.

— Hair Analysis. (Good Health Guides Ser.). 48p. (Orig.). Date not set. pap. 3.95 (*0-87983-658-X*, 3658XK, Keats Publng) NTC Contemp Pub Co.

— Lipoic Acid: The Metabolic Antioxidant. (Good Health Guides Ser.). 48p. (Orig.). 1996. pap. 3.95 (*0-87983-720-9*, 37209K, Keats Publng) NTC Contemp Pub Co.

— The Longevity Factor: Chromium Picolinate. LC 93-5147. Orig. Title: Living Longer, Living Better, Slowing Aging with the Longevity Factor. 88p. (Orig.). 1993. pap. 4.95 (*0-87983-619-9*, 36199K, Keats Publng) NTC Contemp Pub Co.

— New Super Antioxidant Plus. 46p. 1992. pap. 3.95 (*0-87983-589-3*, 35893K, Keats Publng) NTC Contemp Pub Co.

— New Supernutrition. 337p. 1991. mass mkt. 6.99 (*0-671-70071-5*) PB.

— Selenium Against Cancer & AIDS. (Good Health Guides Ser.). 1997. reprint ed. pap. 3.95 (*0-87983-784-5*, 37845K, Keats Publng) NTC Contemp Pub Co.

Passwater, Richard A. & Fuller, John C. Building Muscle Mass, Performance & Health with HMB. (Good Health Guides Ser.). 48p. 1997. pap. 3.95 (*0-87983-867-1*, 38671K, Keats Publng) NTC Contemp Pub Co.

Passwater, Richard A. & Kandaswami, Chithan. Pycnogenol: The Super "Protector" Nutrient. 112p. (Orig.). 1994. pap. 4.95 (*0-87983-648-2*, 36482K, Keats Publng) NTC Contemp Pub Co.

Passwater, Richard A. & Mindell, Earl R. A Beginner's Introduction to Vitamins: The Fundamental Necessities for Growth & Maintenance of Life. (Good Health Guide Ser.). 32p. 1983. pap. 3.95 (*0-87983-338-6*, 33386K, Keats Publng) NTC Contemp Pub Co.

Passwater, Richard A., ed. see Bland, Jeffrey.

Passwater, Richard A., ed. see DiCyan, Erwin.

Passwater, Richard A., ed. see Garrison, Robert, Jr.

Passwater, Richard A., ed. see Goldbeck, Nikki.

Passwater, Richard A., ed. see Heinerman, John.

Passwater, Richard A., ed. see Kalita, Dwight K. & Wunderlich, Ray C.

Passwater, Richard A., ed. see Lee, William H.

Passwater, Richard A., ed. see Light, Marilyn H.

Passwater, Richard A., ed. see Mervyn, Len.

Passwater, Richard A., ed. see Mindell, Earl R.

Passwater, Richard A., ed. see Rosenberg, Harold S.

Passy, Albert. Sephardic Folk Dictionary, English-Ladino/Ladino-English. (ENG & LAD.). Date not set. 49.95 (*0-7859-9593-5*) Fr & Eur.

Passy, Jane. Cued Articulation. (C). 1990. pap. 10.95 (*0-86431-063-3*, Pub. by Aust Council Educ Res) Stylus Pub VA.

— Cued Vowels. (C). 1990. pap. 10.95 (*0-86431-062-5*, Pub. by Aust Council Educ Res) Stylus Pub VA.

Past, Ambar. The Sea on Its Side. Hirschman, Jack, tr. from SPA. & intro. by.Tr. of Mar Inclinida. 30p. (Orig.). 1994. pap. 7.00 (*0-942996-19-4*) Post Apollo Pr.

Pasta & Co. Staff. Pasta & Co., the Cookbook. Rosene, Marcella, ed. 223p. (Orig.). 1987. pap. 12.95 (*0-685-19027-7*) Pasta & Co Inc.

Pastalan, Leon A. Aging in Place: The Role of Housing & Social Supports. LC 90-34022. (Journal of Housing for the Elderly: Vol. 6, Nos. 1-2). 130p. 1990. text 39.95 (*0-86656-981-2*) Haworth Pr.

— Shelter & Service Issues for Aging Populations: International Perspectives. LC 97-16059. 177p. 1997. 49.95 (*0-7890-0314-7*) Haworth Pr.

Pastalan, Leon A., ed. Housing Decisions for the Elderly: To Move or Not to Move. (Journal of Housing for the Elderly: Vol. 11, No. 2). 175p. 1995. 29.95 (*1-56024-713-4*) Haworth Pr.

***Pastalan, Leon A., ed.** Making Aging in Place Work. LC 99-31598. (Journal of Housing for the Elderly: Vol. 16, No. 4). 130p. (C). 1999. 39.95 (*0-7890-0753-3*) Haworth Pr.

Pastalan, Leon A., ed. The Retirement Community Movement: Some Contemporary Issues. 81p. 1989. 24.95 (*0-86656-925-1*) Haworth Pr.

Pastalan, Leon A., intro. Optimizing Housing for the Elderly: Homes Not Houses. (Journal of Housing for the Elderly). 163p. 1991. text 39.95 (*1-56024-076-8*) Haworth Pr.

***Pastan, Amy.** Lure of the West. (Treasures from the Smithsonian American Art Museum). (Illus.). 112p. 2000. pap. 19.95 (*0-8230-0191-1*) Watsn-Guptill.

Pastan, Amy, jt. auth. see National Museum of American Art (U.S.) Staff.

Pastan, Ira H. & Willingham, Mark C., eds. Endocytosis. LC 85-3436. 344p. 1985. 89.50 (*0-306-41853-3*, Plenum Trade) Perseus Pubng.

Pastan, Ira H., jt. ed. see Jakoby, William B.

Pastan, Linda. Carnival Evening: New & Selected Poems, 1968-1998. LC 97-39860. 320p. 1998. 27.50 (*0-393-04631-1*) Norton.

— Carnival Evening: New & Selected Poems, 1968-1998. 1999. pap. 15.00 (*0-393-31927-X*) Norton.

— An Early Afterlife: Poems. 88p. 1996. pap. 10.00 (*0-393-31381-6*) Norton.

— Heroes in Disguise. 96p. 1992. pap. 8.95 (*0-393-30922-3*) Norton.

— The Imperfect Paradise. 1989. pap. 7.95 (*0-393-30524-4*) Norton.

— Pm/Am: New & Selected Poems. 128p. 1982. pap. 9.95 (*0-393-30055-2*) Norton.

Pasteels, J. M., ed. From Individual to Collective Behavior in Social Insects. (BioSeries-EXS: No. 54). 250p. 1987. 124.00 (*0-8176-1859-7*) Birkhauser.

Pastel Society of Canada Staff. Best of Canadian Pastels. (Illus.). 128p. 1999. 25.00 (*0-929552-16-4*, 31507, Pub. by Art Instr Assocs) F & W Pubns Inc.

Pasten-Bedingfeld, Henry. Heraldry. 1993. 15.98 (*1-55521-932-2*) Bk Sales Inc.

Pasten, Laura. The Tarantula Whisperer: A Celebrity Vet Shares Her Secrets to Communicating with Animals. LC 99-24541. 208p. 1999. pap. 11.95 (*1-57324-159-8*) Conari Press.

Pastene, Jerome. Three-Quarter Time: The Life & Music of the Strauss Family of Vienna. LC 76-91768. (Illus.). 307p. 1971. reprint ed. lib. bdg. 38.50 (*0-8371-3991-0*, PATQ, Greenwood Pr) Greenwood.

Paster, Gail K. The Body Embarrassed: Drama & the Disciplines of Shame in Early Modern England. LC 92-36855. (Illus.). 304p. 1993. text 47.50 (*0-8014-2776-2*); pap. text 16.95 (*0-8014-8060-4*) Cornell U Pr.

Paster, L., et al. The Jewish Women's Awareness Guide: Connections for the Second Wave of Jewish Feminism. 132p. (Orig.). 1992. pap. 9.25 (*0-930395-14-X*) Biblio NY.

Paster, Vera S., jt. auth. see Diggs, Anita.

Paster, Zorba & Meltsner, Susan. The Longevity Code: Your Personal Prescription for a Longer, Sweeter Life. 336p. 2001. 25.00 (*0-609-60360-4*) C Potter.

Pasteris, Jill D., jt. ed. see Morris, Ellen M.

Pasterkamp, Wim R. The Tyre As Sensor to Estimate Friction. (Illus.). 147p. 1997. pap. 45.00 (*90-407-1538-6*, Pub. by Delft U Pr) Coronet Bks.

Pasternack, Barbara, jt. auth. see Parisi, Barbara.

Pasternack, Barry A., jt. auth. see Lawrence, John A.

***Pasternack, Bruce A. & Viscio, Albert J.** The Centerless Corporation: A New Model for Transforming Your Organization for Growth & Prosperity. (Illus.). 311p. 1999. pap. 14.00 (*0-684-85199-7*, Fireside) S&S Trade Pap.

Pasternack, Bruce A. & Viscio, Albert J. The Centerless Corporation: Transforming Your Organization for Growth & Prosperity in the New Millenium. LC 97-32984. 320p. 1998. 24.50 (*0-684-83835-4*) S&S Trade.

Pasternack, Carol B. The Textuality of Old English Poetry. (Studies in Anglo-Saxon England: No. 13). (Illus.). 231p. (C). 1995. text 69.95 (*0-521-46549-4*) Cambridge U Pr.

Pasternack, Carol B., jt. ed. see Doane, A. N.

***Pasternack, Steve.** Mass Communication Law in New Mexico. 2nd ed. (State Law Ser.). 70p. 1999. pap. text 12.95 (*0-913507-82-2*) New Forums.

P

Pasternack, Susan, ed. see Mahony, Mary.

Pasternack, Victor & Practising Law Institute. How to Handle Your First Workers' Compensation Case. LC 98-207533. (Litigation Course Handbook Ser.). 160 p. 1998. write for info. (0-87224-435-0) PLI.

Pasternak. Oeuvres. (FRE.). 1990. lib. bdg. 150.00 (0-8288-3570-5, F119390) Fr & Eur.

Pasternak, Alexander. A Vanished Present: The Memoirs of Alexander. Slater, Ann P., ed. & tr. by. LC 88-43305. (Illus.). 238p. 1989. pap. 15.95 (0-8014-9576-8) Cornell U Pr.

— A Vanished Present: The Memoirs of Alexander Pasternak. Slater, Ann P., tr. LC 84-6532. (Helen & Kurt Wolff Bk.). (Illus.). 240p. 1985. 17.95 (0-15-193364-2) Harcourt.

Pasternak, Boris. Le Docteur Jivago. (FRE.). 1972. pap. 17.95 (0-7859-3984-9) Fr & Eur.

— Dr. Zhivago. 544p. 1991. 20.00 (0-679-40759-6) Everymns Lib.

— Doctor Zhivago. 576p. 1987. mass mkt. 5.95 (0-345-34100-7) Ballantine Pub Grp.

— Doctor Zhivago. 592p. 1997. pap. 15.00 (0-679-77438-6) Pantheon.

— Doctor Zhivago. 550p. 1991. reprint ed. lib. bdg. 36.95 (0-89966-839-9) Buccaneer Bks.

— Doctor Zhivago: A Critical Companion. Clowes, Edith W., ed. LC 95-31482. (Northwestern - AATSEEL Critical Companions to Russian Literature Ser.). 160p. (C). 1995. pap. text 14.95 (0-8101-1211-6) Northwestern U Pr.

— I Remember: Sketch for an Autobiography. Magarshack, David, tr. 204p. 1983. pap. 14.00 (0-674-43950-3) HUP.

— Karacsonyi Csillag: Kesei Versek, 1945-1969. LC 64-66430.Tr. of Christmas Star. (HUN.). 1965. pap. 5.00 (0-911050-25-6) Occidental.

— My Sister--Life. Boychuk, Bohdan, ed. & tr. by. from RUS. Rudman, Mark, tr. from RUS. 106p. 1993. reprint ed. pap. 13.95 (0-8101-1090-3) Northwestern U Pr.

— The Poems of Doctor Zhivago. Davie, Donald, ed. & tr. by. LC 76-1980. 204p. 1977. reprint ed. lib. bdg. 38.50 (0-8371-8294-8, PAPDZ, Greenwood Pr) Greenwood.

— Safe Conduct. LC 58-12799. 1958. pap. 9.95 (0-8112-0135-X, NDP77, Pub. by New Directions) Norton.

— Second Nature: Forty Six Poems. Navrozov, A., tr. LC 90-80796. 128p. 1990. 34.00 (0-7206-0751-5) Dufour.

— Seven Poems. 2nd ed. Kline, George L., tr. from RUS. LC 76-134742. (Keepsake Ser.). 1970. 15.00 (0-87775-083-1); pap. 6.95 (0-87775-005-X) Unicorn Pr.

Pasternak, Boris & Bobrov, Sergei. Boris Pasternak i Sergei Bobrov: Pis'ma Chetyrekh Desiatiletii. Rushkovskaia, M. A., ed. (Stanford Slavic Studies: Vol. 10). (RUS.). 163p. (Orig.). 1996. pap. 20.00 (1-57201-017-7) Berkeley Slavic.

***Pasternak, Boris & Pasternak, Leonid.** Pis'ma k Roditeliam i Sestram. Pasternak, E. B. & Pasternak, E. V., eds. (Stanford Slavic Studies: Vols. 18 & 19). (RUS., Illus.). 658p. 1998. pap. 70.00 (1-57201-047-9) Berkeley Slavic.

Pasternak, Boris, jt. auth. see Center for Learning Network Staff.

Pasternak, Boris L., et al. Boris Pasternaks Lehrjahre: Neopublikovannye Filosofskie Konspekty I Zametki Borisa Pasternaka, 2 vols. (Stanford Slavic Studies: Vol. 11, Nos. 1 & 2). (GER & RUS.). 799p. (Orig.). 1996. pap. 130.00 (1-57201-027-4) Berkeley Slavic.

Pasternak, Burton. Guests in the Dragon. LC 83-5194. (Illus.). 224p. 1983. text 68.50 (0-231-05610-9) Col U Pr.

Pasternak, Burton & Ember, Carol R. Sex, Gender & Kinship: A Cross-Cultural Perspective. LC 96-41018. 324p. (C). 1996. pap. text 35.33 (0-13-206533-9) P-H.

***Pasternak, Ceel.** Cool Careers for Girls in Air & Space. (Illus.). (J). 2000. pap. 12.95 (1-57023-146-X) Impact VA.

— Cool Careers for Girls in Computers. (J). 1998. 19.95 (1-57023-106-0) Impact VA.

— Cool Careers for Girls in Health. LC 99-26373. (Illus.). (YA). 1999. 19.95 (1-57023-125-7) Impact VA.

— Cool Careers for Girls in Sports. LC 98-48613. (J). 1998. 19.95 (1-57023-107-9) Impact VA.

Pasternak, Ceel. Cool Careers for Girls in Sports. LC 98-48613. (Cool Careers for Girls Ser.). 135p. (J). 1999. pap. 12.95 (1-57023-104-4, Pub. by Impact VA) Natl Bk Netwk.

***Pasternak, Ceel.** Cool Careers for Girls with Animals. LC 98-48086. 1998. 19.95 (1-57023-108-7) Impact VA.

— In Construction. LC 99-58992. (Cool Careers for Girls Ser.). (Illus.). (YA). 2000. pap. 12.95 (1-57023-131-1) Impact VA.

— In Performing Arts. (Cool Careers for Girls Ser.). (Illus.). (YA). 2000. pap. 12.95 (1-57023-132-X) Impact VA.

***Pasternak, Ceel & Thornbur, Linda.** Cool Careers for Girls in Food. LC 99-43040. (Illus.). 128p. (J). (gr. 5 up). 1999. pap. 12.95 (1-57023-120-6) Impact VA.

***Pasternak, Ceel & Thornburg, Linda.** Cool Careers for Girls Engineering. LC 99-16717. (Cool Careers for Girls Ser.). (Illus.). 132p. (YA). (gr. 5-8). 1999. pap. 12.95 (1-57023-119-2) Impact VA.

Pasternak, Ceel & Thornburg, Linda. Cool Careers for Girls in Computers. (Cool Careers for Girls Ser.). 125p. (J). 1999. pap. 12.95 (1-57023-103-6, Pub. by Impact VA) Natl Bk Netwk.

***Pasternak, Ceel & Thornburg, Linda.** Cool Careers for Girls in Engineering. LC 99-16717. (Cool Careers for Girls Ser.). (Illus.). 132p. (YA). (gr. 5-8). 1999. 19.95 (1-57023-126-5) Impact VA.

Pasternak, Ceel & Thornburg, Linda. Cool Careers for Girls in Health. LC 99-26373. (Cool Careers for Girls Ser.). (Illus.). 146p. (J). (gr. 6-9). 1999. pap. 12.95 (1-57023-118-4) Impact VA.

— Cool Careers for Girls with Animals. LC 98-48086. (Cool Careers for Girls Ser.). 145p. 1999. pap. 12.95 (1-57023-105-2, Pub. by Impact VA) Natl Bk Netwk.

***Pasternak, Charles A.** Biosciences 2000: Current Aspects & Prospects for the Next Millennium. LC 99-34736. (Series on Cell & Molecular Biology). 1999. write for info. (1-86094-195-8, Pub. by Imperial College) World Scientific Pub.

Pasternak, Charles A. Biosciences 2000: Current Aspects & Prospects for the Next Millennium. 300p. 1999. 58.00 (981-02-3780-4) World Scientific Pub.

— The Molecules Within Us: Our Body in Health & Disease. LC 98-26173. (Illus.). 350p. (C). 1998. 26.95 (0-306-45987-6, Plenum Trade) Perseus Pubng.

Pasternak, Charles A., ed. Monovalent Cations in Biological Systems. 408p. 1990. lib. bdg. 268.00 (0-8493-4775-0, QP531) CRC Pr.

— Radioimmunoassay in Clinical Biochemistry. LC 76-675546. 317p. reprint ed. pap. 98.30 (0-608-14059-7, 202402500035) Bks Demand.

Pasternak, Dov & San Pedro, Anthony, eds. Biosalinity in Action: Bioproduction with Saline Water. (Developments in Plant & Soil Sciences Ser.). 1985. text 247.50 (90-247-3159-3) Kluwer Academic.

Pasternak, E. B., ed. see Pasternak, Boris & Pasternak, Leonid.

Pasternak, E. V., ed. see Pasternak, Boris & Pasternak, Leonid.

Pasternak, Gavril W., ed. The Opiate Receptors. LC 87-3095. (Receptors Ser.). (Illus.). 520p. 1988. 125.00 (0-89603-120-9) Humana.

Pasternak, Gavril W., jt. ed. see Kuhar, Michael J.

Pasternak, Grigory I. & Raleigh, Eugene. To Reach This Season: A Russians Odyssey to the West. LC 84-82476. 241p. 1985. pap. 12.95 (0-943376-23-8) Magnes Mus.

Pasternak, Jack J. An Introduction to Human Molecular Genetics: Mechanisms of Inherited Diseases. unabridged ed. LC 99-26154. (Illus.). 500p. (C). 1999. text 59.95 (1-891786-03-2) Fitzgerald Sci.

Pasternak, Jack J., jt. auth. see Glick, Bernard R.

Pasternak, Joseph F., jt. auth. see Holmes, Deborah L.

***Pasternak, Josephine.** Indefinability: An Essay in the Philosophy of Cognition. 141p. 1999. 26.00 (87-7289-531-4, Pub. by Mus Tusculanum) Intl Spec Bk.

Pasternak, Josephine. Pasternak Leonid, 1862-1945. 1982. pap. 20.00 (0-905836-34-0, Pub. by Museum Modern Art) St Mut.

Pasternak, Judith. Dixieland: The Birth of Jazz. (CD Ser.). 1995. pap. 16.98 incl. audio (1-56799-236-6, Friedman-Fairfax) M Friedman Pub Grp Inc.

***Pasternak, Judith.** Paris. LC 99-56402. (Timeless Places Ser.). (Illus.). 96p. 2000. 17.95 (1-56799-926-3, Friedman-Fairfax) M Friedman Pub Grp Inc.

Pasternak, Leonid, jt. auth. see Pasternak, Boris.

Pasternak, Mindy, et al. Universal Trail Assessment Coordinator Training Workshop: Training Manual. rev. ed. (Illus.). 62p. (Orig.). 1996. pap. text 30.00 (1-882632-06-0) PAX Pr.

Pasternak, Monique. Flying on the Wings of Aleph: A Tikkun. 76p. (Orig.). 1988. pap. write for info. (0-945646-07-0) Ocean Star Pubns.

Pasternak, Velvel. Jerusalem in Song. 1997. 39.95 (0-933676-42-5) Tara Pubns.

— The Jewish Fake Book. (Illus.). 184p. pap. 19.95 (0-933676-69-7, HL00330350) H Leonard.

— Jewish Holidays in Song. 1998. pap. 14.95 (0-933676-50-6) Tara Pubns.

— Ultimate Jewish Piano Book. 1999. pap. text 24.95 (0-933676-96-4) Tara Pubns.

— World's Most Popular Jewish Songs Vol. 1. 1998. pap. 14.95 (0-933676-73-5) Tara Pubns.

— World's Most Popular Jewish Songs Vol. 2. 1998. pap. 14.95 (0-933676-74-3) Tara Pubns.

Pasternak, Velvel, ed. see Friedman, Debbie.

Pasternak, Yevgeny, ed. see Rilke, Rainer Maria, et al.

Pasternoster, Raymond, jt. auth. see Bachman, Ronet.

***Pasteur, Frank.** Five Pennies for a Nickel. (Illus.). 228p. 1999. pap. 19.95 (0-938041-46-0) Arc Pr AR.

Pasteur, Louis & Lister, Joseph. Germ Theory & Its Application to Medicine & on the Antiseptic Principle of the Practice. 144p. 1996. pap. text 7.95 (1-57392-065-7) Prometheus Bks.

Pasteur, Nicole, et al. Practical Isozyme Genetics. 215p. 1988. text 52.95 (0-470-21155-5) P-H.

Pastides, Harris. Conducting Epidemiological Research. 1999. 74.95 (0-87371-558-6, L558) Lewis Pubs.

Pastier, John. Cesar Pelli. (Illus.). 120p. 1980. 89.50 (0-8230-7414-5) Elliots Bks.

***Pastime, Publications.** Scotland: Home of Golf. 1999. pap. 9.95 (1-873163-65-7) Pastime Pubns.

***Pastime Publications Staff.** Scotland, Home of Golf 2000. (Illus.). 2000. pap. 9.95 (1-873163-67-3) Pastime Pubns.

Pastin, Mark J. The Hotline Handbook. Brecto, Christina M. & Goldberg, Elisa M., eds. LC 96-72260. 55p. (Orig.). 1996. pap. 125.00 (0-9656061-0-4) Coun of Ethical.

Pastin, Mark J., jt. ed. see Youngstrom, Nina.

Pastine, Maureen, ed. Access in the Virtual Library. LC 97-38860. 225p. 1997. 49.95 (0-7890-0385-6) Haworth Pr.

— Collection Development: Past & Future. LC 96-32318. (Collection Management Ser.: Vol. 21, Nos. 2/3). 248p. (C). 1996. 34.95 (1-56024-825-4) Haworth Pr.

Pastine, Maureen & Katz, Bill, eds. Integrating Library Skills into the General Education Curriculum. (Reference Librarian Ser.: No. 24). 334p. 1994. 49.95 (0-86656-841-7) Haworth Pr.

Pastine, Maureen, jt. ed. see Huston, Mary M.

Pastis, Steven, jt. auth. see Levy, Nathan.

Pastman, Robert A., ed. Randax Graduate School Directory. LC 75-41653. 303p. 1976. lib. bdg. 21.50 (0-914880-06-3) Educ Guide.

Pasto, Daniel G. & Johnson, Carl R. Organic Structure Determination. (C). 1969. text 55.00 (0-13-640854-0) P-H.

Pasto, David, tr. see Juana Ines de la Cruz, Sor.

Paston, George. Social Caricature in the Eighteenth-Century. LC 67-12467. (Illus.). 1972. reprint ed. 54.95 (0-405-08840-X) Ayer.

— A Writer of Books. LC 98-19500. 258p. 1999. pap. 15.00 (0-89733-465-5) Academy Chi Pubs.

***Paston, George.** A Writer of Books. LC 98-19500. 258p. 1999. 35.00 (0-89733-466-3) Academy Chi Pubs.

Paston-Williams, Sara. Art of Dining: A History of Cooking & Eating. (Illus.). 348p. 1994. 49.50 (0-8109-1940-0, Pub. by Abrams) Time Warner.

— A Book of Historical Recipes. (Illus.). 60p. 1996. pap. 17.95 (0-7078-0240-7, Pub. by Natl Trust) Trafalgar.

***Paston-Williams, Sara.** Jams, Preserves & Edible Gifts. (Illus.). 160p. 2000. 24.95 (0-7078-0274-1, Pub. by Natl Trust) Trafalgar.

Paston-Williams, Sara. The National Trust Book of Fish Cookery. (Illus.). 160p. 1988. 17.95 (0-7078-0093-5, Pub. by Natl Trust) Trafalgar.

***Pastor.** Centurys End. 464p. 2000. pap. 18.00 (0-465-05476-5, Pub. by Basic) HarpC.

Pastor, jt. auth. see Frieden.

Pastor, Beatriz. Discursos Narratives de la Conquista: Mitifacacion y Emergencia. limited ed. (Rama Ser.). (SPA.). 400p. 1988. 25.00 (0-910061-36-X, 1507) Ediciones Norte.

— Roberto Arlt y la Rebelion Alienada. LC 80-70560. (SPA.). 128p. 1980. pap. 8.00 (0-935318-05-4) Edins Hispamerica.

***Pastor, Ben.** Liar Moon. 230p. 2001. 25.00 (1-929871-01-5) Van Neste.

Pastor, Ben. Lumen: A Novel. LC 98-40703. 279p. 1999. 24.00 (0-9657639-4-3) Van Neste.

Pastor, Carol. Food Magic: Easy Ideas for Pastry Dishes. LC 95-44990. 112p. 1996. 29.95 (0-470-23606-X) Wiley.

— Pastry Magic. 96p. 1996. 29.95 (0-470-23610-8) Wiley.

Pastor, Irene. Silent Legacy. 208p. 2000. pap. 14.95 (0-88739-290-3) Creat Arts Bk.

Pastor, Iris & Levine, Bev. Slices, Bites & Other Facts of Life. (Illus.). 364p. (Orig.). 1996. pap. 12.95 (0-9652832-0-8) Ladies Ink.

Pastor, Jack. Land & Economy in Ancient Palestine. LC 96-41705. 304p. (C). 1997. 75.00 (0-415-15960-1) Routledge.

Pastor, Jose C., tr. see Smook, Gary A.

Pastor, Larry, jt. auth. see Pastore, Michael.

Pastor, Manuel, Jr. Capital Flight & the Latin American Debt Crisis. 45p. 1990. 12.00 (0-944826-19-9) Economic Policy Inst.

***Pastor, Manuel.** Regions that Work: How Cities & Suburbs Can Grow Together. LC 00-44717. (Globalization & Community Ser.). (Illus.). 2000. pap. write for info. (0-8166-3340-1) U of Minn Pr.

Pastor, Maria A. & Artieda, Julio, eds. Time, Internal Clocks & Movement. LC 96-18161. (Advances in Psychology Ser.: Vol. 115). 324p. 1996. text 142.00 (0-444-82114-7, North Holland) Elsevier.

Pastor, Peter. Hungary Between Wilson & Lenin: The Hungarian Revolution of 1918-1919 & the Big Three. 191p. 1976. text 52.50 (0-914710-13-3, Pub. by East Eur Monographs) Col U Pr.

Pastor, Peter, ed. Revolutions & Interventions in Hungary & Its Neighbor States, 1918-1919. 320p. 1988. text 63.00 (0-88033-137-2, Pub. by East Eur Monographs) Col U Pr.

Pastor, Peter & Williamson, Samuel R., Jr. Essays on World War I: Origins & Prisoners of War. (East European Monographs: No. 126). 264p. 1983. text 59.50 (0-88033-015-5, Pub. by East Eur Monographs) Col U Pr.

Pastor, Peter, ed. see Fodor, Andras, et al.

Pastor, Peter, jt. ed. see Kiraly, B. K.

Pastor, Peter, jt. ed. see Williamson, Samuel R., Jr.

Pastor, Reyna & Carle, M. Historia de Espana Vol. 10: Los Reinos Cristianos en los Siglos XI y XII V.1 Economias, Sociedades, Instituciones. (SPA.). 478p. 1992. 189.50 (84-239-4812-9) Elliots Bks.

Pastor, Reyna, ed. see Pidal, Ramon M.

Pastor, Robert A. Condemned to Repetition: The United States & Nicaragua. LC 88-12663. (Illus.). 446p. 1988. reprint ed. pap. 138.30 (0-608-07640-6, 2059956) Bks Demand.

— Integration with Mexico: Options for U. S. Policy in the 21st Century. LC 92-44930. 1993. 8.95 (0-87078-328-9) Century Foundation.

Pastor, Robert A., ed. A Century's Journey: How the Great Powers Shape the World. LC 99-40493. 400p. 1999. 32.50 (0-465-05475-7, Pub. by Basic) HarpC.

Pastor, Robert A. & Carter, Jimmy, eds. Democracy in the Americas: Stopping the Pendulum. LC 89-1781. 262p. 1989. 49.50 (0-8419-1182-7); pap. 24.50 (0-8419-1183-5) Holmes & Meier.

Pastor, Robert A. & Fernandez de Castro, Rafael, eds. The Controversial Pivot: The U. S. Congress & North America. LC 98-25372. 200p. 1998. 39.95 (0-8157-6924-5); pap. 16.95 (0-8157-6923-7) Brookings.

Pastor, Rodolfo. Historia de Centroamerica (History of Central America) (SPA.). 272p. 1988. pap. 8.99 (968-12-0382-8, Pub. by Fondo) Continental Bk.

Pastor, Xavier. The Ships of Christopher Columbus. (Anatomy of the Ship Ser.). (Illus.). 128p. 1992. 39.95 (1-55750-755-4) Naval Inst Pr.

Pastoral Publications Staff. Your Guide to a Catholic Funeral. LC 97-177328. 24p. 1997. pap. text 2.95 (0-7648-0137-6) Liguori Pubns.

Pastoral Publiction Redemptorist Staff. Catholic Prayers & Devotions. LC 98-66645. 64p. 1998. pap. 1.95 (0-7648-0276-3) Liguori Pubns.

Pastore, Ann L., jt. ed. see Maguire, Kathleen.

Pastore, Garry. You're Not in Mom's Kitchen Anymore! College Cooking for the Dorming Gourmet. 1997. pap. text 9.95 (1-890638-00-5) Ramholtz Bks.

Pastore, Jorqia. Shouting Nothings. (Illus.). 101p. 1997. pap. 10.00 (0-9660921-0-4, 921-0) UNITEL.

Pastore, Jose. Inequality & Social Mobility in Brazil. Oxley, Robert M., tr. from SPA. LC 81-69826. 213p. reprint ed. pap. 66.10 (0-608-07018-1, 206722500009) Bks Demand.

Pastore, Jose & Haller, Archibald O. Inequality & Social Mobility in Brazil. LC 81-69826. 240p. (C). 1982. reprint ed. text 35.00 (0-299-08830-8) U of Wis Pr.

Pastore, Judith L., ed. Confronting AIDS Through Literature: The Responsibilities of Representation. LC 92-31606. 272p. 1993. text 39.95 (0-252-01989-X); pap. text 12.95 (0-252-06294-9) U of Ill Pr.

Pastore, Lisa M. & MacDorman, Marian F. Infant Mortality by Hispanic Origin of Mother, 20 States, 1985-87 Birth Cohorts. LC 95-25370. (Vital & Health Statistics, Series 20, Data from the National Vital Statistics System: No. 27). 1995. write for info. (0-8406-0510-2) Natl Ctr Health Stats.

Pastore, Mary & Deneen, Lawrence J. Escape from Disability: Best Kept Secrets, Injured Workers Win. LC 87-63296. 107p. (Orig.). 1988. pap. 8.95 (0-9614877-2-0) Rehab Pubns.

Pastore, Michael. Dynamite Counselors Don't Explode! A Complete Survival Course for Child-Care Workers & Camp Counselors. LC 92-82030. 128p. (Orig.). 1996. reprint ed. pap. 14.95 (0-927379-64-3, ZP 50) Zorba Pr.

— Lark's Magic. LC 89-51204. (Illus.). 113p. (YA). (gr. 4-12). 1990. pap. 10.00 (0-927379-36-8, ZP36) Zorba Pr.

— You're Ugly & Your Mother Dresses You Funny: 101 Problems in Child Maintenance for Everyone Who Works with Kids. LC 97-61978. 128p. 1998. pap. 20.95 (0-927379-96-1, ZP 101) Zorba Pr.

— Zenlightenment! Insights into the Art of Living Miraculously. Umeboshi, Hokku, tr. LC 89-50097. (Illus.). 104p. (Orig.). 1989. pap. 125.00 (0-927379-00-7) Zorba Pr.

Pastore, Michael & Pastor, Larry. Zen in the Art of Child Maintenance. LC 92-82027. 120p. (Orig.). 1993. pap. 14.95 (0-927379-28-7, ZP 99) Zorba Pr.

Pastore, Michael A. Networking Essentials. LC 97-45352. (Rapid Review Study Guides Ser.). 200p. 1997. pap. 29.95 incl. cd-rom (1-882419-90-1, Pub. by News Four-Hund) IPG Chicago.

— Rapid Review Study Guides, 7 vols. 1997. pap. 29.95 (1-882419-89-8) News Four-Hund.

— Systems Management Server 1.2. LC 98-8862. (Rapid Review Study Guides Ser.). 200p. 1998. pap. 29.95 incl. cd-rom (1-882419-96-0) News Four-Hund.

— TCP/IP for Microsoft Windows NT. LC 97-45458. (Rapid Review Study Guides Ser.). 200p. 1998. pap. 29.95 incl. cd-rom (1-882419-94-4) News Four-Hund.

— Windows 95. LC 97-45353. (Rapid Review Study Guides Ser.). 200p. 1997. pap. 29.95 incl. cd-rom (1-882419-91-X) News Four-Hund.

— Windows NT 4.0 Server. (Rapid Review Study Guides Ser.). 200p. 1998. pap. 29.95 incl. cd-rom (1-882419-93-6, Pub. by News Four-Hund) IPG Chicago.

— Windows NT 4.0 Workstation. LC 97-45354. (Rapid Review Study Guides Ser.). 200p. 1998. pap. 29.95 incl. cd-rom (1-882419-92-8, Pub. by News Four-Hund) IPG Chicago.

— Windows NT Server 4.0 in the Enterprise. (Rapid Review Study Guides Ser.). 200p. 1998. pap. 29.95 incl. cd-rom (1-882419-95-2) News Four-Hund.

Pastore, Michael A. & Karow, Bill. A+ Certification Study System. LC 98-71152. 936p. 1999. student ed. 59.99 (0-7645-3166-2) IDG Bks.

***Pastore, Robert R.** Stock Options: An Authoritative Guide to Incentive & Nonqualified Stock Options. 2nd ed. 150p. 2000. 39.95 (0-9668899-2-4) PCM Cap Pub.

Pastore, Rose M. The True Miracles of God. (Illus.). 128p. 1998. pap. 13.00 (0-8059-4288-2) Dorrance.

Pastore, Stephen, ed. see Crane, Stephen.

Pastore, Stephen, ed. see Lewis, Sinclair & Graham, Tom.

Pastore, Stephen R. & Garry, Angela. Helene Hanff: A Life in Books. Date not set. pap. 19.95 (0-9656275-1-9) S R Pastore.

Pastore, Stephen R. & Hutchisson, James M. Sinclair Lewis: A Descriptive Bibliography. (Illus.). 397p. 1997. 59.95 (0-9656275-0-0) YaleBooks.

Pastore, Stephen R., jt. auth. see Hanff, Helene.

Pastore, Stephen R., jt. auth. see Lewis, Sinclair.

Pastore, Vera A. The Fredericksburg Region: A Leader in Virginia. (Illus.). 184p. 1999. 34.95 (1-890291-09-9) Platinum Pubng.

Pastorek, Joseph G., II, ed. Obstetric & Gynecologic Infectious Disease. LC 93-24716. 858p. 1993. text 129.00 (0-7817-0023-X) Lppncott W & W.

— Obstetric & Gynecologic Infectious Disease. LC 93-24716. (Illus.). 824p. reprint ed. pap. 200.00 (0-608-09764-0, 206993700007) Bks Demand.

Pastorek, Norman J. Blepharoplasty. 3rd ed. LC 94-40392. (Self-Instructional Package Ser.). (Illus.). 137p. 1994. pap. text 25.00 (1-56772-013-7) AAO-HNS.

Pastorek, Sheryl. Caps, Commas, & Other Things. 264p. 1982. pap. 20.00 (0-87879-325-9) Acad Therapy.

Pastorelli, Pietro, ed. Vol. Primo, 1891-1913. (Opera Omnia di - The Complete Works of Sidney Sonnino Ser.). xvi, 592p. 1982. write for info. (0-7006-0225-9) U Pr of KS.

P

An Asterisk (*) at the beginning of an entry indicates that the title is appearing for the first time.

— Vol. Secondo, 1914-1916. (Opera Omnia di - The Complete Works of Sidney Sonnino Ser.). xvi, 776p. 1975. write for info. (*0-7006-0139-2*) U Pr of KS.

— Vol. Terzo, 1916-1922. (Opera Omnia di - The Complete Works of Sidney Sonnino Ser.). (ITA.). xvi, 788p. 1976. write for info. (*0-7006-0150-3*) U Pr of KS.

Pastoret, Paul-Pierre, et al, eds. Handbook of Vertebrate Immunology. LC 97-45873. (Illus.). 704p. 1998. boxed set 150.00 (*0-12-546401-0*) Acad Pr.

— Veterinary Vaccinology. LC 97-11156. 882p. 1997. 200.75 (*0-444-81968-1*) Elsevier.

Pastorino. What Is Psychology? (C). 2001. text. write for info. (*0-15-507333-8*); pap. text, student ed. write for info. (*0-15-507336-2*) Harcourt Coll Pubs.

Pastorino, Torres. Minutos de Sabiduria. large type ed. (SPA., Illus.). 310p. 1997. pap. 5.98 (*968-13-2342-4*, Pub. by Edit Diana) Libros Fronteras.

Pastorius, Francis D. Description of Pennsylvania, Seventeen Hundred. 1993. reprint ed. lib. bdg. 89.00 (*0-7812-5816-2*) Rprt Serv.

Pastorius, Kay. Cruising Cuisine: Fresh Food from the Galley. LC 97-17094. (Illus.). 230p. 1997. pap. 18.95 (*0-07-048703-0*) Intl Marine.

Pastors, Joyce Green, see Holler, Harold J. & Green Pastors, Joyce.

Pastoureau, Michel. Heraldry: An Introduction to a Noble Tradition. Garvie, Francisca, tr. LC 96-49756. (Discoveries Ser.). (Illus.). 144p. 1997. pap. 12.95 (*0-8109-2830-2*, Pub. by Abrams) Time Warner.

Pastoureau, Michel, jt. auth. see Duchet-Suchaux, Gaston.

Pastras, Philip, tr. see Ritsos, Yannis.

Pastre, Olivier. Multinationals: Bank & Corporation Relationships. Altman, Edward I. & Walter, Ingo I., eds. LC 81-80869. (Contemporary Studies in Economic & Financial Analysis: Vol. 28). 316p. 1981. 78.50 (*0-89232-219-5*) Jai Pr.

Pastron, Allen G. & Walsh, Michael R. Archaeological Excavations at CA-SFR-112, the Stevenson Street Shellmound, San Francisco, California. Vol. 21. (Archives of California Prehistory Ser.: No. 21). (Illus.). 137p. (Orig.). (C). 1988. pap. text 15.00 (*1-55567-057-1*) Coyote Press.

— Archaeological Excavations at CA-SFR-113, the Market Street Shell Midden, San Francisco, California. Breschini, G. I. & Haversat, Trudy, eds. (Archives of California Prehistory Ser.: Vol. 25). (Illus.). vi, 92p. (Orig.). (C). 1988. pap. 11.56 (*1-55567-061-X*) Coyote Press.

Pastrovicchi, Angelo. St. Joseph of Copertino. LC 79-91298. 135p. 1994. reprint ed. pap. 6.00 (*0-89555-135-7*) TAN Bks Pubs.

Pastubov, V. D. A Guide to the Practice of International Conferences. (Studies in the Administration of International Law & Organization). 1945. reprint ed. 30.00 (*0-527-00882-6*) Periodicals Srv.

Pastuchiv, Olga. Minas & the Fish. LC 96-24861. (Illus.). 32p. (J). 1997. 14.95 (*0-395-79756-X*) HM.

— Minas Lived by the Sea. LC 97-10126. 96p. (J). (ps-4). 1998. 16.00 (*0-395-72290-X*) HM.

Pasture, Edmee E. De La, see De La Pasture, Edmee E.

Pasture, Patrick. Christian Trade Unionism in Europe Since 1968: Tensions Between Identity & Practice. 208p. 1994. 66.95 (*1-85628-950-8*, Pub. by Avebry) Ashgate Pub Co.

Pasture, Patrick, et al, eds. The Lost Perspective? Trade Unions Between Ideology & Social Action in the New Europe Vol. 1: Ideological Persistence in National Traditions. (Perspectives on Europe Ser.: Vol. 1). 304p. 1996. 72.95 (*1-85972-080-3*, Pub. by Avebry) Ashgate Pub Co.

— The Lost Perspective? Trade Unions Between Ideology & Social Action in the New Europe Vol. 2: Significance of Ideology in European Trade Unionism. (Perspectives on Europe Ser.). 416p. 1996. 85.95 (*1-85972-330-6*, Pub. by Avebry) Ashgate Pub Co.

— The Lost Perspectives? Trade Unions Between Ideology & Social Action in the New Europe, Vol. 1 & 2. (Perspectives on Europe Ser.). 720p. 1996. 149.95 (*1-85972-331-4*, Pub. by Avebry) Ashgate Pub Co.

Pasture, Patrick & Verberckmoes, Johan, eds. Working-Class Internationalism & the Appeal of National Identity: Historical Debates & Current Perspectives. LC 99-191149. 256p. 1998. 65.00 (*1-85973-281-X*, Pub. by Berg Pubs) NYU Pr.

Pastuszek, Eric J. & French, Robert B. Is the Fetus Human? LC 92-82132. (Illus.). 87p. 1993. pap. 7.00 (*0-89555-486-0*) TAN Bks Pubs.

Pastva, Loretta. The Church: A Spirit-Filled People, Teacher's Annotated Edition. rev. ed. (Light of the World Ser.). 1999. pap. write for info. (*0-02-655835-1*, Benzger Pub) Glencoe.

— Great Religions of the World. (Illus.). 190p. 1986. teacher ed. 14.95 (*0-88489-176-3*) St Marys.

— The Hebrew Scriptures: Called by the Father, Teacher's Annotated Edition. rev. ed. (Light of the World Ser.). 1999. pap. write for info. (*0-02-655832-7*, Benzger Pub) Glencoe.

— Jesus of Nazareth: The Mystery Revealed, Teacher's Annotated Edition. rev. ed. (Light of the World Ser.). 1999. pap. write for info. (*0-02-655822-X*, Benzger Pub) Glencoe.

— Living a Moral Life: Gifted & Growing, Teacher's Annotated Edition. rev. ed. (Light of the World Ser.). 1999. pap. write for info. (*0-02-655825-4*, Benzger Pub) Glencoe.

— Worship & Sacraments: We Celebrate, We Praise, Teacher's Annotated Edition. rev. ed. (Light of the World Ser.). 1999. pap. write for info. (*0-02-655828-9*, Benzger Pub) Glencoe.

Pastva, Mary L. Growing up to God: A Guide for Teenagers on the Sacrement of Reconciliation. LC 83-15538. 82p. (Orig.). 1983. pap. 4.95 (*0-8189-0455-0*) Alba.

Pasvolsky, Leo & Viner, Jacob. Current Monetary Issues. LC 82-48212. (Gold, Money, Inflation & Deflation Ser.). 235p. 1983. lib. bdg. 28.00 (*0-8240-5250-1*) Garland.

Paszczyk, Linda. 1999 U. S. Master Employee Benefits Guide. 700p. 1998. pap. 49.00 (*0-8080-0301-1*) CCH INC.

Paszek, Lawrence J. A Guide to Documentary Sources. (Reference Ser.). (Illus.). 245p. 1986. reprint ed. write for info. (*0-912799-21-8*) AFH & MP.

Paszek, Lawrence J., jt. auth. see Dornbusch, Charles E.

Paszkiewicz, Henryk. The Rise of Moscow's Power. 1984. text 84.00 (*0-88033-036-8*, 145, Pub. by East Eur Monographs) Col U Pr.

Paszkiewicz, M. & Kulczycki, J., eds. Herby Rodow Polskich. (POL., Illus.). 1990. 160.00 (*0-614-25050-1*) Szwede Slavic.

Paszkiewicz, T., ed. Physics of Phonons. (Lecture Notes in Physics Ser.: Vol. 285). x, 486p. 1987. 64.95 (*0-387-18244-6*) Spr-Verlag.

Paszkiewicz, T. & Rapcewicz, K. Die Kunst of Phonons: Lectures from the Winter School of Theoretical Physics. (Illus.). 444p. (C). 1994. text 120.00 (*0-306-44677-4*, Kluwer Plenum) Kluwer Academic.

Paszkowski, Jerzy, ed. Homologous Recombination & Gene Silencing in Plants. LC 93-50752. 396p. 1994. text 234.00 (*0-7923-2704-7*) Kluwer Academic.

Pasztor, E. Concise Neurosurgery. (Illus.). 292p. 1980. 81.75 (*3-8055-1431-X*) S Karger.

Pasztor, E., et al, eds. Language & Speech: Proceedings of the Fifth Convention of the Academia Eurasiana Neurochirurgica, Budapest, September 19-12, 1990. (Acta Neurochirugica - Supplementum Ser.: No. 56). (Illus.). 120p. 1993. 119.95 (*0-387-82386-7*) Spr-Verlag.

Pasztor, Eileen M., jt. auth. see Wynne, Suzan F.

Pasztor, Eileen Mayers, et al. Helping Children & Youths Develop Positive Attachments. (Homeworks Ser.). 1993. pap. 9.95 (*0-87868-443-3*) Child Welfare.

— Helping Children & Youths Manage Separation & Loss. (Homeworks Ser.). 1993. pap. 9.95 (*0-87868-442-5*) Child Welfare.

— Helping Children, Youths & Families Manage the Impact of Placement. (Homeworks Ser.). 1993. pap. 9.95 (*0-87868-444-1*) Child Welfare.

— Homeworks: At-Home Training Resources for Foster Parents & Adoptive Families, 3 bks., Set. 1991. pap. 25.00 (*0-87868-447-6*, 4476) Child Welfare.

Pasztory, Esther. Aztec Art. (Illus.). 336p. 1993. 49.50 (*0-8109-0687-2*, Pub. by Abrams) Time Warner.

— Aztec Art. LC 92-38123. (Illus.). 512p. 1998. pap. 29.95 (*0-8061-2536-5*) U of Okla Pr.

— The Iconography of the Teotihuacan Tlaloc. LC 74-16543. (Studies in Pre-Columbian Art & Archaeology: No. 15). (Illus.). 22p. 1974. pap. 6.00 (*0-88402-059-2*) Dumbarton Oaks.

— Pre-Columbian Art. (Illus.). 176p. 1999. pap. 18.95 (*0-521-64551-4*) Cambridge U Pr.

— Teotihuacan: An Experiment in Living. LC 96-32775. 304p. 1997. 49.95 (*0-8061-2847-X*) U of Okla Pr.

***Paszyn, Danuta.** The Soviet Attitude to Political & Social Change in Central America, 1979-90: Case-studies on Nicaragua, El Salvador & Guatemala. LC 99-48853. 208p. 2000. text 65.00 (*0-312-23007-9*) St Martin.

Pat Burke Guild & Garger, Stephen. Marching to Different Drummers. 2nd ed. 193p. 1998. pap. 17.95 (*0-87120-306-5*, 198186) ASCD.

Pat, Jacob. Ashes & Fire. Steinberg, Leo, tr. LC 48-1353. 254p. reprint ed. pap. 78.80 (*0-8357-5784-6*, 201071300070) Bks Demand.

Pata, Jan L. Alaskan Malamute Champions, 1936-1980. (Illus.). 138p. 1987. pap. 36.95 (*0-940808-10-2*) Camino E E & Bk.

— Brittany Champions, 1952-1981. (Illus.). 280p. 1986. 36.95 (*0-940808-20-X*) Camino E E & Bk.

— Clumber Spaniel Champions, 1955-1981. (Illus.). 94p. 1982. pap. 36.95 (*0-940808-15-3*) Camino E E & Bk.

— Doberman Pinscher Champions, 1952-1980. (Illus.). 220p. 1981. pap. 36.95 (*0-940808-01-3*) Camino E E & Bk.

— German Shorthaired Pointer Champions, 1952-1980. (Illus.). 201p. 1986. pap. 36.95 (*0-940808-05-6*) Camino E E & Bk.

— German Wirehaired Pointer Champions, 1959-1980. (Illus.). 75p. 1981. pap. 36.95 (*0-940808-07-2*) Camino E E & Bk.

— Lhasa Apso Champions, 1952-1980. (Illus.). 164p. 1981. pap. 36.95 (*0-940808-09-9*) Camino E E & Bk.

— Pekingese Champions, 1952-1981. (Illus.). 236p. 1987. pap. 36.95 (*0-940808-12-9*) Camino E E & Bk.

— Pointer Champions, 1889-1980. (Illus.). 108p. 1981. pap. 36.95 (*0-940808-00-5*) Camino E E & Bk.

— Rhodesian Ridgeback Champions, 1955-1980. (Illus.). 97p. 1981. pap. 36.95 (*0-940808-04-8*) Camino E E & Bk.

— Siberian Husky Champions, 1952-1980. (Illus.). 151p. 1982. pap. 36.95 (*0-940808-11-0*) Camino E E & Bk.

— Whippet Champions, 1952-1980. (Illus.). 187p. 1987. pap. 36.95 (*0-940808-03-X*) Camino E E & Bk.

— Yorkshire Terrier Champions, 1952-1980. (Illus.). 214p. 1981. pap. 36.95 (*0-940808-08-0*) Camino E E & Bk.

Pata, Jan L. & Johnson, Dorothy L. A Century of Pointers - Field & Show: Show, Vol. 2. (Illus.). 405p. 2001. lib. bdg. 59.95 (*1-55893-056-6*) Camino E E & Bk.

Pata, Jan L., jt. auth. see Johnson, Dorothy L.

Pata, Njali & Miller, Barbara S. Yoga: Discipline of Freedom : The Yoga Sutra Attributed to Patanjali : A Translation of the Text, with Commentary, Introduction & Glossary of Keywords. LC 97-30455. 128p. 1998. pap. 11.95 (*0-553-37428-1*) Bantam.

Pata, Njali & Sankar, Acarya. Meditation Practice & Yoga Techniques: An Authoritative Guide by Sankara, India's Greatest Religious & Philosophical Genius. Leggett, Trevor, ed. & tr. by. LC 97-51367. 275p. 1998. 31.00 (*0-7103-0614-8*, Pub. by Kegan Paul Intl) Col U Pr.

***PATA Staff.** Environment, Culture & Heritage: Best Practice Papers, 1999. 337p. 1999. pap. 125.00 (*1-882866-22-3*) Pac Asia Trvl.

— 1999-2000 PATA Membership Directory. 251p. 1999. pap. 250.00 (*1-882866-21-5*, D-002-99) Pac Asia Trvl.

— PATA Arab Gulf Countries Outbound Market Report: November 1999. 125p. 1999. pap. 415.00 (*1-882866-18-5*) Pac Asia Trvl.

— PATA Israel Outbound Market Report, November 1999. 27p. 1999. pap. 85.00 (*1-882866-19-3*) Pac Asia Trvl.

***Patabendi, Warren.** The Removal. 273p. 1999. pap. write for info. incl. audio (*0-9674608-0-8*) ThreeNineNine.

Patach, Heidi. Monkey Stickers. (Illus.). (J). (gr. k-3). 1993. pap. 1.00 (*0-486-27493-4*) Dover.

Patacsil, Priscila De, see Strom, Kay M. & De Patacsil, Priscila.

Patacsil, Priscila M., tr. see Waldrop, C. Sybil.

Patai, Daphne. Brazilian Women Speak: Contemporary Life Stories. 404p. (Orig.). (C). 1988. pap. 18.00 (*0-8135-1301-4*) Rutgers U Pr.

***Patai, Daphne.** Heterophobia: Sexual Harassment & the Future of Feminism. 276p. 2000. pap. 16.95 (*0-8476-8988-3*) Rowman.

Patai, Daphne. Heterophobia: Sexual Harassment & the Politics of Purity. LC 98-27901. 240p. 1998. 22.95 (*0-8476-8987-5*, Pub. by Rowman) Natl Bk Netwk.

— Myth & Ideology in Contemporary Brazilian Fiction. LC 81-71313. 256p. 1983. 37.50 (*0-8386-3132-0*) Fairleigh Dickinson.

— The Orwell Mystique: A Study in Male Ideology. LC 84-8488. 344p. 1984. pap. 19.95 (*0-87023-447-1*); lib. bdg. 40.00 (*0-87023-446-3*) U of Mass Pr.

Patai, Daphne, ed. Looking Backward, 1988-1888: Essays on Edward Bellamy. LC 88-10621. 240p. (Orig.). (C). 1988. pap. 16.95 (*0-87023-634-2*); lib. bdg. 35.00 (*0-87023-633-4*) U of Mass Pr.

Patai, Daphne, ed. see De Sena, Jorge.

Patai, Daphne, jt. ed. see Gluck, Sherna B.

Patai, Daphne, jt. ed. see Ingram, Angela.

Patai, Jennifer, jt. auth. see Patai, Raphael.

Patai, Joseph. Souls & Secrets: Hasidic Stories. Patai, Raphael, tr. LC 94-45339. (Illus.). 272p. 1995. 40.00 (*1-56821-355-7*) Aronson.

Patai, Ralphael, tr. from ARA. Arab Folktales from Palestine & Israel. LC 98-11614. (Ralphael Patai Series in Jewish Folklore & Anthropology). 298p. (Orig.). 1997. pap. 24.95 (*0-8143-2710-9*) Wayne St U Pr.

Patai, Raphael. Apprentice in Budapest: Memories of a World That Is No More. LC 87-37185. 538p. 1988. pap. 166.80 (*0-7837-8561-5*, 204937600011) Bks Demand.

***Patai, Raphael.** The Children of Noah. 224p. 1999. pap. 14.95 (*0-691-00968-6*, Pub. by Princeton U Pr) Cal Prin Full Svc.

Patai, Raphael. Gates to the Old City: A Book of Jewish Legends. LC 80-66154. 859p. reprint ed. pap. 200.00 (*0-608-15784-8*, 203101700073) Bks Demand.

— The Hebrew Goddess. 3rd enl. ed. LC 89-70488. (Jewish Folklore & Anthropology Ser.). (Illus.). 370p. (C). 1990. reprint ed. pap. text 21.95 (*0-8143-2271-9*) Wayne St U Pr.

— Israel Between East & West: A Study in Human Relations. rev. ed. LC 70-98711. 394p. 1970. 65.00 (*0-8371-3719-5*, PAI/, Greenwood Pr) Greenwood.

— Jadid Al-Islam: The Jewish "New Muslims" of Meshhed. LC 97-2527. (Jewish Folklore & Anthropology Ser.). (Illus.). 352p. 1997. 39.95 (*0-8143-2652-8*) Wayne St U Pr.

— The Jewish Alchemists: A History & Source Book. 633p. (C). 1994. pap. text 24.95 (*0-691-00642-3*, Pub. by Princeton U Pr) Cal Prin Full Svc.

— The Jewish Mind. 650p. 1996. pap. 24.95 (*0-8143-2651-X*) Wayne St U Pr.

— The Jews of Hungary: History, Culture, Psychology. LC 95-21756. (Illus.). 732p. 1996. text 49.95 (*0-8143-2561-0*) Wayne St U Pr.

— The Kingdom of Jordan. LC 83-22723. (Illus.). 315p. 1984. reprint ed. lib. bdg. 49.50 (*0-313-24396-4*, PAKJ, Greenwood Pr) Greenwood.

— Messiah Texts: Jewish Legends of Three Thousand Years. LC 79-5387. 428p. 1988. pap. 21.95 (*0-8143-1850-9*) Wayne St U Pr.

— Nahum Goldmann: His Missions to the Gentiles. LC 85-24518. (Judaic Studies). 325p. 1987. pap. 100.80 (*0-7837-8397-3*, 205920800009) Bks Demand.

— On Culture Contact & Its Working in Modern Palestine. LC 48-4054. (American Anthropological Association Memoirs Ser.: No. 67). 1974. reprint ed. pap. 25.00 (*0-527-00566-5*) Periodicals Srv.

— On Jewish Folklore. LC 82-11034. (Illus.). 512p. reprint ed. pap. 158.80 (*0-608-10593-7*, 207121400009) Bks Demand.

— Robert Graves & the Hebrew Myths: A Collaboration. LC 91-20963. (Jewish Folklore & Anthropology Ser.). (Illus.). 468p. reprint ed. pap. 145.10 (*0-608-10605-4*, 207122700009) Bks Demand.

— The Seed of Abraham: Jews & Arabs in Contact & Conflict. LC 85-29453. 408p. 1986. pap. 126.50 (*0-7837-8560-7*, 204937500011) Bks Demand.

Patai, Raphael, ed. Herzl Year Book: Vol. 5, Studies in the History of Zionism in America. LC 72-117807. (Essay Index Reprint Ser.). 1977. 24.95 (*0-8369-1951-3*) Ayer.

Patai, Raphael & Goldsmith, Emanuel S. Thinkers & Teachers of Modern Judaism. LC 94-16063. 256p. 1995. 18.95 (*1-55778-701-8*) Paragon Hse.

Patai, Raphael & Goldsmith, Emanuel S., eds. Events & Movements in Modern Judaism. 315p. 1995. 18.95 (*1-55778-707-7*) Paragon Hse.

Patai, Raphael & Patai, Jennifer. The Myth of the Jewish Race. rev. ed. LC 88-27721. (Illus.). 470p. reprint ed. pap. 145.70 (*0-608-10631-3*, 207125300009); reprint ed. pap. 145.70 (*0-608-06269-3*, 206659800008) Bks Demand.

Patai, Raphael, et al. The Children of Noah: Jewish Seafaring in Ancient Times. LC 97-40059. (Illus.). 208p. 1998. 24.95 (*0-691-01580-5*, Pub. by Princeton U Pr) Cal Prin Full Svc.

— Studies in Biblical & Jewish Folklore. LC 72-6871. (Studies in Comparative Literature: No. 35). 1972. reprint ed. lib. bdg. 75.00 (*0-8383-1665-4*) M S G Haskell Hse.

Patai, Raphael, ed. see Brauer, Erich.

Patai, Raphael, tr. see Patai, Joseph.

Patai, Saul, ed. The Chemistry of Amino, Nitroso & Nitro Compounds Parts 1 & 2, Vol. 1. LC 97-107218. (Chemistry of Functional Groups Ser.). 756p. 1996. suppl. ed. 1350.00 (*0-471-95171-4*) Wiley.

— The Chemistry of the Hydrazo, Azo, & Azoxy Groups, 2 pts., Pt. 1. LC 75-2194. (Chemistry of Functional Groups Ser.). (Illus.). 611p. 1975. reprint ed. pap. 189.50 (*0-8357-8840-7*, 203332600001) Bks Demand.

— The Chemistry of the Hydrazo, Azo, & Azoxy Groups, Vol. 2. (The Chemistry of Functional Groups). 836p. 1997. 722.00 (*0-471-96885-4*) Wiley.

— Supplement A3: The Chemistry of Double-Bonded Functional Groups, No. A3. LC 97-184943. (Chemistry of Functional Groups Ser.). 1894p. 1997. suppl. ed. 1525.00 (*0-471-95956-1*) Wiley.

Patai, Saul & Rappoport, Zvi. The Chemistry of Organic Derivatives of Gold & Silver. LC 98-14487. (Chemistry of Functional Groups Ser.). 760p. 1999. 595.00 (*0-471-98164-8*) Wiley.

Patai, Saul & Rappoport, Zvi, eds. The Chemistry of Organic Silicon Compounds, Pt. 1. LC 87-31709. (The Chemistry of Functional Groups Ser.). 908p. reprint ed. pap. 200.00 (*0-608-20174-X*, 205280700001) Bks Demand.

— The Chemistry of Sulphonic Acids, Esters & Their Derivatives. LC 89-70729. (Chemistry of Functional Groups Ser.). (Illus.). 1137p. reprint ed. pap. 200.00 (*0-608-20232-0*, 207149100012) Bks Demand.

Patai, Saul, ed. see Breuer, Eli, et al.

Patai, Saul E. Chemistry of Carboxylic Acids & Esters. LC 70-82547. (Chemistry of Functional Groups Ser.). (Illus.). 1169p. 1969. reprint ed. pap. 200.00 (*0-608-08117-5*, 202788800057) Bks Demand.

— Chemistry of Cyanates & Their Thio Derivatives, Pt. 1. LC 75-6913. (Interscience Publication, Chemistry of Functional Groups Ser.). 632p. 1977. reprint ed. pap. 196.00 (*0-608-04765-1*, 202519700001) Bks Demand.

— Chemistry of Cyanates & Their Thio Derivatives, Pt. 2. LC 75-6913. (Interscience Publication, Chemistry of Functional Groups Ser.). 714p. 1977. reprint ed. pap. 200.00 (*0-608-04766-X*, 202519700002) Bks Demand.

— The Chemistry of Doubled-Bonded Functional Groups, Pt. 1. LC 75-6913. (Chemistry of Functional Groups Ser.: Suppl. A). (Illus.). 667p. 1977. reprint ed. pap. 200.00 (*0-8357-8832-6*, 203331900001) Bks Demand.

— The Chemistry of Ether Linkage. LC 66-30401. (Chemistry of Functional Groups Ser.). (Illus.). 795p. 1967. reprint ed. pap. 200.00 (*0-608-08119-1*, 201696900006) Bks Demand.

Patai, Saul E. Patai's 1992 Guide to the Chemistry of Functional Groups. LC 91-28943. (Chemistry of Functional Groups Ser.: No. 1078). 534p. 1992. 235.00 (*0-471-93022-9*) Wiley.

Patai, Saul E., ed. The Chemistry of Acid Derivatives, Pt. 1. LC 75-6913. (Chemistry of Functional Groups Ser.: Suppl. B). (Illus.). 767p. 1979. reprint ed. pap. 200.00 (*0-8357-8829-6*, 203332500001) Bks Demand.

— The Chemistry of Acid Derivatives, Pt. 2. LC 75-6913. (Chemistry of Functional Groups Ser.: Suppl. B). (Illus.). 734p. 1979. reprint ed. pap. 200.00 (*0-8357-8835-0*, 203332500002) Bks Demand.

— The Chemistry of Acyl Halides. LC 70-37114. (Chemistry of Functional Groups Ser.). 561p. reprint ed. pap. 174.00 (*0-8357-8830-X*, 203332400085) Bks Demand.

— The Chemistry of Amidines & Imidates. LC 75-6913. (Chemistry of Functional Groups Ser.). (Illus.). 691p. reprint ed. pap. 200.00 (*0-8357-8831-8*, 203332000085) Bks Demand.

— The Chemistry of Amino Nitroso & Nitro Compounds & Their Derivatives, Pt. 1. LC 81-16153. (Chemistry of Functional Groups Ser.: Supplement F). (Illus.). 728p. reprint ed. pap. 200.00 (*0-608-08114-0*, 203049100001) Bks Demand.

— The Chemistry of Amino Nitroso & Nitro Compounds & Their Derivatives, Pt. 2. LC 81-16153. (Chemistry of Functional Groups Ser.: Supplement F). (Illus.). 739p. reprint ed. pap. 200.00 (*0-608-08115-9*, 203049100002) Bks Demand.

— The Chemistry of Diazonium & Diazo Groups, 2 pts., Pt. 1. LC 75-6913. (Chemistry of Functional Groups Ser.). 524p. 1978. reprint ed. pap. 162.50 (*0-608-04762-7*, 202240400001) Bks Demand.

— The Chemistry of Diazonium & Diazo Groups, 2 pts., Pt. 2. LC 75-6913. (Chemistry of Functional Groups Ser.). 572p. 1978. reprint ed. pap. 177.40 (*0-608-04763-5*, 202240400002) Bks Demand.

— The Chemistry of Doubled-Bonded Functional Groups, Pt. 2. LC 75-6913. (Chemistry of Functional Groups Ser.: Suppl. A). (Illus.). 708p. 1977. reprint ed. pap. 200.00 (*0-8357-8836-9*, 203331900002) Bks Demand.

— The Chemistry of Ethers, Crown Ethers, Hydroxyl Groups & Their Sulphur Analogues, Pt. 1. LC 80-41256.

P

An Asterisk (*) at the beginning of an entry indicates that the title is appearing for the first time.

(Chemistry of Functional Groups Ser.: Supplement E). (Illus.). 622p. 1980. reprint ed. pap. 192.90 (*0-608-08120-5*, 203049000001) Bks Demand.

— The Chemistry of Ethers, Crown Ethers, Hydroxyl Groups & Their Sulphur Analogues, Pt. 2. LC 80-41256. (Chemistry of Functional Groups Ser.: Supplement E). (Illus.). 549p. 1980. reprint ed. pap. 170.20 (*0-608-08121-3*, 203049000002) Bks Demand.

— The Chemistry of Ketenes, Allenes, & Related Compounds, 2 pts., Pt. 1. LC 79-42899. (Chemistry of Functional Groups Ser.). 499p. 1980. reprint ed. pap. 154.70 (*0-608-08124-8*, 203075000001) Bks Demand.

— The Chemistry of Ketenes, Allenes, & Related Compounds, 2 pts., Pt. 2. LC 79-42899. (Chemistry of Functional Groups Ser.). 491p. 1980. reprint ed. pap. 152.30 (*0-608-08125-6*, 203075000002) Bks Demand.

— The Chemistry of Organic Arsenic, Antimony, & Bismuth Compounds. LC 93-3145. (Chemistry of Functional Groups Ser.). 978p. 1994. 975.00 (*0-471-93044-X*) Wiley.

— The Chemistry of Organic Germanium, Tin & Lead Compounds. LC 95-19750. (Chemistry of Functional Groups Ser.). 1014p. 1995. 875.00 (*0-471-94207-3*) Wiley.

— The Chemistry of Peroxides. LC 83-14844. (Chemistry of Functional Groups Ser.). 1020p. 1983. reprint ed. pap. 200.00 (*0-608-08129-9*, 203078500074) Bks Demand.

— The Chemistry of the Amino Group. LC 67-31072. (Chemistry of Functional Groups Ser.). (Illus.). 827p. reprint ed. pap. 200.00 (*0-8357-8833-4*, 203332100085) Bks Demand.

— The Chemistry of the Azido Group. LC 73-149579. (Chemistry of Functional Groups Ser.). (Illus.). 640p. reprint ed. pap. 198.40 (*0-8357-8834-2*, 203332200085) Bks Demand.

— The Chemistry of the Carbon-Carbon Triple Bond, 2 pts., Pt. 1. LC 75-6913. (Chemistry of Functional Groups Ser.). (Illus.). 536p. reprint ed. pap. 166.20 (*0-8357-8837-7*, 203332300001) Bks Demand.

— The Chemistry of the Carbon-Carbon Triple Bond, 2 pts., Pt. 2. LC 75-6913. (Chemistry of Functional Groups Ser.). (Illus.). 558p. reprint ed. pap. 173.00 (*0-8357-8838-5*, 203332300002) Bks Demand.

— The Chemistry of the Carbon-Nitrogen Double Bond, Pt. 1. LC 70-104166. (Chemistry of Functional Groups Ser.). (Illus.). 808p. 1970. reprint ed. pap. 200.00 (*0-8357-8839-3*, 203332700085) Bks Demand.

— The Chemistry of the Hydrazo, Azo, & Azoxy Groups, 2 pts., Pt. 2. LC 75-2194. (Chemistry of Functional Groups Ser.). (Illus.). 607p. 1975. reprint ed. pap. 188.20 (*0-8357-8841-5*, 203332600002) Bks Demand.

— The Chemistry of the Hydroxyl Group, 2 vols., 1. LC 77-116164. (Chemistry of Functional Groups Ser.: Vol. 10). (Illus.). 653p. 1971. reprint ed. pap. 200.00 (*0-608-08134-5*, 205664700001) Bks Demand.

— The Chemistry of the Hydroxyl Group, 2 vols., 2. LC 77-116164. (Chemistry of Functional Groups Ser.: Vol. 10). (Illus.). 604p. 1971. reprint ed. pap. 187.30 (*0-608-08135-3*, 205664700002) Bks Demand.

— The Chemistry of the Quinonoid Compounds, 2 pts., Pt. 1. LC 73-17765. 630p. 1974. reprint ed. pap. 195.30 (*0-608-08136-1*, 205225400001) Bks Demand.

— The Chemistry of the Quinonoid Compounds, 2 pts., Pt. 2. LC 73-17765. 673p. 1974. reprint ed. pap. 200.00 (*0-608-08137-X*, 205225400002) Bks Demand.

— Supplement C2: The Chemistry of Triple-Bonded Functional Groups, Vol. 2. (Chemistry of Functional Groups, Supplementary Ser.: Vol. C2). 1366p. 1994. 1225.00 (*0-471-93559-X*) Wiley.

Patai, Saul E. & Rappoport, Zvi, eds. Supplement S: The Chemistry of Sulphur-Containing Functional Groups. LC 92-23016. (Chemistry of Functional Groups Ser.). 1136p. 1993. 1465.00 (*0-471-93046-6*) Wiley.

Patai, Saul E. & Zabicky, Jacob Z. The Chemistry of Alkenes. LC 64-25218. (Chemistry of Functional Groups Ser.: Vol. 1). (Illus.). 1325p. 1964. reprint ed. pap. 200.00 (*0-608-08111-6*, 205664500001) Bks Demand.

— The Chemistry of Alkenes, Vol. 2. LC 64-25218. (Chemistry of Functional Groups Ser.: Vol. 1). (Illus.). 685p. 1970. reprint ed. pap. 200.00 (*0-608-08112-4*, 205664500002) Bks Demand.

— The Chemistry of the Carbonyl Group, 2 vols., 1. LC 66-18177. (Chemistry of Functional Groups Ser.: Vol. 2). (Illus.). 1039p. 1966. reprint ed. pap. 200.00 (*0-608-08131-0*, 205664600001) Bks Demand.

— The Chemistry of the Carbonyl Group, 2 vols., 2. LC 66-18177. (Chemistry of Functional Groups Ser.: Vol. 2). (Illus.). 464p. 1970. reprint ed. pap. 143.90 (*0-608-08132-9*, 205664600002) Bks Demand.

Patai, Saul E., jt. ed. see Rappoport, Zvi.

Pataki, Eva. Dominican Painting: Masters & Novices. 2nd rev. ed. LC 89-91748. (Illus.). 102p. (C). 1989. pap. 15.00 (*0-9615932-1-0*) E Pataki.

— Haitian Painting: The Naives & the Moderns. rev. ed. LC 87-61494. (Illus.). 71p. (C). 1987. pap. 15.00 (*0-614-13018-2*) E Pataki.

— Haitian Painting, Art & Kitsch. LC 85-73136. (Illus.). x, 172p. 1986. 25.00 (*0-9615932-0-2*) E Pataki.

Pataki, George & Paisner, Daniel. Pataki: Where I Come From. LC 98-9774. 256p. 1998. 24.95 (*0-670-87339-X*, Viking) Viking Penguin.

Pataky-Brestyanszky, Ilona. Margit Kovacs. 196p. 1989. 65.00 (*963-13-2628-4*, Pub. by Corvina Bks) St Mut.

Pataky-Brestyanzky, Ilona. Kovacs, Margit. 194p. (C). 1989. 130.00 (*0-7855-4524-7*, Pub. by Collets) St Mut.

Pataky-Kosove, Joan. The Comedia Lacrimosa & Spanish Romantic Drama 1773-1865. (Monagrafias A Ser.: Vol. LXVII). 148p. (C). 1977. 51.00 (*0-7293-0049-8*, Pub. by Tamesis Bks Ltd) Boydell & Brewer.

Pataky, Mark. Illustrated SNA. LC 98-8273. (Illustrated Network Ser.). (Illus.). 242p. 1998. pap. text 39.99 incl. cd-rom, disk (*0-471-19372-0*) Wiley.

Pataky, Sophie. Lexikon Deutscher Frauen der Feder, 2 vols., Set. 1983. write for info. incl. fiche (*0-318-71938-X*) G Olms Pubs.

Patalano, Giro R. Behind the Iron Horse: The People Who Made the Trains Run in the Bellows Falls, Vermont, Area (1941-1980) (Illus.). 188p. 1997. pap. 16.95 (*0-934720-40-1*) VT Hist Soc.

Patalas, E., jt. auth. see Gregor, U.

Patalon, William, jt. auth. see Gallea.

Patalon, William, jt. auth. see Gallea, Anthony M., III.

Patalon, William, III, jt. auth. see Gallea, Anthony M.

Patan, Federico. Perfiles Ensayos Sobre Literatura Mexicana Reciente. LC 91-68484. (SPA.). 169p. 1992. pap. 36.00 (*0-89295-066-8*) Society Sp & Sp-Am.

***Patanangkura, Asjarin.** Chakri Dynasty: The Legend of Mother Earth of Siam. 288p. 2000. pap. 18.00 (*0-8059-4693-4*) Dorrance.

Patani, A., tr. see Samsonov, G. V., ed.

Patania, Nancy L., et al. Optimization of Filtration for Cyst Removal. LC 96-131392. (Illus.). 158p. 1995. pap. 115.00 (*0-89867-825-0*, 90699) Am Water Wks Assn.

Patanian, Antranik. Arabe-Express Dictionnaire, Guide de Conversation et Grammaire de l'Arabe Moderne. 4th ed. (ARA & FRE.). 159p. 1989. pap. 32.95 (*0-7859-7947-6*, 2716310076) Fr & Eur.

Patanjali, V. Raja Yoga Sutras. Jyotirmayananda, tr. from SAN. & comment by. (Illus.). 1978. pap. 6.99 (*0-934664-38-2*) Yoga Res Foun.

— Thoughts on Indian Mysticism. 226p. 1989. 14.95 (*0-318-36391-7*) Asia Bk Corp.

Patankar, Suhas V. Numerical Heat Transfer & Fluid Flow. 197p. 1980. 66.95 (*0-89116-522-3*) Hemisp Pub.

Patanothai, Aran, ed. Land-Use Sustainability in the Red River Delta of Vietnam: An Intensively Cultivated & Densely Populated Area. LC 96-1721. 1996. write for info. (*0-86638-180-5*) EW Ctr HI.

***Patapievici, Horia-Roman.** Flying Against the Arrow: An Intellectual in Ceausescu's Romania. (Library of Ideas). 280p. 2000. 49.95 (*963-9116-57-2*) Ctrl Europ Univ.

***Patapivici, Horia-Roman.** Flying Against the Arrow: An Intellectual in Ceausescu's Romania. (Central European Library of Ideas Ser.). 2000. pap. text 22.95 (*963-9116-58-0*) Ctrl Europ Univ.

***Patarca-Montero, Roberto.** Phytotherapy of Chronic Fatigue Syndrome: Evidence-Based & Potentially Useful Botanicals in the Treatment of CFS. LC 00-33544. 2000. write for info. (*0-7890-0909-9*, Hawrth Medical) Haworth Pr.

***Patarca-Montero, Roberto, ed.** Chronic Fatigue Syndrome: Advances in Epidemiologic, Clinical & Basic Science Research. LC 99-48701. (Journal of Chronic Fatigue Syndrome: Vol. 5, Nos. 3/4). 338p. 1999. 69.95 (*0-7890-0697-9*); pap. text 29.95 (*0-7890-0821-1*) Haworth Pr.

— Concise Encyclopedia of Chronic Fatigue Syndrome. LC 99-56033. 200p. 2000. 69.95 (*0-7890-0922-6*, Hawrth Medical); pap. text 24.95 (*0-7890-0923-4*, Hawrth Medical) Haworth Pr.

Patarca-Montero, Roberto, jt. ed. see Klimas, Nancy G.

Patarca-Montero, Roberto, jt. ed. see Klimas, Nancy.

Patarca, Roberto. Cytokines & Their Receptors Clinical Applications. 1998. 99.95 (*0-8493-4020-9*) CRC Pr.

Patarca, Roberto, jt. auth. see Levine, Paul H.

Patargias. English-Greek Dictionary of Biology & Medical Terms. (ENG & GRE.). 413p. pap. 95.00 (*0-7859-9051-8*) Fr & Eur.

Patashinskii, A. Z., et al. Fluctuation Theory of Phase Transitions. Shepherd, P. J., ed. (International Series in Natural Philosophy: Vol. 98). (Illus.). 1979. 143.00 (*0-08-021664-1*, Pub. by Pergamon Repr) Franklin.

***Patashnik, Eric M.** Putting Trust in the U. S. Budget: Federal Trust Funds & the Politics of Commitment. LC 99-57404. (Theories of Institutional Design Ser.). (Illus.). 280p. 2000. write for info. (*0-521-77174-9*); pap. write for info. (*0-521-77748-8*) Cambridge U Pr.

Patavino, Rolandino. The Chronicles of the Trevisan March. Berrigan, Joseph R., ed. & tr. by. 1980. 15.00 (*0-87291-133-0*) Coronado Pr.

Patch, Cecilia & Moynihan, Brendan. Con Games 101: A Primer on Avoiding Frauds & Swindles. 71p. 1992. pap. 7.95 (*0-9635794-0-1*) Infrared Pr.

Patch, Diana C. Reflections of Greatness: Ancient Egypt at the Carnegie Museum of Natural History. LC 89-62543. (Illus.). 128p. (Orig.). (C). 1990. pap. text 24.95 (*0-911239-14-6*) Carnegie Mus.

Patch, Diana C. & Haldane, Cheryl W. The Pharaoh's Boat at the Carnegie. LC 89-85819. (Illus.). 52p. (Orig.). (C). 1990. pap. text 7.95 (*0-911239-22-7*) Carnegie Mus.

Patch, Elizabeth P. Plant Closings & Employment Loss in Manufacturing: The Role of Local Economic Conditions. rev. ed. LC 95-18534. (Garland Studies in the History of American Labor). 144p. 1995. text 20.00 (*0-8153-2028-0*) Garland.

Patch, Howard R. Chaucer & the Common People. (Studies in Chaucer: No. 6). (C). 1970. reprint ed. pap. 12.95 (*0-8383-0060-X*) M S G Haskell Hse.

Patch, Robert W. Maya & Spaniard in Yucatan, 1648-1812. LC 92-25923. 344p. 1993. 49.50 (*0-8047-2062-2*) Stanford U Pr.

Patch, Susanne S. & National Museum of Natural History (U.S.) Staff. Blue Mystery: The Story of the Hope Diamond. 2nd ed. LC 98-30700. (Illus.). 92p. 1999. pap. 9.95 (*0-8109-2797-7*, Pub. by Abrams) Time Warner.

Patch, William L., Jr. The Christian Trade Unions in the Weimar Republic, 1918-1933: The Failure of "Corporate Pluralism" LC 84-27150. (Yale Historical Publications: No. 133). 260p. 1985. 37.50 (*0-300-03328-1*) Yale U Pr.

— Heinrich Bruning & the Dissolution of the Weimar Republic. LC 97-43388. 350p. (C). 1998. 59.95 (*0-521-62422-3*) Cambridge U Pr.

Patchan, Scott C. & Hennessy, John J. Second Manassas: The Fight for Chinn Ridge. Seagrave, Pia S., ed. LC 99-16990. (Illus.). 2000. 29.95 (*1-887901-32-9*) Sergeant Kirk.

Patchefsky, Arthur S., jt. auth. see Carter, Darryl.

Patchen, Aletha, jt. auth. see Patchen, Marvin.

Patchen, Kenneth. Awash with Roses: The Collected Love Poems of Kenneth Patchen. Smith, Laura, ed. (Midwest Authors Ser.). (Illus.). 176p. (Orig.). 1991. 19.95 (*0-933087-19-5*); pap. 9.95 (*0-933087-21-7*) Bottom Dog Pr.

— Before the Brave. LC 74-3035. (Studies in Poetry: No. 38). 1974. lib. bdg. 75.00 (*0-8383-2062-7*) M S G Haskell Hse.

— Collected Poems. LC 67-23487. 512p. 1969. pap. 16.95 (*0-8112-0140-6*, NDP284, Pub. by New Directions) Norton.

— Hallelujah Anyway. LC 66-27612. (New Directions Book Ser.). (Illus.). 94p. 1966. reprint ed. pap. 30.00 (*0-608-05912-9*, 206624700008) Bks Demand.

— The Journal of Albion Moonlight. LC 68-28283. 1961. pap. 12.95 (*0-8112-0144-9*, NDP99, Pub. by New Directions) Norton.

— The Memoirs of a Shy Pornographer. rev. ed. LC 98-37235. (New Directions Classic Ser.). 242p. 1999. pap. 14.00 (*0-8112-1411-7*, NDP879, Pub. by New Directions) Norton.

— Selected Poems. LC 58-590. 1964. pap. 10.95 (*0-8112-0146-5*, NDP160, Pub. by New Directions) Norton.

— Still Another Pelican in the Breadbox. Morgan, Richard, ed. LC 80-82905. 96p. 1980. pap. 7.95 (*0-917530-14-4*) Pig Iron Pr.

— What Shall We Do Without Us? LC 84-4891. (Illus.). 112p. (Orig.). 1984. pap. 12.95 (*0-87156-818-7*, Pub. by Sierra) Random.

— Wonderings. LC 79-148535. (Illus.). (Orig.). 1971. pap. 8.95 (*0-8112-0149-X*, NDP320, Pub. by New Directions) Norton.

Patchen, Martin. Black-White Contact in Schools: Its Social & Academic Effects. LC 80-83511. (Illus.). 400p. 1982. 52.95 (*0-911198-61-X*); pap. 19.95 (*0-911198-64-4*) Purdue U Pr.

— Diversity & Unity: Relations Between Racial & Ethnic Groups. LC 97-36611. (Illus.). 380p. (C). 1998. pap. text 45.95 (*0-8304-1441-X*) Thomson Learn.

— Resolving Disputes Between Nations: Coercion or Conciliation? LC 87-26845. xiii, 365p. (C). 1988. text 54.95 (*0-8223-0764-2*); pap. text 22.95 (*0-8223-0819-3*) Duke.

Patchen, Marvin & Patchen, Aletha. Baja Adventures by Land, Air & Sea. 1981. pap. 9.95 (*0-9605712-0-5*) Baja Source.

Patchen, Nancy. The Journey of a Master: Swami Chinmayananda, the Man, the Path, the Teaching. LC 90-82276. 345p. (Orig.). 1989. reprint ed. pap. 107.00 (*0-608-01778-7*, 206243600003) Bks Demand.

— Swami Chinmayananda: Journey of a Master: The Man, the Path, the Teaching. 335p. 1989. pap. 15.00 (*1-880687-17-8*) Chinmaya Pubns.

Patchen, Robin, ed. see Odom, Sara Jo.

Patchett, Ann. The Magician's Assistant. LC 97-2139. 357p. 1997. 23.00 (*0-15-100263-0*) Harcourt.

— The Magician's Assistant. 357p. (C). 1998. pap. 13.00 (*0-15-600621-9*, Harvest Bks) Harcourt.

— The Patron Saint of Liars. 1996. pap. 12.00 (*0-449-91205-1*) Fawcett.

— Taft. LC PS3566.A7756T3 1999. 246p. 1999. pap. 12.00 (*0-345-43353-X*, Ballantine) Ballantine Pub Grp.

Patchett, Arnold N. Hadrian's Magic Stones. 223p. (C). 1989. text 80.00 (*0-7855-6970-7*, Pub. by Pentland Pr) St Mut.

— Some Yorkshire Bridges of Beauty & Romance. 135p. (C). 1989. text 65.00 (*1-872795-86-2*, Pub. by Pentland Pr) St Mut.

Patchett, Craig. Fast Track to Visual Basic Script. 1996. pap. text 24.99 (*0-7821-1988-3*) Sybex.

Patchett, Craig, et al. CGI/Perl Cookbook: Perl & JavaScript. LC 97-13304. 656p. 1997. pap., pap. text 49.99 incl. cd-rom (*0-471-16896-3*) Wiley.

Patchett, Fiona. Rabbits. (First Pets Ser.). (Illus.). 32p. 1999. pap. text 4.95 (*0-7460-2977-2*, Usborne) EDC.

— Rabbits. (First Pets Ser.). 1999. 12.95 (*1-58086-185-7*) EDC.

Patchett, Fiona, ed. Starting Fishing. (First Skills Ser.). (Illus.). 32p. (YA). (ps-3). 1999. pap. text 4.95 (*0-7460-3119-X*, Usborne); lib. bdg. 12.95 (*1-58086-168-7*, Usborne) EDC.

Patchett, J. Barry. Real Estate Math. Hedrick, Rebecca C., ed. 110p. (C). 1989. reprint ed. pap. text 18.95 (*0-317-93337-X*) PDIL.

Patchett, K. W. Recognition of Commercial Judgments & Awards in the Commonwealth. 384p. 1984. boxed set 136.00 (*0-406-40320-1*, U.K., MICHIE) LEXIS Pub.

***Patchett, Ken.** From the Farm to the Occupation of Japan: A Sailor's Story of World War II. (Illus.). 120p. 2000. 9.95 (*0-9654731-1-2*) K Patchett.

Patchett, Ken. Steps for Success in Starting & Operating a Business.Tr. of Pasos Hacia el Exito al Inciar y Administrar una Empresa. (ENG & SPA., Illus.). 90p. 1996. pap. 14.95 (*0-9654731-0-4*) K Patchett.

Patchett, Lynne. Glaciers. LC 91-45080. (Our Planet Ser.). (Illus.). 32p. (J). (gr. 4-6). 1997. pap. 4.95 (*0-8167-2752-X*) Troll Communs.

— Glaciers. LC 91-45080. (Our Planet Ser.). (Illus.). 32p. (J). (gr. 4-6). 1997. lib. bdg. 17.25 (*0-8167-2751-1*) Troll Communs.

Patchett, Monica, ed. see Wilde, David.

Patchett, Stephen, jt. auth. see Ballinger, Anne.

Patchett, Steve, jt. auth. see Ballinger, Ann.

Patchett, Thomas C. & Wolfe, Ernie, 3rd. Dateline Kenya: The Media Paintings of Joseph Bertiers. 72p. 1998. pap. 20.00 (*1-889195-20-0*) Smart Art Pr.

Patchett, Tom, text. Eats: An American Obsession. (Illus.). 42p. (Orig.). 1996. pap. 15.00 (*1-889195-07-3*) Smart Art Pr.

Patchett, Tom, ed. see Gleason, Mat & Robinson, Walter.

Patchev, Vladimir. Steroid-Hormone-Dependent Organization of Neuroendocrine Functions. LC 98-52781. (Neuroscience Intelligence Unit Ser.). 1999. 99.00 (*1-57059-555-0*) Landes Bioscience.

Patching, Keith, jt. auth. see Chatham, Robina.

Patching, Roger, jt. auth. see Masterton, Murray.

Patching, Roger, jt. ed. see Masterton, Murry.

Patchner, Michael A., jt. auth. see Berger, Raymond M.

Patchwork Quilt Tsushin Staff & Liddell, Jill. The Changing Seasons: Quilt Patterns from Japan. LC 92-52873. (Illus.). 160p. 1992. pap. 25.00 (*0-525-48601-1*, Dutton Studio) Studio Bks.

Pate, jt. auth. see Fernambuco.

Pate, jt. auth. see Fernamburg.

Pate, Alexs D. Amistad. 320p. 1997. mass mkt. 6.50 (*0-451-19516-7*, Sig) NAL.

***Pate, Alexs D.** Finding Makeba. 256p. 1999. pap. 12.50 (*0-380-73152-5*, Avon Bks) Morrow Avon.

Pate, Alexs D. Losing Absalom. 320p. 1995. mass mkt. 7.50 (*0-425-15013-5*) Berkley Pub.

— Losing Absalom. LC 93-23686. 220p. 1994. 5.00 (*1-56689-017-9*) Coffee Hse.

***Pate, Alexs D.** The Multicultiboho Sideshow, Vol. 1. LC 99-29476. 256p. 1999. 23.00 (*0-380-97678-1*, Avon Bks) Morrow Avon.

— Multicultiboho Sideshow: A Novel. 2001. write for info. (*0-380-80041-1*, Perennial) HarperTrade.

— West of Rehoboth. 2001. write for info. (*0-380-97679-X*, Wm Morrow) Morrow Avon.

Pate, Antony M., et al. Police Use of Force: Official Reports, Citizen Complaints, & Legal Consequences, 2 vols., Set only. LC 93-86909. (Illus.). 173p. (Orig.). 1993. pap. text. write for info. (*1-884614-01-9*); pap. text. write for info. (*1-884614-02-7*) Police Found.

— Police Use of Force: Official Reports, Citizen Complaints, & Legal Consequences, 2 vols., Vols. 1 - 2. LC 93-86909. (Illus.). 383p. (Orig.). 1993. pap. text 60.00 (*1-884614-00-0*) Police Found.

Pate, C. Marvin. Adam Christology As the Exegetical & Theological Substructure of Second Corinthians 4 7-5 21. 184p. (C). 1991. lib. bdg. 47.50 (*0-8191-8188-9*) U Pr of Amer.

***Pate, C. Marvin.** Communities of the Last Days: The Dead Sea Scrolls & the New Testament. LC 99-87490. 340p. 2000. pap. 21.99 (*0-8308-1597-X*) InterVarsity.

Pate, C. Marvin. The Glory of Adam & the Afflictions of the Righteous: Pauline Suffering in Context. LC 93-16072. (Biblical Press Ser.: Vol. 7). 380p. 1993. text 99.95 (*0-7734-2360-5*) E Mellen.

— Luke. (Gospel Commentaries Ser.). 475p. pap. 22.99 (*0-8024-5622-7*, 517) Moody.

***Pate, C. Marvin.** The Reverse of the Curse: Paul, Wisdom, & the Law. (Wissenshaftliche Untersuchungen zum Neuen Testament Ser.: Vol. 114). 550p. 2000. pap. 110.00 (*3-16-147286-1*, Pub. by JCB Mohr) Coronet Bks.

Pate, C. Marvin & Haines, Calvin B., Jr. Doomsday Delusions: What's Wrong with Predictions about the End of the World. LC 95-24330. 156p. (Orig.). 1995. pap. 9.99 (*0-8308-1621-6*, 1621) InterVarsity.

***Pate, C. Marvin & Pate, Sheryl L.** Behind the Masks: Personality Disorders in the Church. LC 99-45168. 128p. 2000. pap. 9.99 (*0-8054-1843-1*) Broadman.

Pate, Carol. Easy-to-Duplicate Juvenile Borders. (Quick Copy Ser.). (Illus.). 48p. pap. 5.95 (*0-486-27333-4*) Dover.

— Easy-to-Duplicate School & Education Borders: 57 Copyright-Free Forms. (Quick Copy Ser.). (Illus.). 48p. pap. 5.95 (*0-486-28259-7*) Dover.

— Ready-to-Use Illustrations of Toys, Dolls & Games. (Clip Art Ser.). (Illus.). 64p. (Orig.). 1991. pap. 5.95 (*0-486-26671-0*) Dover.

Pate, Charles W. U. S. Handguns of World War II: The Secondary Pistols & Revolvers. LC 97-73400. (Illus.). 368p. 1998. 39.00 (*0-917218-75-2*) A Mowbray.

Pate, Don. 52 Sabbath Activities for Teen Groups. LC 95-44383. 1995. pap. 9.99 (*0-8280-0941-4*) Review & Herald.

— Judean Chronicles. LC 98-114008. 160p. (Orig.). 1997. pap. 10.99 (*0-8280-1253-9*) Review & Herald.

Pate, Ernest. Dreams for a Quiet Night. LC 83-73639. 80p. (Orig.). 1984. pap. 4.95 (*0-87516-535-4*) DeVorss.

***Pate, James L.** Special Forces Close-Quarter Combat Manual. (Illus.). 184p. 1999. pap. 28.00 (*0-87364-824-2*) Paladin Pr.

Pate, James L., et al, eds. No Small Part: A History of Regional Organizations in American Psychology. LC 93-37085. 227p. 1993. text 29.95 (*1-55798-215-5*) Am Psychol.

Pate, James P., jt. auth. see Gaines, George S.

***Pate, Jeff.** Winner Take All: A Novel of Suspense. 358p. 2000. 25.00 (*0-9676528-0-4*) Harlan Pubng.

Pate, J'nell. North of the River: A Brief History of North Fort Worth. (Chisholm Trail Ser.: No. 11). 208p. (Orig.). (C). 1994. pap. 12.95 (*0-87565-133-X*) Tex Christian.

***Pate, J'Nell L.** Hazel Vaughn Leigh & the Fort Worth Boys' Club. LC 99-47283. (Illus.). 184p. 2000. pap. 12.95 (*0-87565-206-9*, Pub. by Tex Christian) Tex A&M Univ Pr.

Pate, J'Nell L. Ranald Slidell Mackenzie: Brave Cavalry Colonel. LC 93-21952. 166p. (J). (gr. 6-7). 1994. 14.95 (*0-89015-901-7*) Sunbelt Media.

An Asterisk (*) at the beginning of an entry indicates that the title is appearing for the first time.

Pate, J'Nell L., ed. Document Sets for Texas & the Southwest in U. S. History. 3rd ed. 171p. (C). 1991. pap. text 7.96 (*0-669-27109-8*) HM Trade Div.

***Pate, Joan, ed.** 1860 Mortality Schedule for State of Michigan. 267p. 1999. pap. 14.00 (*1-879766-32-9*) OCG Society.

Pate, Joan, ed. Eleventh Census of the United States, 1890: Oakland County, Michigan. 118p. (Orig.). 1994. pap. 8.00 (*1-879766-21-3*) OCG Society.

***Pate, Joan, ed.** Harper-Mulligan Funeral Home Records 1933-1942, Vol. I. 146p. 1999. pap. 8.00 (*1-879766-33-7*) OCG Society.

Pate, Joan, ed. Michigan State Census for Oakland County, 1845. 290p. (Orig.). 1985. pap. 15.00 (*1-879766-01-9*) OCG Society.

— Mortality Schedule for State of Michigan, 1850. 150p. (Orig.). 1996. pap. 10.00 (*1-879766-24-8*) OCG Society.

— Rose Township Cemeteries, Oakland County, Michigan. 72p. 1987. pap. 5.00 (*1-879766-09-4*) OCG Society.

— Roseland Park Cemetery (Military Sections) 59p. (Orig.). 1993. pap. text 5.00 (*1-879766-19-1*) OCG Society.

— Southfield United Presbyterian Church, Early Records. 101p. (Orig.). 1985. pap. 10.00 (*1-879766-02-7*) OCG Society.

***Pate, Joan, ed.** Surname Directory - 1999, Vol. VII. 230p. 1999. pap. 11.00 (*1-879766-31-0*) OCG Society.

Pate, Joan, ed. Surname Directory, 1989. 190p. (Orig.). 1989. pap. 10.00 (*1-879766-08-6*) OCG Society.

— Surname Directory, 1986. 194p. (Orig.). 1986. pap. 8.00 (*1-879766-07-8*) OCG Society.

— Surname Directory, 1983. 123p. (Orig.). 1991. pap. 10.00 (*1-879766-06-X*) OCG Society.

— Surname Directory 1997, Vol. VI. 115p. 1997. pap. 8.00 (*1-879766-25-6*) OCG Society.

— Troy Township Cemeteries, Oakland County, Michigan. 105p. (Orig.). 1988. pap. 7.00 (*1-879766-10-8*) OCG Society.

Pate, Joan, ed. Independence Township Cemeteries, Oakland County, Michigan. 309p. (Orig.). 1995. pap. 15.00 (*1-879766-23-X*) OCG Society.

Pate, Joan, intro. Birmingham & West Bloomfield Cemeteries, Oakland County, Michigan. 182p. (Orig.). 1990. pap. 11.00 (*1-879766-15-9*) OCG Society.

— Commerce Township Cemeteries, Oakland County, Michigan. 200p. (Orig.). 1989. pap. 12.00 (*1-879766-11-6*) OCG Society.

— Farmington & Farmington Hills Cemeteries, Oakland County, Michigan. 149p. (Orig.). 1990. pap. 9.00 (*1-879766-14-0*) OCG Society.

— Federal Census & Mortality Schedule, 1860, Oakland County, Michigan. 689p. (Orig.). 1988. pap. 40.00 (*1-879766-05-1*) OCG Society.

— Holly Township Cemeteries, Oakland County, Michigan. 235p. (Orig.). 1991. pap. 18.00 (*1-879766-17-5*) OCG Society.

— St. Mary's & Royal Oak Cemeteries, Oakland County, Michigan. 136p. (Orig.). 1990. pap. 11.00 (*1-879766-16-7*) OCG Society.

— Southfield Township Cemeteries, Oakland County, Michigan. 135p. (Orig.). 1989. pap. 10.00 (*1-879766-12-4*) OCG Society.

— Surname Directory, 1992, No. 4. 182p. (Orig.). 1992. pap. 10.00 (*1-879766-18-3*) OCG Society.

— White Lake Township Cemeteries, Oakland County, Michigan. 109p. (Orig.). 1990. pap. 8.00 (*1-879766-13-2*) OCG Society.

Pate, Joan, ed. see Society Members.

Pate, John & Dixon, Kingsley. Tuberous, Cormous & Bulbous Plants: Biology of an Adaptive Strategy in Western Australia. 39.95 (*0-85564-201-7*, Pub. by Univ of West Aust Pr) Intl Spec Bk.

Pate, John B. History of Turner County. LC 79-10025. (Illus.). 1979. reprint ed. 25.00 (*0-87152-295-0*) Reprint.

— History of Turner County Georgia. (Illus.). 198p. 1997. reprint ed. lib. bdg. 29.00 (*0-8328-7068-4*) Higginson Bk Co.

Pate, John S., jt. ed. see Meney, Kathy A.

Pate, L., ed. Ozark Writers on Writing: Essays on Creativity. LC 95-71608. 151p. (Orig.). 1996. pap. 12.95 (*0-9630829-4-9*) Seven Oaks Pub.

Pate, Larry, et al. Developing Organisations. 1985. 210.00 (*0-903763-42-7*) St Mut.

Pate, Larry D. Misionologia.Tr. of From Every People to Every People. (SPA.). 1996. pap. 14.99 (*0-8297-0470-1*) Vida Pubs.

***Pate, Marvin C.** Four Views on the Book of Revelation. LC 97-33425. (Counterpoints Ser.). 192p. 1998. pap. 16.99 (*0-310-21080-1*) Zondervan.

Pate, P. Elizabeth, et al. Making Integrated Curriculum Work: Teachers, Students, & the Quest for Coherent Curriculum. LC 96-42444. 1996. 34.00 (*0-8077-3598-1*); pap. 16.95 (*0-8077-3597-3*) Tchrs Coll.

Pate, R. Franklin. The Boomerang Poems. LC 90-46508. xiv, 54p. (Orig.). 1990. pap. 6.00 (*0-926487-07-8*) Rowan Mtn Pr.

Pate, Robert H., Jr., jt. auth. see Brown, Jeannette A.

Pate, Russell R. & Hohn, Richard C., eds. Health & Fitness Through Physical Education. LC 93-39707. (Illus.). 240p. 1994. pap. text 29.00 (*0-87322-490-6*, BPAT0490) Human Kinetics.

Pate, Russell R., jt. auth. see Greene, Laurence S.

Pate, Sarah S. Social Studies: Applications for a New Century. LC 95-34828. (Teaching Methods Ser.). 235p. (C). 1995. mass mkt. 36.95 (*0-8273-6637-X*) Delmar.

— Social Studies: Applications for a New Century. (Teaching Methods Ser.). 40p. (C). 1996. text, teacher ed. 14.95 (*0-8273-6638-8*, VNR) Wiley.

Pate, Sheryl L., jt. auth. see Pate, C. Marvin.

Pate, Steve. John David Crow: Heart of a Champion. limited ed. Jenkins, Dan, ed. (Texas College Football Legends Ser.). (Illus.). 160p. 1997. 99.95 (*1-57028-176-9*, Mstrs Pr) NTC Contemp Pub Co.

— UNIX Internals: A Practical Approach. LC 96-223623. (C). 1996. text 46.88 (*0-201-87721-X*) Addison-Wesley.

Pate, Steve, jt. auth. see Martinez, Matt, Jr.

Pate, Susan, et al. A Beginning Actor's Companion. 144p. (C). 1996. spiral bd. 23.04 (*0-7872-1765-4*) Kendall-Hunt.

Patee, James & Otteson, Orlo. Healthcare: How to Heal the Debate & Define the Argument. 1997. 27.50 (*0-614-27862-7*) Best Small Pr.

Patek, Jan. Quilts for Winter Days. LC 93-33043. (Seasons of the Heart & Home Ser.: No. 2). 1993. 18.95 (*0-89145-824-7*, 3796, Am Quilters Soc) Collector Bks.

Patel. The Complete Micropsychology. 1995. pap. text 32.50 (*0-7020-2067-2*, W B Saunders Co) Harcrt Hlth Sci Grp.

Patel & Langdon, eds. Operative Maxillofacial Surgery. (Illus.). 536p. 1999. text 225.00 (*0-412-56000-3*, Pub. by E A) OUP.

Patel, A. N. & Singh, S. Remote Sensing - Principles & Applications. (C). 1992. text 40.00 (*81-7233-037-5*, Pub. by Scientific Pubs) St Mut.

Patel, Alpesh B. The Mind of a Trader: Lessons in Trading Strategies from the World's Leading Traders. 288p. 1997. 34.95 (*0-273-63006-7*) F T P-H.

***Patel, Alpesh B.** Net-Trading: Strategies from the Frontiers of Electronic Day Trading. 256p. 2000. pap. 29.00 (*0-273-64502-1*) F T P H.

— Trading on Line. 2nd ed. (Illus.). 256p. 2000. pap. 26.95 (*0-273-65041-6*, Finc Times) F T P-H.

— Trading Online: A Step-By-Step Guide to Cyber Profits. (Illus.). 362p. 1999. pap. 29.95 (*0-273-63541-7*) F T P-H.

Patel, Arthi, jt. auth. see Goddard, Jane.

Patel, Ashok, jt. ed. see Riddle, Gregory W.

Patel, Ashok G., ed. The Complete MRCPsych. 255p. 1994. pap. text 38.50 (*0-7020-1808-2*, Pub. by W B Saunders) Saunders.

Patel, B. B. Workers of Closed Textile Mills. (C). 1988. 14.50 (*81-204-0290-1*, Pub. by Oxford IBH) S Asia.

Patel, B. B., ed. Problems of Home-Based Workers in India. (C). 1989. 32.50 (*81-204-0395-9*, Pub. by Oxford IBH) S Asia.

Patel, B. R., ed. see American Society of Mechanical Engineers Staff.

Patel, C. B. Dynastic History of Nalas. (C). 1990. text 56.00 (*81-85094-27-6*, Pub. by Punthi Pus) S Asia.

***Patel, C. Kumar.** Firepower in the Lab: Automation in the Fight Against Infectious Diseases & Bioterrorism. (Illus.). 300p. 2000. 69.95 (*0-309-06849-5*, Joseph Henry Pr) Natl Acad Pr.

Patel, Chandra K. Fiscal Reforms in the Least Developed Countries. LC 96-18298. 208p. 1997. 85.00 (*1-85898-513-7*) E Elgar.

Patel, Chandra K. & Gayi, Samuel, eds. Trade Diversification in the Least Developed Countries. LC 96-35157. 272p. 1997. 95.00 (*1-85898-514-5*) E Elgar.

Patel, Charles. Technical Trading Systems for Stocks & Commodities. (Illus.). 204p. 1998. 50.00 (*0-934380-45-7*) Traders Pr.

Patel, Chhaya & Denny, Mary. Cultural Foods & Renal Diets: Section I: For the Clinical Dietitian; Section II: A Multilingual Guide for Renal Patients, 2 vols., Set. 565p. (C). 1988. pap. text 50.00 (*1-883146-53-4*) Coun Renal Nutrit.

Patel, D. Gel Electrophoresis: Essential Data. LC 94-5796. (Essential Data Ser.). 158p. 1994. pap. 39.95 (*0-471-94306-1*) Wiley.

— Liquid Chromatography: Essential Data. LC 96-53627. (Essential Data Ser.). 160p. 1997. pap. 39.95 (*0-471-97270-3*) Wiley.

Patel, D., et al, eds. OOIS '96 Vol. XVII: 1996 International Conference on Object Oriented Information Systems, 16-18 December 1996. LC 96-37812. (Illus.). 515p. 1997. pap. 79.95 (*3-540-76132-2*) Spr-Verlag.

Patel, D., ed. see Sun, Yanqing.

Patel, D. K., jt. ed. see Sutherland, Jeffrey V.

Patel, Dipak, jt. auth. see Rickwood, David.

Patel, Divyesh N., jt. ed. see Graef, Mart.

Patel, Ebrahim. Worker Rights Vol. 1: From Apartheid to Democracy - What Role for Organized Labour? 203p. 1994. pap. text 28.00 (*0-7021-3076-1*, Pub. by Juta & Co) Gaunt.

Patel, Essop & Nakasa, Nat. The World of Nat Nakasa. LC 95-198771. (Writers Ser.). (Illus.). 206p. (C). 1995. reprint ed. pap. text 12.95 (*0-86975-464-5*, Pub. by Ravan Pr) Ohio U Pr.

Patel, Essop, jt. ed. see Couzens, Tim.

Patel, H., jt. ed. see Mehta, Haroobhai.

Patel, Hasu H., jt. auth. see Mazrui, Ali A.

Patel, I. G., ed. Policies for African Development: From the 1890s to the 1990s. LC 92-15526. 293p. 1992. pap. 24.00 (*1-55775-232-X*) Intl Monetary.

Patel, Indu, jt. auth. see Crosby, Neil T.

Patel, Ishwarbhai, ed. Sciences & the Vedas. 1986. 12.50 (*0-8364-1663-5*, Pub. by Somaiya) S Asia.

***Patel, Jagdish.** The Seven Cs of Happiness: How to Be Happy Using Common Sense. LC 99-64393. 1999. 25.00 (*0-7388-0498-3*); pap. 18.00 (*0-7388-0499-1*) Xlibris Corp.

Patel, Jagdish K. & Read, Campbell. Handbook of the Normal Distribution. LC 81-17422. (Statistics, Textbooks & Monographs; No. 40). 351p. reprint ed. pap. 108.90 (*0-7837-3550-2*, 204338700009) Bks Demand.

Patel, Jagdish K. & Read, Campbell B. Handbook of the Normal Distribution. 2nd ed. LC 95-49404. (Statistics: Textbooks & Monographs: Vol. 150). (Illus.). 456p. 1996. text 150.00 (*0-8247-9342-0*) Dekker.

Patel, Jagdish K., et al. Handbook of Statistical Distributions. LC 76-48474. (Statistics, Textbooks & Monographs: No. 20). 324p. reprint ed. pap. 100.50 (*0-608-15919-0*, 203087000071) Bks Demand.

Patel, Janak H., jt. auth. see Choudhary, Alok N.

***Patel, Jashu & Kumar, Krishan.** Libraries & Librarianship in India. LC 00-35454. (Guides to Asian Librarianship Ser.). 2000. lib. bdg. write for info. (*0-313-29423-2*) Greenwood.

***Patel, Jay.** Franchising - Is It Fair? How to Negotiate an Equitable Franchise Agreement. 175p. 1999. pap. 39.95 (*1-57635-054-1*) WeWrite.

Patel, Jay S., jt. ed. see Collings, Peter J.

Patel, Jay V., jt. auth. see Sinskey, Robert M.

Patel, Jayant. Seeking Home: An Immigrant's Realization. 81p. 1991. write for info. (*0-9631583-0-9*) J C Patel.

Patel, Jitendra, jt. ed. see Conn, P. Jeffrey.

Patel, Jitendra, jt. ed. see Pullan, Linda M.

Patel, Kant & Rushefsky, Mark E. Health Care Politics & Policy in America. LC 95-4603. (Illus.). 312p. (C). 1995. pap. text 36.95 (*1-56324-559-0*) M E Sharpe.

— Health Care Politics & Policy in America. LC 95-4603. (Illus.). 312p. (gr. 13). 1995. text 81.95 (*1-56324-558-2*) M E Sharpe.

***Patel, Kant & Rushefsky, Mark E.** Health Care Politics & Policy in America. 2nd ed. LC 98-56200. 480p. 1999. pap. text 32.95 (*0-7656-0390-X*) M E Sharpe.

Patel, Kant & Rushefsky, Mark E. Health Care Politics & Policy in America. 2nd rev. ed. LC 98-56200. (Illus.). 480p. (gr. 13). 1999. text 81.95 (*0-7656-0389-6*) M E Sharpe.

Patel, Kant, jt. auth. see Rushefsky, Mark E.

***Patel-Kanwal, Hansa & Lenderyou, Gill.** Let's Talk about Sex & Relationships: A Policy Framework for Working with Children & Young People in Public Care. 66p. 1999. spiral bd. 24.95 (*1-900990-36-9*, Pub. by Natl Childrens Bur) Paul & Co Pubs.

***Patel, Keyur & McCarthy, Mary Pat.** Digital Transformation: The Essentials of e-Business Leadership. 127p. 2000. 21.95 (*0-07-136408-0*) McGraw.

Patel, Kishor. Multicultural Education in All-White Areas. 352p. 1994. 77.95 (*1-85628-969-9*, Pub. by Avebry) Ashgate Pub Co.

Patel, Lalbhai D. The Magic of Numbers with Joy & Fun. 168p. (YA). (gr. 8-12). 1998. pap. 14.95 (*1-884962-19-X*) BookWorld.

***Patel, M. I.** Agrarian Transformation in Tribal India. (Tribal Studies). 352p. 1998. pap. 225.00 (*81-7533-086-4*, Pub. by Print Hse) St Mut.

Patel, M. I. Awareness in Weaker Section: Perspective Development & Prospects. LC 97-905428. 265p. 1997. pap. 212.50 (*81-7533-029-5*, Pub. by Print Hse) St Mut.

Patel, M. L. Development Dualism of Primitive Tribes: Constraints, Restraints & Fallacies. 298p. (C). 1994. pap. 188.00 (*81-85880-44-1*, Pub. by Print Hse) St Mut.

— Tribal Development Without Tears. LC 94-901362. (C). 1994. 38.00 (*81-210-0320-2*, Pub. by Inter-India Pubns) S Asia.

— Tribal Research in India: Approach, Constraints, Structure & Techniques. (C). 1994. text 34.00 (*81-210-0318-0*, Pub. by Inter-India Pubns) S Asia.

Patel, M. N., ed. see Marshall Editions Staff.

Patel, M. S., et al, eds. Alpha-Keto Acid Dehydrogenase Complexes. (Molecular & Cell Biology Updates Ser.). 321p. 1996. 155.00 (*0-8176-5181-0*, Pub. by Birkhauser); 155.00 (*3-7643-5181-0*) Birkhauser.

Patel, Mahlaqa, ed. see Fannoun, Kathy.

Patel, Mahlaqa, ed. see Ghazi, Abidullah.

Patel, Mahlaqa, ed. see Ghazi, Abidullah & Ghazi, Tasneema.

Patel, Mahlaqa, ed. see Ghazi, Suhaib.

Patel, Mahlaqa, ed. see Ghazi, Suhaib H.

Patel, Mahlaqa, ed. see Shaikh, Khalid M.

Patel, Maitray, jt. auth. see Gamsu, Gordon K.

Patel, Manish, jt. auth. see Lambert, Nevin.

Patel, Manu. Multiple Choice Questions in Preparation for the AP Physics (B&C) Examination. 2nd ed. 1995. pap. 16.95 (*1-878621-31-9*) D & S Mktg Syst.

— Student's Solutions Manual to Accompany Multiple Choice Questions in Preparation for the AP Physics (B&C) Examination. 2nd ed. 1995. pap., student ed. 13.95 (*1-878621-32-7*) D & S Mktg Syst.

***Patel, Mickey.** Story of a Panther. LC 98-903662. 1998. 14.00 (*81-7530-020-5*, Pub. by Ravi Dayal) S Asia.

Patel, Mukund R. Renewable Power System. LC 98-47934. 220p. 1999. lib. bdg. 79.95 (*0-8493-1605-7*) CRC Pr.

Patel, N. T., jt. auth. see Srivastava, U. K.

Patel, Narendra H. Student Transfers from White to Black Colleges. (National Association for Equal Opportunity in Higher Education Ser.: No. 3). 40p. (Orig.). (C). 1988. pap. text 10.00 (*0-8191-6952-8*) U Pr of Amer.

Patel, Nitin R., jt. auth. see Mehta, Cyrus R.

Patel, P. R. Lecture Notes on Radiology. LC 97-10069. (Lecture Notes Ser.). (Illus.). 1997. pap. 32.95 (*0-632-04758-5*) Blackwell Sci.

Patel, Pannalal. Endurance: A Droll Saga. 1995. 30.00 (*81-7201-899-1*) S Asia.

Patel, Pravinchandra J. Patel's Immigration Law Digest, 5 vols. LC 34-82185. (Immigration Law Ser.). 1985. ring bd., suppl. ed. 575.00 (*0-685-59812-8*) West Group.

Patel, Pretik. Java Database Programming with JDBC: Discover the Essentials for Developing Databases. 10th ed. LC 98-123285. 500p. (C). 1997. mass mkt. 39.99 (*1-57610-159-2*) Coriolis Grp.

Patel, R. I. Forest Flora of Melghat. 380p. (C). 1968. 90.00 (*0-7855-3124-6*, Pub. by Intl Bk Distr) St Mut.

Patel, R. V., et al, eds. Numerical Linear Algebra Techniques for Systems & Control. LC 93-27006. (Illus.). 736p. 1993. text 99.95 (*0-7803-0443-8*, PC3400) Inst Electrical.

Patel, Rahul. Ordinary People Extraordinary Lives: A Book of Possibilities. LC 98-100939. (Illus.). 56p. 1997. pap. 14.99 (*0-9661493-0-0*) R Patel.

Patel, Rajeshwari. W. B. Yeats & the Ideal of "Unity of Being" 200p. 1990. text 27.50 (*81-85218-13-7*, Pub. by Prestige) Advent Bks Div.

Patel, Rajnikant V., jt. auth. see Balafoutis, Constantinos A.

Patel, Ramesh C., jt. auth. see Zuman, Petr.

Patel, Ramesh N. Philosophy of the Gita. LC 90-40763. (American University Studies: Philosophy: Ser. V, Vol. 105). X, 311p. (C). 1991. text 47.95 (*0-8204-1416-6*) P Lang Pubng.

***Patel, Ramesh N.** Stereoselective Biocatalysis. LC 99-51468. 932p. 1999. write for info. (*0-8247-8282-8*) Dekker.

Patel, Raojibhai M. Manav Mootra (Auto-Urine Therapy) 6th ed. 252p. 1994. reprint ed. pap. 12.95 (*0-8464-4820-3*) Beekman Pubs.

Patel, Salil, jt. auth. see Maulik, Sunil.

Patel, Sardar V. The Collected Works of Sardar Vallabhbhai Patel, Vol. II (1926-1929) Chopra, P. N., ed. 432p. (C). 1992. text 60.00 (*81-220-0252-8*, Pub. by Konark Pubs Pvt Ltd) Advent Bks Div.

— Collected Works of Sardar Vallabhbhai Patel, 1918-1925, Vol. I. (Illus.). 500p. 1990. text 60.00 (*81-220-0179-3*, Pub. by Konark Pubs Pvt Ltd) Advent Bks Div.

Patel, Sarol K. Cultural History of Early Medieval Orissa. (C). 1991. text 78.00 (*81-85067-71-6*, Pub. by Sundeep Prak) S Asia.

Patel, Satyavrata. Hinduism: Religion & Way of Life. 165p. (gr. 9-12). 1980. 15.95 (*0-940500-25-6*) Asia Bk Corp.

Patel, Satyavrata R. Tribal Education in India: A Case Study of Orrissa. (C). 1991. 14.00 (*81-7099-292-3*, Pub. by Mittal Pubs Dist) S Asia.

Patel, Shilpesh S., et al. Handbook of Cardiovascular Clinical Trials. LC 96-43506. 1996. pap. text 32.95 (*0-443-07925-0*) Church.

Patel, Shriprakas B. Nuclear Physics: An Introduction. 346p. 1991. text 74.95 (*0-470-21130-X*) Halsted Pr.

Patel, Sujata. The Making of Industrial Relations: The Ahmedabad Textile Industry, 1918-1939. 172p. 1988. 18.95 (*0-19-562064-X*) OUP.

Patel, Sujata & Thorner, Alice, eds. Bombay: Metaphor for Modern India. (Illus.). 336p. 1997. reprint ed. pap. 10.95 (*0-19-564086-1*) OUP.

— Bombay: Mosaic of Arts & Letters. (Illus.). 288p. 1995. text 35.00 (*0-19-563689-9*) OUP.

— Bombay: Mosaic of Arts & Letters. (Illus.). 270p. 1997. pap. text 11.95 (*0-19-564085-3*) OUP.

Patel, Surendra J., ed. Africa. (Technological Transformation in the Third World Ser.: Vol. 2). 242p. 1993. 72.95 (*1-85628-470-0*, Pub. by Avebry) Ashgate Pub Co.

— Technological Tranformation, Vol. 5. (Technological Transformation in the Third World Ser.). 304p. 1995. 77.95 (*1-85628-612-6*, Pub. by Avebry) Ashgate Pub Co.

— Technological Transformation in the Third World: Asia, Vol. 1. (Technological Transformation in the Third World Ser.). 344p. 1993. 77.95 (*1-85628-469-7*, Pub. by Avebry) Ashgate Pub Co.

— Technological Transformation in the Third World Vol. 3: Latin America. 346p. 1993. 82.95 (*1-85628-471-9*, Pub. by Avebry) Ashgate Pub Co.

— Technological Transformation in the Third World Vol. 4: Developed Countries. (Technological Transformation in the Third World Ser.: Vol. 4). 310p. 1993. 72.95 (*1-85628-472-7*, Pub. by Avebry) Ashgate Pub Co.

— Trademarks in Developing Countries. 122p. 1979. pap. 29.00 (*0-08-025223-0*, Pergamon Pr) Elsevier.

Patel, T. Dayananda. Kesava Temple at Somanathapura: A Cultural Study. 1990. 74.00 (*0-8364-2522-7*, Pub. by Agam Kala Prakashan) S Asia.

Patel, T. S., tr. see Dubinin, G. N. & Avraamov, Yu S.

Patel, Tara. Development of Education among Tribal Women. 1985. 17.50 (*0-8364-1320-2*, Pub. by Mittal Pubs Dist) S Asia.

Patel, Tara, jt. auth. see Shah, V. P.

Patel, Tulsi. Fertility Behaviour: Population & Society in a Rajasthan Village. (Illus.). 304p. 1995. text 28.00 (*0-19-563539-6*) OUP.

Patel, V., jt. auth. see Desai, Neera.

Patel, V. I., jt. ed. see Evans, D. A.

Patel, V. T., ed. Problems & Issues in Gandhism. 1990. reprint ed. 48.50 (*81-210-0250-8*, Pub. by Inter-India Pubns) S Asia.

Patel, Vikram. Culture & Common Mental Disorders in Sub-Saharan Africa. (Volume in the Maudsley Monograph Ser.). 144p. 1998. write for info. (*0-86377-530-6*, Pub. by Psychol Pr) Taylor & Francis.

Patel, Vilma, jt. ed. see Evans, David A.

Patel, Vimal H. & Friedman, Lawrence. MRI of the Brain: Normal Anatomy & Normal Variants. Valkoff, Sandra, ed. LC 96-41701. 325p. 1996. text 89.00 (*0-7216-6945-X*, W B Saunders Co) Harcrt Hlth Sci Grp.

Patel, Vimla, ed. see Boy, Guy A.

Patel, Vithal A. Numerical Analysis. LC 93-86061. 652p. (C). 1993. text 93.00 (*0-03-098330-4*) SCP.

Patel, Yogesh. Magic Glasses. (Early Reading Ser.). (Illus.). (J). 1995. pap. 4.99 (*0-85953-945-8*) Childs Play.

— Magic Glasses. (Children's Stories Published in Other Lands Ser.). (Illus.). 32p. (J). (gr. k-3). 1996. lib. bdg. 12.95 (*1-56674-146-7*, HTS Bks) Forest Hse.

Patell, Cyrus R. Beyond Hybridity: The Future of U.S. Emergent Literatures. text. write for info. (*0-312-23387-6*) St Martin.

Patell, Cyrus R. Joyce's View of History in Finnegans Wake. (LeBaron Russell Briggs Prize Honors Essays in English Ser.). 96p. 1985. pap. 5.30 (*0-674-48711-7*) HUP.

P

Patell, Cyrus R., jt. ed. see Bercovitch, Sacvan.

Patella, Chris & Oddo, Eileen. Makin Music! (Illus.). 75p. (Orig.). (J). (gr. k-2). 1989. audio, lp. write for info. (*0-318-64483-5*) Musical Munchkins.

— Makin' Music. (Musical Munchkins Are...Ser.). (Illus.). 75p. (J). (gr. k-2). 1989. teacher ed. 9.95 incl. audio (*0-944333-02-8*) Musical Munchkins.

— Marvelous Musical Adventures for Developing Early Musicianship. (Musical Munchkins Presents Ser.). (Illus.). 50p. 1987. pap. 7.95 (*0-944333-00-1*); audio, lp 9.95 (*0-685-19315-2*) Musical Munchkins.

Patella, Rocco. Basic Air Conditioning. 1980. student ed. 7.00 (*0-8064-0333-0*, 830) Bergwall.

Patelson, Alice. Portrait of a Dancer, Memories of Balanchine: An Autobiography. 1995. 17.95 (*0-533-11378-4*) Vantage.

Pateman, Carole. The Disorder of Women: Democracy, Feminism, & Political Theory. LC 89-62425. 236p. 1990. 42.50 (*0-8047-1764-8*); pap. 13.95 (*0-8047-1765-6*) Stanford U Pr.

— Participation & Democratic Theory. LC 71-120193. 122p. 1976. pap. text 20.95 (*0-521-29004-X*) Cambridge U Pr.

— The Problem of Political Obligation: A Critical Analysis of Liberal Theory. LC 78-18460. 217p. reprint ed. pap. 67.30 (*0-608-17556-0*, 203053600069) Bks Demand.

— The Sexual Contract. LC 87-63007. xii, 264p. 1988. 45.00 (*0-8047-1476-2*); pap. 16.95 (*0-8047-1477-0*) Stanford U Pr.

Pateman, Carole & Gross, Elizabeth, eds. Feminist Challenges: Social & Political Theory. (Northeastern Series in Feminist Theory). 225p. (C). 1986. text 45.00 (*1-55553-003-6*); pap. text 17.95 (*1-55553-004-4*) NE U Pr.

Pateman, Carole, jt. ed. see Goodnow, Jacqueline.

Pateman, Carole, jt. ed. see Shanley, Mary L.

Pateman, Neil A. Teaching Mathematics - A Tantalising Enterprise: On the Nature of Mathematics & Mathematics Teaching. (C). 1989. 44.00 (*0-7300-0630-1*, Pub. by Deakin Univ) St Mut.

Pateman, Roy. Eritrea: Even the Stones Are Burning. LC 90-81664. (Illus.). 260p. 1990. 35.00 (*0-932415-61-X*) Red Sea Pr.

— Eritrea: Even the Stones Are Burning. rev. ed. 252p. 1998. 49.95 (*1-56902-026-4*) Red Sea Pr.

— Eritrea: Even the Stones Are Burning. 2nd ed. LC 97-15405. 256p. 1997. pap. write for info. (*1-56902-057-4*) Red Sea Pr.

Pateman, Trevor. Key Concepts: A Guide to Aesthetics, Criticisms, & the Arts in Education. (Falmer Press Library on Aesthetic Education). 300p. 1991. 95.00 (*1-85000-793-4*, Falmer Pr); pap. 34.95 (*1-85000-794-2*, Falmer Pr) Taylor & Francis.

— Language in Mind & Language in Society: Studies in Linguistic Reproduction. 208p. 1987. text 55.00 (*0-19-824213-1*) OUP.

Pateman, Yvonne C. Women Who Dared: American Female Test Pilots, Flight Test Engineers, & Astronauts. (Illus.). 136p. 1996. 29.95 (*0-9654422-0-9*) Norstahr.

***Patenall, Philip.** Learn to Draw People. (Learn to Draw Ser.). (Illus.). 64p. 1999. pap. 14.95 (*0-00-413361-7*, Pub. by HarpC) Trafalgar.

Patenaude, ed. see Shakespeare, William.

Patenaude, Allan, ed. see Shakespeare, William.

Patenaude, Bertrand, jt. ed. see Dallin, Alexander.

Patenaude, Bertrand M., ed. The Russian Revolution. LC 91-45133. (Articles on Russian & Soviet History, 1500-1991 Ser.: Vol. 5). 334p. 1992. text 20.00 (*0-8153-0562-1*) Garland.

Patenaude, Bertrand M., jt. ed. see Dallin, Alexander.

Patenaude, Bertrand M., jt. ed. see Emmons, Terence.

***Patenaude, Branwen C.** Golden Nuggets: Roadhouse Portraits along the Cariboo Gold-Rush Trail. LC 99-188820. (Illus.). 96p. 1998. pap. 19.95 (*1-895811-56-2*) Heritage Hse.

***Patenaude, Joyce A.** Too Tired to Keep Running - Too Scared to Stop: Change Your Beliefs, Change Your Life. 304p. 2000. pap. 9.95 (*1-86204-270-5*) Element MA.

Patenaude, Joyce A. Too Tired to Keep Running, Too Scared to Stop: Change Your Beliefs, Change Your Life. LC 98-13575. 1998. 109.70 (*1-86204-342-6*, Pub. by Element MA) Penguin Putnam.

— Too Tired to Keep Running-Too Tired to Stop: Change Your Beliefs, Change Your Life. 274p. 1998. 21.95 (*1-86204-349-3*, Pub. by Element MA) Penguin Putnam.

***Patenaude, Robert.** Surviving Leukemia: A Practical Guide. (Personal Health Ser.). (Illus.). 248p. 1999. pap. 19.95 (*1-55209-354-9*) Firefly Bks Ltd.

Patenm, Geoff. Handguns: A Collector's Guide. 1993. 17.98 (*1-55521-916-0*) Bk Sales Inc.

Patent & Trademark Office Staff. Manual of Patent Examining Procedure. 16th ed. (IP Ser.). 1993. pap. 60.00 (*0-614-07304-9*) West Group.

Patent, Arnold M. Money & Beyond. 2nd ed. 226p. 1997. 16.95 (*1-885223-24-2*) Beyond Words Pub.

— You Can Have It All. LC 96-42942. 1997. per. 12.00 (*0-671-00076-4*) PB.

— You Can Have it All. 3rd rev. ed. LC 94-41441. (The/Business of Life Ser.). 224p. (C). 1995. 16.95 (*1-885223-05-6*) Beyond Words Pub.

Patent, Dorothy. Great Ice Bear: The Polar Bear & the Eskimo. LC 97-44820. 40p. (J). 1999. 16.00 (*0-688-13767-9*, Wm Morrow) Morrow Avon.

***Patent, Dorothy.** Great Ice Bear: The Polar Bear & the Eskimo. LC 97-44820. 40p. (J). 1999. 15.89 (*0-688-13768-7*, Wm Morrow) Morrow Avon.

Patent, Dorothy H. Alex & Friends: Animal Talk, Animal Thinking. LC 97-26496. (Illus.). (J). 1997. 23.93 (*0-8225-2859-2*) Lerner Pub.

Patent, Dorothy H. The American Alligator. LC 93-37704. (Illus.). 80p. (J). 1994. 15.95 (*0-395-63392-3*, Clarion Bks) HM.

— Apple Trees. LC 96-27581. (Early Bird Nature Bks.). 48p. (J). 1997. lib. bdg. 19.93 (*0-8225-3020-1*, Lerner Publctns) Lerner Pub.

— Baby Horses. (Illus.). 56p. (J). (ps-3). 1991. lib. bdg. 22.60 (*0-87614-690-6*, Carolrhoda) Lerner Pub.

— Back to the Wild. LC 95-43254. (Illus.). 80p. 1997. 18.00 (*0-15-200280-4*) Harcourt.

— Biodiversity. LC 95-49982. (Illus.). 96p. (J). (gr. 4-9). 1996. 18.00 (*0-395-68704-7*, Clarion Bks) HM.

— Bold & Bright, Black & White Animals. LC 98-3364. (Illus.). 32p. (J). (gr. k-4). 1998. 15.95 (*0-8027-8672-3*); lib. bdg. 16.85 (*0-8027-8673-1*) Walker & Co.

— Buffalo: The American Bison Today. (J). 1986. 12.15 (*0-606-05772-2*, Pub. by Turtleback) Demco.

— Cattle. LC 92-32987. (Illus.). (J). (gr. 4-6). 1993. lib. bdg. 19.95 (*0-87614-765-1*, Carolrhoda) Lerner Pub.

— Deer & Elk. LC 93-25894. (Illus.). 80p. (J). 1994. 15.95 (*0-395-52003-7*, Clarion Bks) HM.

— Dogs: The Wolf Within. LC 92-12334. (Understanding Animals Ser.). (Illus.). (J). (gr. 4-6). 1992. lib. bdg. 19.93 (*0-87614-691-4*, Carolrhoda) Lerner Pub.

— Dogs: The Wolf Within. (Illus.). 48p. (J). (gr. 4-6). 1993. pap. 7.95 (*0-87614-604-3*, First Ave Edns) Lerner Pub.

— Eagles of America. LC 95-6083. (Illus.). 40p. (J). (gr. 4-6). 1995. 15.95 (*0-8234-1198-2*) Holiday.

— A Family Goes Hunting. (Illus.). 64p. (J). (gr. 4-9). 1991. 14.95 (*0-395-52004-5*, Clarion Bks) HM.

— Fire: Friend or Foe. LC 98-11754. (Illus.). (J). (gr. 3-7). 1998. 16.00 (*0-395-73081-3*, Clarion Bks) HM.

— Flashy Fantastic Rain Forest Frogs. LC 96-29060. (Illus.). 32p. (J). (gr. k-3). 1997. lib. bdg. 16.85 (*0-8027-8616-2*) Walker & Co.

— Flashy Fantastic Rain Forest Frogs. LC 96-29060. (Illus.). 32p. (J). (gr. 2-5). 1997. 15.95 (*0-8027-8615-4*) Walker & Co.

— Gray Wolf, Red Wolf. (Illus.). 64p. (J). (gr. 4 up). 1990. 16.00 (*0-89919-863-5*, Clarion Bks) HM.

— Gray Wolf, Red Wolf. 64p. (J). (gr. 4-7). 1994. pap. 7.95 (*0-395-69627-5*, Clarion Bks) HM.

— Homesteading: Settling America's Heartland. LC 98-12463. (Illus.). 32p. (J). (gr. 2-5). 1998. 16.95 (*0-8027-8664-2*); lib. bdg. 17.85 (*0-8027-8665-0*) Walker & Co.

— Horses. LC 93-12329. (Understanding Animals Behavior Ser.). (Illus.). (J). (gr. 4-6). 1993. lib. bdg. 19.95 (*0-87614-766-X*, Carolrhoda) Lerner Pub.

— Horses. (Illus.). 48p. (J). (gr. 1-4). 1996. pap. text 7.95 (*0-87614-991-3*) Lerner Pub.

— In Search of the Maiasaurs. LC 97-46733. (Frozen in Time Ser.). 64p. (YA). (gr. 4 up). 1998. lib. bdg. 27.07 (*0-7614-0787-1*, Benchmark NY) Marshall Cavendish.

— Looking at Bears. LC 94-1834. (Illus.). 40p. (J). (gr. k-3). 1994. lib. bdg. 15.95 (*0-8234-1139-7*) Holiday.

— Looking at Penguins. LC 92-37673. (Illus.). 40p. (J). (gr. k-3). 1993. lib. bdg. 16.95 (*0-8234-1037-4*) Holiday.

— Mystery of the Lascaux Cave. LC 97-48276. (Frozen in Time Ser.). (Illus.). 64p. (YA). (gr. 4 up). 1998. 18.95 (*0-7614-0784-7*) Benchmark Books.

— Osprey. LC 92-30103. (Illus.). 64p. (J). (gr. 4-9). 1993. 14.95 (*0-395-63391-5*, Clarion Bks) HM.

— Pigeons. LC 96-42072. (Illus.). 80p. (J). (gr. 3-6). 1997. 16.00 (*0-395-69848-0*, Clarion Bks) HM.

***Patent, Dorothy H.** Prairie Dogs. LC 92-34724. (Illus.). 64p. (J). 1999. 16.00 (*0-395-56572-3*, Clarion Bks) HM.

Patent, Dorothy H. Prairies. LC 96-14125. (Illus.). 40p. (J). (gr. 4-6). 1996. lib. bdg. 15.95 (*0-8234-1277-6*) Holiday.

— The Quetzal: Sacred Bird of the Forest. LC 95-14402. (Illus.). 40p. (J). 1996. 16.00 (*0-688-12662-6*, Wm Morrow); lib. bdg. 15.93 (*0-688-12663-4*, Wm Morrow) Morrow Avon.

— Return of the Wolf. LC 94-26798. (Illus.). 80p. (J). (gr. 4-7). 1995. 15.95 (*0-395-72100-8*, Clarion Bks) HM.

— Return of the Wolf. LC 94-26798. (Illus.). 80p. (gr. 4-7). 1997. pap. 5.95 (*0-395-84519-X*, Clarion Bks) HM.

— Return of the Wolf. LC 94-26798. 1995. 11.05 (*0-606-11790-3*, Pub. by Turtleback) Demco.

— Secrets of the Ice Man. LC 97-49512. (Frozen in Time Ser.). 72p. (YA). (gr. 4 up). 1998. lib. bdg. 27.07 (*0-7614-0782-0*, Benchmark NY) Marshall Cavendish.

— Turkeys. LC 98-20466. (Early Bird Nature Bks.). (Illus.). 48p. (J). (gr. 2-3). 1999. 22.60 (*0-8225-3026-0*, Lerner Publctns) Lerner Pub.

— The Vanishing Feast. LC 94-2227. (Gulliver Green Book Ser.). 192p. (YA). (gr. 7 up). 1994. 17.95 (*0-15-292867-7*, Gulliver Bks) Harcourt.

— West by Covered Wagon: A Journey on the Oregon Trail. LC 94-48233. (Illus.). 32p. (J). (gr. 3-7). 1995. 15.95 (*0-8027-8377-5*); lib. bdg. 16.85 (*0-8027-8378-3*) Walker & Co.

— Where Bald Eagles Gather. 1990. pap. 5.95 (*0-395-53464-X*, Pub. by Ticknor & Fields) HM.

— Where the Bald Eagles Gather. (J). 1984. 11.15 (*0-606-04583-X*, Pub. by Turtleback) Demco.

— Where the Wild Horses Roam. 80p. (J). (gr. 4-7). 1993. pap. 6.95 (*0-395-66506-X*, Clarion Bks) HM.

— Where the Wild Horses Roam. (J). 1989. 15.95 (*0-89919-507-5*, Pub. by Ticknor & Fields) HM.

— The Whooping Crane. (J). (gr. 4-7). 1993. pap. 6.95 (*0-395-66505-1*, Clarion Bks) HM.

Patent, Dorothy H., et al. The Book of Garden Secrets. 2nd rev. ed. (Illus.). 368p. 1997. pap. 19.95 (*1-55209-104-X*) Firefly Bks Ltd.

***Patent, Dorothy Hinshaw.** The Bald Eagle Returns. LC 00-21751. (Illus.). 80p. (J). (gr. 4-7). 2000. 15.00 (*0-395-91416-7*, Clarion Bks) HM.

— Frozen in Time Boxed Set. (Illus.). 64-72p. lib. bdg. 81.21 (*0-7614-0781-2*) Marshall Cavendish.

Patent, Dorothy Hinshaw. Frozen in Time Boxed Set, 3. 2000. 81.21 (*0-7614-0799-5*, Benchmark NY) Marshall Cavendish.

Patent, Dorothy Hinshaw. Gray Wolf, Red Wolf. LC 89-77718. 1990. 12.15 (*0-606-06424-9*, Pub. by Turtleback) Demco.

— Horses. LC 00-8027. (Early Bird Nature Bks.). (Illus.). 2001. lib. bdg. write for info. (*0-8225-3045-7*, Lerner Publctns) Lerner Pub.

— The Incredible Story of China's Buried Warriors. LC 99-34971. (Frozen in Time Ser.). (J). (gr. 4-7). 2000. 27.07 (*0-7614-0783-9*, Benchmark NY) Marshall Cavendish.

— Lost City of Pompeii. LC 99-34980. (Frozen in Time Ser.). (J). (gr. 4-7). 2000. 27.07 (*0-7614-0785-5*, Benchmark NY) Marshall Cavendish.

— A Polar Bear Biologist at Work. LC 00-38151. (Illus.). 2001. write for info. (*0-531-11850-9*) Watts.

— Polar Bears. LC 99-29601. (Nature Watch Ser.). (Illus.). 48p. (J). (gr. 2-7). 2000. 22.60 (*1-57505-020-X*, Carolrhoda) Lerner Pub.

— Slinky, Scaly, Slithery Snakes. (Illus.). 32p. 2000. lib. bdg. write for info. (*0-8027-8744-4*) Walker & Co.

— Slinky, Scaly, Slithery Snakes. (Illus.). 32p. (J). (gr. 2-5). 2000. write for info. (*0-8027-8743-6*) Walker & Co.

— Treasures of the Spanish Main. LC 99-32141. (Frozen in Time Ser.). (J). (gr. 4-7). 2000. 27.07 (*0-7614-0786-3*) Marshall Cavendish.

Patent, Dorothy Hinshaw. Where the Wild Horses Roam. (Clarion Nonfiction Ser.). 1989. 12.15 (*0-606-06092-8*, Pub. by Turtleback) Demco.

***Patent, Dorothy Hinshaw & Munoz, William.** Shaping the Earth. LC 99-37093. 96p. (J). (gr. 4-7). 2000. 18.00 (*0-395-85691-4*, Clarion Bks) HM.

Patent, Dorothy Hinshaw, see Hinshaw Patent, Dorothy.

Patent, Greg. A Is for Apple: More Than 200 Recipes for Eating, Munching & Cooking with America's Favorite Fruit. LC 98-41926. (Illus.). 276p. 1999. pap. 15.00 (*0-7679-0203-3*) Broadway BDD.

— More Big Sky Cooking. (Big Sky Cooking Ser.: No. 2). (Illus.). 151p. (Orig.). 1980. pap. 9.50 (*0-686-29281-2*) Eagle Comm.

Patente, Michelle S. Umbrians Poetica: Poetry & Lyric Myth for Social Reform. 1998. pap. write for info. (*1-57553-632-3*) Watermrk Pr.

Pater, Alan F., ed. Anthology of Magazine Verse for Nineteen Thirty-Five Yearbook of American Poetry. LC 33-27220. 1976. reprint ed. 25.00 (*0-89609-033-7*) Roth Pub Inc.

Pater, Anton S. Personal Education: About General Learning, Motivation, Development & Progress. LC 76-56540. 1977. 20.00 (*0-918210-01-1*, GL-1A); pap. 15.00 (*0-918210-00-3*, GL-1) Multi Spectral.

Pater, Calvin A. Karlstadt As the Father of the Baptist Movements: The Emergence of Lay Protestantism. LC 84-166680. (Illus.). 364p. reprint ed. pap. 112.90 (*0-8357-3783-7*, 203651300003) Bks Demand.

— Karlstadt As the Father of the Baptist Movements: The Emergence of Lay Protestantism. LC 93-32132. (Illus.). 364p. 1993. reprint ed. text 99.95 (*0-7734-9357-3*) E Mellen.

Pater, Calvin Augustine, jt. ed. see Petersen, Rodney L.

Pater, Robert. The Black Belt Manager: Martial Arts Strategies for Power, Creativity, & Control. Orig. Title: Martial Arts & Arts of Management. 224p. 1989. pap. 10.95 (*0-89281-295-8*, Park St Pr) Inner Tradit.

— How to Make High Impact Safety & Health Presentations. 2nd ed. 46p. 1995. pap. 16.95 (*0-614-23298-8*) ASSE.

— Leading from Within: Martial Arts Skills for Enlightened Business & Management. LC 99-24435. 224p. 1999. 16.95 (*0-89281-794-1*, Park St Pr) Inner Tradit.

Pater, Walter. Essays from 'The Guardian' LC 73-99717. (Essay Index Reprint Ser.). 1977. 19.95 (*0-8369-1370-1*) Ayer.

— Essays on Literature & Art. Uglow, Jennifer, ed. 203p. 1996. pap. 7.95 (*0-460-87009-2*, Everyman's Classic Lib) Tuttle Pubng.

— Gaston de Latour: An Unfinished Romance. Shadwell, Charles L., ed. LC 79-8429. reprint ed. 44.50 (*0-404-62093-0*) AMS Pr.

— Gaston de Latour: The Revised Text. rev. ed. Monsman, Gerald, ed. & intro. by. LC 94-62118. (1880-1920 British Authors Ser.: No. 10). (Illus.). 350p. 1995. lib. bdg. 40.00 (*0-944318-09-6*) ELT Pr.

— Imaginary Portraits. LC 75-30036. reprint ed. 29.50 (*0-404-14038-6*) AMS Pr.

— Imaginary Portraits: With The Child in the House & Gaston de Latour. LC 96-79665. (Illus.). 256p. (Orig.). 1997. pap. 18.95 (*1-880559-77-3*) Allworth Pr.

***Pater, Walter.** Imaginary Portraits: With The Child in the House & Gaston de Latour. 213p. (Orig.). 2000. reprint ed. pap. text 19.00 (*0-7881-6929-7*) DIANE Pub.

Pater, Walter. Marius the Epicurean: His Sensations & Ideas. 224p. 1985. reprint ed. pap. 18.95 (*0-948166-02-9*, Pub. by Soho Bk Co) Dufour.

— Plato & Platonism: A Series of Lectures. LC 69-14031. 282p. 1970. reprint ed. lib. bdg. 79.50 (*0-8371-1151-X*, PAPP, Greenwood Pr) Greenwood.

***Pater, Walter.** The Renaissance. (Green Integer Bks.: No. 38). 200p. 1999. pap. text 11.95 (*1-892295-32-6*, Pub. by Green Integer) Consort Bk Sales.

Pater, Walter. The Renaissance: Studies in Art & Poetry. Phillips, Adam, ed. & intro. by. (Oxford World's Classics Ser.). 208p. 1998. pap. 7.95 (*0-19-283553-X*) OUP.

— The Renaissance: Studies in Art & Poetry. LC 77-12308. 239p. 1977. reprint ed. pap. 9.00 (*0-915864-35-5*) Academy Chi Pubs.

— Selected Writings of Walter Pater. Bloom, Harold, ed. & intro. by. LC 81-17099. (Morningside Bk.). 304p. 1982. reprint ed. pap. text 23.00 (*0-231-05481-5*) Col U Pr.

— Sketches & Reviews. LC 77-99718. (Essay Index Reprint Ser.). 1977. 19.95 (*0-8369-1371-X*) Ayer.

Patera, Charlotte. Schoolhouse Applique: Reverse Techniques & More. (Illus.). 80p. 1995. pap. 19.95 (*0-914881-99-X*, 10121) C & T Pub.

Patera, J., jt. auth. see McKay, W. G.

Patera, Jiri, ed. Quasicrystals & Discrete Geometry. LC 98-4530. (Fields Institute Monographs: Vol. 10). 289p. 1998. 79.00 (*0-8218-0682-3*, FIM/10) Am Math.

Patera, Meridith S. Kings & Things: 20 Jewish Plays for Kids 8 to 18. LC 96-84132. 164p. (J). (gr. 3-12). 1996. pap. 11.95 (*0-86705-038-1*) A R E Pub.

Patera, Tatiana, compiled by. A Concordance to the Poetry of Anna Akhmatova. LC 94-7867. 353p. 1995. 60.00 (*0-87501-111-X*) Ardis Pubs.

Paterculus, Velleius. Ad M. Vinicium Consulem Libri duo Curavit Adnotavitque Maria Elefante. (Bibliotheca Weidmanniana Ser.: Vol. III). (GER.). xxxvi, 583p. 1996. 178.00 (*3-487-10257-9*) G Olms Pubs.

— Concordantia in Velleium Paterculum. Elefante, Maria, ed. (Alpha-Omega, Reihe A Ser.: Bd. LXXVI). (GER.). vi, 524p. 1992. write for info. incl. 3.5 hd (*3-487-09506-8*) G Olms Pubs.

— Velleii Paterculi Quae Supersunt Ex Historiae Romanae Libris Duobus. (GER.). cxliv, 638p. reprint ed. write for info. (*0-318-70527-3*) G Olms Pubs.

Paterek, Josephine. Encyclopedia of American Indian Costume. LC 93-39337. 516p. 1994. lib. bdg. 99.50 (*0-87436-685-2*) ABC-CLIO.

— Encyclopedia of American Indian Costume. (Illus.). 536p. 1996. pap. 22.95 (*0-393-31382-4*) Norton.

Patern, Fabio. Model-Based Design & Evaluation of Interactive Applications. LC 99-12334. (Applied Computing Ser.). (Illus.). 205p. 1999. 49.95 (*1-85233-155-0*, Pub. by Spr-Verlag) Spr-Verlag.

Paternain, G. P. Geodesic Flows. LC 99-38332. (Progress in Mathematics Ser.). 168p. 1999. 44.95 (*0-8176-4144-0*, Pub. by Birkhauser) Spr-Verlag.

***Paternain, Gabriel P.** Geodesic Flows LC 99-38332. (Progress in Mathematics Ser.). 1999. write for info. (*3-7643-4144-0*) Birkhauser.

***Paternak, Boris Leonidovich.** Dr. Zhivago. 1999. pap. 16.95 (*5-8370-0375-4*) Distribks Inc.

Paternie, Patrick C. How to Restore & Modify Your Porsche 914 & 914/6. LC 99-26203. (Illus.). 192p. 1999. pap. 24.95 (*0-7603-0584-6*, 128078AP, Pub. by MBI Pubg) Motorbooks Intl.

***Paternie, Patrick C.** Porsche 911 Red Book 1965-1999. (Red Bks.). (Illus.). 160p. 2000. pap. 11.95 (*0-7603-0723-7*, 129810AP, Pub. by MBI Pubg) Motorbooks Intl.

Paternite, David, jt. ed. see Paternite, Stephen.

Paternite, Stephen & Paternite, David, eds. American Infrared Survey. LC 82-6160. (Illus.). 88p. (C). 1982. 21.95 (*0-9609812-0-9*) Photo Survey.

Paterniti, Debora A., jt. ed. see Charmaz, Kathleen.

***Paterniti, Michael.** Driving Mr. Albert: A Trip Across America with Einstein's Brain. LC 00-24030. 192p. 2000. 18.95 (*0-385-33300-5*, Dial Pr) Dell.

Paterno, Cynthia, jt. auth. see Lackner, Marie.

Paterno, Fabio, et al, eds. Interactive Systems: Design, Specification & Verification: 1st Eurographics Workshop, Bocca di Magra, Italy, June 1994, Vol. X. LC 95-32298. (Focus on Computer Graphics Ser.). 447p. 1995. 99.00 (*3-540-59480-9*) Spr-Verlag.

Paterno, Fred. The Literate Bassist. 80p. 1982. pap. 10.95 (*0-87166-958-7*, 93822) Mel Bay.

Paterno, George. Joe Paterno: The Coach from Byzantium. (Illus.). 194p. 1997. 22.95 (*1-57167-153-6*) Sports Pub.

Paterno, Gianfranco, jt. auth. see Barone, Antonio.

Paterno, Jim. Building Cathedrals: A Debate Coaches Resource. (Illus.). v, 330p. (Orig.). 1992. pap. text 75.00 (*1-889510-01-7*) Chmpionship Debate.

Paterno, Jim. Directing Debate Tournaments. (Illus.). i, 77p. (Orig.). 1993. pap. text 38.50 (*1-889510-04-1*) Chmpionship Debate.

Paterno, Jim & Poppen, Nikki. The CDE Lincoln Douglas Dictionary. (Illus.). 140p. (Orig.). (YA). (gr. 7-12). 1993. pap. text 38.00 (*1-889510-06-8*) Chmpionship Debate.

Paterno, Maria E. The Girl Who Fell from the Sky & Other Classic Philippine Legends. (Illus.). (J). (gr. 3-7). 1995. 11.95 (*971-630-025-5*, Pub. by Tahanan Pacific) Paperworks.

Paterno, Salvatore. The Liturgical Context of Early European Drama. 1990. 33.50 (*0-916379-62-0*) Scripta.

Paterno, Susan F., jt. auth. see Stein, M. L.

Paternoster. Juvenile Delinquency & Juvenile Justice. (Criminal Justice). 2002. pap. text 40.00 (*0-534-55917-4*) Thomson Learn.

***Paternoster Publishing Staff.** Discovery Bible. 1999. pap. 17.99 (*1-85078-325-X*) O M Pubng.

Paternoster, Raymond & Bachman, Ronet, eds. Explaining Criminals & Crime: Essays in Contemporary Criminological Theory. LC 99-35826. 250p. (C). 2000. pap. text. write for info. (*1-891487-32-9*) Roxbury Pub Co.

Paternoster, Raymond, jt. auth. see Tittle, Charles R.

Paternosto, Cesar. The Stone & the Thread: Andean Roots of Abstract Art. Allen, Esther, tr. LC 95-22899.Tr. of Piedra Abstracta. (ENG & SPA., Illus.). 296p. 1996. 35.00 (*0-292-76565-7*) U of Tex Pr.

***Paternostro, Silvana.** In the Land of God & Man: A Latin Women's Journey. 336p. 1999. pap. 13.95 (*0-452-28030-3*, Plume) Dutton Plume.

Paternostro, Silvana. In the Land of God & Man: Confronting Our Sexual Culture. LC 98-29084. 336p. 1998. 25.95 (*0-525-94422-2*) NAL.

***Paterra, M. Elizabeth.** Kweisi Mfume: Congressman & NAACP Leader. LC 00-8029. (African-American Biographies Ser.). (Illus.). 2000. write for info. (*0-7660-1237-9*) Enslow Pubs.

An Asterisk (*) at the beginning of an entry indicates that the title is appearing for the first time.

Paterra, Mary E. Cambridge Stratford Study Skills Course, 20 Hour Edition. (Illus.). 108p. (J). (gr. 6-8). 1986. teacher ed. 64.95 (*0-935637-03-6*); student ed. 13.95 (*0-935637-02-8*); audio 40.00 (*0-935637-01-X*); trans. 60.00 (*0-935637-00-1*) Cambridge Strat.

— Cambridge Stratford Study Skills Course, 30 Hour Edition. (Illus.). 159p. (YA). (gr. 9-11). 1986. teacher ed. 64.95 (*0-935637-07-9*); student ed. 16.95 (*0-935637-06-0*); audio 40.00 (*0-935637-05-2*); trans. 120.00 (*0-935637-04-4*) Cambridge Strat.

***Paterson.** Behind the Mask. 376p. 2000. 99.95 (*0-7546-2042-5*) Ashgate Pub Co.

Paterson. Current Topics in Radiography. 1995. pap. text 36.00 (*0-7020-1971-2*, W B Saunders Co) Harcrt Hlth Sci Grp.

— Current Topics in Radiography. 2nd ed. 1996. pap. text 41.00 (*0-7020-2202-0*, W B Saunders Co) Harcrt Hlth Sci Grp.

***Paterson.** Man from Snowy River & Other Verses: Australia's Best Loved Poetry Collection. 2000. pap. 15.95 (*0-207-19173-5*) Collins Angus & Robertson Pubs.

Paterson. New Patricians. LC 97-38224. 168p. 1998. text 55.00 (*0-312-21194-5*) St Martin.

Paterson. Nihilistic Egoist. 336p. 1993. 63.95 (*0-7512-0258-4*) Ashgate Pub Co.

— Physics of Glaciers. 3rd ed. 496p. 1999. text 125.00 (*0-7506-4406-0*) Buttrwrth-Heinemann.

Paterson, A. Amenability. LC 88-14485. (SURV Ser.: No. 29). 452p. 1988. text 39.00 (*0-8218-1529-6*, SURV/29) Am Math.

Paterson, A. & Piggott, J. R. Understanding Natural Flavors. 318p. 1994. 165.00 (*0-8342-1351-6*) Aspen Pub.

Paterson, A., jt. ed. see Piggott, J. R.

Paterson, A. B. The Man from Snowy River & Other Verses. 198p. 1989. reprint ed. lib. bdg. 31.95 (*0-89966-589-6*) Buccaneer Bks.

Paterson, A. K., ed. see De Molina, Tirso.

Paterson, A. R. A First Course in Fluid Dynamics. LC 82-23437. 544p. 1984. pap. text 44.95 (*0-521-27424-9*) Cambridge U Pr.

Paterson, A. Tony. Offshore Fire Safety. LC 93-12103. 300p. 1993. 25.00 (*0-87814-381-5*, S4516) PennWell Bks.

***Paterson, Aileen.** Maisie Goes to a Wedding. (Illus.). 32p. (J). (gr. 1-3). 2000. pap. write for info. (*1-871512-54-9*) Glowworm Bks.

Paterson, Alan. Groupoids, Inverse Semigroups & Their Operator Algebras. LC 98-47617. (Progress in Mathematics Ser.). 1998. 54.50 (*0-8176-4051-7*) Birkhauser.

Paterson, Alan A. & Goriely, Tamara, eds. A Reader on Resourcing Civil Justice. (Oxford Readings in Socio-Legal Studies). (Illus.). 312p. 1997. text 75.00 (*0-19-876462-6*) OUP.

— A Reader on Resourcing Civil Justice. (Oxford Readings in Socio-Legal Studies). (Illus.). 310p. 1997. pap. text 38.00 (*0-19-876461-8*) OUP.

Paterson, Alan J. How Glass Is Made. (How It Is Made Ser.). (Illus.). 32p. (YA). (gr. 7 up). 1985. 14.95 (*0-8160-0038-7*) Facts on File.

Paterson, Alexander H. G., jt. auth. see Dion.

Paterson, Allan, jt. auth. see George, Dick.

Paterson, Allen. Herbs in the Garden. 370p. 1993. pap. 16.95 (*0-460-86015-1*, Pub. by J M Dent & Sons) Trafalgar.

— Plants for Shade: A Complete Guide to What to Grow in Shade & Woodland. (Illus.). 160p. 1994. pap. 17.95 (*0-460-86096-8*, Pub. by J M Dent & Sons) Trafalgar.

Paterson, Andrew H. Genome Mapping in Plants. LC 96-17126. (Biotechnology Intelligence Unit Ser.). 280p. 1996. 79.00 (*1-57059-359-0*) Landes Bioscience.

— Molecular Dissection of Complex Traits. LC 97-12278. 336p. 1997. boxed set 134.95 (*0-8493-7686-6*) CRC Pr.

Paterson, Anna, tr. see Enquist, Per Olov.

Paterson, Arthur G. 400 Trademarks on Glass: With Alphabetical Index. 7th rev. ed. LC 68-12557. (Illus.). 54p. (Orig.). 1996. pap. 9.95 (*0-9605664-1-4*) L-W Inc.

Paterson, Audrey & Price, Richard. Current Topics in Radiology. 3rd ed. (Illus.). 320p. 1999. pap. text 35.00 (*0-7020-2353-1*) W B Saunders.

Paterson, B. Donald, jt. auth. see Govindasamy, Devin.

Paterson, Banjo. Man from Snowy River & Other Verses. 262p. Date not set. 22.95 (*0-8488-2534-9*) Amereon Ltd.

Paterson, Bettina. Baby's Words. (So Tall Board Bks.). (Illus.). 18p. (J). (ps up). 1995. bds. 4.95 (*0-448-40926-7*, G & D) Peng Put Young Read.

— I Go to Preschool. (Illus.). 12p. (J). (ps). 1996. 14.95 (*0-590-84911-5*, Cartwheel) Scholastic Inc.

— My First Animals. LC 89-17275. (Illus.). 32p. (J). (ps). 1990. 8.95 (*0-690-04775-4*) HarpC Child Bks.

— My First Wild Animals. LC 89-17305. (Illus.). 32p. (J). (ps). 1991. 8.95 (*0-690-04771-1*) HarpC Child Bks.

Paterson, Bettina. Baby's ABC. (So Tall Board Bks.). 18p. (J). (ps). 1992. bds. 4.95 (*0-448-40130-4*, G & D) Peng Put Young Read.

— Baby's 1, 2, 3. (So Tall Board Bks.). 18p. (J). (ps). 1992. bds. 4.99 (*0-448-40265-3*, G & D) Peng Put Young Read.

— Busy Witch. 12p. (J). (ps). 1993. bds. 2.50 (*0-448-40573-3*, G & D) Peng Put Young Read.

— Christmas Tree Angel. 12p. (J). (ps). 1995. bds. 2.95 (*0-448-40933-X*, G & D) Peng Put Young Read.

— Duckling's Surprise. 12p. (J). (ps). 1995. bds. 2.95 (*0-448-40587-3*, G & D) Peng Put Young Read.

— Happy Easter, Bunny! 12p. (J). (ps). 1995. bds. 2.95 (*0-448-40588-1*, G & D) Peng Put Young Read.

— Jolly Snowman. 12p. (J). (ps). 1992. bds. 2.95 (*0-448-40575-X*, G & D) Peng Put Young Read.

— Merry ABC. (Wee Pudgy Board Bks.). 24p. (J). (ps). 1993. bds. 2.95 (*0-448-40553-9*, G & D) Peng Put Young Read.

— Merry Christmas, Santa! 12p. (J). (ps). 1992. bds. 2.95 (*0-448-40576-8*, G & D) Peng Put Young Read.

— Potty Time. (Teddy Board Bks.). 12p. (J). (ps). 1993. bds. 4.95 (*0-448-40539-3*, G & D) Peng Put Young Read.

— Who's at the Firehouse? LC 95-77544. (Lift & Look Board Bks.). 12p. (J). (ps). 1996. bds. 4.95 (*0-448-41281-0*, G & D) Peng Put Young Read.

Paterson, Brent G. & Kibler, William L. The Administration of Campus Discipline: Student, Organizational & Community Issues. LC 97-39108. (Higher Education Administration Ser.). xx, 307 p. 1998. 39.95 (*0-912557-22-2*) Coll Admin Pubns.

***Paterson, Brent G. & Kibler, William L.** The Administration of Campus Discipline: Student, Organizational & Community Issues. LC 97-39108. (Higher Education Administration Ser.). 307p. 1998. pap. 26.95 (*0-912557-19-2*) Coll Admin Pubns.

Paterson, Bronwyn. Excellence & Expertise in Nursing. (C). 1995. pap. 22.00 (*0-7300-1266-2*, NPR300, Pub. by Deakin Univ) St Mut.

Paterson-Brown, Simon, ed. General & Emergency Surgery. (Companion Guide to Specialist Surgical Practice Ser.: Vol. 1). (Illus.). 415p. 1997. text 84.00 (*0-7020-2140-7*, Pub. by W B Saunders) Saunders.

Paterson-Brown, Simon & Eckersley, Rupert. Aids to Anatomy. (Illus.). 288p. 1988. pap. text 23.00 (*0-443-03624-1*) Church.

Paterson-Brown, Simon & Garden, James, eds. Principles & Practice of Surgical Laparoscopy. (Illus.). 619p. 1994. pap. text 76.00 (*0-7020-1712-4*, W B Saunders Co) Harcrt Hlth Sci Grp.

Paterson-Brown, Simon, jt. auth. see Ellis, Brian W.

Paterson-Brown, Simon, jt. ed. see Ellis, Brian W.

Paterson Chappell, Ruth. All 'Bout Charleston. LC 97-51146. (Illus.). 54p. (J). 1998. 14.95 (*0-87844-144-1*) Sandlapper Pub Co.

Paterson, Colin R. & MacLennan, W. J. Bone Disease in the Elderly. LC 84-3716. (Wiley Series on Disease Management in the Elderly: No. 3). (Illus.). 224p. reprint ed. pap. 69.50 (*0-8357-3926-0*, 203666100004) Bks Demand.

Paterson, D. G. British Direct Investment in Canada, 1890-1914. LC 76-22429. 159p. reprint ed. pap. 49.30 (*0-8357-7421-X*, 205612200050) Bks Demand.

Paterson, David. The Cape Wrath Trail: A 200-Mile Walk Through the North-West Scottish Highlands. (Illus.). 128p. 1996. pap. 27.50 (*0-9521908-1-8*, Pub. by Peak Pubg Ltd) Trans-Atl Phila.

— Heart of the Himalaya: Journeys in Deepest Nepal. (Illus.). 144p. 1997. pap. 27.50 (*0-9521908-2-6*, Pub. by Peak Pubg Ltd) Trans-Atl Phila.

— London: City on a River. (Illus.). 144p. 1997. pap. 27.50 (*0-9521908-3-4*, Pub. by Peak Pubg Ltd) Trans-Atl Phila.

— A Long Walk on the Isle of Skye: A New 75-Mile Island Trek. (Illus.). 144p. 1999. pap. 27.50 (*0-9521908-4-2*, Pub. by Peak Pubg Ltd) Trans-Atl Phila.

Paterson, David & Palmer, Mary, eds. The Status of Animals: Ethics, Education & Welfare. 268p. (Orig.). 1989. pap. text 39.95 (*0-85198-650-1*) OUP.

Paterson, David E. A Frontier Link with the World: Upson County's Railroad. LC 98-156052. 304p. 1998. text 32.95 (*0-86554-585-5*, H435) Mercer Univ Pr.

Paterson, Debi, jt. auth. see Brown, Cathy J.

Paterson, Diane. Stone Soup. LC 80-27947. 32p. (J). (gr. 1-4). 1996. pap. 3.95 (*0-89375-479-X*) Troll Communs.

Paterson, Don. The Eyes. 64p. 1999. pap. 11.00 (*0-571-20055-9*) Faber & Faber.

Paterson, Donald G. Physique & Intellect. LC 73-98866. 304p. 1970. reprint ed. lib. bdg. 65.00 (*0-8371-2886-2*, PAPI, Greenwood Pr) Greenwood.

Paterson, Ellen R., compiled by. Anabolic Steroids & Sports: A Selective Bibliography with Annotations. LC 90-83684. x, 67p. 1991. 25.00 (*0-87875-389-3*) Whitston Pub.

— Anabolic Steroids & Sports & Drug Testing, 1991-1997: An Annotated Bibliography. LC 97-62104. xii, 90p. 1998. 29.50 (*0-87875-499-7*) Whitston Pub.

Paterson, Evangeline. Lucifer, with Angels. 58p. 1994. pap. 11.95 (*1-873790-64-3*) Dufour.

Paterson, F. William. The Protestants Theologie. LC 77-362661. (English Recusant Literature, 1558-1640 Ser.). 309p. 1976. write for info. (*0-85967-330-8*) Scolar Pr.

Paterson, Fiona & Fewell, Judith, eds. Girls in Their Prime: Scottish Education Revisited. 180p. 1991. reprint ed. pap. 29.95 (*0-7073-0578-0*, Falmer Pr) Taylor & Francis.

Paterson, H., jt. auth. see Roy, J.

Paterson, Helena. The Celtic Lunar Zodiac: How to Interpret Your Moon Sign. LC 97-5648. 157p. 1997. 117.95 (*0-15-671851-0*) Harcourt.

— Celtic Lunar Zodiac: How to Interpret Your Moon Sign. LC 97-5648. (Illus.). 160p. 1999. pap. 17.95 (*1-56718-510-X*) Llewellyn Pubns.

— The Celtic Moon Sign Kit. LC 99-17392. 176p. 1999. per. 24.95 (*0-684-86218-2*) S&S Childrens.

— The Handbook of Celtic Astrology: The 13-Sign Lunar Zodiac of the Ancient Druids. LC 94-42390. (Illus.). 288p. 1999. pap. 15.00 (*1-56718-509-6*) Llewellyn Pubns.

Paterson, Hohn M. Gaelic Made Easy, Vol. 1. 1991. pap. 7.95 (*0-8288-3348-6*, M4308) Fr & Eur.

Paterson, Hugh E. Evolution & the Recognition Concept of Species: Collected Writings. McEvey, Shane F., ed. LC 92-4779. 224p. 1993. text 42.50 (*0-8018-4409-6*) Johns Hopkins.

Paterson, I. B. Geology of the Hamilton District: Memoir for 1:50,000 Geological Sheet 23W (Scotland) (Memoirs of the Geological Survey of Great Brittain (Scotland) Ser.). (Illus.). viii, 94p. 1998. pap. 80.00 (*0-11-884533-0*, 81027261, Pub. by Statnry Office) Balogh.

Paterson, Isabel B. God of the Machine. LC 77-172225. (Right Wing Individualist Tradition in America Ser.). 1972. reprint ed. 25.50 (*0-405-00434-6*) Ayer.

— God of the Machine. LC 72-4510. (Essay Index Reprint Ser.). 1979. reprint ed. 29.95 (*0-8369-2966-7*) Ayer.

Paterson, J. The Homes of Tennyson. LC 72-3621. (Studies in Tennyson: No. 27). (Illus.). 1972. reprint ed. lib. bdg. 75.00 (*0-8383-1579-8*) M S G Haskell Hse.

Paterson, J. D. Primate Behavior: An Exercise Workbook. (Illus.). 105p. (C). 1992. pap. text 12.95 (*0-88133-618-1*) Waveland Pr.

***Paterson, Jacqueline M.** Tree in Your Pocket. 1999. pap. 8.00 (*0-7225-3778-6*) Thorsons PA.

Paterson, James. Commentaries on the Liberty of the Subject & the Laws of England: Relating to the Security of the Person, 2 vols., Set. 1010p. 1980. reprint ed. 95.00 (*0-8377-1005-7*, Rothman) W S Hein.

— Liberty of the Press, Speech & Public Worship: Being Commentaries on the Liberty of the Subject & Laws of England. xxxi, 568p. 1985. reprint ed. 52.00 (*0-8377-1019-7*, Rothman) W S Hein.

Paterson, James M. The Contemporaries of Burns, & the More Recent Poets of Ayrshire, with Selections from Their Writings. LC 70-144468. reprint ed. 57.50 (*0-404-08524-5*) AMS Pr.

Paterson, Jane H. Sign Here. (Illus.). 96p. (Orig.). 1997. pap. 10.95 (*1-85398-106-0*, Pub. by Ashgrove Pr) Words Distrib.

Paterson, Janet M. Postmodernism & the Quebec Novel. Homel, David & Phillips, Charles, trs. (Theory - Culture Ser.). 168p. 1994. text 35.00 (*0-8020-0530-6*); pap. text 14.95 (*0-8020-6968-1*) U of Toronto Pr.

Paterson, Janet M., jt. ed. see Lennox, John.

Paterson, Jennifer. Two Fat Ladies Ride Again. LC 98-25803. (Illus.). 192p. 1998. 25.00 (*0-609-60379-5*) C Potter.

Paterson, Jennifer & Dickson-Wright, Clarissa. Cooking with the Two Fat Ladies. LC 97-38982. 1998. 25.00 (*0-609-60322-1*) C Potter.

— Two Fat Ladies Full Throttle. LC 99-216012. (Illus.) 192p. 1999. 27.50 (*0-609-60423-6*) Random Hse Value.

***Paterson, Jennifer & Wright, Clarissa D.** Two Fat Ladies Obsessions. (Illus.). 240p. 2000. 30.00 (*0-609-60634-4*) C Potter.

Paterson, John. Consider the Lilies: Plants of the Bible. LC 85-43603. (Illus.). 96p. (J). 1998. pap. 7.95 (*0-395-88828-X*, Clarion Bks) HM.

— David Harvey's Geography. LC 83-22293. 232p. 1984. 56.00 (*0-389-20441-2*, N8003) B&N Imports.

— The Edwardians: London Life & Letters, 1901-1914. (Illus.). 352p. 1996. text 27.50 (*1-56663-101-7*) I R Dee.

— Real Truth about Baptism in Jesus' Name. 32p. 1995. reprint ed. pap. 2.00 (*1-56722-035-5*) Word Aflame.

Paterson, John & Paterson, Katherine. Images of God. (J). 1998. pap. 20.00 (*0-395-70729-3*) Ticknor & Fields.

— Images of God: Views of the Invisible. LC 97-21637. (Illus.). 112p. (J). (gr. 3 up). 1998. 20.00 (*0-395-70734-X*, Clarion Bks) HM.

Paterson, John H. North America: A Geography of the United States & Canada. 9th ed. (Illus.). 544p. (C). 1994. text 64.95 (*0-19-508058-0*) OUP.

Paterson, John K. & Burn, Loic. Examination of the Back: An Introduction. 1986. text 73.50 (*0-85200-930-5*) Kluwer Academic.

Paterson, John K. & Burn, Loic, eds. Back Pain: An International Review. (C). 1990. text 244.50 (*0-7923-8912-3*) Kluwer Academic.

Paterson, John M. Gaelic Made Easy. (GAE.). 1992. 89.95 incl. audio (*0-88432-443-5*, AFSG20) Audio-Forum.

— Gaelic Made Easy, Vol. 2. 1991. pap. 7.95 (*0-8288-3349-4*, M4309) Fr & Eur.

— Gaelic Made Easy, Vol. 3. 1991. pap. 7.95 (*0-7859-0644-4*, M4310) Fr & Eur.

Paterson, John M., jt. auth. see Kerr, William W.

Paterson-Jones, Colin. Best Walks of the Garden Route. 1999. pap. 14.95 (*1-86872-115-9*) Struik Pubs.

— Cape Floral Kingdom. 1998. 49.95 (*1-86872-039-X*, Pub. by New Holland) Sterling.

Paterson, Judith H. Sweet Mystery: A Southern Memoir of Family Alcoholism, Mental Illness & Recovery. LC 95-13113. 288p. 1996. 23.00 (*0-374-27226-3*) FS&G.

— Sweet Mystery: A Southern Memoir of Family Alcoholism, Mental Illness, & Recovery. 1997. pap. text 12.00 (*0-374-52499-8*, Noonday) FS&G.

***Paterson, Judy.** The Dwarfie Stane. (Illus.). 32p. (J). (gr. k-4). 1998. pap. write for info. (*1-871512-57-3*) Glowworm Bks.

— The Fisherman's Son. (Illus.). 32p. (J). (gr. k-4). 1999. pap. write for info. (*1-871512-61-1*) Glowworm Bks.

— The History of Scotland for Children. (Illus.). 136p. (J). (gr. 3-6). 1999. write for info. (*1-871512-56-5*); pap. write for info. (*1-871512-63-8*) Glowworm Bks.

— Peerifool. (Illus.). 32p. (J). (gr. k-4). 1998. pap. write for info. (*1-871512-59-X*) Glowworm Bks.

— Spook's Edinburgh - A Child's Guide. (Illus.). 32p. (J). (gr. 1-6). 1997. pap. write for info. (*1-871512-52-2*) Glowworm Bks.

— Tamlane. (Illus.). 32p. (J). (gr. k-4). 1999. pap. write for info. (*1-871512-62-X*) Glowworm Bks.

— Thomas the Rhymer. (Illus.). 32p. (J). (gr. k-4). 1999. pap. write for info. (*1-871512-60-3*) Glowworm Bks.

— The Witch of Fife. (Illus.). 32p. (J). (gr. k-4). 1998. pap. write for info. (*1-871512-58-1*) Glowworm Bks.

Paterson, Katherine. Ame a Jacob.Tr. of Jacob Have I Loved. (ACE.). 1984. 17.05 (*0-606-10376-7*, Pub. by Turtleback) Demco.

— Angels & Other Strangers. LC 79-63797. 128p. (J). (gr. 1 up). 1979. 14.00 (*0-690-03992-1*) HarpC Child Bks.

— Angels & Other Strangers: Family Christmas Stories. LC 79-63797. 128p. (YA). (gr. 7 up). 1991. lib. bdg. 13.89 (*0-690-04911-0*) HarpC Child Bks.

Paterson, Katherine. Angels & Other Strangers: Family Christmas Stories. (J). 1979. 9.05 (*0-606-03962-7*, Pub. by Turtleback) Demco.

Paterson, Katherine. Angels & Other Strangers: Family Christmas Stories. LC 79-63797. (Trophy Bk.). 128p. (J). (gr. 7 up). 1988. reprint ed. pap. 4.95 (*0-06-440283-5*, HarpTrophy) HarpC Child Bks.

— Bridge to Terabithia. (YA). (gr. 5 up). 1987. 10.05 (*0-606-00861-6*, Pub. by Turtleback) Demco.

— Bridge to Terabithia. large type ed. (LRS Large Print Cornerstone Ser.). (Illus.). 250p. (YA). (gr. 5-12). 1999. lib. bdg. 28.95 (*1-58118-053-5*, 22769) LRS.

— Bridge to Terabithia. LC 77-2221. (Illus.). 128p. (J). (gr. 4-7). 1987. reprint ed. lib. bdg. 15.89 (*0-690-04635-9*) HarpC Child Bks.

— Bridge to Terabithia. LC 77-2221. (Trophy Bk.). (Illus.). 144p. (J). (gr. 4-7). 1987. reprint ed. pap. 5.95 (*0-06-440184-7*, HarpTrophy) HarpC Child Bks.

— Bridge to Terabithia: (Puente Hasta Terabithia) (SPA.). (J). (gr. 1-6). 8.95 (*84-204-3633-X*) Santillana.

— Celia & the Sweet, Sweet Water. 32p. (J). (gr. k-3). 1998. 15.00 (*0-395-91324-1*, Clarion Bks) HM.

— Celia & the Sweet, Sweet Water. LC 95-41632. (Illus.). (J). 1999. pap. 14.99 (*0-525-67481-0*, Dutton Child) Peng Put Young Read.

— Come Sing, Jimmy Jo. 192p. (J). (gr. 5 up). 1986. mass mkt. 3.99 (*0-380-70052-2*, Avon Bks) Morrow Avon.

— Come Sing, Jimmy Jo. LC 84-21123. 208p. (J). (gr. 5 up). 1985. 15.99 (*0-525-67167-6*, Dutton Child) Peng Put Young Read.

— Come Sing, Jimmy Jo. 208p. (J). 1995. pap. 4.99 (*0-14-037397-7*, PuffinBks) Peng Put Young Read.

— Come Sing, Jimmy Jo. 1995. 10.09 (*0-606-07386-8*, Pub. by Turtleback) Demco.

— Flip-Flop Girl. 128p. (YA). (gr. 6 up). 1996. pap. 4.99 (*0-14-037679-8*, PuffinBks) Peng Put Young Read.

— Flip-Flop Girl. (YA). (gr. 6 up). 1996. 9.09 (*0-606-08682-X*, Pub. by Turtleback) Demco.

— La Gran Gilly Hopkins. 1994. 15.05 (*0-606-10436-4*, Pub. by Turtleback) Demco.

— The Great Gilly Hopkins. LC 77-27075. 148p. (YA). (gr. 4-7). 1978. 15.95 (*0-690-03837-2*); lib. bdg. 15.89 (*0-690-03838-0*) HarpC Child Bks.

— The Great Gilly Hopkins. LC 92-788634. (J). 1979. 21.33 incl. audio (*0-394-78371-9*) Random.

— The Great Gilly Hopkins. (J). 1987. 10.05 (*0-606-02061-6*, Pub. by Turtleback) Demco.

— The Great Gilly Hopkins. large type ed. (LRS Large Print Cornerstone Ser.). 300p. (YA). (gr. 5-12). 1999. lib. bdg. 29.95 (*1-58118-052-7*, 22770) LRS.

— The Great Gilly Hopkins. LC 77-27075. (Trophy Bk.). 160p. (YA). (gr. 5-9). 1987. reprint ed. pap. 5.95 (*0-06-440201-0*, HarpTrophy) HarpC Child Bks.

— The Great Gilly Hopkins: (La Gran Gilly Hopkins) (SPA.). (J). (gr. 1-6). 8.95 (*84-204-3222-9*) Santillana.

— Jacob Have I Loved. LC 80-668. 224p. (YA). (gr. 7 up). 1980. 15.95 (*0-690-04078-4*) HarpC Child Bks.

— Jacob Have I Loved. LC 80-668. 224p. (YA). (gr. 7 up). 1980. lib. bdg. 15.89 (*0-690-04079-2*) HarpC Child Bks.

— Jacob Have I Loved. LC 80-668. (Trophy Bk.). 256p. (J). (gr. 7-12). 1990. pap. 5.95 (*0-06-440368-8*, HarpTrophy) HarpC Child Bks.

— Jacob Have I Loved. (YA). (gr. 7 up). 1981. pap. 2.95 (*0-380-56499-8*, Avon Bks) Morrow Avon.

— Jacob Have I Loved. (J). 1980. 10.05 (*0-606-04379-9*, Pub. by Turtleback) Demco.

— Jacob Have I Loved. large type ed. 1991. 66.00 (*0-614-09883-1*, L-34040-00) Am Printing Hse.

Paterson, Katherine. Jacob Have I Loved, Set. abr. ed. 256p. (J). (gr. 7-12). 1992. audio 16.95 (*1-55994-611-3*, Caedmon) HarperAudio.

— Jacob Have I Loved (pb repkg) 256p. (J). 1990. mass mkt. 5.95 (*0-06-447059-8*, HarpTrophy) HarpC Child Bks.

Paterson, Katherine. Jip, His Story. LC 96-2680. 208p. (J). (gr. 5-9). 1996. 15.99 (*0-525-67543-4*, Dutton Child) Peng Put Young Read.

— Jip, His Story. LC 96-2680. (Puffin Novels Ser.). 181p. (J). (gr. 5-9). 1998. pap. 4.99 (*0-14-038674-2*) Peng Put Young Read.

Paterson, Katherine. Jip, His Story, Set. unabridged ed. (J). (gr. 2). 1997. 57.99 incl. audio (*0-7887-1711-1*, 40579) Recorded Bks.

Paterson, Katherine. The King's Equal. LC 90-30527. (Illus.). 64p. (J). (gr. 2-5). 1992. 17.00 (*0-06-022496-7*); lib. bdg. 16.89 (*0-06-022497-5*) HarpC Child Bks.

— The King's Equal. LC 90-30527. (Trophy Picture Bk.). (Illus.). 64p. (J). (gr. 2-5). 1996. pap. 6.95 (*0-06-443396-X*, HarpTrophy) HarpC Child Bks.

— The King's Equal. LC 98-7214. (Chapter Bks.). (Illus.). 64p. (J). (gr. 2-5). 1999. pap. 4.25 (*0-06-442090-6*, HarpTrophy) HarpC Child Bks.

— The King's Equal. 1992. 12.15 (*0-606-08791-5*, Pub. by Turtleback) Demco.

— The King's Equal. large type ed. (Illus.). 1993. 17.50 (*0-614-09834-3*, L-34098-00) Am Printing Hse.

***Paterson, Katherine.** Literature Guide: Great Gilly Hopkins. (Illus.). 16p. 1999. pap. 3.95 (*0-590-04116-9*) Scholastic Inc.

Paterson, Katherine. Lyddie. 240p. (YA). (gr. 5-9). 1991. 15.99 (*0-525-67338-5*, Dutton Child) Peng Put Young Read.

— Lyddie. LC 92-20304. 182p. (YA). (gr. 5-12). 1992. pap. 4.99 (*0-14-034981-2*, PuffinBks) Peng Put Young Read.

— Lyddie. 182p. (YA). (gr. 7-12). 1995. pap. 5.99 (*0-14-037389-6*, PuffinBks) Peng Put Young Read.

P

An Asterisk (*) at the beginning of an entry indicates that the title is appearing for the first time.

Paterson, Katherine. Lyddie. (J). 1992. 10.09 (*0-606-00880-2*, Pub. by Turtleback) Demco.

Paterson, Katherine. Lyddie. large type ed. (J). 1995. 49.50 (*0-614-09599-9*, L-81891-00) Am Printing Hse.

— Lyddie. large type ed. 277p. (YA). 1993. reprint ed. lib. bdg. 15.95 (*1-56054-616-6*) Thorndike Pr.

***Paterson, Katherine.** Lyddie, No. 18. Vol. 18. (SPA., Illus.). (J). (gr. 9-12). 1999. pap. 9.95 (*84-239-9015-X*) Espasa Calpe.

— Marvin One Too Many. 48p. (gr. k-3). pap. 3.95 (*0-06-444279-9*) HarpC.

— Marvin One Too Many. (Illus.). 48p. (gr. k-3). 14.95 (*0-06-028769-1*) HarpC.

— Marvin One Too Many. (Illus.). 48p. (J). (gr. k-3). 14.89 (*0-06-028770-5*) HarpC Child Bks.

Paterson, Katherine. Marvin's Best Christmas Present Ever. LC PZ7.P273Mar 1997. (I Can Read Bks.). (Illus.). 48p. (J). (gr. 2-4). 1997. 14.95 (*0-06-027159-0*) HarpC Child Bks.

— Marvin's Best Christmas Present Ever. LC 96-31692. (I Can Read Bks.). (Illus.). 48p. (J). (ps-3). 1997. lib. bdg. 14.89 (*0-06-027160-4*) HarpC Child Bks.

— Marvin's Best Christmas Present Ever. (I Can Read Bks.). (Illus.). 48p. (J). (gr. 2-4). 1999. pap. 3.95 (*0-06-444265-9*) HarpC Child Bks.

— The Master Puppeteer. (Illus.). 180p. (J). (gr. 5 up). 1981. pap. 2.95 (*0-380-53322-7*, Avon Bks) Morrow Avon.

— The Master Puppeteer. (J). 1975. 10.05 (*0-606-04273-3*, Pub. by Turtleback) Demco.

— The Master Puppeteer. LC 75-8614. (Trophy Bk.). (Illus.). 192p. (J). (gr. 7-12). 1989. reprint ed. pap. 4.95 (*0-06-440281-9*, HarpTrophy) HarpC Child Bks.

— Of Nightingales That Weep. LC 74-8294. (Illus.). (J). (gr. 5 up). 1974. 14.00 (*0-690-00485-0*) HarpC Child Bks.

Paterson, Katherine. Of Nightingales That Weep. (J). 1974. 9.60 (*0-606-04039-0*, Pub. by Turtleback) Demco.

Paterson, Katherine. Of Nightingales That Weep. LC 74-8294. (Trophy Bk.). (Illus.). 192p. (J). (gr. 4-7). 1989. reprint ed. pap. 4.95 (*0-06-440282-7*, HarpTrophy) HarpC Child Bks.

— Omnibus. 1999. pap. 12.95 (*0-452-27486-9*, Plume) Dutton Plume.

— Park's Quest. (Horn Book "Fanfare" Ser.). 160p. (J). (gr. 5 up). 1989. pap. 4.99 (*0-14-034262-1*, PuffinBks) Peng Put Young Read.

— Park's Quest. 1988. 9.09 (*0-606-02743-2*, Pub. by Turtleback) Demco.

***Paterson, Katherine.** Parzival: The Quest of the Grail Knight. 144p. (YA). (gr. 5-9). 2000. pap. 4.99 (*0-14-130573-8*, PuffinBks) Peng Put Young Read.

— Preacher's Boy. LC 98-50083. 160p. (YA). (gr. 5-9). 1999. 15.00 (*0-395-83897-5*, Clarion Bks) HM.

— Preacher's Boy. 176p. (YA). (gr. 7 up). 2001. mass mkt. 4.95 (*0-06-447233-7*, HarpTrophy) HarpC Child Bks.

Paterson, Katherine. Un Puente Hasta Terabithia. 1996. 15.05 (*0-606-10524-7*, Pub. by Turtleback) Demco.

— Puzzling Book. Date not set. pap. 1.75 (*0-906731-81-X*, Pub. by Christian Focus) Spring Arbor Dist.

— Rebels of the Heavenly Kingdom. 240p. (J). (gr. 7 up). 1984. pap. 2.95 (*0-380-68304-0*, Avon Bks) Morrow Avon.

— Rebels of the Heavenly Kingdom. 240p. (YA). (gr. 7 up). 1995. pap. 4.99 (*0-14-037610-0*, PuffinBks) Peng Put Young Read.

Paterson, Katherine. Rebels of the Heavenly Kingdom. 1995. 10.09 (*0-606-08063-5*, Pub. by Turtleback) Demco.

Paterson, Katherine. Sal a Cantar Jimmy Jo! (Come Sing, Jimmy Joe!) 1995. pap. text 8.95 (*84-204-4567-3*) Santillana.

— The Sign of the Chrysanthemum. LC 72-7553. 128p. (YA). (gr. 7 up). 1991. lib. bdg. 14.89 (*0-690-04913-7*) HarpC Child Bks.

— Sign of the Chrysanthemum. LC 72-7553. 1973. 10.05 (*0-606-03917-1*, Pub. by Turtleback) Demco.

— The Sign of the Chrysanthemum. LC 72-7553. (Trophy Bk.). (Illus.). 144p. (J). (gr. 4-7). 1988. reprint ed. pap. 4.95 (*0-06-440232-0*, HarpTrophy) HarpC Child Bks.

Paterson, Katherine. The Smallest Cow in the World. LC 90-30521. (I Can Read Bks.). (Illus.). 64p. (J). (ps-3). 1996. pap. 8.95 incl. audio (*0-694-70036-3*) HarpC.

Paterson, Katherine. The Smallest Cow in the World. (I Can Read Bks.). (Illus.). 64p. (J). (gr. 2-4). 1991. lib. bdg. 14.89 (*0-06-024691-X*) HarpC Child Bks.

— The Smallest Cow in the World. LC 90-30521. (I Can Read Bks.). (Illus.). 64p. (J). (ps-3). 1993. pap. 3.95 (*0-06-444164-4*, HarpTrophy) HarpC Child Bks.

— The Smallest Cow in the World. (I Can Read Bks.). (J). (gr. 2-4). 1993. 8.95 (*0-606-05608-4*, Pub. by Turtleback) Demco.

— The Tale of the Mandarin Ducks. LC 88-30484. (Illus.). 34p. (J). (ps-3). 1990. 15.99 (*0-525-67283-4*, Dutton Child) Peng Put Young Read.

Paterson, Katherine. The Tale of the Mandarin Ducks. (J). 1995. 11.19 (*0-606-08261-1*, Pub. by Turtleback) Demco.

Paterson, Katherine. Who Am I? (Illus.). 96p. (Orig.). (J). 1992. pap. 8.00 (*0-8028-5072-3*) Eerdmans.

***Paterson, Katherine, retold by.** Parzival: The Quest of the Grail Knight. LC 97-23891. 144p. (YA). (gr. 5 up). 1998. 15.99 (*0-525-67579-5*, Dutton Child) Peng Put Young Read.

Paterson, Katherine, tr. from JPN. The Crane Wife. large type ed. Orig. Title: Tsuru-Nyobo. (Illus.). 1993. 11.50 (*0-614-09820-3*, L-34116-00) Am Printing Hse.

Paterson, Katherine & Stickney, Elizabeth S. Who Am I? Leader's Guide. 36p. 1994. pap. 10.00 (*0-8028-5093-6*, Eerdmans Bks) Eerdmans.

Paterson, Katherine, jt. auth. see Center for Learning Network Staff.

Paterson, Katherine, jt. auth. see Paterson, John.

Paterson, Kathy, ed. see Kearns, Thomas F.

***Paterson, Kent.** The Hot Empire of Chile. (Illus.). 224p. 2000. 24.00 (*0-927534-91-6*) Biling Rev-Pr.

Paterson, L. E. Evolution of the Rules of Engagement for Southeast Asia, 1960-1965. 86p. 1996. reprint ed. pap. 12.50 (*0-923135-30-8*) Dalley Bk Service.

Paterson, Lee T. Documenting Employee Discipline. 170p. 1994. pap. 42.50 (*0-250-47241-4*, MICHIE) LEXIS Pub.

— Employer's Compliance Audit: California. Johnson, Margaret L., ed. 163p. (Orig.). 1989. pap. 79.50 (*0-932823-02-5*) Am Somerset.

— Employer's Compliance Review: California. 2nd ed. 194p. 1993. pap. 45.00 (*1-55943-198-9*, 83100-10, MICHIE) LEXIS Pub.

— Employer's Compliance Review: Federal. 2nd ed. 160p. 1993. pap. 54.00 (*1-55943-199-7*, MICHIE) LEXIS Pub.

Paterson, Lee T. Employer's Wage Manual: Federal. 2nd ed. pap. 85.00 (*0-327-10219-5*) LEXIS Pub.

Paterson, Lee T. Employer's Wage Manual (Federal) 380p. 1992. pap. 65.00 (*1-55943-172-5*, 80691-10, MICHIE) LEXIS Pub.

— Federal Mandatory Workplace Posters. 3rd ed. (Orig.). 1992. spiral bd. 30.00 (*1-55943-177-6*, 80448-10, MICHIE) LEXIS Pub.

— Mandatory Workplace Posters in California. 4th ed. 1992. pap. 30.00 (*1-55943-094-X*, MICHIE) LEXIS Pub.

Paterson, Lee T. Mandatory Workplace Posters in California. 5th ed. 140p. pap. 35.00 (*0-250-47262-7*) LEXIS Pub.

Paterson, Lee T. Mandatory Workplace Posters in California. 5th ed. 140p. 1994. pap. 35.00 (*0-250-47242-2*) Parker Pubns.

— Negotiating Employee Resignations. 2nd ed. 120p. 1991. pap. 29.50 (*1-55943-125-3*, MICHIE) LEXIS Pub.

— Public Employer's Compliance Audit. Johnson, Margaret L., ed. 156p. 1990. pap. 79.50 (*0-932823-07-6*) Am Somerset.

— Public Employer's Compliance Review. 2nd ed. 182p. 1993. pap. 39.50 (*1-55943-200-4*, MICHIE) LEXIS Pub.

— Public Employer's Wage Manual. 400p. 1991. pap. 39.50 (*1-55943-066-4*, MICHIE) LEXIS Pub.

— Supervisor's Guide to Documenting Employee Discipline. 60p. 1993. pap. 19.00 (*0-250-47232-5*, MICHIE) LEXIS Pub.

Paterson, Lee T. & Deblieux, Michael R. Supervisor's Guide to Documenting Employee Discipline. 3rd ed. 1991. pap. 19.00 (*1-55943-091-5*, MICHIE) LEXIS Pub.

— Supervisor's Guide to Employee Performance Reviews. 2nd ed. 110p. 1993. pap. 19.00 (*1-55943-176-8*, MICHIE) LEXIS Pub.

Paterson, Lee T. & Lerner, Stewart M. California Unemployment Insurance Handbook. 166p. (Orig.). 1991. pap. 39.50 (*1-55943-093-1*, 80270-10, MICHIE) LEXIS Pub.

Paterson, Lee T., jt. auth. see Benton-Powers, Susan.

Paterson, Lee T., jt. auth. see Cowan, Ari.

Paterson, Lee T., jt. ed. see Cowan, Ari.

Paterson, Linda M. Troubadours & Eloquence. (C). 1975. 45.00 (*0-19-815711-8*) OUP.

— The World of the Troubadours: Medieval Occitan Society, c. 1100-c. 1300. (Illus.). 381p. (C). 1995. pap. text 24.95 (*0-521-55832-8*) Cambridge U Pr.

Paterson, Lindsay. The Autonomy of Modern Scotland. 224p. 1995. 50.00 (*0-7486-0520-7*, Pub. by Edinburgh U Pr); pap. 25.00 (*0-7486-0525-8*, Pub. by Edinburgh U Pr) Col U Pr.

***Paterson, Lindsay, ed.** A Diverse Assembly: The Debate on a Scottish Parliament. LC 99-181717. 320p. 1999. (*0-7486-1007-3*) Polygon.

Paterson, Lindsay, jt. auth. see Bechhofer, Frank.

Paterson, M. S., ed. Boolean Function Complexity. (London Mathematical Society Lecture Note Ser.: No. 164). 211p. (C). 1992. pap. text 49.95 (*0-521-40826-1*) Cambridge U Pr.

Paterson, M. S., et al, eds. Automata, Languages & Programming: Proceedings 17th International Colloquium Warwick University, England, July 16-20, 1990. (Lecture Notes in Computer Science Ser.: Vol. 443). ix, 781p. 1990. 85.95 (*0-387-52826-1*) Spr-Verlag.

Paterson, M. S., jt. ed. see Crochemore, M.

Paterson, Matthew. Global Warming & Global Politics. LC 96-5372. (Environmental Politics Ser.). 256p. (C). 1996. 90.00 (*0-415-13871-X*); pap. 24.99 (*0-415-13872-8*) Routledge.

***Paterson, Matthew.** Understanding Global Environmental Politics: Domination, Accumulation, Resistance. LC 99-53110. 208p. 2000. text 49.95 (*0-312-23090-7*) St Martin.

Paterson, Matthew & Grubb, Michael, eds. Sharing the Effort: Options for Differentiating Commitments on Climate Change. 80p. 1996. pap. 14.95 (*1-899658-75-0*, Pub. by Royal Inst Intl Affairs) Brookings.

Paterson, Matthew, jt. auth. see Kassler, Peter.

***Paterson, Michael.** Singing for Our Lives: Positively Gay & Christian. 112p. 1999. pap. 27.00 (*0-85305-420-7*, Pub. by Arthur James) St Mut.

Paterson, Neil. Something Like a Poem. 32p. 1986. 20.00 (*0-7223-1988-6*, Pub. by A H S Ltd) St Mut.

Paterson, R. C. A Land Afflicted: Scotland & the Covenanter Wars, 1638-1690. LC 99-494961. 230p. 1998. pap. 36.00 (*0-85976-486-9*, Pub. by J Donald) St Mut.

Paterson, R. C., et al. Modern Concepts in the Management of Fissure Caries. (Illus.). 80p. 1991. text 42.00 (*1-85097-013-0*) Quint Pub Co.

Paterson, R. R. & Bridge, P. D. Biochemical Techniques for Filamentous Fungi. (IMI Technical Handbks.: No. 1). (Illus.). 144p. 1994. spiral bd. 45.00 (*0-85198-899-7*) OUP.

Paterson, R. W. Philosophy & the Belief in a Life after Death. LC 95-23638. 204p. 1996. text 59.95 (*0-312-12838-X*) St Martin.

***Paterson, Randy J.** The Assertiveness Workbook: How to Express Your Ideas & Stand Up for Yourself at Work & in Relationships. 200p. 2000. pap., wbk. ed. 14.95 (*1-57224-209-4*, Pub. by New Harbinger) Publishers Group.

Paterson, Raymond C. For the Lion: A History of the Scottish Wars of Independence. 220p. 1996. pap. 30.00 (*0-85976-435-4*, Pub. by J Donald) St Mut.

Paterson, Richard, jt. ed. see Smith, Anthony.

Paterson, Robert H. Britain's Strategic Nuclear Deterrent: From Before the V-Bomber to Beyond Trident. LC 96-37620. 208p. 1997. 57.50 (*0-7146-4740-3*, Pub. by F Cass Pubs) Intl Spec Bk.

— Britain's Strategic Nuclear Deterrent: From Before the V-Bomber to Beyond Trident. LC 96-37620. 208p. (C). 1997. pap. 24.50 (*0-7146-4297-5*, Pub. by F Cass Pubs) Intl Spec Bk.

Paterson, Robin. Your Baby Book: Birth to Six Years. (Illus.). 120p. 1993. 32.00 (*0-9638231-0-8*) Pacific Eagle.

***Paterson, Ross.** Continuing Heartcry for China. 240p. 2000. pap. text 14.99 (*1-85240-268-7*) SOV5.

Paterson, Russell. An Introduction to Ion Exchange. LC 75-104789. 117p. reprint ed. pap. 36.30 (*0-608-10840-5*, 202254500027) Bks Demand.

Paterson, S. R., et al, eds. Service Experience, Structural Integrity, Severe Accidents, & Erosion in Nuclear & Fossil Plants. LC 95-77521. (Proceedings of the 1995 ASME/JSME Pressure Vessels & Piping Conference Ser.: PVP-Vol. 303). 428p. 1995. 130.00 (*0-7918-1334-7*, H00966) ASME.

Paterson, Sheila, jt. auth. see Gill, Michael.

Paterson, Simon. Witness to Evolving Void. 1998. pap. write for info. (*1-57553-878-4*) Watermrk Pr.

Paterson, Stanley, jt. auth. see Seaburg, Carl.

***Paterson, Stuart.** Cinderella. (Nick Hern Books, Drama Classics). 64p. 2000. pap. 14.95 (*1-85459-484-2*) Theatre Comm.

— Hansel & Gretel. 64p. 2000. pap. 14.95 (*1-85459-483-4*) Theatre Comm.

— King of the Fields. (Nick Hern Books, Drama Classics). 64p. 2000. pap. 14.95 (*1-85459-477-X*) Theatre Comm.

— The Snow Queen: With Incidental Music. 86p. 1990. pap. 5.95 (*0-87129-065-0*, S84) Dramatic Pub.

***Paterson, Sue.** Skin Diseases of the Cat. (Illus.). 244p. 2000. pap. text 64.95 (*0-632-04805-0*, Pub. by Blckwell Science) Iowa St U Pr.

Paterson, Sue. Skin Diseases of the Dog. LC 98-34064. (Illus.). 310p. (C). 1999. pap. text 59.95 (*0-632-04808-5*, Pub. by Blckwell Science) Iowa St U Pr.

Paterson, Thomas G. Major Problems in American Foreign Policy, 2 Vols. 2nd ed. (C). 1984. pap. text 29.16 (*0-669-06449-1*) HM Trade Div.

— Meeting the Communist Threat: Truman to Reagan. 336p. 1989. pap. text 10.95 (*0-19-504532-7*) OUP.

— On Every Front: The Making & Unmaking of the Cold War. 2nd ed. (C). 1993. pap. text 11.00 (*0-393-96435-3*, Norton Paperbks) Norton.

— On Every Front: The Making & Unmaking of the Cold War. 2nd rev. ed. 256p. 1992. 24.95 (*0-393-03060-1*) Norton.

— The Origins of the Cold War. 2nd ed. (Problems in European Civilization Ser.). (C). 1990. pap. text 18.36 (*0-669-91447-9*) HM Trade Div.

— Soviet-American Confrontation: Postwar Reconstruction & the Origins of the Cold War. LC 73-8120. 302p. reprint ed. pap. 93.70 (*0-7837-5387-X*, 204515100005) Bks Demand.

Paterson, Thomas G., ed. Major Problems in American Foreign Policy: Documents & Essays, 2 vols., Vol. II. 3rd ed. LC 88-80720. (Major Problems in American History Ser.). 721p. (C). 1990. pap. text 29.16 (*0-669-15857-7*) HM Trade Div.

Paterson, Thomas G. & Clifford, J. Garry. American Foreign Policy, Vol. 2: A History since 1900. 3rd rev. ed. LC 90-82956. 502p. (C). 1991. pap. text 35.96 (*0-669-24678-6*) HM Trade Div.

Paterson, Thomas G. & McMahon, Robert J., eds. The Origins of the Cold War. 3rd ed. LC 90-82002. (Problems in American Civilization Ser.). 367p. (C). 1991. pap. text 18.36 (*0-669-24445-7*) HM Trade Div.

Paterson, Thomas G. & Merrill, Dennis J. Major Problems in American Foreign Relations Vol. I: To 1920: Documents & Essays, 2 vols., Vol. I. 4th ed. LC 94-77213. (Major Problems in American History Ser.). 592p. (C). 1995. pap. text 29.16 (*0-669-35077-X*) HM Trade Div.

— Major Problems in American Foreign Relations Vol. 2: Documents & Essays Since 1914, 2 vols., Vol. II. 4th ed. LC 94-77213. (Major Problems in American History Ser.). 592p. (C). 1995. pap. text 29.16 (*0-669-35078-8*) HM Trade Div.

Paterson, Thomas G. & Rabe, Stephen G., eds. Imperial Surge: The United States Abroad, the 1890s-Early 1900s. (Problems in American Civilization Ser.). 211p. (C). 1992. pap. text 17.96 (*0-669-26915-8*) HM Trade Div.

Paterson, Thomas G., et al. American Foreign Policy: A History, 2 vols., Vol. I to 1914. 3rd ed. LC 87-81183. 255p. (C). 1988. pap. text 29.16 (*0-669-12664-0*) HM Trade Div.

— American Foreign Relations Vol. I: A History: To 1920. 4th ed. LC 94-77212. 352p. (C). 1995. pap. text 29.16 (*0-669-35155-5*) HM Trade Div.

— American Foreign Relations Vol. II: A History: Since 1895. 4th ed. LC 94-77212. 554p. (C). 1995. pap. text 35.96 (*0-669-35156-3*) HM Trade Div.

Paterson, Thomas G., jt. ed. see Hogan, Michael J.

Paterson, Thomas G., jt. ed. see Jentleson, Bruce W.

Paterson, Torquil. Eckard's Principles of Civil Procedure in the Magistrates' Courts. 3rd ed. LC 99-457152. 397p. 1996. pap. 52.00 (*0-7021-3718-9*, Pub. by Juta & Co) Gaunt.

Paterson, W., jt. auth. see Guile, A. E.

Paterson, W. F. Inquire Within: For Everything You Need to Know, 1857. Latham, J. D., ed. (Illus.). 500p. 1991. pap. text 35.00 (*0-87556-143-8*) Saifer.

Paterson, W. S. The Physics of Glaciers. (Illus.). vii, 380p. 1981. pap. text 27.00 (*0-08-024004-6*, Pergamon Pr) Elsevier.

— The Physics of Glaciers. 2nd ed. (Illus.). vii, 380p. 1981. text 96.00 (*0-08-024005-4*, Pergamon Pr) Elsevier.

— The Physics of Glaciers. 3rd ed. LC 94-30918. 380p. 1995. text 169.00 (*0-08-037945-1*, Prgamon Press) Buttrwrth-Heinemann.

Paterson, W. S. B. The Physics of Glaciers. 3rd ed. (Illus.). 380p. 1995. pap. 49.95 (*0-08-037944-3*, Prgamon Press) Buttrwrth-Heinemann.

***Paterson, Wendy A.** The Unbroken Home: Single-Parent Mothers Tell Their Stories. 326p. 2000. 69.95 (*0-7890-1139-5*); pap. 27.95 (*0-7890-1140-9*) Haworth Pr.

Paterson, William. The Writings of William Paterson: Of Dumfrieshire, & a Citizen of London, Founder of the Bank of England, & of the Darien Colony, 3 vols., Set. 2nd ed. Bannister, Saxe, ed. LC 68-54311. (Library of Money & Banking History). 1968. reprint ed. 150.00 (*0-678-00427-7*) Kelley.

Paterson, William D. Road Deterioration & Maintenance Effects: Models for Planning & Management. LC 87-22177. (Highway Design & Maintenance Standards Ser.). 352p. (Orig.). 1988. pap. text 32.95 (*0-8018-3590-9*) Johns Hopkins.

Paterson, William E. & Smith, Gordon, eds. West German Model: Perspectives on a Stable State. (Illus.). 184p. 1981. 35.00 (*0-7146-3180-9*, Pub. by F Cass Pubs); pap. 12.50 (*0-7146-4034-4*, Pub. by F Cass Pubs) Intl Spec Bk.

Paterson, William E., jt. ed. see Clemens, Clay.

Paterson, William E., jt. ed. see Gillespie, Richard.

Paterson, William E., jt. ed. see Urwin, Derek W.

Paterson, William P. The Nature of Religion. LC 77-27202. (Gifford Lectures: 1924-25). reprint ed. 75.00 (*0-404-60476-5*) AMS Pr.

Paterson, Wilma. A Fountain of Gardens: Plants & Herbs of the Bible. (Illus.). 160p. 1992. 35.00 (*0-87951-461-2*, Pub. by Overlook Pr) Penguin Putnam.

Paterson, Wilma & Gray, Alasdair. The Songs of Scotland. (Illus.). 208p. 1996. 50.00 (*1-85158-722-5*, Pub. by Mainstream Pubng) Trafalgar.

***Paterson, Yvonne.** Intracellular Bacterial Vaccine Vectors: Immunology Cell Biology & Genetics. LC 98-47838. 267p. 1999. 84.50 (*0-471-17278-2*) Wiley.

Paterson, Yvonne, jt. ed. see Levinson, Arnold I.

Patey, Douglas L. The Life of Evelyn Waugh: A Critical Biography. LC 97-15469. (Critical Biographies Ser.: Vol. 8). (Illus.). 480p. 1998. 47.95 (*0-631-18933-5*) Blackwell Pubs.

Patey, Douglas L. & Keegan, Timothy, eds. Augustan Studies: Essays in Honor of Irvin Ehrenpreis. LC 85-40084. (Illus.). 272p. 1986. 38.50 (*0-87413-272-X*) U Delaware Pr.

Patey, R. L. The Illustrated Rules of Football. (Illustrated Rules of the Game Ser.). (Illus.). 32p. (J). (gr. 1-4). 1996. lib. bdg. 21.27 (*1-884756-11-5*) Davidson Titles.

— The Illustrated Rules of Football. LC 95-8118. (Illustrated Sports Ser.). (Illus.). 32p. (J). (gr. 1-4). 1995. pap., per. 6.95 (*1-57102-049-7*, Ideals Child) Hambleton-Hill.

Patey, Stan. The Coast of New England: A Pictorial Tour from Connecticut to Maine. (Illus.). 192p. 1996. 49.95 (*0-07-048770-7*) McGraw.

— The Coastal Guide to New England. (Illus.). 192p. 1996. 49.99 (*1-56496-280-6*, Quarry Bks) Rockport Pubs.

Patey, Tom. One Man's Mountains. LC 97-223983. (Illus.). 294p. 1998. pap. 15.95 (*0-89886-542-5*) Mountaineers.

Patfield, Fiona M. & University of London Staff. Perspectives on Company Law. LC 95-37403. 1995. 108.00 (*90-411-0852-1*) Kluwer Law Intl.

Patfield, Fiona M., jt. ed. see White, Robin.

Patfoort, Pat. Uprooting Violence: Building Nonviolence. (Illus.). 1995. pap. 10.00 (*0-89166-015-1*) Cobblesmith.

Path to Peace Foundation Staff, jt. auth. see Catholic Church Staff.

Pathak, Aditi. Caste Status & Socialization among the Students. (C). 1989. 20.00 (*0-8364-2468-9*) S Asia.

Pathak, Akhileshwar. Contested Domains: The State, Peasants & Forests in Contemporary India. 244p. 1995. 26.00 (*0-8039-9184-3*) Sage.

Pathak, Avijit. Indian Modernity: Contradiction, Paradoxes & Possibilities. LC 98-908539. 243 p. 1998. write for info. (*81-212-0612-X*) Gian Publng Hse.

Pathak, Bindeshwar. Road to Freedom: A Sociological Study on the Abolition of Scavenging in India. (C). 1991. 34.00 (*81-208-0704-9*, Pub. by Motilal Bnarsidass) S Asia.

Pathak, Bindeshway. Rural Violence in Bihar. (C). 1993. 18.00 (*81-7022-474-8*, Pub. by Concept) S Asia.

Pathak, Dev S., et al, eds. Promotion of Pharmaceuticals: Issues, Trends, Options. LC 92-49617. (Journal of Pharmaceutical Marketing & Management: Vol. 7, No. 1). (Illus.). 203p. 1993. pap. text 19.95 (*1-56024-384-8*); lib. bdg. 49.95 (*1-56024-383-X*) Haworth Pr.

Pathak, Dev S. & Escovitz, Alan, eds. Managed Competition & Pharmaceutical Care: A Challenge for the Profession. LC 96-10194. (Journal of Research in Pharmaceutical Economics: Vol. 7, Nos. 1/2). 169p. (C). 1996. 49.95 (*1-56024-821-1*, Pharmctl Prods) Haworth Pr.

— Managed Competition & Pharmaceutical Care: A Challenge for the Profession. LC 96-10194. (Journal of

P

An Asterisk (*) at the beginning of an entry indicates that the title is appearing for the first time.

Research in Pharmaceutical Economics: Vol. 7, Nos. 1/2). 169p. (C). 1997. pap. 19.95 (0-7890-0211-6, Pharmctl Prods) Haworth Pr.

Pathak, Dev S., jt. ed. see Escovitz, Alan.

Pathak, Dhiraj, jt. ed. see Merrill, Gary.

*Pathak, Haresh. Structural Package Design, 1. 1999. pap. text 21.95 (90-5496-051-5) Pepin Pr.

Pathak, J. P., ed. Insect Immunity. LC 92-41646. (Entomologica Ser.: Vol. 48). 204p. 1993. text 144.00 (0-7923-2086-7) Kluwer Academic.

Pathak, K. K. Nuclear Policy of India. 276p. 1980. 24.95 (0-318-37256-8) Asia Bk Corp.

— Nuclear Policy of India. 1983. 18.50 (0-8364-1024-6, Pub. by Gitanjali Prakashan) S Asia.

Pathak, K. N., jt. auth. see Prakash, Shamsher.

Pathak, Mahesh T., ed. Sardar Sarovar Project. (C). 1991. 12.50 (81-204-0545-5, Pub. by Oxford IBH) S Asia.

Pathak, Manjushree. Crimes, Customs & Justice in Tribal India. (C). 1991. 34.00 (81-7099-283-4, Pub. by Mittal Pubs Dist) S Asia.

Pathak, Mohan, ed. Flood Plains & Agricultural Occupance. (C). 1991. 26.00 (81-7100-289-7, Pub. by Ashish Pub Hse) S Asia.

Pathak, P. K., jt. ed. see Ghosh, M.

Pathak, Pratul. The Infinite Passion of Finite Hearts: Robert Browning & Failure in Love. LC 91-32994. (American University Studies: English Language & Literature: Ser. IV, Vol. 141). 208p. (C). 1992. text 39.95 (0-8204-1776-9) P Lang Pubng.

Pathak, R. C. Bhargava's Concise Hindi-English Dictionary. 6th ed. 1040p. 1981. 22.95 (0-8288-1744-8, M9437) Fr & Eur.

— Concise English Hindi Dictionary. (ENG & HIN.). 1979. 6.00 (0-89744-972-X) Auromere.

— Concise Hindi-English Dictionary. (ENG & HIN.). 1979. 6.00 (0-89744-971-1) Auromere.

— Hindi-English Dictionary. (ENG & HIN.). 1979. 22.00 (0-89744-969-X) Auromere.

Pathak, R. C., compiled by. English-Hindi Dictionary: Large Edition. (ENG & HIN.). 1981. 42.50 (0-87557-034-8) Saphrograph.

— English-Hindi Dictionary: Regular Edition. (ENG & HIN.). 1981. 37.50 (0-87557-115-8) Saphrograph.

Pathak, R. S. Generalized Functions & Their Applications. LC 92-42065. (Illus.). 316p. (C). 1993. 125.00 (0-306-44404-6, Plenum Trade) Perseus Pubng.

Pathak, R. S., jt. ed. see Dhokalia, R. P.

Pathak, Raj K. Environmental Planning Resources & Development. 1990. 40.00 (81-85076-91-X, Pub. by Chugh Pubns) S Asia.

Pathak, Ram S. Integral Transforms of Generalized Functions & Their Applications. 416p. 1997. text 55.00 (90-5699-554-5) Gordon & Breach.

*Pathak, S. How to Survive in the Middle Management Cadre. 1998. pap. 38.00 (81-86982-28-0, Pub. by Business Pubns) St Mut.

Pathak, S. C. Recent Advances in Insect Physiology Morphology & Ecology. (Illus.). xiii, 324p. 1986. 39.00 (1-55528-079-X, Pub. by Today Tomorrow) Scholarly Pubns.

Pathak, V. M. Medicinal Plants of Gwalior. (C). 1987. 130.00 (0-7855-3123-8, Pub. by Intl Bk Distr) St Mut.

Pathak, Vijay & Ramaiah, L. S. Bibliography of Research in Library & Information Science in India. 1986. 18.00 (0-8364-1827-1, Pub. by Indian Doc Serv) S Asia.

Pathan, B. A. Gandhian Concept of Beauty. (C). 1989. 12.75 (81-202-0224-4, Pub. by Ajanta) S Asia.

— Gandhian Myth in English Literature in India. 1987. 29.95 (81-7100-006-1) Asia Bk Corp.

Pathania, B. S. Goldsmith & Sentimental Comedy. 152p. 1989. text 22.50 (81-85218-00-5, Pub. by Prestige) Advent Bks Div.

Pathasarathy, Sampath. Modified Lipoproteins in the Pathogenesis of Atherosclerosis. (Medical Intelligence Unit Ser.). 115p. 1994. 99.00 (1-57059-080-X, LN9080) Landes Bioscience.

Pathelin, Pierre. Farce du Quinzieme Siecle. 131p. 1970. 14.95 (0-8288-7492-1) Fr & Eur.

Pathfinder Press Staff, ed. see Mandel, Ernest.

Pathmanathan, I. & Nik-Safiah, N. I. Training of Trainers for Health Systems Research. 282p. 1992. pap. write for info. (0-88936-589-X) IDRC Bks.

Pathobiology Annual Staff. Pathobiology Annual, Vol. 1. fac. ed. Ioachim, Harry L., ed. LC 78-151816. (Illus.). 368p. pap. 114.10 (0-7837-7231-9, 204706700012) Bks Demand.

Pathria, Mini Nutan & Chan, Karence K. MRI of the Musculoskeletal System. 2nd ed. 256p. text 89.00 (0-7817-2571-2) Lppncott W & W.

Pathria, R. K. Advanced Statistical Mechanics. (International Series on Natural Philsophy). 1972. text 76.00 (0-08-016747-0, Pergamon Pr) Elsevier.

— Statistical Mechanics. 2nd ed. LC 96-1679. (Illus.). 576p. 1996. pap. text 69.95 (0-7506-2469-8, Q175, Prgamon Press) Buttrwrth-Heinemann.

Pathway Press Editors. Evangelical Sunday School Commentary 1998-1999. 1998. 13.99 (0-87148-981-3) Pathway Pr.

Pathway Press Staff. Evangelical Sunday School Lesson Commentary, 1999-2000 Ed. 1999. 13.99 (0-87148-991-0) Pathway Pr.

Pathways Publishing Staff. The Giver. (Pathways to Critical Thinking Ser.). 32p. (YA). 1997. pap. text, student ed. 19.95 (1-58303-025-5) Pthways Pubng.

— The Giver. (Assessment Packs Ser.). 15p. 1998. pap. text, teacher ed. 15.95 (1-58303-043-3) Pthways Pubng.

— Number the Stars. (Assessment Packs Ser.). 15p. 1998. pap. text, teacher ed. 15.95 (1-58303-054-9) Pthways Pubng.

*Pathy, Dinanath, ed. Continuity in the Flux. 1999. 34.00 (81-86622-31-4, Pub. by Harman Pub Hse) S Asia.

Pathy, Jaganath. Anthropology of Development: Demystification & Relevance. 214p. 1987. 13.00 (81-212-0081-4, Pub. by Gian Publng Hse) S Asia.

— Ethnic Minorities in the Process of Development. (C). 1988. 28.50 (81-7033-055-6, Pub. by Rawat Pubns) S Asia.

Pathy, M. S. & Emeritus, eds. Principles & Practice of Geriatric Medicine, 2 Vols. 3rd ed. LC 96-37118. 1688p. 1998. 595.00 (0-471-96348-8) Wiley.

Pathy, M. S. & Finucane, Paul, eds. Geriatric Medicine. (Illus.). xix, 383p. 1989. 121.00 (0-387-19525-4) Spr-Verlag.

Pati, Biswamoy. Resisting Domination: Peasants, Tribals & the Nationalist Movement in Orissa 1920-50. (C). 1993. 22.00 (81-7304-027-3, Pub. by Manohar) S Asia.

*Pati, Biswamoy, ed. Turbulent Times India, 1940-44. LC 98-901513. 1998. 27.00 (81-7154-834-2, Pub. by Popular Prakashan) S Asia.

Pati, Geeta. The Animals' Journey to the Moon. Dageforde, Linda, ed. LC 99-12683. (Illus.). 1999. pap. 15.95 (1-886225-39-7, 2000) Dageforde Pub.

Pati, J. C., et al, eds. Current Topics in Condensed Matter & Particle Physics: Non-Perturbative Phenomena & Strongly Correlated Systems, 19 May-14 June 1991. LC 93-7576. (Kathmandu Summer School Lecture Notes: Vol. 2). 332p. 1993. pap. 58.00 (981-02-1386-7); text 121.00 (981-02-1376-X) World Scientific Pub.

— Current Trends in Condensed Matter, Particle Physics & Cosmology. 400p. (C). 1990. text 86.00 (981-02-0114-1); pap. text 43.00 (981-02-0115-X) World Scientific Pub.

— High Energy Physics & Cosmology. 708p. (C). 1990. pap. 44.00 (981-02-0347-0); text 123.00 (981-02-0174-5) World Scientific Pub.

Pati, J. C., et al. High Energy Physics & Cosmology. (ICTP Ser. in Theoretical Phys.: Vol. 7). 732p. 1991. text 129.00 (981-02-0469-8) World Scientific Pub.

— Superstrings, Unified Theories & Cosmology, 1988. (ICTP Series in Theoretical Physics: Vol. 5). 664p. 1989. pap. 53.00 (9971-5-0871-0); text 151.00 (9971-5-0850-8) World Scientific Pub.

Pati Joshi, Jagat, ed. Facets of Indian Civilization: Recent Perspectives. LC 98-900524. (C). 1997. 225.00 (81-7305-087-2, Pub. by Aryan Bks Intl) S Asia.

Pati, Rabindra N. Health, Environment & Development. (C). 1992. 38.00 (81-7024-460-9, Pub. by Ashish Pub Hse) S Asia.

— Population Family & Culture. 1987. 31.95 (81-7024-151-0) Asia Bk Corp.

— Rehabilitation of Child Labourers in India. (C). 1991. 30.00 (81-7024-361-0, Pub. by Ashish Pub Hse) S Asia.

Pati, Rabindra N., jt. auth. see Jena, Basantibala.

Pati, Rabindra N., jt. ed. see Jena, B.

Pati, Satyabhama. Democratic Movements in India. 280p. (C). 1987. 32.00 (0-8364-2204-X) S Asia.

Patience, Allan, et al. Australian Federalism, Future Tense. LC 83-177942. 1983. pap. text 26.00 (0-19-554207-X) OUP.

Patient Care Publications Staff. Emergency Medical Procedures for the Outdoors. LC 87-18508. (Illus.). 120p. 1987. reprint ed. pap. 6.95 (0-89732-051-4) Menasha Ridge.

Patient, Derrick A. Healthcare Equipment International: Market Trends, Companies, Statistics. 342p. 1989. pap. text 150.00 (0-582-03683-6) Church.

Patient, Matthew, jt. auth. see Fleck, Richard F.

Patil, Abhimanuy O., et al, eds. Functional Polymers: Modern Synthetic Methods & Novel Structures. LC 98-21508. (ACS Symposium Ser.: No. 704). (Illus.). 368p. 1998. text 120.00 (0-8412-3577-5) OUP.

Patil, D. K. Pakistan's Islamic Bomb. 150p. 1979. 14.95 (0-7069-0911-9) Asia Bk Corp.

Patil, G. P. Random Counts in Scientific Work, 3 vols. Incl. Vol. 1. Random Counts in Models & Structures. LC 73-114351. 276p. 1970. 25.00 (0-271-00114-3); Vol. 2. Random Counts in Biomedical & Social Sciences. LC 73-114351. 232p. 1970. 25.00 (0-271-00115-1); Vol. 3. Random Counts in Physical Science, Geoscience, & Business. LC 73-114351. 215p. 1970. 25.00 (0-271-00116-X); LC 73-114351. (Illus.). write for info. (0-318-54929-8) Pa St U Pr.

Patil, G. P., et al, eds. Statistical Distributions in Ecological Work. (Statistical Ecology Ser.: Vol. 4). 1979. 45.00 (0-89974-001-4) Intl Co-Op.

— Statistical Ecology, 3 vols. Incl. Vol. 1. Spatial Patterns & Statistical Distributions. 584p. 26.50 (0-271-00111-9); Vol. 2. Sampling & Modeling Biological Populations & Population Dynamics. 428p. 26.50 (0-271-00112-7); Vol. 3. Many Species Populations, Ecosystems, & Systems Analysis. 470p. 1970. 26.50 (0-271-00113-5); (Illus.). write for info. (0-318-54930-1) Pa St U Pr.

Patil, G. P. & Rao, C. R., eds. Multivariate Environmental Statistics. LC 93-27385. (North-Holland Series in Statistics & Probability: Vol. 6). 608p. 1994. 201.25 (0-444-89804-2, North Holland) Elsevier.

— Statistics & Probability, Management/Monitoring/Policy/ Law, Statistics: Environmental Statistics. LC 93-33430. (Handbook of Statistics Ser.: No. 12). 948p. 1994. 190.00 (0-444-89803-4, North Holland) Elsevier.

Patil, G. P. & Rosenzweig, M. L., eds. Contemporary Quantitive Ecology & Related Ecometrics. (Statistical Ecology Ser.: Vol. 12). 1979. 60.00 (0-89974-009-X) Intl Co-Op.

Patil, Popat N. & Burkman, Allan M. An Introduction to Ocular Pharmacology & Toxicology. (Illus.). 320p. (C). 1995. pap. text 22.00 (1-57074-294-4) Greyden Pr.

Patil, R. B., jt. auth. see Pawar, S. N.

*Patil, S. International Food Indian Style. 1998. pap. 50.00 (81-86982-49-3, Pub. by Business Pubns) St Mut.

— What's in Your Name? Indian Baby Names & Their Meanings. 1998. pap. 150.00 (81-86982-26-4, Pub. by Business Pubns) St Mut.

Patil, S. H. Gandhi & Swaraj. 1984. 12.50 (0-8364-1227-3, Pub. by Deep & Deep Pubns) S Asia.

*Patil, S. H. & Tang, K. T. Asymptotic Methods in Quantum Mechanics: Application to Atoms, Molecules & Nuclei. LC 00-28523. (Series in Chemical Physics: Vol. 64). (Illus.). xi, 171p. 2000. 72.00 (3-540-67240-0) Spr-Verlag.

Patil, V. K., et al. Grape Research in India, 1981-1986. 134p. 1987. 29.95 (81-200-0247-4) Asia Bk Corp.

Patil, V. T. New Dimensions & Perspectives in Gandhism. 1989. 60.00 (81-210-0230-3, Pub. by Inter-India Pubns) S Asia.

Patil, V. T., ed. Explorations in Nehruvian Thought. (C). 1992. 38.00 (81-210-0282-6, Pub. by Inter-India Pubns) S Asia.

Patil, Vimla. Cook's Tour of South India. (C). 1993. write for info. (81-207-0947-0) Sterling Pubs.

— Entertaining Indian Style: Recipes for All Occasions. (C). 1992. pap. 10.00 (81-85674-16-7, Pub. by UBS Pubs Dist) S Asia.

Patilla, Peter. Clixi: Exploring Shape & Space. Stillman, Meg, ed. 48p. (YA). 1994. student ed. 7.99 (1-884461-09-3) NES Arnold.

— Fun with Numbers. LC 98-16664. (Fun with . . . Ser.). (Illus.). 31p. (J). (ps-2). 1998. lib. bdg. 22.40 (0-7613-0957-8, Copper Beech Bks) Millbrook Pr.

— Fun with Patterns. LC 98-16642. (Fun with . . . Ser.). 31p. (J). (gr. k-8). 1998. lib. bdg. 22.40 (0-7613-0960-8, Copper Beech Bks) Millbrook Pr.

— Fun with Shapes. LC 98-16665. (Fun with . . . Ser.). 31p. (J). (gr. k-8). 1998. lib. bdg. 22.40 (0-7613-0958-6, Copper Beech Bks) Millbrook Pr.

— Fun with Sizes. LC 98-16641. (Fun with . . . Ser.). 32p. (J). (ps-2). 1998. lib. bdg. 22.40 (0-7613-0959-4, Copper Beech Bks) Millbrook Pr.

— Length. LC 98-49372. (Measuring up Ser.). 1999. write for info. (0-382-42233-3) Silver Burdett Pr.

— Measuring. LC 99-20367. (Math Links Ser.). 1999. 19.92 (1-57572-965-2) Heinemann Lib.

— Numbers LC 99-20369. (Math Links Ser.). 1999. lib. bdg. write for info. (1-57572-966-0) Heinemann Lib.

— Patterns. LC 99-24955. (Math Links Ser.). 32p. (J). (gr. k-2). 1999. lib. bdg. 13.95 (1-57572-967-9) Heinemann Lib.

— Shapes. LC 99-24957. (Math Links Ser.). 1999. lib. bdg. write for info. (1-57572-968-7) Heinemann Lib.

— Size. LC 99-17737. (Measuring up Ser.). (J). 1999. write for info. (0-382-42231-7) Silver Burdett Pr.

*Patilla, Peter. Sorting: (or Handling Data) LC 99-14552. (Math Links Ser.). 32p. (J). (gr. k-2). 1999. 13.95 (1-57572-969-5) Heinemann Lib.

Patilla, Peter. Time. LC 99-24956. (Math Links Ser.). 1999. lib. bdg. write for info. (1-57572-970-9) Heinemann Lib.

*Patilla, Peter. Time. LC 99-14114. (Measuring up Ser.). 1999. write for info. (0-382-42232-5, New Dscvry Bks) Silver Burdett Pr.

— Weight. LC 98-46863. 1999. write for info. (0-382-42234-1) Silver.

Patilla, Peter & Stone, Bob. Multilink: Rediscovering Fractions. Brady, Cathleen, ed. (Middle School Math Ser.). (Illus.). 37p. (J). (gr. 5-9). 1995. student ed. 8.99 (1-884461-12-3) NES Arnold.

— Multilink: Shape & Space. Brady, Cathleen, ed. (Middle School Math Ser.). (Illus.). 36p. (J). (gr. 5-9). 1995. student ed. 8.99 (1-884461-13-1) NES Arnold.

Patin, jt. auth. see Shean.

*Patin, Douglas & Shean, Owen. Construction Insurance: Coverages & Disputes, 1999 Cumulative Supplement: Pocketpart. 125p. 1999. suppl. ed. write for info. (0-327-01700-7, 6693213) LEXIS Pub.

Patin, Douglas, jt. auth. see Shean, Owen.

Patin, Sally M. Our Dawson Family. 232p. 1981. 20.00 (0-89308-215-5) Southern Hist Pr.

Patin, Stanislav. Environmental Impact of the Offshore Oil & Gas Industry. Cascio, Elena, tr. from RUS. (Illus.). 512p. 1999. 199.00 (0-9671836-0-X) EcoMonitor Pubg.

Patin, Sylvie. Monet: The Ultimate Impressionist. Roberts, Anthony, tr. (Discoveries Ser.). (Illus.). 182p. 1993. pap. 12.95 (0-8109-2883-3, Pub. by Abrams) Time Warner.

Patin, Thomas. Discipline & Varnish: Rhetoric, Subjectivity, & Counter-Memory in the Museum. LC 98-9256. (Hermeneutics of Art Ser.: Vol. 7). (Illus.). 157p. (C). 1999. text 40.95 (0-8204-3806-5) P Lang Pubng.

Patin, Thomas & Mclerran, Jennifer. Artwords: A Glossary of Contemporary Art Theory. LC 96-29274. 176p. 1997. lib. bdg. 65.00 (0-313-29272-8) Greenwood.

Patin, Thomas & McLerran, Jennifer, eds. Artwords: A Glossary of Contemporary Art Theory. 1997. lib. bdg. 75.00 (1-884964-91-5) Fitzroy Dearborn.

Patinkin, Don. Anticipations of the General Theory & Other Essays on Keynes. LC 81-21929. 308p. 1985. pap. text 15.00 (0-226-64874-5) U Ch Pr.

— Anticipations of the General Theory & Other Essays on Keynes. LC 81-21929. 304p. 1997. 30.00 (0-226-64873-7) U Ch Pr.

— Money, Interest, & Prices: An Integration of Monetary & Value Theory. 2nd ed. 576p. 1989. 65.00 (0-262-16114-1) MIT Pr.

Patinkin, Mark. An African Journey. LC 85-15987. (Illus.). 52p. reprint ed. pap. 30.00 (0-8357-5236-4, 203007000067) Bks Demand.

— One Percent Inspiration, 99Desperation. 192p. 1996. 19.95 (0-924771-63-1, Covered Brdge Pr) Douglas Charles Ltd.

— The Pocket R. I. Dictionary. (Illus.). 64p. 2000. 4.95 (1-58066-003-7, Covered Brdge Pr) Douglas Charles Ltd.

— Rhode Island Dictionary. (Illus.). 128p. 1993. pap. 8.95 (0-924771-45-3, Covered Brdge Pr) Douglas Charles Ltd.

— Rhode Island Handbook. (Illus.). 144p. 1994. pap. 9.95 (0-924771-49-6, Covered Brdge Pr) Douglas Charles Ltd.

*Patinkin Rubin, Doralee. Grandma Doralee Patinkin's Jewish Holiday Cookbook. LC 99-15929. 288p. 1999. text 24.95 (0-312-24196-8) St Martin.

*Patinkin, Sheldon. The Second City. 192p. 2000. 45.00 incl. audio compact disk (1-57071-561-0) Sourcebks.

Patino, Diogenes. Asentamientos Prehispanicos en la Costa Pacifica Caucana. (SPA., Illus.). 160p. 1988. pap. 8.50 (1-877812-19-6, BR009) UPLAAP.

Patino, J. M. Rodriguez, jt. ed. see Dickinson, E.

Patino, Manny & Moreno, Jorge. Afro-Cuban Keyboard Grooves. Stang, Aaron, ed. (Illus.). 80p. (Orig.). 1997. pap. text 19.95 (1-57623-911-X, EL9706CD) Wrner Bros.

Patino, Michael. The 1997 Sports Summit Business Directory. 1000p. 1997. pap. text 179.00 (0-9644259-2-0) E J Krause.

Patino, Michael, ed. The 1998 Sport Summit Sports Business Directory. rev. ed. 1152p. (Orig.). 1998. pap. 189.00 (0-9644259-3-9) E J Krause.

*Patino, Michael, ed. The 1999 Sport Summit Sports Business Directory. rev. ed. 1096p. 1999. pap. 189.00 (0-9644259-4-7) E J Krause.

Patire, Thomas J. CDT- The Art of Non-Deadly Force. 2nd rev. ed. (Illus.). 122p. 1996. reprint ed. pap. 19.95 (0-9663316-0-5) CDT Training.

Patitu, Carol L., jt. auth. see Tack, Martha W.

Patitucci, Frank M. & Lichtenstein, Michael H. Improving Cash Management in Local Government: A Comprehensive Approach. LC 76-52518. (Illus.). 1977. pap. 6.00 (0-89125-003-4) Municipal.

Patitucci, J. John Patitucci. 64p. 1992. per. 14.95 (0-7935-0763-4, 00673216) H Leonard.

Patitucci, Karen. Three-Minute Dramas for Worship. LC 89-30342. 272p. (C). 1989. pap. 16.95 (0-89390-143-1) Resource Pubns.

Patkaniowska, M., jt. auth. see Corbridge.

*Patkau Architects Staff. Patkau Architects: Selected Projects 1983-1993. 2nd ed. Carter, Brian & ARUP Associates Staff, eds. LC 94-950012. (Documents in Canadian Architecture Ser.). (Illus.). 120p. 1998. reprint ed. pap. 24.50 (0-929112-28-8, Pub. by Tuns Pr) Baker & Taylor.

Patkau, Karen, jt. auth. see Heidbreder, Robert.

Patki, Rajani. The Concept of Upasana: Worship in Sanskrit Literature. (C). 1996. 38.00 (81-7030-483-0, Pub. by Sri Satguru Pubns) S Asia.

Patkin, Izhar. Mistresses & Wives, Husbands & Other Lives. (Illus.). 288p. 1998. 40.00 (0-8478-5783-2, Pub. by Rizzoli Intl) St Martin.

Patkus, Ronald D. From Generation to Generation II: The Roman Catholic Archbishop of Boston, a Corporation Sole. LC 91-76158. 1992. pap. 10.95 (0-8158-0480-6) Chris Mass.

Patla, Aftab E., ed. Adaptability of Human Gait: Implications for the Control of Locomotion. (Advances in Psychology Ser.: No. 78). 456p. 1991. 185.25 (0-444-88364-9, North Holland) Elsevier.

Patlagean, E. Pauvrete Economique Et Pauvrete Social a Byzance 4e-7e Siecles. 1977. 107.70 (90-279-7933-2) Mouton.

Patler, Louis. Don't Compete... Tilt the Field! 300 Irreverent Lessons for Tomorrow's Business Leaders. 256p. 1999. 24.95 (1-900961-74-1) Capstone Pub NH.

Patler, Louis, jt. auth. see Kriegel, Robert J.

*Patman. Security in a Post Cold War World. LC 98-42207. 1999. text 72.00 (0-312-22062-6) St Martin.

Patman, Robert. The Soviet Union in the Horn of Africa: The Diplomacy of Intervention & Disengagement. (Cambridge Russian, Soviet & Post-Soviet Studies: No. 71). (Illus.). 429p. (C). 1990. text 74.95 (0-521-36022-6) Cambridge U Pr.

*Patman, Robert G. Universal Human Rights in Theory & Practice. LC 99-87200. 2000. text 65.00 (0-312-23265-9) St Martin.

Patmore, Coventry K. Courage in Politics & Other Essays, 1885-1896. LC 68-26464. (Essay Index Reprint Ser.). 1977. reprint ed. 19.95 (0-8369-0774-4) Ayer.

— Rod, the Root & the Flower. Patmore, Derek, ed. LC 68-16966. (Essay Index Reprint Ser.). 1977. 19.95 (0-8369-0775-2) Ayer.

Patmore, Coventry K., ed. The Children's Garland: From the Best Poets. LC 73-167478. (Granger Index Reprint Ser.). 1977. reprint ed. 19.95 (0-8369-6283-4) Ayer.

Patmore, Derek, ed. see Patmore, Coventry K.

Patmore, Emma. Baking. LC 98-15354. (What's Cooking Ser.). (Illus.). 256p. 1998. 15.98 (1-57145-148-X, Thunder Bay) Advantage Pubs.

*Patmore, Emma. Baking. (Portable Chef Ser.). (Illus.). 256p. 1999. 7.98 (0-7651-0874-7) Smithmark.

Patmore, J. Allan. Land & Leisure in England & Wales. LC 75-164656. 332p. 1971. 39.50 (0-8386-1024-2) Fairleigh Dickinson.

— U. K. Recreation & Resources: Leisure Patterns & Leisure Places. (Illus.). 288p. 1999. 55.00 (0-631-17229-7); pap. 55.00 (0-631-19249-2) Blackwell Pubs.

Patmore, Ruth & Ross, Elizabeth. Rossmore Appliances. 50p. (C). 1972. write for info. (0-86766706-9) Macmillan.

Patnaik, B. K., ed. Ageing in Cold-Blooded Vertebrates. (Journal: Gerontology: Vol. 40, Nos. 2-4, 1994). (Illus.). 166p. 1994. pap. 131.50 (3-8055-5995-X) S Karger.

Patnaik, Deba P., jt. auth. see Morgan, Barbara.

Patnaik, Gayatri & Shinseki, Michelle, eds. The Secret Life of Teens: Young People Speak Out About Their Lives. 208p. 2000. pap. 12.95 (0-688-17076-5) Harper SF.

P

Patnaik, Himanshu S. Lord Jagannath: His Temple, Cult & Festivals. (Illus.). 196p. (C). 1994. 67.00 (*81-7305-051-1*, Pub. by Aryan Bks Intl) Nataraj Bks.

Patnaik, Jagadish K. India & the Gatt: Origin, Growth & Development. xiii, 237p. 1997. 36.00 (*81-7024-813-2*, Pub. by APH Pubng) Nataraj Bks.

Patnaik, K. U. Industrial Planning, Productivity & Technical Progress in India. (C). 1991. 25.00 (*0-8364-2661-4*, Pub. by Chugh Pubns) S Asia.

Patnaik, Lalit N. Environmental Impacts of Industrial & Mining Activities. (New World Environment Ser.). 1990. 36.50 (*81-7024-333-5*, Pub. by Ashish Pub Hse) S Asia.

Patnaik, N. R. History & Culture of Khond Tribes. (C). 1992. 44.00 (*81-7169-199-4*, Commonwealth) S Asia.

Patnaik, Nihar Ranjan. The Economic History of Orissa in the Nineteenth Century. LC 98-902460. 389p. 1997. write for info. (*81-7387-075-6*) Indus Pub.

Patnaik, Prabhat. Accumulation & Stability under Capitalism. 330p. (C). 1997. text 75.00 (*0-19-828805-0*) OUP.

Patnaik, Prabhat, ed. Macroeconomics. (Oxford in India Readings Ser.; Themes in Economics). (Illus.). 256p. (C). 1995. 24.00 (*0-19-563534-5*) OUP.

— Macroeconomics. (Oxford in India Readings Ser.). (Illus.). 254p. 1997. reprint ed. pap. text 10.95 (*0-19-564164-7*) OUP.

Patnaik, Pradyot. A Comprehensive Guide to the Hazardous Properties of Chemical Substances. 800p. 1992. text 119.95 (*0-442-00191-6*, VNR) Wiley.

— A Comprehensive Guide to the Hazardous Properties of Chemical Substances. 2nd ed. (Illus.). 750p. 1998. 130.00 (*0-442-02376-6*, VNR) Wiley.

***Patnaik, Pradyot.** A Comprehensive Guide to the Hazardous Properties of Chemical Substances. 2nd ed. LC 98-39972. 984p. 1999. 189.00 (*0-471-29175-7*) Wiley.

Patnaik, Pradyot. Handbook of Environmental Analysis: Chemical Pollutants in Air, Water, Soil & Solid Wastes. LC 96-32647. 608p. 1997. lib. bdg. 85.00 (*0-87371-989-1*) Lewis Pubs.

Patnaik, Priyadarshi. Rasa in Aesthetics: An Application of Rasa Theory to Modern Western Literature. LC 97-900289. (C). 1997. 32.00 (*81-246-0081-3*, Pub. by DK Pubs Ind) S Asia.

Patnaik, Tandra. Sabda: A Study of Bhartrharti's Philosophy of Language. (C). 1994. text 19.00 (*81-246-0028-7*, Pub. by DK Pubs Ind) S Asia.

Patnaik, U. C. & Mishra, A. K. Handloom Industry in Action. LC 97-901602. 128p. 1997. pap. 100.00 (*81-7533-037-6*, Pub. by Print Hse) St Mut.

Patnaik, Utsa, ed. Agrarian Relations & Accumulation: The "Mode of Production" Debate in India. 280p. 1991. 27.00 (*0-19-562565-X*) OUP.

Patnaude, Jeff. Leading from the Maze: A Personal Pathway to Leadership. LC 95-45433. 158p. 1996. text 17.95 (*0-89815-745-5*) Ten Speed Pr.

Patneaude, David. Dark, Starry Morning: Stories of This World & Beyond. LC 95-770. 128p. (J). (gr. 6-9). 1995. lib. bdg. 13.95 (*0-8075-1474-8*) A Whitman.

— Dark, Starry Morning: Stories of This World & Beyond. 128p. (YA). (gr. 6-9). 1998. lib. bdg. 3.95 (*0-8075-1475-6*) A Whitman.

***Patneaude, David.** Dark Starry Morning: Stories of This World & Beyond. 1998. 9.05 (*0-606-13315-1*, Pub. by Turtleback) Demco.

Patneaude, David. Framed in Fire. LC 98-39606. 224p. (YA). (gr. 6-9). 1999. lib. bdg. 14.95 (*0-8075-9098-3*) A Whitman.

***Patneaude, David.** Haunting at Home Plate. LC 99-40607. (J). (gr. 4-8). 2000. lib. bdg. 14.95 (*0-8075-3181-2*) A Whitman.

Patneaude, David. The Last Man's Reward. 192p. (J). (gr. 5-8). 1996. lib. bdg. 14.95 (*0-8075-4370-5*) A Whitman.

— The Last Man's Reward. 192p. (YA). (gr. 5-8). 1998. pap. 4.95 (*0-8075-4371-3*) A Whitman.

***Patneaude, David.** The Last Man's Reward. (J). 1998. 10.05 (*0-606-13564-2*, Pub. by Turtleback) Demco.

Patneaude, David. Someone Was Watching. Mathews, Judith, ed. LC 92-39130. 240p. (J). (gr. 6-9). 1993. lib. bdg. 14.95 (*0-8075-7531-3*) A Whitman.

— Someone Was Watching. (J). (gr. 6-9). 1995. pap. 4.95 (*0-8075-7532-1*) A Whitman.

— Someone Was Watching. (J). 1995. 10.05 (*0-606-13788-2*, Pub. by Turtleback) Demco.

Patneaude, David. Someone Was Watching, Set. unabridged ed. (YA). (gr. 7). 1997. pap. 38.95 incl. audio (*0-7887-1252-7*, 40498) Recorded Bks.

Patner, Andrew, ed. Alternative Futures: Challenging Designs for Arts Philanthropy. LC 94-79005. 117p. (Orig.). 1994. pap. 11.95 (*0-9643011-0-5*) Grantmakers Arts.

Patni, M. J., jt. auth. see Srivastava, C. M.

Patni, M. J., jt. ed. see Srivastava, C. M.

Patnode, Darwin. A History of Parliamentary Procedure. 3rd ed. LC 81-86047. 85p. (Orig.). 1982. pap. 10.95 (*0-942302-00-1*) Parliamentarians.

Patnode, Gladys. Patckwork Quilt: Stories of My Childhood. (Stories We Tell Ser.). 31p. 1993. pap. 4.00 (*1-884983-03-0*) Homegrown Bks.

Patnoe, S. A Narrative History of Experimental Social Psychology. (Recent Research in Psychology Ser.). 295p. 1988. pap. 43.00 (*0-387-96850-4*) Spr-Verlag.

Patnuker, B. W. Grasses of Marathwada. (C). 1980. text 50.00 (*81-85046-05-0*, Pub. by Scientific Pubs) St Mut.

Pato, Hilda. Los Finales Poematicos en la Obra de Luis Cernuda. LC 87-62377. (SPA.). 118p. 1988. pap. 30.00 (*0-89295-052-8*) Society Sp & Sp-Am.

Pato, Michele T. & Zohar, Joseph, eds. Current Treatments of Obsessive-Compulsive Disorder. LC 90-14497. (Clinical Practice Ser.: No. 18). 198p. 1991. text 14.95 (*0-88048-351-2*, 8351) Am Psychiatric.

Patocka, Franz. Satzgliedstellung in den Bairischen Dialekten Osterreichs. (Reihe Schriften zur Deutschen Sprache in Osterreich Ser.: Bd. 20). (GER., Illus.). 433p. 1996. 69.95 (*3-631-30450-1*) P Lang Pubng.

Patocka, J. Le Monde Naturel Comme Probleme Philosophique. (Phaenomenologica Ser.: No. 68). 190p. 1976. lib. bdg. 99.50 (*90-247-1795-7*, Pub. by M Nijhoff) Kluwer Academic.

— Le Monde Naturel et le Mouvement de l'Existence Humaine. (Phaenomenologica Ser.: Vol. 110). (FRE.). 272p. 1988. lib. bdg. 195.50 (*90-247-3577-7*, Pub. by M Nijhoff) Kluwer Academic.

Patocka, Jan. Body Community, Language, World. Dodd, James, ed. Kohak, Erazim, tr. from CZE. LC 97-26040. 208p. 1997. pap. 19.95 (*0-8126-9359-0*) Open Court.

— Body Community, Language, World. Dodd, James, ed. Kohak, Erazim, tr. from CZE. LC 97-26040. 208p. (C). 1997. 42.95 (*0-8126-9358-2*) Open Court.

— Heretical Essays in the Philosophy of History. Dodd, James, ed. Kohak, Erazim V., tr. from CZE. 206p. 1996. 42.95 (*0-8126-9336-1*); pap. 19.95 (*0-8126-9337-X*) Open Court.

— An Introduction to Husserl's Phenomenology. Dodd, James, ed. Kohak, Erazin V., tr. from CZE. LC 96-39052. 216p. 1996. 35.95 (*0-8126-9338-8*) Open Court.

Patokorpi, Erkki. Rhetoric, Argumentative & Divine: Richard Whately & His Discursive Project of the 1820s. Gimpl, Georg & Manninen, Julia, eds. (European Studies in the History of Science & Ideas: Vol. 2). (Illus.). 309p. 1996. pap. 57.95 (*3-631-30235-5*) P Lang Pubng.

— Rhetoric, Argumentative & Divine: Richard Whately & His Discursive Project of the 1820s. Gimpl, Georg & Manninen, Julia, eds. (European Studies in the History of Science & Ideas: Vol. 2). (Illus.). 309p. 1996. pap. 57.95 (*0-8204-3191-5*) P Lang Pubng.

Patom, Thomas R., et al. Soils: A New Global View. LC 95-30335. 213p. 1996. pap. 22.50 (*0-300-06609-0*) Yale U Pr.

Patomaki, Heikki, jt. ed. see Minkkinen, Petri.

Paton. The New Management Reader. 1996. pap. write for info. (*1-86152-200-2*) Thomson Learn.

Paton, et al, eds. Plutarchi Vol. I: De Liberis Educandis. (GRE.). 1993. reprint ed. 100.00 (*3-8154-1678-7*, T1678, Pub. by B G Teubner) U of Mich Pr.

— Plutarchi Vol. II: Regum et Imperatorum Apophthegmata. (GRE.). 1972. reprint ed. 53.50 (*3-322-00200-4*, T1679, Pub. by B G Teubner) U of Mich Pr.

Paton, A. A., et al. Civil Engineering Design for Decommissioning of Nuclear Installations. 104p. 1984. pap. text 95.00 (*0-86010-614-4*) G & T Inc.

Paton, Alan. Cry, the Beloved Country. 23.95 (*0-89190-379-8*) Amereon Ltd.

— Cry, the Beloved Country. (Barron's Book Notes Ser.). 1985. pap. 2.95 (*0-8120-3507-0*) Barron.

— Cry, the Beloved Country. 1985. pap. 12.00 (*0-684-51544-X*, Scribners Ref) Mac Lib Ref.

— Cry, the Beloved Country. 320p. 1995. per. 12.00 (*0-684-81894-9*) S&S Trade.

— Cry, the Beloved Country. 1996. 11.05 (*0-606-00509-9*, Pub. by Turtleback) Demco.

— Cry the Beloved Country. 304p. 1977. 35.00 (*0-684-15559-1*, Scribners Ref) Mac Lib Ref.

— Cry, the Beloved Country. large type ed. 370p. 1987. reprint ed. lib. bdg. 19.95 (*1-55736-004-9*) BDD LT Grp.

— Cry, the Beloved Country. 300p. 1991. reprint ed. lib. bdg. 28.95 (*0-89966-788-0*) Buccaneer Bks.

— Cry, the Beloved Country, 2 vols., Set. large type ed. (YA). (gr. 10 up). reprint ed. 10.00 (*0-89064-021-1*) NAVH.

— Instrument of Thy Peace. 1984. 6.95 (*0-8164-2421-7*) Harper SF.

Paton, Alan. Instrument of Thy Peace. large type ed. 124p. 1985. reprint ed. pap. text 8.95 (*0-8027-2494-9*) Walker & Co.

Paton, Alan. Save the Beloved Country. 336p. 1989. 22.50 (*0-684-19127-X*) S&S Trade.

— Tales from a Troubled Land. 128p. 1996. per. 9.00 (*0-684-82584-8*) S&S Trade.

— Too Late the Phalarope. 23.95 (*0-89190-392-5*) Amereon Ltd.

— Too Late the Phalarope. 1983. pap. 7.95 (*0-684-10455-5*) S&S Trade.

— Too Late the Phalarope. 288p. 1996. per. 11.00 (*0-684-81895-7*) S&S Trade.

Paton, Alan, jt. auth. see Center for Learning Network Staff.

Paton, Alex. ABC of Alcohol. 3rd ed. 48p. 1994. pap. text 18.00 (*0-7279-0812-X*, Pub. by BMJ Pub) Login Brothers Bk Co.

Paton, Andrew. Stendhal. 1972. 59.95 (*0-8490-1124-8*) Gordon Pr.

Paton, B. E. Welding & Surfacing Reviews: Explosion Welding Criteria, Vol. 3. (Welding & Surfacing Reviews Ser: Vol. 3, Pt. 4). 127p. 1994. pap. text 259.00 (*3-7186-5725-2*, Harwood Acad Pubs) Gordon & Breach.

— Welding & Surfacing Reviews: Laser-Arc Discharge, Vol. 3. (Welding & Surfacing Reviews Ser: Vol. 3, Pt. 3). 148p. 1994. pap. text 302.00 (*3-7186-5726-0*, Harwood Acad Pubs) Gordon & Breach.

— Welding & Surfacing Reviews Vol. 3, Pt. 2: Fatigue Strength of Welded Structures, Vol. 3. (Welding & Surfacing Reviews Ser). 100p. 1994. pap. text 204.00 (*3-7186-5724-4*, Harwood Acad Pubs) Gordon & Breach.

Paton, B. E. & Lapchinskii, V. F. Welding in Space & Allied Technologies. 110p. 1997. 72.00 (*1-898326-45-2*, Pub. by CISP) Balogh.

Paton, B. E. & Nazarenko, O. K. Welding & Surfacing Reviews: Electron Beam Welding: Achievements & Problems (a Review), Vol. 1, No. 1. (Soviet Technology Reviews Ser.: Vol. 1, Pt. 1). ii, 54p. 1989. pap. text 63.00 (*3-7186-4946-2*) Gordon & Breach.

Paton, B. E., ed. see Gladkii, P. V., et al.

Paton, B. E., ed. see Kuchuk-Yatsenko, S. I. & Cherednichok, V. T.

Paton, B. E., ed. see Medovar, B. I., et al.

Paton, B. E., ed. see Pokhodnaya, I. K. & Podgaetsky, V. V.

Paton, Barry E. Sensors, Transducers & LabVIEW: An Application Approach to Virtual Instrumentation. LC 98-19173. 350p. 1998. pap., lab manual ed. 60.00 (*0-13-081155-6*) P-H.

Paton, C. R. Competition & Planning in the NHS: The Danger of Unplanned Markets. 174p. 1992. pap. 57.50 (*1-56593-058-4*, 0364) Singular Publishing.

— Health Policy & Management: The Healthcare Agenda in a British Political Context. 400p. 1995. pap. 63.75 (*1-56593-285-4*, 0609) Singular Publishing.

— Lifespan Health Psychology: Nursing Problems & Interventions. 288p. 1992. pap. 43.25 (*1-56593-008-8*, 0249) Thomson Learn.

— U. S. Health Politics: Public Policy & Political Theory. 240p. 1990. text 77.95 (*0-566-07101-0*, Pub. by Avebry) Ashgate Pub Co.

Paton, Calum. Ethics & Politics: Theory & Practice. 139p. 1992. 82.95 (*1-85628-382-8*, Pub. by Avebry) Ashgate Pub Co.

***Paton, Calum R.** World Class Britain: Political Economy, Political Theory & British Politics. LC 99-53010. 2000. 65.00 (*0-312-23109-1*) St Martin.

Paton, Caroline, jt. auth. see Paton, Sandy.

Paton, D. M., ed. The Transport of Neurotransmitters. (Journal: Pharmacology: Vol. 21, No. 2). (Illus.). 74p. 1980. pap. 21.00 (*3-8055-1316-X*) S Karger.

Paton, David, ed. see Allen, Roland.

Paton, David F. Fractures & Orthopaedics. 2nd ed. LC 92-12316. (Student Notes Ser.). (Illus.). 248p. 1992. pap. text 33.95 (*0-443-04707-3*) Church.

Paton, David M., ed. Methods in Pharmacology Vol. 6: Methods Used in Adenosine Research. LC 84-26638. 400p. 1985. 95.00 (*0-306-41872-X*, Plenum Trade) Perseus Pubng.

Paton, Douglas & Violanti, John M. Traumatic Stress in Critical Occupations: Recognition, Consequences, & Treatment. LC 95-47069. (Illus.). 260p. 1996. 62.95 (*0-398-06577-2*); pap. 41.95 (*0-398-06578-0*) C C Thomas.

Paton, Douglas, jt. auth. see Violanti, John M.

Paton, Douglas, jt. ed. see Violanti, John M.

Paton, E. O., jt. ed. see Pokhodnya, I. K.

Paton, Garth, jt. auth. see Haggerty, Terry.

Paton, H. J. Kant's Metaphysics of Experience: A Commentary on the First Half of the Kritik der Reinen Vernunft, 2 vols. 1095p. 1998. 225.00 (*1-85506-528-2*) Thoemmes Pr.

Paton, Herbert J. Kant's Metaphysics of Experience, 2 vols., Set. (Muirhead Library of Philosophy). (C). 1984. reprint ed. pap. 80.00 (*0-391-00673-8*) Humanities.

Paton, Herbert J., tr. see Kant, Immanuel.

Paton, J., jt. auth. see Kuhlmann, P.

Paton, J. E., jt. ed. see Aitchison, Ian J.

Paton, Jessie, jt. ed. see Rickert, Edith.

Paton, John G. L' Aria Barocca: Medium High Voice. 110p. (Orig.). 1986. pap. text 8.95 (*0-9602296-5-5*) Leyerle Pubns.

— L' Aria Barocca: Medium Low Voice. 110p. 1987. pap. text 8.95 (*0-9602296-7-1*) Leyerle Pubns.

— Gateway to German Diction: The Singer's Guide to Pronunciation. (Gateway Ser.). 128p. 1999. pap. 25.95 incl. audio compact disk (*0-7390-0103-5*, 17607) Alfred Pub.

— Gateway to German Diction: Teacher's Supplementary Materials: The Singer's Guide to Pronunciation. (Gateway Ser.). 1999. pap., teacher ed. 29.95 (*0-7390-0105-1*, 17608) Alfred Pub.

— Gateway to German Lieder/High Voice: An Anthology of Songs. (Gateway Ser.). 2000. pap. 19.95 (*0-7390-0106-X*, 17611) Alfred Pub.

— Gateway to German Lieder/High Voice: An Anthology of Songs. (Gateway Ser.). 2000. pap. 34.95 incl. audio compact disk (*0-7390-0107-8*, 17612) Alfred Pub.

— Twenty-Six Italian Songs & Arias, Medium High. 152p. (C). 1991. pap. 8.95 (*0-88284-489-X*, 3402) Alfred Pub.

— Twenty-Six Italian Songs & Arias, Medium Low. 152p. (C). 1991. pap. 8.95 (*0-88284-490-3*, 3403) Alfred Pub.

Paton, John G., ed. 20 Songs by Donizetti, High Voice. 1996. pap. 19.95 (*0-88284-808-9*) Alfred Pub.

— 20 Songs by Donizetti, Low Voice. 1996. pap. 19.95 (*0-88284-809-7*) Alfred Pub.

Paton, John G. & Chiti, Patricia A. Italian Art Songs of the Romantic Era/Medium High. 112p. 1994. pap. 14.95 (*0-7390-0245-7*, 4954) Alfred Pub.

Paton, John G., jt. auth. see Christy, Van Ambrose.

Paton, John G., jt. auth. see Van Christy, A.

Paton, John G., ed. see Mendelssohn, Felix & Mendelssohn, Fanny.

Paton, John G., ed. see Mozart, Wolfgang Amadeus.

Paton, John Glenn. Gateway to German Lieder, Low. 216p. 2000. pap. 34.95 incl. audio compact disk (*0-7390-0274-0*, 17618); pap. 19.95 (*0-7390-0273-2*, 17617) Alfred Pub.

Paton, John J. & Chiti, Patricia A. Songs & Duets of Garcia & Viardot: Medium-Low Voice. 1997. pap. 12.95 (*0-88284-786-4*, 16814) Alfred Pub.

Paton, Joseph N. Poems by a Painter. LC 73-112941. reprint ed. 32.00 (*0-404-04905-2*) AMS Pr.

***Paton, Kathleen.** Santa. LC 98-21581. (Ornaments Ser.). (Illus.). 72p. 1998. 12.98 (*0-7651-0868-2*) Smithmark.

Paton, Kathleen, ed. Poems to Share. (Real Mother Goose Library). (Illus.). 24p. (J). (ps-3). 1990. 4.95 (*1-56288-050-0*) Checkerboard.

Paton, Kevin T., jt. auth. see Thibodeau, Gary A.

Paton, L. A. Studies in the Fairy Mythology of Arthurian Romance. 1972. 69.95 (*0-8490-1150-7*) Gordon Pr.

Paton, Lewis B. Esther: Critical Exegetical Commentary. Driver, Samuel R. et al, eds. LC 08-30156. (International Critical Commentary Ser.). 360p. 1908. 39.95 (*0-567-05009-2*, Pub. by T & T Clark) Bks Intl VA.

— Jerusalem in Bible Times. Davis, Moshe, ed. LC 77-70733. (America & the Holy Land Ser.). (Illus.). 1977. reprint ed. lib. bdg. 23.95 (*0-405-10277-1*) Ayer.

Paton, Lucy A. Elizabeth Cary Agassiz: A Biography. LC 74-3969. (Women in America Ser.). (Illus.). 454p. 1974. reprint ed. 35.95 (*0-405-06117-X*) Ayer.

Paton, Maureen. Alan Rickman: The Unauthorised Biography. (Illus.). 256p. 1997. text 24.95 (*1-85227-630-4*, Pub. by Virgin Bks) London Brdge.

Paton, Mena. System 1032 PCI Guide. Stone, Shirley, ed. 50p. (Orig.). pap. text 20.00 (*0-912055-24-3*) CompuServe Data Tech.

Paton, Neil E., ed. see International Conference on Superplasticity & Supe.

Paton, Neil E., ed. see Metallurgical Society of AIME Staff.

Paton, Norman, et al, eds. Active Rules for Databases. LC 98-17537. (Monographs in Computer Science). (Illus.). 450p. 1998. 64.95 (*0-387-98529-8*) Spr-Verlag.

***Paton, Norman W. & Griffiths, Tony, eds.** User Interfaces to Data Intensive Systems: Proceedings User Interfaces to Data Intensive Systems (UIDS), Edinburgh, Scotland, 1999. LC 99-62797. 166p. 1999. 110.00 (*0-7695-0262-8*) IEEE Comp Soc.

Paton, Norman W. & Williams, M. Howard, eds. Rules in Database Systems: Proceedings of the 1st International Workshop on Rules in Database Systems, Edinburgh, Scotland, 30 August-1 September 1993. LC 93-27566. (Workshops in Computing Ser.). 1994. 84.95 (*0-387-19846-6*) Spr-Verlag.

Paton, Patricia. A Medical Gentleman: James J. Waring, M. D. LC 93-23589. 1993. write for info. (*0-942576-02-0*); pap. write for info. (*0-942576-33-0*) CO Hist Soc.

Paton, Priscilla. Howard & the Sitter Surprise. (Illus.). 32p. (J). (ps-3). 1996. 15.95 (*0-395-71814-7*) HM.

Paton, R. Computing with Biological Metaphors: A Multidisciplinary Approach. 464p. 1994. pap. 99.95 (*0-412-54470-9*) Chapman & Hall.

Paton, Ray & Neilsen, Irene E., eds. Visual Representations & Interpretations. LC 98-49156. x, 406p. 1999. pap. (*1-85233-082-1*) Spr-Verlag.

Paton, Rob. The New Management Reader. 304p. 1996. pap. 27.95 (*1-86152-201-0*) Thomson Learn.

Paton, Rob, ed. The New Management: Readings & Perspectives. LC 95-40497. 304p. 1996. mass mkt. 27.95 (*0-415-13987-2*) Routledge.

Paton, Rob, et al, eds. The New Management: Readings & Perspectives. LC 95-40497. 304p. 1996. pap. 79.95 (*0-415-13986-4*) Thomson Learn.

Paton, Rob, jt. auth. see Boddy, David.

Paton, Rob, ed. see Shiva Tirtha, Sada.

Paton, Robert A., jt. auth. see McCalman, James.

Paton, Roderick. Business Case Studies: French. (ENG & FRE.). 124p. 1980. pap. 19.95 (*0-8288-0986-0*, M 14377) Fr & Eur.

— Business Case Studies: German. (ENG & GER.). 124p. 1980. pap. 17.95 (*0-8288-0991-7*, M 9204) Fr & Eur.

Paton, Sandy & Paton, Caroline. I've Got a Song! A Collection of Songs for Youngsters. 2nd ed. (Illus.). 40p. (Orig.). (J). (gr. k-4). 1989. pap. 10.98 (*0-938702-05-X*) Folk-Legacy.

— Sandy & Caroline Paton: When the Spirit Says Sing. (Illus.). 40p. (J). (gr. k-8). 1989. pap. 9.98 incl. audio (*0-938702-06-8*, C1002) Folk-Legacy.

Paton, Thomas R. Perspectives on a Dynamic Earth. 176p. 1986. text 55.00 (*0-04-550042-8*) Routledge.

— Perspectives on a Dynamic Earth. 176p. (C). 1986. pap. text 21.95 (*0-04-550043-6*) Routledge.

— Soils: A New Global View. LC 95-30335. 213p. 1996. 45.00 (*0-300-06576-0*) Yale U Pr.

Paton, Tricia, jt. auth. see Downes, John.

Paton, W. A. Corporate Profits As Shown by Audit Reports. (General Ser.: No. 28). 165p. 1935. reprint ed. 42.90 (*0-87014-027-2*) Natl Bur Econ Res.

Paton, W. A. & Littleton, Ananias C. An Introduction to Corporate Accounting Standards. (Monograph: No. 3). 156p. 1940. 12.00 (*0-86539-000-2*) Am Accounting.

***Paton, Wally.** Back to Basics: The Alcoholics Anonymous Beginners' Meetings. 2nd rev. ed. LC 99-215281. Orig. Title: Back to Basics - The Alcoholics Anonymous "Beginners' Classes". (Illus.). xi, 160p. 1998. pap. 12.00 (*0-9657720-1-2*) Faith Works.

Paton Walsh, Jill. Birdy & the Ghosties. LC 89-45397. (Illus.). 48p. 1991. pap. 4.95 (*0-374-40675-8*) FS&G.

— A Chance Child. LC 78-21521. (Illus.). 192p. (YA). (gr. 4-7). 1991. pap. 5.95 (*0-374-41174-3*) FS&G.

— A Chance Child. 144p. (YA). (gr. 7 up). 1980. pap. 1.95 (*0-380-48561-3*, 48561-3, Avon Bks) Morrow Avon.

***Paton Walsh, Jill.** Desert in Bohemia. 2000. 23.95 (*0-312-26263-9*) St Martin.

Paton Walsh, Jill. The Emperor's Winding Sheet. LC 73-90970. 288p. (YA). (gr. 7 up). 1992. pap. 4.95 (*0-374-42121-8*) FS&G.

— Fireweed. LC 73-109554. 160p. (YA). (gr. 6 up). 1988. pap. 3.50 (*0-374-42316-4*) FS&G.

— Fireweed. (YA). 1998. 18.50 (*0-8446-6978-4*) Peter Smith.

— Gaffer Samson's Luck. LC 84-10180. (Illus.). 128p. (J). (gr. 4-7). 1990. pap. 4.95 (*0-374-42513-2*) FS&G.

— Gaffer Samson's Luck. (J). 1984. 10.05 (*0-606-04677-1*, Pub. by Turtleback) Demco.

P

An Asterisk (*) at the beginning of an entry indicates that the title is appearing for the first time.

— Goldengrove. LC 72-81484. 130p. (YA). (gr. 7 up). 1985. pap. 3.50 (0-374-42587-6) FS&G.
— Goldengrove. (J). (gr. 4-9). 1993. 17.25 (0-8446-6646-7) Peter Smith.
— Goldengrove Unleaving. 1997. pap. 12.95 (0-552-99655-6) Bantam.
— Grace. LC 91-31054. 256p. (YA). (gr. 7 up). 1992. 16.00 (0-374-32758-0) FS&G.
— Grace. 256p. (YA). 1994. pap. 5.95 (0-374-42792-5) FS&G.
— The Green Book. LC 81-12620. (Illus.). 80p. (J). (ps-3). 1982. 13.00 (0-374-32778-5) FS&G.
— The Green Book. LC 81-12620. (Illus.). 69p. (J). (gr. 4-7). 1986. pap. 3.95 (0-374-42802-6) FS&G.
— The Green Book. (J). 1986. 9.15 (0-606-03220-7, Pub. by Turtleback) Demco.
— The Island Sunrise: Prehistoric Britain. LC 75-327466. (Mirror of Britain Ser.). 128p. 1975. write for info. (0-233-96671-4) Andre Deutsch.
— Matthew & the Sea Singer. LC 92-53467. (Illus.). 48p. (J). (ps-3). 1993. 13.00 (0-374-34869-3) FS&G.
— A Parcel of Patterns. LC 83-48143. 144p. (YA). 1992. pap. 3.95 (0-374-45743-3) FS&G.
Paton Walsh, Jill. A Parcel of Patterns. 137p. (YA). (gr. 7 up). pap. 3.95 (0-8072-1485-X) Listening Lib.
Paton Walsh, Jill. A Parcel of Patterns. 1995. 17.75 (0-8446-6819-2) Peter Smith.
— A Parcel of Patterns. 1992. 9.05 (0-606-02412-3, Pub. by Turtleback) Demco.
— Pepi & the Secret Names. LC 93-48620. (Illus.). 32p. (J). (gr. 1 up). 1995. 15.00 (0-688-13428-9) Lothrop.
— The Serpentine Cave. LC 97-23094. 224p. 1997. text 20.95 (0-312-16999-X) St Martin.
— The Serpentine Cave. large type ed. (Charnwood Large Print Ser.). 272p. 1998. 29.99 (0-7089-9001-0, Charnwood) Ulverscroft.
— Torch. LC 87-45995. 176p. (YA). (gr. 7 up). 1988. 15.00 (0-374-37684-0) FS&G.
— Unleaving. 160p. 1990. pap. 3.50 (0-374-48068-0) FS&G.
Paton Walsh, Jill. When I Was Little Like You. (Illus.). 32p. (J). pap. 9.95 (0-14-055829-2, Pub. by Pnguin Bks Ltd) Trafalgar.
Paton Welding Institute Staff. Underwater Wet Welding & Cutting: Proceedings of TWI International Seminar. 120p. 1998. 153.00 (1-85573-388-9, Pub. by Woodhead Pubng) Am Educ Systs.
Paton, William. Man & Mouse: Animals in Medical Research. 2nd ed. (Illus.). 304p. 1993. pap. 16.95 (0-19-286146-8) OUP.
Paton, William A. Down the Islands: A Voyage to the Caribbees. LC 69-19360. (Illus.). 301p. 1970. reprint ed. lib. bdg. 65.00 (0-8371-1129-3, PAD&) Greenwood.
— Paton on Accounting: Selected Writings of W. A. Paton. Taggart, Herbert F., ed. LC 64-64728. 729p. reprint ed. pap. 180.00 (0-608-13524-0, 2022093) Bks Demand.
Paton, William A. & Dixon, Robert L. Make-or-Buy Decisions in Tooling for Mass Production. LC 61-63325. (Michigan Business Studies: No. 35). 40p. reprint ed. pap. 30.00 (0-608-13526-7, 202209100024) Bks Demand.
Paton, William A. & Stevenson, Russell A. Principles of Accounting. Brief, Richard P., ed. LC 77-87284. (Contemporary Accounting Thought Ser.). 1978. reprint ed. lib. bdg. 59.95 (0-405-10912-1) Ayer.
— Principles of Accounting. LC 75-18479. (History of Accounting Ser.). 1978. reprint ed. 18.95 (0-405-07561-8) Ayer.
Paton, William D., ed. see International Congress of Pharmacology Staff.
Paton, William R. & Hicks, Edward L. The Inscriptions of Cos. (Subsidia Epigraphica Ser.). (GER., Illus.). liv, 407p. 1990. reprint ed. 89.70 (3-487-09288-3) G Olms Pubs.
Patonay, G., ed. HPLC Detection: Newer Methods. 236p. 1993. 139.00 (0-471-18802-6, Wiley-VCH) Wiley.
Patonay, Gabor, ed. Advances in Near-Infrared Measurements, Vol. 1. 144p. 1993. 109.50 (1-55938-173-6) Jai Pr.
— HPLC Detection: Newer Methods. LC 92-26716. 240p. 1993. 95.00 (0-89573-327-7, Wiley-VCH) Wiley.
Patons. Supplement Series, 1974. 1973. 18.00 (0-316-69344-8, Aspen Law & Bus) Aspen Pub.
Patorski, K. Handbook of the Moire Fringe Technique. LC 92-37210. 432p. 1992. 187.25 (0-444-88823-3) Elsevier.
Patorski, Krzysztof, jt. ed. see Jueptner, Werner P.
Patoski, Joe N. Selena: Como la Flor. 1996. 16.95 incl. audio (1-882071-75-1, 634018) B&B Audio.
Patoski, Joe N. Selena: Como la Flor. 368p. 1997. reprint ed. mass mkt. 6.50 (1-57297-246-7) Blvd Books.
— Stevie Ray Vaughan: Caught in the Crossfire. 336p. 1994. pap. 12.95 (0-316-16069-5) Little.
Patoski, Joe Nick. Selena: Como la Flor. 1999. mass mkt. 6.99 (0-425-17124-8) Berkley Pub.
Patoski, Margaret, tr. see Denikin, Anton I.
Patout, Alex. Patout's Cajun Home Cooking. 1986. 27.50 (0-394-54725-X) Random.
Patra, Amit, jt. auth. see Rao, Ganti P.
Patra, Hari Pada & Nath, Sankar Kumar. Schlumberger Geoelectric Sounding in Groundwater: Principles, Interpretation & Application. (Illus.). 160p. (C). 1999. text 45.00 (90-5410-789-8) A A Balkema.
Patraka, Vivian, ed. & intro. see Schenkar, Joan M.
Patraka, Vivian M. Spectacular Suffering: Theatre, Fascism, & the Holocaust. LC 98-43476. (Unnatural Acts Ser.). 168p. 1999. pap. 14.95 (0-253-21292-8) Ind U Pr.
***Patraka, Vivian M.** Spectacular Suffering: Theatre, Fascism, & the Holocaust. LC 98-43476. (Unnatural Acts Ser.). 168p. 1999. text 35.00 (0-253-33532-9) Ind U Pr.
Patraker, Deborah M. & Bernardin, Tom. What Is a Farmers' Market? large type ed. Fastrup, Christian et al, eds. (Illus.). 40p. (Orig.). (J). (ps-6). 1997. pap. 4.75 (0-9658431-0-6) D Patraker.
***Patraker, Joel & Schwartz, Joan.** The Greenmarket Cookbook: Recipes, Tips & Lore from the World Famous Urban Farmer's Market. LC 99-53639. (Illus.). 256p. 2000. 29.95 (0-670-88134-1, Viking) Viking Penguin.
***Patras, Ronald.** Respect Selling: A Quick Guide to Exponential Sales in 45 Days of Less. 104p. 1999. pap. 9.95 (1-890676-45-4) Beavers Pond.
Patrascu, Anghel. Construction Cost Engineering Handbook. (Cost Engineering Ser.: Vol. 12). (Illus.). 520p. 1988. text 199.00 (0-8247-7827-8) Dekker.
Patray, Stuart. The Heroin Highway. Knox, Dahk & Pearson, Keith, eds. LC 97-228605. (Illus.). 360p. (Orig.). 1997. pap. 14.95 (1-881116-84-0, Abenteuer Bks) Black Forest Pr.
Patri, Angelo. Pinocchio in Africa: Cherubini, 1911. Orig. Title: Cherubini. (Illus.). 150p. (J). 1995. pap. 25.00 (0-87556-781-9) Saifer.
Patri, Umesh. Hindu Scriptures & American Transcendentalists. (C). 1987. 21.00 (81-7076-005-4, Pub. by Intellect Pub Hse) S Asia.
***Patriarca, Gianna.** Ciao, Baby. (Essential Poets Ser.: Vol. 97). 96p. 1999. pap. 10.00 (1-55071-096-6, Pub. by Guernica Editions) Paul & Co Pubs.
Patriarca, Gianna. Daughters for Sale. LC 96-78721. 96p. 1997. pap. 10.00 (1-55071-045-1) Guernica Editions.
— Italian Women & Other Tragedies. LC 93-73686. 77p. 1995. pap. 8.00 (1-55071-001-X) Guernica Editions.
Patriarca, Linda. Developing Decimal Concepts: Building Bridges Between Whole Numbers & Decimals. LC 98-162562. 224p. 1997. pap. text 19.95 (0-86651-958-0) Seymour Pubns.
Patriarca, Silvana. Numbers & Nationhood: Writing Statistics in Nineteenth-Century Italy. LC 95-4328. (Studies in Italian History & Culture). 292p. (C). 1996. text 59.95 (0-521-46296-7) Cambridge U Pr.
Patrias, Carmela. Patriots & Proletarians: Politicizing Hungarian Immigrants in Interwar Canada. (McGraw & Arnold's Atlas of Muscle & Musculocutaneous Flaps Ser.). (Illus.). 336p. 1994. 60.00 (0-7735-1174-1, Pub. by McG-Queens Univ Pr) CUP Services.
Patrias, Karen. Thalidomide: Potential Benefits & Risks, CBM 97-4, January 1963 Through July 1997. 78p. 1997. pap. 8.50 (0-16-061586-0) USGPO.
— Trimethylaminuria (Fish-Malodor Syndrome) & the Flavin Monooxygenases, CBM 99-2, January 1966 Through December 1998. 28p. 1999. pap. 3.00 (0-16-050107-5) USGPO.
Patric, Beth S. The Splintered Eye. LC 87-12192. 1987. 15.95 (0-88282-031-1) New Horizon NJ.
Patric, Darlene, ed. see Parke, Elaine.
Patric, John. Yankee Hobo in the Orient: Why Japan Was Strong. 1979. 250.00 (0-685-96533-3) Revisionist Pr.
Patrica Galaz. Padres de Tiempo Completo. 1997. pap. text 7.98 (970-643-079-2) Selector.
Patricca, Nicholas A. The Fifth Sun - Full. 1986. pap. 5.50 (0-87129-207-6, F38) Dramatic Pub.
— The Fifth Sun - One Act. 1993. pap. 3.50 (0-87129-217-3, F53) Dramatic Pub.
— The Idea of Chaos: Sex, Death, Life & Order in Key West. Sturm, Robert, ed. (Illus.). 96p. (Orig.). 1994. pap. 12.00 (0-9640343-5-2) Traditional Arts.
— Oh, Holy Allen Ginsberg. 1995. 5.60 (0-87129-510-5, O52) Dramatic Pub.
— An Uncertain Hour. 1995. 5.60 (0-87129-534-2, U17) Dramatic Pub.
— Where Shadows Fall. Sturm, Robert, ed. 50p. (Orig.). 1994. pap. 12.00 (0-9640343-9-5) Traditional Arts.
Patricca, Nicholas A. & Ronstadt, Karen. El Quinto Sol. (SPA.). 94p. (YA). (gr. 10 up). 1996. pap. 5.50 (0-87129-596-2, E33) Dramatic Pub.
Patricelli, Dick. Nature's Pantry Cookbook. 131p. 1990. spiral bd. 19.95 (0-9629224-0-4) Natures Pantry.
Patricelli, Leslie & Gruening, Michelle. Espresso Served Here: The Official Espresso Humor Book. 60p. 1993. pap. 6.95 (0-9639085-0-2) Good Dog Pr.
Patrich, Joseph. The Formation of Nabatean Art: Prohibition of a Graven Image among the Nabateans. LC 90-1846. (Illus.). 231p. 1990. 72.00 (90-04-09285-4) Brill Academic Pubs.
— Sabas, Leader of Palestinian Monasticism: A Comparative Study in Eastern Monasticism, Fourth to Seventh Centuries. LC 93-49099. (Dumbarton Oaks Studies: No. 32). 1995. 50.00 (0-88402-221-8) Dumbarton Oaks.
Patricia. Jesus I: The Man. Morningland Publications, Inc. Staff, ed. (Series of Three Books Called Jesus). (Illus.). 439p. 1980. pap. 10.00 (0-935146-15-6) Morningland.
— Jesus II: The Mission. Morningland Publications, Inc. Staff, ed. (Series of Three Books Called Jesus). (Illus.). 461p. 1980. pap. 10.00 (0-935146-17-2) Morningland.
— Jesus III: The Return. Morningland Publications, Inc. Staff, ed. (Illus.). 470p. (Orig.). 1980. pap. 10.00 (0-935146-18-0) Morningland.
— Morningland Astrology, Bk. 3. Morningland Publications, Inc. Staff, ed. (Astrology Ser.). (Illus.). 301p. (Orig.). 1980. pap. 7.95 (0-935146-07-5) Morningland.
— Osiris & Isis. (Illus.). 267p. (Orig.). 1980. pap. 7.95 (0-935146-19-9) Morningland.
— Thinis. (Illus.). 330p. (Orig.). 1980. spiral bd. 7.95 (0-935146-12-1) Morningland.
— The Way Out of Vietnam. 166p. (Orig.). 1980. pap. 3.00 (0-935146-21-0) Morningland.
Patricia & Gyan, Gopi. Oneness, Vol. II. (Orig.). 1980. spiral bd. 7.95 (0-935146-24-5) Morningland.
Patricia, De Man, jt. auth. see Van Straten, Roelof.
***Patricia Seybold Group Staff.** Application Integration & Middleware Collection. (Illus.). 420p. 1998. pap. write for info. (1-892815-30-3) Patricia Seybold.
Patricia Seybold Group Staff. Java Collection. 1998. pap. write for info. (1-892815-28-1) Patricia Seybold.
— Patricia Seybold Group's Customers.com Collection. (Illus.). 213p. 1998. pap. 4695.00 (1-892815-00-1) Patricia Seybold.
Patricia, Sri & Gyan, Gopi. Oneness, Vol. I. (Orig.). 1979. pap. 3.95 (0-935146-11-3) Morningland.
Patricios, Nicholas N. Building Marvelous Miami. (Illus.). 376p. 1994. 49.95 (0-8130-1299-6) U Press Fla.
Patricios, Nicholas N., ed. International Handbook on Land Use Planning. LC 84-29018. (Illus.). 699p. 1986. lib. bdg. 175.00 (0-313-23950-9, PHL/, Greenwood Pr) Greenwood.
Patrick. Confession of St. Patrick. 1984. pap. 2.95 (0-89981-014-4) Eastern Orthodox.
— Industrial Process Control Systems. (Mechanical Technology Ser.). 1995. pap., teacher ed. 15.00 (0-8273-6387-7) Delmar.
— Kingdom of the Flies. 19.95 (0-8488-1536-X) Amereon Ltd.
— Treatise on Adhesion & Adhesives, Vol. 5. (Illus.). 416p. 1981. text 195.00 (0-8247-1399-0) Dekker.
Patrick & Fardo, Stephen W. Electricity & Electronics. 2nd ed. 1990. pap. text, lab manual ed. 27.80 (0-13-247891-9) P-H.
Patrick & Fiacc. Writings of St. Patrick, with the Metrical Life of St. Patrick. 1984. pap. 2.95 (0-89981-109-4) Eastern Orthodox.
Patrick, Roger & Water Environment Research Foundation Staff. Benchmarking Wastewater Operations: Collection, Treatment & Biosolids Management. LC 97-61979. 1997. 75.00 (1-57278-121-1) Water Environ.
Patrick, Alison. The Men of the First French Republic: Political Alignments in the National Convention of 1792. LC 72-4018. 425p. reprint ed. pap. 131.80 (0-8357-4329-2, 203712900007) Bks Demand.
Patrick, Ann. Betting on Love. large type ed. (Black Satin Romance Ser.). 288p. 1997. 27.99 (1-86110-037-X) Ulverscroft.
— Let's Make Piano Music with Marvin, Bk. 1. 40p. (J). (gr. k-7). 1985. pap. text 6.95 (0-931759-06-4) Centerstream Pub.
— Let's Make Piano Music with Marvin, Bk. 2. (Illus.). 48p. (J). (gr. k-7). 1986. pap. text 6.95 (0-931759-13-7) Centerstream Pub.
— Let's Make Piano Music with Marvin, Bk. 3. 40p. (J). (gr. k-7). 1985. pap. text 6.95 (0-931759-05-6) Centerstream Pub.
Patrick, Anne E. Liberating Conscience: Feminist Explorations in Catholic Moral Theology. 176p. 1996. 24.95 (0-8264-0891-5) Continuum.
— Liberating Conscience: Feminist Explorations in Catholic Moral Theology. 252p. 1997. pap. 16.95 (0-8264-1051-0) Continuum.
Patrick, Arthur N. Christianity & Culture in Colonial Australia. 324p. 1998. 74.95 (1-57309-225-8); pap. 54.95 (1-57309-224-X) Intl Scholars.
Patrick, B. Allen. SpearFishing & Underwater Hunting Handbook: Beginner Through Advanced. LC 96-79542. (Illus.). 128p. (Orig.). 1996. pap. 17.95 (1-890079-11-1) Active Advent.
Patrick, Bert, ed. see Galindo, Sergio.
Patrick, Beverly H. Uncivil Wars: Men, Women, & Office Etiquette in the 90's. LC 94-239969. 144p. 1994. boxed set 24.95 (0-8403-9261-3) Kendall-Hunt.
Patrick, Brian, jt. auth. see Peat, Neville.
Patrick, Carmen. Making Liqueurs at Home. 74p. (Orig.). 1989. pap 9.95 (0-919574-76-9) Gordon Soules Bk.
Patrick, Charles W., Jr., et al. Frontiers in Tissue Engineering. LC 97-50321. 1997. write for info. (0-08-042689-1, Pergamon Pr) Elsevier.
Patrick, Christian C. Clinical Management of Infections in Immunocompromised Infants & Children. 608p. text 120.00 (0-7817-1718-3) Lppncott W & W.
— Infections in Immunocompromised Infants & Children. (Illus.). 975p. 1992. text 195.00 (0-443-08857-8) Church.
Patrick, Colleen. Mind over Media: Everybody's Ultimate Authority on Media Access from an Insider's Point of View. 184p. (Orig.). 1988. pap. 13.00 (0-935529-04-7) Comprehen Health Educ.
— The One Hundred Percent Solution: Solve Every Problem, Positively! 1992. pap. 11.95 (0-9634281-0-1) Meadow Brook.
***Patrick County Historical Society Staff.** History of Patrick County, Virginia. LC 99-75809. (Illus.). 592p. 1999. 35.00 (0-9648393-9-3) Miona Pubns.
Patrick, Cynthia L., jt. auth. see Calfee, Robert C.
Patrick, Dale. The Rendering of God in the Old Testament. LC 80-2389. (Overtures to Biblical Theology Ser.: No. 10). 174p. (Orig.). reprint ed. pap. 54.00 (0-608-18039-4, 202911000058) Bks Demand.
— The Rhetoric of Revelation in the Hebrew Bible. LC 99-36969. (Overtures to Biblical Theology Ser.). 1999. pap. 20.00 (0-8006-3177-3, Fortress Pr) Augsburg Fortress.
Patrick, Dale & Fardo, Stephen. Understanding DC Circuits. LC 99-16983. 255p. 1998. pap. text 39.95 (0-7506-7110-6, Newnes) Buttrwrth-Heinemann.
Patrick, Dale & Scult, Allen. Rhetoric & Biblical Interpretation. (JSOT Supplement Ser.: Vol. 82). 171p. 1990. 52.50 (1-85075-222-2, Pub. by Sheffield Acad) CUP Services.
Patrick, Dale, jt. auth. see Fardo, Stephen.
Patrick, Dale R. Industrial Process Control Systems. LC 96-22104. (Mechanical Technology Ser.). 1997. pap. 70.95 (0-8273-6386-9) Delmar.
— Introduction to Fluid Power. (Mechanical Technology Ser.). 1996. teacher ed. 15.00 (0-8273-6446-6); text 48.95 (0-8273-6445-8) Delmar.
Patrick, Dale R. & Fardo, Stehen W. Rotating Electrical Machines & Power Systems. 2nd ed. 411p. (C). 1996. 79.00 (0-13-268665-1) P-H.
Patrick, Dale R. & Fardo, Stephen W. Electrical Distribution Systems. LC 98-36065. (Illus.). 1998. 79.00 (0-88173-252-4, 0418) Fairmont Pr.
***Patrick, Dale R. & Fardo, Stephen W.** Electrical Motor Control Systems: Fundamentals & Applications Electronic & Digital Controls. LC 99-42169. 2000. 49.28 (1-56637-701-3) Goodheart.
Patrick, Dale R. & Fardo, Stephen W. Industrial Electrical Experimentation. 2nd ed. (Illus.). 271p. (C). 1983. reprint ed. pap. 14.95 (0-89917-385-3) Tichenor Pub.
***Patrick, Dale R. & Fardo, Stephen W.** Industrial Electronics: Devices & Systems. 2nd ed. LC 00-37543. (Illus.). 2000. pap. write for info. (0-88173-320-2) Fairmont Pr.
Patrick, Dale R. & Fardo, Stephen W. Rotating Electrical Machines & Power Systems. 2nd ed. LC 96-9543. 398p. 1996. 79.00 (0-88173-239-7) Fairmont Pr.
Patrick, Dale R. & Fardo, Stephen W. Understanding Electricity & Electronics. 550p. 1989. pap. text 109.00 (0-13-943242-6) P-H.
Patrick, Dale R. & Patrick, Steven R. Pneumatic Instrumentation. 3rd ed. LC 92-31773. 434p. 1993. mass mkt. 42.50 (0-8273-5482-7) Delmar.
Patrick, Dale R., et al. Electricity & Electronics: A Survey. 4th ed. LC 98-5479. 972p. (C). 1998. 106.00 (0-13-779992-6) P-H.
Patrick, Dale R., jt. auth. see Fardo, Stephen W.
***Patrick, Dan.** Outtakes. LC 99-57923. (Illus.). 160p. 2000. pap. 12.95 (0-7868-8539-4, Pub. by Hyperion) Time Warner.
Patrick, Dan, jt. auth. see Olbermann, Keith.
Patrick, Dave. California's Nude Beaches: Plus Hawaii, Oregon & Washington. 4th ed. 144p. 1994. pap. 15.95 (0-9614880-3-4) Bold Type.
— Radio Control Aerobatics for Everyone. Atwood, Tom, ed. (Illus.). 74p. (Orig.). 1994. pap. 12.95 (0-911295-31-3) Air Age.
Patrick, David R. Facility Manager's Guide to Clean Air Compliance. LC 94-29008. 293p. 1995. 75.00 (0-87179-857-3) BNA Books.
Patrick, David R., ed. Toxic Air Pollution Handbook. LC 93-21545. (Environmental Engineering Ser.). 588p. 1993. text 119.95 (0-442-00903-8, VNR) Wiley.
Patrick, David R., ed. Toxic Air Pollution Handbook. (Environmental Engineering Ser.). 588p. 1993. 140.00 (0-471-28449-1, VNR) Wiley.
Patrick, Denise. Look Inside a Ship. (Poke & Look Learning Ser.). (Illus.). 16p. (J). (ps-3). 1989. spiral bd., bds. 11.95 (0-448-19352-3, G & D) Peng Put Young Read.
Patrick, Denise L. The Adventures of Midnight Son. LC 97-14406. (J). (gr. 4-8). 1995. 15.95 (0-8050-4714-X) H Holt & Co.
— Case of the Missing Cookies. (Gullah Gullah Island Ser.). 24p. (ps-1). 1996. 3.25 (0-689-80398-2) S&S Bks Yung.
Patrick, Denise L. Red Dancing Shoes. LC 91-32666. (Illus.). 32p. (J). (ps up). 1993. 15.89 (0-688-10393-6, Wm Morrow) Morrow Avon.
Patrick, Denise L. Red Dancing Shoes. (Illus.). 32p. (J). (ps-3). 1998. mass mkt. 4.95 (0-688-15850-1, Wm Morrow) Morrow Avon.
— Red Dancing Shoes. 1998. 10.15 (0-606-13023-3, Pub. by Turtleback) Demco.
— Shaina's Garden. 3rd ed. (Gullah Gullah Island Ser.: 3). 24p. (ps-1). 1996. 3.25 (0-689-80397-4) S&S Bks Yung.
Patrick, Denise Lewis. The Car Washing Street. LC 92-9229. (Illus.). 32p. (J). (ps-3). 1993. lib. bdg. 13.93 (0-688-11453-9, Wm Morrow) Morrow Avon.
Patrick di Camillo, Kevin T. Of the Hovrs: A Poem. LC 96-32116. 64p. 1996. pap. 14.95 (0-7734-2679-5, Mellen Poetry Pr) E Mellen.
Patrick, Diane. The Executive Branch. LC 94-963. (First Bks.). 64p. (J). (gr. 4-6). 1994. lib. bdg. 22.00 (0-531-20179-1) Watts.
— Family Celebrations. LC 93-18456. (Family Ties Ser.). (Illus.). 64p. (J). (ps-4). 1993. lib. bdg. 14.95 (1-881889-04-1) Silver Moon.
— Martin Luther King, Jr. LC 89-24800. (First Bks.). (Illus.). 64p. (J). 1990. lib. bdg. 21.00 (0-531-10892-9) Watts.
— The New York Public Library Amazing African American History: A Book of Answers for Kids. LC 97-16938. (NYPL Answer Books for Kids). 176p. (J). 1997. pap. 12.95 (0-471-19217-1) Wiley.
— Terry McM illan: An Unauthorized Biography. 2nd ed. LC 99-23849. 231p. 1999. text 23.95 (0-312-20032-3) St Martin.
Patrick, Donald L. & Erickson, Pennifer. Health Status & Health Policy: Quality of Life in Health Care Evaluation & Resource Allocation. (Illus.). 504p. 1993. text 69.50 (0-19-505027-4) OUP.
Patrick, E. A. Minority Small Business & Capital Ownership Development Program, Vols. 1-2. 2 Bks. (1056p. 1990. ring bd. 38.00 (0-16-027829-5) USGPO.
Patrick, E. A. & Costello, J. P. Unsupervised Estimation & Processing of Unknown Signals. LC 71-136727. 207p. 1970. 19.00 (0-403-04528-2) Scholarly.
Patrick, Edward & Fattu, James. Artificial Intelligence with Statistical Pattern Recognition. 363p. 1986. text 59.95 (0-13-049131-4, Busn) P-H.
Patrick, Edward A. Decision Analysis in Medicine: Methods & Applications. 352p. 1979. 197.00 (0-8493-5255-X, R723, CRC Reprint) Franklin.
Patrick, Elizabeth N., intro. An Interview with William J. Moore. (Illus.). 107p. 1985. lib. bdg. 34.50 (1-56475-296-8); fiche. write for info. (1-56475-297-6) U NV Oral Hist.

P

An Asterisk (*) at the beginning of an entry indicates that the title is appearing for the first time.

Patrick, Ellen. Aunt Sally's Cornpone Remedies & Claptrap Cures: 159 Tonics for What Ails You! 96p. 1995. pap. 2.95 (*1-881548-29-5*) Crane Hill AL.

— A Bunny's Tale. LC 96-144889. (Easter Ornament Bks.). (Illus.). 8p. (J). (ps-3). 1996. 2.95 (*0-689-80783-X*) S&S Childrens.

— Help! I'm Southern & I Can't Stop Eating. LC 94-33287. 96p. 1994. pap. 2.95 (*1-881548-13-9*) Crane Hill AL.

— Magic Easter Egg. LC 96-145410. (Easter Ornament Bks.). (Illus.). 8p. (J). (ps-3). 1996. 2.95 (*0-689-80784-8*) S&S Childrens.

— Three Baby Chicks. LC 96-144895. (Easter Ornament Bks.). (Illus.). 8p. (J). (ps-3). 1996. 2.95 (*0-689-80785-6*) S&S Childrens.

— Very Little Duck. LC 96-144891. (Easter Ornament Bks.). (Illus.). 8p. (J). (ps-3). 1996. 2.95 (*0-689-80786-4*) S&S Childrens.

Patrick, Ellen & Heine, John. Southern Fried: True Views of the South. LC 98-40831. (Illus.). 96p. 1998. pap. 5.95 (*1-57587-095-9*) Crane Hill AL.

Patrick, Floyd A. Personnel - Human Resource Management. 512p. (C). 1994. per. 52.95 (*0-8403-9435-7*) Kendall-Hunt.

***Patrick, G.** Instant Notes in Organic Chemistry. (Instant Notes Series). 352p. 2000. pap. text (*0-387-91603-2*) Spr-Verlag.

Patrick, Gay D. Building the Reference Collection: A How-to-Do-It Manual for School & Public Librarians. (How-to-Do-It Ser.). 192p. 1992. 38.50 (*1-55570-105-1*) Neal-Schuman.

Patrick, George. George Thomas White Patrick. (American Autobiography Ser.). 180p. 1995. reprint ed. lib. bdg. 69.00 (*0-7812-8607-7*) Rprt Serv.

Patrick, George Z. Popular Poetry in Soviet Russia. LC 74-174378. 1972. reprint ed. 20.95 (*0-405-08841-8*, Pub. by Blom Pubns) Ayer.

— Roots of the Russian Language. (RUS & ENG., Illus.). 248p. 1994. pap. 16.95 (*0-8442-4267-5*, 42675, Natl Textbk Co) NTC Contemp Pub Co.

Patrick, Georgie, jt. auth. see Duncan, Cyndi.

Patrick, Gloria. A Bug in a Jug & Other Funny Rhymes. LC 92-246264. 32p. (J). 1993. write for info. (*0-669-30229-5*) HM Trade Div.

Patrick, Graham L. Beginning Organic Chemistry 1, Vol. 1. LC 97-164929. (Workbooks in Chemistry). (Illus.). 184p. 1997. pap. text 25.00 (*0-19-855935-6*) OUP.

— Beginning Organic Chemistry 2, Vol. 2. LC 97-164929. (Workbooks in Chemistry Ser.). (Illus.). 320p. 1997. pap. text 32.00 (*0-19-855936-4*) OUP.

— F. J. A. Hort: Eminent Victorian. 127p. 1988. 36.50 (*1-85075-098-X*, Pub. by Sheffield Acad); pap. 14.95 (*1-85075-097-1*, Pub. by Sheffield Acad) CUP Services.

Patrick, Graham L. An Introduction to Medicinal Chemistry. (Illus.). 350p. 1995. pap. text 45.00 (*0-19-855871-6*) OUP.

Patrick, Heather, jt. auth. see Patrick, Ross.

Patrick, Hilary, jt. auth. see Blackie, John.

Patrick, Hugh & Rosovsky, Henry, eds. Asia's New Giant: How the Japanese Economy Works. LC 75-42304. 957p. reprint ed. pap. 200.00 (*0-8357-5791-9*, 203000200067) Bks Demand.

Patrick, Hugh T., ed. Pacific Basin Industries in Distress. 560p. 1991. text 67.00 (*0-231-07570-7*) Col U Pr.

Patrick, Hugh T. & Aoki, M., eds. The Japanese Main Bank System: Its Relevance for Developing & Transforming Economies. (Illus.). 684p. 1995. text 95.00 (*0-19-828899-9*) OUP.

Patrick, Hugh T. & Meissner, Larry, eds. Japan's High Technology Industries & Industrial Policy. LC 85-40973. 296p. (C). 1986. 40.00 (*0-295-96342-5*) U of Wash Pr.

Patrick, Hugh T. & Park, Yung C., eds. The Financial Development of Japan, Korea & Taiwan: Growth, Repression & Liberalization. LC 93-31448. (Illus.). 400p. 1994. text 70.00 (*0-19-508766-6*) OUP.

Patrick, Hugh T., jt. auth. see Hoshi, Takeo.

Patrick, Isabel. Dark Stranger. 224p. 1999. mass mkt. 4.99 (*0-8217-6155-2*) Kensgtn Pub Corp.

Patrick, J. Mad about the Boys. 1997. pap. 14.95 (*1-877978-78-7*, STARbks Pr) FL Lit Foundation.

Patrick, J., jt. auth. see Heinemann, S.

Patrick, J., jt. ed. see Walker, A.

Patrick, J. Max & Sundell, Roger H., eds. Milton & the Art of Sacred Song: Essays. LC 78-65014. 168p. 1979. reprint ed. pap. 52.10 (*0-7837-9792-3*, 206052100005) Bks Demand.

Patrick, J. Max, ed. see Milton, John.

Patrick, J. Max, ed. see Robert Herrick Memorial Conference, University of.

Patrick, James. Architecture in Tennessee, 1768-1897. LC 80-21089. 1990. pap. 19.50 (*0-87049-631-X*) U of Tenn Pr.

— The Magdalen Metaphysicals: Idealism & Orthodoxy at Oxford, 1901-1945. LC 84-20751. xl, 192p. 1985. 18.95 (*0-86554-145-0*, MUP/H135) Mercer Univ Pr.

Patrick, James, ed. see Lewis, C. S.

Patrick, James B., ed. see Bradley, David.

Patrick, James B., ed. see Dunwell, Steve.

Patrick, James B., ed. see Gannon, Thomas.

Patrick, James B., ed. see Llewellyn, Robert.

Patrick, James B., ed. see McCord, David.

Patrick, James B., ed. see Smith, Clyde H.

Patrick, Jane, ed. A Handwoven Treasury. LC 89-7567. (Illus.). 144p. (Orig.). 1989. pap. 17.95 (*0-934026-46-7*) Interweave.

***Patrick, Jean L. S.** The Girl Who Struck Out Babe Ruth. (On My Own History Ser.). (Illus.). 56p. (gr. 1-3). 2000. pap. 5.95 (*1-57505-455-8*, First Ave Edns) Lerner Pub.

— The Girl Who Struck Out Babe Ruth. LC 99-33322. (On My Own History Ser.). (Illus.). 56p. (J). (gr. 1-3). 2000. lib. bdg. 21.27 (*1-57505-397-7*, Carolrhoda) Lerner Pub.

Patrick, Jerry. How to Develop Successful New Products. LC 96-39370. (Illus.). 172p. 1997. 47.95 (*0-8442-3662-4*, NTC Business Bks) NTC Contemp Pub Co.

Patrick, John. Advanced Craps. (So You Wanna Be a Gambler Ser.). 1994. pap. 29.95 (*0-930911-08-3*) J Patrick.

— Advanced Roulette. (So You Wanna Be a Gambler Ser.). 1997. pap. 19.95 (*0-930911-05-9*) J Patrick.

— Anybody Out There? 1972. pap. 5.25 (*0-8222-0058-9*) Dramatists Play.

— Baccarat. (So You Wanna Be a Gambler Ser.). (Illus.). 246p. 1985. pap. 14.95 (*0-930911-03-2*) J Patrick.

— A Bad Year for Tomatoes. 1975. pap. 5.25 (*0-8222-0089-9*) Dramatists Play.

— A Barrel Full of Pennies. 1970. pap. 5.25 (*0-8222-0095-3*) Dramatists Play.

— Blackjack. (So You Wanna Be a Gambler Ser.). (Illus.). 188p. (Orig.). 1983. pap. 14.95 (*0-930911-01-6*) J Patrick.

— Card Counting. (So You Wanna Be a Gambler Ser.). 1989. pap. 19.95 (*0-930911-04-0*) J Patrick.

— Cheating Cheaters. 1985. pap. 5.25 (*0-8222-0199-2*) Dramatists Play.

— Craps. (So You Wanna Be a Gambler Ser.). (Illus.). 371p. (Orig.). 1984. pap. 19.95 (*0-930911-00-8*) J Patrick.

— Craps for the Clueless: A Beginner's Guide to Playing & Winning. LC 98-22808. (Illus.). 192p. 1998. pap. text 12.00 (*0-8184-0599-6*, L Stuart) Carol Pub Group.

— The Curious Savage. 1950. pap. 5.25 (*0-8222-0260-3*) Dramatists Play.

— The Dancing Mice. 1972. pap. 5.25 (*0-8222-0267-0*) Dramatists Play.

— Db2 Fundamentals. (C). 2000. text 45.00 (*0-13-531187-X*) P-H.

— Divorce-Anyone? 1976. pap. 5.25 (*0-8222-0316-2*) Dramatists Play.

— The Doctor Will See You Now: Four One Act Plays. 1991. pap. 5.25 (*0-8222-0317-0*) Dramatists Play.

— The Enigma. 1974. pap. 5.25 (*0-8222-0361-8*) Dramatists Play.

— Everybody Loves Opal. 1962. pap. 5.25 (*0-8222-0367-7*) Dramatists Play.

— Everybody's Girl. 1968. pap. 5.25 (*0-8222-0368-5*) Dramatists Play.

***Patrick, John.** Fresh N' Frisky. (Illus.). (J). 2000. pap. 14.95 (*1-891855-05-0*, STARbks Pr) FL Lit Foundation.

Patrick, John. The Gay Deceiver. 1988. pap. 5.25 (*0-8222-0433-9*) Dramatists Play.

— The Girls of the Garden Club. 1979. pap. 5.25 (*0-8222-0448-7*) Dramatists Play.

— The Hasty Heart. 1945. pap. 5.25 (*0-8222-0501-7*) Dramatists Play.

***Patrick, John.** Heatwave. 2000. pap. 14.95 (*1-891855-08-5*) FL Lit Foundation.

Patrick, John. It's Been Wonderful. 1976. pap. 5.25 (*0-8222-0580-7*) Dramatists Play.

— John Patrick on Slots: More Than Twenty Ways to Beat the Machine. LC 93-45562. 1994. 12.95 (*0-8184-0574-0*, L Stuart) Carol Pub Group.

— John Patrick's Advanced Blackjack: The Science of Card Counting. 288p. 1995. pap. 19.95 (*0-8184-0582-1*, Citadel Pr) Carol Pub Group.

— John Patricks Advanced Craps: The Sophisticated Players Guide to Winning. 512p. 1995. pap. 18.95 (*0-8184-0577-5*, L Stuart) Carol Pub Group.

— John Patrick's Baccarat. LC 97-45546. 256p. 1997. pap. 18.95 (*0-8184-0595-3*) Carol Pub Group.

— John Patrick's Blackjack. 1991. pap. 12.95 (*0-8184-0555-4*, L Stuart) Carol Pub Group.

— John Patrick's Casino Poker: Professional Gambler's Guide to Winning. 256p. 1996. pap. text 16.95 (*0-8184-0592-9*, L Stuart) Carol Pub Group.

— John Patrick's Craps. 1991. pap. 14.95 (*0-8184-0554-6*, L Stuart) Carol Pub Group.

— John Patrick's Money Management & Discipline: How to Maximize Your Gambling Profits. LC 99-32832. 1999. pap. text 12.95 (*0-8184-0607-0*, L Stuart) Carol Pub Group.

— John Patrick's Roulette: A Pro's Guide to Managing Your Money & Beating the Wheel. 404p. 1996. pap. 19.95 (*0-8184-0587-2*, L Stuart) Carol Pub Group.

— John Patrick's Sports Betting: Proven Winning Systems for Football, Basketball & Baseball. LC 96-47769. 288p. 1996. pap. text 16.95 (*0-8184-0597-X*, L Stuart) Carol Pub Group.

— Love Is a Time of Day. 1970. pap. 5.25 (*0-8222-0692-7*) Dramatists Play.

— Macbeth Did It. 1972. pap. 5.25 (*0-8222-0711-7*) Dramatists Play.

— The Magenta Moth. 1983. pap. 5.25 (*0-8222-0716-8*) Dramatists Play.

— Opal Is a Diamond. 1992. pap. 5.25 (*0-8222-0857-1*) Dramatists Play.

— Opal's Baby. 1974. pap. 5.25 (*0-8222-0858-X*) Dramatists Play.

— Opal's Husband. 1975. pap. 5.25 (*0-8222-0859-8*) Dramatists Play.

— Opal's Million Dollar Duck. 1980. pap. 5.25 (*0-8222-0860-1*) Dramatists Play.

***Patrick, John.** Pleasures of the Flesh. 1999. pap. 14.95 (*1-891855-03-4*) FL Lit Foundation.

Patrick, John. The Reluctant Rogue: or Mother's Day. 1984. pap. 5.25 (*0-8222-0942-X*) Dramatists Play.

— Roulette-Slots. (So You Wanna Be a Gambler Ser.). (Illus.). 234p. (Orig.). 1983. pap. 14.95 (*0-930911-02-4*) J Patrick.

— The Savage Dilemma. 1972. pap. 5.25 (*0-8222-0989-6*) Dramatists Play.

— Scandal Point: Manuscript Edition. 1969. pap. 13.00 (*0-8222-0994-2*) Dramatists Play.

— Sense & Nonsense. 200p. 1990. write for info. (*0-573-64232-X*) French.

— Slots. (So You Wanna Be a Gambler Ser.). 1995. pap. 19.95 (*0-930911-06-7*) J Patrick.

— Sports Handicapping. (So You Wanna Be a Gambler Ser.). 1997. pap. 29.95 (*0-930911-07-5*) J Patrick.

— The Story of Mary Surratt. 1947. pap. 5.25 (*0-8222-1086-X*) Dramatists Play.

— Suicide Anyone? 1976. pap. 5.25 (*0-8222-1096-7*) Dramatists Play.

***Patrick, John.** Sweet Temptations. 1999. pap. 14.95 (*1-891855-02-6*) FL Lit Foundation.

Patrick, John. The Willow & I: Manuscript Edition. 1943. pap. 13.00 (*0-8222-1258-7*) Dramatists Play.

Patrick, John, ed. Barely Legal. 512p. (Orig.). 1995. pap. text 14.95 (*1-877978-71-X*, STARbks Pr) FL Lit Foundation.

***Patrick, John, ed.** Boys on the Prowl. (Illus.). 500p. 2000. pap. 14.95 (*1-891855-06-9*, STARbks Pr) FL Lit Foundation.

Patrick, John, ed. Intimate Strangers. 1998. pap. 14.95 (*1-877978-94-9*, FLF Pr) FL Lit Foundation.

***Patrick, John, ed.** Juniors 2. LC 98-96881. 550p. 1999. pap. 14.95 (*1-891855-01-8*, STARbks Pr) FL Lit Foundation.

Patrick, John, ed. Naughty by Nature. LC 96-70306. 564p. 1998. pap. 14.95 (*1-877978-91-4*) FL Lit Foundation.

— Smooth 'n' Sassy. LC 96-70308. 528p. 1998. pap. 14.95 (*1-877978-90-6*, STARbks Pr) FL Lit Foundation.

— Training Research & Practice. (Illus.). 585p. 1992. text 84.95 (*0-12-546660-9*) Acad Pr.

***Patrick, John.** The Best of the Superstars, 2000 Vol. 11: The Year in Sex. 576p. 1999. pap. 11.95 (*1-891855-14-X*, STARbks Pr) FL Lit Foundation.

Patrick, John. Dreamboys. 528p. 1999. pap. 14.95 (*1-877978-93-0*, STARbks Pr) FL Lit Foundation.

***Patrick, John.** Play Hard, Score Big. 552p. 1999. pap. 14.95 (*1-877978-97-3*, STARbks Pr) FL Lit Foundation.

Patrick, John J. Lessons on the Northwest Ordinance of 1787. (Illus.). 84p. (YA). (gr. 9-12). 1987. spiral bd. 8.50 (*0-941339-02-5*) Ind U SSDC.

— Lessons on the Northwest Ordinance of 1787: Learning Materials for Secondary School Courses in American History, Government, & Civics. 1987. pap. 6.95 (*1-885323-52-2*) IN Hist Bureau.

***Patrick, John J.** SQL Fundamentals. (Illus.). 544p. 1999. pap. text 44.99 (*0-13-096016-0*) P-H.

Patrick, John J. The Young Oxford Companion to the Supreme Court of the United States. LC 93-6467. (Illus.). 368p. (YA). (gr. 7 up). 1994. text 40.00 (*0-19-507877-2*) OUP.

Patrick, John J., ed. Founding the Republic: A Documentary History. LC 95-7537. 304p. 1995. 49.95 (*0-313-29226-4*, Greenwood Pr) Greenwood.

— Ideas of the Founders on Constitutional Government: Resources for Teachers of History & Government. (Project Ser.: No. 87). (Illus.). 159p. (C). 1991. pap. text 12.00 (*1-878147-02-1*) Am Political.

— James Madison & the Federalist Papers. 188p. 1991. pap. text 15.00 (*0-941339-11-4*) Ind U SSDC.

Patrick, John J. & Keller, Clair W. Lessons on the Federalist Papers. (Illus.). 95p. (gr. 9-12). 1987. pap. text 10.00 (*0-941339-00-9*) Ind U SSDC.

Patrick, John J. & Long, Gerald P. Constitutional Debates on Freedom of Religion: Documentary History. LC 99-21819. (Primary Documents in American History & Contemporary Issues). 360p. 1999. 49.95 (*0-313-30140-9*) Greenwood.

Patrick, John J. & Remy, Richard C. Lessons on the Constitution: Supplements to High School Courses in American History, Government & Civics. 302p. (Orig.). 1985. pap. 13.50 (*0-89994-302-0*) Soc Sci Ed.

Patrick, John J., ed. see Pious, Richard M. & Ritchie, Donald A.

Patrick, John W., ed. Porosity in Carbons Characterisation & Applications. 331p. 1994. text 125.00 (*0-470-23454-7*) Halsted Pr.

Patrick, Judy L., jt. auth. see Dunn-Merritt, Sheila.

Patrick, Ken L., ed. Advances in Bleaching Technology. 180p. 1997. pap. 58.00 (*0-87930-522-3*) Miller Freeman.

Patrick, Ken L., ed. Advances in Paper Recycling: New Technology & Marketing Trends. (Illus.). 200p. 1994. pap. 49.00 (*0-87930-351-4*, 528) Miller Freeman.

— Bleaching Technology: For Chemical & Mechanical Pulps. (Illus.). 174p. 1991. pap. 52.00 (*0-87930-246-1*) Miller Freeman.

— Modern Mechanical Pulping: In the Pulp & Paper Industry. LC 89-80421. (Illus.). 246p. (Orig.). 1989. pap. 45.00 (*0-87930-218-6*) Miller Freeman.

— New Maintenance Strategies: Organizing, Implementing & Managing Effective Mill Programs. (Illus.). 223p. 1992. pap. 49.00 (*0-87930-189-9*) Miller Freeman.

— Paper Coating Trends: In the Worldwide Paper Industry. (Illus.). 172p. 1991. pap. 58.00 (*0-87930-247-X*) Miller Freeman.

— Paper Recycling: Strategies, Economics, & Technology. (Illus.). 202p. (Orig.). 1991. pap. 49.00 (*0-87930-231-3*) Miller Freeman.

Patrick, Kevin Joseph, jt. auth. see Butko, Brian A.

Patrick, Laurie & Hill, Janis. From Kids with Love. (J). (ps-2). 1987. pap. 10.99 (*0-8224-3166-1*) Fearon Teacher Aids.

Patrick, Lawrence M., ed. see Stapp Car Crash Conference Staff.

Patrick, Lerissa, ed. see Crane, Thomas G.

Patrick, Linda L., jt. auth. see Patrick, Randy R.

Patrick, Lucille. Caroline Lockhart: Liberated Lady, 1870-1962. (Illus.). 678p. 1998. pap. 19.95 (*0-941875-10-5*) Wolverine Distrib.

Patrick, Lura L., ed. see Galindo, Sergio.

Patrick, Lynn. Wild Thing. (Temptation Ser.: No. 395). 1992. per. 2.99 (*0-373-25495-4*, 1-25495-2) Harlequin Bks.

Patrick, Lynn, ed. see Savannah Junior Auxiliary Staff.

Patrick, Marjory W. Reflections of Christian Women, Vol. 1. (Illus.). 120p. 1998. pap. 10.00 (*1-889743-06-2*) R Dean Pr.

Patrick, Mark. Tiniest Miracle: Angel of Grace. LC 96-96488. 1997. mass mkt. 5.99 (*0-380-78442-4*, Avon Bks) Morrow Avon.

Patrick, Mark A. Lincoln Motor Cars 1946-1960 Photo Archive: Photographs from the Detroit Public Library's National Automotive History Collection. LC 96-76228. (Photo Archive Ser.). (Illus.). 128p. 1996. pap. 29.95 (*1-882256-58-1*) Iconografix.

Patrick, Mark A., ed. Cadillac 1948-1964 Photo Album: Photographs from the National Automotive History Collection of the Detroit Public Library. LC 97-75278. (Photo Album Ser.). (Illus.). 112p. 1998. pap. 19.95 (*1-882256-83-2*, O-006) Iconografix.

— Lincoln Motor Cars 1920-1942 Photo Archive: Photographs from the Detroit Public Library's National Automotive History Collection. LC 96-76227. (Photo Archive Ser.). (Illus.). 128p. 1996. pap. 29.95 (*1-882256-57-3*) Iconografix.

— Packard Motor Cars 1946-1958 Photo Archive: Photographs from the Detroit Public Library's National Automotive History Collection. LC 95-82099. (Photo Archive Ser.). (Illus.). 128p. 1996. pap. 29.95 (*1-882256-45-X*) Iconografix.

— Packard Motor Cars 1935-1942 Photo Archive: Photographs from the Detroit Public Library's National Automotive History Collection. LC 95-82098. (Photo Archive Ser.). (Illus.). 128p. 1996. pap. 29.95 (*1-882256-44-1*) Iconografix.

Patrick, Matthew, jt. auth. see Davenhill, Rachael.

Patrick, Maxine. The Abducted Heart. 1981. mass mkt. 2.75 (*0-451-11220-2*, 1220, Sig) NAL.

Patrick, Maxine, ed. see Carnevali, Doris L.

Patrick, Michael. Cats of the Masters. LC 96-83987. (Illus.). 64p. 1997. 9.95 (*0-8362-2156-7*) Andrews & McMeel.

***Patrick, Michael.** Cats of the Masters. 64p. 1999. 5.98 (*1-56731-335-3*, MJF Bks) Fine Comms.

— Mutts of the Masters. 64p. 1999. 5.98 (*1-56731-336-1*, MJF Bks) Fine Comms.

Patrick, Michael D. & Trickel, Evelyn G. Orphan Trains to Missouri. LC 97-12244. (Illus.). 144p. (J). 1997. pap. 9.95 (*0-8262-1121-6*) U of Mo Pr.

Patrick, Mike, ed. see Harmon, Dick & Cameron, Steve.

Patrick, Morag. Derrida, Responsibility & Politics. LC 97-61065. (Avebury Series in Philosophy). 192p. 1997. text 64.95 (*1-85972-545-7*, Pub. by Ashgate Pub) Ashgate Pub Co.

Patrick, Myra, tr. see Billac, Pete.

Patrick, Natalie. Boot Scootin' Secret Baby. 1998. per. 3.50 (*0-373-19289-4*, 1-19289-7) Silhouette.

— Une Famille Modele. (Horizon Ser.: Bk. 490). 1999. mass mkt. 3.50 (*0-373-39490-X*, 1-39490-7) Harlequin Bks.

***Patrick, Natalie.** His, Hers... Ours? (Romance Ser.). 2000. mass mkt. 3.50 (*0-373-19467-6*, 1-19467-9) Silhouette.

Patrick, Natalie. The Marriage Chase. (Romance Ser.). 1996. per. 2.99 (*0-373-19130-8*, 1-19130-3) Silhouette.

***Patrick, Natalie.** The Millionaire's Proposition, No. 141. (Romance Ser.). 1999. mass mkt. 3.50 (*0-373-19413-7*) Silhouette.

Patrick, Natalie. Three Kids & a Cowboy. (Romance Ser.: No. 1235). 1997. per. 3.25 (*0-373-19235-5*, 1-19235-0) Silhouette.

— Wedding Bells & Diaper Pins. (Romance Ser.). 1995. per. 2.99 (*0-373-19095-6*, 1-19095-8) Silhouette.

Patrick, Owen. The Homeowner's Insurance Kit: How to Ensure Maximum Coverage: The Insider's Guide to Buying & Maximizing the Benefits of Your Homeowner's Insurance. 127p. 1997. 29.95 (*1-882584-50-3*) HOMEFILE.

Patrick, P. K. Glossary on Solid Waste. (EURO Nonserial Publication Ser.). 92p. 1980. 12.00 (*92-9020-199-1*, 1340003) World Health.

Patrick, Pamela, jt. auth. see Ammon, Richard.

Patrick, Pamela, jt. illus. see Ammon, Richard.

Patrick, Peter L., jt. auth. see Schneider, Edgar W.

Patrick, Priscilla. To Life! Yoga with Priscilla Patrick. LC 82-71187. (Illus.). 76p. (Orig.). 1982. pap. 9.95 (*0-943274-00-1*) SC Ed Comm Inc.

Patrick Publishing Staff, jt. auth. see Smith, Jeffrey H.

Patrick, R. S. Colour Atlas of Liver Pathology. (Oxford Color Atlases of Pathology). (Illus.). 176p. 1983. text 85.00 (*0-19-921033-0*) OUP.

Patrick, Randy R. & Blair, Charesa M. Hiking Indiana No. 1: Shades State Park. (Illus.). 64p. (Orig.). 1997. pap. 8.95 (*0-9659927-0-5*, HI1) Memories Forever.

— Hiking Indiana No. 3: McCormick's Creek State Park. (Illus.). 96p. 1998. pap. 8.95 (*0-9659927-2-1*) Memories Forever.

Patrick, Randy R. & Patrick, Linda L. Hiking Indiana No. 4: Spring Mill State Park. unabridged ed. (Illus.). 96p. 1999. pap. 8.95 (*0-9659927-3-X*) Memories Forever.

Patrick, Randy R., jt. auth. see Blair, Charesa M.

Patrick, Rembert W. Jefferson Davis & His Cabinet. LC 83-45832. reprint ed. 43.50 (*0-404-20197-0*) AMS Pr.

— Opinions of the Confederate Attorneys General, 1861-1865. xxiv, 608p. 1950. lib. bdg. 55.00 (*0-89941-617-9*, 500470) W S Hein.

Patrick, Robert. Mutual Benefit Life. 1979. pap. 5.25 (*0-8222-0795-8*) Dramatists Play.

— My Cup Ranneth Over. 1979. pap. 5.25 (*0-8222-0798-2*) Dramatists Play.

— Temple Slave. 1998. mass mkt. 7.95 (*1-56333-635-9*, Hard Candy) Masquerade.

An Asterisk (*) at the beginning of an entry indicates that the title is appearing for the first time.

Patrick, Robert L. Treatise on Adhesion & Adhesives, Vol. 3. LC 66-11285. 271p. reprint ed. pap. 84.10 (*0-8357-3575-3*, 202680800052) Bks Demand.

Patrick, Robert L. Treatise on Adhesion & Adhesives, Vol. 6. (Illus.). 304p. 1988. text 165.00 (*0-8247-7587-2*) Dekker.

Patrick, Robert L., ed. Treatise on Adhesion & Adhesives: Materials, Vol. 2. LC 66-11285. (Illus.). 568p. reprint ed. pap. 176.10 (*0-8357-3574-5*, 202680800002) Bks Demand.

Patrick, Ross & Patrick, Heather. Exiles Undaunted: The Irish Rebels Kevin & Eva O'Doherty. 1989. pap. 17.95 (*0-7022-2223-2*, Pub. by Univ Queensland Pr) Intl Spec Bk.

Patrick, Ruth. Rivers of the United States, 6 vols. 3910p. 1999. 935.00 (*0-471-11501-0*) Wiley.

— Rivers of the United States: Colorado River Part A, Vol. 5. 336p. 2000. text 175.00 (*0-471-30348-8*) Wiley.

— Rivers of the United States: Pollution & Environmental Management, Vol. 6. 500p. 1997. 140.00 (*0-471-30349-6*) Wiley.

— Rivers of the United States: Rivers of the East & Southeast, 3 vols., Vol. 3. LC 93-27583. 848p. 1996. 175.00 (*0-471-30346-1*) Wiley.

— Rivers of the United States: The Mississippi, Vol. 4, Pt. A: The Mississippi. (Rivers of the United States Ser.). 408p. 1998. 175.00 (*0-471-19741-6*) Wiley.

— Rivers of the United States: The Mississippi, Vol. 4, Pt. B: The Mississippi. (Rivers of the United States Ser.). 488p. 1998. 175.00 (*0-471-19742-4*) Wiley.

— Rivers of the United States The Mississippi River: Mississippi Drainage, Vol. 4. (Rivers of the United States Ser.). 896p. 1998. 350.00 (*0-471-30347-X*) Wiley.

— Rivers of the United States Vol. 1: Estuaries, Vol. 1. 825p. 1994. 175.00 (*0-471-30345-3*) Wiley.

— Rivers of the United States Vol. 2: Chemical & Physical Characteristics, Vol. 2. 237p. 1995. 175.00 (*0-471-10752-2*) Wiley.

Patrick, Ruth. Surface Water Quality: Have the Laws Been Successful? (Illus.). 247p. 1992. text 45.00 (*0-691-08769-5*, Pub. by Princeton U Pr) Cal Prin Full Svc.

Patrick, Ruth & Reimer, Charles W. The Diatoms of the United States (Exclusive of Alaska & Hawaii), Set. LC 65-29113. (Monograph: No. 13). (Illus.). 688p. 1966. lib. bdg. 50.00 (*0-910006-19-9*) Acad Nat Sci Phila.

— The Diatoms of the United States (Exclusive of Alaska & Hawaii), Vol. 1. LC 65-29113. (Monograph: No. 13-1). (Illus.). 688p. 1966. lib. bdg. 30.00 (*0-910006-20-2*) Acad Nat Sci Phila.

— The Diatoms of the United States (Exclusive of Alaska & Hawaii), Vol. 2, Pt. 1. (Monograph: No. 13-2). (Illus.). 213p. 1975. lib. bdg. 20.00 (*0-910006-21-0*) Acad Nat Sci Phila.

Patrick, Ruth, et al. The Catherwood Foundation Peruvian-Amazon Expedition: Limnological & Systematic Studies. (Monograph: No. 14). (Illus.). 495p. (Orig.). 1966. pap. 15.00 (*0-910006-22-9*) Acad Nat Sci Phila.

— Groundwater Contamination in the United States. 2nd ed. LC 87-19143. 538p. 1987. 58.95 (*0-8122-8079-2*); pap. 26.50 (*0-8122-1256-8*) U of Pa Pr.

Patrick, Ruth, jt. ed. see Cairns, John, Jr.

Patrick, Ruth, jt. ed. see Paddock, Todd.

Patrick, Ruth A. Colors of Tomorrow. 60p. 1997. pap. 7.95 (*1-57502-522-1*, PO1561) Morris Pubng.

— A Power So Great. 40p. (Orig.). 1996. pap. 7.95 (*1-57502-276-1*, PO975) Morris Pubng.

Patrick, S. & Larkin, M. J. Immunological & Molecular Aspects of Bacterial Virulence. LC 94-24433. 292p. 1995. pap. 79.95 (*0-471-95251-6*) Wiley.

Patrick, Sally, et al. The Month by Month Treasure Box. LC 86-82599. (Illus.). 80p. (Orig.). (J). (ps-1). 1988. 9.95 (*0-86530-124-7*, IP 130-1) Incentive Pubns.

Patrick, Sean. Patrick's Corner. LC 91-33634. 224p. 1992. 18.95 (*0-88289-878-7*) Pelican.

Patrick, Shirley. European Insurance Accounting & Regulatory Handbook. (DYP Textbook Ser.). 176p. 1991. pap. 180.00 (*1-870255-75-5*) LLP.

Patrick, Simmons L, Jr. ERISA Basics: Complying with the Rules for Fiduciary Responsibility. (Building Blocks Ser.: Vol. 30). (Illus.). 32p. (Orig.). 1996. pap. 24.95 (*1-57963-031-6*, A0230) Am Compensation.

Patrick, Steve. Beginning Computers, Applications & Statistics. 168p. (C). 1998. spiral bd. 32.95 (*0-7872-4999-8*, 41499901) Kendall-Hunt.

Patrick, Steven R., et al. Energy Conservation Guidebook. LC 93-13523. 467p. 1993. 74.00 (*0-88173-154-4*) Fairmont Pr.

Patrick, Steven R., jt. auth. see Patrick, Dale R.

Patrick, Stewart, jt. ed. see Forman, Shepard.

Patrick, Terry. Cracking International Markets. 352p. 1998. 59.50 (*0-273-63030-X*, Pub. by Pitman Pub) Trans-Atl Phila.

Patrick, Thomas. Rapture or Renaissance - A View from the Sky. LC 97-95321. 328p. 1998. pap. 15.00 (*0-9662579-6-0*) Anonymous Publ.

Patrick, Thomas S., ed. see Benson, Betty L.

***Patrick, Tim.** The Visual Basic Style Guide. 384p. 2000. pap. 39.99 (*0-13-088361-1*) P-H.

Patrick, Toni. One Hundred One Ways to Make Ramen Noodles: Creative Cooking When You Can Only Afford Ten-for-One-Dollar Pasta. (Illus.). 96p. (Orig.). 1993. spiral bd. 9.95 (*0-9626335-2-6*) C&G Pub CO.

Patrick, Vanessa E., ed. An Illustrated Glossary of Early Southern Architecture & Landscape. (Illus.). 448p. (C). 1994. text 85.00 (*0-19-507992-2*) OUP.

***Patrick, Vincent.** Smoke Screen. 2000. mass mkt. 6.99 (*0-451-40911-6*, Onyx) NAL.

Patrick, Vincent. Smoke Screen: A Novel. LC 98-44614. 352p. 1999. 24.00 (*0-688-15536-7*, Wm Morrow) Morrow Avon.

Patrick, W. B. Letter to the Ghosts. LC 77-17153. 53p. 1977. 3.50 (*0-87886-091-6*, Greenfld Rev Pr) Greenfld Rev Lit.

Patrick, W. H., jt. ed. see DeDatta, S. K.

Patrick-Wexler, Diane. Barbara Jordan. LC 95-12611. (Contemporary African Americans Ser.). (Illus.). 48p. (J). (gr. 4-6). 1996. lib. bdg. 24.26 (*0-8172-3976-6*) Raintree Steck-V.

— Barbara Jordan. large type ed. 54p. (J). (gr. 4-8). pap. 13.50 (*0-614-20565-4*, L-86277-00 APHB) Am Printing Hse.

— Colin Powell. 48p. (J). (gr. 4-7). 1996. pap. 4.95 (*0-8114-9797-6*) Raintree Steck-V.

— Colin Powell. LC 95-11153. (Contemporary African Americans Ser.). (Illus.). 48p. (J). (gr. 4-6). 1996. lib. bdg. 24.26 (*0-8172-3977-4*) Raintree Steck-V.

— Colin Powell. large type ed. 54p. (J). 1996. pap. 13.50 (*0-614-20567-0*, L-86279-00 APHB) Am Printing Hse.

— Toni Morrison. LC 96-45136. (Contemporary African Americans Ser.). (Illus.). 48p. (J). (gr. 3-8). 1997. lib. bdg. 24.26 (*0-8172-3987-1*) Raintree Steck-V.

— Walter Dean Myers. (Contemporary Biographies Ser.). (Illus.). 48p. (J). (gr. 4-8). 1996. lib. bdg. 24.26 (*0-8172-3979-0*) Raintree Steck-V.

— Walter Dean Myers. large type ed. 54p. (J). (gr. 4-8). 1996. pap. 13.50 (*0-614-20569-7*, L-86309-00 APHB) Am Printing Hse.

Patrick, William, ed. see Hall, Lee.

Patrick, William B. Roxa: Voices of the Culver Family. (American Poets Continuum Ser.: No. 16). 181p. 1989. 20.00 (*0-918526-68-X*) BOA Edns.

— Roxa: Voices of the Culver Family. (American Poets Continuum Ser.: No. 16). 181p. 1989. pap. 12.50 (*0-918526-69-8*) BOA Edns.

— These Upraised Hands. (American Poets Continuum Ser.: No. 34). 90p. 1995. 20.00 (*1-880238-26-8*); pap. 12.50 (*1-880238-27-6*) BOA Edns.

— We Didn't Come Here for This: A Memoir in Poetry. LC 98-71252. (American Poets Continuum Ser.: Vol. 52). (Illus.). 96p. 1999. pap. 12.50 (*1-880238-71-3*, Pub. by BOA Edns) Consort Bk Sales.

Patrick, William H., Jr., jt. auth. see Reddy, K. Ramesh.

Patricof, Alan J. Foundation for a New Century: A Report to the President & Congress: The White House Conference on Small Business Commission. 111p. 1997. reprint ed. pap. text 35.00 (*0-7881-3810-3*) DIANE Pub.

Patrides, C. A., ed. Figures in a Renaissance Context. 362p. 1989. text 49.50 (*0-472-10119-6*, 10119) U of Mich Pr.

Patrides, C. A. & Wittreich, Joseph A., eds. The Apocalypse in English Renaissance Thought & Literature. LC 84-71281. 452p. (C). 1985. pap. text 27.50 (*0-8014-9893-7*) Cornell U Pr.

Patrides, C. A., ed. see Donne, John.

Patrides, C. A., ed. see Herbert, George.

Patrides, C. A., ed. see Milton, John.

Patrides, C. A., ed. see Smith, John.

Patrides, C. A., ed. & intro. see Browne, Thomas.

Patrides, G. A., ed. George Herbert: The Critical Heritage. (Critical Heritage Ser.). 390p. 1983. 69.50 (*0-7100-9240-7*, Routledge Thoemms) Routledge.

Patridge, Frances, tr. see Carpentier, Alejo.

Patridge, Ray. The Deer Hunter Log Book. 36p. 1984. pap. 9.95 (*0-9615880-0-4*) Bootstrap Pubns.

Patrignani. A Manual of Practical Devotion to St. Joseph. LC 82-50594. 328p. (J). 1988. reprint ed. pap. 15.00 (*0-89555-175-6*) TAN Bks Pubs.

Patrignani, Roberto, jt. auth. see Colombo, Mario.

***Patrik.** Existential Literature: An Introduction. (Philosophy Ser.). 2000. pap. text 41.95 (*0-534-56705-3*) Thomson Learn.

Patrik, Gary S., et al. Foundations of Casualty Actuarial Science. 2nd ed. LC 97-220305. 600p. (C). 1989. text 75.00 (*0-9624762-0-X*) Casualty Actuarial.

Patrikalakis, N. M., ed. Scientific Visualization of Physical Phenomena. (Illus.). 706p. 1991. 216.95 (*0-387-70081-1*) Spr-Verlag.

Patrikeeff, Felix, jt. auth. see Murphy, Brian.

Patriksson, Michael. Nonlinear Programming & Variational Inequality Problems: A Unified Approach. LC 98-45184. (Applied Optimization Ser.). 12p. 1999. 168.00 (*0-7923-5455-9*) Kluwer Academic.

Patrinacos, Nicon. All That a Greek Orthodox Should Know: An Orthodox Christian Catechism. 2nd ed. 170p. 1986. reprint ed. pap. 14.95 (*1-880971-48-8*) Light&Life Pub Co MN.

Patrinacos, Nicon D. A Dictionary of Greek Orthodoxy. LC 84-80596. (Illus.). 391p. 1984. pap. 19.95 (*1-880971-53-4*) Light&Life Pub Co MN.

Patrino de McVittie, Marina, tr. see Crary, Elizabeth.

***Patrinos, Aristides, ed.** Human Genome Program Report 1997 Pt. 1: Overview & Progress. (Illus.). 108p. (C). 1999. pap. text 25.00 (*0-7881-7984-5*) DIANE Pub.

— Human Genome Program Report 1997 Pt. 2: 1996 Research Abstracts. 98p. (C). 1999. pap. text 25.00 (*0-7881-7983-7*) DIANE Pub.

Patrinos, Harry A. & Ariasingam, David L. Decentralization of Education: Demand-Side Financing. LC 97-15317. (Directions in Development Ser.). 60p. 1997. pap. 22.00 (*0-8213-3930-3*, 13930) World Bank.

Patrinos, Harry A., jt. auth. see Glewwe, Paul.

Patrinos, Harry A., jt. ed. see Psacharopoulos, George.

***Patrizio, Andrew.** Contemporary Sculpture in Scotland. (Illus.). 164p. 1999. text 50.00 (*90-5703-431-X*, Harwood Acad Pubs) Gordon & Breach.

Patrizio, Giorgio, jt. auth. see Abate, Marco.

Patron. Dictionnaire des Communes Vol. 2: Departement du Loiret. fac. ed. (FRE.). 586p. 1991. pap. 115.00 (*0-7859-8248-5*, 2909112012); pap. 125.00 (*0-7859-8249-3*, 2909112020) Fr & Eur.

Patron Lugan, Roger. Un Regalo Excepcional. (SPA., Illus.). 130p. (Orig.). 1997. pap. text 13.98 (*968-409-474-4*) Edamex.

Patron, Lujan Roger. Un Regalo Excepcional. 194p. 1997. pap. text 18.98 (*968-409-785-9*) Edamex.

Patron, Susan. Maybe Yes, Maybe No, Maybe Maybe. LC 92-34067. (Richard Jackson Bk.). (Illus.). 96p. (J). (gr. 3-5). 1993. 15.95 (*0-531-05482-9*) Orchard Bks Watts.

***Patrone, Fioravante, et al.** Game Practice: Contributions from Applied Game Theory. LC 99-46683. (Theory & Decision Library). 2000. write for info. (*0-7923-8661-2*, Kluwer Plenum) Kluwer Academic.

Patrone, Nadia. Principe y Mecenas: Alfonso V En Los "Dichos y Hechos" De A. Beccadelli. (Currents in Comparative Romance Languages & Literatures Ser.: Vol. 17). (SPA.). XII, 106p. (C). 1995. text 36.95 (*0-8204-2150-2*) P Lang Pubng.

Patronis, Jimmy, Jr., jt. auth. see Lapensohn, Lee.

Patronius, Arbiter. Cena Trimalchionis. (Illus.). 270p. 1983. pap. text 27.00 (*0-19-814459-8*) OUP.

Patrons Association of the Collegiate School Staff, ed. Stuffed Cougar. (Illus.). 375p. (Orig.). 1973. pap. 12.95 (*0-681-21703-0*) Collegiate Schls.

— The Stuffed Cougar, Too. (Illus.). 362p. (Orig.). 1992. pap. 12.95 (*0-9634044-0-7*) Collegiate Schls.

Patros, Philip G. Depression & Suicide in Children & Adolescents. LC 88-14448. 360p. (C). 1988. 68.00 (*0-205-11670-1*, H16702) Allyn.

Patros, Philip G., jt. auth. see Shamoo, Tonia K.

***Patrouch, Joseph F.** A Negotiated Settlement: The Counter-reformation in Upper Austria under the Habsburgs. LC 99-98004. (Studies in Central European Histories). 2000. write for info. (*0-391-04099-5*) Humanities.

Patrovici, M., et al, eds. Heavy Ion Physics at Low, Intermediate & Relativistic Energies Using 4PI Detectors: Proceedings of the International Research Workshop. 400p. 1997. text 86.00 (*981-02-3227-6*) World Scientific Pub.

Patrowicz, Lucie J. & Wilk, Kathryn L. North Shore Schools: A Comprehensive Guide to Elementary & Secondary Education. LC 95-72396. 200p. 1996. pap. write for info. (*0-9649203-2-8*) Pigeon Cove Pr.

Patrucco, Armand. The Critics of the Italian Parliamentary System, 1860-1915. LC 91-44848. (Modern European History Ser.). 328p. 1992. text 25.00 (*0-8153-0738-1*) Garland.

Patruno, Nicholas. Understanding Primo Levi. LC 94-18747. (Understanding Modern European & Latin American Literature Ser.). 170p. 1995. text 29.95 (*1-57003-026-X*) U of SC Pr.

Patry, Gilles G. & Chapman, David T. Dynamic Modeling & Expert Systems in Wastewater Engineering. (Illus.). 450p. 1989. lib. bdg. 110.00 (*0-87371-174-2*, L174) Lewis Pubs.

Patry, Robert P. City of the Four Freedoms: A History of Evansville, Indiana. (Illus.). 300p. 1996. 35.00 (*0-940163-04-7*) Friends of Willard Library Pr.

Patry, William F. Copyright & the GATT - an Interpretation & Legislative History of the Uruguay Round Agreements Act: 1995 Supplement to Copyright Law & Practice. LC 95-10477. 1995. pap. 55.00 (*0-87179-886-7*) BNA Books.

— Copyright Law & Practice, Vol. 1. LC 94-12208. 1994. write for info. (*0-87179-854-9*) BNA Books.

— Copyright Law & Practice, Vol. 2. LC 94-12208. 1994. write for info. (*0-87179-855-7*) BNA Books.

— Copyright Law & Practice, Vol. 3. LC 94-12208. 1994. write for info. (*0-87179-856-5*) BNA Books.

— Copyright Law & Practice: 1998 Cumulative Supplement. 445p. 1999. pap., suppl. ed. 125.00 (*1-57018-140-3*, 1140) BNA Books.

— Copyright Law & Practice: 1998 Cumulative Supplement, 3 vols. 7th ed. LC 94-12208. 2272p. 1994. 225.00 (*0-87179-685-6*, 9078) BNA Books.

— The Fair Use Privilege in Copyright Law. 2nd ed. LC 85-4088. 675p. 1995. text 115.00 (*0-87179-831-X*) BNA Books.

Patrylick, Carol. Bank Loan Pools: Financial Structures for Business Development. Murphy, Jenny, ed. 30p. (Orig.). 1987. pap. 17.00 (*0-317-04817-1*) Natl Coun Econ Dev.

— Downtown Retail Revitalization: Strategies to Maximize Your Market. Murphy, Jenny, ed. 42p. (Orig.). 1989. pap. 21.50 (*0-317-04898-8*) Natl Coun Econ Dev.

— Retail Incubators: Linking Entrepreneurship & Commercial Development. Murphy, Jenny, ed. 38p. (Orig.) 1988. pap. 18.00 (*0-317-04810-4*) Natl Coun Econ Dev.

Patsalis, Toula. Joys of Pressure Cooking. Wadlington, Vickie, ed. 245p. 1990. pap. write for info. (*0-318-68123-4*) Kitchen Glamor.

Patsavos, Lewis J. Primacy & Conciliarity: Studies in the Primacy of the See of Constantinople & the Synodal Structure of the Orthodox Church. 57p. 1995. pap. 3.95 (*1-885652-02-X*, Pub. by Holy Cross Orthodox) BookWorld.

Patscheider, Herwig, jt. auth. see Neuhold, Andreas.

Patschke, Steve. Don't Look at It! Don't Touch It! LC 96-205425. (Illus.). 32p. (Orig.). (J). (ps-3). 1996. pap. 3.50 (*0-8167-4120-4*, Whistlstop) Troll Communs.

— Halloween Mix: Happy Halloween/Don't Look at It! Don't Touch It! (Illus.). (J). (ps-3). 1999. pap. text 4.50 (*1-55254-090-1*) Brighter Vision.

***Patschke, Steve.** The Spooky Book. LC 99-13040. (Illus.). 32p. (J). (gr. k-3). 1999. 15.95 (*0-8027-8692-8*); lib. bdg. 16.85 (*0-8027-8693-6*) Walker & Co.

Patsie, Nichols, ed. see Bureau of Deep Mine Safety & Mining & Reclamation.

Patsis, Peter. UNIX, AWK & SED Programmer's Interactive. LC 99-209885. (UNIX Interactive Workbook Ser.). (Illus.). 500p. 1998. pap. text, wbk. ed. 34.99 (*0-13-082675-8*) P-H.

Patsoulis, Toula. The Pressure Cooker Cookbook. 208p. (Orig.). 1994. pap. 12.00 (*1-55788-189-8*, HP Books) Berkley Pub.

Patsouras, Louis. Jean Grace & the Anarchist Tradition in France. LC 94-46629. 152p. (C). 1995. text 29.95 (*0-391-03911-3*) Humanities.

— Simone Weil & the Socialist Tradition. LC 91-42735. 120p. 1992. pap. text 39.95 (*0-7734-9913-X*) E Mellen.

Patsouras, Louis, ed. Debating Marx. LC 93-44821. 280p. 1994. pap. 29.95 (*0-7734-1934-9*) E Mellen.

Patsouras, Louis & Thomas, Jack R., eds. Essays on Socialism. LC 92-32173. 420p. 1992. pap. text 39.95 (*0-7734-9911-3*) E Mellen.

Patsouras, Louis, jt. ed. see Ensign, Russell L.

Patsukov, Vitaly. Forbidden Art: Soviet Nonconformist Art, 1956-1988. LC 98-7458. (Illus.). 326p. 1998. 65.00 (*1-881616-89-4*) Dist Art Pubs.

Patsukov, Viytaly. Forbidden Art: Soviet Nonconformist Art, 1956-1988. LC 98-7458. (Illus.). 326p. 1997. 65.00 (*1-881616-91-6*) Dist Art Pubs.

***Patsula, Peter J.** Successful Business Planning in 30 Days: A Step-by-Step Guide for Writing a Business Plan & Starting Your Own Business. Nowik, William, ed. LC 00-190077. (Illus.). xii, 212p. 2000. pap. 19.95 (*0-9678402-0-1*) Patsula Media.

Patt. The Cancer Pain Handbook. (Illus.). 250p. 1997. spiral bd. 29.95 (*0-397-51479-4*) Lppncott W & W.

— Introduction to Computing. 2000. text 60.95 (*0-07-237690-2*) McGraw.

Patt & Nozick. Generation Eighteen Ninety-Eight & After. (C). 1991. mass mkt. 37.95 (*0-8384-3755-9*) Heinle & Heinle.

Patt, Beatrice & Nozick, Martin, eds. Spanish Literature, 1700-1900. 463p. (C). 1989. reprint ed. pap. text 20.95 (*0-88133-454-5*) Waveland Pr.

Patt, Beatrice P., jt. ed. see Florit, Eugenio.

***Patt, Ben.** The Turtle Who Needed Glasses. (Illus.). 38p. (J). (gr. k-6). 2000. pap. 5.95 (*0-943599-34-2*) OEPF.

Patt, Claudia. Die Strategische Planung als Komponente Eines Controllingsystems im Krankenhaus: Eine Untersuchung fur das Deutsche Krankenhauswesen. (GER., Illus.). 262p. 1996. 51.95 (*3-631-30087-5*) P Lang Pubng.

Patt, David. A Strange Liberation: Tibetan Lives in Chinese Hands. LC 92-44590. 272p. 1992. pap. 12.95 (*1-55939-013-1*) Snow Lion Pubns.

— Wheel of Time. 1983. pap. write for info. (*0-318-62752-3*) Deer Park Bks.

Patt, Gail R. Human Anatomy & Physiology. 3rd ed. (C). 1994. pap. text, student ed. 24.06 (*0-07-011174-X*) McGraw.

Patt, Hans Josef. Relativity for Windows. 1998. 59.95 (*3-540-14735-7*) Spr-Verlag.

Patt, Richard B. Cancer Pain. LC 92-49630. 672p. 1993. text 98.00 (*0-397-51138-8*) Lppncott W & W.

— Manual of Cancer Pain Management. (Illus.). 450p. 1992. write for info. (*0-318-69535-9*) Lppncott W & W.

Patt, Richard B., jt. auth. see Lang, Susan S.

Patt, Richard W. Partners in the Impossible. 1984. 5.00 (*0-89536-678-9*, 4854) CSS OH.

— Sermons for Pentecost II Based on Gospel Texts for Cycle C: All Stirred Up. LC 96-53192. (Sermons Based on the Gospel Texts Ser.). 94p. (Orig.). 1997. pap. 10.75 (*0-7880-1040-9*) CSS OH.

Patt, Ruth M. Uncommon Lives: Eighteen Extraordinary New Jersey Jews. 1994. 17.95 (*0-533-10970-1*) Vantage.

Patta, Debora, jt. auth. see Steyn, Rory.

Patta Pillar, De, see De Patta Pillar.

***Pattabhi Jois, Sri K.** Yoga Mala. Stern, Eddie, ed. 137p. 2000. pap. text 32.00 (*0-9700501-0-0*) Patanjali Yoga.

— Yoga Mala. Stern, Eddie, ed. (Illus.). 137p. 2000. 25.00 (*0-9700501-1-9*) Patanjali Yoga.

Pattabhiraman, P. Handbook of Tax on Salaries. (C). 1990. 110.00 (*0-89771-266-8*) St Mut.

Pattak, Evan M. & Wilson, Andrew G. Pittsburgh: A Portrait of Progress. Robertson, Scott, ed. LC 92-64401. (Illus.). 160p. 1993. text 49.95 (*0-9634100-0-8*, 08) Wyndham Pubns.

Pattakos, Alex, ed. see Harman, Willis, et al.

Pattallo, Polly. Judging Women. (C). 1988. 30.00 (*0-946088-07-1*, Pub. by NCCL) St Mut.

Pattan, Bruno. Robust Modulation Methods & Smart Antennas in Wireless Communications. LC 99-11799. 304p. 1999. 75.00 (*0-13-022029-9*) P-H.

— Satellite-Based Cellular Communications. LC 97-26254. (Telecommunications Ser.). (Illus.). 259p. 1997. 69.00 (*0-07-049417-7*) McGraw.

***Pattanaik, Devdutt.** The Goddess in India: The Five Faces of the Eternal Feminine. (Illus.). 176p. 2000. pap. 19.95 (*0-89281-807-7*) Inner Tradit.

Pattanaik, Manoj, jt. auth. see Human, Joe.

Pattanaik, P., jt. ed. see Gaertner, W.

Pattanaik, P. K., jt. auth. see Suzumura, K.

Pattanayak, Debi P., ed. Multilingualism in India. (Multilingual Matters Ser.: No. 61). 116p. 1990. 69.00 (*1-85359-073-8*); pap. 24.95 (*1-85359-072-X*) Taylor & Francis.

Pattarozzi, Chris. Private Sector Participation in Public Transit Systems. (State Legislative Reports: Vol. 18, No. 4). 7p. 1993. 15.00 (*1-55516-298-3*, 7302-1804) Natl Conf State Legis.

— Recreational Boating Safety: State Policies & Programs. 40p. 1992. pap. text 10.00 (*1-55516-989-9*, 9348) Natl Conf State Legis.

Pattarozzi, Michelle M. Uniquely Yours: A Collection of over 700 Suggestions to Individualize Your Wedding. 104p. 1983. 9.95 (*0-317-00911-7*) M M Pattarozzi.

P

Pattatucci, Angela M. Women in Science: Meeting Challenges & Transcending Boundaries. LC 98-9052. 1998. 51.00 (0-7619-0048-9); pap. 24.50 (0-7619-0049-7) Sage.

***Pattavina, Achille.** Switching Theory: Architectures & Performance in Broadband ATM Networks. 432p. 1998. 155.00 (0-471-96338-0) Wiley.

***Patte, Daniel.** The Challenge of Discipleship: A Critical Study of the Sermon on the Mount as Scripture. LC 99-16380. 288p. 1999. pap. 25.00 (1-56338-286-5) TPI PA.

Patte, Daniel. Discipleship According to the Sermon on the Mount: Four Legitimate Readings, Four Plausible Views of Discipleship, & Their Relative Values. LC 96-46647. 432p. (Orig.). (C). 1996. pap. 30.00 (1-56338-177-X) TPI PA.

— Early Jewish Hermeneutic in Palestine. LC 75-22225. (Society of Biblical Literature. Dissertation Ser.: No. 22). 358p. reprint ed. 111.00 (0-8357-9570-5, 201766600007) Bks Demand.

— Ethics of Biblical Interpretation: A Reevaluation. 160p. (Orig.). 1995. pap. 19.95 (0-664-25568-X) Westminster John Knox.

— The Gospel According to Matthew: A Structural Commentary on Matthew's Gospel. LC 96-41605. 448p. (C). 1996. reprint ed. pap. 26.00 (1-56338-179-6) TPI PA.

— Structural Exegesis for New Testament Critics. LC 96-42565. 144p. 1996. reprint ed. pap. 16.00 (1-56338-178-8) TPI PA.

***Patte, Daniel & Grenholm, Christina, eds.** Reading Israel in Romans: Legitimacy & Plausibility of Divergent Interpretations. LC 99-58583. (Romans Through History & Cultures Ser.: Vol. 1). 265p. 2000. pap. 29.00 (1-56338-308-X) TPI PA.

Pattee, F. L., ed. see Brown, Charles Brockden.

Pattee, Fred L. The Development of the American Short Story. LC 66-13477. 1923. pap. 22.00 (0-8196-0175-6) Biblo.

— The Development of the American Short Story: An Historical Survey. (BCL1-PS American Literature Ser.). 388p. 1992. reprint ed. lib. bdg. 89.00 (0-7812-6638-6) Rprt Serv.

— A History of American Literature since 1870. (BCL1-PS American Literature Ser.). 449p. 1992. reprint ed. lib. bdg. 99.00 (0-7812-6617-3) Rprt Serv.

— The New American Literature, 1890-1930. (BCL1-PS American Literature Ser.). 507p. 1992. reprint ed. lib. bdg. 99.00 (0-7812-6622-X) Rprt Serv.

— Tradition & Jazz. LC 68-22937. (Essay Index Reprint Ser.). 1977. reprint ed. 23.95 (0-8369-0776-0) Ayer.

Pattee, Howard H. Hierarchy Theory: The Challenge of Complex Systems. LC 72-93477. 1973. 7.95 (0-8076-0674-X, Pub. by Braziller) Norton.

Pattee, James J. & Otteson, Orlo J. The Health Care Future Vol. 1: Defining the Argument, Healing the Debate. 227p. 1998. 27.50 (0-9629614-1-8) North Ridge Pr.

— Medical Direction in the Nursing Home: Principles & Concepts for Physician-Administrators. 405p. 1991. 49.50 (0-9629614-0-X) North Ridge Pr.

Pattee, James L. Health Care: How to Heal the Debate & Define the Argument. 1997. 27.50 (1-889279-04-8) Best Small Pr.

Pattee, Richard, tr. see Ramos, Artur.

Pattee, William S. Essential Nature of Law: or The Ethical Basis of Jurisprudence. xxv, 264p. 1982. reprint ed. 38.00 (0-8377-1011-1, Rothman) W S Hein.

***Pattee, William S. & Sullivan, E. Thomas.** Understanding Antitrust & Its Economic Implications 1998. annuals 3rd ed. 1998. text 30.00 (0-8205-3973-2) Bender.

Patten. Auto Ser Basic. 3rd ed. 1997. pap. text, student ed. 36.40 (0-13-359266-9) P-H.

— Catastrophism & the Old Testament. 1996. 19.95 (1-57558-011-X); pap. 14.95 (1-57558-012-8) Hearthstone OK.

— Scaffold at Hangmans Creek. large type ed. LC 98-33775. Date not set. 20.95 (0-7838-0354-0, G K Hall Lrg Type) Mac Lib Ref.

— The Youngerman Guns. large type ed. LC 98-48525. Date not set. 30.00 (0-7838-0446-6, G K Hall Lrg Type) Mac Lib Ref.

***Patten, Bob.** Old Tools - New Eyes: A Primal Primer of Flintknapping. (Illus.). 160p. 1999. pap. 13.95 (0-9668701-0-7) Stone Dagger.

***Patten, Alan.** Hegel's Idea of Freedom. LC 99-15985. 232p. 1999. text 45.00 (0-19-823770-7) OUP.

***Patten, Angela.** Still Listening. 72p. 2000. pap. 12.95 (1-897648-50-2, Pub. by Salmon Poetry) Dufour.

Patten, B. C., ed. Wetlands & Shallow Continental Water Bodies Vol. 1: Natural & Human Relationships. (Illus.). xiii, 759p. 1990. 190.00 (90-5103-046-0, Pub. by SPB Acad Pub) Balogh.

— Wetlands & Shallow Continental Water Bodies Vol. 2: Case Studies. (Illus.). 732p. 1994. 190.00 (90-5103-092-4, Pub. by SPB Acad Pub) Balogh.

Patten, B. E., et al. Pasteurellosis in Production Animals. 256p. (Orig.). 1993. pap. 159.00 (1-86320-081-9) St Mut.

Patten, Barbara. Life's Connections. LC 95-91034. 224p. (Orig.). 1996. pap. 12.95 (0-9651082-7-9) Tenton Pr.

Patten, Barbara J. The Basic Five Food Groups. LC 95-20557. (Read All about Food for Good Health Ser.). 24p. (J). (gr. 1-4). 1996. lib. bdg. 12.95 (0-86593-399-5) Rourke Corp.

— Digestion: Food at Work. LC 95-33537. (Read All about Food for Good Health Ser.). 24p. (J). (gr. 1-4). 1996. lib. bdg. 12.95 (0-86593-403-7) Rourke Corp.

— Food Safety. LC 95-33538. (Read All about Food for Good Health Ser.). 24p. (J). (gr. 1-4). 1995. lib. bdg. 12.95 (0-86593-404-5) Rourke Corp.

— Growing Food We Eat. LC 95-25218. (Read All about Food for Good Health Ser.). 24p. (J). (gr. 1-4). 1996. lib. bdg. 12.95 (0-86593-401-0) Rourke Corp.

— How to Eat to Win. LC 95-33550. (Read All about Food for Good Health Ser.). 24p. (J). (gr. 1-4). 1996. lib. bdg. 12.95 (0-86593-400-2) Rourke Corp.

— Nutrients: Superstars of Good Health. LC 95-33536. (Read All about Food for Good Health Ser.). 24p. (J). (gr. 1-4). 1996. lib. bdg. 12.95 (0-86593-402-9) Rourke Corp.

Patten, Bernard C. & Jorgensen, Sven E. Complex Ecology. 736p. (C). 1994. 120.00 (0-13-161506-8) P-H.

Patten, Bill V., et al. Destinos Homeviewer's Guide & Audiocassettes: An Introduction to Spanish. (C). 1993. pap. text, student ed. 34.38 incl. audio (0-07-911479-2) McGraw.

Patten, Bradley M., et al. Science in Progress. Baitsell, George A., ed. LC 78-37534. (Essay Index Reprint Ser.: 7). 1977. reprint ed. 44.95 (0-8369-2532-7) Ayer.

Patten, Brian. The Blue & Green Ark: An Alphabet for Planet Earth. LC 99-70822. (Illus.). 64p. (J). (ps-3). 2000. 18.95 (0-439-07969-1, Pub. by Scholastic Inc) Penguin Putnam.

***Patten, Brian.** Utter Nutters. 2000. 29.95 (0-593-04307-3, Pub. by Transworld Publishers Ltd) Trafalgar.

Patten, Chris. The Tory Case. LC 82-17085. (Jossey-Bass Higher Education Ser.). 208p. reprint ed. pap. 64.50 (0-608-30941-9, 202252400027) Bks Demand.

Patten, Christen Taylor. Miss O'Keeffe. LC 91-22431. 203p. (C). 1992. 18.95 (0-8263-1322-1) U of NM Pr.

Patten, Christine T. O'Keeffe at Abiquiu. LC 94-39687. (Illus.). 120p. 1995. 39.95 (0-8109-3680-1, Pub. by Abrams) Time Warner.

Patten, Christine T. & Cardona-Hine, Alvaro. Miss O'Keeffe. (Illus.). 203p. 1998. pap. 12.95 (0-8263-1961-0) U of NM Pr.

Patten, Christopher. East & West: China, Power & the Future of Asia. LC 98-24150. (Illus.). 320p. 1998. 25.00 (0-8129-3000-2, Times Bks) Crown Pub Group.

***Patten, Christopher.** East & West: China, Power & the Future of Asia. 320p. 1999. pap. 15.00 (0-8129-3232-3, Times Bks) Crown Pub Group.

Patten, Christopher. Great Britain & the World: Three Talks at Berkeley. LC 89-26964. (Institute of Governmental Studies Lecture Ser.). 66p. reprint ed. pap. 30.00 (0-608-20130-8, 207140200011) Bks Demand.

Patten, Claudius B. The Methods & Machinery of Practical Banking. Bruchey, Stuart, ed. LC 80-1164. (Rise of Commercial Banking Ser.). (Illus.). 1981. reprint ed. lib. bdg. 49.95 (0-405-13673-0) Ayer.

***Patten, Dennis.** The Matchstick Fun Book. (Illus.). 48p. (J). 1999. pap. 9.95 (0-7641-1215-5) Barron.

Patten, Dick & Ferguson, Donald L. Journalism. (VGM Career Planner Ser.). (Illus.). 128p. 1993. pap. 7.95 (0-8442-8690-7, Natl Textbk Co) NTC Contemp Pub Co.

Patten, Donald W. The Mars - Earth Catastrophes. 1988. 19.95 (0-685-20125-2); pap. 14.95 (0-685-20126-0) Pacific Mer.

— Symposium on Creation VI. 1977. pap. 3.95 (0-685-52492-2) Pacific Mer.

Patten, Donald W. & Remling, John. Automotive Service Basics. 3rd ed. LC 95-49552. 609p. (C). 1996. pap. text 70.00 (0-13-359258-8) P-H.

Patten, Edith. Beach Seiners. 1986. pap. 3.00 (0-942396-38-3) Blackberry ME.

Patten, Fred, ed. see Ledoux, Trish & Ranney, Doug.

Patten, G. Z. A Lotta Malarkey. (Illus.). 140p. 1998. pap. text 11.95 (0-9612974-3-3) Patten Pr Inc.

Patten, G. Z., ed. see Meador, Dale.

Patten, G. Z., ed. see Van Flossen, Jacob.

***Patten, H.** Clever Anansi & Boastful Bullfrog. (Illus.). 32p. (J). (gr. k-3). 1999. 13.95 (1-887734-74-0) Star Brght Bks.

Patten, J. P. Neurological Differential Diagnosis: An Illustrated Approach. (Illus.). 292p. 1987. reprint ed. 75.00 (0-387-90264-3) Spr-Verlag.

Patten, James J. Van, see Pulliam, John D. & Van Patten, James J.

Patten, James J. Van, see Van Patten, James J., ed.

Patten, Jim & Ferguson, Donald L. Opportunities in Journalism Careers. (Opportunities In . . . Ser.). (Illus.). 160p. pap. 11.95 (0-8442-4014-1, 40141, VGM Career) NTC Contemp Pub Co.

— Opportunities in Journalism Careers. (Opportunities in...Ser.). 160p. 1995. 14.95 (0-8442-4013-3) NTC Contemp Pub Co.

Patten, Jim, jt. auth. see Ferguson, Donald L.

Patten, Joan F. Van, see Van Patten, Joan F.

Patten, John. Neurological Differential Diagnosis. 2nd ed. LC 95-14336. 350p. 1996. 69.00 (3-540-19937-3) Spr-Verlag.

Patten, John A., jt. ed. see Thompson, Daniel C.

Patten, John M., Jr. Acid Rain. LC 94-24207. (Read All about Eye on the Environment Ser.). 24p. (J). (gr. 1-4). 1995. lib. bdg. 18.60 (1-55916-099-3) Rourke Bk Co.

— Acids & Bases. LC 95-6213. (Read All about Let's Wonder about Science Ser.). 24p. (J). (gr. 1-4). 1995. lib. bdg. 18.60 (1-55916-128-0) Rourke Bk Co.

— Atoms Family. LC 94-47598. (Read All about Let's Wonder about Science Ser.). 24p. (J). (gr. 1-4). 1995. lib. bdg. 18.60 (1-55916-125-6) Rourke Bk Co.

— Canine Companions. LC 96-23069. (Read All about Dogs Ser.). 24p. (J). (gr. 1-4). 1996. lib. bdg. 12.95 (0-86593-455-X) Rourke Corp.

— Dogs with a Job. LC 96-23070. (Read All about Dogs Ser.). 24p. (J). (gr. 1-4). 1996. lib. bdg. 12.95 (0-86593-456-8) Rourke Corp.

— Elements, Compounds & Mixtures: Elements, Compounds & Mixtures. LC 95-4203. (Read All about Let's Wonder about Science Ser.). 24p. (J). (gr. 1-4). 1995. lib. bdg. 18.60 (1-55916-127-2) Rourke Bk Co.

— Hounds on the Trail. LC 96-19942. (Read All about Dogs Ser.). 24p. (J). (gr. 1-4). 1996. lib. bdg. 12.95 (0-86593-459-2) Rourke Corp.

— Liquid to Gas & Back. LC 95-6214. (Read All about Let's Wonder about Science Ser.). 24p. (J). (gr. 1-4). 1995. lib. bdg. 18.60 (1-55916-129-9) Rourke Bk Co.

— Matter Really Matters. LC 94-47601. (Read All about Let's Wonder about Science Ser.). 24p. (J). (gr. 1-4). 1995. lib. bdg. 18.60 (1-55916-124-8) Rourke Bk Co.

— Numbers & Age. (Read All about Numbers Ser.). 24p. (J). (gr. 1-4). 1996. lib. bdg. 12.95 (0-86593-437-1) Rourke Corp.

— Numbers & Counting. (Read All about Numbers Ser.). 24p. (J). (gr. 1-4). 1996. lib. bdg. 12.95 (0-86593-438-X) Rourke Corp.

— Numbers & Measuring. (Read All about Numbers Ser.). 24p. (J). (gr. 1-4). 1996. lib. bdg. 12.95 (0-86593-434-7) Rourke Corp.

— Numbers & Money. (Read All about Numbers Ser.). 24p. (J). (gr. 1-4). 1996. lib. bdg. 12.95 (0-86593-439-8) Rourke Corp.

Patten, John M. Numbers & Speed. LC 96-12625. (Read All about Numbers Ser.). 24p. (J). (gr. 1-4). 1996. lib. bdg. 12.95 (0-86593-436-3) Rourke Corp.

Patten, John M., Jr. Numbers & Sports. (Read All about Numbers Ser.). 24p. (J). (gr. 1-4). 1996. lib. bdg. 12.95 (0-86593-435-5) Rourke Corp.

— Oil Spills. LC 94-37162. (Read All about Eye on the Environment Ser.). 24p. (J). (gr. 1-4). 1995. lib. bdg. 18.60 (1-55916-096-9) Rourke Bk Co.

— Polluted Air. LC 94-38616. (Read All about Eye on the Environment Ser.). 24p. (J). (gr. 1-4). 1995. lib. bdg. 18.60 (1-55916-098-5) Rourke Bk Co.

— Posioned Water. LC 94-37163. (Read All about Eye on the Environment Ser.). 24p. (J). (gr. 1-4). 1995. lib. bdg. 18.60 (1-55916-097-7) Rourke Bk Co.

— Solids, Liquids & Gases: Solids, Liquids & Gases. LC 94-47599. (Read All about Let's Wonder about Science Ser.). 24p. (J). (gr. 1-4). 1995. lib. bdg. 18.60 (1-55916-126-4) Rourke Bk Co.

— Sporting Dogs. LC 96-23078. (Read All about Dogs Ser.). 24p. (J). (gr. 1-4). 1996. lib. bdg. 12.95 (0-86593-460-6) Rourke Corp.

— Terrier Breeds. LC 96-23074. (Read All about Dogs Ser.). 24p. (J). (gr. 1-4). 1996. lib. bdg. 12.95 (0-86593-458-4) Rourke Corp.

— Toxic Wastes. LC 94-38615. (Read All about Eye on the Environment Ser.). 24p. (J). (gr. 1-4). 1995. lib. bdg. 18.60 (1-55916-100-0) Rourke Bk Co.

— Trash. LC 94-42670. (Read All about Eye on the Environment Ser.). 24p. (J). (gr. 1-4). 1995. lib. bdg. 18.60 (1-55916-101-9) Rourke Bk Co.

— The World's Smallest Dogs. LC 96-19943. (Read All about Dogs Ser.). 24p. (J). (gr. 1-4). 1996. lib. bdg. 12.95 (0-86593-457-6) Rourke Corp.

Patten, Karen. Data Networking Made Easy: The Small Business Guide to Getting Wired for Success. (Illus.). 400p. 2000. pap. 19.95 (1-890154-15-6) Aegis Pub Grp.

Patten, Karl. Touch: Poems. LC 98-45090. 128p. 1999. 19.95 (0-8387-5423-6) Bucknell U Pr.

— Yes, of Course, but No. (Press of Appletree Alley Poets Ser.). (Illus.). 12p. 1997. pap. 35.00 (0-916375-32-3) Press Alley.

***Patten, Laurie L. & Haberman, David L.** Notes on a Mandala. 312p. 2000. 40.00 (1-889119-56-3) Seven Bridges.

Patten, Lewis B. Ambush Creek. large type ed. LC 98-15048. (Sagebrush Large Print Westerns Ser.). 1998. 19.95 (1-57490-126-5) T T Beeler.

***Patten, Lewis B.** The Arrogant Guns. large type ed. LC 99-41715. (Thorndike Western Ser.). 1999. 20.95 (0-7862-2192-5) Thorndike Pr.

Patten, Lewis B. The Best Western Stories of Lewis Patten. Greenberg, Martin H. & Pronzini, Bill, eds. LC 86-26144. (Western Writers Ser.). 180p. 1989. reprint ed. pap. 12.95 (0-8040-0925-2) Swallow.

***Patten, Lewis B.** Bounty Man. large type ed. LC 99-39436. 2000. 30.00 (0-7838-8734-5, G K Hall Lrg Type) Mac Lib Ref.

— Cheyenne Drums. large type ed. LC 99-22226. 1999. pap. 19.95 (0-7838-8651-9, G K Hall & Co) Mac Lib Ref.

Patten, Lewis B. The Cheyenne Pool. LC 72-79415. (Western Ser.). 160p. (J). 1972. write for info. (0-385-02262-X) Doubleday.

— The Cheyenne Pool. 272p. 1983. mass mkt. 2.95 (0-451-12492-8, Sig) NAL.

— The Cheyenne Pool. large type ed. 1993. 11.95 (0-8161-3367-0, G K Hall Lrg Type) Mac Lib Ref.

— The Feud at Chimney Rock. large type ed. LC 96-49293. (Sagebrush Large Print Westerns Ser.). 1997. lib. bdg. 18.95 (1-57490-113-3) T T Beeler.

— Gun Proud. large type ed. LC 93-43544. (General Ser.). 243p. 1994. lib. bdg. 16.95 (0-8161-5924-6, G K Hall Lrg Type) Mac Lib Ref.

— Hunt the Man Down. 1984. mass mkt. 3.50 (0-451-13282-3, Sig) NAL.

— Hunt the Man Down. large type ed. (General Ser.). 260p. 1985. 13.95 (0-8161-3899-0, G K Hall Lrg Type) Mac Lib Ref.

— The Killings at Coyote Springs: The Trail of the Apache Kid, 2 vols. in 1. 336p. 1994. pap. text, mass mkt. 4.99 (0-8439-3638-X) Dorchester Pub Co.

— No God in Saguarro. large type ed. (Sagebrush Large Print Westerns Ser.). 176p. 1996. lib. bdg. 18.95 (1-57490-022-6) T T Beeler.

— Posse from Poison Creek. 1981. mass mkt. 1.75 (0-451-09577-4, Sig) NAL.

— Redskin. 1982. mass mkt. 2.75 (0-451-11929-0, AE1929, Sig) NAL.

— Rifles of Revenge. 1979. mass mkt. 1.95 (0-89083-568-3, Zebra Kensgtn) Kensgtn Pub Corp.

***Patten, Lewis B.** The Ruthless Range. large type ed. LC 98-10489. (Western Ser.). 168p. 1998. write for info. (0-7540-3294-9) Chivers N Amer.

Patten, Lewis B. The Ruthless Range. large type ed. LC 98-10489. 185p. 1998. pap. 18.95 (0-7838-8458-3, G K Hall & Co) Mac Lib Ref.

— The Scaffold at Hangman's Creek large type ed. LC 98-33775. 173 p. 1999. write for info. (0-7540-3542-5) Chivers N Amer.

— Tincup in the Storm Country. large type ed. (Five-Star Western Ser.). 200p. 1996. 16.95 (0-7862-0593-8), Thorndike Pr.

— Track of the Hunter. large type ed. LC 98-21083. 191p. 1998. 20.95 (0-7838-0257-9, G K Hall & Co) Mac Lib Ref.

— The Trail of the Apache Kid. large type ed. LC 98-21235. 1998. 18.95 (0-7838-0245-5, G K Hall Lrg Type) Mac Lib Ref.

***Patten, Lewis B.** Trail to Vicksburg: A Western Duo. 256p. 2000. pap. 4.50 (0-8439-4700-4, Leisure Bks) Dorchester Pub Co.

Patten, Lewis B. Trail to Vicksburg: A Western Duo. large type ed. LC 96-53881. 238p. 1997. 17.95 (0-7862-0741-8) Thorndike Pr.

— Trail to Vicksburg: A Western Duo. large type ed. LC 98-5427. 1998. 18.95 (0-7862-0764-7) Thorndike Pr.

— Villa's Rifles. 20.95 (0-89190-420-4) Amereon Ltd.

— Villa's Rifles. large type ed. LC 94-20140. 235p. 1994. pap. 17.95 (0-8161-7424-5, G K Hall Lrg Type) Mac Lib Ref.

***Patten, Lewis B.** The Woman at Ox-Yoke: A Western Duo. LC 00-37130. 2000. pap. write for info. (0-7862-2475-4) Five Star.

Patten, Lewis B. The Younger Man Guns. 1986. pap. 2.75 (0-451-14266-7, Sig) NAL.

Patten, M. N., ed. Information Sources in Metallic Materials. (Guides to Information Sources Ser.). 528p. 1990. lib. bdg. 75.00 (0-408-01491-1) Bowker-Saur.

Patten, Malcolm C. Patten Genealogy: 1 Line Descending from William Patten. LC 90-62211. (Illus.). 402p. 1990. 25.00 (0-9627321-0-9) Powell & Taylor.

Patten, Margaret A. Van, see Monahan, Edward C. & Van Patten, Margaret A., eds.

Patten, Marguerite. Cooking for Today. 256p. 1995. write for info. (1-57215-187-0) World Pubns.

***Patten, Marguerite.** Marguerite Patten's Complete Book of Teas. (Illus.). 144p. 1999. reprint ed. pap. text 17.00 (0-7881-6686-7) DIANE Pub.

Patten, Marguerite. Marguerite Potter's Complete Book of Teas. (Illus.). 144p. (Orig.). 1997. pap. text 14.95 (0-7499-1691-5, Pub. by Piatkus Bks) London Brdge.

Patten, Marjorie. Arts Workshop of Rural America. LC 37-15722. reprint ed. 20.00 (0-404-04907-9) AMS Pr.

***Patten, Mildred L.** Proposing Empirical Research: A Guide to the Fundamentals. 138p. 1999. pap. text 23.95 (1-884585-25-6) Pyrczak Pub.

Patten, Mildred L. Questionnaire Research: A Practical Guide. (Illus.). 144p. (Orig.). (C). 1997. pap. text 21.95 (1-884585-07-8) Pyrczak Pub.

***Patten, Mildred L.** Understanding Research Methods: An Overview of the Essentials. rev. ed. (Illus.). (C). 1999. pap. text 23.95 (1-884585-22-1) Pyrczak Pub.

Patten, Mildred L., ed. Educational & Psychological Research: A Cross Section of Journal Articles for Analysis & Evaluation. 2nd rev. ed. (Illus.). 208p. (C). 1997. pap. text 23.95 (1-884585-03-5) Pyrczak Pub.

Patten, Paul R., jt. auth. see Goldstein, Larry J.

Patten, Priscilla, jt. auth. see Patten, Rebecca.

Patten, Priscilla C. & Patten, Rebecca. The World of the Early Church: A Companion to the New Testament. LC 90-44322. 276p. 1991. lib. bdg. 89.95 (0-88946-598-3) E Mellen.

Patten, Rebecca & Patten, Priscilla. Before the Times. LC 80-36848. (Illus.). 256p. 1980. 15.95 (0-89407-047-9) Strawberry Hill.

Patten, Rebecca, jt. auth. see Patten, Priscilla C.

Patten, Rena. How to Prepare Stuffings & Fillings. 1996. pap. text 19.95 (0-86417-702-X, Pub. by Kangaroo Pr) Seven Hills Bk.

Patten, Richard A. Van, see Van Patten, Richard A.

Patten, Richard H. & Rosengard, Jay K. Progress with Profits: The Development of Rural Banking in Indonesia. 114p. 1991. pap. 14.95 (1-55815-140-0) ICS Pr.

Patten, Robert L. George Cruikshank's Life, Times & Art: 1792-1835, Vol. 1. LC 91-40344. (Illus.). 550p. 1992. 55.00 (0-8135-1813-X) Rutgers U Pr.

— George Cruikshank's Life, Times & Art Vol. II: 1835-1878. (Illus.). 500p. (C). 1996. 75.00 (0-8135-1814-8) Rutgers U Pr.

Patten, Robert L., ed. George Cruikshank: A Revaluation. (Illus.). 258p. 1974. 20.00 (0-87811-018-6) Princeton Lib.

— George Cruikshank: A Revaluation. LC 92-12258. (Illus.). 300p. 1992. pap. text 21.95 (0-691-00293-2, Pub. by Princeton U Pr) Cal Prin Full Svc.

Patten, Robert L., ed. see Dickens, Charles.

Patten, Robert L., jt. ed. see Jordan, John O.

Patten, Simon . The Premises of Political Economy: Being a Re-Examination of Certain Fundamental Principles of Economic Science. LC 68-30540. (Reprints of Economic Classics Ser.). 244p. 1968. reprint ed. 39.50 (0-678-00446-3) Kelley.

Patten, Simon N. The Economic Basis of Protection. LC 73-2528. (Big Business; Economic Power in a Free Society Ser.). 1973. reprint ed. 15.95 (0-405-05107-7) Ayer.

An Asterisk (*) at the beginning of an entry indicates that the title is appearing for the first time.

— New Basis for Civilization. Fox, Daniel M., ed. LC 68-25622. (John Harvard Library). 267p. 1968. 36.50 (*0-674-60901-8*) HUP.

Patten, Terry. Systemic Text Generation As Problem Solving. (Studies in Natural Language Processing). (Illus.). 230p. 1988. text 49.95 (*0-521-35076-X*) Cambridge U Pr.

Patten, Thomas E. Martin Luther: Reformer or Heretic? 1991. pap. 5.50 (*1-55673-407-7*, 9220) CSS OH.

— The Twisted Cross & Dietrich Bonhoffer. 1992. pap. 5.75 (*1-55673-475-1*, 7925) CSS OH.

Patten, Thomas H. Manpower Planning & the Development of Human Resources. LC 76-137109. 747p. reprint ed. pap. 200.00 (*0-608-13285-3*, 205576000037) Bks Demand.

Patten, W. Wayne. Aces. LC 99-218888. (Illus.). 64p. 1998. pap. 14.95 (*0-89747-394-9*, 6077) Squad Sig Pubns.

Pattenden, G. General & Synthetic Methods, Vol. 11. 1989. 352.00 (*0-85186-924-6*) CRC Pr.

— General & Synthetic Methods, Vol. 12. 1990. 362.00 (*0-85186-934-3*) CRC Pr.

— General & Synthetic Methods, Vol. 13. 1992. 325.00 (*0-85186-944-0*) CRC Pr.

— General & Synthetic Methods Vol. 16, Vol. 1. 620p. 1994. 301.00 (*0-85186-834-7*, R6834) CRC Pr.

— General Synthetic Methods, Vol. 10. 1988. 352.00 (*0-85186-914-9*) CRC Pr.

Pattenden, G., ed. General & Synthetic Methods, Vol. 15. 450p. 1993. 294.00 (*0-85186-974-2*) CRC Pr.

Pattenden, G., jt. auth. see Ansell, M. F.

Pattenden, Rosemary. Criminal Appeals in English Courts 1844-1994. (Oxford Monographs on Criminal Law & Justice). (Illus.). 506p. 1996. text 105.00 (*0-19-825405-9*) OUP.

Pattenden, Rosemary. Judicial Discretion & Criminal Litigation. 2nd ed. 496p. 1990. text 95.00 (*0-19-825567-5*) OUP.

Pattengale, P. K., et al, eds. Lymphoproliferative Diseases: Pathogenesis, Diagnosis, Therapy. (Developments in Oncology Ser.). 1985. text 147.00 (*0-89838-725-6*) Kluwer Academic.

Pattenson, Matthew. The Image of Bothe Churches. LC 78-306350. (English Recusant Literature, 1558-1640 Ser.). 461p. 1977. write for info. (*0-85967-430-4*) Scolar Pr.

Patter, Bruce Van, see Samuels, Aurora & Van Patter, Bruce.

Patterns by Alfreda Staff. Crafts & More Rhyming Instructions & Patterns. 1992. pap. text 21.95 (*0-318-04425-0*) Prosperity & Profits.

— Herbal Quilts: A Rhyming Pattern Reference. 1991. pap. text 9.00 (*0-318-04426-9*) Prosperity & Profits.

— Kimono Fashions Poetry Recital. 1984. pap. text 6.00 (*0-318-04427-7*) Prosperity & Profits.

— Mitten Recycling Pattern, Royal Neck Attire & String Potpourri Pattern Poems. 1984. pap. text 5.00 (*0-318-04428-5*) Prosperity & Profits.

Patterson. Blue Guide Java, Bali & Lombok. 512p. 1999. pap. 23.95 (*0-393-31948-2*) Norton.

— Changing Patient Behavior: Improving Outcomes in Health & Disease Management. 1999. 75.00 (*1-55648-246-9*) AHPI.

— Child Development. 2002. 55.50 (*0-07-234795-3*) McGraw.

Patterson. Commercial Timbers of the World. 1988. 96.95 (*0-291-39718-2*) Ashgate Pub Co.

Patterson. Genetic Disease in Dogs: A Guide to Diagnosis & Control. 288p. (C). (gr. 13). 1999. pap. text 44.95 (*0-8151-4380-X*, 31126) Mosby Inc.

Patterson. An Introduction to Crop Science. 640p. (C). 1997. write for info. (*0-02-391801-2*, Macmillan Coll) P-H.

Patterson, Albion W., ed. see Krishnamurti, Jiddu.

Patterson, Alec & Couraud, Louis, eds. Lung Transplantation, No. 3. LC 94-43203. (Current Topics in General Thoracic Surgery Ser.: Vol. 3). 612p. 1994. 281.50 (*0-444-81567-8*) Elsevier.

Patterson, Alex. A Field Guide to Rock Art Symbols of the Greater Southwest. LC 92-883. (Illus.). 250p. (Orig.). 1992. pap. 15.95 (*1-55566-091-6*) Johnson Bks.

— Hopi Pottery Symbols. LC 94-2295. (Illus.). 308p. 1994. pap. 17.95 (*1-55566-120-3*) Johnson Bks.

— Spike Lee. 248p. (Orig.). 1992. mass mkt. 4.99 (*0-380-76994-8*, Avon Bks) Morrow Avon.

Patterson, Alexander. Other Side of Evolution Its Effect & Fallacy (1903) 178p. 1998. reprint ed. pap. 17.95 (*0-7661-0569-5*) Kessinger Pub.

Patterson, Alexander, et al. Antievolutionism Before World War I. Numbers, Ronald L., ed. & intro. by. LC 94-45044. (Creationism in Twentieth-Century America Ser.: Vol. 1). 424p. 1995. text 83.00 (*0-8153-1802-2*) Garland.

Patterson, Andrew. The Hypocrites: An Epic Novel about the Middle East from 1959-1989. 1994. 19.95 (*0-9641679-0-5*) A Patterson.

Patterson, Andrew R. A Celtic Saga: Whithorn, Iona & Lindisfarne. (C). 1989. pap. 32.00 (*0-7855-6838-7*, Pub. by St Andrew) St Mut.

— A Celtic Saga: Whithorn, Iona & Lindisfarne. (C). 1991. pap. text 45.00 (*86-15-30647-8*, Pub. by St Andrew) St Mut.

— A Celtic Saga: Whithorn, Iona & Lindisfarne. 1993. pap. 21.00 (*0-7152-0647-8*) St Mut.

Patterson, Anita H. From Emerson to King: Democracy, Race, & the Politics of Protest. LC 96-38150. (W. E. B. Dubois Institute Ser.). (Illus.). 272p. 1997. text 52.00 (*0-19-510915-5*) OUP.

Patterson, Anna G., ed. Index to American Reference Books Annual, 1990-1994: A Cumulative Index to Subjects, Authors, & Titles. ix, 288p. 1994. lib. bdg. 65.00 (*1-56308-272-1*) Libs Unl.

Patterson, Annabel. Andrew Marvell. (Writers & Their Work Ser.). 95p. 1996. pap. text 15.00 (*0-7463-0715-2*, Pub. by Northcote House) U Pr of Miss.

— Early Modern Liberalism. LC 96-18733. (Ideas in Context Ser.: Vol. 48). (Illus.). 328p. (C). 1997. text 54.95 (*0-521-59260-7*) Cambridge U Pr.

— Fables of Power: Aesopian Writing & Political Theory. LC 90-46299. (Post-Contemporary Interventions Ser.). (Illus.). 184p. 1991. text 39.95 (*0-8223-1106-2*); pap. text 17.95 (*0-8223-1118-6*) Duke.

***Patterson, Annabel.** Marvell: The Writer in Public Life. LC 99-39930. (Medieval & Renaissance Library Ser.). 280p. (C). 1999. pap. 33.86 (*0-582-35675-X*); text 85.95 (*0-582-35676-8*) Longman.

Patterson, Annabel. Reading Between the Lines. LC 92-50257. 350p. (Orig.). (C). 1993. pap. 19.95 (*0-299-13544-6*); lib. bdg. 50.00 (*0-299-13540-3*) U of Wis Pr.

— Reading Holinshed's Chronicles. LC 93-47629. 359p. (C). 1994. pap. text 16.95 (*0-226-64912-1*); lib. bdg. 43.00 (*0-226-64911-3*) U Ch Pr.

Patterson, Annabel, ed. Roman Images. LC 83-17560. (Selected Papers from the English Institute; 1982-83, New Ser.: Vol. 8). (Illus.). 207p. reprint ed. pap. 64.20 (*0-608-07323-7*, 206755100009) Bks Demand.

Patterson, Annabel, intro. John Milton. LC 92-12385. (Longman Critical Readers Ser.). 248p. (C). 1992. text 52.95 (*0-582-04550-9*, 79370) Longman.

Patterson, Annabel, ed. & intro. see Shakespeare, William.

Patterson, Annabel M. Censorship & Interpretation: The Conditions of Writing & Reading in Early Modern England. LC 84-40156. (Illus.). 296p. 1991. pap. 16.95 (*0-299-09954-7*) U of Wis Pr.

— Hermogenes & the Renaissance: Seven Ideas of Style. LC 70-113006. 256p. 1970. reprint ed. pap. 79.40 (*0-608-03361-8*, 206407300008) Bks Demand.

Patterson, Annette H. Fairbanks Blanket Toss: Your Guide to Bed & Breakfasts in Interior Alaska. LC 93-84312. (ENG & JPN., Illus.). 176p. (Orig.). 1993. pap. text 14.95 (*0-9636113-7-2*) RWPP Pr.

Patterson, Archibald L. Public Pension Administration. 116p. (Orig.). 1982. pap. 9.50 (*0-89854-082-8*) U of GA Inst Govt.

Patterson, B. W. & International Federation of Automatic Control, Tri, eds. Modeling & Control in Biomedical Systems: Proceedings of the International Federation of Automatic Control Symposium, Gavelston, Texas, U. S. A., 27-30 March 1994. LC 94-3756. 598p. 1994. pap. 105.75 (*0-08-042224-1*, Pergamon Pr) Elsevier.

Patterson, Barbara A., ed. see Patterson, William P.

Patterson, Barbara A., ed. see Patterson, William Patrick.

Patterson, Becky. Concentration: Strategies for Attaining Focus. 160p. (C). 1994. pap. text, per. 17.95 (*0-8403-8685-0*) Kendall-Hunt.

Patterson, Becky, jt. auth. see Adams, W. Royce.

Patterson, Ben. Deepening Your Conversation with God: The Life-Changing Power of Prayer, Vol. 7. LC 99-6481. (Pastor's Soul Ser.). 176p. 1999. 16.99 (*1-55661-974-X*) Bethany Hse.

— Waiting: Finding Hope When God Seems Silent. LC 89-15342. 170p. 1990. reprint ed. pap. 10.99 (*0-8308-1296-2*, 1296, Saltshaker Bk) InterVarsity.

— Work. (Christian Basics Bible Studies). 64p. (Orig.). 1994. pap., wbk. ed. 4.99 (*0-8308-2007-8*, 2007) InterVarsity.

— Worship. (Christian Basics Bible Studies). 64p. (Orig.). 1994. pap., wbk. ed. 4.99 (*0-8308-2008-6*, 2008) InterVarsity.

Patterson, Benton R. Write to Be Read: A Practical Guide to Feature Writing. LC 85-31842. 155p. reprint ed. pap. 48.10 (*0-608-09710-1*, 206987600007) Bks Demand.

Patterson, Benton R. & Patterson, Coleman E. The Editor-in-Chief: A Practical Management Guide for Magazine Editors. LC 96-29935. (Illus.). 1997. pap. 29.95 (*0-8138-1084-1*) Iowa St U Pr.

Patterson, Benton Rains. A Reporter's Interview with Jesus. LC 99-57370. 1999. pap. 10.99 (*0-8423-7171-0*) Tyndale Hse.

Patterson, Bessie. A Living Sacrifice. 1985. pap. 6.95 (*0-89137-436-1*) Quality Pubns.

— The Wise Woman Builds Her House. 1979. pap. 6.95 (*0-89137-413-2*) Quality Pubns.

— The Wise Woman Knows. 1982. 6.95 (*0-89137-422-1*) Quality Pubns.

— Wisely Train the Younger Women. 1973. pap. 6.95 (*0-89137-406-X*) Quality Pubns.

Patterson, Bette. Physicalizing FE Principle. 44p. 1994. pap. text, per. 9.95 (*0-9643532-0-2*) Teel & Co.

Patterson, Betty. Index to "Memorial & Genealogical Record of Dodge & Jefferson Counties, Wis.", 1894. 15p. (Orig.). 1984. pap. 5.00 (*0-910255-44-X*) Wisconsin Gen.

Patterson, Betty, ed. Some Pioneer Families of Wisconsin, Vol 2. 139p. 1988. pap. 8.00 (*0-910255-49-0*) Wisconsin Gen.

Patterson, Betty, rev. Index to Names in the Portrait & Biographical Record of Waukesha County, Wisconsin, 1894. rev. ed. 42p. 1990. pap. 6.00 (*0-910255-51-2*) Wisconsin Gen.

Patterson, Beverly B. The Sound of the Dove: Singing in Appalachian Primitive Baptist Churches. 1995. 45.00 incl. audio, digital audio (*0-252-02174-6*); text 37.50 (*0-252-02123-1*) U of Ill Pr.

Patterson, Bob E. Who Is Jesus Christ? 128p. 1996. pap. 13.00 (*1-57312-027-8*) Smyth & Helwys.

Patterson, Brad & Patterson, Kathryn, compiled by. New Zealand. (World Bibliographic Ser.: Vol. 18). 416p. 1998. lib. bdg. 98.00 (*1-85109-279-X*) ABC-CLIO.

***Patterson, Bradley H., Jr.** The White House Staff: Inside the West Wing & Beyond. 448p. 2000. 30.00 (*0-8157-6950-4*) Brookings.

Patterson, Brian. Fresh! Seeds from the Past & Food for Tomorrow. 1999. pap. text 14.95 (*1-86448-735-6*, Pub. by Allen & Unwin Pty) IPG Chicago.

Patterson, Bruce. Canadians on Everest. (Illus.). 241p. 1990. text 29.95 (*1-55059-015-4*) Temeron Bks.

Patterson, Bruce D., jt. ed. see Goodman, Steven M.

***Patterson, Bruce K., ed.** Techniques in Quantification & Localization of Gene Expression. LC 99-27046. (Illus.). 200p. 1999. 100.00 (*0-8176-4034-7*, Pub. by Birkhauser) Spr-Verlag.

Patterson, Bruce L. The Lurleen B. Wallace Foundation: A Legacy of Love. (Illus.). 128p. (Orig.). 1996. pap. 9.95 (*0-9652910-0-6*) Comprehen Cancer.

Patterson, Bryan. Early Cretaceous Mammals & the Evolution of Mammalian Molar Teeth. LC 57-979. (Chicago Natural History Museum, Publication 809, Fieldiana, Anthropology Ser.: Vol. 13, No. 1). 107p. reprint ed. pap. 33.20 (*0-608-03776-1*, 206461800009) Bks Demand.

Patterson, C. H. Plato's the Republic Notes. (Cliffs Notes Ser.). 80p. 1963. pap. 4.95 (*0-8220-1129-8*, Cliff) IDG Bks.

— Rehabilitation Counseling: Collected Papers. 1969. pap. 7.80 (*0-87563-015-4*) Stipes.

Patterson, C. H., et al, eds. Epioptics: Linear & Nonlinear Optical Spectroscopy of Surfaces & Interfaces. LC 95-37998. (ESPRIT Basic Research Ser.). 248p. 1995. 64.00 (*3-540-59410-8*) Spr-Verlag.

Patterson, C. H. & Hidore, Suzanne C. Successful Psychotherapy: A Caring, Loving Relationship. LC 95-52030. 280p. 1997. 40.00 (*1-56821-795-1*) Aronson.

Patterson, C. H. & Moses, H. Readings in Rehabilitation Counseling. 1971. pap. 8.60 (*0-87563-034-0*) Stipes.

Patterson, C. H. & Watkins, C. Edward, Jr. Theories of Psychotherapy. 5th ed. LC 95-17191. 608p. (C). 1997. pap. text 75.00 (*0-673-99103-2*) Addson-Wesley Educ.

Patterson, C. H., jt. auth. see Moses, H.

Patterson, C. Stuart, et al. Principles of Chemistry. LC 66-28993. (Illus.). (C). 1967. 40.00 (*0-89197-530-6*) Irvington.

Patterson, Caleb P. The Constitutional Principles of Thomas Jefferson. LC 77-157352. (Select Bibliographies Reprint Ser.). 1977. reprint ed. 24.95 (*0-8369-5813-6*) Ayer.

Patterson, Calvin, Jr. First Step for High School Students. 144p. (YA). (gr. 9-12). 1997. pap. 9.95 (*0-9661722-0-5*) Patterson Pub.

Patterson, Carol. The Business of Ecotourism: The Complete Guide for Eco-Sensitive Tourism Providers. LC 97-60449. (Illus.). 208p. (Orig.). 1997. pap. 24.95 incl. disk (*1-879432-25-0*) Explorers Guide Pub.

— The Cash Producer. 118p. 1995. pap. text 14.95 (*0-9648317-0-8*) Patterson CA.

Patterson, Carol, ed. see Hollis, Claire & Hollis, Paul.

Patterson, Carol B., ed. see Hollis, Paul & Hollis, Claire.

Patterson, Carol Cushard, jt. auth. see McWilliams, Jane Wilson.

Patterson, Carole & Ruffin, Clyde. Commitment: Fatherhood in Black America. LC 97-22908. (Illus.). 128p. 1998. pap. 19.95 (*0-8262-1157-7*) U of Mo Pr.

Patterson, Carolyn B. Of Lands, Legends & Laughter: The Search for Adventure with National Geographic. LC 98-18616. (Illus.). 224p. 1998. 28.95 (*1-55591-332-5*) Fulcrum Pub.

***Patterson, Catherine M.** Urban Patronage in Early Modern England: Corporate Boroughs, The Landed Elite, & The Crown, 15. LC 99-35537. 1999. 60.00 (*0-8047-3587-5*) Stanford U Pr.

Patterson, Ce C., ed. see Loughrin, Judy.

Patterson, Charles. Animal Rights. LC 92-44286. (Illus.). 112p (YA). (gr. 6 up). 1993. lib. bdg. 20.95 (*0-89490-468-X*) Enslow Pubs.

— The Civil Rights Movement. LC 95-3027. (Social Reform Movements Ser.). 144p. (YA). (gr. 7-12). 1995. 19.95 (*0-8150-2968-7*) Facts on File.

— Down with Lawyer Power... Let's Get America Back on Track. LC 93-72960. 284p. 1994. pap. 7.95 (*0-9637926-5-2*) Comm for Pract IPD.

— Eating Disorders. LC 94-32116. (Teen Hotline Ser.). 80p. (J). (gr. 6-7). 1995. lib. bdg. 25.68 (*0-8114-3813-9*) Raintree Steck-V.

— Hafiz Al-Asad of Syria. (Illus.). 128p. (YA). (gr. 8 up). 1991. pap. 7.95 (*0-671-69469-3*); lib. bdg. 13.95 (*0-671-69468-5*, Julian Messner) Silver Burdett Pr.

Patterson, Charles. The Oxford 50th Anniversary Book of the United Nations. (Illus.). 240p. (YA). (gr. 7 up). 1995. 40.00 (*0-19-508280-X*) OUP.

Patterson, Charles B. New Thought Essays. 103p. 1997. pap. 9.00 (*0-89540-271-8*, SB-271) Sun Pub.

— The Will to Be Well. 255p. 1997. pap. 20.00 (*0-89540-275-0*, SB-275) Sun Pub.

Patterson, Charles H. Cliffs Notes on the Bible. (Cliffs Notes Ser.). 228p. 1999. pap. 9.95 (*0-8220-0236-1*, Cliff) IDG Bks.

— Moral Standards: An Introduction to Ethics. 2nd ed. LC 57-6801. 545p. reprint ed. pap. 169.00 (*0-608-30263-5*, 201252300081) Bks Demand.

— New Testament Notes. (Cliffs Notes Ser.). 104p. 1965. pap. 4.95 (*0-8220-0880-7*, Cliff) IDG Bks.

— Old Testament Notes. (Cliffs Notes Ser.). 96p. 1965. pap. 4.95 (*0-8220-0949-8*, Cliff) IDG Bks.

— Plato's Euthyphro, Apology, Crito & Phaedo Notes. (Cliffs Notes Ser.). 64p. (Orig.). 1975. pap. text 4.95 (*0-8220-1044-5*, Cliff) IDG Bks.

Patterson, Charles L., Jr. The Daemonic in the Poetry of John Keats. LC 71-94399. 1970. 20.00 (*0-252-00079-X*) Lib Soc Sci.

Patterson, Charles J. & Tippin, G. Lee. The Heroes Who Fell from Grace: The True Story of Operation Lazarus, the Attempt to Free American POWs from Laos in 1982. (Illus.). 319p. 1998. reprint ed. pap. text 17.00 (*0-7881-5578-4*) DIANE Pub.

Patterson, Charles W. Psychotherapy: The Mystery Solved. LC 84-61941. 118p. (Orig.). 1984. pap. 8.00 (*0-9614334-1-8*) Passages.

— Psychotherapy: The Mystery Solved. 2nd ed. LC 95-68732. 187p. (Orig.). 1995. pap. text 17.95 (*0-9614334-3-4*) Passages.

Patterson, Charlotte J. & D'Augelli, Anthony R., eds. Lesbian, Gay, & Bisexual Identities in Families: Psychological Perspectives. LC 97-44736. 320p. 1998. pap. 29.95 (*0-19-511050-1*); text 60.00 (*0-19-511049-8*) OUP.

Patterson, Charlotte J., jt. ed. see D'Augelli, Anthony R.

Patterson, Christopher S. United States & the States under the Constitution. LC 97-1955. xxxi, 290p. 1997. reprint ed. 45.00 (*0-8377-2559-3*, Rothman) W S Hein.

Patterson, Clair C., jt. auth. see Gilfillan, S. Colum.

Patterson, Claire. It's OK to Be You: A Frank & Funny Guide to Growing Up. LC 94-17791. (Illus.). 70p. (J). (gr. 3-7). 1994. pap. 8.95 (*1-883672-16-3*) Tricycle Pr.

— Let's Celebrate Math. (Illus.). 80p. 1991. pap. 4.95 (*0-9623835-6-2*, CLC0053) Pieces of Lrning.

Patterson, Cleveland S. The Cost of Capital: Theory & Estimation. LC 94-32081. 344p. 1995. 79.50 (*0-89930-862-7*, Quorum Bks) Greenwood.

Patterson, Coleman E., jt. auth. see Patterson, Benton R.

Patterson, Colin. Evolution. 2nd ed. LC 98-41312. 1999. 39.95 (*0-8014-3642-7*) Cornell U Pr.

— Evolution. 2nd ed. LC 98-41312. (Illus.). 1999. pap. 18.95 (*0-8014-8594-0*) Cornell U Pr.

Patterson, Colin & Johnson, G. David. The Intermuscular Bones & Ligaments of Teleostean Fishes. LC 94-10700. (Smithsonian Contributions to Zoology Ser.: Vol. 559). 93p. 1995. reprint ed. pap. 30.00 (*0-608-00510-X*, 206133000008) Bks Demand.

Patterson, Collis D. Dr. Samuel L. Banks Speaks: Selected Writings from 1990-1995. 114p. 1997. pap. 19.95 (*0-9661980-0-X*) C D Patterson.

Patterson, Cynthia. Pericles' Citizenship Law of 451-450 B. C. 25.00 (*0-405-14046-0*) Ayer.

— Pericles' Citizenship Law of 451-450 B. C. 1981. 27.95 (*0-88143-022-6*) Ayer.

Patterson, Cynthia. Second Changes. mass mkt. 5.99 (*1-896329-88-8*) Picasso Publ.

Patterson, Cynthia B. The Family in Greek History. LC 98-9295. 304p. 1999. 35.00 (*0-674-29270-7*) HUP.

Patterson, D. H., jt. auth. see Brenes, Edin.

Patterson, D. J., jt. auth. see Corliss, J. O.

Patterson, D. L. Self Assessment Picture Tests: Clinical Cardiology. 2nd ed. 1997. pap. 15.95 (*0-7234-2591-4*, Pub. by Martin Dunitz) Mosby Inc.

Patterson, D. W. Holmes. Letter of Directions to His Father's Birthplace, by John Holmesm with Notes & a Genealogy. 76p. 1997. reprint ed. pap. 15.00 (*0-8328-9190-8*); reprint ed. lib. bdg. 25.00 (*0-8328-9189-4*) Higginson Bk Co.

Patterson, D. Williams. Brockway Family, Descendants of Wolston Brockway. (Illus.). 167p. 1989. reprint ed. pap. 34.00 (*0-8328-0327-8*); reprint ed. lib. bdg. 44.00 (*0-8328-0326-X*) Higginson Bk Co.

***Patterson, Dale.** What Time of Day Was That? History by the Minute. 2000. pap. 17.95 (*1-55041-123-3*, Pub. by Fitzhenry & W Ltd) Genl Dist Srvs.

Patterson, Dan. Artificial Neural Networks. (Prentice Hall Series in Advanced Communications). 400p. 1998. pap. 58.00 (*0-13-295353-6*) P-H.

— Lancaster: RAF Heavy Bomber. LC 96-75272. (Living History Ser.: No. 4). (Illus.). 64p. 1996. pap. 15.95 (*1-57427-052-4*) Howell Pr VA.

Patterson, Dan, photos by. Full Power: Aircraft Engines That Made History. (Illus.). 144p. 2000. 39.95 (*1-57427-080-X*) Howell Pr VA.

— The Lady: Boeing B-17 Flying Fortress. (Living History Ser.: No. 1). (Illus.). 67p. 1993. pap. 15.95 (*0-943231-58-2*) Howell Pr VA.

— Messerschmitt BF-109: Luftwaffe Fighter. LC 97-73124. (Living History Ser.: No. 5). (Illus.). 64p. 1997. pap. 15.95 (*1-57427-054-0*) Howell Pr VA.

— Mustang: North American P-51. (Living History Ser.: No. 3). (Illus.). 64p. 1995. pap. 15.95 (*0-943231-75-2*) Howell Pr VA.

— The Soldier: Consolidated B-24 Liberator. LC 93-79037. (Living History Ser.: No. 2). (Illus.). 64p. 1993. pap. 15.95 (*0-943231-61-2*) Howell Pr VA.

— Thunderbolt: Republic P-47. (Living History Ser.: No. 7). (Illus.). 64p. 1999. pap. 15.95 (*1-57427-053-2*) Howell Pr VA.

Patterson, Dan & Dick, Ron, eds. American Eagles: A History of the United States Air Force. 456p. 1997. 160.00 (*1-86227-041-4*, Pub. by Spellmnt Pubs) St Mut.

Patterson, Dan & Merva, George E. Shoo-Shoo Baby: A Lucky Lady of the Sky. (Illus.). 1988. pap. 10.00 (*0-9622271-0-2*) Patterson Productions.

Patterson, Daniel, ed. see Cooper, Susan F.

Patterson, Daniel W. Gift Drawing & Gift Song: A Study of Two Forms of Shaker Inspiration. (Illus.). xii, 112p. (Orig.). 1983. 34.95 (*0-915836-17-3*); pap. 24.95 (*0-318-32857-7*) United Soc Shakers.

***Patterson, Daniel W.** A Tree Accurst: Bobby McMillon & Stories of Frankie Silver. (Illus.). 264p. 2000. pap. 18.95 (*0-8078-4873-5*); lib. bdg. 49.95 (*0-8078-2564-6*) U of NC Pr.

Patterson, Daniel W., ed. Sounds of the South. LC 91-30427. (Illus.). 219p. 1991. pap. text 16.95 (*0-8223-1343-X*) Duke.

Patterson, Daniel W. & Zugg, Charles G., III, eds. Arts in Earnest: North Carolina Folklife. LC 89-1212. (Illus.). 324p. (Orig.). 1989. text 54.95 (*0-8223-0943-2*); pap. text 23.95 (*0-8223-1021-X*) Duke.

Patterson, Daryl N. More Than Legend. 238p. 1995. pap. 9.95 (*0-9646761-0-9*) Cabin Bks.

P

Patterson, David. The Affirming Flame: Religion, Language, Literature. LC 87-30026. (Illus.). 192p. 1988. 34.95 (0-8061-2109-2) U of Okla Pr.
— Along New Mexico's Continental Divide Trail. (Illus.). 144p. 2000. pap. 24.95 (1-56579-346-3) Westcliffe Pubs.
— Along the Edge of Annihilation: The Collapse & Recovery of Life in the Holocaust Diary. LC 98-43862. 328p. 1999. 35.00 (0-295-97782-5); pap. 19.95 (0-295-97783-3) U of Wash Pr.
— Exile: The Sense of Alienation in Modern Russian Letters. LC 94-16230. 224p. 1994. 29.95 (0-8131-1888-3) U Pr of Ky.
— The Greatest Jewish Stories Ever Told. LC 97-11943. 1997. 24.95 (0-8246-0399-0) Jonathan David.
— Greatest Jewish Stories Ever Told. 1998. pap. text 16.95 (0-8246-0409-1) Jonathan David.
— The Hebrew Novel in Czarist Russia: A Portrait of Jewish Life in the Nineteenth Century LC 98-44399. 320p. 1998. 21.95 (0-8476-9339-2) Rowman.
***Patterson, David.** Hebrew Novel In Czarist Russia: A Portrait of Jewish Life in the Nineteenth Century. LC 98-44399. 320p. 1998. 55.00 (0-8476-9338-4) Rowman.
— John Cage: Music, Philosophy & Intention, 1933-1950. (Studies in Contemporary Music & Culture Ser.). (Illus.). 2000. 70.00 (0-8153-2995-4) Garland.
Patterson, David. Literature & Spirit: Essays on Bakhtin & His Contemporaries. LC 88-9743. 176p. 1988. 23.00 (0-8131-1647-3) U Pr of Ky.
— A Phoenix with Fetters: Studies in 19th & Early 20th Century Hebrew Fiction. (Oxford Centre for Postgraduate Hebrew Studies). 200p. 1988. 55.00 (0-8476-7564-5) Rowman.
— Pilgrimage of a Proselyte: From Auschwitz to Jerusalem. LC 93-13626. 207 p. 1993. 19.95 (0-8246-0363-X) Jonathan David.
— The Shriek of Silence: A Phenomenology of the Holocaust Novel. LC 91-17269. 192p. 1992. text 25.00 (0-8131-1768-2) U Pr of Ky.
— Sun Turned to Darkness: Memory & Recovery in the Holocaust Memoir. LC 98-24320. 1998. 34.95 (0-8156-0530-7) Syracuse U Pr.
— The Way of the Child. LC 86-83410. 280p. (Orig.). Date not set. pap. 12.95 (0-89896-168-8) Larksdale.
— When Learned Men Murder. LC 95-71479. (Illus.). 181p. 1996. 32.00 (0-87367-484-7) Phi Delta Kappa.
***Patterson, David & Berger, Alan L.** Encyclopedia of Holocaust Literature. 240p. 2001. text 55.00 (1-57356-257-2) Oryx Pr.
Patterson, David & Spicehandler, Ezra, trs. Random Harvest: The Novellas of C. N. Bialik. LC 99-10677. 320p. 1999. 28.00 (0-8133-6711-5, Pub. by Westview) HarpC.
Patterson, David & Wiesel, Elie. In Dialogue & Dilemma with Elie Wiesel. LC 91-3489. 1992. text 30.00 (0-89341-674-6, Longwood Academic) Hollowbrook.
Patterson, David, jt. auth. see Hassold, Terry J.
Patterson, David, jt. auth. see Rock, Joe.
Patterson, David, ed. see Bradley, Pamela.
Patterson, David, ed. & tr. see Tolstoy, Leo.
Patterson, David, tr. see Dostoyevsky, Fyodor.
Patterson, David, tr. see Shamir, Moshe.
Patterson, David, tr. & intro. see Tolstoy, Leo.
***Patterson, David A.** Personal Computer Applications in the Social Services. LC 99-31864. (Illus.). 335p. 1999. pap. 36.00 (0-205-28537-6) P-H.
Patterson, David A. & Hennessy, John L. Computer Architecture: A Quantitative Approach. 2nd ed. LC 95-37027. 760p. 1998. text 83.95 (1-55860-329-8) Morgan Kaufmann.
— Computer Organization & Design: The Hardware/Software Interface. 2nd ed. LC 97-16050. 900p. 1998. text 79.95 (1-55860-428-6) Morgan Kaufmann.
Patterson, David A., et al. Computing Unbound: Using Computers in the Arts & Sciences. 400p. (C). 1988. pap. text 54.25 (0-393-95664-4) Norton.
Patterson, David J. Free-Living Freshwater Protozoa: A Color Guide. (Illus.). 223p. 1996. pap. 59.95 (0-86840-327-X, Pub. by New South Wales Univ Pr) Intl Spec Bk.
— Free-Living Freshwater Protozoa: A Colour Guide. LC 96-38713. (Illus.). 223p. 1996. pap. text 49.95 (0-470-23567-5) Halsted Pr.
— Living Freshwater Protozoa. 1992. 88.00 (0-8493-7735-8, QL366) CRC Pr.
Patterson, David J. & Corliss, John O., eds. Progress in Protistology. (Illus.). 299p. 1989. 70.00 (0-948737-08-5, Pub. by Biopress) Balogh.
Patterson, David J. & Larsen, Jacob, eds. The Biology of Free-Living Heterotrophic Flagellates. (Systematics Association Special Volume Ser.: VOL. 45). (Illus.). 520p. 1992. 140.00 (0-19-857747-8) OUP.
Patterson, David S. Toward a Warless World: The Travail of the American Peace Movement, 1887-1914. LC 75-28916. 350p. reprint ed. pap. 108.50 (0-608-13208-X, 205605000044) Bks Demand.
Patterson, David S., ed. Foreign Relations of the United States, 1964-1968 Vol. 9: International Development & Economic Defense Policy; Commodities. 1997. boxed set 46.00 (0-16-048300-X) USGPO.
Patterson, David S., jt. auth. see Schwar, Harriet D.
Patterson, David S., jt. ed. see Glennon, John P.
Patterson, Debbie, jt. auth. see Ganderton, Lucinda.
Patterson, Deborah, jt. auth. see Evelegh, Tessa.
Patterson, Debra. Macroeconomics: An Integrated Approach, Study Guide to Accompany. 2nd ed. (Illus.). 171p. 1998. pap. text, student ed. 16.95 (0-262-66146-2) MIT Pr.
Patterson, Debra, ed. see Wyman, J. N.
Patterson, Denise, jt. auth. see Kalfayan, Garo.
Patterson, Dennis. Law & Truth. (Illus.). 200p. 1996. text 49.95 (0-19-508323-7) OUP.
— Law & Truth. (Illus.). 200p. 1999. pap. 18.95 (0-19-513247-5) OUP.
— Postmodernism & Law. Campbell, Tom D., ed. (International Library of Essays in Law & Legal Theory). 500p. (C). 1994. lib. bdg. 150.00 (0-8147-6550-5) NYU Pr.
Patterson, Dennis, ed. A Companion to Philosophy of Law & Legal Theory. (Blackwell Companions to Philosophy Ser.). 450p. 1999. reprint ed. pap. 34.95 (0-631-21329-5) Blackwell Pubs.
***Patterson, Dennis, ed.** Philosophy of Law & Legal Theory: An Anthology. (Philosophy Anthologies Ser.). 600p. 1999. 79.95 (0-631-20287-0); pap. 39.95 (0-631-20288-9) Blackwell Pubs.
Patterson, Dennis, ed. A Companion to the Philosophy of Law & Legal Theory. LC 95-46024. (Companions to Philosophy Ser.). 624p. (C). 1993. 89.95 (1-55786-535-3) Blackwell Pubs.
Patterson, Dennis, jt. auth. see White, Jefferson.
Patterson, Dennis J. Indexing Managed Care. LC 97-29562. 225p. 1997. 50.00 (0-7863-1067-7, Irwn Prfssnl) McGraw-Hill Prof.
Patterson, Dennis M. Lender Liability: Definitions - Theories - Applications. 350p. 1990. boxed set 75.00 (0-88063-279-8, 81394-10, MICHIE) LEXIS Pub.
Patterson, Diane A. The Computer Documentation Kit. 176p. 24.95 (0-685-09668-8) P-H.
Patterson, Dianne, jt. auth. see Greenberg, Barbara R.
Patterson, Don. A Child's Trip to Christmas in Santa Fe: A Photographic Documentary. LC 91-62868. (Illus.). 120p. (J). (gr. k-3). 1991. 29.95 (0-9629093-2-7) MyndSeye.
***Patterson, Don.** Fighter Escort. Parenteau, Mary, ed. (Tales of the RAF Ser.). (Illus.). 92p. (J). (gr. 3-8). 1999. pap. 7.95 (1-929031-09-2) Hindsight Ltd.
Patterson, Don. Scramble! Parenteau, Mary, ed. (Tales of the RAF Ser.). (Illus.). 72p. (J). (gr. 3-8). 1999. per. 7.95 (1-929031-00-9) Hindsight Ltd.
— Ski Vacation. (Illus.). 40p. (J). (gr. k-6). 1991. 13.95 (0-9629093-3-5) MyndSeye.
***Patterson, Don.** Spitfire! Parenteau, Mary, ed. (Tales of the RAF Ser.). (Illus.). 104p. (J). (gr. 3-8). 2000. per. 7.95 (1-929031-18-1) Hindsight Ltd.
Patterson, Don. Virginia Democrats: A Photographic Portrait. LC 91-61019. (Illus.). 144p. 1991. 34.95 (0-9629093-0-0); pap. 24.95 (0-9629093-1-9) MyndSeye.
Patterson, Don, jt. auth. see Liskevych, Terry.
Patterson, Donald E., jt. auth. see Frank, James A.
***Patterson, Donald L.** One Handed: A Guide to Piano Music for One Hand, 80. LC 99-36260. (Music Reference Collection). 336p. 1999. lib. bdg. 75.00 (0-313-31179-X, Greenwood Pr) Greenwood.
Patterson, Donald L. & Patterson, Janet L. Vincent Persichetti: A Bio-Bibliography, 16. LC 88-25084. (Bio-Bibliographies in Music Ser.: No. 16). 352p. 1988. lib. bdg. 69.50 (0-313-25334-X, PPE/, Greenwood Pr) Greenwood.
***Patterson, Donald W.** Creating Watercolor Landscapes Using Photographs. LC 99-53782. (Illus.). 128p. 2000. 27.99 (0-89134-973-1, North Lght Bks) F & W Pubns Inc.
***Patterson, Dorothy.** Be Attitudes for Women. 176p. 2000. pap. 9.99 (0-8054-2062-2) Broadman.
Patterson, Dorothy K. A Woman Seeking God. 1992. pap. 12.99 (0-8054-5351-2, 4253-51) Broadman.
***Patterson, Douglas M. & Ashley, Richard A.** A Nonlinear Time Series Workshop. LC 99-46691. (Dynamic Modeling & Econometrics in Economics & Finance Ser.). 1999. write for info. (0-7923-8674-4) Kluwer Academic.
Patterson, Douglas O., ed. Best Practices: How to Avoid Surprises in the World's Most Complicated Technical Process, the Transition from Development to Production. (NAVSO Ser.: No. P-6071). (Illus.). 326p. 1986. pap. 25.00 (0-16-002100-6, S/N 008-050-002) USGPO.
Patterson, Durel R. It's Just the Way I Feel. 56p. 1997. 10.00 (0-8059-4191-6) Dorrance.
Patterson, E. Britt, jt. ed. see Lynch, Michael J.
Patterson, E. M. Great Northern Railway of Ireland. 188p. (C). 1985. 60.00 (0-85361-343-5) St Mut.
Patterson, E. M., tr. see Berge, Claude.
Patterson, Edward. The Pug: An Owner's Guide to a Happy, Healthy Pet. (Illus.). 1996. 12.95 (0-87605-496-3) Howell Bks.
Patterson, Elizabeth B., ed. Saint Francis & the Poet. 163p. 11.95 (0-8159-6802-7) Devin.
Patterson, Elizabeth C. Mary Somerville & the Cultivation of Science, 1815-1840. (International Archives of the History of Ideas Ser.: No. 102). 278p. 1983. lib. bdg. 126.50 (90-247-2823-1) Kluwer Academic.
— Mary Somerville & the Cultivation of Science, 1815-1848. 1983. lib. bdg. 39.50 (90-247-2433-3) Kluwer Academic.
Patterson, Ella. For Women Who Live Alone: A Woman's Guide to Safety. Alle, Sejon, ed. LC 94-75720. 425p. (YA). (gr. 7-12). 1999. lib. bdg. 20.00 (1-884331-31-9, Pub. by Knowledge Concepts) Herveys Bklink.
— Higher Expectations: 12 Steps to Unlimited Success. LC 95-95109. 300p. 1999. pap. 17.95 (1-884331-12-2, Pub. by Knowledge Concepts) Herveys Bklink.
— 1001 Reasons to Think Positive. LC 96-29540. 1997. pap. 10.00 (0-684-83020-5, Fireside) S&S Trade Pap.
— Will the Real Women . . . Please Stand Up! Uncommon Sense about Sex, Sensuality & Self-Discovery. 240p. 1997. per. 12.00 (0-684-83151-1) S&S Trade Pap.
Patterson, Ella M. Easy Alternatives to Healthy Eating: Cookbook. Alle, Sekpm, ed. (Illus.). 450p. 1999. pap. 24.95 (1-884331-26-2, Pub. by Knowledge Concepts) Herveys Bklink.
— For Women Who Live Alone: A Woman's Guide to Safety. Ennix, Lucille & Alle, Sejon, eds. LC 94-75720. 425p. (YA). (gr. 7-12). 1999. 17.95 (1-884331-02-5, 1884331-025) Knowledge Concepts.
— One Thousand Reasons to Think: Special Insights to Achieve a Better Life. LC 94-75365. (Illus.). 200p. (J). (ps-12). 1993. 10.00 (1-884331-00-9) Knowledge Concepts.
— Will the Real Men Please Stand Up! A Nine Step Plan for Lasting Romance & Passion. LC 95-94104. (Illus.). 286p. 2000. pap. 19.95 (1-884331-11-4, Pub. by Knowledge Concepts) ACCESS Pubs Network.
— Will the Real Women... Please Stand Up! Uncommon Sense on Etuquette & Sensuality. 4th rev. ed. Ennix, Lucille & Whaley, Marvin, eds. LC 94-75061. (Illus.). 215p. (C). 1999. reprint ed. 14.95 (1-884331-01-7) Knowledge Concepts.
— A Woman with a Past: Novel. LC 95-95111. 300p. 1999. 14.95 (1-884331-09-2, 1884331092) Knowledge Concepts.
Patterson, Ella M., jt. auth. see Jones, Herbert L., Jr.
Patterson, Ellen T., jt. auth. see Freda, Margaret Comerford.
Patterson, Emma L. Peekskill in the American Revolution. (Illus.). 184p. 1997. reprint ed. lib. bdg. 26.50 (0-8328-6201-0) Higginson Bk Co.
Patterson, Ernest M. & Wilkins, Mira, eds. America's Changing Investment Market. LC 76-29983. (European Business Ser.). (Illus.). 1977. reprint ed. lib. bdg. 31.95 (0-405-09748-4) Ayer.
Patterson, Ernest M., jt. auth. see Conway, Thomas, Jr.
Patterson, Ernestine, ed. see Hill, Luella.
Patterson, F. W. Los Evangelicos Frente al Siglo Veintiuno. (SPA.). 160p. (Orig.). 1992. pap. 4.99 (0-311-29012-4, Edit Mundo) Casa Bautista.
Patterson, Francine. Colloquial Spanish. 1979. pap. 13.95 (0-415-05908-9) Routledge.
***Patterson, Francine.** Koko Love! Conversations with a Signing Gorilla, 1. 32p. (J). (gr. 2-4). 1999. 14.99 (0-525-46319-4, Dutton Child) Peng Put Young Read.
Patterson, Francine. Koko's Kitten. (Illus.). 32p. (J). (gr. k-4). 1985. pap. 14.95 (0-590-40952-2) Scholastic Inc.
— Koko's Kitten. LC 85-2311. 32p. (J). (gr. 2 up). 1987. pap. 4.99 (0-590-44425-5) Scholastic Inc.
Patterson, Francine. Koko's Kitten. (Reading Rainbow Bks.). (J). 1985. 10.19 (0-606-02299-6, Pub. by Turtleback) Demco.
— Koko's Kitten. (Illus.). (J). 1999. 12.25 (0-8085-8825-7) Econo-Clad Bks.
Patterson, Francine. Koko's Story. (J). 1988. 10.90 (0-606-04021-8, Pub. by Turtleback) Demco.
Patterson, Frank A. Middle English Penitential Lyric. LC 11-26002. reprint ed. 31.50 (0-404-04908-7) AMS Pr.
Patterson, Frank E., 3rd. Afghanistan, Its Twentieth Century Postal Issues. (Illus.). 208p. 1965. 18.00 (0-912574-18-6, HE6185,A32P3) Collectors.
Patterson, Frank W. A Short History of Christian Missions. 176p. 1985. pap. 12.50 (0-311-72663-1) Casa Bautista.
Patterson, Franklin K. Colleges in Consort: Institutional Cooperation Through Consortia. LC 73-20964. (Jossey-Bass Higher Education Ser.). 200p. reprint ed. pap. 62.00 (0-608-14794-X, 202566600045) Bks Demand.
Patterson, Frederick C. A Systems Approach to Recreation Programming. LC 87-12682. (Illus.). 181p. (C). 1991. reprint ed. pap. text 15.95 (0-88133-593-2) Waveland Pr.
Patterson, Freeman. Namaqualand: Garden of the Gods. 2nd ed. (Illus.). 128p. 1984. 35.00 (0-919493-37-8) Firefly Bks Ltd.
— Photographing the World Around You: A Visual Design Workshop. (Illus.). 168p. 1994. pap. 18.95 (1-55013-590-2) Firefly Bks Ltd.
— Photography & the Art of Seeing. rev. ed. LC 89-93254. (Illus.). 156p. 1985. pap. 17.95 (1-55013-099-4) Firefly Bks Ltd.
Patterson, Freeman. Photography for the Joy of It. rev. ed. (Illus.). 168p. 1986. pap. 17.95 (1-55013-095-1) Firefly Bks Ltd.
Patterson, Freeman. Photography of Natural Things. (Illus.). 168p. 1989. pap. 17.95 (1-55013-097-8) Firefly Bks Ltd.
— Shadowlight. 1998. pap. 35.00 (0-00-638656-3) HarpC.
Patterson, Freeman, jt. auth. see Canadian Nature Federation Staff.
Patterson, G. The State of Biodiversity in Lake Tanganyika: A Literature Review. 1998. pap. 60.00 (0-85954-492-3, Pub. by Nat Res Inst) St Mut.
Patterson, G. A. Basic Fluid System Analysis: With HP-25 & SR-56 Pocket Calculator Programs. LC 76-21585. 95p. 1977. 12.95 (0-917410-00-9) Basic Sci Pr.
— Energy Analysis with a Pocket Calculator. 2nd ed. LC 77-88128. (Illus.). 138p. 1981. pap. 16.95 (0-917410-04-1) Basic Sci Pr.
— Engine Thermodynamics with a Pocket Calculator. 2nd ed. 149p. 1983. pap. 14.95 (0-917410-07-6) Basic Sci Pr.
Patterson, G. D. Physical Chemistry of Macromolecules. (Illus.). Date not set. text. write for info. (0-8247-9467-2) Dekker.
Patterson, G. E. Tug. LC 98-88483. 71p. 1999. pap. 12.95 (1-55597-285-3, Pub. by Graywolf) SPD-Small Pr Dist.
Patterson, G. R., jt. auth. see Capaldi, D.
Patterson, Gareth. With My Soul Amongst Lions. large type ed. (Ulverscroft Large Print Ser.). (Illus.). 384p. 1997. 27.99 (0-7089-3740-3) Ulverscroft.
Patterson, Gary K., jt. ed. see Ulbrecht, Jaromir J.
Patterson, Geoffrey. All about Bread. (Illus.). 32p. (J). (gr. 3). 1996. pap. 9.95 (0-85236-321-4, Pub. by Farming Pr) Diamond Farm Bk.
— Dairy Farming. (Illus.). 32p. (J). (gr. 3). 1996. pap. 9.95 (0-85236-323-0, Pub. by Farming Pr) Diamond Farm Bk.
— The Lion & the Gypsy. (J). 1990. 14.95 (0-385-44521-0) Doubleday.
— The Naughty Boy & the Strawberry Horse. (Illus.). 32p. (J). (gr. 1-3). 1997. 19.95 (0-09-176547-1, Pub. by Hutchinson) Trafalgar.
— The Story of Hay. (Illus.). 32p. (J). (gr. 3). 1996. pap. 9.95 (0-85236-324-9, Pub. by Farming Pr) Diamond Farm Bk.
— The Story of Wool. (Illus.). 32p. (J). (gr. 3). 1996. pap. 9.95 (0-85236-322-2, Pub. by Farming Pr) Diamond Farm Bk.
— The Working Horse. (Illus.). 32p. (Orig.). (J). (gr. 3). 1996. pap. 9.95 (0-85236-320-6, Pub. by Farming Pr) Diamond Farm Bk.
Patterson, George. The Citizen's Rights Initiative: The Ten-A Amendment. LC 99-191835. 85p. 1998. pap. 19.00 (0-917410-09-2) Basic Sci Pr.
— Patterson of Tibet: Death Throes of a Nation. 600p. 1998. pap. 19.95 (1-57901-026-1, PPA) ProMotion Pub.
Patterson, George & Scoggins, Richard. Church Multiplication Guide: Helping Churches to Reproduce Locally & Abroad. LC 93-40678. 128p. 1994. pap. text 6.95 (0-87808-245-X) William Carey Lib.
Patterson, George J., Jr. The Unassimilated Greeks of Denver. LC 88-36704. (Immigrant Communities & Ethnic Minorities in the U. S. & Canada Ser.: No. 41). 1989. 49.50 (0-404-19451-6) AMS Pr.
Patterson, George S. Preparing Tris (2, 4-Pentanedionato) Iron (III), an Iron Coordination Complex. Neidig, H. Anthony, ed. (Modular Laboratory Program in Chemistry Ser.). 8p. (C). 1993. pap. text 1.50 (0-87540-431-6, SYNT 431-6) Chem Educ Res.
— Synthesizing & Analyzing a Coordination Compound of Nickel (II) Ion, Ammonia, & Chloride Ion. Neidig, H. Anthony, ed. (Modular Laboratory Program in Chemistry Ser.). 16p. (C). 1994. pap. text 1.50 (0-87540-433-2, SYNT 433-2) Chem Educ Res.
Patterson, George S. & Good, William E., Jr. Studying the Effect of Buffering on the Resistance of a Solution to pH Change. Neidig, H. Anthony, ed. (Modular Laboratory Program in Chemistry Ser.). 11p. (C). 1994. pap. text 1.50 (0-87540-443-X, EQUL 443-x) Chem Educ Res.
Patterson, Gerald, et al. Antisocial Boys, Vol. 4. 193p. 1992. pap. 24.95 (0-916154-05-X) Castalia Pub.
Patterson, Gerald G. How to Pass a Road Test for Your Driver's License. 72p. 1994. pap. 8.95 (0-9641406-0-8) Red Rock WI.
Patterson, Gerald H., jt. ed. see Riga, Alan T.
Patterson, Gerald R. Depression & Aggression in Family Interaction. 352p. (C). 1990. text 89.95 (0-8058-0137-5) L Erlbaum Assocs.
— Families: Applications of Social Learning to Family Life. rev. ed. (Illus.). 180p. (Orig.). 1975. pap. text 12.95 (0-87822-156-5, 0020) Res Press.
— Living with Children: New Methods for Parents & Teachers. rev. ed. LC 76-23974. 132p. 1976. pap. text 9.95 (0-87822-130-1, 0003) Res Press.
Patterson, Gerald R. & Forgatch, Marion. Parents & Adolescents Living Together: The Basics, Pt. 1. (Illus.). 286p. (Orig.). 1987. pap. 12.95 (0-916154-16-5) Castalia Pub.
— Parents & Adolescents Living Together Pt. 2: Family Problem Solving. (Illus.). xiii, 299p. (Orig.). 1989. pap. 13.95 (0-916154-12-2) Castalia Pub.
Patterson, Gerald R., et al. Antisocial Boys. (Social Interactional Approach Ser.: Vol. 4). (Illus.). xiii, 193p. (C). 1992. pap. 24.95 (0-916154-03-3) Castalia Pub.
Patterson, Gerard A. Debris of Battle: The Wounded of Gettysburg. LC 97-4996. (Illus.). 240p. 1997. 24.95 (0-8117-0498-X) Stackpole.
***Patterson, Gerard A.** From Blue to Gray: The Life of Confederate General Cadmus M. Wilcox. 2001. 24.95 (0-8117-0682-6) Stackpole.
Patterson, Gerard A. Justice or Atrocity: Gen. George E. Pickett & the Kinston, NC Hangings. LC 98-84401. (Illus.). 152p. 1998. pap. 16.95 (1-57747-027-3) Thomas Publications.
— Justice or Atrocity: Gen. George Pickett & the Kinston, N.C. Hangings. LC 98-84401. (Illus.). 160p. 1998. 24.95 (1-57747-042-7) Thomas Publications.
Patterson, Glenn W. & Nes, W. David, eds. Physiology & Biochemistry of Sterols. 395p. (C). 1992. 85.00 (0-935315-38-1) Am Oil Chemists.
Patterson, Gordon & Morrison, Brian. Invertebrate Animals As Indicators of Acidity in Upland Streams. (Forestry Commission Field Book Ser.: No. 13). (Illus.). 28p. 1993. pap. 25.00 (0-11-710317-9, Pub. by Statnry Office) Balogh.
Patterson, Gordon, jt. auth. see Rodwell, John.
Patterson, Graeme. History & Communications. 258p. 1990. text 40.00 (0-8020-2764-4); pap. text 15.95 (0-8020-6810-3) U of Toronto Pr.
Patterson-Greeb, Patricia. The Denver Job Search: Survive Unemployment & Land the Right Job Fast! 288p. (Orig.). 1996. pap. 24.95 (0-9656263-0-X) LifeChange Pubns.
Patterson, H. B. Bleaching & Purifying Fats & Oils: Theory & Practice. LC 92-30226. 256p. 1993. 70.00 (0-935315-42-X) Am Oil Chemists.
— Hydrogenation of Fats & Oils: Theory & Practice. LC 94-35070. 288p. 1994. 75.00 (0-935315-55-1) Am Oil Chemists.
Patterson, H. R. Tutorials in Management in General Practice: Tutorials in Practice Management. (Illus.). 224p. 1998. pap. write for info. (0-443-05485-1) Church.
Patterson, H. Robert, et al. Current Drug Handbook 1984-1986. 1984. text 42.00 (0-7216-1223-7, W B Saunders Co) Harcrt Hlth Sci Grp.
Patterson, H. W. Small Boat Building. 144p. 1985. reprint ed. pap. 20.00 (0-87556-691-X) Saifer.

An Asterisk (*) at the beginning of an entry indicates that the title is appearing for the first time.

Patterson, Harry. To Catch a King. large type ed. 1981. 27.99 (*0-7089-0612-5*) Ulverscroft.

Patterson, Helen, jt. ed. see Francovich, Riccardo.

Patterson, Henry. The Politics of Illusion: A Political History of the IRA. 320p. 1998. pap. 24.95 (*1-897959-31-1*, Pub. by Serif) IPG Chicago.

Patterson, Henry, jt. auth. see Mead, Michael.

Patterson, Ian, tr. see Vaneigem, Raoul.

Patterson, Ian J. The Theory of the Four Movements. (Cambridge Texts in the History of Political Thought Ser.). 275p. (C). 1992. write for info. (*0-521-35289-4*) Cambridge U Pr.

Patterson, Ian J., ed. see Fourier, Charles.

Patterson, Ippy. Flora, a Book of Days: Forest's Floor. (Illus.). 144p. (Orig.). 1997. pap. 14.95 (*0-9637518-2-4*) Ippy Patterson Pubs.

Patterson, J. H. The Maneaters of Tsavo. 240p. 1996. per. 6.99 (*0-671-00306-2*) PB.

Patterson, J. B., ed. see Black Hawk.

Patterson, J. G. A Zola Dictionary: The Characters of the Rougon-Macquart Novels of Emile Zola. xi, 232p. 1973. reprint ed. 42.90 (*3-487-04854-X*) G Olms Pubs.

Patterson, J. H. The Man-Eaters of Tsavo. 2nd ed. (Peter Capstick Library). (Illus.). 384p. 1985. text 22.95 (*0-312-51010-1*) St Martin.

Patterson, J. W., et al, eds. Nonpoint Pollution & Urban Stormwater Management. LC 95-61552. (Water Quality Management Library: Vol. 9). 435p. 1995. pap. 99.95 (*1-56676-305-3*) Technomic.

Patterson, Jack & Stevenson, George B. Native Trees of the Bahamas. (Illus.). 1977. pap. 5.95 (*0-916224-42-2*) Banyan Bks.

Patterson, James. Along Came a Spider. 512p. 1993. reprint ed. mass mkt. 7.99 (*0-446-36419-3*, Pub. by Warner Bks) Little.

Patterson, James. Along Came a Spider. Set. abr. ed. 1993. audio 18.00 (*1-55994-751-9*, 390336) HarperAudio.

— Black Friday. 480p. 2000. mass mkt. 6.99 (*0-446-60932-3*, Warner Vision) Warner Bks.

— Black Market. large type ed. 440p. 2000. write for info. (*0-7089-9138-6*) Ulverscroft.

Patterson, James. Black Market. large type ed. LC 95-23553. (Large Print Bks.). 1995. pap. 22.95 (*1-56895-243-0*) Wheeler Pub.

— Black Market. 368p. 1994. reprint ed. mass mkt. 5.99 (*0-446-60046-6*, Pub. by Warner Bks) Little.

— Cat & Mouse. 480p. 1998. mass mkt. 7.99 (*0-446-60618-9*, Pub. by Warner Bks) Little.

— Cat & Mouse. large type ed. LC 97-40815. 565p. 1998. 28.95 (*0-7838-8344-7*, G K Hall Lrg Type) Mac Lib Ref.

— Cat & Mouse. large type ed. LC 97-40815. 2001. pap. 30.00 (*0-7838-8345-5*, G K Hall Lrg Type) Mac Lib Ref.

— Cradle & All. LC 99-36037. 368p. 2000. 25.95 (*0-316-69061-9*) Little.

***Patterson, James.** Cradle & All. large type ed. LC 00-40422. (Large Print Book Ser.). 2000. pap. write for info. (*1-56895-879-X*) Wheeler Pub.

Patterson, James. Hide & Seek. large type ed. LC 96-22463. 26.95 (*1-56895-345-3*) Wheeler Pub.

— Hide & Seek. 464p. 1996. reprint ed. mass mkt. 7.99 (*0-446-60371-6*, Pub. by Warner Bks) Little.

Patterson, James. Jack & Jill. 1997. mass mkt. 270.00 (*0-446-16421-6*) Warner Bks.

Patterson, James. Jack & Jill. large type ed. LC 96-44966. 622p. 1998. pap. 25.95 (*0-7862-0939-9*) Thorndike Pr.

— Jack & Jill. 480p. 1997. reprint ed. mass mkt. 7.99 (*0-446-60480-1*, Pub. by Warner Bks) Little.

— Kiss the Girls. 480p. 1995. reprint ed. mass mkt. 7.99 (*0-446-60124-1*, Pub. by Warner Bks) Little.

— The Midnight Club. 256p. 1990. mass mkt. 5.99 (*0-8041-0597-9*) Ivy Books.

***Patterson, James.** The Midnight Club. 400p. 2000. mass mkt. 13.95 (*0-446-67641-1*, Pub. by Warner Bks) Little.

Patterson, James. The Midnight Club. large type ed. LC 99-19337. (Large Print Book Ser.). 1999. pap. 23.95 (*1-56895-716-5*) Wheeler Pub.

— The Midnight Club. 368p. 1999. reprint ed. mass mkt. 6.99 (*0-446-60638-3*, Pub. by Warner Bks) Little.

— Pop Goes the Weasel. LC 99-21473. 432p. (gr. 8). 1999. 26.95 (*0-316-69328-6*) Little.

***Patterson, James.** Pop Goes the Weasel. 480p. 2000. mass mkt. 7.99 (*0-446-60881-5*) Warner Bks.

— Pop Goes the Weasel. large type ed. LC 99-28491. 1999. 25.00 (*0-375-40854-1*) Wheeler Pub.

— Pop Goes the Weasel. large type ed. 2000. pap. 13.95 (*0-375-72793-0*) Random.

— Roses Are Red. 2000. pap. 16.00 (*0-316-66620-3*) Little.

— Roses Are Red. large type ed. 2000. 26.95 (*0-375-43090-3*) Random.

— Roses Are Red: A Novel. 368p. 2002. 26.95 (*0-316-69325-1*) Little.

Patterson, James. The Season of the Machete. large type ed. LC 98-3231. 1998. 23.95 (*1-56895-553-7*, Wheeler) Wheeler Pub.

— The Season of the Machete. 352p. 1995. reprint ed. mass mkt. 7.99 (*0-446-60047-4*, Pub. by Warner Bks) Little.

— See How They Run. 1997. mass mkt. write for info. (*0-316-69382-0*) Little.

— See How They Run. large type ed. LC 97-29615. 1997. 26.95 (*1-56895-480-8*, Compass) Wheeler Pub.

— See How They Run. 336p. 1997. reprint ed. mass mkt. 7.99 (*0-446-60392-9*, Pub. by Warner Bks) Little.

— Simplified Design for Building Fire Safety. LC 93-1037. (Parker Simplified Design Guides Ser.). 344p. 1993. 89.00 (*0-471-57236-5*) Wiley.

— The Thomas Berryman Number. large type ed. LC 97-44468. 1997. 25.95 (*1-56895-511-1*) Wheeler Pub.

— The Thomas Berryman Number. 288p. 1996. reprint ed. mass mkt. 7.50 (*0-446-60045-8*, Pub. by Warner Bks) Little.

— When the Wind Blows. 432p. 1999. mass mkt. 7.99 (*0-446-60765-7*, Pub. by Warner Bks) Little.

— When the Wind Blows. large type ed. LC 98-45065. 1999. 30.00 (*0-7838-0423-7*, G K Hall Lrg Type) Mac Lib Ref.

***Patterson, James.** When the Wind Blows. 416p. 2000. reprint ed. mass mkt. 13.95 (*0-446-67643-8*) Warner Bks.

Patterson, James. When the Wind Blows: A Novel. LC 98-14367. 432p. (gr. 8). 1998. 25.00 (*0-316-69332-4*) Little.

— When the Wind Blows: A Novel. large type ed. LC 98-45065. (Paperback Bestsellers Ser.). 521p. 1999. pap. 27.95 (*0-7838-0424-5*, G K Hall Lrg Type) Mac Lib Ref.

Patterson, James & De Jonge, Peter. Miracle on the 17th Green: A Novel about Life, Love, Family, Miracles...& Golf. 160p. (gr. 8). 1996. 16.95 (*0-316-69331-6*) Little.

— Miracle on the 17th Green: A Novel about Life, Love, Family, Miracles...& Golf. 160p. 1999. pap. 10.00 (*0-316-69335-9*, Back Bay) Little.

Patterson, James, tr. see Gero, Andras.

Patterson, James C., ed. see Tucker, Judy H.

Patterson, James E. Pearl Inlay: An Instruction Manual for Inlaying Abalone & Mother-of-Pearl. 82p. 1991. pap. 13.90 (*0-9644752-2-7*) Stewart MacDonald.

Patterson, James G. Benchmarking Basics: Looking for a Better Way. Keppler, Kay, ed. LC 95-69642. (Fifty-Minute Ser.). (Illus.). 90p. (Orig.). 1995. pap. 10.95 (*1-56052-356-5*) Crisp Pubns.

— How to Become a Better Negotiator. 100p. 1996. pap. text 10.95 (*0-8144-7839-5*) AMACOM.

***Patterson, James G., III.** I-Net+ Exam Prep. (Exam Prep Ser.). (Illus.). 2000. 49.99 (*1-57610-598-9*) Coriolis Grp.

Patterson, James G. ISO 9000: Worldwide Quality Standard. Paris, Janis, ed. LC 93-74236. (Fifty-Minute Ser.). (Illus.). 131p. (Orig.). 1995. pap. 10.95 (*1-56052-291-7*) Crisp Pubns.

Patterson, James H., jt. auth. see Pfaffenberger, Roger C.

Patterson, James M., jt. auth. see Allvine, Fred C.

Patterson, James M., ed. see Obayashi, Alan W. & Gorgan, Joseph M.

Patterson, James T. America in the Twentieth Century: A History. 5th ed. (C). 1999. text 50.00 (*0-15-507860-7*, Pub. by Harcourt Coll Pubs) Harcourt.

— America since 1941: A History. (C). 1994. pap. text 46.00 (*0-15-501113-8*) Harcourt.

— America since 1941: A History. 2nd ed. (C). 1999. text 50.00 (*0-15-507859-3*, Pub. by Harcourt Coll Pubs) Harcourt.

***Patterson, James T.** America's Struggle Against Poverty in the Twentieth Century. LC 00-38277. 2000. 18.95 (*0-674-00434-5*) HUP.

Patterson, James T. America's Struggle Against Poverty, 1900-1985. rev. ed. 320p. 1986. pap. 15.95 (*0-674-03122-9*) HUP.

— America's Struggle Against Poverty, 1900-1994. LC 94-22736. 320p. 1995. pap. text 18.50 (*0-674-03123-7*, PATAMZ) HUP.

— Congressional Conservatism & the New Deal: The Growth of the Conservative Coalition in Congress, 1933 to 1939. LC 81-4195. (Illus.). 369p. 1981. reprint ed. lib. bdg. 65.00 (*0-313-22676-8*, PACC, Greenwood Pr) Greenwood.

— The Dread Disease: Cancer & Modern American Culture. LC 87-160. (Illus.). 416p. 1987. 42.50 (*0-674-21625-3*) HUP.

— The Dread Disease: Cancer & Modern American Culture. (Illus.). 416p. 1987. pap. 20.50 (*0-674-21626-1*) HUP.

— Grand Expectations: The United States, 1945-1974. (Oxford History of the United States Ser.: Vol. X). (Illus.). 880p. (C). 1996. 40.00 (*0-19-507680-X*) OUP.

— Grand Expectations: The United States, 1945-1974, Vol. 10. (Oxford History of the United States Ser.). (Illus.). 880p. 1997. pap. 19.95 (*0-19-511797-2*) OUP.

— The New Deal & the States: Federalism in Transition. LC 80-29606. 226p. 1981. reprint ed. lib. bdg. 55.00 (*0-313-22841-8*, PAND, Greenwood Pr) Greenwood.

Patterson, James T., jt. auth. see Graebner, Norman A.

Patterson, James W. Chlorinated Dioxins & Furans: Exposed Populations 1994. Date not set. 74.95 (*0-87371-879-8*, L879) Lewis Pubs.

Patterson, James W., ed. Metals Speciation, Separation & Recovery, Vol. I. (Illus.). 800p. 1987. lib. bdg. 129.00 (*0-87371-034-7*, L034) Lewis Pubs.

Patterson, James W. & Passino, Roberto, eds. Metals Speciation, Separation & Recovery, Vol. II. (Illus.). 654p. 1990. lib. bdg. 119.00 (*0-87371-268-4*, L268) Lewis Pubs.

Patterson, Jan. SmART Book: The Smart Mart to the Arts. 3rd ed. Date not set. pap. 24.95 (*0-9643197-2-1*) Patterson Mktg.

Patterson, Jane, jt. auth. see Madaras, Lynda.

Patterson, Janet L., jt. auth. see Patterson, Donald L.

Patterson, Janice H., jt. auth. see Patterson, Jerry L.

Patterson, Jay. Grammar Works: Equipping Students with Tools to Master the English Language. (Illus.). 526p. (J). (gr. k-8). 1998. pap. text 49.99 (*1-888306-43-2*, Home School Pr) Holly Hall.

Patterson, Jay W. Grammar Works: Equipping Students with Tools to Master the English Language. Patterson, Jeanne R., ed. (J). (ps-12). 1999. pap. text 49.99 (*0-9649574-0-X*) Holly Hall.

— Reading Works: Gleanings from My Journey along the Writing Road to Reading. Patterson, Jeanne R., ed. 315p. 1998. teacher ed., ring bd. 44.95 (*0-9649574-1-8*) Whittier Assocs.

Patterson, Jeanne R., ed. see Patterson, Jay W.

Patterson, Jeff & Melcher, Ryan. Audio on the Web: The Official IUMA Guide. LC 98-230231. (Illus.). 224p. 1998. pap. 34.95 incl. cd-rom (*0-201-69613-4*) Peachpit Pr.

***Patterson, Jennifer.** Jennifer Patterson's Seasonal Recipes: Over 100 Splendid Recipes for All Seasons. (Illus.). 160p. 2000. 35.00 (*0-7472-2193-6*, Pub. by Headline Bk Pub); 22.95 (*0-7472-7619-6*, Pub. by Headline Bk Pub) Trafalgar.

Patterson, Jerry. The Delta & Other Poems. 90p. 1988. pap., per. 6.95 (*0-89697-312-3*) Intl Univ Pr.

— Fifth Avenue: The Best Address. LC 97-47410. (Illus.). 224p. 1998. 40.00 (*0-8478-2008-4*, Pub. by Rizzoli Intl) St Martin.

***Patterson, Jerry.** The First 400: New York in the Guilded Age. (Illus.). 240p. 2000. 40.00 (*0-8478-2285-0*) Rizzoli Intl.

Patterson, Jerry. Moral of the Story & the Last Hero. 50p. pap., per. 7.95 (*0-89697-311-5*) Intl Univ Pr.

— Teacher, Oh Teacher. 180p. 1988. pap. 8.95 (*0-89697-300-X*) Intl Univ Pr.

Patterson, Jerry E. The Vanderbilts. (Illus.). 304p. 1989. 49.50 (*0-8109-1748-3*, Pub. by Abrams) Time Warner.

***Patterson, Jerry L.** The Anguish of Leadership. LC 00-131246. 80p. 2000. pap. write for info. (*0-87652-246-0*, 234-002) Am Assn Sch Admin.

Patterson, Jerry L. Blackjack: A Winner's Handbook. 208p. 1990. pap. 12.00 (*0-399-51598-4*, Perigee Bks) Berkley Pub.

***Patterson, Jerry L.** Casino Gambling: A Winner's Guide to Blackjack, Craps, Roulette, Baccarat & Casino Poker. LC 99-55268. 2000. pap. 12.95 (*0-399-52511-4*, Perigee Bks) Berkley Pub.

Patterson, Jerry L. Coming Clean about Organizational Change: Leadership in the Real World. 64p. 1997. 13.95 (*0-87652-229-0*, 750) Am Assn Sch Admin.

— Leadership for Tomorrow's Schools. LC 93-19133. 1993. pap. 14.95 (*0-87120-209-3*) ASCD.

— Liderazgo Para las Escuelas del Manana. LC 95-41279. (SPA.). 1996. pap. 14.95 (*0-87120-257-3*) ASCD.

Patterson, Jerry L. & Olsen, Eddie. Break the Dealer: Winning Strategies for Today's Blackjack. 1986. pap. 10.00 (*0-399-51233-0*, Perigee Bks) Berkley Pub.

Patterson, Jerry L. & Patterson, Janice H. Putting Computer Power in School: A Step-by-Step Approach. 1984. 17.95 (*0-317-38248-9*, Parker Publishing Co); pap. 12.95 (*0-317-38249-7*, Parker Publishing Co) P-H.

— Putting Computer Power in Schools: A Step-by-Step Approach. LC 83-8017. 227p. 1983. 17.95 (*0-13-744474-5*, Busn); pap. 12.95 (*0-13-744467-2*, Busn) P-H.

Patterson, Jerry L. & Patterson, Nancy. Casino Gambler's Winning Edge: How to Get in, Get the Money & Get Out. (Illus.). 144p. (Orig.). 1989. pap. text 3.95 (*0-318-42764-8*) Echelon Gaming.

Patterson, Jo, tr. see Dadie, Bernard B.

***Patterson, Joby.** Romanian Wooden Churches from Medieval Maramures. 300p. 1999. 42.00 (*0-88033-428-2*, 530, Pub. by East Eur Monographs) Col U Pr.

Patterson, Joe A. God Will Make This Child a Blessing! The Jamie Coulter Story. 100p. 1994. pap. 12.00 (*0-9641696-2-2*) Heritage TX.

— Pulpit Echoes. 181p. 1988. 12.00 (*0-9641696-0-6*) Heritage TX.

Patterson, JoEllen, et al. Essential Skills in Family Therapy: From the First Interview to Termination. LC 97-41754. (Family Therapy Ser.). 250p. 1998. lib. bdg. 31.00 (*1-57230-307-7*) Guilford Pubns.

Patterson, John. Child Abuse Prevention Primer for Your Organization. LC 95-67770. (Illus.). 1995. pap. 12.00 (*0-9637120-2-0*) Nonprof Risk Mgmt Ctr.

Patterson, John C. Staff Screening Tool Kit: Building a Strong Foundation Through Careful Screening. 2nd ed. LC 99-158829. Orig. Title: Staff Screening Tool Kit: Keeping the Bad Apples Out of Your Organization. 135p. 1998. pap. 30.00 (*1-893210-00-6*) Nonprof Risk Mgmt Ctr.

Patterson, John C., jt. auth. see Boles, Anita B.

Patterson, John M., jt. auth. see Bliss, Edward, Jr.

Patterson-Jones, Colin, text. Namaqualand: A Visual Souvenir. LC 98-214705. 1999. 22.95 (*1-86872-166-3*) Struik Pubs.

Patterson, Jordan. Box Turtles. (Illus.). 64p. 1995. pap. 9.95 (*0-7938-0251-2*, RE101) TFH Pubns.

— Box Turtles: Keeping & Breeding Them in Captivity. LC 98-7657. (Basic Domestic Reptile & Amphibian Library). (Illus.). 64p. (YA). (gr. 3 up). 1999. lib. bdg. 17.95 (*0-7910-5077-7*) Chelsea Hse.

— Newts. (Illus.). 68p. 1995. pap. text 9.95 (*0-7938-0274-1*, RE131) TFH Pubns.

— Newts: Their Care in Captivity. (Basic Domestic Reptile & Amphibian Library). (Illus.). 64p. (YA). (gr. 3 up). 1999. lib. bdg. 17.95 (*0-7910-5131-5*) Chelsea Hse.

— Red Eared Slider Turtles. (Illus.). 64p. 1995. pap. text 9.95 (*0-7938-0253-9*, RE109) TFH Pubns.

Patterson, Jose. Angels, Prophets, Rabbis & Kings: From the Stories of the Jewish People. LC 90-23469. (World Mythology Ser.). (Illus.). 132p. (J). (ps up). 1991. lib. bdg. 24.95 (*0-87226-912-4*, 69124B, P Bedrick Books) NTC Contemp Pub Co.

— Israel. LC 96-36975. (Country Fact Files Ser.). (Illus.). 48p. (J). (gr. 4-8). 1997. lib. bdg. 24.26 (*0-8172-4627-4*) Raintree Steck-V.

Patterson, Joseph, jt. ed. see Lamb, Donald Q.

Patterson, Joseph M. A Little Brother of the Rich. LC 68-57545. (Muckrakers Ser.). (Illus.). reprint ed. lib. bdg. 22.50 (*0-8398-1553-0*) Irvington.

— A Little Brother of the Rich. (Muckrakers Ser.). (C). 1987. reprint ed. pap. text 7.95 (*0-8290-2377-1*) Irvington.

Patterson, Judith E. Feelings of Emotions That Came from Within. LC 95-92534. (Illus.). 69p. (Orig.). 1995. pap. 15.00 (*0-9649066-0-0*) J E Patterson.

Patterson, Judy & Lang, Fiona. The Scottish Cook. (Illus.). 62p. pap. 7.95 (*1-874744-35-1*, Pub. by Birlinn Ltd) Dufour.

Patterson, K. D. The Development of Expectations Generating Schemes Which Are Asymptotically Rational. LC 88-42524. (Bank of England, Discussion Papers: Vol. 12). 24p. 1985. reprint ed. pap. 30.00 (*0-608-01649-7*, 206230100002) Bks Demand.

***Patterson, K. D.** An Introduction to Applied Econometrics. LC 00-35255. 2000. pap. write for info. (*0-312-23513-5*) St Martin.

Patterson, K. D. & Ryding, J. Deriving & Testing Rate of Growth & Higher Order Growth Effects in Dynamic Economic Models. LC HB0141.. (Bank of England. Discussion Papers: No. 21). 40p. pap. 30.00 (*0-608-12740-X*, 202434500037) Bks Demand.

Patterson, K. D., jt. auth. see Hall, S. G.

Patterson, K. David. Health in Colonial Ghana: Disease, Medicine, & Socio-Economic Change, 1900-1955. 187p. 1981. 20.00 (*0-918456-42-8*) African Studies Assn.

— Infectious Diseases in Twentieth-Century Africa: A Bibliography of Their Distribution & Consequences. (Archival & Bibliographic Ser.). 251p. (Orig.). 1979. pap. 25.00 (*0-918456-29-0*, Crossroads) African Studies Assn.

— Pandemic Influenza, 1700-1900: A Study in Historical Epidemiology. (Illus.). 128p. (C). 1987. 45.00 (*0-8476-7512-2*, R7512) Rowman.

Patterson, K. David & Hartwig, Gerald W. Cerebrospinal Meningitis in West Africa & the Sudan in the Twentieth Century. 1984. pap. 15.00 (*0-918456-55-X*) African Studies Assn.

— Schistosomiasis in Twentieth Century Africa: Historical Studies on West Africa & Sudan. 1984. pap. 15.00 (*0-918456-54-1*) African Studies Assn.

***Patterson, Karen A.** Herbs for All Seasons. (Illus.). 160p. 1999. pap. 12.99 (*1-892525-10-0*) ACW Press.

Patterson, Karen F. & Nelson, Angela. Language Builder Picture Cards, No.1. (Illus.). 350p. (ps-3). 1997. 150.00 (*0-9668008-0-X*) Stages Learn.

Patterson, Kathryn, jt. compiled by see Patterson, Brad.

Patterson, Kelly D. Political Parties & the Maintenance of Liberal Democracy. (Illus.). 240p. 1996. pap. 17.50 (*0-231-10257-7*) Col U Pr.

— Political Parties & the Maintenance of Liberal Democracy. Shapiro, Robert Y., ed. (Illus.). 240p. 1996. 47.50 (*0-231-10256-9*) Col U Pr.

***Patterson, Kelly D. & Shea, Daniel.** Contemplating The People's Branch: Legislative Dynamics in The Twenty First Century. LC 99-57666. 360p. (C). 2000. pap. 34.67 (*0-13-040160-9*) P-H.

Patterson, Kerry, et al. Balancing Act: Mastering the Competing Demands of Leadership. 471p. 1996. mass mkt. 42.95 (*0-538-86139-8*) S-W Pub.

Patterson, Kerry D. Growth Coefficients in Error Correction & Autoregressive Distributed Log Models. LC 84-4308. (Bank of England. Discussion Papers. Technical Ser.: No. 2). 33p. reprint ed. pap. 30.00 (*0-608-15635-3*, 203176500076) Bks Demand.

***Patterson, Kevin.** The Water in Between: A Journey at Sea. 304p. 2000. 23.95 (*0-385-49883-7*) Doubleday.

Patterson, L. G. Methodius of Olympus: Divine Sovereignty, Human Freedom, & Life in Christ. LC 96-29371. 270p. (C). 1997. text 59.95 (*0-8132-0875-0*) Cath U Pr.

Patterson, L. Ray. Jurisprudence, Men & Ideas of the Law. 1953. text 28.00 (*0-88277-362-3*) Foundation Pr.

***Patterson, L. Ray & Brock, Pope.** Lawyer's Law: Procedural, Malpractice & Disciplinary Issues, 1999. annuals 4th ed. 1999. text 42.00 (*0-8205-4055-2*) Bender.

Patterson, L. Ray & Metzloff, Thomas B. Legal Ethics: The Law of Professional Responsibility. 3rd ed. 1989. teacher ed. 54.50 (*0-8205-2909-5*) Bender.

Patterson, Lance. Wings of Gold. LC 97-6856. (Illus.). 144p. (YA). 1997. pap. 6.49 (*0-89084-933-1*, 106245) Bob Jones Univ.

Patterson, Lee. Chaucer & the Subject of History. LC 90-50651. 504p. (Orig.). (C). 1991. pap. 21.95 (*0-299-12834-2*) U of Wis Pr.

— Negotiating the Past: The Historical Understanding of Medieval Literature. LC 87-40144. 253p. 1987. reprint ed. pap. 78.50 (*0-608-01860-0*, 206251100003) Bks Demand.

Patterson, Lee, ed. see Thornton, Virden.

Patterson, Lee T. & Deblieux, Michael R. Documenting Employee Discipline. LC 88-61702. 1988. pap. 39.50 (*0-911110-61-5*, MICHIE) LEXIS Pub.

Patterson, Leslie, jt. ed. see Mallow, Frances.

Patterson, Lewis E., jt. auth. see Eisenberg, Sheldon.

Patterson, Lillie. Martin Luther King, Jr. & the Freedom Movement. Scott, John A., ed. (Makers of America Ser.). (Illus.). 192p. (YA). (gr. 7-12). 1989. 19.95 (*0-8160-1605-4*) Facts on File.

— Martin Luther King, Jr. & the Freedom Movement. Scott, John A., ed. (Makers of America Ser.). (Illus.). 192p. (YA). (gr. 7-12). 1993. pap. 8.95 (*0-8160-2997-0*) Facts on File.

Patterson, Lily, jt. auth. see Norman, Winifred L.

Patterson, Lindsay, ed. A Rock Against the Wind: African-American Poems & Letters of Love & Passion. LC 95-30268. 224p. (Orig.). 1996. pap. 12.00 (*0-399-51982-3*, Perigee Bks) Berkley Pub.

Patterson, Lindsey M., jt. auth. see Goddard, Angela.

Patterson, Lois. Teach Yourself Microsoft Excel 97 in 24 Hours. LC 97-66675. (Teach Yourself Ser.). 464p. 1997. 19.99 (*0-672-31116-X*) Sams.

P

An Asterisk (*) at the beginning of an entry indicates that the title is appearing for the first time.

Patterson, Lori A. Self-Publishing Made Simple: Step-by-Step Guide No Thinking Required. LC 94-65050. 320p. (Orig.). 1998. 29.95 (*1-884573-04-5*); pap. 19.95 (*1-884573-15-0*) S-By-S Pubns.

Patterson, Lorne. Tides & Ceremonies. LC 97-13833. 64p. 1997. pap. 14.95 (*0-7734-2820-8*, Mellen Poetry Pr) E Mellen.

Patterson, Lotsee & Snodgrass, Mary E. Indian Terms of the Americas. (Illus.). xvi, 275p. 1994. lib. bdg. 35.00 (*1-56308-133-4*) Libs Unl.

Patterson, Lyman R. Copyright in Historical Perspective. LC 68-22415. 264p. 1968. 22.95 (*0-8265-1120-1*) Vanderbilt U Pr.

Patterson, M., et al. Recommended Nomenclature for Physical Quantities in Medical Application of Light. (Report Ser.: No. 57). 10p. (Orig.). 1996. write for info. (*1-888340-02-9*) AAPM.

Patterson, Margaret C. Literary Research Guide. 2nd fac. ed. LC 82-20386. 685p. 1984. reprint ed. pap. 200.00 (*0-7837-8032-X*, 204778800008) Bks Demand.

Patterson, Margaret J., jt. ed. see Russell, Robert H.

Patterson, Marilyn N. Every Body Can Learn: Engaging the Bodily-Kinesthetic Intelligence in the Everyday Classroom. LC 96-30261. 1996. 30.00 (*1-56976-057-8*) Zephyr Pr AZ.

Patterson, Mark. Divorce Forms for Washington. 2nd ed. 1998. pap. 15.95 (*1-55180-199-X*) Self-Counsel Pr.

***Patterson, Mark.** Washington Divorce Forms. 3rd ed. 1999. pap. 15.95 (*1-55180-272-4*) Self-Counsel Pr.

Patterson, Mark R. Authority, Autonomy, & Representation in American Literature, 1776-1865. LC 88-13999. 279p. 1988. reprint ed. pap. 86.50 (*0-608-07169-2*, 206739400009) Bks Demand.

Patterson, Mark T. Divorce Guide for Washington. 10th ed. (Washington Legal Ser.). 160p. 1997. pap. 18.95 (*1-55180-150-7*) Self-Counsel Pr.

Patterson, Marni C. Doing Business on the World Wide Web. Keppler, Kay, ed. LC 96-85520. 120p. (Orig.). 1996. pap. 12.95 (*1-56052-390-5*) Crisp Pubns.

Patterson, Martha F. The Backyard Bomber of Pacific Palisades: A Love Story. LC 84-52475. (Illus.). 273p. 1984. 9.95 (*0-9614294-0-2*) Seamount Pubns.

Patterson, Martha P. Retirement Plan Basics Vol. 41: Selecting Programs That Support Organization Objectives. LC 98-119177. (Building Blocks Ser.). (Illus.). 1997. pap. 24.95 (*1-57963-046-4*, A0241) Am Compensation.

***Patterson, Martha Priddy.** The New Working Woman's Guide to Retirement Planning: Saving & Investing Now for a Secure Future. 2nd ed. LC 99-36954. 1999. pap. text 19.95 (*0-8122-1703-9*) U of Pa Pr.

Patterson, Marva. Braiding. (Illus.). 192p. 1991. pap. 22.95 (*0-87350-386-4*) Milady Pub.

Patterson, Marvin. Accelerating Innovation. 2nd ed. (Industrial Engineering Ser.). 1995. text 24.95 (*0-442-02065-1*, VNR) Wiley.

Patterson, Marvin L. & Fenoglio, John J., Jr. Leading Product Innovation: Accelerating Growth in a Product-Based Business. LC 99-15417. 434p. 1999. 55.00 (*0-471-34517-2*) Wiley.

Patterson, Marvin L. & Lightman, Sam. Accelerating Innovation: Improving the Process of Product Development. LC 92-34006. 159p. 1992. 34.95 (*0-442-01378-7*, VNR) Wiley.

Patterson, Marvin L. & Lightman, Sam. Accelerating Innovation: Improving the Process of Product Development. 159p. 1992. 34.95 (*0-471-28546-3*, VNR) Wiley.

Patterson, Matthew C. Adolf Hitler, Mother Teresa & the Mercy of God. LC 98-90759. 1999. 18.95 (*0-533-12908-7*) Vantage.

Patterson, Maureen L. South Asian Civilizations: A Bibliographic Synthesis. LC 81-52518. (Illus.). 893p. 1981. lib. bdg. 84.00 (*0-226-64910-5*) U Ch Pr.

Patterson, Maurice, ed. Interlaken Oral History Project: Interviews with Residents about Life & Times of the Area 1900-1950 Including the History of the Hallstead Canning Company. (Illus.). 318p. 1997. pap. 18.00 (*0-9622056-3-X*) Interlaken Hist.

P

Patterson, Maurice, jt. ed. see Covert, William V.

Patterson, Mavis, ed. Ladies' Choice: A Collection of Humor by Maine Women. LC 89-5533. (Illus.). 95p. (Orig.). 1982. pap. 4.95 (*0-945980-15-9*) Nrth Country Pr.

Patterson, Michael. The Bibliography of German Theatre. 1996. 250.00 (*0-7838-1662-6*, G K Hall & Co) Mac Lib Ref.

Patterson, Michael, ed. see Buchner, Georg.

Patterson, Michael S., jt. ed. see Fujimoto, James G.

Patterson, Miles, jt. auth. see Heslin, Richard.

Patterson, Miles L., ed. Non-Verbal Intimacy & Exchange: A Special Issue of Journal of Nonverbal Behavior. (Illus.). 169p. (Orig.). 1985. pap. 14.95 (*0-89885-224-2*, Kluwer Acad Hman Sci) Kluwer Academic.

Patterson, Nancy. South Sound Places. (Illus.). 64p. (Orig.). 1993. pap. 11.95 (*0-9627201-2-7*) Patcha Pubng.

Patterson, Nancy, jt. auth. see Eskew, Mike.

Patterson, Nancy, jt. auth. see Patterson, Jerry L.

Patterson, Nancy-Lou. Apple Staff & Silver Crown. 228p. 1985. pap. write for info. (*0-88984-075-X*) Porcup Quill.

— The Painted Hallway. 208p. 1992. pap. write for info. (*0-88984-142-X*) Porcup Quill.

Patterson, Nancy R. The Shiniest Rock of All. LC 91-12081. (Illus.). 80p. (J). (ps-3). 1991. 13.00 (*0-374-36805-8*) FS&G.

— The Shiniest Rock of All. 80p. (J). (ps-3). 1994. pap. 4.95 (*0-374-46615-7*) FS&G.

Patterson, Neil. Chalkstream Chronicle. (Illus.). 320p. 1995. 35.00 (*1-55821-425-9*) Lyons Pr.

Patterson, Nerys. Cattle Lords & Clansmen: The Social Structure of Early Ireland. 2nd ed. (C). 1994. reprint ed. pap. text 25.50 (*0-268-00800-0*) U of Notre Dame Pr.

Patterson, Olive. Nurse in Torment. large type ed. (Dales Large Print Ser.). 237p. 1998. pap. 19.99 (*1-85389-797-3*, Dales) Ulverscroft.

Patterson-Oriel, Patricia, ed. see Quell, Lawrence A.

Patterson, Orlando. Freedom: Freedom in the Making of Western Culture, Vol. 1. 512p. 1992. pap. 18.00 (*0-465-02532-3*, Pub. by Basic) HarpC.

— Freedom: Freedom in the Modern World, Vol. II. LC 90-55593. 448p. 1992. 30.00 (*0-465-02537-4*, Pub. by Basic) HarpC.

— Freedom in the Modern World, Vol. 2. pap. write for info. (*0-465-02540-4*) Basic.

— The Ordeal of Integration: Progress & Resentment in America's "Racial" Crisis, 3 vols., Vol. 1. 248p. 1998. reprint ed. pap. 15.00 (*1-887178-97-X*, Pub. by Counterpt DC) HarpC.

— Rituals of Blood: Consequences of Slavery in Two American Centuries. 352p. 1999. pap. text 13.00 (*1-58243-039-X*, Pub. by Basic) HarpC.

— Rituals of Blood: Consequences of Slavery in Two American Centuries. LC 98-47778. (Civitas). 330p. 1998. 29.50 (*1-887178-82-1*, Pub. by Counterpt DC) HarpC.

— Slavery & Social Death: A Comparative Study. (Illus.). 528p. 1982. pap. 23.50 (*0-674-81083-X*) HUP.

— Slavery & Social Death: A Comparative Study. LC 82-1072. (Illus.). 528p. 1982. 39.95 (*0-674-81082-1*) HUP.

— Sociology of Slavery. LC 70-84198. 310p. 1975. 35.00 (*0-8386-7469-0*) Fairleigh Dickinson.

Patterson, P. G. & Pettit, D. G. Ciento Cincuenta Cosas Que Hacer Con Papel: 150 Things to Make with Paper. 64p. 1971. reprint ed. pap. 6.99 (*0-311-26604-5*) Casa Bautista.

Patterson, Paige. Cantar de los Cantares.Tr. of Song of Solomon. (SPA.). 120p. 1996. pap. 6.99 (*0-8254-1550-0*, Edit Portavoz) Kregel.

— The Troubled Triumphant Church: An Exposition of I Corinthians. 2nd ed. 326p. 1983. reprint ed. pap. 7.95 (*0-317-93397-3*) Criswell Pubns.

Patterson, Pat, ed. see Sward, Sharon.

***Patterson, Patricia E.** All about Life. 64p. 1999. pap. write for info. (*0-9671062-0-6*) P E Patterson.

Patterson, Patricia J. Way of Faithfulness: Study Guide to Christians in Japan. (Orig.). 1991. pap. 5.95 (*0-377-00220-8*) Friendship Pr.

Patterson, Paul. Backfire Trail. 1999. write for info. (*1-887743-04-9*) Cow Hill Pr.

— Bokay of Biscuits, 3 vols. (Illus.). 1997. pap. 50.00 (*1-887743-02-2*) Cow Hill Pr.

— Pecos River Pilgrim's Poems V. 1996. 6.00 (*1-887743-01-4*) Cow Hill Pr.

— Pecos River Pilgrim's Poems I. 1988. reprint ed. pap. 6.00 (*0-9617714-1-0*) Cow Hill Pr.

— Pecos River Pilgrim's Poems VI. 1998. pap. 10.00 (*1-887743-03-0*) Cow Hill Pr.

— Pecos River Pilgrim's Poems III. (Illus.). 1992. pap. 11.00 (*0-9617714-5-3*) Cow Hill Pr.

— Pecos River Pilgrim's Poems II. (Illus.). 1989. reprint ed. pap. 6.00 (*0-9617714-2-9*) Cow Hill Pr.

— Sam McGoo & Texas Too. 2nd ed. (Illus.). 183p. 1995. pap. 6.00 (*0-9617714-9-6*) Cow Hill Pr.

Patterson, Paul, et al, eds. Psychosocial Aspects of Cystic Fibrosis: A Model for Chronic Lung Disease. LC 72-9893. 234p. 1973. 12.50 (*0-930194-33-0*) Ctr Thanatology.

Patterson, Paul E. Great Plains Cattle Empire: Thatcher Brothers & Associates (1875-1945) (Illus.). 256p. 2000. 28.95 (*0-89672-397-6*) Tex Tech Univ Pr.

***Patterson, Paul E.** Hardhat & Stetson: Robert O. Anderson, Oilman & Cattleman. LC 99-44786. (Illus.). 224p. 1999. pap. 12.95 (*0-86534-301-2*) Sunstone Pr.

Patterson, Paul E. Triple Crown: A Novel. LC 95-44925. 224p. (Orig.). 1996. pap. 14.95 (*0-86534-240-7*) Sunstone Pr.

***Patterson, Paul H., et al, eds.** Neuro-Immune Interactions in Neurologic & Psychiatric Disorders. LC 99-36334. (Research & Perspectives in Neurosciences Ser.). (Illus.). xiv, 180p. 1999. 104.00 (*3-540-66013-5*) Spr-Verlag.

Patterson, Paul R., et al, eds. Psychosocial Aspects of Cystic Fibrosis: A Model for Chronic Lung Disease. LC 72-9893. 246p. reprint ed. pap. 76.30 (*0-8357-4573-2*, 203748200008) Bks Demand.

Patterson, Pernet. The Road to Canaan. 1977. 17.95 (*0-8369-9193-1*, 9062) Ayer.

Patterson, Philip & Wilkins, Lee C. Media Ethics: Issues & Cases. 2nd ed. 304p. (C). 1994. text. write for info. (*0-697-17099-3*) Brown & Benchmark.

Patterson, Philip C., jt. ed. see Wilkins, Lee.

Patterson, Philip D. Come unto Me: The Lives & Stories of Those Who Met Jesus. (Illus.). (Orig.). 1992. pap. 8.99 (*0-89900-613-2*) College Pr Pub.

— The Electronic Millstone: Christian Parenting in a Media Age. 230p. (Orig.). 1992. pap. 9.99 (*0-89900-420-2*) College Pr Pub.

— Redeeming the Time: The Christian Walk in a Hurried World. LC 94-44044. 1995. 8.99 (*0-89900-726-0*) College Pr Pub.

Patterson, Philip D. & Herndon, Michael W. Right-Sizing Your Life: The up Side of Slowing Down. LC 98-6085. 132p. 1998. pap. 9.99 (*0-8308-1942-8*, 1942) InterVarsity.

Patterson, Phillip. Media Ethics: Issues & Cases. 3rd ed. Wilkins, Lee, ed. LC 97-8386. 384p. 1997. pap. 24.69 (*0-697-32717-5*) McGraw.

Patterson, R. D., et al. The Expositor's Bible Commentary, Vol. 4. 1988. 39.99 (*0-88469-192-6*) BMH Bks.

Patterson, R. E. Deadly Revenge. Schwartz, Donna, ed. (Illus.). (Orig.). Date not set. pap. 8.00 (*0-9669837-2-6*) Gotcha Pubns.

— Out of the Darkness. Schwartz, Donna, ed. (Illus.). (Orig.). Date not set. pap. 8.00 (*0-9669837-0-X*) Gotcha Pubns.

— Sometimes Angels Die. Schwartz, Donna, ed. (Illus.). (Orig.). Date not set. pap. 8.00 (*0-9669837-3-4*) Gotcha Pubns.

— Without a Trace. Schwartz, Donna, ed. (Illus.). (Orig.). Date not set. pap. 8.00 (*0-9669837-1-8*) Gotcha Pubns.

Patterson, R. F. Ben Jonson's Conversations with Drummond of Hawthornden. LC 73-22023. (English Literature Ser.: No. 33). 1974. lib. bdg. 55.00 (*0-8383-1835-5*) M S G Haskell Hse.

— Home Medical Dictionary. 256p. (Orig.). 1989. pap. 5.95 (*0-938261-99-1*) PSI & Assocs.

— New Webster's Expanded Dictionary. 384p. (Orig.). 1994. pap. write for info. (*1-884907-01-6*) Paradise Pr FL.

Patterson, R. F., ed. New Webster's Dictionary. 256p. (Orig.). 1993. pap. 5.95 (*0-938261-80-0*) PSI & Assocs.

— New Webster's Dictionary. 256p. (Orig.). 1994. pap. write for info. (*1-884907-02-4*) Paradise Pr FL.

— New Webster's Dictionary - Roget's Thesaurus. 512p. 1994. pap. write for info. (*1-884907-00-8*) Paradise Pr FL.

— New Webster's Dictionary & New Roget's Thesaurus. 512p. (Orig.). 1990. pap. 12.95 (*0-938261-39-8*) PSI & Assocs.

— New Webster's Expanded Dictionary. 384p. (Orig.). 1988. pap. 6.95 (*0-938261-79-7*) PSI & Assocs.

— New Webster's Giant Print Dictionary. 288p. (Orig.). 1990. pap. 5.95 (*0-938261-81-9*) PSI & Assocs.

— New Webster's Large Print Dictionary. large type ed. 256p. 1994. pap. 5.95 (*1-884907-03-2*) Paradise Pr FL.

— New Webster's Pocket Pal Dictionary. 192p. (Orig.). 1989. pap. 3.95 (*0-938261-20-7*) PSI & Assocs.

— Webster's French-English, English-French Dictionary. 256p. (Orig.). 1993. pap. 5.95 (*0-938261-15-0*) PSI & Assocs.

— Webster's Spanish-English - English-Spanish Dictionary. (ENG & SPA.). 192p. (Orig.). 1993. pap. 2.95 (*0-938261-02-9*) PSI & Assocs.

Patterson, R. Gary. Hellhounds on Their Trail: Tales from the Rock n Roll Graveyard. 230p. 1998. pap. 15.95 (*0-9646452-6-2*, DO10032, Pub. by Dowling Pr) Music Sales.

— The Walrus Was Paul: The Great Beatle Death Clues. LC 98-34607. (Illus.). 208p. 1998. pap. 13.00 (*0-684-85062-1*, Fireside) S&S Trade Pap.

— The Walrus Was Paul: The Great Beatle Death Clues of 1969. LC 96-105691. (Illus.). 162p. (Orig.). 1994. pap. 19.95 (*0-9641163-0-8*) Excursion Prods.

Patterson, R. L. S. & Charlwood, B. Bioformation of Flavours, No. 95. 1992. 122.00 (*0-85186-446-5*) CRC Pr.

Patterson, R. M. Dangerous River: Adventure on the Nahanni. (Illus.). 276p. 1999. reprint ed. pap. 18.95 (*1-55046-316-0*) Boston Mills.

— Dangerous River: Adventures on the Nahanni. 1999. pap. 18.95 (*0-7737-2308-0*) Genl Dist Srvs.

***Patterson, R. T., et al.** Atlas of Common Benthic Foraminiferal Species for Quaternary Shelf Environments of Western Canada LC 99-203771. (Bulletin/Geological Survey of Canada Ser.). (ENG & FRE.). 91p. 1998. write for info. (*0-660-17435-9*, Pub. by Can7 Govern Pub) Intl Spec Bk.

Patterson, Ray. House Beautiful. (Illus.). 118p. 1987. pap. 3.95 (*0-936369-05-1*) Son-Rise Pubns.

— Idiopathic Anaphylaxis. LC 97-65405. 100p. 1997. 56.00 (*0-936587-10-5*) OceanSide Pubns.

Patterson, Raymond. The Negro & His Needs. LC 74-178480. (Black Heritage Library Collection). 1977. reprint ed. 25.95 (*0-8369-8929-5*) Ayer.

Patterson, Raymond M. Dangerous River. LC 89-71264. (Illus.). 294p. reprint ed. pap. 91.20 (*0-608-08576-6*, 206909900002) Bks Demand.

Patterson, Raymond R. Elemental Blues. Barkan, Stanley H., ed. (Review Chapbook Ser.: No. 19). (Illus.). 48p. 1983. 15.00 (*0-89304-817-8*); 15.00 (*0-89304-842-9*); 5.00 (*0-89304-843-7*); pap. 5.00 (*0-685-49061-0*) Cross-Cultrl NY.

Patterson, Raymond R., jt. auth. see Barkan, Stanley H.

Patterson, Richard. Aristotle's Modal Logic: Essence & Entailment in the Organon. (Illus.). 303p. (C). 1995. text 69.95 (*0-521-45168-X*) Cambridge U Pr.

— Butch Cassidy: A Biography. LC 98-15765. (Illus.). 372p. 1998. pap. 19.95 (*0-8032-8756-9*) U of Nebr Pr.

***Patterson, Richard.** Changing Patient Behavior: Improving Outcomes in Health & Disease Management. 2000. 74.95 (*0-7879-5279-6*) Jossey-Bass.

Patterson, Richard. Effectively Leading. 96p. 1992. pap. text 9.95 (*0-910566-53-4*) Evang Trg Assn.

***Patterson, Richard.** Harney's Medical Malpractice. 4th ed. LC 93-80116. 800p. 1999. 95.00 (*0-327-04982-0*, 6272011) LEXIS Pub.

Patterson, Richard. Historical Atlas of the Outlaw West. LC 84-82543. (Illus.). 250p. (Orig.). 1984. pap. 17.95 (*0-933472-89-7*) Johnson Bks.

Patterson, Richard. Lawyers' Medical Encyclopedia of Personal Injuries & Allied Specialties, Vols. 3, 4 & 5. 4th ed. LC RA1022.U6L38 1996. 1996. 0.00 (*1-55834-638-4*) LEXIS Pub.

Patterson, Richard, ed. Defense Law Journal, Vol. 47, Issue 4. 216p. 1998. pap. write for info. (*0-327-00709-5*, 7097211) LEXIS Pub.

***Patterson, Richard, ed.** Defense Law Journal, Vol. 48, Issue 3. 235p. 1999. pap. write for info. (*0-327-01681-7*, 7097112) LEXIS Pub.

Patterson, Richard, ed. Lawyers Medical Cyclopedia, 11 vols., Vol. 4B. LC 88-61859. 780p. 1999. write for info. (*0-327-01051-7*, 6204511) LEXIS Pub.

— Lawyers' Medical Cyclopedia, 1999 Cumulative Supplements. 744p. 1999. pap. write for info. (*0-327-01324-9*, 6206616) LEXIS Pub.

— Lawyer's Medical Cyclopedia of Personal Injuries & Allied Specialties. 4th ed. LC 96-75647. 630p. 1998. text. write for info. (*0-327-00284-0*, 62044-11) LEXIS Pub.

— Lawyer's Medical Cyclopedia of Personal Injuries & Allied Specialties: Winter 1998 General Index. 446p. 1998. write for info. (*0-327-00296-4*, 62065-18) LEXIS Pub.

***Patterson, Richard, ed.** Lawyer's Medical Cyclopedia, Summer 1999 General Index. 460p. 1999. write for info. (*0-327-01381-8*, 6206519) LEXIS Pub.

— Lawyers Medical Encyclopedia, Vol. 6A. 4th ed. 715p. 1999. write for info. (*0-327-04962-6*, 6205311) LEXIS Pub.

Patterson, Richard & White, Dana, eds. Electronic Production Techniques. (Illus.). 100p. (Orig.). (C). 1984. reprint ed. pap. 7.95 (*0-935578-04-8*) ASC Holding.

Patterson, Richard B. In Search of the Wounded Healer. 1990. pap. 9.95 (*0-87193-269-5*) Dimension Bks.

Patterson, Richard E. Confident Parenting in Challenging Times: Essential Convictions of Highly Successful Parents. LC 99-60658. 238p. 1999. pap. 12.99 (*0-9664413-3-8*) Tekna Bks.

Patterson, Richard North. Dark Lady. LC 99-23565. 371p. 1999. 25.95 (*0-679-45043-2*) Knopf.

***Patterson, Richard North.** Dark Lady. large type ed. 2000. pap. 14.95 (*0-375-72789-2*) Random Hse Lrg Prnt.

— The Dark Lady. large type ed. LC 99-34269. (Large Print Ser.). 448p. 1999. 25.95 (*0-375-40844-4*) Knopf.

— Dark Lady, Vol. 3. 448p. 2000. 7.99 (*0-345-40478-5*, Ballantine) Ballantine Pub Grp.

Patterson, Richard North. Degree of Guilt. 1998. pap. 7.99 (*0-345-91454-6*) Ballantine Pub Grp.

— Degree of Guilt. 1994. reprint ed. mass mkt. 7.99 (*0-345-38184-X*) Ballantine Pub Grp.

— Escape the Night. 384p. 1986. mass mkt. 6.99 (*0-345-33401-9*) Ballantine Pub Grp.

— Escape the Night. 1997. pap. 12.00 (*0-345-41812-3*) Ballantine Pub Grp.

— Eyes of a Child. 1996. mass mkt. 7.99 (*0-345-38613-2*) Ballantine Pub Grp.

— Eyes of a Child. 1998. pap. 7.99 (*0-345-91463-5*) Ballantine Pub Grp.

— The Final Judgment. 1997. mass mkt. 7.99 (*0-345-40761-X*) Ballantine Pub Grp.

— The Final Judgment. 1998. pap. 7.99 (*0-345-91462-7*) Ballantine Pub Grp.

— The Final Judgment. LC 95-35083. 400p. 1995. 25.00 (*0-679-42989-1*) Knopf.

— The Final Judgment. large type ed. 640p. 1995. 25.95 (*0-7838-1581-6*, G K Hall Lrg Type) Mac Lib Ref.

— The Final Judgment. large type ed. LC 95-35459. 640p. 1995. pap. 25.00 (*0-679-76666-9*) Random Hse Lrg Prnt.

— The Lasko Tangent. 208p. 1985. mass mkt. 6.99 (*0-345-32532-X*) Ballantine Pub Grp.

***Patterson, Richard North.** The Lasko Tangent. large type ed. LC 99-59458. 2000. 25.95 (*1-56895-830-7*) Wheeler Pub.

Patterson, Richard North. No Safe Place. 1999. mass mkt. 7.99 (*0-345-38612-4*) Ballantine Pub Grp.

— No Safe Place. LC 98-14573. 495p. 1998. 25.95 (*0-679-45042-4*) Knopf.

— No Safe Place. large type ed. LC 97-51822. 512p. 1998. pap. 25.95 (*0-375-70296-2*) Random.

— No Safe Place, Vol. 2. 1999. mass mkt. 7.99 (*0-345-40477-7*) Ballantine Pub Grp.

— The Outside Man. 320p. 1982. mass mkt. 6.99 (*0-345-30020-3*) Ballantine Pub Grp.

— The Outside Man. 1997. pap. 12.00 (*0-345-41815-8*) Ballantine Pub Grp.

***Patterson, Richard North.** The Outside Man. large type ed. LC 00-39870. 2000. write for info. (*1-56895-907-9*) Wheeler Pub.

Patterson, Richard North. Private Screening. 448p. 1986. mass mkt. 7.99 (*0-345-31139-6*) Ballantine Pub Grp.

— Private Screening. 1993. pap. 12.00 (*0-345-38572-1*) Ballantine Pub Grp.

— Private Screening. 1997. pap. 6.99 (*0-345-91284-5*) Ballantine Pub Grp.

***Patterson, Richard North.** Protect & Defend. 2001. 26.95 (*0-679-45044-0*) Knopf.

Patterson, Richard North. Silent Witness. large type ed. LC 96-41558. 494p. 1996. pap. 25.95 (*0-679-77416-5*) Random.

— Silent Witness, Vol.1. 1997. mass mkt. 7.99 (*0-345-40476-9*) Ballantine Pub Grp.

Patterson, Robert. Centers of Pedagogy. LC 98-51244. (Agenda for Education in a Democracy Ser.). 1999. pap. text 27.95 (*0-7879-4561-7*) Jossey-Bass.

— While They Died. Mackey, Sharon, ed. (Illus.). 220p. 1999. pap. 18.95 (*0-9668369-0-1*) Patterson Pr.

Patterson, Robert B. The Haskins Society Journal, Vol. I. 1989. 40.00 (*1-85285-031-0*) Hambledon Press.

— The Haskins Society Journal, Vol. II. 1990. 40.00 (*1-85285-059-0*) Hambledon Press.

— The Haskins Society Journal, Vol. III. 1991. 40.00 (*1-85285-061-2*) Hambledon Press.

Patterson, Robert B., ed. The Haskins Society Journal Vol. 4, 1992: Studies in Medieval History, Vol. 4, 1992. (Haskins Society Journal Ser.). (Illus.). 158p. 1993. 60.00 (*0-85115-333-X*) Boydell & Brewer.

— The Haskins Society Journal Vol. 5, 1993: Studies in Medieval History. (Illus.). 140p. (C). 1994. 60.00 (*0-85115-550-2*) Boydell & Brewer.

An Asterisk (*) at the beginning of an entry indicates that the title is appearing for the first time.

P

An Asterisk (*) at the beginning of an entry indicates that the title is appearing for the first time.

— Critical Essay on Donald Barthelme. (Critical Essays on American Literature Ser.). 190p. (C). 1991. 49.00 (*0-8161-7305-2*, G K Hall & Co) Mac Lib Ref.

— A World Outside: The Fiction of Paul Bowles. 167p. 1987. pap. 7.95 (*0-292-79035-X*) U of Tex Pr.

Patteson, Rita, ed. see Browning, Robert.

Patthy, L. & Friedrich, P. Multidomain Proteins: Proceedings of the UNESCO Workshop on Structure & Function of Proteins, Budapest, Sept. 13-15, 1984. 221p. (C). 1986. 100.00 (*963-05-4306-0*, Pub. by Akade Kiado) St Mut.

Patthy, Laszio. Protein Evolution. LC 98-46905. (Illus.). 228p. 1999. pap. 49.95 (*0-632-04774-7*) Blackwell Sci.

Patti, Charles H., et al. Business-to-Business Advertising: A Marketing Management Approach. LC 90-47970. (Illus.). 304p. 1994. 39.95 (*0-8442-3471-0*, NTC Business Bks) NTC Contemp Pub Co.

Patti, Janet, jt. auth. see Lantieri, Linda.

Patti, Nora M. I Am That I Am - Alta Major: Shortcut to Alignment & Enlightenment. Wilson, Eric, tr. from FRE.Tr. of Je Suis Celui Qui Suis - Alta Major. 224p. 1997. pap. 12.95 (*0-9655990-0-0*) Antahkaranah.

Patti, Rino, et al, eds. Managing for Service Effectiveness in Social Welfare Organizations. LC 87-22930. (Administration in Social Work Ser.: Vol. 11, Nos. 3 & 4). 295p. 1989. text 49.95 (*0-86656-687-2*) Haworth Pr.

Patti, Sebastian T., jt. auth. see Zimmerman, John L.

Pattiaratchi, Charitha, ed. Mixing in Estuaries & Coastal Seas. LC 96-175. (Coastal & Estuarine Studies: Vol. 50). 1996. 70.00 (*0-87590-264-2*) Am Geophysical.

Pattie, Alice, jt. auth. see Kreis, Bernardine.

Pattie, Charles, et al, eds. British Elections & Parties Review. (British Elections & Parties Ser.: Vol. 7). 304p. 1997. 64.00 (*0-7146-4860-4*, Pub. by F Cass Pubs); pap. 30.00 (*0-7146-4417-X*, Pub. by F Cass Pubs) Intl Spec Bk.

Pattie, D. A. Poetic Reflections. LC 87-72042. 58p. (Orig.). 1987. pap. 1.95 (*0-911789-02-2*) Pattie Prop Inc.

— To Cock a Cannon: A Pilots View of World War II Through the Eyes of a Naval Aviator. LC 82-91126. (Illus.). 164p. 1983. 7.95 (*0-911789-01-4*); pap. 4.95 (*0-911789-00-6*) Pattie Prop Inc.

***Pattie, Don & Fisher, Chris.** Mammals of Alberta. 240p. 1999. pap. 19.95 (*1-55105-209-1*) Lone Pine.

***Pattie, Don, et al.** Mammals of the Rocky Mountains. (Illus.). 296p. 2000. pap. 18.95 (*1-55105-211-3*) Lone Pine.

Pattie, Frank A. Mesmer & Animal Magnetism: A Chapter in the History of Medicine. LC 93-41168. (Illus.). 303p. 1994. 39.95 (*0-9622393-5-6*) Edmonston Publ.

Pattie, Geoffrey, et al. Making Transatlantic Defense Cooperation Work: Findings & Recommendations of the CSIS Atlantic Partnership Project. LC 96-14000. (CSIS Panel Reports). (C). 1996. pap. text 14.95 (*0-89206-286-X*) CSIS.

Pattie, James O. Personal Narrative of James O. Pattie. Batman, Richard, ed. LC 88-5221. 216p. 1988. pap. 14.00 (*0-87842-205-6*) Scurlock Pub.

— Personal Narrative of James O. Pattie. (American Biography Ser.). 300p. 1991. reprint ed. lib. bdg. 69.00 (*0-7812-8308-6*) Rprt Serv.

— The Personal Narrative of James O. Pattie of Kentucky. Flint, Timothy, ed. LC 72-9464. (Far Western Frontier Ser.). (Illus.). 314p. 1973. reprint ed. 23.95 (*0-405-04992-7*) Ayer.

— The Personal Narrative of James O. Pattie, 1831. unabridged ed. LC 83-27406. 285p. reprint ed. pap. 88.40 (*0-7837-6011-6*, 204582200008) Bks Demand.

Pattie, Jane. Cowboy Spurs & Their Makers. LC 90-10889. (Centennial Series of the Association of Former Students: No. 37). (Illus.). 192p. 1991. 39.95 (*0-89096-343-6*) Tex A&M Univ Pr.

Pattie, Ling-Yuh W. & Cox, Bonnie J., eds. Electronic Resources: Selection & Bibliographic Control. LC 96-27556. (Cataloging & Classification Quarterly Ser.: Vol. 22, Nos. 3 & 4). 268p. (C). 1996. 39.95 (*1-56024-847-5*) Haworth Pr.

P

Pattie, Steven N. For Fathers of Sons. (Illus.). 48p. 1991. 8.95 (*0-8378-1987-3*) Gibson.

Pattie, Susan P. Faith in History: Armenians Rebuilding Community. LC 96-7579. (Smithsonian Series in Ethnographic Inquiry). (Illus.). 352p. 1996. text 49.00 (*1-56098-629-8*) Smithsonian.

Pattie, T. S. Manuscripts of the Bible: Greek Bibles in the British Library. rev. ed. (Illus.). 48p. (C). 1995. pap. 9.95 (*0-7123-0403-7*, Pub. by B23tish Library) U of Toronto Pr.

***Pattie, T. S. & McKendrick, S., eds.** Summary Catalogue of Greek Manuscripts, Vol. I. 500p. 1999. write for info. (*0-7123-4622-8*, Pub. by B23tish Library) U of Toronto Pr.

Pattillo, Craig W. Christmas on Record: Best Selling Xmas Singles & Albums of the Past 40 Years. 220p. 1983. pap. 14.50 (*0-9612044-0-0*) Braemar OR.

— TV Theme Soundtrack Directory & Discography with Cover Versions. 287p. 1990. pap. 14.50 (*0-9612044-2-7*) Braemar OR.

Pattillo, Donald M. A History in the Making: 50 Years of Turbulent History in the General Aviation Industry. LC 98-4213. (Illus.). 300p. 1998. 29.95 (*0-07-049448-7*) McGraw.

Pattillo, Donald M. Pushing the Envelope: The American Aircraft Industry. LC 97-45390. (Illus.). 484p. (C). 1998. text 49.50 (*0-472-10869-7*, 10869) U of Mich Pr.

***Pattillo, Donald M.** Pushing the Envelope: The American Aircraft Industry. (Illus.). 484p. 2000. pap. text 27.95 (*0-472-08671-5*, 08671) U of Mich Pr.

Pattillo, Janice & Vaughan, Elizabeth. Learning Centers for Child-Centered Classrooms. 112p. 1992. pap. 15.95 (*0-8106-0357-8*) NEA.

Pattillo, Manning M., Jr. Private Higher Education in the United States. 46p. (Orig.). (C). 1990. pap. 2.00 (*1-880647-02-8*) U GA Inst High Educ.

Pattillo-McCoy, Mary. Black Picket Fences: Privilege & Peril among the Black Middle Class. LC 99-18913. 248p. 1999. 25.00 (*0-226-64928-8*) U Ch Pr.

***Pattin, Ed & Pattin, Linda.** The Guide to Home Canning. 1999. pap. 8.95 (*0-9667622-1-5*) Schlabach Print.

Pattin, Linda, jt. auth. see Pattin, Ed.

Pattinson, James. Avenger of Blood LC 96-24259. 249 p. 1996. write for info. (*0-7451-4943-X*) Chivers N Amer.

Pattinson, James. Avenger of Blood. large type ed. LC 96-24259. (Nightingale Ser.). 1996. 17.95 (*0-7838-1880-7*, G K Hall Lrg Type) Mac Lib Ref.

— Away with Murder. large type ed. (Linford Mystery Large Print Ser.). 304p. 1998. pap. 17.99 (*0-7089-5267-4*, Linford) Ulverscroft.

***Pattinson, James.** Dangerous Enchantment. large type ed. 288p. 2000. pap. 18.99 (*0-7089-5657-2*, Linford) Ulverscroft.

— Death of a Go-Between. large type ed. 256p. 2000. 31.99 (*0-7089-4174-5*) Ulverscroft.

Pattinson, James. Dishonour among Thieves. large type ed. 224p. 1990. 22.95 (*0-7451-1147-5*, G K Hall Lrg Type) Mac Lib Ref.

— Fat Man from Colombia. large type ed. (Dales Large Print Ser.). 235p. 1997. pap. 18.99 (*1-85389-742-6*) Ulverscroft.

— A Fatal Errand. large type ed. (Dales Large Print Ser.). 292p. 1997. pap. 18.99 (*1-85389-748-5*) Ulverscroft.

***Pattinson, James.** Flight to the Sea. large type ed. 336p. 1999. pap. 18.99 (*0-7089-5602-5*, Linford) Ulverscroft.

— Homecoming. 312p. 2000. 18.99 (*0-7089-5770-6*) Ulverscroft.

Pattinson, James. Last in Convoy. 1958. 10.95 (*0-8392-1060-4*) Astor-Honor.

— Last in Convoy. large type ed. (Ulverscroft Large Print Ser.). 432p. 1998. 29.99 (*0-7089-3931-7*) Ulverscroft.

— One-Way Ticket. large type ed. (Ulverscroft Large Print Ser.). 288p. 1998. 29.99 (*0-7089-3918-X*) Ulverscroft.

***Pattinson, James.** The Petronov Plan. large type ed. 312p. 2000. pap. 18.99 (*0-7089-5674-2*, Linford) Ulverscroft.

Pattinson, James. The Poison Traders. large type ed. LC 95-20451. 250p. 1995. pap. 18.95 (*0-7838-1439-9*, G K Hall Lrg Type) Mac Lib Ref.

— Silent Voyage. 1959. 10.95 (*0-8392-1105-8*) Astor-Honor.

***Pattinson, James.** The Spoilers. large type ed. 296p. 2000. pap. 18.99 (*0-7089-5681-5*, Linford) Ulverscroft.

Pattinson, James. The Stalking-Horse. large type ed. LC 94-12774. 272p. 1994. lib. bdg. 16.95 (*0-8161-7420-2*, G K Hall Lrg Type) Mac Lib Ref.

Pattinson, James. Steel. large type ed. 288p. pap. 18.99 (*0-7089-5446-4*) Ulverscroft.

Pattinson, James. A Wind on the Heath. large type ed. (Ulverscroft Large Print Ser.). 352p. 1998. 29.99 (*0-7089-3907-4*) Ulverscroft.

Pattinson, James A. Across the Narrow Seas. large type ed. (General Ser.). 1993. 20.95 (*0-7089-2811-0*) Ulverscroft.

— The Animal Gang. large type ed. 272p. 1996. pap. 18.99 (*1-85389-600-4*, Dales) Ulverscroft.

— Contact Mr. Delgado. large type ed. 1994. 27.99 (*0-7089-3155-3*) Ulverscroft.

***Pattinson, James A.** The Deadly Shore. large type ed. 320p. 1999. pap. 18.99 (*0-7089-5537-1*, Linford) Ulverscroft.

Pattinson, James A. Devil under the Skin. large type ed. (Dales Large Print Ser.). 1995. pap. 18.99 (*1-85389-577-6*, Dales) Ulverscroft.

— Killer. large type ed. LC 97-32592. (Nightingale Ser.). 1998. pap. 18.95 (*0-7838-8386-2*, G K Hall & Co) Mac Lib Ref.

— Lady from Argentina. large type ed. 320p. 1996. 27.99 (*0-7089-3505-2*) Ulverscroft.

***Pattinson, James A.** The Murmansk Assignment. large type ed. 336p. 1999. pap. 18.99 (*0-7089-5591-6*, Linford) Ulverscroft.

Pattinson, James A. The Saigon Merchant. large type ed. 274p. 1994. pap. 18.99 (*1-85389-468-0*, Dales) Ulverscroft.

— Soldier, Sail North. large type ed. (Large Print Ser.). 448p. 1996. 27.99 (*0-7089-3577-X*) Ulverscroft.

— Squeaky Clean. large type ed. (Large Print Ser.). 336p. 1997. 27.99 (*0-7089-3689-X*) Ulverscroft.

— The Telephone Murders. large type ed. (Linford Mystery Library). 336p. 1996. pap. 16.99 (*0-7089-7875-4*, Linford) Ulverscroft.

— The Wheel of Fortune. large type ed. (Adventure Suspense Ser.). 1991. 11.50 (*0-7089-2376-3*) Ulverscroft.

— Wild Justice. large type ed. (Linford Mystery Library). 1989. pap. 16.99 (*0-7089-6752-3*) Ulverscroft.

Pattinson, Lee, jt. auth. see Wigmore, Ann.

Pattiruhu, Maureen, tr. see Muller, Kal.

Pattis, Anne-Francoise. The French Culture Coloring Book. (The...Culture Coloring Book Ser.). (FRE., Illus.). 64p. (J). 1994. pap. 4.95 (*0-8442-1377-2*, 13772, Passprt Bks) NTC Contemp Pub Co.

— Italian Coloring Book. 2nd ed. (Let's Learn Ser.). (ITA., Illus.). 64p. (J). pap. 9.95 incl. audio (*0-8442-9276-1*) NTC Contemp Pub Co.

— Let's Learn French Coloring Book. (Let's Learn...Coloring Books Ser.). (FRE., Illus.). 16p. (J). (gr. 4 up). 1994. pap. 3.95 (*0-8442-1389-6*, 13896, Passprt Bks) NTC Contemp Pub Co.

Pattis, Anne-Francoise. Let's Learn Spanish. (Let's Learn...Coloring Books Ser.). (SPA., Illus.). 16p. (J). (gr. 4 up). 1995. pap. 4.95 (*0-8442-7549-2*, 75492, Passprt Bks) NTC Contemp Pub Co.

Pattis, Anne-Francoise. The Spanish Culture. (The...Culture Coloring Book Ser.). (SPA., Illus.). 48p. (J). (gr. 4-7). 1996. wbk. ed. 4.95 (*0-8442-7538-7*, 75387, Passprt Bks) NTC Contemp Pub Co.

Pattis, Anne-Francoise, jt. auth. see Hazzan, Anne-Francoise.

Pattis, Richard E. Karel the Robot: A Gentle Introduction to the Art of Programming. 2nd ed. LC 94-8087. 176p. 1994. pap. 25.95 (*0-471-59725-2*) Wiley.

Pattis, Richard E. Karel the Robot: A Gentle Introduction to the Art of Programming. 2nd ed. 1995. text 14.95 (*0-471-10702-6*) Wiley.

Pattis, Richard P., et al. Karel the Robot & IBM Software. 2nd ed. 176p. 1994. pap. text, suppl. ed. 36.90 incl. disk (*0-471-11734-X*) Wiley.

Pattis, S. William. Careers in Advertising. 144p. 1993. pap. 12.95 (*0-8442-8697-4*, VGM Career) NTC Contemp Pub Co.

— Careers in Advertising. 144p. 1994. 16.95 (*0-8442-8696-6*, VGM Career) NTC Contemp Pub Co.

— Careers in Advertising. 2nd ed. LC 96-2131. (Careers for You Ser.). (Illus.). 144p. 1996. 17.95 (*0-8442-4507-0*, 45070, VGM Career); pap. 13.95 (*0-8442-4508-9*, 45089, VGM Career) NTC Contemp Pub Co.

— Let's Learn German Coloring Book. (Let's Learn...Coloring Books Ser.). (GER., Illus.). 16p. (J). (gr. 4 up). 1994. pap. 4.95 (*0-8442-2164-3*, 21643, Passprt Bks) NTC Contemp Pub Co.

— Opportunities in Advertising. (Illus.). 160p. 1993. pap. 10.95 (*0-8442-6272-2*, VGM Career) NTC Contemp Pub Co.

— Opportunities in Advertising Careers. LC 94-49545. (Opportunities In . . . Ser.). (Illus.). 160p. pap. 11.95 (*0-8442-4443-0*, 44430, VGM Career) NTC Contemp Pub Co.

— Opportunities in Advertising Careers. LC 94-49545. (Illus.). 160p. 1995. 14.95 (*0-8442-4442-2*, 44422, VGM Career) NTC Contemp Pub Co.

— Opportunities in Magazine Publishing. (Illus.). 160p. 1987. 13.95 (*0-8442-6141-6*, VGM Career) NTC Contemp Pub Co.

— Opportunities in Magazine Publishing. (Illus.). 160p. 1993. pap. 10.95 (*0-8442-6142-4*, VGM Career) NTC Contemp Pub Co.

— Opportunities in Magazine Publishing Careers. (Opportunities In . . . Ser.). (Illus.). 160p. pap. 12.95 (*0-8442-8180-8*, 297OIMP, VGM Career) NTC Contemp Pub Co.

— Opportunities in Magazine Publishing Careers. (Opportunities in...Ser.). (Illus.). 160p. 1994. 13.95 (*0-8442-8179-4*, VGM Career) NTC Contemp Pub Co.

Pattis, S. William & Carter, Robert A. Opportunities in Publishing Careers. LC 94-49618. (Opportunities In . . . Ser.). (Illus.). 160p. pap. 11.95 (*0-8442-4432-5*, 44325, VGM Career) NTC Contemp Pub Co.

— Opportunities in Publishing Careers. LC 94-49618. (Illus.). 160p. 1995. 14.95 (*0-8442-4431-7*, 44317, VGM Career) NTC Contemp Pub Co.

***Pattis, S. William, et al.** Opportunities in Publishing Careers. rev. ed. LC 00-39272. (Opportunities Ser.). 2000. pap. 11.95 (*0-658-00484-0*) NTC Contemp Pub Co.

Pattishall, Beverly W., et al. Trademarks & Unfair Competition. 2nd ed. LC 94-21711. 592p. (C). 1994. 42.50 (*0-8205-2816-1*) Bender.

— Trademarks & Unfair Competition. 3rd ed. LC 98-34819. (Contemporary Casebook Ser.). 1998. 56.00 (*0-8205-3133-2*) Bender.

Pattishall, Evan G. Behavioral Science. 8th ed. (Basic Sciences: Pretest Self Assessment & Review Ser.). (Illus.). 1998. pap. text 18.95 (*0-07-052689-3*) McGraw-Hill HPD.

Pattison. Peridontal Instrumentation. 3rd ed. (C). 2002. spiral bd. 39.95 (*0-8385-7690-7*) Appleton & Lange.

Pattison, Andrew. M Factor. 1999. pap. text 12.00 (*0-7318-0697-2*) Simon & Schuster.

Pattison, Anna & Pattison, Gordon. Periodontal Instrumentation. 2nd ed. (Illus.). 485p. (C). 1991. pap. text 42.95 (*0-8385-7804-7*, A7804-6) Appleton & Lange.

Pattison, Bruce. Music & Poetry of the English Renaissance. LC 70-127278. (Music Ser.). (Illus.). 1971. reprint ed. lib. bdg. 29.50 (*0-306-71298-9*) Da Capo.

Pattison, Darcy. Let's Quilt: A First Book on Quilt Making. LC 96-33615. (J). 1997. write for info. (*0-8442-2629-7*, Quilt Dgst Pr) NTC Contemp Pub Co.

— The River Dragon. LC 90-49931. (Illus.). 32p. (J). (gr. k up). 1991. 13.95 (*0-688-10426-6*) Lothrop.

Pattison, Darcy. The Wayfinder. LC 99-89401. 160p. (J). (gr. 4-7). 2000. 15.95 (*0-688-17080-3*, Grenwillow Bks) HarpC Child Bks.

***Pattison, Darcy.** The Wayfinder. LC 99-89401. 208p. (J). (gr. 4-7). 2000. 15.89 (*0-06-029157-5*, Grenwillow Bks) HarpC Child Bks.

Pattison, Diana, jt. auth. see Baldwin, Bruce.

Pattison, Diane, jt. auth. see Baldwin, Bruce.

Pattison, E. Mansell, ed. Selection of Treatment for Alcoholics. LC 79-620007. (NIAAA-RUCAS Alcoholism Treatment Ser.: No. 1). 1982. pap. 22.50 (*0-911290-47-8*) Rutgers Ctr Alcohol.

Pattison, E. Mansell & Kaufman, Edward, eds. Encyclopedic Handbook of Alcoholism. LC 81-24196. 1256p. 1982. 120.00 (*0-89876-017-8*) Gardner Pr.

Pattison, E. Mansell, jt. ed. see Galanter, Marc.

Pattison, E. Scott, ed. Fatty Acids & Their Industrial Applications. LC 68-12437. (Illus.). 402p. reprint ed. pap. 124.70 (*0-608-30548-0*, 205500400007) Bks Demand.

Pattison, Eliot. The Skull Mantra: A Minotaur Discovery. LC 99-23847. 352p. 1999. text 24.95 (*0-312-20478-7*, Minotaur) St Martin.

***Pattison, Eliot.** The Skull Mantra. large type ed. LC 99-56339. 709p. 2000. 30.00 (*0-7862-2258-1*) Mac Lib Ref.

Pattison, Eugene, jt. auth. see Howells, William Dean.

Pattison, F. L. Granville Sharp Pattison: Anatomist & Antagonist, 1791-1851. LC 87-10835. (History of American Science & Technology Ser.). 304p. 1987. text 29.95 (*0-8173-0375-8*) U of Ala Pr.

Pattison, Gary. Restructuring Culture: Identification of Difference & the Regulation of Change in Ex-Mining Communities. LC 99-72650. (Urban & Regional Planning & Development Ser.). 218p. 1999. text 65.95 (*1-84014-330-4*, Pub. by Ashgate Pub) Ashgate Pub Co.

Pattison, Gavin, jt. auth. see Villiers, John.

Pattison, George. Anxious Angels. LC 98-30657. 24p. 1999. text 59.95 (*0-312-22011-1*) St Martin.

***Pattison, George.** Art, Modernity & Faith: Restoring the Image. 1998. pap. 22.00 (*0-334-02719-5*) S C M Pr Ltd.

Pattison, George. Poor Paris! Kierkegaard's Critique of the Spectacular City. LC 99-11509. xvi, 152p. 1999. 63.25 (*3-11-016388-8*) De Gruyter.

***Pattison, George.** Routledge Philosophy Guidebook to the Later Heidegger. LC 00-20572. (Philosophy Guidebooks Ser.). 2000. pap. write for info. (*0-415-20195-0*) Routledge.

— Routledge Philosophy Guidebook to the Later Heidegger. 2000. 60.00 (*0-415-20196-9*); pap. 14.95 (*0-415-20197-7*) Routledge.

Pattison, George, jt. auth. see Becket, Wendy.

Pattison, George, jt. auth. see Platten, Stephen.

Pattison, Gordon, jt. auth. see Pattison, Anna.

Pattison, Iain. History of the British Veterinary Profession, 1791-1948. 222p. 1990. 38.00 (*0-85131-379-5*, Pub. by J A Allen) St Mut.

— John McFadyean. 240p. 1990. 40.00 (*0-85131-352-3*, Pub. by J A Allen) St Mut.

— Professor James Beart Simonds: A Great British Veterinarian Forgotten. 172p. 1990. 64.00 (*0-85131-491-0*, Pub. by J A Allen) St Mut.

Pattison, James. Agnosis: Theology in Void. 208p. 1997. text 59.95 (*0-312-16206-5*) St Martin.

Pattison, James B. A Programmed Introduction to Gas-Liquid Chromatography. 2nd ed. LC QD0271.P33. (Illus.). 320p. reprint ed. pap. 99.20 (*0-608-17586-2*, 203042700069) Bks Demand.

Pattison, Jean, jt. auth. see Jordan, Rick.

Pattison, John R., ed. Parvoviruses & Human Disease. 208p. 1988. 117.00 (*0-8493-5956-2*, QR201, CRC Reprint) Franklin.

Pattison, Joseph E. Antidumping & Countervailing Duty Laws. LC 84-14463. (International Business & Law Ser.). 1984. ring bd. 145.00 (*0-87632-446-4*) West Group.

— Breaking Boundaries: Public Policy vs. American Business in the World Economy. (Pacesetter Bks.). 240p. 1996. text 24.95 (*1-56079-611-1*, Petersons Pacesetter) Petersons.

Pattison, Mansell E., ed. Clinical Applications of Social Network Theory: A Special Issue of International Journal of Family Therapy, Vol. 3. LC 81-84340. 88p. 1982. pap. 16.95 (*0-89885-126-2*, Kluwer Acad Hman Sci) Kluwer Academic.

Pattison, Marilyn. ABC Sing with Me. (Illus.). 30p. (J). (ps-1). 1997. spiral bd. 15.95 incl. audio (*0-9663421-0-0*) ABC Sing.

Pattison, Mark. Milton. (BCL1-PR English Literature Ser.). 227p. 1992. reprint ed. lib. bdg. 79.00 (*0-7812-7388-9*) Rprt Serv.

— Suggestions on Academical Organisation with Especial Reference to Oxford. Metzger, Walter P., ed. (Academic Profession Ser.). 1977. lib. bdg. 29.95 (*0-405-10027-2*) Ayer.

Pattison, Mark, ed. The Health of Poultry. 294p. pap. 84.95 (*0-582-06579-8*, Pub. by Addison-Wesley) Longman.

Pattison, Mary A. Buffalo County: A Pictorial History. LC 93-4366. 1993. write for info. (*0-89865-870-5*) Donning Co.

Pattison-Muir, M. M. The Alchemical Essence: An Episode in the Quest for the Unchanging. 1994. pap. 6.95 (*1-55818-291-8*) Holmes Pub.

Pattison, Pat. Managing Lyric Structure. 112p. 1991. pap. 11.95 (*0-7935-1180-1*, 50481582, Berklee Pr) H Leonard.

— Rhyming Techniques & Strategies. 76p. 1991. pap. 10.95 (*0-7935-1181-X*, 50481583, Berklee Pr) H Leonard.

— Writing Better Lyrics. LC 95-20964. 192p. 1995. 19.99 (*0-89879-682-2*, Wrtrs Digest Bks) F & W Pubns Inc.

Pattison, Philippa. Algebraic Models for Social Networks. (Structural Analysis in the Social Sciences Ser.: No. 7). (Illus.). 332p. (C). 1993. text 42.95 (*0-521-36568-6*) Cambridge U Pr.

Pattison, Robert. Fair Housing for the Real Estate Practitioner. LC 96-92039. (Illus.). 158p. 1996. per. 19.95 (*0-9650709-0-5*) Suburban Real Est.

— Tennyson & Tradition. LC 79-13247. 178p. 1980. 31.00 (*0-674-87415-3*) HUP.

Pattison, Ruth. No Way of Escape. large type ed. (Dales Large Print Ser.). 184p. 1997. pap. 18.99 (*1-85389-762-0*, Dales) Ulverscroft.

Pattison, Stephen. The Faith of the Managers: When Managerialism Becomes Religion. 192p. 1997. pap. 19.95 (*0-304-70144-0*) Bks Intl VA.

— Pastoral Care & Liberation Theology. (Cambridge Studies in Ideology & Religion: No. 5). 288p. (C). 1994. text 59.95 (*0-521-41822-4*) Cambridge U Pr.

***Pattison, Stephen.** Shame: Theory, Therapy, Theology. (Illus.). 335p. 2001. write for info. (*0-521-56045-4*); pap. write for info. (*0-521-56863-3*) Cambridge U Pr.

Pattison, Stephen, jt. ed. see Seale, Clive.

Pattison, Stephen, jt. ed. see Woodward, James.

***Pattison, Ted.** Programming Distributed Applications with COM+ & Microsoft Visual Basic. 2nd ed. LC 00-20234. (DV-MPS Programming Ser.). (Illus.). 2000. pap. text 49.99 (*0-7356-1010-X*) Microsoft.

An Asterisk (*) at the beginning of an entry indicates that the title is appearing for the first time.

Pattison, Ted. Programming Distributed Applications with COM & Microsoft Visual Basic 6.0. LC 98-39267. 500p. 1998. 44.99 incl. cd-rom (*1-57231-961-5*) Microsoft.

Pattison, W. T. Life & Works of the Troubadour Raimbaut D'Orange. LC 80-2182. reprint ed. 35.00 (*0-404-19015-4*) AMS Pr.

Pattison, Walter T. Emilia Pardo Bazan. LC 70-120497. (Twayne's World Authors Ser.). 1971. lib. bdg. 20.95 (*0-8057-2120-7*) Irvington.

Pattison, Walter T. & Bleznick, Donald W., eds. Representative Spanish Authors Vol. 1: From the Middle Ages Through the Eighteenth Century. 3rd ed. (C). 1971. text 34.95 (*0-19-501326-3*) OUP.

— Representative Spanish Authors Vol. 2: The Nineteenth Century to the Present. 3rd ed. (Illus.). 500p. (C). 1971. text 37.95 (*0-19-501433-2*) OUP.

Pattison, William D. Beginnings of the American Rectangular Land Survey Systems, 1704-1800. Bruchey, Stuart, ed. LC 78-56654. (Management of Public Lands in the U. S. Ser.). (Illus.). 1979. reprint ed. lib. bdg. 23.95 (*0-405-11350-1*) Ayer.

Pattisson, Rodney. Boatspeed. 64p. (C). 1990. text 59.00 (*0-906754-25-9*, Pub. by Fernhurst Bks) St Mut.

Pattisson, Rodney, ed. Tactics. 2nd ed. 96p. (C). 1993. text 18.95 (*0-906754-75-5*, Pub. by Fernhurst Bks) St Mut.

Pattnaik, Binay K. Scientific Temper: An Empirical Study. (C). 1992. 22.00 (*81-7033-176-5*, Pub. by Rawat Pubns) S Asia.

Pattnaik, D. D. Political Philosophy of Subash Chandra Bose. 1990. text 22.50 (*81-7045-066-7*, Pub. by Assoc Pub Hse) Advent Bks Div.

Pattnayak, Satya R., ed. Globalization, Urbanization, & the State: Selected Studies on Contemporary Latin America. LC 96-16414. 274p. 1996. pap. text 32.00 (*0-7618-0353-X*); lib. bdg. 52.00 (*0-7618-0352-1*) U Pr of Amer.

— Organized Religion in the Political Transformation of Latin America. LC 95-3402. 252p. (Orig.). (C). 1995. pap. text 29.50 (*0-7618-0040-9*); lib. bdg. 54.00 (*0-7618-0039-5*) U Pr of Amer.

Patton. Birthmarks. text 55.00 (*0-8147-6681-1*); pap. text 18.50 (*0-8147-6682-X*) NYU Pr.

Patton. Convergence in Career Development. LC 97-52264. (Counseling Ser.). 1998. mass mkt. 48.95 (*0-534-34813-0*) Brooks-Cole.

— Decision Making: Group Interaction. 4th ed. (C). 2000. pap. write for info. (*0-321-04919-5*) Addison-Wesley.

— Securities Fraud Issue 9: Litigating under Rule 10b-5. 175p. 1998. ring bd. write for info. (*0-327-00723-0*, 8238414) LEXIS Pub.

Patton & Cooper. Ergo. (C). 1994. pap. text, teacher ed. 11.00 (*0-06-502393-5*) HarpC.

Patton & Labarre. Viewer's Choice: A Comprehensive Record Keeping. (BB - Record Keeping I Ser.). 1988. pap. 11.95 (*0-538-02080-6*) S-W Pub.

***Patton & Patton, Sally J., eds.** A Magic Still Dwells: Comparative Religion in the Postmodern Age. LC 99-31468. 250p. 2000. 45.00 (*0-520-21971-6*, Pub. by U CA Pr) Cal Prin Full Svc.

Patton & Ray, Benjamin C., eds. A Magic Still Dwells: Comparative Religion in the Postmodern Age. LC 99-31468. 250p. 2000. pap. 17.95 (*0-520-22105-2*, Pub. by U CA Pr) Cal Prin Full Svc.

Patton & Tangedahl. Sim Strategy - A Computer-Assisted Simulation. (DF - Computer Applications Ser.). 1986. pap. 13.95 (*0-538-10070-2*) S-W Pub.

— Strategy: A Computer Assisted Program. 2nd ed. (BE-Accounting Advanced Ser.). 1991. mass mkt. 12.95 (*0-538-60394-1*) S-W Pub.

Patton & Thibodeau, Gary A. Quick Reference to Anatomy & Physiology. (Illus.). 64p. (C). (gr. 13). 1992. pap. text 9.95 (*0-8016-7530-8*, 07530) Mosby Inc.

Patton & Wolfe. Electronic Classroom, Quiktronic Management. (KG - Filing/Records Management Ser.). 1995. 115.50 (*0-538-63094-9*) S-W Pub.

— Quiktronic Records Management: Practice Set. (KG - Filing/Records Management Ser.). 1995. pap. 18.75 (*0-538-63089-2*) S-W Pub.

Patton, et al. Capstone Office Simulation. 1989. text 125.00 (*0-471-60876-9*) P-H.

Patton, jt. auth. see Shea.

Patton, A. B. Pattons Lehigh County, Pennsylvania. 1997. pap. 10.95 (*1-57381-048-7*, 836801Q) A B Patton.

Patton, Adell. Physicians, Colonial Racism & Diaspora in West Africa. LC 95-45070. 296p. (C). 1996. 49.95 (*0-8130-1432-8*) U Press Fla.

Patton, Aileen, jt. auth. see Shepherd, Caroline M.

Patton, Anthony. Practical LotusScript. LC 99-13034. (Illus.). 488p. 1999. pap. 43.95 (*1-884777-76-7*) Manning Pubns.

***Patton, Anthony S.** Domino Development with Java. (Illus.). 550p. 2000. pap. 49.95 (*1-930110-04-9*, Pub. by Manning Pubns) IPG Chicago.

Patton, Antwoine. Nocturnal Scriptures. 70p. 1997. pap. write for info. (*1-57502-526-4*, P01558) Morris Pubng.

Patton, Barbara W. Introducing Frederic Chopin. (Introducing the Composers Ser.). (Illus.). (Orig.). (J). (gr. 3-9). 1990. pap. 6.95 (*1-878636-00-6*) Soundboard Bks.

— Introducing Johann Sebastian Bach. (Introducing the Composers Ser.). (Illus.). 48p. (Orig.). (J). (gr. 3-9). 1992. pap. 6.95 (*1-878636-01-4*) Soundboard Bks.

— Introducing Wolfgang Amadeus Mozart. (Introducing the Composers Ser.). (Illus.). 48p. (Orig.). (J). (gr. 3-9). 1991. pap. 6.95 (*1-878636-03-0*) Soundboard Bks.

Patton, Beatrice A. Love Without End. (Illus.). 175p. (Orig.). 1987. pap. 10.00 (*0-914916-79-3*) Ku Paa.

Patton, Betty, jt. auth. see Haniford, Beatrice.

Patton, Bobby R. & Giffin, Kim. Interpersonal Communication in Action: Basic Text & Readings. 2nd ed. (Auer Ser.). (C). 1977. pap. text 14.50 (*0-06-042316-1*) Addison-Wesley Educ.

— Problem-solving Group Interaction. LC 73-6230. xii, 264p. 1973. 6.95 (*0-06-045059-2*, HarperHorizon) HarpC.

Patton, Bobby R., et al. Decision-Making Group Interaction. 3rd ed. 240p. (C). 1997. pap. text 57.00 (*0-06-045066-5*) Addson-Wesley Educ.

Patton, Boggs & Blow Staff. Environmental Law Handbook. Vanderver, Timothy A., Jr., ed. LC 93-47638. 725p. 1994. 115.00 (*0-87179-811-5*) BNA Books.

Patton, Brian, ed. Tales from the Canadian Rockies. 304p. Date not set. pap. 19.99 (*0-7710-6948-0*) McCland & Stewart.

***Patton, Brooks & Franklin, Derek.** Flash 4! Creative Web Animation. 3rd ed. (Illus.). 428p. 2000. pap. 39.99 incl. cd-rom (*0-201-35470-5*) Peachpit Pr.

Patton, C. V., jt. ed. see Checkoway, B.

Patton, Carl A. Big Ralph: Reflections of a Black Police Chief. LC 97-65057. (Illus.). 359p. 1997. 19.95 (*0-9656467-0-X*) Psyche Pub.

Patton, Carl V., ed. Spontaneous Shelter: International Perspectives & Prospects. LC 87-10002. (Illus.). 256p. (C). 1987. 49.95 (*0-87722-507-9*) Temple U Pr.

Patton, Carl V. & Sawicki, David S. Basic Methods of Policy Analysis. 2nd ed. 496p. (C). 1993. pap. text 54.00 (*0-13-060948-X*) P-H.

Patton, Carl V., jt. auth. see Page, G. William.

Patton, Cindy. Fatal Advice: How Safe-Sex Education Went Wrong. LC 95-44292. (Series Q). (Illus.). 184p. 1996. pap. 16.95 (*0-8223-1747-8*); text 49.95 (*0-8223-1750-8*) Duke.

— Last Served? Gendering the HIV Pandemic. LC 94-11502. (Social Aspects of AIDS Ser.). 1994. write for info. (*0-7484-0189-X*, Pub. by Tay Francis Ltd) Taylor & Francis.

— Last Served? Gendering the HIV Pandemic. LC 94-11502. (Social Aspects of AIDS Ser.). 1994. pap. 19.95 (*0-7484-0190-3*) Taylor & Francis.

— Sex & Germs: The Politics of AIDS. 182p. write for info. (*0-920057-82-9*); pap. write for info. (*0-920057-80-2*) Black Rose.

***Patton, Cindy & Sbanchez-Eppler, Benigno.** Sexualities on the Move. LC 99-29367. (Series Q). 280p. 2000. pap. 18.95 (*0-8223-2422-9*) Duke.

Patton, Claudia, ed. see Petty, Bill.

Patton, D. Keith. Petroleum Exploration Opportunities in Africa & Countries Beyond. LC 95-3072. 1995. 25.00 (*0-87814-440-4*) PennWell Bks.

Patton, David, ed. see Dake, Finis J., Sr.

Patton, David, ed. see Freeman, H. M. & Tolentino, F.

Patton, David, ed. see Spaeth, George I. & Koch, Douglas D.

Patton, David F. Cold War Politics in Post-War Germany. LC 98-41912. 272p. 1999. text 49.95 (*0-312-21361-1*) St Martin.

Patton, David R. Wildlife Habitat Relationships in Forested Ecosystems. 2nd rev. ed. LC 96-9410. (Illus.). 442p. 1997. 54.95 (*0-88192-371-0*) Timber.

Patton, David R., et al, eds. Management & Utilization of Arid Land Plants: Symposium Proceedings. rev. ed. 124p. 1997. 20.60 (*0-89904-656-8*, Bear Meadows Resrch Grp); pap. 15.60 (*0-89904-657-6*, Bear Meadows Resrch Grp) Crumb Elbow Pub.

Patton, Deborah. Bed & Breakfasts & Country Inns of New England. 2nd ed. 1990. pap. 12.95 (*0-89909-225-X*, 80-650-3) Yankee Bks.

Patton, Diane. From Conception to Healthy Childbirth with Minimal Weight Gain, & Through the Terrible 2's & 3's: Teaching Your Child How to Think Smart, & Not to Cry & Act Like a Baby!: Includes CD-ROM Visual ABC's, Counting & Reading Flash Cards to Jump Start Your Child Understanding Thinking Concepts. 160p. (Orig.). 1999. pap. 27.95 (*1-891950-15-0*, Pub. by Amer Group Pub) Koen Bk Distributors.

Patton, Dick. Life with Wine: A Practical Guide to the Basice. LC 94-92254. (Illus.). 128p. (Orig.). 1994. pap. 9.95 (*0-9642885-0-8*) R J Patton.

Patton, Don. Armadillos. LC 95-7179. (Nature Books Ser.). (Illus.). 32p. (J). (gr. 2-6). 1995. lib. bdg. 22.79 (*1-56766-182-3*) Childs World.

— Pythons. LC 95-7388. (Nature Books Ser.). (Illus.). 32p. (J). (gr. 2-6). 1995. lib. bdg. 22.79 (*1-56766-180-7*) Childs World.

— Sea Turtles. LC 95-7858. (Nature Books Ser.). (Illus.). 32p. (J). (gr. 2-6). 1995. lib. bdg. 22.79 (*1-56766-188-2*) Childs World.

Patton, Donald J., jt. ed. see Fernald, Edward A.

***Patton, Donald L.** Gulf War Illnesses: Procedural & Reporting Improvements Are Needed in DOD's Investigative Processes: Squalene Antibodies in Veterans. 97p. (C). 2000. pap. text 25.00 (*0-7881-8625-6*) DIANE Pub.

Patton, Douglas. Badr al-Din Lu'lu' Atabeg of Mosul, 1211-1259. LC 91-27342. (Occasional Papers, Middle East Center Ser.: No. 3). 122p. (C). 1992. pap. text 12.95 (*0-295-97156-8*) U of Wash Pr.

***Patton, Dwight L.** Andy's Mountain: Fathers Grieve Too. 144p. 1999. pap. 8.95 (*0-7880-1413-7*) CSS.

Patton, Ellen R., ed. see Ferguson, Jeannette S.

Patton, Elota, ed. see Dorsey, Jason Ryan.

Patton, F. Lester. Diminishing Returns in Agriculture. LC 68-57575. (Columbia University. Studies in the Social Sciences: No. 284). reprint ed. 20.00 (*0-404-51284-4*) AMS Pr.

Patton, Fiona. The Granite Shield. 528p. 1999. mass mkt. 6.99 (*0-88677-842-5*, Pub. by DAW Bks) Penguin Putnam.

— Painter Knight. 544p. 1998. mass mkt. 6.99 (*0-88677-780-1*, Pub. by DAW Bks) Penguin Putnam.

— The Stone Prince. 1997. mass mkt. 6.99 (*0-88677-735-6*, Pub. by DAW Bks) Penguin Putnam.

Patton, Frances G. Good Morning, Miss Dove. 21.95 (*0-88411-879-7*) Amereon Ltd.

Patton, Fred. The History of Fort Smith, 1817 Through 1992. 468p. 1993. 24.95 (*0-9614629-0-6*); pap. 14.95 (*0-9614629-1-4*) J F Patton.

Patton, Fred, tr. see Riasanovsky, A. V. & Zubarev, Vera.

Patton, Gary M. & Sale-Tinney, Lindsay, eds. Golfing America: Western Edition. 265p. (Orig.). 1993. pap. 16.95 (*0-9636438-0-0*) Golfing Am.

Patton, Gene. Integrating Technology into the Science Curriculum. 144p. (J). (gr. 3-5). 1997. pap. 14.95 (*1-57690-428-8*) Tchr Create Mat.

Patton, George S. The Patton Papers, 1940-1945. Blumenson, Martin, ed. LC 96-15251. (Illus.). 936p. 1996. reprint ed. pap. 19.95 (*0-306-80717-3*) Da Capo.

Patton, George S., Jr. The Poems of General George S. Patton, Jr. Lines of Fire. Prioli, Carmine A., ed. LC 90-30990. (Studies in American Literature: Vol. 8). 232p. 1991. 89.95 (*0-88946-162-7*) E Mellen.

Patton, George S. War As I Knew It. (War Ser.). 416p. 1983. mass mkt. 7.99 (*0-553-25991-1*) Bantam.

— War As I Knew It: General George S. Patton, Jr. (Illus.). 448p. 1995. pap. 16.95 (*0-395-73529-7*) HM.

Patton, Gerald W. War & Race: The Black Officer in the American Military, 1915 to 1941, 62. LC 80-24629. (Contributions in Afro-American & African Studies: No. 62). (Illus.). 214p. 1981. 55.00 (*0-313-22176-6*, PWR/, Greenwood Pr) Greenwood.

Patton, Grant W., Jr. & Kistner, Robert W. Atlas of Infertility. 368p. 1984. 99.00 (*0-316-69387-1*, Little Brwn Med Div) Lppncott W & W.

Patton, Harold S. Grain Growers' Cooperation in Western Canada. LC 71-100529. reprint ed. 57.50 (*0-404-00630-2*) AMS Pr.

Patton-Hulce, Vicki R. Environment & the Law: A Dictionary. LC 95-46013. (Contemporary World Issues Ser.). 361p. 1995. lib. bdg. 45.00 (*0-87436-749-2*) ABC-CLIO.

Patton, Isolde M. My Three Worlds. 167p. 1985. 9.95 (*0-87770-316-7*) Ye Galleon.

***Patton, James J.** World Trade Organization (WTO) Dispute Settlement Decisions: Bernan's Annotated Reporter. 1999. 90.00 (*0-89059-184-9*) Bernan Pr.

— World Trade Organization (WTO) Dispute Settlement Decisions: Bernan's Annotated Reporter. 1999. 90.00 (*0-89059-185-7*) Bernan Pr.

— World Trade Organization (WTO) Dispute Settlement Decisions: Bernan's Annotated Reporter. 1999. 90.00 (*0-89059-186-5*) Bernan Pr.

— World Trade Organization (WTO) Dispute Settlement Decisions: Bernan's Annotated Reporter. 1999. 90.00 (*0-89059-187-3*) Bernan Pr.

Patton, James J. WTO Dispute Settlement Decisions Reporter, Vol. 2. (Illus.). 535p. 1998. boxed set 90.00 (*0-89059-106-7*, BWTO/1067) Bernan Pr.

***Patton, James J.** WTO Dispute Settlement Decisions Reporter, Vol. 4. Vol. 4. (Illus.). 1999. boxed set 90.00 (*0-89059-163-6*) Bernan Pr.

Patton, James J. WTO Dispute Settlement Decisions Reporter, Vol. 5. Vol. 5. (Illus.). 519p. 1999. boxed set 90.00 (*0-89059-164-4*) Bernan Pr.

***Patton, James J.** WTO Dispute Settlement Decisions Reporter, Vol. 6. (Illus.). 520p. 1999. boxed set 90.00 (*0-89059-183-0*) Bernan Pr.

***Patton, James J. & Bernan Press Staff.** World Trade Organization Dispute Settlement Decisions, Bernan's Annotated Reporter: Annotations Tables & Cumulative Index Volume, 12. 2000. 75.00 (*0-89059-253-5*, Pub. by Bernan Pr) Bernan Associates.

— World Trade Organization Dispute Settlement Decisions, Bernan's Annotated Reporter: Annotations Tables & Cumulative Index Volume, 13. 500p. 2000. 90.00 (*0-89059-254-3*, Pub. by Bernan Pr) Bernan Associates.

— World Trade Organization Dispute Settlement Decisions, Bernan's Annotated Reporter: Annotations Tables & Cumulative Index Volume, II. 2000. 75.00 (*0-89059-209-8*, Pub. by Bernan Pr) Bernan Associates.

— World Trade Organization Dispute Settlement Decisions, Bernan's Annotated Reporter: Bernan's Annotated Reporter, Cumulative Index Volume. 2000. 75.00 (*0-89059-210-1*) Bernan Pr.

Patton, James L. & Smith, Margaret F. The Evolutionary Dynamics of the Pocket Gopher Thomomys bottae, with Emphasis on California Populations. LC 90-11136. (Publications in Zoology: Vol.123). (Illus.). 177p. 1991. pap. 25.00 (*0-520-09761-0*, Pub. by U CA Pr) Cal Prin Full Svc.

Patton, James L., jt. auth. see Mustrangi, Meika A.

Patton, James R. & Blalock, Ginger, eds. Transition & Students with Learning Disabilities: Facilitating the Movement from School to Adult Life. LC 95-52856. 309p. 1996. pap. 32.00 (*0-89079-696-3*, 7818) PRO-ED.

Patton, James R. & Dunn, Caroline. Transition from School to Young Adulthood: Basic Concepts & Recommended Practices. (Series on Transition). 78p. 1998. pap. text 9.00 (*0-89079-782-X*, 8571) PRO-ED.

Patton, James R. & Polloway, Edward A., eds. Learning Disabilities: The Challenges of Adulthood. LC 95-14293. 303p. 1996. pap. text 34.00 (*0-89079-581-9*) PRO-ED.

Patton, James R., et al. Exceptional Individuals in Focus. 6th ed. LC 95-41896. 337p. (C). 1996. pap. 43.67 (*0-13-502352-1*, Merrill Pub Co) Macmillan.

Patton, James R., et al. Infusing Real-life Topics into Existing Curricula: Recommended Procedures & Instructional Examples for the Elementary, Middle, & High School Levels. LC 99-13430. (Pro-Ed Series on Transition). 1999. write for info. (*0-89079-814-1*) PRO-ED.

Patton, James R., jt. auth. see Cronin, Mary E.

Patton, James R., jt. auth. see De Fur, Sharon.

Patton, James R., jt. auth. see Hoover, John J.

Patton, James R., jt. auth. see Polloway, Edward A.

Patton, James R., jt. auth. see Smith, Tom E.

Patton, James R., jt. auth. see Wehmeyer, Michael L.

Patton James, Systems Control, Inc. Staff, jt. auth. see Curtice, David.

Patton, James W., jt. auth. see Simkins, Francis B.

Patton, James W., jt. ed. see Crabtree, Beth G.

Patton, James W., ed. see Greenville Ladies' Association Staff.

Patton, Jeffrey, jt. auth. see Bennett, D. Gordon.

Patton, Jim. Il Basket d'Italia: A Season in Italy with Great food, Good Friends & Some Very Tall Americans. LC 94-16163. (Illus.). 320p. 1994. 22.00 (*0-671-86849-7*) S&S Trade.

***Patton, Jim.** The Shake. 256p. 2000. 24.00 (*0-7867-0737-2*, Pub. by Carroll & Graf) Publishers Group.

Patton, John. From Ministry to Theology: Pastoral Action & Reflection. LC 95-36934. 1995. write for info. (*0-929670-13-2*) JPCP.

— Is Human Forgiveness Possible? A Pastoral Care Perspective. LC 85-9191. 192p. (Orig.). 1985. pap. 15.95 (*0-687-19704-X*) Abingdon.

— Pastoral Care in Context: An Introduction to Pastoral Care. LC 93-3262. 288p. 1993. text 24.95 (*0-664-22034-7*) Westminster John Knox.

Patton, John P. Divine Unity: A Universal Spirituality. 303p. (Orig.). 1994. 24.95 (*0-9639382-3-1*); student ed. 20.00 (*0-9639382-1-5*); pap. 14.95 (*0-9639382-0-7*); lib. bdg. 29.95 (*0-9639382-2-3*) Ctr Creat Power.

Patton, Joseph D. Maintainability & Maintenance Management. 2nd enl. fac. rev. ed. LC 88-13043. (Illus.). 460p. 1994. pap. 142.60 (*0-7837-7633-0*, 204738600007) Bks Demand.

Patton, Joseph D., Jr. Maintainability & Maintenance Management. 3rd ed. LC 94-50673. 452p. 1994. 76.00 (*1-55617-510-8*) ISA.

— Preventive Maintenance. LC 82-48557. (Illus.). 208p. 1983. reprint ed. pap. 64.50 (*0-7837-9043-0*, 204979400003) Bks Demand.

— Preventive Maintenance. 2nd ed. LC 94-47619. 200p. 1995. pap. 56.00 (*1-55617-533-7*) ISA.

Patton, Joseph D., Jr., ed. Instrument Maintenance Managers' Sourcebook. 2nd ed. LC 80-83407. (Illus.). 331p. reprint ed. pap. 102.70 (*0-7837-5148-6*, 204487600004) Bks Demand.

***Patton, Joseph D. & Bleuel, William H.** After the Sale: How to Manage Product Service for Customer Satisfaction & Profit. 406p. 2000. 89.00 (*0-934623-63-5*) Solomon Pr.

Patton, Joseph D. & Feldmann, Herbert C. Service Parts Handbook. LC 96-35417. 1996. write for info. (*0-934623-73-2*) Solomon Pr.

Patton, Joseph D., jt. auth. see Bleuel, William H.

***Patton, Kevin T.** Anatomy & Physiology. 4th ed. (Illus.). 456p. 1998. student ed. write for info. (*0-323-00193-9*); lab manual ed. write for info. (*0-323-00195-5*) Mosby Inc.

— Laboratory Manual to Accompany Anatomy & Physiology. (Illus.). 1998. teacher ed. write for info. (*0-323-00196-3*) Mosby Inc.

Patton, Kevin T. & Schauf, Victoria. Introduction to Human Physiology. 736p. 53.95 (*0-8016-6337-7*) Mosby Inc.

Patton, Kevin T., jt. auth. see Thibodeau, Gary.

Patton, Kevin T., jt. auth. see Thibodeau, Gary A.

***Patton, Laurie L.** Jewels of Authority: Women & Textual Tradition in Hindu India. LC 99-53416. 272p. 2000. text. write for info. (*0-19-513478-8*) OUP.

Patton, Laurie L. Myth As Argument: The Brhaddevata As Canonical Commentary. LC 96-20603. (Religionsgeschichtliche Versuche und Vorarbeiten Ser.: Vol. 41). xxviii, 549p. (C). 1996. lib. bdg. 207.40 (*3-11-013805-0*) De Gruyter.

Patton, Laurie L., ed. Authority, Anxiety, & Canon: Essays in Vedic Interpretation. LC 93-25748. (SUNY Series in Hindu Studies). (Illus.). 334p. (C). 1994. text 64.50 (*0-7914-1937-1*); pap. text 21.95 (*0-7914-1938-X*) State U NY Pr.

Patton, Laurie L. & Doniger, Wendy, eds. Myth & Method. (Studies in Religion & Culture). 448p. (C). 1996. pap. text 22.50 (*0-8139-1657-7*) U Pr of Va.

— Myth & Method. (Studies in Religion & Culture). 448p. (C). 1996. text 57.50 (*0-8139-1656-9*) U Pr of Va.

Patton, Leah. The Donkey Our Brother. 4th ed. 224p. 1998. reprint ed. pap. 15.00 (*0-9659312-2-6*) Am Donkey.

Patton, M. Jersey in Prehistory. 1987. 40.00 (*0-86120-017-9*, Pub. by Aris & Phillips) David Brown.

Patton, Mark. Islands in Time: Island Sociogeography & Mediterranean Prehistory. LC 95-44147. (Illus.). 224p. (C). 1996. 75.00 (*0-415-12659-2*) Routledge.

Patton, Marvyl L. Guide-Lines & God-Lines for Facing Cancer: Mind, Body & Faith Connections. Hermanson, Renee, ed. LC 94-26046. (Illus.). 256p. (Orig.). 1994. pap. 13.95 (*1-880292-12-2*) LangMarc.

Patton, Mary, ed. see Archibald, David.

***Patton, Michael.** The Raven's Way. 1999. pap. 10.95 (*1-881542-58-0*) Blue Star Prodns.

Patton, Michael Q. Grand Canyon Celebration: A Father-Son Journey of Discovery. LC 98-48764. (Illus.). 330p. 1999. 26.95 (*1-57392-266-8*) Prometheus Bks.

P

— How to Use Qualitative Methods in Evaluation. 2nd ed. (Program Evaluation Kit Ser.: Vol. 4). 176p. (C). 1987. pap. text 13.95 (*0-8039-3129-8*) Sage.

— Practical Evaluation. (Illus.). 320p. 1982. 48.00 (*0-8039-1904-2*); pap. 22.50 (*0-8039-1905-0*) Sage.

— Qualitative Evaluation & Research Methods. 2nd ed. (Illus.). 536p. (C). 1990. text 49.95 (*0-8039-3779-2*) Sage.

— Utilization-Focused Evaluation. 2nd ed. LC 85-27817. 352p. (C). 1986. text 52.00 (*0-8039-2779-7*); pap. text 25.00 (*0-8039-2566-2*) Sage.

— Utilization-Focused Evaluation: The New Century Text. 3rd ed. LC 96-25310. 640p. 1996. 69.95 (*0-8039-5264-3*); pap. 29.95 (*0-8039-5265-1*) Sage.

Patton, Michael Q., ed. Family Sexual Abuse: Frontline Research & Evaluation. (Illus.). 248p. 1991. 49.95 (*0-8039-3960-4*); pap. 23.50 (*0-8039-3961-2*) Sage.

***Patton, Pamela.** The Meadows Museum: A Handbook of Spanish Painting & Sculpture. Lunsford, John & Powers, Jackson L., eds. (Illus.). 100p. 2000. pap. write for info. (*0-935937-14-5*) Meadows Mus.

***Patton, Paul.** Deleuze & the Political. LC 99-86552. (Thinking the Political Ser.). 184p. 2000. pap. 20.99 (*0-415-10064-X*) Routledge.

— Deleuze & the Political. LC 99-86552. (Thinking the Political Ser.). 184p. 2000. 65.00 (*0-415-10063-1*) Routledge.

Patton, Paul, ed. Deleuze: A Critical Reader. LC 96-5380. (Blackwell Critical Readers Ser.). 320p. 1996. 60.95 (*1-55786-564-7*); pap. 28.95 (*1-55786-565-5*) Blackwell Pubs.

— Nietzsche, Feminism, & Political Theory. LC 92-33978. 272p. (C). 1993. pap. 24.99 (*0-415-08256-0*, B0699) Routledge.

Patton, Paul, jt. auth. see Bradley, Teresa.

Patton, Paul, tr. see Deleuze, Gilles.

Patton, Paul, tr. & intro. see Baudrillard, Jean.

***Patton, Paula & Hase, Karla Neeley.** Microsoft Word for Terrified Teachers. Humrichouse, Kathy, ed. 304p. 1999. pap., teacher ed. 24.95 (*1-57690-438-5*, TCM2438) Tchr Create Mat.

Patton, Peter C. & Kent, James M. A Moveable Shore: The Fate of the Connecticut Coast. LC 91-9822. (Living with the Shore Ser.). (Illus.). 240p. 1991. text 54.95 (*0-8223-1128-3*) Duke.

— A Moveable Shore: The Fate of the Connecticut Coast. LC 91-9822. (Living with the Shore Ser.). (Illus.). 240p. 1992. pap. text 22.95 (*0-8223-1147-X*) Duke.

Patton, Phil. Dreamland: Travels Inside the Secret World of Roswell & Area 51. LC 97-48659. 512p. 1998. 25.00 (*0-679-45651-1*) Villard Books.

— Dreamland: Travels Inside the Secret World of Roswell & Area 51. 352p. 1999. pap. 12.95 (*0-375-75385-0*) Villard Books.

— Technofollies. 1995. 24.95 (*0-8050-3319-X*) H Holt & Co.

Patton, Phil & Polster, Bernd. Highway: America's Endless Dream. LC 96-29586. (Illus.). 160p. 1997. 29.95 (*1-55670-604-9*) Stewart Tabori & Chang.

Patton, R. J., ed. Fault Detection Supervision & Safety for Technical Processes 1997. LC 98-18269. (IFAC Postprint Ser.). 1998. pap. text. write for info. (*0-08-042381-7*, Pergamon Pr) Elsevier.

***Patton, R. J., et al, eds.** Issues of Fault Diagnosis for Dynamic Systems. xvi, 598p. 2000. pap. 135.00 (*3-540-19968-3*) Spr-Verlag.

Patton, Randall L. & Parker, David B. Carpet Capital: The Rise of a New South Industry. LC 98-53802. (Economy & Society in the Modern South Ser.). 341p. 1999. 35.00 (*0-8203-2110-9*) U of Ga Pr.

***Patton, Richard M.** The American Home Is a Firetrap. (Illus.). 360p. 2000. 49.00 (*0-9700140-0-7*) Crusade Fire Deaths.

***Patton, Robert.** Student Athletic Trainer Manual: An Outline Presentation. 2nd ed. 143p. (C). 1999. spiral bd. 25.95 (*0-7872-5982-9*) Kendall-Hunt.

Patton, Robert D., ed. The American Family: Life & Health. 2nd rev. ed. 704p. 1995. pap. text 19.95 (*0-89914-044-0*) Third Party Pub.

Patton, Robert D. & Cissell, William B., eds. Community Organization: Traditional Principles & Modern Applications. (Illus.). 372p. (C). 1990. pap. text 36.50 (*0-9625490-1-0*) Latchpins Pr.

Patton, Robert F. Sojourners in Faith: The First 35 Years of Covenant Presbyterian Church, Madison, Wisconsin, 1954-1989. 288p. 1994. 19.95 (*1-881576-25-6*) Providence Hse.

Patton, Robert H. Life Between Wars. LC 96-46357. 256p. 1997. 24.00 (*1-877946-97-4*) Permanent Pr.

— The Pattons: A Personal History of an American Family. (Illus.). 352p. 1996. reprint ed. pap. 21.95 (*1-57488-127-2*) Brasseys.

— Up, down & Sideways. LC 96-27409. 1997. 22.00 (*1-877946-91-5*) Permanent Pr.

Patton, Ron, jt. auth. see Chen, J.

Patton, Ron, jt. auth. see Liu, G. P.

Patton, Rosemary, jt. auth. see Cooper, Sheila.

Patton, Sally J. & Maletis, Margaret. Inventors: A Source Guide for Self-Directed Units. 72p. 1989. pap. text, teacher ed. 25.00 (*0-913705-35-7*) Zephyr Pr AZ.

Patton, Sally J., jt. ed. see Patton.

Patton, Sara, ed. see Nielsen, Ashleea.

Patton, Sara, ed. see Taylor, Ted M.

***Patton, Sarah.** A Joy of Old Horses. 95p. 1998. pap. 10.00 (*1-881604-48-9*) Scopcraeft.

Patton, Sarah, ed. see Pysz, Stephen.

Patton, Scott, tr. see Strang, Carl A.

Patton, Sharon F. African-American Art. (Oxford History of Art Ser.). (Illus.). 320p. 1998. 39.95 (*0-19-284254-4*); pap. 16.95 (*0-19-284213-7*) OUP.

***Patton, Sharon F.** Discretion. 98p. 2000. pap. 16.00 (*1-892096-02-1*) Ishai Creat.

Patton, Susan G., ed. Wildwords: A Glossary for the Wildlife Rehabilitator. 64p. 1997. pap. 10.00 (*0-9660923-0-9*) Wldlfe Pubns.

Patton, Temple C. Paint Flow & Pigment Dispersion: A Rheological Approach to Coating & Ink Technology. 2nd ed. LC 78-10774. 656p. 1979. 245.00 (*0-471-03272-7*, Wiley-Interscience) Wiley.

***Patton Thoele, Sue.** The Woman's Book of Confidence: Meditations for Strength & Inspiration. 304p. 1999. 6.98 (*1-56731-301-9*, MJF Bks) Fine Comms.

— The Woman's Book of Courage: Meditations for Empowerment & Peace of Mind. 304p. 1999. 6.98 (*1-56731-300-0*, MJF Bks) Fine Comms.

Patton, Thomas E. & Saunders, Terry R. Securities Fraud: Litigating under Rule 10b-5. 1993. ring bd., suppl. ed. 75.00 (*0-685-74475-2*, MICHIE) LEXIS Pub.

— Securities Fraud: Litigating under Rule 10b-5. 1994. spiral bd. 125.00 (*0-8342-0130-5*, MICHIE) LEXIS Pub.

Patton, Timothy. Summary Judgements in Texas: Practice, Procedure & Review. 2nd ed. 350p. Date not set. text 120.00 (*1-55834-361-X*, 82681-11, MICHIE) LEXIS Pub.

— Summary Judgments in Texas: Practice, Procedure & Review. 1994. ring bd., suppl. ed. 59.00 (*0-685-74458-2*, MICHIE) LEXIS Pub.

— Summary Judgments in Texas: Practice, Procedure & Review. 2nd ed. 400p. Date not set. text 120.00 (*0-409-25573-4*, 82681-11, MICHIE) LEXIS Pub.

***Patton, Timothy.** Summary Judgments in Texas: Practice, Procedure & Review, 1999 Supplement, Pocketpart. 2nd ed. 350p. 1999. write for info. (*0-327-01520-9*, 8268316) LEXIS Pub.

Patton, Venetria K. Women in Chains: The Legacy of Slavery in Black Women's Fiction. LC 99-14973. (SUNY Series in Afro-American Studies). 192p. (C). 1999. text 49.50 (*0-7914-4343-4*); pap. text 16.95 (*0-7914-4344-2*) State U NY Pr.

Patton, Vince, ed. see Ward, Phyllis.

Patton, Vincent, ed. see McNulty, Edward N.

***Patton, Vincent M. & Graham, Stephany.** Faith Journey: Special Edition. rev. ed. LC 00-30413. 2000. write for info. (*1-57895-097-X*) Bridge Resources.

Patton, W. S. & Cragg, F. W. A Text Book of Medical Entomology. 764p. 1984. pap. 175.00 (*0-7855-0400-1*, Pub. by Intl Bks & Periodicals) St Mut.

Patton, Wesley E. Sales Force: A Sales Management Simulation. 110p. (C). 1994. text 25.95 (*0-256-15009-5*, Irwn McGrw-H) McGrw-H Hghr Educ.

Patton, Will. Lassitudes of Fire. (Illus.). 42p. 1999. pap. 5.95 (*0-9666328-4-2*) CUZ Ed.

Patton, William. Bible Wines. 2nd ed. 139p. (Orig.). 1976. reprint ed. pap. 3.95 (*0-933672-04-7*, C-1474) Star Bible.

Patton, William J. Materials in Industry. 3rd ed. (Illus.). 480p. (C). 1986. text 52.00 (*0-13-560749-3*) P-H.

— Mechanical Power Transmission. 1980. text 43.00 (*0-13-569905-3*) P-H.

Pattou, E. Fire Arrow. LC 97-40634. 320p. (J). (gr. 5 up). 1998. 18.00 (*0-15-201635-X*, Harcourt Child Bks) Harcourt.

— Fire Arrow. 352p. (J). 1999. pap. 6.00 (*0-15-202264-3*, Voyager Bks) Harcourt.

— Hero's Song. LC 91-12893. 304p. (J). (gr. 3-7). 1991. 16.95 (*0-15-233807-1*, Harcourt Child Bks) Harcourt.

— Hero's Song. LC 97-30181. 352p. (J). 1998. pap. 6.00 (*0-15-201636-8*, Harcourt Child Bks) Harcourt.

Pattou, Edith. Hero's Song: The First Song of the Eirren. 1998. 11.10 (*0-606-13479-4*, Pub. by Turtleback) Demco.

Pattow, Donald. Communicating Technological Information. 2nd ed. LC 97-11852. 568p. (C). 1997. pap. text 59.00 (*0-13-761271-0*) P-H.

Pattullo, Polly. Last Resorts: The Cost of Tourism in the Caribbean. LC 97-115879. xiii, 220 p. 1996. write for info. (*976-8100-81-8*) Ian Randle.

— Last Resorts: The Cost of Tourism in the Caribbean. (Illus.). 220p. Date not set. pap. 19.00 (*0-85345-977-0*, Pub. by Lat Am Bur) Monthly Rev.

Patty, C. Wayne. Foundations of Topology. (Illus.). 349p. (C). 1997. text 51.95 (*0-88133-955-5*) Waveland Pr.

Patty, C. Wayne, jt. auth. see Fletcher, Peter.

Patty, C. Wayne, ed. see Fletcher, Peter & Hoyle, Hughes B.

Patty, Catherine. Jumbo Science Yearbook: Grade 4. (Jumbo Science Ser.). 96p. (gr. 4). 1978. 18.00 (*0-8209-0025-7*, JSY 4) ESP.

— Jumbo Social Studies Yearbook: Grade 3. (Jumbo Social Studies Ser.). 96p. (gr. 3). 1980. 18.00 (*0-8209-0075-3*, JSSY 3) ESP.

— Jumbo Social Studies Yearbook: Grade 4. (Jumbo Social Studies Ser.). 96p. (gr. 4). 1981. 18.00 (*0-8209-0076-1*, JSSY 4) ESP.

— Jumbo Social Studies Yearbook: Grade 6. (Jumbo Social Studies Ser.). 96p. (gr. 6). 1981. 18.00 (*0-8209-0078-8*, JSSY 6) ESP.

Patty, Del, et al. Reading Resource Handbook for School Leaders. 425p. 1996. pap. 59.95 (*0-926842-50-1*) CG Pubs Inc.

Patty, James S., ed. see Giraudoux, Jean.

***Patty, Sandi.** I've Just Seen Jesus. 64p. 2000. 12.99 (*0-8499-5560-2*) Word Pub.

Patty, Teresa. Discover Your Business Potential: A Comprehensive Self-Evaluation. 96p. 1992. student ed. write for info. (*0-9633989-0-3*) New Start Cnslting.

Patunker, B. W. Grasses of Marathwada. 300p. (C). 1979. 125.00 (*0-7855-1947-5*, Pub. by Scientific) St Mut.

Paturas, James & Weinberg, Andrew D. Advanced Cardiac Life Support: Preparatory Manual. (Emergency Care Ser.). (C). 1995. pap. text 32.50 (*0-86720-819-8*) Jones & Bartlett.

Paturas, James L., et al, eds. Cold Weather Emergencies: Principles of Patient Management. 64p. 1990. pap. text 15.00 (*1-887272-00-3*) Amer Med Pub.

Paturas, James L. & Werdmann, Michael J. First Aid & Safety for Day Care Providers. Reinberg, Steven E., ed. (Illus.). 100p. (C). 1994. pap. text 15.00 (*1-884225-03-9*) Communs Skills.

Paturas, James L., jt. auth. see Weinberg, Andrew D.

Paturas, James L., jt. ed. see Weinberg, Andrew D.

Paturau, J. M. By-Products of the Cane Sugar Industry: An Introduction to Their Industrial Utilization. 3rd rev. ed. (Sugar Ser.: No. 11). 436p. 1989. 242.75 (*0-444-88214-6*) Elsevier.

Patuznik, Dennis D. Sick Building Syndromes & Distressed Employees: Index of New Information. 160p. 1998. 47.50 (*0-7883-1754-7*); pap. 44.50 (*0-7883-1755-5*) ABBE Pubs Assn.

— Smog, Health & Disease: Index of New Information. 160p. 1998. 47.50 (*0-7883-1758-X*); pap. 44.50 (*0-7883-1759-8*) ABBE Pubs Assn.

Patvardhan, V. S. Growth of Indigenous Entrepreneurship Vol. 1: The House of Garwares India. 1990. 28.00 (*0-86132-272-X*, Pub. by Popular Prakashan) S Asia.

***Patwardhan, Sunanda.** Vision of the Sacred: My Personal Journey with Krishnamurti. 1999. pap. 16.00 (*0-14-029447-3*, Pub. by Capital Pub IA)) S Asia.

— A Vision of the Sacred: My Personal Journey with Krishnamurti. Shrinavasan, Malini, ed. (Illus.). 120p. 2000. pap. 16.00 (*0-9649247-6-5*, Pub. by Edwin Hse) IPG Chicago.

Patwari, A. B. Fundamental Rights & Personal Liberty in India, Pakistan & Bangladesh. (C). 1990. 175.00 (*0-89771-200-5*) St Mut.

Paty, Donald W. & Ebers, George C. Multiple Sclerosis, No. 51. LC 97-3052. (Contemporary Neurology Ser.: No. 50). (Illus.). 612p. (C). 1997. text 150.00 (*0-8036-6784-1*) OUP.

Paty, M. La Matiere Derobee: L'Appropriation Critique de l'Objet de la Physique Contemporaine. 442p. 1988. pap. text 61.00 (*2-88124-186-7*) Gordon & Breach.

Paty, Michel, jt. ed. see Lopes, Jose L.

Patyra, M. J. & Mlynek, D. M., eds. Fuzzy Logic: Implementation & Applications. LC 95-45241. 346p. 1996. 155.00 (*0-471-95059-9*) Wiley.

Patyra, Marek J. Fuzzy Hardware Systems Design. 300p. 1999. 54.95 (*0-7803-3401-9*, PC5674-QOE) Inst Electrical.

Patz, Nancy. Moses Supposes His Toeses Are Roses: And 7 Other Silly Old Rhymes. LC 82-3099. (Illus.). 32p. (J). (ps-3). 1989. pap. 6.00 (*0-15-255691-5*) Harcourt.

***Patz, Nancy.** Pumpernickel Tickle & Mean Green Cheese. (Illus.). 40p. 2000. reprint ed. 16.95 (*1-893116-17-4*) Baltimore Sun.

Patz, Nancy. Sarah Bear & Sweet Sidney. LC 88-21300. (Illus.). 32p. (J). (ps-2). 1989. lib. bdg. 13.95 (*0-02-770270-7*, Four Winds Pr) S&S Childrens.

— To Annabella Pelican from Thomas Hippopotamus. LC 90-30038. (Illus.). 32p. (J). (ps-3). 1991. lib. bdg. 13.95 (*0-02-770280-4*, Four Winds Pr) S&S Childrens.

Patz, Naomi & Olitzky, Kerry M. I Am a Reform Jew: A Workbook Diary for Explaining Reform Judaism. 90p. (J). (gr. 6-8). 1995. pap., wbk. ed. 4.95 (*0-87441-448-2*) Behrman.

Patz, Naomi & Perman, Jane. In the Beginning: The Jewish Baby Book. (Illus.). 64p. 1983. 15.00 (*0-8074-0258-3*, 510500) UAHC.

Patz, Naomi, jt. auth. see Borowitz, Eugene B.

Patzelt, Annette. Dissertations Botanicae, Band 297. (GER., Illus.). 215p. 1998. 59.00 (*3-443-64209-8*, Pub. by Gebruder Borntraeger) Balogh.

Patzelt, Lawrence H. & Berends, Nancy L. Coronary Artery Bypass Surgery. Grin, Oliver D. & Bouwman, Dorothy L., eds. (Patient Education Ser.). (Illus.). 34p. (Orig.). 1991. pap. text 3.50 (*0-929689-41-0*) Ludann Co.

— Heart Valve Surgery. Grin, Oliver D. & Bouwman, Dorothy L., eds. (Patient Education Ser.). (Illus.). 30p. (Orig.). 1991. pap. text 4.00 (*0-929689-42-9*) Ludann Co.

Patzer, Andreas, ed. Franz Overbeck - Erwin Rohde: Briefwechsel. (Supplementa Nietzscheana Ser.: Vol. 1). xxxiii, 652p. (C). 1990. lib. bdg. 173.10 (*3-11-011895-5*) De Gruyter.

Patzer, Gordon L. Experiment-Research Methodology in Marketing: Types & Applications. LC 95-24914. 232p. 1996. 59.95 (*0-89930-960-7*, Quorum Bks) Greenwood.

— The Physical Attractiveness Phenomena. LC 85-6593. (Perspectives in Social Psychology Ser.). (Illus.). 320p. (C). 1985. 83.00 (*0-306-41783-9*, Plenum Trade) Perseus Pubng.

— Using Secondary Data in Marketing Research: United States & Worldwide. LC 94-40460. 184p. 1995. 55.00 (*0-89930-961-5*, Quorum Bks) Greenwood.

Patzer, Nancy, jt. auth. see Major, Mike.

Patzert, Rudolph W. Running the Palestine Blockade: The Last Voyage of the Paducah. LC 93-28122. (Illus.). 244p. 1994. 29.95 (*1-55750-679-5*) Naval Inst Pr.

Patzia, Arthur G. Ephesians, Colossians, Philemon: New International Biblical Commentary. 312p. 1991. pap. 11.95 (*0-943575-19-2*) Hendrickson MA.

— The Making of the New Testament: Origin, Collection, Text & Canon. LC 94-45403. 208p. (Orig.). 1995. pap. text 14.99 (*0-8308-1859-6*, 1859) InterVarsity.

Patzig, G. Aristotle's Theory of the Syllogism: A Logico-Philosophical Study of Book 'A' of the Prior Analytics. Barnes, Jonathan, tr. from GER. (Synthese Library: No. 16). 232p. 1968. text 112.50 (*90-277-0030-3*, D Reidel) Kluwer Academic.

***Patzman, Barbara J.** Would You Have Gone with Lewis & Clark? The Story of the Corps of Discovery for Young People. Albers, Everett C., ed. (Illus.). ii, 37p. (YA). (gr. 4 up). 2000. pap. 6.95 (*0-9674002-2-8*) United Printing.

Patzold, Michael, jt. auth. see Gramley, Stephan.

Patzon, Flora, tr. see Saloff-Astakhoff, N. I.

Pau, H. Differential Diagnosis of Eye Disease. 2nd enl. rev. ed. Blodi, Frederick C., tr. from GRE. (Illus.). 560p. 1988. 159.00 (*0-86577-264-9*) Thieme Med Pubs.

Pau, Hana, ed. see Comeau, Rosalin U.

Pau, Hana, tr. see Williams, Julie S.

Pau, Hannah H., ed. see Galuteria, Peter.

Pau, Hannah H., ed. see Lowe, Ruby H.

Pau, Hannah H., ed. see Williams, Julie S.

Pau, L. F. Computer Vision for Electronics Manufacturing. LC 89-22910. (Advances in Computer Vision & Machine Intelligence Ser.). (Illus.). 340p. (C). 1990. 79.50 (*0-306-43182-3*, Plenum Trade) Perseus Pubng.

Pau, L. F. & Olafsson, R. Fish Quality Control by Computer Vision. (Food Science & Technology Ser.: Vol. 43). (Illus.). 320p. 1991. text 150.00 (*0-8247-8426-X*) Dekker.

Pau, L. P. Failure Diagnosis & Performance Monitoring. (Control & Systems Theory Ser.: Vol. 11). 448p. 1981. text 145.00 (*0-8247-1018-5*) Dekker.

Pau-Llosa, Ricardo. Bread of the Imagined. LC 91-11914. 88p. 1992. pap. 9.00 (*0-927534-16-9*) Biling Rev-Pr.

— Cuba. LC 92-71503. (Poetry Ser.). 1993. pap. 11.95 (*0-88748-151-5*) Carnegie-Mellon.

— Humberto Calzada: A Retrospective of Work from 1979-1990. Echerri, Vincente, tr. LC 91-73400. (SPA., Illus.). 96p. (Orig.). 1991. pap. 25.00 (*1-880511-00-2*) Bass Museum.

— Sorting Metaphors. 1983. pap. 8.00 (*0-938078-15-1*) Anhinga Pr.

— Vereda Tropical. LC 97-76751. (Poetry Ser.). 96p. 1999. 24.95 (*0-88748-299-6*, Pub. by Carnegie-Mellon); pap. 12.95 (*0-88748-277-5*) Carnegie-Mellon.

Pau-Llosa, Ricardo, jt. auth. see Escallon, Ana M.

Pau, Louis & Willums, Jan-Olaf, eds. Manufacturing Automation at the Crossroads: Standardization in CIM Software. LC 93-78479. 181p. (gr. 12). 1993. pap. 70.00 (*90-5199-137-1*, Pub. by IOS Pr) IOS Press.

Pau, Louis F., ed. Mapping & Spatial Modelling for Navigation. (NATO ASI Series F: Computer & Systems Sciences, Special Programme AET: Vol. 65). (Illus.). viii, 357p. 1990. 91.95 (*0-387-52711-7*) Spr-Verlag.

Pau, Louis F. & Gianotti, C. Economic & Financial Knowledge-Based Processing. (Illus.). xv, 364p. 1990. 103.95 (*0-387-53043-6*) Spr-Verlag.

Paubert-Braquet, M., et al, eds. Foods, Nutrition & Immunity: Effects of Dairy & Fermented Milk Products. (Dynamic Nutrition Research Ser.: Vol. 1). (Illus.). viii, 126p. 1992. 106.25 (*3-8055-5605-5*) S Karger.

— Lipid Mediators in the Immunology of Shock. LC 87-29239. (NATO ASI Series A, Life Sciences: Vol. 139). (Illus.). 540p. 1988. 135.00 (*0-306-42694-3*, Plenum Trade) Perseus Pubng.

Pauchet, Victor & Dupret, S. Atlas de Anatomia. 6th ed. 520p. 1989. pap. 24.95 (*0-7859-5797-9*) Fr & Eur.

— Pocket Atlas of Anatomy. 3rd ed. (Illus.). 1976. pap. 14.95 (*0-19-263131-4*) OUP.

Pauchet, Victor & Rodrigo, Garcia I. Atlas Manual de Anatomia. 6th ed. (SPA.). 518p. 1978. pap. 29.95 (*0-8288-4863-7*, S12343) Fr & Eur.

Pauchy, Hwang W., jt. ed. see Henley, Ernest M.

Paudel, Mehar M. Agriculture & Industrial Finance in Nepal. 1986. 55.00 (*0-7855-0239-4*, Pub. by Ratna Pustak Bhandar) St Mut.

— Planning for Agriculture Development in Nepal. 1985. 75.00 (*0-7855-0250-5*, Pub. by Ratna Pustak Bhandar) St Mut.

Paudel, Mehar M., ed. Agriculture & Industrial Finance in Nepal. 147p. (C). 1987. 200.00 (*0-89771-046-0*, Pub. by Ratna Pustak Bhandar) St Mut.

— Planning for Agriculture Development in Nepal. 216p. (C). 1985. 250.00 (*0-89771-054-1*, Pub. by Ratna Pustak Bhandar) St Mut.

Paudler, William W., jt. auth. see Newkome, George R.

Paudras, Francis. Dance of the Infidels: A Portrait of Bud Powell. Monet, Rubye, tr. from FRE. Orig. Title: La Danse des Infideles. (Illus.). 368p. 1998. pap. 18.95 (*0-306-80816-1*) Da Capo.

Pauer, Erich. Japan's War Economy. LC 98-4048. 7p. 1998. 85.00 (*0-415-15472-3*) Routledge.

Pauer, Gyula, jt. auth. see Ulack, Richard.

Pauer-Studer, Herlinde, ed. Norms, Values, & Society. (Vienna Circle Institute Yearbook Ser.). 360p. (C). 1994. lib. bdg. 156.00 (*0-7923-3071-4*, Pub. by Kluwer Academic) Kluwer Academic.

Pauerstein, Carl J., ed. Seminar on Tubal Physiology & Biochemistry. (Journal: Gynecologic Investigation: Vol. 6, Nos. 3-4). iv, 160p. 1975. reprint ed. 48.75 (*3-8055-2252-5*) S Karger.

Pauerstein, Carl J., jt. auth. see Woodruff, James D.

Paugam, Serge, jt. ed. see Gallie, Duncan.

Paugh, Jon. Meeting the Challenge: U. S. Industry Faces the 21st Century: The U. S. Biotechnology Industry. Lafrance, John C., ed. (Illus.). 108p. (C). 1998. pap. text 35.00 (*0-7881-7195-X*) DIANE Pub.

Paugh, Jon, ed. see Berg, David R. & Ferrier, Grant.

Paugh, Tom. Loving Life after 60: Celebrating the Autumn of Your Life. LC 99-31679. 176p. 2000. pap. 9.50 (*1-57223-283-8*) Willow Creek Pr.

***Paugh, Tom.** Sports Afield Treasury of Fly Fishing. 2000. 27.95 (*1-58574-201-5*) Lyon Press.

Pauk. Clarifying Devices: Reading Level 10/J. 10th ed. (Single Skills Ser.). 1985. pap. 5.65 (*0-89061-385-0*, Jamestwn Pub) NTC Contemp Pub Co.

— Clarifying Devices: Reading Level 11/K, Vol. 11k. (Single Skills Ser.). 1985. pap. 5.65 (*0-89061-391-5*, Jamestwn Pub) NTC Contemp Pub Co.

— Clarifying Devices: Reading Level 12/L, Vol. 12l. (Single Skills Ser.). 1985. pap. 5.65 (*0-89061-397-4*, Jamestwn Pub) NTC Contemp Pub Co.

P

— Clarifying Devices: Reading Level 3/C. 3rd ed. (Single Skills Ser.). 1985. pap. 5.65 (*0-89061-368-0*, Jamestwn Pub) NTC Contemp Pub Co.

— Clarifying Devices: Reading Level 4/D. 4th ed. (Single Skills Ser.). 1985. pap. 5.65 (*0-89061-374-5*, Jamestwn Pub) NTC Contemp Pub Co.

— Clarifying Devices: Reading Level 5/E. 5th ed. (Single Skills Ser.). 1985. pap. 5.65 (*0-89061-330-3*, Jamestwn Pub) NTC Contemp Pub Co.

— Clarifying Devices: Reading Level 6/F. 6th ed. (Single Skills Ser.). 1985. pap. 5.65 (*0-89061-336-2*, Jamestwn Pub) NTC Contemp Pub Co.

— Clarifying Devices: Reading Level 7/G. 7th ed. (Single Skills Ser.). 1985. pap. 5.65 (*0-89061-342-7*, Jamestwn Pub) NTC Contemp Pub Co.

— Clarifying Devices: Reading Level 8/H. 8th ed. (Single Skills Ser.). 1985. pap. 5.65 (*0-89061-348-6*, Jamestwn Pub) NTC Contemp Pub Co.

— Clarifying Devices: Reading Level 9/I. 9th ed. (Single Skills Ser.). 1985. pap. 5.65 (*0-89061-379-6*, Jamestwn Pub) NTC Contemp Pub Co.

— Conclusions: Reading Level 11/K, Vol. 11k. (Single Skills Ser.). 1985. pap. 5.65 (*0-89061-390-7*, Jamestwn Pub) NTC Contemp Pub Co.

— Conclusions: Reading Level 3/C. 3rd ed. (Single Skills Ser.). 1985. pap. 5.65 (*0-89061-367-2*, Jamestwn Pub) NTC Contemp Pub Co.

— Conclusions: Reading Level 4/D. 4th ed. (Single Skills Ser.). 1985. pap. 5.65 (*0-89061-373-7*, Jamestwn Pub) NTC Contemp Pub Co.

— Conclusions: Reading Level 7/G. 7th ed. (Single Skills Series). Date not set. pap. 5.65 (*0-89061-341-9*, Jamestwn Pub) NTC Contemp Pub Co.

— Conclusions: Reading Level 8/H. 8th ed. (Single Skills Ser.). 1985. pap. 5.65 (*0-89061-347-8*, Jamestwn Pub) NTC Contemp Pub Co.

— Conclusions: Reading Level 9/I. 9th ed. (Single Skills Ser.). 1986. pap. 5.65 (*0-89061-378-8*, Jamestwn Pub) NTC Contemp Pub Co.

— Main Idea: Reading Level 10-J. 10th ed. (Single Skills Ser.). 1993. pap. 5.65 (*0-89061-382-6*, Jamestwn Pub) NTC Contemp Pub Co.

— Main Idea: Reading Level 11-K. 11th ed. (Single Skills Ser.). 1993. pap. 5.65 (*0-89061-388-5*, Jamestwn Pub) NTC Contemp Pub Co.

— Main Idea: Reading Level 3-C. 3rd ed. (Single Skills Ser.). 1993. pap. 5.65 (*0-89061-365-6*, Jamestwn Pub) NTC Contemp Pub Co.

— Main Idea: Reading Level 4-D. 4th ed. (Single Skills Ser.). 1993. pap. 5.65 (*0-89061-371-0*, Jamestwn Pub) NTC Contemp Pub Co.

— Main Idea: Reading Level 5-E. 5th ed. (Single Skills Ser.). 1993. pap. 5.65 (*0-89061-327-3*, Jamestwn Pub) NTC Contemp Pub Co.

— Main Idea: Reading Level 6-F. 6th ed. (Single Skills Ser.). 1993. pap. 5.65 (*0-89061-333-8*, Jamestwn Pub) NTC Contemp Pub Co.

— Main Idea: Reading Level 9-I. 9th ed. (Single Skills Ser.). 1993. pap. 5.65 (*0-89061-376-1*, Jamestwn Pub) NTC Contemp Pub Co.

— Single Skills: Supporting Details. 3rd ed. (Sing). (YA). (gr. 3 up). 1998. 6.33 (*0-89061-366-4*, R0366-4E, Jamestwn Pub) NTC Contemp Pub Co.

— Subject Matter: Reading Level 10-J. 10th ed. (Single Skills Ser.). 1985. pap. 5.65 (*0-89061-381-8*, Jamestwn Pub) NTC Contemp Pub Co.

— Subject Matter: Reading Level 11-K. 11th ed. (Single Skills Ser.). 1985. pap. 5.65 (*0-89061-387-7*, Jamestwn Pub) NTC Contemp Pub Co.

— Subject Matter: Reading Level 12-L, Vol. 12l. (Single Skills Ser.). 1985. pap. 5.65 (*0-89061-393-1*, Jamestwn Pub) NTC Contemp Pub Co.

— Subject Matter: Reading Level 3-C. 3rd ed. (Single Skills Series Ser.). 1985. pap. 5.64 (*0-89061-364-8*, Jamestwn Pub) NTC Contemp Pub Co.

— Subject Matter: Reading Level 4-D. 4th ed. (Single Skills Ser.). 1985. pap. 5.65 (*0-89061-370-2*, Jamestwn Pub) NTC Contemp Pub Co.

— Subject Matter: Reading Level 5-E. 5th ed. (Single Skills Ser.). 1985. pap. 5.65 (*0-89061-326-5*, Jamestwn Pub) NTC Contemp Pub Co.

— Subject Matter: Reading Level 7-G. 7th ed. (Single Skills Ser.). 1985. pap. 5.65 (*0-89061-338-9*, Jamestwn Pub) NTC Contemp Pub Co.

— Subject Matter: Reading Level 8-H. 8th ed. (Single Skills Ser.). 1985. pap. 5.65 (*0-89061-344-3*, Jamestwn Pub) NTC Contemp Pub Co.

— Subject Matter: Reading Level 9-I. 7th ed. (Single Skills Ser.). 1985. pap. 5.65 (*0-89061-375-3*, Jamestwn Pub) NTC Contemp Pub Co.

— Supporting Details: Reading Level 10-J. 10th ed. (Single Skills Ser.). 1985. pap. 5.65 (*0-89061-383-4*, Jamestwn Pub) NTC Contemp Pub Co.

— Supporting Details: Reading Level 11-K. 11th ed. (Single Skills Ser.). 1985. pap. 5.65 (*0-89061-389-3*, Jamestwn Pub) NTC Contemp Pub Co.

— Supporting Details: Reading Level 12-L, Vol. 12l. (Single Skills Ser.). 1985. pap. 5.65 (*0-89061-395-8*, Jamestwn Pub) NTC Contemp Pub Co.

— Supporting Details: Reading Level 4-D. 4th ed. (Single Skills Ser.). 1985. pap. 5.65 (*0-89061-372-9*, Jamestwn Pub) NTC Contemp Pub Co.

— Supporting Details: Reading Level 5-E. 5th ed. (Single Skills Ser.). 1985. pap. 5.65 (*0-89061-328-1*, Jamestwn Pub) NTC Contemp Pub Co.

— Supporting Details: Reading Level 6-F. 6th ed. (Single Skills Ser.). 1985. pap. 5.65 (*0-89061-334-6*, Jamestwn Pub) NTC Contemp Pub Co.

— Supporting Details: Reading Level 7-G. 7th ed. (Single Skills Ser.). 1985. pap. 5.65 (*0-89061-340-0*, Jamestwn Pub) NTC Contemp Pub Co.

— Vocabulary in Context: Reading Level 10-J. 10th ed. (Single Skills Ser.). 1985. pap. 5.65 (*0-89061-386-9*, Jamestwn Pub) NTC Contemp Pub Co.

— Vocabulary in Context: Reading Level 11-K, Vol. 11k. (Single Skills Ser.). 1985. pap. 5.65 (*0-89061-392-3*, Jamestwn Pub) NTC Contemp Pub Co.

— Vocabulary in Context: Reading Level 12-L, Vol. 12l. (Single Skills Ser.). 1985. pap. 5.65 (*0-89061-398-2*, Jamestwn Pub) NTC Contemp Pub Co.

— Vocabulary in Context: Reading Level 3-C. 3rd ed. (Single Skills Ser.). 1985. pap. 5.65 (*0-89061-369-9*, Jamestwn Pub) NTC Contemp Pub Co.

— Vocabulary in Context: Reading Level 4-D. 4th ed. (Single Skills Ser.). 1985. pap. 5.65 (*0-89061-325-7*, Jamestwn Pub) NTC Contemp Pub Co.

— Vocabulary in Context: Reading Level 5-E. 5th ed. (Single Skills Ser.). 1985. pap. 5.65 (*0-89061-331-1*, Jamestwn Pub) NTC Contemp Pub Co.

— Vocabulary in Context: Reading Level 6-F. 6th ed. (Single Skills Ser.). 1985. pap. 5.65 (*0-89061-337-0*, Jamestwn Pub) NTC Contemp Pub Co.

— Vocabulary in Context: Reading Level 7-G. 7th ed. (Single Skills Ser.). 1985. pap. 5.65 (*0-89061-343-5*, Jamestwn Pub) NTC Contemp Pub Co.

— Vocabulary in Context: Reading Level 8-H. 8th ed. (Single Skills Ser.). 1985. pap. 5.65 (*0-89061-349-4*, Jamestwn Pub) NTC Contemp Pub Co.

Pauk, Walter. Book 10: Level 7B, Bk. 10. (Essential Skills Ser.). 109p. 1995. pap., student ed. 8.31 (*0-89061-229-3*, Jamestwn Pub) NTC Contemp Pub Co.

— Book 11: Level 8A, Bk. 11. (Essential Skills Ser.). 109p. 1995. pap., student ed. 8.31 (*0-89061-230-7*, Jamestwn Pub) NTC Contemp Pub Co.

— Book 12: Level 8B, Bk. 12. (Essential Skills Ser.). 109p. 1995. pap., student ed. 8.31 (*0-89061-231-5*, Jamestwn Pub) NTC Contemp Pub Co.

— Book 13: Level 9A, Bk. 13. (Essential Skills Ser.). 109p. 1995. pap., student ed. 8.31 (*0-89061-232-3*, Jamestwn Pub) NTC Contemp Pub Co.

— Book 14: Level 9B, Bk. 14. (Essential Skills Ser.). 109p. 1995. pap., student ed. 8.31 (*0-89061-233-1*, Jamestwn Pub) NTC Contemp Pub Co.

— Book 16: Level 10B, Bk. 16. (Essential Skills Ser.). 109p. 1995. pap., student ed. 8.31 (*0-89061-235-8*, Jamestwn Pub) NTC Contemp Pub Co.

— Book 17: Level 11A, Bk. 17. (Essential Skills Ser.). 109p. 1995. pap., student ed. 8.31 (*0-89061-236-6*, Jamestwn Pub) NTC Contemp Pub Co.

— Book 18: Level 11B, Bk. 18. (Essential Skills Ser.). 109p. 1995. pap., student ed. 8.31 (*0-89061-237-4*, Jamestwn Pub) NTC Contemp Pub Co.

— Book 19: Level 12A, Bk. 19. (Essential Skills Ser.). 109p. 1995. pap., student ed. 8.31 (*0-89061-238-2*, Jamestwn Pub) NTC Contemp Pub Co.

— Book 2: Level 3B, Bk. 2. (Essential Skills Ser.). 109p. 1995. pap., student ed. 8.31 (*0-89061-221-8*, Jamestwn Pub) NTC Contemp Pub Co.

— Book 20: Level 12B, Bk. 20. (Essential Skills Ser.). 109p. 1995. pap., student ed. 8.31 (*0-89061-239-0*, Jamestwn Pub) NTC Contemp Pub Co.

— Book 3: Level 4A, Bk. 3. (Essential Skills Ser.). 109p. 1995. pap., student ed. 8.31 (*0-89061-222-6*, Jamestwn Pub) NTC Contemp Pub Co.

— Book 4: Level 4B, Bk. 4. (Essential Skills Ser.). 109p. 1995. pap., student ed. 8.31 (*0-89061-223-4*, Jamestwn Pub) NTC Contemp Pub Co.

— Book 5: Level 5A, Bk. 5. (Essential Skills Ser.). 109p. 1995. pap., student ed. 8.31 (*0-89061-224-2*, Jamestwn Pub) NTC Contemp Pub Co.

— Book 6: Level 5B, Bk. 6. (Essential Skills Ser.). 109p. 1995. pap., student ed. 8.31 (*0-89061-225-0*, Jamestwn Pub) NTC Contemp Pub Co.

— Book 7: Level 6A, Bk. 7. (Essential Skills Ser.). 109p. 1995. pap., student ed. 8.31 (*0-89061-226-9*, Jamestwn Pub) NTC Contemp Pub Co.

— Book 8: Level 6B, Bk. 8. (Essential Skills Ser.). 109p. 1995. pap., student ed. 8.31 (*0-89061-227-7*, Jamestwn Pub) NTC Contemp Pub Co.

— Book 9: Level 7A, Bk. 9. (Essential Skills Ser.). 109p. 1995. pap., student ed. 8.31 (*0-89061-228-5*, Jamestwn Pub) NTC Contemp Pub Co.

***Pauk, Walter.** Essential Study Strategies. 160p. 2000. pap. 25.33 (*0-13-031416-1*) P-H.

— Essential Study Strategies. rev. ed. LC 99-71819. 162p. (C). 2000. pap. text 29.00 (*0-943202-71-X*) H & H Pub.

Pauk, Walter. How to Study in College, 6 vols. (C). Date not set. pap., student ed. write for info. (*0-395-83065-6*) HM.

— How to Study in College, 5 vols. (C). 1992. pap. 32.36 (*0-395-64326-0*) HM.

— How to Study in College, 6 vols. LC 96-76945. (C). 1996. pap., teacher ed. 31.96 (*0-395-83063-X*); pap., teacher ed. 11.96 (*0-395-83064-8*) HM.

— How to Study in College. 4th ed. 384p. 1989. teacher ed. write for info. (*0-318-63329-9*) HM.

— How To Study in College, 6 vols. 6th ed. LC 96-76945. (C). 1996. pap. text 32.36 (*0-395-83062-1*) HM.

— Six-Way Paragraphs: Advanced Level. 239p. 1983. pap. text 13.30 (*0-89061-303-6*, 731, Jamestwn Pub) NTC Contemp Pub Co.

— Six-Way Paragraphs: Middle Level. 239p. (YA). (gr. 6-12). pap. text 12.97 (*0-89061-302-8*, 730, Jamestwn Pub) NTC Contemp Pub Co.

— Study Skills for College Athletes. LC 96-72549. 136p. 1998. pap. text 29.95 (*0-943202-69-8*) H & H Pub.

— A User's Guide to College - Making Notes & Taking Tests: Conversations with Dr. Walter Pauk. (Illus.). 72p. (C). 1988. pap. text 6.75 (*0-89061-481-4*, Jamestwn Pub) NTC Contemp Pub Co.

Pauk, Walter, ed. see Henry, O.

Pauka, Kirstin. Theater & Martial Arts in West Sumatra: Rundai & Silek of Minangkabau. LC 98-19143. (Monographs in International Studies, Southeast Asia Ser.). (Illus.). 288p. (C). 1998. pap. text 26.00 (*0-89680-205-1*) Ohio U Pr.

Pauken, Thomas W. The Thirty Years War: The Politics of the Sixties Generation. LC 98-105400. 238p. 1995. 22.50 (*0-915463-66-0*) Jameson Bks.

Pauker, G. Y., ed. Energy Efficiency & Conservation in the Asia-Pacific Region: Proceedings of the Fouth Workshop, Honolulu, Hawaii, June 2-5, 1981. 200p. 1983. pap. 28.00 (*0-08-030532-6*, Pergamon Pr) Elsevier.

Pauker, Guy J., ed. Current Attitudes & Reactions to Soviet Policies in the Asia-Pacific Region. 155p. (C). 1986. ring bd. 12.50 (*0-317-91350-6*) Pac Forum.

***Pauker, Joe.** Get Lost! The Cool Guide to Amsterdam. 7th ed. 1999. pap. text 13.00 (*90-802561-0-2*) SCB Intl.

Pauker, John. Angry Candy. (Midwest Writer Ser.). 48p. 1976. pap. 4.95 (*0-917530-01-2*) Pig Iron Pr.

Pauker, Robert, jt. auth. see Krupp, Judy-Arin.

Pauker, Robert, jt. auth. see Portner, Hal.

Pauker, Samuel L., jt. auth. see Arond, Miriam.

Paukert, F. & Robinson, D., eds. Incomes Policies in the Wider Context: Wage, Price & Fiscal Inititiatives in Developing Countries. v, 259p. (Orig.). 1992. pap. 31.50 (*92-2-107749-7*) Intl Labour Office.

Paukert, Liba & Richards, Peter, eds. Defence Expenditure, Industrial Conversion & Local Employment. ix, 228p. 1991. 36.00 (*92-2-107288-6*); pap. 27.00 (*92-2-107287-8*) Intl Labour Office.

Pauketat, Timothy R. The Ascent of Chiefs: Cahokia & Mississippian Politics in Native North America. LC 93-42734. (Illus.). 256p. (C). 1994. pap. text 29.95 (*0-8173-0728-1*) U of Ala Pr.

Pauketat, Timothy R. & Emerson, Thomas E., eds. Cahokia: Domination & Ideology in the Mississippian World. LC 96-28639. (Illus.). ix, 362p. 1997. text 60.00 (*0-8032-3708-1*) U of Nebr Pr.

— Cahokia: Domination & Ideology in the Mississippian World. 362p. 2000. pap. text 25.00 (*0-8032-8765-8*, Bison Books) U of Nebr Pr.

***Pauketat, Timothy R., et al.** An Archaeological Survey of the Horseshoe Lake State Park, Madison County, Illinois LC 99-174055. (Reports of Investigations). vii, 147p. 1998. write for info. (*0-89792-158-5*) Ill St Museum.

Pauketat, Timothy R., et al. The Archaeology of Downtown Cahokia: The Tract 15A & Dunham Tract Excavations. LC 98-52767. (Studies in Archaeology). (Illus.). 444p. 1998. 27.50 (*0-9644881-4-0*) ITARP.

— Temples of Cahokia Lords: Preston Holder's 1955-1956 Excavations of Kunnemann Mound. LC 93-13529. (Memoirs Ser.: No. 26). 1993. pap. 28.00 (*0-915703-33-5*) U Mich Mus Anthro.

Paukovits, Walter. How to Study, 5 vols. (C). Date not set. pap. write for info. (*0-395-64734-7*) HM.

— Pauk How to Study 6E & Dict CMPC 6, 6 vols. 6th ed. (C). Date not set. pap. 40.76 (*0-395-90540-0*) HM.

— Pauk How To Study 6E & ESL Dict, 6 vols. 6th ed. (C). Date not set. 48.76 (*0-395-90541-9*) HM.

— Pauk How To Study 6E & PEJSA, 6 vols. 6th ed. (C). Date not set. pap. 39.96 (*0-395-90539-7*) HM.

— Pauk How To Study 6E & Roget, 6 vols. 6th ed. (C). Date not set. 44.36 (*0-395-90542-7*) HM.

Paukovits, Walter, ed. Growth Regulation & Carcinogenesis, 2 vols., Vol. 1. 328p. 1990. boxed set 217.00 (*0-8493-5960-0*, QH604) CRC Pr.

Paukovits, Walter R., ed. Growth Regulation & Carcinogenesis, 2 vols., Vol. 2. 368p. 1990. boxed set 239.00 (*0-8493-5961-9*, QH604) CRC Pr.

Paul. Accounting Fundamentals. 2nd ed. 1991. pap. text 64.95 (*0-409-10012-9*) Buttrwrth-Heinemann.

— Analysis of Linear Circuits. 1989. 27.50 (*0-07-045920-7*) McGraw.

Paul. Astronomic Gamma Spatiale. 304p. 1997. text 110.00 (*90-5699-073-X*); pap. text 50.00 (*90-5699-064-0*) Gordon & Breach.

Paul. Fighting Fire, Vol. 1. Date not set. write for info. (*0-312-96705-5*) Tor Bks.

— Introduction to Electrical Engineering. 2nd ed. 1992. student ed. 15.93 (*0-07-011323-8*) McGraw.

— Introduction to Electromagnetic Fields. 2nd ed. 1987. 27.50 (*0-07-045909-6*) McGraw.

— Introduction to Electromagnetic Fields. 4th ed. 2000. 77.74 (*0-07-232109-1*) McGraw.

***Paul.** Language & Deafness. 3rd ed. 2001. pap. 47.95 (*1-56593-999-9*) Singular Publishing.

Paul. Peach Blossom Cologne Company. 3rd ed. 1997. pap. text. write for info. (*0-256-21801-3*, Irwn McGrw-H) McGrw-H Hghr Educ.

— Peach Blossum Cologne. 3rd ed. 1998. pap., student ed. 49.06 (*0-256-21672-X*) McGraw.

— Pepito's Fate. 2001. pap. write for info. (*0-15-600613-8*) Harcourt.

Paul & Houng-Lee. Handbook of Hong Kong Tax Statutes. 2nd ed. 120p. 1990. pap. 180.00 (*0-409-99582-7*, MICHIE) LEXIS Pub.

Paul & Solez, Kim, eds. Organ Transplantation: Long-Term Results. LC 92-18547. (Illus.). 432p. 1992. text 190.00 (*0-8247-8599-1*) Dekker.

Paul, jt. auth. see Feder.

Paul, jt. auth. see Haeussler, Ernest F.

Paul, Swraj. Beyond Boundaries: A Memoir. LC 98-901276. xii, 228 p. 1998. write for info. (*0-670-87925-8*) Viking Penguin.

Paul, Terri. Glass Hearts. LC 99-10242. 322p. 1999. 24.95 (*0-89733-470-1*, Academy Chi Pubs.

***Paul, A. J.** Bibliography of Research on Snow Crab (Chionoecetes Opilio) 49p. 2000. pap. 10.00 (*1-56612-063-2*) AK Sea Grant CP.

Paul, A. J., et al. Phytoplankton, Zooplankton, & Ichthyoplankton in Resurrection Bay. (Alaska Sea Grant Report: No. 91-02). 22p. 1991. pap. 4.00 (*1-56612-002-0*) AK Sea Grant CP.

Paul, A. J., jt. auth. see Pinchuk, Alexei I.

Paul, Aileen. Coloring Calendar Cookbook for Kids: Projects & Recipes for Children. (Illus.). 24p. (Orig.). (YA). (gr. 5 up). 1982. pap. 2.95 (*0-913270-90-3*) Sunstone Pr.

Paul, Alexander. Suicide Wall. LC 96-207442. 320p. (Orig.). 1996. pap. 11.95 (*0-9642761-1-9*) PakDonald Pubng.

Paul, Allen. Katyn: Stalin's Massacre & the Seeds of Polish Resurrection. LC 91-4773. (Illus.). 412p. 1996. pap. 19.95 (*1-55750-670-1*) Naval Inst Pr.

— Katyn: The Untold Story of Stalin's Polish Massacre. 352p. 1991. text 24.95 (*0-684-19215-2*, Scribners Ref) Mac Lib Ref.

Paul, Amy C., ed. Managing for Tomorrow: Global Change & Local Futures. (Practical Management Ser.). (Illus.). 188p. 1990. 23.95 (*0-87326-061-9*) Intl City-Cnty Mgt.

Paul, Anand J. & Sobolewski, Michael. Concurrent Engineering: A Global Perspective Conference Proceedings 1995. 676p. 1994. 40.00 (*0-9642449-1-8*) Concurrent Tech.

Paul, Anand J. & Sobolewski, Michael, eds. Concurrent Engineering: Research & Applications Conference Proceedings 1994. 800p. 1994. pap. 40.00 (*0-9642449-0-X*) Concurrent Tech.

Paul, Ann W. All by Herself: 14 Girls Who Made a Difference. LC 97-5871. (Illus.). 40p. (J). (gr. 4-6). 1999. 17.00 (*0-15-201477-2*, Harcourt Child Bks) Harcourt.

— Eight Hands Round: A Patchwork Alphabet. LC 88-745. (Illus.). 32p. (J). (gr. 3 up). 1991. 15.95 (*0-06-024689-8*); lib. bdg. 15.89 (*0-06-024704-5*) HarpC Child Bks.

— Eight Hands Round: A Patchwork Alphabet. LC 88-745. (Trophy Picture Bk.). (Illus.). 32p. (J). (gr. 3 up). 1996. pap. 5.95 (*0-06-443464-8*, HarpTrophy) HarpC Child Bks.

— Hello Toes! Hello Feet! LC 97-31002. (Illus.). 32p. (J). (ps-1). 1998. 15.95 (*0-7894-2481-9*) DK Pub Inc.

— The Seasons Sewn: A Year in Patchwork. LC 94-35358. (Illus.). 40p. (J). (gr. 3-6). 1996. 16.00 (*0-15-276918-8*, Harcourt Child Bks) Harcourt.

— Shadows Are About. (Illus.). 32p. (J). 1992. pap. 13.95 (*0-590-44842-0*, Scholastic Hardcover) Scholastic Inc.

— Shadows Are About. (Illus.). (J). 1996. pap. text 4.95 (*0-590-44843-9*) Scholastic Inc.

Paul, Ann Whitford. Eight Hands Round: A Patchwork Alphabet. LC 88-745. 1991. 10.15 (*0-606-09231-5*, Pub. by Turtleback) Demco.

— Everything to Spend the Night from A to Z. LC 97-43593. 40p. (J). (ps-2). 1999. 15.95 (*0-7894-2511-4*, D K Ink) DK Pub Inc.

***Paul, Ann Whitford.** Hello Toes, Hello Feet. LC 97-31002. (Illus.). 32p. (J). (ps-2). 2000. pap. text 5.95 (*0-7894-2664-1*, D K Ink) DK Pub Inc.

— The Seasons Sewn: A Year in Patchwork Quilt. (Illus.). 40p. (J). (gr. 1-4). 2000. pap. 6.00 (*0-15-202107-8*, Voyager Bks) Harcourt.

Paul, Ann Whitford. Shadows Are About. 1992. 10.15 (*0-606-09848-8*, Pub. by Turtleback) Demco.

— Silly Sadie, Silly Samuel. (Ready-to-Read Ser.). (J). 1999. mass mkt. 3.99 (*0-689-81690-1*) S&S Childrens.

— Silly Sadie, Silly Samuel. LC 97-25146. (Ready-to-Read Ser.). 40p. (J). 2000. per. 15.00 (*0-689-81689-8*) S&S Childrens.

Paul, Anne, ed. Paracas Art & Architecture: Object & Context in South Coastal Peru. LC 91-16740. (Illus.). 455p. 1991. text 42.95 (*0-87745-327-6*) U of Iowa Pr.

Paul, Anthony. The Tiger Who Lost His Stripes. 2nd ed. LC 95-15472. (Illus.). 32p. (J). (gr. 2-5). 1995. 15.00 (*0-15-200992-2*, Harcourt Child Bks) Harcourt.

Paul, Anthony & Rees, Yvonne. The Water Garden. (Illus.). 168p. 1986. pap. 19.95 (*0-14-025150-2*, Penguin Bks) Viking Penguin.

— The Water Garden. 168p. 1996. 19.95 (*2-01-402515-0*, Penguin Bks) Viking Penguin.

Paul, Anthony M., jt. ed. see Olson, Raymond E.

Paul, Arnold M. Conservative Crisis & the Rule of Law: Attitudes of Bar & Bench 1887-1895. 1990. 19.75 (*0-8446-0839-4*) Peter Smith.

Paul, B., ed. see Symposium on Mechanics of Transportation Suspensio.

Paul, Barbara. The Curse of Halewood. large type ed. (General Ser.). 496p. 1993. 27.99 (*0-7089-2926-5*) Ulverscroft.

— Fare Play. (Worldwide Library Mysteries). 1996. per. 5.50 (*0-373-26209-4*, 1-26209-6, Wrldwide Lib) Harlequin Bks.

— Fare Play. LC 95-19983. 256p. 1995. 20.00 (*0-684-19715-4*) S&S Trade.

— Fare Play. large type ed. 400p. 31.50 (*0-7089-3690-3*) Ulverscroft.

— Full Frontal Murder. (WWL Mystery Ser.). 1998. per. 4.99 (*0-373-26284-1*, 1-26284-9, Wrldwide Lib) Harlequin Bks.

— Full Frontal Murder, Bk. 2. LC 96-37258. 256p. 1997. 20.50 (*0-684-19716-2*, Scribner Pap Fic) S&S Trade Pap.

— Full Frontal Murder: A Mystery with Marian Larch. large type ed. LC 97-44299. 329p. 1997. 25.95 (*0-7838-8363-3*, G K Hall & Co) Mac Lib Ref.

— In-Laws & Outlaws. 1992. per. 3.99 (*0-373-26103-9*, 1-26103-1) Harlequin Bks.

— In-Laws & Outlaws. large type ed. (General Ser.). 323p. 1991. lib. bdg. 18.95 (*0-8161-5239-X*, G K Hall Lrg Type) Mac Lib Ref.

— Jack Be Quick & Other Crime Stories. LC 99-22369. 202p. 1999. 20.95 (*0-7862-1919-X*, Five Star MI) Mac Lib Ref.

P

An Asterisk (*) at the beginning of an entry indicates that the title is appearing for the first time.

— Liars & Tyrants & People Who Turn Blue. 179p. 1992. pap. 5.95 (*1-55882-110-4*) Intl Polygonics.
— Paul McCartney. 1981. 24.95 (*0-671-43123-4*) S&S Trade.
— Your Eyelids Are Growing Heavy. LC 92-70413. 188p. 1992. reprint ed. pap. 5.95 (*1-55882-126-0*, Lib Crime Classics) Intl Polygonics.
Paul, Barbara, jt. auth. see Candeloro, Dominic.
Paul, Barbara D. The Germans after WWII. (History-Reference Ser.). 285p. 1990. 45.00 (*0-8161-8994-3*, Hall Reference) Macmillan.
— The Polish-German Boderlands: An Annotated Bibliography, 35. LC 94-13054. (Bibliographies & Indexes in World History Ser.: Vol. 35). 224p. 1994. lib. bdg. 75.00 (*0-313-29162-4*, Greenwood Pr) Greenwood.
***Paul, Barbara Dotts.** Wisconsin History: An Annotated Bibliography, 8. LC 99-14354. (Bibliographies of the States of the United States Ser.: Vol. 8). 448p. 1999. lib. bdg. 79.50 (*0-313-28271-4*, Bergin & Garvey) Greenwood.
Paul, Benjamin D., ed. Health, Culture & Community: Case Studies of Public Reactions to Health Programs. LC 55-10583. 494p. 1955. pap. 22.50 (*0-87154-653-1*) Russell Sage.
Paul, Bette. The A-One Scam. LC 94-79392. (Ten-Minute Mysteries Ser.). 32p. (YA). (gr. 6-12). 1994. pap. 2.95 (*0-7854-0840-1*, 40751); pap. 2.95 (*0-7854-0841-X*, 40754) Am Guidance.
— The A-One Scam Readalong. (Ten-Minute Mysteries Ser.). 32p. (YA). (gr. 6-12). 1994. pap. 12.95 incl. audio (*0-7854-1049-X*, 40753) Am Guidance.
Paul, Bil. The Tri-X Chronicles. LC 73-86842. (Illus.). 1972. pap. 3.45 (*0-9600650-0-8*) Alchemist-Light.
Paul, Bill. Getting In: Inside the College Admissions Process. LC 95-18675. 288p. 1995. 20.00 (*0-201-62256-4*) Addison-Wesley.
— Pro-Engineer Exercise Book: Based on Release 15. 2nd ed. LC 96-136834. 192p. 1995. pap. 44.95 (*1-56690-083-2*, OnWord Pr) High Mtn.
Paul, Bobbi, jt. auth. see Mosteller, Lee.
Paul-Boncour, Joseph. Recollections of the Third Republic. 1957. 15.00 (*0-8315-0050-6*) Speller.
Paul, C. Kegan. William Godwin: His Friends & Contemporaries, 2 vols. LC 73-115359. reprint ed. write for info. (*0-404-04941-9*) AMS Pr.
Paul, C. Kegan, ed. see Huysmans, Joris K.
Paul, C. Kegan, tr. see Huysmans, Joris K.
Paul, C. R. & Smith, A. B., eds. Echinoderm Phylogeny & Evolutionary Biology. (Current Geological Concepts Ser.: No. 1). (Illus.). 392p. 1988. 125.00 (*0-19-854491-X*) OUP.
Paul, Carol. Revitalizing Apathetic Communities. 3rd ed. (GAP Reports: No. 16). 28p. 1996. pap. 17.50 (*0-944715-50-8*) CAI.
— Revitalizing Apathetic Communities. 3rd rev. ed. (GAP Reports: No. 16). 16p. (C). 1994. pap. 17.50 (*0-944715-34-6*) CAI.
Paul, Carol, jt. auth. see Paul, Marcel.
Paul, Carol A., et al, eds. Discovering Neurons: The Experimental Basis of Neuroscience. LC 97-24523. (Illus.). 456p. (C). 1997. text 100.00 (*0-87969-454-8*) Cold Spring Harbor.
— Discovering Neurons: The Experimental Basis of Neuroscience. LC 97-24523. (Illus.). 456p. (C). 1997. pap. text 40.00 (*0-87969-455-6*) Cold Spring Harbor.
***Paul, Carole, et al.** Making a Prince's Museum: Drawings for the Late-Eighteenth-Century Redecoration of the Villa Borghese. LC 99-58367. (Illus.). 180p. 2000. 24.95 (*0-89236-539-0*, Getty Res Inst) J P Getty Trust.
Paul, Caroline. Fighting Fire. LC 98-9791. 288p. 1998. text 23.95 (*0-312-18581-2*) St Martin.
— Fighting Fire. 272p. 1999. mass mkt. 6.99 (*0-312-97000-5*) St Martin.
Paul, Carolyn K. T'shuva. LC 95-37125. 240p. (Orig.). 1996. pap. 10.95 (*0-89407-115-7*) Strawberry Hill.
***Paul, Catherine.** Waterview Manor. West, Kelly, ed. 150p. (gr. 6-10). 1999. pap. 6.50 (*0-9670006-0-2*) FAME Etc.
Paul, Cauvin. Mache Chache: Text Comprehension Exercises in Haitian Creole. Vilsaint, Fequiere, ed. 101p. (YA). (gr. 6-12). Date not set. wbk. ed. 10.00 (*1-881839-44-3*) Educa Vision.
Paul, Cedar, tr. see De Man, Henri.
Paul, Cedar, tr. see Mussolini, Benito.
Paul, Cedar, tr. see Oechsli, Wilhelm.
Paul, Cedar, tr. see Schnitzler, Arthur.
Paul, Cedar, tr. see Sigerist, Henry E.
Paul, Cedar, tr. see Spann, Othman.
Paul, Cedar, tr. see Wittels, Fritz.
Paul, Cedar, tr. see Zweig, Stefan.
Paul, Celia, jt. auth. see Rosen, Stephen.
Paul, Charles R. Fundamentals of Circuit Analysis. 624p. (C). 2000. text. write for info. (*0-471-37195-5*) Wiley.
Paul, Christina, tr. see Glowacki, Janusz.
Paul, Christopher R., jt. auth. see Donavan, Stephen K.
Paul, Clayton R. Analysis of Linear Circuits. 896p. 1989. text 84.95 (*0-07-045919-3*) McGraw.
— Analysis of Linear Circuits. 792p. (C). 1989. text 98.13 incl. disk (*0-07-909340-X*) McGraw.
— Analysis of Multiconductor Transmission Lines. (Microwave & Optical Engineering Ser.). 584p. 1994. text 137.00 incl. disk (*0-471-02080-X*) Wiley.
— Introduction to Electromagnetic Compatibility. LC 91-16016. (Series in Microwave & Optical Engineering: No. 1187). 784p. 1992. 105.00 (*0-471-54927-4*) Wiley.
Paul, Clayton R. & Nasar, Syed A. Introduction to Electrical Engineering. 2nd ed. 816p. (C). 1992. 66.88 (*0-07-011322-X*) McGraw.
— Introduction to Electromagnetic Fields. 2nd ed. (Electrical Engineering "Electromagnetics" Ser.). 760p. (C). 1987. text 79.50 (*0-07-045908-8*) McGraw.
Paul, Clayton R., et al. Introduction to Electromagnetic Fields. 3rd ed. LC 97-34699. 768p. 1997. 105.94 (*0-07-046083-3*) McGraw.
Paul, Clayton R., jt. auth. see Nasar, Syed A.
Paul, D. K. Newtopia: How to Build a Bright New Utopia. LC 96-119926. 120p. (Orig.). (YA). 1995. pap. 9.95 (*0-9642761-0-0*) PakDonald Pubng.
Paul, D. R., jt. ed. see Sperling, Leslie H.
Paul, Dalziel. The New Zealand Macroeconomy: A Briefing on the Reforms. 3rd ed. LC 99-462631. (Illus.). 150p. 1999. pap. text 24.95 (*0-19-558402-3*) OUP.
Paul, Danette, jt. ed. see Hatch, Gary L.
Paul, Daniel N. We Were Not the Savages: A Micmac Perspective on the Collision of European & Aboriginal Civilization. (Illus.). 196p. (Orig.). 1993. pap. 17.95 (*1-55109-056-2*) Nimbus Publ.
Paul, David. Relativities Vol. 3: Pages from a Pillow Book, 3. LC 98-114686. 81 p. 1997. pap. 11.95 (*3-7052-0105-0*, Pub. by Poetry Salzburg) Intl Spec Bk.
— Selected Prose in Three Volumes Vol. 1: Mirrors to Catch Larks. LC 98-105637. 1997. pap. 11.95 (*3-7052-0103-4*, Pub. by Poetry Salzburg) Intl Spec Bk.
— Selected Prose in Three Volumes Vol. 2: The Door of Knowing & Seeing. LC 98-114692. 80p. 1997. pap. 11.95 (*3-7052-0104-2*, Pub. by Poetry Salzburg) Intl Spec Bk.
— A Voice Outside & Other Poems. LC 98-138969. 1997. 15.95 (*1-85421-228-1*, Pub. by Poetry Salzburg) Intl Spec Bk.
Paul, David, tr. see Valery, Paul.
Paul, David B., et al, eds. Slurry Walls: Design, Construction, & Quality Control. LC 92-32908. (Special Technical Publication Ser.: 1129). (Illus.). 430p. 1992. text 47.00 (*0-8031-1427-3*, STP1129) ASTM.
Paul, David C. Six Miles to Town: Vignettes of Early 20th Century Farm Life in Ellis County, Texas. LC 96-61585. (Illus.). xii, 112p. 1996. pap. 10.95 (*0-934955-34-4*) Watercress Pr.
Paul, David M., tr. see Jersild, P. C.
Paul, David W. The Cultural Limits of Revolutionary Politics. rev. ed. 1979. text 72.00 (*0-914710-41-9*, 48) Col U Pr.
— Czechoslovakia: Profile of a Binational Socialist Country. (Nations of Contemporary Eastern Europe Ser.). 196p. 1981. text 38.50 (*0-89158-861-2*) Westview.
Paul, Debjani. Art of Nalanda: Development of Buddhist Sculpture AD 600-1200. LC 95-904334. 1995. 68.00 (*81-215-0628-X*, Pub. by M Manoharial) Coronet Bks.
Paul, Dexter, tr. see Gardner, Garth.
Paul, Diana M. The Buddhist Feminine Ideal. LC 79-12031. (American Academy of Religion. Dissertation Ser.: No. 30). 250p. reprint ed. pap. 77.50 (*0-7837-5404-3*, 204516800005) Bks Demand.
— Women in Buddhism: Images of the Feminine in the Mahayana Tradition. 1985. pap. 17.95 (*0-520-05428-8*, Pub. by U CA Pr) Cal Prin Full Svc.
Paul, Diana Y. Philosophy of Mind in Sixth-Century China: Paramartha's "Evolution of Consciousness" LC 82-42862. 280p. 1984. 39.50 (*0-8047-1187-9*) Stanford U Pr.
Paul, Diane B. Controlling Human Heredity: 1865 to the Present. LC 95-12762. (Control of Nature Ser.). (Illus.). 144p. (C). 1995. pap. 12.50 (*0-391-03916-4*) Humanities.
— Controlling Human Heredity: 1865 to the Present. LC 98-50455. 1998. write for info. (*1-57392-339-7*) Prometheus Bks.
— The Politics of Heredity: Essays on Eugenics, Biomedicine, & the Nature-Nurture Debate. LC 97-45212. (SUNY Series in Philosophy & Biology). 224p. (C). 1998. text 59.50 (*0-7914-3821-X*); pap. text 19.95 (*0-7914-3822-8*) State U NY Pr.
***Paul, Dierdre Glenn.** Raising Black Children Who Love Reading & Writing: A Guide from Birth Through Grade Six. LC 99-40490. 192p. 2000. write for info. (*0-89789-555-X*, Bergin & Garvey) Greenwood.
Paul, Dilip K., ed. Fiber Optics Reliability & Testing: Proceedings of a Conference Held 8-9 September 1993, Boston, Mass. LC 93-46151. (Critical Reviews of Optical Science & Technology Ser.: Vol. CR50). 1994. 30.00 (*0-8194-1342-9*); pap. 30.00 (*0-8194-1343-7*) SPIE.
Paul, Dilip K., ed. see Society of Photo-Optical Instrumentation Engineers Staff.
Paul, Don. AmeriModern. Poems. LC 75-785. 82p. 1982. 5.00 (*0-943096-02-2*); pap. 2.50 (*0-943096-03-0*) Harts Spring Wks.
— Everybody's Knife Bible. 3rd rev. ed. LC 92-80509. (Illus.). 150p. (Orig.). 1992. pap. 12.95 (*0-938263-13-7*) Path Finder.
— Everybody's Outdoor Survival Guide: The Green Beret's Guide to Outdoor Survival. 3rd ed. (Illus.). 150p. 1999. reprint ed. pap. 12.95 (*0-938263-22-6*) Path Finder.
— Good Intentions: A Novel about Revolution. 433p. 1986. 7.00 (*0-943096-04-9*) Harts Spring Wks.
— Great Livin' in Grubby Times Book II: The Green Beret's Guide to Outdoor Survival. 3rd rev. ed. (Illus.). 180p. 1996. pap. 12.95 (*0-938263-21-8*) Path Finder.
— The Green Beret's Compass Course: The New Way to Stay Found (Not Lost) Anywhere. 6th rev. ed. (Illus.). 114p. 1991. reprint ed. pap. 9.95 (*0-938263-00-5*) Path Finder.
— How to Write a Book in Fifty Three Days: The Elements of Speed Writing, Necessity & Benefits, Too! LC 92-80122. (Illus.). 121p. 1992. pap. 14.95 (*0-938263-10-2*) Path Finder.
— Just Like You: Poems & Bits Before Hell. 73p. 1986. 4.00 (*0-943096-05-7*) Harts Spring Wks.
— Lawrence & Mann Overarching: Once Upon the County of Ujamaa; Roll Away der Rock & Other Essays. 360p. 1981. 10.00 (*0-943096-00-6*); pap. 5.00 (*0-943096-01-4*) Harts Spring Wks.
Paul, Don & Smith, David B. Ammo Forever: The Complete What to Shoot & How Manual for Rifles & Shotguns. LC 94-69563. (Illus.). 192p. (Orig.). 1995. pap. 14.95 (*0-938263-15-3*) Path Finder.
— Shooting Forever: The Complete What to Shoot & How Manual for Handguns. LC 96-67855. (Illus.). 172p. (Orig.). 1995. pap. 14.95 (*0-938263-19-6*) Path Finder.
Paul, Donald R. Polymeric Gas Separation Membranes. 640p. 1993. boxed set 178.95 (*0-8493-4415-8*) CRC Pr.
Paul, Donald R. & Harris, F. W., eds. Controlled Release Polymeric Formulations: Symposium, Jointly Sponsored by the Division of Organic Coatings & Plastics Chemistry & the Division of Polymer Chemistry at the 171st Meeting of the American Chemical Society, New York, N.Y., April 7-9, 1976. LC 76-29016. (ACS Symposium Ser.: No. 33). 327p. reprint ed. pap. 101.40 (*0-7837-1450-5*, 205242600018) Bks Demand.
Paul, Donna. The Home Office Book. LC 96-21064. (Illus.). 256p. 1996. 40.00 (*1-885183-30-5*) Artisan.
Paul, Doris A. The Navajo Code Talkers. (Illus.). 176p. (C). 1973. 17.00 (*0-8059-1870-1*) Dorrance.
Paul, Doris H., jt. ed. see Hammer, Carolyn S.
Paul, Douglas J., jt. auth. see Krieger, Larry S.
Paul, Douglas J., jt. auth. see Lawrence, Paul.
Paul, E. Adoption Choices: A Guidebook to National & International Adoption Resources. 1991. 24.95 (*0-8103-9403-0*) Visible Ink Pr.
— The Adoption Directory. 2nd ed. LC 95-7961. 571p. 1995. 70.00 (*0-8103-7495-1*) Gale.
— Adoption Directory: A Guide to Agencies, State Laws on Adoption, Exchanges, Support Groups, & Professional Services in Domestic & International Adoption, Including Foster Parenting, & Biological Options. 800p. 1995. 70.00 (*0-8103-2240-4*) Gale.
Paul, E., et al. Elementary Particle Physics. (Tracts in Modern Physics Ser.: Vol. 79). (Illus.). 1976. 41.00 (*0-387-07778-2*) Spr-Verlag.
Paul, E. A., ed. see McLaren, Arthur D.
Paul, E. C. Fisheries Development & the Food Needs of Mauritius. (Illus.). 224p. 1987. text 123.00 (*90-6191-627-5*, Pub. by A A Balkema) Ashgate Pub Co.
Paul, E. J. Paul: Ancestry of Katharine Choate Paul. (Illus.). 386p. 1991. reprint ed. pap. 60.00 (*0-8328-1763-5*); reprint ed. lib. bdg. 70.00 (*0-8328-1762-7*) Higginson Bk Co.
Paul, E. Robert & Hertzsprung-Kapteyn, Henrietta. The Life & Works of J. C. Kapteyn: An Annotated Translation. 90p. (C). 1994. text 55.50 (*0-7923-2603-2*) Kluwer Academic.
Paul, Eden, tr. see De Man, Henri.
Paul, Eden, tr. see Moll, Albert.
Paul, Eden, tr. see Mussolini, Benito.
Paul, Eden, tr. see Oechsli, Wilhelm.
Paul, Eden, tr. see Schnitzler, Arthur.
Paul, Eden, tr. see Sigerist, Henry E.
Paul, Eden, tr. see Spann, Othman.
Paul, Eden, tr. see Wittels, Fritz.
Paul, Eden, tr. see Zweig, Stefan.
***Paul, Eileen, ed.** Religious Funding Resource Guide: Millennium Issue. 520p. 2000. wbk. ed. 85.00 (*1-883542-10-3*) ResourceWomen.
Paul, Eileen & Clements, Linda, eds. Church Funding Resource Guide, 1994. 11th ed. 500p. 1994. student ed. 75.00 (*1-883542-02-2*) ResourceWomen.
Paul, Eileen & Flores, Andrea, eds. 1995 Religious Funding Resource Guide. 500p. 1995. 75.00 (*1-883542-04-9*) ResourceWomen.
— Religious Funding Resource Guide: 1996 Update. 75p. 1996. wbk. ed. 25.00 (*1-883542-03-0*) ResourceWomen.
Paul, Eileen & Griffith, Jennifer E., eds. 1996 Religious Funding Resource Guide. 500p. 1996. wbk. ed. 75.00 (*1-883542-05-7*) ResourceWomen.
— Religious Funding Resource Guide, 1997-98. 518p. 1997. wbk. ed. 75.00 (*1-883542-08-1*) ResourceWomen.
Paul, Eldor A. & Clark, Francis E. Soil Microbiology & Biochemistry. 2nd ed. (Illus.). 340p. 1996. text 47.00 (*0-12-546806-7*) Acad Pr.
Paul, Eldor A. & McLaren, A. Douglas, eds. Soil Biochemistry, Vol. 3. LC 66-27705. (Books in Soils & the Environment). 352p. reprint ed. pap. 109.20 (*0-8357-3540-0*, 202783300003) Bks Demand.
Paul, Eldor A., et al. Soil Organic Matter in Temperate Agroecosystems: Long Term Experiments in North America. LC 96-23071. 432p. 1996. boxed set 104.95 (*0-8493-2802-0*) CRC Pr.
Paul, Elizabeth, et al. Testing the Waters VIII: Has Your Vacation Beach Cleaned up Its Act. 145p. 1998. pap. 10.50 (*1-893340-01-5*) Natl Resources Defense Coun.
Paul, Ellen. Adoption Choices: A Guidebook to National & International Adoption Resources. 590p. 1998. pap. text 25.00 (*0-7881-5267-X*) DIANE Pub.
Paul, Ellen F. Equity & Gender: The Comparable Worth Debate. 143p. (Orig.). 1988. pap. 21.95 (*0-88738-720-9*) Transaction Pubs.
— Moral Revolution & Economic Science: The Demise of Laissez-Faire in Nineteenth Century British Political Economy, 23. LC 78-73797. (Contributions in Economics & Economic History Ser.: No. 23). 309p. 1979. 65.00 (*0-313-21055-1*, PMR/) Greenwood.
— Property Rights & Eminent Domain. 276p. 1987. 39.95 (*0-88738-094-8*) Transaction Pubs.
Paul, Ellen F., ed. Totalitarianism at the Crossroads. 196p. (C). 1990. 34.95 (*0-88738-351-3*); pap. 21.95 (*0-88738-850-7*) Transaction Pubs.
Paul, Ellen F., et al, eds. Altruism. LC 93-6963. (Social Philosophy & Policy Ser.: No. 10). 256p. (C). 1993. pap. text 19.95 (*0-521-44759-3*) Cambridge U Pr.
— Economic Rights. (Social Philosophy & Policy Ser.: No. 9, pt. 1). 328p. (C). 1992. pap. text 19.95 (*0-521-42873-4*) Cambridge U Pr.
— Human Flourishing. LC 98-50573. (Social Philosophy & Policy Ser.: No. 16.1). 450p. (C). 1999. pap. text 24.95 (*0-521-64471-2*) Cambridge U Pr.
— Liberalism & the Economic Order. (Social Philosophy & Policy Ser.: No. 10: 2). 339p. (C). 1993. pap. text 24.95 (*0-521-45724-6*) Cambridge U Pr.
***Paul, Ellen F., et al, eds.** The Right to Privacy. (Social Philosophy & Policy Ser.). 340p. 2000. pap. write for info. (*0-521-78621-5*) Cambridge U Pr.
Paul, Ellen F., et al, eds. Self-Interest. LC 96-46422. (Social Philosophy & Policy Ser.: No. 14, Pt. 1). 316p. (C). Date not set. pap. text 21.95 (*0-521-59892-3*) Cambridge U Pr.
— Social Philosophy & Policy No. 13:2: Scientific Innovation, Philosophy, & Public Policy. 258p. (C). 1996. pap. text 21.95 (*0-521-58994-0*) Cambridge U Pr.
— Virtue & Vice. LC 97-45966. (Social Philosophy & Policy Ser.: No. 15, Pt. 1). 300p. (C). 1998. pap. text 21.95 (*0-521-63991-3*) Cambridge U Pr.
— The Welfare State. LC 97-14489. (Social Philosophy & Policy Ser.: No. 14:2). 312p. (C). 1998. pap. text 21.95 (*0-521-62731-1*) Cambridge U Pr.
Paul, Ellen F. & Dickman, Howard, eds. Liberty, Property, & Government: Constitutional Interpretation Before the New Deal. LC 88-38771. (SUNY Series in the Constitution & Economic Rights). 303p. (C). 1989. text 64.50 (*0-7914-0086-7*); pap. text 21.95 (*0-7914-0087-5*) State U NY Pr.
— Liberty, Property, & the Foundations of the American Constitution. LC 88-11614. (SUNY Series in the Constitution & Economic Rights). 181p. (C). 1988. pap. text 19.95 (*0-88706-915-0*) State U NY Pr.
— Liberty, Property, & the Future of Constitutional Development. LC 89-21639. (SUNY Series in the Constitution & Economic Rights). 341p. (C). 1990. text 69.50 (*0-7914-0303-3*); pap. text 24.95 (*0-7914-0304-1*) State U NY Pr.
Paul, Ellen F. & Russo, Philip A., eds. Public Policy: Issues, Analysis, & Ideology. LC 81-10027. (Chatham House Series on Change in American Politics). 333p. reprint ed. pap. 103.30 (*0-7837-2600-7*, 204276400006) Bks Demand.
***Paul, Ellen Frankel.** Why Animal Experimentation Matters: The Use of Animals in Medical Research. (New Studies in Social Policy Ser.). 2000. 49.95 (*0-7658-0025-X*) Transaction Pubs.
***Paul, Ellen Frankel, et al, eds.** Democracy. LC 99-51590. (Social Philosophy & Policy Ser.: Vol. 17.1). 330p. 2000. pap. 24.95 (*0-521-78620-7*) Cambridge U Pr.
— Responsibility. (Social Philosophy & Policy Ser.: Vol. 162). 352p. (C). 2000. pap. text 24.95 (*0-521-65450-5*) Cambridge U Pr.
***Paul, Ellen Frankel, et al.** Why Animal Experimentation Matters: The Use of Animals in Medical Research. LC 99-47844. (New Studies in Social Policy). 2000. write for info. (*0-7658-0685-1*) Transaction Pubs.
Paul, Elliot. Ghost Town on the Yellowstone. (American Autobiography Ser.). 341p. 1995. reprint ed. lib. bdg. 89.00 (*0-7812-8608-5*) Rprt Serv.
— The Last Time I Saw Paris. 1993. reprint ed. lib. bdg. 37.95 (*1-56849-157-3*) Buccaneer Bks.
— Linden on the Saugus Branch. (American Autobiography Ser.). 401p. 1995. reprint ed. lib. bdg. 99.00 (*0-7812-8609-3*) Rprt Serv.
— Mayhem in B-Flat: A Homer Evans Murder Mystery. 320p. 1988. reprint ed. pap. 6.95 (*0-486-25621-9*) Dover.
— Narrow Street. (American Autobiography Ser.). 342p. 1995. reprint ed. lib. bdg. 89.00 (*0-7812-8610-7*) Rprt Serv.
Paul, Elliot H. Life & Death of a Spanish Town. LC 79-138171. 427p. (C). 1971. reprint ed. lib. bdg. 35.00 (*0-8371-5628-9*, PAST, Greenwood Pr) Greenwood.
— The Stars & Stripes Forever. LC 74-22802. reprint ed. 32.50 (*0-404-58459-4*) AMS Pr.
Paul, Erich R. The Milky Way Galaxy & Statistical Cosmology, 1890-1924. LC 92-36530. (Illus.). 278p. (C). 1993. text 54.95 (*0-521-35363-7*) Cambridge U Pr.
— Science, Religion, & Mormon Cosmology. (Illus.). 312p. (C). 1992. text 29.95 (*0-252-01895-8*) U of Ill Pr.
Paul, Erik. Australia in Southeast Asia: Regionalism & Democracy. LC 98-217134. 128p. 1998. pap. 19.95 (*87-87062-66-6*, Pub. by NIAS) Paul & Co Pubs.
Paul, Eunice M., tr. from FRE. Jesus-Christ et la Foi (Jesus Christ & the Faith) A Collection of Studies by Philippe H. Menoud. LC 78-15551. (Pittsburgh Theological Monographs: No. 18). 1978. pap. 10.00 (*0-915138-22-0*) Pickwick.
***Paul, Florence Joseph.** Leah's Dream: Leah. LC 00-190641. 209p. 2000. 25.00 (*0-7388-1887-9*); pap. 18.00 (*0-7388-1886-0*) Xlibris Corp.
— Peg - A Dream Betrayed: Peg. LC 00-190639. 387p. 2000. 25.00 (*0-7388-1884-4*); pap. 18.00 (*0-7388-1885-2*) Xlibris Corp.
Paul, Frances. Spruce Root Basketry of the Alaska Tlingit. 80p. 1991. pap. text 5.95 (*1-880475-02-2*) Friends of SJM.
Paul, Frances L. Kahtahah: A Tlingit Girl. (Illus.). 120p. (Orig.). (J). (gr. 1 up). 1976. reprint ed. pap. 13.95 (*0-88240-058-4*, Alaska NW Bks) Gr Arts Ctr Pub.
***Paul, Francis X.** Silo Deep. 208p. 2000. pap. 15.54 (*1-58721-099-1*) First Bks Lib.
Paul, Frank A. & Bahan, Ben. The American Sign Language Handshape Game Cards. rev. ed. 1990. 16.95 (*0-915035-25-1*, 8110) Dawn Sign.
Paul, Frank A., et al. Sign Language Animals. 16p. 1985. pap. 4.50 (*0-915035-01-4*, 4161) Dawn Sign.
— Sign Language House. 16p. (J). 1984. pap. 4.50 (*0-915035-03-0*, 4162) Dawn Sign.

P

Paul, Frederic. John Currin: Works, 1989-1995. 80p. 1996. pap. 20.00 (*2-908257-18-1*, Pub. by F R A C) Dist Art Pubs.
— Steven Pippin, Photo, Videos, Sculpture, 1983-1995. (Illus.). 108p. 1996. pap. 25.00 (*2-908257-17-3*, Pub. by F R A C) Dist Art Pubs.
Paul, Frederic, jt. auth. see Wegman, William.
Paul, Garrett E., jt. auth. see Pasewark, Kyle A.
Paul, Garrett E., tr. see Troeltsch, Ernst.
Paul, George. Summers at the Paul Ranch. Lay, Eldonna, ed. (East County Childhoods Ser.: Vol. 4). (Illus.). 20p. (Orig.). (YA). (gr. 3 up). 1995. pap. 2.50 (*0-9619184-3-8*) E P Lay Assocs.
Paul, George F., jt. auth. see Fabrizio, Timothy C.
Paul, George M. & Ierardi, Michael, eds. Roman Coins & Public Life under the Early Empire: E. Togo Salmon Papers II. LC 98-25518. (Illus.). 216p. 1999. text 42.50 (*0-472-10875-1*, 10875) U of Mich Pr.
Paul, Georgina, tr. see Sigrid, Weigel.
Paul, Gerhard, jt. ed. see Haase, Norbert.
Paul, Gordon L. & Lentz, Robert J. Psycholsocial Treatment of Chronic Mental Patients: Milieu Versus Social-Learning Programs. LC 77-10868. 528p. 1977. reprint ed. pap. 163.70 (*0-7837-4174-X*, 205902300012) Bks Demand.
Paul, Gordon W., jt. auth. see Guiltinan, Joseph P.
Paul, Greg. '60's Flashback. LC 94-35574. (Illus.). 124p. 1995. pap. 19.95 (*0-86636-279-7*) PBC Intl Inc.
Paul, Gregor, jt. ed. see Lenk, Hans.
***Paul, Gregory S., ed.** The Scientific American Book of Dinosaurs. (Illus.). 432p. 2000. 29.95 (*0-312-26226-4*) St Martin.
Paul, Gregory S. & Cox, Earl. Beyond Humanity: Cyberevolution & Future Minds. (Illus.). 300p. 1996. pap. 20.95 (*1-886801-21-5*) Thomson Learn.
Paul, H. Things My Sponsor Taught Me. 1996. pap. 8.00 (*0-89486-444-0*) Hazelden.
Paul, H. B., ed. see De Constant, D'Estaurnelles.
Paul, H. G., jt. ed. see Baldwin, C.
Paul, H. N. Paul: Joseph Paull of Ilminster, Somerset, Eng., & Some Descendants Who Have Resided in Philadelphia. (Illus.). 157p. 1992. reprint ed. pap. 24.00 (*0-8328-2703-7*); reprint ed. lib. bdg. 34.00 (*0-8328-2702-9*) Higginson Bk Co.
Paul, H. W. From Knowledge to Power: The Rise of the Science Empire in France, 1860-1939. 416p. 1985. text 74.95 (*0-521-26504-5*) Cambridge U Pr.
Paul, Harry G. John Dennis. LC 75-181968. reprint ed. 34.50 (*0-404-04918-4*) AMS Pr.
— John Dennis, His Life & Criticism. (BCL1-PR English Literature Ser.). 229p. 1992. reprint ed. lib. bdg. 79.00 (*0-7812-7345-5*) Rprt Serv.
Paul, Harry W. The Edge of Contingency: French Catholic Reaction to Scientific Change from Darwin to Duhem. LC 78-11168. 223p. reprint ed. pap. 69.20 (*0-7837-5087-0*, 204478500004) Bks Demand.
— The Science of Vine & Wine in France, 1750-1990. (Illus.). 364p. (C). 1996. text 64.95 (*0-521-49745-0*) Cambridge U Pr.
— The Second Ralliement: The Rapprochement Between Church & State in France in the Twentieth Century. LC 67-14435. 246p. reprint ed. pap. 76.30 (*0-608-17251-0*, 202950300061) Bks Demand.
— The Sorcerer's Apprentice: The French Scientist's Image of German Science, 1840-1919. LC 77-178986. (University of Florida Monographs: Social Sciences: No. 44). 96p. reprint ed. pap. 30.00 (*0-7837-5086-2*, 204478400004) Bks Demand.
Paul, Hastings, Janofsky & Walker Staff. California OSHA Compliance Handbook. 262p. (Orig.). 1992. pap. text 79.00 (*0-86587-289-9*) Gov Insts.
Paul, Haydn. The Astrological Moon: Aspects, Signs, Cycles & the Mythology of the Goddess in Your Chart. LC 98-23035. Orig. Title: Queen of the Night. 288p. 1998. pap. 16.95 (*1-57863-032-0*) Weiser.
— Gate of Rebirth: Astrology, Regeneration & 8th House Mysteries. LC 92-45557. 320p. (Orig.). 1993. pap. 14.95 (*0-87728-761-9*) Weiser.
— Lord of the Light: Exploring the Astrological Sun. (Illus.). 240p. 1993. pap. 17.95 (*1-85230-188-0*, Pub. by Element MA) Penguin Putnam.
— Your Starchild: An Astrology Guide for You & Your Child. 320p. 1992. mass mkt. 4.99 (*0-380-76355-9*, Avon Bks) Morrow Avon.
***Paul, Henry A.** Parents Make the Best Shrinks: What You Need to Know to Help Your Troubled Child. LC 00-25332. 256p. 2000. pap. 13.00 (*0-440-50887-8*) Dell.
Paul, Henry A. When Kids Are Mad, Not Bad: A Guide to Recognizing & Handling Children's Anger. 256p. (Orig.). 1995. mass mkt. 5.99 (*0-425-14648-0*) Berkley Pub.
— When Kids Are Mad, Not Bad: A Guide to Recognizing & Healing Your Child's Anger. 256p. 1999. pap. text 13.00 (*0-425-16681-3*) Berkley Pub.
Paul, Herbert W. Men & Letters. LC 70-111856. (Essay Index Reprint Ser.). 1977. 21.95 (*0-8369-1622-0*) Ayer.
Paul, Hermann. German Dictionary: Deutches Woerterbuch. 8th ed. (GER.). 841p. 1981. 75.00 (*0-8288-1979-3*, M7335) Fr & Eur.
***Paul, Hilde & Maslova, Nina.** Partizipien und Partizipialsatze Aus Kontrastiver Deutsch-Russischer Sicht: Ubersetzungstraining Mit Grammatischen Schwerpunkten. (Beitrage Zur Slavistik Ser.). 246p. 1999. 45.95 (*3-631-35149-6*) P Lang Pubng.
Paul, I. H. The Craft of Psychotherapy: Twenty-Seven Studies. LC 89-17492. 320p. 1989. 55.00 (*0-87668-826-1*) Aronson.
— The Craft of Psychotherapy: Twenty-Seven Studies. LC 89-17492. 320p. 1996. pap. 55.00 (*1-56821-840-0*) Aronson.
— Letters from Simon. LC 96-444465. 270p. (Orig.). 1996. pap. 29.95 (*0-8236-8130-0*, 23011) Intl Univs Pr.
— Studies in Remembering: The Reproduction of Connected & Extended Verbal Material. (Psychological Issues Monographs: No. 2, Vol. 1, No. 2). 152p. (Orig.). 1959. 27.50 (*0-8236-6240-3*) Intl Univs Pr.
Paul, Iain, jt. ed. see Fennema, Jan.
***Paul, Ileana, et al.** Formal Issues in Austronesian Linguistics. LC 99-51947. (Studies in Natural Language & Linguistic Theory). 276p. 1999. 117.00 (*0-7923-6068-0*) Kluwer Academic.
***Paul, J.** Paul in the Greco-Roman World. 464p. 2001. 40.00 (*1-56338-266-0*, Pub. by TPI PA) Morehouse Pub.
Paul, J. Ellis. Manual of Four-Handed Dentistry. (Illus.). 155p. 1980. text 60.00 (*0-931386-09-8*) Quint Pub Co.
Paul, Jack W. Peach Blossom Cologne Company: A Short Audit Case. 2nd ed. 166p. (C). 1993. text 38.95 (*0-256-09546-9*, Irwn McGrw-H) McGrw-H Hghr Educ.
Paul, James C. & Schwartz, Murray L. Federal Censorship: Obscenity in the Mail. LC 77-10978. 368p. 1977. reprint ed. lib. bdg. 69.50 (*0-8371-9818-6*, PAFC, Greenwood Pr) Greenwood.
Paul, James C., jt. auth. see Coates, Albert.
Paul, James L. Ethics & Decision Making in Local Schools: Inclusion, Policy & Reform. LC 96-53207. 1997. pap. 27.00 (*1-55766-282-7*) P H Brookes.
Paul, James L., ed. The Exceptional Child: A Guidebook for Churches & Community Agencies. LC 82-16914. 176p. 1983. text 45.00 (*0-8156-2287-2*); pap. text 19.95 (*0-8156-2288-0*) Syracuse U Pr.
Paul, James L., et al, eds. Child Advocacy Within the System. (Special Education & Rehabilitation Monograph Ser.: No. 11). (C). 1977. 34.95 (*0-8156-0133-6*) Syracuse U Pr.
Paul, James L. & Epanchin, B. C. Educating Emotionally Disturbed Children & Youth. 2nd ed. 480p. (C). 1991. text 47.20 (*0-675-21211-1*, Merrill Coll) P-H.
Paul, James L. & Simeonsson, Rune J., eds. Children with Special Needs: Family, Culture, & Society. 2nd ed. (Illus.). 352p. (C). 1993. text 29.50 (*0-03-055743-7*) Harcourt Coll Pubs.
***Paul, James L. & Smith, Terry Jo.** Stories Out of School: Memories & Reflections on Care & Cruelty in the Classroom LC 99-36571. (Contemporary Studies in Social & Policy Issues in Education). 1999. pap. write for info. (*1-56750-477-9*) Ablx Pub.
Paul, James L., et al. Foundations of Special Education: Basic Knowledge Informing Research & Practice... LC 96-39237. (Special Education Ser.). 320p. 1997. 62.95 (*0-534-34202-7*) Brooks-Cole.
— Mainstreaming: A Practical Guide. (C). 1977. 29.95 (*0-8156-0136-0*) Syracuse U Pr.
— Special Education Practice: Applying the Knowledge, Affirming the Values... LC 96-39238. (Special Education Ser.). 384p. 1997. 43.00 (*0-534-34201-9*) Brooks-Cole.
Paul, James L., jt. ed. see Pappanikou, A. J.
Paul, James M., et al, eds. Deinstitutionalization: Program & Policy Development. (Special Education & Rehabilitation Monograph Ser.: No. 12). (C). 1977. 34.95 (*0-8156-0132-8*) Syracuse U Pr.
Paul, Jan. Martha's Vineyard ABC's. Rooney, Richard, ed. (Illus.). 32p. (Orig.). (J). 1996. pap. 12.95 (*0-9654165-0-X*) ABC Graphics.
Paul, Jan & Pradier, Claire-Marie, eds. Carbon Dioxide Chemistry: Environmental Issues. (Special Publication Ser.: No. 153). 405p. 1994. 136.00 (*0-85186-634-4*, R6634) CRC Pr.
Paul, Jan S. Hortense. LC 83-45055. (Illus.). 40p. (J). (ps-2). 1984. lib. bdg. 12.89 (*0-690-04371-6*) HarpC Child Bks.
Paul, Janet, jt. ed. see Locke, Elsie Violet.
Paul, Janis M. The Victorian Heritage of Virginia Woolf. 225p. 1987. 29.95 (*0-937664-73-1*) Pilgrim Bks OK.
***Paul, Jay.** Going Home in Flood Time. LC 98-73416. 72p. 1998. pap. 9.95 (*1-880016-28-1*, Ink Drop Pr) Road Pubs.
Paul, Jean. Jean Paul: A Reader. Casey, Timothy J., ed. Casey, Erika, tr. LC 90-25478. (Illus.). 392p. reprint ed. pap. 121.60 (*0-608-06117-4*, 206645000008) Bks Demand.
Paul, Jean, jt. auth. see Von Kleist, Heinrich.
Paul, Jeffrey, jt. ed. see Epstein, Richard A.
Paul, Jennifer L. Nobody Home. 1977. 7.95 (*0-393-08766-2*) Norton.
Paul, Jeremy. The Musgrave Ritual. 48p. (Orig.). 1992. pap. 11.00 (*0-86025-443-7*, Pub. by I Henry Pubns) Empire Pub Srvs.
— The Naval Treaty: The Adventures of Sherlock Holmes. (Illus.). 48p. (Orig.). 1991. pap. 11.00 (*0-86025-435-6*, Pub. by I Henry Pubns) Empire Pub Srvs.
— The Problem of Thor Bridge: The Case-Book of Sherlock Holmes. (Illus.). 50p. (Orig.). 1991. pap. 11.00 (*0-86025-434-8*, Pub. by I Henry Pubns) Empire Pub Srvs.
— The Secret of Sherlock Holmes. 60p. (Orig.). 1991. pap. 11.00 (*0-86025-438-0*, Pub. by I Henry Pubns) Empire Pub Srvs.
— The Secret of Sherlock Holmes. LC 96-36105. 55p. (Orig.). 1996. pap. 11.00 (*0-88734-708-8*) Players Pr.
— The Speckled Band: The Adventures of Sherlock Holmes. (Illus.). 48p. (Orig.). 1991. pap. 11.00 (*0-86025-436-4*, Pub. by I Henry Pubns) Empire Pub Srvs.
Paul, Jeremy, jt. auth. see Fischl, Richard M.
Paul, Jerome, jt. auth. see Berman, Ken.
Paul, Jim. Catapult. LC 97-16080. (J). 1997. pap. 12.00 (*0-15-600556-5*) Harcourt.
— Catapult: Harry & I Build a Siege Weapon. 272p. 1992. pap. 9.00 (*0-380-71840-5*, Avon Bks) Morrow Avon.
— Celtic Symbols: 18 Rubber Stamps. 24p. 1998. 19.95 (*0-8118-2054-8*) Chronicle Bks.
— Medieval in L. A. A Delightful Romp Through Los Angeles as Seen Through the Mind of a Medieval Man. LC 97-25494. 1997. pap. 12.00 (*0-15-600537-9*) Harcourt.
— What's Called Love: A Real Romance. 1993. 19.00 (*0-685-63495-7*) Villard Books.
Paul, Jim & Moynihan, Brendan. What I Learned Losing a Million Dollars. 190p. 28.95 (*0-9635794-9-5*) Infrared Pr.
***Paul, John, II.** Crossing the Threshold of Hope. Messori, Vittorio, ed. Orig. Title: Varcare la Soglia Della Speranza. 244p. 1999. reprint ed. text 20.00 (*0-7881-6825-8*) DIANE Pub.
Paul, John. Porcupine. (Illus.). (J). pap. 3.00 (*1-55500-072-X*) Alaska Native.
Paul, John E. Catherine of Aragon & Her Friends. LC 66-15774. 285p. reprint ed. pap. 88.40 (*0-7837-0461-5*, 204078400018) Bks Demand.
Paul, John J. & Paul, Sheryl R. Achieving Customer Delight in Your Organization: Positioning Your Organization to Stand Out, Field Book. 109p. 1999 pap. 21.95 (*1-893827-00-3*) Assn Works.
Paul, John J., jt. ed. see Yandell, Keith E.
Paul, John R. The Pine Vole in North Carolina. (Reports of Investigations: No. 20). (Illus.). 28p. 1970. pap. 1.00 (*0-89792-044-9*) Ill St Museum.
Paul, John R. & Parmalee, Paul W. Soft Drink Bottling: A History with Special Reference to Illinois. (Illus.). 121p. 1973. pap. 5.00 (*0-89792-079-1*) Ill St Museum.
Paul, John W. Apple Blossom Cologne Co. (Micro Computer Version) (C). 1987. text 39.95 (*0-255-05984-5*, Irwn McGrw-H) McGrw-H Hghr Educ.
— Peach Blossom Cologne Company Microcomputer IBM Version for Use with 1-2-3 from Lotus. 2nd ed. 32p. (C). 1993. text 41.87 incl. 3.5 hd (*0-256-13096-5*, Irwn McGrw-H) McGrw-H Hghr Educ.
Paul, Jordan & Paul, Margaret. Do I Have to Give up Me to Be Loved by You? Orig. Title: From Conflict to Caring. 316p. 1995. 7.98 (*1-56731-067-2*, MJF Bks) Fine Comms.
— Do I Have to Give up Me to Be Loved by You? Orig. Title: From Conflict to Caring. 211p. pap., wbk. ed. 15.95 (*1-56838-051-8*) Hazelden.
— Do I have to Give up Me to Be Loved by You? Orig. Title: From Conflict to Caring. 336p. pap. 14.95 (*1-56838-068-2*, 7605 A) Hazelden.
— Free to Love. LC 74-27653. 160p. 1983. reprint ed. pap. 5.95 (*0-912389-00-1*) Evolving Pubns.
Paul, Jordan, jt. auth. see Paul, Margaret.
***Paul, Joseph.** The System. 332p. 1999. pap. 17.95 (*0-7414-0154-1*) Buy Books.
Paul, Juanita. God in the Flow of Life. LC 96-92982. (Illus.). xii, 288p. (Orig.). 1997. per. 18.00 (*0-9655822-0-5*, G-1) JP Books.
Paul, Juergen. Die Politische und Soziale Bedeutung der Naqsbandiyya in Mittelasien Im 15. Jahrhundert. (Studien zur Sprache, Geschichte und Kultur des Islamischen Orients: Bd. 13). (GER.). x, 275p. (C). 1991. lib. bdg. 136.95 (*3-11-012720-2*) De Gruyter.
Paul, K., jt. auth. see Long, J.
Paul, K., ed. see Salusbury, John.
***Paul, Karen.** Kegginaqa. large type ed.Tr. of My Face. (ESK., Illus.). 8p. (J). (gr. k-3). 2000. pap. text 6.00 (*1-58084-198-8*) Lower Kuskokwim.
— My Face. large type ed. (Illus.). 8p. (J). (gr. k-3). 2000. pap. text 6.00 (*1-58084-197-X*) Lower Kuskokwim.
— My Face (Cup'ik) large type ed. (Illus.). 8p. (J). (gr. k-3). 2000. pap. text 6.00 (*1-58084-199-6*) Lower Kuskokwim.
Paul, Karen, ed. Contemporary Issues in Business & Society in the United States. LC 91-22282. (Mellen Studies in Business: Vol. 8). 324p. 1991. lib. bdg. 99.95 (*0-7734-9733-1*) E Mellen.
— Contemporary Issues in Business Ethics & Politics. LC 91-18939. (Mellen Studies in Business: Vol. 7). 316p. 1991. lib. bdg. 99.95 (*0-7734-9718-8*) E Mellen.
Paul, Karen, jt. ed. see Ludwig, Dean C.
Paul, Karen Dawley. Research Collections of Former United States Senators, 1789-1995. 755p. 1995. per. 55.00 (*0-16-063265-X*) USGPO.
Paul, Kathleen. Sonoran Desert Handbook. 1987. 3.95 (*0-9605656-4-7*) Desert Botanical.
— Whitewashing Britain: Race & Citizenship in the Postwar Era. LC 97-5410. (Illus.). 288p. 1996. text 39.95 (*0-8014-3348-7*); pap. text 16.95 (*0-8014-8440-5*) Cornell U Pr.
Paul, Kees, jt. ed. see Reinders, Reinder.
Paul, Kevin. Chairing a Meeting with Confidence: An Easy Guide to Rules & Procedure. 3rd ed. (Reference Ser.). 96p. 1989. 7.95 (*1-55180-019-5*) Self-Counsel Pr.
— Complete Guide to Canadian Universities. 5th rev. ed. 240p. 1998. pap. 15.95 (*1-55180-200-7*) Self-Counsel Pr.
— Get Your University Degree at Home: Accredited University Education at Home. 1999. pap. 15.95 (*1-55180-209-0*) Self-Counsel Pr.
— Study Smarter, Not Harder: Your Guide to Successful Learning & Studying in Any Situation. 232p. (Orig.). 1996. pap. 16.95 (*1-55180-059-4*) Self-Counsel Pr.
— Your Guide to Canadian Colleges: Select a Program, Choose a College, & Succeed When You Get There. (Reference Ser.). 256p. 1993. pap. 14.95 (*0-88908-291-X*) Self-Counsel Pr.
Paul Klee Foundation Staff, ed. Paul Klee Catalogue Raisonne: The Bauhaus in Weimar (1919-1922), 9 vols. LC 98-61525. (ENG & GER., Illus.). 500p. 1999. 225.00 (*0-500-09281-8*, Pub. by Thames Hudson) Norton.
***Paul Klee Foundation Staff, ed.** Paul Klee Catalogue Raisonne Vol. 2: 1913-1918. LC 98-61082. Vol. 2. (Illus.). 500p. 2000. text 225.00 (*0-500-09280-X*, Pub. by Thames Hudson) Norton.
— Paul Klee Catalogue Raisonne Vol. 4: 1923-1928. LC 98-61082. (Illus.). 500p. 2001. 225.00 (*0-500-09282-6*, Pub. by Thames Hudson) Norton.
Paul, Korky. Pop-Up Book of Ghost Tales. (Illus.). 24p. (J). (gr. 3 up). 1991. 14.95 (*0-15-200589-7*, Harcourt Child Bks) Harcourt.
Paul, Korky. Dinosaur Poems. 32p. (J). (gr. k). 1997. pap. 7.95 (*0-19-276126-9*) OUP.
— Dragons, Dinosaurs & Monster Poems. LC 98-203452. 106p. (J). 1998. 17.00 (*0-19-276195-1*) OUP.
Paul, Korky. Monster Poems. 32p. (J). (gr. k up). 1997. pap. 7.95 (*0-19-276147-1*) OUP.
Paul, Korky, jt. auth. see Agard, John.
Paul, Korky, jt. auth. see Long, Jonathan.
Paul, Korky, jt. auth. see Thomas, Valerie.
Paul, Korky, jt. auth. see Tzannes, Robin.
Paul, Krugman. Peddling Prosperity: Economic Ideas & Ideology in America. 180p. 1994. 22.00 (*0-393-03602-2*) Norton.
Paul, Larry A. ARE Practice Exam: Multiple-Choice Divisions. 2nd ed. 87p. 1999. pap. 34.95 (*1-888577-28-2*) Prof Pubns CA.
Paul, Lauren. PC Week: The Internet Advantage. LC 98-160796. 416p. 1996. pap. text 34.99 (*1-56276-427-6*, Ziff-Davis Pr) Que.
***Paul, Lee.** Frontier Lawmen: Incredible Stories of Incredible Men. (Illus.). 220p. 2000. pap. 14.95 (*0-9657929-5-1*) JONA Bks.
Paul, Lee. Jim Peters: Texas Ranger. LC 97-68451. (Illus.). 216p. 1997. pap. 12.95 (*0-9657929-0-0*) JONA Bks.
***Paul, Lee.** Unsolved Mysteries of the Old West. (Illus.). 200p. 2000. pap. 17.95 (*0-9657929-7-8*) JONA Bks.
Paul, Leendert C. & Issekutz, Thomas B., eds. Adhesion Molecules in Health & Disease. LC 97-12034. (Illus.). 768p. 1997. text 195.00 (*0-8247-9824-4*) Dekker.
Paul, Leslie. Sir Thomas More. LC 75-128882. (Select Bibliographies Reprint Ser.). 1977. reprint ed. 18.95 (*0-8369-5502-1*) Ayer.
Paul, Leslie A. Meaning of Human Existence. LC 73-148642. 1971. reprint ed. lib. bdg. 65.00 (*0-8371-6008-1*, PAHE, Greenwood Pr) Greenwood.
Paul, Linda L., jt. auth. see Sacks, Ann.
***Paul, Linda Leigh.** Cottages by the Sea: The Handmade Homes of Carmel, America's Artist Community. (Illus.). 2000. 35.00 (*0-7893-0495-3*) Universe.
Paul, Lisa. Cowboy Way. 1997. pap. text 12.95 (*0-929526-66-X*) Double B Pubns.
Paul, Lissa. Reading Otherways. LC 98-50187. (Illus.). 100p. 1998. pap. 12.95 (*0-9663233-7-8*) Calendar Islands.
Paul, Lois. Lois' Luscious Low-Fat Creations: A Collection of Recipes by Lois Paul. 111p. (Orig.). 1998. spiral bd. 14.95 (*0-9661869-0-7*) Nutritional Consult.
Paul, M. Finances Publiques A a Z, Dictionnaire du Droit Budgetaire. (FRE.). 1998. 69.95 (*0-320-00287-X*) Fr & Eur.
Paul, M. & Robinet, B., eds. International Symposium on Programming: 6th Colloquium, Toulouse, April 17-19, 1984 Proceedings. (Lecture Notes in Computer Science Ser.: Vol. 167). vi, 262p. 1984. 31.00 (*0-387-12925-1*) Spr-Verlag.
Paul, M. & Siegert, H. J., eds. Distributed Systems. (Lecture Notes in Computer Science Ser.: Vol. 190). vi, 573p. 1988. 55.00 (*0-387-15216-4*) Spr-Verlag.
Paul, M., jt. auth. see Winter, Hans.
Paul, M., jt. ed. see Neuhold, Erich J.
Paul, M. C. Dimensions of Tribal Movements in India. (C). 1989. 18.00 (*81-210-0219-2*, Pub. by Inter-India Pubns) S Asia.
Paul, M. Eden, tr. see Bloch, Iwan.
Paul, Malcolm. Transblepharoplasty Suberiosteal Forehead & Midfacelift. LC 98-4297. (Illus.). 32p. 1998. pap. 185.00 incl. vdisk (*0-387-98482-8*) Spr-Verlag.
Paul, Manfred, jt. ed. see Sommerville, Ian.
Paul, Manmathanath, tr. see Sandilya.
Paul, Mara. Child Secrets: Milford-Haven, 12 vols., Bk. 3. LC 99-71766. (Milford-Haven). 215p. 1999. pap. 13.95 (*0-9659480-3-X*) Haven Bks CA.
Paul, Marcel & Paul, Carol. The Adventures of Elbert Egret & Magnolia Cow: Chicken Soup. LC 94-93863. 17p. (J). (gr. 3-12). 1995. pap. 6.95 (*0-9612822-1-5*) Green Rose.
***Paul, Margaret.** Do I Have to Give Up Me to Be Loved by God? LC 99-43082. 200p. 1999. pap. 11.95 (*1-55874-697-8*) Health Comm.
Paul, Margaret. Inner Bonding: Becoming a Loving Adult to Your Inner Child. LC 91-58163. 240p. 1992. pap. 16.00 (*0-06-250710-9*, Pub. by Harper SF) HarpC.
Paul, Margaret & Chopich, Erika J. Healing Your Aloneness: Finding Love & Wholeness Through Your Inner Child. LC 89-46151. 208p. 1990. pap. 13.00 (*0-06-250149-6*, Pub. by Harper SF) HarpC.
Paul, Margaret & Paul, Jordan. Do I Have to Give Up Me to Be Loved by My Kids? Hesse, Bonnie B., ed. 313p. 1987. pap. 13.99 (*0-89638-307-5*); mass mkt. 5.99 (*0-425-15059-3*) Evolving Pubns.
Paul, Margaret, jt. auth. see Paul, Jordan.
Paul, Margareta, tr. see Jersild, P. C.
Paul, Margot, jt. auth. see Stinchecum, Amanda M.
Paul-Marie of the Cross. Carmelite Spirituality in the Teresian Tradition. rev. ed. Payne, Steven & Sullivan, John, eds. Sullivan, Kathryn, tr. LC 94-27728. (Illus.). 98p. 1997. reprint ed. pap. 8.95 (*0-935216-50-2*) ICS Pubns.
***Paul, Marini.** Broken Tower Pennsylvania. 512p. 2000. pap. 15.95 (*0-393-32041-3*) Norton.
Paul, Martin, tr. see Alberti, Rafael.

P

An Asterisk (*) at the beginning of an entry indicates that the title is appearing for the first time.

Paul, Mary. Her Side of the Story: Readings of Mansfield, Mander & Hyde. (Illus.). 288p. Date not set. pap. 39.95 (*1-877133-71-X*, Pub. by Univ Otago Pr) Intl Spec Bk.

Paul, Mary. Partnership Bidding: A Workbook, 1. 1997. 7.95 (*0-9698461-0-X*) Master Pt Pr.

Paul, Mary E. Organizational Development Tools. 84p. 1993. student ed. 25.00 (*1-883542-01-4*) ResourceWomen.

Paul, Mary E. & Clements, Linda, eds. Church Funding Resource Guide, 1993. 10th ed. 500p. 1993. 80.00 (*0-685-66581-X*); student ed. 65.00 (*1-883542-00-6*) ResourceWomen.

Paul-Matos, Janice. How to Get into College: Step by Step, Vol. 1. 24p. (Orig.). (J). (gr. 9-12). 1985. pap. 5.00 (*0-9615165-0-X*) Coll Acceptance.

***Paul, Matthias.** Success in Referential Communication. LC 99-42471. (Philosophical Studies Ser.). 200p. 1999. text 85.00 (*0-7923-5974-7*) Kluwer Academic.

Paul, Maureen, ed. Occupational & Environmental Reproductive Hazards. LC 92-13719. (Illus.). 448p. 1993. 85.00 (*0-683-06801-6*) Lppncott W & W.

***Paul, Maureen, et al.** A Clinician's Guide to Medical & Surgical Abortion. Schmitt, William, ed. LC 98-43931. (Illus.). 395p. 1999. text. write for info. (*0-443-07529-8*) Church.

Paul, Megan. No Sweeter Conflict. (Scarlet Ser.). 1998. mass mkt. 3.99 (*1-85487-999-5*, Pub. by Scarlet Bks) London Brdge.

Paul, Mercer H. How to Save a Fortune on Your Heating & Air Conditioning. (Illus.). 16p. 1997. pap. 6.00 (*0-8059-4091-X*) Dorrance.

***Paul, Michael.** Living Zen. (Illus.). 160p. 2000. 30.00 (*0-7892-0681-1*) Abbeville Pr.

Paul, Michael. The Plural of Bus Is Buses Isn't It? A Guide to Word Usage. rev. ed. LC 87-91305. (Illus.). 85p. 1988. pap. 5.00 (*0-9616367-2-6*) Michael Paul.

— The Warming Tract: A Guide to Good Writing from Sports Stories. LC 86-90402. 54p. (Orig.). (YA). (gr. 7-12). 1986. pap. 5.00 (*0-9616367-0-X*) Michael Paul.

Paul, Michael I. Before We Were Young: An Exploration of Primordial States of Mind. 224p. 1997. lib. bdg. 35.95 (*1-883881-24-2*, 24-2) S Freud RT&PF.

Paul, Michel. Orchids. 1998. 19.99 (*3-8228-7762-X*) Taschen Amer.

***Paul, Michel.** Orquideas a la Luz de la Luna. 1998. 25.99 (*3-8228-8036-1*) Benedikt Taschen.

Paul, Michele. The Women's Pharmacy. mass mkt. 3.50 (*0-318-23489-0*, Pinncle Kensgtn) Kensgtn Pub Corp.

Paul, N. M., tr. see Bergson, Henri.

Paul, Natalie W., ed. A Guide to Human Chromosome Defects. 2nd ed. LC 68-57287. (March of Dimes Birth Defects Foundation Ser.: Vol. 16, No. 6). 1980. 0.50 (*0-686-30821-2*) March of Dimes.

Paul, Natalie W., jt. auth. see Opitz, John M.

***Paul, Nora M.** Computer Assisted Research: A Guide to Tapping Online Information. 4th ed. LC 99-45331. 207p. 1999. pap. text 12.95 (*1-56625-137-0*) Bonus Books.

Paul of Venice. Logica Magna, Fascicule 8 Pt. 1: Tractatus de Necessititate et Contingentia Futurorum. Williams, C. J., ed. (Classical & Medieval Logic Texts Ser.: No. VIII). 288p. 1991. pap. 45.00 (*0-19-726101-9*) OUP.

Paul-of-Venice. Logica Magna, Fascicule 5 Pt. 2: Capitula de Conditionali et de Rationali. Hughes, G. E., ed. (Classical & Midieval Logic Texts Ser.: Vol. VI). 592p. 1990. pap. 59.00 (*0-19-726094-2*) OUP.

Paul of Venice. Logica Magna, Fascicule 3 Pt. 2: Tractatus de Hypotheticis. Broadie, Alexander, ed. (Classical & Medieval Logic Texts Ser.: Vol. VII). 420p. 1990. pap. 59.00 (*0-19-726095-0*) OUP.

Paul, Oglesby. Take Heart: The Life of Dr. Paul Dudley White. LC 86-3170. (Francis A. Countway Library of Medicine). (Illus.). 336p. 1986. 19.95 (*0-674-86745-9*) HUP.

Paul, P. F., et al, eds. Synthetic Fuels from Coal: Status of the Technology. (C). 1988. pap. text 215.00 (*1-85333-103-1*, Pub. by Graham & Trotman) Kluwer Academic.

Paul, Patty. A New Spirituality - Beyond Religion: With Personal Growth That Leads to Spiritual Growth - The Human Being Becomes a Spiritual Being. LC 94-79198. 208p. 1995. pap. 12.95 (*0-9642726-7-9*) IMDEX Pub.

***Paul, Paul A.** Kia Una Pikau? large type ed.Tr. of Whose Is This?. (ESK., Illus.). 8p. (J). (gr. k-3). 2000. pap. text 6.00 (*1-58084-204-6*) Lower Kuskokwim.

— Whose Is This? large type ed. (Illus.). 8p. (J). (gr. k-3). 2000. pap. text 6.00 (*1-58084-203-8*) Lower Kuskokwim.

— Whose Is This? (Cup'ik) large type ed. (Illus.). 8p. (J). (gr. k-3). 2000. pap. text 6.00 (*1-58084-205-4*) Lower Kuskokwim.

Paul, Paula. Geronimo Chino. 47p. (J). (gr. 3-9). 1980. 4.45 (*0-89992-079-9*) Coun India Ed.

Paul, Penelope. Costume & Clothes. LC 94-44417. (Legacies Ser.). (Illus.). 48p. (J). (gr. 4-6). 1995. lib. bdg. 24.26 (*1-56847-274-9*) Raintree Steck-V.

Paul, Peter C. Easy Pickings: Non-Profits & Charities Regulation in the 50 US States-10 Canadian Provinces, England-Wales & Australia. Fox, L. Christopher, ed. (Selected Directory of Non-profits & Charities Regulation in the U. S., Canada, Australia, England & Wales Ser.). (Illus.). 700p. (Orig.). (C). 1988. pap. 38.95 (*0-318-39969-5*); text 38.95 (*0-318-39968-7*) Verzola.

Paul, Peter V. Literacy & Deafness. LC 97-21431. 358p. 1997. 60.00 (*0-205-17576-7*) P-H.

Paul, Peter V. & Jackson, Dorothy W. Toward a Psychology of Deafness: Theoretical & Empirical Perspectives. LC 92-31126. 476p. 1992. 81.00 (*0-205-14112-9*, H41122) Allyn.

Paul, Peter V. & Quigley, Stephen P. Language & Deafness. 2nd ed. LC 94-4478. (Illus.). 112p. (C). 1994. teacher ed. 24.50 (*1-56593-362-1*, 0695) Singular Publishing.

— Language & Deafness. 2nd ed. LC 94-4478. (Illus.). 394p. (C). 1994. pap. text 45.00 (*1-56593-108-4*, 0411) Thomson Learn.

— Language & Deafness. 2nd ed. 252p. (C). 1994. pap. text, student ed. 29.95 (*1-56593-363-X*, 0700) Thomson Learn.

Paul, Philip C. Where to Find Venture Capital: A Resource Guide. LC 95-815. 296p. (Orig.). 1995. pap. 19.95 (*1-56825-028-2*) Rainbow Books.

Paul, Phyllis, ed. Historic Homes & Buildings in Rancho Santa Fe. (Illus.). 74p. 1999. pap. 10.00 (*0-938711-59-8*) Tecolote Pubns.

Paul, Prem S., et al, eds. Mechanisms in the Pathogenesis of Enteric Diseases: Proceedings of the First International Rushmore Conference Held in Rapid City, South Dakota, September 28-30, 1995. LC 97-5561. (Advances in Experimental Medicine & Biology Ser.: No. 412). (Illus.). 452p. 1997. 125.00 (*0-306-45519-6*, Kluwer Plenum) Kluwer Academic.

Paul, R. E., jt. auth. see Whyte, W. S.

Paul, R. Eli. Autobiography of Red Cloud: War Leader of the Oglalas. LC 96-52849. (Illus.). 240p. 1999. pap. 15.95 (*0-917298-50-0*) MT Hist Soc.

Paul, R. Eli, ed. The Nebraska Indian Wars Reader, 1865-77. LC 97-32942. (Illus.). xii, 289p. 1998. pap. 15.00 (*0-8032-8749-6*, Bison Books) U of Nebr Pr.

Paul, R. Eli, jt. ed. see Buecker, Thomas R.

Paul, R. J., ed. see Graham, Deryn & Barrett, Anthony N.

Paul, R. J., ed. see Hunt, John.

Paul, R. S., jt. auth. see Corson, John J.

Paul, R. W., ed. see Shinn, Charles H.

Paul, Ray J. Simulation in Action. 1998. pap. text 34.95 (*3-540-76236-1*) Spr-Verlag.

Paul, Rhea. Exploring the Speech-Language Connection. LC 97-29523. (Communication & Language Intervention Ser.). 344p. 1998. 42.00 (*1-55766-325-4*) P H Brookes.

— Language Disorders in Children & Adolescents. (Illus.). 624p. (gr. 13). 1995. text 58.00 (*0-8016-7927-3*, 07927) Mosby Inc.

Paul, Rhea, jt. auth. see Miller, Jon F.

Paul, Richard. Critical Thinking: How to Prepare Students for a Rapidly Changing World. Willsen, Jane & Binker, A. J., eds. 572p. (Orig.). 1995. pap. text 29.95 (*0-944583-09-1*) Found Critical Think.

— A Handbook to the Universe: Explorations of Matter, Energy, Space, & Time for Beginning Scientific Thinkers. LC 92-39670. (Illus.). 308p. (Orig.). (J). (gr. 6 up). 1993. pap. 14.95 (*1-55652-172-3*) Chicago Review.

— The Magic Telescope. (Illus.). 32p. (Orig.). (J). (gr. k-3). 1996. pap. 9.95 (*0-9653238-0-3*) Twilght Pr.

— Red Riding Hood Races the Big Bad Wolf. (Illus.). 40p. (J). (gr. k-2). 1998. 12.95 (*0-9653238-1-1*) Twilght Pr.

Paul, Richard C. Orchid Growing Outside in the Kingdom of the Coconut Palm. 16th ed. 24p. 1984. pap. 5.00 (*1-888089-20-2*) Green Nature Bks.

Paul, Richard P. SPARC Architecture Assembly Language Programming. LC 93-10038. 448p. (C). 1993. text 71.00 (*0-13-876889-7*) Prntice Hall Bks.

***Paul, Richard P.** Sparc Architecture, Assembly Language Programming & C. 2nd ed. LC 99-32663. 528p. 1999. pap. 71.00 (*0-13-025596-3*) P-H.

Paul, Richard P., jt. ed. see Brady, Michael.

Paul, Richard S. & Shaevel, M. Leonard. Essentials of Technical Mathematics with Calculus. 2nd ed. 1104p. (C). 1988. text 53.25 (*0-13-289091-7*) P-H.

Paul, Richard S. & Shavel. Essentials of Technical Mathematics. 3rd ed. LC 87-21147. 832p. (C). 1988. 120.00 (*0-13-288812-2*) P-H.

Paul, Richard S., jt. auth. see Haeussler, Ernest F.

Paul, Richard S., jt. auth. see Haeussler, Ernest F., Jr.

Paul, Richard W. Critical Thinking: What Every Person Needs to Survive in a Rapidly Changing World. 3rd rev. ed. Binker, A. J. & Williams, Jane, eds. LC 90-80195. 505p. 1993. pap. text 29.95 (*0-944583-07-5*) Found Critical Think.

— Critical Thinking: What Every Person Needs to Survive in a Rapidly Changing World. 3rd rev. ed. Willson, Jane & Binker, A. J., eds. LC 90-80195. 505p. 1993. pap. text 29.95 (*0-944583-08-3*) Found Critical Think.

— Critical Thinking Handbook--High School: A Guide for Redesigning Instruction. Binker, A. J., ed. LC 89-62293. 381p. (Orig.). 1989. pap. text 19.95 (*0-944583-03-2*) Found Critical Think.

Paul, Richard W., et al. Critical Thinking Handbook: K-Three: A Guide for Remodelling Lesson Plans in Language Arts, Social Studies & Science. 2nd ed. LC 90-82938. (Illus.). 437p. 1995. pap. text 19.95 (*0-944583-05-9*) Found Critical Think.

— Critical Thinking Handbook - 4th-6th Grades: A Guide for Remodelling Lesson Plans in Language Arts, Social Studies, & Science. 2nd ed. Binker, A. J., ed. LC 87-72836. 427p. (Orig.). (C). 1990. reprint ed. pap. text 19.95 (*0-944583-01-6*) Found Critical Think.

***Paul, Rick.** The Experienced Entrepreneur: Marketing & Business Planning to Enable Both Start-Ups & Existing Business to Become More Successful & Profitable. (Illus.). 154p. 1999. pap. text. write for info. (*0-9700206-0-0*) R Paul.

Paul, Rik, jt. auth. see Darlington, Mansur.

Paul, Rik, jt. auth. see Haynes, J. H.

Paul, Robert A. Exercises in Meteorology. 2nd ed. 272p. (C). 1996. pap. text 42.00 (*0-02-393212-0*, Macmillan Coll) P-H.

Paul, Robert A. Moses & Civilization: The Meaning Behind Freud's Myth. LC 95-23585. 268p. 1996. 37.00 (*0-300-06428-4*) Yale U Pr.

— The Tibetan Symbolic World: Psychoanalytic Explorations. LC 81-16505. (Chicago Original Paperback Ser.). (Illus.). 360p. 1982. pap. text 14.00 (*0-226-64987-3*) U Ch Pr.

— The Tibetan Symbolic World: Psychoanalytic Explorations. LC 81-16505. (Illus.). 357p. reprint ed. pap. 110.70 (*0-608-09492-7*, 205429300005) Bks Demand.

Paul, Robert D. & Disney, Diane M., eds. The Sourcebook on Postretirement Health Care Benefits. LC 88-15194. 603p. 1988. 89.00 (*0-916592-76-6*) Panel Pubs.

Paul, Robert S. The Assembly of the Lord: Politics & Religion in the Westminster Assembly & the 'Grand Debate' 624p. 1997. pap. 39.95 (*0-567-08559-7*, Pub. by T & T Clark) Bks Intl VA.

— Whatever Happaned to Sherlock Holmes? Detective Fiction, Popular Theology, & Society. LC 90-23719. 256p. (C). 1991. 26.95 (*0-8093-1722-2*) S Ill U Pr.

Paul, Rodman W. California Gold: The Beginning of Mining in the Far West. LC 47-54111. (Bison Book Ser.). (Illus.). 400p. reprint ed. pap. 124.00 (*0-8357-7974-2*, 202916100058) Bks Demand.

— The Far West & the Great Plains in Transition, 1859-1900. LC 98-6213. (Illus.). 416p. 1998. pap. 17.95 (*0-8061-3023-7*) U of Okla Pr.

Paul, Rodman W. & Etulain, Richard W. The Frontier & the American West. LC 76-11622. (Goldentree Bibliographies Series in American History). (C). 1977. pap. text 14.95 (*0-88295-542-X*) Harlan Davidson.

Paul, Rodman W., ed. see Foote, Mary H.

Paul, Roman. Fontanes Wortkunst: Von "Angstmeierschaft" bis "Zivil-Wallenstein" - Ein Blinder Fleck der Realismusforschung. Schlosser, Horst D., ed. (Frankfurter Forschungen zur Kultur- und Sprachwissenschaft: Band 2). (GER.). 180p. 1998. pap. 37.95 (*3-631-32897-4*) P Lang Pubng.

Paul, Ronald. Fire in Our Hearts: A Study of the Portrayal of Youth in a Selection of Post-War British Working-Class Fiction. (Gothenburg Studies in English: No. 51). 225p. (Orig.). 1982. pap. 45.00 (*91-7346-110-5*, Pub. by Acta U Gothenburg) Coronet Bks.

Paul, Ronald N., jt. auth. see Bernstein, Charles.

Paul, Rothman, jt. auth. see Martha, Pelaez.

Paul, S. Capacity Building for Health Sector Reform No. 5: Forum on Health Sector Reform, Discussion Paper. 19p. 1995. pap. 10.80 (*0-614-32410-6*, 1935076) World Health.

— Dictionary of Aerospace Teledetection: Dictionnaire de Teledetection Aero-Spatiale. (ENG & FRE.). 256p. 1982. 225.00 (*0-8288-0012-X*, M14360) Fr & Eur.

— Illustrator's Reference Manual: Sports. 1992. 22.98 (*1-55521-791-5*) Bk Sales Inc.

— India's Exports: New Imperatives & Newer Vistas. The Emerging Asia-Pacific Nexus. 1992. 64.00 (*81-7169-173-0*, Commonwealth) S Asia.

Paul, S. K. Accountancy, Vol. I. (C). 1989. 110.00 (*0-89771-429-6*, Pub. by Current Dist) St Mut.

— Accountancy, Vol. II. (C). 1989. 110.00 (*0-89771-430-X*, Pub. by Current Dist) St Mut.

— Advanced Accountancy. (C). 1989. 125.00 (*0-7855-6559-0*, Pub. by Current Dist) St Mut.

— Financial Management. (C). 1989. 75.00 (*0-89771-432-6*, Pub. by Current Dist) St Mut.

Paul, Sabine, et al. Non-Governmental Organizations in Malawi: Their Contribution to Development & Democratization. 248p. 1997. pap. text 16.95 (*3-8258-3030-6*) Transaction Pubs.

Paul, Sally. Creative Fabric Frames. (Illus.). 32p. (YA). (gr. 7-12). 1981. pap. 6.00 (*0-932946-06-2*) Burdett CA.

Paul, Samuel. Strategic Management of Development Programmes: Guidelines for Action. (Management Development Ser.: No. 19). vii, 137p. 1990. pap. 18.00 (*92-2-103252-3*) Intl Labour Office.

Paul, Sandra. Baby on the Way. 1997. per. 3.50 (*0-373-52056-5*, 1-52056-8) Silhouette.

— His Accidental Angel. (Romance Ser.). 1995. per. 2.99 (*0-373-19087-5*, 1-19087-5) Silhouette.

— Last Chance for Marriage. large type ed. 239p. 1992. reprint ed. lib. bdg. 13.95 (*1-56054-541-0*) Thorndike Pr.

— The Reluctant Hero. (Silhouette Romance Ser.). 1994. per. 2.75 (*0-373-19016-6*, 5-19016-0) Harlequin Bks.

— The Reluctant Hero. 1997. per. 42.00 (*0-373-91016-9*, 5-91016-1) Harlequin Bks.

Paul, Sandra & Porter, Cheryl A. Head over Heels & Puppy Love. (Duets Ser.: No. 12). 1999. per. 5.99 (*0-373-44078-2*, 1-44078-3) Harlequin Bks.

Paul, Sanjoy. Multicasting on the Internet & Its Applications. LC 98-20100. 421p. 1998. write for info. (*0-7923-8200-5*) Kluwer Academic.

Paul, Sara & Hebra, Jennifer D. The Nurse's Guide to Cardiac Rhythm Interpretation: Implications for Patient Care. Cullen, Barbara N., ed. LC 97-36629. (Illus.). 405p. (C). 1998. pap. text 27.95 (*0-7216-5906-3*, W B Saunders Co) Harcrt Hlth Sci Grp.

Paul, Satya, ed. Trade & Growth: New Theory & the Australian Experience. (Illus.). 320p. 1998. pap. 45.00 (*1-86448-535-3*, Pub. by Allen & Unwin Pty) Paul & Co Pubs.

***Paul, Septimus H.** Anglo-American Cooperation & the Development of the British Atomic Bomb. LC 00-8677. 272p. 2000. 42.50 (*0-8142-0852-5*) Ohio St U Pr.

Paul, Serge, jt. auth. see Association National Staff.

Paul, Shale. Maybe It's Not Your Fault, but You Can Do Something about It: The Blue Book for Personal Survival. 64p. (Orig.). 1993. pap., per. 4.95 (*0-913787-08-6*) Delta G Pr.

— The Warrior Within: A Guide to Inner Power. LC 83-72057. (Illus.). 160p. (Orig.). 1984. 12.95 (*0-913787-01-9*); pap. 9.95 (*0-913787-02-7*) Delta G Pr.

Paul, Shalom. Amos. LC 90-45137. (Hermeneia: A Critical & Historical Commentary on the Bible Ser.). 440p. (Orig.). 1991. 53.00 (*0-8006-6023-4*, 1-6023, Fortress Pr) Augsburg Fortress.

Paul, Shalom M., jt. ed. see Cogan, Mordechai.

Paul, Shannon. Design Presentation. 41p. 1993. pap. 10.00 (*0-614-25158-3*, Sage Prdcls Pr) Sage.

Paul, Sharda. General Elections in India. iv, 205p. 1990. text 27.95 (*81-7045-060-8*, Pub. by Assoc Pub Hse) Advent Bks Div.

Paul, Sharda, jt. auth. see Ahuja, M. L.

Paul, Sherman. Emerson's Angle of Vision: Man & Nature in American Experience. LC 80-2542. reprint ed. 33.50 (*0-404-19267-X*) AMS Pr.

— For Love of the World: Essays on Nature Writers. LC 92-6160. 274p. 1992. pap. 16.95 (*0-87745-396-9*) U of Iowa Pr.

— Hart's Bridge. LC 76-188133. 325p. reprint ed. pap. 100.80 (*0-608-13988-2*, 202226400026) Bks Demand.

— Hewing to Experience: Essays & Reviews on Recent American Poetry & Poetics, Nature & Culture. LC 89-32349. 407p. 1989. text 38.95 (*0-87745-247-4*) U of Iowa Pr.

— In Love with the Gratuitous: Rereading Armand Schwerner. (Illus.). 72p. (Orig.). 1986. pap. 5.00 (*0-940237-01-6*) ND Qtr Pr.

— Randolph Bourne. LC 66-64593. (University of Minnesota Pamphlets on American Writers Ser.: No. 60). 48p. (Orig.). reprint ed. pap. 30.00 (*0-7837-2869-7*, 205758600006) Bks Demand.

— Repossessing & Renewing: Essays in the Green American. LC 75-5351. (Illus.). 314p. reprint ed. pap. 97.40 (*0-7837-8805-3*, 204945100011) Bks Demand.

— The Shores of America: Thoreau's Inward Exploration. LC 58-6998. 447p. reprint ed. pap. 138.60 (*0-608-18047-5*, 201492800093) Bks Demand.

Paul, Sherman, ed. Criticism & Culture: Papers of the Midwest Modern Language Association Presented at the Annual Meeting for 1969, October 23, 24 & 25, in St. Louis, MO. LC 89-643764. (Papers of the Midwest Modern Language Association: No. 2). 133p. 1972. pap. 41.30 (*0-608-05590-5*, 206605000006) Bks Demand.

Paul, Sherry. Blossom Bird Falls in Love. (See How I Read Ser.). (Illus.). 32p. (Orig.). (J). (ps-2). 1981. pap. 14.10 (*0-685-01192-5*); pap. 16.20 (*0-685-01193-3*) CPI Pub.

— Blossom Bird Finds a Family. (See How I Read Ser.). (Illus.). 32p. (Orig.). (J). (ps-2). 1981. 16.20 (*0-685-01194-1*) CPI Pub.

— Blossom Bird Finds a Family, Set. (See How I Read Ser.). (Illus.). 32p. (Orig.). (J). (ps-2). 1981. pap. 14.10 (*0-686-31343-7*) CPI Pub.

— Blossom Bird Goes South. (See How I Read Ser.). (Illus.). 32p. (Orig.). (J). (ps-2). 1981. 16.20 (*0-685-01195-X*) CPI Pub.

— Blossom Bird Goes South, Set. (See How I Read Ser.). (Illus.). 32p. (Orig.). (J). (ps-2). 1981. pap. 14.10 (*0-675-01080-2*, Merrill Coll) P-H.

— Finn the Foolish Fish: Trouble with Bubbles, Set. (See How I Read Ser.). (Illus.). 32p. (Orig.). (J). (ps-2). 16.20 (*0-685-01196-8*); pap. 14.10 (*0-675-01084-5*) CPI Pub.

— Two-B & the Rock 'n' Roll Band. (See How I Read Ser.). (Illus.). 32p. (Orig.). (J). (ps-2). 16.20 (*0-685-01197-6*) CPI Pub.

— Two-B & the Rock 'n' Roll Band, Set. (See How I Read Ser.). (Illus.). 32p. (Orig.). (J). (ps-2). pap. 14.10 (*0-675-01082-9*) CPI Pub.

— Two-B & the Space Visitor. (See How I Read Ser.). (Illus.). 32p. (Orig.). (J). (ps-2). pap. 14.10 (*0-685-01198-4*); pap. 16.20 (*0-685-01199-2*) CPI Pub.

Paul, Sheryl R., jt. auth. see Paul, John J.

Paul, Stella. Twentieth-Century Art at the Metropolitan Museum of Art: A Resource for Educators. LC 99-18306. 173p. 1999. 65.00 (*0-87099-899-4*) Metro Mus Art.

Paul, Stephen C. Illuminations: Visions for Change, Growth, & Self-Acceptance. LC 90-55075. (Illus.). 112p. (Orig.). 1990. pap. 13.00 (*0-06-250681-1*, Pub. by Harper SF) HarpC.

Paul, Stephen C. & Collins, Gary M. Inneractions: Visions to Bring Your Inner & Outer Worlds into Harmony. LC 91-58142. (Illus.). 112p. 1992. pap. 13.00 (*0-06-250711-7*, Pub. by Harper SF) HarpC.

Paul, Stephen M., et al, eds. Neuropharmacology of Ethanol: New Approaches. 280p. 1991. 69.00 (*0-685-48688-5*) Spr-Verlag.

Paul, Sudhir. Autoimmune Reactions. LC 98-28432. (Contemporary Immunology Ser.). (Illus.). 448p. 1998. 125.00 (*0-89603-550-6*) Humana.

Paul, Sudhir, ed. Antibody Engineering Protocols. LC 95-423. (Methods in Molecular Biology Ser.: Vol. 51). (Illus.). 460p. 1995. 89.50 (*0-89603-275-2*) Humana.

Paul, Susan. American Renegade. 224p. pap. 5.99 (*1-55197-164-X*) Picasso Publ.

— Memoir of James Jackson: The Attentive & Obedient Scholar, Who Died in Boston, October 31, 1833, Aged Six Years & Eleven Months, by His Teacher Miss Susan Paul. Brown, Lois, ed. LC 99-51781. 160p. 2000. pap. 14.00 (*0-674-00237-7*) HUP.

Paul, Susan. My Story: A Journal. 130p. (Orig.). 1997. spiral bd. 10.95 (*0-9650231-2-5*) Inner Edge.

— Until Death Do Us Part. 185p. 1999. pap. 8.95 (*1-885478-83-6*, Pub. by Genesis Press) BookWorld.

— Your Story Matters: Introducing the Pleasures of Personal Writing. 3rd rev. ed. Schlahta, Glenda, ed. (Illus.). 160p. 1997. pap. 14.95 (*0-9650231-1-7*) Inner Edge.

Paul, Susan S. Beguiled. (Historical Ser.: Vol. 408). 1998. per. 4.99 (*0-373-29008-X*, 1-29008-9) Harlequin Bks.

— The Bride Thief. (Historical Ser.: No. 373). 1997. per. 4.99 (*0-373-28973-1*, 1-28973-5) Harlequin Bks.

— The Bride's Portion. LC 95-8359. (Historical Ser.). 296p. 1995. per. 4.50 (*0-373-28866-2*, 1-28866-1) Harlequin Bks.

— The Heiress Bride. LC 96-3732. (Historical Ser.). 299p. 1996. mass mkt. 4.50 (*0-373-28901-4*, 1-28901-6) Harlequin Bks.

P

An Asterisk (*) at the beginning of an entry indicates that the title is appearing for the first time.

Paul, Susan Spencer. The Captive Bride. 1999. per. 4.99 (0-373-29071-3, 1-29071-7) Harlequin Bks.
Paul, Susie, jt. ed. see Little, Anne Colclough.
Paul, Swaraj, ed. Surface Coatings: Science & Technology. 2nd ed. 950p. 1996. 425.00 (0-471-95818-2) Wiley.
Paul, T. F. The Law & Administration of Incorporated Societies. 2nd ed. 276p. 1986. pap. 54.00 (0-409-78744-2, NZ, MICHIE) LEXIS Pub.
Paul, T. Otis, jt. auth. see Sardegna, Jill.
Paul, T. V., et al, eds. The Absolute Weapon Revisited: Nuclear Arms & the Emerging International Order. (Illus.). 320p. (C). pap. text 21.95 (0-472-08700-2, 08700) U of Mich Pr.
Paul, T. V., et al, eds. The Absolute Weapon Revisited: Nuclear Arms & the Emerging International Order. LC 97-33943. (Illus.). 320p. (C). 1998. text 49.50 (0-472-10863-8, 10863) U of Mich Pr.
Paul, T. V. & Hall, John A., eds. International Order & the Future of World Politics. LC 98-41843. (Illus.). 416p. (C). 1999. pap. 44.95 (0-521-65832-2) Cambridge U Pr.
— International Order & the Future of World Politics. LC 98-41843. (Illus.). 416p. (C). 1999. 64.95 (0-521-65138-7) Cambridge U Pr.
Paul, Ted. The Christmas Collie. LC 89-17994. (Illus.). 42p. (J). (ps-7). 1989. 12.95 (0-89802-548-6) Beautiful Am.
Paul, Tessa. At the Poles. LC 98-10864. (Animal Trackers Ser.). (Illus.). 32p. (J). (gr. 2-3). 1998. pap. 7.95 (0-86505-598-X) Crabtree Pub Co.
***Paul, Tessa.** At The Poles. LC 98-10864. (Animal Trackers Ser.). (Illus.). 32p. (J). (gr. 2-3). 1998. lib. bdg. 20.60 (0-86505-590-4) Crabtree Pub Co.
Paul, Tessa. Autobiography of Andrew Carnegie. (Animal Trackers Ser.). 1997. 13.15 (0-606-12736-4, Pub. by Turtleback) Demco.
— By Lakes & Rivers. LC 96-49684. (Animal Trackers Ser.). (Illus.). 32p. (J). (gr. 2-3). 1997. pap. 7.95 (0-86505-594-7) Crabtree Pub Co.
Paul, Tessa. By Lakes & Rivers. LC 96-49684. (Animal Trackers Ser.). (Illus.). 32p. (J). (gr. 2-3). 1997. lib. bdg. 20.60 (0-86505-586-6) Crabtree Pub Co.
Paul, Tessa. By Lakes & Rivers. (Animal Trackers Ser.). 1997. 13.15 (0-606-12637-6, Pub. by Turtleback) Demco.
— By the Sea Shore. LC 96-45707. (Animal Trackers Ser.). (Illus.). 32p. (J). (gr. 2-3). 1997. pap. 7.95 (0-86505-595-5) Crabtree Pub Co.
— By the Sea Shore. LC 96-45707. (Animal Trackers Ser.). (Illus.). 32p. (J). (gr. 2-3). 1997. lib. bdg. 20.60 (0-86505-587-4) Crabtree Pub Co.
— By the Seashore. (Animal Trackers Ser.). 1997. 13.15 (0-606-12638-4, Pub. by Turtleback) Demco.
***Paul, Tessa.** Down Under. LC 98-2561. (Animal Trackers Ser.). (Illus.). 32p. (J). (gr. 2-3). 1998. lib. bdg. 20.60 (0-86505-588-2) Crabtree Pub Co.
Paul, Tessa. Down Under. LC 98-2561. (Animal Trackers Ser.). (Illus.). 32p. (J). (gr. 4-7). 1998. pap. 7.95 (0-86505-596-3) Crabtree Pub Co.
— In Fields & Meadows. LC 96-39671. (Animal Trackers Ser.). (Illus.). 32p. (J). (gr. 2-3). 1997. pap. 7.95 (0-86505-593-9); lib. bdg. 20.60 (0-86505-585-8) Crabtree Pub Co.
— In Fields & Meadows. (Animal Trackers Ser.). 1997. 13.15 (0-606-12735-6, Pub. by Turtleback) Demco.
— In the Jungle. LC 98-10863. (Animal Trackers Ser.). (Illus.). 32p. (J). (gr. 1-7). 1998. pap. 7.95 (0-86505-599-8) Crabtree Pub Co.
***Paul, Tessa.** In the Jungle. LC 98-10863. (Animal Trackers Ser.). (Illus.). 32p. (J). (gr. 2-3). 1998. lib. bdg. 20.60 (0-86505-591-2) Crabtree Pub Co.
Paul, Tessa. In Woods & Forests. LC 96-39672. (Animal Trackers Ser.). (Illus.). 32p. (J). (gr. 2-3). 1997. pap. 7.95 (0-86505-592-0); lib. bdg. 20.60 (0-86505-584-X) Crabtree Pub Co.
Paul, Tessa. On Safari. LC 98-10862. (Animal Trackers Ser.). (Illus.). 32p. (J). (gr. 1-7). 1998. pap. 7.95 (0-86505-597-1) Crabtree Pub Co.
***Paul, Tessa.** On Safari. LC 98-10862. (Animal Trackers Ser.). (Illus.). 32p. (J). (gr. 2-3). 1998. lib. bdg. 20.60 (0-86505-589-0) Crabtree Pub Co.
Paul, V. P. & Talwar, Ravindra. Wonderful World of Games & Sports, Bk. I. 1997. pap. 20.00 (81-209-0927-5, Pub. by Pitambar Pub) St Mut.
— Wonderful World of Games & Sports, Bk. II. 1997. pap. 20.00 (81-209-0930-5, Pub. by Pitambar Pub) St Mut.
— Wonderful World of Games & Sports, Bk. III. 1997. pap. 20.00 (81-209-0931-3, Pub. by Pitambar Pub) St Mut.
— Wonderful World of Games & Sports, Bk. IV. 1997. pap. 20.00 (81-209-0934-8, Pub. by Pitambar Pub) St Mut.
Paul, Valerie J. Ecological Roles of Marine Natural Products. LC 91-57899. (Explorations in Chemical Ecology Ser.). (Illus.). 264p. 1992. text 45.00 (0-8014-2727-4) Cornell U Pr.
Paul, Vincent De, see De Paul, Vincent.
Paul, W John. Apple Blossom Cologne Company Audit Case. 4th ed. 352p. (C). 1995. 39.95 (0-614-11233-8, Irwn McGrw-H) McGrw-H Hghr Educ.
Paul, Warren. Brave New World & Brave New World Revisited. (Cliffs Notes Ser.). 72p. (Orig.). 1965. pap. 4.95 (0-8220-0256-6, Cliff) IDG Bks.
Paul, William. Laughing Screaming: Modern Hollywood Horror & Comedy. 512p. 1995. pap. 19.50 (0-231-08465-X) Col U Pr.
— Laughing, Screaming: Modern Hollywood Horror & Comedy. LC 93-27388. (Film & Culture Ser.). 510p. (C). 1994. 40.50 (0-231-08464-1) Col U Pr.
— Sleeping Partner. LC 96-44845. 1997. 19.95 (0-312-15208-6) St Martin.
Paul, William, et al, eds. Homosexuality: Social, Psychological, & Biological Issues. LC 82-5653. 416p. 1982. reprint ed. pap. 129.00 (0-608-01149-5, 205944900001) Bks Demand.
Paul, William, jt. ed. see Suski, Tadeusz.
Paul, William, jt. ed. see Suski.
Paul, William E. Fundamental Immunology. 4th ed. LC 98-3611. 1456p. 1998. text 135.00 (0-7817-1412-5) Lppncott W & W.
— Immunogenetics. LC 84-40126. (Illus.). 223p. 1984. reprint ed. pap. 69.20 (0-608-00621-1, 206120800007) Bks Demand.
— Immunology Recognition & Response from Scientific American. (Illus.). 176p. (C). 1991. pap. text 16.95 (0-7167-2223-2) W H Freeman.
Paul, William E., ed. Annual Review of Immunology, Vol. 12. (Illus.). 1994. text 48.00 (0-8243-3012-9) Annual Reviews.
— Annual Review of Immunology, Vol. 15. 1997. text 64.00 (0-8243-3015-3) Annual Reviews.
— Annual Review of Immunology, Vol. 16. 714p. 1998. text 128.00 (0-8243-3016-1) Annual Reviews.
— Annual Review of Immunology, 1995, Vol. 13. (Illus.). 825p. 1995. 48.00 (0-8243-3013-7) Annual Reviews.
— Fundamental Immunology. 3rd ed. LC 93-9718. 1440p. 1993. text 103.00 (0-7817-0022-1) Lppncott W & W.
Paul, William E., et al, eds. Annual Review of Immunology, Vol. 1. (Illus.). 1983. text 41.00 (0-8243-3001-3) Annual Reviews.
— Annual Review of Immunology, Vol. 2. (Illus.). 1984. text 41.00 (0-8243-3002-1) Annual Reviews.
— Annual Review of Immunology, Vol. 3. (Illus.). 1985. text 41.00 (0-8243-3003-X) Annual Reviews.
— Annual Review of Immunology, Vol. 4. (Illus.). 1986. text 41.00 (0-8243-3004-8) Annual Reviews.
— Annual Review of Immunology, Vol. 5. (Illus.). 1987. text 41.00 (0-8243-3005-6) Annual Reviews.
— Annual Review of Immunology, Vol. 6. 1988. text 41.00 (0-8243-3006-4) Annual Reviews.
— Annual Review of Immunology, Vol. 7. (Illus.). 1989. text 41.00 (0-8243-3007-2) Annual Reviews.
— Annual Review of Immunology, Vol. 8. 1990. text 41.00 (0-8243-3008-0) Annual Reviews.
— Annual Review of Immunology, Vol. 9. 1991. text 41.00 (0-8243-3009-9) Annual Reviews.
— Annual Review of Immunology, Vol. 10. (Illus.). 1992. text 45.00 (0-8243-3010-2) Annual Reviews.
— Annual Review of Immunology, Vol. 11. (Illus.). 1993. text 45.00 (0-8243-3011-0) Annual Reviews.
— Annual Review of Immunology, Vol. 14. 718p. 1996. 56.00 (0-8243-3014-5, QR180) Annual Reviews.
***Paul, William E., et al, eds.** Annual Review of Immunology Vol. 17: 1999. 1031p. 1999. 128.00 (0-8243-3017-X) Annual Reviews.
Paul, William E., jt. auth. see Knowles, Victor.
Paul, William Henry. Getting In. 272p. 1997. pap. 9.00 (0-201-15491-9) Addison-Wesley.
Paul-Wolf, Helen. Personal Lunation Charts. LC 83-71152. 88p. 1984. 11.00 (0-86690-243-0, W2299-014) Am Fed Astrologers.
Paul, Wolfgang. Herman Goring: Hitler's Paladin or Puppet? LC 98-162634. (Illus.). 320p. 1998. 29.95 (1-85409-429-7, Pub. by Arms & Armour) Sterling.
***Paul, Wolfgang & Baschnagel, Jhorg.** Stochastic Processes: From Physics to Finance. LC 99-56371. 300p. 2000. 59.95 (3-540-66560-9) Spr-Verlag.
Paul, Wolfgang J., jt. auth. see Mhuller, Silvia M.
Paul, Wolfgang J., jt. auth. see Muller, Silvia M.
Paula, Frederic De, see De Paula, Frederic.
***Paula, Patricia.** Kitten & Cat Care. 64p. 2000. 12.95 (0-7938-3046-X) TFH Pubns.
Paula, Patricia. Kitten & Cat Care: A Complete & Authoritative Guide. (Illus.). 64p. 1997. 12.95 (0-7938-0244-X, WW-078) TFH Pubns.
Paulaharju, Samuli. Arctic Twilight: Old Finnish Tales. Matson, Robert W., ed. Pitkanen, Allan M., tr. from FIN.Tr. of Tunturien Yopuolta. (Illus.). 1982. 15.00 (0-943478-00-6) Finnish Am Lit.
Paulanka, Betty, jt. auth. see Kee, Joyce.
Paulanka, Betty J., jt. auth. see Kee, Joyce L.
Paulanka, Betty J., jt. ed. see Purnell, Larry D.
Paulapuro, Hannu. Developments in Wet Pressing. 72p. 1993. pap. 100.00 (1-85802-038-7, Pub. by Pira Internatl) Bks Intl VA.
Paulauskas, V. & Rackauskas, A. Approximation Theory in the Central Limit Theorem: Exact Results in Banach Spaces. (C). 1989. text 164.00 (90-277-2825-9) Kluwer Academic.
Paulay, Thomas, jt. auth. see Park, Robert.
Paulay, Tom & Priestley, M. J. Seismic Design of Reinforced Concrete & Masonry Buildings. LC 91-34862. 768p. 1992. 165.00 (0-471-54915-0) Wiley.
Paulding, James E. Ensemble, V: A Collection of Fiction & Poetry. LC 87-90639. 156p. (Orig.). 1987. pap. text 17.50 (0-9618718-0-6) J E Paulding.
Paulding, James K. The Backwoodsman (Verse) (Notable American Authors Ser.). 1999. reprint ed. lib. bdg. 125.00 (0-7812-4742-X) Rprt Serv.
— The Book of St. Nicholas. (Notable American Authors Ser.). 1999. reprint ed. lib. bdg. 125.00 (0-7812-8705-7) Rprt Serv.
— Chronicles of the City of Gotham. (Notable American Authors Ser.). 1999. reprint ed. lib. bdg. 125.00 (0-7812-8700-6) Rprt Serv.
— The Diverting History of John Bull & Brother Jonathan. (Notable American Authors Ser.). 1999. reprint ed. lib. bdg. 125.00 (0-7812-4738-1) Rprt Serv.
— The Dumb Girl. (Notable American Authors Ser.). 1999. reprint ed. lib. bdg. 125.00 (0-7812-4749-7) Rprt Serv.
— The Dutchman's Fireside. O'Donnell, Thomas F., ed. (Masterworks of Literature Ser.). 1966. 19.95 (0-8084-0110-6); pap. 15.95 (0-8084-0111-4) NCUP.
— The Dutchman's Fireside. (Notable American Authors Ser.). 1999. reprint ed. lib. bdg. 125.00 (0-7812-8701-4) Rprt Serv.
— A Gift from Fairy Land. (Notable American Authors Ser.). 1999. reprint ed. lib. bdg. 125.00 (0-7812-8706-5) Rprt Serv.
— John Bull in America: or The New Munchausen. (Notable American Authors Ser.). 1999. reprint ed. lib. bdg. 125.00 (0-7812-4745-4) Rprt Serv.
— Konigsmarke: or The Long Finne. (Notable American Authors Ser.). 1999. reprint ed. lib. bdg. 125.00 (0-7812-4744-6) Rprt Serv.
— Koningsmarke, 2 vols. in 1. LC 71-173932. reprint ed. 45.00 (0-404-04919-2) AMS Pr.
— Koningsmarke: or Old Times in the New World, 2 vols., Set. (BCL1-PS American Literature Ser.). 1992. reprint ed. lib. bdg. 150.00 (0-7812-6824-9) Rprt Serv.
— Koningsmarke, the Long Finne: A Story of the New World. LC 88-80670. 294p. 1988. 24.00 (0-912756-20-9); pap. 7.75 (0-912756-21-7) Union Coll.
— The Lay of the Scottish Fiddle: A Tale of Havrede Grace (Verse) (Notable American Authors Ser.). 1999. reprint ed. lib. bdg. 125.00 (0-7812-4739-X) Rprt Serv.
— Letters from the South: By a Northern Man. (Notable American Authors Ser.). 1999. reprint ed. lib. bdg. 125.00 (0-7812-4741-1) Rprt Serv.
— Letters from the South, Written During an Excursion in the Summer of 1816, 2 vols. in 1. LC 75-173933. reprint ed. 59.50 (0-404-00280-3) AMS Pr.
— Life of Washington. (Notable American Authors Ser.). 1999. reprint ed. lib. bdg. 125.00 (0-7812-8703-0) Rprt Serv.
— Lion of the West. Gado, Frank, ed. (Masterworks of Literature Ser.). 1994. 12.95 (0-8084-0428-8) NCUP.
— The Merry Tales of the Three Wise Men of Gotham. (Notable American Authors Ser.). 1999. reprint ed. lib. bdg. 125.00 (0-7812-4746-2) Rprt Serv.
— New Mirrors for Travelers. (Notable American Authors Ser.). 1999. reprint ed. lib. bdg. 125.00 (0-7812-4747-0) Rprt Serv.
— The Old Continental: or The Price of Liberty. (Notable American Authors Ser.). 1999. reprint ed. lib. bdg. 125.00 (0-7812-8707-3) Rprt Serv.
— Paulding Short Stories. Bendixen, Alfred, ed. (Masterworks of Literature Ser.). 1999. write for info. (0-8084-0442-3) NCUP.
— The Puritan & His Daughter. (Notable American Authors Ser.). 1999. reprint ed. lib. bdg. 125.00 (0-7812-8708-1) Rprt Serv.
— The Puritan & His Daughter, 2 vols., Vols. 1 - 2. LC 78-64087. reprint ed. 75.00 (0-404-17350-0) AMS Pr.
— Salmagundi: Second Series, 2 vols. in 1. LC 70-144669. reprint ed. 49.50 (0-404-04944-3) AMS Pr.
— Salmagundi: Second Series, 2 vols., Set. (BCL1-PS American Literature Ser.). 1992. reprint ed. lib. bdg. 150.00 (0-7812-6825-7) Rprt Serv.
— A Sketch of Old England: By a New England Man. (Notable American Authors Ser.). 1999. reprint ed. lib. bdg. 125.00 (0-7812-4743-8) Rprt Serv.
— Slavery in the United States. (Notable American Authors Ser.). 1999. reprint ed. lib. bdg. 125.00 (0-7812-8704-9) Rprt Serv.
— Stories of St. Nicholas. LC 95-8396. (New York Classics Ser.). Orig. Title: Book of Saint Nicholas. 152p. 1995. 19.95 (0-8156-0325-8) Syracuse U Pr.
— Tales of the Good Woman. (Notable American Authors Ser.). 1999. reprint ed. lib. bdg. 125.00 (0-7812-4748-9) Rprt Serv.
— The United States & England. (Notable American Authors Ser.). 1999. reprint ed. lib. bdg. 125.00 (0-7812-4740-3) Rprt Serv.
— Westward Ho. (Notable American Authors Ser.). 1999. reprint ed. lib. bdg. 125.00 (0-7812-8702-2) Rprt Serv.
— Westward Ho!, 2 vols., Set. (BCL1-PS American Literature Ser.). 1992. reprint ed. lib. bdg. 150.00 (0-7812-6826-5) Rprt Serv.
— Westward Ho: A Tale, 2 vols., Set. LC 06-25598. 1968. reprint ed. 39.00 (0-403-00066-1) Scholarly.
Paulding-Thrasher, Barbara. Cape Cod & the Islands. 64p. 1995. write for info. (1-57215-064-5) World Pubns.
— New England. 64p. 1995. write for info. (1-57215-063-7) World Pubns.
Pauldrach, A., et al. Sprachbruecke Level 2: Lehrbuch. (GER.). 175p. (C). 1989. pap. text 23.50 (3-12-557200-2, Pub. by Klett Edition) Intl Bk Import.
— Sprachbruecke Level 2: Lehrbuch, 2 cass. (GER.). (C). 1990. audio 45.00 (3-12-557215-0, Pub. by Klett Edition) Intl Bk Import.
Paule, Jean. The German Settlement at Anaheim. 74p. (Orig.). 1990. pap. 10.00 (1-877959-02-2) D Henson Bks.
***Paule, Marie & Piednoir, Christian, photos by.** 1000 Photos of Aquarium Fish. (One Thousand Photos Ser.). (Illus.). 128p. 2000. 24.95 (0-7641-5217-3) Barron.
Paule, Marvin R., ed. Transcription of Ribosomal RNA Genes by Eukaryotic RNA Polymerase I. LC 97-44013. (Molecular Biology Intelligence Unit Ser.). 285p. 1998. 159.00 (3-540-64365-6) Spr-Verlag.
Pauleau, Yves, ed. Materials & Processes for Surface & Interface Engineering: Proceedings of the NATO Advanced Study Institute, Chateau de Bonas, Gers, France, July 18-29, 1994. LC 95-11665. (NATO ASI Ser.: Series E, Applied Sciences: Vol. 290). 660p. (C). 1995. text 327.50 (0-7923-3458-2) Kluwer Academic.
— Protective Coatings & Thin Films: Synthesis, Characterization & Applications. LC 96-52351. (NATO Advanced Science Institutes: Partnership Sub-Series: 3 High Technology). 680p. (C). 1997. text 364.50 (0-7923-4380-8) Kluwer Academic.
Paulenoff, Michael J., jt. auth. see Kroll, Stanley.
Paules, Greta F. Dishing It Out: Power & Resistance among Waitresses in a New Jersey Restaurant. (Women in the Political Economy Ser.). (C). 1991. 59.95 (0-87722-887-6); pap. 19.95 (0-87722-888-4) Temple U Pr.
Paulet, Elisabeth. The Role of Banks in Monitoring Firms: The Case of the Credit Mobilier. LC 98-30729. 1999. write for info. (0-415-19539-X) Routledge.
Paulet, J. P. Economic Dictionary. Orig. Title: Dictionnaire d'Economie. 265p. 1992. pap. 45.00 (2-212-00808-2, Pub. by Eyrolles) IBD Ltd.
Paulet, Jean-Pierre. Dictionnaire d'Economie. (FRE.). 265p. 1992. pap. 49.95 (0-7859-7771-6, 2212008082) Fr & Eur.
Paulet, William. The Lord Marques Idlenes: Containing Mainfold Matters of Acceptable Devise. LC 79-84131. (English Experience Ser.: No. 949). 112p. 1979. reprint ed. lib. bdg. 15.00 (90-221-0949-6) Walter J Johnson.
Pauletto, Bruno. Strength Training for Basketball. LC 93-17540. (Illus.). 144p. 1993. pap. 14.95 (0-87322-433-7, PPAU0433) Human Kinetics.
— Strength Training for Coaches. LC 90-13122. (Illus.). 189p. reprint ed. pap. 58.60 (0-608-20831-0, 207193000003) Bks Demand.
— Strength Training for Football. LC 92-12982. (Illus.). 144p. 1992. pap. 14.95 (0-87322-398-5, PPAU0398) Human Kinetics.
Pauletto, Giorgio. Computational Solution of Large-Scale Macroeconometric Models. LC 97-23944. (Advances in Computational Economics Ser.). 1997. lib. bdg. 99.00 (0-7923-4656-4) Kluwer Academic.
Paulev. Physiology. rev. ed. 1996. pap. text, student ed. 26.00 (0-7020-2043-5, W B Saunders Co) Harcrt Hlth Sci Grp.
Pauley, Bruce F. From Prejudice to Persecution: A History of Austrian Anti-Semitism. LC 91-50249. (Illus.). 456p. (C). 1992. 65.00 (0-8078-1995-6) U of NC Pr.
— From Prejudice to Persecution: A History of Austrian Anti-Semitism. (Illus.). 456p. 1998. pap. 22.50 (0-8078-4713-5) U of NC Pr.
— Habsburg Legacy, Eighteen Sixty-Seven to Nineteen Thirty-Nine. LC 76-56401. (Berkshire Studies). 204p. 1977. reprint ed. pap. text 13.50 (0-88275-485-8) Krieger.
— Hitler & the Forgotten Nazis: A History of Austrian National Socialism. LC 80-17006. (Illus.). 318p. reprint ed. pap. 98.60 (0-608-06002-X, 206633000008) Bks Demand.
— Hitler, Stalin & Mussolini: Totalitarianism in the Twentieth Century. Eubank, Keith, ed. LC 96-48121. (European History Ser.). 290p. (C). 1997. pap. text 14.95 (0-88295-935-2) Harlan Davidson.
Pauley, Edward. Footsteps to Follow: Eternal Truths for Christians. 224p. 1998. 12.99 (0-8499-5364-2); pap. 4.99 (0-8499-5365-0) Word Pub.
Pauley, Edward H. & Larson, Robert C. God's Little Promise Book. 144p. 1995. 7.99 (0-8499-5157-7) Word Pub.
— Happiness Is... 144p. 1995. 7.99 (0-8499-5158-5) Word Pub.
— The Mirror Our Children See. 144p. 1995. 7.99 (0-8499-5159-3) Word Pub.
— Together Is Forever. LC 95-18138. 144p. 1995. 7.99 (0-8499-5160-7) Word Pub.
Pauley, Kenneth, ed. Rancho Days in Southern California: An Anthology with New Perspectives. (Westerners - Los Angeles Corral Ser.: Vol. 20). (Illus.). 400p. 1997. text 45.00 (1-890125-00-8) Wsternrs LA Corral.
Pauley, Matthew A. Criminal Law, Its Nature & Sources. LC 98-37482. 177p. 1999. 39.95 (0-918680-72-7, 0-918680-74-3); pap. 19.95 (0-918680-74-3, 0-918680-74-3) Griffon House.
***Pauley, Matthew A.** I Do Solemnly Swear - The President's Constitutional Oath: Its Meaning & Importance in the History of Oaths. LC 99-39996. 272p. 1999. 45.00 (0-7618-1488-4) U Pr of Amer.
Pauley, Penelope J., jt. auth. see Pauley, Thomas L.
Pauley, Steven E. Technical Report Writing. (C). 1995. pap. text 31.56 (0-395-72176-8) HM.
Pauley, Steven E. & Riordan. Technical Report Writing Today, 4 vols. 4th ed. (C). 1989. trans. 19.96 (0-395-52986-7) HM.
— Technical Report Writing Today, 4 vols. 4th ed. (C). 1990. pap. text 2.76 (0-395-52684-1) HM.
Pauley, Thomas K., jt. auth. see Green, N. Bayard.
***Pauley, Thomas L. & Pauley, Penelope J.** I'm Rich Beyond My Wildest Dreams. I Am. I Am. I Am: How to Get Everything You Want in Life. (Illus.). xx, 182p. 2000. pap. 21.95 (1-929177-25-9) RichDreams.
Paulhan, Jean. Progress in Love on the Slow Side. Laennec, Christine M. & Syrotinski, Michael, trs. LC 94-1316. (French Modernist Library). xxii, 146p. 1994. text 35.00 (0-8032-3705-7) U of Nebr Pr.
Pauli & Duchamp. Menu Translator: English/French/German. 17th ed. (ENG, FRE & GER.). 85p. 1996. 39.95 (0-320-00499-6) Fr & Eur.
Pauli, E. Speisekarten-Fuer sie Uebersetzt: Menu Reader. 15th ed. (ENG, FRE & GER.). 86p. 1983. 19.95 (0-8288-1302-7, M15238) Fr & Eur.
Pauli, Eugen. Classical Cooking the Modern Way. 2nd ed. 1989. text 52.95 (0-442-27206-5, VNR) Wiley.
— Classical Cooking the Modern Way, Vol. I. 3rd ed. (Culinary Arts Ser.). 1998. text 49.95 (0-442-01944-0, VNR) Wiley.
— Classical Cooking the Modern Way: Recipes, Vol. 1. 3rd ed. Schmidt, Arno & Dawson-Holt, Hannelore, trs. LC 96-18125. (Culinary Arts Ser.). (Illus.). 350p. 1997. text 49.95 (0-442-01942-4, VNR) Wiley.
***Pauli, Gunter.** Upsizing: The Road to Zero Emissions: More Jobs, More Income & No Pollution. (Illus.). 220p. 2000. pap. 16.95 (1-874719-18-7, Pub. by Greenleaf Pubng) Chelsea Green Pub.

P

***Pauli, Gunter & Vetra.** Grow Your Own House: Bamboo Architecture & Simon Velez. (Illus.). 265p. 2000. pap. 39.00 (*3-931936-25-2*) Chelsea Green Pub.

Pauli, Gunter A. Crusader for the Future: A Portrait of Aurelio Peccei, Founder of the Club of Rome. (Illus.). 152p. 1987. 48.25 (*0-08-034861-0*, Pergamon Pr) Elsevier.

Pauli, Gunter A., jt. auth. see Wright, Richard W.

***Pauli, Hertha.** Bernadette: Our Lady's Little Servant. 1999. pap. 9.95 (*0-89870-760-9*) Ignatius Pr.

Pauli, Karen. The Care & Feeding of Spinning Wheels. LC 81-80903. (Illus.). 84p. 1986. pap. 7.50 (*0-934026-04-1*) Interweave.

Pauli, Lydia, tr. see Ayers, Dottie & Harrison, Donna, eds.

Pauli, Philip. Classical Cooking in the Modern Way: Recipes. 3rd ed. Schmidt, Margaret, ed. Schmidt, Arlo & Dawson-Holt, Hannelore, trs. 432p. 1996. 49.95 (*0-471-28670-2*, VNR) Wiley.

Pauli, Philip. Classical Cooking the Modern Way: Methods & Techniques. LC 99-39547. 432p. 1999. 55.00 (*0-471-29187-0*) Wiley.

Pauli, Reinhold. Life of Alfred the Great. Thorpe, B., tr. LC 68-57869. (Bohn's Antiquarian Library). reprint ed. 46.00 (*0-404-50021-8*) AMS Pr.

Pauli, Ulf. The Baltic States in Facts, Figures & Maps. (Illus.). 72p. 1994. pap. 8.95 (*1-85756-074-4*, Pub. by Janus Pubng) Paul & Co Pubs.

Pauli, W. Scientific Correspondence with Bohr, Einstein, Heisenberg A. O. Vol. 4 Pt. 2: 1953-1954. (Illus.). 1000p. 1998. 169.00 (*3-540-64312-5*) Spr-Verlag.

Pauli, W. & Meyenn, K. V., eds. Scientific Correspondence with Bohr, Einstein, Heisenberg A. O. (Sources in the History of Mathematics & Physical Sciences Ser.: Vol. 14). (Illus.). xxxviii, 1030p. 169.50 (*3-540-59442-6*) Spr-Verlag.

***Pauli, Walt.** Alliance Chronicles: Legacy. 188p. 2000. pap. 12.95 (*1-57532-217-X*) Press-Tige Pub.

Pauli, Wolfgang. General Principles of Quantum Mechanics. 212p. 1990. 38.95 (*0-387-09842-9*) Spr-Verlag.

— Theory of Relativity. 255p. 1981. reprint ed. pap. 8.95 (*0-486-64152-X*) Dover.

Pauli, Wolfgang, et al. Writings on Physics & Philosophy. Schlapp, Robert, tr. LC 94-15098. 1996. 44.95 (*0-387-56859-X*) Spr-Verlag.

Paulian, R. Les Coleopteres Scarabaeoidea de Nouvelle-Caledonie (The Scarab Beetles of New Caledonia) (Faune Tropicale Ser.: Vol. XIX).Tr. of Scarab Beetles of New Caledonia. (FRE., Illus.). 164p. 1991. pap. 22.00 (*2-7099-1030-6*, Pub. by LInstitut Francais) Balogh.

Pauliat, Paul. Dictionnaire Bilingue. (FRE.). 1976. write for info. (*0-7859-7652-3*, 2034017366) Fr & Eur.

Paulick, Raymond S. & Liebman, Dan, eds. Nicks, 1998: The Annual Guide to Sire & Brookmare Sire Crosses. 500p. 1998. pap. 44.95 (*1-58150-005-X*) Blood-Horse.

Paulick, Raymond S. & Mearns, Dan, eds. Breeder's Guide for 1993: Annual Supplements. (Illus.). 1994. 95.00 (*0-939049-69-4*) Blood-Horse.

— Breeder's Guide for 1994. (Illus.). 1995. suppl. ed. 95.00 (*0-939049-75-9*) Blood-Horse.

— Breeder's Guide for 1995. (Illus.). 1996. 95.00 (*0-939049-78-3*) Blood-Horse.

— The Source for North American Racing & Breeding, 1997-1998. (Illus.). 500p. (Orig.). 1997. pap. 19.95 (*0-939049-84-8*) Blood-Horse.

— Stallion Register for 1998. (Illus.). 1600p. (Orig.). 1997. pap. 39.95 (*0-939049-88-0*) Blood-Horse.

Paulien, Gunther. The Divine Prescription/Science of Health & Healing. LC 94-61325. 560p. 1995. otabind 19.95 (*1-57258-017-8*) Teach Servs.

Paulien, Jon. Book of Revelation: Too Good to Be False. Coffen, Richard, ed. 32p. 1991. pap. 0.89 (*0-8280-0591-5*) Review & Herald.

— Decoding Revelation's Trumpets: Literary Allusions & Interpretation of Revelation 8:7-12. (Andrews University Seminary Doctoral Dissertation Ser.: Vol. 11). 506p. 1988. pap. 19.99 (*0-943872-44-8*) Andrews Univ Pr.

***Paulien, Jon.** The Millennium Bug: Is This the End of the World As We Know It? Holt, B. Russell, ed. LC 99-30888. 128p. 1999. pap. 9.99 (*0-8163-1755-0*) Pacific Pr Pub Assn.

Paulien, Jon. Present Truth in the Real World: Can Adventists Keep & Share Their Faith in a Secular Society? LC 92-32316. 1993. pap. 10.99 (*0-8163-1127-7*) Pacific Pr Pub Assn.

Pauligny, G. M. De, see De Pauligny, G. M.

Paulik, Ferenc. Special Trends in Thermal Analysis. 478p. 1995. 330.00 (*0-471-95769-0*) Wiley.

Paulik, Helmut. Lexicon of Education Practice: Lexikon der Ausbildungspraxis. 3rd ed. (GER.). 256p. 1982. pap. 49.95 (*0-8288-1394-9*, M7274) Fr & Eur.

Paulikas, George. Thirteen Years, 1936-1949. LC 98-118753. (Illus.). 120p. 1997. pap. 12.00 (*0-8059-4105-3*) Dorrance.

Paulikova, Zuzana, tr. see Drobna, Olga, et al.

Paulin, Barbara. Path of Promise, Path of Peace: How to Hear Your Higher Self Speak. LC 94-28852. 280p. 1995. pap. 12.95 (*0-87604-328-7*, 397) ARE Pr.

Paulin, George B. Granting Stock Options: An Approach to Designing Long-Term Incentives for Employees. (Building Blocks Ser.: Vol. 32). (Illus.). 24p. (Orig.). 1996. pap. 24.95 (*1-57963-033-2*, A0232) Am Compensation.

Paulin, J. Saint-Jean, jt. ed. see Chipot, Michel.

Paulin, Mary A. Creative Uses of Children's Literature. LC 81-12405. 730p. (C). 1986. pap. text 47.50 (*0-208-01862-X*, Lib Prof Pubns); lib. bdg. 55.00 (*0-208-01861-1*, Lib Prof Pubns) Shoe String.

— More Creative Uses of Children's Literature, Vol. 1 Vol. 1: Introducing Books in All Kinds of Ways. LC 92-8916. xvii, 619p. (C). 1992. pap. text 35.00 (*0-208-02203-1*, Lib Prof Pubns); lib. bdg. 57.50 (*0-208-02202-3*, Lib Prof Pubns) Shoe String.

Paulin, R., ed. Goethe: Die Leiden des Jungen Werthers. (Bristol German Texts Ser.). (GER.). 192p. 1993. pap. 18.95 (*1-85399-323-9*, Pub. by Brist Class Pr) Focus Pub-R Pullins.

Paulin, Roger. The Brief Compass: The Nineteenth Century German Novelle. 180p. 1985. text 49.95 (*0-19-815810-6*) OUP.

— Ludwig Tieck: A Literary Biography. (Illus.). 448p. 1987. reprint ed. pap. text 28.00 (*0-19-815852-1*) OUP.

Paulin, Roger & Hutchinson, Peter, eds. Rilke's Duino Elegies. (Studies in Austrian Literature, Culture, & Thought). (Illus.). xii, 238p. 1996. 37.95 (*1-57241-032-9*) Ariadne CA.

Paulin, Tom. The Day-Star of Liberty: William Hazlitt's Radical Style. (Illus.). 400p. 1999. 30.00 (*0-571-17421-3*) Faber & Faber.

— Ireland & the English Crisis. 224p. 1988. pap. 18.95 (*0-906427-64-9*, Pub. by Bloodaxe Bks) Dufour.

— Minotaur: Poetry & the Nation State. 256p. (C). 1992. 35.50 (*0-674-57637-3*) HUP.

— Thomas Hardy: The Poetry of Perception. LC 75-329438. x, 225p. 1975. write for info. (*0-333-16915-8*) Macmillan.

— Walking a Line. 128p. 1995. pap. 9.95 (*0-571-17081-1*) Faber & Faber.

***Paulin, Tom.** Wind Dog. 96p. 2000. pap. 13.00 (*0-571-20168-7*) Faber & Faber.

Paulin, Tom. Writing to the Moment: Selected Critical Essays, 1980-1995. 384p. 1998. pap. 14.95 (*0-571-17582-1*) Faber & Faber.

Paulin, Tom & Connor, Noel. Book of Juniper. 24p. 1981. pap. 6.95 (*0-906427-16-9*, Pub. by Bloodaxe Bks) Dufour.

Paulin, Tom, ed. see James, Henry.

Paulin, Tony. The Last Computer. Bumpus, Peter, ed. 224p. 1999. pap. 14.95 (*0-9670808-1-9*) Spherical Pub Inc.

Pauline Heinke, Dagmar. Relieving Pain with Acupressure. LC 98-40060. (Illus.). 96p. 1998. pap. 10.95 (*0-8069-4213-4*) Sterling.

Pauline-Morand, Mary B., jt. auth. see Raider, Melvyn.

***Pauling, Chris.** Common New Zealand Marine Fishes. (Illus.). 80p. 1998. pap. 9.95 (*0-908812-74-4*, Pub. by Canterbury Univ) Accents Pubns.

Pauling, Chris. Introducing Buddhism. (Orig.). 1996. text 12.95 incl. audio (*1-899507-01-9*) Weatherhill.

— Introducing Buddhism. 73p. (Orig.). 1996. pap. 6.50 (*0-904766-63-2*) Windhorse Pubns.

Pauling, Linus. General Chemistry. (Illus.). 992p. 1988. reprint ed. pap. text 19.95 (*0-486-65622-5*) Dover.

— General Chemistry. 3rd ed. LC 78-75625. (Books in Chemistry Ser.). (Illus.). 975p. reprint ed. pap. 200.00 (*0-608-10202-4*, 201072600070) Bks Demand.

— How to Live Longer. 416p. 1987. mass mkt. 6.99 (*0-380-70289-4*, Avon Bks) Morrow Avon.

— Linus Pauling on Peace: A Scientist Speaks Out on Humanism & World Survival. Marinacci, Barbara & Krishnamurthy, Ramesh, eds. LC 98-86622. (Illus.). 296p. 1998. pap. 17.95 (*0-933670-03-6*) Rising Star.

— The Nature of the Chemical Bond & the Structure of Molecules & Crystals: An Introduction to Modern Structural Chemistry. 3rd ed. (George Fisher Baker Non-Resident Lectureship in Chemistry at Cornell University Ser.). (Illus.). 644p. 1960. text 69.95 (*0-8014-0333-2*) Cornell U Pr.

— Vitamin C & the Common Cold. 1995. reprint ed. lib. bdg. 18.95 (*1-56849-669-9*) Buccaneer Bks.

Pauling, Linus & Ikeda, Daisaku. A Lifelong Quest for Peace: A Dialogue. 144p. (C). 2000. 30.00 (*0-86720-278-5*) Jones & Bartlett.

Pauling, Linus & Pauling, Peter. Chemistry. LC 74-34071. (Chemistry Ser.). (Illus.). 767p. (C). 1975. text 28.80 (*0-7167-0176-6*) W H Freeman.

Pauling, Linus & Wilson, E. Bright. Introduction to Quantum Mechanics with Applications to Chemistry. (Physics Ser.). 468p. 1985. reprint ed. pap. 12.95 (*0-486-64871-0*) Dover.

Pauling, Linus, jt. auth. see Cameron, Ewan.

Pauling, Peter, jt. auth. see Pauling, Linus.

Pauling, Sharon, jt. auth. see Prendergast, John.

Paulinus, A. S. & Paulinus, A. S. Bartholomaeo. Dissertation on the Sanskrit Language. Rocher, Ludo, tr. & intro. by. (Studies in History of Linguistics: No. 12). xxviii, 224p. 1977. 59.00 (*90-272-0953-7*) J Benjamins Pubng Co.

Paulinus, A. S. Bartholomaeo, jt. auth. see Paulinus, A. S.

Paulinus, Nola, jt. auth. see Quasten, J.

Paulis, Guido De, see De Paulis, Guido.

Paulis, L. Technique & Design of Cluny Lace. Rutgers, M., tr. 1984. 16.50 (*0-903585-18-9*) Robin & Russ.

Paulisch, F. N. The Design of an Extendible Graph Editor. (Lecture Notes in Computer Science Ser.: Vol. 704). xv, 184p. 1993. pap. write for info. (*3-540-57090-X*) Spr-Verlag.

Paulisen, May N., jt. auth. see McQueary, Carl R.

Paulissen, Dirk, jt. auth. see Von Buelow, Heinz.

Paulissen, May N., jt. auth. see McQueary, Carl R.

Paulita, Mary. Half-Pint on Guadalcanal: A Saga of Heroism, Commitment & Love. (Illus.). 144p. (Orig.). (YA). (gr. 8). 1993. pap. 10.00 (*0-9631198-1-8*) Marist Miss Sis.

Paulk, Anne, jt. auth. see Paulk, John.

Paulk, Don. I Laugh . . . I Cry . . . 212p. 1987. 12.95 (*0-917595-17-3*) Kingdom Pubs.

Paulk, Don, jt. auth. see Paulk, Earl.

Paulk, Donald Earl. Finding Sacred in the Secular. 176p. Date not set. lib. bdg. 9.95 (*0-917595-50-5*) Kingdom Pubs.

Paulk, Earl. The Church: Trampled or Triumphant? 240p. (Orig.). 1990. pap. 9.95 (*0-917595-35-1*) Kingdom Pubs.

— El Cuerpo Herido de Cristo. Orig. Title: Wounded Body of Christ. (SPA.). 144p. (Orig.). 1985. pap. 3.50 (*0-917595-05-X*) Kingdom Pubs.

— Divine Runner. LC 78-71967. 142p. (Orig.). 1978. pap. 3.25 (*0-917595-00-9*) Kingdom Pubs.

— Held in the Heavens until . . . 256p. (Orig.). 1985. pap. 7.95 (*0-917595-07-6*) Kingdom Pubs.

— How to Conquer Depression. (Orig.). 1989. mass mkt. 2.50 (*0-917595-30-0*) Kingdom Pubs.

— The Local Church Says "Hell No" 190p. (Orig.). 1991. pap. 9.95 (*0-917595-40-8*) Kingdom Pubs.

— Offspring: The Generation the World Is Waiting For... 126p. (Orig.). 1996. pap. 8.99 (*1-56043-167-9*) Destiny Image.

— One Blood. 152p. 1996. 12.99 (*1-56043-175-X*) Destiny Image.

— The Prophetic Community. 140p. (Orig.). 1995. pap. 9.99 (*1-56043-841-X*, Treasure Hse) Destiny Image.

— The Provoker. Weeks, Tricia, ed. 400p. (Orig.). 1986. pap. 9.95 (*0-917595-09-2*) Kingdom Pubs.

— Satan Unmasked. 344p. (Orig.). 1984. pap. 9.95 (*0-917595-03-3*) Kingdom Pubs.

— Sex Is God's Idea. 175p. (Orig.). 1985. pap. 7.95 (*0-917595-04-1*) Kingdom Pubs.

— Spiritual Megatrends. 293p. 1988. 8.95 (*0-917595-16-5*) Kingdom Pubs.

— That the World May Know. 189p. (Orig.). 1987. pap. 7.95 (*0-917595-15-7*) Kingdom Pubs.

— Thrust in the Sickle & Reap. 141p. (Orig.). 1986. pap. 5.95 (*0-917595-11-4*) Kingdom Pubs.

— Turn on the Light at Christmas. 32p. 1987. mass mkt. 1.50 (*0-917595-23-8*) Kingdom Pubs.

— Twenty-Twenty Vision. 1988. pap. 2.50 (*0-917595-24-6*) Kingdom Pubs.

— Ultimate Kingdom. 2nd ed. 264p. (Orig.). 1987. reprint ed. pap. 7.95 (*0-917595-13-0*) Kingdom Pubs.

— El Ultimo Reino. Orig. Title: The Ultimate Kingdom. (SPA.). 268p. (Orig.). 1987. pap. 3.50 (*0-917595-19-X*) Kingdom Pubs.

— Vision Twenty-Twenty: Una Mirada Clara al Reino de Dios. 50p. 1989. mass mkt. 2.50 (*0-917595-26-2*) Kingdom Pubs.

— Winning Spiritual Warfare in the Family. 21p. 1987. mass mkt. 1.50 (*0-917595-20-3*) Kingdom Pubs.

— Wounded Body of Christ. 2nd ed. 160p. 1985. pap. 4.95 (*0-917595-06-8*) Kingdom Pubs.

— Your Guide to Greatness. 64p. 1990. 3.50 (*0-917595-38-6*) Kingdom Pubs.

Paulk, Earl & Paulk, Don. One Hundred One Questions Your Pastor Hopes You Never Ask. 128p. 1990. 12.95 (*0-917595-36-X*) Kingdom Pubs.

Paulk, Earl & Rhodes, Dan. A Theology for the New Millennium. 192p. Date not set. pap. 10.00 (*0-917595-52-1*) Kingdom Pubs.

Paulk, John. Love Won Out. LC 99-27731. 1999. 17.99 (*1-56179-783-9*) Focus Family.

— Not Afraid to Change: The Remarkable Story of How One Man Overcame Homosexuality. LC 98-60061. (Illus.). 256p. 1998. pap. 12.95 (*1-57921-150-X*, Pub. by WinePress Pub) BookWorld.

***Paulk, John & Paulk, Anne.** Love Won Out. LC 99-27731. 1999. pap. 10.99 (*1-56179-816-9*) Focus Family.

Paull, Barbara & Harrison, Christine. The Athletic Musician: A Guide to Playing Without Pain. LC 97-20326. 175p. 1997. pap. 27.00 (*0-8108-3356-5*) Scarecrow.

Paull, Bonnie E. Winning with Grammar: Basic Workbook I. 2nd ed. 224p. (C). 1993. per. 24.95 (*0-8403-8554-4*) Kendall-Hunt.

— Winning with Grammar: Basic Workbook II. 2nd ed. 240p. (C). 1993. per. 33.95 (*0-8403-8705-9*) Kendall-Hunt.

— Winning with Words: An Introduction to the Dictionary. 128p. (C). 1993. per. 31.95 (*0-8403-8706-7*) Kendall-Hunt.

Paull, Candy. Art of Abundance. 224p. 1998. 14.99 (*1-56292-487-7*) Honor Bks OK.

***Paull, Candy.** Christmas Abundance: A Simple Guide to Discovering the True Meaning of Christmas. 192p. 2000. 15.99 (*0-7852-6750-6*) Nelson.

— Grandfather's Memories to His Grandchild. (Illus.). 96p. (J). 1999. per. 12.99 (*0-8499-5912-8*) Tommy Nelson.

Paull, Donald. Fitness to Stand Trial. LC 92-35105. (American Series in Behavioral Science & Law). (Illus.). 196p. 1993. pap. 37.95 (*0-398-06316-8*); text 54.95 (*0-398-05836-9*) C C Thomas.

Paull, Elisabeth M. Paull-Irwin, a Family Sketch. (Illus.). viii, 198p. 1993. reprint ed. pap. 32.50 (*0-8328-2985-4*); reprint ed. lib. bdg. 42.50 (*0-8328-2984-6*) Higginson Bk Co.

Paull, Frankie & Cary, Bob. Cool Fishin' for Kids Age 5 to 85. LC 97-69906. (Illus.). 60p. 1997. pap. 8.95 (*0-9653027-7-6*) Paper Moon Pub.

Paull, Irving S., et al. Trade Association Activities. (Business Enterprises Reprint Ser.). viii, 381p. 1983. reprint ed. lib. bdg. 47.50 (*0-89941-209-2*, 302950) W S Hein.

Paull, Nancy B. Capital Medicine: A Tradition of Excellence. (Illus.). 128p. 1994. 29.95 (*1-882933-02-8*) Cherbo Pub Grp.

Paull, R. E. & Armstrong, J. W., eds. Insect Pests & Fresh Horticultural Products: Treatment & Responses. (Illus.). 368p. 1994. text 120.00 (*0-85198-872-5*) OUP.

Paull, Rachel K. & Paull, Richard A. Geology of Wisconsin & Upper Michigan: Including Parts of Adjacent States. 2nd ed. 288p. 1980. per. 37.95 (*0-8403-2142-2*) Kendall-Hunt.

Paull, Richard A., jt. auth. see Paull, Rachel K.

Paull, Richard C. Aldabran Tortoise Expert's Guide. (Tortoises of the World Ser.: No. 5). (Illus.). 116p. 1999. pap. 29.95 (*1-888089-31-8*, 31-8) Green Nature Bks.

— Baja's Botanical Beauty. (Illus.). 60p. 1996. pap. 28.95 (*1-888089-14-8*) Green Nature Bks.

— The Eight Great Tortoises: "The Eight Great" 3rd rev. ed. (Tortoises of the World Ser.: Vol. 1). (Illus.). 137p. 1996. pap. 39.95 (*1-888089-13-X*) Green Nature Bks.

— The Eighteen Mile Stretch: A Guided Tour of the Wildlife along Route 1 Between Florida City & Key Largo, Florida. 3rd rev. ed. (Illus.). 27p. 1997. pap. 7.95 (*1-888089-21-0*) Green Nature Bks.

— Galapagos Tortoise Expert's Guide. (Tortoises of the World Ser.: Vol. 6). (Illus.). 136p. 1999. pap. 32.50 (*1-888089-38-5*) Green Nature Bks.

— Galapagos Tortoise Expert's Guide: Special Color Presentation. (Tortoises of the World Ser.: Vol. 6). (Illus.). 136p. 1999. pap. 65.00 (*1-888089-32-6*) Green Nature Bks.

— The Great African Spur-Thighed or Sulcata Tortoise: "The Sulcata" 3rd rev. ed. (Tortoises of the World Ser.: Vol. 3). (Illus.). 52p. 1996. pap. 28.95 (*1-888089-22-9*) Green Nature Bks.

— The Great Red-Foot Tortoise. 3rd rev. ed. (Tortoises of the World Ser.: No. 4). (Illus.). 115p. 1999. pap. 42.50 (*1-888089-37-7*, 37-7) Green Nature Bks.

— Orchids Organic. 3rd ed. (Illus.). 86p. 1996. pap. 39.95 (*1-888089-15-6*) Green Nature Bks.

— The Small & Medium-Sized Tortoises: All the Small & Medium-Sized Tortoises. 2nd expanded rev. ed. (Tortoises of the World Ser.: Vol. 2). (Illus.). 214p. 1997. 59.95 (*1-888089-25-3*) Green Nature Bks.

— Tortoise Dodos: The Mascarene Migration & Massacre. (Tortoises of the World Ser.: Vol. 7). (Illus.). 64p. (C). 1999. pap. 18.95 (*1-888089-35-0*) Green Nature Bks.

— Turtles, Twenty Remarkable. (Illus.). 102p. 1997. 37.50 (*1-888089-28-8*) Green Nature Bks.

***Paull, Richard C. & Palika, Liz.** Leopard Tortoise Guide: She Says; He Says. unabridged ed. (Tortoises of the World Ser.: Vol. 8). (Illus.). 107p. 1999. pap. text 37.95 (*1-888089-42-3*) Green Nature Bks.

Paull, Robert E., jt. auth. see Nakasone, Henry Y.

Paull, Susan G. Teach an Adult to Read: Tutor Training Workbook. Ringo, Betty, ed. 40p. 1987. 6.95 (*0-910475-36-9*) KET.

Paull, Sylvia L. Rainclouds Study the Ten Commandments: A Bible Study Drama. (Illus.). 29p. 1993. pap. 3.25 (*0-88680-393-4*) I E Clark.

Paull, Thelma. Kids Skills: A Resource for Discussion Group Leaders. (C). 1990. 75.00 (*0-86431-084-6*, Pub. by Aust Council Educ Res) St Mut.

— Talk about Problems. (C). 1990. 49.00 (*0-86431-085-4*, Pub. by Aust Council Educ Res) St Mut.

Paulley, J. W. & Pelser, H. E. Psychological Managements for Psychosomatic Disorders. (Illus.). 370p. 1989. 86.95 (*0-387-19298-0*) Spr-Verlag.

Paullin, C. O. & Paxson, F. L. Guide to the Materials in London Archives for the History of the United States Since 1783. (Carnegie Institute Ser.: Vol. 7). 1914. 65.00 (*0-527-00687-4*) Periodicals Srv.

Paullin, Charles. Navy of the American Revolution. LC 73-122997. (American History & Americana Ser.: No. 47). 1970. reprint ed. lib. bdg. 75.00 (*0-8383-1130-X*) M S G Haskell Hse.

Paullin, Charles O. Commodore John Rodgers. LC 79-6127. (Navies & Men Ser.). (Illus.). 1980. reprint ed. lib. bdg. 44.95 (*0-405-13049-X*) Ayer.

— Diplomatic Negotiations of American Naval Officers, 1778-1883. 1990. 16.50 (*0-8446-1342-8*) Peter Smith.

Paulling, John, jt. auth. see Christy, Dennis T.

***Paulman, Paul M.** Precepting Medical Students in the Office. 2000. pap. 19.95 (*0-8018-6366-X*) Johns Hopkins.

Paulmann, Heinz G. Zur Festigkeits-Anisotropie von Gesteinen: Untersuchungen an Gesteinen des Ruhr Karbons. (Geotektonische Forschungen Ser.: Vol. 25). (GER.). iii, 106p. 1967. pap. 25.00 (*3-510-50916-1*, Pub. by E Schweizerbartsche) Balogh.

Paulmier, G. Microplancton des Eaux Marines et Saumatres de la Guyane et des Antilles Francaises (Microplankton in Sea Water & Brackish Water in Guiana & the French West Indies)Tr. of Microplankton in Sea Water & Brackish Water in Guiana & the French West Indies. (FRE., Illus.). 438p. 1993. pap. 28.00 (*2-7099-1131-0*, Pub. by LInstitut Francais) Balogh.

Paulo, Craig J. Being & Conversion: A Phenomenological Ontology of Radical Restlessness. 2nd ed. 239p. (C). 1997. reprint ed. 30.00 (*0-9664204-1-1*) Cath Colleg.

— Out of the Garden: A Collection of Poetry. 52p. 1998. pap. 6.25 (*0-9664204-0-3*) Cath Colleg.

Paulos, Dan. He's Put the Whole World in Her Hands: Silhouette Paper-Cuttings. LC 93-78532. 130p. 1993. 21.95 (*0-89870-466-9*) Ignatius Pr.

Paulos, Daniel T. Behold the Women: A Tribute to Sisters & Nuns of the Catholic Church in the United States & Other Countries. (Illus.). 208p. (YA). (gr. 5 up). 1997. 24.95 (*0-9627900-4-4*) St Bernadette.

Paulos, John A. Beyond Numeracy. 1992. pap. 13.00 (*0-679-73807-X*) Vin Bks.

— Beyond Numeracy: Ruminations of a Numbers Man. 1991. 22.00 (*0-685-48163-8*) Knopf.

— I Think, Therefore I Laugh. LC 89-40602. 1990. pap. 9.00 (*0-679-72954-2*) Vin Bks.

— Innumeracy. 1990. pap. 11.00 (*0-679-72601-2*) Vin Bks.

— A Mathematician Reads the Newspaper. LC 94-48206. (Illus.). 212p. 1995. 18.00 (*0-465-04362-3*, Pub. by Basic) HarpC.

— A Mathematician Reads the Newspaper. LC 95-46049. (Illus.). 224p. 1996. pap. 12.95 (*0-385-48254-X*, Anchor NY) Doubleday.

An Asterisk (*) at the beginning of an entry indicates that the title is appearing for the first time.

— Mathematics & Humor. LC 80-12742. 124p. 1982. pap. 12.95 (0-226-65025-1) U Ch Pr.
— Once upon a Number: A Mathematical Bridges Stories & Statistics. LC 98-39252. 224p. 1998. 23.00 (0-465-05158-8, Pub. by Basic) HarpC.
— Once upon a Number: The Hidden Mathematical Logic of Stories. Date not set. pap. 12.00 (0-465-05159-6, Pub. by Basic) HarpC.
***Paulos, John Allen.** I Think, Therefore I Laugh: The Flip Side of Philosophy. 2000. 14.95 (0-231-11915-1) Col U Pr.
Paulos, Jose. Memorias de Jesus de Nazaret. LC 96-86649. (Coleccion Felix Varela). (SPA.). 166p. (Orig.). 1996. pap. 16.00 (0-89729-815-2) Ediciones.
Paulos, Lonnie E. & Tibone, James E., eds. Operative Techniques in Shoulder Surgery. LC 90-1157. (Illus.). 216p. 1991. reprint ed. pap. 67.00 (0-608-07376-8, 206760300009) Bks Demand.
Paulos, Martha. Insectisides. 64p. 1999. pap. write for info. (0-14-024410-7) Viking Penguin.
Paulos, Nicholas. The Doll in the Window. 250p. pap., per. 9.95 (0-89697-291-7) Intl Univ Pr.
Paulovich, David. Midterm Survey of Churched Development, 1985-1989. Weaver, Irvin D., ed. 87p. 1990. pap. 5.00 (1-877736-09-0) MB Missions.
Paulraj, Arogyaswami, et al, eds. Communications, Computation, Control, & Signal Processing: A Tribute to Thomas Kailath. LC 96-45714. 608p. (C). 1997. text 126.50 (0-7923-9815-7) Kluwer Academic.
***Pauls, Cornelia Anna.** Emotion und Personlichkeit. (Psychophysiologie in Labor und Feld. Bd. 8 Ser.). Xii, 393p. 1999. 52.95 (3-631-34439-2) P Lang Pubng.
Pauls, Julie A. & Reed, Kathlyn L. Quick Reference to Physical Therapy. 688p. 1996. 45.00 (0-8342-0654-4, 20654) Aspen Pub.
Pauls, Julie A., et al. Therapeutic Approaches to Women's Health: A Program of Exercise & Education. LC 95-19712. 350p. 1996. ring bd. 189.00 (0-8342-0564-5) Aspen Pub.
Pauls, Michael, jt. auth. see Facaros, Dana.
Paulse, Michele, jt. auth. see Elwin, Rosamund.
***Paulsell, Patricia Ryan, et al.** German for Business & Economics Vol. 1: Die Volks- und Welwirtschaft (Economics) 2nd rev. ed. (GER.). (C). 2000. pap. 50.00 (0-87013-538-4) Mich St U Pr.
— German for Business & Economics Vol. 1: Die Volks- und Welwirtschaft (Economics) 2nd rev. ed. (GER.). 2000. pap. 25.00 (0-87013-540-6) Mich St U Pr.
— German for Business & Economics Vol. 2: Die Betriebswirtschaft (Business) 2nd rev. ed. (GER.). (C). 2000. pap. 50.00 (0-87013-539-2) Mich St U Pr.
— German for Business & Economics Vol. 2: Die Betriebswirtschaft (Business) 2nd rev. ed. (GER.). 2000. pap. 25.00 (0-87013-541-4) Mich St U Pr.
Paulsell, William & Kelty, Matthew. Letters from a Hermit. 128p. 1978. 7.95 (0-87243-086-3) Templegate.
Paulsell, William O. Disciples at Prayer: The Spirituality of the Christian Church, Disciples of Christ. 104p. (Orig.). 1995. pap. 9.99 (0-8272-0621-6) Chalice Pr.
— Rules for Prayer. LC 93-4387. 160p. 1993. pap. 9.95 (0-8091-3410-1) Paulist Pr.
— Taste & See: A Personal Guide to the Spiritual Life. rev. ed. 128p. 1992. pap. 9.99 (0-8272-3629-8) Chalice Pr.
Paulsell, William O., ed. Sermons in a Monastery: Chapter Talks by Matthew Kelty Ocso, No. 59. (Cistercian Studies). 1983. pap. 9.95 (0-87907-958-4) Cistercian Pubns.
Paulsell, William O., ed. see Kelty, Matthew.
Paulsen. Dogsong. (J). (gr. 4-6). 1998. per. 2.65 (0-689-82165-4) S&S Childrens.
Paulsen & Assoc. Staff, ed. see Schwartz, Linda K.
Paulsen & Associates Staff. How to Use Microsoft Word '97. Maloff, Debbie, ed. (Illus.). 105p. 1998. pap. 225.00 incl. disk (1-56562-095-X) OneOnOne Comp Trng.
— How to Use Microsoft Word 7. unabridged ed. Maloff, Deborah, ed. 90p. 1995. pap. 225.00 incl. disk (1-56562-068-2, 474) OneOnOne Comp Trng.
Paulsen & Associates Staff, ed. see Nance, Kimi.
Paulsen, Albert Chr., jt. auth. see Leach, John.
Paulsen, Arvid, tr. see Strindberg, August.
***Paulsen, Christine.** Pflanzenmedizin in einer Dorfgemeinschaft Im Sudwesten Madagaskars. (Europaische Hochschulschriften Ser.: Bd. 52). 202p. 1999. 37.95 (3-631-35389-8) P Lang Pubng.
Paulsen, David W., jt. auth. see Cederblom, Jerry.
Paulsen, Deborah, ed. see Schwartz, Linda K.
Paulsen, Deirdre, jt. auth. see Rider, Rowland.
Paulsen, Douglas F. Basic Histology: Examination & Board Review. 3rd ed. 368p. (C). 1996. pap. 32.95 (0-8385-2282-3, A2282-0, Apple Lange Med) McGraw.
— Basic Histology & Cell Biology: Examination & Board Review. 4th ed. (Illus.). 432p. (C). 2000. pap. 32.95 (0-8385-0593-7) McGraw.
***Paulsen, Elsa P.** Taking Care of Your Diabetes - Making It Simple & Safe. vi, 90p. 1999. spiral bd. 20.00 (0-9673871-0-8) Elsa Paulsen.
Paulsen, Emily & Paulsen, Faith. Fun with the Family in Pennsylvania: Great Things to See & Do for the Entire Family. 2nd ed. LC 98-13783. (Fun with the Family Ser.). (Illus.). 288p. 1998. pap. 12.95 (0-7627-0247-8) Globe Pequot.
***Paulsen, Emily & Paulsen, Faith.** Fun with the Family in Pennsylvania: Hundreds of Ideas for Day Trips with the Kids. 3rd ed. (Fun with the Family Ser.). (Illus.). 288p. 2000. pap. 12.95 (0-7627-0620-1) Globe Pequot.
Paulsen, Eugene, jt. auth. see Barksdale, Karl.
Paulsen, Faith, jt. auth. see Paulsen, Emily.
Paulsen, Frank R. American Education: Challenges & Images. LC 66-28787. 124p. reprint ed. pap. 38.50 (0-8357-5363-8, 205621200055) Bks Demand.
— Changing Dimensions in International Education. LC 73-76783. 175p. reprint ed. pap. 54.30 (0-608-15197-1, 202738600055) Bks Demand.
Paulsen, Frank R., ed. Contemporary Issues in American Education. LC 66-24302. 130p. reprint ed. pap. 40.30 (0-608-15198-X, 202738700055) Bks Demand.
Paulsen, Friedrich. Autobiography. Lorenz, Theodore, tr. LC 38-38641. reprint ed. 29.50 (0-404-04945-1) AMS Pr.
— Die Deutschen Universitaten und das Universitatsstudium. xii, 575p. 1966. reprint ed. write for info. (0-318-71853-7) G Olms Pubs.
— German Education Past & Present. Lorenz, Theodore, tr. LC 75-41209. reprint ed. 42.50 (0-404-14693-7) AMS Pr.
Paulsen, G. Norsk-Tysk Ordbok: Norwegian-German Dictionary. (GER & NOR.). 416p. 1973. 39.95 (0-8288-6326-1, M-9466) Fr & Eur.
***Paulsen, Gary.** Alida's Song. 96p. 2001. pap. 5.50 (0-440-41474-1) BDD Bks Young Read.
Paulsen, Gary. Alida's Song. LC 98-37015. (YA). 1999. pap. 15.95 (0-385-32586-X) Delacorte.
— Amos & the Alien. (Culpepper Adventures Ser.). 80p. (J). (gr. 3-5). 1994. pap. 3.50 (0-440-40990-X) Dell.
— Amos & the Chameleon Caper. (Culpepper Adventures Ser.). (J). (gr. 3-5). 1996. 9.19 (0-606-11039-9, Pub. by Turtleback) Demco.
— Amos & the Vampire. (Culpepper Adventures Ser.). (J). (gr. 3-5). 1996. 9.19 (0-606-08996-9, Pub. by Turtleback) Demco.
— Amos Binder, Secret Agent. (Culpepper Adventures Ser.). 80p. (J). (gr. 3-5). 1996. pap. 3.99 (0-440-41050-9) Dell.
Paulsen, Gary. Amos Binder, Secret Agent. (Culpepper Adventures Ser.). (J). (gr. 3-5). 1997. 9.19 (0-606-11040-2, Pub. by Turtleback) Demco.
Paulsen, Gary. Amos Gets Married. LC 95-143305. (Culpepper Adventures Ser.). 112p. (J). (gr. 3-5). 1995. pap. 3.50 (0-440-40933-0) Dell.
— Amos Gets Married. (Culpepper Adventures Ser.). (J). (gr. 3-5). 1995. 8.60 (0-606-07187-3, Pub. by Turtleback) Demco.
Paulsen, Gary. Amos Goes Bananas. (Culpepper Adventures Ser.). (J). (gr. 3-5). 1995. 9.19 (0-606-08997-7, Pub. by Turtleback) Demco.
Paulsen, Gary. Amos's Killer Concert Caper. (Culpepper Adventures Ser.). (J). (gr. 3-5). 1995. 8.60 (0-606-07188-1, Pub. by Turtleback) Demco.
***Paulsen, Gary.** Beet Fields: Memories of a Sixteenth Summer. LC 00-23184. 176p. (gr. 8-12). 2000. 15.95 (0-385-32647-5) Delacorte.
Paulsen, Gary. The Boy Who Owned the School. 96p. (YA). 1991. pap. 4.50 (0-440-40524-6, YB BDD) BDD Bks Young Read.
— The Boy Who Owned the School. LC 89-23048. 112p. (J). (gr. 6-9). 1990. 15.95 (0-531-05865-4) Orchard Bks Watts.
Paulsen, Gary. Boy Who Owned the School: A Comedy of Love. (J). 1990. 9.09 (0-606-00327-4, Pub. by Turtleback) Demco.
Paulsen, Gary. Brian's Return. LC 98-24278. 128p. (YA). (gr. 5-9). 1999. 15.95 (0-385-32500-2, Delacorte Pr Bks) BDD Bks Young Read.
— Brian's Winter. 144p. (YA). (gr. 6 up). 1996. 15.95 (0-385-32198-8, Delacorte Pr Bks) BDD Bks Young Read.
— Brian's Winter. (J). 1996. 16.95 (0-385-31736-0) Doubleday.
— Brian's Winter. (J). 1996. 16.95 (0-385-31722-0) Doubleday.
— Brian's Winter. (Assessment Packs Ser.). 15p. (J). 1998. pap. text 15.95 (1-58303-039-5) Pthways Pubng.
— Brian's Winter. (J). 1998. 10.09 (0-606-12898-0, Pub. by Turtleback) Demco.
— Brian's Winter. 144p. (YA). (gr. 7 up). 1998. reprint ed. mass mkt. 5.50 (0-440-22719-4, LLL BDD) BDD Bks Young Read.
— Call Me Frances Tucket. (J). 1995. 19.95 (0-385-44632-2) BDD Bks Young Read.
— Call Me Frances Tucket. 112p. (J). 1995. 15.95 (0-385-32116-3) Delacorte.
— Call Me Frances Tucket. LC 94-33639. 128p. (J). (gr. 4-7). 1996. pap. 4.50 (0-440-41270-6) Dell.
Paulsen, Gary. Call Me Frances Tucket. 1996. 9.09 (0-606-10766-5, Pub. by Turtleback) Demco.
Paulsen, Gary. Canoe Days. LC 97-21542. (Illus.). 32p. (J). (gr. k up). 1999. 16.95 (0-385-32524-X, DD Bks Yng Read) BDD Bks Young Read.
— Canyons. 192p. (J). (gr. 4-7). 1991. mass mkt. 5.50 (0-440-21023-2) Dell.
Paulsen, Gary. Canyons. 1990. 10.09 (0-606-04884-7, Pub. by Turtleback) Demco.
Paulsen, Gary. Captive! 80p. (J). (gr. 3-7). 1995. pap. 3.99 (0-440-41042-8, YB BDD) BDD Bks Young Read.
— Captive! (World of Adventure Ser.). (J). 1995. 9.19 (0-606-07340-X, Pub. by Turtleback) Demco.
— The Car. (J). 1995. mass mkt. 5.99 (0-440-91044-7) BDD Bks Young Read.
— The Car. 180p. (YA). (gr. 7-12). 1995. mass mkt. 4.99 (0-440-21918-3, LLL BDD) BDD Bks Young Read.
— The Car. LC 93-41834. 176p. (YA). (gr. 7 up). 1994. 15.00 (0-15-292878-2) Harcourt.
— The Car. (YA). 1995. 9.60 (0-606-07341-8, Pub. by Turtleback) Demco.
— Christmas Sonata. 80p. (J). 1994. pap. 4.50 (0-440-40958-6) Dell.
Paulsen, Gary. Christmas Sonata. 1994. 9.19 (0-606-06958-5, Pub. by Turtleback) Demco.
Paulsen, Gary. Clabbered Dirt: Sweet Grass. (Illus.). 140p. 1994. pap. 9.95 (0-15-600052-0) Harcourt.
Paulsen, Gary. Coach Amos. (Culpepper Adventures Ser.). (J). (gr. 3-5). 1994. 8.70 (0-606-06284-X, Pub. by Turtleback) Demco.
Paulsen, Gary. The Cookcamp. 128p. (J). (gr. 2-6). 1992. pap. 4.50 (0-440-40704-4, YB BDD) BDD Bks Young Read.
— The Cookcamp. LC 90-7734. 128p. (J). (gr. 5-7). 1991. 15.95 (0-531-05927-8) Orchard Bks Watts.
— The Cookcamp. 1991. 9.09 (0-606-00894-2, Pub. by Turtleback) Demco.
— Cowpokes & Desperadoes. LC 94-146934. (Culpepper Adventures Ser.). 80p. (J). (gr. 3-5). 1993. pap. 3.50 (0-440-40902-0) Dell.
Paulsen, Gary. Cowpokes & Desperadoes. (Culpepper Adventures Ser.). (J). (gr. 3-5). 1994. 8.70 (0-606-05793-5, Pub. by Turtleback) Demco.
Paulsen, Gary. The Creature of Black Water Lake. (World of Adventure Ser.: No. 13). 80p. (gr. 3-7). 1997. pap. 3.99 (0-440-41211-0) Dell.
— The Creature of Black Water Lake. (Mulberry Paperback Bks.= Un Libro Mulbe). 1997. 9.19 (0-606-11224-3, Pub. by Turtleback) Demco.
— The Crossing. 128p. (YA). (gr. k up). 1990. mass mkt. 4.99 (0-440-20582-4, LLL BDD) BDD Bks Young Read.
— The Crossing. (J). 1990. mass mkt. 5.95 (0-440-80156-7) Dell.
— The Crossing. LC 87-7738. 128p. (J). (gr. 6-8). 1987. 15.95 (0-531-05709-7) Orchard Bks Watts.
Paulsen, Gary. Crossing. (J). 1987. 9.60 (0-606-03175-8, Pub. by Turtleback) Demco.
Paulsen, Gary. Culpepper's Cannon. (Culpepper Adventures Ser.). (J). (gr. 3-5). 1992. 8.60 (0-606-00890-X, Pub. by Turtleback) Demco.
— Curse of the Ruins. (Gary Paulsen World of Adventure Ser.: Vol. 17). (J). 1998. pap. 3.99 (0-440-41225-0) Dell.
— Dancing Carl. LC 86-30245. (YA). (gr. 5 up). 1987. pap. 3.95 (0-685-19101-X, PuffinBks) Peng Put Young Read.
— Dancing Carl. LC 83-2663. 112p. (J). (gr. 4-7). 1995. mass mkt. 3.95 (0-689-80410-5) S&S Childrens.
— Dancing Carl. 1995. 9.05 (0-606-07409-0, Pub. by Turtleback) Demco.
— Danger on Midnight River. (Gary Paulsen World of Adventure Ser.). 80p. (J). 1995. pap. 3.99 (0-440-41028-2) Dell.
— Danger on Midnight River. (Gary Paulsen's World of Adventure Ser.). (J). 1995. 9.19 (0-606-07411-2, Pub. by Turtleback) Demco.
— Dogsong. LC 84-20443. 177p. (YA). (gr. 5-9). 1995. pap. 4.50 (0-689-80409-1) Aladdin.
— Dogsong. LC 84-20443. 208p. (YA). (gr. 7 up). 1999. per. 4.50 (0-689-82700-8, 076714004993) Aladdin.
***Paulsen, Gary.** Dogsong. (2000 Kids Picks Ser.). 192p. (J). (gr. 4-7). 2000. mass mkt. 2.99 (0-689-83869-7) Aladdin.
Paulsen, Gary. Dogsong. LC 84-20443. 192p. (YA). (gr. 7 up). 1985. lib. bdg. 16.00 (0-02-770180-8, Bradbury S&S) S&S Childrens.
***Paulsen, Gary.** Dogsong. (J). (gr. 4-7). 2000. per. 16.00 (0-689-83960-X) S&S Childrens.
Paulsen, Gary. Dogsong. 1995. 9.60 (0-606-07437-6, Pub. by Turtleback) Demco.
— Dogteam. (J). 1995. mass mkt. 7.99 (0-440-91061-7) BDD Bks Young Read.
— Dogteam. (Illus.). 32p. (J). (gr. 2 up). 1995. pap. 6.99 (0-440-41130-0, Yearling) BDD Bks Young Read.
— Dogteam. 1995. 11.19 (0-606-07438-4, Pub. by Turtleback) Demco.
— Dunc & Amos Go to the Dogs. (Culpepper Adventures Ser.). (J). (gr. 3-5). 1996. 9.19 (0-606-09218-8, Pub. by Turtleback) Demco.
Paulsen, Gary. Dunc & Amos Meet the Slasher. (Culpepper Adventures Ser.). (J). (gr. 3-5). 1994. 8.70 (0-606-06971-2, Pub. by Turtleback) Demco.
— Dunc & Amos on Thin Ice. (Culpepper Adventures Ser.). (J). (gr. 3-5). 1997. 34.00 (0-606-12684-8, Pub. by Turtleback) Demco.
Paulsen, Gary. Dunc & the Haunted Castle. (Culpepper Adventures Ser.). (J). (gr. 3-5). 1993. 9.19 (0-606-05817-6, Pub. by Turtleback) Demco.
— Dunc's Halloween. (Culpepper Adventures Ser.). (J). (gr. 3-5). 1992. 8.60 (0-606-05245-3, Pub. by Turtleback) Demco.
— Eastern Sun, Winter Moon: An Autobiographical Odyssey. LC 91-47127. 1993. 22.95 (0-15-127260-3) Harcourt.
Paulsen, Gary. Eastern Sun, Winter Moon: An Autobiographical Odyssey. (Illus.). 256p. 1995. pap. 11.00 (0-15-600203-5, Harvest Bks) Harcourt.
Paulsen, Gary. Escape from Fire Mountain. (J). 1994. pap. 4.50 (0-440-91012-9) BDD Bks Young Read.
— Escape from Fire Mountain. (Gary Paulsen World of Adventure Ser.). 80p. (J). (gr. 4-7). 1995. pap. 3.99 (0-440-41025-8) Dell.
— Escape from Fire Mountain. (World of Adventure Ser.). (J). 1995. 9.19 (0-606-07486-4, Pub. by Turtleback) Demco.
— Father Water, Mother. 1995. 21.95 (0-385-30984-8) Doubleday.
— Father Water, Mother Woods: Essays on Fishing & Hunting in the North Woods. (Illus.). 192p. (J). 1996. mass mkt. 4.99 (0-440-21984-1) BDD Bks Young Read.
— Father Water, Mother Woods: Essays on Fishing & Hunting in the North Woods. 1996. 10.09 (0-606-09263-3, Pub. by Turtleback) Demco.
— Flight of the Hawk. (Gary Paulsen World of Adventure Ser.: No. 18). 80p. (J). (gr. 3-7). 1998. pap. 3.99 (0-440-41228-5, YB BDD) BDD Bks Young Read.
— The Foxman. 128p. (J). (gr. 4 up). 1990. pap. 3.99 (0-14-034311-3, PuffinBks) Peng Put Young Read.
— Foxman. (J). 1977. 9.09 (0-606-03296-7, Pub. by Turtleback) Demco.
***Paulsen, Gary.** Guts. (YA). 2001. mass mkt. 16.95 (0-385-32650-5, Pub. by Random Bks Yng Read) Random.
Paulsen, Gary. El Hacha. 1989. 14.05 (0-606-10411-9, Pub. by Turtleback) Demco.
— El Hacha - Hatchet. 1996. pap. text 8.95 (84-279-3206-5) Lectorum Pubns.
— Harris & Me: A Summer Remembered. (J). 1995. pap. 4.99 (0-440-91051-X) BDD Bks Young Read.
— Harris & Me: A Summer Remembered. 160p. (YA). (gr. 7 up). 1995. pap. 4.99 (0-440-40994-2) Dell.
— Harris & Me: A Summer Remembered. LC 93-19788. (Illus.). 160p. (YA). (gr. 7 up). 1993. 13.95 (0-15-292877-4) Harcourt.
— Harris & Me: A Summer Remembered. (J). 1995. 9.35 (0-606-07624-7, Pub. by Turtleback) Demco.
***Paulsen, Gary.** Hatchet. LC 87-6416. 208p. (J). (gr. 5-9). 1999. per. 4.50 (0-689-82699-0, 076714004993) Aladdin.
Paulsen, Gary. Hatchet. (YA). (gr. 6 up). 1995. 9.28 (0-395-73261-1) HM.
Paulsen, Gary. Hatchet. 195p. (J). (gr. 4-6). pap. 4.99 (0-8072-8320-7) Listening Lib.
Paulsen, Gary. Hatchet. (J). 1986. 12.95 (0-02-527403-1) Macmillan.
— Hatchet. LC 87-6416. 208p. (J). (gr. 4-7). 1996. mass mkt. 4.50 (0-689-80882-8) S&S Bks Yung.
— Hatchet. LC 87-6416. 208p. (J). (gr. 6-8). 1987. text 16.00 (0-02-770130-1, Bradbury S&S) S&S Childrens.
***Paulsen, Gary.** Hatchet. (Illus.). (J). 2000. per. 16.95 (0-689-84092-6) S&S Childrens.
Paulsen, Gary. Hatchet. LC 87-6416. (J). 1996. 9.60 (0-606-10206-X, Pub. by Turtleback) Demco.
— Hatchet. large type ed. 220p. (YA). (gr. 6 up). 55.50 (0-614-20593-X, L-38206-00 APHB) Am Printing Hse.
***Paulsen, Gary.** Hatchet. large type ed. (LRS Large Print Cornerstone Ser.). 205p. (YA). (gr. 4-12). 2000. lib. bdg. 28.95 (1-58118-055-1, 23469) LRS.
Paulsen, Gary. The Haymeadow. 208p. (J). (gr. 4-7). 1994. pap. 4.99 (0-440-40923-3) Dell.
— The Haymeadow. (J). 1992. 9.60 (0-606-05869-9, Pub. by Turtleback) Demco.
Paulsen, Gary. The Haymeadow. unabridged ed. 1992. audio 17.99 (0-553-47077-9) BDD Aud Pub.
Paulsen, Gary. Hook 'Em Snotty! (World of Adventure Ser.). 1995. 8.70 (0-606-07659-X, Pub. by Turtleback) Demco.
— The Island. 208p. (YA). (gr. k up). 1990. mass mkt. 4.99 (0-440-20632-4, LLL BDD) BDD Bks Young Read.
— The Island. LC 87-24761. 224p. (J). (gr. 6-9). 1988. 17.95 (0-531-05749-6) Orchard Bks Watts.
Paulsen, Gary. Island. 1988. 9.60 (0-606-04437-X, Pub. by Turtleback) Demco.
Paulsen, Gary. Legend of Red Horse Cavern. 80p. (J). 1994. pap. 3.99 (0-440-41023-1) Dell.
— Legend of Red Horse Cavern. (Gary Paulsen's World of Adventure Ser.). 1994. 8.70 (0-606-07141-5, Pub. by Turtleback) Demco.
***Paulsen, Gary.** Literature Guide: Hatchet. (Illus.). 16p. 1999. pap. 3.95 (0-590-38924-6) Scholastic Inc.
Paulsen, Gary. Mr. Tucket. (J). 1995. pap. 5.99 (0-440-91053-6) BDD Bks Young Read.
— Mr. Tucket. Vol. 1. 192p. (YA). (gr. 5-9). 1995. pap. 4.50 (0-440-41133-5, YB BDD) BDD Bks Young Read.
— Mr. Tucket. (J). 1996. pap. 5.99 (0-440-91097-8) BDD Bks Young Read.
— Mr. Tucket. LC 93-31180. 176p. (J). 1994. 15.95 (0-385-31169-9) Delacorte.
***Paulsen, Gary.** Mr. Tucket. (Illus.). (J). (gr. 4-7). 2000. mass mkt. 2.99 (0-375-80680-6, Pub. by Random Bks Yng Read) Random.
Paulsen, Gary. Mr. Tucket. 1995. 9.85 (0-606-07895-9) Turtleback.
— Monument. 160p. (J). 1991. 15.00 (0-385-30518-4) Delacorte.
— Monument. 160p. (YA). 1993. pap. 4.99 (0-440-40782-6) Dell.
— Monument. (J). 1991. 9.60 (0-606-05471-5, Pub. by Turtleback) Demco.
— My Life in Dog Years. 144p. (J). 1999. pap. 4.99 (0-440-41471-7) BDD Bks Young Read.
— My Life in Dog Years. LC 97-40254. (Illus.). 144p. (YA). (gr. 5 up). 1998. 15.95 (0-385-32570-3) Delacorte.
— Night John. (J). 1994. mass mkt. 4.99 (0-440-82072-3) BDD Bks Young Read.
— Night the White Deer Died. 112p. (YA). 1991. mass mkt. 3.99 (0-440-21092-5, YB BDD) BDD Bks Young Read.
— NightJohn. (J). 1994. mass mkt. 4.99 (0-440-91014-5) BDD Bks Young Read.
— NightJohn. 112p. (YA). (gr. 6 up). 1995. mass mkt. 4.50 (0-440-21936-1) Dell.
— NightJohn. LC 92-1222. 96p. (YA). (gr. 6 up). 1993. 15.95 (0-385-30838-8) Doubleday.
— Nightjohn. 1995. 9.60 (0-606-07951-3, Pub. by Turtleback) Demco.
— Pilgrimage on a Steel Ride: A Memoir about Men & Motorcycles. LC 97-24799. 192p. 1997. 21.00 (0-15-193093-7) Harcourt.
— Popcorn Days & Buttermilk Nights. 112p. (J). (gr. 5-9). 1989. pap. 4.99 (0-14-034204-4, PuffinBks) Peng Put Young Read.
— Popcorn Days & Buttermilk Nights. (J). 1989. 10.09 (0-606-02250-3, Pub. by Turtleback) Demco.
Paulsen, Gary. Prince Amos. (Culpepper Adventures Ser.). (J). (gr. 3-5). 1994. 8.70 (0-606-05979-2, Pub. by Turtleback) Demco.
Paulsen, Gary. Project: A Perfect. (J). 1996. pap. 4.99 (0-440-91113-3) BDD Bks Young Read.
— Project: A Perfect World. (World of Adventure Ser.). 1996. 9.09 (0-606-08851-2, Pub. by Turtleback) Demco.
— Puppies, Dogs, & Blue Northers: Reflections on Being Raised by a Pack of Sled Dogs. LC 95-18981. (Illus.). 81p. (J). 1996. 16.00 (0-15-292881-2) Harcourt.

P

An Asterisk (*) at the beginning of an entry indicates that the title is appearing for the first time.

— Puppies, Dogs, & Blue Northers: Reflections on Being Raised by a Pack of Sled Dogs. 1998. 14.15 (*0-606-13019-5*, Pub. by Turtleback) Demco.

— Puppies, Dogs, & Blue Northers: Reflections on Being Raised by a Pack of Sled Dogs. (Illus.). 96p. (YA). (gr. 7 up). 1998. reprint ed. pap. 9.95 (*0-385-32585-1*, Delacorte Pr Bks) BDD Bks Young Read.

— The Rifle. 105p. (YA). (gr. 7 up). 1997. mass mkt. 4.99 (*0-440-21920-5*, LLL BDD) BDD Bks Young Read.

— The Rifle. LC 95-730. 192p. (YA). (gr. 7 up). 1995. 16.00 (*0-15-292880-4*, Harcourt Child Bks) Harcourt.

— The Rifle. LC 95-730. 1997. 10.25 (*0-606-11800-4*, Pub. by Turtleback) Demco.

— The River. 144p. (YA). (gr. 7-12). 1993. pap. 4.99 (*0-440-40753-2*) Dell.

— The River. LC 90-49294. 144p. (J). (gr. 7-12). 1991. 15.95 (*0-385-30388-2*) Doubleday.

— The River. (J). 1991. 10.09 (*0-606-02872-2*, Pub. by Turtleback) Demco.

— The River. 160p. (J). (gr. 5-9). 1998. reprint ed. mass mkt. 5.50 (*0-440-22750-X*, LLL BDD) BDD Bks Young Read.

— Rock Jockeys. (Gary Paulsen World of Adventure Ser.). 80p. (J). (gr. 4-6). 1995. pap. 3.99 (*0-440-41026-6*) Dell.

— Rock Jockeys. (World of Adventure Ser.). (J). 1995. 9.44 (*0-606-08080-5*) Turtleback.

— Rodomonte's Revenge. (Gary Paulsen's World of Adventure Ser.). 1994. 9.19 (*0-606-07142-3*, Pub. by Turtleback) Demco.

— Sarny, a Life Remembered. 192p. (YA). 1999. mass mkt. 4.99 (*0-440-21973-6*) BDD Bks Young Read.

— Sarny, a Life Remembered. LC 96-53842. 192p. (YA). (gr. 6 up). 1997. 15.95 (*0-385-32195-3*) Delacorte.

— The Schernoff Discoveries. 128p. (J). (gr. 5-9). 1998. pap. 4.50 (*0-440-41463-6*) BDD Bks Young Read.

— The Schernoff Discoveries. LC 96-45390. 112p. (J). 1997. 15.95 (*0-385-32194-5*) Delacorte.

— The Schernoff Discoveries. 1998. 9.60 (*0-606-13761-0*, Pub. by Turtleback) Demco.

— Sentries. LC 85-26978. 160p. (YA). (gr. 7 up). 1986. lib. bdg. 17.00 (*0-02-770100-X*, Bradbury S&S) S&S Childrens.

— Sentries. LC 85-26978. 176p. (J). 1995. 3.95 (*0-689-80411-3*) S&S Childrens.

— Sentries. 1995. 10.34 (*0-606-08146-1*) Turtleback.

— Sentries. (J). (gr. 5-9). reprint ed. pap. 3.95 (*0-317-62279-X*, PuffinBks) Peng Put Young Read.

— Seventh Crystal. (World of Adventure Ser.). 1996. 9.19 (*0-606-09844-5*, Pub. by Turtleback) Demco.

— Sisters - Hermanas. LC 93-13777. 144p. (YA). (gr. 7 up). 1993. 10.95 (*0-15-275323-0*, Harcourt Child Bks) Harcourt.

— Sisters - Hermanas. LC 93-13777. (Illus.). 144p. (YA). (gr. 7 up). 1993. pap. 6.00 (*0-15-275324-9*, Harcourt Child Bks) Harcourt.

— Sisters - Hermanas. 1993. 11.10 (*0-606-06002-2*, Pub. by Turtleback) Demco.

— Skydive! (World of Adventure Ser.). 1996. 9.19 (*0-606-09865-8*, Pub. by Turtleback) Demco.

— A Soldier's Heart. LC 98-10038. 128p. (YA). (gr. 7-10). 1998. 15.95 (*0-385-32498-7*) Doubleday.

***Paulsen, Gary.** Soldier's Heart: Being the Story of the Enlistment & Due Service of the Boy Charley Goddard. LC 98-10038. (Illus.). 128p. (gr. 8-12). 2000. mass mkt. 5.50 (*0-440-22838-7*, LE) Dell.

— Super Amos. (Culpepper Adventures Ser.). (J). (gr. 3-5). 1997. 9.19 (*0-606-12820-4*, Pub. by Turtleback) Demco.

Paulsen, Gary. The Tent: A Parable in One Sitting. 192p. (J). 1996. mass mkt. 4.99 (*0-440-21919-1*) Dell.

— The Tent: A Parable in One Sitting. LC 94-36103. 96p. (YA). (gr. 7 up). 1995. 14.00 (*0-15-292879-0*) Harcourt.

— Tent: A Parable in One Sitting. LC 94-36103. 1996. 10.09 (*0-606-10952-8*, Pub. by Turtleback) Demco.

Paulsen, Gary. Tilt-a-Whirl John. 1990. 9.09 (*0-606-04830-8*, Pub. by Turtleback) Demco.

Paulsen, Gary. Tiltawhirl John. 1992. 18.75 (*0-8446-6535-5*) Peter Smith.

— Time Benders. (World of Adventure Ser.). (J). 1997. 9.19 (*0-606-11991-4*, Pub. by Turtleback) Demco.

— The Tortilla Factory. LC 93-48590. (Illus.). 32p. (J). 1995. 16.00 (*0-15-292876-6*, Harcourt Child Bks) Harcourt.

— The Tortilla Factory. LC 94-48590. (Illus.). 32p. (C). 1998. pap. 7.00 (*0-15-201698-8*, Harcourt Child Bks) Harcourt.

— The Tortilla Factory. (J). 1998. 12.20 (*0-606-13857-9*, Pub. by Turtleback) Demco.

— La Tortilleria. De Aragon Andujar, Gloria, tr. LC 94-18543.Tr. of Tortilla Factory. (Illus.). 32p. (J). 1995. 15.00 (*0-15-200237-5*, Red Wagon Bks) Harcourt.

— La Tortilleria. LC 94-18543.Tr. of Tortilla Factory. (SPA., Illus.). 32p. (J). 1998. pap. 7.00 (*0-15-201714-3*, Harcourt Child Bks) Harcourt.

— La Tortilleria.Tr. of Tortilla Factory. 1998. 12.20 (*0-606-13559-6*, Pub. by Turtleback) Demco.

— Tracker. LC 83-22447. 96p. (J). (gr. 6-8). 1984. mass mkt. 15.00 (*0-02-770220-0*, Bradbury S&S) S&S Childrens.

***Paulsen, Gary.** Tracker. (J). (gr. 7-12). 2000. per. 15.00 (*0-689-84088-8*) S&S Trade.

Paulsen, Gary. Tracker. 1995. 9.05 (*0-606-08316-2*, Pub. by Turtleback) Demco.

— Tracker. (J). (gr. 5-9). reprint ed. pap. 3.95 (*0-317-62280-3*, PuffinBks) Peng Put Young Read.

— Tracker: Sentries. LC 83-22447. 90p. (J). (gr. 4-8). 1995. mass mkt. 3.95 (*0-689-80412-1*) S&S Childrens.

— The Transall Saga. 256p. (YA). 1999. mass mkt. 5.50 (*0-440-21976-0*) Bantam.

***Paulsen, Gary.** The Transall Saga. LC 97-40773. 248p. (YA). (gr. 7-12). 1998. 15.95 (*0-385-32196-1*) Delacorte.

— Transall Saga. 1998. write for info. (*0-385-43196-1*, Delacorte) DELL.

— The Transall Saga. large type ed. LC 99-42435. (Thorndike Young Adult Ser.). (YA). 1999. 21.95 (*0-7862-2187-9*) Thorndike Pr.

Paulsen, Gary. Treasure of El Patron. (World of Adventure Ser.). 1996. 9.19 (*0-606-09990-5*, Pub. by Turtleback) Demco.

***Paulsen, Gary.** Tucket's Gold. 112p. 2001. pap. 4.50 (*0-440-41376-1*) BDD Bks Young Read.

— Tucket's Gold. LC 99-11463. 112p. 1999. 15.95 (*0-385-32501-0*) Bantam.

— Tucket's Home. (Tucket Adventures Ser.: Vol. 5). (Illus.). 112p. (J). (gr. 4-7). 2000. 15.95 (*0-385-32648-3*, Delacorte Pr Bks) BDD Bks Young Read.

Paulsen, Gary. Tucket's Ride. LC 96-21703. 112p. (J). 1997. 15.95 (*0-385-32199-6*, Delacorte Pr Bks) BDD Bks Young Read.

— Tucket's Ride. (Illus.). 112p. (YA). (gr. 5 up). 1998. reprint ed. pap. 4.50 (*0-440-41147-5*, YB BDD) BDD Bks Young Read.

— Tucket's Ride, 3. (Tucket Adventures Ser.). (J). 1998. 9.09 (*0-606-13877-3*, Pub. by Turtleback) Demco.

— Voyage of Frog. (J). 1996. pap. 4.99 (*0-440-91101-X*) BDD Bks Young Read.

— The Voyage of the Frog. LC 88-15261. (Illus.). 160p. (J). (gr. 6-8). 1989. 15.95 (*0-531-05805-0*) Orchard Bks Watts.

— The Voyage of the Frog. 1989. 9.60 (*0-606-04841-3*, Pub. by Turtleback) Demco.

— The Voyage of the Frog. large type ed. LC 93-30238. (YA). (gr. 9-12). 1993. 16.95 (*0-7862-0060-X*) Thorndike Pr.

— The Voyage of the Frog. 160p. (YA). (gr. 5-9). 1990. reprint ed. pap. 4.99 (*0-440-40364-2*) Dell.

— The White Fox Chronicles. LC 98-24274. Vol. 1. 288p. (YA). (gr. 4-9). 2000. 8.95 (*0-385-32254-2*, Delacorte Pr Bks) BDD Bks Young Read.

— The Winter Room. 112p. (J). (gr. 4-7). 1991. pap. 4.50 (*0-440-40454-1*) BDD Bks Young Read.

— The Winter Room. 112p. (YA). 1998. mass mkt. 4.50 (*0-440-22783-6*) BDD Bks Young Read.

— The Winter Room. LC 89-42541. 128p. (J). (gr. 6-9). 1989. 15.95 (*0-531-05839-5*); lib. bdg. 16.99 (*0-531-08439-6*) Orchard Bks Watts.

— The Winter Room. 1991. 7.59 (*0-606-12580-9*, Pub. by Turtleback) Demco.

— Winterdance: The Fine Madness of Running the Iditarod. (Illus.). 240p. (YA). (gr. 9 up). 1994. 21.95 (*0-15-126227-6*) Harcourt.

— Winterdance: The Fine Madness of Running the Iditarod. (Illus.). 264p. (YA). (gr. 9 up). 1995. pap. 15.00 (*0-15-600145-4*, Harvest Bks) Harcourt.

— Woodsong. LC 94-53099. (Illus.). 144p. (YA). (gr. 4-7). 1991. pap. 4.99 (*0-14-034905-7*, PuffinBks) Peng Put Young Read.

***Paulsen, Gary.** Woodsong. (YA). (gr. 6 up). 2000. 19.25 (*0-8446-7152-5*) Peter Smith.

— Woodsong. LC 89-70835. (Illus.). 160p. (YA). (gr. 7 up). 1990. pap. 16.00 (*0-02-770221-9*, Bradbury S&S) S&S Childrens.

Paulsen, Gary. Woodsong. 1991. 10.09 (*0-606-00829-2*, Pub. by Turtleback) Demco.

— Worksong. LC 95-49309. (Illus.). 32p. (J). (ps-3). 1997. 15.00 (*0-15-200980-9*) Harcourt.

***Paulsen, Gary.** Worksong. (Illus.). 32p. (J). (ps-3). 2000. pap. 6.00 (*0-15-202371-2*, Voyager Bks) Harcourt.

— Zero to Sixty: A Motorcycle Journey Through Midlife. Stearns, Michael, ed. 224p. 1999. pap. text 12.00 (*0-15-100478-1*) Harcourt.

Paulsen, Gary. Zero to Sixty: The Motorcycle Journey of a Lifetime. 224p. (C). 1999. pap. 12.00 (*0-15-600704-5*) Harcourt.

Paulsen, Gary & Burks, Brian. Murphy's Ambush. large type ed. LC 95-20828. (Western Ser.). 175p. 1995. 17.95 (*0-7862-0518-0*) Thorndike Pr.

— Murphy's Stand. large type ed. LC 93-48427. (Western Ser.). 177p. 1994. lib. bdg. 19.95 (*0-7862-0169-X*) Thorndike Pr.

— Murphy's Trail. 1996. 18.95 (*0-8027-4154-1*) Walker & Co.

— Murphy's Trail. large type ed. LC 96-38779. 208p. 1997. 18.95 (*0-7862-0899-6*) Thorndike Pr.

Paulsen, Gary & Distribution Media. Dogsong. (J). 1986. 21.33 incl. audio (*0-676-31628-X*) Ballantine Pub Grp.

Paulsen, Gary, et al. Hatchet/Robinson Crusoe: Curriculum Unit. (Novel Ser.). 79p. (YA). (gr. 9-12). 1996. spiral bd. 18.95 (*1-56077-457-6*) Ctr Learning.

Paulsen, George E. A Living Wage for the Forgotten Man: The Quest for Fair Labor Standards, 1933-1941. LC 96-17806. 232p. 1996. 37.00 (*0-945636-91-1*) Susquehanna U Pr.

Paulsen, Jim, pref. Quality Upstream: Quality Concepts Conference & Exposition, 1992. (Illus.). 1992. 50.00 (*1-56378-009-7*) ESD.

Paulsen, Joanna, jt. auth. see Hill, Grace Livingston.

Paulsen, Karl. Video & Media Servers: Technology & Applications. LC 98-10222. 457p. 1998. pap. text 42.95 (*0-240-80296-9*, Focal) Buttrwrth-Heinemann.

Paulsen, Kathryn. The Complete Book of Magic & Witchcraft. 1970. mass mkt. 5.99 (*0-451-16832-1*, E92712, Sig) NAL.

***Paulsen, Lyle.** Poetry. Kozachik, Ann, ed. 106p. 2000. pap. 10.00 (*0-9619354-2-1*) Victoria Productions.

Paulsen, Michael B. College Choice: Understanding Student Enrollment Behavior. Fife, Jonathan D., ed. LC 91-60267. (ASHE-ERIC Higher Education Reports: No. 90-6). 100p. 1990. pap. 24.00 (*1-878380-03-6*) GWU Grad Schl E&HD.

Paulsen, Michael B. & Feldman, Kenneth. Taking Teaching Seriously: Meeting the Challenge of Instructional Improvement. Fife, Jonathan D., ed. LC 96-76558. (ASHE-ERIC Higher Education Reports: No. 95-2). (Illus.). 188p. (Orig.). 1996. pap. 24.00 (*1-878380-66-4*) GWU Grad Schl E&HD.

Paulsen, Michael B., jt. ed. see Feldman, Kenneth A.

Paulsen, Michelle M. What Wells Up: Poems. LC 96-53098. 64p. 1997. pap. 14.95 (*0-7734-2713-9*, Mellen Poetry Pr) E Mellen.

Paulsen, Norman D. The Christ Consciousness: The Pure Self Within You. (Illus.). 496p. (Orig.). 1994. pap. 19.95 (*0-941848-05-1*) Builders Pub.

Paulsen, Norman D. The Sacred Science of Meditation, Transformation, Illumination, Vol. 1. (Illus.). 168p. Date not set. text. write for info. (*0-941848-07-8*) Builders Pub.

Paulsen, P. Dictionary of Production Engineering: Metal Forming, German/English/French. 2nd ed. (ENG, FRE & GER.). 400p. 1996. 295.00 (*0-7859-9534-X*) Fr & Eur.

Paulsen, P., jt. ed. see C. I. R. P. Staff.

Paulsen, Paulsen. Father Water, Mother Water. (J). 1995. mass mkt. 6.99 (*0-440-91088-9*) BDD Bks Young Read.

Paulsen, Richard A. The Role of U. S. Nuclear Weapons in the Post-Cold War Era. (Illus.). 208p. 1994. pap. 23.00 (*1-58566-055-8*) Air Univ.

Paulsen, S. K. Rainbow Slide: Kowanda Kids. (Illus.). 20p. (J). (ps-2). 1994. pap. 3.95 (*0-9638163-2-2*) Hisel Bk Ends.

Paulsen, Thomas D., jt. auth. see Mack, William P.

Paulsen, W., jt. ed. see Schirokauer, A.

Paulson, Alan, jt. auth. see Walter, Paulette.

Paulson, Alan C. Roadside History of Arkansas. McKenna, Gwen & Greer, Dan, eds. LC 98-14017. (Roadside History Ser.). (Illus.). 406p. 1998. 30.00 (*0-87842-334-6*); pap. 18.00 (*0-87842-335-4*) Mountain Pr.

Paulson, Alan C., jt. auth. see Walker, Paulette H.

***Paulson, Arthur C.** Realignment & Party Revival: Understanding American Electoral Politics at the Turn of the Twenty-first Century. LC 99-54877. 376p. 2000. 69.95 (*0-275-96865-0*, Praeger Pubs) Greenwood.

Paulson, Bonnie L., tr. see Kelsen, Hans.

Paulson, Boyd C., jt. auth. see Barrie, Donald S.

Paulson, Buck. Painting with Paulson. 947p. 1996. pap. 11.95 (*1-56770-343-7*) S Scheewe Pubns.

Paulson, C. Robert. Designing Dtv Facilities. 1999. 65.00 (*0-07-049453-3*) Datapro Res.

— Fiber Optic Technology & Applications in Image Transmission. 300p. 1991. 55.00 (*0-8493-7403-0*, CRC Reprint) Franklin.

Paulson, Carl & Janda, Louis. Rookie on Tour: The Education of a PGA Golfer. 272p. 1999. reprint ed. pap. 12.95 (*0-425-16688-0*) Berkley Pub.

Paulson, Carl & Janda, Louis H. Rookie on Tour: The Education of a PGA Golfer. LC 97-13408. 262p. 1998. 22.95 (*0-399-14378-5*, G P Putnam) Peng Put Young Read.

Paulson, Dale G. Allegiance: Fulfilling the Promise of One-to-One Marketing for Associations. LC 98-16695. (Illus.). xi, 78 p. 1998. pap. 24.95 (*0-88034-139-4*) Am Soc Assn Execs.

Paulson, Darryl S. Topical Antimicrobial Testing & Evaluation. LC 99-14707. (Illus.). 224p. 1999. text 145.00 (*0-8247-1957-3*) Dekker.

Paulson, Daryl S. Walking the Point: Male Initiation & the Vietnam Experience. LC 94-8249. 96p. (Orig.). 1995. pap. 8.95 (*0-942963-49-0*) Distinctive Pub.

Paulson, David, ed. see Hamilton, Donna.

Paulson, David F. Genitourinary Cancer I. 1982. text 199.50 (*90-247-2480-5*) Kluwer Academic.

Paulson, David F., ed. Genitourinary Surgery, Vol. 1. LC 83-18969. (Illus.). 422p. reprint ed. pap. 130.90 (*0-8357-4661-5*, 203759100001) Bks Demand.

— Prostatic Disorders. LC 88-9388. 397p. reprint ed. pap. 123.10 (*0-7837-2737-2*, 204311700006) Bks Demand.

Paulson, David F., jt. auth. see DeKernion, Jean B.

Paulson, Dennis. Shorebirds of the Pacific Northwest. LC 92-19050. (Illus.). 422p. 1998. pap. text 27.50 (*0-295-97706-X*) U of Wash Pr.

— Voices of Survival in the Nuclear Age. (Orig.). 1986. pap. text 12.95 (*0-86171-051-7*) Wisdom MA.

Paulson, Don & Simpson, Roger. An Evening at the Garden of Allah: A Gay Cabaret in Seattle. (Between Men - Between Women Ser.). (Illus.). 167p. 1996. 39.00 (*0-231-09698-4*) Col U Pr.

Paulson, Ed. The Complete Communications Handbook. 2nd ed. 296p. (Orig.). 1995. pap. 21.95 (*1-55622-476-1*) Wordware Pub.

***Paulson, Ed.** Complete Idiot's Guide to Starting Your Own Business. 3rd ed. (Complete Idiot's Guides (Lifestyle) Ser.). (Illus.). 384p. 2000. pap. text 18.95 (*0-02-863888-3*, Alpha Ref) Macmillan Gen Ref.

Paulson, Ed. Learn Lotus 1-2-3 Release 4 for Windows in a Day. LC 93-45769. (Popular Applications Ser.). (Illus.). 136p. 1994. pap. 15.95 incl. disk (*1-55622-408-7*) Wordware Pub.

— Learn Microsoft Exchange Server 5.5 Core Technologies. LC 97-44017. 1997. pap. 39.95 (*1-55622-601-2*) Wordware Pub.

— Learn Networking Essentials. 1999. pap. text 29.95 (*1-55622-645-4*) Wordware Pub.

***Paulson, Ed.** The Technology M&A Guidebook. 400p. 2000. 65.00 (*0-471-36010-4*) Wiley.

Paulson, Ed. Using CorelDraw. (Using... Ser.). (Illus.). 696p. (Orig.). 1993. 29.95 (*1-56529-124-7*) Que.

— Using CorelDRAW! 5.0. LC 94-66722. 1994. 39.99 (*1-56529-764-4*) Que.

Paulson, Ed & Layton, Marcia. Complete Idiot's Guide to Starting Your Own Business. 2nd ed. LC 98-84503. (Illus.). 418p. 1998. 18.95 (*0-02-861979-X*, Pub. by Macmillan Gen Ref) S&S Trade.

Paulson, Ed, jt. auth. see Easto, Larry.

Paulson, Gaylen D., jt. ed. see Roloff, Michael E.

Paulson, Gaylord D., et al, eds. Xenobiotic Conjugation Chemistry. LC 85-32553. (ACS Symposium Ser.: No. 299). (Illus.). x, 358p. 1986. 54.95 (*0-8412-0957-X*, Pub. by Am Chemical) OUP.

— Xenobiotic Conjugation Chemistry. LC 85-32553. (ACS Symposium Ser.: Vol. 299). 368p. 1986. reprint ed. pap. 114.10 (*0-608-03845-8*, 206429200008) Bks Demand.

— Xenobiotic Metabolism: In Vitro Methods: A Symposium. LC 79-789. (ACS Symposium Ser.: Vol. 97). 336p. 1979. reprint ed. pap. 104.20 (*0-608-03093-7*, 206354500007) Bks Demand.

— Xenobiotic Metabolism: In Vitro Studies. LC 79-789. (Symposium Ser.: No. 97). 1979. 37.95 (*0-8412-0486-1*) Am Chemical.

Paulson, Gaylord D. & Hutson, D. H., eds. Progress in Pesticide Biochemistry & Toxicology: The Mammalian Metabolism of Agrochemicals, Vol. 8, The Mammalian Metabolism of Agrochemicals. LC 83-647760. (Progress in Pesticide Biochemistry & Toxicology Ser.: Vol. 8). 384p. 1995. 275.00 (*0-471-95155-2*) Wiley.

***Paulson, Genevieve L.** Energy Focused Meditation: Body, Mind, Spirit. 224p. 2000. pap. 12.95 (*1-56718-512-6*) Llewellyn Pubns.

Paulson, Genevieve L. Kundalini & the Chakras: A Practical Manual - Evolution in This Lifetime. LC 90-27422. (New Age Ser.). (Illus.). 224p. (Orig.). 1999. pap. 14.95 (*0-87542-592-5*) Llewellyn Pubns.

— Meditation & Human Growth: A Practical Manual for Higher Consciousness. LC 93-42899. (New Age Ser.). (Illus.). 224p. 1999. pap. 12.95 (*0-87542-599-2*) Llewellyn Pubns.

Paulson, Genevieve L. & Paulson, Stephen J. Reincarnation: Remembering Past Lives. LC 97-20099. (Illus.). 224p. (Orig.). 1999. pap. 7.95 (*1-56718-511-8*, K-511-8) Llewellyn Pubns.

***Paulson, Genevieve Lewis & Paulson, Stephen J.** Chakras, Auras, & the New Spirit: A Complete Guide to Opening the Seven Senses. 2000. pap. 17.95 (*1-56718-513-4*) Llewellyn Pubns.

Paulson, George & Koller, William C., eds. Therapy of Parkinson's Disease. 2nd expanded rev. ed. (Neurological Disease & Therapy Ser.: No. 34). (Illus.). 632p. 1994. text 180.00 (*0-8247-9226-2*) Dekker.

Paulson, Gerald A. Wetlands & Water Quality: A Citizen's Handbook on How to Review & Comment on Section 404 Permits. 47p. 1985. 3.00 (*0-318-18950-X*) Lake Mich Fed.

Paulson, Ivar. Old Estonian Folk Religion. LC 76-63029. (Uralic & Altaic Ser.: Vol. 108). (Orig.). 1971. pap. text. write for info. (*0-87750-154-8*) Curzon Pr Ltd.

Paulson, J. Sig. To Humanity with Love. 2nd ed. LC 74-33594. (Illus.). 124p. 1982. reprint ed. pap. 6.95 (*0-87516-484-6*) DeVorss.

Paulson, Jana. An August Game: A Farm Alphabet. deluxe ed. (Set 1 Ser.: Vol. 4). (Illus.). 32p. (J). (ps-3). 1997. pap. 3.50 (*1-890567-03-5*) Berry Bks Ltd.

— The Making of Strawberry. deluxe ed. (Set 1 Ser.: Vol. 1). (Illus.). 20p. (J). (ps-3). 1997. pap. 2.50 (*1-890567-00-0*) Berry Bks Ltd.

***Paulson, Jane H.** Joy of Christmas. 2000. pap. 8.95 (*0-7407-1152-0*) Andrews & McMeel.

***Paulson, Jerome A.** Pediatrics: Review for USMLE, Step 1. Johnson, Kurt E., ed. (Illus.). 250p. 2000. pap. text (*1-888308-08-7*) J Majors Co.

Paulson, Joann. African Economies in Transition. LC 97-23323. 1999. text 79.95 (*0-312-17751-8*) St Martin.

***Paulson, Joann.** African Economies in Transition. LC 97-23323. 1999. text 79.95 (*0-312-17752-6*) St Martin.

Paulson, Johannes. Index Hesiodeus. 94p. 1972. reprint ed. write for info. (*0-318-70994-5*) G Olms Pubs.

Paulson, Joshua, tr. see Marcos, Subcomandante & David, Comandante.

Paulson, L. C. Logic & Computation: Interactive Proof with Cambridge LCF. (Tracts in Theoretical Computer Science Ser.: No. 2). 320p. 1987. text 69.95 (*0-521-34632-0*) Cambridge U Pr.

— Logic & Computation: Interactive Proof with Cambridge LCF. (Tracts in Theoretical Computer Science Ser.: No. 2). 316p. (C). 1990. pap. text 31.95 (*0-521-39560-7*) Cambridge U Pr.

— ML for the Working Programmer. 2nd ed. (Illus.). 494p. (C). 1996. text 80.00 (*0-521-57050-6*); pap. text 35.95 (*0-521-56543-X*) Cambridge U Pr.

Paulson, Lawrence C. Isabelle: A Generic Theorem Prover. Goos, G. & Hartmanis, J., eds. LC 94-3445. (Lecture Notes in Computer Science Ser.: Vol. 828). 1994. 50.95 (*0-387-58244-4*) Spr-Verlag.

***Paulson, Lucy H. & Van Den Pol, Rick.** Good Talking Words: A Social Communications Skills Program for Preschool & Kindergarten Classes. (Illus.). 104p. (J). (ps-k). 1998. pap. 65.00 (*1-57035-150-3*, 100TALKING) Sopris.

Paulson, Lynda R. & Watson, Tom. The Executive Persuader: How to Be a Powerful Speaker. Misuraca, Karen, ed. 192p. 1991. 19.95 (*0-9628039-6-0*) Success Strat.

Paulson, M. I. The Soulmate Millennium. unabridged ed. Wallis, Martha, ed. LC 84-9545. 277p. 1998. pap. 16.95 (*0-9669790-0-1*, 122030) Lava Reef.

Paulson, Michael G. A Critical Analysis of De La Fayette's "La Princesse De Cleves" As a Royal Novel: Kings, Queens, & Splendor. LC 91-31495. (Studies in French Literature: Vol. 13). 116p. 1991. lib. bdg. 59.95 (*0-7734-9740-4*) E Mellen.

— Facets of a Princess: Multiple Readings of Madame de la Fayette's "La Princesse de Cleves" LC 96-52151.

P

(Currents in Comparative Romance Languages & Literatures Ser.: Vol. 58). XIV, 133p. (C). 1998. text 38.95 (*0-8204-3780-8*) P Lang Pubng.
— The Possible Influence of Montaigne's Essais on Descartes' Treatise on the Passions. 138p. (Orig.). (C). 1988. lib. bdg. 38.00 (*0-8191-7027-5*) U Pr of Amer.
Paulson, Michael G. & Alvarez-Detrell, Tamara. Cervantes, Hardy, & "La Fuerza de la Sangre" 1985. 25.50 (*0-916379-13-2*) Scripta.
— A Critical Edition of Juan Bautista Diamante's "La Reina Maria Estuarda" 1990. 44.50 (*0-916379-64-7*) Scripta.
— Madame de la Fayette's The Princess of Cleves: A New Translation. 204p. (Orig.). (C). 1994. pap. text 35.00 (*0-8191-9732-7*) U Pr of Amer.
Paulson, Michael G., jt. ed. see Alvarez-Detrell, Tamara.
Paulson, Michael W. World Wide Web Site Development with Powerbuilder. 1997. pap. text 49.95 (*1-55622-608-X*) Wordware Pub.
Paulson, Moses, ed. Gastroenterologic Medicine. LC 67-29191. (Illus.). 1645p. reprint ed. pap. 200.00 (*0-8357-9404-0*, 201457500094) Bks Demand.
Paulson, Nancy. Fun-to-Learn Bible Lessons Preschool Vol. 1: 20 Easy-to-Use Programs. LC 93-35769. (Fun-to-Learn Ser.). 1993. 16.99 (*1-55945-263-3*) Group Pub.
— Fun-to-Learn Bible Lessons Preschool Vol. 2: 20 Easy-to-Use Programs. Woods, Paul, ed. (Fun-to-Learn Ser.). (Illus.). 96p. 1995. pap. 16.99 (*1-55945-602-7*) Group Pub.
Paulson, Paul L. Guide to Russian Silver Hallmarks. 1976. pap. 18.00 (*0-685-82101-3*) Quaker.
Paulson, R. Lee. Embracing the Beast: Breaking Free from Anger. LC 98-41474. (Illus.). 224p. 1999. pap. 14.95 (*0-89407-146-7*) Strawberry Hill.
Paulson, Rachael P. Johnny & the Old Oak Tree: A Message about Paper Recycling. (Hands on the World Environmental Ser.). (Illus.). 40p. (Orig.). (J). (gr. k-3). 1994. pap. 9.95 (*0-9642296-0-9*) Crestmont Pubng.
— Sir Johnny's Recycling Adventure: Symbols for Paper Recycling. Hutto, Jackie, ed. LC 99-93535. (Hands on the World Environmental Ser.: Vol. II). (Illus.). 42p. (Orig.). (J). (ps-3). 1999. pap. 9.95 (*0-9642296-2-5*) Crestmont Pubng.
Paulson, Richard J. & Sachs, Judith. Rewinding Your Biological Clock: Motherhood Late in Life. LC 98-36837. 288p. 1998. text 23.95 (*0-7167-3303-X*) W H Freeman.
***Paulson, Richard J. & Sachs, Judith.** Rewinding Your Biological Clock: Motherhood Late in Life. (Illus.). 352p. 2000. pap. text 14.95 (*0-7167-3964-X*) W H Freeman.
Paulson, Richard W. National Water Summary, 1988-89: Hydrologic Events & Floods & Droughts. 601p. 1992. per. 52.00 (*0-16-061614-X*) USGPO.
Paulson, Robert J., jt. auth. see Rippley, LaVern J.
Paulson, Roland. Valley of the Skunk: The Story of a Haven. Ayers, Jim, ed. LC 96-69428. (Illus.). 230p. (Orig.). 1996. pap. 13.95 (*0-88100-091-4*) Natl Writ Pr.
Paulson, Ronald. The Beautiful, Novel, & Strange: Aesthetics & Heterodoxy. (Illus.). 304p. 1995. text 39.95 (*0-8018-5171-8*) Johns Hopkins.
— Book & Painting: Shakespeare, Milton, & the Bible: Literary Texts & the Emergence of English Painting. LC 82-2769. (Hodges Lectures). (Illus.). 248p. 1982. reprint ed. pap. 76.90 (*0-608-07984-7*, 206794900012) Bks Demand.
— Breaking & Remaking: Aesthetic Practice in England, 1700-1820. (Illus.). 363p. (Orig.). (C). 1993. reprint ed. pap. text 19.00 (*0-8135-1440-1*) Rutgers U Pr.
— Don Quixote in England: The Aesthetics of Laughter. LC 97-19114. (Illus.). 320p. 1997. text 35.00 (*0-8018-5695-7*) Johns Hopkins.
— Figure & Abstraction in Contemporary Painting. LC 90-31079. (Illus.). 300p. 1990. 44.95 (*0-8135-1604-8*) Rutgers U Pr.
— Hogarth Vol. 1: The Modern Moral Subject, 1697-1732. LC 90-24569. (Illus.). 552p. (C). 1991. pap. 24.95 (*0-8135-1695-1*); text 65.00 (*0-8135-1694-3*) Rutgers U Pr.
— Hogarth, Vol. III: Art & Politics, 1750-1764. LC 90-24569. (Illus.). 680p. (C). 1993. text 70.00 (*0-8135-1698-6*); pap. text 24.95 (*0-8135-1699-4*) Rutgers U Pr.
— Hogarth, Vol. 2: High Art & Low, 1732-1750. LC 90-24569. (Illus.). 550p. (C). 1992. text 65.00 (*0-8135-1696-X*); pap. text 24.95 (*0-8135-1697-8*) Rutgers U Pr.
— Hogarth's Graphic Works: Catalogue Raisonne. (Illus.). 476p. 1989. 250.00 (*1-55660-804-7*) A Wofsy Fine Arts.
***Paulson, Ronald.** The Life of Henry Fielding. LC 99-43635. (Critical Biographies Ser.). 368p. 2000. 54.95 (*0-631-19146-1*) Blackwell Pubs.
Paulson, Ronald, ed. see Hargarth, William.
Paulson, Ronald, ed. see Hogarth, William.
Paulson, Ross E. Language, Science, & Action: Korzybski's General Semantics--A Study in Comparative Intellectual History, 9. LC 83-5490. (Contributions in Intercultural & Comparative Studies: No. 9). (Illus.). 163p. 1983. 49.95 (*0-313-23732-8*, PAL/) Greenwood.
— Liberty, Equality & Justice: Civil Rights, Women's Rights & the Regulation of Business, 1865-1932. LC 96-53409. 361p. 1997. pap. text 18.95 (*0-8223-1991-8*); lib. bdg. 54.95 (*0-8223-1982-9*) Duke.
Paulson, Ross E., ed. see Jackson, Gregory L.
Paulson, Sally, jt. auth. see Kegley, Melanie.
Paulson, Sean D., jt. auth. see Paulson, Terry.
Paulson, Sean D., jt. auth. see Paulson, Terry L.
Paulson, Stanley L., ed. Normativity & Norms: Critical Perspectives on Kelsenian Themes. 682p. 1999. text 120.00 (*0-19-876315-8*) OUP.
Paulson, Stanley L., tr. see Kelsen, Hans.
Paulson, Stephen J., jt. auth. see Paulson, Genevieve L.
Paulson, Stephen J., jt. auth. see Paulson, Genevieve Lewis.
***Paulson Sternlight, Phyllis.** Journey to the Dark Edge of Time. (Illus.). 29p. (J). (gr. 4-7). 1999. 9.95 (*0-9673505-0-6*) P P Sternlight.
Paulson, Steven K., jt. auth. see Baker, Eugene, III.
Paulson, Suzanne M. William Trevor: A Study of the Short Fiction. LC 93-16606. (Studies in Short Fiction: No. 48). 160p. 1993. 23.95 (*0-8057-0858-8*) Macmillan.
Paulson, Terry. 50 Tips for Speaking Like a Pro. LC 98-73859. (Illus.). 80p. 2000. pap. 9.95 (*1-56052-532-0*, Pub. by Crisp Pubns) Natl Bk Netwk.
— Paulson on Change. (Distilled Wisdom Ser.). 160p. (Orig.). 1995. pap. 12.95 (*1-882180-49-6*) Griffin CA.
Paulson, Terry & Paulson, Sean D. Can I Have the Keys to the Car? How Teens & Parents Can Talk about Things That Really Matter. LC 98-53703. 128 p. 1999. pap. 12.99 (*0-8066-3836-2*, 9-3836, Augsburg) Augsburg Fortress.
Paulson, Terry, jt. auth. see Crisp, Michael G.
Paulson, Terry, jt. ed. see Sanborn, Mark.
Paulson, Terry L. They Shoot Managers, Don't They? Making Conflict Work in a Changing World. 156p. 1991. reprint ed. pap. 11.95 (*0-89815-429-4*) Ten Speed Pr.
— They Shoot Managers, Don't They? Managing Yourself & Leading Others in a Changing World. (Illus.). 156p. (Orig.). pap. 10.95 (*0-939007-15-0*) Canter & Assocs.
Paulson, Terry L. & Paulson, Sean D. Secrets of Life Every Teen Needs to Know. LC 90-63405. (Illus.). 160p. (Orig.). (YA). (gr. 7-12). 1990. pap. 6.95 (*0-939513-42-0*) Joy Pub SJC.
Paulson, Thelma. Remi-Nissen. (Illus.). 304p. (Orig.). 1996. pap. 16.95 (*0-9653934-0-2*) Access Midwest.
Paulson, Tim. The Beanstalk Incident. (Upside Down Tales Ser.). (Illus.). (J). 1992. pap. 8.95 (*0-8065-1313-6*, Citadel Pr) Carol Pub Group.
— Days of Sorrow, Years of Glory, 1831-1850: From the Nat Turner Revolt to the Fugitive Slave Law (1831-1850) LC 93-40851. (YA). (gr. 5 up). 1994. pap. 8.95 (*0-7910-2689-2*) Chelsea Hse.
— Harleys, Popes, & Indian Chiefs: Unfinished Business of the Sixties. 1995. 17.98 (*0-7858-0409-9*) Bk Sales Inc.
— Jack & the Beanstalk. (Upside Down Tales Ser.). (Illus.). (J). (ps-2). 1990. 12.95 (*1-55972-048-4*, Birch Ln Pr) Carol Pub Group.
***Paulson, Tim.** Rainforest ABC. LC 99-37501. 2001. write for info. (*1-890817-44-9*) Winslow Pr.
Paulson, William. Sentimental Education: The Complexity of Disenchantment. (Masterwork Studies: No. 85). 160p. (C). 1992. 23.95 (*0-8057-9428-X*); pap. 13.95 (*0-8057-8568-X*) Macmillan.
Paulson, William, ed. Les Genres de l'Henaurme Siecle. LC 81-50963. (Michigan Romance Studies: Vol. 9). 142p. 1989. pap. 15.00 (*0-939730-08-1*) Mich Romance.
Paulson, William, tr. see Serres, Michael.
Paulson, William, tr. see Serres, Michel.
Paulson, William R. Enlightenment, Romanticism, & the Blind in France. LC 87-2274. 270p. 1987. reprint ed. pap. 83.70 (*0-608-07167-6*, 206739200009) Bks Demand.
— The Noise of Culture: Literary Texts in a World of Information. LC 87-47822. 208p. 1988. text 37.50 (*0-8014-2102-0*) Cornell U Pr.
Paulsson, Martin. The Social Anxieties of Progressive Reform: Atlantic City, 1854-1920. LC 93-47416. (American Social Experience Ser.). (Illus.). 245p. (C). 1994. text 47.50 (*0-8147-6620-X*) NYU Pr.
— The Social Anxieties of Progressive Reform: Atlantic City, 1854-1920. (Illus.). 245p. (C). 1996. pap. text 20.00 (*0-8147-6643-9*) NYU Pr.
Paulston, Christina B. Linguistics & Communicative Competence: Topics in ESL. (Multilingual Matters Ser.: No. 85). 160p. 1992. 74.95 (*1-85359-149-1*, Pub. by Multilingual Matters); pap. 29.95 (*1-85359-148-3*, Pub. by Multilingual Matters) Taylor & Francis.
— Sociolinguistic Perspectives on Bilingual Education. (Multilingual Matters Ser.: No. 84). 180p. 1992. 84.95 (*1-85359-147-5*, Pub. by Multilingual Matters); pap. 34.95 (*1-85359-146-7*, Pub. by Multilingual Matters) Taylor & Francis.
Paulston, Christina B., ed. International Handbook of Bilingualism & Bilingual Education. LC 87-263. 614p. 1988. lib. bdg. 145.00 (*0-313-24484-7*, PIB/, Greenwood Pr) Greenwood.
Paulston, Christina B. & Peckham, Donald. Linguistic Minorities in Central & Eastern Europe. LC 98-6230. (Multilingual Matters Ser.: Vol. 109). 289p. 1998. 59.00 (*1-85359-416-4*) Multilingual Matters.
Paulston, Christina B. & Tucker, G. Richard, eds. The Early Days of Sociolinguistics: Memories & Reflections. LC 97-69165. (Publications in Sociolinguistics: Vol. 2). 400p. 1997. pap. 37.00 (*1-55671-022-4*) S I L Intl.
Paulston, Christina B., et al. Writing: Communicative Activities in English. (Illus.). 288p. (C). 1983. pap. text 14.00 (*0-13-970277-6*) P-H.
Paulston, Christina Bratt. Linguistic Minorities in Multilingual Settings: Implications for Language Policies. LC 93-44796. (Studies in Bilingualism: No. 4). xi, 136p. 1994. pap. 19.95 (*1-55619-540-0*); lib. bdg. 39.00 (*1-55619-347-5*) J Benjamins Pubng Co.
Paulston, Rolland. Social Cartography: Mapping Ways of Seeing Social & Educational Change. Beauchamp, Edward R., ed. LC 96-22198. (Garland Reference Library of Social Science: Vol. 1024). (Illus.). 480p. 1996. text 80.00 (*0-8153-1994-0*) Garland.
Paulston, Rolland G., ed. Non-Formal Education: An Annotated International Bibliography. LC 72-186197. (Special Studies in International Economics & Development). 1972. 42.50 (*0-275-28623-1*) Irvington.
Paulte, Francois. Renoir. (Classic Art Ser.). 1988. 9.98 (*0-671-09412-2*) S&S Trade.
Paulu, Burton. British Broadcasting in Transition. LC 61-8399. 260p. reprint ed. pap. 80.60 (*0-8357-7418-X*, 205589600039) Bks Demand.
— Radio & Television Broadcasting in Eastern Europe. LC 74-79505. 604p. reprint ed. pap. 187.30 (*0-608-15973-5*, 203328000084) Bks Demand.
— Television & Radio in the United Kingdom. LC 80-20870. 490p. reprint ed. pap. 151.90 (*0-7837-2927-8*, 205752700006) Bks Demand.
Paulu, Nancy. Helping Your Child Get Ready for School: With Activities for Children from Birth Through Age 5. Greene, Wilma P., ed. (Illus.). 56p. (Orig.). (C). 1993. pap. text 15.00 (*0-7881-0041-6*) DIANE Pub.
— Helping Your Child with Homework: For Parents of Elementary & Junior High School-Aged Children. Perkinson, Kathryn, ed. (Illus.). 44p. 1999. reprint ed. pap. text 10.00 (*0-7881-7858-X*) DIANE Pub.
***Paulu, Nancy.** Helping Your Students with Homework: A Guide for Teachers. 49p. 1998. per. 5.00 (*0-16-049436-2*) USGPO.
Paulu, Nancy. Improving Math & Science Assessment: Report on the Secretary's 3rd Conference on Mathematics & Science Education. 47p. (Orig.). (C). 1994. pap. text 30.00 (*0-7881-1579-0*) DIANE Pub.
Paulu, Nancy. Improving Mathematics & Science Assessment: Report on the Secretary's Third Conference on Mathematics & Science Education. 53p. 1994. pap. 2.50 (*0-16-045061-6*) USGPO.
Paulu, Nancy & Martin, Margery, eds. Helping Your Child Learn Science. LC 92-40108. 60p. 1993. pap. text 12.95 (*0-8412-2626-1*, Pub. by Am Chemical) OUP.
Paulukonis, Mary A. Partners in Preparation: Training Married Couples for Marriage Preparation Ministry. 112p. (Orig.). 1995. pap. 29.95 (*0-8146-2285-2*, Liturg Pr Bks) Liturgical Pr.
***Paulus.** Applied Pattern Recognition. (C). 1999. text 70.00 (*3-528-15558-2*) Harcourt.
***Paulus, et al.** Effective Human Relations: A Guide to People at Work. 4th ed. LC 99-34613. 492p. 1999. 74.00 (*0-205-29333-6*) Allyn.
Paulus, Ingeborg. Search for Pure Food: A Sociology of Legislation in Britain. (Law in Society Ser.). 144p. 1974. 19.95 (*0-85520-076-6*) W S Hein.
Paulus, Aggie. The Feasibility of Ecological Taxation. 313p. 1995. pap. 74.00 (*90-6215-502-2*, Pub. by Maklu Uitgevr) Gaunt.
Paulus, Christiane. Interreligiose Praxis Postmodern: Eine Untersuchung Muslimisch-Christlicher Ehen in der Brd. 306p. 1998. 51.95 (*3-631-34260-8*) P Lang Pubng.
Paulus, David A., et al. Gas Monitoring in Clinical Practice. 2nd rev. ed. LC 94-32851. (Illus.). 225p. 1994. pap. text 49.50 (*0-7506-9445-9*) Buttrwrth-Heinemann.
Paulus, Gerhard. Foxpro. (C). 1991. text. write for info. (*0-201-55949-8*) Addison-Wesley.
Paulus, Harold E., jt. ed. see Famaey, J. P.
Paulus, Jorg. Der Enthusiast und Sein Schatten: Literarische Schwarmer-und Philisterkritik im Roman um 1800. 382p. 1998. 120.00 (*3-11-015908-2*) De Gruyter.
Paulus, P. B. Prison Crowding: A Psychological Perspective. (Research in Criminology Ser.). (Illus.). 105p. 1988. 96.95 (*0-387-96650-1*) Spr-Verlag.
Paulus, P. B., ed. Basic Group Processes. (Psychology Ser.). (Illus.). 356p. 1983. 64.00 (*0-387-90862-5*) Spr-Verlag.
Paulus, Paul B. Psychology of Group Influence. 2nd ed. 456p. (C). 1989. pap. 36.00 (*0-8058-0545-1*); text 79.95 (*0-8058-0445-5*) L Erlbaum Assocs.
Paulus, Paul B., ed. Psychology of Group Influence. 2nd ed. LC 88-36616. (Illus.). 460p. 1989. pap. 142.60 (*0-608-05186-1*, 206572300001) Bks Demand.
Paulus, Paul B., et al. Effective Human Relations: A Guide to People at Work. 3rd ed. (C). 1995. teacher ed. write for info. (*0-205-16687-3*, H6687-1) Allyn.
Paulus, Stefan. Nostradamus: Quien Sobrevivira? LC 97-48469. (ENG & SPA.). 312p. 1999. pap. text 9.95 (*1-56718-516-9*) Llewellyn Pubns.
— Nostradamus, 1999: Who Will Survive? Rojas, Edgar, ed. LC 96-20696. 304p. (Orig.). 1996. pap. 14.95 (*1-56718-515-0*) Llewellyn Pubns.
Paulus, T. J., jt. auth. see Pierce, J. F.
Paulus, Trina. Esperanza para las Flores. Landsness, Ruthanne N. & Prucha, David J., trs.Tr. of Hope for the Flowers. (SPA.). 160p. 1992. pap. 9.95 (*0-8091-3369-5*) Paulist Pr.
— Hope for the Flowers. LC 74-179985. (Illus.). 160p. 1972. 14.95 (*0-8091-0174-2*); pap. 9.95 (*0-8091-1754-1*) Paulist Pr.
— Hope for the Flowers. 1997. pap. text 19.95 incl. audio (*0-8091-8249-1*) Paulist Pr.
***Paulus, W., ed.** Transcranial Magnetic Stimulation. LC 99-36369. (Supplements to Electroencephalography & Clinical Neurophysiology Ser.: Vol. 50). 386p. 1999. 193.00 (*0-444-50070-7*) Elsevier.
Paulus, Wilfried. Microbicides for the Protection of Materials: A Handbook. LC 92-31479. 1993. write for info. (*1-85166-949-3*) Elsevier.
Pauluzzi, Faust, tr. see Sandri, Giovanna.
Pauly. An Analysis of Medical Savings Accounts: Do Two Wrongs Make a Right? 50p. (Orig.). 1994. pap. 9.95 (*0-8447-7027-2*) Am Enterprise.
Pauly, et al. Responsible National Health Insurance. 50p. (Orig.). (C). 1992. pap. 9.75 (*0-8447-7014-0*) Am Enterprise.
Pauly, A. F. & Wissowa, G. Realencyclopaedie der Classischen Altertumswissenschaft, 68 vols & 15 suppl. vols. write for info. (*3-476-00826-6*) Adlers Foreign Bks.
Pauly, Daniel. Fish Population Dynamics in Tropical Waters: A Manual for Use with Programmable Calculators. (ICLARM Studies & Reviews: No. 8). (Illus.). 325p. 1984. pap. 25.00 (*971-10-2204-4*, Pub. by ICLARM) Intl Spec Bk.
— Growth, Mortality & Recruitment of Commercially Important Fishes & Penaeid Shrimps in Indonesian Waters. (ICLARM Technical Reports: No. 17). 91p. 1986. pap. 8.50 (*971-10-2226-5*, Pub. by ICLARM) Intl Spec Bk.
— Theory & Management of Tropical Multispecies Stock: A Review, with Emphasis on the Southeast Asian Demersal Fisheries. (ICLARM Studies & Reviews: No. 1). (Illus.). 35p. 1983. pap. text 6.50 (*0-89955-398-2*, Pub. by ICLARM) Intl Spec Bk.
Pauly, Daniel, et al, eds. Atlas Demographique des Populations de Poissons d'Eau Douce d'Afrique. (ICLARM Technical Reports: No. 45). 140p. 1995. per. write for info. (*971-8709-65-7*, Pub. by ICLARM) Intl Spec Bk.
— Peruvian Upwelling Ecosystem: Dynamics & Interactions. 438p. 1989. pap. 27.00 (*971-10-2247-8*, Pub. by ICLARM) Intl Spec Bk.
— The Third International Symposium on Tilapia in Aquaculture. (ICLARM Conference Proceedings Ser.: No. 41). 400p. Date not set. per. 37.00 (*971-8709-42-8*, Pub. by ICLARM) Intl Spec Bk.
Pauly, Daniel & Christensen, V., eds. Trophic Models of Aquatic Ecosystems. (ICLARM Conference Proceedings Ser.: No. 26). 390p. 1995. per. 32.00 (*971-10-2284-2*, Pub. by ICLARM) Intl Spec Bk.
Pauly, Daniel & Martosubroto, P., eds. The Fish Resources of Western Indonesia: A Baseline Study of Biodiversity. (ICLARM Studies & Reviews: No. 23). 1995. write for info. (*971-8709-48-7*, Pub. by ICLARM) Intl Spec Bk.
Pauly, Daniel & Mines, Antonio N., eds. Small-Scale Fisheries of San Miguel Bay, Philippines: Biology & Stock Assessment. (ICLARM Technical Reports: No. 7). (Illus.). 124p. (Orig.). 1983. pap. 16.00 (*0-89955-394-X*, Pub. by ICLARM) Intl Spec Bk.
Pauly, Daniel & Morgan, G. R., eds. Length-Based Methods in Fisheries Research. (Conference Proceedings Ser.: No. 13). 1986. text 32.50 (*971-10-2228-1*, Pub. by ICLARM) Intl Spec Bk.
Pauly, Daniel & Tsukayama, I., eds. The Peruvian Anchoveta & Its Upwelling Ecosystem: Three Decades of Change. (ICLARM Studies & Reviews: No. 15). 351p. 1987. 36.00 (*971-10-2234-6*, Pub. by ICLARM) Intl Spec Bk.
Pauly, Daniel & Wade-Pauly, Sandra. An Annotated Bibliography of Slipmouths: Pisces: Leiognathidae. (Bibliographies Ser.: No. 2). 62p. (Orig.). 1983. pap. 7.00 (*0-89955-374-5*, Pub. by ICLARM) Intl Spec Bk.
Pauly, Daniel, et al. Small-Scale Fisheries of San Miguel Bay, Philippines: Options for Management & Research. (ICLARM Technical Reports: No. 11). 80p. 1983. per. write for info. (*971-10-2208-7*, Pub. by ICLARM) Intl Spec Bk.
Pauly, Daniel, jt. auth. see Inglese, Jose.
Pauly, Daniel, jt. ed. see Longhurst, Alan R.
Pauly, Daniel, jt. ed. see Thia-Eng, Chua.
Pauly, Daniel, tr. see Peters, Hans M.
Pauly, Daniele. Le Corbusier: The Chapel at Ronchamp. LC 97-35543. (Corbusier Guides Ser.). (GER & ITA., Illus.). 138p. 1997. pap. 16.95 (*3-7643-5759-2*, Pub. by Birkhauser) Princeton Arch.
Pauly, Edward, et al. Homegrown Lessons: Innovative Programs Linking School & Work. (Education Ser.). 359p. 1995. text 32.95 (*0-7879-0074-5*) Jossey-Bass.
Pauly, Edward S., jt. auth. see Gueron, Judith M.
***Pauly, Hans.** Atom, Molecule & Cluster Beams: Basic Theory, Production & Detection of Thermal Energy Beams. LC 00-38829. (Series in Atomic, Molecular, Optical & Plasma Physics: Vol. 28). (Illus.). xii, 348p. 2000. 82.00 (*3-540-66945-0*) Spr-Verlag.
Pauly, Louis M. Who Elected the Bankers? Surveillance & Control in the World Economy. LC 96-45087. (Cornell Studies in Political Economy). 176p. 1996. text 39.95 (*0-8014-3322-3*) Cornell U Pr.
Pauly, Louis W. Opening Financial Markets: Banking Politics on the Pacific Rim. LC 88-47740. (Cornell Studies in Political Economy). 280p. 1988. 42.50 (*0-8014-2080-6*) Cornell U Pr.
— Opening Financial Markets: Banking Politics on the Pacific Rim. LC 88-47740. (Cornell Studies in Political Economy). (Illus.). 280p. 1990. reprint ed. pap. text 17.95 (*0-8014-9928-3*) Cornell U Pr.
— Who Elected the Bankers? Surveillance & Control in the World Economy. LC 96-45087. 200p. 1997. pap. text 16.95 (*0-8014-8375-1*) Cornell U Pr.
Pauly, Louis W., jt. ed. see Greven, Michael T.
Pauly, Mark V. Doctors & Their Workshops: Economic Models of Physician Behavior. LC 80-16112. (National Bureau of Economic Research Ser.). (Illus.). 144p. 1997. lib. bdg. 20.50 (*0-226-65044-8*) U Ch Pr.
— Doctors & Their Workshops: Economic Models of Physician Behavior. LC 80-16112. (National Bureau of Economic Research Monograph Ser.). 142p. reprint ed. pap. 44.10 (*0-608-09031-X*, 206966600005) Bks Demand.
— Health Benefits at Work: An Economic & Political Analysis of Employment-Based Health Insurance. LC 97-18341. 200p. (C). 1997. text 42.50 (*0-472-10857-3*, 10857) U of Mich Pr.
***Pauly, Mark V.** Health Benefits at Work: An Economic & Political Analysis of Employment-Based Health Insurance. 200p. (C). 1999. pap. text 21.95 (*0-472-08644-8*, 08644) U of Mich Pr.
Pauly, Mark V., ed. National Health Insurance: What Now, What Later, What Never? LC 80-22761. (AEI Symposia Ser.: No. 80C). 399p. reprint ed. pap. 123.70 (*0-8357-4513-9*, 203737100008) Bks Demand.

P

Pauly, Mark V., et al, eds. Lessons from the First 20 Years of Medicare: Research Implications for Public & Private Sector Policy. LC 88-17368. (Health Economics, Health Management, & Health Policy Ser.). 412p. (C). 1989. text 45.00 (*0-8122-8118-7*) U of Pa Pr.
— Supplying Vaccines: An Economic Analysis of Critical Issues. LC 95-7993. 225p. (YA). (gr. 12). 1996. 99.00 (*90-5199-231-9*, 231-9) IOS Press.
***Pauly, Mark V. & Herring, Bradley.** Pooling Health Insurance Risks. LC 99-46267. 115p. 1999. 39.95 (*0-8447-4119-1*, Pub. by Am Enterprise); pap. 19.95 (*0-8447-4120-5*, Pub. by Am Enterprise) Pub Resources Inc.
Pauly, Mark V., jt. auth. see Finsinger, Jorg.
Pauly, Mark V., jt. auth. see Kunreuther, Howard K.
***Pauly, Philip J.** Biologists & the Promise of American Life: From Meriwether Lewis to Alfred Kinsey. LC 00-20896. (Illus.). 312p. 2000. 29.95 (*0-691-04977-7*) Princeton U Pr.
Pauly, Philip J. Controlling Life: Jacques Loeb & the Engineering Ideal in Biology. 1990. pap. 15.95 (*0-520-06974-9*, Pub. by U CA Pr) Cal Prin Full Svc.
Pauly, Rebecca M. Le Berceau et la Bibliotheque: Le Paradoxe de l'Ecriture Autobiographique. LC 89-84500. (Stanford French & Italian Studies: Vol. 62). (FRE.). 116p. 1989. pap. 56.50 (*0-915838-77-X*) Anma Libri.
— The Transparent Illusion: Image & Ideology in French Text & Film. LC 92-16539. (Art of Interpretation Ser.: Vol. 3). (FRE.). IX, 496p. (Orig.). (C). 1993. pap. text 41.95 (*0-8204-1930-3*) P Lang Pubng.
Pauly, Reinhard G. Music in Classic Period. 4th ed. LC 99-30849. 272p. 1999. pap. 39.20 (*0-13-011502-9*) P-H.
Pauly, Reinhard G., ed. see Eberlin, Johann E.
Pauly, Reinhard G., ed. see Haydn, Michael.
Pauly, Reinhard G., tr. see Dickreiter, Michael.
Pauly, Reinhard G., tr. see Fischer-Dieskau, Dietrich.
Pauly, Reinhard G., tr. see Kolneder, Walter.
Pauly, Reinhard G., tr. see Schlosser, Johann A.
Pauly, Thomas H., ed. see Watkins, Maurine A.
Paul, VI, pseud. For the Right Ordering & Development of Devotion to the Blessed Virgin Mary: Marialis Cultus. 56p. pap. 1.95 (*0-8198-1825-9*) Pauline Bks.
— Humanae Vitae. 2nd rev. ed. Calegari, Marc, tr. from LAT. 24p. 1983. pap. 1.95 (*0-89870-000-0*) Ignatius Pr.
Paul, VI, pseud. Humanae Vitae: A Challenge to Love. 57p. 1987. pap. 2.00 (*1-892875-01-2*, 3005, Remnant Israel) New Hope Publicatns.
Paul, VI, pseud. On Evangelization in the Modern World. 62p. 1976. pap. text 2.50 (*0-8198-2325-2*) Pauline Bks.
— On Evangelization in the Modern World. 70p. 1975. pap. 4.95 (*1-55586-129-6*) US Catholic.
— On the Development of Peoples: Populorum Progressio. 53p. 1967. pap. 1.95 (*0-8198-1824-0*) Pauline Bks.
— On the Development of Peoples: Populorum Progressio. 50p. 1987. 2.95 (*1-55586-260-8*) US Catholic.
— Paths of the Church: Ecclesiam Suam. 60p. 1964. pap. 2.25 (*0-8198-5855-2*) Pauline Bks.
Paumgartner, G., et al, eds. Bile Acids & Cholesterol in Health & Disease. 350p. 1983. text 217.50 (*0-85200-729-9*) Kluwer Academic.
— Bile Acids & Hepatobiliary Diseases - Basic Research & Clinical Application, Vol. 93. LC 97-188087. 352p. 1997. text 177.50 (*0-7923-8725-2*) Kluwer Academic.
— Bile Acids & the Liver. (Falk Ser.: No. 45). (C). 1987. text 227.50 (*0-85200-675-6*) Kluwer Academic.
— Bile Acids As Therapeutic Agents from Basic Science to Clinical Practice. (Falk Symposium Ser.). (C). 1991. text 243.00 (*0-7923-8954-9*) Kluwer Academic.
— Eterohepatic Circulation of Bile Acids & Sterol Metabolism. (Falk Ser.: No. 42). 1985. text 225.00 (*0-85200-905-4*) Kluwer Academic.
— Strategies for the Treatment of Hepatobiliary Disease. (Falk Symposium Ser.). (C). 1990. text 138.00 (*0-7923-8903-4*) Kluwer Academic.
— Trends in Bile Acid Research. (Falk Symposium Ser.). (C). 1989. lib. bdg. 173.00 (*0-7462-0112-5*) Kluwer Academic.
Paumgartner, G. & Beuers, U., eds. Bile Acids in Liver Diseases: Proceedings of the International Falk Workshop Held in Munich, Germany, January 26-27, 1995. LC 95-24717. 176p. (C). 1996. text 73.50 (*0-7923-8891-7*) Kluwer Academic.
Paumgartner, G., ed. see Falk Symposium Staff.
Paumier, Cyril, et al. Designing the Successful Downtown. LC 88-50773. 116p. 1988. 47.95 (*0-87420-681-2*, D53) Urban Land.
***Paun, G. & Salomaa, A., eds.** Grammatical Models of Multi-Agent Systems. 360p. 1998. text 70.00 (*90-5699-177-9*) Gordon & Breach.
Paun, G., jt. auth. see Dassow, J.
Paun, Gheorghe, ed. Mathematical Aspects of Natural & Formal Languages. LC 94-30230. (Series in Computer Science: Vol. 43). 500p. 1994. text 124.00 (*981-02-1914-8*) World Scientific Pub.
Paun, Gheorghe, et al, eds. New Trends in Formal Languages: Control, Cooperation, & Combinatorics, Vol. 121. LC 97-12652. (Lecture Notes in Computer Science Ser.: No. 1218). ix, 465p. 1997. pap. 73.00 (*3-540-62844-4*) Spr-Verlag.
Paun, Gheorghe, et al. DNA Computing: New Computing Paradigms. Brauer, W., ed. LC 98-18927. (Texts in Theoretical Computer Science. An EATCS Ser.). xiii, 396p. 1998. 59.95 (*3-540-64196-3*) Spr-Verlag.
***Pauncz, Ruben.** The Construction of Spin Eigenfunctions: An Exercise Book. LC 00-35240. 2000. write for info. (*0-306-46400-4*) Plenum.
Pauncz, Ruben. The Symmetric Group in Quantum Chemistry. 352p. 1995. boxed set 139.95 (*0-8493-8291-2*, 8291) CRC Pr.
Pauncz, Ruben, ed. Spin Eigenfunctions: Construction & Use. LC 78-27632. (Illus.). 386p. 1979. 95.00 (*0-306-40141-X*, Plenum Trade) Perseus Pubng.
Paungger, Johanna & Poppe, Thomas. Moon Time: The Art of Harmony with Nature & Lunar Cycles. (Illus.). 187p. 1995. pap. 19.95 (*0-85207-284-8*, Pub. by C W Daniel) Natl Bk Netwk.
Paunnger, Johanna. Moon Time: The Art of Harmony with Nature & Lunar Cycles. pap. 23.95 (*0-8464-4881-5*) Beekman Pubs.
Paunovic, M., et al, eds. Fundamental Aspects of Electrochemical Deposition & Dissolution Including Modeling. LC 99-161348. (Proceedings Ser.: Vol. 97-27). 1998. 108.00 (*1-56677-180-3*) Electrochem Soc.
— Proceedings of the Symposium on Electrochemical Deposited Thin Films. LC 93-70064. (Proceedings Ser.: Vol. 93-26). 426p. 1993. 60.00 (*1-56677-061-0*) Electrochem Soc.
Paunovic, M. & Scherson, D. A., eds. Electrochemically Deposited Thin Films, No. III. LC 97-152280. (Proceedings Ser.: Vol. 96-19). (Illus.). 310p. 1997. 53.00 (*1-56677-169-2*) Electrochem Soc.
***Paunovic, Milan & Schlesinger, Mordechay.** Fundamentals of Electrochemical Deposition. LC 98-16435. (Electrochemical Society Ser.). 312p. 1998. 74.95 (*0-471-16820-3*, Wiley-Interscience) Wiley.
Paunovic, Milan, ed. see Symposium on Electrochemically Deposited Thin Film.
Paunovic, Milan, ed. see Symposium on Electroless Deposition of Metals & Al.
Paup, Bryce. What's Important Now. LC 97-37871. 200p. 1997. pap. 11.99 (*1-57673-249-5*) Multnomah Pubs.
***Paup, Donald C. & Fernhall, Bo.** Skills, Drills & Strategies for Badminton. Pellett, Tracy L. & Blackman, Claudia, eds. LC 99-56784. (Teach, Coach, Play Ser.). (Illus.). 128p. (C). 1999. pap. 15.00 (*1-890871-12-5*) Holcomb Hath.
Paupert, M.L. Saved! A Guide to Success with Your Shelter Dog. LC 97-7744. (Illus.). 168p. 1997. pap. 9.95 (*0-7641-0062-9*) Barron.
Pauphilet, Albert. Aucassin et Nicolette. 171p. 1971. 9.95 (*0-8288-7472-7*) Fr & Eur.
Pauplis, Mary. Heritage Cooking from the Kitchen of Mary Pauplis. 200p. (Orig.). 1993. pap. write for info. (*0-9635383-0-6*) M Pauplis.
— Heritage Cooking from the Kitchen of Mary Pauplis. rev. ed. LC 94-92169. 200p. (Orig.). 1994. pap. text. write for info. (*0-9635383-1-4*) M Pauplis.
***Paupp, Terrence Edward.** Achieving Inclusionary Governance: Advancing Peace & Developments in First & Third World Nations. (Innovation in International Law Ser.). 400p. 2000. 115.00 (*1-57105-136-8*) Transnatl Pubs.
Paur, Leo. How to Teach Your Children to Say No to Drugs: And Keep Their Friends. 126p. 1992. 12.95 (*0-929753-00-3*) Paramount Bks.
Paur, Sandra O. & Page, Levon B. Topics in Finite Mathematics. 286p. (C). 1996. text 18.00 (*0-536-59640-9*) Pearson Custom.
Pauri, Massimo, jt. auth. see Agazzi, Evandro.
Paus, Susanne. Die Erdflechtenvegetation Nordwestdeutschlands und Einiger Randgebiete: Vegeationsokologische Untersuchungen Unter Besonderer Berucksichtigung des Chemismus Ausgewahlter Arten. (Bibliotheca Lichenologica Ser.: Vol. 66). (Illus.). 222p. 1997. 76.70 (*3-443-58045-9*, Pub. by Gebruder Borntraeger) Balogh.
Pausacker, Jenny. Get a Life. (Livewire Ser.). (YA). (gr. 6-9). pap. 7.95 (*0-7043-4925-6*, Pub. by Womens Press) Trafalgar.
— Getting Somewhere LC 96-175220. 233 p. 1995. write for info. (*1-86330-344-8*) Mdrin Au.
Pausanias. Guide to Greece, Vol. 1. rev. ed. Levi, Peter, tr. & intro. by. (Classics Ser.). (Illus.). 592p. 1984. pap. 14.95 (*0-14-044225-1*, Penguin Classics) Viking Penguin.
***Pausanias.** Pausanias: Travel & Memory in Roman Greece. Alcock, Susan E. & Elsner, Jas, eds. (Illus.). 384p. 2000. text 65.00 (*0-19-512816-8*) OUP.
Pausch, Eberhard M. Wahrheit Zwischen Erschlossenheit und Verantwortung: Die Rezeption und Transformation der Wahrheitskonzeption Martin Heideggers in der Theologie Rudolf Bultmanns. (Theologische Bibliothek Toepelmann Ser.: Bd. 64). (GER.). 380p. (C). 1994. lib. bdg. 136.95 (*3-11-014230-9*) De Gruyter.
Pausch, Georg. Journal of Captain Pausch, Chief of the Hanau Artillery During the Burgoyne Campaign. Stone, William L., tr. LC 79-140876. (Eyewitness Accounts of the American Revolution Ser.). 1971. reprint ed. 24.05 (*0-405-01200-4*) Ayer.
Pausch, Lois M., jt. ed. see Anderson, Nancy D.
Pause, Anette, tr. see Gildemeister, Heide.
Pause, C. A., jt. auth. see Shoukri, M. M.
Pause, Michael, jt. auth. see Clark, Roger H.
Pauser, Alice. Creative Herb Cookery. (Illus.). 1998. pap. 10.95 (*0-9664478-0-8*) Gryphon Gardens.
Pausewang, Gudrun. Final Journey. Crampton, Patricia, tr. LC 98-16338. 160p. (YA). (gr. 7-12). 1998. pap. 4.99 (*0-14-130164-X*, PuffinBks) Peng Put Young Read.
— Final Journey. LC 96-219334. 153p. (J). (gr. 7-12). 1996. 15.99 (*0-670-86456-0*) Viking Penguin.
Pausewang, Siegfried, jt. ed. see Zegeye, Abebe.
Paust, Brian C. Fishing for Octopus: A Guide for Commercial Fishermen. (Report Ser.: No. 88-03). (Illus.). 50p. 1988. pap. 5.00 (*1-56612-042-X*) AK Sea Grant CP.
***Paust, Brian C.** Fishing for Octopus: A Guide for Commercial Fishermen. (Illus.). 51p. 1999. reprint ed. pap. text 20.00 (*0-7881-8548-9*) DIANE Pub.
Paust, Brian C. & RaLonde, Raymond. Guidelines for Shellfish Farming in Alaska. (Aquaculture Note Ser.: Vol. 16). 21p. 1997. pap. 4.00 (*1-56612-050-0*) AK Sea Grant CP.
Paust, Brian C., jt. auth. see Crapo, Chuck.
Paust, Brian C., jt. auth. see RaLonde, R.
Paust, Jordan L., jt. ed. see Bassiouni, M. Cherif.
Paustenbach. Health Risk Assessment. 544p. write for info. (*0-471-14747-8*) Wiley.
Paustenbach, Dennis J., ed. The Risk Assessment of Environmental & Human Health Hazards: Textbook of Case Studies. LC 87-35056. 1184p. 1989. 235.00 (*0-471-84998-7*) Wiley.
Paustian, Henry. Listen! God Is Speaking to You! God's Word for Seniors. LC 92-50172. 205p. (Orig.). 1992. pap. 10.99 (*0-8100-0431-3*, 06N0694) Northwest Pub.
Paustian, Paul W. Canal Irrigation in the Punjab. LC 68-58614. (Columbia University. Studies in the Social Sciences: No. 322). reprint ed. 20.00 (*0-404-51322-0*) AMS Pr.
Paustovsky, Konstantin. Magic Ringlet. pap. 5.00 (*0-201-09277-8*) Addison-Wesley.
Pautet, Marie-Bernadette, jt. auth. see Mouly, Michel.
Pautler, Albert J., Jr., ed. High School to Employment Transition: Contemporary Issues. LC 93-86908. 300p. (Orig.). 1993. pap. 19.50 (*0-911168-88-5*) Prakken.
***Pautler, Albert J., Jr., ed.** Workforce Education: Issues for the New Century. LC 99-70241. 312p. 1999. pap. text 21.95 (*0-911168-95-8*) Prakken.
Pautler, Albert J. & Buffamanti, Deborah M., eds. Winning Ways: Best Practices in Work-Based Learning. 240p. 1997. pap. text 18.95 (*0-911168-94-X*) Prakken.
Pautler, Albert J., jt. auth. see Sugarman, Michael N.
Pautz, Otto. Muhammeds Lehre von der Offenbarung Quellenmassig Untersucht. 304p. reprint ed. write for info. (*0-318-71550-3*) G Olms Pubs.
Pautz, Patrick C., jt. auth. see Adorno, Rolena.
Pautz, Peter D., jt. ed. see Cramer, Kathryn D.
Pauw, B. A. The Second Generation. (Xhosa in Town Ser.). 1973. pap. 15.95 (*0-19-570028-7*) OUP.
Pauw, Berthold A. Religion in a Tswana Chiefdom. LC 85-21881. (Illus.). 258p. 1985. reprint ed. lib. bdg. 95.00 (*0-313-24974-1*, PRTC, Greenwood Pr) Greenwood.
Pauw, John W. De, see De Pauw, John W.
Pauw, Linda Grant De, see Grant De Pauw, Linda.
Pauwee, Theresia, jt. auth. see Gilkerson, Linda.
Pauwels, A. F. Immigrant Dialects & Language Maintenance in Australia: The Cases of the Limburg & Swabia Dialects. (Topics in Sociolinguistics Ser.). 149p. 1986. pap. 42.35 (*90-6765-140-0*) Mouton.
Pauwels, Anne. Cross-Cultural Communication in the Health Sciences: Communicating with Migrant Patients. 206p. 1996. 59.95 (*0-7329-2953-9*, Pub. by Macmill Educ); pap. 29.95 (*0-7329-2954-7*, Pub. by Macmill Educ) Paul & Co Pubs.
— Women Changing Language. LC 97-41151. (Real Language Ser.). 1998. pap. text 64.50 (*0-582-09961-7*) Longman.
Pauwels, Brian E., jt. ed. see Harvey, John.
***Pauwels, Colleen Kristl, et al.** Legal Research: Traditional Sources, New Technologies. LC 99-70205. 97p. 1999. pap. 12.00 (*0-87367-814-1*) Phi Delta Kappa.
Pauwels, E. K. Bone Scintigraphy. 224p. 1981. text 154.00 (*90-6021-476-5*) Kluwer Academic.
Pauwels, F. Atlas: The Biomechanics of the Normal & Diseased Hip. Furlong, R. J. & Maguet, P., trs. from GER. LC 75-31723. (Illus.). 280p. 1976. 287.00 (*0-387-07428-7*) Spr-Verlag.
— Biomechanics of the Locomotor Apparatus. (Illus.). 520p. 1980. 308.00 (*0-387-09131-9*) Spr-Verlag.
Pauwels, Heidi R. Krsna's Round Dance Reconsidered: Hariram Vyas's Hindi Ras-pancadhyayi. (SOAS London Studies on South Asia: No. 12). (Illus.). 220p. (C). 1996. text 40.00 (*0-7007-0426-4*, Pub. by Curzon Pr Ltd) UH Pr.
Pauwels, Jacques R. Women, Nazis, & Universities: Female University Students in the Third Reich, 1933-1945, 50. LC 83-20161. (Contributions in Women's Studies: No. 50). (Illus.). 206p. 1984. 55.00 (*0-313-24203-8*, PWU/, Greenwood Pr) Greenwood.
Pauwels, L. Nzayilu N'ti: Guide des Arbres et Arbustes de la Region de Kinshasa-Brazzaville. (Scripta Botanica Belgica Ser.: Vol. 4). (Illus.). 495p. 1992. 57.00 (*90-72619-10-2*, Pub. by Natl Botanic Grdn Belgium) Balogh.
Pauwels, Louis. Blumroch l'Admirable ou le Dejeuner du Surhomme. (FRE.). 1978. pap. 10.95 (*0-7859-4104-5*) Fr & Eur.
Pauwels, Louis & Bergier, Jacques. Eternal Man. LC 74-188065. 238 p. 1973. write for info. (*0-583-12246-9*) Grfton HrprCllns.
— Eternal Man. LC 73-176568. 246p. 1972. write for info. (*0-285-62057-6*) Souvenir Pr Ltd.
Pauwels, Romain & O'Byrne, Paul M., eds. Beta2-agonists in Asthma Treatment. LC 97-11742. (Lung Biology in Health & Disease Ser.). (Illus.). 472p. 1997. text 180.00 (*0-8247-9496-6*) Dekker.
***Pauwelussen, J. P., ed.** Vehicle Performance: Understanding Human Monitoring & Assessment. 256p. 1999. 87.00 (*90-265-1542-1*) Swets.
Pauwelussen, J. P. & Pacejka, Hans B., eds. Smart Vehicles. xii, 472p. 1995. 104.00 (*90-265-1456-5*) Swets.
Pava, Calvin H. Managing New Office Technology: An Organizational Strategy. LC 83-47519. 224p. (C). 1984. 32.95 (*0-02-924970-8*) Free Pr.
Pava, Moses L. Business Ethics: A Jewish Perspective. LC 97-2737. (Library of Jewish Law & Ethics Ser.). x, 206p. 1997. 25.00 (*0-88125-582-3*) Ktav.
— Search for Meaning in Organizations: Seven Practical Questions for Ethical Managers. LC 99-10407. 176p. 1999. 55.00 (*1-56720-201-2*, Quorum Bks) Greenwood.
Pava, Moses L. & Krausz, Joshua. Corporate Responsibility & Financial Performance: The Paradox of Social Cost. LC 94-45284. 192p. 1995. 57.95 (*0-89930-921-6*, Quorum Bks) Greenwood.
Pava, Moses L. & Levine, Aaron. Jewish Business Ethics: The Firm & Its Stakeholder. LC 98-36490. 2000. 40.00 (*0-7657-6056-8*) Aronson.
Pava, Moses L., jt. auth. see Epstein, Marc J.
Pavalko, Ronald M. Risky Business: America's Fascination with Gambling. LC 98-30872. 220p. (C). 1999. pap. text 36.95 (*0-8304-1526-2*) Thomson Learn.
Pavaloi, Margareta, jt. auth. see Kalter, Johannes.
Pavalon, Eugene I. Human Rights & Health Care Law. LC 80-67574. 250p. reprint ed. pap. 77.50 (*0-608-13465-1*, 201999700016) Bks Demand.
Pavalon, Eugene I., jt. auth. see Inlander, Charles B.
Pavan, Barbara N., jt. auth. see Anderson, Robert.
Pavan-Langston, Deborah. Handbook of Ocular Drug Therapy & Ocular Side Effects of Systemic Drugs. 1990. 42.95 (*0-316-69545-9*, Little Brwn Med Div) Lppncott W & W.
— Manual Ocular, No. 3. 1991. 10.95 (*0-316-69548-3*, Little Brwn Med Div) Lppncott W & W.
— Manual of Ocular Diagnosis & Therapy. 2nd ed. 494p. 1985. 24.50 (*0-316-69544-0*, Little Brwn Med Div) Lppncott W & W.
— Manual of Ocular Diagnosis for Asia. 1995. 32.95 (*0-316-69560-2*) Little.
Pavan, Marcella, jt. auth. see Markandya, Anil.
***Pavan, Shanthi & Tsividis, Yannis.** High Frequency Continuous Time Filters in Digital Cmos Processes. LC 99-86383. 2000. write for info. (*0-7923-7773-7*) Kluwer Academic.
Pavao, Joyce M. The Family of Adoption. LC 97-52346. 138p. 1998. 22.00 (*0-8070-2800-2*) Beacon Pr.
Pavao, Joyce Maguire. The Family of Adoption. LC 97-52346. 160p. 1999. pap. 14.00 (*0-8070-2801-0*) Beacon Pr.
Pavarala, Vinod. Interpreting Corruption: Elite Perspectives in India. LC 96-12244. 232p. 1996. 32.00 (*0-8039-9311-0*) Sage.
Pavarin, Franco. Fold-&-Fly Paper Airplanes. LC 98-18288. (Illus.). 80p. (J). 1998. 19.95 (*0-8069-4257-6*) Sterling.
— Fold-&-Fly Paper Airplanes. (Illus.). 80p. (J). (gr. 3-7). 1998. pap. 12.95 (*0-8069-4836-1*) Sterling.
Pavarini, Peter A., ed. United States Health Care Laws & Rules. 1700p. 1995. 75.00 (*0-314-06827-9*) Am Hlth Lawyers.
***Pavarini, Stefano.** Kengo Kuma: Geometries of Nature. (Illus.). 2000. pap. text 25.00 (*88-7838-068-7*) L'Arca IT.
Pavarotti, Adua & Dallas, Wendy. Pavarotti: Life with Luciano. (Illus.). 159p. 1998. reprint ed. text 35.00 (*0-7881-5200-9*) DIANE Pub.
***Pavarotti, Luciano & Wright, William.** Pavarotti: My World. (Illus.). 345p. 1999. reprint ed. pap. text 15.00 (*0-7881-6793-6*) DIANE Pub.
Pavaskar, Madhav. Saga of the Cotton Exchange. 1985. 18.00 (*0-8364-1405-5*, Pub. by Popular Prakashan) S Asia.
Pavaux, Jacques, ed. Air Transport: Horizon 2020: Key Factors & Future Prospects. (Illus.). 219p. 1996. pap. 49.00 (*2-908537-14-1*, Pub. by Inst Air Transport) Bks Intl VA.
Pavek, Gary, ed. A Guide to the Mind. 378p. 1988. pap. 19.95 (*0-275-93010-6*, B3010, Praeger Pubs) Greenwood.
Pavel, D. Michael. American Indians & Alaskan Natives in Postsecondary Education. LC 98-221867. (Education Department Publication Ser.: Vol. 98-291). (Illus.). 426p. 1998. pap. 33.00 (*0-16-049804-X*) USGPO.
Pavel, D. Michael. Characteristics of American Indian & Alaska Native Education: Results from the 1990-91 & 1993-94 Schools & Staffing Surveys. LC 97-176941. 288p. 1997. per. 21.00 (*0-16-049001-4*) USGPO.
Pavel, L., tr. see Klein, Melanie.
Pavel, Margaret M., jt. auth. see Herbert, Anne.
Pavel, Marilyn. Emergency Exit. (Illus.). 41p. (Orig.). 1988. pap. 7.95 (*0-317-91297-6*) Entrprs Pub.
Pavel, Misha, jt. auth. see Gaylord, Richard J.
Pavel, Monique. Fundamentals of Pattern Recognition. 2nd ed. (Pure & Applied Mathematics Ser.: Vol. 174). (Illus.). 272p. 1993. text 135.00 (*0-8247-8883-4*) Dekker.
Pavel, N. H. Nonlinear Evolution Operators & Semigroups. (Lecture Notes in Mathematics Ser.: Vol. 1260). 285p. 1987. 43.95 (*0-387-17974-7*) Spr-Verlag.
Pavel, N. H., jt. auth. see Motreanu, D.
Pavel, Nicolae H., ed. Optimal Control of Differential Equations. (Lecture Notes in Pure & Applied Mathematics Ser.: Vol. 160). (Illus.). 352p. 1994. pap. text 145.00 (*0-8247-9234-3*) Dekker.
Pavel, Ota. How I Came to Know Fish. Badal, Jindriska & McDowell, Robert, trs. from CZE. LC 90-21045. 160p. 1991. reprint ed. pap. 9.95 (*0-8112-1165-7*, NDP713, Pub. by New Directions) Norton.
— How I Came to Know Fish. 2nd ed. Badal, Jindriska & McDowell, Robert, trs. from CZE. 156p. 1990. 16.95 (*0-934257-41-8*) Story Line.
Pavel, Paraschiva, jt. auth. see Micula, Gheorghe.
Pavel, Thomas G. Fictional Worlds. 192p. 1986. 28.00 (*0-674-29965-5*) HUP.
— Fictional Worlds. 192p. 1989. reprint ed. pap. 15.00 (*0-674-29966-3*) HUP.
— The Poetics of Plot: The Case of English Renaissance Drama. LC 84-15663. (Theory & History of Literature Ser.: Vol. 18). 192p. 1985. pap. 14.95 (*0-8166-1375-3*) U of Minn Pr.

P

An Asterisk (*) at the beginning of an entry indicates that the title is appearing for the first time.

Pavela, Gary. The Dismissal of Students with Mental Disorders: Legal Issues, Policy Considerations & Alternative Responses. Gehring, Donald D. & Parker, D. Young, eds. LC 85-13227. (Higher Education Administration Ser.). 108p. 1994. pap. 18.95 (*0-912557-01-X*) Coll Admin Pubns.

Pavelec, Barry J., jt. auth. see Diclerico, James M.

Pavelek, Diane A., ed. see Pavelek, Michael D., 2nd.

***Pavelek, Michael D., 2nd.** A Circuit Hike of the Susquehannock Trail System. Pavelek, Diane A., ed. (Hiking in Pennsylvania Ser.). (Illus.). 170p. 2000. pap. 12.00 (*0-9677503-1-8*) M D Pavelek.

— End to End on the Horse-Shoe Trail. (Hiking in Pennsylvania Ser.: Vol. 1). (Illus.). 188p. 2000. pap. 12.00 (*0-9677503-0-X*) M D Pavelek.

Pavelich, Matt. Beasts of the Forest, Beasts of the Field. 1990. pap. 12.00 (*0-937669-43-1*) Owl Creek Pr.

Pavelich, Matt. Beasts of the Forest, Beasts of the Field. 1990. 22.00 (*0-937669-44-X*) Owl Creek Pr.

Pavelich, Michael J., jt. auth. see Abraham, Michael R.

***Pavelka, Ed.** Bicycling Magazine's Cycling for Women. rev. ed. LC 99-39466. (Illus.). 128p. 1999. pap. 9.95 (*1-57954-169-0*) Rodale Pr Inc.

— Bicycling Magazine's Nutrition for Peak Performance. 2000. pap. 9.95 (*1-57954-252-2*) Rodale Pr Inc.

— Bicycling Magazine's Training Techniques for Cycling. rev. ed. LC 99-36497. (Illus.). 128p. 1999. pap. 9.95 (*1-57954-168-2*) Rodale Pr Inc.

***Pavelka, Ed, ed.** Bicycling Magazine's Basic Maintanence & Repair. rev. ed. LC 99-35338. 128p. 1999. pap. 9.95 (*1-57954-170-4*) Rodale Pr Inc.

— Bicycling Magazine's Cycling for Health & Fitness. rev. ed. LC 99-56769. (Illus.). 128p. 2000. pap. 9.95 (*1-57954-228-X*) Rodale Pr Inc.

— Bicycling Magazine's Mountain Biking Skills. 2000. pap. 9.95 (*1-57954-250-6*) Rodale Pr Inc.

— Bicycling Magazine's New Cyclist Handbook. 2000. pap. 9.95 (*1-57954-251-4*) Rodale Pr Inc.

— Bicycling Magazine's 900 All-Time Best Tips. rev. ed. LC 99-56768. (Illus.). 128p. 2000. pap. 9.95 (*1-57954-227-1*) Rodale Pr Inc.

Pavelka, Ed, jt. auth. see Burke, Edmund R.

Pavelka, Ed, jt. auth. see Overend, Ned.

***Pavelka, J., et al, eds.** SOFSEM'99: Theory & Practice of Informatics: Proceedings of the 26th Conference on Current Trends in Theory & Practice of Informatics, Milovy, Czech Republic, November 27-December 4, 1999. LC 99-57421. (Lecture Notes in Computer Science Ser.: Vol. 1725). xiii, 498p. 1999. pap. 79.00 (*3-540-66694-X*) Spr-Verlag.

Pavelka, M. Functional Morphology of the Golgi Apparatus. (Advances in Anatomy, Embryology & Cell Biology Ser.: Vol. 106). (Illus.). 100p. 1987. 73.95 (*0-387-18062-1*) Spr-Verlag.

***Pavelka, Patricia.** Create Independent Learners: Teacher-Tested Strategies for All Ability Levels. LC 99-72218. (Illus.). 158p. 1999. pap. 19.95 (*1-884548-24-5*, 5741, Crystal Spgs) Soc Dev Educ.

Pavelka, Patricia. Making the Connection Vol. 1: Learning Skills Through Literature: K-2. Sumner, Deborah, ed. (Illus.). 136p. 1995. pap., teacher ed. 17.95 (*1-884548-03-2*) Soc Dev Educ.

— Making the Connection Vol. 2: Learning Skills Through Literature (3-6) Fredenburg, Aldene, ed. LC 95-71328. (Illus.). 132p. (Orig.). 1997. pap., teacher ed. 17.95 (*1-884548-11-3*, 5022) Soc Dev Educ.

Pavelko, Virginia & Scott, L. B. Five Little Speckled Frogs Big Book: Black & White Nellie Edge I Can Read & Sing Big Book. (Illus.). (J). (ps-2). 1988. pap. text 21.00 (*0-922053-05-7*) N Edge Res.

Pavella, M. & Murthy, P. G. Transient Stability of Power Systems: Theory & Practice. LC 93-32934. 420p. 1994. 295.00 (*0-471-94213-8*) Wiley.

Paven-Langston, Deborah, ed. Manual of Ocular Diagnosis & Therapy. 4th ed. LC 95-31695. 506p. 1995. spiral bd. 35.95 (*0-316-69534-3*, Little Brwn Med Div) Lppncott W & W.

Paver, Chloe E. M. Narrative & Fantasy in the Post-War German Novel: A Study of Novels by Johnson, Frisch, Wolf, Becker & Grass. LC 98-37706. 239p. 1999. text 70.00 (*0-19-815965-X*) OUP.

Paver, William & Wan, Yiping. Postsecondary Institutions of the People's Republic of China: A Comprehensive Guide to Institutions of Higher Education in China. (World Education Ser.). 627p. (Orig.). 1992. pap. text 50.00 (*0-929851-11-0*) Am Assn Coll Registrars.

Paves-Yashinsky, Palomba, tr. see Zola, Emile.

Pavese. Uniform Commercial Code, Official Text with Comments. 1995. text 26.95 (*0-314-08647-1*) West Pub.

Pavese, Cesare. Among Women Only. Paige, D. D., tr. from ITA. 168p. 1979. 24.00 (*0-7206-0350-1*) Dufour.

— Among Women Only. 168p. 1996. pap. 14.95 (*0-7206-1005-2*, Pub. by P Owen Ltd) Dufour.

— Among Women Only. Paige, D. D., tr. from ITA. LC 97-176577. 198p. 1997. pap. 14.95 (*0-7206-1030-3*, Pub. by P Owen Ltd) Dufour.

— The Devil in the Hills. 1978. 26.00 (*0-7206-2795-8*) Dufour.

— Dialogues with Leuco. Arrowsmith, William, tr. from ITA. LC 89-83807. 201p. 1989. 17.95 (*0-941419-38-X*, Eridanos Library) Marsilio Pubs.

— House on the Hill. Strachan, W. J., tr. from ITA. 1977. 25.00 (*0-7206-4286-8*) Dufour.

— La Luna e i Falo. Musa, Mark, ed. LC 68-13431. (ITA., Illus.). (C). 1968. pap. text 6.95 (*0-89197-281-1*) Irvington.

— La Luna e i Falo. Thompson, Doug, ed. 240p. 1995. text 19.95 (*0-7190-4383-2*, Pub. by Manchester Univ Pr) St Martin.

— Le Metier de Vivre, 2 vols., 1. 1977. pap. 10.95 (*0-7859-4082-0*) Fr & Eur.

— Le Metier de Vivre, 2 vols., 2. 1977. pap. 10.95 (*0-685-68142-4*) Fr & Eur.

— Political Prisoner. Strachan, W. J., tr. 237p. 1969. reprint ed. 28.00 (*0-7206-6202-8*) Dufour.

— Selected Letters 1924 to 1950. Murch, A. E., tr. from ITA. 1969. 30.00 (*0-7206-1520-8*) Dufour.

— Stories. Murch, A. E., tr. from ITA. & intro. by. 415p. 1987. pap. 12.95 (*0-88001-124-6*) HarpC.

Pavese, Edith M. & Henry, Judith. TV Mania: A Timeline of Television. LC 98-6423. (Illus.). 144p. 1998. 12.95 (*0-8109-3892-8*, Pub. by Abrams) Time Warner.

Pavese, F. & Molinar, G. Modern Gas-Based Temperature & Pressure Measurements. (International Cryogenics Monographs). (Illus.). 544p. (C). 1992. text 130.00 (*0-306-44167-5*, Kluwer Plenum) Kluwer Academic.

Pavese, Mike. Federal Civil Judicial Procedure & Rules. 985p. 1993. pap. text. write for info. (*0-314-02238-4*) West Pub.

— Federal Criminal Code & Rules. 1277p. 1993. pap. text. write for info. (*0-314-02236-8*) West Pub.

Pavese, Monica, jt. ed. see Thomasson, Bengt E.

Pavese, Phyllis, ed. see Sanford, Charles W., Jr.

Pavesi, Stepano. Stepano Pavesi: Dies Irae Concertato. Longyear, Rey M., ed. (Recent Researches in Music of the Nineties Ser.: Vol. RRN25). (Illus.). xix, 183p. 1998. pap. 65.00 (*0-89579-401-2*) A-R Eds.

Pavesic, David V. Cost Controls: 25 Keys to Profitable Success. LC 98-39300. (Restaurant Manager's Pocket Handbook Ser.). 96p. 1999. pap. 12.95 (*0-86730-751-X*, Pub. by Lebhar Friedman) Natl Bk Netwk.

— Food Cost: 25 Keys to Profitable Success. LC 98-39301. (Restaurant Manager's Pocket Handbook Ser.). 96p. 1999. pap. 12.95 (*0-86730-755-2*, Pub. by Lebhar Friedman) Natl Bk Netwk.

— Fundamental Principles of Restaurant Cost. LC 97-34435. 292p. (C). 1997. pap. text 64.00 (*0-13-747999-9*) P-H.

— Labor Cost: 25 Keys to Profitable Success. LC 98-39299. (Restaurant Manager's Pocket Handbook Ser.). 96p. 1999. pap. 12.95 (*0-86730-753-6*, Pub. by Lebhar Friedman) Natl Bk Netwk.

— Menu Design: 25 Keys to Profitable Success. LC 98-39303. (Restaurant Manager's Pocket Handbook Ser.). 96p. 1999. pap. 12.95 (*0-86730-754-4*, Pub. by Lebhar Friedman) Natl Bk Netwk.

— Menu Pricing: 25 Keys to Profitable Success. LC 98-39304. (Restaurant Manager's Pocket Handbook Ser.). 96p. 1999. pap. 12.95 (*0-86730-752-8*, Pub. by Lebhar Friedman) Natl Bk Netwk.

— Purchasing & Inventory: 25 Keys to Profitable Success. LC 98-39302. (Restaurant Manager's Pocket Handbook Ser.). 96p. 1999. pap. 12.95 (*0-86730-756-0*, Pub. by Lebhar Friedman) Natl Bk Netwk.

Pavesic, David V., jt. auth. see Miller, Jack E.

Pavesic, Max G. & Studebaker, William. Backtracking: Ancient Art of Southern Idaho. (Illus.). 84p. (Orig.). 1993. pap. 19.95 (*0-939696-00-2*) Idaho Mus Nat Hist.

Pavetto, Carl S. The Business Manager's Guide to Controlling Legal Costs. LC 89-90688. (Business Managers Ser.: Vol. 1). (Orig.). 1989. pap. 7.95 (*0-925997-00-5*) CSP Assocs Inc.

Pavey, Graham. Start to Plant: Container Gardens. 1996. 7.98 (*0-7858-0368-8*) Bk Sales Inc.

— Start to Plant: Flower Gardens. 1996. 7.98 (*0-7858-0366-1*) Bk Sales Inc.

— Start to Plant: Herb Garden. 1996. 7.98 (*0-7858-0458-7*) Bk Sales Inc.

— Start to Plant: Rock & Alping Gardens. 48p. 1996. 7.98 (*0-7858-0369-6*) Bk Sales Inc.

Pavey, N. L. Guide to Legionellosis Temperature Measurements for Hot & Cold Water Service. 77p. (C). 1994. pap. 60.00 (*0-86022-366-3*, Pub. by Build Servs Info Assn) St Mut.

Pavey, N. L. Ionisation Water Treatment for Hot & Cold Water Services. 1996. pap. 100.00 (*0-86022-438-4*, Pub. by Build Servs Info Assn) St Mut.

Pavey, N. L. Rules of Thumb. 1995. pap. 100.00 (*0-86022-419-8*, Pub. by Build Servs Info Assn) St Mut.

Pavey, N. L. & Crampton, P. Rules of Thumb UK-Italy. 1995. pap. 100.00 (*0-86022-421-X*, Pub. by Build Servs Info Assn) St Mut.

***Pavey, N. L. & Ropert, M.** Chlorine Dioxide Water Treatment - For Hot & Cold Water Services. 1998. 100.00 (*0-86022-486-4*, Pub. by Build Servs Info Assn) St Mut.

Pavey, N. L., jt. auth. see Compton, P.

Pavey, Roger D. O. F. Harmon: A Reluctant Hero. LC 99-71020. (Illus.). 201p. 2000. 30.00 (*0-9654976-3-1*) Vermil.

Pavey, Shawn C. Talking to Shadows. 40p. 1998. pap. 5.00 (*0-9663293-1-7*) Main St Rag.

***Pavfernov, E. A. & Zaikov, G. E.** Biometals & Ligands for Anti Cancer Drug Design: Molecular Mechanisms of Superoxide Dimutase Models Antitumer Effects. 1998. text 89.00 (*1-56072-542-7*) Nova Sci Pubs.

***Pavia.** Introduction to Organic Laboratory Techniques: A Microscale Approach. 3rd ed. 1999. text 90.00 (*0-03-026566-5*) SCP.

Pavia. Organic Lab Techniques: Small-Scale Approach. LC 97-19525. (Saunders Golden Sunburst Ser.). (Illus.). 976p. (C). 1997. text 84.00 (*0-03-024519-2*, Pub. by SCP) Harcourt.

Pavia, Audrey. Andalusian Spirit. (Spirit of the Horse Ser.: No. 2). (Illus.). 64p. 2001. pap. 16.95 (*1-889540-26-9*) Bowtie Press.

— Appaloosa Spirit. LC 97-32192. (Spirit of the Horse Ser.). (Illus.). 64p. 1998. pap. 16.95 (*1-889540-15-3*) Bowtie Press.

— Careers with Dogs. LC 98-13029. (Illus.). 112p. 1998. pap. 8.95 (*0-7641-0503-5*) Barron.

— The Gecko. LC 98-35546. (Owner's Guide to a Happy, Healthy Pet Ser.). (Illus.). 128p. 1998. 9.95 (*0-87605-212-X*) Howell Bks.

— Guide to Owning a Keeshond. 64p. 1998. pap. text 6.95 (*0-7938-1889-3*, RE339) TFH Pubns.

— The Guinea Pig: An Owner's Guide to a Happy, Healthy Pet. LC 97-198262. (Illus.). 128p. 1997. 12.95 (*0-87605-527-7*) Howell Bks.

***Pavia, Audrey.** Labrador Retriever Handbook. (Pet Handbks.). (Illus.). 2000. pap. text 9.95 (*0-7641-1530-8*) Barron.

Pavia, Audrey. Morgan Spirit. (Spirit of the Horse Ser.: No. 1). (Illus.). 64p. 2001. pap. 16.95 (*1-889540-19-6*) Bowtie Press.

— Paint Spirit. LC 97-32167. (Spirit of the Horse Ser.). (Illus.). 64p. 1998. pap. 16.95 (*1-889540-21-8*) Bowtie Press.

— Saddlebred Spirit. (Spirit of the Horse Ser.: No. 4). (Illus.). 64p. 2001. pap. 16.95 (*1-889540-24-2*) Bowtie Press.

***Pavia, Audrey.** Your German Shepherd's Life. LC 99-35890. (Your ...'s Life Ser.). (Illus.). 294p. 1999. pap. 14.99 (*0-7615-2052-X*) Prima Pub.

Pavia, Audrey & Critter Press Staff. Rabbits in Your Life. LC 97-31097. 1997. write for info. (*0-87605-436-X*) Howell Bks.

Pavia, Audrey & Posnikoff, D.V.M, Janice. Horses for Dummies. (For Dummies Ser.). 384p. 1999. pap. 19.99 (*0-7645-5138-8*, Dummies Trade Pr) IDG Bks.

Pavia, C., jt. auth. see Sempe, M.

Pavia, Donald L. Introduction to Organ Lab Technician. (C). 1990. pap. text, teacher ed. 34.00 (*0-03-025419-1*) Harcourt Coll Pubs.

— Introduction to Organic Lab Techniques. 4th ed. (C). 1912. text 63.50 (*0-03-006234-9*); pap. text, teacher ed. 12.00 (*0-03-006237-3*) Harcourt.

— Introduction to Organic Laboratory Techniques. 2nd ed. (C). 1995. text 87.50 (*0-03-006232-2*, Pub. by Harcourt Coll Pubs) Harcourt.

— Introduction to Organic Laboratory Technology. 3rd ed. (C). 1988. pap. text, teacher ed. 20.75 (*0-03-014814-6*) Harcourt Coll Pubs.

— Introduction to Spectroscopy. 2nd ed. LC 95-71401. (C). 1995. text 51.00 (*0-03-058427-2*) Harcourt Coll Pubs.

— Organic Chemistry. (C). 1999. text 47.50 (*0-03-063986-7*) Harcourt Coll Pubs.

— Spectroscopy. 2nd ed. (C). 1995. pap. text, teacher ed. 26.75 (*0-03-058428-0*) Harcourt Coll Pubs.

Pavia, Donald L., et al. Introduction to Organic Lab Techniques: A Microscale Approach. 650p. (C). 1990. text 86.00 (*0-03-025418-3*) SCP.

— Introduction to Organic Laboratory Techniques, a Microscale Approach. 3rd ed. LC 97-87955. (Illus.). 880p. (C). 1999. text 82.50 (*0-03-023848-X*) SCP.

***Pavia, Donald L., et al.** Introduction to Spectroscopy: A Guide for Students of Organic Chemistry. 3rd ed. LC 00-30101. (Golden Sunburst Ser.). (Illus.). 2000. pap. write for info. (*0-03-031961-7*) SCP.

Pavia, Jerry, photos by. Yosemite National Park. (Tiny Folios Ser.). (Illus.). 320p. 1996. pap. 11.95 (*0-7892-0131-3*) Abbeville Pr.

Pavia, M. R., jt. ed. see Moos, W. H.

Pavia, Maria N. Drama del Siglo de Oro: A Study of Magic: Witchcraft & Occult Beliefs. 116p. 1959. 4.00 (*0-318-22344-9*) Hispanic Inst.

Pavia, Tony. An American Town Goes to War. Cloud, Amy, ed. LC 95-80568. (Illus.). 238p. 1995. 29.95 (*1-56311-276-0*) Turner Pub KY.

Pavic, Milorad. Dictionary of the Khazars: Female Edition. Pribicevic-Zoric, Christina, tr. 1989. pap. 15.00 (*0-679-72754-X*) Vin Bks.

— Dictionary of the Khazars: Male Edition. Pribicevic-Zoric, Christina, tr. 1989. pap. 15.00 (*0-679-72461-3*) Vin Bks.

— Last Love in Constantinople: A Tarot Novel for Divination. 1999. pap. 14.95 (*0-8023-1330-2*) Dufour.

Pavic, Milorad. Last Love in Constantinople: A Tarot Novel for Divination. 176p. 1997. 29.95 (*0-7206-1035-4*, Pub. by P Owen Ltd) Dufour.

Pavic, Milorad & Pribchevich-Zoric, Christina. Last Love in Constantinople: A Tarot Novel for Divination. 184p. 1998. 23.95 (*0-8023-1323-X*) Dufour.

Pavicevic, M., jt. auth. see Dragovic, Ivan.

Pavicevic, M. K., jt. ed. see Boekstein, A.

Pavich, Paul N. Joseph Wood Krutch. LC 89-60063. (Western Writers Ser.: No. 89). (Illus.). 52p. (Orig.). 1989. pap. 4.95 (*0-88430-088-9*) Boise St U W Writ Ser.

Pavich, Robert. After High School, Then What. 1997. pap. 5.95 (*1-57481-000-6*) Foxx Res.

***Pavicic, Liliana & Pirker-Mosher, Gordana.** The Best of Croatian Cooking. 200p. 2000. 24.95 (*0-7818-0804-9*) Hippocrene Bks.

Pavicic, Marko, tr. see Stojanovic, Radmila, ed.

Pavie, A. Contes Populaires du Cambodge. LC 78-20136. (Collection de contes et de chansons populaires: Vol. 27). reprint ed. 49.50 (*0-404-60377-7*) AMS Pr.

Pavie, Theodore. Tales of the Sabine Borderlands: Early Louisiana & Texas Fiction. Klier, Betje B., ed. & tr. by. Marsh, Anne C. et al, trs. LC 98-22081. (Centennial Series of the Association of Former Students: No. 79). (Illus.). 144p. 1998. 29.95 (*0-89096-837-3*); pap. 15.95 (*0-89096-854-3*) Tex A&M Univ Pr.

Pavilis. Grammar Dimensions. 2nd ed. (College ESL Ser.: Bk. 4). (J). 1997. mass mkt., wbk. ed. 13.95 (*0-8384-4140-8*) Heinle & Heinle.

Pavin, Corey. Corey Pavin's Shotmaking. 256p. 1997. per. 14.00 (*0-671-54513-2*) PB.

Pavis, Jose, jt. auth. see Steele, Ross.

Pavis, Patrice. Diccionario del Teatro: Dramaturgia, Estetica, Semiologia. 2nd ed. (SPA.). 605p. 1991. pap. 69.95 (*0-7859-6227-1*, 8475092373) Fr & Eur.

— Dictionary of the Theatre: Terms, Concepts & Analysis. Shantz, Christine, tr. from FRE. 672p. 1998. pap. text 34.95 (*0-8020-8163-0*) U of Toronto Pr.

— Dictionary of the Theatre (Dictionnaire du Theatre) Terms, Concepts & Analysis. Shantz, Christine, tr. from FRE. 672p. 1998. text 80.00 (*0-8020-4342-9*) U of Toronto Pr.

— The Intercultural Performance Reader. LC 95-36625. 280p. (C). 1996. pap. 22.99 (*0-415-08154-8*) Routledge.

— Languages of the Stage: Essays in the Semiology of Theatre. (PAJ Bks.). (Illus.). 206p. (C). 1993. pap. text 16.95 (*0-933826-15-X*) Johns Hopkins.

Pavis, Patrice. Spectacles. (Illus.). (C). text. write for info. (*0-472-09689-3*); pap. text. write for info. (*0-472-06689-7*) U of Mich Pr.

Pavis, Patrice, ed. The Intercultural Performance Reader. LC 95-36625. 280p. (C). 1996. 75.00 (*0-415-08153-X*) Routledge.

Pavis, Patricia. Dictionary of the Theatre: Dictionnaire du Theatre Termes et Concepts de l'Analyse Theatrale. (ENG, FRE, GER & SPA.). 477p. 1987. 150.00 (*0-8288-2188-7*, M15589) Fr & Eur.

Pavisich-Ryan, Olga, tr. see Miravalle, Mark I.

Pavithran, A. K. Bangladesh. LC 70-183008. 122p. 1971. 30.00 (*0-912004-02-9*) Gaunt.

***Pavitra.** Education & the Aim of Human Life. 5th ed. 184p. 1999. pap. 4.00 (*81-7058-245-8*, Pub. by SAA) E-W Cultural Ctr.

— On Meditation & Discipline. 3rd ed. 14p. 1996. pap. 0.50 (*81-7058-282-2*, Pub. by SAA) E-W Cultural Ctr.

Pavitra, ed. see Aurobindo, Sri & Mother.

Pavitrananda, Swami. Hymns & Prayers. 1974. pap. 3.95 (*81-7505-116-7*, Pub. by Advaita Ashrama) Vedanta Pr.

Pavitrananda, Swami. Common Sense about Yoga. pap. 2.00 (*81-7505-048-9*, Pub. by Advaita Ashrama) Vedanta Pr.

Pavitt, Irene, jt. ed. see Murfin, James V.

***Pavitt, Jane, ed.** Brand New. (Illus.). 224p. 2000. 49.50 (*0-691-07061-X*) Princeton U Pr.

Pavitt, Kate, jt. auth. see Thomas, William.

Pavitt, Keith. Technology, Management & Systems of Innovation. LC 99-12825. 272p. 1999. 95.00 (*1-85898-874-8*) E Elgar.

Pavitt, Keith, jt. auth. see Hanson, P.

Pavka, John, jt. auth. see Corcoran, Eileen L.

Pavkov, Thomas W. & Pierce, Kent A. Ready, Set, Go! A Student Guide to SPSS for Windows 7.5. LC 97-24168. viii, 79p. 1997. pap. text, student ed. 15.95 (*0-7674-0025-9*, 0025-9) Mayfield Pub.

— Ready, Set, Go! A Student Guide to SPSS Version 6.1 Workbook for Windows. LC 96-37292. (Illus.). 121p. (C). 1996. pap. text, student ed. 15.95 (*1-55934-841-0*, 1841) Mayfield Pub.

— Ready, Set, Go! A Student Guide to SPSS 8.0 for Windows. rev. ed. LC 98-8475. (Illus.). vii, 87p. (C). 1999. pap. text 15.95 (*0-7674-0515-3*, 0515-3) Mayfield Pub.

***Pavkov, Thomas W. & Pierce, Kent A.** Ready, Set, Go! A Student Guide to SPSS 9.0 for Windows. LC 99-23660. vii, 96p. 1999. 15.95 (*0-7674-1213-3*, 1213-3) Mayfield Pub.

Pavkovic. War in World Histroy. 2001. 68.50 (*0-07-052584-6*) McGraw.

***Pavkovic.** Wars in the World History. 2001. 68.50 (*0-07-052585-4*) McGraw.

Pavkovic, jt. auth. see Morillo.

Pavkovic, Aleksandar. Fragmentation of Yugoslavia. LC 96-25631. 256p. 1997. text 59.95 (*0-312-16342-8*) St Martin.

***Pavkovic, Aleksandar.** The Fragmentation of Yugoslavia: Nationalism & War in the Balkans. 2nd ed. LC 99-51697. 2000. pap. 22.95 (*0-312-23084-2*) St Martin.

Pavkovic, Aleksandar. Slobodan Jovanovic: An Unsentimental Approach to Politics. 231p. 1993. 49.50 (*0-88033-268-9*, 371, Pub. by East Eur Monographs) Col U Pr.

Pavkovic, Aleksandar, ed. Contemporary Yugoslav Philosophy: The Analytic Approach. (Nijhoff International Philosophy Ser.: No. 36). 326p. 1988. text 185.00 (*90-247-3776-1*) Kluwer Academic.

Pavkovic, Aleksandar, et al, eds. Nationalism & Postcommunism: A Collection of Essays. LC 95-8908. 192p. 1995. 77.95 (*1-85521-625-6*, Pub. by Dartmth Pub) Ashgate Pub Co.

Pavkovic, Aleksandar, jt. ed. see Radan, Peter.

Pavlak, Stephen A. Classroom Activities for Correcting Specific Reading Problems. LC 84-19001. 192p. (C). 1984. pap. text 24.95 (*0-13-136219-4*, Busn) P-H.

— Informal Tests for Diagnosing Specific Reading Problems. LC 84-19094. 144p. (C). 1984. pap. text 24.95 (*0-13-464801-3*, Busn) P-H.

Pavlan, Robert C. Pharmacy Law: State/Federal for Massachusetts. LC 98-96264. 1998. write for info. (*0-9664725-0-0*) Belmont Publ.

Pavlat, Leo. Bible Stories: From the Old & New Testament. (J). (gr. 1 up). 1994. 12.98 (*0-7858-0013-1*) Bk Sales Inc.

Pavlath, Attila E., jt. ed. see Hudlicky, Milos.

Pavle, Kalan, jt. auth. see Bajac, Anton.

Pavlenko, Stefan, tr. see Theophan the Recluse.

Pavlenkov, Victor. Russia: Yesterday, Today, Tomorrow - Voice of the Young Generation. Pappas, Peter, ed. (Illus.). 295p. (Orig.). 1997. pap. 12.95 (*0-9637035-5-2*) FC-Izdat.

— Russia No. 1: Yesterday, Today, Tomorrow. The Results of Essay Competition & Survey in Nizhmy, Russia in 1995. Babyonishev, Alexander, ed. 400p. (Orig.). 1996. pap. 12.95 (*0-9637035-4-4*) FC-Izdat.

— Tak . . . Just So . . . LC 95-96060. (Illus.). 70p. (Orig.). 1995. pap. 4.95 (*0-9637035-3-6*) FC-Izdat.

P

An Asterisk (*) at the beginning of an entry indicates that the title is appearing for the first time.

Pavlenkov, Victor, ed. Russia: Yesterday, Today, Tomorrow - 97. (RUS., Illus.). 215p. 1998. pap. 9.95 (*0-9637035-7-9*) FC-Izdat.

Pavlenkov, Victor, ed. see Jones, Eugene.

Pavletic, Michael M. Atlas of Small Animal Reconstructive Surgery. LC 92-15376. (Illus.). 352p. 1993. text 95.00 (*0-397-51119-1*) Lppncott W & W.

— Atlas of Small Animal Reconstructive Surgery. 2nd ed. Kersey, Ray, ed. LC 98-37965. 380p. 1999. text 65.00 (*0-7216-7077-6*, W B Saunders Co) Harcrt Hlth Sci Grp.

Pavlicek, Richard, jt. auth. see Root, W.

Pavlicevic, Mercedes. Music Therapy in Context: Music, Meaning & Relationship. LC 97-202351. 224p. 1997. pap. 26.95 (*1-85302-434-1*, Pub. by Jessica Kingsley) Taylor & Francis.

— Music Therapy Intimate Notes. LC 98-45894. 1999. 24.95 (*1-85302-692-1*) Taylor & Francis.

***Pavlich.** Critique & Radical Discourses on Crime. 240p. 2000. 69.95 (*1-84014-731-8*) Ashgate Pub Co.

Pavlich, George. Justice Fragmented: Mediating Community Disputes under Postmodern Conditions. 216p. (C). 1996. 75.00 (*0-415-11312-1*) Routledge.

Pavlich, Walter. Ongoing Portraits. 52p. (Orig.). 1985. pap. 5.95 (*0-935306-33-1*) Barnwood Pr.

— Theories of Birds & Waters. 32p. 1990. pap. 7.00 (*0-937669-36-9*) Owl Creek Pr.

Pavlichenko, Valerly, ed. see Caslow, Andrew Bruce.

Pavlicin, Karen. Webster's New World Fundamentals: Online Style. 224p. 1999. pap. 9.95 (*0-02-863603-1*) S&S Childrens.

Pavlicin, Karen & Lyon, Christy. Online Style Guide: Terms, Usage, & Tips. LC 98-96126. ix, 214p. 1998. spiral bd. 19.95 (*0-9657483-3-2*) Elva Resa Pub.

Pavlick, Mark, ed. see Chomsky, Noam.

Pavlicko, Marie, jt. auth. see Farr, J. Michael.

Pavlidis, George T. & Fisher, Dennis F., eds. Dyslexia: Its Neuropsychology & Treatment. LC 85-16780. (Illus.). 336p. 1986. reprint ed. pap. 104.20 (*0-608-02599-2*, 206325700004) Bks Demand.

Pavlidis, George T. & Miles, T. R., eds. Dyslexia Research & Its Applications to Education. LC 80-49975. (Illus.). 329p. 1981. reprint ed. pap. 102.00 (*0-7837-8872-X*, 204958300001) Bks Demand.

Pavlidis, Stephen. The Abaco Guide: Including Central Bahamas & the Bight of Abaco. LC 99-46516. (Illus.). 174p. 2000. pap. 29.95 (*1-892399-02-4*) Seaworthy WI.

Pavlidis, Stephen J. The Exuma Guide: A Cruising Guide to the Exuma Cays. 1996. pap. text 24.95 (*0-07-052402-5*) McGraw.

Pavlidis, Stephen J. The Exuma Guide: A Cruising Guide to the Exuma Cays. 2nd ed. LC 97-23745. (Illus.). 224p. 1997. pap. 29.95 (*0-9639566-7-1*, \) Seaworthy WI.

Pavlidis, Stephen J. The Turks & Caicos Guide: A Cruising Guide to the Turks & Caicos Islands. LC 98-50578. (Illus.). 135p. 1999. pap. 22.95 (*1-892399-01-6*) Seaworthy WI.

Pavlidis, Stephen J. & Darville, Ray. A Cruising Guide to the Exuma Cays Land & Sea Park. LC 93-86394. (Illus.). 78p. (Orig.). 1994. pap. 14.95 (*0-685-69186-1*) Night Flyer.

Pavlidis, Stephen V. On & off the Beaten Path: The Central & Southern Bahamas Guide. LC 97-36533. (Illus.). 332p. 1997. pap. 34.95 (*0-9639566-9-8*) Seaworthy WI.

Pavlidis, T. Fundamentals of X Programming: Graphical User Interfaces & Beyond. LC 98-56154. (Series in Computer Science). (Illus.). 367p. (C). 1999. 89.95 (*0-306-46065-3*, Plenum Trade) Perseus Pubng.

— Structural Pattern Recognition. LC 77-21105. (Electrophysics Ser.: Vol. 1). (Illus.). 1977. 51.95 (*0-387-08463-0*) Spr-Verlag.

Pavlik. Friends. 48p. 1997. spiral bd. 7.81 (*0-07-292786-0*) McGraw.

— Love Triangle. 48p. 1997. spiral bd. 7.81 (*0-07-292788-7*) McGraw.

— The Mendozas of Mexico. 48p. 1997. spiral bd. 7.81 (*0-07-292787-9*) McGraw.

— Single Dad. 48p. 1998. spiral bd. 7.81 (*0-07-292785-2*) McGraw.

— Speak Up: Books 1 & 2, Bks. 1 & 2. 2nd ed. (College ESL Ser.). (J). 1995. mass mkt., suppl. ed. 8.95 (*0-8384-5018-0*) Heinle & Heinle.

Pavlik, Bruce M., et al. Oaks of California. (Illus.). 184p. (Orig.). 1992. pap. 21.95 (*0-9628505-1-9*) Cachuma Pr.

Pavlik, Cheryl. FREEWAY BOOK 3, Vol. 3. 1996. pap. text, student ed. 13.65 (*0-582-08593-4*) Addison-Wesley.

— FREEWAY BOOK 4, Vol. 4. 1996. pap. text, student ed. 13.65 (*0-582-08597-7*) Addison-Wesley.

— Intermediate Grammar Teacher's Book: From Form to Meaning & Use. 206p. 1996. pap. text, teacher ed. 18.50 (*0-19-434367-7*) OUP.

— Speak Up. (J). 1982. pap. 15.95 (*0-8384-2959-9*, Newbury) Heinle & Heinle.

— Speak Up, Bk. 2. 2nd ed. (College ESL Ser.). 124p. (J). 1995. mass mkt. 26.95 (*0-8384-4998-0*) Heinle & Heinle.

— Speak Up, Set 4. (J). 1982. audio 59.95 (*0-8384-2960-2*, Newbury) Heinle & Heinle.

— WKBK FREEWAY LEVEL 2. 1996. pap. text 8.75 (*0-582-08590-X*) Addison-Wesley.

— WKBK FREEWAY 1. 1996. pap. text, wbk. ed. 8.75 (*0-582-08586-1*) Addison-Wesley.

— WKBK FREEWAY 3. 1996. pap. text, wbk. ed. 8.75 (*0-582-08594-2*) Addison-Wesley.

Pavlik, Cheryl & Stumpfhauser De Hernandez, Anna. Speak Up, Bk. 1. 2nd ed. LC 94-25204. 112p. (J). 1995. mass mkt. 26.95 (*0-8384-4996-4*) Heinle & Heinle.

Pavlik, Cheryl, jt. see Ediger, Anne.

Pavlik, Cheryl, jt. auth. see Segal, Margaret.

Pavlik, Edward J. Estrogens, Progestins & Their Antagonists. LC 96-3059. Date not set. write for info. (*3-7643-3947-0*) Birkhauser.

— Estrogens, Progestins & Their Antagonists. LC 96-3059. 1996. 95.00 (*0-8176-3947-0*) Birkhauser.

— Estrogens, Progestins, & Their Antagonists. LC 96-30592. 1996. 170.00 (*0-8176-3948-9*) Birkhauser.

Pavlik, Edward J., ed. Estrogens, Progestins & Their Antagonists. LC 96-3059. 344p. 1996. 95.00 (*0-8176-3854-7*) Birkhauser.

Pavlik, Ellen L. & Belkaoui, Ahmed R. Determinants of Executive Compensation: Corporate Ownership, Performance, Size, & Diversification. LC 90-26407. 176p. 1991. 65.00 (*0-89930-633-0*, PEZ/, Quorum Bks) Greenwood.

Pavlik, Ellen L., jt. auth. see Riahi-Belkaoui, Ahmed.

Pavlik, Gregory P., ed. Forgotten Lessons: Selected Essays of John T. Flynn. LC 95-61370. 206p. (Orig.). 1995. pap. 10.95 (*1-57246-015-6*) Foun Econ Ed.

Pavlik, John V. New Media Technology: Cultural & Commercial Perspectives. 2nd ed. LC 97-37599. 450p. 1997. pap. 34.67 (*0-205-27093-X*) Allyn.

— Public Relations: What Research Tells Us. (CommText Ser.: Vol. 16). (C). 1987. text 42.00 (*0-8039-2950-1*); pap. text 18.95 (*0-8039-2951-X*) Sage.

— Public Relations: What Research Tells Us. LC 87-13200. (Sage Commtext Ser.: No. 16). 152p. reprint ed. pap. 47.20 (*0-608-09626-1*, 205278400007) Bks Demand.

Pavlik, John V. & Dennis, Everette E., eds. Demystifying Media Technology: Readings from the Freedom Forum Center. Additional readings avail. on diskette. LC 92-25132. xi, 194p. (C). 1993. pap. text 34.95 (*1-55934-145-9*, 1145) Mayfield Pub.

Pavlik, John V., jt. ed. see Williams, Frederick.

Pavlik, Norene. One of Them. LC 88-61212. (Illus.). 263p. 1988. pap. 8.95 (*0-87973-420-5*, 420) Our Sunday Visitor.

Pavlik, Steve, ed. A Good Cherokee, a Good Anthropologist: Papers in Honor of Robert K. Thomas. LC 98-60444. (Contemporary American Indian Issues Ser.: Vol. 8). 400p. 1998. 40.00 (*0-935626-47-6*); pap. 25.00 (*0-935626-48-4*) U Cal AISC.

Pavlin, Charles J. & Foster, F. Stuart. Ultrasound Biomicroscopy of the Eye. LC 93-40948. (Illus.). 164p. 1994. 120.00 (*0-387-94206-8*) Spr-Verlag.

Pavlin, Igor, jt. ed. see Prokopenko, Joseph.

Pavlinek, Petr. Economic Restructuring & Local Environmental Management in the Czech Republic. LC 97-38957. (Illus.). 444p. 1997. text 109.95 (*0-7734-8447-7*) E Mellen.

Pavliscak, Pamela, et al. Information Technology in Humanities Scholarship - Achievements, Prospects, & Challenges: The American Focus. (Occasional Paper Ser.: No. 37). 60p. (Orig.). 1997. pap. text. write for info. (*0-9632792-3-8*) Am Coun Lrnd Soc.

Pavlock, Barbara. Eros, Imitation, & the Epic Tradition. LC 89-36639. 248p. 1990. text 39.95 (*0-8014-2321-X*) Cornell U Pr.

Pavlock, Ernest J. Financial Management for Medical Groups: A Primer for New Managers & a Refresher for the Experienced. 666p. (Orig.). 1994. text 49.00 (*1-56829-007-1*, 4597) Med Group Mgmt.

Pavloff, George. The Man Who Was It. (Illus.). 72p. (J). (gr. 1 up). 1990. 12.95 (*0-931474-39-6*) TBW Bks.

— A Rainbow for Suzanne. (Illus.). 72p. (J). (gr. 1 up). 1991. 14.95 (*0-931474-40-X*) TBW Bks.

Pavlopoulos, George. The Cellar. Date not set. pap. 14.95 (*0-85646-027-3*, Pub. by Anvil Press) Dufour.

Pavlos, Andrew J. The Cult Experience, 6. LC 81-13175. (Contributions to the Study of Religion Ser.: No. 6). 209p. 1982. 57.95 (*0-313-23164-8*, PEX/, Greenwood Pr) Greenwood.

***Pavloska, Susanna.** Modern Primitives: Race & Language in Gertrude Stein, Ernest Hemingway & Zora Neale Hurston. (Literary Criticism & Cultural Theory Ser.). 200p. 2000. 55.00 (*0-8153-3650-0*) Garland.

Pavloskis, Zoya, ed. The Story of Apollonius: The King of Tyre. 1978. 10.00 (*0-87291-095-4*) Coronado Pr.

Pavlou, Konstantinos N., jt. ed. see Simopoulos, Artemis P.

Pavlou, Konstantinos N., jt. ed. see Simopoulos, A. P.

Pavlov, A. S. Warships of the U. S. S. R. & Russia, 1945-1995. Friedman, Norman, ed. Tokar, Gregory, tr. LC 96-30077. (Illus.). 352p. 1997. 65.00 (*1-55750-671-X*) Naval Inst Pr.

Pavlov, Alexander, ed. Kazakov: Selected Stories (The Smell of Bread, The Plain Girl, The Courage of a Writer: Zapakh Khleba, Nekrasivaya, O Muzhestve Pisatelya) (Bristol Russian Texts Ser.). (RUS.). 103p. (C). 1993. reprint ed. pap. 18.95 (*1-85399-252-6*, Pub. by Brist Class Pr) Focus Pub-R Pullins.

Pavlov, Boris & Terentyev, Alexander. Organic Chemistry. 2nd ed. Mir Publishers Staff, tr. from RUS. (Illus.). 616p. (C). 1975. 29.95 (*0-8464-0690-X*) Beekman Pubs.

Pavlov, D., ed. see Symposium on Advances in Lead-Acid Batteries Staff.

***Pavlov, G. A.** Transport Processes in Plasmas with Strong Coulomb Interactions. 200p. 2000. text 95.00 (*90-5699-210-4*, G & B Science) Gordon & Breach.

Pavlov, Helene. An Orthopedist's Guide to Plain Film Imaging. (Illus.). 336p. 1998. 65.00 (*0-86577-717-9*) Thieme Med Pubs.

***Pavlov, V. I.** Indian Capitalist Class: A Historical Study. 2000. 38.00 (*81-86562-92-3*, Pub. by Manak Pubns Pvt Ltd) S Asia.

Pavlov, V. P., tr. see Kulikov, N. V. & Molchanova, I. V.

Pavlov, Yuri. Soviet-Cuban Alliance, 1959-1991. 2nd ed. LC 95-50925. 320p. (C). 1996. pap. 24.95 (*1-57454-004-1*, Pub. by U Miami N-S Ctr) L Rienner.

Pavlov, Z., ed. see International Congress on Electrocardiology Staff.

Pavlova, Anna. Psychopathology & Psychiatry. LC 93-5454. 550p. (C). 1993. pap. text 29.95 (*1-56000-707-9*) Transaction Pubs.

Pavlova, Karolina. A Double Life. 3rd rev. ed. Heldt, Barbara, tr. from RUS. & intro. by. (Illus.). 133p. (C). 1996. pap. text 8.95 (*0-936041-09-9*) Barbary Coast Bks.

Pavlova, L. M., jt. auth. see Glazov, V. M.

Pavlova, Z. F., et al. Conjugated 1,2- & 1,4-Nitrothio (sulfonyl) alkenes & Dienes, Vol. 16. (Sulfur Reports). 258p. 1995. pap. text 860.00 (*3-7186-5751-1*, Harwood Acad Pubs) Gordon & Breach.

Pavlova, Z. V. & Isakova, M. E. Oncology Reviews, Vol. 3. (Soviet Scientific Reviews Ser.: Vol. 3, Pt. 3). 72, ivp. 1989. pap. text 61.00 (*3-7186-4913-6*) Gordon & Breach.

Pavlovic, Darko. The Austrian Army 1836-66 (1) Infantry. (Men at Arms Ser.: Vol 323). (Illus.). 48p. 1999. pap. text 12.95 (*1-85532-801-1*, Pub. by Ospry) Stackpole.

— Austrian Army (2) Cavalry: 1836-66. (Men at Arms Ser.: Vol. 329). (Illus.). 48p. 1999. pap. 12.95 (*1-85532-800-3*, Pub. by Ospry) Stackpole.

Pavlovic, Karl, jt. auth. see Schaub, James H.

Pavlovic, Karl R., tr. see Lorenzen, Paul.

Pavlovic, M. N., ed. Steel Structures: Recent Research Advances & Their Applications to Design. 604p. 1987. mass mkt. 240.50 (*1-85166-046-1*) Elsevier.

Pavlovic, M. N., jt. auth. see Kotsovos, M. D.

Pavlovic, Vukasin, jt. ed. see Seroka, James.

Pavlovsky, A. A. Vseobshii Illiustrirovannyi Putevoditel' po Sviatym Mestam Rossiiskoi Imperii i Sv. Afonu. LC 88-61819. (RUS., Illus.). 900p. 1988. reprint ed. 85.00 (*0-911971-35-1*); reprint ed. pap. 55.00 (*0-911971-34-3*) Effect Pub.

Pavlovsky, Eduardo. Three Plays by Eduardo Pavlovsky: Slow Motion, Potestad - Paternity, Pablo. Carter, Hilma O., ed. Verdier, Paul, tr. from SPA. & adapted by by. (Illus.). 160p. (Orig.). 1994. pap. 12.95 (*0-9642024-0-9*) Stages Theatre.

Pavlovsky, Evgeny N. Natural Nidality of Transmissible Diseases: With Special Reference to the Landscape Epidemiology of Zooanthroponoses. Levine, Norman D., ed. LC 66-11023. 275p. reprint ed. pap. 85.30 (*0-608-13741-3*, 202024400016) Bks Demand.

Pavlow, Al. Hot Charts Index: Artists, 1940-1959. 60p. 1995. pap. 5.95 (*0-915529-22-X*) Music Hse Pub.

— Hot Charts Index: Titles, 1940-1959. 68p. 1995. pap. 5.95 (*0-915529-21-1*) Music Hse Pub.

— Hot Charts, 1950: Top Records of the Year. 84p. (Orig.). 1990. pap. 5.95 (*0-915529-01-7*) Music Hse Pub.

— Hot Charts, 1940: Top Records of the Year. 88p. 1994. pap. 5.95 (*0-915529-11-4*) Music Hse Pub.

— Hot Charts, 1948: Top Records of the Year. 100p. 1994. pap. 5.95 (*0-915529-19-X*) Music Hse Pub.

— Hot Charts, 1945: Top Records of the Year. 80p. 1994. pap. 5.95 (*0-915529-16-5*) Music Hse Pub.

— Hot Charts, 1944: Top Records of the Year. 72p. 1994. pap. 5.95 (*0-915529-15-7*) Music Hse Pub.

— Hot Charts, 1949: Top Records of the Year. 96p. 1994. pap. 5.95 (*0-915529-20-3*) Music Hse Pub.

— Hot Charts, 1941: Top Records of the Year. 84p. 1994. pap. 5.95 (*0-915529-12-2*) Music Hse Pub.

— Hot Charts, 1947: Top Records of the Year. 96p. 1994. pap. 5.95 (*0-915529-18-1*) Music Hse Pub.

— Hot Charts, 1946: Top Hits of the Year. 92p. 1994. pap. 5.95 (*0-915529-17-3*) Music Hse Pub.

— Hot Charts, 1943: Top Records of the Year. 64p. 1994. pap. 5.95 (*0-915529-14-9*) Music Hse Pub.

— Hot Charts, 1942: Top Records of the Year. 84p. 1994. pap. 5.95 (*0-915529-13-0*) Music Hse Pub.

— Hot Charts, 1951. 84p. (Orig.). 1990. pap. 5.95 (*0-915529-02-5*) Music Hse Pub.

— Hot Charts, 1952. 92p. (Orig.). 1990. pap. 5.95 (*0-915529-03-3*) Music Hse Pub.

— Hot Charts, 1953. 96p. (Orig.). 1990. pap. 5.95 (*0-915529-04-1*) Music Hse Pub.

— Hot Charts, 1954. 84p. (Orig.). 1990. pap. 5.95 (*0-915529-05-X*) Music Hse Pub.

— Hot Charts, 1955. 80p. (Orig.). 1991. pap. 5.95 (*0-915529-06-8*) Music Hse Pub.

— Hot Charts, 1956. 96p. (Orig.). 1991. pap. 5.95 (*0-915529-07-6*) Music Hse Pub.

— Hot Charts, 1957. 96p. (Orig.). 1991. pap. 5.95 (*0-915529-08-4*) Music Hse Pub.

— Hot Charts, 1958. 92p. (Orig.). 1992. pap. 5.95 (*0-915529-09-2*) Music Hse Pub.

— Hot Charts, 1959. 104p. (Orig.). 1992. pap. 5.95 (*0-915529-10-6*) Music Hse Pub.

— The R & B Book: A Disc-History of Rhythm & Blues. (Illus.). 111p. 1983. pap. 15.95 (*0-915529-00-9*) Music Hse Pub.

Pavlowitch, Stevan K. History of the Balkans, 1804-1945. LC 98-46175. 400p. (C). 1999. pap. 33.53 (*0-582-04584-3*) Addison-Wesley.

— History of the Balkans, 1804-1945. LC 98-46175. (C). 1999. 75.50 (*0-582-04585-1*) Addison-Wesley.

— Tito - Yugoslavia's Great Dictator: A Reassessment. LC 92-23760. 119p. 1992. pap. text 15.95 (*0-8142-0601-8*) Ohio St U Pr.

Pavlowitch, Steven K., ed. Unconventional Perceptions of Yugoslavia. 166p. 1985. 55.50 (*0-88033-081-3*, Pub. by East Eur Monographs) Col U Pr.

Pavlu, Charles & Pavlu, Lindy. Selected Poems. 64p. 1998. pap. 8.00 (*0-8059-4389-7*) Dorrance.

Pavlu, Lindy, jt. auth. see Pavlu, Charles.

Pavlu, Ricki. Evolution: When Fact Became Fiction. LC 86-13144. (Illus.). 250p. 2000. reprint ed. pap. 6.95 (*0-932581-51-X*) Word Aflame.

***Pavlyak, Michele M.** Systems Survival Guide: For the Systemically - Challenger Executive. Bryant, LaRee, ed. LC 00-190501. viii, 124p. 2000. pap. write for info. (*0-9665370-6-8*) Ruby Moon Pr.

Pavlychko, Solomea. Letters from Kiev. Kostash, Myrna, tr. 150p. 1992. text 35.00 (*0-312-07588-X*) St Martin.

Pavlychko, Solomea & Keefer, Janice K., eds. Two Lands, New Visions. Carynnyk, Marco & Hoban, Marta, trs. LC 99-179811. 320p. 1999. pap. 13.95 (*1-55050-134-8*) Genl Dist Srvs.

Pavlyshyn, Marko, ed. Glasnost in Context: On the Recurrence of Liberalizations in Central & East European Literatures & Cultures. LC 89-39740. (Berg European Studies). 215p. 1990. 19.50 (*0-85496-598-X*) Berg Pubs.

Pavlyukevich, N. V., et al. Physical Kinetics & Transfer Processes in Phase Transitions. 177p. 1996. 75.00 (*1-56700-044-4*) Begell Hse.

Pavon. El Carnaval: B Level Books. text 8.95 (*0-88436-895-5*) EMC-Paradigm.

— Las Hermanas Coloradas: Level C Books. text 8.95 (*0-88436-295-7*) EMC-Paradigm.

— Los Carros Vacios: Level A. text 7.95 (*0-88436-281-7*) EMC-Paradigm.

***Pavon, Francisco G.** The Crimson Twin. Neve, Susan, tr. 1999. pap. 14.95 (*0-7490-0450-9*) Allison & Busby.

Pavon, J., jt. auth. see Ruiz, H.

Pavon, Max. Amor y Muerte: Bilingual Anthology - Spanish-English Poetry. (ENG & SPA., Illus.). 178p. (Orig.). 1996. pap. 15.00 (*1-57502-325-3*, P01091) Morris Pubng.

***Pavon, Max, tr.** Andalusian Poem: de Andalucia Federico Garcia Lorca's Collection of 18 Classic Gypsy Ballards Romancero Gitano. (Illus.). 112p. (C). 1999. pap. 20.00 (*0-7392-0499-8*, PO3836) Morris Pubng.

Pavon, Milton L., jt. ed. see Hruska, Allan J.

Pavone, Christopher. The Wine Log. LC 98-31309. 112p. 1999. 17.95 (*1-55821-686-3*) Lyons Pr.

Pavone-Macaluso, Michele & DeKernion, Jean B. Tumors of the Kidney. (Surgery Ser.). (Illus.). 340p. 1986. 86.75 (*0-683-02426-4*) Lppncott W & W.

Pavone, P. & Passariello, R. MR Cholangiopancreatography: Techniques, Results & Clinical Indications. LC 96-30464. (Illus.). 173p. 1996. 115.00 (*3-540-61349-8*) Spr-Verlag.

Pavone, P. & Rossi, Plinio. Syllabus - European Seminars on Diagnostic & Interventional Radiology (ESDIR), Rome, Italy: Functional MRI. LC 96-26790. 160p. 1996. pap. 79.50 (*3-540-75025-8*) Spr-Verlag.

Pavoni, David, jt. auth. see Chew, Robert Z.

Pavoni, Joseph, et al, eds. Handbook of Solid Waste Disposal: Materials & Energy Recovery. LC 74-26777. 566p. 1981. reprint ed. 49.50 (*0-442-23027-3*) Krieger.

Pavoni, Rosanna. Reviving the Renaissance: The Use & Abuse of the Past in Nineteenth-Century Italian Art & Decoration. (Cambridge Studies in Italian History & Culture). (Illus.). 295p. 1997. text 69.95 (*0-521-48151-1*) Cambridge U Pr.

Pavord & Fisk. Horse Owner's Veterinary Handbook. 35.00 (*1-85223-682-5*, Pub. by Cro1wood) Trafalgar.

Pavord, Anna. Anna Pavord's Gardening Companion. (Illus.). 298p. 1993. pap. 19.95 (*0-7011-4953-1*, Pub. by Chatto & Windus) Trafalgar.

— The Border Book. LC 93-28347. (Illus.). 160p. 1994. 29.95 (*1-56458-485-2*) DK Pub Inc.

— Flowering Year: A Guide to Seasonal Planting. (Illus.). 168p. 1991. 39.95 (*1-55859-240-7*, Cross Riv Pr) Abbeville Pr.

— The New Kitchen Garden. LC 95-44070. (DK Living Ser.). 208p. 1999. pap. text 13.95 (*0-7894-4119-5*) DK Pub Inc.

— The Tulip: The Story of a Flower That Has Made Men Mad. (Illus.). 439p. 1999. 40.00 (*1-58234-013-7*) Bloomsbury Pubg.

Pavord, Marcy. Endurance: Start to Finish. 256p. 1997. pap. 60.00 (*0-85131-648-4*, Pub. by J A Allen) Trafalgar.

***Pavord, Marcy.** Handling & Understanding the Horse. (Illus.). 176p. 2000. pap. 27.95 (*1-85310-967-3*, Pub. by Swan Hill Pr) Voyageur Pr.

Pavord, Marcy, jt. auth. see Pavord, Tony.

Pavord, Tony & Pavord, Marcy. Complete Equine Veterinary Manual. LC 98-133359. (Illus.). 288p. 1998. 34.95 (*0-7153-0330-9*, Pub. by D & C Pub) Sterling.

***Pavri, Julie M.** Honoring Our Past, Building Our Future: A History of the New York State Nurses Association. State Nurses Association Staff, ed. LC 00-30590. 2000. write for info. (*0-9665228-5-0*) Q Pubng VA.

Pavri, Tinaz. On the Brink of War: India, Pakistan, & the 1990 Kashmir Crisis. (Pew Case Studies in International Affairs). 50p. (C). 1996. text 3.50 (*1-56927-373-1*) Geo U Inst Dplmcy.

Pavri, Tinaz, jt. ed. see Matthews, Lloyd J.

Pavry, Jal D. Zoroastrian Doctrine of a Future Life from Death to the Individual Judgment. 2nd ed. LC 79-10518. reprint ed. 32.50 (*0-404-50481-7*) AMS Pr.

Pavsek, Christopher, tr. see Kluge, Alexander.

Pavuk, Pamela & Pavuk, Stephen. The Story of a Lifetime: A Keepsake of Personal Memoirs. deluxe rev. ed. (Illus.). 384p. 1996. 39.95 (*0-9643032-6-4*) Triangel Pubs.

— The Story of a Lifetime: A Keepsake of Personal Memoirs. 3rd deluxe rev. ed. (Illus.). 383p. 1996. 39.95 (*0-9643032-4-8*, TRIP01102396) Triangel Pubs.

Pavuk, Stephen, jt. auth. see Pavuk, Pamela.

Pavuna, Davor, et al, eds. Superconducting & Related Oxides Vol. 3481: Physics & Nanoengineering III. LC 99-200341. 1998. 116.00 (*0-8194-2936-8*) SPIE.

Pavuna, Davor, jt. auth. see Cyrot, Michel.

***Pavy, Donald A.** Accident & Deception: The Huey Long Shooting. Thornton, Don & Thornton, Suzi, eds. (Illus.). 179p. 1999. per. write for info. (*0-933727-01-1*) Cajun Pubng.

Pawagi, Manjusha. The Girl Who Hated Books. rev. ed. LC 98-41606. (Illus.). 32p. (J). (ps-3). 1999. 14.95 (*1-58270-006-0*) Beyond Words Pub.

Pawagi, Manjusha & Franson, Leanne. The Girl Who Hated Books. 1999. bds. 12.95 (*1-896764-11-8*) Sec Story Pr.

Pawalowski, K., jt. ed. see Jackowski, S.

Pawar, Ravi. Tilting at Windmills: New Welsh Short Fiction. LC 96-146556. 144p. 1995. pap. 9.95 (*0-9521558-1-8*) Dufour.

Pawar, S. N. & Patil, R. B. Sociology of Environment. LC 98-909673. 302p. 1998. write for info. (*81-7033-449-7*) Rawat Pubns.

Pawar, Sarbjit S. University Grants Commission (UGC) & Development of Libraries. LC 98-901508. ix, 204p. 1998. write for info. (*81-7629-092-0*) Deep & Deep Pubns.

Pawel, Ernst. The Labyrinth of Exile: A Life of Theodore Herzl. 1989. text 30.00 (*0-374-18256-6*) FS&G.

— Life in Dark Ages. 1995. 20.95 (*0-88064-168-1*) Fromm Intl Pub.

— The Poet Dying: Heinrich Heine's Last Years in Paris. LC 94-40744. 209p. 1995. 23.00 (*0-374-23538-4*) FS&G.

Pawel, Ernst, tr. see Aron, Raymond.

***Pawel, Jody J.** The Parent's Toolshop: The Universal Blueprint for Building a Healthy Family. 2nd ed. LC 99-65065. (Illus.). 450p. 2000. pap. 24.95 (*0-9659119-4-2*) Ambris Publ.

***Pawel, Jody Johnston.** The Parent's Toolshop: The Universal Blueprint for Building a Healthy Family. 2nd ed. 450p. 2000. pap. 24.95 (*1-929643-34-9*, Pub. by Ambris Publ) ACCESS Pubs Network.

Pawel, Jody Johnston. The Parent's Toolshop: The Universal Blueprint for Building a Healthy Family. 2nd unabridged ed. LC 97-92298. (Illus.). 448p. 1997. pap. 29.95 (*0-9659119-3-4*) Ambris Publ.

Pawelec, W. The Friends of Zofia. 96p. 1985. 24.95 (*0-932735-00-2*) Melrose Pub Inc.

Pawelek, Anne J. American in Poland. 1967. 3.75 (*0-685-09282-8*) Endurance.

***Pawkett, Viola S.** A Child's Book of Poetry. (J). (ps). 2000. pap. 5.95 (*0-533-13505-2*) Vantage.

Pawl, Jeree H. & St. John, Maria. How You Are Is As Important As What You Do. LC 98-60085. (Illus.). 44p. 1998. pap. 10.00 (*0-943657-39-3*) ZERO TO THREE.

Pawl, Lawrence E., jt. auth. see Melton, Jack W., Jr.

Pawl, Ronald P. Chronic Pain Primer. LC 79-22621. (Illus.). 221p. reprint ed. pap. 68.60 (*0-8357-7627-1*, 205695000096) Bks Demand.

Pawlak, Elizabeth A., jt. auth. see Hoag, Phillip M.

Pawlak, Laura. Beyond Estrogen: A Guide for Men & Women. (Illus.). 266p. 1998. pap. 25.00 (*1-893549-15-1*) Biomed Genl.

— A Perfect 10: Phyto "New-trients" Against Cancers. 3rd rev. ed. (Illus.). 264p. 1999. pap. 25.00 (*1-893549-13-5*) Biomed Genl.

— Weight Matters: Appetite - The Brain-Body Connection. (Illus.). 200p. 1998. 20.00 (*1-893549-16-X*) Biomed Genl.

Pawlak, Laura & Albers, Michelle, eds. No Ordinary Vitamin: Vitamin E & Health. 160p. 1999. pap. 15.00 (*1-893549-00-3*) Biomed Genl.

Pawlak, Laura & Freedman, Marjorie, eds. Precious Metals: Minerals & Health. 108p. 1998. pap. 10.00 (*1-893549-05-4*) Biomed Genl.

Pawlak, Laura & Turner, Lisa. Food Smart: A Nutritional Atlas. 256p. 2000. pap. 20.00 (*1-893549-03-8*) Biomed Genl.

Pawlak, Mark. All the News. LC 84-12956. 1984. pap. 4.00 (*0-914610-37-6*) Hanging Loose.

— Special Handling. LC 93-160. 1993. 18.00 (*0-914610-99-6*); pap. 10.00 (*0-914610-57-0*) Hanging Loose.

Pawlak, Mark, et al, eds. Bullseye: Stories & Poems by Outstanding High School Writers. LC 95-9866. (High School Age Writing from the Sixties to Now Ser.: Vol. 2). 256p. 1995. pap. 15.00 (*1-882413-12-1*) Hanging Loose.

Pawlak, Mark, jt. ed. see Lourie, Dick.

***Pawlak, Robert J.** Chess Software Sourcebook: A Comprehensive Guide to Selecting & Using Chess Software. LC 99-64661. (Illus.). 128p. 1999. pap. 16.95 (*0-9673840-0-1*) Treehaus Bks.

Pawlak, Walter A., Jr., jt. auth. see Litt, Jerome Z.

Pawlak, Zdzislaw. Rough Sets: Theoretical Aspects of Reasoning about Data. 248p. 1991. text 166.50 (*0-7923-1472-7*) Kluwer Academic.

***Pawlan, Monica.** Essentials of the Java Programming Language: A Hands-on Guide. 320p. 2000. pap. 34.95 (*0-201-70720-9*) Addison-Wesley.

Pawlas, Andreas. Statistik und Ethik: Zur Problematik der Integration Statistischer Aussagen in der Ethik, Dargestellt an der Sozial- und Wirtschaftsethik Alexander von Oettingens. (Europaische Hochschulschriften Ser.: Reihe 23, Bd. 431). (GER.). XIV, 340p. 1991. 58.80 (*3-631-44101-0*) P Lang Pubng.

Pawlas, George E. The Administrator's Guide to School-Community Relations. LC 94-25310. (Illus.). 300p. 1995. 39.95 (*1-883001-13-7*) Eye On Educ.

Pawlas, George E., jt. auth. see Oliva, Peter F.

Pawlay, M. 20th Century Architecture: A Reader's Guide. 160p. 1995. 34.50 (*0-419-19740-0*, Chap & Hall NY) Chapman & Hall.

Pawlcyn, Cindy. Fog City Diner. (Illus.). 224p. 1998. reprint ed. pap. 21.95 (*0-89815-999-7*) Ten Speed Pr.

Pawlenko, Stephan. Organosilicon Chemistry. (Illus.). xii, 186p. 1986. 153.85 (*3-11-010329-X*) De Gruyter.

Pawlett, Raymond. Tai Chi: A Practical Introduction. LC 99-56796. (Alternative Health Ser.). (Illus.). 112p. 1999. 9.98 (*1-57145-211-7*, Thunder Bay) Advantage Pubs.

Pawley, Bernard C. The Second Vatican Council: Studies by Eight Anglican Observers. 1990. 16.00 (*0-8446-2713-5*) Peter Smith.

Pawley, James B., ed. Handbook of Biological Confocal Microscopy. 2nd ed. LC 94-46208. (Illus.). 656p. (C). 1995. text 95.00 (*0-306-44826-2*, Kluwer Plenum) Kluwer Academic.

***Pawley, Margaret.** In Obedience to Instructions: F.A.N.Y. with the S.O.E. in the Wartime Meditterranean. (Illus.). 1999. 36.95 (*0-85052-633-7*, 526337) Leo Cooper.

Pawley, Martin. Buckminster Fuller. (Design Heroes Ser.). (Illus.). 192p. 1991. 24.95 (*0-8008-1116-X*) Taplinger.

— Future Systems: The Story of Tomorrow. (Illus.). 156p. (C). 1993. pap. 29.95 (*0-7148-2767-3*, Pub. by Phaidon Press) Phaidon Pr.

— Hauer-King House: London, 1995: Future Systems. (Architecture in Detail Ser.). (Illus.). 60p. 1997. pap. 29.95 (*0-7148-3630-3*, Pub. by Phaidon Press) Phaidon Pr.

— Norman Foster: A Global Architecture. LC 99-25469. (Illus.). 240p. 1999. pap. 25.00 (*0-7893-0263-2*, Pub. by Universe) St Martin.

— Terminal Architecture. (Essays in Art & Culture Ser.). (Illus.). 224p. 1998. pap. 24.95 (*1-86189-018-4*, Pub. by Reaktion Bks) Consort Bk Sales.

***Pawley, Martin.** 20th Century Architecture: A Reader's Guide. LC 99-51728. 195p. 2000. text 29.95 (*0-7506-4635-7*) Buttrwrth-Heinemann.

Pawley, Martin, ed. see Burney, Jan.

***Pawley, Ronald.** Red Lancers. (Illus.). 144p. 2000. 90.00 (*1-86126-188-8*, 129762AE, Pub. by Crolwood) Motorbooks Intl.

Pawley, Ronald. Red Lancers. 1998. 75.00 (*1-85915-074-8*, Pub. by W & G) Motorbooks Intl.

Pawley, Thomas D., jt. auth. see Reardon, William R.

Pawlick, Edward. Freedom Will Conquer Racism & Sexism. 340p. 1998. 23.95 (*0-9662949-0-4*) Mustard Seeds.

Pawliczko, Ann L., ed. Ukraine & Ukrainians Throughout the World: A Demographic & Sociological Guide to the Homeland & Its Diaspora. (Illus.). 464p. (C). 1994. text 75.00 (*0-8020-0595-0*); pap. text 35.00 (*0-8020-7200-3*) U of Toronto Pr.

Pawlik, Jonathan, jt. auth. see Chase, Pamela L.

Pawlik, Klaus-Dieter E. Solutions Manual for Guide to Energy Management. 3rd ed. (Illus.). 151p. Date not set. 72.00 (*0-88173-340-7*) Fairmont Pr.

Pawlik, Peter S., jt. auth. see Reismann, Herbert.

***Pawlikowski, John & Perelmuter, Hayim Goren.** Reinterpreting Revelation & Tradition: Jews & Christians in Conversation. (Bernardin Center Ser.: Vol. 1). 256p. 2000. 22.95 (*1-58051-042-6*) Sheed & Ward WI.

Pawlikowski, John & Senior, Donald, eds. Economic Justice: The CTU Commentary on the Bishops Letter on the Economy. 200p. 1988. pap. 12.95 (*0-912405-41-4*, Pastoral Press) OR Catholic.

Pawlikowski, John, ed. see Perelmuter, Hayim G., et al.

Pawlikowski, John T. & Fragomeni, Richard, eds. The Ecological Challenge: Ethical, Liturgical, & Spiritual Responses. 152p. (Orig.). 1994. pap. text 9.95 (*0-8146-5840-7*, M Glazier) Liturgical Pr.

Pawlikowski, John T. & Wilde, James A. When Catholics Speak about Jews: Notes for Homilists & Catechists. 88p. 1987. pap. 5.95 (*0-930467-60-4*, CAJEW) Liturgy Tr Pubns.

Pawlikowski, M., jt. auth. see Dohler, K. D.

Pawling, Christopher, jt. auth. see Baxendale, John.

Pawling, J. F. Surface Mounted Assemblies. 263p. 1997. pap. 220.00 (*0-901150-21-5*) St Mut.

Pawling, Jesse R. Dr. Samuel Guthrie, Discoverer of Chloroform. (Illus.). 123p. 1994. reprint ed. lib. bdg. 22.00 (*0-8328-3628-1*) Higginson Bk Co.

Pawliszyn, J. & Smith, R. M., eds. Applications of Solid Phase Microextraction. (Chromatography Monographs). 520p. 1999. 100.00 (*0-85404-525-2*) Royal Soc Chem.

Pawliszyn, Janusz. Solid Phase Microextraction: Theory & Practice. LC 96-45276. 264p. 1997. 74.95 (*0-471-19034-9*, Wiley-VCH) Wiley.

Pawlitski, Susan Lazarus. Be Your Best Body: Every Woman's Fitness Guide to a Strong & Graceful Body. (Illus.). 128p. 1999. pap. 12.95 (*0-9668504-2-4*) Tone-Up Pubg.

Pawlow, E. A. & Semjonowa, O. I. Deutsch-Russisches Worterbuch der Forstund Holzwirtschaft: German-Russian Dictionary of Forestry of the Lumber Industry. (GER & RUS.). 477p. 1978. 29.95 (*0-8288-4870-X*, M9058) Fr & Eur.

Pawlowitzki, I. H., et al, eds. Genetic Mapping of Disease Genes. LC 97-11844. (Illus.). 288p. 1997. text 75.00 (*0-12-232735-7*) Acad Pr.

Pawlowski. The Science & Engineering of Thermal Spray Coatings. text. write for info. (*0-471-49049-0*); pap. text. write for info. (*0-471-49048-2*) Wiley.

Pawlowski, jt. auth. see Kreuzer.

***Pawlowski, Cheryl.** Glued to the Tube. 2000. 22.95 (*1-57071-459-2*) Sourcebks.

Pawlowski, L., ed. Physiochemical Methods for Water & Wastewater Treatment. (Studies in Environmental Science: Vol. 19). 394p. 1982. 203.75 (*0-444-42067-3*) Elsevier.

Pawlowski, L., et al. Chemistry for the Protection of the Environment. (Environmental Science Research Ser.: Vol. 42). (Illus.). 838p. (C). 1991. 175.00 (*0-306-43904-2*, Plenum Trade) Perseus Pubng.

— Chemistry for the Protection of the Environment, Vol. 2. LC 96-25716. (Environmental Science Research Ser.: Vol. 51). (Illus.). 460p. (C). 1996. 150.00 (*0-306-45373-8*, Plenum Trade) Perseus Pubng.

Pawlowski, L., jt. auth. see Bolto, B. A.

Pawlowski, Lech. The Science & Engineering of Thermal Spray Coatings. LC 94-19287. 432p. 1995. 240.00 (*0-471-95253-2*) Wiley.

Pawlowski, Lucjan, et al, eds. Chemistry for the Protection of the Environment 3: Proceedings of the 11th International Conference Held in Cairo, Assuan, & Luxor, Egypt, September 10-17, 1997. (Environmental Science Research Ser.: No. 55). (Illus.). 356p. (C). 1998. 95.00 (*0-306-46026-2*, Plenum Trade) Perseus Pubng.

Pawlowski, M. & Raczka, R., eds. Gauge Theories of Fundamental Interactions: Proceedings of the XXXII Semester in the Stefan Banach International Mathematical Center, Warsaw, Poland, September 19 to December 3, 1988. 520p. 1990. text 129.00 (*981-02-0365-9*) World Scientific Pub.

Pawlowski, Mark & Brown, James. Q & A Landlord & Tenant. (Q & A Ser.). 230p. 1995. pap. 20.00 (*1-85431-398-3*, Pub. by Blackstone Pr) Gaunt.

Pawlowski, Mark, jt. auth. see Brown, J.

Pawlowski, Tadeusz. Aesthetic Values. (Nijhoff International Philosophy Ser.: No. 31). 148p. 1989. lib. bdg. 111.00 (*0-7923-0418-7*, Pub. by Kluwer Academic) Kluwer Academic.

— Concept Formation in the Humanities & the Social Sciences. (Synthese Library: No. 144). 238p. 1980. text 112.50 (*90-277-1096-1*, D Reidel) Kluwer Academic.

Pawlowski, Z. S., et al. Hookworm Infection & Anaemia: Approaches to Prevention & Control. (ENG, FRE & SPA.). vi, 96p. 1991. pap. text 17.10 (*92-4-154415-5*, 1150350) World Health.

Pawlowsky, Peter. Christianity. Bowden, John, tr. from GER. LC 94-47513. (Basics Ser.: Vol. 1). 112p. (C). 1995. pap. 11.00 (*1-56338-112-5*) TPI PA.

Pawluch, Dorothy. The New Pediatrics: A Profession in Transition. (Social Problems & Social Issues Ser.). 187p. 1996. lib. bdg. 41.95 (*0-202-30534-1*) Aldine de Gruyter.

Pawlucki, W. Points de Nash des Ensembles Sous-Analytiques. LC 89-18471. (Memoirs Ser.: No. 425). 76p. 1990. pap. 18.00 (*0-8218-2430-9*, MEMO/84/425) Am Math.

Pawluk, Juan, ed. see Ehrlich, Geri.

Pawluk, William, jt. auth. see Jerabek, Jiri.

Pawnee (Illinois) Elem. School, Mrs. Kern's 1996-9. Whine Cut. (WeWrite Kids! Ser.: No. 36). (Illus.). 50p. (J). (ps-4). 1997. pap. 3.95 (*1-57635-012-6*) WeWrite.

Pawnee Elementary, Mrs. Kern's Third Grade Class. The Joke Ghost. (WeWrite Kids! Ser.: No. 14). (Illus.). 35p. (J). (ps-3). 1995. pap. 3.95 (*1-884987-46-X*) WeWrite.

Pawnee Elementary, Mrs. Salisbury's Third Grade Class. Our Cool Field Trip. (WeWrite Kids! Ser.: No. 13). (Illus.). 35p. (J). (ps-3). 1995. pap. 3.95 (*1-884987-43-5*) WeWrite.

Pawnee Elementary School Third Graders. Alien Attack. (WeWrite Kids! Ser.: No. 4). (Illus.). 25p. (J). (ps-3). 1994. pap. 3.95 (*1-884987-16-8*) WeWrite.

— The Zookeeper's Bad Day. (WeWrite Kids! Ser.: No. 5). (Illus.). 25p. (J). (ps-3). 1995. pap. 3.95 (*1-884987-19-2*) WeWrite.

***Pawsey, Linda.** Christmas Figures. (Sugar Inspiration Ser.). (Illus.). 48p. 1999. pap. 5.95 (*1-85391-418-5*) Tuttle Pubng.

— New Wedding Cake Designs. 2000. pap. 34.95 (*1-85391-884-9*, Pub. by Merehurst Ltd) Tuttle Pubng.

Pawson, A. J., et al, eds. Protein Modules in Signal Transduction. (Current Topics in Microbiology & Immunology Ser.: Vol. 228). (Illus.). 396p. 1997. text 179.00 (*3-540-63396-0*) Spr-Verlag.

Pawson, D. The Road to Hell. 15.95 (*0-340-53964-X*, Pub. by Hodder & Stought Ltd) Trafalgar.

***Pawson, David & Peck, Andy.** New Testament Bk. 1: The Hinge of History. (Unlocking the Bible Ser.). 2000. pap. 13.00 (*0-551-03187-5*, Pub. by M Pickering) Trafalgar.

— New Testament Bk. 2: The Thirteenth Apostle. (Unlocking the Bible Ser.). 2000. pap. 13.00 (*0-551-03190-5*, Pub. by M Pickering) Trafalgar.

— Old Testament Bk. 1: The Maker's Instructions. (Unlocking the Bible Ser.). 2000. pap. 13.00 (*0-551-03186-7*, Pub. by M Pickering) Trafalgar.

— Old Testament Bk. 2: A Land & a Kingdom. (Unlocking the Bible Ser.). 2000. pap. 13.00 (*0-551-03188-3*, Pub. by M Pickering) Trafalgar.

— Old Testament Bk. 3: Poems of Worship & Wisdom. (Unlocking the Bible Ser.). 2000. pap. 13.00 (*0-551-03189-1*, Pub. by M Pickering) Trafalgar.

Pawson, David L. Molpadiid Sea Cucumbers (Echinodermata: Holothuroidea) of the Antarctic Seas: Paper 3 in Biology of the Antarctic Seas VI. LC 77-2320. (Antarctic Research Ser.: Vol. 26). (Illus.). 28p. 1977. pap. 10.70 (*0-87590-131-X*) Am Geophysical.

Pawson, David L., ed. Biology of the Antarctic Seas Five Paper 3: Bathypelagic Isopid Crustacea from the Antarctic & Southern Seas. (Antarctic Research Ser.: Vol. 23). 59p. 1977. 53.00 (*0-87590-127-1*) Am Geophysical.

— Biology of the Antarctic Seas Seven, 4 papers, Set 27-4. (Antarctic Research Ser.: Vol. 27). 302p. 1978. 62.00 (*0-87590-133-6*) 62.00 (*0-87590-134-4*); 62.00 (*0-87590-135-2*); 62.00 (*0-87590-136-0*) Am Geophysical.

— Biology of the Antarctic Seas Six, Set. (Antarctic Research Ser.: Vol. 26). 1978. 51.00 (*0-87590-144-1*) Am Geophysical.

— Biology of the Antarctic Seas Six Paper Four: Polychaeta from the Weddell Sea Quadrant, Antarctica. (Antarctic Research Ser.: Vol. 26). 60p. 1978. 51.00 (*0-87590-132-8*) Am Geophysical.

— Biology of the Antarctic Seas Twelve. (Antarctic Research Ser.: Vol. 35). (Illus.). 110p. 1982. 20.00 (*0-87590-181-6*) Am Geophysical.

Pawson, David L. & Miller, John E. Systematics & Ecology of the Sea-Urchin Genus Centrostephanus: Echinodermata: Echinodea, from the Atlantic & Eastern Pacific Oceans. LC 83-600054. (Smithsonian Contributions to the Marine Sciences Ser.: No. 20). 20p. reprint ed. pap. 30.00 (*0-608-14403-7*, 202176600022) Bks Demand.

Pawson, David L., ed. see Heron, Gayle A.

Pawson, David L., ed. see Kasyanov, V. L., et al.

Pawson, David L., jt. ed. see Kornicker, Louis S.

Pawson, David L., ed. see Lamb, I. Mackenzie & Zimmerman, Martin H.

Pawson, David L., ed. see Lowry, James K.

Pawson, David L., ed. see Schultz, George A.

Pawson, David L., ed. see Tibbs, John F.

Pawson, Des. The Handbook of Knots. LC 97-38707. (Illus.). 192p. 1998. pap. 16.95 (*0-7894-2395-2*) DK Pub Inc.

Pawson, Ernest. Pigeon Racing: Science & Practice. (Illus.). 98p. 1999. pap. 13.00 (*0-627-02217-0*, Pub. by J L Van Schaik) BHB Intl.

Pawson, Ivan G. Physical Anthropology: Human Evolution. LC 77-2412. (Self-Teaching Guides Ser.). 256p. reprint ed. 79.40 (*0-8357-9954-9*, 201187700079) Bks Demand.

Pawson, John. Minimum. LC 97-190858. (Illus.). 272p. 1996. 95.00 (*0-7148-3262-6*, Pub. by Phaidon Press) Phaidon Pr.

— Minimum: Mini Edition. LC 99-214641. (Illus.). 320p. 1998. 18.00 (*0-7148-3817-9*); 18.00 (*0-7148-5011-X*) Phaidon Pr.

***Pawson, John.** Spatium: Fashion Architecture. 2000. pap. 40.00 (*88-7838-062-8*) L'Arca IT.

Pawson, Ray. A Measure for Measures: A Manifesto for Empirical Sociology. 272p. 1989. 49.95 (*0-415-02870-1*) Routledge.

Pawson, Ray & Tilley, Nick. Realistic Evaluation. LC 97-65723. 256p. 1997. text 69.95 (*0-7619-5008-7*); pap. text 25.95 (*0-7619-5009-5*) Sage.

Pawson, Stuart. The Judas Sheep. 320p. 1997. pap. 11.95 (*0-7472-4947-4*, Pub. by Headline Bk Pub) Trafalgar.

— The Judas Sheep. large type ed. 453p. write for info. (*0-7505-1068-4*, Pub. by Mgna Lrg Print) Ulverscroft.

— The Mushroom Man. 320p. 1997. mass mkt. 11.95 (*0-7472-4897-4*, Pub. by Headline Bk Pub) Trafalgar.

— Normal Christian Birth. 19.95 (*0-340-48972-3*, Pub. by Hodder & Stought Ltd) Trafalgar.

— The Picasso Scam. 320p. 1997. mass mkt. 9.95 (*0-7472-4977-6*, Pub. by Headline Bk Pub) Trafalgar.

Pawson, T., jt. ed. see Parker, P.

Pawtucket Arts Council Annual Poetry Competition S. An Anniversary Collection. 88p. 1988. write for info. (*0-318-64093-7*) Poets Pr.

Pax, C. An Existential Approach to God: A Study of Gabriel Marcel. 128p. 1973. pap. text 67.50 (*90-247-1503-2*, Pub. by M Nijhoff) Kluwer Academic.

Pax, Ferdinand, ed. see Boettger, Caesar.

***Pax, Wolfgang E.** In the Footsteps of Jesus: 2000 Years Later. LC 82-22073. (Illus.). 224p. 1999. 34.50 (*0-8264-1141-X*) Continuum.

Paxia, Gaetano. The Artists & Moral Responsibility: Teachings of Pius XII & John XXIII. LC 98-20476. 108p. 1998. 74.95 (*1-57309-313-0*, Cath Scholar Pr) Intl Scholars.

Paxinos, George. Chemoarchitecture of the Rat Brainstem. LC 98-88279. 240p. (C). 1998. pap. text 149.95 (*0-12-547611-6*) Acad Pr.

— Rat Brain in Stereotaxic Coordinates. 4th ed. (Illus.). 256p. 1998. pap. text 159.95 (*0-12-547617-5*); pap. text 119.95 (*0-12-547619-1*) Acad Pr.

Paxinos, George, et al. The Chemoarchitectonic Atlas of the Rat Forebrain. LC 98-85895. (Illus.). 260p. 1998. pap. text 149.95 (*0-12-547613-2*) Acad Pr.

Paxinos, George T., ed. The Human Nervous System. 1195p. 1990. text 99.00 (*0-12-547625-6*) Acad Pr.

— The Rat Nervous System. 2nd ed. (Illus.). 1136p. 1994. text 207.00 (*0-12-547635-3*) Acad Pr.

Paxinos, George T., et al, eds. Neurotransmitters in the Human Brain: Proceedings of a Conference in Honor of Istyan Tork Held in New South Wales, Sydney, February 5, 1994. (Advances in Behavioral Biology Ser.: Vol. 43). (Illus.). 254p. (C). 1995. text 85.00 (*0-306-44915-3*, Kluwer Plenum) Kluwer Academic.

Paxinos, George T. & Huang, Xu F., eds. Atlas of the Human Brainstem. (Illus.). 149p. (C). 1995. spiral bd. 99.00 (*0-12-547615-9*) Acad Pr.

Paxinos, George T. & Watson, Charles, eds. The Rat Brain in Stereotaxic Coordinates. 3rd ed. (Illus.). 96p. 1996. text 69.95 (*0-12-547623-X*) Morgan Kaufmann.

Paxinos, George T., et al. Atlas of the Developing Rat Nervous System. 2nd ed. Orig. Title: Atlas of the Developing Rat Brain. (Illus.). 438p. 1994. 136.00 (*0-12-547610-8*) Acad Pr.

Paxinos, George T., jt. auth. see Franklin, Keith B.

Paxlox, Norman. Teach Yourself German Grammar: A Modern Guide. (ENG & GER., Illus.). 166p. 1995. pap. 7.95 (*0-8442-3781-7*, Teach Yrslf) NTC Contemp Pub Co.

Paxman, David. A Newcomer's Guide to Hawaii. (Illus.). 144p. 1993. pap. 8.95 (*0-935180-32-X*) Mutual Pub HI.

Paxman, David B. & Black, Dianna M. Writing about the Arts & Humanities. 198p. (C). 1995. text 28.20 (*0-536-59164-4*) Pearson Custom.

Paxman, J. M. & Zuckerman, R. J. Laws & Policies Affecting Adolescent Health. 310p. 1987. pap. text 49.00 (*92-4-156095-9*, 1150263) World Health.

***Paxman, Jeremy.** English: A Portrait of a People. 2000. 29.95 (*1-58567-042-1*, Pub. by Overlook Pr) Penguin Putnam.

P

Paxman, John M., ed. The World Population Crisis: Policy Implications & the Role of Law: Proceedings of the American Society of International Law Regional Meeting & the John Bassett Moore Society of International Law Symposium. LC 80-19753. 179p. 1980. reprint ed. lib. bdg. 59.50 (0-313-22619-9, PAWO) Greenwood.

***Paxson & Martine-Barnes, Adrienne.** Shield Between Two. 2000. 22.00 (0-380-97235-2) HarpC.

Paxson, Charles L., ed. see Van Leeuwen, Gerard.

Paxson, Christina H., jt. auth. see Gersovitz, Mark.

Paxson, Dean & Wood, Douglas. Blackwell Encyclopedic Dictionary of Finance. LC 96-29122. (Blackwell Encyclopedia of Management Ser.). (Illus.). 250p. 1997. 110.00 (1-55786-912-X) Blackwell Pubs.

— Blackwell Encyclopedic Dictionary of Finance. LC 98-26082. (Blackwell Encyclopedia of Management Ser.). 288p. 1999. reprint ed. pap. 29.95 (0-631-21188-8) Blackwell Pubs.

Paxson, Diana L. The Book of the Spear. LC 99-213402. (Hallowed Isle Ser.: 2). 208p. 1999. pap. 10.00 (0-380-80546-4, Eos) Morrow Avon.

— The Dragons of the Rhine. LC 94-3198. 432p. (J). 1995. 22.00 (0-688-13986-8, Avon Bks) Morrow Avon.

— The Dragons of the Rhine. 400p. 1995. mass mkt. 5.99 (0-380-76527-6, Avon Bks) Morrow Avon.

***Paxson, Diana L.** Dragon's of the Rhine. 2000. 23.00 (0-380-97247-6) Morrow Avon.

— The Hallowed Isle: The Book of the Sword & the Book of the Spear. 384p. 2000. mass mkt. 6.50 (0-380-81367-X, Avon Bks) Morrow Avon.

— The Hallowed Isle Book Four: The Book of the Stone. LC 99-39528. (Hallowed Isle Ser.: Vol. 4). 208p. 2000. pap. 11.00 (0-380-80548-0, Avon Bks) Morrow Avon.

Paxson, Diana L. The Hallowed Isle Book One: The Book of the Sword. LC 98-49035. Vol. 1. 192p. 1999. pap. 10.00 (0-380-78870-5, Eos) Morrow Avon.

***Paxson, Diana L.** The Hallowed Isle Book Three: The Book of the Cauldron. LC 99-38405. (Hallowed Isle Ser.: Vol. 3). 192p. 1999. pap. 10.00 (0-380-80547-2, Avon Bks) Morrow Avon.

Paxson, Diana L. The Jewel of Fire. (Westria Ser.: No. 7). 1992. mass mkt. 3.99 (0-8125-1110-7) Tor Bks.

— The Lord of Horses. 1996. 23.00 (0-614-96768-6, Avon Bks); 23.00 (0-614-96938-7, Avon Bks) Morrow Avon.

— The Lord of Horses. 1997. mass mkt. 5.99 (0-380-76528-4, Avon Bks) Morrow Avon.

***Paxson, Diana L.** LORD OF HORSES (HC) 2000. 23.00 (0-380-97265-4) HarpC.

Paxson, Diana L. The Serpent's Tooth. 400p. 1993. mass mkt. 4.99 (0-380-75680-3, Avon Bks) Morrow Avon.

— Sword of Fire & Shadow. 1996. mass mkt. 5.99 (0-380-75803-2, Avon Bks) Morrow Avon.

— The White Raven. 480p. 1989. reprint ed. mass mkt. 4.99 (0-380-75229-8, Avon Bks) Morrow Avon.

— Wind Crystal. 1990. pap. 3.95 (0-8125-0040-7) Tor Bks.

— The Wolf & the Raven. 352p. 1994. mass mkt. 5.99 (0-380-76526-8, Avon Bks) Morrow Avon.

Paxson, Diana L. & Martin-Barnes, Adrienne. Sword of Fire & Shadow. LC 94-49015. 1995. 22.00 (0-688-14156-0, Avon Bks) Morrow Avon.

Paxson, Diana L. & Martine-Barnes, Adrienne. Master of Earth & Water. 416p. 1994. mass mkt. 4.99 (0-380-75801-6, Avon Bks) Morrow Avon.

— Master of Earth & Water. 2000. 22.00 (0-380-97219-0, Avon Bks) Morrow Avon.

***Paxson, Diana L. & Martine-Barnes, Adrienne.** Sword of Fire & Shadow. 2000. 22.00 (0-380-97255-7) Morrow Avon.

Paxson, Diana L., jt. auth. see Martine-Barnes, Adrienne.

Paxson, F. L., jt. auth. see Paullin, C. O.

Paxson, James J. The Poetics of Personification. (Literature, Culture, Theory Ser.: No. 6). 222p. (C). 1994. text 54.95 (0-521-44539-6) Cambridge U Pr.

Paxson, James J., et al, eds. The Performance of Middle English Culture: Essays on Chaucer & the Drama in Honor of Martin Stevens. LC 98-24827. (Illus.). 208p. 1998. 75.00 (0-85991-527-1) Boydell & Brewer.

Paxson, James J. & Gravlee, Cynthia. Desiring Discourse: The Literature of Love, Ovid Through Chaucer. LC 97-39577. 239p. 1998. 41.50 (1-57591-013-6) Susquehanna U Pr.

Paxson, Jeanette R., ed. Casing & Cementing. 2nd rev. ed. (Rotary Drilling Ser.: Unit II, Lesson 4). (Illus.). 53p. (Orig.). 1982. pap. text 16.00 (0-88698-056-9, 2.20420) PETEX.

— Reciprocating Gas Compressors. (Oil & Gas Production Ser.). (Illus.). 107p. (Orig.). 1982. pap. text 15.00 (0-88698-119-0, 3.30210) PETEX.

Paxson, Jeanette R., ed. see Cyrus, Cinda.

Paxson, John. Bones. LC 96-95477. 192p. 1997. 18.95 (0-8034-9228-6, Avalon Bks) Bouregy.

— Bones. 1999. per. 4.99 (0-373-26306-6, 1-26306-0, Wrldwide Lib) Harlequin Bks.

Paxson, Lowell Bud. Threading the Needle: The Pax Net Story. LC 98-19272. 192p. 1998. 25.00 (0-88730-948-8) HarpC.

Paxson, Monica Rix, jt. auth. see Brandenburg, John.

Paxson, Ruth. Como Vivir en el Plano Superior. Orig. Title: Life on the Highest Plane. (SPA.). 254p. 1984. mass mkt. 5.99 (0-8254-1551-9, Edit Portavoz) Kregel.

— Life on the Highest Plane: God's Plan for Spiritual Maturity. 512p. 1996. pap. 16.99 (0-8254-3461-0) Kregel.

Paxson, William C. The New American Guide to Punctuation. 240p. 1996. mass mkt. 5.99 (0-451-62878-0, Sig) NAL.

Paxton. Manufactured Carbon - Self Lubricating/Mechanical Division. 192p. 1979. lib. bdg. 75.00 (0-8493-5655-5) CRC Pr.

— Writing Power. 2nd ed. LC 98-28716. 349p. 1998. pap. text 48.00 (0-13-628785-9) P-H.

— Writing Procedure & Puctuation Study Sheet. 1998. pap. text 3.00 (0-13-081163-7) P-H.

***Paxton, Albert S.** 2000 National Repair & Remodeling Estimator. 23rd ed. O'Grady, J. A., ed. (Illus.). 320p. 1999. pap. 48.50 (1-57218-086-2) Craftsman.

Paxton, Andrea, jt. auth. see Podesta, Sandra.

Paxton, Cecil, jt. auth. see Paxton, Lisa.

Paxton, Collin Wilcox & Carden, Gary. Papa's Angels: A Christmas Story. LC 96-24238. (Illus.). 144p. 1996. 17.00 (1-57731-004-7) New Wrld Lib.

Paxton, E. H., tr. see Husayn, Taha.

Paxton, Frederic L. Independence of the South-American Republics: A Study in Recognition & Foreign Policy. LC 70-126379. 1971. reprint ed. lib. bdg. 50.00 (0-8154-0348-8) Cooper Sq.

Paxton, Frederick S. Christianizing Death: The Creation of a Ritual Process in Early Medieval Europe. (Illus.). 248p. 1996. pap. text 14.95 (0-8014-8386-7) Cornell U Pr.

— Liturgy & Anthropology: A Monastic Death Ritual of the Eleventh Century, Vol. II. LC 93-1787. (Chalice of Repose Project: Studies in Music-Thanatology: Vol. 2). 20p. 1993. pap. text 0.95 (1-882878-87-6) Saint Dunstans.

Paxton, Frederick S., tr. A Medieval Latin Death Ritual: The Monastic Customaries of Bernard & Ulrich of Cluny. (Chalice of Repose Project: Studies in Music-Thanatology: Vol. 1). 115p. (C). 1993. pap. text 23.95 (1-882878-88-4) Saint Dunstans.

Paxton Green, Josephine. Memories from the Mountains: A Collection of Short Stories by a Twin Girl Comparing Life in a Small Paper Town to Country Life. LC 98-61140. (Illus.). 228p. 1998. pap. 14.95 (1-56664-137-3) WorldComm.

Paxton, Harold W. & Bain, Edgar C. Alloying Elements in Steel. 2nd ed. LC 65-29304. 301p. reprint ed. pap. 93.40 (0-8357-5323-9, 202699000053) Bks Demand.

***Paxton, Heather N.** The American Royal, 1899-1999. (Illus.). 125p. 1999. 39.95 (1-886157-23-5, Wallaroo Bks); pap. 19.95 (1-886157-22-7, Wallaroo Bks) BkMk.

Paxton, Ian, jt. ed. see Hancock, Ian.

Paxton, J. M., ed. Manual of Civil Engineering Plant & Equipment. 2nd ed. (Illus.). 592p. 1977. 158.50 (0-85334-500-7) Elsevier.

Paxton, John. Companion to Russian History. fac. ed. LC 82-5192. (Illus.). 515p. 1983. reprint ed. pap. 159.70 (0-7837-7829-5, 204758500007) Bks Demand.

— Encyclopedia of Russian History: From the Christianization of Kiev to the Break-up of the U.S.S.R. 2nd ed. LC 93-29564. 483p. 1993. lib. bdg. 65.00 (0-87436-690-9) ABC-CLIO.

— European Communities. 250p. (C). 1992. 54.95 (1-56000-052-X) Transaction Pubs.

***Paxton, John.** Fitzroy Dearborn Calendar of World History. 400p. 1999. lib. bdg. 75.00 (1-57958-153-6) Fitzroy Dearborn.

— Imperial Russia: A Reference Handbook. LC 00-26867. 2000. write for info. (0-312-23480-5) St Martin.

Paxton, John, ed. The Statesman's Year-Book, 1983-1984. 120th ed. 1749p. 1983. 37.50 (0-317-03872-9) St Martin.

Paxton, John, jt. auth. see Cook, Chris.

Paxton, John, jt. auth. see Walsh, A. E.

Paxton, John, ed. see Steinberg, S. H.

Paxton, John L. From the Collection of John & Mary Lou Paxton. 100p. 1994. pap. 50.00 (0-9642216-0-8) J L Paxton.

Paxton, John R. & Eschmeyer, William N., eds. Encyclopedia of Fishes. (Illus.). 240p. (C). 1995. text 29.95 (0-12-547660-4) Acad Pr.

— Encyclopedia of Fishes. 2nd ed. LC 98-88228. (Illus.). 240p. (C). 1998. text 39.95 (0-12-547665-5) Acad Pr.

***Paxton, Joseph F.** Lost Masterpieces. (Architecture 3s Ser.). 1999. 19.95 (0-7148-3872-1) Phaidon Pr.

Paxton, Joseph F., ed. Oklahoma Anthology for 1929. LC 78-116412. (Granger Index Reprint Ser.). 1977. 16.95 (0-8369-6153-6) Ayer.

Paxton, Kate. Tatyana's Golden Doe: A Musical. (J). 1998. pap. 6.50 (0-87602-363-4) Anchorage.

Paxton, Lenore & Siadi, Phillip. Christmas Time of Year: Sing, Color'n Say. 2nd ed. (World of Language Ser.). (Illus.). 32p. (J). (ps up). 1994. reprint ed. pap. 7.95 incl. audio (1-880449-10-2) Wrldkids Pr.

— Going to Grandma's: Sing, Color'n Say. 2nd ed. (World of Language Activity Pack Ser.). (Illus.). 32p. (J). (ps up). 1994. reprint ed. pap. 7.95 incl. audio (1-880449-08-0) Wrldkids Pr.

— Happy B-I-R-T-H-D-A-Y: Sing, Color'n Say. 2nd ed. (World of Language Activity Pack Ser.). (Illus.). 32p. (J). (ps-3). 1994. reprint ed. pap. 7.95 incl. audio (1-880449-09-9) Wrldkids Pr.

— His Name Was David: Sing, Color'n Say. 2nd ed. (World of Language Bible Story Ser.). (Illus.). 32p. (J). (ps up). 1994. reprint ed. pap. 7.95 incl. audio (1-880449-12-9) Wrldkids Pr.

— Noah & the Ark: Sing, Color'n Say. (World of Language Bible Story Ser.). (Illus.). 32p. (J). (ps-4). 1994. reprint ed. pap. 7.95 incl. audio (1-880449-11-0) Wrldkids Pr.

Paxton, Lisa & Paxton, Cecil. Lisa's Story. McGuire, C. J., ed. 30p. pap. Price not set. (1-881541-19-3, 404) A Wommack.

Paxton, Michael. Ayn Rand: A Sense of Life. LC 97-47219. (Illus.). 192p. 1998. 34.95 (0-87905-845-5) Gibbs Smith Pub.

Paxton, Nancy L. George Eliot & Herbert Spencer: Feminism, Evolutionism & the Reconstruction of Gender. 296p. 1991. text 39.50 (0-691-06841-0, Pub. by Princeton U Pr) Cal Prin Full Svc.

— Writing under the Raj: Gender, Race, & Rape in the British Colonial Imagination, 1830-1947. LC 98-19522. 304p. (C). 1999. text 52.00 (0-8135-2600-0); pap. text 23.00 (0-8135-2601-9) Rutgers U Pr.

Paxton, Norman. Basic German. (Teach Yourself Ser.). (GER., Illus.). 144p. 1995. pap. 7.95 (0-8442-3777-9, Teach Yrslf) NTC Contemp Pub Co.

— Teach Yourself German, Basic. (Teach Yourself Ser.). 1992. 12.95 (0-8288-8339-4) Fr & Eur.

— Teach Yourself German Grammar. (Teach Yourself Ser.). 1992. 15.95 (0-8288-8337-8) Fr & Eur.

Paxton, Patsy. C-Notes: My Journey Through Breast Cancer. 152p. Date not set. pap. 12.95 (1-55197-117-8) Picasso Publ.

Paxton, Paul, jt. auth. see Blenkinsopp, Alison.

***Paxton Price, Lew.** Behind Light's Illusion - Gravity: The Nature & Mathematics of the Driving Force of Our Universe. (Behind Light's Illusion Ser.: Bk. 2). (Illus.). 56p. 1999. pap. 12.00 (0-917578-24-4) L Paxton Price.

— Behind Light's Illusion - Overview: An Explanation of the Principle That Unifies the Forces of Our Universe. (Behind Light's Illusion Ser.: Bk. 1). (Illus.). 62p. 1999. pap. 12.00 (0-917578-23-6) L Paxton Price.

Paxton, Robert O. Europe in the 20th Century. 3rd ed. LC 96-75654. 768p. (C). 1996. pap. text 59.00 (0-15-503779-X, Pub. by Harcourt Coll Pubs) Harcourt.

— French Peasant Fascism: Henry Dorgeres' Greenshirts & the Crises of French Agriculture, 1929-1939. LC 96-46864. (Illus.). 256p. 1997. pap. 19.95 (0-19-511189-3) OUP.

— Parades & Politics at Vichy: The French Officer Corps under Marshall Petain. LC 66-10557. 492p. reprint ed. pap. 152.60 (0-608-30014-4, 201057100069) Bks Demand.

— Vichy France: Old Guard & New Order, 1940-1944. LC 81-15221. (Morningside Bk.). 424p. 1982. reprint ed. pap. text 20.50 (0-231-05427-0) Col U Pr.

Paxton, Robert O., jt. auth. see Marrus, Michael R.

Paxton, Robert O., jt. ed. see Wahl, Nicholas.

Paxton, Roland, ed. One Hundred Years of the Forth Bridge. 166p. 1990. text 29.00 (0-7277-1600-X, Pub. by T Telford) RCH.

Paxton, Ruth. This Man...This Cause...This Hour. pap. 0.10 (1-56632-079-8) Revival Lit.

Paxton, Tom. The Animals' Lullaby. LC 92-18841. (Illus.). 40p. (J). (ps-3). 1993. 15.00 (0-688-10468-1, Wm Morrow) Morrow Avon.

— Elgelbert Joins the Circus. LC 96-14835. (Illus.). 32p. (J). 1997. lib. bdg. 14.93 (0-688-09988-2, Wm Morrow) Morrow Avon.

— Engelbert Joins the Circus. LC 96-14835. (Illus.). 32p. (J). 1997. 15.00 (0-688-09987-4, Wm Morrow) Morrow Avon.

— Engelbert Joins the Circus. (Illus.). (J). (gr. 2 up). 1997. 15.00 (0-614-28866-5, Wm Morrow) Morrow Avon.

— Engelbert Moves the House. 2nd ed. (Let Me Read Ser.). (Illus.). 16p. (J). (ps-2). 1995. pap. 2.95 (0-673-36239-6, GoodYrBooks) Addson-Wesley Educ.

— Engelbert the Elephant. LC 89-9376. (Illus.). 32p. (J). (ps up). 1995. pap. 4.95 (0-688-14395-4, Wm Morrow) Morrow Avon.

— Engelbert the Elephant. 1995. 10.15 (0-606-07484-8, Pub. by Turtleback) Demco.

— Going to the Zoo. (Illus.). 40p. (J). 1996. lib. bdg. 14.93 (0-688-13801-2, Wm Morrow) Morrow Avon.

— Going to the Zoo. (Illus.). 40p. (J). (ps). 1996. 15.00 (0-688-13800-4, Wm Morrow) Morrow Avon.

***Paxton, Tom.** Honor of Your Company. 2000. pap. text 17.95 (1-57560-144-3) Cherry Lane.

Paxton, Tom. Jennifer's Rabbit. (J). Date not set. 15.95 (0-688-15262-7, Wm Morrow) Morrow Avon.

Paxton, Tom. Jennifer's Rabbit. (Illus.). (J). Date not set. lib. bdg. 15.89 (0-06-029216-4, Wm Morrow) Morrow Avon.

— The Jungle Baseball Game. LC 97-6459. (Illus.). 40p. (J). (ps-3). 1999. 15.89 (0-688-13980-9, Wm Morrow) Morrow Avon.

Paxton, Tom. The Jungle Baseball Game. LC 97-6459. (Illus.). 40p. (YA). (ps-3). 1999. 16.00 (0-688-13979-5, Wm Morrow) Morrow Avon.

Paxton, Tom. The Marvelous Toy. LC 95-35384. (Illus.). 32p. (J). 1996. 15.93 (0-688-13880-2, Wm Morrow) Morrow Avon.

Paxton, Tom. The Marvelous Toy. LC 95-35384. (Illus.). 32p. (J). (gr. k up). 1996. 16.00 (0-688-13879-9, Wm Morrow) Morrow Avon.

— The Story of Santa Claus. LC 94-23919. (Illus.). 40p. (J). (ps-3). 1995. 15.00 (0-688-11364-8, Wm Morrow) Morrow Avon.

— The Story of Santa Claus. LC 94-23919. (Illus.). 40p. (J). 1997. mass mkt. 5.95 (0-688-15475-1, Wm Morrow) Morrow Avon.

— The Story of Santa Claus. (J). 1997. 11.15 (0-606-11921-3, Pub. by Turtleback) Demco.

Paxton, Tom. The Story of the Tooth Fairy. LC 95-13266. (Illus.). (J). 1996. lib. bdg. 15.93 (0-688-12988-9, Wm Morrow) Morrow Avon.

Paxton, Tom. The Story of the Tooth Fairy. LC 95-13266. (Illus.). 32p. (J). (ps-3). 1996. 16.00 (0-688-12987-0, Wm Morrow) Morrow Avon.

***Paxton, Tom.** The Story of the Tooth Fairy. LC 95-13266. (Illus.). 32p. (YA). (ps-3). 2000. mass mkt. 5.95 (0-688-17523-6, Wm Morrow) Morrow Avon.

Paxton, Tom. Tom Paxton Ramblin' Boy & Other Songs. (Illus.). pap. 12.95 (0-8256-0007-3, OK61069, Oak) Music Sales.

— Where's the Baby? LC 92-39875. (Illus.). 32p. (J). (ps up). 1993. 16.00 (0-688-10692-7, Wm Morrow) Morrow Avon.

Paxton, Vicki, ed. see Louizos, Dianna.

Paxton, Vivian Gaines Tanner. Transitions: A Treatise on Death & Dying. 80p. Date not set. 9.95 (0-9665755-0-4) Garden of Eden.

Paxton, W. M. Annals of Platte County: From Its Exploration down to June 1, 1897, with Genealogies of Its Noted Families & Sketches of Its Pioneers & Distinguished People. (Illus.). 1182p. 1997. reprint ed. lib. bdg. 115.00 (0-8328-6826-4) Higginson Bk Co.

— Annals of Platte County, Missouri, from Its Exploration down to June 1, 1897: With Genealogies of Its Noted Families, & Sketches of Its Pioneers & Distinguished People. 1188p. 1992. reprint ed. pap. 70.00 (1-55613-520-3) Heritage Bk.

— The Marshall Family: or A Genealogical Chart of the Descendants of John Marshall & Elizabeth Markham, His Wife. (Illus.). 415p. 1989. reprint ed. pap. 62.00 (0-8328-0855-5); reprint ed. lib. bdg. 70.00 (0-8328-0854-7) Higginson Bk Co.

Pay-Costa, M. Dictionnaire Pratique Mercure: Francais-Espagnol, Espagnol-Francais. 2nd ed. (FRE & SPA.). 1024p. 1966. 24.95 (0-7859-0762-9, M-6471) Fr & Eur.

Paya & Revilla. Hypocrites! Legault, Robert, tr. from SPA. LC 98-181001. (Illus.). 48p. 1998. pap. 8.95 (1-56163-201-5, Eurotica) NBM.

Paya, jt. auth. see Noe.

Payack, Peter. Blanket Knowledge. LC 97-9452. 128p. (Orig.). 1997. pap. 11.95 (0-944072-83-6) Zoland Bks.

***Payakalanond, Chuluthat.** Thai Mother of Pearl Inlay. (Illus.). 2000. 39.95 (974-8225-44-5, Pub. by River Books) Weatherhill.

***Payan, Gregory.** Attack Submarine: The SSN Seawolf. LC 99-58094. (High-Tech Military Weapons Ser.). (Illus.). 48p. (J). (gr. 4-7). 2000. pap. 6.95 (0-516-23538-9) Childrens.

— Essential Snowmobiling for Teens. (High Interest Bks.). (Illus.). (YA). 2000. 19.00 (0-516-23358-0) Childrens.

— Essential Snowmobiling for Teens. (High Interest Bks.). (Illus.). 48p. (J). (gr. 4-7). 2000. pap. 6.95 (0-516-23558-3) Childrens.

— Essential Snowmobiling for Teens. LC 99-55437. (Outdoor Life Ser.). (J). 2000. write for info. (0-531-17646-0) Watts.

— Life on a Submarine. (High Interest Bks.). (Illus.). (YA). 2000. 19.00 (0-516-23349-1) Childrens.

Payan, H. M. Lousy Foreigner: A Memoir. 2nd ed. LC 98-75084. 420p. 1998. reprint ed. pap. 12.95 (1-891231-10-3) Word Assn.

Payan, Jack, jt. ed. see Vinson, Ronald W.

Payandeh, Shahram, jt. auth. see Farazmand, Ali.

Payant, Katherine B. Becoming & Bonding: Contemporary Feminism & Popular Fiction by American Women Writers, 134. LC 92-39268. (Contributions in Women's Studies: No. 134). 256p. 1993. 57.95 (0-313-28574-8, PWC/) Greenwood.

Payant, Katherine B. & Rose, Toby, eds. The Immigrant Experience in North American Literature: Carving Out a Niche, 4. LC 98-46823. (Contributions to the Study of American Literature: Vol. 4). 224p. 1999. 55.00 (0-313-30891-8) Greenwood.

Payard, Francois. Simply Sensational Desserts. LC 99-19204. (Illus.). 256p. 1999. 35.00 (0-7679-0358-7) Bantam.

Payaslian, Simon. U. S. Foreign Economic & Military Aid: The Reagan & Bush Administrations. 190p. (Orig.). (C). 1995. pap. text 29.00 (0-7618-0240-1); lib. bdg. 44.00 (0-7618-0239-8) U Pr of Amer.

Payden, Deborah A. & Loving, Laura. Celebrating at Home: Prayers & Liturgies for Families. LC 97-44100. 152p. (Orig.). 1998. pap. 15.95 (0-8298-1250-4) Pilgrim OH.

Payden, Deborah A., jt. auth. see Alberswerth, Roy F.

Paye, Anne, jt. auth. see Wassman, Rose.

Paye, Burrall. The Adjustable Area Man-to-Man Press. LC 97-33181. (Illus.). 128p. (Orig.). 1998. pap. 15.00 (1-890450-00-6) Harding Pr.

— Basketball's Zone Presses: A Complete Coaching Guide. 228p. 1983. 19.95 (0-13-069237-9, Parker Publishing Co) P-H.

— Playing the Post: Basketball Skills & Drills. LC 96-21956. (Illus.). 256p. (Orig.). 1996. pap. 15.95 (0-87322-979-7, PPAY0979) Human Kinetics.

***Paye, Burrall & Paye, Patrick.** Youth Basketball Drills. (Illus.). 2001. pap. write for info. (0-7360-3365-3) Human Kinetics.

Paye, Gabriell D. Ethnobotany Curriculum Guide: Cultural Uses of Plants. Date not set. pap. 18.50 (0-89327-422-4, 422-4) NY Botanical.

Paye, Patrick, jt. auth. see Paye, Burrall.

Paye, Peter. Ely & Stives Railway. (C). 1985. 39.00 (0-85361-272-2) St Mut.

— Hayling Railway. (C). 1985. 45.00 (0-85361-225-0) St Mut.

— Mellis & Eye Railway. (C). 1985. 45.00 (0-85361-256-0) St Mut.

— Sidmouth, Seaton & Lyme Regis Branches. 64p. (C). 1985. 45.00 (0-85361-217-X) St Mut.

***Paye, Won-Ldy & Lippert, Margaret.** Why Leopard Has Spots: Dan Stories from Liberia. (Illus.). 64p. (YA). (gr. 3 up). 1998. pap. 12.95 (1-55591-991-X) Fulcrum Pub.

Payen-Appenseller, Pascal. La Broderie. (Illus.). 127p. 1994. 48.00 (2-200-21448-0, Pub. by C Armand) Lacis Pubns.

Payen, D., jt. ed. see Fink, M. P.

Payen, Louis A. Excavations at Sutter's Fort, 1960. (Publications of the Department of Parks & Recreation: No. 3). (Illus.). 55p. (C). 1961. reprint ed. pap. text 6.56 (1-55567-455-0) Coyote Press.

An Asterisk (*) at the beginning of an entry indicates that the title is appearing for the first time.

Payen, Louis A. & Boloyan, D. S. Archeological Excavations at Chilcoot Rockshelter, Pluma County, California. (Publications of the Department of Parks & Recreation: No. 4). (Illus.). 35p. (C). 1961. reprint ed. pap. text 4.06 (*1-55567-456-9*) Coyote Press.

Payen, Louis A. & Boloyan, David S. TCO SE an Archaeology Study of the Bedrock Mortar-Petroglyph at AMA 14, Near Volcano, California. (Publications of the Department of Parks & Recreation: No. 8). (Illus.). 46p. (C). 1963. reprint ed. pap. text 5.00 (*1-55567-460-7*) Coyote Press.

Payen, Louis A., jt. auth. see Olsen, William H.

Payer, Cheryl. The Debt Trap: The IMF & the Third World. LC 74-24794. 256p. 1975. pap. 15.00 (*0-85345-376-4*, Pub. by Monthly Rev) NYU Pr.

— The World Bank: A Critical Analysis. LC 81-84738. 316p. 1982. pap. 17.00 (*0-85345-602-X*, Pub. by Monthly Rev) NYU Pr.

Payer, I. B. Traite d'Organogenie Comparee de la Fleur. 1966. reprint ed. 132.00 (*3-7682-0346-8*) Lubrecht & Cramer.

Payer, J. H., jt. auth. see Thompson, N. G.

Payer, J. H., ed. see American Society for Testing & Materials Staff.

Payer, Lynn. Disease Mongers: How Doctors, Drug Companies & Insurers Are Making You Feel Sick. LC 92-12513. 292p. 1994. pap. 12.95 (*0-471-00737-4*) Wiley.

— Medicine & Culture. 208p. 1995. pap. 11.95 (*0-8050-4803-0*) H Holt & Co.

Payer, Pierre J. The Bridling of Desire: Views of Sex in the Later Middle Ages. LC 92-95553. 285p. 1993. text 35.00 (*0-8020-2919-1*) U of Toronto Pr.

— Sex & the Penitentials: The Development of a Sexual Code 550-1150. 232p. 1984. text 35.00 (*0-8020-5649-0*) U of Toronto Pr.

Payes, Rachel C. The Dark Towers of Trelochen. 1991. mass mkt. 3.95 (*0-8217-3475-X*, Zebra Kensgtn) Kensgtn Pub Corp.

Payes, Rachel C., jt. auth. see Baum, L. Frank.

Payesko, Bob. Truth about Mary, Vol. I. LC 96-70137. 190p. 1996. pap. text 8.95 (*1-882972-82-1*, 3571) Queenship Pub.

— Truth about Mary, Vol. II. LC 96-70137. 358p. 1996. pap. text 9.95 (*1-882972-83-X*, 3572) Queenship Pub.

— Truth about Mary, Vol. III. LC 96-70137. 422p. 1996. pap. text 10.95 (*1-882972-84-8*, 3573) Queenship Pub.

Payesko, Robert. Anno Antichristi: In the Year of the Antichrist. 160p. 1998. pap. 9.95 (*1-57918-060-4*, 3575) Queenship Pub.

— The Truth about Mary Summary. 160p. 1997. pap. 8.95 (*1-57918-050-7*, 3574) Queenship Pub.

Payesko, Robert J. A Marian Dogma Whose Time Has Come. 100p. 1998. pap. 5.95 (*1-57918-074-4*, 3576) Queenship Pub.

Payette, Douglas A. Advanced Travel. (C). 2001. pap. 40.00 (*0-13-326018-6*, Macmillan Coll) P-H.

Payette, Douglas A. So U Want to Be a Travel Agent: An Introduction to Domestic Travel. LC 94-33705. (Illus.). 224p. 1994. pap. text 61.00 (*0-13-326000-3*) P-H.

Payin, Emil A., jt. auth. see Azrael, Jeremy R.

Payin, Emil A., jt. ed. see Azrael, Jeremy R.

Paykel, E. S., ed. Handbook of Affective Disorders. 2nd ed. LC 92-1553. 699p. 1992. reprint ed. lib. bdg. 85.00 (*0-89862-674-9*) Guilford Pubns.

Paykel, E. S., ed. see Collegium Internationale Neuro-Psychopharmacologic.

Paykel, Eugene S., ed. Handbook of Affective Disorders. 2nd ed. (Illus.). 700p. 1992. text 175.00 (*0-443-04302-7*) Church.

Paykoc, E., jt. ed. see Yuncu, H.

Payle, Howard. The Merry Adventures of Robin Hood. Mattern, Joanne, ed. LC 92-12702. (Illustrated Classics Ser.). (Illus.). 48p. (J). (gr. 3-6). 1996. pap. 5.95 (*0-8167-2859-3*) Troll Communs.

Payler, Frederick. Law Courts, Lawyers & Litigants. xiv, 242p. 1980. reprint ed. 38.50 (*0-8377-1006-5*, Rothman) W S Hein.

— Law Courts Lawyers & Litigants. xiv, 241p. 1997. reprint ed. 76.00 (*1-56169-255-7*) Gaunt.

Paylin, Jolie. Cutover Country: Jolie's Story. LC 76-10245. (Illus.). 174p. reprint ed. pap. 54.00 (*0-608-15515-2*, 202969600063) Bks Demand.

— The Gill Netters. LC 79-89031. 1979. 8.95 (*0-910726-82-5*) Hillsdale Educ.

*__Payling, R. & Larkins, Peter L.__ Optical Emission Lines of the Elements. LC 99-56527. 760p. 2000. 750.00 (*0-471-62378-4*) Wiley.

Payling, R., et al. Glow Discharge Optical Emission Spectrometry. LC 97-2837. 888p. 1997. 389.00 (*0-471-96683-5*) Wiley.

Payling, S. J. Political Society in Lancastrian England: The Greater Gentry in Nottinghamshire. (Oxford Historical Monographs). (Illus.). 290p. 1991. text 72.00 (*0-19-820209-1*) OUP.

Paylor, Ian. Housing Needs of Ex-Offenders. 256p. 1995. 72.95 (*1-85628-996-6*, Pub. by Avebry) Ashgate Pub Co.

Paylor, W. J., ed. see Overbury, Thomas.

Paylore, Patricia. Arid Lands Research Institutions: A World Directory, 1977. rev. ed. LC 77-8982. 333p. 1977. pap. 103.30 (*0-608-05641-3*, 206609500006) Bks Demand.

Paymar, Dan. Video Poker - Optimum Play. LC 98-73292. (Illus.). 1998. pap. 19.95 (*1-886070-11-3*) ConJelCo.

Paymar, Dan, et al. The Professional Poker Dealer's Handbook. Cizmar, Paula, ed. LC 99-163450. (Illus.). 247p. 1998. pap. 19.95 (*1-880685-18-3*) Two Plus NV.

Paymar, Michael. Violent No More: Helping Men End Domestic Abuse. LC 93-18003. 224p. 1993. 21.95 (*0-89793-139-4*); pap. 12.95 (*0-89793-117-3*) Hunter Hse.

Paymar, Michael, jt. auth. see Pence, Ellen.

*__Paymar, Michael J.__ Violent No More: Helping Men End Domestic Abuse. 2nd rev. ed. 256p. 1999. 24.95 (*0-89793-273-0*, Pub. by Hunter Hse) Publishers Group.

— Violent No More: Helping Men End Domestic Abuse. 2nd rev. ed. LC 99-59324. 256p. 1999. pap. 14.95 (*0-89793-268-4*, Pub. by Hunter Hse) Publishers Group.

Payme, Sebastian, ed. Instructing Counsel. 214p. 1994. pap. 210.00 (*0-85459-846-4*, Pub. by Tolley Pubng) St Mut.

Payment & Trudel, eds. Methods & Techniques in Virology. LC 93-1766. (Illus.). 336p. 1993. text 165.00 (*0-8247-9101-0*) Dekker.

Payment, Maggie, jt. auth. see Burn, Bonnie E.

Payment, Maggie, jt. auth. see Stern, Nancy B.

*__Payment, Pierre & Siemiatycki, Jack.__ An Epidemiological Study of Gastrointestinal Health Effects of Drinking Water LC 99-36316. 1999. write for info. (*1-58321-004-0*) Am Water Wks Assn.

Paymer, Marvin. Instrumental Music. (Complete Works of G. B. Pergolesi: No. 3, Vol. XVII). 1993. lib. bdg. 102.00 (*0-945193-46-7*) Pendragon NY.

*__Paymer, Marvin E.__ Out of the Mist: Demystifying & Understanding Other Cultures to Improve International Business. 1999. 48.95 (*1-881907-09-0*) Two Bytes Pub.

Paymer, Marvin E., ed. Facts Behind the Songs: A Handbook of American Popular Music from the Nineties to the 90's. LC 93-24342. (Illus.). 592p. 1993. text 30.00 (*0-8240-5240-4*, H1300) Garland.

Payn, Graham. My Life with Noel Coward. LC 94-42525. (Illus.). 320p. 1996. 24.95 (*1-55783-190-4*) Applause Theatre Bk Pubs.

— My Life with Noel Coward. (Illus.). 320p. 1996. pap. 16.95 (*1-55783-247-1*) Applause Theatre Bk Pubs.

*__Payn, Graham & Morley, Sheridan, eds.__ The Noel Coward Diaries. 2000. pap. 22.50 (*0-306-80960-5*, Pub. by Da Capo) HarpC.

Payn, Graham, ed. see Coward, Noel.

Payn, James. Lost Sir Massingberd: A Romance of Real Life. LC 75-32794. (Literature of Mystery & Detection Ser.). 1976. reprint ed. 28.95 (*0-405-07891-9*) Ayer.

Payn, Terry, jt. auth. see Walker, Bridget.

PayNada.com Editors, jt. auth. see Gershman, Eric W.

Payne. Cognitive Psychology. (C). Date not set. pap., teacher ed. 11.96 (*0-395-68574-5*) HM.

— Cognitive Psychology. (C). 1998. text 65.96 (*0-395-68573-7*) HM.

— Drugs. 1991. 13.75 (*0-697-40328-9*, WCB McGr Hill) McGrw-H Hghr Educ.

Payne. Emotions at Work. pap. text. write for info. (*0-471-49155-1*) Wiley.

Payne. Emotions at Work. 2000. text 84.00 (*0-471-98759-X*) Wiley.

— Geting Started in Public Speaking. 1994. pap., teacher ed. 11.33 (*0-8442-5601-3*) NTC Contemp Pub Co.

— Getting Started in Public Speaking. 3rd ed. LC 93-84615. 128p. 1994. pap., student ed. 15.93 (*0-8442-5597-1*) NTC Contemp Pub Co.

*__Payne.__ How to Prepare for Practice Exam in Speech-language Pathology. 2nd ed. 2000. pap. 40.00 (*0-7693-0160-6*, Pub. by Singular Publishing) Thomson Learn.

— How to Prepare for the Praxis Exam in Audiology. 2000. pap. 40.00 (*0-7693-0161-4*, Pub. by Singular Publishing) Thomson Learn.

Payne. Mechanical Ventilation. 3rd ed. 1999. pap. text, student ed. 18.95 (*0-8151-4376-1*) Mosby Inc.

— Medicolegal Essentials in Health. 1996. pap. text 32.00 (*0-443-05240-9*, W B Saunders Co) Harcrt Hlth Sci Grp.

— Payne on Divorce. 2nd ed. 360p. 1988. 115.00 (*0-409-88849-4*, MICHIE) LEXIS Pub.

— Physical Science. 6th ed. 1991. 18.12 (*0-697-09821-4*, WCB McGr Hill) McGrw-H Hghr Educ.

— Physical Science. 6th ed. 1992. 103.12 (*0-697-09822-2*, WCB McGr Hill) McGrw-H Hghr Educ.

*__Payne.__ Physical Science. 7th ed. 1999. 44.00 (*0-697-15821-7*, WCB McGr Hill) McGrw-H Hghr Educ.

Payne. Pocket Spanish Dictionary. (SPA., Illus.). 32p. (J). (ps-3). 1999. 17.00 (*0-395-97910-2*) HM.

— Spousal Property Rights under the Ontario Family Law Act. 280p. 1987. 72.00 (*0-409-80936-5*, MICHIE) LEXIS Pub.

— Understanding Your Health. 4th ed. 1995. teacher ed. (*0-8151-6803-9*) Mosby Inc.

— Understanding Your Health. 6th ed. LC 99-26520. 1999. 41.00 (*0-07-039235-8*) McGraw.

*__Payne.__ Understanding Your Health. 6th ed. 1999. 8.00 (*0-07-236101-8*) McGraw.

Payne. Understanding Your Health. 7th ed. 2001. 41.00 (*0-07-235323-6*) McGraw.

— Voice & Diction. 1998. 31.25 (*0-07-229971-1*) McGraw.

Payne & Fairmont Press Staff, eds. Utility & Independent Power: Concepts for the New Millenium. LC 97-7709. 368p. (C). 1997. text 89.00 (*0-13-645573-5*) P-H.

*__Payne & Palaci.__ Profession of Dietetics. 2nd ed. LC 99-32799. (Illus.). 192p. 1999. pap. text 32.00 (*0-13-646886-1*) P-H.

*__Payne & Toglia.__ Research Methods in Psychology. 2001. pap. text. write for info. (*1-57259-941-3*) Worth.

Payne, jt. auth. see Kostka.

Payne, Adrian. The Essence of Services Marketing. LC 92-33438. (Essence of Management Ser.). 192p. (C). 1993. pap. text 19.95 (*0-13-284852-X*) P-H.

— Relationship Marketing for Competitive Advantage: Winning & Keeping Customers. 320p. 2000. pap. text 39.95 (*0-7506-4017-0*) Buttrwrth-Heinemann.

Payne, Alfred C. A Community at Prayer. LC 93-39067. (Illus.). 168p. (Orig.). 1993. pap. 9.50 (*0-936015-20-9*) Pocahontas Pr.

— A University at Prayer. LC 86-14613. (Illus.). 1987. 13.95 (*0-9617635-0-7*) VA Tech Found.

Payne, Alfred S. Learning English, a Career Investment for Successful Living. 1995. 14.95 (*0-533-11156-0*) Vantage.

*__Payne, Alina, et al, eds.__ Antiquity & Its Interpreters. LC 98-45686. (Illus.). 336p. 2000. 90.00 (*0-521-59400-6*) Cambridge U Pr.

Payne, Alina A. The Architectural Treatise in the Italian Renaissance: Architectural Invention, Ornament & Literary Culture. LC 98-25694. (Illus.). 320p. (C). 1999. text 75.00 (*0-521-62266-2*) Cambridge U Pr.

Payne, Andrew C., et al. An Introduction to Management for Engineers. 606p. 1996. pap. 79.95 (*0-471-95603-1*) Wiley.

Payne, Andy M. Grande Gold. Date not set. pap. 19.95 (*0-912113-35-9*) Railhead Pubns.

*__Payne, Angela.__ Living Every Single Moment. LC 99-50937. 2000. 9.99 (*1-56309-765-6*, New Hope) Womans Mission Union.

Payne, Anita, et al. The Leydig Cell. Russell, Lonnie D., ed. (Illus.). 800p. (C). 1996. text 137.50 (*0-9627422-7-9*) Cache River Pr.

Payne, Ann. Medieval Beasts. (Illus.). 96p. (C). 1990. 36.00 (*1-56131-018-2*, NAB) I R Dee.

Payne, Annie, tr. see Muggli, Glorianne.

Payne, Anothony J. & Sutton, Paul, eds. Modern Caribbean Politics. LC 92-14475. 400p. 1993. pap. text 16.95 (*0-8018-4435-5*) Johns Hopkins.

Payne, Anthony. Elgar's Third Symphony: The Story of the Reconstruction. 128p. 1999. pap. 14.00 (*0-571-19538-5*, Pub. by Faber & Faber) Penguin Books.

— The International Crisis in the Caribbean. LC 83-49193. 187p. reprint ed. pap. 58.00 (*0-608-06182-4*, 206651400008) Bks Demand.

Payne, Anthony, jt. ed. see Sutton, Paul.

Payne, Anthony J. Politics in Jamaica. 226p. 1995. pap. 21.95 (*0-312-12526-7*) St Martin.

— Politics in Jamaica. 2nd rev. ed. LC 95-125043. 223p. 1995. text 59.95 (*0-312-12525-9*) St Martin.

Payne, Anthony J. & Sutton, Paul, eds. Modern Caribbean Politics. LC 92-14475. 400p. 1993. text 50.00 (*0-8018-4434-7*) Johns Hopkins.

Payne, Anthony J., jt. ed. see Gamble, Andrew.

Payne, B. D., jt. auth. see Sciberras, E.

*__Payne, Betty.__ Shine Annie. 2000. 22.95 (*1-57966-011-8*) Black Belt Communs.

Payne, Beverly C. The Quality of Medical Care: Evaluation & Improvement. LC 75-27157. 1976. 10.00 (*0-87914-029-1*, 669153) Hosp Res & Educ.

Payne, Beverly D., jt. auth. see Manning, Brenda H.

Payne, Bob, jt. auth. see Morris, Reg.

Payne, Brian, jt. ed. see Brown, Louis R.

*__Payne, Brian K.__ Crime & Elder Abuse: An Integrated Perspective. LC 00-25986. 2000. pap. write for info. (*0-398-07057-1*) C C Thomas.

Payne, Burl. Magnetic Healing. (Illus.). 200p. (Orig.). 1997. pap. 19.95 (*1-56550-051-2*) Vis Bks Intl.

Payne, Burt. Burt Payne 3, a Project: The World Is Getting to Be a Funner Place. limited ed. LC 92-90633. (Illus.). 90p. 1995. 40.00 (*0-9633321-0-4*, Pub. by Smart Art Pr) RAM Publications.

Payne, Buryl. The Body Magnetic. large type rev. ed. (Illus.). 216p. 1999. pap. 15.00 (*0-9628569-9-1*) Psycho Physics.

— Getting Started in Magnetic Healing. large type ed. (Illus.). 112p. 1998. pap. 14.00 (*0-9628569-8-3*) Psycho Physics.

— Love & Sex Without Conflict. (Illus.). 64p. 1993. 7.95 (*0-9635600-0-X*) Psycho Physics.

— Magnetic Healing: Advanced Techniques for the Application of Magnetic Forces. LC 98-67862. 234p. 1998. pap. 15.95 (*0-914955-42-X*) Lotus Pr.

*__Payne, C. D.__ Civic Beauties: A Novel with Songs. LC 99-24473. 246p. 1999. pap. 12.95 (*1-882647-20-3*, Pub. by Aivia Pr) Bookpeople.

— Frisco Pigeon Mambo. LC 00-9906. 186p. 2000. pap. 12.95 (*1-882647-24-6*) Aivia Pr.

— Revolting Youth: The Further Journals of Nick Twisp. 278p. 2000. pap. 14.95 (*1-882647-15-7*) Aivia Pr.

Payne, C. D. Youth in Revolt: The Journals of Nick Twisp. 512p. 1996. pap. 15.95 (*0-385-48196-9*, Main St Bks) Doubleday.

Payne, C. H., intro. Akbar & the Jesuits: An Account of the Jesuit Missions to the Court of Akbar. (Curzon Travellers Ser.). (C). 1996. text 65.00 (*0-7007-0349-7*, Pub. by Curzon Pr Ltd) Paul & Co Pubs.

Payne, C. H., tr. Jahangir & the Jesuits. (C). 1997. 29.50 (*81-215-0769-3*, Pub. by M Manoharial) Coronet Bks.

*__Payne, Carleen & Schulman Browning, Mary.__ Getting the Most Out of Your Morning Message. 1999. mass mkt. 12.95 (*0-590-36516-9*) Scholastic Inc.

*__Payne, Carleen D. & Schulman Browning, Mary.__ Guided Reading, Making It Work. (Teaching Strategies Ser.). (Illus.). 260p. (J). 2000. pap. 24.95 (*0-439-11639-2*) Scholastic Inc.

Payne-Carter, David, et al, eds. Gower Champion: Dance & American Musical Theatre, 87. LC 98-21954. (Contributions in Drama & Theatre Studies: Vol. 87). 216p. 1999. 55.00 (*0-313-30451-3*, Greenwood Pr) Greenwood.

Payne, Charles. Petrouchka's Cry: A Biography. 1992. write for info. (*0-679-40045-1*) McKay.

Payne, Charles, jt. auth. see Lawson, Steven F.

Payne, Charles A., et al. Physical Science: Principles & Applications. 6th ed. 688p. (C). 1991. text. write for info. (*0-697-09818-4*, WCB McGr Hill) McGrw-H Hghr Educ.

— Physical Science: Principles & Applications. 6th ed. 688p. (C). 1992. text. write for info. (*0-697-13929-8*, WCB McGr Hill) McGrw-H Hghr Educ.

Payne, Charles M. Getting What We Ask For: The Ambiguity of Success & Failure in Urban Education, 12. LC 83-18623. (Contributions to the Study of Education Ser.: No. 12). 206p. 1984. 55.00 (*0-313-23520-1*, PGW/, Greenwood Pr) Greenwood.

— I've Got the Light of Freedom: The Organizing Tradition & the Mississippi Freedom Struggle. LC 94-24645. 1995. 45.00 (*0-520-08515-9*, Pub. by U CA Pr) Cal Prin Full Svc.

— I've Got the Light of Freedom: The Organizing Tradition & the Mississippi Freedom Struggle. (Centennial Bk.). (Illus.). 506p. (C). 1996. pap. 18.95 (*0-520-20706-8*, Pub. by U CA Pr) Cal Prin Full Svc.

Payne, Charles T. Litchfield & Morris Inscriptions. (Illus.). 330p. 1996. reprint ed. pap. 23.00 (*0-7884-0560-8*, P095) Heritage Bk.

— Litchfield & Morris Inscriptions: Record of Inscriptions upon the Tombstones in the Towns of Litchfield & Morris, Connecticut. (Illus.). 304p. 1997. reprint ed. lib. bdg. 35.00 (*0-8328-5661-4*) Higginson Bk Co.

Payne, Cherron M. Poetic Perception. 127p. 1997. pap. write for info. (*0-9662550-0-3*) C M Payne.

Payne, Chris. Better Services for Older People. (C). 1989. 70.00 (*0-7855-0086-3*, Pub. by Natl Inst Soc Work); pap. 22.00 (*0-902789-60-0*, Pub. by Natl Inst Soc Work) St Mut.

— Evaluating the Quality of Care: A Self-Assessment Manual. 1994. 90.00 (*0-902789-93-7*, Pub. by Natl Inst Soc Work) St Mut.

Payne, Chris & Scott, Tony. Developing Supervision of Teams in Field & Residential Social Work, 2 pts. (C). 1982. 65.00 (*0-7855-0074-X*, Pub. by Natl Inst Soc Work); 35.00 (*0-7855-0075-8*, Pub. by Natl Inst Soc Work) St Mut.

— Developing Supervision of Teams in Field & Residential Social Work, pt.2. National Institute for Social Work Staff, ed. 1985. 12.50 (*0-7855-0831-7*, Pub. by Natl Inst Soc Work) St Mut.

Payne, Chris & Scott, Tony, eds. Developing Supervision of Teams in Field & Residential Social Work, Pt. 1. (C). 1982. pap. 21.00 (*0-902789-24-4*, Pub. by Natl Inst Soc Work) St Mut.

Payne, Chris, jt. auth. see Aplin, Geoff.

Payne, Chris, jt. auth. see Douglas, Robin.

Payne, Chris, jt. auth. see Scott, Tony.

Payne, Chris, jt. ed. see Douglas, Robin.

Payne, Chris, ed. see North Tyneside Social Services Home Managers Staff.

Payne, Chris, jt. ed. see Peretz, Liz.

Payne, Christ & Scott, Tony, eds. Developing Supervision of Teams in Field & Residential Social Work, Pt. 2. (C). 1985. pap. 21.00 (*0-902789-34-1*, Pub. by Natl Inst Soc Work) St Mut.

Payne, Christiana. Rustic Simplicity: Scenes from Cottage Life in Nineteenth-Century Britain. (Illus.). 100p. 1998. pap. 24.95 (*0-85331-747-X*) Lund Humphries.

— Toil & Plenty: Images of the Agricultural Landscape in England, 1780-1890. LC 93-13885. (Agrarian Studies). (Illus.). 272p. 1993. 50.00 (*0-300-05773-3*) Yale U Pr.

Payne, Christine. Tearing down the Walls: An Adult Woman's Guide to Educational Financial Aid. 195p. (Orig.). (C). 1993. pap. text. write for info. (*0-9635930-0-5*) Bibury Court.

Payne, Christopher. Animals in Bronze Reference & Price Guide. (Illus.). 424p. 1993. 89.50 (*0-907462-45-6*) Antique Collect.

— Miller's Collecting Furniture: The Facts at Your Fingertips. (Illus.). 192p. 1996. 19.95 (*1-85732-877-9*, Pub. by Reed Illust Books) Antique Collect.

— 19th Century European Furniture. (Illus.). 348p. 1986. 89.50 (*1-85149-001-9*) Antique Collect.

Payne, Christopher, ed. Sotheby's Concise Encyclopedia of Furniture. (Illus.). 208p. 1995. pap. 29.95 (*1-85029-649-9*, Pub. by Conran Octopus) Antique Collect.

Payne, Christopher & Gleeson, Janet. Miller's Collecting Furniture: The Facts at Your Fingertips. (Miller's Antiques Checklist Ser.). 1998. 19.95 (*1-84000-053-8*, Pub. by Millers Pubns) Antique Collect.

Payne, Christopher T. Strategic Financial Planning for Healthcare Organizations: An Executive Guide to Capital Debt. (C). 1994. text 60.00 (*1-55738-615-3*, Irwn Prfssnl) McGraw-Hill Prof.

*__Payne, Claude E.__ Reclaiming the Great Commission: A Practical Model for Transforming Denominations & Congregations. LC 00-35737. 240p. 2000. 23.00 (*0-7879-5268-0*) Jossey-Bass.

Payne, Claudine & Blanchard, Charles. Archaeology & Environment at the Pineland Site Complex: Information & Activities for 4th & 5th Grade Teachers. (Illus.). 16p. 1997. pap. 3.00 (*1-881448-06-1*) IAPS Bks.

Payne, Claudine, et al. The Apalachee Indians of Florida. 2nd ed. Cole, Vicki, ed. (Series of Lesson Plans: Ser. 2, No. 14). (Illus.). 12p. (J). (gr. k-12). 1997. write for info. (*1-889030-09-0*) FL Div Hist Res.

— The Calusa Indians. 2nd ed. (Series of Lesson Plans: Ser. 1, No. 12). (Illus.). 16p. (J). (gr. k-12). 1997. write for info. (*1-889030-02-3*) FL Div Hist Res.

— Demise of the Native Peoples of Florida. 2nd ed. Cole, Vicki, ed. (Series of Lesson Plans: Ser. 2, No. 13). (Illus.). 12p. (J). (gr. k-12). 1997. write for info. (*1-889030-07-4*) FL Div Hist Res.

— Discovering Florida's Indian Mounds. 2nd ed. (Series of Lesson Plans: Ser. 1, No. 7). (Illus.). 12p. 1996. write for info. (*0-9642289-7-1*) FL Div Hist Res.

— Farm Life in the Early 1800s. 2nd ed. (Series of Lesson Plans: Series 1, No. 3). (Illus.). 12p. 1996. write for info. (*0-9642289-3-9*) FL Div Hist Res.

— Florida Place Names. 2nd ed. (Series of Lesson Plans: Series 1, No. 4). (Illus.). 1996. write for info. (*0-9642289-4-7*) FL Div Hist Res.

P

An Asterisk (*) at the beginning of an entry indicates that the title is appearing for the first time.

— Seminole Indians During the Colonial Period. 2nd ed. Cole, Vicki L., ed. (Series of Lesson Plans: Series 2, No. 17). (Illus.). 16p. (J). (gr. k-12). 1997. write for info. (1-889030-08-2) FL Div Hist Res.
— The Timucua Indians of Florida. 2nd ed. Cole, Vicki, ed. (Series of Lesson Plans: Ser. 2, No. 15). (Illus.). 16p. (J). (gr. k-12). 1997. write for info. (1-889030-06-6) FL Div Hist Res.
— What Buildings Tell Us. 2nd ed. (Series of Lesson Plans: Series 1, No. 6). (Illus.). 12p. 1996. write for info. (0-9642289-6-3) FL Div Hist Res.
— World War II Comes to Florida. 2nd ed. (Series of Lesson Plans: Series 1, No. 5). (Illus.). 12p. 1996. write for info. (0-9642289-5-5) FL Div Hist Res.
Payne, Clive, jt. ed. see O'Muircheartaigh, Colm A.
Payne Consulting Group, jt. auth. see Payne, Donna.
Payne, D., ed. An Easy Guide to the Casio Scientific Calculator. 64p. (C). 1991. 50.00 (1-870941-85-3) St Mut.
Payne, Dana, ed. see Pedersen, Helge.
Payne, Daniel A. History of the African Methodist Episcopal Church. LC 69-18573. (American Negro: His History & Literature. Series 2). 1969. reprint ed. 39.95 (0-405-01885-1) Ayer.
— Recollections of 70 Years. LC 68-29015. (American Negro: His History & Literature, Ser. 1). (Illus.). 1969. reprint ed. 32.95 (0-405-01834-7) Ayer.
— The Semi-Centenary & the Retrospection of the African Methodist Episcopal Church. LC 76-37598. (Black Heritage Library Collection). 1977. reprint ed. 25.95 (0-8369-8974-0) Ayer.
— Sermons & Addresses, 1853-1891. LC 70-38458. (Religion in America, Ser. 2). 1976. 21.95 (0-405-04079-2) Ayer.
— Treatise on Domestic Education. LC 75-157373. (Black Heritage Library Collection). 1977. 21.95 (0-8369-8811-6) Ayer.
Payne, Daniel G. Voices in the Wilderness: American Nature Writing & Environmental Politics. LC 95-39422. 195p. 1996. pap. 17.95 (0-87451-752-4) U Pr of New Eng.
— Voices in the Wilderness: American Nature Writing & Environmental Politics. LC 95-39422. 195p. (C). 1996. text 42.00 (0-87451-751-6) U Pr of New Eng.
***Payne, Danyal.** Cows, 1. 1998. pap. text 10.98 (1-57717-029-6) Todtri Prods.
Payne, Darwin. As Old as Dallas Itself: A History of the Lawyers of Dallas, The Dallas Bar Association & the City They Helped Build. LC 99-90293. (Illus.). 336p. 1999. 35.00 (1-893451-01-1, Pub. by Three Forks) Herveys Bklink.
— Owen Wister: Chronicler of the West, Gentleman of the East. LC 85-1989. (Illus.). 392p. 1985. lib. bdg. 24.95 (0-87074-205-1) SMU Press.
— Texas Chronicles: The Heritage & Enterprise of the Lone Star State. (Illus.). 176p. 1994. 39.95 (1-882933-04-4) Cherbo Pub Grp.
Payne, Darwin, ed. Sketches of a Growing Town: Episodes & People of Dallas from Early Days to Recent Times. 208p. 1991. pap. 12.95 (0-9631492-0-2) S Meth U Mstr Lib Arts.
***Payne, Darwin & Fitzpatrick, Kathy.** From Prairie to Planes: How Dallas & Fort Worth Overcame Politics & Personalities to Build One of the World's Biggest & Busiest Airports. (Illus.). 317p. 1999. 28.00 (1-893451-00-3, Pub. by Three Forks) Herveys Bklink.
Payne, Darwin, jt. ed. see Hlavach, Laura.
Payne, Darwin R. Canterville Ghost: A Full Length Play. 49p. 1963. reprint ed. pap. 3.50 (0-87129-044-8, C71) Dramatic Pub.
— A Christmas Carol: A Playscript. LC 80-18827. (Illus.). 138p. 1981. pap. 11.95 (0-8093-0999-8) S Ill U Pr.
— Computer Scenographics. LC 93-39696. (Illus.). 272p. (C). 1994. 51.95 (0-8093-1904-7); pap. 31.95 (0-8093-1905-5) S Ill U Pr.
— Scenographic Imagination. 3rd ed. LC 92-13216. (Illus.). 400p. (C). 1993. 41.95 (0-8093-1850-4); pap. 26.95 (0-8093-1851-2) S Ill U Pr.
— Theory & Craft of the Scenographic Model. rev. ed. LC 84-5630. (Illus.). 192p. 1985. 31.95 (0-8093-1193-3); pap. 19.95 (0-8093-1194-1) S Ill U Pr.
Payne, Darwin R., ed. see Lash, James.
Payne, David. Cronologia Biblica Portavoz. Orig. Title: The Student Bible Timeline. (SPA., Illus.). 16p. 1994. pap. 9.99 (0-8254-1552-7, Edit Portavoz) Kregel.
— Early from the Dance. 1996. pap. 12.95 (0-345-41025-4) Ballantine Pub Grp.
***Payne, David.** Gravesend Light. LC 99-89408. 342p. 2000. 24.95 (0-385-47338-9) Doubleday.
Payne, David. Island Cycling: A Cycle-Campers Guide to Vancouver Island. (Illus.). 192p. (Orig.). 1996. pap. 14.95 (1-55143-082-7) Orca Bk Pubs.
— Ruin Creek. large type ed. LC 93-45632. 576p. 1994. lib. bdg. 23.95 (0-8161-5948-3, G K Hall Lrg Type) Mac Lib Ref.
Payne, David A. Applied Educational Assessment: IBM Version. LC 96-48410. (Education Ser.). 500p. (C). 1997. 68.95 (0-534-50843-X) Wadsworth Pub.
— Applied Educational Assessment: Macintosh Version. 500p. 1997. 80.95 (0-534-50845-6) Wadsworth Pub.
— Designing Educational Project & Program Evaluations: A Practical Overview Based on Research & Experience. LC 93-38469. (Evaluation in Education & Human Services Ser.). 288p. (C). 1994. lib. bdg. 109.00 (0-7923-9426-7) Kluwer Academic.
***Payne, David A.** Evaluating Service-Learning Activities & Programs. 200p. 2000. pap. text 34.50 (0-8108-3747-1) Scarecrow.
Payne, David C. Psychological Theories of Learning & Teaching: An Analysis of the Use of the Psychology. Lee, Don Y., ed. LC 87-82508. 270p. (C). 1988. 43.50 (0-939758-18-0) Eastern Pr.
Payne, David F. Deuteronomy. 121p. 1993. pap. 22.00 (0-7152-0531-5) St Mut.
— Kingdoms of the Lord: A History of the Hebrew Kingdoms from Saul to the Fall of Jerusalem. LC 81-3197. (Illus.). 340p. reprint ed. pap. 105.40 (0-608-11698-X, 202085200020) Bks Demand.
— Samuel. 292p. 1993. pap. 22.00 (0-7152-0521-8, Pub. by St Andrew) St Mut.
Payne, David F., jt. auth. see Bruce, F. F.
Payne, David G. & Conrad, Frederick G., eds. Intersections in Basic & Applied Memory Research. 368p. 1996. text 69.95 (0-8058-1973-8) L Erlbaum Assocs.
Payne, David S. Myth & Modern Man in Sherlock Holmes: Sir Arthur Conan Doyle & the Uses of Nostalgia. LC 91-70565. 325p. 1992. 25.00 (0-934468-29-X, Pub. by Gaslight) Empire Pub Srvs.
Payne, Diane. Arizona Teacher Proficiency Examination Workbook: ATPE Workbook. rev. ed. 96p. 1998. pap. 11.95 (0-935810-52-8) R H Pub.
Payne, Diane, jt. auth. see VanSant, Sondra.
Payne, Donna. Word 97 for Law Firms. LC 97-76504. (Computer Bks.). 512p. 1997. per. 29.99 (0-7615-1316-7) Prima Pub.
— Word 2000 for Law Firms. 500p. 1999. pap. 29.99 (0-7615-1803-7, Prima Tech) Prima Pub.
Payne, Donna & Lenzo, Fran. The Handel's Messiah: Family Advent Reader. 1999. 19.99 (0-8024-5574-3) Moody.
Payne, Donna & Payne Consulting Group. Outlook 98 Fast & Easy. LC 97-76319. (Fast & Easy Ser.). 336p. 2000. pap. 16.99 (0-7615-1405-8) Prima Pub.
Payne, Donna, jt. auth. see Wempen, Faithe.
Payne, Doris L. The Pragmatics of Word Order: Typological Dimensions of Verb Initial Languages. (Empirical Approaches to Language Typology Ser.: No. 7). xiv, 298p. (C). 1990. lib. bdg. 113.85 (3-11-012207-3) Mouton.
Payne, Doris L., ed. Amazonian Linguistics: Studies in Lowland South American Languages. LC 89-37601. (Illus.). 584p. 1990. text 42.50 (0-292-70414-3) U of Tex Pr.
— Pragmatics of Word Order Flexibility. LC 92-5354. (Typological Studies in Language: No. 22). viii, 320p. 1992. 103.00 (1-55619-408-0); pap. 29.95 (1-55619-409-9) J Benjamins Pubng Co.
Payne, Doris L. & Barshi, Immanuel, eds. External Possession. LC 99-22381. (Typological Studies in Language: Vol. 39). ix, 573p. 1999. 125.00 (1-55619-652-0) J Benjamins Pubng Co.
***Payne, Doris L. & Barshi, Immanuel, eds.** External Possession. LC 99-22381. (Typological Studies in Language: Vol. 39). ix, 573p. 1999. pap. 34.95 (1-55619-655-5) J Benjamins Pubng Co.
Payne, Doris P. Captain Jack, Modoc Renegade. (Illus.). 272p. 1979. pap. 9.95 (0-8323-0340-2) Binford Mort.
Payne, Dorothy. Arkansas Pensioners, Eighteen Eighteen to Nineteen Hundred: Records of Some Arkansas Residents Who Applied to the Federal Government for Benefits Arising from Services in Federal Military Organizations. 226p. 1985. 26.50 (0-89308-537-5) Southern Hist Pr.
— Life after Divorce. (Looking up Ser.). 24p. (Orig.). 1982. pap. 1.95 (0-8298-0610-5) Pilgrim OH.
Payne, Dorothy, jt. auth. see Kostka, Stefan.
Payne, Douglas, et al. Latin America after the Cold War: Implications for U. S. Policy. (Latin American Affairs (Study Groups) Ser.). (Illus.). 96p. (C). 1991. pap. 9.95 (1-879128-01-2) Americas Soc.
Payne, Douglas W. The Democratic Mask: The Consolidation of the Sandinista Revolution. LC 85-81020. (Perspectives on Freedom Ser.: No. 3). 100p. 1985. pap. 13.75 (0-932088-06-6) Freedom Hse.
Payne, E. A. & Payne, William F. Easily Applied Principles of Keypunching. LC 72-118315. (C). 1970. text 18.95 (0-685-03852-1) P-H.
Payne, E. F., tr. see Schopenhauer, Arthur.
Payne, E. J., ed. Select Works of Edmund Burke: A New Imprint of the Payne Edition, 3 vols. Incl. Select Works of Edmund Burke Vol. 1: Thoughts on the Cause of the Present Discontents & the Two Speeches on America. xxi, 406p. 20.00 (0-86597-162-5); Select Works of Edmund Burke Vol. 1: Thoughts on the Cause of the Present Discontents & the Two Speeches on America. xxi, 406p. pap. 10.00 (0-86597-163-3); Select Works of Edmund Burke Vol. 2: Reflections on the Revolution in France. xxxiii, 476p. 1999. 20.00 (0-86597-164-1); Select Works of Edmund Burke Vol. 2: Reflections on the Revolution in France. xxxiii, 476p. 1999. pap. 10.00 (0-86597-165-X); Select Works of Edmund Burke Vol. 3: Letters on a Regicide Peace. xi, 434p. 1999. 20.00 (0-86597-166-8); Select Works of Edmund Burke Vol. 3: Letters on a Regicide Peace. xi, 434p. 1999. pap. 10.00 (0-86597-167-6); LC 97-34325. 1998. 55.00 (0-86597-253-2); Set pap. 27.00 (0-86597-254-0) Liberty Fund.
Payne, Edgar A. Composition of Outdoor Painting. 5th rev. ed. Hatcher, Evelyn P., ed. LC 84-90701. (Illus.). 169p. 1995. 38.00 (0-944699-02-2) DeRus Fine Art.
Payne, Edmund C. & McArthur, Robert. Developing Expert Systems: A Knowledge Engineer's Handbook For Rules & Ojects. LC 89-27383. 401p. 1990. pap. 34.95 (0-471-51413-6) Wiley.
***Payne, Edward J.** History of the New World Called America, 2 vols. (LC History-America-E). 1999. reprint ed. lib. bdg. 180.00 (0-7812-4270-3) Rprt Serv.
***Payne, Elaine B. & Whittaker, Lesley.** Developing Essential Study Skills. LC 99-38844. (Illus.). 2000. pap. write for info. (0-13-955874-8) P-H.
Payne, Elizabeth. The Pharaohs of Ancient Egypt. LC 80-21392. (Landmark Books Ser.). (Illus.). 192p. (J). (gr. 5-9). 1998. pap. 5.99 (0-394-84699-0, Pub. by Knopf Bks Yng Read) Random.
Payne, Elizabeth, ed. see Hunt, John H.
Payne, Elizabeth A. Reform, Labor, & Feminism: Margaret Dreier Robins & the Women's Trade Union League. LC 87-10794. (Women in American History Ser.). (Illus.). 234p. 1988. text 24.95 (0-252-01445-6) U of Ill Pr.
Payne, Elizabeth Ann. Pharaohs of Ancient Egypt. (Landmark Bks.). (J). 1964. 10.09 (0-606-02225-2, Pub. by Turtleback) Demco.
Payne, Elizabeth B., ed. Everything's Relative: Genealogical Taglines: Aphorisms for an Electronic Age. LC 99-217715. (Illus.). 200p. 1998. pap. 8.95 (0-88082-085-3) New Eng Hist.
Payne, Emmy. Katy No-Pocket, 001. LC 44-8099. (Illus.). 32p. (J). (ps-3). 1973. pap. 5.95 (0-395-13717-9, Sandpiper) HM.
— Katy No-Pocket, 001. (Illus.). 32p. (J). (ps-3). 1973. 17.00 (0-395-17104-0) HM.
Payne, Emmy. Katy No-Pocket. (Carry-Along Book & Cassette Favorites Ser.). (Illus.). (J). (ps-3). 1989. pap. 9.95 incl. audio (0-395-71411-7, 492749) HM.
Payne, Emmy. Katy No Tiene Bolsa. (SPA., Illus.). 32p. (J). (ps-3). 1999. pap. 5.95 (0-395-97911-0) HM.
Payne, Eric. I See Through Eyes. 90p. 1999. pap. 9.95 (0-7392-0177-8, PO3143) Morris Pubng.
Payne, Eric F., tr. see Schopenhauer, Arthur.
Payne, Ernest A. The Saktas: An Introductory & Comparative Study. LC 97-24965. (Illus.). 153p. 1997. pap. 6.95 (0-486-29866-3) Dover.
Payne, Ernest A., jt. auth. see Robinson, H. Wheeler.
Payne, F. Anne. Chaucer & Menippean Satire. LC 79-5412. 303p. reprint ed. pap. 94.00 (0-608-09919-8, 206925700003) Bks Demand.
— King Alfred & Boethius: An Analysis of the Old English Version of the Consolation of Philosophy. LC 68-9834. 161p. reprint ed. pap. 50.00 (0-608-10006-4, 201537000093) Bks Demand.
***Payne, F. William.** User's Guide to Natural Gas Purchasing & Risk Management. LC 99-45783. 242p. 1999. 87.00 (0-88173-298-2) Fairmont Pr.
Payne, F. William. User's Guide to Natural Gas Technologies. LC 98-53185. 1999. write for info. (0-88173-299-0) Fairmont Pr.
Payne, F. William. User's Guide to Natural Gas Technologies. LC 98-53185. (Illus.). write for info. (0-13-021552-X) P-H.
Payne, F. William. Utility & Independent Power: Concept for the New Millenium. LC 97-7709. 354p. 1997. 84.00 (0-88173-267-2) Fairmont Pr.
Payne, F. William, ed. Advanced Technologies: Improving Industrial Efficiency. LC 84-48433. 300p. 1985. 39.95 (0-88173-001-7) Fairmont Pr.
— Cogeneration Management Reference Guide. LC 96-48537. 443p. 1997. 68.00 (0-88173-248-6) Fairmont Pr.
— Efficient Boiler Operations Sourcebook. 3rd ed. (Illus.). 266p. 1991. 67.00 (0-88173-135-8, 0275) Fairmont Pr.
Payne, F. William & McGowan, John J. Building Energy Management & Control Systems. 2nd ed. (Illus.). 399p. (gr. 13). 1988. text 82.95 (0-442-23734-0) Chapman & Hall.
Payne, F. William & Thompson, Richard E., eds. Efficient Boiler Operations Sourcebook. 4th ed. LC 95-45496. 309p. 1996. 79.00 (0-88173-222-2) Fairmont Pr.
Payne, F. William, jt. auth. see American Gas Association Staff.
Payne, F. William, ed. see Association of Energy Engineers Staff.
Payne, F. William, ed. see Energy Engineers Associations.
Payne, Fiona, ed. The Human Body. LC 92-54481. (Picturepedia Ser.). (Illus.). (J). (gr. k-3). 1993. 12.95 (1-56458-249-3) DK Pub Inc.
Payne, Frank W. John Donne & His Poetry. LC 70-120991. (Poetry & Life Ser.). reprint ed. 27.50 (0-404-52528-8) AMS Pr.
Payne, Franklin E., Jr. Biblical Healing for Modern Medicine: Choosing Life & Health: Or Disease & Death. LC 93-71420. 240p. (Orig.). 1993. pap. 12.95 (0-9629876-1-1) Covenant Enter.
***Payne, Fred & Parameswaran, Ash M., eds.** Education in Microelectronics & MEMS. 1999. pap. text 50.00 (0-8194-3495-7) SPIE.
Payne, G., et al. Plant Cell & Tissue Culture in Liquid Systems. 368p. 1993. 120.00 (0-471-03726-5) Wiley.
Payne, G. C., jt. ed. see Cuff, E. C.
Payne, G. L. & Wallschutzky, I. G. Tax Questions & Answers, 1994. 1993. pap. 51.00 (0-409-30950-8, Austral, MICHIE) LEXIS Pub.
Payne-Gallway, Ralph. Cross-Bow, Medieval & Modern. 1985. pap. 35.00 (0-87556-232-9) Saifer.
— The Crossbow. (C). 1988. 220.00 (0-900470-69-0, Pub. by New5 Holland) St Mut.
***Payne, Geoff.** Social Divisions. LC 00-30584. 2000. pap. write for info. (0-312-23612-3) St Martin.
Payne, Geoff & Abbott, Pamela. The Social Mobility of Women: Beyond Male Mobility Models. 224p. 1990. 69.95 (1-85000-845-0, Falmer Pr); pap. 34.95 (1-85000-846-9, Falmer Pr) Taylor & Francis.
Payne, Geoff, jt. ed. see Abbott, Pamela.
Payne, Geoff, jt. ed. see Cross, Malcolm.
***Payne, Geoffrey K.** Making Common Ground: Public/Private Partnerships in Land for Housing. 256p. 1999. pap. 25.00 (1-85339-479-3) Intermed Tech.
Payne, Gerrye. The Year-God. Trusky, Tom, ed. LC 91-71533. (Ahsahta Press Modern & Contemporary Poets of the West Ser.). 60p. (Orig.). 1992. pap. 6.95 (0-916272-51-6) Ahsahta Pr.
***Payne, Glen.** Cathedrals: The Story of America's Best-Loved Gospel Quartet. (Illus.). 2000. pap. 12.99 (0-310-23520-0) Zondervan.
Payne, Glen, et al. The Cathedrals: The Story of America's Best-Loved Gospel Quartet. LC 97-50603. 224p. 1998. 18.99 (0-310-20983-8) Zondervan.
Payne, H. E., jt. ed. see Hunt, Gareth.
Payne, Heidi, ed. see Aslett, Grant.
***Payne, Helen.** Ethical Practice & the Abuse of Power in Social Responsibility: Leave No Stone Unturned. LC 99-55429. 240p. 1999. 28.95 (1-85302-743-X) Jessica Kingsley.
Payne, Helen, ed. Dance Movement Therapy: Theory & Practice. LC 91-22938. 296p. (C). 1992. pap. 29.99 (0-415-05660-8, A5956) Routledge.
— One River, Many Currents: A Handbook of Inquiry in the Arts Therapies. 250p. 1993. pap. 29.95 (1-85302-153-9) Taylor & Francis.
Payne, Henry F. Organic Coating Technology, Vol. 1. LC 54-5971. 70.00 (0-471-67286-6) Wiley.
— Organic Coating Technology, Vol. 2. 72.00 (0-471-67353-6) Wiley.
— Organic Coating Technology, 2 vols., Vol. 2. Incl. Vol. 1. Oils, Resins, Varnishes & Polymers. LC 54-5971. 674p. 1954. pap. 200.00 Vol. 1. Pigments, & Pigmented Coatings for Architectural & Industrial Applications., 2 vols. LC 54-5971. 674p. pap. 200.00 (0-608-16081-4, 205553600001); LC 54-5971. (Illus.). 725p. reprint ed. Set pap. 200.00 (0-608-18687-2, 205553600002) Bks Demand.
Payne, Hod. A Man, a Woman & a Dream. 290p. (Orig.). 1994. pap. 11.95 (0-9641574-0-3) Ski-Lak.
Payne, Howard E., et al. As the Storm Clouds Gathered: European Perceptions of American Foreign Policy in the 1930's. LC 78-7074. (Topics in American Diplomatic History Ser.). 173p. 1980. 19.95 (0-941690-06-7) Regina Bks.
— As the Storm Clouds Gathered: European Perceptions of American Foreign Policy in the 1930's. LC 78-7074. (Topics in American Diplomatic History Ser.). 173p. 1980. pap. 11.95 (0-87716-101-1) Regina Bks.
Payne, Ian. The Almain & Other Measures in England: Their History & Choreography. LC 95-359. 220p. 1996. 59.95 (0-85967-965-9, Pub. by Scolar Pr) Ashgate Pub Co.
— The Provision & Practice of Sacred Music at Cambridge Colleges & Selected Cathedrals, c. 1547-c. 1646: A Comparative Study of the Archival Evidence. LC 92-43443. (Outstanding Dissertations in Music from British Universities Ser.). (Illus.). 480p. 1993. text 50.00 (0-8153-0952-X) Garland.
Payne, J. Barton. Encyclopedia of Biblical Prophecy: The Complete Guide to Scriptural Predictions & Their Fulfillment. 758p. (Orig.). (gr. 10). 1996. reprint ed. pap. 29.99 (0-8010-7051-1) Baker Bks.
— Theology of the Older Testament. 1971. pap. 21.99 (0-310-30721-X, 10545P) Zondervan.
Payne, J. F., ed. see Boghurst, William.
Payne, J. H. Cogeneration in the Cane Sugar Industry. (Sugar Ser.: No. 12). 338p. 1990. 222.25 (0-444-88826-8) Elsevier.
— Unit Operations in Cane Sugar Production. (Sugar Technology Ser.: Vol. 4). 204p. 1982. 157.50 (0-444-42104-1) Elsevier.
Payne, J. P. & Severinghaus, J. W., eds. Pulse Oximetry. (Illus.). 225p. 1986. 69.95 (0-387-16857-5) Spr-Verlag.
Payne, J. W. In Vitro Techniques in Research: Recent Advances. 176p. 1991. 339.95 (0-471-93251-5, Wiley-Liss) Wiley.
Payne, J. W., ed. In Vitro Techniques in Research: Recent Advances. 224p. 1989. 113.00 (0-335-15885-4) Wiley.
— Microorganisms & Nitrogen Sources: Transport & Utilization of Amino Acids, Peptides, Proteins, & Related Substrates. LC 79-42900. (Illus.). 884p. reprint ed. pap. 200.00 (0-608-17685-0, 203040400069) Bks Demand.
Payne-Jackson, Arvilla & Lee, John. Folk Wisdom & Mother Wit: John Lee - An African American Herbal Healer, 161. LC 92-46396. (Contributions in Afro-American & African Studies: No. 161). 192p. 1993. 57.95 (0-313-28868-2, GM8868, Greenwood Pr) Greenwood.
Payne-Jame. Key Facts in Clinical Nutrition. 1995. pap. text 14.95 (0-443-05182-8, W B Saunders Co) Harcrt Hlth Sci Grp.
***Payne, James.** Studies in Biology: Lab Guide Biology 1162. 86p. (C). 2000. spiral bd. 14.95 (0-7872-7266-3) Kendall-Hunt.
— Text W/sftw-structured Progr W/quickbasic. (Computer Science Ser.). 363p. (C). 1991. mass mkt. 64.95 (0-534-92563-4) PWS Pubs.
Payne, James, jt. auth. see Carlin, Diana B.
Payne, James A. Introduction to Simulation: Programming Techniques & Methods Analysis. 1982. pap. text, teacher ed. write for info. (0-07-048946-7) McGraw.
Payne, James E. & Desai, Pramod D. Properties of Intermetallic Alloys Vol. 1: Aluminides. LC 94-39757. 1994. 400.00 (0-931682-48-7) Purdue U Pubns.
Payne, James E., jt. auth. see Blum, Kenneth.
Payne, James F., et al. Laboratory Studies in Zoology. 4th ed. 220p. 1990. pap. text 24.95 (0-88725-130-7) Hunter Textbks.
***Payne, James F., et al.** Laboratory Studies in Zoology. 5th ed. (Illus.). 240p. 2000. pap. text 26.95 (0-88725-267-2) Hunter Textbks.
Payne-James, Jason, et al, eds. Artificial Nutrition Support in Clinical Practice. 2nd ed. (Greenwich Medical Media Ser.). (Illus.). 600p. 2000. text 225.00 (1-900151-97-9) OUP.
Payne, James L. The American Threat, National Security & Foreign Policy. 344p. (Orig.). 1981. pap. text 19.95 (0-915728-07-9) Lytton Pub.
— Costly Returns: Burdens of the U. S. Tax System. LC 92-19854. 272p. 1993. 34.95 (1-55815-202-4); pap. 19.95 (1-55815-215-6) ICS Pr.

An Asterisk (*) at the beginning of an entry indicates that the title is appearing for the first time.

— The Culture of Spending: Why Congress Lives Beyond Our Means. 250p. 1991. 29.95 (*1-55815-134-6*) ICS Pr.
— Foundations of Empirical Political Analysis. viii, 151p. 1984. pap. text 9.95 (*0-915728-08-7*) Lytton Pub.
— Incentive Theory & Political Process: Motivation & Leadership in the Dominican Republic. (Illus.). 165p. 1976. reprint ed. 23.95 (*0-915728-01-X*) Lytton Pub.
— Labor & Politics in Peru. LC 65-22335. 1980. reprint ed. 23.95 (*0-915728-05-2*) Lytton Pub.
— Overcoming Welfare: Expecting More from the Poor & from Ourselves. LC 98-5360. 288p. 1998. 26.50 (*0-465-06924-X*, Pub. by Basic) HarpC.
— Princess Navina Visits Mandaat. (Illus.). 56p. 1994. pap. 9.95 (*0-915728-10-9*) Lytton Pub.
— Principles of Social Science Measurement. LC 75-7177. 157p. (Orig.). (C). 1975. pap. text 9.95 (*0-915728-02-8*) Lytton Pub.

Payne, James L., et al. The Motivation of Politicians. LC 83-26853. 216p. 1984. pap. text 24.95 (*0-88229-824-0*) Burnham Inc.

Payne, James L., ed. see Hill, Octavia.

Payne, James P. & Hill, D. W., eds. The Management of the Acutely Ill: A Symposium Held in July, 1976. LC 77-370280. (Chartridge Symposium Ser.). (Illus.). 187p. reprint ed. pap. 58.00 (*0-8357-8943-8*, 203345800086) Bks Demand.
— Real-Time Computing in Patient Management: A Symposium Held in June, 1975. LC 76-367573. (Chartridge Symposium Ser.). 215p. reprint ed. pap. 66.70 (*0-8357-7003-6*, 203345900086) Bks Demand.

Payne, James R. Multicultural Autobiography: American Lives. LC 91-27130. 376p. (C). 1992. pap. text 18.95 (*0-87049-740-5*); lib. bdg. 41.00 (*0-87049-739-1*) U of Tenn Pr.

Payne, James R., ed. Joseph Seamon Cotter, Jr. Complete Poems. LC 88-33073. (Illus.). 224p. 1990. 32.00 (*0-8203-1152-9*) U of Ga Pr.

Payne, James R. & Bazergui, Andre. Evaluation of Test Methods for Asbestos Replacement Gasket Materials. LC 92-180810. (MTI Publication Ser.: No. 36). 397p. 1990. reprint ed. pap. 123.10 (*0-608-06731-8*, 206692800009) Bks Demand.

Payne, James S. Selling Cars, Insurance, & over the Counter Products: Differential Selling in the Real World. 145p. (Orig.). 1996. pap. 25.95 (*1-57171-004-3*) Lincoln-Rembrandt.

Payne, James S., et al. Differential Management & Motivation: An Advanced Understanding of Human Development & Motivation. rev. ed. 197p. 1994. pap. 27.95 (*1-57171-000-0*) Lincoln-Rembrandt.
— Differential Selling. 124p. (Orig.). 1994. pap. 25.95 (*1-57171-001-9*) Lincoln-Rembrandt.
— Differential Selling in the Real World. 145p. 1997. pap. 25.95 (*1-57171-030-2*) Lincoln-Rembrandt.
— Rehabilitation Techniques: Vocational Adjustment for the Handicapped. 208p. (C). 1984. 35.95 (*0-89885-159-9*, Kluwer Acad Hman Sci) Kluwer Academic.

Payne, Jean. Decorative Folk Painting. (Illus.). 128p. (Orig.). 1996. pap. 16.95 (*0-304-34823-6*, Pub. by Cassell) Sterling.

Payne, Jerry. Colloquial Hungarian. 1987. pap. 14.95 (*0-7102-0636-4*, Routledge Thoemms) Routledge.
— Colloquial Hungarian. 2nd ed. (Colloquials Ser.). 240p. 1987. audio 15.95 (*0-7102-0984-3*, 09843, Routledge Thoemms) Routledge.
— Colloquial Hungarian. 2nd ed. (Colloquials Ser.). 368p. 1987. pap. 18.99 (*0-415-04589-4*, 06364, Routledge Thoemms) Routledge.
— Colloquial Hungarian, Set. 2nd ed. (Colloquials Ser.). 240p. 1988. pap. 29.95 incl. audio (*0-415-00777-7*, A2575, Routledge Thoemms) Routledge.

Payne, Jerry & Kolmel, Rainer, eds. Babel: The Cultural & Linguistic Barriers Between Nations. 195p. 1990. pap. text 30.00 (*0-08-037969-9*, Pub. by Aberdeen U Pr) Macmillan.

Payne, Jerry, et al. The History of Costume: From Ancient Mesopotamia Through the Twentieth Century. 2nd ed. 608p. (C). 1997. 116.00 (*0-06-047141-7*) Addson-Wesley Educ.

Payne, Jessie. When Basildon Was Farms & Fields. 1993. pap. 16.00 (*0-86025-416-X*, Pub. by I Henry Pubns) Empire Pub Srvs.

Payne, Jessie K. A Ghost Hunter's Guide to Essex. unabridged ed. (Illus.). 144p. 1995. pap. 15.00 (*0-86025-463-1*, Pub. by I Henry Pubns) Empire Pub Srvs.

***Payne, Jim.** Funk Drumming. 144p. 1999. spiral bd. 29.95 incl. audio compact disk (*0-7866-4814-7*, 93892CDP) Mel Bay.

Payne, Jim. Funk Drumming: All Levels. 156p. 1983. spiral bd. 14.95 (*0-87166-511-5*, 93892) Mel Bay.
— Give the Drummer Some. Weinger, Harry, ed. LC 96-86533. (Illus.). 276p. (Orig.). (YA). 1996. pap. text 29.95 (*1-57623-603-X*, MMBK0068CD) Wrner Bros.
— QuickStart in Works for Windows. 152p. (C). 1995. pap. text 11.55 (*1-881991-40-7*) Scott Jones Pubng.

Payne, Joan. Flying High: The Complete Book of Flyball. (Illus.). 128p. 1996. pap. 15.95 (*0-9652723-0-3*) K D B.

Payne, Joan & Witherspoon, Joan. Education & Training for 16-18 Year Olds: Individual Paths, National Trends. 224p. (C). 1996. pap. 19.95 (*0-85374-655-9*) Brookings.

Payne, Joan C. Adult Neurogenic Language Disorders: Assessment & Treatment - A Comprehensive Ethnobiological Approach. LC 97-6441. 405p. 1997. 55.00 (*1-56593-729-5*, 1418) Thomson Learn.

Payne, Joan C. & Ashmolean Museum. Catalog of the Predynastic Egyptian Collection. LC 93-16134. 416p. 1994. 135.00 (*0-19-951355-4*) OUP.

Payne, Joel, jt. auth. see Diel, Armin.

Payne, John. A Manual of Management Training Exercises. (Illus.). 236p. 1989. ring bd. 245.95 (*1-85904-046-2*, Pub. by Gower) Ashgate Pub Co.
— Poetical Works: Definitive Edition, 2 vols. LC 73-128418. 1973. reprint ed. 110.00 (*0-404-04946-X*) AMS Pr.

Payne, John & Payne, Shirley. Exercises for Developing First-Line Managers. 412p. 1995. 271.95 (*0-566-07519-9*, Pub. by Gower) Ashgate Pub Co.
— The "How to" Guide for Managers. LC 95-49265. 150p. 1996. 56.95 (*0-566-07726-4*, Pub. by Gower) Ashgate Pub Co.
— Management Basics: The How-To Guide for Managers. LC 98-17612. 304p. 1998. pap. 9.95 (*1-58062-023-X*) Adams Media.

Payne, John, tr. see Boccaccio, Giovanni.

Payne, John B. & Zikmund, Barbara B., eds. Reformation Roots. (Living Theological Heritage of the United Church of Christ Ser.: Vol. 2). 696p. 1996. 50.00 (*0-8298-1143-5*) Pilgrim OH.

Payne, John B., tr. see Erasmus, Desiderius.

Payne, John C. The Great Cruising Cookbook: An International Galley Guide. (Illus.). 256p. 1996. 27.50 (*0-924486-92-9*) Sheridan.
— Marine Electrical & Electronics Bible. 2nd rev. ed. LC 98-27298. (Illus.). 432p. 1998. 39.95 (*1-57409-060-7*) Sheridan.

Payne, John H. Brutus: or The Fall of Tarquin. (BCL1-PS American Literature Ser.). 56p. 1992. reprint ed. lib. bdg. 59.00 (*0-7812-6828-1*) Rprt Serv.
— Charles II: or The Merry Monarch. (Notable American Authors Ser.). 1999. reprint ed. lib. bdg. 125.00 (*0-7812-8712-X*) Rprt Serv.
— Clari: or The Maid of Milan. (Notable American Authors Ser.). 1999. reprint ed. lib. bdg. 125.00 (*0-7812-8711-1*) Rprt Serv.
— Plays - Brutus: or The Fall Tarquin. (Notable American Authors Ser.). 1999. reprint ed. lib. bdg. 125.00 (*0-7812-8709-X*) Rprt Serv.
— Richelieu: A Domestic Tragedy. (Notable American Authors Ser.). 1999. reprint ed. lib. bdg. 125.00 (*0-7812-8713-8*) Rprt Serv.
— Therese: The Orphan of Geneva. (Notable American Authors Ser.). 1999. reprint ed. lib. bdg. 125.00 (*0-7812-8710-3*) Rprt Serv.

Payne, John M., jt. ed. see Emerson, Darrel T.

Payne, John W., et al. The Adaptive Decision Maker. LC 92-21581. (Illus.). 346p. (C). 1993. pap. text 21.95 (*0-521-42526-3*) Cambridge U Pr.
— The Adaptive Decision Maker. LC 92-21581. (Illus.). 346p. (C). 1993. text 59.95 (*0-521-41505-5*) Cambridge U Pr.

Payne, John W., jt. auth. see Carroll, John S.

Payne, Johnny. Baja. LC 98-27435. 144p. 1998. pap. 12.95 (*0-9647515-8-5*) Ltd Edits.
— Chalk Lake: A Novel. LC 96-19325. 176p. (Orig.). 1996. 18.95 (*0-9647515-2-6*); pap. 12.95 (*0-9647515-1-8*) Ltd Edits.
— Conquest of the New Word: Experimental Fiction & Translation in the Americas. LC 93-6537. (Texas Pan American Ser.). 304p. (C). 1993. text 35.00 (*0-292-76546-0*) U of Tex Pr.
— Kentuckiana. LC 97-23378. 255p. 1997. 24.95 (*0-8101-5075-1*, TriQuart) Northwestern U Pr.
— Kentuckiana. 272p. 1999. pap. 14.95 (*0-8101-5090-5*, TriQuart) Northwestern U Pr.

***Payne, Johnny.** The She-Calf & Other Quechua Folk Tales. LC 99-43530. 2000. pap. 22.50 (*0-8263-2195-X*) U of NM Pr.

Payne, Joseph A. Befriending: A Self-Guided Retreat for Busy People. LC 92-28398. 176p. 1993. pap. 15.95 (*0-8091-3354-7*) Paulist Pr.

Payne, Joseph F. English Medicine in the Anglo-Saxon Times. LC 75-23749. (Illus.). reprint ed. 30.00 (*0-404-13355-X*) AMS Pr.

Payne, Joseph N., ed. Mathematics for the Young Child. LC 90-42418. (Illus.). 306p. 1990. 38.50 (*0-87353-288-0*) NCTM.

Payne, Judith A. & Fitz, Earl E. Ambiguity & Gender in the New Novel of Brazil & Spanish America: A Comparative Assessment. LC 92-37863. 239p. 1993. text 29.95 (*0-87745-405-1*) U of Iowa Pr.

Payne, Junaidi. This Is Borneo. 1998. 39.95 (*1-85368-329-9*, Pub. by New5 Holland) Sterling.
— Wild Malaysia: The Wildlife & Scenery of Peninsular Malaysia, Sarawak & Sabah. (Illus.). 210p. 1990. 39.95 (*0-262-16078-1*) MIT Pr.

Payne, K. T. & Anderson, Noma B. How to Prepare for the N. E. S. P. A. National Examination in Speech Pathology & Audiology. (Illus.). 188p. (Orig.). (C). 1991. pap. 39.95 (*1-879105-33-0*, 0217) Thomson Learn.

Payne, Karen. Between Ourselves, 001. 432p. 1984. pap. 14.95 (*0-395-36571-6*) HM.

Payne, Kathryn. Longing at Least Is Constant. LC 98-215173. 64p. 1988. pap. 9.75 (*0-921411-68-5*) Genl Dist Srvs.

***Payne, Katy.** Silent Thunder: In the Presence of Elephants. 288p. 1999. pap. 13.95 (*0-14-028596-2*, Penguin Bks) Viking Penguin.

Payne, Katy B. Silent Thunder: In the Presence of Elephants. LC 98-4255. 288p. 1998. 25.00 (*0-684-80108-6*) S&S Trade.

Payne, Kay E. Different but Equal: Communication Between the Sexes. 1999. write for info. (*0-275-96522-8*, Praeger Pubs) Greenwood.

Payne, Keith, jt. auth. see Sharkey, John.

Payne, Keith B. Deterrence in the Second Nuclear Age. 184p. (C). 1996. text 32.00 (*0-8131-1998-7*); pap. text 16.00 (*0-8131-0895-0*) U Pr of Ky.

Payne, Keith B. & Gray, Colin S., eds. The Nuclear Freeze Controversy. LC 84-20835. 194p. 1985. pap. text 17.50 (*0-8191-4365-0*); lib. bdg. 57.00 (*0-8191-4364-2*) U Pr of Amer.

Payne, Kim B. Games Children Play. (Illus.). 256p. 1997. pap. 19.95 (*1-869890-78-7*, Pub. by Hawthorn Press) Anthroposophic.

Payne, L. E. Improperly Posed Problems in Partial Differential Equations. (CBMS-NSF Regional Conference Ser.: No. 22). v, 76p. 1975. pap. text 22.00 (*0-89871-019-7*) Soc Indus-Appl Math.

Payne, L. N., ed. Marek's Disease. (Developments in Veterinary Virology Ser.). 1985. text 146.50 (*0-89838-730-2*) Kluwer Academic.

Payne, Larry. Healthy Back Exercises for High Stress Professionals. 48p. (Orig.). 1986. pap. 5.00 (*0-9617784-0-7*) Samata Multimedia.

Payne, Larry, jt. auth. see Feuerstein, George.

Payne, Lauren M. A Leader's Guide to Just Because I Am: A Child's Book of Affirmation. Espeland, Pamela, ed. (Illus.). 56p. 1994. pap., teacher ed. 13.95 (*0-915793-61-X*) Free Spirit Pub.

Payne, Lauren M. & Rohling, Claudia. Just Because I Am: A Child's Book of Affirmation. Espeland, Pamela, ed. LC 93-30609. (Illus.). 32p. (J). (ps-3). 1994. pap. 8.95 (*0-915793-60-1*) Free Spirit Pub.
— A Leader's Guide to We Can Get Along: A Child's Book of Choices. Espeland, Pamela, ed. (Illus.). 64p. (Orig.). 1997. pap. 14.95 (*1-57542-014-7*) Free Spirit Pub.

Payne, Lauren Murphy, see Murphy Payne, Lauren.

Payne, Laurence. Dead for a Ducat. large type ed. (Mystery Ser.). 439p. 1989. 27.99 (*0-7089-1948-0*) Ulverscroft.
— The Nose on My Face. large type ed. (Mystery Ser.). 560p. 1989. 27.99 (*0-7089-2031-4*) Ulverscroft.

Payne, Laurie, ed. see O'Dell, Carla, et al.

Payne, Laurie, jt. ed. see Powers, Vicki.

Payne, Leanne. The Broken Image: Restoring Personal Wholeness Through Healing Prayer. LC 95-31249. 176p. (YA). (gr. 10). 1995. reprint ed. pap. 12.99 (*0-8010-5334-X*, Hamewith MI) Baker Bks.

Payne, Leanne. Crisis in Masculinity. LC 95-37526. 144p. (Orig.). (YA). (gr. 10). 1995. reprint ed. pap. 10.99 (*0-8010-5320-X*, Hamewith MI) Baker Bks.

Payne, Leanne. Healing Homosexuality. LC 96-11269. 80p. (YA). (gr. 10). 1996. reprint ed. pap. 8.99 (*0-8010-5700-0*, Hamewith MI) Baker Bks.
— The Healing Presence: Curing the Soul Through Union with Christ. LC 95-22766. 288p. (YA). (gr. 10). 1995. reprint ed. pap. 14.99 (*0-8010-5348-X*, Hamewith MI) Baker Bks.
— Listening Prayer: Learning to Hear God's Voice & Keep a Prayer Journal. LC 94-37753. 264p. 1999. pap. 12.99 (*0-8010-5916-X*) Baker Bks.
— Real Presence: The Glory of Christ with Us & Within Us. LC 94-46185. 192p. (YA). (gr. 10). 1995. pap. 14.99 (*0-8010-5172-X*, Hamewith MI) Baker Bks.
— Restoring the Christian Soul: Overcoming Barriers to Completion in Christ Through Healing Prayer. LC 95-50955. 256p. (Orig.). (YA). (gr. 10). 1996. reprint ed. pap. 12.99 (*0-8010-5699-3*, Hamewith MI) Baker Bks.

***Payne, Leigh A.** Uncivil Movements: The Armed Right Wing & Democracy in Latin America. LC 99-45860. 2000. 42.50 (*0-8018-6242-6*) Johns Hopkins.

Payne, Leigh A., jt. ed. see Bartell, Ernest.

Payne, Lina. Rebuilding Communities in a Refugee Settlement: A Casebook from Uganda. (Oxfam Development Casebks.). 96p. 1998. pap. 12.95 (*0-85598-394-9*, Pub. by Oxfam Pub) Stylus Pub VA.

Payne, Linda. Arkansas Historical Math Facts. LC 90-63448. 72p. (J). (gr. 3-6). 1986. spiral bd. 25.00 (*0-914546-84-8*) Rose Pub.

Payne, Linda A., ed. see Larson, Virginia.

Payne, Lisa R. Once upon a Garage Sale: From Fairy Tale to Reality: How to Make More Money, Get Rid of More Stuff, & Otherwise Succeed at Your Garage Sale. LC 97-66241. (Illus.). 168p. (Orig.). 1997. pap. 14.95 (*0-9657137-2-5*) Clover Creat.

Payne, Louisa. Deadline for Murder. 243p. 1998. pap. 15.95 (*1-892896-58-3*) Buy Books.
— The Family Pact. unabridged ed. 287p. 1998. pap. 16.95 (*1-892896-07-9*) Buy Books.
— No Deposit No Return. 254p. 1999. 15.95 (*0-7414-0186-X*) Buy Books.

Payne, Lucille M., jt. auth. see Rice, Dorothy M.

Payne, Lucille V. The Lively Art of Writing. 1969. mass mkt. 6.99 (*0-451-62712-1*, Ment) NAL.

Payne, Lynette R. Fountainheads: Selected Poems. LC 90-91730. 56p. (Orig.). 1990. pap. text 5.40 (*0-9626904-0-6*) Linsu Pr.

Payne, M. G., jt. auth. see Hurst, G. S.

Payne, M. G., ed. see International Symposium on Resonance Ionization Sp.

Payne, Malcolm. Modern Social Work Theory: A Critical Introduction. 2nd rev. ed. LC 96-53614. 354p. (C). 1997. pap. text 33.95 (*0-925065-15-3*) Lyceum IL.
— Teamwork in Multiprofessional Care. 208p. 2000. pap. text 29.95 (*0-925065-36-6*) Lyceum IL.

Payne, Malcolm, jt. auth. see Shardlow, Steven.

***Payne, Mark.** Hayfever: Thorsons Health: How to Beat Hayfever--Permanently. 208p. 1998. pap. 10.00 (*0-7225-3630-5*, Pub. by Thorsons MD) Natl Bk Netwk.

Payne, Mark. How to Take Care of Your Heart: Your Survival & Lifestyle Handbook. (Illus.). 150p. 1989. pap. 19.95 (*0-7463-0563-X*, H563, Pub. by How To Bks) Trans-Atl Phila.

Payne, Marque. The Whole Truth about the Tithe: What the Church Never Told You. (Illus.). 40p. (Orig.). 1996. pap. 5.99 (*1-889208-97-3*) Glad Tidngs Pub.

Payne, Marvin. Love & Oranges. (Keepsake Paperbacks Ser.). 62p. 1988. reprint ed. pap. 3.95 (*0-88494-402-6*) Jackman Pubng.
— Love & Oranges. 2nd ed. 64p. (YA). (gr. 9 up). 1988. reprint ed. pap. 3.95 (*0-929985-08-7*) Jackman Pubng.

Payne, Marvin & Randle, Guy. The Planemaker: A Magical Story with Songs. Date not set. pap. 4.00 (*1-57514-182-5*) Encore Perform Pub.

Payne, Marvin, jt. auth. see Barkdull, Larry.

Payne, Mary B., jt. auth. see O'Tool, Martha N.

Payne, Mary B., jt. auth. see O'Toole, Martha N.

Payne, May D., compiled by. Melodic Index to the Works of Johann Sebastian Bach. LC 74-24035. reprint ed. 37.50 (*0-404-12858-0*) AMS Pr.

Payne, Michael. Messerschmitt Bf109 in the West, 1937-1940. LC 97-38291. (Luftwaffe at War Ser.). 72p. 1998. pap. 12.95 (*1-85367-305-6*, Pub. by Greenhill Bks) Stackpole.
— Reading Knowledge: An Introduction to Foucault, Barthes & Althusser. LC 96-46163. 200p. 1997. 58.95 (*0-631-19566-1*); pap. 25.95 (*0-631-19567-X*) Blackwell Pubs.
— Reading Theory: An Introduction to Lacan, Derrida & Kristeva. (Illus.). 250p. (C). 1993. pap. 26.95 (*0-631-18289-6*) Blackwell Pubs.

Payne, Michael, ed. A Dictionary of Cultural & Critical Theory. LC 95-8003. 644p. 1996. 87.95 (*0-631-17197-5*) Blackwell Pubs.
— A Dictionary of Cultural & Critical Theory. LC 95-8003. 644p. 1997. per. 36.95 (*0-631-20753-8*) Blackwell Pubs.

Payne, Michael & Heath, James M. Text, Interpretation, Theory. LC 85-5893. (Bucknell Review Ser.: Vol. 29. No. 2). 176p. 1985. 22.00 (*0-8387-5097-4*) Bucknell U Pr.

Payne, Michael, ed. see Alvarez, Tom & Morga, Michael.

Payne, Michael, jt. ed. see Fleming, Richard.

Payne, Michael, ed. see Hoecklin, Lisa.

Payne, Michael, ed. see Hunger, J. David & Wheelen, Thomas.

Payne, Michael, ed. see Mendenhall, William, et al.

Payne, Michael, jt. ed. see Neuman, Mark.

Payne, Michael, jt. ed. see Nueman, Mark.

Payne, Michael, ed. see Schon, Argyris.

Payne, Michael, illus. see Hageman, Joan.

Payne, Michael H. The Blood Jaguar. LC 98-23496. 256p. 1998. 22.95 (*0-312-86783-2*, Pub. by Tor Bks) St Martin.

***Payne, Michael H.** The Blood Jaguar. 256p. 1999. mass mkt. 6.99 (*0-8125-6675-0*, Pub. by Tor Bks) St Martin.

Payne, Michael N. & Anderson, Wayne R. Applied Trigonometry. 567p. (C). 1989. pap. text, teacher ed. 28.00 (*0-15-502912-6*) SCP.

***Payne, Michelle.** Bodily Discourses: When Students Write about Abuse & Eating Disorders. LC 99-58722. 160p. 2000. pap. text 20.00 (*0-86709-471-0*, Pub. by Boynton Cook Pubs) Heinemann.

Payne, Muriel A. Oliver Untwisted. 1972. 34.95 (*0-8490-0761-5*) Gordon Pr.

Payne, Nancy H. Widowing: A Guide to Another Life. (Illus.). 56p. (Orig.). 1997. pap. 6.95 (*1-879418-78-9*) Audenreed Pr.

Payne, Neil F. Techniques for Wildlife Habitat Management of Wetlands. 250p. 1992. pap. 34.95 (*0-07-048956-4*) McGraw.
— Wildlife Habitat Management of Wetlands. LC 98-13107. Orig. Title: Techniques for Wildlife Habitat Management of Wetlands. (Illus.). 549p. (C). 1998. reprint ed. text 78.50 (*1-57524-089-0*) Krieger.

Payne, Neil F. & Bryant, Fred C. Wildlife Habitat Management of Forestlands, Rangelands, & Farmlands. LC 98-3251. (Illus.). 840p. (C). 1998. reprint ed. text 98.50 (*1-57524-093-9*) Krieger.

***Payne, Neil F. & Bryant, Fred C.** Wildlife Habitat Management of Wetlands/Wildlife Habitat Management of Forestlands, Rangelands, & Farmlands. (Illus.). 1440p. 1999. reprint ed. text 132.75 (*1-57524-122-6*) Krieger.

Payne, Neil F., jt. auth. see Taber, Richard D.

Payne, Nigel & Hart, Dominic. Everyone Must Leave: The Day They Stopped the National. LC 99-490990. (Illus.). 224p. 1998. 35.00 (*1-84018-053-6*, Pub. by Mainstream Pubng) Trafalgar.

Payne, Niravi B. The Language of Fertility. LC 98-23895. 288p. 1998. pap. 14.00 (*0-609-80198-8*) Crown Pub Group.

***Payne, Niravi B.** The Language of Fertility: A Revolutionary Mind-Body Program for Conscious Conception. 266p. 2000. reprint ed. text 25.00 (*0-7881-6991-2*) DIANE Pub.

Payne, P. A., jt. auth. see Marks, R. M.

Payne, P. L. The Hydro: A Study of the Development of the Major Hydro-Electric Schemes Undertaken by the North of Scotland Hydro-Electric Board. (Illus.). 368p. 1988. text 50.00 (*0-08-036584-1*, Pub. by Aberdeen U Pr) Macmillan.

Payne, P. L., ed. Studies in Scottish Business History. 435p. 1967. 37.50 (*0-7146-1349-5*, Pub. by F Cass Pubs) Intl Spec Bk.

***Payne-Palacio, June & Theis, Monica.** West & Wood's Introduction to Foodservice. 9th ed. 640p. 2000. 66.67 (*0-13-020889-2*, Prentice Hall) P-H.

Payne-Palacio, June & Theis, Monica, eds. West & Wood's Introduction to Foodservice. 8th ed. LC 96-27613. (Illus.). 606p. 1996. 77.00 (*0-13-495425-4*, Merrill Coll) P-H.

Payne, Patrica. Sex Tips from a Dominatrix. LC 99-37321. 224p. 1999. pap. 19.00 (*0-06-039287-8*) HarpC.

Payne, Peggy. Doncaster: A Legacy of Personal Style. LC 97-90225. (Illus.). 300p. (Orig.). 1997. pap. write for info. (*0-9657251-0-3*) Tanner Cos.

Payne, Peggy, ed. see Richardson, Arleta.

Payne, Peter. Martial Arts: The Spiritual Dimension. LC 86-51575. (Art & Imagination Ser.). (Illus.). 1987. pap. 15.95 (*0-500-81025-7*, Pub. by Thames Hudson) Norton.

P

An Asterisk (*) at the beginning of an entry indicates that the title is appearing for the first time.

Payne, Peter A. Concise Encyclopedia of Biological & Biomedical Measurement Systems. (Advances in Systems Control & Information Engineering Ser.: No. 3). 504p. 1991. 263.75 (0-08-036188-9, Pergamon Pr) Elsevier.

Payne, Peter L., ed. Studies in Scottish Business History. LC 67-20815. (Illus.). xviii, 435p. 1967. 49.50 (0-678-05076-7) Kelley.

Payne, Peter L. & Davis, Lance E. The Savings Bank of Baltimore, 1818-1866: A Historical & Analytical Study. LC 75-41778. (Companies & Men: Business Enterprises in America Ser.). (Illus.). 1976. reprint ed. 23.95 (0-405-08093-X) Ayer.

Payne, Philip & Lipton, Michael. How Third World Rural Households Adapt to Dietary Energy Stress: The Evidence & the Issues. LC 94-17153. (Food Policy Review Ser.: Vol. 2). 1994. write for info. (0-89629-501-X) Intl Food Policy.

Payne, Philip, jt. auth. see Gray, Alistair.

Payne, Philip, tr. see Musil, Robert.

Payne, Philip, tr. & selected by see Musil, Robert.

Payne, R. George E. Barnard's Invention of a Mail Marking Machine. (Illus.). 80p. 1994. pap. 15.00 (1-880065-11-8) Machine Cancel Soc.

***Payne, R. & Green, P., eds.** COMPSTAT, 1998: Proceedings in Computational Statistics, 13th Symposium Held in Bristol, Great Britain, 1998. (Illus.). xii, 501p. 1998. pap. 109.00 (3-7908-1131-9) Spr-Verlag.

Payne, R., jt. auth. see Morris, R.

Payne, R. E. Caught in the Crossfire: The R. E. "Gus" Payne Story. Arroyo, Sidney L., ed. (Illus.). 217p. (Orig.). 1995. pap. 9.95 (1-885308-01-9) Sr Polit Action.

Payne, R. E., jt. auth. see Mangiaracina, Greg.

Payne, R. E., ed. see Bellavitis, P.

Payne, R. W. Genstat 5 Reference Manual. (Illus.). 768p. 1987. 79.00 (0-19-852212-6) OUP.

Payne, Ray K. Am I a Baby? Johnson, Desiree, ed. (Illus.). 55p. (Orig.). 1995. pap. 5.00 (1-889732-00-1) Word-For-Word.

Payne, Reba, jt. auth. see Williams, Joe.

Payne, Richard, et al, eds. Assessment & Treatment of Cancer Pain. LC 98-12346. (Progress in Pain Research & Management Ser.: Vol. 12). (Illus.). 331p. 1998. 71.00 (0-931092-21-3) Intl Assn Study Pain.

Payne, Richard & Turner, Drexl. The Woodlands: Into the Woods. (Illus.). 98p. 1994. 40.00 (0-9643743-0-7); pap. 20.00 (0-9643743-1-5) Judson Design.

Payne, Richard, jt. auth. see Goodhart, C. A. E.

Payne, Richard A. Charlie the Shy Cowboy. (Illus.). 36p. (J). (gr. 1-9). 1993. pap. 4.95 (0-9636186-2-8) Blue Sky Grap.

— Collin the Canada Goose. (J). (gr. 1-5). 1993. pap. text 4.95 (0-9636186-0-1) Blue Sky Grap.

— How to Get a Better Job Quicker. 3rd ed. (Illus.). 256p. 1987. 16.95 (0-8008-3965-X) Taplinger.

— Rick & Jim's Real Reel Indians. LC 94-70509. (Illus.). 32p. (Orig.). 1994. pap. text 7.95 (0-9636186-8-7) Blue Sky Grap.

Payne, Richard J. The Clash with Distant Cultures: Values, Interests, & Force in American Foreign Policy. LC 94-47454. 285p. (C). 1995. pap. text 19.95 (0-7914-2648-3) State U NY Pr.

— The Clash with Distant Cultures: Values, Interests, & Force in American Foreign Policy. LC 94-47454. 285p. (C). 1995. text 59.50 (0-7914-2647-5) State U NY Pr.

— Getting Beyond Race: The Changing American Culture. LC 97-51414. 256p. 1998. 25.00 (0-8133-6858-8, Pub. by Westview) HarpC.

— The Nonsuperpowers & South Africa: Implications for U. S. Policy. LC 89-46340. 333p. 1990. reprint ed. pap. 103.30 (0-608-01070-7, 205937800001) Bks Demand.

— Opportunities & Dangers of Soviet-Cuban Expansion: Towards a Pragmatic U. S. Policy. LC 87-26778. 261p. (C). 1988. text 21.50 (0-88706-796-4) State U NY Pr.

— The Third World & South Africa: Post-Apartheid Challenges, 304. LC 92-8847. (Contributions in Political Science Ser.: No. 304). 224p. 1992. 52.95 (0-313-28542-X, PTW, Greenwood Pr) Greenwood.

— The West European Allies, the Third World, & U. S. Foreign Policy: Post-Cold War Challenges. LC 91-2563. (Contributions in Political Science Ser.: No. 282). 256p. 1991. pap. 21.95 (0-275-93626-0, B3626, Praeger Pubs) Greenwood.

— The West European Allies, The Third World, & U. S. Foreign Policy: Post-Cold War Challenges, 282. LC 91-11334. (Contributions in Political Science Ser.: No. 282). 256p. 1991. 65.00 (0-313-27460-6, PWN/, Greenwood Pr) Greenwood.

Payne, Richard K. The Tantric Ritual of Japan. (C). 1991. 90.00 (81-85179-76-X, Pub. by Aditya Prakashan) S Asia.

Payne, Richard K., ed. Re-Visioning "Kamakura" Buddhism. LC 98-9375. (Studies in East Asian Buddhism: Vol. 11). (Illus.). 288p. 1998. text 50.00 (0-8248-2024-X); pap. text 28.95 (0-8248-2078-9) UH Pr.

***Payne, Rob, ed.** Pop Goes the Story! Canadian Fiction Anthology. 256p. 1999. pap. 12.95 (1-55082-233-0) Quarry Pr.

***Payne, Robert.** The Dream & the Tomb: A History of the Crusades. 2000. reprint ed. pap. 19.95 (0-8154-1086-7, Pub. by Cooper Sq) Natl Bk Netwk.

Payne, Robert. The Holy Fire. LC 79-27594. 328p. 1980. reprint ed. pap. 12.95 (0-913836-61-3) St Vladimirs.

Payne, Robert, ed. & tr. see Shen Ts'Ung-Wen.

Payne, Robert, tr. see Chekhov, Anton.

Payne, Robert B. Behavior, Mimetic Songs & Song Dialects, & Relationships of the Parasitic Indigobirds (Vidua) of Africa. 333p. 1973. 10.00 (0-943610-11-7) Am Ornithologists.

— A Distributional Checklist of the Birds of Michigan. LC 83-621944. (University of Michigan, Museum of Zoology, Miscellaneous Publications: No. 164). 75p. reprint ed. pap. 30.00 (0-608-07026-2, 206723300009) Bks Demand.

— Sexual Selection, Lek & Arena Behavior, & Sexual Size Dimorphism in Birds. 52p. 1984. 15.00 (0-943610-40-0) Am Ornithologists.

Payne, Robert J., jt. auth. see Morris, Reg.

Payne, Robert J., ed. see Billings, Bart.

Payne, Robert O. Geoffrey Chaucer. 2nd ed. (Twayne's English Authors Ser.: No. 1). 160p. (C). 1986. 32.00 (0-8057-6908-0) Macmillan.

— The Key of Remembrance, a Study of Chaucer's Poetics. LC 72-12316. 246p. 1973. reprint ed. lib. bdg. 75.00 (0-8371-6694-2, PAKR, Greenwood Pr) Greenwood.

Payne, Roberta L. The Influence of Dante on Medieval English Dream Visions. (American University Studies: Romance Languages & Literature: Ser. II, Vol. 63). 178p. (C). 1989. text 36.30 (0-8204-0505-1) P Lang Pubng.

Payne, Roberta L., tr. from ITA. Il Novellino. LC 94-36773. (Studies in Italian Culture: Vol. 19). XVII, 154p. (C). 1995. text 42.95 (0-8204-2676-8) P Lang Pubng.

Payne, Roberta L., tr. see Boccaccio, Giovanni.

Payne, Rodger M. The Self & the Sacred: Conversion & Autobiography in Early American Protestantism. LC 97-45426. 136p. 1998. text 27.00 (1-57233-015-5) U of Tenn Pr.

Payne, Roger. In the Company of Whales. (Illus.). 288p. 1995. text 24.00 (0-02-595245-5) Macmillan.

Payne, Roger, photos by. Handjobs Reader Vol. 2: Dads Do It, Sons Like It. (Illus.). 100p. (C). 1999. pap. 8.00 (1-886458-22-7) Avenue Servs.

Payne, Rolf. Drainage & Sanitation. LC 82-1455. (Illus.). 192p. reprint ed. pap. 59.60 (0-608-17292-8, 203033000068) Bks Demand.

Payne, Ronald, jt. auth. see Dobson, Christopher.

Payne, Rosemary A. Relaxation Techniques: A Practical Handbook for the Health Care Professional. LC 94-33408. 1995. pap. text 33.95 (0-443-04933-5) Church.

Payne, Roy & Cooper, Cary L., eds. Groups at Work. LC 80-41586. (Wiley Series on Individuals, Groups & Organizations). 278p. reprint ed. pap. 86.20 (0-608-15936-0, 203092900072) Bks Demand.

Payne, Roy & Firth-Cozens, Jenny, eds. Stress in Health Professionals. LC 87-8122. (Illus.). 312p. 1987. reprint ed. pap. 96.80 (0-608-02605-0, 206326300004) Bks Demand.

Payne, Roy, jt. auth. see Firth-Cozens, Jenny.

Payne, Roy, jt. ed. see Cooper, Cary L.

Payne, Roy A. Rainbow in Your Tear. 208p. 1998. 17.95 (1-890622-48-6) Leathers Pub.

Payne, Roy L., jt. ed. see Firth-Cozens, Jenny.

Payne, Roy R. Without Faith It Is Impossible to Please God. 90p. 1999. pap. 15.00 (0-7392-0221-9, PO3249) Morris Pubng.

Payne, Ruby K. A Framework for Understanding & Working with Students & Adults from Poverty. 216p. (Orig.). (C). 1995. pap. text 18.95 (0-9647437-4-4) RFT Pubng.

— A Framework for Understanding Poverty. 3rd rev. ed. Orig. Title: Poverty - A Framework for Understanding & Working with Students & Adults from Poverty. 231p. (C). 1998. pap. text 22.00 (0-9647437-2-8) RFT Pubng.

Payne, Ruby K., jt. auth. see Stailey, Jay.

Payne, Sandra J. Barney's Time for Counting. Davis, Guy, ed. (Barney Ser.). (Illus.). 24p. (J). (ps-3). 1999. pap. 2.99 (1-57064-449-7, Barney Publ) Lyrick Pub.

Payne, Sandra J., et al. Barney's Alphabet Fun with Mother Goose. Davis, Guy, ed. (Barney Ser.). 64p. (J). (ps-k). 1999. pap. 1.99 (1-57064-450-0, Barney Publ) Lyrick Pub.

Payne, Sandra J., ed. see Harman, Chuck.

***Payne, Sandy.** Barney, I Did It Myself! LC 99-69203. (Barney Ser.). (Illus.). 20p. (J). (ps-k). 2000. 5.95 (1-57064-719-4) Lyrick Pub.

— Barney's Neighborhood Friends. (Barney Ser.). (Illus.). 84p. (J). (ps-k). 2000. pap. 1.99 (1-57064-779-8, 97985) Lyrick Pub.

Payne, Scott M. Accelerating Cleanup at Toxic Waste Sites: Fast-Tracking Environmental Actions & Decision Making. LC 97-37138. 320p. 1997. lib. bdg. 69.95 (1-56670-237-2) Lewis Pubs.

Payne, Sebastian, jt. auth. see Bibby, Peter.

Payne, Sebastian, jt. ed. see Sunkin, Maurice.

Payne, Sheila. Delivering Customer Service: How to Win a Competitive Edge Through Managing Customer Relationships Successfully. (Business Basics Ser.). 192p. 1997. pap. 19.95 (1-85703-354-X, Pub. by How To Bks) Trans-Atl Phila.

— How to Work in an Office: Getting Off to a Successful Start. (Illus.). 176p. 1993. pap. 19.95 (1-85703-094-X, Pub. by How To Bks) Trans-Atl Phila.

Payne, Sheila & Walker, Janet. Psychology for Nurses & the Caring Professions. LC 95-14761. (Social Science for Nurses & the Caring Professions Ser.). 192p. 1995. 98.95 (0-335-19411-7); pap. 31.95 (0-335-19410-9) OpUniv Pr.

Payne, Sheila, et al. Loss & Bereavement. LC 99-24181. (Health Psychology Ser.). 1999. 28.95 (0-335-20105-9) OpUniv Pr.

Payne, Shirley, jt. auth. see Payne, John.

Payne, Silvano, ed. World Satellite Directory, 1989. 2nd ed. (Illus.). 225p. 1989. 175.00 (0-936361-10-7) Design Pubs.

— World Satellite Directory, 1990. 3rd ed. (Illus.). 1990. 125.00 (0-936361-11-5) Design Pubs.

Payne, Stacy H., ed. see Shivell, Kirk.

Payne, Stanley G. Basque Nationalism. LC 75-15698. (Basque Ser.). (Illus.). xii, 304p. 1975. text 30.00 (0-87417-042-7) U of Nev Pr.

— Falange: A History of Spanish Fascism. ix, 316p. 1961. pap. 14.95 (0-8047-0059-1) Stanford U Pr.

— Fascism: A Comparative Approach Toward a Definition. LC 79-5413. 248p. 1980. 30.00 (0-299-08060-9) U of Wis Pr.

— Fascism: A Comparative Approach Toward a Definition. LC 79-5413. 248p. 1983. pap. 15.95 (0-299-08064-1) U of Wis Pr.

***Payne, Stanley G.** Fascism in Spain, 1923-1977. LC 99-23078. (Illus.). 648p. 1999. text 65.00 (0-299-16560-4) U of Wis Pr.

— Fascism in Spain, 1923-1977. LC 99-23078. (Illus.). 648p. 2000. pap. text 24.95 (0-299-16564-7) U of Wis Pr.

Payne, Stanley G. The Franco Regime, 1936-1975. LC 87-40139. (Illus.). 704p. (C). 1987. text 35.00 (0-299-11070-2) U of Wis Pr.

— A History of Fascism, 1914-1945. LC 95-16723. 628p. 1996. 39.95 (0-299-14870-X) U of Wis Pr.

— A History of Fascism, 1914-1945. LC 95-16723. (Illus.). 628p. 1996. pap. 24.95 (0-299-14874-2) U of Wis Pr.

— A History of Spain & Portugal, Vol. 1. LC 72-7992. 412p. reprint ed. pap. 127.80 (0-608-16469-0, 202656700001) Bks Demand.

— A History of Spain & Portugal, Vol. 2. LC 72-7992. (Illus.). 422p. reprint ed. pap. 130.90 (0-8357-6143-6, 203428100002) Bks Demand.

— Spain's First Democracy: The Second Republic, 1931-1936. LC 92-56925. (Illus.). 494p. (Orig.). (C). 1993. pap. 24.95 (0-299-13674-4); lib. bdg. 60.00 (0-299-13670-1) U of Wis Pr.

— Spanish Catholicism: An Historical Overview. LC 83-25946. 280p. 1984. text 30.00 (0-299-09800-1) U of Wis Pr.

Payne, Stanley G., ed. see Mosher, J. Randolph.

Payne, Stephen, jt. ed. see Kline, Benjamin.

Payne, Stephen L. & Charnov, Bruce H., eds. Ethical Dilemmas for Academic Professionals. 264p. 1987. 46.95 (0-398-05319-7); pap. 33.95 (0-398-06317-6) C C Thomas.

***Payne, Steve, ed.** West Virginia in Pictures. LC 00-102057. (Illus.). 64p. 2000. pap. 6.95 (1-891852-09-4) Quarrier Pr.

Payne, Steven, ed. see Paul-Marie of the Cross.

Payne, Steven K. St. John of the Cross. 264p. (C). 1990. lib. bdg. 155.00 (0-7923-0707-0, Pub. by Kluwer Academic) Kluwer Academic.

Payne, Suzzy C., jt. auth. see Murwin, Susan A.

Payne, T. R. Rubinstein & the Philosophical Foundations of Soviet Psychology. (Sovietica Ser.: No. 30). 184p. 1968. lib. bdg. 130.50 (90-277-0062-1) Kluwer Academic.

Payne, Thomas E. Describing Morphosyntax: A Guide for Field Linguists. 430p. (C). 1997. text 64.95 (0-521-58224-5); pap. text 25.95 (0-521-58805-7) Cambridge U Pr.

— The Twins Stories: Participant Coding in Yagua Narrative. LC 92-23632. (Publications in Linguistics: Vol. 120). 236p. 1992. pap. 35.00 (0-520-09774-2, Pub. by U CA Pr) Cal Prin Full Svc.

***Payne, Tom.** The A-Z of Great Writers: The World's Leading Authors & Their Works. (Illus.). 400p. 1999. 35.00 (1-85868-322-X, Pub. by Carlton Bks Ltd) Natl Bk Netwk.

Payne, Tom. A Company of One: The Power of Independence in the Workplace. LC 92-91095. 118p. (Orig.). 1993. pap., per. 14.95 (0-9627085-4-2) Perf Pr Albuquerque.

— From the Inside Out: How to Create & Survive a Culture of Change. 3rd ed. LC 90-91985. (Illus.). 256p. (Orig.). 1991. per. 14.95 (0-9627085-2-6) Perf Pr Albuquerque.

— FutureWork: Five Rules for a New Game. LC 95-71195. 160p. 1996. pap., per. 14.95 (0-9627085-6-9) Perf Pr Albuquerque.

— Quotes for a Changing Workplace. LC 97-69849. 136p. (Orig.). 1998. pap. 9.95 (0-9627085-7-7) Perf Pr Albuquerque.

Payne, Tom, jt. auth. see McDonald, Megan.

Payne, Tom, jt. illus. see Dobkin, Bonnie.

Payne, Tony, jt. auth. see Bolt, Peter.

Payne, Tony, jt. auth. see Jensen, Phillip D.

Payne, Tony, jt. ed. see Clarke, Colin.

***Payne-Towler, Christine.** Underground Stream: Esoteric Tarot Revealed. 1999. pap. 24.95 (0-9673043-0-X) Noreah Pr.

Payne, Trevor. Christian Videos for Children & Young People: For Use in Home, Church, Youth Club, School. (C). 1989. 35.00 (0-9510086-9-2, Pub. by Jay Bks) St Mut.

Payne, Trevor & Turner, Elizabeth. A Parents' & Teachers' Guide to Dyslexia. LC 98-27057. 260p. 1998. 44.95 (1-85359-411-3); pap. 15.95 (1-85359-410-5) Multilingual Matters.

Payne, Trip. Crosswords. (Mighty Mini Ser.). 1999. pap. text 4.95 (0-8069-9670-6) Sterling.

— Crosswords for Kids. (Mensa Ser.). 1999. pap. text 4.95 (0-8069-1249-9) Strlng Pub CA.

— 365 Celebrity Crypto-Quotes. (Illus.). 96p. (J). 1998. 7.95 (0-8069-6171-6) Sterling.

Payne, V. Gregory & Isaacs, Larry D. Human Motor Development: A Lifespan Approach. 4th ed. LC 98-13523. xxii, 474p. 1998. pap. text 51.95 (0-7674-0523-4, 0523-4) Mayfield Pub.

Payne, Vicky. Alternative Prospects of Universities & Polytechnics. 1989. 60.00 (0-7045-0288-7) St Mut.

***Payne, Vivette.** The Team-Building Workshop: A Trainer's Guide. 2000. pap. 35.00 (0-8144-7079-3) AMACOM.

Payne, W., ed. see Tusser, Thomas.

Payne, W. H. Australian Plants of the Eighties: Series A. 384p. (C). 1991. text 95.00 (0-7855-0035-9, Pub. by Surrey Beatty & Sons) St Mut.

Payne, W. H., ed. see Compayre, Gabriel.

Payne, W. J. & Hodges, J. Tropical Cattle: Origins, Breeds, & Breeding Policies. LC 96-48732. 448p. 1997. text 99.95 (0-632-04048-3) Iowa St U Pr.

***Payne, W. J. & Wilson, R. Trevor.** An Introduction to Animal Husbandry in the Tropics. 5th ed. LC 98-55555. (Illus.). 826p. 1999. text 139.95 (0-632-04193-5, Pub. by Blckwell Science) Iowa St U Pr.

Payne, Walter R. Hazard & Operability Study Method for General Industry. 1999. 69.95 (1-56670-225-9, L1225) Lewis Pubs.

Payne, Wardell J., ed. Directory of African American Religious Bodies: A Comependium by the Howard University School of Divinity. 2nd ed. LC 95-10152. 1995. 49.95 (0-88258-184-8, PADR); pap. 29.95 (0-88258-185-6, PADRP) Howard U Pr.

Payne, Wardell J., tr. & intro. see Noble, E. Myron & Taylor, Evelyn M.

Payne, Wayne A. Understanding Your Health. 4th ed. 1994. teacher ed. (0-8151-6807-1) Mosby Inc.

Payne, Wayne A. & Hahn, Dale B. Understanding Your Health. 5th ed. LC 97-37412. 1997. 38.50 (0-697-41711-5) McGraw.

Payne, Wayne A., jt. auth. see Hahn, Dale B.

Payne, Weldon, jt. auth. see Bradley, Michael R.

Payne, Will. The Money Captain. LC 68-57546. reprint ed. pap. text 8.95 (0-8290-2381-X); reprint ed. lib. bdg. 32.00 (0-8398-1556-5) Irvington.

Payne, William F. Cogeneration Management Reference Guide. 458p. (C). 1997. 68.00 (0-13-743261-5) P-H.

— Creative Financing for Energy Conservation. LC 83-80094. (Illus.). 250p. 1984. text 43.00 (0-915586-69-X) Fairmont Pr.

***Payne, William F.** Mechanical Engineering: User's Guide to Natural Gas Purchasing & Risk Management. (Illus.). 264p. 2000. 87.00 (0-13-017931-0) P-H.

Payne, William F., jt. auth. see Payne, E. A.

Payne, William H. Sally's Doorbell. LC 98-117242. 160p. 1996. 16.00 (0-8059-3894-X) Dorrance.

Payne, William H., et al. NetWare 5: The Complete Reference. LC 99-229010. (Complete Reference Ser.). 1008p. 1999. 49.99 (0-07-211882-2) Osborne-McGraw.

Payne, William J. Adolescent Chemical Dependency - Study Guide. LC 97-92586. 65p. (C). 1997. pap. text, student ed. 15.00 (0-9661956-0-4) May Twenty-Fifth.

Payne, William L., ed. see Syrian Hamster in Toxicology & Carcinogenesis Rese.

Payne, William M. Greater English Poets of the Nineteenth Century. LC 67-22063. (Essay Index Reprint Ser.). 1977. 20.95 (0-8369-0777-9) Ayer.

— Leading American Essayists: Biographies of Leading Americans. LC 68-26466. (Essay Index Reprint Ser.). 1977. reprint ed. 28.95 (0-8369-0778-7) Ayer.

Payne, William M., ed. American Literary Criticism. LC 68-26465. (Wampum Library of American Literature, Index Reprint Ser.). 1977. reprint ed. 23.95 (0-8369-0779-5) Ayer.

Payne, Willie W. The Todd Road Incident. 89p. 1992. pap. 10.00 (0-9637462-0-0) Alcus Pub.

Payne, Wilson F. Industrial Demands upon the Money Market, 1919-57: A Study in Fund-Flow Analysis. (Technical Papers: No. 14). 159p. 1961. reprint ed. 41.40 (0-87014-420-0) Natl Bur Econ Res.

Paynell, Thomas, tr. see Erasmus, Desiderius.

Paynne, Michael, ed. see Ross, Worley H., et al.

Paynter. Electronic Communications. 1998. teacher ed. 10.00 (0-8273-5104-6); text 45.95 (0-8273-5103-8) Delmar.

***Paynter.** Electronics Student Survival Guide. (C). 2001. pap. 21.75 (0-7668-1968-X) Thomson Learn.

Paynter. Instructor's Resource Manual: Conventional Flow Version. LC 98-29272. 800p. 1998. text 65.00 (0-02-392402-0) Macmillan.

***Paynter.** Lab Manual Introduction to Electric Circuits. 1998. pap. text, lab manual ed. 33.40 (0-02-392501-9) Macmillan.

Paynter. Linear Integrated Circuits. (Electronics Technology Ser.). 1996. teacher ed. 12.00 (0-8273-6384-2) Delmar.

— Linear Integrated Circuits. (Electronics Technology Ser.). 1996. text 52.95 (0-8273-6383-4) Delmar.

— Linear Integrated Circuits. (Electronics Technology Ser.). 2001. pap. 52.50 (0-7668-1270-7) Delmar.

— Microwave Electronics. (Electronics Technology Ser.). 1997. teacher ed. 12.00 (0-8273-6382-6) Delmar.

— Microwave Electronics. (Electronics Technology Ser.). 1997. text 52.95 (0-8273-6381-8) Delmar.

***Paynter, Barbara.** The Grass Widow & Her Cow. large type unabridged ed. 119p. 1999. 25.95 (0-7531-5056-5, 150565, Pub. by ISIS Lrg Prnt) ISIS Pub.

Paynter, Barbara. The Grass Widow & Her Cow: An Enchanting Account of Country Life in Wartime Britain. LC 98-70055. (Illus.). 174p. 1998. 25.95 (1-86105-090-9, Pub. by Robson Bks) Parkwest Pubns.

Paynter, Diane E., jt. auth. see Marzano, Robert J.

Paynter, Elizabeth, ed. see Meyer-Denkmann, Gertrud.

Paynter, G. C., jt. ed. see Murthy, S. N.

Paynter, H. M., jt. ed. see Hedrick, J. Karl.

Paynter, John. Sound & Structure. (Resources of Music Ser.). (Illus.). 224p. (C). 1992. text 84.95 (0-521-35581-8); pap. text 39.95 (0-521-35676-8) Cambridge U Pr.

Paynter, John, et al. Companion to Contemporary Musical Thought, 2 vols., Set. (Companion Encyclopedia Ser.). (Illus.). 1268p. (C). (gr. 13). 1992. 325.00 (0-415-01990-7, A7201) Routledge.

Paynter, John, ed. see Meyer-Denkmann, Gertrud.

Paynter, John, ed. & intro. see Mellers, Wilfrid.

Paynter, John H. Fugitives of the Pearl. LC 72-170846. reprint ed. 32.50 (0-404-00205-6) AMS Pr.

P

An Asterisk (*) at the beginning of an entry indicates that the title is appearing for the first time.

Paynter, Raymond A., Jr. Nearctic Passerine Migrants in South America. (Publications of the Nuttall Ornithological Club: No. 25). (Illus.). 126p. 1995. 13.50 (*1-877973-37-8*, 25) Nuttall Ornith.
— Ornithological Gazetteer of Argentina. 2nd ed. (Illus.). 1045p. 1995. pap. 68.00 (*0-910999-31-7*) Mus Comp Zoo.
— Ornithological Gazetteer of Bolivia. 2nd ed. (Illus.). vi, 187p. 1992. pap. 14.00 (*0-910999-28-7*) Mus Comp Zoo.
— Ornithological Gazetteer of Chile. (Illus.). v, 331p. 1988. pap. 22.00 (*0-910999-25-2*) Mus Comp Zoo.
— Ornithological Gazetteer of Colombia. 2nd rev. ed. (Ornithological Gazetteers of the Neotropics Ser.). (Illus.). 537p. 1997. pap. text 40.00 (*0-910999-32-5*) Mus Comp Zoo.
— Ornithological Gazetteer of Ecuador. 2nd ed. (Illus.). xi, 249p. 1993. pap. 20.00 (*0-910999-29-5*) Mus Comp Zoo.
— Ornithological Gazetteer of Paraguay. 2nd ed. (Illus.). iv, 61p. 1989. pap. 8.00 (*0-910999-26-0*) Mus Comp Zoo.
— Ornithological Gazetteer of Uruguay. 2nd ed. (Illus.). vi, 113p. 1994. pap. 14.00 (*0-910999-30-9*) Mus Comp Zoo.
— Ornithological Gazetteer of Venezuela. (Illus.). iii, 245p. 1982. pap. 18.00 (*0-910999-21-X*) Mus Comp Zoo.
Paynter, Raymond A., Jr., ed. Avian Energetics. (Publications of the Nuttall Ornithological Club: No. 15). (Illus.). 334p. 1974. 17.00 (*1-877973-25-4*) Nuttall Ornith.
Paynter, Raymond A., Jr. & Traylor, Melvin A., Jr. Ornithological Gazetteer of Brazil. (Ornithological Gazetteers of the Neotropics Ser.). (Illus.). xiii, 789p. (Orig.). 1991. pap. 53.00 (*0-910999-27-9*) Mus Comp Zoo.
Paynter, Richard H. & Blanchard, Phyllis. A Study of Educational Achievement of Problem Children. LC 74-160985. (Select Bibliographies Reprint Ser.). 1977. reprint ed. 16.95 (*0-8369-5853-5*) Ayer.
***Paynter, Robert T.** Introduction to Electronic Devices & Circuitry. 5th ed. LC 99-22288. (Illus.). 1069p. 1999. text 91.00 incl. audio compact disk (*0-13-927195-3*) P-H.
Paynter, Robert T. Introductory Electric Circuits. LC 98-7299. 924p. 1998. 97.00 (*0-02-392500-0*) P-H.
— Introductory Electronic Devices & Circuits. 4th ed. LC 96-21803. 1026p. 1996. text 91.67 (*0-13-235912-X*) P-H.
Paynter, Will. British Trade Unions & the Problem of Change. LC 75-123196. 172p. reprint ed. pap. 53.40 (*0-8357-7432-5*, 202383500034) Bks Demand.
Paynton, Clifford T. & Blackey, Robert. Why Revolution? Theories & Analyses. 294p. 1971. pap. 22.95 (*0-87073-133-5*) Schenkman Bks Inc.
Paynton, Clifford T., jt. auth. see Blackey, Robert.
Payoyo, Peter B. Cries of the Sea: World Inequality, Sustainable Development & the Common Heritage of Humanity. LC 97-35080. (Publications on Ocean Development: No. 33). 568p. 1997. 195.00 (*90-411-0504-2*) Kluwer Academic.
Payr, Sabine, jt. ed. see Baumgartner, Peter.
***Payrat, Paul, ed.** California Civil Litigation Forms Manual: 9/99 Update, 2 vols. LC 80-65421. 782p. 1999. ring bd. 72.00 (*0-7626-0359-3*, CP-34471) Cont Ed Bar-CA.
Payrot, Alain H., ed. see National Structural Engineering Conference Staff.
Pays, Isobel. Gardening in Retirement. (C). 1989. 35.00 (*0-86242-039-3*, Pub. by Age Concern Eng) St Mut.
Paysan, Catherine. L' Empire du Taureau. (FRE.). 1982. pap. 10.95 (*0-7859-4177-0*) Fr & Eur.
— Je M'Appelle Jericho. (FRE.). 1979. pap. 10.95 (*0-7859-4125-8*) Fr & Eur.
— Nous Autres les Sanchez. (FRE.). 1976. pap. 8.95 (*0-7859-4061-8*) Fr & Eur.
Payseur, R. Stephen. Selling: Effective Techniques for Getting & Keeping Customers. LC 97-91461. ix, 220p. 1997. pap. 12.95 (*0-9656697-1-8*) Creekside Pub.
Payson, Dale. Almost Twins. 196p. (J). (ps-3). 1999. 5.95 (*0-13-022780-3*) P-H.
Payson, David R., ed. see Bradley, Don J.
Payson, Edward. Complete Works of Edward Payson, 3 vols. 1992. 81.99 (*0-87377-955-X*) GAM Pubns.
Payson, George. Golden Dreams & Leaden Realities. LC 75-104537. reprint ed. lib. bdg. 22.00 (*0-8290-2370-4*) Irvington.
— Golden Dreams & Leaden Realities. 1987. reprint ed. pap. text 9.95 (*0-8290-2120-5*) Irvington.
Payson, Harold. Build the Instant Catboat: With Everyday Woodworking Skills & a Modest Investment. (Illus.). 42p. 1997. reprint ed. pap. 12.95 (*1-887222-04-9*) H H Payson.
— Dory Model Book: Build Three Authentic Working Dory Models. (Illus.). 128p. 1997. pap. text 19.95 (*0-937822-45-0*) WoodenBoat Pubns.
Payson, Harold H. Boat Modeling the Easy Way: A Scratch Builder's Guide. LC 92-38474. (Illus.). 208p. 1995. pap. 19.95 (*1-887222-03-0*) H H Payson.
— Boat Modeling with Dynamite Payson: A Step-by-Step Guide to Building Models of Small Craft. (Illus.). 160p. 1989. pap. text 20.95 (*0-87742-983-9*) Intl Marine.
— Build the New Instant Boats. LC 84-81554. (Illus.). 160p. 1984. pap. text 19.95 (*0-87742-187-0*) Intl Marine.
— Build the New Instant Boats. 160p. 1984. pap. 19.95 (*0-07-155966-3*) McGraw.
— Go Build Your Own Boat. 128p. 1995. pap. 19.95 (*1-887222-00-6*) H H Payson.
— How to Build the Gloucester Light Dory. (Illus.). 32p. 1991. pap. 7.95 (*0-937822-04-3*) WoodenBoat Pubns.
— Instant Boats. LC 78-64738. 152p. 1995. pap. 16.00 (*1-887222-02-2*) H H Payson.
— Keeping the Cutting Edge: Setting & Sharpening Hand & Power Saws. (Illus.). 32p. 1991. pap. 7.95 (*0-937822-02-7*) WoodenBoat Pubns.
Payson, Herb. Advice to the Sealorn. LC 97-28086. (Illus.). 352p. 1997. 35.00 (*1-57409-002-X*) Sheridan.
— Blown Away. 256p. 1995. pap. 14.95 (*0-924486-95-3*) Sheridan.
— You Can't Blow Home Again. LC 99-35150. (Mariner's Library). 208p. 1999. pap. 14.95 (*1-57409-090-9*) Sheridan.
Payson, Herta. The Dragon's Eye: Envisioning Women's Wisdom. LC 97-94239. (Illus.). 272p. 1998. pap. 16.95 (*0-9659389-2-1*) Matrix Pr CT.
Payson, Huldah S. Museum Collections of the Essex Institute. Farnam, Anne & Tolles, Bryant F., eds. LC 78-67991. (E.I. Museum Booklet Ser.). (Illus.). 1978. pap. 5.95 (*0-88389-070-4*, PEMP192, Essx Institute) Peabody Essex Mus.
Payson, Martin F. Avoiding Workplace Litigation: Strategies for Lawyers & Human Resource Professionals. LC 97-148454. (Litigation & Administration Practice Ser.). 608p. 1997. write for info. (*0-87224-321-4*) PLI.
***Payson, Parker L. & Powell, Jody.** Great American Speeches Cancelled: A Century of Political Oratory. (Illus.). 256p. 2000. 24.95 (*1-57500-095-4*, Pub. by TV Bks) HarpC.
Payson, Patricia. Science Fiction: Imagining Worlds. 90p. (J). (gr. 1-8). 1994. spiral bd. 18.00 (*0-913705-18-7*) Zephyr Pr AZ.
***Payson, Steven.** Economics, Science & Technology. LC 99-86197. (Illus.). 288p. 2000. 95.00 (*1-85898-672-9*) E Elgar.
Payson, Steven. Quality Measurement in Economics: New Perspectives on the Evolution of Goods & Services. 256p. 1994. 95.00 (*1-85278-926-3*) E Elgar.
Payson, Susan. Noah Looks At Vol. 2: The Flood. (Illus.). 48p. (J). (gr. 2-5). 1999. pap. 12.95 (*1-929078-14-5*, NLSF2) Gods Kids.
— Noah Looks at Creation, Vol. 1. (Illus.). 40p. (J). (gr. 2-5). 1999. pap. 12.95 (*1-929078-13-7*, NLSC1) Gods Kids.
Paysour, Buck. Bass Fishing in North Carolina. 2nd ed. (Illus.). 244p. 1999. reprint ed. pap. 14.95 (*1-878086-71-5*, Pub. by Down Home NC) Blair.
— Fly Fishing in North Carolina. (Illus.). 288p. 1995. pap. 14.95 (*1-878086-38-3*, Pub. by Down Home NC) Blair.
Payter, Judy P. Dietary Minerals & Dangerous Influences: Index of Modern Authors & Subjects with Guide for Rapid Research. rev. ed. LC 96-3124. 149p. 1996. 47.50 (*0-7883-1120-4*); pap. 44.50 (*0-7883-1121-2*) ABBE Pubs Assn.
***Payton, B. A. & Skipp, Jim.** Cowboy: The Legend & the Legacy. LC 99-87889. (Illus.). 112p. 2000. 17.95 (*1-55054-544-2*, Pub. by DGL) Sterling.
Payton, Brian. Long Beach, Clayoquot & Beyond. LC 96-910695. (Illus.). 96p. (Orig.). 1997. pap. 16.95 (*1-55192-063-8*) Raincoast Bk.
Payton, Charles E., ed. Seismic Stratigraphy: Applications to Hydrocarbon Exploration. LC 77-91023. (American Association of Petroleum Geologists. Memoir Ser.: No. 26). (Illus.). 523p. 1977. reprint ed. pap. 162.20 (*0-608-02951-3*, 206341600006) Bks Demand.
Payton, Crystal. Girlie Collectibles: Kitch, Objects D'Art, Junk, & Hundreds of Other Things You Don't Need in Your Life. LC 96-21447. (Illus.). 192p. 1996. pap. 18.95 (*0-312-14532-2*) St Martin.
— The Story of Silver Dollar City: A Pictorial History of Branson's Famous Ozark Mountain Village Theme Park. LC 98-125785. (Illus.). 128p. 1997. pap. 12.95 (*0-9659983-0-4*) Silver Dollar.
Payton, Crystal & Payton, Leland. Girlie Collectibles. 1996. pap. 18.95 (*0-614-20459-3*, St Martin Griffin) St Martin.
Payton, Crystal, jt. auth. see Klise, Kate.
Payton, Crystal, jt. auth. see Payton, Leland.
Payton, David. Cinderella. (Illus.). 32p. (J). (gr. k-4). 1998. pap. 9.95 (*1-58066-012-6*, Covered Brdge Pr) Douglas Charles Ltd.
Payton, Gary. Confidence Counts. LC 99-19795. 1999. 14.95 (*0-87833-228-6*) Taylor Pub.
Payton, George T. Peace Officer's Promotional Manual. 316p. 1996. pap. 25.00 (*0-9649086-0-3*) Crim Just Serv.
Payton, George T. & Amaral, Mike. Patrol Operations & Enforcement Tactics. 10th ed. (Illus.). 450p. (C). 1996. pap. text 25.00 (*0-9649086-1-1*) Crim Just Serv.
Payton, George T. & Guffey, James. Concepts of California Criminal Law. 7th rev. ed. (Illus.). 303p. (C). 1998. pap. text 22.00 (*0-9649086-5-4*) Crim Just Serv.
Payton, George T. & Guffy, Jim. Peace Officer's Guide to Criminal Law. 19th rev. ed. (Illus.). 244p. (C). 1998. pap. text 20.00 (*0-9649086-4-6*) Crim Just Serv.
Payton, Gordon & Grams, Martin, Jr. The CBS Radio Mystery Theater: An Episode Guide & Handbook to Nine Years of Broadcasting, 1974-1982. 485p. 1999. lib. bdg. 65.00 (*0-7864-0559-7*) McFarland & Co.
***Payton, Leland.** The Beautiful & Enduring Ozarks. (Illus.). 80p. 1999. pap. 19.95 (*0-9673925-0-0*) Lens & Pen Pr.
Payton, Leland & Payton, Crystal. Branson: Country Themes, Neon Dreams. (Illus.). 144p. 1994. text 29.95 (*0-9636666-3-0*) Anderson MO.
Payton, Leland, jt. auth. see Payton, Crystal.
***Payton, Leonard R.** Reforming Our Worship Music. LC 99-47563. (Today's Issues Ser.). 48p. 1999. pap. 4.99 (*1-58134-051-6*) Crossway Bks.
Payton, Otto D. Research: The Validation of Clinical Practice. 3rd ed. LC 93-26828. (Illus.). 355p. (C). 1993. pap. text 24.95 (*0-8036-6800-7*) Davis Co.
Payton, Otto D., et al, eds. Manual of Physical Therapy. (Illus.). 761p. 1989. text 69.95 (*0-443-08499-8*) Church.
Payton, Otto D. & Sullivan, Scott. Research: The Validation of Clinical Practice. 4th ed. LC 93-26828. (Illus.). 355p. (C). 2000. pap. text 24.95 (*0-8036-0458-0*) Davis Co.
Payton, Otto D., et al. Patient Participation in Program Planning: A Manual for Therapists. LC 89-16154. 97p. (Orig.). 1990. pap. text 13.95 (*0-8036-6803-1*) Davis Co.
Payton, Philip. Cornish Carols from Australia. (C). 1989. 45.00 (*0-907566-92-8*, Pub. by Dyllansow Truran) St Mut.
— The Cornish Farmer in Australia. (C). 1989. 90.00 (*1-85022-029-8*, Pub. by Dyllansow Truran) St Mut.
— The Cornish Miner in Australia: Cousin Jack Down Under. (C). 1989. 100.00 (*0-907566-51-0*, Pub. by Dyllansow Truran); 50.00 (*0-907566-52-9*, Pub. by Dyllansow Truran) St Mut.
***Payton, Philip.** Cornish Studies Seven. 1999. pap. 29.95 (*0-85989-644-7*) Univ Exeter Pr.
Payton, Philip. Tregantle & Scraesdon: Their Forts & Railway. (C). 1989. 35.00 (*1-85022-038-7*, Pub. by Dyllansow Truran) St Mut.
Payton, Philip, ed. Cornish Studies. 167p. Date not set. pap. text 25.00 (*0-85989-413-4*, Pub. by Univ Exeter Pr); pap. text 25.00 (*0-85989-454-1*, Pub. by Univ Exeter Pr) Northwestern U Pr.
— Cornish Studies. (Devon & Cornwall Studies: Vol. 5). 176p. 1998. pap. 25.95 (*0-85989-551-3*, Pub. by Univ Exeter Pr) Northwestern U Pr.
— Cornish Studies, Vol. 4. (Devon & Cornwall Studies). 208p. 1997. pap. 25.95 (*0-85989-523-8*, Pub. by Univ Exeter Pr) Northwestern U Pr.
— Cornish Studies Six: Devon & Cornwall Studies. (Devon & Cornwall Studies). 176p. 1999. pap. text 26.95 (*0-85989-610-2*) Univ Exeter Pr.
— Cornish Studies Three. 176p. 1995. pap. text 25.95 (*0-85989-476-2*, Pub. by Univ Exeter Pr) Northwestern U Pr.
— Cornwall since the War. (C). 1993. 45.00 (*1-85022-073-5*, Pub. by Dyllansow Truran) St Mut.
Payton, Philip, jt. ed. see Hale, Amy.
Payton, Philip, ed. see Noall, Cyril.
Payton, Robert L. Major Challenges to Philanthropy. 127p. 1984. 10.00 (*0-318-37631-8*) Ind Sector.
Payton, Rodney J. A Modern Reader's Guide to Dante's Inferno. (American University Studies: Romance Languages & Literature: Ser. II, Vol. 191). 264p. 1993. pap. 31.95 (*0-8204-1827-7*) P Lang Pubng.
Payton, Rodney J., tr. see Huizinga, Johan.
Payton, Stella. Building Relationships for Life Style Evangelism. (Illus.). 170p. 1998. pap. 21.95 (*1-57502-989-8*, PO2694) Morris Pubng.
Payton, Thomas, jt. ed. see Long, Judy.
***Payton, Walter & Yaeger, Don.** Never Die Easy: The Autobiography of Walter Payton. (Illus.). 288p. 2000. 24.95 (*0-679-46331-3*) Villard Books.
Payton, William, jt. ed. see Callahan, Nathan.
***Paytress, Mark.** David Bowie: Bowie Style. (Illus.). 160p. 2000. pap. text 29.95 (*0-7119-7722-4*) Music Sales.
Paytress, Mark. The Rolling Stones. (Complete Guides to the Music Of...Ser.). (Illus.). 168p. (Orig.). 1995. pap. 8.95 (*0-7119-4303-6*, OP 47737) Omnibus NY.
***Paytress, Mark.** Rolling Stones Files: Exclusive! 400 Recently Discovered Photographs from the Daily Mirror Achiv. 1999. 19.99 (*1-84100-261-5*) Quadrillion Pubng.
Payutto, Phra P. Buddhadhamma: Natural Laws & Values for Life. Olson, Grant A., tr. LC 95-15504. (SUNY Series in Buddhist Studies). 302p. (C). 1995. text 59.50 (*0-7914-2631-9*); pap. text 19.95 (*0-7914-2632-7*) State U NY Pr.
Payzant, Geoffrey. Glen Gould: Music & Mind. 192p. 1984. mass mkt. 5.95 (*0-88780-145-5*, Pub. by Formac Publ Co) Formac Dist Ltd.
Payzant, Geoffrey. Glenn Gould: Music & Mind. 6th ed. LC 96-932584. 194p. 1997. pap. 14.95 (*1-55013-858-8*, Pub. by Key Porter) Firefly Bks Ltd.
Payzant, Geoffrey, ed. & tr. see Hanslick, Edward.
Payzant, Joan M. Halifax: Cornerstone of Canada. 224p. 1985. 27.95 (*0-89781-149-6*) Am Historical Pr.
***Paz.** Itinerary. LC 00-37022. 128p. 2000. 22.00 (*0-15-100562-1*) Harcourt.
Paz. Software User's Manual: Computer Application. (DC - Introduction to Computing Ser.). (C). 1989. mass mkt. 25.00 (*0-314-53950-6*) West Pub.
— Software User's Manual: Doing Business. (DC - Introduction to Computers Ser.). 1989. mass mkt. 30.95 (*0-314-53949-2*) S-W Pub.
Paz, Abel. Durruti: The People Armed. MacDonald, Nancy, tr. from FRE. (Illus.). 323p. 1976. 45.99 (*0-919618-73-1*, Pub. by Black Rose); pap. 16.99 (*0-919618-74-X*, Pub. by Black Rose) Consort Bk Sales.
— Spanish Civil War. (Pocket Archives Ser.). 1997. pap. text 12.95 (*2-85025-532-7*) Hazan.
Paz, Carlos F. Practica Para el Examen de Cuidadania. 3rd ed. (SPA.). 128p. 1990. pap. 8.95 (*0-685-54072-3*, Arco) Macmillan Gen Ref.
— Practice for the U. S. Citizenship & Legalization of Status Tests. 3rd ed. 128p. 1991. pap. 9.00 (*0-13-691288-5*, Arco) Macmillan Gen Ref.
— Practice for the U.S. Citizenship & Legalization of Status. 3rd ed. (SPA.). 144p. 1991. per. 9.95 (*0-13-677097-5*, Arco) IDG Bks.
Paz, Carmen A. El Veranito de Maria Isabel y Cuentos para Insomnes Rebeldes. (SPA.). 101p. (Orig.). 1996. pap. 9.95 (*1-882721-11-X*) Edit Ponce de Leon.
Paz, D. G. Nineteenth-Century English Religious Traditions: Retrospect & Prospect, 44. LC 95-9665. (Contributions to the Study of Religion Ser.: 44). 248p. 1995. 59.95 (*0-313-29476-3*, Greenwood Pr) Greenwood.
— Popular Anti-Catholicism in Mid-Victorian England. 368p. (C). 1992. 47.50 (*0-8047-1984-5*) Stanford U Pr.
— The Priesthoods & Apostasies of Pierce Connally: A Study of Victorian Conversion & Anticatholicism. LC 86-2487. (Studies in American Religion: Vol. 18). 418p. 1986. lib. bdg. 109.95 (*0-88946-662-9*) E Mellen.
Paz de Araujo, Carlos. Ferroelectric Thin Films: Synthesis & Basic Properties. (Ferroelectricity & Related Phenomena: Vol. 10). 600p. 1996. pap. text 51.00 (*2-88449-197-X*, TA418) Gordon & Breach.
***Paz, Ireneo.** Joaquin Murrieta: California Outlaw, Vol. 1. Belle, Frances P., tr. LC 99-39122. (Illus.). 256p. 1999. pap. 12.95 (*1-55885-277-8*) Arte Publico.
Paz, Ireneo. Vida y Aventuras del Mas Celebre Bandido Sonorense Joaquin Murrieta: Sus Grandes Proezas en California. (SPA.). 256p. 1999. pap. 12.95 (*1-55885-276-X*) Arte Publico.
Paz, Jacob D., et al. The OSHA Index Compliance & Safety Regulations & Job Classifications. 1999. 49.95 (*1-56670-285-2*, L1285) Lewis Pubs.
Paz, Jaime & Panik, Michele. Acute Care Handbook for Physical Therapists. LC 97-8765. 698p. 1997. pap. text 63.00 (*0-7506-9822-5*) Buttrwrth-Heinemann.
Paz, Maria E. Strategy, Security, & Spies. LC 96-31047. 276p. 1997. pap. 19.95 (*0-271-01666-3*) Pa St U Pr.
— Strategy, Security, & Spies: Mexico. LC 96-31047. 1997. 55.00 (*0-271-01665-5*) Pa St U Pr.
Paz, Mario. Solution Manual for Structural Dynamics. 6th ed. 1991. pap. 21.95 (*0-442-00806-6*, VNR) Wiley.
— Structural Dynamics: Theory & Computation. 3rd ed. 600p. (C). (gr. 13). 1990. mass mkt. 74.95 (*0-412-07141-X*) Chapman & Hall.
Paz, Myrna J. De La, see De La Paz, Myrna J.
Paz, Naomi, tr. see Urian, Dan.
Paz, Octavio. Aguila o Sol? (SPA.). pap. 7.95 (*968-16-0399-0*, Pub. by Fondo) Continental Bk.
— Alternating Current. Lane, Helen, tr. 1991. pap. 9.70 (*1-55970-136-6*, Pub. by Arcade Pub Inc) Time Warner.
— El Arco y la Lira. 1986. pap. text 15.99 (*968-16-0782-1*) Fondo.
— La Casa de la Presencia (The House of the Presence) Poesia e Historia (Poetry & History) 2nd ed. (Complete Works of Octavio Paz: Vol. I). (SPA.). 622p. 1994. 45.99 (*968-16-3897-2*, Pub. by Fondo) Continental Bk.
— Children of the Mire: Modern Poetry from Romanticism to the Avant-Garde. LC 73-88498. (Charles Eliot Norton Lectures: 1970-1971). 192p. 1974. pap. text 5.95 (*0-674-11626-7*) HUP.
— Children of the Mire: Modern Poetry from Romanticism to the Avant-Garde. enl. ed. (Norton Lectures). 192p. 1991. pap. 12.50 (*0-674-11629-1*, PAZCHX) HUP.
— Claridad Errante: Poesia y Prosa. (Fondo 2000 Ser.). (SPA.). pap. 2.99 (*968-16-5121-9*, Pub. by Fondo) Continental Bk.
— The Collected Poems of Octavio Paz, 1957-1987: Bilingual Edition. Weinberger, Eliot, ed. & tr. by. from SPA. Bishop, Elizabeth et al, trs. from SPA. LC 87-23989. 688p. 1991. pap. 22.95 (*0-8112-1173-8*, NDP719, Pub. by New Directions) Norton.
— Configurations. LC 78-145932. (ENG & SPA.). 1971. pap. 11.95 (*0-8112-0150-3*, NDP303, Pub. by New Directions) Norton.
— Conjunctions & Disjunctions. Lane, Helen, tr. 1991. pap. 8.70 (*1-55970-137-4*, Pub. by Arcade Pub Inc) Time Warner.
— Convergences. 320p. 1991. pap. 10.95 (*0-15-622586-7*, Harvest Bks) Harcourt.
— Convergences: Essays on Art & Literature. Lane, Helen, tr. 1987. 19.95 (*0-15-122585-0*) Harcourt.
— The Double Flame: Love & Eroticism. Lane, Helen, tr. LC 94-32282. 1995. 22.00 (*0-15-100103-0*) Harcourt.
— The Double Flame: Love & Eroticism. 1996. pap. 13.00 (*0-614-97648-0*, Harvest Bks) Harcourt.
— The Double Flame: Love & Eroticism. Lane, Helen, tr. from SPA. 288p. 1996. pap. 14.00 (*0-15-600365-1*, Harvest Bks) Harcourt.
— A Draft of Shadows & Other Poems. Weinberger, Eliot et al, trs. from SPA. LC 79-15588. 1980. pap. 10.95 (*0-8112-0738-2*, NDP489, Pub. by New Directions) Norton.
— Eagle or Sun? Weinberger, Eliot, tr. from ENG. LC 76-7229. 1976. pap. 9.95 (*0-8112-0623-8*, NDP422, Pub. by New Directions) Norton.
Paz, Octavio. Early Poems 1935-1955. rev. ed. Rukeyser, Muriel, tr. from SPA. & pref. by. LC 72-93981. 1973. pap. 9.95 (*0-8112-0478-2*, NDP354, Pub. by New Directions) Norton.
Paz, Octavio. An Erotic Beyond: Sade. Weinberger, Eliot, tr. from SPA. LC 97-46048. 96p. (C). 1998. 18.00 (*0-15-100352-1*) Harcourt.
— Essays on Mexican Art. Lane, Helen, tr. 1993. 22.95 (*0-15-129063-6*) Harcourt.
— Essays on Mexican Art. Lane, Helen, tr. (Illus.). 320p. 1995. pap. 12.95 (*0-15-600061-X*) Harcourt.
— Estacion Violenta. 1994. pap. text 6.99 (*968-16-1150-0*) Fondo.
— Excursiones/Incursiones (Excursions/Incursions) Dominio Extranjero (Foreign Domain) 2nd ed. (Complete Works of Octavio Paz: Vol. II). (SPA.). 610p. 1994. 45.99 (*968-16-3898-0*, Pub. by Fondo) Continental Bk.
— Generaciones y Semblanzas (Generations & Differences) Antecesores & Fundadores. (Mexico en la Obra de Octavio Paz Ser.: Vol. 4). (SPA.). 203p. pap. 13.99 (*968-16-3167-6*, Pub. by Fondo) Continental Bk.
— Generaciones y Semblanzas (Generations & Differences) Escritores y letras de Mexico, 3 vols. (Mexico en la Obra de Octavio Paz Ser.: Vols. 4-6). (SPA.). 694p. pap. 27.99 (*968-16-2574-9*, Pub. by Fondo) Continental Bk.
— Generaciones y Semblanzas (Generations & Differences) Literatura Contemporanea. (Mexico en la Obra de Octavio Paz Ser.: Vol. 6). (SPA.). 227p. pap. 13.99 (*968-16-3169-2*, Pub. by Fondo) Continental Bk.
— Generaciones y Semblanzas (Generations & Differences) Modernistas & Modernos. (Mexico en la Obra de Octavio Paz Ser.: Vol. 5). (SPA.). 270p. pap. 13.99 (*968-16-3168-4*, Pub. by Fondo) Continental Bk.
— Generaciones y Semblanzas (Generations & Profiles)

P

Dominio Mexicano (Mexican Domain) 2nd ed. (Complete Works of Octavio Paz: Vol. IV). (SPA.). 432p. 1994. 45.99 (*968-16-3900-6*, Pub. by Fondo) Continental Bk.

— In Light of India. 224p. (C). 1998. pap. 12.00 (*0-15-600578-6*) Harcourt.

— In Light of India: Essays. Weinberger, Eliot, tr. from SPA. LC 96-45756. (SPA & ENG.). 224p. 1997. 22.00 (*0-15-100222-3*) Harcourt.

— In Search of the Present: Nobel lecture, 1990. Stanton, Anthony, tr. 72p. 1991. pap. 10.00 (*0-15-644556-5*) Harcourt.

— Itinerario (Itinerary) (SPA.). 280p. 1993. pap. 13.99 (*968-16-4239-2*, Pub. by Fondo) Continental Bk.

— El Laberinto de la Soledad--Postdata-Vuelta. 1991. pap. text 13.99 (*968-16-3937-5*) Fondo.

— El Laberinto de la Soledad y Otras Obras. (SPA.). 352p. 1997. pap. 13.95 (*0-14-025883-3*) Viking Penguin.

— El Laberinto de Soledad. (SPA.). pap. 15.50 (*968-16-0175-0*, Pub. by Fondo) Continental Bk.

— The Labyrinth of Solitude: The Other Mexico & Return to the Labyrinth of Solitude & The U. S. A. & The Philanthropic Ogre. Kemp, Lysander, tr. from SPA. LC 82-47999. 408p. 1989. pap. 13.95 (*0-8021-5042-X*, Grove) Grove-Atltic.

— Libertad Bajo Palabra (Freedom on Parole) Obras Poetica (1935-1957) 2nd ed. (SPA.). 263p. 1968. 15.99 (*968-16-4425-5*, Pub. by Fondo) Continental Bk.

***Paz, Octavio.** Libertad Bajo Palabra (1935-1957) 1998. 10.95 (*84-376-0775-2*) Ediciones Catedra.

Paz, Octavio. Marcel Duchamp: Appearance Stripped Bare. Phillips, Rachel & Gardner, Donald, trs. 1991. pap. 9.70 (*1-55970-138-2*, Pub. by Arcade Pub Inc) Time Warner.

— Mariposa de Obsidiana (with 33 RPM Recording in Spanish) (Ediciones Especiales y de Bibliofilo Ser.). (ENG & SPA., Illus.). 1993. 200.00 (*84-343-0343-4*) Elliots Bks.

— The Monkey Grammarian. Lane, Helen, tr. Orig. Title: El Mono Gramatico. 1991. pap. 9.70 (*1-55970-135-8*, Pub. by Arcade Pub Inc) Time Warner.

— Obra Poetica I (1935-1970) (Poetic Works I (1937-1970) (Complete Works of Octavio Paz: Vol. XI). (SPA.). 588p. 1997. 45.99 (*968-16-3905-7*, Pub. by Fondo) Continental Bk.

— Octavio Paz en Sus Obras Completas (Octavio Paz in His Complete Works) (SPA.). 77p. 1994. pap. 7.99 (*968-16-4498-0*, Pub. by Fondo) Continental Bk.

— On Poets & Others. Schmidt, Michael, tr. 1991. pap. 9.70 (*1-55970-139-0*, Pub. by Arcade Pub Inc) Time Warner.

— On Poets & Others. Schmidt, Michael, tr. from SPA. LC 86-11904. 1986. text 18.95 (*0-8050-0003-8*) Seaver Bks.

— One Earth, Four or Five Worlds: Reflections on Contemporary History. 228p. 1986. pap. 5.95 (*0-15-668746-1*) Harcourt.

— One Word to the Other. (Illus.). 48p. 1991. pap. 10.00 (*0-941179-15-X*) Latitudes Pr.

— The Other Voice: Essays on Modern Poetry. Lane, Helen, tr. 1991. 16.95 (*0-15-170449-X*) Harcourt.

— The Other Voice: Essays on Modern Poetry. Lane, Helen, tr. 176p. 1992. pap. 9.95 (*0-15-670455-2*, Harvest Bks) Harcourt.

— Pasado en Claro (The Clear Past) 2nd ed. (SPA.). 47p. 1978. pap. 8.99 (*968-16-1800-9*, Pub. by Fondo) Continental Bk.

— Pequena Cronica de Grandes Dias (A Small Chronicle of Great Days) (SPA.). 172p. 1990. pap. 9.99 (*968-16-3458-6*, Pub. by Fondo) Continental Bk.

— El Peregrino en Su Patria (The Pilgrim in His Country), 3 vols. (Mexico en la Obra de Octavio Paz Ser.: Vols. 1-3). (SPA.). 808p. pap. 27.99 (*968-16-3732-1*, Pub. by Fondo) Continental Bk.

— El Peregrino en Su Patria (The Pilgrim in His Country) El Cercado Ajeno. (Mexico en la Obra de Octavio Paz Ser.: Vol. 3). (SPA.). 238p. pap. 13.99 (*968-16-3166-8*, Pub. by Fondo) Continental Bk.

— El Peregrino en Su Patria (The Pilgrim in His Country) Historia & Politica de Mexico. 2nd ed. (Complete Works of Octavio Paz: Vol. VIII). (SPA.). 600p. 1994. 45.99 (*968-16-3902-2*, Pub. by Fondo) Continental Bk.

— El Peregrino en Su Patria (The Pilgrim in His Country) Pasados. (Mexico en la Obra de Octavio Paz Ser.: Vol. 1). (SPA.). 284p. pap. 13.99 (*968-16-3164-1*, Pub. by Fondo) Continental Bk.

— El Peregrino en Su Patria (The Pilgrim in His Country) Presente Fluido. (Mexico en la Obra de Octavio Paz Ser.: Vol. 2). (SPA.). 291p. pap. 13.99 (*968-16-3165-X*, Pub. by Fondo) Continental Bk.

— Los Privilegios de la Vista, I (Privileges of the View, I) Vol. VI: Arte Moderno Universal (Universal Modern Art) 2nd ed. (SPA.). 392p. 1994. 45.99 (*968-16-3895-6*, Pub. by Fondo) Continental Bk.

— Los Privilegios de la Vista (The Privileges of the View), Vol. 1. (Mexico en la Obra de Octavio Paz Ser.: Vol. 7). (SPA., Illus.). 220p. pap. 13.99 (*968-16-3170-6*, Pub. by Fondo) Continental Bk.

— Los Privilegios de la Vista (The Privileges of the View) Arte de Mejico. (Mexico en la Obra de Octavio Paz Ser.: Vols. 7 & 8). (SPA., Illus.). 514p. pap. 27.99 (*968-16-2575-7*, Pub. by Fondo) Continental Bk.

— Los Privilegios de la Vista, II (Privileges of the View, II) Arte de Mejico (Mexican Art) 2nd ed. (Complete Works of Octavio Paz: Vol. VII). (SPA.). 445p. 1994. 45.99 (*968-16-3896-4*, Pub. by Fondo) Continental Bk.

— Rappacini's Daughter: A Play. Dougard, Sebastian, tr. from SPA. 80p. (C). 1996. 14.95 (*1-56886-034-X*); pap. 14.95 (*1-56886-035-8*) Marsilio Pubs.

— Rufino Tamayo: Myth & Magic. Phillips, Rachel, tr. from SPA. LC 79-63734. (Illus.). (Orig.). 1979. pap. 12.95 (*0-89207-019-6*) S R Guggenheim.

— Selected Poems. Aroul, G. et al, trs. from SPA. LC 84-9856. 160p. 1984. pap. 10.95 (*0-8112-0899-0*, NDP574, Pub. by New Directions) Norton.

— Sor Juana: Or, the Traps of Faith. Peden, Margaret Sayers, tr. 560p. 1988. pap. text 18.50 (*0-674-82106-8*) HUP.

— Sor Juana: Or, the Traps of Faith. Peden, Margaret Sayers, tr. from SPA. LC 88-3002. (Illus.). 560p. 1988. 49.95 (*0-674-82105-X*) HUP.

— Sor Juana Ines de la Cruz o las Trampas de la Fe (Sor Juana Ines de la Cruz or the Traps of Faith) 2nd ed. (Complete Works of Octavio Paz: Vol. VI). (SPA.). 630p. 1994. 45.99 (*968-16-3901-4*, Pub. by Fondo) Continental Bk.

— Sunstone - Piedra De Sol. Weinberger, Eliot, tr. from SPA. LC 91-29993. (SPA., Illus.). 64p. 1991. reprint ed. pap. 8.95 (*0-8112-1195-9*, NDP735, Pub. by New Directions) Norton.

— Sunstone - Piedra De Sol: Poem. aut. deluxe limited ed. Weinberger, Eliot, tr. from SPA. LC 91-29993. (Illus.). 64p. 1991. 150.00 (*0-8112-1194-0*, Pub. by New Directions) Norton.

— Sunstone - Piedra De Sol: Poem. Weinberger, Eliot, tr. from SPA. LC 91-29993. (Illus.). 64p. 1991. reprint ed. 18.95 (*0-8112-1197-5*, Pub. by New Directions) Norton.

— A Tale of Two Gardens: Poems from India, 1952-1995. Weinberger, Eliot, ed. & tr. by. from SPA. Bishop, Elizabeth et al, trs. from SPA. LC 96-38111. (New Directions Bibelot Ser.). 96p. 1997. pap. 8.00 (*0-8112-1349-8*, NDP841, Pub. by New Directions) Norton.

***Paz, Octavio.** Tiempo Nublado. 1998. pap. text 17.95 (*84-322-0758-6*) Continental Bk.

Paz, Octavio. A Tree Within: Bilingual Edition. Weinberger, Eliot, tr. LC 88-19666. 176p. 1988. pap. 10.95 (*0-8112-1071-5*, NDP661, Pub. by New Directions) Norton.

Paz, Octavio, ed. Mexican Poetry. Beckett, Samuel, tr. from SPA. LC 85-17684. 224p. (Orig.). 1985. reprint ed. pap. 12.00 (*0-8021-5186-8*, Grove) Grove-Atltic.

Paz, Octavio, jt. auth. see Cowan, Catherine.

Paz, Octavio, jt. auth. see Villaurrutia, Xavier.

Paz, Octavio, jt. auth. see Weinberger, Eliot.

Paz, Orlando De La, see De La Paz, Orlando.

Paz, Orlando De La, see Bollinger, Marilyn.

Paz, Ramon. La Capa Del Morrocy. (SPA., Illus.). (J). (gr. 1-4). 8.95 (*980-257-070-2*, Pub. by Ediciones Ekare) Kane-Miller Bk.

Paz, Senel. Las Hermanas. (Encuento/Literary Encounters Ser.).Tr. of Sisters. 1997. pap. text 10.95 (*968-494-058-0*) Donars.

Pazanin, A. Wissenschaft und Geschichte in der Phanomelogie Edmund Husserls. (Phaenomenologica Ser.: No. 46). 202p. 1972. lib. bdg. 94.00 (*90-247-1194-0*, Pub. by M Nijhoff) Kluwer Academic.

Pazarba Sio Glu Ceyla., jt. auth. see Drees, Burkhard.

Pazdan, Mary M. Joel, Obadiah, Haggai, Zechariah, Malachi. (Collegeville Bible Commentary - Old Testament Ser.: No. 17). 128p. 1986. pap. 4.95 (*0-8146-1424-8*) Liturgical Pr.

***Pazdernik.** Pharmacology Review. 1999. text 29.95 (*0-323-00838-0*) Harcourt.

Pazdur, Richard, ed. Medical Oncology: A Comprehensive Review. 2nd ed. 520p. 1995. 49.95 (*0-9641823-1-9*) PRR.

Pazdur, Richard, et al, eds. Cancer Management: A Multidisciplinary Approach. 500p. (Orig.). 1995. pap. 49.95 (*0-9641823-2-7*) PRR.

— Cancer Management: A Multidisciplinary Approach. 2nd ed. (Illus.). 900p. (Orig.). 1997. pap. 39.95 (*0-9641823-8-6*) PRR.

— Cancer Management: A Multidisciplinary Approach. 3rd rev. ed. (Illus.). 900p. (Orig.). 1998. pap. text 49.95 (*1-891483-01-3*) PRR.

***Pazdur, Richard, et al, eds.** Cancer Management: A Multidisciplinary Approach: Medical, Surgical & Radiation Oncology. 4th rev. ed. LC 99-75070. (Illus.). 1014p. 2000. pap. text 49.95 (*1-891483-05-6*) PRR.

Pazdur, Richard & Royce, Delanie. Myths & Facts about Colorectal Cancer: What You Need to Know. 48p. 1998. pap. text 9.95 (*0-9641823-9-4*) PRR.

Pazdur, Richard, jt. ed. see Jaiyesimi, Ishmael A.

***Pazell, Sara.** Anatomy & Physiology of the Visual System Vol. 1: An Occupational Perspective. 1998. 15.00 incl. audio (*1-58111-071-5*) Contemporary Medical.

— Home Care Visual Rehabilitation Vol. 3: A Step-by-Step "How To" 1998. 15.00 incl. audio (*1-58111-073-1*) Contemporary Medical.

— Visual Rehabilitation: Assessment & Treatment Intervention, Vol. 2. 1998. write for info. incl. audio (*1-58111-072-3*) Contemporary Medical.

— Visual Rehabilitation Vol. 4: One Hundred & One Treatment Techniques. 1998. 15.00 incl. audio (*1-58111-074-X*) Contemporary Medical.

Pazer, ed. Business Stats: A New Approach. (C). 2001. pap. text Price not set. (*0-321-01420-0*) Addison-Wesley.

***Pazery, Paul H.** Rescue the Dream: How to Deal with the Complexities of the Property Tax System. LC 99-93675. 1999. pap. 10.95 (*0-533-13113-8*) Vantage.

***Pazge.** Your Ends Are Raggedy, Girlfriend! A Grass-Root Fiction. LC 99-91534. 2000. 25.00 (*0-7388-0854-7*); pap. 18.00 (*0-7388-0855-5*) Xlibris Corp.

Pazi, Margarita, ed. Max Brod, 1884 to 1984: Untersuchungen Zu Max Brods Literarischen und Philosophischen Schriften. (New Yorker Studien zur Neueren Deutschen Literaturgeschichte Ser.: Vol. 8). 268p. 1987. 52.00 (*0-8204-0571-X*) P Lang Pubng.

Pazicky, Diana L. Cultural Orphans in America. LC 98-15894. 256p. 1998. text 40.00 (*1-57806-089-3*) U Pr of Miss.

***Pazienza, Maria T., ed.** Information Extraction: Towards Scalable, Adaptable Systems. LC 99-51734. (Lecture Notes in Artificial Intelligence Ser.: Vol. 1714). ix, 165p. 1999. pap. 34.00 (*3-540-66625-7*) Spr-Verlag.

Pazienza, Maria T., et al, eds. Information Extraction a Multidisciplinary Approach to an Emerging Information Technology: International Summer School, SCIE-97, Frascati, Italy, July 14-18, 1997, Vol. 129. LC 97-35794. (Lecture Notes in Artificial Intelligence: Vol. 1299). ix, 213p. 1997. pap. 43.00 (*3-540-63438-X*) Spr-Verlag.

Pazig, Christianus. Bibliotheca Curiosa: A Treatise of Magic Incantations (1700) Goldsmid, Edmund, ed. 54p. 1994. reprint ed. pap. 12.95 (*1-56459-437-8*) Kessinger Pub.

Pazman, Andrej. Foundations of Optimum Experimental Design. 1986. text 122.00 (*90-277-1865-2*) Kluwer Academic.

— Nonlinear Statistical Model. LC 93-7412. (Mathematics & Its Applications Ser.: Vol. 254). 1993. text 174.50 (*0-7923-2247-9*) Kluwer Academic.

Pazmany Aircraft Corporation Staff, ed. see Pazmany, Ladislao.

Pazmany, Ladislao. Comprehensive Guide to Airfoil Sections for Light Aircraft. (Illus.). 252p. 35.00 (*0-614-13168-5*, 21-37841) EAA Aviation.

Pazmany, Ladislao. Customs Built Aircraft Owners & Operators Manual. (Illus.). 12p. 1976. reprint ed. pap. 6.50 (*0-9616777-5-9*) Pazmany Aircraft.

Pazmany, Ladislao. Landing Gear Design for Light Aircraft, Vol. 1. Pazmany Aircraft Corporation Staff, ed. (Illus.). 252p. 1986. pap. 45.00 (*0-9616777-0-8*) Pazmany Aircraft.

Pazmany, Ladislao. Light Airplane Contruction. ed. (Illus.). 92p. (YA). (gr. 10 up). 1970. reprint ed. pap. 30.00 (*0-9616777-2-4*) Pazmany Aircraft.

Pazmany, Ladislao. Light Airplane Design. (Illus.). 22.00 (*0-614-13171-5*, 21-37839) EAA Aviation.

Pazmany, Ladislao. Light Airplane Design. rev. ed. (Illus.). 80p. (YA). (gr. 10 up). 1963. pap. 30.00 (*0-9616777-1-6*) Pazmany Aircraft.

Pazmany, Ladislao. Light Plane Construction. (Illus.). 22.00 (*0-614-13172-3*, 21-37840) EAA Aviation.

Pazmany, Ladislao. PL-4A Construction Manual. ed. (Illus.). 104p. (YA). (gr. 10 up). 1974. reprint ed. pap. 30.00 (*0-9616777-3-2*) Pazmany Aircraft.

— PL-4A Exploded Views. (Illus.). 45p. (YA). (gr. 10 up). 1974. pap. 30.00 (*0-9616777-4-0*) Pazmany Aircraft.

— PL-8 Main Gear Design & Trade Offs. ed. (Illus.). 75p. (YA). (gr. 10 up). 1980. reprint ed. pap. 25.00 (*0-9616777-7-5*) Pazmany Aircraft.

Pazmino, Robert W. Basics of Teaching for Christians: Preparation, Instruction & Evaluation. LC 98-8591. 144p. (C). 1998. pap. 12.99 (*0-8010-2173-1*) Baker Bks.

— By What Authority Do We Teach? Sources for Empowering Christian Educators. LC 94-1704. 160p. 1994. pap. 10.99 (*0-8010-7129-1*) Baker Bks.

— Cuestiones Fundamentales de la Educacion Cristiana.Tr. of Foundational Issues in Christian Education. (SPA.). 280p. 1995. 15.99 (*0-89922-435-0*, C096-4350) Caribe Betania.

— Foundational Issues in Christian Education: An Introduction in Evangelical Perspective. 2nd rev. ed. LC 96-40859. (Illus.). 240p. (C). 1997. pap. 17.99 (*0-8010-2106-5*) Baker Bks.

— Principios y Practicas de la Educacion Cristiana.Tr. of Principles & Practices of Christian Education. (SPA.). 180p. 1995. 11.99 (*0-89922-436-9*, C96-4369) Caribe Betania.

— The Seminary in the City: A Study of New York Theological Seminary. LC 88-17250. 146p. (Orig.). (C). 1988. pap. text 16.50 (*0-8191-7074-7*); lib. bdg. 35.50 (*0-8191-7073-9*) U Pr of Amer.

Pazos Alonso, Claudia, ed. Women, Literature & Culture in the Portuguese-Speaking World. LC 96-141923. 210p. 1996. write for info. (*0-7734-8805-7*) E Mellen.

Pazos, Felipe. Chronic Inflation in Latin America. LC 71-180848. (Special Studies in International Economics & Development). 1972. 29.50 (*0-275-28282-1*) Irvington.

Pazos, Luis. Historia Sinoptica De Mexico: De Los Olmecas A Salinas. LC 94-200567. (SPA.). 1997. pap. text 15.98 (*968-13-2560-5*) Libros Fronteras.

— Por Que Chiapas. LC 94-156100. (SPA., Illus.). 156p. 1997. pap. 9.98 (*968-13-2633-4*, Pub. by Edit Diana) Libros Fronteras.

Pazy, A. Semigroups of Linear Operators & Applications to Partial Differential Equations. John, F. et al, eds. (Applied Mathematical Sciences Ser.: Vol. 44). viii, 279p. 1996. 64.95 (*0-387-90845-5*) Spr-Verlag.

Pazzagli, Mario, jt. auth. see Serio, Mario.

***Pazzaglia, F. J. & Lucas, S. G., eds.** Albuquerque Geology. (Guidebook Ser.: No. 50). (Illus.). 448p. 1999. pap. 50.00 (*1-58546-085-0*) NMex Geol Soc.

Pazzaglini, Mario, jt. auth. see Leland, Charles G.

Pazzaglini, Peter R. & Hawks, Catharine A. Consilia: A Bibliography of Holdings in the Library of Congress & Certain Other Collections in the United States. LC 89-600323. 154p. 1990. 19.00 (*0-8444-0672-4*, 030-000-00182-6) Lib Congress.

Pazzani, Michael J. Creating a Memory of Casual Relationships: An Integration of Empirical & Explanation-Based Learning Method. 360p. 1990. write for info. incl. disk (*1-56321-040-1*) L Erlbaum Assocs.

— Creating a Memory of Causal Relationships: An Integration of Empirical & Explanation-Based Learning Methods. 360p. 1990. 79.95 (*0-8058-0629-6*); student ed. 10.95 incl. disk (*1-56321-037-1*); student ed. 10.95 incl. disk (*1-56321-038-X*); student ed. 10.95 incl. disk (*1-56321-039-8*); pap. 34.50 (*0-8058-0789-6*) L Erlbaum Assocs.

Pazzanita, Anthony G. Historical Dictionary of Mauritania. 2nd ed. LC 95-40674. (African Historical Dictionaries Ser.: Vol. 68). 560p. 1996. 69.50 (*0-8108-3095-7*) Scarecrow.

***Pazzanita, Anthony G.** The Maghreb. LC 99-219147. Vol. 208. 368p. 1998. lib. bdg. 85.00 (*1-85109-310-9*) ABC-CLIO.

Pazzanita, Anthony G. Western Sahara. LC 97-180602. (World Bibliographical Ser.: Vol. 190). 322p. 1996. lib. bdg. 87.00 (*1-85109-256-0*, DT346) ABC-CLIO.

Pazzanita, Anthony G. & Hodges, Tony. Historical Dictionary of Western Sahara. 2nd ed. LC 93-48064. (African Historical Dictionaries Ser.: No. 55). (Illus.). 641p. 1994. 73.00 (*0-8108-2661-5*) Scarecrow.

Pazzelli, Raffaele. The Franciscan Sisters: Outlines of History & Spirituality. Mullaney, Aidan, tr. LC 92-38686. 239p. 1993. pap. 15.00 (*0-940535-52-1*, UP152) Franciscan U Pr.

— St. Francis & the Third Order. 235p. 1989. pap. 14.95 (*0-8199-0953-X*, Frncscn Herld) Franciscan Pr.

***PBC International Editors.** The Boutique Hotel Vol. IV: International Hotel & Resort Design. 176p. 1999. 50.00 (*0-86636-775-6*) PBC Intl Inc.

PBC International Editors. Clubs & Resorts. LC 93-30033. 1994. 55.00 (*0-86636-230-4*) PBC Intl Inc.

***PBC International Editors.** Cottages, Cabins & Bungalows. (Illus.). 176p. 2000. text 34.95 (*0-86636-785-3*, Pub. by PBC Intl Inc) St Martin.

— Designing for Small Offices. 176p. 1999. 50.00 (*0-86636-777-2*) PBC Intl Inc.

PBC International Editors. Fashion Graphics & Design. 96p. 1999. pap. 16.95 (*0-86636-779-9*) PBC Intl Inc.

— Menus: Graphics & Design. (Illus.). 104p. 1999. pap. 16.95 (*0-86636-748-9*) PBC Intl Inc.

***PBC International Editors.** Small Stores. (Illus.). 176p. 2000. text 50.00 (*0-86636-782-9*, Pub. by PBC Intl Inc) St Martin.

PBC International Editors. Spa. 176p. 1999. 50.00 (*0-86636-781-0*) PBC Intl Inc.

Pbc International Staff. Bathrooms. 1999. 34.95 (*0-688-16056-5*, Wm Morrow) Morrow Avon.

PBC International Staff. Bedrooms & Private Spaces. 1997. 34.95 (*0-688-14815-8*, Wm Morrow) Morrow Avon.

Pbc International Staff. Book of Childrens Illustration. 2nd ed. 1998. 55.00 (*0-688-15880-3*, Wm Morrow) Morrow Avon.

***PBC International Staff.** The Boutique Hotel. 1999. 50.00 (*0-688-17661-5*, Wm Morrow) Morrow Avon.

PBC International Staff. Color. 1998. 42.50 (*0-688-15456-5*, Wm Morrow) Morrow Avon.

— Colorstyling. 1999. pap. 19.95 (*0-688-16687-3*, Wm Morrow) Morrow Avon.

— Colorstyling: Contrasts in Design. (Illus.). 104p. 2000. pap. 19.95 (*0-86636-740-3*) PBC Intl Inc.

***PBC International Staff.** Cosmetics: Graphics & Design. (Illus.). 2000. pap. 16.95 (*0-86636-747-0*) PBC Intl Inc.

PBC International Staff. Covers & Jackets. 1995. 29.95 (*0-688-14633-3*, Wm Morrow) Morrow Avon.

— Design with Tile, Stone & Brick. 1997. pap. 32.50 (*0-688-14930-8*, Wm Morrow) Morrow Avon.

***PBC International Staff.** Designers at Home. 1999. 42.50 (*0-688-17663-1*, Wm Morrow) Morrow Avon.

— Designing for Small Offices. 2000. 50.00 (*0-688-17668-2*, Wm Morrow) Morrow Avon.

— Designing with Details. 1999. 39.95 (*0-688-17657-7*, Wm Morrow) Morrow Avon.

— Designing with Fabric. 1996. 39.95 (*0-688-14560-4*, Wm Morrow) Morrow Avon.

PBC International Staff. Designing with Glass. 1996. 45.00 (*0-688-14517-5*, Wm Morrow) Morrow Avon.

— Designing with Glass. 1998. pap. 32.50 (*0-688-15371-2*, Wm Morrow) Morrow Avon.

Pbc International Staff. Designing with Light. 1998. 42.50 (*0-688-16029-8*, Wm Morrow) Morrow Avon.

PBC International Staff. Designing with Spiritualists. 1999. 37.50 (*0-688-16681-4*, Wm Morrow) Morrow Avon.

— Divine Design: A Celebration. 1999. 50.00 (*0-688-16682-2*, Wm Morrow) Morrow Avon.

— Empowered Gardens. 1998. pap. 34.95 (*0-688-16145-6*, Wm Morrow) Morrow Avon.

— Entertainment Architecture. 1999. 45.00 (*0-688-16685-7*, Wm Morrow) Morrow Avon.

— Entertainment Architecture: Technology & Design. 2000. 45.00 (*0-86636-728-4*) PBC Intl Inc.

***PBC International Staff.** Fashion: Graphics & Design. 2000. pap. 16.95 (*0-688-17669-0*, Wm Morrow) Morrow Avon.

PBC International Staff. Feng Shui at Home. 1999. 34.95 (*0-688-16037-9*, Wm Morrow) Morrow Avon.

***PBC International Staff.** Feng Shui at Work. 1999. 45.00 (*0-688-17658-5*, Wm Morrow) Morrow Avon.

PBC International Staff. Food Wrap. 1998. pap. 29.95 (*0-688-16146-4*, Wm Morrow) Morrow Avon.

Pbc International Staff. Health Clubs. 1998. 45.00 (*0-688-16051-4*, Wm Morrow) Morrow Avon.

***PBC International Staff.** Home as Haven. 2000. 34.95 (*0-86636-786-1*) Universe.

PBC International Staff. Home 2000. 1999. 42.50 (*0-688-17659-3*, Wm Morrow) Morrow Avon.

— Homestyling: Contrast. 1998. pap. 19.95 (*0-688-16142-1*, Wm Morrow) Morrow Avon.

— Innovations. 1999. pap. 32.50 (*0-688-15047-0*, Wm Morrow) Morrow Avon.

***PBC International Staff.** International Clubs & Resorts. 1998. pap. 32.50 (*0-688-16006-9*, Wm Morrow) Morrow Avon.

PBC International Staff. Kitchens: Lifestyle & Design. 1997. 39.95 (*0-688-15454-9*, Wm Morrow) Morrow Avon.

— Lifestyle Stores. 1999. pap. 29.95 (*0-688-15537-5*, Wm Morrow) Morrow Avon.

An Asterisk (*) at the beginning of an entry indicates that the title is appearing for the first time.

— Lightstyling. 1999. pap. 19.95 (*0-688-16686-5*, Wm Morrow) Morrow Avon.
— New Hotels. 1998. pap. 35.00 (*0-688-15403-4*, Wm Morrow) Morrow Avon.
— The New Modern. 1997. pap. 24.95 (*0-688-14926-X*, Wm Morrow) Morrow Avon.
— The New Office. 1998. pap. 34.95 (*0-688-16144-8*, Wm Morrow) Morrow Avon.
***PBC International Staff.** New York Style. (Illus.). 2000. 42.50 (*0-86636-789-6*) Universe.
PBC International Staff. Newsletters. 1997. pap. 24.95 (*0-688-15885-4*, Wm Morrow) Morrow Avon.
— Pubs & Clubs: Bar Excellence. 1999. 45.00 (*0-688-16055-7*, Wm Morrow) Morrow Avon.
— Restaurant 2000. 1998. 45.00 (*0-688-15886-2*, Wm Morrow) Morrow Avon.
PBC International Staff. The School Visual Arts. 1997. 55.00 (*0-688-15416-6*, Wm Morrow) Morrow Avon.
— Shops & Boutiques. 1999. 45.00 (*0-688-16684-9*, Wm Morrow) Morrow Avon.
— Showhouse. 1998. 50.00 (*0-688-16052-2*, Wm Morrow) Morrow Avon.
***PBC International Staff.** Spa. 2000. 50.00 (*0-688-17670-4*, Wm Morrow) Morrow Avon.
PBC International Staff. Stores: Retail Design. 1999. pap. 32.50 (*0-688-16390-4*, Wm Morrow) Morrow Avon.
PBC International Staff. That's Enterainment. 1997. pap. 32.50 (*0-688-16035-2*, Wm Morrow) Morrow Avon.
***PBC International Staff.** Theme Restaurants. 1999. pap. 29.95 (*0-688-16007-7*, Wm Morrow) Morrow Avon.
PBC International Staff. Timeless Designs. 1997. 34.95 (*0-688-15375-5*, Wm Morrow) Morrow Avon.
— Typeplay. 1997. pap. 29.95 (*0-688-16143-X*, Wm Morrow) Morrow Avon.
***PBC International Staff.** Well-Dressed Table. 2000. 34.95 (*0-86636-787-X*) Universe.
P'Bitek, Okot. African Religions in European Scholarship. (African Heritage Classical Research Studies). 140p. reprint ed. 15.00 (*0-938818-29-5*) ECA Assoc.
— Song of a Prisoner. (Illus.). 128p. 1971. 15.95 (*0-89388-004-3*); pap. 9.95 (*0-685-42289-5*) Okpaku Communications.
— Song of Lawino & Song of Ocol. (African Writers Ser.: No. 266). (Illus.). 151p. (C). 1984. reprint ed. pap. 9.95 (*0-435-90266-0*, 90266) Heinemann.
P'Brien, Robert W. & Iwasaki, Amy. College Nisei Revisited. (Illus.). 232p. 1999. 22.95 (*0-87015-254-8*) Pacific Bks.
PBS Adult Learning Service Staff. Transform Myth Thru Time. (Illus.). 183p. (C). 1989. pap. text, student ed. 24.00 (*0-15-592336-6*, Pub. by Harcourt Coll Pubs) Harcourt.
— Transformations of Myth Through Time. (Illus.). 496p. (C). 1989. pap. text 37.00 (*0-15-592335-8*, Pub. by Harcourt Coll Pubs) Harcourt.
— Transformations of Myth Through Time. (Illus.). 496p. (C). 1989. teacher ed. write for info. (*0-15-592337-4*) Harcourt Coll Pubs.
PBS Engineering Department Staff. Digital Video: Making the Analog to Digital Transition. Butler, Andy, ed. (Video Engineering Ser.). (Illus.). 350p. 1998. 85.95 (*0-07-052719-9*) McGraw-Hill Prof.
PC Learning Labs Staff. PC Learning Lab Teacher 123 for Windows 95. 1996. pap. 29.99 incl. disk (*1-56276-403-9*, Ziff-Davis Pr) Que.
— PC Learning Lab Teaches Wordperfect for Windows 95. 1996. pap. 29.99 incl. disk (*1-56276-398-9*, Ziff-Davis Pr) Que.
— PC Learning Labs Teaches Ami Pro 3.0. (Learning Labs Ser.). (Illus.). 464p. 1993. pap. 22.95 incl. disk (*1-56276-134-X*, Ziff-Davis Pr) Que.
— PC Learning Labs Teaches CC: Mail. (Learning Labs Ser.). (Illus.). 288p. 1993. pap. 22.95 incl. disk (*1-56276-135-8*, Ziff-Davis Pr) Que.
— PC Learning Labs Teaches DOS 5. (Learning Labs Ser.). (Illus.). 346p. (Orig.). 1992. pap. 22.95 incl. disk (*1-56276-042-4*, Ziff-Davis Pr) Que.
— PC Learning Labs Teaches DOS 6. (PC Learning Labs Ser.). (Illus.). 456p. (Orig.). 1993. pap. 22.95 incl. disk (*1-56276-100-5*, Ziff-Davis Pr) Que.
— PC Learning Labs Teaches Excel 4.0 for Windows. (Learning Labs Ser.). (Illus.). 384p. (Orig.). 1992. pap. 22.95 incl. disk (*1-56276-074-2*, Ziff-Davis Pr) Que.
— PC Learning Labs Teaches Microsoft Access 2.0. LC 94-172106. 400p. 1995. 22.95 incl. disk (*1-56276-225-7*, Ziff-Davis Pr) Que.
— PC Learning Labs Teaches Microsoft Office. LC 95-123977. (Learning Labs Ser.). (Illus.). 208p. (Orig.). 1994. pap. 22.95 incl. disk (*1-56276-272-9*, Ziff-Davis Pr) Que.
— PC Learning Labs Teaches Microsoft Project 3.0 for Windows. (Illus.). 399p. (Orig.). 1993. pap. 22.95 incl. disk (*1-56276-124-2*, Ziff-Davis Pr) Que.
— PC Learning Labs Teaches 1-2-3 5.0 for Windows. LC 95-114770. 352p. 1994. 22.95 incl. disk (*1-56276-295-8*, Ziff-Davis Pr) Que.
— PC Learning Labs Teaches 1-2-3 Release 2.3. (Learning Labs Ser.). (Illus.). 307p. (Orig.). 1991. pap. 22.95 incl. disk (*1-56276-033-5*, Ziff-Davis Pr) Que.
— PC Learning Labs Teaches OS-2 2.1. 320p. 1993. pap. 22.95 incl. disk (*1-56276-148-X*, Ziff-Davis Pr) Que.
— PC Learning Labs Teaches PowerPoint for Windows. (Learning Labs Ser.). 464p. 1993. pap. 22.95 incl. disk (*1-56276-154-4*, Ziff-Davis Pr) Que.
— PC Learning Labs Teaches Word for Windows 2.0. (Learning Labs Ser.). (Illus.). 363p. (Orig.). 1992. pap. 22.95 incl. disk (*1-56276-065-3*, Ziff-Davis Pr) Que.
— PC Learning Labs Teaches Word 6.0 for Windows. (Learning Labs Ser.). 432p. 1993. pap. 22.95 incl. disk (*1-56276-139-0*, Ziff-Davis Pr) Que.
PC Learning Labs Staff, jt. auth. see Logical Operations Staff.
PC World Editors. Hands On. write for info. (*0-671-49285-3*) S&S Trade.
PC World Editors, jt. auth. see Myers, David.
PCB Staff. Art & Life of Georgia O'Keefe. 1995. 14.99 (*0-517-03002-0*) Random Hse Value.
Pchiluk, William & Nash, David. Autofacts Yearbook, 1992, Vol. 2. 500p. 1992. text 495.00 (*1-879800-03-9*) Autofacts.
PCI Committee on Parking Marketing & Promotion Staff, jt. auth. see PCI Committee on Parking Structures Staff.
PCI Committee on Parking Structures Staff & PCI Committee on Parking Marketing & Promotion Staff. Parking Structures: Recommended Practice for Design & Construction. 2nd ed. LC 98-159940. (Illus.). 141p. 1998. pap. text 50.00 (*0-937040-58-4*, MNL-129-98) P-PCI.
PCI Staff. Design & Typical Details of Connections for Precast & Prestressed Concrete. 2nd ed. 270p. 1988. 80.00 (*0-937040-40-1*) P-PCI.
— PCI Manual for the Design of Hollow-Core Slabs. 120p. 1985. 60.00 (*0-937040-25-8*) P-PCI.
Pckt Staff. Oxford Pocket Bible: Bonded Leather. 1472p. 1998. 39.99 (*0-19-528202-7*) OUP.
***Pckt Staff.** Pocket Bible. 1998. write for info. (*1-55819-723-0*) Broadman.
PcPhail, Helen, tr. see French Ramblers Association Staff.
PCPS Management of Accounting Practice Committee. The Communications Advantage: How to Effectively Share Information with Clients & Employees. Osborne, Jayne E., ed. LC 98-34337. 250p. 1998. pap. 41.95 (*0-87051-240-4*) Am Inst CPA.
PCPS MAP Committee Staff. MAP Selected Reading, 1999. 1999. pap. 38.75 (*0-87051-254-4*, 090451) Am Inst CPA.
PCPS Staff. The Marketing Advantage II: New Ideas on Getting & Keeping Clients. LC 98-20402. 200p. 1998. pap. 43.95 (*0-87051-225-0*, 090437) Am Inst CPA.
PCPSExecutive Committee. A Roadmap of the Peer Review Process: Getting the Most Value from Your Peer Review. 100p. 1998. pap. write for info. (*0-87051-242-0*) Am Inst CPA.
PCRCW '94 Staff. Parallel Computer Routing & Communication: Proceedings of the First International Workshop, PCRCW '94, Seattle, Washington, U. S. A., May 16-18, 1994. Snyder, Lawrence & Bolding, Kevin, eds. LC 94-33307. (Lecture Notes in Computer Science Ser.: 853). 1994. write for info. (*0-387-58429-3*) Spr-Verlag.
— Parallel Computer Routing & Communication: Proceedings of the First International Workshop, PCRCW '94, Seattle, Washington, U. S. A., May 16-18, 1994. Snyder, Lawrence & Bolding, Kevin, eds. LC 94-33307. (Lecture Notes in Computer Science Ser.: 853). 1994. 50.95 (*3-540-58429-3*) Spr-Verlag.
PCS Associates Staff, ed. Student Version of PC: Solve. (C). 1990. pap. 67.00 incl. 3.5 hd (*1-878437-03-8*) Pac Crest Soft.
PCS Associates Staff & Apple, Daniel K. Faculty PC: SOLVE, 3 vols., Set. (Orig.). (C). 1990. pap. text 40.00 (*1-878437-14-3*) Pac Crest Soft.
PCS Associates Staff, jt. auth. see Apple, Daniel K.
PCS Staff. Battle Arena Toshinden 2 Game Secrets: Unauthorized. LC 96-67728. 1996. pap. text 12.99 (*0-7615-0585-7*) Prima Pub.
— Donkey Kong Country Vol. 2: Diddy's Kong Quest - Unauthorized Game Secrets. 1996. pap. text 12.99 (*0-7615-0353-6*) Prima Pub.
PCS Staff. Doom 64 Unauthorized Game Secrets. LC 97-65822. 96p. 1997. per. 12.99 (*0-7615-1108-3*) Prima Pub.
— Fighting Games Secrets. 336p. 1996. pap., per. 14.99 (*0-7615-0785-X*) Prima Pub.
— Final Doom Unauthorized Secrets. LC 96-68170. 1996. pap., per. 19.99 (*0-7615-0723-X*) Prima Pub.
— Killer Instinct Gold: The Unauthorized Guide, Vol. 2. LC 96-72231. 1996. pap., per. 12.99 (*0-7615-0731-0*) Prima Pub.
PCS Staff. Killer Instinct 2 Arcade Secrets: The Unauthorized Guide. 1996. pap. text 12.99 (*0-7615-0551-2*) Prima Pub.
— MDK: The Official Strategy Guide. 128p. 1997. per. 12.99 (*0-7615-1063-X*) Prima Pub.
PCS Staff. Nights: The Official Strategy Guide. LC 96-69704. 96p. 1996. pap., per. 14.99 (*0-7615-0866-X*) Prima Pub.
PCS Staff. Nintendo 64 Unauthorized Game Secrets. 128p. 1997. per. 12.99 (*0-7615-0970-4*) Prima Pub.
PCS Staff. PlayStation, Vol. 3. 1996. pap., per. 12.99 (*0-7615-0527-X*) Prima Pub.
PCS Staff. Sega Saturn Game Secrets: The Unauthorized Edition. LC 96-67262. 352p. 1996. per. 14.99 (*0-7615-0313-7*) Prima Pub.
— Sega Saturn Pocket Power Guide: Unauthorized. LC 96-70917. 96p. 1996. pap. 7.99 (*0-7615-0972-0*) Prima Pub.
— Suikoden. LC 96-72595. 128p. 1997. per. 14.99 (*0-7615-1068-0*) Prima Pub.
— Super Mario Kart 64 Unauthorized Game Secrets. LC 96-72649. 96p. 1997. per. 12.99 (*0-7615-1078-8*) Prima Pub.
PCS Staff. Super Mario 64: Game Secrets Unauthorized. LC 96-71027. 128p. 1996. pap., per. 12.99 (*0-7615-0892-9*) Prima Pub.
PCS Staff. Tekken 2 Unauthorized, Vol. 2. LC 96-98004. 128p. 1996. pap. 12.99 (*0-7615-0584-9*) Prima Pub.
— Terry Pratchett's Discworld: The Official Strategy Guide. 144p. 1995. pap. text 19.95 (*0-7615-0218-1*) Prima Pub.
— Tobal No. 1: The Official Strategy Guide, No. 1. LC 96-71319. 96p. 1996. pap. 12.99 (*0-7615-0984-4*) Prima Pub.
PCS Staff. Tomb Raider Game Secrets. LC 96-70476 (Secrets of the Games Ser.). (Illus.). 107p. 1996. pap. 12.99 (*0-7615-0931-3*) Prima Pub.
PCS Staff. Ultimate Mortal Kombat 3 Official Arcade Secrets. 96p. 1996. pap. text 9.99 (*0-7615-0586-5*) Prima Pub.
PCS Staff. Virtua Fighter 3 Arcade Secrets. LC 96-68916. 144p. 1997. pap., per. 12.99 (*0-7615-0797-3*) Prima Pub.
— War Gods Official Arcade. LC 96-68687. 128p. 1996. pap., per. 9.99 (*0-7615-0767-1*) Prima Pub.
PDA Research Task Force No. 16 on Dry Heat Process. Validation of Dry Heat Processes Used for Sterlization & Depyrogenation. (Technical Reports: No. 3). 55p. (Orig.). 1981. pap. 30.00 (*0-939459-02-7*) PDA.
PDA Research Task Force on Aseptic Filling. Validation of Aseptic Drug Powder Filling Process. (Technical Reports: No. 6). 30p. 1984. pap. 30.00 (*0-939459-05-1*) PDA.
PDA Research Task Group No. 15 on Aseptic Filling. Validation of Aseptic Filling for Solution Drug Products. rev. ed. (Technical Monographs: No. 2). 28p. (Orig.). 1980. pap. 30.00 (*0-939459-01-9*) PDA.
PDA Research Task Group on Steam Sterilization. Validation of Steam Sterilization Cycles. rev. ed. (Technical Monographs: No. 1). 36p. 1978. pap. 30.00 (*0-939459-00-0*) PDA.
PDA Research Task Group-Quality Control Subcommitt. Design Concepts for the Validation of a Water for Injection System. (Technical Reports: No. 4). 1983. pap. 30.00 (*0-939459-03-5*) PDA.
PDA Task Force on Depyrogenation Staff. Technical Report, No. 7. (Depyrogenation Ser.). 116p. 1985. pap. 35.00 (*0-939459-06-X*) PDA.
Pderzoli, P., ed. Facing the Pancreatic Dilemma: Update of Medical & Surgical Pancreatology. LC 94-35004. 1994. write for info. (*3-540-58284-3*) Spr-Verlag.
Pdez, Ramon T., tr. see Stendal, Russell M. & Bayona, Ricardo T.
PDP Research Group Staff, et al. Parallel Distributed Processing: Explorations in the Microstructure of Cognition, Vol. 1: Foundations. (Computational Models of Cognition & Perception Ser.). (Illus.). 567p. 1986. 65.00 (*0-262-18120-7*, Bradford Bks) MIT Pr.
— Parallel Distributed Processing: Explorations in the Microstructure of Cognition, Vol. 1: Foundations. (Computational Models of Cognition & Perception Ser.). (Illus.). 567p. 1987. pap. text 32.50 (*0-262-68053-X*, Bradford Bks) MIT Pr.
PDR Staff. Dictionary Vidal (French PDR) 1998. (FRE.). 1998. 295.00 (*0-320-00371-X*) Fr & Eur.
— Family Encyclopedia of Medical Care. 1999. mass mkt. 6.99 (*0-345-42009-8*) Ballantine Pub Grp.
PDR Staff, ed. The PDR Pocket Guide to Prescription Drugs. 2nd ed. 1997. per. 6.99 (*0-671-01454-4*) PB.
Pe Maung, Tin, tr. from PLI. The Expositor. (C). 1976. reprint ed. 55.00 (*0-86013-070-3*, Pub. by Pali Text) Elsevier.
— The Path of Purity, 3 vols. in 1. (C). 1975. reprint ed. 71.00 (*0-86013-008-8*, Pub. by Pali Text) Elsevier.
Pe Maung Tin, tr. see Buddhaghosa.
Pea, Roy D. & Sheingold, Karen, eds. Mirrors of Minds: Patterns of Experience in Educational Computing. LC 87-1274. (Cognition & Computing Ser.). 336p. 1987. pap. 39.50 (*0-89391-423-1*); text 73.25 (*0-89391-422-3*) Ablx Pub.
Peabody, Al, tr. see Dianov, Y. M., ed.
Peabody, Al, tr. see Komar, A. A., ed.
Peabody, Al, tr. see Vainshtein, Boris K. & Chernov, A. A., eds.
Peabody Anderson, Cynthia. Pioneer Voices from Plymouth to Breckenridge: The Peabody Family over Eleven Generations. Gilliland, Mary E., ed. (Illus.). 237p. 1999. pap. 22.95 (*0-9666420-0-7*) Summit Books.
Peabody, Andrew P. Harvard Reminiscences. LC 72-39149. (Essay Index Reprint Ser.). 1977. reprint ed. 20.95 (*0-8369-2708-7*) Ayer.
Peabody, Barbara. The Screaming Room: A Mother's Journal of Her Son's Struggle with AIDS. 288p. 1987. mass mkt. 4.99 (*0-380-70345-9*, Avon Bks) Morrow Avon.
Peabody, Charles N. Zab: Brevet Major Zabdiel Boylston Adams, 1829-1902, Physician. 255p. 1984. 17.50 (*0-8139-1066-8*) F A Countway.
Peabody, Elizabeth P. Last Evening with Allston, & Other Papers. LC 72-2953. reprint ed. 47.50 (*0-404-10718-4*) AMS Pr.
— Record of a School. LC 74-89218. (American Education: Its Men, Institutions, & Ideas. Series 1). 1974. reprint ed. 20.95 (*0-405-01457-0*) Ayer.
Peabody, Francis G. Education for Life: The Story of Hampton Institute. LC 77-84106. 464p. 1969. reprint ed. 36.95 (*0-405-30234-7*) Ayer.
— Reminiscences of Present-Day Saints. LC 74-37525. (Essay Index Reprint Ser.). 1977. reprint ed. 25.95 (*0-8369-2576-9*) Ayer.
Peabody, Frederick. Asking about Life. 496p. (C). 1998. per. 21.50 (*0-03-072052-4*) SCP.
Peabody, George. Kings Landing: A Living History Colour Guide. LC 97-950010. (Living History Colour Guide Ser.). (Illus.). 72p. (Orig.). 1997. pap. 10.95 (*0-88780-398-9*, Pub. by Formac Publ Co) Seven Hills Bk.
— School Days: The One-Room Schools of Maritime Canada. (Illus.). 137p. 1992. pap. 14.95 (*0-86492-142-X*, Pub. by Goose Ln Edits) Genl Dist Srvs.
Peabody, George, ed. Best Maritime Short Stories. (Illus.). 232p. 1995. pap. 16.95 (*0-88780-068-8*, Pub. by Formac Publ Co) Formac Dist Ltd.
— East Coast Limericks. (Illus.). 86p. 1989. pap. 5.99 (*0-88780-075-0*, Pub. by Formac Publ Co) Formac Dist Ltd.
Peabody, John W., et al. Policy & Health: Implications for Development in Asia. LC 99-24255. (Rand Studies in Policy Analysis). (Illus.). 464p. (C). 1999. 44.95 (*0-521-66164-1*) Cambridge U Pr.
Peabody, Kathleen L. & Mooney, Margaret L. The Lonely Pain of Cancer: Home Care for the Terminally Ill. Ellison, Bettye, ed. LC 91-90114. (Illus.). 160p. (Orig.). (C). 1991. pap. 15.95 (*0-9629350-1-8*) Sharp Pub.
— Swinging in the Wind: Kids: Survivors of a Crisis. Ellison, Bettye & Libby, Peter, eds. LC 92-50632. (Illus.). 144p. (Orig.). (C). 1992. pap. text 12.95 (*0-9629350-9-3*) Sharp Pub.
Peabody, Kathleen L., et al. Widows Are Special: They Know the Sun Will Rise Again. LC 94-17856. 128p. (Orig.). (C). 1994. pap. write for info. (*0-9629350-7-7*) Sharp Pub.
Peabody, Larry. Secular Word Is Full-Time Service Study Guide. 1976. pap., student ed. 1.50 (*0-87508-449-4*) Chr Lit.
— Secular Work Is Full Time Service. 1974. pap. 5.99 (*0-87508-448-6*) Chr Lit.
Peabody, Larry & Gear, John. How to Write Policies, Procedures & Task Outlines: Sending Clear Signals in Written Directions. (Illus.). 128p. 1996. pap. 29.95 (*0-9650585-0-6*) Writing Services.
Peabody, R. P. History of Shelburne. (Illus.). 127p. 1997. reprint ed. lib. bdg. 22.50 (*0-8328-6024-7*) Higginson Bk Co.
Peabody, Richard. Buoyancy: And Other Myths. LC 94-78592. 70p. (Orig.). 1995. pap. 7.95 (*0-945144-06-7*) Gut Punch Pr.
— Sad Fashions. LC 89-85142. 64p. (Orig.). 1990. pap. 7.95 (*0-945144-01-6*) Gut Punch Pr.
Peabody, Richard, intro. One Thousand One Monday Nights: Stories by Twelve Washington Writers. LC 89-52128. 206p. (Orig.). 1990. pap. 10.00 (*0-9609062-1-5*) WA Expatriates Pr.
Peabody, Richard, jt. auth. see Ebersole, Lucinda.
Peabody, Richard, ed. see Cassady, Carolyn, et al.
Peabody, Richard, jt. ed. see Ebersole, Lucinda.
Peabody, Robert E. Models of American Sailing Ships. rev. ed. Ratte, John, ed. LC 94-78003. (Illus.). 116p. (Orig.). 1994. 18.00 (*1-879886-39-1*) Addison Gallery.
Peabody, Robert L. & Polsby, Nelson W., eds. New Perspectives on the House of Representatives. rev. ed. 392p. 1992. pap. text 17.95 (*0-8018-4158-5*) Johns Hopkins.
Peabody, Robert L., jt. auth. see Huitt, Ralph K.
Peabody, S. Peabody (Paybody, Pabody, Pabodie) Genealogy. (Illus.). 614p. 1989. reprint ed. pap. 92.00 (*0-8328-0943-8*); reprint ed. lib. bdg. 100.00 (*0-8328-0942-X*) Higginson Bk Co.
Peabody, Sue. "There Are No Slaves in France" The Political Culture of Race & Slavery in the Ancien Regime. (Illus.). 224p. 1996. text 45.00 (*0-19-510198-7*) OUP.
Peabody, Susan. Addiction to Love: Overcoming Obsession & Dependency in Relationships. 200p. 1995. pap. 12.95 (*0-89087-715-7*) Celestial Arts.
Peabody, Virginia & Sullivan, Paul. The Medicare As a Secondary Payer Guide: Practical Solutions to Administration & Management. Newman, Barry, ed. LC 96-11272. (Illus.). 200p. (C). 1996. text 50.00 (*0-7863-0533-9*, Irwn Prfssnl) McGraw-Hill Prof.
Peabody, Virginia S., jt. auth. see Newman, Barry M.
Peace and White Staff. Brickyard 400: Five Years of NASCAR at Indy. LC 99-179469. (Illus.). 128p. 1998. 24.95 (*0-7603-0597-8*) MBI Pubg.
Peace, Beverly & Peace, Philip. Planning Ahead: A Positive Act of Love for Family & Friends. 32p. (Orig.). 1992. pap., student ed. 4.95 (*1-881576-00-0*) Providence Hse.
***Peace Colloquy Staff, et al.** Paths of Peace: As the Sky Meets the Earth: Selected Papers from the Peace Colloquy (1999), the Temple, Independence, Missouri. LC 00-25506. 2000. write for info. (*0-8309-0939-7*) Herald Pub Hse.
Peace, D. McClymont. Key for Identification of Mandibles of Stored-Food Insects. (Illus.). vi, 166p. 1985. pap. 62.00 (*0-935584-32-3*) AOAC Intl.
Peace, David. The Agape Conspiracy. 472p. mass mkt. 5.99 (*1-55197-211-5*) Picasso Publ.
— The Agape Solution. 325p. mass mkt. 5.99 (*1-55197-209-3*) Picasso Publ.
Peace, David. Eric Gill: The Inscriptions. (Illus.). 208p. 1995. 50.00 (*1-56792-027-6*) Godine.
***Peace, David.** Nineteen Seventy-Four. 2000. pap. 14.00 (*1-85242-634-9*) Serpents Tail.
— Nineteen Seventy Four. 320p. 2000. pap. 12.00 (*1-85242-741-8*) Serpents Tail.
Peace, G., jt. auth. see Faulkner, A.
Peace, Karl A., ed. Biopharmaceutical Sequential Statistical Applications. (Statistics: Textbooks & Monographs: Vol. 128). (Illus.). 376p. 1992. text 155.00 (*0-8247-8628-9*) Dekker.
— Statistical Issues in Drug Research & Development. (Statistics: Textbooks & Monographs: Vol. 106). (Illus.). 384p. 1989. text 165.50 (*0-8247-8290-9*) Dekker.
Peace, Karl E. Biopharmaceutical Statistics for Drug Development. (Statistics Ser.: Vol. 86). (Illus.). 656p. 1987. text 199.00 (*0-8247-7798-0*) Dekker.
Peace, Martha. Becoming a Titus II Woman. 1997. pap. 10.95 (*1-885904-17-7*) Focus Pubng.
— The Excellent Wife: A Biblical Perspective. 256p. (Orig.). 1995. pap. 11.95 (*1-885904-08-8*) Focus Pubng.
— The Excellent Wife: Study Guide. 104p. 1996. pap., spiral bd. 9.95 (*1-885904-14-2*) Focus Pubng.
— The Excellent Wife: Teacher's Guide. 104p. 1995. teacher ed., spiral bd. 9.95 (*1-885904-15-0*) Focus Pubng.

P

Peace, P. & Maugham, M. Jet Engine Manual. 160p. (C). 1989. 55.00 (*81-7002-014-X*, Pub. by Himalayan Bks) St Mut.

Peace, Philip, jt. auth. see Peace, Beverly.

Peace Pilgrim II Staff. Enjoying the Journey: The Adventures, Travels, & Teachings of Peace Pilgrim II. LC 94-36788. 208p. (Orig.). 1995. pap. 10.00 (*0-931892-94-5*) B Dolphin Pub.

Peace, R. Dostoyevsky's Notes from Underground: Critical Study. (Critical Studies in Russian Literature Ser.). 121p. 1993. pap. 16.95 (*1-85399-343-3*, Pub. by Brist Class Pr) Focus Pub-R Pullins.

Peace, R., ed. Griboyedov: Woe from Wit (Gor ot Uma) (Russian Texts Ser.). (RUS.). 1995. pap. 20.95 (*1-85399-389-1*, Pub. by Brist Class Pr) Focus Pub-R Pullins.

Peace, Richard. Contemplative Bible Reading: Experiencing God Through Scriptures. (Spiritual Disciplines Ser.). 1996. pap. 7.00 (*0-89109-899-2*, 98992) NavPress.

— Conversion in the New Testament: Paul & the Twelve Deciples. LC 99-37660. 390p. 1999. pap. 25.00 (*0-8028-4235-6*) Eerdmans.

— Learning to Love God. (Learning to Love Ser.). 96p. (Orig.). 1994. pap. 7.00 (*0-89109-841-0*) NavPress.

— Learning to Love Others. (Learning to Love Ser.). 96p. (Orig.). 1994. pap. 7.00 (*0-89109-840-2*) NavPress.

— Learning to Love Ourselves. (Learning to Love Ser.). 96p. (Orig.). 1994. pap. 7.00 (*0-89109-842-9*) NavPress.

— Meditative Prayer: Entering God's Presence. (Spiritual Formation Ser.). 1999. pap. 7.00 (*0-89109-901-8*) NavPress.

— Spiritual Autobiography. 1998. pap. text 6.00 (*1-57683-110-8*) NavPress.

— Spiritual Journaling: Recording Your Journey Toward God. LC 96-117340. (Spiritual Disciplines Ser.). 1996. pap. 7.00 (*0-89109-897-6*) NavPress.

— Spiritual Journaling: Recording Your Journey Toward God. LC 99-233010. 1999. pap. text 6.00 (*1-57683-109-4*) NavPress.

— Spiritual Storytelling: Discovering & Sharing Your Spiritual Autobiography. (Spiritual Disciplines Ser.). 1996. pap. 7.00 (*0-89109-898-4*) NavPress.

Peace, Robert & Papanastassiou, Marina. The Technological Competitiveness of Japanese Multinationals: The European Dimension. LC 96-4456. (Thames Essays Ser.). (Illus.). 120p. (C). 1996. text 47.50 (*0-472-10728-3*, 10728) U of Mich Pr.

Peace, Roger C., III. A Just & Lasting Peace: The U. S. Peace Movement from the Cold War to Desert Storm. LC 90-63425. (Illus.). 344p. (Orig.). 1991. pap. 14.95 (*0-9622683-8-0*) Noble Pr.

Peace, S., jt. auth. see Richards, R.

Peace, Sheila M. Researching Social Gerontology: Concepts, Methods & Issues. Norton, Peter G. et al, eds. 224p. (C). 1990. text 47.50 (*0-8039-8284-6*); pap. text 19.95 (*0-8039-8285-2*) Sage.

Peace, Sheila M., et al. Re-Evaluating Residential Care. LC 96-46517. (Rethinking Aging Ser.). 1997. pap. 29.95 (*0-335-19392-7*) OpUniv Pr.

***Peace, Tom.** Sunbelt Gardening: Success in Hot-Weather Climates. LC 99-44967. (Illus.). 288p. 2000. pap. 29.95 (*1-55591-356-3*) Fulcrum Pub.

***Peaceable Kingdom Press Staff.** Celebrating Childrens Books. (Illus.). (J). 1999. pap. 11.95 (*1-56890-023-6*) Peaceable King.

***Peaceable Kingdom Press Staff, ed.** Goodnight Moon. 2000. 18.95 (*1-56890-034-1*) Peaceable King.

— Goodnight Moon Baby Journal. 96p. 2000. 18.95 (*1-56890-033-3*) Peaceable King.

Peacefull, Leonard, ed. A Geography of Ohio. rev. ed. LC 95-40344. Orig. Title: The Changing Heartland: A Geography of Ohio. (Illus.). 400p. (C). 1996. reprint ed. pap. 35.00 (*0-87338-525-X*) Kent St U Pr.

Peacemaker Bounty Staff. Peacemaker Bounty. LC 98-96620. 192p. 1998. 18.95 (*0-8034-9331-2*, Avalon Bks) Bouregy.

Peach. ISO 9000 Handbook. 4th ed. 1999. 99.95 (*0-07-134551-5*) McGraw.

Peach, ed. see Toutain.

Peach, Andrew, jt. auth. see Cohen, Jonathan.

Peach, Bernard, ed. see Hutcheson, Francis.

Peach, Bill. Random Thoughts Left & Right. LC 98-72571. 128p. 1998. pap. 11.95 (*1-57736-078-8*, Hillsboro Pr) Providence Hse.

— The South Side of Boston. LC 95-77743. 128p. (Orig.). 1995. pap. 11.95 (*1-881576-42-6*, Hillsboro Pr) Providence Hse.

Peach, Charles. The Whole Works This Our Home Record Keeping & Joy of Dicscovery Workbook. (Illus.). 200p. 1987. student ed. 30.00 (*0-942751-33-7*) Whole Works.

— Whole Works Wine Tasting & Record Book. 2nd ed. (Illus.). 100p. 1987. student ed. 13.00 (*0-942751-01-9*) Whole Works.

Peach, David A. & Livernash, E. Robert. Grievance Initiation & Resolution: A Study in Steel. 1974. text 10.00 (*0-87584-112-0*) HUP.

Peach, Emily. Tarot for Tomorrow: An Advanced Handbook of Tarot Prediction. (Illus.). 192p. (Orig.). 1989. pap. 12.95 (*0-85030-466-0*, Pub. by Aqrn Pr) Harper SF.

— The Tarot Workbook: Understanding & Using Tarot Symbolism. rev. ed. (Workbook Ser.). (Illus.). 256p. 1985. pap. 14.95 (*0-85030-390-7*) Sterling.

— Things That Go Bump in the Night: How to Investigate & Challenge Ghostly Experiences. 1991. pap. 9.95 (*0-85030-873-9*, Pub. by Aqrn Pr) Harper SF.

Peach, James T. Demographic & Economic Change in Mexico's Northern Frontier: Evidence from the X Censo General de Poblacion y Vivienda. 47p. (Orig.). (C). 1984. pap. text 10.00 (*0-937795-12-7*) Waste-Mgmt Educ.

Peach, James T. & Hughes, William F. Some Implications of the 1984 Tandem Truck Safety Act for the U. S.-Mexico Border Area. 17p. (Orig.). (C). 1985. pap. text 10.00 (*0-937795-07-0*) Waste-Mgmt Educ.

Peach, James T., jt. auth. see Jannuzi, F. Tomasson.

Peach, Josephine M., jt. auth. see Hornby, Michael.

Peach, K. J. & Vick, L. L., eds. High Energy Phenomenology. LC 94-30447. (Scottish Universities Summer School in Physics, a NATO Advanced Study Institute Ser.: No. 42). (Illus.). 496p. 1994. 189.00 (*0-7503-0326-3*) IOP Pub.

Peach, K. J., jt. ed. see Frame, D.

Peach, Linden. Ancestral Lines: Culture & Identity in the Work of Six Contemporary Poets. 175p. 1993. 35.00 (*1-85411-061-6*, Pub. by Seren Bks) Dufour.

— Angela Carter. LC 97-13615. (Modern Novelists Ser.). 192p. 1997. text 35.00 (*0-312-17626-0*) St Martin.

— Toni Morrison. LC 94-46867. (Modern Novelists Ser.). 1995. text 39.95 (*0-312-12595-X*) St Martin.

***Peach, Linden.** Toni Morrison: Historical Perspectives & Literary Contexts. 2nd ed. 2000. text 35.00 (*0-312-23397-3*) St Martin.

— Virginia Woolf. LC 99-43513. (Critical Issues Ser.). 2000. 59.95 (*0-312-22889-9*) St Martin.

— Virginia Woolf. LC 99-43513. (Critical Issues Ser.). 2000. pap. 21.95 (*0-312-22891-0*) St Martin.

Peach, Lucinda J. Women at War: The Ethics of Women in Combat. Cuffel, Victoria J., ed. LC 93-655022. (MacArthur Scholar Series, Occasional Paper: No. 20). 133p. (Orig.). 1993. pap. 4.50 (*1-881157-23-7*) In Ctr Global.

— Women in Culture: A Women's Studies Anthology. LC 97-24516. 480p. (C). 1998. text 68.95 (*1-55786-648-1*); pap. text 32.95 (*1-55786-649-X*) Blackwell Pubs.

Peach, M. E., jt. auth. see Haas, A.

Peach, Robert & Ritter, Diane. The Memory Jogger 9000: A Pocket Guide to Implementing ISO 9000 Quality Systems Standard & QS-9000 Third EditionRequirements. Oddo, Francine, ed. (Illus.). 164p. 1996. spiral bd. 6.95 (*1-879364-82-4*, 1060E) GOAL-QPC.

Peach, Robert W. The ISO 9000 Handbook. 3rd ed. LC 96-23785. xvi, 1008 p. 1996. text 80.00 (*0-7863-0786-2*, Irwn Prfssnl) McGraw-Hill Prof.

Peach, Robert W., ed. The IOS Nine Thousand Handbook. 496p. 1992. pap. 85.00 (*1-883337-27-5*) Ctr Energy Envir.

Peach, S. Running Skills. (Superskills Ser.). (Illus.). 48p. (YA). (gr. 6-10). 1988. pap. 5.95 (*0-7460-0165-7*) EDC.

— Technical Drawing. (Practical Guides Ser.). (Illus.). 48p. (YA). (gr. 6 up). 1987. pap. 7.95 (*0-7460-0094-4*) EDC.

— Technical Drawing. (Practical Guides Ser.). (Illus.). 48p. (YA). (gr. 6 up). 1999. lib. bdg. 14.96 (*0-88110-247-4*) EDC.

Peach, S. & Butterfield, M. Photography. (Practical Guides Ser.). (Illus.). 48p. (J). (gr. 6 up). 1987. pap. 8.95 (*0-7460-0107-X*, Usborne) EDC.

— Photography. (Practical Guides Ser.). (Illus.). 48p. (J). (gr. 6 up). 1999. lib. bdg. 16.95 (*0-88110-292-X*, Usborne) EDC.

Peach, S., jt. auth. see Millard, Anne.

Peach, Terry. Interpreting Ricardo. 332p. (C). 1993. text 64.95 (*0-521-26086-8*) Cambridge U Pr.

Peach, W. Bernard, ed. The Correspondence of Richard Price Vol. III: February 1786 - February 1791. LC 82-14646. 376p. 1993. text 52.95 (*0-8223-1327-8*) Duke.

— Richard Price & the Ethical Foundations of the American Revolution. LC 77-91081. 350p. 1979. text 42.95 (*0-8223-0400-7*) Duke.

Peach, William N. The Security Affiliates of National Banks. LC 78-64180. (Johns Hopkins University. Studies in the Social Sciences. Thirtieth Ser. 1912: 3). 192p. 1983. reprint ed. 34.50 (*0-404-61288-1*) AMS Pr.

— The Security Affiliates of National Banks. LC 75-2660. (Wall Street & the Security Market Ser.). 1975. reprint ed. 19.95 (*0-405-06984-7*) Ayer.

Peacham, Henry. The Art of Drawing with the Pen, & Limning with Water Colours. LC 71-25631. (English Experience Ser.: No. 230). 70p. 1970. reprint ed. 35.00 (*90-221-0230-0*) Walter J Johnson.

— The Garden of Eloquence. LC 54-11900. 280p. 1977. reprint ed. 50.00 (*0-8201-1225-9*) Schol Facsimiles.

— Minerva Britanna: or A Garden of Heroical Devises. LC 73-171783. (English Experience Ser.: No. 407). 232p. 1971. reprint ed. 45.00 (*90-221-0407-9*) Walter J Johnson.

— A Most True Relation of the Affairs of Cleve & Gulick, with the Articles of Peace Propounded at Santen. LC 72-6024. (English Experience Ser.: No. 549). (Illus.). 44p. 1973. reprint ed. 35.00 (*90-221-0549-0*) Walter J Johnson.

Peache, Robert J. & O'Sullivan, Denis, eds. Current Trends in Protective Packaging of Computers & Electronic Components. LC 88-3289. (Special Technical Publication Ser.: No. 994). 80p. 1988. pap. text 19.00 (*0-8031-1171-1*, SPT994) ASTM.

Peacher, Georgiana. Mary Stuart's Ravishment Descending Time: Prose Symphony. LC 75-35307. 117p. 1992. reprint ed. pap. 9.00 (*0-916384-01-2*) P Shedding.

Peachey, J. Lorne. How to Teach Peace to Children. 32p. (Orig.). 1981. pap. 3.99 (*0-8361-1969-X*) Herald Pr.

Peachey, L. D., ed. see Interdisciplinary Conference Staff.

Peachey, Lee D. & Adrian, Richard H., eds. Handbook of Physiology: Section 10, Skeletal Muscle. (American Physiological Society Book). (Illus.). 700p. 1988. text 145.00 (*0-19-520685-1*) OUP.

Peachey, Linda G., jt. auth. see Peachey, Titus.

Peachey, Mal. Wet Wet Wet: Pictured. LC 97-107760. (Illus.). 128p. 1996. text 21.95 (*1-85227-533-2*, Pub. by Virgin Bks) London Brdge.

Peachey, Paul, et al, eds. Abrahamic Faiths, Ethnicity & Ethnic Conflicts. LC 97-20062. (Cultural Heritage & Contemporary Change Ser.: Vol. 7). 250p. 1997. pap. 17.50 (*1-56518-104-2*) Coun Res Values.

Peachey, Titus & Peachey, Linda G. Seeking Peace. LC 91-74053. 238p. 1991. pap. 11.95 (*1-56148-049-5*) Good Bks PA.

Peachin, Michael. Roman Imperial Titulature & Chronology, A. D. 235-284. xxviii, 515p. 1990. 174.00 (*90-5063-034-0*, Pub. by Gieben) J Benjamins Pubng Co.

***Peachlum, Sybil.** Under the Shadow of the Almighty: Developing a Closer Relationship with God & His Son. large type ed. LC 99-93221. 189p. 1999. pap. 19.95 (*0-9671686-0-0*) Peachy News.

Peachment, Allan. The Business of Government Western Australia, 1983-1990. xvi, 240p. 1991. 36.50 (*1-86287-045-4*, Pub. by Federation Pr) Gaunt.

Peachment, Allan, ed. Westminster Inc. A Survey of Three States in the Eighties. 225p. 1995. pap. 39.00 (*1-86287-164-7*, Pub. by Federation Pr) Gaunt.

***Peachment, Corinne.** Feed Your Need: Discover the Simple Food, Hormone & Motivation Facts That Really Make a Difference. Rose, Marc, ed. LC 99-74743. (Illus.). 220p. 2000. pap. 14.00 (*0-9673462-0-7*, 123) Marpel Inc.

Peachtree Road United Methodist Church Preschool S. Flavors & Favors. (Illus.). (Orig.). 1988. 9.50 (*0-9620576-0-6*) Peachtree Rd United Meth Ch.

Peachtree Software Staff, jt. auth. see Yacht, Carol.

Peachy, William, ed. see Ibrahim, I. A.

Peacock. Doing Business God's Way. 1996. pap. 10.00 (*1-887021-00-0*) Rebuild.

Peacock. Pocket PCs Made Simple. 160p. pap. text. write for info. (*0-7506-4900-3*) Buttrwrth-Heinemann.

Peacock. Understanding Earth. (C). 1993. 16.80 (*0-7167-2523-1*) W H Freeman.

— Understanding Earth. 2nd ed. (C). 1997. pap. 16.00 (*0-7167-2795-1*) W H Freeman.

— Walking It Off, Vol. 1. 1995. 24.95 (*0-8050-2533-2*) H Holt & Co.

Peacock & Martin. Where Feminists Come From. 1995. per. write for info. (*0-920813-75-5*) Sister Vis Pr.

Peacock, A. Handbook of Polyethylene. LC 99-58168. (Plastics Engineering Ser.). 2000. write for info. (*0-8247-9546-6*) Dekker.

Peacock, A., ed. X-Ray Astronomy in the Exosat Era. 1985. lib. bdg. 253.50 (*90-277-2099-1*) Kluwer Academic.

Peacock, A. J. Pulmonary Circulation: A Handbook for Clinicians. (Illus.). 528p. 1999. text 99.00 (*0-412-56870-5*, Pub. by E A) OUP.

Peacock, Alan. The Political Economy of Economic Freedom. LC 96-48251. 352p. 1997. 100.00 (*1-85898-535-8*) E Elgar.

Peacock, Alan, ed. Public Choice Analysis in Historical Perspective. (Raffaele Mattioli Lectures on the History of Economic Thought). 246p. 1997. pap. text 19.95 (*0-521-59976-8*) Cambridge U Pr.

Peacock, Alan & Bannock, Graham. Takeovers & the Public Interest: The Hume Report on Corporate Takeovers. (Aberdeen University Press Bks.). 156p. 1991. pap. text 25.90 (*0-08-041206-8*, Pub. by Aberdeen U Pr) Macmillan.

Peacock, Alan & Rizzo, Ilde, eds. Cultural Economics & Cultural Policies. LC 94-15817. 196p. (C). 1994. lib. bdg. 127.50 (*0-7923-2868-X*) Kluwer Academic.

Peacock, Alan, jt. auth. see Bannock, Graham.

Peacock, Alan, jt. auth. see Main, Brian G. M.

Peacock, Alan J., ed. The Achievement of Brian Friel. (A Colin Smythe Publication). 288p. (C). 1997. text 65.00 (*0-86140-349-5*) OUP.

Peacock, Alan J., jt. ed. see Devine, Kathleen.

Peacock, Alan T., ed. Income Redistribution & Social Policy: A Set of Studies. LC 84-29020. 296p. 1985. reprint ed. lib. bdg. 75.00 (*0-313-23867-7*, PINC, Greenwood Pr) Greenwood.

Peacock, Alan T. & Shaw, G. K. The Economic Theory of Fiscal Policy. 2nd ed. LC 76-366919. 192p. reprint ed. pap. 59.60 (*0-608-11929-6*, 202327100032) Bks Demand.

Peacock, Alan T. & Wiseman, Jack. The Growth of Public Expenditure in the United Kingdom. (General Ser.: No. 72). 245p. 1961. reprint ed. 63.70 (*0-87014-071-X*) Natl Bur Econ Res.

Peacock, Alan T., et al. The Growth of Public Expenditure in the United Kingdom. (Modern Revivals in Economics Ser.). 215p. 1994. text 63.95 (*0-7512-0256-8*, Pub. by Gregg Revivals) Ashgate Pub Co.

Peacock, Anthony, ed. Rethinking the Constitution: Perspectives on Canadian Constitutional Reform, Interpretation, & Theory. LC 96-216819. 320p. 1996. pap. text 38.00 (*0-19-541178-1*) OUP.

Peacock, Anthony A., ed. Affirmative Action & Representation: Shaw vs. Reno & the Future of Voting Rights. LC 96-39532. 428p. 1997. 49.95 (*0-89089-883-9*); pap. 25.00 (*0-89089-884-7*) Carolina Acad Pr.

Peacock, Bonnie. Sylvania: Majestic Forests & Deep, Clear Waters. LC 87-401098. 60p. 1986. 9.95 (*0-9620008-0-9*) Peacock MI.

Peacock, Brian & Karwowski, Waldemar, eds. Automotive Ergonomics. LC 92-32799. 300p. 1993. 99.00 (*0-7484-0005-2*, Pub. by Tay Francis Ltd) Taylor & Francis.

***Peacock, Carol Antoinette.** Mommy Far, Mommy Near: An Adoption Story. (Concept Book Ser.). (Illus.). 32p. (J). (ps-2). 2000. lib. bdg. 14.95 (*0-8075-5234-8*) A Whitman.

Peacock, Carol Antoinette, et al. Sugar Was My Best Food: Diabetes & Me. LC 97-27869. (Illus.). 56p. (J). (gr. 3-8). 1998. lib. bdg. 13.95 (*0-8075-7646-8*) A Whitman.

***Peacock, Carol Antoinette, et al.** Sugar Was My Best Food: Diabetes & Me. (Concept Book Ser.). (Illus.). 56p. (J). (gr. 3-8). 2000. pap. 4.95 (*0-8075-7648-4*) A Whitman.

Peacock, Charlie. At the Crossroads: An Insider's Look at the Contemporary Christian Music Dilemma. LC 98-43996. 224p. 1999. 15.99 (*0-8054-1822-9*) Broadman.

Peacock, Christie. Improving Goat Production in the Tropics: A Manual for Development Workers. (Practical Handbooks). (Illus.). 400p. (C). 1996. 47.50 (*0-85598-268-3*, Pub. by Oxfam Pub); pap. 24.95 (*0-85598-269-1*, Pub. by Oxfam Pub) Stylus Pub VA.

Peacock, Christopher M. Rosario Yesterdays. LC 85-51170. (Illus.). 72p. (Orig.). 1985. pap. 9.98 (*0-9614970-0-9*) Rosario Prod.

Peacock, Colin. Teaching Writing: A Systematic Approach. 160p. (Orig.). 1986. pap. 19.95 (*0-7099-4028-9*, Pub. by C Helm) Routldge.

Peacock, Craig. Pocket PC Clear & Simple. Date not set. pap. 12.95 (*0-7506-7354-0*, Digital DEC) Buttrwrth-Heinemann.

— Windows CE Clear & Simple. LC 99-39644. 160p. 1999. pap. text 12.95 (*0-7506-7232-3*, Digital DEC) Buttrwrth-Heinemann.

Peacock, D. Keith. Harold Pinter & the New British Theatre, 77. LC 97-2230. (Contributions in Drama & Theatre Studies: Vol. 77). 248p. 1997. 59.95 (*0-313-29378-3*, Greenwood Pr) Greenwood.

— Radical Stages: Alternative History in Modern British Drama, 43. LC 91-17119. (Contributions in Drama & Theatre Studies: No. 43). 208p. 1991. 57.95 (*0-313-27888-1*, PRP, Greenwood Pr) Greenwood.

— Thatcher's Theatre: British Theatre & Drama in the Eighties, 88. LC 98-38179. (Contributions in Drama & Theatre Studies: Vol. 88). 248p. 1999. 59.95 (*0-313-29901-3*, Greenwood Pr) Greenwood.

Peacock, D. P. & Williams, D. F. Amphorae & the Roman Economy: An Introductory Guide (Longman Archaeology Series) (Archaeology Ser.). 304p. 1986. text 53.95 (*0-582-49304-8*) Longman.

Peacock, D. P., jt. auth. see Fulford, M. G.

Peacock, Derek, jt. auth. see Tribe, Michael A.

Peacock, Don. The Emperor's Guest: A British POW of the Japanese in Indonesia. (Illus.). 220p. 1989. 35.00 (*0-906672-55-4*) Oleander Pr.

Peacock, Donna, jt. auth. see Dechtiarenko, Luba.

Peacock, Doug. Grizzly Years: In Search of the American Wilderness. (Illus.). 304p. 1995. pap. 13.95 (*0-8050-4543-0*, Owl) H Holt & Co.

Peacock, E., ed. John Myrc: Instructions for Parish Priests. (Early English Text Society Original Ser.: No. 31). 1996. reprint ed. 45.00 (*0-85991-818-1*, Pub. by EETS) Boydell & Brewer.

Peacock, E. H. A Game Book for Burma & Adjoining Territories. 292p. 1985. pap. 175.00 (*0-7855-0363-3*, Pub. by Intl Bks & Periodicals) St Mut.

Peacock, Earle E. Wound Repair. 3rd ed. (Illus.). 544p. 1984. text 168.00 (*0-7216-7145-4*, W B Saunders Co) Harcrt Hlth Sci Grp.

Peacock, Edward. A Glossary of Words Used in the Wapentakes of Manley & Corringham, Lincolnshire. (English Dialect Society Publications: No. 15). 1969. reprint ed. pap. 31.00 (*0-8115-0447-6*) Periodicals Srv.

Peacock, Evan & Brookes, Samuel O., eds. Raw Materials & Exchange in the Mid-South: Proceedings of the 16th Annual Mid-South Archaeological Conference. (Archaeological Report Ser.: No. 29). Date not set. pap. 15.00 (*0-938896-81-4*) Mississippi Archives.

Peacock, George. Notes on the Isthmus of Panama & Darien, Also on the River San Juan, Lakes of Nicaragua, Etc.... (Illus.). vii, 96p. 1988. reprint ed. pap. 9.00 (*0-913129-20-8*) La Tienda.

Peacock, Graham. Electricity. LC 93-33258. (Science Activities Ser.). (Illus.). 32p. (J). 1994. lib. bdg. 21.40 (*1-56847-078-9*) Raintree Steck-V.

— Forces. (Science Activities Ser.). (Illus.). 32p. (J). (ps-4). 1994. lib. bdg. 21.40 (*1-56847-192-0*) Raintree Steck-V.

— Geology. 1998. 21.40 (*0-8172-4957-5*) Raintree Steck-V.

— Heat. LC 93-34613. (Science Activities Ser.). (Illus.). 32p. (J). (ps-4). 1994. lib. bdg. 21.40 (*1-56847-075-4*) Raintree Steck-V.

— Meteorology. (Science Activities Ser.). (Illus.). 32p. (J). (ps-4). 1995. lib. bdg. 21.40 (*1-56847-194-7*) Raintree Steck-V.

— Water. LC 93-49799. (Science Activities Ser.). (Illus.). 32p. (J). 1994. lib. bdg. 21.40 (*1-56847-077-0*) Raintree Steck-V.

Peacock, Graham & Ashton, Dennis. Astronomy. (Science Activities Ser.). (Illus.). 32p. (J). (ps-4). 1994. lib. bdg. 19.97 (*1-56847-191-2*) Raintree Steck-V.

Peacock, Graham & Chambers, Cally. The Super Science Book of Materials. LC 93-30779. (Super Science Ser.). (Illus.). 32p. (J). (gr. 2-5). 1993. lib. bdg. 21.40 (*1-56847-096-7*) Raintree Steck-V.

Peacock, Graham & Jesson, Jill. Geology. (Science Activities Ser.). (Illus.). 32p. (J). (ps-4). 1995. lib. bdg. 21.40 (*1-56847-193-9*) Raintree Steck-V.

Peacock, Graham & Smith, Robin. Pulley Activities. rev. ed. Doyle, Connie, ed. (Design & Make Ser.). (Illus.). 33p. (J). (gr. 3-6). 1994. reprint ed. 6.99 (*1-884461-08-5*) NES Arnold.

Peacock, Henry W. Art As Expression. (Illus.). 256p. (Orig.). 1995. pap. 24.95 (*0-929590-14-7*) Whalesback Bks.

***Peacock, Hilda V.** Happy Umbrellas. LC 99-72402. (Illus.). 48p. (J). (gr. k-3). 1999. pap. 12.95 (*1-878647-63-6*) APU Pub Grp.

Peacock, Howard. Nature Lover's Guide to the Big Thicket. LC 93-38508. (W. L. Moody, Jr. Natural History Ser.: No. 15). (Illus.). 192p. 1994. pap. 12.95 (*0-89096-596-X*) Tex A&M Univ Pr.

P

An Asterisk (*) at the beginning of an entry indicates that the title is appearing for the first time.

— Nature Lover's Guide to the Big Thicket. LC 93-38508. (W. L. Moody, Jr. Natural History Ser.: No. 15). (Illus.). 192p. 1994. 29.50 (*0-89096-589-7*) Tex A&M Univ Pr.

Peacock, Howard, ed. The Nature of Texas: A Feast of Native Beauty from Texas Highways Magazine. LC 89-20277. (Louise Lindsey Merrick Texas Environement Ser.: No. 11). (Illus.). 144p. 1990. 24.95 (*0-89096-402-5*) Tex A&M Univ Pr.

Peacock, Ian. Painting & Finishing Models. (Illus.). 160p. (Orig.). 1987. pap. text 19.95 (*0-85242-912-6*, Pub. by Nexus Special Interests) Trans-Atl Phila.

Peacock, J. A., et al, eds. Physics of the Early Universe: Proceedings of the Thirty Sixth Scottish Universities Summer School in Physics, Edinburgh, July 24-August 11, 1989. (Scottish Universities Summer School in Physics, a NATO Advanced Study Institute Ser.: No. 36). (Illus.). 502p. 1990. 189.00 (*0-905945-19-0*) IOP Pub.

Peacock, James. Rites of Modernization: Symbols & Social Aspects of Indonesian Proletarian Drama. LC 68-15931. (Symbolic Anthropology Ser.). (Illus.). xxvi, 332p. (C). 1997. pap. text 19.50 (*0-226-65131-2*) U Ch Pr.

Peacock, James & Chambers, Graham. How to Get Your Children into Television Commercials. LC 81-17112. 190p. 1982. 14.95 (*0-8253-0092-4*) Beaufort Bks NY.

Peacock, James L. The Anthropological Lens: Harsh Light, Soft Focus. 144p. 1987. text 44.95 (*0-521-33160-9*); pap. text 13.95 (*0-521-33748-8*) Cambridge U Pr.

— Rites of Modernization: Symbolic & Social Aspects of Indonesian Proletarian Drama. LC 68-15931. (Symbolic Anthropology Ser.: Vol. 1). (Illus.). 1993. lib. bdg. 26.00 (*0-226-65130-4*) U Ch Pr.

Peacock, Jimmy, ed. see Brister, Darryl S.

Peacock, Jimmy, ed. see Caldwell, Fred G.

Peacock, Jimmy, ed. see Crist, Terry.

Peacock, Jimmy, ed. see Crist, Terry M., Jr.

Peacock, Jimmy, ed. see Hamilton, Margaret W. & Stone, Sophie I.

Peacock, Jimmy, ed. see Speer, Bonnie S.

Peacock, John. Chronicle of Western Fashion: From Ancient Times to the Present Day. (Illus.). 224p. 1991. 39.95 (*0-8109-3953-3*, Pub. by Abrams) Time Warner.

Peacock, John. Costume, 1066-1990s. 2nd rev. ed. LC 94-60271. (Illus.). 136p. 1994. pap. 16.95 (*0-500-27791-5*, Pub. by Thames Hudson) Norton.

— Fashion Accessories: The Complete 20th Century Sourcebook. LC 99-69520. (Illus.). 192p. 2000. 34.95 (*0-500-01997-5*, Pub. by Thames Hudson) Norton.

Peacock, John. Men's Fashion: The Complete Sourcebook. LC 96-60141. (Illus.). 216p. 1996. 29.95 (*0-500-01725-5*, Pub. by Thames Hudson) Norton.

— Multilingual Dictionary of Printing & Publishing Terms. (DUT, ENG, FRE, GER & ITA.). 242p. 1992. 225.00 (*0-8288-7928-1*, 221200808905352) Fr & Eur.

— The 1980s. LC 98-60250. (Fashion Sourcebks.). (Illus.). 64p. 1998. pap. 10.95 (*0-500-28076-2*, Pub. by Thames Hudson) Norton.

— The 1950s. LC 96-61232. (Fashion Sourcebooks Ser.). (Illus.). 64p. (Orig.). 1997. pap. 10.95 (*0-500-27931-4*, Pub. by Thames Hudson) Norton.

— The 1940s. LC 97-61657. (Fashion Sourcebooks Ser.). (Illus.). 64p. 1998. pap. 10.95 (*0-500-28041-X*, Pub. by Thames Hudson) Norton.

— The 1970s. LC 97-60236. (Fashion Sourcebooks Ser.). (Illus.). 64p. (Orig.). 1997. pap. 10.95 (*0-500-27972-1*, Pub. by Thames Hudson) Norton.

— The 1960s. LC 97-61658. (Fashion Sourcebooks Ser.). (Illus.). 64p. 1998. pap. 10.95 (*0-500-28040-1*, Pub. by Thames Hudson) Norton.

— The 1930s. LC 97-60235. (Fashion Sourcebooks Ser.). (Illus.). 64p. (Orig.). 1997. pap. 10.95 (*0-500-27973-X*, Pub. by Thames Hudson) Norton.

— The 1920s. LC 96-61171. (Fashion Sourcebooks Ser.). (Illus.). 64p. (Orig.). 1997. pap. 10.95 (*0-500-27932-2*, Pub. by Thames Hudson) Norton.

— The Stage Designs of Inigo Jones: The European Context. (Illus.). 400p. (C). 1995. text 149.95 (*0-521-41812-7*) Cambridge U Pr.

— Twentieth Century Fashion. LC 93-60138. (Illus.). 240p. 1993. 29.95 (*0-500-01564-3*, Pub. by Thames Hudson) Norton.

Peacock, John, ed. Multilingual Dictionary of Print & Publishing Terms. (DUT, ENG, FRE, GER & ITA.). 192p. (gr. 13). 1991. mass mkt. 73.95 (*0-948905-35-2*) Chapman & Hall.

Peacock, John A. Cosmological Physics. (Illus.). 694p. (C). 1999. text 85.00 (*0-521-41072-X*); pap. text 39.95 (*0-521-42270-1*) Cambridge U Pr.

***Peacock, Judith.** Abstinence: Postponing Sexual Involvement. (Perspectives on Healthy Sexuality Ser.). 64p. (YA). (gr. 7-12). 2000. lib. bdg. 22.60 (*0-7368-0713-6*, LifeMatters Bks) Capstone Pr.

— Asthma. LC 99-32904. (Perspectives on Disease & Illness Ser.). (Illus.). 64p. (YA). (gr. 5-9). 1999. 22.60 (*0-7368-0283-5*) Capstone Pr.

— Bipolar Disorder. LC 99-56078. (Perspectives on Mental Health Ser.). 64p. (YA). (gr. 7-12). 2000. lib. bdg. 22.60 (*0-7368-0434-X*, LifeMatters Bks) Capstone Pr.

— Birth Control & Protection: Choices for Teens. (Perspectives on Healthy Sexuality Ser.). 64p. (YA). (gr. 7-12). 2000. lib. bdg. 22.60 (*0-7368-0715-2*, LifeMatters Bks) Capstone Pr.

Peacock, Judith. Cerebral Palsy. LC 99-31228. (Perspectives on Disease & Illness Ser.). (Illus.). 64p. (YA). (gr. 5-9). 1999. 22.60 (*0-7368-0280-0*) Capstone Pr.

***Peacock, Judith.** Compulsive Overeating. LC 99-54355. (Perspectives on Mental Health Ser.). 64p. (J). (gr. 7-12). 2000. lib. bdg. 22.60 (*0-7368-0437-4*, LifeMatters Bks) Capstone Pr.

— Diabetes. LC 99-23879. (Perspectives on Disease & Illness Ser.). (Illus.). 64p. (YA). (gr. 5-9). 1999. 22.60 (*0-7368-0277-0*) Capstone Pr.

— Epilepsy. LC 99-30562. (Perspectives on Disease & Illness Ser.). (Illus.). 64p. (YA). 1999. 22.60 (*0-7368-0278-9*) Capstone Pr.

— Influences on Sexuality: Making Healthy Choices. 64p. 2000. lib. bdg. 22.60 (*0-7368-0714-4*, LifeMatters Bks) Capstone Pr.

— Juvenile Arthritis. LC 99-23863. (Perspectives on Disease & Illness Ser.). (Illus.). 64p. (YA). (gr. 5-9). 1999. 22.60 (*0-7368-0279-7*) Capstone Pr.

— Leukemia. LC 99-15709. (Perspectives on Disease & Illness Ser.). (Illus.). 64p. (YA). 1999. 22.60 (*0-7368-0282-7*) Capstone Pr.

— Sex & Dating: When I Right for Me? 64p. 2000. lib. bdg. 22.60 (*0-7368-0716-0*, LifeMatters Bks) Capstone Pr.

— Teen Suicide. LC 99-56215. (Perspectives on Mental Health Ser.). 64p. (YA). (gr. 7-12). 2000. lib. bdg. 22.60 (*0-7368-0436-6*, LifeMatters Bks) Capstone Pr.

***Peacock, Judith & Casey, Jackie.** Depression. LC 99-48411. (Perpsectives on Mental Health Ser.). 64p. (YA). (gr. 7-12). 2000. lib. bdg. 22.60 (*0-7368-0435-8*, LifeMatters Bks) Capstone Pr.

***Peacock, Judith & Stutman, Suzanne.** Anger Management. LC 99-45030. (Perspectives on Mental Health Ser.). 1999. write for info. (*0-7368-0440-4*) Capstone Pr.

— Anger Management. LC 99-45030. (Perspectives on Mental Health Ser.). 64p. (YA). (gr. 7-12). 2000. lib. bdg. 22.60 (*0-7368-0433-1*, LifeMatters Bks) Capstone Pr.

Peacock, Judith, jt. auth. see Wheeler, Leslie.

Peacock, Kenneth, jt. auth. see Creighton, Helen.

Peacock, Larry J. Heart & Soul: A Guide for Spiritual Formation in the Local Church. 64p. (Orig.). 1992. pap. 5.00 (*0-8358-0682-0*) Upper Room Bks.

Peacock, Larry J., et al. Source Book of Worship Resources. Purdum, Stan, ed. 232p. 1994. pap. 39.95 (*0-930921-05-4*) Comm Res OH.

Peacock-LeJeune, Harriet. Postscripts for Thinking Flutists: Self-Help Techniques for Individualized Optimum Beauty of Sound. 1993. 12.95 (*0-533-10521-8*) Vantage.

Peacock, Linda & Fitch, Stanley. Insights into Child Development. 212p. (C). 1995. pap. text 17.15 (*1-56226-269-6*) CAT Pub.

***Peacock, Linda & Johnson, Willa.** Pathways to Teaching: A Guide for Beginning Early Childhood Teachers. 3rd ed. 192p. (C). 1999. spiral bd. 36.95 (*0-7872-5998-5*, 41599803) Kendall-Hunt.

Peacock, Lindsay, jt. auth. see Debay, Yves.

Peacock, Lindsey, jt. auth. see Dorr, Robert F.

Peacock, Louise. Crossing the Delaware: History. LC 97-12431. 48p. (J). (gr. 4-7). 1998. 17.00 (*0-689-80994-8*) S&S Trade.

Peacock, Mabel, jt ed. see Gutch, E.

***Peacock, Margaret.** A Poem Called Lost. 222p. 1999. pap. 7.95 (*0-88028-210-X*, 1497) Forward Movement.

Peacock, Martin. Information Technology in Hospitality. LC 95-16299. (Illus.). 192p. 1997. pap. 29.95 (*0-304-33238-0*) Continuum.

— Information Technology in the Hospitality Industry. 192p. 1996. 110.00 (*0-304-33236-4*) Continuum.

Peacock, Mary R. Silversmiths of North Carolina,1696-1860. rev. ed. (Illus.). xxix, 301p. 1984. pap. 15.00 (*0-86526-215-2*) NC Archives.

Peacock, Molly. Animals at the Table. limited ed. Wheatcroft, John, ed. (Series in Contemporary Poetry). (Illus.). 48p. 1995. 150.00 (*0-916375-20-X*) Press Alley.

***Peacock, Molly.** How to Read a Poem: And Start a Poetry Circle. 2000. pap. 12.95 (*1-57322-785-4*, Riverhd Trade) Berkley Pub.

Peacock, Molly. How to Read a Poem . . . And Start a Poetry Circle. LC 98-55132. 224p. 1999. 22.95 (*1-57322-128-7*, Riverhead Books) Putnam Pub Group.

— Original Love. 96p. 1996. pap. 10.00 (*0-393-31466-9*, Norton Paperbks) Norton.

— Paradise, Piece by Piece. LC 97-49965. 384p. 1998. 23.95 (*1-57322-097-3*, Riverhead Books) Putnam Pub Group.

— Paradise, Piece by Piece. 1999. reprint ed. pap. 14.00 (*1-57322-730-7*, Riverhd Trade) Berkley Pub.

Peacock, Molly, frwd. Understory: Poems by Michelle Boisseau. 64p. 1996. pap. text 11.95 (*1-55553-286-1*) NE U Pr.

Peacock, N. A., jt. auth. see Moles, E.

Peacock, N. A., ed. see Moliere.

***Peacock, Nancy.** Chris Rock: Comedian/Actor. LC 99-39931. (Black Americans of Achievement Ser.). (Illus.). 144p. 1999. 19.95 (*0-7910-5277-X*) Chelsea Hse.

Peacock, Nancy. City Smart: Cleveland. 2nd rev. ed. (City Smart Ser.). (Illus.). 208p. 1999. pap. 14.95 (*1-56261-456-8*, City Smart) Avalon Travel.

— Dave Thomas. (Overcoming Adversity Ser.). (Illus.). 128p. 1999. 19.95 (*0-7910-5302-4*) Chelsea Hse.

***Peacock, Nancy.** Home Across the Road. LC 99-61756. 250p. 1999. 18.95 (*1-56352-509-7*) Longstreet.

Peacock, Nancy. Kidding Around Cleveland: A Fun-Filled, Fact-Packed Travel & Activity Book. LC 96-47353. (Kidding Around Ser.). (Illus.). 144p. (gr. 4-7). 1997. pap. 7.95 (*1-56261-335-9*) Avalon Travel.

— Life Without Water. 224p. 1998. pap. 11.95 (*0-553-37929-1*) Bantam.

— Life Without Water. LC 96-76498. 176p. 1996. 16.95 (*1-56352-337-X*) Longstreet.

Peacock, Noel. L'Ecole des Femmes: Critical Monographs in English. 80p. 1993. pap. 45.00 (*0-85261-245-1*, Pub. by Univ of Glasgow) St Mut.

Peacock, Primrose. Discovering Old Buttons. (Handbook Ser.: No. 213). (Illus.). 80p. 1989. pap. 8.50 (*0-85263-445-5*, Pub. by Shire Pubns) Parkwest Pubns.

Peacock, Reginald. The Repressor of Overmuch Blaming of the Clergy, by Sometime Bishop of Chichester, 2 vols. Babington, Churchill, ed. (Rolls Ser.: No. 19). 1974. reprint ed. 140.00 (*0-8115-1025-5*) Periodicals Srv.

Peacock, Richard. The Art of Movie Making. (Mass Communication Ser.). 1998. mass mkt. 35.00 (*0-534-51885-0*) Wadsworth Pub.

Peacock, Richard, jt. auth. see Triere, Lynette.

***Peacock, Richard B.** The Art of Movie Making: Script to Screen. 512p. 2000. pap. write for info. (*0-13-087942-8*) P-H.

Peacock, Richard D., et al. Data for Room Fire Model Comparisons. (Illus.). 52p. (Orig.). (C). 1993. pap. text 30.00 (*0-7881-0058-0*) DIANE Pub.

Peacock, Robert. Light of the Spirit: Portraits of Southern Outsider Artists. LC 98-6663. (Illus.). 120p. 1998. 60.00 (*1-57806-025-7*); pap. 35.00 (*1-57806-015-X*) U Pr of Miss.

Peacock, Robert & Gorman, Roger, eds. Sleep: Bedtime Reading. LC 97-52939. 96p. Date not set. 19.95 (*0-7893-0112-1*, Pub. by Universe) St Martin.

Peacock, Robert & Jenkins, Annibel. Paradise Garden: A Trip Through Howard Finster's Visionary World. LC 95-17481. (Illus.). 120p. 1996. 35.00 (*0-8118-1197-2*); pap. 22.95 (*0-8118-0941-2*) Chronicle Bks.

Peacock, Ronald. The Art of Drama. LC 73-3026. 263p. 1974. reprint ed. lib. bdg. 35.00 (*0-8371-6825-2*, PEAD, Greenwood Pr) Greenwood.

— The Poet in the Theatre. LC 86-22749. 211p. 1986. reprint ed. lib. bdg. 59.50 (*0-313-25220-3*, PPOE, Greenwood Pr) Greenwood.

Peacock, Roy, jt. auth. see Lascelles, David.

Peacock, S. M., jt. ed. see Spear, Frank S.

Peacock, Thomas B. Great Western London Suburban Services. 108p. (C). 1985. 50.00 (*0-85361-230-7*) St Mut.

Peacock, Thomas D. A Forever Story: The People & Community of the Fond du Lac Reservation. 263p. 1999. pap. 15.95 (*0-9670645-0-3*) Fond du Lac Band MN.

Peacock, Thomas D. & Cleary, Linda M. Collected Wisdom. LC 97-1212. 272p. 1997. pap. text 28.00 (*0-205-26757-2*) P-H.

Peacock, Thomas Love. The Four Ages of Poetry. LC 65-26536. 1965. pap. 4.20 (*0-672-60291-1*, LLA98, Bobbs) Macmillan.

— Headlong Hall. LC 97-34626. 96p. 1997. 35.00 (*1-57113-260-0*) Camden Hse.

— Nightmare Abbey, Crotchet Castle. Wright, Raymond, ed. 284p. 1982. pap. 13.95 (*0-14-043045-8*, Penguin Classics) Viking Penguin.

— Nightmare Abbey, 1818. LC 93-3948. (Revolution & Romanticism Ser.). 236p. 1992. 48.00 (*1-85477-123-X*) Continuum.

— Peacock's Memoir of Shelley, with Shelley's Letters to Peacock. (BCL1-PR English Literature Ser.). 219p. 1992. reprint ed. lib. bdg. 79.00 (*0-7812-7655-1*) Rprt Serv.

— Works, 10 vols. Brett-Smith, H. B. & Jones, C. E., eds. LC 71-181967. reprint ed. 925.00 (*0-404-04970-2*) AMS Pr.

— Works, 10 vols., Set. (BCL1-PR English Literature Ser.). 1992. reprint ed. lib. bdg. 900.00 (*0-7812-7616-0*) Rprt Serv.

Peacock, Valerie S. A Family Heritage. 2nd ed. 94p. 1982. reprint ed. 9.95 (*0-939909-00-6*) Scribe Write.

Peacock, Virginia A. Problems in the Interpretation of Jonathan Edwards' The Nature of True Virtue. LC 90-35441. (Studies in American Religion: Vol. 47). 252p. 1991. lib. bdg. 89.95 (*0-88946-643-2*) E Mellen.

Peacock, Virginia T. Famous American Belles of the Nineteenth Century. LC 73-128284. (Essay Index Reprint Ser.). 1977. 23.95 (*0-8369-1893-2*) Ayer.

Peacock, Walter G., et al. Hurricane Andrew: Ethnicity, Gender, & the Sociology of Disasters. LC 97-7146. (Illus.). 304p. (C). 1997. 110.00 (*0-415-16811-2*) Routledge.

Peacock, Wayne, jt. auth. see Gadreau, Roger.

Peacock, William. English Prose, 5 vols., Set. (BCL1-PR English Literature Ser.). 1992. reprint ed. lib. bdg. 375.00 (*0-7812-7153-3*) Rprt Serv.

Peacocke, Alfred. God & the New Biology. 1994. 28.00 (*0-8446-6776-5*) Peter Smith.

Peacocke, Arthur. From DNA to Dean: Reflections & Explorations of a Priest-Scientist. 240p. (Orig.). 1997. pap. 23.95 (*1-85311-132-5*, 832, Pub. by Canterbury Press Norwich) Morehouse Pub.

— Theology for a Scientific Age: Being & Becoming - Natural, Divine, & Human. LC 93-30674. (Theology & the Sciences Ser.). 416p. 1993. pap. 25.00 (*0-8006-2759-8*, 1-2759, Fortress Pr) Augsburg Fortress.

Peacocke, Arthur, ed. Reductionism in Academic Disciplines. 1985. 46.00 (*1-85059-006-0*) Taylor & Francis.

Peacocke, Arthur, jt. ed. see Andersen, Svend.

Peacocke, Christopher. Being Known. LC 98-45921. 368p. 1999. text 65.00 (*0-19-823859-2*); pap. text 19.95 (*0-19-823860-6*) OUP.

— A Study of Concepts. (Bradford Representation & Mind Ser.). (Illus.). 284p. 1992. 35.00 (*0-262-16133-8*, Bradford Bks) MIT Pr.

— A Study of Concepts. (Representation & Mind Ser.). (Illus.). 288p. 1995. reprint ed. pap. text 20.00 (*0-262-66097-0*, Bradford Bks) MIT Pr.

Peacocke, Christopher, ed. Understanding & Sense, 2 vols. (International Research Library of Philosophy). 872p. 1993. 296.95 (*1-85521-292-7*, Pub. by Dartmth Pub) Ashgate Pub Co.

Peacocke, Christopher, jt. ed. see Boghossian, Paul.

Peacocke, Christopher A. Holistic Explanation: Action, Space, Interpretation. 1979. 39.95 (*0-19-824605-6*) OUP.

— Sense & Content: Experience, Thought & Their Relations. (Illus.). 230p. 1984. pap. text 19.95 (*0-19-824702-8*) OUP.

Peacocke, Christopher A., ed. Objectivity, Simulation & the Unity of Consciousness: Current Issues in the Philosophy of Mind. (Proceedings of the British Academy Ser.: Vol. 83). (Illus.). 188p. 1996. reprint ed. pap. text 16.95 (*0-19-726167-1*) OUP.

Peacocke, Iris & Kress, Evan. Savoring Your Sunset Years. (Illus.). 84p. 1998. pap., wbk. ed. 10.45 (*0-9663263-0-X*) Thornton Publ.

Peacocke, T. Atomic & Nuclear Chemistry: Atomic Theory & the Structure of the Atom, Vol. 1. 1967. 75.00 (*0-08-012524-7*, Pub. by Pergamon Repr) Franklin.

Peacocke, T. A. Radiochemistry: Theory & Experiment. (Wykeham Science Ser.: No. 50). 274p. 1978. pap. 18.00 (*0-85109-690-5*) Taylor & Francis.

— Radiochemistry: Theory & Experiment. LC 78-57666. (Wykeham Science Ser.: No. 50). 274p. (C). 1979. pap. 18.00 (*0-8448-1360-5*, Crane Russak) Taylor & Francis.

Peaden, Carroll. Always Tomorrow or the Philosophy of Hope. 314p. 1996. pap. 11.95 (*1-57502-549-3*, PO1201) Morris Pubng.

— Out of the Spider's Web: Love Triumphs. 180p. 1998. pap. 10.95 (*1-57502-852-2*, PO2337) Morris Pubng.

***Peaden, Carroll H.** China Shangri-La: How Some U. S. Army Air Force Personnel Assisted the Missionaries in China. (Illus.). 140p. 1999. pap. write for info. (*0-7392-0476-9*, PO3806) Morris Pubng.

Peaden, Carroll H. Driven by Fear or Clem's Gold. 146p. 1997. pap. write for info. (*1-57502-513-2*, P01521) Morris Pubng.

— The Female Trap or Tears of Ecstasy. 222p. 1998. pap. 10.95 (*1-57502-966-9*, PO2647) Morris Pubng.

Peairs, Frank B., jt. ed. see Quisenberry, Sharron S.

Peak, Caroline. A Perfect Surprise. (Special Edition Ser.). 1995. per. 3.75 (*0-373-09960-6*, 1-09960-5) Silhouette.

Peak, D. W. Developments in the Air Cargo Industry. 98p. (C). 1981. 190.00 (*0-906297-17-6*, Pub. by ICHCA) St Mut.

Peak, David & Frame, Michael. Chaos under Control: The Art & Science of Complexity. LC 94-3092. 432p. (C). 1994. pap. text 24.95 (*0-7167-2429-4*) W H Freeman.

Peak, Elizabeth. Prints & Drawings. (Illus.). 1982. pap. 5.00 (*0-916606-04-X*) Bowdoin Coll.

Peak, Helen. Modifications of the Lid-Reflex by Voluntary Induced Sets. (Psychology Monographs General & Applied: Vol. 42). 1974. reprint ed. pap. 55.00 (*0-8115-1441-2*) Periodicals Srv.

Peak, I., jt. auth. see Gecseg, F.

Peak, John A. Mortal Judgments. LC 98-43846. 352p. 1999. 23.95 (*0-312-19837-X*, Thomas Dunne) St Martin.

Peak, Kenneth J. Justice Administration. 2nd ed. LC 97-10406. 436p. (C). 1997. 76.00 (*0-13-758772-4*) P-H.

***Peak, Kenneth J.** Justice Administration: Police, Courts & Corrections Management. 3rd ed. 496p. 2000. 64.00 (*0-13-020539-7*) P-H.

Peak, Kenneth J. Policing America: Methods, Issues, Challenges. 3rd ed. LC 99-19289. (Illus.). 394p. 1999. 81.00 (*0-13-021884-7*) P-H.

Peak, Kenneth J. & Glensor, Ronald W. Community Policing & Problem Solving: Strategies & Practices. 2nd ed. LC 98-15320. 440p. 1998. 77.00 (*0-13-081417-2*) P-H.

***Peak, Kenneth J. & Peak, Patricia A.** Kansas Temperance: Much Ado About Booze, 1870-1920. (Illus.). 248p. 2000. pap. 22.95 (*0-89745-246-1*) Sunflower U Pr.

Peak, Kenneth J., jt. auth. see O'Brien, Patrick G.

Peak, Lois. Learning to Go to School in Japan: The Transition from Home to Preschool Life. LC 91-13628. (Illus.). 224p. 1991. pap. 15.95 (*0-520-08387-3*, Pub. by U CA Pr) Cal Prin Full Svc.

Peak, Lois & Third International Mathematics & Science Study Staff. Pursuing Excellence: A Study f U. S. Eighth-Grade Mathematics & Science Teaching, Learning, Curriculum & Achievement in International Context. LC 97-156299. 80p. 1996. write for info. (*0-16-048936-9*) USGPO.

Peak Media, Inc. Staff. Salt Lake & Surrounding Area. (Trail Books Ser.). 1998. ring bd. 24.95 (*1-889364-01-0*) Peak Media.

— Santa Barbara & Surrounding Area. (Trail Books Ser.). 1998. ring bd. 24.95 (*1-889364-03-7*) Peak Media.

— The Trail Book: For Boise & the Surrounding Area. LC 96-131930. 210p. 1995. ring bd. 24.95 (*0-9639134-5-X*) Peak Media.

— The Trail Book: For Lake Tahoe & the Surrounding Area. 210p. 1997. ring bd. 24.95 (*1-889364-00-2*) Peak Media.

— The Trail Book: For Monterey & the Surrounding Area. 210p. 1996. ring bd. 24.95 (*0-9639134-8-4*) Peak Media.

— The Trail Book: For Portland & the Surrounding Area. LC 96-164809. 210p. 1996. ring bd. 24.95 (*0-9639134-6-8*) Peak Media.

— The Trail Book: For San Francisco & the Surrounding Area. 210p. 1996. ring bd. 24.95 (*0-9639134-9-2*) Peak Media.

— The Trail Book: For Seattle & the Surrounding Area. LC 96-161276. 210p. 1996. ring bd. 24.95 (*0-9639134-7-6*) Peak Media.

— The Trail Book: For Sun Valley & the Surrounding Area. LC 96-132626. 210p. 1995. ring bd. 24.95 (*0-9639134-4-1*) Peak Media.

Peak, Patricia A., jt. auth. see Peak, Kenneth J.

Peak, Robin, jt. ed. see Lucock, John.

***Peak, S.** Media Guide, 1999. 1998. pap. 29.95 (*1-85702-872-4*, Pub. by Fourth Estate) Trafalgar.

***Peak, Steve.** Media Guide 1997. 2000. pap. 27.50 (*1-85702-491-5*, Pub. by Fourth Estate) Trafalgar.

Peak, Steve. Troops in Strikes. (C). 1988. 59.00 (*0-900137-22-3*, Pub. by NCCL) St Mut.

P

Peak, Steve & Fisher, Paul. The Media Guide, 1998. 384p. 1997. 24.95 (*1-85702-639-X*, Pub. by Fourth Estate) Trafalgar.

Peak, William, ed. Guidelines for Radio Promotion: Best of the Best II. (Illus.). 60p. (Orig.). 1991. 30.00 (*0-89324-156-3*) Natl Assn Broadcasters.

Peakall, David & Kennedy, Sean W. Handbook of Biomarkers. 450p. 1999. 89.95 (*1-56670-310-7*) Lewis Pubs.

Peakall, David B. & Shugart, Lee R., eds. Research & Application in the Assessment of Environmental Health. LC 92-38833. (NATO ASI Series H: Cell Biology: Vol. 68). 1993. 122.95 (*0-387-54612-X*) Spr-Verlag.

Peakall, David B., et al. Biomarkers: A Pragmatic Basis for Remediation of Severe Pollution in Eastern Europe. LC 99-13864. (Nato Science Series. Partnership Sub-Series Environmental Security, 2). 1999. write for info. (*0-7923-5643-8*) Kluwer Academic.

Peake, A. S., et al. Germany in the Nineteenth Century. LC 67-30189. (Manchester University Publications Historical Series No. 13, Essay Index Reprint Ser.: No. 24). 1977. 18.95 (*0-8369-0472-9*) Ayer.

Peake, C. H. James Joyce: The Citizen & the Artist. LC 76-47985. xii, 369p. 1977. reprint ed. pap. 17.95 (*0-8047-1014-7*) Stanford U Pr.

Peake, Charles. Jonathan Swift & the Art of Raillery. (Princess Grace Irish Library Lecture: Vol. 3). 32p. (Orig.). 1987. pap. 8.95 (*0-86140-264-2*, Pub. by Smyth) Dufour.

Peake, Cyrus H. Nationalism & Education in Modern China. LC 72-80580. 1970. reprint ed. 35.00 (*0-86527-138-0*) Fertig.

Peake, Elaine, jt. auth. see Kwasny, Barbara.

Peake, Frank A. The Riddle of the Ages. 80p. 1996. reprint ed. spiral bd. 10.00 (*0-7873-0660-6*) Hlth Research.

— The Riddle of the Ages. 80p. 1996. reprint ed. pap. 8.95 (*1-56459-974-4*) Kessinger Pub.

Peake, Harold J. The English Village, the Origin & Decay of Its Community: An Anthropological Interpretation. LC 76-44774. reprint ed. 37.50 (*0-404-15876-5*) AMS Pr.

— The Origins of Agriculture. LC 76-44776. reprint ed. 27.50 (*0-404-15960-5*) AMS Pr.

Peake, Harold J. & Fleure, Herbert J. The Corridors of Time: New Haven & London, 1927-1956, 10 vols., Set. Incl. Vol. 1. Apes & Men. (*0-404-18251-8*); Vol. 2. Hunters & Artists. (*0-404-18252-6*); Vol. 3. Peasants & Potters. (*0-404-18253-4*); Vol. 4. Priests & Kings. (*0-404-18254-2*); Vol. 5. Steepe & the Sown. (*0-404-18255-0*); Vol. 6. Way of the Sea. (*0-404-18256-9*); Vol. 7. Merchant Venturers in Bronze. (*0-404-18257-7*); Vol. 8. Horse & the Sword. (*0-404-18258-5*); Vol. 9. Law & the Prophets. (*0-404-18259-3*); Vol. 10. Times & Places. (*0-404-18260-7*); write for info. (*0-404-18250-X*) AMS Pr.

Peake, Hayden B., jt. auth. see Allason, Rupert.

Peake, Howard, jt. auth. see Overstreet, Robert M.

Peake, Jacqueline. How to Start a Home-Based Antiques Business. 2nd rev. ed. LC 98-104105. (How to Start a Home-Based Business Ser.). (Illus.). 240p. 1997. pap. 17.95 (*0-7627-0064-5*) Globe Pequot.

Peake, Jacquelyn. How to Recognize & Refinish Antiques: For Pleasure & Profit. 4th rev. ed. LC 97-37289. (Illus.). 256p. 1997. pap. 14.95 (*0-7627-0114-5*) Globe Pequot.

***Peake, Jacquelyn.** How to Start a Home-Based Antiques Business. 3rd ed. (Home-Based Business Ser.). (Illus.). 2000. pap. 17.95 (*0-7627-0814-X*) Globe Pequot.

Peake, Jacquelyn & Petersen, Carol A. The Complete Audio-Visual Guide for Teachers & Media Specialists. 224p. 1989. text 27.95 (*0-13-155441-7*) P-H.

Peake-Jones, Kenneth. The Branch Without a Tree: The Centenary History of the Royal Geographical Society of Australasia (South Australian Br.) Inc. 1885-1985. deluxe ed. 208p. (C). 1985. 125.00 (*0-7855-0329-3*, Pub. by Royal Geograp Soc) St Mut.

Peake, Lilian. Gold Ring of Revenge. (Presents Ser.). 1993. per. 2.99 (*0-373-11580-6*, 1-11580-7) Harlequin Bks.

— Gold Ring of Revenge. large type ed. 1992. reprint ed. 18.95 (*0-263-13100-9*) Mac Lib Ref.

— Innocent Deceiver. large type ed. 288p. 1995. 23.99 (*0-263-14128-4*, Pub. by Mills & Boon) Ulverscroft.

— Irresistible Enemy. large type ed. 1991. reprint ed. lib. bdg. 18.95 (*0-263-12680-3*) Thorndike Pr.

— No Promise of Love. 1994. per. 2.99 (*0-373-11700-0*, 1-11700-1) Harlequin Bks.

— Stranger Passing By. (Presents Ser.). 1994. per. 2.99 (*0-373-11629-2*, 1-11629-2) Harlequin Bks.

— Stranger Passing By. large type ed. 1993. 19.95 (*0-263-13320-6*) Thorndike Pr.

— Undercover Affair. (Presents Ser.). 1993. per. 2.89 (*0-373-11532-6*, 1-11532-8) Harlequin Bks.

— Undercover Affair. large type ed. (Harlequin Ser.). 1992. reprint ed. 18.95 (*0-263-12984-5*) Thorndike Pr.

***Peake, Linda.** Gender Ethnicity & Place: Women & Identity in Guyana. LC 98-43534. 1999. text 75.00 (*0-415-15004-3*) Routledge.

Peake, Linda, jt. ed. see Caulfield, Jon.

Peake, Linda, jt. ed. see Moser, Caroline.

Peake, Luise E. Conradin Kreutzer's Fruhlingslieder & Wanderlieder. LC 85-754791. 200p. 1990. lib. bdg. 64.00 (*0-918728-58-4*) Pendragon NY.

Peake, M. Boy in Darkness. (J). mass mkt. 9.95 (*0-340-67822-4*, Pub. by Hodder & Stought Ltd) Trafalgar.

— Boy in Darkness. (J). 1996. text 22.95 (*0-340-68323-6*, Pub. by Hodder & Stought Ltd) Trafalgar.

Peake, Martin. Pacific People & Society. (Pacific in the Twentieth Century Ser.). (Illus.). 122p. (C). 1991. pap. text 19.95 (*0-521-37628-9*) Cambridge U Pr.

Peake, Mervyn. A Book of Nonsense. LC 75-4108. 1975. 13.95 (*0-7206-0412-5*) Dufour.

***Peake, Mervyn.** Book of Nonsense. 1999. pap. text 16.95 (*0-7206-1059-1*) P Owen Ltd.

Peake, Mervyn. Gormenghast. (Gormenghast Trilogy: Vol. II). (Illus.). 264p. 1982. pap. 13.95 (*0-87951-426-4*, Pub. by Overlook Pr) Penguin Putnam.

— Gormenghast. LC 81-18902. (Gormenghast Trilogy: Vol. II). (Illus.). 524p. 1982. 25.00 (*0-87951-144-3*, Pub. by Overlook Pr) Penguin Putnam.

***Peake, Mervyn.** Gormenghast. 2000. 24.95 (*1-58567-082-0*, Pub. by Overlook Pr) Penguin Putnam.

Peake, Mervyn. The Gormenghast Novels: Titus Groan, Gormenghast, Titus Alone. LC 95-16431. 1172p. 1996. pap. 25.95 (*0-87951-628-3*, Pub. by Overlook Pr) Penguin Putnam.

— The Gormenghast Trilogy, 3 bks. in 1. LC 85-7909. 1032p. 1988. 35.00 (*0-87951-974-6*, Pub. by Overlook Pr) Penguin Putnam.

— The Gormenghast Trilogy, Vol. III. (Illus.). 262p. 1991. pap. 13.95 (*0-87951-427-2*, Pub. by Overlook Pr) Penguin Putnam.

— Mr. Pye. LC 83-19497. (Illus.). 288p. 1984. 15.95 (*0-87951-955-X*, Pub. by Overlook Pr) Penguin Putnam.

— Peake's Progress: Selected Writings & Drawings of Mervyn Peake. Gilmore, Maeve, ed. LC 80-83054. (Illus.). 592p. 1981. 37.50 (*0-87951-121-4*, Pub. by Overlook Pr) Penguin Putnam.

— Rhyme of the Flying Bomb. 43p. 1973. 18.95 (*0-900675-93-4*) Dufour.

— Rhyme of the Flying Bomb. (Illus.). 43p. 1973. 10.95 (*0-317-61324-3*, Pub. by Smyth) Dufour.

— Titus Alone. LC 81-18908. (Gormenghast Trilogy: Vol. III). (Illus.). 264p. 1982. 25.00 (*0-87951-145-1*, Pub. by Overlook Pr) Penguin Putnam.

— Titus Groan. LC 81-18909. (Gormenghast Trilogy: Vol. I). (Illus.). 512p. 1982. 25.00 (*0-87951-143-5*, Pub. by Overlook Pr) Penguin Putnam.

— Titus Groan. (Gormenghast Trilogy: Vol. I). (Illus.). 408p. 1991. pap. 13.95 (*0-87951-425-6*, Pub. by Overlook Pr) Penguin Putnam.

Peake, Pamela. The Complete Book of Dollmaking: A Practical Step-by-Step Guide to More Than 50 Traditional & Contemporary Techniques. LC 97-29785. (Illus.). 144p. 1997. pap. 24.95 (*0-8230-0773-1*) Watsn-Guptill.

Peake, R. J. Cotton: Raw Material to Finished Product. (Illus.). 135p. 1994. pap. 20.00 (*0-87556-797-5*) Saifer.

Peake, Richard B. Memoirs of the Colman Family, 2 vols., Set. LC 68-20242. 906p. 1972. reprint ed. 60.95 (*0-405-08842-6*, Pub. by Blom Pubns) Ayer.

— Memoirs of the Colman Family, 2 vols., Vol. 1. LC 68-20242. 906p. 1972. reprint ed. 30.95 (*0-405-08843-4*, Pub. by Blom Pubns) Ayer.

— Memoirs of the Colman Family, 2 vols., Vol. 2. LC 68-20242. 906p. 1972. reprint ed. 30.95 (*0-405-08844-2*, Pub. by Blom Pubns) Ayer.

Peake, Stephen. Transport in Transition: Lessons from the History of Energy Policy. 144p. (C). 1994. pap. 19.95 (*1-85383-209-X*) Brookings.

Peake, Thomas. Compendium of the Law of Evidence. 3rd rev. ed. xxxii, 460,xcixp. 1996. reprint ed. 75.00 (*0-8377-2556-9*, Rothman) W S Hein.

Peake, Thomas H. Healthy Aging, Healthy Treatment: The Impact of Telling Stories. LC 97-33704. 168p. 1998. 49.95 (*0-275-95922-8*, Praeger Pubs) Greenwood.

Peake, Thomas H. & Ball, John D. Psychotherapy Training: Contextual & Developmental Influences in Settings, Stages & Mind Sets. (Clinical Supervisor Ser.). (Illus.). 230p. 1991. text 6.95 (*1-56024-133-0*); pap. text 19.95 (*1-56024-134-9*) Haworth Pr.

Peake, Thomas H., et al. Brief Psychotherapies: Changing Frames of Mind. 280p. (C). 1988. text 36.00 (*0-8039-2829-7*) Sage.

— Brief Psychotherapies: Changing Frames of Mind. LC 87-28486. (Illus.). 235p. 1988. reprint ed. pap. 72.90 (*0-608-01724-8*, 206238100003) Bks Demand.

Peake, Tom H., et al, eds. Clinical Training in Psychotherapy. LC 84-15873. (Clinical Supervisor Ser.: Vol. 2, No. 4). 129p. 1985. text 4.95 (*0-86656-334-2*); pap. text 19.95 (*0-86656-335-0*) Haworth Pr.

***Peake, Tony.** Derek Jarman: A Biography. 2000. 40.00 (*1-58567-066-9*, Pub. by Overlook Pr) Penguin Putnam.

Peaker, A. R. & Grimmeiss, H. G. Low Dimensional Structures in Semiconductors: From Basic Physics to Applications. (NATO ASI Ser.: Vol. 281). (Illus.). 440p. (C). 1992. text 110.00 (*0-306-44086-5*, Kluwer Plenum) Kluwer Academic.

Peaker, Antony. Economic Growth in Modern Britain. LC 74-174850. (Macmillan Studies in Economics Ser.). 80 p. 1974. write for info. (*0-333-13414-1*) Macmillan.

Peaker, M. & Linzell, J. L. Salt Glands in Birds & Reptiles. LC 75-314900. (Monographs of the Physiological Society: No. 32). 318p. reprint ed. pap. 90.70 (*0-608-13413-9*, 2022465) Bks Demand.

Peakman, Mark & Vergani, Diego. Basic & Clinical Immunology. LC 97-1431. 1997. pap. 42.50 (*0-443-04672-7*) Church.

Peal, David. The America Online Guide to the Internet. 2nd ed. LC 98-161654. 576p. 1998. pap. text 24.99 (*0-07-882516-4*) Osborne-McGraw.

— America Online Internet Guide: AOL Edition. 2nd ed. LC 98-161654. 1998. 24.99 (*0-07-882517-2*) McGraw.

***Peal, David.** Graphic Suite. LC 99-38582. 1999. write for info. (*1-891556-59-2*) Amer Online.

— Picture This. LC 99-40521. 1999. write for info. (*1-891556-58-4*) Amer Online.

Peale, C. George, jt. ed. see Manson, William R.

Peale, Charles W. The Papers of Charles Willson Peale Vol. 2: The Artist as Museum Keeper 1791-1810. Miller, Lillian S., ed. LC 87-10646. 1318p. 1988. 140.00 (*0-300-03422-9*) Yale U Pr.

— The Selected Papers of Charles Wilson Peale & His Family Vol. 1: Charles Wilson Peale: Artist in Revolutionary America, 1735 to 1791. Miller, Lillian B. & Hart, Sidney, eds. LC 82-20155. Vol. 1. (Illus.). 676p. 1983. 85.00 (*0-300-02576-9*) Yale U Pr.

— The Selected Papers of Charles Wilson Peale & His Family Vol. 3: The Belfield Farm Years, 1810-1820, Miller, Lillian B. et al, eds. 832p. (C). 1991. 140.00 (*0-300-04930-7*) Yale U Pr.

***Peale, Charles Willson.** Selected Papers of Charles Willson Peale & His Family: The Autobiography of Charles Willson Peale. (Illus.). 560p. 2000. 75.00 (*0-300-07547-2*) Yale U Pr.

Peale, Constance F. Give Us Forever. large type ed. (Romance Ser.). 480p. 1984. 27.99 (*0-7089-1091-2*) Ulverscroft.

***Peale, Cynthia.** The Death of Colonel Mann: A Beacon Hill Mystery. LC 99-34766. (Beacon Hill Mysteries Ser.). 288p. 2000. 22.95 (*0-385-49636-2*) Doubleday.

Peale, George C., ed. Antiguedad Y Actualidad de Luis Velez de Guevara: Estudios Criticos. (Purdue University Monographs in Romance Languages: Vol. 10). xii, 298p. 1983. 71.00 (*90-272-1720-3*) J Benjamins Pubng Co.

Peale, John S. Biblical History & the Quest for Maturity. LC 85-5067. (Symposium Ser.: Vol. 15). 120p. 1985. lib. bdg. 59.95 (*0-88946-706-4*) E Mellen.

Peale, Norman Vincent. The Amazing Results of Positive Thinking. LC 96-96676. 1996. pap. 10.00 (*0-449-91191-8*) Fawcett.

— Build a Great Future. 1987. 9.95 incl. audio (*0-943371-00-7*, C1AZ) Positive Comns.

— Enthusiasm Makes the Difference. 1986. mass mkt. 5.99 (*0-449-21159-2*, Crest) Fawcett.

— Enthusiasm Makes the Difference. 1996. pap. 10.00 (*0-449-91195-0*) Fawcett.

— A Guide to Confident Living. LC 96-96681. 1996. pap. 10.00 (*0-449-91192-6*) Fawcett.

— In God We Trust: A Positive Faith for Troubled Times. 192p. 1995. 14.99 (*0-7852-7675-0*) Nelson.

— Inspirational Writings of Norman Vincent Peale. 1989. 12.98 (*0-88486-024-8*) Arrowood Pr.

— Inspirational Writings of Norman Vincent Peale. 1991. 12.98 (*0-88486-051-5*, Inspirational Pr) Arrowood Pr.

— My Christmas Treasury. 160p. Date not set. 15.00 (*0-88365-928-X*) Galahad Bks.

— My Favorite Quotations. LC 89-45895. 144p. 1990. 17.00 (*0-06-066483-5*, Pub. by Harper SF) HarpC.

— A New Collection of Three Complete Books. LC 95-18750. 528p. 1996. 13.99 (*0-517-14671-1*) Random Hse Value.

— Norman Vincent Peale: An Inspiring Collection of Three Complete Books. 400p. 1997. 9.99 (*0-517-18661-6*) Random Hse Value.

— Norman Vincent Peale: The Inspirational Writings. 416p. 1996. 12.99 (*0-88486-153-8*, Inspirational Pr) Arrowood Pr.

— Un Pensamiento Positivo para Cada Dia.Tr. of Positive Thinking Everyday. (SPA.). 384p. 1995. per. 10.00 (*0-684-81553-2*, Fireside) S&S Trade Pap.

— Positive Imaging. 1996. pap. 10.00 (*0-449-91164-0*) Fawcett.

Peale, Norman Vincent. Positive Imaging: Peale,&Norman Vincent. abr. ed. 1992. audio 12.00 (*1-55994-472-2*, CPN 5002) HarperAudio.

Peale, Norman Vincent. The Positive Power of Jesus Christ. 266p. 1984. mass mkt. 5.99 (*0-8423-4914-6*) Tyndale Hse.

— The Positive Principle Today: How to Renew & Sustain the Power of Positive Thinking. LC 96-96658. 1996. pap. 10.00 (*0-449-91198-5*) Fawcett.

— Positive Thinking Everyday: An Inspiration for Each Day of the Year. LC 93-22576. 384p. 1993. pap. 10.00 (*0-671-86891-8*, Fireside) S&S Trade Pap.

— The Power of Ethical Management. 1996. pap. 10.00 (*0-449-91975-7*) Fawcett.

— The Power of Positive Living. LC 96-96721. 1996. pap. 10.00 (*0-449-91166-7*) Fawcett.

— The Power of Positive Thinking. 210p. 1982. mass mkt. 5.99 (*0-449-21493-1*, Crest) Fawcett.

— The Power of Positive Thinking. LC 96-96734. 1996. pap. 10.00 (*0-449-91147-0*) Fawcett.

— The Power of Positive Thinking. 226p. 1987. 20.50 (*0-671-76470-5*) S&S Trade.

Peale, Norman Vincent. The Power of Positive Thinking. large type ed. 464p. 1985. reprint ed. pap. 15.95 (*0-8027-2465-5*) Walker & Co.

Peale, Norman Vincent. Reaching Your Potential. LC 96-31514. 176p. 1997. 6.99 (*0-517-18542-3*) Random Hse Value.

— Seis Actitudes para Vencer. (Serie Guia de Bolsillo - Pocket Guides Ser.).Tr. of Six Attitudes for Winners. (SPA.). 1989. pap. 2.79 (*1-56063-001-9*, 498050) Editorial Unilit.

— Six Attitudes for Winners. 88p. 1989. pap. 3.99 (*0-8423-5906-0*) Tyndale Hse.

— Stay Alive All Your Life. 1996. pap. 10.00 (*0-449-91204-3*) Fawcett.

— Three Complete Books. LC 92-19453. 608p. 1992. 13.99 (*0-517-08472-4*) Random.

— The Tough-Minded Optimist. 1996. pap. 10.00 (*0-449-91202-7*) Fawcett.

— The True Joy of Positive Living: An Autobiography. large type ed. (Large Print Inspirational Ser.). 480p. 1985. pap. 16.95 (*0-8027-2503-1*) Walker & Co.

— The True Joy of Positive Living: An Autobiography. 304p. 1998. reprint ed. pap. 12.00 (*0-688-16349-1*, Quil) HarperTrade.

— Why Some Positive Thinkers Get Powerful Results. 1996. pap. 10.00 (*0-449-91213-2*) Fawcett.

— Why Some Positive Thinkers Get Powerful Results. large type ed. (Large Print Inspirational Ser.). 320p. 1987. pap. 12.95 (*0-8027-2569-4*) Walker & Co.

— Words I Have Lived By. 1993. boxed set 8.95 (*0-8378-5301-X*) Gibson.

— You Can If You Think You Can. 320p. 1987. pap. 9.00 (*0-671-76591-4*, Fireside) S&S Trade Pap.

Peale, Norman Vincent & Kauffman, Donald T. Bible Power for Successful Living: Helping You Solve Everyday Problems. 192p. 1996. 7.99 (*0-517-18063-4*) Random Hse Value.

Peale, Norman Vincent, et al. To Father, with Love: Wisdom from Guideposts. LC 94-35286. 128p. 1995. 2.88 (*0-687-00833-6*) Dimen for Liv.

Peale, Norman Vincent, jt. auth. see Blanchard, Kenneth.

Peale, Ruth S. The Adventure of Being a Wife. 1995. reprint ed. lib. bdg. 26.95 (*1-56849-601-X*) Buccaneer Bks.

Peale, Titian R. United States Exploring Expedition During the Years 1838, 1839, 1840, 1841, 1842 under the Command of Charles Wilkes, U.S.N, Vol. 8. Sterling, Keir B., ed. LC 77-81078. (Biologists & Their World Ser.). (Illus.). 1978. reprint ed. lib. bdg. 35.95 (*0-405-10646-7*) Ayer.

Peale, W. B., ed. see Hinkle, Joseph D. & Law, Donald F.

***Pealing, Norman.** Turboprop Commuters. (Illus.). 128p. 1999. pap. 21.95 (*1-85532-871-2*, 128365AE) Motorbooks Intl.

Pealing, Norman & Savage, Mike. Jumbo Jetliners. (Color Classics Ser.: No. 6). (Illus.). 128p. 1999. pap. 10.95 (*1-85532-874-7*, Pub. by Ospry) Motorbooks Intl.

Peall, Keith, jt. auth. see Bridwell, Jim.

Pean, Stanley. L' Emprise De la Nuit. (Novels in the Roman Plus Ser.). (FRE.). 160p. (YA). (gr. 8 up). 1993. pap. 8.95 (*2-89021-203-3*, Pub. by La Courte Ech) Firefly Bks Ltd.

— La Memoire Ensanglantee. (Novels in the Roman Plus Ser.). (FRE.). 160p. (YA). (gr. 8 up). 1994. pap. 8.95 (*2-89021-217-3*, Pub. by La Courte Ech) Firefly Bks Ltd.

Pean, Stanley & Poulin, Stephane. Un Petit Garcon Qui Avait Peur de Tout et de Rien. 24p. (*2-89021-320-X*) La Courte Ech.

Peano, A. & Rosso, R. Advances in Distributed Hydrology: Selected Papers from International Workshop by ISMES. 1994. boxed set 60.00 (*0-918334-81-0*) WRP.

***Peano, G.** Geometric Calculus: According to the Ausdehnungslehre of H. Grassman. Kannenberg, Lloyd C., tr. from ITA. LC 99-51963. 160p. 1999. 64.95 (*0-8176-4126-2*, Pub. by Birkhauser) Spr-Verlag.

Peano, Pierre. Franciscan Sisters: Bearing Christ to the People. LC 96-43400. 1996. 6.95 (*0-940535-89-0*, UP189) Franciscan U Pr.

Peaps, E. The Fall of Constantinople. 432p. 1987. 300.00 (*1-85077-176-6*, Pub. by Darf Pubs Ltd) St Mut.

Pear, Joseph, jt. auth. see Martin, Garry.

Pear, Joseph, jt. auth. see Martin, Garry L.

Pear, Nancy, jt. ed. see Clark, Jerome.

Pear, Tom H. Psychological Factors of Peace & War. 262p. 1977. 18.95 (*0-8369-2290-5*) Ayer.

Pearc, Frank. Falmouth to Helford. (C). 1989. 40.00 (*1-85022-007-7*, Pub. by Dyllansow Truran) St Mut.

Pearce. Brief Style Guide. LC 98-87729. (C). 1998. pap. text 15.00 (*0-15-508433-X*, Pub. by Harcourt Coll Pubs) Harcourt.

— Great Predators of the Land. LC 95-425. (Illus.). 64p. 1999. pap. 12.95 (*0-312-85981-3*) St Martin.

— Great Predators of the Sea & Great Predators of the Land. (Illus.). 64p. 1999. pap. 12.95 (*0-312-85979-1*) St Martin.

— Handbook of Essential Oils. 1996. write for info. (*1-85617-248-1*) Elsevier.

— Museums Objects & Collections. 2000. text. write for info. (*0-7185-1442-4*) St Martin.

— One Man's Odyssey. 187p. 1986. pap. 13.95 (*0-85207-179-5*, Pub. by C W Daniel) Natl Bk Netwk.

— Ready-to-Use Celtic Designs: 96 Different Copyright-Free Designs Printed One Side. (Clip Art Ser.). (Illus.). 64p. pap. 5.95 (*0-486-28986-9*) Dover.

— Ready to Use Celtic Frames. 1998. pap. text 5.95 (*0-486-40235-5*, 881746Q) Dover.

***Pearce.** Strategic Management. 7th ed. LC 99-16363. 1072p. 1999. 88.44 (*0-07-229075-7*) McGraw.

Pearce. Strategic Management: Business Week Edition. 7th ed. 1999. 77.50 (*0-07-229730-1*) McGraw.

— Weekend Territory. (Clipper Fiction Ser.). (J). 1993. pap. text. write for info. (*0-582-80053-6*, Pub. by Addison-Wesley) Longman.

Pearce & Arnold. Collectors Voice, Vol. 2. 70.95 (*1-85928-418-3*) Ashgate Pub Co.

Pearce & Bentley. Togetherness Routines & I Love You Danny Rocc. (Clipper Fiction Ser.). 1991. pap. text. write for info. (*0-582-87552-8*, Pub. by Addison-Wesley) Longman.

Pearce & Bounia. Collectors Voice, Vol. 1. 70.95 (*1-85928-417-5*) Ashgate Pub Co.

Pearce & Flanders. Collectors Voice, Vol. 3. 70.95 (*1-85928-419-1*) Ashgate Pub Co.

Pearce & Kramer. Collectors Voice, Vol. 4. 70.95 (*1-85928-420-5*) Ashgate Pub Co.

Pearce & Yao. Vascular Medicine. (C). 1999. pap. text 145.00 (*0-8385-9378-X*) P-H.

Pearce, et al. Tourism Community Relationships. LC 96-41663. 330p. 1996. 67.00 (*0-08-042395-7*, Pergamon Pr) Elsevier.

Pearce, jt. auth. see Yao.

Pearce, jt. ed. see Lewin.

Pearce, A., jt. auth. see Bailey, C. R.

An Asterisk (*) at the beginning of an entry indicates that the title is appearing for the first time.

***Pearce, Al.** Brickyard 400: 1999 Annual. (Illus.). 128p. 1999. 24.95 (*0-7603-0773-3*, 128997AP, Pub. by MBI Pubg) Motorbooks Intl.
— Unauthorized NASCAR Fan Guide. 3rd ed. 625p. 2000. pap. text 19.95 (*1-57859-102-3*) Visible Ink Pr.
Pearce, Al & Fleischman, Bill. Inside Sports NASCAR: The Ultimate Fan Book. 750p. 1998. pap. 19.95 (*0-614-27174-6*) Visible Ink Pr.
— Inside Sports NASCAR: The Ultimate Fan Book. LC 98-166823. (Illus.). 650p. 1998. 19.95 (*1-57859-033-7*, 00157409) Visible Ink Pr.
Pearce, Al & Hunter, Don. The Illustrated History of Stock Car Racing: From the Sands of Daytona to Madison Avenue. LC 98-7612. (Illus.). 192p. 1998. 24.95 (*0-7603-0416-5*) Motorbooks Intl.
Pearce, Al, jt. auth. see Fleishman, Bill.
Pearce, Alan, jt. auth. see NBC News Division Staff.
Pearce, Amanda. Crafter's Complete Guide to Collage. LC 96-45947. (Illus.). 144p. 1996. 24.95 (*0-8230-0258-6*) Watsn-Guptill.
Pearce, Andrew. Farm Welding. (Illus.). 112p. 1992. text 34.95 (*0-85236-230-7*, Pub. by Farming Pr) Diamond Farm Bk.
Pearce, B. G., ed. Health Hazards of VDTs? LC 82-21841. (Wiley Series in Information Processing). 254p. reprint ed. pap. 78.80 (*0-608-18448-9*, 203266400080) Bks Demand.
Pearce, Barbara. Regionalized Systems As an Approach to Perinatal Health Care: Annotated Bibliography. (CPL Bibliographies Ser.: No. 54). 81p. 1981. 10.00 (*0-86602-054-3*, Sage Prdcls Pr) Sage.
Pearce, Barbara, jt. auth. see Werner, Linda.
Pearce, Barbara B. Cowboy Poetry & Everything Else: From Pearce's Pen. 1999. pap. write for info. (*0-7392-0106-9*, PO2997) Morris Pub.
Pearce, Barry. Arthur Boyd: Retrospective. (Illus.). 200p. (C). 1994. 80.00 (*0-947349-08-1*, Pub. by Lund Humphries) Antique Collect.
— Kevin Connor. (Illus.). 150p. 1989. text 37.00 (*0-947131-24-8*) Gordon & Breach.
Pearce, Benjamin W. Senior Living Communities: Operations Management & Marketing for Assisted Living, Congregate. LC 98-8731. 9p. 1998. pap. text 60.00 (*0-8018-5961-1*) Johns Hopkins.
Pearce, Brian, tr. see Amin, Samir.
Pearce, Brian, tr. see Bettelheim, Charles.
Pearce, Brian, tr. see Chatellier, Louis.
Pearce, Brian, tr. see Ferro, Marc.
Pearce, Brian, tr. see Giraud, Marcel.
Pearce, Brian, tr. see Godelier, Maurice.
Pearce, Brian, tr. see Ladurie, Emmanuel L.
Pearce, Brian, tr. see Mandel, Ernest.
Pearce, Brian, tr. see Mousnier, Roland.
Pearce, Brian, tr. see Mousnier, Roland E.
Pearce, Brian, tr. see Porshnev, B. F.
Pearce, Brian, tr. see Roche, Daniel.
Pearce, Brian L., ed. Varieties of Fervor: Portraits of Victorian & Edwardian Poets. 120p. 1996. pap. 11.95 (*3-7052-0786-5*, Pub. by Poetry Salzburg) Intl Spec Bk.
Pearce, Brian Louis. The Proper Fuss. 105p. pap. write for info. (*3-7052-0785-7*, Pub. by Poetry Salzburg) Intl Spec Bk.
— Thames Listener: Poems 1949-89. 295p. pap. write for info. (*3-7052-0610-9*, Pub. by Poetry Salzburg) Intl Spec Bk.
Pearce, Carol A. Amelia Earhart. LC 87-9102. (Makers of America Ser.). (Illus.). 175p. reprint ed. pap. 54.30 (*0-7837-5340-3*, 204508200005) Bks Demand.
Pearce, Carol A., jt. auth. see Eid, J. Francois.
Pearce, Carol L. The Adventure Starts Here: The Novice Amateur Experience. unabridged ed. LC 96-94632. (Illus.). viii, 104p. (Orig.). 1996. pap. 10.95 (*0-9653082-0-0*) Mayapple Imaging.
Pearce, Celia. The Interactive Book: A Guide to the Interactive Revolution. LC 97-74465. 1997. pap. text 39.99 (*1-57870-028-0*) Macmillan Tech.
Pearce, Charles. The Anatomy of Letters. (Illus.). 128p. 1987. pap. 11.95 (*0-8008-0199-7*) Taplinger.
— The Little Manual of Calligraphy. 32p. 1981. pap. 3.95 (*0-8008-4923-X*) Taplinger.
Pearce, Charles E. Madame Vestris & Her Times. LC 70-77975. (Illus.). 314p. 1972. 26.95 (*0-405-08845-0*, Pub. by Blom Pubns) Ayer.
— Polly Peachum: The Story of Lavinia Fenton - "The Beggar's Opera" LC 68-21222. (Illus.). 1972. reprint ed. 26.95 (*0-405-08846-9*) Ayer.
— Sims Reeves, Fifty Years of Music in England. LC 79-25066. (Music Reprint Ser.). 1980. reprint ed. lib. bdg. 35.00 (*0-306-76007-X*) Da Capo.
Pearce, Charles R. Nurturing Inquiry: Real Science for the Elementary Classroom. LC 98-52475. 5p. 1999. pap. text 21.00 (*0-325-00135-9*) Heinemann.
Pearce, Christopher. Fifties Source Book. 1990. 15.98 (*1-55521-549-1*) Bk Sales Inc.
— Vintage Jukeboxes. 1988. 10.98 (*1-55521-323-5*) Bk Sales Inc.
— Vintage Jukeboxes. 128p. 1997. 12.98 (*0-7858-0785-3*) Bk Sales Inc.
Pearce, Craig, jt. auth. see Luhrmann, Baz.
Pearce, D. Public Sector Decision-Making. 1980. pap. 24.00 (*0-08-025832-8*, Pergamon Pr) Elsevier.
Pearce, D., et al, eds. Logic in Artificial Intelligence, 838. LC 94-228872. (Lecture Notes in Artificial Intelligence Ser.). 413p. 1994. 61.95 (*0-387-58332-7*) Spr-Verlag.
— Nonclassical Logics & Information Processing: International Workshop, Berlin, Germany, November 9-10, 1990 Proceedings. (Lecture Notes in Computer Science, Lecture Notes in Artificial Intelligence Ser.: Vol. 619). vii, 171p. 1992. 38.00 (*0-387-55745-8*) Spr-Verlag.
Pearce, D. & Wagner, G., eds. Logics in AI: European Workshop JELIA '92, Berlin, Germany, September 7-10, 1992, Proceedings. LC 92-26468. (Lecture Notes in Computer Science Ser.: Vol. 633). viii, 410p. 1992. 63.00 (*0-387-55887-X*) Spr-Verlag.
Pearce, D. C. Commonwealth Administrative Law. 1986. 74.00 (*0-409-49088-1*, AT, MICHIE); pap. 58.00 (*0-409-49089-X*, AT, MICHIE) LEXIS Pub.
— Delegated Legislation in Australia & New Zealand. 1977. 76.00 (*0-409-31820-5*, AT, MICHIE) LEXIS Pub.
— Statutory Interpretation in Australia. 3rd ed. 1988. pap. 55.00 (*0-409-30810-2*, MICHIE) LEXIS Pub.
Pearce, D. C., ed. Australian Administrative Law Decisions, 15 vols., Set. 1990. 2239.00 (*0-409-42141-3*, MICHIE) LEXIS Pub.
Pearce, D. C. & Geddes, R. S. Statutory Interpretation in Australia. 4th ed. 344p. 1996. pap. write for info. (*0-409-30729-7*, MICHIE) LEXIS Pub.
Pearce, David. Blueprint No. 3: Msrng. Sustaining Development. 1993. 25.00 (*1-85383-183-2*, Pub. by Escan Pubns) Island Pr.
— Conservation Today. 256p. 1989. 49.95 (*0-415-00778-X*, A3718) Routledge.
Pearce, David. Economics & Environment: Essays on Ecological Economics & Sustainable Development. LC 98-46611. 384p. 1999. 95.00 (*1-85278-772-4*) E Elgar.
***Pearce, David.** Economics & Environment: Essays on Ecological Economics & Sustainable Development. LC 97-39590. 464p. 2000. pap. 40.00 (*1-84064-326-9*) E Elgar.
Pearce, David & Barbier, Edward B. Blueprint No. 4: Sustaining Earth. 1995. 25.00 (*1-85383-184-0*, Pub. by Escan Pubns) Island Pr.
Pearce, David & Morgan, D. Economic Value Biodiversity. 1994. 70.00 (*1-85383-225-1*, Pub. by Escan Pubns); pap. 28.00 (*1-85383-195-6*, Pub. by Escan Pubns) Island Pr.
Pearce, David, et al. Sustainable Development: Economics & Environment in the Third World. (Illus.). 232p. 1990. text 95.00 (*1-85278-167-X*) E Elgar.
Pearce, David A. Roads to Commensurability. (Synthese Library: No. 187). 260p. 1987. lib. bdg. 139.00 (*90-277-2414-8*, Pub. by Kluwer Academic) Kluwer Academic.
Pearce, David W. Economic Values & the Natural World. (Illus.). 143p. 1993. 35.00 (*0-262-16138-9*); pap. text 15.95 (*0-262-66084-9*) MIT Pr.
— Environmental Economics. LC 75-44207. (Modern Economics Ser.). (Illus.). 212p. reprint ed. pap. 65.80 (*0-608-10711-5*, 202097400020) Bks Demand.
— World Without End: Economics, Environment, & Sustainable Development, a Summary. 48p. 1993. pap. 22.00 (*0-8213-2502-7*, 12502) World Bank.
Pearce, David W., ed. The MIT Dictionary of Modern Economics. 4th ed. (Illus.). 486p. 1992. 46.00 (*0-262-16132-X*); pap. text 21.50 (*0-262-66078-4*) MIT Pr.
Pearce, David W. & Rau, Nicholas J., eds. Economic Perspectives: An Annual Survey of Economics, Vol. 4. xii, 374p. 1986. text 146.00 (*3-7186-0362-4*) Gordon & Breach.
Pearce, David W. & Turner, R. Kerry. The Economics of Natural Resources & the Environment. LC 89-19855. 320p. 1990. text 58.00 (*0-8018-3986-6*); pap. text 19.95 (*0-8018-3987-4*) Johns Hopkins.
Pearce, David W. & Warford, Jeremy J. Un Monde Sans Fin - World Without End: Economie, Environnement et Developpement Viable, un Resume - Economics, Environment, & Sustainable Development, a Summary. (FRE.). 52p. 1994. pap. 22.00 (*0-8213-2658-9*, 12658) World Bank.
— World Without End: Economics, Environment, & Sustainable Development. LC 92-39551. (Illus.). 456p. 1993. text 50.00 (*0-19-520881-1*, 60881, Pub. by World Bank) OUP.
Pearce, David W., jt. ed. see Button, Kenneth J.
Pearce, Diana M. Child Care Workers' Salaries. 13p. 1988. pap. 5.00 (*0-685-29947-3*) Inst Womens Policy Rsch.
— The Family Support Act: An Analysis of Key Components, Draft Federal Regulations & State Options. 6p. 1989. pap. 4.00 (*0-685-29944-9*) Inst Womens Policy Rsch.
— The Feminization of Poverty: A Second Look. 40p. 1989. pap. 10.00 (*0-685-29933-3*) Inst Womens Policy Rsch.
— The Invisible Homeless: Women & Children. 6p. 1988. pap. 4.00 (*0-685-29945-7*) Inst Womens Policy Rsch.
— Permanent Housing for the Homeless. 9p. 1989. pap. 4.00 (*0-685-29946-5*) Inst Womens Policy Rsch.
— Welfare Is Not for Women: Toward a Model of Advocacy to Meet the Needs of Women in Poverty. 17p. 1989. pap. 5.00 (*0-685-29943-0*) Inst Womens Policy Rsch.
Pearce, Diana M., jt. auth. see Hartmann, Heidi.
Pearce, Donald. Para Worlds: Entanglements of Art & History. LC 88-43434. 304p. 1990. lib. bdg. 35.00 (*0-271-00667-6*) Pa St U Pr.
Pearce, Donald, jt. ed. see Essick, Robert N.
Pearce, Donn. Cool Hand Luke. 1995. reprint ed. lib. bdg. 24.95 (*1-56849-668-0*) Buccaneer Bks.
— Cool Hand Luke: The Novel, LC 98-55509. 304p. 1999. pap. 13.95 (*1-56025-228-6*, Thunders Mouth) Avalon NY.
Pearce, Douglas. Tourism Today: A Geographical Analysis. 2nd ed. 202p. (C). 1996. pap. 57.00 (*0-582-22822-0*) Longman.
Pearce, Douglas G. & Butler, Richard. Tourism Development: Contemporary Issues. LC 98-52802. 1999. write for info. (*0-415-20691-X*) Routledge.
Pearce, E. A. & Smith, Gordon. The Times Books World Weather Guide. ed. LC 90-50319. (Illus.). 1990. pap. 17.95 (*0-8129-1881-9*, Times Bks) Crown Pub Group.
Pearce, E. Truman. 4 O'Clock Tunes. 16p. (J). (gr. 2 up). 1986. pap. text 3.50 (*0-913277-19-3*) Summy-Birchard.
— Solo Flight. 16p. (J). (gr. 2 up). 1986. pap. text 3.95 (*0-913277-18-5*) Summy-Birchard.
Pearce, Edward J., jt. auth. see Tschudin, Christian.
Pearce, Eli M., jt. auth. see Lin, Shiow-Ching.
Pearce, Elizabeth. Parameters in Old French Syntax: Infinitival Complements. (Studies in Natural Language & Linguistic Theory). 336p. (C). 1990. pap. text 65.50 (*0-7923-0433-0*); lib. bdg. 141.50 (*0-7923-0432-2*) Kluwer Academic.
Pearce, Ellen. Life in (Very) Minor Works: Poems. 1968. 4.50 (*0-8079-0073-7*); pap. 1.95 (*0-8079-0074-5*) October.
Pearce, Ellen, jt. auth. see Ferris, Scott R.
Pearce, Eric. Windows NT in a Nutshell. Denn, Robert J., ed. (Computer Science). (Illus.). 364p. (Orig.). 1997. pap. 24.95 (*1-56592-251-4*) Thomson Learn.
Pearce, Eric, jt. auth. see Mui, Linda.
Pearce, Erica L. The Permissive Garden. 102p. 1987. 75.00 (*0-9511795-0-0*, Pub. by Sweethaws Pr) St Mut
Pearce, F. B. Zanzibar: The Island Metropolis of Eastern Africa. (Illus.). 431p. 1967. reprint ed. 47.50 (*0-7146-1098-4*, Pub. by F Cass Pubs) Intl Spec Bk.
Pearce, Flora. Essie. large type ed. 1991. 27.99 (*0-7089-2377-1*) Ulverscroft.
Pearce, Frank. The Radical Durkheim. 216p. 1989. text 49.95 (*0-04-445269-1*) Routledge.
— Sea War: Great Naval Battles of World War Two. large type ed. (Illus.). 384p. 1991. 21.95 (*1-85089-505-8*, Pub. by ISIS Lrg Prnt) Transaction Pubs.
Pearce, Frank & Snider, Laureen, eds. Corporate Crime: Contemporary Debates. 416p. 1995. text 60.00 (*0-8020-0667-1*); pap. text 19.95 (*0-8020-7621-1*) U of Toronto Pr.
Pearce, Frank & Tombs, Steve. Toxic Capitalism: Corporate Crime & the Chemical Industry. (Socio-Legal Studies). xii, 372 p. 1998. 82.95 (*1-85521-950-6*, HV6768.P43, Pub. by Ashgate Pub) Ashgate Pub Co.
Pearce, Frank & Woodiwiss, Michael, eds. Global Crime Connections: Dynamics & Control. 240p. (Orig.). 1992. text 50.00 (*0-8020-2838-1*); pap. text 16.95 (*0-8020-7716-1*) U of Toronto Pr.
Pearce, Fred. The Damned: Rivers, Dams, & the Coming World Water Crisis. (Illus.). 400p. 1994. 34.95 (*0-370-31609-6*, Pub. by Bodley Head) Trafalgar.
Pearce, G., ed. see University of Western Ontario Conference Staff.
***Pearce, George F.** Pensacola During the Civil War: A Thorn in the Side of the Confederacy. LC 99-43001. (Florida History & Culture Ser.). (Illus.). 304p. 2000. 29.95 (*0-8130-1770-X*) U Press Fla.
Pearce, George F. The U. S. Navy in Pensacola: From Sailing Ships to Naval Aviation, 1825-1930. LC 80-12167. (Illus.). vii, 207p. 1980. 29.95 (*0-8130-0665-1*) U Press Fla.
Pearce, Gerald. Orphans. 192p. 1990. 18.95 (*0-8027-5764-2*) Walker & Co.
Pearce, Helen, jt. ed. see Kaiser, Chester C.
Pearce, Howard. Human Shadows Bright As Glass: Drama As Speculation & Transformation. LC 96-48858. 272p. 1997. 41.50 (*0-8387-5353-1*) Bucknell U Pr.
Pearce, Howard D., jt. ed. see Collins, Robert A.
Pearce, Howard D., jt. ed. see Hokenson, Jan.
Pearce, I. The Assessment & Evaluation of Training. (Financial Times Management Briefings Ser.). 1997. pap. 94.50 (*0-273-63195-0*, Pub. by F T P-H) Trans-Atl Phila.
Pearce, Ian. Holistic Approach to Cancer. 106p. 1989. pap. 11.95 (*0-85207-211-2*, Pub. by C W Daniel) Natl Bk Netwk.
Pearce, J. Programming & Meta-Programming in Scheme. Gries, D. & Schneider, F. B., eds. LC 97-28476. (Undergraduate Texts in Computer Science Ser.). 340p. 1997. 39.95 (*0-387-98320-1*) Spr-Verlag.
Pearce, J. Wisdom & Innocence. pap. text 24.95 (*0-340-69434-3*, Pub. by Hodder & Stought Ltd) Trafalgar.
Pearce, J. A., jt. auth. see Roussy, G.
Pearce, J. E. Tales That Dead Men Tell. 1993. reprint ed. lib. bdg. 75.00 (*0-7812-5972-X*) Rprt Serv.
Pearce, J. G. Telecommunications Switching. LC 80-20586. (Applications of Communications Theory Ser.). (Illus.). 348p. (C). 1981. 85.00 (*0-306-40584-9*, Plenum Trade) Perseus Pubng.
Pearce, J. Malcolm. Parkinson's Disease & Its Management. (Illus.). 160p. 1992. 39.95 (*0-19-262177-7*) OUP.
Pearce, J. Malcolm, ed. Doppler Ultrasound in Perinatal Medicine. 362p. 1992. 98.00 (*0-19-262019-3*) OUP.
Pearce, J. R., jt. ed. see Bachrach, A. L.
Pearce, J. T. Naked Plunder. 1998. pap. text 8.95 (*1-897809-42-5*) Silver Moon.
Pearce, Jack. Reflections of a Rotarian. LC 94-72593. 401p. 1994. 24.95 (*1-885373-03-1*); pap. 19.95 (*1-885373-04-X*) Emerald Ink.
Pearce, Janice, jt. auth. see Gappa, Judith.
Pearce, Jean. Foot-Loose in Tokyo: The Curious Traveler's Guide to the 29 Stages of the Yamanote Line. LC 76-23738. (Exploring Japan Ser.). (Illus.). 212p. 1976. pap. 11.95 (*0-8348-0123-X*) Weatherhill.
— More Foot-Loose in Tokyo: The Curious Traveler's Guide to Shitamachi & Narita. LC 83-51221. (Exploring Japan Ser.). (Illus.). 148p. 1984. pap. 11.95 (*0-8348-0190-6*) Weatherhill.
Pearce, Jean L. Swept under the Rug. 222p. 1998. text 21.00 (*1-887301-05-4*) Palmetto Bookworks.
Pearce, Jenny, jt. auth. see Howell, Jude A.
Pearce, Jim. Wildfowl Carving Vol. 1: Essential Techniques for Carving, Texturing & Painting Wildfowl. (Illus.). 160p. 1995. pap. 16.95 (*0-946819-53-X*, Pub. by Guild Master) Sterling.
— Wildfowl Carving Vol. 2: Power Tools & Painting Techniques, Vol. 2. (Illus.). 192p. 1996. pap. 16.95 (*1-86108-008-5*, Pub. by Guild Master) Sterling.
Pearce, John. Baby & Toddler Sleep Program: How to Get Your Child to Sleep Through the Night, Every Night. LC 98-51783. (Illus.). 160p. 1999. pap. 9.95 (*1-55561-175-3*) Fisher Bks.
Pearce, John & Hunt, Stephen. Radiology Policy & Procedure Guideline Manual. 116p. 1998. spiral bd. 120.00 (*1-879575-95-7*) Acad Med Sys.
Pearce, John A., II & Robinson, Richard B., Jr. Cases in Strategic Management. 3rd ed. LC 93-27424. 519p. (C). 1993. text 44.75 (*0-256-12633-X*, Irwn Prfssnl) McGraw-Hill Prof.
Pearce, John A. & Robinson, Richard B. Cases in Strategic Management. 4th ed. LC 96-28687. 512p. (C). 1996. text 44.75 (*0-256-21659-2*, Irwn McGrw-H) McGrw-H Hghr Educ.
Pearce, John A., II & Robinson, Richard B. Formulation, Implementation & Control of Competitive Strategy. 5th ed. 418p. (C). 1993. text 41.75 (*0-256-12634-8*, Irwn McGrw-H) McGrw-H Hghr Educ.
Pearce, John A. & Robinson, Richard B. Formulation, Implementation & Control of Competitive Strategy. 6th ed. LC 96-28686. 448p. (C). 1996. text 41.75 (*0-256-21660-6*, Irwn McGrw-H) McGrw-H Hghr Educ.
***Pearce, John A. & Robinson, Richard B.** Formulation, Implementation, & Control of Competitive Strategy. 7th ed. LC 99-16362. 2000. write for info. (*0-07-233323-5*) McGrw-H Hghr Educ.
Pearce, John A. & Robinson, Richard B. An Industry Approach to Cases in Strategic Management. 2nd ed. LC 95-23658. 864p. (C). 1995. text 44.95 (*0-256-09933-2*, Irwn Prfssnl) McGraw-Hill Prof.
Pearce, John A., II & Robinson, Richard B., Jr. Strategic Management: Formulation, Implementation & Control. 5th ed. LC 94-41400. 976p. (C). 1994. 68.95 (*0-256-17067-3*, Irwn McGrw-H) McGrw-H Hghr Educ.
Pearce, John A. & Robinson, Richard B. Strategic Management: Formulation, Implementation & Control. 6th ed. LC 96-9674. 960p. (C). 1996. 72.75 (*0-256-15478-3*, Irwn McGrw-H) McGrw-H Hghr Educ.
Pearce, John A., jt. auth. see Robinson, Richard.
Pearce, John E. Days of Darkness: The Feuds of Eastern Kentucky. LC 94-2773. (Illus.). 240p. 1994. 25.00 (*0-8131-1874-3*) U Pr of Ky.
— Divide & Dissent: Kentucky Politics, 1930-1963. LC 86-28978. (Illus.). 256p. 1987. pap. 18.00 (*0-8131-0804-7*) U Pr of Ky.
***Pearce, John E.** Heart of the Pines: Ghostly Voices of the Pine Barrens. (Illus.). 890p. 2000. 50.00 (*0-9679565-0-1*) Batsto Citizens.
Pearce, John E. Ohio River. LC 89-14830. (Illus.). 200p. 1989. 45.00 (*0-8131-1693-7*) U Pr of Ky.
Pearce, John K., jt. auth. see Glantz, Kalman.
Pearce, John L., jt. auth. see Carter, Elizabeth.
Pearce, John N., jt. ed. see McDaniel, George W.
Pearce, John W. & Pezzot-Pearce, Terry D. Psychotherapy of Abused & Neglected Children. LC 96-43650. 368p. 1997. lib. bdg. 40.00 (*1-57230-163-5*) Guilford Pubns.
***Pearce, Jonathan.** The Balona Klongs. 381p. 1999. pap. 14.95 (*0-7414-0285-8*) Buy Books.
Pearce, Jone L. Volunteers: The Organizational Behaviour of Unpaid Workers. (People & Organizations Ser.). 288p. 1993. 39.95 (*0-04-445098-2*, A8219) Routledge.
***Pearce, Joseph.** Literary Converts: Spiritual Inspiration in an Age of Unbelief. 465p. 2000. 24.95 (*0-89870-790-0*) Ignatius Pr.
Pearce, Joseph. The Three Ys Men. 200p. 1998. pap. 24.95 (*1-901157-02-4*) St Augustines Pr.
***Pearce, Joseph.** Tolkien: Man & Myth. 1999. 24.95 (*0-89870-711-0*) Ignatius Pr.
Pearce, Joseph. Wisdom & Innocence: A Life of G. K. Chesterton. 1997. 29.95 (*0-89870-629-7*); pap. 19.95 (*0-89870-700-5*) Ignatius Pr.
Pearce, Joseph C. Evolution's End: Claming the Potential of Our Intelligence. rev. ed. LC 91-58899. 288p. 1993. pap. 15.00 (*0-06-250732-X*, Pub. by Harper SF) HarpC.
— Magical Child: Rediscovering Nature's Plan for Our Children. 276p. 1992. pap. 13.95 (*0-452-26789-7*, Plume) Dutton Plume.
Pearce, Joseph C. Magical Child Magical Adult, Set. 142p. 1995. 16.95 incl. audio (*1-879323-24-9*) Sound Horizons AV.
Pearce, Joseph R. Analytic Sociology: Its Logical Foundations & Relevance to Theory & Empirical Research. LC 94-17653. 210p. (C). 1994. reprint ed. lib. bdg. 37.50 (*0-8191-9578-2*) U Pr of Amer.
Pearce, K. R. Uxbridge, 1950-1970: The Changing Town. LC 99-207439. (Illus.). 128p. 1999. 26.95 (*0-7509-1310-X*, Pub. by Sutton Pub Ltd) Intl Pubs Mktg.
Pearce, Kenn. Shed Side on Merseyside: The Locomotive Depots of Liverpool & Birkenhead. LC 97-158798. (Illus.). 1997. 33.95 (*0-7509-1369-X*, Pub. by Sutton Pub Ltd) Intl Pubs Mktg.
Pearce, L. The Assessment & Evaluation of Training. 1996. pap. 129.00 (*0-946655-99-5*, Pub. by Tech Comm) St Mut.
***Pearce, Linda.** Better Riding Through Exercise. (Threshold Picture Guides Ser.: Vol. 42). (Illus.). 24p. 1999. pap. 12.00 (*1-872119-11-5*, Pub. by Kenilworth Pr) Half Halt Pr.
Pearce, Lynne. Feminism & Politics of Reading. LC 97-48334. (An Arnold Publication). (Illus.). 288p. 1997. text 70.00 (*0-340-70062-9*) OUP.
— Feminism & the Politics of Reading. LC 97-48334. (An Arnold Publication). (Illus.). 288p. 1997. pap. text 19.95 (*0-340-61413-7*) OUP.
— Reading Dialogics. (Interrogating Texts Ser.). 240p. 1994. pap. text 18.95 (*0-340-55052-X*, B2527) OUP.

P

An Asterisk (*) at the beginning of an entry indicates that the title is appearing for the first time.

— Woman - Image - Text: Readings in Pre-Raphaelite Art & Literature. 1991. text 85.00 (*0-8020-5980-5*); pap. text 24.95 (*0-8020-6912-6*) U of Toronto Pr.

Pearce, Lynne & Stacey, Jackie, eds. Romance Revisited. (Illus.). 310p. (C). 1995. text 45.00 (*0-8147-6630-7*); pap. text 18.50 (*0-8147-6631-5*) NYU Pr.

Pearce, Lynne & Wisker, Gina. Fatal Attractions: Rescripting Romance in Contemporary Literature & Film. LC 98-16430. 256p. 1998. 59.95 (*0-7453-1386-8*, Pub. by Pluto GBR) Stylus Pub VA.

***Pearce, Lynne & Wisker, Gina, eds.** Fatal Attractions: Rescripting Romance in Contemporary Literature & Film. 256p. 1998. pap. 19.95 (*0-7453-1381-7*, Pub. by Pluto GBR) Stylus Pub VA.

Pearce, Lynne, jt. auth. see Mills, Sara.

Pearce, M. Laboratory Culture & Experimental Techniques Using Termites. 1997. pap. 60.00 (*0-85954-455-9*, Pub. by Nat Res Inst) St Mut.

Pearce, M. J. The Termite Slide Kit: Termite Pests of Crops, Trees, Rangeland & Foodstores. 1995. pap. 45.00 (*0-85954-390-0*, Pub. by Nat Res Inst) St Mut.

— Termites: Biology & Pest Management. LC 97-13544. (Illus.). 192p. (C). 1998. text 65.00 (*0-85199-130-0*) OUP.

Pearce, M. J., et al. Quarantine Pests for Europe: Quarentine Pests for Europe & Illustrations of Quarentine Pests, 2 vols. 2nd ed. (Illus.). 1660p. 1998. text 265.00 (*0-85199-206-4*) OUP.

Pearce, Malcolm. British Political History, 1867-1995. 2nd ed. (Illus.). 664p. (C). 1996. pap. 25.99 (*0-415-13812-4*) Routledge.

Pearce, Mallory. Celtic Animals Stained Glass Coloring Book. 1999. pap. text 4.50 (*0-486-40572-9*) Dover.

Pearce, Mallory. Celtic Animals Stickers. (Illus.). (J). 1996. pap. 1.00 (*0-486-29397-1*) Dover.

Pearce, Mallory. Celtic Motifs. (Illus.). 1995. pap. 1.00 (*0-486-28408-5*) Dover.

— Celtic Stained Glass Pattern Book. LC 99-14046. (Illus.). 1999. pap. text 6.95 (*0-486-40479-X*) Dover.

Pearce, Mallory. Celtic Stickers & Seals. (Illus.). (J). 1995. pap. 4.50 (*0-486-28419-0*) Dover.

Pearce, Mallory. Easy-to-Duplicate Celtic Borders. (Illus.). 1993. pap. 5.95 (*0-486-27797-6*) Dover.

— Ready-to-Use Celtic Borders on Layout Grids. (Clip Art Ser.). (Illus.). 64p. text 5.95 (*0-486-26518-8*) Dover.

— Ready-to-Use Celtic Borders on Layout Grids. (Illus.). 1992. pap. 5.95 (*0-486-27041-6*) Dover.

— The Ready-to-Use Sea Shore Life Illustrations: 150 Different Copyright-free Designs: Printed One Side. 64p. 1999. pap. text 5.95 (*0-486-40707-1*) Dover.

Pearce, Marion K. Celtic Sacrifice: Pre-Christian Ritual & Religion. (Illus.). 1998. pap. 21.95 (*1-86163-023-9*) Holmes Pub.

Pearce, Martin, ed. Sociology. 250p. (C). 1991. pap. 60.00 (*1-85352-929-X*, Pub. by HLT Pubns) St Mut.

***Pearce, Mary.** Jack Mercybright. large type unabridged ed. (Apple Tree Saga Ser.: No. 2). 1999. 25.95 (*0-7531-6050-1*, 160501, Pub. by ISIS Lrg Prnt) ISIS Pub.

***Pearce, Mary E.** Apple Tree Lean Down. large type unabridged ed. 355p. 1999. 25.95 (*0-7531-6049-8*, 160498, Pub. by ISIS Lrg Prnt) ISIS Pub.

Pearce, Mary E. Cast a Long Shadow. large type ed. 464p. 1988. 27.99 (*0-7089-1790-9*) Ulverscroft.

— The Old House at Railes. large type ed. LC 94-8760. 595p. 1994. lib. bdg. 24.95 (*0-8161-5989-0*, G K Hall Lrg Type) Mac Lib Ref.

Pearce, Maurice. Seven Days to Calvary: The Crucifixion. 177p. 1996. pap. 14.95 (*1-57502-252-4*) Morris Pubng.

Pearce, Maurice L. A Gate Called Beautiful: Simon Bar. 193p. 1998. pap. 22.00 (*1-57502-796-8*, PO200) Morris Pubng.

Pearce, Michael. The Camel of Destruction. large type ed. (Linford Mystery Library). 384p. 1997. pap. 16.99 (*0-7089-5169-4*) Ulverscroft.

— Don't Shoot the Piano Player. Daper, Peter, ed. 203p. (Orig.). 1994. pap. 19.95 (*0-9640555-0-3*) Spin Pubng.

— The Mamur & the Girl in the Nile. 1995. pap. write for info. (*0-446-40316-4*, Mysterious Paperbk) Warner Bks.

— The Mamur Zapt & the Donkey-Vous. 272p. 1992. 17.95 (*0-89296-486-3*) Mysterious Pr.

— The Mamur Zapt & the Donkey-Vous. 272p. 1993. mass mkt. 4.99 (*0-446-40181-1*, Pub. by Warner Bks) Little.

— The Mamur Zapt & the Men Behind. 240p. 1994. mass mkt. 5.50 (*0-446-40183-8*, Pub. by Warner Bks) Little.

— The Mingrelian Conspiracy. 192p. 1998. mass mkt. 8.95 (*0-00-649778-0*, Pub. by HarpC) Trafalgar.

— Non-Standard Collection Management. 250p. 1992. 78.95 (*1-85742-020-9*) Ashgate Pub Co.

— The Snake-Catcher's Daughter. 192p. 1998. mass mkt. 8.95 (*0-00-649036-0*, Pub. by HarpC) Trafalgar.

— The Snake-Catcher's Daughter. large type ed. (Linford Mystery Library). 352p. 1998. pap. 17.99 (*0-7089-5217-8*, Linford) Ulverscroft.

Pearce, Molly. The Little Gearhead Series Boxed Set, 3 bks. (Illus.). (J). 1996. boxed set 8.95 (*1-57098-098-5*) Roberts Rinehart.

Pearce-Moses, Richard, compiled by. Photographic Collections in Texas: A Union Guide. LC 87-9979. (Union Guide Published for Texas Historical Foundation). 400p. 1987. pap. 29.50 (*0-89096-351-7*) Tex A&M Univ Pr.

Pearce, Narsreen. A Guide to Inheritance Claims. 179p. 1989. 48.00 (*1-85190-073-X*, Pub. by Tolley Pubng) St Mut.

Pearce, Nasreen. Adoption: The Law & Practice. 544p. (C). 1991. 120.00 (*1-85190-104-3*, Pub. by Tolley Pubng) St Mut.

— Adoption Practice & Procedure. 133p. 1984. 90.00 (*0-906840-79-1*, Pub. by Fourmat Pub) St Mut.

— Custodianship: The Law & Practice. 77p. 1986. 70.00 (*1-85190-015-2*, Pub. by Fourmat Pub) St Mut.

— Name-Changing: A Practical Guide. 94p. 1990. 55.00 (*1-85190-089-6*, Pub. by Tolley Pubng) St Mut.

— Wardship: The Law & Practice. 126p. 1986. 104.00 (*0-906840-97-X*, Pub. by Fourmat Pub) St Mut.

Pearce, Neil, et al. Asthma Epidemiology: Principles & Epidemiology. (Monographs in Epidemiology & Biostatistics). (Illus.). 288p. 1998. text 49.95 (*0-19-508016-5*) OUP.

Pearce, Nicholas. Harmony & Contrast: A Journey Through East Asian Art. Wilkinson, Jane, ed. (Illus.). 112p. (C). Date not set. pap. 20.00 (*0-7007-0461-2*, Pub. by Natl Mus Scotland) A Schwartz & Co.

Pearce, P. Wings of Courage. mass mkt. 8.95 (*0-340-71510-3*, Pub. by Hodder & Stought Ltd) Trafalgar.

Pearce, P. L. The Social Psychology of Tourist Behaviour. (International Series in Experimental Social Psychology: Vol. 3). 142p. 1982. 80.00 (*0-08-025794-1*, Pub. by Pergamon Repr) Franklin.

— The Ulysses Factor: Evaluating Visitors in Tourist Settings. (Recent Research in Psychology Ser.). (Illus.). 275p. 1990. 71.95 (*0-387-96834-2*) Spr-Verlag.

Pearce, Paul. Construction Marketing: A Professional Approach. 138p. 1992. text 54.00 (*0-7277-1652-2*, Pub. by T Telford) RCH.

Pearce, Paul, jt. auth. see Barber, Michael.

Pearce, Peter. Polyhedra Primer. 1997. pap. text 14.95 (*0-86651-419-8*) Seymour Pubns.

— Structure in Nature Is a Strategy for Design. LC 77-26866. 1980. pap. text 22.50 (*0-262-66045-8*) MIT Pr.

***Pearce, Philippa.** The Battle of Bubble & Squeak. (Illus.). (J). 1999. 16.95 (*0-7540-6059-4*) Chivers N Amer.

Pearce, Philippa. Minnow on the Say. LC 98-52078. (Illus.). 256p. (YA). (gr. 5-9). 2000. 16.95 (*0-688-17098-6*, Grenwillow Bks) HarpC Child Bks.

— The Shadow Cage & Other Tales of the Supernatural. LC 77-3174. (Illus.). (J). (gr. 3-7). 1977. 11.95 (*0-690-01396-5*) HarpC Child Bks.

— Tom's Midnight Garden. LC 69-12008. (Illus.). 240p. (J). (gr. 4-7). 1992. lib. bdg. 15.89 (*0-397-30477-3*) HarpC Child Bks.

— Tom's Midnight Garden. LC 69-12008. (Trophy Bk.). (Illus.). 240p. (J). (gr. 4-7). 1992. mass mkt. 5.95 (*0-06-440445-5*, HarpTrophy) HarpC Child Bks.

— Tom's Midnight Garden. (J). 1992. 10.05 (*0-606-12544-2*, Pub. by Turtleback) Demco.

— Who's Afraid? & Other Strange Stories. LC 86-14299. 160p. (J). (gr. 5-9). 1987. 11.95 (*0-688-06895-2*, Grenwillow Bks) HarpC Child Bks.

Pearce, Philippa, ed. A Century of Children's Ghost Stories: Dread & Delight. LC 97-183531. 368p. (J). 1997. reprint ed. pap. 13.95 (*0-19-288014-4*) OUP.

Pearce, Q. L. Animals. (Illus.). 48p. (J). (gr. 2-6). 1999. pap. 4.95 (*0-7373-0169-4*, 01694W) NTC Contemp Pub Co.

— Backyard Science Experiments. (Kid's Science Ser.). (Illus.). 64p. (J). 1999. pap. 8.95 (*0-7373-0283-6*, 02836W, Pub. by Lowell Hse) NTC Contemp Pub Co.

— Kitchen Science Experiments. (Kid's Science Ser.). (Illus.). 64p. (J). 1999. pap. 8.95 (*0-7373-0285-2*, 02852W, Pub. by Lowell Hse) NTC Contemp Pub Co.

— The Land Before Time: How to Draw Dinosaurs. LC 99-73110. (Illus.). 64p. (YA). (gr. 1 up). 1999. pap. 6.95 (*0-7373-0237-2*, 02372W) NTC Contemp Pub Co.

— The Land Before Time Dinosaur Q & A. (Roxbury Park Bks.). (Illus.). 64p. (J). 1999. pap. 7.95 (*0-7373-0281-X*, 0281XW, Pub. by Lowell Hse) NTC Contemp Pub Co.

— The Science Almanac for Kids. LC 98-25061. (Illus.). 128p. (J). (gr. 3-7). 1998. 12.95 (*1-56565-683-0*, 06830W, Pub. by Lowell Hse Juvenile); pap. 8.95 (*1-56565-684-9*, 06849W, Pub. by Lowell Hse Juvenile) NTC Contemp Pub Co.

— 60 Super Simple More Science Experiments. LC 99-73108. (60 Super Simple Ser.). (Illus.). 80p. (J). (gr. 3-6). 1999. pap. 6.95 (*0-7373-0233-X*, 0233XW) NTC Contemp Pub Co.

— 60 Super Simple Science Experiments. (Sixty Super Simple Ser.). (Illus.). 80p. (J). (gr. 3-7). 1998. pap. 6.95 (*1-56565-688-1*, 06881W, Pub. by Lowell Hse Juvenile) NTC Contemp Pub Co.

***Pearce, Q. L.** 60 Super Simple Still More Science Experiments. (Illus.). (J). 2000. pap. 6.95 (*0-7373-0534-7*) Lowell Hse Juvenile.

Pearce, Q. L. Story Starters: Mysteries. (Gifted & Talented Ser.). (Illus.). 64p. (J). (gr. 1-2). 1999. pap. 5.95 (*0-7373-0204-6*, Pub. by Lowell Hse) NTC Contemp Pub Co.

— Super Science Experiments. Artenstein, Michael, ed. LC 98-75646. (Illus.). 96p. (J). (gr. 3-6). 1999. pap. 7.95 (*0-7373-0073-6*, 00736W) NTC Contemp Pub Co.

Pearce, Q. L. & Rusackas, Francesca. The First-Timer's Guide to Science Fair Projects. LC 97-74874. (Illus.). 80p. (J). (gr. 1-4). 1997. pap. 8.95 (*1-56565-734-9*, 07349W, Pub. by Lowell Hse Juvenile) NTC Contemp Pub Co.

Pearce, Querida L. All about Dinosaurs. (Illus.). (J). (gr. 2 up). 1989. pap. 7.95 (*0-671-64517-X*) Litle Simon.

— Animal Footnotes: A Nature's Footprints Guide. (Illus.). 40p. (J). (ps-3). 1991. lib. bdg. 12.95 (*0-671-69116-3*) Silver Burdett Pr.

— Armadillos & Other Unusual Animals. Steltenpohl, Jane, ed. (Amazing Science Ser.). (Illus.). 64p. (J). (gr. 4-6). 1989. pap. 5.95 (*0-671-68645-3*, Julian Messner) Silver Burdett Pr.

— Atlas of the Strange. LC 94-41537. (Twenty-Five Scariest Ser.). (Illus.). 64p. (J). (gr. 2 up). 1995. 5.95 (*1-56565-223-1*, 02231W, Pub. by Lowell Hse Juvenile) NTC Contemp Pub Co.

— The Checkerboard Press Kids' Science Dictionary. LC 88-71150. (Illus.). 124p. (J). (gr. 4-6). 1991. reprint ed. 12.95 (*1-56288-003-9*) Checkerboard.

— Great Predators of the Land. (YA). 1995. pap. 9.95 (*0-614-08647-7*) Tor Bks.

— Great Predators of the Land. LC 95-425. (Illus.). 64p. (J). 1995. 16.95 (*0-312-85480-3*, Pub. by Tor Bks) St Martin.

— Great Predators of the Sea. (J). 1995. pap. 9.95 (*0-614-08648-5*) Tor Bks.

— Great Predators of the Sea. LC 95-424. (Illus.). 64p. (J). 1995. pap. 12.95 (*0-312-85481-1*, Pub. by Tor Bks) St Martin.

— How to Talk Dinosaur with Your Child. (Illus.). 176p. 1991. pap. 10.95 (*0-929923-48-0*) Lowell Hse.

— Lightning & Other Wonders of the Sky. Steltenpohl, Jane, ed. (Amazing Science Ser.). (Illus.). 64p. (J). (gr. 4-6). 1989. pap. 5.95 (*0-671-68648-8*, Julian Messner) Silver Burdett Pr.

— Piranhas & Other Wonders of the Jungle. (Amazing Science Ser.). (Illus.). 64p. (J). (gr. 4-6). 1990. pap. 5.95 (*0-671-70690-X*, Julian Messner) Silver Burdett Pr.

— Prehistoric Mammals. 48p. 1989. 1.95 (*0-8125-9493-2*, Pub. by Tor Bks) St Martin.

— Rainbow Book of Birds: A Color-by-Number Book. 1989. pap. 1.95 (*0-8125-9442-8*, Pub. by Tor Bks) St Martin.

— Rainbow Book of Snakes, Turtles, Lizards & More: A Color-by-Number Book. 1989. pap. 1.95 (*0-8125-9444-4*, Pub. by Tor Bks) St Martin.

— Saber-Toothed Cats - Prehistoric Worlds. (Amazing Science Ser.). (Illus.). 64p. (J). (gr. 4-6). 1991. pap. 5.95 (*0-671-70692-6*, Julian Messner) Silver Burdett Pr.

— Scary Stories. (Illus.). 128p. (J). (gr. 2-8). 1995. pap., boxed set 14.85 (*0-8431-3956-0*, Price Stern) Peng Put Young Read.

— The Science Almanac for Kids. (Illus.). 128p. (J). (gr. 3-7). 1993. pap. 5.95 (*1-56293-356-6*, McClanahan Book) Learn Horizon.

— Strange Science: Outer Space. 64p. (Orig.). 1994. pap. 3.50 (*0-8125-2364-4*, Pub. by Tor Bks) St Martin.

— Strange Science: Planet Earth. 64p. (Orig.). (YA). 1993. pap. 3.50 (*0-8125-2365-2*, Pub. by Tor Bks) St Martin.

— Tyrannosaurus Rex & Other Dinosaur Wonders. (Amazing Science Ser.). (Illus.). 64p. (J). (gr. 4-6). 1990. pap. 5.95 (*0-671-70688-8*, Julian Messner) Silver Burdett Pr.

— Whales & Other Wonders - Frozen Worlds. (Amazing Science Ser.). (Illus.). 64p. (J). (gr. 4-6). 1991. pap. 5.95 (*0-671-70694-2*, Julian Messner) Silver Burdett Pr.

Pearce, Querida L. & Pearce, W. L. In the Desert. Brook, Bonnie, ed. (Nature's Footprints Ser.). (Illus.). 24p. (J). (ps-1). 1990. lib. bdg. 9.95 (*0-671-68825-1*) Silver Burdett Pr.

— In the Forest. Brook, Bonnie, ed. (Nature's Footprints Ser.). (Illus.). 24p. (J). (ps-1). 1990. lib. bdg. 6.95 (*0-671-68826-X*) Silver Burdett Pr.

Pearce, Querida L., jt. auth. see Pearce, W. J.

Pearce, R. Britain: Industrial Relations & the Economy 1900-1939. (Access to History Ser.). 135p. 1994. pap. 16.50 (*0-340-57374-0*, Pub. by Hodder & Stought Ltd) Lubrecht & Cramer.

Pearce, R. D. Attlee. LC 96-44365. (Profiles in Power Ser.). 224p. (C). 1997. 69.00 (*0-582-25691-7*); pap. 22.26 (*0-582-25690-9*) Longman.

— The Growth & Evolution of Multinational Enterprise: Patterns of Geographical & Industrial Diversification. 192p. 1993. 90.00 (*1-85278-396-6*) E Elgar.

— Turning Point in Africa: British Colonial Policy, 1938-48. 234p. 1982. text 42.50 (*0-7146-3160-4*, Pub. by F Cass Pubs) Intl Spec Bk.

Pearce, R. H., ed. see James, Henry.

Pearce, Rhoda M. Thomas Telford. (Lifelines Ser.: No. 10). (Illus.). 48p. 1989. pap. 7.50 (*0-85263-410-2*, Pub. by Shire Pubns) Parkwest Pubns.

Pearce, Richard. The Politics of Narration: James Joyce, William Faulkner & Virginia Woolf. LC 90-8977. 200p. (C). 1991. text 40.00 (*0-8135-1656-0*) Rutgers U Pr.

— William Styron. LC 74-635458. (University of Minnesota Pamphlets on American Writers Ser.: No. 98). 47p. (Orig.). reprint ed. pap. 30.00 (*0-7837-2868-9*, 205758700006) Bks Demand.

Pearce, Richard, ed. Molly Blooms: A Polylogue on Penelope & Cultural Studies. LC 93-39641. 1994. 45.00 (*0-299-14120-9*); pap. 24.95 (*0-299-14124-1*) U of Wis Pr.

***Pearce, Robert.** The Owens Valley Controversy & A. A. Brierly: The Untold Story. Reiter, Sheila, ed. LC 99-30722. (Illus.). 112p. 1999. pap. 10.95 (*1-886225-37-0*) Dageforde Pub.

Pearce, Robert, ed. Then the Wind Changed in Africa: Nigerian Letters of Robert Hepburn Wright. (Illus.). 256p. (C). 1993. text 39.50 (*1-85043-573-1*, Pub. by I B T) St Martin.

Pearce, Robert, ed. see Thomas, Michael.

Pearce, Robert D. Attlee's Labour Governments, 1945-51. LC 93-15764. (Lancaster Pamphlets Ser.). 96p. (C). 1993. pap. 11.99 (*0-415-08893-3*) Routledge.

Pearce, Robert D. & Papanastassiou, Marina. Multinationals, Technology & National Competitiveness. LC 99-31590. (New Horizons in International Business Ser.). 288p. 1999. 95.00 (*1-85898-822-5*) E Elgar.

Pearce, Robert P., jt. auth. see Pielke, Roger A.

Pearce, Robert R. History of the Inns of Court & Chancery: With Notices of Their Ancient Discipline, Rules, Orders, & Customs, Readings, Moots, Masques, Revels, & Entertainments; Including an Account of the Eminent Men of the Four Learned & Honourable Societies, -Lincoln's Inn, the Inner Temple, the Middle Temple, & Gray's Inn, & c. xi, 440p. 1987. reprint ed. 52.00 (*0-8377-2512-7*, Rothman) W S Hein.

Pearce, Roy H. Gesta Humanorum: Studies in the Historicist Mode. LC 87-5091. (Illus.). 208p. 1987. text 29.95 (*0-8262-0637-9*) U of Mo Pr.

— Historicism Once More: Problems & Occasions for the American Scholar. LC 68-56317. 371p. 1969. reprint ed. pap. 115.10 (*0-7837-9417-7*, 206015800004) Bks Demand.

— Savagism & Civilization: A Study of Indians & the American Mind. 1988. pap. 14.95 (*0-520-06227-2*, Pub. by U CA Pr) Cal Prin Full Svc.

Pearce, Roy H., ed. see Hawthorne, Nathaniel.

Pearce, Ruth L. Russian for Expository Prose Vol. 1: Introductory Course. 413p. (Orig.). (C). 1983. pap. text 18.95 (*0-89357-121-0*) Slavica.

— Russian for Expository Prose Vol. 2: Advanced Course. 255p. (Orig.). 1983. pap. text 16.95 (*0-89357-122-9*) Slavica.

Pearce, S., jt. auth. see Knowlton, J.

Pearce, S. C. & North, P. M., contrib. by. Statistics: A Newcomer's Introduction to the Subject. 146p. 1994. 49.00 (*1-85070-420-1*) Prthnon Pub.

Pearce, Sarah, jt. ed. see Jones, S.

***Pearce, Sharyn.** Shameless Scribblers. LC 98-201909. 1998. pap. 19.95 (*1-875998-50-0*, Pub. by Central Queensland) Accents Pubns.

Pearce, Stanley C. The Agricultural Field Experiment: A Statistical Examination of Theory & Practice. LC 82-13711. 351p. reprint ed. pap. 108.90 (*0-7837-4731-4*, 204451600003) Bks Demand.

— Field Experimentation with Fruit Trees & Other Perennial Plants. 2nd ed. 182p. (Orig.). 1976. pap. text 55.00 (*0-85198-354-5*) OUP.

Pearce, Stephen & Bushnell, Richard. The Bar Code Implementation Guide: Using Bar Codes in Distribution. 159p. 1997. pap. 89.00 (*0-941668-06-1*) Tower Hill Pr.

Pearce, Stephen S. Flash of Insight: Metaphor & Narrative in Therapy. 304p. (C). 1995. 55.00 (*0-205-14572-8*, Longwood Div) Allyn.

***Pearce, Steve.** The 1999 Rugby World Cup Essential Stats & Facts. (Illus.). 160p. 1999. pap. 15.95 (*0-7522-1740-2*, Pub. by Boxtree) Trans-Atl Phila.

Pearce, Stewart. Annals of Luzerne County: A Record of Interesting Events, Traditions & Anecdotes from the First Settlement in Wyoming Valley to 1866. (Illus.). 564p. 1995. reprint ed. lib. bdg. 59.50 (*0-8328-5109-4*) Higginson Bk Co.

Pearce, Susan. Collecting in Contemporary Practice. 221p. 1998. 74.50 (*0-7619-5080-X*); 24.95 (*0-7619-5081-8*) Sage.

Pearce, Susan, ed. Museums & Their Development: The European Tradition, 1700-1900, 8 vols. fac. ed. 3200p. (C). 1999. 980.00 (*0-415-19307-9*, D6391) Routledge.

Pearce, Susan M. Archaeological Curatorship. 224p. 1996. pap. 25.00 (*0-7185-0040-7*) Bks Intl VA.

— Archaeological Curatorship. 224p. 1996. pap. text 19.95 (*1-56098-632-8*) Smithsonian.

— Eskimo Carving. (Ethnography Ser.: No. 2). (Illus.). 64p. 1989. pap. 10.50 (*0-85263-770-5*, Pub. by Shire Pubns) Parkwest Pubns.

— The History of Museums, 8 vols., Set. 2144p. (C). 1997. 980.00 (*0-415-14872-3*) Routledge.

— Museums & Popular Culture: New Research in Museum Studies #7. LC 98-30552. (New Research in Museum Studies: 7). (C). 1997. text 90.00 (*0-485-90007-6*) Humanities.

— Museums, Objects, & Collections: A Cultural Study. (Illus.). 318p. 1993. pap. text 16.95 (*1-56098-330-2*) Smithsonian.

— On Collecting: An Investigation into Collecting in the European Tradition. LC 94-35151. 1995. pap. write for info. (*0-415-07561-0*) Routledge.

— On Collecting: An Investigation into Collecting in the European Tradition. LC 94-35151. (Collecting Cultures Ser.). (Illus.). 304p. (C). (gr. 13). 1995. 75.00 (*0-415-07560-2*, C0035) Routledge.

Pearce, Susan M., ed. Art in Museums. (New Research in Museum Studies: Vol. 5). 264p. (C). 1995. text 85.00 (*0-485-90005-X*, Pub. by Athlone Pr) Humanities.

— Exploring Science in Museums: New Research in Museum Studies. (International Ser.: Vol. 6). 240p. (C). 1996. text 90.00 (*0-485-90006-8*, Pub. by Athlone Pr) Humanities.

— Interpreting Objects & Collections. LC 94-11658. (Leicester Readers in Museums Studies Ser.). (Illus.). 352p. (C). 1994. pap. 34.99 (*0-415-11289-3*, B4595) Routledge.

— Interpreting Objects & Collections. LC 94-11658. (Leicester Readers in Museums Studies Ser.). (Illus.). 352p. (C). (gr. 13). 1994. 110.00 (*0-415-11288-5*, B4591) Routledge.

— Museum Studies in Material Culture. 280p. 1990. text 42.50 (*0-7185-1288-X*, Pub. by Leicester U Pr) Cassell & Continuum.

— Museums & Europe, 1992. LC 92-28225. (New Research in Museum Studies: An International Ser.: Vol. 3). 240p. (C). 1992. text 85.00 (*0-485-90003-3*, Pub. by Athlone Pr) Humanities.

— Museums & the Appropriation of Culture. LC 93-39430. (New Research in Museum Studies: An International Ser.: Vol. 4). 256p. (C). 1994. text 85.00 (*0-485-90004-1*, Pub. by Athlone Pr) Humanities.

— Museums Economics & the Community. LC 91-25711. (New Research in Museum Studies: An International Ser.: Vol. 2). 224p. (C). 1991. text 85.00 (*0-485-90002-5*, Pub. by Athlone Pr) Humanities.

— Objects of Knowledge. LC 90-1021. (New Research in Museum Studies: An International Ser.: Vol. 1). 224p. (C). 1990. text 85.00 (*0-485-90001-7*, Pub. by Athlone Pr) Humanities.

An Asterisk (*) at the beginning of an entry indicates that the title is appearing for the first time.

Pearce, Susan M., ed. Experiencing Material Culture in the Western World. LC 96-26727. 224p. 1997. pap. 28.95 (*0-7185-0022-9*) Bks Intl VA.

Pearce, Sylvia. The Treasure of Darkness. 178p. (Orig.). 1997. pap. 6.00 (*1-57502-395-4*, P01232) Morris Pubng.

Pearce, T. M. Mary Hunter Austin. (Twayne's United States Authors Ser.). 1965. pap. text 4.95 (*0-8290-0003-8*); lib. bdg. 20.95 (*0-89197-837-2*) Irvington.

Pearce, T. M., ed. Literary America, 1903-1934: The Mary Austin Letters, 5. LC 78-67914. (Contributions in Women's Studies: No. 5). (Illus.). 296p. 1979. 55.00 (*0-313-20636-8*, PEL/, Greenwood Pr) Greenwood.

Pearce, Terry. Leading Out Loud: The Authentic Speaker, the Credible Leader. (Management Ser.). 192p. 1995. mass mkt. 22.50 (*0-7879-0111-3*) Jossey-Bass.

Pearce, Terry, jt. auth. see Pottruck, David S.

Pearce, Tim, ed. see Dickens, Charles.

Pearce, Tola O. & Abonja, Simi, eds. Social Change in Nigeria. 262p. (Orig.). (C). 1986. pap. text 13.95 (*0-582-64434-8*) Longman.

Pearce, Tola O., jt. ed. see Afonja, Simi.

Pearce, Virginia H., ed. Glimpses into the Life & Heart of Marjorie Pay Hinckley. LC 99-10317. 224p. 1999. write for info. (*1-57345-523-7*) Deseret Bk.

Pearce, W. Barnett. Communication & the Human Condition. LC 88-30565. 224p. (C). 1989. text 31.95 (*0-8093-1411-8*); pap. text 21.95 (*0-8093-1412-6*) S Ill U Pr.

Pearce, W. Barnett & Littlejohn, Stephen W. Moral Conflict: When Social Worlds Collide. LC 96-51308. 320p. 1997. 48.00 (*0-7619-0052-7*); pap. 22.95 (*0-7619-0053-5*) Sage.

Pearce, W. Barnett, jt. auth. see Narula, Uma.

Pearce, W. Barnett, jt. ed. see Narula, Uma.

Pearce, W. Barnett, jt. ed. see Weiler, Michael.

Pearce, W. J. & Pearce, Querida L. Nature's Footprints Series, 3 vols., Set. (Illus.). 96p. (J). (ps-1). 1990. 14.85 (*0-671-94431-2*); lib. bdg. 27.80 (*0-671-94430-4*) Silver Burdett Pr.

Pearce, W. J., jt. auth. see Rouverol, W. S.

Pearce, W. L., jt. auth. see Pearce, Querida L.

Pearce, William H., jt. auth. see Yao, James S.

Pearce, William H., jt. auth. see Yao, James S. T.

Pearcey, Nancy & Thaxton, Charles. The Soul of Science: Christian Faith & Natural Philosophy. LC 93-42580. (Turning Point Christian Worldview Ser.). 224p. 1994. pap. 15.99 (*0-89107-766-9*) Crossway Bks.

Pearcey, Nancy R., jt. auth. see Colson, Charles.

Pearcey, S., tr. see Dagnini, G.

Pearcey, T., jt. auth. see Hatt, H. H.

Pearch, Sara. Simply Pottery: A Practical Course in Basic Pottery Techniques. LC 98-60565. 144p. 1998. pap. 24.95 (*0-8230-4837-3*) Watsn-Guptill.

Pearcy. Corporate Law. (LQ-Paralegal Ser.). (C). 1998. pap. text, teacher ed. 14.95 (*0-8273-8091-7*) Delmar.

— Corporate Law. (LQ-Paralegal Ser.). (C). 2000. pap. text 49.95 (*0-8273-8090-9*) Delmar.

Pearcy, Arthur. Berlin Airlift. 1998. 29.95 (*1-85310-845-6*) Specialty Pr.

— Lend-Lease Aircraft in World War II: An Operational History. (Illus.). 176p. 1996. 19.98 (*0-7603-0259-6*) MBI Pubg.

— McDonnell Douglas MD-80 & MD-90. LC 99-32255. (Illus.). 128p. 1999. pap. 24.95 (*0-7603-0698-2*, 128432AP) MBI Pubg.

— Sixty Glorious Years: A Tribute to the Douglas DC-3 Dakota. (Illus.). 160p. 1995. 29.98 (*0-7603-0192-1*) MBI Pubg.

— U. S. Coast Guard Aircraft since 1916. LC 91-62723. (Illus.). 330p. 1992. 39.95 (*1-55750-852-6*) Naval Inst Pr.

***Pearcy, Bobbie.** Decorative Painting Color Match Sourcebook. (Illus.). 1999. pap. 19.99 (*1-889937-23-1*) Crescent Hill Bks.

Pearcy, Bobbie, jt. auth. see Pearcy, Neal.

Pearcy, Carl M. Some Recent Developments in Operator Theory. LC 78-8754. (CBMS Regional Conference Series in Mathematics: No. 36). 73p. 1978. reprint ed. pap. 18.00 (*0-8218-1686-1*, CBMS/36) Am Math.

Pearcy, Carl M., ed. Topics in Operator Theory. LC 74-8254. (Mathematical Surveys & Monographs: No. 13). 235p. 1974. reprint ed. pap. 44.00 (*0-8218-1513-X*, SURV/13) Am Math.

Pearcy, Carl M., et al. Nonselfadjoint Operator Algebras, Operator Theory & Related Topics: The Carl M. Pearcy Anniversary Volume. LC 98-22018. (Operator Theory, Advances & Applications Ser.). 1998. 89.50 (*0-8176-5954-4*) Birkhauser.

Pearcy, Carl M., jt. auth. see Brown, A.

Pearcy, Carl M., jt. auth. see Brown, Aren.

***Pearcy, Derek.** In Nomine. Jackson, Steve & Koke, Jeff, eds. (Illus.). 208p. 2000. reprint ed. 24.95 (*1-55634-448-1*) S Jackson Games.

Pearcy, Derek, et al. In Nomine Night Music Vol. 1: Revelations Cycle. Jackson, Steve, ed. (Revelations Cycle Ser.: No. 1). (Illus.). 128p. 1997. pap. 19.95 (*1-55634-289-6*, 3303, Pub. by S Jackson Games) BookWorld.

Pearcy, Derek, jt. auth. see Moore, James A.

Pearcy, Derek, jt. auth. see White Wolf Publishing Staff, Wolf.

Pearcy, Lee T. The Mediated Muse: English Translations of Ovid, 1560-1700. LC 84-16895. xviii, 179p. (C). 1984. lib. bdg. 30.00 (*0-208-02056-X*, Archon Bks) Shoe String.

— The Shorter Homeric Hymns. 53p. (Orig.). (C). 1989. pap. text 6.00 (*0-929524-62-4*) Bryn Mawr Commentaries.

Pearcy, Lee T., jt. auth. see Smith, Peter M.

Pearcy, Neal & Pearcy, Bobbie. Decorative Painting Color Match Sourcebook. LC 97-19592. (Illus.). 96p. 1997. pap. 19.99 (*0-89134-836-0*, North Lght Bks) F & W Pubns Inc.

Pearcy, Robert W., jt. ed. see Caldwell, Martyn M.

Pearcy, Roy D. Studies in the Age of Chaucer, Vol. 1. 1979. 40.00 (*0-933784-00-7*) New Chaucer Soc.

Pearcy, Roy J. Studies in the Age of Chaucer, Vol. 2. 1980. 40.00 (*0-933784-01-5*) New Chaucer Soc.

— Studies in the Age of Chaucer, Vol. 3. 1981. 40.00 (*0-933784-02-3*) New Chaucer Soc.

— Studies in the Age of Chaucer, Vol. 4. 1982. 40.00 (*0-933784-03-1*) New Chaucer Soc.

Pearcy, Thomas L. We Answer Only to God: Politics & the Military in Panama, 1903-1947. LC 98-14669. 232p. 1998. 45.00 (*0-8263-1841-X*) U of NM Pr.

Pearcy, William G. Ocean Ecology of North Pacific Salmonids. LC 92-6564. (Books in Recruitment Fishery Oceanography). (Illus.). 190p. 1992. 25.00 (*0-295-97192-4*) U of Wash Pr.

***Peard, Julyan G.** Race, Place, & Medicine: The Idea of the Tropics in Nineteenth-Century Brazil. LC 99-34867. 240p. 1999. 49.95 (*0-8223-2376-1*) Duke.

Peard, Julyan G. Race, Place & Medicine: The Idea of the Tropics in Nineteenth-Century Brazil. LC 99-34867. 240p. 1999. pap. text 17.95 (*0-8223-2397-4*) Duke.

Peardon, Celeste C., jt. auth. see Gates, Arthur I.

Peardon, Thomas P., ed. The Second Treatise of Government: Locke. 168p. (C). 1952. pap. text 6.00 (*0-02-393300-3*, Macmillan Coll) P-H.

Pearen, Shelley J. Exploring Manitoulin. 176p. 1992. pap. 18.95 (*0-8020-6899-5*) U of Toronto Pr.

— Exploring Manitoulin. rev. ed. 220p. 1996. pap. 18.95 (*0-8020-7961-X*) U of Toronto Pr.

Pearl. Guide to Jewish Knowledge. Date not set. 13.50 (*0-85303-266-1*, Pub. by M Vallentine & Co) Intl Spec Bk.

— Ten Stupid Things Dr. Laura Tells Women to Do to Mess up Their Lives. 177p. 1998. pap. 13.95 (*1-892896-54-0*) Buy Books.

***Pearl, A.** Backstage Pass: 'n Sync: Now & Forever. 2nd ed. (Illus.). 48p. (gr. 2-9). 2000. pap. text 5.99 (*0-439-22220-6*) Scholastic Inc.

Pearl, Art & Knight, Tony. The Democratic Classroom: Theory to Inform Practice. LC 98-51060. (Understanding Education & Policy Ser.). 272p. (C). 1998. 75.00 (*1-57273-218-0*); pap. 29.50 (*1-57273-219-9*) Hampton Pr NJ.

Pearl, Arthur J. & Bergfeld, John A., eds. Extraarticular Reconstruction in the Anterior Cruciate Ligament Deficient Knee. LC 92-16257. (Illus.). 71p. 1992. reprint ed. pap. 30.00 (*0-608-07121-8*, 206734700009) Bks Demand.

Pearl, Arthur J., ed. see American Orthopaedic Society for Sports Medicine S.

Pearl, Arthur J., jt. ed. see Cahill, Bernard R.

Pearl, Barbara N., jt. auth. see Nissenberg, Sandra K.

Pearl, Betty. Betty & Pansy's Severe Queer Review of New York. 2nd rev. ed. LC 97-10283. (Illus.). 200p. (Orig.). 1997. pap. 10.95 (*1-57344-070-1*) Cleis Pr.

Pearl, Betty & Pansy. Betty & Pansy's Severe Queer Review of San Francisco, 6th ed. (Illus.). 200p. 1999. pap. 10.95 (*1-57344-081-7*) Cleis Pr.

Pearl, Betty, jt. auth. see Pansy.

Pearl, Bill. Getting Stronger. 1988. pap. 14.95 (*0-679-73948-3*) Random.

— Keys to the Inner Universe: Encyclopedia on Weight Training. 638p. 1991. reprint ed. pap. 32.95 (*0-9629910-0-7*); reprint ed. text 52.95 (*0-9629910-1-5*) B Pearl Ent.

Pearl, Bill & Moran, Gary. Getting Stronger: Weight Training for Men & Women. Kahn, Lloyd, ed. LC 86-19914. 463p. 1990. pap. 19.95 (*0-936070-04-8*) Shelter Pubns.

Pearl, Brereton O. Software Engineering Environments. LC 87-31113. (Information Technology Ser.). 270p. 1988. text 66.95 (*0-470-21022-2*) P-H.

Pearl, Chaim. From Liverpool to Jerusalem: A Rabbi's Journey. 95p. 1997. 14.95 (*0-88400-199-7*, Pub. by Schreiber Pub) Natl Bk Netwk.

— Theology in Rabbinic Stories. 180p. (Orig.). 1997. pap. 12.95 (*1-56563-285-0*) Hendrickson MA.

Pearl, Cyril. The Girl with the Swansdown Seat: Aspects of Mid-Victorian Morality. 6.95 (*0-686-85784-4*, Pub. by Quartet) Charles River Bks.

***Pearl, David.** Solo Plus: Boogie & Blues for Alto Saxaphone with Piano Accompaniment. (Illus.). 34p. 1999. pap. text 12.95 (*0-8256-1673-5*, AM947375) Music Sales.

— Solo Plus: Boogie & Blues for Clarinet with Piano Accompaniment. 34p. 1999. pap. text 12.95 (*0-8256-1671-9*, AM947353) Music Sales.

— Solo Plus: Boogie & Blues for Flute with Piano Accompaniment. 34p. 1999. pap. text 12.95 (*0-8256-1672-7*, AM947364) Music Sales.

— Solo Plus: Boogie & Blues for Trumpet with Piano Accompaniment. 34p. 1999. pap. text 12.95 (*0-8256-1674-3*, AM947386) Music Sales.

— Solo Plus: Boogie & Blues for Violin with Piano Accompaniment. (Illus.). 34p. 1999. pap. text 12.95 (*0-8256-1762-6*, AM961390) Music Sales.

Pearl, David. Solo Plus: Clarinet with Piano Accompaniment. 32p. 1998. pap. text 12.95 (*0-8256-1648-4*, AM945637) Music Sales.

***Pearl, David.** Solo Plus: My First Recital for Alto Saxophone with Piano Accompaniment. 35p. 1999. pap. text 12.95 incl. cd-rom (*0-8256-1682-4*, AM947452) Music Sales.

— Solo Plus: My First Recital for Clarinet with Piano Accompaniment. 35p. 1999. pap. text 12.95 incl. cd-rom (*0-8256-1680-8*, AM947430) Music Sales.

— Solo Plus: My First Recital for Flute with Piano Accompaniment. 35p. 1999. pap. text 12.95 incl. cd-rom (*0-8256-1681-6*, AM947441) Music Sales.

— Solo Plus: My First Recital for Trumpet with Piano Accompaniment. 35p. 1999. pap. text 12.95 incl. cd-rom (*0-8256-1683-2*, AM947463) Music Sales.

— Solo Plus: My First Recital for Violin with Piano Accompaniment. 35p. 1999. pap. text 12.95 incl. cd-rom (*0-8256-1656-5*, AM945714) Music Sales.

Pearl, David. Solo Plus: Saxaphone with Piano Accompaniments. 32p. 1998. pap. text 12.95 (*0-8256-1650-6*, AM945659) Music Sales.

— Solo Plus: Trumpet with Piano Accompaniment. 32p. 1998. pap. text 12.95 (*0-8256-1651-4*, AM945660) Music Sales.

— Solos Plus Classical Flute: With Piano Accompaniment. 32p. 1998. pap. text 12.95 incl. cd-rom (*0-8256-1649-2*, AM 945648) Music Sales.

— A Textbook on Muslim Personal Law. 304p. 1987. pap. 39.95 (*0-7099-4089-0*, Pub. by C Helm) Routldge.

Pearl, David, contrib. by. Tori Amos from the Choirgirl Hotel. 1998. pap. 24.95 (*0-8256-1664-6*, AM947342) Music Sales.

Pearl, David, et al, eds. Butterworths Immigration Law Service. ring bd. write for info. (*0-406-99646-6*, BILSASET, MICHIE) LEXIS Pub.

Pearl, David. Alto Saxophone with Piano Accompaniment: An Exciting Collection of Ten Swing Tunes Expertly Arranged for the Beginning Soloist with Piano Acc. (Solo Plus Ser.). (Illus.). 32p. (Orig.). 1999. pap. 12.95 incl. audio compact disk (*0-8256-1678-6*, Amsco Music) Music Sales.

— Clarinet with Piano Accompaniment: An Exciting Collection of Ten Swing Tunes Expertly Arranged for the Beginning Soloist with Piano Acc. (Solo Plus Ser.). 32p. (Orig.). 1999. pap. 12.95 incl. audio compact disk (*0-8256-1676-X*, AM947397, Amsco Music) Music Sales.

— Flute with Piano Accompaniment. (Solo Plus Ser.) (Illus.). 32p. (Orig.). 1999. pap. 12.95 (*0-8256-1677-8*, AM947408, Amsco Music) Music Sales.

— Trumpet with Piano Accompaniment: An Exciting Collection of Ten Swing Tunes Expertly Arranged for the Beginning Soloist with Piano Acc. (Solo Plus Ser.). (Illus.). 32p. (Orig.). 1999. pap. 12.95 (*0-8256-1579-4*, AM947420, Amsco Music) Music Sales.

— Violin with Piano Accompaniment: An Exciting Collection of Ten Swing Tunes Expertly Arranged for the Beginning Soloist with Piano Acc. (Solo Plus Ser.). (Illus.). 32p. (Orig.). 1999. pap. 12.95 (*0-8256-1591-3*, AM948981, Amsco Music) Music Sales.

Pearl, David & Gray, Kevin. Social Welfare Law. 308p. 1981. 29.95 (*0-85664-644-X*, Pub. by C Helm); pap. 14.75 (*0-7099-2004-0*, Pub. by C Helm) Routldge.

Pearl, David, jt. auth. see Hoggett, Brenda.

Pearl, Debi, jt. auth. see Pearl, Michael.

Pearl, Diane & Clinton, Ellie. The Smart Woman's Guide: Smart Womans Guide. 224p. 1997. mass mkt. 5.99 (*0-06-101200-9*, Harp PBks) HarpC.

Pearl, Diane & Williams, Ellie. The Smart Woman's Guide to Spending, Saving & Managing Money. (Smart Woman's Guides Ser.). 271p. 1996. lib. bdg. 19.95 (*0-7910-4488-2*) Chelsea Hse.

***Pearl, Eric Scott.** Reconnective Healing. 2001. 23.95 (*1-56170-819-4*) Hay House.

Pearl, Irwin A. The Chemistry of Lignin. LC 67-17005. (Illus.). 352p. 1967. reprint ed. pap. 109.20 (*0-608-08126-4*, 205503400008) Bks Demand.

Pearl, Jack. The Yellow Rolls Royce. 19.95 (*0-88411-443-0*) Amereon Ltd.

Pearl, Jane. Daring Bride: Montclair at the Crossroads, 1932-1939. LC 97-12008. (Brides of Montclair Ser.: Bk. 13). 288p. (Orig.). 1997. pap. 9.99 (*0-310-20209-4*) Zondervan.

Pearl, Jayne, jt. auth. see Cohn, Mike.

Pearl, Jayne A. Kids & Money: Giving Them the Savvy to Succeed Financially. LC 98-35789. (Personal Bookshelf Ser.). (Illus.). 255p. 1998. pap. 12.95 (*1-57660-064-5*) Bloomberg NJ.

Pearl, Jonathan & Pearl, Judith. The Chosen Image: Television's Portrayal of Jewish Themes & Characters. 269p. 1999. lib. bdg. 43.50 (*0-7864-0522-8*) McFarland & Co.

Pearl, Jonathan L. The Crime of Crimes: Demonology & Politics in France, 1560-1620. vii, 160p. 1998. 39.95 (*0-88920-296-6*) W Laurier U Pr.

***Pearl, Judea.** Causality: Models, Reasoning & Inference. 376p. 2000. 39.95 (*0-521-77362-8*) Cambridge U Pr.

Pearl, Judea. Probabilistic Reasoning in Intelligent Systems: Networks of Plausible Inference. (Representation & Reasoning Ser.). 552p. (C). 1991. pap. text 64.95 (*1-55860-479-0*) Morgan Kaufmann.

— Probabilistic Reasoning in Intelligent Systems: Networks of Plausible Inference. (Representation & Reasoning Ser.). 552p. (C). 1998. text 59.95 (*0-934613-73-7*) Morgan Kaufmann.

***Pearl, Judith.** Mother of All Life. LC 98-72538. 212 p. 1998. write for info. (*0-9665792-8-3*) Chalet Magnificat.

Pearl, Judith, jt. auth. see Pearl, Jonathan.

Pearl, Lauren & Kennedy, Doris F., eds. Lingua Latina Mortua Non Est! Latin Is Not Dead. 22p. 1991. pap. text 3.10 (*0-939507-31-5*, B5) Amer Classical.

Pearl, Lizzy. The Story of Flight. LC 91-33412. (Story of Ser.). (Illus.). 32p. (J). (gr. 1-4). 1993. lib. bdg. 18.60 (*0-8167-2709-0*) Troll Communs.

— The Story of Flight. LC 91-33412. (Story of Ser.). (Illus.). 32p. (J). (gr. 1-4). 1997. pap. 4.95 (*0-8167-2710-4*) Troll Communs.

Pearl, Louis. Sudman's Bubble-Ology Guide. (Illus.). 32p. (Orig.). 1985. pap. 11.95 (*0-932165-07-9*) Tangent Pr.

Pearl, Mary, jt. ed. see Western, David.

Pearl, Michael. By Divine Design. 85p. 1999. pap. 4.00 (*1-892112-06-X*) Ch Cane Creek.

— To Train up a Child. unabridged ed. 109p. 1994. pap. 4.00 (*1-892112-00-0*) Ch Cane Creek.

Pearl, Michael & Pearl, Debi. No Greater Joy, Vol. 1. unabridged ed. (Illus.). 104p. 1997. pap. 4.00 (*1-892112-01-9*) Ch Cane Creek.

Pearl, Monica, jt. ed. see Chris, Cynthia.

Pearl, Morris L. William Cobbett: A Bibliographical Account of His Life & Times. LC 78-136079. 266p. 1971. reprint ed. lib. bdg. 59.75 (*0-8371-5229-1*, PEWC, Greenwood Pr) Greenwood.

***Pearl, Nancy, et al.** Now Read This: A Guide to Mainstream Fiction, 1978-1998. LC 99-15280. (Genreflecting Advisory Ser.). 500p. 1999. 65.00 (*1-56308-659-X*) Libs Unl.

Pearl, Patricia. Helping Children Through Books: A Selected Booklist. 24p. 1990. reprint ed. pap. 7.25 (*0-915324-28-8*) CSLA.

— Religious Books for Children: An Annotated Bibliography. rev. ed. 40p. 1988. 8.50 (*0-915324-21-0*) CSLA.

— Small Claims: Practice & Procedure. 120p. 1998. pap. 41.00 (*1-85811-182-X*, Pub. by CLT Prof) Gaunt.

Pearl, Quinn, jt. auth. see Maurer, David W.

Pearl, Raymond. Alcohol & Longevity. Grob, Gerald N., ed. LC 80-1245. (Addiction in America Ser.). (Illus.). 1981. reprint ed. lib. bdg. 30.95 (*0-405-13615-3*) Ayer.

— The Biology of Death: Series of Lectures Delivered at the Lowell Institute in Boston in Dec. 1920. LC 75-38141. (Demography Ser.). (Illus.). 1976. reprint ed. 24.95 (*0-405-07994-X*) Ayer.

— The Biology of Population Growth. Egerton, Frank N., 3rd, ed. LC 77-74245. (History of Ecology Ser.). 1978. reprint ed. lib. bdg. 24.95 (*0-405-10414-6*) Ayer.

Pearl, Raymond & Pearl, Ruth D. The Ancestry of the Long-Lived. Kastenbaum, Robert J., ed. LC 78-22213. (Aging & Old Age Ser.). (Illus.). 1979. reprint ed. lib. bdg. 17.95 (*0-405-11826-0*) Ayer.

Pearl, Rebekah. Rebekah's Diary. 106p. 1997. pap. 4.00 (*1-892112-02-7*) Ch Cane Creek.

Pearl, Richard H. Colorado's Hydrothermal Resource Base-an Assessment: An Assessment. (Resource Ser.: No. 6). (Illus.). 144p. (Orig.). 1979. pap. 3.00 (*1-884216-27-7*) Colo Geol Survey.

— Proceedings of a Symposium on Geothermal Energy & Colorado. (Bulletin Ser.: No. 35). (Illus.). 102p. (Orig.). 1974. pap. 2.00 (*1-884216-01-3*) Colo Geol Survey.

Pearl, Richard H., et al. Bibliography of Geothermal Reports in Colorado. (Bulletin Ser.: No. 44). 24p. (Orig.). 1981. pap. 1.00 (*1-884216-06-4*) Colo Geol Survey.

Pearl, Richard M. California Attorney Fee Awards. 2nd ed. Dworin, Christopher D., ed. LC 94-71538. 650p. 1994. 130.00 (*0-88124-736-7*, CP-32160) Cont Ed Bar-CA.

Pearl, Richard M. California Attorney Fee Awards: 9/96 Update. 2nd ed. Piatt, Norma, ed. LC 94-71538. 484p. 1996. ring bd. 57.00 (*0-7626-0036-5*, CP-32162) Cont Ed Bar-CA.

— California Attorney Fee Awards: 9/97 Update. Johnson, Elizabeth M., ed. LC 94-71538. 424p. 1997. ring bd. 59.00 (*0-7626-0152-3*, CP-32163) Cont Ed Bar-CA.

— California Attorney Fee Awards: 9/99 Update. 2nd ed. Johnson, Elizabeth M., ed. LC 94-71538. 406p. 1999. ring bd. 55.00 (*0-7626-0356-9*, CP-32165) Cont Ed Bar-CA.

— California Attorney Fee Awards - 9/98 Update. 2nd ed. Johnson, Elizabeth M., ed. LC 94-71538. 404p. 1998. ring bd. 54.00 (*0-7626-0262-7*, CP-32164) Cont Ed Bar-CA.

Pearl, Richard M. Colorado Gem Trails & Mineral Guide. 3rd rev. ed. LC 65-16515. (Illus.). 222p. 1972. pap. 16.95 (*0-8040-0956-2*) Swallow.

— Exploring Rocks, Minerals, Fossils in Colorado. rev. ed. LC 64-25339. (Illus.). 215p. 1969. 16.95 (*0-8040-0105-7*) Swallow.

— 1001 Questions Answered About the Mineral Kingdom. unabridged ed. LC 95-6204. (Illus.). 352p. 1995. reprint ed. pap. text 8.95 (*0-486-28711-4*) Dover.

Pearl, Russell K. Gastrointestinal Endoscopy for Surgeons. 225p. 1984. 58.00 (*0-316-69615-3*, Little Brwn Med Div) Lppncott W & W.

Pearl, Ruth D., jt. auth. see Pearl, Raymond.

Pearl, Stephen. The Picture House in East Anglia. 192p. (C). 1988. 60.00 (*0-900963-56-5*, Pub. by T Dalton) St Mut.

Pearl, Sydelle. Elijah's Tears: Stories for the Jewish Holidays. (Illus.). 64p. (J). (gr. 2-4). 1995. 14.95 (*0-8050-4627-5*, B Martin BYR) H Holt & Co.

Pearlberg, Gerry. Women, AIDS & Communities: A Guide for Action. LC 91-17428. (Illus.). 141p. 1991. 29.00 (*0-8108-2470-1*); pap. 20.50 (*0-8108-2450-7*) Scarecrow.

Pearlberg, Gerry G. Key to Everything: Great Lesbian Love Poems. LC 94-36025. 1994. text 10.00 (*0-312-11842-2*) St Martin.

— Marianne Faithfull's Cigarette. LC 97-47575. 144p. 1998. pap. 12.95 (*1-57344-034-5*) Cleis Pr.

Pearlberg, Gerry G., ed. Queer Dog: Homo Pup Poetry, No. 2. LC 97-10978. 100p. (Orig.). 1997. pap. 12.95 (*1-57344-071-X*) Cleis Pr.

Pearlberg, Robert L. & Breth, Steven, eds. Assisting Sustainable Food Production: Action or Apathy? 92p. (Orig.). (C). 1994. pap. text 9.95 (*0-933595-95-6*) Winrock Intl.

Pearlberg, Robert L. & Lipton, Michael. Role of the World Bank in Agricultural Development in the 1990s. large type ed. 56p. 1990. 10.00 (*0-89629-315-7*) Intl Food Policy.

Pearlin, Leonard I., et al. Profiles in Caregiving: The Unexpected Career. LC 95-3498. (Illus.). 408p. 1995. pap. text 42.00 (*0-12-059540-0*) Acad Pr.

Pearlman. Guide to Rapid Revision. 7th ed. (C). 1999. pap. text 23.00 (*0-205-31453-8*) Allyn.

P

Pearlman, Adrienne L. Dysphagia: Competencies, Controversies, & Costs. 1997. 38.00 incl. audio (*1-58041-007-3*, 0112076) Am Speech Lang Hearing.

Pearlman, Alan L. & Collins, Robert C., eds. Neurobiology of Disease. (Illus.). 504p. 1989. text 55.00 (*0-19-505318-4*); pap. text 45.00 (*0-19-505319-2*) OUP.

Pearlman, Alan S., jt. auth. see Otto, Catherine M.

***Pearlman, Alison.** Unpacking the Nineteen Eighties. 1998. 30.00 (*0-226-65145-2*) U Ch Pr.

***Pearlman, Ann.** Infidelity: A Memoir. LC 00-103680. 207p. 2000. 22.00 (*0-9673701-2-4*) MACADAM-CAGE.

***Pearlman, Barbara.** Gardener's Fitness: Weeding Out the Aches & Pains. LC 99-11691. (Illus.). 133p. 1999. pap. text 12.95 (*0-87833-203-0*) Taylor Pub.

Pearlman, Bill. Characters of the Sacred: The World of Archetypal Drama. 96p. (Orig.). 1995. pap. 10.95 (*0-915008-50-5*) Duende.

— Flareup of Twosomes: Poems. LC 96-84340. (Illus.). 64p. Date not set. pap. 11.00 (*0-9631909-9-7*) La Alameda Pr.

— Inzorbital. 1974. pap. 3.00 (*0-685-82998-7*) Duende.

Pearlman, Cari J. Take New York Home: The First 3-Dimensional Pop-up Map of New York. (Illus.). (YA). (gr. 1-12). 1994. 11.50 (*0-929644-01-8*) MultiMap.

Pearlman, Christine, ed. see Thomas, Natalie B.

Pearlman, Dale A., ed. see Ginenthal, Charles, et al.

Pearlman, Daniel. Black Flames. 208p. (Orig.). 1996. pap. 14.00 (*1-877727-63-6*) White Pine.

— The Final Dream & Other Fictions. (Illus.). 272p. (Orig.). (C). 1995. pap. 14.95 (*1-882633-05-9*) Permeable.

***Pearlman, Daniel D.** Guide to Rapid Revision. 7th ed. LC 99-19082. 148p. 1999. pap. text 16.00 (*0-205-30591-1*) Allyn.

Pearlman, Daniel D. & Dubose, Anita. Letter Perfect: An ABC for Business Writers. 112p. (Orig.). (C). 1985. pap. text. write for info. (*0-672-61623-8*) Macmillan.

Pearlman, David S., et al. Allergy, Asthma, & Immunology from Infancy to Adulthood: Management in Infants, Children, & Adults. 3rd ed. (Illus.). 784p. 1995. text 125.00 (*0-7216-5587-4*, W B Saunders Co) Harcrt Hlth Sci Grp.

Pearlman, Della. No Choice: Library Services for the Mentally Handicapped. LC 82-181478. 65p. reprint ed. pap. 30.00 (*0-7837-5320-9*, 204505900005) Bks Demand.

Pearlman, Donn. Breaking into Broadcasting. 156p. 1986. 17.95 (*0-933893-16-7*) Bonus Books.

— Collecting Baseball Cards. 3rd ed. LC 87-73307. (Illus.). 123p. 1987. pap. 7.95 (*0-929387-20-1*) Bonus Books.

Pearlman, Donn & Green, Paul. Making Money with Baseball Cards: A Handbook of Insider Secrets & Strategies. (Illus.). 214p. 1989. pap. 7.95 (*0-933893-77-9*) Bonus Books.

Pearlman, E. William Shakespeare: The Histories. (Twayne's English Authors Ser.). 150p. 1992. 32.00 (*0-8057-7020-8*) Macmillan.

Pearlman, Edith. Vaquita & Other Stories. 208p. 1996. text 22.50 (*0-8229-3962-2*) U of Pittsburgh Pr.

***Pearlman, Eileen M.** Raising Twins: What Parents Want to Know & What Twins Want to Tell Them. 288p. 2000. pap. 16.00 (*0-06-273680-9*, HarpRes) HarpInfo.

Pearlman, Ellen, jt. auth. see Sikes, Alfred C.

Pearlman, Jill. Elvis for Beginners. (Documentary Comic Bks.). (Illus.). 159p. 1991. pap. 7.95 (*0-86316-110-3*) Writers & Readers.

Pearlman, Jill & White, Wayne. Elvis for Beginners. (Writers & Readers Documentary Comic Bks.). (Illus.). 160p. 1986. pap. 7.95 (*0-04-927011-7*) Writers & Readers.

Pearlman, Kenneth, et al, eds. Contemporary Problems in Personnel. LC 82-20316. (Illus.). 588p. reprint ed. pap. 182.30 (*0-7837-3506-5*, 205783900008) Bks Demand.

Pearlman, Kenneth, jt. auth. see Meck, Stuart.

Pearlman, Laurie A. & Saakvitne, Karen W. Trauma & the Therapist: Countertransference & Vicarious Traumatization in Psychotherapy with Incest Survivors. 320p. 1995. 40.00 (*0-393-70183-2*) Norton.

Pearlman, Laurie A., jt. auth. see McCann, I. Lisa.

Pearlman, M. Evangelismo Personal.Tr. of Personal Evangelism. (SPA.). 128p. 1968. pap. 4.99 (*0-8297-0552-X*) Vida Pubs.

— Teologica Biblica y Sistematica.Tr. of Knowing the Doctrines... Bible. (SPA.). 308p. 1992. pap. 9.99 (*0-8297-1372-7*) Vida Pubs.

Pearlman, Mark D. & Tintinalli, Judith E. Emergency Care of the Woman. LC 97-36815. (Illus.). 650p. 1997. text 75.00 (*0-07-049127-5*) McGraw-Hill HPD.

Pearlman, Michael, ed. & tr. see Mariategui, Jose C.

Pearlman, Michael D. To Make Democracy Safe for America: Patricians & Preparedness in the Progressive Era. LC 83-1107. (Illus.). 294p. 1984. text 24.95 (*0-252-01019-1*) U of Ill Pr.

***Pearlman, Michael D.** Warmaking & American Democracy: The Struggle over Military Strategy, 1700 to the Present. LC 98-43993. (Modern War Studies). 464p. 1999. 45.00 (*0-7006-0938-5*) U Pr of KS.

Pearlman, Mickey. A Few Thousand Words about Love. 256p. 1999. pap. 13.95 (*0-312-21788-9*) St Martin.

— Tillie Olsen. (Twayne's United States Authors Ser.: No. 581). 176p. (C). 1991. 32.00 (*0-8057-7632-X*) Macmillan.

— What to Read, Revised edition: The Essential Guide for Reading Group Members & Other Book Lovers. rev. ed. LC 98-53037. 368p. 1999. pap. 14.00 (*0-06-095313-6*) HarpC.

Pearlman, Mickey, ed. American Women Writing Fiction: Memory, Identity, Family, Space. LC 88-18667. 248p. 1988. 34.00 (*0-8131-1657-0*) U Pr of Ky.

— American Women Writing Fiction: Memory, Identity, Family, Space. LC 88-18667. 248p. 1998. pap. 18.00 (*0-8131-0182-4*) U Pr of Ky.

— The Anna Book: Searching for Anna in Literary History, 46. LC 92-8640. (Contributions to the Study of World Literature Ser.: No. 46). 246p. 1992. 59.95 (*0-313-27585-8*, PAK/, Greenwood Pr) Greenwood.

— Between Friends: Writing Women Celebrate Friendship. 251p. 1999. pap. text 14.00 (*0-7881-5995-X*) DIANE Pub.

— Canadian Women Writing Fiction. LC 92-44969. 288p. 1993. text 35.00 (*0-87805-636-X*) U Pr of Miss.

— A Few Thousand Words about Love. LC 97-41490. 256p. 1997. text 22.95 (*0-312-17355-5*) St Martin.

— Mother Puzzle: Daughters & Mothers in Contemporary American Literature, 110. LC 89-11725. (Contributions in Women's Studies: No. 110). 210p. 1989. 55.00 (*0-313-26414-7*, PMC/, Greenwood Pr) Greenwood.

***Pearlman, Mickey, ed.** A Place Called Home: Twenty Writing Women Remember. 257p. 2000. reprint ed. text. write for info. (*0-7881-9046-6*) DIANE Pub.

Pearlman, Mickey & Henderson, Katherine U., eds. Inter-Views: Talks with America's Writing Women. LC 90-33308. (Illus.). 224p. 1990. 23.00 (*0-8131-1780-1*) U Pr of Ky.

Pearlman, Myer. Knowing the Doctrines of the Bible. 400p. 1937. pap. 11.99 (*0-88243-534-5*, 02-0534) Gospel Pub.

— The Minister's Service Book. 147p. 1990. 7.99 (*0-88243-551-5*, 02-0551) Gospel Pub.

— Seeing the Story of the Bible. 128p. 1930. pap. 5.50 (*0-88243-581-7*, 02-0581) Gospel Pub.

— Through the Bible Book by Book Pt. 1: Genesis to Ester. Vol. 1. 112p. 1935. pap. 4.99 (*0-88243-660-0*, 02-0660) Gospel Pub.

— Through the Bible Book by Book Pt. 2: Job to Malichi. 112p. 1935. pap. 4.99 (*0-88243-661-9*, 02-0661) Gospel Pub.

— Through the Bible Book by Book Pt. 3: Matthew to Acts. 96p. 1935. pap. 4.99 (*0-88243-662-7*, 02-0662) Gospel Pub.

— Through the Bible Book by Book Pt. 4: Romans to Revelation. 128p. 1935. pap. 4.99 (*0-88243-663-5*, 02-0663) Gospel Pub.

Pearlman, Rodney & Wang, Y. John, eds. Formulation, Characterization & Stability of Protein Drugs: Case Histories. LC 96-38784. (Pharmaceutical Biotechnology Ser.: Vol. 9). (Illus.). 460p. (C). 1996. text 114.00 (*0-306-45332-0*, Kluwer Plenum) Kluwer Academic.

Pearlman, Rodney, jt. ed. see Wang, Y. J.

Pearlman, Ronald C. Intraoperative Monitoring: Questions/Answers/References. (Illus.). 60p. 1998. pap. text 45.00 (*0-9664927-0-6*) Pearlman Pr.

Pearlmann, P. & Wigzell, Hans, eds. Malaria Immunology. (Progress in Allergy Ser.: Vol. 41). (Illus.). x, 374p. 1988. 228.00 (*3-8055-4672-6*) S Karger.

Pearlson. Managing Information & Systems. 512p. 2000. pap. 73.95 (*0-471-32001-3*) Wiley.

Pearlson, Keri E. & Whinston, Andrew B., eds. Positioning Customer Support for the 21st Century: Theories & Technologies. (C). 1995. pap. 14.95 (*1-887406-05-0*) ICTwo Inst.

Pearlstein, Elinor, et al. Asian Art in the Art Institute of Chicago. (Illus.). 152p. 1993. 24.50 (*0-8109-1916-8*) Abrams.

— Asian Art in the Art Institute of Chicago. (Illus.). 152p. 1993. pap. 17.47 (*0-86559-095-8*) Art Inst Chi.

Pearlstein, Mitchell B. From Moynihan to "My Goodness" Vol. I: What are the Dimensions & Consequences of Contemporary Family Change in the U. S.? 33p. (Orig.). 1996. 15.00 (*1-886306-17-6*) Nevada Policy.

Pearlstein, Mitchell B. & Meeks, Annette. Minnesota Policy Blueprint: A Project of Center of the American Experiment. Benson, Brooke, ed. (Illus.). 400p. 1999. pap. write for info. (*1-892845-00-8*, Pub. by MSP Communs) Bookmen Inc.

Pearlstein, Richard M. The Mind of the Political Terrorist. LC 90-9134. 237p. 1991. 45.00 (*0-8420-2345-3*) Scholarly Res Inc.

Pearlstein, S., ed. Cross-Section Data for Nuclear Reactor Analyses. (Illus.). 216p. 1984. pap. 88.00 (*0-08-031686-7*, Pergamon Pr) Elsevier.

Pearlstein, Toby. Transportation Planning in the Boston Metropolitan Area: A Selected Bibliography, 1930-1982. LC 83-20954. (CPL Bibliographies Ser.: No. 128). 1983. 10.00 (*0-317-00897-8*, Sage Prdcls Pr) Sage.

— Transportation Planning in the Boston Metropolitan Area: A Selected Bibliography, 1930-1982. (CPL Bibliographies Ser.: No. 128). 53p. 1983. 10.00 (*0-86602-128-0*, Sage Prdcls Pr) Sage.

Pearlstone, Zena. Ethnic L. A. (Illus.). 187p. 1990. pap. 12.95 (*0-914589-05-9*) Hillcrest Pr.

Pearlstone, Zena, ed. see Rubin, Arnold.

Pearmain, A. J., jt. auth. see Gallagher, T. J.

Pearmain, Elisa D., ed. Doorways to the Soul: Fifty-Two Wisdom Tales from Around the World. LC 98-35074. 144p. 1998. pap. 9.95 (*0-8298-1286-5*) Pilgrim OH.

Pearman, A. D., jt. auth. see Button, K. J.

Pearman, Donald V. The Termite Report: The Homeowner & Buyer's Guide to Structural Pest Control. (Illus.). 140p. (Orig.). 1988. pap. 19.95 (*0-943743-00-1*) Pear Pub.

Pearman, Hugh. Contemporary World Architecture. LC 99-171240. (Illus.). 511p. 1998. 89.95 (*0-7148-3743-1*, Pub. by Phaidon Press) Phaidon Pr.

***Pearman, Hugh.** Equilibrium: The Work of Nicholas Grimshaw & Partners. (Illus.). 256p. 2000. 75.00 (*0-7148-3958-2*) Phaidon Pr.

Pearman, Richard A. Electric Machinery & Transformer Technology. LC 93-40123. (C). 1994. text 94.50 (*0-03-097713-4*, Pub. by SCP) Harcourt.

Pearman, Roger R. Enhancing Leadership Effectiveness Through Psychological Type. LC 99-29112. 68p. 1999. pap. 11.95 (*0-935652-48-5*) Ctr Applications Psych.

— Hardwired Leadership: Unleashing the Power of Personality to Become a New Millennium Leader. LC 98-16960. 256p. 1998. 27.95 (*0-89106-116-9*, 7785, Pub. by Consulting Psychol) Natl Bk Netwk.

Pearman, Roger R. & Albritton, Sarah C. I'm Not Crazy, I'm Just Not You: The Real Meaning of the 16 Personality Types. LC 96-43662. (Illus.). 208p. (Orig.). 1997. pap. 16.95 (*0-89106-096-0*, 7756, Davies-Black Pub) Consulting Psychol.

Pearman, William A. & Starr, Phillip, eds. Medicare: A Handbook in the History & Issues of Health Care Services for the Elderly. LC 88-2423. 166p. 1988. text 10.00 (*0-8240-8391-1*) Garland.

Pearman, William I. Support of State Educational Programs by Dedication of Specific Revenues & by General Revenue Appropriations: A Study of Certain Factors Which Relate to the Adoption & Use of These General Policies by State Governments. LC 75-177147. (Columbia University. Teachers College. Contributions to Education Ser.: No. 591). reprint ed. 37.50 (*0-404-55591-8*) AMS Pr.

***Pearn & Kandola, R. S.** Job Analysis: A Manager's Guide. 144p. 2000. pap. 47.95 (*0-8464-5098-4*) Beekman Pubs.

Pearn, B. R., ed. see Watson, James K.

Pearn, M. & Kandola, Rajvinder. Job Analysis: A Practical Guide for Managers. 144p. (C). 1988. 60.00 (*0-85292-368-6*, Pub. by IPM Hse) St Mut.

***Pearn, Michael.** Empowering Team Learning: Enabling Ordinary People to do Extraordinary Things. 176p. 2000. pap. 56.95 (*0-8464-5046-1*) Beekman Pubs.

Pearn, Michael & Kandola, Rajvinder. Job Analysis: A Practical Guide for Managers. 144p. 1993. 40.00 (*0-85292-542-5*, Pub. by IPM Hse) St Mut.

Pearn, Michael, et al. Ending the Blame Culture. LC 97-45184. 250p. 1998. 69.95 (*0-566-07996-8*, Pub. by Gower) Ashgate Pub Co.

— Learning Organizations in Practice. LC 95-5588. 1995. write for info. (*0-07-707744-X*) McGraw.

Pearosn, Allen. The Teacher: Theory & Practice in Education. rev. ed. LC 88-92216. 200p. 1989. pap. text 30.00 (*0-9620940-0-5*, A2713) Routledge.

Pearring, Joanne M., ed. When Someone Dies: A Children's Grief Workbook. (Illus.). 16p. (Orig.). 1995. pap., student ed. 1.50 (*0-89622-644-1*) Twenty-Third.

***Pearring, Parker F.** Human Behavior - Analysis, Therapy & Treatments: Index of New Information with Authors, Subjects & Bibliography. rev. ed. 161p. 1999. 47.50 (*0-7883-2132-3*); pap. 44.50 (*0-7883-2133-1*) ABBE Pubs Assn.

***Pearrow, Mark.** Web Site Usability Handbook. (Illus.). 2000. pap. 49.95 (*1-58450-026-3*) Chrles River Media.

Pears, D. F., ed. see Wittgenstein, Ludwig Josef Johann.

Pears, D. F., tr. see Wittgenstein, Ludwig Josef Johann.

Pears, David. The False Prison: A Study of the Development of Wittgenstein's Philosophy, Vol. 1. 224p. 1987. pap. text 19.95 (*0-19-824770-2*) OUP.

Pears, David. The False Prison: A Study of the Development of Wittgenstein's Philosophy, Vol. 2. 340p. 1988. text 60.00 (*0-19-824487-8*); pap. text 22.00 (*0-19-824486-X*) OUP.

— Hume's System: An Examination of the First Book of His Treatise. 216p. 1991. text 60.00 (*0-19-875100-1*); pap. text 18.95 (*0-19-875099-4*) OUP.

— Motivated Irrationality. LC 97-37665. 268p. 1997. reprint ed. 40.00 (*1-890318-41-8*) St Augustines Pr.

Pears, David, frwd. Wittgenstein. 224p. 1986. pap. 12.95 (*0-674-53951-6*) HUP.

Pears, Edwin. Destruction of the Greek Empire & the Story of the Capture of Constantinople by the Turks. LC 68-25259. (World History Ser.: No. 48). (Illus.). 1969. reprint ed. lib. bdg. 75.00 (*0-8383-0227-0*) M S G Haskell Hse.

— Forty Years in Constantinople: Recollections of Sir Edwin Pears, 1873-1915. LC 78-179533. (Select Bibliographies Reprint Ser.). 1977. reprint ed. 26.95 (*0-8369-6662-7*) Ayer.

— Life of Abdul Hamid. LC 73-6296. (Middle East Ser.). 1973. reprint ed. 28.95 (*0-405-05354-1*) Ayer.

— Turkey & Its People. 2nd ed. LC 77-87634. reprint ed. 37.50 (*0-404-16459-5*) AMS Pr.

Pears, Iain. The Bernini Bust. large type ed. 312p. 1995. pap. 19.95 (*0-7862-0367-6*) Thorndike Pr.

— Death & Restoration: A Jonathan Argyll Mystery, No. 3. LC 97-39932. 224p. 1998. 21.50 (*0-684-81461-7*, Scb1) S&S Trade.

— The Discovery of Painting: The Growth of Interest in Painting in England 1680-1760. (Illus.). 301p. (C). 1991. reprint ed. pap. 25.00 (*0-300-05147-6*) Yale U Pr.

***Pears, Iain.** Giotto's Hand. (Prime Crime Mystery Ser.). 2000. mass mkt. 6.50 (*0-425-17358-5*, Prime Crime) Berkley Pub.

Pears, Iain. Giotto's Hand. LC 96-49279. 1997. 20.50 (*0-684-81460-9*) S&S Trade.

***Pears, Iain.** An Instance of the Fingerpost. LC 97-23899. 691p. 2000. pap. 14.95 (*1-57322-795-1*, Riverhd Trade) Berkley Pub.

Pears, Iain. An Instance of the Fingerpost. LC 97-23899. 800p. 1998. 27.00 (*1-57322-082-5*, Riverhead Books) Putnam Pub Group.

— An Instance of the Fingerpost. large type ed. LC 98-23613. (G. K. Hall Core (Large Print) Ser.). 1998. 28.95 (*0-7838-0280-3*, G K Hall Lrg Type) Mac Lib Ref.

— An Instance of the Fingerpost. 752p. 1999. reprint ed. mass mkt. 7.99 (*0-425-16772-0*) Berkley Pub.

— The Last Judgement: A Jonathan Argyll Mystery. 1999. mass mkt. 6.50 (*0-425-17148-5*, Prime Crime) Berkley Pub.

— The Last Judgement: A Jonathan Argyll Mystery. 1995. 21.00 (*1-57283-001-8*) S&S Trade.

— The Last Judgement: A Jonathan Argyll Mystery. LC 95-38120. 224p. 1996. 20.50 (*0-684-81459-5*) S&S Trade.

— The Raphael Affair. LC 92-18790. 1992. 18.95 (*0-15-178912-6*) Harcourt.

— The Raphael Affair. large type ed. (Linford Mystery Library). 1991. pap. 16.99 (*0-7089-7155-5*) Ulverscroft.

— The Raphael Affair. (Prime Crime Mystery Ser.: Bk. 1). 226p. 1998. reprint ed. pap. 5.99 (*0-425-16613-9*, Prime Crime) Berkley Pub.

— The Titian Committee. LC 93-404. 1993. 19.95 (*0-15-190472-3*) Harcourt.

— The Titian Committee. large type ed. LC 93-48428. 317p. 1994. lib. bdg. 18.95 (*0-7862-0170-3*) Thorndike Pr.

— The Titian Committee. 1999. reprint ed. mass mkt. 5.99 (*0-425-16895-6*, Prime Crime) Berkley Pub.

Pears, Pauline & Sherman, Bob. Healthy Fruit & Vegetables. 64p. 1997. pap. 16.95 (*0-85532-689-1*) Srch Pr.

Pears, Peter. The Travel Diaries of Peter Pears, 1936-1978. Reed, Philip, ed. (Aldeburgh Studies in Music: No. 2). (Illus.). 272p. (C). 1995. 60.00 (*0-85115-364-X*) Boydell & Brewer.

Pears, Randolph. British Battleships Eighteen Ninety-Two to Nineteen Fifty-Seven. 1981. 60.00 (*0-906223-14-8*) St Mut.

Pears, Sarah, jt. auth. see Pears, Thomas.

Pears, Thomas & Pears, Sarah. New Harmony, an Adventure in Happiness: Papers of Thomas & Sarah Pears. Pears, Thomas C., Jr., ed. LC 72-77058. 96p. 1973. reprint ed. lib. bdg. 27.50 (*0-678-00908-2*) Kelley.

Pears, Thomas C., Jr., ed. see Pears, Thomas & Pears, Sarah.

Pears, Tim. In a Land of Plenty. 542p. 1998. 25.00 (*0-385-40846-3*) Bantam.

— In a Land of Plenty. LC 97-33402. 544p. 1998. text 25.00 (*0-312-18112-4*) St Martin.

— In a Land of Plenty. 544p. 1999. pap. 15.00 (*0-312-20412-4*, Picador USA) St Martin.

Pearsall, Anthony B. The Lovecraft Lexicon: A Dictionary of People & Places in Lovecraft's Novels. LC 97-65816. 288p. 2000. pap. 16.95 (*1-56184-129-3*) New Falcon Pubns.

Pearsall, Arlene E. Johannes Pauli (1450-1520) on the Church & Clergy. LC 93-48792. 260p. 1994. 89.95 (*0-7734-9108-2*) E Mellen.

Pearsall, Craig. The Check System of Supervision: How to Manage the Human Resource. (Illus.). 73p. 1995. reprint ed. 7.95 (*0-9648282-0-0*) C Pearsall.

***Pearsall, Deborah M.** Paleoethnobotany: A Handbook of Procedures. 2nd ed. 700p. 2000. 89.95 (*0-12-548042-3*) Acad Pr.

Pearsall, Deborah M., jt. auth. see Piperno, Dolores R.

Pearsall, Deborah M., jt. ed. see Voigt, Eric E.

Pearsall, Deborah M., jt. ed. see Zeidler, James A.

Pearsall, Derek. The Canterbury Tales. 380p. (C). 1985. pap. 25.99 (*0-415-09444-5*, A8672) Routledge.

— Chaucer to Spenser: A Critical Reader. LC 99-28389. (Critical Readers Ser.). 720p. 1998. pap. 34.95 (*0-631-19937-3*) Blackwell Pubs.

— Chaucer to Spenser: A Critical Reader. LC 99-28389. (Critical Readers Ser.). 720p. 2000. 66.95 (*0-631-19936-5*) Blackwell Pubs.

— Chaucer to Spenser: An Anthology. (Blackwell Anthologies Ser.). 1000p. 1998. 74.95 (*0-631-19838-5*); pap. 36.95 (*0-631-19839-3*) Blackwell Pubs.

— The Life of Geoffrey Chaucer: A Critical Biography. 336p. 1995. pap. 25.95 (*1-55786-665-1*) Blackwell Pubs.

Pearsall, Derek, ed. Studies in the Vernon Manuscript. (Illus.). 249p. 1990. 75.00 (*0-85991-310-4*) Boydell & Brewer.

Pearsall, Derek & Scott, Kathleen, eds. Piers Plowman: A Facsimile of Bodleian Library, Oxford, MS Douce 104. (Illus.). 336p. (C). 1992. 250.00 (*0-85991-345-7*) Boydell & Brewer.

Pearsall, Derek, ed. see Chaucer, Geoffrey.

Pearsall, Derek, ed. see Langland, William.

Pearsall, Derek A. & Salter, Elizabeth. Landscapes & Seasons of the Medieval World. LC 73-85089. 316p. reprint ed. pap. 98.00 (*0-608-16809-2*, 202640600049) Bks Demand.

***Pearsall, George T. P., ed.** Properties, Processing & Applications of Indium Phosphide. (EMIS Datareviews Ser.: No. 21). 325p. 1999. boxed set 175.00 (*0-85296-949-X*) INSPEC Inc.

Pearsall, Jay. Mystery & Crime: The New York Public Library Book of Answers-Ingriguing & Entertaining Questions & Answers About the Who's Who & What's What of Whodunnits. 192p. 1995. pap. 11.00 (*0-671-87237-0*, Fireside) S&S Trade Pap.

Pearsall, Judith M. & Trumble, William R. The Oxford Encyclopedic English Dictionary. 2nd ed. 1804p. 1995. 35.00 (*0-19-521158-8*) OUP.

***Pearsall, Judy, ed.** The Concise Oxford English Dictionary: Thumb Indexed. 10th ed. LC 99-20834. 1,696p. 1999. 29.95 (*0-19-860287-1*) OUP.

Pearsall, Margaret. The Pearsall Guide to Successful Dog Training. 3rd ed. LC 80-16840. (Illus.). 352p. 1973. 25.95 (*0-87605-759-8*) Howell Bks.

Pearsall, Marilyn. Women & Values: Readings in Recent Feminist Philosophy. 2nd ed. LC 92-13426. 413p. (C). 1992. pap. 32.50 (*0-534-19554-7*) Wadsworth Pub.

— Women & Values: Readings in Recent Feminist Philosophy. 3rd ed. LC 98-11858. (Philosophy Ser.). 1998. pap. 50.95 (*0-534-53469-4*) Wadsworth Pub.

Pearsall, Marilyn, ed. The Other Within Us: Feminist Perspectives on Women & Aging. 1997. 59.00 (*0-614-27690-X*); pap. 18.00 (*0-614-27689-6*) Westview.

— Women & Values: Readings in Recent Feminist Philosophy. 366p. (C). 1985. mass mkt. write for info. (*0-534-05472-2*) Wadsworth Pub.

P

Pearsall, Marilyn, jt. ed. see Garry, Ann.

Pearsall, Marilyn, jt. ed. see Oliver, Kelly.

Pearsall, Marion. Klamath Childhood & Education. fac. ed. Gifford, Edward W. et al, eds. (University of California Publications: No. 9:5). 17p. (C). 1950. reprint ed. pap. 2.19 (*1-55567-098-9*) Coyote Press.

Pearsall, Milo D. & Verbruggen, Hugo. Scent: Training to Track, Search, & Rescue. (Illus.). 240p. 1982. 19.95 (*0-931866-11-1*) Alpine Pubns.

Pearsall, N. M. Solar Electricity: Its Current Role in Overseas Aid (C48) (C). 1987. 100.00 (*0-7855-3807-0*, Pub. by Interntl Solar Energy Soc) St Mut.

Pearsall, N. M., ed. Solar Electricity: Its Current Role in Overseas Aid. (C). 1987. 135.00 (*0-7855-4206-X*, Pub. by Interntl Solar Energy Soc) St Mut.

Pearsall, N. M., jt. auth. see Hill, R.

Pearsall, Nancy N. & Weiser, Russell S. The Macrophage. LC 77-85844. (Illus.). 214p. reprint ed. 66.40 (*0-8357-9410-5*, 201457600090) Bks Demand.

Pearsall, Paul. The Heart's Code: Tapping the Wisdom & Power of Our Heart Energy. LC 97-45968. 304p. 1998. 25.00 (*0-7679-0077-4*) Broadway BDD.

— The Heart's Code: Tapping the Wisdom & Power of Our Heart Energy. 304p. 1999. reprint ed. pap. 13.00 (*0-7679-0095-2*) Broadway BDD.

— The Pleasure Prescription: To Love, to Work, to Play-Life in the Balance. 288p. 1996. pap. 13.95 (*0-89793-207-2*) Hunter Hse.

— The Pleasure Prescription: To Love, to Work, to Play-Life in the Balance. 288p. 1997. 23.95 (*0-89793-208-0*) Hunter Hse.

Pearsall, Paul. The Pleasure Principle: Discovering a New Way to Health. 1995. 16.00 incl. audio (*0-671-52116-0*) S&S Trade.

Pearsall, Paul. Wishing Well: Making Your Every Wish Come True. LC 99-43142. 384p. 2000. 24.95 (*0-7868-6561-X*, Pub. by Hyperion) Time Warner.

***Pearsall, Paul.** Wishing Well: The Art & Science of Wishcraft. 2002. mass mkt. write for info. (*0-7868-8959-4*) Disney Pr.

— Wishing Well: The Art & Science of Wishcraft 2000. pap. write for info. (*0-7868-8473-8*) Disney Pr.

Pearsall, Paul. Write Your Own Pleasure Prescription: 60 Ways to Create Balance & Joy in Your Life. LC 97-18265. (Illus.). 224p. 1997. pap. 12.95 (*0-89793-229-3*) Hunter Hse.

Pearsall, Paul P. Making Miracles: Finding Meaning in Life's Chaos. 320p. 1993. reprint ed. pap. 10.00 (*0-380-71948-7*, Avon Bks) Morrow Avon.

— Ten Laws of Lasting Love. LC 92-42016. 352p. 1993. 22.00 (*0-671-76798-4*) S&S Trade.

Pearsall, Priscilla. An Art Alienated from Itself: Studies in Spanish American Modernism. LC 83-17736. (Romance Monographs: No. 43). 103p. 1984. 19.00 (*84-499-6721-X*) Romance.

Pearsall, Robert B. Frank Harris. LC 74-120526. (Twayne's English Authors Ser.). 196p. (C). 1970. lib. bdg. 20.95 (*0-317-38186-5*) Irvington.

— Robert Browning. (English Authors Ser.: No. 168). 200p. 1974. 22.95 (*0-8057-1065-5*, Twyne) Mac Lib Ref.

Pearsall, Ronald. Connoisseur's Guide to Antique Pottery & Porcelain, 1. 1998. 16.98 (*1-57717-046-6*) Todtri Prods.

— Connoisseur's Guide to Antique Clocks & Watches, 1. 1998. 16.98 (*1-57717-044-X*) Todtri Prods.

***Pearsall, Ronald.** Connoisseur's Guide to Antique Dolls. 1999. 16.95 (*1-57717-150-0*) Todtri Prods.

Pearsall, Ronald. Connoisseur's Guide to Antique Furniture, 1. 1998. pap. text 16.98 (*1-57717-045-8*) Todtri Prods.

***Pearsall, Ronald.** Connoisseur's Guide to Antique Glass. 1999. 16.95 (*1-57717-153-5*) Todtri Prods.

— Connoisseur's Guide to Antique Jewelry. 1999. 16.95 (*1-57717-152-7*) Todtri Prods.

— Connoisseur's Guide to Antique Toys. 1999. 16.95 (*1-57717-151-9*) Todtri Prods.

Pearsall, Ronald. Edwardian Popular Music. LC 75-10734. (Illus.). 207p. 18.00 (*0-8386-1781-6*) Fairleigh Dickinson.

***Pearsall, Ronald.** Illustrated Guide to Collecting Antiques. (Illus.). 1998. 16.98 (*1-57717-000-8*) Todtri Prods.

— Kings & Queens A History of British Monarchy. 1998. pap. text 16.95 (*1-880908-97-2*) Todtri Prods.

— Lost at Sea: Great Shipwrecks of History. (Illus.). 1998. pap. 12.98 (*1-880908-52-2*) Todtri Prods.

— Mysterious Places of the World, 1. 1999. 16.95 (*1-57717-157-8*) Todtri Prods.

Pearsall, Ronald. Myths & Legends of Ireland Tales of a Magical & Mysterious Past. 1998. 16.98 (*1-880908-43-3*) Todtri Prods.

***Pearsall, Ronald.** Romance of Travel. 1999. 16.95 (*1-57717-156-X*) Todtri Prods.

— Silver. 1998. 16.98 (*1-57717-047-4*) Todtri Prods.

Pearsall, Ronald A. Introduction to Drawing. (Illus.). 92p. 1995. write for info. (*1-57215-083-1*) World Pubns.

— Introduction to Oil Painting. (Illus.). 92p. 1995. write for info. (*1-57215-085-8*) World Pubns.

— Introduction to Pastel & Acrylic. (Illus.). 92p. 1995. write for info. (*1-57215-084-X*) World Pubns.

— Introduction to Watercolor, Gouache & Tempera. (Illus.). 92p. 1995. write for info. (*1-57215-082-3*) World Pubns.

***Pearsall, T. P.** Quantum Effects in Semiconductor Materials & Devices. LC 99-89632. (Electronic Materials Ser.). 2000. write for info. (*0-7923-7748-6*) Kluwer Academic.

Pearsall, T. P., et al, eds. Epitaxial Growth Principles & Applications Vol. 570: Materials Research Society Symposium Proceedings. LC 99-26672. 318p. 1999. text 73.00 (*1-55899-477-7*) Materials Res.

Pearsall, Thomas E. Elements in Technical Writing. LC 96-27196. 180p. 1996. pap. 14.00 (*0-205-18895-8*) Allyn.

Pearsall, Thomas E. The Elements of Technical Writing. 3rd ed. 604p. (C). 1996. pap., teacher ed. write for info. (*0-205-26733-5*) Allyn.

— How to Write for the World. 5th ed. (C). 1994. pap. text, teacher ed. 3.75 (*0-15-501196-0*) Harcourt Coll Pubs.

***Pearsall, Thomas E.** How to Write for the World of Work. 6th ed. 2000. pap. text 71.00 (*0-15-507903-4*) Harcourt.

Pearsall, Thomas E. & Cunningham, Donald H. How to Write for the World of Work. 5th ed. LC 93-27792. (C). 1993. pap. text 63.50 (*0-15-501121-9*, Pub. by Harcourt Coll Pubs) Harcourt.

Pearsall, Thomas E., jt. auth. see Brown, James I.

Pearsall, Thomas P. Introduction to Photonics. (C). 2001. pap. text 95.00 (*0-201-36128-0*) Addison-Wesley.

Pearsall, Thomas P., ed. GaInAsP Alloy Semiconductors. LC 81-15922. 480p. reprint ed. pap. 148.80 (*0-7837-5875-8*, 204559500006) Bks Demand.

— Semiconductors & Semimetals Vol. 33: Strained-Layer Superlattices: Materials Science & Technology. 431p. 1990. text 138.00 (*0-12-752133-X*) Acad Pr.

Pearse, A. G. Histochemistry, Vol. 1: Theoretical & Applied. 4th ed. (Illus.). 456p. 1993. text 241.00 (*0-443-01998-3*) Church.

— Histochemistry, Vol 2: Theoretical & Applied. 4th ed. (Illus.). 624p. 1985. text 210.00 (*0-443-02997-0*) Church.

Pearse, Andrew. Latin American Peasant. (Library of Peasant Studies: No. 1). 299p. 1975. 49.50 (*0-7146-3047-0*, Pub. by F Cass Pubs); pap. 15.00 (*0-7146-4021-2*, Pub. by F Cass Pubs) Intl Spec Bk.

Pearse, Cecilia M. & Hird, Frank. The Romance of a Great Singer: Memoir of Mario. Farkas, Andrew, ed. LC 76-29961. (Opera Biographies Ser.). (Illus.). 1977. reprint ed. lib. bdg. 28.95 (*0-405-09701-8*) Ayer.

Pearse, Edward. A Beam of Divine Glory: The Unchangeableness of God. rev. ed. Kistler, Don, ed. 190p. 1998. reprint ed. 18.95 (*1-57358-067-8*) Soli Deo Gloria.

— The Best Match: The Soul's Espousal to Christ. rev. ed. Kistler, Don, ed. LC 97-104425. 216p. 1996. 24.95 (*1-57358-051-1*) Soli Deo Gloria.

Pearse, J. Frets & Fingers Guitar Players Manual. 1986. pap. 11.50 (*0-7935-5552-3*, 50334900) H Leonard.

***Pearse, John.** Carousel. LC 99-91088. iii, 232p. 1999. 13.95 (*0-9617175-1-3*) J Pearse Mus Pub.

Pearse, John. Cooking with Wine. Warde, John, ed. (Illus.). 100p. 1987. pap. 9.95 (*0-318-22777-0*) Buckingham WP.

Pearse, John. The Guitarist's Picture Chord Encyclopedia. (Illus.). 310p. 1978. pap. 21.95 (*0-8256-2199-2*, AM36625) Music Sales.

Pearse, John & Warde, John. Stringalong. (Illus.). 96p. 1986. pap. 10.95 (*0-9617175-0-5*) J Pearse Mus Pub.

Pearse, M. T. Between Known Men & Visible Saints: A Study of Sixteenth Century English Dissent. LC 94-16045. 1995. 42.50 (*0-8386-3563-6*) Fairleigh Dickinson.

***Pearse, Meic.** The Great Restoration: The Religious Radicals of the 16th & 17th Centuries. xi, 320p. 1998. reprint ed. pap. 30.00 (*0-85364-800-X*, Pub. by Paternoster Pub) OM Literature.

Pearse, Meic. Who's Feeding Whom? (Inside Out Meditations Ser.). ix, 113p. 1996. reprint ed. pap. 9.99 (*1-900507-20-X*, Pub. by Solway) Eisenbrauns.

Pearse, Nancy C. John Fletcher's Chastity Plays: Mirrors of Modesty. LC 72-3258. 255p. 1973. 22.50 (*0-8387-1151-0*) Bucknell U Pr.

Pearse, Padraic H. Collected Works of Padraic H. Pearse. LC 75-28838. reprint ed. 35.00 (*0-404-13827-6*) AMS Pr.

— Padraic Pearse: Rogha Danta - Selected Poems. 80p. (Orig.). 1993. reprint ed. pap. 9.95 (*1-874597-50-2*, Pub. by New Island Books) Irish Bks Media.

Pearse, Patricia. See How You Grow. LC 87-33268. (Illus.). 32p. (J). (gr. 1-4). 1988. 14.95 (*0-8120-5936-0*) Barron.

Pearse, Patrick, et al. The 1916 Poets: Pearse, Plunkett, MacDonagh. Ryan, Desmond, ed. 179p. 1995. reprint ed. pap. 15.95 (*0-7171-2294-8*, Pub. by Gill & MacMill) Irish Bks Media.

Pearse, Richard. The Land Beside the Celtic Sea: Aspect of Cornwall's Past. (C). 1989. pap. 30.00 (*0-907566-48-0*, Pub. by Dyllansow Truran) St Mut.

Pearse, Robert F., jt. auth. see Fram, Eugene H.

Pearse, Warren H., jt. auth. see Seltzer, Vicki L.

Pearse, Warren H., jt. ed. see Seltzer, Vicki L.

Pearson. Esophageal Surgery. 2nd ed. (C). Date not set. text. write for info. (*0-443-07605-7*) Church.

— Fiber Optic Cable Installation/Repair. (Electrical Trades Ser.). 1997. pap., teacher ed. 16.95 (*0-8273-7319-8*) Delmar.

— Gender & Communication. 3rd ed. 1995. teacher ed. 15.00 (*0-697-20155-4*, WCB McGr Hill) McGrw-H Hghr Educ.

— International Political Economy. LC 98-45017. 512p. 1999. pap. 37.19 (*0-07-049082-1*) McGraw.

— Introduction to Human Communication. 8th ed. LC 99-30979. 544p. 1999. pap. 44.06 (*0-07-233693-5*) McGraw.

***Pearson.** Marigold Field. 2000. pap. 5.95 (*0-552-10271-7*, Pub. by Transworld Publishers Ltd) Trafalgar.

Pearson. Morning Glory Mother, Vol. 1. 1998. write for info. (*0-312-96508-7*) Tor Bks.

— The Rise & Fall of the Soviet Empire. LC 96-52562. 192p. 1997. text 55.00 (*0-312-17405-5*) St Martin.

***Pearson.** Sarah Whitman. 2000. pap. 8.95 (*0-552-09140-5*, Pub. by Transworld Publishers Ltd) Trafalgar.

Pearson. Stranger for Christmas, Vol. 1. 1997. mass mkt. 4.99 (*0-312-96454-4*, Pub. by Tor Bks) St Martin.

— Teaching Children to Read. 2001. teacher ed. 21.50 (*0-07-049078-3*) McGraw.

— Teaching Children to Read. 2001. 42.00 (*0-07-049077-5*) McGraw.

— Teaching Reading: Comprehension. 2nd ed. (C). 1998. pap. text 25.00 (*0-03-062779-6*) Harcourt Coll Pubs.

— Thoracic Surgery. 2nd ed. (C). Date not set. text. write for info. (*0-443-07595-6*) Church.

Pearson. Unititled Novel. 1994. text 23.00 (*0-8050-3062-X*) St Martin.

Pearson, ed. The William Makepeace Thackeray Library, 6 vols., Set. (Illus.). 2179p. (C). 1996. text, boxed set 825.00 (*0-415-13742-X*) Routledge.

Pearson, et al, eds. Aquatic Toxicology & Hazard Assessment (Fifth Conference)- STP 766. 414p. 1982. 44.50 (*0-8031-0796-X*, STP766) ASTM.

Pearson & Stephens, eds. Didymi. (GRE.). 1983. 57.50 (*3-519-01269-3*, T1269, Pub. by B G Teubner) U of Mich Pr.

Pearson & Trask, eds. Sea Island Seasons Cookbook. (Illus.). 1995. reprint ed. 14.95 (*0-9647460-1-8*) Beaufort County.

Pearson, jt. auth. see Earis.

Pearson, jt. auth. see Nelson.

Pearson, jt. auth. see Winterbone.

Pearson, A. C., ed. The Fragments of Zeno & Cleanthes. LC 72-9299. (Philosophy of Plato & Aristotle Ser.). 1974. reprint ed. 21.95 (*0-405-04854-8*) Ayer.

Pearson, A. J., ed. Iron Compounds in Organic Synthesis. (Best Synthetic Methods Ser.). (Illus.). 224p. 1994. text 59.00 (*0-12-548270-1*) Acad Pr.

Pearson, A. J., jt. auth. see Mileaf, Harry.

Pearson, A. John, ed. see Lindquist, Emory K.

Pearson, A. John, ed. see Lindquist, Emory K., et al.

***Pearson, A. M.** Haccp in Meat, Poultry & Fish Processing: Advances in Meat Research Series. 393p. 1998. 165.00 (*0-8342-1327-3*) Aspen Pub.

Pearson, A. M., jt. auth. see Dutson, T. R.

Pearson, A. W., jt. auth. see Holden, K.

Pearson-Adams, Sandra, jt. auth. see Brown, Sue H.

Pearson, Alan. Nature of Nursing Work. 1996. pap. 40.00 (*0-949823-69-4*, Pub. by Deakin Univ) St Mut.

— Nursing, from Whence to Where? Professorial Lecture. (C). 1991. pap. 21.00 (*0-7300-1448-7*, Pub. by Deakin Univ) St Mut.

— Optimum Staffing Mix in Australian Nursing Homes: A Review of the Literature (DINROO) 92p. 1993. pap. 39.00 (*0-7300-1550-5*, Pub. by Deakin Univ) St Mut.

— The Social Reality of Clinical Nursing in a Rural Hospital. 35p. (C). 1989. pap. 51.00 (*0-7300-0694-8*, NPR803, Pub. by Deakin Univ) St Mut.

Pearson, Alan, ed. Primary Nursing: Nursing in the Burford & Oxford Nursing Development Units. 160p. 1988. pap. text 25.00 (*0-7099-4066-1*, Pub. by C Helm) Routldge.

Pearson, Alan, et al, trs. Inservice Training in Non-Government Nursing Homes (DINROO) (Research Monographs: No. 3). 1992. pap. 33.00 (*0-7300-1484-3*, Pub. by Deakin Univ) St Mut.

Pearson, Alan & Baker, Helen. Compliance or Alliance? Case Study on Introducing Research Papers: No. 9). 1992. pap. text 21.00 (*0-7855-2669-2*, Pub. by Deakin Univ) St Mut.

— Quality of Care: Do Contemporary Nursing Approaches Make a Difference? (Research Monographs: No. 5). 1995. pap. 20.00 (*0-7300-1497-5*, Pub. by Deakin Univ) St Mut.

Pearson, Alan & Vaughan, Barbara. Nursing Models for Practice. 2nd ed. 264p. 1996. pap. text 45.00 (*0-7506-1597-4*, Focal) Buttrwrth-Heinemann.

Pearson, Alan, et al. Food for Thought: Comparing Nurses Assessment of Food Intake. (Research Monographs: No. 4). 1992. pap. 21.00 (*0-7300-1489-4*, Pub. by Deakin Univ) St Mut.

— Hospital Carpets: Comfort, Cosiness & Cleanliness. (Research Monographs: No. 2). 1992. pap. 21.00 (*0-7300-1482-7*, Pub. by Deakin Univ) St Mut.

Pearson, Alan, jt. auth. see Jeyarajasingam, Allen.

Pearson, Alan, jt. auth. see Lambert, Mike.

Pearson, Alan, jt. auth. see McMahon, Richard.

Pearson, Alan, jt. ed. see Baker, Helen.

Pearson, Alan J. A Unified Theory of Refining. (Pulp & Paper Technology Ser.: No. 6). 128p. 1990. 15.00 (*0-919893-79-1*, 0101JT06) TAPPI.

— A Unified Theory of Refining. (Pulp & Paper Technology Ser.: No. 6). (Illus.). reprint ed. pap. 35.40 (*0-8357-4081-1*, 2036771) Bks Demand.

***Pearson, Albert M.** Processed Meats. 464p. 1998. pap. 55.00 (*0-8342-1304-4*) Aspen Pub.

***Pearson, Allen.** Voyages under Sail: From the Log of Francis Dell. 1999. pap. 21.00 (*1-85072-166-1*, Pub. by W Sessions) St Mut.

Pearson, Angela. Scream, My Darling, Scream! 200p. 1997. pap. 19.95 (*1-897767-16-1*, Pub. by Delectus Bks) Xclusiv Distrib.

— The Whipping Club. 258p. 1999. pap. 19.95 (*1-897767-18-8*, Pub. by Delectus Bks) Xclusiv Distrib.

Pearson, Anita, ed. see Clarin, Leo.

Pearson, Anita, ed. see Cruts, Randy.

Pearson, Anna. The Complete Needlepoint Course. (Illus.). 176p. 1991. pap. 27.95 (*0-8019-8227-8*) Krause Pubns.

— Needlepoint: 20 Classic Projects. (Illus.). 128p. 1998. 24.95 (*1-85732-790-X*, Pub. by Mitchell Beazley) Trafalgar.

***Pearson, Anne.** Ancient Greece. (Eyewitness Books). (Illus.). (J). (gr. 4-7). 2000. 19.99 (*0-7894-6586-8*) DK Pub Inc.

— Ancient Greece. (Eyewitness Books). (J). (gr. 4-7). 2000. 15.95 (*0-7894-5750-4*) DK Pub Inc.

Pearson, Anne. What Do We Know about the Greeks? LC 92-9692. (What Do We Know about...? Ser.). (Illus.). 48p. (YA). (gr. 2 up). 1992. lib. bdg. 18.95 (*0-87226-356-8*, 63568B, P Bedrick Books) NTC Contemp Pub Co.

Pearson, Anne M. Because It Gives Me Peace of Mind: Ritual Fasts in the Religious Lives of Hindu Women. LC 95-39811. (McGill Studies in the History of Religions). 315p. (C). 1996. text 68.50 (*0-7914-3037-5*); pap. text 24.95 (*0-7914-3038-3*) State U NY Pr.

Pearson, Anthony, jt. auth. see Labovitz, Arthur J.

Pearson, Anthony J. & Roush, W. R. Handbook of Reagents for Organic Synthesis, 4 vols., Set. 2364p. 1999. 425.00 (*0-471-98789-1*) Wiley.

Pearson, Anthony J., ed. see Roush, W.R.

Pearson, Aval, ed. see Kyte, Shekhem-Cwolde.

Pearson, Barrie. Successful Acquisition of Unquoted Companies. 3rd ed. 192p. 1989. text 63.95 (*0-566-02814-X*, Pub. by Gower) Ashgate Pub Co.

***Pearson, Barrie.** Successful Acquisition of Unquoted Companies: A Practical Guide. 4th ed. LC 98-8751. 150p. 1998. 86.95 (*0-566-08099-0*, Pub. by Gower) Ashgate Pub Co.

Pearson, Barry L. Sounds So Good to Me: The Bluesman's Story. LC 83-14764. (Illus.). 186p. 1984. pap. 19.95 (*0-8122-1171-5*) U of Pa Pr.

— Virginia Piedmont Blues: The Lives & Art of Two Virginia Bluesmen. LC 89-28014. (Publications of the American Folklore Society, Bibliographical & Special Ser.). (Illus.). 300p. (C). 1990. text 42.50 (*0-8122-8209-4*); pap. text 20.95 (*0-8122-1300-9*) U of Pa Pr.

Pearson, Bill. Rifled Sanctuaries: Some Views of the Pacific Islands in Literature to 1900. 1984. pap. 13.95 (*0-19-648029-9*) OUP.

Pearson, Bill, et al. Hands-On Science with Project Smartlab: Science & Math Activity-Related Teaching from Labs in a Box. LC 95-67968. (Illus.). 288p. (J). (gr. 6-8). 1996. ring bd. 39.95 (*89089-852-9*) Carolina Acad Pr.

Pearson, Bill, ed. see Wood, Wally.

Pearson, Birger A. The Emergence of the Christian Religion: Essays on Early Christianity. LC 97-38320. 256p. (Orig.). 1997. pap. 19.00 (*1-56338-218-0*) TPI PA.

Pearson, Birger A., ed. Nag Hammadi Codex VII. (Nag Hammadi & Manichaean Studies: Vol. 30). 1995. 140.50 (*90-04-10451-8*) Brill Academic Pubs.

Pearson, Birger A. & Goehring, James E., eds. The Roots of Egyptian Christianity. LC 85-47736. (Studies in Antiquity & Christianity). 352p. (C). 1998. pap. 20.00 (*0-8006-2706-7*, 1-2706) TPI PA.

Pearson, Brian, jt. auth. see Griffiths, Ronno.

Pearson, Bruce. Alto Saxophone. (Standard of Excellence Ser.: Bk. 2). 1993. 6.45 (*0-8497-5957-9*, W22XE) Kjos.

— Alto Saxophone. (Standard of Excellence Ser.: Bk. 1). 1995. 6.45 (*0-8497-5932-3*, W21XE) Kjos.

— Alto Saxophone. (Standard of Excellence Ser.: Bk. 3). 1996. 6.45 (*0-8497-5981-1*, W23XE) Kjos.

— Baritone B. C. (Standard of Excellence Ser.: Bk. 1). 1993. 6.45 (*0-8497-5940-4*, W21BC) Kjos.

— Baritone B. C. (Standard of Excellence Ser.: Bk. 2). 1993. 6.45 (*0-8497-5965-X*, W22BC) Kjos.

— Baritone B. C. (Standard of Excellence Ser.: Bk. 3). 1996. 6.45 (*0-8497-5988-9*, W23BC) Kjos.

— Baritone Saxophone. (Standard of Excellence Ser.: Bk. 1). 1993. 6.45 (*0-8497-5934-X*, W21XR) Kjos.

— Baritone Saxophone. (Standard of Excellence Ser.: Bk. 2). 1993. 6.45 (*0-8497-5959-5*, W22XR) Kjos.

— Baritone Saxophone. (Standard of Excellence Ser.: Bk. 3). 1996. 6.45 (*0-8497-5983-8*, W23XR) Kjos.

— Baritone T. C. (Standard of Excellence Ser.: Bk. 1). 1993. 6.45 (*0-8497-5941-2*, W21TC) Kjos.

— Baritone T. C. (Standard of Excellence Ser.: Bk. 2). 1993. 6.45 (*0-8497-5966-8*, W22TC) Kjos.

— Baritone T. C. (Standard of Excellence Ser.: Bk. 3). 1996. 6.45 (*0-8497-5989-7*, W23TC) Kjos.

— Bass Clarinet. (Standard of Excellence Ser.: Bk. 1). 1993. 6.45 (*0-8497-5931-5*, W21CLB) Kjos.

— Bass Clarinet. (Standard of Excellence Ser.: Bk. 2). 1993. 6.45 (*0-8497-5956-0*, W22CLB) Kjos.

— Bass Clarinet. (Standard of Excellence Ser.: Bk. 3). 1996. 6.45 (*0-8497-5980-3*, W23CLB) Kjos.

— Bassoon. (Standard of Excellence Ser.: Bk. 1). 1993. 6.45 (*0-8497-5928-5*, W21BN) Kjos.

— Bassoon. (Standard of Excellence Ser.: Bk. 2). 1993. 6.45 (*0-8497-5953-6*, W22BN) Kjos.

— Bassoon. (Standard of Excellence Ser.: Bk. 3). 1996. 6.45 (*0-8497-5977-3*, W23BN) Kjos.

— Clarinet. (Standard of Excellence Ser.: Bk. 2). 1993. 6.45 (*0-8497-5954-4*, W22CL) Kjos.

— Clarinet. (Standard of Excellence Ser.: Bk. 1). 1996. 6.45 (*0-8497-5929-3*, W21CL) Kjos.

— Clarinet. (Standard of Excellence Ser.: Bk. 3). 1996. pap. 6.45 (*0-8497-5978-1*, W23CLB) Kjos.

— Conductor Score. (Standard of Excellence Ser.: Bk. 3). 1996. 49.95 (*0-8497-5974-9*, W23F) Kjos.

— Cornet - Trumpet. (Standard of Excellence Ser.: Bk. 1). 1993. 6.45 (*0-8497-5935-8*, W21TP) Kjos.

— Cornet/Trumpet. (Standard of Excellence Ser.: Bk. 2). 1993. 6.45 (*0-8497-5960-9*, W22TP) Kjos.

— Cornet/Trumpet. (Standard of Excellence Ser.: Bk. 3). 1996. 6.45 (*0-8497-5984-6*, W23TP) Kjos.

— Eb Alto Clarinet. (Standard of Excellence Ser.: Bk. 1). 1993. 6.45 (*0-8497-5930-7*, W21CLE) Kjos.

— Eb Alto Clarinet. (Standard of Excellence Ser.: Bk. 2). 1994. 6.45 (*0-8497-5955-2*, W22CLE) Kjos.

— Eb Alto Clarinet. (Standard of Excellence Ser.: Bk. 3). 1996. 6.45 (*0-8497-5979-X*, W23CLE) Kjos.

— Eb Alto Horn. (Standard of Excellence Ser.: Bk. 1). 1993. 6.95 (*0-8497-5937-4*, W21HE) Kjos.

— Eb Alto Horn. (Standard of Excellence Ser.: Bk. 2). 1994. 6.95 (*0-8497-5962-5*, W22HE) Kjos.

— Eb Alto Horn. (Standard of Excellence Ser.: Bk. 3). 1996. 6.45 (*0-8497-5986-2*, W23HE) Kjos.

P

— Electric Bass. (Standard of Excellence Ser.: Bk. 3). 1996. 6.45 (0-8497-5994-3, W23EBS) Kjos.
— Flute. (Standard of Excellence Ser.: Bk. 1). 1993. 6.45 (0-8497-5926-9, W21FL) Kjos.
— Flute. (Standard of Excellence Ser.: Bk. 2). 1993. 6.45 (0-8497-5951-X, W22FL) Kjos.
— Flute. (Standard of Excellence Ser.: Bk. 3). 1996. 6.45 (0-8497-5975-7, W23FL) Kjos.
— French Horn. (Standard of Excellence Ser.: Bk. 1). 1993. 6.95 (0-8497-5936-6, W21HF) Kjos.
— French Horn. (Standard of Excellence Ser.: Bk. 2). 1994. 6.95 (0-8497-5961-7, W22HF) Kjos.
— French Horn. (Standard of Excellence Ser.: Bk. 3). 1996. 6.95 (0-8497-5985-4, W23HF) Kjos.
— Music Theory Workbook. (Standard of Excellence Ser.: Bk. 3). 1996. wbk. ed. 6.45 (0-8497-0517-7, L23) Kjos.
— Oboe. (Standard of Excellence Ser.: Bk. 1). 1993. 6.45 (0-8497-5927-7, W21OB) Kjos.
— Oboe. (Standard of Excellence Ser.: Bk. 2). 1993. 6.45 (0-8497-5952-8, W22OB) Kjos.
— Oboe. (Standard of Excellence Ser.: Bk. 3). 1996. 6.45 (0-8497-5976-5, W23OB) Kjos.
— Percussion (Drums & Mallets) (Standard of Excellence Ser.: Bk. 3). 1996. 6.95 (0-8497-5991-9, W23PR) Kjos.
— Piano - Guitar. (Standard of Excellence Ser.: Bk. 3). 1996. 6.45 (0-8497-5993-5, W23PG) Kjos.
— Standard of Excellence: Full Score, Bk. 1. 1994. audio 8.95 (0-614-03107-9); audio compact disk 12.95 (0-614-03108-7, W22CD1) Kjos.
— Standard of Excellence: Full Score, Bk. 1. 660p. 1995. 49.95 (0-8497-5948-X, W21F) Kjos.
— Standard of Excellence: Full Score, Bk. 2. 1994. audio 8.95 (0-614-03111-7); audio compact disk 12.95 (0-318-72755-2, W22CD2) Kjos.
— Standard of Excellence: Full Score, Bk. 2. 640p. 1995. 49.95 (0-8497-5950-1, W22F) Kjos.
— Standard of Excellence: Full Score, Bk. 2: Theory & History Workbook. LC 97-184572. 640p. 1995. 5.95 (0-8497-0516-9, L22) Kjos.
— Tenor Saxophone. (Standard of Excellence Ser.: Bk. 1). 1993. 6.45 (0-8497-5933-1, W21XB) Kjos.
— Tenor Saxophone. (Standard of Excellence Ser.: Bk. 2). 1993. 6.45 (0-8497-5958-7, W22XB) Kjos.
— Tenor Saxophone. (Standard of Excellence Ser.: Bk. 3). 1996. 6.45 (0-8497-5982-X, W23XB) Kjos.
— Timpani. (Standard of Excellence Ser.: Bk. 3). 1996. 6.45 (0-8497-5992-7, W23TM) Kjos.
— Trombone. (Standard of Excellence Ser.: Bk. 1). 1993. 6.45 (0-8497-5938-2, W21TB) Kjos.
— Trombone. (Standard of Excellence Ser.: Bk. 2). 1993. 6.45 (0-8497-5963-3, W22TB) Kjos.
— Trombone. (Standard of Excellence Ser.: Bk. 3). 1996. 6.45 (0-8497-5987-0, W23TB) Kjos.
— Tuba. (Standard of Excellence Ser.: Bk. 3). 1996. 6.45 (0-8497-5990-0, W23BS) Kjos.

Pearson, Bruce, et al. Best in Class Bk. 1: Score & Manual, Baritone BC. 1982. 5.45 (0-8497-5846-7, W3BC) Kjos.
— Best in Class Bk. 1: Score & Manual, Baritone TC. 1982. 5.45 (0-8497-5845-9, W3TC) Kjos.
— Best in Class Bk. 1: Score & Manual, Bassoon. 1982. 5.45 (0-8497-5835-1, W3BN) Kjos.
— Best in Class Bk. 1: Score & Manual, Bb Bass Clarinet. 1982. 5.45 (0-8497-5838-6, W3CLB) Kjos.
— Best in Class Bk. 1: Score & Manual, Bb Clarinet. 1982. 5.45 (0-8497-5836-X, W3CL) Kjos.
— Best in Class Bk. 1: Score & Manual, Bb Tenor Sax. 1982. 5.45 (0-8497-5840-8, W3XB) Kjos.
— Best in Class Bk. 1: Score & Manual, Bb Tuba BC. 1982. 5.45 (0-8497-5847-5, W3BS) Kjos.
— Best in Class Bk. 1: Score & Manual, Bb Tuba TC. 1982. 5.45 (0-8497-8341-0, W3BSG) Kjos.
— Best in Class Bk. 1: Score & Manual, C Flute. 1982. 5.45 (0-8497-5833-5, W3FL) Kjos.
— Best in Class Bk. 1: Score & Manual, Eb Alto Clarinet. 1982. 5.45 (0-8497-5837-8, W3CLE) Kjos.
— Best in Class Bk. 1: Score & Manual, Eb Alto Horn. 1982. 5.45 (0-8497-5851-3, W3HE) Kjos.
— Best in Class Bk. 1: Score & Manual, Eb Alto Sax. 1982. 5.45 (0-8497-5839-4, W3XE) Kjos.
— Best in Class Bk. 1: Score & Manual, Eb Baritone Sax. 1982. 5.45 (0-8497-5841-6, W3XR) Kjos.
— Best in Class Bk. 1: Score & Manual, Eb Tuba BC. 1982. 5.45 (0-8497-8342-9, W3BSE) Kjos.
— Best in Class Bk. 1: Score & Manual, Eb Tuba TC. 1982. 5.45 (0-8497-8359-3, W3BSET) Kjos.
— Best in Class Bk. 1: Score & Manual, French Horn. 1982. 5.45 (0-8497-5843-2, W3HF) Kjos.
— Best in Class Bk. 1: Score & Manual, Oboe. 1982. 5.45 (0-8497-5834-3, W3OB) Kjos.
— Best in Class Bk. 1: Score & Manual, Percussion. 1982. 5.45 (0-8497-5849-1, W3PR) Kjos.
— Best in Class Bk. 1: Score & Manual, Piano Accompaniment. 1982. 5.45 (0-8497-5848-3, W3PA) Kjos.
— Best in Class Bk. 1: Score & Manual, Score & Manual. 1981. 19.95 (0-8497-5850-5, W3F) Kjos.
— Best in Class Bk. 1: Score & Manual, Trombone. 1982. 5.45 (0-8497-5844-0, W3TB) Kjos.
— Best in Class Bk. 1: Score & Manual, Trombone TC. 1982. 5.45 (0-8497-8340-2, W3TBG) Kjos.
— Best in Class Bk. 1: Score & Manual, Trumpet. 1982. 5.45 (0-8497-5842-4, W3TP) Kjos.
— Encore: Conductor Score & Manual. 248p. 1985. 19.95 (0-8497-5906-4, W5F) Kjos.
— Encore: Conductor Score & Manual, Alto Horn. 1989. 3.95 (0-8497-5916-1, W5HE) Kjos.
— Encore: Conductor Score & Manual, Alto Sax. 1989. 3.95 (0-8497-5913-7, W5XE) Kjos.
— Encore: Conductor Score & Manual, Baritone Sax. 1989. 3.95 (0-8497-5915-3, W5XR) Kjos.
— Encore: Conductor Score & Manual, Bass Clarinet. 1989. 3.95 (0-8497-5912-9, W5CLB) Kjos.
— Encore: Conductor Score & Manual, Bassoon. 1989. 3.95 (0-8497-5909-9, W5BN) Kjos.
— Encore: Conductor Score & Manual, Bb Clarinet. 1989. 3.95 (0-8497-5910-2, W5CL) Kjos.
— Encore: Conductor Score & Manual, Eb Clarinet. 1989. 3.95 (0-8497-5911-0, W5CLE) Kjos.
— Encore: Conductor Score & Manual, Flute. 1989. 3.95 (0-8497-5907-2, W5FL) Kjos.
— Encore: Conductor Score & Manual, Oboe. 1989. 3.95 (0-8497-5908-0, W5OB) Kjos.
— Encore: Conductor Score & Manual, Tenor Sax. 1989. 3.95 (0-8497-5914-5, W5XB) Kjos.

Pearson, Bruce, jt. auth. see Sorenson, Dean.

Pearson, Brue. BBb Tuba. (Standard of Excellence Ser.: Bk. 2). 1997. 6.45 (0-8497-5968-4, W22BSG) Kjos.
— BBb Tuba T.C. (Standard of Excellence Ser.: Bk. 1). 1997. 6.45 (0-8497-5943-9, W21BSG) Kjos.
— Trombone T. C. (Standard of Excellence Ser.: Bk. 1). 1997. 6.45 (0-8497-5939-0, W21TBG) Kjos.
— Trombone T. C. (Standard of Excellence Ser.: Bk. 2). 1997. 6.45 (0-8497-5964-1, W22TBG) Kjos.

Pearson, C. Safe Thermal Imaging of Electrical Systems (Up to & Including 1000 V A. C.) 1997. pap. 100.00 (0-86022-470-8, Pub. by Build Servs Info Assn) St Mut.

Pearson, C. C. Readjuster Movement in Virginia. 1990. 16.50 (0-8446-1344-4) Peter Smith.

***Pearson, C. C. & Barnard, N.** Guidance & the Stand Specification for Thermal Imaging of LV Electrical Installations. 1999. pap. 100.00 (0-86022-516-X, Pub. by Build Servs Info Assn) St Mut.

Pearson, C. C. & Hendricks, J. Edwin. Liquor & Anti-liquor in Virginia, 1619-1919. LC 67-18530. 354p. reprint ed. pap. 109.80 (0-608-11977-6, 202343300033) Bks Demand.

Pearson, C. E. Above & Below the ABSeas. (Illus.). 56p. (Orig.). (J). (gr. k-5). 1994. pap. 9.95 (0-9640585-0-2) Mt Hope Pubng.

Pearson, C. J. Field Crop Ecosystems. (Ecosystems of the World Ser.: Vol. 18). 576p. 1992. 289.00 (0-444-88675-3) Elsevier.

Pearson, C. J., ed. Control of Crop Productivity. 339p. 1985. text 104.00 (0-12-548280-9) Acad Pr.

Pearson, C. J. & Ison, R. L. Agronomy of Grassland Systems. 2nd ed. LC 96-45572. (Illus.). 234p. (C). 1997. pap. text 32.95 (0-521-56889-7) Cambridge U Pr.

Pearson, C. J. & Ison, Ray L. Agronomy of Grassland Systems. 2nd ed. LC 96-45572. (Illus.). 234p. (C). 1997. text 80.00 (0-521-56010-1) Cambridge U Pr.

Pearson, C. J., et al. The Ecology of Tropical Food Crops. 2nd ed. (Illus.). 440p. (C). 1995. text 74.95 (0-521-41062-2); pap. text 31.95 (0-521-42264-7) Cambridge U Pr.

Pearson, C. W. The Last Generation. 37p. (Orig.). (C). 1997. pap. write for info. (0-9649675-2-9) Gospel Gold.

Pearson, Carl E. Calculus & Ordinary Differential Equations. (Plastics Ser.). 1997. pap. 15.95 (0-340-62530-9, VNR) Wiley.
— Theoretical Elasticity. LC 59-9283. 230p. reprint ed. pap. 65.60 (0-608-30454-9, 2001586) Bks Demand.

Pearson, Carl E., jt. auth. see Carrier, George F.

Pearson, Carlton. Armed for Battle. 48p. 1991. mass mkt. 4.99 (0-89274-890-7, HH-890) Harrison Hse.
— Breaking the Curse. 48p. 1991. mass mkt. 4.99 (0-89274-891-5, HH-891) Harrison Hse.
— Every Single One of You. LC 94-222120. 176p. 1994. pap. 7.99 (0-89274-629-7, HH-629) Harrison Hse.
— Hope. 48p. 1991. mass mkt. 4.99 (0-89274-889-3, HH-889) Harrison Hse.
— Is There a Man in the House? 196p. (Orig.). 1996. pap. 10.99 (1-56043-270-5, Treasure Hse) Destiny Image.
— I've Got a Feelin' Everything's Gonna Be All Right. Date not set. pap. 9.99 (0-89274-911-3) Harrison Hse.

Pearson, Carol L. Don't Count Your Chickens until They Cry Wolf: Musical. (J). 1979. 6.00 (0-87602-122-4) Anchorage.
— I Believe in Make Believe. (J). (gr. k up). 1984. pap. 6.00 (0-87602-255-7) Anchorage.

***Pearson, Carol L.** The Lesson: A Fable for Our Times. LC 98-4353. (Fable for Our Times Ser.). (Illus.). 32p. 1998. 9.95 (0-87905-862-5) Gibbs Smith Pub.

Pearson, Carol L. The Modern Magi: A Christmas Fable. LC 98-18720. 96p. 1999. text 14.95 (0-312-19300-9) St Martin.
— Morning Glory Mother. LC 97-912. 101p. 1997. text 13.95 (0-312-15592-1) St Martin.
— Morning Glory Mother. 1997. 13.95 (0-614-27909-7) St Martin.
— Mother Wove the Morning: A One-Woman Play. LC 92-31236. 1992. write for info. (1-56236-307-7, Pub. by Aspen Bks) Origin Bk Sales.
— Move On! 50p. (Orig.). 1995. pap. 4.50 (1-57514-171-X, 1140) Encore Perform Pub.
— A Stranger for Christmas. LC 96-19004. 112p. 1996. text 13.95 (0-312-14680-9) St Martin.
— A Stranger for Christmas. large type ed. LC 96-27255. 1996. 20.95 (0-7838-1914-5, G K Hall Lrg Type) Mac Lib Ref.
— What Love Is: A Fable for Our Times. LC 99-12670. (Fable for Our Times Ser.: Vol. 2). (Illus.). 32p. 1999. 9.95 (0-87905-918-4) Gibbs Smith Pub.
— Women I Have Known & Been. 1993. 11.95 (1-882723-03-1) Gold Leaf Pr.

Pearson, Carol Lynn. The Christmas Thief. (YA). 1995. pap. 4.95 (1-882723-23-6, Pub. by Gold Leaf Pr) Origin Bk Sales.

***Pearson, Carol Lynn.** Girlfriend, You Are the Best! (Fable for Our Times Ser.: Vol. 4). (Illus.). 32p. 2000. 9.95 (1-58685-008-3) Gibbs Smith Pub.

Pearson, Carol Lynn. Good-bye, I Love You. LC 93-35914. 1995. pap. 9.95 (1-882723-04-X, Pub. by Gold Leaf Pr) Origin Bk Sales.
— Picture Window: A Carol Lynn Pearson Collection. Utley, Jennifer, ed. LC 96-5449. (Illus.). 201p. 1996. 16.95 (1-882723-27-9, Pub. by Gold Leaf Pr) Origin Bk Sales.

***Pearson, Carol Lynn.** Will You Still Be My Daughter? A Fable for Our Times. LC 99-59127. (Illus.). 32p. 2000. 9.95 (0-87905-959-1) Gibbs Smith Pub.

***Pearson, Carol Lynn & Pearson, Emily C.** Fuzzy Red Bathrobe: Questions from the Heart for Mothers & Daughters. LC 00-23761. (Illus.). 80p. 2000. 12.95 (1-58685-003-2) Gibbs Smith Pub.

Pearson, Carol S. Awakening the Heroes Within: Twelve Archetypes to Help Us Find Ourselves & Transform Our World. LC 90-55296. 352p. (Orig.). 1991. pap. 19.00 (0-06-250678-1, Pub. by Harper SF) HarpC.
— Hero Within - Rev. & Expanded Ed. Six Archetypes We Live By. 3rd expanded rev. ed. LC 98-17531. (Illus.). 368p. 1998. pap. 14.00 (0-06-251555-1, Pub. by Harper SF) HarpC.
— Introduction to Archetypes. 1998. pap. write for info. (1-878287-43-5) Type & Temperament.
— Invisible Forces II: Harnessing the Power of Archetypes to Improve Your Career & Workplace. (Orig.). 1997. pap., wbk. ed. 17.95 (1-878287-46-X) Type & Temperament.
— Invisible Forces I: Using the Power of Archetypes to Heal Family Systems. 1999. pap., wbk. ed. write for info. (1-878287-47-8) Type & Temperament.
— Thinking about Business Differently: Organizational Systems & Leadership Archetypes. 1998. pap. text 8.95 (0-9665472-0-9) Innovision.
— Type & Archetype. (Orig.). 1999. pap. write for info. (1-878287-44-3) Type & Temperament.

Pearson, Carol S., et al, eds. Educating the Majority: Improving Higher Education for Women. (C). 1987. write for info. (0-318-63183-0, 2014) Macmillan.

Pearson, Charles, ed. Multinational Corporations, Environment, & the Third World: Business Matters. LC 86-19810. (Duke Press Policy Studies). xvi, 295p. 1987. text 54.95 (0-8223-0707-3); pap. text 21.95 (0-8223-0761-8) Duke.

Pearson, Charles, jt. auth. see Johnson, Nils.

Pearson, Charles E. & Hoffman, Paul E. Last Voyage of el Nuevo Constante: Wreck & Recovery of an Eighteenth Century Spanish Ship off the Louisiana Coast. LC 94-27046. (Illus.). 264p. 1994. 29.95 (0-8071-1918-0) La State U Pr.

Pearson, Charles E., et al. Contributions to the Archeology of the Great Bend Region of the Red River Valley, Southwest Arkansas. Schambach, Frank F. & Rackerby, Frank, eds. (Illus.). 140p. 1982. pap. 4.00 (1-56349-046-3, RS22) AR Archaeol.

***Pearson, Charles S.** Economics & the Global Environment. (Illus.). 608p. (C). 2000. text Price not set. (0-521-77002-5); pap. text Price not set. (0-521-77988-X) Cambridge U Pr.

Pearson, Charles S. & Pryor, Anthony. Environment: North & South; An Economic Interpretation. LC 77-11143. (Illus.). 377p. reprint ed. pap. 116.90 (0-608-10712-3, 202249900027) Bks Demand.

Pearson, Cheryl, ed. see Trostel, Scott D.

Pearson, Claudia, ed. NOLS Cookery. 4th ed. (Illus.). 160p. 1997. pap. 12.95 (0-8117-2860-9) Stackpole.

Pearson, Clifford A. Indonesia Style. LC 98-19131. 10p. 1998. 50.00 (1-58093-012-3, Pub. by Monacelli Pr) Penguin Putnam.

Pearson, Clifford A., ed. Modern American Houses: Four Decades of Award-Winning Design in Architectural Record. LC 95-48352. (Illus.). 240p. 1996. 49.50 (0-8109-3334-9, Pub. by Abrams) Time Warner.

Pearson, Colin. The Conservation of Marine Archaeological Objects. (Conservation & Museology Ser.). (Illus.). 360p. 1988. 235.00 (0-408-10668-9) Buttrwrth-Heinemann.

***Pearson, Craig.** The Complete Book of Yogic Flying: Enjoy Bubbling Bliss, Optimize Brain Functioning & Mind-Body Coordination, Create Peace & Harmony in the World. LC 00-23070. 2000. write for info. (0-923569-27-8) Maharishi U Mgmt Pr.

Pearson, Craig. Make Your Own Games Workshop. (Crafts Workshop Ser.). (J). (gr. 3-8). 1982. pap. 11.99 (0-8224-9782-4) Fearon Teacher Aids.

Pearson, Crystal K. Spicy Singles, Vol. I. (Illus.). 130p. (Orig.). 1992. pap. text 9.50 (0-9631853-0-6) Spicy Singles.

Pearson, Cynthia, jt. auth. see Freidlander, John.

Pearson, Cynthia, jt. auth. see Stubbs, Margaret.

Pearson, D., jt. auth. see Conrah, T.

Pearson, D., jt. auth. see Conrans, T.

Pearson, D. B., ed. Quantum Scattering & Spectral Theory. (Techniques of Physics Ser.). 519p. 1988. text 160.00 (0-12-548260-4) Acad Pr.

Pearson, D. W., et al, eds. Artificial Neural Nets & Genetic Algorithms: Proceedings of the International Conference in Ales, France, 1995. LC 95-10560. 522p. 1995. 140.00 (3-211-82692-0) Spr-Verlag.

Pearson, Daniel. Baseball in 1889: Players vs Owners. LC 92-63282. 234p. (C). 1993. 42.95 (0-87972-618-0) Bowling Green Univ Popular Press.

Pearson, Daniel M. The Americanization of Carl Aaron Swensson. LC 77-151736. (Augustana Historical Society Publications: No.25). 169p. 1977. 5.95 (0-910184-25-9) Augustana.

Pearson, Darrell, jt. auth. see Dickie, Steve.

Pearson, Darryl. Prayer, Vol. 2. Powell, Kara Eckmann, ed. (True Life Ser.: No. 2). 1999. pap. 14.99 (0-8307-2408-7, Gospel Light) Gospel Lght.

Pearson, Dave. Mining in the West. LC 95-20554. 166p. (gr. 10). 1996. pap. 24.95 (0-88740-933-4) Schiffer.

Pearson, David. Earth to Spirit: In Search of Natural Architecture. LC 93-47523. (Illus.). 160p. 1995. 29.25 (0-8118-0702-9); pap. 17.95 (0-8118-0731-2) Chronicle Bks.
— Natural House Catalog: Everything You Need to Create an Environmentally Friendly Home. LC 95-25220. (Illus.). 288p. 1996. per. 23.00 (0-684-80198-1, Fireside) S&S Trade Pap.
— The New Natural House Book. LC 98-228688. 304p. 1998. per. 22.00 (0-684-84733-7) S&S Trade Pap.
— Provenance Research in Book History. deluxe rev. ed. 352p. (C). 1998. reprint ed. 49.95 (1-884718-79-5, 53851RB) Oak Knoll.
— Provenance Research in Book History. 352p. (C). 1998. reprint ed. pap. 29.95 (1-884718-80-9, 53852RB) Oak Knoll.
— Provenance Research in Book History: A Handbook. (The British Library Studies in the History of the Book). (Illus.). 400p. 1994. 100.00 (0-7123-0318-9, Pub. by B23tish Library) U of Toronto Pr.
— Provenance Research in Book History: A Handbook. (British Library Studies in the History of the Book). (Illus.). 336p. 1994. 90.00 (0-7123-0344-8) U of Toronto Pr.

Pearson, David & Middleton, David. The New Key to Ecuador & the Galapagos. 3rd rev. ed. (New Key Guides Ser.). (Illus.). 400p. 1997. pap. 16.95 (1-56975-075-0) Ulysses Pr.
— The New Key to Ecuador & the Galapagos. 3rd rev. ed. (New Key Travel Ser.). (Illus.). 480p. 1999. pap. 17.95 (1-56975-199-4, Pub. by Ulysses Pr) Publishers Group.

***Pearson, David E.** The World Wide Military Command & Control System: Evolution & Effectiveness. LC 99-462377. 2000. write for info. (1-58566-078-7) Air Univ.

Pearson, David P., et al. Handbook of Reading Research, 1. LC 83-26838. 912p. 1989. text 70.33 (0-582-28119-9, 71177) Longman.

Pearson-Davis, Susan, ed. see Zeder, Suzan L.

Pearson, Debora. Alphabake: A Cookbook & Cookie Cutter Set. LC 95-13379. (Illus.). 32p. (J). (ps-3). 1995. pap. 16.99 (0-525-45461-6, Dutton Child) Peng Put Young Read.
— Cookie Count & Bake: A Cookbook & Cookie Cutter Set. (Illus.). 32p. (J). (ps-2). 1998. pap. 16.95 (1-895897-55-6) Somerville Hse.
— Cookie Critters: A Cookbook & Cookie Cutter Set. (Illus.). 32p. (J). (ps-2). 1998. pap. 17.95 (1-895897-97-1) Somerville Hse.

***Pearson, Debora.** Hard Working Wheels. (Mighty Wheels Ser.). (Illus.). 24p. (J). 2000. lib. bdg. 15.95 (1-55037-615-2, Pub. by Annick Pr) Firefly Bks Ltd.
— Hard Working Wheels. (Mighty Wheels Ser.). (Illus.). 24p. (J). 2000. pap. 5.95 (1-55037-614-4, Pub. by Annick Pr) Firefly Bks Ltd.
— Hard Working Wheels. (Illus.). (J). 2000. 11.40 (0-606-18137-7) Turtleback.
— Load 'em up Trucks. (Mighty Wheels Ser.). (Illus.). 24p. (J). (ps-k). 1999. lib. bdg. 15.95 (1-55037-593-8, Pub. by Annick Pr) Firefly Bks Ltd.

Pearson, Debora. Load 'em up Trucks. (Mighty Wheels Ser.). (Illus.). 24p. (J). (ps-3). 1999. pap. 5.95 (1-55037-592-X, Pub. by Annick Pr) Firefly Bks Ltd.
— Ready Set Grow. 1996. 9.95 (0-590-62986-7) Scholastic Inc.
— Ready, Set, Grow! With the Earth Buddies. (Illus.). 48p. (J). (ps-3). 1998. pap. 9.95 (1-895897-56-4) Somerville Hse.

***Pearson, Debora.** Rough Tough Wheels. (Mighty Wheels Ser.). (Illus.). 24p. (J). (ps). 2000. lib. bdg. 17.95 (1-55037-637-3, Pub. by Annick Pr); per. 5.95 (1-55037-636-5, Pub. by Annick Pr) Firefly Bks Ltd.

Pearson, Debora, jt. auth. see Coffey, Maria.

Pearson, Debora, jt. auth. see Raskin, Lawrie.

Pearson, Debora, jt. auth. see Turnbull, Andy.

Pearson, Deborah. Alphabake: A Cookbook & Cookie Cutter Set. (Illus.). 32p. (J). (ps-2). 1998. pap. 16.95 (1-895897-52-1) Somerville Hse.
— Cookie Critters: A Cookbook & Cookie Cutter Set. (Illus.). 32p. (J). (gr. k-4). 1997. pap. 16.99 (0-525-45833-6) NAL.

Pearson, Dennis A. Classic Lanterns. LC 98-12072. 144p. 1998. pap. 29.95 (0-7643-0487-9) Schiffer.

Pearson, Diane. The Loom of the Tancred. large type ed. (Romance Ser.). 1974. 27.99 (0-85456-303-2) Ulverscroft.

***Pearson, Diane.** The Summer of the Barshinskeys. 2000. pap. 8.95 (0-552-12641-1, Pub. by Transworld Publishers Ltd) Trafalgar.

Pearson, Diane. Voices of Summer. large type ed. 524p. 1993. 27.99 (0-7505-0455-2) Ulverscroft.

Pearson, Dorothy M., intro. Perspectives on Equity & Justice in Social Work. LC 93-70219. (Carl A. Scott Memorial Lectures, 1988-1992). (Illus.). 88p. (Orig.). (C). 1993. pap. text 7.00 (0-87293-034-3) Coun Soc Wk Ed.

Pearson, D'Orsay W., ed. The Merry Wives of Windsor: An Annotated Bibliography. (Garland Shakespeare Bibliographies Ser.). 500p. Date not set. text 75.00 (0-8240-4434-7) Garland.

Pearson, D'Orsay W., ed. Pedro Ciruelo's a Treatise Reproving All Superstitions & Forms of Witchcraft: Very Necessary & Useful for All Good Christians Zealous for Their Salvation. Maio, Eugene, tr. LC 74-4979. 366p. 1976. 38.50 (0-8386-1580-5) Fairleigh Dickinson.

Pearson, Douglas, jt. auth. see Gesme, Carole.

Pearson, Drew & Allen, Robert S. The Nine Old Men. LC 73-21727. (American Constitutional & Legal History Ser). 325p. 1974. reprint ed. lib. bdg. 45.00 (0-306-70609-1) Da Capo.

P

An Asterisk (*) at the beginning of an entry indicates that the title is appearing for the first time.

Pearson, Durk & Shaw, Sandy. Freedom of Informed Choice: FDA Versus Nutrient Supplements. 126p. (Orig.). 1994. pap. text 6.95 (*0-9636249-0-3*) Com Sense NJ.

— Life Extension: A Practical Scientific Approach. 1987. mass mkt. 16.99 (*0-446-38735-5*, Pub. by Warner Bks) Little.

— Life Extension: Adding Years to Your Life & Life to Your Years: A Practical Scientific Approach. LC 80-27589. (Illus.). 600p. (Orig.). 1983. mass mkt. 10.95 (*0-446-87990-8*, Pub. by Warner Bks) Little.

— The Life Extension Companion. LC 83-42592. (Illus.). 430p. (Orig.). 1986. mass mkt. 10.95 (*0-446-38560-3*, Pub. by Warner Bks) Little.

— The Life Extension Weight Loss Program. 1994. reprint ed. lib. bdg. 29.95 (*1-56849-543-9*) Buccaneer Bks.

Pearson, E. K., jt. auth. see Neyman, Jerry.

Pearson, Edmund. Queer Books. (Illus.). 298p. 1990. pap. 25.00 (*0-87556-763-0*) Saifer.

Pearson, Edmund L. Books in Black or Red. LC 77-93371. (Essay Index Reprint Ser.). 1977. 23.95 (*0-8369-1267-5*) Ayer.

— Secret Book, Vol. 1. LC 72-3419. (Short Story Index Reprint Ser.). 1977. reprint ed. 20.95 (*0-8369-4159-4*) Ayer.

— Studies in Murder. LC 98-50781. (Illus.). 1999. 35.00 (*0-8142-0819-3*) Ohio St U Pr.

Pearson, Edmund Lester. Studies in Murder. LC 98-50781. (Illus.). 311p. 1999. pap. text 17.95 (*0-8142-5022-X*) Ohio St U Pr.

Pearson, Edward, ed. Designs Against Charleston: The Trial Record of the Denmark Vesey Slave Conspiracy of 1822. LC 98-5871. (Illus.). 408p. 1999. 49.95 (*0-8078-2446-1*) U of NC Pr.

Pearson, Edward S. Law for European Business Studies. 480p. (Orig.). 1994. pap. 62.50 (*0-273-60474-0*, Pub. by Pitman Pub) Trans-Atl Phila.

Pearson, Egon Sharpe. Selected Papers. 327p. 1966. lib. bdg. 35.00 (*0-521-05926-7*) Lubrecht & Cramer.

— Student: A Statistical Biography of William Sealy Gosset. Plackett, Robert L. & Barnard, G. A., eds. (Illus.). 152p. 1990. 35.00 (*0-19-852227-4*) OUP.

Pearson, Egon Sharpe, ed. The History of Statistics in the 17th & 18th Centuries, Against the Changing Background of Intellectual, Scientific & Religious Thought: Lectures Given at the University College London During the Academic Sessions 1921-33. 1978. 45.00 (*0-85264-250-4*) Lubrecht & Cramer.

Pearson, Egon Sharpe & Hartley, H. O., eds. Biometrika Tables for Statisticians, Vol. 1. 3rd ed. 270p. 1976. lib. bdg. 75.00 (*0-904653-10-2*) Lubrecht & Cramer.

— Biometrika Tables for Statisticians: Reprint with Corrections, Vol. 2. 385p. 1976. reprint ed. lib. bdg. 75.00 (*0-904653-11-0*) Lubrecht & Cramer.

Pearson, Elizabeth W., ed. Letters from Port Royal, 1862-1868. LC 69-18547. (American Negro: His History & Literature. Series 2). 1968. reprint ed. 17.95 (*0-405-01886-X*) Ayer.

Pearson, Emily C. Cousin Franck's Household: or Scenes in the Old Dominion, by Pochanontas. LC 72-1517. (Black Heritage Library Collection). 1977. reprint ed. 28.95 (*0-8369-9041-2*) Ayer.

— The Poor White: or The Rebel Conscript. LC 72-1822. (Illus.). 326p. 1977. reprint ed. 28.95 (*0-8369-9042-0*) Ayer.

Pearson, Emily C., jt. auth. see Pearson, Carol Lynn.

Pearson, Eric R. Complete Guide to Fiber Optic Cable System Installation. LC 96-23138. (Electrical Trades Ser.). 224p. 1996. mass mkt. 48.95 (*0-8273-7318-X*) Delmar.

Pearson, Eunice W., ed. see Martin, Janet L.

Pearson, Eunice W., ed. see Martin, Janet L. & Todnem, Allen.

Pearson, Eva Mildred Mykleby. They Did Not Have Horns. The Vikings of Norway. LC 97-95075. (Illus.). xvi, 240p. 1998. pap. 22.95 (*0-9662510-1-6*) Norbakk Pr.

***Pearson, Evelyn Bitner.** Chronicle of a Pittsburg Family. Kidney, Walter C. & Sturgess, Louise, eds. LC 99-70702. (Illus.). 168p. 1999. 8.95 (*0-916670-20-1*) Pitt Hist & Landmks Found.

Pearson, Ewan, jt. auth. see Gilbert, Jeremy.

Pearson, F. C. Pyrogens: Endotoxins & LAL Testing & Depyrogenation. (Advances in Parenteral Science Ser.: Vol. 2). (Illus.). 288p. 1985. text 135.00 (*0-8247-7436-1*) Dekker.

— Pyrogens: Endotoxins, LAL Testing & Depyrogenation. 2nd expanded rev. ed. (Advances in Parenteral Science Ser.). (Illus.). Date not set. write for info. (*0-8247-9362-5*, 9362-5) Dekker.

Pearson, F. Griffith, et al, eds. Thoracic Surgery. LC 94-42025. 1995. text 215.00 (*0-443-08798-9*) Church.

Pearson, F.Griffith, et al. Esophageal Surgery. LC 94-24093. 1995. text 185.00 (*0-443-08832-2*) Church.

Pearson, Fred L., Jr. Spanish-Indian Relations in Florida: A Study of Two Visitas, 1657-1678. LC 90-14048. (Evolution of North American Indians Ser.: Vol. 15). 336p. 1990. reprint ed. text 10.00 (*0-8240-2510-5*) Garland.

Pearson, Fred R., et al. Holistic Health: An Individualized Approach. 3rd ed. 240p. (C). 1995. pap. text, per. 53.95 (*0-7872-1820-0*, 41182001) Kendall-Hunt.

Pearson, Frederic S. & Rochester, J. Martin. International Relations: The Global Condition in the Late 20th Century. 3rd ed. (C). 1991. text 43.00 (*0-07-049079-1*) McGraw.

— International Relations: The Global Condition in the Twenty-First Century. 4th ed. LC 97-9869. (C). 1997. text 41.50 (*0-07-049083-X*) McGraw.

Pearson, Frederic S., jt. auth. see Brzoska, Michael.

Pearson, Frederick, II. Map Projection Methods. Junkins, John L., ed. (Applied Mathematics for Science & Engineering Ser.). (Illus.). 304p. 1984. 31.00 (*0-915313-00-6*) Sigma Sci Inc.

— Map Projection Software. Junkins, John L., ed. (Applied Mathematics for Science & Engineering Ser.). (Illus.). 50p. 1984. 110.00 incl. disk (*0-317-06090-2*) Sigma Sci Inc.

Pearson, G., jt. ed. see Arnold, J.

***Pearson, Gardner W.** Regards of the Massachuetts Volunteer Militia: Called Out by the Governor of Massachusetts to Supress a Threatened Invasion During the War of 1812-14. 464p. 1999. reprint ed. pap. 58.00 (*0-7884-1326-0*, P109) Heritage Bk.

Pearson, Gardner W., contrib. by. Records of the Massachusetts Militia in the War of 1812-14. (Illus.). 448p. 1998. reprint ed. lib. bdg. 49.00 (*0-8328-9604-7*) Higginson Bk Co.

Pearson, Gayle. One Potato, Tu. 112p. (J). (gr. 4-6). 1994. pap. 2.95 (*0-590-47100-7*) Scholastic Inc.

— The Secret Box. LC 96-30459. (Illus.). 128p. (J). (gr. 3-7). 1997. 15.00 (*0-689-81379-1*) Atheneum Yung Read.

Pearson, Gayle & Conway, Timothy. Don't Call It Paradise. LC 98-45338. Orig. Title: The Truth about Buddy Mcbean. 153p. (J). (gr. 4-6). 1999. 15.00 (*0-689-82579-X*) Atheneum Yung Read.

Pearson, Georgene. A Light in the Window. (Orig.). (J). 1996. pap. 10.00 (*1-57502-143-9*) Morris Pubng.

Pearson, Gerald H., jt. auth. see English, Oliver S.

Pearson, Gordon. Strategic Thinking, Strategic Action. 2nd ed. LC 99-17235. 320p. (C). 1999. pap. 44.00 (*0-13-453580-4*) P-H.

***Pearson, Graham S.** The Unscom Saga: Chemical & Biological Weapons Non-Proliferation. LC 99-46377. (Global Issues Ser.). 2000. text 75.00 (*0-312-22959-3*) St Martin.

Pearson, H. M. Pilot, Diplomat & Garage Rat. (C). 1989. 49.00 (*0-7855-6628-7*) St Mut.

Pearson, H. W. & Green, F. B. Waste Stabilisation Ponds & the Reuse of Pond Effluents. (Water Science & Technology Ser.: Vol. 31). 432p. 1995. 115.00 (*0-08-042666-2*, Pergamon Pr) Elsevier.

Pearson, Hayden S. Country Flavor. 1977. 18.95 (*0-8369-7324-0*, 8117) Ayer.

— Country Flavor. (American Autobiography Ser.). 112p. 1995. reprint ed. lib. bdg. 69.00 (*0-7812-8611-5*) Rprt Serv.

— Countryman's Year. (American Autobiography Ser.). 192p. 1995. reprint ed. lib. bdg. 69.00 (*0-7812-8612-3*) Rprt Serv.

— Sea Flavor. LC 68-58809. (Essay Index Reprint Ser.). 1977. 15.95 (*0-8369-0051-0*) Ayer.

— Sea Flavor. (American Autobiography Ser.). 178p. 1995. reprint ed. lib. bdg. 69.00 (*0-7812-8613-1*) Rprt Serv.

Pearson, Heath. Origins of Law & Economics: The Economists' New Science of Law, 1830-1930. (Historical Perspectives on Modern Economics Ser.). 210p. (C). 1997. text 64.95 (*0-521-58143-5*) Cambridge U Pr.

Pearson, Helen B. Do What You Have the Power to Do! Studies of Six New Testament Women. LC 91-65727. 168p. 1992. pap. text 10.00 (*0-8358-0643-X*) Upper Room Bks.

Pearson, Henry G. An American Railroad Builder: John Murray Forbes. LC 72-29. (Select Bibliographies Reprint Ser.). 1977. reprint ed. 18.95 (*0-8369-9968-1*) Ayer.

Pearson, Hesketh. Dizzy: The Life & Nature of Benjamin Disraeli, Earl of Beaconsfield. LC 74-12579. (Illus.). 284p. 1974. reprint ed. lib. bdg. 59.75 (*0-8371-7729-4*, PEDIZ, Greenwood Pr) Greenwood.

— Gilbert: His Life & Strife. LC 78-3698. 276p. 1978. reprint ed. lib. bdg. 59.75 (*0-313-20364-4*, PEGI, Greenwood Pr) Greenwood.

— Gilbert & Sullivan. 22.95 (*0-89190-868-4*) Amereon Ltd.

— Gilbert & Sullivan. LC 70-175706. (Select Bibliographies Reprint Ser.). 1977. reprint ed. 21.95 (*0-8369-6621-X*) Ayer.

— Last Actor-Managers. LC 77-148225. (Biography Index Reprint Ser.). (Illus.). 1977. 23.95 (*0-8369-8072-7*) Ayer.

— The Life of Oscar Wilde. LC 78-6898. (Illus.). 399p. 1978. reprint ed. lib. bdg. 37.50 (*0-313-20491-8*, PEOW, Greenwood Pr) Greenwood.

— The Smith of Smiths Being the Life, Wit & Humor of Sydney Smith. 1988. reprint ed. lib. bdg. 49.00 (*0-7812-0197-7*) Rprt Serv.

— The Smith of Smiths Being the Life, Wit & Humor of Sydney Smith. LC 73-145230. (Literature Ser.). (Illus.). 338p. 1972. reprint ed. 49.00 (*0-403-01146-9*) Scholarly.

Pearson, Hesketh, ed. & intro. see Wilde, Oscar.

Pearson, Hilary & Miller, Clifford. Commercial Exploitation of Intellectual Property. 474p. 1990. pap. 48.00 (*1-85431-044-5*, Pub. by Blackstone Pr) Gaunt.

Pearson, Hilary E. Computer Contracts: An International Guide to Agreements & Software Protection. 312p. 1984. 70.50 (*90-6544-198-0*) Kluwer Academic.

Pearson, Hugh. The Shadow of the Panther: Huey Newton & the Price of Black Power in America. 422p. 1995. pap. 14.00 (*0-201-48341-6*) Addison-Wesley.

— The Shadow of the Panther: Huey Newton, Oakland & the Price of Power. (Illus.). 422p. 1994. 24.00 (*0-201-63278-0*) Addison-Wesley.

***Pearson, Hugh.** Under the Knife: How a Wealthy Negro Surgeon Wielded Power in the Jim Crow South. LC 99-39636. (Illus.). 288p. 2000. 24.00 (*0-684-84651-9*) S&S Trade.

Pearson, Ian. The Atlas of the Future. 128p. 1998. 27.95 (*0-02-862088-7*); pap. 17.95 (*0-02-862089-5*) Macmillan.

— English in Biological Science. (English in Focus Ser.). 1979. teacher ed. 12.00 (*0-19-437505-6*); pap. text, student ed. 9.95 (*0-19-437513-7*) OUP.

Pearson, Ian & Winter, Chris. Where's It Going? Prospects for Tomorrow. LC 99-70825. (Prospects for Tomorrow Ser.). 112p. (Orig.). 1999. pap. 12.95 (*0-500-28137-8*, Pub. by Thames Hudson) Norton.

Pearson, J. D. A Guide to Manuscripts & Documents in the British Isles Relating to South & South-East Asia, Vol. 2. 352p. 1990. text 180.00 (*0-7201-2011-X*) Continuum.

Pearson, J. D., compiled by. A Guide to Manuscripts & Documents in the British Isles Relating to Africa, 2 vols., Set. LC 93-2886. 1993. text 450.00 (*0-7201-2167-1*) Continuum.

— A Guide to Manuscripts & Documents in the British Isles Relating to Africa, 2 vols., Vol. 1: London. LC 93-2886. 320p. 1993. text 200.00 (*0-7201-2088-8*) Continuum.

— A Guide to Manuscripts & Documents in the British Isles Relating to Africa, 2 vols., Vol. 2. LC 93-2886. 1993. 300.00 (*0-7201-2090-X*) Continuum.

***Pearson, J. D., ed.** Vascular Adhesion Molecules & Inflammation. LC 99-27119. (Progress in Inflammation Research Ser.). 300p. 1999. 149.00 (*3-7643-5800-9*, Pub. by Birkhauser) Spr-Verlag.

Pearson, J. D., jt. ed. see Wainwright, Doreen M.

Pearson, J. D., jt. ed. see Wainwright, M. Doreen.

Pearson, J. M. Mathematics for Economists: A First Course. LC 81-14309. (Illus.). 220p. reprint ed. pap. 68.20 (*0-8357-2971-0*, 203923300011) Bks Demand.

— Nuclear Physics - Energy & Matter: Special Student Edition. (Illus.). 264p. 1986. 42.00 (*0-85274-804-3*) IOP Pub.

Pearson, J. Michael. American Cut Glass for the Discriminating Collector. 3rd ed. LC 65-26205. (Illus.). 204p. 1965. 100.00 (*0-916528-00-6*) J M Pearson.

— Encyclopedia of American Cut & Engraved Glass Vol. 1: Geometric Conceptions. LC 74-18615. (Illus.). 272p. 1975. 75.00 (*0-916528-01-4*) J M Pearson.

— Encyclopedia of American Cut & Engraved Glass Vol. 2: Realistic Patterns. LC 74-18615. (Illus.). 172p. 1977. 35.00 (*0-916528-03-0*) J M Pearson.

— Encyclopedia of American Cut & Engraved Glass Vol. 3: Geometric Motifs. LC 74-18615. (Illus.). 260p. 1978. 40.00 (*0-916528-05-7*) J M Pearson.

Pearson, J. R. Pearson on the Orchard-House: Hints on the Construction & Management of Orchard-Houses. (Illus.). 63p. 1994. pap. 10.35 (*1-881763-00-5*) C Barnett Bks.

Pearson, J. R. A., jt. ed. see Durband, D.

Pearson, Jack. Uncle Alphonso & the Frosty, Fibbing Dinosaurs. LC 92-39373. (On My Own Bks.). (Illus.). 32p. (J). 1993. pap. 4.99 (*0-7814-0100-3*, Chariot Bks) Chariot Victor.

— Uncle Alphonso & the Puffy Proud Dinosuar. LC 90-32442. (Illus.). 32p. (J). 1992. pap. 4.99 (*1-55513-562-5*, Chariot Bks) Chariot Victor.

Pearson, Jacqueline. Women's Reading in Britain, 1750-1835: A Dangerous Recreation. LC 98-38078. (Cambridge Studies in Renaissance Literature & Culture). 320p. (C). 1999. text 59.95 (*0-521-58439-6*) Cambridge U Pr.

Pearson, James C., jt. auth. see Turton, Anthony.

Pearson, James D. Bibliography of Africa: Conference Proceedings, 1967. Jones, Ruth, ed. 362p. 1970. 49.50 (*0-7146-2394-6*, Pub. by F Cass Pubs) Intl Spec Bk.

Pearson, James E., ed. Optical Technologies for Aerospace Sensing: Proceedings of a Conference Held 16-17 November 1992, Boston, Massachusetts. LC 93-18557. (Critical Reviews of Optical Science & Technology Ser.: Vol. CR47). 1993. 30.00 (*0-8194-1042-X*); pap. 30.00 (*0-8194-1041-1*) SPIE.

— Selected Papers on Adaptive Optics for Atmospheric Compensation. LC 93-46626. (Milestone Ser.: Vol. MS 92). 1994. pap. 45.00 (*0-8194-1509-X*) SPIE.

— Selected Papers on Adaptive Optics for Atmospheric Compensation. LC 93-46626. (Milestone Ser.: Vol. MS 92/HC). 1994. 55.00 (*0-8194-1510-3*) SPIE.

Pearson, Jane L. & Conwell, Yeates, eds. Suicide & Aging: International Perspectives. LC 96-19793. (Illus.). 248p. 1996. 43.95 (*0-8261-9370-6*) Springer Pub.

Pearson, Jason. Dragon Blood & Guts. (Illus.). 84p. (Orig.). (YA). 1995. pap. 7.95 (*1-887279-10-5*) Image Comics.

Pearson, Jean. On Speaking Terms with Earth. 32p. 1988. pap. 4.50 (*0-945251-42-4*) Great Elm.

— On Speaking Terms with Earth. 32p. 1992. reprint ed. pap. 5.00 (*0-9627741-5-4*) Green World Pr.

Pearson, Jean, tr. see Olofsson, Tommy.

Pearson, Jean E. Kurt Kusenberg: Humorist of the Fantastic. LC 90-42186. (Studies in Modern German Literature: Vol. 19). VIII, 183p. (C). 1992. text 40.95 (*0-8204-0601-5*) P Lang Pubng.

Pearson, Jennifer. Terms in Context. LC 98-15154. (Studies in Corpus Linguistics: Vol. 1). xii, 246p. 1998. 69.00 (*1-55619-342-4*) J Benjamins Pubng Co.

Pearson, Jenny, ed. Discovering the Self Through Drama & Movement: The Sesame Approach. 350p. 1996. pap. text 29.95 (*1-85302-384-1*, Pub. by Jessica Kingsley) Taylor & Francis.

Pearson, Jenny, jt. auth. see Armstrong, Frankie.

***Pearson, Jeremy D.** Vascular Adhesion Molecules & Inflammation. LC 99-27119. (PIR Ser.). 1999. write for info. (*0-8176-5800-9*) Birkhauser.

Pearson, Jeremy D., jt. ed. see Savage, Caroline O.

***Pearson, Jerry.** More Than Muscle: A Fitness Program for Corrections & Law Enforcement, the Variable Cyclic Phase System. LC 99-88643. (Illus.). 2000. pap. write for info. (*1-56991-118-5*) Am Correctional.

Pearson, Joan. Memories of Monday (Wash Day Before Advent of Washing Machine) with Added Chapter on Scotland. (C). 1989. pap. 21.00 (*1-85072-053-3*, Pub. by W Sessions) St Mut.

Pearson, John. Barbara Cartland: Crusader in Pink LC 80-479282. 158 p. 1979. 5.95 (*0-297-77699-1*) Weidenfeld & Nicolson.

***Pearson, John.** Blood Royal: The Story of the Spencers & the Royals. (Illus.). 292p. 1999. 29.95 (*0-00-255934-X*, Pub. by HarpC) Trafalgar.

— Blood Royal: The Story of the Spencers & the Royals. 2000. reprint ed. pap. 15.95 (*0-00-653054-0*, Pub. by HarpC) Trafalgar.

Pearson, John. Eastern Shore Beckonings. 1998. pap. 10.95 (*0-9615995-7-X*) Recover Comns.

***Pearson, John.** Painfully Rich: J. Paul Getty & His Heirs. (Illus.). 349p. 2000. reprint ed. text 30.00 (*0-7881-6919-X*) DIANE Pub.

Pearson, John. Vindiciae Epistolarum Sancti Ignatii, 2 vols. LC 76-173936. (Library of Anglo-Catholic Theology: No. 16). reprint ed. 57.50 (*0-404-52140-1*) AMS Pr.

Pearson, John, ed. see Eklund, Emmet E. & Eklund, Marion L.

Pearson, John C. & Aros, Andrew A. Home Video Yearbook: 1981. 90p. 1980. pap. 7.00 (*0-932352-05-7*) Applause Pubns.

Pearson, John H. The Prefaces of Henry James: Framing the Modern Reader. LC 96-31044. 1997. 28.50 (*0-271-01659-0*) Pa St U Pr.

Pearson, John K. & Smith, R. Pete. A Guide to Challenging Consumer Bankruptcy: A Key Debt Recovery Process. 190p. (Orig.). 1991. pap. text 128.00 (*0-89982-367-X*) Am Bankers.

Pearson, John K., jt. ed. see Tatelbaum, Charles M.

Pearson, John R., ed. Hiker's Guide to Trails of Big Bend National Park. 2nd ed. (Illus.). 32p. 1998. pap. 1.95 (*0-912001-00-3*) Big Bend.

— River Guide to the Rio Grande, 4 vols. (Illus.). 72p. 1982. pap. 10.00 (*0-912001-08-9*) Big Bend.

— River Guide to the Rio Grande, 4 vols., General Information. (Illus.). 72p. 1982. 1.00 (*0-912001-04-6*) Big Bend.

— River Guide to the Rio Grande, 4 vols., Vol. 1: Colorado & Santa Elena Canyons. (Illus.). 72p. 1992. pap. 3.00 (*0-912001-05-4*) Big Bend.

— River Guide to the Rio Grande, 4 vols., Vol. 2: Mariscal & Boquillas Canyons. (Illus.). 72p. 1989. pap. 3.00 (*0-912001-06-2*) Big Bend.

— River Guide to the Rio Grande, 4 vols., Vol. 3: The Lower Canyons. (Illus.). 72p. 1991. pap. 4.50 (*0-912001-07-0*) Big Bend.

— Road Guide to Backcountry Dirt Roads of Big Bend National Park. (Illus.). 40p. 1993. pap. 1.95 (*0-912001-01-1*) Big Bend.

— Road Guide to Paved & Improved Dirt Roads of Big Bend National Park. (Illus.). 48p. 1999. pap. 1.95 (*0-912001-02-X*) Big Bend.

Pearson, John R., ed. see Maxwell, Ross A.

Pearson, John R., ed. see Rudig, Doug.

Pearson, Jon. Energy Conservation in Small Business: Promoting the Use of New Testament. LC 83-21739. (Illus.). 212p. (Orig.). 1984. lib. bdg. 52.50 (*0-8191-3659-X*) U Pr of Amer.

Pearson, Jon, et al. Comprehensive Wellness for Firefighters: Fitness & Health Guide for Fire & Rescue Workers. (Industrial Health & Safety Ser.). 368p. 1995. pap. 46.95 (*0-442-02068-6*, VNR) Wiley.

Pearson, Jon, et al. Comprehensive Wellness for Firefighters: Fitness & Health Guide for Fire & Rescue Workers. (Industrial Health & Safety Ser.). 358p. 1995. 54.95 (*0-471-28709-1*, VNR) Wiley.

Pearson, Jonathan. Contributions for the Genealogies of the Descendants of the First Settlers of the Patent & City of Schenectady N.Y. from 1662 to 1800. LC 76-20240. 324p. 1998. reprint ed. pap. 27.50 (*0-8063-0730-7*) Clearfield Co.

— Early Records of the City & County of Albany, & Colony of Rensselaerswyck, 1656-1675, Translated from the Dutch, with Notes. 523p. 1997. reprint ed. lib. bdg. 55.00 (*0-8328-6099-9*) Higginson Bk Co.

***Pearson, Jonathan.** Early Records of the City & County of Albany (New York) & Colony of Rensselaerswyck: Morgages 1658-1660 & Wills 1684-1765, Vol. 4. 222p. 1999. pap. 20.00 (*0-7884-1296-5*, P106) Heritage Bk.

Pearson, Jonathan. Genealogies of the Descendants of the First Settlers of Schenectady, 1662-1800. 324p. 1992. reprint ed. pap. 29.50 (*0-8328-2372-4*) Higginson Bk Co.

Pearson, Jonathan, et al. History of the Schenectady Patent, in the Dutch & English Times, Being Contributions Toward a History of the Lower Mohawk Valley. MacMurray, J. W., ed. (Illus.). 466p. 1997. reprint ed. lib. bdg. 49.00 (*0-8328-6229-0*) Higginson Bk Co.

Pearson, Joseph, ed. & tr. see Foucault, Michel.

Pearson, Joyce A. & Tull, Pamela. U. S. Government Directories, 1982-1995. LC 97-30589. 200p. 1998. lib. bdg. 45.00 (*1-56308-290-X*) Libs Unl.

Pearson, Judith, jt. auth. see Pam, Alvin.

Pearson, Judith E., jt. auth. see Corsetty, Kathy.

Pearson, Judy. Friday Fun. 265p. 1993. pap. 28.00 (*0-9637103-0-3*) Clear Writing.

— Marriage after Mourning. 256p. 1994. pap. text, per. 18.95 (*0-7872-0205-3*) Kendall-Hunt.

— Myths of Educational Choice. LC 92-19594. 168p. 1992. 42.95 (*0-275-94169-8*, C4169, Praeger Pubs) Greenwood.

Pearson, Judy & Nelson, Paul E. Understanding & Sharing: An Introduction to Speech. 6th ed. 496p. (C). 1993. per. write for info. (*0-697-21450-8*) Brown & Benchmark.

— Understanding & Sharing: An Introduction to Speech Communication. 6th ed. 496p. (C). 1993. text. write for info. (*0-697-13940-9*) Brown & Benchmark.

Pearson, Judy C. Healthy Mind Healthy Body: Using Your Mind Power to Stay Healthy Overcome Illness. Celia, Jean, ed. 155p. 1994. 12.95 (*0-9635179-0-2*) Awe Bks.

P

Pearson, Judy C. & Nelson, Paul E. Confidence in Public Speaking. 6th ed. 304p. (C). 1995. text. write for info. (0-697-24635-3) Brown & Benchmark.

***Pearson, Judy C. & Nelson, Paul E.** An Introduction to Human Communication: Understanding & Sharing 8th ed. LC 99-30979. 2000. write for info. (0-07-233694-3) McGraw.

Pearson, Judy C., et al. Gender & Communication. 3rd ed. 320p. (C). 1994. text. write for info. (0-697-20154-6) Brown & Benchmark.

Pearson, Judy C., jt. auth. see Nelson, Paul E.

Pearson, Judy C., jt. auth. see Spitzberg, Brian H.

***Pearson, Karinn & K. P. Kids & Co. Staff.** Playful Patchwork Projects. LC 99-39262. 1999. 27.95 (0-8069-2039-4) Sterling.

Pearson, Karl. Tables of the Incomplete Beta Function. 205p. 1968. lib. bdg. 100.00 (0-521-05922-4) Lubrecht & Cramer.

— Tables of the Incomplete Beta Function. 505p. 1968. 160.00 (0-85264-704-2) St Mut.

Pearson, Karl, ed. see Clifford, William K.

Pearson, Kathy. Conflicting Loyalties in Early Medieval Bavaria. LC 99-12197. 247p. 1999. text 78.95 (0-7546-0011-4) Ashgate Pub Co.

Pearson, Kazue, tr. see Pearson, Richard J., et al, eds.

Pearson, Keith, ed. see Carr, Betty J.

Pearson, Keith, ed. see Lenart, Curt.

Pearson, Keith, ed. see Patray, Stuart.

Pearson, Keith, ed. see Tuck, Jerri.

Pearson, Ken. Writing Humor: How to Write Funny Articles, Columns & Letters for Profit & Pleasure. 144p. 1998. pap. 19.95 (1-85703-258-6, Pub. by How To Bks) Trans-Atl Phila.

Pearson, Kenneth, ed. Alive to the Love of God: Essays Presented to James M. Houston on His 75th Birthday. 431p. (C). 1998. pap. 31.95 (1-57383-114-X, Regent Coll Pub) Regent College.

***Pearson, Kim.** Animal ABC. (Illus.). v, 54p. (J). (ps). 1999. pap. 4.95 (1-881849-01-5) Primary Srcs WA.

— Common Disguises. v, 284p. 1999. pap. 9.95 (1-881849-00-7) Primary Srcs WA.

Pearson, Kim. Eating Mythos Soup: Poemstories for Laura. LC 99-34915. (Illus.). 160p. 2000. pap. 11.95 (1-56474-319-5) Fithian Pr.

Pearson, Kit. Awake & Dreaming. LC 99-25967. 228p. (gr. 3-7). 1999. pap. 4.99 (0-14-038166-X, PuffinBks) Peng Put Young Read.

— A Handful of Time. (Illus.). 192p. (J). (gr. 3-7). 1991. pap. 6.99 (0-14-032268-X, PuffinBks) Peng Put Young Read.

Pearson, Kit. A Handful of Time. 1988. 12.09 (0-606-04928-2, Pub. by Turtleback) Demco.

Pearson, Kit. The Lights Go on Again. 224p. (J). 1999. pap. 3.99 (0-14-036412-9, Viking) Viking Penguin.

— Looking at the Moon. 224p. (J). (gr. 5 up). 1996. pap. 3.99 (0-14-034852-2, PuffinBks) Peng Put Young Read.

— Looking at the Moon. (J). 1996. 9.09 (0-606-08562-9, Pub. by Turtleback) Demco.

Pearson, Kit. The Sky Is Falling. (Illus.). (J). (gr. 4-7). 1995. pap. 4.99 (0-14-037652-6, PuffinBks) Peng Put Young Read.

— The Sky Is Falling. (J). 1995. 10.09 (0-606-08172-0, Pub. by Turtleback) Demco.

Pearson, Kristin, ed. see Grayslake Historical Society Bk. Committee Staff, et al.

Pearson, L. Butterworths Student Companions: Company Law. 117p. 1986. pap. 14.00 (0-409-30319-4, AT, MICHIE) LEXIS Pub.

Pearson, L. R., ed. see Mid-America Spectroscopy Symposium (16th: 1965, Ch.

***Pearson, Lance.** A Byte of Charity. LC 99-70337. 264p. 1999. pap. 14.95 (1-878044-69-9) Mayhaven Pub.

Pearson, Larry, see Vantress, Sally.

Pearson, Leonard. Death & Dying: Current Issues in the Treatment of the Dying Person. LC 67-11483. 247p. reprint ed. pap. 76.60 (0-608-11370-0, 200226600012) Bks Demand.

Pearson, Lester B. Words & Occasions: An Anthology of Speeches & Articles from His Papers by the Right Honourable Lester B. Pearson. LC 70-135191. (Illus.). 310p. 1970. 34.50 (0-674-95611-7) HUP.

Pearson, Linda. Local Government Law in New South Wales. 352p. 1994. pap. 49.00 (1-86287-127-2, Pub. by Federation Pr) Gaunt.

Pearson, Lionel. Early Ionian Historians. LC 75-136874. 240p. 1975. reprint ed. lib. bdg. 35.00 (0-8371-5314-X, PEIH, Greenwood Pr) Greenwood.

— The Greek Historians of the West: Timaeus & His Predecessors. LC 87-4877. (American Philological Association Philological Monographs). 305p. 1988. 22.00 (1-55540-078-7, 40-00-35) OUP.

— The Local Historians of Attica. LC 81-16556. (American Philological Association Philological Monographs). 167p. 1981. reprint ed. pap. 19.50 (0-89130-540-8, 40 00 11) OUP.

Pearson, Lorentz C. The Diversity & Evolution of Plants. LC 94-37366. 656p. 1995. per. 84.95 (0-8493-2483-1, 2483) CRC Pr.

— The Mushroom Manual - Tops! Complete for College Class: Simple for You & Me. LC 86-21847. (Illus.). 224p. 1987. pap. 9.95 (0-87961-161-8) Naturegraph.

Pearson, Lu E. Elizabethans at Home. LC 57-9305. (Illus.). 640p. 1957. reprint ed. pap. 30.00 (0-608-00252-6, 206076700006) Bks Demand.

Pearson, Lynn F. Amusement Machines. (Album Ser.: No. 285). (Illus.). 32p. (C). 1989. pap. 6.25 (0-7478-0179-7, Pub. by Shire Pubns) Parkwest Pubns.

***Pearson, Lynn F.** British Breweries: An Architectural History. LC 99-26733. (Illus.). 1999. 45.00 (1-85285-191-0) Hambledon Press.

Pearson, Lynn F. Discovering Famous Graves. (Discovering Ser.: Vol. 123). (Illus.). 184p. 1998. pap. 16.75 (0-7478-0371-4, Pub. by Shire Pubns) Parkwest Pubns.

— Lighthouses. (Album Ser.: No. 32). (Illus.). 32p. 1995. pap. 6.25 (0-7478-0275-0, Pub. by Shire Pubns) Parkwest Pubns.

Pearson, M. Dark of the Moon. mass mkt. 8.95 (0-340-70966-9, Pub. by Hodder & Stought Ltd) Trafalgar.

— Owl Light. 1996. mass mkt. 8.95 (0-340-65572-0, Pub. by Hodder & Stought Ltd) Trafalgar.

Pearson, M. L., jt. ed. see Abel, Emily K.

Pearson, M. N. Pious Passengers: The Hajj in Earlier Times. (C). 1994. write for info. (81-207-1601-9) Sterling Pubs.

— The Portuguese in India. (New Cambridge History of India Ser.: I: 1). 202p. 1988. text 54.95 (0-521-25713-1) Cambridge U Pr.

Pearson, M. N., ed. Legitimacy & Symbols: The South Asian Writings of F. W. Buckler. LC 82-72446. (Michigan Papers on South & Southeast Asia: No. 26). xiii, 193p. 1985. 11.95 (0-89148-032-3); pap. 4.99 (0-89148-033-1) Ctr S&SE Asian.

— Spices in the Indian Ocean World. LC 96-238. (Expanding World Ser.: Vol. 11). 400p. 1996. 128.95 (0-86078-510-6, Pub. by Variorum) Ashgate Pub Co.

Pearson, M. N., jt. auth. see Bickerton, Ian J.

Pearson, M. N., jt. auth. see Das Gupta, Ashin.

Pearson, Maggie & Aldous, Kate, eds. A Treasury of Old Testament Stories. LC 95-1351. (Illus.). 1995. pap. 7.95 (1-85697-594-0) LKC.

Pearson, Maggie, jt. auth. see Aesop.

Pearson, Margaret C., jt. auth. see Ferguson, Amelia C.

Pearson, Margaret M. China's New Business Elite: The Political Consequences of Economic Reform. LC 96-26088. (Illus.). 217p. 1997. 35.00 (0-520-20718-1, Pub. by U CA Pr) Cal Prin Full Svc.

***Pearson, Margaret M.** China's New Business Elite: The Political Consequences of Economic Reform. 217p. 2000. pap. 17.95 (0-520-21933-3, Pub. by U CA Pr) Cal Prin Full Svc.

Pearson, Margaret M. Joint Ventures in the People's Republic of China: The Control of Foreign Direct Investment under Socialism. 350p. 1991. pap. text 19.95 (0-691-02768-4, Pub. by Princeton U Pr) Cal Prin Full Svc.

***Pearson, Mark.** Colorado Canyon Country: A Guide to Hiking & Floating BLM Wildlands. rev. ed. 224p. 2000. pap. 22.95 (1-56579-387-0) Westcliffe Pubs.

Pearson, Mark. Colorado's Canyon Country: A Guide to Hiking & Floating BLM Wildlands. 208p. 1995. pap. text 19.95 (1-56579-133-9) Westcliffe Pubs.

— Complete Guide to Colorado's Wilderness Areas. LC 94-60026. 340p. 1994. pap. 24.95 (1-56579-052-9) Westcliffe Pubs.

***Pearson, Mark.** Emotional Healing & Self Esteem. 168p. 1998. pap. 17.95 (0-86431-264-4, Pub. by Aust Council Educ Res) Stylus Pub VA.

Pearson, Mark. The Journalist's Guide to Media Law. LC 98-215285. viii, 272p. 1997. pap. 24.95 (1-86448-434-9, Pub. by Allen & Unwin Pty) Paul & Co Pubs.

— Numbat-His Magic Quest. (C). 1990. 45.00 (0-947333-14-2, Pub. by Pascoe Pub) St Mut.

Pearson, Mark & Nolan, Patricia. Emotional Release for Children. 212p. 1995. pap. 19.95 (0-86431-162-1, Pub. by Aust Council Educ Res) Stylus Pub VA.

***Pearson, Mark & Wilson, Helen.** Sandplay & Symbol Work: Emotional Healing & Personal Development with Children, Adolescents & Adults. 120p. 2000. pap. 19.95 (0-86431-340-3, Pub. by Aust Council Educ Res) Stylus Pub VA.

Pearson, Mark, jt. auth. see Doudeijns, Marco.

Pearson, Mark, jt. ed. see Hennessy, Patrick.

Pearson, Mark A. Christian Healing: A Practical & Comprehensive Guide. 2nd ed. LC 94-16615. 376p. (gr. 10). 1995. pap. 12.99 (0-8007-9221-1) Chosen Bks.

Pearson, Mark L. & Epstein, Henry F., eds. Muscle Development: Molecular & Cellular Control. LC 82-72381. 601p. reprint ed. pap. 186.40 (0-7837-1993-0, 204226700002) Bks Demand.

Pearson, Marlene J. A Fine Day for a Middle-Class Marriage. LC 96-71123. 96p. 1997. pap. 9.95 (1-888996-00-5, Red Hen Press) Valentine CA.

Pearson, Mary. David vs. God. LC 99-39421. (Illus.). 144p. (YA). 2000. 16.00 (0-15-202058-6, Harcourt Child Bks) Harcourt.

***Pearson, Mary.** Donde Esta Max? (Rookie Espanol Ser.). (SPA., Illus.). (J). 2000. 15.00 (0-516-22023-3) Childrens.

Pearson, Mary. Pickles in My Soup. LC 99-22470. (Rookie Readers Ser.). 32p. (J). (gr. 1-2). 1999. 17.50 (0-516-21636-8) Childrens.

***Pearson, Mary.** Pickles in My Soup. (Rookie Readers Ser.). (J). 2000. pap. text 4.95 (0-516-26550-4) Childrens.

— Where Is Max? (Rookie Readers Ser.). (Illus.). (J). 2000. 15.00 (0-516-22019-5) Childrens.

Pearson, Mary D. Recordings in the Public Library. LC 62-20852. 160p. reprint ed. pap. 49.60 (0-608-10873-1, 201114400074) Bks Demand.

Pearson, Mary R. Frogs in Pharaoh's Bed. 220p. (J). 1995. pap. 8.99 (0-8423-1755-4) Tyndale Hse.

***Pearson, Mary R.** Fun Activities for Bible Learning: Creative Teaching Aids for the Church Classroom. 110p. 1999. pap. 21.00 (0-7880-1522-2) CSS OH.

Pearson, Mary R. Perky Puppets with a Purpose: A Complete Guide to Puppetry & Ventriloquism in Christian Ministry. LC 91-42507. (Illus.). 160p. 1992. pap. 12.95 (0-88243-677-5, 02-0677) Gospel Pub.

Pearson, Michael. Dreaming of Columbus: A Boyhood in the Bronx. LC 98-38554. (New York City Ser.). 1999. 24.95 (0-8156-0561-7) Syracuse U Pr.

***Pearson, Michael.** Imagined Places: Journeys into Literary America. LC 00-32226. 352p. 2000. reprint ed. pap. 17.95 (0-8156-0660-5) Syracuse U Pr.

Pearson, Michael. John McPhee. LC 96-36762. 144p. 1997. 32.00 (0-8057-4624-2, Twyne) Mac Lib Ref.

***Pearson, Michael.** Those Damned Rebels: The American Revolution as Seen Through British Eyes. (Illus.). 448p. 2000. reprint ed. pap. 18.00 (0-306-80983-4) Da Capo.

Pearson, Michael & Sullivan, Sharon. Looking after Heritage Places: The Basics of Heritage Planning for Managers, Landowners & Administrators. 412p. 1995. pap. 39.95 (0-522-84554-1, Pub. by Melbourne Univ Pr) Paul & Co Pubs.

Pearson, Michael, jt. auth. see Gay, William.

Pearson, Michael N. Pilgrimage to Mecca: The Indian Experience, 1500-1800. (World History Ser.). (Illus.). 296p. (C). 1996. text 42.95 (1-55876-089-X); pap. text 18.95 (1-55876-090-3) Wiener Pubs Inc.

— Port Cities & Intruders: The Swahili Coast, India & Portugal in the Early Modern Era. LC 97-20627. (Symposia in Comparative History Ser.). (Illus.). 202p. 1998. text 35.95 (0-8018-5692-2) Johns Hopkins.

***Pearson, Michael P.** The Archaeology of Death & Burial. LC 99-32686. (Anthropology Ser.). 256p. 2000. 34.95 (0-89096-926-4) Tex A&M Univ Pr.

Pearson, Michael P. & Richards, Colin, eds. Architecture & Order: Approaches to Social Space. (Material Cultures Ser.). (Illus.). 264p. (C). 1997. pap. 25.99 (0-415-15743-9) Routledge.

Pearson, Michael Parker. Archaeology of Death & Burial. 1999. write for info. (0-7509-1777-6) Bks Intl VA.

Pearson, Mike. Illini Legends, Lists & Lore: 100 Years of Big Ten Heritage. LC 95-70431. (Illus.). 272p. 1995. 29.95 (1-57167-018-1) Sports Pub.

Pearson, Mike P., et al, eds. Between Land & Sea: Excavations at Dun Vulan, South Uist. (Search Ser.: Vol. 3). 450p. 1999. 95.00 (1-85075-880-8, Pub. by Sheffield Acad) CUP Services.

Pearson, Mildred M. God's Gift, Your Blessing: A Guide to Pastor's Aid Committees. 96-120p. (Orig.). 1995. pap. 9.95 (1-882581-10-5) Campbell Rd Pr.

Pearson, Nancy, tr. see Bertela, Giovanna G.

Pearson, Nancy, tr. see Corbin, Henry.

Pearson, Nancy A. Floral Applique: Original Designs & Techniques for Medallion Quilts. Penders, Mary, ed. (Illus.). 96p. 1994. pap. 21.95 (1-881588-11-4, 882670169) EZ Quilting.

Pearson, Nathan W. Goin' to Kansas City. 320p. 1994. 16.95 (0-252-06438-0) U of Ill Pr.

Pearson, Nathan W., Jr. Goin' to Kansas City. LC 87-5987. (Music in American Life Ser.). (Illus.). 276p. 1987. text 24.95 (0-252-01336-0) U of Ill Pr.

Pearson-Nelson. Understanding & Sharing. 7th ed. 1997. pap. 18.75 (0-697-32702-7) McGraw.

— Understanding & Sharing. 7th ed. 1996. 14.06 (0-697-35695-7, WCB McGr Hill) McGrw-H Hghr Educ.

Pearson, Nicholas M. The State & the Visual Arts. 128p. 1982. pap. 40.95 (0-335-10109-7) OpUniv Pr.

Pearson, Noel, jt. auth. see Calley, Karin.

Pearson, Norman H. Decade: A Collection of Poems from the First Ten Years of The Wesleyan Poetry Program. LC 72-82542. 302p. reprint ed. pap. 93.70 (0-7837-0218-3, 204052600017) Bks Demand.

Pearson, Norman H., jt. auth. see H. D., pseud.

Pearson, Norman H., jt. ed. see Auden, W. H.

Pearson, Norman H., ed. see Devos, Anthony.

Pearson, Norman H., ed. see H. D., pseud.

Pearson, Norman H., ed. see Thoreau, Henry David.

Pearson, Olen. The Web Pocket Directory. 80p. 1998. mass mkt. 3.95 (0-931011-48-5) Grapevine Pubns.

Pearson, Olen & Coffin, Chris. The Family Internet Pocket Guide. 80p. 1998. mass mkt. 3.95 (0-931011-47-7) Grapevine Pubns.

Pearson, P. Psycho-Harmonial Philosophy: Music, Mathematics & Geometry. 1991. lib. bdg. 79.95 (0-8490-5012-X) Gordon Pr.

Pearson, P., jt. ed. see MacKerron, G.

Pearson, P., jt. ed. see Van Empel, Martijn.

Pearson, P. David, jt. ed. see Samuels, S. Jay.

Pearson, P. F. An Introduction to Basic Acupuncture: A Practical Guide for GPs & Other Medical Personnel. 84p. (C). 1987. text 73.50 (0-85200-686-1) Kluwer Academic.

Pearson, P. L., jt. ed. see Klinger, H. P.

Pearson, Pat. Stop Self-Sabotage! How to Get Out of Your Own Way & Have an Extraordinary Life. 186p. 1998. pap. 18.00 (0-9665350-0-6) Pearson Prsntatn.

Pearson, Pat, jt. auth. see Van Meter, Roz.

Pearson, Patricia. When She Was Bad: How & Why Women Get Away with Murder. LC 99-192436. 288p. 1998. pap. 13.95 (0-14-024388-7) Viking Penguin.

Pearson, Paul B. & Greenwell, J. Richard, eds. Nutrition, Food, & Man: An Interdisciplinary Perspective. LC 80-10297. (Illus.). 175p. 1980. pap. 54.30 (0-608-05644-8, 206609800006) Bks Demand.

Pearson, Paul L. The Ark of Jack Pots. LC 94-65022. (Boxy Book: No. 1). (Illus.). 73p. (Orig.). 1994. pap. 4.99 (0-9639830-0-8) Rainbow TX.

Pearson, Paul M. The Speaker: A Collection of the Best Orations, Poems, Stories, Debates & One Net Plays for Public Speaking & Voice training, 4 Vols. text 166.95 (0-8369-9361-6, 19732) Ayer.

Pearson, Paul M., ed. The Humourous Speaker: A Book of Humourous Selections for Reading & Speaking. LC 77-167479. (Granger Index Reprint Ser.). 1977. reprint ed. 21.95 (0-8369-6284-2) Ayer.

— Speaker, 1. LC 72-5498. (Granger Index Reprint Ser.). 1977. reprint ed. 26.95 (0-8369-6374-1) Ayer.

— Speaker, Vol. 3. LC 72-5498. (Granger Index Reprint Ser.). 1977. reprint ed. 26.95 (0-8369-6375-X) Ayer.

— Speaker, Vol. 6. LC 72-5498. (Granger Index Reprint Ser.). 1977. reprint ed. 29.95 (0-8369-6376-8) Ayer.

— Speaker, Vol. 8. LC 72-5498. (Granger Index Reprint Ser.). 1977. reprint ed. 34.95 (0-8369-6377-6) Ayer.

Pearson, Pegi C. The Yellow Slicker: A Fable for Women. (Illus.). 28p. 1995. 12.95 (1-879198-16-9) Knwldg Ideas & Trnds.

Pearson, Peter. Between the Mountains & the Sea: Dun Laoghaire-rathdown County LC 98-233918. 381p. 1998. write for info. (0-86278-582-0) OBrien Pr.

Pearson, Peter L., jt. ed. see Cuticchia, A. Jamie.

Pearson, Peter T., jt. auth. see Bader, Ellyn.

***Pearson, Philip R., Jr.** Poetry Is to Be Consumed. LC 99-93872. 1999. pap. 8.95 (0-533-13170-7) Vantage.

Pearson, Premi, ed. see Stoecklein, David R.

Pearson, R. A Pattern in the Heavens. pap. 3.95 (0-88172-170-0) Believers Bkshelf.

Pearson, R. B. Fasting & Man's Correct Diet. 153p. 1993. spiral bd. 12.00 (0-7873-0661-4) Hlth Research.

— Pasteur, Plagiarist, Impostor! The Germ Theory Exploded! 148p. 1996. reprint ed. spiral bd. 18.00 (0-7873-0662-2) Hlth Research.

Pearson, R. C. & Goheen, A. C., eds. Plagas y Enfermedades de la Vid.Tr. of Compendium of Grape Diseases. (SPA., Illus.). 128p. pap. 42.00 (84-7114-607-X) Am Phytopathol Soc.

Pearson, R. S. Commercial Guide to the Forest Economic Products of India. 155p. (C). 1980. text 175.00 (0-89771-619-1, Pub. by Intl Bk Distr) St Mut.

— Commercial Guide to the Forest Economic Products of India. (C). 1988. 40.00 (0-7855-3310-9, Pub. by Scientific) St Mut.

— Commercial Guide to the Forest Economic Products of India. 155p. (C). 1980. reprint ed. 125.00 (0-7855-3122-X, Pub. by Intl Bk Distr) St Mut.

— Commercial Timber of India, Set, Vols. 1 & 2. (C). 1988. 820.00 (0-7855-3309-5) St Mut.

Pearson, R. W. & Boruch, R. F., eds. Survey Research Designs: Towards a Better Understanding of Their Costs & Benefits. (Lecture Notes in Statistics Ser.: Vol. 38). v, 129p. 1986. 43.95 (0-387-96428-2) Spr-Verlag.

Pearson, Ralph, ed. Ohio in Century Three: Quality of Life. (Illus.). 32p. 1977. pap. 1.00 (0-318-00841-6) Ohio Hist Soc.

Pearson, Ralph G. Chemical Hardness. LC 97-11396. 208p. 1997. 105.00 (3-527-29482-1, Wiley-VCH) Wiley.

— Symmetry Rules for Chemical Reactions: Orbital Topology & Elementary Processes. LC 76-10314. 557p. reprint ed. pap. 172.70 (0-608-13357-4, 205577100037) Bks Demand.

Pearson, Ralph G., jt. auth. see Basolo, Fred.

Pearson, Ralph G., jt. auth. see Moore, John W.

Pearson, Ralph M. Modern Renaissance in American Art: Presenting the Work & Philosophy of 54 Distinguished Artists. LC 68-20329. (Essay Index Reprint Ser.). 1977. 42.95 (0-8369-0780-9) Ayer.

Pearson, Randall S. Effective Information Gathering Techniques. Graham-Herring, Chris et al, eds. 32p. pap. write for info. (1-57125-055-7) Help Desk Inst.

Pearson, Ray, et al. Investing in School Technology: Strategies to Meet the Funding Challenge. Ward, Anne, ed. 85p. 1997. pap. 25.00 (0-88364-214-X) Natl Sch Boards.

Pearson, Raymond. Longman Comp Euro Natlsm. LC 92-46026. (Companions to History Ser.). 352p. (C). 1993. text 57.50 (0-582-07229-8, Pub. by Addison-Wesley) Longman.

— The Longman Companion to European Nationalism 1789-1920. LC 92-46026. (Companions to History Ser.). 352p. (C). 1995. pap. 45.00 (0-582-07228-X) Longman.

— The Rise & Fall of the Soviet Empire. LC 96-52562. 192p. 1997. pap. 19.95 (0-312-17407-1) St Martin.

***Pearson, Raymond A., et al, eds.** Toughening of Plastics: Advances in Modeling & Experiments. (ACS Symposium Ser.). (Illus.). 272p. 2000. text 125.00 (0-8412-3657-7) OUP.

Pearson, Richard. A Band of Arrogant & United Heroes: The Story of the Royal Shakespeare Co. Production of the Wars of the Roses. 168p. (C). 1990. 60.00 (1-85634-005-8, Pub. by Excalibur) St Mut.

***Pearson, Richard.** Wm. Thackeray & the Mediated Text: Writing for Periodicals in the Mid-Nineteenth Century. LC 00-38988. (Nineteenth Century Ser.). 2000. write for info. (0-7546-0065-3, Pub. by Ashgate Pub) Ashgate Pub Co.

Pearson, Richard, et al. Criminal Justice Education: The End of the Beginning. 1980. pap. text 5.50 (0-614-07045-7) John Jay Pr.

Pearson, Richard, jt. auth. see Rosenbaum, Barbara.

Pearson, Richard C. The School Library Media Specialist's Tool Kit. LC 98-39810. (Handbook Ser.). (Illus.). 100p. 1999. pap. 19.00 (1-57950-012-9, 95687) Highsmith Pr.

Pearson, Richard D., jt. auth. see Wilson, Paul F.

Pearson, Richard E. Counseling & Social Support: Perspectives & Practice. (Illus.). 240p. (C). 1990. 52.00 (0-8039-3210-3); pap. 24.00 (0-8039-3211-1) Sage.

Pearson, Richard J., et al, eds. Windows on the Japanese Past. Pearson, Kazue & Nishimura, Masao, trs. LC 85-16639. (Illus.). xx, 629p. 1986. pap. 29.95 (0-939512-24-6) U MI Japan.

Pearson, Richard J., jt. auth. see Winterbone, Desmond E.

Pearson, Richard N., jt. auth. see Henderson, James A., Jr.

Pearson, Ridley. The Angel Maker: A Novel. 432p. 1994. mass mkt. 7.50 (0-440-21632-X, Island Bks) Dell.

— The Angel Maker: A Novel. large type ed. LC 93-19761. 614p. 1993. reprint ed. lib. bdg. 23.95 (1-56054-606-9) Thorndike Pr.

— Beyond Recognition. 653p. 1998. mass mkt. 6.99 (0-7868-8928-4, Pub. by Hyperion) Time Warner.

P

An Asterisk (*) at the beginning of an entry indicates that the title is appearing for the first time.

— Beyond Recognition. large type ed. LC 97-12333. 717p. 1997. 27.95 (0-7862-1106-7) Thorndike Pr.
— Blood of the Albatross. 1993. mass mkt. 3.90 (0-312-95183-3, St Martins Paperbacks) St Martin.
— Chain of Evidence. 368p. 1995. 22.95 (0-7868-6172-X, Pub. by Hyperion) Time Warner.
— Chain of Evidence. 512p. 1997. mass mkt. 6.99 (0-7868-8908-X, Pub. by Hyperion) Time Warner.
— Chain of Evidence. large type ed. 1995. 25.95 (1-56895-268-6) Wheeler Pub.
— The First Victim. LC 98-49992. 416p. 1999. 23.95 (0-7868-6440-0, Pub. by Hyperion) Time Warner.
— The First Victim. 416p. 2000. mass mkt. 7.99 (0-7868-8966-7, Pub. by Hyperion) Time Warner.
— Hard Fall. 416p. 1992. mass mkt. 6.99 (0-440-21262-6) Dell.
— Hard Fall. large type ed. 659p. 1992. 21.95 (1-56054-396-5) Thorndike Pr.
— Hard Fall. large type ed. 659p. 1992. 13.95 (1-56054-932-7) Thorndike Pr.
— Hidden Charges. 1993. mass mkt. 5.99 (0-312-92959-5, St Martins Paperbacks) St Martin.
— Hidden Charges. large type ed. (Niagara Large Print Ser.). 539p. 1996. 29.50 (0-7089-5827-3) Ulverscroft.
***Pearson, Ridley.** Middle of Nowhere. LC 99-51670. 416p. 2000. 23.95 (0-7868-6563-6, Pub. by Hyperion) Time Warner.
Pearson, Ridley. Never Look Back. 1993. mass mkt. 6.99 (0-312-92975-7, St Martins Paperbacks) St Martin.
— Never Look Back. large type ed. (Niagara Large Print Ser.). 397p. 1996. 29.50 (0-7089-5844-3) Ulverscroft.
— No Witnesses. 480p. 1996. mass mkt. 7.50 (0-440-22142-0) Dell.
— No Witnesses. 384p. 1994. 22.45 (0-7868-6066-9, Pub. by Hyperion) Time Warner.
***Pearson, Ridley.** Person 2001. mass mkt. write for info. (0-7868-8960-8) Disney Pr.
Pearson, Ridley. The Pied Piper. LC 97-49709. 497p. 1998. 23.45 (0-7868-6300-5, Pub. by Hyperion) Time Warner.
***Pearson, Ridley.** The Pied Piper. large type ed. LC 99-59455. 2000. pap. 22.95 (1-56895-834-X) Wheeler Pub.
Pearson, Ridley. The Pied Piper. 672p. 1999. reprint ed. mass mkt. 7.99 (0-7868-8955-1, Pub. by Hyperion) Time Warner.
***Pearson, Ridley.** Pied Piper/ Beyond Recognition. (J). 1998. write for info. (0-7868-6433-8) Disney Pr.
Pearson, Ridley. Probable Cause. 1991. mass mkt. 6.99 (0-312-92385-6, St Martins Paperbacks) St Martin.
— The Seizing of Yankee Green Mall. 304p. 1988. pap. 4.50 (0-373-97076-5) Harlequin Bks.
— Undercurrents: A Novel. 1992. mass mkt. 6.99 (0-312-92958-7, St Martins Paperbacks) St Martin.
Pearson, Robert A. Policies & Procedures. 1984. reprint ed. pap. write for info. (0-9608378-1-7) B Pearson.
— Success with Parts. (Illus.). 42p. (Orig.). 1976. pap. 4.20 (0-9608378-0-9) B Pearson.
Pearson, Robert H. Cost Effective Decision Making. 1973. 8.95 (0-912164-12-3) Masterco Pr.
Pearson, Robert M. The Application of Nuclear Magnetic Resonance Spectroscopes to Quality-Control Measurements of Asphalt & Asphalt-Aggregate Mixes. 42p. (Orig.). (C). 1994. pap. text 10.00 (0-309-05760-4, SHRP-A-382) SHRP.
Pearson, Robert P. Through Middle Eastern Eyes. (Through Eyes Ser.). (Orig.). (C). 1993. pap., teacher ed. 8.95 (0-614-02977-5) Amer Forum.
— Through Middle Eastern Eyes: Teaching Strategies. 110p. (C). 1993. pap. text 8.95 (0-938960-42-3) CITE.
Pearson, Robert P. & Clark, Leon E. Through Middle Eastern Eyes. 3rd ed. LC 92-44505. (Illus.). 352p. (Orig.). 1993. lib. bdg. 44.00 (0-938960-43-1) CITE.
— Through Middle Eastern Eyes. 3rd rev. ed. LC 92-44505. (Illus.). 352p. (Orig.). 1993. pap. text 21.95 (0-938960-41-5) CITE.
Pearson, Roberta E. Eloquent Gestures: The Transformation of Performance Style in the Griffith Biograph Films. (C). 1992. 45.00 (0-520-07365-7, Pub. by U CA Pr); pap. 17.95 (0-520-07366-5, Pub. by U CA Pr) Cal Prin Full Svc.
Pearson, Roberta E., jt. auth. see Uricchio, William.
Pearson, Roberta E., jt. ed. see Buscombe, Edward.
Pearson, Roberta E., jt. ed. see Hartley, John.
Pearson, Robin, ed. A Black Country Christmas. (Christmas Ser.). (Illus.). 160p. 1992. pap. 13.95 (0-7509-0071-7, Pub. by Sutton Pub Ltd) Intl Pubs Mktg.
Pearson, Robin M., ed. Connecticut Real Estate Law Journal. 1983. ring bd. 105.00 (0-88063-018-3, 80360-10, MICHIE) LEXIS Pub.
Pearson, Rodney. Exposing Manipulation. 175p. 1998. pap. 14.95 (1-881524-21-3) Milligan Bks.
***Pearson, Rodney.** Significantly Single. 150p. 1999. pap. 13.95 (1-881524-55-8, Prof Busn) Milligan Bks.
Pearson, Roger. Anthropological Glossary. LC 85-195. 286p. (Orig.). 1985. 28.50 (0-89874-510-1) Krieger.
— Cultural Anthropology. (Illus.). 186p. 2000. pap. 18.00 (1-878465-32-5) Scott-Townsend Pubs.
— Eastern Interlude: A Social History of the European Community in Calcutta. (Illus.). 192p. 1997. pap. 18.00 (1-878465-22-8) Scott-Townsend Pubs.
— The Fables of Reason: A Study of Voltaires' "Contes Philosophiques" LC 92-39575. 280p. 1993. text 65.00 (0-19-815880-7) OUP.
— Heredity & Humanity: Race, Eugenics & Modern Science. 156p. (C). 1996. pap. text 16.00 (1-878465-15-5) Scott-Townsend Pubs.
— Physical Anthropology. (Illus.). 164p. 2000. pap. 20.00 (1-878465-31-7) Scott-Townsend Pubs.
— Race, Intelligence & Bias in Academe. 2nd rev. ed. Orig. Title: Race, Intelligence & Bias in Academe. 352p. 1997. pap. 28.00 (1-878465-23-6) Scott-Townsend Pubs.
— Stendhal's Violin: A Novelist & His Reader. 310p. 1988. text 74.00 (0-19-815851-3) OUP.
— Unfolding Mallarme: The Development of a Poetic Art. 328p. 1997. text 80.00 (0-19-815917-X) OUP.
Pearson, Roger, ed. Ecology & Evolution. (Mankind Quarterly Monographs: No. 1). 92p. (C). 1981. pap. 12.00 (0-941694-00-3) Inst Study Man.
— Essays in Medical Anthropology. (Mankind Quarterly Monographs: No. 2). (Orig.). (C). 1981. pap. 12.00 (0-941694-01-1) Inst Study Man.
— Perspectives on Indo-European Language, Culture & Religion: Studies in Honor of Edgar C. Polome, Vol. 1. (Journal of Indo-European Studies: No. 7). (Illus.). 256p. (C). 1991. pap. 36.00 (0-941694-37-2) Inst Study Man.
Pearson, Roger, intro. Stendhal: Red & Black Chart. LC 93-30285. (Modern Literatures in Perspective Ser.). (C). 1994. text 56.50 (0-582-09617-0, 76705, Pub. by Addison-Wesley) Longman.
— Stendhal: Red & Black Chart. LC 93-30285. (Modern Literatures in Perspective Ser.). (C). 1995. pap. text 26.50 (0-582-09616-2, 76704, Pub. by Addison-Wesley) Longman.
***Pearson, Roger & Hermans, Majorie, eds.** Alaska in Maps: A Thematic Atlas. (Illus.). 100p. 1998. spiral bd. 35.00 (1-887419-02-0) Univ of AK.
Pearson, Roger, jt. auth. see Voltaire.
Pearson, Roger, ed. see Shockley, William B.
Pearson, Roger, ed. see Stendhal, pseud.
Pearson, Roger, ed. see Zola, Emile.
Pearson, Roger, ed. see Zysk, K. G., et al.
Pearson, Roger, tr. see Maupassant, Guy de.
Pearson, Roger, tr. see Zola, Emile.
Pearson, Roger, tr. & intro. see Voltaire.
Pearson, Roger C. & Goheen, Austin C., eds. Compendium of Grape Diseases. LC 88-70733. (Disease Compendium Ser.). (Illus.). 128p. (Orig.). 1988. pap. 42.00 (0-89054-088-8) Am Phytopathol Soc.
Pearson, Roger W. Alaska: A Modern American Frontier. 1996. text 35.00 (0-89158-903-1) Westview.
— Alaska: A Modern American Frontier. (C). 1996. pap. text 20.00 (0-86531-489-6) Westview.
Pearson, Ronald K. Discretetime Dynamic Models. LC TP155.75.P43 1999. 480p. 1999. text 85.00 (0-19-512198-8) OUP.
Pearson, Ronald W. The American Patented Brace, 1829-1924: An Illustrated Directory of Patents. (Illus.). 192p. (Orig.). 1994. pap. 22.95 (1-879335-48-4) Astragal Pr.
Pearson, Ross A. Australians at War in the Air Vol. 2: 1939-1945. LC 95-233675. 1996. pap. text 24.95 (0-86417-709-7, Pub. by Kangaroo Pr) Seven Hills Bk.
Pearson, Roy. Prayers for All Occasions: For Pastors & Lay Leaders. 144p. (Orig.). 1990. pap. 14.00 (0-8170-1127-7) Judson.
Pearson, Ruth & Jackson, Cecile. Feminist Visions of Development: Gender Analysis & Policy. LC 97-45904. (Studies in Development Economics). 288p. (C). 1998. (0-415-14234-2); pap. 27.99 (0-415-15790-0) Routledge.
Pearson, Ryne D. Capitol Punishment. 352p. 1996. mass mkt. 5.99 (0-380-72228-3, Avon Bks) Morrow Avon.
— October's Ghost. 464p. 1995. reprint ed. mass mkt. 5.99 (0-380-72227-5, Avon Bks) Morrow Avon.
— Simple Simon. 336p. 1997. mass mkt. 5.99 (0-380-72574-6, Avon Bks) Morrow Avon.
— Thunder One. 384p. 1994. reprint ed. mass mkt. 5.50 (0-380-72037-X, Avon Bks) Morrow Avon.
— Top Ten. LC 99-32569. 304p. 1999. 23.95 (0-399-14499-4, G P Putnam) Peng Put Young Read.
Pearson, Ryne Douglas. Mercury Rising. 1998. mass mkt. 6.50 (0-380-80294-5, Avon Bks) Morrow Avon.
***Pearson, Ryne Douglas.** Top Ten. 2000. mass mkt. 6.99 (0-515-12903-8, Jove) Berkley Pub.
Pearson, S. Ghosts. 1988. lib. bdg. write for info. (0-397-32346-8) Lppncott W & W.
Pearson, Sally, jt. auth. see Ashwell, Malcolm.
Pearson, Sam B., III. The Color of Racism: Understanding & Overcoming Discrimination. Fricke, Donna G., ed. LC 95-61793. (Illus.). 172p. (Orig.). 1996. pap. 12.95 (0-9650220-0-5) Transformax.
Pearson, Scott R., et al. Rice Policy in Indonesia. LC 90-55751. (Food Systems & Agrarian Change Ser.). (Illus.). 208p. 1991. text 37.50 (0-8014-2524-7) Cornell U Pr.
Pearson, Scott R., jt. auth. see Monke, Eric.
Pearson, Sharon, jt. auth. see Strong, Marie.
Pearson, Sidney A., jt. auth. see Croly, Herbert.
Pearson, Spencer B. Of Turkeys & Eagles. LC 97-92850. (Illus.). 288p. 1998. 39.95 (0-9646325-3-5) Javelina AZ.
Pearson-Stamps, Pauline. George Sand's Laura: Journey Within the Crystal: A Study & Translation. (American University Studies: Romance Languages & Literature: Ser. II, Vol. 96). XI, 181p. (C). 1992. text 35.95 (0-8204-0771-2) P Lang Pubng.
Pearson, Stanley M. & Sanjabi, Parviz. Casebook of Respiratory Disease. (C). 2000. 24.95 (0-8385-1490-1) Appleton & Lange.
Pearson, Stewart. Building Brands Directly. (Illus.). 288p. (C). 1996. text 42.50 (0-8147-6618-8) NYU Pr.
***Pearson, Sue.** Tools for Citizenship & Life: Using the ITI Lifelong Guidelines & Lifeskills in Your Classroom. 2nd rev. ed. Olsen, Karen D., ed. (Illus.). 278p. 2000. spiral bd. 27.50 (1-878631-60-8, Pub. by S Kovalik) Bks Educators.
***Pearson, Sue & Olsen, Karen.** Family Tools for Teaching Character & Vaues: Using the ITI Lifelong Guidelines & Lifeskills in Your Home. (Illus.). 266p. 2000. spiral bd. 27.50 (1-878631-61-6, Pub. by S Kovalik) Bks Educators.
Pearson, Sue, et al. Signs & Strategies for Educating Children with Brain Injuries: A Practical Guide for Teachers & Schools. LC 95-34228. 112p. (Orig.). 1995. pap., teacher ed. 24.95 (1-882855-33-7) HDI Pubs.
Pearson, Susan. The Bogeyman Caper. (Eagle-Eye Ernie Mysteries Ser.). (Illus.). 80p. (J). (gr. 1-3). 1990. pap. 11.95 (0-671-70565-2) S&S Bks Yung.
— The Campfire Ghosts. (Eagle-Eye Ernie Mysteries Ser.). (Illus.). 96p. (J). (gr. 1-3). 1990. pap. 11.95 (0-671-70567-9) S&S Bks Yung.
— The Day Porkchop Climbed the Christmas Tree. (Illus.). (J). (gr. k-3). 9.95 (0-317-62031-2) P-H.
— Eagle-Eye Ernie Comes to Town. (Eagle-Eye Ernie Mysteries Ser.). (Illus.). 80p. (J). (gr. 1-3). 1990. pap. 11.95 (0-671-70564-4) S&S Bks Yung.
— The Green Magician Puzzle. LC 90-22436. (Eagle-Eye Ernie Mysteries Ser.). (Illus.). (J). 1991. pap. 11.95 (0-671-74054-7) S&S Bks Yung.
— Monday I Was an Alligator. LC 78-23618. (Lippincott-I-Like-to-Read Bks.). (Illus.). (J). (gr. k-2). 1979. lib. bdg. 11.89 (0-397-31830-8) HarpC Child Bks.
— My Favorite Time of Year. LC 87-45296. (Illus.). 32p. (J). (ps-3). 1988. 12.95 (0-06-024681-2) HarpC Child Bks.
— One-Two-Three Zoo Mystery. (J). 1991. pap. 11.95 (0-671-74052-0) S&S Trade.
— Porkchop & Rosie. (J). 1998. 9.95 (0-13-685793-0) S&S Childrens.
— Silver Morning. LC 96-51579. (Illus.). 32p. (J). (gr. k-3). 1998. 16.00 (0-15-274786-9) Harcourt.
— The Spooky Sleepover. (Eagle-Eye Ernie Mysteries Ser.). (Illus.). 64p. (J). (gr. 1-3). 1991. pap. 12.00 (0-671-74070-9) S&S Bks Yung.
— Well, I Never! 46th ed. LC 89-48016. (Illus.). 40p. (J). (ps-1). 1990. pap. 15.00 (0-671-69199-6) S&S Bks Yung.
Pearson, Sybille. Phantasie. 1989. pap. 6.95 (0-88145-079-0) Broadway Play.
— Sally & Marsha: A Play in Two Acts. 1985. pap. 5.25 (0-8222-0980-2) Dramatists Play.
— Unfinished Stories. 1993. pap. 5.25 (0-8222-1351-6) Dramatists Play.
Pearson, T. A., et al. Primer in Preventive Cardiology. (Illus.). 290p. (C). 1994. pap. write for info. (0-87493-006-5) Am Heart.
Pearson, T. H., jt. ed. see Tyson, R. V.
***Pearson, T. R.** Blue Ridge. 240p. 2000. 24.95 (0-670-89269-6, Viking) Viking Penguin.
Pearson, T. R. Call & Response. 432p. 1991. pap. 10.95 (0-380-71163-X, Avon Bks) Morrow Avon.
— Cry Me a River. LC 92-13860. 272p. 1995. 22.00 (0-8050-2200-7) H Holt & Co.
— Gospel Hour. 368p. 1992. pap. 11.00 (0-380-71036-6, Avon Bks) Morrow Avon.
— The Last of How It Was: A Novel. 352p. 1995. pap. 15.00 (0-8050-3757-8, Owl) H Holt & Co.
— Off for the Sweet Hereafter: A Novel. 384p. 1995. pap. 12.00 (0-8050-3756-X, Owl) H Holt & Co.
— A Short History of a Small Place. 1995. pap. 12.00 (0-8050-3320-3) H Holt & Co.
Pearson, Ted. Acoustic Masks. 1994. pap. 7.00 (84-87467-21-0, Pub. by Zasterle Pr) SPD-Small Pr Dist.
— The Blue Table. 1979. pap. 6.00 (0-917588-03-7) Trike.
— Catenary Odes. LC 87-91337. 48p. 1987. 6.00 (0-917588-17-7) O Bks.
— Evidence. 208p. (Orig.). (C). 1989. pap. 12.00 (0-685-26491-2) Gaz NJ.
— Evidence, 1975-1989. 1990. pap. 12.00 (0-9623399-0-3) Gaz NJ.
— The Grit. 1976. pap. 5.00 (0-917588-01-0) Trike.
— Planetary Gear. LC 91-67074. (Roof Bks.). 72p. (Orig.). 1991. pap. 8.95 (0-937804-43-6) Segue NYC.
Pearson, Terry W., ed. Parasite Antigens: Toward New Strategies for Vaccines. LC 86-2141. (Receptors & Ligands in Intercellular Communication Ser.: No. 7). 427p. 1986. reprint ed. pap. 132.40 (0-608-01332-3, 206207500001) Bks Demand.
Pearson, Thomas S. Russian Officialdom in Crisis: Autocracy & Local Self-Government, 1861-1900. (Illus.). 304p. (C). 1989. text 80.00 (0-521-36127-3) Cambridge U Pr.
Pearson, Timothy J., jt. ed. see Zensus, J. Anton.
Pearson, Tom, jt. auth. see American Academy of Dermatology Staff.
Pearson, Tracey C. The Howling Dog. (Illus.). 32p. (J). (ps up). 1991. 13.95 (0-374-33502-8) FS&G.
— The Howling Dog. (Sunburst Ser.). (Illus.). 32p. (J). (ps up). 1995. pap. 3.95 (0-374-43332-1) FS&G.
— The Purple Hat. LC 96-3116. 32p. (J). (ps-1). 1997. 16.00 (0-374-36153-3) FS&G.
Pearson, Tracey Campbell. Howling Dog. 1991. 9.15 (0-606-07681-6, Pub. by Turtleback) Demco.
— Where Does Joe Go? LC 98-37745. (Illus.). 32p. (J). (ps-2). 1999. 16.00 (0-374-38319-7) FS&G.
Pearson, Veronica & Leung, Benjamin K., eds. Women in Hong Kong. (Illus.). 318p. (C). 1995. text 32.00 (0-19-585954-5) OUP.
Pearson, Virginia. Everything but Elephants. (American Autobiography Ser.). 178p. 1995. reprint ed. lib. bdg. 69.00 (0-7812-8614-X) Rprt Serv.
Pearson, W. & Raynor, G. Handbook of Lattice Spacings & Structures, Metals & Alloys, Vol. 2. LC 57-14965. (International Series of Monographs in Metals Physics & Physical Metallurgy: Vol. 8). 1967. 630.00 (0-08-011897-6, Pub. by Pergamon Repr) Franklin.
Pearson, William H., ed. Advances in Heterocyclic Natural Product Synthesis, Vol. 1. 193p. 1990. 109.50 (1-55938-169-8) Jai Pr.
— Advances in Heterocyclic Natural Product Synthesis, Vol. 2. 250p. 1992. 109.50 (1-55938-333-X) Jai Pr.
— Advances in Heterocyclic Natural Product Synthesis, Vol. 3. 1996. 109.50 (1-55938-426-3) Jai Pr.
— Advances in Heterocyclic Natural Product Synthesis, Vol. 4. Date not set. 109.50 (0-7623-0214-3) Jai Pr.
Pearson, Willie, Jr. & Fechter, Alan, eds. Who Will Do Science? Educating the Next Generation. LC 94-9005. 208p. 1994. text 33.00 (0-8018-4857-1) Johns Hopkins.
Pearsons. Esophageal & Thoracic Surgery Atlas. (C). 1995. text 475.00 (0-443-08984-1, W B Saunders Co) Harcrt Hlth Sci Grp.
Pearsons, H. Gilbert & Sullivan. lib. bdg. 49.00 (0-685-95443-9) Scholarly.
Peart, Aston & Peart, Monica. Enchanting Ways To Romance Your Mate. Fox, Ericka, ed. 1997. 8.95 (1-889757-50-0) Inspiration GA.
Peart-Binns, John S. Defender of the Church of England: A Biography of R. R. Williams, Bishop of Leicester. 172p. 1984. 35.00 (0-7855-1030-3, Pub. by Amate Pr Ltd) St Mut.
— Edwin Morris: Arch-Bishop of Wales. 200p. (C). 1990. 39.00 (0-86383-636-4, Pub. by Gomer Pr) St Mut.
***Peart, Jane.** April & May. abr. ed. (Orphan Train West Ser.). 160p. (J). (gr. 5-9). 2000. pap. 5.99 (0-8007-5724-6, All the Lost Ye) Revell.
Peart, Jane. Brides of Montclair, 4 vols. (Brides of Montclair Ser.: Vols. 1-4). 1994. pap. 15.96 (0-310-49206-8) Zondervan.
— Circle of Love. (Love Inspired Ser.). 238p. 2000. per. 12.95 (0-373-87093-0, 1-87093-0) Harlequin Bks.
— Courageous Bride: Montclair in Wartime, 1940-1945. LC 98-5496. (Brides of Montclair Ser.: Bk. 14). 256p. 1998. pap. 9.99 (0-310-20210-8) Zondervan.
— Designs of the Heart. (American Quilt Ser.). 1999. 12.99 (0-88486-223-2) Arrowood Pr.
— A Distant Dawn. LC 95-35737. (Westward Dreams Ser.: Vol. 4). 256p. 1995. 9.99 (0-310-41301-X) Zondervan.
— Dreams of a Longing Heart. LC 90-38382. (Orphan Train West Ser.). 192p. (Orig.). (gr. 11). 1990. pap. 7.99 (0-8007-5373-9) Revell.
***Peart, Jane.** Dreams of a Longing Heart. LC 00-33751. (Orig.). 2000. write for info. (0-7862-2700-1) Thorndike Pr.
— The Edgecliffe Manor Mysteries Library, 4. (Edgecliffe Manor Mysteries Ser.). (gr. 13 up). 1998. pap. 35.95 (0-8007-6393-9) Revell.
Peart, Jane. Folly's Bride, No. 4. (Brides of Montclair Ser.: Vol. 4). 2000. 3.99 (0-310-21466-1) Zondervan.
— Fortune's Bride. 224p. 1987. pap. 5.95 (0-310-47431-0, 15589P) Zondervan.
— Fortunes Bride, No. 3. (Brides of Montclair Ser.: Vol. 3). 2000. 3.99 (0-310-21468-8) Zondervan.
— Gallant Bride. 224p. (Orig.). 1988. pap. 5.95 (0-310-46741-1, 15673P) Zondervan.
— The Harvey Girls. (Westward Dreams Ser.: No. 6). 2000. 9.99 (0-310-22013-0) Zondervan.
— The Heart's Lonely Secret. LC 94-16722. (Orphan Train West Ser.). 312p. (Orig.). (gr. 10). 1994. pap. 9.99 (0-8007-5542-1) Revell.
— Hero's Bride. (Brides of Montclair Ser.: Vol. 11). 108p. 1993. pap. 8.99 (0-310-67141-8) Zondervan.
— Homeward the Seeking Heart. LC 90-8710. (Orphan Train West Ser.). 192p. (gr. 11). 1990. pap. 7.99 (0-8007-5374-7) Revell.
***Peart, Jane.** Homeward the Seeking Heart. large type ed. LC 00-24260. (Christian Fiction Ser.). 263p. 2000. 24.95 (0-7862-2531-9) Thorndike Pr.
— Ivy & Allison. 2nd abr. ed. LC 99-48425. (Orphan Train West Ser.). (Illus.). 160p. (J). (gr. 5-9). 2000. pap. 5.99 (0-8007-5714-9) Chosen Bks.
— Kit. 2nd abr. ed. (Orphan Train West Ser.). (Illus.). 144p. (J). 2000. pap. 5.99 (0-8007-5715-7) Chosen Bks.
— Laurel. 2nd abr. ed. LC PZ7.P32334Lau 2000. (Orphan Train West Ser.). (Illus.). 160p. (J). (gr. 5-9). 2000. pap. 5.99 (0-8007-5713-0) Chosen Bks.
Peart, Jane. Montclair Brides. Date not set. 19.99 (0-310-23043-8) Zondervan.
Peart, Jane. Montclair Brides, Vol. 2. 2nd ed. Date not set. 19.99 (0-310-23044-6) HarpC.
— A Montclair Homecoming. LC 99-88527. (Brides of Montclair Ser.). 2000. 9.99 (0-310-67161-2) Zondervan.
— Orphan Train West Pack, 4. (Orphan Train West Ser.). (gr. 13 up). pap. 29.95 (0-8007-6403-X) Revell.
— Orphan Train West Series for Young Readers 4 vols. (Illus.). (J). 2000. pap. 19.96 (0-8007-6442-0) Chosen Bks.
Peart, Jane. A Perilous Bargain. LC 96-29629. (Edgecliffe Manor Mysteries Ser.). 240p. 1997. pap. 9.99 (0-8007-5626-6) Revell.
***Peart, Jane.** A Perilous Bargain. large type ed. LC 99-58075. (Edgecliffe Manor Mysteries Ser.). 2000. 24.95 (0-7862-2380-4) Thorndike Pr.
Peart, Jane. The Pledge. large type ed. LC 98-4362. 1998. 22.95 (0-7862-1469-4) Thorndike Pr.
— The Promise. large type ed. LC 98-53621. 1999. 23.95 (0-7862-1804-5) Thorndike Pr.
— Promises to Keep. 1998. per. 4.50 (0-373-87043-4, 1-87043-5) Harlequin Bks.
— Quest for Lasting Love. LC 90-40569. (Orphan Train West Ser.). 192p. (Orig.). (YA). (gr. 10 up). 1990. pap. 7.99 (0-8007-5372-0) Revell.
— Ransomed Bride. (Serenade Saga Ser.: No. 36). 1986. pap. 1.49 (0-310-47312-8) Zondervan.
— Ransomed Bride, No. 2. (Brides of Montclair Ser.: Vol. 2). 2000. 3.99 (0-310-21498-X) Zondervan.
— Rebel Bride, No. 14. (Serenade Saga Ser.). 1985. pap. 1.49 (0-310-46692-X, 15529P) Zondervan.
— The Risk of Loving. (Love Inspired Ser.). 1997. per. 4.50 (0-373-87003-5, 1-87003-9, Steeple Hill) Harlequin Bks.
***Peart, Jane.** The Risk of Loving. LC 00-41184. 2000. write for info. (0-7862-2780-X) Thorndike Pr.

P

Peart, Jane. Shadow of Fear. LC 96-14568. (Edgecliffe Manor Mysteries Ser.: No. 2). 176p. (gr. 11). 1996. pap. 9.99 (*0-8007-5597-9*) Revell.

***Peart, Jane.** Shadow of Fear. large type ed. LC 00-24261. (Christian Mystery Ser.). 276p. 2000. 24.95 (*0-7862-2535-1*) Thorndike Pr.

Peart, Jane. Thread of Suspicion. LC 98-8818. (Edgecliffe Manor Mysteries Ser.: Vol. 4). 224p. 1998. pap. 9.99 (*0-8007-5676-2*) Revell.

***Peart, Jane.** Toddy. 2nd abr. ed. LC 99-31962. (Orphan Train West Ser.). 160p. (J). (gr. 5-9). 2000. pap. 5.99 (*0-8007-5716-5*) Revell.

Peart, Jane. Undaunted Spirit. LC 99-15208. (Westward Dreams Ser.: Vol. 5). 208p. 1999. pap. 9.99 (*0-310-22012-2*) Zondervan.

— Valiant Bride, No. 1. (Brides of Montclair Ser.: Vol. 1). 2000. 3.99 (*0-310-21506-4*) Zondervan.

— Valiant Bride, No. 18. (Serenade Saga Ser.). 1985. pap. 2.50 (*0-310-46782-9*, 15537P) Zondervan.

— Web of Deception. LC 95-49284. (Edgecliffe Manor Mystery Ser.: No. 2). 208p. (gr. 11). 1996. pap. 9.99 (*0-8007-5598-7*) Revell.

— Westward Dreams. Date not set. 19.99 (*0-310-23046-2*) HarpC.

Peart, Jane. Where Tomorrow Waits. (Westward Dreams Ser.: Vol. 3). 256p. 1995. reprint ed. 9.99 (*0-310-41291-9*) Zondervan.

Peart, Jane. Yankee Bride. LC 83-15514. (Serenade Saga Ser.: No. 8). 192p. 1984. 1.49 (*0-310-46542-7*, 15514P) Zondervan.

Peart, John. Catalog of Existing Small Tools for Surface Preparation & Support Equipment for Blasters & Painters. (Illus.). 106p. 1984. pap. text 30.00 (*0-938477-14-5*) SSPC.

Peart, Monica, jt. auth. see Peart, Aston.

***Peart, Norman Anthony.** Separate No More: Understanding & Developing Racial Reconciliation in Your Church. 192p. 2000. pap. 12.99 (*0-8010-6337-X*) Baker Bks.

Peart, R. M. & Brook, R. C. Analysis of Agricultural Energy Systems. (Energy in World Agriculture Ser.: Vol. 5). 394p. 1992. 271.75 (*0-444-88660-5*) Elsevier.

Peart, R. M. & Curry, R. Bruce. Agricultural Systems Modeling & Simulation. LC 97-36225. (Books in Soils, Plants & the Environment Ser.: Vol. 60). (Illus.). 728p. 1997. text 195.00 (*0-8247-0041-4*) Dekker.

Peart, Sandra. The Economics of W. S. Jevons. LC 95-51459. (Studies in the History of Economics: Vol. 9). 328p. (C). 1996. 85.00 (*0-415-06713-8*) Routledge.

Peart, Sandra, jt. auth. see Forget, Evelyn L.

Pearton, Maurice. Diplomacy, War & Technology Since 1830. LC 84-7272. (Studies in Government & Public Policy). 288p. 1984. pap. 14.95 (*0-7006-0254-2*) U Pr of KS.

Pearton, S. J. Hydrogen in Compound Semiconductors. (Materials Science Forum Ser.: Vols. 148-9). (Illus.). 546p. (C). 1994. text 200.00 (*0-87849-672-6*, Pub. by Trans T Pub) Enfield Pubs NH.

— Processing of Wide Bandgap Semiconductors LC 99-27325. 1999. 145.00 (*0-8155-1439-5*) Noyes.

Pearton, S. J., et al, eds. Advanced III-V Compound Semiconductor Growth, Processing & Devices. (Symposium Proceedings Ser.: Vol. 240). 905p. 1992. text 30.00 (*1-55899-134-4*) Materials Res.

Pearton, S. J., et al, eds. Power Semiconductor Materials & Devices Vol. 483: Materials Research Society Symposium Proceedings. LC 98-2946. 456p. 1998. text 73.00 (*1-55899-388-6*) Materials Res.

Pearton, S. J., et al. Hydrogen in Crystalline Semiconductors. Gonser, U. et al, eds. (Materials Science Ser.: Vol. 16). (Illus.). 376p. 1992. 54.00 (*0-387-53923-9*) Spr-Verlag.

— Topics in Growth & Device Processing of III-V Semiconductor. 400p. 1996. text 81.00 (*981-02-1884-2*) World Scientific Pub.

Pearton, S. J., jt. auth. see Jalali, B.

Pearton, S. J., jt. ed. see Shul, R. J.

Pearton, Stephen J., et al, eds. GaN & Related Alloys, Vol. 537. LC 99-15966. (Symposium Proceedings Ser.). 1024p. 1999. 89.00 (*1-55899-443-2*) Materials Res.

Pearton, Stephen J., ed. GaN & Related Materials. (Optoelectronic Properties of Semiconducter Ser.: Vol. 2). 456p. 1997. text 150.00 (*90-5699-516-2*); pap. text 45.00 (*90-5699-517-0*) Gordon & Breach.

***Pearton, Stephen J., ed.** Gan & Related Materials II. (Optoelectronic Properties of Semiconductor Ser.: Vol. 7). 692p. 2000. text 163.00 (*90-5699-685-1*, G & B Science); pap. text 89.00 (*90-5699-686-X*, G & B Science) Gordon & Breach.

Peartree, C. Edward, jt. ed. see Henry, Ryan.

Peary, Danny. Baseball's Finest. 383p. 1996. write for info. (*1-57215-209-5*) World Pubns.

— Cult Movies. LC 98-9648. 416p. 1998. 12.99 (*0-517-20185-2*) Random Hse Value.

— Game of Their Lives. LC 97-3904. 320p. 1997. 27.95 (*0-02-860841-0*) Macmillan.

— Super Bowl: The Game of Their Lives: The Definitive Game-by-Game History As Told by the Stars. 464p. 1998. pap. 16.00 (*0-02-862633-8*) Macmillan.

***Peary, Danny, ed.** Super Bowl: The Game of Their Lives: The Definitive Game-by-Game History as Told by the Stars. (Illus.). 448p. 2000. reprint ed. text 28.00 (*0-7881-6908-4*) DIANE Pub.

Peary, Danny, ed. We Played the Game: Sixty-Five Players Remember Baseball's Greatest Era, 1947-1964. (Illus.). 672p. (J). 1995. pap. 19.45 (*0-7868-8091-0*, Pub. by Hyperion) Time Warner.

Peary, Danny, jt. auth. see McCarver, Tim.

Peary, Gerald, ed. Quentin Tarantino: Interviews. LC 98-17837. (Conversations with Filmmakers Ser.). 256p. 1998. pap. 18.00 (*1-57806-051-6*); text 45.00 (*1-57806-050-8*) U Pr of Miss.

Peary, Josephine D. My Arctic Journal: A Year among Ice-Fields & Eskimos. LC 74-5863. reprint ed. 54.50 (*0-404-11669-8*) AMS Pr.

— My Arctic Journal, a Year among Ice-Fields & Eskimos: With an Account of the Great White Journey Across Greenland by Robert E. Peary. (American Biography Ser.). 240p. 1991. reprint ed. lib. bdg. 69.00 (*0-7812-8309-4*) Rprt Serv.

Peary, Robert E. Northward over the Great Ice Vols. 1-2: A Narrative of Life & Work on Greenland, 1886, 1891-97. (Illus.). 1993. reprint ed. lib. bdg. 125.00 (*0-8328-3133-6*) Higginson Bk Co.

Peary, Warren, jt. auth. see Peavy, William S.

Pease. International Organizations. LC 99-35718. 308p. 1999. pap. text 42.00 (*0-13-924697-5*) P-H.

Pease, A. S., jt. auth. see Fiske, D.

Pease, Allan. Signals. 240p. (Orig.). 1984. pap. 12.95 (*0-553-34366-1*) Bantam.

Pease, Allan, jt. auth. see Pease, Barbara.

***Pease, Allison.** Modernism, Mass Culture & the Aesthetics of Obscenity. LC 99-56880. 2000. write for info. (*0-521-78076-4*) Cambridge U Pr.

Pease, Antonella & Bini, Daniela. Italiano in Diretta: An Introductory Course. 2nd ed. LC 92-29537. 512p. (C). 1992. student ed. 71.25 (*0-07-049267-0*); text 64.37 (*0-07-049268-9*) McGraw.

— Italiano in Diretta: An Introductory Course. 2nd ed. (C). 1993. pap., wbk. ed., lab manual ed. 30.63 (*0-07-049269-7*) McGraw.

Pease, Antonella & Carter, Daniela B. Vivere All Italiana. (C). 1985. pap. text 25.25 (*0-07-554713-9*) McGraw.

Pease, Austin S., jt. auth. see Pease, David.

***Pease, Barbara & Pease, Allan.** Why Men Don't Listen & Women Can't Read Maps. (Illus.). 272p. 2000. 24.95 (*1-56649-156-8*) Welcome Rain.

***Pease, Bob & Fook, Jan.** Transforming Social Work Practice: Postmodern Critical Perspectives. LC 99-20553. 1999. pap. write for info. (*0-415-21647-8*) Routledge.

***Pease, Bob & Fook, Jan, eds.** Transforming Social Work Practice: Postmodern Critical Perspectives. LC 99-20553. 240p. (C). 1999. text. write for info. (*0-415-21646-X*) Routledge.

Pease, Clifford A., Jr. Calvin Coolidge & His Family: An Annotated Bibliography. LC 87-71283. (Illus.). 48p. (Orig.). (C). 1987. pap. 12.00 (*0-944951-00-7*) C Coolidge Memorial.

Pease, Daniel C., ed. Cellular Aspects of Neural Growth & Differentiation: Proceedings of a Conference Held November, 1969. LC 73-126760. (UCLA Forum in Medical Sciences Ser.: No. 14). 523p. reprint ed. pap. 162.20 (*0-608-15829-1*, 203131200074) Bks Demand.

***Pease, David & Pease, Austin S.** A Genealogical & Historical Record of the Descendants of John Pease, Sr., Last of Enfield, Connecticut, 2 vols. in 1. 2000. reprint ed. pap. 55.00 (*0-8063-4991-3*, Pub. by Clearfield Co) ACCESS Pubs Network.

— The Pease Record: An Essential Genealogical Reference on the Pease Family of New England, Comprising Rev. David Pease's "A Genealogical & Historical Record of the Descendants of John Pease, Sr." & Austin S. Pease's "The Early History of the Pease Family in America" 551p. 1999. reprint ed. pap. 38.00 (*0-7884-1300-7*, P108) Heritage Bk.

Pease, Deborah. Another Ghost in the Doorway. LC 98-46171. 150p. 1999. 24.95 (*1-55921-272-1*) Moyer Bell.

— Did You Know? Hunting, Constance, ed. 58p. 1993. pap. 8.95 (*0-913006-52-1*) Puckerbrush.

— The Feathered Wind. Hunting, Constance, ed. 80p. (Orig.). 1992. pap. 8.95 (*0-913006-49-1*) Puckerbrush.

— Into the Amazement. Hunting, Constance, ed. 80p. 1993. pap. 8.95 (*0-913006-56-4*) Puckerbrush.

Pease, Donald, ed. & intro. see Cooper, James Fenimore.

Pease, Donald E., ed. National Identities & Post-Americanist Narratives. LC 93-49689. (New Americanists Ser.). 352p. 1994. text 49.95 (*0-8223-1477-0*); pap. text 17.95 (*0-8223-1492-4*) Duke.

— New Essays on "The Rise of Silas Lapham" (American Novel Ser.). 142p. (C). 1991. text 32.95 (*0-521-37311-5*) Cambridge U Pr.

— New Essays on "The Rise of Silas Lapham" (American Novel Ser.). 142p. (C). 1991. pap. text 14.95 (*0-521-37898-2*) Cambridge U Pr.

— Revisionary Interventions into the Americanist Canon. LC 93-49688. (New Americanists Ser.). 368p. 1994. text 49.95 (*0-8223-1478-9*); pap. text 17.95 (*0-8223-1493-2*) Duke.

Pease, Donald E., jt. ed. see Kaplan, Amy.

Pease, Donald E., jt. ed. see Michaels, Walter B.

Pease, Donald E., ed. see Spanos, William V.

Pease, Dudley A. & Pippenger, John E. Basic Fluid Power. 2nd ed. (Illus.). 384p. 1986. pap. text 86.20 (*0-13-061508-0*) P-H.

Pease, E., et al. Paper City. 24p. (C). 1995. pap. 2.00 (*1-886845-02-6*) Penin Fine Arts.

Pease, Edward, jt. ed. see Dennis, Everette E.

Pease, Edward M. & Wadsworth, George P. Calculus: With Analytic Geometry. LC 68-56150. 1087p. reprint ed. pap. 200.00 (*0-8357-7971-8*, 201245700081) Bks Demand.

Pease, Franklin, jt. ed. see Taylor, William B.

Pease, Greg. Sailing with Pride. LC 90-80916. (Illus.). 128p. 1990. 49.95 (*0-9626299-0-1*) C A Baumgartner Pub.

***Pease, Harold W.** The Mind & Will of the Lord: Joseph Smith. (Illus.). 2000. pap. 12.95 (*0-9701358-0-7*) Wstwood Bks.

— The Mind & Will of the Lord: Lorenzo Snow. (Illus.). 2000. pap. 7.95 (*0-9701358-1-5*) Wstwood Bks.

Pease, Jane H. & Pease, William H. Bound with Them in Chains: A Biographical History of the Antislavery Movement, 18. LC 74-175612. (Contributions in American History Ser.: No. 18). 334p. 1972. 65.00 (*0-8371-6265-3*, PEB/, Greenwood Pr) Greenwood.

— A Family of Women: The Carolina Petigrus in Peace & War. LC 99-12599. (Illus.). 384p. 1999. 29.95 (*0-8078-2505-0*) U of NC Pr.

— Ladies, Women, & Wenches: Choice & Constraint in Antebellum Charleston & Boston. LC 89-21450. (Gender & American Culture Ser.). xvi, 218p. (C). 1990. pap. 17.95 (*0-8078-4289-3*) U of NC Pr.

Pease, Jane H. & Pease, William Henry. A Family of Women: The Carolina Petigrus in Peace & War. LC 99-12599. 1999. write for info. (*0-8078-4787-9*) U of NC Pr.

Pease, Jane H., jt. auth. see Pease, William H.

Pease, Jane H., jt. ed. see Pease, William H.

Pease, Jeane H., jt. ed. see Pease, William H.

Pease, Jonathan. Wang An-Kuo's Jade Rewards & Millet Dream. (American Oriental Ser.: Vol. 77). iv, 106p. 1994. 18.00 (*0-940490-77-3*) Am Orient Soc.

Pease, Joseph Gurney. A Wealth of Happiness & Many Bitter Trials. 384p. 1999. pap. 28.00 (*1-85072-107-6*, Pub. by W Sessions) St Mut.

***Pease, Joyce.** Dance of the Jack O'Lanterns. 4p. 1999. pap. 2.50 (*0-7390-0293-7*, 18524) Alfred Pub.

Pease, Kenneth, ed. Uses & Abuse of Criminal Statistics. LC 95-52117. (International Library of Criminology, Criminal Justice & Penology). (Illus.). 417p. 1996. text 157.95 (*1-85521-408-3*, Pub. by Dartmth Pub) Ashgate Pub Co.

Pease, Kenneth, jt. auth. see Bottomley, A. Keith.

***Pease, Lisa.** Advanced HTML Authoring. McKenna, Jill & Lane, Susan M., eds. (Illus.). 1999. pap. write for info. (*1-58143-011-6*, PSG1AHA) Prosoft I-net.

— Creating Intelligent Documents with the Extensible Markup Language (XML) Lane, Susan M., ed. (Illus.). 1999. pap. write for info. (*1-58143-015-9*, PSG1XML) Prosoft I-net.

— HTML Fundamentals: A4, Version 3.07. Stanger, James et al, eds. (CIW Foundations Track A4 Ser.). (Illus.). 1999. pap. write for info. (*1-58143-061-2*) Prosoft I-net.

— JavaScript Fundamentals: Version 2.07. Lane, Susan M., ed. (CIW Application Developer Track Ser.). (Illus.). 1999. pap. write for info. (*1-58143-038-8*) Prosoft I-net.

***Pease, Lisa & Cohen, Ken.** JavaScript Fundamentals. Stranger, James, ed. (Illus.). 272p. (C). 1999. pap. write for info. (*0-7423-0299-7*) ComputerPREP.

***Pease, Lisa & Stanger, James.** JavaScript Fundamentals: A4, Version 2.07. Lane, Susan M., ed. (CIW Application Developer Track A4 Ser.). (Illus.). 1999. pap. write for info. (*1-58143-074-4*) Prosoft I-net.

***Pease, Lisa & Stranger, James.** HTML Fundamentals: Module 1. McKenna, Jill, ed. (Illus.). 256p. (C). 1999. pap. write for info. (*0-7423-0295-4*) ComputerPREP.

***Pease, Lisa, et al.** Advanced HTML Authoring: A4, Version 2.07. McKenna, Jill, ed. (CIW Site Designer Track A4 Ser.). (Illus.). 1999. pap. write for info. (*1-58143-070-1*) Prosoft I-net.

— Advanced HTML Authoring: Version 2.07. Lane, Susan M., ed. (CIW Site Designer Track Ser.). (Illus.). 1999. pap. write for info. (*1-58143-034-5*) Prosoft I-net.

Pease, Mary B., et al. Johnson. Mahlon Johnson Family of Littleton, N. J., Ancestors & Descendants. (Illus.). 133p. 1997. reprint ed. pap. 19.50 (*0-8328-9349-8*); reprint ed. lib. bdg. 29.50 (*0-8328-9348-X*) Higginson Bk Co.

Pease, Otis. The Responsibilities of American Advertising: Private Control & Public Influence, 1920-1940. LC 75-39266. (Getting & Spending: The Consumer's Dilemma Ser.). (Illus.). 1976. reprint ed. 23.95 (*0-405-08039-5*) Ayer.

Pease, Pamela. The Garden is Open. LC 99-70138. (Illus.). 32p. (J). (gr. k-6). 1999. 20.00 (*0-9669433-1-7*, No. 9901) Paintbox Pr.

— The Garden Is Open: Signed Artist's Pop-Up Edition. LC 99-70138. (Illus.). 32p. (J). (gr. k-6). 1999. 24.00 (*0-9669433-0-9*, 9901) Paintbox Pr.

Pease, Patrick F. The Lover's Picnic: How to Prepare the Most Romantic Picnic Ever. 24p. (Orig.). 1989. pap. 3.95 (*0-9624137-0-4*) Spirit Originals.

Pease, Paul R. Building a Small Blue Chip Business: Planning, Starting, Growing, Running & Exiting a Long-Term Business. (Illus.). 150p. 1996. 18.95 (*0-9652157-0-9*) P R Pease.

Pease, Peter. Rostropovic in Red Square: A Selection of Love Poems. LC 95-20575. (Illus.). 80p. 1996. pap. 14.95 (*0-7734-2805-4*, Mellen Poetry Pr) E Mellen.

Pease, R. Book & Page: A Cape Cod Novel. 185p. 1997. per. 12.95 (*1-889455-02-4*) Flagg Mtn Pr.

— Boston-South End 1965-1970. (Voyages Ser.: Pt. III). 235p. 1995. per. 12.95 (*0-9637154-6-1*) Flagg Mtn Pr.

— Cape Cod. (Voyages Ser.: Pt. IV). 220p. 1995. per. 12.95 (*0-9637154-7-X*) Flagg Mtn Pr.

— Dead Ahead: A Cape Cod Novel. 183p. 1994. per. 12.95 (*0-9637154-1-0*) Flagg Mtn Pr.

— Gayle: A Love Story. (Voyages Ser.: Pt. I). 173p. 1995. per. 12.95 (*0-9637154-4-5*) Flagg Mtn Pr.

***Pease, R.** Head in the Sand: Murder on Sandy Neck. 131p. 1999. pap. 12.95 (*1-889455-07-5*) Flagg Mtn Pr.

Pease, R. Invisible Bounds: Short Stories. 195p. 1994. per. 12.95 (*0-9637154-3-7*) Flagg Mtn Pr.

***Pease, R.** Life is a Flower: New Poems. 66p. 1999. per. 9.95 (*1-889455-05-9*) Flagg Mtn Pr.

Pease, R. Liliana: A Marriage. (Voyages Ser.: Pt. II). 295p. 1995. per. 12.95 (*0-9637154-5-3*) Flagg Mtn Pr.

***Pease, R.** More Parts of the Puzzle: You Name it. 346p. 2000. per. 16.95 (*1-889455-06-7*) Flagg Mtn Pr.

Pease, R. Never Let Go: P. I. Jeeter on Cape Cod. 162p. 1996. per. 12.95 (*0-9637154-8-8*) Flagg Mtn Pr.

— Runaway: P. I. Jeeter in Boston. 174p. 1996. per. 12.95 (*1-889455-00-8*) Flagg Mtn Pr.

— The Voice of Reason: Controversial Essays. 87p. 1998. per. 12.95 (*1-889455-04-0*) Flagg Mtn Pr.

— When Blossoms Opened in the Sun: Poems. 110p. 1994. per. 8.95 (*0-9637154-9-6*) Flagg Mtn Pr.

Pease, Rick. Filling Station Collectibles with Price Guide. LC 94-65623. (Illus.). 144p. (Orig.). 1994. pap. 29.95 (*0-88740-643-2*) Schiffer.

— Petroleum Collectibles. LC 96-70896. (Illus.). 160p. 1997. pap. 29.95 (*0-7643-0202-7*) Schiffer.

— Service Station Collectibles. LC 95-42727. 160p. 1996. pap. 29.95 (*0-88740-934-2*) Schiffer.

— A Tour with Texaco. (Schiffer Book for Collectors Ser.). (Illus.). 204p. 1997. pap. 34.95 (*0-7643-0360-0*) Schiffer.

Pease, Rick, jt. auth. see Stenzler, Sonya.

***Pease, Robert & Galante, Steven P., eds.** Private Equity Funds-of-Funds: State of the Market. 105p. 2000. pap. 495.00 (*1-893648-09-5*) Asset Alternatives.

Pease, Robert & Hockins, William. Diablo Shadows: A Visual Collection of the Grandeur of the Diablo-San Ramon Valley: The Sights, Scenes & Images That Encompass Alamo, Blackhawk, Danville, Diablo, San Ramon & Walnut Creek. LC 98-92317. 112p. 1998. 49.95 (*0-9669310-0-9*) R Pease Co.

Pease, Robert A. How to Drive into Accidents - And How Not To. LC 97-91601. (Illus.). 488p. (YA). (gr. 10-12). 1998. 28.95 (*0-9655648-0-0*, PP02) Pease Pub.

— Troubleshooting Analog Circuits. (EDN Series for Design Engineers). (Illus.). 217p. 2000. pap. text 29.95 (*0-7506-9499-8*) Buttrwrth-Heinemann.

Pease, Robert F. O. U. I. Operating under the Influence. 199p. 1993. per. 12.95 (*0-9637154-0-2*) Flagg Mtn Pr.

Pease, Robert W. Modoc County: A Geographic Time Continuum on the California Volcanic Tableland. LC 66-63867. (University of California Publications in Social Welfare: Vol. 17). 320p. reprint ed. pap. 99.20 (*0-608-14158-5*, 202127400022) Bks Demand.

Pease, Sara R. Performance Indicators for Permanent Disability: Low-Back Injuries in New Jersey. 1987. 35.00 (*0-935149-10-4*, WC-87-5) Workers Comp Res Inst.

— Performance Indicators for Permanent Disability: Low-Back Injuries in Texas. 1988. 35.00 (*0-935149-15-5*, WC-88-4) Workers Comp Res Inst.

— Performance Indicators for Permanent Disability: Low-Back Injuries in Wisconsin. 1987. 35.00 (*0-935149-09-0*, WC-87-4) Workers Comp Res Inst.

— Workers' Compensation in Washington: Administrative Inventory. LC 89-39120. 1989. 35.00 (*0-935149-20-1*, WC-89-3) Workers Comp Res Inst.

Pease, Stephen E. Psywar: Psychological Warfare in Korea, 1950-53. LC 92-21511. (Illus.). 192p. 1992. 12.95 (*0-8117-2592-8*) Stackpole.

Pease, Susan, jt. auth. see Fishbein, Diana.

Pease, Suzanne, tr. & illus. see Lancaster, Barbara M.

Pease, T. C. The Leveller Movement. 1988. 16.50 (*0-8446-1345-2*) Peter Smith.

Pease, Theodore C. The Frontier State, 1818-1848. (Sesquicentennial History of Illinois Ser.). 514p. 1987. reprint ed. text 29.95 (*0-252-01338-7*) U of Ill Pr.

— The Story of Illinois. 3rd ed. LC 65-17299. 383p. reprint ed. pap. 118.80 (*0-608-16496-8*, 202673800051) Bks Demand.

Pease, Theodore C., ed. Illinois Election Returns: 1818-1848. LC 24-12338. (Illinois Historical Collections: Vol. 18). 1923. 10.00 (*0-912154-06-3*) Ill St Hist Lib.

Pease, Warren. Strictly for the Record. LC 98-96981. (Illus.). 224p. 1998. 25.95 (*0-9667781-0-3*) Bench Mark.

Pease-Watkin, Catherine, ed. see Bentham, Jeremy.

***Pease, William.** Toxic Ignorance: The Continuing Absence of Basic Health Testing for Top-Selling Chemicals in the United States. (Illus.). 65p. (C). 1999. reprint ed. pap. text 20.00 (*0-7881-7900-4*) DIANE Pub.

Pease, William D. An Uncommon Spring. 1999. pap. write for info. (*0-14-013990-7*, Viking) Viking Penguin.

Pease, William H. & Pease, Jane H. Black Utopia: Negro Communal Experiments in America. LC 73-74404. 204p. 1972. pap. 12.95 (*0-87020-066-6*) State Hist Soc Wis.

Pease, William H. & Pease, Jane H., eds. The Antislavery Argument. LC 64-66072. 492p. 1965. text 39.50 (*0-8290-0153-0*) Irvington.

Pease, William H. & Pease, Jeane H., eds. The Antislavery Argument. LC 64-66072. 492p. (C). 1985. reprint ed. pap. text 12.95 (*0-8290-1663-5*) Irvington.

Pease, William H., jt. auth. see Pease, Jane H.

Pease, William Henry, jt. auth. see Pease, Jane H.

Pease, William S., jt. auth. see Johnson, Ernest W.

Peaselee, David C., ed. Topics in Hadron Spectroscopy, Vol. 2. 247p. (C). 1995. lib. bdg. 165.00 (*1-56072-224-X*) Nova Sci Pubs.

Peaslee, Amos J. Agriculture-Commodities-Fisheries-Food-Plants, Pt. 2. (International Governmental Organizations Constitutional Documents Ser.). 1975. lib. bdg. 277.50 (*90-247-1687-X*) Kluwer Academic.

— Communications, Transport, Travel. (International Governmental Organizations Constitutional Documents Ser.: Pt. 5). 1977. lib. bdg. 302.50 (*90-247-1826-0*) Kluwer Academic.

— Constitutions of Nations, Vol. 2. 4th ed. 1986. lib. bdg. 499.00 (*90-247-2905-X*) Kluwer Academic.

— General & Regional-Political-Economic-Social-Legal-Defense, 2 vols. (International Governmental Organizations Constitutional Documents Ser.: Pt. 1). 1974. lib. bdg. 472.00 (*90-247-1601-2*) Kluwer Academic.

P

An Asterisk (*) at the beginning of an entry indicates that the title is appearing for the first time.

— International Governmental Organizations: Constitutional Documents, Pts. 3 & 4. 3rd rev. ed. 1979. pap. text 311.00 (0-247-2087-7) Kluwer Academic.

Peaslee, Ann & Kille, Jullien. You Can Make It! You Can Do It! 101 E-Z Holiday Craft-Tivities for Children. (Illus.). 120p. (Orig.). (J). (gr. 3-6). 1991. pap. 9.95 (0-89346-337-X) Heian Intl.

***Peaslee, David C., ed.** Science As a Cultural Expression. 201p. 1999. 59.00 (1-56072-589-3) Nova Sci Pubs.

Peaslee, David C., ed. Topics in Hadron Spectroscopy. 285p. (C). 1992. lib. bdg. 175.00 (1-56072-036-0) Nova Sci Pubs.

— Topics in Hadron Spectroscopy, Vol. 3. 202p. (C). 1995. lib. bdg. 165.00 (1-56072-225-8) Nova Sci Pubs.

Peaslee, David C., jt. auth. see Oneda, Susana.

Peaslee, Dixie, tr. see Dougall, Lucy.

Peasley, Amy E., jt. auth. see Thomas, Scott L.

Peasley, Harold. Heartbeat of Evangelism: Keeping the Main Thing, The Main Thing. 82p. 1999. pap. 6.99 (1-889893-32-3) Emerald House Group Inc.

Peasnell, K. V., jt. ed. see Brief, Richard P.

Peason, B. Men Are Dogs, Women Are Cats. LC 98-87198. 365p. 1999. 25.00 (0-7388-0089-9); pap. 15.00 (0-7388-0090-2) Xlibris Corp.

Peaster, Laura L., ed. see Milam, June M.

Peaster, Lillian. Pueblo Pottery Families: Acoma, Cochiti, Hopi, Isleta, Jemez, Laguna, Nambe, Picuris, Pojoaque, San Ildefonso, San Juan, Santa Clara, Santo Domingo, Taos, Tesuque, Zia, Zuni. LC 97-3643. 160p. 1997. pap. 19.95 (0-7643-0233-7) Schiffer.

Peat. Community Based Rehabilitation. 1997. pap. text 50.00 (0-7020-1941-0, W B Saunders Co) Harcrt Hlth Sci Grp.

Peat, Alan & Whitton, Brian A. John Tunnard: A Life & Catalogue of the Work. LC 96-28032. (Illus.). 248p. 1997. 131.95 (1-85928-320-9, Pub. by Scolar Pr) Ashgate Pub Co.

Peat, B. Condensing Boilers. (C). 1986. 105.00 (0-86022-158-X, Pub. by Build Servs Info Assn) St Mut.

Peat, Bette A., jt. auth. see Gillay, Carlyn Z.

Peat, Bette A., jt. auth. see Gillay, Carolyn Z.

Peat, David, jt. auth. see Briggs, John.

Peat, David F., jt. ed. see Buckley, Paul.

***Peat, F. David.** Blackwinged Night: Creativity in Nature & Mind. (Illus.). 240p. 2000. text 26.00 (0-7382-0205-3) Perseus Pubng.

Peat, F. David. In Search of Nikola Tesla. 144p. (Orig.). 1997. pap. 10.95 (1-85398-020-X, Pub. by Ashgrove Pr) Words Distrib.

— Infinite Potential: The Life & Times of David Bohm. (Illus.). 368p. 1997. pap. 16.00 (0-201-32820-8) Addison-Wesley.

— Lighting the Seventh Fire: The Science, Healing & Spiritual Ways of the Native Americans. LC 94-16685. (Illus.). 352p. 1994. 19.95 (1-55972-249-5, Birch Ln Pr) Carol Pub Group.

Peat, F. David. Return of the Sacred. 14.00 (0-06-098764-2) HarpC.

Peat, F. David. Superstrings & the Search for the Theory of Everything. 256p. 1989. pap. 16.95 (0-8092-4257-5, 425750, Contemporary Bks) NTC Contemp Pub Co.

— Synchronicity. 256p. 1987. pap. 14.95 (0-553-34676-8, New Age Bks) Bantam.

Peat, F. David, jt. auth. see Briggs, John.

Peat, F. David, jt. auth. see Buckley, Paul.

Peat, F. David, jt. auth. see Sokdowski, Thomas.

Peat, F. David, jt. ed. see Hiley, Basil.

Peat, John P., jt. auth. see Petit, Ted L.

Peat, Lindsay. Practical Guide to DBMS Selection. 340p. 1982. 138.50 (3-11-008167-9) De Gruyter.

Peat Marwick Auditores Independentes Staff. Investment in Brazil. (Illus.). xiii, 105p. write for info. (0-318-58175-2) Peat Marwick.

Peat Marwick International Staff. Worldwide Financial Reporting & Audit Requirements: A Peat Marwick Inventory. 258p. write for info. (0-318-57848-4) Peat Marwick.

Peat, Marwick, Mitchell & Co. Staff. Public Sale of Securities in the United States: A Guide for Foreign Bankers. iv, 133p. write for info. (0-318-57034-3) Peat Marwick.

Peat, Marwick, Mitchell & Co. Staff, ed. Taxation of Intercompany Transactions in Selected Countries in Europe & the U. S. A. 119p. 1979. pap. 16.00 (90-200-0589-8) Kluwer Academic.

Peat, N. Ross. Salistamba Sutra: Tibetan Original Sanskrit Vreconstruction, English Translation Critical Notes Including Pali Parallels, Chinese Version & Ancient Tibetan Fragments. (C). 1993. 16.00 (81-208-1135-6, Pub. by Motilal Bnarsidass) S Asia.

Peat, Neville. The Catlins: And the Southern Scenic Route. (Illus.). 80p. 1997. pap. 19.95 (1-877133-42-6, Pub. by Univ Otago Pr) Intl Spec Bk.

***Peat, Neville & Patrick, Brian.** Wild Central: A Natural History of Central Otago. (Illus.). 160p. 1999. pap. 49.95 (1-877133-65-5, Pub. by Univ Otago Pr) Intl Spec Bk.

Peat, Neville & Patrick, Brian. Wild Dunedin: Enjoying the Natural History of New Zealand's Wildlife Capital. (Illus.). 144p. 1996. 39.95 (0-908569-94-7, Pub. by Univ Otago Pr) Intl Spec Bk.

— Wild Fiordland: Discovering the Natural History of New Zealand's World Heritage Area. LC 96-225925. (Illus.), 144p. 1997. 39.95 (1-877133-17-5, Pub. by Univ Otago Pr) Intl Spec Bk.

Peat, Patricia B., ed. see Adams, Anne B. & Nash-Cummings, Nancy.

Peat, W. Leslie & Willbanks, Stephanie J. Federal Estate & Gift Taxation. 265p. (C). 1991. pap. text 22.00 (0-314-91649-0) West Pub.

Peat, W. Leslie, jt. auth. see Willbanks, Stephanie J.

Peat, Wilbur D. Indiana Houses of the Nineteenth Century. LC 63-2411. (Illus.). xiv, 195p. 1969. reprint ed. 17.50 (0-253-32990-6) Ind Hist Soc.

Peate, I. C., ed. Studies in Regional Consciousness & Environment: Essays Presented to H. J. Fleure. LC 68-26478. (Essay Index Reprint Ser.). (Illus.). 1977. reprint ed. 23.95 (0-8369-0917-8) Ayer.

***Peate, Mary.** Girl in a CBC Studio. (Illus.). 192p. 1999. pap. 16.95 (1-896754-08-2) Shloreline.

Peate, Wayne F. English-Somali Phrase Book of Common & Medical Terms. 2nd ed. Heald, Phyllis W., ed. 101p. 1993. pap. text 17.95 (1-883023-07-6) Comp Occup.

Peate, Wayne F. & Lunda, Karen A. Cumulative Trauma Disorders: A Practical Guide to Prevention & Control. LC 96-37429. 238p. 1997. pap. text 59.00 (0-86587-553-7) Gov Insts.

Peate, Wayne F., jt. auth. see Hine, James R.

Peatfield, Tony, ed. Network Systems Tutorial for the IEEE Std. 802.3: Repeater Functions & System Design Topology Considerations for Carrier Sense Multiple Access with Collision Detection (CSMA) Local Area Networks (LANs) LC 95-22626. 1995. write for info. (1-55937-524-8) IEEE Standards.

***Peatling, G. K.** From Unionism to Liberal Commonwealth. (Illus.). 240p. 2000. 52.50 (0-7165-2661-1, Pub. by Irish Acad Pr) Intl Spec Bk.

Peatman, Dora. Home Delivery. (Stories We Tell Ser.). 29p. 1993. pap. 4.00 (1-884983-06-5) Homegrown Bks.

Peatman, Dora, et al. Stories We Tell Series, 6 bks., Set. 167p. 1993. pap. 24.00 (1-884983-00-6) Homegrown Bks.

Peatman, John B. Design with Microcontrol. LC 97-3253. 260p. (C). 1997. 56.00 (0-13-759259-0) P-H.

— Design with Microcontrollers. 618p. (C). 1988. 101.56 (0-07-049238-7) McGraw.

Peatman, W. B. Gratings, Mirrors & Slits: Beamline Design for Soft X-Ray Synchrotron Radiation Sources. 228p. 1997. text 39.00 (90-5699-028-4, ECU50) Gordon & Breach.

Peatross, C. Ford, ed. Historic America: Buildings, Structures, & Sites. LC 83-14422. 708p. 1983. 29.00 (0-8444-0431-4, 030-000-00149-4) Lib Congress.

Peatross, Oscar F. Bless 'em All: The Raider Marines of World War II. McCarthy, John P. & Clayborne, John, eds. (Illus.). 306p. (Orig.). 1995. pap. 22.50 (0-9652325-0-6) ReView Pub CA.

Peattie, Antony. The New Kobbe's Opera Book. rev. ed. Earl of Harewood, ed. LC 97-10981. (Illus.). 1008p. 1997. 60.00 (0-399-14332-7, G P Putnam) Peng Put Young Read.

Peattie, Donald C., Jr. Flowering Earth. LC 90-25484. (Illus.). 272p. 1991. 29.95 (0-253-34308-9); pap. 4.25 (0-253-20662-6, MB-662) Ind U Pr.

Peattie, Donald C. A Natural History of Trees of Eastern & Central North America. (Illus.). 624p. 1991. pap. 19.95 (0-395-58174-5) HM.

— A Natural History of Western Trees. (Illus.). 768p. 1991. pap. 19.95 (0-395-58175-3) HM.

— Vence: Immortal Village. 1963. pap. text 1.75 (0-226-65234-3, P147) U Ch Pr.

Peattie, Edward G., jt. auth. see Parker, Marshall E.

Peattie, Elia W. Mountain Woman. LC 79-98590. (Short Story Index Reprint Ser.). 1977. 20.95 (0-8369-3164-5) Ayer.

— Poems You Ought to Know. LC 75-98084. (Granger Index Reprint Ser.). 1977. 20.95 (0-8369-6085-8) Ayer.

— The Precipice. (Prairie State Bks.). 272p. 1989. reprint ed. 14.95 (0-252-06093-8) U of Ill Pr.

— Shape of Fear & Other Ghostly Tales. LC 72-98591. (Short Story Index Reprint Ser.). 1977. 18.95 (0-8369-3165-3) Ayer.

Peattie, Ken. Environmental Marketing Management. 352p. 2000. write for info. (0-273-60279-9) F T P H.

Peattie, Lisa. Thinking about Development. LC 81-15858. (Environment, Development, & Public Policy: Public Policy & Social Services Ser.). 208p. 1981. 45.00 (0-306-40761-2, Plenum Trade) Perseus Pubng.

Peattie, Lisa & Rein, Martin. Women's Claims: A Study in Political Economy. 152p. 1983. 34.00 (0-19-877179-7) OUP.

Peattie, Lisa, jt. auth. see Ronco, W.

Peattie, Lisa R. Planners & Protesters: Airport Opposition As Social Movement. (Urban Studies: No. 9). 40p. 1991. pap. text 6.00 (0-913749-19-2) U MD Urban Stud.

Peattie, Mark R. A Historian Looks at the Pacific War. LC 95-38840. (Hoover Essays Ser.: No. 13). 12p. 1995. pap. 5.00 (0-8179-3762-5) Hoover Inst Pr.

— Nan'yo: The Rise & Fall of the Japanese in Micronesia, 1885-1945. LC 87-19437. (Pacific Islands Monographs: No. 4). (Illus.). 306p. (Orig.). 1992. reprint ed. pap. text 21.00 (0-8248-1480-0) UH Pr.

Peattie, Mark R., jt. auth. see Evans, David C.

Peattie, Mark R., jt. ed. see Myers, Ramon H.

Peattie, Noel. Amy Rose. LC 95-8080. 215p. (Orig.). 1995. pap. 19.95 (0-916147-61-4) Regent Pr.

— Hydra & Kraken or, the Lore & Lure of Lake-Monsters & Sea Serpents. LC 96-20725. 1996. pap. 9.50 (0-916147-99-1) Regent Pr.

***Peattie, Noel.** In the Dome of Saint Laurence Meteor. 118p. 1999. pap. 12.95 (1-889059-76-5) Regent Pr.

Peattie, Noel. Western Skyline. LC 96-218412. 120p. (Orig.). 1995. pap. 11.95 (0-916147-72-X) Regent Pr.

Peattie, Patricia I., jt. ed. see Walker, Stanley.

Peattie, Roderick. Mountain Geography: A Critique & Field Study. LC 70-88918. 1970. lib. bdg. 75.00 (0-8371-2243-0, PEMG, Greenwood Pr) Greenwood.

Peattie, Roger W. Selected Letters of William Michael Rossetti. LC 89-3838. 704p. 1990. lib. bdg. 70.00 (0-271-00678-1) Pa St U Pr.

Peaty. Working with English Idioms. Date not set. pap. text. write for info. (0-17-555418-8) Addison-Wesley.

Peaty, Ian P. You Brew Good Ale: A History of Home-Brewed Ales. (Illus.). 224p. 1997. pap. 22.95 (0-7509-1592-7, Pub. by Sutton Pub Ltd) Intl Pubs Mktg.

Peau, Andrew T. Le, see Le Peau, Andrew T.

Peau, Phyllis J. Women of the New Testament. (LifeGuide Bible Studies). 64p. (Orig.). 1996. pap., wbk. ed. 4.99 (0-8308-1077-3, 1077) InterVarsity.

Peau, Phyllis J. Le, see Le Peau, Phyllis J.

Peau, Phyllis J. Le, see Le Peau, Andrew T. & Le Peau, Phyllis J.

Peau, Phyllis J. Le, see Le Peau, Phyllis J.

Peavey, Bill. Dignity of the Soul: The Story of Filipino Bravery in World War II. LC 95-78453. (Illus.). 222p. 1995. 17.95 (0-9647607-0-3) Bayanihan Pub.

Peavey, Fran. A Shallow Pool of Time: One Woman Grapples with the AIDS Epidemic. (Orig.). 1988. pap. 10.00 (0-317-93395-7) Crabgrass Pubs.

Peavey, Fran, et al. Heart Politics. 192p. write for info. (0-920057-59-4); pap. write for info. (0-920057-60-8) Black Rose.

Peavey, Michael. Fuel from Water: Energy Independence with Hydrogen. rev. ed. LC 88-188956. (Illus.). 255p. (C). 1995. pap. 20.00 (0-945516-04-5) Merit Prods.

Peavey, Morris. MAH & Family Values. LC 98-170607. 128p. 1998. pap. 14.00 (0-8059-4252-1) Dorrance.

Peavler, Daniel L. Fatherhood: A Journey Through. unabridged ed. 176p. (Orig.). 1997. pap. 12.95 (0-9657113-0-7) Living Sprg.

Peavler, Maggie. It's a Jingle Out There: The Poetry of John Seiler. 128p. (Orig.). 1996. pap. 10.95 (1-889937-03-7) Crescent Hill Bks.

Peavler, Terry J. Julio Cortazar. (Twayne's World Authors Ser.: No. 816). 184p. (C). 1990. 28.95 (0-8057-8257-5) Macmillan.

Peavler, Terry J. & Standish, Peter, eds. Structures of Power: Essays on Twentieth-Century Spanish-American Fiction. LC 95-20009. (SUNY Series in Latin American & Iberian Thought & Culture). 193p. (C). 1996. text 49.50 (0-7914-2839-7); pap. text 16.95 (0-7914-2840-0) State U NY Pr.

Peavy. Environmental Engineering. 1985. 30.00 (0-07-049135-6) McGraw.

— Environmental Engineering. 2nd ed. 2002. 7.25 (0-07-049204-2) McGraw.

Peavy, H. S. & Rowe, D. Environmental Engineering. 640p. (C). 1984. 101.56 (0-07-049134-8) McGraw.

Peavy, John W. & Sherrerd, Katrina F. Cases in Portfolio Management. (Orig.). (C). 1991. pap. 30.00 (1-879087-04-9) Assn I M&R.

Peavy, Linda. Allison's Grandfather. large type ed. 40p. (J). (gr. 3-4). 1984. reprint ed. 9.50 (0-317-01866-3, J-00780-00) Am Printing Hse.

Peavy, Linda & Smith, Ursula. Food, Nutrition & You. LC 82-5694. (Illus.). 208p. (YA). (gr. 6 up). 1982. lib. bdg. 16.00 (0-684-17461-8) Scribner.

— The Gold Rush Widows of Little Falls: A Story Drawn from the Letters of Pamelia & James Fergus. LC 89-49409. (Illus.). xxiii, 305p. 1990. 29.95 (0-87351-249-9); pap. 14.95 (0-87351-250-2) Minn Hist.

— Women in Waiting: Life on the Home Frontier. LC 93-38832. (Illus.). 400p. 1994. 39.95 (0-8061-2616-7); pap. 17.95 (0-8061-2619-1) U of Okla Pr.

Peavy, Linda S. & Smith, Ursula. Frontier Children. LC 99-18932. 176p. 1999. 24.95 (0-8061-3161-6) U of Okla Pr.

— Pioneer Women: The Lives of Women on the Frontier. LC 97-40684. (Illus.). 144p. 1998. pap. 17.95 (0-8061-3054-7) U of Okla Pr.

Peavy, R. Vance. SocioDynamic Counselling: A Constructivist Perspective for the Practice of Counselling in the 21st Century. 260p. 1997. spiral bd. 26.00 (1-55212-094-5, 97-0010, Pub. by Tra3fford) Trafford Pub.

Peavy, William S. & Peary, Warren. Super Nutrition Gardening: How to Grow Your Own Powercharged Foods. LC 92-25950. (Illus.). 248p. pap. 14.95 (0-89529-532-6, Avery) Penguin Putnam.

Peay, Cherilyn J. & McArthur, Mary P., eds. New Mexico Computer Resources Directory, 1996. vi, 110p. (Orig.). 1996. pap. 7.95 (0-9655541-0-4) NMex Computer.

Peay, Jill. Tribunals on Trial: A Study of Decision-Making under the Mental Health Act 1983. 272p. 1989. 65.00 (0-19-825249-8) OUP.

Peay, Jill, ed. Criminal Justice & the Mentally Disordered. LC 98-2546. (International Library of Criminology, Criminal Justice, & Penology). 540p. 1998. text 171.95 (1-85521-962-X, Pub. by Dartmth Pub) Ashgate Pub Co.

Peay, Jill, jt. ed. see Eastman, Nigel.

Peberdy, J. F. Penicillium & Acremonium. LC 87-12328. (Biotechnology Handbooks Ser.: Vol. 1). (Illus.). 314p. (C). 1987. text 85.00 (0-306-42345-6, Kluwer Plenum) Kluwer Academic.

Peberdy, John F., et al, eds. Applied Molecular Genetics of Fungi. (British Mycological Society Symposium Ser.: No. 18). (Illus.). 199p. (C). 1991. text 69.95 (0-521-41571-3) Cambridge U Pr.

Peberdy, Max. Third World Conundrum: A Call to Christian Partnership. 188p. 1986. pap. 7.50 (0-85364-463-2, Pub. by Paternoster Pub) McClelland & Stewart.

Peberman Company Staff, contrib. by. Forbidden Destiny. 265p. 1998. pap. write for info. (1-893282-00-7) Pomeroy Pubg.

Pebley, Anne R., et al. Demographic Diversity & Change in the Central American Isthmus. LC 97-31180. 1997. pap. 30.00 (0-8330-2551-1, CF-135) Rand Corp.

Peboli, O. J. & Rivelles, V. O. Particles & Fields: Proceedings of the VII Ja Swieca Summer School. 812p. 1994. text 135.00 (981-02-1597-5) World Scientific Pub.

Pebuy, M., ed. see Peguy, Charles.

Pebworth, Larry, jt. auth. see Summers, Claude J.

Pebworth, Ted L., jt. auth. see Summers, Claude J.

Pebworth, Ted-Larry, jt. auth. see Summers, Claude J.

Pebworth, Ted-Larry, ed. see Jonson, Ben.

Pebworth, Ted-Larry, jt. ed. see Summers, Claude J.

Pec, Karel, jt. auth. see Bursa, Milan.

Pecan, Erene, jt. ed. see Woodwell, George M.

Pecar, Branko. Business Forecasting for Management. Davis, Glyn & Lillystone, Simon, eds. LC 93-47175. 1994. 14.95 (0-07-707865-9) McGraw.

***Pecar, Joseph A.** Telecommunication Factbook. 2000. 34.95 (0-07-135163-9) McGraw.

Pecar, Joseph A., et al. The McGraw-Hill Telecommunications Factbook. LC 92-24340. (Illus.). 1993. pap. 29.95 (0-07-049183-6) McGraw.

Pecara, W. T., ed. see Reed, John C. & Love, J. D.

Pecarich, Mike A. Consuelo. LC 97-90217. 70p. 1998. pap. 8.95 (0-533-12328-3) Vantage.

Pecarve, Reuben. The Hypnosis Book: Mind & Body Power at the Count of Five. (Illus.). 159p. (Orig.). 1998. pap. 14.95 (1-56072-335-1, Nova Kroshka Bks) Nova Sci Pubs.

Pecaut, Cheryl, ed. see Kavanaugh, James.

Peccati, L. & Viren, M. Financial Modeling. 364p. 1994. 71.95 (0-387-91487-0) Spr-Verlag.

***Peccei, Jean S.** Child Language. 2nd ed. 116p. 1999. 16.99 (0-415-19836-4) Routledge.

Peccei, Jean S. Pragmatics LC 99-10322. (Language Workbooks Ser.). 1999. pap. write for info. (0-415-20523-9) Routledge.

Peccei, Roberto, ed. see Bagger, Jonathan, et al.

Peccei, Roberto D., jt. ed. see Laraneta, M.

Pecci, Ernest F. Chess: How to Beat Your Computer. (Illus.). 350p. 1999. pap. 16.95 (0-9642637-8-5) Pavior Pubng.

— The Violence Potential: In Our Society Today. (Illus.). 171p. (Orig.). 1994. pap. 14.95 (0-9642637-2-6) Pavior Pubng.

Pecci, Ernest F., jt. auth. see Meisterfeld, C. W.

Pecci, Ernest F., ed. see Pecci, Mary F.

Pecci, Mary F. At Last! A Reading Method for Every Child. 4th ed. (Illus.). 342p. 1988. teacher ed., spiral bd. 29.95 (0-943220-07-6) Pecci Educ Pubs.

— How to Discipline Your Class for Joyful Teaching. Pecci, Ernest F., ed. 42p. (Orig.). (C). 1982. pap. text, teacher ed. 4.95 (0-943220-08-4) Pecci Educ Pubs.

— Super Seatwork Color Words. (Super Seatwork Ser.). 130p. (J). (gr. k-3). 1981. 12.95 (0-943220-05-X) Pecci Educ Pubs.

— Super Seatwork Content Areas. (Super Seatwork Ser.). (Illus.). 168p. (J). (gr. 1-2). 1978. 12.95 (0-943220-01-7) Pecci Educ Pubs.

— Super Seatwork Letter Recognition. (Super Seatwork Ser.). (Illus.). 104p. (J). (ps-1). 1978. 12.95 (0-943220-02-5) Pecci Educ Pubs.

— Super Seatwork Linguistic Exercises. 2nd ed. (Super Seatwork Ser.). (Illus.). 106p. (J). (gr. 1-3). 1990. 12.95 (0-943220-03-3) Pecci Educ Pubs.

— Super Seatwork Number Words. (Super Seatwork Ser.). (Illus.). 120p. (J). (ps-1). 1982. 12.95 (0-943220-06-8) Pecci Educ Pubs.

— Super Seatwork Phonic Grab Bag. (Super Seatwork Ser.). (Illus.). 138p. (J). (gr. 1-3). 1984. 12.95 (0-943220-09-2) Pecci Educ Pubs.

— Super Seatwork Word Skills. (Super Seatwork Ser.). (Illus.). 238p. (J). (gr. 1-4). 1980. 18.95 (0-943220-04-1) Pecci Educ Pubs.

— Super Spelling Book One. (Illus.). 244p. (J). (gr. 1-2). 1997. pap. 19.95 (0-943220-11-4) Pecci Educ Pubs.

— Why Johnny Ain't Never Gonna Read! A Challenge to the Nation. (Illus.). 148p. (Orig.). 1995. pap., teacher ed. 6.95 (0-943220-10-6) Pecci Educ Pubs.

Peccinotti, Harri. Cairo: The Site & the History. LC 87-82873. (Illus.). 104p. reprint ed. pap. 32.30 (0-608-09831-0, 206999900007) Bks Demand.

Peccorini, Francisco L. Selfhood As Thinking Thought in the Work of Gabriel Marcel: A New Interpretation. LC 86-28549. (Problems in Contemporary Philosophy Ser.: Vol. 3). 200p. 1987. lib. bdg. 79.95 (0-88946-329-8) E Mellen.

Peceny, Mark. Democracy at the Point of Bayonets. 1999. 55.00 (0-271-01882-8) Pa St U Pr.

Pech, Arleta. Painting Fresh Florals in Watercolor. LC 97-38979. (Illus.). 128p. 1998. 27.99 (0-89134-814-X, North Lght Bks) F & W Pubns Inc.

Pech, Gerald. Besteuerung und Staatsverschuldung in der Demokratie Vol. XIX: Zur Dynamischen Analyse Staatlicher Budgetpolitiken. (Kollektive Entscheidungen, Wirtschaftspolitik und Offentliche Finanzen Ser.: Bd. 1). (GER., Illus.). XIX, 211p. 1996. pap. 44.95 (3-631-30325-4) P Lang Pubng.

Pech, J. C., ed. Cellular & Molecular Aspects of the Plant Hormone Ethylene: Proceedings of the International Symposium "Cellular & Molecular Aspects of Biosynthesis & Action Hormone Ethylene," Agen, France August 31 - Sept. 4, 1992. (Current Plant Science & Biotechnology in Agriculture Ser.). 404p. (C). 1993. text 200.50 (0-7923-2169-3) Kluwer Academic.

Pech, Jurgen. Max Ernst: Sculptures. 1996. pap. 45.00 (88-8158-070-5, Pub. by Charta) Dist Art Pubs.

Pech, Maude R., jt. auth. see Hultgren, Thor.

Pech, Maude R., jt. auth. see Kendrick, John W.

Pecham, John. John Pecham & the Science of Optics: Perspectiva Communis. Lindberg, David L., ed. LC 72-98122. (University of Wisconsin Publications in Medieval Science). (Illus.). 320p. reprint ed. pap. 99.20 (0-608-09916-3, 206925400003) Bks Demand.

Pechan, A. Esperanto Hungarian Pocket Dictionary. (ESP & HUN.). 464p. (C). 1988. 30.00 (963-205-210-2, Pub. by Akade Kiado) St Mut.

— Esperanto-Hungarian Pocket Dictionary: Ezperanto-Magyar Szotar. (ESP & HUN.). 464p. 1983. 12.95 (0-8288-1740-5, M13019) Fr & Eur.

P

— Hungarian-Esperanto Pocket Dictionary. 5th ed. (ESP & HUN.). 560p. 1983. 12.95 (0-8288-1656-5, M 13019) Fr & Eur.

Pechan, A., ed. Hungarian-Esperanto Pocket Dictionary. 560p. (C). 1988. 15.00 (963-205-209-9, Pub. by Akade Kiado) St Mut.

Pechar, Gary & Ng, Nelson. Personal Fitness. 2nd ed. 124p. (C). 1999. spiral bd. 13.95 (0-7872-5703-6, 41570304) Kendall-Hunt.

Pechefsky, jt. auth. see Ryding.

Pechenik. Biology of Invertebrates. 4th ed. LC 99-14462. 592p. 1999. 77.50 (0-07-012204-0) McGraw.

Pechenik & Sumich. Marine Biology. 1998. 16.00 (0-697-16520-5, WCB McGr Hill) McGrw-H Hghr Educ.

Pechenik, A. Biology: A Short Guide in Biology. 1996. write for info. (0-201-33209-4) Addison-Wesley.

Pechenik, Alexander & Kalia, Rajiv K., eds. Computer-Aided Design of High-Temperature Materials. LC 99-19662. (Illus.). 538p. 1999. text 95.00 (0-19-512050-7) OUP.

Pechenik, Jan A. Biology of the Invertebrates. 3rd ed. LC 95-76168. 576p. (C). 1995. text 71.05 (0-697-13712-0, WCB McGr Hill) McGrw-H Hghr Educ.

— Biology of the Invertebrates. 3rd ed. 576p. (C). 1997. per. write for info. (0-07-114625-3, WCB McGr Hill) McGrw-H Hghr Educ.

— A Short Guide to Writing about Biology. 3rd ed. LC 96-35994. 265p. (C). 1997. pap. 24.20 (0-673-52503-1) Longman.

Pecherek, Andrea, jt. auth. see Cowie, Helen.

Pecherskaya, Natalia & Coates, R., eds. The Emancipation of Russian Christianity. LC 95-46901. (Toronto Studies in Theology: Vol. 33). 1996. write for info. (0-7734-8871-5) E Mellen.

***Pechlaner.** Atlas of Hand Surgery. (Illus.). 391p. 2000. pap. 34.00 (0-86577-865-5) Thieme Med Pubs.

Pechman, Carl. Regulating Power: The Economics of Electricity in the Information Age. LC 93-10053. (Topics in Regulatory Economics & Policy Ser.: Vol. 15). 256p. (C). 1993. lib. bdg. 127.00 (0-7923-9347-3) Kluwer Academic.

Pechman, Joseph. Fulfilling America's Promise: Social Policies for the 1990s. McPherson, Michael S., ed. LC 91-55562. (Williams College Center for the Humanities & Social Sciences Ser.). (Illus.). 272p. 1992. 39.95 (0-8014-2631-6); pap. 16.95 (0-8014-8059-0) Cornell U Pr.

Pechman, Joseph A. Federal Tax Policy. 4th ed. LC 83-23126. (Studies of Government Finance). 410p. 1984. 26.95 (0-8157-6964-4); pap. 9.95 (0-8157-6963-6) Brookings.

— Federal Tax Policy. 5th ed. LC 87-13159. (Studies in Government Finance). 430p. 1987. 44.95 (0-8157-6962-8) Brookings.

— Tax Reform & the U. S. Economy. LC 87-70178. (Dialogues on Public Policy Ser.). 108p. 1987. pap. 10.95 (0-8157-6959-8) Brookings.

— Who Paid the Taxes, 1966-85? LC 84-45845. (Studies of Government Finance). 84p. 1985. 26.95 (0-8157-6998-9); pap. 9.95 (0-8157-6997-0) Brookings.

Pechman, Joseph A., ed. Agenda for the Nation's 1980. 34.95 (0-8157-6988-1); pap. 14.95 (0-8157-6987-3) Brookings.

— The Budget 1979. 319p. 1978. pap. 14.95 (0-8157-6983-0) Brookings.

— The Budget 1980. 229p. 1979. 34.95 (0-8157-6986-5); pap. 14.95 (0-8157-6985-7) Brookings.

— The Budget 1982. 275p. 1981. 34.95 (0-8157-6990-3) Brookings.

— The Budget 1982. 275p. 1981. pap. 14.95 (0-8157-6989-X) Brookings.

— A Citizen's Guide to the New Tax Reforms: Fair Tax, Flat Tax, Simple Tax. 176p. 1985. 33.00 (0-8476-7403-7) Rowman.

— The 1984 Budget. 248p. 1983. 34.95 (0-8157-6994-6); pap. 14.95 (0-8157-6993-8) Brookings.

— The Nineteen Eighty-Three Budget. 268p. 1982. 34.95 (0-8157-6992-X); pap. 14.95 (0-8157-6991-1) Brookings.

— Options for Tax Reform. LC 84-72269. (Dialogues on Public Policy Ser.). 149p. 1984. pap. 11.95 (0-8157-6995-4) Brookings.

— The Promise of Tax Reform. LC 85-1236. 1985. 15.95 (0-13-731092-7) Am Assembly.

— What Should Be Taxed, Income or Expenditure? A Report of a Conference Sponsored by the Fund for Public Policy Research & the Brookings Institution. LC 79-22733. (Studies of Government Finance). 344p. reprint ed. pap. 106.70 (0-8357-7072-9, 203359100086) Bks Demand.

— World Tax Reform: A Progress Report. LC 88-70469. 294p. 1988. pap. 16.95 (0-8157-6999-7) Brookings.

Pechman, Joseph A. & McPherson, Michael S., eds. Fulfilling America's Promise: Social Policies for the 1990s. LC 91-55562. 272p. reprint ed. pap. 84.40 (0-608-20932-5, 207203100003) Bks Demand.

Pechman, Joseph A. & Timpane, P. Michael, eds. Work Incentives & Income Guarantees: The New Jersey Negative Income Tax Experiment. LC 75-2321. (Studies in Social Experimentation). 232p. 1975. pap. 12.95 (0-8157-6975-X) Brookings.

Pechman, Joseph A., jt. auth. see Break, George F.

Pechman, Joseph A., jt. ed. see Aaron, Henry J.

Pechman, Joseph A., jt. ed. see Brown, Clair.

Pechman, Joseph A., ed. see Okun, Arthur M.

Pechman, Joseph A., jt. ed. see Palmer, John L.

***Pechman, Kenneth J., ed.** Physician Profiling: Background & Practical Experience. 2000. 55.00 (0-924674-74-1) Am Coll Phys Execs.

Pechmann, Connie, jt. ed. see Grewal, Dhruv.

Pechoin, Daniel. Thesaurus Larousse. (FRE.). 1146p. 1991. 125.00 (0-8288-7369-0, 2033201074) Fr & Eur.

Pechota, Terry L., jt. frwd. see Torres, Estaban E.

Pechota, Vratislav. The Right to Know One's Human Rights: A Road Toward Marriage & Family. LC 83-72868. 52p. 1983. pap. 2.50 (0-87495-056-2) Am Jewish Comm.

Pechota, Vratislav, ed. Commercial Arbitration: An International Bibliography. LC 92-23736. 1993. 125.00 (1-56425-002-4) Juris Pubng.

— Foreign Investment in Central & Eastern Europe & Ukraine. LC 97-157198. 1150p. 1992. ring bd. 195.00 (0-929179-45-5) Juris Pubng.

— Privatization in Eastern Europe. LC 94-9413. 264p. 1994. 85.00 (1-56425-023-7) Juris Pubng.

Pechota, Vratislav, jt. auth. see Smit, Hans.

Pechota, Vratislav, jt. auth. see Smith, Hans.

Pechota, Vratislav, jt. ed. see Hazard, John N.

Pechota, Vratislav, jt. ed. see Smit, Hans.

Pechstein, Cricket, ed. see Cranford, Ron.

Pecht, Judy & Pecht, Michael G. Long-Term Non-Operating Reliability of Electronic Products. LC 95-18275. (Electronics & Reliability Ser.). 144p. 1995. per. 44.95 (0-8493-9621-2, 9621) CRC Pr.

Pecht, Michael, et al. The Korean Electronic Industry. LC 97-145. (Electronics Industry Research Ser.). 144p. 1997. lib. bdg. 39.95 (0-8493-3172-2) CRC Pr.

Pecht, Michael, jt. auth. see Lee, Chung-Shing.

Pecht, Michael G. Electronics Industry in China. LC 99-28272. 192p. 1999. per. 44.95 (0-8493-3174-9) CRC Pr.

Pecht, Michael G. Handbook of Electronic Packaging Design. (Mechanical Engineering Ser.: Vol. 76). (Illus.). 904p. 1991. text 245.00 (0-8247-7921-5) Dekker.

Pecht, Michael G. Integrated Circuit, Hybrid & Multichip Module Package Design Guidelines: A Focus on Reliability. 464p. 1994. 110.00 (0-471-59446-6) Wiley.

— Quality Conformance & Qualification of Microelectronic Packages & Interconnects. Evans, John et al, eds. LC 93-9709. 461p. 1994. pap. 110.00 (0-471-59436-9) Wiley.

— Soldering Processes & Equipment. LC 92-3370. 312p. 1993. 110.00 (0-471-59167-X) Wiley.

Pecht, Michael G., ed. Placement & Routing of Electronic Modules. LC 92-44796. (Electrical Engineering & Electronics Ser.: Vol. 82). (Illus.). 352p. 1993. text 175.00 (0-8247-8916-4) Dekker.

Pecht, Michael G., ed. Product Reliability, Maintainability, & Supportability Handbook. LC 95-5257. 448p. 1995. boxed set 104.95 (0-8493-9457-0, 9457) CRC Pr.

Pecht, Michael G., et al, eds. Estimating Influence of Temperature on Microelectronic Device Reliability: A Physics of Failure Approach. LC 96-39038. 336p. 1997. boxed set 84.95 (0-8493-9450-3, 9450) CRC Pr.

***Pecht, Michael G. & McCluskey, Patrick.** Electronic Packaging Materials & Their Properties. LC 98-34479. (Electronic Packaging Ser.). 128p. 1998. boxed set 74.95 (0-8493-9625-5) CRC Pr.

Pecht, Michael G. & Radojcic, Riko. Guidebook for Managing Silicon Chip Reliability. LC 98-24467. (Electronic Packaging Ser.). 224p. 1998. boxed set 74.95 (0-8493-9624-7, 9624) CRC Pr.

Pecht, Michael G. & Wong, Yeun Tsun, eds. Advanced Routing of Electronic Modules. LC 95-34719. (Electronic Packaging Ser.). 480p. 1995. boxed set 99.95 (0-8493-9622-0, 9622) CRC Pr.

Pecht, Michael G., jt. auth. see Pecht, Judy.

Pecht, Michael G., jt. ed. see Nguyen, L. T.

Pecht, Michael G., ed. see Nguyen, Luu T.

Pechter. Othello. 1998. 29.00 (0-8057-7849-7) Mac Lib Ref.

Pechter, Edward. "Othello" & Interpretive Traditions. LC 99-20943. (Studies in Theatre History & Culture). (Illus.). 272p. 1999. text 32.95 (0-87745-685-2) U of Iowa Pr.

— What was Shakespeare? Renaissance Plays & Changing Critical Practice. LC 94-25366. 216p. 1995. pap. text 13.95 (0-8014-8229-1) Cornell U Pr.

Pechter, Edward, ed. Textual & Theatrical Shakespeare: Questions of Evidence. LC 95-50872. (Studies in Theatre History & Culture). (Illus.). 278p. 1996. text 35.00 (0-87745-545-7) U of Iowa Pr.

Pechter Ellis, Janice. Stepping up to Fluency. (Illus.). 127p. 1998. 29.95 (0-937857-78-5, 1360) Speech Bin.

Pechura, Constance M., ed. see Institute of Medicine Staff.

Pecile, A. & De Bernard, B., eds. Bone Regulatory Factors: Morphology, Biochemistry, Physiology & Pharmacology. LC 90-6777. (NATO ASI Series A, Life Sciences: Vol. 184). (Illus.). 302p. 1990. 95.00 (0-306-43500-4, Plenum Trade) Perseus Pubng.

Pecile, A. & Rescigno, A., eds. Pharmacokinetics: Mathematical & Statistical Approaches. LC 87-36043. (NATO ASI Series A, Life Sciences: Vol. 145). (Illus.). 358p. 1988. 105.00 (0-306-42806-7, Plenum Trade) Perseus Pubng.

Pecile, C., et al, eds. Proceedings of the International Conference on the Physics & Chemistry of Low-Dimensional Synthetic Metals: Special Issues of the Journal Molecular Crystals & Liquid Crystals, 5 vols. 2272p. 1985. text 2980.00 (0-677-06665-1) Gordon & Breach.

Pecina, Marko M. Tunnel Syndromes. (Illus.). 184p. 1991. lib. bdg. 115.00 (0-8493-6933-9, RC422) CRC Pr.

Pecina, Marko M., et al. Tunnel Syndromes: Peripheral Nerve Compression Syndromes. 2nd ed. LC 96-21241. 304p. 1996. boxed set 104.95 (0-8493-2629-X) CRC Pr.

Pecina, Marko M., jt. auth. see Bojanic, Ivan.

Pecinkova, Pavla. Contemporary Czech Painting. (Illus.). 236p. 1993. text 32.00 (976-8097-25-6) Gordon & Breach.

Peck. Chemistry. 1994. teacher ed., student ed. 35.31 (0-8151-6502-1) Mosby Inc.

***Peck.** Foundation Engineering. 3rd ed. (C). 2000. pap. text, student ed. write for info. (0-471-32993-2) Wiley.

Peck. Literary Terms & Criticism. 1997. text 14.95 (0-333-58887-8, Pub. by Macmillan) St Martin.

— Measuring Human Problems: A Practical Guide to the Assessment of Adult Psychological Problems. 418p. 1992. pap. text 113.95 (0-471-93482-8) Wiley.

— Organizational Behavior. 588p. (C). 1998. pap. text 59.75 (0-536-01490-6) Pearson Custom.

— Student Solutions Guide to Accompany Chemistry: The Molecule. 200p. (C). 1994. text 14.95 (0-8016-5071-2) Mosby Inc.

— This Family of Women. large type ed. (Charnwood Large Print Ser.). 1984. 27.99 (0-7089-8214-X, Charnwood) Ulverscroft.

— Treasury of North American Folklore. LC 99-17566. 384p. 1999. text 29.95 (0-393-04741-5) Norton.

Peck. Website Professional. 1996. pap. write for info. (1-56592-174-7) Thomson Learn.

Peck, jt. auth. see Devore.

Peck, A. J. C. I. I. Legal Liabilities, No. 210. (C). 1987. 240.00 (0-7855-4289-2, Pub. by Witherby & Co) St Mut.

— Mastering German. (Mastering Languages Ser.). (Illus.). 322p. 1991. pap. 11.95 (0-87052-056-3) Hippocrene Bks.

Peck, A. L. Parts of Animals. (Loeb Classical Library: No. 323). (ENG & GRE.). (C). 15.50 (0-674-99357-8) HUP.

Peck, A. L., tr. Generation of Animals. (Loeb Classical Library: No. 366). 1942. 18.95 (0-674-99403-5) HUP.

— Historia Animalium, Bks. 1-3. (Loeb Classical Library: No. 437). (ENG & GRE.). 344p. 1965. 18.95 (0-674-99481-7) HUP.

— Historia Animalium, Vol. X, Bks. IV-VI. (Loeb Classical Library: No. 438). 422p. 1970. text 18.95 (0-674-99482-5) HUP.

Peck, Abe. Uncovering the Sixties: The Life & Times of the Underground Press. 1991. pap. 12.95 (0-8065-1225-3, Citadel Pr) Carol Pub Group.

Peck, Abraham J., ed. American Jewish Archives, Cincinnati: The Papers of the World Jewish Congress, 1945-1950. LC 89-16915. (Archives of the Holocaust Ser.: Vol. 8). 544p. 1991. text 149.00 (0-8240-5490-3) Garland.

— American Jewish Archives, Cincinnati: The Papers of the World Jewish Congress, 1945-1950. LC 89-16915. (Archives of the Holocaust Ser.: Vol. 9). 448p. 1991. text 132.00 (0-8240-5491-1) Garland.

— The German-Jewish Legacy in America, 1938-1988: From Bildung to the Bill of Rights. LC 89-16561. 268p. (C). 1989. pap. text 19.95 (0-8143-2264-6) Wayne St U Pr.

— The German-Jewish Legacy in America, 1938-1988: From Bildung to the Bill of Rights. LC 89-16561. 268p. (C). 1990. text 35.00 (0-8143-2263-8) Wayne St U Pr.

— Jews & Christians after the Holocaust. LC 81-70665. 127p. reprint ed. pap. 39.40 (0-608-15324-9, 202961100061) Bks Demand.

Peck, Abraham J. & Herscher, Uri D., eds. Queen City Refuge. 270p. 1989. 29.95 (0-87441-486-5) Behrman.

Peck, Abraham J., jt. auth. see Marcus, Jacob R.

Peck, Abraham J., jt. ed. see Berenbaum, Michael.

Peck, Abraham J., jt. ed. see Cohen, Martin A.

Peck, Ada M. A History of the Hanover Society. rev. ed. Swarthout, Douglas, ed. LC 95-77581. (Illus.). 260p. 1995. 35.00 (0-9646900-0-4) Berry Hill NY.

***Peck, Adam.** Turkey Guide. 2nd ed. 576p. 1999. pap. 17.95 (1-892975-03-3) Open Rd Pub.

Peck, Alan. No Time to Lose: The Fast Moving World of Bill Ivy. (Illus.). 184p. 1997. 29.95 (1-899870-21-0, Pub. by Motor Racing) Motorbooks Intl.

Peck, Amelia. American Quilts & Coverlets in the Metropolitan Museum of Art. (Illus.). 264p. 1990. 19.95 (0-87099-592-8) Metro Mus Art.

***Peck, Amelia, et al.** Lyndhurst: A Guide to the House & Landscape. Barr, Pamela T., ed. (Illus.). 51p. 1998. pap. 10.00 (0-9671404-0-4) Lyndhurst.

Peck, Amelia, jt. auth. see Parker, James.

***Peck, Andrew Stevens.** Francis Bacon Tudor Equals William Shakespeare. 103p. 2000. pap. 14.95 (1-56072-734-9, Nova Kroshka Bks) Nova Sci Pubs.

Peck, Andy, jt. auth. see Pawson, David.

Peck, Annie S. Industrial & Commercial South America. 1977. 75.00 (0-8490-2056-5) Gordon Pr.

Peck, Barbara M., et al. The History of Montgomery Illinois: In Words & Pictures. Giles, Wanda H., ed. LC 90-70501. (Illus.). 224p. 1990. 34.95 (0-9626765-0-0) VMHC.

Peck, Bob & Silver, Sandy. Man's Guide to the Justification of Golf. LC 96-86679. 128p. (Orig.). 1997. pap. 6.95 (0-8362-2755-7) Andrews & McMeel.

Peck, Bradford. World a Department Store: A Story of Life Under a Cooperative System. LC 70-154457. (Utopian Literature Ser.). (Illus.). 1979. reprint ed. 23.95 (0-405-03539-X) Ayer.

Peck, Bryan T. Issues in European Education. LC 98-5135. 1998. 65.00 (1-56072-545-1) Nova Sci Pubs.

— Managing Schools: The European Experience. LC 98-23871. 1998. 65.00 (1-56072-572-9) Nova Sci Pubs.

— Teaching & Education for a New Europe: A Challenge for the Countries of the European Union. (Illus.). 137p. (C). 1996. lib. bdg. 75.00 (1-56072-386-6) Nova Sci Pubs.

***Peck, Bryan T.** Teaching & Learning in Lithuania since "Rebirth" A Challenge for School Directors & Teachers. 178p. 1998. text 69.00 (1-56072-537-0) Nova Sci Pubs.

Peck, Carol F., ed. From Deep Within: Poetry Workshops in Nursing Homes. LC 89-30946. (Activities, Adaptation & Aging Ser.: Vol. 13, No. 3). 153p. 1994. 39.95 (0-86656-897-2) Haworth Pr.

— From Deep Within: Poetry Workshops in Nursing Homes. LC 89-30946. (Activities, Adaptation & Aging Ser.: Vol. 13, No. 3). 153p. 1996. pap. 14.95 (1-56024-622-7) Haworth Pr.

Peck, Carole & Bryant, Carolyn H. Buffet Cookbook. LC 96-38747. (Illus.). 320p. 1997. 29.95 (0-670-86516-8) Viking Penguin.

Peck, Charles, et al. Top Executive Compensation in 1996. (Report Ser.: Vol. 1207-97-RR). (Illus.). 97p. 1997. pap. text 160.00 (0-8237-0653-2) Conference Bd.

— Top Executive Compensation in 1997. (Report Ser.: No. 1227-98-RR). (Illus.). 115p. 1998. pap. text 160.00 (0-8237-0673-7) Conference Bd.

Peck, Charles, jt. auth. see Potter, Frank.

Peck, Charles A. Top Executive Compensation: 1994 Edition. (Report: No. 1099-94-RR). (Illus.). 80p. (Orig.). 1994. pap. text 120.00 (0-8237-0546-3) Conference Bd.

Peck, Charles A., et al. Individual Incentive Programs: A Research Report. LC 98-210022. (Report / Conference Board Ser.). 26 p. 1995. write for info. (0-8237-0575-7) Conference Bd.

Peck, Charlotte T., ed. see Forehand, Karl J.

Peck, Chauncey E. History of Wilbraham, Mass. (Illus.). 469p. 1995. reprint ed. lib. bdg. 47.50 (0-8328-4470-5) Higginson Bk Co.

Peck, Chris. A Good Life in the Inland Northwest: A Collection of Columns from The Spokesman-Review. Higgins, Shaun O., ed. 297p. 1998. 23.95 (0-923910-09-3) NMV.

Peck, Christopher E. The Hidden Terror. Hall, Barbara, ed. LC 96-72537. 132p. 1997. pap. text 5.95 (1-57636-035-0) SunRise Pbl.

Peck, Connie. Sustainable Peace: The Role of the U. N. & Regional Organizations in Preventing Conflict. LC 97-26019. (Carnegie Commission on Preventing Deadly Conflict Ser.). 317p. 1997. 65.00 (0-8476-8560-8); pap. 22.95 (0-8476-8561-6) Rowman.

— The United Nations As a Dispute Settlement System: Improving Mechanisms for the Prevention & Resolution of Conflict. LC 96-18022. (Legal Aspects of International Organization Ser.: Vol. 29). 1996. 65.50 (90-411-0248-5) Kluwer Law Intl.

Peck, Connie, Colloquium on Increasing the Effecti & Lee, Roy S. Increasing the Effectiveness of the International Court of Justice: Proceedings of the ICJ Unitar Colloquium to Celebrate the 50th Anniversary of the Court, the Peace Palace, 16-18 April 1996. LC 97-18432. (Legal Aspects of International Organization Ser.). 1997. 149.00 (90-411-0306-6) Kluwer Law Intl.

Peck, Cynthia & Wilkinson, Wendy. Parents at Last: Celebrating Adoption & the New Pathways to Parenthood. LC 98-15737. (Illus.). 160p. 1998. 27.50 (0-609-60290-X) C Potter.

Peck, D. Sound of a Cry. pap. 6.99 (1-85792-134-8, Pub. by Christian Focus) Spring Arbor Dist.

Peck, Dale. Candidates for the Slaughterhouse. 2001. 23.50 (0-688-16758-6, Wm Morrow) Morrow Avon.

— The Garden of Lost & Found. 2001. write for info. (0-688-16759-4, Wm Morrow) Morrow Avon.

— Law of Enclosures. 320p. 1996. text 23.00 (0-374-18419-4) FS&G.

— Law of Enclosures. LC 96-38540. (U Ser.). 1997. per. 12.00 (0-671-00347-X, WSP) PB.

— Martin & John. LC 93-34064. 240p. 1994. reprint ed. pap. 13.00 (0-06-097588-1, Perennial) HarperTrade.

— Martin & John: A Novel. LC 92-1622. 1993. 21.00 (0-374-20311-3) FS&G.

— Now It's Time to Say Goodbye: A Novel. LC 97-26688. 480p. 1998. 25.00 (0-374-22271-1) FS&G.

***Peck, Dale.** Now It's Time to Say Goodbye: A Novel. LC 98-53918. 464p. 1999. pap. 15.95 (0-688-16841-8, Wm Morrow) Morrow Avon.

— Now It's Time to Say Goodbye Readers Guide. student ed. write for info. (0-374-96122-0) FS&G.

Peck, Daniel. Dear Rachel: The Civil War Letters of Daniel Peck. Stanford, Martha G., ed. LC 93-87081. (Illus.). 69p. (Orig.). 1993. pap. 6.00 (0-9639704-0-2) Devon Press.

Peck, Daniel, jt. auth. see Baron, Cynthia.

Peck, Daniel H., ed. see Cooper, James Fenimore.

Peck, David. Novels of Initiation: A Guidebook for Teaching Literature to Adolescents. 224p. 1989. pap. text 17.95 (0-8077-2951-5) Tchrs Coll.

Peck, David, ed. Identities & Issues in Literature, 3 vols. LC 97-11951. (Illus.). 1148p. 1997. lib. bdg. 225.00 (0-89356-920-8) Salem Pr.

Peck, David, jt. compiled by see Bullock, Chris.

Peck, David D. Multimedia: A Hands-On Introduction. LC 97-22709. (Graphic Communications Ser.). 352p. (C). 1997. pap. 55.95 incl. cd-rom (0-8273-7190-X) Delmar.

— Pocket Guide to Multimedia. abr. rev. ed. (Graphic Communications Ser.). (Illus.). 224p. (C). 1998. text 16.95 (0-8273-7383-X) Delmar.

Peck, David R. American Ethnic Literatures. (Magill Bibliographies Ser.). 218p. 1992. 42.00 (0-8108-2792-1) Scarecrow.

Peck, David R., jt. ed. see Maitino, John R.

Peck, David W. Decision at Law. LC 76-56082. 303p. 1977. reprint ed. lib. bdg. 65.00 (0-8371-9419-9, PEDL, Greenwood Pr) Greenwood.

Peck, Demaree C. The Imaginative Claims of the Artist in Willa Cather's Fiction: Possession Granted by a Different Lease. LC 95-40624. 344p. 1996. 48.50 (0-945636-87-3) Susquehanna U Pr.

***Peck, Dennis L. & Dolch, Norman A., eds.** Extraordinary Behavior: A Case Study Approach to Understanding Social Problems. LC 00-29840. 286p. 2000. 64.00 (0-275-97015-9, C7015, Praeger Pubs); pap. write for info. (0-275-97057-4) Greenwood.

P

An Asterisk (*) at the beginning of an entry indicates that the title is appearing for the first time.

Peck, Dennis L. & Hollingsworth, J. Selwyn, eds. Demographic & Structural Change: The Effects of the 1980s on American Society, 114. LC 95-37332. (Contributions in Sociology Ser.: No. 114). 256p. 1996. 69.50 (*0-313-28744-9*, Greenwood Pr) Greenwood.

Peck, Dennis L., jt. ed. see Murphy, John W.

Peck, Donald. Solos for Flute. (Carl Fischer's "All Time Favorites" Music Ser.). 48p. (Orig.). 1984. pap. 16.95 (*0-8258-0346-2*, ATF104) Fischer Inc NY.

Peck, Donald, compiled by. Easy Original Flute Solos, MFM48. (Illus.). 128p. 1967. pap. 14.95 (*0-8256-4048-2*, AM41682) Music Sales.

Peck, Donald M., jt. auth. see Jencks, Stanley M.

Peck, Donna. Nevada: Off the Beaten Path: A Guide to Unique Places. 2nd ed. LC 99-29027. (Off the Beaten Path Ser.). (Illus.). 225p. (Orig.). 1999. pap. text 12.95 (*0-7627-0460-8*) Globe Pequot.

— Romantic Days & Nights in San Francisco: Intimate Escapes in the City by the Bay. 2nd ed. LC 98-29740. (Romantic Cities Ser.). (Illus.). 256p. 1998. pap. 15.95 (*0-7627-0290-7*) Globe Pequot.

Peck, Douglas R. Ponce de Leon & the Discovery of Florida: The Man, the Myth, & the Truth. LC 93-89738. (Illus.). 160p. (Orig.). 1993. pap. 13.95 (*1-880654-02-4*) Pogo Pr.

Peck, Douglas T. Cristoforo Colombo: God's Navigator. LC 94-72094. (Illus.). 148p. (Orig.). 1994. pap. 12.95 (*0-9641798-0-6*); lib. bdg. 23.95 (*0-9641798-1-4*) Columbian Pubs.

Peck, E. J. Eskimo Grammar. 2nd rev. ed. (ESK.). 92p. 1997. reprint ed. 38.50 (*1-895959-21-7*, Pub. by Laurier Bks) IBD Ltd.

Peck, Elisabeth S. & Smith, Emily A. Berea's First 125 Years, 1855-1980. fac. ed. LC 82-6955. (Illus.). 308p. 1994. pap. 95.50 (*0-7837-7596-2*, 204734900007) Bks Demand.

Peck, Elizabeth A., jt. auth. see Montgomery, Douglas C.

Peck, Elizabeth G. & Stephens, JoAnna, eds. Common Ground: Feminist Collaboration in the Academy. LC 96-54244. 298p. (C). 1997. pap. text 21.95 (*0-7914-3512-1*) State U NY Pr.

— Common Ground: Feminist Collaboration in the Academy. LC 96-54244. 298p. (C). 1997. text 65.50 (*0-7914-3511-3*) State U NY Pr.

Peck, Elsie H., et al. Islamic Art from Michigan Collections. Fisher, Alan W., ed. (Illus.). 114p. (Orig.). 1982. pap. 11.00 (*1-879147-04-1*) Kresge Art Mus.

Peck, Ennis. Circles of Light. Dallagiacomo, Gene, ed. (Illus.). 32p. 1997. pap. text 17.00 (*0-9660417-0-4*) Hopenom.

Peck, Epophroditus. A History of Bristol, Connecticut. (Illus.). 362p. 1994. reprint ed. lib. bdg. 39.50 (*0-8328-4022-X*) Higginson Bk Co.

Peck, Eugene L. & Andrus, Regina P. Old Kanawha Baptist Church Minutes--Indexed, Plus Unpublished County Court Records of West Virginia. x, 87p. 1997. pap. 13.00 (*0-7884-0735-X*, P115) Heritage Bk.

Peck, Everett, jt. auth. see Metaxas, Eric.

***Peck, G. Richard.** Chillicothe. (Images of America Ser.). 128p. 1999. pap. 18.99 (*0-7385-0235-9*) Arcadia Publng.

Peck, Gail. New River. (Harperprints Chapbook Competition Ser.). 24p. 1993. 5.00 (*0-9624274-9-7*) NC Writers Network.

Peck, Gene. Chemistry Lab Manual. (C). 1993. student ed. 10.00 (*1-881592-02-2*) Hayden-McNeil.

Peck, Geo W., ed. History of Wisconsin. (Illus.). 423p. 1992. reprint ed. lib. bdg. 42.50 (*0-8328-2577-8*) Higginson Bk Co.

Peck, George. Birdbooks, 8 bks. Incl. Blackbirds. LC 96-19423. (Illus.). 32p. (J). (gr. 3 up). 1996. lib. bdg. 21.30 (*1-887068-14-7*); Doves. LC 96-18155. (Illus.). 32p. (J). (gr. 3 up). 1996. lib. bdg. 21.30 (*1-887068-16-3*); Gulls. LC 96-8376. (Illus.). 32p. (J). (gr. 3 up). 1997. lib. bdg. 21.30 (*1-887068-13-9*); Hawks & Eagles. LC 96-19421. (Illus.). 32p. (J). (gr. 3 up). 1997. lib. bdg. 21.30 (*1-887068-15-5*); Hummingbirds. LC 96-19431. (Illus.). 32p. (J). (gr. 3 up). 1997. lib. bdg. 21.30 (*1-887068-09-0*); Loons. LC 96-18156. (Illus.). 32p. (J). (gr. 3 up). 1996. lib. bdg. 21.30 (*1-887068-10-4*); Robins. LC 96-19422. (Illus.). 32p. (J). (gr. 3 up). 1996. lib. bdg. 21.30 (*1-887068-11-2*); Woodpeckers. LC 96-18154. (Illus.). 32p. (J). (gr. 3 up). 1996. lib. bdg. 21.30 (*1-887068-12-0*); (J). 1999. 170.40 (*1-887068-17-1*) Smart Apple.

— Crystal Reports 7: The Complete Reference. (Complete Reference Ser.). (Illus.). 771p. 1999. pap. 49.99 (*0-07-211978-0*) Osborne-McGraw.

***Peck, George.** Seagate Crystal Reports 8: Complete Reference. (Complete Reference Ser.). 2000. pap. 49.99 (*0-07-212565-9*) Osborne-McGraw.

Peck, George. Simplicity: A Rich Quaker's View. LC 72-97851. (Orig.). 1973. pap. 4.00 (*0-87574-189-4*) Pendle Hill.

— Sketches & Incidents from the Saddlebag of an Itinerant. 1988. pap. 10.99 (*0-88019-237-2*) Schmul Pub Co.

Peck, George K. The Birdbook, 8 vols. in 1. LC 99-71161. (Illus.). 216p. (J). (gr. 2-7). 1999. lib. bdg. 33.25 (*1-887068-98-8*) Smart Apple.

Peck, George K. & James, Ross D. Breeding Birds of Ontario, Nidiology & Distribution: Nonpasserines. (Illus.). 336p. pap. 40.00 (*0-88854-288-7*) Brill Academic Pubs.

Peck, George T. Christian Perfection, Vol. 1. 1990. pap. 11.99 (*0-88019-266-6*) Schmul Pub Co.

— Christian Perfection, Vol. 2. 1991. reprint ed. pap. 11.99 (*0-88019-271-2*) Schmul Pub Co.

— The Psalms Speak. 32p. (Orig.). 1991. pap. 4.00 (*0-87574-298-X*) Pendle Hill.

— The Triple Way. LC 77-79824. 321p. (Orig.). 1977. pap. 4.00 (*0-87574-213-0*) Pendle Hill.

— What Is Quakerism? A Primer. LC 87-63556. (Orig.). 1988. pap. 4.00 (*0-87574-277-7*) Pendle Hill.

Peck, George W. Adventures of One Terence McGrant. (Notable American Authors Ser.). 1999. reprint ed. lib. bdg. 125.00 (*0-7812-8714-6*) Rprt Serv.

— How Private George W. Peck Put Down the Rebellion. LC 71-91090. (American Humorists Ser.). (Illus.). 328p. 1979. reprint ed. lib. bdg. 37.50 (*0-8398-1559-X*) Irvington.

— How Private George W. Peck Put Down the Rebellion, or the Funny Experiences of a Raw Recruit. LC 90-38549. (Illus.). x, 350p. 1990. reprint ed. pap. 9.95 (*0-940473-20-8*) Wm Caxton.

— Peck's Bad Boy & His Pa. (Illus.). 250p. 1991. reprint ed. lib. bdg. 35.95 (*0-89966-750-3*) Buccaneer Bks.

Peck, Girvan. Writing Persuasive Briefs. LC 84-80192. 312p. 1984. 55.00 (*0-316-69666-8*, 96668, Aspen Law & Bus) Aspen Pub.

Peck, Graham. Two Kinds of Time. LC 83-45833. (Illus.). reprint ed. 67.50 (*0-404-20198-9*) AMS Pr.

***Peck, Gunther.** Reinventing Free Labor: Padrone & Immigrant Workers in the North American West, 1880-1930. (Illus.). 320p. 2000. text 54.95 (*0-521-64160-8*) Cambridge U Pr.

— Reinventing Free Labor: Padrone & Immigrant Workers in the North American West, 1880-1930. (Illus.). 320p. (C). 2000. pap. text 19.95 (*0-521-77819-0*) Cambridge U Pr.

Peck, H. Daniel. Thoreau's Morning Work: Memory & Perception in a Week on the Concord & Merrimack Rivers, the Journal & Walden. 208p. (C). 1990. 35.00 (*0-300-04823-8*) Yale U Pr.

— Thoreau's Morning Work: Memory & Perception in A Week on the Concord & Merrimack Rivers, the Journal, & Walden. 208p. 1994. pap. 15.00 (*0-300-06104-8*) Yale U Pr.

— A World by Itself: The Pastoral Moment in Cooper's Fiction. LC 76-25868. 227p. reprint ed. pap. 70.40 (*0-8357-3755-1*, 203648100003) Bks Demand.

Peck, H. Daniel, ed. New Essays on "The Last of the Mohicans" (American Novel Ser.). 153p. (C). 1992. text 32.95 (*0-521-37414-6*); pap. text 14.95 (*0-521-37771-4*) Cambridge U Pr.

Peck, H. Daniel, ed. & intro. see Thoreau, Henry David.

***Peck, Harriet Taylor.** Secrets of the Stone. LC 99-41363. (Illus.). 32p. (ps-3). 2000. text 16.00 (*0-374-36648-9*) FS&G.

Peck, Harry D., Jr. & LeGall, Jean, eds. Inorganic Microbial Sulfur Metabolism. (Methods in Enzymology Ser.: Vol. 243). (Illus.). 682p. 1994. text. write for info. (*0-12-182144-7*) Acad Pr.

Peck, Harry T. The Adventures of Mabel. (Illus.). 236p. (J). (gr. k-5). 1986. reprint ed. 26.95 (*0-9616844-0-2*) Greenhouse Pub.

— The Adventures of Mabel. (Notable American Authors Ser.). 1999. reprint ed. lib. bdg. 125.00 (*0-7812-8717-0*) Rprt Serv.

— Greystone & Porphyry (Verse) (Notable American Authors Ser.). 1999. reprint ed. lib. bdg. 125.00 (*0-7812-8719-7*) Rprt Serv.

— Hilda & the Wishes. (Notable American Authors Ser.). 1999. reprint ed. lib. bdg. 125.00 (*0-7812-8723-5*) Rprt Serv.

— Latin Pronunciation. (Notable American Authors Ser.). 1999. reprint ed. lib. bdg. 125.00 (*0-7812-8716-2*) Rprt Serv.

— Literature. (Notable American Authors Ser.). 1999. reprint ed. lib. bdg. 125.00 (*0-7812-8724-3*) Rprt Serv.

— The New Baedeker. (Notable American Authors Ser.). 1999. reprint ed. lib. bdg. 125.00 (*0-7812-8726-X*) Rprt Serv.

— The Personal Equation. LC 79-39121. (Essay Index Reprint Ser.). 1977. reprint ed. 24.95 (*0-8369-2709-5*) Ayer.

— The Personal Equation. (Notable American Authors Ser.). 1999. reprint ed. lib. bdg. 125.00 (*0-7812-8718-9*) Rprt Serv.

— The Semitic Theory of Creation. (Notable American Authors Ser.). 1999. reprint ed. lib. bdg. 125.00 (*0-7812-8715-4*) Rprt Serv.

— Studies in Several Literatures. LC 68-16967. (Essay Index Reprint Ser.). 1977. 20.95 (*0-8369-0781-7*) Ayer.

— Studies in Several Literatures. (Notable American Authors Ser.). 1999. reprint ed. lib. bdg. 125.00 (*0-7812-8725-1*) Rprt Serv.

— Twenty Years of the Republic. (Notable American Authors Ser.). 1999. reprint ed. lib. bdg. 125.00 (*0-7812-8722-7*) Rprt Serv.

— What Is Good English? And Other Essays. LC 72-39122. (Essay Index Reprint Ser.). 1977. reprint ed. 21.95 (*0-8369-2710-9*) Ayer.

— What Is Good English? & Other Essays. (Notable American Authors Ser.). 1999. reprint ed. lib. bdg. 125.00 (*0-7812-8720-0*) Rprt Serv.

— William Hickling Prescott. LC 69-14033. 186p. 1969. reprint ed. lib. bdg. 55.00 (*0-8371-0614-1*, PEWP, Greenwood Pr) Greenwood.

— William Hickling Prescott. (BCL1-PS American Literature Ser.). 186p. 1992. reprint ed. lib. bdg. 69.00 (*0-7812-6838-9*) Rprt Serv.

— William Hickling Prescott. (Notable American Authors Ser.). 1999. reprint ed. lib. bdg. 125.00 (*0-7812-8721-9*) Rprt Serv.

Peck, Howard. Howard Peck's New Milford: Memories of a Connecticut Town. LC 91-34071. (Illus.). 176p. 1991. 25.00 (*0-914659-54-5*) Phoenix Pub.

Peck, I. A Genealogical History of the Descendants of Joseph Peck Who Emigrated in 1638: Also an Appendix Giving an Account of the Boston & Hingham Pecks, the Descendant of John of Mendon, Mass. (Illus.). 443p. 1989. reprint ed. pap. 56.50 (*0-8328-0947-0*); reprint ed. lib. bdg. 66.50 (*0-8328-0946-2*) Higginson Bk Co.

***Peck, Ira.** Elizabeth Blackwell: The First Woman Doctor. LC 99-59796. (Gateway Biography Ser.). 2000. lib. bdg. write for info. (*0-7613-1854-2*) Millbrook Pr.

Peck, Ira. The Life & Words of Martin Luther King Jr. (Illus.). 112p. (J). (gr. 3-7). 1991. mass mkt. 5.50 (*0-590-43827-1*) Scholastic Inc.

Peck, Ira. Life & Words of Martin Luther King, Jr. 1968. 8.70 (*0-606-03106-5*, Pub. by Turtleback) Demco.

Peck, Ira & Bly, Nellie. Nellie Bly's Book: Around the World in 72 Days. LC 98-5376. 128p. (YA). (gr. 5 up). 1998. 26.90 (*0-7613-0971-3*) TFC Bks NY.

***Peck, Ira B.** A Genealogical History of the Descendants of Joseph Peck Who Emigrated in 1638: Also Records of His Father's & Grandfather's Families in England. 442p. 2000. reprint ed. pap. 43.00 (*0-8063-4978-6*, Pub. by Clearfield Co) ACCESS Pubs Network.

Peck, J. L., et al. Past & Present of O'Brien & Osceola Counties, Iowa, 2 vols., Set. (Illus.). 1319p. 1994. reprint ed. lib. bdg. 135.00 (*0-8328-3827-6*) Higginson Bk Co.

Peck, J. M. A Gazetteer of Illinois in Three Parts: Containing a General View of the State, a General View of Each County, & a Particular Description of Each Town, Settlement, Stream, Prairie, Bottom, Bluff, Etc. Alphabetically Arranged. xii, 356p. (Orig.). 1993. reprint ed. pap. text 24.00 (*1-55613-782-6*) Heritage Bk.

Peck, Jamie. Work-Place: The Social Regulation of Labor Markets. LC 96-1005. (Perspectives on Economic Change Ser.). 320p. 1996. pap. text 21.95 (*1-57230-044-2*, 0044); lib. bdg. 42.50 (*1-57230-043-4*) Guilford Pubns.

Peck, Janet R., jt. ed. see Bailey, Elizabeth E.

Peck, Janice. The Gods of Televangelism: The Crisis of Meaning & the Appeal of Religious Television. Good, Leslie T., ed. LC 92-32476. (Communication Series: Critical Studies in Communication). 288p. (C) 1993. text 59.50 (*1-881303-65-9*); pap. text 26.50 (*1-881303-66-7*) Hampton Pr NJ.

Peck, Jash, jt. auth. see Niemeyer, Pat.

Peck, Jean M. At the Fire's Center: A Story of Love & Holocaust Survival. LC 98-9060. 1998. 24.95 (*0-252-02420-6*) U of Ill Pr.

Peck, Jeffrey M. Culture - Contexture: Explorations in Anthropology & Literary Studies. Daniel, E. Valentine, ed. LC 94-3997. 1995. 55.00 (*0-520-08463-2*, Pub. by U CA Pr); pap. 17.95 (*0-520-08464-0*, Pub. by U CA Pr) Cal Prin Full Svc.

— Hermes Disguised: Literary Hermeneutics & the Interpretation of Literature, Vol. 602. (European University Studies: German Language & Literature: Ser. 1). 347p. 1982. pap. 54.00 (*3-261-03232-4*) P Lang Pubng.

Peck, Jeffrey M., jt. auth. see Borneman, John.

Peck, Jeffrey M., jt. ed. see Cohen, Ralph.

Peck, Jeffrey M., jt. ed. see Milich, Klaus J.

***Peck, Jesse T.** The Central Idea of Christianity. 229p. 1999. pap. 11.99 (*0-88019-390-5*) Schmul Pub Co.

Peck, Jim, ed. see Chomsky, Noam.

Peck, Johanne T., et al. Kindergarten Policies: What Is Best for Children? LC 88-61832. 88p. 1988. pap. text 6.00 (*0-935989-15-3*, NAEYC #141) Natl Assn Child Ed.

Peck, John. M & Other Poems. LC 96-24855. 136p. 1996. 29.95 (*0-8101-5055-7*, TriQuart); pap. 12.95 (*0-8101-5056-5*, TriQuart) Northwestern U Pr.

— Poems & Translations of Hi-Lo. LC 93-38629. 181p. (Orig.). 1993. pap. 14.95 (*1-878818-28-7*, Pub. by Sheep Meadow) U Pr of New Eng.

Peck, John, ed. David Copperfield, Hard Times: Charles Dickens. LC 94-35204. (New Casebooks Ser.). 1995. text 45.00 (*0-312-12492-9*) St Martin.

— Middlemarch. LC 91-36461. (New Casebooks Ser.). 208p. 1992. text 45.00 (*0-312-07567-7*) St Martin.

Peck, John, tr. see Nisetich, Frank J. & Euripides.

Peck, John E., jt. ed. see Swartz, Thomas R.

Peck, John M. Father Clark: Or The Pioneer Preacher. LC 72-104539. 285p. reprint ed. lib. bdg. 31.00 (*0-8398-1560-3*) Irvington.

— Father Clark: Or The Pioneer Preacher. 285p. 1986. reprint ed. pap. text 6.95 (*0-8290-1901-4*) Irvington.

— Forty Years of Pioneer Life: Memoir of John Mason Peck, D.D. (American Biography Ser.). 360p. 1991. reprint ed. lib. bdg. 79.00 (*0-7812-8310-8*) Rprt Serv.

— A Guide for Emigrants: Containing Sketches of Illinois, Missouri, & the Adjacent Parts. LC 75-115. (Mid-American Frontier Ser.). 1975. reprint ed. 28.95 (*0-405-06881-6*) Ayer.

Peck, Josh, jt. auth. see Niemeyer, Pat.

Peck, Judith. Art & Interaction: A Fieldwork Program for Colleges/An Activities Program for Institutions. (Illus.). 179p. (C). 1997. reprint ed. pap. text 19.95 (*0-927351-00-5*) Ramapo College.

— Judith Peck Sculpture Catalog: 50 Years of Sculpture. Messet, David, ed. (Illus.). 36p. 1999. pap. 15.00 (*0-927351-06-4*) Ramapo College.

— Leap to the Sun: Learning Through Dynamic Play. (Illus.). 158p. 1979. 12.95 (*0-13-527275-0*) P-H.

— Sculpture: A Fifteen-Week Multimedia Program. (Illus.). 144p. 1986. pap. 14.95 (*0-671-61426-6*) P-H.

— Sculpture As Experience. LC 88-43308. (Illus.). 208p. 1989. pap. 17.95 (*0-8019-7978-1*) Krause Pubns.

Peck, Kyle L., jt. auth. see Hannafin, Michael J.

Peck, Larry & Irgolic, Kurt. Measurement & Synthesis in the Chemistry Laboratory. 2nd ed. 478p. (C). 1997. pap. text 56.00 (*0-13-905050-7*) P-H.

***Peck, Lib, ed.** Race Discrimination: Developing & Using a New Legal Framework. 250p. 2000. pap. 30.00 (*1-84113-167-9*, Pub. by Hart Pub) Intl Spec Bk.

Peck, Linda L. Court Patronage & Corruption in Early Stuart England. 320p. 1990. text 55.00 (*0-04-942195-6*) Routledge.

— Court Patronage & Corruption in Early Stuart England. LC 92-46114. 336p. (C). 1993. pap. 25.99 (*0-415-09368-6*, B0617) Routledge.

— Northampton: Patronage & Policy at the Court of James I. 288p. (C). 1982. text 55.00 (*0-04-942177-8*) Routledge.

Peck, Lisa J. Dangerous Memories. pap. 12.95 (*1-55517-389-6*) CFI Dist.

Peck, Lisa J. Life with the Kids: A Year's Supply of Family Funnies. 128p. 1998. pap. 6.98 (*0-88290-620-8*, 1086) Horizon Utah.

— Lovin' for a Lifetime: 365 Ways to Keep Romance in Your Marriage. 128p. 1998. pap. 6.98 (*0-88290-640-2*, 1092) Horizon Utah.

***Peck, Lisa J.** More Precious Than Diamonds. 2000. pap. 10.95 (*1-55517-450-7*) CFI Dist.

***Peck, M. Scott.** Abounding Grace: An Anthology of Wisdom. LC 00-29325. 2000. 24.95 (*0-7407-1014-1*) Andrews & McMeel.

Peck, M. Scott. All-American Boy: Growing up Gay in God's Country. 1996. pap. 11.00 (*0-614-12544-8*) Ballantine Pub Grp.

— A Bed by the Window. 320p. 1991. pap. 14.95 (*0-553-35387-X*) Bantam.

— The Different Drum. 1998. per. 14.00 (*0-684-84858-9*, Touchstone) S&S Trade Pap.

***Peck, M. Scott.** The Different Drum: Community Making & Peace. 1999. 9.98 (*0-671-04625-X*) S&S Trade.

Peck, M. Scott. The Different Drum: Community Making & Peace. 336p. 1988. pap. 12.00 (*0-671-66833-1*, Touchstone) S&S Trade Pap.

— The Different Drum: Community Making & Peace. unabridged ed. 1987. 16.00 incl. audio (*0-671-64633-8*, Audioworks) S&S Trade.

— Further along the Road Less Traveled. 252p. 1998. per. 14.00 (*0-684-84723-X*) S&S Trade.

Peck, M. Scott. Further along the Road Less Traveled. 1997. per. 6.99 (*0-684-85016-8*, Touchstone) S&S Trade Pap.

Peck, M. Scott. Further along the Road Less Traveled: Growing up Painfully: Consciousness & the Problem of Pain [sound recording], 1. LC 91-740424. 1990. audio 9.95 (*0-671-70930-5*, Audioworks) S&S Trade.

Peck, M. Scott. Further along the Road Less Traveled: Sexuality & Spirituality, 1. 1988. audio 12.00 (*0-671-66891-9*, Audioworks) S&S Trade.

Peck, M. Scott. Further along the Road Less Traveled: The Unending Journey Toward Spiritual Growth. 252p. 1994. pap. 14.00 (*0-671-89288-6*, Touchstone) S&S Trade Pap.

— Further along the Road Less Traveled: The Unending Journey Toward Spiritual Growth. large type ed. 272p. 1994. pap. 13.95 (*0-8027-2682-8*) Walker & Co.

***Peck, M. Scott.** Golf & the Spirit: Lessons for the Journey. (Illus.). 320p. 2000. pap. 15.00 (*0-609-80566-5*, Three Riv Pr) Crown Pub Group.

Peck, M. Scott. Golf & the Spirit: Lessons for the Journey. LC 99-11240. (Illus.). 352p. 1999. 25.00 (*0-517-70883-3*) Harmony Bks.

***Peck, M. Scott.** Golf & the Spirit: Lessons for the Journey. large type ed. LC 99-32365. 1999. write for info. (*1-56895-751-3*) Wheeler Pub.

Peck, M. Scott. In Heaven As on Earth: A Vision of the Afterlife. LC 95-44662. 240p. 1996. 19.95 (*0-7868-6204-1*, Pub. by Hyperion) Time Warner.

— In Heaven As on Earth: A Vision of the Afterlife. 240p. 1997. mass mkt. 5.99 (*0-7868-8933-0*, Pub. by Hyperion) Time Warner.

— In Heaven As on Earth: A Vision of the Afterlife. 240p. (J). 1997. mass mkt. 5.99 (*0-7868-8921-7*, Pub. by Hyperion) Time Warner.

— In Heaven As on Earth: A Vision of the Afterlife. 24p. 1998. pap. 12.45 (*0-7868-8374-X*, Pub. by Hyperion) Time Warner.

— In Heaven As on Earth: A Vision of the Afterlife. large type ed. LC 96-45002. (Inspirational Ser.). 263p. 1997. lib. bdg. 23.95 (*0-7838-2014-3*, G K Hall Lrg Type) Mac Lib Ref.

***Peck, M. Scott.** In Heaven As on Earth: A Vision of the Afterlife. 224p. 1999. reprint ed. text 20.00 (*0-7881-6332-9*) DIANE Pub.

— In Search of Stones: A Pilgrimage of Faith, Reason & Discovery. (Illus.). 422p. 2000. pap. text 14.00 (*0-7881-9142-X*) DIANE Pub.

Peck, M. Scott. In Search of Stones: A Pilgrimage of Faith, Reason & Discovery. (Illus.). 416p. 1995. 22.45 (*0-7868-6021-9*, Pub. by Hyperion) Time Warner.

— In Search of Stones: A Pilgrimage of Faith, Reason & Discovery. large type ed. LC 95-36055. (Compass Press Large Print Book Ser.). 1995. 26.95 (*1-56895-270-8*, Compass) Wheeler Pub.

— In Search of Stones: A Pilgrimage of Faith, Reason & Discovery. LC 94-36475. (Illus.). 448p. (J). 1996. reprint ed. pap. 13.45 (*0-7868-8164-X*, Pub. by Hyperion) Time Warner.

— The Love you Deserve: Ten Keys to Perfect Love. LC 97-94328. (Illus.). 270p. 1998. pap. 13.95 (*0-9659976-3-4*) Lifepath Pub.

Peck, M. Scott. Meditations from the Road. 1993. audio 12.00 (*0-671-87477-2*) S&S Audio.

Peck, M. Scott. Meditations from the Road: Daily Reflections from The Road Less Traveled & The Different Drum. 384p. 1993. pap. 9.00 (*0-671-79799-9*, Touchstone) S&S Trade Pap.

— Meditations from the Road Less Traveled. 1998. per. 10.00 (*0-684-84729-9*) S&S Trade.

— People of the Lie. 1998. per. 14.00 (*0-684-84859-7*) S&S Trade Pap.

Peck, M. Scott. People of the Lie, Vol. 1. unabridged ed. 1992. audio 12.00 (*0-671-76971-5*) S&S Audio.

Peck, M. Scott. People of the Lie: The Hope for Healing Human Evil. 270p. 1985. pap. 12.00 (*0-671-52816-5*, Touchstone) S&S Trade Pap.

P

— The Road Less Traveled. 320p. 1998. per. 14.00 (0-684-84724-8) S&S Trade.

Peck, M. Scott. The Road Less Traveled. 1997. per. 6.99 (0-684-85015-X, Touchstone) S&S Trade Pap.

Peck, M. Scott. The Road Less Traveled: A New Psychology of Love, Traditional Values & Spiritual Growth. 322p. 1980. pap. 14.00 (0-671-25067-1, Touchstone) S&S Trade Pap.

— The Road Less Traveled: A New Psychology of Love, Traditional Values & Spiritual Growth. 322p. 1988. pap. 14.00 (0-671-67300-9, Touchstone) S&S Trade Pap.

— The Road Less Traveled: A New Psychology of Love, Traditional Values & Spiritual Growth. large type ed. 448p. 1985. pap. 16.95 (0-8027-2498-1) Walker & Co.

— The Road Less Traveled: A New Psychology of Love, Traditional Values & Spiritual Growth. 1995. reprint ed. lib. bdg. 37.95 (1-56849-158-1) Buccaneer Bks.

Peck, M. Scott. The Road Less Traveled & Beyond. 1997. per. 6.99 (0-684-85017-6, Touchstone) S&S Trade Pap.

Peck, M. Scott. The Road Less Traveled & Beyond. 320p. 1998. per. 14.00 (0-684-83561-4, Touchstone) S&S Trade Pap.

— The Road Less Traveled & Beyond: Spiritual Growth in an Age of Anxiety. LC 96-43391. 1997. 22.50 (0-684-81314-9) S&S Trade.

— The Road Less Traveled & Beyond: Spiritual Growth in an Age of Anxiety. large type ed. LC 96-44451. 463p. 1997. 26.95 (0-7862-0943-7) Thorndike Pr.

— The Road Less Traveled & Beyond: Spiritual Growth in an Age of Anxiety. large type ed. LC 96-44451. 1999. pap. 24.95 (0-7862-0944-5) Thorndike Pr.

*Peck, M. Scott. The Road Less Traveled & Beyond: Spiritual Growth in an Age of Anxiety. 314p. 1999. reprint ed. text 23.00 (0-7881-6705-7) DIANE Pub.

Peck, M. Scott. A World Waiting to Be Born: Civility Rediscovered. 384p. 1994. pap. 13.95 (0-553-37317-X) Bantam.

Peck, M. Scott & Peck, Shannon. Liberating Your Magnificence: 25 Keys to Loving & Healing Yourself. 292p. 1999. pap. 13.95 (0-9659976-5-0, Pub. by Lifepath Pub) IPG Chicago.

Peck, M. Scott & Von Waldner, Marilyn. Gifts for the Journey: Treasures of the Chrisitan Life. LC 98-56060. 160p. 1999. pap. 20.00 (1-58063-056-1, Pub. by Renaissance) St Martin.

Peck, M. Scott, et al. What Return Can I Make? The Dimensions of the Christian Experience. LC 85-11945. 96p. 1985. 24.95 (0-317-38030-3) S&S Trade.

Peck, M. Scott, jt. auth. see Pogue, David.

Peck, Malcolm C. Historical Dictionary of the Gulf Arab States. (Asian Historical Dictionaries Ser.: No. 21). (Illus.). 1996. 45.00 (0-8108-3203-8) Scarecrow.

Peck, Margarette R. Souvenir Lives Forever. (Orig.). 1997. pap. write for info. (1-57553-452-5) Watermrk Pr.

Peck, Marie J. Mythologizing Uruguayan Reality in the Works of Jose Pedro Diaz. LC 85-5910. 130p. 1985. pap. 8.00 (0-87918-058-7) ASU Lat Am St.

Peck, Mark A. Integrated Account Management: How Business-to-Business Marketers Maximize Customer Loyalty & Profitability. LC 96-40049. 320p. 1997. 60.00 (0-8144-0333-6) AMACOM.

Peck, Marshall, III, jt. auth. see Berger, Melvin H.

Peck, Mary B. A Full House & Fine Singing: The Diaries & Letters of Sadie Harper. 251p. 1992. pap. 14.95 (0-86492-140-3, Pub. by Goose Ln Edits) Genl Dist Srvs.

Peck, Merton J., ed. World Aluminum Industry in a Changing Energy Era. LC 88-4990. 231p. 1988. 30.00 (0-915707-42-X) Resources Future.

Peck, Merton J. & Richardson, Thomas J. What Is to Be Done? Proposals for the Soviet Transition to the Market. 224p. (Orig.). 1992. 35.00 (0-300-05466-1); pap. 16.00 (0-300-05468-8) Yale U Pr.

Peck, Michael, et al. Youth Suicide. (Death & Suicide Ser.: Vol. 6). 224p. 1986. pap. 33.95 (0-8261-4481-0) Springer Pub.

Peck, Paula. The Art of Fine Baking: Cakes & Pastries, Coffeecakes, Breads with a Continental Flavor. LC 97-10106. (Cook's Classic Library). (Illus.). 320p. 1997. pap. 14.95 (1-55821-594-8) Lyons Pr.

Peck, Pauline C. & Erardi, Glenn. Mustache Cups: Timeless Victorian Treasures. (Illus.). 176p. 1999. 49.95 (0-7643-0924-2) Schiffer.

Peck, Ralph B., et al. Foundation Engineering. 2nd ed. 544p. 1974. text 100.95 (0-471-67585-7) Wiley.

Peck, Rasamond. The Flavor of Waverly. Belin, Susan S., ed. & intro. by. (Illus.). 266p. 1986. 18.95 (0-9616433-0-7) Waverly Comm Hse.

Peck, Richard. Amanda/Miranda. abr. ed. Kane, Cindy, ed. LC 99-12246. (Illus.). 176p. (YA). (gr. 7-12). 1999. 16.99 (0-8037-2489-6, Dial Yng Read) Peng Put Young Read.

— Anonymously Yours. 136p. (YA). (gr. 6 up). 1995. pap. 4.95 (0-688-13702-4, Wm Morrow) Morrow Avon.

Peck, Richard. Anonymously Yours. 1995. 10.05 (0-606-07201-2, Pub. by Turtleback) Demco.

Peck, Richard. Are You in the House Alone? 176p. (YA). (gr. k up). 1977. mass mkt. 4.99 (0-440-90227-4, LLL BDD) BDD Bks Young Read.

*Peck, Richard. Are You in the House Alone? (Illus.). (J). 2000. pap. 5.99 (0-14-130693-9, PuffinBks) Peng Put Young Read.

Peck, Richard. Are You in the House Alone? (Laurel-Leaf Mystery Ser.). (J). 1967. 9.60 (0-606-01121-8, Pub. by Turtleback) Demco.

*Peck, Richard. Are You in the House Alone? (Illus.). (J). 2000. 10.34 (0-606-18388-4) Turtleback.

Peck, Richard. Bel Air Bambi. (J). 1994. mass mkt. 4.99 (0-440-91031-5) BDD Bks Young Read.

— Bel-Air Bambi & the Mall Rats. 192p. (YA). 1995. mass mkt. 3.99 (0-440-21925-6) Dell.

— Bel-Air Bambi & the Mall Rats. 1995. 9.09 (0-606-07274-8, Pub. by Turtleback) Demco.

— Blossom Culp & the Sleep of Death. (J). 1986. 9.09 (0-606-03552-4, Pub. by Turtleback) Demco.

— Don't Look & It Won't Hurt. LC 99-14969. 176p. (gr. 7). 1999. pap. 16.95 (0-8050-6316-1) H Holt & Co.

— Don't Look & It Won't Hurt. 1972. 9.60 (0-606-00920-5, Pub. by Turtleback) Demco.

*Peck, Richard. Dreamland Lake. LC 99-55400. (Illus.). 160p. (YA). (gr. 7-12). 2000. pap. 4.99 (0-14-130812-5, PuffinBks) Peng Put Young Read.

Peck, Richard. Father Figure. (Illus.). 208p. (Orig.). (YA). (gr. 7 up). 1996. pap. 4.99 (0-14-037969-X, PuffinBks) Peng Put Young Read.

Peck, Richard. Father Figure: A Novel. LC 78-7909. 1996. 9.09 (0-606-09262-5, Pub. by Turtleback) Demco.

Peck, Richard. The Ghost Belonged to Me. (YA). 1997. 10.09 (0-606-12708-9, Pub. by Turtleback) Demco.

— The Ghost Belonged to Me. (Illus.). 192p. (J). (gr. 3-7). 1997. pap. 4.99 (0-14-038671-8) Viking Penguin.

— Ghosts I Have Been. 224p. (J). (gr. k-6). 1987. pap. 4.50 (0-440-42864-5, YB BDD) BDD Bks Young Read.

— Ghosts I Have Been: A Novel. 1994. 9.09 (0-606-01635-X, Pub. by Turtleback) Demco.

— The Great Interactive Dream Machine. abr. ed. LC 95-53263. 160p. (YA). (gr. 5 up). 1996. 14.99 (0-8037-1989-2, Dial Yng Read) Peng Put Young Read.

— Great Interactive Dream Machine: Sequel To: Lost in Cyberspace. (Puffin Novels Ser.). 196p. (J). (gr. 5-9). 1998. pap. 4.99 (0-14-038264-X) Peng Put Young Read.

— Last Safe Place. (J). 1996. 20.95 (0-385-30995-3); mass mkt. 4.99 (0-440-91152-4) BDD Bks Young Read.

— The Last Safe Place on Earth. 176p. (YA). (gr. 5 up). 1996. mass mkt. 4.99 (0-440-22007-6, LLL BDD) BDD Bks Young Read.

— Last Safe Place on Earth. LC 94-446. 1996. 9.09 (0-606-09528-4, Pub. by Turtleback) Demco.

— London Holiday. 1999. pap. 12.95 (0-14-027857-5) Viking Penguin.

— London Holiday. large type ed. LC 98-36372. 1998. 26.95 (0-7862-1635-2) Thorndike Pr.

*Peck, Richard. A Long Way from Chicago. LC 98-10953. 148p. (J). (gr. 4-7). 1998. 15.99 (0-8037-2290-7, Dial Yng Read) Peng Put Young Read.

— A Long Way from Chicago. (Illus.). 176p. (J). (gr. 5 up). 2000. pap. 4.99 (0-14-130352-2, PuffinBks) Peng Put Young Read.

— Lost in Cyberspace. (J). 1997. 10.09 (0-606-10985-4, Pub. by Turtleback) Demco.

Peck, Richard. Lost in Cyberspace. LC 94-48330. (Illus.). 160p. (J). (gr. 5-9). 1997. pap. 4.99 (0-14-037856-1) Viking Penguin.

— A Morbid Fascination: White Prose & Politics in Apartheid South Africa, 78. LC 96-27387. (Contributions to the Study of World Literature Ser.). 216p. 1997. 59.95 (0-313-30091-7) Greenwood.

— Remembering the Good Times. 192p. (YA). (gr. 5-12). 1986. mass mkt. 4.99 (0-440-97339-2, LLL BDD) BDD Bks Young Read.

Peck, Richard. Remembering the Good Times. 181p. (YA). (gr. 7 up). pap. 4.50 (0-8072-1380-2) Listening Lib.

— Remembering the Good Times. (J). 1986. 9.60 (0-606-02348-8, Pub. by Turtleback) Demco.

Peck, Richard. Rock: Making Musical Choices. 174p. (Orig.). 1985. pap. 7.95 (0-89084-297-3, 025288) Bob Jones Univ.

Peck, Richard. Secrets of the Shopping Mall. (Laurel-Leaf Contemporary Fiction Ser.). (J). 1979. 9.09 (0-606-02252-X, Pub. by Turtleback) Demco.

Peck, Richard. Something for Joey. 192p. (YA). 1983. mass mkt. 4.99 (0-553-27199-7) Bantam.

— Something for Joey. (Bantam Starfire Bks.). (J). 1978. 9.60 (0-606-01226-5, Pub. by Turtleback) Demco.

Peck, Richard. Soup for the President. (J). 1991. pap. 3.25 (0-440-80255-5) BDD Bks Young Read.

Peck, Richard. Strays Like Us. LC 97-18575. 160p. (YA). (gr. 5-9). 1998. 15.99 (0-8037-2291-5, Dial Yng Read) Peng Put Young Read.

*Peck, Richard. Strays Like Us. (Illus.). 160p. (J). (gr. 5-9). 2000. pap. 4.99 (0-14-130619-X, PuffinBks) Peng Put Young Read.

— Through a Brief Darkness. (J). 1997. 9.09 (0-606-11986-8, Pub. by Turtleback) Demco.

— Voices After Midnight. 1989. 9.60 (0-606-04840-5, Pub. by Turtleback) Demco.

Peck, Richard. Voices after Midnight. 192p. (YA). 1990. reprint ed. pap. 4.50 (0-440-40378-2) Dell.

*Peck, Richard. A Year down Yonder. LC 99-43159. 144p. (J). (gr. 5 up). 2000. 16.99 (0-8037-2518-3, Dial Yng Read) Peng Put Young Read.

Peck, Richard E. The New Mexico Experience: 1598-1998: A Confluence of Cultures. (Illus.). 240p. 1998. 29.95 (0-9661142-0-5) Sierra Pub.

Peck, Rob, jt. auth. see Center for Learning Network Staff.

Peck, Robert A. The Amiga Companion. 256p. 1988. pap. 19.95 (0-928579-00-X) IDG NH.

— The Amiga Companion. 2nd rev. ed. 306p. 1989. pap. 19.95 (0-928579-01-8) IDG NH.

*Peck, Robert B. Libraries, the First Amendment & Cyberspace: What You Need to Know. LC 99-39455. 144p. 1999. pap. 32.00 (0-8389-0773-3) ALA.

Peck, Robert L. American Meditation & Beginning Yoga. 1976. 6.00 (0-917828-05-4) Personal Dev Ctr.

— The Golden Triangle, Vol. 1. (Illus.). 288p. 1998. pap. text 14.95 (0-917828-06-2) Personal Dev Ctr.

Peck, Robert L. & Peck, Thelma M. The Handbook for Goats. 1985. 8.50 (0-917828-00-3) Personal Dev Ctr.

— Philosophy of Patanjali. 1994. 7.95 (0-917828-04-6) Personal Dev Ctr.

— Stone of the Philosophers. 1988. 14.95 (0-917828-02-X) Personal Dev Ctr.

Peck, Robert M. A Celebration of Birds: The Life & Art of Louis Agassiz Fuertes. (Illus.). 192p. 1982. 30.00 (0-8027-0716-5) Walker & Co.

— Headhunters & Hummingbirds: An Expedition into Ecuador. LC 86-15908. (Illus.). 128p. (J). (gr. 11 up). 1987. 14.95 (0-8027-6645-5); lib. bdg. 14.85 (0-8027-6646-3) Walker & Co.

— Land of the Eagle: A Natural History of North America. (Illus.). 288p. 1991. 30.00 (0-671-75596-X) Summit Bks.

Peck, Robert N. A Day No Pigs Would Die, Set. unabridged ed. (J). 1995. pap. 28.98 incl. audio (0-8072-8533-1, LB3SP) Listening Lib.

— A Part of the Sky. unabridged ed. (YA). (gr. 7-12). 1994. 21.95 incl. audio (1-883332-10-9) Audio Bkshelf.

Peck, Robert Newton. Arly. (History Series for Young People). 160p. (J). (gr. 5 up). 1989. 16.95 (0-8027-6856-3) Walker & Co.

— Arly's Run. 160p. (J). (gr. 5-9). 1991. 16.95 (0-8027-8120-9) Walker & Co.

— Cowboy Ghost. LC 98-34915. 208p. (YA). (gr. 7-12). 1999. 15.95 (0-06-028168-5, HarpTrophy) HarpC Child Bks.

— Cowboy Ghost. LC 98-34915. 208p. (YA). (gr. 7-12). 1999. lib. bdg. 15.89 (0-06-028211-8) HarpC Child Bks.

*Peck, Robert Newton. Cowboy Ghost. (YA). 2000. pap. 4.95 (0-06-447228-0, HarpTrophy) HarpC Child Bks.

— Cowboy Ghost. (Illus.). (J). 2000. 10.30 (0-606-18684-0) Turtleback.

— A Day No Pig Would Die. 1999. 19.00 (0-8446-6990-3) Peter Smith.

Peck, Robert Newton. A Day No Pigs Would Die. 1972. 24.00 (0-394-48235-2) Knopf.

Peck, Robert Newton. A Day No Pigs Would Die. 139p. (YA). (gr. 7 up). pap. 4.99 (0-8072-1384-5); pap. 4.99 (0-8072-1357-8) Listening Lib.

Peck, Robert Newton. A Day No Pigs Would Die. LC 72-259. (Illus.). 156p. (YA). (gr. 7 up). 1994. pap. 4.99 (0-679-85306-5, Pub. by Random Bks Yng Read) Random.

— Day No Pigs Would Die. 1994. 10.09 (0-606-06904-6, Pub. by Turtleback) Demco.

— Eagle Fur. large type ed. LC 92-971. 361p. 1992. 16.95 (1-56054-390-6) Thorndike Pr.

Peck, Robert Newton. Extra Innings. 176p. (J). (gr. 5-8). mass mkt. 4.95 (0-06-447229-9) HarpC.

— Extra Innings. 176p. (J). (gr. 5-8). 2000. 15.95 (0-06-028867-1); lib. bdg. 15.89 (0-06-028868-X) HarpC Child Bks.

Peck, Robert Newton. Hallapoosa. 1988. 16.95 (0-8027-1016-6) Walker & Co.

— Higbee's Halloween. 101p. (J). (gr. 5-7). 1990. 13.95 (0-8027-6968-3); lib. bdg. 14.85 (0-8027-6969-1) Walker & Co.

*Peck, Robert Newton. Nine Man Tree. 192p. (gr. 5-9). 2000. pap. 4.99 (0-375-80250-9) Random.

Peck, Robert Newton. Nine Man Tree. LC 97-43624. 170p. (YA). (gr. 5-8). 1998. 17.00 (0-679-89257-5, Pub. by Random Bks Yng Read); lib. bdg. 18.99 (0-679-99257-X, Pub. by Random Bks Yng Read) Random.

— A Part of the Sky. (YA). 1997. pap. 4.99 (0-679-88696-6, Pub. by Random Bks Yng Read) Random.

Peck, Robert Newton. Part of the Sky. (J). 1997. 10.09 (0-606-12149-8, Pub. by Turtleback) Demco.

Peck, Robert Newton. Soup. 112p. (J). (gr. 3 up). 1979. pap. 4.50 (0-440-48186-4, YB BDD) BDD Bks Young Read.

— Soup. LC 73-15117. (Illus.). 104p. (J). (gr. 4-7). 1974. lib. bdg. 15.99 (0-394-92700-1, Pub. by Knopf Bks Yng Read) Random.

— Soup. (Illus.). 112p. (J). (gr. 4-7). 1998. pap. 4.99 (0-679-89261-3, Pub. by Random Bks Yng Read) Random.

— Soup. 1974. 9.09 (0-606-02270-8, Pub. by Turtleback) Demco.

— Soup Ahoy. LC 93-14097. (Illus.). 144p. (J). (gr. 2-6). 1994. lib. bdg. 15.99 (0-679-94978-X, Pub. by Knopf Bks Yng Read) Random.

— Soup Ahoy. 1995. 9.60 (0-606-08610-2, Pub. by Turtleback) Demco.

— Soup for President. (J). (gr. 4-7). 1998. pap. 4.99 (0-679-89259-1, Pub. by Knopf Bks Yng Read) Random.

— Soup for President. (Dell Yearling Bks.). (J). 1978. 9.09 (0-606-03073-5, Pub. by Turtleback) Demco.

— Soup for President. 112p. (J). (gr. 3-6). 1986. reprint ed. pap. 3.99 (0-440-48188-0, YB BDD) BDD Bks Young Read.

— Soup in Love. (J). 1992. 17.95 (0-385-30703-9) Doubleday.

— Soup on Wheels. 112p. (J). (gr. 4-7). 1998. pap. 4.99 (0-679-89260-5, Pub. by Random Bks Yng Read) Random.

— Soup 1776. LC 94-23879. (Illus.). 160p. (J). (gr. 2-6). 1995. 16.00 (0-679-87320-1) Knopf.

— Soup 1776. (J). (gr. 4-7). 1998. pap. 4.99 (0-679-89262-1, Pub. by Random Bks Yng Read) Random.

— Soup's Hoop. 144p. (J). (gr. 4-7). 1992. pap. 4.50 (0-440-40589-0, YB BDD) BDD Bks Young Read.

— Soup's Hoop. 1990. 9.09 (0-606-00926-4, Pub. by Turtleback) Demco.

Peck, Robert S., ed. To Govern a Changing Society: Constitutionalism & the Challenge of New Technology. LC 89-39868. 228p. (Orig.). 1990. pap. text 17.95 (0-87474-783-X) Smithsonian.

Peck, Rodney G. Crack. (Drug Abuse Prevention Library). 64p. (gr. 7 up). 1997. pap. 6.95 (1-56838-165-4, 1757 A) Hazelden.

— Crack. rev. ed. (Drug Abuse Prevention Library). (Illus.). 64p. (YA). (gr. 7-12). 1994. lib. bdg. 17.95 (0-8239-2618-4) Rosen Group.

— Drugs & Sports. (Drug Abuse Prevention Library). 64p. (YA). 1998. reprint ed. pap. 6.95 (1-56838-212-X) Hazelden.

— Drugs & Sports. rev. ed. Rosen, Ruth C., ed. LC 92-12359. (Drug Abuse Prevention Library). (Illus.). 64p. (YA). (gr. 7-12). 1997. lib. bdg. 16.95 (0-8239-2565-X) Rosen Group.

— Working Together Against Human Rights Violations. LC 94-8858. (Library of Social Activism). (Illus.). 64p. (YA). (gr. 7-12). 1995. lib. bdg. 16.95 (0-8239-1778-9) Rosen Group.

Peck, Roxy, et al, eds. Statistical Case Studies: A Collaboration Between Academe & Industry. (ASA-SIAM Series on Statistics & Applied Probability: Vol. 3). (Illus.). xxxi, 282p. 1998. pap. 44.50 (0-89871-413-3, BKSA0003) Soc Indus-Appl Math.

Peck, Roxy, ed. see Haugh, Larry D. & Goodman, Arnold.

Peck, Roxy L., jt. auth. see Devore, Jay.

Peck, Russell, ed. Heroic Women from the Old Testament in Middle English Verse. (TEAMS Middle English Text Ser.). 1991. pap. 9.00 (1-879288-11-7) Medieval Inst.

Peck, Russell A., ed. Chaucer's Romaunt of the Rose & Boece, the Treatise on the Astrolabe, the Equatorie of the Planetis, the Lost Works & the Chaucerian Apocrypha: An Annotated Bibliography, 1900-1985. (Chaucer Bibliographies Ser.). 402p. 1988. text 75.00 (0-8020-2493-9) U of Toronto Pr.

Peck, Russell A., ed. John Gower: Confessio Amantis. Galloway, Andrew, tr. (Teams). xii, 363p. (C). pap. 20.00 (1-58044-057-6) Medieval Inst.

Peck, Russell A., ed. see Gower, John.

Peck, Ruth A. A Century of Ministry: The History of Trinity Lutheran Church. 140p. 1992. pap. 10.00 (0-9632829-0-5) Trinity Evang Luth.

Peck, Samuel M. Alabama Sketches. 299p. 1977. 19.95 (0-8369-9043-9) Ayer.

Peck, Shannon, jt. auth. see Peck, M. Scott.

Peck, Sheila. Planning for Biodiversity: Issues & Examples. LC 98-10504. 256p. 1998. pap. text 27.50 (1-55963-401-4) Island Pr.

Peck, Shelley, jt. ed. see Goetz, Kathy.

Peck, Stephen R. Atlas of Facial Expression. (Illus.). 176p. 1990. pap. 12.95 (0-19-506322-8) OUP.

— Atlas of Human Anatomy for the Artist. (Illus.). 288p. 1982. pap. 17.95 (0-19-503095-8) OUP.

Peck, Steve. Fly Fishing in Middle-Earth. 12p. 1992. pap. 2.50 (1-881799-02-6) Am Tolkien Soc.

Peck, Susan. Build Your Own Website. Arrants, Stephen, ed. 514p. (Orig.). 1997. pap. write for info. (1-56592-340-5) OReilly & Assocs.

Peck, Susan & Scherf, Beverly. Using Web Board 2.0. (Illus.). (Orig.). 1997. pap. write for info. (1-56592-318-9) OReilly & Assocs.

Peck, Susan, ed. see O'Reilly & Associates, Inc. Staff.

Peck, Susan B. & Arrants, Stephen. Building Your Own WebSite: Everything You Need to Reach Your Audience on the Web. 514p. 1996. pap. 59.00 (1-56592-232-8) Thomson Learn.

Peck, Susan B. & Scherf, Beverly M. Build Your Own Web Conference. (Illus.). 265p. 1997. pap. write for info. (1-56592-339-1) OReilly & Assocs.

Peck, T. B. Richard Clarke of Rowley, Mass., & His Descendants in the Line of Timothy Clark of Rockingham, Vermont, 1638-1904. (Illus.). 93p. 1993. reprint ed. lib. bdg. 28.00 (0-8328-1354-0) Higginson Bk Co.

Peck, Ted & Rychkun, Ed A. The 12 Basic Skills of Fly Fishing. (Illus.). 48p. (Orig.). (C). 1996. pap. 6.95 (0-88839-392-X) Hancock House.

Peck, Terrance W., jt. auth. see Heil, Scott.

Peck, Thelma M., jt. auth. see Peck, Robert L.

Peck, Theodore S., compiled by. Revised Roster of Vermont Volunteers & Lists of Vermonters Who Served in the Army & Navy of the United States During the War of the Rebellion, 1861-66. 862p. 1995. reprint ed. lib. bdg. 89.00 (0-8328-5122-1) Higginson Bk Co.

Peck, Thomas B. The Bellows Genealogy: John Bellows, the Boy Emigrant of 1635 & His Descendants. (Illus.). 673p. 1988. reprint ed. pap. 83.50 (0-8328-0231-X); reprint ed. lib. bdg. 93.50 (0-8328-0230-1) Higginson Bk Co.

— Richard Clarke of Rowley, Mass., & His Descendants in the Line of Timothy Clark of Rockingham, Vermont, 1638-1904. (Illus.). 93p. 1993. reprint ed. pap. 18.00 (0-8328-1355-9) Higginson Bk Co.

Peck, Tom, ed. see Youngson, Jeanne.

Peck, Walter E., ed. see Shelley, Percy Bysshe.

Peck, William. A Tidy Universe of Islands. (Illus.). 192p. 1996. pap. 14.95 (1-56647-117-6) Mutual Pub HI.

Peck, William A., ed. Bone & Mineral Research Annual, No. 6. 350p. 1989. 223.25 (0-444-81061-7) Elsevier.

Peck, William A., et al, eds. Engineering Geology of Melbourne: Proceedings of the Seminar on Engineering Geology of Melbourne, Victoria, Australia, 16 September 1992. (Illus.). 418p. (C). 1992. text 123.00 (90-5410-083-4, Pub. by A A Balkema) Ashgate Pub Co.

Peck, William F., et al. Landmarks of Monroe County, Containing an Historical Sketch of Monroe County & the City of Rochester...Followed by Brief Historical Sketches of the Towns, with Biography & Family History. (Illus.). 831p. 1997. reprint ed. lib. bdg. 85.00 (0-8328-6178-2) Higginson Bk Co.

Peck, William H. Dear Mr. & Mrs. Bill. LC 97-95005. (Illus.). 208p. 1998. pap. 8.85 (0-9661787-3-4) Hermits Cave.

— Splendors of Ancient Egypt. (Illus.). 88p. 1998. pap. 14.95 (0-7892-0451-7) Abbeville Pr.

P

— Splendors of Ancient Egypt. LC 97-19806. 1997. pap. 14.95 (*0-89558-148-5*) Det Inst Arts.

Peck, William J., ed. New Studies in Bonhoeffer's Society. LC 87-7944. (Toronto Studies in Theology: Vol. 30). 284p. 1987. lib. bdg. 89.95 (*0-88946-775-7*) E Mellen.

Peck, Willys I. & De Anza College Staff. Saratoga Stereopticon: A Magic Lantern of Memory. LC 97-35256. (Local History Studies). 1997. 8.50 (*0-935089-21-7*) CA History Ctr.

Peck, Wm. E. Selleck & Peck Genealogy. (Illus.). 74p. 1994. reprint ed. pap. 15.00 (*0-8328-4379-2*); reprint ed. lib. bdg. 25.00 (*0-8328-4378-4*) Higginson Bk Co.

Peckarsky, Barbara, et al. Freshwater Macroinvertebrates of Northeastern North America. LC 89-17468. (Illus.). 456p. 1990. text 69.95 (*0-8014-2076-8*); pap. text 29.95 (*0-8014-9688-8*) Cornell U Pr.

Peckel, Floyd A. Impudent Perspectives. Leshe, Leta, ed. (Illus.). 60p. (Orig.). 1995. pap. 5.00 (*0-9645451-2-8*) F Swann Pubns.

— Sunny's Legacy: The Poetry of Floyd Alexander Peckel. Leshe, Leta, ed. & illus. by. 44p. (Orig.). 1997. pap. 5.00 (*0-9645451-7-9*) F Swann Pubns.

Peckenham, Nancy, ed. Sunbelt Blues: Where Have All the Good Jobs Gone? (Illus.). 64p. (Orig.). 1990. pap. 5.00 (*0-943810-46-9*) Inst Southern Studies.

Peckenham, Nancy & Street, Annie, eds. Honduras: Portrait of a Captive Nation. LC 85-9482. 366p. 1985. 55.00 (*0-275-90219-6*, C0219, Praeger Pubs) Greenwood.

Peckenpaugh, Angela. Designs, Like Branches or Arteries. 20p. (Orig.). 1994. pap. 15.00 (*1-880723-01-8*) Morgan Pr WI.

***Peckenpaugh, Nancy J. & Poleman, Charlotte.** Instructor's Manual for Nutrition Essentials & Diet Therapy. Connor, Maura, ed. (Illus.). 110p. 1999. text, teacher ed. write for info. (*0-7216-7693-6*, W B Saunders Co) Harcrt Hlth Sci Grp.

Peckenpaugh, Nancy J. & Poleman, Charlotte M. Nutrition: Essentials & Diet Therapy. 7th ed. (Illus.). 642p. 1995. pap., teacher ed. write for info. (*0-7216-5131-3*, W B Saunders Co) Harcrt Hlth Sci Grp.

— Nutrition: Essentials & Diet Therapy. 7th ed. LC 94-21254. 560p. 1995. pap. text 31.00 (*0-7216-5130-5*, W B Saunders Co) Harcrt Hlth Sci Grp.

— Nutrition Essentials & Diet Therapy. 8th ed. Connor, Maura, ed. (Illus.). 635p. (C). 1998. pap. text 32.95 (*0-7216-7707-X*, W B Saunders Co) Harcrt Hlth Sci Grp.

Pecker, J. Space Observatories. 1970. text 112.00 (*90-277-0168-7*) Kluwer Academic.

Pecker, Jean-Claude. Understanding the Heavens: 30 Centuries of Ideas from Ancient Thinking to Modern Cosmology. Kaufman, S., tr. from FRE. (Illus.). xii, 450p. 2000. 89.95 (*3-540-63198-4*) Spr-Verlag.

Pecker the Cat. A Rug Before My Time: The Memoirs of Pecker the Cat. (Illus.). 32p. (J). 1982. pap. 1.25 (*0-9604894-1-X*) Borf Bks.

Peckerar, Martin C., jt. auth. see Murarka, Shyam P.

Peckett. The Colours of Opaque Minerals. 512p. 1991. text 467.00 (*0-471-93347-3*) Wiley.

Peckett, Andrew. The Colours of Opaque Minerals. (Illus.). 573p. (gr. 13). 1992. mass mkt. 145.95 (*0-442-30808-6*) Chapman & Hall.

Peckett, C. W. & Munday, A. R. Thrasymachus: New Greek Course. 326p. 1965. reprint ed. pap. 27.95 (*0-86292-139-2*, Pub. by Brist Class Pr) Focus Pub-R Pullins.

***Peckham, Anne.** Contemporary Singer: Elements of Vocal Technique. 250p. 2000. pap. 24.95 (*0-634-00797-1*, Berklee Pr) H Leonard.

Peckham, Betty. The Story of a Dynamic Community: York, Pennsylvania. 257p. 1999. 37.50 (*0-8328-6550-8*) Higginson Bk Co.

Peckham, Brian. History & Prophecy: The Development of Late Judaean Literary Traditions. LC 92-11671. (Anchor Bible Reference Library Ser.). 896p. 1993. 35.00 (*0-385-42348-9*) Doubleday.

***Peckham, Colin N.** The Authority of the Bible. 157p. 1999. pap. 7.99 (*1-85792-436-3*) Christian Focus.

Peckham, Colin N. Learning to Resist Temptation: In an Immoral Society. 1999. pap. text 2.99 (*1-85792-247-6*) Christian Focus.

Peckham, Donald, jt. auth. see Paulston, Christina B.

Peckham, Donald C., jt. ed. see O'Shea, Donald C.

Peckham, George. A True Reporte of the Late Discoueries of the Newfound Landes. LC 78-25630. (English Experience Ser.: No. 341). 1971. reprint ed. 20.00 (*90-221-0341-2*) Walter J Johnson.

Peckham, H. C. Van Buren: History of Cornelis Maessen Van Buren. (Illus.). 431p. 1990. reprint ed. pap. 64.50 (*0-8328-1629-9*); reprint ed. lib. bdg. 72.50 (*0-8328-1628-0*) Higginson Bk Co.

Peckham, Herbert, jt. auth. see Luehrmann, Arthur.

Peckham, Herbert D. Hands-on BASIC for the TRS-80 Color Computer. (Personal Programming Ser.). 352p. 1983. pap. text. write for info. (*0-07-049159-3*, BYTE Bks) McGraw.

Peckham, Herbert D., jt. auth. see Luehrmann, Arthur.

Peckham, Howard. Making of the University of Michigan, 1817-1992. 416p. 1994. pap. text 16.95 (*0-472-06594-7*, 06594) U of Mich Pr.

— William Henry Harrison: Young Tippecanoe. 2nd rev. ed. Underdown, Harold, ed. (Young Patriots Ser.: Vol. 2). (Illus.). 115p. (J). (gr. 3-7). 2000. 14.95 (*1-882859-03-0*) Patria Pr.

Peckham, Howard H. Colonial Wars, 1689-1762. LC 64-12606. (Chicago History of American Civilization Ser.). (Illus.). 272p. 1965. pap. text 15.95 (*0-226-65314-5*, CHAC21) U Ch Pr.

— Indiana, a History. (States & the Nation Ser.). (Illus.). 1978. 14.95 (*0-393-05670-8*) Norton.

Peckham, Howard H. The Making of the University of Michigan 1817-1992. (Illus.). 416p. (C). 1994. text 34.95 (*0-472-09594-3*) U of Mich Pr.

Peckham, Howard H. Pontiac & the Indian Uprising. LC 93-36864. 376p. 1994. pap. 16.95 (*0-8143-2469-X*) Wayne St U Pr.

— Sources of American Independence: Selected Manuscripts from the Collection of the William L. Clements Library, 2 vols., Set. LC 77-25964. (Clements Library Bicentennial Studies). 622p. 1996. lib. bdg. 48.00 (*0-226-65321-8*) U Ch Pr.

— War for Independence: A Military History. LC 58-5685. (Chicago History of American Civilization Ser.). 235p. 1958. pap. text 15.95 (*0-226-65316-1*) U Ch Pr.

Peckham, Howard H., ed. Memoirs of the Life of John Adlum in the Revolutionary War. 1968. 12.00 (*0-940550-03-2*) Caxton Club.

Peckham, Howard H. & Gibson, Charles, eds. Attitudes of Colonial Powers Toward the American Indian. LC 77-99793. (University of Utah Publications in the American West: No. 2). 147p. reprint ed. pap. 45.60 (*0-8357-4380-2*, 203721100007) Bks Demand.

Peckham, Howard H., jt. ed. see Brown, Lloyd A.

Peckham, Howard H., ed. see Dann, John C. & Byrd, Cecil K.

Peckham, Howard H., ed. see Dearborn, Henry.

Peckham, Howard H., ed. see Michigan University, William L. Clements Library S.

Peckham, J. Brian. Development of the Late Phoenician Scripts. LC 68-17629. (Semitic Ser.: No. 20). (Illus.). 245p. 1968. 15.00 (*0-674-20050-0*) HUP.

Peckham, Joan, jt. auth. see Jepson, Brian.

Peckham, John M. The Classic American La-France. (Illus.). 128p. Date not set. 34.95 (*0-89404-095-2*) Aztex.

— Fighting Fire with Fire. expanded rev. ed. (Illus.). 330p. Date not set. 44.95 (*0-89404-096-0*) Aztex.

Peckham, L. P. Prise De Defur & le Voyage D'Alexandre au Paradis Terrestre. (Elliott Monographs: Vol. 35). 1974. reprint ed. 24.00 (*0-527-02638-7*) Periodicals Srv.

Peckham, Linda & Walsh, Ray, eds. Through the Years: A Pictorial History of Greater Lansing, 1847-1997. 175p. 1997. 36.95 (*0-9658933-0-8*) Visions Sports.

***Peckham, Linda R. & Heuft, Lori E.** Saw Mills & Sleigh Bells. LC 99-62897. (Illus.). (J). (gr. 2-5). 1999. pap. 11.95 (*0-9671616-1-4*) Catalpa Pubns.

Peckham, Michael, et al, eds. Oxford Textbook of Oncology, 2 vols., Set. (Illus.). 1995. text 275.00 (*0-19-261685-4*) OUP.

Peckham, Michael & Smith, Richard, eds. Scientific Basis of Health Services. 186p. 1996. pap. text 40.00 (*0-7279-1029-9*, Pub. by BMJ Pub) Login Brothers Bk Co.

Peckham, Michael, jt. ed. see Marinker, Marshall.

Peckham, Morse. The Birth of Romanticism: Cultural Crisis, 1790-1815. (Romanticism & Its Consequences: Emergent Culture in the 19th Century Ser.: Vol. I). (Illus.). 400p. 1986. 32.50 (*0-913283-08-8*) Penkevill.

— Humanistic Education for Business Executives: An Essay in General Education. LC 60-9884. 149p. reprint ed. pap. 46.20 (*0-8357-8672-2*, 205682800091) Bks Demand.

— Man's Rage for Chaos: Biology, Behavior & the Arts. 360p. 1997. pap. 19.95 (*0-944624-36-7*) Maisonneuve Pr.

— Romanticism & Ideology. 400p. 1985. lib. bdg. 32.50 (*0-913283-05-3*) Penkevill.

— Romanticism & Ideology. LC 94-45308. 329p. 1995. reprint ed. pap. 25.00 (*0-8195-6285-8*, Wesleyan Univ Pr) U Pr of New Eng.

— The Uses of the Unfashionable: The Pre-Raphaelites in Nineteenth-Century Culture. LC 92-33625. 1993. 10.95 (*0-935061-50-9*) Contemp Res.

Peckham, S. F. & Weeks, Joseph D. Census of the United States: Tenth Decennial Census, 1880: Production, Technology, & Uses of Petroleum & Its Products . . . The Manufacture of Coke . . . Building Stones of the United States & Statistics of Quarry Industry for 1880, 22 vols., Vol. 10, Series 33. LC 07-18862. (Illus.). 908p. 1991. reprint ed. lib. bdg. 575.00 incl. fiche (*0-88354-433-4*) N Ross.

Peckham, Stephen F. Peckham Genealogy: English Ancestors & American Descendants of John Peckham of Newport, RI, 1630. (Illus.). 596p. reprint ed. pap. 91.00 (*0-8328-1651-5*); reprint ed. lib. bdg. 101.00 (*0-8328-1650-7*) Higginson Bk Co.

Peckham, Stewart. From This Earth: The Ancient Art of Pueblo Pottery. 180p. 1990. pap. 39.95 (*0-89013-205-4*) Museum NM Pr.

— I Am Here: Two Thousand Years of Southwest Indian Art & Culture. 256p. 1988. pap. 39.95 (*0-89013-174-0*) Museum NM Pr.

***Peckham, Thomas E.** Writing of Thomas E. Peck, Vol. 3. 421p. 1999. reprint ed. write for info. (*0-85151-769-2*) Banner of Truth.

— Writings of Thomas E. Peck, 3 vol. set. 384p. 1999. reprint ed. 79.99 (*0-85151-770-6*) Banner of Truth.

— Writings of Thomas E. Peck, Vol. 2. 405p. 1999. reprint ed. write for info. (*0-85151-768-4*) Banner of Truth.

***Peckham, Virginia.** Grantmaking with a Purpose: Mission & Guidelines. (Practices in Family Philanthropy Ser.: Vol. 2). 1999. pap. 30.00 (*1-929455-04-6*) Nat Ctr Famly Phil.

Peckinpah, Sandra L. Chester. . . the Imperfect All-Star. LC 92-74057. (Imperfect Angels Ser.). (Illus.). (J). (gr. 1-5). 1993. 15.95 (*0-9627806-1-8*) Dasan Prodns.

— Chester. . . the Imperfect All-Star. LC 92-74057. (Imperfect Angels Ser.). (Illus.). (J). (ps-1). 1993. pap. 8.95 (*0-9627806-2-6*) Dasan Prodns.

— Rosey . . . the Imperfect Angel. LC 90-63058. (Imperfect Angels Ser.). (Illus.). 32p. (J). (ps-4). 1991. 15.95 (*0-9627806-0-X*) Dasan Prodns.

Peckinpaugh, Angela & Hayna, Lois B. A Book of Charms. LC 82-74406. 80p. (Orig.). 1983. pap. 6.95 (*0-935306-19-6*) Barnwood Pr.

Peckinpaugh, Carl J. Government Contracts for Services: The Handbook for Acquisition Professionals. LC 97-72174. 464p. 1997. pap. 89.95 (*1-57073-448-8*, 539-0168, ABA Pub Contract) Amer Bar Assn.

Pecklers, Keith F. The Unread Vision: The Liturgical Movement in the United States of America 1926-1955. LC 97-41220. 336p. 1998. pap. 24.95 (*0-8146-2450-2*) Liturgical Pr.

Peckman, Betty. Christian Midwifery. 3rd rev. ed. (Illus.). 535p. 1997. pap. 24.95 (*0-934426-80-5*) NAPSAC Reprods.

Pecktal, Lynn. Costume Design: Techniques of Modern Masters. LC 98-49867. (Illus.). 256p. 1999. pap. text 29.95 (*0-8230-8812-X*) Watson-Guptill.

— Designing & Drawing for the Theatre. LC 94-21638. 608p. (C). 1994. 80.63 (*0-07-557232-X*) McGraw.

Peckus, Kestutis. Alicija Rugyte: Gyvenimo Kelias. (LIT., Illus.). 170p. 1996. 15.00 (*0-929700-14-7*) Lith Res & Studies.

Peckus, Kestutis & Rackauskas, Jonas. Uzsienio Lietuviu Svietimo Ir Pedagogines Minties Istorijos Metmenys: A Historical Outline of Lithuanian Educational Thought Outside of Lithuania. LC 94-73757. (LIT., Illus.). 78p. 1995. pap. 5.00 (*0-929700-12-0*) Lith Res & Studies.

Peckwas, Edward A. Register of Vital Records of Roman Catholic Parishes from the Region Beyond the Bug River. 44p. 5.95 (*0-317-57777-8*) Polish Genealog.

Pecl, Karel. Fishes of Lakes & Rivers: A Book for Anglers & Anyone Interested in Distribution, Behavior, Feeding & Breeding Habits of Fish. Krojzl, Clare & Krojzl, Jiri, trs. from CZE. (Illus.). 223p. 1999. reprint ed. text 25.00 (*0-7881-6176-8*) DIANE Pub.

Pecock, R. The Donet. (EETS, OS Ser.: No. 156). 1972. reprint ed. 54.00 (*0-527-00153-8*) Periodicals Srv.

— The Folewer to the Donet. (EETS, OS Ser.: No. 164). 1972. reprint ed. 50.00 (*0-527-00161-9*) Periodicals Srv.

— The Reule of Crysten Religioun. (EETS, OS Ser.: No. 171). 1974. reprint ed. 75.00 (*0-527-00168-6*) Periodicals Srv.

Pecor, Charles J. The Ten Year Tour of John Rannie: A Magician-Ventriloquist in Early America. (Illus.). 48p. 1998. 25.00 (*0-916638-89-8*, D M Magic Bks) Meyerbooks.

***Pecora & Berne, Bruce J.** Dynamic Light Scattering: With Applications to Chemistry, Biology & Physics. 2000. pap. 17.95 (*0-486-41155-9*) Dover.

Pecora, Amy J., ed. see Sullivan, Steve.

Pecora, Carol, ed. see Johnson, Richard & Wood, John.

Pecora, David V. Between the Raindrops. LC 97-90260. 243p. 1997. 21.95 (*0-533-12340-2*) Vantage.

Pecora, L. M., jt. ed. see Carroll, T. L.

Pecora, Norma O. The Business of Children's Entertainment. LC 97-40876. (Communication Ser.). 190p. 1997. lib. bdg. 32.00 (*1-57230-280-1*, C0280) Guilford Pubns.

Pecora, Norma Odom, jt. ed. see Mazzarella, Sharon R.

Pecora, Peter J., et al, eds. The Child Welfare Challenge: Policy, Practice & Research. 2nd rev. ed. (Modern Applications of Social Work Ser.). 543p. 1992. lib. bdg. 51.95 (*0-202-36125-X*) Aldine de Gruyter.

— The Child Welfare Challenge: Policy, Practice & Research. 2nd rev. ed. (Modern Applications of Social Work Ser.). 543p. 2000. pap. text 30.95 (*0-202-36126-8*) Aldine de Gruyter.

Pecora, Peter J., et al, eds. Quality Improvement & Evaluation in Child & Family Services: Managing into the Next Century. LC 96-15333. 315p. (Orig.). 1997. pap. 26.95 (*0-87868-606-1*, CWLA Pr) Child Welfare.

Pecora, Peter J. & Austin, Michael J. Managing Human Services Personnel. (Human Services Guides Ser.: Vol. 48). 160p. (Orig.). 1987. pap. text 18.95 (*0-8039-2685-5*) Sage.

Pecora, Peter J., et al. Evaluating Family-Based Services. (Modern Applications of Social Work Ser.). 342p. 1995. pap. text 26.95 (*0-202-36094-6*); lib. bdg. 48.95 (*0-202-36093-8*) Aldine de Gruyter.

Pecora, R. Dynamic Light Scattering: Applications of Photon Correlation Spectroscopy. LC 84-24831. (Illus.). 436p. (C). 1985. text 115.00 (*0-306-41790-1*, Kluwer Plenum) Kluwer Academic.

Pecora, Robert, jt. ed. see Dorfmueller, T.

Pecora, Vincent P. Households of the Soul. LC 96-31069. 344p. 1997. text 49.95 (*0-8018-5427-X*) Johns Hopkins.

— Self & Form in Modern Narrative. LC 88-46067. 336p. 1989. text 49.95 (*0-8018-3768-5*) Johns Hopkins.

Pecora, William T. Memorial Symposium on Remote Se. Satellite Hydrology: Proceedings of the Fifth Annual William T. Pecora Memorial Symposium on Remote Sensing, Sioux Falls SD, June 10-15, 1979. LC 81-65679. (Technical Publications: No. TPS81-1). (Illus.). 744p. reprint ed. pap. 200.00 (*0-8357-4079-X*, 203676900005) Bks Demand.

Pecoraro, George A., et al. Corrosion of Materials by Molten Glass. LC 96-34361. (Ceramic Transactions Ser.: No. 78). 1996. 79.00 (*1-57498-019-X*, CT078) Am Ceramic.

Pecoraro, V. L., ed. Maganese Redox Enzymes. 290p. 1992. 155.00 (*0-471-18743-7*, Wiley-VCH) Wiley.

Pecoraro, Vincent L., ed. Manganese Redox Enzymes. (Illus.). 290p. 1992. 110.00 (*0-89573-729-9*, Wiley-VCH) Wiley.

Pecoraro, Vincent L., ed. see American Chemical Society, Division of Inorganic C.

Pecorella, Robert F. Community Power in a Postreform City: Politics in New York City. LC 93-22409. 240p. (gr. 13). 1993. text 69.95 (*1-56324-136-6*) M E Sharpe.

***Pecorini, Daniele.** Game of Wei-Chi. 2000. pap. 0.00 (*0-89346-922-X*) Heian Intl.

Pecorini, Daniele & Shu, Tong. The Game of Wei-Chi. rev. ed. 165p. 1991. reprint ed. pap. 12.95 (*981-218-015-X*) Heian Intl.

Pecotich. Marketing Behaviour in Asia. 1999. pap. 34.95 (*0-07-470480-X*) McGraw.

***Pecquet, Antoine.** Diverse Thoughts on Man. Sirkis, Murray D. & Gruzinska, Aleksandr, eds. LC 99-19793. (Age of Revolution & Romanticism Ser.: Vol. 27). (Illus.). xxvi, 108p. (C). 1999. text 41.95 (*0-8204-4452-9*) P Lang Pubng.

***Pecseli, Hans L.** Fluctuations in Physical Systems. (Illus.). 200p. (C). 2000. text Price not set. (*0-521-65192-1*); pap. text Price not set. (*0-521-65592-7*) Cambridge U Pr.

Pecsi, Kalman. The Future of Socialist Economic Integration. Hajdu, George & Crane, Keith, trs. LC 81-2524. 207p. reprint ed. pap. 64.20 (*0-608-18130-7*, 203278400081) Bks Demand.

Pecsi, M. & Richter, G., eds. Geomorphology & Geoecology - Applied Geomorphology Vol. 9: Proceedings of the Second International Conference on Geomorphology, Frankfurt/Main, 1989. (Zeitschrift fuer Geomorphologie - Annals of Geomorphology Ser.: Supplementband 87). (Illus.). iv, 194p. 1993. pap. 58.00 (*3-443-21087-2*, Pub. by Gebruder Borntraeger) Balogh.

Pecsi, Marton. Environmental & Dynamic Geomorphology: Contribution to the First International Geomorphological Conference, Manchester, September 1985. No. 17. 220p. (C). 1985. 69.00 (*963-05-4226-9*, Pub. by Akade Kiado) St Mut.

— Geomorphological & Geoecological Essays. (Studies in Geography in Hungary: No. 25). 155p. (C). 1989. 57.00 (*963-05-5710-X*, Pub. by Akade Kiado) St Mut.

— Loess & the Quaternary: Chinese & Hungarian Case Studies. (Studies in Geography in Hungary: No. 18). 125p. (C). 1985. 42.00 (*963-05-4227-7*, Pub. by Akade Kiado) St Mut.

— Studies in Loess. 556p. (C). 1981. 120.00 (*963-05-2871-1*, 41212, Pub. by Akade Kiado) St Mut.

***Pecsi, Marton, ed.** 150 Years of Landform Evolution Studies in Hungary. (Illus.). 210p. 1999. 48.00 (*963-05-7670-8*, Pub. by Akade Kiado) Intl Spec Bk.

Pecsi, Marton & Richter, Gerold. Herkunft, Gliederung, Landschaften: Gewidmet dem 14. INQUA-Kongress in Berlin, 1995. (Zeitschrift fuer Geomorphologie - Annals of Geomorphology Ser.: Supplementband 98). (GER., Illus.). vii, 391p. 1995. pap. 88.00 (*3-443-21098-8*, Pub. by Gebruder Borntraeger) Balogh.

Pecsi, Marton, jt. auth. see Compton, P. A.

Pecsi, Marton, jt. auth. see Kretzoi, M.

Pecsi, Marton, jt. auth. see Lictenberger, E.

Pecsi, Marton, jt. auth. see Schweitzer, F.

Pecsok, Robert L., et al, eds. Chemical Technology Handbook. LC 75-22497. 1975. pap. 14.95 (*0-8412-0578-7*) Am Chemical.

— Chemical Technology Handbook. LC 75-22497. 224p. 1976. text 24.95 (*0-8412-0242-7*, Pub. by Am Chemical) OUP.

Pecsok, Robert L., ed. see Chemical Technician Curriculum Project Staff.

Pecsok, Robert L., jt. ed. see Hajian, Harry G.

Pecuch, Patricia. Ezra Jack Keats. (Favorite Authors Ser.). 112p. 1997. pap. 11.95 (*1-55734-459-0*) Tchr Create Mat.

Peuchet, Jean-Pierre R., jt. ed. see Abdulrab, Habib.

Pecujlit, Miroslav. The University of the Future: The Yugoslav Experience, 22. Lorkovic, Tanja, tr. LC 86-31899. (Contributions to the Study of Education Ser.: No. 22). 211p. 1987. 55.00 (*0-313-25430-3*, PUF/, Greenwood Pr) Greenwood.

Pecura, Constance M., ed. see Institute of Medicine, Committee on a National Neu.

Peczenik, Aleksander. On Law & Reason. abr. ed. (Law & Philosophy Library: No. 8). 456p. 1989. lib. bdg. 166.00 (*0-7923-0444-6*, Pub. by Kluwer Academic) Kluwer Academic.

Peczenik, Aleksander, et al. Theory of Legal Science. 681p. 1984. text 247.50 (*90-277-1834-2*, D Reidel) Kluwer Academic.

***Peczkowski, Robert.** White Eagles: The Aircraft, Men & Operations of the Polish Air Force, 1918-1939. (Illus.). 2000. 49.95 (*1-902109-73-2*) Hikoki Pubns.

***Pedace-Allentuck, Gianna.** Welcome to My Heart: A Journey Through a Young Woman's Heart. (Sharing Hearts Publications). 219p. 2000. pap. 20.00 (*0-9679629-0-0*) Sharing Hearts.

Pedak, Johannes, ed. Korporation Rotalia Voorsil, 1944-1987. 600p. 1988. 50.00 (*0-9621533-0-3*) Korp Rotalia.

Pedan, James A. Vegetarian Cats & Dogs. 2nd rev. ed. LC 90-82536. (Illus.). 240p. 1995. pap. text 14.95 (*0-941319-02-4*) Harbingers New Age.

Pedder, Jonathan R., jt. auth. see Brown, Dennis G.

Pedder, Nancy Shank. A Matter of Heart: One Woman's Story of Triumph. Orloff, Erica, ed. Morrell, Pam, tr. LC 98-61118. 192p. 1998. 19.95 (*1-885843-08-9*) Saturn Press.

Peddg, Shirley. Secrets of the Jungle: Lessons on Survival & Success in Today's Organizations. 1996. pap., boxed set 29.95 incl. audio (*0-9651376-2-7*) Bullion Bks.

***Peddicord, Jo.** Feel Nifty after 50! Top Tips to Help Women Grow Young! LC 98-93704. (Illus.). 160p. 1999. pap. 12.95 (*0-9654434-1-8*) Golden Aspen.

— Feel Nifty after 50! Top Tips to Help Women Grow Young! 2nd rev. ed. Roerden, Chris, ed. (Illus.). 190p. 2000. pap. 14.95 (*0-9654434-2-6*) Golden Aspen.

Peddicord, Jo. Look Like a Winner after 50! With Care, Color & Style. 3rd rev. ed. LC 96-79098. (Illus.). 190p. 1997. pap. 15.95 (*0-9654434-0-X*) Golden Aspen.

P

Peddicord, K. L., et al. Nuclear Materials Safety Management. LC 98-26191. (NATO Science Ser.). 378p. 1998. write for info. (0-7923-5191-6) Kluwer Academic.

Peddicord, Kathleen, ed. The World's Best. 5th enl. rev. ed. 650p. 1992. pap. 29.00 (0-945332-33-5) Agora Inc MD.

***Peddicord, Lou.** But When She Was Bad... 216p. 2000. 24.00 (1-57962-067-1) Permanent Pr.

Peddicord, Richard. Gay & Lesbian Rights: A Question: Sexual Ethics or Social Justice? 209p. (Orig.). 1996. pap. 16.95 (1-55612-759-6) Sheed & Ward WI.

Peddicord, Richard G. & Converse, George. Having Fun Learning Basic: A Workbook Approach. 208p. (C). 1991. per. 19.57 (0-697-14956-0, Irwn McGrw-H) McGrw-H Hghr Educ.

Peddie, J. Cameron, ed. The Forgotten Talent. (C). 1990. pap. 35.00 (0-85305-266-2, Pub. by Arthur James) St Mut.

Peddie, John. Alfred: Warrior King. 1999. 39.95 (0-7509-2105-6) Sutton Pub Ltd.

— Alfred, the Good Soldier: His Life & Campaigns LC 94-185524. 192p. 1992. pap. write for info. (0-948975-31-8) Millstream Bks.

— Conquest: Roman Invasion of Britain. 240p. 1997. pap. 18.95 (0-312-17389-X) St Martin.

— Hannibal's War. (Illus.). 256p. 1997. 44.95 (0-7509-1336-3, Pub. by Sutton Pub Ltd) Intl Pubs Mktg.

— The Roman War Machine. (Medieval Military Library). (Illus.). 169p. 1997. pap. 16.95 (0-938289-85-3, 289853) Combined Pub.

Peddie, Jon. Graphical User Interfaces & Graphic Standards. 320p. 1991. 39.95 (0-8306-2505-4) McGraw-Hill Prof.

Peddie, Mary, et al. Growing & Using Scented Geraniums. Foster, Kim & Parkinson, Connie, eds. (Country Wisdom Bulletin Ser.). (Illus.). 32p. 1991. pap. 2.95 (0-88266-699-1, Storey Pub) Storey Bks.

Peddie, R. A. A Catalogue of the Technical Reference Library of Works on Printing at the Allied Arts Saint Bride Foundation. 999p. 1999. reprint ed. 110.00 (1-57898-135-2) Martino Pubng.

Peddie, Robert A. Place-Names in Imprints: An Index to the Latin & Other Forms Used on Title-Pages. 1968. reprint ed. 35.00 (1-55888-207-3) Omnigraphics Inc.

Peddie, Sandra & Rosenberg, Craig H. The Repetitive Strain Injury Sourcebook. LC 97-34717. (Illus.). 384p. 1998. reprint ed. pap. 17.00 (0-7373-0022-1, 00221W) NTC Contemp Pub Co.

Peddito, Paul. Of All the Wide Torsos in All the Wild Glen. 46p. 1991. pap. 3.50 (0-87129-097-9, O47) Dramatic Pub.

Peddiwell, J. A. The Saber-Tooth Curriculum. (C). 1959. pap. 7.95 (0-07-049151-8) McGraw.

***Peddle, Daniel.** Snow Day. (Illus.). 32p. (J). (ps-k). 2000. 12.95 (0-385-32693-9) Doubleday.

Peddle, Francis K. Cities & Greed: Taxes, Inflation & Land Speculation. LC 96-132774. 255p. 1994. 12.00 (0-9698812-0-7, Pub. by Canadian Res Comm) Schalkenbach.

***Peddle, Michael T.** Does Government Need to Be Involved in Primary & Secondary Education: Evaluating Policy Options Using Market Role Assessment. LC 00-34084. (Reference Library of Social Science). 2000. write for info. (0-8153-2572-X) Garland.

Peddle, Sandra & Rosenberg, Craig H. The Repetitive Strain Injury Sourcebook. LC 97-34717. 224p. 1998. reprint ed. 30.00 (1-56565-791-8, 07918W, Pub. by Lowell Hse) NTC Contemp Pub Co.

Peddler, Mike. The Learning Company: A Strategy for Sustainable Development. 224p. 1994. 24.95 (0-07-707479-3) McGraw.

Peddy, Carolyn P., jt. auth. see Allen, James L.

Peddy, Shirley. The Art of Mentoring: Lead, Follow & Get Out of the Way. LC 98-92757. 188p. 1999. 21.95 (0-9651376-3-5) Bullion Bks.

— Secrets of the Jungle: Lessons in Survival & Success in Today's Organizations. 1996. 14.95 (0-9651376-0-0) Bullion Bks.

Peden. Comparative Records for Health Information Management. (Home Care Aide Ser.). 1998. teacher ed. 14.00 (0-8273-7521-2) Delmar.

Peden, A. J. Egyptian Historical Inscriptions of the Twentieth Dynasty. (Documenta Mundi - Aegyptiaca Ser.: No. 3). (Illus.). 286p. 1994. 78.00 (91-7081-065-6, Pub. by P Astroms) Coronet Bks.

— The Reign of Ramesses IV. LC 95-139298. (Illus.). 148p. 1994. pap. 30.00 (0-85668-622-0, Pub. by Aris & Phillips) David Brown.

Peden, Allan. The Monklands: An Illustrated Architectural Guide. (Illus.). 88p. (C). 1992. pap. 40.00 (1-873190-05-0, Pub. by Rutland Pr) St Mut.

Peden, Ann. Comparative Records for Health Information Management. LC 97-28555. (Health Services Administration Ser.). 576p. (C). 1997. mass mkt. 50.95 (0-8273-7520-4) Delmar.

Peden, Creighton. Civil War Pulpit to World's Parliament of Religion: The Thought of William James Potter. (American Liberal Religious Thought Ser.: Vol. 1). VIII, 395p. (C). 1996. text 59.95 (0-8204-2704-7) P Lang Pubng.

— The Philosopher of Free Religion: Francis Ellingwood Abbot, 1836-1903. LC 91-31769. (American University Studies: Philosophy: Ser. V, Vol. 133). 207p. (C). 1992. text 39.95 (0-8204-1747-5) P Lang Pubng.

Peden, Creighton, ed. Philosophy for a Changing Society. (Orig.). (C). 1985. pap. text 13.95 (0-89894-003-6) Advocate Pub Group.

Peden, Creighton & Axel, Larry E., eds. God, Values & Empiricism: Issues in Philosophical Theology. LC 89-28704. (Highlands Institute Ser.: No. 1). vii, 252p. 1990. text 31.95 (0-86554-360-7, MUP-H298) Mercer Univ Pr.

Peden, Creighton & Hudson, Yeager, eds. Communitarianism, Liberalism, & Social Responsibility. LC 91-35244. (Studies in Social & Political Theory: Vol. 14). 336p. 1991. lib. bdg. 99.95 (0-7734-9656-4) E Mellen.

— Freedom, Dharma, & Rights. LC 93-32109. 464p. 1993. text 109.95 (0-7734-9363-8) E Mellen.

— Liberalism, Oppression, & Empowerment. LC 94-17270. 306p. 1994. text 99.95 (0-7734-9091-4) E Mellen.

— Terrorism, Justice & Social Values. LC 90-24911. (Studies in Social & Political Theory: Vol. 11). 456p. 1991. lib. bdg. 109.95 (0-88946-739-0) E Mellen.

Peden, Creighton & Roth, John K., eds. Rights, Justice, & Community. LC 92-27955. 496p. 1992. text 109.95 (0-7734-9599-1) E Mellen.

Peden, Creighton & Willig, Charles L., eds. Science Serving Faith: Henry Nelson Wieman. LC 87-9441. (American Academy of Religion, Studies in Religion). 200p. 1987. 22.95 (1-55540-131-7, 01-00-46); pap. 16.95 (1-55540-132-5) OUP.

Peden, Creighton, jt. ed. see Hudson, Yeager.

Peden, Creighton, jt. ed. see Speak, David M.

Peden, Creighton, jt. ed. see Sterba, James.

Peden, David, jt. auth. see Richardson, Donna.

***Peden, G. C.** The Treasury & British Public Policy, 1906-1959. (Illus.). 600p. 2000. text 105.00 (0-19-820707-7) OUP.

***Peden, Greg.** Tabletop Hockey: Tips for Kids. (Illus.). 32p. (YA). (gr. 2-5). 2000. pap. 4.95 (1-55074-864-5, Pub. by Kids Can Press) Genl Dist Srvs.

***Peden, Henry C., Jr.** Guide to Genealogical Research in Maryland. 5th rev. enl. ed. (Illus.). 140p. 2000. pap. 18.00 (0-938420-72-0, Pub. by MD Hist) A C Hood.

Peden, J. R. Teaching Materials & Cases on Commercial Transactions. 2nd ed. 560p. 1983. 69.00 (0-409-49364-3, AT, MICHIE) LEXIS Pub.

***Peden, James A.** Vegetarian Cats & Dogs. 3rd rev. ed. (Illus.). 144p. 1999. mass mkt. 18.95 (0-941319-03-2) Harbingers New Age.

Peden, Joseph R & Glahe, Fred R., eds. The American Family & the State. LC 85-63547. (Illus.). 488p. 1984. 34.95 (0-936488-12-3); pap. 14.95 (0-936488-05-0) PRIPP.

Peden, Lauren D. The Healing Arts: Aromatherapy. 60p. 1998. 6.95 (0-446-91201-8) Warner Bks.

— The Healing Arts: Healing Herbs. 60p. 1998. 6.95 (0-446-91202-6) Warner Bks.

— The Healing Arts: Meditation. 60p. 1998. 6.95 (0-446-91204-2) Warner Bks.

— The Healing Arts: Reflexology. 60p. 1998. 6.95 (0-446-91205-0) Warner Bks.

— The Mystical Arts: Dream Interpretation. 60p. 1995. write for info. (0-446-51905-7) Warner Bks.

— The Mystical Arts: I Ching. 60p. 1995. write for info. (0-446-51903-0) Warner Bks.

— The Mystical Arts: Numerology. 60p. 1995. write for info. (0-446-51902-2) Warner Bks.

— The Mystical Arts: Numerology. LC 96-161731. 60p. 1996. 6.95 (0-446-91012-0, Pub. by Warner Bks) Little.

— The Mystical Arts: Palmistry. 60p. 1995. write for info. (0-446-51904-9) Warner Bks.

Peden, Margaret, tr. see Mastretta, Angeles.

Peden, Margaret Sayers. Out of the Volcano: Portraits of Contemporary Mexican Artists. LC 91-52842. (Illus.). 264p. (C). 1991. pap. 34.95 (1-56098-061-3) Smithsonian.

Peden, Margaret Sayers, ed. The Latin American Short Story: A Critical History. (Critical History of the Modern Short Story Ser.). 164p. 1983. 23.95 (0-8057-9351-8, Twyne) Mac Lib Ref.

Peden, Margaret Sayers, tr. A Woman of Genius: The Intellectual Autobiography of Sor Juana de la Cruz. (Illus.). 192p. (C). 1982. 37.50 (0-915998-14-9); pap. 7.95 (0-915998-15-7) Lime Rock Pr.

Peden, Margaret Sayers, tr. from SPA. Sor Juana Ines de la Cruz: Poems. LC 85-71537. (ENG & SPA.). 144p. 1985. pap. text 13.00 (0-916950-60-3) Biling Rev-Pr.

Peden, Margaret Sayers, jt. auth. see Allende, Isabel.

Peden, Margaret Sayers, tr. see Allende, Isabel.

Peden, Margaret Sayers, tr. see De La Cruz, Sor J.

Peden, Margaret Sayers, tr. see Fuentes, Carlos.

Peden, Margaret Sayers, tr. see Mastretta, Angeles.

Peden, Margaret Sayers, tr. see Neruda, Pablo.

Peden, Margaret Sayers, tr. see Paz, Octavio.

Peden, Margaret Sayers, tr. see Quiroga, Horacio.

Peden, Margaret Sayers, tr. see Rodo, Jose E.

Peden, Margaret Sayers, tr. see Saralegui, Cristina.

Peden, Margaret Sayers, tr. see Serrano, Marcela.

Peden, Margaret Sayers, tr. see Velarde, Ramon L.

Peden, Murray. Fall of an Arrow. 192p. 1987. pap. 14.95 (0-7737-5105-X) Genl Dist Srvs.

— A Thousand Shall Fall. (Illus.). 504p. 1998. pap. 19.95 (0-7737-5967-0) Stoddart Publ.

Peden, N. R., jt. auth. see MacLennan, W. J.

Peden, W. Creighton & Axel, Larry E., eds. New Essays in Religious Naturalism. LC 93-37812. (Highlands Institute Ser.). 1994. pap. 29.95 (0-86554-426-3, MUP/H346) Mercer Univ Pr.

Peden, W. Creighton & Stone, Jerome A., eds. The Chicago School of Theology - Pioneers in Religous Inquiry Vol. I: The Early Chicago School, 1906-1959 - G. B. Foster, E. S. Ames, S. Mathews, G. B. Smith, S. J. Case. LC 96-18391. (Studies in American Religion: Vol. 66A). 376p. 1996. text 99.98 (0-7734-8748-4) E Mellen.

— The Chicago School of Theology - Pioneers in Religous Inquiry Vol. II: The Later School, 1919-1988 - A. E. Haydon, H. N. Wieman, D. D. Williams, B. E. Meland, B. M. Loomer. LC 96-18391. (Studies in American Religion: Vol. 66B). 500p. 1996. text 109.95 (0-7734-8750-6) E Mellen.

Peden, W. Creighton & Tarbox, Everett J., Jr., eds. The Collected Essays of Francis Ellingwood Abbot (1836-1903), American Philosopher & Free Religionist, Vol. I. LC 94-49064. (Studies in American Religion: Vol. 63A). 424p. 1995. text 109.95 (0-7734-9007-8) E Mellen.

— The Collected Essays of Francis Ellingwood Abbot (1836-1903), American Philosopher & Free Religionist, Vol. II. LC 94-49064. (Studies in American Religion: Vol. 63B). 444p. 1995. text 109.95 (0-7734-9009-4) E Mellen.

— The Collected Essays of Francis Ellingwood Abbot (1836-1903), American Philosopher & Free Religionist, Vol. III. LC 94-49064. (Studies in American Religion: Vol. 63C). 456p. 1995. text 109.95 (0-7734-9011-6) E Mellen.

— The Collected Essays of Francis Ellingwood Abbot (1836-1903), American Philosopher & Free Religionist, Vol. IV. LC 94-49064. (Studies in American Religion: Vol. 63D). 440p. 1995. text 109.95 (0-7734-9013-2) E Mellen.

Peden, W. Creighton, jt. ed. see Hudson, Yeager.

Peden, William. Fragments & Fictions: Workbooks of an Obscure Writer. 125p. 1990. 14.50 (0-922820-10-4) Watermark Pr.

Peden, William, ed. see Jefferson, Thomas.

Peden, William, ed. & intro. see Jefferson, Thomas.

Pedersen. Current Topics. (C). 1998. text 89.95 (0-12-153144-9) Acad Pr.

Pedersen, Aksel G. NAFCU's Internal Auditing Manual for Credit Unions LC 98-207721. 1997. write for info. (1-55827-240-2) Sheshunoff.

Pedersen, Aksel G. & National Association of Federal Credits Unions Staff. Nafcu's Contingency Planning, Disaster Recovery & Record Retention for Credit Unions. LC 98-213173. 1998. write for info. (1-55827-251-8) Sheshunoff.

***Pedersen, Ann.** Tanchaz: The Hungarian Dance House Movement & Its Use of the Folk Music & Dance from Transylvania. 160p. 2000. 37.00 (87-7289-596-9, Pub. by Mus Tusculanum) Intl Spec Bk.

Pedersen, Anne. Teens: A Fresh Look. Mothering Magazine Staff, ed. (Illus.). 240p. 1991. pap. 10.95 (0-945465-54-8) Avalon Travel.

Pedersen, Annegrethe, jt. auth. see Engberg-Pedersen, Elisabeth.

***Pedersen, Arild.** Portrait of a Hero, or a Theory of the Novel. (Acta Humaniora). 361p. 1998. pap. 48.00 (82-00-12935-7) Scandnvan Univ Pr.

— Theory of David Copperfield, or a Theory of the Novel's Theory. (Acta Humaniora). 730p. 1998. pap. 79.00 (82-00-12936-5) Scandnvan Univ Pr.

Pedersen, B. Martin. Graphis Poster 97: The International Annual Of Poster Art: Das Internationale Jahrbuch Der Plank. 1997. text 69.95 (1-888001-23-2) Graphis US.

***Pedersen, B. Martin.** Advertising's Top 10. (Illus.). 220p. 2000. 70.00 (1-888001-95-X, Pub. by Graphis US) Watsn-Guptill.

Pedersen, B. Martin. Bottle Design: Beer, Wine, Spirits. (Illus.). 224p. 1997. pap. text 39.95 (1-888001-27-5) Watsn-Guptill.

— Design Annual 2000. 256p. 1999. text 70.00 (1-888001-68-2) Graphis US.

— Graphics Diagrams 2. (Illus.). 224p. 1997. 69.95 (1-888001-13-5) Watsn-Guptill.

— Graphis Design 97. (Illus.). 240p. 1997. 69.95 (1-888001-16-X) Graphis US.

— Graphis Nudes. (Illus.). 224p. 1995. pap. 39.95 (0-8230-6459-X, Amphoto) Watsn-Guptill.

— Graphis T-Shirt Design 2. 2nd ed. (Illus.). 256p. 1998. 60.00 (1-888001-40-2) Graphis US.

— Graphis Trademark: Logo Compendium, 2 vols., Set. (Illus.). 304p. 1996. 250.00 (1-888001-07-0) Graphis US.

— Nudes 3. 256p. 1999. text 70.00 (1-888001-66-6) Graphis US.

***Pedersen, B. Martin.** 100 Best Products of the Century. 240p. 1999. 40.00 (1-888001-81-X) Graphis US.

Pedersen, B. Martin. Poster Annual 1999. 256p. 1999. text 70.00 (1-888001-62-3, Pub. by Graphis US) Watsn-Guptill.

***Pedersen, B. Martin.** Poster Annual 2000. (Illus.). 2000. pap. 70.00 (1-888001-67-4) Graphis US.

Pedersen, B. Martin. Shorelines: The Camera at Water's Edge. (Illus.). 104p. 1995. 85.95 (0-8230-6462-X, Amphoto) Watsn-Guptill.

***Pedersen, B. Martin, ed.** Advertising Annual 2000. (Illus.). 256p. 1999. text 70.00 (1-888001-69-0) Graphis US.

— Advertising Annual, 2001. (Illus.). 256p. 2000. 70.00 (1-888001-86-0, Pub. by Graphis US) Watsn-Guptill.

— Annual Reports 7. (Illus.). 256p. 2000. 70.00 (1-888001-89-5, Pub. by Graphis US) Watsn-Guptill.

Pedersen, B. Martin, ed. Counting Sheep: A Book to Fall Asleep With. (Illus.). 111p. 1998. text 15.00 (0-7881-5942-9) DIANE Pub.

***Pedersen, B. Martin, ed.** Design Annual, 2001. (Illus.). 256p. 2000. 70.00 (1-888001-88-7, Pub. by Graphis US) Watsn-Guptill.

Pedersen, B. Martin, ed. Digital Photo 1. (Illus.). 256p. 1998. 70.00 (1-888001-59-3) Graphis US.

— Ferenc Berko. (Illus.). 104p. 1999. text 60.00 (1-888001-44-5, Pub. by Graphis US) Watsn-Guptill.

— Graphis Advertising Annual 1999. (Graphis Advertising Ser.: Vol. 99). (Illus.). 256p. 1998. 70.00 (1-888001-50-X) Graphis US.

— Graphis Amateur Photography I. (Illus.). 224p. 1997. pap. 39.95 (1-888001-34-8) Graphis US.

— Graphis Annual Reports 6. 6th ed. (Illus.). 256p. 1998. 70.00 (1-888001-55-0) Graphis US.

— Graphis Book Design 2. (Illus.). 256p. 1998. 70.00 (1-888001-45-3) Graphis US.

— Graphis Brochures 3. 3rd ed. (Illus.). 256p. 1998. 70.00 (1-888001-49-6) Graphis US.

— Graphis Brochures 2. (Illus.). 224p. 1996. 75.00 (1-888001-12-7) Graphis US.

— Graphis Corporate Identity, Vol. 3. 3rd ed. (Illus.). 256p. 1998. 70.00 (1-888001-43-7) Graphis US.

— Graphis Design Annual 1999. (Graphis Design Ser.: Vol. 99). (Illus.). 256p. 1998. 70.00 (1-888001-48-8) Graphis US.

— Graphis Design 98. (Illus.). 272p. 1997. 69.95 (1-888001-31-3) Graphis US.

— Graphis Fine Art Photography 97. (Illus.). 224p. 1997. 69.95 (1-888001-14-3) Graphis US.

— Graphis Human Condition 95: The Year in Photojournalism. (Illus.). 224p. 1996. 49.95 (1-888001-04-6) Graphis US.

— Graphis Letterhead 4. 4th ed. (Illus.). 256p. 1998. 70.00 (1-888001-57-7) Graphis US.

— Graphis Letterhead 3. (Illus.). 224p. 1996. 75.00 (1-888001-03-8) Graphis US.

— Graphis Logo 4. 4th ed. (Illus.). 256p. 1998. 60.00 (1-888001-58-5) Graphis US.

— Graphis Logo 3. (Illus.). 224p. 1996. 49.95 (1-888001-02-X) Graphis US.

— Graphis New Media 96. (Illus.). 224p. 1996. 69.95 (1-888001-06-2) Graphis US.

— Graphis Nudes II. 2nd ed. (Illus.). 240p. 1997. 50.00 (1-888001-30-5) Graphis US.

— Graphis Packaging 7. (Illus.). 224p. 1996. 69.95 (1-888001-17-8) Graphis US.

— Graphis Photo Annual 1998. (Graphis Photo Ser.: Vol. 98). (Illus.). 256p. 1998. 70.00 (1-888001-46-1) Graphis US.

— Graphis Photo 97. (Illus.). 240p. 1997. 69.95 (1-888001-28-3) Graphis US.

— Graphis Photography 96. (Illus.). 224p. 1996. 69.95 (1-888001-18-6) Graphis US.

— Graphis Poster Annual, 1998. (Poster Ser.). (Illus.). 256p. 1998. 70.00 (1-888001-41-0) Graphis US.

— Graphis Poster '96. (Illus.). 224p. 1996. 69.95 (1-888001-00-3) Graphis US.

— Graphis Product Design 2. 2nd ed. (Illus.). 240p. 1997. 69.95 (1-888001-33-X) Graphis US.

— Graphis Student Design Annual, 1998, Vol. 3. (Illus.). 256p. 1998. 60.00 (1-888001-39-9) Graphis US.

— Graphis Student Design '96. 224p. 1996. pap. 44.95 (1-888001-01-1) Graphis US.

***Pedersen, B. Martin, ed.** Magazine Design 2. (Illus.). 256p. 2000. 70.00 (1-888001-91-7, Pub. by Graphis US) Watsn-Guptill.

Pedersen, B. Martin, ed. New Media, Vol. 2. 256p. 1998. 69.95 (1-888001-42-9) Graphis US.

— New Talent Design 1999. 4th ed. (Illus.). 256p. 1999. text 60.00 (1-888001-60-7, Pub. by Graphis US) Watsn-Guptill.

***Pedersen, B. Martin, ed.** Packaging Design 8. (Illus.). 256p. 2000. 70.00 (1-888001-87-9, Pub. by Graphis US) Watsn-Guptill.

— Photo Annual 1999. (Illus.). 256p. 1999. text 70.00 (1-888001-65-8) Graphis US.

— Photography Annual, 2001. (Illus.). 256p. 2000. 70.00 (1-888001-90-9, Pub. by Graphis US) Watsn-Guptill.

Pedersen, B. Martin, ed. Promotion Design, Vol. 1. (Illus.). 256p. 1999. text 70.00 (1-888001-61-5, Pub. by Graphis US) Watsn-Guptill.

***Pedersen, B. Martin, ed.** Surface Fetish: The Art & Design of Bridget De Socio. (Illus.). 256p. 2000. 70.00 (1-888001-97-6, Pub. by Graphis US) Watsn-Guptill.

Pedersen, B. Martin, ed. Typography, Vol. 2. 2nd ed. (Illus.). 256p. 1999. 70.00 (1-888001-26-7, Pub. by Graphis US) Watsn-Guptill.

— Water Dance. (Illus.). 192p. 1996. pap. 24.95 (1-888001-20-8) Graphis US.

Pedersen, B. Martin & Calderhead, Richard, eds. Graphis Advertising 97. (Illus.). 224p. 1996. 69.95 (1-888001-15-1) Graphis US.

Pedersen, B. Martin, jt. ed. see Balog, James.

Pedersen, B. Martin, ed. see Schmidt, Klaus.

Pedersen, Bente Klarlund, jt. auth. see Nieman, David C.

Pedersen, Bjorn. Face to Face with God in Your Church: Establishing a Prayer Ministry. LC 95-2308. 128p. 1995. pap. 19.99 (0-8066-2766-2, 1-27662, Fortress Pr) Augsburg Fortress.

Pedersen, Carl T. The Physical Chemistry of 1,2-Dithiole Compounds: The Question of Aromaticity, Vol.1. (Sulfur Reports). 96p. 1980. pap. text 142.00 (3-7186-0031-5) Gordon & Breach.

Pedersen, Carl T., jt. ed. see Becher, J.

Pedersen, Cindy. Family Night: Book of Mormon Lessons That Teach with Treats. 1996. pap. 7.95 (1-55503-761-5, 01111752) Covenant Comms.

Pedersen, Cindy & Sidwell, Rhea. Bible Stories: Family Night Lessons That Teach with Treats. LC 97-149197. 1996. pap. 8.95 (1-55503-930-8, 01112333) Covenant Comms.

Pedersen, Cort A., et al, eds. Oxytocin in Maternal, Sexual, & Social Behaviors, Vol. 652. 492p. 1992. 125.00 (0-89766-699-2) NY Acad Sci.

Pedersen, Curtis. Cooling & Heating: Load Calculation Principles. Geshwiler, Mildred, ed. 240p. (C). 1998. pap. text 95.00 (1-883413-59-1, 90395) Am Heat Ref & Air Eng.

Pedersen, Darlene, ed. see Rakel, Robert E.

Pedersen, David L. Cameral Analysis: A Method of Treating the Psychoneuroses Using Hypnosis. LC 93-37852. (Illus.). 240p. (C). 1994. 75.00 (0-415-10424-6, B3806); pap. 24.99 (0-415-10425-4, B3910) Routledge.

***Pedersen, Dianne.** 21st Century Woman of Virtue. 230p. 1999. pap. 10.00 (0-7392-0423-8, P-03690) Morris Pubng.

An Asterisk (*) at the beginning of an entry indicates that the title is appearing for the first time.

Pedersen, Donald B. & Meyer, Keith G. Agricultural Law in a Nutshell. (Nutshell Ser.). 440p. (C). 1995. pap. 22.95 (*0-314-06454-0*) West Pub.

Pedersen, F. B. Environmental Hydraulics: Stratified Flows. (Lecture Notes on Coastal & Estuarine Studies: Vol. 18). vii, 278p. 1986. pap. 42.00 (*0-387-16792-7*) Spr-Verlag.

Pedersen, Frank A., ed. The Father-Infant Relationship: Observational Studies in the Family Settings. LC 79-20514. (Praeger Special Studies). 185p. 1980. 35.95 (*0-275-90535-7*, C0535, Praeger Pubs) Greenwood.

Pedersen, Frank A., jt. ed. see Berman, Phyllis W.

Pedersen, Franklin D. Modern Algebra: A Conceptual Approach. 224p. (C). 1992. text 53.75 (*0-697-11926-2*, WCB McGr Hill) McGrw-H Hghr Educ.

Pedersen, G. Analysis Now. (Graduate Texts in Mathematics Ser.: Vol. 118). xiv, 277p. 1995. 59.95 (*0-387-96788-5*) Spr-Verlag.

***Pedersen, Gloria.** Gabriel's Fire. 320p. (Orig.). 2000. pap. 4.99 (*0-8439-4669-5*, Leisure Bks) Dorchester Pub Co.

Pedersen, Gordon, jt. auth. see Wilson, Mary Lou.

Pedersen, Gorm. Afghan Nomads in Transition. LC 94-61394. (Carlsberg Nomad Ser.). (Illus.). 320p. 1995. 50.00 (*0-500-01639-9*, Pub. by Thames Hudson) Norton.

Pedersen, Gunnar. The Highway Angler: Fishing Southcentral Alaska. (Illus.). 258p. (Orig.). 1989. pap. 19.95 (*0-9621551-0-1*) Alaska Viking Pr.

Pedersen, H. B. & Balslev, H. Ecuadorean Palms for Agroforestry. (AAU Reports: No. 23). (Illus.). 122p. (C). 1990. pap. 12.95 (*87-87600-30-7*, Pub. by Aarhus Univ Pr) David Brown.

Pedersen, Helge. 10 Years on 2 Wheels: A Photographers Journey Around the World. 3rd ed. Payne, Dana & Squire, Scott, eds. LC 98-70088. 208p. 1998. reprint ed. 48.00 (*0-944958-38-9*) Elfin Cove Pr.

Pedersen, Henry F., Jr. Sadness in Sunshine: The Flood of Estes Park, an Illustrated Journal. (Illus.). 64p. (Orig.). 1995. pap. 8.50 (*0-9641585-3-1*) H F Pedersen.

Pedersen, Herbert L. A Deacon Ministry That Works. 1993. 186.95 incl. VHS (*0-941005-75-5*) Chrch Grwth VA.

Pedersen, Holger, ed. A Glance at the History of Lingustics with Particular Regard to the Historical Study of Phonology. (Studies in History of Linguistic Sciences: No. 7). xxxii, 100p. 1983. 35.00 (*90-272-0898-0*) J Benjamins Pubng Co.

Pedersen, J. H. & Runestad, J. A. Concrete Manure Storages Handbook. Huffman, C. J., ed. LC 91-26955. (Illus.). 80p. (Orig.). 1994. pap. 20.00 (*0-89373-082-3*, MWPS-36) MidWest Plan Serv.

Pedersen, Jean J. New Twist: Developing Arithmetic Skills Through Problem Solving. 1979. text 16.00 (*0-201-05712-3*) Addison-Wesley.

Pedersen, Jean J., et al. Mathematical Reflections: In a Room with Many Mirrors. LC 96-14274. (Undergraduate Texts in Mathematics Ser.). 351p. 1996. 34.00 (*0-387-94770-1*) Spr-Verlag.

Pedersen, Jean J., jt. auth. see Hilton, Peter J.

Pedersen, Jens A., ed. Handbook of EPR Spectra from Natural & Synthetic Quinones & Quinols. 392p. 1985. 155.00 (*0-8493-2955-8*, QC463) CRC Pr.

Pedersen, Jesper S. & Sorensen, Jesper S., eds. Organizational Cultures in Theory & Practice. (Illus.). 135p. 1989. text 72.95 (*0-566-07090-1*, Pub. by Avebry) Ashgate Pub Co.

Pedersen, Jesper S., et al. Teach Yourself Emacs in 24 Hours With CDROM. LC 98-83136. (Sams Teach Yourself ... in 24 Hours Ser.). (Illus.). 445p. (Orig.). 1999. pap. 24.99 (*0-672-31594-7*) Sams.

Pedersen, John, jt. auth. see Mills, Robert.

Pedersen, John K. Sincerity Meets the Truth. (Illus.). 70p. 1997. pap. 9.95 (*1-889058-04-1*) Old Paths Pubns.

Pedersen, Jon E. & Digby, Annette D. Secondary Schools & Cooperative Learning: Theories, Models & Strategies. LC 94-15326. (Source Books on Education: Vol. 40). 488p. 1995. text 76.00 (*0-8153-0421-8*, SS788) Garland.

Pedersen, Jon E., jt. ed. see Totten, Samuel.

***Pedersen, Judy.** When Nighttime Comes Near. LC 98-44366. (Illus.). 40p. (J). (ps-2). 1999. 15.99 (*0-670-88259-3*, Viking) Viking Penguin.

Pedersen, Judy. On the Road of Stars: Native American Night Poems & Sleep Charms. LC 92-20001. 40p. (J). (gr. 1 up). 1994. mass mkt. 15.95 (*0-02-709735-8*, Mac Bks Young Read) S&S Childrens.

Pedersen, Kai R. The United States & European Reconstruction: The Case of Norway, 1945-1953. 286p. 1998. 74.95 (*1-57292-079-3*); pap. 54.95 (*1-57292-078-5*) Austin & Winfield.

Pedersen, Kristin. The Shadow Shop. Thatch, Nancy R., ed. (Books for Students by Students). (Illus.). 29p. (J). (gr. 3-6). 1994. lib. bdg. 15.95 (*0-933849-53-2*) Landmark Edns.

Pedersen, Lars. Newer Islamic Movements in Western Europe. LC 98-74759. (Research in Migration & Ethnic Relations Ser.). 296p. 1999. text 69.95 (*1-84014-388-6*) Ashgate Pub Co.

Pedersen, Laura. Going Away Party. 256p. 1999. 24.95 (*0-947993-77-0*, Pub. by Mlvrn Pubg Co) Brit Bk Co Inc.

***Pedersen, Layna, ed.** ADA Case Digest. 1998. pap. 89.00 (*1-58012-028-8*) James Pub Santa Ana.

Pedersen, Lee G., jt. auth. see Johnson, Charles S., Jr.

Pedersen, Liz. Edge of Desire. (Rainbow Romances Ser.). 160p. 1994. 14.95 (*0-7090-5022-4*, 912) Parkwest Pubns.

Pedersen, Liz. The Perfect Gentleman. large type ed. 256p. pap. 18.99 (*0-7089-5450-2*) Ulverscroft.

Pedersen, Lloyd. The Vintage: A Novel. LC 97-93805. 885p. 1998. 26.00 (*0-9657029-0-1*) Joyce & Co.

Pedersen, Marguerite. The Cruise of the Skuld. LC 87-61085. 160p. (Orig.). 1987. pap. 7.00 (*0-914752-25-1*) Sovereign Pr.

— Life's Meaning. LC 89-60446. 112p. (Orig.). 1989. pap. 7.00 (*0-914752-27-8*) Sovereign Pr.

Pedersen, Marialyce, ed. see Harmonious Technologies Staff.

***Pedersen, Marika & Hall, Mikele.** Mommy Works, Daddy Works. (Illus.). 32p. (J). (ps-1). 2000. lib. bdg. 17.95 (*1-55037-657-8*, Pub. by Annick Pr); per. 5.95 (*1-55037-656-X*, Pub. by Annick Pr) Firefly Bks Ltd.

Pedersen, Mark. Nutritional Herbology: A Reference Guide to Herbs. rev. ed. LC 94-60830. 336p. 1994. pap. text 19.95 (*1-885653-03-4*) W W Whitman.

— Nutritional Herbology: A Reference Guide to Herbs. 3rd rev. ed. 352p. 1998. pap. 21.95 (*1-885653-07-7*) W W Whitman.

Pedersen, Martha. Trees of the Pacific Northwest. LC 96-70516. (Illus.). 72p. (Orig.). 1996. pap. write for info. (*0-9639462-1-8*) Portland Garden.

— Wildflowers & Weeds of the Pacific Northwest. 64p. 1993. pap. 9.95 (*0-9639462-0-X*) Portland Garden.

Pedersen, Mary J. & Burney, Joan R. Sharing the Faith with Your Child: From Age Seven to Fourteen. LC 92-81360. 160p. 1992. pap. 6.95 (*0-89243-444-9*, Liguori Lifespan) Liguori Pubns.

***Pedersen, Mary Jo, et al.** More Than Meets the Eye: Finding God in the Creases & Folds of Family Life. 160p. (YA). 2000. pap. 14.95 (*0-88489-594-7*) St Marys.

Pedersen, Michael. Functional Analysis in Applied Math & Engineering. LC 99-37641. (Studies in Advanced Mathematics). 312p. 1999. boxed set 69.95 (*0-8493-7169-4*) CRC Pr.

Pedersen, N. F. Nonlinear Superconducting Devices & High-TC Materials: Proceedings of the International Conference. 500p. 1995. text 150.00 (*981-02-2091-X*) World Scientific Pub.

Pedersen, Niels C., et al. Feline Husbandry: Disease & Management in the Multiple-Cat Environment. LC 90-81326. (Illus.). 453p. 1991. text 43.95 (*0-939674-29-7*) Am Vet Pubns.

Pedersen, Nils A. Studies in the Sermon on the Great War: Investigations of a Manichaean-Coptic Text from the Fourth Century. 512p. 1996. 40.00 (*87-7288-559-9*, Pub. by Aarhus Univ Pr) David Brown.

Pedersen, Norman. What Is This Book? LC 89-61804. (Illus.). 104p. (Orig.). 1989. pap. text 5.95 (*0-685-26789-X*) Sol-Earth.

Pedersen, Olaf. The Book of Nature. (C). 1992. pap. 8.00 (*0-268-00690-3*) U of Notre Dame Pr.

— Early Physics & Astronomy. 2nd ed. (Illus.). 423p. (C). 1993. pap. text 31.95 (*0-521-40899-7*) Cambridge U Pr.

— The First Universities: Studium Generale & the Origins of University Education in Europe. LC 97-7037. 326p. (C). 1998. text 64.95 (*0-521-59431-6*) Cambridge U Pr.

Pedersen, Olof. Archives & Libraries in the Ancient near East 1500-300 B. C. LC 98-4337. (Illus.). 312p. (C). 1998. 42.00 (*1-883053-39-0*) CDL Pr.

Pedersen, Ove K., jt. ed. see Campbell, John L.

Pedersen, P. A. Monash As Military Commander. 380p. 1992. pap. 24.95 (*0-522-84504-5*, Pub. by Melbourne Univ Pr) Paul & Co Pubs.

***Pedersen, Paul.** A Handbook for Developing Multicultural Awareness. 3rd ed. LC 99-55851. 230p. 2000. pap. text 39.95 (*1-55620-177-X*, 72692) Am Coun Assn.

Pedersen, Paul. Multiculturalism As a Fourth Force. LC 98-42486. 300p. 1998. pap. 29.95 (*0-87630-930-9*); boxed set 59.95 (*0-87630-929-5*) Brunner-Mazel.

Pedersen, Paul B. Culture-Centered Counseling Interventions: Striving for Accuracy. LC 96-35663. 304p. (C). 1997. 52.00 (*0-7619-0249-X*, 0249X); pap. 24.95 (*0-7619-0250-3*, 02503) Sage.

— The Five Stages of Culture Shock: Critical Incidents Around the World, 25. LC 93-49711. (Contributions in Psychology Ser.: Vol. 25). 296p. 1994. 65.00 (*0-313-28782-1*, Greenwood Pr) Greenwood.

— A Handbook for Developing Multicultural Awareness. 2nd ed. LC 93-33195. 320p. 1994. pap. text 40.95 (*1-55620-133-8*, 72586) Am Coun Assn.

Pedersen, Paul B., ed. Handbook of Cross-Cultural Counseling & Therapy. LC 84-12832. xv, 353p. 1985. pap. 19.95 (*0-685-10209-2*, Greenwood Pr); lib. bdg. 59.95 (*0-313-23914-2*, PRH/, Greenwood Pr) Greenwood.

— Handbook of Cross-Cultural Counseling & Therapy. LC 87-9337. 376p. 1987. pap. 24.95 (*0-275-92713-X*, B2713, Praeger Pubs) Greenwood.

Pedersen, Paul B., et al, eds. Counseling Across Cultures. 4th ed. 484p. (Orig.). 1995. 54.00 (*0-8039-5748-3*); pap. 25.00 (*0-8039-5749-1*) Sage.

— Mental Health Services: The Cross-Cultural Context. LC 83-26945. (Cross-Cultural Research & Methodology Ser.). 311p. 1984. reprint ed. pap. 96.50 (*0-608-01180-0*, 205947800001) Bks Demand.

Pedersen, Paul B. & Hernandez, Daniel. Decisional Interviewing in a Cultural Context: Structured Exercises. 195p. (C). 1996. pap. 17.95 (*0-7619-0303-8*) Sage.

Pedersen, Paul B. & Locke, Don C., eds. Cultural & Diversity Issues in Counseling. 159p. (C). 1998. pap. text 19.95 (*1-56109-071-9*, EC212) CAPS Inc.

Pedersen, Paul B., jt. auth. see Ivey, Allen E.

Pedersen, Paul B., jt. auth. see Ponterotto, Joseph G.

Pedersen, Paul B., jt. ed. see Jandt, Fred E.

Pedersen, Paul B., jt. ed. see Lefley, Harriet P.

Pedersen, Paul B., jt. ed. see Tyson, Lawrence E.

Pedersen, Paul M. Build It & They Will Come! The Arrival of the Tampa Bay Devil Rays. LC 97-94499. (Illus.). 1997. pap. write for info. (*0-9660520-0-5*) Florida Sports Pr.

Pedersen, Peder J. & Lund, Reinhard, eds. Unemployment: Theory, Policy & Structure. (Studies in Organization: No. 10). 353p. (C). 1987. lib. bdg. 113.85 (*3-11-011071-7*) De Gruyter.

Pedersen, Poul, jt. ed. see Baker, Jonathan.

Pedersen, Poul O. The Maussolleion at Halikarnassos, Reports of the Danish Archaeological Expedition to Bodrum Vol. 3: The Maussolleion Terrace & Accessory Structures. 2 vols., Set. (Jutland Archaeological Society Publications: No. 15). (Illus.). 342p. (C). 1992. 54.00 (*87-7288-563-7*, Pub. by Aarhus Univ Pr) David Brown.

— The Parthenon & the Origin of the Corinthian Capital. (Illus.). 48p. (Orig.). 1989. pap. 27.50 (*87-7492-708-6*) Coronet Bks.

— Small African Towns - Between Rural Networks & Urban Hierarchies. LC 97-70636. (Making of Modern Africa Ser.). (Illus.). 234p. 1997. text 73.95 (*1-85972-589-9*, Pub. by Ashgate Pub) Ashgate Pub Co.

Pedersen, Poul O., jt. ed. see Baker, Jonathan.

Pedersen, Rita & Andersen, Flemming G., eds. The Concept of Tradition in Ballad Research. 130p. (Orig.). 1985. pap. text 36.50 (*87-7492-562-8*) Coronet Bks.

Pedersen, Roger A. Current Topics in Developmental Biology. 234p. 1999. 99.95 (*0-12-153146-5*) Acad Pr.

Pedersen, Roger A., ed. Current Topics in Developmental Biology, Vol. 29. (Illus.). 369p. (C). 1994. text. write for info. (*0-12-153129-5*) Acad Pr.

Pedersen, Roger A., et al, eds. Animal Applications of Research in Mammalian Development. (Current Communications in Cell & Molecular Biology Ser.: No. 4). (Illus.). 334p. (C). 1991. pap. text 44.00 (*0-87969-333-9*) Cold Spring Harbor.

Pedersen, Roger A. & Schatten, Gerald A., eds. Current Topics in Developmental Biology, Vol. 35. (Illus.). 277p. (C). 1997. text 79.00 (*0-12-153135-X*) Morgan Kaufmann.

Pedersen, Roger A. & Schatten, Gerald P. Current Topics in Developmental Biology, Vol. 40. (Illus.). 300p. (C). 1998. boxed set 89.95 (*0-12-153140-6*) Acad Pr.

Pedersen, Roger A. & Schatten, Gerald P., eds. Current Topics in Developmental Biology, Vol. 32. (Illus.). 244p. (C). 1996. text 75.00 (*0-12-153132-5*) Acad Pr.

— Current Topics in Developmental Biology, Vol. 33. (Illus.). 307p. (C). 1996. text 75.00 (*0-12-153133-3*) Acad Pr.

— Current Topics in Developmental Biology, Vol. 34 (Illus.). 287p. (C). 1996. text 75.00 (*0-12-153134-1*) Acad Pr.

— Current Topics in Developmental Biology, Vol. 38. (Illus.). 301p. (C). 1997. text 79.95 (*0-12-153138-4*) Morgan Kaufmann.

— Current Topics in Developmental Biology, Vol. 39. (Illus.). 317p. (C). 1998. text 89.95 (*0-12-153139-2*) Morgan Kaufmann.

— Current Topics in Developmental Biology, Vol. 43. (Illus.). 303p. 1998. boxed set 89.95 (*0-12-153143-0*) Acad Pr.

— Current Topics in Developmental Biology, Vol. 45. Vol. 45. (Illus.). 261p. 1999. 99.95 (*0-12-153145-7*) Acad Pr.

***Pedersen, Roger A. & Schatten, Gerald P., eds.** Current Topics in Developmental Biology Vol. 47. Vol. 47. 512p. 1999. 99.95 (*0-12-153147-3*) Acad Pr.

Pedersen, Roger A., ed. see Ordahl.

Pedersen, Roger A., jt. ed. see Rossant, J.

Pedersen, Roy N. One Europe - One Hundred Nations. 150p. 1992. 39.00 (*1-85359-123-8*, Pub. by Multilingual Matters) Taylor & Francis.

Pedersen, Scott C., jt. auth. see Adams, Rick A.

Pedersen, Sigfred, ed. New Directions in Biblical Theology Vol. 76: Papers of the Aarhus Conference, 16-19 September, 1993. LC 94-28789. xiii, 290p. 1994. 116.00 (*90-04-10120-9*) Brill Academic Pubs.

Pedersen, Sigfred, jt. ed. see Nissen, Johannes.

Pedersen, Solveig S. A Glimpse of Heaven. 80p. (Orig.). 1996. pap. 5.00 (*1-57502-370-9*, P01179) Morris Pubng.

Pedersen, Steffan. The Dutch for the Attacking Player. LC 96-78266. (New American Batsford Chess Library). 160p. 1997. pap. 20.95 (*1-879479-44-3*) ICE WA.

***Pedersen, Steffen.** The Botvinnik Semi-Slav. (Illus.). 192p. 2000. pap. 21.95 (*1-901983-26-9*, Pub. by Gambit) BHB Intl.

— The Meran System. 192p. 2000. pap. 21.95 (*1-901983-28-5*, Pub. by Gambit) BHB Intl.

— Test Your Chess. 2000. pap. 19.95 (*1-901983-35-8*, Pub. by Gambit) BHB Intl.

Pedersen, Stefi. Psychoanalysis in Our Time. LC 70-173220. 1973. 5.95 (*0-672-51411-7*, Bobbs) Macmillan.

***Pedersen, Stephanie.** Dong Quai: Women's Wonder Drug. LC 99-43067. (Natural Cure Library). 64p. 2000. pap. 3.95 (*0-7894-5193-X*, D K Ink) DK Pub Inc.

— Echinacea: Amazing Immunity. LC 99-40021. (Natural Cure Library). 64p. 2000. pap. 3.95 (*0-7894-5199-9*, D K Ink) DK Pub Inc.

— Garlic: Immunity Booster & Inflammation Reducer. LC 99-43068. (Natural Cure Library). 64p. 2000. pap. 3.95 (*0-7894-5192-1*, D K Ink) DK Pub Inc.

— Ginkgo Biloba: Ease Anxiety & Increase Intellect. LC 99-41997. (Natural Cure Library). 64p. 2000. 3.95 (*0-7894-5188-3*, D K Ink) DK Pub Inc.

— Ginseng: Energy Enhancer. LC 99-41998. (Natural Cure Library). 64p. 2000. pap. 3.95 (*0-7894-5190-5*, D K Ink) DK Pub Inc.

— Kava: Relax Your Muscles & Your Mind. LC 99-43070. (Natural Cure Library). 64p. 2000. pap. 3.95 (*0-7894-5191-3*, D K Ink) DK Pub Inc.

— Saw Palmetto. (Natural Cure Library). 64p. (YA). 2000. pap. 3.95 (*0-7894-5335-5*, D K Ink) DK Pub Inc.

— Saw Palmetto: Men's Health Enhancer. LC 99-43069. (Natural Cure Library). 2000. pap. write for info. (*0-7894-5194-8*) DK Pub Inc.

— St. John's Wort: Improve Your Moods & Immunity. LC 99-43066. (Natural Cure Library). 64p. 2000. pap. 3.95 (*0-7894-5189-1*, D K Ink) DK Pub Inc.

— Vitamin B. (Natural Cure Library). 64p. 2000. pap. 3.95 (*0-7894-5195-6*, D K Ink) DK Pub Inc.

— Vitamin C: Building Flexibility & Fighting Infection. (Natural Cure Library). 64p. 2000. pap. 3.95 (*0-7894-5196-4*, D K Ink) DK Pub Inc.

— Vitamin D: Maximizing Minerals. LC 99-45774. (Natural Cure Library). 64p. 2000. pap. 3.95 (*0-7894-5197-2*, D K Ink) DK Pub Inc.

— Vitamin E: Anti Aging & Anti Oxidant. LC 99-45779. (Natural Cure Library). 64p. 2000. pap. 3.95 (*0-7894-5198-0*, D K Ink) DK Pub Inc.

Pedersen, Stephanie, jt. auth. see Simon, John M.

Pedersen, Stephen F., jt. auth. see Rygle, Kathy J.

Pedersen, Susan. Family, Dependence & the Origins of the Welfare State: Britain & France, 1914-1945. (Illus.). 492p. (C). 1995. pap. text 21.95 (*0-521-55834-4*) Cambridge U Pr.

Pedersen, Susan, jt. ed. see Mandler, Peter.

Pedersen, Ted. Gypsy World. (Star Trek: Deep Space Nine Ser.: No. 7). (J). (gr. 3-6). 1996. pap. 3.99 (*0-671-51115-7*) PB.

***Pedersen, Ted.** How to Find Almost Anything on the Internet: A Kid's Guide to Safe Searching. (Illus.). 96p. (J). (gr. 4-7). 2000. pap. 4.99 (*0-8431-7593-1*, Price Stern) Peng Put Young Read.

— How to Find Almost Anything on the Internet: A Kid's Guide to Safe Searching. (Illus.). (J). 2000. 10.34 (*0-606-18468-6*) Turtleback.

Pedersen, Ted. Internet for Kids: A Beginner's Guide to Surfing the Net. (J). 1997. 14.05 (*0-606-12741-0*, Pub. by Turtleback) Demco.

— Make Your Own Web Page: A Guide for Kids. LC 98-30511. (Illus.). 96p. (J). (gr. 8 up). 1998. pap. 4.99 (*0-8431-7459-5*) Putnam Pub Group.

— The Tale of the Virtual Nightmare. (Are You Afraid of the Dark? Ser.: No. 9). (YA). (gr. 4-7). 1996. pap. 3.99 (*0-671-00080-2*) PB.

— Trapped in Time. (Deep Space Nine Ser.: No. 12). (J). 1998. per. 3.99 (*0-671-01440-4*, Star Trek) PB.

Pedersen, Ted & Moss, Francis. Internet for Kids. rev. ed. LC 96-38116. (Illus.). 224p. (YA). (gr. 3-7). 1997. pap. 8.99 (*0-8431-7937-6*, Price Stern) Peng Put Young Read.

Pedersen, Ted, jt. auth. see Gilden, Mel.

Pedersen, Thomas. European Union & the EFTA Countries: Enlargement & Integration. LC 94-1947. 1994. 49.00 (*1-85567-148-4*) St Martin.

— Germany, France & the Integration of Europe: A Realist Interpretation. LC 97-52770. 224p. 1998. 59.95 (*1-85567-537-4*, Pub. by P P Pubs) Cassell & Continuum.

Pedersen, Tom A. & Curtis, James T. Soil Vapor Extraction Technology. LC 91-12465. (Pollution Technology Review Ser.: No. 204). (Illus.). 316p. 1991. 98.00 (*0-8155-1284-8*) Noyes.

Pedersen, Torben, jt. auth. see Holm, Ulf.

***Pedersen, Vernon L.** Bolsheviks in Baltimore, 1919-57. 256p. 2001. text 29.95 (*0-252-02321-8*) U of Ill Pr.

Pederson. New Deal & Public Policy. LC 97-41742. 288p. 1998. text 49.95 (*0-312-17540-X*) St Martin.

Pederson, jt. auth. see Hilton.

Pederson, A., jt. auth. see Dever, S. M.

***Pederson, Ann.** God, Creation & All That Jazz. 2001. pap. 18.99 (*0-8272-1246-1*) Chalice Pr.

Pederson, Ann. Where in the World Is God? Variations on a Theme. LC 98-41531. 160p. 1998. pap. 14.99 (*0-8272-4237-9*) Chalice Pr.

Pederson, Ann, et al. Health Promotion in Canada: Provincial, National & International Perspectives. (Illus.). 401p. 1994. pap. 40.00 (*0-920513-09-3*, W B Saunders Co) Harcrt Hlth Sci Grp.

Pederson, Ann, jt. auth. see Farr, Gail E.

Pederson, April. What about Hooters: America's Introduction to the Hilarious Reality of Hooters. LC 98-91656. (Illus.). 246p. 1998. pap. 19.95 (*0-9665306-0-8*) New Park Pr.

Pederson, Cynthia, jt. auth. see Daniels, Celia.

Pederson, Daniel J. Savings Bonds: When to Hold, When to Fold & Everything in Between. LC 99-191285. Orig. Title: U. S. Savings Bonds: A Comprehensive Guide for Bond Owners & Financial Professionals. 272p. 1998. pap. 19.95 (*1-890394-29-7*, Pub. by Rhodes & Easton) TSBI.

— U. S. Savings Bonds: The Definitive Guide for Financial Professionals. LC 99-209897. Orig. Title: U. S. Savings Bonds: A Comprehensive Guide for Bond Owners & Financial Professionals. 288p. 1998. pap. 29.95 (*1-890394-28-9*, Pub. by Rhodes & Easton) TSBI.

***Pederson, David H. & Sieber, William Karl, eds.** National Occupational Exposure Survey Vol. III: Analysis of Management Interview Responses. (Illus.). 720p. (C). 1999. reprint ed. pap. text 60.00 (*0-7881-8385-0*) DIANE Pub.

Pederson, David S. & Heintz, Nicholas H. Transcription Factors & DNA Replication. LC 94-33851. (Molecular Biology Intelligence Unit Ser.). 125p. 1994. 99.00 (*1-57059-069-9*, LN9069) Landes Bioscience.

Pederson, Donald, jt. auth. see Coates, Marvin.

Pederson, Donald E. Mental Laxatives for a Constipated Mind. LC 98-91714. (Illus.). 262p. 1999. pap. 14.95 (*0-9665819-0-3*) Galactic Enterp.

Pederson, Donald O. & Mayaram, Kartikeya. Analog Integrated Circuits for Communications: Principles, Simulation & Design. 592p. (C). 1990. lib. bdg. 129.00 (*0-7923-9089-X*) Kluwer Academic.

Pederson, Duane E., jt. auth. see Cook, Harvey A.

Pederson, Eric, jt. ed. see Nuyts, Jan.

Pederson, Gunnar, jt. auth. see Limeres, Rene.

Pederson, Helen S. Prairie Needles. (Illus.). 57p. 1997. pap. 7.95 (*0-942323-27-0*) N Amer Heritage Pr.

P

Pederson, Jane M. Between Memory & Reality: Family & Community in Rural Wisconsin, 1870-1970. LC 91-45787. (History of American Thought & Culture Ser.). (Illus.). 320p. (Orig.). (C). 1992. pap. 24.95 (*0-299-13284-6*); lib. bdg. 21.95 (*0-299-13280-3*) U of Wis Pr.

Pederson, Jay. International Directory of Company Histories, Vol. 25. 725p. 1998. 175.00 (*1-55862-367-1*, GML00197-200287) Gale.

Pederson, Jay P. St. James Guide to Science-Fiction Writers, Vol. 1. 4th rev. ed. LC 95-36171. (St. James Guide Ser.). 1175p. 1995. 140.00 (*1-55862-179-2*) Gale.

Pederson, Jay P., ed. St. James Guide to Science Fiction Writers. 3rd ed. (St. James Guide Ser.). 1300p. (C). 1991. 135.00 (*1-55862-111-3*, 200195) St James Pr.

Pederson, Jay P. & Benbow-Pfalzgraf, Taryn. St. James Guide to Crime & Mystery Writers. 4th ed. LC 96-18661. (St. James Guide to Writers Ser.). 1261p. 1996. 140.00 (*1-55862-178-4*) St James Pr.

Pederson, Jay P. & Estell, Kenneth, eds. African-American Almanac, 3 vols., Set. LC 94-30210. (Illus.). 609p. (J). (gr. 4-7). 1994. text 95.00 (*0-8103-9239-9*, GML00597-021503, UXL) Gale.

Pederson, Jay P. & Estell, Kenneth, eds. African-American Almanac, Vol. 2. (African-American Reference Library). (Illus.). (J). (gr. 6-9). 1994. write for info. (*0-8103-9241-0*, UXL) Gale.

— African-American Almanac, Vol. 3. (African-American Reference Library). (Illus.). (J). (gr. 6-9). 1994. write for info. (*0-8103-9242-9*, UXL) Gale.

— African-American Almanac, Vol.1. (African-American Reference Library). (Illus.). 576p. (J). (gr. 6-9). 1994. write for info. (*0-8103-9240-2*, UXL) Gale.

Pederson, Jay P., jt. ed. see Henderson, Helene.

Pederson, Jean. Geometric Playthings. 1997. text 11.95 (*0-86651-351-5*) Seymour Pubns.

Pederson, Joan, ed. see Bradkin, Cheryl G.

Pederson, Judith, jt. auth. see Ayuso, Agnes.

Pederson, Judith, jt. auth. see Dolin, Eric J.

Pederson, Judith, jt. ed. see Dorsey, Eleanor M.

Pederson, Judy. Dream Journal: Notebook of Visions. 160p. 1996. spiral bd. 15.95 (*1-55670-521-2*) Stewart Tabori & Chang.

***Pederson, Julia & Weinig, Katrina.** Safe & Smart: Making the After-School Hours Work for Kids. (Illus.). 93p. 2000. reprint ed. pap. text 25.00 (*0-7881-8848-8*) DIANE Pub.

Pederson, Lee, et al. From the Gulf States & Beyond: The Legacy of Lee Pederson & Lags. LC 98-35175. 1998. write for info. (*0-8173-0948-9*) U of Ala Pr.

Pederson, Lee A. The Pronunciation of English in Metropolitan Chicago. (Publications of the American Dialect Society: No. 44). 87p. 1967. pap. text 8.70 (*0-8173-0644-7*) U of Ala Pr.

Pederson, Lucille M. Katherine Cornell: A Bio-Bibliography, 46. LC 93-32102. (Bio-Bibliographies in the Performing Arts Ser.: No. 46). 264p. 1993. lib. bdg. 69.50 (*0-313-27718-4*, Greenwood Pr) Greenwood.

Pederson, Lucille M. & Trigg, Janet M. Breast Cancer: A Family Survival Guide. LC 94-37836. 304p. 1995. 65.00 (*0-89789-293-3*, Bergin & Garvey) Greenwood.

— Breast Cancer: A Family Survival Guide. LC 94-37836. 304p. 1995. pap. 21.95 (*0-89789-438-3*, Bergin & Garvey) Greenwood.

Pederson, Poul Ove, et al, eds. Flexible Specialization: The Dynamics of Small-Scale Industries in the South. 186p. 1994. pap. 27.50 (*1-85339-217-0*, Pub. by Intermed Tech) Stylus Pub VA.

Pederson, Rolf A. Our Wild Harvest: Sowing, Reaping, Cooking, Eating. Carlson, Nancy, ed. (Illus.). 174p. (Orig.). 1982. pap. 9.95 (*0-910579-00-8*) Rolfs Gall.

— Waterfowl, Vol. 2. (Orig.). 1983. pap. 9.95 (*0-910579-01-6*) Rolfs Gall.

Pederson, Steve. Drama Ministry. LC 99-21608. 2000. pap. 19.99 (*0-310-21945-0*) Zondervan.

Pederson, Steve, ed. Sunday Morning Live: A Collection of Drama Sketches, Vol. 5. 64p. 1994. 19.99 (*0-310-61541-0*) Zondervan.

— Sunday Morning Live: A Collection of 6 Drama Sketches, Vol. 7. 64p. 1998. pap. 19.99 (*0-310-22156-0*) Zondervan.

— Sunday Morning Live: A Collection of 6 Drama Sketches, Vol. 8. 64p. 1998. pap. 19.99 (*0-310-22157-9*) Zondervan.

Pederson, Steve, ed. see Demel, Mark.

Pederson, Steve, ed. see Willow Creek Staff.

Pederson, Steven I. The Tournament Tradition & Staging the Castle of Perseverance. LC 86-25050. (Theater & Dramatic Studies: No. 38). (Illus.). 148p. 1987. reprint ed. pap. 45.90 (*0-8357-1768-2*, 207056800001) Bks Demand.

Pederson, Ted. Buried Alive! (True Fright Ser.: No. 2). (YA). 1996. mass mkt. 3.99 (*0-8125-4396-3*, Pub. by Tor Bks) St Martin.

— True Fright No. 1: Trapped under the Ice, No. 01. 128p. (J). (gr. 3). 1996. pap., mass mkt. 3.99 (*0-8125-4395-5*, Pub. by Tor Bks) St Martin.

Pederson, Trudy R. A Pioneer Experience. (Illus.). 116p. (Orig.). 1982. 10.00 (*0-686-95352-5*) Directed Media.

Pederson, Westley M. Take Five. 1983. pap. 3.50 (*0-87129-268-8*, T64) Dramatic Pub.

Pederson, William D. The Barberian Presidency: Theoretical & Empirical Readings. (American University Studies: Political Science: Ser. X, Vol. 14). XII, 265p. (C). 1989. text 37.60 (*0-8204-0693-7*) P Lang Pubng.

Pederson, William D., ed. Congressional-Presidential Relations in the United States: Studies in Governmental Gridlock. LC 91-41686. 164p. 1991. lib. bdg. 79.95 (*0-7734-9742-0*) E Mellen.

***Pederson, William D., et al, eds.** The M. E. Sharpe Library of Franklin D. Roosevelt Studies, 2 vols., Set. Incl. Franklin D. Roosevelt & Congress: The New Deal & Its Aftermath. Wolf, Thomas Phillip, ed. LC 99-87719. (Illus.). 288p. 2000. text 69.95 (*0-7656-0622-4*); Franklin D. Roosevelt & the Shaping of American Political Culture. Young, Nancy Beck, ed. LC 99-88090. 224p. 2000. text 56.95 (*0-7656-0620-8*); 2000. Set text 119.95 (*0-7656-0648-8*) M E Sharpe.

Pederson, William D. & Prozier, Norman W., eds. Great Justices of the U. S. Supreme Court: Ratings & Case Studies. LC 92-40142. (American University Studies: Political Science: Ser. X, Vol. 39). 388p. (Orig.). (C). 1993. pap. text 32.95 (*0-8204-2066-2*) P Lang Pubng.

Pederson, William D., jt. ed. see Rozell, Mark J.

Pederson, William D., jt. ed. see Williams, Frank J.

Pederson, William O. & McLaurin, Ann M., eds. The Rating Game in American Politics: An Interdisciplinary Approach. LC 87-4145. 425p. (C). 1987. text 39.50 (*0-8290-1812-3*); pap. text 19.95 (*0-685-16492-6*) Irvington.

Pederzoli, Giorgio, jt. ed. see Eiselt, H. A.

Pederzoli, P., et al, eds. Facing the Pancreatic Dilemma: Update of Medical & Surgical Pancreatology. LC 94-35004. 528p. 1994. 174.00 (*0-387-58284-3*) Spr-Verlag.

— Pancreatic Fistulas. LC 92-49618. 1992. 139.00 (*0-387-55338-X*) Spr-Verlag.

Pedhazur, E. & Schmelkin, L. Measurement, Design, & Analysis: An Integrated Approach. 849p. (C). 1991. pap., student ed. 49.95 (*0-8058-1063-3*) L Erlbaum Assocs.

Pedhazur, Elazar J. Multiple-Regression in Behavioral Research: Explanation & Prediction. 3rd ed. LC 96-78486. 1074p. (C). 1997. text 91.50 (*0-03-072831-2*, Pub. by Harcourt Coll Pubs) Harcourt.

***Pediani, Ramon.** Patient Controlled Epidural Analgesia. 128p. 2000. pap. text 25.00 (*0-7506-4299-8*) Buttrwrth-Heinemann.

Pediatric Nephrology International Symposium Staff. Pediatric Nephrology: Proceedings of the Pediatric Nephrology International Symposium, 5th, 1980, No. 3. Gruskin, Alan B. & Norman, Michael E., eds. 530p. 1981. text 211.50 (*90-247-2514-3*) Kluwer Academic.

Pedicini, John G. Slow Moe. Serino, John, ed. (Nantucket Nanny & Friends Ser.). (Illus.). 32p. (J). (gr. k-2). 1991. 9.95 (*0-9627436-7-4*) Je Suis Derby.

Pedicino, Teresa. What's Left? Who's Left? The Layman's Handbook for Estate Property Management, with Accounting Records & Survivor's Guide to Personal & Financial Well-Being. LC 96-90816. (Illus.). 384p. 1997. pap. 24.95 (*0-9652846-0-3*) Tristus Pub.

Pedicord, Harry W. & Bergmann, Fredrick L., eds. The Plays of David Garrick Vol. 1: Garrick's Own Plays, 1740-1766. LC 79-28443. (Plays of David Garrick). (Illus.). 480p. 1980. 49.95 (*0-8093-0862-2*) S Ill U Pr.

— The Plays of David Garrick Vol. 2: Garrick's Own Plays, 1767-1775. LC 79-28443. (Illus.). 444p. 1980. 49.95 (*0-8093-0863-0*) S Ill U Pr.

— The Plays of David Garrick Vol. 3: Garrick's Adaptations of Shakespeare, 1744-1756. LC 80-28443. (Illus.). 496p. 1981. 49.95 (*0-8093-0968-8*) S Ill U Pr.

— The Plays of David Garrick Vol. 4: Garrick's Adaptations of Shakespeare, 1759-1773. LC 80-28443. (Illus.). 490p. 1981. 49.95 (*0-8093-0969-6*) S Ill U Pr.

— The Plays of David Garrick Vol. 5: Garrick's Alterations of Others, 1742-1750. LC 80-28443. 485p. 1982. 51.95 (*0-8093-0993-9*) S Ill U Pr.

— The Plays of David Garrick Vol. 6: Garrick's Alterations of Others, 1751-1756. LC 80-28443. 453p. 1982. 51.95 (*0-8093-0994-7*) S Ill U Pr.

— The Plays of David Garrick Vol. 7: Garrick's Alterations of Others, 1757-1773. LC 80-28443. 399p. 1982. 50.00 (*0-8093-1051-1*) S Ill U Pr.

Pedigo, Alan. International Encyclopedia of Violin-Keyboard Sonatas & Composer Biographies. 2nd enl. rev. ed. LC 95-77999. (Illus.). 341p. 1995. 85.00 (*0-9606356-2-9*) Arriaga Pubns.

Pedigo, Kate. When Even the Cows Were Up: Kate's Book of Childhood in the Early 1900s & After. LC 90-71867. (Illus.). 64p. (Orig.). 1990. pap. text 6.95 (*1-877675-06-7*) Midmarch Arts.

Pedigo, Larry P. Analyses in Insect Ecology & Management. LC 95-32003. (Illus.). 1995. text 74.95 (*0-8138-2861-9*) Iowa St U Pr.

— Entomology & Pest Management. 3rd ed. LC 98-10927. 688p. (C). 1998. 105.00 (*0-13-780024-X*) P-H.

— Handbook of Sampling Methods for Arthropod Pests in Agriculture. 736p. 1993. boxed set 250.95 (*0-8493-2923-X*, SB933) CRC Pr.

Pedigo, Larry P. & Zeiss, Michael R. Analyses in Insect Ecology & Management Teacher's Manual: Answer Key. 98p. 1996. pap., teacher ed. write for info. (*0-8138-2860-0*) Iowa St U Pr.

Pedigo, Larry P., jt. auth. see Higley, Leon G.

Pedigo, Lewis G., jt. auth. see Pedigo, Virginia G.

***Pedigo, Patricia & DeSanti, Roger.** Math & Test Taking Grade 4. (Kelley Wingate Ser.). 128p. (J). (gr. 4). 2000. pap. 10.95 (*0-88724-535-8*, CD-3754) Carson-Dellos.

— Math & Test Taking Grade 1. (Kelley Wingate Ser.). 128p. (J). (gr. 1). 2000. pap. 10.95 (*0-88724-532-3*, CD-3751) Carson-Dellos.

— Math & Test Taking Grade 3. (Kelley Wingate Ser.). 128p. (J). (gr. 3). 2000. pap. 10.95 (*0-88724-534-X*, CD-3753) Carson-Dellos.

— Math & Test Taking Grade 2. (Kelley Wingate Ser.). 128p. (J). (gr. 2). 2000. pap. 10.95 (*0-88724-533-1*, CD-3752) Carson-Dellos.

— Phonics Basics. (Kelley Wingate Ser.). (Illus.). 131p. (J). (gr. 1-3). 1996. pap. text 10.95 (*0-88724-444-0*, CD-3726) Carson-Dellos.

— Phonics Fun. (Kelley Wingate Ser.). (Illus.). 128p. (J). (gr. 2-3). 1996. pap. text 10.95 (*0-88724-443-2*, CD-3725) Carson-Dellos.

— Reading Comprehension Test Taking Skills Grade 1. (Kelley Wingate Ser.). (Illus.). viii, 130p. (J). (gr. 1). 1998. pap. text 10.95 (*0-88724-474-2*, CD-3733) Carson-Dellos.

— Reading Comprehension Test Taking Skills Grade 2. (Kelley Wingate Ser.). (Illus.). viii, 130p. (J). (gr. 2). 1998. pap. text 10.95 (*0-88724-475-0*, CD-3734) Carson-Dellos.

— Reading Comprehension Test Taking Skills Grade 3. (Kelley Wingate Ser.). (Illus.). viii, 130p. (J). (gr. 3). 1998. pap. text 10.95 (*0-88724-476-9*, CD-3735) Carson-Dellos.

— Reading Comprehension Test Taking Skills Grade 4. (Kelley Wingate Ser.). (Illus.). viii, 130p. (J). (gr. 4). 1998. pap. text 10.95 (*0-88724-477-7*, CD-3736) Carson-Dellos.

— Reading Comprehension Test Taking Skills Grade 5. (Kelley Wingate Ser.). (Illus.). viii, 110p. (J). (gr. 5). 1998. pap. text 10.95 (*0-88724-478-5*, CD-3737) Carson-Dellos.

— Reading Comprehension Test Taking Skills Grade 6. (Kelley Wingate Ser.). (Illus.). viii, 110p. (J). (gr. 6). 1998. pap. text 10.95 (*0-88724-479-3*, CD-3738) Carson-Dellos.

— Reading Comprehension Test Taking Skills Grade 7. (Kelley Wingate Ser.). (Illus.). viii, 110p. (YA). (gr. 7). 1998. pap. text 10.95 (*0-88724-480-7*, CD-3739) Carson-Dellos.

— Reading Comprehension Test Taking Skills Grade 8. (Kelley Wingate Ser.). (Illus.). viii, 110p. (YA). (gr. 8). 1998. pap. text 10.95 (*0-88724-481-5*, CD-3740) Carson-Dellos.

Pedigo, Patricia, ed. see Drumm, Susan T.

Pedigo, Patricia, ed. see Jacobi, Dawn T.

Pedigo, Patricia, ed. see Notarianni, Barbara.

Pedigo, Patricia, ed. see Roberson, Rae Anne.

Pedigo, Virginia G. & Pedigo, Lewis G. History of Patrick & Henry Counties, Virginia. LC 76-53104. (Illus.). 400p. 1990. reprint ed. 27.00 (*0-8063-8010-1*) Clearfield Co.

Peditto, C. Natale, ed. see Bivins, Charles.

Peditto, C. Natale, ed. see Priestley, Eric.

Peditto, Paul. 1,001 Afternoons in Chicago. 94p. 1998. pap. 5.60 (*0-87129-836-8*, 060) Dramatic Pub.

Pedlar, Alison, et al. A Textured Life: Empowerment & Adults with Developmental Disabilities. xi, 104p. 1999. pap. 24.95 (*0-88920-335-0*) W Laurier U Pr.

Pedlar, Dorothy. Divorce Guide for Manitoba: Step-by-Step Guide to Obtaining Your Own Divorce. 2nd ed. (Legal Ser.). 120p. (Orig.). 1991. pap. 14.95 (*0-88908-516-1*) Self-Counsel Pr.

Pedlar, Neil. The Imported Pioneers: Westerners Who Helped Build Modern Japan. (Illus.). 248p. (C). 1996. text 42.00 (*0-904404-51-X*, Pub. by Curzon Pr Ltd) UH Pr.

Pedler, Margaret. The Hermit of Far End. 1976. lib. bdg. 15.75 (*0-89968-216-2*, Lghtyr Pr) Buccaneer Bks.

— The Lamp of Fate. 1976. lib. bdg. 15.25 (*0-89968-217-0*, Lghtyr Pr) Buccaneer Bks.

— Splendid Family. 14.95 (*0-8488-1444-4*) Amereon Ltd.

— The Splendid Folly. 1976. lib. bdg. 13.75 (*0-89968-218-9*, Lghtyr Pr) Buccaneer Bks.

Pedler, Melvin. Concise Guide to the Learning Organization, 1. 1998. pap. text 17.95 (*1-898001-43-X*) Lemos & Crane.

Pedler, Mike. Action Learning in Practice. 3rd enl. ed. LC 97-20724. 403p. 1997. text 96.95 (*0-566-07795-7*, Pub. by Arena) Ashgate Pub Co.

Pedler, Mike, et al, eds. Towards the Learning Company: Concepts & Practices. LC 94-103167. 1994. write for info. (*0-07-707802-0*) McGraw.

Pedler, Mike & Aspinwall, Kath. Perfect Pic? The Purpose & Practice of Organizational Learning. LC 95-24732. (Developing Organizations Ser.). 1995. write for info. (*0-07-709130-2*) McGraw.

Pedler, Robin & VanSchendelen, M., eds. Lobbying in the European Union: Companies, Trade Associations & Issue Groups. 328p. 1994. 77.95 (*1-85521-609-4*) Ashgate Pub Co.

Pedley. Recent Advances in Epilepsy. 6th ed. 1995. text 78.00 (*0-443-05125-9*, W B Saunders Co) Harcrt Hlth Sci Grp.

Pedley, A. J. The Manuscript Collections of the Maryland Historical Society. LC 68-23074. 1968. 20.00 (*0-938420-08-9*) MD Hist.

Pedley, Carolyn F., et al. Mnemonics Rhetoric & Poetics for Medics, Vol. II. (Illus.). 175p. (Orig.). 1984. pap. 10.95 (*0-9612242-3-1*) Harbinger Med Pr NC.

Pedley, Carolyn F., jt. auth. see Bloomfield, Robert L.

***Pedley, David E. & Pedley, Mark L.** The Melchizedek Bible. unabridged ed. 589p. 1999. reprint ed. pap. 24.95 (*1-893107-29-9*, Pub. by Healing Unltd) Assoc Pubs Grp.

Pedley, Evan David, jt. auth. see Vinedresser, Branch.

Pedley, John G. Ancient Literary Sources on Sardis. LC 72-172327. (Archaeological Exploration of Sardis Monograph: No. 2). 108p. 1972. 25.50 (*0-674-03375-2*) HUP.

— Greek Art & Archaeology. 2nd ed. LC 97-6881. (Illus.). 384p. 1997. 55.00 (*0-8109-3398-5*, Pub. by Abrams) Time Warner.

— Greek Art & Archaeology. 2nd ed. (Illus.). 384p. (C). 1997. pap. text 59.33 (*0-13-874520-X*) P-H.

— Paestum: Greeks & Romans in Southern Italy. LC 89-51868. (New Aspects of Antiquity Ser.). (Illus.). 184p. 1990. 35.00 (*0-500-39027-4*, Pub. by Thames Hudson) Norton.

— Sardis in the Age of Croesus. LC 67-64447. (Centers of Civilization Ser.). 155p. reprint ed. pap. 48.10 (*0-608-13516-X*, 20162470002) Bks Demand.

***Pedley, John Griffiths.** Sardis in the Age of Croesus. (Centers of Civilization Ser). (Illus.). 76p. 2000. pap. text 13.95 (*0-8061-3248-5*) U of Okla Pr.

Pedley, Mark L., jt. auth. see Pedley, David E.

Pedley, T. J. The Fluid Mechanics of Large Blood Vessels. LC 78-73814. (Cambridge Monographs on Mechanics & Applied Mathematics). (Illus.). 464p. 1980. text 160.00 (*0-521-22626-0*) Cambridge U Pr.

Pedley, Timothy A., jt. auth. see Daly, David D.

Pedley, Timothy A., jt. auth. see Ebersole, John S.

Pedlosky, Joseph. Geophysical Fluid Dynamics: Springer Study Edition. 2nd ed. (Illus.). 710p. 1995. 54.95 (*0-387-96387-1*) Spr-Verlag.

— Ocean Circulation Theory. LC 96-13298. 1996. write for info. (*0-387-60489-8*); 89.95 (*3-540-60489-8*) Spr-Verlag.

***Pedlow, Gregory W.** The CIA & the U-2 Program, 1954-1974. 343p. 1999. per. 29.00 (*0-16-058823-5*) USGPO.

Pedlow, Gregory W. The Survival of the Hessian Nobility, 1770-1870. LC 87-25720. 318p. 1988. reprint ed. pap. 98.60 (*0-608-02915-7*, 206397900008) Bks Demand.

***Pedlow, Gregory W. & Welzenbach, Donald E.** The CIA & the U-2 Program, 1954-1974. (Illus.). 333p. (C). 1999. pap. text 50.00 (*0-7881-8326-5*) DIANE Pub.

Pedlow, J. C. Windows on the Holy Land. (Illus.). 150p. 1980. pap. 12.50 (*0-227-67839-7*) Attic Pr.

Pedneau, Dave. Dead Witness. 208p. 1987. pap. 2.95 (*0-380-75214-X*, Avon Bks) Morrow Avon.

Pedoe, Dan. Geometry. 464p. 1988. pap. 14.95 (*0-486-65812-0*) Dover.

Pedoe, Daniel. Circles: A Mathematical View. 2nd ed. LC 95-77405. (Spectrum Ser.). 144p. 1995. pap. text, suppl. ed. 18.95 (*0-88385-518-6*, CIRCLES) Math Assn.

— The Gentle Art of Mathematics. (Illus.). 143p. 1973. reprint ed. pap. 6.95 (*0-486-22949-1*) Dover.

— Geometry & the Visual Arts. (Illus.). 320p. 1983. reprint ed. pap. 8.95 (*0-486-24458-X*) Dover.

Pedoe, Daniel & Hodge, W. V. Methods of Algebraic Geometry, Vol. 2. (Cambridge Mathematical Library). (Illus.). 404p. (C). 1994. pap. text 27.95 (*0-521-46901-5*) Cambridge U Pr.

— Methods of Algebraic Geometry, Vol. 3. (Cambridge Mathematical Library). (Illus.). 346p. (C). 1994. pap. text 27.95 (*0-521-46775-6*) Cambridge U Pr.

Pedoe, Daniel & Sneddon, Ian N. Introduction to Projective Geometry. LC 62-22053. (International Series of Monographs on Pure & Applied Mathematics: Vol. 33). 1963. 101.00 (*0-08-009920-3*, Pub. by Pergamon Repr) Franklin.

Pedoe, Nadine T., et al, eds. Environmental Management at Airports: Liabilities & Social Responsibilities. 260p. 61.00 (*0-7277-2520-3*, Pub. by T Telford) RCH.

Pedolsky, Andrea, jt. auth. see Turock, Betty J.

Pedone, F. Stephen & Donlon, James I., eds. Roman Replies & CLSA Advisory Opinions, 1998. viii, 114p. pap. text 14.00 (*0-943616-82-4*) Canon Law Soc.

***Pedone, F. Stephen & Donlon, James I., eds.** Roman Replies & CLSA Advisory Opinions, 1999. 150p. 1999. pap. 14.00 (*0-943616-84-0*) Canon Law Soc.

Pedoto, Constance A. Painting Literature: Dostoevsky, Kafka, Pirandello, & Garcia Marquez in Living Color. 122p. (C). 1993. lib. bdg. 32.50 (*0-8191-9099-3*) U Pr of Amer.

Pedotti, Antonio, ed. Electrophysiological Kinesiology: Proceedings of ISEK Conference, Florence, Italy 28-6 - 2-7. LC 92-53264. (Studies in Health Technology & Informatics: Vol. 5). 438p. (gr. 12). 1992. 130.00 (*90-5199-095-2*, Pub. by IOS Pr) IOS Press.

Pedotti, Antonio & Zanchetti, Alberto. Blood Pressure & Heart Rate Variability: Computer Analysis, Methodology & Clinical Applications. LC 91-59040. (Studies in Health Technology & Informatics: Vol. 4). 293p. (gr. 12). 1993. 110.00 (*90-5199-077-4*, Pub. by IOS Pr) IOS Press.

Pedotti, Antonio, jt. ed. see Ferrarin, Maurizio.

Pedowitz, James M. Title Insurance, 1990: The Basics & Beyond. 633p. 1990. pap. 17.50 (*0-685-69506-9*) PLI.

Pedowitz, James M., ed. Real Estate Titles. 2nd ed. 65p. 1994. reprint ed. pap. text 25.00 (*0-942954-58-0*) NYS Bar.

Pedowitz, James M., ed. & pref. see New York State Bar Association Staff.

Pedraja, Luis G. Jesus Is My Uncle: Christology from a Hispanic Perspective. LC 99-10158. 1999. 15.00 (*0-687-05996-8*) Abingdon.

Pedraja, Rene de la, see De La Pedraja, Rene.

Pedram, Massoud, jt. auth. see Chang, Jui-Ming.

Pedram, Massoud, jt. auth. see Iman, Sasan.

Pedram, Massoud, jt. auth. see Rabaey, Jan M.

Pedras, Melvin J. The Experience of Teaching. 128p. (C). 1995. pap. text, spiral bd. 19.95 (*0-7872-1886-3*) Kendall-Hunt.

Pedraz, Martin A. Diccionario de la Exportacion. (SPA.). 928p. 1986. 150.00 (*0-7859-6212-3*, 8472991709) Fr & Eur.

— Diccionario Medieval Espanol, 2 vols. (SPA.). 784p. 1986. 150.00 (*0-7859-6213-1*, 8472991717) Fr & Eur.

— Diccionario Militar, Vol. 2. (SPA.). 1712p. 1986. 295.00 (*0-7859-6211-5*, 8472991695) Fr & Eur.

Pedraza, Jesus S., jt. auth. see Bernard, Harvey R.

Pedraza Jimenez, Felipe B. & Rodriguez Caceres, Milagros. Manual de Literatura Espanola, 12 vols. Cenlit Ediciones Staff, ed. (SPA., Illus.). 628.00 (*0-8485-1104-2*) Cenlit Ediciones.

— Manual de Literatura Hispanoamericana, Vols. 1-3. Cenlit Ediciones Staff, ed. (SPA.). 180.00 (*84-85511-26-3*) Cenlit Ediciones.

Pedraza, Jorge A. Estampillas de Colores. LC 85-82322. (SPA.). 94p. (Orig.). 1986. pap. 9.95 (*0-89729-386-X*) Ediciones.

Pedraza, Pedro, Jr. An Ethnographic Analysis of Language Use in the Puerto Rican Community of East Harlem. 65p. 1987. lib. bdg. 5.00 (*1-878483-44-7*) Hunter Coll CEP.

Pedraza, Silvia & Rumbaut, Ruben. Origins & Destinies: Immigration, Race & Ethnicity in America. 575p. (C). 1995. 48.95 (*0-534-21444-4*) Wadsworth Pub.

Pedrazas, Allan. Angel's Cove: A Harry Rice Mystery. (Worldwide Library Mysteries: No. 302). 1999. per. 4.99 (*0-373-26302-3*, 1-26302-9, Wrldwide Lib) Harlequin Bks.

— Angel's Cove: A Harry Rice Mystery. LC 97-14692. 272p. 1997. 21.95 (*0-312-16773-3*, Thomas Dunne) St Martin.

Pedrazzoli, S., jt. ed. see Obertop, H.

Pedregal, P. Parametrized Measures & Variational Principles. LC 97-16343. 1997. write for info. (*0-8176-5697-9*) Birkhauser.

Pedregal, Pablo. Parametrized Measures & Variational Principles. LC 97-16343. (Progress in Nonlinear Differential Equations & Their Applications Ser.). 1997. write for info. (*3-7643-5697-9*) Birkhauser.

***Pedregal, Pablo.** Variational Methods in Nonlinear Elasticity. LC 99-54264. (Miscellaneous Titles in Applied Mathematics Ser.: No. 70). 97p. 2000. pap. 32.00 (*0-89871-452-4*, OT0070) Soc Indus-Appl Math.

Pedregon, Cynthia C. Peach Tree Family Cookbook. LC 94-66692. 1994. 19.95 (*0-9627590-0-7*) Peach Tree & Tea.

— Peach Tree Tea Room. 1990. 19.95 (*0-9627590-7-4*) Peach Tree & Tea.

Pedreira, Antonio S. Bibliografia Puertorriquena, 2 vols. 1976. lib. bdg. 400.00 (*0-8490-1495-6*) Gordon Pr.

— Hostos, Citizen of America. (Puerto Rico Ser.). 1979. lib. bdg. 59.95 (*0-8490-2939-2*) Gordon Pr.

— Insularism. (Puerto Rico Ser.). 1979. lib. bdg. 59.95 (*0-8490-2949-X*) Gordon Pr.

Pedreira, Frank. Doctor's Prescription for Life: A Christian Perspective on Life's Most Challenging Decisions. LC 98-87119. 174p. 1999. pap. 17.95 (*1-58501-007-3*) CeShore Pubg.

Pedrero, Enrique G. Pais de un Solo Hombre (Land of One Man) Vol. 1: El Mexico de Santa Anna (Santa Anna's Mexico) (SPA., Illus.). 690p. 1993. 49.99 (*968-16-3962-6*, Pub. by Fondo) Continental Bk.

***Pedrero, J. I., et al.** Theoretical Model for Load Distribution on Cylindrical Gears: Application to Contact Stress Analysis. (Technical Papers: Vol. 99FTM15). 13p. 1999. pap. 30.00 (*1-55589-753-3*) AGMA.

Pedrero, Jose I., et al. On the Location of the Tooth Critical Section for the Determination of the AGMA J-Factor. (Technical Papers: Vol. 97FTM6). (Illus.). 7p. 1997. pap. text 30.00 (*1-55589-700-2*) AGMA.

Pedrero, Manuel, tr. see Mike Byrnes & Associates Staff.

Pedrero, Paloma. Parting Gestures: Three by Pedrero (El Color De Agosto, La Noche Dividida, Resguardo Personal) Halsey, Martha T., ed. Zatlin, Phyllis, tr. from SPA. LC 93-73773. xvi, 67p. 1994. pap. 6.00 (*0-9631212-5-1*) Estreno.

— Parting Gestures with a Night in the Subway. rev. exp. ed. Zatlin, Phyllis, tr. from SPA. LC 98-73219. (Contemporary Spanish Plays Ser.: Vol. 6). (Illus.). xiv, 60p. 1999. pap. 8.00 (*1-888463-06-6*) Estreno.

Pedreschi, Dino & Zaniolo, Carlo. Logic in Databases: International Workshop LID 96, San Miniato, Italy, July 1996: Proceedings. LC 96-41820. (Lecture Notes in Computer Science Ser.: Vol. 1154). 497p. 1996. text 81.00 (*3-540-61814-7*) Spr-Verlag.

Pedretti, Carlo. Leonardo Da Vinci: Nature Studies from the Royal Library at Windsor Castle. 1981. pap. 14.95 (*0-15-149848-2*) Harcourt.

— Leonardo da Vinci: The Royal Palace at Romorantin. LC 76-102673. 176p. 1972. 45.00 (*0-674-52455-1*) Belknap Pr.

Pedretti, Erica. Stones. Black, Judith, tr. from GER. (Swiss Library). 220p. (Orig.). 1982. pap. 9.95 (*0-7145-3942-2*) Riverrun NY.

Pedretti, Lorraine W. Occupational Therapy: Practice Skills for Physical Dysfunction. 4th ed. (Illus.). 384p. (gr. 13). 1995. pap. text, student ed. 20.95 (*0-8151-7214-1*, 27650) Mosby Inc.

Pedretti, Lorraine W., ed. Occupational Therapy: Practice Skills for Physical Dysfunction. 4th ed. (Illus.). 896p. (C). (gr. 13). 1995. text 64.00 (*0-8151-6812-8*, 25289) Mosby Inc.

Pedrick, Cherry, jt. auth. see Hyman, Bruce M.

Pedrick, Gale, ed. see Dunn, Henry T.

Pedrick, George. A First Course in Analysis. LC 93-5141. (Undergraduate Texts in Mathematics Ser.). (Illus.). 280p. (C). 1994. 47.95 (*0-387-94108-8*) Spr-Verlag.

Pedrick, Jean. Pride & Splendor. LC 75-23818. 72p. 1976. pap. 3.95 (*0-914086-10-3*) Alice James Bks.

— Wolf Moon. LC 73-94067. 72p. 1974. pap. 3.95 (*0-914086-03-0*) Alice James Bks.

Pedrick, Katharine F. Practical Mystic or How to Make Perfection Appear (1915) 224p. 1998. reprint ed. pap. 17.95 (*0-7661-0573-3*) Kessinger Pub.

Pedrini, Arnold. St. Francis de Sales: Don Bosco's Patron. Klauder, Francis J., ed. Cornell, Wallace L., tr.Tr. of San Francesco di Sales e Don Bosco. 149p. 1988. 13.95 (*0-89944-096-7*); pap. 8.95 (*0-89944-092-4*) Salesiana Pubs.

Pedrini, Arnold, jt. auth. see Archenti, Augustine.

Pedrini, Duilio T., jt. auth. see Pedrini, Lura.

Pedrini, Lura & Pedrini, Duilio T. Serpent Imagery & Symbolism. 1966. pap. 15.95 (*0-8084-0274-9*) NCUP.

Pedrizet, P. & Lefebvre, G., eds. Inscriptiones Graecae Aegypti No. 3: Abydos. xxvi, 125p. 1978. 30.00 (*0-89005-243-3*) Ares.

Pedro, IV. Chronicle. Hillgarth, Mary & Hillgarth, J. N., trs. from CAT. (Illus.). xviii, vi 1980p. pap. 46.29 (*0-88844-272-6*) Brill Academic Pubs.

Pedro, Anthony San, see Pasternak, Dov & San Pedro, Anthony, eds.

Pedro, Daniele C. Oro Plata: Embroidered Costumes of the Bullfight. LC 98-116084. (Illus.). 162p. 1997. 75.00 (*2-84323-035-7*, Pub. by Assouline) Rizzoli Intl.

Pedro Hernandez, Aquillino De, see De Pedro Hernandez, Aquillino.

***Pedro, J. O., ed.** Arch Dams: Designing & Monitoring for Safety. (CISM International Centre for Mechanical Sciences Ser.: Vol. 367). vi, 403p. 2000. pap. (*3-211-83149-5*) Spr-Verlag.

Pedro, M. Del, see Del Pedro, M.

Pedro, Michael J., jt. auth. see Tiernan, S. Gregory.

Pedro, Nunes. Pedro Nunes, 1502-1578: His Lost Algebra & Other Discoveries. Martyn, John R., ed. & tr. by. from GRE. (American University Studies: Series 9, Vol. 182). 158p. (C). 1996. text 35.95 (*0-8204-3060-9*) P Lang Pubng.

Pedro Silva Ruiz. Derecho Notarial: Casos y Materiales. 2nd rev. ed. LC 89-38006. 629p. (C). 1994. pap. text 27.00 (*0-8477-3032-8*) U of PR Pr.

Pedrocco, Filippo. Canaletto & Venetian Vedutisti. Evans, Christopher, tr. from ITA. LC 97-174095. (Library of Great Masters). (Illus.). 80p. (Orig.). 1995. pap. 12.99 (*1-878351-49-4*) Riverside NY.

— Canaletto y Los Vedutistas Venecianos. (Grandes Maestros del Arte Ser.). (SPA., Illus.). 80p. 1995. pap. 12.99 (*1-878351-50-8*) Riverside NY.

— Titian. Madocks, Susan, tr. from ITA. LC 98-132140. (Library of Great Masters). (Illus.). 80p. (Orig.). 1993. pap. 12.99 (*1-878351-14-1*) Riverside NY.

— Tiziano. (Grandes Maestros del Arte Ser.). (SPA., Illus.). 80p. 1995. pap. 12.99 (*1-878351-35-4*) Riverside NY.

***Pedrocco, Filippo & Nava, Simonetta.** Painting in Renaissance Italy. (Illus.). 312p. 2000. 60.00 (*0-8478-2255-9*, Pub. by Rizzoli Intl) St Martin.

Pedrocco, Filippo, jt. auth. see Pignatti, Terisio.

***Pedroli, Hubert.** Let the Big Dog Eat. LC 99-58054. (Illus.). 96p. 2000. 18.00 (*0-688-17576-7*, Hearst) Hearst Commns.

Pedrolo, Manuel De, see De Pedrolo, Manuel.

Pedroncini, Guy, ed. see Corvisier, Andre.

Pedroni, Peter N. The Anti-Naturalist Experience: Federigo Tozzi. (Explorations in the Humanities Ser.: Vol. 1). 93p. (C). 1989. 25.00 (*0-9624254-1-9*) DeSoto Pr Inc.

Pedroni, Peter N., tr. & intro. see Volponi, Paolo.

Pedrosa, Carmen N. The Rise & Fall of Imelda Marcos 3rd ed. LC 97-946873. 230p. 1988. write for info. (*971-13-4031-3*) C A Reitzel.

Pedrosa, Fbabio O., jt. auth. see International Congress on Nitrogen Fixation Staff.

Pedrosa, Gary L., tr. see Taylor, Eldon.

Pedrosa, Jose R. Memorias de un Desmemoriado: Lena Para el Fuego de la Historia de Cuba. LC 78-67007. (Coleccion Cuba y sus Jueces). 1979. 13.00 (*0-89729-207-3*) Ediciones.

Pedroso de Lima, Maria C., et al, eds. Trafficking of Intercellular Membranes: From Molecular Sorting to Membrane Fusion. LC 94-49441. (NATO ASI Series: Subseries H: Cell Biology: Vol. 91). 1995. 188.95 (*3-540-58915-5*) Spr-Verlag.

Pedroti, F., jt. ed. see Gehu, Jean-Marie.

Pedrotti, Frank L. & Pedrotti, Leno S. Introduction to Optics. 2nd ed. 672p. (C). 1992. 91.00 (*0-13-501545-6*) P-H.

Pedrotti, Frank L. & Pedrotti, Leon S. Optics & Vision. LC 97-26179. 395p. (C). 1997. 78.00 (*0-13-242223-9*) P-H.

Pedrotti, Leno S., jt. auth. see Pedrotti, Frank L.

Pedrotti, Leon S., jt. auth. see Pedrotti, Frank L.

Pedrotti, Louis. Jozef-Julian Sekowski: The Genesis of a Literary Alien. LC 65-63974. (U. C. Publ. in Modern Philology Ser.: Vol. 73). 233p. reprint ed. pap. 72.30 (*0-8357-9630-2*, 201379800087) Bks Demand.

Pedrotti, Louis, tr. see Senkovskii, Osip I.

Pedrycz, W. & Peters, J. F. Computational Intelligence in Software Engineering. (Advances in Fuzzy Systems Ser.: Vol. 16). 400p. 1998. 68.00 (*981-02-3503-8*) World Scientific Pub.

Pedrycz, Witold. Computational Intelligence. 1998. ring bd. write for info. (*0-8493-0577-2*) CRC Pr.

— Computational Intelligence: An Introduction. LC 97-26964. 304p. 1997. boxed set 74.95 (*0-8493-2643-5*) CRC Pr.

— Fuzzy Evolutionary Computation. LC 97-15286. 1997. text 145.00 (*0-7923-9942-0*) Kluwer Academic.

Pedrycz, Witold, ed. Fuzzy Modelling: Paradigms & Practices. LC 96-1147. (International Intelligent Technologies Ser.: No. 7). 416p. (C). 1996. text 151.50 (*0-7923-9703-7*) Kluwer Academic.

Pedrycz, Witold & Gomide, Fernando. An Introduction to Fuzzy Sets: Analysis & Design. LC 97-34598. (Complex Adaptive Systems Ser.). (Illus.). 475p. 1998. 60.00 (*0-262-16171-0*, Bradford Bks) MIT Pr.

***Pedrycz, Witold & Vasilakos, Athanasios.** Computational Intelligence in Telecommunications Networks. LC 00-30342. 2000. pap. write for info. (*0-8493-1075-X*) CRC Pr.

Pedrycz, Witold & Zadeh, Lofti A. Fuzzy Sets Engineering. LC 94-22949. 352p. 1995. boxed set 89.95 (*0-8493-9402-3*) CRC Pr.

Pedrycz, Witold, jt. auth. see Peters, James F.

Pedrys, R., jt. auth. see Szymonski, M.

Pedulla, Albert. Creating Architectural Working Drawings. 300p. (C). 2001. pap. 51.33 (*0-13-716333-9*, Macmillan Coll) P-H.

***Peduzzi, Kelli.** Clip It: A Paper Clip Jewelry Workshop. LC 00-21294. (Illus.). 2000. write for info. (*1-58485-040-X*) Pleasant Co.

Peduzzi, Kelli. Shaping a President: Sculpting the Roosevelt Memorial. 1997. pap. text 6.95 (*0-7613-0325-1*) Millbrook Pr.

— Shaping a President: Sculpting the Roosevelt Memorial. LC 97-7331. (Illus.). 48p. (J). (gr. 3-6). 1997. lib. bdg. 22.40 (*0-7613-0207-7*) Millbrook Pr.

Peduzzi, Kelli, ed. The Katalan Collection of Italian Drawings. (Illus.). 142p. (Orig.). 1995. pap. 30.00 (*0-9644263-1-5*) F L Loeb Art Ctr.

Peduzzi, Kelli, ed. see Frances Lehman Loeb Art Center Staff.

Pedziwiatr, A. T. Twenty-Fifth Zakopane School on Physics: Proceedings, 2 vols., 1. Stanek, J., ed. 852p. (C). 1990. text. write for info. (*981-02-0340-3*) World Scientific Pub.

— Twenty-Fifth Zakopane School on Physics: Proceedings, 2 vols., Set. Stanek, J., ed. 852p. (C). 1990. text 189.00 (*981-02-0339-X*) World Scientific Pub.

Peeaver, Richard, tr. see Bychkov, Victor.

Peebles Burch, Sharon. Collective Absolute Presuppostions: Tectonic Plates for Churches. LC 93-37634. (American University Studies, VII Ser.: Vol. 164). 129p. (C). 1999. 34.95 (*0-8204-2258-4*) P Lang Pubng.

Peebles, Catherine & Edge, Denzil. A Natural Curiosity: Taffy's Search for Self. LC 87-36882. (Illus.). (Orig.). (J). 1988. pap. 6.95 (*0-939991-01-2*) Learning KY.

Peebles, Christopher, jt. ed. see Gardin, Jean-Claude.

Peebles, Christopher S., ed. see Gardin, Jean-Claude.

***Peebles, Curtis.** Asteroids: A History. LC 00-20733. (Illus.). 2000. 29.95 (*1-56098-389-2*) Smithsonian.

Peebles, Curtis. Dark Eagles: A History of Top Secret U. S. Aircraft. rev. ed. (Illus.). 368p. 1999. pap. 19.95 (*0-89141-696-X*) Presidio Pr.

— High Frontier: The United States Air Force & the Military Space Program. (Illus.). 80p. (C). 1998. pap. text 25.00 (*0-7881-4800-1*) DIANE Pub.

— High Frontier: The United States Air Force & the Military Space Program. LC 97-121560. 82p. 1997. pap. 7.50 (*0-16-048945-8*) USGPO.

***Peebles, Curtis.** Shadow Flights: America's Secret War Against the Soviet Union: A Cold War History. (Illus.). 368p. 2000. 27.95 (*0-89141-700-1*) Presidio Pr.

Peebles, Curtis. Watch the Skies! A Chronicle of the Flying Saucer Myth. 432p. (Orig.). 1995. mass mkt. 6.99 (*0-425-15117-4*) Berkley Pub.

— Watch the Skies! A Chronicle of the Flying Saucer Myth. LC 93-26819. 368p. (Orig.). 1994. 26.95 (*1-56098-343-4*) Smithsonian.

Peebles, Curtis, jt. auth. see Thompson, Milton O.

Peebles, Curtis L. The Corona Project: America's First Spy Satellites. LC 97-12272. (Illus.). 351p. 1997. 36.95 (*1-55750-688-4*) Naval Inst Pr.

Peebles, David. Study Guide for Introductory Genetics. 2nd ed. 324p. (C). 1997. spiral bd. 42.95 (*0-7872-3669-1*, 41366901) Kendall-Hunt.

Peebles, Dorothy. Harvest of Gold. LC 72-92720. 96p. 1973. 9.50 (*0-8378-1760-9*) Gibson.

Peebles, Douglas. Landmark Hawaii: Favorite Postcard Views of the Islands. 112p. 1989. pap. 11.95 (*0-935180-81-8*) Mutual Pub HI.

— Viewbook: Island of Hawaii. (Illus.). 32p. (Orig.). 1991. pap. 6.95 (*0-9627294-6-9*) Hawaiian Resources.

— Viewbook Hawaii's Volcanos. (Illus.). 32p. (Orig.). 1994. pap. 6.95 (*0-9627294-9-3*) Hawaiian Resources.

— Viewbook Kauai. (Illus.). 32p. (Orig.). 1991. pap. 6.95 (*0-9627294-5-0*) Hawaiian Resources.

— Viewbook Maui. (Illus.). 32p. 1988. pap. 6.95 (*0-9627294-7-7*) Hawaiian Resources.

— Viewbook Oahu. (Illus.). 32p. (Orig.). 1989. pap. 6.95 (*0-9627294-8-5*) Hawaiian Resources.

Peebles, Douglas, photos by. Capturing Hawai'i Birds Eye View. (Capturing Hawai'i Ser.). (Illus.). 32p. pap. 7.95 (*1-56647-212-1*) Mutual Pub HI.

— Capturing Hawai'i Flowers. (Capturing Hawai'i Ser.). (Illus.). 32p. 1998. pap. 7.95 (*1-56647-215-6*) Mutual Pub HI.

— From the Skies of Paradise Kauai. (Illus.). 112p. 1992. 25.95 (*0-935180-51-6*) Mutual Pub HI.

— From the Skies of Paradise Maui. (Illus.). 112p. 1991. 25.95 (*0-935180-74-5*) Mutual Pub HI.

***Peebles, Douglas, photos by.** Hawaii. (Illus.). 144p. 1999. 29.95 (*1-56647-279-2*) Mutual Pub HI.

Peebles, Douglas, photos by. Hawaii: A Floral Paradise (Illus.). 64p. 1995. pap. 9.95 (*1-56647-071-4*) Mutual Pub HI.

Peebles, Evelyn R., ed. see Peebles, Joseph.

Peebles, Evelyn Rice, ed. see Peebles, Joseph.

Peebles, G. & Wilson, P. The Singapore Economy. 304p. 1996. pap. 30.00 (*1-85898-389-4*) E Elgar.

Peebles, Gavin. Hong Kong's Economy: An Introductory Macroeconomic Analysis. (Illus.). 288p. 1988. pap. 14.95 (*0-19-584227-8*) OUP.

— Money in the People's Republic of China: A Comparative Perspective. 1992. text 45.00 (*1-86373-033-8*, Pub. by Allen & Unwin Pty) Paul & Co Pubs.

— A Short History of Socialist Money. 192p. 1992. text 34.95 (*1-86373-113-X*, Pub. by Allen & Unwin Pty); pap. text 19.95 (*1-86373-071-0*, Pub. by Allen & Unwin Pty) Paul & Co Pubs.

Peebles, Gavin & Wilson, Peter. The Singapore Economy. LC 95-36676. (Illus.). 304p. 1996. 100.00 (*1-85898-286-3*) E Elgar.

***Peebles, Hugh B.** Warship Building on the Clyde. 2000. reprint ed. pap. 19.95 (*0-85976-530-X*, Pub. by J Donald) Dufour.

Peebles, J. M. The General Principles & the Standard Teachings of Spiritualism. 29p. 1996. reprint ed. spiral bd. 10.00 (*0-7873-0664-9*) Hlth Research.

— What Is Spiritualism, Who Are These Spiritualists, & What Has Spiritualism Done for the World? 131p. 1996. reprint ed. spiral bd. 14.00 (*0-7873-0663-0*) Hlth Research.

— Who Are These Spiritualists? 129p. 1972. reprint ed. spiral bd. 9.00 (*0-7873-1080-8*) Hlth Research.

Peebles, Jane. The Handbook of International Philanthropy. LC 98-9485. 138p. 1998. 49.00 (*1-56625-096-X*) Bonus Books.

Peebles, Joseph. The Adventures of New Jack Swing, Vol. 1. Peebles, Evelyn R., ed. LC 96-82017. 260p. 1996. pap. 19.95 (*0-9644758-2-0*) Peebco Pub.

***Peebles, Joseph.** Hannibal: The Ultimate Warrior. 2000. pap. 10.95 (*1-930097-09-3*) Lushena Bks.

Peebles, Joseph. Hannibal: The Ultimate Warrior: The Untold Story. LC 94-93928. (Illus.). 110p. 1994. 19.95 (*0-9644758-0-4*) Peebco Pub.

***Peebles, Joseph.** Tuscaloosa. large type ed. Peebles, Evelyn Rice, ed. 166p. 2000. pap. 10.95 (*0-9644758-3-9*) Peebco Pub.

Peebles, Kelly, photos by see Bizar, Jodi.

Peebles, L. H., Jr. Carbon Fibers: Information, Structure, & Properties. LC 94-7765. 224p. 1994. boxed set 115.95 (*0-8493-2450-5*) CRC Pr.

Peebles, Mario Van, see Van Peebles, Mario.

Peebles, Marvin L. Directory of Consultants & Management Training Programs Intended for Local Non-Profit Groups, 1985. 100p. 1985. ring bd. 20.00 (*0-939020-27-0*) MLP Ent.

— Directory of Management Resources for Community Based Organizations. 6th ed. 125p. 1987. ring bd. 20.00 (*0-939020-06-8*) MLP Ent.

— Own Worst Enemies: Local Charity Unmasked. 300p. 1984. ring bd. 32.50 (*0-939020-50-5*) MLP Ent.

Peebles, Melvin Van, see Van Peebles, Melvin.

Peebles, P. J. Principles of Physical Cosmology. LC 92-33370. (Physics Ser.). 736p. (C). 1993. text 79.50 (*0-691-07428-3*, Pub. by Princeton U Pr); pap. text 35.00 (*0-691-01933-9*, Pub. by Princeton U Pr) Cal Prin Full Svc.

— Quantum Mechanics. 408p. 1992. text 45.00 (*0-691-08755-5*, Pub. by Princeton U Pr) Cal Prin Full Svc.

Peebles, P. J., jt. ed. see Abell, George O.

Peebles, Patrick. Social Change in 19th Century Ceylon. (C). 1995. 30.00 (*81-7013-141-3*, Pub. by Navarang) S Asia.

Peebles, Paul. Oh, My Gosh, We're Pregnant. unabridged ed. LC 97-92729. (Parent's Survival Kit Ser.: Bk. 1). (Illus.). v, 92p. 1998. pap. 16.95 (*0-9660853-0-2*) Pediatric Care.

Peebles, Peyton Z. Probability, Random Variables, & Random Signal Principles. 3rd ed. 424p. (C). 1993. 87.81 (*0-07-049273-5*) McGraw.

***Peebles, Peyton Z.** Probability, Random Variables & Random Signal Principles. 4th ed. LC 00-34881. (Series in Electrical & Computer Engineering). 448p. 2000. 85.63 (*0-07-366007-8*) McGraw.

Peebles, Peyton Z., Jr. Radar Principles. LC 97-39470. 794p. 1998. 125.00 (*0-471-25205-0*) Wiley.

Peebles, Peyton Z., Jr. & Giuma, Tayeb A. Principles of Electrical Engineering. (C). 1991. text 64.50 (*0-07-049252-2*) McGraw.

Peebles, Robert W. Leonard Covello: A Study of an Immigrants Contribution to New York City. Cordasco, Francesco, ed. LC 77-90551. (Bilingual-Bicultural Education in the U. S. Ser.). 1978. lib. bdg. 41.95 (*0-405-11090-1*) Ayer.

Peed, Joseph W., ed. see Citation Directories, Ltd., Inc. Staff.

Peed, Joseph W., ed. see Citation Directories, Ltd. Inc. Staff.

Peedle, Ian. Belize in Focus. LC 99-18563. 1999. pap. 12.95 (*1-56656-284-8*) Interlink Pub.

Peek. This Is San Quentin. (Illus.). 50p. (Orig.). 1991. pap. 3.95 (*0-9630115-0-2*) San Quentin Mus.

Peek, Andrea, compiled by. ASTC Salary Survey, 1993. 68p. 1993. 125.00 (*0-944040-33-0*) AST Ctrs.

Peek, Charles A. Catch-22 Notes. (Cliffs Notes Ser.). 48p. 1976. pap. 4.95 (*0-8220-0296-5*, Cliff) IDG Bks.

Peek, Charles A., jt. ed. see Hamblin, Robert W.

Peek, Chester L. The First Cub. (Illus.). 90p. 1996. pap. 17.95 (*1-886196-02-8*) Three Peaks.

— Resurrection of a Jenny. (Illus.). 120p. (Orig.). 1994. pap., per. 19.95 (*1-886196-00-1*) Three Peaks.

Peek, Chet. The Taylorcraft Story. (Illus.). 220p. 1993. pap. text 24.95 (*0-943691-08-7*) Aviation Heritage.

— The Taylorcraft Story. (Illus.). 236p. 1995. pap. 24.95 (*1-886196-01-X*) Three Peaks.

Peek, Fran. The Real Rain Man. Anderson, Stevens, ed. Date not set. pap. 11.95 (*0-9651163-0-1*) Harkness Pubng.

Peek, Francis. The Real Rainman: Kim Peek. Anderson, Stevens W., ed. (Illus.). 180p. (Orig.). 1996. pap. 12.00 (*0-614-14631-3*) Harkness Publishing Co.

Peek, Glenna. ACT! 2.0 for Windows at a Glance. (At a Glance Ser.). 112p. (Orig.). 1995. pap. 15.95 (*1-55622-450-8*) Wordware Pub.

Peek, Jeannette M. Stepping into Time. 128p. 1994. boxed set 19.95 (*1-56647-024-2*) Mutual Pub HI.

— Stepping into Time: A Guide to Honolulu's Historic Landmarks. 144p. 1994. pap. 19.95 (*1-56647-052-8*) Mutual Pub HI.

Peek, Jerry. MH & XMH: E-Mail for Users & Programmers. 3rd ed. O'Reilly, Tim & Willison, Frank, eds. (Illus.). 750p. (Orig.). 1995. pap. 34.95 (*1-56592-093-7*) Thomson Learn.

P

— UNIX Power Tools. 2nd ed. LC 97-209552. 1120p. 1997. pap. write for info. (1-56592-260-3) Thomson Learn.

Peek, Jerry, et al. Learning the UNIX Operating System. 4th ed. Estabrook, Gigi, ed. (Illus.). 92p. 1997. reprint ed. pap. 12.95 (1-56592-390-1) OReilly & Assocs.

Peek, Jerry, jt. auth. see Lamb, Linda.

Peek, Merle. Mary Wore Her Red Dress. (Carry-Along Book & Cassette Favorites Ser.). (Illus.). 1p. (J). (ps-1). 1993. bds. 9.95 incl. audio (0-395-61577-1, Clarion Bks) HM.

— Mary Wore Her Red Dress & Henry Wore His Green Sneakers. LC 84-12733. 32p. (J). (ps-3). 1988. pap. 5.95 (0-89919-701-9, Clarion Bks) HM.

— Mary Wore Her Red Dress & Henry Wore His Green Sneakers. LC 84-12733. (Illus.). 22p. (ps). 1998. bds. 5.95 (0-395-90022-0, Clarion Bks) HM.

— Roll Over! A Counting Song, 001. (Illus.). 32p. (J). (ps-2). 1981. 15.00 (0-395-29438-X, Clarion Bks) HM.

***Peek, Merle.** Roll Over! A Counting Song. (Illus.). (J). (ps-3). 1999. pap. 9.95 incl. audio (0-395-95754-0) HM.

— Roll Over! A Counting Song. (Illus.). 24p. (J). (ps-k). 1999. 5.95 (0-395-98037-2, Clarion Bks) HM.

Peek, Merle. Roll Over! A Counting Song. (Illus.). 32p. (J). (ps). 1991. reprint ed. pap. 5.95 (0-395-58105-2, Clarion Bks) HM.

Peek, Merle. Roll Over! A Counting Song. (Carry-Along Book & Cassette Favorites Ser.). (Illus.). 32p. (J). (ps). 1991. reprint ed. pap. 9.95 incl. audio (0-395-60117-7, 111276, Clarion Bks) HM.

— Three Little Kittens. (Illus.). (J). (ps-3). 1999. pap. 9.95 incl. audio (0-395-89901-X) HM.

Peek, P. Cary. One Winter in the Wilderness. LC 97-26236. (Illus.). 224p. 1998. 24.95 (0-89301-210-6) U of Idaho Pr.

Peek, Philip M., ed. African Divination Systems: Ways of Knowing. LC 90-39421. (African Systems of Thought Ser.). (Illus.). 240p. 1991. 39.95 (0-253-34309-7); pap. 16.95 (0-253-20653-7, MB-653) Ind U Pr.

***Peek, Robin P. & Newby, Gregory B.** Scholarly Publishing: The Electronic Frontier. (Illus.). 365p. 2000. pap. 39.95 (0-262-66168-3) MIT Pr.

Peek, Werner. Greek Verse Inscriptions. (GER & GRE.). 740p. (Orig.). 1988. reprint ed. pap. 50.00 (0-89005-479-7) Ares.

Peeke, Graham. Mission & Change: Institutional Mission & Its Application to the Management of Further & Higher Education. LC 94-19796. 146p. 1994. pap. 39.95 (0-335-19338-2) OpUniv Pr.

— Mission & Change: Institutional Mission & Its Application to the Management of Further & Higher Education. LC 94-19796. 160p. 1994. 122.00 (0-335-19337-4) Taylor & Francis.

Peeke, Margaret B. Born of a Flame (1892) 300p. 1996. reprint ed. pap. 24.95 (1-56459-836-5) Kessinger Pub.

— Born of Flame: A Rosicrucian Story. 299p. 1971. reprint ed. spiral bd. 18.50 (0-7873-1139-1) Hlth Research.

— Numbers & Letters: or The Thirty-Two Paths of Wisdom. 191p. 1986. reprint ed. pap. 21.00 (0-7873-0666-5) Hlth Research.

— Numbers & Letters: or The Thirty-Two Paths of Wisdom, 1908. 215p. 1996. reprint ed. pap. 17.95 (1-56459-816-0) Kessinger Pub.

— Zenia, the Vestal: The Problem of Vibrations. 355p. 1965. reprint ed. spiral bd. 23.00 (0-7873-0665-7) Hlth Research.

***Peeke, Pamela.** Fight Fat after Forty: The Revolutionary Three-pronged Approach That Will Break Your Stress-fat Cycle & Make You Healthy, Fit, & Trim for Life. LC 99-54167. (Illus.). 352p. 2000. 24.95 (0-670-88919-9) Viking Penguin.

Peekel, Gerhard. Grammatik der Neu-Mecklenburgischen Sprache, Speziell der Pala-Sprache. LC 75-35147. reprint ed. 35.00 (0-404-14163-3) AMS Pr.

Peel. Descubra Su Destino.Tr. of Discover Your Destiny. (SPA.). 1997. 10.99 (0-88113-490-2, B031-4902) Caribe Betania.

Peel, Bill C. What God Does When Men Pray. 96p. (Orig.). 1993. pap. 6.00 (0-89109-729-5) NavPress.

Peel, Billy & Peel, Kathy. Donde Esta Moises Cuando Mas lo Necesitamos.Tr. of Where Is Moses When We Need Him?. (SPA.). 1997. pap. text 12.99 (0-311-46147-6) Casa Bautista.

***Peel Board of Education Teachers Staff & Corney, Bob.** Mathematics, Science & Technology Connections. 148p. (YA). (gr. 6-9). 2000. pap., teacher ed. 31.95 (1-895579-37-6, Pub. by Trifolium Inc) ACCESS Pubs Network.

Peel, Bruce, compiled by. Bibliography of the Prairie Provinces to Nineteen Fifty Three: With Biographical Index. 2nd ed. LC 72-97930. 1973. text 85.00 (0-8020-1972-2) U of Toronto Pr.

Peel, Colin D. Blood of Your Sisters. LC 96-48768. 1997. 20.95 (0-312-15065-2, Thomas Dunne) St Martin.

— Blood of Your Sisters. large type ed. (Ulverscroft Large Print Ser.). 400p. 1997. 27.99 (0-7089-3867-1) Ulverscroft.

***Peel, Colin D.** Cherry Red & Dangerous. large type ed. 400p. 1999. 31.99 (0-7089-4103-6, Linford) Ulverscroft.

Peel, Colin D. Flameout. large type ed. (Linford Mystery Library). 384p. 1995. pap. 16.99 (0-7089-7658-1, Linford) Ulverscroft.

Peel, Don. The Phoenix Solutions. 256p. 1990. per. write for info. (0-8187-0131-5) Harlo Press.

Peel, Dorothy. The Eat-Less-Meat Book. 220p. 1973. 250.00 (0-87968-071-7) Gordon Pr.

Peel, Edith, ed. see Wharton, Edith.

Peel, Edward. Cream School from Sixteen Forty-Five. (C). 1988. 40.00 (0-904110-02-8, Pub. by Thornhill Pr) St Mut.

Peel, Fred W., et al. Consolidated Tax Returns: A Treatise on the Law of Consolidated Federal Income Tax Returns, 2 vols., Set. 3rd ed. LC 84-23688. 1990. 245.00 (0-317-14545-2) West Group.

Peel, Fred W., Jr., jt. auth. see Oliver, Philip D.

Peel, J. D. Herbert Spencer. (Modern Revivals in Sociology Ser.). 352p. 1993. 61.95 (0-7512-0094-8, Pub. by Gregg Pub) Ashgate Pub Co.

Peel, J. D., jt. ed. see Adeajayi, J. F.

Peel, J. D., ed. see Spencer, Herbert.

***Peel, J. D. Y.** Religious Encounter & the Making of the Yoruba. LC 00-37031. (African Systems of Thought Ser.). 2000. write for info. (0-253-33794-1) Ind U Pr.

Peel, John. The Addams Family Programme Guide. 304p. (Orig.). 1996. mass mkt. 5.95 (0-86369-837-9, Pub. by Virgin Bks) London Brdge.

Peel, John. Alien Invasion from Hollyweird. (Outer Limits Ser.: No. 10). 128p. pap. text 3.99 (0-8125-7567-9) Tor Bks.

Peel, John. Avengers: Too Many Targets. 1998. mass mkt. 5.99 (0-8125-8909-2, Pub. by Tor Bks) St Martin.

***Peel, John.** Betrayal (2099, 2), Vol. 2. 1999. mass mkt. 4.99 (0-439-06031-1) Scholastic Inc.

Peel, John. Beware the Metal Children, 9. 128p. 1999. mass mkt. 3.99 (0-8125-7566-0, Pub. by Tor Bks) St Martin.

— Book of Earth. (Diadem Ser.: Vol. 5). (gr. 4-7). 1998. pap. text 3.99 (0-590-14965-2) Scholastic Inc.

***Peel, John.** Book of Earth, 5. (Diadem Ser.). (J). 1998. 9.09 (0-606-12913-8, Pub. by Turtleback) Demco.

Peel, John. Book of Nightmares. (Diadem Ser.: No. 6). (J). 1998. pap. 3.99 (0-590-14966-0, Apple Paperbacks) Scholastic Inc.

***Peel, John.** Book of Nightmares. (Diadem Ser.). 1998. 9.09 (0-606-13329-1, Pub. by Turtleback) Demco.

Peel, John. Book 1: Doomsday. (2099 Ser.: Bk. 1). 192p. (J). (gr. 4-7). 1999. pap. 4.99 (0-439-06030-3, Pub. by Scholastic Inc) Penguin Putnam.

Peel, John. Bureau of Lost. (Eerie Indiana Ser.: No. 2). (J). (gr. 3-7). 1997. mass mkt. 3.99 (0-380-79775-5, Avon Bks) Morrow Avon.

Peel, John. Bureau of Lost. (Eerie Indiana Ser.: No. 2). (J). (gr. 3-7). 1997. 9.09 (0-606-12687-2, Pub. by Turtleback) Demco.

— Change: Outer Limits, Vol.12. 128p. 1999. pap. text 3.99 (0-8125-7569-5, Pub. by Tor Bks) St Martin.

— Choice. (Outer Limits Ser.). 1997. 9.09 (0-606-13686-X, Pub. by Turtleback) Demco.

— Dances with Werewolves. (Tombstones Ser.). 1995. 9.09 (0-606-08647-1, Pub. by Turtleback) Demco.

— Death of Princes. (Star Trek Next Generation Ser.: No. 44). 1997. per. 5.99 (0-671-56808-6, Star Trek) PB.

— Diadem, No. 1. (J). (gr. 4-7). 1997. mass mkt. 3.99 (0-590-05947-5) Scholastic Inc.

— Diadem, No. 2. (J). (gr. 4-7). 1997. mass mkt. 3.99 (0-590-05948-3) Scholastic Inc.

— Diadem, No. 3. (J). (gr. 4-7). 1997. mass mkt. 3.99 (0-590-05949-1) Scholastic Inc.

— Diadem, Vol. 4. (J). (gr. 4-7). 1997. pap. 3.99 (0-590-05950-5, Apple Classics) Scholastic Inc.

Peel, John. Diadem #4. (Diadem Ser.). 1997. 9.09 (0-606-11255-3, Pub. by Turtleback) Demco.

Peel, John. Diadem #1. (Diadem Ser.). 1997. 9.09 (0-606-11252-9, Pub. by Turtleback) Demco.

— Diadem #2. (Diadem Ser.). 1997. 9.09 (0-606-11253-7, Pub. by Turtleback) Demco.

— Diadem #3. (Diadem Ser.). 1997. 9.09 (0-606-11254-5, Pub. by Turtleback) Demco.

— Doomsday. 1999. pap. text 59.88 (0-439-09277-9) Scholastic Inc.

***Peel, John.** Dragonhome. 1998. pap. text 4.99 (0-590-59680-2) Scholastic Inc.

Peel, John. Field Trip. (Star Trek Ser.: No. 6). (J). (gr. 3-6). 1995. pap. 3.99 (0-671-88287-2, Minstrel Bks) PB.

— Fight for Justice: By Luke Skywalker. (Star Wars Journals). (J). (gr. 3-7). 1998. pap. 3.99 (0-590-18902-6) Scholastic Inc.

— Fight for Justice: By Luke Skywalker. (Star Wars Journals). 1998. 9.09 (0-606-13810-2, Pub. by Turtleback) Demco.

— Fire. (The Outer Limits Ser.). 1998. pap. 3.99 (0-8125-7564-4, Pub. by Tor Bks) St Martin.

***Peel, John.** Firestorm. (2099 Ser.: Vol. 6). (Illus.). 160p. (J). (gr. 4-7). 2000. pap. 4.99 (0-439-06035-4) Scholastic Inc.

Peel, John. Hangman. (Foul Play Ser.). (J). 1992. 8.09 (0-606-01703-8, Pub. by Turtleback) Demco.

— Here There Be Dragons. Ryan, Kevin, ed. (Star Trek: The Next Generation Ser.: No. 28). 288p. (Orig.). 1993. mass mkt. 5.99 (0-671-86571-4) PB.

— Hide & Seek. (Puffin High Flyer Ser.). (J). 1993. 8.09 (0-606-02671-1, Pub. by Turtleback) Demco.

— Hot Rock. (Mystery Files of Shelby Woo Ser.: No. 3). 144p. (J). (gr. 4-7). 1997. pap. 3.99 (0-671-01154-5) PB.

— I Spy! (Secret World of Alex Mack Ser.: Vol. 13). (J). (gr. 3-6). 1997. pap. 3.99 (0-671-00356-9, Minstrel Bks) PB.

— Independence. (Quantum Leap Ser.). 1996. mass mkt. 5.99 (1-57297-150-9) Blvd Books.

— Innocent. (Outer Limits Ser.). 1998. 9.09 (0-606-13690-8, Pub. by Turtleback) Demco.

— The Invaders. (The Outer Limits Ser.). 128p. (YA). (gr. 3 up). 1998. pap. 3.99 (0-8125-9068-6, Pub. by Tor Bks) St Martin.

— The Invaders, 5. (Outer Limits Ser.). 1998. 9.09 (0-606-13689-4, Pub. by Turtleback) Demco.

— The Last Drop. (Tombstones Ser.: No. 2). (J). (gr. 7 up). 1995. mass mkt. 3.99 (0-671-53530-7) PB.

— Last Drop. (Tombstones Ser.). 1995. 9.09 (0-606-08648-X, Pub. by Turtleback) Demco.

— The Lost. LC 98-113364. (Outer Limits Ser.: No. 4). 128p. (J). (gr. 3 up). 1997. mass mkt. 3.99 (0-8125-9067-8, Pub. by Tor Bks) St Martin.

— The Lost. (Outer Limits Ser.). 1997. 9.09 (0-606-13688-6, Pub. by Turtleback) Demco.

— Lost in Vegas! (Secret World of Alex Mack Ser.: No. 23). (J). (gr. 3-6). 1984. pap. 3.99 (0-671-00710-6) PB.

— Making 4-Track Music. 3rd rev. ed. (Illus.). 114p. 1989. pap. 12.95 (0-933224-51-6, T033) Bold Strummer Ltd.

— Maniac. (YA). (gr. 7 up). 1995. mass mkt. 3.50 (0-671-88735-1, Archway) PB.

***Peel, John.** Meltdown. (2099 Ser.: Vol. 5). 160p. (J). (gr. 4-7). 2000. pap. 4.99 (0-439-06034-6) Scholastic Inc.

Peel, John. Mountain Biking Durango. LC 97-50138. (Illus.). 1998. pap. 10.95 (1-56044-531-9) Falcon Pub Inc.

— Objective Bajor. (Star Trek: Deep Space Nine Ser.: No. 15). 288p. 1996. per. 5.99 (0-671-56811-6) S&S Trade.

— The Outer Limits, 11. 1999. mass mkt. 3.99 (0-8125-7568-7, Pub. by Tor Bks) St Martin.

— Outer Limits: The Nightmare. (The Outer Limits Ser.). 1998. mass mkt. 3.99 (0-8125-7565-2, Pub. by Tor Bks) St Martin.

— Outer Limits Innocent. (Outer Limits Ser.: No. 6). (J). 1998. pap. text 3.99 (0-8125-6455-3, Pub. by Tor Bks) St Martin.

— Outer Limits 2, Vol. 1. 1997. pap. text 3.99 (0-8125-9064-3, Pub. by Tor Bks) St Martin.

— Prisoners of Peace. Clancy, Lisa, ed. (Star Trek: Deep Space Nine Ser.: No. 3). 128p. (J). (gr. 3-6). 1994. pap. 3.99 (0-671-88288-0, Minstrel Bks) PB.

— Realtime, Shadowtime. (J). 14.00 (0-671-79894-4) S&S Bks Yung.

***Peel, John.** Revolution, Vol. 4. Vol. 4. (Illus.). 160p. (J). (gr. 4-7). 2000. mass mkt. 4.99 (0-439-06033-8) Scholastic Inc.

Peel, John. Shattered. 224p. (Orig.). (J). (gr. 6 up). 1993. mass mkt. 3.50 (0-671-79406-X, Archway) PB.

— Simon & Marshall's Excellent Adventure. (Eerie Indiana Ser.: No. 4). (J). (gr. 3-7). 1997. pap. 3.99 (0-380-79777-1, Avon Bks) Morrow Avon.

— Simon & Marshall's Excellent Adventure. (Eerie Indiana Ser.: No. 4). (J). (gr. 3-7). 1997. 9.09 (0-606-12689-9, Pub. by Turtleback) Demco.

— The Tale of the Restless House. (Are You Afraid of the Dark? Ser.: No. 3). (YA). (gr. 4-7). 1995. pap. 3.99 (0-671-52547-6, Minstrel Bks) PB.

— The Tale of the Sinister Statues, Clancy, Lisa, ed. (Are You Afraid of the Dark? Ser.: No. 1). 128p. (Orig.). (YA). (gr. 5-8). 1995. pap. 3.99 (0-671-52545-X, Minstrel Bks) PB.

— The Tale of the Three Wishes. (Are You Afraid of the Dark? Ser.: No. 13). (YA). (gr. 5-8). 1997. pap. 3.99 (0-671-00358-5, Minstrel Bks) PB.

— The Tale of the Zero Hero. (Are You Afraid of the Dark? Ser.: No. 11). 128p. (YA). (gr. 3-6). 1997. pap. 3.99 (0-671-00357-7) PB.

— Talons. 224p. (Orig.). (YA). (gr. 6 up). 1993. mass mkt. 3.50 (0-671-79405-1, Archway) PB.

— The Time Shifter. (Outer Limits Ser.). 1997. 9.09 (0-606-13687-8, Pub. by Turtleback) Demco.

— The Time Shifter, Vol. 1. LC 98-113362. (The Outer Limits Ser.). 1997. pap. text 3.99 (0-8125-9065-1, Pub. by Tor Bks) St Martin.

— Tombstones: Dances with Werewolves. (J). (gr. 7 up). 1995. mass mkt. 3.99 (0-671-53529-3, Archway) PB.

***Peel, John.** Traitor. (2099 Ser.: Vol. 3). (Illus.). 160p. (J). (gr. 4-7). 2000. pap. 5.99 (0-439-06032-X, Apple Paperbacks) Scholastic Inc.

Peel, John. The Zanti Misfits, 1. (Outer Limits Ser.). 1997. 9.09 (0-606-13685-1, Pub. by Turtleback) Demco.

— The Zanti Misfits, Vol. 2. (The Outer Limits Ser.). (J). pap. 3.99 (0-8125-9063-5, Pub. by Tor Bks) St Martin.

Peel, John D. Fundamentals of Training for Security Officers: A Comprehensive Guide to What You Should Be, Know, & Do to Have a Successful Career As a Private Patrolman or Security Officer. 6th rev. ed. (Illus.). 344p. 1980. text 40.95 (0-398-03966-6) C C Thomas.

Peel, Kathy. Be Your Best: The Family Manager's Guide to Personal Success. LC 97-52298. 224p. 2000. pap. 12.95 (0-345-41984-7, Ballantine) Ballantine Pub Grp.

— Do Plastic Surgeons Take VISA? 192p. 1992. pap. 9.99 (0-8499-3348-X) Word Pub.

— The Family Manager. LC 96-9084. 304p. 1996. pap. 14.99 (0-8499-3937-2) Word Pub.

— The Family Manager's Everyday Survival Guide. LC 98-22166. 303p. 1998. pap. 12.00 (0-345-41985-5) Ballantine Pub Grp.

— The Family Manager's Guide for Working Moms: Balance Your Family & Work Demands & Live to Tell about It. LC 97-20386. 224p. 1997. pap. 12.00 (0-345-41311-3) Ballantine Pub Grp.

— Stomach Virus & Other Forms of Family Bonding. 1993. pap. 9.99 (0-8499-3477-X) Word Pub.

Peel, Kathy & Byrd, Judie. A Mother's Manual for Holiday Survival. (Orig.). 1991. pap. 9.99 (1-56179-040-0) Focus Family.

Peel, Kathy & Mahaffey, Joy. A Mother's Manual for Summer Survival. LC 89-1348. (Illus.). 72p. 1989. reprint ed. pap. 9.99 (0-929608-31-3) Focus Family.

Peel, Kathy, jt. auth. see Peel, Billy.

Peel, Lee S. Farmington: A Pictorial History. 2nd rev. ed. (Illus.). 256p. 1993. 45.00 (0-9626618-1-3) L S Peel.

— Speak Easy - Read Write. (Illus.). 128p. (Orig.). 1988. pap. 7.95 (0-9626618-0-5); pap. 5.95 (0-685-41319-5) L S Peel.

***Peel, Lucy.** Family Garden. LC 99-31345. 112p. 2000. 13.95 (0-7641-0932-4) Barron.

Peel, Lucy. The Ultimate Sunflower Book. LC 97-12546. (Illus.). 112p. 1997. 18.00 (0-06-270212-2) HarpC.

Peel, Lucy, jt. auth. see Powell, Paula.

Peel, Lynette. The Henty Diaries. LC 96-187923. (Miegunyah Press Ser.: No. 2). 272p. 1996. 49.95 (0-522-84666-1, Pub. by Melbourne Univ Pr) Paul & Co Pubs.

Peel, Malcolm. Improving Your Communications Skills. 160p. 1990. 50.95 (0-8464-1388-4); pap. 29.95 (0-8464-1389-2) Beekman Pubs.

Peel, Margaret M., jt. auth. see Gardner, Joan F.

Peel, Mark. Food of Campanile. LC 96-36962. 320p. 1997. 35.00 (0-679-40906-8) Villard Books.

— Good Times, Hard Times: The Past & Future in Elizabeth. 328p. 1996. pap. 24.95 (0-522-84628-9, Pub. by Melbourne Univ Pr) Paul & Co Pubs.

— A Little History of Australia. (Illus.). 96p. 1997. 9.95 (0-522-84757-9, Pub. by Melbourne Univ Pr) Paul & Co Pubs.

Peel, Paul H., Jr., ed. Hugh Smithwick Descendants. LC 97-73367. 350p. 1997. 50.00 (0-9626609-5-7) MCH Soc NC.

Peel, Robert. Christian Science: Its Encounter with American Culture. 1986. pap. 9.95 (0-933062-24-9) R H Sommer.

Peel, Robin & Bell, Mary. The Primary Language Leader's Book: A Handbook for English Curriculum Leaders at Key Stages 1 & 2. 160p. 1994. pap. 27.50 (1-85346-249-7, Pub. by David Fulton) Taylor & Francis.

***Peel, Robin, et al.** Questions of English: Ethics, Aesthetics, Rhetoric & the Formation of the Subject in England, Australia & the United States. LC 99-36308. 312p. 2000. write for info. (0-415-19119-X) Routledge.

Peel, Roy V. The Campaign, 1932: An Analysis. (History - United States Ser.). 242p. 1993. reprint ed. lib. bdg. 79.00 (0-7812-4926-0) Rprt Serv.

Peel, Roy V. & Donnelly, Thomas C. 1932 Campaign: An Analysis. LC 73-454. (FDR & the Era of the New Deal Ser.). 252p. 1973. reprint ed. lib. bdg. 29.50 (0-306-70567-2) Da Capo.

— The 1928 Campaign: An Analysis. LC 73-19170. (Politics & People Ser.). (Illus.). 196p. 1974. reprint ed. 17.95 (0-405-05892-6) Ayer.

— The 1928 Campaign: An Analysis. LC 74-12758. (Illus.). 183p. 1975. reprint ed. lib. bdg. 45.00 (0-8371-7749-9, PENC, Greenwood Pr) Greenwood.

Peel, S. Granulated Metrial Gland Cells. (Advances in Anatomy, Embryology & Cell Biology Ser.). (Illus.). 120p. 1989. 96.95 (0-387-50390-0) Spr-Verlag.

Peel, V. A. Somaliland. 368p. 1986. 265.00 (1-85077-086-7, Pub. by Darf Pubs Ltd) St Mut.

Peel, Val, jt. auth. see Barrett, Daniel.

Peel, Victoria, et al. Hawthorn: A History. (Illus.). 352p. 1994. 49.95 (0-522-84507-X, Pub. by Melbourne Univ Pr) Paul & Co Pubs.

Peel, William C. Living in a Lions' Den Without Being Eaten. LC 94-11890. 252p. (Orig.). 1994. pap. 12.00 (0-89109-794-5) NavPress.

— Lo Que Hace Dios Cuando Hombre. (SPA.). 1998. pap. 5.99 (0-8297-0469-8) Vida Pubs.

Peel, William C., et al. Discover Your Destiny: Finding the Courage to Follow Your Dreams. LC 96-43266. 192p. 1996. pap. 14.00 (0-89109-983-2) NavPress.

Peel, William C., jt. auth. see Larimore, Walter L.

Peelaert, Guy & Cohn, Nik. Rock Dreams. LC 73-7289. (Illus.). 176p. 1982. 19.95 (0-394-52870-0) Knopf.

Peele, Carol C., jt. auth. see Gentry, Atron A.

Peele, Carolyn C., jt. auth. see Gentry, Atron A.

Peele, George. The Chronicle of King Edward the First: Surnamed Longshanks with the Life of Lleullen, Rebel in Wales. Dreher, George K., ed. LC 74-79524. (Illus.). 224p. 1997. reprint ed. pap. 10.95 (0-9601000-1-6) Longshanks Bk.

— The Chronicle of King Edward the First: Surnamed Longshanks with the Life of Lluellen, Rebel in Wales. 2nd ed. Dreher, George K., ed. (Illus.). 224p. 1998. reprint ed. 19.50 (0-9601000-7-5) Longshanks Bk.

— The Old Wives Tale. Binnie, Patricia, ed. LC 79-48011. (Revels Plays Ser.). 107p. reprint ed. pap. 33.20 (0-608-06036-4, 206636700008) Bks Demand.

— Samples from the Love of King David & Fair Bethsabe: With Reference Portions of the Bible. LC 79-56834. 71p. (Orig.). 1980. pap. 4.95 (0-9601000-2-4) Longshanks Bk.

Peele, Gillian. Governing the U. K. 3rd ed. LC 96-143072. 1996. text 71.95 (0-631-19886-5); pap. text 28.95 (0-631-16742-0) Blackwell Pubs.

Peele, Gillian, et al, eds. Developments in American Politics. 3rd ed. LC 98-23826. (Illus.). 448p. (C). 1998. pap. text 26.95 (1-56643-048-8, Chatham House Pub) Seven Bridges.

Peele, Stanton. Diseasing of America: How We Allowed Recovery Zealots & the Treatment Industry to Convince Us We Are out of Control. LC 95-6377. 321p. 1995. pap. 15.95 (0-02-874014-9) Lxngtn Bks.

— Diseasing of America: How We Allowed Recovery Zealots & the Treatment Industry to Convince Us We Are Out of Control. LC 98-30568. 321p. 1999. pap. 19.95 (0-7879-4643-5) Jossey-Bass.

— The Meaning of Addiction: An Unconventional View. LC 98-19896. (Psychology Ser.). 224p. 1998. reprint ed. pap. 24.95 (0-7879-4382-7) Jossey-Bass.

— The Meaning of Addiction: Compulsive Experience & Its Interpretations. LC 79-4750. 203p. 1985. pap. 27.95 (0-669-13835-5) Jossey-Bass.

— Visions of Addiction: Major Contemporary Perspectives on Addiction & Alcoholism. LC 86-45054. 244p. 1987. 37.00 (0-669-13092-3) Lxngtn Bks.

Peele, Stanton & Brodsky, Archie. Love & Addiction. LC 74-5818. 284p. 1975. 16.95 (0-8005-5041-6) Taplinger.

***Peele, Stanton & Grant, Marcus.** Alcohol & Pleasure: A Health Perspective LC 99-12975. (Series on Alcohol in Society). 1999. boxed set. write for info. (1-58391-015-8) Brunner-Mazel.

An Asterisk (*) at the beginning of an entry indicates that the title is appearing for the first time.

Peele, Stanton, et al. Resisting 12-Step Coercion: How to Fight Forced Participation in AA, NA or 12-Step Treatment. LC 99-91322. 204p. 2000. pap. 14.95 (*1-884365-17-5*) See Sharp Pr.
— The Truth about Addiction & Recovery. 432p. 1992. pap. 13.00 (*0-671-75530-7*, Fireside) S&S Trade Pap.
Peelen, Julie, ed. see Capes, Richard.
Peeler, Alexandra. Parish Social Ministry: A Vision & Resource. 194p. 1986. 14.95 (*0-318-20492-4*) Catholic Charities.
Peeler, Damon E. Mapas de Monte Alban: Proyecto Especial Monte Alban, 1992-1994. (SPA., Illus.). 162p. 1994. pap. 70.00 (*1-877812-75-7*, UC006) UPLAAP.
Peeler, Damon E. & Winter, Marcus. Tiempo Sagrado, Espacio Sagrado: Astronomia, Calendario y Arquitectura en Monte Alban y Teotihuacan. 2nd ed. (SPA.). 26p. 1996. pap. 3.00 (*1-877812-74-9*, UC005) UPLAAP.
Peeler, David, jt. auth. see Jain, Vijay.
Peeler, David K. & Marra, James C., eds. Environmental Issues & Waste Management Technologies in the Ceramic & Nuclear Industries III. (Ceramic Transactions Ser.: Vol. 87). (Illus.). 710p. 1998. 95.00 (*1-57498-035-1*, CT087) Am Ceramic.
Peeler, E. F., tr. see Gurian, Waldemar.
Peeler, George. Selling in the Quality Era. (C). 1995. pap. text 22.95 (*1-55786-666-X*) Blackwell Pubs.
Peeler, J. Yorke, Jr. Talking with Your Child about the Presence of God. LC 94-40774. (Growing Together Ser.). 32p. (Orig.). 1995. pap. 2.25 (*0-8298-0995-3*) Pilgrim OH.
Peeler, John. Building Democracy in Latin America. LC 97-30554. 240p. 1998. pap. text 19.95 (*1-55587-781-8*); lib. bdg. 55.00 (*1-55587-758-3*) L Rienner.
Peeler, John A. Latin American Democracies: Colombia, Costa Rica, Venezuela. LC 84-13209. xiii, 193p. (C). 1985. pap. 17.95 (*0-8078-4153-6*) U of NC Pr.
Peeler, Keith. Thoughts. (Orig.). 1996. pap. write for info. (*1-57553-215-8*) Watermrk Pr.
***Peeler, Tim.** Touching All the Bases: Poems from Baseball. 128p. 1999. pap. 18.95 (*0-7864-0705-0*) McFarland & Co.
Peeling, Rosanna & Sparling, P. Frederick. Sexually Transmitted Diseases: Methods & Protocols. LC 98-18197. (Methods in Molecular Medicine Ser.: No. 20). (Illus.). 256p. 1998. 89.50 (*0-89603-535-2*) Humana.
Peeling, W. B., ed. Questions & Uncertainties in Prostate Cancer. 320p. 1996. pap. 79.95 (*0-86542-965-0*) Blackwell Sci.
Peeling, W. B., et al, eds. Progress in Diagnostics & Therapy of Prostatic Cancer. (Illus.). 80p. 1996. pap. 49.00 (*3-540-60195-3*) Spr-Verlag.
Peellaert, G., jt. auth. see Cohn, N.
Peellaert, Guy. Twentieth-Century Dreams. LC 99-30626. 1999. pap. 25.00 (*0-375-70708-5*) Knopf.
Peelman, Achiel. Christ Is a Native American. LC 95-22933. 285p. (Orig.). 1995. pap. 20.00 (*1-57075-047-5*) Orbis Bks.
Peelo, Maira T. Helping Students with Study Problems. LC 94-27677. 160p. 1994. pap. text 31.95 (*0-335-19307-2*) OpUniv Pr.
Peelo, Richard. Multiply Your Profits: A Common-Sense Approach for Small to Midsize Businesses. LC 97-46410. xii, 155p. 1999. 24.00 (*0-9661609-0-8*) Inverness Pubs.
Peels, Hendrik G. The Vengeance of God: The Meaning of the Root NQM & the Function of the NQM-Texts in the Context of Divine Revelation in the Old Testament. LC 94-35317. (Oudtestamentische Studien: Vol. 31). xiv, 326p. 1994. 101.50 (*90-04-10164-0*) Brill Academic Pubs.
Peen, Bud, jt. auth. see Browning, Robert.
Peenen, Dirk Van, see Van Peenen, John & Van Peenen, Dirk.
Peenen, John Van, see Van Peenen, John.
Peeno, Larry, ed. Adaptations of the National Visual Arts Standards. 64p. (Orig.). 1995. pap. text 20.00 (*0-937652-91-1*, 259) Natl Art Ed.
Peeperkorn, David, ed. Limitation of Free Bargaining & Sanctity of Contracts with Performing Artists & Composers. 122p. 1987. pap. 76.00 (*90-6215-169-8*, Pub. by Maklu Uitgev) Gaunt.
— Merchandising & Sponsorship in the Music Business. 120p. 1986. pap. 76.00 (*90-6215-167-1*, Pub. by Maklu Uitgev) Gaunt.
Peeperkorn, David & Van Rij, Cees, eds. Collecting Societies in the Music Business. 160p. 1989. pap. 95.00 (*90-6215-228-7*, Pub. by Maklu Uitgev) Gaunt.
Peeples. Edgar Allan Poe Revisited. LC 98-29014. 1998. 32.00 (*0-8057-4572-6*) Mac Lib Ref.
***Peeples, Donna K. & Peeples, Minor.** Texas Real Estate Agency. 4th ed. LC 99-87480. 2000. pap. 34.95 (*0-7931-3585-0*) Dearborn.
Peeples, Edwin A. Hole in the Hill. LC 77-82913. 1969. 6.50 (*0-9600080-2-0*) Peeples.
— Planting an Inheritance: Life on a Pennsylvania Farm. 224p. 1994. 19.95 (*0-8117-1206-0*) Stackpole.
— Professional Storywriter's Handbook. LC 60-6901. 1960. 8.50 (*0-9600080-0-4*) Peeples.
Peeples, Mary G. All We Like Sheep. 104p. 1989. 15.00 (*0-9634836-0-9*) Sheep Shoppe.
Peeples, Mary G. & Peeples, Sam L., Jr. Parenting, an Heir Raising Experience: Raising Your Child with Confidence. Lee, Betsy, ed. (Illus.). 190p. 1993. 17.00 (*0-9634836-1-7*) Sheep Shoppe.
Peeples, Minor, jt. auth. see Peeples, Donna K.
Peeples, S. Elise. The Emperor Has a Body: Body-Politics in the Between. LC 98-67875. 300p. 1998. 25.00 (*0-9654418-9-X*); pap. 16.95 (*0-9654418-2-2*) Javelina Bks.
Peeples, Sam L., Jr. Depression: A Way Out a Christian Biblical View. (Illus.). 125p. 1999. pap. 12.00 (*0-9634836-3-3*) Sheep Shoppe.
Peeples, Sam L., Jr., jt. auth. see Peeples, Mary G.
Peeples, Samuel. The Man Who Died Twice. 252p. 1984. pap. 6.00 (*0-89733-121-4*) Academy Chi Pubs.
Peeples, Susan L., jt. auth. see Seabury, Debra L.
Peeps, Claire. American Activists Reflect Process. text. write for info. (*0-312-22978-X*) St Martin.
Peer, Charles. Celebrating the Master's Christmas. LC 96-69683. 72p. 1996. boxed set 14.95 (*0-89221-328-0*) New Leaf.
PEER Consultants & CalRecovery, Inc. Staff. Material Recovery Facility Design Manual. 176p. 1993. boxed set 94.95 (*0-87371-944-1*, TD794) CRC Pr.
Peer, Kurt. TV Tie-Ins: A Bibliography of American TV Tie-In Paperbacks. LC 96-92907. (Illus.). 384p. 1997. 55.00 (*0-9654536-4-2*); pap. 24.95 (*0-9654536-3-4*) Neptune Pub.
— TV Tie-Ins: A Bibliography of American TV Tie-In Paperbacks. (Illus.). 384p. 1999. pap. 24.95 (*1-57500-073-3*, Pub. by TV Bks) HarpC.
Peer, Larry H. The Romantic Manifesto: An Anthology. (American University Studies: Comparative Literature: Ser. III, Vol. 23). 156p. (C). 1988. text 36.50 (*0-318-37856-6*) P Lang Pubng.
— Romanticism Across the Disciplines. LC 98-16034. 272p. (C). 1998. 57.00 (*0-7618-1103-6*); pap. 34.50 (*0-7618-1104-4*) U Pr of Amer.
Peer, Larry H. & Hoeveler, Diane L., eds. Comparative Romanticisms: Power, Gender, Subjectivity. LC 97-46703. (Studies in German Literature, Linguistics, & Culture). 220p. 1998. 55.00 (*1-57113-170-1*) Camden Hse.
Peer, Larry H., jt. auth. see Matteo, Sante.
Pe'er, M. The Story of Maran BetYosef: R'Yosef Karo - Author of the Shulman Aruch. (ArtScroll Youth Ser.). (Illus.). 96p. 1986. 11.95 (*0-89906-400-0*) Mesorah Pubns.
Peer, P. Van, see Vermeersch, P., ed.
Peer, P. Van, see Vermeersch, P. & Van Peer, P., eds.
Peer, Shanny. France on Display: Peasants, Provincials, & Folklore in the 1937 Paris World's Fair. LC 97-30996. (SUNY Series in National Identities). (Illus.). 265p. (C). 1998. text 65.50 (*0-7914-3709-4*); pap. text 21.95 (*0-7914-3710-8*) State U NY Pr.
Peera, Aziem. Secrets of America's Rich & Successful "Damn" Foreigners! (Illus.). 20p. (Orig.). 1996. pap. 3.95 (*0-9652988-2-5*) Asante Intl.
— Welcome to America: What a Wonderful Country! (Illus.). 78p. (Orig.). 1996. pap. 6.95 (*0-9652988-0-9*) Asante Intl.
Peerage. The Peerage of Scotland. (Illus.). 339p. 1995. reprint ed. pap. 25.00 (*0-7884-0289-7*) Heritage Bk.
Peerbolt, Anna, ed. see Hofemann, Peggy.
Peerbolte, Lambertus J. The Antecedents of Antichrist: A Traditio-Historical Study of the Earliest Christian Views on Eschatological Opponents. LC 96-1524. (Supplements to the Journal for the Study of Judaism Ser.: Vol. 49). 350p. 1996. 128.00 (*90-04-10455-0*) Brill Academic Pubs.
***Peerce, Donna & Allen, Jackie.** Dream Messages: How to Make the Connection Between Heaven & Earth. 2000. 19.95 (*1-56072-781-0*) Nova Sci Pubs.
Peerce, Donna & Cochran, Chuck. Heart & Soul Resumes: 7 Never-Before-Published Secrets to Capturing "Heart & Soul" in Your Resume. LC 97-46374. 232p. 1998. pap. 15.95 (*0-89106-113-4*, Davies-Black Pub) Consulting Psychol.
Peerce, Donna, jt. auth. see Cochran, Chuck.
Peercy, Mark S., jt. auth. see Friedhoff, Richard M.
Peerdeman, Ida & Kunzli, Josef. The Messages of the Lady of All Nations. LC 96-70128. 152p. 1996. pap. text 4.95 (*1-882972-87-2*) Queenship Pub.
Peerenboom, Ellen, tr. see Westhoff, Peter, et al.
Peerenboom, R. P. Law & Morality in Ancient China: The Silk Manuscripts of Huang-Lao. (SUNY Series in Chinese Philosophy & Culture). 380p. (C). 1993. text 19.50 (*0-7914-1237-7*) State U NY Pr.
Peerkins, William E., ed. Droppin' Science: Critical Essays on Rap Music & Hip Hop Culture. LC 95-1532. (Critical Perspectives on the Past Ser.). (Illus.). 240p. (C). 1996. pap. 22.95 (*1-56639-362-0*) Temple U Pr.
Peerlinck, K. Von Willebrand's Disease & Hemophilia: Clinical & Genetic Aspects. No. 74. 95p. (Orig.). 1994. pap. 30.00 (*90-6186-593-X*, Pub. by Leuven Univ) Coronet Bks.
Peers, Allison, tr. see Lull, Ramon, pseud.
Peers, Chris. Warlords of China 700 BC to AD 1662. (Illus.). 176p. 1998. 27.95 (*1-85409-401-7*, Pub. by Arms & Armour) Sterling.
Peers, Chris & Hook, Christa. Late Imperial Chinese Armies, 1520-1840. (Men-at-Arms Ser.: Vol. 307). (Illus.). 48p. 1997. pap. 12.95 (*1-85532-655-8*, Pub. by Ospry) Stackpole.
Peers, Chris J. Ancient Chinese Armies, 1500 BC-200 BC. (Men-at-Arms Ser.: No. 218). (Illus.). 48p. 1990. pap. 11.95 (*0-85045-942-7*, 9175, Pub. by Ospry) Stackpole.
— Imperial Chinese Armies No. 2: 590-1260 AD. (Men-at-Arms Ser.: No. 295). (Illus.). 48p. 1996. pap. 12.95 (*1-85532-599-3*, Pub. by Ospry) Stackpole.
— Imperial Chinese Armies 100 BC-AD 589. (Men-at-Arms Ser.). (Illus.). 48p. 1995. pap. 12.95 (*1-85532-514-4*, Pub. by Ospry) Stackpole.
— Medieval Chinese Armies, 1260-1520. (Men-at-Arms Ser.: No. 251). (Illus.). 48p. 1992. pap. 11.95 (*1-85532-254-4*, 9222, Pub. by Ospry) Stackpole.
Peers, Douglas M. Between Mars & Mammon: Colonial Armies & the Garrison State in 19th-Century India. (Illus.). 224p. 1995. text 65.00 (*1-85043-954-0*, Pub. by I B T) St Martin.
Peers, Douglas M., ed. Warfare & Empires: Contact & Conflict Between European & Non-European Military & Maritime Forces & Cultures. LC 96-40443. (Expanding World Ser.: Vol. 24). 420p. 1997. text 138.95 (*0-86078-528-9*, Pub. by Variorum) Ashgate Pub Co.
Peers, Douglas M., jt. auth. see Finkelstein, David.
Peers, E. A., ed. From Cadalso to Ruben Dario. LC 75-41176. (Liverpool Studies in Spanish Literature 3rd Ser.). reprint ed. 50.00 (*0-404-15031-4*) AMS Pr.
Peers, E. Allison. Dark Night of the Soul. 192p. 1996. pap. 45.00 (*0-86012-036-8*, Pub. by Srch Pr) St Mut.
— The Life of Teresa of Jesus. 400p. 1991. pap. 14.95 (*0-385-01109-1*, Image Bks) Doubleday.
— The Mystics of Spain. 1977. lib. bdg. 59.95 (*0-8490-2322-X*) Gordon Pr.
— St. John of the Cross & Other Lectures & Addresses. 1977. lib. bdg. 250.00 (*0-8490-2558-3*) Gordon Pr.
— Studies of the Spanish Mystics, 3 vols. 1977. lib. bdg. 300.00 (*0-8490-2706-3*) Gordon Pr.
Peers, E. Allison, ed. Liverpool Studies in Spanish Literature, 4 vols. reprint ed. write for info. (*0-404-15030-6*) AMS Pr.
Peers, E. Allison, tr. The Way of Perfection. 288p. 1991. pap. 10.95 (*0-385-06539-6*, D176, Image Bks) Doubleday.
Peers, Edgar A. Behind That Wall. LC 72-90672. (Essay Index Reprint Ser.). 1977. 18.95 (*0-8369-1210-1*) Ayer.
— Catalonia Infelix. LC 77-109819. 326p. 1970. reprint ed. lib. bdg. 35.00 (*0-8371-4310-1*, PECI, Greenwood Pr) Greenwood.
— The Church in Spain, Seventeen Thirty-Seven to Nineteen Thirty-Seven. 1980. lib. bdg. 44.95 (*0-8490-3149-4*) Gordon Pr.
— A Handbook to the Study & Teaching of Spanish. 1980. lib. bdg. 69.95 (*0-8490-3105-2*) Gordon Pr.
— Ramon Lull: A Biography. 1980. lib. bdg. 75.00 (*0-8490-3186-9*) Gordon Pr.
— St. John of the Cross & Other Lectures & Addresses, 1920-1945. LC 70-136650. (Biography Index Reprint Ser.). 1977. 18.95 (*0-8369-8045-X*) Ayer.
— A Short History of the Romantic Movement in Spain. LC 76-28478. reprint ed. 32.50 (*0-404-15034-9*) AMS Pr.
— Spanish Golden Age in Poetry & Drama. LC 76-28691. reprint ed. 32.50 (*0-404-15032-2*) AMS Pr.
— The Spanish Tragedy, 1930-1936. LC 75-8724. 247p. 1975. reprint ed. lib. bdg. 35.00 (*0-8371-8048-1*, PEST, Greenwood Pr) Greenwood.
Peers, Edgar A., ed. Cassell's Spanish Dictionary: Spanish-English, English-Spanish. LC 77-7403. (ENG & SPA.). 464p. 1977. 13.00 (*0-02-522660-6*) Macmillan.
— Cassell's Spanish Dictionary: Spanish-English, English-Spanish. rev. ed. LC 77-7403. (ENG & SPA.). 1100p. 1978. 22.95 (*0-02-522910-9*, Pub. by Macmillan); 19.95 (*0-02-522900-1*) Macmillan.
— Critical Anthology of Spanish Verse. LC 69-10145. 1741p. 1969. reprint ed. lib. bdg. 45.50 (*0-8371-0190-5*, PESV, Greenwood Pr) Greenwood.
Peers, Frank W. The Politics of Canadian Broadcasting, 1920-1951. LC 78-430275. 474p. reprint ed. pap. 147.00 (*0-608-15413-X*, 202934200060) Bks Demand.
— The Public Eye: Television & the Politics of Canadian Broadcasting, 1952-68. LC 79-311230. 475p. reprint ed. pap. 147.30 (*0-8357-6400-1*, 203575800096) Bks Demand.
Peers, George. Appomattox County & Its People: Recollections & Reminiscenses. Schroeder, Patrick A., ed. (Illus.). 40p. 1999. pap. 5.00 (*1-889246-12-3*) P A Schroeder.
Peers, Ian. Statistical Analysis for Education & Psychology Researchers. LC 96-12659. 224p. 1996. pap. 34.95 (*0-7507-0506-X*, Falmer Pr) Taylor & Francis.
Peers, Judi. Home Base. unabridged ed. (Illus.). 112p. (Orig.). (YA). (gr. 3 up). 1991. pap. 4.95 (*0-7736-7346-6*) STDK.
— Shark Attack. 74p. (J). (gr. 3-8). 1998. text 6.95 (*1-55028-620-X*, Pub. by J Lorimer) Formac Dist Ltd.
Peers, Ken. History of East Oxford Township, Ontario. (Illus.). 80p. 1997. reprint ed. pap. 15.00 (*0-8328-7188-5*) Higginson Bk Co.
Peers, Laura. The Ojibwa of Western Canada, 1780 to 1870. LC 94-31544. (Manitoba Studies in Native History 7). (Illus.). xviii, 288p. 1994. 32.95 (*0-87351-310-X*) Minn Hist.
— The Ojibwa of Western Canada, 1780 to 1870. LC 94-31544. (Manitoba Studies in Native History: Vol. 7). (Illus.). xviii, 288p. 1994. pap. 15.95 (*0-87351-311-8*) Minn Hist.
Peers, Paloma, ed. Tenga una Actitud Mental Positiva. (SPA.). 130p. (Orig.). 1995. pap. 6.95 (*1-884864-04-X*) Am Success Inst.
Peers, Robert. Adult Education - A Comparative Study. (C). 1972. 45.00 (*0-7100-7410-7*, Pub. by Univ Nottingham) St Mut.
***Peers, Robin & Hawkins, Richard.** Asset Based Working Capital Finance. 288p. 2000. pap. 80.00 (*0-85297-516-3*, Pub. by Chartered Bank) St Mut.
Peers, Tom. Fit Function & Flourish. 78p. 1987. pap. 3.50 (*0-88144-077-9*) Christian Pub.
Peers, William R., et al. The Peers Inquiry of the Massacre at My Lai. LC 97-42604. (Vietnam War Research Collections). 1997. write for info. (*1-55655-660-8*) U Pubns Amer.
Peerse Weaver, Marlow. In Our Own Words: Generation X Poetry. 160p. 1999. pap. 9.95 (*0-9654136-2-4*) MW Enter.
***Peery, Brady.** Pantone Colors & Black: Duotone Guide for Adobe Photoshop. (Illus.). 300p. 1998. pap. 129.95 (*0-9651388-5-2*) PickerBook.
— Pantone Colors & Black Studio Edition: Duotone Guide for Adobe Photoshop. (Illus.). 300p. 1999. pap. 199.00 (*0-9651388-4-4*) PickerBook.
Peery, Brady. Photoshop Quadtones: Process Quadtones, Tritones, & Duotones. (Illus.). 192p. 1996. pap. 109.95 (*0-9651388-3-6*) PickerBook.
Peery, David J. & Azar, J. J. Aircraft Structures. 2nd ed. (Illus.). 454p. (C). 1982. text 125.00 (*0-07-049196-8*) McGraw.
Peery, Harry E. & Singer, Margaret A. Basic Microbiology Study Guide. 288p. 1986. pap. text 14.25 (*0-02-304410-1*, Macmillan Coll) P-H.
Peery, J. C., et al, eds. Music & Child Development. (Illus.). 315p. 1987. 59.00 (*0-387-96422-3*) Spr-Verlag.
Peery, Janet. Alligator Dance. LC 97-36081. 224p. (Orig.). 1998. pap. 12.00 (*0-312-18038-1*) St Martin.
— Alligator Dance: Stories. LC 93-18694. (Southwest Life & Letters Ser.). 224p. 1993. 22.50 (*0-87074-353-8*) SMU Press.
— The River Beyond the World. 304p. 1997. pap. 13.00 (*0-312-16986-8*) St Martin.
Peery, Nelson. Black Fire: The Making of a Revolutionary. 352p. 1995. pap. 11.95 (*1-56584-159-X*, Pub. by New Press NY) Norton.
Peery, Susan M. Potluck Plain & Fancy: Our Favorite Recipes from "Quick 'n' Easy" to Masterpieces. LC 96-22085. 256p. 1996. pap. 14.95 (*0-911469-13-3*) A C Hood.
Pees, Samuel T. Pennsylvania's Oil Heritage Vol. 1: Columbia Farm. Stewart, Anne W., ed. (Self Guided Tours Ser.: Vol. 1). (Illus.). 32p. (Orig.). Date not set. pap. 5.00 (*0-614-12696-7*) Colonel PA.
Peesch, R. Ornament in European Folk Art. (Illus.). 210p. (C). 1982. text 303.00 (*0-7855-5872-1*, Pub. by Collets) St Mut.
— Ornament in European Folk Art. (Illus.). 210p. (C). 1988. 300.00 (*0-569-19823-2*, Pub. by Collets) St Mut.
Peeschansky, V. G., jt. auth. see Gokhfel'd, V.
Peeslee, Amos G. Constitutions of Nations. Incl. No. 2. Asia, Australia, & Oceania., 2 pts. 1974. lib. bdg. 280.00 (*90-247-0444-8*); write for info. (*0-318-53996-9*) Kluwer Academic.
Peet, Bill. The Ant & the Elephant. (J). 1972. pap. text. write for info. (*0-395-13733-0*) HM.
— The Ant & the Elephant, 001. LC 74-179918. (Illus.). 48p. (J). (gr. k-3). 1980. 16.00 (*0-395-16963-1*) HM.
Peet, Bill. The Ant & the Elephant, 001. LC 74-179918. (Illus.). 48p. (J). (gr. k-3). 1980. pap. 8.95 (*0-395-29205-0*) HM.
Peet, Bill. Ant & the Elephant. (J). 1972. 12.15 (*0-606-02019-5*, Pub. by Turtleback) Demco.
— Big Bad Bruce, 001. LC 76-62502. (Illus.). 48p. (J). (ps-3). 1977. 16.00 (*0-395-25150-8*) HM.
— Big Bad Bruce, 001. LC 76-62502. (Illus.). 40p. (J). (ps-3). 1982. pap. 7.95 (*0-395-32922-1*) HM.
— Big Bad Bruce. (J). 1977. 12.15 (*0-606-02722-X*, Pub. by Turtleback) Demco.
— Big Bad Bruce. unabridged ed. (Carry-Along Book & Cassette Favorites Ser.). (Illus.). 40p. (J). (gr. 3 up). 1987. pap. 10.95 incl. audio (*0-395-45741-6*, 493317) HM.
— Bill Peet: An Autobiography. (Illus.). 192p. (J). (gr. 3 up). 1989. 20.00 (*0-395-50932-7*) HM.
— Bill Peet: An Autobiography. 192p. (J). (gr. 4-7). 1994. pap. 12.00 (*0-395-68982-1*) HM.
Peet, Bill. Bill Peet: An Autobiography. LC 88-37067. 1989. 17.10 (*0-606-06232-7*, Pub. by Turtleback) Demco.
— Bill Peet Menagerie. 2000. 30.00 (*0-618-08859-8*); pap. 19.95 (*0-618-08711-7*) HM.
Peet, Bill. Buford, the Little Bighorn, 001. (Illus.). 48p. (J). (gr. k-3). 1975. 16.00 (*0-395-20337-6*) HM.
— Buford, the Little Bighorn, 001. (Illus.). 48p. (J). (gr. k-3). 1983. pap. 7.95 (*0-395-34067-5*) HM.
— The Caboose Who Got Loose, 001. LC 79-155554. (Illus.). 48p. (J). (gr. k-3). 1971. 16.00 (*0-395-14805-7*) HM.
— The Caboose Who Got Loose, 001. LC 79-155554. (Illus.). 48p. (J). (gr. k-3). 1980. pap. 7.95 (*0-395-28715-4*) HM.
— The Caboose Who Got Loose. (Snuggle & Read Story Bks.). (J). 1971. 12.15 (*0-606-02054-3*, Pub. by Turtleback) Demco.
Peet, Bill. Capyboppy, 001. (Illus.). 62p. (J). (gr. 2-4). 1985. pap. 8.95 (*0-395-38368-4*) HM.
Peet, Bill. Capyboppy. 1966. 12.15 (*0-606-00778-4*, Pub. by Turtleback) Demco.
— Chester the Wordly Pig. (Illus.). 48p. (J). (ps-3). 1997. 10.95 incl. audio (*0-395-85758-9*, 493007) HM.
— Chester the Worldly Pig, 001. (Illus.). 48p. (J). (gr. k-3). 1978. pap. 7.95 (*0-395-27271-8*) HM.
— Chester the Worldly Pig, 001. (Illus.). 48p. (J). (gr. k-3). 1980. 16.00 (*0-395-18470-3*) HM.
— Chester the Worldly Pig. 1965. 12.15 (*0-606-02060-8*, Pub. by Turtleback) Demco.
— Cock-a-Doodle Dudley. (Illus.). 48p. (J). (gr. k-3). 1990. 16.00 (*0-395-55331-8*) HM.
— Cock-a-Doodle Dudley. (Illus.). 48p. (J). (gr. k-3). 1993. pap. 8.95 (*0-395-65745-8*) HM.
Peet, Bill. Cock-a-Doodle Dudley. 1990. 11.15 (*0-606-05209-7*, Pub. by Turtleback) Demco.
— Cowardly Clyde. (Illus.). (J). 1999. pap. 15.65 (*0-8085-3560-9*) Econo-Clad Bks.
Peet, Bill. Cowardly Clyde, 001. (Illus.). 48p. (J). (gr. k-3). 1984. pap. 7.95 (*0-395-36171-0*) HM.
Peet, Bill. Cowardly Clyde. (J). 1979. 12.15 (*0-606-03196-0*, Pub. by Turtleback) Demco.
Peet, Bill. Cyrus the Unsinkable. (Carry-Along Book & Cassette Favorites Ser.). (Illus.). 48p. (J). (gr. k-3). 1995. 10.95 incl. audio (*0-395-72025-7*, 492975) HM.
— Cyrus the Unsinkable Sea Serpent, 001. LC 74-20646. (Illus.). 48p. (J). (gr. k-3). 1975. 16.00 (*0-395-20272-8*) HM.

P

An Asterisk (*) at the beginning of an entry indicates that the title is appearing for the first time.

— Cyrus the Unsinkable Sea Serpent, 001. LC 74-20646. (Illus.). 48p. (J). (gr. k-3). 1982. pap. 7.95 (*0-395-31389-9*) HM.

Peet, Bill. Cyrus the Unsinkable Sea Serpent. (J). 1975. 12.15 (*0-606-03334-3*, Pub. by Turtleback) Demco.

Peet, Bill. Eli, 001. LC 77-17500. (Illus.). 48p. (J). (gr. k-3). 1984. pap. 8.95 (*0-395-36611-9*) HM.

— Eli. 1978. 14.15 (*0-606-03378-5*, Pub. by Turtleback) Demco.

— Ella, 001. (Illus.). 48p. (J). (gr. k-3). 1978. pap. 7.95 (*0-395-27269-6*) HM.

Peet, Bill. Encore for Eleanor Pa, 001. 48p. (J). (ps-3). 1985. pap. 8.95 (*0-395-38367-6*) HM.

Peet, Bill. Farewell to Shady Glade, 001. (Illus.). 48p. (J). (gr. k-3). 1966. 16.00 (*0-395-18975-6*) HM.

— Farewell to Shady Glade, 001. (Illus.). 48p. 1981. pap. 7.95 (*0-395-31128-4*) HM.

— Farewell to Shady Glade. (Carry-Along Book & Cassette Favorites Ser.). (Illus.). 48p. (J). (gr. k-3). 1991. pap. 10.95 incl. audio (*0-395-60166-5*, 492989) HM.

Peet, Bill. Farewell to Shady Glade. (J). 1966. 12.15 (*0-606-03324-6*, Pub. by Turtleback) Demco.

— Fly Homer Fly, 001. (Illus.). 64p. (J). (gr. k-3). 1979. pap. 8.95 (*0-395-28005-2*) HM.

Peet, Bill. The Gnats of Knotty Pine, 001. LC 75-17024. (Illus.). 48p. (J). (gr. k-3). 1975. 16.00 (*0-395-21405-X*) HM.

— The Gnats of Knotty Pine, 001. LC 75-17024. (Illus.). 48p. (J). (gr. k-3). 1984. pap. 7.95 (*0-395-36612-7*) HM.

— Gnats of Knotty Pine. 1975. 12.15 (*0-606-03385-8*, Pub. by Turtleback) Demco.

***Peet, Bill.** How Droofus the Dragon. (Illus.). (J). 1999. pap. 15.75 (*0-8085-3078-X*) Econo-Clad Bks.

Peet, Bill. How Droofus the Dragon Lost His Head, 001. LC 75-135136. (Illus.). 48p. (J). (gr. k-3). 1983. pap. 7.95 (*0-395-34066-7*) HM.

— How Droofus the Dragon Lost His Head. (J). 1971. 12.15 (*0-606-03769-1*, Pub. by Turtleback) Demco.

— Hubert's Hair-Raising Adventure, 001. (Illus.). 40p. (J). (gr. k-3). 1979. pap. 7.95 (*0-395-28267-5*) HM.

— Hubert's Hair-Raising Adventure. (J). 1959. 12.15 (*0-606-02137-X*, Pub. by Turtleback) Demco.

— Huge Harold, 001. (Illus.). 48p. (J). (gr. k-3). 1974. 16.00 (*0-395-18449-5*) HM.

— Huge Harold, 001. (Illus.). 48p. (J). (ps-3). 1982. pap. 7.95 (*0-395-32923-X*) HM.

— Jennifer & Josephine, 001. (Illus.). 48p. (J). (gr. k-3). 1980. pap. 7.95 (*0-395-29608-0*) HM.

— Jennifer & Josephine. (J). 1967. 12.15 (*0-606-02143-4*, Pub. by Turtleback) Demco.

— Jethro & Joel Were a Troll. LC 86-20879. (Illus.). 32p. (J). (gr. k-3). 1990. pap. 7.95 (*0-395-53968-4*) HM.

— Jethro & Joel Were a Troll. (J). 1987. 11.15 (*0-606-04450-7*, Pub. by Turtleback) Demco.

— Kermit the Hermit, 001. (Illus.). 48p. (J). (gr. k-3). 1973. 16.00 (*0-395-15084-1*) HM.

— Kermit the Hermit, 001. LC 65-20482. (Illus.). 48p. (J). (ps-3). 1980. pap. 8.95 (*0-395-29607-2*) HM.

— Kermit the Hermit. (J). 1965. 12.15 (*0-606-02147-7*, Pub. by Turtleback) Demco.

— The Kweeks of Kookatumdee. (Illus.). 32p. (J). (gr. k-3). 1988. pap. 7.95 (*0-395-48656-4*, Sandpiper) HM.

— The Luckiest One of All, 001. (Illus.). 32p. (J). (gr. k-3). 1982. 16.00 (*0-395-31863-7*) HM.

— The Luckiest One of All, 001. (Illus.). 32p. (J). (gr. k-3). 1985. pap. 7.95 (*0-395-39593-3*) HM.

— Luckiest One of All. (J). 1982. 12.15 (*0-606-02818-8*, Pub. by Turtleback) Demco.

— Merle the High Flying Squirrel, 001. (Illus.). 30p. (J). (gr. k-3). 1983. reprint ed. pap. 7.95 (*0-395-34923-0*) HM.

— No Such Things, 001. LC 82-23234. (Illus.). 32p. (J). (gr. k-3). 1983. 16.00 (*0-395-33888-3*) HM.

— No Such Things, 001. LC 82-23234. (Illus.). 32p. (J). (gr. k-3). 1985. pap. 7.95 (*0-395-39594-1*) HM.

Peet, Bill. No Such Things. (J). 1983. 12.15 (*0-606-04490-6*, Pub. by Turtleback) Demco.

Peet, Bill. Pamela Camel. (Illus.). 32p. (J). (gr. 4-8). 1986. pap. 7.95 (*0-395-41670-1*, Sandpiper) HM.

— Pinkish, Purplish, Bluish Egg, 001. (Illus.). 48p. (J). (gr. k-3). 1984. pap. 7.95 (*0-395-36172-9*) HM.

Peet, Bill. Pinkish, Purplish, Bluish Egg. (J). 1963. 11.15 (*0-606-03199-5*, Pub. by Turtleback) Demco.

Peet, Bill. Randy's Dandy Lions, 001. (Illus.). 48p. (J). (gr. k-3). 1979. pap. 6.95 (*0-395-27498-2*) HM.

Peet, Bill. Randy's Dandy Lions. (J). 1964. 12.15 (*0-606-02238-4*, Pub. by Turtleback) Demco.

Peet, Bill. Smokey, 001. (Illus.). 40p. (J). (gr. k-3). 1962. 16.00 (*0-395-15992-X*) HM.

Peet, Bill. Smokey, 001. (Illus.). 48p. (J). (gr. k-3). 1983. reprint ed. pap. 8.95 (*0-395-34924-9*) HM.

Peet, Bill. The Spooky Tail of Prewitt Peacock, 001. LC 72-7930. (Illus.). 32p. (J). (gr. k-3). 1973. 16.00 (*0-395-15494-4*) HM.

— The Spooky Tail of Prewitt Peacock, 001. (Illus.). 32p. (J). (gr. k-3). 1979. pap. 6.95 (*0-395-28159-8*) HM.

— Spooky Tail of Prewitt Peacock. (J). 1973. 11.15 (*0-606-02276-7*, Pub. by Turtleback) Demco.

— Whingdingdilly, 001. LC 71-98521. (Illus.). 64p. (J). (gr. k-3). 1977. 16.00 (*0-395-24729-2*) HM.

— Whingdingdilly, 001. LC 71-98521. (Illus.). 64p. (J). (gr. k-3). 1982. pap. 7.95 (*0-395-31381-3*) HM.

— Whingdingdilly. (J). 1970. 12.15 (*0-606-00652-4*, Pub. by Turtleback) Demco.

— Whingdingsilly. (Carry-Along Book & Cassette Favorites Ser.). (J). (ps-3). 1994. pap. 9.95 incl. audio (*0-395-68981-3*, 492955) Ticknor & Flds Bks Yng Read.

— Wump World, 001. LC 72-124999. (Illus.). 48p. (J). (gr. 3-5). 1974. 16.00 (*0-395-19841-0*) HM.

— Wump World, 001. LC 72-124999. (Illus.). 48p. (J). (gr. 3-5). 1981. pap. 6.95 (*0-395-31129-2*) HM.

— Wump World. 1970. 12.15 (*0-606-02427-1*, Pub. by Turtleback) Demco.

— The Wump World. (Carry-Along Book & Cassette Favorites Ser.). (Illus.). 1p. (J). 1991. pap. 10.95 incl. audio (*0-395-58412-4*, 492998) HM.

— Zella, Zack & Zodia, 001. 1986. 16.00 (*0-395-41069-X*) HM.

— Zella, Zack, & Zodiac. (Illus.). 32p. (J). (gr. k-3). 1989. pap. 6.95 (*0-395-52207-2*) HM.

— Zella, Zack, & Zodiac. (J). 1986. 12.15 (*0-606-04434-5*, Pub. by Turtleback) Demco.

Peet, Eric. Egypt & the Old Testament. 244p. 1990. pap. text 18.00 (*0-916157-83-0*) African Islam Miss Pubns.

Peet, Eric T. A Comparative Study of the Literatures of Egypt, Palestine & Mesopotamia. (British Academy, London, Schweich Lectures on Biblical Archaeology Series, 1930). 1972. reprint ed. pap. 25.00 (*0-8115-1271-1*) Periodicals Srv.

Peet, Harvey P. Notions of the Deaf & Dumb Before Instruction. 1973. 59.95 (*0-8490-0740-2*) Gordon Pr.

— Scripture Lessons for the Deaf & Dumb. 1972. 59.95 (*0-8490-1007-1*) Gordon Pr.

Peet, Jennifer. Chiropractic Pediatric & Prenatal Reference Manual. 2nd rev. ed. Marko, Stephanie K., ed. (Illus.). (C). 1992. 49.95 (*0-614-29608-0*) Baby Adjusters.

Peet, Jennifer B. & Peet, Palmer M. Pediatric Chiropractic Practice Management. 2nd ed. (Illus.). 187p. (C). 1993. 45.00 (*0-9638642-5-3*) Baby Adjusters.

Peet, John. Energy & the Ecological Economics of Sustainability. LC 91-41207. 311p. 1992. text 45.00 (*1-55963-161-9*); pap. text 25.00 (*1-55963-160-0*) Island Pr.

Peet, John, jt. auth. see Benton, John.

Peet, John, tr. see Marx, Karl & Engels, Friedrich.

Peet, Louise J. Science Fundamentals: A Background for Household Equipment. LC 70-171171. (Illus.). 140p. 1972. reprint ed. pap. 43.40 (*0-608-00157-0*, 206093800006) Bks Demand.

Peet, Marceline N. The New Life Cookbook: Based on the Health & Nutritional Philosophy of the Edgar Cayce Readings. LC 97-31082. 180p. 1998. pap. 12.95 (*0-87604-400-3*, 522) ARE Pr.

Peet, Margaret S., jt. auth. see Lad, Vasant D.

Peet, Mary. Sustainable Practices for Vegetable Production in the South. (Illus.). 184p. 1996. pap. text 32.95 (*0-941051-55-2*) Focus Pub-R Pullins.

Peet, Palmer M., jt. auth. see Peet, Jennifer B.

Peet, R. C. A Monologue with God: In Remembrance of the Holocaust. LC 95-95112. (Illus.). 20p. (Orig.). 1996. write for info. (*0-9649871-0-4*) Remembrnce Hse.

Peet, Richard. Modern Geographic Thought: Richard Peet. LC 97-27639. 1998. 73.95 (*1-55786-206-0*); pap. 31.95 (*1-55786-378-4*) Blackwell Pubs.

Peet, Richard, ed. International Capitalism & Industrial Restructuring. LC 86-28870. 256p. 1987. text 39.95 (*0-04-338132-4*); pap. text 21.95 (*0-04-338133-2*) Routledge.

***Peet, Richard & Hartwick, Elaine.** Theories of Development. LC 99-28968. 240p. 1999. pap. text 22.95 (*1-57230-489-8*) Guilford Pubns.

Peet, Richard & Thrift, Nigel J., eds. New Models in Geography: The Political-Economy Perspective, 1. 448p. 1989. text 75.00 (*0-685-44712-X*) Routledge.

Peet, Richard & Watts, Michael, eds. Liberation Ecologies: Environment, Development, Social Movements. LC 95-45381. 288p. (C). 1996. pap. 25.99 (*0-415-13362-9*) Routledge.

— Liberation Ecologies: Environment, Development, Social Movements. LC 95-45381. 288p. (C). 1996. 85.00 (*0-415-13361-0*) Routledge.

Peet, Richard H. Manufacturing Industries & Economic Development in the SADCC Countries. (Energy, Environment & Development in Africa Ser.: No. 5). 119p. 1984. write for info. (*91-7106-233-5*, Pub. by Nordic Africa) Transaction Pubs.

Peet, Stephen D. Prehistoric America, 5 vols., Set. LC 74-7993. 1905. 295.00 (*0-404-11930-1*) AMS Pr.

***Peet, Stephen D.** The Sources of Information As to the Prehistoric Condition of America. (LC History-America-E). 30p. 1999. reprint ed. lib. bdg. 69.00 (*0-7812-4271-1*) Rprt Serv.

Peet, T. Eric. Egypt & the Old Testament. (African Heritage Classical Research Studies). 236p. reprint ed. 25.00 (*0-938818-43-0*) ECA Assoc.

Peet, T. Eric, tr. The Rhind Mathematical Papyrus. 1990. reprint ed. 85.00 (*3-262-00839-7*) Periodicals Srv.

Peete, Gary R. Business, Government & Law on the Internet: A Hands-on Workshop. 2nd ed. LC 99-187519. (Internet Workshop Ser.: Vol. 3). (Illus.). 170p. 1999. pap. text 45.00 incl. disk (*1-882208-24-2*) Library Solns.

***Peeters.** The Lexicon-Encyclopedia Interface. 2000. 90.00 (*0-08-043591-2*, Pergamon Pr) Elsevier.

Peeters & Schuiten, Peeters. Stories of the Fantastic: The Tower. Lofficier, Jean-Marc & Lofficier, R., trs. from FRE. (Stories of the Fantastic Ser.). 112p. 1993. pap. 14.95 (*1-56163-070-5*) NBM.

Peeters, Benoit. Tintin & the World of Herge: An Illustrated History. (Illus.). 161p. (J). (gr. 5 up). 1992. 45.00 (*0-316-69752-4*, Joy St Bks) Little.

Peeters, C. & Wergeland, T. European Shortsea Shipping - 3: Proceedings from the Third European Research Roundtable, Bergen, Norway. (Illus.). 564p. 1997. 142.50 (*90-407-1408-8*, Pub. by Delft U Pr) Coronet Bks.

Peeters, C., jt. ed. see Wijnolst, N.

Peeters, Eric, jt. ed. see French, Patrick J.

Peeters, F. L., jt. ed. see Valk, J.

Peeters, F. M., jt. ed. see Devresse, J. T.

Peeters, Flor. Jubilate Deo Omnis Terra: Psalm 99, Score & Brass Parts Accompaniment 1954. LC M 2079.L45P3. 43p. reprint ed. pap. 30.00 (*0-608-10798-0*, 200340700021) Bks Demand.

— Little Organ Book for Beginners in Organ Playing. 114p. (Orig.). (gr. 3-12). 1957. pap. text 14.95 (*0-87487-600-1*) Summy-Birchard.

— Magnificat, Opus One Hundred Eight, Score & Eight Parts, (Trumpet, Trombone, Bass Tuba, Kettle Drum, Cymbals) LC M 1528.M3. 45p. reprint ed. pap. 30.00 (*0-608-10722-0*, 200438900058) Bks Demand.

— Thirty-Five Miniatures & Other Pieces for Organ. 64p. (Orig.). (gr. 7-12). 1975. pap. text 10.95 (*0-87487-602-8*) Summy-Birchard.

Peeters, Hans, jt. auth. see Jameson, E. W., Jr.

Peeters, Hans J., jt. auth. see Jameson, E. W., Jr.

Peeters, Marga. Time-to-Build: Interrelated Investments & Labour Demand Modelling with Applications to Six OECD Countries. LC 94-43958. (Lecture Notes in Economics & Mathematical Systems Ser.: Vol. 420). 1995. write for info. (*0-387-58809-4*) Spr-Verlag.

***Peeters, Marguerite A.** Hijacking Democracy: The Power Shift to the Unelected. 2000. 29.95 (*0-8447-4135-3*, Pub. by Am Enterprise); pap. 16.95 (*0-8447-4136-1*, Pub. by Am Enterprise) Pub Resources Inc.

Peeters, Paul, jt. auth. see Meijer, Anton.

Peeters, Peter. The Four Phases of Society: Where Are We Going in the 21st Century? LC 97-34756. 192p. 1998. 49.95 (*0-275-96143-5*, Praeger Pubs) Greenwood.

Peeters Publishers Staff. Pentateuchal & Deuteronomy Studies. 1998. 46.95 (*90-6831-306-1*, Pub. by Peeters Pub) Bks Intl VA.

Peeters, T. W. Turbulence, Heat & Mass Transfer 2: Proceedings of the 2nd International Symposium Delft, June 9-12, 1997. Hanjalic, K., ed. (Illus.). 922p. 1997. 147.50 (*90-407-1465-7*, Pub. by Delft U Pr) Coronet Bks.

Peeters, Theo. Autism: From Theoretical Understanding to Educational Intervention. LC 97-10245. (Illus.). 198p. (Orig.). 1997. pap. 39.95 (*1-56593-846-1*, 1652) Singular Publishing.

— Autism: Medical & Educational Aspects. 2nd ed. 1998. pap. text 26.95 (*1-86156-093-1*) Whurr Pub.

Peeters, Theo, jt. ed. see Fratianni, Michele U.

***Peeters, Vital.** Stained Glass. 1999. pap. 29.95 (*1-86126-299-X*, Pub. by Crolwood) Trafalgar.

Peetoom, Adrian. Shared Reading: Safe Risks with Whole Books. (J). 1993. pap. 7.95 (*0-590-71698-0*) Scholastic Inc.

Peetoom, Adrian, tr. see Stilma, Lize.

Peetre, J., et al, eds. Function Spaces & Applications. (Lecture Notes in Mathematics Ser.: Vol. 1302). vi, 445p. 1988. 59.95 (*0-387-18905-X*) Spr-Verlag.

Peetre, J., jt. auth. see Cwikel, Michael.

Peetre, J., jt. auth. see Lumiste, V.

Peetre, J., tr. see Ashurov, R. R., et al.

Peetre, J., tr. see Nikol'skii, N. K.

Peetre, J., tr. see Nikol'skij, S. M. & Gamkrelidze, R. V., eds.

Peets, Leonora. Women of Marrakesh. Taagepera, Rein, tr. from EST. LC 87-26536. 200p. 1988. text 38.95 (*0-8223-0812-6*) Duke.

Peetz, David. Unions in a Contrary World: The Future of the Australian Trade Union Movement. LC 98-7189. (Reshaping Australian Institutions Ser.). (Illus.). 256p. (C). 1998. text 64.95 (*0-521-63055-X*); pap. text 25.95 (*0-521-63950-6*) Cambridge U Pr.

Peetz, Michael, jt. auth. see Boyne, Philip J.

Peetz, Richard H. Improving the Performance & Handling of Your Sporty Car: A Guide & Source Book. LC 97-14817. (Illus.). 100p. (Orig.). 1997. 25.00 (*1-56216-254-3*); pap. 18.00 (*1-56216-255-1*) Systems Co.

Peetz, Richard H. & Peetz, Tuttie. ABCs of Retiring Early: A Guide to Changing Your Life-Style Before Traditional Age. LC 97-20928. (Illus.). 60p. (Orig.). 1997. 23.00 (*1-56216-252-7*); pap. 14.00 (*1-56216-253-5*) Systems Co.

Peetz, Tuttie. Basic Budgeting & Money Management: A Guide for Taking Control of Your Spending. LC 97-20924. (Illus.). 75p. 1997. 23.00 (*1-56216-250-0*); pap. 14.00 (*1-56216-251-9*) Systems Co.

Peetz, Tuttie, jt. auth. see Peetz, Richard H.

Peeva, K. & Delijska, B., compiled by. Elsevier's Dictionary of Computer Science & Mathematics. LC 95-32300.Tr. of Mnogoezichen Rechik po Informatika i Kompiutarna Tekhnika. (ENG, FRE, GER & RUS.). 800p. 1995. 215.50 (*0-444-81816-2*) Elsevier.

Peeva, K. G. & Peeva, P. N. Elsevier's Dictionary of Mathematics. LC 99-89650. 800p. 2000. write for info. (*0-444-82953-9*) Elsevier.

Peeva, P. N., jt. auth. see Peeva, K. G.

Peeved, I. M. & Strand, Ed. 701 Things That P-ss Me off about Work. LC 96-5344. 288p. 1996. pap. 7.95 (*0-399-52231-X*, Perigee Bks) Berkley Pub.

Peeved, I.M. One Thousand Four Hundred & One Things That P*Ss Me Off. 1991. pap. 5.95 (*0-399-51670-0*, Perigee Bks) Berkley Pub.

Peevers, David, jt. auth. see Shulte-Peevers, Andrea.

***Peez, Carl, et al.** Maria-Theresien-Thaler. (Social Research on Africa Ser.: Vol. 5). 128p. 1999. pap. 22.95 (*3-8258-3765-3*, Pub. by CE24) Transaction Pubs.

Pef. Belles Lisses Poires de France. (Folio - Cadet Bleu Ser.: No. 216). (FRE.). 56p. (J). (gr. 1-5). 1990. pap. 8.95 (*2-07-031216-X*) Schoenhof.

— Dictionnaires des Mots Tordus. (Folio - Cadet Bleu Ser.: No. 192). (FRE.). 79p. (J). (gr. 1-5). 1989. pap. 10.95 (*2-07-031192-9*) Schoenhof.

— Ivre de Francais. (Folio - Cadet Bleu Ser.: No. 246). (FRE.). 48p. (J). (gr. 1-5). 1986. pap. 7.95 (*2-07-031246-1*) Schoenhof.

— Livre de Nattes. (Folio - Cadet Bleu Ser.: No. 240). (FRE.). 78p. (J). (gr. 1-5). 1990. pap. 7.95 (*2-07-031240-2*) Schoenhof.

Pefanis, Julian. Heterology & the Postmodern: Bataille, Baudrillard & Lyotard. LC 90-3381. 200p. (C). 1991. text 36.00 (*0-8223-1075-9*); pap. text 39.95 (*0-8223-1093-7*) Duke.

Pefanis, Julian, ed. see Lyotard, Jean F.

Pefanis, Julian, tr. see Guattari, Felix.

Pefaur, Jaime E. & Hoffmann, Robert S. Studies of Small Mammal Populations at Three Sites on the Northern Great Plains. (Occasional Papers: No. 37). 27p. 1975. pap. 1.00 (*0-317-04897-X*) U KS Nat Hist Mus.

Pefaur, Jaime E., jt. auth. see Humphrey, Philip S.

Peffer, E. Louise. The Closing of the Public Domain: Disposal & Reservation Policies, 1900-50. LC 72-2862. (Use & Abuse of America's Natural Resources Ser.). 388p. 1972. reprint ed. 25.95 (*0-405-04528-X*) Ayer.

— The Closing of the Public Domain: Disposal & Reservation Policies, 1900-50. LC HD0216.P37. 383p. reprint ed. pap. 30.00 (*0-608-08249-X*, 205195800016) Bks Demand.

Peffer-Engels, John. Chewa. LC 96-7634. (Heritage Library of African Peoples). (Illus.). 64p. (J). (gr. 7-12). 1996. lib. bdg. 16.95 (*0-8239-2010-0*) Rosen Group.

Peffer, George. Personal Effects. 56p. (Orig.). 1993. pap. 8.00 (*0-9637849-1-9*) Bacchae Pr.

Peffer, George & Murcko, Terry. Orphan Trees. LC 79-91911. (Midwest Writer Ser.). 80p. 1980. pap. 4.95 (*0-917530-08-X*) Pig Iron Pr.

Peffer, George Anthony. If They Don't Bring Women Here: Chinese Female Immigration Before Exclusion. LC 98-58013. 184p. 1999. 35.00 (*0-252-02469-9*); pap. 17.95 (*0-252-06777-0*) U of Ill Pr.

Peffer, John. The Benin Kingdom of West Africa, 6 vols., Set. LC 96-7580. (Celebrating the Peoples & Civilizations of Africa Ser.). (Illus.). 24p. (J). (gr. k-4). 1996. lib. bdg. 15.93 (*0-8239-2334-7*, PowerKids) Rosen Group.

— States of Ethiopia. LC 97-37354. (African Civilizations Ser.). (J). 1998. 22.00 (*0-531-20278-X*) Watts.

Peffer, Nathaniel. The White Man's Dilemma: Climax of the Age of Imperialism. LC 72-4288. (World Affairs Ser.: National & International Viewpoints). 320p. 1972. reprint ed. 23.95 (*0-405-04580-8*) Ayer.

***Peffer, Randall.** Logs of the Dead Pirates Society: A Schooner Adventure Around Buzzards Bay. LC 99-86721. 256p. 2000. 23.95 (*1-57409-095-X*) Sheridan.

— Puerto Rico. (Illus.). 304p. 1999. pap. 15.95 (*0-86442-552-X*) Lonely Planet.

Peffer, Randall S. Watermen. LC 79-9896. (Maryland Paperback Bookshelf Ser.). 208p. 1985. reprint ed. pap. 12.95 (*0-8018-2737-X*) Johns Hopkins.

Peffer, Randall S., et al. New York & Pennsylvania & New Jersey. LC 97-22435. (Driving Guides to America Ser.). 1997. write for info. (*0-7922-3431-6*) Natl Geog.

***Peffer, Randy, et al.** Lonely Planet Virginia & the Capital Region. (Travel Guides Ser.). (Illus.). 624p. 2000. pap. 21.95 (*0-86442-769-7*) Lonely Planet.

Peffer, Rodney G. Marxism, Morality, & Social Justice. LC 89-38899. (Studies in Moral, Political, & Legal Philosophy). 540p. reprint ed. pap. 167.40 (*0-608-08019-5*, 206798400001) Bks Demand.

Peffer, William A. Populism, Its Rise & Fall. annot. ed. LC 91-18795. (Illus.). viii, 208p. 1992. 25.00 (*0-7006-0509-6*) U Pr of KS.

Pefferkorn, ed. Interfacial Phenomena in Chromatography. LC 99-17313. (Surfactant Science Ser.). (Illus.). 456p. 1999. text 175.00 (*0-8247-1947-6*) Dekker.

Peffers, Hopkins S. Aurora-Elgin Area Streetcars & Interurbans, 4 vols., Set. (Illus.). 776p. 1993. 198.00 (*1-883461-05-7*) Am Slide-Chart.

— Aurora-Elgin Area Streetcars & Interurbans Vol. 1: Fox River Division. (Illus.). 168p. 1993. 49.50 (*1-883461-01-4*) Am Slide-Chart.

— Aurora-Elgin Area Streetcars & Interurbans Vol. 2: Aurora Elgin & Fox River Electric. (Illus.). 184p. 1993. 49.50 (*1-883461-02-2*) Am Slide-Chart.

— Aurora-Elgin Area Streetcars & Interurbans Vol. 3: The Third Rail Line. (Illus.). 224p. 1993. 49.50 (*1-883461-03-0*) Am Slide-Chart.

— Aurora-Elgin Area Streetcars & Interurbans Vol. 4: The Connecting Lines. (Illus.). 200p. 1993. 49.50 (*1-883461-04-9*) Am Slide-Chart.

Peffers, Ken, jt. auth. see Dos Santos, Brian L.

***Peffley, Ellen, et al.** Introductory Horiculture Laboratory Manual. 104p. (C). 1999. spiral bd. 23.95 (*0-7872-6218-8*, 41621801) Kendall-Hunt.

Peffley, Mark, jt. ed. see Hurwitz, Jon.

***Peffley, Mary.** Woman of Faith: The Life of Edel Quinn. (Illus.). 64p. 2000. 3.00 (*1-892875-08-X*, 3019) New Hope Publicatns.

Pefkaros, Kenneth. Fundamentals of IFPS. 66p. 1996. wbk. ed. 16.95 (*1-885587-67-8*) Bridge Lrn Systs.

Pefkaros, S., jt. auth. see O'Donnell, K.

Pefla, Ramon O. Sanchez, see Sanchez Pefla, Ramon O.

Pefley, Richard K. Mechancial Engineering Problems & Solutions. 6th rev. ed. Orig. Title: Mechanical Engineering License Review Problems & Solutions. (Illus.). 378p. 1996. 39.50 (*1-57645-008-2*) Engineering.

Pefley, Richard K., jt. ed. see Hirao, Osamu.

Pegalis, Steven E. & Wachsman, Harvey F. American Law of Medical Malpractice, 3 vols., Set. 2nd ed. LC 92-90712. 1992. 365.00 (*0-685-59872-1*) West Group.

Pegasus Learning Company Staff. Science Anytime Videodisc Series Library, Set. (J). (gr. k-6). 1996. write for info. incl. vdisk (*1-881259-37-4*) Pegasus Lrn.

Pegden, C. Dennis, et al. Introduction to Simulation Using SIMAN. (C). 1991. text 83.50 (*0-07-049217-4*) McGraw.

An Asterisk (*) at the beginning of an entry indicates that the title is appearing for the first time.

— Introduction to Simulation Using SIMAN. 2nd ed. LC 94-41386. 640p. (C). 1995. 98.13 *(0-07-049320-0)* McGraw.

Pegels, C. Carl. Handbook of Strategies & Tools for the Learning Company. LC 98-28751. 496p. 1998. 65.00 *(1-56327-210-5)* Productivity Inc.

— Systems Analysis for Production Operations, Vol. 3. (Studies in Operations Research). xvi, 472p. 1976. text 304.00 *(0-677-04710-X)* Gordon & Breach.

Pegels, C. Carl, ed. Management & Industry in China. LC 86-25260. 294p. 1986. 65.00 *(0-275-92553-6,* C2553, Praeger Pubs) Greenwood.

Pegels, C. Carl, jt. auth. see Goldberg, Alvin.

Pegels, C. Carl, jt. auth. see Lofti, Vahid.

Pegels, C. Carl, ed. see Cerveny, Robert P.

Pegels, C. Carl, jt. ed. see Mahajan, Vijay.

Pegg, A. E., ed. Biochemical Journal Reviews 1994. (Illus.). 200p. (C). 1995. text 51.00 *(1-85578-084-4,* Pub. by Portland Pr Ltd) Ashgate Pub Co.

— Biochemical Journal Reviews 1995. (Illus.). 200p. (C). 1996. text 51.00 *(1-85578-107-7,* Pub. by Portland Pr Ltd) Ashgate Pub Co.

Pegg, A. E., jt. ed. see Evans, W. H.

Pegg, Anthony E., jt. ed. see Zappia, V.

Pegg, Carl H. Evolution of the European Idea, 1914-1932. LC 82-24796. 238p. reprint ed. pap. 73.80 *(0-7837-7076-6,* 204688800004) Bks Demand.

***Pegg, Carole.** Mongolian Music, Dance, & Oral Narrative: Performing Diverse Identities. LC 00-42308. 2001. write for info. *(0-295-98030-3)* U Pr of Amer.

Pegg, Connie J. Snow Bound: Pen & Ben Youth Adventures. 112p. (J). (gr. 6-10). 1999. pap. 7.95 *(1-929078-17-X,* CPB01) Gods Kids.

Pegg, David E., jt. ed. see Karow, Armand M., Jr.

Pegg, Leonard. Family Law in Hong Kong. 3rd ed. 305p. 1994. pap. text, student ed. write for info. *(0-409-99688-2,* MICHIE) LEXIS Pub.

***Pegg, Mary Christina.** The Poetical Works, Pt. I. 48p. 1999. pap. 4.95 *(1-885206-79-8)* Cader Pubng.

Pegg, P. F., jt. auth. see Jespersen, Ellen.

Pegg, Scott. International Society & the De Facto State. LC 98-37112. 9p. 1998. text 68.95 *(1-84014-478-5,* Pub. by Ashgate Pub) Ashgate Pub Co.

Pegge, S. Two Collections of Derbicisms Containing Words & Phrases in a Great Measure... Derby. Hallum, T. & Skeat, Walter W., eds. (English Dialect Society Publications: No. 78). 1974. reprint ed. pap. 30.00 *(0-8115-0496-4)* Periodicals Srv.

Pegge, Samuel. An Assemblage of Coins Fabricated by the Authority of the Archbishops of Canterbury. (Illus.). 1975. pap. 15.00 *(0-916710-23-8)* Obol Intl.

Peggs, Ian D., ed. Geosynthetics: Microstructure & Performance. LC 90-36990. (Special Technical Publication (STP) Ser.: STP 1076). (Illus.). 170p. 1990. text 30.00 *(0-8031-1298-X,* STP1076) ASTM.

Peggs, L. A. Underground Piping Handbook. LC 83-19906. 296p. 1985. lib. bdg. 32.50 *(0-89874-616-7)* Krieger.

Peggy, Ned, contrib. by. So Many Bridges. large type ed. 1994. 27.99 *(0-7089-3209-6)* Ulverscroft.

Pegington, John, jt. auth. see Dean, Christopher.

Pegis, Anton C. St. Thomas & Philosophy. LC 64-17418. (Aquinas Lectures). 1964. 15.00 *(0-87462-129-1)* Marquette.

— St. Thomas & the Greeks. (Aquinas Lectures). 1939. 15.00 *(0-87462-103-8)* Marquette.

— St. Thomas & the Problem of the Soul in the Thirteenth Century. 213p. pap. text 18.29 *(0-88844-406-0)* Brill Academic Pubs.

Pegis, Anton C., ed. see Aquinas, Thomas, Saint.

Pegleer, Martin. Stores of the Year. 1997. 59.95 *(0-07-049399-5)* McGraw.

Pegler, D. N. The Agarics of Sao Paulo, Brazil. (Illus.). iv, 114p. 1997. pap. 46.00 *(1-900347-16-4,* Pub. by Royal Botnic Grdns) Balogh.

— The Genus Lentinus: A World Monograph. (Kew Bulletin Additional Ser.: Vol. X). (Illus.). 281p. 1983. pap. 20.00 *(0-11-242627-1,* Pub. by Royal Botnic Grdns) Balogh.

Pegler, David. British Chanterelles & Tooth-Fungi: An Account of the British Cantharelloid & Stipitate Hydnoid Fungi. (Illus.). iv, 114p. 1997. pap. 46.00 *(1-900347-15-6,* Pub. by Royal Botnic Grdns) Balogh.

Pegler, David N. Agaric Flora of Sri Lanka. (Kew Bulletin Additional Ser.: Vol. XII). (Illus.). 519p. 1986. pap. 42.00 *(0-11-250004-8,* Pub. by Royal Botnic Grdns) Balogh.

— Agaric Flora of the Lesser Antilles. (Kew Bulletin Additional Ser.: Vol. IX). 668p. 1983. pap. 70.00 *(0-11-241180-0,* Pub. by Royal Botnic Grdns) Balogh.

— Preliminary Agaric Flora of East Africa. (Kew Bulletin Additional Ser.: Vol. VI). (Illus.). 615p. 1977. pap. 60.00 *(0-11-241101-0,* Pub. by Royal Botnic Grdns) Balogh.

Pegler, David N., et al, eds. Fungi of Europe: Investigation, Recording & Conservations. (Illus.). x, 322p. 1993. pap. 36.00 *(0-947643-54-0,* Pub. by Royal Botnic Grdns) Balogh.

Pegler, David N., et al. British Puffballs, Earthstars & Stinkhorns: An Account of the British Gasteroid Fungi. (Illus.). x, 270p. 1995. pap. 60.00 *(0-947643-81-8,* Pub. by Royal Botnic Grdns) Balogh.

— British Truffles: A Revision of British Hypogeous Fungi. (Illus.). viii, 216p. 1993. pap. 40.00 *(0-947643-39-7,* Pub. by Royal Botnic Grdns) Balogh.

— Genera of Endogonales. (Illus.). iv, 229p. 1996. pap. 42.00 *(0-947643-92-3,* Pub. by Royal Botnic Grdns) Balogh.

Pegler, Martin. British Tommy, 1914-1918. (Illus.). 64p. 1996. pap. 12.95 *(1-85532-541-1,* Pub. by Ospry) Stackpole.

— Live Firing Classic Weapons: Powder & Ball Small Arms. 1998. 39.95 *(1-85915-069-1,* Pub. by W & G) Motorbooks Intl.

***Pegler, Martin.** Powder & Ball Small Arms. (Illus.). 128p. 1999. write for info. *(1-86126-185-3,* Pub. by Cro1wood) Trafalgar.

Pegler, Martin. U. S. Cavalryman, 1865-90. (Warrior Ser.). (Illus.). 64p. 1993. pap. 12.95 *(1-85532-319-2,* 9603, Pub. by Ospry) Stackpole.

***Pegler, Martin M.** Cafe Design. (Illus.). 176p. 2000. 49.95 *(1-58471-020-9,* Pub. by Visual Refer) Watsn-Guptill.

Pegler, Martin M. Cafes & Bistros. (Illus.). 176p. 1998. 49.95 *(0-934590-95-8)* Visual Refer.

***Pegler, Martin M.** Cafes & Coffee Shops. rev. ed. (Illus.). 208p. 1999. pap. 34.95 *(1-58471-009-8)* Visual Refer.

— Contemporary Exhibit Design. (Illus.). 176p. 2000. 49.95 *(1-58471-002-0)* Visual Refer.

Pegler, Martin M. Dictionary of Interior Design. (Illus.). 217p. (C). 1983. 43.00 *(0-87005-447-3)* Fairchild.

***Pegler, Martin M.** Entertainment Destinations. (Illus.). 176p. 2000. 49.95 *(1-58471-012-8)* Visual Refer.

— Entertainment Dining. (Illus.). 176p. 1999. 49.95 *(1-58471-005-5)* Visual Refer.

Pegler, Martin M. Food Presentation & Display. (Illus.). 224p. 1991. 41.95 *(0-934590-41-9)* Visual Refer.

— Food Retail Design & Display, No. 2. (Illus.). 240p. 1992. 49.95 *(0-934590-51-6)* Visual Refer.

— Lifestyle Stores. LC 96-15789. 176p. 1996. 37.50 *(0-86636-498-6)* PBC Intl Inc.

— Lifestyle Stores. LC 96-15789. (Illus.). 176p. 1998. pap. 29.95 *(0-86636-499-4)* PBC Intl Inc.

— Retail Entertainment. 176p. 1996. 49.95 *(0-934590-89-3)* Visual Refer.

— Specialty Food Store Design. (Illus.). 176p. 1999. 49.95 *(0-934590-77-X)* Visual Refer.

— Store Fronts & Facades, No. 3. (Illus.). 224p. 1990. 49.95 *(0-934590-38-9)* Visual Refer.

— Store Fronts & Facades, No. 4. (Illus.). 240p. 1992. 49.95 *(0-934590-48-6)* Visual Refer.

***Pegler, Martin M.** Store Windows, No. 11. (Illus.). 176p. 2000. 49.95 *(1-58471-018-7,* Pub. by Visual Refer) Watsn-Guptill.

— Store Windows, No. 11. 176p. 2000. 49.95 *(1-58471-014-4)* Visual Refer.

Pegler, Martin M. Store Windows, Vol. 10. 1999. text 49.95 *(0-934590-17-6)* Visual Refer.

— Store Windows 8. 224p. 1995. 59.95 *(0-934590-72-9)* Visual Refer.

— Store Windows That Sell, No. 5. (Illus.). 1990. 49.95 *(0-934590-39-7)* Visual Refer.

— Store Windows That Sell, No. 6. (Illus.). 224p. 1992. 49.95 *(0-934590-47-8)* Visual Refer.

— Storefronts & Facades, No. 5. 240p. 1994. 59.95 *(0-934590-67-2)* Visual Refer.

— Stores of the Year, Bk. 7. 1993. 49.95 *(0-934590-53-2)* Visual Refer.

— Stores of the Year, Bk. 11. (Illus.). 192p. 1999. 59.95 *(0-934590-98-2)* Visual Refer.

— Stores of the Year, No. 6. (Illus.). 224p. 1991. 49.95 *(0-934590-42-7)* Visual Refer.

— Stores of the Year, No. 9. 224p. 1995. 59.95 *(0-934590-71-0)* Visual Refer.

***Pegler, Martin M.** Stores of the Year, No. 12. (Illus.). 192p. 1999. text 59.95 *(1-58471-001-2)* Visual Refer.

Pegler, Martin M. Stores of the Year V. (Illus.). 256p. 1989. 34.98 *(0-934590-31-1)* Visual Refer.

— Visual Merchandising & Display: The Business of Presentation. (Illus.). 1998. teacher ed. write for info. *(1-56367-174-3)* Fairchild.

— Visual Merchandising & Display: The Business of Presentation. 4th rev. ed. LC 98-72982. (Illus.). 368p. (C). 1998. 52.00 *(1-56367-173-5)* Fairchild.

— Visual Merchandising & Display Student Set: The Business of Presentation & Study Guide. 3rd ed. (Illus.). 375p. 1995. student ed., wbk. ed. 35.00 *(1-56367-084-4)* Fairchild.

Pegler, Martin M., ed. Food Retail Design & Display, No. 3. (Illus.). 240p. 1994. 49.95 *(0-934590-61-3)* Visual Refer.

— Market Supermarket & Hypermarket Design, No. 2. (Illus.). 224p. 1992. 49.95 *(0-934590-44-3)* Visual Refer.

— The Power of Visual Presentation: Retail Design/Kiosks/Exhibit Design/Environmental Design. (Illus.). 176p. 2000. 39.95 *(1-58471-007-1)* Visual Refer.

— Store Fronts & Facades, No. 2. (Illus.). 192p. 1988. 44.95 *(0-934590-26-5)* Visual Refer.

— Store Windows, No. 9. (Illus.). 192p. 1997. 49.95 *(0-934590-93-1)* Visual Refer.

— Store Windows That Sell, No. 3. (Illus.). 176p. 1985. 39.95 *(0-934590-12-5)* Visual Refer.

— Store Windows That Sell, No. 4. (Illus.). 192p. 1988. 44.95 *(0-934590-27-3)* Visual Refer.

— Store Windows That Sell, No. 7. (Illus.). 240p. 1994. 49.95 *(0-934590-57-5)* Visual Refer.

— Storefronts & Facades, No. 6. (Illus.). 208p. 1996. 59.95 *(0-934590-84-2)* Visual Refer.

— Stores of the Year, No. 8. (Illus.). 240p. 1994. 49.95 *(0-934590-60-5)* Visual Refer.

— Stores of the Year, No. 10. (Illus.). 208p. 1996. 59.95 *(0-934590-85-0)* Visual Refer.

— Stores of the Year, Vol. II. (Illus.). 176p. 1981. 39.95 *(0-934590-07-9)* Visual Refer.

— Stores of the Year, Vol. III. (Illus.). 176p. 1984. 39.95 *(0-934590-11-7)* Visual Refer.

— Stores Windows, No. 10. (Illus.). 192p. 1999. 49.95 *(0-934590-01-X)* Visual Refer.

— Streetscapes. (Illus.). 176p. 1998. 49.95 *(0-934590-78-8,* 886971) Visual Refer.

— Successful Food Merchandising & Display. (Illus.). 192p. 1989. 49.95 *(0-934590-24-9)* Visual Refer.

— Supermarket Design, No. 1. (Illus.). 208p. 1996. 59.95 *(0-934590-79-6)* Visual Refer.

Pegler, Martin M., intro. Home Furnishings Merchandising & Store Design. (Illus.). 224p. 1990. 39.95 *(0-934590-36-2)* Visual Refer.

— Market Supermarket & Hypermarket Design. (Illus.). 224p. 1990. 49.95 *(0-934590-33-8)* Visual Refer.

— Stores of the Year, Vol. IV. (Illus.). 192p. 1987. 44.95 *(0-934590-22-2)* Visual Refer.

Pegler, Westbrook. George Spelvin, American: And Fireside Chats. LC 75-39112. (Essay Index Reprint Ser.). 1977. reprint ed. 18.95 *(0-8369-2711-7)* Ayer.

Pegley, Rob. The Virgin Book of Golf Records. (Illus.). 1998. text 24.95 *(1-85227-771-8,* Pub. by Virgin Bks) London Brdge.

Pegoda, Dan, jt. auth. see Sims, Tim.

***Pegoles, Margaret L.** One Life Moving Toward the Light. Voices of Truths Staff, ed. 96p. 1999. pap. 10.95 *(0-9666777-2-2)* Voice of Truths.

Pegoraro, Laura. We'll Practice Addition I. (Powertools for Kids Ser.). (Illus.). 4p. (J). (ps-2). 1998. pap., wbk. ed. 4.95 *(1-58220-000-9,* 32101, PowerTools for Kids) Navigator.

— We'll Practice Addition 2. (Powertools for Kids Ser.: No. 5). (Illus.). 4p. (J). (gr. 1-4). 1998. pap., wbk. ed. 4.95 *(1-58220-004-1,* 32105, PowerTools for Kids) Navigator.

— We'll Practice Cursive. (Powertools for Kids Ser.: No. 9). (Illus.). 4p. (J). (gr. 1-3). 1998. pap., wbk. ed. 4.95 *(1-58220-008-4,* 32109, PowerTools for Kids) Navigator.

— We'll Practice Division. (Powertools for Kids Ser.: No. 4). (Illus.). 4p. (J). (gr. k-4). 1998. pap., wbk. ed. 4.95 *(1-58220-003-3,* 32104, PowerTools for Kids) Navigator.

— We'll Practice More Math. (Powertools for Kids Ser.: No. 8). (Illus.). 4p. (J). (gr. 2-5). 1998. pap., wbk. ed. 4.95 *(1-58220-007-6,* 32108, PowerTools for Kids) Navigator.

— We'll Practice Multiplication 2. (Powertools for Kids Ser.: No. 7). (Illus.). 4p. (J). (gr. 1-4). 1998. pap., wbk. ed. 4.95 *(1-58220-006-8,* 32107, PowerTools for Kids) Navigator.

— We'll Practice Printing. (Powertools for Kids Ser.: No. 10). (Illus.). 4p. (J). (ps-3). 1998. pap., wbk. ed. 4.95 *(1-58220-009-2,* 32110, PowerTools for Kids) Navigator.

— We'll Practice Subtraction I. (Powertools for Kids Ser.: No. 2). (Illus.). 4p. (J). (ps-3). 1998. pap., wbk. ed. 4.95 *(1-58220-001-7,* 32102, PowerTools for Kids) Navigator.

— We'll Practice Subtraction 2. (Powertools for Kids Ser.: No. 6). (Illus.). 4p. (J). (gr. 1-4). 1998. pap., wbk. ed. 4.95 *(1-58220-005-X,* 32106, PowerTools for Kids) Navigator.

Pegoraro, Laura, ed. We'll Practice Multiplication I. (Powertools for Kids Ser.: No. 3). (Illus.). 4p. (J). (gr. 1-3). 1998. pap., wbk. ed. 4.95 *(1-58220-002-5,* 32103, PowerTools for Kids) Navigator.

Pegoraro, Olinto, jt. ed. see McLean, George F.

Pegoretti, Giovanni, jt. ed. see Dallago, Bruno.

Pegram, Billy. Fashion Model Photography: Professional Techniques & Images. LC 98-72987. (Illus.). 120p. 1999. pap. 29.95 *(0-936262-78-8)* Amherst Media.

Pegram, Amelia B. Echoes Across a Thousand Hills: Poems. (Illus.). 96p. 1994. 29.95 *(0-86543-417-4)*; pap. 9.95 *(0-86543-418-2)* Africa World.

Pegram, Kay L. Marketing & Promotion from A to Z: For Home Fashions Retailers & Interior Designers. 157p. (Orig.). 1992. pap. 22.95 *(0-9634747-0-7)* Kaymar Bks.

Pegram, Laura. Daughter's Day Blues. LC 94-41555. (Illus.). 32p. (J). 2000. 15.99 *(0-8037-1557-9,* Dial Yng Read) Peng Put Young Read.

— Rainbow Is Our Face. (Illus.). 12p. (J). (ps). 1994. 5.95 *(0-86316-217-7)* Writers & Readers.

— Windy Day. LC 94-70952. (Illus.). 12p. (J). (ps). 1994. 5.95 *(0-86316-218-5)* Writers & Readers.

Pegram, Linda, ed. see Hamm, Tanya.

Pegram, Thomas R. Battling Demon Rum: The Struggle for a Dry America, 1800-1933. LC 98-15875. (American Ways Ser.). 224p. 1998. 24.95 *(1-56663-208-0,* Pub. by I R Dee) Natl Bk Netwk.

— Battling Demon Rum: The Struggle for a Dry America, 1800-1933. LC 98-15875. (American Ways Ser.). 224p. 1999. pap. 12.95 *(1-56663-209-9,* Pub. by I R Dee) Natl Bk Netwk.

— Partisans & Progressives: Private Interest & Public Policy in Illinois, 1870-1922. 312p. 1992. text 42.50 *(0-252-01847-8)* U of Ill Pr.

***Pegrum, Brenda.** Painted Ceramics: Colour & Imagery on Clay. (Illus.). 160p. 2000. 50.00 *(1-86126-236-1,* Pub. by Cro1wood) Trafalgar.

***Pegrum, Juliet.** The Vastu Vidya Handbook: The Indian Feng Shui. (Illus.). 160p. 2000. pap. 18.95 *(0-609-80578-9,* Three Riv Pr) Crown Pub Group.

Pegrum. Mark A. Challenging Modernity: Dada Between Modern & Postmodern. 352p. 2000. 69.95 *(1-57181-130-3)* Berghahn Bks.

Peguero, Leone. Creative Locker Hooking. (Illus.). 48p. 1993. per. 12.00 *(0-916896-95-1,* LE52) Lacis Pubns.

— Lionel & Amelia. LC 95-49117. (Illus.). 32p. (J). (gr. 2-6). 1996. pap. 4.95 *(1-57255-197-6)* Mondo Pubng.

Pegues, Beverly, ed. see Agthe, Dale.

Pegues, Beverly, jt. ed. see Ebert, Michael.

Pegues, Deborah S. Confronting Without Offending. pap. 7.99 *(0-927936-75-5)* Vincom Pubng Co.

Pegues, Guy. The Illustrated SuperCalc Book. (Illus.). 200p. 17.95 *(0-317-13063-3)* P-H.

Pegues, Lillian. Family Tales: Curse or Happenstance? (Illus.). 208p. 1998. text 21.95 *(1-56167-392-7)* Noble Hse MD.

Pegues, R. P. Catechism of the Summa Theologica of Saint Thomas Aquinas. Whitacre, Aelred, tr. from FRE. 315p. 1993. reprint ed. text 17.95 *(0-912141-03-4)* Roman Cath Bks.

Peguilhan, Aimeric De, see Aimeric De Peguilhan.

Peguy, Charles. L' Argent. (FRE.). 252p. 1932. pap. 34.95 *(0-7859-1292-4,* 2070249743) Fr & Eur.

— La Ballade du Coeur: Poeme Inedit. (FRE.). 274p. 1973. pap. 24.95 *(0-7859-1461-7,* 2252015381) Fr & Eur.

— Cing Prieres dans la Cathedrale de Chartres. (FRE.). 48p. 1947. pap. 10.95 *(0-7859-1295-9,* 2070249921) Fr & Eur.

— Clio. (FRE.). 276p. 1931. pap. 13.95 *(0-7859-1293-2,* 2070249751) Fr & Eur.

— De Jean Coste. (FRE.). 228p. 1937. pap. 10.95 *(0-7859-1294-0,* 2070249832) Fr & Eur.

— Deuxieme Elegie. (FRE.). 440p. 1955. pap. 16.95 *(0-7859-1298-3,* 2070250024) Fr & Eur.

— Les Enfants. (FRE.). 96p. 1952. pap. 10.95 *(0-7859-1296-7,* 2070249972) Fr & Eur.

— L' Esprit de Systeme. (FRE.). 340p. 1953. pap. 11.95 *(0-7859-1297-5,* 2070249999) Fr & Eur.

— Eve. Les Tapisseries. (FRE.). 160p. 1968. pap. 10.95 *(0-7859-1352-1,* 2070302148) Fr & Eur.

— Eve Premiere Mortelle. (FRE., Illus.). 328p. 1933. pap. 13.95 *(0-7859-1291-6,* 2070249697) Fr & Eur.

— Jeanne d'Arc: Cinq Poemes. pap. 3.95 *(0-685-37025-9)* Fr & Eur.

— Jeanne d'Arc: Theatre. 8.95 *(0-685-37026-7)* Fr & Eur.

— Lettres et Entretiens. 13.95 *(0-685-37027-5)* Fr & Eur.

— Lumieres d'Homme. pap. 6.25 *(0-685-37052-6)* Fr & Eur.

— Marcel: Premier Dialogue de la Cite Harmonieuse. (FRE.). 208p. 1973. pap. 11.95 *(0-686-54858-2,* 2070284638) Fr & Eur.

— Morceaux Choisis: Poesie. pap. 6.95 *(0-685-37014-3)* Fr & Eur.

— Le Mystere de la Charite de Jeanne D'Arc. (Gallimard Ser.). (FRE.). pap. 11.95 *(2-07-010656-X)* Schoenhof.

— Note Conjointe: Note sur M. Bergson et la Philosophie Bergsonienne, Note Conjointe sur Descartes et la Philosophie Cartesienne. pap. 8.75 *(0-685-37030-5)* Fr & Eur.

— Notre Jeunesse de la Raison. (Folio Essais Ser.: No. 232). (FRE.). pap. 15.95 *(2-07-032786-8)* Schoenhof.

— Un Nouveau Theologien, M. Laudet. pap. 3.95 *(0-685-37044-5)* Fr & Eur.

— Oeuvres Completes: Paris, 1917-1955, 20 vols. 9827p. 1974. 1995.00 *(0-7859-5391-4)* Fr & Eur.

— Oeuvres en Prose: 1909-1914, Vol. 2: 1905-1909. deluxe ed. Peguy, Marcel, ed. (Pleiade Ser.). (FRE.). 1957. 99.95 *(2-07-011134-2)* Schoenhof.

— Oeuvres en Prose: 1909-1914, Vol. 3. Peguy, Marcel, ed. (Pleiade Ser.). (FRE.). 1957. 129.95 *(2-07-011231-4)* Schoenhof.

— Oeuvres en Prose Completes, 1900-1914: Index. Burac, Robert, ed. (FRE.). 1988. lib. bdg. 225.00 *(0-7859-3881-8)* Fr & Eur.

— Oeuvres en Prose, 1898-1908, Vol. 1. deluxe ed. Pebuy, M., ed. (Pleiade Ser.). (FRE.). 1959. 98.95 *(2-07-011114-8)* Schoenhof.

— Oeuvres Poetiques Completes. deluxe ed. Peguy, Marcel, ed. (FRE.). 1664p. 1941. 130.00 *(0-7859-3779-X,* 2070104389) Fr & Eur.

— Oeuvres Poetiques Completes. deluxe ed. Peguy, P. & Peguy, Marcel, eds. (Pleiade Ser.). (FRE.). 1939. 76.95 *(2-07-010438-9)* Schoenhof.

— Par Ce Demi-Clair Matin. pap. 5.95 *(0-685-37033-X)* Fr & Eur.

— Peguy et les Cahiers. pap. 6.95 *(0-685-37034-8)* Fr & Eur.

— Un Poet L'a Dit. pap. 5.95 *(0-685-37045-3)* Fr & Eur.

— Le Porche du Mystere de la Deuxieme Vertu. (FRE.). 1986. pap. 11.95 *(0-7859-2850-2)* Fr & Eur.

— Precis de Climatologie. (FRE., Illus.). 468p. 1970. 150.00 *(0-686-54865-5,* 2225615233) Fr & Eur.

— La Republique . . . Notre Royaume de France. pap. 7.95 *(0-685-37037-2)* Fr & Eur.

— Sainte Genevieve. pap. 4.50 *(0-685-37038-0)* Fr & Eur.

— Saints de France. pap. 1.95 *(0-685-37039-9)* Fr & Eur.

— Situations. (FRE.). pap. 4.50 *(0-685-37040-2)* Fr & Eur.

— Souvenirs. pap. 1.95 *(0-685-37041-0)* Fr & Eur.

— Les Tapisseries. (Poesie Ser.). (FRE.). pap. 7.95 *(2-07-030214-8)* Schoenhof.

— La These. pap. 4.95 *(0-685-37043-7)* Fr & Eur.

— Veronique, Dialogue de l'Histoire et de l'Ame Charnelle. 12.75 *(0-685-37046-1)* Fr & Eur.

— Victor-Marie, Comte Hugo. pap. 5.95 *(0-685-37047-X)* Fr & Eur.

Peguy, Charles & Basstaire, Jean. Pour l'Honneur de l'Esprit: Correspondance, 1898-1914. (FRE.). 352p. 1973. pap. 13.95 *(0-7859-5392-2)* Fr & Eur.

Peguy, Charles & Burac, Robert. Oeuvres en Prose Complete, 1897-1899, 1900-1905, Vol. 1. (FRE.). 1987. lib. bdg. 160.00 *(0-7859-3876-1)* Fr & Eur.

Peguy, Charles & Roche, Anne. Charles Peguy: De Jean Coste: Edition Critique avec le Roman d'Antonin Lavergne. (FRE.). 670p. 1976. pap. 69.95 *(0-7859-1463-3,* 2252017406) Fr & Eur.

Peguy, Charles, jt. auth. see Rolland, Romain.

Peguy, Charles P. Basic Verities: Prose & Poetry. Green, Ann & Green, Julian, trs. LC 72-4493. (Essay Index Reprint Ser.). 1977. reprint ed. 21.95 *(0-8369-2967-5)* Ayer.

Peguy, Marcel, ed. see Peguy, Charles.

Peguy, P., ed. see Peguy, Charles.

Pehe, Jiri, ed. The Prague Spring: A Mixed Legacy. LC 88-16261. (Perspectives on Freedom Ser.: No. 10). (Illus.). 236p. (Orig.). (C). 1988. pap. text 20.50 *(0-932088-28-7)*; lib. bdg. 45.50 *(0-932088-27-9)* Freedom Hse.

Peheim, E., tr. see Eastham, R. C.

***Pehilka, Olena, et al.** For a Crust of Bread. Morris, Sonia, ed. Franko, Roma, tr. from UKR. (Women's Voices in Ukrainian Literature Ser.: Vol. VI). (Illus.). 480p. 2000. pap. 12.95 *(0-9683899-5-3)* LLPI.

P

— Warm the Children, O Sun. Morris, Sonia, ed. Franko, Roma, tr. from UKR. (Women's Voices in Ukrainian Literature Ser.: Vol. V). (Illus.). 480p. 2000. pap. 12.95 (*0-9683899-4-5*) LLPI.

Pehl, Erich. Microwave Technology. LC 85-70815. (Artech House Microwave Library). (Illus.). 230p. reprint ed. pap. 71.30 (*0-608-17721-0*, 203012900067) Bks Demand.

Pehle, Walter H., ed. November, 1938: From the Reichskristallnacht to Genocide. Templer, William, tr. 269p. 1991. 37.50 (*0-85496-687-0*) Berg Pubs.

Pehle, Walter H., jt. ed. see Benz, Wolfgang.

Pehlke, R. D. Continuous Casting of Steel. Date not set. write for info. (*0-8247-9556-3*) Dekker.

Pehlke, R. D., jt. auth. see Harabuchi, T. B.

Pehnke, Andreas. Einblicke in Reformorientierte Schulpraxis der Neuen Bundeslander. (Illus.). 279p. 1996. 31.95 (*3-631-30548-6*) P Lang Pubng.

***Pehnke, Andreas, et al.** Anregungen International Verwirklichter Reformpadagogik: Traditionen, Bilanzen, Visionen. (Greifswalder Studien zur Erziehungswissenschaft). 731p. 1999. 79.95 (*3-631-35645-5*) P Lang Pubng.

Pehnt, Wolfgang. Gottfried Bohm. LC 99-10836. (Studiopaperback Ser.). (Illus.). 176p. 1999. pap. 29.95 (*3-7643-5965-X*, Pub. by Birkhauser) Princeton Arch.

— Rudolph Steiner Goetheanum, Dornach. 95p. 1993. 45.00 (*0-685-67851-2*, Pub. by Ernst & Sohn) Wiley.

Pehnt, Wolfgang & Bhohm, G. Gottfried Bhohm. LC 99-10836. 1999. write for info. (*0-8176-5965-X*) Birkhauser.

Pehnt, Wolfgang & Forster, Kurt W. Karl Friedrich Schinkel, 1781-1841: The Drama of Architecture. Zukowsky, John, ed. & intro. by. LC 94-5313. (Illus.). 176p. 1994. 60.00 (*3-8030-2822-1*) Art Inst Chi.

Pehoski, Charlane, jt. auth. see Henderson, Anne.

Pehoski, Charlane, jt. ed. see Case-Smith, Jane.

Pehrson, Bjorn, jt. auth. see Holzmann, Gerard.

Pehrson, John B. & Mehrtens, Susan E. Intuitive Imagery: A Resource at Work. LC 96-47499. 200p. 1997. pap. text 17.95 (*0-7506-9805-5*) Buttrwrth-Heinemann.

Pehrsson, Robert S. Language & Literacy. 228p. (C). 1996. pap. text, per. 28.95 (*0-7872-2740-4*, 41274001) Kendall-Hunt.

Pehu, jt. auth. see Watanabe.

Pei An. Practical Guide to Centronic, RS232 & Game Ports. (Illus.). 352p. 1998. pap. text 32.95 (*0-7506-3637-8*, Newnes) Buttrwrth-Heinemann.

Pei Fen, Chen. Ancient Chinese Bronzes in the Shanghai Museum. (Illus.). 96p. 1996. 30.00 (*1-85759-114-3*) Scala Books.

***Pei, I. M. & Von Boehm, Gero.** I. M. Pei "Light Is the Key" Conversations with Gero Von Boehm. (Illus.). 128p. 2000. 29.95 (*3-7913-2176-5*) Prestel Pub NY.

Pei, Mario. Swords of Anjou. 310p. 1953. 8.95 (*0-913298-66-2*) S F Vanni.

Pei, Mario A. French Precursors of the Chanson De Roland. LC 48-9636. reprint ed. 20.00 (*0-404-04967-2*) AMS Pr.

— One Language for the World & How to Achieve It. LC 68-56449. 1958. pap. 22.00 (*0-8196-0218-3*) Biblo.

— Voices of Man. LC 71-173940. reprint ed. 20.00 (*0-404-07928-8*) AMS Pr.

Pei, Mario A., ed. see Miles, Preston.

Pei, Mario A., tr. see De Fiori, Vittorio E.

Pei, Minxin. From Reform to Revolution: The Demise of Communism in China & the Soviet Union. LC 93-50948. (Illus.). 256p. 1994. text 44.50 (*0-674-32563-X*, PEIFRO) HUP.

— From Reform to Revolution: The Demise of Communism in China & the Soviet Union. (Illus.). 264p. 1998. pap. text 16.95 (*0-674-32564-8*) HUP.

Pei, Richard, jt. auth. see Webb, Timothy.

Peich, Michael. The Red Ozier: A Literacy Fine Press. (Illus.). 102p. 1993. 130.00 (*1-882916-00-X*) Yellow Barn.

Peich, Michael, jt. auth. see McCurdy, Michael.

Peich, Michael, ed. see Berger, Suzanne E.

Peich, Michael, ed. see Steiner, Robert.

Peichl, Gustav. Buildings & Projects. (Illus.). 224p. 60.00 (*3-7757-0399-3*, Pub. by Gerd Hatje) Dist Art Pubs.

Peierls, R., ed. Nuclear Physics, 1929-1952. (Niels Bohr Collected Works). 694p. 1986. 350.75 (*0-444-86929-8*, North Holland) Elsevier.

Peierls, Rudolf. Selected Scientific Papers of Sir Rudolf Peierls. LC 96-32743. 850p. 1997. lib. bdg. 104.00 (*981-02-2692-6*); lib. bdg. 53.00 (*981-02-2693-4*) World Scientific Pub.

— Surprises in Theoretical Physics. LC 79-84009. (Physics Ser.). 176p. 1979. pap. text 16.95 (*0-691-08242-1*, Pub. by Princeton U Pr) Cal Prin Full Svc.

Peierls, Rudolf E., et al. Atomic Histories. Corson, D. et al, eds. LC 96-22298. (Masters of Modern Physics Ser.). (Illus.). 394p. 1996. reprint ed. 29.95 (*1-56396-243-8*) Spr-Verlag.

Peierls, Rudolph. More Surprises in Theoretical Physics. (Physics Ser.). 115p. 1991. text 39.50 (*0-691-08576-5*, Pub. by Princeton U Pr) Cal Prin Full Svc.

Peifer, Charles, Jr. George Patton: Soldier of Destiny: A Biography of George Patton. LC 88-20265. (People in Focus Ser.). (Illus.). 128p. (YA). (gr. 5 up). 1988. lib. bdg. 13.95 (*0-87518-395-6*, Dillon Silver Burdett) Silver Burdett Pr.

— Houston. LC 88-20197. (Downtown America Ser.). (Illus.). 60p. (J). (gr. 3 up). 1988. pap. 7.95 (*0-382-24787-6*, Dillon Silver Burdett); text 13.95 (*0-87518-387-5*, Dillon Silver Burdett) Silver Burdett Pr.

Peifer, Jane. The Biggest Popcorn Party Ever in Center County. LC 86-27063. (Illus.). 32p. (Orig.). (J). (ps-1). 1987. pap. 4.99 (*0-8361-3435-4*) Herald Pr.

Peifer, Jane H. & Stahl-Wert, John. Welcoming New Christians: A Guide for the Christian Initiation of Adults. LC 94-74576. 142p. 1995. pap. 24.95 (*0-87303-298-5*) Faith & Life.

***Peiff, Katrina Schimmoeller.** Coyote at Large: Humor in American Nature Writing. 240p. 2000. 19.95 (*0-87480-664-X*) U of Utah Pr.

Peiffer. Small Animal Ophthalmology: A Problem Oriented Approach. 2nd ed. 205p. 1996. pap. text 49.00 (*0-7020-2017-6*, Pub. by W B Saunders) Saunders.

Peiffer, Jules. I Lost My Bear. LC 97-34475. (Illus.). 40p. (J). (ps-3). 1998. 16.00 (*0-688-15147-7*, Wm Morrow) Morrow Avon.

Peiffer, Vera. Duty Trap: How to Say "No" When You Feel You Ought to Say "Yes" 160p. 1997. pap. 12.95 (*1-85230-856-7*, Pub. by Element MA) Penguin Putnam.

— The Energy Technique: Simple Secrets for a Lifetime of Vitality & Energy. 174p. 1999. pap. 8.00 (*0-7225-3792-1*) Thorsons PA.

— Positive Thinking: Everything You Have Always Known about Positive Thinking but Were Afraid to Put into Practice. 1994. pap. 7.95 (*1-85230-554-1*, Pub. by Element MA) Penguin Putnam.

— Positive Thinking: Everything You Have Always Known about Positive Thinking But Were Afraid to Put into Practice. 192p. 1999. pap. 12.95 (*1-86204-528-3*, Pub. by Element MA) Penguin Putnam.

— Positively Fearless: Breaking Free of the Fears That Hold You Back. 1993. pap. 12.95 (*1-85230-389-1*, Pub. by Element MA) Penguin Putnam.

***Peiffer, Vera.** Positively Fearless: Breaking Free of the Fears That Hold You Back. 176p. 1999. pap. 10.95 (*1-86204-622-0*, Pub. by Element MA) Penguin Putnam.

Peiffer, Vera. Positively Single: The Art of Being Single & Happy. 176p. 1991. pap. 12.95 (*1-85230-241-0*, Pub. by Element MA) Penguin Putnam.

— Positively Single: The Art of Being Single & Happy. 160p. 1995. pap. 7.95 (*1-85230-712-9*, Pub. by Element MA) Penguin Putnam.

— Positively Single: The Art of Being Single & Happy. 160p. 1999. pap. 10.95 (*1-86204-578-X*, Pub. by Onewrld Pubns) Penguin Putnam.

— Principles of Stress Management, 1. 1997. pap. 11.00 (*0-7225-3243-1*) Thorsons PA.

Peigler, Richard S. A Revision of the Indo-Australian Genus Attacus. LC 88-82574. (Illus.). 168p. (Orig.). (C). 1989. pap. text 30.00 (*0-9611464-2-7*) Lepidoptera.

Peigne, Jean. Grande Encyclopedie des Histoires Droles. (FRE.). 447p. 1993. pap. 49.95 (*0-7859-5664-6*, 2877061787) Fr & Eur.

Peijan, Achim. Die Beziehung Zwischen Aktien- und Anleihenrenditen: Eine Theoretische und Empirische Analyse. (Europaische Hochschulschriften: Reihe 5: Bd. 2017). (GER., Illus.). 200p. 1996. pap. 42.95 (*3-631-31165-6*) P Lang Pubng.

Peiji, ed. see Huenemann.

Peijnenburg, Willie J., ed. Biodegradability Prediction: Proceedings of the NATO Advanced Research Workshop on QSAR Biodegradation II: QSARs for Biotransformation & Biodegradation Luhacovice, Czech Republic, May 2-3, 1996. LC 96-49530. (NATO ASI Series: Partnership Sub-Series 2). 160p. (C). 1996. text 102.50 (*0-7923-4341-7*) Kluwer Academic.

Peik, Leander. Camper's Guide to San Diego County. 1992. pap. 3.50 (*0-9620402-6-6*) Sunbelt Pubns.

— Discover San Diego. 16th ed. 1991. pap. 3.50 (*0-9620402-5-8*) Sunbelt Pubns.

Peik, Leander & Peik, Rosalie. Discover San Diego. 15th rev. ed. (Illus.). 136p. 1988. pap. 2.50 (*0-9620402-0-7*) Sunbelt Pubns.

Peik, Rosalie, jt. auth. see Peik, Leander.

Peiken, Steven. Gastrointestinal Health, rev ed: Completely New & Revised. rev. ed. LC RC806.P45 1999. (Illus.). 368p. 1999. pap. 15.00 (*0-06-095318-7*) HarpC.

***Peikin, Steven R.** The Complete Book of Diet Drugs. 2000. pap. 14.00 (*1-57566-492-5*, Knsington) Kensgtn Pub Corp.

Peikin, Steven R. Gastrointestinal Health: A Self-Help Nutritional Program to Prevent, Cure or Alleviate Irritable Bowel Syndrome, Ulcers, Heartburn, Gas, Constipation, & Many Other Digestive Disorders. LC 90-55547. 304p. 1992. reprint ed. pap. 13.50 (*0-06-098405-8*, Perennial) HarperTrade.

Peikoff, Leonard. Objectivism: The Philosophy of Ayn Rand. 512p. 1993. pap. 16.95 (*0-452-01101-9*, Mer) NAL.

Peikoff, Leonard, ed. Ominous Parallels. 1983. pap. 13.95 (*0-452-01117-5*, Mer) NAL.

Peikoff, Leonard, jt. auth. see Rand, Ayn.

Peikoff, Leonard, ed. see Rand, Ayn.

Peikoff, Leonard, ed. & intro. see Rand, Ayn.

Peil, Jan. Adam Smith & Economic Science: A Methodological Reinterpretation. LC 99-15588. 224p. (C). 1999. 80.00 (*1-85898-919-1*) E Elgar.

Peil, Margaret. Cities & Suburbs: Urban Life in West Africa. LC 80-26440. (New Library of African Affairs). 330p. (C). 1982. 49.50 (*0-8419-0685-8*) Holmes & Meier.

— Consensus & Conflict in African Societies: An Introduction to Sociology. LC 78-312566. (Illus.). 412p. reprint ed. pap. 127.80 (*0-8357-6073-1*, 203449200090) Bks Demand.

— Lagos: The City Is the People. (World Cities Ser.). 256p. 1991. 40.00 (*0-8161-7299-4*, Hall Reference) Macmillan.

Peil, Margaret & Sada, Pius O. African Urban Society. LC 84-5092. (Social Development in the Third World Ser.). 404p. reprint ed. pap. 125.30 (*0-8357-5242-9*, 203176100076) Bks Demand.

Peile, Colin. The Creative Paradigm: Insight, Synthesis & Knowledge Development. (Avebury Series in Philosophy). 320p. 1994. 82.95 (*1-85628-629-0*, Pub. by Avebry) Ashgate Pub Co.

Peile, James H. The Reproach of the Gospel: An Inquiry into the Apparent Failure of Christianity As a General Rule of Life & Conduct. 1977. lib. bdg. 59.95 (*0-8490-2516-8*) Gordon Pr.

Peillon, Michel. The Concept of Interest in Social Theory. LC 90-22627. (Studies in Sociology: Vol. 9). 200p. 1990. lib. bdg. 79.95 (*0-88946-722-6*) E Mellen.

Peimani, Hooman. Iran & the United States: The Rise of the West Asian Regional Grouping. LC 98-56627. 152p. 1999. 59.95 (*0-275-96454-X*) Greenwood.

***Peimani, Hooman.** Nuclear Proliferation in the Indian Subcontinent: The Self-Exhausting 'Superpowers' & Emerging Alliances. LC 99-88509. 2000. write for info. (*0-275-96704-2*, Praeger Pubs) Greenwood.

Peimani, Hooman. Regional Security & the Future of Central Asia: The Competition of Iran, Turkey & Russia. LC 97-32943. 168p. 1998. 59.95 (*0-275-96021-8*, Praeger Pubs) Greenwood.

Peimbert, Luis M. La Cara Oculta de las Esferas. (Ciencia para Todos Ser.). (SPA.). pap. 6.99 (*968-16-3037-8*, Pub. by Fondo) Continental Bk.

Peimbert, Manuel & Jugaku, Jun, eds. Star Forming Regions. 1986. pap. text 110.00 (*90-277-2389-3*); lib. bdg. 259.00 (*90-277-2388-5*) Kluwer Academic.

Peimer, Clayton A. Surgery of the Hand & Upper Extremity, 1. write for info. (*0-07-049388-X*) McGraw.

— Surgery of the Hand & Upper Extremity, 2. write for info. (*0-07-049389-8*) McGraw.

Peimer, Clayton A., ed. Surgery of the Hand & Upper Extremity, 2 vols., Set. LC 95-32395. 2336p. 1996. text 295.00 (*0-07-049293-X*) McGraw-Hill HPD.

Pein, Malcolm. Guide to Chess. 88p. 1995. pap. 14.00 (*0-8050-4225-3*, Pub. by Batsford Chess) H Holt & Co.

Pein, Malcolm, jt. auth. see Mikhalchishin, Adrian.

Pein, Malcolm, jt. auth. see Przewoznik, J.

Pein, Roland, jt. ed. see Kuo, Kenneth K.

Peinado, Monica, ed. see Riesen, Janet.

Peinador, E. M., ed. Geometric Aspects of Banach Spaces. (London Mathematical Society Lecture Note Ser.: No. 140). 206p. (C). 1989. pap. text 44.95 (*0-521-36752-2*) Cambridge U Pr.

Peindao, M., et al. Vegetation of Southeastern Spain. (Flora et Vegetatio Mundi Ser.: Vol. 10). (Illus.). 487p. 1992. pap. text 105.00 (*3-443-66002-9*, Pub. by Gebruder Borntraeger) Balogh.

Peine, Ira. Quality Assurance Compliance: Procedures for Pharmaceutical & Biotechnology Manufacturers. 279p. 1994. ring bd. 199.00 (*0-935184-51-1*) Interpharm.

***Peine, Jan Muir.** Journey with Jay. LC 99-96750. 2000. pap. 8.95 (*0-533-13335-1*) Vantage.

Peine, John. Ecosystem Management for Sustainability: Illustrated by an International Biosphere Reserve Cooperative. LC 98-15035. (Illus.). 528p. 1998. boxed set 74.95 (*1-57444-053-5*) St Lucie Pr.

Peinke, J., et al. Chaos in Experiment: Self-Organized Hierachical Complexity in Semiconductor Experiments. LC 92-25600. (Illus.). 320p. 1993. write for info. (*3-540-55647-8*); 66.95 (*0-387-55647-8*) Spr-Verlag.

— Encounter with Chaos: Self-Organized Hierarchial Complexity in Semiconductor Experiments. LC 92-30273. 1993. 49.95 (*0-387-55845-4*) Spr-Verlag.

***Peinkofer, Jim.** 101 Ways to Soothe a Crying Baby. LC 99-88337. (Illus.). 112p. 2000. pap. 8.95 (*0-8092-9842-2*, Contemporary Bks) NTC Contemp Pub Co.

Peins, Maryann. Aspects of Communion & the Mentally Retarded Population: A Selected Annotated Bibliography: 1970-1993. 368p. 1998. 75.00 (*0-931510-66-X*) Hi Willow.

Peiny, David C. Fabulae Romanae: Stories of Famous Romans. 1993. pap., student ed. 16.55 (*0-685-66000-1*) Longman.

***Peiper, Howard & Anderson, Nina.** Natural Solutions for Sexual Enhancement. large type ed. LC 98-61668. (Illus.). 88p. 1999. pap. 9.95 (*1-884820-42-5*) SAFE GOODS.

Peiper, Howard, jt. auth. see Anderson, Nina.

Peiper, Howard, jt. auth. see Bell, Rachel.

Peipers, Jeanne. Le Peintre du Maitre-Autel de Lautenbach, l'Atelier de Durer et l'Art du Rhin Superieur. (Publications Universitaires Europeennes, Serie 28: Vol. 245). (FRE., Illus.). 538p. 1996. 88.95 (*3-631-47885-2*) P Lang Pubng.

Peiqi, Xie. The Dao of Writing: Chinese Calligraphy. Nugent-Head, Andrew, tr. 44p. pap. 12.00 (*1-888179-53-8*) Assn For Tradit.

— The Eight Healing Sounds of Yin Style Ba Gua. Nugent-Head, Andrew, tr. 180p. 1995. pap. 15.00 (*1-888179-50-3*) Assn For Tradit.

— The Twelve Guiding Energy Sitting Mediations of Yin Style Ba Gua. Nugent-Head, Andrew, tr. 108p. 1995. pap. 13.50 (*1-888179-51-1*) Assn For Tradit.

Peiqi, Yue. China Red Data Book of Endangered Animals: Pisces. Yigu, Chen, ed. (CHI & ENG., Illus.). 247p. 1998. pap. text 49.90 (*1-880132-36-2*) Sci Pr NY.

Peiqing, Pan. Ethico-Strategie et Bio-Strategie, Vol. 572. (Publications Universitaires Europeennes: Serie 20, Vol. 572). xxxiv, 653p. 1998. 57.95 (*3-906761-49-5*) P Lang.

Peirce, Andrea. The Apha Practical Guide to Natural Medicines: The First Authoritative Home Reference For Herbs And Natural Remedies, From TheNation's Largest And. LC 98-26810. (American Pharmaceutical Association Guide Ser.). (Illus.). 752p. 1999. 35.00 (*0-688-16151-0*, Wm Morrow) Morrow Avon.

Peirce, Andrea & American Pharmaceutical Association Staff, eds. American Pharmaceutical Association's Parent's Guide to Childhood Medications. 624p. (Orig.). 1997. pap. 16.95 (*0-8362-2138-9*) Andrews & McMeel.

Peirce, Benjamin. An Elementary Treatise on Algebra. (Notable American Authors Ser.). 1999. reprint ed. lib. bdg. 125.00 (*0-7812-8728-6*) Rprt Serv.

— An Elementary Treatise on Curves, Functions & Forces. (Notable American Authors Ser.). 1999. reprint ed. lib. bdg. 125.00 (*0-7812-8731-6*) Rprt Serv.

— An Elementary Treatise on Plane & Solid Geometry. (Notable American Authors Ser.). 1999. reprint ed. lib. bdg. 125.00 (*0-7812-8729-4*) Rprt Serv.

— An Elementary Treatise Plane & Sperical Trigonometry. (Notable American Authors Ser.). 1999. reprint ed. lib. bdg. 125.00 (*0-7812-8730-8*) Rprt Serv.

— An Elementary Treatiseon Sound. (Notable American Authors Ser.). 1999. reprint ed. lib. bdg. 125.00 (*0-7812-8727-8*) Rprt Serv.

— Ideality in the Physical Sciences. (Notable American Authors Ser.). 1999. reprint ed. lib. bdg. 125.00 (*0-7812-8736-7*) Rprt Serv.

— Linear Associative Alegebra. (Notable American Authors Ser.). 1999. reprint ed. lib. bdg. 125.00 (*0-7812-8735-9*) Rprt Serv.

— A System of Analytic Mechanics. (Notable American Authors Ser.). 1999. reprint ed. lib. bdg. 125.00 (*0-7812-8733-2*) Rprt Serv.

— Tables of the Moon. (Notable American Authors Ser.). 1999. reprint ed. lib. bdg. 125.00 (*0-7812-8732-4*) Rprt Serv.

— Tables of the Moon's Parallax. (Notable American Authors Ser.). 1999. reprint ed. lib. bdg. 125.00 (*0-7812-8734-0*) Rprt Serv.

Peirce, Bradford K. Half Century with Juvenile Delinquents: Or, the New York House of Refuge & Its Times. LC 69-16242. (Criminology, Law Enforcement, & Social Problems Ser.: No. 91). (Illus.). 1969. reprint ed. 25.00 (*0-87585-091-X*) Patterson Smith.

Peirce, Charles Sanders. Chance, Love, & Logic: Philosophical Essays. Cohen, Morris R., ed. & intro. by. Ketner, Kenneth L., intro. LC 97-53232. (Illus.). xlv, 318p. 1998. pap. 15.00 (*0-8032-8751-8*, Bison Books) U of Nebr Pr.

— Charles S. Peirce: Selected Writings. Wiener, Philip P., ed. 446p. 1966. pap. text 11.95 (*0-486-21634-9*) Dover.

Peirce, Charles Sanders. Collected Papers of Charles Sanders Peirce, 8 Vol. Hartshorne, Charles et al, eds. 3746p. 1997. 995.00 (*1-85506-556-8*) Thoemmes Pr.

Peirce, Charles Sanders. Collected Papers of Charles Sanders Peirce, Vols. 1-2. Hartshorne, Charles & Weiss, Paul, eds. LC 60-9172. (Illus.). 959p. 1960. reprint ed. pap. 200.00 (*0-7837-1682-6*, 205721300001) Bks Demand.

— Collected Papers of Charles Sanders Peirce, Vols. 5-6. Hartshorne, Charles & Weiss, Paul, eds. LC 60-9172. (Illus.). 942p. 1960. reprint ed. pap. 200.00 (*0-7837-1683-4*, 205721300005) Bks Demand.

— Philosophical Writings of Peirce. Buchler, Justus, ed. 386p. 1940. pap. 9.95 (*0-486-20217-8*) Dover.

— The Philosophy of Peirce: Selected Writings. Buchler, Justus, ed. LC 75-41210. reprint ed. 39.50 (*0-404-14694-5*) AMS Pr.

— Pragmatism As a Principle & Method of Right Thinking: The 1903 Harvard Lectures on Pragmatism. Turrisi, Patricia A., ed. LC 96-14144. 305p. (C). 1997. text 57.50 (*0-7914-3265-3*); pap. text 19.95 (*0-7914-3266-1*) State U NY Pr.

— Reasoning & the Logic of Things. 297p. 1993. pap. 22.50 (*0-674-74967-7*) HUP.

— Writings of Charles S. Peirce Vol. 1: A Chronological Edition: Vol. 1, 1857-1866. Moore, Edward C. et al, eds. LC 79-1993. (Illus.). 738p. 1982. 57.50 (*0-253-37201-1*) Ind U Pr.

— Writings of Charles S. Peirce Vol. 2: A Chronological Edition: Vol. 2, 1867-1871. Kloesel, Christian J. et al, eds. LC 79-1993. (Illus.). 704p. 1984. 57.50 (*0-253-37202-X*) Ind U Pr.

— Writings of Charles S. Peirce Vol. 3: A Chronological Edition: Vol. 3, 1872-1878. Kloesel, Christian J. et al, eds. LC 79-1993. (Illus.). 672p. 1986. 57.50 (*0-253-37203-8*) Ind U Pr.

— Writings of Charles S. Peirce Vol. 4: A Chronological Edition, Vol. 4: 1879-1884. LC 79-1993. 768p. 1989. 67.50 (*0-253-37204-6*) Ind U Pr.

— Writings of Charles S. Peirce Vol. 5: A Chronological Edition, Vol. 5, 1884-1886. LC 79-1993. (Illus.). 592p. 1993. 75.00 (*0-253-37205-4*) Ind U Pr.

Peirce, Charles Sanders, ed. Studies in Logic: By Members of the Johns Hopkins University (1883) (Foundations of Semiotics Ser.: No. 1). xl, 203p. (C). 1983. reprint ed. 65.00 (*90-272-3271-7*) J Benjamins Pubng Co.

***Peirce, David, ed.** Irish Writing in the Twentieth Century: A Reader. 800p. 2000. 39.95 (*1-85918-208-9*, Pub. by Cork Univ) Stylus Pub VA.

Peirce, Donald. Art & Enterprise: American Decorative Art 1825-1917, the Virginia Carroll Crawford Collection. LC 99-22014. (Illus.). 464p. 1999. 60.00 (*0-939802-87-2*) High Mus Art.

Peirce, Donald C. English Ceramics: Frances & Emory Cocke Collection. LC 88-82295. (Illus.). 255p. (Orig.). 1988. pap. 24.95 (*0-939802-51-1*) High Mus Art.

Peirce, Donald C. & Alswang, Hope. American Interiors: New England & the South. (Illus.). 62p. pap. 4.87 (*0-87273-095-6*) Bklyn Mus.

Peirce, Ebenezer W. Indian History, Biography & Genealogy. LC 72-4336. (Select Bibliographies Reprint Ser.). 1977. reprint ed. 23.95 (*0-8369-6890-5*) Ayer.

— The Peirce Family of the Old Colony: or the Lineal Descent of Abraham Peirce, Who Came to America As Early As 1623. (Illus.). 510p. 1989. reprint ed. pap. 76.50 (*0-8328-0949-7*); reprint ed. lib. bdg. 84.50 (*0-8328-0948-9*) Higginson Bk Co.

Peirce, Ebenezer W., jt. auth. see Dean, G.

Peirce, Ebenezer W., jt. auth. see Dean, Gardner.

An Asterisk (*) at the beginning of an entry indicates that the title is appearing for the first time.

Peirce Edition Project Staff, ed. The Essential Peirce Vol. 2: Selected Philosophical Writings (1893-1913) 640p. 1998. 39.95 (*0-253-33397-0*); pap. 24.95 (*0-253-21190-5*) Ind U Pr.

Peirce, H. W., jt. ed. see Weber, R. H.

Peirce, Hayford. Dinosaur Park Vol. 1. 1994. pap. 4.99 (*0-8125-5040-4*, Pub. by Tor Bks) St Martin.

— Phylum Monsters. 1989. pap. 3.95 (*0-8125-4894-9*, Pub. by Tor Bks) St Martin.

Peirce, Henry A. Biography. 25p. 1976. pap. 3.95 (*0-87770-160-1*) Ye Galleon.

Peirce, Henry B., jt. auth. see Durrant, Samuel W.

***Peirce, J. Jeffrey & Vallero, Daniel.** Hazardous Waste Risk Management. (Illus.). 384p. 2001. 75.00 (*0-7506-7318-4*) Buttrwrth-Heinemann.

Peirce, J. Jeffrey, et al. Environmental Pollution & Control. 4th ed. LC 97-20292. 400p. 1997. pap. 39.95 (*0-7506-9899-3*) Buttrwrth-Heinemann.

Peirce, Kathleen. Mercy. LC 91-50110. (Poetry Ser.). 64p. (C). 1991. pap. 10.95 (*0-8229-5457-5*); text 19.95 (*0-8229-3686-0*) U of Pittsburgh Pr.

— The Oval Hour. LC 98-44842. (Iowa Poetry Prize Ser.). 86p. 1999. pap. 10.95 (*0-87745-664-X*) U of Iowa Pr.

Peirce, Leslie P. The Imperial Harem: Women & Sovereignty in the Ottoman Empire. (Studies in Middle Eastern History). (Illus.). 400p. 1993. pap. text 24.95 (*0-19-508677-5*) OUP.

Peirce, Lincoln C. Vegetables: Characteristics, Production & Marketing. LC 86-32625. 448p. 1987. text 100.95 (*0-471-85022-5*) Wiley.

Peirce, Liz. Activity Assemblies for Multi-Racial Schools 5-11. 160p. 1992. pap. 29.95 (*0-7507-0049-1*, Falmer Pr) Taylor & Francis.

Peirce, Neal. Citistates: How Urban America Can Prosper in a Competitive World. LC 93-18709. 359p. 1993. text 24.95 (*0-929765-16-8*) Seven Locks Pr.

Peirce, Neal & Johnson, Curtis. Boundary Crossers: Community Leadership for a Global Age. LC 98-130034. (Illus.). 72p. 1997. pap. 10.50 (*1-891464-04-3*) J M Burns Academy.

Peirce, Neal R. Over New England. Fraser, Jane & Wertz, Laurie, eds. (Wings over America Ser.). (Illus.). 256p. 1995. reprint ed. pap. 35.00 (*1-887451-05-6*) Weldon Owen.

Peirce, Pam. Golden Gate Gardening: The Complete Guide to Year-Round Food Gardening in the San Francisco Bay Area & Coastal California. 2nd rev. ed. (Illus.). 416p. 1998. pap. 24.95 (*1-57061-136-X*) Sasquatch Bks.

Peirce, Pamela K. Environmentally Friendly Gardening Controlling Vegetable Pests. Lang, Susan, ed. LC 90-86161. 160p. 1996. 14.95 (*0-89721-359-9*, Ortho Bks) Meredith Bks.

Peirce, Paul S. The Freedmen's Bureau: A Chapter in the History of Reconstruction. (BCL1 - U. S. History Ser.). 200p. 1991. reprint ed. lib. bdg. 69.00 (*0-7812-6082-5*) Rprt Serv.

***Peirce, Penney.** El Camino de la Intuicion. 2000. pap. 15.95 (*968-19-0514-8*) Aguilar.

— Dreams for Dummies. 2000. pap. 19.99 (*0-7645-5297-X*) IDG Bks.

Peirce, Penney. The Intuitive Way: A Guide to Living from Inner Wisdom. LC 97-21813. 272p. 1997. pap. 16.95 (*1-885223-55-2*) Beyond Words Pub.

***Peirce, Penney.** The Intuitive Way: A Guide to Living from Inner Wisdom. 272p. 1999. 8.98 (*1-56731-315-9*, MJF Bks) Fine Comms.

— The Present Moment: A Daybook of Clarity & Intuition. LC 99-88335. 416p. 2000. pap. 14.95 (*0-8092-2475-5*, 247550, Contemporary Bks) NTC Contemp Pub Co.

Peirce, Susan P., compiled by. Gift Club Programs: A Survey of How Forty-Four Institutions Raise Money. 60p. 1992. pap. 12.00 (*0-89964-292-6*, 28302) Coun Adv & Supp Ed.

Peirce, William S. TheEconomics of the Energy Industries. 2nd ed. LC 96-912. 336p. 1996. text 49.95 (*0-275-95626-1*, Praeger Pubs) Greenwood.

Peires, J. B. The Dead Will Arise: Nongqawuse & the Great Xhosa Cattle-Killing Movement of 1856-57. LC 88-32799. (Illus.). 364p. 1989. 39.95 (*0-253-34338-0*); pap. 18.95 (*0-253-20524-7*, MB-524) Ind U Pr.

Peiris, H. A. Political Parties in Sri Lanka since Independence: A Bibliography. (C). 1988. 22.50 (*81-7013-027-1*, Pub. by Navarang) S Asia.

Peiris, Kamala. Weaving a Future Together: Women & Participatory Development. LC 97-177438. 96p. (Orig.). 1997. pap. 14.95 (*90-6224-972-8*, Pub. by Uitgeverij Arkel) LPC InBook.

Peiris, William. The Western Contribution to Buddhism. 372p. 1974. lib. bdg. 79.95 (*0-87968-550-6*) Krishna Pr.

Peirson, jt. auth. see Henderson.

Peisach, Max, jt. auth. see Alfassi, Zeev B.

Peischl, Margaret T., jt. auth. see Godwin-Jones, Robert.

Peiser, Brett M., jt. auth. see Armor, David J.

Peiser, H., jt. auth. see Air Force Cambridge Research Staff.

***Peiser, Ken & Sandry, Martin.** The Universal 12-Step Program. LC 99-15776. 224p. 1999. pap. 10.95 (*1-58062-213-5*) Adams Media.

Peiser, Kenneth B. The Thinker's Guide to Recovery: A Rational Approach. 1993. pap. 9.95 (*0-8306-4218-8*) McGraw-Hill Prof.

Peiser, Kenneth B. & Sandry, Martin. The Thinker's Guide to Recovery: A Rational Approach. 1993. pap. 9.95 (*0-07-049290-5*) McGraw-Hill Prof.

Peiser, Richard B. Reducing Crime Through Real Estate Development & Management. LC 98-87159. 160p. 1998. pap. 39.95 (*0-87420-823-8*, R01) Urban Land.

Peiser, Richard B., jt. auth. see Porter, Douglas R.

Peiser, Richard B., jt. auth. see Schwanke, Dean.

Peishan, Zhang, et al. Mineralogy & Geology of Rare Earths in China. 242p. 1996. 99.50 (*90-6764-220-7*, Pub. by VSP) Coronet Bks.

Peisker, Armor D., ed. see Caldwell, Wayne E.

Peiss, Kathy. Cheap Amusements: Working Women & Leisure in Turn-of-the-Century New York. LC 85-14783. 256p. 1987. pap. 18.95 (*0-87722-500-1*) Temple U Pr.

— Hope in a Jar: The Making of America's Beauty Culture. LC 97-42706. (Illus.). 318p. 1998. 25.00 (*0-8050-5550-9*, Metropol Bks) H Holt & Co.

— Hope in a Jar: The Making of America's Beauty Culture. 352p. 1999. pap. 16.00 (*0-8050-5551-7*, Pub. by H Holt & Co) VHPS.

Peiss, Kathy, et al, eds. Passion & Power: Sexuality in History. LC 88-21670. (Critical Perspectives on the Past Ser.). (Illus.). 326p. (C). 1989. pap. 22.95 (*0-87722-637-7*) Temple U Pr.

Peiss, Kathy & Clark Smith, Barbara. Men & Women: A History of Costume, Gender, & Power. (Illus.). 80p. (Orig.). 1989. pap. 6.95 (*0-929847-02-4*) Natl Mus Am.

Peiss, Kathy, jt. auth. see Horowitz, Helen L.

Peissel, M. Mustang, a Lost Tibetan Kingdom. (C). 1993. 120.00 (*0-7855-0193-2*, Pub. by Ratna Pustak Bhandar) St Mut.

Peissel, Michel. The Last Barbarians. 1995. pap. 14.95 (*0-8050-4535-X*) H Holt & Co.

— The Last Barbarians: The Discovery of the Source of the Meking in Tibet. LC 97-27534. 320p. 1995. 27.50 (*0-8050-4534-1*) H Holt & Co.

Peissel, Michel & Allen, Missy. Dangerous Environments. (Encyclopedia of Danger Ser.). (Illus.). 120p. (J). (gr. 5 up). 1993. lib. bdg. 19.95 (*0-7910-1793-1*) Chelsea Hse.

— Dangerous Mammals. 120p. (YA). (gr. 5 up). 1992. pap. 9.95 (*0-7910-1935-7*) Chelsea Hse.

— Dangerous Mammals. (Encyclopedia of Danger Ser.). (Illus.). 120p. (J). (gr. 5 up). 1993. lib. bdg. 19.95 (*0-7910-1790-7*) Chelsea Hse.

— Dangerous Natural Phenomena. (Encyclopedia of Danger Ser.). (Illus.). 120p. (J). (gr. 5 up). 1993. lib. bdg. 19.95 (*0-7910-1794-X*) Chelsea Hse.

— Dangerous Professions. (Encyclopedia of Danger Ser.). (Illus.). 120p. (J). (gr. 5 up). 1993. lib. bdg. 19.95 (*0-7910-1792-3*) Chelsea Hse.

— Dangerous Reptilian Creatures. (Encyclopedia of Danger Ser.). (Illus.). 120p. (J). (gr. 5 up). 1993. lib. bdg. 19.95 (*0-7910-1789-3*) Chelsea Hse.

— Dangerous Sports. (Encyclopedia of Danger Ser.). (Illus.). 120p. (J). (gr. 5 up). 1993. lib. bdg. 19.95 (*0-7910-1791-5*) Chelsea Hse.

— Dangerous Water Creatures. (Encyclopedia of Danger Ser.). (Illus.). 120p. (YA). (gr. 5 up). 1992. pap. 9.95 (*0-7910-1932-2*) Chelsea Hse.

— Dangerous Water Creatures. (Encyclopedia of Danger Ser.). (Illus.). 120p. (J). (gr. 5 up). 1993. lib. bdg. 19.95 (*0-7910-1788-5*) Chelsea Hse.

— The Encyclopedia of Danger, 10 vols., Set. (Illus.). (YA). (gr. 5 up). 1993. lib. bdg. 199.59 (*0-7910-1784-2*) Chelsea Hse.

Peissel, Michel, jt. auth. see Allen, Missy.

Peissner, Elias. American Question in Its National Aspect. LC 71-152928. (Black Heritage Library Collection). 1977. 17.95 (*0-8369-8772-1*) Ayer.

Peitersen, Birger, jt. auth. see Bangsbo, Jens.

Peitgen, H. O., et al. The Beauty of Fractals Labs. 2nd ed. 12p. 1993. 53.95 (*0-387-14212-6*) Spr-Verlag.

— Fractals for the Classroom Vol. 3: Strategic Activities. 113p. 1998. pap. 24.95 (*0-387-98420-8*) Spr-Verlag.

Peitgen, Heinz-Otto, ed. Newton's Method & Dynamical Systems. (C). 1989. text 160.00 (*0-7923-0113-7*) Kluwer Academic.

Peitgen, Heinz-Otto & Richter, P. H. Beauty of Fractals: Images of Complex Dynamical Systems. (Illus.). 199p. 1991. 54.95 (*0-387-15851-0*) Spr-Verlag.

Peitgen, Heinz-Otto & Saupe, Dietmar. The Science of Fractal Images. (Illus.). xiv, 312p. 1991. 53.95 (*0-387-96608-0*) Spr-Verlag.

Peitgen, Heinz-Otto, et al. Chaos & Fractals: New Frontiers of Science. LC 92-23277. 1992. write for info. (*0-387-97345-1*) Spr-Verlag.

— Chaos & Fractals: New Frontiers of Science. (Illus.). 984p. 1992. 59.95 (*0-387-97903-4*) Spr-Verlag.

— Fractals for the Classroom: Complex Systems & Mandelbrot Set, Pt. 2. (Illus.). 448p. 1992. 34.95 (*0-387-97722-8*) Spr-Verlag.

— Fractals for the Classroom: Introduction to Fractals & Chaos. (Illus.). 450p. (C). 1997. 39.95 (*0-387-97041-X*) Spr-Verlag.

— Fractals for the Classroom: Introduction to Fractals & Chaos, 2 vols. 2nd ed. (Illus.). xv, 450p. 1993. write for info. (*3-540-97041-X*) Spr-Verlag.

— Fractals for the Classroom: Strategic Activities, 2 vols., Vol. 1. (Illus.). xii, 128p. 1993. 24.95 (*0-387-97346-X*) Spr-Verlag.

— Fractals for the Classroom: Strategic Activities, 2 vols., Vol. 2. (Illus.). 160p. 1993. 29.95 (*0-387-97554-3*) Spr-Verlag.

— The Game of Fractal Images. 2nd ed. 1989. 39.00 incl. disk (*0-387-14203-7*) Spr-Verlag.

Peitgen, Heinz-Otto, jt. auth. see Nussbaum, Roger.

Peithman, Stephen, et al, eds. The Stage Direction Guide to Auditions. LC 98-28883. 144p. 1998. pap. text 12.95 (*0-325-00083-2*) Heinemann.

***Peithman, Stephen & Offen, Neil.** Stage Directions Guide to Shakespeare. 128p. 2000. pap. 14.95 (*0-325-00233-9*) Heinemann.

Peithman, Stephen & Offen, Neil, eds. Stage Directions Guide to Directing. LC 98-56058. (Orig.). 1999. pap. 14.95 (*0-325-00112-X*) Heinemann.

— Stage Directions Guide to Getting & Keeping Your Audience. LC 98-55260. (Orig.). 1999. pap. 13.95 (*0-325-00113-8*) Heinemann.

— The Stage Directions Guide to Publicity. LC 98-51139. 144p. 1999. pap. 13.95 (*0-325-00082-4*, Pub. by Heinemann) Natl Bk Netwk.

***Peithman, Stephen & Offen, Neil, eds.** The Stage Directions Guide to Working Back Stage. 2000. pap. 14.95 (*0-325-00244-4*) Heinemann.

Peitro, Silvio San, see San Peitro, Silvio.

Peitsch, Helmut, et al. European Memories of World War Two: New Perspectives on Postwar Literature. LC 97-31897. 1999. 59.95 (*1-57181-936-3*) Berghahn Bks.

Peitsch, Helmut, ed. see Mann, Heinrich.

Peitz, Darlene A. Solidarity As Hermeneutics: A Revisionist Reading of the Theology of Walter Rauschenbusch. LC 91-865. (American University Studies: Theology & Religion: Ser. VII, Vol. 122). 236p. (C). 1992. text 46.95 (*0-8204-1753-X*) P Lang Pubng.

Peitz, Mary. Romeo & Juliet - Study Guide. Friedland, Joyce & Kessler, Rikki, eds. (Novel-Ties Ser.). (YA). (gr. 9-12). 1993. pap. text 15.95 (*0-88122-127-9*) Lrn Links.

***Peitzer, Bernice.** Forever Flowers: A Flower Lover's Guide to Selecting, Pressing & Designing. LC 99-66141. (Illus.). 128p. 2000. pap. 21.95 (*0-87341-805-0*, PRFLO) Krause Pubns.

Peitzman, Andrew, et al. The Trauma Manual. LC 97-29878. (Illus.). 250p. 1997. spiral bd. 37.95 (*0-316-69834-2*, Little Brwn Med Div) Lppncott W & W.

Peitzman, Faye & Gadda, George, eds. With Different Eyes: Insights into Teaching Language Minority Students Across the Disciplines. LC 93-33727. 1994. 17.95 (*0-8013-1311-2*) Longman.

***Peitzman, Steven J.** A New & Untried Course: Woman's Medical College & Medical College of Pennsylvania, 1850-1998. LC 99-45850. 272p. 2000. text 60.00 (*0-8135-2815-1*); pap. text 22.00 (*0-8135-2816-X*) Rutgers U Pr.

Peixoto, Aldo J., jt. ed. see Schneiderman, Henry.

Peixoto, J. P., et al. Physics of Climate. 560p. 1992. 97.00 (*0-88318-711-6*); pap. 49.95 (*0-88318-712-4*) Spr-Verlag.

***Peixotto, Ernest.** A Revolutionary Pilgrimage. (Illus.). 399p. 2000. reprint ed. pap. 30.00 (*0-7884-1402-X*, P139) Heritage Bk.

Peixotto, Jessica B. Getting & Spending at the Professional Standard of Living: A Study of the Costs of Living an Academic Life. LC 75-39267. (Getting & Spending: The Consumer's Dilemma Ser.). (Illus.). 1976. reprint ed. 28.95 (*0-405-08040-9*) Ayer.

Pejcic, Bogdan & Meyer, Rolf. Pocket Billiards: Fundamentals of Technique & Play. LC 93-8557. (Illus.). 80p. 1993. pap. 9.95 (*0-8069-0458-5*) Sterling.

Pejdvich, Svetozar, ed. The Economic Foundations of Property Rights: Selected Readings. LC 97-14361. 320p. (C). 1997. text 95.00 (*1-85898-543-9*) E Elgar.

Pejovich, Steve. Industrial Democracy: Conflict or Cooperation. Dethloff, Henry, ed. (Series on Public Issues: No. 12). 10p. 1984. pap. 2.00 (*0-86599-022-0*) PERC.

— Karl Marx in One Lesson (1818-1883) Dethloff, Henry, ed. (Series on Public Issues: No. 6). 10p. (Orig.). 1983. pap. 2.00 (*0-86599-016-6*) PERC.

Pejovich, Steve, ed. see Auernheimer, Leonardo.

Pejovich, Steve, ed. see Dethloff, Henry C. & Bryant, Keith L., Jr.

Pejovich, Steve, ed. see Fraser, Donald R.

Pejovich, Steve, ed. see Greenhut, Melvin L.

Pejovich, Steve, ed. see Greenhut, Melvin & Smithson, Charles W.

Pejovich, Steve, ed. see Hamilton, Billy.

Pejovich, Steve, ed. see Keim, Gerald D.

Pejovich, Steve, ed. see Maurice, S. Charles & Smithson, Charles W.

Pejovich, Steve, ed. see Moore, John H.

Pejovich, Steve, ed. see Reynolds, Morgan O.

Pejovich, Steve, ed. see Saving, Thomas R.

Pejovich, Steve, ed. see Walker, Deborah.

Pejovich, Steve, ed. see Wiggins, Steven N.

Pejovich, Svetovar. The Economics of Property Rights: Towards a Theory of Comparative Systems. (C). 1990. lib. bdg. 155.00 (*0-7923-0878-6*) Kluwer Academic.

Pejovich, Svetozar. Economic Analysis of Institutions & Systems. LC 94-40239. (International Studies in Economics & Econometrics). 244p. (C). 1995. lib. bdg. 118.00 (*0-7923-3214-8*) Kluwer Academic.

— Economic Analysis of Institutions & Systems. LC 97-34978. (International Studies in Economics & Econometrics). 240p. 1997. lib. bdg. 99.00 (*0-7923-8031-2*) Kluwer Academic.

— The Market-Planned Economy of Yugoslavia. LC 66-18868. (Illus.). 172p. reprint ed. pap. 53.40 (*0-608-15974-3*, 203328100084) Bks Demand.

Pejovich, Svetozar, ed. Governmental Controls & the Free Market: The U. S. Economy in the 1970s. LC 76-17976. 240p. 1976. 24.95 (*0-89096-020-8*) Tex A&M Univ Pr.

— Governmental Controls & the Free Market: The U. S. Economy in the 1970s. LC 76-17976. 240p. 1987. pap. 15.95 (*0-89096-309-6*) Tex A&M Univ Pr.

Pejovich, Svetozar, ed. see Greenhut, Melvin.

Pejovich, Svetozar, ed. see Maurice, S. Charles & Hobson, Jane.

Pejovich, Svetozar, ed. see Maurice, S. Charles & Smithson, Charles W.

Pejovich, Svetozar, jt. ed. see Maurice, S. Charles.

Pejovich, Svetozar, ed. see Saving, Thomas R.

Pejsa, Arthur J. Modern Practical Ballistics. LC 88-84150. (Illus.). 200p. 1989. 19.95 (*0-9612776-1-0*) Kenwood Pub.

— Modern Practical Ballistics. 2nd ed. LC 88-84150. (Illus.). 224p. (C). 1991. pap. 19.95 (*0-9612776-3-7*) Kenwood Pub.

— Strong Club Standard: Bidding in Contract Bridge. 66p. (Orig.). 1991. pap. 8.95 (*0-9612776-4-5*) Kenwood Pub.

Pejsa, Jack. Success in College Using the Internet. 196p. (C). 1997. pap. text 14.36 (*0-395-83016-8*) HM.

Pejsa, Jane. Gratia Countryman: Her Life, Her Loves & Her Library. LC 95-67415. (Illus.). 341p. (Orig.). 1995. pap. 14.95 (*0-931714-66-4*, Pub. by Nodin Pr) Bookmen Inc.

— Matriarch of Conspiracy: Ruth Von Kleist, 1867-1945. 2nd ed. LC 90-92033. (Illus.). 432p. 1998. pap. 22.95 (*0-9612776-9-6*) Kenwood Pub.

— Mission to Pomerania Where Bonhoeffer Met the Holocaust: A History & Traveler's Journal. 2nd expanded ed. LC 00-91150. (Illus.). 100p. 2000. pap. 14.95 (*0-9612776-7-X*) Kenwood Pub.

— The Molineux Affair. LC 83-82593. (Illus.). 240p. 1984. pap. 12.95 (*0-9612776-0-2*) Kenwood Pub.

— Romanoff--Prince of Rogues: The Life & Times of a Hollywood Icon. LC 97-93226. (Illus.). 230p. 1997. 22.95 (*0-9612776-8-8*) Kenwood Pub.

Pejsachowicz, Jacobo, jt. auth. see Fitzpatrick, Patrick.

Pekacz, Jolanta T. Conservative Tradition in Pre-Revolutionary France: Parisian Salon Women. LC 98-25160. (The Age of Revolution & Romanticism Ser.: Vol. 25). 256p. (C). 1999. text 51.95 (*0-8204-4138-4*, 41384) P Lang Pubng.

Pekala, Beverly. Don't Settle for Less: A Woman's Guide to Getting a Fair Divorce & Custody Settlement. 288p. 1996. pap. 12.95 (*0-385-48211-6*, Main St Bks) Doubleday.

Pekala, R. J. Quantifying Consciousness: An Empirical Approach. (Illus.). 448p. (C). 1990. 59.50 (*0-306-43750-3*, Plenum Trade) Perseus Pubng.

Pekalski, A., jt. auth. see Galasiewicz, Z. M.

Pekalski, A., jt. ed. see Turko, L.

Pekalski, Andrzej, ed. Diffusion Processes Vol. 438: Experiment, Theory, Simulations: Proceedings of the Fifth Max Born Symposium, Held at Kudowa, Poland, 1-4 June 1994. LC 94-39108. 1994. 72.95 (*3-540-58653-9*) Spr-Verlag.

Pekalski, Andrzej & Sznajk- Weron, Katarzyna, eds. Anomalous Diffusion: From Basics to Applications: Proceedings of the XIth Max Born Symposium Held at Warsaw, Poland, 20-27 May, 1998. LC 98-53206. xviii, 378p. 1999. 86.00 (*3-540-65416-X*) Spr-Verlag.

Pekar, Athanasius. The History of the Church in the Carpathian Rus' Hierarchical Structure. Magosi, Paul R. & Krafcik, Patricia A., eds. 320p. 1993. text 49.00 (*0-88033-219-0*, Pub. by East Eur Monographs) Col U Pr.

Pekar, George M. & Oettmeier, Timothy N. Advanced Short Baton Techniques: Modern Methods Made Easy. fac. ed. (Illus.). 112p. (C). 1984. pap., spiral bd. 23.95 (*0-398-04897-5*) C C Thomas.

— Techniques with a Thirty-Six Inch Baton: Modern Methods Made Easy. (Illus.). 82p. (C). 1983. 17.95 (*0-398-04751-0*) C C Thomas.

Pekar, Harvey. American Splendor Presents Bob & Harv's Comics. (Illus.). 96p. (Orig.). 1996. pap. 16.00 (*1-56858-101-7*) FWEW.

— The New American Splendor Anthology. LC 91-2987. (Illus.). 300p. (Orig.). 1991. pap. 18.95 (*0-941423-64-6*) FWEW.

Pekar, Harvey & Brabner, Joyce. Our Cancer Year. LC 94-10523. (Illus.). 252p. (Orig.). 1994. pap. 17.95 (*1-56858-011-8*) FWEW.

Pekar, Jack P. Total Quality Management: Guiding Principles for Application. LC 95-12661. (Manual Ser.: MNL 22). 1995. 54.00 (*0-8031-2062-1*, MNL22) ASTM.

Pekar, Peter, Jr., jt. auth. see Harbison, John R.

Pekar, Thomas B. & Keeler, Patricia. Creation, the Diary of Lothemur: An Autobiographical Journey from the Place of No Time to the Present. 170p. 1998. spiral bd. 20.00 (*1-879559-10-2*) Galaxy OH.

Pekarcik, Karin. Bridges of the Inner Heart. Stites, Trisha, ed. (Illus.). 300p. 1997. pap. 14.95 (*1-888298-04-9*) Native Planet.

***Pekarck, Daniel L.** Ultimate Adventure. 1999. pap. 18.95 (*0-89716-900-X*, Peanut Btr Pubng) Elton-Wolf Pub.

Pekarek, Art L. The End-Time Holocaust: A Revealing Text Book on Biblical Prophecy. LC 94-73689. (Illus.). 176p. (Orig.). 1994. pap. 8.95 (*0-9639482-3-7*) Lamb Pubns.

— Gay Rights Deception: The Drastic Goals of the Gays! 160p. (C). 1996. pap. 8.95 (*0-9639482-2-9*) Lamb Pubns.

— The Naked Truth about Gays: A Text Book on the Past, Present & Future of Homosexuality. 346p. 1993. pap. 7.95 (*0-9639482-0-2*) Lamb Pubns.

— Satan's Superman in the 21st Century. (Illus.). 208p. (C). 1998. pap. 8.95 (*0-9639482-4-5*) Lamb Pubns.

Pekarik, Andrew. Japanese Ceramics from Prehistoric Times to the Present. LC 78-61434. (Illus.). 103p. (C). 1978. pap. 10.00 (*0-943526-31-0*) Parrish Art.

— Painting. LC 92-52987. (Behind the Scenes Ser.). (Illus.). 64p. (J). (gr. 3-7). 1992. 18.95 (*1-56282-296-9*, Pub. by Hyprn Child); lib. bdg. 18.89 (*1-56282-297-7*, Pub. by Hyprn Child) Little.

— Painting. LC 92-52987. (Behind the Scenes Ser.). (Illus.). 64p. (J). (gr. 3-7). 1995. pap. 8.70 (*0-7868-1031-9*, Pub. by Hyprn Ppbks) Little.

— Painting: Behind the Scenes. (J). 1992. 14.15 (*0-606-07987-4*) Turtleback.

— Sculpture. LC 92-52988. (Behind the Scenes Ser.). (Illus.). 64p. (J). (gr. 3-7). 1995. pap. 8.70 (*0-7868-1032-7*, Pub. by Hyprn Ppbks) Little.

— Sculpture: Behind the Scenes. (J). 1992. 14.15 (*0-606-08138-0*) Turtleback.

Pekarik, Andrew J. The Thirty-Six Immortal Women Poets. (Illus.). 192p. 1991. 45.00 (*0-8076-1256-1*); pap. 24.95 (*0-8076-1257-X*) Braziller.

P

Pekarik, Andrew J., ed. Ukifune: Love in the Tale of Genji. LC 82-1157. 264p. 1983. text 57.50 (*0-231-04598-0*) Col U Pr.

Pekarik, Gene. Psychotherapy Abbreviation: A Practical Guide. LC 95-42382. (Illus.). 191p. 1996. 39.95 (*1-56024-934-X*) Haworth Pr.

***Pekarkova, Iva.** Gimme the Money. 2000. 15.00 (*1-85242-658-6*) Serpents Tail.

Pekarkova, Iva. Truck Stop Rainbows: A Czech Road Novel. Powelstock, David, tr. LC 92-13734. 1992. 22.00 (*0-374-24065-5*) FS&G.

— The World Is Round. Powelstock, David, tr. LC 94-653.Tr. of Kulaty Svet. (RUS.). 224p. 1994. 22.00 (*0-374-29287-6*) FS&G.

Pekas, Mary. Telephone Mastery: Skills for Business Productivity. 1990. text 72.00 incl. audio (*1-56118-018-1*) Paradigm MN.

— Telephone Mastery: Skills for Business Productivity. (C). 1990. teacher ed. 8.00 (*1-56118-020-3*) Paradigm MN.

Pekelis, Alexander H. Law & Social Action: Selected Essays of Alexander H. Pekelis. Konvitz, Milton R., ed. LC 77-87376. (American Constitutional & Legal History Ser). (Illus.). 1970. reprint ed. lib. bdg. 37.50 (*0-306-71600-3*) Da Capo.

Pekhlivanova, K. I. Russian Grammar in Illustrations. (Illus.). 352p. 1987. text 18.75 (*0-8285-3735-6*) Firebird NY.

Pekic, Borislav. The Houses of Belgrade. Johnson, Bernard, tr. from SER. LC 93-47920. (Writings from an Unbound Europe). 220p. (C). 1994. reprint ed. pap. 12.95 (*0-8101-1141-1*) Northwestern U Pr.

— The Time of Miracles: A Legend. Edwards, Lovett F., tr. from SER. LC 93-45889. (Writings from an Unbound Europe). 332p. (C). 1994. reprint ed. pap. 13.95 (*0-8101-1117-9*) Northwestern U Pr.

Pekier, Alter. From Kletz to Siberia: A Students Wanderings During the Holocaust. Hirschler, Gertrude, ed. (ArtScroll History Ser.). (Illus.). 160p. 1985. 16.99 (*0-89906-470-1*); pap. 13.99 (*0-89906-471-X*) Mesorah Pubns.

Peking University staff. Modern Chinese: A Basic Course. LC 78-169835. 249p. 1971. reprint ed. pap. text 6.95 (*0-486-22755-3*) Dover.

— Modern Chinese: A Basic Course. 16th ed. LC 78-169835. 249p. 1984. reprint ed. pap. 18.95 incl. audio (*0-486-99910-6*) Dover.

Peking University staff. Modern Chinese: A Basic Course by the Faculty of Peking University. 1971. 14.95 (*0-486-98832-5*) Dover.

Peking University staff. Modern Chinese: A Second Course. rev. ed. (Illus.). 472p. (C). 1981. reprint ed. pap. 11.95 (*0-486-24155-6*) Dover.

Peking University staff, tr. see Ho, Kan-Chih.

***Pekish, Christie.** Mystical Illusions. 1999. write for info. (*1-58235-449-9*) Watermrk Pr.

Pekka, Peltola, jt. auth. see Soiri, Iina.

Pekkarinen, Jukka, et al, eds. Social Corporatism: A Superior Economic System? (WIDER Studies in Development Economics). (Illus.). 444p. 1992. text 105.00 (*0-19-828380-6*) OUP.

Pekonen, O., jt. ed. see Mickelsson, J.

Pelaccio, Mario. Love in a Bare Room. Barkan, Stanley H., ed. Scammacca, Nat & Scammacca, Nina, trs. (Review Italian-American Writers Ser.: No. 1). 48p. 1992. 15.00 (*0-685-49050-5*); 15.00 (*0-685-49051-3*); pap. 5.00 (*0-89304-668-X*); pap. 5.00 (*0-685-49052-1*) Cross-Cultrl NY.

Peladeau, Marius B. Stephen R. Deane: Early Maine Folk Calligrapher. Howells, Jean, ed. (Illus.). 128p. 1991. 24.95 (*0-933858-04-3*); pap. 19.95 (*0-933858-03-5*) Kennebec River.

Pelaez, Jose A. Arqueologia. (Aqui y Ahora Ser.). 70p. 1997. pap. 6.95 (*0-8477-0283-9*) U of PR Pr.

Pelaez, Martha, jt. auth. see Dluhy, Milan J.

Pelaez, Martha B., ed. see Dluhy, Milan J.

Pelagatti, Susanna. Structured Development of Parallel Programs. 248p. 1997. pap. text 44.95 (*0-7484-0759-6*, Pub. by Tay Francis Ltd) Taylor & Francis.

Pelagius. Peagius's Commentary on St. Paul's Epistle to the Romans. De Bruyn, Theodore, tr. & intro. by. (Oxford Early Christian Studies). 248p. 1998. reprint ed. pap. text 24.95 (*0-19-826980-3*) OUP.

Pelan, John, ed. Darkside: Horror for the Next Millennium. 352p. 1998. mass mkt. 5.99 (*0-451-45662-9*, ROC) NAL.

Pelan, John, jt. auth. see Lee, Edward.

Pelan, John, ed. see Wellman, Manly W.

Pelassy, Dominique, jt. auth. see Dogan, Mattei.

Pelc, Jerzy. Studies in Functional Logical Semiotics of Natural Languages. (Janua Linguarum, Ser. Minor: No. 90). 1971. text 52.35 (*90-279-1599-7*) Mouton.

Pelc, Jerzy, et al, eds. Sign, System & Function: Papers of the First & Second Polish-American Semiotics Colloquia. LC 84-3288. (Approaches to Semiotics Ser.: No. 67). xiii, 503p. 1984. 180.80 (*90-279-3270-0*) Mouton.

Pelc, Jerzy & Wojtasiewicz, Olgierd, eds. Semiotics in Poland, 1894-1969. (Synthese Library: No. 119). 526p. 1978. text 171.00 (*90-277-0811-8*, D Reidel) Kluwer Academic.

Pelchen, Arthur, jt. auth. see Hacker, Jhurgen.

Pelcher, Rosemary L. Just a Dream. (Illus.). 117p. 1997. ring bd. 15.00 (*0-9657924-1-2*, 1002) Write Prodns.

Pelcovits, Nathan A. Security Guarantees in a Middle East Settlement. LC 76-2219. (Foreign Policy Papers: Vol. 2, No. 5). 76p. reprint ed. pap. 30.00 (*0-7837-1987-6*, 204226100002) Bks Demand.

Pelczar, Michael J., Jr., et al. Microbiology: Concepts & Applications. (C). 1993. pap. text, student ed. 28.12 (*0-07-049260-3*) McGraw.

— Microbiology: Concepts & Applications. (C). 1993. text 72.50 (*0-07-049258-1*) McGraw.

— Microbiology: Concepts & Applications. 6th ed. 576p. (C). 1993. pap. 47.19 (*0-07-049264-6*) McGraw.

Pelczynski, Aleksander. Banach Spaces of Analytic Functions & Absolutely Summing Operators. LC 77-9884. (CBMS Regional Conference Series in Mathematics: No. 30). 91p. 1977. reprint ed. pap. 17.00 (*0-8218-1680-2*, CBMS/30) Am Math.

Peldyak, John. SweetSmart Xylitol: Sweeten Your Smile. (Illus.). 52p. (Orig.). 1996. pap. write for info. (*1-57502-341-5*) Morris Pubng.

Pelecanos, George P. The Big Blowdown. 320p. 1999. pap. 14.95 (*0-312-24291-3*) St Martin.

***Pelecanos, George P.** Down by the River Where the Dead Men Go. 1999. pap. 12.00 (*1-85242-716-7*, Pub. by Serpents Tail) Consort Bk Sales.

— A Firing Offense. 1999. pap. 12.00 (*1-85242-715-9*, Pub. by Serpents Tail) Consort Bk Sales.

Pelecanos, George P. King Suckerman: A Novel. 336p. 1998. mass mkt. 6.50 (*0-440-22595-7*) Dell.

***Pelecanos, George P.** Nick's Trip. 1999. pap. 12.00 (*1-85242-714-0*, Pub. by Serpents Tail) Consort Bk Sales.

— Right as Rain: A Novel. 304p. 2000. 24.95 (*0-316-69526-2*) Little.

— Shame the Devil: A Novel. LC 99-29854. 336p. 2000. 24.95 (*0-316-69523-8*) Little.

Pelecanos, George P. The Sweet Forever: A Novel. 384p. 1999. mass mkt. 6.50 (*0-440-23493-X*) Dell.

— The Sweet Forever: A Novel. LC 97-41963. 304p. 1998. 23.95 (*0-316-69109-7*) Little.

Peled, Abraham & Liu, Bede. Digital Signal Processing. LC 85-7984. 320p. 1985. reprint ed. lib. bdg. 35.50 (*0-89874-864-X*) Krieger.

Peled, Alon. A Question of Loyalty: Military Manpower Policy in Multiethnic States. LC 97-51489. (Cornell Studies in Security Affairs). (Illus.). 224p. 1998. text 32.50 (*0-8014-3239-1*) Cornell U Pr.

Peled, D., jt. ed. see Halbwachs, N.

Peled, Einat, et al, eds. Ending the Cycle of Violence: Community Responses to Children of Battered Women. 264p. 1994. 48.00 (*0-8039-5368-2*); pap. 22.95 (*0-8039-5369-0*) Sage.

Peled, Einat & Davis, Diane. Groupwork with Children of Battered Women: A Practitioner's Manual. (Interpersonal Violence: the Practice Ser.: Vol. 10). 160p. 1994. 48.00 (*0-8039-5514-6*); pap. 21.50 (*0-8039-5515-4*) Sage.

Peled, Mattityahu. Religion, My Own: The Literary Works of Najib Mahfuz. LC 82-17582. 268p. 1983. 44.95 (*0-87855-135-2*) Transaction Pubs.

Peled, U. N., jt. auth. see Mahadev, N. V.

Peled, Yoav, jt. ed. see Shafir, Gershon.

***Peleg, David.** Distributed Computing: A Locality-Sensitive Approach. (Discrete Mathematics & Applications Ser.: Vol. 5). 2000. 106.00 (*0-89871-464-8*) Soc Indus-Appl Math.

Peleg, Dorith E., jt. auth. see Sweetgall, Robert.

Peleg, Ilan. Begin's Foreign Policy, 1977-1983: Israel's Move to the Right, 164. LC 86-15020. (Contributions in Political Science Ser.: No. 164). 247p. 1987. 49.95 (*0-313-24938-5*, PGF/, Greenwood Pr) Greenwood.

Peleg, Ilan. Human Rights in the West Bank & Gaza. LC 96-25627. (Studies on Peace & Conflict Resolution). 240p. 1995. 39.95 (*0-8156-2682-7*) Syracuse U Pr.

Peleg, Ilan, ed. The Middle East Peace Process: Interdisciplinary Perspectives. LC 97-1208. (SUNY Series in Israeli Studies). 312p. (C). 1997. text 59.50 (*0-7914-3541-5*); pap. text 19.95 (*0-7914-3542-3*) State U NY Pr.

***Pelegri, Assimina A., ed.** Durability & Damage Tolerance of Composite Materials & Structures, 1999. LC 99-75419. (MD Ser.: Vol. 86). 178p. 1999. 90.00 (*0-7918-1641-9*) ASME Pr.

Pelegrimas, Marthayn & Dowd, Joseph. Thirteen Doors: Doors I & II, Vols. I & II. unabridged ed. 1993. pap. 7.95 incl. audio (*1-882071-45-X*) B&B Audio.

Pelegrin-Genel, Elisabeth. The Office. (Illus.). 216p. 1996. 45.00 (*2-08-013589-9*, Pub. by Flammarion) Abbeville Pr.

Pelegrin, Marc & Hollister, Walter M., eds. Concise Encyclopedia of Aeronautics & Space Systems. LC 93-10616. (Advances in Systems Control & Information Engineering Ser.). 492p. 1993. 321.75 (*0-08-037049-7*, Pergamon Pr) Elsevier.

Peleminsky, S. V., jt. auth. see Akhiezer, A. I.

Pelen, Marc M. Latin Poetic Irony in the Roman de la Rose. v. LC 87-10242. (Vinaver Studies in French). 1987. write for info. (*0-905205-32-4*) F Cairns Pubns.

Pelenski, Jaroslaw. The Contest for the Legacy of Kievan Rus' LC 96-84141. 300p. 1996. 42.00 (*0-88033-274-3*, 377, Pub. by East Eur Monographs) Col U Pr.

— Studies in Ukrainian History. 300p. 1993. 47.00 (*0-88033-275-1*, 378, Pub. by East Eur Monographs) Col U Pr.

Pelensky, Olga A. Isak Dinesen: The Life & Imagination of a Seducer. LC 90-45735. (Illus.). 243p. 1991. reprint ed. pap. 19.95 (*0-8214-1008-3*) Ohio U Pr.

Pelensky, Olga A., ed. Isak Dinesen: Critical Views. LC 93-7023. 371p. (C). 1993. text 39.95 (*0-8214-1055-5*) Ohio U Pr.

Pelereants, C., jt. ed. see Cavalloro, R.

Pelerents, C., jt. ed. see Cavalloro, R.

Peles, John D., jt. ed. see Barrett, Gary W.

Peletminskii, S. V., jt. auth. see Akhiezev, A. I.

Peletskaya, E. N. Virology Reviews Vol. 4, Pt. 3: Viral Hepatitides A & E Part B, Vol. 4. (Soviet Medical Reviews Ser.: Section E). 83p. 1992. pap. text 84.00 (*3-7186-5260-9*, Harwood Acad Pubs) Gordon & Breach.

Peletskii, V. E., et al. Thermophysical Properties of Titanium & Its Alloys: A Handbook. 110p. 1990. 85.00 (*0-89116-752-8*) Begell Hse.

Peletz, Michael G. Reason & Passion: Representations of Gender in a Malay Society. LC 94-45698. (Illus.). 371p. 1996. pap. 22.50 (*0-520-20070-5*, Pub. by U CA Pr) Cal Prin Full Svc.

— Reason & Passion: Representations of Gender in a Malay Society. LC 94-45698. (Illus.). 371p. (C). 1996. 55.00 (*0-520-20069-1*, Pub. by U CA Pr) Cal Prin Full Svc.

— A Share of the Harvest: Kinship, Property, & Social History among the Malays of Rembau. 448p. 1988. 55.00 (*0-520-06153-5*, Pub. by U CA Pr) Cal Prin Full Svc.

— A Share of the Harvest: Kinship, Property & Social History among the Malays of Rembau. 1992. pap. 17.95 (*0-520-08086-6*, Pub. by U CA Pr) Cal Prin Full Svc.

Peletz, Michael G., jt. ed. see Ong, Aihwa.

***Pelevin, Victor.** The Blue Lantern. Bromfield, Andrew, tr. from RUS. 2000. pap. 12.95 (*0-8112-1434-6*, Pub. by New Directions) Norton.

— Buddha's Little Finger. Bromfield, Andrew, tr. LC 99-89565. 352p. 2000. 25.95 (*0-670-89168-1*, Viking) Viking Penguin.

Pelevin, Victor. The Life of Insects. 192p. 1999. pap. 11.95 (*0-14-027972-5*) Viking Penguin.

— The Life of Insects: A Novel. Bromfield, Andrew, tr. from RUS. LC 97-11106. 179p. 1998. 22.00 (*0-374-18625-1*) FS&G.

— Omon Ra. LC 95-47618. 154p. 1996. 21.00 (*0-374-22592-3*) FS&G.

— Omon Ra. Bromfield, Andrew, tr. from RUS. LC 97-34302. 160p. 1998. pap. 9.95 (*0-8112-1364-1*, NDP851, Pub. by New Directions) Norton.

— A Werewolf Problem in Central Russia & Other Stories. Bromfiel, Andrew, tr. LC 98-17488. 213p. 1998. 23.95 (*0-8112-1394-3*, Pub. by New Directions) Norton.

— The Yellow Arrow. Bromfield, Andrew, tr. from RUS. LC 96-773.Tr. of Aheltaia Strela. 96p. 1996. 17.95 (*0-8112-1324-2*, Pub. by New Directions) Norton.

— The Yellow Arrow. Bromfield, Andrew, tr. from RUS.Tr. of Aheltaia Strela. 96p. 1997. pap. 8.95 (*0-8112-1355-2*, NDP845, Pub. by New Directions) Norton.

***Pelevin, Victoria.** Life of Insects. 1999. pap. 5.00 (*5-7027-0773-7*) Distribks Inc.

Pelfer, P. G., jt. auth. see Navarria, F. L.

***Pelfrey, Evelyn, ed.** The Heritage of Barbour County, Alabama. (Heritage of Alabama Ser.: Vol. 3). 320p. 2001. 50.00 (*1-891647-36-9*) Herit Pub Consult.

Pelfrey, Robert. Art & Mass Media. 376p. (C). 1996. pap. text 49.95 (*0-7872-0488-9*) Kendall-Hunt.

Pelfrey, Sandra H. Basic Accounting for Hospital Based Non-Financial Managers. 1993. text 31.50 (*0-8273-4894-0*) Delmar.

***Pelger, Ned.** Joyful Living: Build Yourself a Great Life! 2000. pap. 9.95 (*0-9624569-8-5*) ATA Pub Co.

Pelgrin, Mark. And a Time to Die. Moon, Sheila & Howes, Elizabeth, eds. LC 75-26836. 159p. 1976. reprint ed. pap. 5.25 (*0-8356-0305-9*, Quest) Theos Pub Hse.

Pelgrom, Els. The Acorn Eaters. Prins, Johanna H. & Prins, Johanna W., trs. from DUT. LC 93-34210.Tr. of Eikelvreters. 224p. (J). (gr. 7-12). 1997. 16.00 (*0-374-30029-1*) FS&G.

Pelgrum, Willem J. The IEA Study of Computers in Education II. (International Studies in Educational Achievement: Vol. 14). 1995. write for info. (*0-08-042565-8*, Pergamon Pr) Elsevier.

Pelgrum, Willem J. & Plomp, Tjeerd, eds. The IEA Study of Computers in Education. LC 93-23567. (International Studies in Educational Achievement: Vol. 2). 344p. 1993. text 102.50 (*0-08-041935-6*, Pergamon Pr) Elsevier.

Pelham. Conducting Experiments in Psychology: Measuring the Weight of Smoke. LC 98-27537. (Psychology Ser.). 1998. pap. 29.50 (*0-534-35718-0*) Brooks-Cole.

Pelham, Brett W. Conducting Research in Psychology: Measuring the Weight of Smoke. LC 98-27537. xvi, 334p. 1998. 39.95 (*0-534-36358-X*) Brooks-Cole.

Pelham, David. A Is for Animals. (Illus.). 14p. (J). (ps-1). 1991. 16.95 (*0-671-72495-9*) S&S Bks Yung.

— Applebee Cat's ABC Fun. LC 97-229066. (Illus.). 26p. (J). 1997. 10.99 (*0-525-45827-1*) NAL.

***Pelham, David.** Kites. LC 99-86856. (Illus.). 227p. 2000. pap. 14.95 (*1-58567-017-0*, Pub. by Overlook Pr) Penguin Putnam.

Pelham, David. Nightmare. 1999. pap. 19.95 (*0-670-82402-X*) Viking Penguin.

***Pelham, David.** A Piece of Cake: A Delectable Pop-Up Book. (Illus.). (J). 2000. 12.95 (*1-929766-02-5*) Handprint.

Pelham, David. Sam's Pizza. LC 96-222155. (Illus.). 11p. (J). (ps up). 1996. 12.99 (*0-525-45594-9*) NAL.

— Sam's Sandwich. (Illus.). 22p. (J). (ps-4). 1991. 10.99 (*0-525-44751-2*, Dutton Child) Peng Put Young Read.

— Sam's Sandwich. 1990. 4.99 (*0-224-03011-6*) Random.

— Sam's Snack. (Illus.). 16p. (J). (ps-4). 1994. pap. 11.99 (*0-525-45266-4*, Dutton Child) Peng Put Young Read.

— Worms Wiggle. (Illus.). 20p. (J). (ps-3). 1989. pap. 9.95 (*0-671-67218-5*) Litle Simon.

Pelham, David. The Sensational Samburger. 10p. (J). (ps). 1995. 13.99 (*0-525-45426-8*, Dutton Child) Peng Put Young Read.

***Pelham, David & Miller, Jonathan.** Facts of Life. (Illus.). 12p. (YA). (gr. 3 up). 2000. 16.95 (*1-58117-093-9*, Piggy Toes Pr) Intervisual Bks.

— Human Body. (Illus.). 12p. (YA). (gr. 3 up). 2000. 16.95 (*1-58117-092-0*, Piggy Toes Pr) Intervisual Bks.

Pelham, Erra, jt. auth. see Axsom, Dora.

Pelham, Henry, jt. auth. see Copley, John S.

Pelham, Jackie, ed. Food for Thought: Ez Recipes & Poetry by Texas Poets. (Illus.). 232p. 1990. pap. 12.95 (*0-9627844-0-0*) Page One TX.

***Pelham, Jackie, ed.** Suddenly: Prose Poetry & Sudden Fiction. LC 98-66716. viii, 180 p. 1998. pap. 10.00 (*0-9627844-2-7*) Page One TX.

— Suddenly III: Prose Poetry & Sudden Fiction. 200p. 2000. pap. 10.00 (*0-9627844-4-3*) Page One TX.

Pelham, Jackie, ed. Suddenly II: Prose Poetry & Sudden Fiction. 156p. 1999. pap. 10.00 (*0-9627844-3-5*) Page One TX.

Pelham, Jackie, jt. ed. see Jackson, Guida.

Pelham, Jackie, ed. see Stahl, Carmine A.

Pelham, Lawrence. I Am Indian American. LC 96-40530. (Our American Family Ser.). (J). (gr. k-3). 1997. lib. bdg. 15.93 (*0-8239-5008-5*, PowerKids) Rosen Group.

***Pelham, Raydon.** Shame. 240p. 1998. mass mkt. 9.95 (*0-352-33302-2*) Virgin Games.

Pelham, Thomas G. State Land-Use Planning & Regulation: Florida, the Model Code & Beyond. LC 79-2390. 224p. reprint ed. pap. 69.50 (*0-7837-5773-5*, 204543800006) Bks Demand.

Peli, Eli. Vision Models for Target Detection & Recognition - In Memory of Arthur Menedez. (World Scientific Series on Information Display). 432p. 1995. text 69.00 (*981-02-2149-5*) World Scientific Pub.

***Peli, Pinchas, ed.** On Repentance. LC 96-22665. 336p. 2000. pap. 30.00 (*0-7657-6140-8*) Aronson.

***Pelias, Ronald J.** Performance Studies: The Interpretation of Aesthetic Texts. 272p. (Orig.). (C). 1999. per. 39.95 (*0-7872-6219-6*, 41621901) Kendall-Hunt.

Pelias, Ronald J. Writing Performance: Poeticizing the Researcher's Body. LC 98-37551. 1999. 34.95 (*0-8093-2235-8*) S Ill U Pr.

Pelican, Fred. From Dachau to Dunkirk. LC 92-21684. 1993. pap. text 19.50 (*0-85303-253-X*, Pub. by M Vallentine & Co) Intl Spec Bk.

Pelican Publishing Staff. Cowboy: Texas Night Before Christmas. 1998. audio 9.95 (*1-56554-385-8*) Pelican.

***Pelican Publishing Staff, ed.** Country Inns & Selected Hotels in Great Britain & Ireland 1999. 60th ed. 400p. 1999. pap. 17.95 (*1-56554-638-5*) Pelican.

Pelican, Suzanne & Bachman-Carter, Karen. Navajo Food Practices, Customs, & Holidays. (Ethnic & Regional Food Practices Ser.). 1992. pap. 10.00 (*0-88091-083-6*, 0867) Am Dietetic Assn.

Pelicier, Yves, ed. Univers de la Psychologie, 1: Champ, Histoire et Methodes de la Psychologie. (FRE.). 512p. 1977. 150.00 (*0-8288-5525-0*, M6537) Fr & Eur.

— Univers de la Psychologie, 3: Le Development Psychologique Normale, Lavie Psychologie Pathologique. (FRE.). 523p. 1977. 150.00 (*0-8288-5527-7*, M6539) Fr & Eur.

— Univers de la Psychologie, 2: La Vie Psychologique Normale. (FRE.). 509p. 1977. 150.00 (*0-8288-5526-9*, M6538) Fr & Eur.

Peligeot, Joal. Be Your Own Investment Advisor: It's a Piece of Cake! (Illus.). 186p. (Orig.). 1996. pap. 9.95 (*0-9655538-0-9*) Moneycare.

Pelikaan, R., et al, eds. Arithmetic, Geometry & Coding Theory: Proceedings of the International Conference Held at Centre International de Recontres Mathematiques (CIRM), Luminy, France, June 28 - July 2, 1993. xii, 288p. 1996. lib. bdg. 129.95 (*3-11-014616-9*) De Gruyter.

Pelikan. Applications of Numerical Methods: Molecular Spectroscopy. 368p. 1994. boxed set 115.95 (*0-8493-7322-0*, QD96) CRC Pr.

Pelikan, E., jt. ed. see Novak, M.

Pelikan, Jaroslav. Jesus Through the Centuries: His Place in the History of Culture. (Illus.). 320p. 1999. pap. 13.95 (*0-300-07987-7*) Yale U Pr.

— What Has Athens to Do with Jerusalem? Timaeus & Genesis in Counterpoint. LC 97-4244. 21. 160p. (C). 1997. text 29.95 (*0-472-10807-7*, 10807) U of Mich Pr.

Pelikan, Jaroslav J. The Christian Tradition - a History of the Development of Doctrine Vol. 1: Emergence of the Catholic Tradition, 100-600. LC 79-142042. 420p. 1997. 36.00 (*0-226-65370-6*) U Ch Pr.

— The Christian Tradition - a History of the Development of Doctrine Vol. 1: The Emergence of the Catholic Tradition, 100-600. LC 79-142042. 420p. 1975. pap. 16.00 (*0-226-65371-4*, P644) U Ch Pr.

— The Christian Tradition - a History of the Development of Doctrine Vol. 2: The Spirit of Eastern Christendom, 600-1700. LC 79-142042. xxv, 358p. 1996. 36.00 (*0-226-65372-2*) U Ch Pr.

— The Christian Tradition - a History of the Development of Doctrine Vol. 2: The Spirit of Eastern Christendom, 600-1700. LC 79-142042. 358p. 1977. reprint ed. pap. 14.95 (*0-226-65373-0*, P738) U Ch Pr.

— The Christian Tradition - a History of the Development of Doctrine Vol. 3: The Growth of Medieval Theology, 600-1300. LC 78-1501. 364p. 1978. 40.50 (*0-226-65374-9*) U Ch Pr.

— The Christian Tradition - a History of the Development of Doctrine Vol. 3: The Growth of Medieval Theology, 600-1300. LC 78-1501. 368p. 1980. pap. 16.00 (*0-226-65375-7*) U Ch Pr.

— The Christian Tradition - a History of the Development of Doctrine Vol. 4: Reformation of Church & Dogma, 1300-1700. LC 79-142042. Vol. 4. lii, 480p. 1984. 34.95 (*0-226-65376-5*) U Ch Pr.

— The Christian Tradition - a History of the Development of Doctrine Vol. 4: Reformation of Church & Dogma, 1300-1700. LC 79-142042. iii, 478p. 1985. pap. 17.00 (*0-226-65377-3*) U Ch Pr.

— The Christian Tradition - a History of the Development of Doctrine Vol. 5: Christian Doctrine & Modern Culture, since 1700. LC 88-23658. 416p. 1989. 34.95 (*0-226-65378-1*) U Ch Pr.

— The Christian Tradition - a History of the Development of Doctrine Vol. 5: Christian Doctrine & Modern Culture, since 1700. 417p. 1991. pap. 14.95 (*0-226-65380-3*) U Ch Pr.

— Christianity & Classical Culture: The Metamorphosis of Natural Theology in the Christian. 1995. pap. 18.00 (*0-300-06255-9*) Yale U Pr.

— Confessor Between East & West: A Portrait of Ukrainian Cardinal Josyf Slipyj. fac. ed. LC 89-27536. (Illus.). 262p. 1990. reprint ed. pap. 81.30 (*0-7837-7970-4*, 204772600008) Bks Demand.

— Eternal Feminines: Three Theological Allegories in Dante's Paridiso. LC 90-8261. 150p. (C). 1990. pap. text 15.00 (*0-8135-1603-X*) Rutgers U Pr.

— Faust the Theologian. LC 94-37989. 158p. 1995. 30.00 (*0-300-06288-5*) Yale U Pr.

— Faust the Theologian. 158p. 1997. pap. 14.00 (*0-300-07064-0*) Yale U Pr.

— The Idea of the University: A Reexamination. 288p. (C). 1992. 37.50 (*0-300-05725-3*); pap. 16.00 (*0-300-05834-9*) Yale U Pr.

— The Illustrated Jesus Through the Centuries. LC 97-7360. (Illus.). 256p. 1997. 35.00 (*0-300-07268-6*) Yale U Pr.

— Imago Dei: The Byzantine Apologia for Icons. (Bollingen Ser.). (Illus.). 196p. (C). 1990. text 49.50 (*0-691-09970-7*, Pub. by Princeton U Pr) Cal Prin Full Svc.

— Jesus Through the Centuries: His Place in the History of Culture. LC 86-45679. (Illus.). 304p. (C). 1987. pap. 14.00 (*0-06-097080-4*, PL 7080, Perennial) HarperTrade.

— Mary Through the Centuries: Her Place in the History of Culture. LC 96-24726. (Illus.). 240p. 1998. 30.00 (*0-300-06951-0*); pap. 14.00 (*0-300-07661-4*) Yale U Pr.

— The Melody of Theology: A Philosophical Dictionary. 320p. 1988. pap. text 10.95 (*0-674-56473-1*) HUP.

— The Melody of Theology: A Philosophical Dictionary. LC 88-690. 320p. 1988. 29.95 (*0-674-56472-3*) HUP.

— The Mystery of Continuity: Time & History, Memory & Eternity in the Thought of Saint Augustine. LC 86-7788. (Richard Lectures, University of Virginia: No. 1984). 189p. reprint ed. pap. 58.60 (*0-608-20051-4*, 207132300011) Bks Demand.

— The Shape of Death: Life, Death, & Immortality in the Early Fathers. LC 78-6030. 128p. 1978. reprint ed. lib. bdg. 38.50 (*0-313-20458-6*, PESD, Greenwood Pr) Greenwood.

— The Vindication of Tradition. LC 84-5132. 94p. 1984. pap. 12.00 (*0-300-03638-8*) Yale U Pr.

Pelikan, Jaroslav J., ed. Luther the Expositor. 286p. 1959. 29.00 (*0-570-06431-7*, 15-1741) Concordia.

Pelikan, Jaroslav J. & Schick, George V. Luther's Works: Genesis Chapters 1-5, Vol. 1. LC 55-9893. 1958. 29.00 (*0-570-06401-5*, 15-1743) Concordia.

Pelikan, Jaroslav J., ed. see Luther, Martin.

Pelikan, Jaroslav J., ed. see Luther, Martin H.

Pelikan, Jaroslav J., tr. see Luther, Martin.

Pelikan, Judy. Great Girl Food: Easy Eats & Tempting Treats for Girls to Make. 1996. 13.15 (*0-606-10833-5*, Pub. by Turtleback) Demco.

— The Heart's Journey. LC 95-20550. (Illus.). 32p. 1996. 5.95 (*0-7892-0088-0*) Abbeville Pr.

— The Light's Way. (Illus.). 32p. 1997. 5.95 (*0-7892-0138-0*) Abbeville Pr.

Pelikan, Judy, jt. auth. see Levy, Judith.

Pelikan, Maria, tr. see Lorenz, Juliane, ed.

Pelillo, Marcello, et al, eds. Energy Minimization Methods in Computer Vision & Pattern Recognition: International Workshop EMMCVPRAE97, Venice, Italy, May 21-23, 1997, Proceedings, Vol. 122. LC 97-15187. (Lecture Notes in Computer Science Ser.: No. 1223). xii, 549p. 1997. pap. 85.00 (*3-540-62909-2*) Spr-Verlag.

Pelillo, Marcello, jt. ed. see Hancock, Edwin R.

Pelinka, Anton. Austria: Out of the Shadow of the Past. LC 98-22740. (Nations of the Modern World Ser.). 272p. 1998. text 75.00 (*0-8133-2918-3*, Pub. by Westview) HarpC.

— Politics of the Lesser Evil: Leadership, Democracy, & Jaruzelski's Poland. LC 97-51254. 1998. 44.95 (*1-56000-367-7*) Transaction Pubs.

— Social Democratic Parties in Europe. LC 82-18940. 190p. 1983. 57.95 (*0-275-91057-1*, C1057, Praeger Pubs) Greenwood.

Pelinka, Anton & Bischof, Gunter, eds. Austria in the New Europe. (Contemporary Austrian Studies: Vol. 1). 250p. (C). 1992. pap. 35.00 (*1-56000-597-1*) Transaction Pubs.

Pelinka, Anton, jt. auth. see Reinalter, Helmut.

Pelinka, Anton, jt. ed. see Bischof, Gunter.

Pelinka, Anton, jt. ed. see Reinalter, Helmut.

Pelissier, Alain. Reichen & Robert: Transforming Space. (Illus.). 120p. 1994. pap. 60.00 (*3-7643-5052-0*, Pub. by Birkhauser) Princeton Arch.

Pelissier, Michel, jt. auth. see Lupson, Peter.

Pelissier, Rene, jt. auth. see Wheeler, Douglas L.

Peliti, L. Biologically Inspired Physics. (NATO ASI Ser.: Vol. 263). (Illus.). 408p. (C). 1991. text 129.50 (*0-306-44000-8*, Kluwer Plenum) Kluwer Academic.

— Disordered Systems & Biological Models. 210p. (C). 1989. text 77.00 (*9971-5-0948-2*) World Scientific Pub.

Peliti, L. & Vulpiani, Angelo, eds. Measures of Complexity. (Lecture Notes in Physics Ser.: Vol. 314). vii, 150p. 1988. 45.95 (*0-387-50316-1*) Spr-Verlag.

Pelizza, John J. The Answer. Niles, Phillip, ed. (Personal Growth Ser.). (Illus.). 34p. 1995. pap. 3.95 (*0-9614872-4-0*) Pelizza & Assocs.

— The Big Secret. Niles, Phillip, ed. (Children's Bks.). (Illus.). 114p. (J). 1994. pap. 10.95 (*0-9614872-3-2*) Pelizza & Assocs.

— Foot in the Door. (Stress Management & Personal Growth Ser.). (Illus.). 152p. (Orig.). 1985. pap. 10.95 (*0-9614872-0-8*) Pelizza & Assocs.

— There's Magic in Discovery! Niles, Phillip, ed. (Illus.). 165p. 1993. pap. 11.95 (*0-9614872-2-4*) Pelizza & Assocs.

— Thoughts to Make You Think & Feel Better. 87p. 1988. pap. 11.95 (*0-9614872-1-6*) Pelizza & Assocs.

Pelizzetti, Ezio, ed. Fine Particles Science & Technology: From Micro to Nanoparticles. (NATO ASI Ser.: Vol. 12). 1996. text 438.50 (*0-7923-4047-7*) Kluwer Academic.

Pelizzetti, Ezio & Schiavello, Mario, eds. Photochemical Conversion & Storage of Solar Energy. (C). 1991. text 316.50 (*0-7923-1194-9*) Kluwer Academic.

Pelizzetti, Ezio & Serpone, Nick, eds. Homogeneous & Heterogeneous Photocatalysis. 1986. text 326.00 (*90-277-2221-8*) Kluwer Academic.

Pelizzetti, Ezio, jt. auth. see Serpone, Nick.

Pelizzoli, Francesca. Far & Away: A Notebook for Travellers. 164p. 1992. 14.95 (*0-948751-04-5*) Interlink Pub.

***Pelizzon, V. Penelope.** Nostos. LC 99-36767. 80p. 1999. 24.95 (*0-8214-1298-1*); pap. 12.95 (*0-8214-1299-X*) Ohio U Pr.

Pelka, Fred. The ABC-CLIO Companion to the Disability Rights Movement. LC 97-7662. (Companions to Key Issues in American History & Life Ser.). 422p. 1997. lib. bdg. 65.00 (*0-87436-834-0*, FN-1654) ABC-CLIO.

Pelkey, Charles, jt. auth. see Wilcockson, John.

Pelkey, Eddie J. & Getz, Irene. Self-Esteem: Encouraging Self & Others. (Intersections: Small Group Ser.). 1995. pap. 5.49 (*0-8066-0137-X*) Augsburg Fortress.

Pelkey, Rod. Satori. 279p. mass mkt. 4.99 (*1-55197-194-1*) Picasso Publ.

Pelkey, Rosemary M. The Adirondack Bridgebuilder from Charleston: Life & Times of Robert Cogdell Gilchrist. LC 93-6165. 1993. pap. 15.00 (*0-925168-23-8*) North Country.

Pelkey, William L., jt. auth. see Koga, Robert K.

Pelkmans, Jacques. Economics European Integ. LC 96-39223. 320p. (C). 1996. pap. text 30.00 (*0-582-27759-0*, Pub. by Addison-Wesley) Longman.

— Market Integration in the European Community. LC 84-8138. (Studies in Industrial Organization: Vol. 5). 1984. lib. bdg. 122.50 (*90-247-2978-5*) Kluwer Academic.

Pelkmans, Jacques, jt. ed. see Alting Von Gesau, Frans A.

Pelkmans, Jacques, jt. ed. see Brenton, Paul.

Pelkmans, Jaques, jt. ed. see Galli, Giampaolo.

Pelkonen, Eeva-Liisa. Achtung Architektur! Image & Phantasm in Contemporary Austrian Architecture. LC 96-10497. (Illus.). 203p. 1996. 42.00 (*0-262-16159-1*) MIT Pr.

Pell, Arthur. Complete Idiot's Guide to Managing People. 352p. 1995. 18.95 (*0-02-861036-9*) Macmillan Gen Ref.

***Pell, Arthur R.** Complete Idiot's Guide to Recruiting the Right Stuff. (Complete Idiot's Guides (Lifestyle) Ser.). (Illus.). 384p. 2000. pap. 18.95 (*0-02-863901-4*, Alpha Ref) Macmillan Gen Ref.

Pell, Arthur R. Getting the Most from Your People. 64p. 1990. audio. write for info. (*0-318-67224-3*) P-H.

***Pell, Arthur R.** The Pocket Idiot's Guide to One-Minute Managing. LC 99-64050. (Pocket Idiot's Guides Ser.). (Illus.). 202p. 1999. pap. 9.95 (*0-02-863343-1*, Pub. by Macmillan Gen Ref) S&S Trade.

Pell, B. Ernest Buckler's the Mountain & the Valley. LC 96-111790. (Canadian Fiction Studies: No. 31). 120p. (C). 1994. pap. text 14.95 (*1-55022-180-9*, Pub. by ECW) Genl Dist Srvs.

Pell, Barbara. Faith & Fiction: A Theological Critique of the Narrative Strategies of Hugh MacLennan & Morley Callaghan. No. 23. (Editions SR Ser.: Vol. 23). 148p. 1998. pap. 24.95 (*0-88920-307-5*) W Laurier U Pr.

Pell, Barney, jt. ed. see Musliner, David.

Pell, Derek. Assassination Rhapsody. (Illus.). 124p. 1989. pap. 6.00 (*0-936756-54-3*) Autonomedia.

— Bewildering Beasties. LC 96-3900. (Pictorial Archive Ser.). (Illus.). 64p. 1996. 2.50 (*0-486-29126-X*) Dover.

— The Marquis de Sade's Elements of Style. (Illus.). 64p. (Orig.). 1996. pap. 5.95 (*1-882633-20-2*) Permeable.

— Scar Mirror. (Illus.). 1979. pap. 2.50 (*0-916866-05-X*) Cats Pajamas.

— X-Texts. 158p. Date not set. 7.00 (*1-57027-005-8*) Autonomedia.

Pell, E. J. Invention & Discovery of Reality: The Acquisition of Conservation of Amount. LC 74-10243. 211p. reprint ed. pap. 65.50 (*0-608-30625-8*, 201615900098) Bks Demand.

Pell, Elsie, ed. see Gide, Andre.

Pell, J. M., jt. ed. see Loughna, P. T.

Pell, Jerry, jt. auth. see Hanna, Steven R.

Pell, John. Ethan Allen. LC 72-5515. (Select Bibliographies Reprint Ser.). (Illus.). 1977. reprint ed. 31.95 (*0-8369-6919-7*) Ayer.

Pell, M. Gas Fluidization. (Handbook of Powder Technology Ser.: No. 8). 126p. 1990. 136.00 (*0-444-88335-5*) Elsevier.

Pell, Malcolm, ed. Handbook of Stereotaxy Using the CRW Apparatus. LC 94-1716. (Illus.). 256p. 1994. 95.00 (*0-683-06835-0*) Lppncott W & W.

Pell, Patty. Esther: Character under Pressure. (Life Guide Bible Studies). 64p. (Orig.). 1995. pap., wbk. ed. 4.99 (*0-8308-1039-0*) InterVarsity.

Pell, Sarah, jt. auth. see Welker, Matthew.

***Pell, Steve.** Over 200 Proven Ways & Places to Pick up Girls by an Average Looking Guy. 2nd rev. ed. LC 99-229485. 1999. pap. 19.95 (*0-9668698-0-X*) S A Pell.

Pell, Wilbur F. Obstacle's Overcome. LC 98-90864. 1999. 18.95 (*0-533-12953-2*) Vantage.

Pella Historical Society Staff. Pella Community, Iowa, Vol. I. (Illus.). 682p. 1988. 45.00 (*0-88107-106-4*) Curtis Media.

Pella, J. & Peterson, T. Ribbons of Steel, Vols. 1-3. (Ribbons of Steel Ser.). (J). 1998. pap., boxed set 32.99 (*0-7642-8309-X*, 258309) Bethany Hse.

Pella, Jerome, et al. Stock Composition of Some Sockeye Salmon, Oncorhynchus Nerka, Catches in the Southeast Alaska, Based on Incidence of Allozyme Variants, Freshwater Ages, & a Brian-Tissue Parasite. 32p. 1998. reprint ed. pap. 4.20 (*0-89904-774-2*, Cascade Geog Soc) Crumb Elbow Pub.

Pella, Judith. Beloved Stranger. 32p. 1998. pap. 9.99 (*0-7642-2040-3*) Bethany Hse.

***Pella, Judith.** Beloved Stranger. large type ed. LC 98-48263. 456p. 1999. 27.95 (*0-7838-8495-8*) Macmillan Gen Ref.

Pella, Judith. Blind Faith. LC 96-35649. (Portraits Ser.). 34p. 1996. pap. 8.99 (*1-55661-880-8*) Bethany Hse.

— Dawning of Deliverance. (Russians Ser.: Bk. 5). 432p. 1995. pap. 10.99 (*1-55661-359-8*) Bethany Hse.

— Frontier Lady. (Lone Star Legacy Ser.: Bk. 1). 4p. (Orig.). 1993. pap. 10.99 (*1-55661-293-1*) Bethany Hse.

***Pella, Judith.** Heaven's Road. (Illus.). 352p. (J). 2000. pap. 10.99 (*0-7642-2279-1*) Bethany Hse.

Pella, Judith. Heirs of the Motherland. 384p. 1993. pap. 10.99 (*1-55661-358-X*) Bethany Hse.

— A Hope Beyond. LC 97-21036. (Ribbons of Steel Ser.: No. 2). 32p. 1997. pap. 10.99 (*1-55661-863-8*) Bethany Hse.

— Passage into Light. (Russians Ser.). 34p. 1998. pap. 10.99 (*1-55661-869-7*) Bethany Hse.

— Russians, Vol. 1-5. 1995. boxed set 54.99 (*1-55661-795-X*) Bethany Hse.

— Separate Roads, 2. LC 99-6609. (Ribbons West Ser.). 320p. 1999. pap. 10.99 (*0-7642-2072-1*) Bethany Hse.

— Stoner's Crossing. LC 94-4891. (Lone Star Legacy Ser.: Bk. 2). 384p. 1994. pap. 10.99 (*1-55661-294-X*) Bethany Hse.

***Pella, Judith.** Texas Angel. LC 99-6544. 320p. (Orig.). 1999. pap. 10.99 (*0-7642-2278-3*) Bethany Hse.

Pella, Judith. Warrior's Song. LC 95-45622. (Lone Star Softly Ser.: Vol. 3). 384p. (Orig.). 1996. pap. 10.99 (*1-55661-655-4*) Bethany Hse.

— White Nights, Red Morning. LC 96-25282. (Russians Ser.: Bk. 6). 416p. 1996. pap. 10.99 (*1-55661-360-1*) Bethany Hse.

Pella, Judith & Peterson, Tracie. Distant Dreams. LC 95-45906. (Ribbons of Steel Ser.: Bk. 1). 352p. 1997. pap. 10.99 (*1-55661-862-X*) Bethany Hse.

— A Promise for Tomorrow. LC 97-45442. (Ribbons of Steel Ser.). 368p. 1998. pap. 10.99 (*1-55661-864-6*) Bethany Hse.

***Pella, Judith & Peterson, Tracie.** Ribbons West: Westward the Dream; Separate Roads; Ties That Bind, Vols. 1-3. 2000. pap., boxed set 32.99 (*0-7642-8649-8*) Bethany Hse.

— Ties That Bind. LC 99-50592. (Ribbons West Ser.: Vol. 3). 320p. 2000. pap. 10.99 (*0-7642-2073-X*) Bethany Hse.

Pella, Judith & Peterson, Tracie. Westward the Dream. LC 99-6614. (Ribbons West Ser.). 352p. 1999. pap. 10.99 (*0-7642-2071-3*) Bethany Hse.

Pella, Judith, jt. auth. see Phillips, Michael.

Pella, Judith, jt. auth. see Phillips, Michael R.

Pellam, Janet. Three Faces of the River. 67p. (Orig.). 1994. pap. write for info. (*1-879294-06-0*) Warm Spring Pr.

***Pellam, John L.** The Asia 500: Leaders for the New Century. 2000. 395.00 (*1-882292-19-7*) Barons Whos Who.

— The Barons 500: Leaders for the New Century. 2000. 395.00 (*1-882292-18-9*) Barons Whos Who.

— The Europe 500: Leaders for the New Century. 2000. 395.00 (*1-882292-21-9*) Barons Whos Who.

— The Financial 500: Leaders for the New Century. 2000. 395.00 (*1-882292-20-0*) Barons Whos Who.

Pellam, John L. Great Designers of the World. (Illus.). 178p. 1998. 115.00 (*1-882292-08-1*) Barons Whos Who.

— Great Designers of the World. 2nd ed. (Illus.). 2000. 45.00 (*1-882292-15-4*) Barons Whos Who.

— 100 Designers' Favorite Rooms: Selected Projects of the World's Finest Designers & Architects. (Illus.). 236p. 1993. 30.00 (*1-882292-00-6*) Barons Whos Who.

— 100 Designers' Favorite Rooms: Selected Projects of the World's Finest Designers & Architects. 2nd ed. (Illus.). 236p. 1994. 45.00 (*1-882292-03-0*) Barons Whos Who.

— 100 Designers' Favorite Rooms: Selected Projects of the World's Finest Designers & Architects. 3rd ed. (Illus.). 236p. 1996. 45.00 (*1-882292-06-5*) Barons Whos Who.

— Who's Who in Global Banking & Finance: 2000-2001 Edition. 1999. 280.00 (*1-882292-16-2*) Barons Whos Who.

— Who's Who in Interior Design: 2000-2001 Edition. 1999. 280.00 (*1-882292-17-0*) Barons Whos Who.

— Who's Who of the Asian Pacific Rim: 1997-1998 Edition. 464p. 1996. 210.00 (*1-882292-09-X*) Barons Whos Who.

Pellam, John L., ed. Who's Who in Asian Banking & Finance: The International Directory of Asia's Leaders in Banking, Investment & Finance. 304p. 1997. 210.00 (*1-882292-12-X*) Barons Whos Who.

— Who's Who in Interior Design: 1994-1995 Edition. 512p. 1994. 175.00 (*1-882292-02-2*) Barons Whos Who.

— Who's Who in Interior Design, 1998-1999. 540p. 1998. 210.00 (*1-882292-10-3*) Barons Whos Who.

— Who's Who in Vietnam: The International Directory of Vietnam's Leaders in Business, Commerce, Government & Industry. xviii, 365p. 1997. 210.00 (*1-882292-11-1*) Barons Whos Who.

— Who's Who of the Asian Pacific Rim: 1993-1994 Edition. 403p. 1993. 175.00 (*1-882292-01-4*) Barons Whos Who.

— Who's Who of the Asian Pacific Rim: 1995-1996 Edition. 381p. 1995. 210.00 (*1-882292-05-7*) Barons Whos Who.

***Pellant, Chris.** The Best Book of Fossils, Rocks, & Minerals. (Illus.). 32p. (J). (gr. k-3). 2000. 12.95 (*0-7534-5274-X*, Kingfisher) LKC.

Pellant, Chris. Fossils of the World, 11 vols. Charman, Andrew, ed. LC 93-46144. (Science Nature Guides Ser.). (Illus.). 80p. (J). (gr. 3-6). 1994. 12.95 (*1-85028-262-5*, Thunder Bay) Advantage Pubs.

— Rocks & Minerals. LC 91-58222. (Eyewitness Handbooks Ser.). (Illus.). 256p. 1992. 29.95 (*1-56458-033-4*) DK Pub Inc.

— Rocks & Minerals. LC 91-58222. (Eyewitness Handbooks Ser.). (Illus.). 256p. (J). 2000. pap. 18.95 (*1-56458-061-X*, D K Ink) DK Pub Inc.

— Rocks, Minerals, & Fossils of the World. 175p. 1990. pap. 25.00 (*0-316-69796-6*) Little.

Pellant, Christopher. Collecting Gems & Minerals. LC 98-22851. (Illus.). 80p. (YA). (gr. 5 up). 1998. 14.95 (*0-8069-9760-5*) Sterling.

Pellaprat, Henri P. The Great Book of French Cuisine. (Illus.). 1173p. 1994. text 45.00 (*0-86565-025-X*) Vendome.

Pellat, C. H., jt. auth. see Chouemi, Moustafa.

Pellaton, Jackie, ed. see Grayson, Stan.

Pellatt, A. H., jt. auth. see Freeman, M. A.

Pellatt, M. G., jt. auth. see Ando, D. J.

Pellatz, David W., jt. auth. see Pellatz, Karla S.

Pellatz, Karla S. & Pellatz, David W. Tastes & Tours of Wyoming. (Illus.). 296p. 1997. 25.95 (*0-9661976-0-7*) WY Homestay.

Pellauer, David, tr. see Ricoeur, Paul.

Pellauer, David, tr. see Ricoeur, Paul & Lacocque, Andre.

Pellauer, David, tr. see Ricouer, Paul.

Pellauer, David, tr. see Sartre, Jean-Paul.

Pellauer, David, tr. see Veyne, Paul.

Pellcovitz, Raphael. Sforno: Commentary on the Torah. (ArtScroll Mesorah Ser.). 1993. 31.99 (*0-89906-238-5*) Mesorah Pubns.

Pelle, Kimberly D., jt. ed. see Findling, John E.

Pelle, Marie P. & Mauries, Patrick. Valentino's Magic. rev. ed. LC 91-10337. (Illus.). 304p. 1998. 75.00 (*0-7892-0463-0*) Abbeville Pr.

Pelle, Marie-Paule & Mauries, Patrick. Valentino: Thirty Years of Magic. (Illus.). 336p. 1991. 95.00 (*1-55859-237-7*) Abbeville Pr.

Pelle, Marie-Paule, jt. auth. see Laurent, Yves Saint.

Pellecchia, Michael. Fort Worth, a Sesquicentennial Celebration. Rogers, Truitt, tr. LC 99-13128. (Millennium Ser.). (Illus.). 320p. 1999. 45.00 (*1-58192-000-8*) Community Comm.

Pellecchia, Michael, jt. ed. see Bangs, David H., Jr.

Pellech, Christine. Die Ersten Entdecker Amerikas: Der Kulturdiffusionismus. (Illus.). 579p. 1997. pap. 79.95 (*3-631-30723-3*) P Lang Pubng.

Pellechet, M. Catalogue des Incunables et des Livres Imprimes de MD A MDXX. viii, 302p. reprint ed. write for info. incl. 3.5 hd (*0-318-71386-1*) G Olms Pubs.

— Catalogue des Incunables et des Livres Imprimes de MD a MDXX. (FRE.). viii, 302p. reprint ed. write for info. (*0-318-71854-5*) G Olms Pubs.

***Pellechia, Thomas.** Garlic, Wine & Olive Oil: Historical Anecdotes & Recipes. (Illus.). 220p. 2000. pap. 15.95 (*0-88496-444-2*) Capra Pr.

Pelleg, Amir & Belardinelli, Luiz. Effects of Extracellular Adenosine & ATP on Cardiomyocytes. LC 97-46653. (Molecular Ser.). 218p. 1999. 99.00 (*1-57059-524-0*) Landes Bioscience.

Pellegreno, Ann H. Iowa Takes to the Air, 1845-1918, Vol. 1. LC 79-55458. (Illus.). 288p. (J). (gr. 4 up). 1981. 19.95 (*0-935092-01-3*) Aerodrome Pr.

— Iowa Takes to the Air, 1919-1941, Vol. 2. LC 79-55458. (Illus.). 336p. (J). (gr. 4 up). 1986. 24.95 (*0-935092-02-1*) Aerodrome Pr.

Pellegrin, Jean-Pierre, jt. auth. see Giguere, Sylvain.

Pellegrin, Karen L. Fat-Free Desserts. (Illus.). 192p. 1995. pap. 12.95 (*0-8092-3444-0*, 344400, Contemporary Bks) NTC Contemp Pub Co.

***Pellegrin, Pierre.** Greek Thought: A Guide to Classical Knowledge. Brunschwig, Jacques & Lloyd, Geoffrey E. R., eds. LC 00-36032. (Harvard University Press Reference Library). (Illus.). 1112p. 2000. 49.95 (*0-674-00261-X*) Belknap Pr.

Pellegrin, Pierre, jt. auth. see Wittern, Renate.

Pellegrin-Resci, jt. auth. see Levi.

Pellegrin, Roland J., jt. auth. see Coates, Charles H.

Pellegrini. Observational Methods. (C). 1995. pap. text. write for info. (*0-15-501217-7*) Harcourt Coll Pubs.

Pellegrini, A., et al, eds. The Role of Medroxyprogesterone in Endocrine-Related Tumors, Vol. 3. fac. ed. LC 80-5550. (Progress in Cancer Research & Therapy Ser.: No. 15). (Illus.). 191p. pap. 59.30 (*0-7837-7150-9*, 204714600003) Bks Demand.

Pellegrini, Alessandro. Friedrich Hoelderlin: Sein Bild in der Forschung. (C). 1965. 115.40 (*3-11-000338-4*) De Gruyter.

Pellegrini, Angelo. Vintage Pellegrini: The Collected Wisdom of an American Buongustaio. Ingle, Schuyler, ed. 262p. 1991. text 18.95 (*0-912365-45-5*) Sasquatch Bks.

Pellegrini, Angelo M. Food Lover's Garden. (Cook's Classic Library). (Illus.). 272p. 1999. reprint ed. pap. 14.95 (*1-55821-025-3*) Lyons Pr.

— The Unprejudiced Palate: Classic Thoughts on Food & the Good Life. LC 83-60691. (Cook's Classic Library). 256p. 1997. pap. 14.95 (*1-55821-199-3*) Lyons Pr.

Pellegrini, Ann. Performance Anxieties. 198p. (C). 1996. pap. 18.99 (*0-415-91686-0*) Routledge.

***Pellegrini, Anthony & Blatchford, Peter.** The Child in School. (Texts in Development Psychology Series). (Illus.). 256p. 2000. text 75.00 (*0-340-73181-8*); pap. text 25.00 (*0-340-73182-6*) E A.

Pellegrini, Anthony D. Observing Children in Their Natural Worlds: A Methodological Primer. 232p. 1996. pap. 29.95 (*0-8058-2152-X*) L Erlbaum Assocs.

P

— Observing Children in Their Natural Worlds: A Primer in Quantitative Observational Methods. 272p. 1996. text 55.00 (*0-8058-2151-1*) L Erlbaum Assocs.

— Psychological Bases for Early Education. fac. ed. LC 87-18995. (Wiley Series in Developmental Psychology & Its Applications). 296p. 1988. reprint ed. pap. 91.80 (*0-7837-8275-6*, 204905500009) Bks Demand.

— School Recess & Playground Behavior: Educational & Developmental Roles. LC 93-50547. (SUNY Series, Children's Play in Society). 187p. (C). 1994. text 59.50 (*0-7914-2183-X*); pap. text 19.95 (*0-7914-2184-8*) State U NY Pr.

Pellegrini, Anthony D., ed. Applied Child Study: A Developmental Approach. 2nd ed. 264p. (C). 1991. pap. 29.95 (*0-8058-0723-3*); text 49.95 (*0-8058-0722-5*) L Erlbaum Assocs.

— The Future of Play Theory: A Multidisciplinary Inquiry into the Contributions of Brian Sutton-Smith. LC 94-41396. (SUNY Series, Children's Play in Society). 306p. (C). 1995. text 74.50 (*0-7914-2641-6*); pap. text 24.95 (*0-7914-2642-4*) State U NY Pr.

Pellegrini, Anthony D., et al, eds. The Development of Oral & Written Language in Social Contexts. LC 84-369. (Advances in Discourse Processes Ser.: Vol. 13). 288p. (Orig.). (C). 1984. pap. 42.50 (*0-89391-172-0*); text 78.50 (*0-89391-171-2*) Ablx Pub.

Pellegrini, Anthony D. & Bjorklund, David. Applied Child Study: A Developmental Approach. 3rd ed. LC 98-11806. 265p. 1998. write for info. (*0-8058-2756-0*); pap. write for info. (*0-8058-2757-9*) L Erlbaum Assocs.

Pellegrini, Anthony D. & Galda, Lee. The Development of School-Based Literacy: A Social Ecological Perspective. LC 98-14912. (International Library of Psychology). (Illus.). 160p. (C). 1998. 75.00 (*0-415-15393-X*) Routledge.

Pellegrini, Anthony D., jt. auth. see Smith, Peter K.

Pellegrini, Anthony D., jt. ed. see Bloch, Marianne N.

Pellegrini, Anthony D., jt. ed. see Britton, B. K.

Pellegrini, Anthony D., jt. ed. see Galda, Lee.

Pellegrini, Anthony D., jt. ed. see Yawkey, Thomas D.

Pellegrini, Anthony L., jt. ed. see Bernardo, Aldo S.

Pellegrini, C., ed. Beam-Beam & Beam-Radiation Interactions: High Intensity & Nonlinear Effects: Proceedings of the 7th ICFA Workshop on Beam Dynamics, U.C.L.A., U. S. A. 13-16 May 1991. 200p. 1992. text 98.00 (*981-02-0838-3*) World Scientific Pub.

Pellegrini, C., jt. auth. see Cooper, R. K.

Pellegrini, Carlos A., jt. auth. see Way, Lawrence M.

Pellegrini, Claudio, et al, eds. Free Electron Generation of Extreme Ultraviolet Coherent Radiation (Brookhaven-OSA, 1983) AIP Conference Proceedings No. 118. LC 84-71539. (Optical Science & Engineering Ser.: No. 4). 319p. 1984. lib. bdg. 40.50 (*0-88318-317-X*) Am Inst Physics.

Pellegrini, Claudio & Sessler, Andrew M., eds. The Development of Colliders. 1995. 54.95 (*1-56396-349-3*) Spr-Verlag.

Pellegrini, Frank. Organic Chemistry I Quick Review. (Cliffs Quick Reviews Ser.). (Illus.). 101p. (C). 1997. pap. text 9.95 (*0-8220-5326-8*, Cliff) IDG Bks.

Pellegrini, Nina. Families Are Different. LC 90-22876. (Illus.). 32p. (J). (gr. k-3). 1991. lib. bdg. 16.95 (*0-8234-0887-6*) Holiday.

Pellegrini, Nina, jt. auth. see Garcia, Edward.

Pellegrini, Vincent D. & Evarts, C. McColister. Operative Orthopaedics. (C). 2000. 295.00 (*0-8385-7400-9*) Appleton & Lange.

***Pellegrino, Anna Maria.** Diary of a Rapist. Veggian, Henry, tr. LC 00-101957. 174p. 2000. pap. 14.00 (*1-892323-24-9*) Vivisphere.

Pellegrino, Charles. Dust. LC 97-26936. 400p. 1998. mass mkt. 15.95 (*0-380-97308-1*, Avon Bks) Morrow Avon.

— Dust. 464p. 1999. mass mkt. 6.99 (*0-380-78742-3*, Avon Bks) Morrow Avon.

Pellegrino, Charles R. Flying to Valhalla. LC 92-45642. 338p. 1993. 22.00 (*0-688-12506-9*, Wm Morrow) Morrow Avon.

— Flying to Valhalla. 2000. 22.00 (*0-380-97220-4*, Avon Bks) Morrow Avon.

***Pellegrino, Charles R.** Ghosts of the Titanic: New Discoveries from the Depths of the Ocean Floor. LC 00-24552. 2000. write for info. (*0-380-72472-3*) Morrow Avon.

Pellegrino, Charles R. The Killing Star. 1996. mass mkt. 5.99 (*0-380-77026-1*, Avon Bks) Morrow Avon.

— Return to Sodom & Gomorr. 424p. 1995. pap. 13.50 (*0-380-72633-5*, Avon Bks) Morrow Avon.

— Time Gate: Hurtling Backward Through History. LC 84-23955. 1985. pap. 16.95 (*0-8306-1863-5*, 1863P) McGraw-Hill Prof.

Pellegrino, Charles R. & Stoff, Joshua. Chariots for Apollo: The Untold Story Behind the Race to the Moon. (Illus.). 320p. (YA). (gr. 8 up). 1999. pap. 13.50 (*0-380-80261-9*, Avon Bks) Morrow Avon.

***Pellegrino, Charles R. & Zebrowski.** The Killing Star. 2000. 22.00 (*0-380-97250-6*) Morrow Avon.

Pellegrino, Charles R., jt. auth. see Stoff, Jesse A.

Pellegrino, Charles R., jt. auth. see Zebrowski, George.

Pellegrino, Edmund D. Humanism & the Physician. LC 78-23174. 263p. reprint ed. pap. 81.60 (*0-7837-3026-8*, 204291400006) Bks Demand.

Pellegrino, Edmund D., et al, eds. Catholic Perspectives on Medical Morals: Foundational Issues. 314p. (C). 1989. lib. bdg. 127.50 (*1-55608-083-2*, Pub. by Kluwer Academic) Kluwer Academic.

— Ethics, Trust, & the Professions: Philosophical & Cultural Aspects. LC 90-46368. 298p. 1991. reprint ed. pap. 92.40 (*0-7837-9251-4*, 204989000005) Bks Demand.

— Transcultural Dimensions in Medical Ethics. 225p. 1992. 35.00 (*1-55572-015-3*) Univ Pub Group.

***Pellegrino, Edmund D. & Faden, Alan I.** Jewish & Catholic Bioethics: An Ecumenical Dialogue LC 99-12407. 1999. pap. write for info. (*0-87840-746-4*) Georgetown U Pr.

***Pellegrino, Edmund D. & Faden, Alan I., eds.** Jewish & Catholic Bioethics: An Ecumenical Dialogue. LC 99-12407. (Moral Traditions & Moral Arguments Ser.). 256p. 1999. 55.00 (*0-87840-745-6*) Georgetown U Pr.

Pellegrino, Edmund D. & Thomasma, David C. The Christian Virtues in Medical Practice. LC 94-11007. 176p. 1996. 27.95 (*0-87840-566-6*) Georgetown U Pr.

— For the Patient's Good: The Restoration of Beneficence in Health Care. 256p. 1988. text 41.50 (*0-19-504319-7*) OUP.

— Helping & Healing: Religious Commitment in Health Care. LC 96-46598. 176p. 1997. pap. 15.95 (*0-87840-643-3*) Georgetown U Pr.

— The Virtues in Medical Practice. LC 92-49073. 224p. 1993. text 42.50 (*0-19-508289-3*) OUP.

***Pellegrino, Edmund D., et al.** The Health Care Professional as Friend & Healer: Building on the Work of Edmund D. Pellegrino. Thomasma, David C. & Kissell, Judith Lee, eds. LC 00-26362. 384p. 2000. pap. text 24.95 (*0-87840-810-X*) Georgetown U Pr.

Pellegrino, Frank W. & Rao's Restaurant Staff. Rao's Cookbook: One Hundred Years of Traditional Italian Home Cooking. LC 97-34543. 183p. 1998. 40.00 (*0-679-45749-6*) Random.

Pellegrino, James, et al, eds. Setting Consensus Goals for Academic Achievement: A Special Issue of Applied Measurement in Education. 115p. 1997. pap. write for info. (*0-8058-9850-6*) L Erlbaum Assocs.

Pellegrino, James W., et al. Grading the Nation's Report Card: Evaluating NAEP & Transforming the Assessment of Educational Progress. LC 98-40150. 296p. 2000. pap. text 42.95 (*0-309-06285-3*) Natl Acad Pr.

Pellegrino, James W., jt. ed. see Dillon, Ronna F.

Pellegrino, John M., jt. ed. see Berg, Norman J.

Pellegrino, Louis, jt. auth. see Dormans, John P.

Pellegrino, Louis J., et al. A Stereotaxic Atlas of the Brain. 2nd ed. LC 79-9438. (Illus.). 157p. reprint ed. pap. 48.70 (*0-608-09367-X*, 205411200002) Bks Demand.

Pellegrino, Maria, jt. auth. see Pellegrino, Mark J.

Pellegrino, Mario. Postkommunismus und Zivilrecht: Das Obligationenrecht Georgiens. 364p. 1997. 76.95 (*3-631-31679-8*) P Lang Pubng.

***Pellegrino, Marjorie White.** My Grandma's the Mayor. LC 99-16771. (Illus.). 32p. (J). (gr. k-8). 1999. 14.95 (*1-55798-608-8*, 441-6088, Magination Press) Am Psychol.

Pellegrino, Mark J. Fibromyalgia - Managing the Pain: Understanding the Syndrome & Managing Its Pain. 2nd ed. LC 97-205620. (Illus.). 102p. (Orig.). 1997. pap. 12.45 (*1-890018-10-4*) Anadem Pubng.

— The Fibromyalgia Chef. (Illus.). 203p. 1997. pap. 15.50 (*1-890018-16-3*) Anadem Pubng.

— The Fibromyalgia Supporter. (Illus.). 90p. 1997. pap. 15.50 (*1-890018-11-2*) Anadem Pubng.

— The Fibromyalgia Survivor. LC 97-205623. (Illus.). 119p. (Orig.). 1995. pap. 19.50 (*0-9646891-2-X*) Anadem Pubng.

— Laugh at Your Muscles: A Light Look at Fibromyalgia. (Illus.). 92p. (Orig.). 1995. pap. 5.95 (*0-9646891-4-6*) Anadem Pubng.

***Pellegrino, Mark J.** A Sunnier Tomorrow. 155p. 1998. 14.95 (*1-890018-32-5*) Anadem Pubng.

Pellegrino, Mark J. Understanding Post-Traumatic Fibromyalgia: A Medical Perspective. LC 97-205619. (Illus.). 130p. 1996. pap. 16.25 (*0-9646891-8-9*) Anadem Pubng.

Pellegrino, Mark J. & Dawkins, Barbara. Laugh at Your Muscles II: A Second Light Look at Fibromyalgia. (Illus.). 97p. 1997. pap. 5.95 (*1-890018-15-5*) Anadem Pubng.

Pellegrino, Mark J. & Pellegrino, Maria. Mommy's Fibromonster. (Illus.). 16p. (J). 1997. pap. 4.75 (*1-890018-00-7*) Anadem Pubng.

Pellegrino, Michele. The True Priest: The Priesthood As Preached & Practiced by Saint Augustine. Rotelle, John E., ed. LC 87-71970. (Illus.). 144p. 1988. reprint ed. pap. 7.95 (*0-941491-08-0*) Augustinian Pr.

Pellegrino, Victor C. Maui Art Thoughts: Expressions & Visions. LC 88-92541. (Illus.). 112p. 1988. pap. 9.95 (*0-945045-01-8*) Maui Arthoughts.

— A Slip of Bamboo: A Collection of Haiku from Maui. LC 95-94392. (Illus.). 136p. 1996. pap. 7.95 (*0-945045-04-2*) Maui Arthoughts.

— A Writer's Guide to Transitional Words & Expressions. 6th rev. ed. LC 83-34726. 48p. 1995. pap. 9.95 (*0-945045-02-6*) Maui Arthoughts.

— A Writer's Guide to Using Eight Methods of Transition. LC 93-77683. 52p. (Orig.). (C). 1993. pap. 5.95 (*0-945045-03-4*) Maui Arthoughts.

Pelleier, Linda. English - French Vocabulary of Microwave Ovens. (ENG & FRE.). 52p. 1987. pap. 24.95 (*0-8288-9381-0*) Fr & Eur.

Pelleier, Susann. Immigrant Dream & Other Poems. 48p. 1989. pap. 7.95 (*0-685-46223-4*) Soleil Pr.

Pellengahr, I., tr. see Faber, Malte, et al.

Pellengahr, Ingo. The Austrian Subjectivist Theory of Interest: An Investigation into the History of Thought. (Illus.). 95p. 1996. pap. 29.95 (*3-631-48607-3*) P Lang Pubng.

— The Austrian Subjectivist Theory of Interest: An Investigation into the History of Thought. (Illus.). 95p. 1996. pap. 29.95 (*0-8204-2944-9*) P Lang Pubng.

Pellens, Mildred, jt. auth. see Terry, Charles E.

Peller, Beth. The Family under the Bridge: A Study Guide. Friedland, J. & Kessler, R., eds. (Novel-Ties Ser.). (J). (gr. 3-5). 1995. pap. text, student ed. 15.95 (*1-56982-286-7*) Lrn Links.

Peller, Jane E., jt. auth. see Walter, John L.

Peller, Julie R. Exploring Chemistry in General, Organic & Biological Chemistry. LC 97-29684. 380p. 1997. pap. text, lab manual ed. 47.00 (*0-13-857426-X*) P-H.

Pellerin. Spinning Gold. 2001. pap. text. write for info. (*0-13-459074-0*) P-H.

Pellerin, Bill & Neidhardt, Ralph. Bicycling the Houston Area. 70p. 1987. pap. 9.95 (*1-882358-01-5*) TX Bicycle Map.

— Bicycling the Texas Hill Country & West Texas. 72p. 1988. pap. 9.95 (*1-882358-00-7*) TX Bicycle Map.

— Bicycling the Texas Hill Country & West Texas. rev. ed. 1988. reprint ed. pap. 10.95 (*1-882358-04-X*) TX Bicycle Map.

— Mountain Biking the Houston Area. 72p. (Orig.). 1993. pap. text. write for info. (*1-882358-03-1*) TX Bicycle Map.

Pellerin, Cheryl. Trips: How Hallucinogens Work in Your Brain. (Illus.). 224p. (Orig.). 1998. pap. 23.95 (*1-888363-34-7*) Seven Stories.

Pellerin, Dave. Practical Design: Using Programmable Logic. 400p. 1991. text 43.60 (*0-13-723834-7*) P-H.

Pellerin, David & Holley, Michael. Digital Design Using ABEL. LC 93-39558. 320p. (C). 1994. 77.00 incl. disk (*0-13-605874-4*) P-H.

Pellerin, David & Taylor, Douglas. VHDL Made Easy! LC 96-26999. 432p. 1996. pap. 73.00 (*0-13-650763-8*) P-H.

Pellerin, J. M., jt. auth. see Foley, Shelia.

Pellerite, James J. A Handbook of Literature for the Flute. 3rd rev. ed. LC 77-85443. 1978. pap. text 20.00 (*0-931200-69-5*) Zalo.

— A Modern Guide to Fingerings for the Flute. LC 72-76260. 1972. pap. text 15.00 (*0-931200-68-7*) Zalo.

— A Modern Guide to Fingerings for the Flute. 64p. 1988. reprint ed. pap. text 16.50 (*0-88284-449-0*, 2887) Alfred Pub.

— A Notebook of Techniques for a Flute Recital. 1967. pap. text 3.50 (*0-931200-50-4*) Zalo.

— Performance Methods for Flutists. 1968. pap. text 4.95 (*0-931200-51-2*) Zalo.

Pellerito. Women's Imaging. 1998. text 150.00 (*0-443-07611-1*, W B Saunders Co) Harcrt Hlth Sci Grp.

Pellet, Lizz, jt. auth. see Bouchard, P. J.

Pelletan, Camille. Semaine de Mai. LC 75-173941. (FRE.). reprint ed. 54.00 (*0-404-07163-5*) AMS Pr.

Pelleti, Lisa, tr. see Valcanover, Francesco.

Pelletier. Techniques & Strategies Coach. 2nd ed. LC 99-36246. 297p. 1999. pap. text 33.00 (*0-205-30361-7*, Longwood Div) Allyn.

Pelletier, Alain J. Beech Aircraft & Their Predecessors. LC 95-69497. (Putnam Aviation Ser.). (Illus.). 256p. 1995. 49.95 (*1-55750-062-2*) Naval Inst Pr.

— Bell Aircraft since Nineteen Thirty-Five. (Putnam Aviation Ser.). (Illus.). 288p. 1992. 49.95 (*1-55750-056-8*) Naval Inst Pr.

Pelletier, B. R., jt. ed. see Schafer, C. T.

***Pelletier, Carol Marra.** Strategies for Successful Student Teaching: A Comprehensive Guide. LC 99-36853. 270p. 1999. pap. text 35.33 (*0-205-30163-0*) Allyn.

Pelletier, Cathie. Beaming Sonny Home. 288p. 1996. 22.00 (*0-614-15955-5*) Crown Pub Group.

— Beaming Sonny Home. 288p. 1997. per. 12.00 (*0-671-00175-2*, WSP) PB.

— The Bubble Reputation. 304p. 1994. reprint ed. pap. 12.00 (*0-671-89010-7*, WSP) PB.

— The Funeral Makers. 1997. per. 11.00 (*0-684-82614-3*, Scribner Pap Fic) S&S Trade Pap.

— A Marriage Made at Woodstock. Ng, Donna, ed. 288p. 1995. reprint ed. pap. 14.00 (*0-671-51694-9*, WSP) PB.

— Once upon a Time. 1999. pap. write for info. (*0-14-012087-4*) Viking Penguin.

— Once upon a Time on the Banks. Rosenman, Jane, ed. 384p. 1991. reprint ed. pap. 14.00 (*0-671-72447-9*, WSP) PB.

— The Weight of Winter. LC 92-39708. 432p. 1993. reprint ed. pap. 14.00 (*0-671-79387-X*, WSP) PB.

Pelletier, Cathie, jt. auth. see Davis, Skeeter.

Pelletier, Christine, jt. auth. see Holmes, Wayne.

Pelletier, Claire, jt. auth. see Martin, Helene.

Pelletier, Darlene. A Tip of the Scales. 64p. 1997. pap. 7.00 (*0-8059-4190-8*) Dorrance.

Pelletier, David L. An Analysis of the Uses & Limitations of Information in the Iringa Nutrition Program, Tanzania. (Working Papers). (C). 1991. pap. text 7.00 (*1-56401-105-4*) Cornell Food.

— The Graphic Alphabet. LC 96-4001. (Illus.). 32p. 1996. 17.95 (*0-531-36001-6*) Orchard Bks Watts.

— The Relationship Between Child Antropometry & Mortality in Developing Countries: Implications for Policy, Progress, & Future Research. (Monographs). (Illus.). 72p. (C). 1991. pap. text 12.00 (*1-56401-012-0*) Cornell Food.

Pelletier, David L. & Msukwa, Louis A. Intervention Planning in Response to Disasters: A Case Study of the Mealy Bug Disaster in Malawi. (Monographs). (Illus.). 54p. (C). 1990. pap. text 12.00 (*1-56401-006-6*) Cornell Food.

Pelletier, Donald H., tr. see Cori, Rene & Lascar, Daniel.

Pelletier, Francis Jeffry. Parmenides, Plato & the Semantics of Not-Being. LC 89-27650. 188p. 1997. 35.95 (*0-226-65390-0*) U Ch Pr.

Pelletier, Francis Jeffry, ed. Mass Terms: Some Philosophical Problems. (Studies in Linguistics & Philosophy: No. 6). 316p. 1979. text 121.50 (*90-277-0931-9*) Kluwer Academic.

Pelletier, Francis Jeffry, jt. ed. see Carlson, Greg N.

Pelletier, Henry L. Favorite Patchwork Patterns: Full-Size Templates & Instructions for Twelve Quilts. 56p. 1984. pap. 4.50 (*0-486-24753-8*) Dover.

Pelletier, Henry P. Nature's Endless Pulsations: Poems. LC 91-36603. 96p. 1992. pap. 8.95 (*0-86534-168-0*) Sunstone Pr.

Pelletier, Ida O. Dynamic Nurse-Patient Relationship. 128p. 1990. 12.50 (*0-88737-489-1*) Natl League Nurse.

Pelletier, J. P., et al, eds. Osteoarthritis: Clinical & Experimental Aspects. LC 98-33430. (Illus.). 480p. 1999. pap. 99.00 (*3-540-65127-6*) Spr-Verlag.

Pelletier, J. W., jt. auth. see Kaijser, S. G.

Pelletier, Jacques, jt. ed. see Moisan, Michel.

Pelletier, James L. Mariner's Directory & Guide, 1998-1999 - Worldwide Maritime Source Book (Directory & Guide) 2nd expanded rev. ed. Levine, Aaron, ed. LC 97-94345. (Periodic Chapter/Serial Updates Ser.: No. 1). Orig. Title: Mariner's Employment Guide. (Illus.). 1212p. 1999. pap. 350.00 (*0-9644915-1-6*) Marine Techn.

— Mariner's Employment Guide - 1997/1998 Edition. 5th expanded rev. ed. LC 94-96822. (Illus.). 357p. 1999. 85.00 (*0-9644915-0-8*) Marine Techn.

Pelletier, James L., compiled by. Deep-Draft Vessel Owners, Operators & Managers Vol. 7: Foreign Companies Only. LC 97-93954. 275p. 1999. 85.00 (*0-9644915-8-3*) Marine Techn.

— Deep-Draft Vessel Owners, Operators & Managers (U. S. A. Only) Fishing Vessels - Shallow & Deep-Draft (U. S. A. Companies Only), Vol. 5. LC 97-93954. 220p. 1999. 85.00 (*0-9644915-6-7*) Marine Techn.

— Offshore Oil Platforms (Rigs) & Offshore Oil Support Vessels Directory Owners, Operators & Managers Vol. 6: Foreign Companies Only. LC 97-93954. 220p. 1999. 85.00 (*0-9644915-7-5*) Marine Techn.

— Offshore Oil Platforms (Rigs) & Offshore Oil Support Vessels, Owners, Operators & Managers Vol. 3: U. S. A. Companies Only. LC 97-93954. 215p. 1999. 85.00 (*0-9644915-4-0*) Marine Techn.

— Shallow-Draft Vessel Owners, Operators & Managers Vol. 2: U. S. A. Companies Only. LC 97-93954. 170p. 75.00 (*0-9644915-3-2*) Marine Techn.

— Shallow-Draft Vessel Owners, Operators & Managers Vol. 8: Foreign Companies Only. LC 97-93954. 35p. 55.00 (*0-9644915-9-1*) Marine Techn.

— Worldwide Cruise Ships, & Inland & Coastal Waterways Entertainment Vessels Directory Vol. 4: Foreign & U. S. A. Companies, 1998-1999, Yachts, Sail & Motor (U. S. A. & Foreign) LC 97-93954. 151p. 1999. 65.00 (*0-9644915-5-9*) Marine Techn.

— Worldwide Ship & Boat Repair Facilities Vol. 1: Shipyards, Repair Yards & Dry Docks. (Foreign & U. S. A. Companies) 1997-1998 Edition. LC 97-93954. 230p. 75.00 (*0-9644915-2-4*) Marine Techn.

Pelletier, Joseph A. Queen of Peace Visits Medugorie. 1998. pap. text 7.50 (*5-551-70100-X*) Ambasdr Bks.

Pelletier, Kenneth R. Best Alternatives: Sorting Fact from Fiction in Complementary & Alternative Medicine. LC 99-26629. 448p. 2000. 25.50 (*0-684-84207-6*) S&S Trade.

— Holistic Medicine: From Stress to Optimum Health. 1984. 25.00 (*0-8446-6092-2*) Peter Smith.

— A New Age: Problems & Potential. (Broadside Editions Ser.). 44p. (Orig.). (C). 1985. pap. 4.95 (*0-931191-02-5*) Rob Briggs.

Pelletier, Louis Le, see Le Pelletier, Louis.

Pelletier, Louise & Perez-Gomez, Alberto, eds. Architecture, Ethics & Technology. LC 93-90630. (Illus.). 256p. 1994. 65.00 (*0-7735-1148-2*, Pub. by McG-Queens Univ Pr) CUP Services.

Pelletier, Louise, jt. auth. see Perez-Gomez, Alberto.

Pelletier, Louise, jt. auth. see Perez Gomez, Alberto.

Pelletier, Louise, jt. compiled by see Perez-Gomez, Alberto.

Pelletier, Maryse. Duo for Obstinate Voices. 146p. 1990. pap. 10.00 (*0-920717-16-0*) Guernica Editions.

Pelletier, Michael J. Analytical Applications of Raman Spectroscopy. LC 98-51403. 1999. 195.00 (*0-632-05305-4*) Blackwell Sci.

Pelletier, Nicole, jt. ed. see Merlio, Gilbert.

Pelletier, Paul A. Prominent Scientists: An Index to Collective Biographies. 3rd ed. 390p. 1994. 65.00 (*1-55570-114-0*) Neal-Schuman.

Pelletier, Paula, jt. auth. see Rattenbury, Judith.

Pelletier, Ray. Permission to Win. LC 96-8180. (Illus.). 201p. 1996. 22.95 (*1-886939-10-1*, Pub. by OakHill Pr VA) ACCESS Pubs Network.

Pelletier, Robert. Planets in Aspect: Understanding Your Inner Dynamics. LC 74-82711. (Planets Ser.). 364p. 1974. pap. 19.95 (*0-914918-20-6*, Whitford) Schiffer.

— Planets in Houses: Experiencing Your Environment Planets. Anderson, Margaret, ed. (Planets Ser.). (Illus.). 372p. 1978. pap. 19.95 (*0-914918-27-3*, Whitford) Schiffer.

Pelletier, Robert, jt. auth. see Cataldo, Leonard.

***Pelletier, S. W., ed.** Alkaloids. 410p. 1999. 264.00 (*0-08-043403-7*, Pergamon Pr) Elsevier.

Pelletier, S. W., ed. Alkaloids: Chemical & Biological Perspectives, Vol. 12. 384p. 1998. 224.00 (*0-08-042805-3*, Pergamon Pr) Elsevier.

Pelletier, S. William. Alkaloids: Chemical & Biological Perspectives. (Alkaloids Chemical & Biological Ser.: No. 10). 406p. 1996. text. write for info. (*0-08-042791-X*, Pergamon Pr) Elsevier.

— Alkaloids: Chemical & Biological Perspectives, Vol. 4. (Chemical & Biological Perspectives Ser.). 460p. 1986. text 100.00 (*0-471-89301-3*) Krieger.

— Alkaloids: Chemical & Biological Perspectives, Vol. 9. (Alkaloids Chemical & Biological Ser.). 272p. 1994. text 142.00 (*0-08-042089-3*, Pergamon Pr) Elsevier.

— GMOA Bulletin Vol. 17: John Taylor Arms, His World & Work. Phagan, Patricia, ed. (Illus.). 124p. 1993. pap. 10.00 (*0-685-66927-0*) Georgia Museum of Art.

Pelletier, S. William, ed. Alkaloids: Chemical & Biological Perspectives, Vol. 2. LC 82-11071. 504p. 1984. text 68.50 (*0-471-89299-8*) Krieger.
— Alkaloids: Chemical & Biological Perspectives, Vol. 3. 336p. 1985. text 75.00 (*0-471-89302-1*) Krieger.
— Alkaloids: Chemical & Biological Perspectives, Vol. 5. 730p. 1987. text 125.00 (*0-471-85372-0*) Krieger.
— Alkaloids: Chemical & Biological Perspectives, Vol. 6. 542p. 1988. 265.00 (*0-471-60298-1*) Wiley.
— Alkaloids Vol. 7: Chemical & Biological Perspectives. (Illus.). 624p. 1991. 190.00 (*0-387-97290-0*) Spr-Verlag.
— Alkaloids Vol. 11: Chemical & Biological Perspectives. 376p. 1996. 188.50 (*0-08-042797-9*, Pergamon Pr) Elsevier.
— Alkaloids, Vol. 8: Chemical & Biological Perspectives. (Illus.). 344p. 1992. 238.00 (*0-387-97787-2*) Spr-Verlag.
Pelletier, S. William, et al. Adriaen Van Ostade: Etchings of Peasant Life in Holland's Golden Age. Phagan, Patricia, ed. LC 93-45388. (Illus.). 284p. 1994. pap. 30.00 (*0-915977-14-1*) Georgia Museum of Art.
Pelletier, S. William, jt. auth. see Eiland, William U.
Pelletier, Sophie & Magnaint-Lopez, Bernard. Les Petits Points de Casa Lopez. (Illus.). 176p. 1993. 35.00 (*2-200-21331-X*, Pub. by C Armand) Lacis Pubns.
Pelletier, Stephen G., ed. see Sigmon, Robert L., et al.
Pelletier, Theo, photos by. River of Song: A Musical Journey down the Mississippi. LC 98-45508. (Illus.). 352p. 1998. text 35.00 (*0-312-20059-5*) St Martin.
Pelletiere, Stephen C. The Iran-Iraq War: Chaos in a Vacuum. LC 91-28089. 192p. 1992. 52.95 (*0-275-93843-3*, C3843, Praeger Pubs) Greenwood.
— The Iran-Iraq War: Chaos in a Vacuum. (WVSS on the Middle East Ser.). 1996. text 31.50 (*0-8133-7490-1*) Westview.
— The Kurds: An Unstable Element in the Gulf. (Middle East Ser.). 250p. 1984. text 39.00 (*0-89158-689-X*) Westview.
***Pelletiere, Stephen C.** Landpower & Dual Containment: Rethinking America's Policy in the Gulf. 36p. 1999. pap. write for info. (*1-58487-010-9*) SSI US Army.
Pelletiere, Stephen C. & Johnson, Douglas V., II. Lessons Learned: The Iran-Iraq War. (Illus.). 119p. (Orig.). (C). 1994. pap. text 35.00 (*0-7881-0601-5*) DIANE Pub.
Pelletreau, Robert H., et al. Advancing Common Purposes in the Broad Middle East. 40p. 1998. pap. 6.00 (*0-930503-77-5*) Trilateral Comm.
Pelletreau, William S. Historic Homes & Institutions & Genealogical & Family History of New York, 4 vols. (Illus.). 1663p. 1998. reprint ed. pap. 150.00 (*0-8063-4779-1*, 9268) Clearfield Co.
— Records of the Town of Smithtown, Long Island, with Other Ancient Documents of Historic Value, with Notes & Introduction. (Illus.). 503p. 1997. reprint ed. lib. bdg. 52.50 (*0-8328-6243-6*) Higginson Bk Co.
— Smith: Wills of the Smith Families of NY & Long Island, 1664-1794, with Genealogy & History Notes. 151p. 1991. reprint ed. pap. 27.50 (*0-8328-1832-1*); reprint ed. lib. bdg. 37.50 (*0-8328-1831-3*) Higginson Bk Co.
— Suffolk County, Early Long Island Wills of Suffolk County, 1691-1703, with Genealogical & Historical Notes. (Illus.). 289p. 1995. reprint ed. lib. bdg. 37.50 (*0-8328-4714-3*) Higginson Bk Co.
***Pellett, Tracy L. & Lox, Curt.** Skills, Drills & Strategies for Volleyball. Rutherford, Jack & Blackman, Claudia, eds. LC 99-14472. (Teach, Coach, Play Ser.). 80p. (C). 1999. pap. 13.50 (*1-890871-13-3*) Holcomb Hath.
Pellett, Tracy L., ed. see Nix, Charlie.
Pellett, Tracy L., ed. see Paup, Donald C. & Fernhall, Bo.
Pellett, Tracy L., ed. see Rutherford, Jack.
Pellett, Tracy L., ed. see Stephens, Kenneth P. & Stephens, Joni M.
Pellett, Tracy L., ed. see Walker, David.
Pellett, W., et al. Otoneurosurgery. (Illus.). 256p. 1990. 238.00 (*0-387-50979-8*) Spr-Verlag.
Pelletti, Lisa C., tr. see Angelini, Alessandro.
Pelletti, Lisa C., tr. see Fossi, Gloria.
Pelletti, Lisa C., tr. see Heusinger, Lutz.
Pelletti, Lisa C., tr. see Jannella, Cecilia.
Pelletti, Lisa C., tr. see Paolieri, Annarita.
Pelletti, Lisa C., tr. see Paolucci, Antonio.
***Pellettieri, L.** Plazas. (C). 2000. pap., wbk. ed., lab manual ed. 3.50 (*0-8384-1182-7*) Heinle & Heinle.
— Plazas. (C). 2000. pap., wbk. ed., lab manual ed. 25.00 (*0-8384-1129-0*) Heinle & Heinle.
Pellev, John W. & Dalley, Bernell K. SuccessTypes for Medical Students: A Program for Improving Academic Performance. unabridged ed. (SuccessTypes Ser.: Vol. 1). (Illus.). 242p. 1997. pap. 23.95 (*0-9665049-0-9*) Extend Studies.
Pellew, George. John Jay. Morse, John T., Jr., ed. LC 70-128973. (American Statesmen Ser.: No. 9). reprint ed. 45.00 (*0-404-50859-6*) AMS Pr.
Pellew, Jill. The Home Office, Eighteen Forty-Eight to Nineteen Fourteen: From Clerks to Bureaucrats. LC 82-1533. 261p. 1982. 37.50 (*0-8386-3165-7*) Fairleigh Dickinson.
Pelley. Biochemistry Review. 2000. text. write for info. (*0-323-00835-6*) Harcourt.
Pelley, Charles. Paydirt: Canadian Mining. LC 97-137490. (Illus.). 144p. 1996. 32.00 (*1-55046-085-4*, Pub. by Boston Mills) Genl Dist Srvs.
Pelley, John W. Biochemistry: Mosby's USMLE Step 1 Reviews. LC 96-41726. (Ace the Boards Ser.). (Illus.). 400p. (C). (gr. 13). 1996. pap. text 29.95 (*0-8151-8652-5*, 28894); pap. text 29.95 (*0-8151-8668-1*, 28947) Mosby Inc.
Pelley, Nicolette Le, see Le Pelley, Nicolette.
***Pelham, Brian.** Games for Naughty People. Neary, Sally, ed. (Illus.). 112p. 1999. pap. 9.95 (*0-9649678-3-9*, Pub. by Kheper Pubg) Partners-West.
Pellham, Brian L. Egyptian Hieroglyphics & Their Meanings. (Illus.). 12p. 1995. pap. 3.00 (*0-9649678-1-2*, 6002) Kheper Pubg.
— A Partier's Guide to 51 Drinking Games. Neises, Amy, ed. (Illus.). 104p. (Orig.). 1995. pap. 9.95 (*0-9649678-0-4*, B106) Kheper Pubg.
Pellham, Brian L. & Kent, Allison. Outrageous Party Games. unabridged ed. Neary, Sally, ed. (Illus.). 128p. 1998. pap. 8.95 (*0-9649678-2-0*) Kheper Pubg.
Pelli. Getting by in Hebrew, 2 cassettes. (Getting by Ser.). (HEB & ENG.). 90p. 1983. pap. 18.95 incl. audio (*0-8120-7151-4*) Barron.
— Getting by in Hebrew. (Getting by Ser.). (HEB.). 90p. 1984. pap. 4.95 (*0-8120-2662-4*) Barron.
Pelli, Cesar. Observations for Young Architects. LC 98-52134. 207p. 1999. pap. 35.00 (*1-58093-031-X*, Pub. by Monacelli Pr) Penguin Putnam.
Pelli, Cesar, jt. auth. see Crosbie, Michael J.
Pellicane, Patricia. Darkest Heart. 320p. 1994. mass mkt. 4.50 (*0-8217-4565-4*, Zebra Kensgtn) Kensgtn Pub Corp.
— Endless Night. 352p. 1996. mass mkt. 4.99 (*0-8217-5408-4*, Zebra Kensgtn) Kensgtn Pub Corp.
— Sweet Revenge. 1986. pap. 3.50 (*0-317-61761-3*) PB.
Pellicani, Luciano. The Genesis of Capitalism & the Origins of Modernity. Milliron, Kerry, ed. Colbert, James G., tr. 1994. 26.00 (*0-914386-25-5*); pap. 16.00 (*0-914386-26-3*) Telos Pr.
Pellicano, John M. Conquer or Die: The 39th New York Volunteer Infantry: Garibaldi Guard. LC 96-93117. (Illus.). 240p. (Orig.). 1997. pap. 14.95 (*0-9656276-0-8*) J M Pellicano.
Pellicano, Tony A. History of War: Index of Foreign Medical Literature. rev. ed. 153p. 1998. 47.50 (*0-7883-2112-9*); pap. 44.50 (*0-7883-2113-7*) ABBE Pubs Assn.
— Medical Psychosomatics: Index of Modern Authors & Subjects with Guide for Rapid Research. LC 90-56289. 160p. 1991. 47.50 (*1-55914-382-7*); pap. 44.50 (*1-55914-383-5*) ABBE Pubs Assn.
— Psycho-Physiology & Biofeedback: Index of New Information with Authors & Subjects. rev. ed. LC 94-31239. 237p. 1994. write for info. (*0-7883-0258-2*); pap. write for info. (*0-7883-0259-0*) ABBE Pubs Assn.
Pellicci, Paul M., jt. auth. see Padgett, Douglas E.
Pellicci, Paul M., ed. see Cornell University Medical College Staff.
Pelliccia, A., et al. Advances in Sports Cardiology. 186p. 1997. pap. 63.00 (*3-540-75036-3*) Spr-Verlag.
Pelliccioni, Louis, Jr., jt. auth. see Scott, Michael.
Pellicciotti, Joseph M. Handbook of Basic Trial Evidence: A College Introduction. LC 91-50745. xx, 462p. (C). 1992. pap. 28.00 (*1-55605-191-3*) Wyndham Hall.
— Handbook on Basic Trial Evidence. 2nd ed. 246p. (Orig.). (C). 1988. lib. bdg. 45.00 (*0-8191-6715-0*) U Pr of Amer.
— Title VII Liability for Sexual Harassment in the Workplace. 3rd ed. (Public Employee Relations Library: Vol. 77). (Orig.). 1997. pap. 18.00 (*0-914945-14-9*) Intl Personnel Mgmt.
Pellicer, Carlos. Antologia Breve (Brief Anthology) (SPA.). 176p. 1992. reprint ed. pap. 9.99 (*968-16-2049-6*, Pub. by Fondo) Continental Bk.
— Julieta y Su Caja de Colores (Julieta & Her Box of Colors) (SPA., Illus.). 36p. (J). (gr. 1-3). 1993. 12.99 (*968-16-4127-2*, Pub. by Fondo) Continental Bk.
Pellicer, D. Olga. U. S. Concerns Regarding Mexico's Oil & Gas: Evolution of the Debate, 1977-1980. (Research Reports: No. 10). 21p. (Orig.). (C). 1981. pap. 5.00 (*0-935391-09-6*, RR-10) UCSD Ctr US-Mex.
— U. S. Trade Policy Toward Mexico: Are There Reasons to Expect Special Treatment? (Research Reports: No. 9). 24p. (Orig.). (C). 1981. pap. 5.00 (*0-935391-08-8*, RR-09) UCSD Ctr US-Mex.
Pellicer, Leonard O. Caring Enough to Lead: Schools & the Sacred Trust. LC 99-6312. (One-Off Ser.). 144p. 1999. pap. 21.95 (*0-8039-6755-1*); lib. bdg. 49.95 (*0-8039-6754-3*) Sage.
Pellicer, Leonard O. & Anderson, Lorin W. A Handbook for Teacher Leaders. LC 95-2535. (Illus.). 264p. 1995. 65.95 (*0-8039-6172-3*); pap. 29.95 (*0-8039-6173-1*) Corwin Pr.
Pellicer, Leonard O. & Stevenson, Kenneth R., eds. The Best of the NASSP Bulletin: Readings in Secondary School Administration. 288p. (Orig.). (C). 1985. pap. text 12.00 (*0-88210-168-4*) Natl Assn Principals.
Pellicer, Olga, ed. Regional Mechanisms & International Security in Latin America. 172p. 1998. pap. 14.95 (*92-808-0967-9*, Pub. by UN Univ Pr) Brookings.
Pellicer, Olga, jt. ed. see Fagen, Richard R.
Pellicone, Patricia. Only for Love. 384p. 1998. pap. 4.99 (*0-8217-5927-2*) Kensgtn Pub Corp.
Pellier, P. Programming Real Time Games on the TRS-80. Martres, Laurent, tr. from FRE. 112p. write for info. (*0-318-57946-4*) Blue Cat.
***Pelligrino, Charles R.** Ghosts of the Titanic: New Discoveries from the Depths of the Ocean Floor. (Illus.). 304p. 2000. 26.00 (*0-688-13955-8*, Wm Morrow) Morrow Avon.
Pelligrino, Charles R. Her Name, Titanic: The Untold Story of the Sinking & Finding of the Unsinkable Ship. LC 88-13212. (Illus.). 304p. 1990. mass mkt. 6.50 (*0-380-70892-2*, Avon Bks) Morrow Avon.
Pelligrino, James W., jt. ed. see Dillon, Ronna R.
Pelligrino, Richard. Improving Your IQ. LC 98-88701. (Complete Idiot's Guide Ser.). (Illus.). 352p. 1998. pap. 16.95 (*0-02-862724-5*) Macmillan Gen Ref.
Pellikaan, Maja & Schroder, Hannelore, eds. Against Patriarchal Thinking: Women Philosophers in Europe 1992; a Future Without Discrimination? 400p. (Orig.). 1993. pap. text 45.00 (*90-5383-102-9*, Pub. by VU Univ Pr) Paul & Co Pubs.
***Pelling.** The Common Lot: Sickness, Medical Occupations & the Urban Poor in Early Modern England. 288p. (C). 1998. pap. 38.00 (*0-582-23182-5*) Addison-Wesley.
Pelling. The Common Lot: Sickness, Medical Occupations & the Urban Poor in Early Modern England. 288p. (C). 1998. text 77.00 (*0-582-23183-3*, Pub. by Longman) Longman.
***Pelling, C. B.** Literary Texts & Greek Historian. LC 99-33324. 336p. 1999. pap. 24.99 (*0-415-07351-9*) Routledge.
Pelling, Christopher. Greek Tragedy & the Historian. LC 96-9814. (Illus.). 280p. 1997. text 75.00 (*0-19-814987-5*) OUP.
Pelling, Christopher B., ed. Characterization & Individuality in Greek Literature. 280p. 1990. text 69.00 (*0-19-814058-4*) OUP.
***Pelling, Christopher B. R.** Literary Texts & Greek Historian. LC 99-33324. 336p. (C). 2000. text 65.00 (*0-415-07350-2*) Routledge.
Pelling, Christopher B. R., ed. see Plutarch.
***Pelling, George.** Beginning Your Family History in Great Britain. 7th rev. ed. LC 98-75210. (Illus.). 96p. 1999. pap. 9.95 (*0-8063-1585-7*) Genealog Pub.
Pelling, Henry. American Labor. LC 60-7247. (Chicago History of American Civilization Ser.). (Illus.). 1994. lib. bdg. 15.00 (*0-226-65392-7*) U Ch Pr.
— American Labor. LC 60-7247. (Chicago History of American Civilization Ser.). (Illus.). 1995. pap. text 10.95 (*0-226-65393-5*, CHAC16) U Ch Pr.
— American Labor. LC 60-7247. (Chicago History of American Civilization Ser.). (Illus.). 255p. reprint ed. pap. 79.10 (*0-608-09032-8*, 206966700005) Bks Demand.
***Pelling, Henry.** Churchill. (Illus.). 1999. pap. 12.99 (*1-84022-218-2*, Pub. by Wrdsworth Edits) Combined Pub.
Pelling, Henry. Churchills Peace Ministry, 1951. LC 96-2994. (Illus.). 224p. 1997. text 59.95 (*0-312-16271-5*) St Martin.
Pelling, Henry. History of British Trade Unionism. 352p. 1992. pap. 22.95 (*0-14-013640-1*, Pub. by Pnguin Bks Ltd) Trafalgar.
Pelling, Henry. A Short History of the Labour Party. 10th ed. LC 93-16705. (Illus.). 225p. 1993. text 45.00 (*0-312-09676-3*) St Martin.
— Social Geography of British Elections, 1885-1910. (Modern Revivals in History Ser.). 488p. (C). 1994. text 83.95 (*0-7512-0278-9*, Pub. by Gregg Revivals) Ashgate Pub Co.
Pelling, Henry & Reid, Alistair J. A Short History of the Labour Party. 11th ed. 224p. 1996. text 65.00 (*0-312-15934-X*, Pub. by E A) St Martin.
Pelling, Henry, jt. auth. see Bealey, Frank W.
Pelling, M., jt. ed. see Marland, H.
Pellingell, Noel. The Pellingell Book of Birding Records. 2nd ed. LC 91-76702. (Illus.). 152p. (Orig.). 1992. pap. 12.95 (*1-878788-27-2*) Amer Birding Assn.
Pellini, William S. Guidelines for Fracture-Safe & Fatigue-Reliable Design of Steel Structure. (Illus.). 148p. 1983. pap. 89.95 (*0-85300-166-9*, Pub. by Woodhead Pubng) Am Educ Systs.
Pelliot, Paul. Les Mongols et la Papaute, 3 pts. in 1 vol. LC 80-2365. reprint ed. 34.50 (*0-404-18913-X*) AMS Pr.
Pelliot, Paul, ed. see Huc & Gabet.
Pellis, Mark, jt. auth. see Ringel, William E.
Pellisier, Georges. The Literary Movement in France During the Nineteenth Century. LC 71-150197. 504p. reprint ed. lib. bdg. 28.00 (*0-8290-0508-0*) Irvington.
Pellissier, Georges. Les Ecrivains Politiques en France Avant le Revolution. Mayer, J. P., ed. LC 78-67374. (European Political Thought Ser.). (FRE.). 1980. reprint ed. lib. bdg. 15.95 (*0-405-11724-8*) Ayer.
— The Literary Movement in France During the Nineteenth Century. LC 71-150197. (Select Bibliographies Reprint Ser.). 1977. reprint ed. 31.95 (*0-8369-5710-5*) Ayer.
Pellissier, R., tr. see De Musset, Alfred.
Pellitero, Ana M., ed. Teatro Medieval. (Nueva Austral Ser.: No. 157). (SPA.). 1991. pap. text 24.95 (*84-239-1957-9*) Elliots Bks.
Pellitte, Chris. The Martial Arts Information Guide. (Illus.). 77p. 1998. spiral bd. 7.95 (*0-9668079-0-1*) C Pellitteri Martial Arts.
***Pellitteri, Phillip.** Endocrine Surgery of the Head & Neck. 2001. pap. 150.00 (*0-7693-0091-X*) Singular Publishing.
Pellizari, Edo, ed. Proceedings of the Workshop on General Population Exposure to Gasoline: (Gasoline Assessment of Human Exposure) (Journal of Exposure Analysis & Environmental Epidemiology Ser.: Vol. 2, No. 1). (Illus.). 1992. pap. text 65.00 (*0-911131-28-0*) Specialist Journals.
Pellizzari, Edo, ed. National Human Exposure Assessment Survey (NHEXAS) (Journal of Exposure Analysis & Environmental Epidemiology Ser.: Vol. 5, No. 3). (Illus.). 1995. pap. text. write for info. (*0-911131-72-8*) Specialist Journals.
Pellizzari, Edo, et al, eds. Measuring, Understanding, & Predicting Exposures in the 21st Century. (Journal of Exposure Analysis & Environmental Epidemiology Ser.: Vol. 2 Suppl. 1). (Illus.). 244p. 1992. 65.00 (*0-911131-84-1*) Specialist Journals.
— Measuring, Understanding, & Predicting Exposures in the 21st Century. (Journal of Exposure Analysis & Environmental Epidemiology Ser.: Vol. 2, Suppl. 2). (Illus.). 204p. 1992. 65.00 (*0-911131-83-3*) Specialist Journals.
Pellizzari, Fausta, jt. auth. see Curzio, Alberto Q.
Pellizzari, Piero. Italian-Spanish - Spanish-Italian Technical & Commercial Dictionary, 2 vols. (ITA & SPA.). 1500p. 1990. 250.00 (*0-8288-7348-8*, 8885158021) Fr & Eur.
Pellizzetti, E., jt. auth. see Pramauro, E.
***Pellizzi, Francesco, ed.** Architecture. (RES Journal Monographs: Vol. 34). (Illus.). 216p. 1999. pap. 30.00 (*0-87365-829-9*) Peabody Harvard.
— Pre-Columbian States of Being. (RES Journal Monographs: Vol. 33). (Illus.). 256p. 1998. pap. 30.00 (*0-87365-826-4*) Peabody Harvard.
Pellizzi, Francesco, ed. RES 27 Spring 1995: Anthropology & Aesthetics. (RES Monographs on Anthropology & Aesthetics: Vol. 27). (Illus.). 154p. (C). 1996. pap. text 25.95 (*0-521-48373-5*) Cambridge U Pr.
— Res 26 Autumn 1994: Anthropology & Aesthetics. (RES Monographs on Anthropology & Aesthetics: Vol. 26). (Illus.). 144p. (C). 1996. pap. text 25.95 (*0-521-47722-0*) Cambridge U Pr.
— Res 23 Spring 1993: Anthropology & Aesthetics. (RES Monographs on Anthropology & Aesthetics: Vol. 23). (Illus.). 152p. (C). 1993. pap. text 25.95 (*0-521-44741-0*) Cambridge U Pr.
— Res 22 Autumn 1992: Anthropology & Aesthetics. (RES Monographs on Anthropology & Aesthetics: Vol. 22). (Illus.). 160p. (C). 1992. pap. text 24.95 (*0-521-43760-1*) Cambridge U Pr.
— Res 25: Anthropology & Aesthetics. (RES Monographs on Anthropology & Aesthetics: Vol. 25). (Illus.). 145p. (C). 1994. pap. text 25.95 (*0-521-46663-6*) Cambridge U Pr.
— Res 28: Anthropology & Aesthetics. (RES Monographs on Anthropology & Aesthetics: Vol. 28). 194p. (C). 1996. pap. text 25.95 (*0-521-55858-1*) Cambridge U Pr.
Pellizzi, Francesco & Tambiah, Stanley J., eds. Ethnicities & Nations: Processes of Interethnic Relations in Latin America, Southeast Asia, & the Pacific. LC 88-6471. 416p. (C). 1988. 22.50 (*0-945472-01-3*) Rothko Chapel.
Pellizzi, Francescso, ed. Res 24: Anthropology & Aesthetics. (RES Monographs on Anthropology & Aesthetics: Vol. 24). (Illus.). 160p. (C). 1993. pap. text 25.95 (*0-521-44742-9*) Cambridge U Pr.
Pellman, Kathryn A., jt. auth. see Rafalovich, Danita.
Pellman, Kenneth & Pellman, Rachel T. A Treasury of Amish Quilts. deluxe ed. LC 90-82488. (Illus.). 128p. 1990. pap. 19.95 (*1-56148-000-2*) Good Bks PA.
— A Treasury of Mennonite Quilts. deluxe ed. LC 92-26505. (Illus.). 128p. 1992. pap. 19.95 (*1-56148-059-2*) Good Bks PA.
— The World of Amish Quilts. deluxe ed. LC 84-80651. (Illus.). 128p. 1984. pap. 19.95 (*0-934672-22-9*) Good Bks PA.
Pellman, Kenneth, jt. auth. see Pellman, Rachel T.
Pellman, Kenneth, jt. auth. see Scott, Stephen.
Pellman, Leonard J., jt. auth. see Shimabukuro, Shihan M.
Pellman, Rachel T. Amish Quilt Patterns. rev. ed. 128p. 1998. pap. 14.95 (*1-56148-190-4*) Good Bks PA.
— Dahlia Quilts & Projects: Complete Patterns & Instructions. LC 95-41599. (Illus.). 98p. 1995. pap. 16.95 (*1-56148-179-3*) Good Bks PA.
— Small Amish Quilt Patterns: For Crib Quilts & Wall Hangings. rev. ed. LC 85-70280. (Illus.). 128p. 1997. pap. 14.95 (*1-56148-236-6*) Good Bks PA.
— Tips for Quilters: A Handbook of Hints, Shortcuts, & Practical Suggestions from Experienced Quilters. LC 93-24758. 236p. 1993. pap. 9.95 (*1-56148-080-0*) Good Bks PA.
Pellman, Rachel T. & Pellman, Kenneth. The World of Amish Quilts. deluxe ed. LC 84-80651. (Illus.). 128p. 1997. pap. 21.95 (*1-56148-237-4*) Good Bks PA.
Pellman, Rachel T. & Ranck, Joanne. Quilts among the Plain People. LC 81-82209. (People's Place Book Ser.: No. 4). (Illus.). 96p. 1981. pap. 5.95 (*0-934672-03-2*) Good Bks PA.
Pellman, Rachel T., jt. auth. see Benner, Cheryl A.
Pellman, Rachel T., jt. auth. see Good, Phyllis Pellman.
Pellman, Rachel T., jt. auth. see Pellman, Kenneth.
Pellman, Ron, jt. auth. see Pinchot, Gifford.
Pellman, Samuel. An Introduction to the Creation of Electroacoustic Music. 441p. 1994. 42.75 (*0-534-21450-9*) Wadsworth Pub.
Pellock, John M. & Myer, Edwin C. Neurologic Emergencies in Infancy & Childhood. 2nd ed. (Illus.). 425p. 1993. text 95.00 (*0-7506-9419-X*) Buttrwrth-Heinemann.
Pellock, John M., jt. ed. see Dodson, W. Edward.
Pellon, Dick & Raphel, Murray. The Idea Book. 1998. 200.00 (*0-9624808-7-8*) Raphel Mktg.
Pellon, Gustavo. Jose Lezama Lima's Joyful Vision: A Study of Paradiso & Other Prose Works. LC 89-4856. (Texas Pan American Ser.). (Illus.). 165p. 1989. text 22.50 (*0-292-74020-4*) U of Tex Pr.
Pelloso, Pierre. Practical Digital Electronics. Nelson, John C., tr. from FRE. LC 85-15524. 229p. reprint ed. pap. 71.00 (*0-7837-4408-0*, 204415100012) Bks Demand.
Pelloutier, F. Histoire des Bourses du Travail. (Publications Gramma Ser.). ii, 340p. 1971. pap. text 33.00 (*0-677-50725-9*) Gordon & Breach.
Pelloux, R. M., ed. see Metallurgical Society of AIME Staff.
Pellow, C. Kenneth. Films As Critiques of Novels: Transformational Criticism. LC 94-31631. 380p. 1995. text 99.95 (*0-7734-9067-1*) E Mellen.
Pellow, C. Kenneth, jt. ed. see Blackburn, Alexander.
Pellow, Deborah. Women in Accra: Options for Autonomy. Kitchen, Cole, ed. LC 77-78740. (Illus.). 1977. 24.00 (*0-917256-03-4*) Ref Pubns.
Pellow, Deborah, ed. Setting Boundaries: The Anthropology of Spatial & Social Organization. LC 95-12840. 256p. 1996. 59.95 (*0-89789-428-6*, Bergin & Garvey) Greenwood.
Pellow, George. Issues of Faith & Morals. LC 97-70813. 1997. pap. text 12.95 (*0-89870-634-3*) Ignatius Pr.
— John Jay. Schlesinger, Arthur Meier, Jr., ed. LC 96-51598. (American Statesmen Ser.). 500p. 1997. lib. bdg. 34.95 (*0-7910-4544-7*, Chelsea Juniors) Chelsea Hse.

P

Pellow, Harry C. The ABCs & Nine Twelves of Porsche Engines: Porsche Engines & the Future of the Human Race. rev. ed. (Illus.). 700p. 1981. per. 29.95 (*0-941210-04-9*) HCP Res.
— The Maestro Chronicles. 1984p. per. 19.50 (*0-941210-08-1*) HCP Res.
— The Maestro's Newsletter. 200p. (Orig.). 1989. 19.95 (*0-941210-12-X*) HCP Res.
— The Maestro's Spec Book & Emergency Breakdown Procedures. 1984. per. 19.95 (*0-941210-09-X*) HCP Res.
— Murphy Is My Co-Pilot. (Illus.). 407p. 1983. 29.95 (*0-941210-07-3*) HCP Res.
— Secrets of the Inner Circle. 3rd ed. 450p. 1983. per. 29.95 (*0-941210-06-5*) HCP Res.
Pellow, Randall A. Pennsylvania Geography. (Illus.). 64p. (J). (gr. 4-8). 1999. pap. text 8.35 (*0-931992-55-9*) Penns Valley.
Pellow, Sandy. Too Much Noise. (Literature Unit Ser.). (Illus.). 48p. 1998. pap., teacher ed. 7.95 (*1-55734-568-6*) Tchr Create Mat.
Pellowe, Susan. Saffron & Currants: A Cornish Heritage Cookbook. 2nd rev. ed. (Illus.). 52p. 1998. pap. 6.00 (*0-9623507-2-9*) Renard Prodns.
Pellowe, Susan L., ed. A Wesley Family Book of Days. LC 94-68425. (Illus.). 172p. (Orig.). 1994. pap. 12.00 (*0-9623507-1-0*) Renard Prodns.
Pellowski, Anne. Betsy's Up-&-Down Year, Vol. 5. rev. ed. LC 98-165351. (Polish American Girls Ser.). (Illus.). 160p. (J). (gr. 3-5). 1997. pap. 9.95 (*0-88489-539-4*) St Marys.
— First Farm in the Valley Vol. 1: Anna's Story. rev. ed. LC 98-144044. (Polish American Girls Ser.). (Illus.). 192p. (J). (gr. 3-5). 1997. pap. 9.95 (*0-88489-537-8*) St Marys.
— Hidden Stories in Plants: Unusual & Easy-to-Tell Stories from Around the World Together with Creative Things to Do While Telling Them. LC 89-37166. (Illus.). 176p. (J). (ps up). 1990. text 15.95 (*0-02-770611-7*, Mac Bks Young Read) S&S Childrens.
— Stairstep Farm Vol. 3: Anna Rose's Story. rev. ed. LC 98-165275. (Polish American Girls Ser.). (Illus.). 176p. (J). (gr. 3-6). 1997. pap. 9.95 (*0-88489-536-X*) St Marys.
— The Story Vine: A Source Book of Unusual & Easy-to-Tell Stories from Around the World. LC 83-26756. (Illus.). 128p. (J). 1984. lib. bdg. 15.95 (*0-02-770590-0*, Mac Bks Young Read) S&S Childrens.
— The Storytelling Handbook: A Young People's Collection of Unusual Tales & Helpful Hints on How to Tell Them. LC 95-2991. (Illus.). 128p. (YA). (gr. 3-7). 1995. per. 16.00 (*0-689-80311-7*) Aladdin.
— Willow Wind Farm Vol. 4: Betsy's Story. rev. ed. Nagel, Steve, ed. (Polish American Girls Ser.). (Illus.). 176p. (J). (gr. 3-5). 1997. pap. 9.95 (*0-88489-525-4*) St Marys.
— Winding Valley Farm Vol. 2: Annie's Story. rev. ed. (Polish American Girls Ser.). (Illus.). 192p. (J). (gr. 3-6). 1997. pap. 9.95 (*0-88489-538-6*) St Marys.
— The World of Storytelling: A Practical Guide to the Origins, Development, & Applications of Storytelling. enl. rev. ed. 322p. 1990. 40.00 (*0-8242-0788-2*) Wilson.
Pellowski, Anne, ed. A World of Children's Stories. LC 93-13509. (Children's World Ser.). (Illus.). 192p. (Orig.). (J). (gr. 3-6). 1993. pap. 19.95 (*0-377-00259-3*) Friendship Pr.
Pellowski, Anne, jt. auth. see Miller, Teresa.
***Pellowski, Michael.** Amphetamine Drug Dangers. LC 99-36152. (Drug Dangers Ser.). (Illus.). 64p. (gr. 4-10). 2000. lib. bdg. 19.95 (*0-7660-1321-9*) Enslow Pubs.
Pellowski, Michael. Football's Wackiest Moments. (Illus.). 96p. 1998. pap. 5.95 (*0-8069-1363-0*) Sterling.
— Totally Loony Jokes & Riddles. LC 99-13664. (J). 1999. 4.95 (*0-8069-9897-0*) Sterling.
Pellowski, Michael J. Bad News Boyfriend, No. 2. LC 91-19659. (Riverdale High Ser.). (Illus.). 128p. (YA). (gr. 4-8). 1991. pap. 2.99 (*1-56282-108-3*) Hyprn Child.
— Baseball's Funniest People. LC 96-39060. (Illus.). 96p. 1997. 5.95 (*0-8069-9442-8*) Sterling.
— The Funny Side of Sports. LC 95-51511. (Illus.). 96p. 1996. pap. 5.95 (*0-8069-3892-7*) Sterling.
— Ghost in the Library. LC 88-1236. (Fiddlesticks Ser.). (Illus.). 48p. (Orig.). (J). (gr. 1-4). 1989. pap. text 3.50 (*0-8167-1338-3*) Troll Communs.
— Joke & Riddle Bonanza. (Illus.). 96p. (J). 1996. pap. 4.95 (*0-8069-0961-7*) Sterling.
— Not-So-Great Moments in Sports. (Illus.). 96p. (Orig.). 1995. pap. 5.95 (*0-8069-1257-X*) Sterling.
— One Hundred Two Cat & Dog Jokes. LC 91-42769. (Illus.). 64p. (J). (gr. 2-6). 1997. pap. 2.95 (*0-8167-2790-2*) Troll Communs.
— Wackiest Jokes in the World. (Illus.). 96p. (J). 1995. pap. 4.95 (*0-8069-0494-1*) Sterling.
Pellowski, Michael M. The Art of Making Comic Books. (Illus.). 80p. (J). (gr. 4 up). 1995. lib. bdg. 21.27 (*0-8225-2304-3*) Lerner Pub.
Pellowski, Morgan M. Art of Making Comic Books. (Illus.). 80p. (J). 1995. pap. 8.95 (*0-8225-9672-5*) Lerner Pub.
Pells, Edward G. European, Coloured & Native Education in South Africa, 1652-1928. LC 74-15077. reprint ed. 29.50 (*0-404-12126-8*) AMS Pr.
— Three Hundred Years of Education in South Africa. LC 71-90156. 152p. 1970. reprint ed. lib. bdg. 59.50 (*0-8371-2217-1*, PEEA, Greenwood Pr) Greenwood.
Pells, P. J., ed. Engineering Geology of the Sydney Region. 407p. (C). 1985. text 125.00 (*0-318-32581-0*, Pub. by A A Balkema) Ashgate Pub Co.
— Structural Foundations on Rock: Proceedings of the International Conference, Sydney, 7-9th May 1980, 2 vols., Set. 494p. (C). 1981. text 272.00 (*90-6191-072-2*, Pub. by A A Balkema) Ashgate Pub Co.
Pells, Richard H. The Liberal Mind in a Conservative Age: American Intellectuals in the 1940s & 1950s. 2nd ed. LC 89-14676. 488p. 1989. pap. 24.95 (*0-8195-6225-4*, Wesleyan Univ Pr) U Pr of New Eng.
— Not Like Us: How Europeans Loved, Hated & Transformed American Culture Since WWII. 400p. 1998. pap. 18.00 (*0-465-00163-7*, Pub. by Basic) HarpC.
— Radical Visions & American Dreams. LC 98-21404. xxi, 424p. 1998. pap. 19.95 (*0-252-06743-6*) U of Ill Pr.
Pells, T., jt. auth. see Somerville, L.
Pelltreau, William S. & Brown, John H., eds. American Families of Historic Lineage, Long Island Edition, 2 vols. (Illus.). 714p. 1997. reprint ed. lib. bdg. 76.00 (*0-8328-6088-3*) Higginson Bk Co.
Pelly, David. Illustrated Encyclopedia to World Sailing. LC 65-18206. 1989. 16.95 (*0-671-10146-3*) S&S Trade.
Pelly, David F. Thelon: A River Sanctuary. (Illus.). 202p. 1999. pap. 24.95 (*1-895465-21-4*) CNR Canoe.
Pelly, Lewis. Report on a Journey to Riyadh (1865) (Arabia Past & Present Ser.: Vol. 6). (Illus.). 1978. reprint ed. 26.95 (*0-902675-64-8*) Oleander Pr.
Pelly, M. E. & Yasamee, H. J., eds. Eastern Europe August 1945-April 1946. (Documents on British Policy Overseas Ser.: Vol. 6). (Illus.). xiii, 395p. 1991. boxed set 94.00 (*0-11-591687-3*, Pub. by Statnry Office) Balogh.
Pelly, M. E., jt. ed. see Butler, Rohan.
Pelly, T. M. Doctor Minor-a Sketch of the Life of Dr. Thomas T. Minor, 1844-1889. (Shorey Historical Ser.). 142p. reprint ed. pap. 10.00 (*0-8466-0204-0*, S204) Shoreys Bkstore.
Pelmear, Kenneth. Carols of Cornwall. (C). 1989. 40.00 (*0-907566-22-7*, Pub. by Dyllansow Truran) St Mut.
— Salute to Truro. (C). 1989. 30.00 (*0-907566-31-6*, Pub. by Dyllansow Truran) St Mut.
— Songs of Cornwall. (C). 1989. 30.00 (*1-85022-010-7*, Pub. by Dyllansow Truran) St Mut.
Pelmear, P. L. & Wasserman, D. E., eds. Hand-Arm Vibration: A Comprehensive Guide for Occupational Health Professionals. 2nd ed. LC 98-66605. 272p. 1998. text 80.00 (*1-883595-22-3*, 23049, OEM Pr) OEM Health.
Pelnar, Premysl V. Health Effects of Asbestos & of Other Minerals & Fibres: An Annotated Compilation of the Worlds' Literature on Asbestos 1906-1986, 3 vols., Set. Scherr, George H., ed. 2400p. 1988. 362.00 (*0-930376-46-3*) Chem-Orbital.
***Pelo, Ann & Davidson, Fran.** That's No Fair! A Teacher's Guide to Activism with Young Children. LC 99-55729. (Illus.). 288p. 2000. pap. 29.95 (*1-884834-74-4*, 409901, Pub. by Redleaf Pr) Gryphon Hse.
Pelofsky, Arnold H. Coal Conversion Technology: Problems & Solutions. LC 79-17936. (ACS Symposium Ser.: Vol. 110). 270p. 1979. reprint ed. pap. 83.70 (*0-608-03088-0*, 206354000007) Bks Demand.
Pelofsky, Arnold H., ed. Coal Conversion Technology: Problems & Solutions. LC 79-17936. (ACS Symposium Ser.: No. 110). 257p. 1979. 36.95 (*0-8412-0516-7*) Am Chemical.
— Heavy Oil Gasification. LC 77-24338. (Energy, Power, & Environment Ser.: No. 1). (Illus.). 175p. reprint ed. pap. 54.30 (*0-7837-0846-7*, 204115800019) Bks Demand.
— Synthetic Fuels Processing: Comparative Economics. LC 76-41472. (Illus.). 487p. reprint ed. pap. 151.00 (*0-7837-3351-8*, 204330900008) Bks Demand.
***Peloquin, Albert.** Barrier-Free Residential Design. (Illus.). 239p. 1999. reprint ed. text 30.00 (*0-7881-6768-5*) DIANE Pub.
Peloquin, Claude. A Dive into My Essence. 96p. 1990. pap. 8.00 (*0-920717-44-6*) Guernica Editions.
— Les Mers Detroublees: Poisies et Textes, 1963-1969. (FRE.). 364p. 1993. pap. write for info. (*2-89135-045-6*) Guernica Editions.
— Pellucid Waters: Selected Poems. Ranger, Lucie, tr. from FRE. LC 97-72261. (Essential Poets Ser.: Vol. 81). 64p. 1998. pap. 8.00 (*1-55071-066-4*) Guernica Editions.
— Une Plongee dans Mon Essentiel.Tr. of Dive into My Essence. (FRE.). 119p. 1985. pap. 10.00 (*2-89135-011-1*) Guernica Editions.
Peloquin, Suzanne, jt. auth. see Davidson, Deborah.
Peloquin, Suzanne, jt. auth. see Punwar, Alice.
Pelosi. Doing Statistics: Data, Inference & Decision Making for Managers. pap. text, teacher ed. write for info. (*0-471-14008-2*) Wiley.
— Doing Statistics: Data, Inference & Decision Making for Managers. 107p. 1999. pap., student ed. 26.95 (*0-471-14011-2*) Wiley.
Pelosi, Giuseppe, et al. Quick Finite Element Method for Electromagnetic Waves. LC 98-16279. 216p. 1998. 95.00 incl. cd-rom (*0-89006-848-8*) Artech Hse.
Pelosi, Giuseppe, jt. ed. see Silvester, Peter P.
Pelosi, Marilyn & Sandifer, Theresa M. Doing Statistics with Minitab for Windows Release 10: An Introductory Course Supplement for Explorations in Data Analysis. 1997. pap. text. write for info. (*0-471-14754-0*) Wiley.
***Pelosi, Marilyn K.** Doing Statistics with MINITAB for Windows Release 11. LC 98-137618. 302p. 1998. pap. 34.95 (*0-471-25170-4*) Wiley.
***Pelosi, Marilyn K. & Sandifer, Theresa M.** Doing Statistics for Business: Data, Inferences & Decision Making. LC 98-24484. 896p. 1999. pap. 78.95 incl. disk (*0-471-12208-4*) Wiley.
Pelosi, Marilyn K. & Sandifer, Theresa M. Doing Statistics with Minitab for Windows Release 10: An Introductory Course Supplement for Explorations in Data Analysis. LC 96-101733. 320p. 1995. pap. 31.95 (*0-471-30471-9*) Wiley.
— Pelosi Doing Statistics with Minitab for Windows Release: An Introductory Course Supplement for Explorations in Data Analysis & Minitab Mini-Manual. 904p. 1996. 53.95 (*0-471-17441-6*) Wiley.
Pelosi, Marilyn K., et al. Doing Statistics with Excel for Windows Version 5.0: An Introductory Course Supplement for Explorations in Data Analysis. LC 96-155376. 359p. 1996. pap. 28.95 (*0-471-14899-7*) Wiley.
***Pelosi, Marilyn K., et al.** Doing Statistics with Excel 97: Software Instruction & Exercise Activity Supplement. LC 98-138197. (Illus.). 338p. 1998. pap. write for info. (*0-471-25171-2*) Wiley.
— Research & Evaluation for Business. 992p. (C). 2000. write for info. incl. cd-rom (*0-471-39088-7*) Wiley.
Pelosi, Paolo. Odoriferous Molecules. 1999. 74.95 (*0-8493-8965-8*) CRC Pr.
Peloso, Vincent C. Peasants on Plantations: Subaltern Strategies of Labor & Resistance in the Pisco Valley, Peru. LC 98-27846. (Latin America Otherwise Ser.). 1998. pap. 17.95 (*0-8223-2246-3*) Duke.
— Peasants on Plantations: Subaltern Strategies of Labor & Resistance in the Pisco Valley, Peru. LC 98-27846. (Latin America Otherwise Ser.). (Illus.). 248p. 1998. lib. bdg. 49.95 (*0-8223-2229-3*) Duke.
Peloso, Vincent C. & Tenenbaum, Barbara A., eds. Liberals, Politics, & Power: State Formation in Nineteenth-Century Latin America. LC 95-32602. (C). 1996. 50.00 (*0-8203-1777-2*); pap. 25.00 (*0-8203-1800-0*) U of Ga Pr.
Pelote, Vincent P., jt. auth. see Strongwater, Steven L.
Peloubet, Don, ed. Wheelmaking: Wooden Wheel Design & Construction. LC 96-86030. (Illus.). 248p. (Orig.). 1996. pap. 29.95 (*1-879335-73-5*) Astragal Pr.
Peloubet, F. N., ed. see Smith, William.
Peloubet, F. N., ed. see Smith, William, Jr.
Peloubet, M. A., ed. see Smith, William.
Peloubet, M. A., ed. see Smith, William, Jr.
Peloubet, S. S. Collection of Legal Maxims in Law & Equity: With English Translations. (Illus.). ix, 332p. 1985. reprint ed. 46.00 (*0-8377-1020-0*, Rothman) W S Hein.
Pelphrey, Jo A. Into the Think Tank with Literature. Keeling, Jan, ed. (Illus.). 160p. (Orig.). (J). (gr. k-3). 1992. pap. text 14.95 (*0-86530-192-1*, IP193-6) Incentive Pubns.
Pelras, Christian. The Bugis. LC 95-42827. (Peoples of South-East Asia & the Pacific Ser.). 352p. (C). 1996. 66.95 (*0-631-17231-9*) Blackwell Pubs.
Pelrine, Diane M. Affinities of Form: Art of Africa, Oceania, & the Americas. (Illus.). 232p. 1996. 65.00 (*3-7913-1669-9*, Pub. by Prestel) te Neues.
Pelrine, Eleanor W. Morgentaler: The Doctor Who Couldn't Turn Away. 2nd ed. 222p. 1975. mass mkt. 4.95 (*0-88780-119-6*, Pub. by Formac Publ Co) Formac Dist Ltd.
***Pelrine, Joseph, et al.** Mastering ENVY/Developer. (Advances in Object Technology Ser.: No. 25). 350p. (C). 2000. pap. text. write for info. (*0-521-66650-3*) Cambridge U Pr.
Pelroy, R. A., jt. ed. see Park, J. F.
Pels, David, jt. auth. see Kaner, Cem.
***Pels, Dick.** The Intellectual as Stranger: Studies in Spokespersonship. LC 00-42467. 2000. write for info. (*0-415-20584-0*) Routledge.
Pels, Dick. Property & Power in Social Theory: A Study in Intellectual Rivalry. LC 98-23828. (Studies in Social & Political Thought : No. 14). (Illus.). 336p. (C). (gr. 13). 1998. 100.00 (*0-415-18780-X*, D6275) Routledge.
Pels, Jacquelin R. Unga Island Girl (Ruth's Book) LC 94-96375. (Illus.). 312p. (Orig.). 1995. pap. 24.50 (*0-9625429-7-0*) Hardscratch Pr.
Pels, Peter. A Politics of Presence: Contacts Between Missionaries & Waluguru in Late Colonial Tanganyika. (Studies in Anthropology & History: Vol. 22). 372p. 1998. text 58.00 (*90-5702-304-0*, ECU49) Gordon & Breach.
Pels, Peter & Salemink, Oscar. Colonial Subjects. LC 99-6129. 432p. 1999. text 49.50 (*0-472-11017-9*, 11017) U of Mich Pr.
Pels, Peter & Salemink, Oscar, eds. Colonial Subjects: Essays on the Practical History of Anthropology. (Illus.). 432p. (C). pap. text 24.95 (*0-472-08746-0*, 08746) U of Mich Pr.
Pels, Peter, jt. auth. see Molendijk, Arie L.
Pels, Peter, jt. ed. see Nencel, Lorraine.
Pelser, Caroline, ed. see Field, Stuart.
Pelser, Frederick. Prayer Made Practical. 1998. pap. 9.99 (*1-873796-65-X*) Review & Herald.
Pelser, Frederick & Pelser, Marcia E. Freedom Bridge. (Illus.). 100p. (Orig.). 1984. pap. 5.95 (*0-9612348-0-6*) Fremar Pr.
Pelser, H. E., jt. auth. see Paulley, J. W.
Pelser, Marcia E., jt. auth. see Pelser, Frederick.
***Pelsmacker, Patrick de, et al.** Marketing Communications: Cornerstones, Instruments, & Applications. LC 99-49461. 472p. 2000. write for info. (*0-273-63871-8*) F T P H.
***Pelsser, Antoon.** Efficient Methods for Valuing Interest Rate Derivatives. LC 00-33821. (Finance Ser.). 2000. write for info. (*1-85233-304-9*) Spr-Verlag.
Pelt, Adrian. Libyan Independence & the United Nations: A Case of Planned Decolonization. LC 72-99836. 1046p. reprint ed. pap. 200.00 (*0-8357-8208-5*, 203385300087) Bks Demand.
Pelt, Chester H., Sr. Pelt: A Genealogical History of the Pelt Family Branch of the Van Pelt Family Tree. (Illus.). 140p. 1992. pap. 22.00 (*0-8328-2383-X*); lib. bdg. 32.00 (*0-8328-2382-1*) Higginson Bk Co.
Pelt, Gertrude W. Van, see Van Pelt, Gertrude W.
Pelt, Katie van, see Van Pelt, Katie.
Pelt, Ken A. Farewell to Freedom. 124p. (Orig.). 1985. pap. 7.95 (*0-936527-00-5*) Amer Sec Bill.
— Life. (Pocket Library). 73p. (Orig.). 1987. pap. 4.95 (*0-943139-00-7*) Heritage Heirloom.
Pelt, Michael R. A History of Original Free Will Baptists. LC 93-80106. (Illus.). 400p. 1996. pap. 21.95 (*1-880994-26-7*) Mt Olive Coll Pr.
Pelt, Mogens. Tobacco, Arms & Politics: Greece & Germany from World Crisis to World War, 1929-1941. LC 98-235478. 344p. 1998. pap. 57.50 (*87-7289-450-4*, Pub. by Almqvist Wiksell) Coronet Bks.
Pelt, Nancy L. Van, see Van Pelt, Nancy L.
Pelt, Nancy Van, see Van Pelt, Nancy.
Pelt, Rich Van, see Van Pelt, Rich.
Pelt, Robert J. Van, see Van Pelt, Robert J.
Pelt, Robert J. Van, see Dwork, Deborah & Van Pelt, Robert J.
Pelt, Robert Jan van, see Dwork, Deborah & Jan van Pelt, Robert.
Pelt, Robert Van, see Van Pelt, Robert.
Pelt, Sydney J. Van, see Van Pelt, Sydney J.
Pelt, William V. Van, see Schuster, Charles I. & Van Pelt, William V.
Pelta, Kasthy. Cattle Trails: "Get Along Little Doggies" LC 96-36876. (American Trails Ser.). (Illus.). 96p. (J). (gr. 6-9). 1997. lib. bdg. 28.55 (*0-8172-4073-X*) Raintree Steck-V.
Pelta, Kathy. Alexander Graham Bell. (Pioneers in Change Ser.). (Illus.). 144p. (J). (gr. 5-9). 1989. lib. bdg. 13.95 (*0-382-09529-4*) Silver Burdett Pr.
— California. LC 93-1497. (Hello U. S. A. Ser.). (Illus.). 72p. (J). (gr. 3-6). 1993. lib. bdg. 19.93 (*0-8225-2738-3*, Lerner Publctns) Lerner Pub.
— California. (Illus.). 72p. 1995. pap. text 5.95 (*0-8225-9668-7*) Lerner Pub.
— Discovering Christopher Columbus: How History Is Invented. (How History Is Invented Ser.). 96p. (J). (gr. 4-9). 1991. lib. bdg. 21.27 (*0-8225-4899-2*, Lerner Publctns) Lerner Pub.
— Idaho. LC 94-2235. (Hello U. S. A. Ser.). (Illus.). 72p. (J). (gr. 3-6). 1995. lib. bdg. 19.93 (*0-8225-2734-0*, Lerner Publctns) Lerner Pub.
***Pelta, Kathy.** Rediscovering Easter Island. LC 00-9163. (How History is Invented Ser.). 2001. write for info. (*0-8225-4890-9*) Lerner Pub.
Pelta, Kathy. The Royal Roads: Spanish Trails in North America. LC 96-37369. (American Trails Ser.). (Illus.). 96p. (J). (gr. 6-9). 1997. lib. bdg. 28.55 (*0-8172-4074-8*) Raintree Steck-V.
— Texas. LC 93-33390. (Hello U. S. A. Ser.). (Illus.). 72p. (J). (gr. 3-6). 1994. lib. bdg. 19.95 (*0-8225-2749-9*, Lerner Publctns) Lerner Pub.
— Texas. (Illus.). 72p. (J). (gr. 3-6). 1995. pap. text 5.95 (*0-8225-9667-9*) Lerner Pub.
— Trails to the West: Beyond the Mississippi. LC 96-39483. (American Trails Ser.). (Illus.). 96p. (J). 1997. lib. bdg. 28.55 (*0-8172-4072-1*) Raintree Steck-V.
— The U. S. Navy. (Armed Services Ser.). (Illus.). 88p. (YA). (gr. 5 up). 1990. lib. bdg. 22.95 (*0-8225-1435-4*, Lerner Publctns) Lerner Pub.
Pelta, Kathy. Vermont. LC 93-33389. (Hello U. S. A. Ser.). (Illus.). 72p. (J). (gr. 3-6). 1994. lib. bdg. 19.95 (*0-8225-2729-4*, Lerner Publctns) Lerner Pub.
— Vermont. (Hello U. S. A. Ser.). (Illus.). 72p. (J). (gr. 3-6). 2000. pap. 5.95 (*0-8225-9784-5*, First Ave Edns) Lerner Pub.
Pelta, R. & Vivas, E. Piel y Alergia. (SPA.). 211p. 1997. pap. 33.00 (*84-7978-298-6*, Pub. by Ediciones Diaz) IBD Ltd.
***Peltason & Burns.** Government by the People, National Version: Interactive Edition. 18th ed. 400p. 2000. pap. write for info. (*0-13-030722-X*) P-H.
Peltason, J. W. Understanding the Constitution. 2nd ed. LC 98-137910. 512p. (C). 1997. pap. text 21.00 (*0-15-599717-3*, Pub. by Harcourt Coll Pubs) Harcourt.
Peltason, Jack W. Fifty-Eight Lonely Men: Southern Federal Judges & School Desegregation. LC 61-12350. 288p. 1971. reprint ed. pap. text 15.95 (*0-252-00175-3*) U of Ill Pr.
Peltason, Timothy. Reading in Memoriam. LC 85-42698. (Princeton Essays in Literature Ser.). 193p. 1985. reprint ed. pap. 59.90 (*0-7837-9418-5*, 206015900004) Bks Demand.
Peltenburg, E. J. Lembra Archaeological Project Vol. I: Excavations at Lembra Lakkous, 1976-1983. (Studies in Mediterranean Archaeology: Vol. LXX:1). (Illus.). 356p. (Orig.). 1985. pap. 165.00 (*91-86098-27-6*, Pub. by P Astroms) Coronet Bks.
— Recent Developments in the Later Prehistory of Cyprus. (Studies in Mediterranean Archaeology & Literature: No. 16). (Illus.). 145p. (Orig.). 1982. pap. 39.50 (*91-86098-02-0*, Pub. by P Astroms) Coronet Bks.
Peltenburg, Edgar. Western Asiatic Antiquities. 1992. text 110.00 (*0-7486-0224-0*, Pub. by Edinburgh U Pr) Col U Pr.
Peltenburg, Edgar, et al. Lembra Archaeological Project Vol. II.2: A Ceremonial Area at Kissonerga. (Studies in Mediterranean Archaeology: Vol. LXX:3). (Illus.). 135p. (Orig.). 1991. pap. 97.50 (*91-7081-011-7*, Pub. by P Astroms) Coronet Bks.
Pelteret, David A. Catalogue of English Post-Conquest Vernacular Documents. 152p. 1990. 75.00 (*0-85115-259-7*) Boydell & Brewer.
***Pelteret, David A.** The History of Anglo-Saxon England: Basic Readings. LC 00-23328. (Reference Library of the Humanities). 2000. write for info. (*0-8153-3140-1*) Garland.
Pelteret, David A. Slavery in Early Medieval England from the Reign of Alfred to the Twelfth Century. (Studies in Anglo-Saxon History: Vol. 7). 390p. (C). 1995. 75.00 (*0-85115-399-2*) Boydell & Brewer.
Peltier, A. P., jt. auth. see Kahn, M. F.
Peltier, Althea Y. Psychology & Its Practice: Index of Modern Information. LC 89-78057. 150p. 1990. 47.50 (*1-55914-202-2*); pap. 44.50 (*1-55914-203-0*) ABBE Pubs Assn.

P

Peltier-Draine, Elsaida. What's Up Girlfriend? (Illus.). 170p. (Orig.). 1994. pap., per. 11.95 (*0-9643320-0-0*) Zenon Pubn.

— What's Up Girlfriend? large type ed. LC 95-106674. (Illus.). 170p. (Orig.). 1994. 17.95 (*0-9643320-1-9*); 17.95 (*0-9643320-2-7*) Zenon Pubn.

Peltier-Draine, Elscuda. Black Male. (Illus.). 197p. (Orig.). 1995. pap. 14.95 (*0-9643320-3-5*) Zenon Pubn.

Peltier, Gary L. Perspectives on Education. 5th ed. (C). 1991. pap. 52.00 (*0-536-57907-5*) Pearson Custom.

Peltier, Jerome. Antoine Plante: Mountain Man, Rancher, Miner, Guide, Hosteler & Ferryman. 1983. 9.95 (*0-87770-286-1*) Ye Galleon.

— Black Harris. 158p. 1986. 19.95 (*0-87770-388-4*) Ye Galleon.

— A Brief History of the Coeur d'Alene Indians, 1806-1909. 94p. 1987. pap. 8.95 (*0-87770-256-X*) Ye Galleon.

— Felix Warren, Pioneer Stage Driver. 66p. 1988. pap. 5.95 (*0-87770-441-4*) Ye Galleon.

— The Fur Trade Was Equitable. 53p. 1991. pap. 9.95 (*0-87770-503-8*) Ye Galleon.

— Madame Dorion. 44p. 1981. pap. 6.95 (*0-87770-240-3*) Ye Galleon.

— Northwest History: Articles from the Pacific Northwest Quarterly. LC 96-52910. 1996. pap. 14.95 (*0-87770-602-6*) Ye Galleon.

Peltier, Jerome, ed. Banditti of the Rockies: And Vigilance Committee in Idaho. 1964. 15.00 (*0-87018-048-7*) Ross.

— Journal of Edward Cavileer Hinde. 84p. 1983. 15.95 (*0-87770-313-2*) Ye Galleon.

***Peltier, Jerome, ed.** Ratification of Coeur d'Alene Indian Treaties. 117p. 1999. reprint ed. pap. 10.95 (*0-87770-689-1*) Ye Galleon.

Peltier, Leonard. Prison Writings: My Life is My Sun Dance. 2nd ed. Arden, Harvey, ed. LC 99-21283. 256p. 1999. text 23.95 (*0-312-20354-3*) St Martin.

Peltier, Leonard F. Fractures: A History & Iconography of Their Treatment. (Illus.). 273p. 1990. 225.00 (*0-930405-16-1*) Norman SF.

— Orthopedics: A History & Iconography. (Illus.). 305p. 1993. 225.00 (*0-930405-47-1*) Norman SF.

***Peltier, Leonard F. & Arden, Harvey.** Prison Writings: My Life is My Sun Dance. (Illus.). 272p. 2000. pap. 13.95 (*0-312-26380-5*, St Martin Griffin) St Martin.

Peltier, Leonard F. & Aust, J. Bradley. L' Etoile du Nord: An Account of Owen Harding Wangensteen (1898-1981), Surgeon-Teacher-Scholar. LC 94-78654. (Illus.). 165p. (Orig.). 1994. pap. text 20.00 (*1-880696-07-X*) Am Coll Surgeons.

Peltier, Leslie. Binocular Stargazer: A Beginner's Guide to Exploring the Sky. 160p. 1995. per. 19.95 (*0-913135-25-9*, 18544) Kalmbach.

***Peltier, Leslie C.** Starlight Nights: The Adventures of a Star-Gazer. LC 99-46982. 240p. 1999. write for info. (*0-933346-94-8*) Sky Pub.

Peltier, Thomas R. Information Security Policies & Procedures: A Practitioner's Reference. LC 98-44238. 20p. 1998. lib. bdg. 245.00 (*0-8493-9996-3*) CRC Pr.

Peltier, W. Richard. Mantle Convection: Plate Tectonics & Global Dynamics, Vol. 4. viii, 882p. 1989. text 383.00 (*0-677-22120-7*) Gordon & Breach.

Peltier, W. Richard, ed. Ice in the Climate System. LC 93-29039. (NATO ASI Series I: Global Environmental Change: Vol. 12). 1994. 310.95 (*0-387-57167-1*) Spr-Verlag.

— Mantle Convection: Plate Tectonics & Global Dynamics. 882p. 1988. 198.00 (*0-677-22102-9*) Gordon & Breach.

Pelto, Pertti J., et al, eds. Listening to Women Talk about Their Health: Issues & Evidence from India. (C). 1994. text 34.00 (*81-241-0274-0*, Pub. by Har-Anand Pubns) S Asia.

Pelton. Marketing Channels. 2nd ed. 1999. 67.50 (*0-07-289512-8*) McGraw.

Pelton, Alan, et al. Proceedings of the 2nd International Conference on Shape Memory & Superelastic Technologies (SMST-97) 636p. (C). 1997. 100.00 (*0-9660508-1-9*) MIAS.

Pelton, Alan R., et al. Proceedings of the 1st International Conference on Shape Memory & Superelastic Technologies (SMST-94) 527p. (C). 1995. 100.00 (*0-9645943-0-7*) MIAS.

Pelton, Albert L. Creed of the Conquering Chief an Experiment in Psychology (1917) 60p. 1998. reprint ed. pap. 7.95 (*0-7661-0628-4*) Kessinger Pub.

Pelton, Barry C. Tennis Edition. 4th ed. (Physical Activities Ser.). (C). 1986. 15.00 (*0-673-16665-1*) Addson-Wesley Educ.

Pelton, Charles L. Doctor, My Bill Is Too High. (Illus.). 1978. 18.00 (*0-931470-01-3*); pap. 14.95 (*0-931470-00-5*) Fam Health Media.

— How to Get Rid of Fat. 45p. 1986. pap. 5.00 (*0-931470-02-1*) Fam Health Media.

— The Sex Book for Those Who Think They Know It All. Klinkel, Sheryl, ed. (Illus.). 227p. 1980. pap. 14.95 (*0-931470-04-8*); lib. bdg. 24.95 (*0-931470-03-X*) Fam Health Media.

Pelton, Charles L. & Myers, Lois. How to Emotionally Survive Difficult Times. 103p. 1986. pap. 6.00 (*0-931470-07-2*) Fam Health Media.

Pelton, Charles L. & Myers-Pelton, Lois. Pelton Family in America: 375 Years of Genealogy. 1167p. 1992. lib. bdg. 84.95 (*0-931470-10-2*) Fam Health Media.

Pelton, Dan. God Invented Safe Sex: He Created Families. Pelton, Jeanette, ed. 50p. (Orig.). 1993. pap. 5.00 (*1-879564-03-3*) Long Acre Pub.

Pelton, Dan, ed. see Pelton, Jeanette.

Pelton, Dan, ed. see Pelton, Jeanette & Pelton, Fawn.

Pelton, Donald. My Love for You. (Illus.). 1984. pap. 5.95 (*0-933169-00-0*) Heldon Pr.

— My Sense of Self. (Illus.). 1984. pap. 7.95 (*0-933169-01-9*) Heldon Pr.

— Spiritual Quest: Variations on a Theme. (Illus.). (Orig.). 1986. pap. 8.95 (*0-933169-02-7*) Heldon Pr.

Pelton, Fawn, jt. auth. see Pelton, Jeanette.

Pelton, Howard K. Noise Control Management. (Industrial Health & Safety Ser.). 267p. 1992. 89.95 (*0-471-28433-5*, VNR) Wiley.

Pelton, Howard K. Noise Control Management. LC 92-18950. 288p. 1993. text 70.95 (*0-442-00763-9*, VNR) Wiley.

Pelton, J. M. Genealogy of the Pelton Family in America, Being a Record of the Descendants of John Pelton, Who Settled in Boston about 1630-1632. (Illus.). 722p. 1989. reprint ed. pap. 113.00 (*0-8328-0951-9*); reprint ed. lib. bdg. 121.00 (*0-8328-0950-0*) Higginson Bk Co.

Pelton, Jeanette. Don't Call Me Emmy! 94p. (J). (gr. 5-8). 1991. pap. 3.50 (*1-879564-02-5*) Long Acre Pub.

— Folks I Wish I'd Known. Pelton, Dan, ed. (Illus.). 75p. (J). (gr. 5-8). 1993. pap. 4.00 (*1-879564-05-X*) Long Acre Pub.

— God Wanted to Write a Best Seller, So in the Beginning Was the Word. LC 91-90003. 52p. (YA). (gr. 6 up). 1991. pap. 5.95 (*1-879564-00-9*, GWBS101) Long Acre Pub.

— Kids Grow in My Garden. LC 91-90004. (Growing with God Ser.: No. I). (Illus.). 88p. (J). (gr. 4-6). 1991. pap. 3.50 (*1-879564-01-7*, GWG1) Long Acre Pub.

— Natural Morning. Pelton, Dan, ed. (Illus.). 100p. (Orig.). (J). (gr. 5-7). 1993. pap. 6.00 (*1-879564-06-8*) Long Acre Pub.

Pelton, Jeanette & Pelton, Fawn. Crafts for a Long, Boring, What-Do-I-Do-Now Afternoon. Pelton, Dan, ed. (Illus.). 50p. (Orig.). (J). (gr. 4-7). 1993. pap. 4.00 (*1-879564-04-1*) Long Acre Pub.

Pelton, Jeanette, ed. see Pelton, Dan.

Pelton, Jeffrey J., jt. auth. see Murphy, Kent R.

Pelton, John T., jt. ed. see Huggins, John P.

Pelton, Joseph N. Cyberspace Chronicles. (C). 2001. 24.95 (*0-13-594748-0*) P-H.

***Pelton, Joseph N.** e-Sphere: The Rise of the World-Wide Mind. LC 00-25251. 250p. 2000. 67.00 (*1-56720-390-6*, Q390, Quorum Bks) Greenwood.

Pelton, Joseph N. Future Talk. (Illus.). 300p. 1990. pap. 24.95 (*0-685-34870-9*) Smith Micro.

— Futuretalk. 1991. pap. 19.95 (*0-923426-90-6*) Smith Micro.

— Global Communications Satellite Policy: INTELSAT, Politics & Functionalism. LC 74-77978. 183p. 1974. 24.50 (*0-912338-32-6*); fiche 11.50 (*0-912338-33-4*) Lomond.

— The Satellite Revolution: The Shift to Direct Consumer Access & Mass Markets. (Illus.). 1998. pap. 1295.00 (*0-933217-42-0*) Prof Educ Intl.

— Wireless & Satellite Telecommunications: The Technology, the Market & the Regulations. 2nd ed. LC 95-7049. (Digital & Wireless Communication Ser.). 400p. (C). 1995. 84.00 (*0-13-140493-8*) P-H.

— The Wireless Industry & the Coming Personal Communications Services Revolution. (Illus.). 300p. 1997. pap. 995.00 (*0-933217-30-7*) Prof Educ Intl.

Pelton, Joseph N., jt. ed. see Edelson, Burton I.

Pelton, Leroy H. Doing Justice: Liberalism, Group Constructs, & Individual Realities. LC 98-39113. (SUNY Series in Deviance & Social Control). 288p. (C). 1999. text 65.50 (*0-7914-4179-2*); pap. text 21.95 (*0-7914-4180-6*) State U NY Pr.

Pelton, Leroy H., ed. The Social Context of Child Abuse & Neglect. LC 80-13922. 331p. 1981. 45.95 (*0-87705-504-1*, Kluwer Acad Hman Sci) Kluwer Academic.

Pelton, Leroy J. For Reasons of Poverty: A Critical Analysis of the Public Child Welfare System in the United States. LC 89-33968. 220p. 1989. 55.00 (*0-275-93073-4*, C3073, Praeger Pubs) Greenwood.

Pelton, Linda. The Hatha Yoga Workbook. 224p. (Orig.). 1989. pap. 6.95 (*0-931454-15-8*) Timeless Bks.

Pelton, Lou E. & Strutton, David. Channels Management: A Relationship Marketing Approach. 864p. (C). 1996. text 71.95 (*0-256-17802-X*, Irwn McGrw-H) McGrw-H Hghr Educ.

Pelton, Mary H. Reading Is Not a Spectator Sport. (Illus.). xix, 264p. 1993. pap. text 23.00 (*1-56308-118-0*) Teacher Ideas Pr.

Pelton, Mary H. & DiGennaro, Jacqueline. Images of a People: Tlingit Myths & Legends. LC 92-20564. (World Folklore Ser.). (Illus.). xvii, 170p. 1992. lib. bdg. 22.00 (*0-87287-918-6*) Libs Unl.

Pelton, Mary H., jt. auth. see Kinghorn, Harriet R.

Pelton, Mimi, ed. see D'Aquila, Ignatus.

Pelton, Robert. Circling the Sun: Meditations on Christ in Liturgy & Time. 1986. 13.95 (*0-912405-14-7*, Pastoral Press) OR Catholic.

— Complete Book of Voodoo. 1999. pap. 17.95 (*0-942272-51-X*) Original Pubns.

— Complete Book of White Magic. 1998. pap. 5.95 (*0-942272-53-6*) Original Pubns.

Pelton, Robert. Legal Lunacies 1996. 13.95 (*0-939251-50-7*) Accord CO.

Pelton, Robert. Voodoo Charms & Talismans. 148p. 1997. pap. 8.95 (*0-942272-50-1*) Original Pubns.

Pelton, Robert D. The Trickster in West Africa: A Study of Mythic Irony & Sacred Delight. LC 77-75396. (Hermeneutics: Studies in the History of Religions: No. 8). 1980. pap. 15.95 (*0-520-06791-6*, Pub. by U CA Pr) Cal Prin Full Svc.

Pelton, Robert S. From Power to Communion: Toward a New Way of Being Church Based on the Latin American Experience. LC 93-40435. (C). 1994. text 25.50 (*0-268-00989-9*); pap. text 14.00 (*0-268-00990-2*) U of Notre Dame Pr.

— Small Christian Communities: Imagining Future Church. LC 97-34882. 1997. pap. 14.00 (*0-268-01761-1*) U of Notre Dame Pr.

Pelton, Robert W. Dead or Alive? LC 92-90483. 208p. (Orig.). 1993. pap. 11.95 (*0-918751-31-4*) Delta Pr.

— X-Rated Media Bloopers & Messups: A Choice Collection of Sexy Newsworthy Boners. LC 93-74665. 120p. (Orig.). 1994. pap. 10.00 (*0-918751-38-1*, 38) Delta Pr.

Pelton, Robert W., jt. auth. see Lynn, Kristie.

Pelton, Robert Y. Fielding's Hot Spots: Travel in Harm's Way. Knoles, Kathy, ed. (Illus.). 256p. 1997. pap. 16.95 (*1-56952-166-2*) Fielding Wrldwide.

— Fielding's Indiana Jones Adventure & Survival Guide. Knoles, Kathy, ed. (Illus.). 256p. 1998. pap. 15.95 (*1-56952-144-1*) Fielding Wrldwide.

— Fielding's Los Angeles. 1996. pap. text 16.95 (*1-56952-117-4*) Fielding Wrldwide.

— Fielding's the World's Most Dangerous Places. Knoles, Kathy, ed. (Illus.). 1048p. 1997. pap. 21.95 (*1-56952-140-9*) Fielding Wrldwide.

***Pelton, Robert Young.** The Adventurist: My Life in Dangerous Places. LC 99-87243. (Illus.). 352p. 2000. 24.95 (*0-385-49567-6*) Doubleday.

***Pelton, Robert Young, et al.** The World's Most Dangerous Places, 4th ed. LC 99-56716. (Illus.). 1040p. 2000. pap. 21.95 (*0-06-273738-4*, HarpRes) HarpInfo.

***Pelton, Ross.** The Nutritional Cost of Prescription Drugs. Lavalle, James B., ed. 262p. 2000. pap. 14.95 (*0-89582-548-1*) Morton Pub.

Pelton, Ross & Overholser, Lee C. Alternatives in Cancer Therapy: The Complete Guide to Current Alternative Treatments. LC 93-30140. 304p. 1994. pap. 12.00 (*0-671-79623-2*, Fireside) S&S Trade Pap.

Pelton, Ross & Pelton, Taffy C. Mind Food & Smart Pills: A Sourcebook for the Vitamins, Herbs & Drugs That Can Increase Intelligence, Improve Memory & Prevent Brain Aging. 336p. 1989. pap. 13.95 (*0-385-26138-1*) Doubleday.

Pelton, Ross, et al. How to Prevent Breast Cancer. 352p. 1995. pap. 13.00 (*0-684-80022-5*, Fireside) S&S Trade Pap.

Pelton, Ross R. Mind Food & Smart Pills. 1989. mass mkt. 13.95 (*0-385-26139-X*) Doubleday.

Pelton, Sonya T. Awake Savage Heart. 1983. mass mkt. 3.75 (*0-8217-1279-9*, Zebra Kensgtn) Kensgtn Pub Corp.

— Forbidden Dawn. 1985. mass mkt. 3.75 (*0-8217-1602-6*, Zebra Kensgtn) Kensgtn Pub Corp.

— Love Hear My Heart. 1990. mass mkt. 4.50 (*0-8217-2913-6*, Zebra Kensgtn) Kensgtn Pub Corp.

— Passion's Paradise. 544p. (Orig.). 1981. mass mkt. 3.25 (*0-89083-765-1*, Zebra Kensgtn) Kensgtn Pub Corp.

— Phantom Love. (Orig.). 1982. mass mkt. 3.50 (*0-89083-950-6*, Zebra Kensgtn) Kensgtn Pub Corp.

— Wild Island Sands. 1983. mass mkt. 3.75 (*0-8217-1135-0*, Zebra Kensgtn) Kensgtn Pub Corp.

Pelton, Taffy C., jt. auth. see Pelton, Ross.

Pelton, Walter J., et al. Epidemiology of Oral Health. LC 77-88811. (Vital & Health Statistics Monographs, American Public Health Association). (Illus.). 189p. 1969. 27.50 (*0-674-25885-1*) HUP.

Peltonen, K., et al, eds. Butadiene & Styrene: Assessment of Health Hazard. (IARC Scientific Publications: No. 127). (Illus.). 424p. 1994. pap. text 95.00 (*92-832-2127-3*) OUP.

Peltonen, Markku. Classical Humanism & Republicanism in English Political Thought 1570-1640. (Ideas in Context Ser.: No. 36). 371p. (C). 1995. text 69.95 (*0-521-49695-0*) Cambridge U Pr.

Peltonen, Markku, ed. The Cambridge Companion to Bacon. (Companions to Philosophy Ser.). 387p. (C). 1996. text 64.95 (*0-521-43498-X*); pap. text 20.95 (*0-521-43534-X*) Cambridge U Pr.

Peltonen, S. Teitotekniikan Artikkelisanakirja. (FIN.). 276p. 1985. 195.00 (*0-8288-1368-X*, M 356) Fr & Eur.

Peltre, Christine. Orientalism in Art. LC 98-28579. (Illus.). 295p. 1998. 95.00 (*0-7892-0459-2*) Abbeville Pr.

Peltre, G., jt. auth. see Paraf, A.

Pelts, Roman & Alburt, Lev. Comprehensive Chess Course Vol. 1: Learn Chess in 12 Lesssons. 4th ed. (Comprehensive Chess Course). (Illus.). 144p. 1996. pap. 16.95 (*1-889323-00-4*) L Alburt.

— Comprehensive Chess Course Vol. 2: From Beginner to Tournament Player. 4th ed. LC 96-85860. (Comprehensive Chess Course). (Illus.). 320p. (Orig.). 1996. pap. 28.95 (*1-889323-01-2*) L Alburt.

Peltsman, Michael, see Armalinskii, Mikhail, pseud.

Peltsman, Michael, ed. see Armalinskii, Mikhail, pseud.

Pelttari, Carole. Amos Fortune, Free Man Study Guide. 66p. (J). (gr. 5-7). 1996. student ed., ring bd. 12.99 (*1-58609-147-6*) Progeny Pr WI.

— Bridge to Terabithia Study Guide. 52p. (YA). (gr. 6-8). 1996. student ed., ring bd. 12.99 (*1-58609-148-4*) Progeny Pr WI.

— The Bronze Bow Study Guide. 68p. (YA). (gr. 6-8). 1996. student ed., ring bd. 12.99 (*1-58609-145-X*) Progeny Pr WI.

— Carry On, Mr. Bowditch Study Guide. 64p. (J). (gr. 5-7). 1995. student ed., ring bd. 12.99 (*1-58609-142-5*) Progeny Pr WI.

Peltu, Malcolm, jt. auth. see Otway, Harry J.

Peltz, jt. auth. see Shapiro.

Peltz, Carl F. Walking in the Kingdom of God: A Lenten Meditation for the Busy Christian. LC 96-128274. 80p. (Orig.). 1994. pap. 4.95 (*0-8146-2256-9*, Liturg Pr Bks) Liturgical Pr.

— Walking in the Kingdom of God: An Advent Meditation for the Busy Christian. 48p. (Orig.). (C). 1993. pap. 3.95 (*0-8146-2238-0*) Liturgical Pr.

Peltz, Diane, ed. see Kommedahl, Thor.

Peltz, Donna E. Gifts from a Healing Heart. (Illus.). 100p. 1998. pap. 9.95 (*0-9667266-0-X*) Harmony Pr OH.

Peltz, Leslie R. Fashion Accessories. LC 74-10891. 1974. teacher ed. 5.00 (*0-672-96411-2*, Bobbs); pap. text 8.50 (*0-672-96109-1*, Bobbs) Macmillan.

— Fashion Accessories. 2nd ed. 1980. pap. write for info. (*0-672-97275-1*) Macmillan.

— Fashion Color, Line & Design. LC 79-142515. 1971. teacher ed. 5.00 (*0-672-96057-5*, Bobbs); pap. text 9.90 (*0-672-96056-7*, Bobbs) Macmillan.

— Fashion, Color, Line & Design. 2nd ed. 1980. write for info. (*0-672-97277-8*); teacher ed. write for info. (*0-672-97278-6*) Macmillan.

— Merchandising Mathematics. LC 79-494. 1979. pap. 9.49 (*0-672-97273-5*) Macmillan.

Peltz, Lucy, jt. ed. see Myrone, Martin.

Peltz, Mary E., jt. auth. see Goldovsky, Boris.

Peltz, Rakhmiel. From Immigrant to Ethnic Culture: American Yiddish in South Philadelphia. LC 97-11999. (Studies in Jewish History & Culture). 1998. write for info. (*0-8047-3020-2*) Stanford U Pr.

— From Immigrant to Ethnic Culture: American Yiddish in South Philadelphia. LC 97-11999. (Studies in Jewish History & Culture). (Illus.). 350p. 1998. pap. 18.95 (*0-8047-3167-5*) Stanford U Pr.

Peltzer, Gerard R., jt. auth. see Glackin, David L.

Peltzer, Karl. Enzyklopaedisches Handbuch der Werbung und Publikation, Vol. 1. (GER.). 1961. 49.95 (*0-8288-6821-2*, M-7081) Fr & Eur.

— Enzyklopaedisches Handbuch der Werbung und Publikation, Vol. 2. (GER.). 1963. 49.95 (*0-8288-6790-9*, M-7082) Fr & Eur.

— Das Treffende Reim. 7th ed. (GER.). 148p. 1993. 39.95 (*0-7859-8690-1*, 372256123x) Fr & Eur.

— Das Treffende Wort. 23rd ed. (GER.). 792696p. 1993. 75.00 (*0-8288-1980-7*, M15518) Fr & Eur.

Peltzman. Political Participation Goverment. LC 98-14276. 1998. pap. text 22.00 (*0-226-65417-6*) U Ch Pr.

— Political Participation Government. LC 98-14276. 1998. lib. bdg. 60.00 (*0-226-65416-8*) U Ch Pr.

Peltzman, Adam. Blue's Big Pajama Party. LC 99-71057. (Blue's Clues Ser.). (Illus.). 24p. (J). (ps-2). 1999. pap. 9.99 (*0-689-82896-9*, Simon Spot) Litle Simon.

— It's Spring Blue! 16p. (gr. k-3). 2000. pap. 3.99 (*0-689-83097-1*) S&S Trade.

Peltzman, Barbara R. Pioneers of Early Childhood Education. (Source Books on Education). Date not set. text 40.00 (*0-8153-0032-8*) Garland.

— Pioneers of Early Childhood Education: A Bio-Bibliographical Guide. LC 97-26907. 160p. 1998. lib. bdg. 65.00 (*0-313-30404-1*, Greenwood Pr) Greenwood.

Peltzman, Sam, jt. ed. see Fiorentini, Gianluca.

***Pelucir, Talis.** The Gillian Anderson Internet Guide. 50p. 1999. pap. 10.00 (*1-883573-24-6*, Lightning Rod) Pride & Imprints.

— The Men of Star Trek Internet Guide. 50p. 2000. pap. 10.00 (*1-883573-30-0*, Lightning Rod) Pride & Imprints.

Pelucir, Talis. The Sandra Bullock Internet Guide. 50p. 1999. pap. 10.00 (*1-883573-10-6*, Lightning Rod) Pride & Imprints.

***Pelucir, Talis.** The Unofficial Blair Witch Project Internet Guide. 40p. 2000. pap. 10.00 (*1-886383-48-0*, Lightning Rod) Pride & Imprints.

— The Unofficial Buffy the Vampire Slayer New & Improved Internet Guide. 40p. 1999. pap. 10.00 (*1-883573-48-3*, Lightning Rod) Pride & Imprints.

— The Unofficial Farscape Episode & Internet Guide. 60p. 1999. pap. 12.95 (*1-883573-47-5*, Lightning Rod) Pride & Imprints.

— The Unofficial Farscape Episode & Internet Guide Seasons 1 & 2. 80p. 2000. pap. 14.95 (*1-883573-55-6*, Lightning Rod) Pride & Imprints.

— The Unofficial Farscape Episode Guide Supplement Season 2. 40p. 2000. pap., suppl. ed. 12.95 (*1-883573-56-4*, Lightning Rod) Pride & Imprints.

Pelucir, Talis. The Unofficial Pokemon Internet Guide. 50p. 1999. pap. 10.00 (*1-883573-11-4*, Lightning Rod) Pride & Imprints.

— The Unofficial Star Trek Deep Space Nine Internet Guide. 50p. 2000. pap. 10.00 (*1-883573-28-9*, Lightning Rod) Pride & Imprints.

— The Unofficial X-Files Internet Guide. 50p. 1999. pap. 10.00 (*1-883573-27-0*, Lightning Rod) Pride & Imprints.

***Pelucir, Talis.** The Women of Star Trek Internet Guide. 50p. 2000. pap. 10.00 (*1-883573-29-7*, Lightning Rod) Pride & Imprints.

Peluffo, Ana Luisa, tr. see McGovern, Ann.

***Pelupessy, Wim.** Agrarian Policies in Central America. LC 99-33838. 2000. text 69.95 (*0-312-22426-5*) St Martin.

Pelupessy, Wim. The Limits of Economic Reform in El Salvador. LC 96-49057. 256p. 1997. text 69.95 (*0-312-17323-7*) St Martin.

Peluso, Angelo. Tia, the Story of a Mouse & an Eagle. LC 97-75073. (Illus.). 40p. (J). (gr. k up). 1997. pap. 8.95 (*0-9646576-3-5*) Cherubic Pr.

Peluso, Anthony P., et al. Basic BASIC Programming: Self-Instructional Manual & Text. (Computer Science Ser.). (C). 1971. pap. write for info. (*0-201-05845-6*) Addison-Wesley.

Peluso, Emanuel. Good Day. 1966. pap. 3.25 (*0-8222-0461-4*) Dramatists Play.

— Hurricane of the Eye. 1969. pap. 3.25 (*0-8222-0544-0*) Dramatists Play.

— Little Fears. 1967. pap. 3.25 (*0-8222-0675-7*) Dramatists Play.

Peluso, Gary, jt. auth. see Portaro, Sam.

Peluso, Luigi A., jt. auth. see Recardo, Ronald J.

Peluso, Nancy L. Rich Forests, Poor People: Resource Control & Resistance in Java. 1992. pap. 17.95 (*0-520-08931-6*, Pub. by U CA Pr) Cal Prin Full Svc.

P

An Asterisk (*) at the beginning of an entry indicates that the title is appearing for the first time.

— Rich Forests, Poor People: Resource Control & Resistance in Java. 336p. (C). 1992. 55.00 (*0-520-07377-0*, Pub. by U CA Pr) Cal Prin Full Svc.

Peluso, Nancy L., jt. ed. see Padoch, Christine.

Peluso, Samuel L. To Live & Die with Dignity: A Guide to Living Wills. Diecker, Mary L., ed. LC 91-75021. (Illus.). 160p. 1991. pap. 19.95 (*1-880254-01-8*) Vista.

Peluso, Vincenzo, et al. Design of Low-voltage Low-power Cmos [delta Sigma] A/d Converters / LC 98-51572. (Analog Circuits & Signal Processingineering & Computer Science Ser.). 22p. 1999. write for info. (*0-7923-8417-2*) Kluwer Academic.

Pelyas, Istvan, jt. ed. see Gyordydeak, Zoltan.

Pelyvas, Peter. Subjectivity in English: Generative Grammar vs. the Cognitive Theory of Epistemic Grounding. LC 96-7171. (MetaLinguistica Ser.: Bd. 3). (Illus.). 208p. 1996. pap. 42.95 (*0-8204-2955-4*, PE1369) P Lang Pubng.

— Subjectivity in English: Generative Grammar vs. the Cognitive Theory of Epistemic Grounding. Kertesz, Andras, ed. LC 96-7171. (Metalinguistica, Debrecen Studies in Linguistics: Vol. 3). (Illus.). 208p. 1996. 42.95 (*3-631-49534-X*) P Lang Pubng.

Pelz, Bruce, ed. see White, James.

***Pelz, Dave.** Dave Pelz's Putting Bible. (Illus.). 320p. 2000. 30.00 (*0-385-50024-6*) Doubleday.

***Pelz, Dave & Frank, James A.** Dave Pelz's Putting Bible: The Complete Guide to Mastering the Green. LC 00-39773. (Dave Pelz Scoring Game Ser.). 2000. write for info. (*0-7679-0345-5*) Broadway BDD.

Pelz, Dave & Mastroni, Nick. Putt Like the Pros: Dave Pelz's Scientific Way to Improve Your Stroke Reading the Greens, & Lowering Your Score. LC 86-46095. (Illus.). 240p. 1991. reprint ed. pap. 15.00 (*0-06-092078-5*, Perennial) HarperTrade.

Pelz, G. C., jt. ed. see Winnewisser, G.

***Pelz, Manfred.** Sprachbegegnung und Begegnungssprache: Zur Experimentellen Untersuchung des Programms Lerne die Sprache des Nachbarn. (Freiburger Beitrage Zur Erziehungswissenschaft und Fachdidaktik Ser.). vii, 323p. 1999. 48.95 (*3-631-34163-6*) P Lang Pubng.

Pelz, R. B., et al, eds. Parallel Computational Fluid Dynamics, '92: Proceedings of the Conference on Parallel CFD '92 - Implementations & Results Using Parallel Computers, New Brunswick, NJ, 18-20 May, 1992. LC 93-16448. 438p. 1993. 177.25 (*0-444-89986-3*, North Holland) Elsevier.

Pelz, Ruth. Black Heroes of the Wild West. LC 89-63500. (Illus.). (gr. 4-12). 1989. 12.95 (*0-940880-25-3*); pap. 6.95 (*0-940880-26-1*) Open Hand.

— Women of the Wild West: Biographies from Many Cultures. (Contributions Ser.). (Illus.). 64p. (Orig.). (J). (gr. 4 up). 1994. pap. text 6.95 (*0-940880-50-4*) Open Hand.

Pelz, Stephen E. Race to Pearl Harbor: The Failure of the Second London Naval Conference & the Onset of World War II. LC 73-89711. (Studies in American-East Asian Relations: No. 5). 416p. 1974. text 25.50 (*0-685-02135-1*) HUP.

Pelz, William. Basic Keyboard Skills: An Introduction to Accompaniment Improvisation, Transposition & Modulation, with an Appendix on Sight Reading. LC 80-22820. 173p. 1981. reprint ed. lib. bdg. 38.50 (*0-313-22882-5*, PEBK) Greenwood.

— Wilhelm Liebknecht & German Social Collections: A Documentary History. Hahn, Erich, tr. LC 93-31636. (Documentary Reference Collections). 480p. 1994. lib. bdg. 105.00 (*0-313-28200-5*, Greenwood Pr) Greenwood.

Pelz, William A. The Spartakusbund & the German Working Class Movement, 1914-1919. LC 87-5637. (Studies in German Thought & History: Vol. 1). (Illus.). 423p. 1987. lib. bdg. 109.95 (*0-88946-355-7*) E Mellen.

Pelzel, Suzanne, tr. & rev. see Voss, Hermann.

Pelzel, Thomas, jt. auth. see Barkin, Kenneth.

Pelzer, Birgit, et al. Michael Asher. 96p. Date not set. 32.00 (*3-85780-104-2*) Kunsthalle Bern.

Pelzer, Birgit, text see Richter, Gerhard.

Pelzer, Chris, jt. prod. see Brown, Jeff.

Pelzer, Dave. A Child Called "It" One Child's Courage to Survive. 195p. (Orig.). 1995. pap. 9.95 (*1-55874-366-9*, 3669) Health Comm.

***Pelzer, Dave.** Help Yourself: Celebrating the Daily Rewards of Resilience & Gratitude. 320p. 2000. 21.95 (*0-525-94557-1*, Dutt) Dutton Plume.

Pelzer, Dave. The Lost Boy: A Foster Child's Search for the Love of a Family. LC 97-17614. 250p. 1997. pap. 10.95 (*1-55874-515-7*) Health Comm.

— The Lost Boy: A Foster Child's Search for the Love of a Family. 3 Vols., Vol. 2. LC 94-66665. 190p. 1994. pap. text 10.00 (*0-929099-03-6*) Omaha Pr Pub.

— A Man Named Dave: A Story of Triumph & Forgiveness. LC 99-38433. 288p. 1999. 19.95 (*0-525-94521-0*, Dutt) Dutton Plume.

***Pelzer, Dave.** A Man Named Dave: A Story of Triumph & Forgiveness. large type ed. LC 99-86695. 2000. 26.95 (*1-56895-842-0*) Wheeler Pub.

— A Man Named Dave: A Story of Triumph & Forgiveness. 2000. reprint ed. pap. 11.00 (*0-452-28190-3*) Penguin Books.

Pelzer, David J. Structure, Function & Modulation of Striated Muscle Calcium Channels. (Molecular Biology Intelligence Unit Ser.). 115p. 1994. 89.95 (*1-57059-057-5*) CRC Pr.

Pelzer, Karl J. Pioneer Settlement in the Asiatic Tropics: Studies in Land Utilization & Agricultural Colonization in Southeastern Asia, 29. LC 83-1484. (American Geographical Society Ser.-Special publication). (Illus.). 288p. 1983. reprint ed. lib. bdg. 65.00 (*0-313-23853-7*, PEPI) Greenwood.

— West Malaysia & Singapore: A Selected Bibliography. LC 72-87853. (Bibliographies Ser.). 400p. 1971. 30.00 (*0-87536-235-4*) HRAFP.

Pelzer, Linda C. Erich Segal. LC 96-53849. (Critical Companions to Popular Contemporary Writers Ser.). 160p. 1997. 29.95 (*0-313-29930-7*, Greenwood Pr) Greenwood.

— Mary Higgins Clark: A Critical Companion. LC 95-4660. (Critical Companions to Popular Contemporary Writers Ser.). 192p. 1995. 29.95 (*0-313-29413-5*, Greenwood Pr) Greenwood.

***Pelzer, Linda C.** Student Companion to F. Scott Fitzgerald. LC 99-462058. (Student Companions to Classic Writers Ser.). 184p. 2000. 29.95 (*0-313-30594-3*, GR0594, Greenwood Pr) Greenwood.

Pelzer, Louis. Marches of the Dragoons in the Mississippi Valley, 1833-1850. LC 75-116. (Mid-American Frontier Ser.). 1975. reprint ed. 26.95 (*0-405-06882-4*) Ayer.

Pelzer, Louis, ed. & intro. see Carleton, James H.

Pelzer, Peter. Der Proze der Organisation. 194p. 1995. text 81.00 (*3-7186-5773-2*, Harwood Acad Pubs); pap. text 40.00 (*3-7186-5703-1*, Harwood Acad Pubs) Gordon & Breach.

Pelzer, Trudy, jt. auth. see Gulutzan, Peter.

Pelzl, J., jt. ed. see Hess, P.

Pelzmann, Joy & Rosoff, Myrna. Decisions to Make Paths to Take: A Guide for Caregivers. LC 97-94562. 170p. 1997. pap. 13.95 (*0-9661189-0-1*) Decision Pr.

Pema, Jetsun. Tibet: My Story: An Autobiography. LC 97-18273. (Illus.). 304p. 1997. 24.95 (*1-86204-124-5*, Pub. by Element MA) Penguin Putnam.

— Tibet: My Story: An Autobiography. (Illus.). 275p. 1999. pap. 14.95 (*1-86204-361-2*, Pub. by Element MA) Penguin Putnam.

***PEMA Staff & Pennsafe Staff.** 2000 Hazard Communications Standard & Sara Title III. Pennsylvania Chamber of Business & Industry Educational Foundation Staff, ed. 381p. 1999. pap. 90.00 (*1-929744-05-6*) Penn Chamber of Bus.

Pemantle, Robin, jt. auth. see Aldous, David.

Pember. Mass Media Law. 9th ed. 1997. 16.00 (*0-697-35370-2*) McGraw.

— Mass Media Law. 11th ed. 664p. 1999. pap. 58.75 (*0-07-230009-4*) McGraw.

***Pember, Ann.** Painting Close-Focus Flowers in Watercolor. LC 00-20370. (Illus.). 128p. 2000. 27.99 (*0-89134-947-2*) F & W Pubns Inc.

Pember, Don R. Mass Media Law. 10th ed. 664p. 1998. pap. 52.19 (*0-697-35371-0*); pap., student ed. 17.19 (*0-697-35372-9*) McGraw.

Pember, Donald R. Mass Media in America. 6th ed. LC 91-11193. (Illus.). 608p. (C). 1991. pap. text 67.00 (*0-02-393780-7*, Macmillan Coll) P-H.

— Mass Media Law. 7th ed. 656p. (C). 1995. text. write for info. (*0-697-24600-0*) Brown & Benchmark.

— Mass Media Law. 7th ed. 656p. (C). 1995. text, student ed. 16.87 (*0-697-24603-5*) Brown & Benchmark.

— Mass Media Law. 8th ed. 656p. (C). 1996. text. write for info. (*0-697-28904-4*) Brown & Benchmark.

— Mass Media Law. 9th ed. 672p. (C). 1997. per. write for info. (*0-697-32716-7*, WCB McGr Hill) McGrw-H Hghr Educ.

— Privacy & the Press: The Law, the Mass Media, & the First Amendment. LC 79-152335. (Washington Paperback Ser.: No. 64). (Illus.). 312p. 1972. reprint ed. pap. 10.00 (*0-295-95265-2*) U of Wash Pr.

Pember, Donald R. & Cohen, Jeremy. Mass Media Law. 8th ed. 128p. (C). 1996. text, student ed. 15.00 (*0-697-28906-0*) Brown & Benchmark.

Pember, G. H. Earth's Earliest Ages. LC 75-13928. 336p. 1975. pap. 14.99 (*0-8254-3533-1*, Kregel Class) Kregel.

Pember, Harry E. Sikorsky VS-44 Flying Boat. (Illus.). 72p. 1998. pap. 19.95 (*1-891268-02-3*) Flying Machines.

Pember, Phoebe Y. A Southern Woman's Story. Wiley, Bell I., ed. 242p. 1987. pap. 3.95 (*0-89176-024-5*, 6024, Mckingbird) R Bemis Pub.

Pemberton. Mathematics for Economists. 240p. Date not set. pap. 24.95 (*0-7190-3341-1*, Pub. by Manchester Univ Pr); text 79.95 (*0-7190-3340-3*, Pub. by Manchester Univ Pr) St Martin.

Pemberton, C., ed. Elizabeth, Queen of England: Queen Elizabeth's Englishings of Boethius. (EETS, OS Ser.: No. 113). 1972. reprint ed. 40.00 (*0-527-00113-9*) Periodicals Srv.

Pemberton, Carol. Writing Essays. LC 92-14216. 400p. 1992. pap. text 41.00 (*0-205-13986-8*) Allyn.

— Writing Paragraphs. 3rd ed. LC 96-13650. 254p. 1996. pap. text 35.00 (*0-205-26079-9*) Allyn.

— Writing Paragraphs. 3rd ed. 254p. (C). 1996. pap., teacher ed. write for info. (*0-205-26541-3*) Allyn.

Pemberton, Carol A. Lowell Mason: A Bio-Bibliography, 11. LC 87-37569. (Bio-Bibliographies in Music Ser.: No. 11). 219p. 1988. lib. bdg. 55.00 (*0-313-25881-3*, PLL/, Greenwood Pr) Greenwood.

***Pemberton, Carole.** Strike a New Career Deal: Build a Great Future in the Changing World of Work. rev. ed. (Career Tactics Ser.). 270p. 1998. pap. 40.00 (*0-273-63544-1*, Pub. by Pitman Pbg) Trans-Atl Phila.

Pemberton, Carole, jt. auth. see Herriot, Peter.

Pemberton, Caroline H. Stephen the Black. LC 72-1520. (Black Heritage Library Collection). 1977. reprint ed. 28.95 (*0-8369-9044-7*) Ayer.

Pemberton, Cintra. Soulfaring: Celtic Pilgrimage Then & Now. LC 99-23925. 240p. 1999. pap. 17.95 (*0-8192-1780-8*, 4896) Morehouse Pub.

***Pemberton, D., et al.** Managing Career Dilemmas. (Financial Times Management Briefings Ser.). 1998. pap. 94.50 (*0-273-63731-2*, Pub. by F T P-H) Trans-Atl Phila.

Pemberton, Deloras, jt. auth. see Pemberton, L. Beaty.

Pemberton, Elizabeth G. The Sanctuary of Demeter & Kore, the Greek Pottery. LC 89-15004. (Corinth Ser.: Vol. 18, Pt. 1). (Illus.). xx, 235p. 1989. 65.00 (*0-87661-181-1*) Am Sch Athens.

Pemberton, Gayle. The Hottest Water in Chicago: Notes of a Native Daughter. LC 97-42988. 280p. 1998. reprint ed. pap. 14.95 (*0-8195-6337-4*, Wesleyan Univ Pr) U Pr of New Eng.

Pemberton, Gregory, ed. see Edwards, Peter.

Pemberton, Gwen. Regarding Rita. (Love & Laughter Ser.: Vol. 49). 1998. per. 3.50 (*0-373-44049-9*, 1-44049-4) Harlequin Bks.

— Wooing Wanda, Vol. 30. (Love & Laughter Ser.). 1997. per. 3.50 (*0-373-44030-8*) Harlequin Bks.

Pemberton, Gwen, jt. auth. see Gabriel, Kristin.

Pemberton, H. Brent, et al. Production of Pot Roses. LC 96-27599. (Growers Handbook Ser.). 130p. 1997. 17.95 (*0-88192-379-6*) Timber.

Pemberton, Henry. Shakespeare & Sir Walter Raleigh. LC 76-174688. (Studies in Shakespeare: No. 24). 1971. reprint ed. lib. bdg. 75.00 (*0-8383-1340-X*) M S G Haskell Hse.

Pemberton, J. Michael & Prentice, Ann, eds. Information Science: The Interdisciplinary Context. 189p. (Orig.). 1990. pap. text 45.00 (*1-55570-048-9*) Neal-Schuman.

Pemberton, J. Michael, ed. see Ruffner, Henry.

Pemberton, Jane, jt. auth. see Dyck, Norma.

***Pemberton, John.** Insight & Artistry in African Divination. LC 99-59622. 2000. pap. 29.95 (*1-56098-884-3*) Smithsonian.

Pemberton, John. On the Subject of "Java" (Illus.). 320p. 1994. text 45.00 (*0-8014-2672-3*); pap. text 18.95 (*0-8014-9963-1*) Cornell U Pr.

***Pemberton, John, ed.** Insight & Artistry in African Divination. LC 99-59622. 2000. 65.00 (*1-56098-859-2*) Smithsonian.

Pemberton, John, III & Afolayan, Funso S. Yoruba Sacred Kingship: A Power Like That of the Gods. LC 95-26789. 256p. 1996. text 55.00 (*1-56098-631-X*) Smithsonian.

Pemberton, John, III, et al. The Artist's Eye, the Diviner's Insight: African Art in the Barry D. Maurer Collection. LC 98-14013. (Illus.). 43p. 1998. pap. 9.95 (*0-914337-20-3*) Mead Art Mus.

Pemberton, Judy. Let's Get Cooking. (Illus.). 103p. (Orig.). (J). (gr. 3-12). 1984. text 7.95 (*0-317-02695-X*) King Fisher Pr.

Pemberton, Kermit. Sport Marketing: The Money Side of Sports. Myfois, Kevin & Steele, DeAnn, eds. 344p. 1967. pap. 29.95 incl. VHS (*0-9656421-8-6*) Sports Servs.

— Sports Marketing: The Money Side of Sports. 330p. (Orig.). 1997. pap. 22.95 (*0-9656421-9-4*) Sports Servs.

— Sports Marketing: The Money Side of Sports (Educational Program; includes video "Famous People Sell Famous Products" & tapes "Media Attention with Sports Celebrity" & "Increase Profits, Motivate Customers, Employees & Distributors through Sports") 330p. 1997. pap. 177.50 incl. audio, VHS (*0-9656421-6-X*) Sports Servs.

Pemberton, L. Beaty & Pemberton, Deloras. Treatment of Water, Electrolyte, & Acid-Base Disorders in the Surgical Patient. 432p. 1993. pap. text 32.00 (*0-07-049363-4*) McGraw-Hill HPD.

Pemberton, L. Beaty, et al. Workbook of Surgical Anatomy. (Pretest Specialty Level Ser.). (Illus.). 320p. 1990. pap. text 45.00 (*0-07-049349-9*) McGraw-Hill HPD.

Pemberton, Larry, ed. Unto the Least of These: A Caring Church in a Hurting World. 146p. 1993. pap. 8.99 (*0-87148-936-8*) Pathway Pr.

Pemberton, LeRoy A., jt. auth. see Archer, E. C.

Pemberton, Loftus L. The Judgments & Orders of the High Court of Justice & Court of Appeal: Chiefly in Reference to Actions Assigned to the Chancery Division. 3rd ed. LC 97-77306. lix, 602p. 1998. reprint ed. 195.00 (*1-56169-356-1*, 15153) Gaunt.

Pemberton, Lyn, jt. auth. see Connolly, John H.

***Pemberton, Lynn, ed.** Words on the Web: Computer Mediated Communication. 128p. 2000. pap. 24.95 (*1-871516-56-0*, Pub. by Intellect) Intl Spec Bk.

***Pemberton, Margaret.** Coronation Summer. 2000. 29.95 (*0-593-03412-0*, Pub. by Transworld Publishers Ltd); pap. 10.95 (*0-552-14125-9*, Pub. by Transworld Publishers Ltd) Trafalgar.

— The Far Morning. large type ed. 496p. 1999. 31.99 (*0-7505-1407-8*, Pub. by Mgna Lrg Print) Ulverscroft.

Pemberton, Margaret. The Girl Who Knew Too Much. 192p. 24.00 (*0-7278-5211-6*) Severn Hse.

— The Girl Who Knew Too Much. large type ed. (Dales Large Print Ser.). 304p. 1998. pap. 19.99 (*1-85389-840-6*, Dales) Ulverscroft.

— The Last Letter. LC 99-490220. 192p. 1998. 22.00 (*0-7278-5325-2*) Severn Hse.

***Pemberton, Margaret.** Undying Love. 1999. 25.00 (*0-7278-5453-4*, Pub. by Severn Hse) Chivers N Amer.

— A Year to Eternity. 448p. 26.00 (*0-7278-5516-6*) Severn Hse.

Pemberton, Margaret. Yorkshire Rose. large type ed. (Magna Large Print Ser.). 526p. 1997. 27.99 (*0-7505-0772-1*) Ulverscroft.

Pemberton, Margaret A. Forever. large type ed. (Dales General Fiction Ser.). 293p. 1993. pap. 18.99 (*1-85389-419-2*, Dales) Ulverscroft.

— Forget-Me-Not-Bride. 1994. 20.00 (*0-7278-4703-1*) Severn Hse.

— Forget-Me-Not Bride. large type ed. 1996. 11.50 (*0-7505-0771-3*, Pub. by Mgna Lrg Print) Ulverscroft.

— The Guilty Secret. large type ed. 1996. pap. 18.99 (*1-85389-491-5*, Dales) Ulverscroft.

***Pemberton, Margaret A.** The Londoners. 2000. pap. 8.95 (*0-552-14123-2*, Pub. by Transworld Publishers Ltd) Trafalgar.

Pemberton, Margaret A. The Londoners. large type ed. (Magna Large Print Ser.). 675p. 1996. 27.99 (*0-7505-0907-4*, Pub. by Mgna Lrg Print) Ulverscroft.

— Moonflower Madness. large type ed. 386p. 1994. 27.99 (*0-7505-0588-5*, Pub. by Mgna Lrg Print) Ulverscroft.

— Party in Peking. large type ed. 319p. 1993. 27.99 (*0-7505-0464-1*, Pub. by Mgna Lrg Print) Ulverscroft.

— Rendezvous with Death. large type ed. (Dales Large Print Ser.). 1994. pap. 18.99 (*1-85389-493-1*, Pub. by Mgna Lrg Print) Ulverscroft.

— Tapestry of Fear. large type ed. (Dales Large Print Ser.). 268p. 1995. pap. 18.99 (*1-85389-492-3*, Dales) Ulverscroft.

— Vengeance in the Sun. large type ed. (Dales Large Print Ser.). 306p. 1995. pap. 18.99 (*1-85389-490-7*, Dales) Ulverscroft.

— Zadruga. large type ed. (Magna Large Print Ser.). 631p. 1996. 27.99 (*0-7505-0946-5*, Pub. by Mgna Lrg Print) Ulverscroft.

Pemberton, Max. Jewel Mysteries I Have Known: From a Dealer's Note Book. LC 75-32772. (Literature of Mystery & Detection Ser.). (Illus.). 1976. reprint ed. 24.95 (*0-405-07892-7*) Ayer.

— Queen of the Jesters & Her Strange Adventures in Old Paris. LC 76-101818. (Short Story Index Reprint Ser.). 1977. 21.95 (*0-8369-3206-4*) Ayer.

— Signors of the Night. LC 74-132123. (Short Story Index Reprint Ser.). 1977. 20.95 (*0-8369-3680-9*) Ayer.

— Ward's 1994 Worldwide Vehicle Parc. (Illus.). (Orig.). (C). pap. 950.00 (*0-910589-50-X*) Wards Comm.

— Ward's Worldwide Automotive Decade of Data - Production, 1994: Passenger Car & Commercial Vehicle Production, 1984-1993. (Worldwide Automotive Decade of Data, 1994 Ser.). (Illus.). (Orig.). (C). 1994. pap. 450.00 (*0-910589-98-4*) Wards Comm.

— Ward's Worldwide Automotive Decade of Data - Sales, 1994: Passenger Car & Commercial Vehicle Sales, 1984-1993. (Worldwide Automotive Decade of Data, 1994 Ser.). (Illus.). (Orig.). (C). 1994. pap. 450.00 (*0-910589-99-2*) Wards Comm.

— Ward's Worldwide Automotive Decade of Data, 1994. (Illus.). (Orig.). (C). 1994. pap. 750.00 (*0-910589-97-6*) Wards Comm.

***Pemberton, Michael A.** The Ethics of Writing Instruction: Issues in Theory & Practice. LC 99-16404. (Perspectives on Writing Ser.). 1999. pap. 73.25 (*1-56750-471-X*) Ablx Pub.

Pemberton, Robert. The Happy Colony. Richardson, Benjamin W. et al, eds. LC 84-48277. (Rise of Urban Britain Ser.). 264p. 1985. 35.00 (*0-8240-6279-5*) Garland.

***Pemberton, Robert L.** A History of Pleasants County, West Virginia. (Illus.). 293p. 1999. reprint ed. pap. 24.50 (*0-7884-1207-8*, P150) Heritage Bk.

***Pemberton, S. C.** Murder in Winnetka. LC 99-65316. 192p. 2000. pap. 11.95 (*1-56315-251-7*, Pub. by SterlingHse) Natl Bk Netwk.

Pemberton, S. George, ed. Applications of Ichonology to Petroleum Exploration: A Core Workshop. LC 92-247160. (SEPM Core Workshop Ser.: No. 17). (Illus.). 441p. 1992. pap. 136.80 (*0-608-05570-0*, 206603000006) Bks Demand.

Pemberton, Scott, jt. ed. see Andersen, Kim.

Pemberton, Steven & Daniels, Martin. Pascal Implementation: The P4 Compiler, 2 vols. LC 81-20184. 172p. 1983. pap. text 52.95 (*0-470-27386-0*) P-H.

Pemberton, T. Edgar. Dicken's London: Or, London in the Works of Charles Dickens. LC 71-39694. (Studies in Dickens: No. 52). 1972. reprint ed. lib. bdg. 75.00 (*0-8383-1404-X*) M S G Haskell Hse.

Pemberton, Thomas E. The Life of Bret Harte. LC 74-133530. (Select Bibliographies Reprint Ser.). 1977. reprint ed. 23.95 (*0-8369-5562-5*) Ayer.

Pemberton, V. Taking Control: Autonomy in Language Learning. LC 97-143401. 352p. (Orig.). 1996. pap. 52.50 (*962-209-407-4*, Pub. by HK Univ Pr) Coronet Bks.

Pemberton, William E. Bureaucratic Politics: Executive Reorganization During the Truman Administration. LC 78-2990. 270p. reprint ed. pap. 83.70 (*0-7837-8850-9*, AU0045400001) Bks Demand.

— Exit with Honor: The Life & Presidency of Ronald Reagan. LC 97-7269. (The Right Wing in America Ser.). (Illus.). 312p. (C). (gr. 13). 1997. 35.95 (*0-7656-0095-1*) M E Sharpe.

— Exit with Honor: The Life & Presidency of Ronald Reagan. LC 97-7269. (The Right Wing in America Ser.). (Illus.). 312p. (gr. 13). 1998. pap. 21.95 (*0-7656-0096-X*) M E Sharpe.

— George Bush. LC 92-46768. (World Leaders Ser.). 112p. (YA). 1993. lib. bdg. 25.27 (*0-86625-478-1*) Rourke Pubns.

— Harry S. Truman. 1988. 26.95 (*0-8057-7767-9*); pap. 15.95 (*0-8057-7783-0*) Macmillan.

— Ronald Reagan: A Biography. 1997. pap. 21.95 (*1-56324-303-2*) M E Sharpe.

Pemble, John. The Mediterranean Passion: Victorians & Edwardians in the South. LC 86-33183. (Illus.). 326p. 1987. reprint ed. text 65.00 (*0-19-820100-1*) OUP.

— The Raj, the Indian Mutiny, & the Kingdom of Oudh, 1801-1859. LC 76-55892. 303p. 1977. 39.50 (*0-8386-2092-2*) Fairleigh Dickinson.

— Venice Rediscovered. (Illus.). 250p. 1995. 30.00 (*0-19-820501-5*) OUP.

— Venice Rediscovered. (Illus.). 256p. 1996. reprint ed. pap. 14.95 (*0-19-285328-7*) OUP.

Pemble, William. A Brief Introduction to Geography. LC 77-7420. (English Experience Ser.: No. 883). 1977. reprint ed. lib. bdg. 20.00 (*90-221-0883-X*) Walter J Johnson.

Pembleton, Aaron, jt. auth. see Vorreux, Damien.

Pembleton, Seliesa. The Armadillo. LC 91-43731. (Remarkable Animals Ser.). (Illus.). 60p. (J). (gr. 4 up). 1992. lib. bdg. 13.95 (*0-87518-507-X*, Dillon Silver Burdett) Silver Burdett Pr.

— The Pileated Woodpecker. LC 88-20220. (Remarkable Animals Ser.). (Illus.). 60p. (J). (gr. 3 up). 1988. lib. bdg. 13.95 (*0-87518-392-1*, Dillon Silver Burdett) Silver Burdett Pr.

Pembrey, Erin. Land Predators of North America. 1999. pap. text 6.95 (*0-531-15945-0*) Watts.

Pembrey, M. E., jt. auth. see Roberts, J. A.

Pembrey Swan, Erin. Primates: From Howler Monkeys to Humans. (Animals in Order Ser.). (Illus.). 48p. (J). (gr. 3-5). 1999. pap. text 6.95 (*0-531-15921-3*) Watts.

***Pembroke.** Card Games for Smart Kids. LC 98-30848. (Illus.). 128p. (J). (gr. 4-7). 1998. pap. 5.95 (*0-8069-4887-6*) Sterling.

Pembroke, Lynne. The Caterpillarian Chronicles. mass mkt. 4.99 (*1-896329-98-5*) Picasso Publ.

Pement, Isleta L., jt. auth. see Edwards, Paul M.

Pement, Jack, jt. auth. see Keller, Paul.

Pemno, Karen, ed. see Neff, Rena.

Pempel, T. J. Japan: The Dilemmas of Success. LC 86-50478. (Headline Ser.: No. 277). (Illus.). 80p. (Orig.). 1986. pap. 5.95 (*0-87124-106-4*) Foreign Policy.

— Policy & Politics in Japan: Creative Conservatism. LC 81-14464. (Policy & Politics in Industrial States Ser.). 330p. 1982. pap. 22.95 (*0-87722-250-9*) Temple U Pr.

— Regime Shift: Comparative Dynamics of the Japanese Political Economy. LC 98-30185. (Studies in Political Economy). (Illus.). 288p. 1998. text 49.95 (*0-8014-3532-3*); pap. text 17.95 (*0-8014-8529-0*) Cornell U Pr.

***Pempel, T. J., ed.** The Politics of the Asian Economic Crisis. LC 99-38107. 1999. 49.95 (*0-8014-3722-9*); pap. 19.95 (*0-8014-8634-3*) Cornell U Pr.

Pempel, T. J., jt. auth. see Ilgen, Thomas L.

Pemsler, J. Paul, ed. see International Symposium on Molten Salts Staff.

***Pen & Sword Publishing Staff, ed.** Battlestations. (Illus.). 2000. 29.95 (*0-85052-749-X*) Pen & Sword.

Pen, Hired, ed. see Lee, Brenda.

Pen, J., jt. auth. see Owen, Meran R.

Pen Notes Staff. Learn Handwriting. (J). (gr. 2 up). 1986. spiral bd. 13.00 (*0-939564-00-9*) Pen Notes.

— Learn to Print Spanish (Aprendiendo a Escribir las Letras) (J). (ps up). 1989. spiral bd. 12.00 (*0-939564-17-3*) Pen Notes.

— Learn to Tell Time. (J). (gr. 1 up). 1995. spiral bd. 13.00 (*0-939564-13-0*) Pen Notes.

— Learn to Write Numbers. (J). (ps up). 1997. spiral bd. 13.00 (*0-939564-19-X*) Pen Notes.

— Learning to Print. (J). (ps up). 1984. spiral bd. 13.00 (*0-939564-01-7*) Pen Notes.

Pen Pals for Peace Program Staff, jt. auth. see Korpivaara, Ari.

Pen, Polly, jt. auth. see Klavan, Laurence.

Pen, Ronald. Introduction to Music. 348p. (C). 1992. pap. 12.95 (*0-07-038068-6*) McGraw.

Pen, Samantha. WordPerfect 6 for Windows. 2nd ed. LC 94-68906. 293p. 1995. student ed. 29.99 (*0-7897-0008-5*) Que.

Pena, A. An Atlas of Surgical Management of Anorectal Malformations. (Illus.). xiii, 104p. 1992. 120.00 (*0-387-97067-3*, 3064) Spr-Verlag.

Pena, A. S., ed. Recent Advances in Crohn's Disease: Developments in Gastroenterology One. 549p. 1981. text 229.00 (*90-247-2475-9*) Kluwer Academic.

Pena, A. S., jt. auth. see Hekkens, W. T.

Pena, Abe M. Memories of Cibola: Stories from New Mexico Villages. LC 96-25288. (Illus.). 240p. 1997. pap. 16.95 (*0-8263-1773-1*) U of NM Pr.

Pena, Alfredo C. & Cardona-Hine, Alvaro. Dos Elegias-Two Elegies. 1977. per. 2.50 (*0-685-04493-9*) Invisible-Red Hill.

Pena, Alvaro Ruiz de la, see Palacio Valdes, Armando.

Pena, Anthony. Carmageddon II - Carpocalypse Now: Prima's Official Strategy Guide. LC 98-67931. (Prima Games Ser.). 240p. 1998. per. 19.99 (*0-7615-1949-1*) Prima Pub.

— WCW Nitro N64: Prima's Official Strategy Guide. 96p. 1998. per. 12.99 (*0-7615-1864-9*) Prima Pub.

Pena, Anthony, jt. auth. see Kramer, Greg.

Pena, Antonio. Como Funciona una Celula? (Ciencia para Todos Ser.). (SPA.). pap. 6.99 (*968-16-4365-8*, Pub. by Fondo) Continental Bk.

— La Energia y la Vida Bioenergia. (Ciencia Para Todos Ser.). (SPA.). pap. 6.99 (*968-16-3479-9*, Pub. by Fondo) Continental Bk.

— Las Membranas de las Celulas. (Ciencia para Todos Ser.). (SPA.). pap. 6.99 (*968-16-2463-7*, Pub. by Fondo) Continental Bk.

Pena, Augustin De La, see De la Pena, Augustin.

Pena, Betty W. Las Tres Llaves del Exito. Montoya, Ana M., tr. (Illus.). 64p. 1992. pap. text 6.75 (*1-882462-00-9*) Surpass Your Limit.

Pena, Brent A., jt. auth. see Pena, L. W.

Pena, Carlos G. History of Mexican Literature. 3rd enl. rev. ed. LC 68-24078. 552p. reprint ed. pap. 171.20 (*0-8357-8908-X*, 203342000086) Bks Demand.

***Pena, Charlene.** Gifts & Graces. (Illus.). 72p. 2000. pap. 10.50 (*1-56770-475-1*) S Scheewe Pubns.

Pena, Christopher G. Touched by War: Battles Fought in the Lafourche District. LC 98-91509. (Illus.). xviii, 454p. 1998. 28.75 (*0-9667287-0-X*) CGP Pr.

***Pena, Daniel, et al.** A Course in Time Series Analysis. 448p. 2000. 115.00 (*0-471-36164-X*) Wiley.

***Pena, David S.** Economic Barbarism & Managerialism. Vol. 221. 2000. write for info. (*0-313-31469-1*) Greenwood.

Pena, Devon G. Chicano Culture, Ecology, Politics: Subversive Kin. LC 98-25479. (Society, Environment & Place Ser.). 295p. 1998. pap. 19.95 (*0-8165-1873-4*); lib. bdg. 40.00 (*0-8165-1872-6*) U of Ariz Pr.

Pena, Devon S. The Terror of the Machine: Technology, Work, Gender, & Ecology on the U. S.-Mexico Border. LC 96-2352. (Border & Migration Studies). (Illus.). 412p. 1995. pap. 19.95 (*0-292-76562-2*) U of Tex Pr.

Pena, Elena de la, jt. auth. see Chong, Ada.

***Pena, Evelyn.** Michigan. (Illus.). 64p. (gr. 1-5). 2000. pap. 5.95 (*1-892920-48-4*) G H B Pubs.

Pena, Federico, ed. Accelerating Cleanup: Paths to Closure. (Illus.). 320p. (C). 1999. pap. text 35.00 (*0-7881-7613-7*) DIANE Pub.

Pena, Flora, tr. see Fine, Anne.

Pena, German A. Exploraciones Arqueologicas en la Cuenca Media del Rio Bogota. (SPA., Illus.). 138p. 1991. pap. 8.50 (*1-877812-22-6*, BR020) UPLAAP.

Pena, Gladys, ed. For a Permanent Public Art: An Exhibition of Murals Commissioned for New York City Hospitals under President Roosevelt's New Deal. (Illus.). 36p. (Orig.). (C). 1988. pap. text. write for info. (*0-318-63770-7*) Hlth & Hosp Corp.

Pena, Guillermo De La, see De la Pena, Guillermo.

Pena, Humberto J. La Casa del Mortalista. LC 96-81336. (Coleccion del Chichereku). (SPA.). 137p. (Orig.). 1996. pap. 13.00 (*0-89729-807-1*) Ediciones.

— El Hijo Del Hijo. 200p. (Orig.). 1991. pap. text 12.00 (*0-685-54524-5*) Saeta.

***Pena, J., et al, eds.** Tropical Fruit Pests & Pollinators: Biology, Economic Importance, Natural Enemies & Control. (CABI Publishing Ser.). (Illus.). 400p. 2000. text 120.00 (*0-85199-434-2*) OUP.

Pena, J. T., et al. Carthage Papers: The Early Colony's Economy, Water Supply, a Public Bath, & the Mobilization of State Olive Oil. LC 99-185368. (Supplementary Ser.: No. 28). (Illus.). 238p. 1998. 79.50 (*1-887829-28-8*) Jour Roman Arch.

Pena, Jake. Eight Highly Successful Tips for Breaking into the Modeling & Commercial Business. 192p. 1993. pap. text 19.95 (*0-8403-8463-7*) Kendall-Hunt.

Pena, Jesus J. Justicia Poetica - Poetic Justice: Memorias de un Abogado de Barrio - Memoirs of a Neighborhood Lawyer. (SPA.). 279p. 1995. pap. 13.00 (*1-884912-04-4*) Latino Pr.

Pena, Jose, jt. ed. see Solana, Rafael.

Pena, Jose A. Blasphemies of the Flute (Blasfemias de la Flauta) Essential Icon Press Staff, ed. Radcliff, Joni R., tr. from SPA. (Illus.). 128p. 1999. pap. 14.99 (*0-7392-0297-9*, PO3417) Morris Pubng.

***Pena, Juan M.** Shaping Preserving Representation in Computer Aided Geometric Design. LC 99-31025. 233p. 1999. lib. bdg. 79.00 (*1-56072-691-1*) Nova Sci Pubs.

Pena, Julia. 150 Songs with Just 3 Chords. 184p. (YA). pap. 16.95 (*0-943748-47-X*, PF0723) Ekay Music.

Pena, L. W. & Pena, Brent A. TV Video Systems: The How-To Guide to Installation, Operation & Troubleshooting. rev. ed. LC 97-133591. (Illus.). 124p. 1996. reprint ed. pap. 19.95 (*0-7906-1082-5*) Prompt Publns.

Pena, Luis De La, see De La Pena, Luis.

Pena, Luis M. Gonzalez, see Gonzalez Pena, Luis M.

Pena, Lydia M. The Life & Times of Agnes Tait. (Illus.). (Orig.). 1983. pap. text 14.95 (*0-9612982-0-0*) Pena Lydia.

Pena, Manuel. Criminal Investigation. 4th ed. LC 82-70470. (Illus.). 416p. (C). 1996. pap. 31.95 (*0-942728-75-0*) Copperhouse.

— The Mexican American Orquesta: Music, Culture & the Dialectic of Conflict. LC 99-6098. 384p. 1999. pap. 19.95 (*0-292-76587-8*) U of Tex Pr.

***Pena, Manuel.** The Mexican American Orquesta: Music, Culture & the Dialectic of Conflict. LC 99-6098. 384p. 1999. 45.00 (*0-292-76586-X*) U of Tex Pr.

Pena, Manuel. Musica Tejana: The Cultural Economy of Artistic Transformation. LC 98-47951. (University of Houston Series in Mexican American Studies: Vol. 1). (Illus.). 224p. 1999. 27.95 (*0-89096-877-2*); pap. 15.95 (*0-89096-888-8*) Tex A&M Univ Pr.

— The Texas-Mexican Conjunto: History of a Working-Class Music. (Mexican American Monographs: No. 9). (Illus.). 238p. 1985. pap. 14.95 (*0-292-78080-X*) U of Tex Pr.

Pena McCook, Kathleen De La, see De La Pena McCook, Kathleen.

Pena, Michelle V., ed. see Arnold, Eugene D., Jr., et al.

Pena, Paco. Toques Flamencos. 1997. pap. text 22.95 (*0-86175-306-2*) EMI Pubng.

Pena, S. D., et al, eds. DNA Fingerprinting: State of the Science. LC 93-22711. 466p. 1993. 165.50 (*0-8176-2781-2*); 110.00 (*0-8176-2906-8*) Birkhauser.

Pena, Terri De La, see Chin-Lee, Cynthia & De la Pena, Terri.

Pena, Terri De La, see De La Pena, Terri.

Pena, Victor de la, see De La Pena, Victor.

Pena, William. Problem Seeking: An Architectural Programming Primer. 202p. 1987. pap. 21.95 (*0-913962-87-2*) AIA Press.

Penabad, Carie, ed. see Plater-Zyberk, Elizabeth, et al.

Penafiel, Karen W. Power Shopping: A Guide for Building Owners & Managers to Prepare for the Deregulated Electricity Marketplace. (Illus.). 108p. 1996. pap. 50.00 (*0-614-31137-3*, 135-PWRSHP) Build Own & Man.

Penal, Dylan G. 1 Way Microsoft Marches Strong... A Case Study of Law, Judicial Power & Constitutional Corruption in America: Includes Coupon for up to Date CD-ROM with Linux Red Hat 5.2 Based O/S with the 2.2 Kernel That Runs MS-Windows Apps. 268p. 1999. mass mkt. 27.95 (*1-891950-13-4*) Amer Group Pub.

Penalba, Rene. Problems of Daily Living. (SPA.). 1999. pap. 7.99 (*0-8297-1977-6*) Vida Pubs.

Penalosa, Fernando. El Cuento Popular Maya: Una Introduccion. (SPA.). 128p. (Orig.). 1996. pap. 9.95 (*1-886502-08-0*, Ediciones Yax Te) Yax Te Found.

— The Mayan Folktale: An Introduction. 128p. (Orig.). 1996. pap. 9.95 (*1-886502-09-9*) Yax Te Found.

Penalosa, Fernando, ed. Tales & Legends of the Q'anjob'al Maya. (Illus.). 178p. (Orig.). 1995. pap. 8.95 (*1-886502-03-X*) Yax Te Found.

Penalosa, Fernando, ed. see Juan, Jose & Andres, Domingo.

Penalosa, Fernando, tr. see Gonzalez, Gaspar P.

Penalosa, Fernando, tr. see La Farge, Oliver.

Penalosa, Fernando, jt. tr. see Rascon, Susan G.

Penalosa, Fernando, tr. see Sappersa, Karl, et al.

Penalosa, Fernando, tr. see Siegel, Morris & Grollig, Francis X.

Penaranda, Ricardo, ed. see Sanchez, George J. & Sanchez, Gonzalo J.

Penaskovic, Richard. Critical Thinking & the Academic Study of Religion. LC 97-9824. (Studies in the Humanities). 190p. 1997. pap. 19.95 (*0-7885-0360-X*, 000122) Duke.

Penate, Juan, jt. auth. see Escarpanter, Jose.

Penbera, Joseph J., jt. auth. see Betts, Chris A.

Penberthy, Ian. Building Your Garden. 1989. text 17.95 (*0-02-595491-1*) Macmillan.

— Mustang. 72p. 1995. 10.98 (*0-7858-0226-6*) Bk Sales Inc.

Penberthy, Jenny. Niedecker & the Correspondence with Zukofsky, 1931-1970. LC 92-34643. (Illus.), 395p. (C). 1993. text 74.95 (*0-521-44369-5*) Cambridge U Pr.

Penberthy, Jenny, ed. Lorine Niedecker: Woman & Poet. (Man & Poet Ser.). (Illus.). 439p. 1996. 45.00 (*0-943373-38-7*); pap. 22.95 (*0-943373-39-5*) Natl Poet Foun.

Penberthy, John. To Bee or Not to Bee. 119p. 1987. pap. 7.95 (*0-945153-13-9*) Sound Pub CO.

Penberthy, Stephen & Jones, Gary. Step-by-Step to a Classic Fireplace Mantel. LC 94-65609. (Illus.). 64p. (Orig.). 1994. pap. 12.95 (*0-88740-653-X*) Schiffer.

Pencak, Richard. Common Sense Importing: Nineteen Eighty-Eight Edition. Bogue, Jeanne, ed. 206p. pap. 35.00 (*0-945663-00-5*) Pencak & Co.

***Pencak, Richard.** Pencak's Complete Yet Concise Guide to Successful & Profitable Importing Purchases into These United States of America. 99p. 1999. 15.00 (*0-945663-25-0*) Pencak & Co.

Pencak, William. History, Signing In: Essays in History & Semiotics. LC 92-4143. (Semiotics & the Human Sciences Ser.: Vol. 4). 448p. (C). 1993. text 68.95 (*0-8204-1838-2*) P Lang Pubng.

Pencak, William, ed. Worldmaking. (Critic of Institutions Ser.: Vol. 6). VII, 408p. (C). 1996. text 59.95 (*0-8204-2804-3*) P Lang Pubng.

Pencak, William, et al, eds. Immigration to New York. LC 89-13757. 259p. 1991. 38.50 (*0-944190-09-X*) Balch IES Pr.

Pencak, William, jt. auth. see Blair, William Alan.

Pencak, William, jt. auth. see Frantz, John B.

Pencak, William, jt. ed. see Frantz, John B.

Pencak, William, jt. ed. see Freidel, Frank.

Pencak, William, jt. ed. see Gilje, Paul A.

Pencak, William A. & Lindgren, Ralph, eds. New Approaches to Semiotics & the Human Sciences: Essays in Honor of Roberta Kevelson. LC 97-12496. (Semiotics & the Human Sciences Ser.: Vol. 13). XI, 360p. (C). 1998. text 58.95 (*0-8204-3814-6*) P Lang Pubng.

Pence. Classic Cases in Medical Ethics. 3rd ed. LC 99-24647. 528p. 1999. pap. 30.00 (*0-07-303986-1*) McGraw.

Pence, Alan R., ed. Ecological Research with Children & Families: From Concepts to Methodology. (Illus.). 256p. (C). 1988. pap. text 18.95 (*0-8077-2913-2*) Tchrs Coll.

Pence, Alan R., jt. ed. see Moss, Peter.

Pence, Alan R., jt. ed. see Peters, Donald F.

Pence, Barbara C. & Dunn, Dale M. Nutrition & Women's Cancers. (Modern Nutrition Ser.). 192p. 1998. boxed set 84.95 (*0-8493-8562-8*) CRC Pr.

***Pence, Caprial.** Caprial Cooks for Friends. LC 99-86283. 240p. 2000. 27.95 (*1-58008-152-5*) Ten Speed Pr.

— Caprial's Bistro-Style Cuisine. LC 97-36444. (Illus.). 208p. 1998. 24.95 (*0-89815-946-6*) Ten Speed Pr.

Pence, Caprial. Caprial's Cafe Favorites. (Illus.). 160p. 1994. 21.95 (*0-89815-600-9*) Ten Speed Pr.

— Caprial's Soups & Sandwiches. LC 98-38815. (Illus.). 144p. 1997. pap. 17.95 (*1-58008-025-1*) Ten Speed Pr.

— Cooking with Caprial. (Illus.). 224p. 1995. 27.95 (*0-89815-788-9*) Ten Speed Pr.

Pence, Danny B. Keys, Species & Host List, & Bibliography for Nasal Mites of North American Birds: Acarina: Rhinonyssinae, Turbinoptinae, Speleognathinae, & Cytoditidae. (Special Publications: No. 8). (Illus.). 148p. (Orig.). 1975. pap. 6.00 (*0-89672-033-0*) Tex Tech Univ Pr.

Pence, Dennis. Calculus Activities for Graphic Calculators. 280p. (C). 1990. pap. 27.25 (*0-534-92431-X*) PWS Pubs.

— Calculus Activities for the TI-81 Graphic Calculator. 280p. (C). 1992. pap. 22.95 (*0-534-92709-2*) PWS Pubs.

Pence, Donna & Wilson, Charles. The Role of Law Enforcement in the Response to Child Abuse & Neglect. 78p. (Orig.). (C). 1995. pap. text 25.00 (*0-7881-1667-3*) DIANE Pub.

— The Team Investigation of Child Sexual Abuse: The Uneasy Alliance. (Interpersonal Violence: the Practice Ser.: Vol. 6). 176p. 1994. 48.00 (*0-8039-5169-8*); pap. 21.50 (*0-8039-5170-1*) Sage.

Pence, Doug & Hawkins, Ron. Power RPG III: Advanced Concepts, Tips, & Techniques. (Illus.). 374p. (Orig.). 1995. pap. 99.00 (*1-883884-26-8*, 529) Midrange Comput.

— Power RPG IV: Advanced Concepts, Tips, & Techniques, Including ILE. LC 98-105330. (Illus.). 500p. (Orig.). 1996. pap. 99.00 (*1-883884-32-2*, 560) Midrange Comput.

Pence, Ellen & Paymar, Michael. Education Groups for Men Who Batter: The Duluth Model. LC 92-35954. 212p. 1993. 28.95 (*0-8261-7990-8*) Springer Pub.

Pence, Ellen, jt. auth. see Shepard, Melanie.

Pence, Ellen L., jt. ed. see Shepard, Melanie F.

Pence, Gregory, jt. auth. see Stephens, G. Lynn.

Pence, Gregory E. Classic Cases in Medical Ethics: Accounts of Cases That Have Shaped Medical Ethics, with Philosophical, Legal, & Historical Backgrounds. 2nd ed. LC 94-41691. 428p. (C). 1994. pap. 34.69 (*0-07-038094-5*) McGraw.

— Classical Works in Medical Ethics: Core Philosophical Readings. LC 97-1300. 384p. 1997. pap. 28.75 (*0-07-038115-1*) McGraw.

***Pence, Gregory E.** Re-Creating Medicine: Ethical Issues at the Frontiers of Medicine. 192p. 2000. 22.95 (*0-8476-9690-1*) Rowman.

Pence, Gregory E. Who's Afraid of Human Cloning? LC 97-38513. 192p. 1998. 47.50 (*0-8476-8781-3*); pap. 14.95 (*0-8476-8782-1*) Rowman.

Pence, Gregory E., ed. Flesh of My Flesh: The Ethics of Cloning Humans: A Reader. LC 98-11287. 160p. 1998. 35.00 (*0-8476-8981-6*); pap. 12.95 (*0-8476-8982-4*) Rowman.

Pence, Heather, jt. auth. see Bradley, Patrick.

Pence, I. W., Jr., jt. ed. see White, J. A.

Pence, I. W., jt. ed. see White, J. A., Jr.

Pence, Irene. A Clue from the Grave. 320p. 1997. mass mkt. 5.99 (*0-7860-0409-6*, Pinncle Kensgtn) Kensgtn Pub Corp.

— Triangle. 320p. 1998. mass mkt. 5.99 (*0-7860-0473-8*, Pinncle Kensgtn) Kensgtn Pub Corp.

Pence, Jerry. Knowing Us Better: A Guide to Membership in the Wesleyan Church Leader's Book. Higle, David, ed. (Illus.). 160p. 1995. teacher ed., spiral bd., wbk. ed. 14.95 (*0-89827-137-1*, GMH37) Wesleyan Pub Hse.

— Knowing Us Better: A Guide to Membership in the Wesleyan Church Student's Book. Higle, David, ed. LC 96-157142. 104p. 1995. pap., student ed. 4.95 (*0-89827-135-5*, GMH38) Wesleyan Pub Hse.

— Knowing Us Better: A Guide to Membership in the Wesleyan Church Study Guide. Higle, David, ed. (Illus.). 38p. 1995. pap., student ed., wbk. ed. 1.95 (*0-89827-147-9*, GMH39) Wesleyan Pub Hse.

Pence, Joanne. Cook in Time: An Angie Amalfi Mystery. 352p. 1999. mass mkt. 5.99 (*0-06-104454-7*) HarpC.

— Cooking Most Deadly. 256p. 1998. mass mkt. 5.99 (*0-06-104395-8*, Harp PBks) HarpC.

— Cooking up Trouble. 320p. 1998. mass mkt. 5.99 (*0-06-108200-7*, Harp PBks) HarpC.

— Cook's Night Out. (Angie Amalfi Mystery Ser.). 304p. 1998. mass mkt. 5.99 (*0-06-104396-6*) HarpC.

— Cooks Overboard. (Angie Amalfi Mystery Ser.). 304p. 1998. mass mkt. 5.99 (*0-06-104453-9*, Harp PBks) HarpC.

— Something's Cooking. 650th ed. 336p. 1998. mass mkt. 5.99 (*0-06-108096-9*, Harp PBks) HarpC.

***Pence, Joanne.** To Catch a Cook: An Angie Amalfi Mystery. 320p. 2000. mass mkt. 5.99 (*0-06-103085-6*, Avon Bks) Morrow Avon.

Pence, Joanne. Too Many Cooks. 352p. 1998. mass mkt. 5.99 (*0-06-108199-X*, Harp PBks) HarpC.

Pence, Judy. A Helmet Away from Heaven. iii, 130p. (J). (gr. 5-9). 1998. pap. text 9.95 (*0-9665453-0-3*) Pence Pubg.

Pence, Katherine M. . . . And a Time to Knit Stockings. (Illus.). 36p. 1997. reprint ed. ring bd. 14.00 (*0-9661475-0-2*) Pence Design.

Pence, Laura, ed. Interpharm Pharmaceutical Manager's Compliance Guide. 3rd ed. 140p. 1997. pap. 39.00 (*1-57491-044-2*) Interpharm.

Pence, Mary L. Boswell: The Story of a Frontier Lawman. (Illus.). 186p. 1978. 15.00 (*0-931271-06-1*) Hi Plains Pr.

Pence, Patricia. Equine Dentistry & Oral Surgery. 352p. 79.00 (*0-683-30403-8*) Lppncott W & W.

Pence, Richard A. & Dahl, Patrick, eds. The Next Greatest Thing: Fifty Years of Rural Electrification. (Illus.). 256p. 1984. 29.85 (*0-917599-00-4*) Natl Rural.

Pence, Roger, jt. auth. see Monypenny, Julian.

Pence, Roy, jt. auth. see Forester, Mildred.

Pence, Shari A. Beanbag Bonanza. (Illus.). 64p. (J). (gr. 1-7). 1999. pap. 3.50 (*0-8167-5654-6*) Troll Communs.

— Beanie Bonanza: A Gold Mine of Accessories, Crafts, Games & Toys for Your Beloved Beanies. LC 97-94622. (Illus.). 63p. 1997. pap. 7.95 (*0-9645771-3-5*) Funcastle Pubns.

Pence, Shari A. Games Galore for Children's Parties & More: 80 Fun Games & Activities for Parties, Classroom, Youth Groups, Carnivals, Company Picnics, Rainy Days & Special Occasions. 2nd rev. ed. Stearns, Debra & Kohout, Rosemary, eds. LC 95-90818. (Illus.). 121p. (J). (ps-7). 1996. pap. 11.95 (*0-9645771-1-9*) Funcastle Pubns.

Pence, Shari A. A Tumbleweed Christmas. LC 96-96223. (Illus.). 33p. (Orig.). 1999. pap. 6.95 (*0-9645771-2-7*) Funcastle Pubns.

Pence, Sharon, ed. see Classey, Pat.

Pence-Smith, Penny. Under a Maui Sun: A Celebration of the Island of Maui. (JPN., Illus.). 188p. 1989. 24.95 (*0-89610-181-9*) Island Heritage.

Pence, T. J., jt. auth. see Duxbury, P. M.

Pence, Terry. Ethics in Nursing: An Annotated Bibliography. 2nd ed. 255p. 1986. pap. 12.95 (*0-88737-192-2*, 20-1936) Natl League Nurse.

P

Pence, Terry & Cantrall, Janice, eds. Ethics in Nursing: An Anthology. 352p. 1990. 15.50 (*0-88737-461-1*) Natl League Nurse.

Pence, Wanda J. Be Still & Know That I Am God. 1987. pap. 6.95 (*0-89137-332-2*) Quality Pubns.

— The Guest. 1994. pap. 4.95 (*1-56794-058-7*) Star Bible.

***Penceny, Mark.** Democracy at the Point of Bayonets. LC 98-37146. 438p. 1999. 19.00 (*0-271-01883-6*) Pa St U Pr.

Pench, Lucio R., ed. see European Commission, et al.

Penchansky, David. What Rough Beast? Images of God in the Hebrew Bible. LC 99-27859. 144p. 1999. pap. 16.95 (*0-664-25645-7*) Westminster John Knox.

***Penchansky, David & Redditt, Paul L., eds.** Shall Not the Judge of All the Earth Do What Is Right? Studies on the Nature of God in Tribute to James L. Crenshaw. LC 99-59709. xxxv, 268p. 2000. text 32.50 (*1-57506-043-4*) Eisenbrauns.

Penchansky, Roy, ed. Health Services Administration: Policy Cases & the Case Method. LC 68-15640. 475p. 1968. 44.00 (*0-674-38550-0*) HUP.

Penchant Publishing Staff. Skipper's Challenge: 900 Nautical Puzzlers. LC 98-91659. 306p. 1999. pap. text 19.95 (*0-9643108-3-X*) Penchant Pubng

Penchoen, Thomas G. Tamazight of the Ayt Ndhir. LC 73-91702. (Afroasiatic Dialects Ser.: Vol. 1). (Illus.). 124p. 1973. pap. 21.00 (*0-89003-000-6*) Undena Pubns.

Pencik, Regina. Latente Adipositas: Ein Vergleich Latent und Manifest Ausgepragter Ebsucht. (Psychologie Ser.: Bd. 599). (Illus.). 157p. 1997. 31.95 (*3-631-32117-1*) P Lang Pubng.

Pencil Point Press, Inc. Staff, ed. What Your English Teacher Told You ... But You Never Remember! Mechanics for Writing & Usage. 1998. pap. 9.95 (*1-881641-71-6*) Pencil Point.

Pencom International Staff. Pump up Your Profits: 52 Cost-Saving Ideas to Build Your Bottom Line. (Illus.). 132p. 1996. pap. 19.95 (*1-879239-08-6*) Pencom.

Pencraft, Nancy, ed. see Weber, Nancy O.

Penczek, S., et al. Cationic Ring-Opening Polymerization. (Advances in Polymer Science Ser.: Vols. 68 & 69). (Illus.). 300p. 1985. 131.00 (*0-387-13781-5*) Spr-Verlag.

Penczek, Stanislaw, ed. Models of Biopolymers by Ring-Opening Polymerization. 384p. 1989. lib. bdg. 286.00 (*0-8493-5077-8*, QP801) CRC Pr.

Penczek, Wojciech & Szaas, Andrzej, eds. Mathematical Foundations of Computer Science, 1996: 21st International Symposium, MFCS '96, Crakow, Poland, September 2-6, 1996: Proceedings. LC 96-27444. (Lecture Notes in Computer Science Ser.: Vol. 111). 592p. 1996. pap. 94.00 (*3-540-61550-4*) Spr-Verlag.

Penczer, Peter R. Washington, D. C., Past & Present. LC 98-91447. (Illus.). 264p. 1998. pap. 19.95 (*0-9629841-1-6*) Oneonta Pr.

Pendagast, Edward L., Jr., jt. auth. see Butman, Alexander M.

Pendakur, Manjunath. Canadian Dreams & American Control: The Political Economy of the Canadian Film Industry. LC 90-12144. (Contemporary Film & Television Ser.). 332p. (C). 1990. pap. 19.95 (*0-8143-1999-8*) Wayne St U Pr.

— Canadian Dreams & American Control: The Political Economy of the Canadian Film Industry. LC 90-12144. (Contemporary Film & Television Ser.). 332p. (C). 1991. 49.95 (*0-8143-1998-X*) Wayne St U Pr.

***Pendakur, Ravi.** Immigrants & the Labour Force: Policy, Regulation & Impact. 224p. 2000. 60.00 (*0-7735-2058-9*, Pub. by McG-Queens Univ Pr) CUP Services.

Pendar, Kenneth. Adventure in Diplomacy. LC 76-5479. (World War II Ser.). 1976. reprint ed. lib. bdg. 29.50 (*0-306-70774-8*) Da Capo.

Pendaries, Yveline. Les Proces de Rastatt (1946-1954) Le Jugement des Crimes de Guerre en Zone Francaise d'Occupation en Allemagne. (Contacts Ser.: Series II, Vol. 16). (FRE.). 396p. 1995. 55.95 (*3-906754-18-9*, Pub. by P Lang) P Lang Pubng.

Pendarvis. Net Quest: Exploring A&P. LC 97-225291. 1997. 5.74 (*0-697-41894-4*, McGrw-H College) McGrw-H Hghr Educ.

Pendarvis. Net Quest Exploring Zoology. 1997. 8.74 (*0-697-38670-8*, WCB McGr Hill) McGrw-H Hghr Educ.

Pendarvis, Edwina, ed. see Bailey, Rebecca.

Pendarvis, Edwina D., et al. Out of Our Minds: Anti-Intellectualism & Talent Development in American Schooling. LC 94-44979. (Education & Psychology of the Gifted Ser.: Vol. 9). 288p. (C). 1995. text 50.00 (*0-8077-3417-9*) Tchrs Coll.

Pendarvis, Patrick & Ferguson, Barry. Biology: It's All about Life: Zoology. (C). 1994. pap. text, lab manual ed. write for info. (*0-07-038106-2*) McGraw.

Pendas, Miguel. dBASE IV: A Tutorial to Accompany Peter Norton's Introduction to Computers. LC 93-23741. 1994. write for info. (*0-02-801327-1*) Glencoe.

Pendas, Miguel. Lotus 1-2-3, Release 2.4. (Step-by-Step Ser.). 1995. teacher ed. write for info. (*0-02-800956-8*) Glencoe.

Pendas, Miguel. Microsoft Word, Version 5.5. LC 92-17123. (Increasing Your Productivity Ser.). 1992. disk. write for info. (*0-02-800683-6*) Glencoe.

— Microsoft Word, Version 5.5. LC 92-17123. (Increasing Your Productivity Ser.). 1993. write for info. (*0-02-800682-8*) Glencoe.

— Microsoft Word, Version 5.5. large type ed. 1993. 124.00 (*0-614-09561-1*, L-31415-00) Am Printing Hse.

— Step-by-Step Lotus 1-2-3. LC 94-8944. 1994. write for info. (*0-02-800955-X*) Macmillan.

Pendell, Dale. City Limits Blues. 20p. 1986. 5.00 (*1-882623-02-9*) Exiled-Am Pr.

— Pharmako/Gnosis: Plant Teachers & the Poison Path. (Illus.). 304p. 1999. pap. 19.95 (*1-56279-104-4*, Pub. by Mercury Hse Inc) Consort Bk Sales.

— Pharmako/Poeia: Plant Powers, Poisons & Herbcraft. 304p. 1995. pap. 19.95 (*1-56279-069-2*) Mercury Hse Inc.

— Physics for the Heart. 20p. 1986. 5.00 (*1-882623-01-0*) Exiled-Am Pr.

— Rough Cuts & Kindling. 40p. 1986. 5.00 (*1-882623-03-7*) Exiled-Am Pr.

— Swirling. 44p. 1986. boxed set 5.00 (*1-882623-04-5*) Exiled-Am Pr.

Pendell, Dale & Sanfield, Steve. Chasing the Cranes: A Cycle of Linked Hoops. 32p. 1986. 5.00 (*1-882623-00-2*) Exiled-Am Pr.

Pendell, Dale, tr. see Mokujiki.

Pendell, Elmer. Why Civilizations Self-Destruct. LC 76-40801. 196p. 1977. pap. 13.00 (*0-914576-07-0*) Howard Allen.

Pendelton, Don. Moving Target. (Superbolan Ser.: No. 14). 352p. (Orig.). 1989. mass mkt. 3.95 (*0-373-61414-4*) Harlequin Bks.

***Pendelton, Don.** Point of Impact. (Executioner Ser.: Vol. 256). 2000. per. 4.50 (*0-373-64256-3*) Harlequin Bks.

Pendelton, Don. Precision Kill. LC 96-2389. (Superbolan Ser.: Vol. 46). 349p. 1996. per. 4.99 (*0-373-61446-2*, 1-61446-0, Wrldwide Lib) Harlequin Bks.

— Sudden Death. (Mack Bolan Ser.: No. 7). 384p. 1987. mass mkt. 3.95 (*0-373-61407-1*) Harlequin Bks.

***Pendelton, Don, creator.** War Season. (Superbolan Ser.: Vol. 74). 352p. 2000. mass mkt. 5.99 (*0-373-61474-8*, 1-61474-2, Wrldwide Lib) Harlequin Bks.

Pender, Daniel J. Practical Otology. (Illus.). 348p. 1992. text 45.00 (*0-397-51016-0*) Lppncott W & W.

Pender, Harold & Del Mar, William A., eds. Electrical Engineers' Handbook, Vol. 2. 4th ed. LC 49-11664. (Wiley Engineering Handbook Ser.). 1647p. reprint ed. pap. 200.00 (*0-608-15381-8*, 205635700060) Bks Demand.

Pender, J., et al. Impact of Tsetse Control on Land Use in the Semi-Arid Zone of Zimbabwe Phase 2: Analysis of Land Use Change by Remote Sensing Imagery. 1997. pap. 60.00 (*0-85954-469-9*, Pub. by Nat Res Inst) St Mut.

Pender, J. Anne, ed. see Harvard Family Research Project Staff.

Pender, Jennifer. English on Cue: Developing Skills in English Language: Speaking, Level 2. (Illus.). 115p. 1997. pap. 24.95 (*0-949414-63-8*, Pub. by U Sthrn Queenslnd) Accents Pubns.

Pender, Karen. Rover SD1. (Illus.). 200p. 1998. 34.95 (*1-86126-111-X*, Pub. by Crolwood) Motorbooks Intl.

Pender, Ken. Digital Colour in Graphic Design. LC 98-28810. (Illus.). 224p. 1998. 42.95 incl. cd-rom (*0-240-51527-7*, Focal) Buttrwrth-Heinemann.

— Digital Video for the Desktop. LC 00-265129. (Illus.). 224p. 1999. pap. 47.95 (*0-240-51552-8*, Focal) Buttrwrth-Heinemann.

Pender, Kenneth R. Digital Graphic Designer. LC 96-233451. (Illus.). 336p. 1996. pap. 36.95 (*0-240-51477-7*, Focal) Buttrwrth-Heinemann.

Pender, Laura. Dangerous Vintage. 1993. per. 2.89 (*0-373-22212-2*, 1-22212-4) Harlequin Bks.

— Garden of Deceit. (Intrigue Ser.). 1993. per. 2.99 (*0-373-22240-8*, 1-22240-5) Harlequin Bks.

— Melodie Fatale. (Amours d'Aujourd'Hui Ser.: Bk. 313). 1999. mass mkt. 4.99 (*0-373-38313-4*, 1-38313-2) Harlequin Bks.

— Midnight Rider. 1994. per. 2.99 (*0-373-22280-7*, 1-22280-1) Harlequin Bks.

— Mindgame. (Intrigue Ser.: No. 177). 1992. per. 2.79 (*0-373-22177-0*, 1-22177-9) Harlequin Bks.

— Music in the Mist. (Intrigue Ser.). 1993. per. 2.99 (*0-373-22249-1*, 1-22249-6) Harlequin Bks.

— The Pirate Ghost (Dreamscape) (Intrigue Ser.). 1996. per. 3.75 (*0-373-22368-4*, 1-22368-4) Harlequin Bks.

Pender, Lesley. Marketing Management for Travel & Tourism. (Illus.). 320p. 1999. pap. 45.00 (*0-7487-2783-3*, Pub. by S Thornes Pubs) Trans-Atl Phila.

Pender, Malcolm. Biedermann & die Brandstifter, Frisch: Critical Monographs in English. 68p. 1993. pap. 32.00 (*0-85261-258-3*, Pub. by Univ of Glasgow) St Mut.

— Contemporary Images of Death & Sickness: Aspects of a Theme in German-Swiss Literature. (SAP Title Ser.). 250p. 1998. pap. 24.50 (*1-85075-831-X*, Pub. by Sheffield Acad) CUP Services.

Pender, Malcolm, jt. auth. see Charnley, Joy.

Pender, Malcolm, jt. ed. see Butler, Michael.

Pender, Malcolm, jt. ed. see Charnley, Joy.

Pender, Michael P. & McCombe, Pamela A. Autoimmune Neurological Disease. (Cambridge Reviews in Clinical Immunology Ser.). 385p. (C). 1995. text 110.00 (*0-521-46113-8*) Cambridge U Pr.

Pender, Nola J. Health Promotion in Nursing Practice. 3rd ed. LC 96-143912. 320p. (C). 1996. pap. text 39.95 (*0-8385-3659-X*, A3659-8) Appleton & Lange.

Pender, Robert H., jt. auth. see Miller, Glenn A.

Pender, Rose. A Lady's Experiences in the Wild West in 1883. LC 78-17690. xiii, 136p. 1978. reprint ed. pap. 7.95 (*0-8032-8711-9*, Bison Books) U of Nebr Pr.

***Pender, Seamus, ed.** A Census of Ireland, Circa 1659: With Supplementary Material from the Poll Money Ordinances (1660-1661) xix, 946p. 1999. reprint ed. pap. 70.00 (*0-8063-4715-5*, Pub. by Clearfield Co) ACCESS Pubs Network.

Pender, William C. Revelation. (Interpretation Bible Studies). 112p. 1999. pap. 7.00 (*0-664-50039-0*) Geneva Press.

Pendergast, Carol Stamatis, jt. auth. see Valdez del Alamo, Elizabeth.

Pendergast, David M. Excavations at Altun Ha, Belize, 1964-1970, Vol. 1. (Illus.). 240p. 1994. boxed set. write for info. (*0-88854-219-4*) Royal Ontario.

— Excavations at Altun Ha, Belize, 1964-1970, Vol. 2. (Illus.). 320p. 1994. boxed set. write for info. (*0-88854-290-9*) Royal Ontario.

— Excavations at Altun Ha, Belize, 1964-1970, Vol. 3. (Illus.). 432p. 1994. boxed set. write for info. (*0-88854-355-7*) Royal Ontario.

Pendergast, James F. The Massawomeck: Raiders & Traders into the Chesapeake Bay in the Seventeenth Century. LC 90-56111. (Transactions Ser.: Vol. 81, Pt. 2). (Illus.). 93p. (C). 1991. pap. 15.00 (*0-87169-812-9*, T812-PEJ) Am Philos.

Pendergast, John. The Bend in the River: A Prehistory & Contact Period History, Lowell, Dracut, Chelmsford, Tyngsborough & Dunstable (Nashua, NH), Massachusetts 17,000 BP to AD1700. (Illus.). xvii, 92p. (Orig.). 1991. pap. text 14.95 (*0-9629338-0-5*) Merrimac River.

— Dracut. (Images of America Ser.). 1997. pap. 16.99 (*0-7524-0506-3*) Arcadia Publng.

— Lowell. (Images of America Ser.). 128p. 1996. pap. 16.99 (*0-7524-0410-5*) Arcadia Publng.

— Lowell, Vol. II. (Images of America Ser.). 1997. pap. 16.99 (*0-7524-0539-X*) Arcadia Publng.

Pendergast, John, ed. Life along the Merrimac: Collected Histories of the Native Americans Who Lived on Its Banks. LC 95-81901. (Illus.). 192p. (Orig.). (C). 1996. pap. 19.95 (*0-9629338-2-1*) Merrimac River.

Pendergast, Mark. Uncommon Grounds: The History of Coffee & How it Transformed Our World. 400p. 1999. 27.50 (*0-465-03631-7*, Pub. by Basic) HarpC.

***Pendergast, Ned.** Creation. 12p. 1999. pap. 7.00 (*0-9674487-8-6*) Good SAMAR.

— Game of Love. 8p. 1999. pap. 7.00 (*1-930714-00-9*) Good SAMAR.

— Seasons. 1999. pap. 7.00 (*1-930714-02-5*) Good SAMAR.

Pendergast, Richard A. Learn to Use Your Modem in a Day. (Popular Applications Ser.). 136p. (Orig.). 1995. pap. 15.95 (*1-55622-445-1*) Wordware Pub.

Pendergast, Richard J. Cosmos. LC 72-82897. 223p. reprint ed. pap. 69.20 (*0-7837-0462-3*, 204078500018) Bks Demand.

Pendergast, Sara & Pendergast, Tom, eds. St. James Guide to Children's Writers. 5th ed. LC 99-188753. 1406p. 1999. 140.00 (*1-55862-369-8*) St James Pr.

Pendergast, Sara, jt. auth. see Pendergast, Tom.

Pendergast, Susan, jt. auth. see Devencenzi, Jayne.

Pendergast, T. H. & Rosenow, Diane. Pen Pictures from the Second Minnesota: Personal Recollections by a Private Soldier & Marching Thro' Georgia. LC 98-11012. 1998. pap. 15.00 (*0-915709-58-9*) Pk Geneal Bk.

***Pendergast, Tom.** Creating the Modern Man: American Magazines & Consumer Culture, 1900-1950. 2000. write for info. (*0-8262-1280-8*) U of Mo Pr.

***Pendergast, Tom & Pendergast, Sara.** St. James Encyclopedia of Popular Culture, 5 vols. LC 99-46540. (Illus.). 3250p. 1999. 675.00 (*1-55862-405-8*) St James Pr.

Pendergast, Tom, jt. ed. see Pendergast, Sara.

Pendergast, William B. The Catholic Voter in American Politics: The Passing of the Democratic Monolith. LC 98-44649. (Illus.). 260p. 1999. 35.00 (*0-87840-724-3*) Georgetown U Pr.

Penderghast, Thomas F. & Abrams, Lois M. Journey to Couples' Conflict Resolution Using Game Theory: A Manual. (Illus.). 200p. 1998. pap. 19.95 (*0-9664377-0-5*) Guidance Facil.

Pendergr, Donald. Collision Repair Estimating. 1985. pap. 32.36 (*0-02-681230-4*) Macmillan.

— Collision Repair Estimating. 1987. 21.28 (*0-02-679910-3*) Macmillan.

Pendergraft, Patricia. Miracle at Clements' Pond. LC 86-30283. 192p. (J). (gr. 5 up). 1987. pap. 13.95 (*0-399-21438-0*, Philomel) Peng Put Young Read.

Pendergraph, Cynthia B., jt. auth. see Pendergraph, Garland E.

Pendergraph, Garland E. Handbook of Phlebotomy. 3rd ed. (Illus.). 126p. 1992. pap. text 25.95 (*0-8121-1564-3*) Lppncott W & W.

***Pendergraph, Garland E. & Pendergraph, Cynthia B.** Handbook of Phlebotomy & Patient Service Techniques. 4th ed. LC 98-13761. 245p. 1998. pap. 22.00 (*0-683-30556-5*) Lppncott W & W.

Pendergrass, Bonnie B. Public Power, Politics & Technology in the Eisenhower & Kennedy Years: The Hanford Dual-Purpose Reactor Controversy, 1956-1962. Bruchey, Stuart, ed. LC 78-22705. (Energy in the American Economy Ser.). 1979. lib. bdg. 19.95 (*0-405-12007-9*) Ayer.

Pendergrass, Carol R. Writing Right! Bk. 1: Manuscript. 96p. 1994. pap. 4.75 (*0-88323-261-8*, 149) Pendergrass Pub.

— Writing Right! Bk. 2: Cursive. 96p. (J). (gr. 1 up). 1994. pap. text 4.75 (*0-88323-262-6*, 150) Pendergrass Pub.

Pendergrass, Donald H. Collision Repair Estimating. 160p. (Orig.). (C). 1985. teacher ed. write for info. (*0-672-98387-7*); pap. text. write for info. (*0-672-98386-9*) Macmillan.

***Pendergrass, Lela.** Life Experiences. 1999. pap. write for info. (*1-58235-273-9*) Watermrk Pr.

Pendergrass, Paula & Riggs, Sherry. 20th Century Candle Holders: Roaring 20s, Depression Era & Modern Collectible Candle Holders. LC 98-88789. (Illus.). 160p. 1999. pap. 29.95 (*0-7643-0748-7*) Schiffer.

Pendergrass, Teddy & Romanowski, Patricia. Truly Blessed. LC 98-28962. (Illus.). 320p. 1998. 23.95 (*0-399-14420-X*, G P Putnam) Peng Put Young Read.

— Truly Blessed, 1 vol. 1999. reprint ed. mass mkt. 6.99 (*0-425-17110-8*) Blvd Books.

***Pendergrass, Tess.** Colorado Shadows. LC 99-89979. (Colorado Ser.). 2000. 25.95 (*0-7862-2372-5*) Five Star.

***Pendergrast.** Mirror Mirror. 2000. 26.00 (*0-465-05470-6*, Pub. by Basic); pap. 15.00 (*0-465-05471-4*, Pub. by Basic) HarpC.

Pendergrast, James. My Foolish Heart. LC 97-136642. 96p. 1997. per. 12.00 (*0-671-53666-4*, PB Trade Paper) PB.

***Pendergrast, Mark.** For God, Country & Coca-Cola: The Definitive History of the Great American Soft Drink & the Company That Makes It. 2nd ed. 2000. pap. 16.50 (*0-465-05468-4*, Pub. by Basic) HarpC.

Pendergrast, Mark. For God, Country & Coca-Cola: The Unauthorized History of the Great American Soft Drink & the Company That Makes It. (Illus.). 576p. 1994. pap. 14.00 (*0-02-036035-5*) Macmillan.

— For God, Country & Coca-Cola: The Unauthorized History of the Great American Soft Drink & the Company That Makes It. 1997. per. 14.00 (*0-684-82679-8*) S&S Trade.

***Pendergrast, Mark.** Uncommon Grounds: The History of Coffee & How It Transformed Our World. 2000. pap. 18.00 (*0-465-05467-6*, Pub. by Basic) HarpC.

Pendergrast, Mark. Victims of Memory: Sex Abuse Accusations & Shattered Lives. 2nd ed. 603p. (Orig.). 1996. pap. 24.95 (*0-942679-18-0*) Upper Access.

Pendergrast, Mick, jt. auth. see Neich, Roger.

Penders, C. L. The Life & Times of Sukarno. LC 74-369. 224p. 1974. 32.50 (*0-8386-1546-5*) Fairleigh Dickinson.

Penders, Ken & Kanterovich, Mike. Sonic the Hedgehog. (Look & Find Ser.). (Illus.). 24p. (J). (gr. k-6). 1996. lib. bdg. 14.95 (*1-56674-125-4*, HTS Bks) Forest Hse.

Penders, Mary, ed. see Cory, Pepper & McKelvey, Susan.

Penders, Mary, ed. see Pearson, Nancy A.

Penders, Mary C. Color & Cloth: The Quiltmaker's Ultimate Workbook. LC 89-10448. (Illus.). 144p. 1989. pap. 24.95 (*0-8442-2620-3*, Quilt Dgst Pr) NTC Contemp Pub Co.

Penders, Mary C., ed. see Donaldson, Beth.

Penders, Mary C., ed. see Kough, Lynn G.

Penders, Mary C., ed. see Sienkiewicz, Elly.

Penderson, Jean, jt. auth. see Hilton, Peter.

Pendey, Rekha. Women in India, Past & Present. (C). 1990. 32.00 (*0-685-49091-2*, Pub. by Chugh Pubns) S Asia.

Pendharkar, Sumant S. & Biegel, Richard A. dBASE IV Programming. LC 94-1530. 1994. 30.00 (*0-02-800424-8*) Glencoe.

Pendharkar, Sumant S., jt. auth. see Biegel, Richard A.

Pendharker, Sumant S. & Biegel, Richard A. dBASE IV Programming. 1995. teacher ed. write for info. (*0-02-800425-6*) Glencoe.

— Visual dBase 5.5 for Windows. 1997. teacher ed. write for info. (*0-02-802619-5*) Glencoe.

Pendias, Alina K. & Pendias, Henry K., eds. Trace Elements in Soils & Plants. 336p. 1984. 176.00 (*0-8493-6639-9*, S592) CRC Pr.

Pendias, Henry K., jt. ed. see Pendias, Alina K.

Pendias, Henryk, jt. ed. see Kabata-Pendias, Alina.

Pendl, G. Pineal & Midbrain Lesions. (Illus.). 280p. 1985. 126.00 (*0-387-81858-8*) Spr-Verlag.

Pendland, Jacquelyn C., jt. auth. see Boucias, Drion G.

Pendle, George. Paraguay: A Riverside Nation. 1976. lib. bdg. 59.95 (*0-8490-2409-9*) Gordon Pr.

— Uruguay. LC 85-24780. 136p. 1986. reprint ed. lib. bdg. 55.00 (*0-313-24981-4*, PEUR, Greenwood Pr) Greenwood.

Pendle, Karin. Eugene Scribe & French Opera of the Nineteenth Century. Buelow, George, ed. LC 79-20451. (Studies in Musicology: No. 6). 635p. 1979. reprint ed. pap. 196.90 (*0-8357-1004-1*, 207003900063) Bks Demand.

Pendle, Karin, ed. American Women Composers. (Contemporary Music Review Ser.). 128p. 1997. pap. text 22.00 (*90-5702-145-5*, Harwood Acad Pubs) Gordon & Breach.

— Women & Music: A History. LC 91-8413. (Illus.). 372p. 1991. 29.95 (*0-253-34321-6*) Ind U Pr.

***Pendlebury & Groves.** Company Accounts. 5th ed. (ITBP Textbooks Ser.). 2000. write for info. (*1-86152-595-8*, Pub. by ITBP) Thomson Learn.

Pendlebury, David & Jalbani, G. N., trs. The Sacred Knowledge: The Altaf Al-Quds of Shah Waliullah. 103p. 1982. 22.00 (*0-900860-93-6*, Pub. by Octagon Pr) ISHK.

Pendlebury, John, et al. The Ten Keys to Successful Change Management. LC 97-46626. 318p. 1998. 54.95 (*0-471-97930-9*) Wiley.

Pendlebury, John D. The Archaeology of Crete. LC 63-18049. (Illus.). 1969. 32.00 (*0-8196-0121-7*) Biblo.

— Handbook to the Palace of Minos at Knossos. 1979. reprint ed. pap. 10.00 (*0-89005-312-X*) Ares.

Pendlebury, Maurice & Groves, Roger. Company Accounts. 3rd ed. 256p. (C). 1994. pap. 26.95 (*0-415-10602-8*, B4059) Thomson Learn.

Pendlebury, Maurice, jt. auth. see Jones, Rowan.

Pendlebury, M.W. & Groves, R. E. Company Accounts: Analysis, Interpretation, & Understanding. 4th ed. LC 98-219160. viii, 272 p. 1998. 18.99 (*1-86152-262-2*) Thomson Learn.

Pendlebury, P., jt. auth. see Abbott, A.

Pendleton. Betrayal: Stony Man. (Stonyman Ser.: Bk. 40). 1999. per. 5.99 (*0-373-61924-3*, 1-61924-6, Harlequin) Harlequin Bks.

— Cloud of Death: Super Bolan, No. 65. (Four Horsemen Trilogy Ser.). 1999. per. 5.99 (*0-373-61465-9*, 1-61465-0, Wrldwide Lib) Harlequin Bks.

— Judas Kill: The Executioner, Vol. 244. 1999. per. 3.99 (*0-373-64244-X*, 1-64244-6, Wrldwide Lib) Harlequin Bks.

— Rage for Justice. (Superbolan Ser.: No. 58). 1998. per. 5.99 (*0-373-61458-6*, 1-61458-5, Wrldwide Lib) Harlequin Bks.

P

— Virtual Destruction. (Executioner Ser.: No. 245). 1999. per. 3.99 (*0-373-64245-8*, 1-64245-3, Harlequin) Harlequin Bks.

Pendleton, tr. see Hahnemann, Samuel.

Pendleton, Amena. The Golden Heart & Other Stories. (Illus.). 79p. 1987. reprint ed. pap. 4.30 (*0-910557-19-5*) Acad New Church.

***Pendleton, Andrew.** Employee Ownership, Participation & Governance: A Study of ESOPS in the UK. LC 00-42463. 2000. write for info. (*0-415-20424-0*) Routledge.

Pendleton, Andrew & Winterton, Jonathon, eds. Public Enterprise in Transition: Industrial Relations in State & Privatized Corporations. LC 92-44127. 288p. (C). (gr. 13). 1993. pap. 74.95 (*0-415-07572-6*) Thomson Learn.

Pendleton, Austin. Uncle Bob. 1995. pap. 5.25 (*0-8222-1476-8*) Dramatists Play.

Pendleton, Bonnie & Mehling, Betty. Relax! With Self Therap-Ease: A Simple Illustrated Course. (Illus.). 176p. 1984. pap. 7.95 (*0-13-772187-0*) P-H.

— Relax! with Self-Therap-Ease: Whole-Body Acupressure. (Illus.). 171p. 1976. lib. bdg. 15.95 (*0-917306-01-5*) Calif Pubns.

Pendleton, Brian F., jt. auth. see Poloma, Margaret M.

Pendleton, David & Hasler, John, eds. Professional Development in General Practice. (Oxford General Practice Ser.: No. 37). (Illus.). 192p. 1996. pap. text 55.95 (*0-19-262532-2*) OUP.

Pendleton, David, et al. The Consultation: An Approach to Learning & Teaching. (Oxford General Practice Ser.). (Illus.). 117p. 1984. pap. 22.95 (*0-19-261349-9*) OUP.

Pendleton, Don. Ambush. 1994. mass mkt. 4.99 (*0-373-61438-1*, 1-61438-7) Harlequin Bks.

— Armed Force: (The Arms Trilogy) (Executioner Ser.). 1995. per. 3.50 (*0-373-61197-8*, 1-61197-9) Harlequin Bks.

— Asian Crucible. (Executioner Ser.: No. 209). 1996. per. 3.75 (*0-373-64209-1*, 1-64209-9, Wrldwide Lib) Harlequin Bks.

— Asian Storm. (Stony Man Ser.: Vol. 27). 352p. 1997. per. 5.50 (*0-373-61911-1*, 1-61911-3, Wrldwide Lib) Harlequin Bks.

— Assault Reflex. (Executioner Ser.: No. 243). (Orig.). 1999. per. 3.99 (*0-373-64243-1*, 1-64243-8, Wrldwide Lib) Harlequin Bks.

— Baja Blitz. (Executioner Ser.). 1993. per. 3.50 (*0-373-61170-6*, 1-61170-6) Harlequin Bks.

— Battle Force. (Superbolan Ser.). 1993. mass mkt. 4.99 (*0-373-61432-2*, 1-61432-0) Harlequin Bks.

— Bird of Prey. (Stony Man Ser.: No. 24). 1996. per. 5.50 (*0-373-61908-1*, Wrldwide Lib) Harlequin Bks.

— Black Dawn Rising: (The Executioner #247) (Executioner Ser.: Bk. 247). 1999. per. 3.99 (*0-373-64247-4*, 1-64247-9, Wrldwide Lib) Harlequin Bks.

— Blind Eagle. (Stony Man Ser.). 1994. mass mkt. 4.99 (*0-373-61896-4*, 1-61896-6) Harlequin Bks.

— Blood & Fire. 1997. per. 3.75 (*0-373-64221-0*, 1-64221-4, Wrldwide Lib) Harlequin Bks.

— Blood Circle. (Executioner Ser.: No. 227). 1997. per. 3.75 (*0-373-64227-X*, 1-64227-1, Wrldwide Lib) Harlequin Bks.

— Blood Debt. (Stony Man Ser.). 1995. mass mkt. 4.99 (*0-373-61899-9*, 1-61899-0) Harlequin Bks.

— Blood Feud. (Superbolan Ser.). 1998. per. 5.99 (*0-373-61461-6*, 1-61461-9, Wrldwide Lib) Harlequin Bks.

— Blood Harvest. (The Executioner Ser.: No. 213). 1996. per. 3.75 (*0-373-64213-X*, Wrldwide Lib) Harlequin Bks.

— Blood of the Earth. (Executioner Ser.: No. 246). 1999. per. 3.99 (*0-373-64246-6*, 1-64246-1, Wrldwide Lib) Harlequin Bks.

— Blood Price. 1992. mass mkt. 3.50 (*0-373-61168-4*, 1-61168-0) Harlequin Bks.

— Blood Rules. (Executioner Ser.: No. 149). 1991. mass mkt. 3.50 (*0-373-61149-8*, Wrldwide Lib) Harlequin Bks.

— Blood Star. 1997. per. 5.50 (*0-373-61912-X*, 1-61912-1, Wrldwide Lib) Harlequin Bks.

— Blood Strike. (Superbolan Ser.). 1994. per. 4.99 (*0-373-61439-X*, 1-61439-5) Harlequin Bks.

— Body Armor. 1997. per. 3.75 (*0-373-64225-3*, 1-64225-5, Wrldwide Lib) Harlequin Bks.

— Breach of Trust. (Stony Man Ser.: No. 39). 1999. per. 5.99 (*0-373-61923-5*, 1-61923-8, Wrldwide Lib) Harlequin Bks.

— Call to Arms. 1997. per. 3.75 (*0-373-64224-5*, 1-64224-8, Wrldwide Lib) Harlequin Bks.

— Capitol Hit. 1993. per. 3.50 (*0-373-61173-0*, 1-61173-0) Harlequin Bks.

— Cayman Strike. (Executioner Ser.: No. 157). 1992. mass mkt. 3.50 (*0-373-61157-9*) Harlequin Bks.

— Chicago Wipeout. (Executioner Ser.: No. 8). 1988. mass mkt. 3.50 (*1-55817-067-7*, Pinncle Kensgtn) Kensgtn Pub Corp.

— Cleansing Flame. (Executioner Ser.). 1994. mass mkt. 3.50 (*0-373-61187-0*, 1-61187-0) Harlequin Bks.

— Code of Bushido. Vol. 55. 48p. 1997. per. 5.50 (*0-373-61455-1*, 1-61455-1, Wrldwide Lib) Harlequin Bks.

— Code of Conflict. 352p. 1999. per. 5.99 (*0-373-61468-3*, Wrldwide Lib) Harlequin Bks.

— Colors of Hell. (Executioner Ser.: No. 162). 1992. mass mkt. 3.50 (*0-373-61162-5*, 1-61162-3) Harlequin Bks.

— Combat Zone. LC 95-22688. 219p. 1995. per. 3.50 (*0-373-64202-4*, 1-64202-4) Harlequin Bks.

***Pendleton, Don.** Conflict Imperative. 2000. mass mkt. 5.99 (*0-373-61932-4*, 1-61932-9, Wrldwide Lib) Harlequin Bks.

Pendleton, Don. Crimson Tide. (Executioner Ser.: Vol. 238). 1998. per. 3.99 (*0-373-64238-5*, 1-64238-8, Wrldwide Lib) Harlequin Bks.

— Crisis Point. LC 95-22671. (Executioner Ser.). 220p. 1995. per. 3.50 (*0-373-61200-1*, 1-61200-1) Harlequin Bks.

— Dark Emblem. (Deathlands Ser.: Vol. 43). 1998. per. 5.99 (*0-373-62543-X*, 1-62543-3, Wrldwide Lib) Harlequin Bks.

— Day of the Vulture. (Superbolan Ser.). 352p. 1997. per. 5.50 (*0-373-61452-7*, 1-61452-8, Wrldwide Lib) Harlequin Bks.

— Dead Center. (Superbolan Ser.: No. 48). 1996. per. 5.50 (*0-373-61448-9*, 1-61448-6, Wrldwide Lib) Harlequin Bks.

— Dead Easy. (Mack Bolan Ser.: No. 6). 384p. 1986. per. 3.95 (*0-373-61406-3*) Harlequin Bks.

— Deadfall. (Superbolan Ser.). 1993. per. 4.99 (*0-373-61430-6*, 1-61430-4) Harlequin Bks.

— Deadly Agent. (Stony Man Ser.). 1994. per. 4.99 (*0-373-61898-0*, 1-61898-2) Harlequin Bks.

— Death Force. (Executioner Ser.: No. 216). 1996. per. 3.75 (*0-373-64216-4*, 1-64216-4, Wrldwide Lib) Harlequin Bks.

— Death Load. (Executioner Ser.: No. 150). 1991. mass mkt. 3.50 (*0-373-61150-1*, Wrldwide Lib) Harlequin Bks.

— Death Trail. (Executioner Ser.: No. 164). 1992. mass mkt. 3.50 (*0-373-61164-1*) Harlequin Bks.

— Death Whisper. (Executioner Ser.: Vol. 208). 1996. per. 3.75 (*0-373-64208-3*, 1-64208-1, Wrldwide Lib) Harlequin Bks.

— Deep Alert. (Stony Man Ser.). 1995. mass mkt. 4.99 (*0-373-61900-6*, 1-61900-6) Harlequin Bks.

— Deep Attack. (Executioner Ser.: No. 230). 1998. per. 3.99 (*0-373-64230-X*, 1-64230-5, Wrldwide Lib) Harlequin Bks.

— Devil's Guard. (Executioner Ser.: No. 240). 1998. per. 3.99 (*0-373-64240-7*, 1-64240-4, Wrldwide Lib) Harlequin Bks.

— Dirty War. (Mack Bolan Ser.: No. 5). 384p. 1985. per. 3.95 (*0-373-61404-7*) Harlequin Bks.

— Don Pendleton's Mack Bolan: Anvil of Hell. (Gold Eagle Ser.). 352p. 1988. pap. 3.95 (*0-373-61411-X*) Harlequin Bks.

— Doomsday Conspiracy. (Executioner Ser.: No. 242). 1999. per. 3.99 (*0-373-64242-3*) Harlequin Bks.

— Double Action. (Executioner Ser.). 1992. per. 3.50 (*0-373-61167-6*, 1-61167-2) Harlequin Bks.

— Edge of Night. (Stonyman Ser.: No. 42). 1999. mass mkt. 5.99 (*0-373-61926-X*, 1-61926-1, Wrldwide Lib) Harlequin Bks.

— End Game. (Executioner Ser.). 1997. per. 3.75 (*0-373-64218-0*, 1-64218-0, Wrldwide Lib) Harlequin Bks.

— Enemy Within No. 38: Stony Man. 1998. per. 5.99 (*0-373-61922-7*, 1-61922-0) Harlequin Bks.

— Evil Kingdom. (Superbolan Ser.: No. 23). 1991. mass mkt. 4.50 (*0-373-61423-3*) Harlequin Bks.

— Evil Reborn: The/Executioner. 1998. per. 3.99 (*0-373-64241-5*, 1-64241-2, Mira Bks) Harlequin Bks.

— Executioner No. 35: Wednesday's Wrath. 1990. mass mkt. 3.50 (*1-55817-425-7*, Pinncle Kensgtn) Kensgtn Pub Corp.

— Extreme Force. 1994. per. 3.50 (*0-373-61191-9*, 1-61191-2) Harlequin Bks.

— Eye of the Ruby. (Stony Man Ser.: No. 29). 1997. per. 5.50 (*0-373-61913-8*, 1-61913-9, Wrldwide Lib) Harlequin Bks.

— Fast Strike. (Executioner Ser.). 1993. mass mkt. 3.50 (*0-373-61172-2*, 1-61172-2) Harlequin Bks.

— Fight or Die. (Executioner Ser.: No. 217). 1997. mass mkt. 3.75 (*0-373-64217-2*, 1-64217-2, Wrldwide Lib) Harlequin Bks.

— Fire Burst. 1994. mass mkt. 3.50 (*0-373-61186-2*, 1-61186-2) Harlequin Bks.

— Fire Hammer. (The Executioner Ser.: No. 215). 1996. per. 3.75 (*0-373-64215-6*, 1-64215-6, Wrldwide Lib) Harlequin Bks.

— Fire Lash. (Executioner Ser.: No. 210). 1996. per. 3.75 (*0-373-64210-5*, 1-64210-7, Wrldwide Lib) Harlequin Bks.

— Fire Sweep. 1992. mass mkt. 3.50 (*0-373-61165-X*, 1-61165-6) Harlequin Bks.

— Fission Fury. (Executioner Ser.: No. 214). 1996. per. 3.75 (*0-373-64214-8*, 1-64214-9, Wrldwide Lib) Harlequin Bks.

— Flames of Wrath. 1997. per. 5.50 (*0-373-61453-5*, 1-61453-6, Wrldwide Lib) Harlequin Bks.

— Flash Point. (Superbolan Ser.: No. 12). 352p. 1988. per. 3.95 (*0-373-61412-8*) Harlequin Bks.

— Freedom Strike. LC 96-2383. (Executioner Ser.: Vol. 207). 221p. 1996. per. 3.75 (*0-373-64207-5*, 1-64207-3, Wrldwide Lib) Harlequin Bks.

— Hard Contact. LC 95-22664. (Executioner Ser.). 221p. 1995. per. 3.50 (*0-373-64203-2*, 1-64203-2, Wrldwide Lib) Harlequin Bks.

— Hawaiian Heat. (Executioner Ser.: No. 155). 1991. mass mkt. 3.50 (*0-373-61155-2*) Harlequin Bks.

— Hell Road. LC 95-22659. (Executioner Ser.). 218p. 1996. per. 3.50 (*0-373-64205-9*, 1-64205-7, Wrldwide Lib) Harlequin Bks.

— Hellfire Strike. (Superbolan Ser.: Vol. 67). 1999. per. 5.99 (*0-373-61467-5*, Wrldwide Lib) Harlequin Bks.

— Hellfire Trigger. (Executioner Ser.: Vol. 237). 1998. per. 3.99 (*0-373-64237-7*, 1-64237-0, Wrldwide Lib) Harlequin Bks.

— Hellground. 1994. mass mkt. 4.99 (*0-373-61436-5*, 1-61436-1) Harlequin Bks.

— High Aggression. (Superbolan Ser.: No. 54). 1997. per. 5.50 (*0-373-61454-3*, 1-61454-4, Wrldwide Lib) Harlequin Bks.

— Hostile Action. (Executioner Ser.). 1995. mass mkt. 3.50 (*0-373-61193-5*, 1-61193-8) Harlequin Bks.

***Pendleton, Don.** Hostile Instinct: Stony Man. 2000. per. 5.99 (*0-373-61930-8*) Harlequin Bks.

Pendleton, Don. Hostile Proximity. 1998. per. 3.99 (*0-373-64239-3*, 1-64239-6, Wrldwide Lib) Harlequin Bks.

— Hour of Conflict. (Executioner Ser.: No. 223). 1997. per. 3.75 (*0-373-64223-7*, 1-64223-0, Wrldwide Lib) Harlequin Bks.

— Hunting Cry. LC 96-2386. (Executioner Ser.: Vol. 206). 219p. 1996. per. 3.75 (*0-373-64206-7*, 1-64206-5, Wrldwide Lib) Harlequin Bks.

— Inferno. (Superbolan Ser.). 1994. mass mkt. 4.99 (*0-373-61437-3*, 1-61437-9) Harlequin Bks.

— Initiation Bk. 1: The Four Horsemen Trilogy. (Superbolan Ser.: No. 64). 1999. per. 5.99 (*0-373-61464-0*) Harlequin Bks.

— Intercept. (Superbolan Ser.: No. 428). 1992. per. 4.99 (*0-373-61428-4*) Harlequin Bks.

— Jackal Hunt. (Executioner Ser.). 1998. per. 3.99 (*0-373-64232-6*, 1-64232-1, Wrldwide Lib) Harlequin Bks.

— Judgment in Stone. (Superbolan Ser.: No. 57). 1997. per. 5.50 (*0-373-61457-8*, 1-61457-7, Wrldwide Lib) Harlequin Bks.

— Jungle Law. (Superbolan Ser.: Vol. 47). 1996. per. 4.99 (*0-373-61447-0*, 1-61447-8, Wrldwide Lib) Harlequin Bks.

— Kill Radius. (Executioner Ser.: No. 251). 1999. per. 3.99 (*0-373-64251-2*, 1-64251-1, Wrldwide Lib) Harlequin Bks.

— Killing Range. 1994. mass mkt. 3.50 (*0-373-61190-0*, 1-61190-4) Harlequin Bks.

***Pendleton, Don.** Killsport. (Superbolan Ser.: 71). 352p. 2000. per. 5.99 (*0-373-61471-3*, Wrldwide Lib) Harlequin Bks.

Pendleton, Don. Law of Last Resort. (Stony Man Ser.: No. 32). 1998. per. 5.50 (*0-373-61916-2*, 1-61916-2, Wrldwide Lib) Harlequin Bks.

— Lethal Agent. (Executioner Ser.). 1994. per. 3.50 (*0-373-61182-X*, 1-61182-1) Harlequin Bks.

— Lethal Impact. 1992. per. 4.99 (*0-373-61429-2*, 1-61429-6) Harlequin Bks.

— Mack Bolan: Terminal Velocity. (Gold Eagle Ser.: No. 2). 384p. 1984. pap. 2.95 (*0-373-61402-0*) Harlequin Bks.

— Mack Bolan: The Executioner. 1998. 63.88 (*0-373-96225-8*) Harlequin Bks.

— Message to America. (Stony Man Ser.). 1998. per. 5.99 (*0-373-61919-7*, 1-61919-6, Wrldwide Lib) Harlequin Bks.

— New Orleans Knockout. (Executioner Ser.: No. 20). 1989. mass mkt. 3.50 (*1-55817-219-X*, Pinncle Kensgtn) Kensgtn Pub Corp.

— Night Hit. (Executioner Ser.: No. 154). 1991. mass mkt. 3.50 (*0-373-61154-4*) Harlequin Bks.

— Nightmare in New York. (Executioner Ser.: No. 7). 1988. mass mkt. 3.50 (*1-55817-066-9*, Pinncle Kensgtn) Kensgtn Pub Corp.

— Nuclear Nightmare. LC 95-22341. (Stony Man Ser.). 349p. 1995. per. 4.99 (*0-373-61903-0*, 1-61903-0, Wrldwide Lib) Harlequin Bks.

— Omega Game. LC 95-22346. (Superbolan Ser.). 346p. 1995. per. 4.99 (*0-373-61443-8*, 1-61443-7) Harlequin Bks.

— Patriot Gambit. (Executioner Ser.: No. 222). 1997. per. 3.75 (*0-373-64222-9*, 1-64222-2, Wrldwide Lib) Harlequin Bks.

— The Perishing Game. (Stony Man Ser.: No. 23). 1996. per. 5.50 (*0-373-61907-3*, 1-61907-1, Wrldwide Lib) Harlequin Bks.

— Plague Wind. (Executioner Ser.). 1998. per. 3.99 (*0-373-64235-0*, 1-64235-4, Wrldwide Lib) Harlequin Bks.

***Pendleton, Don.** Precision Play: The Executioner. 2000. per. 4.50 (*0-373-64257-1*) Harlequin Bks.

Pendleton, Don. The Prime Target. (Executioner Ser.: No. 201). 1995. per. 3.50 (*0-373-64201-6*) Harlequin Bks.

— Punitive Measures. (Stony Man Ser.: No. 33). 1998. per. 5.99 (*0-373-61917-0*, 1-61917-0, Wrldwide Lib) Harlequin Bks.

— Rampage. (Superbolan Ser.). 1993. mass mkt. 4.99 (*0-373-61433-0*, 1-61433-8) Harlequin Bks.

— Ransom Run. (Executioner Ser.). 1993. per. 3.50 (*0-373-61176-5*, 1-61176-3) Harlequin Bks.

— Rebels & Hostiles. (Superbolan Ser.). 1998. per. 5.99 (*0-373-61459-4*, 1-61459-3, Wrldwide Lib) Harlequin Bks.

— Red Heat. (Superbolan Ser.: No. 50). 1996. per. 5.50 (*0-373-61450-0*, 1-61450-2, Wrldwide Lib) Harlequin Bks.

— Red Horse. 1997. per. 3.75 (*0-373-64226-1*, 1-64226-3, Wrldwide Lib) Harlequin Bks.

— Renegade Force. (Superbolan Ser.: Vol. 62). 1998. per. 5.99 (*0-373-61462-4*, 1-61462-7, Wrldwide Lib) Harlequin Bks.

— Reprisal. (Stony Man Ser.). 1998. per. 5.99 (*0-373-61918-9*, 0-61918-9, Wrldwide Lib) Harlequin Bks.

— Rescue Run. LC 95-22662. 221p. 1995. per. 3.50 (*0-373-64204-0*, 1-64204-0, Wrldwide Lib) Harlequin Bks.

— Resurrection Day. (Mack Bolan Ser.: No. 3). 384p. 1985. per. 3.95 (*0-373-61403-9*) Harlequin Bks.

— Retribution. (Superbolan Ser.: No. 63). 1999. mass mkt. 5.99 (*0-373-61463-2*, 0-61463-6, Wrldwide Lib) Harlequin Bks.

— Ride the Beast. (Executioner Ser.: No. 212). 1996. per. 3.75 (*0-373-64212-1*, 1-64212-3, Wrldwide Lib) Harlequin Bks.

— Risk Factor: The Executioner #253. 1999. per. 3.99 (*0-373-64253-9*) Harlequin Bks.

— Rogue Agent. (Executioner Ser.). 1995. per. 3.50 (*0-373-61199-4*, 1-61199-5) Harlequin Bks.

— Rolling Death. (The Executioner Ser.: Vol. 248). 1999. per. 3.99 (*0-373-64248-2*, Wrldwide Lib) Harlequin Bks.

— Satan's Thrust. LC 96-2391. (Stony Man Ser.: Vol. 21). 346p. 1996. per. 4.99 (*0-373-61905-7*, 1-61905-5, Wrldwide Lib) Harlequin Bks.

— Secret Arsenal. 1994. mass mkt. 4.99 (*0-373-61894-8*) Harlequin Bks.

— Select Fire: (The Arms Trilogy) (Executioner Ser.). 1995. mass mkt. 3.50 (*0-373-61195-1*, 1-61195-3) Harlequin Bks.

— Shadow Target. (Executioner Ser.: No. 249). 1999. mass mkt. 3.99 (*0-373-64249-0*, 1-64249-5, Wrldwide Lib) Harlequin Bks.

— Shifting Target. (Executioner Ser.). 1994. per. 3.50 (*0-373-61181-1*, 1-61181-3) Harlequin Bks.

— Shock Tactic. LC 95-22344. 349p. 1995. per. 4.99 (*0-373-61444-6*, 1-61444-5) Harlequin Bks.

— Shoot Down. (Executioner Ser.). 1995. per. 3.50 (*0-373-61198-6*, 1-61198-7) Harlequin Bks.

— Showdown. LC 95-22685. 348p. 1995. per. 4.99 (*0-373-61445-4*, 1-61445-2, Wrldwide Lib) Harlequin Bks.

— Silent Invader: (Stony Man #41) (Stonyman Ser.: Bk. 41). 1999. per. 5.99 (*0-373-61925-1*, 1-61925-3, Wrldwide Lib) Harlequin Bks.

— Silhouette Christmas Stories. 1987. mass mkt. 3.95 (*0-373-48212-4*) Harlequin Bks.

— Skylance. (Stony Man Ser.: No. 52). 1996. per. 5.50 (*0-373-61909-X*, 1-61909-7, Wrldwide Lib) Harlequin Bks.

— Slaughter Squad. (Executioner Ser.: No. 231). 1998. per. 3.99 (*0-373-64231-8*, 1-64231-3, Wrldwide Lib) Harlequin Bks.

— Stalk Line. 1995. per. 4.99 (*0-373-61442-X*, 1-61442-9) Harlequin Bks.

***Pendleton, Don.** Star Venture. 2000. per. 5.99 (*0-373-61929-4*) Harlequin Bks.

Pendleton, Don. Steel & Flame. (Executioner Ser.: No. 159). 1992. mass mkt. 3.50 (*0-373-61159-5*, 1-61159-9) Harlequin Bks.

— Steel Claws. (Executioner Ser.: No. 211). 1996. per. 3.75 (*0-373-64211-3*, 1-64211-5, Wrldwide Lib) Harlequin Bks.

— Stony Man, No. III. 1991. mass mkt. 4.99 (*0-373-61887-5*) Harlequin Bks.

— Stony Man V. (Stony Man Ser.). 1992. mass mkt. 4.99 (*0-373-61889-1*, 1-61889-1) Harlequin Bks.

— Stony Man IV. (Stony Man Ser.: No. 888). 1992. per. 4.99 (*0-373-61888-3*, 1-61888-3) Harlequin Bks.

— Stony Man VII. 1993. mass mkt. 4.99 (*0-373-61891-3*, 1-61891-7) Harlequin Bks.

— Stony Man II. 1991. per. 4.50 (*0-373-61886-7*) Harlequin Bks.

— Stranglehold. (Stony Man Ser.: Vol. 36). 1998. per. 5.99 (*0-373-61920-0*, 1-61920-4, Wrldwide Lib) Harlequin Bks.

— Stringer. (Stony Man Ser.: Vol. 18). 1995. mass mkt. 4.99 (*0-373-61902-2*) Harlequin Bks.

— Sunflash. (Stony Man Ser.: No. 22). 1996. per. 5.50 (*0-373-61906-5*, 1-61906-3, Wrldwide Lib) Harlequin Bks.

— Takedown. (Superbolan Ser.). 1994. mass mkt. 4.99 (*0-373-61434-9*, 1-61434-6) Harlequin Bks.

— Target Command. (Executioner Ser.). 1998. per. 3.99 (*0-373-64234-2*, 1-64234-7, Wrldwide Lib) Harlequin Bks.

— Terminal Option. (Executioner Ser.: No. 228). 1997. per. 3.75 (*0-373-64228-8*, 1-64228-9, Wrldwide Lib) Harlequin Bks.

— Termination Point: Four Horsemen Trilogy. (Superbolan Ser.: No. 66). 1999. per. 5.99 (*0-373-61466-7*, 1-61466-8, Wrldwide Lib) Harlequin Bks.

— Terms of Survival. LC 95-22686. (Stony Man Ser.). 349p. 1996. per. 4.99 (*0-373-61904-9*, 1-61904-8, Wrldwide Lib) Harlequin Bks.

— Terror Intent. (Executioner Ser.). 1997. per. 3.75 (*0-373-64219-9*, 1-64219-8, Wrldwide Lib) Harlequin Bks.

— Terror Spin. 1997. per. 5.50 (*0-373-61456-X*, 1-61456-9, Wrldwide Lib) Harlequin Bks.

— Thermal Strike. (Superbolan Ser.: No. 51). 1996. per. 5.50 (*0-373-61451-9*, 1-61451-0, Wrldwide Lib) Harlequin Bks.

***Pendleton, Don.** Thirst for Power. (Stony Man Ser.: # 44). 2000. per. 5.99 (*0-373-61928-6*) Harlequin Bks.

Pendleton, Don. Tiger Stalk. 1997. per. 3.75 (*0-373-64220-2*, 1-64220-6, Wrldwide Lib) Harlequin Bks.

— Tightrope. (Superbolan Ser.: No. 15). 352p. (Orig.). 1989. mass mkt. 3.95 (*0-373-61415-2*) Harlequin Bks.

— To Dance with Angels: An Amazing Journey to the Heart with the Phenomenal Thomas Jacobson. 400p. 1995. mass mkt. 5.99 (*0-7860-0095-3*, Pinncle Kensgtn) Kensgtn Pub Corp.

— Tooth & Claw. (Superbolan Ser.: No. 49). 1996. per. 5.50 (*0-373-61449-7*, 1-61449-4, Wrldwide Lib) Harlequin Bks.

— Tough Justice. (Executioner Ser.). 1998. per. 3.99 (*0-373-64233-4*, 0-64233-0, Wrldwide Lib) Harlequin Bks.

— Triburst: (The Arms Trilogy) (Executioner Ser.). 1995. per. 3.50 (*0-373-61196-X*, 1-61196-1) Harlequin Bks.

— Triple Strike. 352p. 1998. per. 5.99 (*0-373-61921-9*, 1-61921-2, Wrldwide Lib) Harlequin Bks.

— Ultimate Game. (Superbolan Ser.). 1998. per. 5.99 (*0-373-61460-8*, 1-61460-1, Wrldwide Lib) Harlequin Bks.

— Vendetta. (Superbolan Ser.). 1995. per. 4.99 (*0-373-61441-1*, 1-61441-1) Harlequin Bks.

P

— Vengeance Rising. (Executioner Ser.). 1998. per. 3.99 (0-373-64236-9, 1-64236-2, Wrldwide Lib) Harlequin Bks.
— Virtual Peril. 1997. per. 5.50 (0-373-61914-6, 1-61914-7, Wrldwide Lib) Harlequin Bks.
— Vortex. (Stony Man Ser.). 1995. per. 4.99 (0-373-61901-4, 1-61901-4) Harlequin Bks.
— War Against the Mafia. 1988. pap. 3.50 (1-55817-024-3) Kensgtn Pub Corp.
***Pendleton, Don.** War Bird. 2000. per. 4.50 (0-373-64255-5, Harlequin) Harlequin Bks.
Pendleton, Don. War Paint. (Executioner Ser.). 1994. per. 3.50 (0-373-61188-9, 1-61188-8) Harlequin Bks.
— Warhead. 1994. mass mkt. 4.99 (0-373-61897-2, 1-61897-4) Harlequin Bks.
— Warning Shot. (Executioner Ser.: No. 250). 1999. mass mkt. 3.99 (0-373-64250-4, 1-64250-3, Wrldwide Lib) Harlequin Bks.
— Wellfire. (Executioner Ser.). 1994. per. 3.50 (0-373-61189-7, 1-61189-6) Harlequin Bks.
— Zero Hour. (Stonyman Ser.: No. 43). 1999. per. 5.99 (0-373-61927-8, 1-61927-9, Wrldwide Lib) Harlequin Bks.
— Zero Tolerance. (Executioner Ser.: No. 229). 1997. per. 3.75 (0-373-64229-6, 1-64229-7, Wrldwide Lib) Harlequin Bks.
Pendleton, Don & Pendleton, Linda. To Dance with Angels. 1992. pap. 10.00 (0-8217-3755-4, Zebra Kensgtn) Kensgtn Pub Corp.
— To Dance with Angels. 400p. 1995. mass mkt. 5.99 (0-8217-0095-2, Zebra Kensgtn) Kensgtn Pub Corp.
— To Dance with Angels. 288p. 1996. pap. 12.00 (1-57566-105-5, Knsington) Kensgtn Pub Corp.
Pendleton, Don, jt. auth. see Pendleton, Laura.
Pendleton, E. H. Holloway: William Holloway of Taunton, Mass. (Illus.). 356p. 1991. reprint ed. pap. 55.00 (0-8328-2222-1); reprint ed. lib. bdg. 65.00 (0-8328-2221-3) Higginson Bk Co.
Pendleton, Howard. Criminal Justice in England: A Study in Law Administration. LC 87-81959. xv, 436p. 1987. reprint ed. lib. bdg. 42.00 (0-89941-579-2, 305340) W S Hein.
Pendleton, James H. Christian Doctrines: A Compendium of Theology. 1957. 22.00 (0-8170-0037-2) Judson.
Pendleton, James M. Baptist Church Manual. rev. ed. 1966. reprint ed. 16.99 (0-8054-2510-1, 4225-10) Broadman.
Pendleton-Jullian, Ann M. Road That Is Not a Road & the Open City, Ritoque, Chile. (Graham Foundation/MIT Press Series in Contemporary Discourse). (Illus.). 196p. (C). 1996. pap. text 18.50 (0-262-66099-7) MIT Pr.
Pendleton, Laura & Pendleton, Don. Night of the Jaguar. (Stony Man Ser.: No. 31). 1997. per. 5.50 (0-373-61915-4, 1-61915-4, Wrldwide Lib) Harlequin Bks.
Pendleton-Lee, Shaun & Belinorlec. ABCs of Aerobics. 112p. 1993. pap. 15.95 (0-8403-8608-7) Kendall-Hunt.
Pendleton, Leila A. A Narrative of the Negro. LC 78-178481. (Black Heritage Library Collection). 1977. reprint ed. 22.95 (0-8369-8930-9) Ayer.
Pendleton, Leila A. & Wilkes, Laura E. Narrative of the Negro: African-American Women Writers, 1910-1940 by Pendleton & Wilkes. 1996. 24.95 (0-7838-1418-6, Hall Reference) Macmillan.
Pendleton, Leslie. One Dough, Fifty Cookies: Baking Favorite & Festive Cookies in a Snap. LC 98-17818. (Illus.). 112p. 1998. 13.00 (0-688-15443-3, Wm Morrow) Morrow Avon.
Pendleton, Linda, jt. auth. see Pendleton, Don.
Pendleton, Linda D. Flying Jets. (Illus.). 301p. 1995. 49.95 (0-07-049296-4) McGraw.
Pendleton, Lorann, et al. Cultural Resource Overview, Carson City District, West Central Nevada. (Bureau of Land Management, Cultural Resource, Nevada Ser.: No. 5, Pt. 1). 324p. (C). 1982. reprint ed. pap. 34.38 (1-55567-624-3) Coyote Press.
Pendleton, Lorann, jt. auth. see Thomas, David H.
Pendleton, Louis. In the Okefenokee: A Story of War Time & the Great Georgia Swamp. LC 72-1558. (Black Heritage Library Collection). 1977. reprint ed. 20.95 (0-8369-9045-5) Ayer.
— The Wedding Garment: A Tale of the Life to Come. 191p. 1987. reprint ed. pap. 5.20 (0-910557-17-9) Acad New Church.
Pendleton, Michalene & Barnes, F. A. Canyon Country Prehistoric Indians. (Canyon Country Ser.). (Illus.). (Orig.). 1979. pap. 9.50 (0-915272-24-5) Wasatch Pubs.
Pendleton, Moses & Richards, Terri. Children on the Hill: Labanotation Score. (Educational Performance Collection). 99p. 1987. pap. write for info. (0-932582-52-4) Dance Notation.
Pendleton, Nathaniel D. The Glorification: Sermons & Papers. 2nd ed. 221p. 1985. reprint ed. 7.00 (0-910557-10-1) Acad New Church.
— Selected Papers & Addresses. 251p. 1985. 7.00 (0-910557-09-8) Acad New Church.
Pendleton, Phillip E. Oley Valley Heritage: The Colonial Years, 1700-1775, Vol. 28. Yoder, Don, ed. (Illus.). 232p. 1995. write for info. (0-911122-59-1) Penn German Soc.
Pendleton, Robert. Graham Greene's Conradian Masterplot: The Arabesques of Influence. LC 94-44448. 220p. 1996. text 59.95 (0-312-12571-2) St Martin.
Pendleton, Scott. The Ultimate Guide to Student Contests: Grades 7-12. LC 97-19244. 280p. (YA). (gr. 7 up). 1997. pap. 15.95 (0-8027-7512-8) Walker & Co.
— The Ultimate Guide to Student Contests, Grades K-6. LC 97-25545. (Illus.). 288p. (Orig.). (J). (gr. k-6). 1998. pap. 14.95 (0-8027-7513-6) Walker & Co.
Pendleton, Scott, ed. see Symonds, Walter S., Jr.

***Pendleton, Thomas A.** Henry VI: Critical Essays. (Shakespeare Criticism Ser.: 22). 300p. 2000. 65.00 (0-8153-3301-3) Garland.
Pendleton, Thomas A. I'm Sorry about the Clock: Chronology, Composition, & Narrative Technique in The Great Gatsby. LC 91-51135. 160p. 1993. 29.50 (0-945636-38-5) Susquehanna U Pr.
Pendleton, Thomas A., jt. ed. see Mahon, John.
Pendleton, W. C. History of Tazewell County & Southwest Virginia, 1748-1920. (Illus.). 720p. 1989. reprint ed. 32.50 (0-932807-39-9) Overmountain Pr.
Pendleton, Wade C. Katutura: A Place Where We Stay: Life in a Post-Apartheid Towns. LC 95-51498. (Monographs in International Studies, Africa: No. 65). (Illus.). 238p. (Orig.). (C). 1995. pap. text 20.00 (0-89680-188-8) Ohio U Pr.
Pendleton, Wendell. Estate Planning with the Living Trust. LC 95-68483. 120p. (Orig.). 1995. pap. 19.95 (1-884570-30-5) Research Triangle.
Pendleton, Willard D. Education for Use. 290p. 1985. 12.00 (0-910557-11-X) Acad New Church.
Pendleton, William C. History of Tazewell County & Southwest Virginia. rev. ed. (Illus.). xvi, 700p. 1997. pap. 44.00 (0-7884-0618-3, P151) Heritage Bk.
— History of Tazewell County & Southwest Virginia, 1748-1920. (Illus.). 700p. 1999. reprint ed. pap. 50.00 (0-8063-4833-X) Clearfield Co.
Pendleton, William C. History of Tazewell County & Southwest Virginia, 1748-1920. (Illus.). 700p. 1994. reprint ed. lib. bdg. 69.50 (0-8328-4021-1) Higginson Bk Co.
Pendleton, William N. Memoirs of William Nelson Pendleton. 1992. 30.99 (0-87377-926-6) GAM Pubns.
Pendleton, Winston K. Handbook of Inspirational & Motivational Stories, Anecdotes & Humor. LC 82-2279. 350p. 1986. 19.95 (0-13-378604-8, Parker Publishing Co) P-H.
— Speaker's Handbook of Successful Openers & Closers. 261p. 1984. pap. 7.95 (0-13-824517-7, Busn) P-H.
Pendleton, Yvonne J. & Tielens, A. G., eds. From Stardust to Planetesimals: Proceedings of a Symposium Held As Part of the 108th Annual Meeting of the ASP Held at Santa Clara, California, June 24-26, 1996. LC 97-72932. (ASP Conference Series Proceedings: Vol. 122). 470p. 1997. 34.00 (1-886733-42-2) Astron Soc Pacific.
Pendley, William P. It Takes a Hero: The Grassroots Battle Against Environmental Oppression. Arnold, Ron, ed. xviii, 326p. (Orig.). 1994. pap. 14.95 (0-939571-16-1) Free Enter Pr.
— War on the West: Government Tyranny on America's Great Frontier. 314p. 1995. 21.95 (0-89526-482-X) Regnery Pub.
Pendley, William T., jt. auth. see Martel, William C.
Pendlington, Mark, et al. West Coast Steelhead. (Illus.). 128p. 1999. 100.00 (0-88839-459-4); pap. 14.95 (0-88839-457-8) Hancock House.
***Pendlum, David W.** So, Who Do You Think You Are? Face Your Wounds, Heal Them & Change Your Life. Chinn, Susan & Macaluso, Nora, eds. LC 99-68285. 160p. 2000. pap. 9.95 (0-9672942-1-5) Grnlf Ent.
Pendo, Stephen. Aviation in the Cinema. LC 84-14169. 414p. 1985. 37.00 (0-8108-1746-2) Scarecrow.
Pendofunda, Liviu. Magicians of the Emptiness. 148p. (C). 1997. pap. write for info. (0-9623183-5-3) Moonfall Pr VA.
Pendola, Angelo. Poesie per I Romeni: Italian Poetry.Tr. of Poetry for the Romanians. (ITA.). 99p. 1990. 20.00 (0-89304-539-X); pap. 10.00 (0-89304-538-1) Cross-Cultrl NY.
— Zabut: Italian Poetry. Scammacca, Nat, ed. 40p. 1983. pap. 5.00 (0-89304-565-9) Cross-Cultrl NY.
Pendola, Richard. Lab Manual for General Biology - Zoology. (C). 1993. student ed. 12.54 (1-56870-069-5) RonJon Pub.
Pendray, E. The Earth-Tube. LC 74-15967. (Science Fiction Ser.). 316p. 1975. reprint ed. 25.95 (0-405-06287-7) Ayer.
Pendreigh, Brian. Ewan McGregor. LC 99-61809. (Illus.). 256p. 1999. pap. 14.95 (1-56025-239-1, Thunders Mouth) Avalon NY.
— On Location: The Film Fan's Guide to Britain & Ireland. (Illus.). 208p. 1996. 29.95 (1-85158-729-2, Pub. by Mainstream Pubng) Trafalgar.
Pendrell, Ernest. Seven Times Monday. 1961. pap. 5.25 (0-8222-1016-9) Dramatists Play.
Pendrill, David, jt. auth. see Lewis, Richard.
Pendry, J. D. The Three Meter Zone: Common Sense Leadership for NCOs. LC 98-46937. 256p. 1999. 24.95 (0-89141-679-X) Presidio Pr.
Pendry, Pattie. Lord, Teach Me How to Pray. McDougal, Harold, ed. 112p. 1998. pap. 7.99 (1-884369-88-X, Serenity Bks) McDougal Pubng.
Pendse, G. S., ed. Recent Advances in Cytochalasans. 202p. (gr. 13). 1987. text 150.95 (0-412-29350-1) Chapman & Hall.
Pendse, Shripad G., ed. Perspectives on an Economic Future: Forms, Reforms, & Evaluations, 116. LC 90-37841. (Contributions in Economics & Economic History Ser.: No. 116). 216p. 1991. 57.95 (0-313-26288-8, PCG/, Greenwood Pr) Greenwood.
Pendziwol, Jean. No Dragons for Tea: Fire Safety for Kids (And Dragons) unabridged ed. (Illus.). 32p. (J). (ps-2). 1999. 14.95 (1-55074-569-7, Pub. by Kids Can Pr) Genl Dist Srvs.
Pene Du Bois, Henri, tr. see France, Anatole, pseud.
Pene Du Bois, William. The Twenty-One Balloons. (Illus.). (J). (gr. 5-9). 1947. 16.99 (0-670-73441-1, Viking Child) Peng Put Young Read.
Pene Du Bois, William, jt. auth. see Caudill, Rebecca.
***Penelhum, Terence.** Christian Ethics & Human Nature. 2000. pap. 16.00 (1-56338-327-6) TPI PA.

Penelhum, Terence. David Hume: An Introduction to His Philosophical System. LC 91-9096. (Series in the History of Philosophy). 240p. (C). 1992. 36.95 (1-55753-012-2) Purdue U Pr.
— Faith. (Philosophical Topics Ser.). (C). 1988. pap. text 12.00 (0-02-393721-1, Macmillan Coll) P-H.
— God & Skepticism. 200p. 1983. text 112.50 (90-277-1550-5, D Reidel) Kluwer Academic.
***Penelhum, Terence.** Themes in Hume: The Self, the Will, Religion. 296p. 2000. text 55.00 (0-19-823898-3) OUP.
Penelis, G. G. & Kappos, A. J. Earthquake Resistant Concrete Structures. LC 96-70571. (Illus.). 592p. (C). (gr. 13). 1996. 120.00 (0-419-18720-0, E & FN Spon) Routledge.
Penella, Robert J. The Private Orations of Themistius. LC 99-30092. (The Transformation of the Classical Heritage Ser.: Vol. Xxix). 287p. 1999. 55.00 (0-520-21821-3, Pub. by U CA Pr) Cal Prin Full Svc.
Penelope, tr. William of St. Thierry: On Contemplating God, Prayer, Meditations. (Cistercian Fathers Ser.: No. 3). 1970. pap. 7.95 (0-87907-903-7) Cistercian Pubns.
Penelope, Allison M. Archaeology of Household Activities. LC 98-46371. 1999. pap. 29.99 (0-415-20597-2) Routledge.
Penelope, Julia. Flinging Wide the Eyed Universe. 84p. 1998. pap. 8.00 (1-884540-34-1) Haleys.
— Speaking Freely: Unlearning the Lies of the Fathers' Tongues. (Athene Ser.). 370p. 1990. text 37.50 (0-08-036556-6, Pub. by PPI); pap. text 16.95 (0-08-036555-8, Pub. by PPI) Elsevier.
— Speaking Freely: Unlearning the Lies of the Fathers' Tongues. (Athene Ser.). 328p. (C). 1990. text 37.50 (0-8077-6245-8); pap. text 19.95 (0-8077-6244-X) Tchrs Coll.
Penelope, Julia & Wolfe, Susan J., eds. The Original Coming Out Stories. 2nd enl. rev. ed. (Illus.). 312p. 1989. pap. 14.95 (0-89594-339-5) Crossing Pr.
Penelope, Julia, jt. ed. see Wolfe, Susan J.
***Penenberg, Adam L. & Barry, Marc.** Spooked: Espionage in Corporate America. 2000. pap. 26.00 (0-7382-0271-1, Pub. by Perseus Pubng) HarpC.
Peneneau, Taylor. Dan Walker: The Glory & the Tragedy. 1993. 29.95 (0-9623414-7-9) Smith Collins.
Peneneau, Taylor & Ellis, Bob. Dan Walker: The Glory & the Tragedy. 352p. 1993. pap. 15.95 (0-9623414-6-0) Smith Collins.
Pener, Degen. The Swing Book. LC 99-42126. (Illus.). 288p. 1999. pap. 14.95 (0-316-69802-4, Back Bay) Little.
Pener, Michael A. Discovery: Interviewing & Investigation. 3rd ed. 352p. (C). 1998. per. 36.50 (0-929563-43-3) Pearson Pubns.
Penetrante, Bernie M. & Schultheis, Shirley E., eds. Non-Thermal Plasma Techniques for Pollution Control, 2 vols. LC 93-21307. (NATO ASI Series G: Ecological Sciences: Vol. 34). (Illus.). lxxii, 790p. 1994. 437.95 (0-387-57174-4) Spr-Verlag.
Penfield. Bon Voyage. 135p. 1992. 15.00 (0-86690-406-9) Am Fed Astrologers.
Penfield, A. Jefferson. Outpatient Gynecologic Surgery. LC 96-49541. (Illus.). 304p. 1997. 69.00 (0-683-30176-4) Lppncott W & W.
Penfield, Elizabeth. Short Takes: Model Essays for Composition. 4th ed. LC 92-22100. (C). 1992. pap. 18.50 (0-673-46598-5) HarperTrade.
Penfield, Elizabeth. Short Takes: Model Essays for Composition. 6th ed. 108p. 1998. 12.00 (0-321-02666-7) Addson-Wesley Educ.
***Penfield, Elizabeth.** Short Takes: Model Essays for Composition. 6th ed. LC 97-44941. 350p. (C). 1998. pap. 33.53 (0-321-01470-7) Longman.
Penfield, Elizabeth & Hill. Quick Takes: Short Model Essays for Composition. LC 94-20373. 352p. (C). 1997. pap. text 36.93 (0-06-501338-7) Addson-Wesley Educ.
Penfield, Florence B. Penfield: Genealogy of the Descendants of Samual Penfield, with a Supplement of Dr. Levi Buckingham Line & the Gridley, Dwight, Burlingham, Dewey & Pyncheon Collateral Lines. 320p. 1994. reprint ed. pap. 49.50 (0-8328-4369-5); reprint ed. lib. bdg. 59.50 (0-8328-4349-0) Higginson Bk Co.
Penfield, Joyce. Communicating with Quotes: The Igbo Case, 8. LC 82-15626. (Contributions in Intercultural & Comparative Studies: No. 8). (Illus.). 138p. 1983. 55.00 (0-313-23767-0, PEN/, Greenwood Pr) Greenwood.
Penfield, Joyce, ed. Women & Language in Transition. LC 86-23113. 208p. (C). 1987. text 74.50 (0-88706-485-X); pap. text 24.95 (0-88706-486-8) State U NY Pr.
Penfield, Kate, ed. Into a New Day: Exploring a Baptist Journey of Division, Diversity, Dialogue. LC 96-38530. 96p. 1997. pap. 11.00 (1-57312-049-9) Smyth & Helwys.
Penfield, Marc. Horoscopes of U. S. & Canada. 1996. spiral bd. 41.00 (0-86690-465-4, P3617-014) Am Fed Astrologers.
— Solar Returns in Your Face. 1996. 19.95 (0-86690-460-3, P3618-014) Am Fed Astrologers.
Penfield, Marjorie P. & Campbell, Ada M. Experimental Food Science. 3rd ed. (Food Science & Technology Ser.). 541p. 1990. text 61.00 (0-12-157920-4) Acad Pr.
Penfield, Mark. Stars over England. 1996. spiral bd. 12.95 (0-86690-453-0, P3589-014) Am Fed Astrologers.
Penfield, Paul, Jr., ed. see Conference on Advanced Research in VLSI (1984: MIT.
Penfield, Paul, Jr., ed. see Massachusetts Institute of Technology, Conference.
Penfield, Thomas. Directory of Buried or Sunken Treasures & Lost Mines of the United States. (True Treasure Ser.). (Illus.). 134p. (Orig.). 1979. reprint ed. pap. text 8.95 (0-941620-06-9) Carson Ent.
— A Guide to Treasure in Arizona. (True Treasure Ser.). 134p. 1982. reprint ed. pap. 9.95 (0-941620-01-8) Carson Ent.

— A Guide to Treasure in California. (Treasure Guide Ser.). 160p. (Orig.). 1983. reprint ed. pap. 9.95 (0-941620-23-9) Carson Ent.
— A Guide to Treasure in Missouri. (Treasure Guide Ser.). 60p. 1974. pap. 7.95 (0-941620-13-1) Carson Ent.
— A Guide to Treasure in Montana & Wyoming. (True Treasure Ser.). 84p. (Orig.). 1975. pap. 6.95 (0-941620-28-X) Carson Ent.
— Treasure Guide to Nebraska, Kansas, North & South Dakota. (Treasure Guide Ser.). 87p. 1971. pap. 7.95 (0-941620-18-2) Carson Ent.
— Treasure Guide to Nevada. (Treasure Guide Ser.). 74p. 1974. pap. 8.95 (0-941620-15-8) Carson Ent.
— Treasure Guide to New Mexico. (Treasure Guide Ser.). 104p. 1974. pap. 8.95 (0-941620-24-7) Carson Ent.
— Treasure Guide to Texas. (Treasure Guide Ser.). 141p. 1988. pap. 9.95 (0-941620-02-6) Carson Ent.
Penfield, Wilder. The Mystery of the Mind: A Critical Study of Consciousness & the Human Brain. LC 74-25626. 154p. reprint ed. pap. 47.80 (0-7837-0102-0, 204038000016) Bks Demand.
Penfield, Wilder & Roberts, Lamar. Speech & Brain-Mechanisms. LC 59-5602. 300p. 1959. reprint ed. pap. 93.00 (0-608-02929-7, 206399500008) Bks Demand.
Penfold, Nita. The Woman with the Wild Grown Hair. 32p. 1998. pap. 7.95 (0-944754-49-X) Pudding Hse Pubns.
— The Woman with the Wild-Grown Hair. (Illus.). 32p. 1998. pap. 7.95 (0-944754-64-3) Pudding Hse Pubns.
Penfold, P. Susan. Sexual Abuse by Health Professionals: A Personal Search for Meaning & Healing. 224p. 1998. text 50.00 (0-8020-4269-4); pap. text 18.95 (0-8020-8106-1) U of Toronto Pr.
Penfold, R. A. Advanced MIDI User's Guide. 2nd ed. (Illus.). 192p. 1995. pap. 15.95 (1-870775-39-2) Cimino Pub Grp.
— Audio Amplifier Projects. (Illus.). 196p. 1997. pap. 15.95 (1-878427-60-1, XC8031) Cimino Pub Grp.
— Computers & Music. 2nd ed. 180p. 1995. pap. 13.95 (1-870775-32-5) Cimino Pub Grp.
— Electronic Music & Midi Projects. (Illus.). 160p. 1994. pap. 15.95 (1-870775-24-4, Pub. by PC Pubg) Cimino Pub Grp.
— Electronic Projects for Guitar. (Illus.). 128p. 1996. pap. 15.95 (1-870775-31-7, Pub. by PC Pubg) Cimino Pub Grp.
— Electronics: Build & Learn. 1990. 15.00 (1-870775-15-5) CRC Pr.
— Practical MIDI Handbook. 3rd ed. (Illus.). 135p. 1995. pap. 15.95 (1-870775-36-8) Cimino Pub Grp.
— Video Projects - For the Home Constructor. (Illus.). 128p. 1999. pap. 29.95 (1-878427-74-1) Cimino Pub Grp.
Penfold, R. R. C., comment. Computer Security: Businesses at Risk. 192p. 1999. 24.95 (0-7090-6253-2, Pub. by R Hale Ltd) Seven Hills Bk.
***Penfold, Sharon.** Change Management for Information Services. 239p. 1999. 60.00 (1-85739-281-7) Bowker-Saur.
Peng. Risk Management Life Insurance Products. 1997. 65.00 (0-7863-0882-6) McGraw-Hill Prof.
***Peng, Chengzhi.** Design through Digital Interaction. 192p. 2000. text 34.95 (1-84150-007-0, Pub. by Intellect) Intl Spec Bk.
Peng, David D., ed. Insurance & Legal Issues in the Oil Industry. LC 93-23158. (International Energy & Resources Law & Policy Ser.). 208p. (C). 1993. lib. bdg. 104.50 (1-85333-913-X, Pub. by Graham & Trotman) Kluwer Academic.
Peng, Fang. The Geopotential: Modeling Techniques & Physical Implications with Case Studies in the South & East China Sea & Fennoscandia. (Uppsala Science Dissertations Ser.: No. 25). (Illus.). 146p. (Orig.). 1989. pap. 45.50 (91-554-2365-5) Coronet Bks.
Peng, Fei. Chinese Mulian Plays: Resources for Studies of Ritual & Performance. Seaman, Gary, ed. LC 94-71629. (Monographs Ser.). 300p. (Orig.). (C). 1994. pap. text 15.00 (1-878986-05-8) Ethnographics Pr.
Peng, H. & Freeman, J. S., eds. Advanced Automotive Technologies - 1995. (1995 ASME International Mechanical Engineering Congress & Exposition Ser.: DSC-Vol. 56/DE-Vol. 86). 220p. 1995. 88.00 (0-7918-1741-5, H01023) ASME.
Peng, H. L., ed. see Liu, Lily.
Peng, Jin-Sheng & Li, Gao-Xiang. Introduction to Modern Quantum Optics. 580p. 1998. 76.00 (981-02-3448-1) World Scientific Pub.
Peng, Kok L. & Tseng, Wen-Shing, eds. Suicidal Behavior in the Asia-Pacific Region. 267p. 1992. 49.50 (9971-69-165-5, Pub. by Sngapore Univ Pr) Coronet Bks.
Peng, Kok L., et al. Diminished Responsibility: With Special Reference to Singapore. 340p. (Orig.). 1990. pap. 42.50 (9971-69-138-8, Pub. by Sngapore Univ Pr) Coronet Bks.
— Mental Disorders & the Law. LC 94-943831. 360p. (Orig.). 1994. pap. 42.50 (9971-69-188-4, Pub. by Sngapore Univ Pr) Coronet Bks.
***Peng, Lam & Tan, Kevin, eds.** Lee's Lieutenants. 272p. 2000. 49.95 (1-86508-172-8, Pub. by Allen & Unwin Pty); 35.00 (1-86448-639-2, Pub. by Allen & Unwin Pty) Paul & Co Pubs.
***Peng, Leif.** Pokemon: Gotta Catch 'em All! 48p. (J). 1999. pap. 3.99 (0-307-10313-7, Goldn Books) Gldn Bks Pub Co.
Peng, Mike W. Behind the Success & Failure of U. S. Export Intermediaries: Transactions, Agents & Resources. LC 97-22747. 232p. 1998. 65.00 (1-56720-152-0, Quorum Bks) Greenwood.

***Peng, Q.** Auslandische Direktinvestitionen im chinesischen TransformationsprozeB.Tr. of Foreign Direct Investments in Chinese Transformation Process. (GER.). 244p. 1999. pap. text 37.00 (*90-5708-052-4*, Verlag Fakultas) Gordon & Breach.

Peng, S., et al, eds. Climate Change & Rice, Vol. XVI. LC 95-12491. (Illus.). 370p. 1995. 130.95 (*3-540-58906-6*) Spr-Verlag.

Peng, Samuel S. & Hill, Susan T. Understanding Racial-Ethnic Differences in Secondary School Science & Mathematics Achievement. (Illus.). 80p. 1996. reprint ed. pap. text 25.00 (*0-7881-3292-X*) DIANE Pub.

Peng Shi-Kaung & Morin, Robert J. Biological Effects of Cholesterol Oxides. (Illus.). 224p. 1991. lib. bdg. 189.00 (*0-8493-6776-X*, QP752) CRC Pr.

P'eng Shu-Tse. The Chinese Communist Party in Power. Evans, Leslie, ed. LC 79-92214. 508p. 1980. lib. bdg. 65.00 (*0-913460-75-3*) Pathfinder NY.

Peng, Soh Y., jt. auth. see Soon, Tan Y.

Peng, Syd S. Surface Subsidence Engineering. LC 92-80558. 170p. (C). 1992. 73.50 (*0-87335-114-2*, 114-2) SMM&E Inc.

— Surface Subsidence Engineering. LC 92-80558. (Illus.). 169p. reprint ed. pap. 52.40 (*0-608-09126-X*, 206975800006) Bks Demand.

Peng, T. A., jt. ed. see Nagata, M.

Peng, Wendy W. & Wallace, Dolores R. Software Error Analysis. LC 94-24763. 1994. write for info. (*0-929306-18-X*) Silicon Pr.

Peng, Xinwei. A Monetary History of China. Kaplan, Edward H., tr. from CHI. (East Asian Research Aids & Translations Ser.: Vol. 5). l, 932p. (C). 1994. pap. 50.00 (*0-914584-81-2*) WWUCEAS.

Peng Xizhe. Demographic Transition in China: Fertility Trends in China since the 1950s. (Studies on Contemporary China). (Illus.). 334p. 1991. 85.00 (*0-19-828715-1*) OUP.

Peng, Y. & Reggia, J. A. Abductive Inference Models for Diagnostic Problem Solving. Loveland, D. W. et al, eds. (Symbolic Computation - Artificial Intelligence Ser.). (Illus.). xii, 284p. 1990. 65.95 (*0-387-97343-5*) Spr-Verlag.

Pengelley, Eric T. Sex & Human Life. 2nd ed. LC 77-77720. (Life Sciences Ser.). (Illus.). 1978. pap. text. write for info. (*0-201-05770-0*) Addison-Wesley.

Pengelly, Andrew. The Constituents of Medicinal Plants: An Introduction to the Chemistry & Therapeutics of Herbal Medicines. 2nd rev. ed. 109p. 1996. pap. 30.00 (*0-646-31595-1*, Pub. by Sunflower Herbals) Herbalist & Alchemist.

Pengelly, Paul & Woodhouse, Douglas. Anxiety & the Dynamics of Collaboration. (Aberdeen University Press Bks.). 176p. (C). 1991. pap. text 25.00 (*0-08-040912-1*, Pub. by Aberdeen U Pr) Macmillan.

Pengelly, Paul, jt. ed. see Hughes, Lynette.

Pengelly, Raymond S. Microwave Field-Effect Transistors: Theory, Design & Applications. 3rd ed. Hammond, Crawford, ed. (Illus.). 704p. 1996. reprint ed. 79.00 (*1-884932-50-9*) Noble Pubng.

Pengilly, John, jt. auth. see Lyon, Rod.

Penglase, Charles. Greek Myths & Mesopotamia: Parallels & Influence in the Homeric Hymns & Hesiod. 292p. (C). 1997. pap. 25.99 (*0-415-15706-4*) Routledge.

Penglis, Gregory M. The Complete Guide to Flight Instruction. LC 93-38698. 550p. 1994. pap. 29.95 (*1-56825-012-6*) Rainbow Books.

Pengra, Nancy L. Family Histories: An Easy Step-by-Step Guide to Capturing Your Family's Precious Memories Now...Before They're Lost! abr. ed. 150p. 1995. spiral bd. 19.95 (*0-9645211-0-5*) Fam Hist MN.

Penguin. Snowman Coloring Book. (J). 1998. pap. 2.75 (*0-679-89215-X*, Pub. by Random Bks Yng Read) Random.

Penguin Books. Venice. 288p. 1999. pap. 14.95 (*0-14-028406-0*) Viking Penguin.

***Penguin Books Staff.** Amsterdam. 6th ed. (Time Out Travel Guides Ser.). (Illus.). 2000. pap. text 14.95 (*0-14-028944-5*) Penguin Putnam.

Penguin Books Staff. Boston. 288p. 1999. pap. 14.95 (*0-14-028405-2*) Viking Penguin.

— Dublin Guide. (Time Out Ser.). 278p. 1998. pap. 14.95 (*0-14-026687-9*, Penguin Bks) Viking Penguin.

***Penguin Books Staff.** London. 7th ed. 352p. 1999. pap. 14.95 (*0-14-027449-9*) Viking Penguin.

— New York. 8th ed. (Time Out Travel Guides Ser.). (Illus.). 2000. pap. 14.95 (*0-14-028943-7*) Penguin Putnam.

Penguin Books Staff. New York Guide. 5th ed. (Time Out Ser.). 352p. 1998. pap. 14.95 (*0-14-026441-8*, Penguin Bks) Viking Penguin.

— Paris. 7th ed. 352p. 1999. pap. 14.95 (*0-14-027451-0*) Viking Penguin.

***Penguin Books Staff.** Paris Short Stories. (Time-Out Book of... Ser.). 2000. pap. 12.95 (*0-14-028121-5*) Viking Penguin.

Penguin Books Staff. Rome Guide. 3rd ed. (Time Out Ser.). 288p. 1998. pap. 14.95 (*0-14-026688-7*, Penguin Bks) Viking Penguin.

— San Francisco Guide. 2nd ed. (Time Out Ser.). 288p. 1998. pap. 14.95 (*0-14-026746-8*, Penguin Bks) Viking Penguin.

***Penguin Books Staff.** Time Out Guide Brussels. 3rd ed. (Time Out Travel Guides Ser.). (Illus.). 2000. pap. 14.95 (*0-14-028942-9*) Viking Penguin.

— Time Out Guide Edinburgh & Glasgow. 2nd ed. (Time Out Travel Guides Ser.). (Illus.). 2000. pap. 14.95 (*0-14-028945-3*) Viking Penguin.

Penguin Books Staff. Vehicles. (Learners Ser.). 48p. (J). text 3.50 (*0-7214-1704-3*, Ladybrd) Penguin Putnam.

Penguin Books Staff, ed. Amsterdam Guide. 5th ed. (Time Out Travel Guides Ser.). 296p. 1998. pap. 14.95 (*0-14-027311-5*) Viking Penguin.

— Animals. (Learners Ser.). 48p. (J). text 3.50 (*0-7214-1705-1*, Ladybrd) Penguin Putnam.

— The Big Secret. (Read with Me Key Words to Reading Ser.: No. 9010-11). (Illus.). (J). (ps-2). 1990. teacher ed. 3.95 (*0-7214-4203-X*, Ladybrd) Penguin Putnam.

— Brussels Guide. 2nd ed. (Time Out Travel Guides Ser.). 296p. 1998. pap. 14.95 (*0-14-027316-6*) Viking Penguin.

— Bunnikin's Picnic Party. (Rhyming Stories Ser.: No. 401-1). (Illus.). (J). (ps-k). pap. 3.50 (*0-7214-0206-2*, Ladybrd) Penguin Putnam.

— Dinosaurs. (Learners Ser.). 48p. (J). text 3.50 (*0-7214-1701-9*, Ladybrd) Penguin Putnam.

— The Dragon Den. (Read with Me Key Words to Reading Ser.: No. 9010-2). (Illus.). (J). (ps-2). 1990. 3.50 (*0-7214-1315-3*, Ladybrd) Penguin Putnam.

— The Dragon Den, Vol. 2. (Series 9011-2: No. 2). (Illus.). (J). (ps-2). 1990. student ed. 2.95 (*0-7214-3221-2*, Ladybrd) Penguin Putnam.

— The Earth. (Learners Ser.). (Illus.). 48p. (J). 1994. text 3.50 (*0-7214-1708-6*, Ladybrd) Penguin Putnam.

— Ecology. (Learners Ser.). 48p. (J). text 3.50 (*0-7214-1710-8*, Ladybrd) Penguin Putnam.

— Edinburgh Guide. (Time Out Travel Guides Ser.). 288p. 1998. pap. 14.95 (*0-14-026684-4*) Viking Penguin.

— First Words. (Read with Me Key Words to Reading Ser.: No. 9010-0). (Illus.). (J). (ps-2). 1990. pap., teacher ed. 3.95 (*0-7214-3219-0*, Ladybrd) Penguin Putnam.

— Heidi. (Classics Ser.). (Illus.). 56p. (J). text 3.50 (*0-7214-1751-5*, Ladybrd) Penguin Putnam.

— Mustang. 1999. pap. 6.99 (*0-7214-5688-X*, Ladybrd) Penguin Putnam.

— My Alphabet Book. (Early Readers Ser.: No. S8711-5). (Illus.). (J). (ps-2). 3.95 (*0-7214-5145-4*, Ladybrd) Penguin Putnam.

— New Orleans Guide. (Time Out Travel Guides Ser.). 296p. 1998. pap. 14.95 (*0-14-027448-0*) Viking Penguin.

— Plants. (Learners Ser.). 48p. (J). text 3.50 (*0-7214-1709-4*, Ladybrd) Penguin Putnam.

— Puppy Tales. (Two Minute Tales Ser.). 48p. (J). 1996. 2.99 (*0-7214-5445-3*, Ladybrd) Penguin Putnam.

— Sam to the Rescue, Series 9011-4, No. 4. (Read with Me Key Words to Reading Ser.: No. 9010-4). (Illus.). 1990. student ed. 2.95 (*0-7214-3223-9*, Ladybrd) Penguin Putnam.

— The Sea. (Information Activity Ser.). 24p. (J). 3.50 (*0-7214-3442-8*, Ladybrd) Penguin Putnam.

— Skeletons. 1999. pap. 4.99 (*0-7214-5656-1*, Ladybrd) Penguin Putnam.

— Space. (Learners Ser.). 48p. (J). text 3.50 (*0-7214-1702-7*, Ladybrd) Penguin Putnam.

— The Space Boat, Vol. 3. (Series 9011-3: No. 3). (Illus.). (J). (ps-2). 1990. student ed. 2.95 (*0-7214-3222-0*, Ladybrd) Penguin Putnam.

— The Stuarts. (History of Britain Ser.: No. F895-5). (Illus.). (YA). (gr. 5 up). 1990. pap. 3.95 (*1-85543-010-X*, Ladybrd) Penguin Putnam.

— Tales from the Arabian Nights. (Classics Ser.). (Illus.). 56p. (J). 1997. text 3.50 (*0-7214-1759-0*, Ladybrd) Penguin Putnam.

— Things That Fly. (Information Activity Ser.). 24p. (J). 3.50 (*0-7214-3443-6*, Ladybrd) Penguin Putnam.

— The Three Billy Goats Gruff. (Fairy Tale Fun Ser.). (J). 3.95 (*0-7214-5430-5*, Ladybrd) Penguin Putnam.

— The Three Little Pigs. (Fairy Tale Fun Ser.). (J). 3.95 (*0-7214-5431-3*, Ladybrd) Penguin Putnam.

— The Three Musketeers. (Classics Ser.). 56p. (J). text 3.50 (*0-7214-1753-1*, Ladybrd) Penguin Putnam.

— Weather. (Illus.). 32p. 1999. pap. 4.99 (*0-7214-5604-9*, Ladybrd) Penguin Putnam.

— Your Body. (Information Activity Ser.). 24p. (J). 3.50 (*0-7214-3441-X*, Ladybrd) Penguin Putnam.

Penguin, Inky. The Writing Book. (Illus.). 44p. (J). (gr. 3-6). 1986. pap., student ed. 8.95 (*0-915924-66-8*) Tchrs & Writers Coll.

***Penguin Staff.** Budapest Guide. 3rd ed. (Time Out Guide Ser.). (Illus.). 296p. 1999. pap. 14.95 (*0-14-028633-0*, Penguin Bks) Viking Penguin.

— Dublin Guide. 2nd ed. (Time Out Guide Ser.). (Illus.). 296p. 1999. pap. 14.95 (*0-14-028173-8*, Penguin Bks) Viking Penguin.

— Florence & Tuscany Guide. 2nd ed. (Time Out Guide Ser.). (Illus.). 296p. 1999. pap. 14.95 (*0-14-027453-7*, Penguin Bks) Viking Penguin.

— New York Guide. 7th ed. (Time Out Guide Ser.). (Illus.). 352p. 1999. pap. 14.95 (*0-14-027452-9*, Penguin Bks) Viking Penguin.

— Rome Guide. 4th ed. (Time Out Guide Ser.). (Illus.). 296p. 1999. pap. 14.95 (*0-14-028755-8*) Viking Penguin.

— Time Out Barcelona Guide. 3rd ed. (Illus.). 296p. 2000. pap. 14.95 (*0-14-028941-0*, Penguin Bks) Viking Penguin.

— Time Out London Guide. 8th ed. (Illus.). 352p. 2000. pap. 14.95 (*0-14-028937-2*) Viking Penguin.

— Time Out Paris Guide. 8th ed. (Illus.). 352p. 2000. pap. 14.95 (*0-14-028938-0*) Viking Penguin.

— Time Out San Francisco Guide. 3rd ed. (Illus.). 296p. 2000. pap. 14.95 (*0-14-028936-4*, Penguin Bks) Viking Penguin.

— Time Out Sydney Guide. 2nd ed. (Time Out Guide Ser.). (Illus.). 318p. 2000. pap. 14.95 (*0-14-027446-4*, Penguin Bks) Viking Penguin.

— Time Out Vienna Guide. (Illus.). 296p. 2000. pap. 14.95 (*0-14-028067-7*) Viking Penguin.

— Tokyo Guide. (Time Out Guide Ser.). (Illus.). 296p. 1999. pap. 14.95 (*0-14-028460-5*, Penguin Bks) Viking Penguin.

— Washington, D. C. Guide. (Time Out Guide Ser.). (Illus.). 296p. 1999. pap. 14.95 (*0-14-028459-1*, Penguin Bks) Viking Penguin.

Penguin Staff & Time Out Magazine Staff. Time Out London 5. 2nd ed. (Illus.). 352p. 1997. reprint ed. pap. 14.95 (*0-14-026440-X*) Viking Penguin.

Penhale, Bridget, jt. auth. see Parker, Jonathan.

Penhale, Bridget, jt. auth. see Stanley, Nicky.

Penhale, Bridget, jt. ed. see Phillips, Judith.

***Penhale, Ken.** Helena. LC 98-88697. (Images of America Ser.). 1998. 18.99 (*0-7524-1398-8*) Arcadia Publng.

Penhale, Polly A., jt. ed. see Weiler, C. Susan.

Penhaligon, Susan. For the Children. 108p. 1996. pap. 13.95 (*1-899344-10-1*, Pub. by Do-Not Pr) Dufour.

Penhaligon, Susan, jt. auth. see Kestelman, Sara.

Penhall, Joe. Love & Understanding. 1998. pap. 5.25 (*0-8222-1688-4*) Dramatists Play.

— Pale Horse. 1996. pap. 9.95 (*0-413-70410-6*, Methuen Drama) Methn.

— Some Voices & Pale Horse. (Methuen Modern Plays Ser.). 1996. pap. 15.95 (*0-413-70440-8*, A0821, Methuen Drama) Methn.

Penhall, Melissa McFarland. Student Companion to Nathaniel Hawthorne. LC 98-54111. (Student Companions to Classic Writers Ser.). 192p. (YA). (gr. 9 up). 1999. 29.95 (*0-313-30595-1*, GR0595, Greenwood Pr) Greenwood.

***Penhallow, David.** After the Ball. 576p. 1999. pap. 24.95 (*0-9674147-0-9*) Rice Street.

Penhallurick, R. D. Tin in Antiquity. 272p. 1986. pap. 59.90 (*0-904357-81-3*, Pub. by Inst Materials) Ashgate Pub Co.

Penick, Douglas J. The Warrior Song of King Gesar. LC 96-20173. (Illus.). 176p. 1996. pap. 16.95 (*0-86171-113-0*) Wisdom MA.

Penick, Harvey. And If You Play Golf, You're My Friend: Further Reflections of a Grown Caddie. 176p. 1999. pap. 10.00 (*0-684-86733-8*, Fireside) S&S Trade Pap.

***Penick, Harvey.** For All Who Love the Game: Lessons & Teachings for Women. 192p. 1999. per. 10.00 (*0-684-86734-6*) S&S Trade.

Penick, Harvey. The Game for a Lifetime: More Lessons & Teachings. 208p. 1999. per. 10.00 (*0-684-86735-4*) S&S Trade.

— Harvey Penick's Little Red Book: And if You Play Golf, You're My Friend, 2 vols., Set. 1994. 40.00 (*0-671-99842-0*) S&S Trade.

Penick, Harvey & Shrake, Bud. And If You Play Golf, You're My Friend: Further Reflections of a Grown Caddie. 173p. 1993. 21.00 (*0-671-87188-9*) S&S Trade.

— For All Who Love the Game: Lessons & Teachings for Women. 176p. 1995. 19.50 (*0-684-80058-6*) S&S Trade.

— The Game for a Lifetime: More Lessons & Teachings. 208p. 1996. 20.50 (*0-684-80059-4*) Simon & Schuster.

— Harvey Penick's Little Red Book: Lessons & Teachings from a Lifetime in Golf. 176p. 1992. 20.50 (*0-671-75992-2*) S&S Trade.

***Penick, Harvey & Shrake, Bud.** The Little Red Book: Lessongs & Teachings from a Lifetime in Golf. LC 92-202. 176p. 1999. per. 10.00 (*0-684-85924-6*) S&S Trade.

Penick, Harvey & Shrake, Bud. The Wisdom of Harvey Penick: Lessons & Thoughts from the Collected Writings of Golf's Best-Loved Teacher. LC 97-28126. (Illus.). 352p. 1997. 25.50 (*0-684-84508-3*) S&S Trade.

Penick, James L. The New Madrid Earthquakes. rev. ed. LC 81-50531. 192p. (C). 1981. pap. 16.95 (*0-8262-0344-2*) U of Mo Pr.

Penick, James L., et al. The Politics of American Science: 1939 to the Present. rev. ed. 250p. 1972. reprint ed. pap. text 12.50 (*0-262-66014-8*) MIT Pr.

Penick, Michael. Beginning Bridge Complete. 176p. 1991. pap. 8.95 (*0-910791-06-6*) Devyn Pr.

— Beginning Bridge Quizzes. 1989. pap. 6.95 (*0-910791-67-8*) Devyn Pr.

***Penick, Robert L.** Blue Forms: Selected Poems, 1990-1998. Hathaway, Michael, ed. 48p. 1999. pap. 10.00 (*0-943795-37-0*) Chiron Rev.

Penick, S. Barksdale, jt. ed. see Braden, John R.

Peniel, Jon. The Lost Teachings of Atlantis. (Illus.). 371p. Date not set. pap. 17.95 (*0-9660015-0-8*, 2001) Windsor-Hill.

***Peniel, Jon & D'Esprit, Jean.** The Golden Rule Workbook: A Manual for the New Millenium. 76p. 1999. pap., wbk. ed. 17.95 (*0-9660015-1-6*, 2001, Pub. by Windsor-Hill) ACCESS Pubs Network.

Penikis, Janis J. Latvia: Independence Renewed. 1997. pap. 17.95 (*0-8133-1838-6*) Westview.

— Latvia: Independence Renewed. (Post-Soviet Republics Ser.). 2000. pap. 49.95 (*0-8133-0013-4*) Westview.

Peninger, Betsy, compiled by. Clip Art Classics: A Revised Collection of Old Favorites, Vol. I. (Illus.). 96p. 1998. pap text 10.95 (*0-88724-457-2*, CD-2016) Carson-Dellos.

— Clip Art Classics: A Revised Collection of Old Favorites, Vol. II. (Illus.). 96p. 1998. pap. text 10.95 (*0-88724-458-0*, CD-2017) Carson-Dellos.

— Clip Art Classics: A Revised Collection of Old Favorites, Vol. III. (Illus.). 96p. 1998. pap. text 10.95 (*0-88724-459-9*, CD-2018) Carson-Dellos.

— Clip Art for Fall. (Illus.). 32p. 1998. pap. text 4.95 (*0-88724-469-6*, CD-0995) Carson-Dellos.

Penington, Graeme & Burry, Hugh C. Introduction to Medical Rehabilitation: An Australian Perspective. 196p. 1990. pap. 24.95 (*0-522-84391-3*, Pub. by Melbourne Univ Pr) Paul & Co Pubs.

Penington, Isaac. The Inward Journey of Isaac Penington. Leach, Robert J., ed. LC 44-280. (Orig.). 1944. pap. 4.00 (*0-87574-029-4*) Pendle Hill.

Penington, M. Basil, ed. Towards an Integrated Humanity: Thomas Merton's Journey. 1988. pap. 17.95 (*0-87907-603-8*) Cistercian Pubns.

***Peninou, Ernest P.** History of the Sonoma Viticultural District: The Grape Growers, the Wine Makers & the Vineyards. LC 98-68600. (Illus.). 456p. 1999. 55.00 (*0-9626543-1-0*) Nomis Pr.

Penionzhkevich, Yu E. & Kalpakchieva, R. Exotic Nuclei: Proceedings of the International Conference. 516p. 1992. text 102.00 (*981-02-1104-X*) World Scientific Pub.

***Penisten, Gary D.** Pentagon Appointment: A Mid-Career Adventure. LC 99-56578. 240p. 2000. pap. 15.00 (*1-58151-066-7*, Pub. by BookPartners) Midpt Trade.

Penisten, John. Adventure Guide to Hawaii. (Adventure Guides Ser.). (Illus.). 300p. 1998. pap. 15.95 (*1-55650-841-7*) Hunter NJ.

— Hawaii: The Big Island: Making the Most of Your Family Vacation. 4th ed. LC 94-28554. (Illus.). 288p. 1994. pap. 14.00 (*1-55958-562-5*) Prima Pub.

— Honolulu. LC 89-11973. (Downtown America Ser.). (Illus.). 60p. (J). (gr. 3 up). 1990. lib. bdg. 13.95 (*0-87518-416-2*, Dillon Silver Burdett) Silver Burdett Pr.

Peniston, A. C. Search for Sybil. Hilovsky, Judy, ed. LC 89-316. 1990. 22.95 (*0-87949-291-0*) Ashley Bks.

Peniston-Bird, C. M. Vienna. LC 98-113366. (World Bibliographical Ser.). (Illus.). 198p. 1997. lib. bdg. 62.00 (*1-85109-275-7*) ABC-CLIO.

Peniston-Bird, C. M., jt. auth. see DeGroot, Gerard J.

Peniston, Bradley. Around the World with the U. S. Navy: A Reporter's Travels. LC 99-27320. 1999. 25.95 (*1-55750-665-5*) Naval Inst Pr.

***Peniston, John.** Hawai'i, the Big Island: Making the Most of Your Family Vacation. 6th ed. (Paradise Family Guides Ser.). (Illus.). 344p. 1999. pap. 15.00 (*0-7615-1622-0*) Prima Pub.

Peniston, Lorraine. Developing Recreational Skills in Persons with Learning Disabilities. 1998. pap. 27.95 (*1-57167-134-X*) Sagamore Pub.

Peniston, William A., ed. see Dana, John Cotton.

Penix, Sherry. San Diego Activity & Coloring Book for All Ages. (Illus.). (J). Date not set. pap. write for info. (*0-9670612-0-2*); pap. write for info. (*0-9670612-1-0*) Sher-A-Craft.

Penix, Sherry, jt. auth. see Berman, Linda.

Penjam, Jaan, jt. auth. see Tyugu, Enn.

Penjam, Jaan, jt. ed. see Bruynooghe, Maurice.

Penjam, Jean & Hermenegildo, M., eds. Programming Language Implementation & Logic Programming: Proceedings of the Sixth International Symposium, PHLILP '94, Madrid, Spain, September 14-16, 1994. (Lecture Notes in Computer Science Ser.: Vol. 844). 469p. 1994. 65.95 (*3-540-58402-1*) Spr-Verlag.

Penke, Botond & Torok, Angela, eds. Peptides: Chemistry-Biology-Interactions with Proteins. 467p. (C). 1988. lib. bdg. 211.55 (*3-11-011546-8*) De Gruyter.

Penker, Magnus, jt. auth. see Eriksson, Hans-Erik.

Penkert, Kathleen S. Marketing to Managed Care Organizations. LC 97-42357. 1998. pap. 9.95 (*0-87868-727-0*, CWLA Pr) Child Welfare.

Penkiln, Burn. Penkiln Burn. pap. 15.00 (*1-84166-001-9*, Pub. by Ellipsis) Norton.

Penkower, Monty N. The Emergence of Zionist Thought. LC 91-3416. (American University Studies: History: Ser. IX, Vol. 111). 159p. (C). 1991. text 33.95 (*0-8204-1600-2*) P Lang Pubng.

— From Catastrophe to Sovereignty: The Holocaust & Israel Reborn. LC 93-41078. 376p. 1994. text 47.50 (*0-252-02087-1*) U of Ill Pr.

— From Catastrophe to Sovereignty: The Holocaust & Israel Reborn. LC 93-41078. 360p. 1994. pap. text 19.95 (*0-252-06378-3*) U of Ill Pr.

— The Jews Were Expendable: Free World Diplomacy & Holocaust. LC 87-24638. 432p. (C). 1987. reprint ed. pap. 22.95 (*0-8143-1952-1*) Wayne St U Pr.

— The Jews Were Expendable: Free World Diplomacy & the Holocaust. LC 82-17490. 446p. 1983. text 34.95 (*0-252-00747-6*) U of Ill Pr.

Penland, Ken, jt. auth. see Alexander, George.

Penland, Patrick R. Communication Science & Technology. LC 74-77108. (Communication Science & Technology Ser.: No. 1). (Illus.). 228p. reprint ed. pap. 70.70 (*0-8357-6064-2*, 203456000090) Bks Demand.

Penland, Patrick R. & Fine, Sara F. Group Dynamics & Individual Development. LC 74-77110. (Communication Science & Technology Ser.: No. 3). 167p. reprint ed. pap. 51.80 (*0-7837-0911-0*, 204121600019) Bks Demand.

Penland, Patrick R. & Mathai, Aleyamma. Interpersonal Communication: Counseling, Guidance & Retrieval for Media, Library & Information Specialists. LC 74-77109. (Communication Science & Technology Ser.: No. 2). (Illus.). 187p. reprint ed. pap. 58.00 (*0-8357-6163-0*, 203456200090) Bks Demand.

— The Library As a Learning Service Center. LC 78-13491. (Books in Library & Information Science: No. 24). 255p. reprint ed. pap. 79.10 (*0-8357-6191-6*, 203456100090) Bks Demand.

Penland, Patrick R. & Williams, James G. Community Psychology & Coordination. LC 74-77111. (Communications Science & Technology Ser.: No. 4). 200p. reprint ed. pap. 62.00 (*0-7837-0727-4*, 204105100019) Bks Demand.

Penland, Patrick R., ed. see McCardle, Ellen S.

Penland, Patrick R., ed. see Williams, James G.

Penley, C., ed. Feminism & Film Theory. 224p. (C). 1988. pap. 18.99 (*0-415-90108-1*) Routledge.

Penley, Constance. Close Encounters: Film, Feminism, & Science Fiction. Speigel, Lynn et al, eds. (Camera Obscura Bks.). (Illus.). 313p. (C). 1990. reprint ed. pap. 18.95 (*0-8166-1912-3*) U of Minn Pr.

— The Future of an Illusion: Film, Feminism & Psychoanalysis. (Media & Society Ser.). (Illus.). 207p. (Orig.). 1989. pap. 16.95 (*0-8166-1772-4*) U of Minn Pr.

P

— NASA/Trek: Popular Science & Sex in America. LC 97-10902. (Illus.). 280p. (C). 1997. pap. 17.00 (*0-86091-617-0*, B4283, Pub. by Verso) Norton.
Penley, Constance & Ross, Andrew. Technoculture. (Cultural Politics Ser.: Vol. 3). (Illus.). 312p. (C). 1991. pap. 19.95 (*0-8166-1932-8*); text 47.95 (*0-8166-1930-1*) U of Minn Pr.
Penley, Constance & Willis, Sharon, eds. Male Trouble. LC 92-25407. (Camera Obscura Bks.: Vol. 3). 336p. (C). 1993. pap. 18.95 (*0-8166-2172-1*) U of Minn Pr.
Penley, Constance, ed. see Bellour, Raymond.
Penley, Gary N. Rivers of Wind: A Western Boyhood Remembered. LC 98-85764. (Illus.). 220p. 1998. pap. 12.95 (*0-86541-044-5*) Filter.
Penley, Janet P. & Stephens, Diane W. The M. O. M. S. Handbook: Understanding Your Personality Type in Mothering. 2nd ed. 64p. (Orig.). 1999. pap. text 14.00 (*0-9646974-0-8*, Mothers of Many Styles) Penley & Assocs.
***Penman, A. D., et al, eds.** Instrumentation, Monitoring & Surveillance: Embankment Dams. (Illus.). 288p. 1999. 68.00 (*90-5410-299-3*, Pub. by A A Balkema) Ashgate Pub Co.
Penman, A. D., tr. from FRE. Deterioration of Dams & Reservoirs: Examples & Their Analysis. 368p. (C). 1984. text 168.00 (*90-6191-546-5*, Pub. by A A Balkema) Ashgate Pub Co.
Penman, Bruce, tr. see Tusquets, Esther.
Penman, Bruce, tr. & intro. see Manzoni, Alessandro.
Penman, Cynthia E. Tangerine Moon. 1998. pap. write for info. (*1-57553-977-2*) Watermrk Pr.
Penman, Emily J., jt. auth. see Penman, W. Robert.
Penman, Ian. Vital Signs: Music, Movies & Other Manias. 374p. 1998. pap. 15.99 (*1-85242-523-7*) Serpents Tail.
Penman, Kay S. The Queen's Man. 288p. 1999. mass mkt. 6.99 (*0-345-42316-X*) Ballantine Pub Grp.
Penman, Laurie. The Clock Repairer's Handbook. (Illus.). 176p. 1994. 29.95 (*0-7153-0054-7*, Pub. by D & C Pub) Sterling.
***Penman, Laurie.** Gear Cutting on the Lathe. (Illus.). 51p. 1999. pap. 22.00 (*0-907868-70-3*) Clockwks Pr.
— Making Clocks. (Illus.). 122p. 1999. pap. 35.00 (*0-907868-71-1*) Clockwks Pr.
— Practical Clock Escapements. (Illus.). 245p. 1998. 42.50 (*0-9523270-4-X*) Clockwks Pr.
***Penman, Robyn.** Reconstructing Communicating: Looking to a Future. (Communication Ser.). 200p. 2000. write for info. (*0-8058-3648-9*) L Erlbaum Assocs.
***Penman, Sarah.** Honoring the Grandmothers: Dakota & Lakota Elders Tell Their Stories. LC 00-21324. 2000. pap. write for info. (*0-87351-385-1*) Minn Hist.
Penman, Sharon K. Cruel as the Grave. 256p. 1999. pap. 12.00 (*0-345-43422-6*, Ballantine) Ballantine Pub Grp.
Penman, Sharon Kay. Cruel As the Grave: A Medieval Mystery. LC 98-13085. 245p. (J). (gr. 7 up). 1998. 22.00 (*0-8050-5608-4*, Marian Wood) H Holt & Co.
— Falls the Shadow. 1989. pap. 12.50 (*0-345-36033-8*) Ballantine Pub Grp.
— Here Be Dragons. 720p. 1993. pap. 12.50 (*0-345-38284-6*) Ballantine Pub Grp.
— Here Be Dragons. 784p. 1987. mass mkt. 4.95 (*0-380-70181-2*, Avon Bks) Morrow Avon.
— The Queen's Man. 304p. 1998. pap. 12.00 (*0-345-41718-6*) Ballantine Pub Grp.
— The Queen's Man: A Medieval Mystery. 240p. 1995. 20.00 (*0-8050-3885-X*) H Holt & Co.
— The Reckoning. 608p. 1992. pap. 12.50 (*0-345-37888-1*) Ballantine Pub Grp.
— The Reckoning. 592p. 1995. 24.95 (*0-8050-1014-9*) H Holt & Co.
— The Sunne in Splendour. 944p. 1990. pap. 14.00 (*0-345-36313-2*) Ballantine Pub Grp.
— When Christ & His Saints Slept. (Eleanor of Aquitaine Trilogy Ser.: Bk. 1). 768p. 1996. pap. 14.00 (*0-345-39668-5*) Ballantine Pub Grp.
Penman, Sue, jt. ed. see Crossley, D. A.
Penman, Susanna, jt. auth. see Emily, Peter.
Penman, W. Robert & Penman, Emily J. Dr. William Goodell & Camp Paoli: The Goodell Collection at West Chester University Including Camp Paoli Documents (Camp Parole) (Illus.). 104p. 1987. pap. 19.95 (*0-9619411-1-1*) Serpentine Pr.
Penmann, Scott, ed. see Ingram, Julia & Hardin, G. W.
Penn. Mortal Term. 1985. 12.95 (*0-684-18317-X*, Scribners Ref) Mac Lib Ref.
— Where Have I Been All My Life. pap. 10.00 (*0-06-251350-8*) HarpC.
Penn & Edwards. Multivariable Calculus with Analytic Geometry. 5th ed. 560p. (C). 1997. pap. text 65.00 (*0-13-793084-4*, Prentice Hall) P-H.
Penn, Alan. Religious Education in a Pluralist Society: Drill, Militarism & Imperialism. LC 98-35315. (Education Ser.). 224p. 1999. pap. 24.50 (*0-7130-4038-6*, Pub. by Woburn Pr) Intl Spec Bk.
— Targeting Schools: Drill, Militarism & Imperialism. LC 98-46124. (Education Ser.). 224p. 1999. 54.50 (*0-7130-0217-4*, Pub. by Woburn Pr) Intl Spec Bk.
Penn, Alexandra & Williams, Dennis. Integrating Academic & Vocational Education: A Model for Secondary Schools. LC 96-37841. 71p. (Orig.). 1997. pap. 10.95 (*0-87120-276-X*, 197019) ASCD.
Penn, Alfred W., jt. auth. see Piekalkiewicz, Jaroslaw.
Penn, Audrey. Feathers & Fur. LC 98-23366. (Illus.). (J). (gr. k-5). 1999. 8.95 (*0-87868-710-6*, 7106, Child-Family Pr) Child Welfare.
— The Kissing Hand. LC 93-36159. (Illus.). 32p. (J). (gr. k-6). 1993. 16.95 (*0-87868-585-5*, Child-Family Pr) Child Welfare.
— No Bones about Driftiss. LC 89-13326. (Illus.). viii, 146p. (J). (gr. 2-6). 1989. 14.95 (*0-939923-11-4*); pap. 7.95 (*0-939923-12-2*) M & W Pub Co.
— Sassafras. (Illus.). 32p. (J). (ps-3). 1995. 16.95 (*0-87868-578-2*, Child-Family Pr) Child Welfare.
Penn, Audrey S., et al, eds. Myasthenia Gravis & Related Disorders: Experimental & Clinical Aspects. LC 93-8239. (Annals Ser.: Vol. 681). 1993. write for info. (*0-89766-755-7*); pap. 165.00 (*0-89766-756-5*) NY Acad Sci.
Penn-Brown, Adelle. Surviving Your Seasons of Change. Mackell, Phyllis, ed. (Orig.). 1991. pap. 1.95 (*0-9629630-0-3*) V I Christian Min.
Penn, Charles. Finding God. 1990. pap. 5.00 (*1-57836-084-6*, BW-065) Sathya Sai Bk Ctr.
— My Beloved. 1981. pap. 4.75 (*1-57836-085-4*, BW-105) Sathya Sai Bk Ctr.
Penn, Charles & Penn, Faith. Sai Ram. 1992. pap. 4.50 (*1-57836-086-2*, BW-165) Sathya Sai Bk Ctr.
Penn, Christopher N. Noise Control. 1979. 110.00 (*0-7219-0830-6*, Pub. by Scientific) St Mut.
Penn, Eric. Children of Chaotics: Breaking the Cycle of Family & Social Dysfunctionalism. unabridged ed. (Illus.). 160p. (Orig.). 1995. pap. 10.00 (*1-56411-118-0*, 4BBG0123) Untd Bros & Sis.
Penn, Faith, jt. auth. see Penn, Charles.
Penn, Garlene. Enrollment Management in the 21st Century: Delivering Institutional Goals, Accountability & Fiscal Responsibility. LC 99-61127. (ASHE-ERIC Report Ser.: Vol. 26-7). 15p. 1999. 24.00 (*1-878380-87-7*) GWU Grad Schl E&HD.
Penn, Gary, ed. see Institute of Medicine Staff.
Penn, Geneva. Jelly Bee. (Illus.). 16p. (J). (gr. k-1). 1998. pap. 6.00 (*0-8059-4151-7*) Dorrance.
Penn, Geoffrey. Fisher, Churchill & the Dardanelles. 1999. 36.95 (*0-85052-646-9*) Leo Cooper.
— HMS Thunderer. 208p. 1987. 60.00 (*0-85937-321-5*, Pub. by K Mason Pubns Ltd) St Mut.
Penn, Graham. Banking Supervision - The Regulation of the U. K. Banking Sector under the Banking Act 1987. 391p. 1989. boxed set 116.00 (*0-406-13603-3*, U.K., MICHIE) LEXIS Pub.
— Penn: Banking Supervision. 2nd ed. 1997. write for info. (*0-406-05212-3*, PBS2, MICHIE) LEXIS Pub.
— Practice & Law of International Banking. 1985. 114.00 (*0-85297-137-0*, Pub. by Chartered Bank) St Mut.
Penn, Gregory E. Freedom: The Essence of Life. LC 78-75026. 1979. pap. 5.95 (*0-87516-288-6*) DeVorss.
— The Love of Your Life. 1996. 20.00 (*0-614-96867-4*) Harper SF.
Penn, Helen. Comparing Nurseries: Staff & Children in Italy, Spain & the U. K. LC 97-196507. (One-Off Ser.). (Illus.). 160p. 1997. pap. (*1-85396-357-7*) Corwin Pr.
***Penn, Helen & University of Toronto School of Graduate Studies.** How Should We Care for Babies & Toddlers? An Analysis of Practice in Out-of-Home Care for Children under Three. 66p. 1999. pap. write for info. (*1-896051-11-1*) CRRU.
Penn, Helen, jt. auth. see Moss, Peter.
Penn, I., jt. ed. see Schmahl, Dietrich.
Penn, I. Garland. Afro-American Press & Its Editors. LC 69-18574. (American Negro: His History & Literature. Series 2). 1969. reprint ed. 36.95 (*0-405-01887-8*) Ayer.
Penn, Ira A., et al. Records Management Handbook. 2nd ed. 1994. 99.95 (*0-566-07510-5*, Pub. by Gower) Ashgate Pub Co.
Penn, Irvine Garland. The Reason Why the Colored American is Not in the World's Columbian Exposition: The Afro-American's Contribution to Columbian Literature. Rydell, Robert W., ed. & intro. by. LC 98-58021. (Illus.). 81p. 1999. 29.95 (*0-252-02473-7*) U of Ill Pr.
Penn, Irving. The Astronomers Plan a Voyage to Earth. (Illus.). 36p. 1999. 75.00 (*0-9665480-1-9*) Apparition.
— Drawings: Irving Penn. (Illus.). 128p. 1998. 65.00 (*0-9665480-0-0*) Apparition.
Penn, Irving, et al. Irving Penn Regards the Work of Issey Miyake. (Illus.). 160p. 1999. 75.00 (*0-8212-2629-0*, Pub. by Bulfinch Pr) Little.
Penn, James R. Encyclopedia of Geographical Features in World History: Europe & the Americas. LC 97-24437. 344p. 1997. lib. bdg. 65.00 (*0-87436-760-3*) ABC-CLIO.
***Penn, James R.** Rivers of the World: A Social, Geographical, & Environmental Sourcebook. 2001. lib. bdg. 60.00 (*1-57607-042-5*) ABC-CLIO.
Penn, Jean, ed. see Goodwin, Betty.
Penn, John. Accident Prone. large type ed. (Mystery Ser.). 1990. 27.99 (*0-7089-2159-0*) Ulverscroft.
— Barren Revenge. large type ed. (Mystery Ser.). 299p. 1989. 11.50 (*0-7089-1965-0*) Ulverscroft.
— Death's Long Shadow. large type ed. (Mystery Ser.). 304p. 1993. 27.99 (*0-7089-2959-1*) Ulverscroft.
— A Feast of Death. large type ed. (Linford Mystery Library). 384p. 1992. pap. 16.99 (*0-7089-7158-X*) Ulverscroft.
— A Haven of Danger. large type ed. 1994. 27.99 (*0-7089-3207-X*) Ulverscroft.
— Mortal Term. large type ed. (Mystery Ser.). 352p. 1988. 27.99 (*0-7089-1822-0*) Ulverscroft.
— Notice of Death. large type ed. 1983. 27.99 (*0-7089-1060-2*) Ulverscroft.
— Outrageous Exposures. large type ed. (Mystery Ser.). 1991. 27.99 (*0-7089-2350-X*) Ulverscroft.
— Sterner Stuff. large type ed. LC 97-52101. 262 p. 1998. write for info. (*0-7540-3246-9*) Chivers N Amer.
— Sterner Stuff. large type ed. 1998. 21.95 (*0-7862-1384-1*) Thorndike Pr.
— Widow's End. large type ed. 352p. 1995. 27.99 (*0-7089-3246-0*) Ulverscroft.
— A Will to Kill. large type ed. (Mystery Ser.). 272p. 1988. 27.99 (*0-7089-1764-X*) Ulverscroft.
Penn, John I. Rediscovering Our Spiritual Gifts: A Workbook. 64p. 1996. pap., wbk. ed. 8.00 (*0-8358-0771-1*) Upper Room Bks.
Penn, Julia M. Linguistic Relativity vs. Innate Ideas. LC 77-170003. (Janua Linguarum, Ser. Minor: No. 120). 62p. (Orig.). 1972. pap. text 30.80 (*90-279-2003-6*) Mouton.
Penn-Lewis. Thru the Bible - Revelation S-S, Pt. II. (Thru the Bible Commentary Ser.: Vol. 59). pap. 6.97 (*0-7852-0900-X*) Nelson.
Penn-Lewis, Jessie. All Things New. rev. ed. LC 97-228509. 161p. 1997. pap. 5.99 (*0-87508-733-7*) Chr Lit.
— Awakening in Wales. rev. ed. 128p. 1993. mass mkt. 5.99 (*0-87508-937-2*) Chr Lit.
— The Battle for the Mind. (Vital Ser.). 1997. pap. 0.75 (*0-87508-527-X*) Chr Lit.
— Centrality of the Cross. 1993. mass mkt. 5.99 (*0-87508-939-9*) Chr Lit.
— Climax of the Risen Life. 1992. mass mkt. 5.99 (*0-87508-941-0*) Chr Lit.
— Communion with God. 1997. mass mkt. 5.99 (*0-87508-734-5*) Chr Lit.
— Conquest of Canaan. 1992. mass mkt. 5.99 (*0-87508-943-7*) Chr Lit.
— Cross: Touchstone of Faith. 1990. mass mkt. 5.99 (*0-87508-730-2*) Chr Lit.
— Cross of Calvary & Its Message. 1979. mass mkt. 5.99 (*0-87508-725-6*) Chr Lit.
— Dying to Live. 1991. mass mkt. 5.99 (*0-87508-945-3*) Chr Lit.
— Face to Face. 1972. mass mkt. 5.99 (*0-87508-942-9*) Chr Lit.
— Fruitful Living. 137p. 1992. mass mkt. 5.99 (*0-87508-946-1*) Chr Lit.
— Hints for Workers. (Vital Ser.). 1997. pap. 0.75 (*0-87508-526-1*) Chr Lit.
— Life in the Spirit. 1979. pap. 5.99 (*0-87508-956-9*) Chr Lit.
— Life Out of Death. 1979. mass mkt. 5.99 (*0-87508-950-X*) Chr Lit.
— Power for Service. rev. ed. LC 98-210095. 94p. 1988. pap. 5.99 (*0-87508-732-9*, Discov Hse) Chr Lit.
— Prayer & Evangelism. 1979. mass mkt. 5.99 (*0-87508-960-7*) Chr Lit.
— Releasing Your Spirit. LC 98-126710. 122p. (Orig.). 1997. mass mkt. 5.99 (*0-88368-424-1*) Whitaker Hse.
— Soul & Spirit. 1993. mass mkt. 5.99 (*0-87508-953-4*) Chr Lit.
— Spiritual Warfare. LC 98-65365. 1991. pap. 5.99 (*0-87508-962-3*) Chr Lit.
— The Story of Job. LC 97-195636. 240p. 1996. pap. 9.99 (*0-87508-736-1*, 736) Chr Lit.
— Thy Hidden Ones. 210p. 1995. mass mkt. 6.99 (*0-87508-735-3*) Chr Lit.
— War on the Saints. 1993. pap. 9.99 (*0-87508-963-1*) Chr Lit.
— War on the Saints. LC 97-221545. 324p. 1996. mass mkt. 5.99 (*0-88368-455-1*) Whitaker Hse.
— The Warfare with Satan. 111p. 1993. pap. text 5.99 (*0-87508-731-0*) Chr Lit.
— The Work of the Holy Spirit. 58p. 1992. pap. text 5.99 (*0-87508-961-5*) Chr Lit.
Penn-Lewis, Jessie & Roberts, Evan. War on the Saints. 325p. 1998. reprint ed. 16.80 (*0-913926-04-3*) T E Lowe.
Penn, M. De la, see De la Penn, M.
Penn, M. J., jt. auth. see Kuhn, J. R.
Penn, Malka. The Hanukkah Ghosts. LC 94-15257. 80p. (J). (gr. 4-6). 1995. 14.95 (*0-8234-1145-1*) Holiday.
Penn, Malka. The Hanukkah Ghosts. 1997. 9.19 (*0-606-12718-6*, Pub. by Turtleback) Demco.
Penn, Margaret. Manchester Fourteen Miles. LC 80-40707. 247p. reprint ed. pap. 70.40 (*0-608-15763-5*, 2031706) Bks Demand.
Penn, Michael. Studies in Philemon. 32p. 1999. pap. 3.00 (*1-880573-75-X*) Bible Search Pubns.
Penn, Michael L. Desecration of the Temple: The Global Problem of Violence Against Women & Girls. 275p. (Orig.). 1997. pap. 17.95 (*0-8476-8465-2*); text 60.00 (*0-8476-8464-4*) Rowman.
Penn, Nate & LaRose, Lawrence. The Code. LC 96-52077. 144p. 1996. pap. 5.99 (*0-684-84225-4*, Fireside) S&S Trade Pap.
Penn, Norgina W., jt. auth. see Starkey, Carolyn M.
Penn, Norgina Wright, jt. auth. see Starkey, Carolyn M.
Penn, Preston L. Little Pee-Wee Christmas Tree. LC 98-92074. (Illus.). 24p. (J). (ps-6). 1998. text 14.95 incl. cd-rom (*0-9667210-0-4*) Little Pee-Wee.
Penn, Raymond G. Medicine on Ancient Greek & Roman Coins. (Illus.). 192p. 1994. pap. 50.00 (*0-7134-7670-2*) S J Durst.
Penn, Richard A. Mom & Pop Stores: A Country Stores Compendium of Merchandising Tools for Display & Value Guide. LC 98-96452. 320 p. 1998. write for info. (*0-9664576-0-9*) Pennyfield Pub.
Penn, Robert E. Gay Men's Wellness Guide. 624p. 1998. pap. 19.95 (*0-8050-4772-7*) St Martin.
Penn, Roger, et al, eds. Skill & Occupational Change. (Social Change & Economic Life Initiative Ser.). (Illus.). 382p. 1994. text 69.00 (*0-19-827914-0*) OUP.
Penn, Sarah & Davenport, Tony. Principles & Practice of Day Surgery Nursing. LC 96-34126. (Illus.). 244p. (Orig.). 1996. pap. text 34.95 (*0-632-03973-6*) Blackwell Sci.
Penn, Shana, et al. The Women's Guide to the Wired World: A User-Friendly Handbook & Resource Directory. LC 97-10031. 320p. 1997. pap. 18.85 (*1-55861-167-3*) Feminist Pr.
Penn State, College of Education Staff. Student Teaching Handbook. 2nd ed. 192p. (C). 1996. spiral bd. 23.95 (*0-7872-2930-X*) Kendall-Hunt.
Penn State Univeristy (Physics) Staff. General Physics 202/204. 178p. (C). 1996. pap. text, per. 26.95 (*0-7872-2392-1*) Kendall-Hunt.
Penn State University Staff. General Physics 202/204 Lab Manual. 3rd ed. 188p. (C). 1998. spiral bd., lab manual ed. 33.95 (*0-7872-5070-8*, 41507001) Kendall-Hunt.
— Introduction to Physics 215/265 Lab Manual. 3rd ed. 180p. (C). 1998. spiral bd. 33.95 (*0-7872-5240-9*, 41524001) Kendall-Hunt.
Penn, Sue. Quick & Easy Bloomin' Country Cottons: Using Quilted Muslin. Johnston, Becky, ed. LC 99-25671. (Illus.). 64p. 1999. pap. 16.95 (*1-890621-02-1*) Landauer Bks IA.
Penn, Thomas A. & Foltz, Ramon D. Understanding Patents & Other Protection for Intellectual Property. (Illus.). 100p. (Orig.). (C). 1990. pap. 15.00 (*0-944606-07-5*) Penn Inst.
Penn, Thomas A., jt. auth. see Foltz, Ramon D.
Penn, V. Mother Load. 1999. pap. text 5.95 (*1-56245-356-4*) Great Quotations.
Penn, W. S. The Absence of Angels: A Novel. LC 94-34607. (American Indian Literature & Critical Studies: Vol. 14). 272p. 1995. pap. 13.95 (*0-8061-2714-7*) U of Okla Pr.
— All My Sins Are Relatives. LC 94-36937. (North American Indian Prose Award Ser.). (Illus.). viii, 268p. 1995. pap. 12.00 (*0-8032-8738-0*, Bison Books) U of Nebr Pr.
— As We Are Now: Mixblood Essays on Race & Identity. LC 97-12057. 282p. 1998. 45.00 (*0-520-21072-7*, Pub. by U CA Pr); pap. 17.95 (*0-520-21073-5*, Pub. by U CA Pr) Cal Prin Full Svc.
***Penn, W. S.** Killing Time with Strangers. LC 99-50962. 280p. 2000. 22.95 (*0-8165-2052-6*); pap. write for info. (*0-8165-2053-4*) U of Ariz Pr.
***Penn, W. S., ed.** The Telling of the World: Native American Stories & Art. (Illus.). 240p. 2000. reprint ed. text 45.00 (*0-7881-9043-1*) DIANE Pub.
— This Is the World. 256p. 2000. pap. 19.95 (*0-87013-561-9*) Mich St U Pr.
Penn Warren, Robert, see Brooks, Cleanth & Warren, Robert Penn.
Penn Warren, Robert, see Warren, Robert Penn.
Penn Warren, Robert, see Center for Learning Network Staff & Warren, Robert Penn.
Penn, William. The Absence of Angels. LC 93-27526. 274p. 1994. 24.00 (*1-877946-42-7*) Permanent Pr.
— Collection of the Works of William Penn, 2 vols. LC 79-173942. reprint ed. 495.00 (*0-404-04982-6*) AMS Pr.
— Correspondence Between William Penn & James Logan & Others, 2 vols. Logan, Deborah & Armstrong, Edward A., eds. LC 72-173943. reprint ed. 115.00 (*0-404-04985-0*) AMS Pr.
— An Essay Towards the Present & Future Peace in Europe: By the Establishment of a European Dyet, Parliament or Estates. (United Nations Library, Geneva, Sources on the History of International Organization: Series F, Vol. 1). 108p. 1983. reprint ed. 19.37 (*3-487-07345-5*) G Olms Pubs.
— No Cross, No Crown. (C). 1989. reprint ed. pap. 32.00 (*0-900657-57-X*, Pub. by W Sessions) St Mut.
— No Cross No Crown. 1999. reprint ed. pap. 30.00 (*0-900657-58-8*, Pub. by W Sessions) St Mut.
— La Paix de l'Europe c. 1700. 1999. pap. 21.00 (*1-85072-016-9*, Pub. by W Sessions) St Mut.
— The Peace of Europe, the Fruits of Solitude: And Other Writings. 376p. 1993. pap. 6.95 (*0-460-87302-4*, Everyman's Classic Lib) Tuttle Pubng.
— The Rise & Progress of the People Called Quakers. (C). 1988. 75.00 (*0-913408-32-8*, Pub. by W Sessions) St Mut.
— Some Fruits of Solitude. 124p. (C). 1978. pap. 6.95 (*0-913408-39-5*) Friends United.
— Some Fruits of Solitude. 96p. 1996. reprint ed. pap. 9.95 (*1-55709-433-0*) Applewood.
Penn, William, ed. Magnetic Resonance: Symposium, Utrech, April 1985. (Journal: Diagnostic Imaging in Clinical Medicine: Vol. 55, No. 1-2, 1986). (Illus.). 108p. (Orig.). 1986. pap. 76.75 (*3-8055-4259-3*) S Karger.
Penn, William & Brinton, Anna. No Cross, No Crown. 1944. pap. text 4.00 (*0-87574-030-8*) Pendle Hill.
Penn, William, ed. see Microsymposium Staff.
Penn, William, jt. pref. see Nickalls, John L.
Penn, William A. Rattling Spurs & Broad-Brimmed Hats: The Civil War in Cynthiana & Harrison County, Kentucky. 240p. 1995. lib. bdg. 26.00 (*0-9646989-1-9*) Battle Grove.
Penna, Anthony N. Nature's Bounty: Historical & Modern Environmental Perspectives. LC 98-42514. 320p. 1999. text 70.95 (*0-7656-0187-7*) M E Sharpe.
— Nature's Bounty: Historical & Modern Environmental Perspectives. (Illus.). 320p. 1999. pap. text 29.95 (*0-7656-0188-5*) M E Sharpe.
Penna, David, jt. ed. see Shepherd, George W., Jr.
Penna, Judith A., jt. auth. see Bittinger, Marvin L.
Penna, La, see Luzzatto & La Penna, eds.
Penna, Lucille R. Landing at Plymouth. 1996. 13.00 (*0-679-83201-7*) McKay.
— Westward Ho! The Story of the Pioneers. LC 97-281. (Landmark Ser.). 1997. lib. bdg. 15.99 (*0-679-94776-0*) Random.
Penna, Richard P., jt. ed. see Knowlton, David H.
Penna, Romano. Paul the Apostle: Jew & Greek Alike, Vol. 1. Wahl, Thomas P., tr. 344p. (Orig.). 1996. pap. 34.95 (*0-8146-5835-0*, M Glazier) Liturgical Pr.
— Paul the Apostle: Wisdom & Folly of the Cross, Vol. 2. Wahl, Thomas P., tr. from ITA. LC 95-37825. 304p. (Orig.). 1996. pap. text 34.95 (*0-8146-5912-8*, M Glazier) Liturgical Pr.
— Paul the Apostle 2 vols. A Theological & Exegetical Study. Wahl, Thomas P., tr. 1996. pap. 64.95 (*0-8146-5913-6*, M Glazier) Liturgical Pr.
Penna, Sandro. Confused Dream. Scrivani, George, tr. from ITA. 92p. 1988. 5.95 (*0-937815-15-2*) Hanuman Bks.

P

An Asterisk (*) at the beginning of an entry indicates that the title is appearing for the first time.

Penna, Sue, et al. Job Satisfaction & Dissatisfaction: A Study of Residential Care Work. 1995. pap. 41.00 (*1-899942-02-5*, Pub. by Natl Inst Soc Work) St Mut.

Penna, Sue, jt. auth. see O'Brien, Martin.

Pennac, Daniel. The Fairy Gunmother. 1998. 26.00 (*1-86046-325-8*) Harvill Press.

— The Fairy Gunmother. Monk, Ian, tr. from FRE. 256p. 1998. pap. 12.00 (*1-86046-445-9*, Pub. by Harvill Press) FS&G.

— The Scapegoat. Monk, Ian, tr. from FRE. 256p. 1998. 23.00 (*1-86046-442-4*, Pub. by Harvill Press) FS&G.

***Pennac, Daniel.** Write to Kill. 2000. pap. 12.00 (*1-86046-726-1*) Harvill Press.

Pennac, Daniel. Write To Kill. Monk, Ian, tr. 277p. 1999. text 23.00 (*1-86046-535-8*, Pub. by Harvill Press) FS&G.

Pennacchia, Yvette M. Healing the Whole. LC 96-176870. 1995. 55.00 (*0-304-33106-6*); pap. 15.95 (*0-304-33111-2*) LPC InBook.

Pennak, Robert W. Collegiate Dictionary of Zoology. LC 85-23983. 594p. (C). 1988. reprint ed. pap. text 36.50 (*0-89874-921-2*) Krieger.

— Fresh-Water Invertebrates of the United States: Protozoa to Mollusca. 3rd ed. LC 88-18570. 656p. 1989. 110.00 (*0-471-63118-3*) Wiley.

Pennance, F. G., jt. auth. see Seldon, Arthur.

Pennanen, Judi. Heads or Tails. (J). (ps-8). 1989. pap. 7.95 (*0-921254-11-3*, Pub. by Penumbra Pr) U of Toronto Pr.

Pennant, Edmund. Askance & Strangely: New & Selected Poems. LC 93-18473. 176p. 1993. 24.95 (*0-914061-35-6*) Orchises Pr.

— Dream's Navel. 80p. (Orig.). 1982. pap. 4.95 (*0-931642-08-6*) Lintel.

— Misapprehensions & Other Poems. 80p. (Orig.). 1984. pap. 5.95 (*0-931642-15-9*) Lintel.

— The Wildebeest of Carmine Street. LC 90-31457. 72p. (Orig.). 1990. pap. 10.00 (*0-914061-17-8*) Orchises Pr.

Pennant-Rea, Rupert, contrib. by. The Ostrich & the EMU: Policy Choices Facing the UK. 112p. 1997. pap. 12.00 (*1-898128-31-6*, Pub. by Ctr Econ Policy Res) Brookings.

Pennant-Rea, Rupert & Emmott, William. The Pocket Economist. LC 83-15054. (Illus.). 194p. 1984. text 31.95 (*0-521-26070-1*) Cambridge U Pr.

Pennant, Thomas. Arctic Zoology, 2 vols. LC 73-17835. (Natural Sciences in America Ser.). (Illus.). 1012p. 1974. reprint ed. 76.95 (*0-405-05758-X*) Ayer.

— Tour in Scotland & Voyage to the Hebrides 1772, 1. 1999. pap. text 29.95 (*1-874744-88-2*) Dufour.

***Pennant, Thomas.** Tour in Scotland, 1769. 256p. 2000. pap. 25.95 (*1-874744-70-X*, Pub. by Birlinn Ltd) Dufour.

Pennant, Thomas. A Tour of Scotland in 1769. 388p. 1989. pap. 24.00 (*0-9505884-9-0*, Pub. by Mercat Pr Bks) St Mut.

— A Tour of Scotland (1796) 496p. (C). 1986. 42.00 (*0-7855-3812-7*, Pub. by Mercat Pr Bks) St Mut.

Pennar, Jaan, jt. ed. see Bereday, George Z.

Pennar, Margaret, ed. The Middle East: Five Perspectives. (Information Papers: No. 7). 33p. (Orig.). (C). 1973. pap. 1.00 (*0-937694-23-1*) Assn Arab-Amer U Grads.

***Pennartz, Paul & Niehof, Anke.** The Domestic Domain: Chances, Choices & Strategies of Family Households. 250p. (C). 1999. text 65.95 (*0-7546-1011-X*) Ashgate Pub Co.

Pennartz, Peter. Open Borders Behind Closed Doors: The European Union & the South. (Illus.). 80p. (Orig.). 1997. pap. 12.95 (*90-5727-005-6*, Pub. by Uitgeverij Arkel) LPC InBook.

Pennbrook, Lloyd. A Method to Our Madness. 176p. (Orig.). 1992. pap. 5.95 (*0-9632330-3-3*) Pennywise.

Penndorf, Ursula. Das Problem der "Reichseinheitsidee" Nach der Teilung von Verdun (843) (GER.). viii, 204p. 1974. 39.80 (*3-615-00154-0*, Pub. by Weidmann) Lubrecht & Cramer.

Penne, R. Leo, et al. The Economics of Amenity: Community Futures & Quality of Life. LC 85-6545. (Illus.). 160p. (Orig.). 1985. pap. 15.00 (*0-941182-15-0*) Partners Livable.

Penne, Saxon. Improve Your English. (Improve Your...Ser.). 1995. audio 69.95 (*0-8442-5679-X*, 5679X, Natl Textbk Co) NTC Contemp Pub Co.

— Practice & Improve Your English. (Practice & Improve Ser.). pap. 39.95 incl. audio (*0-8442-5682-X*, 5682X, Natl Textbk Co) NTC Contemp Pub Co.

— Practice & Improve Your English Plus. (Practice & Improve Ser.). pap. 39.95 incl. audio (*0-8442-5696-X*, 5696X, Natl Textbk Co) NTC Contemp Pub Co.

Penneau, Brad, ed. see Keller, J. J., & Associates, Inc. Staff.

***Pennebaker, D. A.** Spinning. LC 99-58442. 160p. 2000. text 16.95 (*0-8050-6105-3*) St Martin.

Pennebaker, Elizabeth, tr. see Freundlich, Elisabeth.

Pennebaker, James W. Opening Up: The Healing Power of Confiding in Others. 240p. 1991. pap. 8.95 (*0-380-70849-3*, Avon Bks) Morrow Avon.

— Opening Up: The Healing Power of Expressing Emotions. LC 97-20544. 249p. 1997. pap. text 15.95 (*1-57230-238-0*, 0238) Guilford Pubns.

— The Psychology of Physical Symptoms. (Illus.). 192p. 1982. 47.00 (*0-387-90730-0*) Spr-Verlag.

Pennebaker, James W., ed. Emotion, Disclosure, & Health. LC 95-16989. 337p. 1995. text 29.95 (*1-55798-308-9*) Am Psychol.

Pennebaker, James W., et al, eds. Collective Memory of Political Events: Social Psychological Perspectives. 225p. (C). 1997. text 69.96 (*0-8058-2182-1*) L Erlbaum Assocs.

Pennebaker, James W., jt. ed. see Traue, Harald C.

Pennebaker, James W., jt. ed. see Wegner, Daniel M.

***Pennebaker, Ruth.** Conditions of Love. 2000. mass mkt. 4.99 (*0-440-22834-4*, LE) Dell.

Pennebaker, Ruth. Conditions of Love. LC 98-39979. (gr. 9 up). 1999. 16.95 (*0-8050-6104-5*) H Holt & Co.

— Don't Think Twice. LC 95-20499. 272p. (YA). (gr. 7-12). 1995. 15.95 (*0-8050-4407-8*) H Holt & Co.

— Don't Think Twice. 1998. 9.09 (*0-606-13341-0*, Pub. by Turtleback) Demco.

— Don't Think Twice. 272p. (YA). (gr. 7 up). 1998. reprint ed. mass mkt. 3.99 (*0-440-22697-X*, LLL BDD) BDD Bks Young Read.

Pennebaker, W. Facsimile Compression Standards. (Electrical Engineering Ser.). 1997. text 59.95 (*0-442-01871-1*, VNR) Wiley.

Pennee, Donna. Moral Metafiction: The Novels of Timothy Findley. 140p. (C). 1991. pap. 20.00 (*1-55022-138-8*, Pub. by ECW) Genl Dist Srvs.

— Praying for Rain: Timothy Findley's Not Wanted on the Voyage. (Canadian Fiction Studies: No. 21). 120p. (C). 1993. pap. text 14.95 (*1-55022-121-3*, Pub. by ECW) Genl Dist Srvs.

Pennekamp, Marianne, jt. auth. see Freeman, Edith M.

Pennell, jt. auth. see Doyal, Lesley.

Pennell, Allison A., et al, eds. Business & the Environment: A Resource Guide. LC 91-38369. 364p. 1992. text 65.00 (*1-55963-159-7*) Island Pr.

Pennell, C. R. Morocco Since 1830: A History. 1999. pap. text 20.00 (*0-8147-6677-3*) NYU Pr.

***Pennell, C. R.** Morocco Since 1830: A History. LC 99-33567. 1999. text 60.00 (*0-8147-6676-5*) NYU Pr.

***Pennell, C. R., ed.** Bandits at Sea: A Pirates Reader. 408p. 2000. pap. 23.95 (*0-8147-6678-1*); text 65.00 (*0-8147-6679-X*) NYU Pr.

Pennell, C. R., ed. Piracy & Diplomacy in 17th Century North Africa: The Journal of Thomas Baker, English Consul in Tripoli, 1677-1685. LC 86-45999. (Illus.). 264p. 1989. 39.50 (*0-8386-3302-1*) Fairleigh Dickinson.

***Pennell, Elizabeth.** Self Defense for Women. LC 99-88320. 192p. 2000. pap. 10.95 (*1-58062-340-9*) Adams Media.

Pennell, Elizabeth R. Charles Godfrey Leland: A Biography, 2 vols, Set. LC 76-140370. (Select Bibliographies Reprint Ser.). 1977. reprint ed. 60.95 (*0-8369-5613-3*) Ayer.

Pennell, Elizabeth R. & Pennell, Joseph. Life of James McNeill Whistler, 2 vols. LC 70-148285. (Illus.). reprint ed. 135.00 (*0-404-04988-5*) AMS Pr.

***Pennell, Elizabeth Robins.** The Delights of Delicate Eating. 288p. 2000. reprint ed. pap. 15.00 (*0-252-06920-X*) U of Ill Pr.

Pennell, Francis W. The Scrophulariaceae of Eastern Temperate North America. (Monograph: No. 1). (Illus.). 650p. (Orig.). 1935. pap. 7.00 (*0-910006-08-3*) Acad Nat Sci Phila.

— The Scrophulariaceae of the Western Himalayas. (Monograph: No. 5). (Illus.). 163p. (Orig.). 1943. pap. 5.00 (*0-910006-14-8*) Acad Nat Sci Phila.

Pennell, Jeffrey N. Cases & Materials on Income Taxation of Trusts, Estates, Grantors & Beneficiaries. LC 87-10563. (American Casebook Ser.). 460p. (C). 1987. 45.50 (*0-314-42565-9*) West Pub.

Pennell, Joan, jt. auth. see Ristock, Janice L.

Pennell, Joe E. From Anticipation to Transfiguration. 1989. pap. 8.75 (*1-55673-126-4*, 9851) CSS OH.

Pennell, Joseph. Haunts of Old London. LC 71-164620. (Select Bibliographies Reprint Ser.). 1977. reprint ed. 17.95 (*0-8369-5903-5*) Ayer.

— The Jew at Home: Impressions of Jewish Life in Russia & Austria. 1976. lib. bdg. 134.95 (*0-8490-2098-0*) Gordon Pr.

— Pen Drawings & Pen-Draughtsmen. LC 76-30462. (Quality Paperbacks Ser.). 1977. reprint ed. pap. 10.95 (*0-306-80064-0*) Da Capo.

Pennell, Joseph & Bryant, Edward. Pennell's New York City Etchings: 91 Prints. (Illus.). 112p. (Orig.). 1981. pap. 7.95 (*0-486-23913-6*) Dover.

Pennell, Joseph, jt. auth. see Pennell, Elizabeth R.

Pennell, Joseph Judd, jt. auth. see Shortridge, James R.

Pennell, Joseph S. The History of Rome Hanks & Kindred Matters. LC 81-85726. 363p. (C). 1981. reprint ed. 22.00 (*0-933256-32-9*) Second Chance.

— The History of Rome Hanks & Kindred Matters. LC 81-85726. 363p. (C). 1981. reprint ed. pap. 16.00 (*0-933256-33-7*) Second Chance.

Pennell, Paul. Children's Car. (C). 1989. pap. 35.00 (*0-85263-833-7*, Pub. by Shire Pubns) St Mut.

Pennell, R. Obsolete Banknotes of North Carolina. LC 83-71430. 1985. reprint ed. pap. 10.00 (*0-942666-29-1*) S J Durst.

Pennell, Rhett B. Excuse Me, Are You a Dragon? LC 98-71909. (Illus.). 32p. (J). (gr. k-3). 1998. 16.95 (*1-880851-34-2*) Greene Bark Pr.

Pennell, Rosemary V., jt. auth. see Vari, Frank D.

Pennell, W. E. Heavy-section Steel Technology Program: Semiannual Progress Report For April-September 1995. 99p. 1997. per. 14.00 (*0-16-062805-9*) USGPO.

— Heavy Section Steel Technology Program: Semiannual Progress Report for April-September 1996. 106p. 1998. per. 8.50 (*0-16-062948-9*) USGPO.

— Heavy-Section Steel Technology Program: Semiannual Progress Report for October 1995-March 1996. 101p. 1997. per. 8.50 (*0-16-054739-3*) USGPO.

— Heavy-Section Steel Technology Program: Semiannual Progress Report for October 1996-March 1997. 100p. 1998. per. 8.00 (*0-16-062980-2*) USGPO.

Pennell, W. E., ed. Pressure Vessel Integrity - 1993. (PVP Ser.: Vol. 250). 304p. 1993. 60.00 (*0-7918-0977-3*, H00809) ASME.

Pennell, William & Barton, Bruce A. Principles of Salmonid Culture. LC 96-31360. (Developments in Aquaculture & Fisheries Ser.: No. 29). 1070p. 1996. 222.25 (*0-444-82152-X*) Elsevier.

Pennella, C. Robert. Managing the Metrology System. 2nd ed. LC 97-10667. 176p. 1997. 28.00 (*0-87389-421-9*, H0964) ASQ Qual Pr.

Pennella, John J., jt. ed. see Malotky, Lyle O.

Pennells, Geoffrey. Butterworths International Taxation of Financial Instruments & Transactions. 2nd ed. 610p. 1994. boxed set. write for info. (*0-406-10660-6*, U.K., MICHIE) LEXIS Pub.

Pennells, Margaret, jt. auth. see Smith, Susan C.

Penner. El Hombre y la Sexualidad.Tr. of Men & Sex. (SPA.). 1997. 10.99 (*0-88113-475-9*, B001-4759) Caribe Betania.

— Microbiology Lm. 2nd ed. 1999. 31.74 (*0-07-013774-9*) McGraw.

***Penner, et al.** Updating American Soc Contract. 2000. pap. text 12.00 (*0-393-97579-7*) Norton.

Penner, Adrienne. Le Gimmick, Francais Parle. 1977. pap. 9.95 (*0-393-04474-2*) Norton.

— Gimmick I: Gesprochenes Deutsch. 161p. 1977. pap. 8.95 (*0-393-04480-7*) Norton.

***Penner, Archie.** The New Testament, the Christian & the State. (Mennonite Reprint Series: 3). 128p. (YA). 2000. pap. text 6.95 (*1-883453-07-0*) Deutsche Buchhandlung.

Penner, Barbara. Managing Fibromyalgia: A Six-Week Course on Self Care. 80p. 1997. 55.00 (*0-9644848-3-8*) Meerkat Graph.

Penner, Carol, ed. Women & Men: Gender in the Church. LC 98-72959. 152p. 1998. pap. 11.99 (*0-8361-9079-3*) Herald Pr.

Penner, Charlene. Behold Your Body: Anatomy & Physiology Anyone Can Enjoy, 3 vols., Set. (C). 1996. pap. text. write for info. (*1-888515-43-0*) Rose Bud Trust.

— Dry Bones or Wet Noodles: Anatomy & Physiology Anyone Can Enjoy. (Behold Your Body Ser.: Vol. 1). 400p. (C). 1996. pap. text 34.95 (*1-888515-53-8*) Rose Bud Trust.

Penner, Clifford. Fifty-Two Ways to Have Fun, Fantastic Sex: A Guidebook for Married Couples. 142p. 1994. pap. 7.99 (*0-8407-3484-0*) Nelson.

— Men & Sex: Discovering Greater Love, Passion & Intimacy with Your Wife. 224p. 1997. 17.99 (*0-8407-7790-6*) Nelson.

Penner, Clifford & Penner, Joyce. 52 Maneras de Tener Relaciones Sexuales Divertidas y Fabulosas. (Serie "52 Maneras"). (SPA.). 160p. 7.99 (*0-88113-233-0*, B001-2330) Caribe Betania.

— What Every Wife Wants Her Husband to Know about Sex. LC 97-28999. 160p. 1998. pap. 5.99 (*0-7852-7067-1*, Oliver-Nelson) Nelson.

Penner, Clifford & Penner, Joyce J. Getting Your Sex Life Off to a Great Start: A Guide for Engaged & Newlywed Couples. LC 94-28374. 1994. pap. 12.99 (*0-8499-3515-6*) Word Pub.

Penner, Clifford, jt. auth. see Penner, Joyce.

Penner, Cornelia. Games That Byte: Helping Youth Evaluate Computer Games. 41p. (YA). (gr. 6-12). 1998. pap. 8.95 (*0-87303-331-0*) Faith & Life.

Penner, David A., jt. auth. see Best, George W.

Penner, Diane. Elder Fit: A Health & Fitness Guide for Older Adults. 66p. (Orig.). 1990. pap. 16.00 (*0-88314-475-1*, A4751) AAHPERD.

Penner, Dick. Countries of the Mind: The Fiction of J. M. Coetzee, 32. LC 88-34731. (Contributions to the Study of World Literature Ser.: No. 32). 167p. 1989. 49.95 (*0-313-26684-0*, PCD/, Greenwood Pr) Greenwood.

Penner, Donald. The Project Manager's Survival Guide: The Handbook for Real-World Project Management. LC 93-4016. 100p. 1994. pap. text 14.95 (*0-935470-72-7*) Battelle.

Penner, Erwin. The Power of God in a Broken World: Studies in Ephesians. (Luminaire Studies). 196p. (C). 1990. pap. 7.95 (*0-921788-11-8*) Kindred Prods.

Penner, Fred. Fred Penner's Sing along - Play Along. (Illus.). 112p. (Orig.). (J). (ps-4). 1991. pap. 14.95 (*0-89524-625-2*) Cherry Lane.

— Proud. (Illus.). 32p. (J). (ps-1). 1997. 10.95 (*1-56352-441-4*) Longstreet.

Penner, Hans H. Impasse & Resolution: A Critique of the Study of Religion. (Toronto Studies in Religion: Vol. 8). 249p. (C). 1989. text 38.95 (*0-8204-0976-6*) P Lang Pubng.

Penner, James. Goliath. 2000. 6.99 (*0-310-21477-7*) Zondervan.

— Goliath: The Life of Robert Schuller. Baltzell, Richard & Adams, Linda, eds. (Illus.). 448p. 1992. 24.95 (*1-879989-06-9*) New Hope Pub.

— Goliath: The Life of Robert Schuller. (Illus.). 440p. 1998. reprint ed. text 20.00 (*0-7881-5208-4*) DIANE Pub.

***Penner, James.** The Idea of Property in Law. 304p. 2000. pap. text 29.95 (*0-19-829926-5*) OUP.

Penner, James E. The Idea of Property in Law. LC 96-44689. 250p. 1997. text 75.00 (*0-19-826029-6*) OUP.

Penner, Jonathan. The Intelligent Traveler's Guide to Chiribosco. LC 83-81252. (Orig.). 1984. 6.00 (*0-913123-03-X*); pap. 4.00 (*0-913123-01-3*) Galileo.

— Private Parties. LC 83-47825. (Drue Heinz Literature Prize Ser.). 197p. 1983. text 22.50 (*0-8229-3488-4*) U of Pittsburgh Pr.

***Penner, Joyce.** What to Pray When You're Expecting: Hopes, Prayers & Dreams During Pregnancy - For Mom & the Whole Family. LC 00-26719. 144p. 2000. pap. 9.99 (*1-56955-135-9*, Vine Bks) Servant.

Penner, Joyce & Penner, Clifford. The Gift of Sex: A Guide to Sexual Fulfillment. 352p. 1981. pap. 12.99 (*0-8499-2893-1*) Word Pub.

Penner, Joyce, et al. Aviation & the Global Atmosphere: Special Report of the Intergovernmental Panel on Climate Change. (Illus.). 400p. 1999. 90.00 (*0-521-66300-8*); pap. 39.95 (*0-521-66404-7*) Cambridge U Pr.

Penner, Joyce, jt. auth. see Penner, Clifford.

Penner, Joyce J., jt. auth. see Penner, Clifford.

Penner, Laurie. Best Mysteries. (Illus.). 36p. 1991. reprint ed. pap. text 3.95 (*1-893916-08-1*, 2001) Project Pr.

— Bible Terms Made Easy: A Bible Dictionary. (Illus.). 72p. 1992. reprint ed. pap. text 6.95 (*1-893916-00-6*, 1000) Project Pr.

— The Blue Cup: And Other Stories. (Illus.). 28p. 1990. reprint ed. pap. text 3.50 (*1-893916-09-X*, 2003) Project Pr.

Penner, Laurie, ed. The Book of John: A Simplified Version of the Gospel of John. (Illus.). 100p. 1990. reprint ed. pap. text 6.95 (*1-893916-18-9*, 1001) Project Pr.

— Favorite Psalms: A Simplified Version of Favorite Bible Psalms. (Illus.). 64p. 1992. reprint ed. pap. text 5.95 (*1-893916-05-7*, 1007) Project Pr.

— Genesis Pt. 1: A Simplified Version of the Bible Book of Genesis. (Illus.). 104p. 1990. reprint ed. pap. text 6.95 (*1-893916-19-7*, 1002) Project Pr.

— A Letter from James: A Simplified Version of the Bible Book of James. (Illus.). 20p. 1992. reprint ed. pap. text 3.50 (*1-893916-01-4*, 1003) Project Pr.

— Matthew: A Simplified Version of the Gospel of Matthew, Pt. 1. (Illus.). 76p. 1993. reprint ed. pap. text 5.95 (*1-893916-02-2*, 1004) Project Pr.

— Matthew: A Simplified Version of the Gospel of Matthew, Pt. 2. (Illus.). 76p. 1994. reprint ed. pap. text 5.95 (*1-893916-03-0*, 1005) Project Pr.

— Paul's Letter to the Philippians: A Simplified Version of the Bible Book of Philippians. (Illus.). 16p. 1992. reprint ed. pap. text 3.50 (*1-893916-04-9*, 1006) Project Pr.

— Paul's Letter to the Romans: A Simplified Version of the Bible Book of Romans. (Illus.). 64p. 1992. reprint ed. pap. text 5.95 (*1-893916-06-5*, 1008) Project Pr.

— Samuel & Saul: A Bible Study from the First Book of Samuel. (Illus.). 50p. 1993. reprint ed. pap. text 4.75 (*1-893916-07-3*, 1009) Project Pr.

Penner, Laurie, ed. see Young, Mike, et al.

Penner, Louis A., et al, eds. The Challenge in Mathematics & Science Education: Psychology's Response. LC 93-21336. 379p. 1993. text 29.95 (*1-55798-207-4*) Am Psychol.

Penner, Lucille R. Baby Elephant. (All Aboard Bks.). (Illus.). 32p. (Orig.). (J). (ps-3). 1997. pap. 2.95 (*0-448-41497-X*, G & D) Peng Put Young Read.

— Big Birds. LC 98-51748. (Step into Reading Ser.: A Step 1 Book). (Illus.). 32p. (J). (gr. k-3). 2000. pap. 3.99 (*0-679-88968-X*) Random.

***Penner, Lucille R.** Big Birds. LC 98-51748. (Step into Reading Ser.: A Step 1 Book). (Illus.). 32p. (J). (ps-1). 2000. lib. bdg. 11.99 (*0-679-98968-4*, Pub. by Random Bks Yng Read) Random.

Penner, Lucille R. Celebration: The Story of American Holidays. LC 92-25871. (Illus.). 80p. (J). (gr. 1 up). 1993. lib. bdg. 15.95 (*0-02-770903-5*, Mac Bks Young Read) S&S Childrens.

— Cowboys. LC 94-35463. (All Aboard Bks.). (Illus.). 32p. (J). (ps-3). 1996. pap. 2.95 (*0-448-40947-X*, G & D) Peng Put Young Read.

— Cowboys. 1996. 8.15 (*0-606-09167-X*, Pub. by Turtleback) Demco.

— Dinosaur Babies. LC 90-36045. (Step into Reading Ser.: A Step 1 Book). (Illus.). 32p. (J). (ps-3). 1991. pap. 3.99 (*0-679-81207-5*, Pub. by Random Bks Yng Read) Random.

— Dinosaur Babies. (Step into Reading Ser.: A Step 1 Book). (J). (ps-1). 1991. 9.19 (*0-606-12254-0*, Pub. by Turtleback) Demco.

— Eating the Plates: A Pilgrim Book of Food & Manners. 128p. (J). (gr. 2-6). 1997. per. 5.99 (*0-689-81541-7*) Aladdin.

— Eating the Plates: A Pilgrim Book of Food & Manners. LC 90-5918. (Illus.). 128p. (J). (gr. 1-5). 1991. lib. bdg. 16.00 (*0-02-770901-9*, Mac Bks Young Read) S&S Childrens.

— Eating the Plates: A Pilgrim Book of Food & Manners. 1997. 11.09 (*0-606-12685-6*, Pub. by Turtleback) Demco.

— Inside Your Outside. LC 97-52316. (Illus.). (J). 1998. 7.99 (*0-679-87302-3*) Random.

— Is a Camel a Mammal? LC 97-52316. 1998. lib. bdg. 11.99 (*0-679-97302-8*, Pub. by Random Bks Yng Read) Random.

— The Liberty Tree: The Beginning of the American Revolution. LC 95-23715. (Picture Landmark Ser.). 1998. lib. bdg. 15.99 (*0-679-93482-0*) Random.

— The Liberty Tree: The Beginning of the American Revolution. LC 95-23715. (Picture Landmark Ser.). 48p. (J). (gr. 2-4). 1998. 14.00 (*0-679-83482-6*) Random.

***Penner, Lucille R.** Lights Out! LC 99-42678. (Math Matters Ser.). (Illus.). 32p. (J). (gr. k-2). 2000. pap. 4.95 (*1-57565-092-4*) Kane Pr.

— Lights Out! (Math Matters Ser.). (Illus.). (J). 2000. 10.40 (*0-606-18220-9*) Turtleback.

Penner, Lucille R. Monster Bugs. LC 95-347. (Step into Reading Ser.: A Step 2 Book). (Illus.). 48p. (J). (ps-3). 1996. pap. 3.99 (*0-679-86974-3*) Random.

— Monster Bugs. LC 95-347. (Step into Reading Ser.: A Step 2 Book). (Illus.). (J). (ps-3). 1996. lib. bdg. 11.99 (*0-679-96974-8*) Random.

— Monster Bugs. LC 95-347. (Step into Reading Ser.: A Step 2 Book). (J). (gr. 1-3). 1996. 9.19 (*0-606-09626-4*, Pub. by Turtleback) Demco.

***Penner, Lucille R.** A Native American Feast. (Illus.). 99p. 1999. reprint ed. text 15.00 (*0-7881-6557-7*) DIANE Pub.

Penner, Lucille R. On Beyond Bugs: All about Insects. (J). 1999. lib. bdg. 11.99 (*0-679-97303-6*, Pub. by Random Bks Yng Read) Random.

— The Pilgrims at Plymouth. 1996. lib. bdg. 14.99 (*0-679-93201-1*) McKay.

P

An Asterisk (*) at the beginning of an entry indicates that the title is appearing for the first time.

— S-s-snakes! LC 93-46799. (Step into Reading Ser.: A Step 2 Book). (Illus.). 48p. (J). (gr. 1-3). 1994. lib. bdg. 11.99 (*0-679-94777-9*, Pub. by Random Bks Yng Read) Random.

— S-s-snakes! LC 93-46799. (Step into Reading Ser.: A Step 2 Book). (Illus.). 48p. (J). (ps-3). 1994. pap. 3.99 (*0-679-84777-4*, Pub. by Random Bks Yng Read) Random.

— S-s-snakes! (Step into Reading Ser.: A Step 2 Book). (J). (gr. 1-3). 1994. 9.19 (*0-606-06706-X*, Pub. by Turtleback) Demco.

— Sitting Bull. LC 94-46766. (All Aboard Reading Ser.: Level 2). (Illus.). 48p. (J). (gr. 1-3). 1995. pap. 3.99 (*0-448-40937-2*, G & D) Peng Put Young Read.

— Sitting Bull. (All Aboard Reading Ser.). 1995. 9.15 (*0-606-09859-3*, Pub. by Turtleback) Demco.

— The Statue of Liberty. LC 95-1854. (Step into Reading Ser.: A Step 1 Book). (Illus.). 32p. (J). (ps-3). 1995. pap. 3.99 (*0-679-86928-X*) Random.

Penner, Lucille R. The Statue of Liberty. (Step into Reading Ser.: A Step 1 Book). (J). (ps-1). 1995. 10.19 (*0-606-08618-8*, Pub. by Turtleback) Demco.

— Super Dinosaurs. 2000. pap. 3.99 (*0-679-89356-3*, Pub. by Random Bks Yng Read) Random.

Penner, Lucille R. The Tea Party Book. LC 91-52093. (Illus.). 48p. (J). (ps-4). 1993. 12.95 (*0-679-82440-5*, Pub. by Random Bks Yng Read) Random.

— The True Story of Pocahontas. LC 93-45709. (Step into Reading Ser.: A Step 2 Book). (Illus.). 48p. (J). (ps-3). 1994. pap. 3.99 (*0-679-86166-1*, Pub. by Random Bks Yng Read); lib. bdg. 11.99 (*0-679-96166-6*, Pub. by Random Bks Yng Read) Random.

Penner, Lucille R. The True Story of Pocahontas. (Step into Reading Ser.: A Step 2 Book). (J). (gr. 1-3). 1994. 9.19 (*0-606-06828-7*, Pub. by Turtleback) Demco.

Penner, Lucille R. Twister! LC 96-19352. (Step into Reading Ser.: A Step 2 Book). 45p. (J). (gr. 1-3). 1996. pap. 3.99 (*0-679-88271-5*) McKay.

— Twister! LC 96-19352. (Step into Reading Ser.: A Step 2 Book). (J). (gr. 1-3). 1996. lib. bdg. 11.99 (*0-679-98271-X*) McKay.

Penner, Lucille R. Twister! LC 96-19352. (Step into Reading Ser.: A Step 2 Book). (J). (gr. 1-3). 1996. 9.19 (*0-606-12020-3*, Pub. by Turtleback) Demco.

Penner, Lucille R. Westward Ho! The Story of the Pioneers. LC 97-281. (Landmark Ser.). (J). (gr. 1). 1997. 14.00 (*0-679-84776-6*) Random.

***Penner, Lucille R.** Where's That Bone? LC 99-88840. (Math Matters Ser.). (Illus.). 32p. (J). (ps-1). 2000. pap. 4.95 (*1-57565-097-5*) Kane Pr.

***Penner, Lucille R. & Billin-Frye, Paige.** Clean Sweep Campers. LC 99-88838. (Math Matters Ser.). 32p. (J). (gr. 1-3). 2000. pap. 4.95 (*1-57565-096-7*) Kane Pr.

Penner, Marci, jt. auth. see Penner, Mil.

Penner, Mary. Creative Bible Lessons. LC 99-30189. 128p. 1999. pap. 12.99 (*0-310-23094-2*) HarpC.

Penner, Maurice J. Capitation in California: A Study of Physician Organizations Managing Risk. LC 96-39279. 281p. 1997. pap. 44.00 (*1-56793-051-4*) Health Admin Pr.

Penner, Michael H., jt. ed. see Saddler, John N.

Penner, Mil. Exploring Kansas: A New Look at the Sunflower State. Campbell, Mary, ed. (Illus.). 128p. 1996. pap. 14.95 (*0-9615597-8-0*) Sounds Kansas.

Penner, Mil & Penner, Marci. Kansas Event Guide. (Kansas Guide Ser.). (Illus.). 128p. 1991. pap. 12.95 (*0-9615597-4-8*); spiral bd. 12.95 (*0-9615597-5-6*) Sounds Kansas.

Penner, Mil & Schmidt, Carol. Prairie: The Land & Its People. Nielsen, Mary, ed. LC 89-91644. (Illus.). 224p. 1990. 39.95 (*0-9615597-1-3*) Sounds Kansas.

Penner, N. Canadian Left: A Critical Analysis. 1977. pap. 13.67 (*0-13-113126-5*) P-H.

Penner, Nadine R., jt. ed. see Infeld, Donna L.

Penner, Peter. The Patronage Bureaucracy in North India: The Robert M. Bird & James Thomason School, 1820-1870. 380p. 1986. 35.00 (*81-7001-017-9*, Pub. by Chanakya) S Asia.

— Robert Needham Cust, 1821-1909: A Personal Biography. LC 86-23821. (Studies in British History: Vol. 5). (Illus.). 360p. 1987. lib. bdg. 99.95 (*0-88946-456-1*) E Mellen.

— Russians, North Americans & Telugus: The Mennonite Brethren Mission in India, 1885-1975. LC 98-106073. (Perspectives on Mennonite Life & Thought Ser.: No. 10). (Illus.). 445p. 1997. pap. 29.95 (*0-921788-40-1*) Kindred Prods.

Penner, Peter & MacLean, Richard. The Rebel Bureaucrat: Frederick John Shore 1799-1837 as Critic of William Bentinck's India. 1982. 24.00 (*0-8364-0920-5*, Pub. by Chanakya) S Asia.

***Penner, R. C.** Discrete Mathematics: Proof Techniques & Mathematical Structures. LC 99-44793. 1999. 58.00 (*981-02-4088-0*) World Scientific Pub.

Penner, R. C. & Harer, J. L. Combinatorics of Train Tracks. (Annals of Mathematics Studies: No. 125). 216p. 1992. pap. text 29.95 (*0-691-02531-2*, Pub. by Princeton U Pr) Cal Prin Full Svc.

Penner, Randy. A Harvest of Memories. Van Etten, Rick, ed. LC 96-67870. 116p. 1996. 14.95 (*0-89821-170-0*, 20390) Reiman Pubns.

Penner, Richard H. Conference Center Planning & Design: A Guide for Architects, Designers, Meeting Planners, & Facility Managers. LC 90-22581. 256p. reprint ed. pap. 79.40 (*0-608-08065-9*, 206903000002) Bks Demand.

Penner, Rob, jt. auth. see Smith, Ron.

Penner, Robert, jt. ed. see Yau, S. T.

Penner, Rudolph G., ed. The Congressional Budget Process After Five Years. LC 81-8000. (AEI Symposia Ser.: No. 81H). 216p. reprint ed. pap. 67.00 (*0-8357-4453-1*, 203729100008) Bks Demand.

— The Great Fiscal Experiment. LC 90-43204. (Illus.). 250p. 1990. pap. text 16.00 (*0-87766-485-4*) Urban Inst.

Penner, S. S. Chemical Rocket Propulsion & Combustion Research. (Illus.). xii, 158p. 1962. text 220.00 (*0-677-00710-8*) Gordon & Breach.

Penner, S. S., ed. Coal Gasification: Direct Applications & Synthesis of Chemicals & Fuels. (International Journal of Energy: Vol. 12). 296p. 1987. 75.00 (*0-317-66175-2*, Pergamon Pr) Elsevier.

Penner, Samuel. The Four Dimensions of Paradise. LC 92-74667. 200p. 1992. 27.95 (*0-9627145-0-X*, Cyrus Pr) Waterside Prodns.

Penner, Terry. The Ascent from Nominalism: Some Existence Arguments in Plato's Middle Dialogues. (Philosophical Studies: No. 37). 480p. 1987. text 168.00 (*90-277-2427-X*) Kluwer Academic.

Penner, Todd C. The Epistle & James & Eschatology: Re-reading an Ancient Christian Letter. LC 96-165119. (JSNT Supplement Ser.: No. 121). 331p. 1996. 85.00 (*1-85075-574-4*, Pub. by Sheffield Acad) CUP Services.

Penner, Todd C., jt. auth. see Johnson, Luke Timothy.

Penner, Zvi, jt. ed. see Dittmar, Norbert.

Pennewell, John L. Your Family's Financial Survival Guide: How to Organize Your Estate & Provide a Valuable Guide for Your Heirs. 44p. (Orig.). 1995. pap. 8.95 (*0-9647207-0-1*) Lakeside FL.

Penney. Appleton & Lange's Review of Physiology - USMLE 1. LC 97-33321. (Illus.). 277p. (C). 1997. pap. 32.95 (*0-8385-0274-1*, A-0274-9, Apple Lange Med) McGraw.

Penney, jt. auth. see Edwards.

Penney, Alexandra. How to Make Love to a Man. 160p. 1982. mass mkt. 5.99 (*0-440-13529-X*) Dell.

— How to Make Love to a Man. write for info. (*0-318-59623-7*) S&S Trade.

Penney, Alexandria. How to Make Love to a Man. 144p. 1989. 7.99 (*0-517-60109-5*) Random Hse Value.

Penney, Allen. Houses of Nova Scotia. (Illus.). 160p. 1995. pap. 12.95 (*0-88780-072-6*) Formac Dist Ltd.

Penney, Barbara, compiled by. Music in British Libraries: A Directory of Resources. LC 92-16596. 109p. Date not set. reprint ed. pap. 33.80 (*0-608-20732-2*, 207183000002) Bks Demand.

Penney, Bridget. Honeymoon with Death. 1991. pap. 12.95 (*0-7486-6102-6*, Pub. by Edinburgh U Pr) Col U Pr.

Penney, Bridget & Holman, Paul, eds. The Invisible Reader. 108p. 1995. 16.00 (*0-9521256-1-7*, Pub. by Invisible Bks) SPD-Small Pr Dist.

Penney, C., jt. auth. see Dugas, H.

Penney, Charles R. New Guinea Art & Crafts: The Charles Rand Penney Collection. (Illus.). 80p. 1988. 25.00 (*0-9620346-0-6*) C R Penney.

Penney, Clara L. Printed Books, 1468-1700 in the Hispanic Society of America. (Illus.). 614p. 1965. 15.00 (*0-87535-106-9*) Hispanic Soc.

Penney, D. Andrew. Freewill or Predestination? The Battle over Saving Grace in Mid-Tudor England. (Royal Historical Society: Studies in History). 261p. 1991. 75.00 (*0-86193-219-6*) Boydell & Brewer.

Penney, David E., jt. auth. see Edwards.

Penney, David E., jt. auth. see Edwards, C. H., Jr.

Penney, David E., jt. auth. see Edwards, C. H.

Penney, David E., jt. auth. see Edwards, C. H., Jr.

***Penney, David G.** Carbon Monoxide Toxicity. 584p. 2000. boxed set 99.95 (*0-8493-2065-8*) CRC Pr.

Penney, David G. Physiology: MEPC. 9th ed. (Illus.). 255p. (C). 1996. pap. text 21.95 (*0-8385-6222-1*, A6222-2, Apple Lange Med) McGraw.

Penney, David G., ed. Carbon Monoxide. 304p. 1996. boxed set 119.95 (*0-8493-4796-3*) CRC Pr.

Penney, David W. Art of the American Indian Frontier: A Portfolio. LC 94-42820. 24p. 1995. pap. 18.95 (*1-56584-251-0*, Pub. by New Press NY) Norton.

— Art of the American Indian Frontier: The Chandler-Pohrt Collection. LC 91-37736. (Illus.). 368p. 1994. pap. 39.95 (*0-295-97318-8*) U of Wash Pr.

— Native American Art Masterpieces. LC 97-140157. (Illus.). 120p. 1996. 35.00 (*0-88363-496-1*) S&S Trade.

— Native Arts of North America. (Illus.). 208p. 1998. pap. text 27.50 (*2-87939-190-3*, Pub. by Pierre Terrail) Rizzoli Intl.

Penney, David W. & Longfish, George C. Native American Art. (Illus.). 320p. 1999. 40.00 (*0-88363-479-1*) H L Levin.

Penney, David W., jt. auth. see Pohrt, Richard, Jr.

Penney, Edmund F. The Facts on File Dictionary of Film & Broadcast Terms. 272p. 1991. 29.95 (*0-8160-1923-1*) Facts on File.

— The Facts on File Dictionary of Film & Broadcast Terms. LC 88-7023. 267p. 1991. reprint ed. pap. 82.80 (*0-608-02834-7*, 206390100007) Bks Demand.

***Penney, Elaine.** Soul Ties. 100p. 2000. 9.95 (*0-9700449-0-9*) Chrisma Train.

Penney, Elaine, jt. auth. see Crowe, Suzy.

Penney, Electa K. Ketcham Family: Descendants of John Ketcham & His Wife Sarah Matthews of Mt. Hope Township, Orange County, N. Y. (Illus.). 110p. 1997. reprint ed. pap. 19.00 (*0-8328-9409-5*); reprint ed. lib. bdg. 29.00 (*0-8328-9408-7*) Higginson Bk Co.

Penney, Frances. I Was There. Griffen, Zofia, tr. LC 87-43136. 152p. 1988. pap. 13.95 (*0-88400-128-8*, Shengold Bks) Schreiber Pub.

Penney, Grace J. Moki. LC 96-34478. 176p. 1997. pap. 4.99 (*0-14-038430-8*) Viking Penguin.

Penney, Grace Jackson. Moki, a Classic Story of a Young Cheyenne Girl. (J). 1997. 10.09 (*0-606-11631-1*, Pub. by Turtleback) Demco.

Penney, Ian. Ian Penney's Book of Nursery Rhymes. (Illus.). 40p. (J). (ps-2). 1994. 14.95 (*0-8109-3733-6*, Pub. by Abrams) Time Warner.

— The Maine Road Encyclopedia. 208p. 1996. pap. 17.95 (*1-85158-710-1*, Pub. by Mainstream Pubng) Trafalgar.

Penney, Ian. Ian Penney's ABC. LC 98-224251. 36p. (J). (ps-k). 1998. 16.95 (*0-8109-4350-6*, Pub. by Abrams) Time Warner.

Penney, Ian. Ian Penney's Book of Fairy Tales. LC 96-133536. 48p. (J). (gr. k-3). 1995. 14.95 (*0-8109-3740-9*, Pub. by Abrams) Time Warner.

Penney, J. C. Fifty Years with the Golden Rule. 1993. reprint ed. lib. bdg. 21.95 (*1-56849-162-X*) Buccaneer Bks.

Penney, Jacqueline. Painting Greeting Cards in Watercolor. LC 96-36396. (Illus.). 128p. 1997. pap. 22.99 (*0-89134-715-1*, North Lght Bks) F & W Pubns Inc.

Penney, Jane, jt. auth. see Currier, Glenn.

Penney, John M. The Missionary Emphasis of Lukan Pneumatology. (JPTS Ser.: Vol. 12). 143p. 1997. pap. 13.95 (*1-85075-800-X*, Pub. by Sheffield Acad) CUP Services.

Penney, M. Politics, Policy & Practice in Physical Education. LC 98-38800. 208p. 1998. pap. 24.95 (*0-419-21950-1*) Thomson Learn.

Penney, Mary B., ed. & photos by see Brubaker, Donald.

Penney, Norman, et al. Land Financing, Cases & Materials On. 3rd ed. LC 84-24645. (University Casebook Ser.). 1052p. 1984. text 40.95 (*0-88277-199-X*) Foundation Pr.

Penney, Richard C. Linear Algebra: Ideas & Applications. LC 97-17169. 400p. 1997. text 95.95 (*0-471-18179-X*) Wiley.

Penney, Russell, jt. auth. see Couch, Mal.

Penney, Sue. Buddhism. LC 96-3733. (Discovering Religions Ser.). 48p. (J). 1997. lib. bdg. 24.26 (*0-8172-4395-X*) Raintree Steck-V.

***Penney, Sue.** Christianity. LC 00-29590. (World Beliefs & Cultures Ser.). 2000. lib. bdg. write for info. (*1-57572-355-7*) Heinemann Lib.

Penney, Sue. Christianity. LC 96-3730. (Discovering Religions Ser.). 48p. (J). 1997. lib. bdg. 24.26 (*0-8172-4396-8*) Raintree Steck-V.

— Hinduism. LC 96-6981. (Discovering Religions Ser.). 48p. (J). 1997. lib. bdg. 24.26 (*0-8172-4397-6*) Raintree Steck-V.

***Penney, Sue.** Islam. LC 00-24007. (J). 2000. lib. bdg. write for info. (*1-57572-357-3*) Heinemann Lib.

Penney, Sue. Islam. LC 96-3729. (Discovering Religions Ser.). 48p. (J). 1997. lib. bdg. 24.26 (*0-8172-4394-1*) Raintree Steck-V.

***Penney, Sue.** Judaism. LC 00-23230. (World Beliefs & Cultures Ser.). (J). 2000. lib. bdg. write for info. (*1-57572-358-1*) Heinemann Lib.

Penney, Sue. Judaism. LC 96-33727. (Discovering Religions Ser.). 48p. (J). 1997. lib. bdg. 24.26 (*0-8172-4393-3*) Raintree Steck-V.

— Sikhism. (Discovering Religions Ser.). 48p. (J). 1996. lib. bdg. 24.26 (*0-8172-4398-4*) Raintree Steck-V.

Penneys, Neal S. Skin Manifestations of AIDS. LC 89-80849. 220p. 1989. reprint ed. pap. 68.20 (*0-608-04706-6*, 206542700004) Bks Demand.

Penneys, Neal S. Skin Manifestations of AIDS. 2nd ed. 1995. write for info. (*1-85317-242-1*, Pub. by Martin Dunitz) Mosby Inc.

Pennicd, Nigel. Haindl Rune Oracle. LC 97-41146. 1997. pap. text 14.00 (*1-57281-025-4*, BK165) US Games Syst.

Pennick, Nigel. The Celtic Cross: An Illustrated History & Celebration. (Illus.). 160p. pap. 16.95 (*0-7137-2758-6*, Pub. by Blandford Pr) Sterling.

— Celtic Saints: An Illustrated & Authoritative Guide to These Extraordinary Men & Women. (Illus.). 128p. 1998. 14.95 (*0-8069-9601-3*) Sterling.

— The Complete Illustrated Guide to Runes: How to Intrepret the Ancient Wisdom of the Runes. LC 99-17661. (Illus.). 192p. 1999. pap. 19.95 (*1-86204-100-8*, Pub. by Element MA) Penguin Putnam.

— Crossing the Borderlines: Guising, Masking & Ritual Animal Disguises in the European Tradition. (Illus.). 1998. pap. 23.95 (*1-86163-043-3*) Holmes Pub.

— Dragons of the West. (Illus.). (Orig.). 1997. pap. 23.95 (*1-86163-007-7*, Pub. by Capall Bann Pubng) Holmes Pub.

— Earth Harmony: Places of Power, Holiness, & Healing. 1997. pap. 23.95 (*1-898307-97-0*, Pub. by Capall Bann Pubng) Holmes Pub.

— Haindl Rune Oracle Deck & Book Set. (Illus.). 224p. 1998. pap. 26.00 (*1-57281-030-0*, HROS99) US Games Syst.

— Inner Mysteries of the Goths: Rune Lore & Secret Wisdom of the Northern Tradition. (Illus.). 210p. (Orig.). 1995. pap. 22.95 (*1-898307-51-2*, Pub. by Capall Bann Pubng) Holmes Pub.

— Lost Cities & Sunken Lands. 1997. pap. 22.95 (*1-898307-83-0*, Pub. by Capall Bann Pubng) Holmes Pub.

— Magical Alphabets. LC 92-7859. (Illus.). 256p. 1992. pap. 14.95 (*0-87728-747-3*) Weiser.

— Oracle of Geomancy: The Divinatory Arts of Raml, Geomantia, Sikidy, & the I Ching. 1995. pap. 19.95 (*1-898307-16-4*) Holmes Pub.

— The Pagan Book of Days: Celebrating Festivals & Sacred Days Through the Millenium. (Illus.). 160p. 1992. pap. 9.95 (*0-89281-369-5*) Inner Tradit.

— Practical Magic in the Northern Tradition. (Illus.). 288p. 1988. pap. 14.95 (*0-85030-757-0*, Pub. by Aqrn Pr) Harper SF.

— Runic Astrology. (Illus.). 270p. (Orig.). 1995. pap. 22.95 (*1-898307-45-8*, Pub. by Capall Bann Pubng) Holmes Pub.

Pennick, Nigel. Sacred Geometry: Symbolism & Purpose in Religious Structures. 1994. pap. 19.95 (*1-898307-15-6*, Pub. by Capall Bann Pubng) Holmes Pub.

Pennick, Nigel. The Sacred World of the Celts: An Illustrated Guide to Celtic Spirituality & Mythology. LC 97-24736. (Illus.). 144p. 1997. 28.00 (*0-89281-654-6*, Inner Trad) Inner Tradit.

***Pennick, Nigel.** The Sacred World of the Celts: An Illustrated Guide to Celtic Spirituality & Mythology. LC 97-24736. (Illus.). 144p. 2000. pap. 19.95 (*0-89281-701-1*) Inner Tradit.

Pennick, Nigel. Secret Games of the Gods: Ancient Ritual Systems in Board Games. 1997. pap. text 12.95 (*0-88079-589-1*, BK120) US Games Syst.

Pennick, Nigel. Secret Signs, Symbols & Sigils. 1996. pap. 21.95 (*1-898307-55-5*, Pub. by Capall Bann Pubng) Holmes Pub.

Pennick, Nigel. Secrets of the Runes, 1, 1. 1999. pap. 16.00 (*0-7225-3784-0*) Thorsons PA.

Pennick, Nigel & Field, Helen. The God Year. (Orig.). 1997. pap. 19.95 (*1-898307-64-4*, Pub. by Capall Bann Pubng) Holmes Pub.

— The Goddess Year. (Orig.). 1996. pap. 23.95 (*1-898307-63-6*, Pub. by Capall Bann Pubng) Holmes Pub.

Pennick, Nigel & Jackson, Nigel. The New Celtic Oracle. (Orig.). 1997. pap. 22.95 (*1-898307-56-3*, Pub. by Capall Bann Pubng) Holmes Pub.

Pennick, Nigel, jt. auth. see Jones, Prudence.

Pennick, Nigel C. Celtic Sacred Landscapes. LC 95-60273. (Illus.). 224p. 1996. 24.95 (*0-500-01666-6*, Pub. by Thames Hudson) Norton.

Pennick, Nigel C., jt. auth. see Jackson, Nigel.

Pennie, Michael. African Assortment, African Art in Museums in England & Scotland. (Illus.). 303p. (Orig.). 1991. pap. 39.95 (*0-9513023-2-9*, Pub. by Bath Coll High Educ) Knopf.

Pennig, Dietmar, jt. ed. see Court-Brown, Charles.

Pennigstore, Werner, jt. auth. see Davidson, Ken.

Penniman, Clara. State Income Taxation. LC 79-20081. 310p. reprint ed. pap. 96.10 (*0-608-06183-2*, 206651500008) Bks Demand.

Penniman, Howard R., ed. Australia at the Polls: The National Elections of 1980 & 1983. LC 82-73669. 361p. reprint ed. pap. 112.00 (*0-8357-4435-3*, 203726900008) Bks Demand.

— Britain at the Polls 1979: A Study of the General Election. LC 80-27536. (AEI Studies: No. 296). (Illus.). 368p. reprint ed. pap. 114.10 (*0-8357-4439-6*, 203727300008) Bks Demand.

— Canada at the Polls, Nineteen Seventy-Nine & Nineteen Eighty: A Study of the General Elections. LC 81-19144. (Illus.). 448p. reprint ed. pap. 138.90 (*0-8357-4443-4*, 203727800008) Bks Demand.

— Canada at the Polls, 1984: A Study of the Federal General Elections. LC 87-27252. (At the Polls Ser.). xiii, 218p. (C). 1988. text 62.95 (*0-8223-0805-3*); pap. text 23.95 (*0-8223-0821-5*) Duke.

— France at the Polls, 1981 & 1986. LC 87-35743. (At the Polls Ser.). xvi, 368p. (C). 1988. text 62.95 (*0-8223-0833-9*); pap. text 23.95 (*0-8223-0845-2*) Duke.

— The French National Assembly Elections of, 1978. LC 79-28590. (AEI Studies: No. 269). 272p. reprint ed. pap. 84.40 (*0-8357-4483-3*, 203733500008) Bks Demand.

— Greece at the Polls: The National Elections of 1974 & 1977. LC 81-8026. (AEI Studies: No. 317). (Illus.). 236p. reprint ed. pap. 73.20 (*0-8357-4485-X*, 203733700008) Bks Demand.

— Italy at the Polls: The Parliamentary Elections of 1976. LC 77-90425. (American Enterprise Institutes Studies in Political & Social Processes: No. 169). 402p. reprint ed. pap. 124.70 (*0-8357-4497-3*, 203735000008) Bks Demand.

— Italy at the Polls, 1983: A Study of the National Elections. LC 87-6716. (At the Polls Ser.). (Illus.). xii, 216p. (C). 1987. text 62.95 (*0-8223-0755-3*); pap. text 23.95 (*0-8223-0787-1*) Duke.

— Italy at the Polls, 1979: A Study of the Parliamentary Elections. LC 81-8106. (AEI Studies: No. 321). (Illus.). 356p. reprint ed. pap. 110.40 (*0-8357-4498-1*, 203735100008) Bks Demand.

— New Zealand at the Polls: The General Election of 1978. LC 80-16464. (AEI Studies: No. 273). (Illus.). 312p. reprint ed. pap. 96.80 (*0-8357-4514-7*, 203737200008) Bks Demand.

Penniman, Howard R. & Farrell, Brian, eds. Ireland at the Polls, 1981, 1982, & 1987: A Study of Four General Elections. LC 87-13513. xv, 275p. 1987. pap. text 23.95 (*0-8223-0786-3*) Duke.

— Ireland at the Polls, 1981, 1982, & 1987: A Study of Four General Elections. LC 87-13513. xv, 275p. 1987. text 62.95 (*0-8223-0754-5*) Duke.

Penniman, Howard R. & Mujal-Leon, Eusebio M., eds. Spain at the Polls, Nineteen Seventy-Seven, Nineteen Seventy-Nine & Nineteen Eighty-Two: A Study of the National Elections. LC 85-20523. (Illus.). 392p. reprint ed. pap. 121.60 (*0-8357-4536-8*, 203741700008) Bks Demand.

— Spain at the Polls, 1977, 1979, & 1982: A Study of the National Elections. LC 85-20523. (At the Polls Ser.). xviii, 372p. 1985. text 54.95 (*0-8223-0663-8*) Duke.

— Spain at the Polls, 1977, 1979, & 1982: A Study of the National Elections. LC 85-20523. (At the Polls Ser.). xviii, 372p. 1985. pap. text 21.95 (*0-8223-0695-6*) Duke.

Penniman, Howard R., jt. auth. see Ranney, Austin.

Penniman, Josiah H. War of the Theatres. LC 73-126649. reprint ed. 32.50 (*0-404-04992-3*) AMS Pr.

Penniman, T. K., ed. see Spencer, Baldwin.

Pennimo. Myself Has Come Home. (Illus.). 75p. 1997. 24.95 (*0-9661543-1-2*); pap. 11.95 (*0-9661543-0-4*) D A Meaux.

Penning de Vries, F. W., jt. auth. see Stein, A.

P

An Asterisk (*) at the beginning of an entry indicates that the title is appearing for the first time.

Penning-De Vries, F.W.T., et al. Soil Erosion at Multiple Scales: Principles & Methods for Assessing Causes & Impacts. LC 98-22770. 416p. 1998. 110.00 (*0-85199-290-0*) OUP.

Penning, F. M. Electrical Discharges in Gases. x, 118p. 1957. text 123.00 (*0-677-61230-3*) Gordon & Breach.

Penning, James M. & Smidt, Corwin E., eds. Sojourners in the Wilderness: The Christian Right in Comparative Perspective. LC 97-18546. 320p. 1997. 71.50 (*0-8476-8644-2*); pap. 26.95 (*0-8476-8645-0*) Rowman.

Penning, L. & Thijn, C. J. Liber Amicorum Presented to Prof. Dr. J. R. Blickman. (Journal: Diagnostic Imaging in Clinical Medicine: Vol. 53, No. 4). (Illus.). 56p. 1984. 38.50 (*3-8055-3934-7*) S Karger.

Penning, Martin J., jt. auth. see Humphries, John.

Penning-Roswell, Edmund. The Wines of Bordeaux. 704p. (Orig.). 1983. pap. 12.95 (*0-932664-51-2*) Wine Appreciation.

Penning-Roswell, Edmund C. & Lowenthal, D., eds. Landscape Meanings & Values. (Illus.). 160p. 1986. text 39.95 (*0-04-710003-6*) Routledge.

Penning-Rowsell, Edmund, ed. The Economics of Coastal Zone Management: A Manual of Assessment Techniques "The Yellow Manual" 368p. 1992. text 104.95 (*1-85293-161-2*, Pub. by P P Pubs) CRC Pr.

Penning-Rowsell, Edmund, jt. auth. see Handmer, John.

Penning-Rowsell, Edmund C., et al. Economics of Coastal Management: A Manual of Benefit Assessment Techniques. 368p. 1994. 200.00 (*0-471-94744-X*) Wiley.

— Floods & Drainage: British Policies for Hazard Reduction, Agricultural Improvement & Wetland Conservation. (Risks & Hazards Ser.: No. 2). (Illus.). 192p. (C). 1985. text 80.00 (*0-04-627001-9*) Routledge.

Penning, William H. Gold & Diamonds: South African Facts & Inferences. LC 72-4212. 100p. 1977. reprint ed. 18.95 (*0-8369-9101-X*) Ayer.

Penninger, Frieda E. Chaucer's Troilus & Criseyda & the Knight's Tale: Fictions Used. LC 93-25225. 126p. (C). 1993. lib. bdg. 39.50 (*0-8191-9218-X*) U Pr of Amer.

Penninger, Harold. Walking with God. LC 96-60487. 128p. 1996. per. 7.95 (*1-57258-114-X*) Teach Servs.

Penningroth, Kathy, jt. auth. see Anderson, Lee.

Pennings, F. Benefits of Doubt: A Comparative Study of the Unemployment Benefit Schemes & Reintegration Opportunities of Great Britain, France, the Federal Republic of Germany & the Netherlands. 512p. 1991. pap. 79.00 (*90-6544-512-9*) Kluwer Law Intl.

— Introduction to European Social Security Law. 2nd ed. LC 98-27174. (Studies in Social Policy). 1998. 108.00 (*90-411-1033-X*) Kluwer Law Intl.

— Introduction to Social Security. LC 96-152473. 1994. pap. text 121.00 (*90-6544-840-3*) Kluwer Academic.

Pennings, F., et al. Telework in the Netherlands: Labour Law, Social Security Law & Occupational Health & Safety Aspects, No. 1. (Studies & Reports of the Hugo Sinzheimer Instituut: Vol. 2). 109p. 1996. pap. 35.00 (*90-73868-11-4*) Gaunt.

Pennings, Johannes M. Interlocking Directorates: Origins & Consequences of Connections Among Organizations' Boards of Directors. LC 80-8001. (Jossey-Bass Social & Behavioral Science Ser.). 238p. reprint ed. pap. 73.80 (*0-8357-6883-X*, 203793500009) Bks Demand.

Pennings, Johannes M. & Buitendam, Arend, eds. New Technology As Organizational Innovation: The Development & Diffusion of Microelectronics. LC 86-32110. 328p. 1987. text 32.00 (*0-88730-186-X*, HarpBusn) HarpInfo.

Pennings, Johannes M., et al. Organizational Strategy & Change. LC 84-47994. (Jossey-Bass Social & Behavioral Science Ser.). 597p. reprint ed. pap. 185.10 (*0-7837-0186-1*, 204048200017) Bks Demand.

Pennings, Paul & Lane, Jan E., eds. Comparing Party System Change. LC 97-38740. (European Political Science Ser.). (Illus.). 272p. (C). 1998. 90.00 (*0-415-16550-4*) Routledge.

Pennington, A. A. Nearer My God to Thee. LC 98-90133. 1998. pap. 9.95 (*0-533-12708-4*) Vantage.

Pennington, Albert. Big Boy: The Story of a Dog. 320p. 1971. 3.00 (*0-685-04706-7*); pap. 1.00 (*0-685-04707-5*) Pennington.

Pennington, Anna, jt. auth. see Pennington, Krista.

Pennington, Anne, tr. see Popa, Vasko, et al.

Pennington, Arthur R. The Life & Character of Erasmus. 1977. lib. bdg. 59.95 (*0-8490-2159-6*) Gordon Pr.

Pennington, Basil. The Cistercians. (Religious Orders Ser.). 144p. (Orig.). 1992. 18.95 (*0-8146-5720-6*, M Glazier) Liturgical Pr.

— The Eucharist Yesterday & Today. (C). 1988. 39.00 (*0-85439-241-6*, Pub. by St Paul Pubns) St Mut.

— Monastic Journey to India. 2nd rev. ed. LC 81-14422. 178p. 1999. pap. 13.95 (*1-56907-009-1*) Beacon Pt Pr.

Pennington, Basil M. Called. 1984. pap. 8.95 (*0-86683-877-5*) Harper SF.

— Thomas Merton, Brother Monk: The Quest for True Freedom. LC 97-65115. 208p. 1997. pap. 16.95 (*0-8264-1012-X*) Continuum.

***Pennington, Bonnie.** Tommy's Train Ride: On the Alaska Railroad. LC 99-63819. (Illus.). 16p. (J). (gr. k-3). 1999. pap. 12.95 (*1-888125-51-9*) Publ Consult.

Pennington, Bruce F. Diagnosing Learning Disorders: A Neuropsychological Framework. LC 91-9558. 224p. 1991. lib. bdg. 31.00 (*0-89862-563-7*) Guilford Pubns.

Pennington, Bruce F., ed. Reading Disabilities: Genetic & Neurological Influences. 240p. (C). 1992. lib. bdg. 153.00 (*0-7923-1606-1*) Kluwer Academic.

Pennington, C. R. Therapeutic Nutrition: A Practical Guide. (Illus.). 288p. (Orig.). (C). (gr. 13). 1991. pap. text 43.50 (*0-412-29230-0*) Chapman & Hall.

Pennington, Campbell W. The Pima Bajo of Central Sonora Mexico, 2 vols., 1. LC 79-89878. 430p. reprint ed. pap. 133.30 (*0-8357-8986-1*, 203336300001) Bks Demand.

— The Pima Bajo of Central Sonora Mexico, 2 vols., 2. LC 79-89878. 159p. pap. 49.30 (*0-8357-8987-X*, 203336300002) Bks Demand.

— The Tarahumar of Mexico: Their Environment & Material Culture. LC 64-1645. 299p. reprint ed. pap. 92.70 (*0-608-14479-7*, 202528100042) Bks Demand.

— The Tepehuan of Chihuahua: Their Material Culture. LC 73-99792. (Illus.). 427p. reprint ed. pap. 132.40 (*0-8357-7051-6*, 203336400085) Bks Demand.

Pennington, Carole, ed. see Vance, Vince.

Pennington, Carolyn Ingram. The Modernisation of Medical Teaching in the Nineteenth Century LC 95-159417. (Quincentennial Studies). ix, 116p. 1994. write for info. (*1-85752-215-X*) Macmillan.

Pennington, D. D., jt. auth. see Pennington, Eunice A.

Pennington, D. H. Europe in the Seventeenth Century. 2nd ed. 640p. (C). 1989. pap. 48.00 (*0-582-49388-9*, 78027) Longman.

Pennington, Daniel. Cherokee ABC Coloring Book. 28p. (J). (gr. 1-6). 1997. pap. 4.00 (*0-935741-18-6*, Pub. by Cherokee Pubns) Book Pub Co.

— Itse Selu: Cherokee Harvest Festival. LC 93-27147. (Illus.). 32p. (J). (ps-3). 1994. 15.95 (*0-88106-851-9*, Talewinds); pap. 6.95 (*0-88106-850-0*, Talewinds) Charlesbridge Pub.

Pennington, Daniel. Itse Selu: Cherokee Harvest Festival. 1994. 12.15 (*0-606-06501-6*, Pub. by Turtleback) Demco.

Pennington, Donald C. Essential Social Psychology. 288p. 1995. pap. text 18.95 (*0-7131-6483-2*, Pub. by E A) St Martin.

***Pennington, Donald C.** Social Cognition. LC 00-32172. (Modular Psychology Ser.). 2000. write for info. (*0-415-21705-9*) Routledge.

Pennington, Donald C., et al. Essential Social Psychology. 2nd ed. 464p. 1999. pap. text 24.95 (*0-340-54846-0*) OUP.

Pennington, Dorothy L. African American Women Quitting the Workplace. LC 99-20544. (Black Studies: Vol. 5). 142p. 1999. text 69.95 (*0-7734-8183-4*) E Mellen.

Pennington, Elisabeth, ed. Curriculum Revisited: An Update of Curriculum Design. 48p. 1986. 14.95 (*0-88737-338-0*, 15-2165) Natl League Nurse.

Pennington, Estill C. Antiquarian Pursuits. LC 92-71543. (Illus.). 88p. (Orig.). 1992. pap. 20.00 (*0-9632836-0-X*) R M Hicklin.

— Downriver: Currents of Style in Louisiana Painting, 1800-1950. LC 90-6932. (Illus.). 208p. 1991. 49.95 (*0-88289-800-0*) Pelican.

— Echoes & Late Shadows: The Larger World of Southern Impressionism. (Illus.). 18p. 1996. pap. 4.95 (*0-9638753-8-8*) Morris Mus Art.

— Frontier Sublime: Alaskan Art from the Juneau Empire Collection. LC 98-128708. (Illus.). 112p. 1997. 29.95 (*1-890021-00-8*) Morris Mus Art.

— Gracious Plenty: American Still-Life Art from Southern Collections. (Illus.). 128p. 1995. pap. 36.95 (*0-9638753-5-3*) Morris Mus Art.

— Heirs of Magic Realism: Representation in Current Dutch Art. (Illus.). 32p. 1999. pap. 12.95 (*1-890021-06-7*) Morris Mus Art.

— The Last Meeting's Lost Cause. LC 88-91008. (Illus.). 67p. (Orig.). 1988. pap. 20.00 (*0-9632836-4-2*) R M Hicklin.

— Light of Touch: Select Works on Paper from the Permanent Collection. (Illus.). 1993. 19.95 (*0-9638753-0-2*) Morris Mus Art.

— Look Away: Reality & Sentiment in Southern Art. LC 89-8731. (Illus.). 200p. 1989. 50.00 (*0-934601-92-5*) Saraland Pr.

— Passage & Progress in the Works of William Tylee Ranney. (Illus.). 1993. pap. 14.95 (*0-9638753-1-0*) Morris Mus Art.

— A Southern Collection. LC 92-23560. (Illus.). 1992. 39.95 (*0-9618270-5-X*); pap. 24.95 (*0-9618270-6-8*) Morris Mus Art.

— A Southern Collection: A Publication of the Morris Museum of Art. LC 92-23560. 248p. (C). 1992. 39.95 (*0-8203-1534-6*); pap. 24.95 (*0-8203-1535-4*) U of Ga Pr.

— Stars for His Crown: A Memorial Exhibition for William Joseph Petrie (1951-1995) (Illus.). 32p. 1996. pap. 9.95 (*0-9638753-6-1*) Morris Mus Art.

— Victorian Visionary: The Art of Elliott Daingerfield. (Illus.). 1994. 29.95 (*0-9638753-2-9*) Morris Mus Art.

— Will Henry Stevens: From the Mountains to the Sea. (Illus.). 32p. (Orig.). 1994. pap. 8.00 (*0-9641350-0-0*) Blue Spiral.

— With Joy & Wonder: Ante-Bellum Taste in the Bluegrass. (Illus.). 24p. 1992. pap. text 3.50 (*1-882007-04-2*) Univ KY Art Mus.

Pennington, Estill C. & Gruber, J. Richard. Celebrating Southern Art: A Fifth Anniversary Exhibition. Claussen, Louise K., ed. (Illus.). 1997. pap. 9.95 (*1-890021-02-4*) Morris Mus Art.

Pennington, Estill C. & Kiehl, David. Ida Kohlmeyer: Recent Works. LC 96-77770. (Illus.). 62p. 1996. 21.95 (*0-9638753-9-6*) Morris Mus Art.

Pennington, Estill C., jt. auth. see Speakes, Vera J.

Pennington, Estill Curtis. John Bodeker Savage, 1928-1986: A Georgia Painter Rediscovered. (Illus.). 24p. 1993. pap. 10.95 (*0-9618270-8-4*) Morris Comms.

***Pennington, Estill Curtis.** Subdued Hues: Mood & Scene in Southern Landscape Painting, 1865-1925. (Illus.). 60p. 1999. 29.95 (*1-890021-09-1*) Morris Mus Art.

Pennington, Estill Curtis. Will Henry Stevens, 1881-1949: An Eye Transformed, a Hand Transforming... LC 93-22164. (Illus.). 40p. 1993. 10.95 (*0-9618270-7-6*) Morris Comms.

Pennington, Eunice A. History of the Ozarks. (Illus.). 5.00 (*0-685-19373-X*); pap. 2.00 (*0-911120-01-7*) Pennington.

— The Ladybird Mystery. 1974. 4.50 (*0-685-42423-5*); pap. 2.50 (*0-685-42424-3*) Pennington.

— Master of the Mountain. 1971. 4.50 (*0-685-47078-4*); pap. 2.50 (*0-685-47079-2*) Pennington.

— Perry, the Pet Pig. (Illus.). (J). (gr. 4-7). 1966. 3.00 (*0-685-19374-8*, 911120-06-8) Pennington.

Pennington, Eunice a. Perry, the Pet Pig. (Illus.). (J). (gr. 4-7). 1966. pap. 1.00 (*0-685-19375-6*) Pennington.

Pennington, Eunice A. & Pennington, D. D. Ozark National Scenic Riverways. (Illus.). 80p. (Orig.). 1967. 3.00 (*0-685-09252-6*); pap. 1.00 (*0-685-09253-4*) Pennington.

Pennington, G. W. & Naik, Sandra. Hormone Analysis: Methodology & Clinical Intrepretation, 2 vols., I. 320p. 1981. 174.00 (*0-8493-5539-7*, RD48, CRC Reprint) Franklin.

— Hormone Analysis: Methodology & Clinical Intrepretation, 2 vols., II. 320p. 1981. 163.00 (*0-8493-5540-0*, RB48, CRC Reprint) Franklin.

Pennington, H. C. The Year-Round Messier Marathon Field Guide: With Complete Maps, Charts & Tips to Guide You to Enjoying the Most Famous List of Deep-Sky Objects. LC 97-18168. 1998. 19.95 (*0-943396-54-9*) Willmann-Bell.

Pennington, Hank. Marine Survival Equipment & Maintenance. (Education Publication: No. 6). (Illus.). 30p. 1990. pap. text 4.00 (*1-56612-030-6*) AK Sea Grant CP.

Pennington, Harvard C. TRS-80 Disk & Other Mysteries. (TRS-80 Information Ser.: Vol. I). (Illus.). 128p. (Orig.). 1979. pap. 22.50 (*0-936200-00-6*) Blue Cat.

Pennington, Harvard C. & Shrayer, Michael. The Electric Pencil Operating Manual, Version 2.0. (Illus.). 123p. (Orig.). 1981. pap. 29.95 (*0-936200-04-9*) Blue Cat.

— Electric Pencil PC Word Processing System. (Illus.). 240p. 1983. 29.95 (*0-932679-06-4*); disk 149.95 (*0-317-38060-5*) Blue Cat.

Pennington, Harvard C., et al. Getting Started on the Sharp 1500 & Radio Shack PC-2. 280p. 16.95 (*0-936200-11-1*) Blue Cat.

***Pennington, Havoc.** GTK+/Gnome Application Development. (Illus.). 350p. 1999. pap. 34.99 (*0-7357-0078-8*) New Riders Pub.

Pennington, Hilary, jt. auth. see Kazis, Richard.

Pennington, James. Textbook of the Origin & History of the Colored People. LC 77-92437. 1841. 29.00 (*0-403-00169-2*) Scholarly.

Pennington, James E., ed. Respiratory Infections: Diagnosis & Management. 3rd ed. LC 93-48578. 832p. 1994. spiral bd. 99.00 (*0-7817-0173-2*) Lppncott W & W.

Pennington, Janice & De Abreu, Carlos. Husband, Lover, Spy: A True Story. LC 93-72895. (Illus.). 304p. 1994. 21.95 (*1-884025-03-X*); pap. 14.95 (*1-884025-00-5*) Custos Morum.

Pennington, Jean A.T. Bowes & Church's Food Values of Portions Commonly Used. 17th ed. LC 97-24666. 512p. 1997. text 34.00 (*0-397-55435-4*) Lppncott W & W.

Pennington, Judith A. Creating a Sales Culture in a Community Bank. 1991. per. 42.50 (*1-55520-079-6*, Irwn Prfssnl) McGraw-Hill Prof.

***Pennington, Judy.** Baton Rouge - Painting the Town Red: A Celebration of 300 Years. LC 99-43645. (American Enterprise Ser.). (Illus.). 160p. 1999. 39.00 (*1-885352-61-1*) Community Comm.

Pennington, Kenneth. Popes, Canonists, & Texts, 1100-1550. (Collected Studies: Vol. 412). 352p. 1993. 122.95 (*0-86078-387-1*, Pub. by Variorum) Ashgate Pub Co.

— The Prince & the Law, 1200-1600: Sovereignty & Rights in the Western Legal Tradition. LC 92-40544. 1993. 55.00 (*0-520-07995-7*, Pub. by U CA Pr) Cal Prin Full Svc.

Pennington, Krista & Pennington, Anna. Bartholomew's Blunder. (Illus.). 32p. (J). (gr. k-4). 1998. pap. 9.99 (*0-9659654-1-4*) Terpsichore Pubns.

Pennington, Kristina. The Amazing Snail. (Illus.). 28p. (J). (gr. k-6). 1997. pap. 7.95 (*0-9659654-0-6*) Terpsichore Pubns.

Pennington, L. A., jt. ed. see Berg, Irwin A.

Pennington, Lee. The Actor's Edge. LC 95-81869. 181p. 1996. 14.95 (*0-9650309-0-3*) Marble Falls.

— Songs of Bloody Harlan. 1975. pap. 10.00 (*0-87423-017-9*) Westburg.

— Thigmotropism. O'Dell, Mary E., ed. (Green River Writers - Poetry Ser.). 54p. 1993. 17.50 (*0-9623666-3-3*); pap. 11.95 (*0-9623666-4-1*) Green Rvr Writers.

Pennington, Lillian B. Snafu: The Littlest Clown. LC 73-90113. (Illus.). 32p. (J). (gr. 1-6). 1972. lib. bdg. 9.95 (*0-913532-00-2*); audio 7.94 (*0-87783-225-0*) Oddo.

Pennington, Lucinda W. The Hundred Forty-Nine Ways to Profit from Your Divorce. LC 82-17789. 324p. 1983. write for info. (*0-672-52744-8*) Macmillan.

Pennington, M., ed. see Carter, Elizabeth.

Pennington, M. Basil. Awake in the Spirit. 168p. 1995. pap. 12.95 (*0-8245-1516-1*) Crossroad NY.

— Awake in the Spirit: A Practical Handbook on Prayer. 160p. (C). 1996. pap. 39.95 (*0-85439-421-4*, Pub. by St Paul Pubns) St Mut.

— Bernard of Clairvaux: A Lover Teaching the Way of Love. LC 96-46247. (Spirituality Throughout the Ages Ser.). 123p. (Orig.). 1997. pap. 9.95 (*1-56548-089-9*) New City.

— Call to the Center: The Gospel's Invitation to Deeper Prayer. 3rd ed. 168p. 1995. reprint ed. pap. 9.95 (*1-56548-070-8*) New City.

— Centered Living: The Way of Centering Prayer. LC 99-30498. 224p. 1999. pap. 14.95 (*0-7648-0495-2*, Liguori Triumph) Liguori Pubns.

— Centering Prayer: Renewing an Ancient Christian Prayer Form. LC 82-45077. 256p. 1982. pap. 9.95 (*0-385-18179-5*, Image Bks) Doubleday.

— Daily We Touch Him: Practical Religious Experiences. LC 97-6104. 176p. (Orig.). 1997. pap. 12.95 (*1-55612-980-7*, LI1980) Sheed & Ward WI.

***Pennington, M. Basil.** The Eucharist: Wine of Faith, Bread of Life. LC 99-56807. 224p. 2000. pap. 14.95 (*0-7648-0596-7*, Liguori Triumph) Liguori Pubns.

Pennington, M. Basil. Lectio Divina: Renewing the Ancient Practice of Praying with the Scriptures. LC 97-45159. 112p. 1998. pap. 13.95 (*0-8245-1736-9*, Crsrd) Crossroad NY.

***Pennington, M. Basil.** Living in the Question: Meditations in the Style of the Lectio Divina. LC 99-34434. 1999. pap. 14.95 (*0-8264-1206-8*) Continuum.

Pennington, M. Basil. Monastic Journey to India. 144p. (Orig.). 1984. 9.95 (*0-8164-2398-9*) Harper SF.

— A Place Apart Series 1: Monastic Prayer & Practice for Everyone. LC 98-11820. (Illus.). 192p. 1998. reprint ed. pap. 12.95 (*0-7648-0258-5*, Liguori Triumph) Liguori Pubns.

— Praying by Hand: Rediscovering the Rosary As a Way of Prayer. LC 90-55775. 144p. 1995. pap. 10.00 (*0-06-066541-6*, Pub. by Harper SF) HarpC.

***Pennington, M. Basil.** So, What's the Go(o)d Word for Today? LC 00-34033. 2000. write for info. (*0-8264-1287-4*) Continuum.

Pennington, M. Basil. Thomas Merton, My Brother: His Journey into Freedom, Compassion, & Final Integration. 2nd ed. LC 95-34530. 208p. 1996. pap. 10.95 (*1-56548-039-2*) New City.

***Pennington, M. Basil.** True Self/False Self: Unmasking the Spirit Within. 128p. 2000. pap. 14.95 (*0-8245-1845-4*, Pub. by Crossroad NY) Natl Bk Netwk.

Pennington, M. Basil. Vatican II: It Has Only Just Begun! 176p. 1994. pap. 13.95 (*0-8245-1410-6*) Crossroad NY.

— William of Saint Thierry - the Way of Divine Union: Selected Spiritual Writings. LC 97-52200. 176p. 1998. pap. 9.95 (*1-56548-106-2*) New City.

Pennington, M. Basil, ed. The Cistercian Spirit: A Symposium in Memory of Thomas Merton. (Cistercian Studies: No. 3). xvi, 286p. 1973. reprint ed. 5.00 (*0-87907-803-0*) Cistercian Pubns.

— St. Bernard of Clairvaux: Essays Commemorating the Eighth Centenary of His Canonization. LC 77-4487. (Cistercian Studies: No. 28). 1977. 14.95 (*0-87907-828-6*) Cistercian Pubns.

Pennington, M. Basil, jt. auth. see Bolshakoff, Sergius.

Pennington, M. Basil, ed. see Bolshakoff, Serge.

Pennington, M. J. The Stories in Her Eyes. Bakker, Dave, ed. LC 95-70928. (Illus.). 302p. (Orig.). 1995. per. 14.00 (*0-9648049-0-5*) N Hrzns Publns.

Pennington, Malcolm W., jt. ed. see Allio, Robert J.

***Pennington, Mark.** Better Spelling in 5 Minutes a Day: Fun Spelling Activities for Kids & Parents on the Run. (Five Minutes a Day Ser.). (Illus.). 144p. (J). 2000. pap. text 9.99 (*0-7615-2430-4*) Prima Pub.

— Better Test-Taking Skills in 5 Minutes a Day: Fun Activities to Boost Test Scores for Kids & Parents. (Five Minutes a Day Ser.). (Illus.). 144p. (J). 2000. pap. 9.99 (*0-7615-2429-0*) Prima Pub.

Pennington, Mark. Conservation & the Countryside: By Quango or Market? LC 97-103056. (IEA Studies on the Environment: No. 6). 68p. 1996. pap. 17.95 (*0-255-36379-6*, Pub. by Inst Economic Affairs) Coronet Bks.

***Pennington, Mark.** Planning & the Political Market: Public Choice & the Politics of Government Failure. LC 00-31308. 2000. pap. write for info. (*0-485-00606-5*, Pub. by Athlone Pr) Transaction Pubs.

Pennington, Martha C. The Computer & the Non-Native Writer: A Natural Partnership. Farr, Marcia, ed. 240p. (Orig.). (C). 1997. text 49.50 (*1-57273-040-4*); pap. text 23.95 (*1-57273-041-2*) Hampton Pr NJ.

— Language in Hong Kong at Century's End. 449p. 1998. pap. 52.50 (*962-209-418-X*, Pub. by HK Univ Pr) Coronet Bks.

— Phonology in English Language Teaching. LC 95-31239. (Applied Linguistics & Language Ser.). 1996. pap. text 31.49 (*0-582-22571-X*, Pub. by Addison-Wesley) Longman.

— The Power of Call. (Illus.). 224p. 1996. 47.95 (*0-940753-04-9*); pap. 24.95 (*0-940753-03-0*) Athelstan Pubns.

Pennington, Martha C., ed. Building Better English Language Programs: Perspectives on Evaluation in ESL. 259p. (Orig.). 1991. pap. text 19.00 (*0-912207-57-4*) NAFSA Washington.

— New Ways in Teaching Grammar. 205p. 1995. pap. 22.95 (*0-939791-56-0*) Tchrs Eng Spkrs.

Pennington, Martha C. & Stevens, Vance, eds. Computers in Applied Linguistics: An International Perspective. (Multilingual Matters Ser.: No. 75). 300p. 1991. 99.00 (*1-85359-120-3*, Pub. by Multilingual Matters); pap. 39.95 (*1-85359-119-X*, Pub. by Multilingual Matters) Taylor & Francis.

***Pennington, Mary A.** On Quakers, Medicine & Property: The Autobiography of Mray Pennington, 1624-1682. 61p. 2000. reprint ed. pap. 10.50 (*1-889298-14-X*) Rhwymbooks.

Pennington, Michael. Appraisal for Language Teachers. 1994. pap. 24.00 (*1-85234-532-2*, Pub. by S Thornes Pubs) Trans-Atl Phila.

— Hamlet: A User's Guide. 256p. (Orig.). 1996. pap. 16.95 (*0-87910-083-4*) Limelight Edns.

***Pennington, Michael.** Twelfth Night: A User's Guide. 224p. 2000. reprint ed. pap. 17.95 (*0-87910-950-5*) Limelight Edns.

Pennington, Michael W. & Dunn, Ben M., eds. Peptide Analysis Protocols. LC 94-22663. (Methods in Molecular Biology Ser.: Vol. 36). (Illus.). 352p. 1994. 89.50 (*0-89603-274-4*) Humana.

P

An Asterisk (*) at the beginning of an entry indicates that the title is appearing for the first time.

— Peptide Synthesis Protocols. LC 94-26326. (Methods in Molecular Biology Ser.: Vol. 35). (Illus.). 336p. 1994. spiral bd. 79.50 (*0-89603-273-6*) Humana.

Pennington, Patience. A Woman Rice Planter. (Illus.). 496p. (C). 1991. reprint ed. write for info. (*0-318-68580-9*) Seajay Society.

— A Woman Rice Planter. Sproat, John G., ed. LC 91-35167. (Southern Classics Ser.). (Illus.). 501p. 1992. reprint ed. pap. 16.95 (*0-87249-826-3*) U of SC Pr.

Pennington, Patsy. Friends Make the Difference. LC 99-203436. (Charming Petites Ser.). 80p. 1998. 4.95 (*0-88088-838-5*) Peter Pauper.

Pennington, Randy & Bockman, Marc. On My Honor, I Will. rev. ed. 210p. (Orig.). 1995. pap. 10.99 (*1-56043-846-0*, Treasure Hse) Destiny Image.

Pennington, Renee & Harpending, Henry. The Structure of an African Pastoralist Community: Demography, History, & Ecology of the Ngamiland Herero. (Research Monographs on Human Population Biology: No. 11). (Illus.). 284p. 1993. text 75.00 (*0-19-852286-X*) OUP.

Pennington, Richard. For Texas, I Will: The History of Memorial Stadium. (Illus.). 252p. 1992. 19.95 (*1-881825-01-9*) Hist Pubns TX.

— Longhorn Hoops: The History of Texas Basketball. LC 98-60912. (Illus.). 480p. 1998. 35.00 (*0-292-76585-1*) U of Tex Pr.

Pennington, Richard, ed. see Berry, Margaret C.

Pennington, Robert. A Gift of Life. 192p. 1998. pap. 12.95 (*1-884570-84-4*) Research Triangle.

Pennington, Robert R. The Law of Investment Markets. 928p. (C). 1990. text 225.00 (*0-632-02372-4*) Blackwell Sci.

— Pennington's Company Law. 6th ed. 750p. 1990. pap. 60.00 (*0-406-51041-5*, U.K., MICHIE) LEXIS Pub.

— Pennington's Corporate Insolvency Law. 484p. 1991. pap. 42.00 (*0-406-00141-3*, U.K., MICHIE) LEXIS Pub.

— Pennington's Corporate Insolvency Law. 2nd ed. 1997. pap. write for info. (*0-406-08177-8*, PCIL2, MICHIE) LEXIS Pub.

***Pennington, S. & Dunn, M. J.** Proteomics: From Protein Sequence to Function. (Illus.). 304p. 2000. pap. 45.95 (*0-387-91589-3*) Spr-Verlag.

***Pennington, Sandra.** Introduction to Genetics. LC 99-25401. (11th Hour Ser.). (Illus.). 1999. pap. 18.95 (*0-632-04438-1*) Blackwell Sci.

***Pennington Shannon, Marcia & Manch, Susan G.** Recruiting Lawyers: How to Hire the Best Talent. 115p. 2000. pap. 49.95 (*1-57073-772-X*, Pub. by Amer Bar Assn) IPG Chicago.

***Pennington, Susan.** Italy. (Alastair Sawday's Special Places to Stay Ser.). (Illus.). 192p. 2000. pap. 14.95 (*0-7627-0721-6*) Globe Pequot.

***Pennington, T. D. & Fernandes, E. C.** Genus Inga: Utilization. (Illus.). 167p. 1998. pap. 36.00 (*1-900347-58-X*, Pub. by Royal Botnic Grdns) Balogh.

Pennington, T. D. & Revelo, H. El Genero Inga en el Ecuador: Morfologia, Distribucion y Usos. (Illus.). viii, 185p. 1997. pap. text 44.00 (*1-900347-20-2*, Pub. by Royal Botnic Grdns) Balogh.

Pennington, T. D., jt. auth. see Reynel, C.

Pennington, Terence D. The Genera of the Sapotaceae. (Illus.). xi, 296p. 1991. pap. 40.00 (*0-947643-34-6*, Pub. by Royal Botnic Grdns) Balogh.

— The Genus Inga - Botany. x, 844p. 1997. 120.00 (*1-900347-12-1*, Pub. by Royal Botnic Grdns) Balogh.

— Sapotaceae: Palynology. (Flora Neotropica Monographs: No. 52). (Illus.). 770p. 1990. pap. 136.00 (*0-89327-344-9*) NY Botanical.

***Penninx, Rinus & Roosblad, Judith, eds.** Trade Unions, Immigration & Immigrants, 1960-1993: A Comparative Study of the Actions of Trade Unions in Seven West European Countries. LC HD6657.T69 2000. (International Studies in Social History: Vol. 1). 304p. 2000. 69.95 (*1-57181-764-6*) Berghahn Bks.

***Penniston, Gordon V.** United States Supreme Court Reports: Lawyers Edition 2D, 144, No. 3. 250p. 1999. Price not set. (*0-327-09091-X*, 7075912) LEXIS Pub.

Penniston, Gordon V. United States Supreme Court Reports Vol. 143, No. 1: Lawyers' Edition. 2nd ed. 250p. 1999. pap. write for info. (*0-327-07957-6*, 70758-10) LEXIS Pub.

— United States Supreme Court Reports Vol. 143, No. 2: Lawyers' Edition. 2nd ed. 250p. 1999. pap. write for info. (*0-327-07958-4*, 70758-11) LEXIS Pub.

— United States Supreme Court Reports Vol. 143, No. 3: Lawyers' Edition. 2nd ed. 250p. 1999. pap. write for info. (*0-327-07959-2*, 70758-12) LEXIS Pub.

— United States Supreme Court Reports Vol. 143, No. 4: Lawyers' Edition. 2nd ed. 250p. 1999. pap. write for info. (*0-327-07960-6*, 70758-13) LEXIS Pub.

— United States Supreme Court Reports Vol. 143, No. 5: Lawyers' Edition. 2nd ed. 250p. 1999. pap. write for info. (*0-327-07961-4*, 70758-14) LEXIS Pub.

— United States Supreme Court Reports Vol. 143, No. 6: Lawyers' Edition. 2nd ed. 250p. 1999. pap. write for info. (*0-327-07962-2*, 70758-15) LEXIS Pub.

— United States Supreme Court Reports Vol. 143, No. 7: Lawyers' Edition. 2nd ed. 250p. 1999. pap. write for info. (*0-327-07963-0*, 70758-16) LEXIS Pub.

Penniston, Gordon V., ed. United States Supreme Court Digest No. 21: Lawyers' Edition. 650p. 1998. write for info. (*0-327-05799-8*, 76042-11) LEXIS Pub.

Pennock, Dee. Who Is God? Who Am I? Who Are You? Introduction to Basic Christian Psychology. (Illus.). 160p. (Orig.). 1973. pap. 4.95 (*1-878997-08-4*) St Tikhons Pr.

Pennock, J. Roland. Responsiveness, Responsibility, & Majority Rule. (Reprint Series in Social Sciences). (C). 1993. reprint ed. pap. text 5.00 (*0-8290-3603-2*, PS-226) Irvington.

Pennock, J. Roland & Chapman, John W., eds. Criminal Justice. LC 84-14776. (Nomos Ser.: Vol. 27). 384p. (C). 1985. text 45.00 (*0-8147-6588-2*) NYU Pr.

— Due Process. LC 76-40511. (Nomos Ser.: Vol. 18). (C). 1977. text 45.00 (*0-8147-6569-6*) NYU Pr.

— Religion, Morality, & the Law. (Nomos Ser.: Vol. 30). 356p. (C). 1988. text 50.00 (*0-8147-6606-4*) NYU Pr.

Pennock, J. Roland, jt. ed. see Chapman, John W.

Pennock, James R. Liberal Democracy: Its Merits & Prospects. LC 77-13903. 403p. 1978. reprint ed. lib. bdg. 38.50 (*0-8371-9865-8*, PELD, Greenwood Pr) Greenwood.

Pennock, James R., ed. Self-Government in Modernizing Nations. LC 77-167401. (Essay Index Reprint Ser.). 1977. reprint ed. 18.95 (*0-8369-2517-3*) Ayer.

Pennock, Jonathan R., jt. ed. see Bryant, Tracey L.

Pennock, Keith. Rescuing Brain Injured Children. 1998. 17.95 (*1-85398-111-7*, Pub. by Ashgrove Pr) Words Distrib.

Pennock, Margaret T. & Bardwell, Lisa V. Approaching Environmental Issues in the Classroom. Monroe, Martha C. & Cappaert, David, eds. (EEToolbox Workshop Resource Manual Ser.). (Illus.). 60p. 1994. 8.00 (*1-884782-05-1*) Natl Consort EET.

Pennock, Margaret T., jt. auth. see Corcoran, Peter B.

***Pennock, Michael.** Catholic Social Teaching: Learning & Living Justice. 2000. pap. text, teacher ed. 24.95 incl. disk (*0-87793-699-4*) Ave Maria.

— Catholic Social Teaching: Learning & Living Justice Student Book. (Illus.). 288p. 2000. pap. text, student ed. 16.95 (*0-87793-698-6*) Ave Maria.

Pennock, Michael. This Is Our Faith: A Catholic Catechism for Adults. rev. ed. LC 98-4077. 368p. 1998. pap. 11.95 (*0-87793-653-6*) Ave Maria.

Pennock, Michael F. Being Catholic: Believing, Living, Praying. LC 93-73883. (Friendship in the Lord Ser.). (Illus.). 232p. (YA). (gr. 11-12). 1994. pap. text, teacher ed. 16.95 (*0-87793-528-9*); pap. text, student ed. 14.95 (*0-87793-527-0*) Ave Maria.

— Discovering the Promise of the Old Testament. LC 91-76778. (Friendship in the Lord Ser.). (Illus.). 224p. (YA). (gr. 11-12). 1992. pap. text, student ed. 12.95 (*0-87793-472-X*) Ave Maria.

— Discovering the Promise of the Old Testament. LC 91-76778. (Friendship in the Lord Ser.). (Illus.). 192p. (YA). (gr. 11-12). 1999. pap. text, teacher ed. 19.95 (*0-87793-473-8*) Ave Maria.

— Forming a Catholic Conscience. LC 90-84839. (Friendship in the Lord Ser.). (Illus.). 168p. (YA). (gr. 10-11). 1991. pap. text, teacher ed. 16.95 (*0-87793-445-2*); pap. text, student ed. 11.95 (*0-87793-444-4*) Ave Maria.

— Growing in Catholic Faith. LC 89-82328. (Friendship in the Lord Ser.). (Illus.). 200p. (YA). (gr. 9-10). 1990. pap. text, student ed. 10.95 (*0-87793-418-5*) Ave Maria.

— Growing in Catholic Faith. LC 89-82328. (Friendship in the Lord Ser.). (Illus.). 168p. (YA). (gr. 9-10). 1999. pap. text, teacher ed. 16.95 (*0-87793-419-3*) Ave Maria.

— Jesus Friend & Savior. LC 89-82459. (Friendship in the Lord Ser.). 176p. (YA). (gr. 9-10). 1990. pap. text, teacher ed. 16.95 (*0-87793-421-5*); pap. text, student ed. 10.95 (*0-87793-420-7*) Ave Maria.

— Living the Message of the New Testament. LC 91-77474. (Friendship in the Lord Ser.). (Illus.). 184p. (YA). (gr. 11-12). 1992. pap., teacher ed. 16.95 (*0-87793-468-1*); pap. text, student ed. 12.95 (*0-87793-469-X*) Ave Maria.

— Ready for College: Doing Laundry, Writing Papers, Keeping Your Faith, Passing Exams, Avoiding Alcohol, Making Friends, Managing Time, Going on Dates, Eating Healthy, Staying Safe. LC 96-40426. 128p. 1997. pap. 8.95 (*0-87793-607-2*) Ave Maria.

— The Sacraments: Celebrating the Signs of God's Love. LC 92-75347. (Friendship in the Lord Ser.). (Illus.). 240p. (YA). (gr. 11-12). 1993. pap., student ed. 14.95 (*0-87793-503-3*) Ave Maria.

— The Sacraments: Celebrating the Signs of God's Love. LC 92-75347. (Friendship in the Lord Ser.). (Illus.). 240p. (YA). (gr. 11-12). 1999. pap., teacher ed. 16.95 (*0-87793-504-1*) Ave Maria.

— The Seeker's Catechism: The Basics of Catholicism. LC 94-71886. 132p. (Orig.). 1994. pap. 5.50 (*0-87793-539-4*) Ave Maria.

— What We Really Want to Know... Answers to 101 Questions Teens Always Ask. LC 95-83180. 224p. (YA). (gr. 9-12). 1996. pap. 9.95 (*0-87793-573-4*) Ave Maria.

— Why Pray? Director's Manual. Sawyer, Kieran, ed. LC 98-205382. (Developing Faith Ser.). 136p. 1997. pap. text, teacher ed. 16.95 (*0-87793-619-6*) Ave Maria.

— Why Pray? Participant Book. Sawyer, Kieran, ed. (Developing Faith Ser.). 80p. (YA). (gr. 9-12). 1997. pap. text 5.95 (*0-87793-618-8*) Ave Maria.

Pennock, Robert T. Tower of Babel: The Evidence Against the New Creationism. LC 98-27286. (Illus.). 456p. 1999. 35.00 (*0-262-16180-X*) MIT Pr.

***Pennock, Robert T.** Tower of Babel: The Evidence Against the New Creationism. (Illus.). 456p. 2000. reprint ed. pap. 18.95 (*0-262-66165-9*) MIT Pr.

Pennock, S. R. & Shepherd, P. R. Microwave Engineering: With Wireless Applications. 352p. 1998. 65.00 (*0-07-049722-2*) McGraw.

Pennsafe Staff, jt. auth. see PEMA Staff.

***Pennsylvania Chamber of Business & Industry Educational Foundation Staff.** Comprehensive Guide to Pennsylvania Legislators 1999-2000. rev. ed. 500p. 1999. pap. 250.00 (*1-929744-14-5*) Penn Chamber of Bus.

— Critical Waste Management Strategies Guide. 2000. pap. 75.00 (*1-929744-16-1*) Penn Chamber of Bus.

— The 1999/2000 Legislative Directory. rev. ed. 96p. 1999. pap. 15.00 (*1-929744-06-4*) Penn Chamber of Bus.

***Pennsylvania Chamber of Business & Industry Educational Foundation Staff, ed.** The Electronic Commerce Handbook: Preparing Your Business for the New Frontier of Commerce. 274p. 1998. pap. 85.00 (*1-929744-03-X*) Penn Chamber of Bus.

— Human Resources Emerging Trends & Hottest Issues, No. 2. 180p. 1999. pap. 85.00 (*1-929744-11-0*) Penn Chamber of Bus.

— Solving Today's Toughest HR Problems, No. 1. 199p. 1998. pap. 75.00 (*1-929744-02-1*) Penn Chamber of Bus.

— 2000 OSHA Handbook. rev. ed. 359p. 1999. pap. 99.00 (*1-929744-12-9*) Penn Chamber of Bus.

***Pennsylvania Chamber of Business & Industry Educational Foundation Staff & Bond, Thomas R., eds.** 2000 Pennsylvania Workers' Compensation Guide. rev. ed. 373p. 1999. pap. 95.00 (*1-929744-07-2*) Penn Chamber of Bus.

Pennsylvania Chamber of Business & Industry Educational Foundation Staff, ed. see Boslet, Joseph M. & Inservco Insurance Service, Inc. Staff.

Pennsylvania Chamber of Business & Industry Educational Foundation Staff, ed. see McNees, Wallace & Nurick Staff.

Pennsylvania Chamber of Business & Industry Educational Foundation Staff, ed. see Miller, Christopher W.

Pennsylvania Chamber of Business & Industry Educational Foundation Staff, ed. see Parente Randolph Orlando Carey & Associates Staff.

Pennsylvania Chamber of Business & Industry Educational Foundation Staff, ed. see PEMA Staff & Pennsafe Staff.

Pennsylvania Colony Staff. Colonial Records of Pennsylvania, 16 vols., Set. LC 01-10370. reprint ed. 1520.00 (*0-404-05000-X*) AMS Pr.

— General Index to the Colonial Records in 16 Volumes & to the Pennsylvania Archives in 12 Volumes First Series, 16 vols. LC 01-10370. student ed. 47.50 (*0-404-05020-4*) AMS Pr.

Pennsylvania Department of Corrections Staff & Toll, Sheldon S. Pennsylvania Crimes Code Annotated. LC 98-154128. xxix, 811p. 1998. write for info. (*0-314-23112-9*) West Pub.

Pennsylvania Economy League Staff. Industrial Tax Burdens in Philadelphia & Twenty-Seven Other Municipalities in Southeastern Pa. write for info. (*0-318-61045-0*) PA Econ League.

***Pennsylvania Field Office of Rails-Trails Staff.** Pennsylvania's Rail-Trails: 1999 Edition. 5th ed. 1999. pap. text 13.95 (*0-925794-15-5*) Rails Trails.

Pennsylvania Genealogical Magazine Staff. Genealogies of Pennsylvania Families from the Pennsylvania Genealogical Magazine, 3 vols. LC 81-85694. (Illus.). 2894p. 1982. 99.95 (*0-8063-0974-1*) Genealog Pub.

Pennsylvania Health Law Project Staff. Health Care for the Poor in Pennsylvania: An Outline for 1986. 67p. 1986. pap. 7.00 (*0-685-23176-3*, 41,211) NCLS Inc.

Pennsylvania Historical Society Staff. Pennsylvania Historical Society Memoirs, 14 vols., Set. Incl. Vol. 1. LC 72-14378. (*0-404-11076-2*); Vol. 2. LC 72-14378. (*0-404-11077-0*); Vol. 3. LC 72-14378. (*0-404-11078-9*); Vol. 4. LC 72-14378. (*0-404-11079-7*); Vol. 5. LC 72-14378. (*0-404-11080-0*); Vol. 6. LC 72-14378. (*0-404-11081-9*); Vol. 7. LC 72-14378. (*0-404-11082-7*); Vol. 8. LC 72-14378. (*0-404-11083-5*); Vol. 9. LC 72-14378. (*0-404-11084-3*); Vol. 10. LC 72-14378. (*0-404-11085-1*); Vol. 11. LC 72-14378. (*0-404-11086-X*); Vol. 12. LC 72-14378. (*0-404-11087-8*); Vol. 13. LC 72-14378. (*0-404-11088-6*); Vol. 14. LC 72-14378. (*0-404-11089-4*); LC 72-14378. reprint ed. write for info. (*0-404-11075-4*) AMS Pr.

Pennsylvania Historical Society, Works Projects Administration Staff. Inventory of Church Archives Society of Friends in Pennsylvania. 397p. 1996. reprint ed. pap. 35.00 (*0-8063-4650-7*, 9288, Pub. by Clearfield Co) ACCESS Pubs Network.

Pennsylvania Horticultural Society Staff. Great Recipes from Great Gardeners. LC 93-72675. 1993. write for info. (*0-9637494-0-4*) Favorite Recipes.

Pennsylvania. Insurance Dept, et al. Pennsylvania Regulations: Containing Insurance Department Regulations, Statements of Policy, & Notices & Selected Attorney General's Opinions. LC 97-63898. (Illus.). 1997. write for info. (*0-89246-477-1*); write for info. (*0-89246-478-X*) NILS Pub.

Pennsylvania Legislative Reference Bureau Staff. Pennsylvania Consolidated Statutes: Title 75, Vehicles, 1997 Edition. rev. ed. 378p. (C). 1997. pap. 12.24 (*0-8182-0013-8*) Commonweal PA.

Pennsylvania P. U. C. Staff. Pennsylvania Public Utility Commission Decisions, April 1987-August 1987. Sophy, Kathryn G., ed. (PA P.U.C. Decisions Ser.: Vol. 64). 565p. 1987. text 36.95 (*0-8182-0100-2*) Commonweal PA.

Pennsylvania Poetry Society, Inc. Wallace Stevens. Chiaroscuro. Gasser, Ann, ed. & intro. by. 59p. (Orig.). 1994. pap. 2.00 (*1-884257-02-X*) AGEE Keyboard.

— Visions in Verse. Gasser, Ann, ed. & illus. by. 72p. (Orig.). 1995. pap. 3.00 (*1-884257-09-7*) AGEE Keyboard.

Pennsylvania Public Utility Commission. Pennsylvania Public Utility Commission Decisions - August 1994-December 1994, Vol. 83. Leming, Shirley, ed. 757p. 1994. 235.61 (*0-8182-0212-2*) Commonweal PA.

— Pennsylvania Public Utility Commission Decisions - March 1994-August 1994, Vol. 82. Leming, Shirley, ed. 692p. 1994. 235.62 (*0-8182-0211-4*) Commonweal PA.

Pennsylvania Special Grand Jury Staff. Investigation of Vice, Crime & Law Enforcement. LC 74-3856. (Criminal Justice in America Ser.). 1974. reprint ed. 23.95 (*0-405-06164-1*) Ayer.

Pennsylvania State Data Center Staff. Detailed Income Characteristics, 1990: Pennsylvania. 261p. 1992. pap. 25.00 (*0-939667-17-7*) Penn State Data Ctr.

— General Income Characteristics 1990: Pennsylvania. 276p. 1992. pap. 25.00 (*0-939667-16-9*) Penn State Data Ctr.

— General Population & Housing Characteristics, 1990: Pennsylvania. 291p. 1991. pap. 25.00 (*0-939667-15-0*) Penn State Data Ctr.

— Marketers Handbook, 1990: Pennsylvania, Vol. I. 160p. 1993. pap. text 35.00 (*0-939667-31-2*) Penn State Data Ctr.

— Pennsylvania School District Report, 1990. 1994. pap. 45.00 (*0-939667-22-3*) Penn State Data Ctr.

Pennsylvania State Department Staff. Corporate Guide: A Manual for Filing Corporate Documents in Pennsylvania. 31p. 1985. write for info. (*0-318-58006-3*) Penna Secy.

Pennsylvania State Federation of Labor Staff. American Cossack. LC 76-154583. (Police in America Ser.). (Illus.). 1978. reprint ed. 22.95 (*0-405-03380-X*) Ayer.

Pennsylvania State Grange Staff. The Pennsylvania State Grange Cookbook. LC 92-30345. 1992. pap., spiral bd. write for info. (*0-87197-350-2*) Favorite Recipes.

Pennsylvania State Legislature Staff. Second Class Township Code. 176p. (Orig.). 1995. text 2.25 (*0-8182-0001-4*) Commonweal PA.

Pennsylvania State Library Staff. Index to Main Families, Persons, Places & Subjects in Egle's Notes & Queries. 81p. 1993. reprint ed. pap. 15.00 (*0-8063-4897-6*) Clearfield Co.

Pennsylvania State University Staff. Electrodeposition of Copper from Fused Salts. 128p. 1966. 19.20 (*0-317-34520-6*, 44) Intl Copper.

— Thermodynamic Properties of Copper-Base Alloys. 134p. 1981. write for info. (*0-318-60071-4*, 245) Intl Copper.

Pennsylvania University - Department of History St. Translations & Reprints from the Original Sources of European History, 6 vols. rev. ed. LC 75-143179. reprint ed. lib. bdg. 207.00 (*0-404-08970-4*) AMS Pr.

Pennsylvania University, Babylonian Expedition. The Babylonian Expedition of the University of Pennsylvania: Researches & Treatises. Hilprecht, H. V., ed. LC 18-5954. (Series D: Vol. 4). 355p. reprint ed. pap. 110.10 (*0-8357-5937-7*, 202665300050) Bks Demand.

Pennsylvania University Library Staff. Changing Patterns of Scholarship & the Future of Research Libraries. LC 68-14910. (Essay Index Reprint Ser.). 1977. 19.95 (*0-8369-0782-5*) Ayer.

Pennsylvania Writers' Project Staff. Northampton County Guide. 1993. reprint ed. lib. bdg. 89.00 (*0-7812-5817-0*) Rprt Serv.

— Picture of Lycoming County. 1993. reprint ed. lib. bdg. 89.00 (*0-7812-5818-9*) Rprt Serv.

Pensylvania Academy of Fine Arts Staff. Searching Out the Best: A Tribute to the Morris Gallery of the Pennsylvania Academy of the Fine Arts. (Illus.). 212p. (Orig.). 1988. pap. 19.95 (*0-943836-09-3*) Penn Acad Art.

Pennwell Publishing Company Staff. Glossary of the Petroleum Industry: English-Spanish & Spanish-English. 3rd ed. LC 96-43711. (ENG & SPA.). 1996. 59.95 (*0-87814-616-4*) PennWell Bks.

Penny, A. J. Studies in Jacob Boehme. 503p. 1992. reprint ed. pap. 30.00 (*1-56459-290-1*) Kessinger Pub.

Penny, Benjamin. Religion & Biography in China & Tibet. 320p. (C). 1999. text 55.00 (*0-7007-1177-5*, Pub. by Curzon Pr Ltd) UH Pr.

Penny, Charles, ed. Channel Tunnel Transport System: Proceedings of the Conference Organized by the Institution of Civil Engineers, Held in London, England, October 4-5, 1994. LC 96-172801. 262p. 1996. 67.00 (*0-7277-2515-7*) Am Soc Civil Eng.

Penny, David E., et al. Molecular Evolution. 450p. 1984. 62.50 (*0-86720-021-9*) Jones & Bartlett.

Penny, David E., jt. auth. see Edwards, C. H.

Penny, Edward B., tr. see Saint-Martin, Louis Claude de.

Penny, F. E. Southern India Land, People & Culture. (C). 1992. 75.00 (*81-7305-029-5*, Pub. by Aryan Bks Intl) S Asia.

Penny, Gillian N., et al, eds. Health Psychology: A Lifespan Perspective. LC 93-17400. 228p. 1994. text 59.00 (*3-7186-5416-4*); pap. text 25.00 (*3-7186-5415-6*) Gordon & Breach.

Penny, Ian. Shop Full of Kittens. 32p. 1991. 15.95 (*0-385-25299-4*) Doubleday.

Penny, J. E., jt. auth. see Indfield, G. R.

Penny, J. E., jt. auth. see Lindfield, G. R.

Penny, James S., Jr. Archaeological Investigations for the Hard Times Timber Sale, Union County, Illinois. LC 87-71350. (Center for Archaeological Investigations Research Paper Ser.: No. 56). (Illus.). viii, 52p. 1987. pap. 8.50 (*0-88104-067-3*) Center Archaeol.

— Archaeological Survey of Mineral Prospecting Lands in the Shawnee National Forest, Southern Illinois, 1983. (Center for Archaeological Investigations Research Paper Ser.: No. 45). (Illus.). vii, 86p. 1984. pap. 7.50 (*0-88104-017-7*) Center Archaeol.

— The Prehistoric Peoples of Southern Illinois. (Illus.). ix, 70p. (Orig.). 1986. pap. 3.50 (*0-88104-062-2*) Center Archaeol.

Penny, John, jt. auth. see Linfield, George.

Penny, Malcolm. Birds of Prey. (Exciting & Unusual Animals Ser.). (Illus.). 48p. (J). (gr. 3-8). 1996. lib. bdg. 24.26 (*1-56847-414-8*) Raintree Steck-V.

***Penny, Malcolm.** Giant Panda. (Natural World Ser.). (Illus.). (J). 2000. pap. 7.95 (*0-7398-2028-1*) Raintree Steck-V.

An Asterisk (*) at the beginning of an entry indicates that the title is appearing for the first time.

— Giant Panda: Habitats, Life Cycles, Food Chains & Threats. LC 99-43257. (Natural World Ser.). (Illus.). 48p. (gr. 4-7). 2000. lib. bdg. 25.69 (*0-7398-1063-4*) Raintree Steck-V.
— The Indian Ocean. LC 96-40996. (Seas & Oceans Ser.). (Illus.). 48p. (J). (gr. 5-9). 1997. lib. bdg. 24.26 (*0-8172-4514-6*) Raintree Steck-V.
Penny, Malcolm. Night Creatures. (Remarkable World Ser.). (Illus.). 48p. (J). (gr. 3-8). 1996. lib. bdg. 24.26 (*1-56847-371-0*) Raintree Steck-V.
***Penny, Malcolm.** Polar Bear: Habitats, Life Cycles, Food Chains, Threats. LC 99-32666. (Natural World Ser.). (Illus.). 48p. (J). (gr. 4-7). 2000. lib. bdg. 25.69 (*0-7398-1060-X*) Raintree Steck-V.
Penny, Malcolm. The Polar Seas. LC 96-27732. (Seas & Oceans Ser.). 48p. (J). 1997. lib. bdg. 24.26 (*0-8172-4513-8*) Raintree Steck-V.
***Penny, Malcolm.** Your Environment. LC 99-13727. 32p. (J). 1999. 22.83 (*0-8172-5889-2*) Raintree Steck-V.
Penny, Martin, jt. ed. see Penny, Susan.
Penny, Michael. Approaching the Bible. LC 92-70157. 348p. (Orig.). 1992. pap. 15.00 (*1-880573-03-2*) Bible Search Pubns.
— David's Son & the Son of David. 20p. (Orig.). 1994. pap. 2.50 (*1-880573-19-9*) Bible Search Pubns.
***Penny, Michael.** Death: Fearing It or Facing It? 32p. 2000. pap. 2.50 (*1-880573-55-5*) Bible Search Pubns.
Penny, Michael. 40 Problem Passages. LC 96-49910. 288p. (Orig.). 1997. pap. 15.00 (*1-880573-35-0*) Bible Search Pubns.
***Penny, Michael.** The Last Days! When? 28p. 2000. pap. 3.00 (*1-880573-59-8*) Bible Search Pubns.
Penny, Michael. Love in the Bible. 48p. (Orig.). 1997. pap. 3.00 (*1-880573-34-2*) Bible Search Pubns.
— The Mark of the Beast & the Jerusalem Temple. (Illus.). 24p. (Orig.). 1993. pap. text 2.50 (*1-880573-08-3*) Bible Search Pubns.
— Paul's Three Ministries. 2nd rev. ed. 32p. 1999. pap. 3.00 (*1-880573-48-2*) Bible Search Pubns.
— The Place of Prayer in an Age of Grace. 56p. 1999. pap. 4.00 (*1-880573-43-1*) Bible Search Pubns.
— Studies in First Thessalonians. 40p. (Orig.). 1992. pap. text 3.00 (*1-880573-02-4*) Bible Search Pubns.
— Studies in Jude. 32p. (Orig.). 1995. pap. 3.00 (*1-880573-26-1*) Bible Search Pubns.
— The Work of the Spirit in an Age of Grace. 40p. 1997. pap. 4.00 (*1-880573-40-7*) Bible Search Pubns.
Penny, Michael, jt. auth. see Penny, Sylvia.
***Penny, Morris M. & Laine, Gary J.** Struggle for the Round Tops: Law's Alabama Brigade at the Battle of Gettysburg, July 2-3, 1863. (Illus.). 272p. 2000. pap. 17.95 (*1-57249-223-6*, Burd St Pr) White Mane Pub.
Penny, Morris M. & Laine, J. Gary. Law's Alabama Brigade: In the War Between the Union & the Confederacy. LC 96-44654. (Illus.). 458p. 1997. 37.50 (*1-57249-024-1*) White Mane Pub.
— Struggle for the Round Tops: Law's Alabama Brigade at the Battle of Gettysburg, July 2-3, 1863. LC 99-18426. (Illus.). 272p. 1999. 24.95 (*1-57249-063-2*, Burd St Pr) White Mane Pub.
Penny, Nicholas. Catalogue of European Sculpture in the Ashmolean Museum: 1540 to the Present Day: British, Vol. III. (Illus.). 300p. 1998. text 135.00 (*0-19-951350-3*) OUP.
— Catalogue of European Sculpture in the Ashmolean Museum: 1540 to the Present Day: French & Other European Sculpture (Excluding Italian & British), Vol. II. (Illus.). 252p. 1998. text 135.00 (*0-19-951348-1*) OUP.
— Catalogue of European Sculpture in the Ashmolean Museum: 1540 to the Present Day: Italian, Vol. I. LC 92-21820. (Illus.). 360p. (C). 1998. text 135.00 (*0-19-951329-5*, Clarendon Pr) OUP.
— Frames. LC 97-67666. (National Gallery Pocket Guides Ser.). 80p. 1997. pap. text 10.00 (*0-300-07319-4*) Yale U Pr.
— The Materials of Sculpture. 1996. pap. 32.50 (*0-300-06581-7*) Yale U Pr.
— Saints. (Illus.). 80p. 1999. pap. text 10.00 (*0-300-07924-9*) Yale U Pr.
Penny, Nicholas, intro. David Levine: Caricatures & Watercolours. (Illus.). 28p. 1987. pap. 6.95 (*0-907849-83-0*, 830, Pub. by Ashmolean Mus) A Schwartz & Co.
Penny, Nicholas, jt. auth. see Haskell, Francis.
Penny, Nicholas, jt. auth. see Jones, Roger.
Penny, Norman D. & Arias, Jorge R. Insects of an Amazon Forest. LC 81-7665. (Illus.). 328p. 1982. text 80.00 (*0-231-05266-9*) Col U Pr.
Penny, R., jt. ed. see Stuart-Harris, Charles H.
Penny, R. K. Risk, Economy & Safety, Failure Minimisation & Analysis-Failures, 1996: Proceedings of the Second International Symposium, Pilanesberg, South Africa, 22-26 July 1996. 388p. 1996. 123.00 (*90-5410-823-1*, Pub. by A A Balkema) Ashgate Pub Co.
Penny, R. K., ed. Ageing of Materials & Methods for the Assessment of Lifetimes of Engineering Plant - Cape '97: Proceedings of the 4th International Colloquium, Cape Town, SA, 21-25 April 1997. (Illus.). 328p. (C). 1997. text 123.00 (*90-5410-874-6*, Pub. by A A Balkema) Ashgate Pub Co.
***Penny, R. K., ed.** Risk, Economy & Safety, Failure Minimization & Analysis - Failure'98: Proceedings of the 3rd International Symposium, Pilanesberg, South Africa, 6-10 July 1998. (Illus.). 370p. (C). 1998. text 90.00 (*90-5410-977-7*, Pub. by A A Balkema) Ashgate Pub Co.
Penny, Ralph. A History of the Spanish Language. 335p. (C). 1991. pap. text 22.95 (*0-521-39784-7*) Cambridge U Pr.
***Penny, Ralph.** Variation & Change in Spanish. (Illus.). 280p. (C). 2000. write for info. (*0-521-78045-4*) Cambridge U Pr.
Penny, Ralph J. El Habla Pasiega: Ensayo de Dialectologia Mantanesa. (Monagrafias A Ser.: Vol. XIII). (SPA., Illus.). 256p. (Orig.). (C). 1969. pap. 69.00 (*0-900411-05-8*, Pub. by Tamesis Bks Ltd) Boydell & Brewer.
Penny, Richard. The Whitewater Sourcebook: A Sourcebook of Information on American Whitewater Rivers. 3rd rev. ed. (Illus.). 400p. 1997. pap. 24.95 (*0-89732-245-2*) Menasha Ridge.
Penny, Rogene N. & Vaughn, Patricia A. Seasonal Phonics Fun: Grades K-3. 1989. pap. 5.95 (*0-89108-209-3*, 8905) Love Pub Co.
Penny, Selwyn & Jones, Philip. Operation Fire-Operation Tan. (C). 1988. 21.00 (*0-7855-6070-X*, Pub. by NCCL) St Mut.
Penny, Simon, ed. Critical Issues in Electronic Media. LC 94-30826. (SUNY Series in Film History & Theory). 298p. (C). 1995. text 59.50 (*0-7914-2317-4*); pap. text 21.95 (*0-7914-2318-2*) State U NY Pr.
Penny, Susan. Glass Painting Made Easy. LC 99-162192. (Made Easy Ser.). (Illus.). 64p. 1998. 12.95 (*0-7153-0563-8*, Pub. by D & C Pub) Sterling.
***Penny, Susan.** Painted Crafts Made Easy. (Illus.). 64p. 2000. 12.95 (*0-7153-0976-5*) D & C Pub.
— Paper Mache Made Easy. 64p. 1999. 12.95 (*0-7153-0932-3*) Strlng Pub CA.
Penny, Susan. Silk Painting Made Easy. LC 99-162185. (Made Easy Ser.). (Illus.). 64p. 1998. 12.95 (*0-7153-0564-6*, Pub. by D & C Pub) Sterling.
— Stamping Made Easy. LC 99-162143. (Made Easy Ser.). (Illus.). 64p. 1998. 12.95 (*0-7153-0565-4*, Pub. by D & C Pub) Sterling.
— Stencilling Made Easy. LC 99-162199. (Made Easy Ser.). (Illus.). 64p. 1998. 12.95 (*0-7153-0562-X*, Pub. by D & C Pub) Sterling.
***Penny, Susan.** 3-D Decoupage Made Easy. 64p. 1999. 12.95 (*0-7153-0931-5*) Strlng Pub CA.
***Penny, Susan & Penny, Martin, eds.** Candle Making Made Easy. (Illus.). 64p. 2000. 12.95 (*0-7153-0975-7*, Pub. by D & C Pub) Sterling.
***Penny, Sylvia.** Forgiveness. 36p. 2000. pap. 4.00 (*1-880573-57-1*) Bible Search Pubns.
Penny, Sylvia. Lying. 24p. (Orig.). 1995. pap. text 2.00 (*1-880573-23-7*) Bible Search Pubns.
— Theories of Creation. 60p. 1999. pap. 5.00 (*1-880573-41-5*) Bible Search Pubns.
Penny, Sylvia & Penny, Michael. Resurrection! When? 48p. 1999. pap. 5.00 (*1-880573-45-8*) Bible Search Pubns.
Penny, Timothy J. & Schier, Steven E. Payment Due: A Nation in Debt, a Generation in Trouble. (Dilemmas in American Politics Ser.). 2p. (C). 1996. pap. 65.00 (*0-8133-2598-6*, Pub. by Westview) HarpC.
Penny, Timothy J., jt. auth. see Garrett, Major.
Penny, Virginia. How Women Can Make Money, Married or Single, in All Branches of the Arts & Sciences, Professions, Trades, Agricultural & Mechanical Pursuits. LC 75-156439. (American Labor Ser., No. 2). (Illus.). 1975. reprint ed. 47.95 (*0-405-02937-3*) Ayer.
— Think & Act: A Series of Articles Pertaining to Men & Women, Work & Wages, 2 vols. LC 75-156420. (American Labor Ser.: No. 2). 1977. reprint ed. 26.95 (*0-405-02938-1*) Ayer.
Penny, William M., ed. see American Micro Systems Staff.
Pennybacker, Mindy & Ikramuddin, Aisha. Mothers & Others for a Livable Planet: Guide to Natural Baby Care. LC 98-31591. 320p. 1999. pap. 16.95 (*0-471-29333-4*) Wiley.
Pennybacker, Mindy, ed. see Lydon, Betsy.
Pennycook, Alastair. English & the Discourses of Colonialism. LC 98-11146. (Politics of Language Ser.). 240p. (C). 1998. 75.00 (*0-415-17847-9*, D5864) Routledge.
— English & the Discourses of Colonialism. LC 98-11146. (Politics of Language Ser.). 240p. (C). 1998. pap. 22.99 (*0-415-17848-7*, D5868) Routledge.
Pennycook, Bob, jt. auth. see Worthington, Julian.
Pennycook, Joan. Terminal Arrangements. large type ed. (Dales Mystery Ser.). 255p. 1993. pap. 18.99 (*1-85389-395-1*) Ulverscroft.
Pennycook, K. A. Installation, Commissioning & Maintenance of Fire & Security Systems Pt. 1: General. (C). 1992. pap. 260.00 (*0-86022-310-8*, Pub. by Build Servs Info Assn) St Mut.
***Pennycook, K. A. & Hamilton, G.** Specifying Building Management Systems. 1998. pap. 80.00 (*0-86022-496-1*, Pub. by Build Servs Info Assn) St Mut.
Pennycook, K. A., jt. auth. see Pike, P. G.
Pennycook, S. R. Plant Diseases Recorded in NZ, 3 vols., Set. 1990. 66.00 (*0-477-02547-1*, Pub. by Manaaki Whenua) Balogh.
Pennycook, Stephen, jt. ed. see Browning, Nigel.
Pennycuick, C. J. Newton Rules Biology: A Physical Approach to Biological Problems. (Illus.). 128p. 1992. pap. text 25.00 (*0-19-854021-3*) OUP.
Pennycuick, Colin J. Conversion Factors: SI Units & Many Others. 19th ed. LC 87-30145. 48p. 1988. pap. text 8.95 (*0-226-65507-5*) U Ch Pr.
Pennypacker, Bert. Reading Pacifics. (Classic Power Ser.: No. 10). (Illus.). 80p. 1999. pap. write for info. (*0-934088-36-5*) NJ Intl Inc.
***Pennypacker, Bert.** Trackside Around Philadelphia. (Illus.). 128p. 1999. 54.95 (*1-58248-035-4*) Morning NJ.
Pennypacker, C. Hands-On Astronomy for Education: Proceedings of the Workshop. 172p. 1992. text 33.00 (*981-02-1135-X*) World Scientific Pub.
Pennypacker, Eliza, ed. see Nadenicek, Daniel J.
Pennypacker, Henry S., jt. auth. see Johnston, James M.
Pennypacker, Isaac R. General Meade. 402p. 1987. reprint ed. 30.00 (*0-942211-19-7*) Olde Soldier Bks.
Pennypacker, James S., ed. see Project Management Institute Staff.
***Pennypacker, Morton.** General Washington's Spies: On Long Island & in New York. 304p. 1999. reprint ed. pap. 38.80 (*0-89412-281-9*, I-17) Aegean Park Pr.
Pennypacker, Samuel W. Settlement of Germantown & the Beginning of German Emigration to North America. (Illus.). 310p. 1997. reprint ed. lib. bdg. 38.50 (*0-8328-6414-5*) Higginson Bk Co.
— Settlement of Germantown, Pennsylvania, & the Beginning of German Emigration to North America. LC 69-13248. (Illus.). 1972. reprint ed. 26.95 (*0-405-08847-7*) Ayer.
Pennypacker, Samuel W., tr. see Dock, Christopher.
Penoff, R. E., ed. Aircrew Survival. (Illus.). 121p. (Orig.). 1995. pap. text 30.00 (*0-7881-2144-8*) DIANE Pub.
Penoncello, S. G., ed. Computerized Thermophysical Property Packages. (HTD Ser.: Vol. 225). 44p. 1992. 25.00 (*0-7918-1070-4*, G00714) ASME.
Penot-Demetry, Josee, tr. see Bonnemaison, Joel.
Penot, J. P. New Methods in Optimization & Their Industrial Uses. (International Series of Numerical Mathematics: No. 87). 240p. 1989. 91.00 (*0-8176-2286-1*) Birkhauser.
Penoyar, William F. Fed Speak Vol. 1: U. S. Contracting & Grantsmanship Made Easier. unabridged ed. 185p. (Orig.). pap. 12.95 (*0-9615112-2-2*) Grp DAP-USA.
Penoyer, Flyn L. Sales Manager's Guide to Performance Measurement. 275p. 1998. 85.95 (*0-8144-0412-X*) AMACOM.
— Teleselling Techniques That Close the Sale. LC 97-5372. 192p. (Orig.). 1997. pap. 19.95 (*0-8144-7939-1*) AMACOM.
Penoyer, Raymond L. The Winds of Time: The VerNooy Family in the New World. LC 96-77525. (Illus.). xiv, 454p. 1996. 40.00 (*0-9653363-4-4*) Grandview Pr.
Penrice, James. Crossing Home: The Spiritual Lessons of Baseball. LC 93-4222. 118p. (Orig.). 1993. pap. 5.95 (*0-8189-0675-8*) Alba.
— Goal to Go: The Spiritual Lessons of Football. LC 94-17292. 112p. 1994. pap. 5.95 (*0-8189-0702-9*) Alba.
— God Could Be a Teen...No One Understands Him Either: The Truth & Freedom of Catholic Morality. LC 96-40936. 104p. (Orig.). (YA). (gr. 9-12). 1997. mass mkt. 4.95 (*0-8189-0777-0*) Alba.
— If There Is a God, Why Do I Need Braces? An Adolescent Journey to Adult Faith. LC 95-31459. 96p. (Orig.). (YA). (gr. 8-12). 1995. pap. 4.95 (*0-8189-0735-5*) Alba.
Penrice, John. A Dictionary & Glossary of Koran. 167p. 1991. 19.95 (*0-318-37174-X*) Asia Bk Corp.
— Dictionary & Glossary of the Kor'an. (ARA & ENG.). 166p. 1968. 20.00 (*0-86685-088-0*, LDL0880, Pub. by Librairie du Liban) Intl Bk Ctr.
— A Dictionary & Glossary of the Koran. 176p. (C). 1985. text 45.00 (*0-7007-0001-3*, Pub. by Curzon Pr Ltd) Paul & Co Pubs.
— A Dictionary & Glossary of the Koran. (ARA & ENG.). 166p. 1987. 49.95 (*0-8288-1201-2*, M9962) Fr & Eur.
— A Dictionary & Glossary of the Koran. (C). 1995. reprint ed. 25.00 (*81-206-1142-X*, Pub. by Asian Educ Servs) S Asia.
— Dictionary & Glossary of the Koran, with Copious Grammatical References & Explanations. LC 70-90039. (ARA.). 1969. reprint ed. pap. 20.00 (*0-8196-0252-3*) Biblo.
— A Dictionary & Glossary of the Koran with Grammatical References & Explanations. 1980. lib. bdg. 55.00 (*0-8490-3123-0*) Gordon Pr.
— Dictionary & Glossary of the Quran. rev. ed. 166p. (J). 1997. 16.95 (*0-934905-09-6*) Kazi Pubns.
***Penrith, James.** Madagascar, Mayotte & Comoros. (Travellers Survival Kit Ser.). 2000. pap. 18.95 (*1-85458-241-0*) Vac Wrk Pubns.
— Mauritius, Seychelles & Reunion. (Travellers Survival Kit Ser.). 2000. pap. 18.95 (*1-85458-240-2*) Vac Wrk Pubns.
***Penrod.** Microsoft Works 2000. (New Perspectives Ser.). (C). 2000. text 49.95 (*0-619-01945-X*) Course Tech.
Penrod, Diane. Miss Grundy Doesn't Teach Here Anymore: Popular Culture & the Composition Classroom. LC 97-25941. 1997. pap. 25.00 (*0-86709-438-9*, Pub. by Boynton Cook Pubs) Heinemann.
Penrod, Glen A. How to Become President Without Really Lying. 53p. 1998. pap. text 5.95 (*0-9637742-1-2*) Dymon Pubns.
— Touchy Situations: An Advanced Conversation Text for ESL Students. rev. ed. (Illus.). 160p. (C). 1993. pap. text 16.75 (*0-9637742-0-4*) Dymon Pubns.
Penrod, James & Plastino, Janice G. Dancer Prepares: Modern Dance for Beginners. 4th ed. LC 97-18848. (Illus.). viii, 104p. 1997. pap. text 15.95 (*1-55934-675-2*, 1675) Mayfield Pub.
Penrod, James T., jt. auth. see Chaffee, Clarence L.
Penrod, Joan D., jt. auth. see Kane, Roaslie A.
Penrod, Joan D., jt. auth. see Kane, Rosalie A.
***Penrod, John.** The Best Basic & Easy Recipes of Michigan. Hanley, Lucy, ed. 32p. 1999. pap. 5.95 (*0-942618-89-0*) Penrod-Hiawatha.
Penrod, John. Copper Country: Michigan's Historic Wilderness. 1998. pap. 4.95 (*0-942618-69-6*) Penrod-Hiawatha.
***Penrod, John.** Holland, Michigan: Dutch Heritage. 56p. 1999. 19.95 (*0-942618-88-2*) Penrod-Hiawatha.
Penrod, John. Indiana, the Hoosier State: A Pictorial Guide. rev. ed. (YA). (gr. 9 up). 1990. pap. 4.95 (*0-942618-21-1*) Penrod-Hiawatha.
— Lighthouses of Michigan: Historic Landmarks. LC 99-169794. 72p. 1998. pap. 14.95 (*0-942618-78-5*) Penrod-Hiawatha.
***Penrod, John.** Michigan. 32p. 1999. pap. 5.95 (*0-942618-90-4*) Penrod-Hiawatha.
— Michigan Lighthouses: 75 Color Pictures Covering Michigan's Most Scenic Lighthouses. 1992. pap. 5.95 (*0-942618-36-X*) Penrod-Hiawatha.
Penrod, John. Michigan State University: East Lansing Michigan. 1997. pap. 5.45 (*0-942618-68-8*) Penrod-Hiawatha.
***Penrod, John.** Michigan Upper Peninsula: Scenic North Country. 1999. pap. 5.95 (*0-942618-87-4*) Penrod-Hiawatha.
Penrod, John. Ships of the Great Lakes. rev. ed. 1996. pap. 4.95 (*0-942618-63-7*) Penrod-Hiawatha.
***Penrod, John.** Silver Lake Sand Dunes. 1999. pap. 5.95 (*0-942618-86-6*) Penrod-Hiawatha.
Penrod, John. Straits of Mackinac & Mackinac Island. rev. ed. (YA). (gr. 7 up). 1989. pap. 5.95 (*0-942618-20-3*) Penrod-Hiawatha.
— Tahquamenon in Michigan's Upper Peninsula. (YA). (gr. 7 up). 1988. pap. 4.95 (*0-942618-12-2*) Penrod-Hiawatha.
— Whitefish Point Light Station: Michigan's Most Famous Lighthouse. 1998. pap. 5.95 (*0-942618-76-9*) Penrod-Hiawatha.
Penrod, John S. Michigan's Land & Song of Hiawatha. 1986. pap. 5.95 (*0-942618-05-X*) Penrod-Hiawatha.
Penrod, Lynn. Helene Cixious. 1996. 32.00 (*0-8057-8284-2*, Twyne) Mac Lib Ref.
***Penrod, Lynn.** Mise en Pratique. 3rd ed. (FRE.). 208p. 2000. pap. text, wbk. ed. write for info. (*0-201-65413-X*) Addison-Wesley.
Penrod, Paul. Developing Windows Applications Using Borland's Delphi. LC 95-15112. 353p. 1995. pap. 29.95 (*0-471-11017-5*) Wiley.
Penrod, Samantha. Windows '95: Acumen Series. (DF - Computer Applications Ser.). 1996. pap. 20.95 (*0-7895-0349-2*) Course Tech.
— Word 97 Proficient annot. ed. (Illus.). 502p. 1999. pap. write for info. incl. cd-rom (*1-58076-060-0*) Que Educ & Trng.
— WordPerfect 6 for Windows SmartStart: The Step-by-Step Approach. LC 93-86972. 244p. 1994. 25.99 (*1-56529-403-3*) Que.
Penrod, Sigrid, tr. see Imhauser, Hedwig.
Penrod, Steven D., jt. auth. see Cutler, Brian L.
Penrose, A. H., jt. auth. see Hough, M. P.
Penrose, Ann M. & Katz, Stephen B. Writing in the Sciences: Exploring Conventions of Scientific Discourse. 1998. pap. text, teacher ed. 5.00 (*0-312-11968-2*) St Martin.
Penrose, Ann M. & Sitko, Barbara M., eds. Hearing Ourselves Think: Cognitive Research in the College Writing Classroom. LC 92-23469. (Social & Cognitive Studies in Writing & Literacy). 232p. 1993. text 50.00 (*0-19-507833-0*) OUP.
Penrose, Antony. The Lives of Lee Miller. 2nd ed. LC 88-51525. (Illus.). 216p. 1999. reprint ed. pap. 24.95 (*0-500-27509-2*, Pub. by Thames Hudson) Norton.
Penrose, B. Tudor & Early Stuart Voyaging. LC 79-65985. (Folger Guides to the Age of Shakespeare Ser.). 1979. pap. 4.95 (*0-918016-12-6*) Folger Bks.
Penrose, Boies, jt. auth. see Allinson, Edward P.
Penrose, Dina. Occupational Therapy for Orthopaedic Conditions. LC 92-49578. (Therapy in Practice Ser.: Vol. 36). 219p. 1992. 44.75 (*1-56593-044-4*, 0292) Singular Publishing.
Penrose, Edith T. The Large International Firm in Developing Countries. LC 76-7581. (Illus.). 311p. 1976. reprint ed. lib. bdg. 65.00 (*0-8371-8850-4*, PELI, Greenwood Pr) Greenwood.
— The Theory of the Growth of the Firm. LC 79-91109. 304p. reprint ed. pap. 94.30 (*0-608-17083-6*, 202762300055) Bks Demand.
— The Theory of the Growth of the Firm. 3rd ed. 296p. 1995. pap. text 26.00 (*0-19-828977-4*) OUP.
Penrose, Ernest F. European Imperialism & the Partition of Africa. 180p. 1975. 45.00 (*0-7146-3058-6*, Pub. by F Cass Pubs) Intl Spec Bk.
Penrose Family Staff. A Traveler's Guide to 100 Eastern Great Lakes Lighthouses: American & Canadian Lighthouses of the Eastern Great Lakes. (Illus.). 136p. (Orig.). 1994. pap. 14.95 (*0-923756-09-4*) Friede Pubns.
— A Traveler's Guide to 116 Western Great Lakes Lighthouses: American & Canadian Lighthouses of the Western Great Lakes. (Illus.). 176p. (Orig.). 1995. pap. 14.95 (*0-923756-12-4*) Friede Pubns.
Penrose, Francis C. An Investigation of the Principles of Athenian Architecture. 1982. 92.95 (*0-8434-0142-7*) McGrath NH.
Penrose, Gordon. Dr. Zed's Dazzling Book of Science Activities. (Illus.). 48p. (YA). (gr. k up). 1993. pap. 7.95 (*0-919872-78-6*, Pub. by Greey dePencier) Firefly Bks Ltd.
— Dr. Zed's Sensational Science Activities. (Illus.). 48p. (J). (gr. 3 up). 1996. pap. 9.95 (*0-920775-53-5*, Pub. by Greey dePencier) Firefly Bks Ltd.
— Magic Mud & Other Great Experiments: The Best of Dr. Zed's Brilliant Science Activities. (Illus.). 48p. (YA). (gr. 3 up). 1994. pap. 8.95 (*0-920775-18-7*, Pub. by Owl Bks) Firefly Bks Ltd.
— More Science Surprises from Dr. Zed. (Illus.). 32p. (J). (gr. 3-9). 1996. pap. 8.95 (*0-920775-70-5*, Pub. by Greey dePencier) Firefly Bks Ltd.
Penrose, Gordon & Chicadee Magazine Editors. Dr. Zed's Science Surprises. (Illus.). 32p. (J). (gr. 3 up). 1996. pap. 8.95 (*0-920775-42-X*, Pub. by Greey dePencier) Firefly Bks Ltd.
Penrose, Harald. No Echo in the Sky. LC 78-169433. (Literature & History of Aviation Ser.). 1979. reprint ed. 35.95 (*0-405-03776-7*) Ayer.
Penrose, Jan, jt. ed. see Jackson, Peter.
Penrose, John M. & Lahiff, James M. Business Communication. 5th ed. LC 96-16405. 704p. (C). 1996. text 70.00 (*0-13-531112-8*) P-H.

P

Penrose, John M., Jr., et al. Advanced Business Communications. (SWC-Business Communication). 432p. (C). 1989. pap. 59.50 (*0-534-91765-8*) S-W Pub.
— Advanced Business Communication. 2nd ed. LC 92-28661. 430p. 1993. text 53.00 (*0-534-93259-2*) S-W Pub.

Penrose, John M., jt. auth. see Rasberry, Robert W.

Penrose, Laurie. A Guide to 199 Michigan Waterfalls. rev. ed. (Illus.). 168p. (Orig.). 1996. pap. 14.95 (*0-923756-15-9*) Friede Pubns.
— A Traveler's Guide to 116 Michigan Lighthouses. (Illus.). 136p. 1992. pap. 14.95 (*0-923756-03-5*) Friede Pubns.

Penrose, Mary. Roots, Deep & Strong: Great Men & Women of the Church. LC 94-39477. 224p. (Orig.). (C). 1995. pap. 12.95 (*0-8091-3538-8*) Paulist Pr.

Penrose, Maryly B. Compendium of Early Mohawk Valley Families, 2 vols., Set. 1173p. 1990. 55.00 (*0-8063-1279-3*, 4558) Clearfield Co.

Penrose, Nancy L., jt. auth. see Khoo S. Hwa.

Penrose, O. Foundations of Statistical Mechanics: A Deductive Treatment. LC 70-89513. (International Series in Natural Philosophy: Vol. 22). (Illus.). 1970. 112.00 (*0-08-013314-2*, Pub. by Pergamon Repr) Franklin.

Penrose, Pamela. Breaking Free: The Death of Her Brother Sends a Woman in Search of His Killers & Her Identity. LC 98-71011. 192p. 1998. pap. 15.00 (*1-58151-006-3*) BookPartners.

Penrose, Roger. The Emperor's New Mind. 1994. pap. write for info. (*0-09-977170-5*, Pub. by Random) Random House.

Penrose, Roger. The Emperor's New Mind: Concerning Computers, Minds, & the Laws of Physics. (Illus.). 480p. 1989. 30.00 (*0-19-851973-7*) OUP.
— The Emperor's New Mind: Concerning Computers, Minds, & the Laws of Physics. (Illus.). 480p. 1991. pap. 17.95 (*0-14-014534-6*) Viking Penguin.
— Emperor's Tour of the Physical Universe. 1998. pap. write for info. (*0-679-77631-1*) Vin Bks.
— The Large, the Small & the Human Mind. Longair, Malcolm S., ed. LC 96-35837. (Illus.). 203p. (C). 1997. text 20.95 (*0-521-56330-5*) Cambridge U Pr.

***Penrose, Roger.** The Large, the Small & the Human Mind. Longair, Malcolm, ed. (Illus.). 128p. (C). 1999. pap. 12.95 (*0-521-65538-2*) Cambridge U Pr.
— The Large, the Small & the Human Mind. Longair, Malcolm, ed. (Canto Book Ser.). (Illus.). 220p. 2000. pap. 13.95 (*0-521-78572-3*) Cambridge U Pr.

Penrose, Roger. Shadows of the Mind: A Search for the Missing Science of Consciousness. (Illus.). 480p. 1996. reprint ed. pap. 17.95 (*0-19-510646-6*) OUP.
— Shadows of the Mind: On Consciousness, Computation, & the New Physics of the Mind. (Illus.). 480p. 1994. 30.00 (*0-19-853978-9*) OUP.
— Techniques of Differential Topology in Relativity. (CBMS-NSF Regional Conference Ser.: No. 7). viii, 72p. 1972. reprint ed. pap. text 19.00 (*0-89871-005-7*) Soc Indus-Appl Math.

Penrose, Roger & Rindler, Wolfgang. Spinors & Space-Time: Two-Spinor Calculus & Relativistic Fields, Vol. 1. (Monographs on Mathematical Physics). 478p. 1987. pap. text 52.95 (*0-521-33707-0*) Cambridge U Pr.
— Spinors & Space-Time, Vol. 2: Spinor & Twistor Methods in Space-Time Geometry, Vol. 2. (Monographs on Mathematical Physics). (Illus.). 512p. 1986. text 150.00 (*0-521-25267-9*) Cambridge U Pr.
— Spinors & Space-Time, Vol. 2: Spinor & Twistor Methods in Space-Time Geometry, Vol. 2. (Monographs on Mathematical Physics). (Illus.). 512p. 1988. pap. text 52.95 (*0-521-34786-6*) Cambridge U Pr.

Penrose, Roger, jt. auth. see Aldiss, Brian W.

Penrose, Roger, jt. auth. see Hawking, Stephen W.

Penrose, Roland. Antoni Tapies. (Grandes Monografias). (SPA., Illus.). 280p. 1993. 75.00 (*84-343-0257-8*) Elliots Bks.
— Miro. LC 85-50751. (World of Art Ser.). (Illus.). 1985. pap. 14.95 (*0-500-20099-8*, Pub. by Thames Hudson) Norton.
— Picasso. (Color Library). (Illus.). 128p. (C). 1994. reprint ed. pap. 14.95 (*0-7148-2708-8*, Pub. by Phaidon Press) Phaidon Pr.
— Picasso: His Life & Work. 3rd ed. (Illus.). 550p. 1981. pap. 17.95 (*0-520-04207-7*, Pub. by U CA Pr) Cal Prin Full Svc.

Penrose, Roland, jt. ed. see Mesens, E. L.

Penrose, Sandra E. Agatha's Journey, 1828-1998. LC 98-93181. 200p. 1998. pap. 11.95 (*0-9664590-0-8*) Custom Sensor.

***Penrose, Valentine.** The Bloody Countess: The Crimes of Elizabeth Bathory. Trocchi, Alexander, tr. (Illus.). 160p. 2000. pap. 13.95 (*1-84068-056-3*, Pub. by Creation Bks) Subterranean Co.

Penrose, Valentine. The Bloody Countess: The Crimes of Elizabeth Bathory. Trocchi, Alexander, tr. from FRE. (True Crime Ser.). 160p. 1997. pap. 13.95 (*1-871592-64-X*) Creation Books.

Penruddocke, Andrea. English for the Real. LC 99-36008. 1999. 29.95 (*0-609-60507-0*); 29.95 (*0-609-60508-9*); 29.95 (*0-609-60509-7*) Liv Lang.

Penry, Huw. Bird Atlas of Botswana. (Illus.). 320p. 1994. 55.75 (*0-86980-894-X*, Pub. by Univ Natal Pr) Intl Spec Bk.

Penry, Huw. Bird Atlas of Botswana. LC 95-131420. (Illus.). 340p. 1994. pap. 45.00 (*0-86980-895-8*, Pub. by Univ Natal Pr) Intl Spec Bk.

Penry, J. Kiffin, ed. Epilepsy: Diagnosis, Management, Quality of Life. LC 86-3289. 54p. 1986. reprint ed. pap. 30.00 (*0-608-07260-5*, 206748800009) Bks Demand.

Penry, J. Kiffin, ed. see International Symposium on Epilepsy Staff.

Penry, J. Kiffin, jt. ed. see Levy, Rene H.

Penry, J. Kiffin, jt. ed. see Newmark, Michael E.

Pensacola Junior Woman Club Staff. Fiesta. LC 87-62721. (Illus.). 302p. 1987. 12.95 (*0-9619266-0-0*) Pensacola Jr Womans Club.

Pensaert, M. B. & Horzinek, M. C., eds. Virus Infections of Porcines. (Virus Infections of Vertebrates Ser.: Vol. 2). 284p. 1989. 223.50 (*0-444-42909-3*) Elsevier.

Pensak, Myles L., jt. auth. see Hughes, Gordon B.

***Pensanti, Helen.** Better Sex for You. 2000. pap. 12.99 (*0-88419-687-9*) Creation House.

Pensare, C. Rape of Nations: A Study in Societal Economics. LC 73-88364. (C). 1969. 52.75 (*0-912010-01-0*); spiral bd. 35.00 (*0-912010-00-2*) Goss.

Pensee, Clive La, see La Pensee, Clive.

Penshansky, David. The Politics of Biblical Theology: A Postmodern Reading. LC 95-5759. (Studies in American Biblical Hermeneutics: Vol. 10). 1995. 18.00 (*0-86554-462-X*, MUP-P115) Mercer Univ Pr.

Pensiero, Laura, et al. The Strang Program for Cancer Prevention: A Complete Nutrition & Lifestyle Plan to Dramatically Lower Your Cancer Risk. 352p. 1998. 29.95 (*0-525-94313-7*) NAL.

Pensinger, Glen, ed. Digital Video Background & Implementation 4: 2: 2. 160p. 1989. pap. 35.00 (*0-940690-16-0*) Soc Motion Pic & TV Engrs.

***Pension Provision Group & Great Britain. Dept. of Social Security.** We All Need Pensions: The Prospects for Pension Provision : Report. LC 99-202368. (Illus.). 1998. write for info. (*0-11-762607-4*) Statnry Office.

Pensky, Max. The Actuality of Adorno: Critical Essays on Adorno & the Postmodern. LC 96-22721. (SUNY Series in Contemporary Continental Philosophy). 199p. (C). 1997. pap. text 17.95 (*0-7914-3332-3*) State U NY Pr.
— Melancholy Dialectics: Walter Benjamin & the Play of Mourning. LC 92-42229. 296p. 1993. lib. bdg. 32.50 (*0-87023-853-1*) U of Mass Pr.

Pensky, Max, ed. The Actuality of Adorno: Critical Essays on Adorno & the Postmodern. LC 96-22721. (SUNY Series in Contemporary Continental Philosophy). 199p. (C). 1997. text 54.50 (*0-7914-3331-5*) State U NY Pr.

Pensky, Max, tr. see Habermas, Jurgen.

Pensl, G., et al, eds. Silicon Carbid, III-Nitrides & Related Materials: Proceedings of the 7th International Conference on Silicon Carbide, III-Nitrides & Related Materials, Stockholm, Sweden, September, 1997, 2 vols. (Materials Science Forum Ser.: Vols. 264-268). 1606p. 1998. 398.00 (*0-87849-790-0*, Pub. by Scitec Pubns) Enfield Pubs NH.

Penslar, Derek J. Anti-Semitism: The Jewish Response. Siegel, Adam, ed. (Illus.). 62p. (Orig.). 1989. pap. text 6.95 (*0-87441-494-6*) Behrman.
— Zionism & Technocracy: The Engineering of Jewish Settlement in Palestine, 1870-1918. LC 90-25043. (Modern Jewish Experience Ser.). (Illus.). 224p. 1991. 10.95 (*0-253-34290-2*) Ind U Pr.

Penslar, Derek J., jt. ed. see Brenner, Michael.

Penslar, Robin L., ed. Research Ethics: Cases & Materials. LC 94-5971. 320p. 1995. pap. 13.95 (*0-253-20906-4*) Ind U Pr.

Penso Cortes, Josette, jt. auth. see Harrington, Karen.

Penso, Dorothy E. Keyboard, Graphic & Handwriting Skills: Helping People with Motor Disabilities. Campling, Jo, ed. (Therapy in Practice Ser.: No. 15). 160p. 1990. pap. 23.00 (*0-412-32210-2*, A4415) Chapman & Hall.
— Keyboarding Skills for Children with Disabilities. 1998. pap. text. write for info. (*1-86156-106-7*) Whurr Pub.
— Perceptuo-Motor Difficulties: Theory & Strategies to Help Children, Adolescents, & Adults. LC 92-49040. (Therapy in Practice Ser.: Vol. 34). 179p. 1992. 41.50 (*1-56593-025-8*, 0268) Thomson Learn.

Penso, Kia. Wallace Stevens, Harmonium, & the Whole of Harmonium. LC 91-22649. 128p. (C). 1991. lib. bdg. 28.50 (*0-208-02305-4*, Archon Bks) Shoe String.

***Pensom, Roger.** Accent & Metre in French: A Theory of the Relation Between Linguistic Accent & Metrical Practice in French, 1100-1900. 2nd ed. LC 99-56656. 177p. (C). 1999. pap. text 28.95 (*0-8204-4610-6*) P Lang Pubng.

Pensom, Roger. Aucassin et Nicolete: The Poetry of Gender & Growing Up in the French Middle Ages. 160p. 1998. pap. text 27.95 (*0-8204-4211-9*) P Lang Pubng.

***Pensom, Roger.** Aucassin et Nicolete: The Poetry of Gender & Growing up in the French Middle Ages. 160p. 1999. pap. 27.95 (*3-906761-41-X*, Pub. by P Lang) P Lang Pubng.

Pensom, Roger. Reading Beroul's "Tristran" A Poetic Narrative & the Anthropology of Its Reception. LC 96-116242. 116p. 1995. 29.95 (*3-906753-49-2*, Pub. by P Lang) P Lang Pubng.

Pensom, William, et al. The Birmingham Roller Pigeon. rev. ed. Fancier, J. A., ed. (Illus.). 140p. 1989. reprint ed. write for info. (*0-9622998-7-1*) WFancier Pubns.

Penson & Capps. Introduction to Agricultural Economics. 2nd ed. LC 98-34928. (Illus.). 572p. (C). 1998. 93.00 (*0-13-901190-0*) P-H.

Penson, Chuck. Heathkit a Guide to the Amateur Radio Products. (Illus.). 248p. 1995. pap. text 24.95 (*0-9663433-1-X*) Elec Rad Pr.

Penson, Jenny & Fisher, Ronald A. Palliative Care for People with Cancer. 2nd ed. 336p. 1995. pap. text 38.25 (*1-56593-598-5*, 1224) Singular Publishing.

Penson, John B., Jr., et al. Introduction to Agricultural Economics. (Illus.). 496p. (C). 1986. text 51.00 (*0-13-477712-3*) P-H.

Penson, Lillian M. Colonial Agents of the British West Indies: A Study in Colonial Administration, Mainly in the Eighteenth Century. 128p. 1971. reprint ed. 45.00 (*0-7146-1944-2*, Pub. by F Cass Pubs) Intl Spec Bk.

Penson, Lillian M., jt. auth. see Temperley, H. W.

Pensoneau, Taylor. Governor Richard Ogilvie: In the Interest of the State. LC 97-3816. (Illus.). 416p. 1997. 35.00 (*0-8093-2148-3*) S Ill U Pr.

***Penszіwol, Jean.** No Dragons for Tea: Fire Safety for Kids (And Dragons) (Illus.). (J). 1999. pap. 5.95 (*1-55074-571-9*) Kids Can Pr.

Pentagram Partnership Staff. More Puzzlegrams: A Colorful, Beguiling Collection of 148 More Classic Puzzles Designed by Pentagram. (Illus.). 160p. 1994. per. 18.00 (*0-671-51059-2*) S&S Trade Pap.

Pentagram Partnership Staff, compiled by. Puzzlegrams: A Colorful Challenging Collection of 178 Classic Puzzles. 192p. 1989. per. 18.00 (*0-671-68740-9*, Fireside) S&S Trade Pap.

Pentagram Partnership Staff, des. Pentamagic: An Eye-Opening Collection of Optical Illusions & Visual Magic. LC 92-15505. 160p. 1993. per. 16.99 (*0-671-79185-0*, Fireside) S&S Trade Pap.

Pentagram Staff. Pentagram V, Vol. 5. 1998. 45.00 (*1-58093-042-5*) Monacelli Pr.

Pentauk, Keri, ed. Rearing a Husband: The Modern Woman's Guide to Marital Bliss. 128p. 1997. pap. 14.95 (*1-928568-00-9*) Retro Sys.

***Pentauk, Keri & Flannery, Susan.** Spanked Husbands Satisfied Wives. (Illus.). 1998. pap. 11.95 (*1-928568-01-7*) Retro Sys.

Pentecost, Allan. Introduction to Freshwater Algae. (Illus.). 247p. (C). 1984. pap. 20.95 (*0-916422-49-6*) Mad River.

***Pentecost, David.** Parenting the ADHD Child: Can't Do? Want Do? LC 99-43195. (Illus.). 1999. pap. 23.95 (*1-85302-811-8*) Jessica Kingsley.

Pentecost, Don. Put 'Em down, Take 'Em Out: Knife Fighting Techniques from Folsom Prison. (Illus.). 64p. 1988. pap. 14.00 (*0-87364-484-0*) Paladin Pr.

Pentecost, Dwight. Profecias Para el Mundo Moderno.Tr. of Prophecy for Today. (SPA.). 1990. 4.99 (*0-945792-86-7*, 497703) Editorial Unilit.

Pentecost, Dwight J. A Harmony of the Words & Works of Jesus Christ. 208p. 1981. pap. 18.99 (*0-310-30951-4*, 17016P) Zondervan.
— A Harmony of the Words & Works of Jesus Christ. 272p. 1983. 15.95 (*0-310-30950-6*, 17016) Zondervan.
— The Parables of Jesus: Lessons in Life from the Master Teacher. LC 98-41466. 176p. 1998. pap. 9.99 (*0-8254-3458-0*) Kregel.

Pentecost, E. J. A Model of U. K. Non-Oil ICCs' Direct Investment. LC HG4502.. (Bank of England. Discussion Papers: No. 30). 58p. reprint ed. pap. 30.00 (*0-7837-5374-8*, 204513800005) Bks Demand.

Pentecost, Emily, jt. ed. see Keeling, Shirley.

Pentecost, Eric J. Exchange Rate Dynamics: A Modern Analysis of Exchange Rate Theory & Evidence. LC 92-28723. 240p. 1993. 95.00 (*1-85278-138-6*) E Elgar.
— Exchange Rate Dynamics: A Modern Analysis of Exchange Rate Theory & Evidence. 240p. 1994. pap. 35.00 (*1-85278-903-4*) E Elgar.

Pentecost, Eric J., jt. auth. see Button, Kenneth.

Pentecost, Eric J., jt. ed. see Mizen, Paul.

Pentecost, Hugh. Bargain with Death. 224p. 1989. reprint ed. mass mkt. 3.50 (*0-373-26018-0*) Harlequin Bks.
— The Cannibal Who Overate. 191p. 1990. mass mkt. 3.95 (*0-88184-614-7*) Carroll & Graf.
— Deadly Trap. large type ed. (Linford Mystery Library). 368p. 1997. pap. 16.99 (*0-7089-5170-8*) Ulverscroft.
— Fourteen Dilemma. 1990. mass mkt. 3.50 (*0-373-26045-8*) Harlequin Bks.
— Kill & Kill Again. large type ed. (Mystery Ser.). 1990. 27.99 (*0-7089-2243-0*) Ulverscroft.
— Murder As Usual. large type ed. (Linford Mystery Library). 368p. 1997. pap. 16.99 (*0-7089-5103-1*, Linford) Ulverscroft.
— Murder Goes Round & Round. large type ed. (Linford Mystery Library). 304p. 1998. pap. 17.99 (*0-7089-5218-6*, Linford) Ulverscroft.
— Murder in High Places. (Worldwide Library Mysteries: No. 94). 1992. mass mkt. 3.99 (*0-373-26094-6*, 1-26094-2) Harlequin Bks.
— Murder in Luxury. 224p. 1991. mass mkt. 3.50 (*0-373-26069-5*) Harlequin Bks.
— Nightmare Time: A Pierre Chambrun Mystery Novel. large type ed. (Linford Mystery Library). 304p. 1988. pap. 16.99 (*0-7089-6563-6*, Linford) Ulverscroft.
— The Party Killer. large type ed. (Linford Mystery Library). 368p. 1997. pap. 16.99 (*0-7089-5099-X*, Linford) Ulverscroft.
— Pattern for Terror. large type ed. LC 92-30149. (Nightingale Ser.). 208p. 1993. pap. 14.95 (*0-8161-5637-9*, G K Hall Lrg Type) Mac Lib Ref.
— Walking Dead Man. large type ed. (Linford Mystery Library). 368p. 1997. pap. 16.99 (*0-7089-5158-9*) Ulverscroft.

Pentecost, J. Dwight. Design for Discipleship: Discovering God's Blueprint for the Christian Life. LC 95-33414. 128p. 1996. pap. 8.99 (*0-8254-3451-3*) Kregel.

***Pentecost, J. Dwight.** Design for Living: Lessons in Holiness from the Sermon on the Mount. LC 99-12418. 208p. 1999. pap. 10.99 (*0-8254-3457-2*) Kregel.

Pentecost, J. Dwight. The Divine Comforter: The Person & Work of the Holy Spirit. LC 97-30360. 256p. 1998. pap. 12.99 (*0-8254-3456-4*) Kregel.
— Eventas Del Porvinu.Tr. of Things to Come. (SPA.). 472p. 1984. pap. 22.99 (*0-8297-1410-3*) Vida Pubs.
— A Faith That Endures: The Book of Hebrews Applied to the Real Issues of Life. LC 92-26390. 256p. 1992. pap. 11.99 (*0-929239-66-0*) Discovery Hse Pubs.
— Una Fe Que Perdura.Tr. of Faith That Endures. (SPA.). 271p. 1995. 12.99 (*0-89922-529-2*, C001-5292) Caribe Betania.
— The Joy of Fellowship: A Study of First John. 1990. pap. 7.99 (*0-310-30921-2*, 17013P) Zondervan.
— The Joy of Intimacy with God: A Bible Study Guide to I John. rev. ed. LC 95-32309. 144p. 1996. pap. 10.99 (*1-57293-006-3*) Discovery Hse Pubs.

***Pentecost, J. Dwight.** Joy of Intimacy with God: A Devotional Study of 1 John. 144p. 2000. pap. 8.99 (*0-8254-3459-9*) Kregel.

Pentecost, J. Dwight. The Joy of Living: A Devotional Study of Philippians. LC 96-28267. 256p. 1996. pap. 12.99 (*0-8254-3453-X*) Kregel.
— Life's Problems, God's Solutions: Answers to 15 of Life's Most Perplexing Problems. LC 96-46398. 192p. 1998. pap. 10.99 (*0-8254-3454-8*) Kregel.
— Marchando Hacia la Madurez Espiritual. (SPA.). 384p. 1979. mass mkt. 8.99 (*0-8254-1554-3*, Edit Portavoz) Kregel.
— Prophecy for Today: God's Purpose & Plan for Our Future. 224p. 1989. pap. 10.99 (*0-929239-11-3*) Discovery Hse Pubs.
— El Sermon del Monte. Orig. Title: The Sermon on the Mount. (SPA.). 256p. 1995. mass mkt. 6.99 (*0-8254-1555-1*, Edit Portavoz) Kregel.
— Things to Come. 633p. 1965. 29.99 (*0-310-30890-9*, 6355) Zondervan.
— Things Which Become Sound Doctrine. 1970. reprint ed. mass mkt. 7.99 (*0-310-30901-8*, 6504P) Zondervan.
— Things Which Become Sound Doctrine: Doctrinal Studies of Fourteen Crucial Words of Faith. 160p. 1996. pap. 9.99 (*0-8254-3452-1*) Kregel.
— Thy Kingdom Come. 360p. 1995. pap. 15.99 (*0-8254-3450-5*) Kregel.
— Will Man Survive? The Bible Looks at Man's Future. 192p. 1990. pap. 10.99 (*0-310-30931-X*) Zondervan.
— The Words & Works of Jesus Christ. 629p. 1981. 29.99 (*0-310-30940-9*, 17015) Zondervan.
— Your Adversary, the Devil. LC 96-46395. 192p. 1997. pap. 10.99 (*0-8254-3455-6*) Kregel.

Pentecost, John D. Profecias para el Mundo Moderno.Tr. of Prophecy for Today. (SPA.). 228p. 1989. pap. write for info. (*0-614-27118-5*) Editorial Unilit.

Pentecost, Michael J., jt. ed. see Baum, Stanley.

***Pentecoste, Eric J.** Macroeconomics: An Open Economy Approach. 2000. text 72.00 (*0-312-23368-X*) St Martin.

Pentelodimos, jt. auth. see Lust, Barbara.

Pentenero, P. First Dictionary of Welding. (ENG & ITA.). 436p. 1988. 135.00 (*0-8288-7929-X*) Fr & Eur.

Penthouse Magazine Editors. Erotica from Penthouse. Heidenry, John, ed. 224p. (Orig.). 1990. mass mkt. 7.50 (*0-446-34517-2*, Pub. by Warner Bks) Little.
— Erotica from Penthouse III. 224p. (Orig.). 1994. mass mkt. 5.99 (*0-446-60057-1*, Pub. by Warner Bks) Little.
— Feel the Heat. (Letters to Penthouse Ser.: Vol. VI). 368p. (Orig.). 1996. mass mkt. 7.99 (*0-446-60196-9*, Pub. by Warner Bks) Little.

***Penthouse Magazine Editors.** Letters to Penthouse XI. 2000. mass mkt. 7.99 (*0-446-60850-5*) Warner Bks.

Penthouse Magazine Editors. Letters to Penthouse III. 240p. (Orig.). 1992. mass mkt. 7.50 (*0-446-36296-4*, Pub. by Warner Bks) Little.
— Letters to Penthouse IV. 224p. (Orig.). 1994. mass mkt. 7.99 (*0-446-60056-3*, Pub. by Warner Bks) Little.
— Letters to Penthouse IX. 352p. 1999. mass mkt. 7.50 (*0-446-60640-5*, Pub. by Warner Bks) Little.

***Penthouse Magazine Editors.** Letters to Penthouse X. 352p. 2000. mass mkt. 7.99 (*0-446-60641-3*) Warner Bks.

Penthouse Magazine Editors. Letters to Penthouse V. 224p. (Orig.). 1995. mass mkt. 7.50 (*0-446-60195-0*, Pub. by Warner Bks) Little.
— Letters to Penthouse VIII. 352p. (Orig.). 1998. mass mkt. 7.50 (*0-446-60419-4*, Pub. by Warner Bks) Little.
— More Erotica from Penthouse. 224p. (Orig.). 1992. mass mkt. 7.50 (*0-446-36297-2*, Pub. by Warner Bks) Little.
— More Letters from Penthouse. 224p. (Orig.). 1989. mass mkt. 7.50 (*0-446-34515-6*, Pub. by Warner Bks) Little.
— Celebrate the Rites of Passion, No. VII. LC 97-186071. (Letters to Penthouse Ser.). 368p. (Orig.). 1997. mass mkt. 7.99 (*0-446-60418-6*, Pub. by Warner Bks) Little.

***Penthouse Magazine Editors.** Penthouse Uncensored. 592p. 2000. pap. 14.95 (*0-446-67735-3*) Warner Bks.

Pentico, David W. Introduction to Management Science. (Business Statistics Ser.). 2001. pap. 54.95 (*0-534-92477-8*) Wadsworth Pub.

Pentico, David W., jt. auth. see Morton, Thomas E.

Pentikaeinen, Juha, ed. Shamanism & Northern Ecology. LC 95-46624. (Religion & Society Ser.: Vol. 36). ix, 386p. (C). 1996. lib. bdg. 131.85 (*3-11-014186-8*) Mouton.

Pentikainen, Juha, ed. Religion: Global & Arctic Perspectives. 176p. 1997. 45.00 (*1-874312-35-4*, Pub. by Hisarlik Pr) Intl Spec Bk.
— Starovery - Old Believers: Studies on Old Ritualism in Eastern Christianity. 192p. 1997. 70.00 (*1-874312-34-6*, Pub. by Hisarlik Pr) Intl Spec Bk.

***Pentikainen, Juha & Poom, Ritva.** Kalevala Mythology. expanded ed. LC 99-34168. (Folklore Studies in Translation). 1999. write for info. (*0-253-33661-9*) Ind U Pr.

Pentikainen, Juha Y. Kalevala Mythology. rev. ed. Poom, Ritva, ed. & tr. by. (Folklore Studies in Translation). (Illus.). 288p. 1999. pap. 18.95 (*0-253-21239-1*) Ind U Pr.

***Pentikhainen, Juha & Poom, Ritva.** Kalevala Mythology. expanded ed. LC 99-34168. (Folklore Studies in Translation). 1999. 18.95 (*0-253-21352-5*) Ind U Pr.

Pentiuc, Eugen & Blackwell, John A. Symposium Vol. III: Divine Creation & Human Responsibility in the Context of Contemporary Ecological Preoccupations. The Third Ecumenical Theological Symposium. Damian, Theodor et al, eds. 99p. 1996. pap. text 8.00 (*1-888067-03-9*) Romanian Inst.

Pentkovsky, Aleksei, ed. The Pilgrim's Tale. Smith, T. Allan, tr. from RUS. LC 99-35236. (Classics of Western Spirituality Ser.: No. 90). 176p. 1999. pap. 19.95 (*0-8091-3709-7*) Paulist Pr.

P

An Asterisk (*) at the beginning of an entry indicates that the title is appearing for the first time.

— The Pilgrim's Tale. Smith, T. Allan, tr. from RUS. LC 99-35236. (Classics of Western Spirituality Ser.: No. 91). 176p. 1999. 28.95 (*0-8091-0486-5*) Paulist Pr.

Pentland, Alexander, jt. ed. see Cipolla, Roberto.

Pentland, John. Exchanges Within: Questions from Everyday Life, Selected from Gurdjieff Group Meetings with John Pentland in California, 1955-1984. LC 61-11935. 416p. 1997. 29.95 (*0-8264-1025-1*) Continuum.

Pentland Press Ltd. Staff. Lu Gwei-Djen: A Commemoration. (C). 1989. text 59.00 (*1-85821-034-8*, Pub. by Pentland Pr) St Mut.

***Pentland, W. E., et al, eds.** The Application of Time Use Methodology in the Social Sciences. LC 98-47892. (Illus.). 281p. (C). 1999. 59.50 (*0-306-45951-5*, Plenum Trade) Perseus Pubng.

Pentney, jt. auth. see Berlin.

Penton, Carl J., ed. see Gluck, Jay & Gluck, Sumi H.

Penton, Jill, tr. see Beintema, Rita.

Penton, M. James. Apocalypse Delayed: The Story of Jehovah's Witnesses. LC 85-244517. (Illus.). 428p. reprint ed. pap. 132.70 (*0-8357-4733-6*, 203765000009) Bks Demand.

— Apocalypse Delayed: The Story of Jehovah's Witnesses. 2nd rev. ed. LC 97-189457. (Illus.). 464p. 1997. pap. text 20.95 (*0-8020-7973-3*) U of Toronto Pr.

Penton Overseas Inc. Staff. Dutch/English, Level 1. unabridged ed. (VocabuLearn Ser.). (DUT & ENG.). 1992. 15.95 incl. audio (*0-939001-42-X*) Penton Overseas.

— Dutch/English, Level 2. unabridged ed. (VocabuLearn Ser.). (DUT & ENG.). 1997. pap. 15.95 incl. audio (*0-939001-44-6*) Penton Overseas.

— French Around Town. (Immersion Plus Ser.). (ENG & FRE.). 1995. pap. 10.95 incl. audio (*1-56015-559-0*) Penton Overseas.

— Greek (Modern)/English, Level 2. unabridged ed. (VocabuLearn Ser.). (ENG & GER.). 1993. 15.95 incl. audio (*0-939001-51-9*) Penton Overseas.

— Hebrew/English, Level 1. (VocabuLearn Ser.). (ENG & HEB.). 1990. pap. 15.95 incl. audio (*0-939001-00-4*) Penton Overseas.

— Hebrew/English, Level 2. (VocabuLearn Ser.). (ENG & HEB.). 1990. pap. 15.95 incl. audio (*0-939001-03-9*) Penton Overseas.

— Let's Talk French Today. (Immersion Plus Ser.). (FRE.). 1994. pap. 10.95 incl. audio (*1-56015-550-7*) Penton Overseas.

— Let's Talk German Today. (Immersion Plus Ser.). (ENG & GER.). 1995. pap. 10.95 incl. audio (*1-56015-552-3*) Penton Overseas.

— Let's Talk Italian Today. (Immersion Plus Ser.). (ENG & ITA.). 1995. pap. 10.95 incl. audio (*1-56015-553-1*) Penton Overseas.

— Let's Talk Spanish Today. (Immersion Plus Ser.). (SPA.). 1994. pap. 10.95 incl. audio (*1-56015-551-5*) Penton Overseas.

— Polish/English, Level 1. (VocabuLearn Ser.). (ENG & POL.). 1990. pap. 15.95 incl. audio (*0-939001-04-7*) Penton Overseas.

— Polish/English, Level 2. unabridged ed. (VocabuLearn Ser.). (ENG & POL.). 1990. pap. 15.95 incl. audio (*0-939001-05-5*) Penton Overseas.

— Spanish Around Town. (Immersion Plus Ser.). (ENG & SPA.). 1995. pap. 10.95 incl. audio (*1-56015-560-4*) Penton Overseas.

Penton Overseas Inc. Staff. Swahili/English, Level I. (VocabuLearn Ser.). (ENG & SWA.). 1995. pap. 15.95 incl. audio (*0-939001-85-3*) Penton Overseas.

— Tagalog/English, Level I. LC 97-701697. (VocabuLearn Ser.). (ENG & TAG.). 1995. pap. 15.95 incl. audio (*0-939001-84-5*) Penton Overseas.

Penton Overseas Inc. Staff. Ukranian/English, Level 1. (VocabuLearn Ser.). (ENG & UKR.). 1994. pap. 15.95 incl. audio (*0-939001-83-7*) Penton Overseas.

— Vietnamese/English, Level 2. unabridged ed. (VocabuLearn Ser.). (VIE & ENG.). 1993. 15.95 incl. audio (*0-939001-95-0*) Penton Overseas.

— VocabuLearn: Chinese/English, 3 Levels, Set. unabridged ed. (CHI.). 1993. pap. 39.95 incl. audio (*0-939001-16-0*) Penton Overseas.

— VocabuLearn - Anfanger Englisch, Level 1. unabridged ed.Tr. of VocabuLearn - Beginner's English. (ENG & GER.). 10.95 incl. audio (*1-56015-476-4*) Penton Overseas.

— Vocabulearn - Beginners: French - English, Level 1. (ENG & FRE.). (YA). 1992. 10.95 incl. audio (*1-56015-450-0*) Penton Overseas.

— VocabuLearn - Beginners: French - English, Level 2. unabridged ed. (FRE & ENG.). (YA). (gr. 8-12). 1993. 10.95 incl. audio (*1-56015-454-3*) Penton Overseas.

— VocabuLearn - Beginners: German - English, Level 1. (ENG & GER.). (YA). 1992. 10.95 incl. audio (*1-56015-451-9*) Penton Overseas.

Penton Overseas Inc. Staff. VocabuLearn - Beginners: German - English, Level 2. unabridged ed. (GER.). (YA). (gr. 8-12). 1993. 10.95 incl. audio (*1-56015-455-1*) Penton Overseas.

Penton Overseas Inc. Staff. VocabuLearn - Beginners: Italian - English, Level 1. (ITA & ENG.). (YA). (gr. 8-8). 1992. 10.95 incl. audio (*1-56015-452-7*) Penton Overseas.

— VocabuLearn - Beginners: Italian - English, Level 2. (ITA.). (YA). (gr. 8-12). 1993. 10.95 incl. audio (*1-56015-456-X*) Penton Overseas.

— VocabuLearn - Beginners: Spanish - English, Level 1. (ENG & SPA.). (YA). 1992. 10.95 incl. audio (*1-56015-453-5*) Penton Overseas.

— Vocabulearn - Beginners: Spanish - English, Level 2. unabridged ed. (SPA & ENG.). (YA). (gr. 8-12). 1993. 10.95 incl. audio (*1-56015-457-8*) Penton Overseas.

— VocabuLearn - Debutants Anglais, Level 2.Tr. of VocabuLearn - Beginner's English. (ENG & FRE.). 10.95 incl. audio (*1-56015-479-9*) Penton Overseas.

— VocabuLearn - Principiantes Ingles, Level 1.Tr. of VocabuLearn - Beginner's English. (ENG & SPA.). 10.95 incl. audio (*1-56015-478-0*) Penton Overseas.

***Penton Overseas Inc. Staff.** VocabuLearn - Principiantes Ingles, Series 2.Tr. of VocabuLearn - Beginner's English. (ENG & SPA.). 1999. 10.95 incl. audio (*1-56015-482-9*) Penton Overseas.

Penton Overseas Inc. Staff. VocabuLearn - Principianti Inglese, Level 1.Tr. of VocabuLearn - Beginner's English. (ENG & ITA.). 10.95 incl. audio (*1-56015-477-2*) Penton Overseas.

Penton Research Services. Industry Inquiry Trends: A Study of the Methods Used by Purchase Decision Makers to Obtain Information from Advertisers. LC 97-76533. 232 p. 1998. write for info. (*0-9611182-8-8*) Gov Prod News.

Penton, Rhona & Chapman, Stephen, eds. Medicines Management. (Illus.). 196p. 1998. pap. 29.00 (*0-7279-1274-7*, Pub. by BMJ Pub) Login Brothers Bk Co.

Pentony, B. Commercial Transactions: Cases & Materials. 700p. 1991. pap. 90.00 (*0-409-30814-5*, Austral, MICHIE) LEXIS Pub.

Pentony, B., et al. Understanding Business Law. 550p. 1995. pap. write for info. incl. disk (*0-409-30408-5*, MICHIE) LEXIS Pub.

— Understanding Business Law Workbook. LC 95-202144. 184p. 1995. pap., wbk. ed. write for info. (*0-409-30523-5*, MICHIE) LEXIS Pub.

Pentony, B., jt. auth. see Tomasic, R.

Pentreath, R. J. Nuclear Power, Man & the Environment. (Wykeham Science Ser.: No. 51). 268p. 1977. pap. 18.00 (*0-85109-840-1*) Taylor & Francis.

— Nuclear Power, Man & the Environment. LC 80-20173. (Wykeham Science Ser.: No. 51). 250p. (C). 1981. pap. 18.00 (*0-8448-1381-8*, Crane Russak) Taylor & Francis.

Pentreath, V. & O'Hare, S., eds. Experimental In Vitro Neurotoxicology. 300p. 1998. text 89.95 (*0-7484-0388-4*, Pub. by Tay Francis Ltd) Taylor & Francis.

Penttonen, Martti, jt. ed. see Farinas del Cerro, Luis.

Pentz, Croft M. The Complete Book of Zingers. 374p. 1990. pap. 9.99 (*0-8423-0467-3*) Tyndale Hse.

— Outlines on the Holy Spirit. (Sermon Outline Ser.). 64p. 1978. pap. 4.99 (*0-8010-7029-5*) Baker Bks.

— Outlines on the Parables of Jesus. (Sermon Outline Ser.). 48p. 1980. pap. 4.99 (*0-8010-7055-4*) Baker Bks.

— Sermon Outlines for Special Days. (Sermon Outline Ser.). 64p. 1986. pap. 4.99 (*0-8010-7046-5*) Baker Bks.

Pentz, Jane. If You Don't Take Care of Your Body Where Are You Going to Live? Teaching Individuals How to Take Charge of Their Health. unabridged ed. Greenwood, Elaine, ed. 214p. 1998. ring bd. 19.95 (*1-892426-01-3*) LMA Publishing.

***Pentz, Jane.** Nutrition for Professionals: The Nutrition Specialist Course. 5th unabridged ed. Greenwood, Elaine & Bonczek, Lindy, eds. (Illus.). 220p. 1999. pap. text 75.00 (*1-892426-03-X*) LMA Publishing.

Pentz, Jane. Nutrition for Professionals: The Nutrition Specialist Manual. 4th unabridged ed. Greenwood, Elaine & Bonczek, Lindy, eds. (Illus.). 175p. 1998. ring bd. 75.00 (*1-892426-00-5*) LMA Publishing.

— Truth in Marketing: What's a Body to Believe? unabridged ed. 64p. 1999. lib. bdg. 9.95 (*1-892426-02-1*) LMA Publishing.

Pentz, Luncy. The Biolab Book: Twenty-Six Laboratory Exercises for Biology Students. 2nd rev. ed. (Illus.). 168p. (C). 1989. pap. text 14.95 (*0-8018-3707-3*) Johns Hopkins.

Pentz, Lundy. The Biolab Book. LC 82-49066. (Illus.). 144p. reprint ed. pap. 44.70 (*0-8357-6040-5*, 203414500089) Bks Demand.

Pentz, Mike & Shott, Milo. Handling Experimental Data. Aprahamian, Francis, ed. 96p. 1988. pap. 25.95 (*0-335-15824-2*) OpUniv Pr.

Pentz, Peter. The Invisible Conquest: The Ontogenesis of Sixth & Seventh Century Syria. Dietz, Soren, ed. (Illus.). 96p. (C). 1992. pap. text 12.95 (*87-7288-504-1*, Pub. by Aarhus Univ Pr) David Brown.

Pentz, Peter, jt. auth. see Sorensen, Lone W.

Penuel, Arnold. Intertextuality in Garcia Marquez. LC 93-84976. 80p. (C). 1994. 24.00 (*0-938972-20-0*) Spanish Lit Pubns.

Penuelas, Marcelino C. Jacinto Benavente. LC 68-9515. (Twayne's World Authors Ser.). 1968. lib. bdg. 20.95 (*0-8057-2136-3*) Irvington.

Penven, Yves Le, see Le Penven, Yves.

Penvenne, Jeanne. African Workers & Colonial Racism: Mozambican Strategies for Survival in Lourenco Marques, 1877-1962. LC 94-10574. (Social History of Africa Ser.). 229p. 1994. 50.00 (*0-435-08952-8*, 08952); pap. 22.95 (*0-435-08954-4*, 08954) Heinemann.

Penwarden, James F., tr. see Larson, Richard P., et al, eds.

Penwell, Dan. 101 Things to Do in the Year 2000. 224p. 1999. pap. 9.99 (*1-56292-802-3*) Honor Bks OK.

Penwell, Dan, ed. World's Compact Bible Dictionary & Concordance, Slim. 96p. 1990. pap. 4.99 (*0-529-06936-9*, WDC) World Publng.

Penwell, Dan, ed. Tiny Bible Promises. 1995. kivar 1.09 (*0-529-10387-7*, TBP3); kivar 1.09 (*0-529-10388-5*, TBP3BL3); kivar 1.09 (*0-529-10389-3*, TBP3G); kivar 1.09 (*0-529-10390-7*, TBP3W); kivar 1.09 (*0-529-10391-5*, TBP3R) World Publng.

Penwell, Danny L. Bible Brain Quest. (Brain Quest Ser.). (Illus.). 150p. (J). 1997. pap. text 10.95 (*0-7611-0954-4*) Workman Pub.

Penwell, Ellen S. & Kulles, George N. The Morton D. Barker Paperweight Collection. (Handbook of Collections: No. 5). (Illus.). 72p. 1985. pap. 15.00 (*0-89792-106-2*) Ill St Museum.

Penwill, Roger. Cue Pixels - Action! Ivie, Judith, ed. (Illus.). 100p. (Orig.). 1995. pap. 9.95 (*0-9639305-1-6*) A-E-C Systs.

Penycate, John, jt. auth. see Mangold, Tom.

***Penyeh, Tsao, ed.** Tradition & Change in the Performance of Chinese Music Part 1. (Illus.). 96p. 1998. pap. text 25.00 (*90-5755-040-7*, Harwood Acad Pubs) Gordon & Breach.

— Tradition & Change in the Performance of Chinese Music Part II. (Illus.). 96p. 1998. pap. text 25.00 (*90-5755-041-5*, Harwood Acad Pubs) Gordon & Breach.

Penz. Computers in Architecture. 1992. text. write for info. (*0-582-09386-4*, Pub. by Addison-Wesley) Longman.

Penz, Alton. Finding Hidden Profits in Occupancy Analysis. 56p. (Orig.). 1989. pap. text 55.00 (*0-943130-11-5*) Build Own & Man.

Penz, Francois & Thomas, Maureen, eds. Cinema & Architecture: Melies, Mallet-Stevens, Multimedia. LC 98-111604. (Illus.). 192p. 1997. 29.95 (*0-85170-578-2*, Pub. by British Film Inst) Ind U Pr.

Penz, Kathryn & Wandersee, Claire. Living in Space. (Illus.). 48p. (J). 1997. pap. 8.00 (*0-8059-4077-4*) Dorrance.

Penza, John. Sicilian Vegetarian Cooking: 99 More Recipes You Can't Refuse. LC 96-8210. (Illus.). 160p. 1997. pap. 16.95 (*0-89815-868-0*) Ten Speed Pr.

Penza, John, et al. Sicilian American Pasta. (Illus.). 173p. 1994. pap. 16.95 (*0-89815-621-1*) Ten Speed Pr.

***Penza, Pietro & Bansal, Vipul K.** Measuring Market Risk with Value-at-Risk. LC 00-38207. (Series in Financial Engineering). (Illus.). 336p. 2000. 79.95 (*0-471-39313-4*) Wiley.

Penzato, Sadie. Growing up Sicilian & Female: "In America, in a Small Town, in the 30s" (Illus.). 336p. (Orig.). 1991. pap. 14.95 (*0-9632331-0-6*) Penzato Ent.

***Penzel, Fred.** Obsessive-Compulsive Disorders: Getting Well & Staying Well. (Illus.). 448p. 2000. 30.00 (*0-19-514092-3*) OUP.

***Penzella, Victor.** Why Johnny Can't Think (It's Electric) LC 98-90494. 1999. pap. 14.95 (*0-533-12805-6*) Vantage.

***Penzer.** Nursing Care of the Skin. 256p. 2000. pap. text 35.00 (*0-7506-2834-0*) Buttrwrth-Heinemann.

Penzer, Norman M. An Annotated Bibliography of Sir Richard Francis Burton. (Illus.). 351p. 1994. reprint ed. 75.00 (*1-888262-58-3*) Martino Pubng.

— The Harem. LC 77-180304. (Illus.). reprint ed. 49.50 (*0-404-56316-3*) AMS Pr.

— Poisen-Damsels & Other Essays in Folklore & Anthropology. Dorson, Richard M., ed. LC 80-669. (Folklore of the World Ser.). 1981. reprint ed. lib. bdg. 34.95 (*0-405-13336-7*) Ayer.

Penzer, Victor, tr. see Schimmel, Helmut W.

Penzer, William N. Getting Back up from an Emotional Down. Gross, Myra, ed. (Illus.). 256p. (Orig.). 1989. pap. 11.95 (*0-9622658-0-2*) William Penzer.

Penzer, William N. & Goodman, Bonnie. You Have Choices: Recovering from Anxiety, Panic & Phobia. Gross, Myra, ed. Orig. Title: Overcoming Anxiety, Panic, Phobias Through a Support Group. (Illus.). 256p. (Orig.). 1991. pap. 11.95 (*0-9622658-1-0*) William Penzer.

Penzes, Bethen & Tolg, Istvan. Goldfish & Ornamental Carp. 1986. pap. 16.95 (*0-8120-9286-4*) Barron.

Penzi, James. Scenes in Black & White. (Chapbook Ser.). (Illus.). 32p. (Orig.). 1982. pap. 3.00 (*0-936556-05-4*) Contact Two.

Penzias, Arno. Harmony: Business, Technology & Life after Paperwork. LC 94-47435. 320p. 1995. 23.00 (*0-88730-724-8*, HarpBusn) HarpInfo.

Penzias, Arno A. Computer Enhanced Human Beings. (Grace A. Tanner Lecture in Human Values Ser.). 29p. 1987. 7.50 (*0-910153-04-3*) E T Woolf.

Penzien, Joseph, jt. auth. see Clough, Ray W.

Penzin, Olga W. Do You See What I See? Poems for Ordinary People. 64p. 1997. pap. 5.95 (*1-890644-13-7*) Union Cnty.

Penzler, Otto. The 50 Greatest Mysteries of All Time. deluxe ed. 448p. 1996. 18.95 (*0-7871-0963-0*, NewStar Pr) NewStar Media.

— Murder for Love. 368p. 1999. mass mkt. 5.99 (*0-440-22105-6*) Dell.

— Murder for Revenge. 400p. 1999. mass mkt. 5.99 (*0-440-22321-0*) Dell.

***Penzler, Otto.** The 101 Greatest Mystery Films. 2000. per. 14.00 (*0-7434-0717-2*, Pub. by ibooks) S&S Trade.

Penzler, Otto, ed. The Best American Mystery Stories, 1998. 352p. 1998. 27.50 (*0-395-83586-0*); pap. 13.00 (*0-395-83585-2*) HM.

— The Greatest Mysteries of All Time, 4 cass., Vol. 1. abr. ed. 1996. write for info. incl. audio (*0-7871-0913-4*, Dove Audio) NewStar Media.

— Murder & Obsession: New Original Stories. LC 98-41039. 416p. 1999. 22.95 (*0-385-31800-6*) Delacorte.

***Penzler, Otto, ed.** Murder & Obsession: 15 New Original Stories. 455p. 2000. mass mkt. 5.99 (*0-440-22318-0*, Dell Trade Pbks) Dell.

Penzler, Otto, ed. Murder for Love. 1997. mass mkt. 5.50 (*0-440-22315-6*) Dell.

Penzler, Otto, et al. Detectionary. Date not set. lib. bdg. 23.95 (*0-8488-2155-6*) Amereon Ltd.

Penzler, Otto, jt. ed. see Hillerman, Tony.

Penzler, Otto, jt. ed. see Parker, Robert B.

Penzler, Otto, jt. ed. see Westlake, Donald E.

Penzlin, Gustav, jt. auth. see Fuhrhop, Jurgen-Hinrich.

Penzo, Paul A., et al, eds. AAS/AIAA Astrodynamics Conference, Jun. 25-27, 1979, Provincetown, MA, Pt. 1. LC 57-43769. (Advances in the Astronautical Sciences Ser.: Vol. 40). (Illus.). 494p. 1980. 45.00 (*0-87703-107-X*, Am Astronaut Soc); pap. 35.00 (*0-87703-108-8*, Am Astronaut Soc) Univelt Inc.

— AAS/AIAA Astrodynamics Conference, Jun. 25-27, 1979, Provincetown, MA, Pt. 2. LC 57-43769. (Advances in the Astronautical Sciences Ser.: Vol. 40). (Illus.). 502p. 1980. 45.00 (*0-87703-109-6*, Am Astronaut Soc); pap. 35.00 (*0-87703-110-X*, Am Astronaut Soc) Univelt Inc.

Penzo, Paul A., jt. ed. see Rector, William F.

***People for the Ethical Treatment of Animals Staff.** Shopping Guide for Caring Consumers, 2000 Edition. rev. ed. (Illus.). 128p. 1999. pap. 8.95 (*1-57067-089-7*) Book Pub Co.

People for the Ethical Treatment of Animals Staff. We're All Animals Coloring Book. (Illus.). 16p. (Orig.). (J). (gr. k-5). pap. text 3.35 (*0-9622101-0-2*) Peta Pubns.

People for the Ethical Treatment of Animals Staff & Newkirk, Ingrid. The Compassionate Cook: Or Please Don't Eat the Animals! A Vegetarian Cookbook. 256p. (Orig.). 1993. mass mkt. 12.95 (*0-446-39492-0*, Pub. by Warner Bks) Little.

People for the Ethical Treatment of Animals Staff, jt. auth. see Newkirk, Ingrid.

People Magazine Editors. People: Private Lives. (Annual Ser.). (Illus.). 144p. 1993. write for info. (*1-883013-00-3*) Tme Inc.

— People Entertainment Almanac, 1995. 1994. pap. 12.95 (*0-316-69885-7*) Little.

***People Magazine Staff.** People Entertainment Almanac. 610p. 2000. write for info. (*1-929049-07-2*) Tme Inc.

— People Entertainment Almanac: 2000 Edition. 608p. 1999. pap. text 11.95 (*1-883013-50-X*, People Bks) Tme Inc.

— People Yearbook, 1vol. 2000. 24.95 (*1-883013-85-2*) Tme Inc.

People of Kent Staff, photos by. From Garden to Gateway the Changing Face of Kent. (Illus.). 128p. (C). 1993. 65.00 (*1-874344-00-0*, Pub. by Heathrow Pubns) St Mut.

Peoples. Readings in Cultural Anthropology. LC 98-27936. 1998. pap. 52.95 (*0-314-02820-X*) West Pub.

Peoples & Jurmain, Robert. Anthropology for College of Misercordia. (Adaptable Courseware-Softside Ser.). Date not set. pap. 44.00 (*0-534-15956-7*) Wadsworth Pub.

People's Bridge Action Inc. Staff. All My Heroes Are Crazy. 104p. 1992. pap. 9.00 (*1-881467-00-7*) Peoples Bdge Act.

People's Court, Munich Staff & Hitler, Adolf. Hitler Trial: Before the People's Court in Munich, 3 vols., Set. Freniere, H. Francis et al, trs. LC 75-24633. 420p. 1976. lib. bdg. 150.00 (*0-313-27110-0*, U7110) Greenwood.

— Hitler Trial: Before the People's Court in Munich, 3 vols., Vol. 1. Freniere, H. Francis et al, trs. LC 75-24633. 420p. 1976. lib. bdg. 55.00 (*0-313-27111-9*, U7111) Greenwood.

— Hitler Trial: Before the People's Court in Munich, 3 vols., Vol. 2. Freniere, H. Francis et al, trs. LC 75-24633. 420p. 1976. lib. bdg. 55.00 (*0-313-27112-7*, U7112) Greenwood.

— Hitler Trial: Before the People's Court in Munich, 3 vols., Vol. 3. Freniere, H. Francis et al, trs. LC 75-24633. 420p. 1976. lib. bdg. 55.00 (*0-313-27113-5*, U7113) Greenwood.

Peoples, D. What to Expect When You're Experiencing Infertility: How to Cope with the Emotional Crisis & Survive. LC 97-42847. 288p. 1998. 25.00 (*0-393-04104-2*) Norton.

Peoples, David A. Presentations Plus: David Peoples' Proven Techniques. 2nd rev. ed. LC 92-57. 304p. 1992. 49.95 (*0-471-55926-1*) Wiley.

— Presentations Plus: David Peoples' Proven Techniques. 2nd rev. ed. LC 92-57. (Illus.). 304p. 1992. pap. 18.95 (*0-471-55956-3*) Wiley.

— Selling to the Top: David Peoples' Executive Selling Skills. LC 93-526. (Illus.). 256p. 1993. pap. 22.95 (*0-471-58105-4*) Wiley.

— Selling to the Top: David Peoples' Executive Selling Skills. LC 93-526. 256p. 1993. 55.00 (*0-471-58104-6*) Wiley.

Peoples, Debby & Ferguson, Harriette R. Experiencing Infertility: An Essential Resource. LC 99-47605. 320p. 2000. pap. 17.00 (*0-393-32000-6*, Norton Paperbks) Norton.

Peoples, Edward E. Criminal Procedures in California. 225p. 1997. pap. text 19.95 (*0-9641857-4-1*) Meadow Crest.

— Juvenile Procedures in California. 240p. (Orig.). (C). 1994. pap. text 15.95 (*0-9641857-0-9*) Meadow Crest.

— Juvenile Procedures in California. 2nd ed. 249p. (Orig.). 1996. spiral bd. write for info. (*0-9641857-2-5*) Meadow Crest.

People's Insurance Company of China Staff & Beijing Normal University Staff, compiled by. Atlas of Natural Disasters in China. (Illus.). 166p. 1996. 148.00 (*7-03-003393-0*, Pub. by Sci Pr) Lubrecht & Cramer.

Peoples, James, ed. Regulatory Reform & Labor Markets. LC 97-38459. (Recent Economic Thought Ser.: No. 61). 390p. 1997. 137.50 (*0-7923-8065-7*, D Reidel) Kluwer Academic.

Peoples, James G. Humanity: An Introduction To Cultural Antrhopology. 5th ed. LC 99-20288. (Anthropology). 1999. pap. 70.95 (*0-534-51455-3*) Wadsworth Pub.

Peoples, James G. & Bailey, Garrick A. Humanity: An Introduction to Cultural Anthropology. 4th ed. LC 96-32431. 450p. 1997. 45.00 (*0-314-20064-9*) West Pub.

Peoples, James G., jt. auth. see Bailey, Garrick.

Peoples, Lorraine. You Can Teach Someone to Read: A How-To Book for Friends, Parents & Teachers, Step by Step Detailed Directions to Provide Anyone the Necessary Tools to Easily Teach Someone to Read. (Illus.). 304p. 2000. otabind 22.95 (*0-9670984-5-9*) GLoBooks Pubg.

Peoples, M. B., et al, eds. Methods for Evaluating Nitrogen Fixation by Nodulated Legumes in the Field. 76p. 1988. pap. 81.00 (*0-949511-90-0*) St Mut.

People's Medical Society (U. S.) Staff. Dial 800 for Health. rev. ed. LC 97-12305. 128p. 1997. pap. 10.95 (*1-882606-30-2*) Peoples Med Soc.

People's Medical Society (U. S.) Staff, jt. auth. see Inlander, Charles B.

Peoples Medical Society Staff. Blood Pressure: Questions You Have, Answers You Need. LC 95-46873. 96p. 1996. pap. 9.95 (*1-882606-61-2*) Peoples Med Soc.

People's Medical Society Staff. Over-the-Counter-Doctor. (Illus.). 352p. (Orig.). 1997. pap. 14.95 (*0-614-30550-0*, Cader Bks) Andrews & McMeel.

Peoples Medical Society Staff. People's Medical Society Men's Health & Wellness Encyclopedia. 518p. 1998. pap. text 29.95 (*0-02-862295-2*) Macmillan.

People's Medical Society Staff. People's Medical Society Men's Health Desk Reference: Everything a Man Needs. LC 97-40601. 480p. 1999. 29.95 (*0-02-862153-0*) Macmillan.

— Your Complete Medical Record. 208p. 1993. pap. 12.95 (*1-882606-00-0*) Peoples Med Soc.

Peoples Medical Society Staff. Your Heart: Questions You Have--Answers You Need. 4th rev. ed. LC 95-49182. 222p. 1996. 13.95 (*1-882606-60-4*) Peoples Med Soc.

People's Medical Society Staff & Inlander, Charles B. The People's Medical Society Health Desk Reference: Information Your Doctor Can't or Won't Tell You - Everything You Need to Know for the Best in Health Care. Orig. Title: The Consumer's Medical Desk Reference. 672p. (J). 1996. pap. 19.45 (*0-7868-8167-4*, Pub. by Hyperion) Time Warner.

People's Medical Society Staff, jt. auth. see Craze, Richard.

People's Medical Society Staff, jt. auth. see Inlander, Charles B.

People's Medical Society Staff, jt. auth. see Maraldo, Pamela.

People's Medical Society Staff, jt. auth. see Norwood, Janet W.

Peoples' Publishing Group. For the People, by the People: A History of the United States, Beginnings to Present. LC 98-179276. xxvii, 708 p. 1997. 30.99 (*1-56256-091-3*) Peoples Pub Grp.

Peoples Republic of China Staff, jt. auth. see Kuo Chia T'ung Chi Chii.

People's Republic of China, State Council Staff & Chinese Academy of Sciences, Institute of the Hist, eds. The Population Atlas of China. LC 87-675262. (Illus.). 216p. 1987. text 275.00 (*0-19-584092-5*) OUP.

Peoples, Rick. Poetry with a Porpoise. (J). (gr. 1-6). 1998. 12.95 (*0-9668328-0-9*) Appenzell Pr.

— Poetry with a Porpoise. (Illus.). 128p. (J). (ps-6). 1998. reprint ed. 21.95 incl. cd-rom (*0-9668328-3-3*) Appenzell Pr.

Peoples, Susan H., ed. see Donahue, Charles.

Peoples, Susan H., ed. see Thornley, Isobel D. & Bestor, Jane F.

Peoples, Tommy. Fifty Irish Fiddle Tunes. 48p. 1986. pap. 17.95 (*0-7866-1587-7*, 95172WW) Mel Bay.

Peoples, William L. Genealogy of the Corrigan Families, Vol. 1. LC 88-62132. (Illus.). 121p. (C). 1988. write for info. (*0-9621801-1-4*) W L Peoples.

— Genealogy of the Peoples Families, Vol. 1: The Irish Genealogy of the Peoples Families. LC 88-63768. (Illus.). 116p. (C). 1988. write for info. (*0-9621801-0-6*) W L Peoples.

Peoria Newspaper Guild Staff. Peoria People. Knight, Bill, ed. (Illus.). 96p. (Orig.). 1988. pap. 5.95 (*0-9621356-0-7*) Peoria Newspaper Guild.

***Peou, Sorpong.** Cambodia: Change & Continuity in Contemporary Politics. LC 00-32270. (Illus.). 2000. write for info. (*0-7546-2119-7*, Pub. by Ashgate Pub) Ashgate Pub Co.

Peou, Sorpong. Conflict Neutralization in the Cambodia War: From Battlefield to Ballot Box. LC 96-8990. (South-East Asian Social Science Monographs). (Illus.). 380p. 1997. text 60.00 (*983-56-0011-2*) OUP.

***Peou, Sorpong.** Foreign Intervention & Regime Change in Cambodia: Prospects for Democracy. LC 99-34595. 600p. 1999. text 59.95 (*0-312-22717-5*) St Martin.

Pepe, jt. auth. see McKay.

Pepe, Edward C., ed. & tr. see Fock, Gustav.

Pepe, John, ed. see Wilson, Steven K. & Mobley, David F.

Pepe, Phil. The Wit & Wisdom of Yogi Berra. 2nd rev. ed. 150p. 1988. 16.95 (*0-88736-318-0*) Mecklermedia.

— Yankees. LC 96-233462. 240p. 1995. 39.95 (*0-87833-095-X*) Taylor Pub.

— The Yankees. LC 97-30428. (Illus.). 256p. (Orig.). 1997. pap. 24.95 (*0-87833-142-5*) Taylor Pub.

— The Yankees: An Authorized History of the New York Yankees. LC 97-30428. 1997. write for info. (*0-87833-094-1*) Taylor Pub.

— Yankees: An Authorized History of the New York Yankees, 3rd Edtion. 3rd ed. 1999. pap. text 24.95 (*0-87833-234-0*) Taylor Pub.

— Yankees: Limited. 240p. 1995. 75.00 (*0-87833-096-8*) Taylor Pub.

Pepe, Phil, jt. auth. see Hurley, Bob, Sr.

Pepe, Philip. Biology 182 Lab Guide. (C). 1995. pap. text, lab manual ed. 16.01 (*1-56870-212-4*) RonJon Pub.

Pepe, Philip S. Personal Typing 30. 5th ed. 64p. 1974. text 15.96 (*0-07-049299-9*) McGraw.

Pepe, Stephen P. & Dunham, Scott H. Avoiding & Defending Wrongful Discharge Claims, 2 vols. LC 87-10345. 1990. 210.00 (*0-685-18521-4*); suppl. ed. write for info. (*0-318-62083-9*) West Group.

***Pepelnjak, Ivan.** EIGRP Network Design Solutions. 400p. 1999. 55.00 (*1-57870-165-1*) Cisco Press.

Pepels, Werner. Kleines Lexikon Marketing-Management. (GER.). 240p. 1994. 49.95 (*0-7859-8571-9*, 3928860046) Fr & Eur.

Peper, E. & Williams, E. A. From the Inside Out: A Self-Teaching & Laboratory Manual for Biofeedback. LC 80-20551. (Illus.). 446p. (C). 1981. spiral bd. 49.50 (*0-306-40535-0*, Plenum Trade) Perseus Pubng.

Peper, E., et al. Mind/Body Integration: Essential Readings in Biofeedback. LC 78-27224. (Illus.). 606p. (C). 1979. 90.00 (*0-306-40102-9*, Plenum Trade) Perseus Pubng.

***Peper, Elisabeth.** Evaluation der Effekte und Erfolge Von Stationaren Heilfastenmaanahmen. 419p. 1999. 52.95 (*3-631-35594-7*) P Lang Pubng.

Peper, Eric & LaFontaine, Gary. Fly Fishing the Beaverkill. LC 99-13747. (River Book Ser.: No. 1). (Illus.). 128p. 1999. pap. 12.95 (*1-890373-03-6*) Greycliff Pub.

Peper, Erik & Holt, C. F. Creating Wholeness: A Self-Healing Workbook Using Dynamic Relaxation, Images, & Thoughts. (Illus.). 232p. (C). 1993. spiral bd. 37.50 (*0-306-44172-1*, Plenum Trade) Perseus Pubng.

***Peper, George.** The 500 World's Greatest Golf Holes. Golf Magazine Editors, ed. (Illus.). 448p. 2000. 60.00 (*1-57965-162-3*, 85162) Artisan.

Peper, George. Golf Courses of the PGA Tour. LC 94-4099. (Illus.). 304p. 1994. 49.50 (*0-8109-3380-2*, Pub. by Abrams) Time Warner.

— Golfwatching: A Viewer's Guide to the World of Golf. (Illus.). 272p. 1997. reprint ed. 19.98 (*0-8109-8165-3*, Pub. by Abrams) Time Warner.

— The Story of Golf. (Illus.). 224p. 1999. 45.00 (*1-57500-039-3*, Pub. by TV Bks) HarpC.

Peper, George, ed. Golf in America: The First One Hundred Years. 2nd ed. LC 94-4490. (Illus.). 304p. 1994. reprint ed. pap. 24.98 (*0-8109-8123-8*, Pub. by Abrams) Time Warner.

***Peper, George, et al.** Golf Magazine's Complete Book of Golf Instruction. (Illus.). 352p. 2000. 19.98 (*0-8109-8156-4*, Pub. by Abrams) Time Warner.

Peper, George, jt. auth. see Murray, Bill.

Peper, George, jt. auth. see Norman, Greg.

Peperzak, Adriaan. To the Other: An Introduction to the Philosophy of Emmanuel Levinas. LC 91-44845. (Series in the History of Philosophy). 240p. 1992. 45.95 (*1-55753-023-8*) Purdue U Pr.

Peperzak, Adriaan T. Before Ethics. LC 96-53420. (Contemporary Studies in Philosophy & the Human Sciences). 160p. (C). 1997. text 45.00 (*0-391-04034-0*) Humanities.

— Beyond: The Philosophy of Emmanuel Levinas. LC 97-17519. (Northwestern University Studies in Phenomenology & Existential Philosophy). 232p. 1997. 79.95 (*0-8101-1480-1*); pap. 22.50 (*0-8101-1481-X*) Northwestern U Pr.

— Ethics As First Philosophy: The Significance of Emmanuel Levinas for Philosophy, Literature, & Religion. 288p. (C). 1995. pap. 21.99 (*0-415-91143-5*, B4922) Routledge.

— Philosophy & Politics. 150p. 1986. pap. text 59.00 (*90-247-3338-3*, Pub. by M Nijhoff) Kluwer Academic.

— Philosophy & Politics. 150p. 1987. lib. bdg. 87.00 (*90-247-3337-5*, Pub. by M Nijhoff) Kluwer Academic.

— Platonic Transformations: With & after Hegel, Heider & Levinas. LC 96-46160. 280p. 1997. 71.00 (*0-8476-8428-8*); pap. 26.95 (*0-8476-8429-6*) Rowman.

— The Reason in Faith, on the Relevance of Christian Spirituality for Philosophy. LC 98-53544. 168p. 1999. pap. 15.95 (*0-8091-3857-3*) Paulist Pr.

— System & History in Philosophy: On the Unity of Thought & Time, Text & Explanation, Solitude & Dialogue, Rhetoric & Truth in the Practice of Philosophy & Its History. LC 85-27679. (SUNY Series in Contemporary Continental Philosophy). 172p. (Orig.). (C). 1986. pap. text 21.95 (*0-88706-275-X*) State U NY Pr.

Peperzak, Adriaan T., et al, eds. Emmanuel Levinas: Basic Philosophical Writings. LC 95-49540. (Studies in Continental Thought). 224p. (C). 1996. pap. 14.95 (*0-253-21079-8*); text 35.00 (*0-253-33078-5*) Ind U Pr.

Peperzak, Adrian T. Before Ethics. LC 98-54281. 1998. write for info. (*1-57392-402-4*, Humanity Bks) Prometheus Bks.

Pepetela & Wolfers, Michael. Mayombe. (African Writers Ser.). 1996. pap. 11.95 (*0-435-90595-3*) Heinemann.

Pepeu, G., jt. auth. see Hanin, I.

Pepeu, Giancarlo, et al, eds. New Trends in Aging Research. (FIDIA Research Ser.: Vol. 15). viii, 237p. 1989. 79.00 (*0-387-96911-X*) Spr-Verlag.

Pepi, Jerome S. Design Characteristics of Quick Response Sprinklers. 1986. pap. 7.50 (*0-318-22365-1*, TR 86-3) Society Fire Protect.

Pepicello, W. J. & Green, Thomas A. The Language of Riddles: New Perspectives. LC 84-3551. (Illus.). 175p. reprint ed. pap. 54.30 (*0-608-09864-7*, 206982900006) Bks Demand.

Pepin, David. Discovering Cathedrals. (Discovering Bks.: Vol. 112). (Illus.). 112p. pap. 14.75 (*0-7478-0173-8*, Pub. by Shire Pubns) Parkwest Pubns.

Pepin, David & Pepin, Susan. Oracle Resource Guide, 1994-1995. 1168p. 1994. pap. 30.00 (*0-9643092-3-8*) Visionary Sftware.

Pepin, Jacques. Good Life Cooking: Light Classics from Today's Gourmet. LC 92-27810. Orig. Title: Today's Gourmet II. (Illus.). 192p. (Orig.). 1992. pap. 15.95 (*0-912333-17-0*) BB&T Inc.

— Happy Cooking! More Light Classics from "Today's Gourmet" LC 94-29076. (Illus.). 208p. (Orig.). 1994. pap. 17.95 (*0-912333-27-8*) BB&T Inc.

— Jacques Pepin's Kitchen: Cooking with Claudine. LC 96-42377. 1996. 27.95 (*0-912333-84-7*) BB&T Inc.

— Jacques Pepin's Kitchen: Cooking with Claudine. LC 96-42377. (Illus.). 288p. 1996. pap. 18.95 (*0-912333-87-1*) BB&T Inc.

— Jacques Pepin's Kitchen: Encore with Claudine. LC 98-19862. (Illus.). 280p. 1998. 27.95 (*0-912333-86-3*, Bay-Bks) BB&T Inc.

— Jacques Pepin's Simple & Healthy Cooking. LC 94-29177. (Illus.). 354p. 1994. text 27.50 (*0-87596-234-3*) Rodale Pr Inc.

***Pepin, Jacques.** Jacques Pepin's Simple & Healthy Cooking. (Illus.). 368p. 1999. pap. 18.95 (*0-87596-362-5*) Rodale Pr Inc.

Pepin, Jacques. Jacques Pepin's Table: The Complete Today's Gourmet. LC 95-24062. (Illus.). 544p. 1995. 39.95 (*0-912333-19-7*) BB&T Inc.

— Sweet Simplicity: Jacques Pepin's Fruit Desserts. LC 99-12868. (Illus.). 224p. 1999. 29.95 (*0-912333-98-7*) BB&T Inc.

— La Technique. 1989. pap. 25.00 (*0-671-70711-6*) S&S Trade.

— Today's Gourmet: Light & Healthy Cooking for the '90s. LC 90-92204. (Illus.). 176p. (Orig.). 1991. pap. 15.95 (*0-912333-08-1*) BB&T Inc.

Pepin, Marcel, intro. Quebec Labour. 2nd rev. ed. 251p. 1972. 36.99 (*0-919618-14-6*, Pub. by Black Rose); pap. 7.99 (*0-919618-15-4*, Pub. by Black Rose) Consort Bk Sales.

Pepin, Pierre-Yves. American Stories. LC 94-77151. (Prose Ser.: No. 28). 128p. (C). 1995. pap. 10.00 (*0-920717-96-9*) Guernica Editions.

Pepin Press Design Book Staff. Hats: Hute, Chapeaux, Capelli, Sombreros, Hoeden. (Illus.). 352p. 1998. pap. 19.95 (*0-89676-231-9*, Costume & Fashion Pr) QSMG Ltd.

— 1920s Fashion Design. (Illus.). 240p. 1998. pap. 29.95 (*0-89676-232-7*, Costume & Fashion Pr) QSMG Ltd.

Pepin Press Design Book Staff, ed. Fashion Design, 1850-1895. (Illus.). 376p. (Orig.). 1997. pap. 29.95 (*0-89676-223-8*, By Design Pr) QSMG Ltd.

— A Pictorial History of Costume. (Illus.). 224p. 1998. pap. 29.95 (*0-89676-227-0*, Costume & Fashion Pr) QSMG Ltd.

Pepin, Ronald. Literature of Satire in the Twelfth Century: A Neglected Mediaeval Genre. (Studies in Medieval Literature: Vol. 2). 150p. 1989. write for info. (*0-88946-316-6*) E Mellen.

***Pepin, Ronald E.** An English Translation of Auctores Octo, a Medieval Reader. LC 99-43564. (Medieval Studies). 268p. 1999. text 89.95 (*0-7734-7951-1*) E Mellen.

Pepin, Ronald E., ed. & tr. see Bernard of Cluny.

Pepin, Ronald E., tr. see Sergardi, Lodovico.

Pepin, Susan, jt. auth. see Pepin, David.

Pepine, Carl J., et al. Diagnostic & Therapeutic Cardiac Catheterization. 3rd ed. LC 97-21511. (Illus.). 950p. 1998. 99.00 (*0-683-30125-X*) Lppncott W & W.

Pepinsky, Harold E. The Geometry of Violence & Democracy. LC 90-4704. (Illus.). 156p. 1991. 27.50 (*0-253-34343-7*) Ind U Pr.

Pepinsky, Harold E. & Jesilow, Paul. Myths That Cause Crime. 3rd rev. ed. LC 92-18307. 186p. 1992. pap. 12.95 (*0-932020-91-7*) Seven Locks Pr.

Pepinsky, Harold E. & Quinney, Richard, eds. Criminology As Peacemaking. LC 90-42361. (Illus.). 350p. 1991. 39.95 (*0-253-34357-7*); pap. 17.50 (*0-253-20659-6*, MB-659) Ind U Pr.

— Criminology as Peacemaking. LC 90-42361. (Illus.). 348p. Date not set. reprint ed. pap. 107.90 (*0-608-20567-2*, 205448100002) Bks Demand.

Pepinsky, Pauline N. Worlds of Common Sense: Equality, Identity & Two Modes of Impulse Management, 26. LC 94-7432. (Contributions in Psychology Ser.: No. 26). 232p. 1994. 62.95 (*0-313-28991-3*, Greenwood Pr) Greenwood.

Pepitone, James S. Future Training: A Roadmap for Restructuring the Training Function. 250p. 1995. pap. 18.50 (*0-9635822-1-6*) AddVantage Lrn.

***Pepitone, James S.** Human Performance Consulting: Transforming Human Potential into Productive Business Performance. (Improving Human Performance Ser.). 280p. 2000. 37.95 (*0-87719-352-5*) Gulf Pub.

Pepitone, James S. & Barker, Edwin N. How to Make a Smart Decision - A True Story. 122p. 1992. pap. 7.95 (*0-9635822-0-8*) AddVantage Lrn.

Pepitone, James S., jt. auth. see Bruce, Anne.

Pepitone-Rockwell, Fran, ed. Dual-Career Couples. LC 80-15747. (Sage Focus Editions Ser.: No. 24). 294p. 1980. reprint ed. pap. 91.20 (*0-608-01127-4*, 205943100001) Bks Demand.

Peplau, Hildegard E. Interpersonal Relations in Nursing: A Conceptual Frame of Reference for Psychodynamic Nursing. LC 91-4846. 360p. 1991. 41.95 (*0-8261-7910-X*) Springer Pub.

Peplau, Letitia A. Gender, Culture & Ethnicity: Current Research about Women & Men. LC 98-19788. xii,363p. 1998. pap. text 29.95 (*0-7674-0521-8*) Mayfield Pub.

Peplau, Letitia A. & Perlman, Daniel, eds. Loneliness: A Sourcebook of Current Theory, Research, & Therapy. LC 81-16272. (Wiley Series on Personality Processes). 447p. reprint ed. pap. 138.60 (*0-7837-2807-7*, 205766500006) Bks Demand.

Peplau, Letitia A. & Taylor, Shelley E. Sociocultural Perspectives in Solcial Psychology: Current Readings. LC 96-36173. 411p. 1996. pap. text 37.00 (*0-13-241860-6*) P-H.

Pepler, C. The Basis of the Mysticism of St. Thomas Aquinas. 1977. lib. bdg. 59.95 (*0-8490-1479-4*) Gordon Pr.

Pepler, Debra & Rubin, Kenneth H., eds. The Development & Treatment of Childhood Aggression. 488p. 1991. 95.00 (*0-8058-0370-X*) L Erlbaum Assocs.

Peploe, Frances. Love Untangled. large type ed. (Linford Romance Library). 1989. pap. 16.99 (*0-7089-6789-2*, Linford) Ulverscroft.

Peplow, Elizabeth. Encyclopedia of the Horse. LC 98-29371. 1998. 19.98 (*1-57145-165-X*, Thunder Bay) Advantage Pubs.

Peplow, Evelyn. The Philippines. 3rd ed. LC 98-53867. (Odyssey Passport Ser.). (Illus.). 360p. 1999. pap. 19.95 (*962-217-614-3*) Norton.

— The Philippines: Tropical Paradise. (Asian Guides Ser.). (Illus.). 316p. 1994. pap. 15.95 (*0-8442-9690-2*, Passprt Bks) NTC Contemp Pub Co.

— Philippines: Tropical Paradise. 2nd ed. (Asia Guides Ser.). (Illus.). 316p. 1997. pap. 17.95 (*0-8442-4854-1*, 48541, Passprt Bks) NTC Contemp Pub Co.

Peplow, Mary, jt. ed. see Shipley, Debra.

Peponi, Inc. Staff. Beanosaurs Collectors Book. (Illus.). 32p. (J). (ps up). 1998. pap. 6.00 (*0-9662990-0-0*) Peponi Inc.

Pepose, Jay S., ed. see Holland, Gary, et al.

Peppall. Theory & Practice of Industrial Organizations. LC 98-2649. (HU - Industrial Organization Ser.). 1998. pap. 97.95 (*0-538-85948-2*) S-W Pub.

Peppard, Joe. Essence of Business Process Re-Engineering. 224p. (C). 1995. pap. text 19.95 (*0-13-310707-8*, Pub. by P-H) S&S Trade.

Peppard, Judy. Guide to Connected Curriculum & Action Research. LC 97-134937. 122p. (Orig.). 1997. pap. text 27.00 (*1-57337-037-1*, 7177) WI Dept Pub Instruct.

Peppard, Nancy R. Special Needs Dementia Units: Design, Development & Operations. LC 91-12278. 152p. 1991. 29.95 (*0-8261-5950-8*) Springer Pub.

Peppard, Victor. The Poetics of Yury Olesha. (University of Florida Humanities Monographs: No. 63). 176p. 1989. 49.95 (*0-8130-0950-2*) U Press Fla.

Peppas, Nicholas A., et al, eds. Polymer-Inorganic Interfaces II. (Symposium Proceedings Ser.: Vol. 385). 255p. 1995. text 74.00 (*1-55899-288-X*) Materials Res.

Peppas, Nicholas A. & Langer, R. S., eds. Biopolymers II. (Advances in Polymer Science Ser.: Vol.122). (Illus.). 379p. 1995. 188.95 (*3-540-58788-8*) Spr-Verlag.

Peppas, Nicholas A., jt. ed. see Buchholz, Fredric L.

Peppas, Nicholas A., jt. ed. see Cooper, Stuart L.

Peppas, Nikolaos A., ed. Hydrogels in Medicine & Pharmacy, Vol. I: Fundamentals. 192p. 1986. 112.00 (*0-8493-5546-X*, R857, CRC Reprint) Franklin.

— Hydrogels in Medicine & Pharmacy, Vol. II: Polymers. LC 86-4195. 184p. 1987. 107.00 (*0-8493-5547-8*, R857) Franklin.

— Hydrogels in Medicine & Pharmacy, Vol. III: Properties & Applications. 240p. 1987. 120.00 (*0-8493-5548-6*, CRC Reprint) Franklin.

Peppe, Holly, ed. & intro. see Millay, Edna St. Vincent.

Peppe, Rodney. The Magic Toy Box. LC 95-26136. (Illus.). 32p. (J). (ps-k). 1996. 15.99 (*0-7636-0010-5*) Candlewick Pr.

***Peppe, Rodney.** Three Little Pigs. 2000. pap. write for info. (*0-688-17718-2*, Wm Morrow) Morrow Avon.

Pepper. Communicating in Organizations. 1994. 20.93 (*0-07-049287-5*) McGraw.

Pepper, A. T., jt. ed. see Currie, J. C.

Pepper, Allan. Managing the Training & Development Function. 350p. 1994. 83.95 (*0-566-02977-4*, Pub. by Gower) Ashgate Pub Co.

Pepper, Art & Pepper, Laurie. Straight Life: The Story of Art Pepper. 2nd rev. ed. (Illus.). 610p. 1994. reprint ed. pap. 17.95 (*0-306-80558-8*) Da Capo.

Pepper, Barbara, jt. auth. see Levy, Jerrold E.

Pepper, Barrie. International Book of Beer: A Guide to the World's Most Popular Drink, 1. 1998. 16.98 (*1-880908-46-8*) Todtri Prods.

***Pepper, Barrie.** The International Book of Beer: A Guide to the World's Most Popular Drink. (Illus.). 143p. 2000. reprint ed. 25.00 (*0-7881-9259-0*) DIANE Pub.

Pepper, Bert & Ryglewicz, Hilary. Lost Souls: Helping Young Adult Chronic Patients. 300p. 1996. 29.95 (*0-02-924965-1*) Free Pr.

Pepper, Bert & Ryglewicz, Hilary, eds. The Young Adult Chronic Patient. LC 81-48483. (New Directions for Mental Health Services Ser.: No. MHS 14). 1982. pap. 25.00 (*0-87589-908-0*) Jossey-Bass.

Pepper, Bert, jt. auth. see Ryglewicz, Hilary.

Pepper Bird Staff. Copasetic: Adventures of Bojangles Robinson. (Multicultural Historical Fiction Ser.). (Illus.). 48p. (Orig.). (J). (gr. 4-7). 1993. pap. 3.95 (*1-56817-000-9*) Pepper Bird.

— Frozen Fury: Adventures of Matthew Henson. (Multicultural Historical Fiction Ser.). (Illus.). 48p. (Orig.). (J). (gr. 4-7). 1993. pap. 4.95 (*1-56817-001-7*) Pepper Bird.

— Pea Island Rescue. (Multicultural Historical Fiction Ser.). (Illus.). 48p. (Orig.). (J). (gr. 4-7). 1993. pap. 4.95 (*1-56817-002-5*) Pepper Bird.

— Wild Frontier: Adventures of Jean Baptiste Du Sable. (Multicultural Historical Fiction Ser.). (Illus.). 48p. (Orig.). (J). (gr. 4-7). 1993. pap. 4.95 (*1-56817-003-3*) Pepper Bird.

Pepper, Bob. Mother Goose Favorites: With Matching Foam Play Pieces. 8p. (J). 1999. 9.99 (*1-58476-002-8*) Innovative Kids.

***Pepper, Choral.** Baja's Vanishing Missions, Mysteries & Myths. Lindsay, Lowell, ed. (Illus.). 160p. 2000. pap. 14.95 (*0-932653-40-5*) Sunbelt Pubns.

Pepper, Choral. Desert Lore of Southern California. 2nd rev. ed. LC 98-27669. (Illus.). 192p. 1999. pap. 14.95 (*0-932653-26-X*) Sunbelt Pubns.

— Western Treasure Tales. LC 97-48731. (Illus.). 144p. 1998. pap. 17.50 (*0-87081-489-3*) Univ Pr Colo.

Pepper, Choral, jt. auth. see Williams, Brad.

An Asterisk (*) at the beginning of an entry indicates that the title is appearing for the first time.

Pepper, Christina A., ed. see Munzert, Alfred W.

Pepper, Claude D. & Gorey, Hays. Pepper: Eyewitness to a Century. 1987. 17.95 (*0-15-171695-1*) Harcourt.

***Pepper, Clayton.** Church Growth Today. unabridged ed. 244p. 1998. pap. 14.95 (*0-89137-120-6*, 71206) Quality Pubns.

Pepper, Clayton. First Steps in Faith. 1982. pap. 4.35 (*0-89137-206-7*) Quality Pubns.

Pepper, Clayton, ed. Introduction to Soul Winning. 1982. pap. 4.35 (*0-89137-204-0*) Quality Pubns.

— Total Evangelism. 1982. pap. 4.35 (*0-89137-203-2*) Quality Pubns.

Pepper, Clayton, jt. ed. see Dyer, Jerry.

Pepper, Clement. Digital IC Gallery. LC 98-67315. (Illus.). 304p. 1999. pap. 39.95 (*0-7906-1167-8*) Prompt Publns.

Pepper, Clement S. Build Your Own Home Lab. LC 97-69162. (Illus.). 314p. 1997. pap. 29.95 (*0-7906-1108-2*) Prompt Publns.

Pepper, Corey & Porter, Stephen. Best of Times: Lyrics & Score. 1997. pap. 35.00 (*0-88734-039-3*) Players Pr.

Pepper, Corey & Porter, Steven. The Best of Times. 98p. (Orig.). 1996. pap. 35.00 (*0-88734-038-5*) Players Pr.

Pepper, D. W., et al, eds. ASME Heat Transfer Division: Proceedings, ASME International Mechanical Engineering Congress & Exposition, Atlanta, GA, 1996, Vol. 4. LC 96-78665. (HTD Ser.: Vol. 335). 424p. 1996. pap. 110.00 (*0-7918-1523-4*, QC320) ASME.

Pepper, D. W. & Heinrich, Juan C. Finite Element Methods: Basic Concepts & Applications. (Computational Methods in Mechanics & Thermal Sciences Ser.). 250p. 1992. 62.95 incl. disk (*1-56032-104-0*) Hemisp Pub.

Pepper, D. W., jt. auth. see Baker, A. J.

Pepper, D. W., jt. auth. see Heinrich, Juan C.

Pepper, D. W., jt. ed. see Blackwell, B.

Pepper, David. Eco-Socialism: From Deep Ecology to Social Justice. LC 93-16565. 288p. (C). (gr. 13). 1993. pap. 25.99 (*0-415-09719-3*, B2347); text 49.95 (*0-415-09718-5*, B2343) Routledge.

— Modern Environmentalism: An Introduction. (Illus.). 384p. (C). 1996. pap. 25.99 (*0-415-05745-0*) Routledge.

— The Roots of Modern Environmentalism. LC 84-19867. 246p. 1986. pap. text 19.95 (*0-685-30336-5*, Pub. by C Helm) Routldge.

***Pepper, David M., ed.** Process Control & Sensors for Manufacturing II. 188p. 1999. pap. text 62.00 (*0-8194-3059-5*) SPIE.

Pepper, David M., jt. ed. see Bossi, Richard H.

Pepper, Dennis. The Oxford Christmas Storybook. (Illus.). 166p. (J). (gr. 1-5). 1998. reprint ed. pap. 12.95 (*0-19-278136-7*) OUP.

— The Young Oxford Book of Aliens. LC 99-184108. (Illus.). 224p. (J). (gr. 4-7). 1999. 22.95 (*0-19-278155-3*) OUP.

— The Young Oxford Book of Nasty Endings. (Illus.). 224p. (YA). 2000. pap. 12.95 (*0-19-278158-8*) OUP.

Pepper, Dennis, ed. The New Young Oxford Book of Ghost Stories. (Illus.). 224p. (YA). (gr. 8 up). 1999. 22.95 (*0-19-278154-5*) OUP.

***Pepper, Dennis, ed.** The New Young Oxford Book of Ghost Stories, 2 vols., Vol. 2. (Illus.). 224p. (YA). 2000. pap. 12.95 (*0-19-278178-2*) OUP.

Pepper, Dennis, ed. The Oxford Book of Animal Stories. (Illus.). 304p. (YA). (gr. 5-9). 1999. pap. 12.95 (*0-19-278160-X*) OUP.

— The Oxford Book of Christmas Stories. (Illus.). 224p. (YA). 1999. pap. 12.95 (*0-19-278161-8*) OUP.

— The Oxford Book of Scary Tales. (J). Date not set. 14.95 (*0-614-19310-9*) OUP.

***Pepper, Dennis, ed.** The Young Oxford Book of Aliens. (Illus.). 224p. (YA). 2000. pap. 12.95 (*0-19-278177-4*) OUP.

Pepper, Dennis, ed. The Young Oxford Book of Ghost Stories. (Illus.). 320p. (YA). (gr. 5 up). 1997. pap. 14.95 (*0-19-278145-6*) OUP.

Pepper, Dennis, selected by. The Oxford Book of Animal Stories. LC 94-234038. (Illus.). 320p. (YA). (gr. 4 up). 1994. 25.00 (*0-19-278134-0*) OUP.

Pepper, Doug, ed. see Kozol, Jonathan.

Pepper, Edith. Lessons from the Field: Unlocking Economic Potential with an Environmental Key - 20 Case Studies. 230p. 1997. pap. 40.00 (*1-882061-64-0*) Northeast-Midwest.

***Pepper, Elizabeth.** Celtic Tree Magic. (Illus.). 2000. pap. 6.95 (*1-881098-13-3*) Witches Almanac.

— Witches' Almanac: The Complete Guide to Lunar Harmony. 2001. pap. 7.95 (*1-881098-16-8*) Witches Almanac.

Pepper, Elizabeth. Witches' Almanac (Spring 1999-Spring 2000) The Complete Guide to Lunar Harmony. 96p. 1999. pap. text 7.95 (*1-881098-08-7*, Pub. by Witches Almanac); pap. text 95.40 (*1-881098-09-5*) Witches Almanac.

***Pepper, Elizabeth.** Witches Almanac 2000-2001: The Complete Guide to Lunar Harmony. 2000. pap. 7.95 (*1-881098-10-9*) Witches Almanac.

Pepper, Elizabeth & Wilcock, John. Magical & Mystical Sites: Europe & the British Isles. LC 92-28748. (Illus.). 304p. 2000. reprint ed. pap. 16.95 (*0-933999-44-5*) Phanes Pr.

— The Witches' Almanac: Aries, 1992 to Pisces, 1993. (Illus.). 96p. 1992. 5.95 (*1-881098-00-1*) Witches Almanac.

— The Witches Almanac: Complete Astrological Guide, Spring 1995 to Spring 1996. 1995. pap. text 6.95 (*1-881098-06-0*) Witches Almanac.

— The Witches' Almanac: Spring 1993 to Spring 1994. 1992. pap. 5.95 (*1-881098-02-8*) Witches Almanac.

***Pepper, Gene.** Business Owners Manual.Com: The Secrets to a Profitable Company. 120p. 1999. pap. 18.95 (*1-891689-78-9*) Gabriel Pubns.

Pepper, George B. The Boston Heresy Case in View of the Secularization of Religion: A Case Study in the Sociology of Religion. LC 88-9311. (Studies in Religion & Society: Vol. 18). 260p. 1988. lib. bdg. 89.95 (*0-88946-856-7*) E Mellen.

Pepper, George H. Pueblo Bonito. 398p. 1996. 45.00 (*0-8263-1735-9*); pap. 19.95 (*0-8263-1736-7*) U of NM Pr.

Pepper, George H. & Wilson, Gilbert L. Hidatsa Shrine & the Beliefs Respecting It. LC 09-5503. (American Anthropological Association Memoirs Ser.). 1908. pap. 25.00 (*0-527-00509-6*) Periodicals Srv.

Pepper, Gerald L. Communicating in Organizations: A Cultural Approach. LC 94-6694. 314p. (C). 1994. pap. 48.13 (*0-07-049286-7*) McGraw.

Pepper, G.H., et al. Indian Notes. (Museum of the American Indian, Heye Foundation - Quarterly Ser.: No. 1:4). (Illus.). 94p. (C). 1924. pap. text 10.31 (*1-55567-755-X*) Coyote Press.

Pepper, Gordon T. Inside Thatcher's Monetarist Revolution. LC 97-28271. 224p. 1998. text 65.00 (*0-312-21040-X*) St Martin.

— Money, Credit & Inflation: An Historical Indictment of U. K. Monetary Policy & a Proposal for Change. (IEA Research Monographs: No. 44). 80p. (Orig.). (C). 1991. pap. 19.95 (*0-255-36228-5*, Pub. by Inst Economic Affairs) Coronet Bks.

Pepper, Howard. Children - Standing Them on Our Shoulders: Family & Church in a Nurturing Network. LC 92-62036. 183p. (Orig.). 1993. pap. 9.95 (*0-9634519-2-8*) Nurture Pr.

Pepper, Ian L., et al, eds. Environmental Microbiology: A Laboratory Manual. LC 95-23680. (Illus.). 179p. 1995. pap., lab manual ed. 32.00 (*0-12-550655-4*) Acad Pr.

— Pollution Science. LC 96-12826. (Illus.). 397p. 1996. text 63.00 (*0-12-550660-0*) Acad Pr.

Pepper, James, ed. & intro. see Welles, Orson.

Pepper, Jan, ed. Opening: Selected Writings of William Segal, 1985-1997. LC 80-5337. 172p. (C). 1998. 25.00 (*0-8264-1103-7*) Continuum.

Pepper, Jane G. Jane Pepper's Garden: Getting the Most Pleasure & Growing Results from Your Garden Every Month of the Year. LC 96-44183. (Illus.). 224p. (Orig.). 1997. pap. 14.95 (*0-940159-39-2*) Camino Bks.

Pepper, Jeff, ed. Smart Support: How to Transform Your Support Organization by Leveraging What You Know. LC 98-89841. (Illus.). 118p. 1999. pap. 49.00 (*0-9668901-0-8*) ServiceWare.

Pepper, Jeff, ed. see Soucie, Ralph.

Pepper, Jeffrey. The Golden Retriever. (Dog Breed Ser.: No. 3). (Illus.). 320p. 1984. 23.95 (*0-87666-668-3*, PS-786) TFH Pubns.

— Petit Basset Griffon Vendeen. (KW Ser.). (Illus.). 192p. 1993. text 9.95 (*0-86622-578-1*, KW-208) TFH Pubns.

Pepper, John. How to Be Happy. 3rd ed. 166p. 1992. reprint ed. pap. write for info. (*0-946551-79-0*) ACCESS Pubs Network.

— Seeing the Light: The Art of Becoming Beautiful. LC 93-36316. 1994. pap. 11.95 (*1-85230-445-6*, Pub. by Element MA) Penguin Putnam.

Pepper, Laurie, jt. auth. see Pepper, Art.

***Pepper, Letitia.** Handling Civil Appeals Pts. 1 & 2: Spring 2000 Action Guide, 2 vols., Set. Waxman, Robert, ed. 140p. 2000. pap. 58.00 (*0-7626-0426-3*) Cont Ed Bar-CA.

Pepper, Mae J., jt. auth. see Leddy, Susan.

Pepper, Margot. At This Very Moment - En Este Preciso Momento. Clarke, Ben, ed. Lopez, Adriana F. & Torres, Javier, trs. (Poetry & Prose from San Francisco's Tenderloin District Ser.). (ENG & SPA., Illus.). 77p. (Orig.). 1992. pap. text 5.95 (*0-9625153-3-7*) Freedom Voices Pubns.

Pepper, P., ed. Program Transformation & Programming Environments. (NATO ASI Series F: Computer & Systems Sciences, Special Programme AET: No. 8). 400p. 1984. 82.95 (*0-387-12932-4*) Spr-Verlag.

***Pepper, Rachel.** The Ultimate Guide to Pregnancy for Lesbians: Tips & Techniques from Conception Through Birth - How to Stay Sane & Care for Yourself. LC 99-22669. (Illus.). 200p. 1999. pap. 14.95 (*1-57344-080-9*, Pub. by Cleis Pr) Publishers Group.

Pepper, Richard. Sounds for Sax Vol. 2: Alto - Tenor. 1984. pap. 8.95 (*0-7119-2056-7*, CH55658) Shawnee Pr.

Pepper, Robert C. & Nordgren, Mary J. Behavioral Vision: A Multi-Sensory Approach to Processing Information & Learning. LC 98-14541. (Illus.). 100p. 1998. pap. 39.95 (*0-943599-95-4*) OEPF.

Pepper, Robert D., ed. Four Tudor Books on Education. LC 66-10027. 270p. 1976. lib. bdg. 50.00 (*0-8201-1271-2*) Schol Facsimiles.

Pepper, Robert M. The Formation of the Public Broadcasting Service. Sterling, Christopher H., ed. LC 78-21732. (Dissertations in Broadcasting Ser.). 1980. lib. bdg. 37.95 (*0-405-11769-8*) Ayer.

Pepper, Roger S. Pressure Groups among "Small Businessmen" Bruchey, Stuart & Carosso, Vincent P., eds. LC 78-18973. (Small Business Enterprise in America Ser.). 1979. lib. bdg. 15.95 (*0-405-11476-1*) Ayer.

Pepper, Simon & Adams, Nicholas. Firearms & Fortifications: Military Architecture & Siege Warfare in Sixteenth Century Siena. LC 85-24673. (Illus.). 272p. 1996. 29.95 (*0-226-65534-2*) U Ch Pr.

Pepper, Stephen. Bob Jones University Collection of Religious Art: Italian Paintings. (Illus.). 336p. (Orig.). 1984. pap. 55.00 (*0-89084-263-9*) Bob Jones Univ.

Pepper, Stephen C. Aesthetic Quality: A Contextualistic Theory of Beauty. LC 79-110052. 255p. 1970. reprint ed. lib. bdg. 45.00 (*0-8371-4437-X*, PEAQ, Greenwood Pr) Greenwood.

— World Hypotheses: A Study in Evidence. (C). 1970. pap. 18.95 (*0-520-00994-0*, Pub. by U CA Pr) Cal Prin Full Svc.

Pepper, Suzanne. China's Education Reform in the 1980s: Policies, Issues, & Historical Perspectives, No. 36. (China Research Monographs). 195p. (Orig.). 1990. pap. 12.00 (*1-55729-020-2*) IEAS.

— China's Universities: Post-Mao Enrollment Policies & Their Impact on the Structure of Secondary Education. LC 83-25277. (Michigan Monographs in Chinese Studies: No. 46). xvi, 155p. (C). 1984. text 30.00 (*0-89264-050-2*); pap. text 15.00 (*0-89264-046-4*) Ctr Chinese Studies.

— Radicalism & Education Reform in 20th-Century China: The Search for an Ideal Development Model. (Illus.). ix, 610p. (C). 1996. text 59.95 (*0-521-49669-1*) Cambridge U Pr.

***Pepper, Suzanne.** Radicalism & Education Reform in 20th-Century China: The Search for an Ideal Development Model. (Illus.). 609p. (C). 1999. pap. 24.95 (*0-521-77860-3*) Cambridge U Pr.

Pepper, Suzanne, ed. Civil War in China: The Political Struggle, 1945-1949. LC 99-10885. 544p. 1999. 69.00 (*0-8476-9133-0*); pap. 29.95 (*0-8476-9134-9*) Rowman.

Pepper, Terence. Dorothy Wilding, The Pursuit of Perfection. (Illus.). 120p. 1991. 35.00 (*1-85514-052-7*, Pub. by Natl Port Gall) Antique Collect.

— Lewis Morley: Photographer of the '60s. (Illus.). 96p. 1989. pap. 29.50 (*1-85514-003-9*, Pub. by Natl Port Gall) Antique Collect.

— Limelight: Photographs by James Abbe. (Illus.). 120p. 1996. pap. 18.95 (*1-85514-176-0*, Pub. by Natl Port Gall) Antique Collect.

Pepper, Terence, jt. auth. see Gibson, Robin.

Pepper, Thomas. Singularities: Extremes of Theory in the Twentieth Century. (Literature, Culture, Theory Ser.: No. 22). 268p. (C). 1997. text 64.95 (*0-521-57382-3*); pap. text 19.95 (*0-521-57478-1*) Cambridge U Pr.

Pepper, Thomas, ed. Yale French Studies, 93: The Place of Maurice Blanchot. Vol. 93. 224p. 1998. 18.00 (*0-300-07375-5*) Yale U Pr.

Pepper, Thomas, et al. The Competition: Dealing with Japan. LC 85-6304. 396p. 1985. 55.00 (*0-275-91754-1*, C1754, Praeger Pubs) Greenwood.

Pepper, Timothy, jt. auth. see Beattie, Andrew.

Pepper, Wendy J. Travel-Concerning Health Benefits & Dangers, Risks, Warnings & Strategies for Survival & Enjoyment: Index of New Information. (Illus.). 150p. 1994. 47.50 (*0-7883-0016-4*); pap. 44.50 (*0-7883-0017-2*) ABBE Pubs Assn.

Pepper, William. The Medical Side of Benjamin Franklin. (Illus.). 137p. 1970. reprint ed. 15.00 (*0-87266-039-7*) Argosy.

— Orders to Kill: The Truth about the Murder of Martin Luther King. (Illus.). 576p. 1995. 28.00 (*0-7867-0253-2*) Carroll & Graf.

Pepper, William F. Orders to Kill: The Truth Behind the Murder of Martin Luther King. LC 97-26202. 592p. 1998. mass mkt. 16.00 (*0-446-67394-3*, Pub. by Warner Bks) Little.

Pepperberg, Irene M. The Alex Studies: Cognitive & Communicative Abilities in Grey Parrots. LC 99-29630. 448p. 2000. 39.95 (*0-674-00051-X*) HUP.

Peppercorn, David. Les Vins de Bordeaux. (FRE.). 312p. 1993. lib. bdg. 49.95 (*0-7859-3635-1*, 2082005755) Fr & Eur.

— Wines of Bordeaux. (Mitchell Beazley Pocket Guides Ser.). (Illus.). 176p. 1998. write for info. (*1-84000-017-1*, Pub. by Mitchell Beazley) Antique Collect.

***Peppercorn, David.** The Wines of Bordeaux. (Illus.). 248p. 2000. 14.95 (*1-84000-250-6*, Pub. by Mitchell Beazley) Antique Collect.

Peppercorn, Lisa M. Villa-Lobos. (Illustrated Lives of the Great Composers Ser.). (Illus.). 144p. 1996. 17.95 (*0-7119-1688-8*, OP 45061) Omnibus NY.

Peppercorn, Lisa M. Villa-Lobos: Collected Studies by L. M. Peppercorn. 200p. 1992. 86.95 (*0-85967-906-3*, Pub. by Scolar Pr) Ashgate Pub Co.

— Villa-Lobos the Music: An Analysis of His Style. De Haan, Stefan, tr. 136p. 1992. 21.75 (*0-912483-36-9*) Pro-Am Music.

— The World of Villa-Lobos in Pictures & Documents. LC 95-44199. (Illus.). 336p. 1997. 61.95 (*1-85928-261-X*, Pub. by Scolar Pr) Ashgate Pub Co.

Peppercorn, Mark A. Contemporary Diagnosis & Management of Ulcerative Colitis & Proctitis. LC 94-74425. 1995. pap. 39.95 (*1-884065-08-2*) Assocs in Med.

Pepperday, Mike. Celestial Navigation with the S Table: A Complete Sight Reduction Method for All Bodies in Nine Pages. (Illus.). 32p. (Orig.). 1992. reprint ed. pap. 9.95 (*0-939837-09-9*) Paradise Cay Pubns.

Pepperell, Robert. Beyond Chaos: The Post-Human Condition. 224p. (Orig.). 1994. pap. text 22.95 (*1-871516-45-5*, Pub. by Intellect) Cromland.

***Pepperl, Jo-Ann Cipriano & Lezotte, Lawrence W.** What the Effective Schools Research Says: Safe & Orderly Environment. 110p. 1999. pap. 28.00 (*1-883247-14-4*) Effect Schls.

Pepperl, Jo-Ann Cipriano, jt. auth. see Lezotte, Lawrence W.

Peppers, jt. auth. see Jensen.

Peppers, Cheryl, jt. auth. see Briskin, Alan.

***Peppers, Don.** One to One B2B. 2001. 22.95 (*0-385-49409-2*) Doubleday.

Peppers, Don & Rogers, Martha. Enterprise One to One. 464p. 1999. pap. 15.95 (*0-385-48755-X*) Doubleday.

— The One to One Future: Building Relationships One Customer at a Time. 464p. 1996. pap. 17.95 (*0-385-48566-2*) Doubleday.

— The One to One Manager: A Management Guide to Implementing a 1-to-1 Customer Relationship. LC 99-26835. 288p. 1999. 21.95 (*0-385-49408-4*) Doubleday.

Peppers, Don, et al. The One to One Fieldbook: The Complete Toolkit for Implementing a Tool Marketing Program. LC 98-38165. 432p. 1999. pap. 19.95 (*0-385-49369-X*) Doubleday.

Peppers, Jerome G. History of United States Military Logistics 1935-1985. Crowe, Elizabeth P. & Nesmith, Alisa A., eds. (Illus.). 300p. (Orig.). (C). 1988. pap. text 27.95 (*0-945488-00-9*) Soc Logistics Engrs.

Peppers, Larry C., jt. auth. see Bails, Dale G.

Peppers, Larry G. & Knapp, Ronald J. Motherhood & Mourning: Perinatal Death. LC 80-286. 165p. 1980. 49.95 (*0-275-91760-6*, C1760, Praeger Pubs) Greenwood.

Peppers, Russel A. Palynological Correlation of Major Pennsylvanian (Middle & Upper Carboniferous) Chronostratigraphic Boundaries in the Illinois & Other Coal Basins. (Memoir Ser.: No. 188). (Illus.). 1996. 55.00 (*0-8137-1188-6*) Geol Soc.

Peppiatt, Michael. Francis Bacon: Anatomy of an Enigma. LC 97-7554. (Illus.). 366p. 1997. text 30.00 (*0-374-10494-8*) FS&G.

— Francis Bacon: Anatomy of an Enigma. 1998. pap. text 20.00 (*0-8133-3520-5*, Pub. by Westview) HarpC.

Peppin, Anthea. Nature in Art. (YA). 1992. pap. 6.70 (*0-395-64555-7*) HM.

— Nature in Art. LC 91-35014. (Millbrook Arts Library). (Illus.). 48p. (J). (gr. 2-6). 1992. lib. bdg. 22.90 (*1-56294-173-9*) Millbrook Pr.

— Nature in Art. (Millbrook Arts Library). 1992. 14.15 (*0-606-02804-8*, Pub. by Turtleback) Demco.

— People in Art. (J). (gr. 4-7). 1992. pap. 6.70 (*0-395-64556-5*) HM.

— People in Art. LC 91-34983. (Millbrook Arts Library). (Illus.). 48p. (J). (gr. 2-6). 1992. pap. 8.95 (*1-56294-818-0*) Millbrook Pr.

— Places in Art. (J). (gr. 4-7). 1992. pap. 6.70 (*0-395-64557-3*) HM.

— Places in Art. LC 91-34978. (Millbrook Arts Library). (Illus.). 48p. (J). (gr. 2-6). 1992. pap. 8.95 (*1-56294-819-9*); lib. bdg. 22.90 (*1-56294-172-0*) Millbrook Pr.

— Story of Painting. (Fine Arts Ser.). (Illus.). 32p. (J). (gr. 5 up). 1980. pap. 6.95 (*86020-441-3*); lib. bdg. 14.95 (*0-88110-030-7*) EDC.

Peppin, Anthea, jt. auth. see Armstrong, Carole.

Pepping, Ernst. Seven Pieces for SATB Recorders. Ballinger, Peter, ed. (Contemporary Consort Ser.: No. 4). 34p. 1989. pap. text 10.00 (*1-56571-009-6*) PRB Prods.

Peppis, Paul. In Literature, Politics & the English Avant-Garde: Nation & Empire, 1901-1918. LC 99-22648. (Illus.). 243p. (C). 2000. 59.95 (*0-521-66238-9*) Cambridge U Pr.

***Pepple, Scott.** CCNA Study System: Routing & Switching. (Illus.). 350p. 2000. pap. text 39.99 (*0-7645-4717-8*) IDG Bks.

Pepple, Ted. Expect a Miracle: The Story of Matt Young - A Quadriplegic's Amazing Comeback & the Incredible Faith that Made It Happen. 150p. 1991. pap. 11.95 (*0-9630054-0-5*) T Pepple.

***Pepple, Ted.** The Last Face-Off: The Doug Wickenheiser Story. (Illus.). 72p. 2000. 20.00 (*0-9655980-1-2*) T Pepple.

Pepple, Ted. Walking on Water: Reflections on Life & Faith from a Writer's Notebook. 112p. (Orig.). 1997. pap. 7.95 (*0-9655980-0-4*) T Pepple.

Pepple, Ted, ed. see Arteaga, Robert.

Peppler, Cord. Die Borstgrasrasen (Nardetalia) Westdeutschlands. (Dissertationes Botanicae Ser.: Band 193). (GER., Illus.). vi, 205p. 1992. pap. 112.00 (*3-443-64105-9*, Pub. by Gebruder Borntraeger) Balogh.

Peppler, Ellen & Wellington, Charmaine E., frwds. Emerald Coast Review Vol. IV: West Florida Authors & Artists. (Illus.). 192p. 1991. pap. 9.95 (*0-614-20060-1*) W FL Lit Fed.

Peppler, Ellen G., ed. see Hood, Mary A.

Peppler, Henry J., ed. Microbial Technology. LC 67-26866. 464p. reprint ed. pap. 143.90 (*0-608-11278-X*, 200581100054) Bks Demand.

Peprník, J. Dictionary of Americanisms for Czech Speakers. 620p. (C). 1985. 60.00 (*0-89771-908-5*, Pub. by Collets) St Mut.

Pepusch, John C. A Treatise on Harmony. 2nd fac. ed. (Monuments of Music & Music Literature in Facsimile, II Ser.: Vol. 28). (Illus.). 1966. lib. bdg. 42.50 (*0-8450-2228-8*) Broude.

— A Treatise on Harmony: Containing the Chief Rules for Composing in Two, Three & Four Parts. 2nd ed. 227p. 1976. reprint ed. 50.70 (*3-487-05930-4*) G Olms Pubs.

Pepys, M. B., ed. Acute Phase Proteins in the Acute Phase Response. (Argenteuil Symposia Ser.). (Illus.). xviii, 210p. 1989. 118.00 (*0-387-19582-3*, 3483) Spr-Verlag.

Pepys, Samuel. The Diary of Samuel Pepys. Morshead, O. F., ed. (Illus.). 1960. 26.25 (*0-8446-2727-5*) Peter Smith.

— The Diary of Samuel Pepys, 10 vols. Wheatley, Henry B., ed. Bright, Mynors, tr. LC 68-57227. reprint ed. lib. bdg. 825.00 (*0-404-05030-1*) AMS Pr.

***Pepys, Samuel.** Diary of Samuel Pepys, Vol. 4. (Illus.). 476p. 2000. pap. 19.95 (*0-520-22694-1*) U CA Pr.

— Diary of Samuel Pepys, Vol. 5. (Illus.). 397p. 2000. pap. 19.95 (*0-520-22696-8*) U CA Pr.

— Diary of Samuel Pepys, Vol. 6. (Illus.). 379p. 2000. pap. 19.95 (*0-520-22697-6*) U CA Pr.

— Diary of Samuel Pepys, Vol. 7. (Illus.). 461p. 2000. pap. 19.95 (*0-520-22698-4*) U CA Pr.

— The Diary of Samuel Pepys, Vol. 8. (Illus.). 637p. 2000. pap. 19.95 (*0-520-22699-2*) U CA Pr.

P

— Diary of Samuel Pepys, Vol. 9. (Diary of Samuel Pepys Ser.). (Illus.). 601p. 2000. pap. 19.95 (0-520-22701-8) U CA Pr.

— Diary of Samuel Pepys, Vol. 10. (Illus.). 649p. 2000. pap. 19.95 (0-520-22715-8) U CA Pr.

— Diary of Samuel Pepys, Vol. 11. (Illus.). 361p. 2000. pap. 19.95 (0-520-22716-6) U CA Pr.

Pepys, Samuel. The Diary of Samuel Pepys Vol. 1: 1660. Latham, Robert & Matthews, William, eds. 1970. 55.00 (0-520-01575-4, Pub. by U CA Pr) Cal Prin Full Svc.

— The Diary of Samuel Pepys Vol. 2: 1661. Latham, Robert & Mathews, William, eds. 1970. 50.00 (0-520-01576-2, Pub. by U CA Pr) Cal Prin Full Svc.

— The Diary of Samuel Pepys Vol. 3: 1662. Latham, Robert & Mathews, William, eds. 1971. 50.00 (0-520-01577-0, Pub. by U CA Pr) Cal Prin Full Svc.

— The Diary of Samuel Pepys Vol. 5: 1664. Latham, Robert & Mathews, William, eds. 1971. 50.00 (0-520-01858-3, Pub. by U CA Pr) Cal Prin Full Svc.

— The Diary of Samuel Pepys Vol. 6: 1665. Latham, Robert & Mathews, William, eds. 1972. 50.00 (0-520-01859-1, Pub. by U CA Pr) Cal Prin Full Svc.

— The Diary of Samuel Pepys Vol. 7: 1666. Latham, Robert & Mathews, William, eds. 1972. 50.00 (0-520-02094-4, Pub. by U CA Pr) Cal Prin Full Svc.

— The Diary of Samuel Pepys vol. 8: 1667. Latham, Robert & Mathews, William, eds. 1974. 55.00 (0-520-02095-2, Pub. by U CA Pr) Cal Prin Full Svc.

— The Diary of Samuel Pepys Vol. 9: 1668-1669. Latham, Robert & Matthews, William, eds. 1976. 50.00 (0-520-02096-0, Pub. by U CA Pr) Cal Prin Full Svc.

— The Diary of Samuel Pepys Vol. 10: The Companion. Latham, Robert & Matthews, William, eds. 1983. 50.00 (0-520-02097-9, Pub. by U CA Pr) Cal Prin Full Svc.

— The Diary of Samuel Pepys Vol. 11: Index. Latham, Robert & Mathews, William, eds. 1983. 50.00 (0-520-02098-7, Pub. by U CA Pr) Cal Prin Full Svc.

***Pepys, Samuel.** Diary of Samuel Pepys 1660. 349p. 2000. pap. 19.95 (0-520-22579-1, Pub. by U CA Pr) Cal Prin Full Svc.

— Diary of Samuel Pepys 1661. 267p. 2000. pap. 19.95 (0-520-22580-5, Pub. by U CA Pr) Cal Prin Full Svc.

— Diary of Samuel Pepys 1662. 329p. 2000. pap. 19.95 (0-520-22581-3, Pub. by U CA Pr) Cal Prin Full Svc.

Pepys, Samuel. The Diary of Samuel Pepys, 1660, Vol. 1. 1993. 38.00 (0-7135-1551-1) Bell & Hyman.

— The Diary of Samule Pepys Vol. 4: 1663. Latham, Robert & Mathews, William, eds. 1971. 50.00 (0-520-01857-5, Pub. by U CA Pr) Cal Prin Full Svc.

— A Pepys Anthology. Latham, Robert & Latham, Linnet, eds. 350p. 1988. 34.95 (0-520-06354-6, Pub. by U CA Pr) Cal Prin Full Svc.

— A Pepys Anthology. Latham, Robert & Latham, Linnet, trs. 350p. 2000. pap. 18.95 (0-520-22167-2, Pub. by U CA Pr) Cal Prin Full Svc.

— Pepys Ballads, 5 vols., Vols. I-V. fac. ed. Day, W. G., ed. 2327p. 1987. 985.00 (0-85991-256-6) Boydell & Brewer.

— Pepys' Memoires of the Royal Navy. LC 68-25260. (English Biography Ser.: No. 31). 1969. reprint ed. lib. bdg. 75.00 (0-8383-0228-9) M S G Haskell Hse.

— Pepys on the Restoration Stage. McAfee, Helen, ed. LC 63-23195. (Illus.). 1972. 20.95 (0-405-08848-5) Ayer.

— A Pepysian Garland: Black-Letter Broadside Ballads of the Years 1595-1639, Chiefly from the Collection of Samuel Pepys. Rollins, Hyder E., ed. LC 74-176041. (Illus.). 527p. 1971. 32.50 (0-674-66185-0) HUP.

— The Shorter Pepys. Latham, Robert, ed. & selected by by. LC 85-40210. 1152p. 1985. 55.00 (0-520-03426-0, Pub. by U CA Pr) Cal Prin Full Svc.

Pepys, Walter C. Pepys. Genealogy of the Pepys Family, 1273-1887. (Illus.). 102p. 1996. reprint ed. pap. 19.50 (0-8328-5422-0); reprint ed. lib. bdg. 29.50 (0-8328-5421-2) Higginson Bk Co.

Pequeño, Mercedes R. Los Formalistas Rusos y la Teoria de los Generos Literarios. 43.50 (0-685-69528-X) Scripta.

Pequegnat, Willo & Stover, Ellen, eds. How to Write a Successful Research Grant Application: A Guide for Social & Behavioral Scientists. LC 95-23003. (Illus.). 266p. (C). 1995. text 42.00 (0-306-44965-X, Kluwer Plenum) Kluwer Academic.

***Pequegnat, Willo & Szapocznik, Jose.** Working with Families in the Era of HIV: My Partner's Brother's Girlfriend's Grandmother. LC 00-8360. 2000. write for info. (0-7619-2217-2) Sage.

Pequeno, Salvatore S. Social Psychology: Index of Modern Authors & Subjects with Guide for Rapid Research. LC 90-56329. 160p. 1991. 47.50 (1-55914-454-8); pap. 44.50 (1-55914-455-6) ABBE Pubs Assn.

Pequeux, A. & Gilles, R., eds. High Pressure Effects on Selected Biological Systems. (Illus.). xiv, 145p. 1985. 54.95 (0-387-15630-5) Spr-Verlag.

Pequigney, Joseph. Such Is My Love: A Study of Shakespeare's Sonnets. LC 85-984. x, 264p. 1993. lib. bdg. 22.50 (0-226-65563-6) U Ch Pr.

— Such Is My Love: A Study of Shakespeare's Sonnets. LC 85-984. x, 264p. 1996. pap. 11.95 (0-226-65564-4) U Ch Pr.

***Per, Fredriksson & World Bank Staff.** Trade, Global Policy, & the Environment. LC 99-10251. (World Bank Discussion Papers). 1999. pap. 30.00 (0-8213-4458-7) World Bank.

Per Noste Staff. Petit Dictionnaire Francais-Occitan (Bearn) (FRE.). 134p. 1984. pap. 19.95 (0-7859-8163-2, 2868660002) Fr & Eur.

Per Olov Enquist. The Night of the Tribades. Shideler, Ross, tr. 1978. pap. 5.25 (0-8222-0824-5) Dramatists Play.

Per, Schelde. Androids, Humanoids, & Other Folklore Monsters: Science & Soul in Science Fiction Films. LC 93-274. (Illus.). 288p. (C). 1993. text 45.00 (0-8147-7930-1) NYU Pr.

***Pera, Brian.** Troublemaker. LC 00-27122. 224p. 2000. text 22.95 (0-312-25232-3) St Martin.

Pera, Cristobal. Modernistas en Paris. (Perspectivas Hispanicas Ser.: Tomo 8). 207p. 1997. 31.95 (3-906757-46-3, Pub. by P Lang) P Lang Pubng.

Pera, George Le, see Le Pera, George, ed.

Pera, Marcello. The Ambiguous Frog: The Galvani-Volta Controversy on Animal Electricity. Mandelbaum, Jonathan, tr. (Illus.). 262p. 1992. text 37.50 (0-691-08512-9, Pub. by Princeton U Pr) Cal Prin Full Svc.

— The Discoures of Science. Botsford, Clarissa, tr. LC 94-14169. 262p. 1994. 29.95 (0-226-65617-9) U Ch Pr.

Pera, Marcello, ed. Persuading Science: The Art of Scientific Rhetoric. 224p. 1991. 39.95 (0-88135-071-0, Sci Hist) Watson Pub Intl.

Pera, Marcello, jt. ed. see Pitt, Joseph C.

Pera, Pia. The Diary of Love. Date not set. pap. write for info. (0-679-76862-9) McKay.

— Lo's Diary. Goldstein, Ann, tr. from ITA. 336p. 1999. 22.95 (1-56025-243-X, Thunders Mouth) Avalon NY.

— Lo's Diary. Goldstein, Ann, tr. 293p. 1999. 22.95 (0-9643740-1-3) FoxRock.

***Perabo, Susan.** Who I Was Supposed to Be: Short Stories. 2000. pap. 11.00 (0-684-87361-3, Scribner Pap Fic) S&S Trade Pap.

— Who I Was Supposed to Be: Short Stories. LC 99-12256. 192p. 1999. 19.50 (0-684-86233-6) Simon & Schuster.

Perabo, Susan. Writers in the Schools: A Guide to Teaching Creative Writing in the Classroom. LC 97-39768. 1998. pap. 18.00 (1-55728-492-X) U of Ark Pr.

Peracchi. Econometrics. 600p. 2000. text. write for info. (0-471-98764-6) Wiley.

***Peracchia, Camillo.** Gap Junctions: Molecular Basis of Cell Communication in Health & Disease. (Current Topics in Membranes Ser.: Vol. 49). (Illus.). 648p. 2000. pap. text 79.95 (0-12-550645-7) Acad Pr.

Peracchia, Camillo, ed. Biophysics of Gap Junction Channels. 416p. 1990. 229.00 (0-8493-6337-3, QP603, CRC Reprint) Franklin.

***Peracchia, Camillo, ed.** Current Topics in Membranes Vol. 49: Gap Junctions. 400p. 1999. 95.00 (0-12-153349-2) Acad Pr.

Peracci, R. Geometry of Nonlinear Field Theories. 268p. 1986. text 43.00 (9971-5-0079-5) World Scientific Pub.

Perachio, Joseph J., jt. auth. see Young, Edna C.

***Peradotto, John.** Contextualizing Classics: Ideology, Performance, Dialogue: Essays in Honor of John J. Peradotto. Falkner, Thomas M. et al, eds. LC 99-41472. (Greek Studies: Interdisciplinary Approaches). 384p. 1999. pap. 27.95 (0-8476-9733-9) Rowman.

Peradotto, John & Sullivan, J. P., eds. Women in the Ancient World. LC 83-4975. 377p. (C). 1987. pap. text 21.95 (0-87395-773-3) State U NY Pr.

Peradzynski, Z. Asympotiotic Methods in Reaction Diffusion Equations. (Engineering Mathematics Ser.). 1999. 83.95 (0-8493-8513-X) CRC Pr.

Peragine, Diane. Bingo Math: Fun-Filled Reproducible Games That Reinforce Essential Math Skills. (Illus.). 96p. 1998. pap. text 10.95 (0-590-10962-6) Scholastic Inc.

Perahya, C. Dictionary French to Judeo-Spanish. (FRE & LAD.). 1998. 75.00 (0-320-00234-9) Fr & Eur.

***Perahya, K.** Dictionary French-Judeo-Espanol (Ladino) (FRE & SPA.). 297p. 1998. 69.95 (0-320-00955-6) Fr & Eur.

Perakis, Anastassios N., jt. auth. see Nikolaidis, Efstratios.

Perakis, Eva M. The Adventures of Lauralee. Keppel, Wilma, ed. LC 95-61154. (Illus.). 88p. (J). (gr. 1-3). 1995. 4.95 (1-56550-029-6) Vis Bks Intl.

Perakyla, Anssi. AIDS Counselling: Institutional Interaction & Clinical Practice. (Studies in Interactional Sociolinguistics: No. 11). 380p. (C). 1996. text 64.95 (0-521-45463-8) Cambridge U Pr.

Perala, Robert & Stubbs, Tony. The Divine Blueprint: Roadmap for the New Millennium. LC 98-8123. (Illus.). 272p. 1998. pap. 14.95 (0-9663130-7-0, United Lght Pub) United Light.

Peralas, Jorge. Oracional Bilingue Para Ninos: A Children's Prayerbook in Spanish-English. (ENG & SPA.). 1998. pap. text 4.95 (0-8146-2459-6) Liturgical Pr.

Peraldi, Francois, ed. Polysexuality. 300p. Date not set. 12.00 (1-57027-011-2) Autonomedia.

Perales, Alonso S. Are We Good Neighbors? LC 73-14213. (Mexican American Ser.). (Illus.). 298p. 1975. reprint ed. 24.95 (0-405-05687-7) Ayer.

Perales, Cesar A. & Young, Lauren S. Women, Health, & Poverty. LC 87-26274. (Women & Health Ser.: Vol. 12, Nos. 3-4). 259p. 1989. text 49.95 (0-86656-684-8) Haworth Pr.

Perales, Cesar A. & Young, Lauren S., eds. Too Little, Too Late: Dealing with the Health Needs of Women in Poverty. LC 88-908. (Women & Health Ser.: Vol. 12, Nos. 3-4). 259p. 1988. text 17.95 (0-918393-50-7, Harrington Park) Haworth Pr.

Perales, Jorge, ed. Oracional Bilingue: A Prayer Book for Spanish-English Communities. (ENG & SPA.). 96p. 1994. pap. 7.95 (0-8146-2094-9) Liturgical Pr.

Perales, T. English-Spanish Dictionary of Video Terms. (ENG & SPA.). 95p. 1992. pap. 15.00 (0-7859-8859-9) Fr & Eur.

Perales, T. & Monroy, C. English-Spanish Dictionary of Video Terms. (ENG & SPA.). 95p. 1992. pap. 15.75 (84-283-1458-6, Pub. by Paraninfo) IBD Ltd.

Peralta, Araceli. Hallazgos en el Metro de la Ciudad de Mexico: Arqueologia y Acervos. (SPA., Illus.). 144p. 1996. pap. 9.00 (968-29-5248-4, IN72, Pub. by Dir Gen Pubicaiones) UPLAAP.

Peralta, Armando De, see De Peralta, Armando.

Peralta, Carlos I. Fuentes y Proceso de Investigaciun Juridica. (SPA.). 660p. 1991. 55.00 (0-88063-587-8, 82875-10, MICHIE) LEXIS Pub.

Peralta-Fabi, Ramon. Fluidos Apellido de Liquidos y Gases. (Ciencia para Todos Ser.). (SPA.). pap. 6.99 (968-16-4215-5, Pub. by Fondo) Continental Bk.

***Peralta, Ismael.** Inspirational of Poetry. 2000. write for info. (1-58235-453-7) Watermrk Pr.

Peralta, Jose Grave De, see Aguiar, Ricardo J.

Peralta, R. & Varea, C., eds. Statistical Physics. 248p. (C). 1988. text 66.00 (9971-5-0776-5) World Scientific Pub.

Peralta, Tina. Afternoon Tea & Other Stories. 102p. (Orig.). 1993. pap. 8.75 (971-10-0457-7, Pub. by New Day Pub) Cellar.

Peralta y Fabi, Ricardo. Del Espacio Al Subsuelo. (Ciencia para Todos Ser.). (SPA.). pap. 6.99 (968-16-4806-4, Pub. by Fondo) Continental Bk.

Perangelo, Julie. A Competitive Analysis of Electronic Wire & Cable End-Use Markets: Copper vs. Fiber, 1988-1996 Analysis. (Illus.). 60p. 1991. pap. text 1600.00 (1-878218-23-9) World Info Tech.

— Electronic Inductors-U. S. Markets, Competitors, & Opportunities: 1995-2000 Analysis & Forecasts. 35p. 1996. pap. text 2900.00 (1-878218-65-4) World Info Tech.

— Electronic Transformers - U. S. Markets & Opportunities: 1997-2002 Analysis & Forecasts. 150p. 1997. pap. text 3900.00 (1-878218-79-4) World Info Tech.

— Electronic Wire & Cable - U. S. Markets, Technologies, & Opportunities: 1991-1996 Analysis. (Illus.). 160p. 1991. pap. text 2400.00 (1-878218-20-4) World Info Tech.

— Optical Ground Wire - U. S. Markets, Competitors, & Opportunities: 1997-2002 Analysis & Forecasts. 45p. 1998. pap. text 2400.00 (1-878218-86-7) World Info Tech.

— Power & Distribution Transformers - U. S. & Canadian Markets, Competitors, & Materials: 1989-1996 Analysis. (Illus.). 300p. 1992. pap. text 3000.00 (1-878218-28-X) World Info Tech.

Perani, Judith & Smith, Fred T. Visual Arts of Africa: Gender, Power, & Life Cycle Rituals. LC 97-807. 385p. 1997. pap. 50.00 (0-13-442328-3) P-H.

Perani, Judith M. & Wolff, Norma H. Cloth, Dress & Art Patronage in Africa. LC 99-229402. (Dress, Body, Culture Ser.). (Illus.). 224p. 1998. 55.00 (1-85973-290-9, Pub. by Berg Pubs); pap. 19.50 (1-85973-295-X, Pub. by Berg Pubs) NYU Pr.

Peranteau, Paul M., et al, eds. Proceedings: Papers from the 8th Regional Meeting. 615p. 1972. pap. 7.00 (0-914203-02-9) Chicago Ling.

Perard, Victor & Hagman, Rune. Drawing People. (Illus.). 96p. 1987. pap. 9.95 (0-399-51385-X, Perigee Bks) Berkley Pub.

***Peraro, James S., ed.** Limitations of Test Methods for Plastics. LC 99-57208. (Illus.). 225p. 2000. pap. text 45.00 (0-8031-2850-9, STP1369) ASTM.

Perason, Carol S. The Hero Within: Six Archetypes We Live By. LC 85-51996. 240p. 1989. pap. 13.00 (0-06-254862-X, Perennial) HarperTrade.

***Perat, M. Velickovic & Neville, B.G., eds.** Cerebral Palsy. 1999. write for info. (0-444-82961-X) Elsevier.

Perata, David. Black on Steel. 1996. pap. 16.95 (0-8057-7829-2, Hall Reference) Macmillan.

— Those Pullman Blues: An Oral History of the African American Railroad Attendant. (Illus.). 250p. 1996. pap. 33.00 (0-8057-4520-3) Macmillan.

***Perata, David D.** The Orchards of Perseverance: Conversations with Trappist Monks about God, Their Lives & the World. (Illus.). 224p. 2000. pap. 17.95 (0-9672135-0-9) St Thereses Pr.

Perata, David D. Those Pullman Blues: An Oral History of the African-American Railroad Attendant. (Twayne's Oral History Ser.). (Illus.). 219p. 1999. pap. 16.95 (1-56833-124-X, Pub. by Madison Bks UPA) Natl Bk Netwk.

Peratis, Kathleen W., jt. auth. see Gary, Eve.

Peratt, Anthony L. Physics of the Plasma Universe. (Illus.). 250p. 1991. 79.00 (0-387-97575-6) Spr-Verlag.

— Plasma Universe: Beyond the Big Bang. 1999. text. write for info. (0-312-09362-4) St Martin.

Peratt, Anthony L., ed. Plasma Astrophysics & Cosmology: Proceedings of the 2nd IEEE International Workshop, Princeton, New Jersey, May 10-12, 1993. 297p. 1995. reprint ed. text 250.00 (0-7923-3784-0) Kluwer Academic.

***Peray, Kurt E.** Mutual Fund Investments by Fuzzy Logic LC 99-12298. 1999. 39.95 (1-57444-264-3) St Lucie Pr.

Peraza, Elena V. Bio-Bibliografia de Fermin Peraza Sarausa. LC 90-82804. (SPA.). 118p. (Orig.). 1990. pap. 19.00 (0-89729-572-2) Ediciones.

Perazza, George, tr. see Saenz, Gilbert.

Perazzo, John. The Myths That Divide Us: How Lies Have Poisoned American Race Relations. LC 96-60240. 544p. 1998. pap. 19.95 (0-9651268-0-3) Wrld Studies.

***Perazzo, John.** The Myths That Divide Us: How Lies Have Poisoned American Race Relations. LC 99-73860. 629p. 1999. pap. 24.00 (0-9651268-1-1) Wrld Studies.

Perbellini, Maria Rita, jt. auth. see Pongraz, Christian.

Perbix, Todd W. & Noson, Linda L. B. F. Day Elementary School. (Design Decisions, Methods, & Procedures Ser.: Vol. 2). (Illus.). 33p. 1996. pap. 7.00 (0-943198-57-7, DS-2) Earthquake Eng.

Percan, S. T. The Complete Book on Housetraining Rabbits: The Only Rabbit Book You'll Need. (Illus.). 37p. (Orig.). 1984. pap. 3.95 (0-916005-01-1) Silver Sea.

Percas de Ponseti, Helena. Cervantes the Writer & Painter of Don Quijote. LC 88-10609. 128p. 1989. text 24.95 (0-8262-0689-1) U of Mo Pr.

Perce, John A., II & Robinson, Richard B., Jr. Strategic Management: Formulation, Implementation & Control. 5th ed. LC 93-5598. 960p. (C). 1993. text 72.75 (0-256-11362-9, Irwn McGrw-H) McGrw-H Hghr Educ.

Percefull, Aaron. The Cambridge Program for the GED Writing Skills Test. (GED Preparation Ser.). 304p. (Orig.). 1988. pap. text 6.45 (0-8428-9387-3) Cambridge Bk.

Percefull, Aaron. New GED Writing Skills. (Illus.). pap. 9.15 (0-8428-8701-6) Cambridge Bk.

***Percelay, James & Deutchman, Jeremy.** Whiplash! America's Most Frivolous Lawsuits. LC 99-40325. 2000. pap. 9.95 (0-7407-0496-6) Andrews & McMeel.

Percelay, James, et al. Double Snaps: For Advanced Snappers & Those Who Like the Dozens Raw...An All New Book of More Than 500 of the Funniest, Rudest, & Most Creative Snaps, Caps, & Insults for Playing the Dozens. LC 94-24792. (Illus.). 176p. 1995. pap. 9.95 (0-688-14011-4, Quil) HarperTrade.

— Snaps: The African American Art of Verbal Warfare. LC 93-34484. 175p. 1994. pap. 8.95 (0-688-12896-3, Wm Morrow) Morrow Avon.

— Triple Snaps: The Latest Word Off the Street on the Hot Game of Snapping...an All-New Book... 1996. pap. 9.95 (0-688-14591-4, Quil) HarperTrade.

***Percelay, Jim.** Snaps 4: More Than 500 Of The Most Ruthless, Raw, And Hard-Core Snaps, Caps, And Disses From The Official Sna, Vol. 4. LC 97-24140. 160p. 1998. pap. 9.95 (0-688-15014-4, Quil) HarperTrade.

Perception, Inc. Staff. Microsoft Office 97 at a Glance, Updated Edition. LC 98-9289. (At A Glance Ser.). 352p. 16.99 (1-57231-891-0) Microsoft.

Perception Staff. Microsoft Internet Explorer 4 at a Glance: The Easy Way to Find the Right Answers, Right Now. LC 97-37610. 288p. pap. 16.99 (1-57231-740-X) Microsoft.

— Microsoft Office 98 MacIntosh Edition at a Glance. LC 98-9351. 256p. 16.99 (1-57231-916-X) Microsoft.

Perces, Marjorie, et al. The Dance Technique of Lester Horton. (Illus.). 205p. 1992. pap. 24.95 (0-87127-164-8, Dance Horizons) Princeton Bk Co.

Percesepe, Gary J. Future(s) of Philosophy: The Marginal Thinking of Jacques Derrida. (American University Studies: Philosophy: Ser. V, Vol. 67). 237p. (C). 1988. text 36.00 (0-8204-0804-2) P Lang Pubng.

— Introduction to Ethics: Personal & Social Responsibility in a Diverse World. LC 94-4826. 608p. (C). 1995. pap. text 57.00 (0-02-393891-9, Macmillan Coll) P-H.

Percesepe, Gary J. & Mehuron, Kate. Free Spirits: Feminist Philosophers on Culture. LC 94-6867. 521p. (C). 1994. pap. text 29.00 (0-02-380135-2, Macmillan Coll) P-H.

Perceval, Andre. La Vision. (Breviarios Ser.). (SPA.). pap. 6.99 (968-16-4965-6, Pub. by Fondo) Continental Bk.

Perceval, Edward, tr. see Huysmans, J. K.

Perceval, Edward, tr. see Huysmans, Joris K.

Perceval, John. Perceval's Narrative: A Patient's Account of His Psychosis, 1830-1832. Bateson, Gregory, ed. LC 61-14652. 353p. 1961. reprint ed. pap. 30.00 (0-7837-1223-5, 204175400023) Bks Demand.

Perceval-Maxwell, M. The Outbreak of the Irish Rebellion of 1641. 408p. 1994. 60.00 (0-7735-1157-1, Pub. by McG-Queens Univ Pr) CUP Services.

Perceval, W. B., pref. Pictorial New Zealand, 1895. 316p. (C). 1986. 85.00 (0-85091-239-3) St Mut.

Perch, David & Lee, Leonard. How to Make Wooden Planes. (Illus.). 48p. 1981. pap. 4.95 (0-9691019-0-2, Pub. by LVTL) Veritas Tools.

Perch, Karen L., jt. auth. see Toby, Milton C.

Perchan, Robert J. Perchan's Chorea. 1991. 17.50 (0-922820-15-5) Watermark Pr.

Percheron, Daniel. Flavia & Her Fabulous Friends. LC 97-34844. (Illus.). 32p. (J). (ps-1). 1998. 14.95 (0-7892-0302-2, Abbeville Kids) Abbeville Pr.

Percheron, G., et al, eds. The Basal Ganglia 4: New Ideas & Data on Structure & Function. (Advances in Behavioral Biology Ser.: Vol. 41). (Illus.). 630p. (C). 1994. text 145.00 (0-306-44639-1, Kluwer Plenum) Kluwer Academic.

Percheron, Maurice. Buddha & Buddhism. Stapleton, Edmund, tr. from FRE. LC 82-3471. (Spiritual Masters Ser.). (Illus.). 192p. 1984. 18.95 (0-87951-157-5, Pub. by Overlook Pr); pap. 9.95 (0-87951-193-1, Pub. by Overlook Pr) Penguin Putnam.

Perchia, Alexander La, see La Perchia, Alexander.

Perchik, Simon. Birthmark. limited ed. (Illus.). 12p. 1992. bds. 65.00 (1-880392-00-3) Flockophobic Pr.

— The Gandolf Poems. 1988. pap. 7.00 (0-934834-31-8) White Pine.

— Letters to the Dead. 64p. 1994. pap. 8.95 (1-879934-08-6) St Andrews Pr.

Perchuk, Andrew, et al. The Masculine Masquerade: Masculinity & Representation. Posner, Helaine, ed. (Illus.). 160p. 1995. pap. text 27.50 (0-262-16154-0) MIT Pr.

Perchuk, L. L., ed. Progress in Metamorphic & Magmatic Petrology: A Memorial Volume in Honour of D. S. Korzhinskiy. (Illus.). 519p. (C). 1991. text 140.00 (0-521-39077-X) Cambridge U Pr.

Perchuk, L. L. & Kushiro, I., eds. Physical Chemistry of Magmas. (Advances in Physical Geochemistry Ser.: Vol. 9). (Illus.). x, 341p. 1991. 118.95 (0-387-97500-4) Spr-Verlag.

Perciasepe, Bob, ed. The Index of Watershed Indicators. (Illus.). 56p. 1999. reprint ed. pap. text 30.00 (0-7881-7879-2) DIANE Pub.

Perciasepe, Robert. Draft Framework for Watershed-Based Trading. (Illus.). 136p. (C). 1998. pap. text 35.00 (0-7881-4946-6) DIANE Pub.

Perciasepe, Robert, ed. Response to Biosolids Questions & Current Public Acceptance Issues. 148p. (C). 1998. pap. text 30.00 (0-7881-7467-3) DIANE Pub.

Percier, Charles. Empire Stylebook of Interior Design. 96p. 1991. pap. 8.95 (0-486-26754-7) Dover.

P

An Asterisk (*) at the beginning of an entry indicates that the title is appearing for the first time.

Percier, Charles & Fontaine, Pierre F. Palais, Maisons et Autres Edifices Modernes Dessines a Rome. 1980. reprint ed. write for info. (*3-487-06920-2*) G Olms Pubs.
— Residences des Souverains, 2 vols. in 1. xi, 354p. 1973. reprint ed. write for info. (*3-487-04796-9*) G Olms Pubs.
Percifield, Glen, ed. Developing Dynamic Disciples: Pentecostal Faith, Prayer & Commitment. LC 94-76668. 144p. 1994. pap. 2.95 (*0-88243-335-0*, 02-0335) Gospel Pub.
Percival, Anthony. Galdos & His Critics. (Romance Ser.: No. 53). 548p. 1985. text 45.00 (*0-8020-5601-6*) U of Toronto Pr.
— Galdos & His Critics. LC 86-215749. (University of Toronto Romance Ser.: No. 53). 547p. reprint ed. pap. 169.60 (*0-8357-4146-X*, 203691900006) Bks Demand.
Percival, C. S. & Percival, Elizabeth, eds. History of Buchanan County: With Illustrations & Biographical Sketches, 1842-1881. (Illus.). 437p. 1997. reprint ed. lib. bdg. 47.50 (*0-8328-6673-3*) Higginson Bk Co.
Percival, C. T., et al. European Charts of Accounts with English Translation of France-Germany-Spain. 207p. 1995. spiral bd. 119.00 (*0-9507949-4-5*) IBD Ltd.
Percival, Donald B. & Walden, Andrew T. Spectral Analysis for Physical Applications: Multitaper & Conventional Univariate Techniques. (Illus.). 611p. (C). 1993. text 110.00 (*0-521-35532-X*); pap. text 49.95 (*0-521-43541-2*) Cambridge U Pr.
— Wavelet Methods for Time Series Analysis. (Series in Statistical & Probabilistic Mathematics: No. 4). (Illus.). 625p. (C). 2000. write for info. (*0-521-64068-7*) Cambridge U Pr.
Percival, Elizabeth, jt. ed. see Percival, C. S.
Percival, Florence. Chaucer's Legendary Good Women. LC 97-40828. (Cambridge Studies in Medieval Literature: No. 38). 300p. (C). 1998. 69.95 (*0-521-41655-8*) Cambridge U Pr.
Percival, Fred, et al. A Handbook of Educational Technology. 3rd ed. LC 93-8129. 276p. (C). 1993. pap. 39.95 (*0-89397-389-0*) Nichols Pub.
— Handbook of Educational Technology. 3rd ed. 276p. 1993. pap. 29.95 (*0-7494-0849-9*, Kogan Pg Educ) Stylus Pub VA.
Percival, Gwen, jt. auth. see Kulesa, Chester.
Percival, Harold W. Adepts, Masters & MAHATMAS. LC 92-82024. (Illus.). 184p. (Orig.). 1993. reprint ed. pap. 14.95 (*0-911650-11-3*, 113) Word Foun.
— Democracy Is Self-Government: A Guide for Right Living in the New Age. LC 52-30629. (Illus.). 234p. 1989. reprint ed. pap. 9.95 (*0-911650-10-5*, 105) Word Foun.
— Man & Woman, & Child. LC 52-6126. 1992. reprint ed. pap. 9.95 (*0-911650-08-3*) Word Foun.
— Masonry & Its Symbols, in Light of "Thinking & Destiny" LC 52-2237. 1991. reprint ed. pap. 5.95 (*0-911650-07-5*) Word Foun.
— Thinking & Destiny: Being the Science of Man. 11th ed. LC 47-1811. (Illus.). 1000p. (C). 1995. 29.95 (*0-911650-09-1*, 091); pap. 19.95 (*0-911650-06-7*) Word Foun.
Percival, Ian. Quantum State Diffusion. LC 98-7168. (Illus.). 160p. (C). 1999. 49.95 (*0-521-62007-4*) Cambridge U Pr.
Percival, James. The Essiac Handbook. (Illus.). 24p. 1994. pap. 5.00 (*0-9651484-9-1*) Rideout Pub.
Percival, John. Great Famine: Ireland's Potato Famine, 1845-51. 192p. 1996. 24.95 (*1-57500-002-4*, Pub. by TV Bks) HarpC.
Percival, Joyce. Architecture for Dolls' Houses. (Illus.). 160p. 1996. pap. 19.95 (*0-946819-98-X*, Pub. by Guild Master) Sterling.
Percival, K., et al. Orthopaedics: A Problem Solving Approach for Physiotherapists. (Illus.). 288p. (C). 1998. pap. write for info. (*0-443-05074-0*) Church.
Percival, Lloyd. The Hockey Handbook. 320p. 1992. 24.95 (*1-895246-03-2*); 19.99 (*1-895246-09-1*) McCland & Stewart.
— The Hockey Handbook. 2nd rev. ed. LC 98-105406. (Illus.). 260p. 1997. pap. 19.95 (*1-55209-127-9*) Firefly Bks Ltd.
***Percival, Lloyd.** The Hockey Handbook: The Book That Taught the Russians Hockey. rev. ed. Major, Wayne & Thom, Robert, eds. (Illus.). 260p. 1999. reprint ed. pap. text 20.00 (*0-7881-6824-X*) DIANE Pub.
Percival, M. O., jt. ed. see Andrews, C. E.
Percival, Milton O. William Blake's Circle of Destiny. 340p. 1993. reprint ed. pap. 21.00 (*1-56459-315-0*) Kessinger Pub.
Percival, Monica, ed. see Houston, Bud & Mah, Stuart.
Percival, Monica, ed. see Mah, Stuart.
Percival, Monica, ed. & photos by see Hobday, Ruth.
Percival, Olive. Mexico City. 1976. lib. bdg. 59.95 (*0-8490-0625-2*) Gordon Pr.
Percival, P. English-Tamil Dictionary. (ENG & TAM.). 446p. 1993. 21.95 (*0-7859-9809-8*) Fr & Eur.
— Percival's English-Tamil Dictionary. (C). 1993. reprint ed. 22.00 (*81-206-0817-8*, Pub. by Asian Educ Servs) S Asia.
— Tamil - English Dictionary. (ENG & TAM.). 297p. 1993. 21.95 (*0-7859-9810-1*) Fr & Eur.
Percival, Philip H. Hunting, Settling & Remembering. limited ed. LC 95-62009. (Illus.). 243p. 1997. 85.00 (*1-882458-12-5*) Trophy Rm Bks.
Percival, Robert V. Environmental Law. 1992. 53.00 (*0-316-69901-2*, Aspen Law & Bus) Aspen Pub.
— Environmental Law Supplement 1995. 1995. 18.95 (*0-316-69915-2*, Aspen Law & Bus) Aspen Pub.
Percival, Robert V. & Alevizatos, Dorothy C. Law & the Environment: An Interdisciplinary Reader. LC 96-41366. 464p. 1997. 69.95 (*1-56639-523-2*); pap. 29.95 (*1-56639-524-0*) Temple U Pr.
Percival, Robert V., et al. Environmental Regulation: Law, Science, & Policy. 2nd ed. LC 96-75338. 1512p. 1996. teacher ed. write for info. (*0-316-69056-2*, 90562) Aspen Law.
Percival, Robert V., jt. auth. see Friedman, Lawrence M.
Percival, Ronald, tr. see Roques, Henri.
***Percival, Steven Lane, et al.** Microbiological Aspects of Biofilms & Drinking Water: Public Health Effects & Implications. LC 99-98186. (Microbiology of Unusual & Extreme Environments Ser.). 240p. 2000. boxed set 119.95 (*0-8493-0590-X*, Chap & Hall CRC) CRC Pr.
Percival, Thomas. Percival's Medical Ethics. Leake, Chauncey D., ed. LC 75-23750. reprint ed. 39.50 (*0-404-13356-8*) AMS Pr.
Percoco, Ida, ed. see Foster, Dave.
Percoco, James A. A Passion for the Past: Creative Teaching of United States History. LC 98-21451. 1998. write for info. (*0-325-00061-1*) Heinemann.
Percom & Evans, Alastair. How to Comply with the Data Protection Act: Policies, Practice & Procedures. 200p. 1986. text 78.95 (*0-566-02632-5*, Pub. by Gower) Ashgate Pub Co.
Percopo & Kaplan. GEP & Multiple Neuroendocrine Tumors, 2 vols. 600p. 1996. text 156.00 (*88-299-1201-8*, Pub. by Piccin Nuova) Gordon & Breach.
***Percus, Jerome K.** Mathematics of Genome Analysis. (Cambridge Studies in Mathematical Biology: Vol. 17). 200p. 2001. write for info. (*0-521-58517-1*); pap. write for info. (*0-521-58526-0*) Cambridge U Pr.
Percussive Arts Society Education Committee Staff. Percussion Education: A Source Book of Concepts & Information. Whaley, Garwood, ed. (Illus.). 89p. 1990. pap. 12.95 (*0-9664928-0-3*) Percussive OK.
Percy. Positive Aging: Essays In Educational & Social Groups. 52.95 (*1-84014-340-1*) Ashgate Pub Co.
Percy, jt. auth. see Frantzich.
Percy, Ann, jt. auth. see Rosenthal, Mark.
Percy, Ann, jt. ed. see Hiesinger, Ulrich W.
Percy, Ann, ed. see Kerrigan, Maurie.
Percy, C., et al, eds. International Classification of Diseases for Oncology (ICD-O) 2nd rev. ed. (CHI.). xlvii, 144p. 1991. text 50.00 (*92-4-154414-7*, 1150350) World Health.
Percy, Carol E., et al. Synchronic Corpus Linguistics: Papers from the 16th International Conference on English Language Research on Computerized Corpora (ICAME 16) LC 96-178739. (Language & Computers Ser.). 289p. 1996. pap. write for info. (*90-420-0027-9*) Editions Rodopi.
Percy, Donna S. A Visit to Forest Lawn: Educator's Handbook. (Illus.). 54p. (Orig.). 1996. pap. text 5.00 (*0-9652756-2-0*) Forest Lawn.
Percy, E. C., et al. Sport Medicine: Incidence & Treatment of Athletic Injuries. LC 73-10382. (Sport Medicine Ser.: Vol. 1). 1973. 32.00 (*0-8422-7142-2*) Irvington.
Percy, Edward & Denham, Reginald. Ladies in Retirement. 1943. pap. 5.25 (*0-8222-0624-2*) Dramatists Play.
Percy, Graham. The Cock, the Mouse, & the Little Red Hen. LC 91-71857. (Illus.). 32p. (J). (ps up). 1994. pap. 5.99 (*1-56402-268-4*) Candlewick Pr.
— The Cock, the Mouse, & the Little Red Hen: A Traditional Tale. LC 91-71857. (Illus.). 32p. (J). (ps up). 1992. 14.95 (*1-56402-008-8*) Candlewick Pr.
— The Farm. (Press & Lift Bks.). (Illus.). 16p. (J). (gr. 1-5). 1989. write for info. (*1-881469-27-1*) Safari Ltd.
— Favorite Fable Special. (J). 1995. 129.50 (*0-8050-3083-2*) H Holt & Co.
— The Mailbox Mice Mystery. (J). 1999. 12.99 (*0-679-88603-6*, Pub. by Random Bks Yng Read) Random.
— Max & the Very Rare Bird. (Meg & Max Bks.). (Illus.). 32p. (J). (ps-3). 1991. lib. bdg. 22.79 (*0-89565-786-4*) Childs World.
— Meg & Her Circus Tricks. (Meg & Max Bks.). (Illus.). 32p. (J). (ps-3). 1991. lib. bdg. 22.79 (*0-89565-785-6*) Childs World.
— Meg & the Great Race. LC 92-44851. (Meg & Max Bks.). (Illus.). 32p. (J). (ps-3). 1994. lib. bdg. 22.79 (*1-56766-077-0*) Childs World.
— The Mountains. (Press & Lift Bks.). (Illus.). 16p. (J). (gr. 1-5). 1989. 6.50 (*1-881469-11-5*) Safari Ltd.
Percy, Harold. Following Jesus: First Steps on the Way. LC 96-930192. 112p. 1993. 10.95 (*1-55126-154-5*) Forward Movement.
— Good News People: An Introduction to Evangelism for Tongue-Tied Christians. LC 96-931673. (Illus.). 144p. 1996. pap., student ed. 9.95 (*1-55126-165-0*) Forward Movement.
***Percy, Ian.** Going Deep: Exploring Spirituality in Life & Leadership. (Illus.). 260p. 1999. pap. 17.00 (*1-891850-24-5*) Med Bear.
Percy, Jane. The Phantom of Harley Grange. (C). 1989. 42.00 (*0-7223-2308-5*, Pub. by A H S Ltd) St Mut.
***Percy, John & Millar, Graham.** Kenmore. (Images of America Ser.). 1999. pap. 18.99 (*0-7524-1216-7*) Arcadia Publng.
Percy, John R., ed. Astronomy Education: Current Developments, Future Coordination. (ASP Conference Series Proceedings: Vol. 89). 315p. 1996. 34.00 (*1-886733-10-4*) Astron Soc Pacific.
— The Study of Variable Stars Using Small Telescopes. (Illus.). 272p. 1987. text 80.00 (*0-521-33300-8*) Cambridge U Pr.
Percy, John W. The Town of Tonawanda. LC 97-158198. (Images of America Ser.). 1997. pap. 16.99 (*0-7524-0423-7*) Arcadia Publng.
Percy, Keith & Ramsden, Paul. Independent Study: Two Examples from English Higher Education. 79p. 1980. 28.00 (*0-900868-75-9*) Taylor & Francis.
Percy, Keith, jt. auth. see Withnall, Alexandra.
Percy, Kevin E., et al, eds. Air Polutants & the Leaf Cuticle. LC 94-21967. (NATO ASI Series G: Ecological Sciences: 36). (Illus.). ix, 395p. 1994. 219.95 (*0-387-58146-4*) Spr-Verlag.
Percy, Larry. Strategies for Implementing Integrated Marketing Communications. (Illus.). 272p. 1997. 39.95 (*0-8442-3583-0*, NTC Business Bks) NTC Contemp Pub Co.
Percy, Larry, ed. Marketing Research That Pays Off: Case Histories of Marketing Research Leading to Success in the Marketplace. LC 96-25516. (Illus.). 266p. (C). 1997. pap. text 24.95 (*0-7890-0197-7*); lib. bdg. 49.95 (*1-56024-949-8*) Haworth Pr.
Percy, Larry & Rossiter, John R. Advertising Strategy: A Communication Theory Approach. LC 79-25228. 301p. 1980. 57.95 (*0-275-91692-8*, C1692, Praeger Pubs) Greenwood.
Percy, Larry, jt. auth. see Rossiter, John R.
Percy, Martyn. Power & the Church: Ecclesiology in an Age of Transition. LC 98-203042. 224p. 1998. 49.95 (*0-304-70107-6*); pap. 24.95 (*0-304-70105-X*) Continuum.
***Percy, Martyn, ed.** Calling Time: Religion & Change at the Turn of the Millenium. (Lincoln Studies in Religion & Society : No. 2). 280p. 2000. 45.00 (*1-84127-063-6*, Pub. by Sheffield Acad) CUP Services.
Percy, Martyn, jt. ed. see Evans, G. R.
Percy, Melanie S. Not Just a Shelter Kid: How Homeless Children Find Solace. rev. ed. LC 96-30013. (Children of Poverty Ser.). (Illus.). 104p. 1997. text 33.00 (*0-8153-2618-1*) Garland.
Percy, Michael B. & Yoder, Christian. The Softwood Lumber Dispute & Canada & U. S. Trade in Natural Resources. 1989. pap. text 20.00 (*0-88645-057-8*, Pub. by Inst Res Pub) Ashgate Pub Co.
Percy, Rachel, jt. auth. see Ansell, Rod.
Percy, Richard. The 345th. 88p. 1998. pap. 10.00 (*0-8059-4469-9*) Dorrance.
***Percy-Smith, Janie.** Policy Responses to Social Exclusion. LC 99-88206. 2000. write for info. (*0-335-20474-0*) Taylor & Francis.
— Policy Responses to Social Exclusion Towards Inclusion? LC 99-88206. 2000. pap. text 28.95 (*0-335-20473-2*) OpUniv Pr.
Percy-Smith, Janie, ed. Needs Assessments in Public Policy. 192p. 1996. 108.95 (*0-335-19596-2*); pap. 29.95 (*0-335-19595-4*) OpUniv Pr.
Percy, Stephen L. & Scott, Eric J. Demand Processing & Performance in Public Service Agencies. LC 83-9325. 170p. 1985. pap. 52.70 (*0-608-05150-0*, 206571100005) Bks Demand.
Percy, Stephen L., jt. auth. see Frantzich, Stephen E.
Percy, Susan, jt. auth. see Buckingham-Hatfield, Susan.
Percy, Thomas. The Correspondence of Thomas Percy & John Pinkerton: The Percy Letters, Vol. 8. Wood, Harriet H. & Brooks, Cleanth, eds. LC 84-2916. Vol. 8. 129p. 1985. 40.00 (*0-300-03344-3*) Yale U Pr.
Percy, Thomas. The Correspondence of Thomas Percy & Robert Anderson, Vol. 9. LC 88-2074. (C). 1989. 70.00 (*0-300-03814-3*) Yale U Pr.
Percy, Thomas. Reliques of Ancient English Poetry, 2 vols. (BCL1-PR English Literature Ser.). 1992. reprint ed. lib. bdg. 150.00 (*0-7812-7132-0*) Rprt Serv.
Percy, Thomas & Bowle. Cervantine Correspondence. Eisenberg, ed. (Exeter Hispanic Text Ser.: No. 40). (SPA.). 97p. Date not set. pap. text 17.95 (*0-85989-288-3*, Pub. by Univ Exeter Pr) Northwestern U Pr.
Percy, Walker. Lancelot. 256p. 1989. mass mkt. 5.99 (*0-8041-0380-1*) Ivy Books.
— Lancelot: Novel. LC 99-16418. 272p. 1999. pap. 14.00 (*0-312-24307-3*) St Martin.
Percy, Walker. The Last Gentleman. LC 66-18861. 409p. 1966. text 22.95 (*0-374-18372-4*) FS&G.
— The Last Gentleman. 336p. 1989. mass mkt. 5.99 (*0-8041-0379-8*) Ivy Books.
— The Last Gentleman. LC 97-15381. 560p. 1998. 18.50 (*0-679-60272-0*) Modern Lib NY.
***Percy, Walker.** The Last Gentleman: A Novel. LC 99-16417. 416p. 1999. pap. 15.00 (*0-312-24308-1*) St Martin.
Percy, Walker. The Last Gentlemen. 320p. 1978. mass mkt. 4.50 (*0-380-37796-9*, Avon Bks) Morrow Avon.
— Lost in the Cosmos: The Last Self-Help Book. 262p. 1992. pap. 13.00 (*0-374-52346-0*) FS&G.
***Percy, Walker.** Lost in the Cosmos: The Last Self-Help Book. LC 99-87846. 272p. 2000. pap. 14.00 (*0-312-25399-0*, Picador USA) St Martin.
Percy, Walker. Love in the Ruins. LC 71-143301. 416p. 1971. 27.95 (*0-374-19302-9*) FS&G.
— Love in the Ruins. 352p. 1989. mass mkt. 5.99 (*0-8041-0378-X*) Ivy Books.
***Percy, Walker.** Love in the Ruins: Novel. LC 99-32173. 384p. 1999. pap. 15.00 (*0-312-24311-1*) St Martin.
Percy, Walker. The Message in the Bottle. LC 75-5846. 262p. 1975. pap. 14.00 (*0-374-51338-4*) FS&G.
***Percy, Walker.** Message in the Bottle: How Queen Man Is, How Queer Language Is, & What One Has to Do with the Other. LC 99-89027. 272p. 2000. pap. 14.00 (*0-312-25401-6*, Picador USA) St Martin.
Percy, Walker. The Moviegoer. LC 96-96687. 1996. pap. 12.00 (*0-449-91170-5*) Fawcett.
— The Moviegoer. 1961. 26.00 (*0-394-43703-9*) Knopf.
— The Moviegoer. 242p. 1998. pap. 12.00 (*0-375-70196-6*) Vin Bks.
— The Second Coming. 336p. 1990. mass mkt. 5.99 (*0-8041-0542-1*) Ivy Books.
***Percy, Walker.** The Second Coming: Novel. LC 99-32172. 368p. 1999. pap. 15.00 (*0-312-24324-3*) St Martin.
Percy, Walker. Signposts in a Strange Land. 1991. 25.00 (*0-374-26391-4*) FS&G.
— Signposts in a Strange Land. 432p. 1992. pap. 16.00 (*0-374-52345-2*) FS&G.
***Percy, Walker.** Signposts in a Strange Land. LC 99-89573. 432p. 2000. pap. 14.00 (*0-312-25419-9*, Picador USA) St Martin.
Percy, Walker. State of the Novel: Dying Art or New Science. (Illus.). 20p. 1988. 50.00 (*0-917905-05-9*); 125.00 (*0-317-66751-3*) Faust Pub Co.
— The Thanatos Syndrome. 1987. 17.95 (*0-374-27354-5*) FS&G.
— The Thanatos Syndrome. 416p. 1988. reprint ed. mass mkt. 6.99 (*0-8041-0220-1*) Ivy Books.
— Thanatos Syndrome: Novel. LC 99-32174. 384p. 1999. pap. 15.00 (*0-312-24332-4*, Picador USA) St Martin.
Percy, Walker & Letner, Kenneth L. A Thief of Peirce: The Letters of Kenneth Laine Ketner & Walker Percy. Samway, Patrick H., ed. LC 95-14835. 350p. 1995. text 45.00 (*0-87805-810-9*) U Pr of Miss.
Percy, Walker, jt. auth. see Foote, Shelby.
Percy, William, jt. auth. see Johansson, Warren.
Percy, William A. Lanterns on the Levee: Recollections of a Planter's Son. LC 73-90687. (Library of Southern Civilization). xxii, 376p. 1974. 29.95 (*0-8071-1184-8*); pap. 16.95 (*0-8071-0072-2*) La State U Pr.
Percy, William A., III. Pederasty & Pedagogy in Archaic Greece. LC 95-12864. (Illus.). 296p. 1996. 29.95 (*0-252-02209-2*) U of Ill Pr.
Percy, William A. Pederasty & Pedagogy in Archaic Greece. 1998. pap. text 18.95 (*0-252-06740-1*) U of Ill Pr.
— Sewanee. LC 82-60214. (Illus.). 40p. 1982. 14.95 (*0-913720-37-2*) Beil.
— Sewanee. 16p. 1941. pap. 7.50 (*0-918769-35-3*) Univ South Pr.
Percy, William A., jt. auth. see Johnson, Jerah.
Percy, William A., ed. see O'Shaughnessy, Arthur E.
Perczel, Csilla F., ed. Ethiopia: Folk Art of a Hidden Empire. LC 83-62245. (Illus.). 72p. 1983. pap. 15.00 (*0-914155-00-8*) Mingei Intl Mus.
***Perczel, Csilla Ottlik.** A History of Architecture in the Carpathian Basin (1000 A.D.-1920) 300p. 2000. text 49.50 (*0-88033-460-6*) Col U Pr.
Perczynski, Maciej, et al, eds. After the Market Shock: Central & East European Economies in Transition. 320p. 1994. 65.95 (*1-85521-594-2*, Pub. by Dartmth Pub) Ashgate Pub Co.
Perdang, J. M. & LeJeune, A. Cellular Automata: Prospects in Astronomy & Astrophysics. 416p. 1993. text 109.00 (*981-02-1346-8*) World Scientific Pub.
Perdew, Carol & Stiles, Monica. Bubble Trouble. (Illus.). 20p. (ps-5). 1998. pap. 10.95 (*0-9657505-2-3*) Staircase Pub.
Perdew, Suzanne. Jesus Is My Best Friend: Activity, Story & Coloring Book for Children Ages 3 to 7. (Illus.). 32p. (J). 1995. pap. 2.99 (*0-945460-19-8*) Upward Way.
— Story Time with Jesus: Activity, Story & Coloring Book for Children Ages 3 to 7. (Illus.). 32p. (J). 1995. pap. 2.99 (*0-945460-20-1*) Upward Way.
Perdichizzi, Elizabeth M. & Kirk, Katherine S. A Girl Called Tommie: Queen of Marco Island. (Illus.). 176p. Date not set. 24.95 (*0-9677281-5-0*); pap. 19.95 (*0-9677281-6-9*) Caxambas.
Perdigo, Luisa M. The Origins of Vicente Huidobro's Creacionismo (1911-1916) & Its Evolution (1917-1947) LC 93-39318. 360p. 1993. text 99.95 (*0-7734-2299-4*) E Mellen.
Perdigon, G., jt. auth. see Fuller, R.
Perdikaris, George A. Computer Controlled Systems: Theory & Applications. 496p. (C). 1991. lib. bdg. 178.50 (*0-7923-1422-0*) Kluwer Academic.
Perdikis, N., jt. auth. see Kerr, W.
Perdikis, Nicholas & Kerr, William A. Trade Theories & Empirical Evidence. LC 97-48662. 256p. 1998. 69.95 (*0-7190-5409-5*, Pub. by Manchester Univ Pr) St Martin.
Perdomo, Jose E. Lexico Tabacalero Cubano: Con Vocabulario Espanol-Ingles with Spanish-English Vocabulary. (ENG & SPA., Illus.). 265p. 1998. pap. 24.95 (*0-89729-846-2*) Ediciones.
Perdomo, Willie. Where a Nickel Costs a Dime. Date not set. write for info. (*0-393-31415-4*, Norton Paperbks) Norton.
— Where a Nickel Costs a Dime. LC 95-13225. 128p. 1996. pap. 14.95 (*0-393-31383-2*) Norton.
Perdowsi, Abdul. The Tragedy of Sohrab & Rostam: From the Persian National Epic, the Shahname of Abu'l-Qasem Ferdowsi. rev. ed. Clinton, Jerome W., tr. from PER. LC 96-19208. (Publications on the Near East: Vol. 3). 224p. 1996. pap. text 14.95 (*0-295-97567-9*) U of Wash Pr.
Perdrizet, George & Smally, Alan J. Emergent Care in Transplant Patients. (Vademecum Ser.). 2001. spiral bd. 45.00 (*1-57059-581-X*) Landes Bioscience.
Perdrizet, Marie-Pierre. The Cathedral Builders. Raycraft, Mary B., tr. from FRE. LC 91-24233. (Peoples of the Past Ser.). (Illus.). 64p. (J). (gr. 4-6). 1992. lib. bdg. 22.40 (*1-56294-162-3*) Millbrook Pr.
Perdu, Charles. Echoes of Valor. (Illus.). 96p. (Orig.). 1993. pap. 10.00 (*0-9638779-0-9*) Perdido Pr.
Perdue. Farmers Cookbook. 1995. 7.98 (*0-89009-813-1*) Bk Sales Inc.
Perdue, Charles L., Jr., ed. Outwitting the Devil: Jack Tales from Wise County, Virginia. LC 87-71657. (New Deal & Folk Culture Ser.). (Illus.). 129p. 1987. pap. 10.95 (*0-941270-42-4*) Ancient City Pr.
— Pigsfoot Jelly & Persimmon Beer: Foodways from Virginia's Writer's Project. LC 92-9356. (New Deal & Folk Culture Ser.). (Illus.). 128p. (Orig.). 1992. pap. 11.95 (*0-941270-74-2*) Ancient City Pr.
Perdue, Charles L., Jr., et al, eds. Weevils in the Wheat: Interviews with Virginia Ex-Slaves. LC 79-65433. (Midland Bks.: No. 237). (Illus.). 405p. (C). 1992. reprint ed. pap. text 19.50 (*0-8139-1370-5*) U Pr of Va.

P

An Asterisk (*) at the beginning of an entry indicates that the title is appearing for the first time.

Perdue, Charles L., Jr., jt. auth. see Martin-Perdue, Nancy J.

Perdue, Clive, ed. Adult Language Acquisition Vol. 1: Crosslinguistic Perspectives: Field Methods. LC 92-35757. (Illus.). 269p. (C). 1993. text 69.95 (*0-521-41708-2*) Cambridge U Pr.

— Adult Language Acquisition Vol. 2: Crosslinguistic Perspectives: The Results. (Illus.). 298p. (C). 1993. text 69.95 (*0-521-41709-0*) Cambridge U Pr.

Perdue, Clive, jt. auth. see Klein, Wolfgang.

Perdue, Daniel. Debate in Tibetan Buddhism. 1025p. 1992. 45.00 (*0-937938-84-X*); pap. 38.95 (*0-937938-76-9*) Snow Lion Pubns.

Perdue, E. M. & Gjessing, E. T., eds. Organic Acids in Aquatic Ecosystems. LC 89-29728. 360p. 1990. 335.00 (*0-471-92631-0*) Wiley.

Perdue, E. M., jt. auth. see Chameides, William L.

Perdue, Gervaise W. James A. Perdue & Descendants. 540p. (C). 1984. text. write for info. (*0-9613474-0-6*) Wolfe Pubng.

Perdue, Jim M. The Law of Texas Medical Malpractice. LC 85-8205. 660p. 39.50 (*0-913797-08-1*) Houston Law Review.

— Who Will Speak for the Victim? A Practical Treatise on Plaintiff's Jury Argument. LC 88-63945. 420p. 1989. 74.00 (*0-938160-54-0*, 6231) State Bar TX.

Perdue, Joe, ed. Contemporary Club Management. LC 97-25007. 535p. 1997. pap. 65.95 (*0-86612-168-4*) Educ Inst Am Hotel.

Perdue, Joe, et al. Club Manager's Guide to Private Parties & Club Functions. LC 97-41087. 336p. 1998. 54.95 (*0-471-02978-5*) Wiley.

Perdue, Leo G. The Collapse of History: Reconstructing Old Testament Theology. LC 94-2824. (Overtures to Bibical Theology Ser.). 336p. 1994. pap. 18.00 (*0-8006-1563-8*, 1-1563, Fortress Pr) Augsburg Fortress.

— Introduction to the Hebrew Bible. 656p. 1999. 67.95 (*0-687-01980-X*) Abingdon.

***Perdue, Leo G.** Proverbs: Interpretation. 2000. write for info. (*0-8042-3116-8*) Westminster John Knox.

Perdue, Leo G. Wisdom & Creation: The Theology of Wisdom Literature. LC 94-17507. 208p. (Orig.). 1994. pap. 21.95 (*0-687-45626-6*) Abingdon.

Perdue, Leo G. Wisdom in Revolt: Metaphorical Theology in the Book of Job. (JSOT Supplement Ser.: No. 112). 296p. 1991. 85.00 (*1-85075-283-4*, Pub. by Sheffield Acad) CUP Services.

Perdue, Leo G., ed. A Companion to the Hebrew Bible. 600p. 2000. 99.95 (*0-631-21071-7*) Blackwell Pubs.

Perdue, Leo G., et al, eds. In Search of Wisdom: Essays in Memory of John G. Gammie. 352p. (Orig.). 1993. pap. 28.95 (*0-664-25295-8*) Westminster John Knox.

Perdue, Leo G., jt. ed. see Gammie, John G.

Perdue, Leo G., tr. see Preuss, Horst D.

Perdue, Lewis. Country Inns of Maryland, Virginia & West Virginia. 4th ed. (Illus.). 210p. 1996. pap. 10.95 (*0-915168-14-6*) Wash Bk Trad.

***Perdue, Lewis.** Daughter of God. LC 99-51786. 320p. 2000. 24.95 (*0-312-89074-5*, Pub. by Forge NYC) St Martin.

— Lewis Perdue 2. 2001. text. write for info. (*0-312-85238-X*) St Martin.

Perdue, Lewis. The Wrath of Grapes: The coming Wine Industry Shakeout & How to Take Advantage of It. LC 99-94863. 272p. 1999. pap. 13.50 (*0-380-80151-5*, Avon Bks) Morrow Avon.

— Zaibatsu. 400p. (Orig.). 1988. spiral bd. 4.95 (*0-373-97085-4*) Harlequin Bks.

Perdue, Lewis, et al. The French Paradox & Beyond: Live Longer with Wine & the Mediterranean Lifestyle. (Illus.). 244p. (Orig.). (C). 1992. pap. 12.95 (*0-9625271-1-4*) Renais CA.

Perdue, Mitzi. The Perdue Chicken Cookbook. Grose, Bill, ed. 296p. 1991. 18.95 (*0-671-69143-0*) PB.

***Perdue, Mitzi.** Perdue Chicken Cookbook. (Illus.). 2000. 9.99 (*0-7858-1200-8*) Bk Sales Inc.

Perdue, Pamela D. Plan Termination Answer Book, 1. annuals 964p. 1999. boxed set 125.00 (*1-56706-810-3*, 68103) Panel Pubs.

Perdue, Pamela D. & Wilson, Michelle. Qualified Pension & Profit-Sharing Plans. 2nd ed. LC 98-86484. 1998. write for info. (*0-7913-3544-5*) Warren Gorham & Lamont.

Perdue, Peggy K. Diving into Science, Grades Two-Four. 96p. 1989. pap. 7.95 (*0-673-38965-0*, GoodYrBooks) Addson-Wesley Educ.

— Schoolyard Science: Grades 2-4. (J). (gr. 2-4). 1990. pap. 8.95 (*0-673-38967-7*, GoodYrBooks) Addson-Wesley Educ.

— Science Is an Action Word! Grades 1-3. (J). (gr. 1-3). 1990. pap. 8.95 (*0-673-38968-5*, GoodYrBooks) Addson-Wesley Educ.

— Small Wonders: Hands-on Science Activities for Young Children. (Illus.). 66p. (Orig.). 1988. pap. 8.95 (*0-673-38198-6*, GoodYrBooks) Addson-Wesley Educ.

Perdue, Peggy K., jt. auth. see Vaszily, Diane A.

Perdue, Peter C. Exhausting the Earth: State & Peasant in Hunan 1500-1850. (East Asian Monographs: No. 150). 400p. 1987. 30.00 (*0-674-27504-7*) HUP.

Perdue, Terry A. Heath Nostalgia. LC 93-93530. (Illus.). 124p. 1992. pap. text 15.00 (*0-9637627-0-2*) Taptron.

Perdue, Theda. Cherokee Editor: The Writings of Elias Boudinot. LC 95-23379. 256p. 1996. pap. 15.95 (*0-8203-1809-4*) U of Ga Pr.

— Cherokee Women: Gender & Culture Change, 1700-1835. LC 97-30486. (Indians of the Southeast Ser.). 253p. 1998. text 45.00 (*0-8032-3716-2*) U of Nebr Pr.

***Perdue, Theda.** Cherokee Women: Gender & Culture Change, 1700-1835. LC 97-30486. (Indians of the Southeast Ser.). 253p. 1999. pap. 14.95 (*0-8032-8760-7*) U of Nebr Pr.

Perdue, Theda. Nations Remembered: An Oral History of the Cherokees, Chickasaws, Choctaws, Creeks. LC 92-50726. (Illus.). 246p. 1993. pap. 14.95 (*0-8061-2523-3*) U of Okla Pr.

— Nations Remembered: An Oral History of the Five Civilized Tribes, 1865-1907, 1. LC 79-6828. (Contributions in Ethnic Studies: No. 1). 221p. 1980. 55.00 (*0-313-22097-2*, PFN/, Greenwood Pr) Greenwood.

— Native Carolinians: The Indians of North Carolina. (Illus.). xiv, 73p. 1995. reprint ed. pap. 8.00 (*0-86526-217-9*) NC Archives.

— Slavery & the Evolution of Cherokee Society, 1540-1866. LC 78-16284. 222p. 1979. pap. 15.95 (*0-87049-530-5*) U of Tenn Pr.

***Perdue, Theda, ed.** Sifters: Native American Women's Lives. 282p. 2001. pap. 19.95 (*0-19-513081-2*); text 49.95 (*0-19-513080-4*) OUP.

Perdue, Theda & Green, Michael. The Cherokee Removal. 208p. 1995. pap. text 11.95 (*0-312-08658-X*) St Martin.

Perdue, Tito. Lee. LC 91-9477. 145p. 1991. 18.95 (*0-941423-39-5*) FWEW.

— The New Austerities. 224p. 1993. 20.00 (*1-56145-086-3*) Peachtree Pubs.

— Opportunities in Alabama Agriculture. 222p. 1994. 18.00 (*1-880909-24-3*) Baskerville.

Perdue, Wendy C., jt. auth. see Freer, Richard D.

Perdue, William D. Modernization Crisis: The Transformation of Poland. Borkowski, Tadeusz, tr. & contrib. by by. Palka, Stanislaw et al, contrib. by. LC 95-2491. 264p. 1995. 67.95 (*0-275-95009-3*, Praeger Pubs) Greenwood.

— Paradox of Change: The Rise & Fall of Solidarity in Poland. LC 95-7551. 144p. 1995. 55.00 (*0-275-95295-9*, Praeger Pubs) Greenwood.

— Terrorism & the State. LC 88-34029. 240p. 1989. 59.95 (*0-275-93140-4*, Greenwood Pr) Greenwood.

Pere, Vernice W. Electre. Dunkley, ed. (Exeter French Texts Ser.: Vol. 39). (FRE.). 128p. Date not set. pap. text 19.95 (*0-85989-191-7*, Pub. by Univ Exeter Pr) Northwestern U Pr.

— Mahanga: Pacific Poems. 40p. (C). 1978. pap. 4.50 (*0-939154-02-1*) Inst Polynesian.

Pere, Vernice W., jt. auth. see Craig, Robert D.

Perea, Floresmiro. Salvemos la Familia de Hoy.Tr. of Let's Salve Today's Family. (SPA.). 201p. 1991. pap. 4.99 (*1-56063-302-6*, 498423) Editorial Unilit.

Perea, Hector, tr. see Sharpe, Susan.

Perea, Juan F., ed. Immigrants Out! The New Nativism & the Anti-Immigrant Impulse in the United States. 340p. (C). 1996. text 55.00 (*0-8147-6627-7*); pap. text 22.00 (*0-8147-6642-0*) NYU Pr.

Perea, Karen M., jt. auth. see Guthrie, Jeanne.

Perea, M. A., jt. ed. see Goldsmith, P. A.

Perea, Robert L. Stacey's Story. 70p. (Orig.). 1995. pap. 8.95 (*0-931122-80-5*) West End.

Perea, Roberto R. Callando Amores. (Aqui y Ahora Ser.). 54p. 1996. pap. 6.95 (*0-8477-0263-4*) U of PR Pr.

Pereboom, Derk, ed. Free Will. LC 97-27677. (Hackett Readings in Philosophy Ser.). 312p. (C). 1997. pap. 14.95 (*0-87220-372-7*); lib. bdg. 34.95 (*0-87220-373-5*) Hackett Pub.

Pereboom, Derk, jt. ed. see Guignon, Charles B.

Pereboom, Dirk, ed. The Rationalists: Critical Essays on Descartes, Spinoza & Leibniz. LC 99-16484. 384p. 1999. pap. 18.95 (*0-8476-8911-5*); text 65.00 (*0-8476-8910-7*) Rowman.

Pereboom, Maarten L. Democracies at the Turning Point: Britain, France & the End of the Postwar Order, 1928-1933. 2nd ed. (Studies in Modern European History: Vol. 13). X, 239p. (C). 1997. pap. text 39.95 (*0-8204-3796-4*) P Lang Pubng.

Perec, Georges. Un Cabinet d'Amateur. (FRE.). 1989. pap. 6.95 (*0-7859-3151-1*, 2253050598) Fr & Eur.

— Les Choses. (FRE.). 1987. pap. 8.95 (*0-7859-3222-4*, 2266025791) Fr & Eur.

— Les Choses: Une Histoire des Annees Soixante. Leblon, Jean M., ed. LC 71-84473. (FRE., Illus.). (Orig.). (C). 1969. pap. text 14.95 (*0-89197-078-9*) Irvington.

— Disparition. (Imaginaire Ser.). (FRE.). pap. 15.95 (*2-07-071523-X*) Schoenhof.

— La Disparition. (FRE.). 1989. pap. 19.95 (*0-7859-3394-8*) Fr & Eur.

— 53 Days. Mathews, Harry & Roubaud, Jacques, eds. Bellos, David, tr. from FRE. LC 98-33645. (Verba Mundi Ser.). 270p. 1999. 23.95 (*1-56792-088-8*) Godine.

— Homme Qui Dort. (Folio Ser.: No. 2197). (FRE.). 190p. 1990. pap. 8.95 (*2-07-038288-5*) Schoenhof.

— Un Homme Qui Dort. (FRE.). 1990. pap. 12.95 (*0-7859-2921-5*) Fr & Eur.

— Life: A User's Manual. Bellos, David, tr. from FRE. LC 87-8782. 600p. 1987. reprint ed. pap. 19.95 (*0-87923-751-1*) Godine.

— Quel Petit Velo a Guidon Chrome au Fond de la Cour? (FRE.). 1982. pap. 10.95 (*0-7859-2902-9*) Fr & Eur.

— Quel Petit Velo a Guidon Chrome au Fond de la Cour? (Folio Ser.: No. 1413). (FRE.). pap. 8.95 (*2-07-037413-0*) Schoenhof.

— Species of Spaces & Other Pieces. Sturrock, John, ed. & tr. by. from FRE. LC 98-165819. xv, 288p. 1998. pap. 14.95 (*0-14-018986-6*) Viking Penguin.

— Things: A Story of the Sixties. Bellos, David & Leak, Andrew, trs. from FRE.Tr. of Les Choses. 224p. 1990. 19.95 (*0-87923-857-7*) Godine.

***Perec, Georges.** Things: A Story of the Sixties, &, a Man Asleep. Bellos, David & Leak, Andrew, trs. from FRE. 2000. reprint ed. pap. 16.95 (*1-56792-157-4*) Godine.

Perec, Georges. La Vie Mode d'Emploi. (FRE.). 1980. pap. 17.95 (*0-7859-3100-7*) Fr & Eur.

***Perec, Georges.** W, Or the Memory of Childhood. Bellos, David, tr. from FRE. 2000. reprint ed. pap. 16.95 (*1-56792-158-2*) Godine.

Perec, Georges & Bober, Robert. Ellis Island. Mathews, Harry, tr. from FRE. (Illus.). 160p. 1995. pap. 16.95 (*1-56584-318-5*, Pub. by New Press NY) Norton.

Perechi, Reuben O. What's in a Name? Including African Names & Their Meanings. 102p. (Orig.). 1996. pap. 14.95 (*0-9653372-0-0*) Sina Invest.

Perecman, Ellen. Integrating Theory & Practice in Clinical Neuropsychology. 464p. 1989. 95.00 (*0-8058-0285-1*) L Erlbaum Assocs.

Perecman, Ellen, ed. The Frontal Lobes Revisited. 312p. 1988. 79.95 (*0-8058-0288-6*) L Erlbaum Assocs.

Pereda, Jose M. De, see De Pereda, Jose M.

Pereda, Rafael C. Textos y Pretextos. LC 85-14137. (SPA.). 114p. 1986. pap. 6.00 (*0-8477-3516-8*) U of PR Pr.

Pereda Valdes, Ildefonso, ed. Antologia de la Poesia Negra Americana. (B. E. Ser.: No. 9). (POR.). 1953. 35.00 (*0-8115-2960-6*) Periodicals Srv.

Perednik, Jorge S. & Grosman, Ernesto L., eds. The Xul Reader: An Anthology of Argentine Poetry (1981-1996) (ENG & SPA., Illus.). 167p. (Orig.). 1996. pap. 14.95 (*0-937804-67-3*) Segue NYC.

Peredo, Hernan L., jt. auth. see Butin, Heinz.

***Perego, Giacomo.** Interdisciplinary Atlas of the Bible: Scripture, History, Geography, Archaeology & Theology. deluxe ed. Foster, Stewart, tr. LC 99-23092. (Illus.). 118p. 1999. 24.95 (*0-8189-0875-0*) Alba.

Perego, Maria. Comes to Life Storyplayer & Topo Gigio & the Friends of the Forest Book Set: Comes to Life Storyplayer & Topo Gigio e Gli Animaletti del Bosco. Preziosi, Giochi, tr. from ENG. (Comes to Life Bks.). (ITA.). 16p. (J). (ps-2). 1994. write for info. (*1-57234-004-5*) YES Ent.

— Topo Gigio e il Pirata (Topo Gigio & the Pirate with the Beard) Preziosi, Giochi, tr. from ENG. (Comes to Life Bks.). (ITA.). 16p. (J). (ps-2). 1994. write for info. (*1-57234-005-3*) YES Ent.

Peregoy, Suzanne F. & Boyle, Owen F. Reading, Writing, & Learning in ESL: A Resource Book for K-12 Teachers. 2nd ed. (C). 1997. pap. text, teacher ed. write for info. (*0-8013-1548-4*) Longman.

Peregrin, Jaroslav. Doing Worlds with Words. LC 95-36953. (Synthese Library SYLI: Vol. 253). 256p. (C). 1995. text 107.00 (*0-7923-3742-5*) Kluwer Academic.

***Peregrin, Jaroslav, ed.** Truth & Its Nature (If Any) LC 99-38082. (Synthese Library). 240p. 1999. 115.00 (*0-7923-5865-1*) Kluwer Academic.

Peregrinacao Publications Staff, ed. see Brites, Jose.

Peregrinacao Publications Staff, ed. see Dias, Eduardo M.

Peregrinacao Publications Staff, ed. see Dias, Eduardo Mayone.

Peregrinacao Publications Staff, ed. see Gomes, Luis.

Peregrinacao Publications Staff, ed. see Lameiro, Carlos.

Peregrinacao Publications Staff, ed. see Lopes, Emilia.

Peregrinacao Publications Staff, ed. see Melo, Gloria.

***Peregrine.** Archaelogical Research. LC 99-462089. (Illus.). 272p. 2000. pap. 40.00 (*0-13-081127-0*) P-H.

Peregrine, Peter, et al. Cultural Anthropology: An Introduction Using Explorit. (Illus.). 224p. (C). 1998. pap., wbk. ed. 18.00 (*0-922914-25-7*) Thomson Learn.

Peregrine, Peter N. Archaeology of the Mississippian Culture: A Research Guide. LC 95-19358. (Research Guide to Ancient Civilizations Ser.). 240p. 1995. text 50.00 (*0-8153-0336-X*, H1457) Garland.

Peregrine Publishers Staff. The Biology Place Guidebook Package. 1998. text 15.00 (*0-8053-6686-5*) Addison-Wesley.

Peregrinos & Extranjeros. El Buen Pastor: Libro para Colorear.Tr. of Good Shepherd/Pilgrims Club Coloring Book. (SPA.). (J). 1.59 (*1-56063-854-0*, 494016) Editorial Unilit.

Pereira. General Education Statistics. 1999. text 14.00 (*0-07-235754-1*) McGraw.

— Rappers Delights: African American Cook. 96p. Date not set. pap. 16.95 (*0-7893-0141-5*, Pub. by Universe) St Martin.

Pereira, A. Ethanol, Employment & Development: Lessons from Brazil. xiv, 195p. (Orig.). 1986. pap. 22.50 (*92-2-105380-6*) Intl Labour Office.

Pereira, Anthony, jt. auth. see Lovett, Etheridge G.

Pereira, Anthony W. End of the Peasantry: The Rural Labor Movement in Northeast Brazil, 1961-1988. LC 96-45889. (Latin American Ser.). 232p. 1997. pap. 19.95 (*0-8229-5618-7*); text 45.00 (*0-8229-3964-9*) U of Pittsburgh Pr.

Pereira, Antonio. Cuentos para Lectores Complices. (Nueva Austral Ser.: Vol. 101). (SPA.). 1991. pap. text 24.95 (*84-239-1901-3*) Elliots Bks.

Pereira, Bernardo F., tr. see Calvet De Magalhaes, Jose.

Pereira, C. E., jt. ed. see Kopacek, P.

Pereira, Carlos & Baylis, Bayard. Elementary Statistics: A Motivational Approach. Wetherington, Judy, ed. 392p. 1998. pap. 20.00 (*0-07-234342-7*) McGraw.

Pereira, Carlos E. & Halang, Wolfgang A., eds. Real-Time Programming, 1996. (IFAC Postprint Ser.). 162p. 1997. pap. text 62.50 (*0-08-042614-X*, Pergamon Pr) Elsevier.

Pereira, Carlos E., jt. auth. see Finney, Douglas M.

Pereira, Carmo J., jt. ed. see Becker, E. Robert.

Pereira, D. F., jt. auth. see Rao, T. V.

Pereira, Ernest. Contemporary South African Plays. LC 78-302989. 293 p. 1977. write for info. (*0-86975-064-X*) Ravan Pr.

Pereira, Ernest, ed. see Pringle, Thomas.

Pereira, Ernest, ed. see Smith, Pauline.

Pereira, Fernando C. & Gross, Barbara J., eds. Natural Language Processing. LC 93-39575. (Artificial Intelligence Special Issues Ser.). (Illus.). 537p. 1994. pap. text 39.00 (*0-262-66092-X*, Bradford Bks) MIT Pr.

Pereira, Fernando C. & Shieber, Stuart M. Prolog & Natural Language Analysis. LC 87-70774. (Center for the Study of Language & Information-Lecture Notes Ser.: No. 10). 268p. (Orig.). 1987. 39.95 (*0-937073-17-2*); pap. 18.95 (*0-937073-18-0*) CSLI.

Pereira, Filomena M. Lilith: The Edge of Forever. LC 97-46143. (Woman in History Ser.: Vol. 18). (Illus.). xvi, 215p. 1998. pap. 20.00 (*0-86663-222-0*) Ide Hse.

Pereira, H. C. Policy & Practice in the Management of Tropical Watersheds. 237p. 1989. pap. 180.00 (*81-7089-123-X*, Pub. by Intl Bk Distr) St Mut.

Pereira, Helen. Birds of Paradise: And Other Stories. LC 98-113455. 160p. 1997. pap. 9.95 (*1-895387-79-5*) Creative Bk Pub.

Pereira, Helen. The Home We Leave Behind. 160p. 1992. pap. 6.35 (*1-895387-06-X*) Creative Bk Pub.

— Magpie in the Tower. 128p. 1990. pap. 6.35 (*0-920021-74-3*) Creative Bk Pub.

— Wild Cotton. 160p. 1994. pap. 6.35 (*1-895387-31-0*) Creative Bk Pub.

Pereira, Helena B. Michaelis Pequeno Dicionario Espanhol-Portugues - Portugues-Espanhol. (POR & SPA.). 636p. 1992. 24.95 (*0-7859-9316-9*) Fr & Eur.

— Michaelis Pequeno Dicionario Frances-Portugues - Portugues-Frances. (FRE & POR.). 680p. 1992. 24.95 (*0-7859-9315-0*) Fr & Eur.

Pereira, J. C., jt. ed. see Hanjalic, K.

Pereira, J. G., jt. auth. see Aldrovandi, R.

Pereira, J. S. & Landsberg, J. J., eds. Biomass Production by Fast-Growing Trees. (C). 1989. text 175.00 (*0-7923-0208-7*) Kluwer Academic.

Pereira, Joao C. Portuguese Tiles: From the National Museum of Azulejo, Lisbon. (Illus.). 128p. 1996. 35.00 (*0-302-00661-3*) Scala Books.

***Pereira, John W.** Off-Broadway Daring. 1999. text. write for info. (*0-312-22624-1*) St Martin.

Pereira, John W. Opening Nights: 25 Years of the Manhattan Theatre Club, Vol. 17. LC 93-9525. (American University Studies: Series 26, Vol. 17). (Illus.). X, 520p. (C). 1996. 29.95 (*0-8204-2027-1*) P Lang Pubng.

— Opening Nights: 25 Years of the Manhattan Theatre Club, Vol. 17. 2nd ed. LC 93-9525. (American University Studies: Series 26, Vol. 17). (Illus.). X, 520p. (C). 1996. 18.95 (*0-8204-3381-0*) P Lang Pubng.

Pereira, Jose. Elements of Indian Architecture. 1987. 30.00 (*81-208-0064-8*, Pub. by Motilal Bnarsidass) S Asia.

— Elements of Indian Architecture. 1986. 48.00 (*0-8364-0868-3*) S Asia.

— Islamic Sacred Architecture: A Stylistic History. (C). 1994. 165.00 (*81-85016-37-2*, Pub. by Aditya Prakashan) S Asia.

— Monolithic Jinas. 1977. 8.50 (*0-8426-1027-8*, Pub. by Motilal Bnarsidass) S Asia.

— Monolithic Jinas: The Iconography of the Jain Temples of Ellora. (C). 1977. 11.00 (*0-8364-2632-0*, Pub. by Motilal Bnarsidass) S Asia.

***Pereira, Jose.** Song of Goa: Mandos of Yearning. 2000. 32.00 (*81-7305-166-6*, Pub. by Aryan Bks Intl) S Asia.

Pereira, Jose, ed. Hindu Theology: Themes Texts & Structures. (C). 1991. 28.00 (*81-208-0715-4*, Pub. by Motilal Bnarsidass) S Asia.

Pereira, Kim. August Wilson & the African-American Odyssey. LC 94-25855. 136p. 1995. pap. text 12.95 (*0-252-06429-1*) U of Ill Pr.

Pereira, L. M. Gomes, see Gomes Pereira, L. M.

Pereira, L. S., et al, eds. Sustainability of Irrigated Agriculture: Proceedings of the NATO Advanced Research Workshop, Vimeiro, Portugal, March 21-26, 1994. LC 96-205. (NATO ASI Series E: Applied Sciences: Vol. 213). 644p. (C). 1996. text 331.50 (*0-7923-3936-3*) Kluwer Academic.

Pereira, Linda. Computers Don't Byte. 80p. (J). (gr. 1-3). 1996. pap. 9.95 (*1-55734-936-3*) Tchr Create Mat.

— Computers Don't Byte. 80p. (J). (gr. 3-5). 1996. pap. 9.95 (*1-55734-937-1*) Tchr Create Mat.

— Computers Don't Byte. 80p. (J). (gr. 5-8). 1996. pap. 9.95 (*1-55734-938-X*) Tchr Create Mat.

Pereira, Linda. Computers Don't Byte! Creative Kids. (Illus.). 160p. (J). (gr. 2 up). 1996. pap., wbk. ed. 14.95 (*1-55734-813-8*) Tchr Create Mat.

Pereira, Luis M. & Nerode, Anil, eds. Logic Programming & Non-Monotonic Reasoning: Proceedings of the Second International Workshop. (Illus.). 500p. 1993. pap. text 38.50 (*0-262-66083-0*) MIT Pr.

Pereira, Luis M. & Siekmann, Joerg H. Non-Monotonic Extensions of Logic Programming: ICLP '94 Workshop, Santa Margherita Ligure, Italy, June 17, 1994, Selected Papers. LC 95-20072. (Lecture Notes in Computer Science Ser.: Vol. 927). 229p. 1995. 43.00 (*3-540-59467-1*) Spr-Verlag.

Pereira, Luis M., jt. auth. see Alferes, Jose J.

Pereira, Luis S., et al, eds. Water & Environment: Innovative Issues in Irrigation & Drainage. LC 98-26951. (Illus.). 496p. (C). (gr. 13). 1998. 125.00 (*0-419-23710-0*, D6605, E & FN Spon) Routledge.

Pereira, Luiz C., et al. Economic Reforms in New Democracies: A Social-Democratic Approach. LC 92-17342. (Illus.). 237p. (C). 1993. text 64.95 (*0-521-43259-6*); pap. text 18.95 (*0-521-43845-4*) Cambridge U Pr.

***Pereira, Malin.** Embodying Beauty: 20th Century American Women Writers' Aesthetics. LC 99-55079. (Literary Criticism & Cultural Theory Ser.). 200p. 2000. 55.00 (*0-8153-3732-9*) Garland.

Pereira, Manuel F., ed. Computer-Aided Analysis of Rigid & Flexible Mechanical Systems: Proceedings of the NATO Advanced Study Institute, Troia, Portugal, June 27 - July 9, 1993. (NATO Advanced Study Institutes Series E: Applied Sciences Ser.). 640p. (C). 1994. text 382.50 (*0-7923-2839-6*) Kluwer Academic.

P

Pereira, Manuel F. & Ambrosio, Jorge A.C., eds. Computational Dynamics in Multibody Systems. LC 94-45512. (Diverse Ser.). 324p. (C). 1995. text 166.00 (*0-7923-3304-7*) Kluwer Academic.

Pereira-Maxwell, Filomena. A-Z of Medical Statistics: A Companion for Critical Appraisal. LC 99-173194. (Arnold Publications). (Illus.). 128p. (Orig.). 1998. pap. text 26.50 (*0-340-71940-0*) OUP.

Pereira, Michael A. Effect of Dichloracetic Acid & Trichloroacetic Acid on Cell Proliferation in B6C3F1 Mice. LC 96-203954. (Illus.). 29p. 1995. pap. 42.00 (*0-89867-826-9*, 90700) Am Water Wks Assn.

Pereira, Michael E. & Fairbanks, Lynn A., eds. Juvenile Primates: Life History, Development, & Behavior. (Illus.). 400p. (C). 1993. text 75.00 (*0-19-507206-5*) OUP.

Pereira, N. G. White Siberia: The Politics of Civil War. (Illus.). 320p. 1995. 60.00 (*0-7735-1349-3*, Pub. by McG-Queens Univ Pr) CUP Services.

Pereira, Nancy. Creative Drama in the Library. 2nd ed. 94p. 1976. 10.95 (*0-932720-14-5*); pap. 8.95 (*0-932720-13-7*) New Plays Inc.

Pereira, Nino, et al, eds. Dense Z-Pinches. (AIP Conference Proceedings Ser.: No. 195). 568p. 1989. lib. bdg. 80.00 (*0-88318-396-X*) Am Inst Physics.

Pereira, Nino R., et al, eds. Dense Z-Pinches: Fourth International Conference. LC 97-76959. (AIP Conference Proceedings Ser.: Vol. 409). (Illus.). xvi, 628p. 1997. 145.00 (*1-56396-610-7*) Am Inst Physics.

Pereira, Norman C., jt. ed. see Wang, Lawrence K.

Pereira, Patricia, jt. auth. see Dibbs, Owen.

Pereira, Patricia L. Arcturian Songs of the Masters of Light: Intergalactic Seed Messages for the People of Planet Earth: A Manual to Aid in Understanding Matters Pertaining to Personal & Planetary Evolution. LC 99-27436. (Arcturian Star Chronicles Ser.: No. IV). 250p. 1999. pap. 13.95 (*1-885223-69-2*, Pub. by Beyond Words Pub) Publishers Group.

— Eagles of the New Dawn Vol. 2: Intergalactic Seed Messages for the People of Planet Earth: A Manual to Aid in Understanding Matters Pertaining to Personal & Planetary Evolution. LC 97-17957. 264p. (Orig.). 1997. pap. 12.95 (*1-885223-59-5*) Beyond Words Pub.

— Songs of Malantor: Intergalactic Seed Messages for the People of Planet Earth: A Manual to Aid in Understanding Matters Pertaining to Personal & Planetary Evolution. LC 98-22008. (Arcturian Star Chronicles Ser.: Vol. III). 320p. 1998. pap. 13.95 (*1-885223-70-6*) Beyond Words Pub.

— Songs of the Arcturians Bk. 1: Intergalactic Seed Messages for the People of Planet Earth: A Manual to Aid in Understanding Matters Pertaining to Personal & Planetary Evolution. (Arcturian Star Chronicles Ser.). (Illus.). 257p. 1996. pap. 13.95 (*1-885223-43-9*) Beyond Words Pub.

Pereira, Paulo. Pena Palace, Sintra. 1998. 35.00 (*1-85759-175-5*) Scala Books.

Pereira, Paulo R., tr. see Larsson, Goran.

Pereira, Pedro T. & Mata, Maria E., eds. Urban Dominance & Labour Market Differentiation of a European Capital City: Lisbon 1890-1990. LC 96-46652. 200p. (C). 1996. lib. bdg. 97.00 (*0-7923-9830-0*) Kluwer Academic.

***Pereira, Peter.** The Lost Twin. 37p. 2000. pap. 14.95 (*1-58249-006-6*) Grey Spider.

— The Lost Twin. limited deluxe ed. 37p. 2000. 45.00 (*1-58249-005-8*) Grey Spider.

Pereira, Peter, et al, eds. Pontoon: An Anthology of Washington State Poets. (Number One Ser.). 80p. 1997. pap. 7.00 (*0-9647199-3-2*) Floating Bridge Pr.

***Pereira, Peter, et al, eds.** Pontoon No. 3: An Anthology of Washington State Poets. 96p. 1999. pap. 7.00 (*0-9647199-8-3*) Floating Bridge Pr.

— Pontoon, Number Two: An Anthology of Washington State Poets. 96p. 1998. pap. 7.00 (*0-9647199-5-9*) Floating Bridge Pr.

Pereira, Peter, ed. see Van Winckel, Nance.

Pereira, Sam. Brittle Water. (Illus.). 1987. 50.00 (*0-318-41022-2*); pap. 27.50 (*0-318-41023-0*) Abattoir.

— The Marriage of the Portuguese. LC 78-71826. 53p. (Orig.). 1978. pap. 3.75 (*0-934332-09-6*) LEpervier Pr.

Pereira, Winin. Inhuman Rights: The Western System & Global Human Rights Abuse. 258p. 1997. pap. 17.50 (*0-945257-79-1*) Apex Pr.

Pereiras, Manuel. Bebo & the Band. 77p. 1993. pap. text 4.95 (*1-885901-05-4*) Presbyters Peartree.

— It Is It Is Not. 57p. 1994. pap. text 3.95 (*1-885901-14-3*) Presbyters Peartree.

— Santiago. 26p. 1993. pap. text 2.95 (*1-885901-03-8*) Presbyters Peartree.

— Still Still. 57p. 1993. pap. text 3.95 (*1-885901-04-6*) Presbyters Peartree.

Pereiras, Manuel, ed. Jose Marti: Simply Rhymes & Poems from "The Golden Age" 54p. 1998. 3.95 (*1-885901-92-5*, Liberts) Presbyters Peartree.

— Jose Marti: Versos Sencillos Y De La Edad De Oro. (SPA.). 52p. 1998. 3.95 (*1-885901-91-7*, Liberts) Presbyters Peartree.

Pereiras, Manuel, ed. from SPA. Jose Marti, Vol. 2. 106p. 1998. 7.50 (*1-885901-93-3*, Liberts) Presbyters Peartree.

Pereiras, Manuel, tr. see Corrales, Jose.

***Pereire, Anita.** Gardens for the 21st Century. (Illus.). 216p. 2000. 45.00 (*1-85410-639-2*, Pub. by Aurum Pr) London Brdge.

Pereiro, James. Cardinal Manning: An Intellectual Biography. 376p. 1998. text 82.00 (*0-19-815089-X*) OUP.

Perejda, Andrew, ed. see Uitto, Jouni.

Perek, L., ed. see International Astronomical Union Staff.

Perekrestov, Peter, compiled by. Man of God, St. John of Shanghai & San Francisco. 254p. 12.95 (*1-879066-06-8*) Conciliar Pr.

Perel, Azriel & Stock, M. Christine. Handbook of Mechanical Ventilatory Support. (Illus.). 328p. 1991. 40.00 (*0-683-06856-3*) Lppncott W & W.

Perel, Azriel, jt. auth. see Stock, M. Christine.

Perel, Earl J. The Case Against Socrates. LC 98-86008. 325p. 1998. 25.00 (*0-7388-0017-1*); pap. 15.00 (*0-7388-0045-7*) Xlibris Corp.

— Kings in Crisis. LC 98-85967. (Illus.). 325p. 1998. 25.00 (*0-7388-0008-2*); pap. 15.00 (*0-7388-0035-X*) Xlibris Corp.

— Romantic Odyssey: A Quixotic Poet's Random Memoirs. LC 98-85965. 325p. 1998. 25.00 (*0-7388-0006-6*); pap. 15.00 (*0-7388-0037-6*) Xlibris Corp.

— Sequestered Soliloquies. 96p. 1994. 10.00 (*0-932616-46-1*) Brick Hse Bks.

Perel, Solomon. Europa, Europa. Dembo, Margot B., tr. from GER. LC 96-46844. (Illus.). 240p. 1997. 24.95 (*0-471-17218-9*) Wiley.

— Europa, Europa: A Memoir of World War II. Dembo, Margot B., tr. 240p. 1999. pap. 16.95 (*0-471-28364-9*) Wiley.

Perelberg, Rosine J., ed. Psychoanalytic Understanding of Violence & Suicide. LC 98-25639. (New Library of Psychoanalysis Ser.). 200p. (C). (gr. 13). 1999. 95.00 (*0-415-19931-X*, D6659); pap. 29.99 (*0-415-19932-8*, D6663) Routledge.

Perelberg, Rosine J., jt. ed. see Raphael-Leff, Joan.

Pereleshin, Valeriy. Iz Glubiny Vozzvakh. LC 87-61471.Tr. of From Deepness of My Soul. (RUS.). 160p. 1987. pap. text 18.00 (*0-914265-60-1*) New Eng Pub MA.

— Poema Bez Predmeta. Levin, Roman, ed. LC 89-92891.Tr. of Poem with No Point. (RUS., Illus.). 422p. 1989. pap. text 25.00 (*0-914265-28-8*) New Eng Pub MA.

Perelishin, Valeriy. Dvoe I Snova Odin.Tr. of Together & Again Lonely. (RUS.). 48p. 1987. pap. text 16.00 (*0-914265-09-1*) New Eng Pub MA.

— Vdogonku. Levin, Lubov, ed.Tr. of Chase. (RUS.). 48p. 1988. pap. text 16.00 (*0-914265-10-5*) New Eng Pub MA.

Perell. Remedies & the Sale of Land. 352p. 1988. boxed set 81.00 (*0-409-80534-3*, MICHIE) LEXIS Pub.

Perella, Nicholas J. The Kiss, Sacred & Profane: An Interpretative History of Kiss Symbolism & Related Religio-Erotic Themes. LC 75-83292. (Illus.). 370p. reprint ed. pap. 114.70 (*0-608-17984-1*, 202905800058) Bks Demand.

Perella, Nicholas J., tr. see Palazzeschi, Aldo.

Perella, Nicolas J. The Midday in Italian Literature: Variations on an Archetypal Theme. LC 78-70313. 347p. reprint ed. pap. 107.60 (*0-8357-7895-9*, 203631400002) Bks Demand.

Perella, Nicolas J., tr. & intro. see Collodi, Carlo.

Perelli, Carina, et al. Paraguay: Pre-Election Technical Assessment, June 1995. ii, 194p. 1996. pap. text 21.00 (*1-879720-25-6*) Intl Fndt Elect.

Perello, C., et al. Equadiff '91: International Conference on Differential Equations, 2 vols., Set. 1000p. 1993. text 178.00 (*981-02-1023-X*) World Scientific Pub.

Perello, Jennifer Twomey & Gilman, Allison. Seasons in Blue's Backyard. 14p. 1999. pap. 5.99 (*0-689-82396-7*, Simon Spot) Litle Simon.

Perello, Jennifer Twomey, et al. Blue's Guess Who! (Blue's Clues Ser.). (Illus.). 16p. (J). (ps-2). 1999. pap. 3.99 (*0-689-82951-5*, Simon Spot) Litle Simon.

Perello, Jorge. Lexicon de Comunicologia - Diccinario para Audiologos, Audioprotesistas, Fonitras, Logopedas, Profesores de Sordos y Psicolinguistas: Lexicon of Communications Science. (ENG, FRE, GER & SPA.). 856p. 1977. 75.00 (*0-8288-5485-8*, S50096) Fr & Eur.

Perelman, Bob. Braille. LC 75-319972. 61p. 1975. 3.50 (*0-87886-057-6*, Greenfld Rev Pr) Greenfld Rev Lit.

— Captive Audience. 1988. per. 7.50 (*0-935724-36-2*) Figures.

— Face Value. (Roof Bks.). 60p. (Orig.). 1987. pap. 60.00 (*0-937804-26-6*) Segue NYC.

— The Future of Memory. 120p. 1998. 14.95 (*0-937804-75-4*) Segue NYC.

— The Marginalization of Poetry: Language, Writing & Literary History. 224p. 1996. text 39.50 (*0-691-02139-2*, Pub. by Princeton U Pr); pap. text 15.95 (*0-691-02138-4*, Pub. by Princeton U Pr) Cal Prin Full Svc.

— Ten to One: Selected Poems. LC 99-34281. 234p. 1999. pap. 16.95 (*0-8195-6388-9*, Wesleyan Univ Pr) U Pr of New Eng.

***Perelman, Bob.** Ten to One: Selected Poems. LC 99-34281. (Wesleyan Poetry Ser.). 234p. 1999. text 35.00 (*0-8195-6387-0*, Wesleyan Univ Pr) U Pr of New Eng.

Perelman, Bob. Virtual Reality. LC 92-63354. (Roof Bks.). 80p. (Orig.). 1993. pap. 9.95 (*0-937804-49-5*) Segue NYC.

Perelman, Chaim. Justice, Law & Argument: Essays on Moral & Legal Reasoning. (Synthese Library: No. 142). 194p. 1980. lib. bdg. 78.00 (*90-277-1089-9*, D Reidel) Kluwer Academic.

— The Realm of Rhetoric. Kluback, William, tr. LC 79-66378. (C). 1982. pap. text 11.50 (*0-268-01605-4*) U of Notre Dame Pr.

Perelman, Chaim & Olbrechts-Tyteca, L. The New Rhetoric: A Treatise on Argumentation. Wilkinson, John & Weaver, Purcell, trs. LC 68-20440. (C). 1969. pap. text 23.00 (*0-268-00446-3*) U of Notre Dame Pr.

***Perelman, Dale R.** Centenarians: One Hundred Years Old Who Made a Difference. LC 99-41761. 193p. 1999. pap. 15.95 (*0-929765-70-2*) Seven Locks Pr.

Perelman, J. The Perfect Harmonica Method. 1992. pap. 15.95 incl. audio (*0-931759-64-1*, 00000147) H Leonard.

Perelman, Jerry. The Perfect Harmonica Method. (Illus.). 64p. 1992. pap. text 17.95 incl. cd-rom (*1-57424-064-1*) Centerstream Pub.

Perelman, Leslie C., et al. The Mayfield Handbook of Technical & Scientific Writing. LC 97-20849. xxvii, 508p. 1997. spiral bd. 29.95 (*1-55934-647-7*, 1647) Mayfield Pub.

Perelman, Lewis J. The Learning Enterprise: Adult Learning, Human Capital & Economic Development. 62p. 1984. 10.00 (*0-934842-44-2*) CSPA.

— School's Out: The End of Education & the New Technology. 368p. 1993. reprint ed. pap. 12.50 (*0-380-71748-4*, Avon Bks) Morrow Avon.

Perelman, Michael. Class Warfare in the Information Age. LC 97-53280. 160p. 1998. text 35.00 (*0-312-17758-5*) St Martin.

***Perelman, Michael.** Class Warfare in the Information Age. 2000. pap. 16.95 (*0-312-22477-X*) St Martin.

Perelman, Michael. The End of Economics. LC 95-46225. (Frontiers of Political Economy Ser.: Vol. 4). 216p. (C). 1996. 75.00 (*0-415-13737-3*) Routledge.

— Farming for Profit in a Hungry World: Capital & the Crisis in Agriculture. LC 76-43229. 250p. 1978. text 31.00 (*0-916672-88-3*) Rowman.

— Information, Social Relations & the Economics of High Technology. 256p. 1991. text 55.00 (*0-312-05676-1*) St Martin.

***Perelman, Michael.** The Invention of Capitalism: Classical Political Economy & the Secret History of Primitive Accumulation. LC 99-45625. 432p. 2000. pap. 22.95 (*0-8223-2491-1*) Duke.

Perelman, Michael. Marx's Crises Theory: Scarcity, Labor, Finance. LC 87-6936. 256p. 1987. 55.00 (*0-275-92372-X*, C2372, Praeger Pubs) Greenwood.

***Perelman, Michael.** Natural Instability of Capitalism: Expectations, Increasing Returns & the Collapse of Capitalism. LC 98-48413. 188p. 1999. 39.95 (*0-312-22121-5*) St Martin.

Perelman, Michael. The Pathology of the U. S. Economy: The Costs of a Low-Wage System. 250p. 1996. pap. 18.95 (*0-312-12685-9*) St Martin.

***Perelman, Michael.** Transcending the Economy: On the Potential of Passionate Labor & the Wastes of the Market. LC 99-55566. 2000. 39.95 (*0-312-22977-1*) St Martin.

Perelman, N. Autumn Leaves. Orlov, Henry, tr. 64p. 1994. pap. 10.00 (*0-929647-06-8*) H A Frager & Co.

— Osenniye List'ya: Autumn Leaves. (RUS.). 64p. (Orig.). 1994. pap. 10.00 (*0-929647-05-X*) H A Frager & Co.

Perelman, Richard B. Perelman's College Football Companion. (Illus.). 1998. pap. 14.95 (*0-9649258-7-7*) Perelman Pioneer.

— Perelman's Pocket Cyclopedia of Cigars. 296p. 1995. pap. 8.95 (*0-9649258-2-6*) Perelman Pioneer.

***Perelman, Richard B.** Perelman's Pocket Cyclopedia of Cigars. 1999. pap. 12.95 (*1-893273-00-8*) Perelman Pioneer.

Perelman, Richard B. Perelman's Pocket Cyclopedia of Cigars: 1999 Edition. (Illus.). 832p. 1998. pap. 12.95 (*0-9649258-8-5*) Perelman Pioneer.

— Perelman's Pocket Cyclopedia of Cigars, 1997 Edition. (Illus.). 442p. 1996. pap. 9.95 (*0-9649258-3-4*) Perelman Pioneer.

— Perelman's Pocket Cyclopedia of Cigars, 1998 Edition. 4th ed. (Illus.). 608p. 1997. pap. 9.95 (*0-9649258-5-0*) Perelman Pioneer.

— Perelman's Pocket Cylopedia of Havana Cigars. (Illus.). 108p. (Orig.). 1996. pap. 9.95 (*0-9649258-4-2*) Perelman Pioneer.

***Perelman, Richard B., compiled by.** Perelman's College Football Companion: 1999 Edition. (Illus.). 646p. 1999. pap. 14.95 (*0-9649258-9-3*) Perelman Pioneer.

Perelman, Richard B., ed. American Athletics Annual, 1980. 694p. (Orig.). 1980. pap. 15.00 (*0-686-29735-0*) Athletics Cong.

— American Athletics Annual, 1981. 1981. write for info. (*0-318-57618-X*) Athletics Cong.

Perelman, Richard B. & Meyers, Mark. Unforgettable! The 100 Greatest Moments in Los Angeles Sports History. LC 95-36666. (Moments in Sports Ser.). (Illus.). 224p. 1995. 39.95 (*1-881096-21-1*) Towery Pub.

Perelman, S. J. Acres & Pains. LC 94-24655. (Illus.). 128p. 1995. pap. 12.95 (*1-58080-016-5*) Burford Bks.

— Baby, It's Cold Inside: Thirty-Two Side-Splitting Stories by America's Master Humorist. 256p. 2000. pap. 16.95 (*1-58574-117-5*) Lyons Pr.

— Eastward Ha! LC 98-19503. (Illus.). 128p. 1998. reprint ed. pap. 12.95 (*1-58080-068-8*) Burford Bks.

— 1897 Sears, Roebuck & Co. Catalogue: 100th Anniversary Edition. (Illus.). 786p. 1997. pap. 19.95 (*0-7910-4626-5*) Chelsea Hse.

***Perelman, S. J.** The Last Laugh: The Final Word from the First Name in Satire. 192p. 2000. pap. 16.95 (*1-58574-152-3*) Lyons Pr.

— Most of the Most of S. J. Perelman. LC 99-462419. 544p. 2000. pap. 15.95 (*0-679-64037-1*) Modern Lib NY.

— The Rising Gorge: America's Master Humorist Takes on Everything from Monomania to Ernest Hemingway. 288p. 2000. pap. 16.95 (*1-58574-172-8*) Lyons Pr.

— The Swiss Family Perelman: A Rollicking International Road Trip with America's Greatest Humorist. (Illus.). 216p. 2000. pap. 16.95 (*1-58574-181-7*) Lyons Pr.

— Westward Ha! LC 98-19493. (Illus.). 128p. 1998. reprint ed. pap. 12.95 (*1-58080-067-X*) Burford Bks.

Perelman, S. J., et al. The Marx Brothers: Monkey Business, Duck Soup, A Day at the Races. (Classic Screenplay Ser.). (Illus.). 224p. (Orig.). 1993. pap. 16.95 (*0-571-16647-4*) Faber & Faber.

Perelman, Sidney J. Favorites of S. J. Perelman. 24.95 (*0-8488-1123-2*) Amereon Ltd.

— Listen to the Mockingbird. 18.95 (*0-89190-422-0*) Amereon Ltd.

— Vinegar Puss. 21.95 (*0-89190-421-2*) Amereon Ltd.

Perelman, Vladimir. How to Turn a Technical Interview into a Winning Battle: For Computer Professionals. 1991. pap. 25.00 (*0-9631774-0-0*) VSP Mgmt Cnslts.

Perelman, Yakov. Mathematics Can Be Fun. 400p. (C). 1985. 50.00 (*0-7855-4982-X*, Pub. by Collets) St Mut.

Perelmuter, Hayim G., et al. Harvest of a Dialogue: Reflections of a Rabbi Scholar on a Catholic Faculty. Bergant, Dianne & Pawlikowski, John, eds. LC 97-3093. 1997. 39.50 (*0-88125-570-X*) Ktav.

Perelmuter, Hayim Goren, jt. illus. see Pawlikowski, John.

Perelomov, A. Generalized Coherent States & Their Applications. (Texts & Monographs in Physics). 320p. 1986. 123.95 (*0-387-15912-6*) Spr-Verlag.

Perelomov, A. M. Integrable Systems of Classical Mechanics & Lie Algebras, Vol. I. 320p. 1990. 139.50 (*0-8176-2336-1*) Birkhauser.

Perelomov, Askold M. & Zel ' dovich, Yakov B. Quantum Mechanics: Selected Topics. (Selected Topics Ser.). 350p. 1999. 48.00 (*981-02-3550-X*) World Scientific Pub.

Perelson, Alan. The Warriors Within. 1998. write for info. (*0-201-44215-9*) Addison-Wesley.

***Perelson, Alan.** Warriors Within. 2000. 25.00 (*0-7382-0194-4*, Pub. by Perseus Pubng) HarpC.

Perelson, Alan S., et al, eds. Cell Surface Dynamics: Concepts & Models. LC 84-9464. (Receptors & Ligands in Intercellular Communication Ser.: Vol. 3). (Illus.). 572p. reprint ed. pap. 177.40 (*0-608-08972-9*, 206960700005) Bks Demand.

Perelson, Alan S. & Weisbuch, Gerard, eds. Theoretical & Experimental Insights into Immunity. LC 92-27863. (NATO ASI Series H: Cell Biology: Vol. 95). xvii, 480p. 1992. 207.95 (*0-387-54614-6*) Spr-Verlag.

Perelson, Alan S., jt. auth. see Macken, C. A.

Perelson, Ruth & Union of American Hebrew Congregations Department. An Invitation to Shabbat: A Beginner's Guide to Weekly Celebration. LC 96-48518. 96p. 1997. pap. 16.95 (*0-8074-0632-5*, 386501) UAHC.

Perelson, Ruth & Union of American Hebrew Congregations Staff. An Invitation to Shabbat: A Beginner's Guide to Weekly Celebration. LC 96-48518. 1997. pap. 12.95 (*0-8074-0611-2*, 386501) UAHC.

***Pereni, Angelo & Bonfanti, Mario.** The Complete Book of Soccer Restart Plays. (Illus.). 185p. 1999. pap. 14.95 (*1-890946-14-1*) Reedswain.

***Pereni, Angelo & Dicesare, Michele.** Soccer Zone Play: A Technical & Tactical Handbook. (Illus.). 266p. 1999. pap. 14.95 (*1-890946-18-4*) Reedswain.

Perennou, Marie, jt. auth. see Nuridsany, Claude.

Perenyi, Constance. Wild Wild West: Wildlife Habitats of Western North America. LC 92-46995. (Illus.). 32p. (J). (gr. 1 up). 1993. pap. 8.95 (*0-912365-90-0*) Sasquatch Bks.

Perenyi, Eleanor. Green Thoughts. 1992. 25.00 (*0-8446-6629-7*) Peter Smith.

— Green Thoughts: A Writer in the Garden. LC 83-47805. 304p. 1983. pap. 14.00 (*0-394-71714-7*) Vin Bks.

Perenyi, Imre. Town & Environs: Recreation in Town Planning. 152p. (C). 1978. 85.00 (*963-05-1493-1*, Pub. by Akade Kiado) St Mut.

Perepelkin, et al. Collective Phenomena in Current-Carrying Plasmas. xx, 248p. 1985. text 332.00 (*2-88124-016-X*) Gordon & Breach.

Perepelkin, Lev, jt. ed. see Mastyugina, Tatiana.

Perera, Audrey. The Simple Guide to Customs & Etiquette in Singapore. 64p. 1996. pap. text 8.95 (*1-86034-040-7*) MAGI1 UK.

Perera, Audrey, jt. auth. see Murray, Geoffrey.

Perera, Domingo M. Fraternidad Entre Alambradas. LC 98-91717. (SPA., Illus.). 317p. 1998. pap. 19.95 (*0-9666803-0-8*) Domingo M Perera.

Perera, E. S. The Origin & Development of Dhrupad & Its Bearing on Instrumental Music. LC 94-902446. (C). 1995. 28.50 (*81-7074-111-4*, Pub. by KP Bagchi) S Asia.

Perera, Eve L., jt. auth. see Salitan, Lucille.

Perera, Frederica, jt. ed. see Schulte, Paul A.

Perera, H. R. Buddhism in Sri Lanka: A Short History. 96p. 1988. 3.75 (*955-24-0017-1*, Pub. by Buddhist Pub Soc) Vipassana Res Pubns.

Perera, Heidi. The Fine Art of Porcelain Painting. unabridged ed. Tubbs, John & Tubbs, Pat, eds. (Illus.). 115p. 1998. spiral bd. 38.00 (*0-9673244-0-8*) Porclain Artist.

***Perera, Hilda.** El Automovil de Mi Abuelo. (SPA.). 2000. 12.95 (*84-241-3332-3*) Everest SP.

— El Burrito Que Queria Ser Azul. (SPA.). 2000. 12.95 (*84-241-3334-X*) Everest SP.

Perera, Hilda. Cuentos de Apolo. 3rd ed. (SPA., Illus.). 103p. (YA). (gr. 6 up). 1975. pap. 5.00 (*0-89729-438-6*) Ediciones.

— De Encuentros y Despedidas. Hiriart, Rosario, ed. (SPA.). 98p. 1997. 10.00 (*1-887175-02-4*) ECV NY.

— El Duende Del Mar (The Goblin of the Sea) (Encuento/Literary Encounters Ser.). (SPA., Illus.). (gr. 3 up). 1997. pap. text 10.95 (*968-494-071-8*) Donars.

— Froggie Froggette. Sklar, Janet, tr. LC 96-41304. (J). (gr. 1-3). 1996. 12.95 (*1-880507-27-7*); pap. 6.95 (*1-880507-28-5*) Lectorum Pubns.

— Idapo. (SPA.). 1971. pap. 10.00 (*0-89729-088-7*) Ediciones.

— Javi. 1996. 11.95 (*84-241-3335-8*); pap. text 11.95 (*84-241-3355-2*) Lectorum Pubns.

— Kike. 8th ed. (Barco de Vapor Ser.). (SPA.). (J). 1990. 11.05 (*0-606-05393-X*, Pub. by Turtleback) Demco.

Perera, Hilda. La Pata Pita. 1995. pap. 7.95 (*0-8056-0134-1*) Minerva Bks Ltd.

P

An Asterisk (*) at the beginning of an entry indicates that the title is appearing for the first time.

Perera, Hilda. Perdido (Lost) (SPA., Illus.). (YA). 1993. pap. 5.99 (*968-16-4234-1*, Pub. by Fondo) Continental Bk.

— Plantado: Una Cronica Desnuda y Terrible de la Experiencia de las Carceles Castristas. (SPA.). 183p. (Orig.). 1981. pap. 7.95 (*84-320-3612-9*) Ediciones.

***Perera, Hilda.** Rana Ranita. 1999. 12.95 (*84-241-3330-7*) Everest SP.

Perera, Hilda. El Sitio de Nadie. 3rd ed. (SPA.). 329p. (Orig.). 1973. 15.00 (*84-320-5271-X*) Ediciones.

Perera, Lydia, tr. see Soik, Helmut M.

Perera, M. H. Accounting for State Industrial & Commercial Enterprises in a Developing Country. Brief, Richard P., ed. LC 80-1516. (Dimensions of Accounting Theory & Practice Ser.). 1980. lib. bdg. 35.95 (*0-405-13495-9*) Ayer.

Perera, Nihal. Society & Space: Colonialism, Nationalism & Postcolonial Identity in Sri Lanka. LC 97-50122. (Transitions: Asia & Asian America Ser.). 217p. (C). 1998. text 69.00 (*0-8133-2979-5*, Pub. by Westview) HarpC.

Perera, Peter A. The Sales Un-Process. (Illus.). 50p. 1997. pap. 9.95 (*0-9659757-0-3*) iP Squared.

Perera, S. C., tr. from POR. The Temporal & Spiritual Conquest of Ceylon: Sixteenth & Seventeenth Century Account of Ceylon, 3 vols., Set. (C). 1992. reprint ed. 105.00 (*81-206-0764-3*, Pub. by Asian Educ Servs) S Asia.

Perera, Suvendrini. Reaches of Empire. 224p. 1991. text 46.00 (*0-231-07578-2*) Col U Pr.

Perera, Sylvia B. Descent to the Goddess. 213p. 1981. pap. 16.00 (*0-919123-05-8*, Pub. by Inner City Bks) BookWorld.

— The Scapegoat Complex. 128p. 1995. pap. 16.00 (*0-919123-22-8*, Pub. by Inner City Bks) BookWorld.

Perera, Sylvia B., jt. auth. see Whitmont, Edward C.

Perera, Sylvia Brinton. Queen Maeve & Her Lovers: A Celtic Archetype of Ecstacy, Addition & Healing. 490p. 1999. 39.00 (*0-8290-5211-9*) Ardent Media.

Perera, T. & Khing. Perinatal Mortality & Morbidity Including Low Birth Weight: A South-East Asia Regional Profile. (SEARO Regional Health Papers: No. 3). 72p. 1984. pap. text 8.00 (*92-9022-172-0*) World Health.

Perera, Victor. The Cross & the Pear Tree: A Sephardic Journey. (Illus.). 282p. (C). 1996. pap. 15.95 (*0-520-20652-5*, Pub. by U CA Pr) Cal Prin Full Svc.

— Of Whales & Men. 1998. write for info. (*0-375-40013-3*) Random.

— Rites: A Guatemalan Boyhood. 192p. 1986. 15.95 (*0-15-177678-4*) Harcourt.

— Rites: A Guatemalan Boyhood. LC 94-13776. 208p. 1994. reprint ed. pap. 12.95 (*1-56279-065-X*) Mercury Hse Inc.

— Unfinished Conquest: The Guatemalan Tragedy. LC 93-12054. (Illus.). 297p. 1993. 40.00 (*0-520-07965-5*, Pub. by U CA Pr) Cal Prin Full Svc.

— Unfinished Conquest: The Guatemalan Tragedy. LC 93-12054. (Illus.). 297p. 1995. pap. 19.95 (*0-520-20349-6*, Pub. by U CA Pr) Cal Prin Full Svc.

Perera, Victor & Bruce, Robert D. The Last Lords of Palenque: The Lacandon Mayas of the Mexican Rain Forest. (Illus.). 320p. 1985. pap. 15.95 (*0-520-05309-5*, Pub. by U CA Pr) Cal Prin Full Svc.

Perera, Victor, tr. see Montejo, Victor.

Perers, Kristin. Color: Color. LC 98-26895. (Illus.). 128p. (gr. 11). 1999. 19.95 (*0-7370-0017-1*) T-L Custom Pub.

— Seasonal Home: Seasonal Home. LC 98-26911. (Illus.). 128p. (gr. 11). 1999. 19.95 (*0-7370-0019-8*) T-L Custom Pub.

— Storage: Storage. LC 98-28076. (Illus.). 128p. (gr. 11). 1999. 19.95 (*0-7370-0018-X*) T-L Custom Pub.

Peres, ed. Neuronal Factors. 216p. 1987. 123.00 (*0-8493-5241-X*, QP363, CRC Reprint) Franklin.

Peres, Asher. Quantum Theory: Concepts & Methods. LC 93-32994. (Fundamental Theories of Physics Ser.). 460p. (C). 1993. lib. bdg. 155.00 (*0-7923-2549-4*, Pub. by Kluwer Academic) Kluwer Academic.

— Quantum Theory: Concepts & Methods, Vol. 72. LC 95-34044. (Fundamental Theories of Physics Ser.). 1995. pap. text 73.00 (*0-7923-3632-1*, Pub. by Kluwer Academic) Kluwer Academic.

P

Peres, Constanze & Schmidt, Diether. Erneuerung Als Tradition: Dresdner Kunst und 100 Jahre Kunstakademie Im (Inter)Nationalen Kontext. (GER., Illus.). 230p. 1996. pap. text 20.50 (*90-5705-014-5*) Gordon & Breach.

Peres, Edward R. Tendrils of the Eye. 58p. (Orig.). 1993. pap. text. write for info. (*0-9639765-0-8*) Haiku Moments.

Peres, Phyllis. Transculturation & Resistance in Lusophone African Narrative. LC 96-20868. 168p. 1997. 39.95 (*0-8130-1492-1*) U Press Fla.

Peres, Richard. Writing in the Information Age: A Sales & Marketing Approach. 224p. (C). 1991. teacher ed. 8.00 (*1-56118-326-1*); pap. text 13.25 (*1-56118-324-5*) Paradigm MN.

Peres, Shimon. The Imaginary Voyage. LC 99-24365. 216p. 1999. 24.95 (*1-55970-468-3*, Pub. by Arcade Pub Inc) Time Warner.

***Peres, Shimon.** The Imaginary Voyage: With Theodor Herzl in Israel. LC 99-89428. 224p. 2000. pap. 16.00 (*1-58195-017-9*) Zoland Bks.

Peres, Shimon. The New Middle East. 240p. 1995. pap. 14.95 (*0-8050-3811-6*, Owl) H Holt & Co.

Peres, Shimon & Littell, Robert. For the Future of Israel. LC 97-47041. (Illus.). 224p. 1998. 22.95 (*0-8018-5928-X*) Johns Hopkins.

Peres, Wilson, jt. auth. see Stallings, Barbara.

Peres, Yochanan & Yuchtman-Yaar, Ephraim. Trends in Israeli Democracy: The Public's View. LC 91-43887. (Israel Democracy Institute Policy Studies). 62p. 1992. pap. text 9.95 (*1-55587-308-1*) L Rienner.

Peress, Gilles. Farewell to Bosnia. (Illus.). 160p. 1994. 60.00 (*1-881616-22-3*, Pub. by Scalo Pubs) Dist Art Pubs.

— Rwanda - The Silence. (Illus.). 160p. 1995. pap. 29.50 (*1-881616-38-X*, Pub. by Scalo Pubs) Dist Art Pubs.

Peress, Gilles, photos by. Telex Iran. (Illus.). 102p. 1996. 58.00 (*3-931141-36-5*, 620301, Pub. by Scalo Pubs) Dist Art Pubs.

Peress, Gilles & Stover, Eric. The Graves: Forensic Efforts at Srebrenica & Vukovar. (Illus.). 224p. 1998. pap. 24.95 (*3-931141-76-4*, 810221, Pub. by Scalo Pubs) Dist Art Pubs.

Peressini, A. L., et al. The Mathematics of Nonlinear Programming. (Undergraduate Texts in Mathematics Ser.). (Illus.). x, 325p. 1996. 49.95 (*0-387-96614-5*) Spr-Verlag.

— The Mathematics of Nonlinear Programming. 2nd ed. (Undergraduate Texts in Mathematics Ser.). x, 273p. 1993. write for info. (*3-540-96614-5*) Spr-Verlag.

Pereszlenyi-Pinter, Martha. Advanced Hungarian 1: Student Manual. (HUN., Illus.). 380p. (C). 1987. pap. text, student ed. 30.00 (*0-87415-123-6*, 51) Foreign Lang.

— Advanced Hungarian 1: Instructor Manual. (HUN., Illus.). 111p. (Orig.). (C). 1987. pap., teacher ed. 12.00 (*0-87415-124-4*, 51A) Foreign Lang.

Pereszlenyi-Pinter, Martha & Ludanyi, Julianna N. Elementary Hungarian No. 1: Instructor Manual. (OSU Foreign Language Publications). (HUN., Illus.). 133p. (C). 1984. pap., teacher ed. 13.50 (*0-87415-038-8*, 20A) Foreign Lang.

— Elementary Hungarian No. 1: Student Manual. (OSU Foreign Language Publications). (HUN., Illus.). 372p. (Orig.). (C). 1984. pap. text, student ed. 27.00 (*0-87415-037-X*, 20) Foreign Lang.

— Elementary Hungarian No. 2: Instructor Manual. (OSU Foreign Language Publications). (HUN., Illus.). 140p. (Orig.). (C). 1984. pap., teacher ed. 14.00 (*0-87415-041-8*, 21A) Foreign Lang.

— Elementary Hungarian No. 2: Student Manual. (OSU Foreign Language Publications). (HUN., Illus.). 312p. (Orig.). (C). 1984. pap. text, student ed. 24.00 (*0-87415-040-X*, 21) Foreign Lang.

— Intermediate Hungarian 1: Instructor Manual. (OSU Foreign Language Publications). (HUN., Illus.). 124p. (C). 1984. pap., teacher ed. 13.00 (*0-87415-044-2*, 22A) Foreign Lang.

— Intermediate Hungarian 1: Student Manual. (OSU Foreign Language Publications). (HUN., Illus.). 434p. (C). 1988. pap. text, student ed. 30.00 (*0-87415-043-4*, 22) Foreign Lang.

— Intermediate Hungarian 2: Instructor Manual. (OSU Foreign Language Publications). (HUN., Illus.). 398p. (C). 1984. pap., teacher ed. 14.00 (*0-87415-047-7*, 23A) Foreign Lang.

— Intermediate Hungarian 2: Student Manual. (OSU Foreign Language Publications: No. 23). (HUN., Illus.). 328p. (C). 1984. pap. text, student ed. 25.00 (*0-87415-046-9*) Foreign Lang.

— Reading Hungarian 1: Instructor Manual. (HUN., Illus.). 119p. (C). 1987. pap., teacher ed. 12.50 (*0-87415-149-X*, 60A) Foreign Lang.

— Reading Hungarian 1: Student Manual. (HUN., Illus.). 332p. (C). 1987. pap. text, student ed. 26.00 (*0-87415-148-1*, 60) Foreign Lang.

Peret, Benjamin. Death to the Pigs, & Other Writings. Stella, Rachel et al, trs. from FRE. LC 88-27731. (French Modernist Library). (Illus.). 219p. reprint ed. pap. 67.90 (*0-608-20138-3*, 207141000011) Bks Demand.

— From the Hidden Storehouse: Selected Poems of Benjamin Peret. Hollaman, Keith, tr. from FRE. 150p. (C). 1981. 10.95 (*0-932440-10-X*) Oberlin Coll Pr.

— Marvelous World, Poems. Jackson, Elizabeth R., tr. from FRE. LC 80-13631. 97p. 1985. text 25.00 (*0-8071-0664-X*) La State U Pr.

Peretti, Barbara. Seasons of My Heart. (Illus.). 128p. 1998. 14.99 (*0-8499-5373-1*) Word Pub.

Peretti, Barbara, et al. Secrets of a Fulfilled Woman. LC 97-68956. 200p. 1997. pap. 12.95 (*0-89221-367-1*) New Leaf.

Peretti, Brian J. Debt Collection Manual: Regulation, Law, & Best Practices. LC 99-168559. 1998. write for info. (*1-55827-271-2*) Sheshunoff.

Peretti, Burton W. The Creation of Jazz: Music, Race, & Culture in Urban America. (Music in American Life Ser.). (Illus.). 304p. (C). 1992. text 29.95 (*0-252-01708-0*) U of Ill Pr.

— Jazz in American Culture. LC 96-35596. (American Ways Ser.). 208p. 1997. 23.50 (*1-56663-142-4*, Pub. by I R Dee) Natl Bk Netwk.

— Jazz in American Culture. LC 96-35596. (American Ways Ser.). 208p. 1998. pap. text 12.95 (*1-56663-143-2*, Pub. by I R Dee) Natl Bk Netwk.

Peretti, Frank. Escape from the Island of Aquarius. (Cooper Kids Ser.: Vol. 2). (RUS.). 206p. (J). (gr. 4-12). 1998. per. write for info. (*0-7361-0038-5*) Life Pubs Intl.

— Flying Blind. LC 97-24275. (Cooper Kids Adventure Ser.: Vol. 8). 160p. (Orig.). (J). (gr. 5-10). 1998. pap. 5.99 (*0-8499-3646-2*) Tommy Nelson.

— The Oath. 1995. audio 23.00 (*0-8499-6214-5*, 6146) Word Pub.

***Peretti, Frank.** This Present Darkness/Piercing the Darkness. 816p. 2000. 15.99 (*1-58134-214-4*) Crossway Bks.

— Tombs of Anak: Russian Language Edition. Life Publishers International Staff, tr. (Cooper Kids Adventure Ser.: Vol. 4). (Illus.). 206p. (J). (gr. 3-12). 1999. pap. write for info. (*0-7361-0127-6*) Life Pubs Intl.

— Trapped at the Bottom of the Sea: Russian Language Edition. Life Publishers International Staff, tr. (Cooper Kids Adventure Ser.: Vol. 3). (RUS., Illus.). 206p. (gr. 3-12). 1999. pap. write for info. (*0-7361-0126-8*) Life Pubs Intl.

Peretti, Frank E. Atrapada en el Fonda Del Mar.Tr. of Trapped at the Bottom of the Sea. 1995. 15.60 (*0-606-10533-6*, Pub. by Turtleback) Demco.

Peretti, Frank E,. Cooper Kids Adventure Series. (Cooper Kids Adventure Ser.). (J). (gr. 5-7). 1990. pap. 23.96 (*0-89107-901-7*) Crossway Bks.

Peretti, Frank E. The Deadly Curse of Toco-Rey. LC 96-15641. (Cooper Kids Adventure Ser.: Vol. 6). 160p. (J). (gr. 5-9). 1996. pap. 5.99 (*0-8499-3644-6*) Tommy Nelson.

— Escape from the Island of Aquarius. LC 85-72915. (Cooper Kids Adventure Ser.: No. 2). (J). (gr. 4-7). 1990. pap. 5.99 (*0-89107-592-5*) Crossway Bks.

— Esta Patente Oscuridad. (SPA.). 442p. 1989. pap. 10.99 (*0-8297-0854-5*) Vida Pubs.

— Este Mundo Tenebroso.Tr. of This Present Darkness. (SPA.). 420p. 1990. pap. 14.95 (*0-8297-1650-5*) Vida Pubs.

— The Legend of Annie Murphy. LC 96-41694. (Cooper Kids Adventure Ser.). (J). (gr. 5-9). 1997. pap. 5.99 (*0-8499-3645-4*) Tommy Nelson.

— The Oath. 560p. 1996. pap. 12.99 (*0-8499-3863-5*) Word Pub.

— Oath: Inside: Exclusive excerpt from Peretti's 1999 Novel, Sneak Preview Edition. 1998. pap. write for info. (*0-8499-3723-X*) Word Pub.

— Penetrando la Oscuridad.Tr. of Piercing the Darkness. (SPA.). 468p. 1990. pap. 14.99 (*0-8297-0753-0*) Vida Pubs.

— Piercing the Darkness. LC 89-50338. 442p. 1989. pap. 12.99 (*0-89107-527-5*) Crossway Bks.

— Piercing the Darkness. large type ed. LC 93-16771. 771p. 1993. lib. bdg. 22.95 (*0-8161-5699-9*, G K Hall Lrg Type) Mac Lib Ref.

— Profeta.Tr. of Prophet. (SPA.). 480p. 1993. pap. 14.99 (*0-8297-1840-0*) Vida Pubs.

— Prophet. LC 92-4850. 416p. 1992. pap. 12.99 (*0-89107-618-2*) Crossway Bks.

— The Secret of the Desert Stone. LC 96-1919. (Cooper Kids Adventure Ser.: Vol. 5). 160p. (J). (gr. 5-9). 1996. pap. 5.99 (*0-8499-3643-8*) Tommy Nelson.

— This Present Darkness. LC 86-70282. 375p. 1986. pap. 12.99 (*0-89107-390-6*) Crossway Bks.

— This Present Darkness. large type ed. LC 92-35902. (General Ser.). 713p. 1993. lib. bdg. 23.95 (*0-8161-5698-0*, G K Hall Lrg Type) Mac Lib Ref.

— This Present Darkness & Piercing the Darkness: Two Bestselling Novels Complete in One Volume, 2 vols. in 1. 816p. 1997. 14.99 (*0-88486-178-3*, Inspirational Pr) Arrowood Pr.

— This Present Darkness & Piercing the Darkness: Two Bestselling Novels Complete in One Volume, 2. 1998. pap. 12.99 (*1-58134-057-5*) Crossway Bks.

— Tilly. LC 88-70700. 128p. 1988. pap. 8.99 (*0-89107-496-1*) Crossway Bks.

— Tilly. (FRE.). 112p. 1990. pap. 2.95 (*0-8297-1468-5*) Vida Pubs.

— The Tombs of Anak. LC 86-73183. (Cooper Kids Adventure Ser.: No. 3). 144p. (J). (gr. 4-7). 1990. pap. 5.99 (*0-89107-593-3*) Crossway Bks.

— Trapped at the Bottom of the Sea. (Cooper Kids Adventure Ser.: No. 4). (J). (gr. 4-7). 1990. pap. 5.99 (*0-89107-594-1*) Crossway Bks.

***Peretti, Frank E.** The Visitation. LC 99-23074. 400p. 1999. 24.99 (*0-8499-1179-6*) Word Pub.

Peretti, Frank E., et al. The Door in the Dragon's Throat. LC 85-70469. (Cooper Kids Adventure Ser.: No. 1). (J). (gr. 4-7). 1990. pap. 5.99 (*0-89107-591-7*) Crossway Bks.

***Peretti, Marilyn.** Crack the Rifle in Two: Poems for the Oppressed. 27p. 1999. pap. 5.00 (*0-9673333-3-4*, No. 4) Splendid Pr.

— Now a Bridge: Poems from Central America. (Illus.). 8p. 1997. pap. 4.00 (*0-9673333-1-8*, 2) Splendid Pr.

— Poems of a Woman. (Illus.). 32p. 1999. pap. 5.00 (*0-9673333-2-6*) Splendid Pr.

— This Haven Telluride: Little Poems about This Place. (Illus.). 9p. 1995. pap. 3.00 (*0-9673333-0-X*, 1) Splendid Pr.

— To Love Cranes: Little Poems in Praise of All Beautiful Cranes That Grace Our Earth. (Illus.). 21p. 2000. pap. 8.00 (*0-9673333-5-0*) Splendid Pr.

***Peretti, Terri J.** In Defense of a Political Court. LC 99-12206. 384p. 1999. 27.50 (*0-691-00905-8*, Pub. by Princeton U Pr) Cal Prin Full Svc.

Peretto, Pierre. An Introduction to the Modelling of Neural Networks. (Collection Alea - Saclay: Monographs & Texts in Statistical Physics: No. 2). (Illus.). 491p. (C). 1992. text 135.00 (*0-521-41451-2*); pap. text 47.95 (*0-521-42487-9*) Cambridge U Pr.

Peretyat'kin, M. G. Finitely Axiomatizable Theories. LC 97-33255. (Siberian School of Algebra & Logic Ser.). (Illus.). 308p. (C). 1997. text 138.00 (*0-306-11062-8*, Kluwer Plenum) Kluwer Academic.

***Peretz, David.** The Mosel Legacy. rev. ed. 272p. 1999. pap. 15.95 (*1-58444-098-8*) DiscUs Bks.

Peretz, Don. The Arab-Israel Dispute. LC 96-4362. (Library in a Book). (Illus.). 304p. 1996. 26.95 (*0-8160-3186-X*) Facts on File.

— Israel & the Palestine Arabs. LC 80-1915. reprint ed. 31.00 (*0-404-18984-9*) AMS Pr.

— The Middle East Today. 6th ed. LC 93-26376. 608p. 1994. 85.00 (*0-275-94575-8*, Praeger Pubs); pap. 26.95 (*0-275-94576-6*, Praeger Pubs) Greenwood.

— Palestinians, Refugees, & the Middle East Peace Process. LC 93-37820. 1993. pap. text 12.95 (*1-878379-32-1*) US Inst Peace.

Peretz, Don & Doron, Gideon. The Government & Politics of Israel. 3rd ed. LC 96-35240. 320p. (C). 1997. pap. 30.00 (*0-8133-2409-2*, Pub. by Westview) HarpC.

Peretz, Don, et al. Islam: Legacy of the Past, Challenge of the Future. 1984. 12.95 (*0-88427-048-3*) New Horizon NJ.

Peretz, Isaac L. Bontshe the Silent. Rappoport, Angelo S., tr. from YID. LC 77-178454. (Short Story Index Reprint Ser.). 1977. reprint ed. 18.95 (*0-8369-4055-5*) Ayer.

— Peretz. Liptzin, Solomon, ed. & tr. by. LC 72-5689. (Biography Index Reprints - YIVO Bilingual Ser.). 1977. reprint ed. 23.95 (*0-8369-8137-5*) Ayer.

Peretz, Liz & Payne, Chris, eds. Developing Mental Health Services: A Foundation Training for Residential & Community Based Support Workers. 1994. 78.00 (*0-902789-89-9*, Pub. by Natl Inst Soc Work) St Mut.

***Peretz, Martin, et al, texts.** Josef Sudek: Pigment Prints. (Illus.). 160p. 1998. 50.00 (*1-58821-072-3*) Salander OReilly.

Peretz, Paul. The Political Economy of Inflation in the United States. LC 82-24738. 264p. 1993. lib. bdg. 30.00 (*0-226-65671-3*) U Ch Pr.

— The Political Economy of Inflation in the United States. LC 82-24738. 280p. 1996. pap. text 17.00 (*0-226-65672-1*) U Ch Pr.

Peretz, Paul, ed. The Politics of American Economic Policy Making. LC 87-12827. 464p. (C). (gr. 13). 1987. text 83.95 (*0-87332-406-4*); pap. text 32.95 (*0-87332-407-2*) M E Sharpe.

— The Politics of American Economic Policy Making. 2nd ed. LC 95-41956. (Illus.). 520p. (C). (gr. 13). 1996. text 79.95 (*1-56324-566-3*); pap. text 38.95 (*1-56324-567-1*) M E Sharpe.

Pereverzev, Sergei V. Optimization of Methods for Approximate Solution of Operator Equations. LC 93-25889. (Computational Mathematics & Analysis Ser.). 330p. (C). 1994. lib. bdg. 145.00 (*1-56072-140-5*) Nova Sci Pubs.

Perevodchikova, N. I., et al, eds. Tegafur-Ftorafur. (Beitraege Zur Onkologie, Contributions to Oncology Ser.: Vol. 14). (Illus.). viii, 146p. 1983. pap. 40.00 (*3-8055-3653-4*) S Karger.

Perey, Christine. The Art of Visual Collaboration & Video Conferencing Desktop to Desktop. (C). 2001. 24.95 (*0-13-598400-9*, Macmillan Coll) P-H.

Pereyra, V., ed. Numerical Methods. (Lecture Notes in Mathematics Ser.: Vol. 1005). 296p. 1983. 42.95 (*0-387-12334-2*) Spr-Verlag.

Perez. Camilo Jose Cela Revisited. 2000. 28.95 (*0-8057-1640-8*, Twyne) Mac Lib Ref.

— Learning In Two Worlds: An Integrated Spanish/English Biliteracy Approach. 3rd ed. (C). 2000. pap. text. write for info. (*0-8013-3077-7*) Addison-Wesley.

***Perez.** Lesbians Guide to Spain. (Illus.). 2000. pap. text 13.00 (*84-605-9197-2*) Fundacion EFE.

Perez. Tlacotalpan, la Virgen de la Candelaria. (SPA.). pap. 7.99 (*968-16-3506-X*, Pub. by Fondo) Continental Bk.

— Wireless Communications Design. (C). 1998. text 79.00 (*0-12-550723-2*); text 79.00 (*0-12-550722-4*) Acad Pr.

Perez & Weltman, Dennis. Intermediate Algebra. 3rd ed. (Mathematics Ser.). 1993. mass mkt., student ed. 19.50 (*0-534-93729-2*) PWS Pubs.

Perez, et al. Beginning Algebra: A Worktext. (Mathematics Ser.). 1994. mass mkt., student ed. 18.50 (*0-534-17947-9*) PWS Pubs.

Perez, jt. auth. see Weltman.

Perez, A., jt. auth. see Valle, J. W.

Perez-Abreu, Marilyn, ed. see Levy-Konesky, Nancy & Daggett, Karen.

Perez-Abreu, Victor, jt. ed. see Houdre, Christian.

***Perez, Adrian.** Advanced 3-D Game Programming with Directx 7.0. 2000. pap. text 59.95 (*1-55622-721-3*) Wordware.

***Perez, Amada Irma.** My Very Own Room. LC 00-20769. (Illus.). 32p. (J). (ps-3). 2000. 15.95 (*0-89239-164-2*) Childrens Book Pr.

Perez-Amor, M., jt. ed. see Soares, Oliverio D.

Perez, Andrea, pseud. Die Landstortzerin Lustina Dietzin Picara Genandt, 2 vols. in 1. (Barockromane Ser.). 1082p. 1975. reprint ed. write for info. (*3-487-05470-1*) G Olms Pubs.

Perez, Angeles, et al. Cassell's Contemporary Spanish. (SPA., Illus.). 512p. 1994. 25.00 (*0-02-595915-8*) Macmillan.

Perez, Anna L. Valdez, see Valdez Perez, Anna L.

Perez, Antonio C., jt. auth. see Pierret, Antonio P.

Perez-Arriaga, Jesus, jt. auth. see Catedra, Manuel F.

Perez, Arturo. Earmarking State Taxes. 3rd ed. 108p. 1994. 20.00 (*1-55516-524-9*, 5322) Natl Conf State Legis.

— Legislative Oversight of Federal Funds. (Legislative Finance Papers: No. 5101-98). 13p. 1995. 10.00 (*0-614-10575-7*) Natl Conf State Legis.

— State & Local Levels: FY 1993. (Legislative Finance Papers). 12p. 1996. 30.00 (*1-55516-522-2*, 5101-0105) Natl Conf State Legis.

Perez, Arturo & Snell, Ronald K. State Early Retirement Programs in Fiscal Years, 1992 & 1993. (State Legislative Reports: Vol. 18, No. 5). 6p. 1993. 5.00 (*1-55516-225-8*, 7302-1805) Natl Conf State Legis.

— State Fiscal Outlook for 1995. (Legislative Finance Papers: No. 97). 21p. 1994. 25.00 (*1-55516-006-9*, 5101-90) Natl Conf State Legis.

Perez, Arturo, jt. auth. see Eckl, Corina.

Perez, Atayde. Pathlogy Pediatric Tumors. 1999. pap. text 195.00 (*0-8385-7802-0*, Medical Exam) Appleton & Lange.

Perez, Barbara, ed. see Moore, Michael.

Perez, Bendito D. & Silva, M. Majer. Kinetic Methods in Analytical Chemistry. 340p. 1988. text 78.95 (*0-470-21181-4*) P-H.

An Asterisk (*) at the beginning of an entry indicates that the title is appearing for the first time.

Perez-Bendito, D. & Rubino, S. Environmental Analytical Chemistry. LC 98-52378. (Comprehensive Analytical Chemistry Ser.). 1999. 279.00 (*0-444-82205-4*) Elsevier.

Perez, Benny. Pacesetters: Setting the Standard, Not Following the Trend. LC 97-100155. 176p. 1996. pap. 10.00 (*1-883893-69-0*, Pub. by WinePress Pub) BookWorld.

Perez, Bernard. The First Three Years of Childhood. Christie, Alice M., ed. LC 74-21425. (Classics in Child Development Ser.). 330p. 1975. reprint ed. 29.95 (*0-405-06474-8*) Ayer.

Perez, Bertha, ed. Sociocultural Contexts of Language & Literacy. LC 97-27915. 256p. 1997. write for info. (*0-8058-2256-9*); pap. write for info. (*0-8058-2257-7*) L Erlbaum Assocs.

Perez, Bertha & Torres-Guzman, Maria E. Learning in Two Worlds. 2nd ed. LC 95-4930. 232p. (C). 1995. pap. 52.00 (*0-8013-1572-7*) Longman.

Perez-Blanco, H. & Stoecker, Wilbert F. Refrigeracion Industrial. LC 91-45884.Tr. of Industrial Refrigeration. (SPA.). 352p. 1992. 39.95 (*0-912524-68-5*) Busn News.

Perez Bowie, Jose A., ed. see Baroja, Y Nessi, Pio.

Perez-Brignoll, Hector. A Brief History of Central America. 1989. pap. 15.95 (*0-520-06832-7*, Pub. by U CA Pr) Cal Prin Full Svc.

Perez Bustamante, Ciriaco. Historia de Espana No. 24: La Espana de Felipe III: La Politica Interior y los Problemas Internacionales. 660p. 1992. 189.50 (*84-239-4832-3*) Elliots Bks.

Perez-Bustillo, Camilo, tr. see Espada, Martin.

Perez-Bustillo, Camilo, tr. see Velez, Clemente S.

Perez, C. Les Prelevements en Biologie Medicale. 82p. 1991. pap. 45.00 (*2-906077-17-8*) Elsevier.

Perez, Candi, jt. auth. see Goodwin, Bob.

Perez, Carla B., ed. see Houston, Juanita C.

Perez, Carlos A. & Brady, Luther, eds. Principles & Practice of Radiation Oncology. 3rd ed. (Illus.). 2000p. 1997. text 225.00 (*0-397-58416-4*) Lppncott W & W.

Perez, Carlos A. & Brady, Luther W. Principles & Practice of Radiation Oncology. 3rd ed. 2368p. 1997. 325.00 (*0-7817-1691-8*) Lppncott W & W.

Perez, Carlos A., et al. Radiation Oncology: Management Decisions. LC 98-22422. 512p. 1998. pap. text 49.95 (*0-397-58468-7*) Lppncott W & W.

Perez-Castrillo, J. David, jt. auth. see Macho-Stadler, Ines.

Perez-Collins, Yvonne. Beading by Machine. LC 96-46069. 128p. 1997. pap. 19.95 (*0-8019-8642-7*) Krause Pubns.

Perez, Concha, jt. auth. see Truman, Michael.

Perez, Crisostomo N. Land Grants in Alta, California: A Compilation of Spanish & Mexican Private Land Claims in the State of California. 264p. (C). 1996. 55.00 (*0-910845-55-7*) Landmark Ent.

Perez, Cristelia, jt. auth. see Kanellos, Nicolas.

Perez, Cristina Z. The Awakening to Supreme Knowledge: The Zaramela Codex. (Illus.). vi, 56p. (Orig.). 1996. pap. write for info. (*0-9654938-0-6*, 1017195, East Collns Bks) Zeiss Inst.

— The Awakening to Supreme Knowledge: The Zaramela Codex, Calendar Edition. (Illus.). vi, 56p. (Orig.). 1996. pap. write for info. (*0-9654938-1-4*, 1017195, East Collns Bks) Zeiss Inst.

Perez-Cruz, Ignacio H. Graciela. LC 93-70607. (Coleccion Caniqui). (SPA.). 146p. (Orig.). 1993. pap. 16.00 (*0-89729-672-9*) Ediciones.

Perez, Daniel E. Big Footnotes: A Comprehensive Bibliography Concerning Bigfoot, The Abominable Snowmen & Related Beings. 189p. (Orig.). 1988. pap. 16.00 (*0-9618380-0-0*) D Perez.

Perez, Dario E., jt. auth. see Moro, Oscar P.

Perez, David. Capitalism, Genetics & the Natural Order. 26p. 1993. pap. 2.50 (*0-89567-121-2*) World View Forum.

— Las Clases Sociales - Raices del Racismo. 26p. 1989. pap. 0.50 (*0-89567-100-X*) World View Forum.

— Destruction of the Environment: Racism & the Profit System. 26p. 1993. pap. 2.50 (*0-614-02749-7*) World View Forum.

— La Politica de las Drogas: Quin Sufre, Quien Trafica, Quien Se Lucra. 26p. 1989. pap. 0.50 (*0-89567-098-4*) World View Forum.

Perez, David, et al. The Politics of Drugs: Who Suffers, Who Deals, Who Profits. 26p. 1988. pap. 0.50 (*0-89567-093-3*) World View Forum.

Perez de Ayala, Juan, jt. ed. see Diaz Agen, Manzani.

Perez De Ayala, Ramon. Tigre Juan, el Curandero de su Honra. Lozano Marcos, Miguel A., ed. (Nueva Austral Ser.: Vol. 122). (SPA.). 1991. pap. text 24.95 (*84-239-1922-6*) Elliots Bks.

Perez De Cuellar, Javier. Anarchy or Order: Annual Report, 1982-1991. 362p. pap. 9.95 (*92-1-100466-7*, 91.I.52) UN.

— Anarchy or Order: Annual Report, 1982-1991. 362p. 1991. pap. 9.95 (*0-685-53675-0*) UN.

***Perez De Cuellar, Javier & Choue, Young-Seek.** World Encyclopedia of Peace, 8 vols. 2nd ed. LC 99-34811. 1999. text 550.00 (*0-379-21398-2*) Oceana.

Perez de Guzman, Fernan. Generaciones & Semblanzas. LC 73-173946. reprint ed. 41.50 (*0-404-04993-1*) AMS Pr.

Perez de Mendiola, Marina. Gender & Identity Formation in Contemporary Mexican Literature. LC 98-35873. (Latin American Studies: Vol. 12). 176p. 1998. 49.00 (*0-8153-3194-0*) Garland.

Perez De Montalban, Juan. Para Todos Exemplos Morales, Humanos y Divinos. 592p. reprint ed. write for info. (*0-318-71628-3*) G Olms Pubs.

Perez, Demetrio, Jr. Citizens Training Handbook-Manual de Formacion Ciudadana: Discipline-Moral-Covism-Urbanity. (ENG & SPA., Illus.). 315p. (J). 1991. 25.00 (*0-9628780-0-6*) Ed Lncln-Mrt.

— La Escuela Privada Cubana. (SPA.). 1994. 20.00 (*0-9628780-1-4*) Ed Lncln-Mrt.

Perez, Diana. Roberto Clemente, Athlete & Hero. (Illus.). (J). (gr. 1-4). 1994. pap. 6.35 (*0-8136-5273-1*); lib. bdg. 17.50 (*0-8136-5267-7*) Modern Curr.

— Roberto Clemente, Atleta y Heroe. (SPA., Illus.). (J). (gr. 1-4). 1994. pap. 6.35 (*0-8136-5301-0*) Modern Curr.

Perez-Diaz, Victor. Spain at the Crossroads: Civil Society, Politics & the Rule of Law. LC 99-20486. 256p. 1999. 39.95 (*0-674-00052-8*) HUP.

— Structure & Change of Castilian Peasant Community: A Sociological Inquiry into Rural Castile, 1550-1990. LC 91-22825. (Harvard Studies in Sociology). 266p. 1992. text 22.00 (*0-8240-8473-X*) Garland.

Perez-Diaz, Victor M. The Return of Civil Society: The Emergence of Democratic Spain. LC 92-29941. 432p. 1993. 43.50 (*0-674-76688-1*) HUP.

— Return of Civil Society: The Emergence of Democratic Spain. 368p. 1998. pap. text 24.95 (*0-674-76689-X*) HUP.

Perez, Douglas A. Paradoxes of Police Work. LC 96-86235. 101p. (C). 1996. pap. 14.95 (*0-942728-72-6*) Copperhouse.

Perez, Douglas W. Common Sense about Police Review. LC 93-11192. 328p. 1994. 54.95 (*1-56639-132-6*) Temple U Pr.

— Common Sense about Police Review. (C). 1994. pap. text 22.95 (*1-56639-336-1*) Temple U Pr.

Perez, Efrain Rivera, see Rivera Perez, Efrain.

Perez, Emma. The Decolonial Imaginary: Writing Chicanas into History. LC 98-51190. (Theories of Representation & Difference Ser.). 240p. 1999. pap. 16.95 (*0-253-21283-9*); text 35.00 (*0-253-33504-3*) Ind U Pr.

— Mexican American Women in Houston: Work, Family, & Community, 1990-1940. 67p. write for info. (*0-614-06975-0*) Univ Houston Mex Amer.

Perez-Erdelyi, Mireya. La Picara y la Dama: La Imagen de las Nujeres en las Novelas Picaresco Cortesanas de Maria de Zayas y Sotomayor. LC 78-74597. (SPA., Illus.). 128p. 1979. pap. 10.00 (*0-89729-216-2*) Ediciones.

Perez Esclarin, Antonio. Atheism & Liberation. Drury, John, tr. LC 78-731. 208p. reprint ed. pap. 64.50 (*0-8357-4074-9*, 203676400005) Bks Demand.

Perez Esquivel, Adolfo. Christ in a Poncho: Testimonials of the Nonviolent Struggles in Latin America. Antoine, Charles, ed. Barr, Robert R., tr. from FRE. LC 82-18760. 143p. reprint ed. pap. 44.40 (*0-8357-8550-5*, 203489200091) Bks Demand.

***Perez-Esteva, Salvador & Villegas-Blas, Carlos.** Quantization, the Segal-Bargmann Transform & Semiclassical Analysis: First Summer School in Analysis & Mathematical Physics, Cuernavaca Morelos, Mexico, June 8-18, 1998. LC 00-34991. 2000. write for info. (*0-8218-2115-6*) Am Math.

Perez, Esther, ed. see Liebmann, Lisa.

Perez, Eulalia, jt. auth. see Barron's Educational Editors.

Perez, F. Corripio. Diccionario de Sinonimos y Antonimos. (SPA & ITA.). 1128p. 1997. 19.95 (*0-320-01578-5*) Fr & Eur.

Perez Fabo, J. A. Espanol Paso a Paso, Nivel 1. 8th ed. (Paso a Paso Ser.). (SPA.). 112p. (Orig.). (J). (gr. 1). 1991. reprint ed. pap. text 7.95 (*1-56328-011-6*) Edit Plaza Mayor.

— Espanol Paso a Paso, Nivel 2. 9th ed. (Paso a Paso Ser.). (SPA.). 160p. (Orig.). (J). (gr. 2). 1991. reprint ed. pap. text 8.95 (*1-56328-012-4*) Edit Plaza Mayor.

— Espanol Paso a Paso, Nivel 3. 9th ed. (Paso a Paso Ser.). (SPA.). 224p. (Orig.). (J). (gr. 3). 1991. reprint ed. pap. text 9.95 (*1-56328-013-2*) Edit Plaza Mayor.

— Espanol Paso a Paso, Nivel 4. 9th ed. (Paso a Paso Ser.). (SPA.). 256p. (Orig.). (J). (gr. 4). 1991. pap. text 7.95 (*1-56328-014-0*) Edit Plaza Mayor.

— Espanol Paso a Paso, Nivel 5. 10th ed. (Paso a Paso Ser.). (SPA.). 288p. (Orig.). (J). (gr. 5). 1991. reprint ed. pap. text 11.95 (*1-56328-015-9*) Edit Plaza Mayor.

— Espanol Paso a Paso, Nivel 6. 9th ed. (Paso a Paso Ser.). (SPA.). 304p. (Orig.). (J). (gr. 6). 1991. reprint ed. pap. text 12.95 (*1-56328-016-7*) Edit Plaza Mayor.

Perez, Felicita. Child Care Handbook: Tips for Young Parents. (Illus.). 80p. (YA). (gr. 8 up). 1997. pap. text 15.95 (*0-9670887-0-4*, CCH-1) Printrite.

Perez Fernandez, M., jt. auth. see Bosque, I.

Perez Fernandez, Miguel. An Introductory Grammar of Rabbinic Hebrew. Elwolde, John, tr. from SPA. LC 97-2536. (HEB.). 360p. 1997. 112.50 (*90-04-10890-4*) Brill Academic Pubs.

Perez, Fernando. Poemas. LC 88-81563. (Coleccion Espejo de Paciencia). (SPA.). 89p. (Orig.). 1989. pap. 9.95 (*0-89729-496-3*) Ediciones.

Perez, Fernando C. Dictionary of Related Ideas: Diccionario de Ideas Afines. 3rd ed. (ENG & SPA.). 912p. 1990. pap. write for info. (*0-7859-4950-X*) Fr & Eur.

— Gran Diccionario de Sinonimos y Antonimos. (SPA.). 1128p. 1990. 39.95 (*0-8288-8170-7*, S3383) Fr & Eur.

Perez, Fernando Coripio, see Coripio Perez, Fernando.

Perez Firmat, Gustavo. Do the Americas Have a Common Literature? LC 90-33990. 404p. (C). 1990. text 59.95 (*0-8223-1054-6*); pap. text 23.95 (*0-8223-1072-4*) Duke.

— Idle Fictions: The Hispanic Vanguard Novel, 1926-1934. LC 82-12773. 200p. 1993. pap. text 17.95 (*0-8223-1423-1*) Duke.

— Life on the Hyphen: The Cuban-American Way. LC 93-33590. (Illus.). 231p. (C). 1994. pap. 15.95 (*0-292-76551-7*) U of Tex Pr.

— Literature & Liminality: Festive Readings in the Hispanic Tradition. LC 85-13077. xxi, 182p. 1986. text 37.95 (*0-8223-0658-1*) Duke.

***Perez Firmat, Gustavo.** My Own Private Cuba: Essays on Cuban Literature & Culture. LC 99-71350. 260p. 1999. pap. 25.00 (*0-89295-096-X*) Society Sp & Sp-Am.

Perez-Fournon, Ismael, jt. ed. see Clements, David L.

Perez, Francisco G. Como Leer el Lazarillo. 43.00 (*0-685-69535-2*) Scripta.

Perez, Frank. Dolores Huerta. LC 95-18207. (Contemporary Biographies Ser.). (Illus.). 48p. (J). (gr. 4-8). 1995. lib. bdg. 24.26 (*0-8172-3981-2*) Raintree Steck-V.

— Dolores Huerta. LC 95-18207. 48p. (J). (gr. 5-7). 1996. pap. 5.95 (*0-8114-9789-5*) Raintree Steck-V.

— Dolores Huerta. large type ed. 54p. (J). (gr. 4-8). pap. 13.50 (*0-614-32390-8*, L-86283-00 APHB) Am Printing Hse.

Perez, Frank & Weil, Ann. Raul Julia. (Contemporary Hispanic Americans Ser.). (Illus.). 48p. (J). (gr. 4-6). 1995. lib. bdg. 24.26 (*0-8172-3984-7*) Raintree Steck-V.

— Raul Julia. LC 95-18549. 48p. (J). (gr. 5-7). 1996. pap. 5.95 (*0-8114-9786-0*) Raintree Steck-V.

— Raul Julia. large type ed. 54p. Date not set. write for info. (*0-614-24688-1*, L-86308-00 APHB) Am Printing Hse.

Perez, G. Yvonne, et al. Let's Learn English: Second Language Activities for the Primary Grades, K-3. (Illus.). 91p. (Orig.). 1987. pap. 9.95 (*0-673-18371-8*, GoodYrBooks) Addson-Wesley Educ.

Perez Galdos. Marianela. 1995. pap. text 6.95 (*968-416-731-8*) Fernandez USA.

Perez Galdos, Benito. Dona Perfecta: Misericordia. (SPA.). 1989. 7.95 (*0-8288-2572-6*) Fr & Eur.

— Miau y Marianela. (SPA.). 1989. 7.95 (*0-8288-2573-4*) Fr & Eur.

— Las Novelas de Torquemada: Torquemada en la Hoguera, Torquemada en la Cruz. (SPA.). 1989. 18.50 (*0-8288-2584-X*) Fr & Eur.

— La Sombra de Galdos: Libra De Lectura, Repaso y Conversacion. Cardona, Rudolph, ed. (C). 1964. audio. write for info. (*0-393-99114-8*) Norton.

Perez Galdos, Benito, adapted by. Marianela, Level 3. (Leer en Espanol Ser.). (SPA.). (C). 1998. pap. 5.95 (*84-294-3433-X*) Santillana.

Perez, Genaro J. Narrativa de Concha Alos: La Texto, Pretexto y Contexto. (Monagrafias A Ser.: No. 157). (SPA.). 95p. (C). 1994. pap. 51.00 (*1-85566-032-6*, Pub. by Tamesis Bks Ltd) Boydell & Brewer.

Perez, Gilbert, jt. auth. see Weltman, Dennis.

Perez, Gilberto. The Material Ghost: Films & Their Medium. LC 97-16877. (Illus.). 482p. 1998. 29.95 (*0-8018-5673-6*) Johns Hopkins.

***Perez, Gilberto.** The Material Ghost: Films & Their Medium. (Illus.). 448p. 2000. reprint ed. pap. 18.95 (*0-8018-6523-9*) Johns Hopkins.

Perez Gomez, Alberto. Architecture & the Crisis of Modern Science. (Illus.). 416p. 1985. reprint ed. pap. text 21.00 (*0-262-66055-5*) MIT Pr.

Perez-Gomez, Alberto. Chora 2: Intervals in the Philosophy of Architecture, Vol. 2. 336p. 1996. pap. text 24.95 (*0-7735-1407-4*, Pub. by McG-Queens Univ Pr) CUP Services.

Perez-Gomez, Alberto & Parcell, Stephen. Chora 3: Intervals in the Philosophy of Architecture. (Illus.). 416p. 1998. text 60.00 (*0-7735-1711-1*, Pub. by McG-Queens Univ Pr); pap. text 24.95 (*0-7735-1712-X*, Pub. by McG-Queens Univ Pr) CUP Services.

Perez-Gomez, Alberto & Parcell, Stephen, eds. Chora 1: Intervals in the Philosophy of Architecture. (Illus.). 288p. 1994. 65.00 (*0-7735-1193-8*, Pub. by McG-Queens Univ Pr) CUP Services.

Perez-Gomez, Alberto & Parcell, Stephen, eds. Chora 1: Intervals in the Philosophy of Architecture, Vol. 1. (Illus.). 288p. 1994. pap. 24.95 (*0-7735-1276-4*, Pub. by McG-Queens Univ Pr) CUP Services.

Perez-Gomez, Alberto & Parcell, Stephen, eds. Chora 2: Intervals in the Philosophy of Architecture, Vol. 2. 336p. 1996. 65.00 (*0-7735-1406-6*, Pub. by McG-Queens Univ Pr) CUP Services.

Perez-Gomez, Alberto & Pelletier, Louise. Architectural Representation & the Perspective Hinge. LC 97-11186. (Illus.). 525p. 1997. 52.50 (*0-262-16169-9*) MIT Pr.

***Perez Gomez, Alberto & Pelletier, Louise.** Architectural Representation & the Perspective Hinge. (Illus.). 536p. (C). 2000. reprint ed. pap. 34.95 (*0-262-66113-6*) MIT Pr.

Perez-Gomez, Alberto & Pelletier, Louise, compiled by. Anamorphosis: An Annotated Bibliography. (Illus.). 152p. 1996. 55.00 (*0-7735-1450-3*, Pub. by McG-Queens Univ Pr) CUP Services.

Perez-Gomez, Alberto, jt. ed. see Pelletier, Louise.

Perez, Guillermo H. Lo Que los Jovenes Deben Saber Acerca de las Drogas: What Youth Should Know about Drugs. 80p. 1977. reprint ed. pap. 3.99 (*0-311-46070-4*) Casa Bautista.

Perez, H. R. El Ministerio de la Diaconia.Tr. of Deacon's Ministry. (SPA.). pap. 10.99 (*0-7899-0326-1*, 491048) Editorial Unilit.

Perez, Herb. The Complete Tae Kwon Do For Kids. (Martial Arts Ser.). (Illus.). 128p. (J). (gr. 3-7). 1999. pap. 7.95 (*1-56565-959-7*, 09597W, Pub. by Lowell Hse) NTC Contemp Pub Co.

Perez, Humberto. El Maestro y la Forma de la Verdad.Tr. of Teacher & the Truth. (SPA.). 240p. 1995. 12.99 (*0-89922-493-8*, C091-4938) Caribe Betania.

Perez, Isaac L. Stories & Pictures. Frank, Helena, tr. from YID. LC 75-152953. (Short Story Index Reprint Ser.). 1977. reprint ed. 25.95 (*0-8369-3868-2*) Ayer.

Perez, Isabelle & Lang, Margaret A. Modern French Grammar: A Practical Guide to Grammar & Usage. LC 95-39756. (ENG & FRE.). 368p. (C). 1996. pap. 25.99 (*0-415-09852-1*) Routledge.

Perez, Isabelle, et al. Modern French Grammar: A Practical Guide to Grammar & Usage. LC 95-39756. (Modern Grammars Ser.). (ENG & FRE.). 368p. (C). 1996. 75.00 (*0-415-09851-3*) Routledge.

Perez, Isabelle, ed. see Lang, Margaret A.

Perez, J. Guillent. A Case of Conscience. 370p. (Orig.). 1985. pap. 12.95 (*0-9607590-2-6*) Action Life Pubns.

Perez, Janet. Modern & Contemporary Spanish Women Poets. 1996. 32.00 (*0-8057-4627-7*, Twyne) Mac Lib Ref.

Perez, Janet & Aycock, Wendell M., eds. Climate & Literature: Reflections of Environment. LC 95-36736. (Studies in Comparative Literature: No. 25). 134p. 1995. 30.00 (*0-89672-354-2*) Tex Tech Univ Pr.

— The Spanish Civil War in Literature. LC 90-10999. (Studies in Comparative Literature: No. 21). 1990. 24.95 (*0-89672-196-5*) Tex Tech Univ Pr.

Perez, Janet & Horn, Paul W. Contemporary Women Writers of Spain. (World Authors Ser.: No. 798). 256p. 1988. 26.95 (*0-8057-8229-X*, Twyne) Mac Lib Ref.

Perez, Janet & Miller, Stephen, eds. Critical Studies on Gonzalo Torrente Ballester. LC 88-61594. (ENG & SPA.). 196p. 1989. pap. 40.00 (*0-89295-054-4*) Society Sp & Sp-Am.

Perez, Jeannine. Bulletin Board Basics: Hands on Science. Stranich, Helen & Hogan, Eric, eds. (Illus.). 96p. 1991. pap. 9.95 (*1-878727-09-5*) First Teacher.

— Explore & Experiment. Durkin, Lisa L. & Hayes, Martha A., eds. (Illus.). 120p. 1988. pap. 10.95 (*0-9615005-8-1*) First Teacher.

Perez, Jo. Physics & Mechanics of Amorphous Polymers. LC 99-227348. (Illus.). 324p. (C). 1998. text 87.00 (*90-5410-766-9*, Pub. by A A Balkema) Ashgate Pub Co.

***Perez, Joey.** I Lived to Tell about It. 192p. 2000. pap. 10.99 (*1-930027-09-5*, 921-025, Pub. by Insght Pub) BookWorld.

Perez, Jose & Alsina, Ramon. Diccionario de Vinos Espanoles. (SPA.). 238p. 1991. reprint ed. 19.95 (*0-7859-5894-0*, 8430781358) Fr & Eur.

Perez, Jose & Spence, Wayman R. Perez on Medicine. (Illus.). 64p. 1993. 29.95 (*1-56796-005-7*) WRS Group.

— Perez on Sports. (Illus.). 64p. 1995. text 29.95 (*1-56796-125-8*) WRS Group.

Perez, Jose A. & Mejias, Antonio I. La Historia del Cantante, Hector Lavoe, Vol. 2. Beauchamp, Darsi D., ed. Romano, Herminia H., tr. from ENG. LC 98-86804. Orig. Title: Hector Lavoe Story. (SPA., Illus.). 156p. 1999. pap. 12.95 (*0-9661557-2-6*) Infante Pubns Inc.

Perez, Jose A. & Mejinas, Antonio I. The Hector Lavoe Story. LC 97-92741. (Illus.). 110p. (Orig.). 1997. pap. 12.95 (*0-9661557-1-8*) Infante Pubns Inc.

Perez, Jose G. Puerto Rico: U. S. Colony in the Caribbean. 23p. 1976. reprint ed. pap. 2.50 (*0-87348-380-4*) Pathfinder NY.

Perez, Joseph F. Counseling the Alcoholic Group. 145p. 1986. text 22.95 (*0-89876-131-X*) Gardner Pr.

— Relationships: Adult Children of Alcoholics. LC 87-21105. 1989. 23.95 (*0-89876-150-6*) Gardner Pr.

— Tales of an Italian American Family. 1991. 17.95 (*0-89876-167-0*) Gardner Pr.

Perez, Juan M. Latin America Bibliography. LC 98-21207. (Scarecrow Area Bibliographies Ser.: No. 16). 544p. 1999. 79.50 (*0-8108-3496-0*) Scarecrow.

Perez, Kelly. Emergency Medical Services for Children. LC 98-213930. 60p. 1998. 20.00 (*1-55516-604-0*, 6663) Natl Conf State Legis.

Perez, L. King. Ghoststalking. LC 93-41576. (Middle Grade Fiction Ser.). (Illus.). 48p. (J). (gr. 2-5). 1994. lib. bdg. 19.93 (*0-87614-821-6*, Carolrhoda) Lerner Pub.

Perez, L. L., et al. Trade Policy Developments in Industrial Countries. (Occasional Papers: No. 5). 56p. 1981. pap. 5.00 (*1-55775-082-3*) Intl Monetary.

Perez, L. M. Guide to the Materials for American History in Cuban Archives. (Carnegie Institute Ser.: Vol. 16). 1907. 40.00 (*0-527-00696-3*) Periodicals Srv.

Perez, Laura, jt. auth. see Taylor, Macey.

Perez, Laura M., tr. see Doumerc, Beatriz & Alcantara, Ricardo.

Perez Leroux, Ana T. & Glass, William R. Contemporary Perspectives on the Acquisition of Spanish: 2 Volume Set, 2. LC 97-27686. 1997. pap. 42.00 (*1-57473-015-0*) Cascadilla Pr.

— Contemporary Perspectives on the Acquisition of Spanish Vol. 1: Developing Grammars. LC 97-27686. 1997. pap. 28.95 (*1-57473-016-9*) Cascadilla Pr.

— Contemporary Perspectives on the Acquisition of Spanish Vol. 2: Production, Processing & Comprehension. LC 97-27686. 1997. pap. 28.95 (*1-57473-017-7*) Cascadilla Pr.

Perez Leroux, Ana T. & Glass, William R., eds. Contemporary Perspectives on the Acquisition of Spanish, 2 vols. (Illus.). xi, 383p. (C). 1997. lib. bdg. 92.00 (*1-57473-115-7*) Cascadilla Pr.

— Contemporary Perspectives on the Acquisition of Spanish Vol. 1: Production, Processing & Comprehension. (Illus.). xi, 217p. (C). 1997. pap. 28.95 (*1-57473-116-5*) Cascadilla Pr.

— Contemporary Perspectives on the Acquisition of Spanish Vol. 2: Production, Processing & Comprehension. (Illus.). xi, 166p. (C). 1997. lib. bdg. 58.95 (*1-57473-117-3*) Cascadilla Pr.

Perez, Lisandro & De Aragon, Uva, eds. Cuban Studies 30. (Pitt Latin American Ser.). (ENG & SPA.). 280p. (C). 1999. text 40.00 (*0-8229-4114-7*) U of Pittsburgh Pr.

***Perez, Lisandro & De Aragon, Uva, eds.** Cuban Studies 31, 31 vols., Vol. 31. (Pitt Latin American Ser: Vool. 31). 272p. 2001. 40.00 (*0-8229-4138-4*) U of Pittsburgh Pr.

Perez, Livian, ed. see Graham, Dennis.

Perez-Lizaur, Marisol, jt. auth. see Lomnitz, Larissa A.

Perez, Loida Maritza. Geographies of Home. LC 98-26440. 321p. 1999. 23.95 (*0-670-86889-2*) Viking Penguin.

***Perez, Loida Maritza.** Geographies of Home. 288p. 2000. pap. 12.95 (*0-14-025371-8*, Penguin Bks) Viking Penguin.

P

Perez-Lopez, Jorge & Travieso-Diaz, Matias F. Perspectives on Cuban Economic Reforms. LC 97-49289. (Special Studies: Vol. 30). (Illus.). 190p. (Orig.). (C). 1998. pap. 35.00 (*0-87918-087-0*) ASU Lat Am St.

Perez-Lopez, Jorge, jt. auth. see Diaz-Briquets, Sergio.

Perez-Lopez, Jorge F. Cuban Studies, Vol. 27. 460p. 1998. text 40.00 (*0-8229-4046-9*) U of Pittsburgh Pr.

— Cuba's Second Economy: From Behind the Scenes to Center Stage. 172p. (C). 1994. 34.95 (*1-56000-189-5*) Transaction Pubs.

— The Economics of Cuban Sugar. LC 90-40875. (Latin American Ser.). 336p. (C). 1991. text 49.95 (*0-8229-3663-1*) U of Pittsburgh Pr.

— The 1982 Cuban Joint Venture Law: Context, Assessment, & Prospects. 93p. (C). 1985. pap. text 14.95 (*1-56000-662-5*, CP307) Transaction Pubs.

Perez-Lopez, Jorge F., ed. Cuba at a Crossroads: Politics & Economics after the Fourth Party Congress. LC 94-16203. 288p. 1994. 49.95 (*0-8130-1310-0*) U Press Fla.

— Cuban Studies Bk. No. XXIII. (Pitt Series in Cuban Studies). 288p. (C). 1994. text 39.95 (*0-8229-3765-4*) U of Pittsburgh Pr.

Perez Lopez, Manuel M., ed. see De Torres Villarroel, Diego.

Perez, Louis A. Army Politics in Cuba, 1898-1958. LC 75-35440. (Pitt Latin American Ser.). 256p. reprint ed. pap. 79.40 (*0-8357-5750-1*, 202544300043) Bks Demand.

Perez, Louis A., Jr. Cuba: Between Reform & Revolution. 2nd ed. (Latin American Histories Ser.). (Illus.). 560p. (C). 1995. text 64.00 (*0-19-509481-6*); pap. text 24.95 (*0-19-509482-4*) OUP.

— Cuba & the United States: Ties of Singular Intimacy. 2nd ed. LC 97-16850. (United States & the Americas Ser.). (Illus.). 352p. (C). 1997. pap. text 20.00 (*0-8203-1936-8*) U of Ga Pr.

— Cuba Between Empires, 1878-1902. (Pitt Latin American Ser.). 510p. 1998. pap. 22.95 (*0-8229-5687-X*) U of Pittsburgh Pr.

— Cuba under the Platt Amendment, 1902-1934. LC 85-26451. (Latin American Ser.). 430p. (C). 1991. pap. 19.95 (*0-8229-5446-X*) U of Pittsburgh Pr.

— Essays on Cuban History: Historiography & Research. LC 94-29231. 318p. (C). 1995. 49.95 (*0-8130-1329-1*) U Press Fla.

— A Guide to Cuban Collections in the United States, 1. LC 91-6684. (Reference Guides to Archival & Manuscript Sources in World History Ser.: No. 1). 192p. 1991. lib. bdg. 49.95 (*0-313-26858-4*, PGC, Greenwood Pr) Greenwood.

Perez, Louis A. Intervention, Revolution, & Politics in Cuba, 1913-1921. LC 78-53601. (Pitt Latin American Ser.). 216p. reprint ed. pap. 67.00 (*0-608-20007-7*, 207128300010) Bks Demand.

— Lords of the Mountain: Social Banditry & Peasant Protest in Cuba, 1878-1918. LC 88-19815. (Pitt Latin American Ser.). 288p. reprint ed. pap. 89.30 (*0-608-20008-5*, 207128400010) Bks Demand.

Perez, Louis A., Jr On Becoming Cuban: Identity, Nationality & Culture. LC 98-42664. (Illus.). 608p. 1999. 39.95 (*0-8078-2487-9*) U of NC Pr.

— The War of 1898: The United States & Cuba in History & Historiography. LC 98-2615. (Illus.). 192p. 1998. 34.95 (*0-8078-2437-2*); pap. 16.95 (*0-8078-4742-9*) U of NC Pr.

Perez, Louis A., Jr., compiled by. Cuba: An Annotated Bibliography, 10. LC 87-28017. (Bibliographies & Indexes in World History Ser.: No. 10). 314p. 1988. lib. bdg. 79.50 (*0-313-26162-8*, PZC/, Greenwood Pr) Greenwood.

Perez, Louis A., Jr., ed. Cuban Studies, Vol. 21. LC 75-64935. (Latin American Ser.). 320p. 1992. text 39.95 (*0-8229-3691-7*) U of Pittsburgh Pr.

— Cuban Studies Bk. No. XXV. (Latin American Ser.). 295p. (C). 1996. text 39.95 (*0-8229-3911-8*) U of Pittsburgh Pr.

— Impressions of Cuba in the Nineteenth Century: The Travel Diary of Joseph J. Dimock. LC 97-34086. (Latin American Silhouettes Ser.). 112p. (C). 1998. 45.00 (*0-8420-2657-6*, SR Bks); pap. 16.95 (*0-8420-2658-4*, SR Bks) Scholarly Res Inc.

— Jose Marti in the United States: The Florida Experience. LC 95-15740. (Special Studies: No. 28). 114p. (Orig.). (C). 1995. per. 25.00 (*0-87918-081-1*) ASU Lat Am St.

— Slaves, Sugar, & Colonial Society: Travel Accounts of Cuba, 1801-1899. LC 91-44977. (Latin American Silhouettes Ser.). 259p. 1992. 45.00 (*0-8420-2354-2*, SR Bks); pap. 17.95 (*0-8420-2415-8*, SR Bks) Scholarly Res Inc.

Perez, Louis C., ed. see Sabato, Ernesto.

Perez, Louis G. The Dalai Lama. LC 92-38325. (World Leaders Ser.). 112p. (YA). 1993. lib. bdg. 25.27 (*0-86625-480-3*) Rourke Pubns.

— The History of Japan. LC 97-45657. (The Greenwood Histories of the Modern Nations Ser.). 272p. 1998. 35.00 (*0-313-30296-0*, Greenwood Pr) Greenwood.

— Japan Comes of Age: Mutsu Munemitsu & the Revision of the Unequal Treaties. LC 98-45890. 248p. 1999. 41.50 (*0-8386-3804-X*) Fairleigh Dickinson.

Perez Lugin, Alejandro, adapted by. La Casa de la Troya, Level 3. (Leer en Espanol Ser.). (SPA.). (C). 1998. pap. 5.95 (*84-294-4047-X*) Santillana.

Perez, Luis Hipolito Serrano, jt. ed. see Stoner, K. Lynn.

Perez, Lynne B. Frommer's Cancun, Cozumel & Yucatan 99. 99th ed. 336p. 1998. pap. 14.95 (*0-02-862306-1*, Pub. by Macmillan) S&S Trade.

— Frommer's Mexico 99. 99th ed. 720p. 1998. 19.95 (*0-02-862305-3*, Pub. by Macmillan) S&S Trade.

Perez, M. A., jt. auth. see Heurta, R.

***Perez, M. L. & Atanasson, K., eds.** Definitions, Conjectures, Unsolved Problems on Smarandache Notions. rev. ed. (Illus.). 100p. 1999. pap. 19.50 (*1-879585-74-X*) American Res Pr.

Perez, M. L., ed. see Atanasson, Krassimir T.

Perez-Mallaina, Pablo E. Spain's Men of the Sea: Daily Life on the Indies Fleets in the Sixteenth Century. Phillips, Carla R., tr. from SPA. LC 97-42172. (Illus.). 320p. 1998. 29.95 (*0-8018-5746-5*) Johns Hopkins.

Perez, Manuel S. Quien Manda En Cuba? Las Estructuras Del Polder. La Elite. LC 89-83374. (Coleccion Cuba y sus Jueces). (SPA., Illus.). 255p. 1989. 35.00 (*0-89729-551-X*) Ediciones.

Perez-Marchand, Monelisa L. History of Ideas in Puerto Rico. (Puerto Rico Ser.). 1979. lib. bdg. 59.95 (*0-8490-2935-X*) Gordon Pr.

Perez, Maria E. Lo Americano en el Teatro de Sor Juana Ines de la Cruz. 1975. 14.00 (*0-88303-020-9*); pap. 11.00 (*0-685-73221-5*) E Torres & Sons.

Perez, Maritza, jt. auth. see Robins, Perry.

Perez-Mato, J. M., et al, eds. Methods of Structural Analysis of Modulated Structures & Quasicrystals. 600p. (C). 1991. text 128.00 (*981-02-0692-5*) World Scientific Pub.

Perez, Maya & Latterman, Terry. Born with a Veil: The Life of a Spiritual Mystic. 234p. 1991. pap. 9.95 (*1-878901-04-4*) Hampton Roads Pub Co.

***Perez-Mercado, Mary Margaret.** Splat! (Rookie Readers Ser.). (J). 2000. pap. text 4.95 (*0-516-26543-1*) Childrens.

Perez, Miguel. The Earth & the Universe. (Universe Ser.). (Illus.). 36p. (J). (ps-3). 1998. pap. 5.95 (*0-7641-0687-2*) Barron.

— Estrellas y Galaxias. (Universe Ser.).Tr. of Stars & Galaxies. (SPA., Illus.). 36p. (J). 1998. pap. 5.95 (*0-7641-0760-7*) Barron.

— El Sistema Solar. (Universe Ser.).Tr. of Solar System. (SPA., Illus.). 36p. (J). 1998. pap. 5.95 (*0-7641-0759-3*) Barron.

— The Solar System. (Universe Ser.). (Illus.). 36p. (J). 1998. pap. 5.95 (*0-7641-0685-6*) Barron.

— Stars & Galaxies. (Universe Ser.). (Illus.). 36p. (J). 1998. pap. 5.95 (*0-7641-0686-4*) Barron.

— La Tierra y el Universo. (Universe Ser.).Tr. of Earth & the Universe. (SPA., Illus.). 36p. (J). 1998. pap. 5.95 (*0-7641-0761-5*) Barron.

— The Universe: The Solar System, Stars & Galaxies, The Earth & the Universe, 3 bks. (Universe Ser.: No. 3). (Illus.). 36p. (J). (ps-2). 1998. pap. 17.95 (*0-7641-7203-4*) Barron.

Perez, Miguel E., jt. ed. see Guzman, Carmen.

Perez Moro, Oscar. Rumores de Mi Bohio. (SPA.). 1972. pap. 7.95 (*0-89729-066-6*) Ediciones.

Perez-Munuzuri, Vincent, et al, eds. Discretely-Coupled Dynamical Systems. LC 97-159561. 400p. 1997. lib. bdg. 64.00 (*981-02-2912-7*) World Scientific Pub.

Perez, N. A. The Breaker. LC 87-33891. 216p. (J). (gr. 5-9). 1988. 16.00 (*0-395-45537-5*) HM.

— The Slopes of War. LC 83-26436. (Illus.). 224p. (J). (gr. 7 up). 1990. pap. 5.95 (*0-395-54979-5*) HM.

Perez, Nelida, et al, eds. Julia de Burgos (1914-1953) (Puerto Rican Bibliographies Ser.). 25p. (C). 1986. reprint ed. pap. 1.00 (*1-878483-41-2*) Hunter Coll CEP.

Perez, Nelida & Tirado, Amilcar. Boricuas En el Norte. (Centro Library). 39p. 1987. reprint ed. pap. 5.00 (*1-878483-26-9*) Hunter Coll CEP.

— Boricuas En el Norte, Set. (Centro Library). 39p. 1987. reprint ed. pap. 1.00 (*1-878483-39-0*) Hunter Coll CEP.

Perez, Nelida & Tirado, Amilcar, eds. Pedro Albizu Campos, 1891-1965. (Puerto Rican Bibliographies Ser.). (Illus.). 30p. (C). 1986. reprint ed. pap. 1.00 (*1-878483-43-9*) Hunter Coll CEP.

Perez, Nelida, jt. ed. see Tirado, Amilcar.

Perez, Nicole, jt. auth. see Horrigan, Carol.

Perez, Nicostrato D., ed. see Agcaoili-Sombilla, Mercedita.

***Perez, Orlando J., ed.** Post-Invasion Panama: The Challenges of Democratization in the New World Order. LC 99-86082. 208p. 2000. 55.00 (*0-7391-0120-X*) Lxngtn Bks.

Perez-Palacios, G., jt. ed. see Van Look, P. F.

Perez, Paulina. The Nurturing Touch at Birth: A Labor Support Handbook. LC 97-91542. (Illus.). 84p. 1997. pap. 11.95 (*0-9641159-8-0*) Doubleday.

Perez, Paulina & Snedeker, Cheryl. Special Women: The Role of the Professional Labor Assistant. (Illus.). 157p. 1994. pap. 12.95 (*0-937604-10-0*, Pennypr) Intl Childbirth.

— Special Women: The Role of the Professional Labor Assistant. 2nd ed. LC 94-94211. (Illus.). 157p. 1994. pap. 9.95 (*0-9641159-9-9*) Doubleday.

Perez, Paulina & Thelen, Deaun. Doula Programs: How to Start & Run a Private or Hospital-Based Program with Success! LC 98-92531. xi, 190 p. 1998. write for info. (*0-9641159-7-2*) Cutting Edge.

***Perez-Periera, Miguel.** Language Development & Social Interaction in Blind Children. 200p. 1999. 39.95 (*0-86377-795-3*) L Erlbaum Assocs.

Perez, Phil. Official Little League Baseball Rules in Pictures. (J). 1989. 14.15 (*0-606-04288-1*, Pub. by Turtleback) Demco.

Perez, Pilar, ed. see Gonzalez, Rita.

Perez-Polo, Jose R., jt. ed. see Conn, P. Michael.

Perez Prendes, Jose M., et al. Historia de Espana Vol. 3: Espana Visigoda V. 2 la Monarquia, la Cultura, las Artes. (SPA.). 510p. 1992. 189.50 (*84-239-4996-6*) Elliots Bks.

Perez-Prendes, Jose M., ed. see Garcia de Valdeavellano, Luis.

Perez Priego, Miguel A., ed. see De Mena, Juan.

Perez Priego, Miguel A., ed. see Manrique, Jorge.

Perez, Priscila E. Servant's Heart. 1999. pap. text 9.00 (*0-9664870-0-1*) Roca.

Perez, Rachel. Odd Women. (Orig.). 1997. mass mkt. 6.50 (*1-56333-526-3*, Rosebud) Masquerade.

Perez, Rachel L. Ms. Pea's Pet Store & Other Children's Tales. (J). 1994. 7.95 (*0-533-10836-5*) Vantage.

Perez, Ramon. Diary of a Guerrilla. Reavis, Dick J., tr. LC 99-24884. 208p. 1999. 19.95 (*1-55885-282-4*) Arte Publico.

— Garabandal: The Village Speaks. Orhelein, Ann, ed. Mathews, Annette L., tr. from FRE. LC 81-51901.Tr. of Garabandal: Le Village Parle. (Illus.). 352p. (Orig.). 1981. pap. 5.00 (*0-686-32902-3*) Workers Lady Mt Carmel.

Perez, Ramon B., jt. ed. see Rodriguez, Camille.

Perez-Ramon, Joaquin. Self & Non-Self in Early Buddhism. (Religion & Society Ser.: No. 17). 1980. 84.65 (*90-279-7987-1*) Mouton.

Perez, Ramon T. Diary of an Undocumented Immigrant. Reavis, Dick J., tr. LC 91-7869. 237p. 1991. pap. 10.95 (*1-55885-032-5*) Arte Publico.

Perez, Reinaldo. Wireless Communications Design Handbook: Aspects of Noise, Interference, & Environmental Concerns. LC 98-16901. (C). 1998. text 79.00 (*0-12-550721-6*) Acad Pr.

Perez, Reinaldo, ed. Handbook of Electromagnetic Compatibility. LC 94-31850. (Illus.). 1098p. 1995. text 158.00 (*0-12-550710-0*) Acad Pr.

Perez-Reverte, Artaro. The Club Dumas. Soto, Sonia, tr. (Illus.). 362p. 1996. 23.00 (*0-15-100182-0*) Harcourt.

Perez-Reverte, Arturo. El Capitan Alatriste. (Capitan Alatriste Ser.: Vol. 1). 251p. (YA). 1997. pap. 14.95 (*968-19-0324-2*) Santillana.

Perez-Reverte, Arturo. The Club Dumas. (SPA.). 1998. pap. 13.00 (*0-375-70228-8*) Vin Bks.

— The Club Dumas: A Novel. Soto, Sonia, tr. from SPA. LC 97-50179. (International Ser.). 362p. 1998. pap. 13.00 (*0-679-77754-7*) Vin Bks.

— The Fencing Master. Costa, Margaret J., tr. from SPA. LC 98-35536. 256p. 1999. 24.00 (*0-15-100181-2*) Harcourt.

***Perez-Reverte, Arturo.** Fencing Master. (Illus.). 256p. (J). 2000. pap. 13.00 (*0-15-600684-7*, Harcourt Child Bks) Harcourt.

Perez-Reverte, Arturo. The Flanders Panel. Costa, Margaret J., tr. from SPA. LC 95-39573.Tr. of Tabla de Flandes. 304p. 1996. pap. 12.95 (*0-553-37786-8*) Bantam.

— The Flandes Panel. Costa, Margaret J., tr. from SPA. (ENG.). 1994. write for info. (*0-318-71665-8*) Harcourt.

***Perez-Reverte, Arturo.** Limpieza de Sangre. (Capitan Alatriste Ser.: Vol. 2). 251p. (YA). 1998. pap. 14.95 (*84-204-8359-1*) Santillana.

— El Maestro de Esgrima. 356p. 1999. pap. 4.95 (*84-204-4198-8*) Santillana.

— La Piel del Tambor. LC 96-125309. (SPA.). 2000. pap. 16.95 (*84-204-8201-3*) Alfaguara Ediciones.

Perez-Reverte, Arturo. The Seville Communion. Soto, Sonia, tr. from SPA. LC 97-33050. (Illus.). 400p. 1998. 24.00 (*0-15-100283-5*) Harcourt.

— The Seville Communion. Soto, Sonia, tr. from SPA. (Illus.). 375p. (C). 1999. pap. 14.00 (*0-15-600639-1*, Harvest Bks) Harcourt.

***Perez-Reverte, Arturo.** El Sol de Breda. (Capitan Alatrista Ser.: Vol. 3). (SPA.). 254p. (YA). 2000. pap. 14.95 (*84-204-8312-5*) Santillana.

— La Tabla de Flandes. 416p. 1999. pap. 16.95 (*968-19-0372-2*) Santillana.

Perez Rioja, Jose A. Diccionario Literario Universal. (SPA.). 994p. 1977. 89.95 (*0-8288-5351-7*, S31441) Fr & Eur.

Perez, Robert C. Clarence Dillon: Wall Street Enigma. 1995. 29.95 (*1-56833-048-0*) Madison Bks UPA.

— Inside Investment Banking. LC 84-11713. 203p. 1984. 45.00 (*0-275-91242-6*, C1242, Praeger Pubs) Greenwood.

— Inside Investment Banking. LC 84-11713. 1984. 33.95 (*0-03-072062-1*) Holt R&W.

— Inside Venture Capital: Past, Present, & Future. LC 86-30146. 202p. 1986. 55.00 (*0-275-92118-2*, C2118, Praeger Pubs) Greenwood.

— Marketing Financial Services. LC 83-4230. 175p. 1983. 52.95 (*0-275-91723-1*, C1723, Praeger Pubs) Greenwood.

Perez, Robert C. & Willett, Edward F. A Will to Win: The Biography of Ferdinand Eberstadt, 96. LC 89-1898. (Contributions in Economics & Economic History Ser.: No. 96). 181p. 1989. 49.95 (*0-313-26738-3*, PWB, Greenwood Pr) Greenwood.

Perez, Roberto M. & Encinosa, Enrique G. The Castro Revolution: Crime Without Punishment. Kvederas, Robert, ed. 250p. 1992. 25.00 (*0-944273-10-6*) U S Cuba Pr.

Perez, Rolando. The Divine Duty of Servants: A Book of Worship (Based on the Artwork of Bruno Schulz) deluxe ed. (Illus.). 228p. 1999. 22.95 (*1-887276-13-0*); pap. write for info. Cool Grove Pub.

— The Divine Duty of Servants: A Book of Worship (Based on the Artwork of Bruno Schulz) deluxe ed. (Illus.). 168p. 2000. 22.95 (*1-887276-17-3*); pap. 12.95 (*1-887276-16-5*, Pub. by Cool Grove Pub) SPD-Small Pr Dist.

***Perez, Rolando.** The Electric Comedy. (Illus.). 108p. 2000. 22.95 (*1-887276-24-6*, Pub. by Cool Grove Pub); pap. 12.95 (*1-887276-23-8*, Pub. by Cool Grove Pub) LPC Group.

Perez, Rolando. On Anarchy & Schizoanalysis. (Illus.). 160p. (Orig.). (C). 1990. pap. text 8.00 (*0-936756-39-X*) Autonomedia.

Perez, Roman C. & Ferrie, Michel F. Introduction to Business Translation: A Handbook in English - Spanish Contrastive Linguistics. 2nd rev. ed. LC 85-8581. 163p. (C). 1985. pap. 7.00 (*0-8477-3342-4*) U of PR Pr.

Perez, Rosita. The Music Is You. (Illus.). 1994. audio 29.95 (*0-9611354-2-5*) T Knox Pub.

Perez, Rosita. The Music Is You: A Guide to Thinking Less & Feeling More. 4th ed. (Illus.). 124p. (Orig.). 1994. pap. 12.50 (*0-9611354-7-6*) T Knox Pub.

***Perez, Ruperto M., et al, eds.** Handbook of Counseling & Psychotherapy with Lesbian, Gay & Bisexual Clients. LC 99-32399. 1999. text 49.95 (*1-55798-610-X*, 431-736A) Am Psychol.

Perez-Sabido, Jesus. Spanish - English Handbook for Medical Professionals: Compendio en Ingles y Espanol Para Profesionales de la Medicine. 4th ed. Rogers, Gregg, ed. LC 93-37022. (ENG & SPA.). 378p. 1993. spiral bd. 29.95 (*1-878487-61-2*, ME054) Practice Mgmt Info.

Perez Sainz, Juan P. From the Finca to the Maquila: Labor & Capitalist Development in Central America. LC 98-34576. 189p. 1998. 75.00 (*0-8133-3519-1*, Pub. by Westview) HarpC.

Perez-Sala, Paulino. Interferencia Linguistica Del Ingles En el Espanol Hablado En Puerto Rico. LC 72-93776. (Working Papers: No. 77-3). (SPA.). 132p. 1973. 7.50 (*0-913480-10-X*) Inter Am U Pr.

***Perez-Salva, Abilio.** Title Insurance 101: Principles & Fundamentals of the Title Insurance Process. LC 99-73456. 282p. 1999. pap. 65.00 (*1-890622-93-1*) Leathers Pub.

Perez-Sanchez, Alfonso E. & Gallego, Julian. Goya: The Complete Etchings & Lithographs. (Illus.). 264p. 1997. 75.00 (*3-7913-1432-7*, Pub. by Prestel) te Neues.

Perez Sanchez, Delia, tr. see Stonecipher, Philip.

***Perez Sarduy, Pedro & Stubbs, Jean.** Afro-Cuban Voices: On Race & Identity in Contemporary Cuba. LC 99-53467. (Contemporary Cuba Ser.). 312p. 2000. 24.95 (*0-8130-1735-1*) U Press Fla.

Perez-Segura, E. & Jacques-Ayala, Cesar, eds. Studies of Sonoran Geology. (Special Papers: No. 254). (Illus.). 136p. 1991. pap. 15.00 (*0-8137-2254-3*) Geol Soc.

Perez, Sofia A. Banking on Privilege: The Politics of Spanish Financial Reform. LC 97-17554. (Illus.). 248p. 1997. text 29.95 (*0-8014-3323-1*) Cornell U Pr.

Perez-Soler, A. Inflammatory & Artresia-Inducing Disease of the Liver & Bile Ducts. (Monographs in Pediatrics: Vol. 8). (Illus.). 1976. 68.00 (*3-8055-2257-6*) S Karger.

Perez-Stable, Maria A., jt. auth. see Cordier, Mary H.

Perez-Stable, Marifeli. The Cuban Revolution: Origins, Course & Legacy. 2nd ed. LC 98-20278. 288p. (C). 1998. pap. 22.95 (*0-19-512749-8*) OUP.

Perez, Steve, ed. see Adamson, Bruce Campbell.

Perez-Tamayo, Ruy. Mechanisms of Disease: An Introduction to Pathology. 2nd ed. LC 84-25728. (Illus.). 668p. reprint ed. pap. 200.00 (*0-8357-6315-3*, 203558800096) Bks Demand.

Perez-Tamayo, Ruy & Rojkind, Marcos, eds. Molecular Pathology of Connective Tissues. LC 72-86611. (Biochemistry of Disease Ser.: No. 3). (Illus.). 416p. reprint ed. pap. 129.00 (*0-7837-0887-4*, 204119300019) Bks Demand.

Perez Taylor, Rafael & Ramirez, Felipe. Cuadernos de Trabajo No. 6: Fuentes Bibliograficas de Xochimilco. (SPA.). 81p. 1997. pap. 7.00 (*968-36-6003-7*, UN55, Pub. by Instit de Invest) UPLAAP.

Perez, Theresa, jt. auth. see Marquez, Nancy.

Perez, Tommaso. Multinational Enterprises & Technological Spillovers. LC 98-172285. (Studies in Global Competition: Vol. 6). 202p. 1998. text 56.00 (*90-5702-295-8*, ECU40, Harwood Acad Pubs) Gordon & Breach.

Perez, Tony. Dios Busca Adoradores: En Espiritu y en Verdad. (SPA.). 184p. (Orig.). 1996. pap. 9.00 (*0-9652224-0-3*) Alabanzas Llamada.

— Soundscape with Humans. (Orig.). 1974. pap. 1.50 (*0-915242-02-8*) Pygmalion Pr.

Perez, Tony, ed. "Inspiracion" Himnario. 136p. 1997. pap. 9.00 (*0-9652224-1-1*) Alabanzas Llamada.

Perez-Torres, Rafael. Movements in Chicano Poetry: Against Myths, Against Margins. (Studies in American Literature & Culture: No. 88). 348p. (C). 1995. pap. text 21.95 (*0-521-47803-0*) Cambridge U Pr.

Perez-Vega, Ivette. El Cielo & la Tierra en Sus Manos: Los Grandes Propietarios de Ponce, 1816-1830. LC 85-81454. (SPA.). 123p. 1985. pap. 6.95 (*0-940238-22-5*) Ediciones Huracan.

Perez-Venero, Alex. Before the Five Frontiers: Panama from 1821-1903. LC 77-78317. 32.50 (*0-404-16003-4*) AMS Pr.

Perez-Vicente, Conrado, jt. auth. see Rubi, J. M.

Perez, Victor. La Pulga y el Piojo (The Flea & the Louse) (SPA.). 24p. (J). (ps-1). pap. 6.95 (*980-257-106-7*, Pub. by Ediciones Ekare) Kane-Miller Bk.

Perez-Vidal, Angel. Historia Intima de la Revolucion Cubana. LC 97-60682. (Coleccion Cuba y Sus Jueces Ser.). (SPA.). 257p. (Orig.). 1997. pap. 19.95 (*0-89729-840-3*, 840-3) Ediciones.

— Muchas Gracias . . . Marielitos . . . Siete Anos Despues: Una Historia Verdadera y Siete Cuentos Imaginados. LC 87-83680. (Coleccion Caniqui). (SPA.). 151p. (Orig.). 1988. pap. 12.00 (*0-89729-473-4*) Ediciones.

Perez-Wilson, Mario. The Design of Experiments: A Seven-Stage Methodology. (Variation Reduction Program Ser.). 400p. 1993. 95.00 (*1-883237-05-X*) Adv Systs Cnslts.

— M - PCpS-Cpk Software: Software for Machine - Process Capability Studies. (Variation Reduction Program Ser.). 120p. 1993. 800.00 incl. disk (*1-883237-02-5*) Adv Systs Cnslts.

— Machine - Process Capability Study: A Five Stage Methodology for Optimizing Manufacturing Processes. rev. ed. (Variation Reduction Program Ser.). 238p. 1993. reprint ed. 74.95 (*1-883237-00-9*) Adv Systs Cnslts.

An Asterisk (*) at the beginning of an entry indicates that the title is appearing for the first time.

— Multi-Vari Chart & Analysis. (Variation Reduction Program Ser.). 86p. 1993. 35.00 (*1-883237-01-7*) Adv Systs Cnslts.

— Positrol Plans & Logs: A Plan for Controlling Variation During Production. (Illus.). 1999. pap. 45.00 (*1-883237-15-7*) Adv Systs Cnslts.

— Six Sigma: Understanding the Concept, Implications & Challenges. 308p. 1999. 88.00 (*1-883237-68-8*) Adv Systs Cnslts.

***Perez y Gonzalez, Maria.** Puerto Ricans in the United States. LC 99-55207. 2000. write for info. (*0-313-29748-7*) Greenwood.

Perez y Mena, Andres I. Speaking with the Dead: Development of Afro-Latin Religion among Puerto Ricans in the United States. LC 91-8469. (Immigrant Communities & Ethnic Minorities in the U. S. & Canada Ser.: No. 75). 1991. 55.00 (*0-404-19485-0*) AMS Pr.

Perez y Mena, Andres I., jt. ed. see Stevens-Arroyo, Anthony M.

Perez, Yvonne & Haglund, Jill. The Idea Book for Scrapbooking: Featuring Rubber Stamping, Vol. 1. Haglund, Rob, ed. LC 98-96812. (Illus.). 160p. 1999. mass mkt. 19.95 (*1-891898-02-7*) Tweety Jill.

Perez, Zobeida. Orchestral Library Series, No. 2. (Orig.). (YA). 1994. pap. 189.00 (*0-89898-774-1*) Wrner Bros.

Perez, Zobeida, prod. Aaron Piano Course. 64p. (Orig.). (J). (gr. k-5). 1994. pap. 5.50 (*0-7692-1498-3*) Wrner Bros.

— American Scenes. 12p. (Orig.). (J). 1994. pap. 17.00 (*0-89898-747-4*, BMR05074) Wrner Bros.

— Animals & Circus. (Illus.). 12p. (Orig.). (J). 1994. pap. 17.00 (*0-89898-748-2*, BMR05064) Wrner Bros.

— Art of Bop Drumming. 48p. (Orig.). 1994. pap. 24.95 incl. audio compact disk (*0-89898-890-X*, MMBK0056CD) Wrner Bros.

— Band Today Pt. 1: Flute. 32p. (Orig.). (YA). 1985. pap. 5.95 (*0-7692-1485-1*, CBC00021) Wrner Bros.

— Belwin Master Duets Vol. 2: Fl. Int. 32p. (Orig.). 1991. pap. 6.95 (*0-7692-1490-8*, EL03640) Wrner Bros.

— The Book of Great Movie Themes. 208p. (Orig.). 1997. pap. 14.95 (*0-7692-0117-2*, MF9724) Wrner Bros.

— Bradley Kids Meth-Blue: A Book. 64p. (Orig.). (J). 1994. pap. 6.95 (*0-89898-889-6*, BP3231A) Wrner Bros.

— Christmas at the Piano. 32p. (Orig.). 1985. pap. 5.50 (*0-89898-938-8*, EL01527) Wrner Bros.

— Christmas Greatest Hits. rev. ed. 72p. (YA). 1997. pap. 9.95 (*0-7692-0146-6*, F3357ASA) Wrner Bros.

— Classroom Concert. (Orig.). 1994. pap. 17.00 (*0-89898-787-3*, BMR05081) Wrner Bros.

— Concert Matinee. 16p. (Orig.). (J). 1994. pap. 17.00 (*0-89898-788-1*, BMR05076) Wrner Bros.

— Dances, Pt. 1. 20p. (Orig.). 1994. pap. 17.00 (*0-89898-752-0*, BMR05068) Wrner Bros.

— Dances, Pt. 2. 16p. (Orig.). 1994. pap. 17.00 (*0-89898-743-1*, BMR05069) Wrner Bros.

— Fairy Tales in Music. 12p. (Orig.). (J). 1994. pap. 17.00 (*0-89898-742-3*, BMR05070) Wrner Bros.

— Fantasy in Music. 16p. (Orig.). 1994. pap. 17.00 (*0-89898-794-6*, BMR05080) Wrner Bros.

— Festival of Christmas: Duets. 56p. (Orig.). 1988. pap. 10.00 (*0-89898-931-0*, EL03299) Wrner Bros.

— First Class Recorder Solos: Ensemble. 32p. (Orig.). (J). 1994. pap. 4.95 (*0-89898-904-3*, BMP334) Wrner Bros.

— 1st Division Method, No. 2. 32p. (Orig.). (YA). 1985. pap. 5.95 (*0-7692-1491-6*, FDL00095) Wrner Bros.

— 1st Division Method No. 1: Trumpet, No. 1. 32p. (Orig.). (YA). 1985. pap. 5.95 (*0-7692-1432-0*, FDL00012) Wrner Bros.

— 1st Division Method No. 3: Tuba. 32p. (Orig.). (YA). 1985. pap. 5.95 (*0-7692-1492-4*, FDL00182) Wrner Bros.

— 1st Division Method No. 4: Flute. 32p. (Orig.). (YA). 1985. pap. 5.95 (*0-7692-1493-2*, FDL00221) Wrner Bros.

— Folk Dances Around the World. 20p. (Orig.). (J). 1994. pap. 19.95 (*0-89898-776-8*, BMR05114) Wrner Bros.

— Folk Dances of Hawaii. (Illus.). 36p. (Orig.). (J). Date not set. pap. 19.95 (*0-89898-755-5*, BMR05116) Wrner Bros.

— Fun with Five Finger Christmas Carols. 32p. (Orig.). 1987. pap. 6.95 (*0-89898-957-4*, F2860PFX) Wrner Bros.

— Great Keyboard Composers, Bk. 2. 48p. (Orig.). (YA). 1994. pap. 6.95 (*0-89898-946-9*, BMP004) Wrner Bros.

— Jazz Style of Clifford Brown. 120p. (Orig.). 1982. pap. 14.95 (*0-7692-1484-3*, SB104) Wrner Bros.

— Jazz Style of Miles Davis. 68p. (Orig.). 1991. pap. 12.95 (*0-7692-0982-3*, SB97) Wrner Bros.

— Legends in Music. 12p. (Orig.). 1994. pap. 17.00 (*0-89898-746-6*, BMR05072) Wrner Bros.

— Liturgical Organist, Vol. 7. 122p. (Orig.). 1985. pap. 16.95 (*0-7692-1433-9*, FE08910) Wrner Bros.

— Marches. 16p. (Orig.). (J). 1994. pap. 17.00 (*0-89898-753-9*, BMR05067) Wrner Bros.

— MFAO - International Favorites. 112p. (Orig.). 1997. pap. 12.95 (*0-7692-0067-2*, FB9705) Wrner Bros.

— Miniatures in Music. 20p. (Orig.). (J). 1994. pap. 17.00 (*0-89898-749-0*, BMR05077) Wrner Bros.

— Mosaics - New Age Piano: Easy Piano. 20p. (Orig.). (YA). 1989. pap. 5.95 (*0-89898-653-2*, F2981P2X) Wrner Bros.

— Music of the Dance: Stravinsky. 16p. (Orig.). (YA). 1994. pap. 17.00 (*0-89898-799-7*, BMR05084) Wrner Bros.

— Music U. S. A. 16p. (Orig.). (YA). 1994. pap. 17.00 (*0-89898-790-3*, BMR05078) Wrner Bros.

— Musical Kaleidoscope. 20p. (Orig.). (J). 1994. pap. 17.00 (*0-89898-786-5*, BMR05093) Wrner Bros.

— Nature & Make Believe. 16p. (Orig.). (YA). 1991. pap. 17.00 (*0-89898-659-1*, BMR04065) Wrner Bros.

— Nightworks. 20p. (Orig.). 1993. pap. 5.50 (*0-89898-652-4*, F3313P9X) Wrner Bros.

— 101 Rhythmic Rest Patterns: Trombone. 24p. (Orig.). (YA). 1985. pap. 5.95 (*0-7692-1486-X*, EL00557) Wrner Bros.

— Orchestral Library Series, No. 1. (Orig.). 1994. pap. 189.00 (*0-89898-773-3*, BMR05111) Wrner Bros.

— Oriental Scenes. 16p. (Orig.). 1994. pap. 17.00 (*0-89898-785-7*) Wrner Bros.

— Pat Martino, Pt. 2. 72p. (Orig.). 1994. pap. 21.95 incl. audio compact disk (*0-89898-945-0*, REHBK007CD) Wrner Bros.

— Pictures & Patterns. (Illus.). 16p. (Orig.). (J). 1994. pap. 17.00 (*0-89898-745-8*, BMR05066) Wrner Bros.

— Read & Play Recorder Book. 32p. (Orig.). (YA). 1985. pap. 5.50 (*0-7692-1488-6*, EL02938) Wrner Bros.

— Rehearsal Fundamentals: Cornet. 32p. (Orig.). (YA). 1985. pap. 5.95 (*0-7692-1487-8*, EL00957) Wrner Bros.

— Rhythm Etudes: Cornet. 52p. (Orig.). (YA). 1985. pap. 5.95 (*0-7692-1494-0*, SCHBK09624F) Wrner Bros.

— Rhythm Etudes: Trombone. 32p. (Orig.). (YA). 1985. pap. 5.95 (*0-7692-1499-1*, SCHBK09624H) Wrner Bros.

— Rush: Bass Anthology Series. 144p. (Orig.). 1997. pap. write for info. (*0-7692-0071-0*, 0138B) Wrner Bros.

— Solos for Marimba. 64p. (Orig.). (YA). 1985. pap. 10.00 (*0-7692-1489-4*, EL03200) Wrner Bros.

— Stories in Ballet & Opera. 16p. (Orig.). (J). 1994. pap. 17.00 (*0-89898-751-2*, BMR05071) Wrner Bros.

— Under Many Flags. 12p. (Orig.). (J). 1994. pap. 17.00 (*0-89898-750-4*, BMR05073) Wrner Bros.

Perez, Zobeida & DeLisa, Jeannette, eds. Los Grandes Boleros de Mario Clavell. 68p. (Orig.). (YA). 1996. pap. text 14.95 (*1-57623-473-8*, PF9601) Wrner Bros.

Perez, Zobeida, tr. see Cuellar, Carol & Stang, Aaron, eds.

PERF (Police Executive Research Forum) Staff & BJA (Bureau of Justice Assistance) Staff. National Guns First: Training for Law Enforcement Officers to Help Reduce Illegal Trafficking of Firearms. rev. ed. 1999. pap. 20.00 (*1-878734-63-6*) Police Exec Res.

Perfecky, George A. The Galician-Volhynian Chronicle, Vol. 9. (Illus.). 220p. Date not set. text 35.00 (*0-916458-70-9*) Harvard Ukrainian.

Perfect, Christopher. The Complete Typographer. LC 93-131242. 224p. 1992. pap. 54.67 (*0-13-045667-5*) P-H.

Perfect, John R., jt. auth. see Casadevall, Arturo.

***Perfect, Timothy J. & Maylor, Elizabeth A., eds.** Models of Cognitive Aging. LC 99-15924. (Debates in Psychology Ser.). (Illus.). 320p. 2000. pap. 34.95 (*0-19-852437-4*); text 85.00 (*0-19-852438-2*) OUP.

Perfect, William. Annals of Insanity: Comprising a Selection of Curious & Interesting Cases in the Different Species of Lunacy, Melancholy, or Madness. LC 75-16726. (Classics in Psychiatry Ser.). 1976. reprint ed. 28.95 (*0-405-07449-2*) Ayer.

Perfecto, Ivette, jt. auth. see Vandermeer, John.

Perfetti, Bruno M. Metal Surface Characteristics Affecting Organic Coatings. (Illus.). 70p. 1994. pap. 30.00 (*0-934010-32-3*) Fed Soc Coat Tech.

Perfetti, Charles A., et al, eds. Learning to Spell. LC 96-51911. 352p. 1997. 79.95 (*0-8058-2160-0*); pap. 45.00 (*0-8058-2161-9*) L Erlbaum Assocs.

Perfetti, Charles A., et al. Text-Based Learning & Reasoning: Studies in History. 232p. 1995. text 49.95 (*0-8058-1643-7*) L Erlbaum Assocs.

Perfetti, Charles A., jt. auth. see Rieben, Laurence.

Perfetti, Charles A., jt. ed. see Lesgold, Alan M.

Perfetti, Patricia B., jt. auth. see Terrell, Charles R.

Perfetto, Edda, jt. auth. see Ettinger, Blanche.

Perfil'ev, Boris V., et al. Applied Capillary Microscopy: The Role of Microorganisms in the Formation of Iron-Manganese Desposits. LC 65-15003. 130p. reprint ed. pap. 40.30 (*0-8357-5674-2*, 202066900018) Bks Demand.

Performance Solutions Staff. Supervisory Training Program: Student Modules. rev. ed. Watson, Gail, ed. 380p. 1993. teacher ed. write for info. (*0-318-72221-6*); text. write for info. (*0-89982-323-8*) Am Bankers.

Perfumo, Pamela, jt. ed. see Calfee, Robert C.

Pergamit, Gayle, jt. auth. see Peterson, Chris.

Pergamon-Infotech Staff. Computer State of the Art Reports. write for info. (*0-318-57470-5*, Pergamon Pr) Elsevier.

Pergamon Press Staff, ed. Information Mongolia: The Comprehensive Reference Source of the People's Republic of Mongolia (MPR) Mongolian People's Republic Academy of Sciences St, tr. & compiled by. (World Information Ser.: No. 6). (Illus.). 500p. 1990. 150.00 (*0-08-036193-5*, Pergamon Pr) Elsevier.

Pergaud, Louis. De Goupil a Margot. (FRE.). 1982. pap. 10.95 (*0-7859-4162-2*) Fr & Eur.

— Guerre des Boutons. (Folio Ser.: No. 758). (FRE.). 1987. pap. 8.95 (*2-07-036758-4*) Schoenhof.

— La Guerre des Boutons. (FRE.). 1976. pap. 10.95 (*0-7859-4056-1*) Fr & Eur.

— Le Roman de Miraut: Chien de Chasse. (FRE.). 1978. pap. 11.95 (*0-7859-4102-9*) Fr & Eur.

Pergerson, Forest J., jt. auth. see Wellingham-Jones, Patricia.

Pergler, Charles. Judicial Interpretation of International Law in the United States. viii, 222p. 1983. reprint ed. 39.50 (*0-8377-1016-2*, Rothman) W S Hein.

Pergolesi. Stabat Mater in Full Score. 1998. pap. 7.95 (*0-486-29633-4*) Dover.

Pergolesi, Giovanni Battista. Stabat Mater. 1999. 9.95 (*963-9155-82-9*) Konemann.

***Pergolizzi, Carl Milo.** The Terminal Private. Caso, Adolph, ed. 224p. 2000. pap. 16.95 (*0-8283-2055-1*) Branden Bks.

Pergrin, David. The Carver's Handbook I: Woodcarving the Wonders of Nature. LC 84-51192. (Illus.). 60p. 1984. pap. 5.95 (*0-88740-015-9*) Schiffer.

— The Carver's Handbook II: Carving the Wild Life of the Forest & Jungle. LC 84-52153. (Illus.). 60p. 1985. pap. 5.95 (*0-88740-029-9*) Schiffer.

— The Carver's Handbook III: Woodcarving Wild Animals. LC 85-50298. (Illus.). 48p. 1985. pap. 5.95 (*0-88740-039-6*) Schiffer.

— Engineering the Victory: The Battle of the Bulge: A History. LC 96-68183. (Illus.). 320p. 1996. 35.00 (*0-7643-0163-2*) Schiffer.

Perguson, Barbara P. Basic Bible Commentary Vol. 4: Joshua, Judges, & Ruth. Deming, Lynne M., ed. LC 94-10965. 160p. (Orig.). 1994. pap. 5.95 (*0-687-02623-7*) Abingdon.

Perham, Canon M. Revised Common Lectionary in NRSV: For Sundays & Holidays. cd-rom 50.00 (*0-264-67456-1*) Continuum.

— Revised Common Lectionary in NRSV: For Sundays & Holidays. LC 98-120536. 1024p. 1997. 140.00 (*0-304-33697-1*) Continuum.

Perham, Margery. Pacific Prelude: A Journey to Samoa & Australasia, 1929. LC 88-70563. 272p. 1988. 40.00 (*0-7206-0683-7*, Pub. by P Owen Ltd) Dufour.

— West African Passage: A Journey Through Nigeria, Chad & the Cameroons. 245p. 1983. 40.00 (*0-7206-0609-8*, Pub. by P Owen Ltd) Dufour.

Perham, Margery F. The Colonial Reckoning: End of Imperial Rule in Africa in the Light of British Experience. LC 76-25998. 203p. 1976. reprint ed. lib. bdg. 59.50 (*0-8371-9016-9*, PECR, Greenwood Pr) Greenwood.

— The Economics of Tropical Dependency, 2 vols. 1976. lib. bdg. 200.00 (*0-8490-1748-3*) Gordon Pr.

— Native Administration in Nigeria. LC 74-15078. reprint ed. 32.50 (*0-404-12127-6*) AMS Pr.

Perham, Margery F., jt. auth. see Proudfoot, Mary M.

Perham, Michael, ed. The Book of the Gospels: Revised Common Lectionary in NRSV. LC 98-197769. 1998. 110.00 (*0-264-67468-5*, Pub. by G Chapman) Bks Intl VA.

Perham, Michael & Lloyd, Trevor. Enriching the Christian Year. 288p. (Orig.). 1993. 29.95 (*0-8146-2242-9*, Liturg Pr Bks) Liturgical Pr.

Perham, Molly. Cooking for One: Quick & Easy. 192p. 1994. pap. 12.95 (*0-572-01980-7*, Pub. by W Foulsham) Trans-Atl Phila.

— North American Totem Poles: Secrets & Symbols of North America. (Illus.). 16p. (J). (gr. 3-8). 1999. boxed set 14.95 (*1-55209-325-5*) Firefly Bks Ltd.

Perham, Molly & Rowe, Julian. Food. LC 94-39692. (MapWorlds Ser.). 32p. (J). (gr. 5-8). 1996. lib. bdg. 20.00 (*0-531-14374-0*) Watts.

— People. LC 95-2727. (MapWorlds Ser.). (Illus.). 32p. (J). (gr. 5-8). 1995. lib. bdg. 20.00 (*0-531-14362-7*) Watts.

— Water. LC 94-39691. (MapWorlds Ser.). (Illus.). 32p. (J). (gr. 5-8). 1996. lib. bdg. 20.00 (*0-531-14361-9*) Watts.

— Wildlife. LC 95-18170. (MapWorlds Ser.). (J). 1997. lib. bdg. 20.00 (*0-531-14388-0*) Watts.

Perham, Molly, jt. auth. see Ingpen, Robert.

Perham, Molly, jt. auth. see Ingpen, Robert R.

Perham, Molly, jt. auth. see Rowe, Julian.

***Peri, Camille & Moses, Kate, eds.** Mothers Who Think: Tales of Real Life Parenthood. 304p. 2000. reprint ed. pap. 12.95 (*0-671-77468-9*, WSP) PB.

Peri, Camille, jt. ed. see Moss, Kate.

Peri, David, et al. Ethnobotanical Mitigation: Warm Springs Dam-Lake Sonoma, California. (Illus.). 139p. (C). 1983. reprint ed. pap. text 15.00 (*1-55567-433-X*) Coyote Press.

Peri, Jacopo. Jacopo Peri: Euridice: An Opera in One Act, 5 Scenes. Brown, Howard Mayer, ed. (Recent Researches in the Music of the Baroque Era Ser.: Vols. RRB 36-37). (Illus.). xxxvii, 211p. 1981. pap. 80.00 (*0-89579-137-4*) A-R Eds.

— Jacopo Peri: Le Varie Musiche & Other Songs. Carter, Tim, ed. (Recent Researches in Music of the Baroque Era Ser.: Vol. RRB50). (Illus.). xxxvi, 112p. 1985. pap. 50.00 (*0-89579-205-2*) A-R Eds.

Peri, Paolo. The Handkerchief. (Twentieth Century-Histories of Fashion Ser.). (Illus.). 135p. 1996. 29.95 (*0-89676-205-X*, Costume & Fashion Pr) QSMG Ltd.

Peri, Vittorio. Rita of Cascia: Priceless Pearl of Umbria. Rotelle, John E., ed. O'Connell, Matthew J., tr. (Illus.). 174p. 1995. 21.95 (*0-941491-90-0*); pap. 15.95 (*0-941491-89-7*) Augustinian Pr.

***Peri, Yoram, ed.** The Assassination of Yitzhak Rabin. 409p. 2000. pap. 19.95 (*0-8047-3837-8*) Stanford U Pr.

— Assassination of Yitzhak Rabin. (Illus.). 409p. 2000. 55.00 (*0-8047-3835-1*) Stanford U Pr.

Periam, Jonathan. The Groundswell: A History of the Origins, Aims, & Progress of the Farmers' Movement Embracing an Authoritative Account of the Farmers' Clubs Granges Etc. LC 72-89080. (Rural America Ser.). 1973. reprint ed. 40.00 (*0-8420-1493-4*) Scholarly Res Inc.

Periasamy, K., ed. Histochemistry, Development & Structural Anatomy of Angiosperm: A Symposium. 305p. 1980. 40.00 (*1-55528-211-3*, Pub. by Today Tomorrow) Scholarly Pubns.

Periaux, J., et al, eds. Computational Fluid Dynamics '94: Proceedings of the Second European Conference, Stuttgart, Germany. 1324p. 1995. 550.00 (*0-471-95063-7*) Wiley.

Periaux, J., et al. Domain Decomposition Methods in Sciences & Engineering. LC 97-154605. 524p. 1997. 220.00 (*0-471-96560-X*) Wiley.

Periaux, J., ed. see Desideri, J. A.

Peric, M., jt. auth. see Ferziger, Joel H.

Perica, Esther. The American Woman: Her Role During the American Revolution. 2nd ed. LC 80-28294. (Cameo Series of Notable Women). (Illus.). 62p. (Orig.). 1980. reprint ed. pap. 8.50 (*0-912526-28-9*) Lib Res.

Perica, Esther, jt. auth. see Northcutt, Vicki.

Pericak-Vance, Margaret, jt. ed. see Haines, Jonathan L.

Perich, Richard, ed. see Grear, Robert D.

Perich, Shawn. Fly Fishing the North Country. (Illus.). 160p. (Orig.). 1995. pap. 12.95 (*1-57025-063-4*) Pfeifer-Hamilton.

Perich, Shawn & Ellis, Gord. 1997 Northern Ontario Outdoor Guide Book. 160p. (Orig.). Date not set. pap. 8.95 (*0-9649257-3-7*) Outdoor News.

Perich, Shawn C. Fishing Lake Superior: A Complete Guide to Stream, Shoreline, & Open-Water Angling. LC 94-4000. (Illus.). 192p. (Orig.). 1994. pap. 12.95 (*1-57025-022-7*) Pfeifer-Hamilton.

— The North Shore: A Four Season Guide to Minnesota's Favorite Destination. LC 92-70990. (Illus.). 208p. (Orig.). 1992. pap. 14.95 (*0-938586-67-X*) Pfeifer-Hamilton.

Perich, Shawn C. & Ellis, Gord. Northern Ontario Outdoor Guide. 300p. 1995. pap. write for info. (*0-9649257-0-2*) Outdoor News.

Peridans, Dominique F., tr. see Philippe Op, Marie Dominique.

Peridy, Nicolas, jt. auth. see Fontagne, Lionel.

Perie, E. Gabriel & Williams, John T. The Publishing Law Handbook, 2 vols. 2nd ed. 1675p. ring bd. 285.00 (*0-13-739525-6*, 44225) Aspen Law.

Perie, Marianne. International Education Indicators: A Time Series Perspective. 115p. 1997. pap. 12.00 (*0-16-048949-0*) USGPO.

— Job Satisfaction Among America's Teachers: Effects of Workplace Conditions, Background Characteristics & Teacher Compensation. 144p. 1997. pap. 15.00 (*0-16-063638-8*) USGPO.

— Time Spent Teaching Core Academic Subjects in Elementary Schools: Comparisons Across Community, School, Teacher & Student Characteristics. LC 97-168581. 83p. 1997. pap. 10.00 (*0-16-048998-9*) USGPO.

Perie, Marianne, et al. Time Spent Teaching Core Academic Subjects in Elementary Schools: Comparisons Across Community, School, Teacher, & Student Characteristics. (Illus.). 73p. (C). 1997. pap. text 25.00 (*0-7881-4735-8*) DIANE Pub.

Periegeta, Dionysius. Concordantia in Dionysii Periegetae Descriptionem Orbis Terrarum. Tsavari, Isabelle, ed. (Alpha-Omega, Reihe A Ser.: Bd. CXXX). (GER.). 273p. 1992. write for info. (*3-487-09601-3*) G Olms Pubs.

Periegeta, Pausanias. Graeciae Descriptio, 6 vols. in 3, Set. (GER.). xli, 2758p. 1983. reprint ed. write for info. (*3-487-07394-3*) G Olms Pubs.

Periers, Bonaventure des. Cymbalum Mundi: Four Very Ancient Joyous & Facetious Poetic Dialogues. Knapp, Bettina L., tr. from LAT. LC 65-14414. 1965. lib. bdg. 27.50 (*0-8057-5631-0*) Irvington.

Perifield, Glen. Focus on Youth: A Handbook for Teachers. (Focus On Ser.). 128p. 1993. pap. 4.50 (*0-88243-406-3*) Gospel Pub.

Perigo, Grace, tr. Letters of Adam of Perseigne. LC 76-15486. (Cistercian Fathers Ser.: No. 21). 1976. 12.95 (*0-87907-621-6*) Cistercian Pubns.

Perigord, Michel. Dictionnaire De la Qualite: French-English. (FRE.). 351p. 1993. pap. 105.00 (*0-7859-7739-2*, 2124678116) Fr & Eur.

Perikhanian, Anahit. The Book of a Thousand Judgements - A Sasanian Law-Book: Introduction, Transcription & Translation of the Pahlavi Text, Notes, Glossary & Indexes. Garsoian, Nina, tr. from RUS. LC 97-10185. (Persian Heritage Ser.: Vol. 39). (PAL & RUS.). 432p. 1997. text 45.00 (*1-56859-061-X*) Bibliotheca Persica.

***Peril, Lynn.** Pink Think. 2000. 26.50 (*0-688-17534-1*, Wm Morrow) Morrow Avon.

Perilli, Barry, jt. auth. see Weddington, Michael.

Perillo, jt. auth. see Corbin.

Perillo, G. M., ed. Geomorphology & Sedimentology of Estuaries. LC 95-15247. (Developments in Sedimentology Ser.: Vol. 53). 488p. 1995. 297.75 (*0-444-88170-0*) Elsevier.

— Geomorphology & Sedimentology of Estuaries. LC 96-35223. (Developments in Sedimentology Ser.: Vol. 53). 488p. 1996. pap. 103.25 (*0-444-82561-4*) Elsevier.

Perillo, G. M., et al, eds. Estuaries of South America: Their Geomorphology & Dynamics. LC 99-35156. (Environmental Science Ser.). (Illus.). 245p. 1999. 124.00 (*3-540-65657-X*) Spr-Verlag.

Perillo, Gregory. Gregory Perillo: And the Masters of American Western Art. 1998. 90.00 (*1-889097-27-6*) Hard Pr MA.

Perillo, Joseph M. Corbin on Contracts: (SS1-108), Vol. 1. rev. ed. LC 93-60572. 700p. 1993. text. write for info. (*0-314-01881-6*) West Pub.

Perillo, Joseph M., ed. Corbin on Contracts. 1951. im. lthr. write for info. (*0-327-00069-4*) LEXIS Pub.

Perillo, Joseph M., jt. auth. see Calamari, John D.

Perillo, Joseph M., jt. auth. see Corbin, Arthur L.

Perillo, Joseph M., jt. auth. see McAuliffe, Catherine.

Perillo, Joseph M., ed. see Kniffin, Margaret N.

Perillo, Lucia. The Body Mutinies. LC 95-45711. 114p. (Orig.). 1996. pap. 14.95 (*1-55753-083-1*) Purdue U Pr.

— The Oldest Map with the Name America: New & Selected Poems. LC 98-34561. 160p. 1999. 19.95 (*0-375-50160-6*) Random.

Perillo, Lucia M. Dangerous Life. 61p. 1989. pap. text 11.95 (*1-55553-059-1*) NE U Pr.

***Perimeter, Georgia.** The Polishing Cloth. 8th ed. 212p. (C). 1999. per. 12.95 (*0-7872-6103-3*, 41610301) Kendall-Hunt.

Perimutter, Bruce, jt. auth. see Zarkower, Jonathan L.

P

Perin, Constance. Belonging in America: Reading Between the Lines. LC 87-40371. (New Directions in Anthropological Writing Ser.). 320p. 1990. pap. 17.95 (*0-299-11584-4*) U of Wis Pr.

Perin, James C. Atman. (Orig.). 1994. pap. 5.95 (*0-9644656-0-4*) Deep Lingo.

Perin, James C. & Sharp, Joseph. Master's Apprentice. 250p. 1996. 19.95 (*0-9644656-1-2*); pap. 5.95 (*0-9644656-2-0*) Deep Lingo.

Perin, James C., ed. see Sharp, Joseph.

Perin, Marie-Madeleine. English - French Business Dictionary. 92p. 1990. pap. 14.95 (*0-8288-9446-9*) Fr & Eur.

Perin, Robert. Rome in Canada: The Vatican & Canadian Affairs in the Late Victorian Age. 300p. 1990. pap. 20.95 (*0-8020-6762-X*); text 45.00 (*0-8020-5854-X*) U of Toronto Pr.

Perin, Roberto & Sturino, Franc. Arrangiarsi: The Italian Immigration Experience in Canada-Essays. 2nd ed. 256p. 1992. pap. 13.00 (*0-920717-45-4*) Guernica Editions.

Perin, Roberto, ed. see Crowley, Terry, et al.

Perin, Romane. The Human Heart. 40p. (Orig.). 1983. pap. 3.00 (*0-917061-17-9*) Top Stories.

Perina, Jan. Coherence of Light. (Orig.). 1985. text 220.00 (*90-277-2004-5*) Kluwer Academic.

— Quantum Optics & Fundamentals of Physics. (Fundamental Theories of Physics Ser.). 352p. (C). 1994. text 186.50 (*0-7923-3000-5*) Kluwer Academic.

— Quantum Statistics of Linear & Nonlinear Optical Phenomena. 1984. text 185.50 (*90-277-1512-2*) Kluwer Academic.

— Quantum Statistics of Linear & Nonlinear Optical Phenomena. 2nd rev. ed. (C). 1991. text 272.50 (*0-7923-1171-X*) Kluwer Academic.

Perina, Jan, ed. Selected Papers on Photon Statistics & Coherence in Nonlinear Optics. (Milestone Ser.: Vol. MS39). 512p. 1991. pap. 35.00 (*0-8194-0739-9*) SPIE.

— Selected Papers on Photon Statistics & Coherence in Nonlinear Optics. (Milestone Ser.: Vol. MS 39/HC). 512p. 1991. 45.00 (*0-8194-0738-0*) SPIE.

Perinatal Loss Project Staff, ed. see Schwiebert, Pat & Kirk, Paul.

Perinbam, B. Marie. Holy Violence: The Revolutionary Thought of Frantz Fanon. LC 81-51664. 182p. 1982. 15.95 (*0-89410-175-7*, Three Contnts) L Rienner.

Perinbanayagam, R. S. Discursive Acts. (Communication & Social Order Ser.). 223p. 1991. pap. text 26.95 (*0-202-30367-5*); lib. bdg. 47.95 (*0-202-30366-7*) Aldine de Gruyter.

Perinbanayagam, Robert S. The Presence of Self. LC 99-35069. 304p. 1999. 67.00 (*0-8476-9384-8*) Rowman.

— The Presence of Self. LC 99-35069. 304p. 2000. pap. 27.95 (*0-8476-9385-6*) Rowman.

Perinchief, Richard. The New Breed Church: In Your Face. 96p. 1994. pap. 6.00 (*1-879993-18-X*) Albury Pub.

Perinchief, Robert. Drug-Free Word Spree. 58p. (J). (ps-12). 1993. 19.95 (*1-882809-01-7*) Perry Innovat.

— Hamel the Camel: A Different Mammal. (Illus.). 21p. (J). (ps-5). 1993. 12.95 (*1-882809-00-9*) Perry Innovat.

Perine, P., et al. Handbook of Endemic Treponematoses: Yaws, Endemic Syphilis & Pinta. (Nonserial Publication). 59p. 1984. pap. text 20.00 (*92-4-154176-8*, 1150226) World Health.

Perine, Robert. The California Romantics: Harbingers of Watercolorism. LC 86-73257. (Illus.). 96p. 1987. 18.95 (*0-936725-01-X*) Artra Pub.

— The Characters We Know: A to Z. (Illus.). 16p. 1978. ring bd. 15.00 (*0-932300-00-6*, AP00) Artra Pub.

— Chouinard: An Art Vision Betrayed. LC 86-70036. (Illus.). 260p. 1986. 37.50 (*0-936725-00-1*) Artra Pub.

— Nola Figen Perla Draws the Figure. (Illus.). 64p. (Orig.). 1993. pap. 20.00 (*0-936725-08-7*) Artra Pub.

Perine, Robert & Andrea, I. San Diego Artists. LC 88-70826. (Illus.). 224p. 1988. 35.00 (*0-936725-02-8*) Artra Pub.

Perine, Robert, et al. James Hubbell. LC 97-78197. (Illus.). 48p. 1998. pap. 20.00 (*0-936725-09-5*) Artra Pub.

Perine, Roy, ed. see Danjo, Yari.

Peringian, Lynda. Physical & Occupational Therapists' Job Search Handbook: Your Complete Job Search Strategy: How to Hire; How to Be Hired. LC 89-50592. (Illus.). 160p. (C). 1989. text 25.00 (*0-9622773-0-4*) Peringian & Assocs.

***Perini, Tom.** Texas Cowboy Cooking. LC 99-89478. (Illus.). 176p. (gr. 8). 2000. 24.95 (*0-7370-2037-7*) T-L Custom Pub.

Perino, Gregory. The Banks Village Site, Crittenden County, Arkansas. Chapman, Carl H., ed. (Memoir Ser.: No. 4). (Illus.). 161p. (Orig.). 1966. pap. 4.50 (*0-943414-19-9*) MO Arch Soc.

Perino, Joseph G. I Think I'm Hopeless...but I Could be Wrong: A Guide to Building Self-Confidence. LC 95-70119. 208p. (Orig.). 1995. pap. 15.95 (*0-9647432-0-5*) Riv Pr NY.

Perinova, Vlasta, et al, eds. Phase in Optics. LC 98-28356. 330p. 1997. text 58.00 (*981-02-3208-X*) World Scientific Pub.

Periodical Publication Department Staff, jt. compiled by see American Society for Metals Staff.

Perior, Tim, jt. auth. see David, Scott.

Perios, Sylvaine. Mariquita. (SPA.). 13.00 (*84-348-3467-7*, Pub. by SM Ediciones) IBD Ltd.

Peripatos. Der Fruhe Peripatos. 400p. write for info. (*0-318-70995-3*) G Olms Pubs.

Periples Editions Staff. Cambodia: Country Travel Map 1997. (Travel Maps Ser.). 1997. pap. 7.95 (*0-945971-87-7*) Periplus.

Periplus Editions. Cairns: Austrialia Regional. 1997. 7.95 (*962-593-048-5*) Periplus.

— China, 1997: Country Travel Map. 1997. 7.95 (*962-593-107-4*) Periplus.

Periplus Editions. Kathmandu, 1997: Nepal Regional. LC 97-688713. 1997. 7.95 (*962-593-063-9*) Periplus.

— Ko Samui ,1997: Thailand Regional. LC 97-688711. 1997. 7.95 (*962-593-036-1*) Periplus.

Periplus Editions. Malaysia ,1997: Country Travel Map. 1997. 7.95 (*962-593-043-4*) Periplus.

— Ujung Pandang: Indonesia Regional. 1997. 7.95 (*962-593-138-4*) Periplus.

Periplus Editions. West Malaysial, 1997: Malaysia Regional. 1997. 7.95 (*962-593-129-5*) Periplus.

Periplus Editions Staff. Auckland: Australia Regional, 1999 Ed. (Periplus Travel Maps Ser.). 1999. pap. 7.95 (*962-593-130-9*, Periplus Eds) Tuttle Pubng.

— Bintan: Indonesia Regional. 1997. 7.95 (*962-593-139-2*) Periplus.

— Brisbane: Australia Regional. 1997. 7.95 (*962-593-049-3*) Periplus.

— Darwin: Australia Regional, 1999 Ed. (Periplus Travel Maps Ser.). 1999. pap. 7.95 (*962-593-089-2*, Periplus Eds) Tuttle Pubng.

— The Food of Australia. (Periplus World Cookbooks). (Illus.). 144p. 1996. pap. text 12.95 (*962-593-024-8*) Periplus.

— Food of China. (Periplus World Cookbooks). 1996. pap. text 12.95 (*962-593-009-4*) Periplus.

— Food of India. (Periplus World Cookbooks). 1996. pap. text 12.95 (*962-593-011-6*) Periplus.

— Food of Indonesia. (Periplus World Cookbooks). 1996. pap. text 12.95 (*962-593-008-6*) Periplus.

— Food of Japan. 1996. pap. text 12.95 (*962-593-010-8*) Periplus.

— Food of Singapore. 1996. pap. text 12.95 (*962-593-007-8*) Periplus.

— Java: Indonesia Regional. (Periplus Travel Maps Ser.). 1997. 7.95 (*962-593-040-X*) Periplus.

— Melbourne: Australia Regional. (Periplus Travel Maps Ser.). 1997. 7.95 (*962-593-050-7*) Periplus.

— Sydney: Australia Regional. (Periplus Travel Maps Ser.). 1997. pap. 7.95 (*962-593-087-6*) Periplus.

Periplus Editions Staff. Thailand: Country Travel Map, 1997 Ed. LC 96-685727. (Periplus Travel Maps Ser.). 1997. 7.95 (*962-593-044-2*) Periplus.

***Periplus Editions Staff & Lwin, Claudia Saw.** Food of Malaysia, 1 vol. (Illus.). 144p. 2000. 18.95 (*962-593-386-7*) Periplus.

Periplus Staff. The Food of Vietnam: Authentic Recipes from the Heart of Indochina. (Periplus World Cookbooks Ser.). (Illus.). 90p. 1997. pap. 12.95 (*962-593-012-4*, Periplus Eds) Tuttle Pubng.

Periplus Staff, ed. French: Phrase Book. (Essential Phrase Bks.). 160p. 2000. pap. 6.95 (*962-593-801-X*) Tuttle Pubng.

— German: Phrase Book. (Essential Phrase Bks.). 160p. 2000. pap. 6.95 (*962-593-802-8*) Tuttle Pubng.

— Italian: Phrase Book. (Essential Phrase Bks.). 160p. 2000. pap. 6.95 (*962-593-803-6*) Tuttle Pubng.

— Japanese: Phrase Book. (Essential Phrase Bks.). 160p. 2000. pap. 6.95 (*962-593-804-4*) Tuttle Pubng.

— Russian: Phrase Book. (Essential Phrase Bks.). 160p. 2000. pap. 6.95 (*962-593-806-0*) Tuttle Pubng.

— Spanish: Phrase Book. (Essential Phrase Bks.). 160p. 2000. pap. 6.95 (*962-593-805-2*) Tuttle Pubng.

Perira, Wilf. RAF Lyneham: Hercules. (Super Station in Action Ser.). (Illus.). 192p. 1991. 32.95 (*0-85429-767-7*, Pub. by GT Foulis) Haynes Manuals.

Peris, Carme. Goldilocks & the Three Bears. (Fairy Tale Theater Ser.). (Illus.). 32p. (J). (gr. k-3). 1998. pap. 8.95 (*0-7641-5116-9*); pap. 8.95 (*0-7641-5148-7*) Barron.

— Little Red Riding Hood. (Fairy Tale Theater Ser.). (Illus.). 32p. (J). (gr. k-3). 1998. pap. 8.95 (*0-7641-5114-2*); pap. 8.95 (*0-7641-5146-0*) Barron.

Peris, Carme. Blanca Nieves y los Siete Enanitos (Snow White & the Seven Dwarfs) (SPA.). 32p. (J). (ps-3). 1999. 8.95 (*0-7641-5152-5*) Barron.

— El Gato con Botas (Puss 'n Boots) (SPA.). 32p. (J). (ps-3). 1999. 8.95 (*0-7641-5157-6*) Barron.

— Puss 'n Boots. 32p. (J). (ps-3). 1999. 8.95 (*0-7641-5156-8*) Barron.

Peris, Carme, jt. auth. see Sanchez, Isidro.

Peris, Carmie. Snow White & the Seven Dwarfs: Snow White & the Seven Dwarfs. 32p. (J). (ps-3). 1999. 8.95 (*0-7641-5151-7*) Barron.

Peris, Daniel. Storming the Heavens: The Soviet League of the Militant Godless. LC 98-22595. (Illus.). 256p. 1998. 39.95 (*0-8014-3485-8*) Cornell U Pr.

Peris, Jose A. Diccionario de Fisica. (SPA.). 464p. 1987. pap. 110.00 (*0-7859-3337-9*, 8420515299) Fr & Eur.

Perish, Melanie. Notes of a Daughter from the Old Country. 15p. (Orig.). (C). 1978. pap. 1.75 (*0-934238-04-9*) Motheroot.

Perisic, Zoran. Visual Effects Cinematography. LC 99-42963. (Illus.). 240p. 2000. pap. 36.95 (*0-240-80351-5*, Focal) Buttrwrth-Heinemann.

***Perison, Eben Paul.** Seventh Sin. 2000. mass mkt. 6.99 (*0-451-40912-4*, Onyx) NAL.

Perissat, J. Operative Manual of Endoscopic Surgery, Vol. 2. Cuschieri, Alfred & Buess, G. F., eds. LC 92-2421. (Illus.). 265p. 1994. text 175.00 (*3-540-56810-7*) Spr-Verlag.

Perissinotto, Giorgia, ed. Documenting Everyday Life in Early Spanish California: The Santa Barbara Presidio Memorias y Facturas, 1779-1810. Rudolph, Catherine E. & Miller, Elaine, trs. from SPA. LC 98-60517. (ENG & SPA., Illus.). 408p. 1998. 49.95 (*1-879208-03-2*) SB Trust Hist.

Perissinotto, Giorgio. Reconquista y Literatura Medieval: Cuatro Ensayos. 127p. 1990. 29.50 (*0-916379-48-5*) Scripta.

Perissinotto, Giorgio, ed. Research in Humanities Computing Vol. 5: Selected Papers from the 1995 ACH-ALLC Conference. (Illus.). 280p. 1996. text 75.00 (*0-19-823626-3*) OUP.

Peritore, N. Patrick. Socialism, Communism, & Liberation Theology in Brazil: An Opinion Survey Using Q-Methodology. LC 90-36505. (Monographs in International Studies, Latin America Ser.: No. 15). 274p. reprint ed. pap. 85.00 (*0-7837-6474-X*, 204647800001) Bks Demand.

— Third World Environmentalism: Case Studies from the Global South. LC 99-28827. (Illus.). 328p. 1999. 49.95 (*0-8130-1688-6*) U Press Fla.

Peritore, N. Patrick & Galve-Peritore, Ana. Biotechnology in Latin America: Politics, Impact & Risks. LC 95-16955. (Latin American Silhouette Ser.). 229p. 1995. pap. 17.95 (*0-8420-2557-X*) Scholarly Res Inc.

— Biotechnology in Latin America: Politics, Impacts & Risks. LC 95-16955. (Latin American Silhouette Ser.). 229p. 1995. 45.00 (*0-8420-2556-1*) Scholarly Res Inc.

Peritti, Burton W. Creation of Jazz: Music, Race, & Culture in Urban America. 304p. 1994. 15.95 (*0-252-06421-6*) U of Ill Pr.

Peritts, Vivian. Fresh Paint. (Illus.). 32p. (Orig.). 1994. pap. 8.95 (*1-884555-02-0*) P Depke Bks.

***Peritz, Judith, et al.** ARIES Exploring the Moon & Stars: Cycles, Phases & Patterns. (Aries Ser.). (Illus.). 2000. teacher ed., ring bd. 95.00 (*1-57091-264-5*) Charlesbridge Pub.

— ARIES Exploring the Moon & Stars: Cycles, Phases & Patterns: Science Journal. (Aries Ser.). (Illus.). (J). (gr. 3-8). 2000. pap. text 3.80 (*1-57091-256-4*) Charlesbridge Pub.

Peritz, Rudolph. Competition Policy in America, 1888-1992: History, Rhetoric, Law. 384p. 1996. text 55.00 (*0-19-507461-0*) OUP.

Periu, Omar. Investigative Selling: How to Master the Art, Science & Skills of Professional Selling. deluxe ed. 235p. 1997. 29.95 (*1-893444-00-7*) Pub & Prof Ghost Writers.

***Perivolaris, John & James, Conrad.** The Cultures of the Hispanic Caribbean. LC 99-88123. 2000. write for info. (*0-8130-1794-7*) U Press Fla.

***Perivolaris, John Dimitri.** Puerto Rican Cultural Identity & the Work of Luis Rafael Sanchez (RLS #268) (North Carolina Studies in the Romance Languages). 224p. 2001. pap. text 32.50 (*0-8078-9272-6*) U of NC Pr.

Periwal, Sukumar, ed. Notions of Nationalism. LC 95-233799. (Central European University Press Bks.). 258p. (C). 1995. text 51.95 (*1-85866-021-1*); pap. text 21.95 (*1-85866-022-X*) Ctrl Europ Univ.

Periyasamy, K., jt. auth. see Alagar, V. S.

Perjes, Z., ed. Relativity Today. 308p. (C). 1992. text 175.00 (*1-56072-028-X*) Nova Sci Pubs.

— Relativity Today: Proceedings of the 2nd Hungarian Relativity Workshop. 288p. (C). 1988. pap. 47.00 (*9971-5-0517-7*); text 100.00 (*9971-5-0513-4*) World Scientific Pub.

Perjes, Z., jt. auth. see Hoenselaers, C. A.

Perjes, Z., ed. see Kerr, Roy P. & Zoltan, P. P.

Perjovschi, Dan. Postcards from America. (Illus.). 70p. (Orig.). 1995. pap. write for info. (*1-878635-02-6*) Pont La Vue Pr.

Perk, Jeff. Moon Handbooks: Boston. (Illus.). 250p. 1999. pap. 13.95 (*1-56691-136-2*, Moon Handbks) Avalon Travel.

***Perk, Jeff.** Moon Handbooks: Massachusetts: Including Boston, the Berkshires & Cape Cod. (Illus.). 490p. 1998. pap. 18.95 (*1-56691-083-8*, Moon Handbks) Avalon Travel.

Perkal, Adam, jt. ed. see Wilkie, James W.

Perkal, Stephanie. Midnight: A Cinderella Alphabet. LC 96-38241. (Illus.). 32p. (J). (gr. k-4). 1997. 15.95 (*1-885008-05-8*) Shens Bks.

Perkampus, Heinz-Helmut. Encyclopedia of Spectroscopy. Grinter, Heide-Charlotte & Grinter, Roger, trs. LC 95-7227. 674p. 1995. 185.00 (*3-527-29281-0*, Wiley-VCH) Wiley.

— UV-VIS Atlas of Organic Compounds. 2nd ed. (Illus.). 1892p. 1992. 925.00 (*3-527-28510-5*, Wiley-VCH) Wiley.

— UV-VIS Spectroscopy & Its Applications. Grinter, Heide-Charlotte & Threlfall, T. L., trs. LC 92-20077. (Illus.). ix, 240p. 1994. 139.95 (*0-387-55421-1*) Spr-Verlag.

Perkell, Christine. The Poet's Truth: A Study of the Poet in Virgil's Georgics. 1989. 45.00 (*0-520-06323-6*, Pub. by U CA Pr) Cal Prin Full Svc.

— Reading Vergils Aeneid. LC 99-18499. 1999. pap. text 18.95 (*0-8061-3139-X*) U of Okla Pr.

Perkell, Christine G. Reading Vergil's Aeneid: An Interpretive Guide. LC 99-18499. (Series in Classical Culture). 1999. write for info. (*0-8061-3138-1*) U of Okla Pr.

Perkell, Joseph S. & Klatt, D. H., eds. Invariance & Variability in Speech Processes. 632p. (C). 1986. text 125.00 (*0-89859-545-2*) L Erlbaum Assocs.

Perker, L. Craig, Jr. Finnish Criminal Justice: An American Perspective. LC 92-32881. 162p. (C). 1992. lib. bdg. 44.90 (*0-8191-8910-3*) U Pr of Amer.

Perkes, Alden. The Santa Claus Book. (Illus.). 132p. 1996. reprint ed. pap. 16.95 (*0-8184-0381-0*, L Stuart) Carol Pub Group.

Perkes, Alona S. Quick & Easy Cooking: A Busy Person's Guide to Simple, Nutritious Meals. LC 89-83432. 64p. 1991. pap. 6.98 (*0-88290-348-9*) Horizon Utah.

Perket, Cary L., ed. Quality Control in Remedial Site Investigation: Hazardous & Industrial Solid Waste Testing, Vol. 5. LC 86-25873. (Special Technical Publication Ser.: No. 925). (Illus.). 227p. 1986. text 29.00 (*0-8031-0451-0*, STP925) ASTM.

Perkey, Elton A. Perkey's Nebraska Place Names. LC 82-80300. (Illus.). 227p. 1990. reprint ed. pap. 12.95 (*0-934904-19-7*) J & L Lee.

Perkin. Color Atlas & Test Neurology. 1997. text 39.95 (*0-7234-2497-7*) Wolfe Pubng AZ.

Perkin, G. D. An Atlas of Parkinson's Disease & Related Disorders. LC 97-37265. (The Encyclopedia of Visual Medicine Ser.). (Illus.). 96p. 1998. 78.00 (*1-85070-943-2*) Prthnon Pub.

Perkin, Harold. Origins of Modern English Society. (Studies in Social History). 480p. (C). 1985. pap. 24.99 (*0-415-05922-4*) Routledge.

— The Rise of Professional Society: England since 1880. 480p. 1989. 49.95 (*0-415-00890-5*) Routledge.

— The Rise of Professional Society: England since 1880. 624p. (C). 1990. pap. 29.99 (*0-415-04975-X*) Routledge.

— The Structured Crowd: Essays in English Social History. 250p. 1981. 44.00 (*0-389-20116-2*, N6890) B&N Imports.

— The Third Revolution: Professional Society in International Perspective. LC 95-44146. 272p. (C). 1996. pap. 25.99 (*0-415-14338-1*) Routledge.

Perkin, Harold J. Key Profession: The History of the Association of University Teachers. LC 73-81990. 268p. 1969. 39.50 (*0-678-06506-3*) Kelley.

— Origins of Modern English Society, 1780-1880. 480p. pap. 13.95 (*0-7448-0026-9*) Routledge.

— The Origins of Modern English Society, 1780-1880. LC 76-384509. (Canadian University Paperbooks Ser.: No. 115). 479p. reprint ed. pap. 148.50 (*0-8357-4165-6*, 203693900007) Bks Demand.

Perkin, Joan. Victorian Women. (Illus.). 273p. (C). 1995. text 50.00 (*0-8147-6624-2*); pap. text 19.00 (*0-8147-6625-0*) NYU Pr.

— Women & Marriage in Nineteenth Century England. LC 89-8066. 342p. (C). 1989. reprint ed. text 49.95 (*0-925065-18-8*); reprint ed. pap. text 28.95 (*0-925065-16-1*) Lyceum IL.

Perkin, John. Crosswords New Penguin Guardian. 1995. pap. 7.95 (*0-14-024807-2*, Pub. by Pnguin Bks Ltd) Trafalgar.

— Crosswords New Penguin Guardian, No. 4. 144p. pap. 9.95 (*0-14-017645-4*, Pub. by Pnguin Bks Ltd) Trafalgar.

— Penguin Book of the Guardian, 8 Quick Crosswords. 160p. 1999. pap. 9.95 (*0-14-027751-X*, Pub. by Pnguin Bks Ltd) Trafalgar.

Perkin, John. Resurrecting Hope. 168p. 1995. pap. 10.99 (*0-8307-1810-9*, Regal Bks) Gospel Lght.

Perkin, Judy E. Food Allergies & Adverse Reactions. LC 90-684. 294p. 1991. 64.00 (*0-8342-0170-4*) Aspen Pub.

Perkin, Michael, jt. auth. see Cross, Robert.

***Perkin, Norah-Jean.** Outrageous. 1999. 6.99 (*1-57343-018-8*) LionHearted.

Perkins. Activities for the Internet: Introductory Course. (Computer Applications Ser.). 1997. mass mkt. 12.95 (*0-538-71828-5*) S-W Pub.

— Activities for the Internet: Mastery Course. (DF - Computer Applications Ser.). 1997. mass mkt. 12.95 (*0-538-71830-7*) S-W Pub.

— Consumer Representive Best Travel Deal 1998, Vol. 1. 320p. 1998. pap. 8.99 (*0-89043-892-7*) St Martin.

— Created to Praise. 1996. pap. 6.95 (*0-7601-0664-9*) Brentwood Music.

— Created to Praise: Band Charts. 1996. pap. 95.00 (*0-7601-0733-5*) Brentwood Music.

— Easy Rules: Spelling. (EC - HS Communication/English Ser.). 1990. mass mkt. 9.95 (*0-538-60336-4*) S-W Pub.

— Easy Rules: Spelling. (EC - HS Communication/English Ser.). 1991. 22.95 (*0-538-40816-2*) S-W Pub.

— Easy Rules: Spelling Compact Spelling. (EC - HS Communication/English Ser.). 1990. 0.95 (*0-538-60698-3*) S-W Pub.

— Easy Rules: Spelling Software Apple Product. (EC - HS Communication/English Ser.). 1994. 127.95 (*0-538-60587-1*) S-W Pub.

— Marxism & the Proletariat: A Lukacsian Perspective. LC 93-20550. (C). 54.95 (*0-7453-0492-3*, Pub. by Pluto GBR); pap. 19.95 (*0-7453-0499-0*, Pub. by Pluto GBR) Stylus Pub VA.

— Mineralogy. LC 97-36445. 484p. (C). 1997. 86.00 (*0-02-394501-X*, Macmillan Coll) P-H.

— Modern Industrial Hygiene VII, Vol. 2. (Occupational Health & Safety Ser.). 1998. text 59.95 (*0-442-02569-6*, VNR) Wiley.

— New Conceptions. (Educational Psychology Ser.: Vol. 28, No. 1). 1993. 20.00 (*0-8058-9992-8*) L Erlbaum Assocs.

Perkins. Nuclear Medicine Science & Safety. 200p. 49.00 (*0-86196-470-5*, Pub. by J Libbey Med) Bks Intl VA.

Perkins. Punctuation: A Simplified Approach. 3rd ed. (EC - HS Communication/English Ser.). 1989. mass mkt. 15.95 (*0-538-60122-1*) S-W Pub.

— Reform of Macroeconomic Policy. LC 99-38849. 2000. text 69.95 (*0-312-22609-8*) St Martin.

Perkins, ed. American Traditional Literature, Vol. 19. 9th ed. LC 98-13368. 1998. pap. 37.74 (*0-07-049421-5*) McGraw.

Perkins, ed. Brief Testbank Principal Speech. 12th ed. 1997. pap. text 11.00 (*0-673-55906-8*) P-H.

Perkins & Morris. Remembering My Brother. 1997. 11.95 (*0-7136-4541-5*, Pub. by A & C Blk) Midpt Trade.

Perkins, et al. The Complete Communicator: Media Writing : Now & the Future. (Mass Communication Ser.). 2001. pap. text 30.00 (*0-534-56799-1*) Thomson Learn.

Perkins, jt. auth. see Lemay.

Perkins, jt. auth. see Shaeffer.

Perkins, Margarette. Building Wealth Using the Tin Can Method. LC 98-74502. 256p. 1999. 14.99 (*0-88419-561-9*) Creation House.

An Asterisk (*) at the beginning of an entry indicates that the title is appearing for the first time.

Perkins, Dwight H., et al. Rural Development. (East Asian Monographs: No. 89). 493p. 1980. 25.00 (0-674-78042-6) HUP.

Perkins, Dwight H., ed. see Harvard Institute for International Development St.

Perkins, Dwight H., jt. ed. see Koo, Bon-Ho.

Perkins, E. G. & Sebedio, J. L., eds. New Trends in Lipid & Lipoprotein Analyses. 384p. 1995. 90.00 (0-935315-59-4) Am Oil Chemists.

Perkins, E. J. The Life & Work of Harold Palmer. 144p. (C). 1988. 90.00 (0-7855-2245-X, Pub. by Domino Bks Ltd); pap. 100.00 (1-85122-025-9, Pub. by Domino Bks Ltd) St Mut.

Perkins, E. S., et al. Atlas of Diseases of the Eye. 3rd ed. (Illus.). 208p. (Orig.). 1986. pap. text 50.00 (0-443-02961-X) Church.

***Perkins, Ed.** Online Travel. 300p. 2000. pap. 19.99 (0-7356-1110-6) Microsoft.

***Perkins, Edna Brush & Wild, Peter.** The White Heart of the Mojave: An Adventure with the Outdoors of the Desert. LC 00-32715. (American Land Classics Ser.). (Illus.). (C). 2001. pap. write for info. (0-8018-6505-0) Johns Hopkins.

Perkins, Edward G., ed. Analyses of Fats, Oils & Derivatives. 448p. 1993. pap. 45.00 (0-935315-47-0) Am Oil Chemists.

— Analyses of Fats, Oils, & Lipoproteins. 664p. (C). 1991. 130.00 (0-935315-36-5) Am Oil Chemists.

— Lipoproteins. 176p. 1993. pap. 35.00 (0-935315-48-9) Am Oil Chemists.

Perkins, Edward G. & Erickson, M. D., eds. Deep Frying: Chemistry, Nutrition, & Practical Applications. LC 96-18003. (Illus.). 357p. 1996. 60.00 (0-935315-75-6) Am Oil Chemists.

Perkins, Edward G. & Visek, Willard, eds. Dietary Fats & Health. 978p. 1983. 40.00 (0-935315-07-1) Am Oil Chemists.

Perkins, Edward J., jt. ed. see Boren, David L.

Perkins, Edwin. On the Martingale Problem for Interactive Measure-Valued Branching Diffusions. LC 95-3279. (Memoirs Ser.: Vol. 549). 89p. 1995. pap. 33.00 (0-8218-0358-1, MEMO/115/549) Am Math.

Perkins, Edwin, ed. see Mercer, Lloyd J.

Perkins, Edwin A., jt. auth. see Dawson, Donald A.

Perkins, Edwin C., Jr., jt. auth. see Southerton, Alan.

Perkins, Edwin J. American Public Finance & Financial Services, 1700-1815. LC 93-28736. (Historical Perspectives on Business Enterprise Ser.). 448p. 1994. pap. write for info. (0-8142-0620-4) Ohio St U Pr.

— American Public Finance & Financial Services, 1700-1815. LC 93-28736. (Historical Perspectives on Business Enterprise Ser.). 443p. 1997. text 60.00 (0-8142-0619-0) Ohio St U Pr.

— The Economy of Colonial America. 2nd ed. (Illus.). 304p. 1988. pap. text 19.00 (0-231-06339-3) Col U Pr.

— Financing Anglo-American Trade: The House of Brown, 1800-1880. LC 74-34543. (Harvard Studies in Business History: No. 28). 340p. 1975. reprint ed. pap. 105.40 (0-7837-2310-5, 205739800004) Bks Demand.

— Wall Street to Main Street: Charles Merrill & Middle-Class Investors. LC 99-219960. (Illus.). 320p. 1999. 29.95 (0-521-63029-0) Cambridge U Pr.

Perkins, Edwin J., jt. auth. see Adams, Judith A.

Perkins, Elizabeth, jt. ed. see Headon, David.

Perkins, Emily. Leave Before You Go LC 99-19031. 1999. write for info. (0-88001-690-6, Ecco Press) HarperTrade.

***Perkins, Emily.** Leave Before You Go. LC 99-19031. 304p. 2000. 23.00 (0-06-019661-0, Ecco Press) HarperTrade.

Perkins, Emily. Not Her Real Name. LC 97-3574. 272p. 1997. pap. 12.00 (0-385-48664-2, Anchor NY) Doubleday.

Perkins, Ethel R., ed. see Vogue, Adalbert de.

Perkins, Ethel R., tr. see De Vogue, Adalbert.

Perkins, F. T. & Hennessen, W., eds. Standardization & Control of Biologicals Produced by Recombinant DNA Technology. (Developments in Biological Standardization Ser.: Vol. 59). (Illus.). viii, 216p. 1985. pap. 61.00 (3-8055-4027-2) S Karger.

Perkins, F. T., ed. see International Association of Biological Standardiz.

Perkins, F. T., ed. see Permanent Section of Microbiological Standardizati.

Perkins, Fionna. The Horse Orchard: Poems. (Illus.). 75p. (Orig.). 2000. pap. 9.00 (0-9649497-2-5) Floreant Pr.

Perkins, Frank. Travel Adventures on the Company's Nickel: Fun on Business Trips. LC 95-92462. (Illus.). 1996. pap. 14.95 (0-9648512-0-2) Oak Pubng.

Perkins, Frank O. & Cheng, Thomas C., eds. Pathology in Marine Science. 538p. 1990. text 115.00 (0-12-550755-0) Acad Pr.

Perkins-Frederick, Pamela M. A Leaf Gnawed to Lace. (Illus.). 36p. (Orig.). 1992. pap. 5.00 (0-9625348-4-6) P Goodrich.

Perkins, G., jt. auth. see Drummond, David A.

Perkins, G., jt. auth. see Holzman, R.

Perkins, G. A. The Family of John Perkins of Ipswich, Massachusetts. (Illus.). 499p. 1989. reprint ed. pap. 50.00 (0-8328-0953-5); reprint ed. lib. bdg. 60.00 (0-8328-0952-7) Higginson Bk Co.

Perkins, Gareth K., ed. see Guro, Elena.

Perkins, Gareth K., ed. see Mirsky, Dimitry S.

Perkins, Gary. Silly Animal Jokes. LC 92-20776. (Illus.). (J). 1992. pap. 2.50 (0-8167-2966-2) Troll Communs.

— Silly School Jokes. LC 92-20437. (Illus.). 64p. (J). (gr. 2-6). 1992. pap. text 2.50 (0-8167-2964-6) Troll Communs.

Perkins, Geoff, ed. Employee Communications in the Public Sector. 96p. (C). 1986. 45.00 (0-85292-369-4, Pub. by IPM Hse) St Mut.

***Perkins, George.** Readers Encyclopedia of American Literature. 2nd ed. 2000. 50.00 (0-06-019815-X) HarpC.

Perkins, George & Perkins, Barbara, eds. The American Tradition in Literature. 8th ed. LC 93-42292. 2048p. (C). 1993. 60.38 (0-07-049369-3); pap. 49.13 (0-07-049370-7) McGraw.

— The American Tradition in Literature, 2 vols., Vol. 2. 8th ed. LC 93-11009. (C). 1993. pap. text 37.74 (0-07-049366-9) McGraw.

— The American Tradition in Literature, 2 vols., Vol. 2. 8th ed. LC 93-11009. 1800p. (C). 1994. 60.38 (0-07-049365-0) McGraw.

— The American Tradition in Literature, 2 vols., Vol. 3. 8th ed. LC 93-11009. 1960p. (C). 1993. 60.38 (0-07-049367-7); pap. text 37.74 (0-07-049368-5) McGraw.

Perkins, George, jt. auth. see Perkins, Barbara.

***Perkins, George A.** Early Times on the Susquehanna. 302p. 1999. reprint ed. pap. 24.50 (0-7884-1298-1, P164) Heritage Bk.

Perkins, George A. Early Times on the Susquehanna (Athens, Bradford Co.) (Illus.). 285p. 1996. reprint ed. lib. bdg. 35.00 (0-8328-5172-8) Higginson Bk Co.

Perkins, George B. & Perkins, Barbara. The American Tradition in Literature. 9th ed. LC 98-13389. 1998. 47.43 (0-07-049420-7) McGraw.

***Perkins, George B. & Perkins, Barbara.** The American Tradition in Literature. 9th ed. LC 98-13368. (Illus.). 1999. write for info. (0-07-049423-1) McGrw-H Hghr Educ.

Perkins, George G. Gilpin Family, from Richard de Gylpyn in 1206 . . . to Joseph Gilpin, Emigrant to America, & Something of the Kentucky Gilpins & Their Descendants to 1916. 130p. 1997. reprint ed. pap. 25.00 (0-8328-8751-X); reprint ed. lib. bdg. 35.00 (0-8328-8750-1) Higginson Bk Co.

Perkins, George H. Letters of Capt. Geo. Hamilton Perkins, U. S. N. LC 78-107825. (Select Bibliographies Reprint Ser.). 1977. 23.95 (0-8369-5219-7) Ayer.

— Letters of Capt. Geo. Hamilton Perkins, U. S. N. (American Biography Ser.). 254p. 1991. reprint ed. lib. bdg. 69.00 (0-7812-8311-6) Rprt Serv.

Perkins, George R., jt. auth. see Bowen, Carolyn M.

Perkins, George W., tr. from JPN. The Clear Mirror: A Chronicle of the Japanese Court During the Kamakura Period (1185-1333) LC 97-49585. 1998. 49.50 (0-8047-2953-0) Stanford U Pr.

Perkins, Ginny & Morris, Leon. Remembering Mum. 24p. (J). (gr. 1-5). 1998. pap. 6.95 (0-7136-4432-X, Pub. by A & C Blk) Midpt Trade.

Perkins, Gloria O., jt. auth. see Wheat, Ed.

***Perkins, Graham.** Killer CVs & Hidden Approaches: Give Yourself an Unfair Advantage in the Executive Job Market. rev. ed. (Career Tactics Ser.). 301p. 1998. pap. 33.50 (0-273-63543-3, Pub. by Pitman Pbg) Trans-Atl Phila.

Perkins, H. R., et al. Microbial Cell Walls. 575p. 1980. 85.00 (0-412-12030-5, NO. 6415) Chapman & Hall.

Perkins, Hattie L. Humanities: Lecture-Discussion Syllabus. 1977. pap. 7.95 (0-317-17265-4) Banner Pr AL.

Perkins, Hazlehurst B., jt. auth. see Betts, Edwin M.

Perkins, Helen L. Electronic Imaging: In Admissions, Records & Financial Aid Offices. LC 95-39076. 181p. 1996. per. 60.00 (0-929851-73-0) Am Assn Coll Registrars.

Perkins, Henry C., jt. auth. see Reynolds, William C.

***Perkins, Hilary, ed.** GIS Technologies for the Transportation Industry. (Illus.). xii, 370p. 1999. pap. 69.00 (0-916848-04-3) Urban & Regional Information Systems.

Perkins, Howard C. Northern Editorials on Secession, 2 vols., Set. 1990. 31.00 (0-8446-1347-9) Peter Smith.

— Northern Editorials on Secession, 2 vols., Set. (History - United States Ser.). 1993. reprint ed. lib. bdg. 150.00 (0-7812-4891-4) Rprt Serv.

Perkins, J., jt. auth. see Wayman, C. M.

Perkins, J. Alan. An Appeal to Heaven. 300p. 1998. 22.95 (0-9668817-0-2) Blue Sky Pubng.

Perkins, J. D., ed. Interactions Between Process Design & Process Control: Preprints of the IFAC Workshop, London, U. K., 7-8 September 1992. LC 92-40440. 248p. 1992. pap. 97.75 (0-08-042063-X, Pergamon Pr) Elsevier.

Perkins, J. O. The Deregulation of the Australian Financial System: The Experience of the 1980s. 128p. 1989. pap. 17.95 (0-522-84378-6, Pub. by Melbourne Univ Pr) Paul & Co Pubs.

— The Wallis Report & the Australian Financial System. LC 99-180763. x, 68p. 1998. pap. 17.95 (0-522-84824-9, Pub. by Melbourne Univ Pr) Paul & Co Pubs.

Perkins, J. R. Trails, Rails, & War: The Life of General G. M. Dodge. Bruchey, Stuart, ed. LC 80-1338. (Railroads Ser.). (Illus.). 1981. reprint ed. lib. bdg. 38.95 (0-405-13810-5) Ayer.

Perkins, Jack. Acadia: Visions & Verse. LC 99-17158. (Illus.). 112p. 1999. 26.95 (0-89272-469-2) Down East.

— Parasols of Fern: A Book about Wonder. LC 93-10874. (Illus.). 1993. 18.95 (0-934745-17-X) Acadia Pub Co.

Perkins, James. Building up Zion's Walls: Ministry for Empowering the African American Family. Elster, Jean A., ed. LC 99-27907. 176p. 1999. pap. 17.00 (0-8170-1337-7) Judson.

Perkins, James, jt. auth. see Crain, Ernest.

Perkins, James A. The University in Transition. LC 66-15804. (Stafford Little Lectures: No. 1965). 100p. reprint ed. pap. 31.00 (0-8357-4651-8, 203758200008) Bks Demand.

Perkins, James A., ed. see Drake, Robert.

Perkins, James A., jt. ed. see Folks, Jeffrey J.

***Perkins, James B.** France in the American Revolution. 2nd unabridged ed. 564p. 1999. reprint ed. pap. 21.95 (0-87928-129-4) Corner Hse.

Perkins, James B. Richelieu & the Growth of French Power. LC 70-157353. (Select Bibliographies Reprint Ser.). 1977. reprint ed. 35.95 (0-8369-5814-4) Ayer.

***Perkins, James E.** Tom Tobin: Frontiersman. (Illus.). x, 323p. 2000. pap. 17.75 (0-9675562-0-1) Herodotus Pr.

Perkins, James S. Through Death to Rebirth. LC 61-13301. (Illus.). 124p. 1982. pap. 4.25 (0-8356-0451-9, Quest) Theos Pub Hse.

— Visual Meditations on the Universe. LC 83-40233. (Illus.). 136p. 1984. 16.95 (0-8356-0233-8, Quest) Theos Pub Hse.

Perkins, Jane & Blyle, Nancy Roundy. Narrative & Professional Communication. LC 99-19561. (ATTW Contemporary Studies in Technical Communications). 1999. pap. 24.95 (1-56750-449-3) Ablx Pub.

Perkins, Jane & Wulsin, Lucien. An Advocate's Guide to the Medically Needy Program. (Illus.). 120p. 1985. pap. 10.00 (0-941077-01-2, 40,250) NCLS Inc.

Perkins, Jeff. Materials, Science & Engineering. (C). 2000. text. write for info. (0-201-53848-2) Addison-Wesley.

— Sams Teach Yourself SQL in 21 Days. 2nd ed. LC 97-66196. 624p. 1997. 39.99 (0-672-31110-0) Sams.

***Perkins, Jennifer, ed.** Business Phone Book USA 2001. 23rd ed. 2200p. 2000. lib. bdg. 175.00 (0-7808-0341-8) Omnigraphics Inc.

— FaxUSA 2000: A Directory of Facsimile Numbers for Businesses & Organizations Nationwide. 7th ed. 1600p. 1999. pap. 135.00 (0-7808-0346-9) Omnigraphics Inc.

— Fax USA 2001. 8th ed. 1700p. 2000. lib. bdg. 145.00 (0-7808-0424-4) Omnigraphics Inc.

— Toll-Free Phone Book U. S. A., 2000: A Directory of Toll-Free Numbers for Businesses & Organizations Nationwide. 4th ed. 1400p. (Orig.). 1999. pap. 125.00 (0-7808-0349-3) Omnigraphics Inc.

— Toll-Free Phone Book USA 2001. 5th ed. 1500p. 2000. lib. bdg. 135.00 (0-7808-0427-9) Omnigraphics Inc.

Perkins, Jill, intro. Joyce & Hauptmann: Before Sunrise - James Joyce's Translation. LC 77-87870. (Illus.). 177p. 1978. reprint ed. pap. 54.90 (0-608-03167-4, 206362000007) Bks Demand.

Perkins, Jimmy L. Modern Industrial Hygiene: Recognition & Evaluation of Chemical Agents, Vol. I. LC 96-16834. (Industrial Health & Safety Ser.). (Illus.). 864p. 1997. text 49.95 (0-442-02105-4, VNR) Wiley.

Perkins, Jimmy L. & Rose, Vernon E., eds. Case Studies in Industrial Hygiene. LC 86-15709. 208p. 1987. 105.00 (0-471-84263-X) Wiley.

Perkins, Jody M. & Jones, Russell O. Superfund Liability & Taxes: Petroleum Industry Shares in Their Historical Context. (Illus.). 79p. (Orig.). (C). 1997. pap. text 30.00 (0-7881-3776-X) DIANE Pub.

Perkins, John. Build Your Own Birdhouses. (Illus.). 128p. 1997. 17.98 (0-7858-0741-1) Bk Sales Inc.

***Perkins, John.** Build Your Own Birdhouses: From Simple, Natural Designs to Spectacular, Customized Houses. LC QL676.5.P427 1997. (Illus.). 144p. 2000. pap. 19.95 (1-55209-135-X) Firefly Bks Ltd.

Perkins, John. Malice in Wonderland. 1993. pap. 15.00 (0-9636328-0-9) ProMotion Pub.

— Morphosis: Architectural Projects. Krause, Carolyn, ed. (Illus.). 7p. 1989. pap. 2.50 (0-917562-53-4) Contemp Arts.

— El Mundo Es Como uno lo Suena-The World Is As You Dream It. (SPA., Illus.). 238p. 1995. pap. 12.95 (0-89281-465-9) Inner Tradit.

— A Prescription for Life: The Jason Winters Story, a Cancer Survivor. 290p. (Orig.). 1997. pap. 16.95 (1-57901-016-4) Intl Promotions.

— Psiconavegacion: Tecnicas Para Viajar Ma's All a Del Tiempo.Tr. of Psychonavigation. (SPA.). 136p. 1995. pap. 10.95 (0-89281-461-6) Inner Tradit.

— Psychonavigation: Techniques for Travel Beyond Time. expanded rev. ed. (Orig.). 1999. pap. 12.95 (0-89281-800-X) Inner Tradit.

— Shape Shifting: Shamanic Techniques for Self-Transformation. LC 97-27280. (Illus.). 176p. 1997. pap. 12.95 (0-89281-663-5) Inner Tradit.

— The World Is As You Dream It: Shamanic Teachings from the Amazon & Andes. LC 93-39493. (Illus.). 140p. (Orig.). 1994. pap. 10.95 (0-89281-459-4) Inner Tradit.

Perkins, John, et al, eds. The Historic Taf Valleys, Vol. 2: In the Brecon Beacons National Park. 190p. (C). 1989. 59.00 (0-905928-21-0, Pub. by D Brown & Sons Ltd) St Mut.

***Perkins, John, et al.** Attack Proof: The Ultimate Guide to Personal Protection. LC 99-59762. (Illus.). 192p. 2000. pap. 19.95 (0-7360-0351-7) Human Kinetics.

Perkins, John A. The Prudent Peace: Law As Foreign Policy. LC 81-1200. (C). 1993. 28.00 (0-226-65873-2) U Ch Pr.

Perkins, John E., Jr. Leon Rausch: The Voice of the Texas Playboys. LC 94-12045. (Illus.). 266p. 1996. 29.95 (0-9654101-0-2) Swing Pubng.

Perkins, John H. Geopolitics & the Green Revolution: Wheat, Genes & the Cold War. LC 96-8885. (Illus.). 352p. 1997. text 65.00 (0-19-511013-7) OUP.

Perkins, John H. Insects, Experts, & the Insecticide Crisis: The Quest for New Pest Management Strategies. LC 81-22658. 322p. 1982. 65.00 (0-306-40770-1, Plenum Trade) Perseus Pubng.

Perkins, John J. Principles & Methods of Sterilization in Health Sciences. 2nd ed. (Illus.). 580p. 1983. 55.95 (0-398-01478-7) C C Thomas.

Perkins, John M. Beyond Charity: The Call to Christian Community Development. LC 93-18862. 192p. (gr. 11). 1993. pap. 12.99 (0-8010-7122-4) Baker Bks.

— The Stress-Free Habit: Powerful Techniques for Health & Longevity from the Andes, Yucatan, & Far East. LC 89-1670. 128p. 1989. pap. 8.95 (0-89281-292-3, Heal Arts VT) Inner Tradit.

Perkins, John M., ed. Restoring At-Risk Communities: Doing It Together & Doing It Right. LC 95-35456. (Illus.). 272p. 1996. pap. 12.99 (0-8010-5463-X) Baker Bks.

Perkins, John M., et al. He's My Brother: Former Racial Foes Offer Strategy for Reconciliation. LC 94-4075. 240p. (Orig.). (gr. 10). 1994. pap. 14.99 (0-8007-9214-9) Chosen Bks.

Perkins, John P., ed. The Beta-Adrenergic Receptors. LC 90-15616. (Receptors Ser.). (Illus.). 415p. 1991. 125.00 (0-89603-173-X) Humana.

Perkins, Joseph. Saving G. I. Joe: The International Committee of the Red Cross & American Prisoners of War in World War II. 280p. 2000. 24.95 (0-89526-318-1) Regnery Pub.

Perkins, Judith. The Suffering Self: Pain & Narrative Representation in Early Christianity. LC 94-42650. 240p. (C). 1995. 75.00 (0-415-11363-6); pap. 24.99 (0-415-12706-8) Routledge.

Perkins, Judith, ed. see Singh, Ajaib.

Perkins, Julie, jt. auth. see Fleming, Ian.

Perkins, Julie, jt. auth. see Townsend, John.

Perkins, Juliet. The Feminine in the Poetry of Herberto Helder. (Monografias A Ser.: No. 144). 184p. (C). 1991. 58.00 (1-85566-006-7, Pub. by Tamesis Bks Ltd) Boydell & Brewer.

***Perkins, Karl A.** Off the Top of My Mind. LC 00-190636. 121p. 2000. 25.00 (0-7388-1874-7); pap. 18.00 (0-7388-1875-5) Xlibris Corp.

Perkins, Kathryn. Stamp with Style: More Than 50 Creative Cards & Projects. LC 98-7869. (Illus.). 96p. 1998. pap. 24.95 (1-56477-224-1, PasTimes) Martingale & Co.

Perkins, Kathy A., ed. Black Female Playwrights: An Anthology of Plays Before 1950. LC 88-46040. (Blacks in the Diaspora Ser.). (Illus.). 298p. (Orig.). 1990. pap. 18.95 (0-253-20623-5, MB-623) Ind U Pr.

— Black South African Women: An Anthology of Plays. LC 98-18547. (Illus.). 192p. (C). 1999. 80.00 (0-415-18243-3); pap. 22.99 (0-415-18244-1) Routledge.

Perkins, Kathy A. & Uno, Roberta. Contemporary Plays by Women of Color: An Anthology. LC 95-7465. (Illus.). 336p. (C). 1996. pap. 27.99 (0-415-11378-4) Routledge.

— Contemporary Plays by Women of Color: An Anthology. LC 95-7465. (Illus.). 336p. (C). (gr. 13). 1996. 90.00 (0-415-11377-6) Routledge.

Perkins, Kathy A., jt. ed. see Stephens, Judith L.

Perkins, Kelly A., jt. auth. see Perkins, Craig R.

Perkins, Ken & Benoit, John. The Future of Volunteer Fire & Rescue Services: Taming the Dragons of Change. Smith, Carol M., ed. (Illus.). 268p. 1996. pap. text 15.00 (0-87939-131-6, 35939) IFSTA.

Perkins, Kenneth, tr. see Valensi, Lucette.

Perkins, Kenneth J. Historical Dictionary of Tunisia. 2nd ed. LC 96-51075. (African Historical Dictionaries Ser.: No. 45). (Illus.). 448p. 1997. 64.50 (0-8108-3286-0) Scarecrow.

— Qaids, Captains, & Colons: French Military Administration in the Colonial Maghrib 1844-1934. LC 80-13114. 278p. (C). 1981. 45.00 (0-8419-0564-9, Africana) Holmes & Meier.

Perkins, Kenneth J., jt. ed. see Le Gall, Michel.

***Perkins, Kevin, et al.** Golf Everyone. (Everyone Ser.). 208p. 1999. pap. text 21.95 (0-88725-284-2) Hunter Textbks.

Perkins, Kris. Indycar. (Osprey Colour Library). (Illus.). 128p. 1993. pap. 15.95 (1-85532-399-0, Pub. by Osprey) Motorbooks Intl.

Perkins, Kyle, ed. see Teachers of English to Speakers of Other Languages.

Perkins, Lanny & Perkins, Sara. Multiple Sclerosis: Your Legal Rights. 2nd ed. LC 99-22996. 224p. 1999. pap. 21.95 (1-888799-31-5) Demos Medical.

Perkins, Larry D. Impressions of Forty Years: The Prints of Kenneth Kerslake. 32p. (Orig.). (C). 1996. pap. write for info. (0-9629384-2-4) Harn Mus Art.

Perkins, Laura L. Dancing on the Podium. 106p. (Orig.). 1997. pap. 16.50 (0-9655808-1-4) Focus on Excell.

Perkins, Leeman L. Music in the Age of the Renaissance. LC 98-28961. (Illus.). 750p. 1999. 49.95 (0-393-04608-7) Norton.

Perkins, Leialoha A. Cyclone Country: Poems of Tonga (Poetry Collection) (Illus.). 46p. 1987. pap. write for info. (1-892174-03-0) Kamalu uluolele.

— The Firemakers & Other Stories about Hawaii, the Samoas, & Tonga. 107p. 1987. write for info. (1-892174-05-7) Kamalu uluolele.

— Histories in Stone, Wood, Bone, 2 vols., Set. (ENG & HAW.). 224p. (Orig.). 1998. pap. 34.00 (1-892174-00-6) Kamalu uluolele.

— Natural: And Other Stories about Contemporary Hawaiians. 43p. 1995. reprint ed. pap. write for info. (1-892174-07-3) Kamalu uluolele.

— Natural: Short Stories of Contemporary Hawaiians. iv, 43p. 1979. pap. write for info. (1-892174-08-1) Kamalu uluolele.

— Other Places in the Turnings of a Mind: Poetry Collection. 48p. 1987. pap. write for info. (1-892174-04-9) Kamalu uluolele.

— The Oxridge Woman. (ENG, FRE & HAW.). (Orig.). 1998. pap. 28.00 (1-892174-02-2) Kamalu uluolele.

***Perkins, Leigh & Norman, Geoffrey.** A Sportsman's Life: How I Built Orvis by Mixing Business & Sport. LC 99-26364. (Illus.). 192p. 1999. 24.00 (0-87113-757-7, Atlntc Mnthly) Grove-Atltc.

Perkins, Llewellyn R., ed. see Robinson, Rowland E.

Perkins, Lori. Cheapskate's Guide to Entertaining: How to Throw Fabulous Parties on a Modest Budget. LC 98-35548. xi, 180p. 1998. pap. 19.92 (0-8065-2038-8, Citadel Pr) Carol Pub Group.

P

An Asterisk (*) at the beginning of an entry indicates that the title is appearing for the first time.

P

An Asterisk (*) at the beginning of an entry indicates that the title is appearing for the first time.

***Perkins, Russell, contrib. by.** 2000 Dorland's Medical Directory, Northern Florida. 424p. 1999. pap. 49.95 (*1-880874-59-8*) Dorland Hlthcare.
— 2000 Dorland's Medical Directory, Southern Florida. 431p. 1999. pap. 49.95 (*1-880874-60-1*) Dorland Hlthcare.
— 2000 Dorland's Medical Directory, Eastern Pennsylvania. 1000p. 2000. pap. 79.95 (*1-880874-61-X*) Dorland Hlthcare.

Perkins, Russell, ed. Third World Tour of Kirpal Singh. (Illus.). 1974. pap. 2.50 (*0-89142-008-8*) Sant Bani Ash.

Perkins, Russell, ed. see Kabir.

Perkins, Russell, ed. see Oberoi, A. S.

Perkins, Russell, ed. see Singh, Ajaib.

Perkins, Russell, ed. see Singh, Kirpal.

Perkins, Russell A. Directory Publishing: A Practical Guide. 4th ed. 248p. (Orig.). 1996. pap. 44.95 (*0-614-25716-6*) Simba Info.

***Perkins, Russell A.** Directory Publishing: A Practical Guide. 5th rev. ed. 196p. (Orig.). 2000. pap. 43.95 (*1-893683-12-5*) Havestraw.
— Info Commerce: Internet Strategies for Database Publishers. LC 00-190691. 186p. 2000. pap. 43.95 (*1-893683-11-7*) Havestraw.

Perkins, Ruth. Off-Centered Riding: or Not So Swift. (Illus.). 192p. 1993. pap. 9.95 (*0-943955-81-5*) Trafalgar.

Perkins, Salvador T., jt. auth. see Norris, Jeffrey A.

Perkins, Salvador T., jt. auth. see Williams, Robert E.

Perkins, Samuel. Historical Sketches of the United States: From the Peace of 1815 to 1830. LC 72-31. (Select Bibliographies Reprint Ser.). 1977. reprint ed. 28.95 (*0-8369-9969-X*) Ayer.

Perkins, Samuel L. Basic Contracts & Checklists for Petroleum Marketing. 1995. 69.95 (*0-9644877-0-5*) Petrol Pub Grp.

Perkins, Sara, jt. auth. see Perkins, Lanny.

***Perkins, Sean.** Experience: Challenging Visual Indifference Through New Sensory Experience. 2000. pap. 39.95 (*1-86154-000-0*, Pub. by Abrams) Time Warner.

Perkins, Simeon. Diary of Simeon Perkins, 1780-1789, Vol. 36. Harvey, D. C., ed. LC 69-14503. 531p. 1969. reprint ed. lib. bdg. 75.00 (*0-8371-5068-X*, PEDJ, Greenwood Pr) Greenwood.
— Diary of Simeon Perkins, 1766-1780, Vol. 29. Innes, Harold A., ed. LC 69-14503. 298p. 1969. reprint ed. lib. bdg. 55.00 (*0-8371-5067-1*, PEDI, Greenwood Pr) Greenwood.

Perkins, Simon. The Audubon Society Pocket Guide to North American Birds of Sea & Shore. LC 93-21251. (Audubon Society Pocket Guides Ser.). (Illus.). 1994. pap. 9.00 (*0-679-74921-7*) Random.
— Guide to Backyard Birds of Eastern North America. Leahy, Christopher, ed. (Habitat Ser.). (Illus.). 8p. 1996. 3.95 (*0-932691-17-X*) MA Audubon Soc.

***Perkins, Spencer & Rice, Chris.** More Than Equals: Racial Healing for the Sake of the Gospel. 2nd rev. enl. ed. LC 99-86863. 2000. pap. 14.99 (*0-8308-2256-9*) InterVarsity.

Perkins, Spencer, jt. auth. see Rice, Chris.

Perkins, Stanley C. Arvilla & the Tattler Tree: The Fur Trader. (Illus.). 702p. (J). 1994. pap. 25.00 (*0-9620249-4-5*); boxed set 30.00 (*0-9614640-9-7*) Broadblade Pr.
— The Genesee County Fair since 1850. Gleason, Maryann, ed. LC 95-103097. (Illus.). 100p. (Orig.). 1986. pap. 10.00 (*0-9614640-8-9*) Broadblade Pr.
— The House Coveted. (Illus.). 300p. (Orig.). (J). 1996. 18.00 (*0-9620249-9-6*); pap. 14.00 (*0-9620249-8-8*) Broadblade Pr.
— Itinerant Auctioneering. 2nd rev. ed. LC 81-51758. (Illus.). 349p. 1983. 16.00 (*0-9614640-0-3*) Broadblade Pr.
— Lore of Wolverine Country. 2nd ed. (Illus.). 244p. 1984. 15.00 (*0-940404-08-7*); pap. 12.00 (*0-9614640-3-8*) Broadblade Pr.
— Perk's Path. Scheidemantel, Marylin, ed. (Illus.). 538p. 1999. 30.00 (*0-9620249-6-1*, 846730F); pap. 25.00 (*0-9620249-5-3*, 846730F) Broadblade Pr.
— We're from Duffield. 3rd ed. (Illus.). 147p. 1982. pap. 7.50 (*0-9614640-2-X*) Broadblade Pr.
— We're from Duffield. 4th ed. (Illus.). 147p. 1982. 10.00 (*0-9614640-1-1*) Broadblade Pr.

Perkins, Stephen. Efficient Transport for Europe: Policies for Internalisation of External Costs. LC 98-181020. 264p. 1998. pap. 40.00 (*92-821-1226-8*, 75 98 03 1 P, Pub. by European Conference Ministers Transp) OECD.
— Internationalization: The People Dimension. LC 98-183257. 1998. 39.95 (*0-7494-2464-8*) Kogan Page Ltd.

***Perkins, Stephen J.** Globalization-The People Dimension: Human Resources Strategies for Global Expansion. 2000. pap. 39.95 (*0-7494-3124-5*) Kogan Page Ltd.

Perkins, Terry M., jt. auth. see Bock, Douglas G.

Perkins, Thornton. Junior High Champs. (Illus.). 49p. (Orig.). (YA). (gr. 6-9). 1989. pap. 3.00 (*0-9623407-0-7*) NVEM.

***Perkins, Tony.** The Internet Bubble. 2000. pap. 15.00 (*0-06-664001-6*) HarpC.

Perkins, Uradell. They Came Out of the Trees. 40p. 1997. pap. 8.00 (*0-8059-4120-7*) Dorrance.

Perkins, Useni. The Black Fairy & Other Plays for Children. LC 92-60054. (Illus.). 200p. (Orig.). (J). 1993. pap. 13.95 (*0-88378-077-1*) Third World.

Perkins, Useni E. Afrocentric Self Inventory & Discovery Workbook for African American Youth. 56p. (J). (gr. 7-10). 1990. 5.95 (*0-88378-043-7*) Third World.
— Explosion of Chicago's Black Street Gangs, 1900 to Present. (Orig.). 1987. pap. 6.95 (*0-88378-120-4*) Third World.
— Harvesting New Generations: The Positive Development of Black Youth. (Orig.). 1986. pap. 12.95 (*0-88378-116-6*) Third World.
— Home Is a Dirty Street: The Social Oppression of Black Children. LC 74-78322. (Orig.). 1975. pap. 9.95 (*0-88378-048-8*) Third World.

Perkins, V. F. Film As Film: Understanding & Judging Movies. LC 93-25278. 204p. 1993. reprint ed. pap. 12.95 (*0-306-80541-3*) Da Capo.

***Perkins, V. F.** Magnificent Ambersons. 1999. pap. 10.95 (*0-85170-373-9*) British Film Inst.

Perkins, Verna, ed. see Wampler, Joice.

Perkins, Walter W., ed. Ceramic Glossary. 100p. 1984. pap. text 12.00 (*0-916094-61-8*, G007) Am Ceramic.

Perkins, Warren S. Textile Coloration & Finishing. LC 96-2516. (Illus.). 248p. 1996. boxed set 75.00 (*0-89089-885-5*) Carolina Acad Pr.

***Perkins, Wayne.** How to Hypnotize Yourself Without Losing Your Mind: A Self-Hypnosis Training Program for Students & Educators. (How to Hypnotize Ser.). 192p. 2000. cd-rom 16.95 (*1-929695-23-3*) W F Perkins.

Perkins, Wayne F. How to Hypnotize Yourself Without Losing Your Mind: A Self-Hypnosis Training Program for Students & Educators. 183p. 1998. spiral bd. 26.95 (*1-55212-220-4*, No. 98-0039) Trafford Pub.

Perkins, Wendy. Midwifery & Medicine in Early Modern France: Louise Bourgeois. 240p. 1996. text 55.00 (*0-85989-471-1*, Pub. by Univ Exeter Pr) Northwestern U Pr.
— Temporarily Yours, Vol. I. (Illus.). 112p. (Orig.). (C). 1989. pap. 11.95 (*0-9622980-3-4*) Permanently Collectible.

Perkins, Whitney T. Constraint of Empire: The United States & Caribbean Interventions, 8. LC 80-27269. (Contributions in Comparative Colonial Studies: No. 8). 320p. 1981. 75.00 (*0-313-22266-5*, PCE/, Greenwood Pr) Greenwood.

Perkins, Wil. Scat! LC 97-41899. (Open Mouth Poetry Ser.). 93p. (Orig.). 1997. pap. 9.95 (*1-884773-04-4*) Heat Press.

***Perkins, Wilder.** Hoare & the Headless Captains: A Maritime Mystery Featuring Captain Bartholomew Hoare. 256p. 2000. text 22.95 (*0-312-25248-X*, Minotaur) St Martin.

Perkins, Wilder. Hoare & the Portsmouth Atrocities. LC 98-22255. 224p. 2000. 21.95 (*0-312-19283-5*, Thomas Dunne) St Martin.

Perkins, William. The Art of Prophesying. 191p. 1996. reprint ed. pap. 6.99 (*0-85151-689-0*) Banner of Truth.
— General Principles of Therapy: Current Therapy of Communication Disorders, Vol. 1. 98p. 1982. 24.00 (*0-86577-401-3*) Thieme Med Pubs.
— How to Pick Up Women in the 90s: A Handbook for Men. 150p. (Orig.). 1996. pap. 15.00 (*0-9648476-4-7*) HOWL CA.
— How to Pick up Women in the 90's! Instruction in the Art of Meeting, Dating & Seducing Women. 208p. (Orig.). 1997. pap. 15.95 (*0-9648476-6-3*) HOWL CA.
— Three Years in California: William Perkins' Journal of Life at Sonora, 1849-1852. (With an Introduction & Annotations by Dale L. Morgan & James P. Scobie) LC 64-21141. (Illus.). 442p. reprint ed. pap. 137.10 (*0-608-18060-2*, 202905900058) Bks Demand.
— The Whole Treatise of the Cases of Conscience. LC 74-38218. (English Experience Ser.: No. 482). 690p. 1972. reprint ed. 75.00 (*90-221-0482-6*) Walter J Johnson.
— Works of William Perkins, 3 vols. LC 74-144670. reprint ed. lib. bdg. 285.00 (*0-404-05050-6*) AMS Pr.

Perkins, William, jt. auth. see Doyle, William.

Perkins, William D. Chestnuts, Galls, & Dandelion Wine: Useful Wild Plants of the Boston Harbor Islands. LC 81-19867. (Illus.). (Orig.). 1982. pap. 6.95 (*0-940960-00-1*) Plant Pr MA.

Perkins, William H. Language Handicaps in Adults. (Current Therapy of Communication Disorders Ser.: Vol. 3). 1983. 24.00 (*0-86577-406-4*) Thieme Med Pubs.
— Stuttering & Science. 156p. 1995. pap. 35.00 (*1-56593-284-6*, 1244) Thomson Learn.
— Stuttering Disorders Vol. 8: Current Therapy of Communication Disorders. 255p. 1985. text 24.00 (*0-86577-403-X*) Thieme Med Pubs.
— Stuttering Prevented: A Guide for Parents. (Illus.). 204p. (Orig.). (C). 1991. pap. text 39.95 (*1-879105-50-0*, 0235) Thomson Learn.

Perkins, William H., ed. Hearing Disorders. LC 84-51456. (Current Therapy of Communication Disorders Ser.). 170p. 1984. 24.00 (*0-86577-088-3*) Thieme Med Pubs.
— Language Handicaps in Children: Current Therapy of Communication Disorders, Vol. 7. 187p. 1984. 24.00 (*0-86577-405-6*) Thieme Med Pubs.
— Phonologic-Articulatory Disorders: Current Therapy of Communication Disorders, Vol. 5. 114p. 1983. 24.00 (*0-86577-402-1*) Thieme Med Pubs.
— Voice Disorders: Current Therapy of Communication Disorders, Vol. 4. 160p. 1983. 24.00 (*0-86577-407-2*) Thieme Med Pubs.

Perkins, William H. & Kent, Raymond D. Functional Anatomy of Speech, Language, & Hearing: A Primer. 512p. (C). 1991. pap. text 82.00 (*0-205-13572-2*) Allyn.

Perkins, William H., jt. ed. see Fraser, Jane.

Perkins, William H., jt. ed. see McNeil, Malcolm R.

Perkins, William M. & Perkins, Nancy M. Hijos Sanos en un Mundo Ivadido por Las Drogas.Tr. of Drug Free Kids in a Drug-Filled World. (SPA.). 146p. pap. 10.00 (*968-39-0639-7*, 6299) Hazelden.

Perkins, William P., jt. auth. see Barbier, John.

Perkins, William R. & Wick, Barthinius L. History of the Amana Society: Or, Community of True Inspiration. LC 75-117. (Mid-American Frontier Ser.). 1975. reprint ed. 15.95 (*0-405-06883-2*) Ayer.

Perkins, Zoe A., jt. auth. see Hedlund, Ann L.

Perkinsj. Modern Industrial Hygiene, Vol. 4. (Occupational Health & Safety Ser.). 1998. text 59.95 (*0-442-02543-2*, VNR) Wiley.

Perkinson, Gary & McCormick, Michael J. The 1996 Midsummer Classic. (Illus.) 112p. 1996. 24.95 (*0-9638222-2-5*) Maj Leag Baseball.

Perkinson, Henry. Getting Better: Television & Moral Progress. 296p. (C). 1991. 39.95 (*0-88738-397-1*) Transaction Pubs.
— Getting Better: Television & Moral Progress. 336p. (C). 1995. pap. text 24.95 (*1-56000-864-4*) Transaction Pubs.
— No Safety in Numbers: How the Computer Quantified Everything & Made People Risk-Aversive. Strate, Lance, ed. (Communication Ser.). 208p. (C). 1996. text 45.00 (*1-57273-062-5*); pap. text 21.95 (*1-57273-063-3*) Hampton Pr NJ.

Perkinson, Henry J. The Imperfect Panacea: American Faith in Education. 4th ed. 256p. (C). 1995. 33.75 (*0-07-049371-5*) McGraw.
— Learning from Our Mistakes: A Reinterpretation of Twentieth-Century Educational Theory, 14. LC 83-26670. (Contributions to the Study of Education Ser.: No. 14). (Illus.). 224p. 1984. 59.95 (*0-313-24239-9*, PEM/) Greenwood.
— Teachers Without Goals, Students Without Purposes. LC 92-26491. 128p. (C). 1993. pap. 23.44 (*0-07-049372-3*) McGraw.
— Two Hundred Years of American Educational Thought. 342p. 1987. reprint ed. pap. text 27.00 (*0-8191-6124-1*) U Pr of Amer.

Perkinson, Kathryn, ed. see Cullinan, Bernice & Bagert, Brad.

Perkinson, Kathryn, ed. see Paulu, Nancy.

***Perkinson, Margaret A. & Braun, Kathryn, eds.** Teaching Students Geriatric Research. LC 00-23164. 110p. 2000. 39.95 (*0-7890-0996-X*); pap. text 24.95 (*0-7890-0997-8*) Haworth Pr.

Perkinson, Richard C. Data Analysis: The Key to Data Base Design. LC 83-63212. 303p. reprint ed. pap. 94.00 (*0-7837-5887-1*, 204561000006) Bks Demand.

Perkinson, Robert R. Chemical Dependency Counseling: A Practical Guide. LC 96-51207. 464p. (C). 1997. pap. 38.95 (*0-7619-0859-5*, 08595) Sage.

Perkinson, Robert R. & Jongsma, Arthur E., Jr. The Chemical Dependence Treatment Planner. LC 97-35792. 256p. 1997. pap. 39.95 (*0-471-23795-7*) Wiley.

Perkinson, Robert R. & Jongsma, Arthur E., Jr. The Chemical Dependence Treatment Planner. LC 97-35792. 256p. 1997. pap. text 175.00 incl. disk (*0-471-23794-9*) Wiley.

Perkinson, Roy L., jt. auth. see Dolloff, Francis W.

Perkio, L. Swedish & Finnish Glossary of Gastronomy: Gastronomisk Ordlista. (FIN & SWE.). 90p. 1985. 35.00 (*0-8288-0846-5*, F34200) Fr & Eur.

Perkis, Philip, photos by. Warwick Mountain Series. LC 78-61647. (Illus.). 1978. 24.00 (*0-932526-01-2*) Nexus Pr.

Perko, F. Michael, ed. Enlightening the Next Generation: Catholics & Their School 1830-1980. LC 88-24523. (Heritage of American Catholicism Ser.). 448p. 1988. 20.00 (*0-8240-4078-3*) Garland.

Perko, Lawrence. Differential Equations & Dynamical Systems. 2nd ed. LC 96-14281. (Probability & Its Applications Ser.: Vol. 7). 519p. 1996. 49.95 (*0-387-94778-7*) Spr-Verlag.

Perko, Lawrence M. Differential Equations & Dynamical Systems. (Texts in Applied Mathematics Ser.: Vol. 7). (Illus.). xii, 403p. 1993. 43.95 (*0-387-97443-1*) Spr-Verlag.

***Perko, Sandra J.** The Homeopathic Treatment of Influenza: Surviving Influenza Epidemics & Pandemics Past, Present & Future with Homeopathy. LC 99-95502. 395p. 1999. pap. 24.95 (*0-9653187-1-0*) Benchmark Homeopathic.

Perko, Sandra J. Homeopathy for the Modern Pregnant Woman & Her Infant: A Therapeutic Practice Guidebook for Midwives, Physicians & Practitioners. LC 96-96765. xiv, 460p. 1997. 59.95 (*0-9653187-0-2*) Benchmark Homeopathic.

Perkoff, David, et al. Processionals & Recessionals for Traditional Weddings: Guidebook & Cassette. (Illus.). 20p. (Orig.). 1990. pap. 15.95 (*0-9631377-0-0*) Seven Veils Recs.

Perkoff, G., tr. see Afanasiev, Aleksandr, ed.

Perkoff, Gerald, ed. see Perkoff, Stuart Z.

Perkoff, Stuart Z. Alphabet. 1973. 4.00 (*0-88031-010-3*) Invisible-Red Hill.
— Love Is the Silence: Poems, 1948-1974. 1975. pap. 4.00 (*0-88031-018-9*) Invisible-Red Hill.
— Voices of the Lady: Collected Poems. Perkoff, Gerald, ed. (Phoenix Poets Ser.). 486p. 1998. 50.00 (*0-943373-49-2*) Natl Poet Foun.
— Voices of the Lady: Collected Poems. Perkoff, Gerald, ed. (Phoenix Poets Ser.). 486p. 1998. pap. 22.95 (*0-943373-48-4*) Natl Poet Foun.

Perkov, Yury, tr. & intro. see Afanasiev, Aleksandr A., ed.

***Perkovich, Dave.** Complete Visual Basic Database Training Course. 1998. pap., student ed. 71.93 (*0-13-083030-5*, Prentice Hall) P-H.

Perkovich, Dave. Microsoft MCSE Readiness Review Exam 70-098: Implementing & Supporting Microsoft Windows 98. LC 99-10772. 322p. 1999. pap. 29.99 (*0-7356-0671-4*) Microsoft.

Perkovich, David. A Complete Visual Basic Database Training Course: The Ultimate Cyber Classroom. (Prentice Hall PTR Interactive Ser.). (Illus.). 600p. 1998. pap. text 99.95 (*0-13-779653-6*, Prentice Hall) P-H.

Perkovich, George. India's Nuclear Bomb. LC 99-37464. 673p. 1999. text 39.95 (*0-520-21772-1*, Pub. by U CA Pr) Cal Prin Full Svc.

Perkowitz, S. Optical Characterization of Semiconductors. (Techniques of Physics Ser.). (Illus.). 220p. 1993. text 81.00 (*0-12-550770-4*) Acad Pr.

Perkowitz, S., et al. Optical Characterization in Microelectronics Manufacturing. (Illus.). 34p. (Orig.). (C). 1994. pap. text 25.00 (*0-7881-1539-1*) DIANE Pub.

Perkowitz, Sidney. Empire of Light: A History of Discovery in Science & Art. 227p. 1996. 27.50 (*0-8050-3211-8*) H Holt & Co.
— Empire of Light: A History of Discovery in Science & Art. (Illus.). 248p. 1998. pap. 16.95 (*0-309-06556-9*) Natl Acad Pr.

***Perkowitz, Sidney.** Universal Foam: From Cappuccino to the Cosmos. LC 99-86482. (Illus.). 224p. 2000. 24.00 (*0-8027-1357-2*) Walker & Co.

Perkowski, Jan L. The Darkling: A Treatise on Slavic Vampirism. 169p. (Orig.). 1996. reprint ed. pap. 19.95 (*0-89357-200-4*) Slavica.
— Kashubian Idiolect in the United States. LC 68-64529. (Language Science Monographs: Vol. 2). 1969. pap. text 21.50 (*0-87750-135-1*) Res Inst Inner Asian Studies.

Perks, Anne-Marie. The Tortoise Who Bragged: A Trigram Tale. 32p. (J). (gr. 2-4). 1999. pap. 8.50 (*0-914534-18-1*, 120) Stokes.

Perks, Micah. We Are Gathered Here. 304p. 1997. pap. 13.95 (*0-312-15294-9*) St Martin.

Perks, R. Accounting & Society. 232p. 1993. mass mkt. 32.95 (*0-412-47330-5*) Chapman & Hall.

Perks, Rob & Smith, Graham. Ukraine's Forbidden History. (Illus.). 108p. 1998. pap. 24.95 (*1-899235-56-6*, Pub. by Dewi Lewis) Dist Art Pubs.

Perks, Robert & Thomson, Alistair. The Oral History Reader. LC 97-12846. 486p. (C). 1998. 90.00 (*0-415-13351-3*); pap. 25.99 (*0-415-13352-1*) Routledge.

Perks, Robert C. The Flight of a Lifetime! A Journey of Discovery for a Person of Importance...You! LC 97-67739. 90p. 1997. pap. 9.95 (*0-9657935-2-4*) Sparrow Publishing.

Perktold, K. & Verdonck, P., eds. Intra & Extra-Corporeal Cardiovascular Fluid Dynamics Vol. 2: Computational Fluid-Structure Interaction in the Cardiovascular System. (Advances in Fluid Mechanics Ser.: Vol. 23). 280p. 2000. 134.00 (*1-85312-655-1*, 6551, Pub. by WIT Pr) Computational Mech MA.

***Perl.** New Art City. 2000. 26.00 (*0-465-05522-2*, Pub. by Basic); pap. 15.00 (*0-465-05523-0*, Pub. by Basic) HarpC.

Perl. New Art City. 1997. 25.00 (*0-684-19575-5*) S&S Trade.

Perl, Arnold. Tevya & His Daughters. 1957. pap. 5.25 (*0-8222-1125-4*) Dramatists Play.
— The World of Sholom Aleichem. 1955. pap. 5.25 (*0-8222-1277-3*) Dramatists Play.

Perl, Gisella. I Was a Doctor in Auschwitz. LC 79-12470. 1979. reprint ed. lib. bdg. 25.95 (*0-405-12300-0*) Ayer.

***Perl, Jed.** Eyewitness. 2000. pap. 15.00 (*0-465-05521-4*, Pub. by Basic) HarpC.
— Eyewitness: Reports from an Art World in Crisis. 30.00 (*0-8133-3700-3*) Westview.

Perl, Jed. Man Ray. 2nd ed. (Masters of Photography Ser.). (Illus.). 96p. (Orig.). 1997. reprint ed. 18.95 (*0-89381-743-0*) Aperture.

***Perl, Jed, et al.** Louisa Matthiasdottir. (Illus.). 198p. 2000. 65.00 (*1-55595-197-X*) Hudson Hills.

***Perl, Jeff.** Eyewitness: The Crisis in the Art World & What Can Be Done about It. LC 99-49794. (Illus.). 384p. 2000. 35.00 (*0-465-05520-6*, Pub. by Basic) HarpC.

Perl, Jeffery P. Pollution Prevention & Waste Minimization. (C). 2000. 48.00 (*0-13-369091-1*, Macmillan Coll) P-H.

Perl, Jeffrey M. Skepticism & Modern Enmity: Before & after Eliot. LC 89-11057. 252p. reprint ed. pap. 78.20 (*0-608-06184-0*, 206651600008) Bks Demand.
— The Tradition of Return: The Implicit History of Modern Literature. LC 84-42567. (Illus.). 338p. 1984. reprint ed. pap. 104.80 (*0-608-02548-8*, 206319200004) Bks Demand.

Perl, Lila. Dumb Like Me, Olivia Potts. (J). 19.95 (*0-8164-3178-7*) HM.
— Four Perfect Pebbles: A Holocaust Story. LC 95-9752. (Illus.). 144p. (gr. 7-12). 1999. mass mkt. 3.99 (*0-380-73188-6*, Avon Bks) Morrow Avon.
— Four Perfect Pebbles: A Holocaust Story. (Illus.). (J). 1999. 9.34 (*0-606-17971-2*) Turtleback.

Perl, Lila. The Great Ancestor Hunt. LC 88-36211. (Illus.). 112p. (J). (gr. 3-6). 1989. 16.00 (*0-89919-745-0*, Clarion Bks) HM.
— The Great Ancestor Hunt: The Fun of Finding Out Who You Are. 112p. (J). (gr. 3-6). 1990. pap. 7.95 (*0-395-54790-3*, Clarion Bks) HM.
— It Happened in America: True Stories from the Fifty States. 304p. (J). (gr. 4-7). 1995. pap. 14.95 (*0-8050-4707-7*) H Holt & Co.
— It Happened in America: True Stories from the Fifty States. LC 92-6742. (ITA., Illus.). 304p. (J). (gr. 4-7). 1995. 22.50 (*0-8050-1719-4*, Bks Young Read) H Holt & Co.
— Mummies, Tombs, & Treasure: Secrets of Ancient Egypt. LC 86-17646. (Illus.). 128p. (J). (gr. 4 up). 1987. 16.00 (*0-89919-407-9*, Clarion Bks) HM.
— Mummies, Tombs, & Treasure: Secrets of Ancient Egypt. LC 86-17646. (Illus.). 128p. (J). (gr. 2-5). 1990. pap. 8.95 (*0-395-54796-2*, Clarion Bks) HM.
— Mummies, Tombs, & Treasure: Secrets of Ancient Egypt. (J). 1987. 12.15 (*0-606-04483-3*, Pub. by Turtleback) Demco.

Perl, Lila. Pinatas & Paper Flowers (Pinatas y Flores de Papel) Holidays of the Americas in English & Spanish. (ENG & SPA.). (J). 1983. 12.15 (*0-606-02983-4*, Pub. by Turtleback) Demco.

An Asterisk (*) at the beginning of an entry indicates that the title is appearing for the first time.

Perl, Lila. Slumps, Grunts, & Snickerdoodles: What Colonial America Ate & Why, 001. LC 75-4894. (Illus.). 128p. (J). (gr. 6 up). 1979. 16.00 (*0-395-28923-8*, Clarion Bks) HM.

Perl, Lila & Ada, Alma F. Pinatas & Paper Flowers-Pinatas y Flores de Papel: Holidays of the Americas in English & Spanish. LC 82-12211. (Illus.). 91p. (J). (gr. 3-6). 1983. pap. 7.95 (*0-89919-155-X*, Clarion Bks) HM.

Perl, Lila & Lazan, Marian Blumenthal. Four Perfect Pebbles: A Holocaust Story. LC 95-9752. 130p. (YA). (gr. 7-12). 1996. 15.95 (*0-688-14294-X*, Grenwillow Bks) HarpC Child Bks.

Perl, Martin L. Reflections on Experimental Science. LC 95-48852. (World Scientific Series in 20th Century Mathematics: Vol. 14). 580p. 1995. text 84.00 (*981-02-2429-X*, GPPh-BR2901) World Scientific Pub.

— Reflections on Experimental Science: Selected Papers. 1995. pap. text 38.00 (*981-02-2574-1*) World Scientific Pub.

Perl, Martin L., ed. Physics Careers, Employment & Education. LC 77-9403. (AIP Conference Proceedings Ser.: No. 39). (Illus.). 1978. lib. bdg. 18.50 (*0-88318-138-X*) Am Inst Physics.

Perl, Michael. KSU Student Teaching Handbook. 128p. (C). 1993. 10.95 (*0-8403-8446-7*) Kendall-Hunt.

— Teacher Aide Handbook. 64p. (C). 1994. teacher ed. 10.95 (*0-8403-8288-X*) Kendall-Hunt.

Perl, Michael & Burton, Sharon. Working in a Windows World. 2nd ed. 216p. (C). 1996. pap. text, ring bd. 27.95 (*0-7872-2598-3*) Kendall-Hunt.

Perl, Raphael, jt. auth. see Bowers, Jean M.

Perl, Sheri. Healing from the Inside Out. LC 96-49827. 1997. 15.95 (*1-889828-03-3*) SethNet Pub.

Perl, Sondra, ed. Landmark Essays on Writing Process. (Landmark Essays Ser.: Vol. 7). 264p. (Orig.). (C). 1994. pap. 21.00 (*1-880393-13-1*, Hermagoras) L Erlbaum Assocs.

Perl, Sondra & Wilson, Nancy. Through Teachers' Eyes: Portraits of Writing Teachers at Work. rev. ed. LC 98-16243. (Illus.). 296p. 1998. pap. text 20.00 (*0-9663233-3-5*, 323335) Calendar Islands.

Perl, Susan, jt. auth. see Bayley, Monica.

Perl, Susan, jt. auth. see Dutton, June.

Perl, Teri. Math Equals, Biographies of Women Mathematicians & Related Activities. 1978. text 18.95 (*0-201-05709-3*) Addison-Wesley.

— Women & Numbers: Lives of Women Mathematicians Plus Discovery Activities. 2nd ed. LC 93-10535. (Illus.). 192p. 1993. pap. 15.95 (*0-933174-87-X*) Wide World-Tetra.

Perl, Teri, jt. auth. see Freedman, Miriam.

Perl, Teri, jt. ed. see Morrow, Charlene.

Perla, Georges, jt. auth. see Russo.

Perla, Georges, jt. auth. see Russo, Gloria.

Perla, Peter P., III. The Art of Wargaming. LC 89-28818. (Illus.). 416p. 1990. 32.95 (*0-87021-050-5*) Naval Inst Pr.

Perlbach, Max. Die Statuten des Deutschen Ordens. (GER.). lix, 354p. 1975. reprint ed. write for info. (*3-487-05690-9*) G Olms Pubs.

Perlberg, Deborah. The Case of the U. S. Navy Adventure. (Adventures of Mary-Kate & Ashley Ser.). (J). (gr. 2-4). 1997. pap. 3.99 (*0-590-88015-2*) Scholastic Inc.

***Perlberg, Deborah.** Problems in Paradise. (Full House Sisters Ser.: Vol. 5). 112p. (J). (gr. 4-7). 1999. per. 3.99 (*0-671-04057-X*) S&S Trade.

***Perlberg, Mark.** The Impossible Toystore. LC 00-28727. 72p. 2000. 22.50 (*0-8071-2614-4*) La State U Pr.

Perlberg, Mark, ed. see Bailey, David H. & Gottlieb, Louise.

Perlberg, Mark, ed. see Bailey, David H., et al.

Perlberger, Norman. Pennsylvania Divorce Code, with Forms & Form Disks. rev. ed. LC 97-74127. 1998. ring bd. 95.00 (*1-887024-47-6*); disk 69.50 (*1-887024-48-4*) Bisel Co.

Perle, Art. A New Owner's Guide to English Springer Spaniels: AKC Rank #25. (New Owner's Guide to Ser.). (Illus.). 160p. 1997. 12.95 (*0-7938-2763-9*, JG-114) TFH Pubns.

Perle, E. Gabriel & Williams, John T. The Publishing Law Handbook, 2 vols. 2nd ed. 1675p. 1993. 285.00 (*0-13-109364-9*) Aspen Law.

***Perle, E. Gabriel, et al.** Perle & Williams on Publishing Law. 3rd ed. LC 99-26810. 1999. ring bd. 295.00 (*0-7355-0448-2*) Panel Pubs.

Perle, George. The Listening Composer. 1990. 40.00 (*0-520-06991-9*, Pub. by U CA Pr) Cal Prin Full Svc.

— The Listening Composer. LC 89-20436. (Ernest Bloch Lectures: Vol. 7). (Illus.). 202p. (C). 1996. pap. 15.95 (*0-520-20518-9*, Pub. by U CA Pr) Cal Prin Full Svc.

— The Operas of Alban Berg Vol. II: Lulu. LC 76-52033. (Illus.). 352p. 1984. pap. 21.95 (*0-520-06616-2*, Pub. by U CA Pr) Cal Prin Full Svc.

— The Right Notes: Twenty-Three Selected Essays by George Perle on Twentieth-Century Music. 400p. 1995. lib. bdg. 46.00 (*0-945193-37-8*) Pendragon NY.

— Serial Composition & Atonality: An Introduction to the Music of Schoenberg, Berg, & Webern. 6th rev. ed. (Illus.). 178p. 1991. 45.00 (*0-520-07430-0*, Pub. by U CA Pr) Cal Prin Full Svc.

— Style & Idea in the Lyric Suite of Alban Berg. LC 95-16154. (Illus.). 68p. 1995. 36.00 (*0-945193-65-3*) Pendragon NY.

— Twelve-Tone Tonality. 2nd ed. LC 94-40067. 1995. 48.00 (*0-520-20142-6*, Pub. by U CA Pr) Cal Prin Full Svc.

***Perle, Quimetta.** Demon Slayer. (Illus.). 41p. 1999. spiral bd. 50.00 (*1-893125-10-6*) Womens Studio Wrkshop.

Perle, Richard N. Hard Line: A Novel. 300p. 1992. 21.00 (*0-614-16682-9*, AEI Pr) Am Enterprise.

Perlee, Clyde, ed. see Adams, Lynn & Goldbloom, Erwin.

Perlee, Clyde, ed. see Ahrens, C. Donald.

Perlee, Clyde, ed. see Arnold, Roger A.

Perlee, Clyde, ed. see Bagley, Constance E.

Perlee, Clyde, ed. see Ballatore, Ron & Miller, William.

Perlee, Clyde, ed. see Baumann, Susan K. & Mandell, Steven L.

Perlee, Clyde, ed. see Bohlman, Herbert M. & Dundas, Mary J.

Perlee, Clyde, ed. see Brinkerhoff, David B. & White, Lynn K.

Perlee, Clyde, ed. see Brinkerhoff, David B., et al.

Perlee, Clyde, ed. see Carper, Donald L., et al.

Perlee, Clyde, ed. see Casten, Carole M.

Perlee, Clyde, ed. see Casten, Carole M. & Jordan, Peg.

Perlee, Clyde, ed. see Clarkson, Kenneth W., et al.

Perlee, Clyde, ed. see Conover, Theodore E.

Perlee, Clyde, ed. see Coon, Dennis.

Perlee, Clyde, ed. see Cox, Frank D.

Perlee, Clyde, ed. see Cross, Frank B. & Miller, Roger L.

Perlee, Clyde, ed. see Dunikoski, Robert H.

Perlee, Clyde, ed. see Dunphy, Marv & Wilde, Rod.

Perlee, Clyde, ed. see Dworetzky, John P.

Perlee, Clyde, ed. see France, Diane L. & Horn, Arthur D.

Perlee, Clyde, ed. see Jentz, Gaylord A., et al.

Perlee, Clyde, ed. see Kraemer, Richard H. & Newell, Charldean.

Perlee, Clyde, ed. see Kriegel, Lorraine P. & Chandler-Vaccaro, Kimberly.

Perlee, Clyde, ed. see Lamare, James W.

Perlee, Clyde, ed. see Mandell, Steven L.

Perlee, Clyde, ed. see Miller, Roger L. & Jentz, Gaylord A.

Perlee, Clyde, ed. see Miller, Roger L. & Sttafford, Alan D.

Perlee, Clyde, ed. see Nelson, Harry, et al.

Perlee, Clyde, ed. see Pagano, Robert R.

Perlee, Clyde, ed. see Peterson, Brent D., et al.

Perlee, Clyde, ed. see Rowe, Bruce M.

Perlee, Clyde, ed. see Schmidt, Steffen W., et al.

Perlee, Clyde, ed. see Timm, Paul R. & Peterson, Brent D.

Perlee, Clyde, ed. see Turnbaugh, William A., et al.

Perlee, Clyde, ed. see Wadood, Tariq & Tan, Karlyne.

Perlee, Clyde, ed. see Wyrick, Thomas.

Perlee, Simon, ed. see Ahrens, C. Donald.

Perlee, Simon, ed. see Jurmain, Robert & Nelson, Harry.

Perlee, Simon, ed. see Mathis, Robert L. & Jackson, John H.

Perleman, Bob. The Trouble with Genius: Reading Pound, Joyce, Stein, & Zukofsky. LC 93-37181. 1994. pap. 17.95 (*0-520-08755-0*, Pub. by U CA Pr) Cal Prin Full Svc.

Perlemuter, Leon. Practical Dictionary of Clinical Medicine: Dictionnaire Pratique de Medecine Clinique. 2nd ed. (FRE.). 1856p. 1982. 195.00 (*0-8288-1821-5*, M6440) Fr & Eur.

— Practical Dictionary of Medical Therapy (Dictionnaire Pratique de Therapeutique Medicale) 6th ed. (FRE.). 1824p. 1990. ring bd. 150.00 (*0-7859-4566-0*) Fr & Eur.

Perlemuter, Leon, jt. auth. see Apfelbaum, Marian.

Perlemuter, Leon, jt. auth. see Quevauvilliers, J.

Perlemuter, Leon, jt. auth. see Roucoules, Gil.

Perlemuter, Leon, jt. auth. see Touitou, Yvan.

Perlemuter, Vlado & Jourdan-Morhange, Helene. Ravel According to Ravel. Taylor, Harold, ed. Tanner, Frances, tr. 92p. 1988. 16.50 (*0-912483-19-9*) Pro-Am Music.

Perler, Bruce A. & Becker, Gary J. Vascular Intervention: A Clinical Approach. LC 97-30187. 1997. write for info. (*3-13-108041-8*) Thieme Med Pubs.

Perler, Bruce A. & Becker, Gary J., eds. Vascular Intervention: A Clinical Approach. LC 97-30187. (Illus.). 608p. 1997. 129.00 (*0-86577-694-6*) Thieme Med Pubs.

Perler, Dominik. Pradestination, Zeit und Kontingenz: Philosophisch-Historische Untersuchungen zu Wilhelm von Ockhams. Tractatus de praedestinatione et de praescientia dei Repectu Futurorum Contingentium. (Bochumer Studien zur Philosophie Ser.: Vol. 12). (GER.). x, 322p. 1988. 63.00 (*90-6032-310-6*, Pub. by B R Gruner) Humanities.

— Der Propositionale Wahrheitsbegriff im 14. Jahrundert. (Quellen und Studien zur Philosophie: Bd. 33). (GER.). x, 387p. (C). 1992. lib. bdg. 144.65 (*3-11-013415-2*) De Gruyter.

Perles, jt. auth. see Freund.

Perles, Catherine. Les Industries Lithiques Taillees de Franchthi (Argolide, Grece), Tome 2: Fascicle Five, Tome 1. LC 86-46039. (Excavations at Franchthi Cave, Greece Ser.: No. 3). (Illus.). 372p. 1989. pap. 57.50 (*0-253-31972-2*) Ind U Pr.

Perles, Catherine, et al. Fascicle Five: Les Industries Lithiques Taillees de Franchthi (Argolide, Grece), Tome 2: LC 86-46039. (Excavations at Franchthi Cave, Greece Ser.). (Illus.). 296p. 1991. pap. 57.50 (*0-253-31973-0*) Ind U Pr.

Perles, George J. & Gregurian, Vahe. George Perles: The Ride of a Lifetime. (Illus.). 221p. 1995. 22.95 (*1-57167-022-X*) Sports Pub.

Perlesz, A., jt. auth. see Flaskas, Carmel.

Perleth, Matthias. Historical Aspects of American Trypanosomiasis (Chagas' Disease) LC 96-51844. (Medizin in Entwicklungslandern, Schriftenreihe zur Medizin und zu Gesundheitsproblemen in Landern der Dritten Welt Ser.: Bd. 43). (Illus.). 171p. 1996. pap. 35.95 (*0-8204-3232-6*) P Lang Pubng.

— Historical Aspects of American Trypanosomiasis (Chagas' Disease) LC 96-51844. (Medizin in Entwicklungslandern, Schriftenreihe zur Medizin und zu Gesundheitsproblemen in Landern der Dritten Welt Ser.: Bd. 43). (Illus.). 171p. 1997. pap. 35.95 (*3-631-31063-3*) P Lang Pubng.

Perley, Arthur, jt. auth. see Goldstone, Bruce.

Perley, M. V. The History & Genealogy of the Perley Family. (Illus.). 770p. 1989. reprint ed. pap. 115.00 (*0-8328-0955-1*); reprint ed. lib. bdg. 123.00 (*0-8328-0954-3*) Higginson Bk Co.

— A Short History of the Salem Village Witchcraft Trials. 86p. 1997. reprint ed. pap. 12.95 (*0-7661-0043-X*) Kessinger Pub.

Perley, M. V. & Waters, Thomas. Linebrook Parish Church Records, 1747-1819. 135p. (Orig.). 1995. pap. 25.00 (*1-878545-02-7*) ACETO Bookmen.

Perley, R., jt. ed. see Cornwell, T.

Perley, R. A., et al, eds. Synthesis Imaging in Radio Astronomy: A Collection of Lectures from the Third NRAO Synthesis Imaging Summer School. (ASP Conference Series Proceedings: Vol. 6). 509p. 1989. 34.00 (*0-937707-23-6*) Astron Soc Pacific.

Perley, Sidney. The History of Boxford from the Earliest Settlement to the Present Time, a Period of about 230 Years. (Illus.). 418p. 1989. reprint ed. lib. bdg. 42.00 (*0-8328-0809-1*, MA0020) Higginson Bk Co.

Perlgut, Mark. Electricity Across the Border: The U. S.-Canadian Experience. LC 78-65560. (Canadian-American Committee Ser.). 76p. 1978. pap. 4.00 (*0-89068-047-7*) Natl Planning.

Perlick, Deborah, jt. auth. see Silverstein, Brett.

***Perlick, Volker.** Ray Optics, Fermat's Principle & Applications to General Relativity. LC 99-89303. (Lecture Notes in Physics - Monographs: No. 61). x, 220p. 2000. 52.80 (*3-540-66898-5*) Spr-Verlag.

***Perlin.** Quick Review Family Law. 3rd ed. (Sum & Substance Quick Review Ser.): 1999. pap. 18.95 (*0-314-24285-4*) West Pub.

Perlin, D. E. Father Miguel Hidalgo: A Cry for Freedom. LC 90-27375. (ENG & SPA., Illus.). 32p. (J). (ps-4). 1991. pap. 5.95 (*0-937460-67-2*) Hendrick-Long.

Perlin, Doris E. Eight Bright Candles. LC 95-14089. (Women of the West Ser.). 184p. 1995. pap. 12.95 (*1-55622-390-0*, Rep of TX Pr) Wordware Pub.

Perlin, Frank. The Invisible City: Monetary, Administrative & Popular Infrastructures in Asia & Europe, 1500-1900. (Collected Studies: No. CS387). 380p. 1992. 115.95 (*0-86078-342-1*, Pub. by Variorum) Ashgate Pub Co.

— Unbroken Landscape: Commodity, Category, Sign & Identity: Their Production as Myth & Knowledge from 1500. (Collected Studies). 376p. 1994. 115.95 (*0-86078-431-2*, Pub. by Variorum) Ashgate Pub Co.

Perlin, George C. The Tory Syndrome: Leadership Politics in the Progressive Conservative Party. LC 80-474879. 262p. reprint ed. pap. 81.30 (*0-7837-1025-9*, 204133600020) Bks Demand.

Perlin, John. A Forest Journey: The Role of Wood in the Development of Civilization. LC 90-19301. (Illus.). 448p. 1991. pap. text 17.50 (*0-674-30892-1*, PERFOX) HUP.

— From Space to Earth: The Story of Solar Electricity. LC 99-23830. (Illus.). 250p. 1999. 32.00 (*0-937948-14-4*) aatec Pubns.

***Perlin, John.** From Space to Earth: The Story of Solar Electricity LC 99-23830. 1999. write for info. (*0-937948-15-2*) aatec Pubns.

Perlin, John, jt. auth. see Butti, Ken.

Perlin, Marc G. Family Law. 2nd rev. ed. LC 98-160106. (Quick Review Ser.). 152p. (C). 1997. pap. text 18.95 (*1-57793-007-X*) Sum & Substance.

— Mottla's Proof of Cases in Massachusetts. 3rd ed. LC 92-74614. 1992. 230.00 (*0-317-05377-9*) West Group.

Perlin, Marc G., ed. Massachusetts Actions & Remedies: Family Law. 480p. 1991. ring bd. 95.00 (*0-88063-446-4*, MICHIE) LEXIS Pub.

— The Rules Book & Update Service. 1990. 102.10 (*0-318-18709-4*) Lawyers Weekly.

Perlin, Marc G. & Connors, John M. Handbook of Civil Procedure in the Massachusetts District Courts. 2nd ed. (C). 1995. suppl. ed. 37.50 (*0-614-13743-8*) Lawyers Weekly.

— Handbook of Civil Procedure in the Massachusetts District Courts, Incl. 1995 suppl. 2nd ed. 341p. (C). 1990. 110.00 (*0-318-03524-3*) Lawyers Weekly.

Perlin, Michael. Mental Disability: 1990 Supplement. 3rd ed. 1990. write for info. (*0-87473-705-2*, 65814-10, MICHIE) LEXIS Pub.

Perlin, Michael, ed. see Seass, Robert P.

***Perlin, Michael L.** The Hidden Prejudice: Mental Disability on Trial. LC 99-37963. (Law & Public Policy Ser.). 329p. 1999. text 49.95 (*1-55798-616-9*, 431-627A) Am Psychol.

Perlin, Michael L. The Jurisprudence of the Insanity Defense. LC 93-72952. 468p. (C). 1993. 49.95 (*0-89089-555-4*) Carolina Acad Pr.

— Law & Mental Disability. 698p. 1994. 50.00 (*1-55834-153-6*, 12695-10, MICHIE) LEXIS Pub.

— Mental Disability Law: Cases & Materials. LC 98-89959. 1080p. 1999. boxed set 85.00 (*0-89089-882-0*) Carolina Acad Pr.

— Mental Disability Law: Civil & Criminal, 3 vols. 2nd ed. LC 98-87895. 1999. write for info. (*0-327-00493-2*) LEXIS Pub.

— Mental Disability Law: Civil & Criminal, 3 vols., Set. 1989. 240.00 (*0-87473-422-3*, 65810-10, MICHIE) LEXIS Pub.

— Mental Disability Law Vol. 1: Civil & Criminal, 3 vols. 2nd ed. LC 98-87895. 500p. 1998. 240.00 (*0-327-00524-6*, 6581111) LEXIS Pub.

***Perlin, Michael L.** Mental Disability Law Vol. 2: Civil & Criminal. 2nd ed. 600p. 1999. write for info. (*0-327-04964-2*, 6581211) LEXIS Pub.

Perlin, Michael L. Mental Disability Law Vols. 2 & 3: Civil & Criminal, 1998 Cumulative Supplement. 900p. 1998. pap. 90.00 (*0-327-00791-5*, 6581616) LEXIS Pub.

Perlin, Neil. Business Technology for Managers: An Office Automation Handbook. LC 85-223. (Professional Librarian Ser.). 206p. 1986. 30.00 (*0-86729-123-0*, Hall Reference) Macmillan.

Perlin, Rae & White, Marian F. Not a Still Life: The Art & Writings of Rae Perlin. (Illus.). 212p. 1991. pap. 9.55 (*1-895387-00-0*) Creative Bk Pub.

Perlin, Terry M. Clinical Medical Ethics: Cases in Practice. LC 92-12544. 1992. 33.95 (*0-316-69959-4*, Little Brwn Med Div) Lppncott W & W.

Perlin, Terry M., ed. Contemporary Anarchism. LC 74-20197. 294p. 1979. 39.95 (*0-87855-097-6*) Transaction Pubs.

Perlin, Terry M., jt. auth. see Cottell, Philip G., Jr.

Perlina, Nina. Varieties of Poetic Utterance: Quotation in the Brothers Kramazov. LC 84-20959. 236p. (Orig.). 1985. pap. text 24.00 (*0-8191-4372-3*) U Pr of Amer.

Perline, Ronald, ed. see Jameson, William J.

Perling, Joseph J. Presidents' Sons: The Prestige of Name in a Democracy. LC 70-148226. (Biography Index Reprint Ser.). 1977. 29.95 (*0-8369-8073-5*) Ayer.

Perlis, Alan. Wallace Stevens: A World of Transforming Shapes. LC 74-19631. 160p. 1975. 27.50 (*0-8387-1651-2*) Bucknell U Pr.

Perlis, Alan D. A Return to the Primal Self: Identity in the Fiction of George Eliot. (American University Studies: English Language & Literature: Ser. IV, Vol. 71). 221p. (C). 1989. text 35.50 (*0-8204-0637-6*) P Lang Pubng.

Perlis, Alan J. The Unofficial Guide to Buying a Home. 400p. 1998. pap. 22.95 (*0-02-862461-0*, Pub. by Macmillan) S&S Trade.

Perlis, Alan J., et al, eds. Software Metrics. (Computer Science Ser.). (Illus.). 416p. 1981. 50.00 (*0-262-16083-8*) MIT Pr.

Perlis, Linda, jt. auth. see Burt, Sandra.

Perlis, R., jt. auth. see Connor, P. E.

Perlis, Sam. Theory of Matrices. xiv, 237p. 1991. reprint ed. pap. 8.95 (*0-486-66810-X*) Dover.

Perlis, Vivian. Two Men for Modern Music. (I.S.A.M. Monographs: No. 9). (Illus.). 35p. 1978. pap. 10.00 (*0-914678-09-4*) Inst Am Music.

Perlis, Vivian, jt. auth. see Copland, Aaron.

Perlis, Vivian, ed. see Charles Ives Centennial Festival Conference Staff.

Perlman, jt. auth. see Kitch.

Perlman, jt. auth. see Wrightsman.

Perlman, Adrienne & Schulze-Delrieu, Konrad, eds. Deglutition & Its Disorders: Anatomy, Physiology, Clinical Diagnosis, & Management. LC 96-17369. 546p. 1996. pap. 79.95 (*1-56593-621-3*, 1290) Thomson Learn.

Perlman, Alan. Write Your Own Speech. LC 97-228602. 194p. (C). 1997. pap. text 12.00 (*0-205-27300-9*) P-H.

Perlman, Alan, ed. see Lief, Stephen J.

Perlman, Anne S. Sorting It Out. LC 82-70744. 1982. pap. 11.95 (*0-915604-73-6*) Carnegie-Mellon.

Perlman, Barbara H. Allan Houser: Ha-o-zous. LC 86-26605. (Illus.). 266p. (C). 1992. reprint ed. 75.00 (*1-56098-102-4*) Smithsonian.

Perlman, Baron & McCann, Lee I. Recruiting Good College Faculty: Practical Advice for a Successful Search. 224p. 1996. 35.95 (*1-882982-11-8*) Anker Pub.

Perlman, Baron, et al. The Academic Intrapreneur: Strategy, Innovation, & Management in Higher Education. LC 88-6609. 224p. 1988. 57.95 (*0-275-92951-5*, C2951, Praeger Pubs) Greenwood.

Perlman, Bennard B. The Lives, Loves & Art of Arthur B. Davies. LC 98-5205. (Illus.). 512p. (C). 1999. pap. text 29.95 (*0-7914-3836-8*) State U NY Pr.

— Robert Henri: His Life & Art. (Illus.). 208p. 1991. pap. 15.95 (*0-486-26722-9*) Dover.

Perlman, Bennard B., ed. see Sloan, John & Henri, Robert.

Perlman, Bernard B. The Immortal Eight & Its Influence. 108p. 10.00 (*0-318-17801-X*) Art Students.

— Painters of the Ashcan School: The Immortal Eight. (Illus.). 224p. 1990. pap. 12.95 (*0-486-25747-9*) Dover.

Perlman, Bob. Life & Love All Not Spectator Sports. 1986. write for info. (*0-318-62747-7*) Dan Eli Pr.

Perlman, Dan L. & Adelson, Glenn. Biodiversity: Exploring Values & Priorities in Conservation. LC 97-11468. (Illus.). 208p. 1997. pap. text 39.95 (*0-86542-439-X*) Blackwell Sci.

Perlman, Daniel & Duck, Steve, eds. Intimate Relationships: Development, Dynamics & Deterioration. LC 85-26248. (Sage Focus Editions Ser.: No. 80). 320p. 1987. reprint ed. pap. 99.20 (*0-608-01531-8*, 205957500002) Bks Demand.

Perlman, Daniel & Duck, Steven. Intimate Relationships: Development, Dynamics & Deterioration. LC 84-51532. (Focus Editions Ser.; Vol. 80). 340p. 1986. text 59.95 (*0-8039-2609-X*); pap. text 26.00 (*0-8039-2610-3*) Sage.

Perlman, Daniel, jt. ed. see Jones, Warren H.

Perlman, Daniel, jt. ed. see Peplau, Letitia A.

Perlman, Debbie. Flames to Heaven: New Psalms for Healing & Praise. LC 98-65464. (Illus.). 224p. 1998. pap. 14.00 (*0-9644570-5-9*) RAD Publ.

Perlman, Eileen, jt. auth. see Bertin, Phyllis.

Perlman, Elliot. Three Dollars. LC 99-14355. 358p. 1999. 22.00 (*1-878448-88-9*) MacMurray & Beck.

Perlman, Fredy. Against His-Story, Against Leviathan! (Illus.). 1983. pap. 5.00 (*0-934868-25-5*) Black & Red.

— Against History. 1986. lib. bdg. 79.95 (*0-8490-3849-9*) Gordon Pr.

— Anti-Semitism & the Beirut Program. 16p. (Orig.). 1983. pap. 2.00 (*0-939306-07-7*) Left Bank.

— Anything Can Happen. 128p. (Orig.). 1995. pap. 9.95 (*0-948984-22-8*, Pub. by Phoenix Pr) AK Pr Dist.

— Continuing Appeal of Nationalism. 58p. 1985. pap. 1.50 (*0-934868-27-1*) Black & Red.

P

— Plunder: A Play. 1962. pap. 1.50 (*0-934868-18-2*) Black & Red.

— The Reproduction of Daily Life. 1969. pap. 1.00 (*0-934868-17-4*) Black & Red.

— The Strait: Book of Obenabi, His Songs. 1988. pap. 5.00 (*0-934868-29-8*) Black & Red.

Perlman, Fredy, jt. auth. see Gregoire, R.

Perlman, Fredy, tr. see Arshinov, Peter.

Perlman, Fredy, tr. see Rubin, I. I.

Perlman, Fredy, tr. see Voline.

Perlman, Gary, et al, eds. Human Factors Perspectives on Human-Computer Interaction: Selections from Proceedings of Human Factors & Ergonomics Society Annual Meetings 1983-1994. LC 95-36293. (Illus.). 400p. (Orig.). (C). 1995. pap. text 58.00 (*0-945289-05-7*) Human Factors.

Perlman, Harvey S. & Kitch, Edmund W. Competitive Process, Cases, Materials & Notes on Unfair Business Practices, Trademarks, Copyrights & Patents, 1996 Case Supplement to the Legal Regulation of The. 4th rev. ed. (University Casebook Ser.). 410p. 1996. pap. text. write for info. (*1-56662-412-6*) Foundation Pr.

Perlman, Harvey S., jt. auth. see Ketch, Edmund W.

Perlman, Harvey S., jt. auth. see Kitch, Edmund W.

Perlman, Heidi, ed. see Clay, J. E.

Perlman, Helen H. The Dancing Clock & Other Childhood Memories. (Illus.). 204p. 1989. 20.00 (*0-89733-343-8*) Academy Chi Pubs.

— Looking Back to See Ahead. LC 89-31900. 244p. 1989. pap. text 15.95 (*0-226-66038-9*); lib. bdg. 47.00 (*0-226-66037-0*) U Ch Pr.

— Persona: Social Role & Personality. LC 68-21892. 256p. 1986. pap. text 18.00 (*0-226-66028-1*) U Ch Pr.

— Persona: Social Role & Personality. LC 68-21892. 1992. lib. bdg. 16.00 (*0-226-66030-3*) U Ch Pr.

— Relationship: The Heart of Helping People. LC 78-19064. x, 246p. 1983. pap. text 12.00 (*0-226-66036-2*) U Ch Pr.

— Relationship: The Heart of Helping People. LC 78-19064. x, 236p. 1993. lib. bdg. 16.00 (*0-226-66035-4*) U Ch Pr.

— Social Casework: A Problem-Solving Process. LC 57-6270. 283p. 1957. lib. bdg. 14.50 (*0-226-66033-8*) U Ch Pr.

Perlman, Helen H., ed. see Towle, Charlotte.

Perlman, Ian & Chamber, Karen, trs. Dale Chihuly: Japan, 1990. (ENG & JPN., Illus.). 80p. 1990. pap. 20.00 (*1-57684-025-5*) Portland Pr.

Perlman, James, ed. see Kottler, Dorian B.

Perlman, James, ed. see McGrath, Thomas.

Perlman, James S. Science Without Limits: Toward a Theory of Interaction Between Nature & Knowledge. LC 95-19752. 358p. 1995. 30.95 (*0-87975-962-3*) Prometheus Bks.

Perlman, Janet. Cinderella Penguin. (Illus.). 32p. (J). 1995. pap. 5.99 (*0-14-055552-8*, PuffinBks) Peng Put Young Read.

Perlman, Janet. The Emperor Penguin's New Clothes. (Illus.). 32p. (J). 1994. pap. 5.95 (*1-55074-290-6*) Kids Can Pr.

Perlman, Janet. Cinderella Penguin. 32p. (J). 1992. pap. 4.95 (*1-55074-181-0*) Kids Can Pr.

— The Emperor Penguin's New Clothes. 32p. (J). 1994. 11.95 (*1-55074-191-8*) Kids Can Pr.

Perlman, Jim. Walt Whitman: The Measure of His Song. 2nd ed. LC 98-14190. 536p. 1998. pap. text 20.00 (*0-930100-78-6*) Holy Cow.

Perlman, John. Beacons Imaging Within - As Promises. (Chapbook Ser.). 25p. (Orig.). 1990. pap. 5.00 (*0-945112-08-4*) Generator Pr.

Perlman, K. Fingerstyle Guitar. 1980. 16.95 (*0-13-317214-7*) P-H.

Perlman, Kalman I. The Leasing Handbook: Everything Purchasing Managers Need to Know - Complete with Facts, Figures, Forms & Checklists. 350p. 1991. text 45.00 (*1-55738-242-5*, Irwn Prfssnl) McGraw-Hill Prof.

Perlman, Ken. Basic Clawhammer Banjo Solos. 36p. 1996. 17.95 incl. audio compact disk (*0-7866-2374-8*, 95548BCD) Mel Bay.

Perlman, Ken. Clawhammer Style Banjo: A Complete Guide for Beginning & Advanced Banjo Players. 2nd ed. 194p. 1989. reprint ed. pap. text 15.95 (*0-931759-33-1*) Centerstream Pub.

— Contemporary Fingerstyle Guitar. 2nd ed. 218p. 1989. pap. text 14.95 (*0-931759-37-4*) Centerstream Pub.

— The Fiddle Music of Prince Edward Island. 216p. 1996. pap. 22.95 (*0-7866-0363-1*, MB95393) Mel Bay.

Perlman, Ken. The Fiddle Music of Prince Edward Island. 216p. 1996. pap. 37.95 incl. audio compact disk (*0-7866-1310-6*, 95393CDP) Mel Bay.

Perlman, Ken. Fingerstyle Guitar. rev. ed. 242p. 1989. reprint ed. pap. 16.95 (*0-931759-11-0*) Centerstream Pub.

— Melodic Clawhammer. 1979. pap. 15.95 (*0-8256-0226-2*, OK63644, Oak) Music Sales.

Perlman, Lorraine. Having Little, Being Much: A Chronicle of Fredy Perlman's Fifty Years. (Illus.). 155p. 1989. pap. 3.50 (*0-934868-30-1*) Black & Red.

Perlman, Lorraine, tr. see Arshinov, Peter.

Perlman, Mark. The Character of Economic Thought, Economic Characters, & Economic Institutions: Selected Essays. LC 96-7707. 552p. (C). 1996. text 85.00 (*0-472-10711-9*, 10711) U of Mich Pr.

***Perlman, Mark.** Conceptual Flux - Mental Representation, Misrepresentation, & Concept Change. 464p. 2000. 196.00 (*0-7923-6215-2*) Kluwer Academic.

Perlman, Mark. Labor Union Theories in America. LC 76-8925. 313p. 1976. reprint ed. lib. bdg. 65.00 (*0-8371-8916-0*, PELU, Greenwood Pr) Greenwood.

— Machinists: A New Study in American Trade Unionism. LC 61-16695. (Wertheim Publications in Industrial Relations). (Illus.). 350p. 1961. 22.50 (*0-674-54050-6*) HUP.

— A Nurturing Father's Journal: Developing Attitudes & Skills for Male Nurturance. (Illus.). x, 125p. 1998. pap. text 12.00 (*0-9662927-0-7*) CGD Inc.

***Perlman, Mark.** A Nurturing Father's Journal: The Workbook for Strengthening Men's Parenting Skills & Attitudes. 2nd rev. ed. (Illus.). 152p. 2000. pap., wbk. ed. 22.00 (*0-9662927-2-3*) CGD Inc.

Perlman, Mark. The Nurturing Father's Program: Facilitator Manual. (Illus.). xvii, 98p. 1998. pap. text 45.00 (*0-9662927-1-5*) CGD Inc.

Perlman, Mark, ed. Human Resources in the Urban Economy. LC 63-22775. 279p. reprint ed. pap. 86.50 (*0-608-13103-2*, 205210400034) Bks Demand.

***Perlman, Mark & McCann, Charles R.** The Pillars of Economic Understanding: The Factor Markets. LC 99-53550. (Illus.). 400p. (C). 2000. text 79.50 (*0-472-11110-8*, 11110) U of Mich Pr.

Perlman, Mark & McCann, Charles R., Jr., eds. The Pillars of Economic Understanding: Ideas & Traditions. LC 98-8953. 680p. 1998. text 79.50 (*0-472-10907-3*, 10907) U of Mich Pr.

Perlman, Mark, jt. auth. see Baker, Timothy D.

Perlman, Mark, jt. ed. see Heertje, Arnold.

Perlman, Mark, jt. ed. see Helmstadter, Ernst.

Perlman, Mark, jt. ed. see Louca, Francisco.

Perlman, Mark, jt. ed. see Scherer, Frederic M.

Perlman, Mark, jt. ed. see Shionoya, Yuichi.

Perlman, Mark, jt. ed. see Weiermair, Klaus.

Perlman, Martin M., ed. see International Conference on Electrets, Charge Storage, & Transport in Dielectrics Staff.

Perlman, Max, et al. Residents Handbook of Neonatology. 2nd ed. 500p. 1999. pap. 34.95 (*1-55009-071-2*) DEKR.

Perlman, Meg & Dean, Kevin. Syd Solomon: A Dialogue with Nature. Chilson, Kathleen G., ed. LC 90-63244. (Illus.). 1990. pap. 9.95 (*0-916758-31-1*) Ringling Mus Art.

Perlman, Melissa, jt. auth. see Jackson, Joyce.

Perlman, Michael. Hiroshima Forever: The Ecology of Mourning. LC 95-16610. 160p. 1995. 19.95 (*1-886449-14-7*) Barrytown Ltd.

— Imaginal Memory & the Place of Hiroshima. LC 87-22322. 214p. (C). 1988. pap. text 21.95 (*0-88706-747-6*) State U NY Pr.

— The Power of Trees: The Reforesting of the Soul. LC 94-4552. 266p. (Orig.). 1994. pap. 17.00 (*0-88214-362-X*) Spring Pubns.

Perlman, Moshe. Yiddish As a Language of the People. 17.85 (*0-317-58555-X*) P-H.

***Perlman, P. & Wigzell, H., eds.** Vaccines. (Illus.). 550p. 1999. 375.00 (*3-540-64740-6*) Spr-Verlag.

Perlman, Peter. Annotated Opening Statements. rev. ed. ATLA Press Staff, ed. LC 94-15354. (Illus.). 165p. 1994. pap. 42.00 (*0-941916-69-3*) West Group.

— Components of a Trial: Opening Statements. 100p. 23.00 (*0-941916-57-X*) West Group.

Perlman, Radia. Interconnections: Bridges, Routers & Switches. 2nd ed. LC 99-37086. 560p. 1999. 59.95 (*0-201-63448-1*) Addison-Wesley.

Perlman, Richard. Couch Potato Mashes on Simpson Trials: A Fresh Perspective on the Simpson Circus by a Man Born to Watch. Shelly, Tim & Ivone, Sal, eds. (Illus.). vii, 156p. (Orig.). 1996. pap., per. 7.95 (*0-9654611-0-6*) Pearl Productions.

Perlman, Richard, jt. auth. see Hughes, James J.

Perlman, Robert. Bridging Three Worlds: Hungarian-Jewish Americans, 1848-1914. LC 90-11224. 320p. (C). 1991. lib. bdg. 40.00 (*0-87023-468-4*) U of Mass Pr.

— Consumers & Social Services. LC 73-89037. 716p. reprint ed. pap. 200.00 (*0-608-08671-1*, 206919400003) Bks Demand.

Perlman, Robert, ed. Family Home Care: Critical Issues for Services & Policies. LC 83-81. (Home Health Care Services Quarterly Ser.: Vol. 3, Nos. 3 & 4). 294p. 1983. text 49.95 (*0-86656-220-6*) Haworth Pr.

Perlman, Robert L., jt. ed. see Dun, Nae J.

Perlman, Robert W. & Furst, Arthur Y., eds. Architectural Design Collaborators, No. 3. (Illus.). 256p. 1992. pap. write for info. (*0-9624219-4-4*) Perlman Stearns.

Perlman, Ruthie. Daniel My Son. LC 94-70750. 200p. 1994. 16.95 (*1-56062-258-X*) CIS Comm.

— Getting It Right. LC 90-84360. 225p. 1990. 15.95 (*1-56062-050-1*); pap. 12.95 (*1-56062-051-X*) CIS Comm.

— Working It Out. LC 90-82185. (YA). (gr. 7 up). 1990. 15.95 (*1-56062-033-1*); pap. 12.95 (*1-56062-035-8*) CIS Comm.

Perlman, Sandra. Nightwalking: Voices from Kent State. 80p. (Orig.). 1995. pap. 10.00 (*1-885663-01-3*) Franklin Mills.

Perlman, Selig. Selig Perlman's Lectures on Capitalism & Socialism. LC 74-27312. 203p. reprint ed. pap. 63.00 (*0-8357-6791-4*, 203546800095) Bks Demand.

— A Theory of the Labor Movement. LC 66-18323. (Reprints of Economic Classics Ser.). xii, 321p. 1966. reprint ed. 25.00 (*0-678-00025-5*) Kelley.

Perlman, Seth. Fund-Raising Regulation: A State-by-State Handbook of Registration Forms; Requirements & Procedures 1999 Supplement. 440p. 1999. pap., suppl. ed. 135.00 (*0-471-29877-8*) Wiley.

— Fund-Raising Regulation No. 2: A State-by-State Handbook Registration Forms, Requirements & Procedures, 1997 Cumulative Supplement, No. 2. 320p. 1997. pap., suppl. ed. 125.00 (*0-471-16617-0*, AC04) Wiley.

Perlman, Seth & Bush, Betsy H. Fund-Raising Regulation: A State-By-State Handbook of Registration Forms, Requirements & Procedures, Vol. 1. 1996. write for info. (*0-471-14248-4*) Wiley.

— Fund-Raising Regulation: A State-by-State Handbook of Registration Forms, Requirements & Procedures, 2 vols., Vol. 2. LC 95-23810. (Nonprofit Law, Finance, & Management Ser.). 1024p. 1996. 395.00 (*0-471-14253-0*) Wiley.

— Fund-Raising Regulation: A State-By-State Handbook of Registration Forms, Requirements & Procedures, Vol. 2. 1996. write for info. (*0-471-14251-4*) Wiley.

Perlman, Seth & Bush, Betsy Hills. Fund-Raising Regulation: A State-by-State Handbook of Registration Forms, Requirements, & Procedures, 2 vols. 208p. 1998. pap., suppl. ed. 125.00 (*0-471-15926-3*) Wiley.

***Perlman, Seth & Bush, Betsy Hills.** Fund-raising Regulation: A State-by-state Handbook of Registration Forms, Requirements, & Procedures. 528p. 1999. pap. 145.00 (*0-471-36132-1*) Wiley.

Perlman-Stearns Inc. Staff, ed. Architectural Design Collaborators Two: The Comprehensive Sourcebook for the Architectural & Design Communities. (Illus.). 320p. 1991. write for info. (*0-318-68296-6*); write for info. (*0-318-68298-2*); spiral bd. write for info. (*0-318-68297-4*) Perlman Stearns.

Perlman, Stuart D. The Therapist's Emotional Survival. LC 98-23701. (Illus.). xiv, 254 p. 1998. 40.00 (*0-7657-0175-8*) Aronson.

Perlman, Susan, ed. see Mendelsohn, Bob.

Perlman, William J., ed. The Movies on Trial: The Views & Opinions of Outstanding Personalities Anent Screen Entertainment Past & Present. LC 78-160245. (Moving Pictures Ser.). xi, 254p. 1971. reprint ed. lib. bdg. 31.95 (*0-89198-046-6*) Ozer.

Perlman, William S. No Bull: Object Technology for Executives. LC 99-18286. (Managing Object Technology Ser.: No. 18). (Illus.). 211p. (C). 1999. pap. 24.95 (*0-521-64548-4*) Cambridge U Pr.

Perlmann, Joel. Ethnic Differences: Schooling & Social Structure among the Irish, Italians, Jews & Blacks in an American City, 1880-1935. (Interdisciplinary Perspectives on Modern History Ser.). (Illus.). 339p. (C). 1989. pap. text 18.95 (*0-521-38975-5*) Cambridge U Pr.

— Reflecting the Changing Face of America. (Public Policy Brief Highlights Ser.: Vol. 35A). 6p. 1997. pap. text. write for info. (*0-941276-32-5*) J Levy.

— Reflecting the Changing Face of America: Multiracials, Racial Classification, & American Intermarriage. (Public Policy Briefs Ser.: Vol. 35). 48p. 1997. pap. text. write for info. (*0-941276-33-3*) J Levy.

Perlmann, Joel, jt. auth. see Vermeulen, Hans.

Perlmann, Mose, tr. see Brockelmann, Carl.

Perlmann, Moshe, ed. The History of al-Tabari Vol. 4: The Ancient Kingdoms. LC 85-17282. (SUNY Series in Near Eastern Studies). 205p. (C). 1987. text 57.50 (*0-88706-181-8*); pap. text 20.95 (*0-88706-182-6*) State U NY Pr.

Perlmann, Moshe, tr. see Al-Tabari.

Perlmann, Moshe, tr. see Yushmanov, N. V.

Perlmann, Peter, jt. ed. see Wahlgren, Mats.

Perlmon, Selig, et al. History of Labor in the United States: Labor Movements, Vol. 4. LC 66-18557. (Reprints of Economic Classics Ser.). v, 683p. 1966. reprint ed. 75.00 (*0-678-04039-7*) Kelley.

Perlmutt, David, jt. auth. see Peterson, Michael.

Perlmutter. Visions of War. 1999. text 26.95 (*0-312-20045-5*) St Martin.

Perlmutter, A., jt. ed. see Kursunoglu, Behram N.

Perlmutter, Amos. Egypt: The Praetorian State. LC 73-85100. (Third World Ser.). 232p. 1974. 39.95 (*0-87855-085-2*) Transaction Pubs.

— FDR & Stalin: A Not So Grand Alliance, 1943-1945. LC 93-4866. (Illus.). 352p. (C). 1993. 34.95 (*0-8262-0910-6*) U of Mo Pr.

— Making The World Safe for Democracy: A Century of Wilsonianism & Its Totalitarian Challengers. LC 97-9883. 216p. (C). (gr. 13). 1997. 34.95 (*0-8078-2365-1*) U of NC Pr.

— Military & Politics in Israel, 1948-1967: Nation Building & Role Expansion. 2nd rev. ed. (Illus.). 161p. 1977. 42.50 (*0-7146-2392-X*, Pub. by F Cass Pubs) Intl Spec Bk.

— Modern Authoritarianism: A Comparative Institutional Analysis. LC 81-3403. 208p. reprint ed. pap. 64.50 (*0-7837-3306-2*, 205770800006) Bks Demand.

— Political Roles & Military Rulers. 314p. 1981. 42.50 (*0-7146-3122-1*, Pub. by F Cass Pubs) Intl Spec Bk.

— Politics & the Military in Israel, 1967-1977. 1978. 27.50 (*0-7146-3079-9*, Pub. by F Cass Pubs) Intl Spec Bk.

Perlmutter, Amos & Bennett, Valerie P. The Political Influence of the Military: A Comparative Reader. LC 78-26154. 518p. reprint ed. pap. 160.60 (*0-8357-8275-1*, 203385500087) Bks Demand.

Perlmutter, Amos & Gooch, John, eds. Strategy & the Social Sciences: Issues in Defense Policy. 102p. 1981. 32.50 (*0-7146-3157-4*, Pub. by F Cass Pubs) Intl Spec Bk.

Perlmutter, Amos, jt. ed. see Gooch, John.

***Perlmutter, David.** BrainRecovery.com: Powerful Therapy for Challenging Brain Disorders. 2000. pap. 15.95 (*0-9635874-1-2*) D Perlmutter.

Perlmutter, David D. Photojournalism & Foreign Policy: Icons of Outrage in International Crises. LC 98-16908. (Praeger Series in Political Communication). 192p. 1998. 55.00 (*0-275-95812-4*, Praeger Pubs); pap. 17.95 (*0-275-96362-4*, Praeger Pubs) Greenwood.

***Perlmutter, David D.** Policing the Media: Street Cops & Public Perceptions of Law Enforcement. LC 99-50428. 160p. 2000. 69.95 (*0-7619-1104-9*) Sage.

Perlmutter, David D., ed. Manship School Guide to Political Communication. LC 99-23661. (Illus.). 400p. 1999. text 49.95 (*0-8071-2480-X*); pap. text 24.95 (*0-8071-2481-8*) La State U Pr.

Perlmutter, David M., ed. Studies in Relational Grammar 1. LC 82-6945. xvi, 428p. 1983. lib. bdg. 41.00 (*0-226-66050-8*) U Ch Pr.

— Studies in Relational Grammar 1. LC 82-6945. xvi, 428p. 1986. pap. text 19.50 (*0-226-66052-4*) U Ch Pr.

Perlmutter, David M., et al. Studies in Relational Grammar 2, No. 2. LC 82-6945. 404p. 1984. 42.00 (*0-226-66051-6*) U Ch Pr.

***Perlmutter, Dawn & Koppman, Debra.** Reclaiming the Spiritual in Art: Contemporary Cross-Cultural Perspectives. LC 98-30050. (Suny Series in Aesthetics & the Philosophy of Art). (C). 1999. text 54.50 (*0-7914-4161-X*) State U NY Pr.

Perlmutter, Dawn & Koppman, Debra. Reclaiming the Spiritual in Art: Contemporary Cross-Cultural Perspectives. LC 98-30050. (SUNY Series in Aesthetics & the Philosophy of Art). 168p. (C). 1999. pap. text 17.95 (*0-7914-4162-8*) State U NY Pr.

Perlmutter, Donna. Shadowplay: The Life of Antony Tudor. LC 94-39957. (Illus.). 432p. 1995. pap. 18.95 (*0-87910-189-X*) Limelight Edns.

Perlmutter, Felice D. Changing Hats: From Social Work Practice to Administration. LC 90-6436. 161p. 1990. pap. text 23.95 (*0-87101-184-0*) Natl Assn Soc Wkrs.

— From Welfare to Work: Corporate Initiatives & Welfare Reform. (Illus.). 144p. (C). 1997. pap. 18.95 (*0-19-511016-1*); text 36.95 (*0-19-511015-3*) OUP.

Perlmutter, Felice D., ed. Women & Social Change: Nonprofits & Social Policy. 188p. (Orig.). (C). 1994. lib. bdg. 24.95 (*0-87101-239-1*, 2391) Natl Assn Soc Wkrs.

Perlmutter, Felice D., intro. Alternative Social Agencies: Administrative Strategies. LC 88-4414. (Administration in Social Work Ser.: Vol. 12, No. 2). (Illus.). 128p. 1989. text 39.95 (*0-86656-783-6*) Haworth Pr.

Perlmutter, Felice D. & Slavin, Simon, eds. Leadership in Social Administration: Perspectives for the 1980s. 268p. 1980. pap. 19.95 (*0-87722-201-0*) Temple U Pr.

***Perlmutter, Felice Davidson, et al.** Managing Human Resources in the Human Services: Supervisory Challenges. LC 99-39955. (Illus.). 256p. 2000. text. write for info. (*0-19-512027-2*); pap. text. write for info. (*0-19-513707-8*) OUP.

Perlmutter, Gail, jt. auth. see Perlmutter, Rick.

Perlmutter, Gayle, jt. auth. see Perlmutter, Rick.

Perlmutter, Haim. Tools for Tosafos. LC 99-208853. 147p. 1996. 14.95 (*1-56871-093-3*) Targum Pr.

Perlmutter, Howard V. & Sagafi-Nejad, Tagi. International Technology Transfer: Guidelines, Codes & a Muffled Quadrilogue. LC 80-28322. (Policy Studies on Business & Economics). (Illus.). 250p. 1981. 68.00 (*0-08-027519-2*, Pergamon Pr) Elsevier.

Perlmutter, Marian, ed. Cognitive Perspectives on Children's Social & Behavioral Development: The Minnesota Symposia on Child Psychology, Vol. 18. 352p. (C). 1986. text 69.95 (*0-89859-546-0*) L Erlbaum Assocs.

Perlmutter, Marion, ed. Development & Policy Concerning Children with Special Needs. (Minnesota Symposia on Child Psychology Ser.: Vol. 16). 272p. (C). 1983. text 59.95 (*0-89859-261-5*) L Erlbaum Assocs.

— Parent-Child Interaction & Parent-Child Relations. (Minnesota Symposia on Child Psychology Ser.: Vol. 17). 208p. 1984. text 39.95 (*0-89859-380-8*) L Erlbaum Assocs.

— Perspectives on Intellectual Development. (Minnesota Symposia on Child Psychology Ser.: Vol. 19). 280p. (C). 1986. text 59.95 (*0-89859-784-6*) L Erlbaum Assocs.

Perlmutter, Marion & Hall, Elizabeth. Adult Development & Aging. 2nd ed. 608p. (C). 1992. text 80.95 (*0-471-51846-8*) Wiley.

Perlmutter, Marion, jt. ed. see Weinert, Franz E.

Perlmutter, Mark. Why Lawyers (& the Rest of Us) Lie. 1998. pap. 16.95 (*1-880092-47-6*) Bright Bks TX.

Perlmutter, Martin. Producer's Guide to Interactive Videodiscs. 160p. 1991. pap. text 56.95 (*0-86729-173-7*, Focal) Buttrwrth-Heinemann.

Perlmutter, P. Conjugate Addition Reactions in Organic Synthesis. (Organic Chemistry Ser.: No. 9). 394p. 1992. text 129.25 (*0-08-037066-7*, Pergamon Pr); pap. text 50.00 (*0-08-037067-5*, Pergamon Pr) Elsevier.

Perlmutter, Philip. Divided We Fall: A History of Ethnic, Religious, & Racial Prejudice in America. LC 90-20153. 414p. 1992. text 54.95 (*0-8138-0644-5*) Iowa St U Pr.

— The Dynamics of American Ethnic, Religious, & Racial Group Life: An Interdisciplinary Overview. LC 95-50470. 256p. 1996. 65.00 (*0-275-95533-8*, Praeger Pubs) Greenwood.

***Perlmutter, Philip.** Legacy of Hate: A Short History of Ethnic, Religious & Racial Prejudice in America. LC 99-11648. 344p. 1999. text 34.95 (*0-7656-0406-X*) M E Sharpe.

Perlmutter, Richard A. A Family Approach to Psychiatric Disorders. 416p. 1996. text 52.95 (*0-88048-714-3*, 8714) Am Psychiatric.

***Perlmutter, Rick & Gayle.** Walt Disney World for Couples. 1999. pap. 16.00 (*0-7615-2219-0*) Prima Pub.

Perlmutter, Rick & Perlmutter, Gail. Walt Disney World for Lovers. 336p. 1996. pap. 14.95 (*0-7615-0321-8*) Prima Pub.

Perlmutter, Rick & Perlmutter, Gayle. Walt Disney World for Couples. 2nd rev. ed. LC 97-5569. 368p. 1997. per. 15.00 (*0-7615-0940-2*) Prima Pub.

— Walt Disney World for Couples, 1999-2000: With or Without Kids. 400p. 1998. pap. 16.00 (*0-7615-1633-6*) Prima Pub.

Perlo, Ber Van, see Van Perlo, Ber.

Perlo, Ber Van, see Taylor, Barry.

Perlo, Victor. American Labor Today. 1968. pap. 0.25 (*0-87898-029-6*) New Outlook.

— Dollar Crisis: What It Means to You. 1969. pap. 0.40 (*0-87898-033-4*) New Outlook.

An Asterisk (*) at the beginning of an entry indicates that the title is appearing for the first time.

— Economics of Racism, U. S. A. Roots of Black Inequality. LC 75-9911. (Illus.). 296p. reprint ed. pap. 91.80 (*0-8357-4763-8*, 203769000009) Bks Demand.
— End Fascist Terror & U. S. Imperialism in Chile! 56p. 1974. pap. 0.75 (*0-87898-110-1*) New Outlook.
— Marines in Santo Domingo! 1965. pap. 0.20 (*0-87898-004-0*) New Outlook.
— Superprofits & Crises: Modern U. S. Capitalism. LC 88-2925. (Illus.). 568p. (C). 1988. 21.00 (*0-7178-0665-0*); pap. 9.95 (*0-7178-0662-6*) Intl Pubs Co.
Perlo, Victor, et al. The Economics of Racism II. LC 96-7304. (Illus.). 320p. 1996. pap. 9.75 (*0-7178-0698-7*) Intl Pubs Co.
— The Economics of Racism II: The Roots of Inequality, USA. LC 96-7304. (Illus.). 320p. 1996. lib. bdg. 18.50 (*0-7178-0697-9*) Intl Pubs Co.
Perloff. Clinical Recognition of Congenital Heart Disease. 4th ed. (C). 1998. text. write for info. (*0-8089-2148-7*, Grune & Strat) Harcrt Hlth Sci Grp.
— Congenital Heart Disease in Adults. 2nd ed. (C). 1998. text. write for info. (*0-8089-2149-5*, Grune & Strat) Harcrt Hlth Sci Grp.
PERLOFF. Perloff's Instructors Manual. (C). 1998. pap. text 24.00 (*0-201-83421-9*) Addison-Wesley.
***Perloff.** Wittgenstein's Ladder. 1999. pap. 16.00 (*0-226-66060-5*) U Ch Pr.
Perloff, Carol B. The Asylum: The History of Friends Hospital & the Quaker Contribution to Psychiatry. LC 94-72152. (Illus.). 55p. 1994. write for info. (*0-9642252-0-4*) Frnds Hosp.
Perloff, Harvey S. Puerto Rico's Economic Future: A Study in Planned Development. LC 74-14240. (Puerto Rican Experience Ser.). (Illus.). 484p. 1975. reprint ed. 52.95 (*0-405-06228-1*) Ayer.
Perloff, Harvey S., ed. The Quality of the Urban Environment: Essays on "New Resources" in an Urban Age. LC 69-16858. 332p. 1969. pap. 14.95 (*0-8018-1028-0*) Resources Future.
Perloff, Harvey S. & Dodds, Vera W. How a Region Grows: Area Development in the U. S. Economy. LC 84-691. 147p. (C). 1984. lib. bdg. 55.00 (*0-313-23152-4*, PEHG, Greenwood Pr) Greenwood.
Perloff, Harvey S. & Wingo, Lowdon, eds. Issues in Urban Economics. 680p. 1968. 30.00 (*0-8018-0528-7*) Johns Hopkins.
— Issues in Urban Economics. 668p. 1968. pap. 20.00 (*0-8018-0529-5*) Resources Future.
Perloff, Harvey S., ed. see Heller, Walter, et al.
***Perloff, James.** Tornado in a Junkyard: The Relentless Myth of Darwinism. LC 98-92197. (Illus.). 321p. 1999. pap. 16.95 (*0-9668160-0-5*) Refuge Bks.
Perloff, Janet D., et al. Medicaid & Pediatric Primary Care. LC 87-3164. (Johns Hopkins Series in Contemporary Medicine & Public Health). 208p. reprint ed. pap. 64.50 (*0-608-06185-9*, 206651700008) Bks Demand.
Perloff, Jeff. Intermediate Microeconomics. 304p. (C). 1998. pap. text, student ed. 25.00 (*0-201-38069-2*); pap. text, student ed. 139.00 (*0-201-38071-4*) Addison-Wesley.
***Perloff, Jeffrey M.** Microeconomics: Incentives in an Imperfect World. LC 98-23043. 800p. (C). 1998. 98.00 (*0-201-59137-5*); pap. text 67.00 (*0-201-38063-3*) Addison-Wesley.
— Microeconomics: Incentives in an Imperfect World. (C). 1999. write for info. (*0-201-70254-1*) Addison-Wesley.
— Microeconomics: Incentives in an Imperfect World. 2nd ed. LC 00-33190. 2001. write for info. (*0-201-63773-1*) Addison-Wesley.
Perloff, Joseph K. The Clinical Recognition of Congenital Heart Disease. 4th ed. LC 93-32195. 1994. text 135.00 (*0-7216-5504-1*, W B Saunders Co) Harcrt Hlth Sci Grp.
— Physical Examination of the Heart & Circulation. 2nd ed. (Illus.). 304p. 1989. pap. text 39.00 (*0-7216-7189-6*, W B Saunders Co) Harcrt Hlth Sci Grp.
***Perloff, Joseph K.** Physical Examination of the Heart & Circulation. 3rd ed. LC 99-49763. (Illus.). 300p. 2000. pap. text. write for info. (*0-7216-8321-5*, W B Saunders Co) Harcrt Hlth Sci Grp.
Perloff, Joseph K. & Child, John S. Congenital Heart Disease in Adults. 2nd ed. LC 96-50089. (Illus.). 352p. 1997. text 110.00 (*0-7216-2998-9*, W B Saunders Co) Harcrt Hlth Sci Grp.
Perloff, Joseph K., jt. auth. see Carlton, Dennis.
Perloff, Marjorie. The Dance of the Intellect: Studies in the Poetry of the Pound Tradition. (Avant-Garde & Modernism Studies). 256p. 1996. pap. text 16.95 (*0-8101-1380-5*) Northwestern U Pr.
— Frank O'Hara. LC 97-36184. 234p. 1997. pap. text 16.95 (*0-226-66059-1*) U Ch Pr.
— The Futurist Moment: Avant-Garde, Avant Guerre & the Language of Rupture. LC 86-3147. (Illus.). 288p. (C). 1994. 24.95 (*0-226-65731-0*) U Ch Pr.
— The Futurist Moment: Avant-Garde, Avant Guerre & the Language of Rupture. LC 86-3147. (Illus.). 312p. (C). 1997. pap. 19.95 (*0-226-65732-9*) U Ch Pr.
— Poetic License: Essays on Modernist & Postmodernist Lyric. (Illus.). 352p. 1990. 49.95 (*0-8101-0843-7*); pap. 18.95 (*0-8101-0844-5*) Northwestern U Pr.
— The Poetics of Indeterminacy: Rimbaud to Cage. LC 99-46824. 368p. 1999. pap. 18.95 (*0-8101-1764-9*) Northwestern U Pr.
— The Poetics of Indeterminacy: Rimbaud to Cage. 346p. 1981. reprint ed. pap. 18.95 (*0-8101-0661-2*) Northwestern U Pr.
— The Poetics on Indeterminacy: Rimbaud to Cage. LC 80-8569. (Illus.). 363p. 1981. reprint ed. pap. 112.60 (*0-608-02540-2*, 206318400004) Bks Demand.
— Poetry on & off the Page: Essays for Emergent Occasions. LC 97-50432. (Avant-Garde & Modernism Studies). 320p. 1998. 79.95 (*0-8101-1560-3*); pap. 19.95 (*0-8101-1561-1*) Northwestern U Pr.
— Radical Artifice: Writing Poetry in the Age of Media. (Illus.). 264p. 1992. 32.50 (*0-226-65733-7*) U Ch Pr.
— Radical Artifice: Writing Poetry in the Age of Media. xvi, 264p. 1994. pap. text 15.00 (*0-226-65734-5*) U Ch Pr.
— Rhyme & Meaning in the Poetry of Yeats. LC 78-102959. (De Proprietatibus Litterarum, Ser. Practica). (Illus.). 1970. pap. text 53.85 (*90-279-0510-X*) Mouton.
— Wittgenstein's Ladder: Poetic Language & the Strangeness of the Ordinary. LC 95-47873. (Illus.). 300p. (C). 1996. 27.95 (*0-226-66058-3*) U Ch Pr.
Perloff, Marjorie, ed. Postmodern Genres. LC 89-40220. (Oklahoma Project for Discourse & Theory Ser.). (Illus.). 288p. 1995. pap. 14.95 (*0-8061-2715-5*) U of Okla Pr.
Perloff, Marjorie & Junkerman, Charles, eds. John Cage: Composed in America. LC 93-36325. 296p. (C). 1994. pap. 16.95 (*0-226-66057-5*) U Ch Pr.
— John Cage: Composed in America. LC 93-36325. (C). 1995. lib. bdg. 45.00 (*0-226-66056-7*) U Ch Pr.
Perloff, Nancy. Art & the Everyday: Popular Entertainment & the Circle of Erik Satie. (Illus.). 238p. 1994. reprint ed. pap. text 19.95 (*0-19-816398-3*) OUP.
Perloff, Richard. The Dynamics of Persuasion. (LEA's Communication Ser.). 424p. (C). 1993. pap. 36.00 (*0-8058-1377-2*) L Erlbaum Assocs.
— Political Communication: Issues, Ideas, Impact. LC 97-21794. (Communication Ser.). 375p. 1997. write for info. (*0-8058-1794-8*) L Erlbaum Assocs.
— Political Communication: Politics, Press, & Public in America. LC 97-21794. (Communication Ser.). 1997. pap. 45.00 (*0-8058-1795-6*) L Erlbaum Assocs.
***Perloff, Richard M.** Persuading People to Have Safer Sex: Application of Social Science to the AIDS Crisis. (A Volume in LEA's Communication Series). 280p. 2000. write for info. (*0-8058-3380-3*); pap. write for info. (*0-8058-3381-1*) L Erlbaum Assocs.
Perloff, Richard M., jt. ed. see Kraus, Sidney.
Perloff, Robert, jt. ed. see Pallak, Michael S.
Perloff, Robert O., jt. ed. see Pallak, Michael S.
Perloff, Stephen & Callaghan, Charles, photos by. Anthonisen: Woodmere Art Museum Exhibit. (Illus.). 36p. (Orig.). 1992. pap. 12.00 (*0-9634109-0-3*) Anthonisen.
Perloff, Susan. Pennsylvania: Off the Beaten Path. 5th ed. LC 99-48818. (Off the Beaten Path Ser.). (Illus.). 192p. 1999. pap. text 12.95 (*0-7627-0462-4*) Globe Pequot.
Perlongo, Bob. Early American Advertising. LC 84-71519. 192p. 1985. pap. 9.95 (*0-88108-015-2*) Art Dir.
Perlot, Jean-Nicolas. Gold Seeker: Adventures of a Belgian Argonaut During the Gold Rush Years. Lamar, Howard R., ed. Bretnor, Helen H., tr. (Yale Western Americana Ser.). (Illus.). 452p. 1985. pap. 18.00 (*0-300-07645-2*) Yale U Pr.
Perlov, N. I. English-Russian Metallurgical Dictionary. 842p. (C). 1985. 200.00 (*0-7855-5005-4*, Pub. by Collets) St Mut.
— English Russian Metallurgical Dictionary. (ENG & RUS.). 1985. 150.00 (*0-8288-3927-1*, F35840) Fr & Eur.
Perlov, N. I., et al. English - Russian Metallurgical Dictionary. 2nd ed. (ENG & RUS.). 841p. (C). 1985. reprint ed. 37.95 (*0-8285-5246-0*) Firebird NY.
Perlove, Shelley. Bernini & the Idealization of Death: The Blessed Ludovica Albertoni & the Altieri Chapel. LC 89-16336. (Illus.). 152p. 1990. lib. bdg. 38.50 (*0-271-00684-6*) Pa St U Pr.
— Bernini & the Idealization of Death: The "Blessed Ludovica Albertoni" & the Altieri Chapel. (Illus.). 152p. 1990. pap. 25.00 (*0-271-01477-6*) Pa St U Pr.
Perlove, Shelley K. Impressions of Faith: Rembrandt's Biblical Etchings. (Illus.). 80p. (Orig.). 1989. pap. text 10.00 (*0-933691-02-5*) U Mich-Dearborn.
— Renaissance, Reform, Reflections in the Age of Durer, Bruegel, & Rembrandt. (Illus.). 152p. (Orig.). 1994. pap. 18.00 (*0-933691-05-X*) U Mich-Dearborn.
Perlovsky, Leonid. Neural Networks & Intellect: Using Model Based Concepts. (Illus.). 640p. (C). 2000. pap. 79.00 (*0-19-511162-1*) OUP.
Perlow, Gilbert J., ed. Workshop on New Directions in Mossbauer Spectroscopy, Argonne National Lab, June 1977. LC 77-90635. (AIP Conference Proceedings Ser.: No. 38). (Illus.). 1977. lib. bdg. 15.00 (*0-88318-137-1*) Am Inst Physics.
Perlow, Jon. The Thinking Person's Guide to Permanent Weight Loss. LC 85-52342. 190p. (Orig.). 1986. pap. 9.95 (*0-936877-02-2*) Twining Pr.
Perlow, Leslie A. Finding Time: New Work Practice. LC 97-14969. (Collection on Technology & Work Ser.). 176p. 1997. pap. 13.95 (*0-8014-8445-6*) Cornell U Pr.
Perlow, Meir. Understanding Mental Objects. LC 94-45147. (New Library of Psychoanalysis Ser.). 224p. (C). 1995. pap. 27.99 (*0-415-12179-5*, C0225) Routledge.
— Understanding Mental Objects. LC 94-45147. (New Library of Psychoanalysis Ser.). 224p. (C). (gr. 13). 1995. 85.00 (*0-415-12178-7*, C0224) Routledge.
Perlowin, David. General Care & Maintenance of Common Kingsnakes. 71p. 1993. pap. text 11.50 (*1-882770-20-X*) Adv Vivarium.
— General Care & Maintenance of Garter Snakes & Water Snakes. 71p. 1994. pap. text 7.50 (*1-882770-26-9*) Adv Vivarium.
***Perlowin, Michael.** Music Theory in the Real World - A Practical Guide - Todays Music. 48p. 2000. pap. 9.95 (*0-7866-4526-1*, 98207) Mel Bay.
Perlroth, Karen, jt. auth. see Perlroth, Karen A.
Perlroth, Karen A. & Perlroth, Karen. Freedom from Back Pain: The Mensendieck System. 141p. 10.95 incl. audio (*1-880688-05-0*) New Life Opt.
Perlroth, Mark G. & Weiland, Douglass J. Fifty Diseases, Fifty Diagnoses. LC 81-3318. 346p. reprint ed. pap. 107.30 (*0-8357-7598-4*, 205691900096) Bks Demand.
Perls, Frederick. Ego, Hunger, & Aggression: A Revision of Freud's Theory & Method. 286p. 1992. reprint ed. pap. 22.00 (*0-939266-18-0*) Gestalt Journal.
— Gestalt Therapy Verbatim. rev. ed. Wysong, Joe, ed. 304p. 1992. pap. 22.00 (*0-939266-16-4*) Gestalt Journal.
— In & Out the Garbage Pail. (Illus.). 288p. 1992. reprint ed. pap. 20.00 (*0-939266-17-2*) Gestalt Journal.
Perls, Frederick, et al. Gestalt Therapy: Excitement & Growth in the Human Personality. rev. ed. (Illus.). 496p. 1994. pap. 28.00 (*0-939266-24-5*) Gestalt Journal.
Perls, Fritz. The Gestalt Approach & Eyewitness to Therapy. 1973. pap. 13.95 (*0-8314-0034-X*) Sci & Behavior.
Perls, Jeffrey, jt. auth. see Woodsmall, Marilyne.
Perls, Laura P. Living at the Boundary: The Collected Works of Laura Perls. 240p. 1991. text 35.00 (*0-939266-15-6*) Gestalt Journal.
Perls, Thomas, et al. Living to Be 100: Life Lessons from the Landmark Harvard Medical School Study. (Illus.). 31p. 2000. 25.00 (*0-465-04142-6*, Pub. by Basic) HarpC.
***Perls, Thomas T.** Living to 100: Lessons in Living to Your Maximum Potential at Any Age. 2000. pap. 14.00 (*0-465-04143-4*, Pub. by Basic) HarpC.
***Perls, Thomas T., et al.** Living to 100: Lessons in Living to Your Maximum Potential at Any Age. large type ed. LC 99-45855. 1999. 26.95 (*0-7862-2221-2*) Thorndike Pr.
Perlson, Michael R. How to Understand & Influence People & Organizations: Practical Psychology for Goal Achievement. LC 81-69357. 300p. reprint ed. pap. 93.00 (*0-608-12862-7*, 202357700033) Bks Demand.
Perlstein, Gary R., jt. auth. see Vetter, Harold J.
***Perlstein, Rick.** Before the Storm: Barry Goldwater & the Unmaking of the American Consensus. (Illus.). 400p. 2001. 25.00 (*0-8090-2859-X*) Hill & Wang.
Perlstein, Ruth & Thrall, Gloria. Ready-to-Use Conflict Resolution Activities for Secondary Students: Strategies for Dealing with Conflict in Real-Life Situations, Plus Guidelines for Creating a Peer Mediation Program. LC 95-23617. 368p. 1995. pap. text 29.95 (*0-87628-195-1*) Ctr Appl Res.
Perlstein, Scott. Essential Tennis. (Illus.). 192p. 1993. pap. 13.95 (*1-55821-220-5*) Lyons Pr.
— Winning Doubles. (Illus.). 224p. 1995. pap. 18.95 (*1-55821-330-9*) Lyons Pr.
— Winning Tennis. McConnell, Joanne, ed. LC 98-48034. (Illus.). 160p. 1999. pap. 16.95 (*1-55821-900-5*) Lyons Pr.
Perlstein, Steve. Rebel Baseball: The Summer the Game Was Returned to the Fans. LC 94-42570. 1995. pap. 12.95 (*0-8050-3953-8*, Owl) H Holt & Co.
Perlwitz, Ellen C. Charlie's Little Moon Trip. LC 91-77577. (Illus.). 32p. (J). (gr. k-3). 1992. 7.95 (*1-880851-01-6*) Greene Bark Pr.
Perly, Daniel R. Implementing Open Systems. LC 95-1106. 1995. text 40.00 (*0-07-707948-5*) McGraw.
Perlzweig, Judith. Lamps from the Athenian Agora. (Excavations of the Athenian Agora Picture Bks.: No. 9). (Illus.). 32p. 1964. pap. 3.00 (*0-87661-609-0*) Am Sch Athens.
— Lamps of the Roman Period, First to Seventh Century after Christ. (Athenian Agora Ser.: Vol. 7). (Illus.). xv, 240p. 1971. reprint ed. 35.00 (*0-87661-207-9*) Am Sch Athens.
Permaloff, Anne & Grafton, Carl. Political Power in Alabama: The More Things Change. LC 94-38515. 1995. 50.00 (*0-8203-1721-7*) U of Ga Pr.
Perman, Jane, jt. auth. see Patz, Naomi.
Perman, Jay A., et al. Clinical Trials in Infant Nutrition: Methodology, Statistics, & Ethical Issues. LC 97-24179. (Nestle Nutrition Workshop Ser.). 352p. 1998. text 70.00 (*0-7817-1564-4*) Lppncott W & W.
Perman, Lauri. The Other Side of the Coin: The Nonmonetary Characteristics of Jobs. LC 90-29089. (Harvard Studies in Sociology: Outstanding Dissertations & Monographs Twenty-Two Distinguished Works from the Past Fifty Years). 392p. 1991. text 30.00 (*0-8240-9265-1*) Garland.
Perman, Michael. Emancipation & Reconstruction, 1862-1879. Eisenstadt, A. S. & Franklin, John H., eds. LC 86-19889. (American History Ser.). 168p. (C). 1987. pap. text 11.95 (*0-88295-836-4*) Harlan Davidson.
***Perman, Michael.** Major Problems in the Civil War & Reconstruction: Documents & Essays. 2nd ed. LC 97-72533. (Major Problems in American History Ser.). 1998. 31.56 (*0-395-86849-1*) HM.
Perman, Michael. Perspective on the American Past Vol. 1: Readings & Commentary, 1620-1877. 2nd ed. LC 95-76581. 326p. (C). 1996. pap. text 29.16 (*0-669-39720-2*) HM Trade Div.
— Perspectives on the American Past Vol. 2: Readings & Commentary: Since 1865. 2nd ed. LC 95-76581. 363p. (C). 1996. pap. text 29.16 (*0-669-39721-0*) HM Trade Div.
— The Road to Redemption: Southern Politics, 1869-1879. LC 83-12498. (Fred W. Morrison Series in Southern Studies). xiv, 353p. 1985. pap. text 14.95 (*0-8078-4141-2*) U of NC Pr.
***Perman, Michael.** Struggle for Mastery: Disfranchisement in the South, 1888-1908. LC 00-41773. (Fred W. Morrison Series in Southern Studies). 2001. pap. write for info. (*0-8078-4909-X*) U of NC Pr.
Perman, Michael, ed. The Coming of the American Civil War. 3rd ed. (Problems in American Civilization Ser.). 322p. (C). 1993. pap. text 18.36 (*0-669-27106-3*) HM Trade Div.
— Major Problems in the Civil War & Reconstruction: Documents & Essays. LC 90-81121. (Major Problems in American History Ser.). 598p. (C). 1991. pap. text 29.16 (*0-669-20148-0*) HM Trade Div.
Perman, Roger. Natural Resource & Environmental Economics. 2nd ed. LC 99-21560. 1999. pap. text. write for info. (*0-582-36876-6*) Addison-Wesley.
Perman, Roger & Scouller, John. Business Economics. LC 98-37832. (Illus.). 336p. 1999. text 75.00 (*0-19-877525-3*); pap. text 35.00 (*0-19-877524-5*) OUP.
Perman, Victor, et al. Cytology of the Dog & Cat. 159p. 1979. pap. text 35.00 (*0-9616498-1-X*) Am Animal Hosp Assoc.
Permane, Terry, jt. photos by see Mitton, David.
Permanent Bureau of the Hague Conference on Privat, ed. Recueil des Conventions: Collection of Conventions, 1951-1996. 407p. 1997. pap. 34.00 (*90-6215-558-8*) Kluwer Academic.
Permanent Commission & International Association S, jt. auth. see IUPAC Staff.
***Permanent Court of Arbitration Staff & Carnegie Endowment for International Peace Staff.** Great Britain, Spain & France Versus Portugal in the Matter of the Expropriated Religious Properties in Portugal. LC 99-47541. 2000. write for info. (*1-57588-590-5*) W S Hein.
Permanent Court of International Justice Staff. Hague, Permanent Court of International Justice, 9 bks. 1996. reprint ed. 995.00 (*1-57588-181-0*, 310820) W S Hein.
Permanent International Altaistic Conference Staff. Aspects of Altaic Civilization: Proceedings, Vol. 23. Francis, David & Sinor, Denis, eds. LC 80-28299. (Uralic & Altaic Ser.: Vol. 23). 263p. 1981. reprint ed. lib. bdg. 65.00 (*0-313-22945-7*, PIAA) Greenwood.
— Aspects of Altaic Civilization II: Proceedings. Draghi, Paul A. & Clark, Larry V., eds. (Uralic & Altaic Ser.: Vol. 134). 212p. 1978. 34.00 (*0-933070-02-0*) Res Inst Inner Asian Studies.
Permanent International Committee on Linguistics S, ed. Bibliographie Linguistique 1939-1975. 1986. lib. bdg. write for info. (*90-247-3320-0*) Kluwer Academic.
Permanent Section of Microbiological Standardizati. Interferon & Interferon Inducers. Perkins, F. T. & Regamey, R. H., eds. (Immunobiological Standardization Symposia Ser.: Vol. 14). 1970. 26.25 (*3-8055-0637-6*) S Karger.
Permanente, Kaiser. Health Counts: A Fat & Calorie Guide. LC 90-38128. 272p. 1991. pap. 16.95 (*0-471-52949-4*) Wiley.
Permanyer, Lluis. Barcelona Art Nouveau. Rees, Richard, tr. (Illus.). 159p. 1999. 50.00 (*0-8478-2220-6*, Pub. by Rizzoli Intl) St Martin.
— Clave: Sculptor. (Great Monographs). (Illus.). 288p. 1993. 250.00 (*84-343-0633-6*) Elliots Bks.
— Tapies y la Nueva Cultura. (Grandes Monografias). (SPA., Illus.). 216p. 1993. 350.00 (*84-343-0470-8*) Elliots Bks.
Permanyer, Lluis & Levick, Melba. Gaudi of Barcelona. LC 97-67801. (Illus.). 188p. 1997. 50.00 (*0-8478-2062-9*, Pub. by Rizzoli Intl) St Martin.
Permenter, Diane. Oh Those Little Rascals. 100p. 1991. pap. text 10.50 (*1-56770-247-3*) S Scheewe Pubns.
Permenter, P. & Bigley, J. Antigua, Barbuda, St. Kitts & Nevis Alive! (Alive Guides Ser.). 400p. 1999. pap. 16.95 (*1-55650-880-8*) Hunter NJ.
— Jamaica Adventure Guide. 4th rev. ed. (Adventure Guides Ser.). (Illus.). 360p. 1999. pap. 16.95 (*1-55650-885-9*) Hunter NJ.
— Jamaica Alive. (Alive Guides Ser.). 400p. 1999. pap. 15.95 (*1-55650-882-4*) Hunter NJ.
— Nassau & the Best of the Bahamas Alive! (Alive Guides Ser.). 400p. 1999. pap. write for info. (*1-55650-883-2*) Hunter NJ.
Permenter, Paris. Caribbean for Lovers. 320p. 1996. pap., per. 15.00 (*0-7615-0627-6*) Prima Pub.
Permenter, Paris. Caribbean with Kids. 360p. 1998. pap. text 14.95 (*1-883323-82-7*) Open Rd Pub.
Permenter, Paris & Bigley, John. Adventure Guide to the Cayman Islands. 280p. (Orig.). 1997. pap. 16.95 (*1-55650-786-0*) Hunter NJ.
— Adventure Guide to the Leeward Islands. (Illus.). 320p. (Orig.). 1997. pap. 14.95 (*1-55650-788-7*) Hunter NJ.
***Permenter, Paris & Bigley, John.** Antigua, Barbuda, Nevis, St. Barts, St. Kitts & St. Martin. 2nd expanded ed. (Adventure Guides Ser.). (Illus.). 360p. 2000. pap. 16.95 (*1-55650-909-X*) Hunter NJ.
Permenter, Paris & Bigley, John. The Cayman Islands. (Alive Guides Ser.). (Illus.). 360p. 1999. pap. 16.95 (*1-55650-862-X*) Hunter NJ.
***Permenter, Paris & Bigley, John.** The Cayman Islands. 2nd ed. (Adventure Guides Ser.). (Illus.). 320p. 2000. pap. 17.95 (*1-55650-915-4*) Hunter NJ.
Permenter, Paris & Bigley, John. Gourmet Getaways: A Taste of North America's Top Resorts. (Illus.). 176p. 1997. pap. 24.95 (*1-896511-07-4*) Callawind.
***Permenter, Paris & Bigley, John.** Gourmet Getaways: A Taste of North America's Top Resorts. (Illus.). 176p. (C). 1999. reprint ed. pap. text 25.00 (*0-7881-6674-3*) DIANE Pub.
— National Parks with Kids. 360p. 1999. pap. 14.95 (*1-892975-06-8*) Open Rd Pub.
— Romantic Escapes in the Caribbean: Lovetrippers Guide. 2nd ed. (Romantic Weekends Ser.). (Illus.). 320p. 2000. pap. 15.95 (*1-55650-914-6*) Hunter NJ.
Permenter, Paris & Bigley, John. Shifra Stein's Day Trips from Austin: Getaways Less Than Two Hours Away. LC 99-47442. (Day Trips Ser.). (Illus.). 176p. 1999. pap. text 14.95 (*0-7627-0543-4*) Globe Pequot.
— Shifra Stein's Day Trips from San Antonio: Getaways Less Than Two Hours Away. LC 99-45058. (Day Trips Ser.). 176p. 1999. pap. text 14.95 (*0-7627-0542-6*) Globe Pequot.
— A Taste of Jamaica: Where to Find the Very Best Jamaican Food. (Taste of . . . Ser.). (Illus.). 276p. 1998. pap. 15.95 (*1-55650-833-6*) Hunter NJ.
— A Taste of the Bahamas: Where to Find the Very Best Bahamian Food. (Taste of . . . Ser.). (Illus.). 276p. 1998. pap. 15.95 (*1-55650-832-8*) Hunter NJ.
— Texas Barbeque. 160p. (Orig.). 1994. pap. 14.95 (*0-925175-20-X*) Pig Out Pubns.

P

— Texas Gateways for Two. (Illus.). 200p. (Orig.). 1996. pap. 14.95 (1-878686-24-0) Pig Out Pubns.

Permiakov, Eugene A. Luminescent Spectroscopy of Proteins. 176p. 1992. lib. bdg. 110.00 (0-8493-4553-7, QP551) CRC Pr.

Permin, A., jt. ed. see Uilenberg, G.

Perminov, A. M., tr. see Divin, V. A., et al.

***Perminov, V. G.** Difficult Road to Mars: A Brief History of Mars Exploration in the Soviet Union. 79p. 1999. pap. 9.00 (0-16-058859-6) USGPO.

***Permut, Bess S.** Heaven on Earth Is a Mission. LC 87-92255. (Living on the Pathway to Heaven Ser.). 300p. 1998. pap. 16.95 (0-9672184-1-1) Pesha Pubg.

— How to Find Your Way Back Home. LC 87-92255. 220p. 1984. reprint ed. pap. 16.95 (0-9672184-0-3) Pesha Pubg.

Permut, Joanna B. Embracing the Wolf: A Lupus Victim & Her Family Learn to Live with Chronic Disease. Selph, Alexa M., ed. LC 88-9193. 192p. 1989. 14.95 (0-87797-166-8) Cherokee.

Permut, Steven E., ed. American Academy of Advertising Annual Meeting: 21st Proceedings. 1979. pap. 25.00 (0-931030-02-1) Am Acad Advert.

Permut, Steven E., ed. see Mauser, Gary A.

Permut, Steven E., jt. ed. see Mokwa, Michael P.

Permut, Steven E., ed. see Mokwa, Michael P., et al.

Permutt. Photographing the Spirit World. 1988. 12.95 (0-85030-762-7, Pub. by Aqrn Pr) Harper SF.

Permutt, Cyril. Collecting Old Cameras. LC 76-14888. (Photography Ser.). 1977. lib. bdg. 29.50 (0-306-70855-8) Da Capo.

Permutt, S., jt. ed. see Macklem, Peter T.

Pern, Stephen. The Great Divide: A Walk Through America along the Continental Divide of the United States. large type ed. (Non-Fiction Ser.). 512p. 1989. 27.99 (0-7089-2044-6) Ulverscroft.

Perna, D. Chickadee Book of Puzzles & Fun. 1994. pap. text 4.95 (0-920445-82-9, Pub. by Owl Bks) Firefly Bks Ltd.

Perna, Debi. Super Puzzles & Fun. (Illus.). 32p. 1995. pap. 4.95 (1-895688-25-6, Pub. by Owl Bks) Firefly Bks Ltd.

Perna, Laura W., ed. see Heller, Donald E., et al.

Perna, Michael. Remembering Lake Quinsigamond: From Steamboats to White City. LC 97-60311. 116p. (Orig.). 1998. pap. 19.95 (1-886284-02-4, Tatnuck) Chandler Hse.

Perna, Paula Di, see Di Perna, Paula.

Perna, Phyllis A., jt. ed. see Masterpasqua, Frank.

Perna, Rita. Fashion Forecasting. (Illus.). 327p. 1987. text 45.00 (0-87005-468-6) Fairchild.

Perna, Sharon. Country Cross-Stitch. (Illus.). 144p. 1992. pap. 12.95 (0-8069-5769-7) Sterling.

— Cross-Stitch a Beautiful Gift. (Illus.). 144p. 1993. pap. 12.95 (0-8069-8401-5) Sterling.

Pernak, Janine M., et al, eds. Selected Proceedings from the First & Second Delft Pain Symposia: Journal: Applied Neurophysiology, Vol. 47, No. 4-6. (Illus.). 112p. 1986. pap. 64.50 (3-8055-4044-2) S Karger.

Pernal, Andrew B., tr. see Le Vasseur, Guillaume & De Beauplan, Sieur.

Pernanen, Kai. Alcohol in Human Violence. LC 91-16338. (Substance Abuse Ser.). 279p. 1991. lib. bdg. 40.00 (0-89862-171-2) Guilford Pubns.

Pernecky, Jack. Teaching the Fundamentals of Violin Playing. 184p. 1998. pap. text 26.95 (0-87487-771-7) Summy-Birchard.

Perneczky, Alex. The Keyhole Concept in Neurosurgery. (Illus.). 264p. 1999. 199.00 (0-86577-709-8) Thieme Med Pubs.

Perneczky, Alex, et al. Endoscopic Anatomy for Neurosurgery. (Illus.). 350p. 1993. text 399.00 (0-86577-490-0) Thieme Med Pubs.

Perner, Bernard & Perner, Majorie. Mount to the Sky Like Eagles. (Heritage Ser.: Vol. 9). 1986. 10.95 (0-911802-64-9); pap. 8.95 (7-100-07622-6) Free Church Pubns.

Perner, F., et al, eds. Transplant International Official Journal of the European Society for Organ Transplantation, Supp. 1. xviii, 534p. 1998. pap. 129.00 (3-540-64661-2) Spr-Verlag.

Perner, Josef. Understanding the Representational Mind. (Bradford LDCC Ser.). (Illus.). 362p. 1991. 47.50 (0-262-16124-9, Bradford Bks) MIT Pr.

— Understanding the Representational Mind. (Learning, Development & Conceptual Change Ser.). (Illus.). 362p. 1993. reprint ed. pap. text 22.00 (0-262-66082-2, Bradford Bks) MIT Pr.

Perner, Lars, ed. see Haug, Elisabeth.

Perner, Majorie, jt. auth. see Perner, Bernard.

***Perner, P. & Petrou, M., eds.** Machine Learning & Data Mining in Pattern Recognition: Proceedings of the First International Workshop, MLDM'99, Leipzig, Germany, September 16-18, 1999. rev. ed. (Lecture Notes in Artificial Intelligence Ser.: Vol. 1715). viii, 215p. 1999. pap. 45.00 (3-540-66599-4) Spr-Verlag.

Perner, Petra, et al. Advances in Structural & Syntactical Pattern Recognition: 6th International Workshop, SSPR '96, Leipzig, Germany, August 1996, Proceedings. LC 96-29231. (Lecture Notes in Computer Science Ser.: Vol. 1121). 393p. 1996. 68.00 (3-540-61577-6) Spr-Verlag.

Pernetta, John C., ed. Atlas of the Oceans. rev. ed. LC 94-22176. 208p. 1994. 29.95 (0-528-83703-6) Rand McNally.

— Marine Protected Areas Needs in the South Asian Seas Region Vol. 4: Pakistan. 42p. (C). 1993. pap. text 13.50 (2-8317-0177-5, Pub. by IUCN) Island Pr.

— Marine Protected Areas Needs in the South Asian Seas Region Vol. 5: Sri Lanka. 67p. (C). 1993. pap. text 13.50 (2-8317-0178-3, Pub. by IUCN) Island Pr.

Pernety, Antoine-Joseph. Le Dictionnaire Mytho-Hermetique. (FRE.). 548p. 1980. pap. 150.00 (0-8288-2191-7, M6441) Fr & Eur.

Pernety, Antoine-Joseph. Dictionnaire Portatif de Peinture, Sculpture et Gravure. (FRE.). 1972. write for info. (0-7859-8649-9, 282660242X) Fr & Eur.

Pernia, Ernesto D. Urbanization, Population Growth & Economic Development in the Philippines, 3. LC 77-24588. (Studies in Population & Urban Demography: No. 3). 213p. 1977. 57.95 (0-8371-9721-X, PEU/, Greenwood Pr) Greenwood.

Pernia, Ernesto M. Urban Poverty in Asia: A Survey of Critical Issues. (Illus.). 324p. 1995. text 55.00 (0-19-586770-X) OUP.

Pernici, B., et al, eds. Automatic Tools for Designing Office Information Systems: The TODOS Approach. (Research Reports ESPRIT, Project 813, TODOS: Vol. 1). ix, 321p. 1990. 39.00 (0-387-53284-6) Spr-Verlag.

Pernici, Barbara, et al, eds. Advanced Information Systems Engineering: 10th International Conference, CAiSE '98, Pisa, Italy, June 8-12, 1998, Proceedings, Vol. 141. LC 98-22152. (Lecture Notes in Computer Science Ser.: Vol. 1413). x, 423p. 1998. pap. 67.00 (3-540-64556-X) Spr-Verlag.

Pernick, B. J. Handbook of Modern Optics, Vol. 2. (Illus.). 40p. (Orig.). 1994. pap. 11.00 (0-9636539-3-8) Peconic Pubs.

Pernick, Benjamin J. Handbook of Modern Optics, Vol. 1. (Illus.). 40p. (Orig.). 1993. pap. 11.00 (0-9636539-1-1) Peconic Pubs.

***Pernick, Benjamin J.** Handbook of Modern Optics, Vol. 4. 130p. (Orig.). 2000. pap. 18.00 (0-9636539-5-4) Peconic Pubs.

Pernick, Benjamin J., et al. Handbook of Modern Optics, Vol. 3. 47p. (Orig.). 1996. pap. 12.00 (0-9636539-4-6) Peconic Pubs.

***Pernick, Martin S.** The Black Stork: Eugenics & the Death of 'Defective' Babies in American Medicine & Motion Pictures since 1915. (Illus.). 328p. 1999. pap. 24.95 (0-19-513539-3) OUP.

Pernick, Martin S. The Black Stork: Eugenics & the Death of "Defective" Babies in American Medicine & Motion Pictures Since 1945. (Illus.). 312p. 1996. text 29.95 (0-19-507731-8) OUP.

Pernicka, E. & Wagner, G., eds. Archaeometry, '90. 880p. 1990. 163.50 (0-8176-2522-4) Birkhauser.

Pernicone, Nunzio. Italian Anarchism, 1864-1892. LC 92-46661. (Illus.). 336p. 1993. text 49.50 (0-691-05692-7, Pub. by Princeton U Pr) Cal Prin Full Svc.

Pernin, A., jt. auth. see Comte, R.

Pernin, Peter. The Great Peshtigo Fire: An Eyewitness Account. (Wisconsin Stories Ser.). (Illus.). 28p. 1971. pap. 3.95 (0-87020-194-8, GRPE) State Hist Soc Wis.

***Pernin, Peter & State Historical Society of Wisconsin Staff.** The Great Peshtigo Fire: An Eyewitness Account 2nd ed. LC 99-27393. 1999. pap. write for info. (0-87020-310-X) State Hist Soc Wis.

***Perniola, Maria.** Ritual Thinking: Sexuality, Death, World. Verdicchio, Massimo, tr. 220p. 2001. 54.95 (1-57392-869-0) Prometheus Bks.

Perniola, Mario. Enigmas: The Egyptian Moment in Art & Society. Woodall, Christopher, tr. 144p. 1995. pap. 19.00 (1-85984-061-2, C0511, Pub. by Verso) Norton.

— Enigmas: The Egyptian Moment in Art & Society. Woodall, Christopher, tr. 144p. (C). 1995. 60.00 (1-85984-966-0, C0510, Pub. by Verso) Norton.

Pernis, B., jt. auth. see Celada, F.

Pernis, Benvenuto, jt. ed. see Ferrerini, M.

Pernis, Maria G., jt. auth. see Adams, Laurie S.

Pernkopf, Eduard. Atlas of Topographical & Applied Human Anatomy, 2 vols., Set. 3rd enl. rev. ed. Platzer, Werner, ed. Monsen, Harry, tr. from GER. Orig. Title: Atlas der Topographischen und Angewamdten Anatomie Des Menschen. (Illus.). 804p. 1990. 295.00 (0-683-06854-7) Lppncott W & W.

— Atlas of Topographical & Applied Human Anatomy Vol. 1: Head & Neck, 1. 3rd enl. rev. ed. Platzer, Werner, ed. Monsen, Harry, tr. from GER.Tr. of Atlas der Topographischen und Angewnadten Anatomie Des Menschen. (Illus.). 380p. 1989. 175.00 (0-683-06852-0) Lppncott W & W.

— Atlas of Topographical & Applied Human Anatomy Vol. II: Thorax, Abdomen & Extremities, 2. 3rd enl. rev. ed. Platzer, Werner, ed. Monson, Harry, tr. from GER. (Illus.). 424p. 1989. text 175.00 (0-683-06853-9) Lppncott W & W.

Pernoll, Martin L., jt. auth. see Benson, Ralph C.

Pernon, Gerard. Dictionnaire de la Musique. (FRE.). 448p. 1992. 75.00 (0-7859-8013-X, 2737311853) Fr & Eur.

Pernon, Laure-Diane. Nouveau Dictionnaire des Synonymes. (FRE.). 289p. 1986. 32.95 (0-7859-8658-8, 285882925x) Fr & Eur.

Pernot, Laurent. Les "Discours Siciliens" d'Aelius Aristede. rev. ed. Connor, W. R., ed. LC 80-2662. (Monographs in Classical Studies). 1981. lib. bdg. 43.95 (0-405-14047-9) Ayer.

Pernot, Michel, ed. see De Retz, Jean-Francois.

Pernotto, James. Chuck Close Editions: A Catalogue Raissone. (Illus.). 32p. (Orig.). (C). 1989. pap. text. write for info. (0-9624401-0-8) Butler Inst.

Pernoud, R. Egine & Clift, Dominique. A Day with a Medieval Troubadour. LC 96-38952. (Day With Ser.). (Illus.). (J). 1997. lib. bdg. 22.60 (0-8225-1915-1) Lerner Pub.

Pernoud, Regine. A Day with a Noblewoman. LC 96-47107. (Illus.). (J). (gr. 5-8). 1997. lib. bdg. 22.60 (0-8225-1916-X) Lerner Pub.

— Hildegard of Bingen. LC 98-4719. 224p. 1998. 22.95 (1-56924-727-7) Marlowe & Co.

— Joan of Arc: By Herself & Her Witnesses. LC 66-24807. 1966. pap. 16.95 (0-8128-1260-3, Scrbrough Hse) Madison Bks UPA.

— A Miller. Clift, Dominique, tr. from ITA. LC 96-28160. (Day With Ser.). (Illus.). (YA). 1997. lib. bdg. 22.60 (0-8225-1914-3, Runestone Pr) Lerner Pub.

— A Stonecutter. Clift, Dominique, tr. from ITA. LC 96-9519. (Day With Ser.). (Illus.). (J). 1997. lib. bdg. 22.60 (0-8225-1913-5, Lerner Publctns) Lerner Pub.

— Women in the Days of the Cathedrals. 1998. pap. text 15.95 (0-89870-642-4) Ignatius Pr.

Pernoud, Regine & Clin, Marie-Veronique. Joan of Arc: Her Story. Adams, Jeremy D., tr. from FRE. LC 98-45059. (Illus.). 300p. 1999. text 27.95 (0-312-21442-1) St Martin.

— Joan of Arc: Her Story. Adams, Jeremy Du Quesnay, tr. (Illus.). 336p. 1999. pap. 14.95 (0-312-22730-2, St Martins Paperbacks) St Martin.

Pernow, Bengt, jt. ed. see Carlson, Lars A.

Pernow, Bengt, ed. see Nobel Symposium Staff.

Perntagram Partners Staff. Pentagram: The Compendium. (Illus.). 304p. 1998. pap. 39.95 (0-7148-3769-5, Pub. by Phaidon Press) Phaidon Pr.

Pernu, Dennis. Hot Rods. (Cruisin' Ser.). (Illus.). 48p. (J). (gr. 3-6). 1995. 19.00 (0-516-35253-9) Childrens.

Pernul, G. & Tjoa, A. M., eds. Entity-Relationship Approach, ER '92: Eleventh International Conference. LC 92-32250. (Lecture Notes in Computer Science Ser.: Vol. 645). 1992. 63.95 (0-387-56023-8) Spr-Verlag.

Pero, Alice. Thawed Stars. Salamon, Russell, ed. (Illus.). 160p. 1999. pap. 12.00 (0-931104-47-5) SunInk Pubn.

Pero, Jose E. Aqui Washington D. C. (SPA., Illus.). 60p. 1998. pap. write for info. (0-9662392-0-2) Titos Pubg.

Pero, Robert, jt. auth. see Axelrod, David B.

Perol, C., ed. see CLAROM Staff.

Perol, Lucette, jt. auth. see Diderot, Denis.

Perols, S., jt. illus. see Valat, P. M.

Perols, Sylvaine. The Human Body. (First Discovery Book). 30p. (J). (ps-2). 1996. 11.95 (0-590-73876-3, Cartwheel) Scholastic Inc.

Perols, Sylvaine & Gallimard Jeunesse. Farm Animals. LC 97-27032. (First Discovery Book). (Illus.). 24p. (J). (ps-2). 1998. 11.95 (0-590-11618-5) Scholastic Inc.

Peron, Dennis, jt. auth. see Rathbun, Mary.

Peron, Eva D. In My Own Words: Evita. LC 96-69626. (Illus.). 128p. 1996. pap. 8.95 (1-56584-353-3, Pub. by New Press NY) Norton.

Peron, Juan D. Peron Speaks: Speeches & Addresses of Juan Peron. 1996. lib. bdg. 259.95 (0-8490-6351-5) Gordon Pr.

— The Speeches of Juan Domingo Peron. 698p. 1973. 300.00 (0-8490-1108-6) Gordon Pr.

Peron, Juan D., et al. Peron's Argentina. 429p. 1973. 250.00 (0-8490-0814-X) Gordon Pr.

Peron, Michel. Larousse Dictionnaire des Affairs: French-English, English-French. (ENG & FRE.). 512p. 1969. 45.00 (0-7859-7631-0, 2030206091) Fr & Eur.

Peron, Michel, et al. French-English - English-French Dictionary of Business, Finance & Legal Terms. (ENG & FRE.). 1022p. 1992. 69.00 (2-85036-146-1) IBD Ltd.

Perone, ed. Scientific Methods & Behavioral Analysis. (C). 1999. text. write for info. (0-321-01186-4) Addison-Wesley Educ.

Perone, Christopher, jt. auth. see Manard, Barbara.

Perone, James E. Carole King: A Bio-Bibliography, 71. LC 99-10091. (Bio-Bibliographies in Music Ser.: Vol. 88). 240p. 1999. lib. bdg. 65.00 (0-313-30711-3) Greenwood.

— Elvis Costello: A Bio-Bibliography, 70. LC 98-41644. (Bio-Bibliographies in Music Ser.: Vol. 70). 224p. 1998. lib. bdg. 65.00 (0-313-30399-1, Greenwood Pr) Greenwood.

— Harmony Theory: A Bibliography, 57. LC 96-29815. (Music Reference Collection: Vol. 57). 264p. 1997. lib. bdg. 69.50 (0-313-29593-X, Greenwood Pr) Greenwood.

— Howard Hanson: A Bio-Bibliography, 47. LC 93-2589. (Bio-Bibliographies in Music Ser.: No. 17). 352p. 1993. lib. bdg. 69.50 (0-313-28644-2, Greenwood Pr) Greenwood.

— Orchestration Theory: A Bibliography, 52. LC 95-52948. (Music Reference Collection: Vol. 52). 200p. 1996. lib. bdg. 67.95 (0-313-29596-4, Greenwood Pr) Greenwood.

***Perone, James E.** Paul Simon: A Bio-bibliography, 78. (Bio-Bibliographies in Music Ser.: Vol. 78). 200p. 2000. lib. bdg. 69.50 (0-313-31016-5, Greenwood Pr) Greenwood.

Perone, James E., compiled by. Form & Analysis Theory: A Bibliography, 67. LC 97-42481. (Music Reference Collection: Vol. 67). 264p. 1998. lib. bdg. 65.00 (0-313-29594-8, Greenwood Pr) Greenwood.

— Musical Anthologies for Analytical Study: A Annotated Bibliography, 48. LC 95-21762. (Music Reference Collection: Vol. 48). 200p. 1995. lib. bdg. 59.95 (0-313-29595-6, Greenwood Pr) Greenwood.

Perone, Jerry & Sanow, Arnold. Entrepreneur's Boot Camp. 272p. 1995. boxed set 24.95 (0-7872-0253-3) Kendall-Hunt.

Perone, Karen L. Lukas Foss: A Bio-Bibliography, 37. LC 90-29280. (Bio Bibliographies in Music Ser.: No. 37). 296p. 1991. lib. bdg. 65.00 (0-313-26811-8, PLB, Greenwood Pr) Greenwood.

Perone, M., jt. auth. see Lattal, K. A.

Perone, Nicola. Principles of Real-Time Sonography in Modern Obstetrics: A Handbook for the Practicing Physician. LC 83-42848. (Illus.). 173p. 1984. reprint ed. pap. 53.70 (0-7837-9536-X, 206028500005) Bks Demand.

Perone, Tony. The Perrone Plan. Date not set. mass mkt. 7.99 (0-06-109789-6) HarpC.

Peroni, Gwen. Canadian Insurance Claims Directory 1998. annuals 66th ed. 400p. 1998. pap. text 40.00 (0-8020-4915-X) U of Toronto Pr.

Peroni, Gwen, ed. Canadian Insurance Claims Directory 1999, Vol. 67. annuals 67th ed. 400p. 1999. pap. text. write for info. (0-8020-4935-4) U of Toronto Pr.

— Canadian Insurance Claims Directory 1995. annuals 63rd ed. 400p. (C). 1995. pap. text 37.00 (0-8020-4042-X) U of Toronto Pr.

— Canadian Insurance Claims Directory 1996. annuals 64th ed. 400p. 1996. pap. text 40.00 (0-8020-4986-9) U of Toronto Pr.

Peroni, Peter A. The Burg: An Italian-American Community at Bay in Trenton. LC 79-63258. 1979. pap. text 19.00 (0-8191-0724-7) U Pr of Amer.

Peroni, Robert J., jt. auth. see Kuntz, Joel D.

Peronnet, Benjamin, jt. ed. see Fredericksen, Burton B.

Peronnet, Louise. Le Parler Acadien du Sud-Est du Nouveau-Brunswick: Elements Gammaticaux et Lexicaux. (American University Studies: Foreign Language Instruction: Ser. VI, Vol. 8). (FRE.). 275p. (C). 1988. text 37.50 (0-8204-0794-1) P Lang Pubng.

Perosa, Alessandro & Sparrow, John, eds. Renaissance Latin Verse: An Anthology. LC 78-10969. 590p. reprint ed. pap. 182.90 (0-7837-0301-5, 204062300018) Bks Demand.

***Perosa, S.** From Islands to Portraits: Four Literary Variations. (Veneto Institute of Sciences, Letters & Arts Sciences: Vol. 5). 114p. 2000. 54.00 (1-58603-055-8) IOS Press.

Perot, Ross. Save Your Job, Save Our Country: Why NAFTA Must Be Stopped - Now! 160p. (J). 1993. pap. 6.70 (1-56282-711-1, Pub. by Hyperion) Time Warner.

Perotta, Tom. Election. 208p. 1998. pap. 12.00 (0-425-16728-3) Berkley Pub.

Perotti, Robert, et al. Sustainability of Public Finances. 80p. 1998. pap. 14.95 (1-898128-35-9, Pub. by Ctr Econ Policy Res) Brookings.

Perotto, Aldo O. Anatomical Guide for the Electromyographer: The Limbs & Trunk. 3rd ed. (Illus.). 328p. 1994. pap. 34.95 (0-398-06320-6) C C Thomas.

— Anatomical Guide for the Electromyographer: The Limbs & Trunk. 3rd ed. (Illus.). 328p. (C). 1994. text 50.95 (0-398-05900-4) C C Thomas.

Perouse de Montclos, Jean-Marie. Chateaux of the Loire Valley. (Illus.). 360p. 1997. 19.95 (3-89508-598-7, 520352) Konemann.

Perouse, Jean F. De La, see De La Perouse, Jean F.

Peroutka, Stephen J., ed. Ecstasy: The Clinical Pharmacological & Neurotoxicological Effects of the Drug MDMA. (Topics in Neurosciences Ser.). (C). 1989. text 160.50 (0-7923-0305-9) Kluwer Academic.

— Handbook of Receptors & Channels: G Protein-Coupled Receptors, Vol. 1. 368p. 1993. boxed set 166.95 (0-8493-8321-8) CRC Pr.

— Serotonin Receptor Subtypes: Basic & Clinical Aspects. LC 90-12804. (Receptor Biochemistry & Methodology Ser.: Vol. 15). 246p. 1990. 235.00 (0-471-56840-6) Wiley.

Perova, Natasha & Tait, Arch, eds. Beyond the Looking Glass: Russian Grotesque Revisited. (Glas: No. 14). (Illus.). 224p. 1997. pap. 14.95 (1-56663-182-3) I R Dee.

— Booker Winners & Others. (Glas Ser.: No. 7). (Illus.). 224p. 1994. pap. 14.95 (0-939010-43-7) I R Dee.

— Booker Winners & Others II. (Glas Ser.: No. 10). (Illus.). 224p. pap. 14.95 (0-939010-50-X) I R Dee.

— Bulgakov & Mandelstam. (Glas Ser.: No. 5). (Illus.). 224p. 1993. pap. 14.95 (0-939010-40-2) I R Dee.

— Captives. (Glas Ser.: No. 11). (Illus.). 224p. 1996. pap. 14.95 (0-939010-54-2) I R Dee.

— Jews & Strangers. (Glas Ser.: No. 6). (Illus.). 224p. (Orig.). pap. 14.95 (0-939010-42-9) I R Dee.

— Love & Fear. (Glas Ser.: No. 4). (Illus.). 224p. 1993. pap. 14.95 (0-939010-35-6) I R Dee.

— Love Russian Style. (Glas Ser.: No. 8). (Illus.). 224p. pap. 14.95 (0-939010-44-5) I R Dee.

— Revolution - Inaugural Issue. (Glas Ser.: No. 1). (Illus.). 224p. 1993. pap. 14.95 (0-939010-46-1) I R Dee.

— The Scared Generation. (Glas Ser.: No. 9). (Illus.). 224p. 1995. pap. 14.95 (0-939010-49-6) I R Dee.

— Soviet Grotesque. (Glas Ser.: No. 2). 224p. pap. 14.95 (0-939010-47-X) I R Dee.

— Women's View. (Glas Ser.: No. 3). (Illus.). 224p. pap. 14.95 (0-939010-48-8) I R Dee.

Perova, Natasha, jt. auth. see Kagal, Ayesha.

Perovich, Anthony N., ed. see Donagan, Alan.

Perovitch, Milosh. Radiological Evaluation of the Spinal Cord, 2 vols., Vol. 1. 256p. 1981. 145.00 (0-8493-5041-7, RC402, CRC Reprint) Franklin.

— Radiological Evaluation of the Spinal Cord, 2 vols., Vol. 2. 192p. 1981. 108.00 (0-8493-5043-3, CRC Reprint) Franklin.

Perowine, Stuart. Hadrian. (Classical Lives Ser.). (Illus.). 192p. (Orig.). (C). 1987. reprint ed. pap. text 14.95 (0-7099-4048-3, Pub. by C Helm) Routldge.

Perowne, J. J. Commentary on the Psalms, 2 vols. LC 89-11054. Orig. Title: Book of Psalms. 1144p. 1989. pap. 29.99 (0-8254-3485-8, Kregel Class) Kregel.

Perozziello, Michael J., jt. auth. see Ruffa, Stephen A.

Perozzo, James. Assembling & Troubleshooting Microcomputers. 2nd ed. 352p. 1990. mass mkt. 56.95 (0-8273-3986-0) Delmar.

— Assembling & Troubleshooting Microcomputers. 2nd ed. 352p. 1991. pap., teacher ed. 16.00 (0-8273-3987-9) Delmar.

— The Complete Guide to Electronics Troubleshooting. 850p. 1993. mass mkt. 81.95 (0-8273-5045-7) Delmar.

— The Complete Guide to Electronics Troubleshooting: Instructor's Guide. 29p. 1993. pap. 19.00 (0-8273-5046-5) Delmar.

— Microcomputer Troubleshooting. 352p. 1986. pap. 26.95 (0-8273-2500-2) Delmar.

— Microcomputer Troubleshooting. (Electronics Technology Ser.). 1987. pap., teacher ed. 15.00 (0-8273-2501-0) Delmar.

P

An Asterisk (*) at the beginning of an entry indicates that the title is appearing for the first time.

— Practical Electronics Troubleshooting. LC 84-28626. 256p. (C). 1985. pap. 36.95 (*0-8273-2433-2*) Delmar.

— Practical Electronics Troubleshooting. LC 84-28626. 256p. (C). 1985. teacher ed. 16.00 (*0-8273-2434-0*) Delmar.

— Practical Electronics Troubleshooting. 2nd ed. 1990. pap., teacher ed. 16.00 (*0-8273-4054-0*) Delmar.

— Practical Electronics Troubleshooting. 2nd rev. ed. 448p. 1992. pap. text 38.50 (*0-8273-4053-2*) Delmar.

— Systematic Electronic: Troubleshooting. (Electronics Technology Ser.). 1989. mass mkt. 38.50 (*0-8273-3288-2*) Delmar.

Perper, Joshua A. & Wecht, Cyril H. Microscopic Diagnosis in Forensic Pathology. (Illus.). 488p. 1980. 87.95 (*0-398-03969-0*) C C Thomas.

Perper, Timothy, jt. auth. see Cornog, Martha.

Perpetua. Passion of the Holy Martyrs Sts. Perpetua & Felicity. Wallis, R. E., tr. 1991. pap. 2.95 (*0-89981-133-7*) Eastern Orthodox.

Perpetual. Beginnings: Prayers & Promises for Each New Day. 1998. pap. 9.99 (*0-8423-8818-4*) Tyndale Hse.

Perpetual. Bible Promises for Each New Day. 1992. pap. 9.99 (*0-8423-9618-7*) Tyndale Hse.

Perpetual. Cal-Prescriptions for Strength. LC 98-100419. 1997. pap. text 5.99 (*0-310-97376-7*) Zondervan.

Perpetual. Family Circus. 1996. pap. 9.99 (*0-8423-8856-7*) Tyndale Hse.

— Just the Two of Us... 365 Secrets for Lifelong Love. 1998. pap. 9.99 (*0-8423-8822-2*) Tyndale Hse.

Perpetual. Personal Prayer. 1998. pap. 9.99 (*0-8423-8815-X*) Tyndale Hse.

***Perpetual.** Pure Patsy: A Lighthearted Look at Life. 1998. pap. 9.99 (*0-8423-8821-4*) Tyndale Hse.

— Renewing the Heart: Spiritual Refreshment for Each New Day. 1998. pap. 9.99 (*0-8423-8820-6*) Tyndale Hse.

Perpetual. Song of the Thrush. LC 99-236641. 101p. 1997. spiral bd. 5.99 (*1-57051-146-2*) Brownlow Pub Co.

Perpetual. 365 Days of Folk Wisdom. 1997. pap. 9.95 (*0-7611-0833-5*) Workman Pub.

— 365 Days of Love & Friendship. 1997. pap. 9.95 (*0-7611-0834-3*) Workman Pub.

— 365 Great Hymns of the Faith. 1999. pap. 9.99 (*0-8423-3741-5*) Tyndale Hse.

— When God Doesn't Make Sense. 1996. pap. 9.99 (*0-8423-8851-6*) Tyndale Hse.

Perpetual Press Staff. Winning Advice for Conquering College Costs: Essential Tips & Creative Strategies for Financing College Without Excess Strain on Your Pocketbook. 32p. 1998. pap. 7.95 (*1-881199-05-3*) Perptual Pr.

Perpetual, S. M. God Is... (Small Inspirations Ser.). 1997. pap. write for info. (*0-8423-8866-4*) Tyndale Hse.

Perpetual Staff. Family Love, 1. 1999. 9.99 (*0-8423-3738-5*) Tyndale Hse.

— Sensational Marriage Secrets: 365 Keys to Keeping Love Alive, 1. 1999. 9.99 (*0-8423-3740-7*) Tyndale Hse.

***Perpetual Staff.** 365 Bible Promises. 1999. 9.99 (*0-8423-3734-2*) Tyndale Hse.

Perpetual Staff. Women's Bodies, Women's Health: The Mind/Body Connection. 1999. 11.95 (*0-945923-48-1*) J Wilson & Assocs.

Perpetual Staff. Zig Ziglar's Secrets to Success. 1996. pap. 9.99 (*0-8423-8859-1*) Tyndale Hse.

Perpich, George, jt. auth. see Gladstone, John.

Perpich, Sandra W. A Hermeneutic Critique of Structuralist Exegesis: With Specific Reference to Lk. 10.29-37. LC 83-21737. (Illus.). 264p. (Orig.). (C). 1984. pap. text 23.00 (*0-8191-3669-7*) U Pr of Amer.

***Perpilus Editions Staff.** Exciting Bali, 1 vol. (Illus.). 80p. 2000. pap. text 9.95 (*962-593-210-0*) Periplus.

Perquel, Francois E. Financial Markets of Eastern Europe & the Former Soviet Union. 256p. 1998. 155.00 (*1-85573-340-4*, Pub. by Woodhead Pubng) Am Educ Systs.

Perr, Harvey. Rosebloom. 1972. pap. 5.25 (*0-8222-0969-1*) Dramatists Play.

Perram, John W., jt. ed. see Muller, J. P.

Perram, John W., jt. ed. see Van de Velde, Walter.

Perras, Galen R. Franklin Roosevelt & the Origins of the Canadian-American Security Alliance, 1933-1945: Necessary, but Not Necessary Enough. LC 97-39773. 176p. 1998. 57.95 (*0-275-95500-1*, Praeger Pubs) Greenwood.

***Perraton, H. D.** Open & Distance Learning in Developing Countries. LC 99-16902. (Studies in Distance Education). 224p. 2000. pap. write for info. (*0-415-19419-9*) Routledge.

Perraton, Hilary. Alternative Routes to Formal Education. LC 82-7233. 344p. 1982. 38.95 (*0-8018-2587-3*) Johns Hopkins.

Perraton, Jean & Baxter, Richard, eds. Models, Evaluations & Information Systems for Planners. LC 75-326945. (Cambridge University Centre for Land Use & Built Form Studies Conference Proceedings: No. 1). 316p. reprint ed. pap. 98.00 (*0-608-13086-9*, 202521500043) Bks Demand.

Perraud, Louis, jt. ed. see Thomson, Ian.

Perraudin, Michael. Heinrich Heine: Poetry in Context - A Study of Buch der Lieder. LC 88-9512. (Berg Monographs in German Literature). 304p. 1989. 19.50 (*0-85496-028-7*) Berg Pubs.

Perrault, Anna H., jt. auth. see Blazek, Ronald.

Perrault, Charles. Le Chat Botte. adapted ed. LC 95-941619. (Best-Sellers Ser.).Tr. of Puss 'n' Boots. (FRE., Illus.). (J). (ps-2). 2000. pap. 9.95 incl. audio (*2-921997-02-9*) Coffragants.

— Cinderella. (FRE.). 55p. (J). (gr. 3-8). 1990. pap. 10.95 (*0-7859-1354-8*, 2070312224) Fr & Eur.

— Cinderella. Bell, Anthea, tr. from GER. LC 98-38994. (Illus.). (J). (gr. k-3). 1999. lib. bdg. 15.88 (*0-7358-1052-4*, Pub. by North-South Bks NYC) Chronicle Bks.

— Cinderella. LC 78-18067. (Illus.). 32p. (J). (gr. k-3). 1979. pap. 3.95 (*0-89375-098-0*); lib. bdg. 11.89 (*0-89375-120-0*) Troll Communs.

***Perrault, Charles.** Cinderella. LC 99-29918. (Illus.). 48p. (YA). 2000. 17.95 (*1-56846-130-5*, Creative Eds) Creative Co.

Perrault, Charles. Cinderella. Bell, Anthea, tr. from FRE. LC 98-38994. (ENG & GER., Illus.). 32p. (J). (gr. k-3). 1999. 15.95 (*0-7358-1051-6*, Pub. by North-South Bks NYC) Chronicle Bks.

— Cinderella: A Fairy Tale. LC 98-35942. (Little Pebbles Ser.). (Illus.). 32p. (J). (ps-1). 1999. 6.95 (*0-7892-0512-2*, Abbeville Kids) Abbeville Pr.

— Cinderella: And Other Tales from Perrault. (Illus.). 78p. (J). (ps-2). 1995. 18.95 (*0-8050-1004-1*, Bks Young Read) H Holt & Co.

— Cinderella, or, the Little Glass Slipper. 2nd ed. (J). 1988. 10.15 (*0-606-02064-0*, Pub. by Turtleback) Demco.

— Cinderella, Puss in Boots & Other Favorite Tales. Johnson, A. E., tr. from FRE. LC 98-53961. (Illus.). 168p. (J). (ps-3). 1999. 24.95 (*0-8109-4014-0*, Pub. by Abrams) Time Warner.

— The Commedia Puss in Boots. (Commedia Plays Ser.). 27p. (Orig.). (J). (gr. 3-8). 1993. pap. 3.00 (*1-57514-216-3*, 1153) Encore Perform Pub.

— Contes. Rouger, ed. (FRE.). 586p. 1981. pap. 10.95 (*0-7859-1374-2*, 2070372812) Fr & Eur.

— Contes. (Folio Ser.: No. 1281). (FRE.). 1989. pap. 9.95 (*2-07-037281-2*) Schoenhof.

— Contes. unabridged ed. (FRE.). 1999. pap. 5.95 (*2-87714-165-9*, Pub. by Bookking Intl) Distribks Inc.

— Contes de ma Mere l'Oye. (Folio - Junior Ser). (FRE.). pap. 9.95 (*2-07-033028-1*) Schoenhof.

— Contes de Ma Mere l'Oye. (Folio - Junior Ser.: No. 443). (FRE., Illus.). 223p. (J). (gr. 5-10). 1988. pap. 8.95 (*2-07-033443-0*) Schoenhof.

— El Gato con Botas. Marcuse, Aida, tr. from ENG.Tr. of Puss in Boots. (SPA., Illus.). 32p. (J). 1998. pap. 8.95 (*0-374-61856-9*) FS&G.

— El Gato Con Botas: (Puss in Boots) Marcuse, Aida E., tr. LC 91-12754. (Mirasol Ser.). (SPA., Illus.). 32p. (J). (gr. 2 up). 1991. 16.00 (*0-374-36158-4*) FS&G.

***Perrault, Charles.** Little Red Riding Hood. LC 99-32221. (Illus.). 32p. (YA). (gr. 5 up). 2000. lib. bdg. 13.95 (*1-56846-131-3*, Creat Educ) Creative Co.

— Perrault's Complete Fairy Tales. (Classics for Young Readers Ser.). (Illus.). (J). 2000. pap. 4.99 (*0-14-130651-3*, PuffinBks) Peng Put Young Read.

Perrault, Charles. Perrault's Fairy Tales. LC 72-79522. (Illus.). 117p. (J). (gr. 4-6). 1969. reprint ed. pap. 6.95 (*0-486-22311-6*) Dover.

— Le Petit Chaperon Rouge. adapted ed. LC 95-941620. (Best-Sellers Ser.).Tr. of Little Red Riding Hood. (FRE., Illus.). (J). (ps-2). 2000. pap. 9.95 incl. audio (*2-921997-00-2*) Coffragants.

— Popular Tales. Dorson, Richard M., ed. LC 77-70607. (International Folklore Ser.). (Illus.). 1977. reprint ed. lib. bdg. 23.95 (*0-405-10118-X*) Ayer.

— Le Pull-over Rouge. (FRE.). 1980. pap. 12.95 (*0-7859-3104-X*, 2253025437) Fr & Eur.

***Perrault, Charles.** Puss in Boots. Bell, Anthea, tr. from GER. LC 99-17366. (Illus.). 32p. (J). (gr. k-3). 1999. lib. bdg. 15.88 (*0-7358-1159-8*, Pub. by North-South Bks NYC) Chronicle Bks.

Perrault, Charles. Puss in Boots. Arthur, Malcolm, tr. (Illus.). 32p. (J). 1990. 16.00 (*0-374-36160-6*) FS&G.

— Puss in Boots. (Illus.). 32p. (J). (ps up). 1998. pap. 8.95 (*0-374-46034-5*) FS&G.

— Puss in Boots. Bell, Anthea, tr. LC 96-15963. (Illus.). 48p. (J). (gr. k-3). 1996. lib. bdg. 15.88 (*1-55858-643-1*, Pub. by North-South Bks NYC) Chronicle Bks.

***Perrault, Charles.** Puss in Boots. Bell, Anthea, tr. from FRE. LC 99-17366. (Illus.). 32p. (J). (gr. k-3). 1999. 15.95 (*0-7358-1158-X*, Pub. by North-South Bks NYC) Chronicle Bks.

Perrault, Charles. Puss in Boots. LC 78-18061. (Illus.). 32p. (J). (gr. k-3). 1997. pap. 3.95 (*0-89375-108-1*) Troll Communs.

— Puss in Boots: A Fairy Tale by Perrault. LC 97-23047. (Little Pebbles Ser.). (Illus.). 32p. (J). (ps-1). 1999. 6.95 (*0-7892-0422-3*, Abbeville Kids) Abbeville Pr.

— The Sleeping Beauty. Walker, David, tr. & illus. by. LC 76-22697. (J). (gr. k-5). 1977. lib. bdg. 11.89 (*0-690-01279-9*) HarpC Child Bks.

— Tales from Perrault. Lawrence, Ann, tr. (Illus.). 128p. (J). (gr. 1 up). 1997. reprint ed. pap. 11.95 (*0-19-274175-6*) OUP.

— Three Wishes. LC 78-18060. (Illus.). 32p. (J). (gr. k-3). 1979. pap. 3.95 (*0-89375-107-3*); lib. bdg. 15.85 (*0-89375-129-4*) Troll Communs.

— Three Wishes. 1979. 8.70 (*0-606-02720-3*, Pub. by Turtleback) Demco.

— Tom Thumb & Other Stories. 1996. 13.95 (*0-679-45103-X*) McKay.

Perrault, Charles, jt. auth. see Beckett, Sheilah.

Perrault, Charles, jt. auth. see Brown, Marcia.

Perrault, Charles, jt. auth. see Leprince de Beaumont, Marie.

Perrault, Claude. Ordonnance for the Five Kinds of Columns after the Method of the Ancients. McEwen, Indra K., tr. LC 92-4649. (Texts & Documents Ser.). (Illus.). 208p. 1993. 34.95 (*0-89236-232-4*, Pub. by J P Getty Trust); pap. 19.95 (*0-89236-233-2*, Pub. by J P Getty Trust) OUP.

***Perrault, Dominique.** Aplix. Muller, Lars, ed. (Illus.). 108p. 2000. 45.00 (*3-907078-13-6*, Pub. by Lars Muller) Princeton Arch.

Perrault, Dominique. Dominique Perrault: Furniture & Fabrics. LC 97-26442. (Illus.). 144p. 1997. 42.00 (*3-7643-5661-8*, Pub. by Birkhauser) Princeton Arch.

Perrault, Gilles. Le Derapage. (FRE.). 1989. pap. 10.95 (*0-7859-2919-3*) Fr & Eur.

— Notre Ami le Roi. (Folio-Actuel Ser.). (FRE.). 1990. pap. 14.95 (*2-07-032695-0*) Schoenhof.

— L' Orchestre Rouge. (FRE.). 573p. 1989. pap. 65.00 (*0-7859-3451-0*, 2213023883) Fr & Eur.

Perrault, John & Piche, Thomas, Jr. Walter Zimmerman: Past, Present, Future Tense. LC 98-70641. (Illus.). 32p. 1998. pap. text 5.00 (*0-914407-20-1*) Everson Mus.

Perrault, John, jt. auth. see Yassin, Robert A.

Perrault, Mark. Cowboy Memories from Montana. LC 96-51484. 1997. 24.95 (*0-89301-207-6*) U of Idaho Pr.

Perrault-Mattison, Patricia. The Art of Bill Alexander & Robert Warren, Series 7. (Illus.). 84p. 1989. pap. text. write for info. (*1-883576-06-7*) Alexander Art.

— The Art of Bill Alexander & Robert Warren, Series 8. (Illus.). 84p. 1989. pap. text. write for info. (*1-883576-07-5*) Alexander Art.

— The Art of Bill Alexander & Robert Warren, Series 9. (Illus.). 78p. 1990. pap. text. write for info. (*1-883576-08-3*) Alexander Art.

— The Art of Buck Paulson, Series 1. (Illus.). 96p. 1989. pap. text. write for info. (*1-883576-16-4*) Alexander Art.

— The Art of Buck Paulson, Series 2. (Illus.). 88p. 1990. pap. text. write for info. (*1-883576-17-2*) Alexander Art.

Perrault, Robert D., ed. Paper Machine Steam & Condensate Systems. 4th ed. 40p. 1990. pap. 18.00 (*0-89852-504-7*, 0101R096) TAPPI.

Perre, Van de, see Van de Perre.

Perreau & Langford. Concise French-American Dictionary of Figurative & Idiomatic Language. (ENG & FRE.). 17.95 (*0-685-36686-3*) Fr & Eur.

Perreault. Basic Marketing. 12th ed. 1997. 64.25 (*0-07-561022-1*) McGraw.

— Essentials of Marketing. 7th ed. 1998. student ed. 61.50 (*0-07-013552-5*) McGraw.

— Essentials of Marketing. 8th ed. 1999. student ed. 51.00 (*0-07-228323-8*) McGraw.

***Perreault, Bruce A.** Radiant Energy the Holy Grail. (Illus.). 55p. 1999. pap. 25.00 (*1-930216-01-7*) Nu Energy.

Perreault, George. Curved Like an Eye. Trusky, Tom, ed. LC 87-14656. (Ahsahta Press Modern & Contemporary Poets of the West Ser.). 59p. (Orig.). 1988. pap. 6.95 (*0-916272-35-4*) Ahsahta Pr.

— Trying to Be Round. 64p. 1994. pap. 9.50 (*1-880286-20-3*) Singular Speech Pr.

Perreault, Jeanne. Writing Selves: Contemporary Feminist Autography. LC 95-8529. 176p. 1995. pap. 17.95 (*0-8166-2655-3*) U of Minn Pr.

Perreault, John. Hotel Death. (New American Fiction Ser.: No. 16). 213p. 1990. 16.95 (*0-940650-87-8*) Sun & Moon CA.

— Hotel Death. deluxe ed. (New American Fiction Ser.: No. 16). 216p. 1990. 30.00 (*0-940650-86-X*) Sun & Moon CA.

— Luck. 7.00 (*0-686-09743-2*); pap. 3.50 (*0-686-09744-0*) Kulchur Foun.

Perreault, John, jt. auth. see Nahas, Dominique.

Perreault, William, jt. auth. see McCarthy, Jerome E.

***Perreault, William D., Jr.** Basic Marketing Learning Aid. 464p. (C). 1998. pap. 29.38 (*0-07-000569-9*) McGrw-H Hghr Educ.

***Perreault, William D.** Essentials of Marketing. 8th ed. LC 99-40845. 1999. text 61.50 (*0-07-289482-2*) McGraw.

Perreault, William D., Jr. & McCarthy, E. Jerome. Basic Marketing. 13th ed. LC 98-6853. 1998. 71.25 (*0-256-20982-0*) McGraw.

Perreault, William D. & McCarthy, Jerome E. Applications in Basic Marketing: 1995-1996 Edition Clippings from the Popular Business Press. 6th ed. 192p. (C). 1995. text 15.50 (*0-256-18834-3*, Irwn McGrw-H) McGrw-H Hghr Educ.

— Basic Marketing International. 11th ed. 816p. (C). 1992. student ed., per. 33.50 (*0-256-12877-4*, Irwn McGrw-H) McGrw-H Hghr Educ.

— Essentials of Marketing: With Applications in Basic Marketing 1996-1997. 6th ed. (C). 1996. pap. text 63.95 (*0-256-24979-2*, Irwn McGrw-H) McGrw-H Hghr Educ.

— Essentials of Marketing Learning Aid. 6th ed. 400p. (C). 1993. text 24.37 (*0-256-12898-7*, Irwn McGrw-H) McGrw-H Hghr Educ.

— Essentials of Marketing Learning Aid. 7th ed. 432p. (C). 1996. text 24.37 (*0-256-18982-X*, Irwn McGrw-H) McGrw-H Hghr Educ.

— Fundamentos de Marketing. 11th ed. (C). 1996. text 33.50 (*84-8086-180-0*, Irwn McGrw-H) McGrw-H Hghr Educ.

Perreault, William D., et al. Essentials of Marketing: Canadian Version. 3rd ed. 672p. (C). 1990. per. 46.95 (*0-256-09420-9*, Irwn McGrw-H) McGrw-H Hghr Educ.

Perreault, William D., jt. auth. see McCarthy, E. Jerome, Jr.

Perreault, William D., jt. auth. see McCarthy, E. Jerome.

Perreault, William D., jt. auth. see McCarthy, Jerome E.

Perreault, Yves. Using BaanERP. 1999. 59.99 (*0-7897-2015-9*) Que.

Perreiah, Alan R., ed. Paul of Venice: A Bibliographical Guide. (Bibliographies of Famous Philosophers Ser.). 175p. (C). 1986. 14.25 (*0-912632-83-6*) Philos Document.

— Paul of Venice. Logica Magna (Tractatus de Suppositionibus) xiv, 121p. 1971. pap. 16.00 (*1-57659-052-6*) Franciscan Inst.

Perreira, Hiapo K., tr. see Beaver, Margaret.

Perreira, Hiapo K., tr. see Jimmie, Elsie.

***Perrella, Stephen, ed.** Hypersurface Architecture. (Illus.). 112p. 1998. pap. 39.95 (*0-471-97809-4*) Wiley.

Perrella, Stephen, ed. see Hejduk, John, et al.

Perrella, Stephen, ed. see Riley, Terence.

Perrella, Stephen, ed. see Stern, Robert A., et al.

Perrels, Adriaan, jt. auth. see Nijkamp, Peter.

***Perremans, Sabine.** Physiological & Ethological Responses of Pigs During Simulation of Transport. (Acta Biomedica Lovaniensia Ser.: No. 201). (Illus.). 156p. 1999. pap. 46.50 (*90-6186-974-9*, Pub. by Leuven Univ) Coronet Bks.

Perren, L., jt. auth. see Partridge, M.

Perren, Richard. Agriculture in Depression, 1870-1940. (New Studies in Economic & Social History: Vol. 26). 92p. (C). 1995. text 34.95 (*0-521-55285-0*); pap. text 10.95 (*0-521-55768-2*) Cambridge U Pr.

Perren, S. M. & Schneider, E., eds. Biomechanics: Current Interdisciplinary Research. (Developments in Biomechanics Ser.). 1985. lib. bdg. 299.00 (*0-89838-755-8*) Kluwer Academic.

Perrera, Gloria & Walls, Jerry G. Apple Snails. (Illus.). 128p. 1996. 19.95 (*0-7938-2085-5*, TS260) TFH Pubns.

Perrero, Laurie. World of Tropical Flowers. LC 76-12926. (Illus.). 64p. (Orig.). 1976. pap. 4.95 (*0-89317-008-9*) Windward Pub.

Perrero, Laurie & Perrero, Louis. Tarantulas: In Nature & As Pets. (Illus.). 1979. pap. 2.95 (*0-89317-029-1*) Windward Pub.

Perrero, Louis, jt. auth. see Perrero, Laurie.

Perret. On the 8th Day God Laughed. 1995. mass mkt. 5.95 (*0-929292-81-2*) Hannibal Bks.

Perret, Annick. Painting on Porcelain: Oriental Designs. (Illus.). 96p. (Orig.). 1995. pap. 22.50 (*0-85532-786-3*, 786-3, Pub. by Srch Pr) A Schwartz & Co.

— Painting on Porcelain: Traditional & Contemporary Design. (Illus.). 96p. (Orig.). (YA). 1994. pap. 22.50 (*0-85532-766-9*, 766-9, Pub. by Srch Pr) A Schwartz & Co.

Perret, B. A., et al, eds. Long-Term Intravenous Immunoglobulin Treatment in Patients with AIDS-Related Complex: Journal: Vox Sanguinis, Vol. 59, Suppl. 1, 1990. (Illus.). iv, 60p. 1990. pap. 19.25 (*3-8055-5256-4*) S Karger.

Perret, Brian. Megiddo 1918: The Last Great Cavalry Victory. (Campaign Ser.: Vol. 61). (Illus.). 96p. 1999. pap. 16.95 (*1-85532-827-5*, Pub. by Ospry) Stackpole.

Perret, C., jt. ed. see Bossart, H.

***Perret-Catipovic, Maja & Ladame, F.** Adolescence & Psychoanalysis: The Story & The History. 200p. 1998. pap. text 30.00 (*1-85575-199-2*, Pub. by H Karnac Bks Ltd) Other Pr LLC.

Perret, Claude, et al. The Pulmonary Artery Catheter in Critical Care: A Concise Handbook. 2nd ed. (Illus.). 360p. 1997. 125.00 (*0-632-04212-5*) Blackwell Sci.

Perret, Claude, jt. ed. see Vincent, J. L.

Perret-Clermont, A. N., et al. Thinking Time: A Multidisciplinary Perspective on Time. (Swiss Monographs in Psychology: Vol. 4). (Illus.). 220p. 2000. pap. 35.00 (*0-88937-202-0*) Hogrefe & Huber Pubs.

Perret-Clermont, Anne N. Social Interaction & Cognitive Development in Children. (European Monographs in Social Psychology: No. 19). 1980. text 139.95 (*0-12-551950-8*) Acad Pr.

Perret-Clermont, Anne-Nelly. La Construction de l'Intelligence dans l'Interaction Sociale: Nouvelle Edition, Revue et Augmentee avec la Collaboration de Michele Grossen, Michel Nicolet et Maria Luisa Schubauer-Leoni. (Exploration Ser.). (FRE.). 312p. 1996. 36.95 (*3-906754-54-5*, Pub. by P Lang) P Lang Pubng.

Perret-Gallix, D. New Computing Techniques in Physics 2. 804p. 1992. text 178.00 (*981-02-1122-8*) World Scientific Pub.

Perret-Gallix, D., jt. auth. see Becks, K-H.

Perret-Gallix, D., jt. ed. see Denby, B.

Perret, Gene. Become a Richer Writer: Shift Your Writing Career into High Gear. 234p. 1996. pap. 14.95 (*1-888688-01-7*) Jester Press.

— Best Back-to-School Jokes. (Illus.). 96p. (J). (gr. 3-7). 1998. pap. text 4.95 (*0-8069-9939-X*) Sterling.

— Business Humor. LC 98-21161. 192p. 1998. 10.95 (*0-8069-9904-7*) Sterling.

— Comedy Writing Step by Step: How to Write & Sell Your Sense of Humor. 2nd ed. LC 90-2907. 281p. 1990. reprint ed. pap. 11.95 (*0-573-60605-6*) S French Trade.

— Comedy Writing Workbook. LC 94-20150. 192p. 1994. reprint ed. pap. 25.00 (*0-88734-647-2*) Players Pr.

— Great Book of Zany Insults. (Illus.). 96p. (J). 1996. pap. 4.95 (*0-8069-9408-8*) Sterling.

***Perret, Gene.** Growing Older Is So Much Fun Everybody's Doing It. LC 99-68960. 144p. 2000. pap. 6.95 (*1-893860-10-8*) Ariz Hwy.

— Someday I'd Like to go to All the Places My Luggage Has Been. LC 99-62103. 144p. 2000. pap. 7.95 (*1-893860-01-9*) Ariz Hwy.

Perret, Gene. Successful Stand-Up Comedy: Advice from a Comedy Writer. LC 94-13671. 270p. (Orig.). 1994. pap. 13.95 (*0-573-69916-X*) S French Trade.

— Super Funny School Jokes. LC 91-22501. (Illus.). 96p. (J). (gr. 2-10). 1991. 14.95 (*0-8069-8294-2*) Sterling.

Perret, Gene & Bolton, Martha. Talk about Hope: Two Bob Hope Writers Trade Stories. 96p. 1998. pap. 6.95 (*1-888688-02-5*) Jester Press.

Perret, Gene & Martin, Terry. The Little Giant Encyclopedia of One-Liners. LC 99-31374. (Little Giant Ser.). 512p. 1999. pap. 9.95 (*0-8069-1905-1*) Sterling.

Perret, Gene & Martin, Terry P. Hilarious One-Liners. LC 95-39432. (Illus.). 96p. (J). 1996. 5.95 (*0-8069-1352-5*) Sterling.

— Roasts & Toasts: Snappy One-Liners for Every Occasion. LC 96-37008. (Illus.). 96p. 1997. 5.95 (*0-8069-9444-4*) Sterling.

Perret, Gene & Perret Martin, Terry. Classic One-Liners. LC 94-28144. (Illus.). 128p. (J). 1994. pap. 5.95 (*0-8069-0722-3*) Sterling.

P

An Asterisk (*) at the beginning of an entry indicates that the title is appearing for the first time.

*Perret, Geoffrey. Eisenhower. 688p. 2000. pap. 15.95 (1-58062-431-6) Adams Media.

— Eisenhower. LC 99-20101. 672p. 1999. 35.00 (0-375-50046-4) Random.

Perret, Geoffrey. Old Soldiers Never Die: The Life of Douglas MacArthur. LC 97-8759. 1997. pap. text 14.95 (1-55850-723-X) Adams Media.

— Ulysses S. Grant: Soldier & President. LC 98-23883. 560p. 1999. pap. 15.00 (0-375-75220-X) Modern Lib NY.

— Winged Victory. (Illus.). 544p. 1997. pap. 15.00 (0-375-75047-9) Random.

Perret, Jacques. Bande a Part. (FRE.). 1973. pap. 8.95 (0-7859-4000-6) Fr & Eur.

— Les Bifflins de Gonesse. (FRE.). 1979. pap. 8.95 (0-7859-4103-7) Fr & Eur.

— Le Caporal Epingle. (FRE.). 1972. pap. 17.95 (0-7859-3993-8) Fr & Eur.

— Les Origines de la Legende Troyenne de Rome (281-31) xxxii, 678p. reprint ed. write for info. (0-318-71387-X) G Olms Pubs.

— Role de Plaisance. (FRE.). 1975. pap. 10.95 (0-7859-4037-5) Fr & Eur.

— Roucou. (FRE.). 1984. pap. 11.95 (0-7859-4202-5) Fr & Eur.

— Le Vent dans les Voiles. (FRE.). 1983. pap. 11.95 (0-7859-4182-7) Fr & Eur.

Perret Martin, Terry, jt. auth. see Perret, Gene.

Perret, Patti. The Faces of Fantasy. 240p. 1996. pap. 22.95 (0-312-86216-4) St Martin.

— The Faces of Science Fiction. (Illus.). 164p. 1984. pap. 11.95 (0-685-10347-1) St Martin.

— The Faces of Science Fiction. deluxe ed. (Illus.). 164p. 1985. 35.00 (0-685-10348-X) St Martin.

Perret, Patti, photos by. The Faces of Fantasy. (Illus.). 231p. 1999. reprint ed. pap. text 23.00 (0-7881-5681-0) DIANE Pub.

Perrett, Angelina, jt. auth. see Daines, Brian.

Perrett, Bryan. At All Costs! (Cassell Military Classics Ser.). (Illus.). 223p. 1998. pap. 9.95 (0-304-35054-0) Sterling.

— The Battle Book: Crucial Conflicts in History from 1469 BC. 352p. 1996. pap. 19.95 (1-85409-328-2, Pub. by Arms & Armour) Sterling.

— Churchill Infantry Tank 1941-51. (New Vanguard Ser.: No. 4). (Illus.). 48p. pap. 12.95 (1-85532-297-8, 9339, Pub. by Osprey) Stackpole.

— German Armored Cars & Reconnaissance Half-Tracks, 1939-1945. (New Vanguard Ser.: Vol. 29). (Illus.). 48p. 1999. pap. text 12.95 (1-85532-849-6) Osprey.

— German Light Panzers, 1932-42. (New Vanguard Ser.: Vol. 26). (Illus.). 48p. 1999. pap. text 12.95 (1-85532-844-5, Pub. by Osprey) Stackpole.

— German Light Panzers 1932-42. (Vanguard Ser.: No. 33). (Illus.). 48p. pap. 10.95 (0-85045-483-2, 9330, Pub. by Osprey) Stackpole.

— A Hawk at War: The Peninsular War Reminiscences of General Sir Thomas Brotherton, CB. 84p. (C). 1986. 84.00 (0-948251-22-0, Pub. by Picton) St Mut.

— The Hawks: A Short History of the 14-20th King's Hussars. 151p. (C). 1984. pap. 45.00 (0-902633-94-5, Pub. by Picton) St Mut.

— Impossible Victories: Ten Unlikely Battlefield Successes. (Illus.). 240p. pap. 16.95 (1-85409-462-9, Pub. by Arms & Armour) Sterling.

— Impossible Victories: Ten Unlikely Battlefield Successes. LC 97-132756. (Illus.). 240p. 1997. 29.95 (1-85409-314-2, Pub. by Arms & Armour) Sterling.

*Perrett, Bryan. Impossible Victories: Ten Unlikely Battlefield Successes. (Military Classics). (Illus.). 2000. pap. 9.95 (0-304-35458-9) Continuum.

Perrett, Bryan. Iron Fist: Classic Armoured Warfare Case Studies. (Cassell Military Classics Ser.). 1999. pap. text 9.99 (0-304-35128-8) Continuum.

— Last Stand! (Cassell Military Classics Ser.). (Illus.). 240p. 1998. pap. 9.95 (0-304-35055-9) Sterling.

— Last Stand! Famous Battles Against the Odds. (Illus.). 240p. 1993. pap. 16.95 (1-85409-188-3) Sterling.

— Mechanised Infantry. (Vanguard Ser.: No. 38). (Illus.). 48p. pap. 10.95 (0-85045-526-X, 9327, Pub. by Osprey) Stackpole.

— The PzKpfw V Panther. (Vanguard Ser.: No. 21). (Illus.). 48p. pap. 10.95 (0-85045-397-6, 9310, Pub. by Osprey) Stackpole.

— PzKpfw III. (New Vanguard Ser.: Vol. 27). (Illus.). 48p. 1999. pap. text 12.95 (1-85532-845-3, Pub. by Osprey) Stackpole.

— The Real Hornblower: The Life & Times of Admiral Sir James Gordon, GCB. LC 97-75762. (Illus.). 168p. 1998. 29.95 (1-55750-697-3) Naval Inst Pr.

*Perrett, Bryan. The Real Hornblower: The Life & Times of Admiral Sir James Gordon, GCB. (Illus.). 168p. 2000. pap. 19.95 (1-55750-968-9) Naval Inst Pr.

— Seize & Hold: Master Strokes on the Battlefield. (Military Classics). (Illus.). 240p. 1999. pap. 9.95 (0-304-35170-9, Pub. by Cassell) Sterling.

— Sturmartillerie & Panzerjager, 1939-1945. (New Vanguard Ser.: Vol. 34). 48p. 2000. pap. 12.95 (1-84176-004-8) Osprey.

Perrett, Geoffrey. Days of Sadness, Years of Triumph: The American People, 1939-1945. LC 72-87594. 512p. 1985. reprint ed. pap. 24.95 (0-299-10394-3) U of Wis Pr.

Perrett, Jan. Job Hunting. 180p. 1996. ring bd. 199.00 (0-7494-1870-2, Kogan Pg Educ) Stylus Pub VA.

Perrett, Jan. Job Hunting after University or College. 128p. 1996. student ed., boxed set 14.95 (0-7494-1869-9, Kogan Pg Educ) Stylus Pub VA.

Perrett, Jeanne. Word Bird & the Whirlies. (English Language Teaching Ser.). (Illus.). (J). 1994. 7.50 (0-13-100256-2) P-H Intl.

Perrett, K. E., jt. auth. see Walmsley, D. A.

Perrett, Roy W. Death & Immortality. (Studies in Philosophy & Religion: No. 10). 230p. 1986. text 153.00 (90-247-3440-1) Kluwer Academic.

— Hindu Ethics: A Philosophical Study. LC 98-28560. (Monographs of the Society for Asian & Comparative Philosophy: Vol. 17). 110p. 1998. pap. text 20.00 (0-8248-2085-1) UH Pr.

— Indian Philosophy of Religion. 216p. (C). 1989. lib. bdg. 132.50 (0-7923-0437-3, Pub. by Kluwer Academic) Kluwer Academic.

Perrett, Roy W., jt. ed. see Oddie, Graham.

Perrett, Thomas I. Gold Book of Photography Price 1992. 294p. 1992. pap. 29.95 (0-915827-14-X); pap. 39.95 (0-915827-15-8) Photo Res Inst Carson Endowment.

— Gold Book of Photography Prices 1987. LC 86-18756. 300p. (Orig.). 1987. spiral bd. 29.95 (0-915827-04-2) Photo Res Inst Carson Endowment.

— Gold Book of Photography Prices 1988. 300p. (Orig.). 1988. pap. 39.95 (0-915827-06-9) Photo Res Inst Carson Endowment.

— Gold Book of Photography Prices 1990. 300p. 1990. 39.95 (0-915827-11-5); pap. 29.95 (0-915827-10-7) Photo Res Inst Carson Endowment.

— Gold Book of Photography Prices 1991. 300p. 1991. pap. 29.95 (0-915827-12-3); pap. 39.95 (0-915827-13-1) Photo Res Inst Carson Endowment.

— Gold Book of Photography Prices 1993. 342p. 1993. pap. 39.95 (0-915827-16-6) Photo Res Inst Carson Endowment.

— Gold Book of Photography Prices 1994. 325p. 1994. pap. 39.95 (0-915827-17-4) Photo Res Inst Carson Endowment.

— 1988 Gold Book of Photography Prices. 300p. (Orig.). 1988. pap. text 29.95 (0-915827-07-7) Photo Res Inst Carson Endowment.

— 1989 Gold Book of Photography Prices. 300p. 1989. spiral bd. 39.95 (0-915827-09-3) Photo Res Inst Carson Endowment.

— 1998 Gold Book of Photography Prices. 328p. 1998. pap. 49.95 (0-915827-20-4) Photo Res Inst Carson Endowment.

— 1995 Gold Book of Photography Prices. (Illus.). 328p. 1995. pap. 39.95 (0-915827-18-2) Photo Res Inst Carson Endowment.

— 1996 Gold Book of Photography Prices. 328p. 1996. pap. 39.95 (0-915827-19-0) Photo Res Inst Carson Endowment.

*Perrett, Thomas I. 2000 Goldbook of Photography Prices. 2000. pap. 69.95 (0-915827-22-0, 220) Photo Res Inst Carson Endowment.

Perrett, Thomas I., ed. Gold Book of Photography Prices 1989. 300p. 1989. pap. write for info. (0-915827-08-5) Photo Res Inst Carson Endowment.

Perrewe, Pamela L., jt. ed. see Crandall, Rick.

Perrey, Bob. The Decisive Heart. LC 96-90388. iii, 336p. 1996. 25.00 (0-9653211-0-X) R Travers Pr.

Perrez, Meinrad & Reicherts, Michael. Stress, Coping, & Health: A Situation-Behavior Approach - Theory, Methods, Applications. LC 91-35352. (Illus.). 233p. 1992. pap. text 24.00 (0-88937-065-6) Hogrefe & Huber Pubs.

Perri, Lynne, ed. see Curtis, Richard A.

Perri, Matthew. Guidelines for Improving Communications in Pharmacy Practice. 2nd ed. 24p. 1995. 20.00 (0-910769-29-X) Am Coll Apothecaries.

Perri, Michael G., et al. Improving the Long-Term Management of Obesity: Theory, Research, & Clinical Guidelines. LC 92-92. 320p. 1992. 99.95 (0-471-52899-4) Wiley.

Perri, Vincent L. Language of the Archetype: Explorations of the Unconscious in Movement, Speech, & Development. LC 97-66789. 160p. 1997. 15.95 (1-887750-64-9) Rutledge Bks.

Perri, William D. A Radical Challenge for Priesthood Today. LC 96-60952. 144p. (Orig.). 1996. pap. 14.95 (0-89622-710-3) Twenty-Third.

Perri 6 & Randon, Anita. Liberty, Charity & Politics: Non-Profit Law & Freedom of Speech. (Illus.). 240p. 1995. text 82.95 (1-85521-507-1, Pub. by Dartmth Pub) Ashgate Pub Co.

Perriam, Chris. Desire & Dissent: An Introduction to Luis Antonio de Villena. Flower, John E., ed. LC 95-183447. (New Directions in European Writing Ser.). 152p. 1995. 40.00 (1-85973-057-4) Berg Pubs.

*Perriam, Chris, et al. A New History of Spanish Writing, 1939 to the 1990s. 240p. 2000. pap. 24.95 (0-19-871517-X); text 65.00 (0-19-871516-1) OUP.

*Perriam, Wendy. Lying. 2000. 32.95 (0-7206-1108-3, Pub. by P Owen Ltd) Dufour.

*Perriand, Charlotte. Charlotte Perriand: A Life of Creation. (Illus.). 400p. 2000. pap. 40.00 (1-58093-074-3, Pub. by Monacelli Pr) Penguin Putnam.

Perriard, J., jt. ed. see Eppenberger, H. M.

*Perrick, Penny. Evermore. 2000. 29.95 (0-593-03696-4, Pub. by Transworld Publishers Ltd) Trafalgar.

Perrick, Penny. Impossible Things. 1997. pap. 12.95 (0-552-99693-9) Bantam.

Perricone, Jack. I Like to Dream. (Illus.). 16p. (J). (ps-2). 1993. lib. bdg. 10.95 (1-879567-16-4, Valeria Bks) Wonder Well.

— Me Gusta Sonar. (Illus.). 16p. (J). (ps-2). 1993. lib. bdg. 10.95 (1-879567-17-2, Valeria Bks) Wonder Well.

*Perricone, Jack. Melody in Songwriting. 2000. pap. 19.95 (0-634-00638-X, Berklee Pr) H Leonard.

Perricone, Mike. From Deadlines to Diapers: Journal of an At-Home Father. LC 92-50437. 224p. (Orig.). 1992. pap. 11.95 (1-879360-22-5) Noble Pr.

*Perricone, Nicholas. The Wrinkle Cure: Unlock the Power of Cosmeceuticals for Supple, Youthful Skin. LC 00-24808. (Illus.). 152p. 2000. 22.95 (1-57954-237-9) Rodale Pr Inc.

Perrie, D. W. Cloud Physics. LC 51-9779. (Scholarly Reprint Ser.). 155p. reprint ed. pap. 48.10 (0-608-31004-2, 202051200018) Bks Demand.

Perrie, Maureen. The Agrarian Policy of the Russian Socialist-Revolutionary Party from Its Origins Through the Revolution of 1905-1907. LC 76-644. (Soviet & East European Studies). 228p. reprint ed. pap. 65.00 (0-8357-5263-1, 2030613) Bks Demand.

— Pretenders & Popular Monarchism in Early Modern Russia: The False Tsars of the Time of Troubles. (Illus.). 287p. (C). 1995. text 64.95 (0-521-47274-1) Cambridge U Pr.

Perrie, W., ed. Nonlinear Ocean Waves. LC 97-80258. (Advances in Fluid Mechanics Ser.: Vol. 17). 272p. 1997. 135.00 (1-85312-414-1, 4141) Computational Mech MA.

Perrier, Donald, jt. auth. see Gibaldi, M.

Perrier, Edmond. The Earth Before History: Man's Origin & the Origin of Life. LC 76-44777. reprint ed. 32.50 (0-404-15962-1) AMS Pr.

Perrier, Eugene R. & Salkini, Abdul B., eds. Supplemental Irrigation in the Near East & North Africa. 628p. 1991. text 292.50 (0-7923-1006-3) Kluwer Academic.

Perrier, F., jt. auth. see Kayser, B.

Perrier, Georges & Green, Aliza. Georges Perrier Le Bec-Fin Recipes. (Illus.). 224p. 1997. 35.00 (0-7624-0170-2) Running Pr.

Perrier, Joseph. Wind of Change: Cardinal Lavigerie, 1825-1892. 142p. 1993. 29.00 (0-85439-435-4, Pub. by St Paul Pubns) St Mut.

Perrier, Joseph L. Revival of Scholastic Philosophy in the Nineteenth Century. LC 09-10966. reprint ed. 32.50 (0-404-04994-X) AMS Pr.

Perriere, Guillaume D. La, see La Perriere, Guillaume D.

Perrig, Alexander. Michelangelo's Drawings: The Science of Attribution. Joyce, Michael, tr. from GER. (Illus.). 320p. (C). 1991. 65.00 (0-300-03948-4) Yale U Pr.

Perrig, Walter J., jt. ed. see Grob, Alexander.

Perrigo, Eileen M., jt. auth. see Gaut, Deborah A.

Perrigo, Evelyn L. Grandies Are Great. (Illus.). 88p. 1980. pap. 5.00 (0-933992-11-4) Coffee Break.

*Perrigo, L. D., et al, eds. Cold Climate Corrosion: Special Topics. (Illus.). 150p. 1999. 75.00 (1-57590-047-5, 37404) NACE Intl.

Perrigo, Lynn, ed. see Cionca, John.

Perrigo, Lynn I. Hispanos: Historic Leaders in New Mexico. LC 85-489. 128p. (Orig.). 1985. pap. 9.95 (0-86534-011-0) Sunstone Pr.

Perrigo, O. E. Lathe Design-Construction & Operation. 1984. reprint ed. pap. 24.95 (0-917914-18-X) Lindsay Pubns.

Perrill, John H., jt. auth. see Dunlap, Franklin.

Perrim, Jim. Games Climbers Play II: Mirrors in the Cliffs. (Illus.). 706p. (Orig.). 1999. pap. 19.95 (0-89732-296-7) Menasha Ridge.

Perriman, Wendy. Free Fall. 88p. 1998. pap. 8.50 (1-57502-933-2, PO2569) Morris Pubng.

Perriman, Wendy K. Collected Experience. 108p. (Orig.). 1996. pap. 8.50 (1-57502-110-2) Morris Pubng.

*Perrin. Ethics. (Nursing Concepts Ser.). 2000. 22.95 (1-889325-52-X, Pub. by Fence Crk Pubng) Blackwell Sci.

Perrin. General Statutes of North Carolina. write for info. (0-614-05826-0, MICHIE) LEXIS Pub.

— Perrin Beacon Hd Bk & Desk Ref. 5th ed. Date not set. pap. text 19.17 (0-395-98207-3) HM.

— Switching Machines. 1972. text 155.50 (90-277-0196-2) Kluwer Academic.

— Switching Machines. 2nd ed. 1972. text 162.50 (90-277-0197-0) Kluwer Academic.

*Perrin & Webber, T. Organisational Health: Diagnosis & Treatment. (Financial Times Management Briefings Ser.). 1998. pap. 94.50 (0-273-63396-1, Pub. by F T P-H) Trans-Atl Phila.

Perrin, A. F. & Meeker, M. F. Purdy: Allied Families of Purdy, Fauconnier (Falconer), Archer & Perrin. 114p. 1991. reprint ed. pap. 16.50 (0-8328-1759-7) Higginson Bk Co.

*Perrin, Anne Elliott. Soliloquy of a Farmer's Wife: The Diary of Annie Elliot Perrin. Randall, Dale B., ed. LC 98-49756. (Illus.). 304p. 1999. 39.95 (0-8214-1266-3) Ohio U Pr.

*Perrin, Annie Elliott. Soliloquy of a Farmer's Wife: The Diary of Annie Elliot Perrin. Randall, Dale B., ed. LC 98-49756. (Illus.). 304p. 1999. pap. 19.95 (0-8214-1267-1) Ohio U Pr.

Perrin, Arnold. The Care & Feeding of the Prostate. 1980. pap. 1.00 (0-939736-49-7) Wings ME.

— The Essentials of Writing Poetry. 40p. 1992. pap. 7.95 (0-911666-50-8) Wings ME.

— Noah. 1993. pap. 4.00 (0-939736-50-0) Wings ME.

— Out of Bondage. (Illus.). 52p. 1983. pap. 4.95 (0-939736-45-4) Wings ME.

— View from Hill Cabin. 1979. pap. 2.95 (0-89002-119-8) Wings ME.

— The Wind's Will. 24p. 1993. pap. 4.00 (0-939736-05-5) Wings ME.

— You Were Designed to Live for One Hundred & Forty Years. 1979. pap. 1.00 (0-939736-06-3) Wings ME.

Perrin, Arnold, ed. The Best of Nineteen-Eighty. 32p. (Orig.). 1981. pap. 2.95 (0-939736-20-9) Wings Bks.

— Black Washed & Ghost Bright. 1981. pap. 2.00 (0-939736-22-5) Wings ME.

— Bury Me Sioux. 1982. pap. 2.00 (0-939736-46-2) Wings ME.

— Ecossaise. 1983. pap. 2.00 (0-939736-47-0) Wings ME.

— Fingers of the Wind. 1980. pap. 2.00 (0-939736-13-6) Wings ME.

Perrin, Beradotte, tr. Plutarch, the Parallel Lives Vol. IV: Alcibiades & Coriolanus, Lysander & Sulla. 1989. text 18.95 (0-674-99089-7) HUP.

Perrin, Carl. Successful Resumes & Interviews: Instructor's Guide. 23p. 1994. teacher ed. 13.00 (0-8273-5992-6) Delmar.

Perrin, Carl & Dublin, Peter. Successful Resumes & Interviews. LC 93-4925. (C). 1994. mass mkt. 28.00 (0-8273-5991-8) Delmar.

Perrin, Cathy J. Recipes from America's Farm Kitchens. 1995. 11.90 (0-9646525-0-1) Perrin Prod.

Perrin, Charles E. La Societe Feodale Allemande et Ses Institutions du Xe au XIIe Siecle. LC 80-2013. reprint ed. 38.50 (0-404-18583-5) AMS Pr.

*Perrin, D. Well Completion & Servicing: Oil & Gas Field Development Techniques. 325p. 1999. 85.00 (2-7108-0765-3) Edits Technip.

Perrin, D., jt. ed. see Gross, M.

Perrin, D., jt. ed. see Nivat, Maurice.

Perrin, D. D. Dissociation Constants of Organic Bases in Aqueous Solution, Vol. 12. 524p. 1972. 516.00 (0-08-020827-4, Pub. by Pergamon Repr) Franklin.

Perrin, D. D., ed. Ionization Constants of Inorganic Acids & Bases in Aqueous Solution, No.29. 2nd ed. (Chemical Data Ser.). 194p. 1982. 91.00 (0-08-029214-3, Pub. by Pergamon Repr) Franklin.

— Stability Constants of Metal-Ion Complexes Pt. B: Organic Ligands. (Chemical Data Ser.: No. 22). 1280p. 1979. 552.00 (0-08-020958-0, Pub. by Pergamon Repr) Franklin.

Perrin, D. D. & Dempsey, B. Buffers for Pich & Metal Ion Control. 1979. pap. 25.00 (0-412-21890-9, NO.6218) Chapman & Hall.

Perrin, D. D., et al. Purification of Laboratory Chemicals. 2nd ed. LC 79-41708. 580p. 1980. 110.00 (0-08-022961-1, Pergamon Pr) Elsevier.

Perrin, D. D., jt. auth. see Armarego, W. L.

Perrin, David. The Injured Athlete. 3rd ed. LC 98-26849. 640p. 1998. text 98.00 (0-397-51534-0) Lppncott W & W.

Perrin, David B. Canciones Entre el Alma y el Esposo of Juan de la Cruz: A Hermeneutical Interpretation. 430p. 1996. 74.95 (1-57309-095-6) Intl Scholars.

— For Love of the World: The Old & New Self of John of the Cross. LC 96-49320. 146p. 1997. 74.95 (1-57309-146-4, Cath Scholar Pr); pap. 54.95 (1-57309-145-6, Cath Scholar Pr) Intl Scholars.

— The Sacrament of Reconciliation: An Existential Approach. LC 98-44214. (Roman Catholic Studies: Vol. 11). 180p. 1998. text 79.95 (0-7734-8245-8) E Mellen.

Perrin, David Brian. Canciones Entre el Alma y el Esposo of Juan de la Cruz: A Hermeneutical Interpretation. 430p. 1996. pap. 54.95 (1-57309-094-8) Intl Scholars.

Perrin, David H. Athletic Taping & Bracing. LC 95-1519. 120p. 1995. pap. text 26.00 (0-87322-502-3, BPER0502) Human Kinetics.

*Perrin, Dennis. American Fan: Sports Mania & the Culture That Feeds It. LC 99-41417. 240p. 2000. 23.00 (0-380-97732-X, Avon Bks) Morrow Avon.

— Mr. Mike: The Life & Work of Michael O'Donoghue. (Illus.). 448p. 1999. pap. 13.50 (0-380-72832-X, Avon Bks) Morrow Avon.

Perrin, Don. Theros Ironfeld. (DragonLance Warriors Ser.: Vol. 4). 1996. pap. 5.99 (0-7869-0481-X, Pub. by TSR Inc) Random.

Perrin, Don, jt. auth. see Weis, Margaret.

Perrin, Don, ed. see Smith, Lester.

Perrin, Edward B., et al, eds. Assessment of Performance Measures for Public Health, Substance Abuse, & Mental Health. LC 97-4915. 160p. 1997. pap. 25.00 (0-309-05796-5) Natl Acad Pr.

Perrin, Edward B., ed. see National Research Council Staff.

Perrin, Eugene, jt. auth. see Lewis, Steven H.

Perrin, Fern B. To Make a Dream Come True. 198p. (Orig.). pap. 8.95 (0-927022-04-4) CHJ Pub.

Perrin, Guy-Ren E. & Darte, Alain. The Data Parallel Programming Model: Foundations, HPF Realization & Scientific Applications, Vol. 113. LC 96-41753. (Lecture Notes on Computer Science Ser.). xv, 284p. 1996. 49.00 (3-540-61736-1) Spr-Verlag.

Perrin, J. P., ed. Control, Computers, Communications in Transportation: Selected Papers from the IFAC - IFIP - IFORS Symposium, Paris, France, 19-21 September 1989. (IFAC Symposia Ser.: No. 9012). 300p. 1990. 142.00 (0-08-037025-X, Pergamon Pr) Elsevier.

Perrin, J. R., ed. Roman Pottery from Excavation at & Near to the Roman Small Town of Durobrivae, Water Newton, Cambridgeshire, 1956-58. (Journal of Roman Pottery Studies: Vol. 8). (Illus.). 145p. (Orig.). 1999. pap. 36.00 (1-900188-84-8, Pub. by Oxbow Bks) David Brown.

Perrin, J. S., jt. auth. see Garner, F. A.

Perrin, James M., et al. Home & Community Care for Chronically Ill Children. 176p. (C). 1993. text 39.50 (0-19-507120-4) OUP.

Perrin, James M., jt. auth. see Bruner, Charles.

Perrin, James M., jt. ed. see Hobbs, Nicholas.

*Perrin, Janet T. Annie's Favorite Home Decor Projects. (Illus.). 2000. 19.96 (0-9655269-6-8) Annies Attic TX.

Perrin-Jassy, Marie F. Basic Community in the African Churches. LC 72-93342. (Illus.). 275p. reprint ed. pap. 85.30 (0-8357-8813-X, 203346600086) Bks Demand.

Perrin, Jean. Atoms. Hammick, D. L., tr. from FRE. LC 90-42918. xvi, 232p. 1990. reprint ed. 42.00 (0-918024-78-1); reprint ed. pap. 19.95 (0-918024-79-X) Ox Bow.

Perrin, Jean P. History of the Ancient Christians Inhabiting the Valleys of the Alps. 1991. reprint ed. 32.00 (0-685-40812-4) Church History.

Perrin, Jim. Spirits of Place. (Illus.). 1997. 52.95 (0-8464-4575-1) Beekman Pubs.

— Spirits of Place. (Illus.). 1997. 53.00 (1-85902-482-3, Pub. by Gomer Pr) St Mut.

P

Perrin, Jim, ed. Eric Shipton: The Six Mountain-Travel Books. LC 84-62263. (Illus.). 800p. 1985. 38.00 (*0-89886-075-X*) Mountaineers.

Perrin, J.S., jt. ed. see Brager.

***Perrin, Kalya.** The Disappearance of Allison Jones. (J). (gr. 4-7). 2000. pap. 5.95 (*1-58571-022-9*, 909-099, Pub. by Genesis Press) BookWorld.

Perrin, Kayla. Again, My Love. 1999. mass mkt. 5.99 (*0-345-43255-X*) Ballantine Pub Grp.

— Again, My Love. LC 98-142446. 212p. 1998. pap. 10.95 (*1-885478-23-2*, Pub. by Genesis Press) BookWorld.

— Arabesque: Sweet Honesty. pap. 4.99 (*1-58314-011-5*) BET Bks.

— Everlasting Love. 304p. 1998. pap. 4.99 (*0-7860-0533-5*) Kensgtn Pub Corp.

***Perrin, Kayla.** Holiday of Love. (Arabesque Ser.). 2000. mass mkt. 5.99 (*1-58314-187-1*) BET Bks.

— Midnight Dreams. 1999. mass mkt. 4.99 (*1-58314-044-1*) BET Bks.

Perrin, Lionel, tr. see Fulcanelli.

Perrin, Marshall L., tr. see Von Sybel, Heinrich.

***Perrin, Michel.** Magnificent Molas: The Art of the Kuna Indians. (Illus.). 208p. 2000. text 45.00 (*2-08-013674-7*, Pub. by Flammarion) Abbeville Pr.

Perrin, Michel. The Way of the Dead Indians: Guajiro Myths & Symbols. Fineberg, Michael, tr. from FRE. (Sourcebooks in Anthropology: No. 13). (Illus.). 229p. 1987. pap. 14.95 (*0-292-79039-2*); text 30.00 (*0-292-79032-5*) U of Tex Pr.

Perrin, N. Making Maple Syrup. 1983. pap. 2.95 (*0-88266-226-0*, Storey Pub) Storey Bks.

Perrin, Nat. Celebration: Manuscript Edition. 1964. pap. 13.00 (*0-8222-0194-1*) Dramatists Play.

Perrin, Noel. Amateur Sugar Maker. anniversary ed. LC 91-50818. (Illus.). 120p. 1992. pap. 10.95 (*0-87451-579-3*) U Pr of New Eng.

— A Child's Delight. LC 97-28220. 177p. 1997. 19.95 (*0-87451-840-7*) U Pr of New Eng.

— Dr. Bowdler's Legacy: A History of Expurgated Books in England & America. 346p. 1992. pap. 14.95 (*0-87923-861-5*) Godine.

— First Person Rural: Essays of a Sometime Farmer. LC 77-94109. 124p. 1990. reprint ed. pap. 13.95 (*0-87923-833-X*) Godine.

— Giving up the Gun. LC 80-50744. 122p. 1980. pap. 6.95 (*0-394-73949-3*) Random.

— Giving up the Gun: Japan's Reversion to the Sword, 1543-1879. LC 78-74252. (Nonpareil Bks.). (Illus.). 136p. 1979. pap. 11.95 (*0-87923-773-2*) Godine.

— A Noel Perrin Sampler: Elegant Humor & Lighthearted Essays by the Author of First Person Ruran & a Reader's Delight. LC 90-50907. 160p. Date not set. reprint ed. pap. 49.60 (*0-608-20688-1*, 207179600002) Bks Demand.

— A Reader's Delight. LC 87-40507. 220p. 1988. pap. 14.95 (*0-87451-432-0*) U Pr of New Eng.

— Second Person Rural: More Essays of a Sometime Farmer. LC 80-66193. 176p. 1980. reprint ed. pap. 13.95 (*0-87923-834-8*) Godine.

— Third Person Rural: Further Essays of a Sometime Farmer. (Illus.). 208p. 1983. reprint ed. pap. 13.95 (*1-56792-057-8*) Godine.

Perrin, Noel, ed. see Lindbergh, Anne M.

Perrin, Norman. What Is Redaction Criticism? Via, Dan O., Jr., ed. LC 72-81529. (Guides to Biblical Scholarship Ser.). 96p. (Orig.). 1969. pap. 12.00 (*0-8006-0181-5*, 1-181, Fortress Pr) Augsburg Fortress.

Perrin, Norman, jt. auth. see Duling, Dennis C.

Perrin, Pat, ed. Architecture: An Image for America. LC 97-77595. (Perspectives on History Ser.: Pt. III). (Illus.). 64p. 1998. pap. 6.95 (*1-57960-010-7*) Disc Enter Ltd.

***Perrin, Pat, intro.** The Underground Railroad: Life on the Road to Freedom. LC 99-62411. (Perspectives on History Ser.). (Illus.). 66p. (YA). (gr. 5-12). 1999. pap. 6.95 (*1-57960-051-4*) Disc Enter Ltd.

Perrin, Pat, jt. auth. see Coleman, Wim.

Perrin, Pat, jt. ed. see Coleman, Wim.

Perrin, Penelope. Russia. LC 93-30422. (Discovering Science Ser.). (Illus.). 32p. (J). (gr. 4 up). 1994. lib. bdg. 13.95 (*0-89686-775-7*, Crstwood Hse) Silver Burdett Pr.

Perrin, Randy, et al. Time Like a River. 140p. (YA). (gr. 4 up). 1997. pap. 8.95 (*1-57143-083-0*) RDR Bks.

Perrin, Randy, et al. Time Like a River. 128p. (YA). (gr. 4 up). 1997. pap. 8.95 (*1-57143-067-9*) RDR Bks.

— Time Like a River. LC 97-67391. 144p. (YA). (gr. 5 up). 1999. 14.95 (*1-57143-061-X*) RDR Bks.

***Perrin-Riou, Bernadette.** P-Adic L-Functions of P-Adic Representations. LC 99-56550. (SMF Texts & Monographs: Vol. 3). 150p. 2000. 49.00 (*0-8218-1946-1*) Am Math.

Perrin, Rob, ed. Journal of Roman Pottery Studies, Vol. 2. annuals (Illus.). 130p. 1989. pap. 22.00 (*0-946897-26-3*, Pub. by Oxbow Bks) David Brown.

— Journal of Roman Pottery Studies, Vol. 3. annuals (Illus.). 130p. 1990. pap. 22.00 (*0-946897-24-7*, Pub. by Oxbow Bks) David Brown.

— Journal of Roman Pottery Studies, Vol. 5, 1992. annuals (Illus.). 160p. 1993. pap. 27.00 (*0-946897-65-4*, Pub. by Oxbow Bks) David Brown.

— Journal of Roman Pottery Studies, Vol. 6, 1993. annuals (Illus.). 125p. 1995. pap. 27.00 (*0-946897-88-3*, Pub. by Oxbow Bks) David Brown.

— Journal of Roman Pottery Studies, Vol. 7. annuals 1996. pap. 35.00 (*0-614-21877-2*, Pub. by Oxbow Bks) David Brown.

Perrin, Robert. Beacon Handbook, 3 vols. (C). 1993. text 19.16 (*0-395-69262-8*) HM.

— Beacon Handbook, 4 vols. (C). 1996. pap., teacher ed. 11.96 (*0-395-77993-6*) HM.

— The Beacon Handbook, 2 vols. 2nd ed. (C). 1989. text 22.76 (*0-395-52686-8*) HM.

— The Beacon Handbook, 2 vols. 2nd ed. (C). 1990. pap. text 7.16 (*0-395-52688-4*) HM.

— The Beacon Handbook, 2 vols. 2nd ed. (C). 1990. pap. text 1.16 (*0-395-53278-7*); 89.56 (*0-395-52987-5*) HM.

— Handbook for College Research. 352p. (C). 1996. pap. text 17.96 (*0-395-73869-5*) HM.

— Piggy's Luck & More Tales of Evildoing. LC 98-74578. 244p. 1998. pap. 14.95 (*0-9668151-0-6*) Claybanks Pr.

Perrin, Robert G. Herbert Spencer: A Primary & Secondary Bibliography, 2 vols., Set. LC 93-12108. 1024p. 1993. text 40.00 (*0-8240-4597-1*, H1061) Garland.

Perrin, Robin D., jt. auth. see Miller-Perrin, Cindy L.

Perrin, Steve. Acadia: The Soul of a National Park. Orig. Title: Hiking the Living Trails of Acadia National Park. (Illus.). 360p. 1998. pap. 28.30 (*0-9651058-4-9*) Earthling Pr.

— Charlemagne's Paladins: Historical Reference. 1992. 15.00 (*1-56076-393-0*) TSR Inc.

— Hiking the Living Trails of Acadia National Park, Bk. 1. (Illus.). 160p. (Orig.). 1996. pap. 12.95 (*0-9651058-1-4*) Earthling Pr.

***Perrin, Steve.** The Shore Path, Bar Harbor, Maine. (Illus.). 96p. 2000. pap. 8.95 (*0-9651058-6-5*) Earthling Pr.

Perrin, Stuart. The Dancing Man: A Deeper Sense of Surrender. 145p. (Orig.). (YA). 1993. pap. 15.00 (*0-9638401-0-X*) Carvalhosa Grap.

Perrin, Suzanne M. Comparable Worth & Public Policy: The Case of Pennsylvania. LC 85-51721. (Labor Relations & Public Policy Ser.: No. 29). 136p. reprint ed. pap. 42.20 (*0-8357-3155-3*, 203941800012) Bks Demand.

Perrin, Towers. Handbook of Executive Benefits. LC 94-32794. 336p. 1995. text 75.00 (*0-7863-0185-6*, Irwn Prfssnl) McGraw-Hill Prof.

— Handbook of 401(k) Plan Management. 2nd rev. ed. 360p. 1996. 70.00 (*0-7863-1117-7*, Irwn Prfssnl) McGraw-Hill Prof.

Perrin, Ursula. Cool's Ridge. LC 95-4583. 320p. 1996. 24.00 (*1-877946-68-0*) Permanent Pr.

— The Looking-Glass Lover: A Novel. 256p. 1989. 17.95 (*0-316-69961-6*) Little.

Perrin, W. H., et al. Kentucky, a History of the State, 10 vols. Incl. Fifth Edition. (Illus.). 164p. 1992. reprint ed. 25.00 (*0-89308-137-X*); First Edition. (Illus.). 440p. 1992. reprint ed. 32.50 (*0-89308-133-7*); Second Edition. (Illus.). 507p. 1992. reprint ed. 37.50 (*0-89308-134-5*); 1992. reprint ed. write for info. (*0-318-55756-8*) Southern Hist Pr.

Perrin, Wendy. Wendy Perrin's Secrets Every Smart Traveler Should Know. LC 96-48213. 240p. 1996. pap. 15.00 (*0-679-03351-3*) Fodors Travel.

Perrin, Wes. Advertising Realities: A Practical Guide to Agency Management. 184p. (C). 1991. pap. text 27.95 (*0-87484-999-3*, 999) Mayfield Pub.

Perrin, William H. County of Christian, Kentucky. (Illus.). 656p. 1993. reprint ed. lib. bdg. 66.00 (*0-8328-2943-9*) Higginson Bk Co.

— History of Todd County, Kentucky. Battle, J. H., ed. 385p. 1979. reprint ed. 35.00 (*0-89308-162-0*) Southern Hist Pr.

— History of Trigg County, Historical & Biographical. (Illus.). 293p. 1979. 32.50 (*0-89308-164-7*) Southern Hist Pr.

— History of Trigg County, Kentucky. (Illus.). 324p. 1994. reprint ed. pap. text 22.50 (*0-7884-0040-1*) Heritage Bk.

— Southwest Louisiana: Biographical & Historical. 1971. 35.00 (*0-87511-094-0*) Claitors.

Perrin, William H., ed. History of Alexander, Union & Pulaski Counties. (Illus.). 926p. 1995. reprint ed. lib. bdg. 95.00 (*0-8328-4995-2*) Higginson Bk Co.

— History of Effingham County, Illinois. (Illus.). 628p. 1993. reprint ed. lib. bdg. 65.00 (*0-8328-3232-4*) Higginson Bk Co.

— History of Summit County Ohio. 1050p. 1993. reprint ed. lib. bdg. 99.50 (*0-8328-3462-9*) Higginson Bk Co.

Perrin, William H., jt. ed. see Hill, H. H.

Perrine. Limerick's Always a Verse. (C). 1989. pap. text 21.00 (*0-15-551003-7*) Harcourt Coll Pubs.

Perrine, Daniel M. The Chemistry of Mind-Altering Drugs: History, Pharmacology, & Cultural Context. LC 96-28908. (An American Chemical Society Publication). (Illus.). 500p. 1996. pap. text 42.00 (*0-8412-3253-9*, Pub. by Am Chemical) OUP.

Perrine, Doug. Sharks. LC 94-42427. (WorldLife Library). (Illus.). 72p. (YA). 1995. pap. 16.95 (*0-89658-270-1*) Voyageur Pr.

— Sharks & Rays of the World. LC 99-25791. (Illus.). 132p. 1999. 29.95 (*0-89658-448-8*) Voyageur Pr.

Perrine, H. D. Daniel Perrin, "the Huguenot", & His Descendants in America of the Surnames Perrine, Perine, & Prine, 1665-1910. (Illus.). 553p. 1989. reprint ed. pap. 69.00 (*0-8328-0957-8*); reprint ed. lib. bdg. 79.00 (*0-8328-0956-X*) Higginson Bk Co.

Perrine, James O. Slide Rule Handbook. 112p. (C). 1965. 45.00 (*0-677-01060-5*) Gordon & Breach.

***Perrine, Jane Myers.** The Mad Herringtons. 200p. 2000. 19.95 (*1-929085-22-2*); 17.95 (*1-929085-23-0*); mass mkt. 4.95 (*1-929085-21-4*) Rgncy Pr.

— The Mad Herringtons. large type ed. 336p. 2000. 23.95 (*1-929085-24-9*); per. 19.95 (*1-929085-25-7*) Rgncy Pr.

Perrine, Laurence. Literature: Structure, Sound, & Sense. 6th ed. (C). 1993. pap. text, teacher ed. 30.00 (*0-15-500299-6*) Harcourt Coll Pubs.

— Perrine's Story & Structure. 9th ed. (C). 1997. pap. text, teacher ed. 28.00 (*0-15-503722-6*) Harcourt Coll Pubs.

— Sense & Nonsense: Original Limericks by Laurence Perrine. LC 93-42068. 64p. (Orig.). 1994. pap. 10.00 (*0-914061-41-0*) Orchises Pr.

— Sound & Sense. 8th ed. (C). 1992. pap. text, teacher ed. 32.00 (*0-15-582611-5*) Harcourt Coll Pubs.

— Sound & Sense: An Introduction to Poetry. 9th ed. (C). 1996. pap. text, teacher ed. 28.00 (*0-15-503743-9*) Harcourt Coll Pubs.

— Story & Structure. 8th ed. (C). 1993. pap. text, teacher ed. 33.75 (*0-15-500300-3*) Harcourt Coll Pubs.

Perrine, Laurence & Arp, Thomas R. Sound & Sense: An Introduction to Poetry. 3rd ed. 350p. (C). 1992. pap. text 4.50 (*0-15-565732-1*) Harcourt Coll Pubs.

— SOUND & SENSE 8E (SCHOOL EDITI. 8th ed. 350p. (C). 1992. pap. text 37.00 (*0-15-582610-7*) Harcourt Coll Pubs.

Perrine, Laurence, jt. auth. see Arp, Thomas R.

Perrine, Mary. Nannabah's Friend. (Illus.). 32p. (J). (gr. k-3). 1989. pap. 5.95 (*0-395-52020-7*) HM.

Perrine, Robert C., Sr. Design Handbook for PM Motors & Tachometers. 140.00 (*1-881855-05-8*) Motorsoft.

Perrine, Susie. Follow the Fun: Places to Go, Things to Do: Las Vegas. (Illus.). 100p. (Orig.). (J). 1995. pap. 9.95 (*1-885511-00-0*) Las Vegas Pubng.

Perrine, Toni A. Film & the Nuclear Age: Representing Cultural Anxiety. LC 97-31934. (Studies in American Popular History & Culture). 304p. 1997. text 68.00 (*0-8153-2932-6*) Garland.

***Perring, Chris, ed.** Ports of Call: A Distinguished Companion to the Harbours & Marinas of the British Isles. (Illus.). 224p. 2000. 24.95 (*1-871349-98-2*, Pub. by Kensington West) Midpt Trade.

Perring, Christine M. The Experience of Psychiatric Hospital Closure: An Anthropological Study. (Studies of Care in the Community). 231p. 1993. 67.95 (*1-85628-422-0*, Pub. by Avebry) Ashgate Pub Co.

Perring, Dominic, jt. auth. see Perring, Stefania.

Perring, Stefania. Then & Now. 1999. 15.99 (*0-7858-1116-8*) Bk Sales Inc.

Perring, Stefania & Perring, Dominic. Then & Now: The Wonders of the Ancient World Brought to Life in Vivid See-Through Reproductions. (Illus.). 144p. 1991. 29.95 (*0-02-599461-1*) Macmillan.

Perrings, C. A., et al, eds. Biodiversity Conservation: Problems & Policies. LC 94-32553. (Ecology, Economy & Environment Ser.: Vol. 4). 416p. (C). 1994. lib. bdg. 186.50 (*0-7923-3140-0*) Kluwer Academic.

— Biodiversity Conservation: Problems & Policies. LC 95-30108. (Ecology, Economy & Environment Ser.: Vol. 4). 1995. text 195.00 (*0-7923-3616-X*) Kluwer Academic.

Perrings, Charles. Black Mineworkers in Central Africa. LC 78-11413. 302p. 1979. 49.50 (*0-8419-0462-6*, Africana) Holmes & Meier.

— Economics of Ecological Resources: Selected Essays. LC 96-52255. (New Horizons in Environmental Economics Ser.). 288p. 1997. 95.00 (*1-85898-473-4*) E Elgar.

— Economy & Environment: A Theoretical Essay on the Interdependence of Economics & Environmental Systems. 200p. 1987. text 80.00 (*0-521-34081-0*) Cambridge U Pr.

Perrings, Charles, ed. The Economics of Biodiversity Conservation in Sub-Saharan Africa: Mending the Ark. LC 99-22821. 384p. 2000. 110.00 (*1-84064-150-9*) E Elgar.

Perrings, Charles, et al, eds. Biodiversity Loss: Economic & Ecological Issues. (Illus.). 348p. (C). 1995. text 64.95 (*0-521-47178-8*) Cambridge U Pr.

***Perrings, Charles, et al.** The Economics of Biological Invasions. LC 00-26460. 2000. write for info. (*1-84064-378-1*) E Elgar.

Perrino, Anthony F. Holyquest. LC 88-63124. 162p. (Orig.). (C). 1988. pap. 8.00 (*0-931104-24-6*) SunInk Pubn.

— The Numbering of Our Days. (Mediation Manuals Ser.). (Illus.). (Orig.). 1988. pap. 3.00 (*0-933840-33-0*) Unitarian Univ.

Perrino, Karen, jt. auth. see Neff, Rena.

Perrins, Bryan. Trade Union Law. 1985. 70.00 (*0-406-25830-9*, UK, MICHIE); pap. 48.00 (*0-406-25831-7*, UK, MICHIE) LEXIS Pub.

Perrins, Bryn. Introduction to Land Law. 192p. 1995. pap. 18.00 (*1-85941-029-4*, Pub. by Cavendish Pubng) Gaunt.

Perrins, Bryn, et al, eds. Harvey on Industrial Relations & Employment Law. ring bd. write for info. (*0-406-04811-8*, HIREASET, MICHIE) LEXIS Pub.

Perrins, C. M., jt. ed. see Snow, D. W.

Perrins, Christopher M. New Generation Guide to the Birds of Britain & Europe. (Corrie Herring Hooks Ser.: No. 8). (Illus.). 320p. 1987. 16.95 (*0-292-75532-5*) U of Tex Pr.

Perrins, Christopher M., et al, eds. Bird Population Studies: Relevance to Conservation & Management. (Ornithology Ser.: No. 1). (Illus.). 700p. 1993. pap. text 45.00 (*0-19-854082-5*) OUP.

Perrins, Christopher M. & Middleton, Alex L., eds. The Encyclopedia of Birds. (Illus.). 480p. 1985. 50.00 (*0-8160-1150-8*) Facts on File.

Perrins, Gerald L., ed. Occupational Compensation Survey: National Summary, 1996. (Illus.). 256p. (C). 1998. pap. text 50.00 (*0-7881-7560-2*) DIANE Pub.

Perris, Arnold. Music As Propaganda: Art to Persuade, Art to Control. 8. LC 84-27969. (Contributions to the Study of Music & Dance Ser.: No. 8). 247p. 1985. 49.95 (*0-313-24505-3*, PMP/, Greenwood Pr) Greenwood.

Perris, C. Cognitive Therapy with Schizophrenic Patients. LC 88-24467. 240p. 1989. lib. bdg. 34.95 (*0-89862-737-0*) Guilford Pubns.

Perris, C., ed. Clinical Neurophysiological Aspects of Psychopathological Coniditions. (Advances in Biological Psychiatry Ser.: Vol. 4). (Illus.). viii, 192p. 1980. pap. 53.25 (*3-8055-0604-X*) S Karger.

Perris, C., et al, eds. Cognitive Psychotherapy. (Illus.). 480p. 1988. 137.00 (*0-387-18870-3*) Spr-Verlag.

— Neurophysiological Correlates of Normal Cognition & Psychopathology. (Advances in Biological Psychiatry Ser.: Vol. 13). (Illus.). viii, 232p. 1984. pap. 85.25 (*3-8055-3737-9*) S Karger.

— Parental & Psychopathology. LC 94-11557. (Clinical Psychology Ser.). 360p. 1995. 250.00 (*0-471-94226-X*) Wiley.

Perris, Carlo & McGorry, Patrick D. Cognitive Psychotherapy of Psychotic Disorders: Handbook of Theory & Practice. LC 98-3825. 468p. 1999. 131.95 (*0-471-98221-0*) Wiley.

Perris, P.Harold & Lutz, Norma Jean. A Matter of Conscience: Court-Martialed for his Faith. LC 97-47005. 164p. (Orig.). 1997. pap. 9.99 (*0-8280-1087-0*) Review & Herald.

Perrissoud, D. & Testa, B., eds. Liver Drugs: From Experimental Pharmacology to Therapeutic Application. 288p. 1988. 218.00 (*0-8493-6734-4*, RC846) CRC Pr.

Perritt. Human & Envionmental Interchange. LC 97-170265. (C). 1997. pap. text 20.50 (*0-03-020307-4*, Pub. by Harcourt Coll Pubs) Harcourt.

Perritt, Gerald W. Dollars & Sense: Financial Wisdom in 101 Doses. 312p. 1986. pap. 18.95 (*0-685-14685-5*) Invest Info.

— Expand Your Investment Horizons & Increase Your Stock Market Profits. 288p. 1987. 24.95 (*0-930369-02-5*); pap. 19.95 (*0-930369-03-3*) Invest Info.

— Mutual Funds & Your Investment Portfolio. 2nd ed. 129p. 1987. pap. 8.95 (*0-930369-18-1*) Invest Info.

Perritt, Gerald W. & Lavine, Alan. Diversify Your Way to Wealth: How to Customize Your Investment Portfolio to Protect & Build. 2nd rev. ed. LC 94-119080. 200p. 1993. text 24.95 (*1-55738-546-7*, Irwn Prfssnl) McGraw-Hill Prof.

Perritt, Henry H. Americans with Disabilities Act Handbook, 3 vols., Vol. 3. 3rd ed. LC 97-6383. 1720p. 1997. boxed set 395.00 (*0-471-16754-1*, LA45) Wiley.

Perritt, Henry H., Jr. Employee Dismissal: Law & Practice, 3. 1760p. 1997. boxed set 295.00 (*0-7355-1150-0*) Aspen Pub.

Perritt, Henry H., Jr. Everything Solo Practitioners Need to Know about Computers. 104p. 1995. pap. 29.95 (*0-614-17119-9*, G1-1023) PLI.

— How to Practice Law with Computers. 1217p. 1992. suppl. ed. 110.00 (*0-685-69450-X*, G1-1018) PLI.

Perritt, Henry H. How to Practice Law with Computers. 3rd ed. LC 97-76202. xxxv, 626 p. 1998. 135.00 (*0-87224-111-4*) PLI.

— How to Practice Law with Computers 3rd ed. LC 97-76202. xxxv, 626p. 1998. write for info. (*0-08-722403-8*) Elsevier.

— How to Practice Law with Computers Plus 1990 Supplement. 779p. 1988. text 110.00 (*0-685-46012-6*, G6-1014) PLI.

Perritt, Henry H., Jr. Trade Secrets: A Practitioner's Guide. 700p. 1994. 125.00 (*0-614-17115-6*, G1-1021) PLI.

— Your Rights in the Workplace: Everything Employees Need to Know. 250p. 1993. pap. 14.95 (*0-87224-049-5*) PLI.

*** Perritt Jr., Henry H.** 1999 Employment Law Update, 1. 544p. 1999. pap. text 150.00 (*0-7355-0348-6*) Panel Pubs.

Perrizo, E. W. 11th International Conference on Computer Applications in Industry & Engineering Procedures: Caine-98, November 11-13, 1998, Las Vegas, Nevada, U. S. A. LC 99-181341. 314p. (C). 1998. write for info. (*1-880843-26-9*) Int Soc Comp App.

Perro, Robert S. How to Find Your Upswing after You've Been Downsized. 187p. (Orig.). 1997. pap. 19.95 (*0-9658880-0-2*) R S Perro.

Perrolle, Pierre M., ed. Fundamentals of the Chinese Communist Party. Richardson, Lloyd & Richardson, Chung, trs. from CHI. LC 75-46228. (China Book Project Ser.). 253p. reprint ed. 78.50 (*0-8357-9435-0*, 201613400098) Bks Demand.

Perrolle, Pierre M., ed. see Liang-Ying Hsu & Dainian, Fan.

Perron. Lessons for New Teachers. LC 99-32561. 208p. 1999. pap. 29.36 (*0-07-232446-5*) McGraw.

Perron, Brandon A. Uncovering Reasonable Doubt: The Component Method - A Comprehensive Guide for the Criminal Defense Investigator. LC 98-93137. (Illus.). 110p. 1998. pap. 38.00 (*0-9670615-0-4*, 001) Invest Support Spec.

Perron, Donna W. Flowers for Grampa. LC 97-93425. (Illus.). 24p. (J). (ps-6). 1997. 17.95 (*0-9657986-7-4*) Just Good.

Perron, E. Du, see Du Perron, E.

Perron, Lee. Seeking the Hills. 64p. 1992. pap. 10.00 (*0-9620634-3-6*); lib. bdg. 25.00 (*0-9620634-5-2*) Sun Moon Bear Pr.

— Seeking the Hills. limited ed. (Illus.). 64p. 1992. 50.00 (*0-9620634-4-4*) Sun Moon Bear Pr.

— The White Bones of the Year Are Scattered among Jonquils. (Illus.). 52p. 1988. pap. 35.00 (*0-9620634-0-1*) Sun Moon Bear Pr.

Perron, Madeleine. French - English Vocabulary Related to Tax Returns. (ENG & FRE.). 37p. 1988. pap. 19.95 (*0-8288-9408-6*) Fr & Eur.

Perron, Paul & Collins, Frank, eds. Paris School Semiotics I: Theory. LC 88-24058. (Semiotic Crossroads Ser.: Vol. 2). xxviii, 258p. 1989. 76.00 (*1-55619-040-9*) J Benjamins Pubng Co.

— Paris School Semiotics II: Practice. LC 88-24058. (Semiotic Crossroads Ser.: No. 3). xvi, 225p. 1989. 71.00 (*1-55619-041-7*) J Benjamins Pubng Co.

Perron, Paul, ed. see Ubersfeld, Anne.

Perron, Paul J. Semiotics & the Modern Quebec Novel: A Greimassian Analysis of Thiriault's Agaguk. (Toronto Studies in Semiotics). 192p. 1996. text 40.00 (*0-8020-0926-3*) U of Toronto Pr.

Perron, Paul J., tr. see Greimas, Algirdas Julien & Maupassant, Guy de.

Perron, Paul J., tr. see Greimas, Algirdas J. & Fontanille, Jacques.

P

Perron, Robert, jt. auth. see Gauthier-Lafaye, Jean.

Perrone, Bobette, et al. Medicine Women, Curanderas, & Women Doctors. LC 89-4901. (Illus.). 272p. 1993. pap. 14.95 (0-8061-2512-8) U of Okla Pr.

Perrone, Charles A. Masters of Contemporary Brazilian Song: MPB, 1965-1985. (Illus.). 293p. 1989. 27.95 (0-292-75102-8) U of Tex Pr.

— Masters of Contemporary Brazilian Song: MPB, 1965-1985. (Illus.). 293p. (C). 1993. pap. 15.95 (0-292-76550-9) U of Tex Pr.

— Seven Faces: Brazilian Poetry since Modernism. LC 96-78. (Illus.). 280p. 1996. text 49.95 (0-8223-1807-5); pap. text 16.95 (0-8223-1814-8) Duke.

Perrone, Charles A., tr. see Espinola, Adriano.

Perrone, Ed. Astrology: A New Age Guide. LC 83-70690. 219p. 1983. pap. 8.95 (0-8356-0579-5, Quest) Theos Pub Hse.

Perrone, Jeff. Ken Price. Thomas, Sissy & Thompson, Lauri, eds. (Illus.). 40p. 1989. 15.00 (0-942779-01-0) Greenberg Van Doren.

Perrone, Jeff, contrib. by. Jennifer Bartlett - Recent Work. LC 88-61642. (Illus.). 40p. (Orig.). 1988. pap. 8.00 (0-944110-16-9) Milwauk Art Mus.

Perrone, Jeff & Schjehldahl, Peter. Adrian Saxe. (Illus.). 19p. (Orig.). 1987. pap. text 8.00 (0-914489-05-4) Univ Miss-KC Art.

Perrone, Joe, Jr. & Luftglass, Manny. Gone Fishin' with Kids. (Gone Fishin' Ser.: Vol. 5). (Illus.). 100p. 1997. reprint ed. pap. 9.99 (0-9650261-4-0) Gone Fishin.

Perrone, Lisbeth. Country Christmas Cross-Stitch. (Illus.). 192p. 1986. write for info. (0-02-595920-4) Macmillan.

Perrone, Nicholas. Dynamic Response of Biomechanical Systems: Papers Presented at the Winter Annual Meeting of the ASME, New York, NY, Dec. 2, 1970. LC 78-143213. 156p. reprint ed. pap. 48.40 (0-608-30744-0, 201691300005) Bks Demand.

Perrone, Nicholas & Pilkey, W., eds. Structural Mechanics Software Series, 5 vols., Vol. 1. LC 77-641779. (Software Ser.). 640p. 1977. reprint ed. pap. 198.40 (0-8357-2719-X, 203983300001) Bks Demand.

— Structural Mechanics Software Series, 5 vols., Vol. 2. LC 77-641779. (Software Ser.). 466p. 1978. reprint ed. pap. 144.50 (0-8357-2720-3, 203983300002) Bks Demand.

— Structural Mechanics Software Series, 5 vols., Vol. 3. LC 77-641779. (Software Ser.). 352p. 1980. reprint ed. pap. 109.20 (0-8357-2721-1, 203983300003) Bks Demand.

— Structural Mechanics Software Series, 5 vols., Vol. 4. LC 77-641779. (Software Ser.). 476p. 1982. reprint ed. pap. 147.60 (0-8357-2722-X, 203983300004) Bks Demand.

— Structural Mechanics Software Series, 5 vols., Vol. 5. LC 77-641779. (Software Ser.). 350p. 1984. reprint ed. pap. 108.50 (0-8357-2723-8, 203983300005) Bks Demand.

Perrone, Nicholas, ed. see Applied Mechanics, Bioengineering & Fluids Enginee.

Perrone, Nicholas, ed. see Symposium on Naval Structural Mechanics Staff.

***Perrone, Santina, ed.** Violence in the Wrokplace. 115p. 1999. pap. 75.00 (0-642-24132-5, Pub. by Aust Inst Criminology) St Mut.

Perrone, Santina, jt. auth. see White, Rob.

Perrone, Steve, ed. New Jersey Lake Survey Fishing Maps Guide. annuals 5th rev. ed. (Illus.). 132p. 1997. per. 10.95 (1-887544-01-1) NJ Sportsmens Guides.

Perrone, Tony. Dr. Tony Perrone's Body-Fat Breakthru: 10 Personalized Plans for Mega HealthPerrone. LC 99-228521. 304p. 1999. 24.00 (0-06-039274-6) HarpC.

***Perrone, Tony.** Dr. Tony Perrone's Body Fat Breakthru: 10 Personalized Plans for Mega HealthPerrone,&Tony, Set. 1999. audio 18.00 (0-694-52126-4) HarperAudio.

— Hollywood's Healthiest Diets: Ten Healthy Fat-Fighting Diets. 304p. 2000. pap. 14.00 (0-06-098848-7, ReganBks) HarperTrade.

Perrone, Vito. A Letter to Teachers: Reflections on Schooling & the Art of Teaching. LC 90-19890. (Education-Higher Education Ser.). 166p. 1991. pap. text 17.95 (1-55542-313-2) Jossey-Bass.

— 101 Educational Conversations You Should Have with Your Child, 6 vols. (Illus.). 112p. 1993. lib. bdg. 95.70 (0-7910-1917-9) Chelsea Hse.

— 101 Educational Conversations You Should Have with Your Fourth Grader. (101 Educational Conversations You Should Have with Your Child Ser.). (Illus.). 96p. 1993. lib. bdg. 15.95 (0-7910-1920-9) Chelsea Hse.

— 101 Educational Conversations You Should Have with Your Sixth Grader. (101 Educational Conversations You Should Have with Your Child Ser.). (Illus.). 96p. 1993. pap. 5.95 (0-7910-1989-6) Chelsea Hse.

— 101 Educational Conversations You Should Have with Your Sixth Grader. (101 Educational Conversations You Should Have with Your Child Ser.). (Illus.). 96p. 1994. lib. bdg. 15.95 (0-7910-1922-5) Chelsea Hse.

— 101 Educational Conversations You Should Have with Your Kindergartner-First Grader. (101 Educational Conversations You Should Have with Your Child Ser.). (Illus.). 96p. 1992. pap. 5.95 (0-7910-1981-0) Chelsea Hse.

— 101 Educational Conversations You Should Have with Your Kindergartner-First Grader. (101 Educational Conversations You Should Have with Your Child Ser.). (Illus.). 96p. 1993. lib. bdg. 15.95 (0-7910-1918-7) Chelsea Hse.

— 101 Educational Conversations You Should Have with Your Second Grader. (101 Educational Conversations You Should Have with Your Child Ser.). (Illus.). 96p. 1992. pap. 5.95 (0-7910-1982-9) Chelsea Hse.

— 101 Educational Conversations You Should Have with Your Second Grader. (101 Educational Conversations You Should Have with Your Child Ser.). (Illus.). 96p. 1992. lib. bdg. 15.95 (0-7910-1937-3) Chelsea Hse.

— 101 Educational Conversations You Should Have with Your Third Grader. (101 Educational Conversations You Should Have with Your Child Ser.). (Illus.). 96p. 1993. lib. bdg. 15.95 (0-7910-1919-5) Chelsea Hse.

— 101 Educational Conversations You Should Have with Your Third Grader. LC 92-28529. (101 Educational Conversations You Should Have with Your Child Ser.). (Illus.). 96p. 1993. pap. 5.95 (0-7910-1984-5) Chelsea Hse.

— 101 Educational Conversations You Should Have with Your Fifth Grader. (101 Educational Conversations You Should Have with Your Child Ser.). (Illus.). 96p. 1993. lib. bdg. 15.95 (0-7910-1921-7) Chelsea Hse.

— 101 Educational Conversations You Should Have with Your Fifth Grader. (101 Educational Conversations You Should Have with Your Child Ser.). (Illus.). 96p. 1993. pap. 5.95 (0-7910-1987-X) Chelsea Hse.

— Teacher with a Heart: Reflections on Leonardo Covello & Community. LC 98-29612. 160p. 1998. 43.00 (0-8077-3778-X); pap. 19.95 (0-8077-3777-1) Tchrs Coll.

— Working Papers: Reflections on Teachers, Schools & Communities. 256p. (C). 1989. pap. text 19.95 (0-8077-2944-2) Tchrs Coll.

Perrone, Vito, contrib. by. Chelsea House Library of Biography. Incl. Barbara Bush. Heiss, Arleen M. LC 91-7829. (Illus.). 120p. (YA). (gr. 5 up). 1992. pap. 8.95 (0-7910-1634-X); Norman Schwarzkopf. Stefoff, Rebecca. (Illus.). 120p. (YA). (gr. 5 up). 1995. pap. 8.95 (0-7910-1726-5); 1995. Set 5.25 hd 23.85 (0-7910-3761-4) Chelsea Hse.

Perrone, Vito, ed. Visions of Peace. (Illus.). 90p. 1988. pap. 5.00 (0-940237-02-4) ND Qtr Pr.

Perronet, Vincent. A Second Vindication of Mr. Locke: 1738 Edition. 158p. 1996. reprint ed. 55.00 (1-85506-118-X) Bks Intl VA.

Perrons, Diane, jt. ed. see Shaw, Jenny.

Perros, Harry G. Queuing Networks with Blocking: Exact & Approximate Solutions. (Illus.). 304p. 1994. text 75.00 (0-19-508580-9) OUP.

Perros, Harry G., ed. High-Speed Communication Networks. LC 92-26600. (Illus.). 284p. (C). 1992. 114.00 (0-306-44257-4, Plenum Trade) Perseus Pubng.

Perros, Harry G., et al, eds. Modelling & Performance Evaluation of ATM Technology: Proceedings of the IFIP TC6 Task Group - WG6.4 International Workshop on Performance of Communication Systems, Martinique, French Caribbean Island. LC 93-22898. (IFIP Transactions C: Communication Systems Ser.: Vol. 15). 500p. 1993. 163.75 (0-444-81512-0, North Holland) Elsevier.

Perrot, Dominique, jt. auth. see Preiswork, Roy.

Perrot, George, et al. Exploration Archeologique de la Galatie et de la Bithynie, d'une Partie de la Mysie, de la Phrygie, de la Cappadocie et du Pont. Set. 394p. reprint ed. write for info. (3-487-07404-4) G Olms Pubs.

— Exploration Archeologique de la Galatie et de la Bithynie, d'une Partie de la Mysie, de la Phrygie, de la Cappadocie et du Pont. Vol. 1. 394p. 1983. reprint ed. write for info. (3-487-07405-2) G Olms Pubs.

— Exploration Archeologique de la Galatie et de la Bithynie, d'une Partie de la Mysie, de la Phrygie, de la Cappadocie et du Pont, Vol. 2. 394p. reprint ed. write for info. (3-487-07406-0) G Olms Pubs.

Perrot, Georges. A History of Art in Ancient Egypt, 2 vols. Armstrong, Walter, ed. 1976. lib. bdg. 200.00 (0-8490-1969-9) Gordon Pr.

Perrot, Jean-Claude & Woolf, Stuart J. State & Statistics in France, Seventeen Eighty-Nine to Eighteen Fifteen. (Social Orders Ser.: Vol. 2). xii, 206p. 1984. text 112.00 (3-7186-0201-6) Gordon & Breach.

Perrot, Maryvonne, ed. see Kopper, Joachim.

Perrot, Maryvonne, ed. see Steinfeld, Patricia.

Perrot, Michelle. A History of Private Life, Vol. 4: From the Fires of Revolution to the Great War, Vol. 4. 736p. (C). 1994. text 19.95 (0-674-40003-8) HUP.

Perrot, Michelle, et al, eds. A History of Private Life, Vol. 4: From the Fires of Revolution to the Great War, Vol. 4. Goldhammer, Arthur, tr. from FRE. (Illus.). 736p. 1990. text 39.95 (0-674-39978-1) Belknap Pr.

— A History of Women Vol. IV: Emerging Feminism from Revolution to World War. (History of Women Ser.: Vol. 4). (Illus.). 640p. (Orig.). (C). 1995. pap. 16.95 (0-674-40366-5) Belknap Pr.

Perrot, Michelle, jt. auth. see Duby, Georges.

Perrot, Michelle, ed. see Duby, Georges.

Perrot, Michelle, jt. ed. see Fraisse, Genevieve.

Perrot, Philippe & Bienvenu, Richard, trs. The Bourgeoisie Inside Out: A History of Clothing in the Nineteenth Century. LC 93-40094. 296p. 1994. text 39.50 (0-691-03383-8, Pub. by Princeton U Pr); pap. text 15.95 (0-691-00081-6, Pub. by Princeton U Pr) Cal Prin Full Svc.

Perrot, Pierre. A to Z of Thermodynamics. (Illus.). 336p. 1998. pap. text 29.95 (0-19-856552-6) OUP.

Perrott Cartographics Staff. Good Beer Guide to Belgium & Holland: The Best Bars & All the Breweries. 232p. 1992. per. 18.99 (1-85249-110-8, Pub. by Camra Bks) All About Beer.

Perrott, D. V. Concise Swahili & English Dictionary. (Teach Yourself Bks. Ser.). 184p. 1993. text 18.00 (0-340-54695-6, Pub. by Hodder & Stought Ltd) Lubrecht & Cramer.

— Teach Yourself Swahili. (Teach Yourself Ser.). 1992. 15.95 (0-8288-8404-8) Fr & Eur.

— Teach Yourself Swahili: A Complete Course for Beginners. (SWA.). 224p. 1995. pap. 14.95 (0-8442-3837-6, Teach Yrslf) NTC Contemp Pub Co.

— Teach Yourself Swahili Complete Course. (Teach Yourself Ser.). (SWA & ENG.). 324p. 1997. pap. 24.95 incl. audio (0-8442-3835-X, Teach Yrslf) NTC Contemp Pub Co.

— Teach Yourself Swahili Dictionary. (Teach Yourself Ser.). 1992. 15.95 (0-8288-8405-6) Fr & Eur.

— Teach Yourself Swahili Dictionary. (ENG & SWA., Illus.). 184p. 1995. pap. 15.95 (0-8442-3838-4, Teach Yrslf) NTC Contemp Pub Co.

Perrott, David. Guide to the Western Islands of Scotland. 96p. 1991. pap. 29.00 (0-9511003-2-7, Pub. by Kittiwake Pr) St Mut.

— The Western Islands Handbook. 160p. 1995. pap. 39.95 (0-9511003-4-3, Pub. by Kittiwake Pr) St Mut.

Perrott, David L. & Pogany, Istvan S. Current Issues in International Business Law. 1988. text 89.95 (0-566-05473-6, Pub. by Dartmth Pub) Ashgate Pub Co.

Perrott, Jeff, ed. see Krakow, Barbara.

Perrott, Louis A. Reinventing Your Practice As a Business Psychologist: A Step-by-Step Guide. LC 98-40286. 1999. 32.95 (0-7879-4349-5) Jossey-Bass.

***Perrott, Mark.** Hope Abandoned: Eastern State Penitentiary. (Illus.). 105p. 2000. 28.00 (0-9670455-0-9, Pub. by PA Prison Soc) Howell Pr VA.

Perrott, Michael. Newman's Mariology. 104p. 1997. pap. 15.95 (1-901157-45-8) St Austin.

***Perrotta, Kevin.** Jonah/Ruth: Love Crosses Boundaries. (Catholic Perspectives Six Weeks with the Bible). 83p. 2000. pap. 6.95 (0-8294-1433-9) Loyola Pr.

— Luke: The Good News of God's Mercy. (Catholic Perspectives Six Weeks with the Bible). 83p. 2000. pap. 6.95 (0-8294-1370-7) Loyola Pr.

— Psalms: An Invitation to Pray. (Catholic Perspectives Six Weeks with the Bible). 83p. 2000. pap. 6.95 (0-8294-1434-7) Loyola Pr.

— Revelation: God's Gift of Hope. (Catholic Perspectives Six Weeks with the Bible). 83p. 2000. pap. 6.95 (0-8294-1435-5) Loyola Pr.

— Your One-Stop Guide to the Bible. 2000. pap. 9.99 (1-56955-208-8) Servant.

Perrotta, Kevin, jt. auth. see Groeschel, Benedict J.

Perrotta, Louise. All You Need to Know about Prayer, You Can Learn from the Poor. LC 96-46519. 1996. 11.99 (1-56955-028-X, Charis) Servant.

***Perrotta, Louise.** Praying the Catechism: Opening Your Heart to Divine Wisdom. 174p. 2000. pap. 9.99 (1-56955-207-X) Servant.

***Perrotta, Louise Bourassa.** Saint Joseph: His Life & His Role in the Church Today. LC 99-75024. 240p. 2000. pap. 11.99 (0-87973-573-2) Our Sunday Visitor.

Perrotta, Mary, ed. see Brown, Fern G.

Perrotta, Tom. Bad Haircut: Stories of the Seventies. 256p. 1995. mass mkt. 6.99 (0-425-14942-0) Berkley Pub.

— Bad Haircut: Stories of the Seventies. LC 93-33687. 197p. 1994. 18.95 (1-882593-05-7) Bridge Wrks.

— Bad Haircut: Stories of the Seventies. 240p. 1997. reprint ed. pap. 12.00 (0-425-15954-X) Berkley Pub.

***Perrotta, Tom.** Joe College. 320p. 2000. 23.95 (0-312-26184-5) St Martin.

Perrotta, Tom. The Wishbones. 304p. 1998. pap. 12.00 (0-425-16314-8) Berkley Pub.

— The Wishbones. 288p. 1999. reprint ed. mass mkt. 6.99 (0-425-16971-5) Berkley Pub.

Perrottet, Oliver. The Visual I Ching: A New Approach to the Ancient Chinese Oracle Cards & Commentary. (Illus.). 96p. 1997. 18.95 (0-8048-3102-5) Tuttle Pubng.

Perrotti, Luisa, jt. ed. see Wright, Vincent.

Perroux, F., jt. ed. see Schuhl, Pierre M.

Perrow, Angeli. Captain's Castaway. LC 98-34914. (Illus.). 32p. (J). (gr. k-5). 1998. 15.95 (0-89272-419-6) Down East.

***Perrow, Angeli.** Lighthouse Dog to the Rescue. (Illus.). 32p. (J). (gr. k-3). 2000. 14.95 (0-89272-487-0) Down East.

Perrow, Charles. Complex Organizations. 3rd ed. 320p. (C). 1986. pap. 34.38 (0-07-554799-6) McGraw.

— Normal Accidents: Living with High-Risk Technologies. LC 83-45256. 400p. 1985. pap. 20.00 (0-465-05142-1, Pub. by Basic) HarpC.

***Perrow, Charles.** Normal Accidents: Living with High Risk Technologies. LC 99-32990. 1999. pap. 19.95 (0-691-00412-9, Pub. by Princeton U Pr) Cal Prin Full Svc.

Perrow, Charles & Guillen, Mauro F. The AIDS Disaster: The Failure of Organizations in New York & the Nation. 208p. (C). 1990. pap. 15.00 (0-300-04880-7) Yale U Pr.

Perroy, D. Diplomatic Correspondence of Richard II. (Camden Third Ser.). 63.00 (0-86193-048-7) David Brown.

Perroy, Edouard. La Feodalite En France Du X. Au XII. Siecle. LC 80-2012. reprint ed. 28.00 (0-404-18584-3) AMS Pr.

Perrucci & Wysong, Earl. The New Class Society. LC 99-11242. 320p. 1999. pap. 21.95 (0-8476-9173-X) Rowman.

Perrucci, Carolyn C., jt. ed. see Haas, Violet B.

Perrucci, Robert. Japanese Auto Transplants in the Heartland: Capital & Community in Transition. LC 93-50053. (Social Institutions & Social Change Ser.). 198p. 1994. pap. text 21.95 (0-202-30529-5); lib. bdg. 41.95 (0-202-30528-7) Aldine de Gruyter.

Perrucci, Robert & Potter, Harry R., eds. Networks of Power. (Social Institutions & Social Change Ser.). 144p. 1989. pap. text 24.95 (0-202-30343-8); lib. bdg. 47.95 (0-202-30342-X) Aldine de Gruyter.

Perrucci, Robert & Targ, Dena B. Mental Patients & Social Networks. LC 81-20630. 174p. 1982. 39.95 (0-86569-095-2, Auburn Hse) Greenwood.

Perrucci, Robert & Wysong, Earl. The New Class Society. LC 99-11242. 320p. 1999. 69.00 (0-8476-9172-1) Rowman.

Perrucci, Robert, et al. Plant Closings: International Context & Social Costs. (Social Institutions & Social Change Ser.). 203p. 1988. lib. bdg. 48.95 (0-202-30338-1) Aldine de Gruyter.

— Plant Closings: International Context & Social Costs. (Social Institutions & Social Change Ser.). 203p. (C). 1988. pap. text 25.95 (0-202-30339-X) Aldine de Gruyter.

Perrucci, Robert, jt. auth. see Trachtman, Leon E.

***Perruchot, Henri.** Toulouse - Lautrec. Hare, Humphrey, tr. (ENG & FRE., Illus.). 317p. 1999. reprint ed. pap. text 20.00 (0-7881-6536-4) DIANE Pub.

Perruchoud, A. P., ed. Herzog, Heinrich W. on the Occasion of his 65th Birthday. (Journal: Respiration: Vol. 48 No. 3). (Illus.). 92p. 1985. pap. 39.25 (3-8055-4256-9) S Karger.

Perruchoud, A. P., jt. ed. see Herzog, H.

Perrusquia, Gina, jt. auth. see Moore, Daphna R.

Perry. Advanced Programming in C. LC 97-31818. 640p. (C). 1998. mass mkt. 53.95 (0-534-95140-6) PWS Pubs.

— Alain Locke. 1997. 26.95 (0-8057-4023-6) Macmillan.

— Apartheid: A History. 1992. pap. text. write for info. (0-582-66385-7, Pub. by Addison-Wesley) Longman.

Perry. Biology. (Adaptable Courseware-Hardside Ser.). Date not set. pap., lab manual ed. 15.50 (0-534-16003-4) Wadsworth Pub.

Perry. Biology, Vol. 1. (Adaptable Courseware-Hardside Ser.). Date not set. lab manual ed. 15.50 (0-534-15893-5) Wadsworth Pub.

— Biology, Vol. 2. (Adaptable Courseware-Hardside Ser.). Date not set. lab manual ed. 15.50 (0-534-15911-7) Wadsworth Pub.

***Perry.** Building Accounting Systems Using Window 98. LC 99-20789. 300p. 1999. 45.95 (0-324-01617-4) Sth-Wstrn College.

Perry. Care of the Ophthalmic Patient. 2nd ed. 480p. 1995. pap. 79.75 (1-56593-334-6, 0664) Singular Publishing.

***Perry.** College Vocabulary Building. 10th ed. 1998. 33.95 (0-538-71762-9) Thomson Learn.

— Flight of the Romanovs. 2000. pap. 16.00 (0-465-02463-7, Pub. by Basic) HarpC.

Perry. From Theology to History. 1974. lib. bdg. 106.00 (90-247-1578-4, Pub. by M Nijhoff) Kluwer Academic.

— A Handbook for Calculus + 2nd ed. (C). 1988. pap. text, teacher ed. 13.50 (0-03-008883-6) Harcourt Coll Pubs.

— Intercultural Communication. 2000. pap. text 11.97 (0-395-97223-X) HM.

— Lab Manual for Biology 121. Date not set. pap., lab manual ed. 20.50 (0-534-32037-6) Wadsworth Pub.

Perry. Law & Practice Relating Banking. 5th ed. 1987. pap. write for info. (0-416-38230-4) Thomson Learn.

— Make Your Own Riding Clothes. 2000. pap. 14.95 (0-85131-718-9, Pub. by J A Allen) Trafalgar.

Perry. Marriage & the Family. (C). 2000. text 48.00 (0-205-18544-4) Allyn.

— MasterCases: Orthopaedic Trauma. (Illus.). 456p. 1998. 95.00 (0-86577-782-9) Thieme Med Pubs.

— Microbiology. (C). 1997. pap. text, teacher ed. 28.00 (0-03-019452-0) Harcourt.

— Microbiology. 1996. 246.00 (0-03-019454-7) Harcourt Coll Pubs.

— Microbiology. LC 96-69306. (C). 1997. text 99.00 (0-03-053893-9, Pub. by Harcourt Coll Pubs) Harcourt.

— Modern Era Filler. Date not set. write for info. (0-395-69111-7) HM.

— Modern Era Shipper. Date not set. write for info. (0-395-69109-5) HM.

— Netscape Navigator 5.0. (Computer Applications Ser.). 1998. mass mkt. 22.00 (0-538-68593-X) S-W Pub.

— New Persectives on the Internet. (C). 1998. mass mkt. 21.95 (0-7600-6973-5) Course Tech.

— Perry Sources 20th Century Eur. Date not set. pap. text 24.57 (0-395-92568-1) HM.

— Perry Western Civ Complete. 6th ed. 1999. pap. text 54.27 (0-395-95935-7) HM.

— Perry Western Civ V1. 6th ed. 1999. pap. text 39.57 (0-395-95936-5) HM.

— Perry Western Civ V2. 6th ed. 1999. pap. text 39.57 (0-395-95937-3) HM.

— Photo Atlas for Botany. LC 98-121287. 1998. 35.95 (0-534-52938-0) Brooks-Cole.

— Sisters of Henry VIII. LC 99-39126. (Orig.). 1999. text 23.95 (0-312-24241-7) St Martin.

***Perry.** Sisters of Henry VIII. 2000. mass mkt. 13.00 (0-306-80989-3, Pub. by Da Capo) HarpC.

— Software Testing. 2nd ed. LC 99-44927. 812p. 2000. 59.99 (0-471-35418-X) Wiley.

Perry. Sources Vol. 2. 4th ed. LC 98-71766. 1998. pap. text 25.17 (0-395-89202-3) HM.

***Perry.** Spelling Reference. 5th ed. 2000. pap. 18.95 (0-538-69120-4) Sth-Wstrn College.

Perry. Standards for Auditing Computer Applications. 144p. 1998. per. 295.00 (0-8493-9985-8) CRC Pr.

— Umbrella Conspiracy, Vol. 1. (Resident Evil Ser.). 262p. 1998. per. 6.50 (0-671-02439-6) S&S Trade.

***Perry.** Western Civilization. 6th ed. 1999. pap. text 8.97 (0-395-95940-3) HM.

Perry. Word Studies. 8th ed. (Communication-English Ser.). 1988. teacher ed. 27.25 (0-538-28141-3) S-W Pub.

Perry & Morton. Biology. (Adaptable Courseware-Hardside Ser.). Date not set. lab manual ed. 22.00 (0-534-55479-2) Wadsworth Pub.

Perry & Schneider. Business Information Systems. (Introduction to Computing Ser.). 1997. 50.95 (0-7895-0697-1) Course Tech.

***Perry & Schneider.** E-Commerce: An Introductory. (New Perspectives Ser.). (C). 2000. text 31.95 (0-619-01929-8) Course Tech.

— The Internet. 2nd ed. (New Perspectives Ser.). (C). 2000. text 21.95 (0-619-01937-9) Course Tech.

***Perry, et al.** Internet: Comprehensive. 2nd ed. (New Perspectives Ser.). (C). 2000. text 44.95 (0-619-01938-7) Course Tech.

Perry, jt. auth. see Levy.

An Asterisk (*) at the beginning of an entry indicates that the title is appearing for the first time.

Perry, jt. auth. see Shelp.

Perry, jt. auth. see Starr, Cecie.

Perry, ed. see Lemercier.

Perry, A. Icebreaking 101: Getting to Know You in One FUN Question. 2nd ed. 1996. pap. 11.95 (*1-887879-01-3*) Perry Prods.

— People Are Just Desserts . . . Experience the Sweet Rewards. rev. ed. LC 97-171196. (Illus.). 112p. 1995. pap. 14.95 (*1-887879-00-5*) Perry Prods.

— Thank You for Listening, But I Wasn't Quite Through. 80p. (Orig.). 1995. pap. 11.95 (*1-887879-03-X*) Perry Prods.

Perry, A. J. Salvador. 1990. pap. text 2.25 (*0-921411-12-X*) Genl Dist Srvs.

Perry, A. S., et al. Insecticides in Agriculture & Environment: Retrospects & Prospects. LC 97-28341. (Applied Agriculture Ser.). (Illus.). 230p. 1998. 119.00 (*3-540-62729-4*) Spr-Verlag.

Perry, A. Thompson, 2nd. Brief Field of View & Elderly Drivers: A Research Study. (Illus.). 109p. (Orig.). (C). 1995. pap. text 40.00 (*0-7881-1615-0*) DIANE Pub.

Perry, Aaren Y. Poetry across the Curriculum: An Action Guide for Elementary Teachers. LC 96-42531. 192p. 1996. pap. text 30.00 (*0-205-19807-4*) Allyn.

Perry, Abbie, ed. Sociology: Insights in Health Care. (Illus.). 320p. (Orig.). 1996. pap. 38.25 (*1-56593-770-8*, 1498) Singular Publishing.

Perry, Abigayl. Nursing: A Knowledge Base for Practice. 2nd ed. (Illus.). 400p. 1997. pap. 34.95 (*1-56593-819-4*, 1610) Singular Publishing.

***Perry, Adrienne.** Fetching a Life with Your Dog. LC 99-39213. 1999. pap. 16.95 (*0-87719-354-1*, 9354) Gulf Pub.

Perry, Alan & Perry, Linda. The Baby Jesus: A Touch & Feel Book. Augustine, Peggy, ed. (J). 1995. bds. 8.95 (*0-687-00127-7*) Abingdon.

Perry, Albert J. History of Knox County Illinois, Its Cities, Towns & People, 2 vols. (Illus.). 1957p. 1997. reprint ed. lib. bdg. 165.00 (*0-8328-5756-4*) Higginson Bk Co.

Perry, Allen H., jt. auth. see Thompson, Russell D.

Perry, Allen H., jt. auth. see Walker, J. M.

***Perry, Andrea J.** Stink Stoppers Spider Spotters & Other Uninvented Invention. LC 99-46463. (J). (gr. k-3). 2000. 16.00 (*0-689-83067-X*) Atheneum Yung Read.

Perry, Angela. The AMA Essential Guide to Asthma. LC 98-15733. 320p. 1998. per. 14.00 (*0-671-01013-1*, Pocket Books) PB.

— The AMA Essential Guide to Depression. LC 98-19507. 256p. 1998. per. 14.00 (*0-671-01016-6*) PB.

— The AMA Essential Guide to Hypertension. LC 98-19506. 256p. 1998. per. 14.00 (*0-671-01015-8*) PB.

— The AMA Essential Guide to Menopause. LC 98-15034. 256p. 1998. per. 14.00 (*0-671-01014-X*, Pocket Books) PB.

Perry, Angie, jt. auth. see Anderson, Mike.

***Perry, Anne.** Ashworth Hall. 1998. mass mkt. 6.99 (*0-449-00086-9*, Crest) Fawcett.

— Bedford Square. LC 98-29854. (Charlotte & Thomas Pitt Novel Ser.). 330p. (YA). 1999. 24.95 (*0-345-43298-3*) Ballantine Pub Grp.

— Bedford Square. 327p. 2000. mass mkt. 6.99 (*0-449-00582-8*, Ballantine) Ballantine Pub Grp.

— Bedford Square. 2000. write for info. (*0-449-00696-4*, Crest) Fawcett.

— Bedford Square. large type ed. LC 99-27471. (Basic Ser.). 1999. 29.95 (*0-7862-2018-X*) Mac Lib Ref.

Perry, Anne. Belgrave Square. 1993. mass mkt. 6.99 (*0-449-22227-6*, Crest) Fawcett.

— Belgrave Square. large type ed. 657p. 1992. reprint ed. lib. bdg. 21.95 (*1-56054-446-5*) Thorndike Pr.

— Bethlehem Road. 1991. mass mkt. 6.99 (*0-449-21914-3*) Fawcett.

— Bluegate Fields. 1986. mass mkt. 6.99 (*0-449-20766-8*) Fawcett.

***Perry, Anne.** Bluegate Fields. large type ed. LC 99-48810. 400p. 2000. lib. bdg. 28.95 (*1-58547-017-1*) Ctr Point Pubg.

Perry, Anne. A Breach of Promise. 1998. mass mkt. 6.99 (*0-8041-1888-4*) Ivy Books.

— A Breach of Promise. 1999. mass mkt. 6.99 (*0-8041-1855-8*) Ivy Books.

— A Breach of Promise. large type ed. LC 98-41227. 1999. 27.95 (*0-7862-1465-1*) Thorndike Pr.

— Brunswick Gardens. 402p. 1999. mass mkt. 6.99 (*0-449-00318-3*, Crest) Fawcett.

— Brunswick Gardens. (Basic Ser.). 1998. 28.95 (*0-7862-1464-3*) Thorndike Pr.

— Brunswick Gardens, No. 2. LC 97-38441. (Illus.). 389p. (YA). 1998. 25.00 (*0-449-90845-3*) Fawcett.

— Cain His Brother. 1996. mass mkt. 6.99 (*0-8041-1507-9*) Ivy Books.

— Cain His Brother. large type ed. (Cloak & Dagger Ser.). 1996. 24.95 (*0-7862-0607-1*) Thorndike Pr.

— Callander Square. 1986. pap. 2.25 (*0-449-24365-6*); mass mkt. 6.99 (*0-449-20999-7*, Crest) Fawcett.

— Callander Square. large type ed. 1981. 12.00 (*0-7089-0718-0*) Ulverscroft.

***Perry, Anne.** Cardington Crescent. LC 00-31508. 2001. write for info. (*1-58547-015-5*) Ctr Point Pubg.

Perry, Anne. Cardington Crescent. 304p. 1988. reprint ed. mass mkt. 6.99 (*0-449-21442-7*, Crest) Fawcett.

— The Cater Street Hangman. 1985. mass mkt. 6.99 (*0-449-20867-2*, Crest) Fawcett.

***Perry, Anne.** The Cater Street Hangman. large type ed. 364p. 2000. lib. bdg. 27.95 (*1-58547-002-3*) Ctr Point Pubg.

Perry, Anne. A Dangerous Mourning. 1992. mass mkt. 6.99 (*0-8041-1037-9*) Ivy Books.

***Perry, Anne.** Death in the Devil's Acre. LC 00-31507. 2001. lib. bdg. write for info. (*1-58547-016-3*) Ctr Point Pubg.

Perry, Anne. Death in the Devil's Acre. 272p. 1987. mass mkt. 6.99 (*0-449-21095-2*, Crest) Fawcett.

— Defend & Betray. 1993. mass mkt. 6.99 (*0-8041-1188-X*) Ivy Books.

— Defend & Betray. large type ed. (Cloak & Dagger Ser.). 737p. 1993. reprint ed. lib. bdg. 21.95 (*1-56054-625-5*) Thorndike Pr.

— The Face of a Stranger. 1991. mass mkt. 6.99 (*0-8041-0858-7*) Ivy Books.

— The Face of a Stranger. large type ed. 556p. 1991. reprint ed. lib. bdg. 20.95 (*1-56054-113-X*) Thorndike Pr.

— Farriers' Lane. 1994. mass mkt. 6.99 (*0-449-21961-5*) Fawcett.

— Farriers' Lane. large type ed. LC 93-10504. 672p. 1993. lib. bdg. 23.95 (*1-56054-626-3*) Thorndike Pr.

***Perry, Anne.** Half Moon Street. LC 99-55232. 336p. 2000. 25.00 (*0-345-43327-0*, Ballantine) Ballantine Pub Grp.

— Half Moon Street. large type ed. LC 00-23134. 2000. 26.95 (*1-56895-857-9*, Compass) Wheeler Pub.

Perry, Anne. Highgate Rise. 1992. mass mkt. 6.99 (*0-449-21959-3*) Fawcett.

— Highgate Rise. large type ed. (Ulverscroft). 672p. 1994. 21.95 (*0-7089-3013-1*) Ulverscroft.

— The Hyde Park Headsman. 1995. mass mkt. 6.99 (*0-449-22350-7*, Crest) Fawcett.

— The Hyde Park Headsman. large type ed. LC 94-13813. 682p. 1994. lib. bdg. 24.95 (*0-7862-0240-8*) Thorndike Pr.

— Paragon Walk. 1986. mass mkt. 5.99 (*0-449-45319-7*) Fawcett.

— Paragon Walk. 1986. mass mkt. 6.99 (*0-449-21168-1*) Fawcett.

***Perry, Anne.** Paragon Walk. large type ed. LC 99-46443. 308p. 2000. lib. bdg. 27.95 (*1-58547-005-8*) Ctr Point Pubg.

Perry, Anne. Pentecost Alley. 1997. mass mkt. 6.99 (*0-449-22566-6*, Crest) Fawcett.

— Pentecost Alley. large type ed. LC 96-22225. (Cloak & Dagger Ser.). 683p. 1996. 25.95 (*0-7862-0812-0*) Thorndike Pr.

— Resurrection Row. 192p. 1986. mass mkt. 6.99 (*0-449-21067-7*, Crest) Fawcett.

***Perry, Anne.** Resurrection Row. large type ed. LC 99-48815. 312p. 2000. lib. bdg. 27.95 (*1-58547-009-0*) Ctr Point Pubg.

Perry, Anne. Rutland Place. 1986. pap. 2.50 (*0-449-20474-X*); mass mkt. 6.99 (*0-449-21285-8*) Fawcett.

***Perry, Anne.** Rutland Place. large type ed. LC 99-48816. 320p. 2000. lib. bdg. 27.95 (*1-58547-013-9*) Ctr Point Pubg.

Perry, Anne. The Silence in Hanover Close. 1989. mass mkt. 6.99 (*0-449-21686-1*, Crest) Fawcett.

— The Silence in Hanover Close. large type ed. (Mystery Ser.). 1990. 27.99 (*0-7089-2324-0*) Ulverscroft.

***Perry, Anne.** The Silent Cry. 1998. mass mkt. 6.99 (*0-8041-1793-4*) Ivy Books.

Perry, Anne. The Silent Cry. large type ed. LC 97-32571. (Basic Ser.). 1998. 28.95 (*0-7862-1301-9*) Thorndike Pr.

— The Sins of the Wolf. 1995. mass mkt. 6.99 (*0-8041-1383-1*) Ivy Books.

— A Sudden, Fearful Death: A William Monk Mystery. 1994. mass mkt. 6.99 (*0-8041-1283-5*) Ivy Books.

— A Sudden, Fearful Death: A William Monk Mystery. large type ed. LC 93-42207. 714p. 1994. lib. bdg. 22.95 (*0-7862-0130-4*) Thorndike Pr.

***Perry, Anne.** Tathea. LC 99-32538. 460p. 1999. 21.95 (*1-57345-536-9*, Shadow Mount) Deseret Bk.

Perry, Anne. Traitor's Gate. 1996. mass mkt. 6.99 (*0-449-22439-2*) Fawcett.

***Perry, Anne.** The Twisted Root. LC 99-34689. 320p. 1999. 25.00 (*0-345-43325-4*, Ballantine) Ballantine Pub Grp.

— The Twisted Root. (William Monk Novels Ser.). 368p. 2000. mass mkt. 6.99 (*0-8041-1936-8*) Ballantine Pub Grp.

— The Twisted Root. large type ed. LC 99-28490. 1999. 25.00 (*0-375-40857-6*) Wheeler Pub.

Perry, Anne. Weighed in the Balance. 1997. mass mkt. 6.99 (*0-8041-1562-1*) Ivy Books.

Perry, Anne, ed. Malice Domestic Vol. 6: An Anthology of Original Traditional Mystery Stories. 6th ed. 1997. per. 5.99 (*0-671-89633-4*) PB.

Perry, Anne C. The Evolution of U. S. Trade Intermediaries: The Changing International Environment. LC 92-882. 200p. 1992. 55.00 (*0-89930-708-6*, PEI/, Quorum Bks) Greenwood.

Perry, Anne G. Pocket Guide to Basic Skills & Procedures, Vol. 4. 4th ed. LC 99-187163. (Illus.). 576p. (C). (gr. 13). 1998. text 22.95 (*0-8151-2714-6*, 31635) Mosby Inc.

***Perry, Anne G. & Potter, Patricia A.** Clinical Nursing Skills & Techniques. 4th ed. 1392p. 1998. write for info. (*0-8151-4308-7*) Mosby Inc.

Perry, Anne G., jt. auth. see Potter, Patricia A.

Perry, Anne M. Bluebonnet Books: Activities for 1993. 144p. (Orig.). 1993. pap. 16.95 (*0-944459-72-2*) ECS Lrn Systs.

Perry, Anne M., ed. see Clarke, A. B.

Perry, Anthony F. & Sion, Mike. The Expert from Out of Town: Marketing a Business Nationwide. LC 97-92201. (Illus.). 175p. write for info. (*0-9652694-1-8*) Nationwide Mktging.

***Perry, Art.** The Tibetans: Photographs. (Illus.). 176p. 1999. 35.00 (*0-670-88645-9*) Viking Penguin.

Perry, Arthur L. Origin of Williamstown, MA. 2nd ed. (Illus.). 650p. reprint ed. lib. bdg. 65.00 (*0-8328-2554-9*) Higginson Bk Co.

— Origins in Williamstown, Massachusetts, 2 vols. (Illus.). viii, 631p. 1993. reprint ed. pap. text 36.50 (*1-55613-766-4*) Heritage Bk.

Perry, Arthur W. Are You Considering Cosmetic Surgery? 256p. 1997. mass mkt. 5.99 (*0-380-79159-5*, Avon Bks) Morrow Avon.

Perry, B. E. Origin of the Book of Sindbad. (C). 1960. 35.00 (*3-11-000538-7*) De Gruyter.

Perry, B. E., tr. see Babrius.

Perry, Barbara. American Ceramics Now: The Twenty-Seventh Ceramic National Exhibition. Piche, Thomas E., Jr., ed. LC 87-80542. (Illus.). 84p. (Orig.). 1987. pap. write for info. (*0-914407-08-2*) Everson Mus.

— Magnetic Connections. (Illus.). 198p. (Orig.). 1985. pap. 12.50 (*0-9616312-0-1*, TXV-101-598) Arkbridge Assn.

Perry, Barbara, et al. The Twenty-Eighth Ceramic National: Clay, Color, Content. Piche, Thomas E., ed. LC 90-81161. (Illus.). 88p. 1990. pap. text 15.00 (*0-914407-13-9*) Everson Mus.

Perry, Barbara, jt. auth. see Abraham, Henry J.

Perry, Barbara, jt. auth. see Anderson, Ross.

Perry Barbara, A. American Art Pottery: From the Collection of Everson Museum of Art. LC 96-36452. (Illus.). 144p. 1997. 39.95 (*0-8109-1971-0*, Pub. by Abrams) Time Warner.

Perry, Barbara A. The Priestly Tribe: The Supreme Court's Image in the American Mind. LC 99-13438. 184p. 1999. 59.95 (*0-275-96598-8*, C6598, Praeger Pubs); pap. 17.95 (*0-275-96599-6*, C6598, Praeger Pubs) Greenwood.

— A Representative Supreme Court? The Impact of Race, Religion, & Gender on Appointments, 66. LC 91-14336. (Contributions in Legal Studies: No. 66). 176p. 1991. 52.95 (*0-313-27777-X*, PRC, Greenwood Pr) Greenwood.

***Perry, Barbara A.** The Supremes: Essays on the Current Justices of the Supreme Court of the United States. LC 99-33948. (Teaching Texts in Law & Politics Ser.: Vol. 6). 159p. (C). 1999. pap. 24.95 (*0-8204-4046-9*) P Lang Pubng.

Perry Barbara, A. Unfounded Fears: Myths & Realities of a Constitutional Convention, 55. LC 89-7502. (Contributions in Legal Studies: No. 55). 189p. 1989. 55.00 (*0-313-26717-0*, WKC, Greenwood Pr) Greenwood.

Perry Barbara, A., jt. auth. see Abernathy, M. Glenn.

Perry, Barbara A., jt. auth. see Weber, Paul J.

Perry, Ben, jt. auth. see Girard, Frank.

Perry, Ben Edwin. Studies in the Text History of the Life & Fables of Aesop. LC 81-13575. (American Philological Association Philological Monographs). 240p. 1981. reprint ed. pap. 23.50 (*0-89130-534-3*, 40 00 07) OUP.

Perry, Ben Edwin, et al. Index Apuleianus. li, 490p. 1979. reprint ed. lib. bdg. 89.70 (*3-487-06678-5*) G Olms Pubs.

Perry, Ben Edwin, ed. see Aesop.

Perry, Bernard J. Instructional Guide for Introduction to Employee Involvement Teams for Potential Members: The Zero Meeting. rev. ed. 31p. 1992. pap. 15.00 (*0-937670-30-8*) QCI Intl.

Perry, Bert. The Fight Goes On. (Illus.). 250p. (Orig.). 1996. pap. 14.95 (*0-9643786-2-0*) Media Pubng.

Perry, Bill. Add to Your Faith. 138p. 1995. wbk. ed. 8.95 (*0-9633645-1-0*) Multi-Lang Media.

— American Holidays. 48p. 1995. pap. 2.50 (*0-9633645-2-9*) Multi-Lang Media.

— Crossing over with Parables. 109p. 1997. pap. text 8.95 (*0-9633645-3-7*) Multi-Lang Media.

— Robert & Oliver. (Illus.). 1995. 9.00 (*1-86371-486-3*) Harper SF.

— Rocky Mountain Wildlife of Yellowstone & Grand Teton National Parks. (Illus.). 68p. 1995. pap. 10.95 (*0-943972-41-8*) Homestead WY.

— Storyteller's Bible Study for Internationals. 160p. 1992. pap. 8.95 (*0-9633645-0-2*) Multi-Lang Media.

— They're Not Christian?? 48p. 1998. pap. 3.25 (*0-9633645-4-5*) Multi-Lang Media.

Perry, Bliss. Amateur Spirit. LC 70-84332. (Essay Index Reprint Ser.). 1977. 17.95 (*0-8369-1102-4*) Ayer.

— American Spirit in Literature: A Chronicle of Great Interpreters. (BCL1-PS American Literature Ser.). 281p. 1992. reprint ed. lib. bdg. 79.00 (*0-7812-6605-X*) Rprt Serv.

— And Gladly Teach: Reminiscences. (BCL1-PS American Literature Ser.). 315p. 1993. reprint ed. lib. bdg. 89.00 (*0-7812-6998-9*) Rprt Serv.

— Life & Letters of Henry Lee Higginson. LC 72-37905. (Select Bibliographies Reprint Ser.). 1977. reprint ed. 35.95 (*0-8369-6743-7*) Ayer.

— Park-Street Papers. LC 73-117826. (Essay Index Reprint Ser.). 1977. 21.95 (*0-8369-2012-0*) Ayer.

— Powers at Play. LC 74-110209. (Short Story Index Reprint Ser.). 1977. 20.95 (*0-8369-3360-5*) Ayer.

— The Praise of Folly: And Other Papers. (BCL1-PS American Literature Ser.). 230p. 1992. reprint ed. lib. bdg. 79.00 (*0-7812-6829-X*) Rprt Serv.

— Salem Kittredge, & Other Stories. LC 71-133165. (Short Story Index Reprint Ser.). 1977. 19.95 (*0-8369-3689-2*) Ayer.

— Walt Whitman. 1998. 34.95 (*0-7910-4540-4*) Chelsea Hse.

— Walt Whitman: His Life & Work. (BCL1-PS American Literature Ser.). 318p. 1992. reprint ed. lib. bdg. 89.00 (*0-7812-6899-0*) Rprt Serv.

— Walt Whitman, His Life & Work. LC 79-86165. reprint ed. 35.00 (*0-404-04995-8*) AMS Pr.

Perry, Bliss, ed. see Emerson, Ralph Waldo.

Perry, Bob. Landscape Plants for Western Regions: An Illustrated Guide to Plants for Water Conservation. (Illus.). 318p. 1994. 62.00 (*0-9605988-3-9*) Land Design.

Perry, Bonnie. Gifts of the Heart. 1994. pap. 4.95 (*0-8217-4547-6*) NAL.

Perry, Bonnie, jt. auth. see Truesdale, Albert.

Perry, Bonnie J. Bare Essentials. 224p. 1994. mass mkt. 4.50 (*0-7860-0036-8*, Pinncle Kensgtn) Kensgtn Pub Corp.

— Twice in a Lifetime. 320p. 1996. mass mkt. 4.99 (*0-7860-0213-1*, Pinncle Kensgtn) Kensgtn Pub Corp.

***Perry, Brad.** Content-Based Access to Multimedia Information: From Technology Trends to State of the Art. LC 99-20231. (International Series in Engineering & Computer Science). 143 p. 1999. write for info. (*0-7923-8495-4*) Kluwer Academic.

***Perry, Brian D., Sr.** Algiers Point: A Shocking Story of Murder & Corruption in the N. O. Police Dept. LC 99-91246. 1999. 25.00 (*0-7388-0704-4*); pap. 18.00 (*0-7388-0705-2*) Xlibris Corp.

Perry, Bridgett T., jt. auth. see Berndt, Thomas J.

Perry, Bruce. Biography of Cesar Chavez. 1998. write for info. (*0-679-45020-3*) Pantheon.

— Malcolm: The Life of the Man Who Changed Black America. (Illus.). 560p. 1991. 24.95 (*0-88268-103-6*) Station Hill Pr.

Perry, Bruce, ed. see Malcolm X.

Perry, Bruce D. Maltreated Children: Experience, Brain Development, & the Next Generation. 240p. 1998. 29.00 (*0-393-70212-X*) Norton.

Perry, Bruce W. Clean Air Act Compliance Guide, 3 vols., Set. rev. ed. LC 96-156195. 1994. ring bd. 249.00 (*1-55645-014-1*, 160002) Busn Legal Reports.

— Environmental Manager's Guide to ISO 14000. LC 96-156288. 1995. ring bd. 395.00 (*1-55645-034-6*, 160008) Busn Legal Reports.

Perry, Bryon A. Seventy-Five Years at Oakland Hills: A Jubilee Celebration. Cook, Shelby, ed. (Illus.). 120p. 1991. 55.00 (*0-9629299-0-5*) B A Perry & Assocs.

Perry, C. Seat Weaving. 1940. pap. 7.67 (*0-02-665670-1*) Glencoe.

Perry, C. B. Charles d'Wolf of Guadalupe, His Ancestors & Descendants, Being a Complete Genealogy of the "RI de Wolf's", the Descendants of Simon, with Their Common Descent from Balthasar of Lyme, Conn., 1668. (Illus.). 325p. 1989. reprint ed. pap. 49.00 (*0-8328-0477-0*); reprint ed. lib. bdg. 59.00 (*0-8328-0476-2*) Higginson Bk Co.

— The Perrys of Rhode Island, & Tales of Silver Creek. (Illus.). 115p. reprint ed. pap. 23.00 (*0-8328-1655-8*); reprint ed. lib. bdg. 33.00 (*0-8328-1654-X*) Higginson Bk Co.

Perry, C. Dianne, jt. ed. see Herumin, Wendy W.

Perry, C. Martin. Bones of Contention. 228p. 1998. 5.99 (*1-55197-236-0*) Picasso Publ.

Perry, C. Michael. Christmas Dreams: A Musical. 48p. 1993. pap. 4.00 (*1-57514-212-0*, 0063) Encore Perform Pub.

— Remember When? Monologs of the Middle School Experience. (Scene Bks.). 32p. (YA). (gr. 7-12). 1994. pap. 6.95 (*1-57514-006-3*, 5015) Encore Perform Pub.

Perry, C. Michael, ed. Christmas Programs for Sacrament Meetings. (LDS Theatre Ser.). 60p. 1997. pap. 8.95 (*1-57514-166-3*) Encore Perform Pub.

— Scenes & Monologues for Teenaged Actors, Vol. 1. (Scene Bks.). 60p. (YA). (gr. 7-12). 1994. pap. 8.95 (*1-57514-001-2*, 5006) Encore Perform Pub.

— Scenes & Monologues for Teenaged Actors, Vol. 2. (Scene Bks.). 67p. (YA). (gr. 7-12). 1994. pap. 8.95 (*1-57514-000-4*, 5009) Encore Perform Pub.

— Scenes for Young Actors: From the World of Literature & Modern Day Plays. (Scene Bks.). 51p. (J). (gr. 3-10). 1993. pap. 8.95 (*1-57514-002-0*, 5007) Encore Perform Pub.

Perry, C. Michael & Lewis, Susan. Of Babylon: A Musical. 1997. pap. 4.00 (*1-57514-302-X*, 0100) Encore Perform Pub.

Perry, C. Michael, jt. auth. see Lambert, James G.

Perry, C. Michael, jt. auth. see Martin, Rod.

Perry, C. Michael, jt. auth. see Zelenak, Nancy.

Perry, C. Michael, jt. contrib. by see Bean, Mimi.

Perry, C. R. The Victorian Post Office: The Growth of a Bureaucracy. (Royal Historical Society: Studies in History: No. 64). 320p. (C). 1992. 75.00 (*0-86193-220-X*, Royal Historical Soc) Boydell & Brewer.

Perry, Campbell, jt. auth. see Laurence, Jean-Roch.

Perry, Candy M., jt. ed. see Mackey, Howard.

Perry, Carla. Laughing Like Dogs. unabridged ed. LC 96-70940. (Illus.). 76p. (Orig.). 1996. pap. 5.00 (*1-888934-23-9*, Cape Perpetua) Central OR Coast.

Perry, Carla, ed. Talus & Scree No. 4: An International Literary Journal. (Illus.). 164p. 1998. pap. 9.00 (*1-892076-00-4*) Dancing Moon.

— Talus & Scree No. 5: International Literary Journal. (Illus.). 164p. 1998. pap. 9.00 (*1-892076-05-5*) Dancing Moon.

Perry, Carla, ed. see Berger-Kiss, Andres.

Perry, Carmen, ed. & tr. see De La Pena, Jose E.

Perry, Carol D. Dangerous to Love. LC 96-595. (Superromance Ser.). 297p. 1995. per. 3.75 (*0-373-70652-9*, 1-70652-2) Harlequin Bks.

— Wings of Time. (Superromance Ser.). 1993. mass mkt. 3.39 (*0-373-70537-9*, 1-70537-5) Harlequin Bks.

Perry, Carol J. Introduction to Amateur Radio. (Illus.). 155p. 1986. ring bd. 99.95 (*0-939863-00-6*) Media Mentors.

— Travel Smart: Florida Gulf Coast. 2nd ed. (Illus.). 240p. 1999. pap. 15.95 (*1-56261-441-X*, Travel Smart) Avalon Travel.

Perry, Carol J., ed. see Clegg, Jeanette.

Perry, Carol R. The Fine Art of Technical Writing: Key Points to Help You Think Your Way Through Scientific or Technical Publications, Theses, Term Papers & Business Reports. 112p. (Orig.). 1991. pap. 7.95 (*0-936085-24-X*) Blue Heron OR.

Perry, Carolyn, jt. auth. see Hunt, Douglas G.

P

Perry, Carolyn, jt. ed. see Weaks, Mary L.

Perry, Cassandra J. Body Smart: Have Fun As You Learn about the Parts of the Body. (Illus.). 33p. (YA). (gr. 4 up). 1994. pap. 7.99 (0-9642365-6-7) CarSan Pubng.

Perry, Cecilia, ed. see Amidei, Nancy.

***Perry, Charles, Jr.** Burned Out: Why Me? 2nd rev. ed. Orig. Title: Why Christians Burn Out. 173p. 2000. pap. 9.95 (0-9677054-5-2) Nethope Pub.

— The Caregiver. (Illus.). 128p. 2000. 9.95 (0-9677054-4-4) Nethope Pub.

Perry, Charles. Portrait of a Young Man Drowning. LC 95-39541. (Old School Bks.). 296p. 1996. pap. 11.00 (0-393-31462-6) Norton.

— Up the Rough Side. LC 85-61878. (Illus.). 96p. 1985. pap. 5.95 (0-9615139-0-X) C Perry Pub.

— The West, Japan, & Cape Route Imports: The Oil & Non-Fuel Mineral Trades. LC 82-80947. (Special Reports). 88p. 1982. 11.95 (0-89549-042-0) Inst Foreign Policy Anal.

***Perry, Charles E., Jr.** Dangerous Dispositions. 120p. 2000. pap. 9.95 (0-9677054-2-8) Nethope Pub.

— Growing Weary in the Work of Love. 120p. 2000. pap. 9.95 (0-9677054-1-X) Nethope Pub.

Perry, Charles E., ed. Founders & Leaders of Connecticut, Sixteen Thirty-Three to Seventeen Eighty-Three. LC 78-177965. (Essay Index Reprint Ser.). 1977. reprint ed. 23.95 (0-8369-2518-1) Ayer.

***Perry, Charles E., Jr. & Robbins, Georgia.** The Treasure of Our Heritage: The Sam Via Story. 91p. 2000. pap. 9.95 (0-9677054-0-1) Nethope Pub.

Perry, Charles E., jt. auth. see Perry, Louise K.

Perry, Charles E., Jr., ed. see Moore, Ruth.

Perry, Charles L. Purchasing Transportation. LC 96-30411. (Illus.). 100p. (Orig.). 1998. pap. 14.95 (0-945456-45-X) PT Pubns.

Perry, Charles M. Henry Philip Tappan: Philosopher & University President. LC 71-165723. (American Education Ser., No. 2). 1972. reprint ed. 26.95 (0-405-03715-5) Ayer.

— Toward a Dimensional Reality. LC 39-11737. 188p. reprint ed. pap. 58.30 (0-608-30018-7, 201624900002) Bks Demand.

Perry, Charles M., ed. The St. Louis Movement in Philosophy: Some Source Material. LC 31-8773. (Illus.). 150p. reprint ed. pap. 46.50 (0-608-10334-9, 201624800002) Bks Demand.

Perry, Charles M., et al. Airpower Synergies in the New Strategic Era: The Complementary Roles of Long-Range Bombers & Carrier-Based Aircraft. (Institute for Foreign Policy Anaylsis Ser.). (Illus.). 116p. 1997. pap. 15.00 (1-57488-160-4) Brasseys.

— Strategic Dynamics in the Nordic/Baltic Region. (IFPA Special Reports Ser.). 120p. 1999. pap. 15.00 (1-57488-196-5) Brasseys.

Perry, Charles M., jt. ed. see Praaning, Rio D.

Perry, Charles R. Union Corporate Campaigns. LC 86-82727. (Major Industrial Research Unit Study Ser.: Vol. 66). 211p. (Orig.). 1987. pap. 30.00 (0-89546-065-3) U PA Ctr Hum Res.

Perry, Charles R. & Kegley, Delwyn H. Disintegration & Change: Labor Relations in the Meat Packing Industry. LC 88-83309. (Labor Relations & Public Policy Ser.: No. 35). 240p. 1989. pap. 35.00 (0-89546-073-4) U PA Ctr Hum Res.

Perry, Charles R. & Northrup, Herbert R., frwds. Collective Bargaining & the Decline of the United Mine Workers. LC 84-47503. (Major Industrial Research Unit Studies: No. 60). 273p. 1984. 30.00 (0-89546-043-2) U PA Ctr Hum Res.

Perry, Charles R. & Rowan, Richard L. The Impact of Government Manpower Programs in General & on Minorities & Women. LC 74-13177. (Major Industrial Research Unit Ser.: No. 4). 543p. reprint ed. pap. 168.40 (0-608-14846-6, 202590800047) Bks Demand.

Perry, Charles R., et al. Employee Financial Participation: An International Survey. LC 90-70533. (Multinational Industrial Relations Ser.: Vol. 12). 222p. 1990. 35.00 (0-89546-077-7, MUL12) U PA Ctr Hum Res.

— Operating During Strikes: Company Experience, NLRB Policies & Governmental Regulations. LC 82-80521. (Labor Relations & Public Policy Ser.: No. 23). 163p. 1982. pap. 20.00 (0-89546-036-X) U PA Ctr Hum Res.

Perry, Cheryl. Creating Health Behavior Change: How to Develop Community-Wide Programs for Youth. LC 99-6239. (Developmental Clinical Psychology & Psychiatry Ser.). 1999. write for info. (0-7619-1227-4) Sage.

— The Story of the Bible: How the World's Bestselling Book Came to Be. 1998. pap., boxed set 59.95 (1-55145-298-7, Pub. by Wood Lake Bks) Logos Prods.

Perry, Cheryl, compiled by. Live the Story: Short Simple Plays for Church Groups. (Whole People of God Library). 144p. Date not set. pap. 15.95 (1-55145-245-6, Pub. by Wood Lake Bks) Logos Prods.

— Youth Spirit: Program Ideas for Church Groups. (Illus.). 192p. Date not set. pap. 19.95 (1-55145-247-2, Pub. by Wood Lake Bks) Logos Prods.

Perry, Cheryl & Faulkner, Hal. Holiday Mathemagic. (Illus.). 56p. (J). (gr. 4-10). 1977. pap. text 8.50 (0-918932-50-5, AE-1537) Activity Resources.

***Perry, Cheryl L.** Creating Health Behavior Change: How to Develop Community-Wide Programs for Youth. LC 99-6239. (Developmental Clinical Psychology & Psychiatry Ser.: Vol. 43). 140p. 1999. 60.00 (0-7619-1226-6) Sage.

Perry, Chrsitopher. Listen to the Voice Within. 1991. pap. 15.95 (0-687-85683-3) Abingdon.

Perry, Chuck, ed. see Caruso, Gary.

Perry, Cindy. Activities That Build Young Women, Vol. 1. 48p. (YA). 1993. pap. 7.98 (0-88290-456-6) Horizon Utah.

Perry, Claire. Pacific Arcadia: Images of California, 1600-1915. LC 98-17283. (Illus.). 256p. 1999. 40.00 (0-19-510936-8); pap. 25.00 (0-19-510937-6) OUP.

Perry, Clark, jt. auth. see Rowan, Robin H.

***Perry, Clay & Perry, Maggie.** A World of Flowers. LC 00-40486. 2001. write for info. (0-312-27182-4) St Martin.

Perry, Clay, et al. Old English Villages. (Country Ser.). (Illus.). 160p. 1997. pap. 17.95 (0-7538-0263-5, Pub. by Weidenfeld & Nicolson) Trafalgar.

Perry, Clay, jt. auth. see Innes, Miranda.

***Perry, Clayton R.** MasterCases: Orthopaedic Trauma. 1998. write for info. (3-13-115121-8) Thieme Med Pubs.

Perry, Clayton R., et al, eds. Handbook of Fractures. (Illus.). 356p. 1994. pap. text 34.00 (0-07-048590-9) McGraw-Hill HPD.

Perry, Clayton R., et al. Handbook of Fractures. 2nd ed. LC 99-38946. (Illus.). 432p. 1999. pap. text 32.95 (0-07-048624-7) McGraw-Hill HPD.

Perry, Corinna, ed. see Barron, Leanna.

Perry, Curtis. The Making of Jacobean Culture: James I & the Renegotiation of Elizabethan Literary Practice. (Illus.). 296p. (C). 1997. text 59.95 (0-521-57406-4) Cambridge U Pr.

***Perry, Cynthia S.** All Things Being Equal: One Woman's Journey. Fowler, Alice S. & Ward, James, eds. (Illus.). vii, 286p. 2000. 25.00 (0-9675571-1-9, 5); per. 19.95 (0-9675571-0-0, 5) Stonecrest.

Perry, D., ed. Legislation on Dangerous Substances: Classification & Labelling in the European Communities, 2 vols., Vol. 1-2. (C). 1987. lib. bdg. 153.00 (0-86010-960-7, Pub. by Graham & Trotman) Kluwer Academic.

Perry, D. L. Materials Synthesis & Characterization: Based on the Proceedings of an American Chemical Society Symposium Held in San Diego, California, March 13-17, 1994. LC 97-31218. 226p. (C). 1997. 95.00 (0-306-45377-0, Kluwer Plenum) Kluwer Academic.

Perry, D. L., ed. Instrumental Surface Analysis of Geologic Materials. (Illus.). ix, 373p. 1990. 65.00 (0-89573-758-2, Wiley-VCH) Wiley.

Perry, D. L., ed. Instrumental Surface Analysis of Geologic Materials. 373p. 1990. 99.95 (0-471-18729-1, Wiley-VCH) Wiley.

Perry, D. R., jt. auth. see Farnfield, Carolyn A.

Perry, Dal, jt. auth. see Perry, Steve.

Perry, Dale L. Applications of Analytical Techniques to the Characteristics. (Illus.). 208p. (C). 1992. text 95.00 (0-306-44189-6, Kluwer Plenum) Kluwer Academic.

Perry, Dale L., et al, eds. Applications of Synchrotron Radiation Techniques to Materials Science, Vol. 307. (Symposium Proceedings Ser.). 357p. 1993. text 30.00 (1-55899-203-0) Materials Res.

Perry, Dale L., et al, eds. Applications of Synchrotron Radiation Techniques to Materials Science III. LC 96-47201. (MRS Symposium Proceedings Ser.: Vol. 437). 252p. 1996. 76.00 (1-55899-340-1, 437-H6) Materials Res.

Perry, Dale L. & Phillips, Sidney L., eds. Handbook of Inorganic Compounds. 584p. 1995. boxed set 145.00 (0-8493-8671-3) CRC Pr.

Perry, Dame & Co. Staff. Women's & Children's Fashions of 1917: The Complete Perry, Dame & Co., Catalog. LC 92-12621. Orig. Title: New York Styles - Spring & Summer 1917 Catalog, No. 67. (Illus.). 160p. 1992. reprint ed. pap. 12.95 (0-486-27128-5) Dover.

***Perry, Dan.** Israel & the Quest for Permanence. LC 99-22620. (Illus.). 216p. 1999. 24.95 (0-7864-0645-3) McFarland & Co.

Perry, Dave. Dave Perry's 100 Best Racing Rules Quizzes. 168p. 1994. pap. text 16.95 (1-882502-19-1) US Sail Assn.

— Little Fox's Airbrush Stencil Techniques. (Illus.). 125p. (Orig.). 1982. pap. text 14.95 (0-9603530-8-9) US Screen.

— Understanding the Racing Rules of Sailing Through 2000. 4th rev. ed. Orig. Title: Understanding the Yacht Racing Rules. (Illus.). 140p. 1997. pap. 25.00 (1-882502-44-2) US Sail Assn.

— Understanding the Yacht Racing Rules - 1993-96. rev. ed. 306p. 1993. pap. 19.95 (1-882502-02-7) US Sail Assn.

— Winning in One Designs. 2nd ed. (Illus.). 293p. 1992. pap. text 16.95 (1-882502-00-0) US Sail Assn.

Perry, David. The Long Night. (Vampire: The Dark Ages). (Illus.). (Orig.). 1997. pap. 10.95 (1-56504-509-2, 5008) White Wolf.

Perry, David, contrib. by. Jazz Greats. LC 96-196298. (20th Century Composers Ser.). (Illus.). 240p. (Orig.). (C). 1996. pap. 19.95 (0-7148-3204-9, Pub. by Phaidon Press) Phaidon Pr.

Perry, David & Gifford, Barry. Hot Rod. LC 96-26779. 1997. pap. 22.95 (0-8118-1593-5) Chronicle Bks.

Perry, David, jt. auth. see Neal, Bill.

Perry, David A. Forest Ecosystems. LC 94-10796. 1995. pap. text 49.95 (0-8018-4987-X) Johns Hopkins.

Perry, David A., ed. Maintaining the Longterm Productivity of Pacific Northwest Forest Ecosystems. LC 89-20168. (Illus.). 256p. 1989. text 44.95 (0-88192-144-0) Timber.

Perry, David B. Bike Cult: The Ultimate Guide to Human-Powered Vehicles. LC 95-5128. (Illus.). 570p. (Orig.). 1995. pap. 23.95 (1-56858-027-4) FWEW.

Perry, David C., ed. Building the Public City: The Politics, Governance & Finance of Public Infrastructure. (Urban Affairs Annual Review Ser.: Vol. 43). 280p. 1994. 62.00 (0-8039-4432-2); pap. 26.00 (0-8039-4433-0) Sage.

Perry, David C. & Watkins, Alfred J., eds. The Rise of the Sunbelt Cities. LC 77-93698. (Urban Affairs Annual Reviews Ser.: No. 14). 309p. reprint ed. pap. 95.80 (0-8357-8504-1, 203478300091) Bks Demand.

Perry, David C., jt. auth. see Liggett, Helen.

Perry, David G. Brachiopoda & Biostratigraphy of the Silurian-Devonian Delorme Formation in the District of Mackenzie. (Illus.). 243p. pap. 29.71 (0-88854-304-2) Brill Academic Pubs.

Perry, David J. & Pasi, K. John, eds. Hemostasis & Thrombosis Protocols. LC 99-10466. (Methods in Molecular Medicine Ser.: Vol. 31). (Illus.). 384p. 1999. 89.50 (0-89603-419-4) Humana.

Perry, David J., jt. auth. see Lebet, Philip E.

***Perry, David K.** American Pragmatism & Communication Research. LC 00-34735. (Communication Ser.). 2000. write for info. (0-8058-3590-3) L Erlbaum Assocs.

Perry, David K. Theory & Research in Mass Communication: Contexts & Consequences. (LEA's Communication Ser.). 240p. 1996. pap. 24.50 (0-8058-1924-X); text 45.00 (0-8058-1923-1) L Erlbaum Assocs.

Perry, David M. Dave Perry's 100 Best Racing Rules Quizzes: Based on the 1997-2000 Racing Rules of Sailing. (Illus.). 160p. 1998. pap. 16.95 (1-882502-62-0) US Sail Assn.

***Perry, David M.** Winning in One Designs. 3rd ed. (Illus.). 2000. pap. write for info. (1-882502-78-7) US Sail Assn.

Perry, Devern J. College Vocabulary Building. 9th ed. LC 92-15515. (C). 1992. mass mkt. 24.50 (0-538-61413-7) S-W Pub.

— Word Division & Spelling. 4th ed. (KM - Office Procedures Ser.). 1993. mass mkt. 11.75 (0-538-62750-6) S-W Pub.

Perry, Devern J. Word Division & Spelling Manual. 4th ed. 1993. pap. 11.50 (0-538-61995-3) S-W Pub.

Perry, Devern J. Word Studies. 8th ed. (PS - Communication/English Ser.). 1988. mass mkt. 14.75 (0-538-05811-0) S-W Pub.

— Word Studies. 8th ed. (C). 1988. mass mkt. 16.00 (0-538-05813-7, E81U) S-W Pub.

— Word Studies. 9th ed. (PS - Communication/English Ser.). (C). 1995. mass mkt., wbk. ed. 15.50 (0-538-71274-0) S-W Pub.

— Word Studies, Tests. 9th ed. (PS - Communication/English Ser.). (C). 1995. 5.00 (0-538-71300-3) S-W Pub.

Perry, Donald D. Moak 4 State Regional Exhibition, 1996. (Illus.). 16p. (Orig.). 1996. pap. 3.00 (0-934306-15-X) Springfield.

Perry, Donald G. Managing a Wildland Fire: A Practical Perspective. Brooks, Carol C., ed. LC 89-84092. (Illus.). 145p. (Orig.). (C). 1989. pap. text 14.95 (0-941943-01-1) Fire Pubns.

— Wildland Firefighting: Fire Behavior, Tactics & Command. 2nd rev. ed. Brooks, Carol C., ed. (Illus.). 412p. 1990. pap. text 29.95 (0-941943-02-X, 35390) Fire Pubns.

Perry, Donna. Backtalk: Women Writers Speak Out. (Illus.). 360p. 1995. pap. 16.95 (0-8135-2199-8) Rutgers U Pr.

Perry, Donna, ed. Backtalk: Women Writers Speak Out. LC 92-41201. (Illus.). 360p. (C). 1993. 40.00 (0-8135-1991-8) Rutgers U Pr.

Perry, Donna & Maglin, Nan B., eds. Bad Girls - Good Girls: Women, Sex, & Power in the Nineties. (Illus.). (C). 1996. pap. 17.95 (0-8135-2251-X); text 50.00 (0-8135-2250-1) Rutgers U Pr.

Perry, Doreen. Restoring Dolls: A Practical Guide. (Illus.). 94p. 1987. 15.95 (0-900873-59-0, Pub. by Bishopsgte Pr); pap. 11.95 (0-900873-61-2, Pub. by Bishopsgte Pr) Intl Spec Bk.

— Restoring Toys: A Practical Guide. (C). 1988. 35.00 (1-85219-002-7, Pub. by Bishopsgate Pr Ltd) St Mut.

Perry, Dorothy A., et al. Periodontology for the Dental Hygienist. Ozmat, Selma, ed. LC 95-19487. (Illus.). 336p. 1995. pap. text 36.00 (0-7216-4063-X, W B Saunders Co) Harcrt Hlth Sci Grp.

Perry, Dorothy A., jt. auth. see Carranza, Fermin A., Jr.

***Perry, Douglas L.** Immortal Colossus. 112p. 1999. 6.95 (0-9677115-0-9) Retro Vision.

Perry, Douglas L. VHDL. 3rd ed. LC 98-16663. 1998. 60.00 (0-07-049436-3) McGraw.

Perry, Duncan M. The Politics of Terror: The Macedonian Revolutionary Movements, 1893-1903. LC 87-33062. (Illus.). 275p. (C). 1988. text 39.95 (0-8223-0813-4) Duke.

— Stefan Stambolov & the Emergence of Modern Bulgaria, 1870-1895. LC 92-34704. (Illus.). 328p. 1993. text 46.95 (0-8223-1313-8) Duke.

Perry, Dwight. Breaking Down the Barriers: A Black Evangelical Explains the Black Church. LC 98-8102. 176p. (gr. 10). 1998. pap. 12.99 (0-8010-5709-4) Baker Bks.

Perry, E. Eugene. It Works for Everybody Else: Playscript. LC 98-31257. 1984. pap. 5.00 (0-88734-312-0) Players Pr.

Perry, Earl, ed. Geometry: Axiomatic Developments with Problem Solving. (Pure & Applied Mathematics Ser.: Vol. 160). (Illus.). 376p. 1992. text 55.00 (0-8247-8727-7) Dekker.

Perry, Earl & Perry, Wilma. Puppets Go to Church. 88p. 1975. pap. 6.99 (0-8341-0385-0) Beacon Hill.

Perry, Edmond S., et al, eds. Separation & Purification Methods, Vol. 3. LC 73-77000. (Illus.). 479p. reprint ed. pap. 148.50 (0-608-18044-0, 202900800003) Bks Demand.

Perry, Edmund F., jt. auth. see Reat, N. Ross.

Perry, Edvard D. Sanskrit Primer. 2nd ed. 230p. (Orig.). 1986. reprint ed. 13.95 (81-208-0206-3, Pub. by Motilal Bnarsidass); reprint ed. pap. 9.00 (81-208-0207-1, Pub. by Motilal Bnarsidass) S Asia.

Perry, Edward. Descriptive Analyses of Piano Works. 1977. lib. bdg. 59.95 (0-8490-1708-4) Gordon Pr.

— Movies, Me, & Us. LC 99-19624. 1996. 22.95 (0-8050-4917-7) H Holt & Co.

Perry, Edward L. Luyties Homeopathic Practice. 165p. 1974. pap. 1.95 (0-89378-052-9) Formur Intl.

Perry, Edward L., jt. auth. see Chapman, J. B.

Perry, Elaine, et al, eds. Dementia with Lewy Bodies: Clinical, Pathological, & Treatment Issues. LC 96-16710. (Illus.). 541p. (C). 1996. text 130.00 (0-521-56188-4) Cambridge U Pr.

Perry, Eleanor. Keeping Our Heads on Straight. LC 97-104261. 112p. (Orig.). 1996. pap. 12.95 (1-886094-46-2) Chicago Spectrum.

— The Swimmer. LC 67-17163. 127p. 1967. 16.95 (0-910278-70-9) Boulevard.

Perry, Elisabeth I. Women in Action: Rebels & Reformers, 1920-1980. 60p. 1995. pap. 6.95 (0-89959-389-5, 1019) LWVUS.

***Perry, Elisabeth Israels.** Belle Moskowitz: Feminine Politics & the Exercise of Power in the Age of Alfred E. Smith. LC 99-52901. (Illus.). 279p. 2000. reprint ed. pap. text 22.00 (1-55553-424-4) NE U Pr.

Perry, Elizabeth & Li, Xun. Proletarian Power: Shanghai in the Cultural Revolution. LC 96-42940. (Transitions: Asia & Asian America Ser.). (C). 1996. pap. 25.00 (0-8133-2165-4, Pub. by Westview) HarpC.

Perry, Elizabeth A. A Brief History of the Town of Glocester Rhode Island. (Illus.). 175p. 1996. pap. 18.50 (0-7884-0389-3, P167) Heritage Bk.

Perry, Elizabeth J. The Contentious Chinese. (Asia & the Pacific Ser.). 352p. 2000. 69.95 (0-7656-0444-2, East Gate Bk) M E Sharpe.

— Rebels & Revolutionaries in North China, 1845-1945. LC 79-65179. xvi, 324p. 1980. 45.00 (0-8047-1055-4); pap. 15.95 (0-8047-1175-5) Stanford U Pr.

— Shanghai on Strike: The Politics of Chinese Labor. LC 92-17774. 352p. (C). 1993. 45.00 (0-8047-2063-0) Stanford U Pr.

— Shanghai on Strike: The Politics of Chinese Labor. (Illus.). 344p. (C). 1995. pap. 16.95 (0-8047-2491-1) Stanford U Pr.

Perry, Elizabeth J., ed. Chinese Perspectives on the Nien Rebellion. LC 81-9300. 147p. 1981. reprint ed. pap. 45.60 (0-7837-9989-6, 206071600006) Bks Demand.

— Putting Class in Its Place: Worker Identities in East Asia. LC 95-50860. (China Research Monographs: Vol. 48). 1996. pap. 18.50 (1-55729-050-4) IEAS.

***Perry, Elizabeth J. & Selden, Mark.** Chinese Society: Change Conflict & Resistance. LC 99-38813. (Asia's Transformations Ser.). 240p. 1999. text 90.00 (0-415-20490-9) Routledge.

***Perry, Elizabeth J. & Selden, Mark, eds.** Contemporary Chinese Society: Change, Conflict & Resistance. (Asia's Transformations Ser.). 240p. 2000. pap. 27.99 (0-415-22334-2) Routledge.

Perry, Elizabeth J., jt. ed. see Lu, Xiaobo.

Perry, Elizabeth S., ed. see Perry, Floyd D.

Perry, Elizabeth W. We Left Because the Creek Went Dry: The People of the First Creek District Lake Chelaw, Washington, 1888-1932. LC 99-60367. 144p. 1999. pap. 16.95 (0-9663560-1-2, 99-0300) Point Publ.

Perry, Ellen L. Ward Management & Teaching. 3rd ed. (Illus.). 304p. 1988. 26.00 (0-685-32962-3) Bailliere Tindall.

Perry, Elliot. Pat Paragraphs. Turner, George T. & Stanton, Thomas E., eds. LC 81-68198. (Illus.). 648p. 1982. 55.00 (0-930412-05-2) Bureau Issues.

Perry, Erna K. Contemporary Society. 7th ed. (C). 1997. 64.00 (0-673-99034-6) Addson-Wesley Educ.

Perry, Erna K., jt. auth. see Perry, John A.

Perry, Estelle S. Streamlining the United Nations Pt. A: Wanted: A U. N. Personnel System That Works. (Monograph in CURE Ser.: No. 12A). 68p. 1993. pap. text 5.00 (1-881520-02-1) Ctr U N Reform Educ.

Perry, Evan. Corkscrews & Bottle Openers. (Album Ser.). (Illus.). 32p. 1980. pap. text 5.25 (0-85263-534-6, Pub. by Shire Pubns) Lubrecht & Cramer.

— Corkscrews & Bottle Openers. (Album Ser.: No. 59). (Illus.). 32p. 1998. pap. 6.25 (0-7478-0281-5, Pub. by Shire Pubns) Parkwest Pubns.

Perry, Floyd D. Floyd Perry's Pictorial Guide to Quality Groundskeeping Bk. 1: Covering All the Bases. 2nd ed. (Illus.). 104p. 1993. reprint ed. pap. 35.95 (1-891250-00-0) Grounds Maint.

— Floyd Perry's Pictorial Guide to Quality Groundskeeping Bk. 2: There Ain't No Rules. Perry, Elizabeth S., ed. (Illus.). 109p. 1994. pap. 35.95 (1-891250-01-9) Grounds Maint.

— Floyd Perry's Pictorial Guide to Quality Groundskeeping Bk. 3: Maintain It Easy - Keep It Safe. Perry, Elizabeth S., ed. (Illus.). 124p. 1997. pap. 35.95 (1-891250-02-7) Grounds Maint.

Perry, Foster. The Violet Forest: Shamanic Journeys in the Amazon. LC 97-52709. 256p. 1998. pap. 14.00 (1-879181-43-6) Bear & Co.

— When Lightning Strikes a Hummingbird: The Awakening of a Healer. LC 93-10285. (Illus.). 224p. (Orig.). 1993. pap. 10.95 (1-879181-10-X) Bear & Co.

Perry, Frances, ed. Simon & Schuster's Complete Guide to Plants & Flowers. (Illus.). 1976. per. 15.00 (0-671-22247-3) S&S Trade.

Perry, Frances B., ed. Let's Sing Together: Favorite Primary Songs. (Illus.). 96p. (J). (ps-6). 1984. 12.98 (0-941518-02-7) Perry Enterprises.

— Let's Sing Together: Favorite Primary Songs of Members of the Church of Jesus Christ of Latter-day Saints. (Illus.). 96p. (J). (ps-6). 1981. 10.98 (0-941518-00-0) Perry Enterprises.

Perry, Frank, Jr. Afro-American Vocal Music: A Select Guide to Fifteen Composers. LC 91-751616. 142p. (C). 1991. 18.95 (0-9628916-2-2) Vande Vere.

Perry, Frank. History of Pigeon Point Lighthouse. (Illus.). 88p. 1995. pap. 7.95 (0-9617681-2-6) Otter B Bks.

Perry, Frank A. East Brother: History of an Island Light Station. LC 84-82389. (Illus.). 109p. 1984. pap. 10.00 (0-9614254-0-7) East Brother.

P

— Fossil Invertebrates & Geology of the Marine Cliffs at Capitola, California. 30p. 1993. pap. 3.95 (*0-9632480-2-2*) Santa Cruz Mus Assn.

— Fossil Sharks & Rays of the Southern Santa Cruz Mountains, California. (Illus.). 48p. (Orig.). 1994. pap. 4.95 (*0-9632480-1-4*) Santa Cruz Mus Assn.

Perry, Fred. Elements of Banking. 4th ed. 1984. 100.00 (*0-416-36630-9*, Pub. by Chartered Bank) St Mut.

Perry, Frederick. St. Louis: Louis IX of France, the Most Christian King. LC 73-14462. reprint ed. 49.50 (*0-404-58280-X*) AMS Pr.

Perry, Frederick J. A Reconstruction-Analysis of "Buried Child" by Playwright Sam Shepard. LC 92-865. 172p. 1992. lib. bdg. 79.95 (*0-7734-9810-9*) E Mellen.

Perry, Fredi & Thomas, Berwyn B. Shelton: The First Century Plus Ten. abr. rev. ed. (Illus.). 112p. 1996. lib. bdg. 20.00 (*0-935693-17-3*) Mason Cty Hist.

Perry, G., ed. Alterations in the Neuronal Cytoskeleton in Alzheimer's Disease. LC 87-29256. (Advances in Behavioral Biology Ser.: Vol. 34). 240p. 1987. 69.50 (*0-306-42766-4*, Plenum Trade) Perseus Pubng.

Perry, G. E., jt. auth. see Wilson, J. G.

Perry, G. G., ed. Religious Pieces in Prose & Verse from R. Thornton's MS. (Early English Text Society Original Ser.: No. 26). 1996. reprint ed. 36.00 (*0-85991-813-0*, Pub. by EETS) Boydell & Brewer.

Perry, G. G., ed. see Rolle, Richard.

Perry, G. W., jt. ed. see Lowe, A. L.

Perry, Gai. Color from the Heart: Seven Great Ways to Make Quilts with Colors You Love. Aneloski, Liz & Koolish, Lynn, eds. LC 99-6063. (Illus.). 112p. 1999. pap. 24.95 (*1-57120-071-1*, 10191) C & T Pub.

***Perry, Gai.** Color in Quilts Gift Wrap. 1999. 12.95 (*1-57120-082-7*) C & T Pub.

Perry, Gai. Impressionist Palette: Quilt Color & Design. Kuhn, Barb, ed. LC 97-6598. (Illus.). 128p. (Orig.). 1997. pap. 25.95 (*1-57120-030-4*, 10155) C & T Pub.

— Impressionist Quilts. (Illus.). 128p. 1995. pap. 24.95 (*1-57120-003-7*, 10125) C & T Pub.

Perry, Gail. Complete Idiot's Guide to Doing Your Income Taxes. 434p. 1997. pap. text 12.95 (*0-02-862000-3*) Macmillan Gen Ref.

— Complete Idiot's Guide to Doing Your Income Taxes 200t. 2000th ed. 528p. 2000. pap. text 12.95 (*0-02-863688-0*) S&S Trade.

— Excel 2000 Answers! (Certified Tech Support Ser.). 1999. pap. text 24.99 (*0-07-211883-0*) Osborne.

***Perry, Gail & Brandon, Bill.** Word for Windows 95 Essentials, Level Iii. 2nd ed. 194p. (C). 1998. pap. text 18.67 (*1-58076-154-2*) Que Educ & Trng.

***Perry, Gail & Duru, Mary S., eds.** Resources for Developmentally Appropriate Practice: Recommendations from the Profession. LC 99-67612. 239p. 1999. pap. text 10.00 (*0-935989-91-9*, NAEYC 233) Natl Assn Child Ed.

Perry, Gail A. The Complete Idiot's Guide to Doing Your Income Taxes: 1999 Edition. (Complete Idiot's Guide to Doing Your Income Tax). 520p. 1998. pap. 12.95 (*0-02-862682-6*, Pub. by Macmillan) S&S Trade.

***Perry, Gail A.** Using QuickBooks & QuickBooks Pro 99. LC 99-60354. (Special Edition Using... Que Ser.). 1999. pap. text 29.99 (*0-7897-1965-7*) Que.

— Wordperfect Suite 8 Fast & Easy: Visual Learning Guide. LC 97-67397. 400p. 1997. pap. text 16.99 (*0-7615-1188-1*) Prima Pub.

Perry, Gail R. The Complete Idiot's Guide to Doing Your 1995 Taxes. 350p. 1995. 14.99 (*1-56761-586-4*, Alpha Ref) Macmillan Gen Ref.

— The Complete Idiot's Guide to Preparing Your 1996 Taxes. 350p. 1995. 14.99 (*0-614-03572-4*, Alpha Ref) Macmillan Gen Ref.

— Turbo Tax for Windows for Dummies. 384p. 1994. pap. 19.99 (*1-56884-228-7*) IDG Bks.

Perry, Garland. An American Saga William George Hughes (1859-1902) A Pioneer Texas Rancher: His Life, His Times, His Story. LC 95-75913. 250p. 1995. 24.95 (*0-9646196-0-1*) Perry TX.

Perry, Garry P. & Orchard, Janet. Assessment & Treatment of Adolescent Sex Offenders. LC 92-14135. 160p. (Orig.). 1992. pap. 22.95 (*0-943158-75-3*, ATABP, Prof Resc Pr) Pro Resource.

Perry, Gayle. Alphabet, No. 2428. Friedman, Susan, ed. (Primary Theme Ser.). (Illus.). 48p. (J). (gr. k-1). 1999. pap. 6.98 (*1-57471-541-0*) Creat Teach Pr.

***Perry, Gayle.** Numbers. Wolkoff, Stacey, ed. (Primary Theme Ser.: Vol. 2431). (Illus.). 32p. (J). (gr. k-2). 2000. pap. 6.98 (*1-57471-683-2*) Creat Teach Pr.

Perry, George. The Complete Phantom of the Opera. 168p. 1995. pap. 19.95 (*0-8050-1722-4*, Owl) H Holt & Co.

— The Complete Phantom of the Opera. (Illus.). 176p. 1995. 29.95 (*0-8050-0657-5*) H Holt & Co.

— The Life of Python: And Now for Something Completely Different. (Illus.). 192p. (Orig.). 1984. pap. 12.95 (*0-316-70015-0*) Little.

— The Life of Python: The History of Something Completely Different. (Illus.). 192p. 1995. pap. 16.95 (*1-56138-568-9*) Running Pr.

***Perry, George.** Magic Movie Moments: Classic Scenes from Cinema. (Illus.). 176p. 2000. 30.00 (*0-670-88932-6*, Viking Studio) Studio Bks.

Perry, George. Steven Speilberg - Close Up: The Making of His Movies. LC 98-86827. (Close Ups Ser.). (Illus.). 144p. 1998. pap. 13.95 (*1-56025-195-6*, Thunders Mouth) Avalon NY.

— Sunset Boulevard: The Making of the Musical. (Illus.). 89p. 1995. 29.95 (*0-8050-2927-3*) H Holt & Co.

Perry, George, jt. ed. see Morgan, Robin.

Perry, George G., ed. Religious Pieces in Prose & Verse. (EETS, OS Ser.: No. 26). 1974. reprint ed. 35.00 (*0-527-00026-4*) Periodicals Srv.

***Perry, George L.** Economic Events, Ideas & Policies: The 1960s & After. 224p. 2000. pap. 20.95 (*0-8157-7011-1*) Brookings.

Perry, George L., jt. ed. see Okun, Arthur M.

Perry, George S. Cities of America. LC 70-128286. (Essay Index Reprint Ser.). 1977. 26.95 (*0-8369-1840-1*) Ayer.

— Walls Rise Up: A Novel. LC 93-37785. (Texas Tradition Ser.: No. 21). 154p. 1994. 19.95 (*0-87565-126-7*) Tex Christian.

Perry, George Sessions. Hold Autumn in Your Hand. LC 75-7473. (Zia Bks.). 260p. 1975. reprint ed. pap. 14.95 (*0-8263-0377-3*) U of NM Pr.

***Perry, Georgette.** Bramblecrown. iv, 28p. 2000. pap. 5.00 (*1-891812-25-4*, 00-025) Cedar Hill Pubns.

Perry, Gill & Cunningham, Colin, eds. Academies, Museums, & Canons of Art. LC 98-23735. (Illus.). 272p. 1998. pap. 27.50 (*0-300-07743-2*) Yale U Pr.

— Academies, Museums, & Canons of Art. LC 98-23735. Vol. 1. (Illus.). 272p. 1998. 50.00 (*0-300-07741-6*) Yale U Pr.

Perry, Gill, et al. Primitivism, Cubism, Abstraction: The Early Twentieth Century. LC 92-50988. (Illus.). 280p. (C). 1993. 60.00 (*0-300-05515-3*); pap. 30.00 (*0-300-05516-1*) Yale U Pr.

Perry, Gillian. Gender & Art. LC 98-34691. (Art & Its Histories Ser.). 1999. 50.00 (*0-300-07759-9*) Yale U Pr.

— Gender & Art. LC 98-34691. (Art & Its Histories Ser.: Vol. 3). (Illus.). 272p. 1999. pap. 27.50 (*0-300-07760-2*) Yale U Pr.

Perry, Gillian, jt. auth. see Brady, Charles.

Perry, Glen C. Dear Bart: Washington Views of World War II, 31. LC 81-13418. (Contributions in Military History Ser.: No. 31). 341p. 1982. 65.00 (*0-313-23265-2*, PED/, Greenwood Pr) Greenwood.

Perry, Glenn & Fiorenza, Joseph. How to Start a Jukebox & Pinball Business with Little or No Money: Part-Time, Full-Time or Absentee: A Guide to the Electronic Amusement Game Business. LC 80-83931. (Illus.). (Orig.). 1985. 31.95 (*0-9602586-5-5*); pap. 25.95 (*0-9602586-4-7*) Perry Omega.

Perry, Glenn E. The Middle East: Fourteen Islamic Centuries. 3rd ed. LC 96-33631. 362p. (C). 1996. pap. text 52.00 (*0-13-266339-2*) P-H.

— The Palestine Question: An Annotated Bibliography. (Bibliography Ser.: No. 6). 138p. (Orig.). 1990. pap. 6.95 (*0-937694-86-X*) Assn Arab-Amer U Grads.

Perry, Glenn E., et al. Palestine: Continuing Dispossession. LC 85-20031. (AAUG Monographs: No. 21). 145p. (Orig.). 1986. pap. 10.00 (*0-937694-72-X*) Assn Arab-Amer U Grads.

Perry, Graham. The Numbers Game. 128p. (Orig.). 1993. mass mkt. 3.99 (*0-446-60040-7*, Pub. by Warner Bks) Little.

Perry, Grant E. Musings & Forebodings. LC 93-71088. (Illus.). 60p. (Orig.). 1993. pap. 7.95 (*1-878149-22-9*) Counterpoint Pub.

Perry, Greg. Sams Teach Yourself Beginning Programming in 24 Hours. LC 98-85492. (Teach Yourself Ser.). 1998. pap. 19.99 (*0-672-31355-3*) Sams.

— Sams Teach Yourself PC's in 24 Hours. 432p. 1997. pap. 19.99 (*0-672-31163-1*) Sams.

— Sams Teach Yourself PCs in 24 Hours. 2nd ed. LC 98-87065. 400p. 1999. pap. 19.99 (*0-672-31447-9*) Sams.

— Teach Yourself Microsoft Office 97 in 24 Hours. 2nd ed. 1998. 19.99 (*0-672-31338-3*) Sams.

***Perry, Greg.** Teach Yourself Visual Basic 6 in 24 Hours: Starter Kit. (Teach Yourself... in 24 Hours Ser.). (Illus.). 1999. pap. 19.99 (*0-672-31533-5*) Sams.

Perry, Greg. Sams Teach Yourself Visual Basic 6 in 21 Days: Complete Training Kit. (Teach Yourself . . . in 21 Days Ser.). 1999. 39.99 (*0-672-31512-2*) Sams.

— Sam's Teach Yourself Windows 98 in 24 Hours. 3rd ed. LC 97-69137. 384p. 1998. 19.99 (*0-672-31223-9*, Pub. by Macmillan) S&S Trade.

— Visual Basic 5 Night School. 3rd ed. LC 97-65534. 912p. 1997. 39.99 (*0-7897-0921-X*) Que.

— Visual Basic X Night School. 1997. pap. 39.99 (*0-614-28482-1*) Que.

Perry, Greg, et al. Teach Yourself Visual Studio 6 Megabundle. (Teach Yourself Ser.). (Illus.). 1999. boxed set 79.99 (*0-672-31596-3*) Sams.

Perry, Greg M. Absolute Beginners Guide to Programming. 448p. 1993. 19.95 (*0-672-30269-1*) Sams.

— Access Programming by Example. (By Example Ser.). (Illus.). 478p. (Orig.). 1993. 27.95 (*1-56529-305-3*) Que.

— C by Example: Special Edition. 634p. 1993. 24.95 (*1-56529-438-6*) Que.

— C by Example Academic Edition. 1994. 41.99 (*1-56529-453-X*) Que.

— C++ Programming 101. 631p. 1992. pap. 29.95 incl. disk (*0-672-30200-4*) Sams.

— C Programming in 12 Easy Lessons. (Illus.). 603p. (Orig.). 1994. 39.99 (*0-672-30522-4*) Sams.

— The Complete Idiot's Guide to Visual Basic. (Illus.). 300p. 1994. 19.95 (*1-56761-486-8*, Alpha Ref) Macmillan Gen Ref.

— The Complete Idiot's Guide to Visual Basic. 2nd ed. 400p. 1995. 19.95 (*1-56761-520-1*, Alpha Ref) Macmillan Gen Ref.

— Managing Rental Properties for Maximum Profit. 288p. 1995. pap. 15.95 (*1-55958-572-2*) Prima Pub.

Perry, Greg M. Managing Rental Properties for Maximum Profit. 2nd rev. ed. LC 96-52171. 336p. 1997. pap., per. 18.00 (*0-7615-0841-4*) Prima Pub.

— Managing Rental Properties for Maximum Profit: Prima's Official Strategy Guide. 3rd rev. ed. LC 99-59675. 2000. pap. 24.95 (*0-7615-2531-9*) Prima Pub.

Perry, Greg M. Managing Your Rental Properties for Maximum Profit: Save Time & Money with Greg Perry's Fool-Proof System. 288p. 1993. 22.95 (*1-55958-314-2*) Prima Pub.

— 1001 Windows 95 Tips. LC 96-142663. 544p. 1996. pap. 39.95 (*1-884133-15-0*, Jamsa Press) Gulf Pub.

— QBASIC by Example: Special Edition. (Illus.). 620p. (Orig.). 1993. 29.99 (*1-56529-439-4*) Que.

— QBASIC by Example Academic Edition. LC 93-86968. 620p. 1994. 46.99 (*1-56529-454-8*) Que.

— Sams Teach Yourself Office 97 in 24 Hours: Small Business Edition. (Teach Yourself Ser.). 416p. 1998. pap. text 19.99 (*0-672-31280-8*) Sams.

— Sams Teach Yourself Visual Basic 6 in 24 Hours. LC 98-84138. (Teach Yourself Ser.). 400p. 1998. pap. 19.99 (*0-672-31306-5*) Sams.

***Perry, Greg M.** Sams Teach Yourself Windows Millenium Edition in 24 Hours. (Teach Yourself... in 24 Hours Ser.). (Illus.). 400p. 2000. pap. text 19.99 (*0-672-31953-5*) Sams.

— Teach Yourself Microsoft Office 2000 in 24 Hours. (Teach Yourself Ser.). 1999. pap. text 19.99 (*0-672-31446-0*) Sams.

Perry, Greg M. Teach Yourself Microsoft Office 2000 in 24 Hours. LC 99-227074. (Teach Yourself Ser.). (Illus.). 494p. 1999. pap. 19.99 (*0-672-31439-8*) Sams.

— Teach Yourself Microsoft Office 2000 in 24 Hours: Small Business Edition. LC 98-89231. (Teach Yourself Ser.). (Illus.). 416p. 1999. pap. 19.99 (*0-672-31568-8*) Sams.

— Teach Yourself Office 97 in 10 Minutes. LC 98-84598. (Teach Yourself Ser.). 208p. 1998. pap. 12.99 (*0-672-31321-9*) Sams.

— Sams Teach Yourself Visual Basic 6 in 21 Days. LC 98-84132. (Teach Yourself Ser.). 700p. 1998. pap. 29.99 (*0-672-31310-3*) Sams.

— Teach Yourself Windows 95 in 24 Hours. (Illus.). 560p. 1994. 25.00 (*0-672-30504-6*) Sams.

— Teach Yourself Windows 95 in 24 Hours. 2nd ed. LC 95-70716. 568p. 1997. 19.99 (*0-672-31006-6*) Sams.

— Turbo C++ Programming in 12 Easy Lessons. (Illus.). 603p. (Orig.). 1994. 39.99 (*0-672-30523-2*) Sams.

— Using Visual J++ LC 96-69611. 408p. 1996. pap. text 34.99 (*0-7897-0899-X*) Que.

Perry, Greg M., jt. auth. see Spencer, Ian.

Perry, Gregg, ed. see Farah, Andy.

Perry, Gregory. Graphics & Sound on the Commodore 64. (Illus.). 304p. 1986. disk 18.95 (*0-13-363169-9*) P-H.

Perry, Guillermo & Herrera, Ana M. Finanzas Publicas, Estabilizacion y Reforma Estructural en America Latina.Tr. of Public Finances, Stabilization & Structural Reform in Latin America. (SPA.). 146p. 1994. pap. text 12.50 (*0-940602-74-1*) IADB.

— Public Finances, Stabilization & Structural Reform in Latin America. (Inter-American Development Bank Ser.). 140p. 1994. 12.50 (*0-940602-92-X*) IADB.

Perry, Guillermo & Lederman, Daniel. Financial Vulnerability, Spillover Effects & Contagion: Lessons from the Asian Crises for Latin America. LC 98-20908. (Latin American & Caribben Studies). 80p. 1998. pap. 22.00 (*0-8213-4228-2*) World Bank.

***Perry, Guillermo, et al.** Fiscal Reform & Structural Change in Developing Countries. LC 00-33331. 2000. write for info. (*0-312-23580-1*) St Martin.

Perry, Guillermo, jt. auth. see Burki, Shahid J.

Perry, Guillermo E., ed. Currency Boards & External Shocks: How Much Pain, How Much Gain? LC 96-51060. 32p. 1997. pap. 22.00 (*0-8213-3864-1*, 13864) World Bank.

***Perry, Guillermo E. & Lederman, Daniel.** Adjustments after Speculative Attacks in Latin America & Asia: A Tale of Two Regions? LC 99-34548. (Latin America & the Caribbean Region Viewpoints Ser.: No. 14541). 52p. 1999. pap. 22.00 (*0-8213-4541-9*, 14541) World Bank.

***Perry, Guillermo E. & Leipziger, Danny M., eds.** Chile: Recent Policy Lessons & Emerging Challenges. (World Bank Institute Development Studies). 452p. 1999. 35.00 (*0-8213-4500-1*, 14500) World Bank.

Perry, Guillermo E., jt. auth. see Burki, Shahid J.

Perry, Guillermo E., jt. ed. see Burki, Shahid J.

Perry, Guy, ed. see Lowe, Brian.

Perry, Guy A., et al. Fundamentals of Digital Semiconductor Testing. Lowe, Brian, ed. & illus. by. 300p. (Orig.). 1996. pap. 100.00 (*0-9658797-0-4*) Soft Test.

***Perry, H. Bradlee.** Winning the Investment Marathon: A Simple Path to Financial Success. LC 99-73441. (Illus.). 272p. 1999. 25.00 (*0-9673138-0-5*, 1234) Midas Pr.

Perry, H. Mitchell. Lifelong Management of Hypertension. (Developments in Cardiovascular Medicine Ser.). 1983. text 176.50 (*0-89838-582-2*) Kluwer Academic.

Perry, H. W. Deciding to Decide: Agenda Setting in the United States Supreme Court. (Illus.). 320p. (C). 1992. 52.00 (*0-674-19442-X*) HUP.

— Deciding to Decide: Agenda Setting in the United States Supreme Court. (Illus.). 328p. 1994. pap. 21.50 (*0-674-19443-8*) HUP.

Perry, Harold T. & Forbes, David P. Understanding Orthodontics. LC 96-27508. (Illus.). 56p. (J). 1996. pap. 28.00 (*0-86715-315-6*) Quint Pub Co.

Perry, Helen S. Psychiatrist of America: The Life of Harry Stack Sullivan. LC 81-7066. (Illus.). 74p. 1982. 36.50 (*0-674-72076-8*) Belknap Pr.

— Psychiatrist of America: The Life of Harry Stack Sullivan. 474p. 1987. pap. 16.95 (*0-674-72077-6*) Belknap Pr.

Perry, Helga J., ed. see Sullivan, Arthur & Gilbert, W. S.

Perry, Henry B. & Breitner, Bina. Physician Assistants: Their Contribution to Health Care. LC 81-6260. 331p. 1982. 45.95 (*0-89885-066-5*, Kluwer Acad Hman Sci) Kluwer Academic.

Perry, Henry B., jt. auth. see Carter, Reginald.

Perry, Henry T., ed. see Congreve, William.

Perry, Hilda. Broken Engagement. large type ed. (Linford Romance Library). 1989. pap. 16.99 (*0-7089-6659-4*, Linford) Ulverscroft.

— Depths of Love. large type ed. (Linford Romance Library). 1990. pap. 16.99 (*0-7089-6912-7*) Ulverscroft.

Perry, Horace M., III, et al, eds. Aging & Musculoskeletal Disorders. LC 93-1426. 392p. 1993. 48.95 (*0-8261-7930-4*) Springer Pub.

Perry, Huey L., ed. Race, Politics, & Governance in the United States. LC 96-19925. (Illus.). 240p. 1997. 49.95 (*0-8130-1456-5*); pap. 21.95 (*0-8130-1481-6*) U Press Fla.

Perry, Huey L. & Parent, Wayne S., eds. Blacks & the American Political System. LC 95-5917. (Illus.). 312p. 1995. pap. 21.95 (*0-8130-1373-9*) U Press Fla.

Perry, Huey L., jt. auth. see Parent, Wayne S.

Perry, I. Mac. Black Conquistador: The Story of the First Black Man in America. LC 98-96193. 224p. 1998. pap. 9.95 (*0-9663628-4-5*) Boca Bay Bks.

— Children of the Sun: The Cabeza de Vaca Expedition Across America. LC 99-61992. 220p. 1999. pap. 9.95 (*0-9663628-5-3*, Pub. by Boca Bay Bks) Great Outdoors.

— Indian Mounds You Can Visit: 165 Aboriginal Sites on Florida's West Coast. rev. ed. LC 98-17991. (Illus.). 320p. 1998. pap. 14.95 (*0-8200-1039-1*) Great Outdoors.

Perry, Inez E. & Carey, George W. Twelve Lessons in the Astro Biochemic System of Body Building. 80p. 1996. reprint ed. spiral bd. 18.50 (*0-7873-0668-1*) Hlth Research.

Perry, Inez E., jt. auth. see Carey, George W.

Perry, J. A., ed. RPL Dosimetry: Radiophotoluminescence in Health Physics. (Medical Science Ser.). (Illus.). 192p. 1987. 106.00 (*0-85274-272-X*) IOP Pub.

Perry, J. B. A Season Till Spring. 120p. 1991. pap. 7.99 (*0-8341-1393-7*) Beacon Hill.

Perry, J. Mitchell & Griggs, Richard E. The Road to Optimism Vol. 1: Change Your Language, Change Your Life. Norman, Fred, ed. LC 96-33893. (Illus.). 208p. 1997. 25.00 (*0-922530-02-5*) Tantalus Bks.

Perry, J. Mitchell & Jamison, Steve. In the Zone. (Illus.). 224p. 1998. pap. 14.95 (*0-8092-2952-8*, 295280, Contemporary Bks) NTC Contemp Pub Co.

Perry, Jack. Clarion Chronicles, a Garden Along the Railroad Tracks: And Other Recollections of Growing Up in a Small Midwestern Town During the Depression. Scherban, Debra, ed. & pref. by. (Illus.). 64p. (Orig.). 1994. pap. 7.95 (*0-9618052-5-0*) Daily Hampshire.

— Light from Light. 208p. 1987. 11.95 (*0-310-23850-1*, 11418) Zondervan.

Perry, Jack O. Come Ride with Me. (Illus.). 8p. (Orig.). 1996. pap. 10.00 (*1-887804-08-0*) Cent Mont Pubng.

Perry, Jacquelin. Gait Analysis: Normal & Pathological Function. LC 90-50830. 556p. 1992. 55.00 (*1-55642-192-3*) SLACK Inc.

Perry, Jacques. Vie d'un Paien. (FRE.). 1984. pap. 15.95 (*0-7859-4217-3*) Fr & Eur.

Perry, James. Fortunes Child: Travels on the Open Road. 166p. (Orig.). 1997. pap. 12.00 (*1-888550-02-3*) Champions Pubng.

— How to Change Your Life Positively. unabridged ed. 26p. 1998. pap. 9.95 (*1-892896-29-X*) Buy Books.

— New Perspectives on the Internet: Comprehensive. (C). 1998. pap. 44.95 (*0-7600-7010-5*) Course Tech.

Perry, James A. & Vanderklein, Elizabeth. Water Quality: Management of a Natural Resource. LC 96-857. (Illus.). 450p. 1996. 64.95 (*0-86542-469-1*) Blackwell Sci.

Perry, James L., ed. Handbook of Public Administration. 2nd rev. ed. LC 95-25769. (Public Administration Ser.). 830p. 1996. 59.95 (*0-7879-0194-6*) Jossey-Bass.

— Research in Public Administration, Vol. 1. 232p. 1991. 73.25 (*1-55938-114-0*) Jai Pr.

— Research in Public Administration, Vol. 2. 270p. 1993. 73.25 (*1-55938-433-6*) Jai Pr.

— Research in Public Administration, Vol. 3. 338p. 1994. 73.25 (*1-55938-734-3*) Jai Pr.

— Research in Public Administration, Vol. 5. Date not set. 73.25 (*0-7623-0526-6*) Jai Pr.

Perry, James M. Arrogant Armies: Great Military Disasters & the Generals Behind Them. LC 95-38345. 314p. 1996. 27.95 (*0-471-11976-8*) Wiley.

— The Bohemian Brigade: The Civil War Battlefield Correspondents Mostly Rough, Sometimes Ready. LC 99-39101. (Illus.). 320p. 2000. text 27.95 (*0-471-32009-9*) Wiley.

Perry, James R. The Formation of a Society on Virginia's Eastern Shore, 1615-1655. LC 90-11980. (Institute of Early American History & Culture Ser.). 266p. (C). 1997. 45.00 (*0-8078-1927-1*) U of NC Pr.

Perry, James R., jt. auth. see Marcus, Maeva.

Perry, James R., jt. ed. see Marcus, Maeva.

Perry, James T. Building Accounting Systems Using Access '97. 3rd ed. LC 99-169960. 498p. 1998. pap. 60.95 (*0-324-00076-6*) Sth-Wstrn College.

— Select Quattro Pro 7 Projects for Windows 95. 3rd ed. (C). 1996. pap. text. write for info. (*0-8053-1239-0*) Benjamin-Cummings.

Perry, James T., ed. International Survey of Trademark Anti-Counterfeiting Procedures. 192p. 1994. pap. 35.00 (*0-939190-11-7*) Intl Trademark.

Perry, James T. & Schneider, Gary P. Building Accounting Systems: A Transaction Cycle Approach. 1994. write for info. (*0-538-84454-X*) S-W Pub.

— Building Accounting Systems: A Transaction Cycle Approach. LC 97-20713. 1997. pap. write for info. (*0-538-87494-5*) S-W Pub.

— Building Accounting Systems Access Ed. A Transaction Cycle Approach. LC 95-1160. 1996. pap. 37.95 (*0-538-84897-9*) S-W Pub.

— Building Accounting Systems Using Access for Windows 95. 2nd ed. LC 97-20713. 544p. 1997. pap. 38.95 (0-538-87493-7) Thomson Learn.

Perry, James T., et al. Select Quattro Pro Seven Point O: Win 95 Standalone. (C). 1996. pap. text 26.00 (0-8053-6772-1) Benjamin-Cummings.

Perry, James W., jt. auth. see Morton, David.

Perry, Jan F. The Kinesiology Workbook. 2nd ed. 206p. 1995. pap. 25.95 (0-8036-0046-1) Davis Co.

Perry, Jane G., jt. auth. see Perry, John.

Perry, Janet. Counselling for Women. LC 93-15402. (Counselling in Context Ser.). 128p. 1993. pap. 29.95 (0-335-19034-0) OpUniv Pr.

Perry, Janet & Gentle, Victor. Monsters, 9 bks. Incl. Aliens. LC 99-14720. (Illus.). 24p. (YA). (gr. 2 up). 1999. lib. bdg. 18.60 (0-8368-2435-0); Dragons & Dinosaurs. LC 99-25566. (Illus.). 24p. (YA). (gr. 2 up). 1999. lib. bdg. 18.60 (0-8368-2436-9); Giants & Wild Hairy Monsters. LC 99-14719. (Illus.). 24p. (YA). (gr. 2 up). 1999. lib. bdg. 18.60 (0-8368-2437-7); Mad Scientists. LC 99-25418. (Illus.). 24p. (YA). (gr. 2 up). 1999. lib. bdg. 18.60 (0-8368-2438-5); Manmade Monsters. LC 99-14713. (Illus.). 24p. (YA). (gr. 2 up). 1999. lib. bdg. 18.60 (0-8368-2439-3); Monsters of the Deep. LC 99-22864. (Illus.). 24p. (YA). (gr. 2 up). 1999. lib. bdg. 18.60 (0-8368-2440-7); Morph Monsters. LC 99-14714. (Illus.). 24p. (YA). (gr. 2 up). 1999. lib. bdg. 18.60 (0-8368-2441-5); Vampires. LC 99-22509. (YA). (gr. 2 up). 1999. lib. bdg. 18.60 (0-8368-2442-3); Zombies. LC 99-22510. (Illus.). 24p. (YA). (gr. 2 up). 1999. lib. bdg. 18.60 (0-8368-2443-1); (Illus.). (J). (gr. 2 up). Set lib. bdg. 167.40 (0-8368-2434-2) Gareth Stevens Inc.

Perry, Janet, jt. auth. see Gental, Victor.

Perry, Janette, ed. see Shawl, Kathy A.

Perry, Jason L. Bag Visitors. LC 95-60149. 112p. 1995. pap., per. 6.95 (1-883889-16-2) TWanda.

Perry, Jean. Make Your Own Horse Clothing. 112p. (C). 1990. pap. 21.00 (0-85131-383-3, Pub. by J A Allen) Trafalgar.

— Make Your Own Horse Equipment. 111p. (C). 1990. pap. 35.00 (0-85131-393-0, Pub. by J A Allen) Trafalgar.

Perry, Jeb H. Screen Gems: A History of Columbia Pictures Television from Cohn to Coke, 1948-1983. LC 91-33388. 385p. 1991. 47.50 (0-8108-2487-6) Scarecrow.

Perry, Jesse, Jr., jt. auth. see Worley, Demetrice A.

Perry, Jim. Sleeper Awakes: A Journey to Sleep-Awareness. 138p. 1992. pap. 11.95 (0-945806-06-X) Summit CA.

Perry, Jo Ellen. An Introduction to Object-Oriented Design in C++ (P Copy) (C). 1995. pap. text. write for info. (0-201-42003-1) Addison-Wesley.

Perry, Joan. A Girl Needs Cash: Banish the White Knight Myth & Take Charge of Your Financial Life. LC 97-12704. 256p. 1997. 23.00 (0-8129-2840-7, Times Bks) Crown Pub Group.

***Perry, Joan & Barclay, Dolores.** A Girl Needs Cash. LC 97-12704. 244p. 1999. pap. 13.00 (0-8129-3135-1, Times Bks) Crown Pub Group.

***Perry, Joe N., et al.** Chaos in Real Data: Analysis of Non-linear Dynamics in Short Ecological Space. (Population & Community Biology Ser.: Vol. 27). 236p. 2000. 122.00 (0-412-79690-2, Pub. by Kluwer Academic) Kluwer Academic.

***Perry, Joel.** Funny That Way: Adventures in Fabulousness. 288p. 2000. pap. 12.95 (1-55583-557-0, Pub. by Alyson Pubns) Consort Bk Sales.

Perry, Joey A., Sr. Parenting Lessons from God, the Perfect Parent. 180p. (Orig.). 1997. pap. 11.95 (0-9653365-5-7) Albatross Pub.

Perry, John. Dialogue on Good, Evil & the Existence of God. LC 99-30951. (Hackett Dialogues in Philosophy Ser.). 80p. (C). 1999. pap. text 4.95 (0-87220-460-X); lib. bdg. 19.95 (0-87220-461-8) Hackett Pub.

— Doing Fieldwork: Eight Personal Accounts of Social Research. 155p. (C). 1995. pap. 65.00 (0-7300-0786-3, Pub. by Deakin Univ) St Mut.

— Encyclopedia of Acting Techniques. (Illus.). 160p. 1997. 26.99 (1-55870-456-6, Betrwy Bks) F & W Pubns Inc.

— Forty Cords of Wood. (American Autobiography Ser.). 459p. 1995. reprint ed. lib. bdg. 99.00 (0-7812-8615-8) Rprt Serv.

— The Problem of the Essential Indexical: And Other Essays. LC 92-33242. (Illus.). 352p. (C). 1993. text 65.00 (0-19-504999-3) OUP.

***Perry, John.** The Problems of the Essential Indexical: And Other Essays. expanded rev. ed. 300p. (C). 2000. pap. 22.95 (1-57586-246-8, Pub. by CSLI) Cambridge U Pr.

— Sgt. York: His Life, Legend & Legacy: The Remarkable Untold Story of Sgt. Alvin C. York. LC 97-15736. (Illus.). 320p. 1997. 16.99 (0-8054-6074-8) Broadman.

Perry, John. The Sierra Club Guide to Natural Areas of California. 352p. 1997. pap. 15.00 (0-87156-850-0, Pub. by Sierra) Random.

— The Sierra Club Guide to the Natural Areas of New England. rev. ed. (Illus.). 400p. 1997. pap. 15.00 (0-87156-940-X, Pub. by Sierra) Random.

— The Sierra Club Guide to the Natural Areas of Oregon & Washington. 352p. 1997. pap. 15.00 (0-87156-939-6, Pub. by Sierra) Random.

***Perry, John.** Unshakable Faith. LC 99-43357. 300p. 1999. 21.99 (1-57673-493-5) Multnomah Pubs.

Perry, John, ed. Contemporary Society: Custom Edition CB. (C). 1997. pap. text 55.00 (0-321-01290-9) Addison-Wesley.

— Personal Identity. (Topics in Philosophy Ser.: Vol. 2). 246p. 1975. pap. 16.95 (0-520-02960-7, Pub. by U CA Pr) Cal Prin Full Svc.

Perry, John & Bratman, Michael, eds. Introduction to Philosophy: Classical & Contemporary Readings. 3rd ed. 848p. (C). 1998. pap. text 46.00 (0-19-511204-0) OUP.

Perry, John & Hughes, Jenny. Anthropology: Voices from the Margins. 1996. pap. 74.00 (0-949823-46-5, Pub. by Deakin Univ) St Mut.

Perry, John & Perry, Jane G. The Natural Areas of Oregon & Washington. LC 82-16937. (Guides to the Natural Areas of the United States Ser.). (Illus.). 360p. 1983. pap. 12.00 (0-87156-334-7, Pub. by Sierra) Random.

— The Nature of Florida. LC 97-36054. 1998. pap. 17.95 (0-8203-2008-0) U of Ga Pr.

— The Sierra Club Guide to the Natural Areas of Florida. LC 92-905. (Guides to the Natural Areas of the United States Ser.). 416p. (Orig.). 1992. pap. 12.00 (0-87156-551-X, Pub. by Sierra) Random.

— The Sierra Club Guide to the Natural Areas of New Mexico, Arizona, & Nevada. LC 85-18481. (Guides to the Natural Areas of the United States Ser.). (Illus.). 448p. 1986. pap. 12.00 (0-87156-753-9, Pub. by Sierra) Random.

***Perry, John & Perry, Kathy.** The Complete Guide to Home Schooling. 2000. pap. 17.95 (0-7373-0422-7, Pub. by Lowell Hse) NTC Contemp Pub Co.

Perry, John, jt. auth. see Barwise, Jon.

Perry, John, jt. auth. see Dotterweich, Kass.

Perry, John, jt. auth. see Rogers, Adrian.

Perry, John, ed. see Berkeley, George.

Perry, John, ed. see Henry, Philip.

Perry, John, ed. see Meskoob, Shahrokh.

Perry, John, ed. see Newcomb, Jack.

Perry, John, tr. see Alavi, Bozorg, et al.

Perry, John A. Social Web. 6th ed. (C). 1997. pap., student ed. 17.00 (0-06-501647-5) Addson-Wesley Educ.

Perry, John A. & Perry, Erna K. Contemporary Society: An Introduction to Social Science. 9th ed. LC 99-29811. 539p. (C). 1999. pap. text 59.00 (0-321-04462-2) Addison-Wesley.

Perry, John A., jt. auth. see Scott, Raymond P.

Perry, John A., jt. ed. see Domsky, Irving I.

Perry, John C. Facing West: Americans & the Opening of the Pacific. LC 94-11302. 400p. 1994. 75.00 (0-275-94920-6, Praeger Pubs); pap. 21.95 (0-275-94965-6, Praeger Pubs) Greenwood.

Perry, John C. & Pleshakov, Constantine V. Flight of the Romanovs: A Family Saga. (Illus.). 424p. 1999. 30.00 (0-465-02462-9, Pub. by Basic) HarpC.

Perry, John H. Adventures of Freddie. (C). 1989. 30.00 (0-7223-2347-6, Pub. by A H S Ltd) St Mut.

Perry, John H., Jr. Never Say Impossible: The Life & Times of an American Entrepreneur. LC 96-1882. 1996. write for info. (1-56566-099-4) Thomasson-Grant.

Perry, John M. Exploring the Evolution of the Lord's Supper in the New Testament. 160p. (Orig.). 1994. pap. 9.95 (1-55612-721-9) Sheed & Ward WI.

***Perry, John M.** Exploring the Evolving View of God: From Ancient Israel to the Risen Jesus. LC 99-16893. 222p. 1999. 14.95 (1-58051-067-1) Sheed & Ward WI.

Perry, John M. Exploring the Genesis Creation & Fall Stories. LC 92-5024. (Exploring Scripture Ser.). 64p. (Orig.). (C). 1992. pap. 5.95 (1-55612-553-4, LL1553) Sheed & Ward WI.

— Exploring the Identity & Mission of Jesus. LC 95-45045. (Exploring Scripture Ser.: No. 5). 304p. (Orig.). 1996. pap. 14.95 (1-55612-820-7, LL1820) Sheed & Ward WI.

— Exploring the Messianic Secret in Mark's Gospel. LC 97-29746. (Exploring Scripture Ser.). 168p. 1997. pap. 15.95 (1-55612-924-6, LL1924) Sheed & Ward WI.

— Exploring the Resurrection of Jesus. LC 93-29160. 160p. 1993. pap. 12.95 (1-55612-670-0) Sheed & Ward WI.

— Exploring the Transfiguration Story. LC 92-26971. (Exploring Scripture Ser.). 64p. (Orig.). (C). 1993. pap. 5.95 (1-55612-574-7, LL1574) Sheed & Ward WI.

Perry, John O., ed. Voices of Emergency: An All India Anthology of Protest Poetry of the 1975-77 Emergency, India. 1983. 28.50 (0-317-05076-1, Pub. by Popular Prakashan) S Asia.

Perry, John R. A Dialogue on Personal Identity & Immortality. LC 78-52943. 60p. (C). 1978. pap. text 4.95 (0-915144-53-0); lib. bdg. 24.95 (0-915144-91-3) Hackett Pub.

— Karim Khan Zand: A History of Iran, 1747-1779. LC 78-26553. (Publications of the Center for Middle Eastern Studies: No. 12). (Illus.). 1993. lib. bdg. 23.00 (0-226-66098-2) U Ch Pr.

— Karim Khan Zand: A History of Iran, 1747-1779. LC 78-26553. (Publications of the Center for Middle Eastern Studies: No. 12). (Illus.). 352p. reprint ed. pap. 109.20 (0-608-09493-5, 205429400005) Bks Demand.

Perry, John R. & Lehr, Rachel. The Sands of Oxus: Boyhood Reminiscences of Sadriddin Aini. LC 98-39882. (Bibliotheca Iranica Ser.: Vol. 6). (Illus.). 284p. 1998. pap. text 24.95 (1-56859-078-4) Mazda Pubs.

Perry, John W. The Far Side of Madness. LC 89-21572. (Jungian Classics Ser.: No. 12). 180p. 1974. reprint ed. pap. 17.00 (0-88214-511-8) Spring Pubns.

— The Heart of History: Individuality in Evolution. LC 86-14428. (SUNY Series in Transpersonal & Humanistic Psychology). 249p. (C). 1987. pap. text 19.95 (0-88706-400-0) State U NY Pr.

— Lord of the Four Quarters: The Mythology of Kingship. 1991. pap. 12.95 (0-8091-3252-4) Paulist Pr.

— Roots of Renewal in Myth & Madness: The Meaning of Psychotic Episodes. LC 76-19500. (Jossey-Bass Behavioral Science Ser.). 268p. reprint ed. pap. 83.10 (0-608-15166-1, 205216400045) Bks Demand.

— Trials of the Visionary Mind: Spiritual Emergency & the Renewal Process. LC 98-23483. (SUNY Series in Transpersonal & Humanistic Psychology). 200p. (C). 1998. text 59.50 (0-7914-3987-9); pap. text 19.95 (0-7914-3988-7) State U NY Pr.

Perry, Joseph M. The Impact of Immigration on Three American Industries, 1865-1914. LC 77-14788. (Dissertations in American Economic History Ser.). 1978. 23.95 (0-405-11052-9) Ayer.

Perry, Kate. Gerbils. LC 94-26049. (First Pets Ser.). (Illus.). 24p. (J). (ps-3). 1995. pap. 3.95 (0-8120-9081-0) Barron.

— Horse Heroes: True Stories of Amazing Horses. LC 98-50745. (Eyewitness Readers). (J). (gr. 2-4). 1999. 12.95 (0-7894-4001-6); pap. 3.95 (0-7894-4000-8) DK Pub Inc.

— Pieces of Earth. Lyons Graphic Designs Staff, ed. (Illus.). 159p. (Orig.). 1994. pap. text 12.95 (0-9626823-5-7) Perry ME.

Perry, Kathleen. The Everyday Gourmet. 176p. 1986. mass mkt. 8.95 (0-446-38095-4, Pub. by Warner Bks) Little.

Perry, Kathleen A. Another Reality. LC 89-12639. (American University Studies: Classical Languages & Literature: Ser. XVII, Vol. 10). IX, 260p. 1989. text 43.50 (0-8204-1112-4) P Lang Pubng.

Perry, Kathy, jt. auth. see Perry, John.

Perry, Katy. The Laughing Lighthouse. Lyons Graphic Design Staff, ed. (Illus.). 16p. (Orig.). (J). (gr. 1-4). 1995. pap. 7.50 (0-9626823-6-5) Perry ME.

— Mad Tuesdays. Lyons, Lisa, ed. (Illus.). 160p. (Orig.). 1992. pap. 12.95 (0-9626823-3-0) Perry ME.

— My Grandmother Wears Crazy Hats. Minor, Mary E., ed. (Illus.). 16p. (J). (gr. k-5). 1993. pap. 4.95 (0-9626823-4-9) Perry ME.

Perry, Kenneth. Act-Up in Pole Town. 285p. 1999. mass mkt. 6.99 (1-57532-138-6) Press-Tige Pub.

***Perry, Kenneth A.** The Fitch Gazetteer: An Annotated Index to the Manuscript History of Washington County, New York. LC 99-199264. 592p. 1999. pap. 47.00 (0-7884-1143-8, P170) Heritage Bk.

Perry, Kenneth A. The Fitch Gazetteer: An Annotated Index to the Manuscript History of Washington County NY. LC 99-199264. 601p. 1999. pap. 49.00 (0-7884-1182-9, P171) Heritage Bk.

— The Fitch Gazetteer Vol. I: An Annotated Index to the Manuscript History of Washington County New York. LC 99-199264. 640p. 1999. pap. 47.00 (0-7884-1090-3, P165) Heritage.

Perry, Kenneth D., ed. The Museum Forms Book. 3rd ed. 463p. 1999. pap. 50.00 (0-935260-05-6) Tex Assn Mus.

Perry, Kirk. Mechanics & Owners Guide to 1941-1959 Harley-Davidson Big Twins, Vol. 1. (Illus.). 200p. 1997. spiral bd. write for info. (0-9672744-0-0) Vintage Twin.

Perry, L. Tom. Living with Enthusiasm. LC 96-580. viii, 136p. 1996. 14.95 (1-57345-136-3) Deseret Bk.

Perry, Larry. Islam, Christianity & Other Religions of the World: What They Believe & How They Worship. 150p. 1997. 14.95 (0-614-29852-0) Perry Publns.

— Self Sufficient Woman: Things Every Woman Must Know but Men Won't Tell You. 2nd rev. ed. 150p. 1997. pap. 19.95 (0-942442-00-8) Perry Publns.

Perry, Larry & Arthur, Ernie. Nichemanship: How to Carve Your Niche in Life & Business. 2nd rev. ed. 150p. 1996. 14.95 (0-942442-06-7) Perry Publns.

Perry, Larry D. One Hour Bible. Boughner, Eloise, ed. 120p. 1996. 10.00 (0-942442-01-6) Perry Publns.

Perry, Larry L. Guide to Quality & Efficiency for Prentice Hall's Accounting & Auditing Manual. 148p. 1988. pap. text 19.95 (0-13-370628-1, Busn) P-H.

— Guide to Quality & Efficiency for Prentice Hall's Compilation & Review Manual. 64p. 1987. pap. text 19.95 (0-13-370644-3, Busn) P-H.

— Guide to Quality & Efficiency for Prentice Hall's Small Business Audit Manual. 116p. 1987. pap. text 24.95 (0-13-370677-X) P-H.

— Prospective Financial Statements Documentation Manual. 432p. 1988. ring bd. 69.95 (0-13-731373-X, Busn) P-H.

— Reporting Manual. 248p. 1987. ring bd. 95.00 (0-13-773490-5, Busn) P-H.

— Small Business Audit Manual, Vol. 2. 344p. 1987. 140.00 (0-13-813155-4) P-H.

— Small Business Audit Manual Documentation. 176p. 1987. pap. 50.00 (0-13-813106-6) P-H.

Perry, Larry L., jt. auth. see Marthinuss, George.

Perry, Le R. Now & Then, Vol. 8. (Illus.). 60p. 1998. pap. 10.50 (1-56770-428-X) S Scheewe Pubns.

Perry Leacock, Cynthia. Roswell: Have You Wondered?: Understanding the Evidence at the International UFO Museum & Research Center. LC 98-85669. (Illus.). 192p. 1998. 24.95 (0-9661329-1-2, 526); pap. 19.95 (0-9661329-0-4, 526) Novel Writing.

Perry, Lee T. Offensive Strategy: Forging a New Competitiveness in the Fires of Head-to-Head Competition. 1990. 24.95 (0-88730-435-4, HarpBusn) HarpInfo.

Perry, Lee T., et al. Real-Time Strategy: Improvised Team-Based Planning for a Fast Changing World. LC 92-34982. 272p. 1993. 34.95 (0-471-58564-5) Wiley.

Perry, Leonard P. Herbaceous Perennials Production: A Guide from Propagation to Marketing. LC 98-18961. (NRAES Ser.: Vol. 93). (Illus.). 220p. 1998. pap. text 27.00 (0-935817-29-8, NRAES-93) NRAES.

Perry, Lewis. Boats Against the Current: American Culture Between Revolution & Modernity, 1820-1860. LC 92-11094. 352p. (C). 1993. text 35.00 (0-19-506091-1) OUP.

— Childhood, Marriage & Reform: Henry Clarke Wright, 1797-1870. LC 79-13649. 373p. reprint ed. pap. 115.70 (0-608-09494-3, 205429500005) Bks Demand.

— Radical Abolitionism: Anarchy & the Government of God in Antislavery Thought. LC 95-4355. 362p. (C). 1995. pap. text 18.00 (0-87049-899-1) U of Tenn Pr.

Perry, Lewis, jt. ed. see Halttunen, Karen.

Perry, Lewis C. Childhood Marriage & Reform: Henry Clarke Wright, 1797-1870. LC 79-13649. 1995. lib. bdg. 34.00 (0-226-66100-8) U Ch Pr.

— Intellectual Life in America: A History. LC 88-27770. xxii, 484p. 1989. pap. text 18.95 (0-226-66101-6) U Ch Pr.

Perry, Linda, jt. auth. see Perry, Alan.

Perry, Linda A., et al, eds. Constructing & Reconstructing Gender: The Links among Communication, Language, & Gender. LC 91-29718. (SUNY Series in Feminist Criticism & Theory). 320p. (C). 1992. text 21.50 (0-7914-1009-9) State U NY Pr.

Perry, Linda A. & Geist, Patricia, eds. Courage of Conviction: Women's Words, Women's Wisdom. LC 96-40937. (Illus.). (C). 1997. pap. text 33.95 (1-55934-716-3, 1716) Mayfield Pub.

Perry, Linda W., ed. see Pinto, George Frederick.

***Perry, Lloyd M. & Strubhar, John R.** Evangelistic Preaching. 216p. 2000. pap. 20.00 (1-57910-427-4) Wipf & Stock.

Perry, Lo Sun, jt. auth. see Teng, Shou-hsin.

Perry, Lora, jt. auth. see Perry, Steve.

Perry, Lorne, jt. auth. see Mackay, Donald.

***Perry, Lorraine.** God Is Love. 1999. pap. write for info. (1-58235-333-6) Watermrk Pr.

***Perry, Louise K. & Perry, Charles E.** The Treasure on Orchard Hill. 292p. 1999. pap. 12.95 (0-7392-0446-7, PO3730) Nethope Pub.

Perry, Lynette & Skolnick, Manny. Keeper of the Delaware Dolls. LC 98-39896. (Illus.). 1999. pap. 12.00 (0-8032-8759-3, Bison Books) U of Nebr Pr.

Perry, Lynn. Perry. A Branch of the Peery Family Tree: Ancestors & Descendants of James Peery Who Came to Delaware about 1730. (Illus.). 125p. 1995. reprint ed. pap. 19.50 (0-8328-4818-2); reprint ed. lib. bdg. 29.50 (0-8328-4817-4) Higginson Bk Co.

Perry, Lynn E. Sacramental Cocoa & Other Stories from the Parish of the Poor. LC 94-43406. 164p. (Orig.). 1995. pap. 15.95 (0-664-25521-3) Westminster John Knox.

Perry, Mac. Landscaping in Florida: A Photo Idea Book. LC 88-28875. (Illus.). 256p. 1993. pap. 21.95 (1-56164-057-3) Pineapple Pr.

— Mac Perry's Florida Lawn & Garden Care. LC 84-80148. (Illus.). 128p. 1984. pap. 6.95 (0-9613236-0-4) Florida Flair Bks.

***Perry, Mac, et al.** Mac Perry's Florida Lawn & Garden Care. LC 99-64731. (Illus.). 128p. 1999. pap. 8.95 (0-8200-0417-0) Great Outdoors.

Perry, Maggie, jt. auth. see Perry, Clay.

***Perry, Malcolm.** Polar Bear. (Natural World Ser.). (J). 2000. pap. 7.95 (0-7398-1816-3) Raintree Steck-V.

Perry, Margaret. Bio-Bibliography of Countee P. Cullen, 1903-1946, 8. LC 75-105995. 134p. 1970. 49.95 (0-8371-3325-4, PCC&) Greenwood.

Perry, Margaret. Silence to the Drums, 18. LC 74-19806. (Contributions in Afro-American & African Studies: No. 18). 194p. 1976. 27.50 (0-8371-7847-9, PSD/, Greenwood Pr) Greenwood.

Perry, Margaret, ed. The Short Fiction of Rudolph Fisher, 107. LC 86-29580. (Contributions in Afro-American & African Studies: No. 107). 242p. 1987. 55.00 (0-313-21348-8, FPF, Greenwood Pr) Greenwood.

Perry, Marge, jt. auth. see Ochs, Cathy.

Perry, Maria. Knightsbridge Woman. (Illus.). 118p. 1995. 19.95 (0-233-98940-4, Pub. by Andre Deutsch) Trafalgar.

— The Word of a Prince: A Life of Elizabeth I from Contemporary Documents. (Illus.). 280p. (C). 1999. pap. 29.95 (0-85115-633-9) Boydell & Brewer.

Perry, Marilyn. Our Baby's Being Baptized. (Illus.). 16p. (J). Date not set. pap. 3.95 (0-929032-70-5, Pub. by Wood Lake Bks) Logos Prods.

Perry, Mark. Conceived in Liberty: Joshua Chamberlain, William Oates, & the American Civil War. 1999. pap. 15.95 (0-14-024797-1) Viking Penguin.

***Perry, Mark.** Walking the Color Line: The Art & Practice of Anti-Racist Teaching. LC 00-23416. (Teaching for Social Justice Ser.). (Illus.). 2000. write for info. (0-8077-3964-2) Tchrs Coll.

Perry, Mark, et al. Army Medical Support for Operations Other Than War. LC 96-22136. (Illus.). 183p. 1996. pap. 15.00 (0-8330-2413-2, MR-773-A) Rand Corp.

Perry, Mark, jt. auth. see Baker, Danny.

Perry, Mark C. Morigu: The Desecration. 336p. (Orig.). 1986. mass mkt. 3.50 (0-445-20300-5, Pub. by Warner Bks) Little.

***Perry, Marta.** Desperately Seeking Dad: Hometown Heroes. 2000. per. 4.50 (0-373-87097-3) Harlequin Bks.

— The Doctor Next Door. (Love Inspired Ser.: Bk. 104). 2000. per. 4.50 (0-373-87110-4, 1-87110-2, Steeple Hill) Harlequin Bks.

Perry, Marta. A Father's Promise. (Love Inspired Ser.: Vol. 41). 1998. per. 4.50 (0-373-87041-8, 1-87041-9) Harlequin Bks.

— Since You've Been Gone. (Love Inspired Ser.). 1999. mass mkt. 4.50 (0-373-87075-2, 1-87075-7) Harlequin Bks.

Perry, Martin. Small Business & Network Economies. Knapp, A. Bernard & Piggott, Vincent C., eds. LC 98-44077. (Studies in Small Business: No. 6). (Illus.). 256p. (C). (gr. 13). 1998. 90.00 (0-415-18392-8, D6309) Routledge.

Perry, Martine H. Arithmetic Arithmetic: Solve the Puzzle Pictures by Colouring. 32p. (J). (gr. 2-6). 1997. pap. 8.50 (1-899618-14-7, Pub. by Tarquin Pubns) Parkwest Pubns.

Perry, Marvin. Arnold Toynbee & the Western Tradition. (American University Studies Series V: Philosophy: Vol. 169). XII, 145p. (C). 1996. text 36.95 (0-8204-2671-7) P Lang Pubng.

— History of the World. Date not set. pap., teacher ed., suppl. ed. write for info. (0-395-56239-2) HM.

P

An Asterisk (*) at the beginning of an entry indicates that the title is appearing for the first time.

— History of the World. 1989. text, teacher ed. 95.12 (*0-395-49230-0*); text, student ed. 72.20 (*0-395-46130-8*) HM.

— History of the World. 1989. pap., teacher ed. 15.84 (*0-395-49257-2*); pap., suppl. ed. 10.52 (*0-395-52413-X*); pap., wbk. ed. 9.88 (*0-395-52412-1*) HM.

— History of the World. 1989. pap., teacher ed. 17.60 (*0-395-49247-5*) HM.

— History of the World. 1989. pap., teacher ed., wbk. ed. 17.28 (*0-395-49234-3*); pap., wbk. ed. 15.84 (*0-395-49233-5*) HM.

— History of the World. (C). 1990. pap., teacher ed. 17.92 (*0-395-56258-9*) HM.

— History of the World. 1991. text, teacher ed. 95.12 (*0-395-59103-1*); text, student ed. 72.20 (*0-395-59092-2*) HM.

— History of the World. (C). 1991. pap., teacher ed. 18.48 (*0-395-59258-5*); pap., teacher ed., wbk. ed. 17.28 (*0-395-59263-1*); pap., wbk. ed. 15.84 (*0-395-59262-3*) HM.

— History of the World. (C). 1991. pap., suppl. ed. 36.12 (*0-395-59820-6*) HM.

— History of the World. 1992. text, teacher ed. 93.36 (*0-395-63219-6*); text, student ed. 72.20 (*0-395-63218-8*) HM.

— History of the World. (C). 1992. pap., teacher ed. 10.64 (*0-395-64577-8*); pap., teacher ed. 18.16 (*0-395-63229-3*); pap., teacher ed., suppl. ed. 16.92 (*0-395-63228-5*); pap., wbk. ed. 15.64 (*0-395-63227-7*) HM.

— History of the World. 1994. text 65.28 (*0-395-68827-2*); text, teacher ed. 96.04 (*0-395-68828-0*) HM.

Perry, Marvin. A History of the World, 001. 1984. text 77.08 (*0-395-33299-0*) HM.

— A History of the World, 001. 1984. pap., teacher ed. 33.28 (*0-395-33300-8*); pap., teacher ed., wbk. ed. 17.44 (*0-395-33302-4*); pap., wbk. ed. 15.08 (*0-395-33301-6*) HM.

Perry, Marvin. A History of the World. 1987. text, teacher ed. 72.72 (*0-395-42710-X*) HM.

— History of the World: Framework Studies. (C). 1990. pap., teacher ed. 14.32 (*0-395-56257-0*) HM.

— History of the World: Modern Era. (C). 1990. pap., student ed. 77.80 (*0-395-54340-1*) HM.

— History of the World: Modern Era. 1991. text, teacher ed. 101.12 (*0-395-59817-6*) HM.

— History of the World: Modern Era. 1993. text, teacher ed. 96.04 (*0-395-67052-7*); text, student ed. 62.64 (*0-395-67051-9*) HM.

— An Intellectual History of Modern Europe. 512p. (C). 1992. pap. text 39.16 (*0-395-65348-7*) HM.

— West Civilization: Testbank, 3 vols. (C). 1996. pap., teacher ed. 11.96 (*0-395-81114-7*) HM.

— Western Civilization, 2 vols. (C). 1992. pap., teacher ed. 4.76 (*0-395-63788-0*) HM.

— Western Civilization, 5 vols. (C). 1995. pap., teacher ed. 11.96 (*0-395-75048-2*) HM.

— Western Civilization, 5 vols. (C). 1995. pap., teacher ed., suppl. ed. 11.96 (*0-395-75049-0*) HM.

— Western Civilization, 2 vols. 2nd ed. (C). 1992. pap. text, student ed. 33.16 (*0-395-63787-2*) HM.

— Western Civilization, 2 vols. 2nd ed. (C). 1992. pap. text, student ed. 17.16 (*0-395-63882-8*) HM.

— Western Civilization, 4 vols. 4th ed. (C). 1991. pap. text, teacher ed. 3.96 (*0-395-59336-0*) HM.

— Western Civilization, 4 vols. 4th ed. (C). 1992. pap. text, teacher ed., suppl. ed. 5.96 (*0-395-59337-9*) HM.

— Western Civilization, 5 vols. 5th ed. (C). 1995. pap. text, student ed. 18.36 (*0-395-75046-6*) HM.

— Western Civilization, 2 vols., Vol. 2. 2nd ed. (C). 1992. pap. text 33.16 (*0-395-63881-X*) HM.

— Western Civilization, 5 vols., Vol. 2. 5th ed. (C). 1995. pap. text, student ed. 18.36 (*0-395-75047-4*) HM.

— Western Civilization: A Brief History, 3 vols. 3rd ed. (C). 1996. pap. text, student ed. 17.16 (*0-395-81113-9*) HM.

— Western Civilization: A Brief History, Complete. (C). 1990. pap. text 2.76 (*0-395-52690-6*) HM.

— Western Civilization: A Brief History: To 1789, 3 vols. 3rd ed. LC 96-76985. 340p. (C). 1997. pap. text 33.16 (*0-395-81111-2*) HM.

— Western Civilization Vol. II: A Brief History: From the 1400s, 3 vols. 3rd ed. LC 96-76985. 460p. (C). 1997. pap. text 33.16 (*0-395-81112-0*) HM.

Perry, Marvin & Scweitzer, Frederick M., eds. Jewish-Christian Encounters over the Centuries: Symbiosis, Prejudice, Holocaust, Dialogue, Vol. 136. LC 93-31044. (American University Studies: History: Ser. IX, Vol. 136). X, 436p. (C). 1994. text 52.95 (*0-8204-2082-4*) P Lang Pubng.

Perry, Marvin, et al. Sources of the Western Tradition, 3 vols. 3rd ed. (C). 1995. text, teacher ed. 11.96 (*0-395-68975-9*) HM.

— Sources of the Western Tradition, 3 vols., Vol. I. 3rd ed. 464p. (C). 1994. pap. text 30.36 (*0-395-68973-2*) HM.

— Sources of the Western Tradition, Vol. 2. LC 86-81593. (C). 1987. pap. text 19.16 (*0-685-17245-7*) HM.

— Sources of the Western Tradition, 3 vols., Vol. II. 3rd ed. 464p. (C). 1994. pap. text 30.36 (*0-395-68974-0*) HM.

— Western Civilization: Ideas, Politics, & Society. 3rd ed. 1989. student ed., lab manual ed. write for info. (*0-318-63330-2*) HM.

— Western Civilization: Ideas, Politics, & Society, 5 vols. 5th ed. LC 95-76972. 900p. (C). 1995. pap. text 65.16 (*0-395-74575-6*) HM.

— Western Civilization: Ideas, Politics & Society: From the 1400s, 4 vols. 4th ed. (C). 1991. pap. text 57.56 (*0-395-59333-6*) HM.

— Western Civilization: Ideas, Politics, & Society: From the 1400s, 5 vols. 5th ed. 604p. (C). 1995. pap. text 48.36 (*0-395-74460-1*) HM.

— Western Civilization Vol. I: Ideas, Politics, & Society: To 1789, 5 vols. 5th ed. 457p. (C). 1995. pap. text 47.16 (*0-395-74458-X*) HM.

— Western Civilization Vol. II: Ideas, Politics, & Society: From the 1600s, 5 vols. 5th ed. 524p. (C). 1995. pap. text 47.16 (*0-395-74459-8*) HM.

Perry, Marvin, jt. ed. see McIntire, C. T.

Perry, Mary E. Crime & Society in Early Modern Seville. LC 79-66452. 311p. reprint ed. pap. 96.50 (*0-7837-2617-1*, 204295200006) Bks Demand.

— Gender & Disorder in Early Modern Seville. (Illus.). 202p. (C). 1990. text 45.00 (*0-691-03143-6*, Pub. by Princeton U Pr) Cal Prin Full Svc.

— Gender & Disorder in Early Modern Seville. LC 90-32784. (Illus.). 220p. reprint ed. pap. 68.20 (*0-608-09116-2*, 206974800005) Bks Demand.

Perry, Mary E. & Cruz, Anne J., eds. Cultural Encounters: The Impact of the Inquisition in Spain & the New World. LC 90-22450. (Publications of the Center for Medieval & Renaissance Studies: No. 24). (Illus.). 320p. 1991. 40.00 (*0-520-07098-4*, Pub. by U CA Pr) Cal Prin Full Svc.

Perry, Mary E., jt. auth. see Green, Harvey.

Perry, Mary E., jt. ed. see Cruz, Anne J.

***Perry, Matthew.** Bread & Work. LC 99-40488. 288p. 2000. 69.95 (*0-7453-1486-4*, Pub. by Pluto GBR); pap. 22.50 (*0-7453-1481-3*, Pub. by Pluto GBR) Stylus Pub VA.

Perry, Matthew C. Narrative of the Expedition of an American Squadron to the China Seas & Japan, 3 vols. Hawks, Francis L., ed. LC 01-4228. (Illus.). reprint ed. write for info. (*0-404-05060-3*) AMS Pr.

***Perry, Matthew C.** Narrative of the Expedition to the China Seas Japan: 1852-1854. 2000. pap. 34.95 (*0-486-41133-8*) Dover.

Perry, Matthew C., et al. Narrative of the Expedition of an American Squadron to the China Seas & Japan Performed in the Years 1852, 1853, & 1854 under the Command of Commodore M. C. Perry, United States Navy, by Order of the Government of the United States, Vol. 1. 1968. 60.95 (*0-405-18940-0*, 17148) Ayer.

— Narrative of the Expedition of an American Squadron to the China Seas & Japan Performed in the Years 1852, 1853 & 1854, Under the Command of Commodore M. C. Perry, United States Navy, by Order of the Government of the United States, Vol. 3. 1968. 60.95 (*0-405-18942-7*, 17150) Ayer.

— Narrative of the Expedition of an American Squadron to the China Seas & Japan Performed in the Years 1852, 1853, & 1854 under the Command of Commodore M. C. Perry, United States Navy, by Order of the Government of the United States, Vol. 4. 1968. 60.95 (*0-405-18943-5*, 17151) Ayer.

— Narrative of the Expedition of an American Squadron to the China Seas & Japan Performed in the Years 1852, 1853, 1854, under the Command of Commodore M. C. Perry, United States Navy, by Order of the Government of the United States, Vol. 2. 1968. 60.95 (*0-405-18941-9*, 17149) Ayer.

Perry, Melissa, jt. auth. see Lloyd, Stephen.

***Perry, Michael.** Big Rigs, Elvis & the Grand Dragon Wayne. (Illus.). 1999. pap. 16.95 (*0-9631695-6-4*) Whist & Jugg.

Perry, Michael. The Dramatized Old Testament Vol. 1: Genesis to Esther, 1. LC 94-5701. 520p. 1994. pap. 22.99 (*0-8010-7136-4*) Baker Bks.

— Handbook for Freelance Writing. LC 97-287. (Handbook for...Ser.). (Illus.). 224p. 1997. 24.95 (*0-8442-3255-6*, 32556) NTC Contemp Pub Co.

— Handbook for Freelance Writing. (Handbook for...Ser.). (Illus.). 224p. 1998. pap. 12.95 (*0-8442-3256-4*, 32564, NTC Business Bks) NTC Contemp Pub Co.

***Perry, Michael.** Planning Your Retirement. (Cliffs Notes Ser.). 128p. 1999. pap. text 8.99 (*0-7645-8542-8*) IDG Bks.

Perry, Michael. Singing to God. LC 95-79497. 312p. 1995. pap. 18.95 (*0-916642-59-3*, 1207) Hope Pub.

— Why They Killed Big Boy: And Other Stories. (Orig.). 1996. pap. 9.95 (*0-9631695-3-X*) Whist & Jugg.

Perry, Michael, et al, eds. Come Rejoice! 107p. (Orig.). 1989. pap. 12.95 (*0-916642-38-0*, 899) Hope Pub.

Perry, Michael C. The Chemotherapy Source Book. (Illus.). 1192p. 1991. 140.00 (*0-683-06859-8*) Lppncott W & W.

— The Chemotherapy Source Book. 2nd ed. LC 96-685. (Illus.). 1184p. 1996. 149.00 (*0-683-06868-7*) Lppncott W & W.

Perry, Michael C., et al. Companion Handbook to the Chemotherapy Sourcebook. LC 98-42010. 534p. 1998. pap. 45.00 (*0-683-30248-5*) Lppncott W & W.

Perry, Michael D. & Corkum, Paul B., eds. Short Wavelength V: Physics with Intense Laser Pulses. LC 92-62909. (Proceedings Ser.: Vol. 17). 350p. (Orig.). 1993. lib. bdg. 75.00 (*1-55752-298-7*) Optical Soc.

Perry, Michael J. The Constitution in the Courts: Law or Politics? 288p. 1996. pap. 19.95 (*0-19-510464-1*) OUP.

— The Idea of Human Rights: Four Inquiries. LC 97-12764. 176p. (C). 1998. 35.00 (*0-19-511636-4*) OUP.

***Perry, Michael J.** The Idea of Human Rights: Four Inquiries. 176p. 2000. pap. 14.95 (*0-19-513828-7*) OUP.

Perry, Michael J. Love & Power: The Role of Religion & Morality in American Politics. 240p. 1993. reprint ed. pap. text 19.95 (*0-19-508355-5*) OUP.

— Morality, Politics & Law. 336p. 1990. reprint ed. pap. text 21.00 (*0-19-506456-9*) OUP.

— Religion in Politics: Constitutional & Moral Perspectives. 176p. 1999. pap. 18.95 (*0-19-513095-2*) OUP.

— We the People: The Fourteenth Amendment & the Supreme Court. LC 98-48865. 288p. 1999. 35.00 (*0-19-512362-X*) OUP.

Perry, Michael P. Low Frequency Electromagnetic Design. (Electrical Engineering & Electronics Ser.: Vol. 28). (Illus.). 256p. 1985. text 150.00 (*0-8247-7453-1*) Dekker.

Perry, Michael R. The Couple's Wedding Survival Manual: How to Tie the Knot Without Coming Unraveled. LC 98-51028. 224p. 1999. pap. 14.00 (*0-671-53790-3*, PB Trade Paper) PB.

— The Groom's Survival Manual. Marrow, Linda, ed. 224p. (Orig.). 1991. pap. 12.00 (*0-671-69357-3*) PB.

— Skelter. Chellus, Jane, ed. 560p. (Orig.). 1994. mass mkt. 5.99 (*0-671-73496-2*, Pocket Star Bks) PB.

— The Stranger Returns. Marrow, Linda, ed. 432p. (Orig.). 1992. mass mkt. 5.50 (*0-671-73495-4*, Pocket Star Bks) PB.

Perry, Michael W., jt. auth. see Balfour, Arthur James.

Perry, Michael W., jt. auth. see Sanger, Margaret.

Perry, Michael W., ed. see Chesterton, G. K.

Perry, Michael W., ed. see U.S. Seventh Army Staff.

***Perry, Mike.** Rural Rescue. 2000. 25.00 (*0-06-019852-4*); pap. 14.00 (*0-06-095807-3*) HarpC.

Perry, Milton F. Infernal Machines: The Story of Confederate Submarine & Mine Warfare. LC 85-9706. (Illus.). 231p. 1985. pap. 16.95 (*0-8071-1285-2*) La State U Pr.

Perry, Milton F., et al. The Kansas City Archaeologist. (Kansas City Archaeologists Special Bulletin Ser., 1986: No. 1). (Illus.). 104p. (Orig.). 1986. pap. 5.95 (*0-318-22802-5*) KC Archaeol Soc.

Perry, Murvin H. Murv's Motoring Memories. (Illus.). 160p. 1993. pap. 9.95 (*0-932807-72-0*) Overmountain Pr.

Perry, Nancy W. & Wrightsman, Lawrence S. The Child Witness: Legal Issues & Dilemmas. (Illus.). 280p. 1991. text 52.00 (*0-8039-3771-7*); pap. text 24.00 (*0-8039-3772-5*) Sage.

Perry, Nell, ed. see Barnes, T. W. & Freeman, Nona.

Perry, Nell, ed. see Freeman, Nona.

***Perry, Nellie M. & Teichmann, Sandra Gail.** Woman of the Plains: The Journals & Stories of Nellie M. Perry. LC 99-57743. Vol. 4. (Illus.). 224p. 2000. 24.95 (*0-89096-935-3*) Tex A&M Univ Pr.

Perry, Newman S. Business, Government & Society: Managing Competitiveness, Ethics & Social Issues. (Illus.). 736p. (C). 1994. 54.80 (*0-02-393401-8*, Macmillan Coll) P-H.

Perry, Nicholas. Hyperreality. LC 97-43299. 208p. (C). 1998. 65.00 (*0-415-10514-5*); pap. 22.99 (*0-415-10515-3*) Routledge.

— Ruskin's Drawings in the Ashmolean Museum. (Illus.). 79p. 1995. text 19.95 (*1-85444-039-X*, 741) A Schwartz & Co.

— Ruskin's Drawings in the Ashmolean Museum. (Illus.). 79p. 1995. pap. 17.95 (*0-907849-74-1*, 741P, Pub. by Ashmolean Mus) A Schwartz & Co.

Perry, Nicholas & Echeverria, Loreto. Under the Heel of Mary. 336p. 1989. 39.95 (*0-415-01296-1*) Routledge.

Perry, Nicolette. Symbiosis: Close Encounters of the Natural Kind. LC 83-190953. 1983. 16.95 (*0-7137-1229-5*) Blandford Pr.

Perry, Oliver H. Hunting Expeditions of Oliver Hazard Perry: As Recorded in the Diaries Kept from 1836 Through 1855 by Oliver Hazard Perry of Cleveland, Ohio. deluxe ed. LC 94-4228. (Illus.). 299p. 1994. lthr. 150.00 (*0-9633094-3-9*) St Huberts Pr.

— Hunting Expeditions of Oliver Hazard Perry: As Recorded in the Diaries Kept from 1836 Through 1855 by Oliver Hazard Perry of Cleveland, Ohio. LC 94-4228. (Illus.). 299p. 1994. reprint ed. 45.00 (*0-9633094-2-0*) St Huberts Pr.

Perry, P. Scattering Theory by the Enss Method, Vol. 1. (Mathematical Reports: Vol. 1, No. 1). xiv, 348p. 1983. text 332.00 (*3-7186-0093-5*) Gordon & Breach.

Perry, Patricia. Welcome to Your Bible. (Little Library Ser.). 48p. (J). (gr. 4-8). 1998. pap. 0.99 (*1-57748-439-8*) Barbour Pub.

Perry, Patricia, jt. auth. see Lynch, Marietta.

Perry, Paul. Fasting Safely. LC 78-68564. 128p. (Orig.). 1980. pap. 4.95 (*0-89037-217-9*) Anderson World.

Perry, Paul & Babbs, Ken. On the Bus: The Complete Guide to the Legendary Trip of Ken Kesey & the Merry Pranksters & the Birth of the Counterculture. 2nd ed. 205p. 1997. pap. text 22.95 (*1-56025-114-X*, Thunders Mouth) Avalon NY.

— On the Bus: The Legendary Trip of Ken Kesey & the Merry Pranksters. (Non-Fiction - Photo Ser.). (Illus.). 224p. 1990. pap. 22.95 (*0-685-37673-7*, Thunders Mouth) Avalon NY.

Perry, Paul, jt. auth. see Brinkley, Dannion.

Perry, Paul, jt. auth. see Cherewatenko, Vern.

Perry, Paul, jt. auth. see Clifford, Barry.

Perry, Paul, jt. auth. see Liu, Hong.

Perry, Paul, jt. auth. see Moody, Raymond.

Perry, Paul, jt. auth. see Morse, Melvin.

Perry, Paul, jt. auth. see Steiner, Claude.

Perry, Paul E., jt. auth. see Webster, Alan C.

Perry, Paul J. Creating Cool Web Applets with Java. 350p. 1996. pap. 29.99 (*1-56884-881-1*) IDG Bks.

Perry, Paul J. World Wide Web Secrets. 744p. 1995. pap. 39.99 (*1-56884-456-5*) IDG Bks.

Perry, Paul J., et al. Psychotropic Drug Handbook. 6th ed. LC 90-71835. (Illus.). vi, 358p. 1991. pap. text 4.00 (*0-929375-06-8*) H W Bks.

— Psychotropic Drug Handbook. 7th ed. 757p. 1997. spiral bd. 44.50 (*0-88048-851-4*, 8851) Am Psychiatric.

Perry, Paul J., jt. auth. see Callahan, Roger.

Perry, Paul J., jt. auth. see Morse, Melvin L.

Perry, Peter C. Hours into Minutes. (C). 1983. pap. 40.00 (*0-905675-02-9*, Pub. by IPM Hse) St Mut.

Perry, Peter J. Political Corruption & Political Geography. LC 97-1226. (Illus.). 176p. 1997. text 72.95 (*1-85521-901-8*, Pub. by Ashgate Pub) Ashgate Pub Co.

Perry, Philip. Opportunities in Banking Careers. (Opportunities In . . . Ser.). (Illus.). 160p. pap. 11.95 (*0-8442-4050-8*, 40508, VGM Career) NTC Contemp Pub Co.

— Opportunities in Banking Careers. (Opportunities in...Ser.). (Illus.). 160p. 1994. 14.95 (*0-8442-4049-4*, 40494, VGM Career) NTC Contemp Pub Co.

Perry, Philip, jt. auth. see Weber, Robert M.

Perry, Philip A. Opportunities in Mental Health Careers. (VGM Opportunities Ser.). (Illus.). 160p. 1996. 14.95 (*0-8442-4429-5*, 44295, VGM Career) NTC Contemp Pub Co.

Perry, Philip A. & Simons, Virginia. Opportunities in Mental Health Careers. (Opportunities In . . . Ser.). (Illus.). 160p. pap. 11.95 (*0-8442-4430-9*, 44309, VGM Career) NTC Contemp Pub Co.

Perry, Philippa. How to Be Animal Friendly: Choose the Kindest Ways to Eat, Shop & Have Fun! (Illus.). 96p. (gr. 4-7). 1999. pap. 4.95 (*1-901881-74-1*, Pub. by Element MA) Penguin Putnam.

Perry, Phillip & Weber, Robert M. Opportunities in Automotive Services. LC 96-27797. (Opportunities in... Ser.). (Illus.). 160p. 1996. 14.95 (*0-8442-4672-7*, 46727, Natl Textbk Co) NTC Contemp Pub Co.

Perry, Phillip A., ed. see Calhoun, W. L.

Perry, Phillis Jean. Myths, Legends & Tales. LC 98-48773. 102p. 1999. pap. text 16.95 (*1-57950-017-X*) Highsmith Pr.

***Perry, Phyllis A.** Stigmata. LC 98-5324. 224p. (J). 1998. 21.45 (*0-7868-6408-7*, Pub. by Hyperion) Time Warner.

Perry, Phyllis Alesia. Stigmata: A Novel. LC 99-16322. 256p. 1999. pap. 12.95 (*0-385-49635-4*, Anchor NY) Doubleday.

Perry, Phyllis J. Armor to Venom: Animal Defenses. LC 96-37289. (First Bk.). (Illus.). 63p. (J). (gr. 4-6). 1997. 22.00 (*0-531-20299-2*) Watts.

— Armor to Venom: Animal Defenses. (First Bks.). 1998. pap. 6.95 (*0-531-15884-5*) Watts.

— Ballooning. LC 96-7229. (First Books-Sports & Recreation). (Illus.). 64p. (J). (gr. 4-6). 1996. lib. bdg. 22.00 (*0-531-20234-8*) Watts.

— Ballooning. (First Bks.). 64p. (J). 1997. pap. 6.95 (*0-531-15807-1*) Watts.

— Bats: The Amazing Upside-Downers. LC 97-4048. (First Book Ser.). 64p. (J). 1997. 22.00 (*0-531-20342-5*) Watts.

— Bats: The Amazing Upside-Downers. (First Book--Animals). (Illus.). 64p. (J). (gr. 4 up). 1998. pap. 6.95 (*0-531-15903-5*) Watts.

— Crafty Canines: Coyotes, Foxes, & Wolves. LC 98-22023. (Watts Library: Animals). 63p. (J). (gr. 5-7). 1999. 24.00 (*0-531-11680-8*) Watts.

***Perry, Phyllis J.** Crafty Canines: Coyotes, Foxes & Wolves. (Illus.). (J). 2000. pap. 8.95 (*0-531-16422-5*) Watts.

Perry, Phyllis J. The Crocodilians: Reminders of the Age of Dinosaur. LC 96-25875. (First Bk.). (J). 1997. lib. bdg. 22.00 (*0-531-20254-2*) Watts.

— Crocodilians: Reminders of the Age of Dinosaurs. (First Books). (YA). (gr. 9 up). 1997. pap. text 6.95 (*0-531-15856-X*) Watts.

— Exploring Our Country's History: Linking Fiction to Nonfiction. LC 98-20275. (Literature Bridges to Social Studies Ser.). 133p. 1998. pap. 23.50 (*1-56308-622-0*) Teacher Ideas Pr.

— Exploring the World of Animals: Linking Fiction to Nonfiction. (Literature Bridges to Science Ser.). 200p. 1997. lib. bdg. 24.50 (*1-56308-517-8*) Teacher Ideas Pr.

— Exploring the World of Sports: Linking Fiction to Nonfiction. LC 97-43558. 150p. 1998. pap. 24.00 (*1-56308-570-4*) Libs Unl.

— The Fiddlehoppers: Crickets, Katydids, & Locusts. (First Bks.). (Illus.). 64p. (J). (gr. 4-6). 1995. lib. bdg. 22.00 (*0-531-20209-7*) Watts.

***Perry, Phyllis J.** Freshwater Giants. LC 98-25123. (Watts Library: Animals). 63p. (J). (gr. 5-7). 1999. 24.00 (*0-531-11681-6*) Watts.

— Freshwater Giants: Hippopotamuses, River Dolphins & Manatees. (Watts Library). (Illus.). (J). 2000. pap. 8.95 (*0-531-16424-1*) Watts.

Perry, Phyllis J. Getting Started in Science Fairs: From Planning to Judging. LC 94-44103. (Illus.). 192p. (J). (gr. 1-6). 1995. pap. 14.95 (*0-07-049526-2*) McGraw-Hill Prof.

— Guide to Math Materials: Grades K-5. LC 96-33101. 120p. 1997. pap. text, teacher ed. 20.00 (*1-56308-491-0*) Teacher Ideas Pr.

— Hide & Seek: Creatures in Camouflage. LC 96-37290. (First Bk.). (J). (gr. 4-6). 1997. 22.00 (*0-531-20306-9*) Watts.

***Perry, Phyllis J.** Keeping the Traditions: A Multicultural Resource. (Illus.). 272p. (YA). (gr. 4-9). 2000. pap. 19.95 (*1-55591-975-8*) Fulcrum Pub.

Perry, Phyllis J. Rainy, Windy, Snowy, Sunny Days: Linking Fiction to Nonfiction. (Literature Bridges to Science Ser.). xviii, 145p. 1996. pap. text 22.00 (*1-56308-392-2*) Teacher Ideas Pr.

— Reading Activities & Resources That Work. LC 97-9859. 206p. (J). 1997. pap. 25.00 (*0-917846-94-X*) Highsmith Pr.

— Science Fair Success with Plants. LC 98-25944. (Science Fair Success Ser.). 104p. (YA). (gr. 6 up). 1999. lib. bdg. 20.95 (*0-7660-1170-4*) Enslow Pubs.

— Sea Stars & Dragons. (First Bks.). (Illus.). 64p. (J). (gr. 4-6). 1996. lib. bdg. 22.00 (*0-531-20223-2*) Watts.

— The Snow Cats. LC 96-25873. (First Bks.). (J). 1997. lib. bdg. 22.00 (*0-531-20267-4*) Watts.

— The Snow Cats. (First Books). 1997. pap. text 6.95 (*0-531-15859-4*) Watts.

P

— Soaring. LC 96-41075. (First Bk.). (J). 1997. lib. bdg. 22.00 (0-531-20258-5) Watts.

— Soaring. (First Bks.). (J). 1997. pap. text 6.95 (0-531-15852-7) Watts.

— A Teacher's Science Companion: Resources & Activities in Science & Math. LC 93-43620. (Illus.). 128p. 1994. 14.95 (0-07-049518-1) McGraw-Hill Prof.

— The World of Water: Linking Fiction to Nonfiction. LC 94-44426. (Literature Bridges to Science Ser.). xvi, 149p. 1995. pap. text 21.50 (1-56308-321-3) Teacher Ideas Pr.

— The World's Regions & Weather: Linking Fiction to Nonfiction. (Literature Bridges to Science Ser.). xvi, 157p. 1996. pap. text 22.00 (1-56308-338-8) Teacher Ideas Pr.

Perry, Phyllis J. & Hoback, John R. A Guide to Independent Research. 69p. 1986. pap. 9.97 (0-937659-33-9) GCT.

***Perry, Phyllis Jean.** Boardsailing. LC 99-53161. (Extreme Sports Ser.). (Illus.). 49p. (YA). (gr. 5 up). 2000. lib. bdg. 21.26 (0-7368-0481-1, Capstone Bks) Capstone Pr.

Perry, R., ed. see Institute of Criminology, University of Cambridge,.

***Perry, R. Ross.** Common-Law Pleading: Its History & Principles: Including Dicey's Rules Concerning Parties to Actions & Stephen's Rules of Pleading. LC 00-36239. 2000. write for info. (1-58477-105-4) Lawbk Exchange.

Perry, R. S., jt. auth. see Haugk, Kenneth C.

Perry, R. Scott, ed. see Fischer, Fred.

Perry, R. Scott, ed. see McKay, William J. & Haugk, Kenneth C.

Perry, Rachel. Reverse the Aging Process of Your Face: A Simple Technique That Works. LC 95-18688. (Illus.). 196p. pap. 13.95 (0-89529-625-X, Avery) Penguin Putnam.

Perry, Ralph B. Characteristically American. LC 73-134125. (Essay Index Reprint Ser.). 1977. 20.95 (0-8369-2013-9) Ayer.

— The Free Man & the Soldier. LC 73-24250. (Select Bibliographies Reprint Ser.). 1977. reprint ed. 18.95 (0-8369-5438-6) Ayer.

— General Theory of Values: Its Meaning & Basic Principles Construed in Terms of Interest. LC BD0232.P4. 720p. reprint ed. pap. 200.00 (0-608-30641-X, 200642200059) Bks Demand.

— In the Spirit of William James. LC 78-31937. 211p. 1979. reprint ed. lib. bdg. 59.50 (0-313-20715-1, PEIN, Greenwood Pr) Greenwood.

— Philosophy of the Recent Past: An Outline of European & American Philosophy Since 1860. LC 75-3314. reprint ed. 37.50 (0-404-59295-3) AMS Pr.

— Present Philosophical Tendencies. LC 68-21328. 383p. 1968. reprint ed. lib. bdg. 69.50 (0-8371-0191-3, PEPT, Greenwood Pr) Greenwood.

— Puritanism & Democracy. 1980. 24.50 (0-8149-0180-8) Random.

— The Thought & Character of William James. LC 96-32306. (Library of American Philosophy). 424p. 1996. reprint ed. pap. 21.95 (0-8265-1279-8) Vanderbilt U Pr.

Perry, Raymond E., ed. Accounting for Derivatives. LC 96-20983. 360p. 1996. 95.00 (0-7863-0541-X, Irwn Prfssnl) McGraw-Hill Prof.

Perry, Raymond M. Jobs & Careers in Hawaii: "Your Job - Career Search Begins Here in Hawaii" 148p. 1997. 19.95 (0-9663583-0-9) Aspen Co.

Perry, Raymond P., ed. see McKeachie, William J. & Feldman, Kenneth A.

Perry, Raymond P., ed. see McKeachie, William J., et al.

Perry, Rebecca. Lots of Limericks. LC 91-329. 128p. (J). (gr. 4-7). 1991. 16.00 (0-689-50531-0) McElderry Bks.

— Riddle-Me Rhymes. LC 93-25179. 96p. (J). (gr. 3-7). 1994. mass mkt. 16.00 (0-689-50602-3) McElderry Bks.

Perry, Rex, ed. see LaBelle, Dave.

Perry, Richard. The Broken Land. 1997. mass mkt. 5.50 (0-312-95777-7) St Martin.

— Changes. LC 73-13224. 1974. 6.95 (0-672-51850-3, Bobbs) Macmillan.

— Mexico's Fortress Monasteries. (Illus.). 224p. (Orig.). 1992. pap. 19.95 (0-9620811-6-5) Espadana Pr.

— Montgomery's Children. LC 98-233109. 282p. 1998. pap. 14.95 (1-885478-25-9, Pub. by Genesis Press) BookWorld.

Perry, Richard & Perry, Rosalind W. Maya Missions: Exploring the Spanish Colonial Churches of Yucatan. (Illus.). 256p. (Orig.). 1988. pap. 12.95 (0-9620811-0-8) Espadana Pr.

***Perry, Richard A., Jr.** The Series 7 & 63 Secrets of Preparation, a Bullish Approach. 33p. 1999. mass mkt. 29.95 (0-9674107-0-3) R A Perry.

Perry, Richard D. Blue Lakes & Silver Cities: The Colonial Arts & Architecture of West Mexico. LC 97-60544. (Illus.). 272p. (Orig.). 1997. pap. 25.00 (0-9620811-3-2) Espadana Pr.

— More Maya Missions: Exploring Colonial Chiapas. LC 93-72945. (Illus.). 128p. (Orig.). (C). 1994. pap. 12.95 (0-9620811-2-4) Espadana Pr.

Perry, Richard J. Apache Reservation: Indigenous Peoples & the American State. LC 92-37253. (Illus.). 276p. (C). 1993. text 37.50 (0-292-76542-8) U of Tex Pr.

— From Time Immemorial: Indigenous Peoples & State Systems. LC 96-903. (Illus.). 312p. 1996. pap. 16.95 (0-292-76599-1); text 37.50 (0-292-76598-3) U of Tex Pr.

Perry, Richard L., ed. Sources of Our Liberties. LC 78-67316. xxii, 466p. 1991. reprint ed. 47.50 (0-89941-752-3, 305030) W S Hein.

Perry, Ritchie. The Runton Werewolf. large type ed. (J). 1997. 16.95 (0-7451-6908-2, Galaxy Child Lrg Print) Chivers N Amer.

***Perry, Robert.** Artificial Intelligence. (Computer Science Library). (Illus.). (YA). 2000. pap. 8.95 (0-531-16468-3) Watts.

— Build Your Own Website. (Computer Science Library). (Illus.). (YA). 2000. pap. 8.95 (0-531-16469-1) Watts.

Perry, Robert. Jack May's War. (Illus.). 1998. pap. 14.95 (1-57072-071-1) Overmountain Pr.

***Perry, Robert.** Matrix. (Doctor Who Ser.). (Illus.). 1998. mass mkt. 5.95 (0-563-40596-1) BBC Bks.

— Multimedia Magic. (Computer Science Library). (Illus.). (J). 2000. pap. 8.95 (0-531-16472-1) Watts.

— Personal Computer Communications. (Computer Science Library). (Illus.). (YA). 2000. pap. 8.95 (0-531-16483-7) Watts.

Perry, Robert & Ashcraft-Eason, Lillian. Inside Ethnic America: An Ethnic Studies Reader. 284p. (C). 1996. pap. text, per. 39.95 (0-7872-2098-1, 41209801) Kendall-Hunt.

***Perry, Robert H.** Sailing Designs, Vol. 5. (Illus.). 1999. pap. 39.95 (1-929006-04-7) Port Pubns.

Perry, Robert H. Sailing Designs Vol. 1: The Design Reviews of Robert H. Perry As Published in Sailing Magazine. (Illus.). 96p. 1977. pap. write for info. (1-929006-00-4) Port Pubns.

— Sailing Designs Vol. 2: The Design Reviews of Robert H. Perry As Published in Sailing Magazine. (Illus.). 120p. 1980. pap. write for info. (1-929006-01-2) Port Pubns.

— Sailing Designs Vol. 3: The Design Reviews of Robert H. Perry As Published in Sailing Magazine. (Illus.). 207p. 1986. pap. write for info. (1-929006-02-0) Port Pubns.

— Sailing Designs Vol. 4: The Design Reviews of Robert H. Perry As Published in Sailing Magazine. (Illus.). 240p. 1994. pap. write for info. (1-929006-03-9) Port Pubns.

Perry, Robert H. & Green, Don W. Perry's Chemical Engineers' Handbook. 7th ed. LC 96-51648. (Illus.). 2640p. 1991. 150.00 (0-07-049841-5) McGraw.

Perry, Robert H., jt. ed. see Jones-Parker, Janet.

Perry, Robert J. Life with the Little People. (Frank Waters Memorial Ser.: No. 3). 161p. 1998. pap. 14.95 (0-912678-98-4) Greenfld Rev Lit.

***Perry, Robert L.** Artificial Intelligence. LC 99-88785. (Computer Science Library). 2000. 24.00 (0-531-11757-X) Watts.

— Build Your Own Website. LC 99-88786. (Computer Science Library). 2000. 24.00 (0-531-11756-1) Watts.

Perry, Robert L. The Fifty Best Low-Investment, High-Profit Franchises. 2nd ed. LC 94-1569. 384p. (C). 1994. pap. 14.95 (0-13-300393-0) P-H.

***Perry, Robert L.** Multimedia Magic. LC 99-88787. (Computer Science Library). 2000. 24.00 (0-531-11755-3) Watts.

— Personal Computer Communications. (Computer Science Library). 2000. 24.00 (0-531-11758-8) Watts.

***Perry, Roland.** Bold Warnie: Shane Warne & Australia's Rise to Cricket Dominance. LC 99-487754. (Illus.). 1999. write for info. (0-09-184001-5); write for info. (0-09-184043-0) Trafalgar.

Perry, Roland. Lethal Hero: The Mel Gibson Biography. 256p. 1993. 22.95 (1-870049-79-9) Oliver Bks.

Perry, Roland N. & Wright, Denise J. The Physiology & Biochemistry of Free-Living & Plant-Parasitic Nematodes. LC 98-23906. (Illus.). 464p. 1998. text 120.00 (0-85199-231-5) OUP.

Perry, Ronald F. & Hoover, Stewart V. Simulation: A Problem Solving Approach. (Illus.). 700p. (C). 1989. 91.00 (0-201-16880-4) Addison-Wesley.

Perry, Ronald W. & Greene, Marjorie. Citizen Response to Volcanic Eruption: The Case of Mt. St. Helens. 145p. 1983. text 22.50 (0-8290-1050-5) Irvington.

Perry, Ronald W. & Hirose, Hirotada. Volcano Management in the United States & Japan, Vol. 7. Levy, Judith A., ed. LC 91-15558. (Contemporary Studies in Applied Behavioral Science). 230p. 1991. 73.25 (1-55938-275-9) Jai Pr.

Perry, Ronald W. & Levy, Judith A., eds. Comprehensive Emergency Management Vol. 3: Evacuating Threatened Populations. LC 84-12616. (Contemporary Studies in Applied Behavioral Science: Vol. 3). 173p. 1985. 73.25 (0-89232-436-8) Jai Pr.

Perry, Ronald W. & Lindell, Michael K. Behavioral Foundations of Community Emergency Response Planning. (Illus.). 630p. 1992. 99.95 (0-89116-620-3) Hemisp Pub.

— Living with Mt. St. Helens: Human Adjustment to Volcano Hazards. LC 90-59721. (Illus.). x, 220p. 1990. pap. text 9.95 (0-87422-053-X) Wash St U Pr.

Perry, Ronald W. & Mushkatel, Alvin H. Disaster Management: Warning Response & Community Relocation. LC 83-17729. (Illus.). 280p. 1984. 65.00 (0-89930-078-2, PDM/, Quorum Bks) Greenwood.

Perry, Rosalie S. Charles Ives & the American Mind. LC 74-620003. (Illus.). 157p. reprint ed. 48.70 (0-8357-9360-5, 201729600007) Bks Demand.

Perry, Rosalind W. & Frolli, Marty. A Joy Forever: Marie Webster's Quilt Patterns. LC 92-80786. (Illus.). 96p. (Orig.). 1992. pap. 19.50 (0-9620811-7-5) Pract Patchwk.

Perry, Rosalind W., jt. auth. see Perry, Richard.

Perry, Rosemary. Teaching Practice: A Guide for Early Years. LC 97-473. (Illus.). 208p. (C). 1998. pap. 20.99 (0-415-14882-0) Routledge.

Perry-Rudolph, Polly S. Home Cookin' Cookin' Like Grandma. 113p. 1992. spiral bd. 10.00 (0-9636540-0-4) P S Perry-Rudolph.

Perry, Rufus L. The Cushite: The Children of Ham (the Negro Race) Obaba, Al I., ed. (YA). 1991. pap. text 6.00 (0-916157-32-6) African Islam Miss Pubns.

— The Cushite: or The Children of Ham. 49p. (Orig.). 1887. pap. 4.00 (0-916157-20-2) African Islam Miss Pubns.

Perry, Ruth. The Celebrated Mary Astell: An Early English Feminist. LC 82-28922. (Illus.). 576p. 1994. lib. bdg. 45.00 (0-226-66093-1) U Ch Pr.

— The Celebrated Mary Astell: An Early English Feminist. LC 82-28922. (Illus.). 564p. 1999. pap. text 24.00 (0-226-66095-8) U Ch Pr.

— Women, Letters & the Novel. LC 79-8637. (Studies in the Eighteenth Century: No. 4). (Illus.). 1980. 39.50 (0-404-18025-6) AMS Pr.

Perry, Ruth & Brownley, Martine Watson, eds. Mothering the Mind: Twelve Studies of Writers & Their Silent Partners. LC 83-10849. (Illus.). 261p. (C). 1984. 39.95 (0-8419-0892-3); pap. 19.95 (0-8419-0893-1) Holmes & Meier.

Perry, Ruth & Kelly, Tim. Ladies of the Tower. 1971. 3.50 (0-87129-586-5, L11) Dramatic Pub.

Perry, Ruth & Milne, A. A. The Red House Mystery. 96p. 1956. pap. 5.50 (0-87129-115-0, R34) Dramatic Pub.

Perry, Ruth & Welty, Eudora. Lily Daw & the Three Ladies. 39p. 1972. pap. 3.50 (0-87129-692-6, L22) Dramatic Pub.

Perry, Ruth, et al. Joy! - Christmas Musical. 1973. pap. 5.95 (0-87129-138-X, J01) Dramatic Pub.

Perry, Ruth, ed. see Ballard, George.

Perry, Ruth F. & Baum, Frank. Christmas in the Land of Oz. 55p. 1987. pap. 3.50 (0-87129-986-0, C43) Dramatic Pub.

Perry, S., jt. auth. see Tatlock, John S.

Perry, S. D. Aliens Go Berserk. (Aliens Ser.). 240p. 1998. mass mkt. 4.99 (0-553-57731-X, Spectra) Bantam.

— City of the Dead, Vol. 3. (Resident Evil Ser.: Vol. 3). 338p. (Orig.). 1999. per. 6.50 (0-671-02441-8) PB.

***Perry, S. D.** Nemesis. (Resident Evil Ser.: No. 5). 288p. 2000. 6.50 (0-671-78496-X) PB.

Perry, S. D. Underworld. 1999. per. 6.50 (0-671-02442-6) PB.

— Virus. 224p. 1998. mass mkt. 5.99 (0-8125-4158-8, Pub. by Tor Bks) St Martin.

— War: Aliens vs. Predator. 288p. 1999. mass mkt. 5.50 (0-553-57732-8, Spectra) Bantam.

***Perry, S. D.** Xena Warrior Princess Prophecy. (Xena Warrior Princess Ser.). (Illus.). 1999. mass mkt. 5.99 (0-425-17084-5) Berkley Pub.

Perry, S. V. Molecular Mechanisms in Striated Muscle. (Lezioni Lincee Lectures). (Illus.). 176p. (C). 1996. text 59.95 (0-521-57001-8); pap. text 21.95 (0-521-57916-3) Cambridge U Pr.

Perry, Sam M. Capers: Tales from an Himalayan Boarding School. (Illus.). 338p. 1999. 26.50 (1-85776-396-3, Pub. by Book Guild Ltd) Trans-Atl Phila.

Perry, Samuel, et al. A DSM-III-R Casebook of Treatment Selection. 2nd ed. LC 90-1317. 416p. 1990. text 49.95 (0-87630-572-9) Brunner-Mazel.

Perry, Samuel W., jt. ed. see Price, Richard W.

Perry, Sara. Christmastime Recipes & Crafts for the Whole Family. LC 98-53662. (Illus.). 96p. 1999. pap. 14.95 (0-8118-2491-8) Chronicle Bks.

— Great Gingerbread. LC 97-6173. 1997. pap. 14.95 (0-8118-1613-3) Chronicle Bks.

***Perry, Sara.** Guardian Career Guide. 2000. pap. 19.95 (1-85702-751-5, Pub. by Fourth Estate) Trafalgar.

Perry, Sara. Summertime Treats: Recipes & Crafts for the Whole Family. LC 98-33815. (Illus.). 96p. 1999. pap. 14.95 (0-8118-2323-7) Chronicle Bks.

***Perry, Sara.** Valentine Treats: Recipes & Crafts for the Whole Family. LC 99-88462. 2001. pap. 14.95 (0-8118-2592-2) Chronicle Bks.

Perry, Sarah. The Book of Herbal Teas: A Guide to Gathering, Brewing, & Drinking. LC 96-1605. (Illus.). 120p. 1996. 17.95 (0-8118-1337-1) Chronicle Bks.

— If... LC 94-35108. (Illus.). 46p. (J). (gr. k-8). 1995. 16.95 (0-89236-321-5, Pub. by J P Getty Trust) OUP.

— Living with Multiple Sclerosis: Personal Accounts of Coping & Adaptation. (Developments in Nursing & Health Care Ser.). 272p. 1994. 72.95 (1-85628-893-5, Pub. by Avebry) Ashgate Pub Co.

— The Tea Book: A Gourmet Guide to Buying, Brewing, & Cooking. LeBlond, Bill, ed. LC 92-38967. (Illus.). 96p. 1993. pap. 12.95 (0-8118-0336-8) Chronicle Bks.

— Y Si... (SPA., Illus.). 44p. (J). 1999. 16.95 (0-89236-542-0, Pub. by J P Getty Trust) OUP.

Perry, Sarah, et al. The Complete Coffee Book. (Illus.). 96p. (Orig.). 1991. 19.95 (0-87701-899-5); pap. 12.95 (0-87701-820-0) Chronicle Bks.

***Perry, Schneider.** An Introduction to Internet. (Illustrated Ser.). (Illus.). (C). 1999. text 21.95 (0-7600-6158-0) Course Tech.

Perry, Scott. Bookends: A Play LC 99-166424. 34p. 1997. write for info. (0-573-14208-4) S French Trade.

***Perry, Scott L.** 1999 Pro Football Ultimate Statistics. 152p. 1999. pap. 19.95 (0-9674386-0-8) Perry Rating.

Perry, S.D. Caliban Cove, Vol. 2. (Resident Evil Ser.). 242p. 1998. per. 6.50 (0-671-02440-X, Pocket Books) PB.

Perry, Seamus. Coleridge & the Uses of Division. LC 99-28843. (Oxford English Monographs). 320p. 1999. text 72.00 (0-19-818397-6) OUP.

Perry, Shannon E. Bone & Joint Infections. 200p. 1996. write for info. (1-85317-132-8) Mosby Inc.

Perry, Shannon E. & Wong, Donna L. Maternal-Child Nursing Care. LC 97-8667. (Illus.). 1848p. (C). (gr. 13). 1997. text 79.00 (0-8151-2837-1, 29893) Mosby Inc.

Perry, Shannon E., jt. auth. see Wong, Donna L.

Perry, Shauneille & Jackson, Donald. Mio & Other Plays for Young People. LC 73-92790. (J). (gr. 4 up). 1976. 5.95 (0-89388-154-6) Okpaku Communications.

Perry, Sheila. Aspects of Contemporary France. LC 96-32445. 288p. (C). 1997. 75.00 (0-415-13179-0); pap. 24.99 (0-415-13180-4) Routledge.

Perry, Sheila, jt. auth. see Cross, Maire.

Perry, Sherry Ann. The Complete Help Your Child Learn to Read Books. (Illus.). ix, 296p. (Orig.). 1997. pap. 21.95 (0-9659958-0-1) P-ALS.

Perry, Simon D. & John Deaver Drinko Academy for American Political Institutions. Morality, Self-interest, & the Cities. LC 98-216556. 106 p. 1997. write for info. (1-891607-01-4) Drinko Acad.

Perry, Steve. Albino Knife. 1991. mass mkt. 4.99 (0-441-01391-0) Ace Bks.

— Aliens No. 7: Labyrinth. 256p. 1996. mass mkt. 5.50 (0-553-57491-4, Spectra) Bantam.

— Aliens 1: Earth Hive. (Aliens Ser.: No. 1). 288p. 1992. mass mkt. 5.50 (0-553-56120-0, Spectra) Bantam.

— Aliens vs. Predator: Prey. 272p. 1994. mass mkt. 5.50 (0-553-56555-9) Bantam.

Perry, Steve. Aliens 2: Nightmare Asylum. (Aliens Ser.: No. 2). 288p. 1993. mass mkt. 5.50 (0-553-56158-8) Bantam.

— Aliens 3: The Female War. (Aliens Ser.: No. 3). 304p. 1993. mass mkt. 5.50 (0-553-56159-6) Bantam.

— Breaking Point, Vol. 4. 2000. mass mkt. 7.99 (0-425-17693-2) Berkley Pub.

Perry, Steve. Conan the Defiant. 256p. 1987. pap. 6.95 (0-8125-4264-9) Tor Bks.

— Conan the Formidable. 1990. pap. text 7.95 (0-8125-0998-6) Tor Bks.

— Conan the Formidable. 288p. 1991. mass mkt. 3.99 (0-8125-1377-0, Pub. by Tor Bks) St Martin.

— Conan the Free Lance. 1990. pap. 3.95 (0-8125-0690-1, Pub. by Tor Bks) St Martin.

— Conan the Indomitable. 1989. pap. 7.95 (0-8125-0295-7) Tor Bks.

— Conan the Indomitable. 1990. pap. 3.95 (0-8125-0860-2, Pub. by Tor Bks) St Martin.

— The Digital Effect. 272p. 1997. mass mkt. 5.99 (0-441-00439-3) Ace Bks.

— The Forever Drug. 304p. (Orig.). 1995. mass mkt. 5.50 (0-441-00142-4) Ace Bks.

— Leonard Nimoy's Primortals: Target Earth. 304p. 1998. mass mkt. 6.50 (0-446-60510-7, Pub. by Warner Bks) Little.

— Machiavelli Interface. (Matador Trilogy Ser.: No. 3). 208p. 1986. mass mkt. 4.99 (0-441-51356-5) Ace Bks.

— Man Who Never Missed. (Matador Trilogy Ser.: No. 1). 1986. mass mkt. 4.99 (0-441-51918-0) Ace Bks.

— Men in Black. 240p. 1997. mass mkt. 5.99 (0-553-57756-5) Bantam.

— Shadows of the Empire. (Star Wars Ser.). 1996. 22.95 (0-614-96771-6); 22.95 (0-614-96941-7) Bantam.

— Shadows of the Empire. (Star Wars Ser.). 416p. (YA). (gr. 5 up). 1997. mass mkt. 5.99 (0-553-57413-2, Spectra) Bantam.

— Shadows of the Empire. (Star Wars Ser.). 1997. mass mkt. 5.99 (0-614-27717-5) Bantam.

***Perry, Steve.** Shadows of the Empire. (Star Wars Ser.). (Illus.). 2000. pap. 14.95 (1-56971-441-X) Dark Horse Comics.

Perry, Steve. Shadows of the Empire. LC 95-34660. (Star Wars Ser.). 1996. 11.09 (0-606-11895-0, Pub. by Turtleback) Demco.

— Spindoc. 272p. (Orig.). 1994. mass mkt. 5.50 (0-441-00008-8) Ace Bks.

— Stellar Ranger. 224p. (Orig.). 1994. mass mkt. 4.99 (0-380-77301-5, Avon Bks) Morrow Avon.

— Time Cop. 208p. (Orig.). 1994. mass mkt. 4.99 (0-425-14652-9) Berkley Pub.

— Trinity Vector. 1996. mass mkt. 5.99 (0-441-00350-8) Ace Bks.

Perry, Steve, ed. Another Dimension: The Big Book. (Illus.). 16p. (Orig.). 1994. pap. 12.95 (0-9640954-4-0, 2136691022) TFCP.

***Perry, Steve & Perry, Dal.** Titan A. E. 240p. 2000. mass mkt. 5.99 (0-441-00736-8) Ace Bks.

Perry, Steve & Perry, Lora. Boating Fiascos: Adventures in Yachting. 232p. 1989. pap. 12.95 (0-9624131-0-0) Robinhood Pub Co.

***Perry, Steve & Solomon, Ed.** Men in Black. large type ed. (G. K. Hall Science Fiction Ser.). 2000. 25.95 (0-7838-8986-0, G K Hall Lrg Type) Mac Lib Ref.

Perry, Steve, ed. see Twenty-First Century Publishing Staff.

Perry, Steve F., et al, eds. Fish Respiration. (Fish Physiology Ser.: Vol. 17). (Illus.). 356p. (C). 1998. boxed set. write for info. (0-12-350441-4) Acad Pr.

Perry, Stewart E. Building a Model Black Community: The Roxbury Action Program. 100p. 1978. pap. text 17.95 (0-87855-773-3) Transaction Pubs.

— Communities on the Way: Rebuilding Local Economies in the United States & Canada. LC 86-30069. 254p. (C). 1987. pap. text 21.95 (0-88706-525-2) State U NY Pr.

Perry, Stewart E. & Russell, Raymond. Collecting Garbage: Dirty Work, Clean Jobs, Proud People. LC 97-23173. 1997. pap. write for info. (0-7658-0410-7) Transaction Pubs.

Perry, Stuart. Las Vegas Blackjack Diary. 3rd rev. ed. LC 96-72324. 214p. 1997. pap. 19.95 (1-886070-08-3) ConJelCo.

Perry-Sumwalt, Jo, jt. auth. see Sumwalt, John.

Perry, Susan. The Body Bandits. (Umbrella Bks.). (Illus.). 32p. (J). (gr. 2-6). 1993. lib. bdg. 21.36 (0-89565-875-5) Childs World.

— A Cold Is Nothing to Sneeze At. (Umbrella Bks.). (Illus.). 32p. (J). (gr. 2-6). 1993. lib. bdg. 21.36 (0-89565-819-4) Childs World.

— Getting In Step. (Umbrella Bks.). (Illus.). 32p. (J). (gr. 2-6). 1993. lib. bdg. 21.36 (0-89565-872-0) Childs World.

— How Are You Feeling Today? (Umbrella Bks.). (Illus.). 32p. (J). (gr. 2-6). 1993. lib. bdg. 21.36 (0-89565-876-3) Childs World.

P

An Asterisk (*) at the beginning of an entry indicates that the title is appearing for the first time.

Perry, Susan & O'Hanlan, Katherine A. Natural Menopause: The Complete Guide to a Woman's Most Misunderstood Passage. (Illus.). 224p. 1993. pap. 10.95 (*0-201-62477-X*) Addison-Wesley.

Perry, Susan & O'Hanlon, Katherine. Natural Menopause: The Complete Guide. 2nd rev. ed. Broll, James, ed. 272p. 1997. pap. 15.00 (*0-201-47987-7*) Addison-Wesley.

Perry, Susan, jt. auth. see Ross, Joel E.

Perry, Susan, ed. see Brennan, Ed & Weng, Larry.

***Perry, Susan K.** Catch the Spirit: Teen Volunteers Tell How They Made a Difference. (Illus.). (YA). 2000. 33.00 (*0-531-11883-5*); pap. write for info. (*0-531-16499-3*) Watts.

Perry, Susan K. Playing Smart: A Parent's Guide to Enriching, Offbeat Learning Activities for Ages 4-14. Espeland, Pamela, ed. LC 90-40224. (Illus.). 224p. (Orig.). 1990. pap. 14.95 (*0-915793-22-9*) Free Spirit Pub.

— Writing in Flow: Keys to Enhanced Creativity. LC 99-19820. 272p. 1999. 19.99 (*0-89879-929-5*, 10622, Wrtrs Digest Bks) F & W Pubns Inc.

Perry, Susan K. & Chesman, Andrea. Fun Time, Family Time: More Than 700 Activities, Adventures, Recipes & Rituals to Help Bring Parents & Children Closer Together. LC 96-9262. (Illus.). 224p. (Orig.). 1996. pap. 14.00 (*0-380-78772-5*, Avon Bks) Morrow Avon.

Perry, Susan K., jt. auth. see Herman, Barry.

Perry, Susanna M. Test Yourself Abnormal Psychology. LC 98-23395. (Test Yourself Ser.). (Illus.). 192p. 1997. pap. 14.95 (*0-8442-2384-0*, 23840) NTC Contemp Pub Co.

Perry, T. A. Wisdom Literature & the Structure of Proverbs. LC 92-33650. 160p. 1993. 35.00 (*0-271-00929-2*) Pa St U Pr.

Perry, T. A., tr. Dialogues with Kohelet: The Book of Ecclesiastes, Translation & Commentary. LC 92-16256. 256p. (C). 1993. 32.00 (*0-271-00882-2*) Pa St U Pr.

Perry, T. Anthony, ed. Proverbios Morales de Santob de Carrion. (Spanish Ser.: No. 21). (SPA.). xiii, 233p. 1986. 17.00 (*0-942260-63-5*) Hispanic Seminary.

Perry, T. Anthony, et al, eds. Estudios Literarios en Honor de Gustavo Correa. (SPA.). 229p. 25.00 (*0-916379-14-0*) Scripta.

Perry, T. M. Music Lessons for Children with Special Needs. 140p. 1995. pap. 19.95 (*1-85302-295-0*) Taylor & Francis.

***Perry, Ted.** My Reel Story. 2001. 26.00 (*1-58465-076-1*) U Pr of New Eng.

Perry, Ted, ed. Performing Arts Resources, Vol. 3. 175p. 1976. 25.00 (*0-910482-84-5*) Theatre Lib.

Perry, Ted, ed. see Bowser, et al.

Perry, Theodore, jt. auth. see Parkhill, Joe M.

Perry, Theresa, ed. Teaching Malcolm X: Popular Culture & Literacy. 256p. (C). (gr. 13). 1995. pap. 19.99 (*0-415-91155-9*, B4929) Routledge.

Perry, Theresa & Delpit, Lisa, eds. The Real Ebonics Debate: Power, Language, & the Education of African-American Children. LC 97-46828. 192p. 1998. pap. 14.00 (*0-8070-3145-3*) Beacon Pr.

Perry, Theresa & Fraser, James W., eds. Freedom's Plow: Teaching in the Multicultural Classroom. LC 92-29648. 352p. (C). (gr. 13). 1993. pap. 20.99 (*0-415-90700-4*, A9790) Routledge.

***Perry, Thomas.** Blood Money: A Novel of Suspense. LC 99-18340. 352p. 1999. 24.95 (*0-679-45304-0*) Random.

Perry, Thomas. Dance for the Dead. 1997. mass mkt. 6.99 (*0-8041-1425-0*) Ivy Books.

— Dance for the Dead. large type ed. LC 96-2991. 416p. 1996. lib. bdg. 24.95 (*1-57490-065-X*, Beeler LP Bks) T T Beeler.

— Dance for the Dead. large type ed. 608p. 1997. 34.50 (*0-7089-8938-1*) Ulverscroft.

***Perry, Thomas.** Death Benefits. 2001. 24.95 (*0-679-45305-9*) Random.

Perry, Thomas. The Face-Changers. LC 98-96637. (Jane Whitefield Novels Ser.). 421p. 1999. mass mkt. 6.99 (*0-8041-1540-0*) Ivy Books.

— The Face-Changers. large type ed. LC 98-33601. 742p. 1998. 30.00 (*0-7862-1611-5*, G K Hall Lrg Type) Mac Lib Ref.

— Shadow Woman. (Jane Whitfield Novel Ser.). 416p. 1998. mass mkt. 6.99 (*0-8041-1539-7*) Ivy Books.

***Perry, Thomas.** Shadow Woman. large type ed. 480p. 1999. 31.99 (*0-7089-9098-3*) Ulverscroft.

— Shadow Woman. large type ed. LC 97-32442. (Large Print Book Ser.). 1997. 23.95 (*1-56895-513-8*) Wheeler Pub.

Perry, Thomas. Sleeping Dogs: A Novel of Suspense. 1993. mass mkt. 5.99 (*0-8041-1160-X*) Ivy Books.

— Vanishing Act. 1996. mass mkt. 5.99 (*0-8041-1387-4*) Ivy Books.

— Vanishing Act. large type ed. LC 95-17067. (Large Print Bks.). 1995. pap. 21.95 (*1-56895-234-1*) Wheeler Pub.

Perry, Thomas A. From These Roots & Other Poems. LC 96-68830. 39p. (Orig.). 1996. pap. 11.95 (*1-57197-027-4*) Pentland Pr.

Perry, Thomas A., ed. Evidence & Argumentation in Linguistics. (Grundlagen der Kommunikation Ser.). (C). 1979. 108.50 (*3-11-007272-6*) De Gruyter.

Perry, Thomas D. Professional Philosophy. 256p. 1985. pap. text 61.50 (*90-277-2072-X*, D Reidel); lib. bdg. 107.50 (*90-277-2071-1*, D Reidel) Kluwer Academic.

Perry, Thomas K. Textile League Baseball: South Carolina's Mill Teams, 1880-1955. LC 92-56680. (Illus.). 327p. 1993. lib. bdg. 29.95 (*0-89950-875-8*) McFarland & Co.

Perry, Thomas K., jt. auth. see Kirkpatrick, Mac C.

Perry, Thomas L., ed. Peacemaking in the 1990s: A Guide for Canadians. (Illus.). 312p. (Orig.). 1991. pap. 14.95 (*0-919574-93-9*) Gordon Soules Bk.

Perry, Thomas L. & Foulks, James G., eds. End the Arms Race : Fund Human Needs: Proceedings of the 1986 Vancouver Centennial Peace & Disarmament Symposium. 240p. 1986. 14.95 (*0-919574-96-3*) Gordon Soules Bk.

Perry, Thomas S. English Literature in the Eighteenth Century. LC 70-39124. (Essay Index Reprint Ser.). 1977. reprint ed. 26.95 (*0-8369-2712-5*) Ayer.

— English Literature of the Eighteenth Century. (Notable American Authors Ser.). 1999. reprint ed. lib. bdg. 125.00 (*0-7812-8740-5*) Rprt Serv.

— The Evolution of a Snob. (Notable American Authors Ser.). 1999. reprint ed. lib. bdg. 125.00 (*0-7812-8742-1*) Rprt Serv.

— From Opitz to Lessing. (Notable American Authors Ser.). 1999. reprint ed. lib. bdg. 125.00 (*0-7812-8741-3*) Rprt Serv.

— History of Greek Literature. (Notable American Authors Ser.). 1999. reprint ed. lib. bdg. 125.00 (*0-7812-8743-X*) Rprt Serv.

— The Life & Letters of Francis Lieber. (Notable American Authors Ser.). 1999. reprint ed. lib. bdg. 125.00 (*0-7812-8739-1*) Rprt Serv.

— Selections from the Letters of Thomas Sergeant Perry. (American Biography Ser.). 255p. 1991. reprint ed. lib. bdg. 69.00 (*0-7812-8312-4*) Rprt Serv.

— Selections from the Letters of Thomas Sergeant Perry. (BCL1-PS American Literature Ser.). 255p. 1992. reprint ed. lib. bdg. 79.00 (*0-7812-6830-3*) Rprt Serv.

— Selections from the Letters of Thomas Sergeant Perry. Robinson, Edwin Arlington, ed. LC 78-131797. 1971. reprint ed. 25.00 (*0-403-00684-8*) Scholarly.

Perry, Thomas W. Public Opinion, Propaganda & Politics in Eighteenth Century England: A Study of the Jew Bill of 1753. LC 62-17222. (Historical Monographs: No. 51). (Illus.). 215p. 1962. 20.00 (*0-674-72400-3*) HUP.

Perry, Tilden W. Animal Life Cycle Feeding & Nutrition. (Animal Feeding & Nutrition Ser.). 1984. text 79.00 (*0-12-552060-3*) Acad Pr.

Perry, Tilden W. & Cecava, Michael, eds. Beef Cattle Feeding & Nutrition. 2nd ed. (Animal Feeding & Nutrition Ser.). (Illus.). 389p. 1995. text 79.00 (*0-12-552052-2*) Acad Pr.

Perry, Tim. Basic Patrol Procedures. 2nd rev. ed. LC 98-219275. 215p. 1998. pap. text 22.95 (*1-879215-36-5*) Sheffield WI.

Perry, Timothy A. The Practical Mock Scene Manual. 60p. 1986. student ed. 59.95 (*0-915837-02-1*) T Perry.

Perry, Todd. Kevin Costner. LC 91-77802. 256p. 1991. 20.00 (*1-870049-34-9*) Oliver Bks.

Perry-Trauthig, Howard, tr. see Klaiber, Walter.

Perry-Trauthig, Howard F. Story und Ethik: Eine Untersuchung Aus Christlich-Theologischer Perspektive. (Europaische Hochschulschriften Ser.: Reihe 23, Bd. 580). (GER.). xvi, 333p. 1997. 57.95 (*3-631-49621-4*) P Lang Pubng.

Perry, V. G., ed. see Society of Nematologists Staff.

Perry, V. Hugh. Macrophages & the Nervous System. (Molecular Biology Intelligence Unit Ser.). 118p. 1994. 99.00 (*1-57059-044-3*, LN9044); 99.00 (*1-57059-173-3*) Landes Bioscience.

Perry, Victor. Stolen Art. (Illus.). 80p. 1999. pap. text 12.95 (*965-229-187-0*, Pub. by Gefen Pub Hse) Gefen Bks.

Perry, Victoria. Built for a Better Future: The Brynmawr Rubber Factory. (Illus.). 96p. 1995. pap. 25.00 (*1-873487-04-5*, Pub. by White Cockade) Paul & Co Pubs.

Perry, Vincent J., intro. Ken Keeley: Is It Real? (Illus.). 68p. (Orig.). 1993. write for info. (*1-883269-03-2*); pap. write for info. (*1-883269-04-0*) Sunstorm Arts.

Perry, W. Brian. Irish Ice. LC 99-62359. 288p. 2000. pap. 15.95 (*0-88739-272-5*) Creat Arts Bk.

Perry, W. J. Gods & Men: The Attainment of Immortality. 86p. 1996. reprint ed. spiral bd. 9.00 (*1-885395-83-3*) Book Tree.

Perry, W. J., Jr., jt. ed. see Schmidt, C. J.

Perry, Walter. The Open University. 320p. 1988. pap. 19.99 (*0-335-15828-5*) OpUniv Pr.

— The Open University. LC 76-55917. (Illus.). 316p. reprint ed. pap. 98.00 (*0-8357-4693-3*, 205234800008) Bks Demand.

***Perry, Walter, et al.** The Future of Warfare: Issues from the 1999 Army after Next Study Cycle. LC 00-38717. (Illus.). 2000. pap. write for info. (*0-8330-2824-3*) Rand Corp.

Perry, Walter, et al. Issues Raised During the 1998 Army after Next Spring Wargame. LC 98-52861. (Illus.). 106p. 1999. pap. text 15.00 (*0-8330-2688-7*, MR-1023-A) Rand Corp.

Perry, Walter J. Walt Perry: An Early-Day Forest Ranger in New Mexico & Oregon. Joslin, Les, ed. LC 99-70812. (Illus.). 208p. 1999. pap. 15.95 (*0-9647167-2-0*, Pub. by Wilderness Assocs) Maverick Dist.

Perry, Walter L. & Millot, Marc D. Issues from the 1997 Army after Next Winter Wargames. LC 98-27334. (Illus.). 70p. 1998. pap. 15.00 (*0-8330-2636-4*, MR-988-A) Rand Corp.

***Perry, Warren R.** Landscape Transformation & the Archaeology of Impact: Disruption & State Formation in Southern Africa. LC 99-37714. 182p. 1999. 62.00 (*0-306-45955-8*, Kluwer Plenum) Kluwer Academic.

***Perry, Wendell.** Mars/Venus Affair: Astrology's Sexiest Planets. LC 99-54273. (Illus.). 480p. 2000. pap. 17.95 (*1-56718-517-7*) Llewellyn Pubns.

Perry, Whitall N. Challenges of a Secular Society. 240p. (C). 2000. pap. 13.95 (*0-9629984-3-5*, Pub. by Foun Trad Studies) Kazi Pubns.

— A Treasury of Traditional Wisdom, Vol. 1. 111p. 1991. pap. 18.95 (*1-870196-08-2*, Pub. by Islamic Texts) Intl Spec Bk.

— The Widening Breach: Evolutionism in the Mirror of Cosmology. (Illus.). 111p. (Orig.). 1995. pap. 9.95 (*1-870196-13-9*, Pub. by Islamic Texts) Intl Spec Bk.

— The Widening Breach: Evolutionism in the Mirror of Cosmology. 110p. (Orig.). 1996. pap. 9.95 (*0-614-21613-3*, 1403) Kazi Pubns.

Perry, Wilhelmina. Sociology of Minority Groups Courses: Syllabi & Related Materials. 145p. 1981. 9.50 (*0-317-36345-X*) Am Sociological.

Perry, Williaim. West Wind Properties: Problem Solving Using Computer Applications. 1997. pap. 24.95 (*0-538-71727-0*) Sth-Wstrn College.

Perry, William. How to Develop Competency-Based Vocational Education. LC 82-80093. (Illus.). 180p. 1982. pap. 8.95 (*0-911168-48-6*) Prakken.

— The Revolution in Military Affairs: Peace or War in the 21st Century. (New Ser.: Vol. 14). 30p. 1997. pap. 15.00 (*0-86682-105-8*) Ctr Intl Relations.

Perry, William. A Standard for Testing Application Software. 1997. ring bd. 190.00 (*0-7913-0975-4*) Warren Gorham & Lamont.

— Year 2000 Software Testing. 432p. 1998. 49.99 (*0-471-31428-5*) Wiley.

Perry, William & Bailey, Norman A. Venezuela, 1994: Challenges for the Caldera Administration. LC 94-44043. (CSIS Panel Reports). 24p. (C). 1994. pap. 10.95 (*0-89206-310-6*) CSIS.

Perry, William E. Effective Methods for Software Testing. 1997. 55.00 (*0-614-29665-X*) Quality Assurance.

— Effective Methods for Software Testing. 3rd ed. LC 95-16910. 560p. 1995. 69.99 (*0-471-06097-6*) Wiley.

— Hatching the EDP Quality Assurance Function. 2nd ed. (Illus.). 104p. 1986. pap. 24.95 (*0-318-20490-8*) Quality Assurance.

— Managing Systems Maintenance. LC 81-51630. (Illus.). 382p. reprint ed. pap. 118.50 (*0-8357-8573-4*, 203493900091) Bks Demand.

— Orchestrating Your Career. 1997. 10.00 (*0-614-29666-8*) Quality Assurance.

— Quality Assurance for Information Systems: Methods, Tools & Techniques. 848p. 1993. 84.99 (*0-471-58804-0*, GD3470) Wiley.

— Quality Assurance System Development Reviews. (Illus.). 1981. pap. 24.95 (*0-318-20493-2*) Quality Assurance.

— Report Writing for Quality Assurance Analysts. (Illus.). 1981. pap. 24.95 (*0-318-20494-0*) Quality Assurance.

— Standards for Auditing Computer Applications. 2nd ed. 1990. ring bd., suppl. ed. 182.00 (*0-87769-288-2*) Warren Gorham & Lamont.

— Standards for Auditing Computer Applications, No. 1. 2nd ed. 1991. suppl. ed. 49.00 (*0-685-45022-8*) Warren Gorham & Lamont.

— Standards for Auditing Computer Applications, No. 2. 2nd ed. 1991. suppl. ed. 54.00 (*0-685-45023-6*) Warren Gorham & Lamont.

Perry, William E. & Birenbaum, Eric, eds. EDP Auditing. 1992. ring bd. 464.00 (*0-87769-268-8*) Warren Gorham & Lamont.

Perry, William E. & Kuong, Javier F. Developing & Implementing an Integrated Test Facility for Testing Computerized Systems. 1979. 40.00 (*0-940706-09-1*, MAP-12) Management Advisory Pubns.

— EDP Risk Analysis & Controls Justification. 1981. 50.00 (*0-940706-10-5*) Management Advisory Pubns.

— Generalized Computer Audit Software-Selection & Application. 1980. 40.00 (*0-940706-15-6*, MAP-14) Management Advisory Pubns.

— How to Test Internal Control & Integrity in Computerized Systems. 1980. 40.00 (*0-940706-13-X*, MAP-15) Management Advisory Pubns.

Perry, William E. & Rice, Randall W. Surviving the Top Ten Challenges of Software Testing: A People-Oriented Approach. LC 97-44565. 216p. 1997. pap. 27.95 (*0-932633-38-2*) Dorset Hse Pub Co.

Perry, William G., Jr. Forms of Intellectual & Ethical Development in the College Years: A Scheme. LC 98-33543. (Education Ser.). 304p. 1998. reprint ed. pap. 24.95 (*0-7879-4118-2*) Jossey-Bass.

— Learn to Love to Learn. 300p. (YA). (gr. 8-12). Date not set. pap. write for info. (*1-887946-01-2*) Comp Age Educ.

Perry, William J. Children of the Sun: A Study in the Early History of Civilization. 551p. 1968. reprint ed. 59.00 (*0-403-00065-3*) Scholarly.

— The Megalithic Culture of Indonesia. LC 77-86999. (Manchester, University. Publications. Ethnological Ser.: No. 3). reprint ed. 32.50 (*0-404-16773-X*) AMS Pr.

— Proliferation: Threat & Response. (Illus.). 63p. 1997. pap. text 25.00 (*0-7881-4219-4*) DIANE Pub.

Perry, William J., jt. auth. see Carnegie Commission on Science, Technology, & Gove.

Perry, William J., jt. auth. see Carter, Ashton B.

Perry, William S. Historical Collections Relating to the American Colonial Church, 5 pts. in 4 vols. LC 75-99948. reprint ed. 375.00 (*0-404-05070-0*) AMS Pr.

Perry, William T., jt. ed. see Eckley, H. J.

Perry, William W. & Dreher, Jacob. Monitorial Instructions for the Use of Symbolic Lodges of Free & Accepted Masons (1915) 192p. 1998. reprint ed. pap. 17.95 (*0-7661-0709-4*) Kessinger Pub.

Perry, Williams & Wehner, Peter, eds. The Latin American Policies of U. S. Allies: Balancing Global Interests & Regional Concerns. LC 85-12259. 206p. 1985. 57.95 (*0-275-90220-X*, C0220, Praeger Pubs) Greenwood.

Perry, Wilma, jt. auth. see Perry, Earl.

Perry, Yvonne N. The Other Side of the Island: Stories. LC 93-45278. (Illus.). 112p. (Orig.). 1994. pap. 10.00 (*1-880284-06-5*) J Daniel.

Perryman, Anne D. & Thompson, Patricia J., eds. The Mayakovsky Centennial, 1893-1993: A Commemoration of the Life, Work, & Times of Vladimir Mayakovsky: Proceedings of a Symposium. 196p. (C). Date not set. write for info. (*0-9640564-0-2*) Lehman College.

***Perryman, Bob L., frwd.** The Narrow Way. 89p. 1999. pap. 7.49 (*0-9679090-0-7*) Lghthse Bapt.

Perryman, Ellen M., jt. auth. see Blank, Rolf.

Perryman, Eunice & Waddell, Pam. Simply His: A Missionary Story of Love, Commitment, & a Willing Heart. Nelson, Becky, ed. 144p. 1996. pap. text 9.95 (*1-56309-172-0*, W964120) Womans Mission Union.

Perryman, F. J. How to Resist the Devil. 48p. pap. 1.50 (*0-686-29122-0*) Faith Pub Hse.

Perryman, J. Smoke-Fired Pottery. (Illus.). 176p. 1995. text. write for info. (*976-641-037-2*) Gordon & Breach.

Perryman, Jane. Smoke Fired Pottery. (Illus.). 128p. 1995. reprint ed. 39.95 (*0-9650786-7-1*) Gentle Br.

***Perryman, Jane.** Traditional Pottery of India. 192p. 2000. 64.95 (*0-7136-4521-0*, Pub. by A & C Blk) Midpt Trade.

Perryman, M. Ray. The Measurement of Monetary Policy. 1983. lib. bdg. 73.50 (*0-89838-117-7*) Kluwer Academic.

— Regional Econometric. 1987. lib. bdg. 115.50 (*0-89838-216-5*) Kluwer Academic.

Perryman, Mark. The Blair Agenda. LC 97-129991. (C). 1996. pap. 18.50 (*0-85315-843-6*, Pub. by Lawrence & Wishart) NYU Pr.

***Perryman, Mark.** Philosophy Football: Eleven Great Thinks Play It Deep. 144p. 1998. pap. 13.95 (*0-14-026843-X*, Pub. by Pnguin Bks Ltd) Trafalgar.

Perryman, Mark, ed. Altered States: Postmodernism, Politics, Culture. 192p. (C). 1994. pap. 25.00 (*0-85315-793-6*, Pub. by Lawrence & Wishart) NYU Pr.

Perryman, Mark, jt. ed. see Coddington, Anne.

Perryman, Michael A., jt. auth. see Sinnott, Roger W.

Perryman, Wayne. 1993 Trail on the Curse of Ham. 1995. pap. 6.99 (*1-56229-423-7*) Pneuma Life Pub.

Perryman, Wayne R. & Wilkas, Lenore R. International Subscription Agents: An Annotated Directory. 5th ed. LC 85-26830. 142p. 1986. reprint ed. pap. 44.10 (*0-7837-9686-2*, 206041600005) Bks Demand.

Pers, Jessica S. Government As Parent: Administering Foster Care in California. LC 76-25050. 136p. reprint ed. pap. 42.20 (*0-608-20129-4*, 207140100011) Bks Demand.

Pers, Mona. Willa Cather's Swedes: The Literary Significance of Swedish Immigrants. (Illus.). 118p. (Orig.). 1995. pap. 52.50 (*91-88834-00-X*) Coronet Bks.

Persac, A. Plantations on the Mississippi River: From Natchez to New Orleans. 1931. 26.00 (*0-911116-26-5*) Pelican.

***Persadsingh, Neil.** Acne in Black Women. (Illus.). 64p. 1999. pap. 10.00 (*976-8138-86-6*) N Persadsingh.

Persak, James. Savage Trail. 1985. mass mkt. 2.25 (*0-8217-1594-1*, Zebra Kensgtn) Kensgtn Pub Corp.

Persall, Holli C. The Magic Corn. (Illus.). 24p. (J). (gr. k-4). 1990. 10.95 (*0-9628486-0-3*) Rhyme Time.

Persall, Kathy, jt. auth. see Thoms, Ray.

***Persaran, Mohammad.** Energy Demand in Asian Developing Economies. 256p. 1999. text 70.00 (*0-19-730020-0*) OUP.

Persaud, Arabella. Domine el Espanol: Ejercicios Sencillos & Practicos. (SPA.). 248p. (C). 1996. per. 24.95 (*0-7872-2226-7*) Kendall-Hunt.

Persaud, Bishnodat, jt. ed. see Cable, Vincent.

***Persaud, Lakshmi.** Butterfly in the Wind. 208p. 1999. reprint ed. pap. (*0-948833-36-X*, Pub. by Peepal Tree Pr) Paul & Co Pubs.

— For the Love of My Name. 324p. 2000. pap. 18.95 (*1-900715-42-2*, Pub. by Peepal Tree Pr) Paul & Co Pubs.

— Sastra. 273p. 1999. reprint ed. pap. (*0-948833-71-8*, Pub. by Peepal Tree Pr) Paul & Co Pubs.

Persaud, Rajen. Making It Through College: The Multicultural Guide for Success & Surviving the Real Deal. 182p. (Orig.). (YA). (gr. 9-12). 1995. pap. 7.95 (*0-9642713-8-9*) D & R Pub CA.

— Making It Through College: Your Passport to the Information Age. rev. ed. LC 96-86248. (Illus.). 290p. 1996. pap. 19.95 (*0-9642713-6-2*) D & R Pub CA.

***Persaud, Rajen.** Staying Sane: How to Make Your Mind Work for You. 478p. 1999. pap. 19.95 (*1-900512-38-6*, Pub. by Metro Bks) Trafalgar.

***Persaud, Randolph B.** Hegemony & Foreign Policy: The Dialectics of Marginalized & Global Forces in Jamaica. (C). 2001. pap. text 22.95 (*0-7914-4920-3*) State U NY Pr.

— Hegemony & Foreign Policy: The Dialectics of Marginalized & Global Forces in Jamaica. (C). 2001. text 68.50 (*0-7914-4919-X*) State U NY Pr.

Persaud, S. Canada Geese & Apple Chutney. LC 99-203007. 159p. 1998. pap. 15.95 (*0-920661-72-6*) TSAR Pubns.

Persaud, Sasenarine. A Surf of Sparrows' Songs. LC 97-156778. 104p. 1997. pap. 11.95 (*0-920661-60-2*, Pub. by TSAR Pubns) LPC InBook.

***Persaud, Sasenarine.** The Wintering Kundalini. 72p. 1999. pap. (*0-948833-79-3*, Pub. by Peepal Tree Pr) Paul & Co Pubs.

Persaud, Sharda, jt. auth. see Giordano, Francesco.

Persaud, T. V. A History of Anatomy: The Post-Vesalian Era. LC 97-3002. (Illus.). 372p. 1997. text 92.95 (*0-398-06772-4*); pap. text 75.95 (*0-398-06773-2*) C C Thomas.

Persaud, T. V., jt. auth. see Moore, Keith L.

Persaud, Tara. O. J. Simpson Murder Case: The Story of the Mystery Woman. LC 97-147716. 168p. 1997. pap. 10.99 (*1-56043-280-2*, Treasure Hse) Destiny Image.

P

Persaud, Thakoor. Conflicts Between Multinational Corporations & Less Developed Countries: The Case of Bauxite Mining in the Caribbean with Special Reference to Guyana. Bruchey, Stuart, ed. LC 80-587. (Multinational Corporations Ser.). 1981. lib. bdg. 31.95 (*0-405-13378-2*) Ayer.

Persaud, Winston D. The Theology of the Cross & Marx's Anthropology: A View from the Caribbean. LC 90-40423. (American University Studies: Theology & Religion: Ser. VII, Vol. 84). XI, 298p. (C). 1991. text 48.95 (*0-8204-1409-3*) P Lang Pubng.

Perschbacher, Peter W., et al, eds. Recirculation - Aeration: Bibliography for Aquaculture. 78p. (Orig.). (C). 1995. pap. text 30.00 (*0-7881-2394-7*) DIANE Pub.

Perschbacher, Rex R., et al. Cases & Materials on Civil Procedure. 1987. teacher ed. write for info. (*0-8205-0032-1*); write for info. (*0-8205-0035-6*) Bender.

— Cases & Materials on Civil Procedure. 1990. suppl. ed. write for info. (*0-8205-0034-8*) Bender.

Perschbacher, Rex R., jt. auth. see Berger, Moise E.

Perschbacher, Rex R., jt. auth. see Oakley, John.

Perschbacher, Rex R., jt. auth. see Wydick, Richard C.

Perschbacher, Rex R., ed. see Schwartz, Mortimer D.

Perschbacher, Rex R., ed. see Schwartz, Mortimer D. & Wydick, Richard C.

Perschbacher, Rex R., ed. see Wydick, Richard C.

Perschbacher, Ruth. Assessment: The Cornerstone of Activity Programs. LC 93-85327. 145p. (C). 1993. pap. 24.95 (*0-910251-62-2*) Venture Pub PA.

Perschbacher, Wesley J., ed. The New Analytical Greek Lexicon. LC 90-23777. 450p. 1990. 29.95 (*0-943575-33-8*) Hendrickson MA.

Perschuk, Louis P. & Lee, Sin H., eds. Localization of Putative Steroid Receptors, 2 vols., Vol. II: Clinically Oriented Studies. 184p. 1985. 106.00 (*0-8493-6049-8*, CRC Reprint) Franklin.

Perschy, Mary K. Helping Teens Work Through Grief. LC 96-48297. 150p. 1997. pap. write for info. (*1-56032-558-5*) Hemisp Pub.

***Perse, Elizabeth.** Media Effects & Society. (A Volume in LEA's Communication Series). 320p. 2000. write for info. (*0-8058-2505-3*); pap. write for info. (*0-8058-2506-1*) L Erlbaum Assocs.

Perse, Elizabeth, jt. auth. see Courtright, John.

Perse, Elizabeth M., jt. auth. see Courtright, John A.

Perse, Saint-John, pseud. Amers & Oiseaux. (Poesie Ser.). (FRE.). 256p. 1970. 9.95 (*2-07-030248-2*) Schoenhof.

— Amers, Oiseaux, Poesie. (FRE.). 1970. pap. 12.95 (*0-8288-3873-9*, F123891) Fr & Eur.

— Chant pour une Equinoxe. (FRE.). 36p. 1976. pap. 16.95 (*0-7859-1344-0*, 2070293300) Fr & Eur.

— Eloges & Gloire des Rois, Anabase, Exil. (Poesie Ser.). (FRE.). pap. 11.95 (*2-07-030246-6*) Schoenhof.

— Eloges, la Gloire des Rois, Anabase, Exil. (FRE.). 1966. pap. 10.95 (*0-8288-3874-7*, F123880) Fr & Eur.

— Exil. 2nd ed. Little, Roger, ed. (Critical Editions Ser.). (FRE.). 124p. (C). 1995. pap. 12.50 (*0-485-12706-7*, Pub. by Athlone Pr) Humanities.

Perse, Saint-John, pseud. Oeuvre Poetique, 2 tomes, Tome II. (Coll. Soleil Ser.). 1960. 16.95 (*0-685-35911-5*) Schoenhof.

— Oeuvres Completes. (FRE.). 1987. lib. bdg. 110.00 (*0-7859-3818-4*) Fr & Eur.

— Oeuvres Completes. deluxe ed. (Pleiade Ser.). (FRE.). 1972p. 1982. 70.95 (*2-07-010736-1*) Schoenhof.

Perse, Saint-John, pseud. Oiseaux. pap. 10.50 (*0-685-36544-1*) Fr & Eur.

— Poesie. (FRE.). 16p. 1961. pap. 10.95 (*0-7859-1315-7*, 2070256790) Fr & Eur.

— Selected Poems. Caws, Mary A., ed. Eliot, T. S. et al, trs. from FRE. LC 82-8305. 160p. (Orig.). (C). 1982. pap. 10.95 (*0-8112-0855-9*, NDP547, Pub. by New Directions) Norton.

— Vent, Chronique, Chant pour un Equinoxe. (FRE.). 1968. pap. 10.95 (*0-8288-3825-9*, F123930) Fr & Eur.

— Vents Chroniques. (Poesie Ser.). (FRE.). pap. 6.95 (*2-07-030247-4*) Schoenhof.

Perseghetti, Jackie. Caution: Dangerous Devotions: An Exciting Journey Through the New Testament. LC 98-51341. 384p. 1995. pap. 10.99 (*0-7814-0250-6*, Lion) Chariot Victor.

— Caution: MORE Dangerous Devotions: Exploring the Nooks & Crannies of the Old Testament. LC 98-51341. 384p. 1999. pap. text 11.99 (*0-7814-3061-5*) Chariot Victor.

Persell, Caroline H. Quality, Careers & Training in Educational & Social Research. LC 76-9294. (Illus.). 321p. 1976. pap. text 22.95 (*0-930390-31-8*) Gen Hall.

Persell, Caroline H., jt. auth. see Cookson, Peter W., Jr.

Persell, Caroline H., jt. auth. see Maisel, Richard.

Persell, Stuart M. Neo-Lamarckism & the Evolution Controversy in France, 1870-1920. LC 98-48633. (Studies in French Civilization: Vol. 14). 300p. 1999. text 89.95 (*0-7734-8275-X*) E Mellen.

Persellin, Diane, jt. auth. see Kenney, Susan H.

Pershad, Guru, ed. see Aurobindo, Sri.

Pershan, P. S. Structure of Liquid Crystal Phases. (Lecture Notes in Physics Ser.: Vol. 23). 440p. 1988. text 93.00 (*9971-5-0668-8*); pap. text 55.00 (*9971-5-0705-6*) World Scientific Pub.

Pershing, Betty, jt. auth. see Hirschmann, Maria A.

Pershing, Diane. First Date: Honeymoon. (Yours Truly Ser.). 1997. per. 3.50 (*0-373-52040-9*, 1-520402) Silhouette.

***Pershing, Diane.** Una Noche Juntos. Vol. 224. (SPA.). 2000. per. 3.50 (*0-373-35354-5*) S&S Trade.

Pershing, Diane. Un Rendez-Vous Avec l'Amour. (Rouge Passion Ser.: Vol. 470). 1998. mass mkt. 3.50 (*0-373-37470-4*, 1-37470-1) Harlequin Bks.

— Third Date's the Charm. 1997. per. 3.50 (*0-373-52050-6*, 1-52050-1) Silhouette.

— The Tough Guy & the Toddler: Men in Blue. (Intimate Moments Ser.: No. 928). 1999. per. 4.25 (*0-373-07928-1*, 1-07928-4) Silhouette.

— While She Was Sleeping. rev. ed. (Intimate Moments Ser.). 1998. per. 4.25 (*0-373-07863-3*, 1-07863-3) Silhouette.

Pershing, John J. My Experiences in the First World War. (Illus.). 868p. 1995. reprint ed. pap. 19.95 (*0-306-80616-9*) Da Capo.

— My Experiences in the First World War. (Military Classics Ser.: Vol. 2). 472p. 1989. reprint ed. 24.95 (*0-8306-9407-2*) McGraw-Hill Prof.

***Pershing, Karen E.** Contemporary Mallet Duets. 36p. 1999. pap. 7.50 (*0-7390-0377-1*, 17322) Alfred Pub.

— Contemporary Mallet Duets. 1999. pap. 18.00 incl. audio compact disk (*0-7390-0378-X*, 17323) Alfred Pub.

— Mallet Duets for the Student & Teacher. 40p. 1999. pap. 7.95 (*0-7390-0531-6*, 17325) Alfred Pub.

Pershing, Karen E., ed. see Garris, Anne.

Pershing, Linda. The Ribbon Around the Pentagon: Peace by Piecemakers. LC 95-32486. (Publications of the American Folklore Society Ser.). (Illus.). 242p. 1996. pap. text 22.50 (*0-87049-923-8*); lib. bdg. 45.00 (*0-87049-922-X*) U of Tenn Pr.

— Sew to Speak: The Fabric Art of Mary Milne. LC 95-12151. (Folk Art & Artists Ser.). (Illus.). 72p. 1995. 32.50 (*0-87805-786-2*); pap. 16.95 (*0-87805-787-0*) U Pr of Miss.

Persia, A. Trent De, see DePersia, A. Trent.

Persia, Juan De, see De Persia, Juan.

Persic, Massimo & Salucci, Paolo, eds. Dark & Visible Matter in Galaxies: Proceedings of a Conference Held in Sesto Puseria, Italy, July 2-5, 1996. (ASP Conference Series Proceedings: Vol. 117). 597p. 1997. 34.00 (*1-886733-37-6*) Astron Soc Pacific.

Persic, Milena, jt. auth. see Jordan, Peter.

Persichetti, Vincent. Twentieth-Century Harmony. (Illus.). (C). 1961. 28.00 (*0-393-09539-8*) Norton.

Persico, Deborah A. Mapp vs. Ohio: Evidence & Search Warrants. LC 96-21295. (Landmark Supreme Court Cases Ser.). (Illus.). 128p. (YA). (gr. 6 up). 1997. lib. bdg. 20.95 (*0-89490-857-X*) Enslow Pubs.

— New Jersey vs. T. L. O. Drug Searches in Schools. LC 97-38667. (Landmark Supreme Court Cases Ser.). (Illus.). 128p. (YA). (gr. 6 up). 1998. lib. bdg. 20.95 (*0-89490-969-X*) Enslow Pubs.

— Vernonia School District vs. Acton: Drug Testing in Schools. LC 98-48872. (Landmark Supreme Court Cases Ser.). (Illus.). 128p. (YA). (gr. 7 up). 1999. lib. bdg. 20.95 (*0-7660-1087-2*) Enslow Pubs.

Persico, Enrico, ed. see Levi-Civita, Tullio.

Persico, John, Jr., ed. The TQM Transformation: A Model for Organizational Change. 224p. 1992. text 24.95 (*0-527-91654-4*, 916544) Productivity Inc.

Persico, John, Jr & Morris, Patricia R. The New Business Values for Success in the 21st Century: Improvement, Innovation, Inclusion, Incentives, Information. LC 96-51808. 312p. 1997. 49.95 (*0-7890-0155-1*); pap. 24.95 (*0-7890-0239-6*) Haworth Pr.

***Persico, Joseph E.** Nuremberg: Infamy on Trial. 2000. pap. 15.95 (*0-14-029815-0*) Penguin Putnam.

Persico, Joseph E. My Enemy, My Brother: Men & Days of Gettysburg. LC 95-45864. (Illus.). 288p. 1996. reprint ed. pap. 16.00 (*0-306-80692-4*) Da Capo.

Persico, Joseph E. Nuremberg: Infamy on Trial. 544p. 1995. pap. 15.95 (*0-14-016622-X*, Penguin Bks) Viking Penguin.

Persico, Joseph E., jt. auth. see Powell, Colin L.

Persico, V. Richard, Jr., jt. auth. see Platt, Larry A.

***Persidsky, Andre.** Director X. 5th ed. (Visual QuickStart Guides Ser.). 400p. 2000. pap. 19.99 (*0-201-70258-4*) Peachpit Pr.

Persidsky, Andre. Director 4 for Windows: Visual Quickstart. 1995. pap. text. write for info. (*0-201-88422-4*) Addison-Wesley.

— Director Seven for Macintosh & Windows: Visual QuickStart Guide. LC 99-236302. (Visual QuickStart Guides). 400p. (C). 1999. pap. text 19.99 (*0-201-35398-9*, Pub. by Peachpit Pr) Addison-Wesley.

— Director 6 for Macintosh: Visual QuickStart Guide. LC 97-210561. 264p. (C). 1997. pap. text 18.95 (*0-201-68895-6*) Peachpit Pr.

— Director 6 for Windows: Visual QuickStart Guide. LC 97-207491. 264p. (C). 1997. pap. text 18.95 (*0-201-68896-4*) Peachpit Pr.

Persidsky, Andre, jt. auth. see Kahn, Richard.

Persigout, Jean-Paul. Dictionnaire de Mythologie Celte Dieux et Heros. 2nd ed. (FRE.). 319p. 1990. pap. 55.00 (*0-7859-7879-8*, 2268009688) Fr & Eur.

— Dictionnaire de Mythologie Celtique. (FRE.). 1985. pap. 32.95 (*0-7859-7876-3*, 2268003507) Fr & Eur.

Persily. Reinventing the IDS. 1999. 55.00 (*0-07-134218-4*) McGraw.

Persily, Andrew K., jt. ed. see Modera, Mark P.

Persin. Beacon Handbook, 4 vols. 4th ed. LC 96-76947. (C). 1996. pap. text 15.96 (*0-395-77992-8*) HM.

Persin, Margaret H. Getting the Picture: The Ekphrastic Principle in Twentieth-Century Spanish Poetry. LC 96-44360. (Illus.). 256p. 1997. 39.50 (*0-8387-5335-3*) Bucknell U Pr.

— Recent Spanish Poetry & the Role of the Reader. LC 85-43247. 176p. 1987. 36.50 (*0-8387-5100-8*) Bucknell U Pr.

Persing, David H., ed. PCR Protocols for Emerging Infectious Diseases. 180p. 1996. spiral bd., suppl. ed. 39.95 (*1-55581-108-6*) ASM Pr.

Persing, David H., et al, eds. Diagnostic Molecular Microbiology: Principles & Applications. LC 92-38523. (Illus.). 700p. 1993. spiral bd. 79.95 (*1-55581-056-X*) ASM Pr.

Persing, Gary. Advanced Practitioner Respiratory Care Review: Written Registry & Clinical Simulation Exam. LC 93-20774. 1994. pap. text 43.00 (*0-7216-4963-7*, W B Saunders Co) Harcrt Hlth Sci Grp.

— Entry-Level Respiratory Care Review: Study Guide & Workbook. 2nd ed. Biello, Lisa, ed. (Illus.). 272p. 1995. pap. text, student ed., wbk. ed. 40.95 (*0-7216-6426-1*, W B Saunders Co) Harcrt Hlth Sci Grp.

***Persing, Gary.** Respiratory Care Exam Guide: Review for the Entry-Level & Advanced Exams. 3rd ed. (Illus.). 510p. 2000. pap. text. write for info. (*0-7216-8288-X*, W B Saunders Co) Harcrt Hlth Sci Grp.

Persing, Louisa, ed. Ever, Never & Sometimes: A Collection of Modern Poetry. (Illus.). 1978. 5.95 (*0-686-24291-2*) Palomar.

— Life Is a Moody Rainbow: A Collection of Modern Poetry. LC 72-87102. (Illus.). 130p. 1972. 5.50 (*0-686-01303-4*) Palomar.

— Shades & Shadows: An Anthology of Modern Poetry. (Illus.). 1973. 5.50 (*0-686-05276-5*) Palomar.

— Stepping Stones: A Collection of Modern Poetry. (Illus.). 1977. 5.95 (*0-686-20028-4*) Palomar.

— To Banbury Cross & Back: A Collection of Modern Poetry. (Illus.). 1976. 5.95 (*0-686-17956-0*) Palomar.

— Windfall: A Collection of Modern Poetry. 1975. 5.95 (*0-686-10961-9*) Palomar.

Persinger, Joseph. The Life of Jacob Persinger. 23p. 1983. pap. 4.95 (*0-87770-296-9*) Ye Galleon.

Persinger, Michael A. Neuropsychological Bases of God Beliefs. LC 87-14689. 175p. 1987. 59.95 (*0-275-92648-6*, C2648, Praeger Pubs) Greenwood.

— The Paranormal: Mechanisms & Models, Pt. 2. LC 74-19227. 195p. 1974. 30.50 (*0-8422-5211-8*); pap. text 12.95 (*0-8422-0476-8*) Irvington.

— The Paranormal: The Patterns, Pt. 1. LC 74-19227. 248p. (C). 1974. 29.50 (*0-8422-5212-6*); pap. text 13.95 (*0-8422-0477-6*) Irvington.

— Weather Matrix & Human Behavior. LC 80-18422. 327p. 1980. 65.00 (*0-275-90536-5*, C0536, Praeger Pubs) Greenwood.

Persinger, Michael A., et al. Tm & Cult Mania. 208p. 1980. 12.95 (*0-8158-0392-3*) Chris Mass.

Persinos, John F., ed. see Monea, Michael J.

Persius. Auli Persii Flacci Lexicon. Bo, Domenico, ed. xiii, 199p. 1967. write for info. (*0-318-71191-5*) G Olms Pubs.

— Index Verborum Quae in Saturis Auli Persi Flacci Reperiuntur. Berkowitz, Luci & Brunner, Theodore F., eds. xvi, 160p. 1967. write for info. (*0-318-71192-3*) G Olms Pubs.

Persius. Persius Flaccus, Aulus: Konkordanz zu den Satiren des Persius Flaccus. Fleury, P. et al, eds. (Alpha-Omega, Reihe A Ser.: Bd. XXXVI). 280p. 1978. write for info. (*3-487-06557-6*) G Olms Pubs.

Persius. Satirarum Liber. ccxvi, 418p. 1967. reprint ed. write for info. (*0-318-71193-1*) G Olms Pubs.

— The Satires of A. Persius Flaccus. Nettleship, H., ed. xxxix, 149p. 1987. reprint ed. 29.12 (*3-487-01781-4*) G Olms Pubs.

Persius. The Satires of Persius Flaccus. Connor, W. R. & Gildersleeve, Basil L., eds. LC 78-67138. (Latin Texts & Commentaries Ser.). (ENG & LAT.). 1979. reprint ed. lib. bdg. 19.95 (*0-405-11605-5*) Ayer.

Persius, jt. auth. see Jenkinson, J.

Persius, jt. auth. see Juvenal.

Perske, Martha. Perske Pencil Portraits, 1971-1990. LC 98-217952. 120p. 1998. 20.00 (*0-687-05080-4*) Abingdon.

Perske, Robert. Circles of Friends: People with Disabilities & Their Friends Enrich the Lives of One Another. LC 88-14616. (Illus.). 96p. 1988. pap. 12.95 (*0-687-08390-7*) Abingdon.

— Deadly Innocence. 128p. (Orig.). 1995. pap. 12.95 (*0-687-00615-5*) Abingdon.

— Don't Stop the Music. LC 86-17426. (YA). (gr. 12 up). 1986. pap. 11.95 (*0-687-11060-2*) Abingdon.

— Hope for the Families: New Directions for Parents of Persons with Retardation or Other Disabilities. LC 81-5700. (Illus.). 112p. (Orig.). 1981. pap. 5.98 (*0-687-17380-9*) Abingdon.

— New Life in the Neighborhood: How Persons with Retardation & Other Disabilities Can Help Make a Good Community Better. LC 80-15517. (Illus.). 80p. (Orig.). 1997. pap. 3.59 (*0-687-27800-7*) Abingdon.

— Show Me No Mercy: A Compelling Story of Remarkable Courage. LC 83-21384. 144p. (Orig.). (YA). (gr. 12 up). 1984. pap. 2.99 (*0-687-38435-4*) Abingdon.

— Unequal Justice. 1991. pap. 3.59 (*0-687-42983-8*) Abingdon.

Perski, J. & Witt, Ulrich. SMS: A Program Package for Simulation & Gaming of Stochastic Market Processes & Learning Behavior. (Lecture Notes in Economics & Mathematical Systems Ser.: Vol. 202). (Illus.). 266p. 1982. 38.00 (*0-387-11551-X*) Spr-Verlag.

Perskin, Pamela S., jt. auth. see Noblitt, James R.

Persky, Barry & Golubchick, Leonard H., eds. Early Childhood Education. 2nd ed. 424p. (Orig.). (C). 1991. pap. text 34.50 (*0-8191-8296-6*) U Pr of Amer.

Persky, Harold. Psychoendocrinology of Human Sexual Behavior, 6. LC 87-6976. (Sexual Medicine Ser.: Vol. 6). 280p. 1987. 95.00 (*0-275-92526-9*, C2526, Praeger Pubs) Greenwood.

Persky, Hilary R. NAEP 1994 Geography Report Card, Findings from the National Assessment of Educational Progress. 134p. 1996. pap. 11.00 (*0-16-048680-7*) USGPO.

— NAEP 1997 Arts Report Card: Eighth-Grade Findings from the National Assessment of Educational Progress. 240p. 1999. per. 19.00 (*0-16-049863-5*) USGPO.

Persky, John. Maximizing Agency Value: A Guide for Buying, Selling & Perpetuating Insurance Agencies. 190p. 1998. pap. text 55.00 (*1-878204-57-2*) APIS Inc.

***Persky, Joseph & Wiewel, Wim.** When Corporations Leave Town: The Costs & Benefits of Metropolitan Job Sprawl. (Illus.). 192p. 2000. 39.95 (*0-8143-2907-1*); pap. 19.95 (*0-8143-2908-X*) Wayne St U Pr.

Persky, Joseph, et al. Does America Need Cities? An Urban Investment Strategy for National Prosperity. 1992. 12.00 (*0-944826-47-4*) Economic Policy Inst.

Persky, Joseph J. The Burden of Dependency: Colonial Themes in Southern Economic Thought. LC 92-10844. 192p. 1993. text 32.50 (*0-8018-4422-3*) Johns Hopkins.

Persky, Margaret. Living in God's Time: A Primer for Nurturing the Spiritual Life of Children Throughout the Christian Year. Miller, JoAnn, ed. LC 98-55212. 176p. 1999. pap. 10.00 (*0-8358-0875-0*) Upper Room Bks.

Persky, Robert S. The Artist's Guide to Getting & Having a Successful Exhibition. LC 85-72702. 120p. (Orig.). 1985. pap. 24.95 (*0-913069-04-3*) Consultant Pr.

Persky, Robert S., ed. Big Apple Street Smarts. 128p. 1992. pap. 14.95 (*0-913069-33-7*) Consultant Pr.

Persky, Robert S. & Levy, Susan P. The Photographer's Guide to Getting & Having a Successful Exhibition. 124p. (Orig.). 1987. pap. 24.95 (*0-913069-10-8*) Consultant Pr.

Persky, Robert S., jt. auth. see Cisek, Eugene.

Persky, Serge M. Contemporary Russian Novelists. Eisemann, Frederick, tr. LC 68-26468. (Essay Index Reprint Ser.). 1977. 20.95 (*0-8369-0784-1*) Ayer.

Persky, Stan. Autobiography of a Tattoo. 256p. 1997. pap. 15.00 (*0-921586-62-0*, Pub. by New Star Bks) Genl Dist Srvs.

Persky, Stan. Boyopolis: Essays from Gay Eastern Europe. LC 96-21522. 400p. 1996. 26.95 (*0-87951-690-9*, Pub. by Overlook Pr) Penguin Putnam.

— Buddy's: Meditations on Desire. 2nd rev. ed. 150p. 1991. pap. 9.95 (*0-921586-19-1*, Pub. by New Star Bks) Genl Dist Srvs.

Persky, Stan, jt. ed. see Jackson, Ed.

***Persley, G. J.** Investment Strategies for Agricultural & Natural Resources: Investing in Knowledge for Development. LC 98-8806. 336p. 1999. text 90.00 (*0-85199-280-3*) OUP.

Persley, Gabrielle J. Agricultural Biotechnology: Country Case Studies. 350p. 2000. 100.00 (*0-85198-816-4*) OUP.

— Agricultural Biotechnology: Opportunities for International Development. (Biotechnology in Agriculture Ser.: No. 2). (Illus.). 528p. 1990. text 150.00 (*0-85198-643-9*) OUP.

— Replanting the Tree of Life: Towards An International Agenda for Coconut Palm Research. (Illus.). 172p. 1992. text 65.00 (*0-85198-815-6*) OUP.

— Tropical Legume Improvement. 78p. (Orig.). 1984. pap. 42.00 (*0-949511-13-7*) St Mut.

Persley, Gabrielle J., ed. Biotechnology & Integrated Pest Management. LC 97-103837. (Biotechnology in Agriculture Ser.: No. 15). 496p. 1996. text 110.00 (*0-85198-930-6*) OUP.

Persley, Gabrielle J., jt. ed. see DeLanghe, E. A.

Persley, Gabrielle J., jt. ed. see Doyle, John J.

Persley, Gabrielle J., jt. ed. see Ferrar, P.

Persloe, C., jt. auth. see Hejab, M.

Person, Ann. Stretch & Sew Guide to Sewing on Knits. (Illus.). 160p. 1994. pap. 19.95 (*0-8019-8593-5*) Krause Pubns.

Person, Ann B., jt. auth. see Schiff, Isaac.

Person, Carl E. The Lizard's Trail. LC 74-22755. (Labor Movement in Fiction & Non-Fiction Ser.). reprint ed. 38.50 (*0-404-58508-6*) AMS Pr.

Person, David K., et al. The Alexander Archipelago Wolf: A Conservation Assessment. (Illus.). 52p. 1997. reprint ed. 12.00 (*0-89904-552-9*); reprint ed. pap. 7.00 (*0-89904-553-7*) Crumb Elbow Pub.

Person, Diane G., jt. auth. see Freeman, Evelyn B.

Person, Diane G., jt. ed. see Cullinan, Bernice E.

Person, Diane G., jt. ed. see Freeman, Evelyn B.

Person, Ethel S. By Force of Fantasy: How We Make Our Lives. 288p. Date not set. pap. 24.00 (*0-465-02360-6*) Basic.

— Dreams of Love & Fateful Encounters: The Power of Romantic Passion. 384p. 1989. pap. 14.95 (*0-14-012055-6*, Penguin Bks) Viking Penguin.

***Person, Ethel S.** Power Struggles. 2001. write for info. (*0-688-17577-5*, Wm Morrow) Morrow Avon.

Person, Ethel S., et al, eds. On Freud's "Creative Writers & Day-Dreaming" LC 94-48270. (Contemporary Freud Ser.). 1995. 25.00 (*0-300-06266-4*) Yale U Pr.

— On Freud's "Observations on Transference-Love" LC 92-41560. (Contemporary Freud Turning Points & Critical Issues Ser.). 202p. 1993. reprint ed. pap. 62.70 (*0-608-07844-1*, 205402000011) Bks Demand.

Person, Ethel S., et al. On Freud's "A Child Is Being Beaten" LC 97-8960. (Contemporary Freud). 1997. pap. write for info. (*0-300-07162-0*) Yale U Pr.

— On Freud's "A Child Is Being Beaten" LC 97-8960. (Contemporary Freud Turning Points & Critical Issues Ser.: Vol. 5). 256p. 1997. 25.00 (*0-300-07161-2*) Yale U Pr.

Person, Ethel S., jt. ed. see Stimpson, Catherine R.

***Person, Ethel Spector.** The Sexual Century. LC 99-34598. 377p. 1999. 35.00 (*0-300-07604-5*) Yale U Pr.

Person, Hara, ed. see Motzkin, Linda.

Person, Jack. All of a Sudden. (Illus.). 192p. 1999. pap. 35.00 (*1-57687-029-4*, pwerHse Bks) pwerHse Cultrl.

Person, James E. Essentials of Mathematics. 5th ed. 880p. 1997. 72.80 (*0-13-284191-6*) P-H.

Person, James E., Jr. Literary Criticism from 1400 to 1800, Vol. 16. 500p. 1991. text 150.00 (*0-8103-6115-9*) Gale.

— Literary Criticism from 1400 to 1800, Vol. 17. 500p. 1991. text 150.00 (*0-8103-6116-7*) Gale.

An Asterisk (*) at the beginning of an entry indicates that the title is appearing for the first time.

— Literary Criticism from 1400 to 1800, Vol. 18. 500p. 1992. text 150.00 (*0-8103-7960-0*) Gale.
— Literary Criticism from 1400 to 1800, Vol. 21. 500p. 1993. text 150.00 (*0-8103-7963-5*) Gale.
— Literary Criticism from 1400 to 1800, Vol. 22. 500p. 1993. text 150.00 (*0-8103-7964-3*) Gale.
— Literary Criticism from 1400 to 1800, Vol. 23. 500p. 1993. text 150.00 (*0-8103-7965-1*) Gale.
— Literary Criticism from 1400 to 1800, Vol. 24. 500p. 1994. text 150.00 (*0-8103-8462-0*) Gale.
— Literary Criticism from 1400 to 1800, Vol. 25. 500p. 1994. text 150.00 (*0-8103-8463-9*) Gale.
— Literary Criticism from 1400 to 1800, Vol. 26. 500p. 1994. text 150.00 (*0-8103-8464-7*) Gale.
— Literature Criticism from 1400 to 1800, Vol. 14. 500p. 1990. text 150.00 (*0-8103-6113-2*) Gale.
— Literature Criticism from 1400 to 1800, Vol. 15. 500p. 1991. text 150.00 (*0-8103-6114-0*) Gale.
— Literature Criticism from 1400 to 1800, Vol. 19. 500p. 1992. text 150.00 (*0-8103-7961-9*) Gale.
— Literature Criticism from 1400 to 1800, Vol. 20. 500p. 1992. text 150.00 (*0-8103-7962-7*) Gale.

Person, James E. Nineteenth Century Literature, Vol. 52. 500p. 1996. text 150.00 (*0-8103-9298-4*) Gale.
— Nineteenth-Century Literature Criticism, Vol. 54. 400p. 1996. text 150.00 (*0-8103-6437-9*) Gale.
— Nineteenth-Century Literature Criticism, Vol. 55. 400p. 1996. text 150.00 (*0-8103-5518-3*) Gale.

Person, James E., Jr. Russell Kirk: A Critical Biography of a Conservative Mind. LC 99-39707. (Illus.). 208p. 1999. 26.95 (*1-56833-131-2*, Pub. by Madison Bks UPA) Natl Bk Netwk.

Person, James E., Jr., ed. Literature Criticism from 1400 to 1800, Vol. 1. 500p. 1984. text 150.00 (*0-8103-6100-0*) Gale.
— Literature Criticism from 1400 to 1800, Vol. 2. 600p. 1985. text 150.00 (*0-8103-6101-9*) Gale.
— Literature Criticism from 1400 to 1800, Vol. 3. 600p. 1986. text 150.00 (*0-8103-6102-7*) Gale.
— Literature Criticism from 1400 to 1800, Vol. 4. 567p. 1986. text 150.00 (*0-8103-6103-5*) Gale.
— Literature Criticism from 1400 to 1800, Vol. 5. 555p. 1987. text 150.00 (*0-8103-6104-3*) Gale.
— Literature Criticism from 1400 to 1800, Vol. 6. 545p. 1987. text 150.00 (*0-8103-6105-1*) Gale.
— Literature Criticism from 1400 to 1800, Vol. 7. LC 83-20504. 600p. 1988. text 150.00 (*0-8103-6106-X*) Gale.
— Literature Criticism from 1400 to 1800, Vol. 8. 600p. 1988. text 150.00 (*0-8103-6107-8*) Gale.
— Literature Criticism from 1400 to 1800, Vol. 9. 600p. 1988. text 150.00 (*0-8103-6108-6*) Gale.
— Literature Criticism from 1400 to 1800, Vol. 10. 500p. 1989. text 150.00 (*0-8103-6109-4*) Gale.

Person, James E., ed. Literature Criticism from 1400 to 1800, Vol. 27. 535p. 1995. text 150.00 (*0-8103-8943-6*) Gale.
— Literature Criticism from 1400 to 1800, Vol. 28. 500p. 1995. text 150.00 (*0-8103-8944-4*, 001412) Gale.
— Nineteenth Century Literary Criticism: Criticism of the Works of Novelists, Poets, Playwrights, Short Story Writers, Philosophers, & Other Creative Writers Who Died Between 1800 & 1899, from the First Published Critical Appraisals to Current Evaluations, Vol. 5. 450p. 1995. text 150.00 (*0-8103-9295-X*, 002315) Gale.

Person, James E., ed. The Unbought Grace of Life: Essays in Honor of Russell Kirk. Date not set. pap. 19.95 (*0-89385-043-8*) Sugden.

Person, James E., Jr. & Draper, James P., eds. Literature Criticism from 1400-1800, Vol. 12. 500p. 1990. text 150.00 (*0-8103-6111-6*) Gale.

Person, James E., Jr. & Williamson, Sandra L., eds. Literature Criticism from 1400-1800, Vol. 11. 535p. 1989. text 150.00 (*0-8103-6110-8*) Gale.
— Shakespearean Criticism, Vol. 10. 400p. 1989. text 155.00 (*0-8103-6134-5*) Gale.

Person, James E., Jr., jt. ed. see Draper, James P.

Person, James E., Jr., jt. ed. see Williamson, Sandra L.

Person-Lynn, Kwaku. First Word: Black Scholars, Thinkers & Warriors: Knowledge, Wisdom & Mental Liberation. LC 96-41295. 224p. 1996. 22.00 (*0-86316-335-1*) Writers & Readers.

Person, Matthew M., III. The Smart Hospital: A Case Study in Hospital Computerization. LC 88-71149. 244p. 1988. lib. bdg. 29.95 (*0-89089-338-1*) Carolina Acad Pr.
— The Zero-Base Hospital: Survival & Success in America's Evolving Healthcare System. LC 96-36383. 248p. 1997. 44.00 (*1-56793-049-2*) Health Admin Pr.

Person, May W. Better Than You Know Yourself. 134p. (Orig.). 1996. pap. 7.95 (*1-888813-00-8*, 001) Brghtside.

Person, May W., ed. see Taylor, Tina.

Person, Peter M. Zigger Zagger Mooney & His Caravans. (Illus.). 192p. (J). pap. 15.95 (*0-14-048122-2*, Pub. by Pnguin Bks Ltd) Trafalgar.

Person, Raymond F., Jr. In Conversation with Jonah: Conversation Analysis, Literary Criticism, & the Book of Jonah. (JSOTS Ser.: No. 220). 204p. 1996. 57.50 (*1-85075-619-8*, Pub. by Sheffield Acad) CUP Services.

Person, Raymond F. The Kings: Isaiah & Kings - Jeremiah Recensions. LC 97-18658. (Beiheft zur Zeitschrift fuer die Alttestamentliche Wissenschaft Ser.: Vol. 252). viii, 127p. (C). 1997. lib. bdg. 65.35 (*3-11-015457-9*) De Gruyter.

Person, Raymond F., Jr. Second Zechariah & the Deuteronomic School. (JSOTS Ser.: Vol. 167). 230p. 1993. 65.00 (*1-85075-455-1*, Pub. by Sheffield Acad) CUP Services.

***Person, Raymond F., Jr.** Structure & Meaning in Conversation & Literature. LC 99-36110. 168p. 1999. 38.00 (*0-7618-1472-8*) U Pr of Amer.

Person, Robert B., jt. auth. see Trenk, Henry C.

Person, Robert J., jt. ed. see Theis, R.

Person, Robert J., jt. ed. see Thies, R.

Person, Roland C. A New Path: Undergraduate Libraries at United States & Canadian Universities, 1949-1987, 17. LC 87-29553. (New Directions in Information Management Ser.: No. 17). (Illus.). 173p. 1988. 45.00 (*0-313-25303-X*, PNU/) Greenwood.

Person, Ron. Using Excel for Windows 95: Special Edition. (Illus.). 1211p. (Orig.). 1995. pap. 34.99 (*0-7897-0112-X*) Que.
— Using Windows 98: Platinum Edition. 400p. 1997. pap. 19.99 (*0-7897-1487-6*) Que.
— Using Windows 98: Platinum Edition. LC 97-75460. 912p. 1998. pap. 39.99 (*0-7897-1488-4*); pap. 49.99 (*0-7897-1489-2*) Que.
— Using Windows 95. LC 97-68680. 360p. 1997. 19.99 (*0-7897-1462-0*) Que.
— Using Windows 95: Platinum Edition. LC 96-71431. 1464p. 1996. 65.00 (*0-7897-1052-8*) Que.
— Windows 95 at Work. 700p. 1998. 29.99 (*0-7897-1190-7*) Que.

Person, Ron & Acklen, Laura. Windows QuickStart, 3.11 Edition. LC 95-129969. 301p. 1994. 29.99 (*1-56529-866-7*) Que.

Person, Ron & Que Development Group Staff. Special Edition Using Microsoft Word 97. 1296p. 1996. 34.99 (*0-7897-0962-7*) Que.

Person, Ron & Tow, Tim. Browsing the World Wide Web with Word for Windows. LC 95-69249. (Illus.). 393p. (Orig.). 1995. 29.99 (*0-7897-0243-6*) Que.

Person, Ron & Voss, Robert. Using Windows 95: Special Edition. 2nd ed. LC 97-68670. 1232p. 1997. pap. 39.99 incl. cd-rom (*0-7897-1381-0*) Que.

Person, Ron, et al. Using Windows 95: Special Edition. (SPA., Illus.). 1344p. 1995. 39.99 (*1-56529-921-3*) Que.

Person, Russell V. Essentials of Mathematics. 4th ed. LC 79-10708. 865p. 1980. pap. text 8.00 (*0-471-07752-6*) P-H.

Person, Ruth J., ed. The Management Process: A Selection of Readings for Librarians. LC 83-3788. 431p. reprint ed. pap. 133.70 (*0-7837-5923-1*, 204572200007) Bks Demand.

Person, Ruth J. & Newman, George Charles. Selection of the University Librarian. (Occasional Papers: Vol. 13). 28p. 1988. pap. 25.00 (*0-918006-56-2*, OP#13) ARL.

Person, Ruth J., jt. auth. see Rogers, Sharon.

Person, Ruth J., jt. ed. see McCabe, Gerard B.

Person, Sarah. A Book for Betsy. (Illus.). 24p. (J). (gr. k-6). 1998. pap. 3.95 (*0-9668635-0-X*) Gtr Mankato Area.

Person, Willis B., jt. auth. see Mulliken, Robert S.

Personal Counselors, Inc. Staff. Postulates of Re-Evaluation Counseling. rev. ed. 1990. pap. 2.00 (*0-913937-43-6*) Rational Isl.

Personal Investor Recovery, Inc. Staff. Winning Your Rightful Recompense: A Do-It-Yourself Manual to Arbitration Procedures. LC 97-75596. 78p. 1997. pap. 99.95 (*0-9661331-0-2*) Personal Investor.

Personal Narratives Group Staff. Interpreting Women's Lives: Feminist Theory & Personal Narratives. LC 88-45445. (Illus.). 286p. 1989. 42.00 (*0-253-33070-X*); pap. 15.95 (*0-253-20501-8*, MB-501) Ind U Pr.

Personal Reference Group Staff. New King James Version Giant Print Personal Size Bonded Leather Blue Indexed, Supersaver ed. 1998. 32.97 (*0-7852-0399-0*) Nelson.
— New King James Version Giant Print Personal Size Bonded Leather Blue, Supersaver ed. 1998. 24.97 (*0-7852-0397-4*) Nelson.

***Personal Stamp Exchange Staff.** Rubber Stamp Celebrations: Dazzling Projects from Personal Stamp Exchange. 128p. 1999. pap. text 14.95 (*0-8069-6291-7*) Sterling.

Personal Strengths Publishing, Inc., Staff. Strength Deployment Inventory Facilitation Guide. (Illus.). 100p. 1998. 350.00 incl. cd-rom (*0-9628732-2-5*) Prsnl Strengths.

Personick, S. D. Fiber Optics: Technology & Applications. LC 85-12370. (Applications of Communications Theory Ser.). (Illus.). 270p. (C). 1985. text 79.50 (*0-306-42079-1*, Kluwer Plenum) Kluwer Academic.
— Optical Fiber Transmission Systems. LC 80-20684. (Applications of Communications Theory Ser.). (Illus.). 192p. (C). 1981. text 59.50 (*0-306-40580-6*, Kluwer Plenum) Kluwer Academic.

Personick, Stewart D. Fiber Optics: Technology & Applications. 1996. 59.50 (*0-614-18443-6*, B10018) Info Gatekeepers.
— Fiber Optics: Technology & Applications. 270p. 1985. teacher ed. write for info. (*0-318-60148-6*, Plenum Trade) Perseus Pubng.

Personius, Stephen F. Paleoseismic Analysis of the Wasatch Fault Zone at the Brigham City Trench Site, Brigham City, Utah & the Pole Patch Trench Site, Pleasant View, Utah. LC TN24.U8 A322. (Special Study Ser.: Vol. 76). (Illus.). 39p. 1991. pap. 6.00 (*1-55791-195-9*, SS-76) Utah Geological Survey.

Personke, Carl R., jt. auth. see Kean, John M.

Personnel & Professional Concerns Cmte Staff. Position Classification for Wisconsin Public Libraries. (FRE.). 303p. 1994. 30.00 (*0-614-04669-6*) Wisc Lib Assn.
— Salary & Fringe Benefit Survey. 274p. 1996. 20.00 incl. cd-rom (*0-614-04670-X*) Wisc Lib Assn.

Personnel Management Services, Ltd. Staff. Recruitment. 150p. (C). 1990. 125.00 (*0-85292-449-6*, Pub. by IPM Hse) St Mut.

Persons, Benjamin S. Relieved of Command. (Illus.). 264p. 1996. pap. 20.95 (*0-89745-204-6*) Sunflower U Pr.

Persons, Billie, jt. auth. see Holman, David.

Persons, Georgia, ed. Race & Ethnicity in Comparative Perspective. (National Political Science Review Ser.). 380p. 1999. pap. text 24.95 (*0-7658-0435-2*) Transaction Pubs.
— Race & Representation. (National Political Science Review Ser.: Vol. 6). 300p. (Orig.). 1997. pap. text 24.95 (*1-56000-959-4*) Transaction Pubs.

Persons, Georgia A. The Making of Energy & Telecommunications Policy. LC 94-34318. 208p. 1995. 59.95 (*0-275-95039-5*, Praeger Pubs) Greenwood.

Persons, Hal. The How-To of Great Speaking: Stage Techniques to Tame Those Butterflies. 1992. 18.95 (*0-9632786-1-4*); pap. 12.95 (*0-9632786-0-6*) Black & Taylor.

Persons, Jacqueline B. Cognitive Therapy in Practice: A Case Formulation Approach. (C). 1989. 29.00 (*0-393-70077-1*) Norton.

***Persons, Jacqueline B., et al.** Essential Components of Cognitive-Behavior Therapy for Depression. LC 00-38045. 2000. write for info. (*1-55798-697-5*) Am Psychol.

***Persons, Marjorie Kiel.** Themes to Remember, Vol. 1. LC 99-96104. (Illus.). xiv, 110p. 2000. 29.95 incl. cd-rom (*0-9675997-0-9*, Pub. by Classical) BookMasters.

Persons, Mark D., ed. Personnel Record Keeper. (Illus.). 400p. 1991. ring bd. 86.00 (*1-878375-31-8*) Panel Pubs.

Persons, Mark D., jt. auth. see DeLuca, Matthew J.

Persons, Mark D., jt. auth. see McNeil, Bruce J.

Persons, Mark D., ed. see Castagnera, James O. & Derewicz, Kristine G.

Persons, Mark D., ed. see Chadwick, Joseph T., Sr.

Persons, Mark D., ed. see Farber, Phillip.

Persons, Mark D., ed. see McNeil, Bruce J.

Persons, Mark D., ed. see Shrader, J. Carl & Weisberg, Stuart A.

Persons, Mark D., ed. see Wertman, Janet A. & Kuraitis, V. P.

Persons, Stow. American Minds: A History of Ideas. rev. ed. LC 74-12326. 540p. 1975. 57.50 (*0-88275-203-0*) Krieger.
— The Decline of American Gentility. LC 73-534. 336p. 1976. pap. text 25.50 (*0-231-08347-5*) Col U Pr.
— Ethnic Studies at Chicago, Nineteen Five to Nineteen Forty-Five. LC 86-11416. 168p. 1987. text 24.95 (*0-252-01344-1*) U of Ill Pr.
— The University of Iowa in the Twentieth Century: An Institutional History. LC 90-10771. (Illus.). 354p. 1990. 38.95 (*0-87745-282-2*) U of Iowa Pr.

Persons, Stow, jt. ed. see Egbert, Donald D.

Persons, W. Scott. American Ginseng: Green Gold. rev. ed. LC 93-46283. (Illus.). 224p. (Orig.). 1994. pap. 17.95 (*0-914875-23-X*) Bright Mtn Bks.

Persoon, Gerard, jt. ed. see Kalland, Arne.

Persoon, J. G., et al, eds. Series of Revisions of Apocynaceae Vol. XXXIV: The African Species of Landolphia P. Beauv. (Wageningen Agricultural University Papers: No. 92-2). 250p. 1992. 63.00 (*90-6754-234-2*, Pub. by Backhuys Pubs) Balogh.

***Persoon, James.** Hardy's Early Poetry: Romanticism through a "Dark Bilberry Eye" 128p. 2000. 50.00 (*0-7391-0152-8*) Lxngtn Bks.

Persoon, James. Modern British Poetry, 1900-1939. LC 99-29212. 207p. 1999. 29.95 (*0-8057-1681-5*, Twyne) Mac Lib Ref.

***Persoone, Guido, et al.** New Microbiotests for Routine Toxicity Screening. 210p. 2000. 99.50 (*0-306-46406-3*, Kluwer Plenum) Kluwer Academic.

***Perspecti.** Microsoft Internet Explorer. LC 98-31457. 1998. pap. 16.99 (*1-57231-964-X*) Microsoft.

Perspecti. MS Access 2000 at a Glance. LC 98-48183. 1998. pap. 19.99 (*1-57231-946-1*) Microsoft.
— MS Excel 2000 at a Glance. LC 98-31458. 256p. 1998. pap. 19.99 (*1-57231-942-9*) Microsoft.
— MS Office 2000 Professional at a Glance. LC 98-48182. 352p. 1998. pap. 19.99 (*1-57231-937-2*) Microsoft.

Perspection, Inc. Staff. Microsoft Access 97 at a Glance. LC 96-36628. 1996. pap. text 16.95 (*1-57231-369-2*) Microsoft.
— Microsoft Excel 97 at a Glance. LC 96-36632. 1996. pap. text 16.95 (*1-57231-367-6*) Microsoft.
— Microsoft Office 2000 at a Glance: Small Business Edition. LC 98-43584. (At A Glance Ser.). 352p. 1999. pap. 19.99 (*0-7356-0546-7*) Microsoft.
— Microsoft PowerPoint for Windows 95 Step by Step. (Step by Step Ser.). 352p. 1995. 29.95 incl. disk (*1-55615-829-7*) Microsoft.
— Microsoft PowerPoint 97 at a Glance. LC 96-36629. 1996. pap. text 16.95 (*1-57231-368-4*) Microsoft.
— Microsoft PowerPoint 97 Step by Step. LC 96-38987. 352p. 29.95 (*1-57231-315-3*) Microsoft.
— Microsoft PowerPoint 2000 Step by Step With CDROM. LC 98-49818. (Step by Step Ser.). (Illus.). 328p. 1999. pap. 29.99 (*1-57231-972-0*) Microsoft.
— Microsoft Publisher 2000 at a Glance. LC 99-13361. 1998. 16.99 (*1-57231-950-X*) Microsoft.
— Microsoft Works 2000 Step by Step. LC 99-40199. (Step by Step Ser.). 1999. pap. text 29.99 (*0-7356-0836-9*) Microsoft.
— MS PowerPoint 2000 at a Glance. LC 98-48186. 1998. pap. 19.99 (*1-57231-944-5*) Microsoft.

***Perspection Staff.** Microsoft Powerpoint 2000 Step by Step Courseware Core Skills. 300p. 2000. pap., student ed. 25.00 (*0-7356-1115-7*) Microsoft.

Perspective Press Inc. Staff. Home Care Aide. 304p. (gr. 13). 1995. pap. text 24.95 (*0-8151-4748-1*, 24903) Mosby Inc.
— Long-Term Care Nursing Assistant. (Illus.). 320p. (gr. 13). 1995. pap. text 24.95 (*0-8151-4550-0*, 25772) Mosby Inc.

Perspective Press Staff. Nursing Assistant. 304p. 1995. write for info. (*0-8151-6698-2*) Mosby Inc.

Perspective Press Staff. Nursing Assistant. (Illus.). 304p. (gr. 13). 1995. write for info. (*0-8151-4747-3*, 24904) Mosby Inc.

***Perspective Publishing Staff.** Guilt-Free Guide to Your New Life as a Mom: Practical Ways to Take Care of Yourself. 2000. pap. 14.95 (*1-930085-01-X*) Prspctive Pub.

***Persse, James R.** Kiss, Boo, Bang: Film Analysis & Criticism from the 1998-1999 Theatrical Review. 253p. 2000. pap. 9.95 (*0-9676821-0-X*) LightTouch Syst.

Persson, Agnetta, jt. auth. see Persson, Bengt.

Persson, Ake, ed. This Fellow with the Fabulous Smile: A Tribute to Brendan Kennelly. 128p. 1996. pap. 17.95 (*1-85224-367-8*, Pub. by Bloodaxe Bks) Dufour.

Persson, Ake, ed. see Kennelly, Brendan.

Persson, Alfred V. & Skudder, Paul A., Jr., eds. Visceral Vascular Surgery. fac. ed. LC 87-6882. (Science & Practice of Surgery Ser.: No. 13). 303p. 1987. reprint ed. pap. 94.00 (*0-7837-8326-4*, 204911300010) Bks Demand.

Persson, Alison Noel, ed. see Boyadjian, Berge.

Persson, Axel W. Staat und Manufaktur im Romischen Reiche. Finley, Moses I., ed. LC 79-4998. (Ancient Economic History Ser.). (GER.). 1979. reprint ed. lib. bdg. 17.95 (*0-405-12387-6*) Ayer.

Persson, B. N. Sliding Friction: Physical Principles & Applications. Von Klitzing, K. & Wiesendanger, R., eds. LC 97-28561. (Nanoscience & Technology Ser.). (Illus.). ix, 256p. 1998. text 79.95 (*3-540-63296-4*) Spr-Verlag.

Persson, B. N. & Tosatti, E., eds. Physics of Sliding Friction: Proceedings of the NATO Advanced Research Workshop & Adriatico Research Conference, Miramare, Trieste, Italy, June 20-23, 1995. (NATO ASI Series E: Applied Sciences: Series E, Vol. 311). 472p. (C). 1996. text 247.00 (*0-7923-3935-5*) Kluwer Academic.

***Persson, B. N. J.** Sliding Friction: Physical Principles & Applications. 2nd ed. LC 00-27993. (Nanoscience & Technology Ser.). (Illus.). xii, 514p. 2000. 79.95 (*3-540-67192-7*) Spr-Verlag.

Persson, Bengt & Persson, Agnetta. Swedish Residential Yards, 1930-1959: Qualities for the Future. (Illus.). 117p. 1995. 97.50 (*91-540-5683-7*) Coronet Bks.

Persson, Bertil R. & Stahlberg, Freddy. Health & Safety of Clinical NMR Examinations. 208p. 1988. 110.00 (*0-8493-6096-X*, RC78, CRC Reprint) Franklin.

Persson, C. G., et al, eds. Inflammatory Indices in Chronic Bronchitis. (Agents & Actions Supplements Ser.: Vol. 30). 296p. 1990. 79.50 (*0-8176-2370-1*) Birkhauser.

Persson, C. G., jt. auth. see O'Donnell, S.

Persson, Conrad. Complete Guide to HDTV. 217p. 1999. pap. text 34.95 (*0-7906-1166-X*) Prompt Publns.

Persson, Dorothy M. & Winter, Michael F., eds. Psychology & Psychiatry Serials: A Bibliographic Aid for Collection Development. LC 90-39559. (Behavioral & Social Sciences Librarian Ser.: Vol. 9, No. 2). 121p. 1990. text 39.95 (*1-56024-048-2*) Haworth Pr.

Persson, Elwy, jt. auth. see Blomqvist, Gun.

Persson, Gunnar. Meanings, Models & Metaphors: A Study in Lexical Semantics in English. (Umea Studies in the Humanities: No. 92). (Illus.). 205p. (Orig.). 1990. pap. 43.50 (*91-7174-478-9*) Coronet Bks.

Persson, Gunnar & Jansson, Mats, eds. Phosphorus in Freshwater Ecosystems. (Developments in Hydrobiology Ser.). (C). 1989. text 292.50 (*90-6193-657-8*) Kluwer Academic.

Persson, Gunnar, jt. auth. see Magnusson, Ulf.

Persson, Gunnar, jt. ed. see Edlund, Lars-Erik.

Persson, Gunnar, jt. ed. see Odenstedt, Bengt.

Persson, Inga, jt. auth. see Jonung, Christina M.

Persson, Jonas & Jungert, Erland. Generation of Multi-Resolution Maps. (Illus.). 66p. (Orig.). (C). 1993. pap. text 35.00 (*0-7881-0158-7*) DIANE Pub.

***Persson, Karl Gunnar.** Grain Markets in Europe, 1500-1900: Integration & Deregulation. (Cambridge Studies in Modern Economic History: No. 7). (Illus.). 193p. (C). 2000. 59.95 (*0-521-65096-8*) Cambridge U Pr.

Persson, Karl Gunnar, ed. The Economic Development of Denmark & Norway since 1870. (Economic Development of Modern Europe since 1870 Ser.: Vol. 2). 672p. 1993. 270.00 (*1-85278-683-3*) E Elgar.

Persson, L., jt. ed. see Benman, B. E.

Persson, Lars E., jt. ed. see Gyllenberg, Mats.

Persson, Lars O., jt. auth. see Lundgvist, Lars.

Persson, Leonard N. The Handbook of Job Evaluations & Job Pricing. rev. ed. 60p. 1982. per. 27.95 (*1-55645-401-5*, 401) Busn Legal Reports.

Persson, Leonard N., jt. auth. see Brady, Robert L.

Persson, Magnus. Great Britain, the United States & the Security of the Middle East: The Formation of the Baghdad Pact. (Lund Studies in International History: No. 35). 368p. 1998. pap. 44.50 (*91-7966-523-3*, Pub. by Almqvist Wiksell) Coronet Bks.

Persson, Olle. The Chanterelle Book. LC 97-15957. (Illus.). 120p. (Orig.). 1997. pap. 16.95 (*0-89815-947-4*) Ten Speed Pr.

Persson, P. World Forest Resources. (C). 1992. 287.50 (*81-7136-034-3*, Pub. by Periodical Expert) St Mut.

Persson, P. B. & Kirchheim, H. R., eds. Baroreceptor Reflexes: Integrative Functions & Clinical Aspects. xi, 322p. 1991. 163.00 (*0-387-53588-8*) Spr-Verlag.

Persson, P. E., et al, eds. Taste & Odor in Waters & Aquatic Organisms. (Water Science & Technology Ser.: No. 15). (Illus.). 340p. 1983. pap. 91.00 (*0-08-029713-7*, Pergamon Pr) Elsevier.

Persson, P. E., et al. Off-Flavours in Drinking Water & Aquatic Organisms. (Water Science & Technology Ser.: Vol. 25). 368p. 1992. 147.00 (*0-08-041861-9*, Pergamon Pr) Elsevier.
— Off-Flavours in the Aquatic Environment: Proceedings of the 2nd IAWPRC International Symposium held in

P

Kagoshima, Japan, 14-16 October, 1987. LC 82-645900. (Water Science & Technology Ser.: No. 20). (Illus.). 294p. 1988. pap. 112.00 (*0-08-036887-5*, Pergamon Pr) Elsevier.

Persson, Richard J. The Stock Photographer's Marketing Guide. (Illus.). (Orig.). 1984. pap. 2.50 (*0-9608486-0-6*) R J Persson Ent.

Persson, Sune, jt. ed. see Ozdalga, Elisabeth.

Persson, Sverker. Mechanics of Cutting Plant Material. LC 87-70989. 280p. (C). 1987. 58.25 (*0-916150-86-0*, M0487) Am Soc Ag Eng.

Persson, Torsten. Macroeconomic Policy, Credibility & Politics, Vol. 38. (Fundamentals of Pure & Applied Economics Ser.). 187p. 1990. pap. text 71.00 (*3-7186-5029-0*) Gordon & Breach.

— Nobel Lectures in Economic Sciences 1991-1995 - The Sveriges Riksbank (Bank of Sweden) Prize in Economics. 220p. 1997. pap. text 19.00 (*981-02-3060-5*) World Scientific Pub.

Persson, Torsten & Tabellini, Guido, eds. Monetary & Fiscal Policy: Politics, Vol. 2. LC 93-35772. (Illus.). 471p. 1994. pap. text 27.50 (*0-262-66088-1*) MIT Pr.

— Monetary & Fiscal Policy Vol. 1: Credibility. LC 93-35772. 1994. pap. text 27.50 (*0-262-66087-3*) MIT Pr.

***Persson, Torsten & Tabellini, Guido Enrico.** Political Economics: Explaining Economic Policy. LC 00-28245. (Zeuthen Lecture Ser.). (Illus.). 544p. 2000. 55.00 (*0-262-16195-8*) MIT Pr.

Persson, U. On Degenerations of Algebraic Surfaces. LC 77-8972. (Memoirs Ser.: No. 11/189). 144p. 1977. pap. 22.00 (*0-8218-2189-X*, MEMO/11/189) Am Math.

Persson, W., jt. ed. see Svanberg, Sune.

Persson, Walter. Free & United: The Story of the International Federation of Free Evangelical Churches. 336p. 1990. pap. 14.95 (*0-910452-84-9*) Covenant.

***Persuitte, David.** Joseph Smith & the Origins of the Book of Mormon. 2nd ed. (Illus.). 312p. 2000. 29.95 (*0-7864-0826-X*) McFarland & Co.

***Persun, Morgan R.** No Pets Allowed. LC 98-18971. (Illus.). 30p. (J). (ps-4). 1998. pap. 5.49 (*1-57924-077-1*) Bob Jones Univ.

Persun, Terry L. Barn Tarot. 62p. 1999. pap. 10.95 (*0-9664667-3-X*) Implos Pr.

— Plant-Animal-I. Bixby, Robert, ed. 26p. 1994. pap. text 6.00 (*1-882983-17-3*) March Street Pr.

— The Witness Tree. 213p. 1999. pap. 13.95 (*0-9664667-1-3*) Implos Pr.

— The Witness Tree. aut. num. ed. 213p. 1998. 29.95 (*0-9664667-0-5*) Implos Pr.

Perszyk, Kenneth J. Nonexistent Objects: Meinong & Contemporary Philosophy. LC 93-11875. (Nijhoff International Philosophy Ser.). 324p. (C). 1993. lib. bdg. 174.50 (*0-7923-2461-7*, Pub. by Kluwer Academic) Kluwer Academic.

Pert, Candace B. Molecules of Emotion: The Science Behind Mind-Body Medicine. 368p. 1999. per. 14.00 (*0-684-84634-9*) S&S Trade.

— Molecules of Emotion: Why You Feel the Way You Feel. LC 97-17463. 304p. 1997. 24.50 (*0-684-83187-2*) S&S Trade.

Pert, G. J., jt. auth. see Wolfson, M. M.

Pertersen, Rodney L., ed. Christianity & Civil Society: Theological Education for Public Life. LC 94-43405. (Boston Theological Institute Ser.: Vol. 4). 184p. (Orig.). 1995. pap. 18.00 (*1-57075-009-2*) Orbis Bks.

Pertes, Richard A. & Gross, Sheldon G., eds. Clinical Management of Temporomandibular Disorders & Orofacial Pain. LC 95-23861. (Illus.). 368p. (Orig.). 1995. pap. text 58.00 (*0-86715-298-2*, B2982) Quint Pub Co.

Perth, James D. Letters from James, Earl of Perth, Lord Chancellor of Scotland, to His Sister the Countess of Erroll, & Other Members of His Family. Jerdan, William, ed. (Camden Society, London. Publications, First Ser.: No. 33). reprint ed. 30.00 (*0-404-50133-8*) AMS Pr.

Perthame, B. Advances in Kinetic Theory: Selected Papers. (Series on Advances in Mathematics). 200p. 1994. text 61.00 (*981-02-1671-8*) World Scientific Pub.

Perthes, Clemens T. Das Deutsche Staatssleban Vor der Revolution. Mayer, J. P., ed. LC 78-67375. (European Political Thought Ser.). (GER.). 1979. lib. bdg. 28.95 (*0-405-11725-6*) Ayer.

Perthes, Volker. Political Economy of Syria under ASAD. 272p. 1995. text 65.00 (*1-85043-910-9*, Pub. by I B T) St Martin.

— Political Economy of Syria under ASAD. 272p. 1997. text 19.95 (*1-86064-192-X*, Pub. by I B T) St Martin.

— Scenarios for Syria: Socio-Economic & Political Choices. LC 99-159731. (Aktuelle Materialien Zur Internationalen Politik Ser.). 130 p. 1998. 5.25 (*3-7890-5722-3*) Intl Bk Import.

Perthuis, E., jt. auth. see Leboue, F.

Perthuisot, J. P. & Sonnenfeld, Peter, eds. Brines & Evaporites. (Short Course Ser.: Vol. 3). 126p. 1989. 21.00 (*0-87590-707-5*) Am Geophysical.

Perticarnini, Romano. Via Diaz. 153p. 1989. pap. 10.00 (*0-920717-36-5*) Guernica Editions.

Perticone, Eugene X. The Clinical & Projective Use of the Bender-Gestalt Test. LC 97-43203. (Illus.). 150p. 1998. text 36.95 (*0-398-06834-8*); pap. text 23.95 (*0-398-06835-6*) C C Thomas.

Pertierra, Raul. Explorations in Social Theory & Philippine Ethnography. LC 97-946621. 276p. (C). 1999. pap. text 25.00 (*971-542-134-2*) UH Pr.

— Philippine Localities & Global Perspectives: Essays on Society & Culture. LC 95-94378. 228p. 1997. pap. text 20.00 (*971-550-148-6*, Pub. by Ateneo de Manila Univ Pr) UH Pr.

Pertierra, Raul, ed. Remittances & Returnees: The Cultural Economy of Migration in Ilocos. (Illus.). 162p. (Orig.). 1992. pap. 15.00 (*971-10-0476-3*, Pub. by New Day Pub) Cellar.

Pertierra, Raul & Ugarte, Eduardo F., eds. Cultures & Texts: Representations of Philippine Society. LC 96-946151. 184p. (C). 1995. pap. text 16.00 (*971-542-044-3*, Pub. by U of Philippines Pr) UH Pr.

Pertile, Lino, jt. ed. see Baranski, Zygmunt G.

Pertile, Lino, jt. ed. see Brand, Peter.

***Pertman, Adam.** Adoption Nation: How the Adoption Revolution Is Transforming America. 2000. 25.00 (*0-465-05650-4*, Pub. by Basic) HarpC.

***Pertman, Judith.** Adoption Revolution. 2000. pap. 15.00 (*0-465-05651-2*, Pub. by Basic) HarpC.

Pertman, Judith. Bad Blood: Crisis in the American Red Cross. (Illus.). 352p. 1998. pap. 6.99 (*0-7860-0508-4*, Pinncle Kensgtn) Kensgtn Pub Corp.

***Perton, Irwin.** The Hamptons: Cartoons over the Edge. (Illus.). 64p. 2000. pap. 12.95 (*0-615-11858-5*) A-Muse.

Pertsch, Erich. Langenscheidt Latin-German Dictionary: Langenscheidt Handwoerterbuch Lateinisch-Deutsch. (GER & LAT.). 703p. 1983. 59.95 (*0-8288-1029-X*, F58020) Fr & Eur.

Pertsch, Wilhelm. Die Orientalischen Handschriften der Herzoglichen Bibliothek Zu Gotha, 5 vols. xlviii, 2601p. reprint ed. write for info. (*0-318-71551-1*) G Olms Pubs.

— Verzeichnib der Persischen Handschriften. (GER.). xvi, 1279p. 1989. reprint ed. write for info. (*3-487-09143-7*) G Olms Pubs.

Pertschuk, Louis P. Immunocytochemistry for Steroid Receptors. 240p. 1990. lib. bdg. 179.00 (*0-8493-6943-6*, RC280) CRC Pr.

Pertschuk, Louis P. & Lee, Sin H., eds. Localization of Putative Steroid Receptors, 2 vols., Vol. I: Experimental Systems. 200p. 1985. 116.00 (*0-8493-6048-X*, RC268, CRC Reprint) Franklin.

Pertschuk, Mark, ed. Major Local Tobacco Control Ordinances in the U. S. (Illus.). 139p. (Orig.). (C). 1994. pap. text 30.00 (*0-7881-1457-3*) DIANE Pub.

Pertschuk, Michael. Giant Killers. 1987. pap. 7.95 (*0-393-30435-3*) Norton.

— Revolt Against Regulation: The Rise & Pause of the Consumer Movement. LC 82-40108. 192p. 1982. pap. 14.95 (*0-520-05074-6*, Pub. by U CA Pr) Cal Prin Full Svc.

Pertsin, A. J. & Kitaigorodsky, A. I. The Atom-Atom Potential Method for Organic Molecular Solids. (Chemical Physics Ser.: Vol. 43). (Illus.). 400p. 1987. 102.95 (*0-387-16246-1*) Spr-Verlag.

Pertsov, Nikolaj V., jt. auth. see Mel'cuk, Igor K.

Perttu, K. L. Modelling of Energy Forestry: Growth, Water Relations & Economics. 209p. (C). 1991. pap. 175.00 (*81-7089-134-5*, Pub. by Intl Bk Distr) St Mut.

Perttula, Timothy K. The Caddo Nation: Archaeological & Ethnohistoric Perspectives. 2nd ed. (Illus.). 352p. 1997. pap. 19.95 (*0-292-76574-6*) U of Tex Pr.

Pertuiset, Nicole, tr. see Le Corbusier Staff.

Pertusati, Linda. In Defense of Mohawk Land: Ethnopolitical Conflict in Native North America. LC 96-15322. (SUNY Series in Ethnicity & Race in American Life). (Illus.). 166p. (C). 1997. text 44.50 (*0-7914-3211-4*); pap. text 14.95 (*0-7914-3212-2*) State U NY Pr.

— Race Ethnic Relations Us. 2000. 36.25 (*0-07-234183-1*) McGraw.

Pertwee, Bill. Dad's Army: The Making of a Television Legend. (Illus.). 208p. 1997. 29.95 (*1-86205-176-3*, Pub. by Pavilion Bks Ltd) Trafalgar.

Pertwee, Ernest. Reciters Treasury of Verse: Serious & Humerous. LC 77-37018. (Granger Index Reprint Ser.). 1977. reprint ed. 42.95 (*0-8369-6317-2*) Ayer.

Pertz, Emma. Through the Fire. (Folktales for Children Ser.). 58p. (J). (gr. 6-8). 1994. pap. 9.95 (*1-882427-18-1*) Aspasia Inc.

Pertzig, Faigy. Messes of Dresses. 2nd ed. Rosenfeld, Dina, ed. LC 94-80242. (Illus.). 32p. (J). (ps-3). 1999. reprint ed. 9.95 (*0-922613-75-3*) Hachai Pubng.

Perucca, Fabien & Pouradier, Gerard. The Rubbish on Our Plates. 192p. 1997. pap. 14.95 (*1-85375-223-1*) Prion.

Perucci, Dorianne, jt. auth. see Connors, Patricia.

Perucho, Juan. Rosas, Diablos y Sonrisas. La Sonrisa de Eros. (Nueva Austral Ser.: Vol. 137). (SPA.). 1991. pap. text 24.95 (*84-239-1937-4*) Elliots Bks.

Peruggia, Mario. Discrete Iterated Function Systems. LC 93-20664. (Illus.). 200p. (C). 1993. text 49.00 (*1-56881-015-6*) AK Peters.

Perugorria, Ricardo, tr. see Stewart, Deborah D.

Perun, Thomas, jt. auth. see Propst, C.

Perun, Thomas, jt. ed. see Propst, C.

Perusek, Glenn & Worcester, Kent, eds. Trade Union Politics: American Unions & Economic Change, 1960s-1990s. LC 94-37802. 264p. (C). 1995. pap. 17.50 (*0-391-03887-7*) Humanities.

— Trade Union Politics: American Unions & Economic Change, 1960s-1990s. LC 94-37802. 264p. (C). 1995. text 49.95 (*0-391-03886-9*) Humanities.

Perushek, Diane E., ed. The Griffis Collection of Japanese Books: An Annotated Bibliography. LC 82-874115. (Cornell East Asia Ser.: No. 28). 118p. 1982. pap. 8.50 (*0-939657-28-7*) Cornell East Asia Pgm.

Peruski, Anne H., jt. auth. see Peruski, Leonard F.

Peruski, Leonard F. & Peruski, Anne H. The Internet & the New Biology: Tools for Genomic & Molecular Research. LC 96-46766. 320p. 1997. 34.95 (*1-55581-119-1*) ASM Pr.

Perusse, Roland I. Haitian Democracy Restored, 1991-1995. LC 95-8761. 240p. (C). 1995. pap. text 28.50 (*0-8191-9952-4*); lib. bdg. 52.00 (*0-8191-9951-6*) U Pr of Amer.

— The United States & Puerto Rico: Decolonization Options & Prospects. 192p. (Orig.). (C). 1987. pap. text 22.00 (*0-8191-6658-8*) U Pr of Amer.

— The United States & Puerto Rico: The Struggle for Equality. LC 89-48583. (Anvil Ser.). 188p. (C). 1990. pap. 12.50 (*0-89464-396-7*) Krieger.

Perusse, Roland I., ed. Directory of Caribbean Scholars. 1978. lib. bdg. 300.00 (*0-8490-1394-1*) Gordon Pr.

Perutz, Kathrin, jt. auth. see Linden, Anne.

Perutz, Leo. The Master of the Day of Judgement. Mosbacher, Eric, tr. from GER. LC 94-14353. 148p. 1994. 19.45 (*1-55970-171-4*, Pub. by Arcade Pub Inc) Time Warner.

— The Master of the Day of Judgement: An Arcade Mystery. Mosbacher, Eric, tr. 192p. 1996. pap. 10.45 (*1-55970-334-2*, Pub. by Arcade Pub Inc) Time Warner.

— The Swedish Cavalier. 192p. 1993. 19.45 (*1-55970-170-6*, Pub. by Arcade Pub Inc) Time Warner.

Perutz, Max F. I Wish I'd Made You Angry Earlier: Essays on Science, Scientists, & Humanity. LC 97-31786. 354p. 1998. 42.00 (*0-87969-524-2*) Cold Spring Harbor.

— Protein Structure. LC 92-928. (C). 1992. text 36.80 (*0-7167-7021-0*) W H Freeman.

Perutz, Max F., jt. auth. see Fermi, G.

Perutz, Vivien. Edouard Manet: The Janus of Mid-Nineteenth-Century French Painting. LC 89-46405. (Illus.). 284p. 1993. 95.00 (*0-8387-5195-4*) Bucknell U Pr.

Peruvian Bishops' Commission for Social Action. Between Honesty & Hope: Documents from & about the Church in Latin America. LC 78-143185. (Maryknoll Documentation Ser.). 271p. reprint ed. pap. 84.10 (*0-8357-7150-4*, 205211600042) Bks Demand.

Peruzzi, L., jt. ed. see Coppo, R.

Peryan, Tomislav. Reina de la Paz: Eco de la Palabra Eterna. 55p. 1988. pap. 3.50 (*0-940535-16-5*, UP114) Franciscan U Pr.

Pervan, V. Oncology for Health-Care Professionals. 1995. pap. 63.50 (*0-7021-2669-1*, Pub. by Juta & Co) Gaunt.

***Pervanic, Kemal.** Killing Days: My Journey Through the Bosnian War. 2000. 26.00 (*1-85782-363-X*) Blake Publng.

Perveen, Talot. Growth of Soviet Technical Intelligentsia. 1987. 21.00 (*0-8364-2244-9*, Pub. by Mittal Pubs Dist) S Asia.

Pervical, Mary B., jt. auth. see Cohen, Stan B.

Pervin. Pervin's Science of Personality. 256p. 1996. pap. text, teacher ed. 25.00 (*0-471-16082-2*) Wiley.

Pervin, David J. & Spiegel, Steven L. Practical Peacemaking in the Middle East Vol. 1: Arms Control & Regional Security. LC 94-40942. 262p. 1995. text 15.00 (*0-8153-1999-1*, SS1026) Garland.

Pervin, David J., jt. auth. see Spiegel, Steven L.

Pervin, David J., jt. ed. see Spiegel, Steven L.

Pervin, Lawrence A. Current Controversies & Issues in Personality. LC 78-15361. 323p. reprint ed. pap. 100.20 (*0-7837-3499-9*, 205783200008) Bks Demand.

— Current Controversies & Issues in Personality. 2nd ed. LC 83-23246. 368p. (C). 1984. pap. 55.95 (*0-471-88086-8*) Wiley.

— Personality: Theory & Research. 7th ed. LC 96-7678. 608p. 1996. text 89.95 (*0-471-12804-X*) Wiley.

— The Science of Personality. LC 95-5144. 496p. 1995. text 89.95 (*0-471-57850-9*) Wiley.

Pervin, Lawrence A., ed. Goal Concepts in Personality & Social Psychology. 520p. 1989. pap. 45.00 (*0-8058-0383-1*) L Erlbaum Assocs.

— Handbook of Personality: Theory & Research. LC 90-37936. 738p. 1992. pap. text 39.95 (*0-89862-593-9*) Guilford Pubns.

Pervin, Lawrence A., et al, eds. The College Dropout & the Utilization of Talent. LC 66-11976. (Illus.). 268p. reprint ed. pap. 83.10 (*0-8357-8849-0*, 203338500085) Bks Demand.

Pervin, Lawrence A. & John, Oliver P., eds. Handbook of Personality: Theory & Research. 2nd ed. LC 99-25807. 738p. 1999. 65.00 (*1-57230-483-9*, C0483) Guilford Pubns.

Pervin, Lawrence A., jt. auth. see Cooper, Cary L.

***Pervola, Cindy & Hobgood, Debby.** How to Get a Job If You're a Teenager. 2nd rev. ed. 68p. (YA). (gr. 6-13). 2000. pap. 13.95 (*1-57950-059-5*, Alleyside) Highsmith Pr.

Pervozvanskii, A. A. & Gaitsgori, V. G. Theory of Suboptimal Decisions: Decomposition & Aggregation. (C). 1988. text 226.50 (*90-277-2401-6*) Kluwer Academic.

Pervukhina, Natalie. Anton Chekhov: The Sense & the Nonsense. 200p. 1993. pap. 20.00 (*0-921252-28-5*) LEGAS.

Perweiler, Gary. Secrets of Studio Still Life Photography. (Illus.). 144p. 1984. pap. 22.50 (*0-8174-5898-0*, Amphoto) Watsn-Guptill.

Pery, Charles, ed. see Goldbeck, Anneliese.

Peryer, Peter. Peter Peryer, Second Nature. (Illus.). 140p. 1995. pap. 39.95 (*3-905514-56-7*, Pub. by Edit Stemmle) Dist Art Pubs.

Peryt, T. M., ed. Coated Grains. (Illus.). 600p. 1983. 107.00 (*0-387-12071-8*) Spr-Verlag.

— Evaporite Basins. (Lecture Notes in Earth Sciences Ser.: Vol. 13). v, 188p. 1988. 38.95 (*0-387-18679-4*) Spr-Verlag.

— The Zechstein Facies in Europe. (Lecture Notes in Earth Sciences Ser.: Vol. 10). x, 272p. 1987. 62.95 (*0-387-17710-8*) Spr-Verlag.

Peryt, T. M., jt. ed. see Scholle, Peter A.

Peryt, Tadeusz, jt. ed. see Fuechtbauer, Hans.

Perzaao, Jose M., tr. see Carruthers, Peter.

Perzow, Sidney, jt. ed. see Kets de Vries, Manfred F.

Perzyna, P., ed. Localization & Fracture Phenomena in Inelastic Solids. (CISM International Centre for Mechanical Sciences Ser.: Suppl. 386). (Illus.). vii, 468p. 1998. pap. 84.95 (*3-211-82918-0*) Spr-Verlag.

PES Staff, jt. auth. see ARI Staff.

Pesala, Bhikkhu. The Debate of King Milinda. (C). 1991. 14.00 (*81-208-0893-2*, Pub. by Motilal Bnarsidass) S Asia.

Pesando, James E. & Rea, Samuel A. Public & Private Pensions in Canada: An Economic Analysis. LC 77-376564. (Ontario Economic Council Research Studies: No. 9). 193p. reprint ed. pap. 59.90 (*0-8357-4001-3*, 203670200005) Bks Demand.

Pesando, Paolo, jt. auth. see Lovisolo, Carlo.

Pesantubbee, Michelene A. Encyclopedia of Native American Ceremonies. 1996. lib. bdg. 65.00 (*0-87436-780-8*) ABC-CLIO.

Pesaran, A. A., jt. ed. see Worek, W. M.

Pesaran, B. & Wright, C. B. Using & Assessing CBI Data at the Bank of England. LC HG2993.. (Bank of England Technical Ser.: Vol. 37). 28p. 1991. reprint ed. pap. 30.00 (*0-608-00690-4*, 206146100009) Bks Demand.

Pesaran, Bahram & Robinson, Gary. The Statistical Distribution of Short-Term Labor Rates under Two Monetary Regimes. (Bank of England, Economics Division: Vol. 16). (Illus.). 36p. 1993. reprint ed. pap. 30.00 (*0-608-07935-9*, 206790800012) Bks Demand.

Pesaran, Hashem, jt. ed. see Lawson, Tony.

Pesaran, M. H. & Schmidt, P., eds. Handbook of Applied Econometrics Vol. 2: Microeconometrics. 416p. (C). 1997. text 115.95 (*1-55786-209-5*) Blackwell Pubs.

Pesaran, M. Hashem, ed. Handbook of Applied Econometrics: Microeconomics. (Handbooks in Economics Ser.). (Illus.). 482p. 1999. pap. 34.95 (*0-631-21558-1*) Blackwell Pubs.

Pesaran, M. Hashem & Potter, Simon M., eds. Nonlinear Dynamics, Chaos & Econometrics. 256p. 1993. 140.00 (*0-471-93942-0*) Wiley.

Pesaran, M. Hashem & Schmidt, Peter, eds. Handbook of Applied Econometrics Vol. Ii: Microeconomics. 416p. pap. 34.95 (*0-631-21633-2*) Blackwell Pubs.

Pesaran, M. Hashem & Wickers, Mike, eds. Handbook of Applied Econometrics Vol. I: Macroeconomics & Finance. LC 94-47425. (Illus.). 360p. (C). 1995. 104.95 (*1-55786-208-7*) Blackwell Pubs.

Pesaresi, M. & Glenn, S. Search & Rescue. LC 96-90774. 1997. mass mkt. 5.99 (*0-449-22578-X*, Crest) Fawcett.

Pesaresi, Marco. Underground. LC 97-76791. (Illus.). 128p. 1998. pap. 53.00 (*0-89381-753-8*) Aperture.

Pesaresi, Mary, jt. auth. see Glen, Samantha.

***Pesaresi, Massimo.** Grecian Vista: Giacomo Leopardi & Romantic Hellas. 140p. 1999. pap. 25.00 (*0-913298-97-2*) S F Vanni.

Pesatrice, Terri, ed. see Musser, Sandra K.

Pesavento, Larry. Artificial Intelligence: A New Era of Technical Analysis. (Illus.). 300p. 1995. pap. 49.95 (*1-883272-17-3*) Traders Lib.

— Astro-Cycles: The Trader's Viewpoint. (Illus.). 189p. 1997. reprint ed. pap. 49.00 (*0-934380-31-7*, 263) Traders Pr.

— Fibonacci Ratios with Pattern Recognition. Shapiro, Steven, ed. LC 97-204230. (Illus.). 184p. 1997. pap. 49.00 (*0-934380-36-8*, 1098) Traders Pr.

— Harmonic Vibrations: A Metamorphosis from Traditional Cycle Theory to Astro-Harmonics. Shapiro, Steven, ed. (Illus.). 172p. 1997. reprint ed. pap. 49.00 (*0-934380-33-3*, 390) Traders Pr.

— Planetary Harmonics of Speculative Markets. (Illus.). 202p. 1997. reprint ed. pap. 49.00 (*0-934380-32-5*, 336) Traders Pr.

— Profitable Patterns for Stock Trading. (Illus.). 224p. 1999. 49.00 (*0-934380-47-3*) Traders Pr.

Pescador de Umpierre, Paquita. Manual de Bailes Folkloricos. 290p. (C). 1981. pap. 5.00 (*0-8477-2501-4*) U of PR Pr.

Pescador, Manuel L., jt. auth. see Berner, Lewis.

Pescar, Susan C. & Nelson, Christine A. Where Does It Hurt? A Guide to Symptoms & Illnesses. LC 83-5663. 323p. reprint ed. pap. 100.20 (*0-7837-1573-0*, 204186500024) Bks Demand.

Pescatello, Ann M. Charles Seeger: A Life in American Music. LC 92-4679. (Illus.). 360p. (C). 1992. text 34.95 (*0-8229-3713-1*) U of Pittsburgh Pr.

— Power & Pawn: The Female in Iberian Families, Societies & Cultures, 1. LC 75-35352. (Council on Intercultural & Comparative Studies: No. 1). 281p. 1976. 38.50 (*0-8371-8583-1*, PPP/, Greenwood Pr) Greenwood.

Pescatello, Ann M., ed. Old Roots in New Lands: Historical & Anthropological Perspectives on Black Experiences in the Americas, 31. LC 76-50409. (Contributions in Afro-American & African Studies: No. 31). (Illus.). 301p. 1977. 55.00 (*0-8371-9476-8*, PEA/) Greenwood.

***Pescatore, Fred.** Feed Your Kids. LC 98-13103. (Illus.). 290p. 1999. pap. 14.95 (*0-471-34963-1*) Wiley.

Pescatore, Fred. Feed Your Kids Well: How to Help Your Child Lose Weight & Get Healthy. LC 98-13103. 304p. 1998. 22.95 (*0-471-24855-X*) Wiley.

***Pescatore, Fred.** Thin for Good: The One-Low Carb Diet That Will Finally Work for You. LC 99-54631. 304p. 2000. 24.95 (*0-471-36267-0*) Wiley.

Pescatore, Joseph F., jt. ed. see Schneeweis, Thomas.

Pescatore, Pierre. WTO/GATT Dispute Settlement: Digest with Key Words & Summaries. LC 97-220138. 1997. 95.00 (*1-57105-075-2*) Transnatl Pubs.

Pescatore, Pierre, et al. Handbook of GATT (WTO) Dispute Settlement, 2 vols. 1991. ring bd. 321.00 (*90-6544-953-1*) Kluwer Law Intl.

Pescatore, Pierre, et al. Handbook of WTO/GATT Dispute Settlement. 1991. ring bd. 325.00 (*1-57105-032-9*) Transnatl Pubs.

P

An Asterisk (*) at the beginning of an entry indicates that the title is appearing for the first time.

Pesce, Amadeo J., et al, eds. Fluorescence Spectroscopy: An Introduction for Biology & Medicine. LC 76-154611. 262p. reprint ed. pap. 81.30 (*0-608-14174-7*, 202150900022) Bks Demand.

Pesce, Amadeo J. & First, Martin R. Proteinuria: An Integrated Review. LC 79-20352. (Kidney Disease Ser.: No. 1). (Illus.). 310p. reprint ed. pap. 96.10 (*0-7837-0633-2*, 204097700019) Bks Demand.

Pesce, Amadeo J., jt. auth. see Pesce, John.

Pesce, Amadeo J., jt. ed. see Kaplan, Lawrence A.

Pesce, Angelo. Colours of the Arab Fatherland. (Illus.). 144p. (C). 1995. 75.00 (*0-907151-16-7*, Pub. by IMMEL Pubng) St Mut.

— Jiddah: Portrait of an Arabian City. 240p. (C). 1995. 85.00 (*0-907151-25-6*, Pub. by IMMEL Pubng) St Mut.

— Taif: The Summer Capital of Saudi Arabia. 120p. (C). 1995. 100.00 (*0-907151-27-2*, Pub. by IMMEL Pubng) St Mut.

Pesce, Angelo, ed. Makkah a Hundred Years Ago. 128p. (C). 1995. 66.00 (*0-907151-36-1*, Pub. by IMMEL Pubng); 66.00 (*0-907151-44-2*, Pub. by IMMEL Pubng) St Mut.

Pesce, Angelo & Pesce, Elvira G. Marvel of the Desert: The Camel in Saudi Arabia. 112p. (C). 1995. 75.00 (*0-907151-21-3*, Pub. by IMMEL Pubng) St Mut.

Pesce, Angelo, jt. auth. see Ward, Philip.

Pesce, Angelo, ed. see Guarmani, Carlo.

Pesce, Celestino. Oil Palms & Other Oilseeds of the Amazon. 2nd ed. Johnson, Dennis V., ed. & tr. by. from POR. LC 85-11958. (Studies in Economic Botany).Tr. of Oleaginosas da Amazonia. (Illus.). 200p. 1985. 29.00 (*0-917256-28-X*) Ref Pubns.

Pesce, Dolores. The Affinities & Medieval Transposition. LC 86-45398. (Music: Scholarship & Performance Ser.). (Illus.). 256p. 1987. 24.95 (*0-253-30460-1*) Ind U Pr.

Pesce, Dolores, ed. Hearing the Motet: Essays on the Motet of the Middle Ages & Renaissance. (Illus.). 392p. 1998. pap. 19.95 (*0-19-512905-9*) OUP.

Pesce, Elvira G., jt. auth. see Pesce, Angelo.

Pesce, G. Costs & Taxations in Family Law. xxi, 201p. 1988. 45.50 (*0-455-20796-8*, Pub. by LawBk Co) Gaunt.

Pesce, John & Pesce, Amadeo J. The Lead Paint Primer: Questions & Answers on Lead Paint Poisoning. (Illus.). 150p. (Orig.). 1991. pap. 9.95 (*0-9628220-1-9*) Star Industries.

***Pesce, Mark.** The Playful World: Interactive Toys & the Future of Imagination. 256p. 2000. 24.00 (*0-345-43943-0*) Ballantine Pub Grp.

Pesce, Mark. VRML Browsing & Building Cyberspace: Browsing & Building Cyberspace. LC 95-24793. (Illus.). 320p. (Orig.). 1995. 40.00 (*1-56205-498-8*) New Riders Pub.

Pesce, Vince. Renaissance Selling: Enduring Wisdom from the Italian Masters. LC 95-90608. 176p. 1996. 24.95 (*1-887951-11-3*) Fish Pubng.

Pescetti, Luis Maria. Caperucita Roja: Tal Como Se Lo Contaron a Jorge. 1. 1998. pap. text 9.95 (*84-204-4490-1*) Santillana.

Pescetto, Gioia, jt. ed. see Lewis, Alfred.

Pesch, Barbara B., jt. auth. see Whiting, Susan B.

Pesch, E., et al, eds. Learning in Automated Manufacturing: A Local Search Approach. (Production & Logistics Ser.). 257p. 1994. 61.95 (*3-7908-0792-3*) Spr-Verlag.

Pesch, Heinrich. Heinrich Pesch on Solidarist Economics: Excerpts from the Lehrbuch der National Okonomie. Ederer, Rupert J., tr. LC 98-38624. 1998. write for info. (*0-7618-1246-6*) U Pr of Amer.

***Pesch, Heinrich.** Liberalism, Socialism & Christian Social Order Bk. 1: The Philosophical Roots of Economic Liberalism. Ederer, Rupert J., tr. from GER. LC 99-88233. (Studies in Economics: Vol. 3). 300p. 2000. text 89.95 (*0-7734-7798-5*) E Mellen.

Pesch, Ludwig. The Illustrated Companion to South Indian Classical Music. LC 99-932759. (Illus.). 394p. 1999. text 39.95 (*0-19-564382-8*) OUP.

Pesch, Martin & Weisbeck, Markus, eds. Techno Style: Graphics, Fashion, Culture. (ENG & GER., Illus.). 132p. 1996. pap. 39.95 (*3-283-00290-8*) Gingko Press.

***Pesch, Martin & Welsbeck, Marcus.** Discstyle: The Graphic Arts of Electronic Music & Club Culture. (Illus.). 136p. 1999. pap. 39.95 (*3-283-00369-6*, Pub. by Olms Verlag) Gingko Press.

Pesch, Michael. Effiziente Verkaufsplanung im Investitionsgutermarketing. (Entscheidungsunterstutzung fur Okonomische Probleme Ser.: Bd. 13). (GER., Illus.). 313p. 1996. pap. 57.95 (*3-631-31064-1*) P Lang Pubng.

***Pesch, Otto Hermann.** What Big Ears You Have! The Theologians' Red Riding Hood. 144p. 2000. pap. 14.95 (*0-8146-5898-9*, M Glazier) Liturgical Pr.

Pesch, Rudolf. The Trial of Jesus Continues. Wagner, Doris G., tr. from GER. LC 96-47382. (Princeton Theological Monographs: Vol. 43).Tr. of Prozess Jesu Geht Weiter. 106p. 1996. pap. 12.00 (*1-55635-033-3*) Pickwick.

***Peschanski, Denis, et al.** Collaboration & Resistance: Images of Life in Vichy France, 1940-44. LC 99-54637. (Illus.). 220p. 2000. 49.50 (*0-8109-4123-6*, Pub. by Abrams) Time Warner.

Peschansky, V. G. Physics Reviews Vol. 16, Pt. 1: Kinetic Size Effects in Metals in a Magnetic Field, Vol. 16. (Soviet Scientific Reviews Ser.: Section A). 111p. 1991. text 110.00 (*3-7186-5170-X*, Harwood Acad Pubs) Gordon & Breach.

Peschar, J., jt. auth. see Niessen, M.

Peschar, J., jt. ed. see Niessen, M.

Peschar, Jules L. & Waslander, Siteske. Prepared for Life? How to Measure Cross-Curricular Competencies. LC 97-181101. 196p. (Orig.). 1997. pap. 20.00 (*92-64-05259-3*, 96-97-01-3, Pub. by Org for Econ) OECD.

Peschek-Bohmer, Flora & Schreiber, Gisela. Urine Therapy: Nature's Elixir for Good Health. LC 99-18418. 160p. 1999. pap. 9.95 (*0-89281-799-2*, Heal Arts VT) Inner Tradit.

Peschek, Gunter A., et al, eds. The Phototrophic Prokaryotes: Proceedings of the 9th International Symposium Held in Vienna, Austria, September 6-12, 1997. LC 98-35189. (Illus.). 852p. (C). 1999. text 130.00 (*0-306-45923-X*, Kluwer Plenum) Kluwer Academic.

Peschek, Joseph G., jt. auth. see Grover, William F.

Peschel & Spurgeon. Federal Taxation of Trust Grantors & Beneficiaries, No. 2734. rev. ed. 608p. 1989. boxed set 160.00 (*0-7913-0370-5*) Warren Gorham & Lamont.

Peschel, Enid R., ed. Medicine & Literature. 1980. 17.95 (*0-685-03475-5*) Watson Pub Intl.

Peschel, Enid R., jt. auth. see Peschel, Richard E.

Peschel, Enid R., tr. see Rimbaud, Arthur.

Peschel, G., jt. ed. see Rehage, H.

***Peschel, Ingo, et al, eds.** Density-Matrix Renormalization - a New Numerical Method in Physics: Lectures of a Seminar & Workshop at the Max-Planck-Institut fur Physik Komplexer Systeme, Dresden, Germany, August 24 to September 18, 1998. LC 99-34219. (Lecture Notes in Physics Ser.: Vol. 528). (Illus.). xvi, 355p. 1999. 86.00 (*3-540-66129-8*) Spr-Verlag.

Peschel, John L. & Spurgeon, Edward D. Federal Taxation of Trust Grantors & Beneficiaries, 2. rev. ed. 608p. 1989. 170.00 (*0-318-67196-4*, UTP) Warren Gorham & Lamont.

Peschel, K., ed. Infrastructure & the Space-Economy: Essays in Honor of Rolf Funck. (Illus.). xiv, 447p. 1990. 119.95 (*0-387-52388-X*) Spr-Verlag.

— Regional Growth & Regional Policy Within the Framework of European Integration. (Contributions to Economics Ser.). (Illus.). 197p. 1996. pap. 67.00 (*3-7908-0957-8*) Spr-Verlag.

Peschel, Keewaydinoquay. Puhpohwee for the People: A Narrative Account of Some Uses of Fungi among the Ahnishinaabeg. LC 96-9321. (Illus.). 70p. 1998. pap. 24.95 (*1-879528-18-5*) Ed Studies Pr.

Peschel, Lisa. A Practical Guide to the Runes: Their Uses in Divination & Magic. LC 89-2246. (New Age Ser.). (Illus.). 192p. (Orig.). 1999. mass mkt. 4.99 (*0-87542-593-3*) Llewellyn Pubns.

Peschel, M. & Mende, W. The Predator-Prey Model: Do We Live in a Volterra World? (Illus.). 260p. 1986. 53.95 (*0-387-81848-0*) Spr-Verlag.

Peschel, Max, jt. auth. see Mercurio, Gian.

Peschel, Maxymilian L., jt. auth. see Mercurio, Gian.

Peschel, Richard E. Prostate Cancer. Ernstoff, Marc S. & Heaney, John A., eds. 240p. 1998. 75.00 (*0-632-04317-2*) Blackwell Sci.

Peschel, Richard E., et al, eds. Urologic Cancer. 500p. (C). 1995. write for info. (*0-393-71029-7*, Norton Medical Bks) Norton.

Peschel, Richard E. & Peschel, Enid R. When a Doctor Hates a Patient: Chapters from a Young Physician's Life. (C). 1986. pap. 13.95 (*0-520-06343-0*, Pub. by U CA Pr) Cal Prin Full Svc.

Peschka, V. Die Eigenart des Rechts. 199p. (C). 1989. pap. 45.00 (*963-05-4987-5*, Pub. by Akade Kiado) St Mut.

Peschka, W. Liquid Hydrogen-Fuel of the Future. Wilhelm, E., tr. from GER. (Illus.). 256p. 1992. 147.95 (*0-387-82250-X*) Spr-Verlag.

Peschke, Donald B. Woodsmith, 4 vols., Set. (Illus.). 2000p. write for info. (*0-9634375-0-X*) August Home.

***Peschke, Egon & von Olshausen, Rainer.** Cable Systems for High & Ultra High Voltages: Cable Designs & Accessories - Dimensions, Development & Testing. 296p. 2000. 94.95 (*3-89578-118-5*) Wiley.

Peschke, Erhard, ed. August Hermann Francke: Schriften und Predigten. (Texte zur Geschichte des Pietismus Ser.: Vol. 10, Sec. 2). xxvi, 639p. (C). 1989. lib. bdg. 273.10 (*3-11-007143-6*) De Gruyter.

Peschke, J., tr. see Fritsch, R. & Fritsch, G.

Peschke, Michael, jt. compiled by see Horn-Sauder, Erdmunte.

***Peschko, Edward S.** Perl Developer's Guide. (Application Development Ser.). 2000. pap. 49.99 (*0-07-212630-2*) Osborne-McGraw.

Peschko, Edward S. & DeWolfe, Michele. Perl 5 Complete. 1232p. 1998. pap. 54.95 incl. cd-rom (*0-07-913698-2*) McGraw.

***Peschl, Fred.** I'm "Fred" The Fred Peschl Story. unabridged ed. Goreham, Gary, ed. (Illus.). 144p. 1999. mass mkt. 7.00 (*0-9673814-0-1*) Harold Prntg.

Pesci, David. Amistad: A Novel. 292p. 1998. pap. text 12.95 (*1-56924-703-X*) Marlowe & Co.

— Amistad: The Thunder of Freedom. LC 96-54050. 240p. 1997. 22.95 (*1-56924-748-X*) Marlowe & Co.

Pesci, David, ed. see Connolly, Frank B.

Pescia, D., jt. auth. see Rettori, A.

Pescia, G. & Nguyen The, H., eds. Chorionic Villi Sampling (CVS) (Contributions to Gynecology & Obstetrics Ser.: Vol. 15). (Illus.). viii, 116p. 1986. 69.75 (*3-8055-4326-3*) S Karger.

Pescio, Claudio. Rembrandt: And Dutch Painting of the 17th Century. LC 95-34387. (Masters of Art Ser.). (Illus.). 64p. (J). (gr. 4-7). 1995. lib. bdg. 22.50 (*0-87226-317-7*, 63177B, P Bedrick Books) NTC Contemp Pub Co.

***Pescio, Claudio, et al.** Rembrandt & 17th Century Holland. 2nd ed. LC 00-39746. (Masters of Art Ser.). (Illus.). 2000. write for info. (*0-87226-642-7*, P Bedrick Books) NTC Contemp Pub Co.

Pescod, M. B., jt. auth. see FAO Staff.

Pescod, Michael. Takeover Bids. 1989. write for info. (*0-406-10369-0*, MICHIE) LEXIS Pub.

Pescosolido, Bernice A. & Aminzade, Ronald. The Social Worlds of Higher Education: Handbook for Teaching in a New Century. LC 98-25533. 1999. 54.95 (*0-8039-9045-6*) Pine Forge.

— The Social Worlds of Higher Education: Handbook for Teaching in a New Century. LC 98-25533. 1999. pap. 89.95 (*0-7619-8613-8*) Sage.

Pescosolido, Carl A. & Gleason, Pamela. The Proud Italians: Our Great Civilizers. LC 90-64028. (Illus.). 200p. 1991. 19.95 (*0-9628757-0-8*) Latium Pub.

— The Proud Italians: Our Great Civilizers. 2nd ed. (Illus.). 210p. 1995. pap. 11.95 (*0-9628757-1-6*) Latium Pub.

Pesovitz, David, jt. ed. see Wieners, Brad.

Pesek, Boris P. Gross National Product of Czechoslovakia in Monetary & Real Terms, 1946-58. LC 65-14429. (Studies in Economics of the Economics Research Center of the University of Chicago). 72p. reprint ed. pap. 30.00 (*0-608-15105-X*, 202578700046) Bks Demand.

Pesek, J., jt. ed. see Gayer, R.

Pesek, Jiri & Hojda, Zdenek. The Palaces of Prague. LC 94-24176. (Illus.). 216p. 1995. text 65.00 (*0-86565-958-3*) Vendome.

Pesek, Joseph J. & Leigh, Ivan E., eds. Chemically Modified Surfaces. 240p. 1994. 89.00 (*0-85186-595-X*, R6595) CRC Pr.

Pesek-Marous, Eduard. Salvatore: Bull of Salvation. Tau Editors, ed. LC 76-49340. (Illus.). 111p. 1976. pap. 4.95 (*0-916453-00-6*) TAU Pr.

Pesek-Marous, Georgia. The Bull: A Religious & Secular History of Phallus Worship & Male Homosexuality. (Illus.). 185p. (Orig.). 1984. pap. 9.95 (*0-916453-01-4*) TAU Pr.

Peselnick, jt. auth. see Highland.

Peselnick, Charles, jt. auth. see Highland, Esther H.

Peseroff, Joyce. A Dog in the Lifeboat. LC 90-84778. (Poetry Ser.). 64p. (Orig.). (C). 1991. pap. 11.95 (*0-88748-114-0*) Carnegie-Mellon.

***Peseroff, Joyce.** Hardness Scale. (Classic Contemporaries Ser.). 2000. pap. text 12.95 (*0-88748-322-4*) Carnegie-Mellon.

— Mortal Education. LC 99-72502. (Poetry Ser.). 80p. 2000. pap. 12.95 (*0-88748-326-7*, Pub. by Carnegie-Mellon) CUP Services.

Peseroff, Joyce, ed. The Ploughshares Poetry Reader. LC 86-6319. 336p. 1987. 25.00 (*0-933277-02-4*) Ploughshares.

Peset, Jose L., ed. The Ethics of Diagnosis. (Philosophy & Medicine Ser.). 320p. (C). 1992. lib. bdg. 171.00 (*0-7923-1544-8*, Pub. by Kluwer Academic) Kluwer Academic.

Peset, Z., jt. auth. see Rous, J.

Pesetsky, Bette. Cast a Spell. 1993. 21.95 (*0-15-116072-4*) Harcourt.

Pesetsky, David. Zero Syntax: Experiences & Cascades. (Current Studies in Linguistics: No. 27). 369p. 1994. 43.00 (*0-262-16145-1*) MIT Pr.

— Zero Syntax: Experiences & Cascades. (Current Studies in Linguistics: No. 27). (Illus.). 369p. 1996. pap. text 21.50 (*0-262-66100-4*) MIT Pr.

Pesetsky, David Michael. Phrasal Movement & Its Kin. (Linguistic Inquiry Monographs: No. 37). (Illus.). 144p. (C). Date not set. 45.00 (*0-262-16196-6*) MIT Pr.

— Phrasal Movement & Its Kin. LC 00-38695. (Linguistic Inquiry Monographs: No. 37). (Illus.). 144p. (C). 2000. pap. 18.00 (*0-262-66166-7*) MIT Pr.

Pesez, Maurice & Bartos, J. Colorimetric & Fluorimetric Analysis of Organic Compounds & Drugs. LC 73-84815. (Clinical & Biochemical Analysis Ser.: No. 1). 688p. reprint ed. pap. 200.00 (*0-7837-5176-1*, 204490600004) Bks Demand.

Peshawaria, Reeta. Managing Behavior Problems in Children: A Guide for Parents. 1991. pap. text 4.95 (*0-7069-5322-3*, Pub. by Vikas) S Asia.

Peshef, Robert J. TMJ Therapy Balances Body Chemistry. 1983. 65.00 (*0-9605902-6-9*) Color Coded Charting.

Peshek, Robert J. Clinical Nutrition Using the Seven Lines of Defense Against Disease. 1980. 10.00 (*0-9605902-3-4*) Color Coded Charting.

— Cross Index. 1982. 10.00 (*0-9605902-5-0*) Color Coded Charting.

— Nutrition for a Healthy Heart. (Illus.). 1979. 20.00 (*0-9605902-2-6*) Color Coded Charting.

— Searching for Health. 1982. 15.95 (*0-9605902-4-2*) Color Coded Charting.

— Student's Manual for Balancing Body Chemistry with Nutrition. 1977. 20.00 (*0-9605902-1-8*) Color Coded Charting.

Peshev, Tsolo C., et al. The International History of Mammalogy. Sterling, Keir B., ed. LC 82-18865. (Eastern Europe & Fennoscandia Ser.: Vol. I). (Illus.). 200p. (C). 1987. pap. 25.00 (*0-910485-01-1*) One World Pr.

Peshine, John H. Peshine Family in Europe & America: Notes & Suggestions for a Genealogical Tree from the Beginning of the 14th Century to the Present Day, with Some Biographical Sketches & Much Data Relating to the Ball, Mulford & Pye Families. 109p. 1996. reprint ed. pap. 19.00 (*0-8328-5328-3*); reprint ed. lib. bdg. 29.00 (*0-8328-5327-5*) Higginson Bk Co.

Peshkin, Alan. The Color of Strangers, the Color of Friends: The Play of Ethnicity in School & Community. LC 90-19765. 318p. 1991. pap. text 18.00 (*0-226-66201-2*) U Ch Pr.

— The Color of Strangers, the Color of Friends: The Play of Ethnicity in School & Community. LC 90-19765. 320p. 1995. lib. bdg. 52.00 (*0-226-66200-4*) U Ch Pr.

— God's Choice: The Total World of a Fundamentalist Christian School. LC 85-24524. x, 360p. (C). 1988. pap. text 17.95 (*0-226-66199-7*) U Ch Pr.

— God's Choice: The Total World of a Fundamentalist Christian School. LC 85-24524. x, 360p. (C). 1997. 29.95 (*0-226-66198-9*) U Ch Pr.

— Growing up American: Schooling & the Survival of Community. LC 78-5849. 1994. pap. text 10.95 (*0-226-66197-0*) U Ch Pr.

— Growing up American: Schooling & the Survival of Community. (Illus.). 256p. (C). 1994. reprint ed. pap. text 11.95 (*0-88133-825-7*) Waveland Pr.

— The Imperfect Union: School Consolidation & Community Conflict. LC 82-16104. (Illus.). 224p. (C). 1994. lib. bdg. 19.00 (*0-226-66166-0*) U Ch Pr.

***Peshkin, Alan.** Permissible Advantage? The Moral Consequences of Elite Schooling. 200p. 2000. write for info. (*0-8058-2466-9*) L Erlbaum Assocs.

— Permissible Advantage? The Moral Consequences of Elite Schooling. 200p. 2000. pap. write for info. (*0-8058-2467-7*) L Erlbaum Assocs.

Peshkin, Alan. Places of Memory: Whiteman's Schools & Native American Communities. LC 97-5612. 1997. write for info. (*0-8058-2468-5*); pap. write for info. (*0-8058-2469-3*) L Erlbaum Assocs.

Peshkin, Alan, jt. ed. see Eisner, Elliot W.

Peshkin, M. & Tonomura, A. The Aharonov-Bohm Effect. (Lecture Notes in Physics Ser.: Vol. 340). vi, 152p. 1989. 34.95 (*0-387-51567-4*, 3455) Spr-Verlag.

PeshKova, I. M. The Art of the Kasli Masters: Iskusstvo Kaslinskikh Masterov, 2 vols. (RUS.). 1983. write for info. (*0-7855-2562-9*) St Mut.

— The Art of the Kasli Masters: Iskusstvo Kaslinskikh Masterov, 2 vols., Vol. I. (RUS.). 160p. 1983. 212.00 (*0-7855-1557-7*) St Mut.

Peshut, Jeffrey J. Golf's Timeless Fundamental Vol. 1: Discover Techniques to Improve Your Game. LC 97-20051. (Illus.). 96p. 1997. pap. 10.95 (*1-57034-083-8*) Globe Pequot.

***Pesic, Peter.** Labyrinth: A Search for the Hidden Meaning of Science. LC 99-46389. (Illus.). 160p. 2000. 21.95 (*0-262-16190-7*) MIT Pr.

Pesic, Slobodan, jt. auth. see Gottlieb, Annie.

Pesic, Slobodan D., jt. auth. see Gottlieb, Annie.

Pesin. Dimension Theory Dynamical Systems. LC 97-16686. 312p. 1997. lib. bdg. 56.00 (*0-226-66221-7*) U Ch Pr.

Pesin, Yakov B. Dimension Theory Dynamical Systems. LC 97-16686. 312p. 1997. pap. text 19.95 (*0-226-66222-5*) U Ch Pr.

Pesina, Jaroslav. The Master of the Hohenfurth Alterpiece. (Illus.). 260p. 1989. 95.00 (*0-85667-339-0*) Sothebys Pubns.

Pesiri, Evelyn. The Thesaurus for Kids. LC 98-20848. (Illus.). 144p. (J). (gr. 3-7). 1998. pap. 8.95 (*1-56565-694-6*, 06946W, Pub. by Lowell Hse Juvenile) NTC Contemp Pub Co.

— The Thesaurus for Kids. LC 98-20848. (Illus.). 144p. (J). (gr. 3-8). 1998. 12.95 (*1-56565-693-8*, 06938W, Pub. by Lowell Hse Juvenile) NTC Contemp Pub Co.

Pesiri, Salina, jt. auth. see Ventimiglia, Sebastian B.

Peske, Gretchen C., et al. Patient Education: Strategies & Skills for Living Well. LC 95-76320. (Illus.). 300p. (Orig.). 1996. pap. 12.00 (*1-887109-00-5*) Blue Path Pr.

Peske, Nancy & West, Beverly. Frankly Scarlett, I Do Give a Damn! Classic Romances Retold. 99p. 1999. reprint ed. text 10.00 (*0-7881-6222-5*) DIANE Pub.

Peske, Nancy, jt. auth. see West, Beverly.

Peskett, Howard. Isaiah: Trusting God in Troubled Times. (LifeGuide Bible Studies). 112p. (Orig.). 1991. pap., wbk. ed. 4.99 (*0-8308-1029-3*, 1029) InterVarsity.

Peskett, Pamela, jt. auth. see Wycherley Gibson, Jeremy Sumner.

Peskin, Allan. Garfield. rev. ed. LC 77-15630. (Illus.). 720p. 1998. 45.00 (*0-87338-210-2*) Kent St U Pr.

Peskin, Allan, ed. North into Freedom: The Autobiography of John Malvin, Free Negro, 1795-1880. 2nd ed. 93p. 1996. reprint ed. pap. 7.95 (*0-911704-48-5*) Western Res.

Peskin, Brian S. Beyond the Zone. LC 96-71593. (Illus.). 480p. 2000. pap. 19.95 (*0-9651551-3-7*, Noble Pub) Dynamic Pubng.

Peskin, C. S., jt. auth. see Hoppensteadt, Frank C.

Peskin, Dean B. The Corporate Casino: How Managers Win & Lose at the Biggest Game in Town. LC 78-12779. 251p. reprint ed. pap. 77.90 (*0-608-11910-5*, 202357000033) Bks Demand.

— Human Behavior & Employment Interviewing. LC 78-130915. (Illus.). 256p. reprint ed. pap. 79.40 (*0-608-10773-5*, 201173600079) Bks Demand.

— Sacked! What to Do When You Lose Your Job. LC 79-13522. 191p. reprint ed. pap. 59.30 (*0-608-11906-7*, 202357500033) Bks Demand.

— Womaning: Overcoming Male Dominance of Executive Row. Ashton, Sylvia, ed. LC 80-13060. 1981. 22.95 (*0-87949-165-5*) Ashley Bks.

Peskin, Henry M., et al, eds. Environmental Regulation & the U. S. Economy. LC 81-47620. 163p. 1981. 21.95 (*0-8018-2711-6*); pap. 14.95 (*0-8018-2712-4*) Resources Future.

***Peskin, Hy & Thorn, John.** A Life in the Shadows: The Sports Photography of Hy Peskin. (Illus.). 192p. 2000. 40.00 (*1-892129-40-X*) Total Sprts.

Peskin, Michael E. & Schroeder, Daniel V. An Introduction to Quantum Field Theory. 656p. (C). 1994. pap. write for info. (*0-201-50934-2*) Addison-Wesley.

— An Introduction to Quantum Field Theory. 656p. (C). 1995. 55.00 (*0-201-50397-2*) Addison-Wesley.

Peskin, Michael W. Asset-Liability Management for Corporate Pensions: Analysis & Strategy for Effective Plans. (Illus.). 200p. 1997. 50.00 (*0-7863-1146-0*, Irwn Prfssnl) McGraw-Hill Prof.

Peskin, Nancy, ed. Angle of Repose. 100p. 1986. pap. 5.95 (*0-936739-01-0*) Hallwalls Inc.

Peskin, Stephan. How to Settle for Top Dollar: 1991 Supplement. 90p. 1992. write for info. (*0-87473-830-X*, 65833-10, MICHIE) LEXIS Pub.

Peskin, Stephan H. How to Settle for Top Dollar: 1990 Supplement. 1990. write for info. (*0-87473-703-6*, 65832-10, MICHIE) LEXIS Pub.

P

Peskine, Christian. An Algebraic Introduction to Complex Projective Geometry Vol. 1: Commutative Algebra. (Studies in Advanced Mathematics: No. 47). 238p. (C). 1996. text 44.95 (*0-521-48072-8*) Cambridge U Pr.

Peskoff, Joel. Beat NYC Parking Tickets - Z System: Beat the Pub at Its Own Game. Bolofsky, Glen, ed. 8p. 1992. student ed. write for info. (*0-931579-25-2*) J F Caroll Pub.

— The Original - How to Beat a Parking Ticket - NYC Edition. Ornstein, Judy, ed. 40p. (Orig.). 1991. pap. write for info. (*0-931579-16-3*) J F Caroll Pub.

Peskowitz, Miriam. Spinning Fantasies: Rabbis, Gender & History. LC 96-43149. (Contraversions Ser.). 263p. 1997. 45.00 (*0-520-20831-5*, Pub. by U CA Pr); pap. 17.95 (*0-520-20967-2*, Pub. by U CA Pr) Cal Prin Full Svc.

Peskowitz, Miriam & Levitt, Laura, eds. Judaism since Gender. LC 96-42109. 241p. (C). 1996. 70.00 (*0-415-91460-4*); pap. 18.99 (*0-415-91461-2*) Routledge.

Pesman, Curtis. What She Wants. 1992. pap. 10.00 (*0-345-36653-0*) Ballantine Pub Grp.

— When a Man Turns Forty: The Ultimate Mid-Life Manual. LC 99-12006. viii, 248p. 1999. 19.95 (*1-57954-022-8*) Rodale Pr Inc.

— Your First Year of Marriage. LC 95-17631. 240p. 1995. pap. 11.00 (*0-684-80246-5*, Fireside) S&S Trade Pap.

Pesman, M. Walter. Meet the Natives: The Amateur's Field Guide to Rocky Mountain Wildflowers, Trees, & Shrubs. 9th ed. (Illus.). 244p. 1992. pap. 12.95 (*1-879373-31-9*) Roberts Rinehart.

Pesman, Roslyn. Duty Free: Australia Women Abroad. LC 96-134237. (Illus.). 280p. (C). 1996. text 45.00 (*0-19-553639-8*) OUP.

Pesman, Roslyn, et al, eds. The Oxford Book of Australian Travel Writing. LC 97-108823. 352p. 1997. 49.95 (*0-19-553640-1*) OUP.

Pesmatzoglou, Haris. Die Harmonisierung der Kapitaleinkommensbesteuerung in der Europaischen Union. (Europaische Hochschulschriften: Reihe 5: Bd. 1970). (GER.). 230p. 1996. pap. 44.95 (*3-631-30419-6*) P Lang Pubng.

***Pesmen, Dale.** Russia & Soul: An Exploration. 2000. 19.95 (*0-8014-8709-9*) Cornell U Pr.

Pesmen, Sandra. Writing for the Media. LC 82-72510. (Illus.). 172p. 1994. pap. 24.95 (*0-8442-3076-6*, NTC Business Bks) NTC Contemp Pub Co.

Pesola, Carol A., jt. auth. see Curtain, Helena.

Pesola, Mike. The Bedrock Guide to Remodeling Success. (Illus.). 64p. 1998. pap. 14.00 (*0-8059-4455-9*) Dorrance.

Pesolu, Marilyn, ed. see Still, Tom & Leigh-Kendall, T. A.

Pesonen, Niilo & Ponteva, E. Laaketieteen Sanakirja. 8th ed. (ENG, FIN, FRE & SWE.). 525p. 1987. 250.00 (*0-8288-1886-X*, M9984) Fr & Eur.

Pesonen, Pertti. An Election in Finland: Party Activities & Voter Reactions. LC 68-13925. 436p. reprint ed. pap. 135.20 (*0-608-14026-0*, 202202900024) Bks Demand.

Pesonen, Pertti, et al, eds. To Join or Not to Join: Three Nordic Referendums on Membership in the European Union. 368p. 1998. text 49.00 (*82-00-12843-1*) Scandnvan Univ Pr.

Pesotta, Rose. Bread upon the Waters. 464p. (Orig.). 1987. reprint ed. text 39.95 (*0-87546-126-3*, ILR Press); reprint ed. pap. text 16.95 (*0-87546-127-1*, ILR Press) Cornell U Pr.

— Bread upon the Waters. (American Autobiography Ser.). 435p. (Orig.). 1995. reprint ed. lib. bdg. 99.00 (*0-7812-8616-6*) Rprt Serv.

Pesquera, Beatriz M., jt. ed. see De La Torre, Adela.

Pesquera, L. & Bermejo, F. J., eds. Dynamics of Non-Linear Optical Systems. 350p. (C). 1989. text 93.00 (*9971-5-0814-1*) World Scientific Pub.

Pesquera, L. & Rodriguez, M. A., eds. International School on Stochastic Processes Applied to Physics: Proceedings, 1984. 332p. 1985. 70.00 (*9971-978-20-2*) World Scientific Pub.

Pessagno, E. A., Jr. Radiolarian Zonation & Stratigraphy of the Upper Cretaceous Portion of the Great Valley Sequence, California Coast Ranges. (Micropaleontology Special Publications: No. 2). 95p. 1976. 20.00 (*0-686-84250-2*) Am Mus Natl Hist.

Pessagno, E. A., Jr., et al. Bulletins of American Paleontology Vol. 87, No. 320: A Revised Radiolarian Zonation for the Upper Jurassic of Western North America. 52p. 1984. 10.00 (*0-87710-396-8*) Paleo Res.

— Bulletins of American Paleontology Vol. 91: Jurassic Nassellariina (Radiolaria) from North American Geologic Terranes. 75p. 1986. 25.00 (*0-87710-406-9*) Paleo Res.

***Pessah, Suzanne.** I Remember the Schwabs. 2000. pap. write for info. (*0-8059-5043-5*) Dorrance.

Pessanha, Ricardo, jt. auth. see McGowan, Chris.

Pessano, Laurie, jt. auth. see Marolf, Stacey.

Pessar, Patricia R. A Visa for a Dream: Dominicans in the United States. Foner, Nancy, ed. LC 96-185888. (Immigrants Ser.). 100p. (C). 1996. pap. 20.00 (*0-205-16675-X*) Allyn.

Pessar, Patricia R., ed. When Borders Don't Divide: Labor Migration & Refugee Movements in the Americas. LC 87-20856. 300p. 1988. 19.50 (*0-934733-26-0*); pap. 14.50 (*0-934733-27-9*) CMS.

Pessar, Patricia R., jt. auth. see Grasmuck, Sherri.

***Pessarakli, Mohammad.** Handbook of Plant & Crop Stress. 2nd ed. LC 99-14997. (Books in Soils, Plants & the Environment Ser.). (Illus.). 1256p. 1999. text 235.00 (*0-8247-1948-4*) Dekker.

Pessarakli, Mohammad, ed. Handbook of Photosynthesis. LC 96-31583. (Books in Soils, Plants & the Environment: Vol. 51). (Illus.). 1056p. 1996. text 215.00 (*0-8247-9708-6*) Dekker.

— Handbook of Plant & Crop Physiology. LC 94-32077. (Books in Soils, Plants & the Environment: Vol. 36). (Illus.). 1024p. 1994. text 199.00 (*0-8247-9250-5*) Dekker.

Pesselhoy, Arnulf. Dem Kapitalismus eine Chance. (Zur Diskussion - Thesen - Erfahrungen - Urteile Ser.: Bd. 2). (GER.). 270p. 1996. 35.00 (*3-487-08376-0*) G Olms Pubs.

Pessemier, Edgar A., jt. auth. see Moore, William L.

Pessen, David W. Industrial Automation: Circuit Design & Components. LC 88-28002. 528p. 1989. 140.00 (*0-471-60071-7*) Wiley.

— Industrial Automation: Circuit Design & Components. 1989. pap. text, teacher ed. write for info. (*0-471-50793-8*) Wiley.

Pessen, David W. & Hubl, Werner. The Design & Application of Programmable Sequence Controllers for Automation Systems. LC 78-40456. 128p. reprint ed. pap. 39.70 (*0-608-30507-3*, 202097600020) Bks Demand.

Pessen, Edward. Jacksonian America: Society, Personality, & Politics. LC 85-1100. 400p. (C). 1985. reprint ed. pap. text 17.95 (*0-252-01237-2*) U of Ill Pr.

— Losing Our Souls: The American Experience in the Cold War. LC 93-11241. 256p. 1993. text 24.95 (*1-56663-037-1*) I R Dee.

— Losing Our Souls: The American Experience in the Cold War. LC 95-32551. 256p. 1995. pap. text 12.95 (*1-56663-096-7*, Elephant Paperbacks) I R Dee.

— The Many-Faceted Jacksonian Era: New Interpretations, 67. LC 77-24621. (Contributions in American History Ser.: No. 67). (Illus.). 331p. 1977. 59.95 (*0-8371-9720-1*, PJE/, Greenwood Pr) Greenwood.

— Riches, Class, & Power: The United States Before the Civil War. 467p. 1989. pap. 24.95 (*0-88738-806-X*) Transaction Pubs.

Pessen, Edward, ed. Jacksonian Panorama. LC 75-20140. (AHS Ser: No. 85). 1976. pap. 8.95 (*0-672-60142-7*, Bobbs) Macmillan.

Pessereau, Jennifer, ed. see Ripoche, Bokar.

Pessey, Christian & Samson, Remy. Bonsai Basics: A Step-by-Step Guide to Growing, Training & General Care. LC 92-38557. (Illus.). 120p. 1993. pap. 10.95 (*0-8069-0327-9*) Sterling.

Pessin, Allan H. Fundamentals of the Securities Industries. rev. ed. (Illus.). 1985. text 35.00 (*0-317-01037-9*) NY Inst Finance.

— Fundamentals of the Securities Industry: An Inside View from Wall Street. 1986. 39.95 (*0-13-349062-9*) S&S Trade.

— Securities Law Compliance: A Guide for Brokers, Dealers & Investors. 320p. 1989. text 70.00 (*1-55623-228-4*, Irwn Prfssnl) McGraw-Hill Prof.

Pessin, Andrew & Goldberg, Sanford, eds. The Twin Earth Chronicles: Twenty Years of Reflection. LC 95-10001. 432p. (gr. 13). 1996. text 76.95 (*1-56324-873-5*) M E Sharpe.

— The Twin Earth Chronicles: Twenty Years of Reflection on Hilary Putnam's "The Meaning of 'Meaning'" LC 95-10001. 448p. 1995. 49.95 (*1-55778-720-4*); pap. 19.95 (*1-55778-721-2*) M E Sharpe.

Pessin, Andrew & Goldberg, Sanford, eds. The Twin Earth Chronicles: Twenty Years of Reflection on Hilary Putnam's the Meaning of 'Meaning' LC 95-10001. 432p. (gr. 13). 1996. pap. text 32.95 (*1-56324-874-3*) M E Sharpe.

Pessin, Andrew, jt. auth. see Goldberg, Sanford.

Pessin, Deborah. Aleph-Bet Story Book. (Illus.). (J). (gr. 1-3). 1989. pap. 7.95 (*0-8276-0337-1*) JPS Phila.

— History of the Jews in America. (Illus.). (J). (gr. 8-10). 1957. pap. 4.95 (*0-8381-0189-5*) USCJE.

— Jewish People, 3 vols. (Illus.). (J). (gr. 5-8). 1953. write for info. (*0-318-56293-6*); 4.25 (*0-318-56294-4*) USCJE.

— Jewish People, 3 Vols, I. (Illus.). (J). (gr. 5-8). 1953. 4.25 (*0-8381-0182-8*) USCJE.

— Jewish People, Vol. I. (Illus.). (J). (gr. 5-8). 1953. student ed. 4.25 (*0-8381-0183-6*) USCJE.

— Jewish People, Vol. II. (Illus.). (J). (gr. 5-8). 1953. 4.25 (*0-8381-0185-2*); student ed. 4.25 (*0-8381-0186-0*) USCJE.

— Jewish People, Vol. III. (Illus.). (J). (gr. 5-8). 1953. 4.25 (*0-8381-0187-9*); student ed. 4.25 (*0-8381-0188-7*) USCJE.

Pessino, Catherine, jt. auth. see Hussey, Lois J.

Pessireron, Sylvia, tr. see Caldwell, Ian & Volkman, Toby A., eds.

Pessis. Cinema-Video-Sound-Multimedia-Electronic Web Dictionary French-English - English-French. (ENG & FRE.). 451p. 1997. pap. 55.00 (*2-906587-67-2*, Pub. by Dixit Editions) IBD Ltd.

Pessis, G. Dictionnaire Francais-Anglais, Anglais-Francais de l'Audiovisuel. (FRE.). 432p. 1995. 95.00 (*0-7859-9898-5*) Fr & Eur.

Pessis, George. Dictionnaire Cinema, Audiovisuel, Multimedia, Reseaux Anglais-Francais/Francais-Anglais. (ENG & FRE.). 452p. 1997. pap. 95.00 (*0-7859-9505-6*) Fr & Eur.

Pessis-Pasternak, Guitta. Dictionnaire de l'Audio-Visuel: Francais-Anglais, Anglais-Francais. (ENG & FRE.). 384p. 1976. pap. 39.95 (*0-8288-5639-7*, M6442) Fr & Eur.

Pessissiron, Sylvia, tr. see Oey, Eric, ed.

Pesso, Albert, ed. see Crandell, John S.

Pessoa, Fernando. Always Astonished: Selected Prose. Honig, Edwin, tr. from POR. 160p. 1988. pap. 12.95 (*0-87286-228-3*) City Lights.

— Antologia Poetica. El Poeta es un Fingidor. Crespo, Angel, ed. & tr. by. (Nueva Austral Ser.: Vol. 67). (SPA.). 1991. pap. text 24.95 (*84-239-1867-X*) Elliots Bks.

— The Book of Disquiet. MacAdam, Alfred, tr. from POR. 1998. pap. text 15.95 (*1-878972-27-8*) Exact Change.

— The Book of Disquietude by Bernardo Soares, Assistant Bookkeeper in the City of Lisbon. Zenith, Richard, ed. & tr. by. from POR. LC 97-179124. 339p. 1997. pap. 17.95 (*1-878818-65-1*, Pub. by Sheep Meadow) U Pr of New Eng.

— Fernando Pessoa & Co. Selected Poems. Zenith, Richard, ed. & tr. by. from POR. LC 97-50201. 304p. 1998. reprint ed. 25.00 (*0-8021-1628-0*, Grove) Grove-Atltic.

***Pessoa, Fernando.** Fernando Pessoa & Co. Selected Poems. Zenith, Richard, ed. 304p. 1999. reprint ed. pap. 14.00 (*0-8021-3627-3*, Grove) Grove-Atltic.

Pessoa, Fernando. The Keeper of Sheep: Bilingual Edition. Honig, Edwin & Brown, Susan M., trs. from POR. LC 97-37487. Orig. Title: O Guardador de Rabanhos. (ENG & POR.). 137p. 1997. pap. 12.95 (*1-878818-45-7*, Pub. by Sheep Meadow) U Pr of New Eng.

— Mensagem - Poemas Esotericos: Edicao Critica. (Coleccion Archivos de Ediciones Criticas). (SPA.). 30.99 (*84-88344-04-X*, Pub. by Fondo) Continental Bk.

— The Poems of Fernando Pessoa. (Modern European Poets Ser.). 215p. 1988. pap. 10.50 (*0-88001-123-8*) HarpC.

— The Poems of Fernando Pessoa. Honig, Edwin & Brown, Susan M., eds. LC 98-11043. 236p. 1998. reprint ed. pap. 15.95 (*0-87286-342-5*) City Lights.

Pessoa, Fernando. Selected Poems. 1996. pap. 14.95 (*0-14-018845-2*, Pub. by Pnguin Bks Ltd) Trafalgar.

Pessoa, Fernando. The Surprise of Being: Twenty-Five Poems : Dual Text. Greene, James & Azevedo Mafra, Clara de, trs. from POR. LC 86-82063. 64p. 1987. 25.00 (*0-946162-23-9*, Pub. by Angel Bks); pap. 13.95 (*0-946162-24-7*, Pub. by Angel Bks) Dufour.

Pessolano, F. John, jt. ed. see Mendell, Jay S.

Pessoneaux, Emile. Dictionnaire Grec-Francais.Tr. of Greek-French Dictionary. (FRE & GRE.). 896p. 1953. 59.95 (*0-8288-6877-8*, M-6443) Fr & Eur.

Pest & Pathogen Control Through Mgmt. of Bio. Cont. Ecologically Based Pest Management: New Solutions for a New Century. LC 96-4946. 160p. 1996. text 37.95 (*0-309-05330-7*) Natl Acad Pr.

Pest Publications Staff. Organic Pest Control Handbook. rev. ed. LC 97-48311. (Illus.). 96p. 1998. pap. 10.95 (*1-57067-052-8*) Book Pub Co.

Pesta, Otto. Der Hochgebirgssee der Alpen: Versuch einer Limnologischen Charakteristik. (Binnengewaesser Ser.: Band VIII). (GER., Illus.). xi, 156p. 1929. 23.00 (*3-510-40708-3*, Pub. by E Schweizerbartsche) Balogh.

Pestalozzi, anno. Band 29 (Nachtrag) Anonyme Drucke und Nachgelassene Texte Aus Den Jahren 1781 Bis 1818. 1997. 56.00 (*3-11-015538-9*) De Gruyter.

Pestalozzi, Johann H. Buch der Mutter: 1803 Edition. Stern, Jeffrey, ed. & intro. by. (Classics in Education Ser.). (GER.). 182p. 1996. reprint ed. 75.00 (*1-85506-305-0*) Bks Intl VA.

— Education of Man, Aphorisms. LC 79-88920. 93p. 1969. reprint ed. lib. bdg. 49.50 (*0-8371-2107-8*, PEEM, Greenwood Pr) Greenwood.

— How Gertrude Teaches Her Children: How Mothers Teach Their Own Children. 1973. 250.00 (*0-87968-066-0*) Gordon Pr.

— Leonard & Gertrude. 1976. lib. bdg. 250.00 (*0-8490-0507-8*) Gordon Pr.

— Pestalozzi. Anderson, Lewis F., ed. LC 73-10877. 283p. 1975. reprint ed. lib. bdg. 35.00 (*0-8371-7046-X*, PEP, Greenwood Pr) Greenwood.

— Pestalozzi's Educational Writings, 2. Green, John A., tr. from GER. LC 77-72191. (Contributions to the History of Psychology Ser.: Vol. II, Pt. B, Psychometrics). 424p. 1977. reprint ed. lib. bdg. 85.00 (*0-313-26937-8*, U6937, Greenwood Pr) Greenwood.

— Wie Gertrud Ihre Kinder Lehrt: 1801 Edition. Stern, Jeffrey, ed. & intro. by. (Classics in Education Ser.). 392p. 1996. reprint ed. 95.00 (*1-85506-304-2*) Bks Intl VA.

***Pestalozzi, Julia, et al.** Psychoanalytic Psychotherapy in Institutional Settings. 256p. 1998. pap. 32.00 (*1-85575-198-4*, Pub. by H Karnac Bks Ltd) Other Pr LLC.

Pestalozzi, Karl, jt. ed. see Mueller-Lauter, Wolfgang.

***Pestalozzi, Tina.** Life Skills 101: A Practical Guide to Leaving Home & Living on Your Own. LC 00-133460. 160p. 2000. pap. 12.95 (*0-9701334-4-8*, 004796) Stonewood.

Pestana, Carla G. Liberty of Conscience & the Growth of Religious Diversity in Early America, 1636-1786. (Illus.). 102p. 1986. pap. 30.00 (*0-916617-02-5*) J C Brown.

— Quakers & Baptists in Colonial Massachusetts. 211p. (C). 1991. text 64.95 (*0-521-41111-4*) Cambridge U Pr.

Pestana, Carla Gardina & Salinger, Sharon V., eds. Inequality in Early America. LC 99-25050. (Reencounters with Colonialism Ser.). (Illus.). 343p. 1999. pap. 19.95 (*0-87451-927-6*); text 40.00 (*0-87451-926-8*) U Pr of New Eng.

***Pestana, Carlos.** Fluids & Electrolytes in the Surgical Patient. 5th ed. LC 99-40625. 1999. write for info. (*0-7817-2425-2*) Lppncott W & W.

Pestana, Carlos. Fluids & Electrolytes in the Surgical Patients. 4th ed. (Illus.). 240p. 1989. pap. text 34.00 (*0-683-06862-8*) Lppncott W & W.

Pestana, Emily. Circles. Bixby, Robert, ed. 17p. 1993. pap. 6.00 (*1-882983-03-3*) March Street Pr.

Pestana, Joseph P. Gold Street. Holian, Gail C., ed. (Illus.). 136p. (Orig.). 1996. pap. 11.95 (*0-9655828-0-9*, GS5637, Nauvoo Pr) Nauvoo Ent.

***Pestana, Linda Lambert.** Two Faces of Love: A Memoir. (Illus.). 176p. 2000. pap. 19.95 (*0-9632793-9-4*) Annedawn Pub.

Pestana, Mark. Moral Virtue or Mental Health? LC 96-38658. (San Francisco State University Series in Philosophy: Vol. 10). XVI, 152p. (C). 1998. text 39.95 (*0-8204-3687-9*) P Lang Pubng.

Pestel. Keith Haring. (Prestel Postcard Bks.). (Illus.). 18p. 1994. pap. 8.95 (*3-7913-1359-2*, Pub. by Prestel) te Neues.

Pestelli, Giorgio, jt. ed. see Bianconi, Lorenzo.

Pester, Martin M., ed. Theme Restaurant Design, No. 9. (Illus.). 178p. 1997. 59.95 (*0-934590-87-7*) Visual Refer.

Pestereau, Gilbert. Dictionnaire des Personnages Vian. (FRE.). 426p. 1993. pap. 28.95 (*0-7859-7874-7*, 2267012006) Fr & Eur.

Pestieau, Caroline. The Quebec Textile Industry in Canada. LC 79-302341. (Accent Quebec Ser.). 90p. 1978. reprint ed. pap. 30.00 (*0-608-01370-6*, 206211000002) Bks Demand.

Pestieau, Caroline, jt. auth. see Maxwell, Judith B.

Pestieau, Caroline, jt. ed. see Culpepper, Roy.

Pestieau, Joseph. Essai Contre le Defaitisme Politique: Imagination Politique et Intelligence Economique. LC 74-180539. (FRE.). 255p. reprint ed. pap. 79.10 (*0-7837-6939-3*, 204676800003) Bks Demand.

Pestis, Gene. Raising Healthy Poultry under Primitive Conditions. rev. ed. 1994. pap. text 7.50 (*1-886532-02-8*) Christian Vet.

Pestka, Sidney, ed. Cytokine Yearbook, Vol. 1. 104p. (C). 1996. text 95.50 (*0-7923-3876-6*) Kluwer Academic.

Pestka, Sidney, jt. ed. see Colowick, Sidney P.

Pestman, P. W., ed. The New Papyrological Primer. 5th ed. (Illus.). xxii, 318p. 1990. pap. 46.50 (*90-04-10019-9*) Brill Academic Pubs.

Pestman, P. W. & Rupprecht, H. A. Berichtigungsliste. (Berichtigungsliste der Griechischen Papyrusurkunden aus Agypten Ser.: Vol. 10). (GER.). 400p. 1998. 129.50 (*90-04-11133-6*) Brill Academic Pubs.

Pestman, P. W., jt. auth. see Vleeming, S. P.

Pestman, Wiebe R. Mathematical Statistics. LC 98-18771. 546p. 1998. pap. 49.00 (*3-11-015356-4*) De Gruyter.

— Mathematical Statistics: An Introduction. LC 98-18771. 545p. 1997. 80.00 (*3-11-015357-2*) De Gruyter.

Pestman, Wiebe R. & Alberink, Ivo B. Mathematical Statistics: Problems & Detailed Solutions. LC 98-20084. 325p. 1998. 80.00 (*3-11-015359-9*) De Gruyter.

— Mathematical Statistics: Problems & Detailed Solutions. LC 98-20084. 326p. 1998. pap. 49.00 (*3-11-015358-0*) De Gruyter.

Pestoff, Victor A. Beyond the Market & State: Social Enterprise & Civil Democracy in a Welfare Society. LC 98-72797. 287p. 1998. text 69.95 (*1-84014-575-7*, Pub. by Ashgate Pub) Ashgate Pub Co.

Peston, Maurice H., jt. auth. see Corry, Bernard.

Peston, Maurice H., jt. ed. see Quandt, Richard E.

Pestonjee, D. M. Second Handbook of Psychological & Social Instruments. (C). 1990. 56.00 (*81-7022-193-5*, Pub. by Concept) S Asia.

— Stress & Coping: The Indian Experience. 224p. (C). 1992. 32.00 (*0-8039-9400-1*) Sage.

***Pestonjee, D. M.** Stress & Coping: The Indian Experience. 2nd ed. LC 98-32120. 1998. write for info. (*0-7619-9312-6*) Sage.

Pestonjee, D. M. Stress & Coping: The Indian Experience 2nd ed. LC 98-32120. 1998. write for info. (*0-7619-9313-4*) Sage.

Pestonjee, Shirin F. Nurse's Handbook of Patient Education. LC 99-36721. 274p. 1999. text 29.95 (*1-58255-018-2*) Springhouse Corp.

Pestre, D. Physique et Physiciens en France, 1918-1940. 2nd ed. (FRE.). xvi, 356p. 1992. pap. text 60.00 (*2-903928-08-8*) Gordon & Breach.

Pestre, Dominique, jt. ed. see Krige, John.

Pestrikov, Dmitri & Dikansky, Nikolai. The Physics of Intense Beams & Storage Rings. LC 93-19889.Tr. of Fizika Intensivnykh Puchkov v Nakopiteliakh. 1994. 79.95 (*1-56396-107-5*) Spr-Verlag.

***Pestritto, Ronald J.** Founding the Criminal Law: Punishment & Political Thought in the Origins of America LC 99-32841. 2000. 36.00 (*0-87580-260-5*) N Ill U Pr.

Pestryakov, E. M., tr. see Dobrovolsky, V. N. & Litovchenko, V. G.

Pestum, Jo. Maya y el Truco Para Hacer la Tarea. (SPA.). (J). (gr. 3-4). 1995. pap. 5.99 (*968-16-4727-0*, Pub. by Fondo) Continental Bk.

Pestureau, Gilbert, tr. see De Beaumarchais, Pierre-Augustin C.

Pesut, Herman. Clinical Reasoning: The Art & Science of Critical & Creative Thinking. 2nd ed. LC 98-37445. (Professional Reference - Nursing Ser.). 272p. (C). 1999. pap. 31.95 (*0-8273-7869-6*) Delmar.

Pesut, Robert N., jt. auth. see Thomasson, Joanne.

Peszke, Michael A. Battle for Warsaw: 1939-1944. 400p. 1995. 56.00 (*0-88033-324-3*, 427, Pub. by East Eur Monographs) Col U Pr.

***Peszke, Michael A.** Longing for a Kiss: Treasury of Love Poems. 128p. 1999. 19.95 (*0-7818-0671-2*) Hippocrene Bks.

Peszke, Michael A. Poland's Navy, 1918-1945. (Illus.). 250p. 1999. reprint ed. 29.95 (*0-7818-0672-0*) Hippocrene Bks.

Pet-Edwards, J., et al. Risk Assessment & Decision Making Using Test Results: The Carcinogenicity Prediction & Battery Selection Approach. (Illus.). 220p. (C). 1989. 85.00 (*0-306-43067-3*, Plenum Trade) Perseus Pubng.

Pet-Edwards, J., jt. auth. see Mollaghasemi, Mansooreh.

PETA Staff, ed. Cooking with PETA: Great Vegetarian Recipes for a Compassionate Kitchen. LC 97-17909. 244p. (Orig.). 1997. pap. 14.95 (*1-57067-044-7*) Book Pub Co.

Petaccia, Mario A. Walking on Water. (Illus.). 64p. 1986. 15.00 (*0-89304-075-4*, CCC195); pap. 7.50 (*0-89304-076-2*) Cross-Cultrl NY.

Petach, Heidi. Daniel & the Lions Den. (Happy Day Bks. Ser.). (Illus.). 24p. (J). (ps). 1995. pap. 1.99 (*0-7847-0347-7*, 04227) Standard Pub.

P

— Frog Sticker Paper Doll, Vol. 80. (Illus.). (J). (gr. k-3). 1993. pap. 1.00 (0-486-27252-4) Dover.
— Frog Stickers. (Illus.). (J). (gr. k-3). 1994. pap. 1.00 (0-486-28067-5) Dover.
***Petach, Heidi.** Goldilocks & the Three Hares. (ps-3). 1999. pap. 5.99 (0-698-11760-3) Putnam Pub Group.
Petach, Heidi. Jonah, the Inside Story. (Happy Day Bks.). (Illus.). 24p. (J). (ps). 1995. pap. 1.99 (0-7847-0351-5, 04231) Standard Pub.
Petach, Heidi. Monkey. (Little Activity Bks.). (Illus.). (J). 1995. pap. 1.00 (0-486-26992-2) Dover.
***Petaelio, Justin L.** Maturity: Evolution of the Self. LC 00-190513. 276p. 2000. 15.95 (0-9700245-0-9) DualGems.
Petaja, Emil. Stardrift & Other Fantastic Flotsam. 6.50 (0-686-00172-9) Fantasy Pub Co.
Petak, Joseph A. Never Plan Tomorrow. LC 91-78112. (Illus.). 524p. (Orig.). 1992. pap. 19.95 (0-9631609-6-6) Aquataur.
Petak, William J., ed. Emergency Management: A Challenge for Public Administration. 176p. 1985. 9.50 (0-685-25269-8) Am Soc Pub Admin.
Petak, William J., jt. auth. see Alesch, Daniel J.
Petak, William J., jt. auth. see Atkisson, A. A.
Petar, Prince, 2nd. The Mountain Wreath of P. P. Nyegosh, Prince Bishop of Montenegro. Wiles, James W., tr. LC 71-109820. 250p. 1970. reprint ed. lib. bdg. 47.50 (0-8371-4311-X, PEMW, Greenwood Pr) Greenwood.
Petaschnick, Joann. Patient Account Manager's 1999 Sourcebook. LC 98-48637. 1999. 89.00 (0-8342-1155-6) Aspen Pub.
Petch, Alison, jt. auth. see Fuller, Roger.
Petch, D. A., jt. auth. see Singleton, G. R.
Petch, James R., jt. auth. see Haines-Young, Roy H.
Petchenkine, Youry. Buying a Business in Russia: A Handbook for Westerners on Russian Privatization. 182p. 1993. 89.00 (0-9637388-0-1) D N Yng & Assocs.
— Ghana: In Search of Stability, 1957-1992. LC 92-9113. 264p. 1993. 57.95 (0-275-94326-7, C4326, Praeger Pubs) Greenwood.
— The United Nations Industrial Development Organization: UNIDO & Problems of International Industrial Development. LC 93-2859. 224p. 1993. 62.95 (0-275-94496-4, C4496, Praeger Pubs) Greenwood.
Petchesky. Negotiating Reproductive Right: Women's Perspectives Across Countries & Cultures, Vol. 1. LC 98-19802. 320p. 1998. pap. 25.00 (1-85649-536-1, Pub. by Zed Books) St Martin.
Petchesky, Rosalind. Negotiating Reproductive Right: Women's Perspectives Across Countries & Cultures. LC 98-19802. 320p. 1998. text 69.95 (1-85649-535-3, Pub. by Manchester Univ Pr) St Martin.
Petchesky, Rosalind P. Abortion & Woman's Choice: The State, Sexuality & Reproductive Freedom. rev. ed. (Northeastern Series in Feminist Theory). 412p. 1990. pap. text 18.95 (1-55553-075-3) NE U Pr.
Petchsiri, Apirat. Eastern Importation of Western Criminal Law: Thailand As a Case Study. LC 86-24821. (Comparative Criminal Law Project Publications Ser.: Vol. 17). xix, 208p. 1987. reprint ed. 37.50 (0-8377-1054-5, Rothman) W S Hein.
Petee, Frank, jt. auth. see Stauffer, Carol.
Peteet, Julie M. Gender in Crisis: Women & the Palestinian Resistance Movement. 224p. 1991. text 52.50 (0-231-07446-8) Col U Pr.
— Gender in Crisis: Women & the Palestinian Resistance Movement. 245p. (C). 1992. pap. text 18.00 (0-231-07447-6) Col U Pr.
Petegorsky, David W. Left-Wing Democracy in the English Civil War. LC 72-2021. (British History Ser.: No. 30). 1972. reprint ed. lib. bdg. 75.00 (0-8383-1472-4) M S G Haskell Hse.
— Left-Wing Democracy in the English Civil War: Gerrard Winstanley & the Digger Movement. 352p. 1996. pap. 26.95 (0-7509-1053-4, Pub. by Sutton Pub Ltd) Intl Pubs Mktg.
Petek, Daniel J. Spokane Centennial Cookbook. (Illus.). 144p. (Orig.). 1988. pap. 6.95 (0-9615201-5-9) BCG Ltd.
— Spokane Light Cookbook. (Illus.). 144p. (Orig.). 1987. pap. 5.95 (0-9615201-4-0) BCG Ltd.
— Spokane Style Cookbook. (Illus.). 72p. (Orig.). 1985. pap. 4.95 (0-9615201-0-8) BCG Ltd.
— Spokane Too! Cookbook. (Illus.). 120p. (Orig.). 1986. pap. 4.95 (0-9615201-3-2) BCG Ltd.
Petek, Danita, jt. auth. see Kile, Sibyl.
Petelin, Carol. The Creative Guide to Dried Flowers. (Illus.). 108p. 1990. pap. 18.95 (0-7181-3392-7) Viking Penguin.
Petelin, Joseph B., jt. auth. see Klaiber, Christian.
***Petelin, S.** Result of Bethsy Test 9.1B Using RELAP5/MOD3. 76p. 1998. pap. 9.00 (0-16-063222-6) USGPO.
Petellat, John. Journey Beyond Trauma. Jaeger, Joseph, ed. LC 95-61474. 133p. 1995. pap. 12.95 (1-880254-24-7) Vista.
Petelle, Joey D., ed. The Rocky Mountain Creative Sourcebook, 1996. (Illus.). 300p. 1996. spiral bd. 50.00 (1-886295-06-9) Everest Pubng.
— Southwest Creative Sourcebook, 1996. (Illus.). 1996. pap., spiral bd. 50.00 (1-886295-01-8) Everest Pubng.
— Texas Creative Sourcebook, 1996-1997. (Illus.). 350p. 1996. 50.00 (1-886295-07-7) Everest Pubng.
Peteni, R. L. Hill of Fools. (African Writers Ser.). 151p. (C). 1976. pap. 8.95 (0-435-90178-8, 90178) Heinemann.
— Towards Tomorrow: The Story of the African Teachers Association of South Africa. Kitchen, Cole, ed. LC 78-59714. 1979. pap. 9.00 (0-917256-08-5) Ref Pubns.
Peter. Elementary Algebra. Date not set. pap. text, teacher ed. write for info. (0-314-09190-4) West Pub.
— Elementary Algebra: Cooperative Learning Worksheet. (Mathematics Ser.). 1995. 8.25 (0-314-07008-7) Brooks-Cole.
— Historicirum Romanorum Reliquiae, Vol. I. Kroymann-Schaub, ed. (LAT.). 395p. 1993. reprint ed. 125.00 (3-519-04228-2, T4228, Pub. by B G Teubner) U of Mich Pr.
— Historicirum Romanorum Reliquiae, Vol. II. Kroymann, ed. (LAT.). 234p. 1993. reprint ed. 92.50 (3-519-04229-0, T4229, Pub. by B G Teubner) U of Mich Pr.
— Intermediate Algebra. Date not set. pap. text, teacher ed. write for info. (0-314-08972-1) West Pub.
— Intermediate Algebra Graph. 1996. mass mkt., lab manual ed. 10.50 (0-314-08758-3) West Pub.
— Preface Marketing Management. 8th ed. LC 99-10058. 336p. 1999. pap. 48.75 (0-07-366151-1) McGraw.
— Saunders Manual for Veterinary Technology. Date not set. text. write for info. (0-7216-4193-8, W B Saunders Co) Harcrt Hlth Sci Grp.
Peter, Beate, tr. see Wiesmuller, Dieter.
***Peter, Bill.** As the Soul Teaches: Living Life to Achieve Peace of Mind. (Peace of Mind Ser.). (Illus.). 244p. 2000. pap. 14.95 (1-890676-60-8, Pub. by Beavers Pond) Bookman Bks.
Peter, Bill. I'm Moving: Eliminating the Anxiety of Buying or Selling a Home. (Illus.). 176p. 1998. pap. 12.95 (1-890676-26-8) Beavers Pond.
Peter Bros. Staff. Where Science Went Wrong: Tracking Four Centuries of Misconceptions. (Copernican Ser.: Vol. 7). 215p. (Orig.). 1997. pap. 16.95 (0-9627769-7-1) Fin Bk Partners.
Peter, Bruce. 100 Years of Glasgow's Amazing Cinemas. 256p. 1996. 24.00 (0-7486-6210-3, Pub. by Polygon) Subterranean Co.
Peter, Chris M. Human Rights in Africa: A Comparative Study of the African Human & People's Rights Charter & the New Tanzanian Bill of Rights, 10. LC 89-17126. (Studies in Human Rights: No. 10). 153p. 1990. 45.00 (0-313-26863-0, PHR/, Greenwood Pr) Greenwood.
Peter Collin Publishers. Check Your Vocabulary for Business. 2nd ed. 1999. pap. text 9.95 (1-901659-27-5) P Collin.
— Dictionary of English. 1999. pap. text, wbk. ed. 9.95 (1-901659-11-9) P Collin.
Peter Collin Publishing Staff. Bradford's Crossword Solver's Dictionary. 3rd ed. 1998. pap. write for info. (1-901659-03-8, Pub. by Peter Collin) IBD Ltd.
— Catalan Business Glossary. (Business Glossaries Ser.). 1997. pap. 9.95 (0-948549-57-2, Pub. by Peter Collin) IBD Ltd.
— Check Your Vocabulary for Banking & Finance. 1997. pap. text 9.95 (0-948549-96-3, Pub. by Peter Collin) IBD Ltd.
— Check Your Vocabulary for Law. 2nd ed. 1999. pap. text 9.95 (1-901659-21-6) IPG Chicago.
— Computing & IT: English - German with German - English Glossary. 2nd ed. 1998. 49.95 (1-901659-00-3, Pub. by Peter Collin) IBD Ltd.
— Dictionary of Aeronautical Terms. 1999. pap. text 15.95 (1-901659-10-0) IPG Chicago.
— Dictionary of Agriculture. 2nd ed. 1997. pap. 15.95 (0-948549-78-5, Pub. by Peter Collin) IBD Ltd.
Peter Collin Publishing Staff. Dictionary of Banking & Finance. 278p. 15.95 (1-901659-30-5, Pub. by P Collin) IPG Chicago.
— Dictionary of Chinese Hotels. 400p. 1999. 49.95 (1-901659-08-9, Pub. by P Collin) IPG Chicago.
— Dictionary of Chinese Law. 588p. 49.95 (1-901659-07-0, Pub. by P Collin) IPG Chicago.
— Dictionary of Chinese Multimedia. 1999. (1-901659-02-X) P Collin.
Peter Collin Publishing Staff. Dictionary of Computing. 3rd ed. 1998. pap. 15.95 (1-901659-04-6, Pub. by Peter Collin) IBD Ltd.
— Dictionary of Ecology & the Environment. 3rd ed. 1997. pap. 15.95 (0-948549-74-2, Pub. by Peter Collin) IBD Ltd.
— Dictionary of Government & Politics. 2nd ed. 1997. pap. 15.95 (0-948549-89-0, Pub. by Peter Collin) IBD Ltd.
— Dictionary of Information Technology. 2nd ed. 1997. pap. 15.95 (0-948549-88-2, Pub. by Peter Collin) IBD Ltd.
— Dictionary of Marketing. 2nd ed. 1997. pap. 15.95 (0-948549-73-4, Pub. by Peter Collin) IBD Ltd.
***Peter Collin Publishing Staff.** Dictionary of Medicine. 3rd ed. 460p. 2000. pap. text 15.95 (1-901659-45-3) P Collin.
Peter Collin Publishing Staff. Dictionary of Multimedia. 2nd ed. 1998. pap. 17.95 (1-901659-01-1, Pub. by Peter Collin) IBD Ltd.
— Dictionary of Printing & Publishing. 2nd ed. LC 98-127212. 1998. pap. write for info. (0-948549-99-8, Pub. by Peter Collin) IBD Ltd.
— Dutch Business Glossary. (Business Glossaries Ser.). 1997. pap. 9.95 (0-948549-56-4, Pub. by Peter Collin) IBD Ltd.
***Peter Collin Publishing Staff.** English Dictionary of Computing. 4th ed. 2000. pap. text 15.95 (1-901659-46-1, Pub. by P Collin) IPG Chicago.
Peter Collin Publishing Staff. English-Greek Business Glossary. 1999. 9.95 (1-901659-29-1) IPG Chicago.
Peter Collin Publishing Staff. Estonian English Business Glossary. 196p. 9.95 (0-948549-94-7, Pub. by P Collin) IPG Chicago.
Peter Collin Publishing Staff. French Business Glossary. (Business Glossaries Ser.). 196p. 1997. pap. 9.95 (0-948549-52-1, Pub. by Peter Collin) IBD Ltd.
— German Business Glossary. (Business Glossaries Ser.). (GER.). 1997. pap. 9.95 (0-948549-53-X, Pub. by Peter Collin) IBD Ltd.
— Italian Business Glossary. (Business Glossaries Ser.). (ITA.). 1997. pap. 9.95 (0-948549-55-6, Pub. by Peter Collin) IBD Ltd.
Peter Collin Publishing Staff. Spanish English Business Glossary. 196p. pap. 9.95 (0-948549-54-8, Pub. by P Collin) IPG Chicago.
Peter Collin Publishing Staff. Spanish/German Business Glossary. 1999. pap. text 9.95 (0-948549-98-X) Peter Collin.
Peter Collin Publishing Staff, jt. auth. see Collin, Peter.
Peter Collins Publishing Staff. Hungarian Law Dictionary. 1999. 49.95 (0-948549-95-5) Peter Collin.
Peter-Contesse, Rene & Ellington, John. A Handbook on Leviticus. LC 92-20509. (UBS Handbook Ser.). Orig. Title: Translator's Handbook on Leviticus. ix, 458p. 1990. pap. 20.99 (0-8267-0110-8, 104588) Untd Bible Soc.
— A Handbook on the Book of Daniel. LC 93-33287. (UBS Handbook Ser.). viii, 365p. 1994. pap. 17.99 (0-8267-0126-4, 105036) Untd Bible Soc.
Peter Damian, St. Letters, 1-30. Blum, Owen, tr. LC 88-25802. (Fathers of the Church: Mediaeval Continuation Ser.: Vol. 1). 312p. 1989. 39.95 (0-8132-0702-9) Cath U Pr.
Peter, Diana. Claire & Emma. LC 77-629. (Illus.). (J). (gr. k-4). 1977. lib. bdg. 11.89 (0-354-11415-8) HarpC Child Bks.
***Peter, Donnelly.** CTB Marketing Management. 8th ed. 1999. 25.00 (0-07-228388-2, McGrw-H College) McGrw-H Hghr Educ.
***Peter, Edwin A.** Cosmic Keys to Perfect Health: Lessons on How to Achieve Wholeness Through the Transformational Properties of the Fourteen Cosmic Minerals & Universal Laws. Day-Schmal, Linda, ed. LC 00-104451. (Illus.). 180p. 2000. pap. 15.00 (1-929341-01-6) SpiritPassage.
Peter, Emmett. Lake County, Florida: A Pictorial History. LC 94-24867. 1994. write for info. (0-89865-905-1) Donning Co.
***Peter, Frances D.** A Union Woman in Civil War Kentucky: The Diary of Frances Peter. Smith, John David & Cooper, William J., Jr., eds. LC 99-23203. (Illus.). 176p. 2000. 22.50 (0-8131-2144-2) U Pr of Ky.
Peter, Gilbert M. & Welch, C. Lee. Algebra for College Students. (C). 1988. 72.00 (0-673-18798-5) Addson-Wesley Educ.
— Intermediate Algebra. 740p. (C). 1996. text 58.75 (0-314-04158-3) West Pub.
Peter, Gilbert M., jt. auth. see Welch, C. Lee.
Peter Glenn Staff. The Image Makers Source, Vol. 1. 1999. 59.95 (0-87314-250-0) Peter Glenn.
— Miami Model Agency Directory, Vol. 1. 1998. pap. 12.95 (0-87314-225-X) Peter Glenn.
— The National Casting Guide. 1998. 17.95 (0-87314-154-7) Peter Glenn.
— New York City Model Agency Directory, Vol. 9. 1998. pap. 13.95 (0-87314-131-8) Peter Glenn.
— The Production Makers Source, Vol. 1. 1998. 44.95 (0-87314-275-6) Peter Glenn.
Peter, Herbert, jt. auth. see Schiffer, Nancy N.
Peter, Hermann. Die Geschichtliche Literatur Uber die Romische Kaiserzeit Bis Theodosius I. und Ihre Quellen, 2 vols., Set. xxii, 888p. 1967. reprint ed. write for info. (0-318-71194-X) G Olms Pubs.
— Wahrheit und Kunst, Geschichtsschreibung und Plagiat Im Klassischen Altertum. xii, 490p. 1965. reprint ed. write for info. (0-318-70813-2) G Olms Pubs.
Peter, J., Frost, et al, eds. Managerial Reality: Balancing Technique, Practice & Values. 2nd ed. LC 94-27813. 425p. (C). 1997. pap. text 51.00 (0-673-99183-0) Addson-Wesley Educ.
Peter, J. H., et al, eds. Sleep & Health Risk. (Illus.). 560p. 1991. pap. 126.00 (0-387-53083-5) Spr-Verlag.
Peter, J. Paul. Marketing for the Manufacturer. (APICS Ser.). 270p. 1992. 47.50 (1-55623-648-4, Irwn Prfssnl) McGraw-Hill Prof.
— Marketing Management: Knowledge & Skills. 6th ed. 896p. 2000. 85.63 (0-07-231557-1) McGraw.
Peter, J. Paul & Donnelly, James H. Marketing Management: Knowledge & Skills. 5th ed. LC 97-20733. (Irwin Series in Marketing). (C). 1997. text 95.14 (0-256-22633-4, Irwn Prfssnl) McGraw-Hill Prof.
Peter, J. Paul & Donnelly, James H., Jr. A Preface to Marketing Management. 6th ed. LC 93-19853. (Marketing Ser.). 368p. (C). 1993. text 37.50 (0-256-12251-2, Irwn McGrw-H) McGrw-H Hghr Educ.
— A Preface to Marketing Management. 7th ed. LC 95-51535. (Series in Marketing). 368p. (C). 1997. text 37.50 (0-256-20281-8, Irwn McGrw-H) McGrw-H Hghr Educ.
Peter, J. Paul & Olson, Jerry C. Consumer Behavior. 5th ed. LC 98-16996. 576p. (C). 1998. 83.13 (0-256-26190-3) McGraw.
— Consumer Behavior & Marketing Strategy. 4th ed. LC 95-22713. (Irwin Series in Marketing). 736p. (C). 1995. text 71.95 (0-256-13904-0, Irwn McGrw-H) McGrw-H Hghr Educ.
— Understanding Consumer Behavior. LC 93-13484. 512p. (C). 1993. text 68.95 (0-256-12278-4, Irwn McGrw-H) McGrw-H Hghr Educ.
Peter, J. Paul, et al. Marketing Management: Knowledge & Skills CPS - Finance 1 Course (Pace University) 3rd ed. (C). 1994. 15.95 (0-256-19142-5, Irwn McGrw-H) McGrw-H Hghr Educ.
— Marketing Management & Cases in Marketing Management: Select Chapters. 3rd ed. (C). 1994. text 36.95 (0-256-18210-8, Irwn McGrw-H) McGrw-H Hghr Educ.
Peter, J. Paul, jt. auth. see Certo, Samuel C.
Peter, J. Paul, jt. auth. see Churchill, Gilbert A.
Peter, J. Paul, jt. auth. see Donnelly, James H., Jr.
Peter, J. Raymond, jt. auth. see Oblitas, Keith Robert A.
Peter, James B. & Shoenfeld, Yehuda, eds. Autoantibodies. LC 96-13604. 910p. 1996. 148.25 (0-444-82383-2) Elsevier.
Peter, Jennifer A. & Crosier, Louis M., eds. The Cultural Battlefield: Art Censorship & Public Funding. LC 94-71656. 220p. 1995. 19.95 (0-9627671-7-4) Avocus Pub.
***Peter, John.** The Oral History of Modern Architecture: Interviews with the Greatest Architects of the Twentieth Century. 320p. 2000. pap. 34.95 (0-8109-2746-2, Pub. by Abrams) Time Warner.
Peter, John. Vladimir's Carrot: Modern Drama & the Modern Imagination. LC 87-5838. xii, 384p. 1987. 29.95 (0-226-66265-9) U Ch Pr.
Peter, K. Deenaadai' Gwich'in Gwandak (Stories of Long Ago) 12p. 1975. pap. 2.00 (1-55500-010-X) Alaska Native.
— Deenaadai Gwich'in Oozhri' (Old-Time Gwich'in Names) 14p. 1978. pap. 2.00 (1-55500-011-8) Alaska Native.
— Gineerinlyaa (Poems) 17p. 1974. pap. 2.50 (1-55500-006-1) Alaska Native.
— Gwich'in ABC Dehtlly'aa (Gwich'in ABC Book) (Illus.). 47p. 1974. pap. 3.00 (0-933769-99-7) Alaska Native.
— Gwich'in Gwitr'it Dehtlly'aa (Gwich'in Workbook) 16p. 1975. pap., wbk. ed. 2.50 (1-55500-001-0) Alaska Native.
— Olti'Daga'at Dik Haa (Olti' & His Wife Dik) 11p. 1975. pap. 2.00 (1-55500-003-7) Alaska Native.
— Shih Doo Daazhyaa (The Four Food Groups) 13p. 1974. pap. 2.00 (1-55500-005-3) Alaska Native.
— Three Stories (Vasaagihdzak/Shoh Deetrya' Haa Gwandak/Tr'injaa) 17p. 1975. pap. 2.50 (1-55500-007-X) Alaska Native.
— Vak'aandaii (Touch It) 21p. 1974. pap. 2.00 (1-55500-002-9) Alaska Native.
***Peter, Katalin, ed.** Beloved Children: History of Childhood in Hungary in the Early Modern Age. 180p. (C). 2000. 36.95 (963-9116-77-7) Ctrl Europ Univ.
Peter, Katherine. Nats'ahts'a' Ch'adhah' Ahkhii: How I Tan Hides.Tr. of How I Tan Hides. (ESK., Illus.). 22p. 1980. pap. 6.50 (1-55500-012-6) Alaska Native.
— Neets'aii Gwiindaii: Living in the Chandalar Country. Raboff, Adeline, tr. from ENG. (Illus.). xii, 108p. (Orig.). 1992. pap. 14.00 (0-933769-11-3) Alaska Native.
Peter, Katherine, ed. see Sapir, Edward.
Peter, Laszlo, ed. Historians & the History of Transylvania. 280p. 1993. text 43.50 (0-88033-229-8, 332, Pub. by East Eur Monographs) Col U Pr.
Peter, Laszlo, ed. see Macartney, C. A.
Peter, Laurence J. Peter's Quotations: Ideas for Our Time. 1993. pap. 12.00 (0-688-11909-3, Quil) HarperTrade.
— El Principio de Peter. 1998. pap. 6.50 (84-01-45124-8) Lectorum Pubns.
Peter, Laurence J. & Hull, Raymond. The Peter Principle. Date not set. lib. bdg. 19.95 (0-8488-2156-4) Amereon Ltd.
— The Peter Principle. 1993. reprint ed. 29.95 (1-56849-161-1) Buccaneer Bks.
***Peter, Laurence J. & Hull, Raymond.** The Peter Principle: Why Things Always Go Wrong. (Illus.). 192p. 1998. pap. 13.00 (0-688-27544-3, Quil) HarperTrade.
Peter, Margo I., jt. auth. see Darling, Rosalyn B.
Peter, Melanie. Art for All II - the Practice: Developing Art in the Curriculum with Pupils with Special Education Needs. 96p. 1996. pap. text 24.95 (1-85346-418-X, Pub. by David Fulton) Taylor & Francis.
— Drama for All: Developing Drama in the Curriculum with Pupils with Special Educational Needs. 96p. 1994. pap. 19.95 (1-85346-315-9, Pub. by David Fulton) Taylor & Francis.
— Making Dance Special. LC 98-153340. 160p. 1997. pap. 160.00 (1-85346-434-1, Pub. by David Fulton) Taylor & Francis.
— Making Drama Special: Developing Drama Practice for Special Educational Needs. 176p. 1995. pap. 24.95 (1-85346-316-7, Pub. by David Fulton) Taylor & Francis.
Peter, Melanie, ed. Art for All I - The Framework: Developing Art in the Curriculum with Students with Special Educational Needs. 96p. 1996. pap. text 24.95 (1-85346-317-5, Pub. by David Fulton) Taylor & Francis.
Peter, Melanie, jt. auth. see Wills, Peter.
Peter Nahum Ltd. Staff. Burne-Jones - A Quest for Love: Works by Sir Edward Burne-Jones BT & Related Works by Contemporary Artists. (Illus.). (C). 1993. pap. 60.00 (1-872508-03-0) St Mut.
Peter, Nancy & Schiffer, Herbert F. The Brass Book: American, English & European, 15th Century Thru 1850. LC 78-63428. 447p. 1978. 60.00 (0-916838-17-X) Schiffer.
Peter Norton Computing Group Staff & Mueller, John. Peter Norton's Complete Guide to Windows 95. (Illus.). 848p. 1995. 29.99 (0-672-30791-X) Sams.
Peter, O. Herder-Lexikon Chemie. 3rd ed. (GER.). 256p. 1975. pap. 35.00 (0-8288-5896-9, M7454) Fr & Eur.
Peter, Paul J. & Donnelly, James. Marketing Management: Knowledge & Skills CPS Selected. 4th ed. (C). 1994. 29.95 (0-256-19134-4, Irwn McGrw-H) McGrw-H Hghr Educ.
Peter, Paul J., jt. auth. see Donnelly, James.
***Peter Pauper Press Staff.** Baby's Own Photo Album/Memory Box. (Illus.). 1998. 24.95 (0-88088-150-X) Peter Pauper.
Peter Pauper Press Staff. Baby's Record Keeper & Memory Box. 1999. 24.95 (0-88088-165-8) Peter Pauper.
***Peter Pauper Press Staff.** History of Our Family: Record Keeper & Memory Box. (Illus.). 48p. 1999. 24.95 (0-88088-166-6) Peter Pauper.

P

An Asterisk (*) at the beginning of an entry indicates that the title is appearing for the first time.

— Honeymooner's Photo Album/Memory Box. 1998. 24.95 (*0-88088-154-2*) Peter Pauper.

Peter Pauper Press Staff. To Teach Is to Touch Lives Forever. LC 99-170266. (Pocket Gift Editions Ser.). 1998. 4.95 (*0-88088-073-2*) Peter Pauper.

***Peter Pauper Press Staff.** Treasured Photo Album/Memory Box. 1998. 24.95 (*0-88088-152-6*) Peter Pauper.

Peter, Rozsa. Playing with Infinity: Mathematical Explorations & Excursions. LC 75-26467. (Illus.). 268p. 1976. reprint ed. pap. text 7.95 (*0-486-23265-4*) Dover.

Peter, Salm. The Poem as a Plant: A Biological View of Goethe's Faust. LC 71-141461. 169p. reprint ed. pap. 52.40 (*0-608-30811-0*, 200325900021) Bks Demand.

***Peter Seldin & Associates Staff.** Changing Practices in Evaluating Teaching: A Practical Guide to Improved Faculty Performance & Promotion. 275p. 1999. 35.95 (*1-882982-28-2*) Anker Pub.

Peter Seldin & Associates Staff. Improving College Teaching. 288p. (C). 1995. text 35.95 (*1-882982-08-8*) Anker Pub.

Peter, Stephen. AutoCAD Professional's Toolkit. 400p. (YA). (gr. 9 up). 1999. pap. 49.95 (*1-889671-19-3*) Advice Pr.

Peter, T. Xootsx X'ayakuwdligadee Shaawat. 34p. 1973. pap. 3.00 (*1-55500-013-4*) Alaska Native.

Peter, T. J., et al, eds. Ophiolites - Genesis & Evolution of Oceanic Lithosphere. (C). 1991. text 50.00 (*0-7923-1176-0*) Kluwer Academic.

Peter The Venerable. Letters of Peter the Venerable, 2 vols., Set. Constable, Giles, ed. LC 67-10086. (Historical Studies: No. 78). 897p. 1967. 60.00 (*0-674-52775-5*) HUP.

Peter, Ulrich. Der Bund der Religiosen Sozialisten in Berlin von 1919 Bis 1933: Geschichte - Struktur - Theologie und Politik. (Europaische Hochschulschriften Ser.: Reihe 23, Bd. 532). (GER.). 696p. 1995. 97.95 (*3-631-48604-9*) P Lang Pubng.

Peter, Val, et al, contrib. by. The Well-Managed Classroom for Catholic Schools: Promoting Student Success Through the Teaching of Social Skills & Christian Values. LC 98-195020. 173p. 1997. pap. text, teacher ed. 24.95 (*1-889322-06-7*, 48-006) Boys Town Pr.

***Peter, Val J.** Dealing with Your Kids' 7 Biggest Troubles. 2000. pap. 4.95 (*0-938510-97-5*) Boys Town Pr.

Peter, Val J. I Think of My Homelessness: Stories from Boys Town. 102p. 1991. pap. 2.99 (*0-938510-26-6*, 19-004) Boys Town Pr.

***Peter, Val J.** Parents & Kids Talking about School Violence. 2000. pap. 4.95 (*0-938510-74-6*) Boys Town Pr.

— What Makes Boys Town Successful. 159p. 1999. pap. 5.95 (*1-889322-26-1*) Boys Town Pr.

Peter, Val J., ed. Boys Town Prayer Book: Prayers by & for the Boys & Girls of Boys Town. rev. ed. 176p. 1989. pap. 6.99 (*0-938510-88-6*, 19-008) Boys Town Pr.

***Peter, Val J. & Herron, Ron.** A Good Friend: How to Make One, How to Be One. 84p. (YA). 1998. pap. 8.99 (*1-889322-19-9*, 25-010) Boys Town Pr.

— What's Right for Me? Making Good Choices in Relationships. 160p. (YA). 1998. pap. 8.99 (*1-889322-21-0*, 25-012) Boys Town Pr.

— Who's in the Mirror? Finding the Real Me. 137p. (YA). 1998. pap. 8.99 (*1-889322-20-2*, 25-011) Boys Town Pr.

Peter, Val J., jt. auth. see Daly, Daniel L.

Peter Warlock Society Staff, jt. auth. see Parrott, Ian.

Peter, Wolfgang. Arbitration & Renegotiation of International Investment Agreements: A Study with Particular Reference to Means of Conflict Avoidance under Natural Resources Investment Agreements. 2nd enl. rev. ed. LC 95-15795. 1995. lib. bdg. 195.00 (*90-411-0037-7*) Kluwer Academic.

Peteraitis, Vilius. Lithuanian - English Dictionary. 1991. 49.95 (*0-8288-2626-9*, F58440) Fr & Eur.

— Lithuanian-English Dictionary. (ENG & LIT.). 42.50 (*0-87559-037-3*) Shalom.

Peterborough Field Naturalists. Kawarthas Nature. Hudson, Noel, ed. (Illus.). 120p. (Orig.). 1995. pap. 19.95 (*1-55046-058-7*, Pub. by Boston Mills) Genl Dist Srvs.

***Peterfalvi, T.** Character Theory for the Odd Order Theorem. LC 99-25752. (London Mathematical Society Lecture Note Ser.: No. 272). 180p. 2000. pap. 39.95 (*0-521-64660-X*) Cambridge U Pr.

Peterfreund, Emanuel. Information, Systems & Psychoanalysis. LC 71-141662. (Psychological Issues Monographs: No. 25-26, Vol. 8, No. 1-2). 397p. 1971. 57.50 (*0-8236-2658-X*); pap. 45.00 (*0-8236-2659-8*) Intl Univs Pr.

Peterfreund, Herbert & McLaughlin, Joseph M. New York Practice, Cases & Other Materials. 4th ed. (University Casebook Ser.). 1583p. 1991. reprint ed. text 38.50 (*0-88277-434-4*) Foundation Pr.

Peterfreund, Sheldon P., jt. auth. see Denise, Theodore C.

Peterfreund, Stuart. The Hanged Knife & Other Poems. 52p. 1970. 2.95 (*0-87886-000-2*, Greenfld Rev Pr) Greenfld Rev Lit.

— Harder Than Rain. LC 77-23857. 82p. 1977. 3.50 (*0-87886-084-3*, Greenfld Rev Pr) Greenfld Rev Lit.

— William Blake in a Newtonian World: Essays on Literature As Art & Science. LC 97-40080. (Oklahoma Project for Discourse & Theory: Vol. 2). xv, 272p. 1998. 34.95 (*0-8061-3042-3*) U of Okla Pr.

Peterfreund, Stuart, ed. Literature & Science: Theory & Practice. 248p. 1999. reprint ed. text 22.00 (*0-7881-6387-6*) DIANE Pub.

— Literature & Science Theory & Practice. (Illus.). 248p. 1989. text 47.50 (*1-55553-058-3*) NE U Pr.

***Peteri, Gyorgy.** Academia under State Socialism: Essays on the Political History of Academic Life in Post-1945 Hungary & East Central Europe. LC 97-76980. 296p. 1998. text 35.00 (*0-88033-398-7*, 501, Pub. by East Eur Monographs) Col U Pr.

Peteri, Gyorgy. The Effects of World War I: War Communism in Hungary. 229p. 1984. text 53.50 (*0-88033-059-7*, Pub. by East Eur Monographs) Col U Pr.

Peteri, Gyorgy, jt. ed. see David-Fox, Michael.

Peteri, Z. Legal Theory - Comparative Law: Studies in Honour of Professor Imre Szabo. (ENG & FRE.). 463p. (C). 1984. 125.00 (*963-05-3992-6*, Pub. by Akade Kiado) St Mut.

Peteri, Z. & Lamm, V. Legal Development & Comparative Law, 1986: Selected Essays for the 12th International Congress of Comparative Law. (FRE.). 330p. (C). 1986. 90.00 (*963-05-4434-2*, Pub. by Akade Kiado) St Mut.

Peteri, Z., jt. auth. see Szabo, I.

Peteri, Zoltan & Lamm, Vanda, eds. General Reports to the Tenth International Congress of Comparative Law, 8 Vols. 1050p. 1981. 230.00 (*0-569-08701-5*) St Mut.

Peterich, Eckart, ed. Athens. (Panorama Bks.). (FRE., Illus.). 1966. 3.95 (*0-685-11018-4*) Fr & Eur.

Petering, John, ed. & tr. see Von Mackinsen, Manfred.

***Peterjohn, Bruce G.** The Birds of Ohio: With the Ohio Breeding Bird Atlas. LC 99-58312. 400p. 2000. pap. 18.95 (*1-888683-88-0*) Wooster Bk.

Peterjohn, Bruce G., et al. Abundance & Distribution of the Birds of Ohio. LC 86-63244. (Biological Notes Ser.). (Illus.). 52p. 1987. pap. 7.00 (*0-86727-103-5*) Ohio Bio Survey.

Peterken, George. Natural Woodlands. LC 94-20760. (Illus.). 536p. (C). 1996. text 135.00 (*0-521-36613-5*); pap. text 47.95 (*0-521-36792-1*) Cambridge U Pr.

Peterkiewicz, Jerzy, tr. see John Paul, II, pseud.

Peterkin, Allan. What about Me? When Brothers & Sisters Get Sick. LC 92-20035. (Illus.). 32p. (J). (ps-3). 1992. pap. 8.95 (*0-945354-49-5*) Am Psychol.

Peterkin, Allan D. The Bald-Headed Hermit & The Artichoke: An Erotic Thesaurus. 150p. 1999. pap. 13.95 (*1-55152-063-X*, Pub. by Arsenal Pulp) LPC InBook.

— Staying Human During Residency Training. 2nd ed. LC 98-167109. 162p. 1998. pap. 15.00 (*0-8020-8148-7*) U of Toronto Pr.

***Peterkin, Genevieve C.** Heaven Is a Beautiful Place: A Memoir of the South Carolina Coast. LC 00-8174. (Illus.). 240p. 2000. 19.95 (*1-57003-361-7*) U of SC Pr.

Peterkin, Julia. Black April. 24.95 (*0-89190-527-8*) Amereon Ltd.

— Black April. LC 97-30012. 328p. 1998. reprint ed. pap. 15.95 (*0-8203-1953-8*) U of Ga Pr.

— Bright Skin. 21.95 (*0-89190-676-2*) Amereon Ltd.

— Bright Skin. LC 97-37356. 360p. 1998. reprint ed. pap. 15.95 (*0-8203-1954-6*) U of Ga Pr.

— Green Thursday. LC 97-23317. 200p. 1998. reprint ed. pap. 15.95 (*0-8203-1955-4*) U of Ga Pr.

— A Plantation Christmas. LC 72-4563. (Black Heritage Library Collection). (Illus.). (YA). (gr. 7 up). 1977. reprint ed. 13.95 (*0-8369-9119-2*) Ayer.

— A Plantation Christmas. LC 78-22014. (Illus.). (J). (gr. 6 up). 1978. reprint ed. pap. 2.95 (*0-89783-007-5*) Cherokee.

— Scarlet Sister Mary. LC 97-28924. 352p. 1998. reprint ed. pap. 15.95 (*0-8203-1956-2*) U of Ga Pr.

Peterkin, Karen & Black, Donald V. The Directory of Online Healthcare Databases. 5th rev. ed. 80p. 1990. spiral bd. 35.00 (*0-931712-10-6*) Alpine Guild.

Peterkin, Mike. Hercules Pop-Up Book. LC 96-71093. 12p. (J). (gr. k-2). 1997. 13.95 (*0-7868-3128-6*, Pub. by Disney Pr) Time Warner.

— Who's Afraid of the Big Bad Wolf? LC 93-70940. 10p. (J). (ps-3). 1993. 11.95 (*1-56282-513-5*, Pub. by Disney Pr) Little.

Peterkofsky, Alan, jt. auth. see Reizer, Jonathan.

Peterkops, Raimonds. Theory of Ionization of Atoms by Electron Impact. Hummer, D. G., ed. Aronson, Elliot, tr. LC 77-81310. (Illus.). 273p. reprint ed. pap. 84.70 (*0-608-10333-0*, 201220300081) Bks Demand.

Peterle, Tony J., ed. International Congress of Game Biologists: Proceedings, 13th, Atlanta, 11-15 March 1977. (Illus.). 538p. (Orig.). 1977. pap. 6.00 (*0-933564-04-X*) Wildlife Soc.

Peterlin, Davorin. Paul's Letter to the Philippians in the Light of Disunity in the Church. (Supplements to Novum Testamentum Ser.: Vol. 79). xi, 272p. 1995. 116.50 (*90-04-10305-8*) Brill Academic Pubs.

Peterman. Integrating Clinical Practice text. write for info. (*0-471-49156-X*); pap. text. write for info. (*0-471-49157-8*) Wiley.

Peterman. On Aristotle. (Philosophy Ser.). 1999. pap. text 13.95 (*0-534-57607-9*) Brooks-Cole.

— On Plato. (Philosophy Ser.). 1999. pap. text 13.95 (*0-534-57608-7*) Brooks-Cole.

Peterman, Barbara S. Origins of Piaget's Concept of Decentration: Developmental Theory in Piaget & Habermas. LC 96-72015. 104p. (Orig.). (C). 1997. pap. text 12.95 (*1-889767-00-X*) Custos Pr.

Peterman, Dennis A. The 1890 Tax List of Phelps County Missouri. xxvii, 208p. 1988. pap. 35.00 (*1-893474-16-X*) Phelps Cnty Gene.

Peterman, G. W. Paul's Gift from Philippi: Conventions of Gift-Exchange & Christian Giving. LC 96-7897. (Society for New Testament Studies Monographs: No. 92). 257p. 1997. text 59.95 (*0-521-57220-7*) Cambridge U Pr.

Peterman, James F. Philosophy As Therapy: An Interpretation & Defense of Wittgenstein's Later Philosophical Project. LC 91-18277. (SUNY Series in Philosophy & Psychotherapy). 158p. (C). 1992. text 24.50 (*0-7914-0981-3*) State U NY Pr.

***Peterman, John.** Peterman Rides Again: The True Story of the Real "J. Peterman" & the Unconventional Catalog Company He Built. 288p. 2001. 25.00 (*0-7352-0199-4*) PH Pr.

Peterman, Larry L. & Weschler, Louis F., eds. American Political Thought: Readings. LC 78-184069. (C). 1972. pap. text 16.95 (*0-89197-015-0*) Irvington.

Peterman, Michael. This Great Epoch of Our Lives No. 33: Susanna Moodie's Roughing It in the Bush. (Canadian Fiction Studies). 1996. pap. 14.95 (*1-55022-182-5*, Pub. by ECW) Genl Dist Srvs.

Peterman, Mindy. Quantum Leap: Song & Dance. 256p. 1998. pap. 6.99 (*0-425-16577-9*) Berkley Pub.

Peterman, Peggy M., ed. see Cotman, Sochitl S.

***Peterman, William.** Neighborhood Planning & Community-Based Development. LC 99-50429. (Cities & Planning Ser.). 2000. write for info. (*0-7619-1198-7*) Sage.

Petermann, Erwin. Lehmbruck (Wilhelm) The Complete Graphic Work. (GER., Illus.). 428p. 1985. 275.00 (*1-55660-005-4*) A Wofsy Fine Arts.

Petermann, Franz, jt. ed. see Essau, Cecilia A.

Petermann, J. Kleines Woerterbuch der Kroatisch-Serbischen Idiomatischen Redewendungen: Small Dictionary of Croatian & Serbian Idiomatic Expressions. (GER & SER.). 144p. 1980. 35.00 (*0-8288-1052-4*, M15172) Fr & Eur.

Petermann, K. Laser Diode Modulation & Noise. (C). 1991. pap. text 102.00 (*0-7923-1204-X*) Kluwer Academic.

Peternel, Carolyn R. & Ahern, James. The I Like to Go to School Book. (Illus.). 36p. (Orig.). (J). (gr. k-2). 1983. pap. 2.95 (*0-9612060-0-4*) Primary Progs.

Peternel, Joan. Hampton Sampler. 48p. (Orig.). 1995. pap. 1.00 (*0-9646718-0-8*) Whelks Walk Pr.

— Howl & Hosanna. LC 97-165694. 132p. (Orig.). 1997. pap. 7.95 (*0-9646718-1-6*) Whelks Walk Pr.

***Peternel, Joan.** The Language of Yes: Poems. 96p. 2001. pap. 12.00 (*1-56474-354-3*) Fithian Pr.

Peternel, Joan. Nintotem: Indiana Stories. 1999. pap. 10.00 (*0-9646718-3-2*) Whelks Walk Pr.

Peternell, T., jt. auth. see Miyaoka, Yoichi.

Peternell, T., jt. auth. see Yoichi Miyaoka.

Peternell, Thomas, jt. ed. see Andreatta, Marco.

Peteros, Randall G., jt. auth. see Fiszel, Geoffrey L.

Peters. Akathistos Hymn. (Illus.). 35p. 1990. pap. 4.95 (*1-879516-01-2*) Betterpub Pr.

— Biotechnology. 1992. teacher ed. 13.75 (*0-697-12321-9*, WCB McGr Hill) McGrw-H Hghr Educ.

— Chemical Skills. 4th ed. 1992. student ed. 15.31 (*0-07-049569-2*) McGraw.

— Chemotherapy in Malaria, 2 vols. 2nd ed. 1987. 395.00 (*0-12-552720-9*) Acad Pr.

— College Accounting with Student Guide. 1998. pap. text 18.27 (*0-395-89138-8*) HM.

— Computing with Standard Pascal. (C). 1985. pap. text 25.00 (*0-03-069794-8*) Harcourt Coll Pubs.

— Cpsq Coll Acct 1-29 Rev 02 Ed. 2nd ed. 1998. pap. 65.31 (*0-07-229128-1*) McGraw.

— Culture Sketches. 3rd ed. 1999. pap. 13.13 (*0-07-228598-2*) McGraw.

Peters. The Elder Pitt. LC 97-18992. 304p. (C). 1997. pap. 23.53 (*0-582-25957-6*) Addison-Wesley.

Peters. Elder Pitt. LC 97-18992. (C). 1998. text 69.00 (*0-582-25958-4*) Addison-Wesley.

— Elementary Chemical Engineering. 2nd ed. 1984. text, student ed. 21.75 (*0-07-049588-2*) McGraw.

— Flames of Heaven: Export Edition. 1993. mass mkt. 5.99 (*0-671-88063-2*) PB.

— Flex Text. LC 96-71009. (Illus.). 728p. (C). 1997. pap. text 47.50 (*0-03-019978-6*, Pub. by SCP) Harcourt.

***Peters.** Generation Xx. 2000. pap. 25.00 (*0-7382-0346-7*, Pub. by Perseus Pubng) HarpC.

Peters. Geological Reasoning. 2000. pap. text. write for info. (*0-7167-3145-2*) W H Freeman.

— Herpetological Contributions of Wilhelm C. H. Peters. LC 94-74599. 1995. write for info. (*0-916984-35-4*) SSAR.

— An Introduction to Chemistry: Preliminary Edition. (Illus.). 144p. 1997. text. write for info. (*0-03-024556-7*) SCP.

— Introduction to Chemistry Principles. 6th ed. (C). 1994. pap. text, teacher ed. 33.75 (*0-03-096812-7*) Harcourt Coll Pubs.

— Introduction to Logic. (Philosophy Ser.). 1999. pap. 42.00 (*0-534-57398-3*) Wadsworth Pub.

— Introductory Chemistry. (C). 1997. pap. text, teacher ed. 31.50 (*0-03-023523-5*, Pub. by Harcourt Coll Pubs) Harcourt.

— Israel & Africa. 1992. text 59.50 (*1-870915-10-0*, Pub. by I B T) St Martin.

— It's Never Too Late to Discipline. 208p. 1999. pap. 12.95 (*1-58238-034-1*, Whitman Coin) St Martin.

— It's Never Too Soon. 1999. pap. write for info. (*0-312-24568-8*) St Martin.

— The Leishmaniases in Biology & Medicine, 2 vols. 1987. 157.00 (*0-12-552103-0*) Acad Pr.

— Maid for Marriage. 1993. per. 2.99 (*0-373-17159-5*) Harlequin Bks.

— New Security Challenges. LC 96-17549. 216p. 1996. text 59.95 (*0-312-16262-6*) St Martin.

— No Stone Unturned & Under Earth. 2000. 51.00 (*0-7167-3133-9*) W H Freeman.

***Peters.** Plant Design Economy Chemical Engineer. 5th ed. 2001. text 68.00 (*0-07-239266-5*) McGraw.

Peters. Revenge of the Snobs. LC 97-42168. 128p. (YA). (gr. 5 up). 1998. 13.95 (*0-316-70603-5*) Little.

— Rural Environment. LC 96-143871. Date not set. pap. 8.95 (*0-7453-0935-6*, Pub. by Pluto GBR) Stylus Pub VA.

— Sourcebook on Asbestos Disease, Vol. 16. 474p. 1998. text. write for info. (*0-88063-774-9*, 82427-10, MICHIE) LEXIS Pub.

Peters & Golden. Culture Sketches. 2nd ed. 192p. 1996. pap. 14.69 (*0-07-049715-X*) McGraw.

Peters & Macleod. X Peters - Macleod. 1989. 179.50 (*0-89296-700-5*) Mysterious Pr.

Peters, et al. California. 2nd ed. LC 98-110522. 400p. (C). 1997. per. 48.24 (*0-7872-3622-5*) Kendall-Hunt.

***Peters, et al.** California. 3rd ed. LC 99-462541. 444p. 1999. per. 51.95 (*0-7872-5577-7*, 41557701) Kendall-Hunt.

Peters, jt. auth. see Johnson.

Peters, jt. auth. see Weiner.

Peters, jt. ed. see Zodhiates, Spiros.

Peters & Peters Staff, jt. auth. see Cannon, Raymond.

Peters, A. & Jones, E. G. Cerebral Cortex: Association & Auditory Cortices, Vol. 4. LC 84-1982. (Illus.). 376p. (C). 1985. text 105.00 (*0-306-42040-6*, Kluwer Plenum) Kluwer Academic.

— Cerebral Cortex: Cellular Components of the Cerebral Cortex, Vol. 1. LC 84-1982. (Illus.). 580p. (C). 1984. text 120.00 (*0-306-41544-5*, Kluwer Plenum) Kluwer Academic.

— Cerebral Cortex: Visual Cortex, Vol. 3. LC 84-1982. (Illus.). 438p. (C). 1985. text 105.00 (*0-306-42025-2*, Kluwer Plenum) Kluwer Academic.

— Cerebral Cortex Vol. 7: Development & Maturation of Cerebral Cortex. LC 84-1982. (Illus.). 536p. (C). 1988. text 120.00 (*0-306-42881-4*, Kluwer Plenum) Kluwer Academic.

— Cerebral Cortex Vol. 9: Normal & Altered States of Function. LC 84-1982. (Illus.). 552p. (C). 1991. text 120.00 (*0-306-43648-5*, Kluwer Plenum) Kluwer Academic.

***Peters, A. & Morrison, J. H.** Cerebral Cortex Vol. 14: Neurodegenerative & Age-Related Changes in Structure & Function of Cerebral Cortex. 745p. 1999. write for info. (*0-306-45966-3*, Kluwer Plenum) Kluwer Academic.

Peters, A. & Rockland, K. S. Cerebral Cortex Vol. 10: Primary Visual Cortex in Primates. (Illus.). 576p. (C). 1994. text 125.00 (*0-306-44605-7*, Kluwer Plenum) Kluwer Academic.

Peters, A., jt. auth. see Jones, E. G.

Peters, A., jt. ed. see Brebbia, Carlos A.

Peters, A. J. British Further Education. 1967. 176.00 (*0-08-011893-3*, Pub. by Pergamon Repr) Franklin.

Peters, A. M. & Myers, M. J. Physiological Measurements with Radionuclides in Clinical Practice. LC 97-21585. (Illus.). 318p. 1998. text 73.00 (*0-19-261994-2*) OUP.

Peters, A. R., ed. Vaccines for Vet Applications. (Illus.). 304p. 1993. 115.00 (*0-7506-1126-X*) Buttrwrth-Heinemann.

Peters, A. T., jt. auth. see Freeman, H. S.

Peters, A. T., jt. ed. see Lampman.

***Peters, Alan.** The Paranoia Factor. Hunter, Ann A., ed. (Illus.). 272p. 1999. 24.95 (*1-893846-51-2*) Loft Pr.

Peters, Alan A., et al. The Fine Structure of the Nervous System: The Neurons & Their Supporting Cells. 3rd ed. (Illus.). 528p. 1990. text 69.50 (*0-19-506571-9*) OUP.

Peters, Alan A., jt. auth. see Jones, Edward G.

Peters, Alan A., jt. ed. see Jones, Edward G.

Peters, Alan H., jt. auth. see Fisher, Peter S.

Peters, Alexander, et al, eds. Computational Methods in Water Resources X, 2 vols. LC 94-17902. (Water Science & Technology Library). 1600p. (C). 1994. lib. bdg. 489.50 (*0-7923-2937-6*) Kluwer Academic.

Peters, Allan, ed. Recollections: Nathaniel Hailes's Adventurous Life in Colonial South Australia. (Illus.). 182p. 1999. pap. 14.95 (*1-86254-467-0*, Pub. by Wakefield Pr) BHB Intl.

Peters, Andrew. Sheep Don't Go to School. 1997. pap. 13.95 (*1-85224-408-9*, Pub. by Bloodaxe Bks) Dufour.

Peters, Andrew F. Strange & Spooky Stories. LC 97-3270. (Illus.). 80p. (J). (gr. 3-6). 1997. lib. bdg. 23.90 (*0-7613-0321-9*) Millbrook Pr.

***Peters Angelica, Marion.** Resolving Conflict in Nonprofit Organizations: The Leader's Guide to Finding Constructive Solutions. Hyman, Vincent & Thompson, Dale, eds. LC 99-50373. (Illus.). 192p. 1999. per. 28.00 (*0-940069-16-4*) A H Wilder.

Peters, Angie. Celebrate Home: Great Ideas for Stay-at-Home Moms. LC 97-38687. 160p. 1997. pap. 10.99 (*0-570-05316-1*, 12-3366) Concordia.

***Peters, Angie.** Celebrate Kids: More Great Ideas for Stay-at-Home Moms. LC 99-55105. (Illus.). 176p. 1999. pap. 10.99 (*0-570-05229-7*, 12-4036) Concordia.

Peters, Ann. Rings of Green. 84p. 1982. 19.95 (*0-86140-124-7*, Pub. by Smyth); pap. 9.95 (*0-86140-129-8*, Pub. by Smyth) Dufour.

Peters, Anna, jt. auth. see Ney, Philip G.

Peters, Anne. Accidental Dad. (Romance Ser.). 1993. pap. 2.75 (*0-373-08946-5*, 5-08946-1) Silhouette.

— Along Comes Baby (First Comes Marriage) 1995. per. 2.99 (*0-373-19116-2*, 1-19116-2) Silhouette.

— Une Famille pour la Vie. (Horizon Ser.). 1999. mass mkt. 3.50 (*0-373-39510-8*, 1-39510-2) Harlequin Bks.

— Green Card Wife: Wedding Month First Comes Marriage. 1995. per. 2.99 (*0-373-19104-9*) Harlequin Bks.

— His Only Deception. (Romance Ser.). 1994. per. 2.75 (*0-373-08995-3*, 5-08995-8) Silhouette.

— Love, Marriage & Family 101. 1997. per. 3.25 (*0-373-19254-1*, 1-19254-1) Silhouette.

— McCullough's Bride. (Silhouette Romance Ser.). 1994. pap. 2.75 (*0-373-19031-X*, 1-19031-3) Harlequin Bks.

— My Baby, Your Son. (Fabulous Fathers Ser.). 1997. per. 3.25 (*0-373-19222-3*, 1-19222-8) Silhouette.

— The Pursuit of Happiness. 1993. per. 2.69 (*0-373-08927-9*, 5-08927-1) Silhouette.

— The Pursuit of Happiness. large type ed. LC 93-30342. 227p. 1993. lib. bdg. 13.95 (*0-7862-0058-8*) Thorndike Pr.

— Stand-in Husband. 1995. per. 2.99 (*0-373-19110-3*, 1-19110-5) Silhouette.

— Storky Jones Is Back in Town. (Romance Ser.: No. 850). 1992. per. 2.69 (*0-373-08850-7*, 5-08850-5) Silhouette.

An Asterisk (*) at the beginning of an entry indicates that the title is appearing for the first time.

— Wanted: A Family Forever. (Romance Ser.). 1998. per. 3.50 (*0-373-19309-2*, 1-19309-3) Silhouette.

Peters, Anne L. A Life. 1992. pap. 5.50 (*0-87129-143-6*, L73) Dramatic Pub.

Peters, Arlene, jt. auth. see Peters, David, pseud.

Peters, Arnold T., ed. see Freeman, Harold.

Peters, Arthur K. Seven Trails West. (Illus.). 252p. 1996. 39.95 (*1-55859-782-4*) Abbeville Pr.

Peters, Arthur K., ed. Jean Cocteau & the French Scene. LC 83-73421. (Illus.). 224p. 1984. 19.98 (*0-89659-412-2*) Abbeville Pr.

***Peters, Arthur King.** Seven Trails West. (Illus.). 2000. pap. 29.95 (*0-7892-0678-1*) Abbeville Pr.

Peters, B. Practical Timber Formwork. 1991. pap. 44.95 (*0-442-31386-1*) Chapman & Hall.

Peters, B. F., jt. auth. see Barer, R. D.

Peters, B. Guy. American Public Policy: Promise & Performance. 5th ed. LC 98-40204. (Illus.). 528p. (C). 1999. pap. text 42.95 (*1-56643-067-4*, Chatham House Pub) Seven Bridges.

— Comparative Politics: Theory & Methods. LC 98-18784. 1998. text 55.00 (*0-8147-6667-6*); pap. text 18.50 (*0-8147-6668-4*) NYU Pr.

— Comparing Public Bureaucracies: Problems of Theory & Method. LC 87-5077. 240p. 1988. pap. text 17.95 (*0-8173-0368-5*) U of Ala Pr.

— European Politics Reconsidered. 2nd expanded rev. ed. LC 98-40363. 344p. (C). 1999. pap. text 19.95 (*0-8419-1364-1*) Holmes & Meier.

— The Future of Governing: Four Emerging Models. (Studies in Government & Public Policy). 184p. 1996. 35.00 (*0-7006-0793-5*); pap. 14.95 (*0-7006-0794-3*) U Pr of KS.

— Institutional Theory in Political Science: The New Institutionalism. LC 98-23045. 12p. Date not set. 65.00 (*1-85567-425-4*, Pub. by P P Pubs); pap. 24.95 (*1-85567-426-2*, Pub. by P P Pubs) Cassell & Continuum.

— Politics of Bureaucracy. 3rd ed. 300p. (C). 1989. pap. text 26.95 (*0-8013-0066-5*, 75730) Longman.

— Taking Stock: Assessing Public Sector Reforms. 432p. 1998. pap. text 22.95 (*0-7735-1743-X*, Pub. by McG-Queens Univ Pr) CUP Services.

Peters, B. Guy & Hollifield, James F., eds. Democracy & the State: The Rise of Administrative Politics in Britain, France & the United States. 288p. (C). 1999. pap. 65.00 (*0-8133-8319-6*) Westview.

Peters, B. Guy & Rockman, Bert A., eds. Agenda for Excellence No. 2: Administering the State. LC 95-41827. (Festschriften in Honor of Charles H. Levine: Vol. 2). 192p. (C). 1996. pap. text 27.95 (*1-56643-016-X*, Chatham House Pub) Seven Bridges.

Peters, B. Guy & Savoie, Donald I., eds. Taking Stock: Assessing Public Sector Reforms. 432p. 1998. text 65.00 (*0-7735-1742-1*, Pub. by McG-Queens Univ Pr) CUP Services.

Peters, B. Guy & Savoie, Donald J., eds. Governance in a Changing Environment. LC 96-128122. (Canadian Centre for Management Development Governance & Public Management Ser.). 352p. 1995. pap. 22.95 (*0-7735-1321-3*, Pub. by McG-Queens Univ Pr) CUP Services.

***Peters, B. Guy & Van Nispen, Frans K., eds.** Public Policy Instruments: Evaluating the Tools of Public Administration. LC 97-47513. (New Horizons in Public Policy Ser.). 264p. 1998. 85.00 (*1-85898-744-X*) E Elgar.

***Peters, B. Guy, et al.** Administering the Summit: Administration of the Core Executive in Developed Countries. LC 99-48155. (Transforming Government Ser.). 288p. 2000. text 69.95 (*0-312-23033-8*) St Martin.

Peters, B. Guy, jt. auth. see Ball, Alan R.

Peters, B. Guy, jt. auth. see Hogwood, Brian W.

Peters, B. Guy, jt. auth. see Pierre, Jon.

Peters, B. Guy, jt. ed. see Christensen, Tom.

Peters, B. Guy, jt. ed. see Hood, Christopher.

Peters, B. Guy, jt. ed. see Olsen, Johan P.

Peters, B. Guy, jt. ed. see Savoie, Donald J.

***Peters, Barbara.** Az Murder Goes . . . Artful. rev. ed. 182p. 1999. pap. 15.95 (*1-890208-26-4*) Poisoned Pen.

Peters, Barbara J., contrib. by. The Head Start Mother: Low-Income Mothers' Empowerment Through Participation. rev. ed. (Children of Poverty Ser.). 246p. 1998. 58.00 (*0-8153-3178-9*) Garland.

Peters, Barbara J., jt. auth. see Peters, George A.

Peters, Barbara J., jt. ed. see Peters, George A.

Peters, Barbarba & Samuels, Victoria, eds. Dialogue on Diversity: A New Agenda for Women. 88p. 1978. pap. 1.95 (*0-87495-003-1*) Am Jewish Comm.

Peters, Barry, ed. see Peters, Ronnie.

Peters, Basil, jt. auth. see Edwards, Anthony J.

Peters, Becky S. Building Faith One Child at a Time. 184p. (J). 1997. pap. 9.99 (*0-570-01552-9*, 22-2544) Concordia.

Peters, Bernard C. Lake Superior Place Names: From Bawating to the Montreal. (Illus.). 111p. 1996. 21.95 (*0-918616-16-6*); pap. 11.95 (*0-918616-18-2*) Northern Mich.

Peters, Bernard C., ed. Lake Superior Journal: Bela Hubbard's Account of the 1840 Houghton Expedition. LC 82-60622. (Illus.). 113p. 1982. 8.95 (*0-918616-11-5*) Northern Mich.

***Peters, Beth.** Girl Next Door: All about Katie Holmes. (Illus.). 2000. mass mkt. 5.99 (*0-345-43828-0*) Ballantine Pub Grp.

— Pop Princesses. 2000. mass mkt. 5.50 (*0-345-43829-9*) Ballantine Pub Grp.

— True Brit: The Story of Singing Sensation Britney Spears. LC 99-90436. 1999. mass mkt. 4.99 (*0-345-43687-3*) Ballantine Pub Grp.

Peters, Bette D., et al. Denver's City Park. rev. ed. (Illus.). 67p. 1986. pap. 7.95 (*0-937859-01-X*) Univ CO Dept Hist.

Peters, Betty A. Returning Back to Eden. LC 94-61583. 128p. (Orig.). 1994. spiral bd. 9.95 (*0-945383-55-X*, 945-5838) Teach Servs.

Peters, Bill. First Force Reconaissance Company. LC 98-93276. 1999. mass mkt. 6.99 (*0-8041-1873-6*) Ivy Books.

Peters, Bill, jt. auth. see Dent, Martin.

Peters, Bonnie H. & McDonald, Winnie P. Union County (TN) Faces of War: A Pictorial History of Union Countians Involvement in the Military Service of Our Country. LC 95-92282. (Illus.). 256p. 1995. lib. bdg. 35.00 (*0-9636662-1-5*) Peters McDonald.

Peters, Bonnie H., jt. auth. see McDonald, Winnie P.

Peters, Brent R., jt. auth. see Feltman, Linda C.

Peters, Byron. Ethnic Encounter: Race Relations. (Inter Acta Ser.). (Illus.). 6p. (C). 1994. teacher ed., ring bd. 1.25 (*1-885702-25-6*, 741-021t, Inter Acta); student ed., ring bd. 3.25 (*1-885702-24-8*, 741-021s, Inter Acta) WSN Pr.

Peters, Byron G., et al. Pocket Guide to Injectable Chemotherapeutic Agents: Drug Information & Dosages. 2nd rev. ed. xiii, 152p. 1998. pap. 24.95 (*0-9663138-0-1*) Oncology Educ.

***Peters, Byron G., et al.** Pocket Guide to Injectable Chemotherapeutic Agents: Drug Information & Dosages. 3rd rev. ed. xvi, 168p. 2000. pap. 24.95 (*0-615-11127-0*) Midwest Bk.

Peters, C. Mathematics, the Gas Laws & the Respiratory Practitioner. 33p. (C). 1988. pap. 15.00 (*0-933195-37-0*) CA College Health Sci.

Peters, C., et al, eds. Research & Advanced Technology for Digital Libraries: 1st European Conference, ECDL '97, Pisa, Italy, September 1-3, 1997 : Proceedings. LC 97-37055. (Lecture Notes in Computer Science Ser.: Vol. 1324). xi, 423p. 1997. pap. 67.00 (*3-540-63554-8*) Spr-Verlag.

Peters, C. H., tr. see Husserl, Edmund.

Peters, C. J. Clinical Simulations - The Right Way! The Complete Guide to Respiratory Care. 370p. 1990. pap. text 49.95 (*0-931657-20-2*) Learning Proc Ctr.

Peters, C. J. & Olshaker, Mark. Virus Hunter: Thirty Years of Battling Hot Viruses Around the World. LC 97-977. (Illus.). 336p. 1997. 23.95 (*0-385-48557-3*, Anchor NY) Doubleday.

— Virus Hunter: Thirty Years of Battling Hot Viruses Around the World. LC 97-977. (Illus.). 352p. 1998. pap. 14.95 (*0-385-48558-1*, Anchor NY) Doubleday.

Peters, C. R., et al. Edible Wild Plants of Subsaharan Africa. 240p. 1992. pap. 30.00 (*0-947643-51-6*, Pub. by Royal Botnic Grdns) Balogh.

Peters, Calvin B., jt. ed. see Loy, James.

Peters, Carl. Diary of a House Husband. 240p. 1998. pap. 10.95 (*1-874509-60-3*, Pub. by X Pr) LPC InBook.

— Eldorado of the Ancients: Archaeology, Ethnology & History of Africa. 1976. lib. bdg. 69.95 (*0-8490-1754-8*) Gordon Pr.

Peters, Carl C. The Handbook of Managed Futures & Hedge Funds: Performance, Evaluation, & Analysis. 2nd ed. LC 96-29592. 504p. 1996. 70.00 (*1-55738-917-9*, Irwn Prfssnl) McGraw-Hill Prof.

Peters, Carl C., ed. Managed Futures: Performance, Evaluation & Analysis of Commodity Funds, Pools & Accounts. 400p. 1992. text 65.00 (*1-55738-291-3*, Irwn Prfssnl) McGraw-Hill Prof.

Peters, Carmichael C. A Gadamerian Reading of Karl Rahner's Theology of Grace & Freedom. 392p. 1998. 64.00 (*1-57309-135-9*); pap. 44.50 (*1-57309-134-0*) U Pr of Amer.

Peters, Carol Heher. John Elliott Tapan & Origins. text. write for info. (*0-312-23398-1*) St Martin.

Peters, Carolyn R., jt. auth. see Wilksten, Denise.

Peters, Carolyn R., ed. see Peters, Vincent F.

Peters, Cash. Instant Insight: Secrets of Life, Love & Destiny Revealed in Your Handwriting. LC 97-29937. (Illus.). 256p. 1998. mass mkt. 11.99 (*0-446-67355-2*, Pub. by Warner Bks) Little.

Peters, Catharine, ed. see Collins, Wilkie.

***Peters, Catherine.** Byron. (Pocket Biographies Ser.). 128p. 2000. pap. 9.95 (*0-7509-2124-2*) Sutton Publng.

Peters, Catherine. Charles Dickens. (New Pocket Biographies Ser.). (Illus.). 128p. 1998. pap. 9.95 (*0-7509-1619-2*, Pub. by Sutton Pub Ltd) Intl Pubs Mktg.

— The King of Inventors: A Life of Wilkie Collins. (Illus.). 523p. 1993. text 45.00 (*0-691-03392-7*, Pub. by Princeton U Pr) Cal Prin Full Svc.

***Peters, Catherine.** Thackeray: His Life & His Work. 2000. pap. text 21.95 (*0-7509-2306-7*) Sutton Pub Ltd.

Peters, Catherine, ed. see Collins, Wilkie.

Peters, Catherine, ed. see Gasson, Andrew.

***Peters, Celeste, contrib. by.** Asthma, Antibiotics, & Exercise: The Science of Health. LC 99-27289. (Science at Work Ser.). 48p. 2000. lib. bdg. 25.69 (*0-7398-0140-6*) Raintree Steck-V.

Peters, Celeste A. Circuits, Shocks & Lightning: The Science of Electricity. LC 99-24771. (Science at Work Ser.). 48p. 2000. lib. bdg. 25.69 (*0-7398-0143-0*) Raintree Steck-V.

— Don't Be SAD: Fight the Winter Blues-Your Guide to Conquering Seasonal Affective Disorder. (Illus.). 243p. 1994. pap. 14.95 (*1-896015-01-8*) Script Pubng Inc.

***Peters, Celeste A., contrib. by.** Peppers, Popcorn & Pizza: The Science of Food. LC 99-10179. (Science at Work Ser.). (Illus.). (J). 2000. lib. bdg. write for info. (*0-7398-0136-8*) Raintree Steck-V.

Peters, Charles. How Washington Really Works. LC 82-20629. 160p. (Orig.). (C). 1983. pap. 8.61 (*0-201-14661-4*) Addison-Wesley.

— How Washington Really Works. 3rd ed. (Orig.). 1992. pap. write for info. (*0-201-57085-8*) Addison-Wesley.

— How Washington Really Works. 4th ed. LC 92-44602. (Illus.). 192p. (Orig.). 1993. pap. 13.00 (*0-201-62470-2*) Addison-Wesley.

— Tilting at Windmills: An Autobiography. Washington Monthly Staff, ed. LC 87-35903. 1988. 18.22 (*0-201-05657-7*) Addison-Wesley.

***Peters, Charles & Dillon, Kenneth.** Poetry H2O. Demings, Patricia, ed. LC 99-90525. (Illus.). 109p. 1999. pap. 12.95 (*1-891601-17-2*) Ladies Caliber.

Peters, Charles, jt. illus. see Lock, Andrew.

Peters, Charles C. Motion Pictures & Standards of Morality. LC 72-124030. (Literature of Cinema Ser.). 1970. reprint ed. 15.95 (*0-405-01648-4*) Ayer.

***Peters, Charles L. & Dillon, Kenneth C.** Perceptions. LC 98-68492. 168p. 1998. pap. 16.00 (*1-57579-137-4*) Pine Hill Pr.

Peters, Charles M. The Ecology & Management of Non-Timber Forest Resources. LC 96-2417. (Technical Papers: No. 322). 168p. 1996. pap. 22.00 (*0-8213-3619-3*, 13619) World Bank.

Peters, Charles R., jt. ed. see Lock, Andrew J.

Peters, Charles S. & Yoder, Paul. Advanced Harmony & Arranging, Bk. 6. (Master Theory Ser.). 1968. pap. text 3.45 (*0-8497-0159-7*, L185) Kjos.

— Advanced Theory, Bk. 3. (Master Theory Ser.). 1965. pap. text 3.45 (*0-8497-0156-2*, L175) Kjos.

— Beginning Theory, Bk. 1. (Master Theory Ser.). 1963. pap. text 3.45 (*0-8497-0154-6*, L173) Kjos.

— Elementary Harmony, Bk. 4. (Master Theory Ser.). 1986. pap. text 3.45 (*0-8497-0157-0*, L179) Kjos.

— Intermediate Harmony & Arranging, Bk. 5. (Master Theory Ser.). 1967. pap. text 3.45 (*0-8497-0158-9*, L181) Kjos.

— Intermediate Theory, Bk. 2. (Master Theory Ser.). 1964. pap. text 3.45 (*0-8497-0155-4*, L174) Kjos.

***Peters, Charlie.** Chicken Chaser. 160p. 2000. reprint ed. pap. 5.95 (*1-930535-05-8*) Star Dists.

Peters, Cherie A. A Miracle from the Streets. LC 96-34387. 160p. 1997. pap. 10.99 (*0-8163-1360-1*) Pacific Pr Pub Assn.

Peters, Cheryl D. & Peters, James A. More Choices for a Healthy Low-Fat You: Tasty Meals in 30 Minutes or Less. LC 97-13418. 144p. 1997. ring bd. 12.99 (*0-8280-1306-3*) Review Pr.

Peters, Chester & Beemer. Ford Model 9N, 2N & 8N. LC 96-50422. (Original Ser.). (Illus.). 128p. 1997. 24.95 (*0-7603-0289-8*) MBI Pubg.

Peters, Chris. AS/400 Client-Server Programming with Visual Basic 5.0. LC 98-222216. (Illus.). 444p. 1998. pap. 99.00 (*1-883884-47-0*, 578) Midrange Comput.

— AS/400 Client/Server Programming with Visual Basic 4.0. 2nd ed. LC 97-178499. (Illus.). 400p. 1996. pap. 99.00 (*1-883884-27-6*, 534) Midrange Comput.

— Peer Networking on the AS/400: Practical Networking Solutions for Today's Business Applications. LC 97-186148. (Illus.). 380p. (Orig.). 1997. pap. 79.00 (*1-883884-39-X*, 565) Midrange Comput.

— Sudan: A Nation in the Balance. (Oxfam Country Profiles Ser.). (Illus.). 64p. (C). 1996. pap. 9.95 (*0-85598-316-7*, Pub. by Oxfam Pub) Stylus Pub VA.

Peters, Chris, jt. auth. see Strachan, Peter.

Peters, Clarice. The Absentee Earl. large type ed. 350p. 1995. 23.99 (*0-263-14428-3*, Pub. by Mills & Boon) Ulverscroft.

Peters, Claude D., jt. auth. see Moses, Elbert R.

Peters, Colette. Colette's Birthday Cakes. LC 99-36425. (Illus.). 192p. 2000. 34.95 (*0-316-70274-9*) Little.

— Colette's Cakes: The Art of Cake Decorating. 163p. (gr. 8). 1991. 28.95 (*0-316-70205-6*) Little.

— Colette's Christmas: Spectacular Holiday Cookies, Cakes, Pies & Other Edible Art. (Illus.). 176p. 1999. pap. 19.95 (*0-316-70276-5*) Little.

— Colette's Wedding Cakes. LC 94-5299. (Illus.). 192p. (gr. 8). 1995. 39.95 (*0-316-70256-0*) Little.

— Colette's Wedding Cakes. 192p. 1997. pap. 24.95 (*0-316-70270-6*) Little.

Peters-Corbett, David, ed. Wyndham Lewis & the Art of Modern War. LC 97-6746. (Illus.). 262p. (C). 1998. text 64.95 (*0-521-56118-3*) Cambridge U Pr.

Peters Corporation, Gerald Peters Gallery Staff. Modernist Themes in New Mexico: Works by Early Modernist Painters. Rowley, Michael C., ed. LC 89-84573. (Illus.). 56p. 1989. pap. text 12.00 (*0-935037-29-2*) G Peters Gallery.

Peters, Cortez. Championship Keyboarding Drills. 3rd ed. 1998. pap. 47.50 (*0-02-801209-7*) Glencoe.

Peters, Cortez. Cortez Peters Championship Formatting. 1993. teacher ed. write for info. (*0-02-802301-3*) Glencoe.

Peters, Cortez W. Cortex Peters' Championship Keyboarding Drills: An Individualized Diagnostic & Prescriptive Method for Developing Accuracy & Speed. 3rd ed. 1996. 24.65 (*0-02-801199-6*); write for info. incl. audio compact disk (*0-02-801200-3*) Glencoe.

Peters, Cortez W., Jr. Cortez Peters Championship Formatting. LC 92-21574. 1993. 29.00 (*0-02-802300-5*) Glencoe.

— Cortez Peters Championship Keyboarding. (Illus.). 192p. 1988. text 19.96 (*0-07-049635-8*) McGraw.

— The Cortez Peters Championship Typing Drills. 2nd ed. 112p. 1987. pap. text 13.84 (*0-07-049637-4*) McGraw.

***Peters, Craig.** Navigating Toward Home: Charting Your Course Toward Biblical Manhood. 192p. 2000. pap. 10.95 (*1-58169-047-9*, Evergrn Pr AL) Genesis Comm Inc.

— Star Cars. (Illus.). 64p. 2000. 12.98 (*0-7651-1764-9*) Smithmark.

Peters, Curtis H. Kant's Philosophy of Hope. LC 90-35439. (American University Studies: Philosophy: Ser. V, Vol. 103). XV, 190p. (C). 1994. text 37.95 (*0-8204-1386-0*) P Lang Pubng.

Peters, Cynthia, ed. Collateral Damage: The New World Order at Home & Abroad. 433p. 1992. 40.00 (*0-89608-423-X*); pap. 16.00 (*0-89608-422-1*) South End Pr.

***Peters, Cynthia L.** Deaf American Literature: From Carnival to the Canon. 2000. 55.00 (*1-56368-094-7*) Gallaudet Univ Pr.

Peters, D., ed. Geology in Coal Resource Utilization. (Illus.). 850p. (C). 1991. text 121.00 (*1-878907-22-0*) TechBooks.

Peters, D. E. Brown: Genealogical Record of the Descendants of Brown, Runyan, Peters, Needham & Ackerman Families, with Historical & Biographical Sketches. 137p. 1993. reprint ed. pap. 21.00 (*0-8328-3275-8*); reprint ed. lib. bdg. 31.00 (*0-8328-3274-X*) Higginson Bk Co.

Peters, D. K., ed. Advanced Medicine Twelve: Proceedings of the 12th Annual Symposium of Advanced Medicine, 1976. (Illus.). 1976. 32.00 (*0-8464-0117-7*) Beekman Pubs.

Peters, Dan. Birth & Growth of the Early Church: Draw Your Way Through the Bible. (Picturethis! Ser.: No. 7). (Illus.). 50p. 1997. ring bd. write for info. (*1-890598-21-6*) PictureThis.

— General to Judges: Draw Your Way Through the Bible. (Picturethis! Ser.: No. 2). 50p. 1997. ring bd. write for info. (*1-890598-06-2*) PictureThis.

— In the Easement of Absent Ties. deluxe limited ed. (Working Signs Ser.: No. 2). (Illus.). 56p. 1998. pap. 10.86 (*0-911287-29-9*) Blue Begonia.

— Rise & Fall of the Kingdom: Draw Your Way Through the Bible. (Picturethis! Ser.: No. 3). (Illus.). 60p. 1997. ring bd. write for info. (*1-890598-09-7*) PictureThis.

— Watchmen: Draw Your Way Through the Bible. (Picturethis! Ser.: No. 5). (Illus.). 70p. 1997. ring bd. write for info. (*1-890598-15-1*) PictureThis.

— Wisemen: Draw Your Way Through the Bible. (Picturethis! Ser.: No. 4). 50p. 1997. ring bd. write for info. (*1-890598-12-7*) PictureThis.

Peters, Daniel. The Incas: A Magical Epic about a Lost World. (Illus.). 1060p. write for info. (*0-318-68908-1*) Random.

Peters, Daniel J. Rising from the Ruins. 1995. 24.00 (*0-614-32043-7*) Random.

Peters, Danny. Wings of Morning. 160p. (Orig.). 1996. pap. 9.95 (*1-57502-140-4*) Morris Pubng.

Peters, Dave. Surviving Church Conflict. LC 96-40869. 160p. (Orig.). 1997. pap. 12.99 (*0-8361-9051-3*) Herald Pr.

Peters, David, jt. auth. see Woodham, Anne.

Peters, David A. The Probability of Addiction: Legal, Medical & Social Implications. LC 96-46207. 166p. 1997. 69.95 (*1-57292-053-X*); pap. 49.95 (*1-57292-052-1*) Austin & Winfield.

***Peters, David H., et al.** Health Expenditures, Services & Outcomes in Africa: Basic Data & Cross-National Comparisons, 1990-1996. LC 99-22639. (Health, Nutrition, & Population Ser.). 63p. 1999. pap. 22.00 (*0-8213-4438-2*, 14438) World Bank.

***Peters, David, pseud.** Encyclopedia Of Natural Healing. (Illus.). 336p. 2000. 40.00 (*0-7894-6784-4*) DK Pub Inc.

Peters, David, pseud. Sky Kings. (J). 1998. write for info. (*0-316-70269-2*) Little.

Peters, David, pseud & Peters, Arlene. By an Unfamiliar Path: The Story of David & Arlene Peters. LC 94-69126. (Jaffray Collection of Missionary Portraits: Bk. 13). 164p. 1995. pap. 9.99 (*0-87509-580-1*) Chr Pubns.

***Peters, David, pseud & Woodham, Anne.** The Complete Guide to Integrative Medicine. LC 99-50060. 2000. 29.95 (*0-7894-5177-8*) DK Pub Inc.

Peters, Deanna, jt. auth. see Strohm, Richard L.

Peters, DeWitt C. Life & Adventures of Kit Carson, the Nestor of the Rocky Mountains from Facts Narrated by Himself. LC 76-109631. (Select Bibliographies Reprint Ser.). 1977. 36.95 (*0-8369-5240-5*) Ayer.

Peters, Diana L. S., tr. see Von Kleist, Heinrich.

Peters, Diane M., jt. auth. see Rosenbluth, Hal F.

Peters, Donald C. The Democratic System in the Eastern Caribbean, 298. LC 91-33502. (Contributions in Political Science Ser.: No. 298). 256p. 1992. 59.95 (*0-313-28428-8*, PDN, Greenwood Pr) Greenwood.

Peters, Donald F. & Pence, Alan R., eds. Family Day Care: Current Research for Informed Policy. (Early Childhood Education Ser.). 304p. (C). 1992. text 36.00 (*0-8077-3202-8*) Tchrs Coll.

Peters, Donald J. A Contrarian Strategy for Growth Stock Investing: Theoretical Foundations & Empiracal Evidence. LC 92-1748. 208p. 1992. 57.95 (*0-89930-803-1*, Q803, Quorum Bks) Greenwood.

Peters, Donald L., et al, eds. Professionalism & the Early Childhood Practitioner. (Early Childhood Education Ser.). 216p. (C). 1988. text 36.95 (*0-8077-2896-9*); pap. text 18.95 (*0-8077-2895-0*) Tchrs Coll.

Peters, Donna A. & McKeon, Tad. Transforming Home Care: Quality, Cost, & Data Management. LC 98-15281. 450p. 1998. 59.00 (*0-8342-1072-X*, 1072X) Aspen Pub.

***Peters, Dorothy L.** Taking Cues from Kids: How They Think, What to Do about It. LC 99-42847. 2000. pap. text 18.00 (*0-325-00210-X*) Heinemann.

Peters, E. Adamantius=Gnostica. 1998. 25.95 (*90-6831-893-4*, Pub. by Peeters Pub) Bks Intl VA.

— L' Affaire Bosman. 1998. 50.00 (*90-6831-804-7*, Pub. by Peeters Pub) Bks Intl VA.

— Die Agtyptischen Motive in Glyptik. 1998. 63.95 (*90-6831-775-X*, Pub. by Peeters Pub) Bks Intl VA.

— Les Allemands en Perse Pendant. 1998. 28.95 (*90-6831-914-0*, Pub. by Peeters Pub) Bks Intl VA.

P

— Analytiques du Sens. 1998. 22.95 (*90-6831-816-0*, Pub. by Peeters Pub) Bks Intl VA.
— Annus Platonicus: Study of World. 1998. 65.95 (*90-6831-876-4*, Pub. by Peeters Pub) Bks Intl VA.
— Apocryphal Acts of Peter. 1999. 34.95 (*90-390-0162-6*, Pub. by Peeters Pub) Bks Intl VA.
— Aramaic Language Achaemenid Semitique. 1998. 119.00 (*90-6831-740-7*, Pub. by Peeters Pub) Bks Intl VA.
— Arguments for Immortality of Soul. 1998. 75.00 (*90-6831-759-8*, Pub. by Peeters Pub) Bks Intl VA.
— L' Augustinisme, No. Betl 111. 1998. 75.00 (*90-6831-573-0*, Pub. by Peeters Pub) Bks Intl VA.
— Babylonian Topographical Texts. 1998. 200.00 (*90-6831-410-6*, Pub. by Peeters Pub) Bks Intl VA.
— Begin with the Body. LC 98-221748. 1998. 40.00 (*90-6831-997-3*, Pub. by Peeters Pub) Bks Intl VA.
— Belgen in Perzie, 1915-1941. 1998. 26.95 (*90-6831-850-0*, Pub. by Peeters Pub) Bks Intl VA.
— Biblio. Anal. L'Archeologie, S. 2 & 3. 1998. 23.95 (*90-6831-867-5*, Pub. by Peeters Pub) Bks Intl VA.
— Book of Daniel, No. Betl 106. 1998. 93.95 (*90-6831-467-X*, Pub. by Peeters Pub) Bks Intl VA.
— Book of Genesis in Jewish=Teg. 1998. 65.95 (*90-6831-920-5*, Pub. by Peeters Pub) Bks Intl VA.
— Book of Jeremiah, No. Betl 128. 1998. 75.00 (*90-6831-815-2*, Pub. by Peeters Pub) Bks Intl VA.
— Book of Job, No. Betl 114. LC 96-138410. 1998. 75.00 (*90-6831-652-4*, Pub. by Peeters Pub) Bks Intl VA.
— Cain & Abel in Syr, No. SUBS 95. LC 98-186285. 1998. 100.00 (*90-6831-909-4*, Pub. by Peeters Pub) Bks Intl VA.
— Cardinal Mercier: A Memoir. 1998. 46.95 (*90-6831-862-4*, Pub. by Peeters Pub) Bks Intl VA.
— Catalogus Van de Middeleeuwse. 1998. 75.00 (*90-6831-935-3*, Pub. by Peeters Pub) Bks Intl VA.
— La Chaine sur la Genese. 4th ed. 1998. 131.95 (*90-6831-817-9*, Pub. by Peeters Pub) Bks Intl VA.
— Chalkedon: Geschichte und Aktualit. 1998. 35.95 (*90-6831-984-1*, Pub. by Peeters Pub) Bks Intl VA.
— Civil Calendar & Lunar Calendar. LC 99-195345. 1998. 75.00 (*90-6831-908-6*, Pub. by Peeters Pub) Bks Intl VA.
— Clemente di Alessandria. 1998. 59.95 (*90-6831-794-6*, Pub. by Peeters Pub) Bks Intl VA.
— Collecties Op Orde, Vol. 1. 1998. 115.00 (*90-6831-975-2*, Pub. by Peeters Pub) Bks Intl VA.
— Collecties Op Orde, Vol. II. 1998. 115.00 (*90-6831-974-4*, Pub. by Peeters Pub) Bks Intl VA.
— Commentum Medium Super Libro. 1998. 150.00 (*90-6831-859-4*, Pub. by Peeters Pub) Bks Intl VA.
— Constitution du Picard. 1998. 28.95 (*90-6831-905-1*, Pub. by Peeters Pub) Bks Intl VA.
— Coptic Grammatical Chrestomathy. 1998. 62.95 (*90-6831-139-5*, Pub. by Peeters Pub) Bks Intl VA.
— Corinthian Correspondence, No. Betl 125. 1998. 75.00 (*90-6831-774-1*, Pub. by Peeters Pub) Bks Intl VA.
— Creation et Evenement-Jean Ladrier. 1998. 50.00 (*90-6831-869-1*, Pub. by Peeters Pub) Bks Intl VA.
— Cultural Inter Ancient near East. LC 97-227516. 1998. 50.00 (*90-6831-786-5*, Pub. by Peeters Pub) Bks Intl VA.
— Cura Aquarium in Campania. 1998. 68.95 (*90-6831-844-6*, Pub. by Peeters Pub) Bks Intl VA.
— De Beste Arts Zij Oook Een Filos. 1998. 26.95 (*90-6831-906-X*, Pub. by Peeters Pub) Bks Intl VA.
— De Bosman Case. 1998. 50.00 (*90-6831-796-2*, Pub. by Peeters Pub) Bks Intl VA.
— De Faculteit Godgeleerdheid. 1998. 46.95 (*90-6831-910-8*, Pub. by Peeters Pub) Bks Intl VA.
— De Waarheid Van de Kunst. 1998. 17.95 (*90-6831-886-1*, Pub. by Peeters Pub) Bks Intl VA.
— Deontology & Teleology, No. Betl 120. LC 96-211987. 1998. 90.95 (*90-6831-721-0*, Pub. by Peeters Pub) Bks Intl VA.
— Deuteronomy & Deut. Lit., No. Betl 133. 1998. 93.95 (*90-6831-936-1*, Pub. by Peeters Pub) Bks Intl VA.
— Dictionnaire Abzakh. 1998. 50.00 (*90-6831-742-3*, Pub. by Peeters Pub) Bks Intl VA.
— Dictionnaire de Logopedie. 1998. 13.95 (*90-6831-897-7*, Pub. by Peeters Pub) Bks Intl VA.
— Dictionnaire des Racines Semitique. 1998. 34.95 (*90-6831-811-X*, Pub. by Peeters Pub) Bks Intl VA.
— Les Dictionnaires Specialises et l'Analyse de la Valeur. 1998. 30.95 (*90-6831-898-5*, Pub. by Peeters Pub) Bks Intl VA.
— Dying, Death & Bereavement. LC 98-221622. 1998. 34.95 (*90-6831-976-0*, Pub. by Peeters Pub) Bks Intl VA.
— Dynamique dans la Langue et Cultur. 1998. 23.95 (*90-6831-852-7*, Pub. by Peeters Pub) Bks Intl VA.
— E. M. Uhlenbeck. 1998. 15.95 (*90-6831-884-5*, Pub. by Peeters Pub) Bks Intl VA.
— East & West Crusader States. LC 94-173231. 1998. 39.00 (*90-6831-792-X*, Pub. by Peeters Pub) Bks Intl VA.
— L' Ecclesiologie, No. Betl 107. 1998. 81.95 (*90-6831-451-3*, Pub. by Peeters Pub) Bks Intl VA.
— L' Ecrit Argumente. 1998. 29.95 (*90-6831-918-3*, Pub. by Peeters Pub) Bks Intl VA.
— Encomiastica Morgan, Lib 1, CSCO 544. 1998. 60.00 (*90-6831-576-5*, Pub. by Peeters Pub) Bks Intl VA.
— Encomiastica Morgan, Lib 2, CSCO 545. 1998. 60.00 (*90-6831-575-7*, Pub. by Peeters Pub) Bks Intl VA.
— L' Enonciation Mediatisee. 1998. 43.95 (*90-6831-861-6*, Pub. by Peeters Pub) Bks Intl VA.
— L' Enseignement, No. Betl 109. 1998. 39.00 (*90-6831-513-7*, Pub. by Peeters Pub) Bks Intl VA.
— Essai sur l'Evolution Subjonctif. 1998. 37.95 (*90-6831-882-9*, Pub. by Peeters Pub) Bks Intl VA.
— Essays on John. 1998. 32.95 (*90-6831-444-0*, Pub. by Peeters Pub) Bks Intl VA.
— L' Etre et Dieu Chez Gustav Siewert. 1998. 43.95 (*90-6831-872-1*, Pub. by Peeters Pub) Bks Intl VA.
— Europees Sociale-Zekerheidsrecht. 1998. 56.95 (*90-6831-864-0*, Pub. by Peeters Pub) Bks Intl VA.
— Europese Unie. 1998. 71.95 (*90-6831-732-6*, Pub. by Peeters Pub) Bks Intl VA.
— Evangelica II, 1982-91. 1998. 87.95 (*90-6831-312-6*, Pub. by Peeters Pub) Bks Intl VA.
— Finding of the True Cross, No. SUBS 93. 1998. 43.95 (*90-6831-891-8*, Pub. by Peeters Pub) Bks Intl VA.
— From Malines to Arcic, No. Betl 130. 1998. 56.95 (*90-6831-916-7*, Pub. by Peeters Pub) Bks Intl VA.
— Il Gadla Absadi, No. AETH.103. 1998. 40.95 (*90-6831-800-4*, Pub. by Peeters Pub) Bks Intl VA.
— Il Gadla Absadi, No. AETH.104. 1998. 28.95 (*90-6831-801-2*, Pub. by Peeters Pub) Bks Intl VA.
— Geschichte des Zweiten Vatika. 1998. 63.95 (*90-6831-841-1*, Pub. by Peeters Pub) Bks Intl VA.
— Gezelles "Gouden EEUW" 1998. 51.00 (*90-6831-877-2*, Pub. by Peeters Pub) Bks Intl VA.
— God's Self-Confident Daughters. 1998. 34.95 (*90-390-0272-X*, Pub. by Peeters Pub) Bks Intl VA.
— Grammaire du Berbere de Figuig. Date not set. write for info. (*90-6831-875-6*, Pub. by Peeters Pub) Bks Intl VA.
— Grammaire Fondamentale du Latin. 1998. 75.00 (*90-6831-895-0*, Pub. by Peeters Pub) Bks Intl VA.
— Greek-English Lexicon - 12 Prophets. 1998. 65.95 (*90-6831-495-5*, Pub. by Peeters Pub) Bks Intl VA.
— Griffe des Aieux. 1998. 38.95 (*90-6831-806-3*, Pub. by Peeters Pub) Bks Intl VA.
— Het Einde Van de Alpha-Tekst. 1998. 50.00 (*90-6831-987-6*, Pub. by Peeters Pub) Bks Intl VA.
— Het Vouwbeen Van de Lezer. 1998. 20.00 (*90-6831-887-X*, Pub. by Peeters Pub) Bks Intl VA.
— Histoire de Claude Simon: Ecriture. Date not set. write for info. (*90-6831-851-9*, Pub. by Peeters Pub) Bks Intl VA.
— Historia Romana. 1998. 46.95 (*90-6831-888-8*, Pub. by Peeters Pub) Bks Intl VA.
— Ik Hadde de Nieusgierigheid. 1998. 32.95 (*90-6831-927-2*, Pub. by Peeters Pub) Bks Intl VA.
— Ioannis Buridani Exposito. 1998. 155.95 (*90-6831-797-0*, Pub. by Peeters Pub) Bks Intl VA.
— Isaac of Ninevah, No. SYR225. 1998. 50.00 (*90-6831-709-1*, Pub. by Peeters Pub) Bks Intl VA.
— L' Ivresse Linguistique. 1998. 25.00 (*90-6831-812-8*, Pub. by Peeters Pub) Bks Intl VA.
— Jean Perrot. 1998. 15.95 (*90-6831-946-9*, Pub. by Peeters Pub) Bks Intl VA.
— Les Juifs en Roumanie. 1998. 56.95 (*90-6831-829-2*, Pub. by Peeters Pub) Bks Intl VA.
— Kaffa Lives Desert Fathers, No. SUBS94. LC 98-186271. 1998. 78.95 (*90-6831-874-8*, Pub. by Peeters Pub) Bks Intl VA.
— Ktaba D'Durrasa, No. SYR 226. 1998. 121.95 (*90-6831-776-8*, Pub. by Peeters Pub) Bks Intl VA.
— Ktaba D'Durrasa, No. SYR 227. 1998. 87.95 (*90-6831-777-6*, Pub. by Peeters Pub) Bks Intl VA.
— Languages & Linguists. 1998. 37.95 (*90-6831-948-5*, Pub. by Peeters Pub) Bks Intl VA.
— Lexique Encyclopedique & Them. Iran. 1998. 28.95 (*90-6831-923-X*, Pub. by Peeters Pub) Bks Intl VA.
— Linguistique Naturaliste en France. 1998. 57.95 (*90-6831-878-0*, Pub. by Peeters Pub) Bks Intl VA.
— Lire Descartes Aujourd'Hui. 1998. 35.95 (*90-6831-870-5*, Pub. by Peeters Pub) Bks Intl VA.
— Literatuur Als Systeem. 1998. 20.00 (*90-6831-818-7*, Pub. by Peeters Pub) Bks Intl VA.
— Living with God. 1998. 34.95 (*90-6831-966-3*, Pub. by Peeters Pub) Bks Intl VA.
— Le Livre de Jeremie, No. Betl 54. 1998. 56.95 (*90-6831-941-8*, Pub. by Peeters Pub) Bks Intl VA.
— Magistri Petri de Ybernia Exposito. 1998. 68.75 (*90-6831-819-5*, Pub. by Peeters Pub) Bks Intl VA.
— Manuscripts Speculum Humanae. 1998. 118.95 (*90-6831-773-3*, Pub. by Peeters Pub) Bks Intl VA.
— Mark & Q. 1998. 56.95 (*90-6831-712-1*, Pub. by Peeters Pub) Bks Intl VA.
— Martyrium, No. Betl 117. 1998. 93.95 (*90-6831-680-X*, Pub. by Peeters Pub) Bks Intl VA.
— Matrices, Etymons, Racines. 1998. 43.95 (*90-6831-917-5*, Pub. by Peeters Pub) Bks Intl VA.
— Memling Studies. LC 98-209367. 1998. 87.95 (*90-6831-950-7*, Pub. by Peeters Pub) Bks Intl VA.
— Mens en Recht. 1998. 38.95 (*90-6831-896-9*, Pub. by Peeters Pub) Bks Intl VA.
— Missing Century. LC 99-223615. 1998. 43.95 (*90-6831-985-X*, Pub. by Peeters Pub) Bks Intl VA.
— Morale de la Foi, No. Betl 119. 1998. 93.95 (*90-6831-665-6*, Pub. by Peeters Pub) Bks Intl VA.
— Morpheme-Ant. 1998. 50.00 (*90-6831-924-8*, Pub. by Peeters Pub) Bks Intl VA.
— Mt. Sinai Arabic Version, No. AR 48. 1998. 50.00 (*90-6831-838-1*, Pub. by Peeters Pub) Bks Intl VA.
— Mt. Sinai Arabic Version, No. AR49. 1998. 50.00 (*90-6831-839-X*, Pub. by Peeters Pub) Bks Intl VA.
— Les Moyens D'Expression du Pouvoir. 1998. 37.95 (*90-6831-871-3*, Pub. by Peeters Pub) Bks Intl VA.
— Mythe et Roman en Egypte Ancienne. 1998. 63.95 (*90-6831-890-X*, Pub. by Peeters Pub) Bks Intl VA.
— Mytho-Cycle Heroique dans l'Aire. 1998. 60.95 (*90-6831-813-6*, Pub. by Peeters Pub) Bks Intl VA.
— Nature & Grace Theol. Occ., No. Betl 127. 1998. 56.95 (*90-6831-832-2*, Pub. by Peeters Pub) Bks Intl VA.
— Ndroje Balendro: Musiques, Terrain. 1998. 50.00 (*90-6831-785-7*, Pub. by Peeters Pub) Bks Intl VA.
— Neologie Lexicale Berbere. 1998. 46.95 (*90-6831-810-1*, Pub. by Peeters Pub) Bks Intl VA.
— 1996 Europese Ondernemingsgraad. 1998. 56.95 (*90-6831-857-8*, Pub. by Peeters Pub) Bks Intl VA.
— Nominal Anaphors. LC 97-227407. 1998. 28.95 (*90-6831-798-9*, Pub. by Peeters Pub) Bks Intl VA.
— Nous Deux, 1947-1997. 1998. 17.95 (*90-6831-957-4*, Pub. by Peeters Pub) Bks Intl VA.
— Old Babylonian Legal & Adm. Texts. 1998. 42.95 (*90-6831-063-1*, Pub. by Peeters Pub) Bks Intl VA.
— Old Nubian Dict. Appendic, No. SUBS 92. LC 97-179785. 1998. 43.95 (*90-6831-925-6*, Pub. by Peeters Pub) Bks Intl VA.
— Old Nubian Dictionary, No. SUBS90. LC 97-103160. 1998. 93.95 (*90-6831-787-3*, Pub. by Peeters Pub) Bks Intl VA.
— Omne Ens Est Aliquid. 1998. 18.95 (*90-6831-814-4*, Pub. by Peeters Pub) Bks Intl VA.
— 1 4:1-113,16 Temptations of Jesus. 1998. 56.95 (*90-6831-880-2*, Pub. by Peeters Pub) Bks Intl VA.
— Origeniana Quinta, No. Betl 105. 1998. 84.95 (*90-6831-423-8*, Pub. by Peeters Pub) Bks Intl VA.
— Origeniana Sexta, No. Betl 118. LC 96-204051. 1998. 122.00 (*90-6831-725-3*, Pub. by Peeters Pub) Bks Intl VA.
— Paul Ricoeur. 1998. 93.95 (*90-6831-793-8*, Pub. by Peeters Pub) Bks Intl VA.
— Pauline Studies, No. Betl 115. LC 95-208618. 1998. 78.00 (*90-6831-622-2*, Pub. by Peeters Pub) Bks Intl VA.
— Perception et Langage. 1998. 50.00 (*90-6831-902-7*, Pub. by Peeters Pub) Bks Intl VA.
— Perspectives Arabes et Medievales. 1998. 75.00 (*90-6831-783-0*, Pub. by Peeters Pub) Bks Intl VA.
— Peters of New England: A Genealogy & Family History. (Illus.). 470p. 1989. reprint ed. pap. 70.00 (*0-8328-0959-4*); reprint ed. lib. bdg. 78.00 (*0-8328-0958-6*) Higginson Bk Co.
— Petrofina. 1998. 28.95 (*90-6831-900-0*, Pub. by Peeters Pub) Bks Intl VA.
— Plotinus' Theory of Matter-Evil. 1998. 90.95 (*90-6831-752-0*, Pub. by Peeters Pub) Bks Intl VA.
— Proto-Gbaya. 1998. 51.00 (*90-6831-743-1*, Pub. by Peeters Pub) Bks Intl VA.
— Ptolemaic Lexikon, No. Ola 78. LC 98-218348. 1998. 171.95 (*90-6831-933-7*, Pub. by Peeters Pub) Bks Intl VA.
— Q 11:2B-4 The Lord's Prayer=Q. LC 96-207580. 1998. 25.00 (*90-6831-788-1*, Pub. by Peeters Pub) Bks Intl VA.
— Q12:8-12 Confessing. 1998. 87.95 (*90-6831-990-6*, Pub. by Peeters Pub) Bks Intl VA.
— Q 12:49-59 Children vs. Parents. 1998. 56.95 (*90-6831-931-0*, Pub. by Peeters Pub) Bks Intl VA.
— Question de l'Essence. 1998. 56.95 (*90-6831-894-2*, Pub. by Peeters Pub) Bks Intl VA.
— Repercussion Phonologiques & Morph. 1998. 37.95 (*90-6831-951-5*, Pub. by Peeters Pub) Bks Intl VA.
— Rezeption der Christologischen For. Date not set. write for info. (*90-390-0311-4*, Pub. by Peeters Pub) Bks Intl VA.
— Rise of Yahwism, No. BETL 91. 1998. 43.95 (*90-6831-901-9*, Pub. by Peeters Pub) Bks Intl VA.
— Sayat'-Nova, No. SUBS.91. 1998. 131.95 (*90-6831-795-4*, Pub. by Peeters Pub) Bks Intl VA.
— Schizofrenie-Het Raadsel Opgelost? 1998. 17.95 (*90-6831-938-8*, Pub. by Peeters Pub) Bks Intl VA.
— Scriptures in the Gospels, No. Betl 131. 1998. 75.00 (*90-6831-932-9*, Pub. by Peeters Pub) Bks Intl VA.
— Secte des Soeurs Bacchus. 1998. 17.95 (*90-6831-944-2*, Pub. by Peeters Pub) Bks Intl VA.
— Self-Determination & Moral Act. 1998. 36.95 (*90-6831-699-0*, Pub. by Peeters Pub) Bks Intl VA.
— Semitic Languages Outline. LC 98-218350. 1998. 115.00 (*90-6831-939-6*, Pub. by Peeters Pub) Bks Intl VA.
— Signs Source in 4th Gospel, No. Betl 116. 1998. 78.00 (*90-6831-649-4*, Pub. by Peeters Pub) Bks Intl VA.
— Le Sort de la Bulle, No. Betl 104. 1998. 62.50 (*90-6831-452-1*, Pub. by Peeters Pub) Bks Intl VA.
— Stoffige Geesten. 1998. 17.95 (*90-6831-955-8*, Pub. by Peeters Pub) Bks Intl VA.
— Structuration Conceptuelle Langage. 1998. 25.95 (*90-6831-907-8*, Pub. by Peeters Pub) Bks Intl VA.
— Studia Patristica, No. XXX. 1998. 110.00 (*90-6831-840-3*, Pub. by Peeters Pub) Bks Intl VA.
— Studia Patristica, No. XXXI. 1998. 110.00 (*90-6831-847-0*, Pub. by Peeters Pub) Bks Intl VA.
— Studia Patristica, No. XXXII. LC 98-209567. 1998. 110.00 (*90-6831-854-3*, Pub. by Peeters Pub) Bks Intl VA.
— Studia Patristica, No. XXXIII. LC 98-209567. 1998. 110.00 (*90-6831-868-3*, Pub. by Peeters Pub) Bks Intl VA.
— Studia Patristica, Vol. XXIX. 1998. 110.00 (*90-6831-836-5*, Pub. by Peeters Pub) Bks Intl VA.
— Studies Book Isaiah, No. BETL 132. 1998. 93.95 (*90-6831-926-4*, Pub. by Peeters Pub) Bks Intl VA.
— Studies Book of Exodus, No. BETL 126. 1998. 75.00 (*90-6831-825-X*, Pub. by Peeters Pub) Bks Intl VA.
— Studies in Ancient Hebrew Semantic. LC 96-137016. 1998. 43.95 (*90-6831-755-5*, Pub. by Peeters Pub) Bks Intl VA.
— Studies on 2 Corinthians. LC 95-172329. 1998. 93.95 (*90-6831-612-5*, Pub. by Peeters Pub) Bks Intl VA.
— Suivre la Divinite. 1998. 18.95 (*90-6831-873-X*, Pub. by Peeters Pub) Bks Intl VA.
— Synoptic Gospels, No. Betl 110. 1998. 93.95 (*90-6831-493-9*, Pub. by Peeters Pub) Bks Intl VA.
— Syriac Gospel Translation, No. CSCO 548. LC 95-126704. 1998. 68.95 (*90-6831-642-7*, Pub. by Peeters Pub) Bks Intl VA.
— Syrian in Greek Dress=Teg. 1998. 75.00 (*90-6831-958-2*, Pub. by Peeters Pub) Bks Intl VA.
— Le Temoignage Veritable, No. NH IX, 3. Date not set. write for info. (*90-6831-834-9*, Pub. by Peeters Pub) Bks Intl VA.
— Terminologie & Intre-Disciplinarit. 1998. 17.95 (*90-6831-949-3*, Pub. by Peeters Pub) Bks Intl VA.
— Theodore Abu Qurrah=ECTT. 1998. 25.95 (*90-6831-928-0*, Pub. by Peeters Pub) Bks Intl VA.
— Tibi Soli Peccavi TIU3. 1998. 28.95 (*90-6831-885-3*, Pub. by Peeters Pub) Bks Intl VA.
— Tradition & Communion, No. BETL 129. 1998. 93.95 (*90-6831-892-6*, Pub. by Peeters Pub) Bks Intl VA.
— Two Cardinals, No. Betl 123. LC 96-178683. 1998. 56.00 (*90-6831-771-7*, Pub. by Peeters Pub) Bks Intl VA.
— Utraque Lingua. 1998. 46.95 (*90-6831-889-6*, Pub. by Peeters Pub) Bks Intl VA.
— Vers l'Invention de la Rhetorique. 1998. 36.95 (*90-6831-942-6*, Pub. by Peeters Pub) Bks Intl VA.
— Le Voyage Initiatique en Terre. 1998. 37.95 (*90-6831-846-2*, Pub. by Peeters Pub) Bks Intl VA.
— Worterverzeichnis, No. SUBS 96. 1998. 87.95 (*90-6831-911-6*, Pub. by Peeters Pub) Bks Intl VA.

Peters, E. & Goris, Harm J. M. J. Free Creatures of an Eternal God. 1998. 38.95 (*90-6831-866-7*, Pub. by Peeters Pub) Bks Intl VA.

Peters, Edgar E. Chaos & Order in the Capital Markets: A New View of Cycles, Prices & Market Volatility. 2nd ed. LC 96-18533. (Illus.). 274p. 1996. 65.00 (*0-471-13938-6*) Wiley.
— Fractal Market Analysis: Applying Chaos Theory to Investment & Economics. (Financial Editions Ser.). 336p. 1994. 69.95 (*0-471-58524-6*) Wiley.

***Peters, Edgar E.** Patterns in the Dark: Understanding Risk & Financial Crisis with Complexity Theory. LC HB95.P42 1999. (Wiley Investment Classics Ser.). (Illus.). 222p. 1999. 39.95 (*0-471-23947-X*) Wiley.

Peters, Edward. Europe & the Middle Ages. 3rd ed. LC 96-7267. 433p. (C). 1996. pap. text 51.00 (*0-13-105982-3*) P-H.
— The First Crusade: Chronicle of Fulcher of Chartres & Other Source Materials. 2nd ed. LC 98-12687. (Middle Ages Ser.). 336p. 1998. pap. 19.95 (*0-8122-1656-3*) U of Pa Pr.
— The Magician, the Witch & the Law. LC 78-51341. (Middle Ages Ser.). 216p. 1982. pap. text 16.95 (*0-8122-1101-4*) U of Pa Pr.
— Torture. expanded ed. 304p. 1996. pap. 16.95 (*0-8122-1599-0*) U of Pa Pr.

Peters, Edward, ed. Christian Society & the Crusades, 1198-1229: Sources in Translation, Including the Capture of Damietta. LC 78-163385. (Middle Ages Ser.). 192p. (C). 1971. pap. text 16.95 (*0-8122-1024-7*) U of Pa Pr.
— Heresy & Authority in Medieval Europe. LC 79-5262. (Middle Ages Ser.). 312p. 1980. pap. text 20.95 (*0-8122-1103-0*) U of Pa Pr.

Peters, Edward, jt. ed. see Kors, Alan Charles.

Peters, Edward H., jt. auth. see Krochalis, Jeanne.

Peters, Edward I. Basic Chemical Principles. (C). 1988. pap. text, teacher ed. 16.00 (*0-03-004812-5*) Harcourt Coll Pubs.
— Basic Chemical Principles. 2nd ed. LC 93-83231. (C). 1994. text 69.50 (*0-03-096811-9*) Harcourt Coll Pubs.

Peters, Edward I. & Scroggins, William T. Chemical Skills. 4th ed. 512p. (C). 1992. pap. 42.81 (*0-07-049562-9*) McGraw.

Peters, Edward M. Inquisition. 1989. pap. 17.95 (*0-520-06630-8*, Pub. by U CA Pr) Cal Prin Full Svc.

Peters, Edward N. Home Schooling & the New Code of Canon Law. 48p. (Orig.). 1988. pap. 2.95 (*0-931888-29-8*) Christendom Pr.
— 100 Answers to Your Questions on Annullments. 250p. 1997. 24.99 (*0-9642610-7-3*) Basilica Pr.

Peters, Edward N. 100 Answers to Your Questions on Annulments. LC 97-224547. 240p. (C). 1997. text 8.00 (*0-536-00172-3*) Pearson Custom.

Peters, Elana. Hard Questions, Simple Answers Vol. I: A Workbook to Take the Crisis Out of Caregiving. v, 120p. 1999. pap., wbk. ed. 29.95 (*1-893775-00-3*) Care Giving.

Peters, Eleanor B. Bradley of Essex County: Early Records, 1643-1746. (Illus.). 213p. 1991. reprint ed. pap. 35.00 (*0-8328-2100-4*); reprint ed. lib. bdg. 45.00 (*0-8328-2099-7*) Higginson Bk Co.

Peters, Elisabeth T., intro. Gerald Gleeson (1915-1986) California Watercolorist. (Illus.). 30p. (Orig.). 1990. pap. text 10.00 (*0-9626611-1-2*) Montgomery Gallery.

***Peters, Elizabeth.** The Dead Sea Cipher. large type ed. 305p. 2000. lib. bdg. 25.95 (*1-58547-039-2*) Ctr Point Pubg.
— The Jackal's Head. large type ed. LC 00-30975. 281p. 2000. 26.95 (*1-58547-040-6*) Ctr Point Pubg.
— Night of Four Hundred. Date not set. mass mkt. write for info. (*0-380-73120-7*) Morrow Avon.

Peters, Elizabeth, pseud. The Ape Who Guards the Balance. (Amelia Peabody Mystery Ser.). 400p. (YA). (gr. 8 up). 1999. mass mkt. 6.99 (*0-380-79856-5*, Avon Bks) Morrow Avon.
— The Ape Who Guards the Balance. LC 98-42756. (Amelia Peabody Mystery Ser.). 1999. 25.95 (*1-56895-597-9*) Wheeler Pub.
— The Ape Who Guards the Balance: An Amelia Peabody Mystery. LC 97-44189. (Amelia Peabody Mystery Ser.). 384p. 1998. mass mkt. 24.00 (*0-380-97657-9*, Avon Bks) Morrow Avon.
— Borrower of the Night: A Vicky Bliss Mystery. 1990. mass mkt. 4.99 (*0-8125-2355-5*, Pub. by Tor Bks) St Martin.

***Peters, Elizabeth, pseud.** Borrower of the Night: The First Vicky Bliss Mystery. 352p. 2000. mass mkt. 6.99 (*0-380-73339-0*, Avon Bks) Morrow Avon.

Peters, Elizabeth, pseud. The Camelot Caper. 320p. 1990. mass mkt. 4.99 (*0-8125-1241-3*, Pub. by Tor Bks) St Martin.
— The Camelot Caper. 320p. 1996. reprint ed. 24.00 (*0-7278-4936-0*) Severn Hse.

P

An Asterisk (*) at the beginning of an entry indicates that the title is appearing for the first time.

Peters, Elizabeth, pseud. The Copenhagen Connection. 1990. mass mkt. 4.99 (*0-8125-2227-3*) Tor Bks.

Peters, Elizabeth, pseud. The Copenhagen Connection. 224p. 1994. mass mkt. 5.50 (*0-446-36483-5*, Pub. by Warner Bks) Little.

— Crocodile on the Sandbank. (Amelia Peabody Mystery Ser.). 262p. 1988. mass mkt. 6.99 (*0-445-40651-8*, Pub. by Warner Bks) Little.

— The Curse of the Pharaohs. (Amelia Peabody Mystery Ser.). 285p. 1988. mass mkt. 6.99 (*0-445-40648-8*, Pub. by Warner Bks) Little.

— The Dead Sea Cipher. 224p. 1988. pap. 4.99 (*0-8125-0756-8*, Pub. by Tor Bks) St Martin.

***Peters, Elizabeth, pseud.** The Deeds of the Disturber, (Amelia Peabody Mystery Ser.). 400p. 2000. mass mkt. 6.99 (*0-380-73195-9*, Avon Bks) Morrow Avon.

Peters, Elizabeth, pseud. The Deeds of the Disturber. (Amelia Peabody Mystery Ser.). 304p. 1989. mass mkt. 5.99 (*0-446-35333-7*) Warner Bks.

— Devil-May-Care. 1989. mass mkt. 4.50 (*0-8125-0789-4*, Pub. by Tor Bks) St Martin.

— Devil-May-Care. large type ed. (General Ser.). 381p. 1990. 19.95 (*0-8161-4907-0*, G K Hall Lrg Type) Mac Lib Ref.

— Die for Love. 288p. 1992. mass mkt. 4.50 (*0-8125-2470-5*, Pub. by Tor Bks) St Martin.

***Peters, Elizabeth, pseud.** The Falcon at the Portal: An Amelia Peabody Mystery. LC 99-19595. (Amelia Peabody Mystery Ser.). 384p. (YA). (gr. 8 up). 1999. 24.00 (*0-380-97658-7*, Avon Bks) Morrow Avon.

— The Falcon at the Portal: An Amelia Peabody Mystery. LC 99-19595. (Amelia Peabody Mystery Ser.). 464p. 2000. mass mkt. 6.99 (*0-380-79857-3*, Avon Bks) Morrow Avon.

— The Falcon at the Portal: An Amelia Peabody Mystery. large type ed. LC 99-37995. 1999. 26.95 (*1-56895-765-3*, Wheeler) Wheeler Pub.

Peters, Elizabeth, pseud. The Geese Fly High. 1999. pap. 13.95 (*0-8166-0311-1*) U of Minn Pr.

***Peters, Elizabeth, pseud.** He Shall Thunder in the Sky: An Amelia Peabody Mystery. LC 00-25807. (Amelia Peabody Mystery Ser.). 400p. 2000. 25.00 (*0-380-97659-5*) Morrow Avon.

Peters, Elizabeth, pseud. The Hippopotamus Pool. (Amelia Peabody Mystery Ser.). 464p. 1997. reprint ed. mass mkt. 6.99 (*0-446-60398-8*, Pub. by Warner Bks) Little.

— The Jackal's Head. 1988. pap. 3.95 (*0-8125-0002-4*, Pub. by Tor Bks) St Martin.

— The Last Camel Died at Noon. large type ed. (Amelia Peabody Mystery Ser.). 574p. 1992. lib. bdg. 21.95 (*0-8161-5357-4*, G K Hall Lrg Type) Mac Lib Ref.

— The Last Camel Died at Noon. large type ed. (Amelia Peabody Mystery Ser.). 576p. 1992. pap. 24.95 (*0-8161-5358-2*, G K Hall Lrg Type) Mac Lib Ref.

— The Last Camel Died at Noon. (Amelia Peabody Mystery Ser.). 480p. 1992. reprint ed. mass mkt. 6.99 (*0-446-36338-3*, Pub. by Warner Bks) Little.

— Legend in Green Velvet. 1989. mass mkt. 4.50 (*0-8125-2441-1*, Pub. by Tor Bks) St Martin.

— Legend in Green Velvet. 256p. 1995. reprint ed. 20.00 (*0-7278-4721-X*) Severn Hse.

***Peters, Elizabeth, pseud.** Lion in the Valley. 384p. 1999. mass mkt. 6.99 (*0-380-73119-3*, Avon Bks) Morrow Avon.

Peters, Elizabeth, pseud. Lion in the Valley. (Amelia Peabody Mystery Ser.). 320p. 1990. reprint ed. mass mkt. 4.99 (*0-8125-1242-1*, Pub. by Tor Bks) St Martin.

— The Love Talker. 1990. pap. 4.99 (*0-8125-0727-4*, Pub. by Tor Bks) St Martin.

— The Mummy Case. (Amelia Peabody Mystery Ser.). 336p. 1995. mass mkt. 6.99 (*0-446-60193-4*, Pub. by Warner Bks) Little.

— The Murders of Richard III. 230p. 1986. mass mkt. 5.99 (*0-445-40229-6*, Pub. by Warner Bks) Little.

— Naked Once More. 1990. mass mkt. 6.99 (*0-446-36032-5*, Pub. by Warner Bks) Little.

— Naked Once More. large type ed. (General Ser.). 550p. 1990. lib. bdg. 20.95 (*0-8161-4939-9*, G K Hall Lrg Type) Mac Lib Ref.

— The Night of Four Hundred Rabbits. 1989. mass mkt. 4.50 (*0-8125-0773-8*, Pub. by Tor Bks) St Martin.

— The Night of Four Hundred Rabbits. 1996. mass mkt. 5.99 (*0-8125-6360-3*, Pub. by Tor Bks) St Martin.

— Night Train to Memphis. 368p. 1995. mass mkt. 6.99 (*0-446-60248-5*, Pub. by Warner Bks) Little.

— Night Train to Memphis. unabridged ed. (Vicky Bliss Mysteries Ser.). 1997. 28.95 incl. audio (*1-885608-26-8*) Airplay.

— Seeing a Large Cat, Vol. 9. LC 96-37998. (Amelia Peabody Mystery Ser.). 416p. 1997. 24.00 (*0-446-51834-4*, Pub. by Warner Bks) Little.

— Seeing a Large Cat, Vol. 9. (Amelia Peabody Mystery Ser.). 432p. 1998. mass mkt. 7.50 (*0-446-60557-3*, Pub. by Warner Bks) Little.

— The Seventh Sinner. 243p. 1989. mass mkt. 5.99 (*0-445-40778-6*, Pub. by Warner Bks) Little.

— The Seventh Sinner. 1990. mass mkt. 3.95 (*0-445-77323-5*, Pub. by Warner Bks) Little.

***Peters, Elizabeth, pseud.** Silhouette in Scarlet: A Vicky Bliss Mystery. 320p. 2000. mass mkt. 6.99 (*0-380-73337-4*, Avon Bks) Morrow Avon.

Peters, Elizabeth, pseud. The Snake, the Crocodile & the Dog. large type ed. LC 92-35900. (Amelia Peabody Mystery Ser.). 555p. 1993. 24.95 (*0-8161-5681-6*, G K Hall Lrg Type) Mac Lib Ref.

— The Snake, the Crocodile & the Dog. large type ed. LC 92-35900. (Amelia Peabody Mystery Ser.). 555p. 1994. pap. 17.95 (*0-8161-5682-4*, G K Hall Lrg Type) Mac Lib Ref.

— The Snake, the Crocodile & the Dog. (Amelia Peabody Mystery Ser.). 448p. 1994. reprint ed. mass mkt. 6.99 (*0-446-36478-9*, Pub. by Warner Bks) Little.

***Peters, Elizabeth, pseud.** Street of the Five Moons: A Vicky Bliss Mystery. (Vicky Bliss Mysteries Ser.). 384p. 2000. mass mkt. 6.99 (*0-380-73121-5*, Avon Bks) Morrow Avon.

Peters, Elizabeth, pseud. Street of the Five Moons: A Vicky Bliss Mystery. 256p. 1990. mass mkt. write for info. (*0-8125-1244-8*, Pub. by Tor Bks) St Martin.

Peters, Elizabeth, pseud. Summer of the Dragon. Date not set. mass mkt. write for info. (*0-380-73122-3*) Morrow Avon.

Peters, Elizabeth, pseud. Summer of the Dragon. 288p. 1989. pap. 4.99 (*0-8125-0754-1*, Pub. by Tor Bks) St Martin.

***Peters, Elizabeth, pseud.** Trojan Gold: A Vicky Bliss Mystery. (Vicky Bliss Mysteries Ser.). 368p. 2000. mass mkt. 6.99 (*0-380-73123-1*) Morrow Avon.

Peters, Elizabeth, pseud. Trojan Gold: A Vicky Bliss Mystery. 1988. mass mkt. 5.99 (*0-8125-2357-1*, Pub. by Tor Bks) St Martin.

Peters, Elizabeth, pseud, et al. Az Murder Goes . . . Artful. (AZ Murder Goes... Ser.). 200p. 1998. 24.95 (*1-890208-07-8*) Poisoned Pen.

Peters, Ellie R. Home Child Care: The Tender Business. LC 90-82384. 105p. (Orig.). 1990. pap. 5.95 (*0-937779-16-4*) Greenlawn Pr.

Peters, Ellis. Black is the Colour of My True Love's Heart. 208p. 1992. mass mkt. 5.99 (*0-446-40072-6*, Pub. by Warner Bks) Little.

— Brother Cadfael's Penance. 272p. 1996. mass mkt. 6.50 (*0-446-40453-5*, Pub. by Warner Bks) Little.

— Brother Cadfael's Penance: The Twentieth Chronicle of Brother Cadfael. 1994. 18.95 (*0-89296-599-1*) Mysterious Pr.

— The Confession of Brother Haluin. 1989. mass mkt. 5.99 (*0-445-40855-3*, Pub. by Warner Bks) Little.

— The Confession of Brother Haluin. large type ed. LC 90-32780. (General Ser.). 282p. 1990. lib. bdg. 20.95 (*0-8161-4859-7*, G K Hall Lrg Type) Mac Lib Ref.

— Dead Man's Ransom. 288p. 1997. mass mkt. 5.99 (*0-446-40516-7*, Pub. by Warner Bks) Little.

***Peters, Ellis.** Dead Man's Ransom: The Ninth Chronicle of Brother Cadfael. LC 99-11733. 1999. 23.95 (*0-7862-1829-0*) Thorndike Pr.

Peters, Ellis. Death & the Joyful Woman: An Inspector George Felse Mystery. 224p. 1995. mass mkt. 5.50 (*0-446-40068-8*, Pub. by Warner Bks) Little.

— The Devil's Novice. 288p. 1997. mass mkt. 6.50 (*0-446-40515-9*, Pub. by Warner Bks) Little.

— The Devil's Novice: The Eighth Chronicle of Brother Cadfael. large type ed. LC 98-41992. 1999. 30.00 (*0-7862-1668-9*) Thorndike Pr.

— An Excellent Mystery. 224p. 1997. mass mkt. 6.50 (*0-446-40532-9*, Pub. by Warner Bks) Little.

— Fallen into the Pit. 336p. 1996. mass mkt. 5.99 (*0-446-40318-0*, Pub. by Warner Bks) Little.

— Fallen into the Pit. large type ed. LC 94-19116. 1994. 23.95 (*1-56895-116-7*) Wheeler Pub.

— Flight of a Witch: An Inspector George Felse Mystery. 240p. 1992. mass mkt. 5.99 (*0-446-40146-3*, Pub. by Warner Bks) Little.

— The Heretic's Apprentice. 1991. mass mkt. 5.99 (*0-446-40000-9*, Pub. by Warner Bks) Little.

— The Hermit of Eyton Forest. 1989. mass mkt. 6.50 (*0-445-40347-0*, Pub. by Warner Bks) Little.

— The Hermit of Eyton Forest. large type ed. (General Ser.). 329p. 1989. lib. bdg. 19.95 (*0-8161-4677-2*, G K Hall Lrg Type) Mac Lib Ref.

Peters, Ellis. The Hermit of Eyton Forest: The Fourteenth Chronicle of Brother Cadfael. LC 88-135624. 224p. 1987. write for info. (*0-7472-0037-8*) Headline Bk Pub.

Peters, Ellis. The Holy Thief. 256p. 1993. 17.95 (*0-89296-524-X*) Mysterious Pr.

— The Holy Thief. 256p. 1994. mass mkt. 5.99 (*0-446-40363-6*, Pub. by Warner Bks) Little.

— The Horn of Rowland. large type ed. (Magna Mystery Ser.). 1992. 18.95 (*0-7505-0380-7*, Pub. by Mgna Lrg Print) Ulverscroft.

— The Knocker on Death's Door: An Inspector George Felse Mystery. 208p. 1992. mass mkt. 5.99 (*0-446-40016-5*, Pub. by Warner Bks) Little.

— The Leper of St. Giles. 1995. mass mkt. 5.99 (*0-446-40437-3*, Pub. by Warner Bks) Little.

— The Leper of St. Giles: The Fifth Chronicle of Brother Cadfael. large type ed. LC 97-42553. 1998. 22.95 (*0-7862-1375-2*) Thorndike Pr.

— Monk's Hood. 224p. 1992. mass mkt. 5.99 (*0-446-40300-8*, Pub. by Warner Bks) Little.

— Monk's Hood: The Third Chronicle of Brother Cadfael. large type ed. LC 97-1199. 1997. pap. 23.95 (*0-7862-1073-7*) Thorndike Pr.

— A Morbid Taste for Bones. 208p. 1994. mass mkt. 6.50 (*0-446-40015-7*, Pub. by Warner Bks) Little.

— A Nice Derangement of Epitaphs. 208p. 1992. mass mkt. 5.99 (*0-446-40069-6*, Pub. by Warner Bks) Little.

— A Nice Derangement of Epitaphs. large type ed. 1993. 18.95 (*0-7505-0311-4*, Pub. by Mgna Lrg Print) Ulverscroft.

— One Corpse Too Many. 224p. 1994. mass mkt. 6.50 (*0-446-40051-3*, Pub. by Warner Bks) Little.

— The Pilgrim of Hate. 256p. 1997. mass mkt. 5.99 (*0-446-40531-0*, Pub. by Warner Bks) Little.

***Peters, Ellis.** The Pilgrim of Hate: The Tenth Chronicle of Brother Cadfael. large type ed. LC 99-14891. 257p. 1999. pap. text 23.95 (*0-7862-1945-9*, G K Hall Lrg Type) Mac Lib Ref.

Peters, Ellis. The Piper on the Mountain: An Inspector George Felse Mystery. 208p. 1996. mass mkt. 5.99 (*0-446-40071-8*, Pub. by Warner Bks) Little.

— The Piper on the Mountain: An Inspector George Felse Mystery. large type ed. 342p. 1993. 27.99 (*0-7505-0584-2*, Pub. by Mgna Lrg Print) Ulverscroft.

— The Potter's Field. 1991. mass mkt. 5.99 (*0-446-40058-0*, Pub. by Warner Bks) Little.

— The Potter's Field: The Seventeenth Chronicle of Brother Cadfael. large type ed. LC 91-15480. (General Ser.). 303p. 1991. lib. bdg. 19.95 (*0-8161-5194-6*, G K Hall Lrg Type) Mac Lib Ref.

— Rainbow's End. 208p. 1992. mass mkt. 5.99 (*0-446-40017-3*, Pub. by Warner Bks) Little.

— A Rare Benedictine. 1989. 19.45 (*0-89296-397-2*) Mysterious Pr.

— A Rare Benedictine. 1991. mass mkt. 5.99 (*0-446-40088-2*, Pub. by Warner Bks) Little.

— The Raven in the Foregate. 240p. 1997. mass mkt. 5.99 (*0-446-40534-5*, Pub. by Warner Bks) Little.

***Peters, Ellis.** The Raven in the Foregate. large type ed. (General Ser.). 2000. pap. 24.95 (*0-7862-2494-0*) Thorndike Pr.

Peters, Ellis. The Rose Rent. 240p. 1997. mass mkt. 6.50 (*0-446-40533-7*, Pub. by Warner Bks) Little.

***Peters, Ellis.** The Rose Rent: The 13th Chronicle of Brother Cadfael. LC 00-28684. 2000. write for info. (*0-7862-2569-6*) Thorndike Pr.

— St. Peter's Fair: The Fourth Chronicle of Brother Cadfael. LC 82-119472. 220p. 1981. write for info. (*0-333-31050-0*) Macmillan.

Peters, Ellis. St. Peter's Fair: The Fourth Chronicle of Brother Cadfael. large type ed. LC 97-1202. (General Ser.). 1998. pap. 22.95 (*0-7862-1074-5*) Thorndike Pr.

***Peters, Ellis.** The Sanctuary Sparrow. (Brother Cadfael Ser.). 1999. audio 9.95 (*1-56938-268-9*, AMP-2689) Acorn Media.

Peters, Ellis. The Sanctuary Sparrow. 1995. mass mkt. 5.99 (*0-446-40429-2*, Pub. by Warner Bks) Little.

— The Sanctuary Sparrow: The Seventh Chronicle of Brother Cadfael. large type ed. LC 98-28857. 286p. 1999. 30.00 (*0-7862-1599-2*) Thorndike Pr.

— St. Peter's Fair. 224p. 1992. mass mkt. 5.99 (*0-446-40301-6*, Pub. by Warner Bks) Little.

— The Summer of the Danes. 256p. 1992. mass mkt. 5.99 (*0-446-40018-1*, Pub. by Warner Bks) Little.

— The Virgin in the Ice. 208p. 1995. mass mkt. 6.50 (*0-446-40428-4*, Pub. by Warner Bks) Little.

— The Virgin in the Ice: The Sixth Chronicle of Brother Cadfael. large type ed. LC 98-6680. 1998. 22.95 (*0-7862-1479-1*) Thorndike Pr.

Peters, Ellis & Morgan, Roy. Shropshire: Photographed Memoir. LC 92-13684. 168p. 1993. 34.00 (*0-89296-516-9*, Pub. by Mysterious Pr) Little.

— Strongholds & Sanctuaries: The Borderland of England & Wales. LC 93-17979. (Illus.). 192p. 1993. 30.95 (*0-7509-0200-0*, Pub. by Sutton Pub Ltd) Intl Pubs Mktg.

Peters, Ellis, jt. auth. see Pargeter, Edith.

Peters, Emilie. Muffin, a Palm Beach Pooch. (Muffin Ser.: No. 1). 30p. (J). (gr. 3-8). 1992. pap. write for info. (*0-9635568-0-0*) Muffin Pubns.

Peters, Emma. Alien Chemistry. (Illus.). 24p. (J). (gr. 3-9). 1999. pap. 8.95 (*0-8167-5036-X*) Troll Communs.

***Peters, Enrique Dussel.** Polarizing Mexico: The Impact of Liberalization Strategy. (Critical Perspectives on Latin America's Economy & Society Ser.). 210p. 2000. lib. bdg. 49.95 (*1-55587-861-X*) L Rienner.

Peters, Erskine. African Americans in the New Millennium: Blueprinting the Future. (Orig.). 1991. pap. 9.95 (*0-916147-18-5*) Regent Pr.

— Fundamentals of Essay Writing: An Orientation Manual. 53p. (Orig.). (C). 1987. pap. text 9.95 (*0-916147-05-3*) Regent Pr.

— Lyrics of the Afro-American Spiritual: A Documentary Collection. LC 92-27574. (Encyclopedia of Black Music Ser.). 480p. 1993. lib. bdg. 75.00 (*0-313-26238-1*, PLY/, Greenwood Pr) Greenwood.

Peters, Eugene H. Hartshorne & Neoclassical Metaphysics: An Interpretation. LC 77-116531. 153p. reprint ed. pap. 47.50 (*0-8357-8683-8*, 205684000092) Bks Demand.

Peters, F. E. The Children of Abraham: Judaism, Christianity, Islam. LC 81-47941. 240p. 1982. pap. text 14.95 (*0-691-02030-2*, Pub. by Princeton U Pr) Cal Prin Full Svc.

— Greek Philosophical Terms: A Historical Lexicon. LC 67-25043. 234p. (C). 1970. pap. text 21.00 (*0-8147-6552-1*) NYU Pr.

— Hajj: The Muslim Pilgrimage to Mecca & the Holy Places. 430p. 1994. pap. text 19.95 (*0-691-02619-X*, Pub. by Princeton U Pr) Cal Prin Full Svc.

— The Hajj: The Muslim Pilgrimage to Mecca & the Holy Places. 424p. 1996. 30.95 (*0-614-21111-5*, 371) Kazi Pubns.

— The Hajj: The Muslim Pilgrimmage to Mecca & the Holy Places. LC 93-47292. 456p. 1994. text 55.00 (*0-691-02120-1*, Pub. by Princeton U Pr) Cal Prin Full Svc.

— Jerusalem: The Holy City in the Eyes of Chroniclers, Visitors, Pilgrims & Prophets from The... 672p. (C). 1985. pap. text 19.95 (*0-691-00641-5*, Pub. by Princeton U Pr) Cal Prin Full Svc.

— Judaism, Christianity, & Islam, Vol. I. 1200p. 1996. pap. 18.95 (*0-614-21671-0*, 681) Kazi Pubns.

— Judaism, Christianity, & Islam, Vol. II. 1200p. 1996. pap. 18.95 (*0-614-21672-9*, 681) Kazi Pubns.

— Judaism, Christianity, & Islam, Vol. III. 1200p. 1996. pap. 18.95 (*0-614-21673-7*, 681) Kazi Pubns.

— Judaism, Christianity & Islam: The Classical Texts & Their Interpretation, 3 vols., Vol. I. 436p. 1990. pap. text 18.95 (*0-691-02044-2*, Pub. by Princeton U Pr) Cal Prin Full Svc.

— Judaism, Christianity & Islam: The Classical Texts & Their Interpretation, 3 vols., Vol. II. 434p. 1990. pap. text 18.95 (*0-691-02054-X*, Pub. by Princeton U Pr) Cal Prin Full Svc.

— Judaism, Christianity & Islam: The Classical Texts & Their Interpretation, 3 vols., Vol. III. 450p. 1990. pap. text 18.95 (*0-691-02055-8*, Pub. by Princeton U Pr) Cal Prin Full Svc.

— Mecca: A Literary History of the Muslim Holy Land. 500p. 1996. 29.95 (*0-614-21159-X*, 769) Kazi Pubns.

— Mecca: A Literary History of the Muslim Holy Land. LC 94-20923. 504p. 1994. text 35.00 (*0-691-03267-X*, Pub. by Princeton U Pr) Cal Prin Full Svc.

***Peters, F. E.** Muhammad: A Life & a Guide. 252p. (C). 2000. pap. text 19.95 (*1-889119-01-6*) Seven Bridges.

Peters, F. E. Muhammad & the Origins of Islam. 355p. 1996. pap. 19.95 (*0-614-21161-1*, 809) Kazi Pubns.

— Muhammad & the Origins of Islam. LC 93-10568. (SUNY Series in Near Eastern Studies). 334p. (C). 1994. pap. text 24.95 (*0-7914-1876-6*) State U NY Pr.

— The Quest: The Search for the Historical Jesus & Muhammad. (Illus.). 252p. 2000. pap. text 19.95 (*1-889119-04-0*) Seven Bridges.

— A Reader on Classical Islam. 430p. 1996. pap. 19.95 (*0-614-21069-0*, 1060) Kazi Pubns.

— A Reader on Classical Islam. 440p. 1994. text 70.00 (*0-691-03394-3*, Pub. by Princeton U Pr); pap. text 22.95 (*0-691-00040-9*, Pub. by Princeton U Pr) Cal Prin Full Svc.

— The Two Hundred Dollar Look. 1987. 14.95 (*0-8184-0434-5*) Carol Pub Group.

Peters, F. J., ed. see International Conference, ParCo93, Staff.

Peters, Francis E. The Distant Shrine: The Islamic Centuries in Jerusalem. LC 89-45876. (Studies in Modern Society: No. 22). 275p. 1993. 39.50 (*0-404-61629-1*) AMS Pr.

Peters, Frank, ed. The Arabs & Arabia on the Eve of Islam. LC 98-6040. (Formation of the Classical Islamic World Ser.). 410p. 1998. text 129.95 (*0-86078-702-8*, DS38.A73, Pub. by Ashgate Pub) Ashgate Pub Co.

Peters, Frank, jt. auth. see McCue, George.

Peters, Fred E., jt. auth. see West, Bryan N.

Peters, Frederick G., tr. see Von Kleist, Heinrich.

Peters, Fritz. My Journey with a Mystic. Weaver, Richard & Baron, Ron, eds. 312p. 1989. reprint ed. 22.50 (*0-942139-00-3*); reprint ed. pap. 11.95 (*0-942139-10-0*) Tale Weaver.

Peters, G. David. Musical Skills: A Computer-Based Assessment. 1992. 8.00 (*0-317-05525-9*) U IL Sch Music.

Peters, G. David & Eddins, John M. A Planning Guide to Successful Computer Instruction. rev. ed. (C). 1995. 19.95 (*0-942132-00-9*) Electron Course.

Peters, G. H. Agriculture. (Reviews of U. K. Statistical Sources Ser.). 224p. (gr. 13). 1988. lib. bdg. 109.95 (*0-412-31670-6*) Chapman & Hall.

Peters, G. H., et al. Sustainable Agricultural Development: The Role of International Cooperation: Proceedings of the Twenty-First International Conference of Agricultural Economists. (International Association of Agricultural Economists Ser.). 736p. 1992. 72.95 (*1-85521-272-2*, Pub. by Dartmth Pub) Ashgate Pub Co.

Peters, G. H., ed. see International Conference of Agricultural Economist.

Peters, G. H., ed. see Von Braun, Joachim & International Association of Agricultural Librarians Staff.

Peters, Gary L. American Winescapes: The Cultural Landscape of America's Wine Country. LC 97-9125. (Geographies of Imagination Ser.). 230p. (C). 1997. pap. text 21.00 (*0-8133-2856-X*, Pub. by Westview) HarpC.

— California. 416p. (C). 1995. pap. text, per. 48.95 (*0-7872-1018-8*) Kendall-Hunt.

— Wines & Vines of California. (Illus.). 200p. (Orig.). 1989. pap. 16.95 (*0-89863-136-X*) Star Pub CA.

— Wines & Vineyards: Inside California's Wine Regions. (Illus.). 270p. pap. write for info. (*0-89863-203-X*) Star Pub CA.

Peters, Gary L. & Larkin, Robert P. Population Geography. 6th ed. LC 98-75500. 316p. 1999. per. 46.95 (*0-7872-5672-2*, 41567201) Kendall-Hunt.

Peters, Gary L., jt. auth. see Larkin, Robert P.

Peters, Geoff, jt. auth. see Fortune, Joyce.

Peters, George. A Theology of Church Growth. 283p. 1981. pap. 11.95 (*0-310-43101-8*, 11285P) Zondervan.

Peters, George. The Complete Rokkaku Kite Chronicles & Training Manual. (Best of Kite Lines Ser.). 20p. (Orig.). 1991. reprint ed. pap. 6.95 (*0-937315-00-1*) Aeolus Pr.

Peters, George & Greuter, Henri. Novi Vol. 2: The Legendary Indianapolis Race Car, 1961-1966. (Illus.). 222p. (Orig.). 1998. pap. 32.95 (*0-9630227-1-7*) Bar Jean Enter.

Peters, George A. Diary of "G. Peters, High Private" LC 98-93826. 70 p. 1998. write for info. (*0-9667100-0-2*) Family Time Bks.

— Sourcebook on Asbestos Diseases. 3500p. 1989. boxed set 500.00 (*0-614-05965-8*, MICHIE) LEXIS Pub.

Peters, George A. & Peters, Barbara J. Sourcebook on Asbestos Disease, 18 vols. 1998. 500.00 (*0-327-01028-2*, 82410-10, MICHIE) LEXIS Pub.

— Sourcebook on Asbestos Diseases: Asbestos Abatement, Vol. 5. 800p. 1991. boxed set 85.00 (*0-88063-792-7*, MICHIE) LEXIS Pub.

— Sourcebook on Asbestos Diseases: Asbestos Control & Medical Treatment, Vol. 7. 1993. 95.00 (*0-88063-797-8*, MICHIE) LEXIS Pub.

— Sourcebook on Asbestos Diseases: Asbestos Medical Research, Vol. 4. 1989. boxed set 75.00 (*0-88063-759-5*, MICHIE) LEXIS Pub.

— Sourcebook on Asbestos Diseases Vol. Medical, Legal & Engineering Aspects, Vol. 1. 1980. boxed set 75.00 (*0-88063-756-0*, MICHIE) LEXIS Pub.

P

— Sourcebook on Asbestos Diseases Vol. Medical, Legal & Engineering Aspects, Vol. 2. 1986. boxed set 75.00 (*0-88063-757-9*, MICHIE) LEXIS Pub.

— Sourcebook on Asbestos Diseases Vol. Medical, Legal & Engineering Aspects, Vol. 3. 1988. boxed set 75.00 (*0-88063-758-7*, MICHIE) LEXIS Pub.

— Sourcebook on Asbestos Diseases Vol. 9: Medical, Legal & Engineering Aspects. 61p. 1994. boxed set 95.00 (*0-614-03169-9*, MICHIE) LEXIS Pub.

— Sourcebook on Asbestos Diseases, 1980-1993: Medical, Legal & Engineering Aspects, 8 vols., Set. 7100p. 1993. boxed set 500.00 (*0-8240-7175-1*, 82410-10, MICHIE) LEXIS Pub.

— Warnings, Instructions & Technical Communications. LC 98-52233. (Law, Engineering & Medicine Book Ser.). (Illus.). 450p. 1999. pap. 89.00 (*0-913875-61-9*, 5619) Lawyers & Judges.

Peters, George A. & Peters, Barbara J., eds. Sourcebook on Asbestos Diseases: International Asbestos Medical Research, Vol. 6. 600p. 1991. boxed set 95.00 (*0-88063-796-X*, MICHIE) LEXIS Pub.

***Peters, George A. & Peters, Barbara J., eds.** Sourcebook on Asbestos Diseases Vol. 19: Social Consequences & Cellular Biology. 450p. 1999. write for info. (*0-327-01303-6*, 8360210) LEXIS Pub.

Peters, George F. Der Grosse Heide Nr. 2: Heinrich Heine & the Levels of His Goethe Reception. (North American Studies in Nineteenth-Century German Literature: Vol. 4). XIII, 322p. (C). 1989. text 49.95 (*0-8204-0880-8*) P Lang Pubng.

***Peters, George F.** The Poet As Provocateur: Heinrich Heine & His Critics. LC 99-49775. (Literary Criticism in Perspective Ser.). (Illus.). 256p. 2000. 55.00 (*1-57113-161-2*) Camden Hse.

Peters, George F., tr. see Thon, Eleonore, et al.

Peters, George H., ed. Agricultural Economics. LC 95-13218. (International Library of Critical Writings in Economics: Vol. 55). 672p. 1995. 285.00 (*1-85278-301-X*) E Elgar.

Peters, George W. Biblical Theology of Missions. 384p. pap. 19.99 (*0-8024-0706-4*, 92) Moody.

Peters, Gerald P. Classic Western American Paintings. LC 78-58003. (Illus.). 45p. 1979. pap. 15.00 (*0-933052-00-6*) G Peters Gallery.

— The Mutilating God: Authorship & Authority in the Narrative of Conversion. LC 93-22151. 192p. 1993. lib. bdg. 29.95 (*0-87023-891-4*) U of Mass Pr.

Peters, Gerald P., III, intro. George Carlson: The Strength of the Spirit. LC 92-73101. (Illus.). 60p. 1992. pap. 15.00 (*0-935037-45-4*) G Peters Gallery.

Peters, Gerald P., intro. Georgia O'Keeffe. LC 90-63231. (Illus.). 47p. 1990. pap. 20.00 (*0-935037-39-X*) G Peters Gallery.

Peters, Gerald P., 3rd & Fox, Megan. Paul Strand: An Extraordinary Vision. LC 94-75850. (Illus.). 40p. (Orig.). 1994. pap. 28.00 (*0-935037-56-X*) G Peters Gallery.

Peters, Gerald P. & Maxon, Gayle, intros. Helen Frankenthaler: Santa Fe Series - Pastels & Other Works on Paper. LC 90-63314. (Illus.). 32p. 1990. pap. 10.00 (*0-935037-35-7*) G Peters Gallery.

Peters, Gerald R., ed. Healthcare Integration: A Legal Manual for Constructing Integrated Organizations. 615p. 1995. 75.00 (*0-918945-17-8*) Am Hlth Lawyers.

— Healthcare Joint Ventures: The Next Generation. 369p. 1991. 45.00 (*0-918945-12-7*) Am Hlth Lawyers.

Peters, Gil, ed. & intro. see Koplow, James.

Peters, Glen. Benchmarking Customer Service. (Financial Times Management Ser.). 256p. 1995. 77.50 (*0-273-61069-4*, Pub. by Pitman Pub) Trans-Atl Phila.

— Beyond the Next Wave: Imagining the Next Generation of Customers. (Illus.). 225p. 1996. pap. text 17.95 (*0-273-62417-2*) F T P-H.

***Peters, Glen.** Waltzing with the Raptors: A Practical Roadmap to Protecting Your Company's Reputation. LC 98-31701. (Illus.). 304p. 1999. 27.95 (*0-471-32732-8*) Wiley.

Peters, Gloria & Mohan, Cynthia. The Complete Guide to Shield & Liberty Head Nickels. LC 95-71800. (Illus.). 224p. 1995. pap. 37.00 (*1-880731-52-5*) S J Durst.

Peters, Gordon & Vousden, Karen H., eds. Oncogenes & Tumour Suppressors. (Frontiers in Molecular Biology Ser.: No. 19). (Illus.). 352p. 1997. text 120.00 (*0-19-963595-1*); pap. text 55.00 (*0-19-963594-3*) OUP.

Peters, Greg. The Graphic Art of Paul Fournier. 96p. 1981. pap. write for info. (*0-88984-045-8*) Porcup Quill.

— Images of Vulnerability: The Art of George Wallace. (Illus.). 128p. 1995. pap. 14.95 (*0-88962-225-6*) Mosaic.

***Peters, H. Elizabeth & Day, Randal D., eds.** Fatherhood: Research, Interventions & Policies. LC 00-25431. 375p. 2000. 49.95 (*0-7890-1015-1*) Haworth Pr.

— Fatherhood: Research, Interventions & Policies. LC 00-25431. 375p. 2000. pap. text 24.95 (*0-7890-1016-X*) Haworth Pr.

Peters, H. F. Rainer Maria Rilke: Masks & the Man. LC 77-24731. 240p. 1977. reprint ed. 50.00 (*0-87752-198-0*) Gordian.

Peters, H. F., et al, eds. Speech Motor Control & Stuttering: Proc. of the 2nd Internat. Conf., Held in Nijmegen, The Netherlands, June 13-16, 1990. (International Congress Ser.: No. 950). 582p. 1991. 273.50 (*0-444-81408-6*, Excerpta Medica) Elsevier.

Peters, H. F. & Hulstijn, W., eds. Speech Motor Dynamics in Stuttering. (Illus.). xv, 420p. 1987. 87.95 (*0-387-81971-1*) Spr-Verlag.

Peters, H. J. Axiomatic Bargaining Game Theory. LC 92-21620. (Theory & Decision Library: No. C). 1992. lib. bdg. 171.00 (*0-7923-1873-0*) Kluwer Academic.

Peters, Hans F. Zarathustra's Sister: The Case of Elizabeth & Friedrich Nietzsche. LC 85-40728. 260p. 1999. reprint ed. pap. text 9.95 (*0-910129-37-1*) Wiener Pubs Inc.

Peters, Hans J. The Maritime Transport Crisis. LC 93-41296. (Discussion Paper Ser.). 60p. 1993. pap. 22.00 (*0-8213-2714-3*, 12714) World Bank.

Peters, Hans M. Fecundity, Egg Weight & Oocyte Development in Tilapias: Cichlidae, Teleostei. Pauly, Daniel, tr. (ICLARM Translations Ser.: No. 2). (Illus.). 28p. (Orig.). 1983. pap. 5.50 (*0-89955-381-8*, Pub. by ICLARM) Intl Spec Bk.

Peters, Harold E. The Foreign Debt of the Argentine Republic. LC 78-64290. (Johns Hopkins University. Studies in the Social Sciences. Thirtieth Ser. 1912: 21). 200p. 1983. reprint ed. 37.50 (*0-404-61390-X*) AMS Pr.

Peters, Harry B. Woodwind Music in Print. LC 97-25679. (Music-in-Print Ser.). 1997. 165.00 (*0-88478-045-7*) Musicdata.

Peters, Harry T. America on Stone: The Other Printmakers to the American People. LC 75-22832. (America in Two Centuries Ser.). (Illus.). 1977. reprint ed. 71.95 (*0-405-07703-3*) Ayer.

— California on Stone. LC 75-22833. (America in Two Centuries Ser.). (Illus.). 1977. reprint ed. 55.95 (*0-405-07704-1*) Ayer.

— Currier & Ives: Printmakers to the American People, 2 Vols., Set. LC 75-22834. (America in Two Centuries Ser.). (Illus.). 1977. reprint ed. 137.95 (*0-405-07741-6*) Ayer.

— Currier & Ives: Printmakers to the American People, 2 vols., Vol. 1. LC 75-22834. (America in Two Centuries Ser.). (Illus.). 1977. reprint ed. 66.95 (*0-405-07742-4*) Ayer.

— Currier & Ives: Printmakers to the American People, 2 vols., Vol. 2. LC 75-22834. (America in Two Centuries Ser.). (Illus.). 1977. reprint ed. 71.95 (*0-405-07743-2*) Ayer.

— Printmakers: Currier & Ives; American on Stone; California on Stone. 240.00 (*0-405-07705-X*, 93) Ayer.

Peters, Heather, jt. auth. see Lyons, Elizabeth.

Peters, Helen, ed. The Plays of Codco. LC 92-3833. (Illus.). XL, 446p. (Orig.). (C). 1993. pap. text 26.95 (*0-8204-1861-7*) P Lang Pubng.

— Stars in the Sky Morning. 576p. 1996. pap. 19.95 (*1-895387-74-4*) Creative Bk Pub.

Peters, Helen J., ed. Ground Water in the Pacific Rim Countries. LC 91-21069. 192p. 1991. pap. text 5.00 (*0-87262-812-4*) Am Soc Civil Eng.

Peters, Helene. The Existential Woman. LC 90-41034. (American University Studies: Feminist Studies: Ser. XXVII, Vol. 3). XIX, 152p. (C). 1991. text 32.95 (*0-8204-1331-3*) P Lang Pubng.

Peters, Henrietta. Mary Ward. 658p. 1995. 40.00 (*0-85244-268-8*, 948, Pub. by Gra1cewing) Morehouse Pub.

Peters, Howard K., Jr., jt. auth. see Peters, Jean M.

Peters, Howard M., jt. auth. see Maynard, John T.

Peters, J., jt. auth. see Bauschinger, J.

Peters, J. Douglas, jt. auth. see Gilbert, Ronald R.

Peters, J. E. Discovering Traditional Farm Buildings. 1989. pap. 25.00 (*0-85263-556-7*, Pub. by Shire Pubns) St Mut.

Peters, J. F., jt. auth. see Pedrycz, W.

Peters, J. H. & Baumgarten, H., eds. Monoclonal Antibodies: A Practical Guide. LC 92-30163. (Laboratory Ser.). (Illus.). 480p. 1992. 74.95 (*0-387-50843-0*) Spr-Verlag.

Peters, J. M., compiled by. Bow Angle Tables. (C). 1987. 40.00 (*0-85174-135-5*) St Mut.

Peters, J. M., et al. Ubiquitin & the Biology of the Cell. LC 98-18550. (Illus.). 442p. (C). 1998. text 115.00 (*0-306-45649-4*, Kluwer Plenum) Kluwer Academic.

Peters, J. Rose. Economics of the Canadian Corporate Bond Market. LC 78-135414. 133p. reprint ed. pap. 41.30 (*0-608-12259-9*, 202383700034) Bks Demand.

Peters, J. S. & Wolper, Andrea, eds. Women's Rights, Human Rights: International Feminist Perspectives. LC 94-15775. (Illus.). 450p. (gr. 13). 1994. pap. 25.99 (*0-415-90995-3*, B3886) Routledge.

Peters, Jacob & Smith, Doreen L. Organizational & Interorganizational Dynamics: An Annotated Bibliography. LC 92-10773. (Library of Sociology: Vol. 25). 288p. 1992. text 20.00 (*0-8240-5304-4*, SS641) Garland.

Peters, Jacqueline S. Music Therapy: An Introduction. 186p. 1987. pap. 25.95 (*0-398-06321-4*) C C Thomas.

— Music Therapy: An Introduction. 186p. (C). 1987. text 37.95 (*0-398-05284-0*) C C Thomas.

***Peters, Jacqueline Schmidt.** Music Therapy: An Introduction. 2nd ed. LC 99-88599. 2000. pap. write for info. (*0-398-07043-1*) C C Thomas.

Peters, James. The Arab World Handbook. 156p. 1995. pap. 19.95 (*0-905743-82-2*, Pub. by Stacey Intl) Intl Bk Ctr.

— Very Simple Arabic. (ARA., Illus.). 120p. 1994. pap. 12.95 (*0-905743-71-7*, Pub. by Stacey Intl) Intl Bk Ctr.

— Very Simple Arabic/Simple Etiquette. (ARA.). 109p. 1994. pap. 10.95 (*0-86685-709-5*, STA3717, Pub. by Librairie du Liban) Intl Bk Ctr.

Peters, James, jt. auth. see Boswell, Jonathan.

Peters, James, jt. auth. see Pittman, Thomas.

Peters, James, jt. auth. see Salloum, Habeeb.

Peters, James, ed. see Coultoff, Eric.

Peters, James A. Dictionary of Herpetology. 1985. 16.95 (*0-02-850230-2*) Macmillan.

Peters, James A., jt. auth. see Peters, Cheryl D.

Peters, James E. Arlington National Cemetery: Shrine to America's Heroes. LC 86-50284. 335p. 1988. pap. 13.95 (*0-933149-04-2*) Woodbine House.

***Peters, James Edward.** Arlington National Cemetery, Shrine to America's Heroes. 2nd ed. LC 00-43286. 2000. pap. write for info. (*1-890627-14-3*) Woodbine House.

Peters, James F., III. Introduction to VAX-VMS. 500p. 1989. pap. 30.00 (*0-13-502808-6*) P-H.

— UNIX Programming: Methods & Tools. 464p. (C). 1995. pap. text 42.95 (*0-15-593021-4*) OUP.

Peters, James F. & Pedrycz, Witold. Software Engineering: An Engineering Approach. LC 99-16026. 720p. 1999. text 88.95 (*0-471-18964-2*) Wiley.

Peters, James S., II. The Epic of a Proud Black Family: An Allegorical History. 200p. 1994. 64.95 (*1-883255-79-1*); pap. 44.95 (*1-883255-78-3*) Intl Scholars.

Peters, James S., 2nd. The Saga of Black Navy Veterans of World War II: An American Triumph. LC 96-47070. 160p. 1996. pap. 12.95 (*1-57309-122-7*) Intl Scholars.

Peters, James S., II. Socio-Egocentrism: Theory, Research & Practice. 76p. (Orig.). 1997. pap. 49.95 (*1-57309-034-4*); pap. 69.95 (*1-57309-035-2*) Intl Scholars.

Peters, James S., et al. Mace Bowman: Texas Feudist, Western Lawman. (Illus.). 230p. 1996. 39.95 (*0-614-13835-3*) Hartmann Heritage.

— Mace Bowman: Texas Feudist, Western Lawman - Collector's Edition. (Illus.). 230p. 1996. 79.95 (*0-614-28587-9*) Hartmann Heritage.

Peters, James Sedalia, II. The Saga of Black Navy Veterans of World War II: An American Triumph. LC 96-47070. 160p. 1996. text 24.95 (*1-57309-123-5*) Intl Scholars.

Peters, Jane. Cancer: A Beginner's Guidebook of Hope. rev. ed. 96p. 1991. pap. 6.95 (*0-9628806-1-2*) Encouraging Words.

Peters, Jane S., ed. The Illustrated Bartsch Vol. 18: German Masters 1550-1600. LC 79-50679. 1982. lib. bdg. 149.00 (*0-89835-018-2*) Abaris Bks.

— The Illustrated Bartsch Vol. 19-1: German Masters 1550-1600. 1987. lib. bdg. 149.00 (*0-89835-019-0*) Abaris Bks.

— The Illustrated Bartsch Vol. 19-2: German Masters 1550-1600. 1988. lib. bdg. 149.00 (*0-89835-316-5*) Abaris Bks.

— The Illustrated Bartsch Vol. 20-1: German Masters 1550-1600. 1985. lib. bdg. 149.00 (*0-89835-119-7*) Abaris Bks.

***Peters, Jane S., ed.** The Illustrated Bartsch Vol. 20-2: German Masters, 1550-1600. 1998. lib. bdg. 149.00 (*0-89835-020-4*) Abaris Bks.

Peters, Janice G., jt. ed. see Peters, William L.

Peters, Jean. Representing Children in Child Protective Proceedings: Ethical & Practical Dimensions. LC 97-71968. 885p. 1997. 85.00 (*1-55834-504-3*, 66690-10, MICHIE) LEXIS Pub.

***Peters, Jean K.** Representing Children in Child Protective Proceedings, 1999 Cumulative Supplement: Ethical & Practical Dimensions: Pocketpart. 250p. 1999. suppl. ed. write for info. (*0-327-01699-X*, 6669111) LEXIS Pub.

Peters, Jean Kob. Representing Children in Child Protective Proceedings: Ethical & Practical Dimensions. 1997. 85.00 (*1-55834-545-0*, 66690) LEXIS Pub.

Peters, Jean M. & Peters, Howard K., Jr. The Flexibility Manual. 2nd ed. LC 92-85429. (Illus.). 100p. 1995. 32.00 (*0-9633896-0-2*) Spts Kinetics.

Peters, Jeffrey H. & DeMeester, Tom R., eds. Minimally Invasive Surgery of the Foregut. LC 94-31703. (Illus.). 334p. 1994. text 115.00 (*0-942219-62-7*) Quality Med Pub.

Peters, Jens. Lonely Planet Philippines. 6th ed. (Illus.). 528p. 1997. pap. 19.95 (*0-86442-466-3*) Lonely Planet.

Peters, Jim. Market It Write: Entrepreneur's Guide to Publicity in the Chicago Area Press. LC 95-90279. 149p. (Orig.). 1995. pap. 15.95 (*0-9646583-0-5*) Eastview Pub.

— The Nigerian Military & the State. (Military & Security Studies). 224p. 1997. text 59.50 (*1-85043-874-9*) St Martin.

Peters, Jim, jt. auth. see Davidson, Jonathan.

Peters, Jim B. Catacombs of the Bear Cult. 1981. 3.95 (*0-940244-55-1*) Flying Buffalo.

— Dungeon of the Bear Set. 1982. 6.95 (*0-940244-58-6*) Flying Buffalo.

— Grimtooth's Dungeon of Doom. (Illus.). 80p. (Orig.). 1992. pap. 9.95 (*0-940244-88-8*) Flying Buffalo.

Peters, Jo, jt. auth. see Boucher Stetson, Debi.

Peters, Joan. From Time Immemorial: The Origins of the Arab-Jewish Conflict over Palestine. LC 93-77505. xii, 601p. (C). 1993. pap. 16.95 (*0-9636242-0-2*) JKAP Pubns.

Peters, Joan K. When Mothers Work: Loving Our Children Without Sacrificing Our Selves. LC 98-86287. 272p. 1968. reprint ed. pap. text 12.00 (*0-7382-0028-X*) Perseus Pubng.

Peters, Joan K., jt. auth. see Carter, Betty.

***Peters, Joel.** Scripture Alone: 21 Reasons to Reject "Sola Scriptura" LC 98-61405. 72p. 1999. pap. 2.00 (*0-89555-640-5*, 1545) TAN Bks Pubs.

Peters, Joel, jt. ed. see Kyle, Keith.

Peters, Johannes A. Metaphysics, a Systematic Survey. LC 63-8144. (Duquesne Studies, Philosophical Ser.: No. 16). 547p. reprint ed. pap. 169.60 (*0-608-30013-6*, 205134200096) Bks Demand.

Peters, John. Elements of Critical Reading. LC 90-46144. 90p. (C). 1990. pap. text 15.00 (*0-02-394601-6*, Macmillan Coll) P-H.

— Getting Laid for $17.95. 24p. 1996. pap. 11.95 (*0-8059-4058-8*) Dorrance.

Peters, John & Guttridge, Roger, eds. Bournemouth Then & Now: A Pictorial Past. (C). 1989. 39.00 (*1-85455-024-1*, Pub. by Ensign Pubns & Print) St Mut.

Peters, John, ed. see Whitehawk.

Peters, John D. Speaking into the Air: A History of the Idea of Communication. LC 98-50308. 280p. 1999. 26.00 (*0-226-66276-4*) U Ch Pr.

Peters, John E. CFE & Military Stability in Europe. LC 97-32076. (Illus.). 92p. 1997. pap. 15.00 (*0-8330-2559-7*, MR-911-OSD) Rand Corp.

***Peters, John E.** The Changing Quality of Stability in Europe: The CFE Treaty Toward 2001. LC 99-52261. (Illus.). vii, 32p. (C). 1999. pap. 7.50 (*0-8330-2783-2*, MR-1104-JS) Rand Corp.

Peters, John E. The U. S. Military: Ready for the New World Order?, 133. LC 92-25627. (Contributions in Military Studies Ser.: No. 133). 192p. 1993. 55.00 (*0-313-28591-8*, PUM, Greenwood Pr) Greenwood.

Peters, John E. & Deshong, Howard. Out of Area or Out of Reach? European Military Support for Operations in Southwest Asia. LC 95-44672. 148p. (Orig.). 1995. pap. text 15.00 (*0-8330-2329-2*, MR-629-OSD) Rand Corp.

Peters, John E., et al. Futures Intelligence: Assessing Intelligence Support to Three Army Long-Range Planning Communities. LC 98-36061. (Illus.). 63p. 1998. pap. 15.00 (*0-8330-2649-6*, MR-995-A) Rand Corp.

Peters, John E., jt. auth. see Taw, Jennifer M.

Peters, John F. Life among the Yanomani. LC 98-205033. 148p. 1998. pap. 16.95 (*1-55111-193-4*) Broadview Pr.

Peters, John F., jt. auth. see Early, John D.

Peters, John G., Jr. Defensive Tactics with Flashlights. (Illus.). 179p. 1982. pap. 9.00 (*0-923401-02-4*) Reliapon Police Prods.

Peters, John G., Jr. Tactical Handcuffing for Chain & Hinged-Style Handcuffs. (Illus.). 304p. (Orig.). (C). 1989. pap. 15.50 (*0-923401-00-8*) Reliapon Police Prods.

Peters, John G., Jr. & Kuboata, Takayuki. Realistic Defensive Tactics. (Illus.). 104p. 1981. pap. 10.50 (*0-923401-04-0*) Reliapon Police Prods.

Peters, John G., Jr. & Peters, Laurie A. Afraid of the Dark? Lite Your Way to Safety. (Illus.). 35p. 1984. pap. 3.00 (*0-923401-03-2*) Reliapon Police Prods.

Peters, John G., Jr., jt. auth. see Kubota, Takayuki.

Peters, John G., ed. see Defoe, Daniel, et al.

Peters, John L. Christian Perfection & American Methodism. 256p. 1985. pap. 7.95 (*0-310-31241-8*, 17034P) Zondervan.

— Christian Perfection & American Methodism. 252p. 1995. reprint ed. pap. 12.99 (*0-88019-341-7*) Schmul Pub Co.

— Cry Dignity! 1988. 5.00 (*0-942716-06-X*) World Neigh.

Peters, John M., et al. Adult Education: Evolution & Achievements in a Developing Field of Study. LC 91-13977. (Higher & Adult Education Ser.). 525p. 1991. text 47.00 (*1-55542-381-7*) Jossey-Bass.

— Building an Effective Adult Education Enterprise. LC 78-62573. (Adult Education Association Handbook Series in Adult Education). 200p. reprint ed. pap. 62.00 (*0-8357-4959-2*, 203789100009) Bks Demand.

Peters, John M., jt. ed. see Bierbaum, Philip J.

Peters, John O., jt. auth. see Peters, Margaret T.

Peters, Jon, jt. auth. see Sonnenfeld, Barry.

Peters, Jonathan A. A Dance of Masks: Senghor, Achebe, & Soyinka. LC 77-3839. 270p. 1978. 10.00 (*0-914478-23-0*, Three Contnts) L Rienner.

Peters, Jos H., et al, eds. Artificial Recharge of Groundwater: Proceedings of the Third International Symposium - TISAR '98 Amsterdam, Netherlands, 21-25 September, 1998. (Illus.). 492p. (C). 1998. text 87.00 (*90-5809-017-5*, Pub. by A A Balkema) Ashgate Pub Co.

Peters, Joseph J., jt. auth. see Harlow, George E.

Peters, Joseph M., jt. auth. see Gega, Peter C.

Peters, Joseph P., compiled by. Indian Battles & Skirmishes on the American Frontier 1790-1898. LC 66-29882. 256p. 1972. 33.95 (*0-405-03676-0*) Ayer.

Peters, Joyce & Teaching Research Early Childhood Training Departm. Supporting Children with Disabilities in Community Programs: The Teaching Research Integrated Preschool. (Illus.). 165p. (Orig.). (C). 1993. pap. text 20.00 (*0-685-64739-0*) Teaching Res.

Peters, Juan K. Representing Children in Child Protective Proceedings, 1998 Supplement. 120p. 1998. suppl. ed. write for info. (*0-327-00562-9*, 6669110) LEXIS Pub.

Peters, Judith M. College Accounting: Holiday Health Club Practice Set. 2nd ed. 160p. (C). 1995. text 17.50 (*0-256-17103-3*, Irwn McGrw-H) McGrw-H Hghr Educ.

— College Accounting: John Webster, Attorney at Law Practice Set. 2nd ed. 112p. (C). 1996. text 16.95 (*0-256-17104-1*, Irwn McGrw-H) McGrw-H Hghr Educ.

— College Accounting: Ready Notes - Chapters 1-10. 2nd ed. 152p. (C). 1995. text, suppl. ed. 20.00 (*0-256-21173-6*, Irwn McGrw-H) McGrw-H Hghr Educ.

— College Accounting: Ready Notes - Chapters 1-15. 2nd ed. 240p. (C). 1995. text, suppl. ed. 20.00 (*0-256-21174-4*, Irwn McGrw-H) McGrw-H Hghr Educ.

— College Accounting: Ready Notes - Chapters 16-29. 2nd ed. 328p. (C). 1995. text, suppl. ed. 20.00 (*0-256-21310-0*, Irwn McGrw-H) McGrw-H Hghr Educ.

— College Accounting: Wheeler Dealer Practice Set. 2nd ed. 128p. (C). 1995. text 18.95 (*0-256-17105-X*, Irwn McGrw-H) McGrw-H Hghr Educ.

***Peters, Judith M.** College Accounting with Excel & Peachtree for Microsoft Windows Release 5.0 Judith M. Peters, Robert M. Peters, Carol Yacht. LC 98-72073. 547p. 1999. pap. text. write for info. incl. disk (*0-395-93230-0*) HM.

Peters, Judith M. CPS College Accounting, Vol. 1. 2nd ed. 264p. (C). 1995. 19.95 (*0-256-21513-8*, Irwn McGrw-H) McGrw-H Hghr Educ.

Peters, Judith M. & Peters, Robert M. College Accounting. 2nd ed. LC 95-10475. (Introductory Accounting Ser.). 1056p. (C). 1995. text 57.95 (*0-256-09053-X*, Irwn McGrw-H) McGrw-H Hghr Educ.

— College Accounting. 2nd ed. LC 95-10475. (Introductory Accounting Ser.). (C). 1995. text, teacher ed. write for info. (*0-256-19476-9*, Irwn McGrw-H) McGrw-H Hghr Educ.

— College Accounting. 2nd ed. LC 95-10475. (Introductory

P

Peters, O. E. Peters: Conrad Peters & Wife Clara Snidow: Their Descendants & Ancestry. (Illus.). 229p. 1991. reprint ed. pap. 35.00 (0-8328-1885-2); reprint ed. lib. bdg. 45.00 (0-8328-1884-4) Higginson Bk Co.

Peters, Otto. Learning & Teaching in Distance Education: Analyses & Interpretations from an International Perspective. LC 99-234365. (Illus.). 320p. 65.00 (0-7494-2855-4, Kogan Pg Educ) Stylus Pub VA.

Peters, P. A., tr. see Ines De La Cruz, Sor Juana.

***Peters, P. Stefan.** A Rainbow for Venus: A Multi-Seasoned Cookbook for Lovers. 90p. 2001. pap. 12.95 (1-930185-05-7, 106) Joan of Arc Pubng.

Peters, P. W., ed. Congenital Malformations Worldwide: A Report from the International Clearing House for Birth Defects Monitoring Systems. 220p. 1991. 143.25 (0-444-89137-4) Elsevier.

Peters, Pam. The Cambridge Australian English Style Guide. (Illus.). 862p. (C). 1995. text 85.00 (0-521-43401-7) Cambridge U Pr.

Peters, Pamela. Strategies for Student Writers: Guide to Writing Essays, Tutorial Papers, Exam Papers & Reports. 152p. 1987. text 9.95 (0-471-33406-5) Wiley.

Peters, Pamela M. Biotechnology: A Guide to Genetic Engineering. 272p. (C). 1992. text. write for info. (0-697-12063-5, WCB McGr Hill) McGrw-H Hghr Educ.

Peters, Patricia & Lazzari, Andrea M. HELP Elementary (Handbook of Exercising for Language Processing) 207p. 1993. spiral bd. 39.95 (1-55999-259-X) LinguiSystems.

Peters, Patricia, tr. see Ines De La Cruz, Sor Juana.

Peters, Patricia C. Early Morning on Castaway Street. LC 94-32411. 64p. 1996. pap. 14.95 (0-7734-0001-X, Mellen Poetry Pr) E Mellen.

— Tributaries from a Well: Poems. LC 98-8424. 68p. 1998. pap. 14.95 (0-7734-2843-7) E Mellen.

— Water under a Film of Ice. LC 96-42368. 64p. 1997. pap. 14.95 (0-7734-2685-X, Mellen Poetry Pr) E Mellen.

— When Last I Saw You: Poems. Schultz, Patricia, ed. LC 91-34456. (Lewiston Poetry Ser.: Vol. 18). 78p. 1992. pap. 14.95 (0-7734-9619-X) E Mellen.

***Peters, Patricia Claire.** From My Desk at Skip's Place. LC 00-32438. 56p. 2000. pap. 14.95 (0-7734-1258-1) E Mellen.

— Round the Bend & over the Hill. LC 00-32437. 60p. 2000. pap. 14.95 (0-7734-1256-5) E Mellen.

Peters, Patricia M. & Lazzari, Andrea M. HELP 1 (Handbook of Exercises for Language Processing) 2nd ed. 163p. 1987. spiral bd. 39.95 (1-55999-045-7) LinguiSystems.

— HELP 3 (Handbook of Exercises for Language Processing) 194p. 1988. spiral bd. 39.95 (1-55999-047-3) LinguiSystems.

— HELP 2 (Handbook of Exercises for Language Processing) 2nd ed. 175p. 1987. spiral bd. 39.95 (1-55999-046-5) LinguiSystems.

Peters, Patricia M., jt. auth. see Lazzari, Andrea M.

Peters, Patrick, jt. ed. see Cafruny, Alan.

Peters, Paul, jt. auth. see Ball, Robert.

Peters, Paulette. Basic Quiltmaking Techniques for Curved Piecing. (Basic Quiltmaking Techniques Ser.). (Illus.). 80p. 1999. pap. 14.95 (1-56477-252-7, B359, That Patchwrk Pl) Martingale & Co.

— Basic Quiltmaking Techniques for Strip Piecing. LC 98-20252. (Basic Quiltmaking Techniques Ser.: No. 3). (Illus.). 80p. 1998. pap. 14.95 (1-56477-232-2, B341, That Patchwrk Pl) Martingale & Co.

Peters, Paulette. Borders by Design: Creative Ways to Border Your Quilts. White, Janet, ed. LC 94-36946. (Joy of Quilting Ser.). (Illus.). 56p. (Orig.). 1994. pap. 12.95 (1-56477-082-6, B208) Martingale & Co.

Peters, Paulhans. AS & P Albert Speer & Partner: Urbanism & Architecture. LC 97-4316. (GER., Illus.). 148p. 1997. pap. 45.00 (3-7643-5265-5, Pub. by Birkhauser) Princeton Arch.

***Peters, Pauline E.** Development Encounters: Sites of Participation & Knowledge. (Harvard Studies in International Development). 2000. pap. 19.95 (0-674-00260-1) HUP.

Peters, Pauline E. Dividing the Commons: Politics, Policy, & Culture in Botswana. 320p. (C). 1994. pap. text 19.50 (0-8139-1551-1) U Pr of Va.

Peters, Plym, tr. see Dunselman, Ron.

Peters, Plym, tr. see Locher, Kees & Van Der Brug, Jos.

Peters, Plym, tr. see Van Haren, Wil & Kischnick, Rudolf.

Peters, Plym, tr. see Zoeteman, Kees.

***Peters-Pries, Pam.** Go for Broke: Using the Gifts God Gave You, Vol. 4.5. (Generation Why Ser.: Vol. 4.5). 34p. (YA). (gr. 9-12). 1999. pap. 12.95 (0-87303-285-3) Faith & Life.

Peters-Pries, Pam. Living Unplugged: Young Adults, Faith & the Uncommon Life. LC 95-83909. 144p. (C). 1996. pap. 10.95 (0-87303-251-9) Faith & Life.

Peters, R., jt. auth. see Schmidt, W.

Peters, R. D., jt. ed. see McMahon, Robert J.

Peters, R. H., jt. auth. see Hakanson, L.

Peters, R. W., jt. ed. see Cohen, Y.

Peters, Ralph. The Devil's Garden. LC 97-28603. 400p. 1998. mass mkt. 15.95 (0-380-97362-6, Avon Bks) Morrow Avon.

— Devil's Garden. 368p. 1999. mass mkt. 6.99 (0-380-78900-0, Avon Bks) Morrow Avon.

***Peters, Ralph.** Fighting for the Future: Will America Triumph? LC 98-45281. 192p. 1999. 19.95 (0-8117-0651-6) Stackpole.

Peters, Ralph. Flames of Heaven. McCarthy, Paul, ed. 464p. 1994. reprint ed. mass mkt. 5.99 (0-671-73739-2) PB.

— The Perfect Soldier. LC 94-45908. 320p. 1995. 23.00 (0-671-86583-8, PB Hardcover) PB.

— The Perfect Soldier. 1996. mass mkt. 6.99 (0-671-86584-6) PB.

— Red Army. McCarthy, Paul, ed. 416p. 1990. mass mkt. 6.99 (0-671-67669-5) PB.

— Traitor. LC 98-46862. 320p. 1999. 23.00 (0-380-97641-2, Avon Bks) Morrow Avon.

***Peters, Ralph.** Traitor. LC 98-46862. 384p. 2000. mass mkt. 6.99 (0-380-79738-0, Avon Bks) Morrow Avon.

Peters, Ralph. Twilight of Heroes. 464p. 1997. mass mkt. 6.50 (0-380-78898-5, Avon Bks) Morrow Avon.

— The War in 2020. McCarthy, Paul, ed. 624p. 1992. reprint ed. mass mkt. 6.50 (0-671-75172-7, Pocket Star Bks) PB.

Peters, Ray. The Lafitte Case. 256p. 1997. 22.95 (1-885173-27-X) Write Way.

Peters, Ray D. & McMahon, Robert J. Aggression & Violence Throughout the Life Span. (Illus.). 342p. (C). 1992. 55.00 (0-8039-4550-7); pap. 25.00 (0-8039-4551-5) Sage.

Peters, Ray D. & McMahon, Robert J., eds. Preventing Childhood Disorders, Substance Abuse, & Delinquency. LC 96-4477. (Banff International Behavioral Science Ser.: Vol. 3). (Illus.). 344p. 1996. 54.00 (0-7619-0014-4); pap. 24.95 (0-7619-0015-2) Sage.

Peters, Raymond H. Textile Chemistry, Vols. 2 & 3. Incl. Impurities in Fibres. 374p. 1967. 100.00 (0-444-40452-X); write for info. (0-318-51826-0) Elsevier.

Peters, Raymond R. Foothills to Mountaintops: My Pilgrimage to Wholeness. LC 93-229691. 387p. 1990. reprint ed. pap. 120.00 (0-608-02167-9, 206283600004) Bks Demand.

Peters, Reiner, ed. Nucleo-Cytoplastic Transport. 184p. 1989. pap. text 52.00 (0-12-552100-6) Acad Pr.

Peters, Reiner & Trendelenburg, M., eds. Nucleo-Cytoplasmic Transport. (Illus.). 315p. 1986. 79.95 (0-387-17050-2) Spr-Verlag.

Peters, Richard, jt. auth. see Agazarian, Yvonne.

Peters, Richard M. & Toledo, Jose, eds. Perioperative Care. LC 92-49794. (Current Topics in General Thoracic Surgery: an International Ser.: Vol. 2). 462p. 1992. 163.75 (0-444-89660-0) Elsevier.

Peters, Richard M., jt. ed. see Ying-Kai, Wu.

***Peters, Rick.** Air Tools: How to Choose, Use & Maintain Them. (Illus.). 128p. 2000. pap. 14.95 (0-8069-3692-4) Sterling.

— Drills & Drill Presses: How to Choose, Use, ND Maintain Them. LC 99-86642. 2000. 14.95 (0-8069-3691-6) Sterling.

— Electrical Basics. LC 99-86645. 2000. 14.95 (0-8069-3667-3) Sterling.

— Flooring Basics. LC 00-30817. (Illus.). 2000. write for info. (0-8069-5897-9) Sterling.

— Plumbing Basics. LC 99-86644. (Illus.). 128p. 2000. pap. 14.95 (0-8069-3669-X) Sterling.

— Woodworker's Guide to Wood: Softwoods, Hardwoods, Plywoods, Composites, Veneers. LC 99-86641. 2000. 24.95 (0-8069-3687-8) Sterling.

Peters, Rob. Beech Forests. LC 97-7522. (Geobotany Ser.). 1997. lib. bdg. 141.00 (0-7923-4485-5) Kluwer Academic.

Peters, Robert. The Blood Countess, Erzebet of Hungary (1560-1614) LC 86-17570. (Illus.). 120p. 1987. 16.00 (0-916156-80-X); pap. 8.00 (0-916156-81-8) Cherry Valley.

— Connections. Date not set. pap. 7.95 (0-900977-44-2, Pub. by Anvil Press) Dufour.

— Cool Zebras of Light. LC 73-87666. (Hip-Pocket Ser.: No. 4). (Illus.). 64p. (Orig.). 1974. pap. 2.75 (0-685-38810-7) Christophers Bks.

— Crunching Gravel: A Wisconsin Boyhood in the Thirties. LC 93-19801. (North Coast Bks.). 128p. 1993. reprint ed. pap. 12.95 (0-299-14104-7); reprint ed. lib. bdg. 12.95 (0-299-14100-4) U of Wis Pr.

— Feather: A Child's Death & Life. LC 96-43213. (Illus.). 232p. 1997. 19.95 (0-299-15360-6) U of Wis Pr.

— For You, Lili Marlene: A Memoir of World War II. LC 95-13155. (Illus.). 120p. (Orig.). 1995. 19.95 (0-299-14810-6) U of Wis Pr.

— For You, Lili Marlene: A Memoir of World War II. LC 95-13155. (North Coast Bk.). (Illus.). 120p. (Orig.). 1996. pap. 12.95 (0-299-14814-9) U of Wis Pr.

— The Gift to Be Simple: A Garland for Mother Ann Lee. LC 75-9974. 114p. (Orig.). 1975. pap. 4.95 (0-87140-103-7, Pub. by Liveright) Norton.

— Good Night, Paul. 75p. (Orig.). 1992. pap. 8.95 (1-879194-06-6) GLB Pubs.

— The Great American Poetry Bake-Off. LC 79-16090. 290p. 1979. 29.00 (0-8108-1231-2) Scarecrow.

— The Great American Poetry Bake-Off. LC 91-12621. (Illus.). 306p. 1991. 34.50 (0-8108-2410-8) Scarecrow.

— The Great American Poetry Bake-Off: Second Series. LC 81-18536. 409p. 1982. 31.00 (0-8108-1502-8) Scarecrow.

— Hawker. 116p. (Orig.). 1984. 20.00 (0-87775-165-X); pap. 10.95 (0-87775-166-8) Unicorn Pr.

— Hawthorne: Poems Adapted from Journals. (Illus.). 1977. 15.00 (0-88031-048-0); 6.00 (0-88031-047-2) Invisible-Red Hill.

— Haydon. (Illus.). 110p. 1989. 24.95 (0-87775-219-2); pap. 14.95 (0-87775-220-6) Unicorn Pr.

— Holy Cow: Parable Poems. 1974. pap. 2.50 (0-88031-014-6) Invisible-Red Hill.

— Hunting the Snark: American Poetry at Century's End: Classifications & Commentary. rev. ed. 288p. (C). 1997. reprint ed. pap. 20.00 (1-888105-16-X) Avisson Pr.

— Kane. (Illus.). 110p. (Orig.). 1985. 20.00 (0-87775-168-4); pap. 10.95 (0-87775-169-2) Unicorn Pr.

— Ludwig of Bavaria: A Verse Biography & a Play for Single Performer. 128p. (Orig.). 1986. pap. 7.00 (0-916156-82-6) Cherry Valley.

— Peters Third Black & Blue Guide to Literary Journals. 3rd ed. 164p. 1987. pap. 5.95 (0-916685-03-9) Dustbooks.

— Poems: Selected & New, 1967-1991. LC 92-71208. 190p. (Orig.). 1992. 20.00 (1-878580-30-2); pap. 11.95 (1-878580-31-0) Asylum Arts.

— Shaker Light. 127p. 1987. 25.00 (0-87775-200-1); pap. 14.95 (0-87775-201-X) Unicorn Pr.

— Snapshots for a Serial Killer: A Fiction & a Play. 125p. (Orig.). 1992. pap. 10.95 (1-879194-07-4) GLB Pubs.

— The Sow's Head & Other Poems. LC 68-24447. 91p. reprint ed. 30.00 (0-608-16984-6, 202760000055) Bks Demand.

— Where the Bee Sucks: Workers, Drones & Queens of Contemporary American Poetry. LC 94-70673. 300p. (Orig.). 1994. pap. 14.95 (1-878580-63-9) Asylum Arts.

— Zapped: Two Novellas: Asbestos: a Book for Lepers, How to Make Love to a Foot. 135p. (Orig.). 1993. pap. 11.95 (1-879194-10-4) GLB Pubs.

Peters, Robert, jt. auth. see Peters, Nell.

Peters, Robert, ed. see Murphy, Dan.

Peters, Robert, illus. see Brown, George H.

Peters, Robert B., ed. see Ratch, Jerry.

Peters, Robert B., ed. see Ratner, Rochelle.

Peters, Robert C., ed. see Prokop, Michael S.

Peters, Robert H. A Critique for Ecology. (Illus.). 382p. (C). 1991. text 95.00 (0-521-40017-1); pap. text 37.95 (0-521-39588-7) Cambridge U Pr.

Peters, Robert L. The Crowns of Apollo: Swinburne's Principles of Literature & Art: A Study in Victorian Criticism & Aesthetics. LC 65-10769. (Illus.). 226p. reprint ed. pap. 70.10 (0-7837-3610-X, 204347600009) Bks Demand.

Peters, Robert L. Getting What You Came For: The Smart Student's Guide to Earning a Masters or a Ph.D. 400p. 1997. pap. text 14.00 (0-374-52477-7, Noonday) FS&G.

Peters, Robert L. Getting What You Came For: The Smart Student's Guide to Earning an M.A. or a Ph.D. LC 92-27763. 1992. pap. 12.00 (0-374-52361-4, Noonday) FS&G.

Peters, Robert L. & Lovejoy, Thomas E. Global Warming & Biological Diversity. (Illus.). 407p. (C). 1994. pap. 20.00 (0-300-05930-2) Yale U Pr.

Peters, Robert L., ed. see Symonds, John A.

Peters, Robert M. College Accounting: Treads & Threads Practice Set. 2nd ed. 152p. (C). 1995. text 18.95 (0-256-21450-6, Irwn McGrw-H) McGrw-H Hghr Educ.

Peters, Robert M., jt. auth. see Peters, Judith M.

Peters, Robert W. Coprecipitation, Absorption & Coremoval Phenomena. Date not set. 125.00 (0-87371-401-6) Lewis Pubs.

Peters, Robert W. & Bennett, Gary F. Industrial Wastewater Pretreatment. Date not set. 45.00 (0-87371-656-6) Lewis Pubs.

Peters, Roger, jt. auth. see Wold, Geoffrey H.

Peters, Roger, ed. see Michigan Legislative Council Staff.

Peters, Roger W., intro. Michigan Administrative Code, 1979: 1988 Annual Supplement. (Illus.). 1050p. 1988. pap. 27.00 (1-878210-01-7) Legis Serv Bur.

Peters, Roger W., ed. see Michigan Legislative Council Staff.

Peters, Ronald M., Jr. The American Speakership: The Office in Historical Perspective. LC 89-20025. 352p. 1990. text 55.00 (0-8018-3955-6) Johns Hopkins.

— The American Speakership: The Office in Historical Perspective. 2nd ed. LC 97-16988. 408p. 1997. text 48.50 (0-8018-5751-1); pap. text 16.95 (0-8018-5758-9) Johns Hopkins.

— The Massachusetts Constitution of 1780: A Social Compact. LC 77-90730. 256p. 1978. 30.00 (0-87023-143-X) U of Mass Pr.

— The Next Generation: Dialogues Between Leaders & Students. LC 92-54133. 320p. 1992. pap. 9.95 (0-8061-2430-X) U of Okla Pr.

Peters, Ronald M., Jr., jt. ed. see Hertzke, Allen D.

Peters, Ronnie. Ultimate Claris Works Solutions! for Education. Peters, Barry, ed. (Illus.). 270p. (C). 1994. spiral bd. 36.95 (0-9643120-0-X); ring bd. 425.00 (0-9643120-1-8) EduPress Pubng.

— Ultimate Claris Works Solutions 4.0. Peters, Barry, ed. (Illus.). 352p. 1995. spiral bd. 49.95 incl. disk (0-9643120-9-3, 2001) EduPress Pubng.

Peters, Rudolph. Islam & Colonialism. (Religion & Society Ser.). 1984. pap. 32.95 (3-11-010022-3) Mouton.

— The Jihad in Classical & Modern Islam. LC 95-20943. (Princeton Series on the Middle East). (Illus.). 220p. (C). 1996. pap. 18.95 (1-55876-109-8) Wiener Pubs Inc.

— The Jihad in Classical & Modern Islam. LC 95-20943. (Princeton Series on the Middle East). (Illus.). 220p. (C). 1996. 44.95 (1-55876-108-X) Wiener Pubs Inc.

Peters, Rudolph, jt. auth. see Zwaini, Laila A.

Peters, Russell M. Clambake: A Wampanoag Tradition. (We Are Still Here: Native Americans Today Ser.). (Illus.). 48p. (J). (gr. 3-6). 1992. lib. bdg. 21.27 (0-8225-2651-4, Lerner Publctns) Lerner Pub.

— Clambake: A Wampanoag Tradition. (Illus.). (J). (gr. 3-6). 1992. pap. 6.95 (0-8225-9621-0, Lerner Publctns) Lerner Pub.

Peters, Ruth. Don't Be Afraid to Discline. 1999. pap. 12.00 (1-58238-025-2, Whitman Coin) St Martin.

— It's Never Too Soon. unabridged ed. LC 98-2880. (Illus.). 216p. 1998. text 19.00 (0-307-44002-8, Whitman Coin) St Martin.

***Peters, Ruth Allen.** Overcoming Underachieving: A Simple Plan to Boost Your Kids' Grades & Their Homework Blahs. LC 00-24990. 256p. 2000. 12.95 (0-7679-0458-3) Broadway BDD.

Peters, S. Activated Carbon Technology. (General Engineering Ser.). 1999. text. write for info. (0-442-00810-4, VNR) Wiley.

Peters, S., et al. Celebrate the States. (Illus.). 144p. (YA). (gr. 4 up). 178.21 (0-7614-0643-3) Marshall Cavendish.

Peters, S. M. Cyberotica: On-Line Dominant & Submissive Play. LC 96-20799. (Orig.). Date not set. pap. write for info. (0-945456-34-4) PT Pubns.

Peters, Sally. Bernard Shaw: The Ascent of the Superman. LC 95-37248. 344p. 1996. 37.00 (0-300-06097-1) Yale U Pr.

— Bernard Shaw: The Ascent of the Superman. (Illus.). 344p. 1998. pap. 18.00 (0-300-07500-6) Yale U Pr.

Peters, Sally, ed. see Alexis, Katina.

Peters, Sally, ed. see Bernstein, Patricia.

Peters, Sally, ed. see Bronte, Emily Jane.

Peters, Sally, jt. ed. see Campbell, Ramsey.

Peters, Sally, ed. see Chiel, Deborah.

Peters, Sally, ed. see Cooper, James Fenimore.

Peters, Sally, ed. see Dershowitz, Alan M.

Peters, Sally, ed. see Ellison, James.

Peters, Sally, ed. see Engel, Lewis & Ferguson, Tom.

Peters, Sally, ed. see Engelhard, Jack.

Peters, Sally, ed. see Ferguson, Tom & Graedon, Joe.

Peters, Sally, ed. see Geiberger, Al.

Peters, Sally, ed. see Graham, Janis.

Peters, Sally, ed. see Henry, Diane & Horrock, Nicholas.

Peters, Sally, ed. see Hunter, Linda M.

Peters, Sally, ed. see Keane, Maureen B.

Peters, Sally, ed. see Late Night with David Letterman Writers Staff & Letterman, David.

Peters, Sally, ed. see Levin, Ira.

Peters, Sally, ed. see Maclean, Norman F.

Peters, Sally, ed. see Malone, Michael.

Peters, Sally, ed. see March, Ray A.

Peters, Sally, ed. see McCammon, Robert R.

Peters, Sally, ed. see Minninger, Joan & Dugan, Eleanor.

Peters, Sally, ed. see Morton, Andrew.

Peters, Sally, ed. see Nadel, Jack.

Peters, Sally, ed. see Natow, Annette B. & Heslin, Jo-Ann.

Peters, Sally, ed. see Natow, Annette B. & Heslin, Joann.

Peters, Sally, ed. see Natow, Annette B. & Hesun, Jo-Ann.

Peters, Sally, ed. see Natow, Annette B. & Hesun, JoAnn.

Peters, Sally, ed. see Palmer, Jessica.

Peters, Sally, ed. see Riccero, Delores & Bingham, Joan.

Peters, Sally, ed. see Rincover, Arnold.

Peters, Sally, ed. see Storm, Jordan.

Peters, Sally, ed. see Taski, Bob & Flick, Jim.

Peters, Sally, ed. see Toshi, Bob & Flich, Jim.

Peters, Sally, ed. see Watson, Tom & Seitz, Nick.

Peters, Sally, ed. see Weinberg, Robert.

Peters, Sally, ed. see Wilson, F. Paul.

Peters, Samuel A. General History of Connecticut. LC 77-104540. 285p. reprint ed. lib. bdg. 27.50 (0-8398-1562-X) Irvington.

— General History of Connecticut, from Its First Settlement Under George Fenwick to Its Latest Period of Amity with Great Britain Prior to the Revolution. LC 71-95073. (Select Bibliographies Reprint Ser.). 1977. 30.95 (0-8369-5073-9) Ayer.

Peters, Sarah W. Becoming O'Keeffe: The Early Years. (Illus.). 400p. 1991. 24.95 (0-89659-907-8) Abbeville Pr.

Peters, Selton L. Emergent Materialism: A Proposed Solution to the Mind-Body Problem. 104p. (C). 1995. lib. bdg. 28.50 (0-7618-0060-3) U Pr of Amer.

Peters, Sharon. Champ on Ice. LC 87-10908. (Giant First Start Reader Ser.). (Illus.). 32p. (J). (gr. k-2). 1997. pap. 3.95 (0-8167-1094-5) Troll Communs.

— Contento Juan. 1995. pap. 2.50 (0-89375-952-X) Troll Communs.

— Feliz Cumpleanos. (SPA., Illus.). 32p. (J). (gr. k-2). 1997. pap. 2.50 (0-89375-955-4) Troll Communs.

— Five Little Kittens. LC 81-2317. (Illus.). 32p. (J). (gr. k-2). 1981. lib. bdg. 17.25 (0-89375-503-6) Troll Communs.

— Five Little Kittens. LC 81-2317. (Illus.). 32p. (J). (gr. k-2). 1997. pap. 3.95 (0-89375-504-4) Troll Communs.

— Fun at Camp. (Illus.). 32p. (J). (gr. k-2). 1980. lib. bdg. 13.05 (0-89375-378-5) Troll Communs.

— Fun at Camp. (Illus.). 32p. (J). (gr. k-2). 1997. pap. 2.50 (0-89375-278-9) Troll Communs.

— Una Funcion Titeres. 1995. pap. 2.50 (0-89375-956-2) Troll Communs.

— The Goofy Ghost. LC 81-2573. (Illus.). 32p. (J). (gr. k-2). 1997. pap. 3.95 (0-89375-534-6) Troll Communs.

— Happy Birthday. (Illus.). 32p. (J). (gr. k-2). 1996. pap. 2.50 (0-89375-279-7) Troll Communs.

— Happy Jack. (Illus.). 32p. (J). (gr. k-2). 1997. pap. 2.50 (0-89375-280-0) Troll Communs.

— Listos, en Sus Marcas, Adelante! (SPA., Illus.). 32p. (J). (gr. k-2). 1995. pap. 2.50 (0-89375-957-0) Troll Communs.

— Messy Mark. (Illus.). 32p. (J). (gr. k-2). 1997. pap. 2.50 (0-89375-281-9) Troll Communs.

— Messy Mark: Big Book Edition. 1999. pap. text 16.95 (0-8167-2664-7) Troll Communs.

— On a Roll: A Conversation & Listening Text. 160p. (C). 1990. pap. text 26.93 (0-13-155326-7) P-H.

— Puppet Show. (Illus.). 32p. (J). (gr. k-2). 1997. pap. 2.50 (0-89375-286-X) Troll Communs.

— Ready, Get Set, Go! (Illus.). 32p. (J). (gr. k-2). 1997. pap. 2.50 (0-89375-285-1) Troll Communs.

— The Rooster & the Weather Vane. LC 86-30838. (Illus.). 32p. (J). (gr. k-2). 1988. lib. bdg. 13.05 (0-8167-0980-7) Troll Communs.

— The Rooster & the Weather Vane. LC 86-30838. (Illus.). 32p. (J). (gr. k-2). 1997. pap. 2.50 (0-8167-0981-5) Troll Communs.

— Rooster & the Weather Vane, Big Book ed. 1999. pap. text 16.95 (0-8167-2666-3) Troll Communs.

— Rub-a-Dub Suds. LC 86-30856. (Illus.). 32p. (J). (gr. k-2). 1997. pap. 2.50 (0-8167-0985-8) Troll Communs.

— Santa's New Sled. LC 81-5028. (Illus.). 32p. (J). (gr. k-2). 1997. pap. 3.95 (0-89375-524-9) Troll Communs.

— Stop That Rabbit. (Illus.). 32p. (J). (gr. k-2). 1980. lib. bdg. 13.05 (*0-89375-388-2*) Troll Communs.

— Stop That Rabbit. (Illus.). 32p. (J). (gr. k-2). 1997. pap. 2.50 (*0-89375-288-6*) Troll Communs.

— The Tiny Christmas Elf. LC 86-30849. (Illus.). 32p. (J). (gr. k-2). 1988. lib. bdg. 13.05 (*0-8167-0988-2*) Troll Communs.

— The Tiny Christmas Elf. LC 86-30849. (Illus.). 32p. (J). (gr. k-2). 1997. pap. 2.50 (*0-8167-0989-0*) Troll Communs.

— The Tooth Fairy. LC 81-5100. (Illus.). 32p. (J). (gr. k-2). 1997. pap. 3.95 (*0-89375-520-6*) Troll Communs.

— Trick or Treat Halloween. (Illus.). 32p. (J). (gr. k-2). 1980. lib. bdg. 13.05 (*0-89375-392-0*) Troll Communs.

— Trick or Treat Halloween. (Illus.). 32p. (J). (gr. k-2). 1997. pap. 2.50 (*0-89375-292-4*) Troll Communs.

***Peters, Sharon L.** Caught in the Middle: How to Improve the Lives & Performance of Newspaper Middle Managers. 72p. 1999. pap. 17.00 (*0-9656018-9-7*) NMC.

Peters, Sharon L. In Their Prime: Motivating Senior Reporters. 76p. 1997. pap. 8.00 (*0-9656018-4-6*) NMC.

***Peters, Sharon L.** Managing Newsroom Employees: A Guide to Solving Common Personnel Problems. 52p. 1999. pap. 12.50 (*1-930341-00-8*) NMC.

***Peters, Shawn Francis.** Judging Jehovah's Witnesses: Religious Persecution & the Dawn of the Rights Revolution. LC BX8525.7.P48 2000. (Illus.). 352p. 2000. text 34.95 (*0-7006-1008-1*) U Pr of KS.

Peters, Sherry. Making Cents Out of Signs. 2nd rev. ed. (Illus.). 160p. 1997. pap. 12.95 (*0-9659990-0-9*) Ein Gavar Pub.

Peters, Sonja. A Family from Germany. LC 97-15582. (Families Around the World Ser.). (Illus.). 32p. (J). 1998. 22.83 (*0-8172-4905-2*) Raintree Steck-V.

Peters, Stanley. Semantic Ambiguity & Underspecification. Van Deemter, Kees, ed. 294p. (C). 1996. 69.95 (*1-57586-029-5*); pap. 24.95 (*1-57586-028-7*) CSLI.

Peters, Stanley & Saarinen, Esa, eds. Processes, Beliefs & Questions: Essays on Formal Semantics of Natural Language & Natural Language Processing. 252p. 1981. text 149.50 (*90-277-1314-6*, D Reidel) Kluwer Academic.

Peters, Stanley, jt. auth. see Gawron, Jean M.

Peters, Stephanie T. Gary Paulsen. Clark, Kimberley, ed. LC 98-54725. (Meet the Author Ser.). (Illus.). 112p. (J). (gr. 3-6). 1999. pap. 6.95 (*0-88160-324-4*, LW387) Learning Wks.

Peters, Stephanie T. & Mitter, Kathy. My First Raggedy Ann: Raggedy Ann & the Birthday Surprise. LC 99-24899. 2000. per. 15.00 (*0-689-83136-6*) S&S Bks Yung.

Peters, Stephen. Grateful Dead: What a Long, Strange Trip - The Stories Behind Every Song. LC 99-60902. (Illus.). 256p. 1999. pap. 22.95 (*1-56025-233-2*, Thunders Mouth) Avalon NY.

***Peters, Stephen.** Pennsylvania, 5 vols. , Set. LC 99-16414. (Celebrate the States Ser.). 144p. (J). 2000. 35.64 (*0-7614-0644-1*) Marshall Cavendish.

***Peters, Stephen G.** Inspired to Learn: Why We Must Give Children Hope. 2000. pap. 15.95 (*1-880463-08-3*) Rising Sun.

Peters, Suan, jt. see Bird, Chuck.

Peters, Sue. Maid for Marriage. large type ed. 1992. reprint ed. lib. bdg. 18.95 (*0-263-13134-3*) Mac Lib Ref.

— Marriage in Haste. large type ed. (Linford Romance Library). 384p. 1985. pap. 16.99 (*0-7089-6100-2*, Linford) Ulverscroft.

— Weekend Wife. large type ed. 1992. reprint ed. 18.95 (*0-263-13038-X*) Mac Lib Ref.

Peters, Susan & Bird, Chuch. Christmas Songs for Folk Harp. 128p. 1994. spiral bd. 21.95 incl. audio (*0-7866-1140-5*, 95307P) Mel Bay.

Peters, Susan, jt. auth. see Bird, Chuck.

Peters, Susan J., ed. Education & Disability in Cross-Cultural Perspective. LC 92-41906. (Reference Library of Social Science, Reference Books in International Education: Vol. 25). 328p. 1993. text 59.00 (*0-8240-6988-9*) Garland.

Peters, Susanne. The Germans & the INF Missiles: Getting Their Way in NATO's Strategy of Flexible Response. 334p. 1990. pap. 62.00 (*3-7890-2236-5*, Pub. by Nomos Verlags) Intl Bk Import.

Peters, T. M., et al. Fourier Transforms & Biomedical Engineering. LC 97-30101. (Illus.). 200p. 1997. 49.50 (*0-8176-3941-1*) Birkhauser.

Peters, Ted. Cosmos as Creation: Theology & Science in Consonance LC 88-39258. 1989. write for info. (*0-687-09655-3*) Abingdon.

— For the Love of Children: Genetic Technology & the Future of the Family. (Studies in the Family, Religion, & Culture). 248p. 1996. pap. 18.00 (*0-664-25468-3*) Westminster John Knox.

— God-The World's Future: Systematic Theology for a Postmodern Era. LC 91-43158. 400p. 1992. pap. 24.00 (*0-8006-2542-0*, 1-2542, Fortress Pr) Augsburg Fortress.

— Playing God? Genetic Determinism & Human Freedom. 218p. (C). 1996. pap. 19.99 (*0-415-91522-8*) Routledge.

— Playing God? Genetic Determinism & Human Freedom. 218p. (C). 1996. 70.00 (*0-415-91521-X*) Routledge.

***Peters, Ted.** Sin: Radical Evil in Soul & Society. 348p. 1998. pap. 35.00 (*1-57910-181-X*) Wipf & Stock.

Peters, Ted, ed. Genetics: Issues of Social Justice. LC 97-45113. (Pilgrim Library of Ethics). 208p. (Orig.). 1998. pap. 18.95 (*0-8298-1251-2*) Pilgrim OH.

— Science & Theology: The New Consonance. 264p. 1999. pap. text 26.00 (*0-8133-3259-1*, Pub. by Westview) HarpC.

Peters, Thelma. Biscayne Country, 1870-1926. LC 81-13030. (Illus.). viii, 323p. 1981. pap. 14.95 (*0-916224-65-1*) Banyan Bks.

— Lemon City, 1850-1925: Pioneering on Biscayne Bay. LC 76-48058. (Illus.). 1976. 14.95 (*0-916224-12-0*) Banyan Bks.

Peters, Thelma B., ed. & intro. see Maloney, Walter C.

Peters, Theodore, Jr. All about Albumin: Biochemistry, Genetics, & Medical Applications. (Illus.). 414p. 1995. text 85.00 (*0-12-552110-3*) Acad Pr.

Peters, Theodore, jt. auth. see Guitar, Barry.

Peters, Theodore J. & Guitar, Barry. Stuttering: An Integrated Approach to Its Nature & Treatment. (Illus.). 392p. 1991. 42.00 (*0-683-06870-9*) Lppncott W & W.

— Stuttering: An Integration of Contemporary Therapies, No. 16. LC 80-51679. 1980. pap. 2.00 (*0-933388-15-2*) Stuttering Fnd Am.

***Peters, Thomas A.** The Use of Computers to Monitor Human-Computer Interactions. LC 99-32116. 414p. 1999. lib. bdg. 65.00 (*0-7864-0706-9*) McFarland & Co.

Peters, Thomas A., jt. ed. see Kurth, Martin.

Peters, Thomas C. Battling for the Modern Mind: A Beginner's Chesterton. LC 94-5963. (Concordia Scholarship Today Ser.). 176p. (Orig.). 1994. pap. 17.00 (*0-570-04664-5*, 12-3236) Concordia.

***Peters, Thomas C.** The Christian Imagination: G. K. Chesterton on the Arts. 154p. 2000. pap. 12.95 (*0-89870-757-9*) Ignatius Pr.

Peters, Thomas C. Simply C. S. Lewis: A Beginner's Guide to His Life & Works. LC 97-8203. 272p. 1997. pap. 12.99 (*0-89107-948-3*) Crossway Bks.

Peters, Thomas R., Jr. Over the Roofs of the World. Daniel, Darrin, ed. (Spike Ser.: No. 7). (Illus.). 80p. 2000. pap. 7.95 (*1-885089-04-X*, Pub. by Cityful Pr) SPD-Small Pr Dist.

Peters, Tim. Asthma & Chronic Obstructive Pulmonary Disease (COPD) (Humanatomy Board Bks.). 10p. 1996. bds. 9.95 (*1-879874-49-0*) T Peters & Co.

— Common Disorders of the Nasal Cavity. (Humanatomy Board Bks.). (Illus.). 12p. 1994. bds. 9.95 (*1-879874-02-4*) T Peters & Co.

— A Guide to Middle Ear Infection. (Humanatomy Board Bks.). (Illus.). 12p. 1998. bds. 9.95 (*1-879874-11-3*) T Peters & Co.

— A Guide to the Human Eye. (Humanatomy Board Bks.). (Illus.). 12p. 1993. bds. 9.95 (*1-879874-16-4*) T Peters & Co.

— A Guide to Understanding Stroke. Smith, Shane, ed. (Humanatomy Board Bks.). (Illus.). 12p. 1996. bds. 9.95 (*1-879874-32-6*) T Peters & Co.

— A Patient's Guide to COPD & Lung Cancer. (Humanatomy Board Bks.). (Illus.). 12p. 1991. bds. 9.95 (*1-879874-03-2*) T Peters & Co.

Peters, Timothy. Alcohol & Cardiovascular Disease, Vol. 216. LC 98-27198. (Novartis Foundation Symposium Ser.). 280p. 1998. 95.00 (*0-471-97769-1*) Wiley.

Peters, Timothy J., ed. Alcohol Misuse: A European Perspective. 208p. 1996. text 41.00 (*3-7186-5814-3*, Harwood Acad Pubs); pap. text 16.00 (*3-7186-5869-0*, Harwood Acad Pubs) Gordon & Breach.

Peters, Tom. Beyond Hierarchy: Organizations in the 1990s. 1991. 30.00 (*0-685-58667-7*) Knopf.

***Peters, Tom.** The Brand You50. 1999. 15.95 (*0-375-40772-3*) Knopf.

Peters, Tom. Circle of Innovation: You Can't Shrink Your Way to Greatness. 544p. 1998. pap. 14.00 (*0-679-75765-1*) Vin Bks.

— The Circle of Inovation: You Can't Shrink Your Way to Greatness. LC 97-74755. 1997. 35.00 (*0-375-40157-1*) Knopf.

***Peters, Tom.** The Design + Identity50. 240p. 2001. 15.95 (*0-375-40775-8*) Knopf.

Peters, Tom. Fragile People: Stories from Betterway. Scrivo, William, ed. (Illus.). 291p. 1991. pap. 9.95 (*1-879516-02-0*) Betterpub Pr.

— Hard Time Prayers. (Illus.). 104p. (Orig.). 1991. pap. 3.95 (*1-879516-03-9*) Betterpub Pr.

— In Search of Excellence. 1993. 13.95 (*0-446-77805-2*) Warner Bks.

— Liberation Management. 1994. pap. text 12.00 (*0-449-90910-7*) Fawcett.

— Liberation Management: Necessary Disorganization for the Nanosecond Nineties. 880p. 1994. pap. 15.00 (*0-449-90888-7*, Columbine) Fawcett.

— Liberation Management: Necessary Disorganization for the Nanosecond Nineties. LC 90-53071. 928p. 1992. 27.50 (*0-394-55999-1*) Knopf.

— Naked I Came . . . And Naked I Shall Go: The Growth & Ending of an Organization. 240p. (Orig.). 1992. pap. write for info. (*1-879516-05-5*) Betterpub Pr.

— O Felix Culpa . . . O Happy Fault: How Bad Guys Keep Good Guys Going. (Illus.). 200p. (Orig.). 1991. pap. write for info. (*1-879516-07-1*) Betterpub Pr.

— O My Soul: The Inside Story. Scrivo, William, ed. (Illus.). 250p. (Orig.). 1991. pap. 15.00 (*1-879516-00-4*) Betterpub Pr.

***Peters, Tom.** The Power + Action50. 240p. 2001. 15.95 (*0-375-40774-X*) Knopf.

Peters, Tom. The Professional Service Firm 50. LC 99-33616. 1999. 15.95 (*0-375-40771-5*) Knopf.

***Peters, Tom.** The Project50. LC 99-33615. 208p. 1999. 15.95 (*0-375-40773-1*) Knopf.

Peters, Tom. The Pursuit of Wow! Every Person's Guide to Topsy-Turvy Times. 349p. 1995. pap. 15.00 (*0-679-75555-1*) Vin Bks.

***Peters, Tom.** Reinventing Work, Vol. 15. 1999. text 239.25 (*0-676-59306-2*) Knopf.

Peters, Tom. The Skunk Camp Promises. 1987. 9.95 (*0-317-56480-3*) Knopf.

— Thriving on Chaos: Handbook for a Management Revolution. LC 88-45121. 736p. 1991. pap. 20.00 (*0-06-097184-3*, Perennial) HarperTrade.

— Thriving on Chaos: Handbook for a Management Revolution. LC 87-45575. 561p. 1987. 35.00 (*0-394-56784-6*) Knopf.

Peters, Tom & Austin, Nancy K. A Passion for Excellence. 608p. 1989. mass mkt. 16.99 (*0-446-38639-1*, Pub. by Warner Bks) Little.

Peters, Tom & Waterman, Robert H., Jr. In Search of Excellence. pap. write for info. (*0-446-36578-5*) Warner Bks.

— In Search of Excellence. 384p. 1988. mass mkt. 15.99 (*0-446-38507-7*, Pub. by Warner Bks) Little.

Peters, Tom & Waterman, Robert H. In Search of Excellence: Lessons from America's Best Run Companies. write for info. (*0-317-17653-6*) Macmillan.

Peters, Tom F. Building the Nineteenth Century. (Illus.). 551p. 1996. 49.50 (*0-262-16160-5*) MIT Pr.

Peters, Tom F. Transitions in Engineering: Guillaume Henri Dufour & the Early 19th Century Cable Suspension Bridges. 252p. 1987. 110.00 (*0-8176-1929-1*) Birkhauser.

Peters, Tom F. Transitions in Engineering: Guillaume Henri Dufour & the Early 19th Century Cable Suspension B. 1996. 122.00 (*3-7643-1929-1*) Birkhauser.

Peters, Uwe. Pflanzenoekologische und Bodenkundliche Untersuchungen an Quellwaldstandorten in Bochum. (Dissertationes Botanicae Ser.: Band 122). (GER., Illus.). 211p. 1988. pap. 48.00 (*3-443-64034-6*, Pub. by Gebruder Borntraeger) Balogh.

Peters, Uwe H. Anna Freud: A Life Dedicated to Children. LC 84-1278. (Illus.). 384p. 1985. 24.95 (*0-8052-3910-3*) Schocken.

— Dictionary of Psychiatry & Medical Psychology: Woerterbuch der Psychiatrie und Medizinischen Psychologie. 4th ed. (ENG, FRE & GER.). 676p. 1990. 69.95 (*0-8288-0586-5*, M 6972) Fr & Eur.

Peters, V. A. Pete. Consumers Guide to Remodeling & Construction: For the General Public & Profession, Vol. 5,000. Brin, Susannah, ed. 104p. 1998. pap. 24.95 (*0-9664292-0-6*) Peters-Jillore.

Peters, Vicki. Salonovations' Nail Question & Answer Book. (NAILS). 224p. (C). 1996. pap. 29.95 (*1-56253-266-9*) Thomson Learn.

Peters, Victor. All Things Common: The Hutterian Way of Life. LC 65-28661. (Illus.). 245p. reprint ed. pap. 76.00 (*0-8357-5315-8*, 203328200084) Bks Demand.

Peters, Vincent F. New Wave Pharmaceutical Selling. Peters, Carolyn R., ed. (Illus.). ii, 50p. (Orig.). 1996. pap. 29.95 (*0-9656231-0-6*) Black Dog Pub.

***Peters, Vincent F. & Yeats, Thomas B.** Pharmaceutical Sales Management in a Changeable Market Place. (Illus.). v, 220p. 2000. pap. 49.95 (*0-9656231-2-2*) Black Dog Pub.

Peters, Vincent F., jt. auth. see Magnani, Joseph L.

Peters, Virginia B. Women of the Earth Lodges: Tribal Life on the Plains. LC 94-9251. (Illus.). xvi, 217p. (C). 1994. lib. bdg. 39.50 (*0-208-02219-8*, Archon Bks) Shoe String.

***Peters, Virginia Bergman.** Women of the Earth Lodges: Tribal Life on the Plains. LC 99-55160. (Illus.). 240p. 2000. pap. text 14.95 (*0-8061-3243-4*) U of Okla Pr.

Peters, W. Chemotherapy & Drug Resistance in Malaria, 2 vols., Vol. 1. 2nd ed. 542p. 1987. text 209.00 (*0-12-552721-7*) Acad Pr.

— Chemotherapy & Drug Resistance in Malaria, 2 vols., Vol. 2. 2nd ed. 650p. 1987. text 209.00 (*0-12-552722-5*) Acad Pr.

— Peritrophic Membranes. (Zoophysiology Ser.: Vol. 30). (Illus.). xi, 238p. 1992. 207.95 (*0-387-53635-3*) Spr-Verlag.

Peters, W. & Killick-Kendrick, R., eds. The Leishmaniases: Clinical Aspects & Control, Vol. 2. 400p. 1987. text 104.00 (*0-12-552102-2*) Acad Pr.

— The Leishmaniases I: Biology & Epidemiology, Vol. 1. 550p. 1987. text 104.00 (*0-12-552101-4*) Acad Pr.

Peters, W. & Richards, W. H., eds. Antimalarial Drugs. (Handbook of Experimental Pharmacology Ser.: Vol. 68, Pt. 1). (Illus.). 540p. 1984. 295.00 (*0-387-12616-3*) Spr-Verlag.

— Antimalarial Drugs II: Current Antimalarials & New Drug Developments. (Handbook of Experimental Pharmacology Ser.: Vol. 68). (Illus.). xxiii, 520p. 1984. 312.00 (*0-387-12617-1*) Spr-Verlag.

Peters, W., et al. Chemotherapy of Malaria. 2nd ed. (Monographs: No. 27). 261p. 1986. pap. text 39.60 (*92-4-140127-3*, 1142027) World Health.

Peters, W. L., jt. auth. see Hubbard, M. D.

Peters, W. S. Counting for Something: Statistical Principles & Personalities. (Texts in Statistics Ser.). (Illus.). 305p. 1986. 58.95 (*0-387-96364-2*) Spr-Verlag.

Peters, Wallac. Color Atlas of Arthropods in Clinical Medicine. (Illus.). 256p. (C). (gr. 13). 1992. text 165.00 (*0-8151-6679-6*, 21938) Mosby Inc.

Peters, Wallace. A Color Atlas of Tropical Medicine & Parasitology. 4th ed. 1995. mass mkt. 49.95 (*0-7234-2069-6*) Mosby Inc.

Peters, Wallace & Gilles, Herbert M. A Color Atlas of Tropical Medicine & Parasitology. 3rd ed. (Illus.). 1989. 104.00 (*0-7234-1535-8*) CRC Pr.

Peters, Warren. Mystical Medicine. LC 95-61242. 96p. 1995. per. 7.95 (*1-57258-044-5*) Teach Servs.

Peters, Werner. Society on the Run: A European View of Life in America. LC 95-25770. (Illus.). 312p. (C). (gr. 13). 1996. 77.95 (*1-56324-585-X*, HN59); pap. 32.95 (*1-56324-586-8*) M E Sharpe.

Peters, William. A Class Divided. expanded ed. LC 87-50411. 172p. 1987. pap. 12.00 (*0-300-04048-2*) Yale U Pr.

Peters, William, jt. auth. see Evers, Myrlie.

Peters, William C. Exploration & Mining Geology. 2nd ed. LC 86-29005. 706p. 1987. text 105.95 (*0-471-83864-0*) Wiley.

— Fire Apparatus Purchasing Handbook. 382p. 1994. 49.95 (*0-912212-33-0*) Fire Eng.

Peters, William E. Ohio Lands & Their History. 3rd ed. Bruchey, Stuart, ed. LC 78-53541. (Development of Public Land Law in the U. S. Ser.). (Illus.). 1979. reprint ed. lib. bdg. 30.95 (*0-405-11383-8*) Ayer.

Peters, William L. & Peters, Janice G., eds. Ephemeroptera: Proceedings of the First International Conference Held at the Florida Agricultural & Mechanical University, August 1970. (Illus.). 312p. 1973. lib. bdg. 124.00 (*90-04-06461-3*) Lubrecht & Cramer.

Petersdorf, Robert G., ed. see Institute of Medicine Staff.

***Petersdorff, Charles.** A Practical Compendium of the Law of Master & Servant in General & Especially of Employers & Workmen under the Acts of 1875 with Suggestions for Its Improvement. vii, 147p. 1999. reprint ed. 48.00 (*1-56169-548-3*, 18112) Gaunt.

Peterse, Arie, jt. auth. see Kuitert, Wybe.

Peterse, O. J., jt. ed. see Wierenga, H. K.

Peterseil, Gedalia. Children's Passover Haggadah: The Energizing Haggadah for Children. (Illus.). 48p. 1998. pap. text 7.95 (*0-943706-28-9*) Pitspopany.

— Energizing Jewish Holidays for Children. (Illus.). 48p. 1999. pap. text 7.95 (*0-943706-92-0*) Pitspopany.

— Genesis/Exodus. (Tell It from the Torah Ser.). 1997. pap. text 12.95 (*0-943706-82-3*) Pitspopany.

— Tell It from the Torah: Genesis/Exodus, Vol. 1. 1997. 18.95 (*0-943706-95-5*) Pitspopany.

Peterseil, Gedalia. Tell it from the Torah: Torah Thoughts to Read & Repeat. 488p. (YA). 34.95 (*0-943706-98-X*); pap. 24.95 (*0-943706-99-8*) Pitspopany.

Peterseil, Tamar. Zap It! A Microwave Cookbook Just for Kids. (J). (gr. 4-7). 1993. 12.95 (*0-943706-13-0*) Pitspopany.

Peterseil, Tehila. The Safe Place. (Illus.). 144p. (J). (gr. 4-8). 1996. 16.95 (*0-943706-71-8*); pap. 12.95 (*0-943706-72-6*) Pitspopany.

— Secret Files of Lisa Weiss. (J). 1990. 11.95 (*0-87306-549-2*); pap. 9.95 (*0-87306-550-6*) Feldheim.

— Secret Files of Lisa Weiss. 208p. 1998. pap. text 8.95 (*0-943706-39-4*) Pitspopany.

— Secret Files of Lisa Weiss. rev. ed. (J). (gr. 3-8). 1998. 14.95 (*0-943706-30-0*) Pitspopany.

— Unjust Cause. 144p. (J). (gr. 4-8). 1997. 16.95 (*0-943706-94-7*) Pitspopany.

— Unjust Cause. 144p. (J). (gr. 4-8). 1997. pap. text 12.95 (*0-943706-83-1*) Pitspopany.

Peterseil, Yaacov. The Gang of Four: Kung-Fooey to the Rescue. (Illus.). 192p. (YA). 1995. pap. text 7.95 (*0-943706-51-3*) Pitspopany.

— The Gang of Four: Nest of the Jerusalem Eagle. (Illus.). 144p. (YA). 1996. pap. 4.95 (*0-943706-53-X*) Pitspopany.

— Jewish Sci-Fi Stories for Kids: An Anthology of Short Stories. 208p. 1999. pap. 12.95 (*0-943706-74-2*) Pitspopany.

— Jewish Sci-Fi Stories for Kids: An Anthology of Short Stories. 208p. (gr. 3-7). 1999. 16.95 (*0-943706-73-4*) Pitspopany.

— Leviticus, Numbers, Deuteronomy. (Tell It from the Torah Ser.). 1998. 18.95 (*0-943706-97-1*); pap. text 12.95 (*0-943706-84-X*) Pitspopany.

— Noah's Family Carousel. (Illus.). (J). (ps). 1993. 12.95 (*0-943706-10-6*) Pitspopany.

Peterseil, Yaacov. Princess Alopecia. (Illus.). 32p. (J). (gr. k-3). 1999. 14.95 (*0-943706-26-2*) Pitspopany.

***Peterseil, Yaacov.** Princess Alopecia. (Illus.). 32p. (J). (gr. k-3). 1999. pap. 8.95 (*0-943706-25-4*) Pitspopany.

Petersen. Economics: The Free Enterprise System. (HB - Economics Ser.). 1988. 171.95 (*0-538-28722-5*) S-W Pub.

— Economics: The Free Enterprise System. (HB - Economics Ser.). 1988. 171.95 (*0-538-28723-3*); 171.95 (*0-538-28724-1*) S-W Pub.

— Economics of Work. (HB - Economics Ser.). 1983. pap. 20.95 (*0-538-07620-8*) S-W Pub.

— Experiments General Chemistry. 2nd ed. 1998. pap. 18.12 (*0-07-233275-1*) McGraw.

— On the Track of the Dixie Limited. (Illus.). 64p. 10.00 (*0-936610-00-X*) Colophon Bk Shop.

Petersen, et al. Binder Characterization & Evaluation Vol. 4: Test Methods. 193p. (Orig.). (C). 1994. pap. text 15.00 (*0-309-05806-6*, SHRP-A-370) SHRP.

Petersen, jt. auth. see Kelley.

Petersen, Ian R. & Savkin, Andrey V. Robust Kalman Filtering for Signals & Systems with Large Uncertainties. LC 98-46010. (Illus.). 250p. 1999. 69.00 (*0-8176-4089-4*) Birkhauser.

Petersen, Alan. Health Matters: A Sociology of Illness, Prevention & Care. 1998. 85.00 (*0-335-20261-6*); pap. text 29.95 (*0-335-20260-8*) Taylor & Francis.

— In a Critical Condition: Health & Power Relations in Australia. 208p. 1994. pap. 22.95 (*1-86373-530-5*, Pub. by Allen & Unwin Pty) Paul & Co Pubs.

Petersen, Alan & Lupton, Deborah. The New Public Health: Health & Self in the Age of Risk. 224p. (C). 1997. 69.95 (*0-7619-5403-1*, 54031); pap. 25.95 (*0-7619-5404-X*, 5404X) Sage.

Petersen, Alan & Waddell, Charles, eds. Health Matters: A Sociology of Illness, Prevention & Care. LC 98-194038. 384p. 1998. 39.95 (*1-86448-564-7*, Pub. by Allen & Unwin Pty) Paul & Co Pubs.

Petersen, Alan R. Poststructuralism, Citizenship, & Social Policy. LC 99-19521. 1999. pap. write for info. (*0-415-18288-3*) Routledge.

***Petersen, Alan R.** Poststructuralism, Citizenship & Social Policy. LC 99-19521. 1999. write for info. (*0-415-18287-5*) Routledge.

P

An Asterisk (*) at the beginning of an entry indicates that the title is appearing for the first time.

Petersen, Alan R. & Bunton, Robin. Foucault, Health & Medicine. LC 96-43375. 288p. (C). 1997. 80.00 (*0-415-15177-5*); pap. 22.99 (*0-415-15178-3*) Routledge.

***Petersen, Allan Rosengren.** The Royal God: Enthronement Festivals in Ancient Israel & Ugarit? LC 98-170997. (JSOT Supplement Ser.: No. 259). 121p. 1998. 46.50 (*1-85075-864-6*, Pub. by Sheffield Acad) CUP Services.

Petersen, Andrew. Dictionary of Islamic Architecture. 352p. 1996. pap. 75.00 (*0-614-21574-9*, 201) Kazi Pubns.

— Dictionary of Islamic Architecture. (Illus.). 352p. (C). (gr. 13). 1995. 140.00 (*0-415-06084-2*, B0381) Routledge.

Petersen, Andrew, jt. auth. see Arcangelo, Virginia Poole.

Petersen, Anne C., ed. Women & Science: Celebrating Achievements, Charting Challenges: Conference Report. (Illus.). 155p. (C). 1999. reprint ed. text 25.00 (*0-7881-7886-5*) DIANE Pub.

Petersen, Anne C. & Mortimer, Jeylan T., eds. Youth Unemployment & Society. (Illus.). 337p. (C). 1994. text 49.95 (*0-521-44473-X*) Cambridge U Pr.

Petersen, Anne C., jt. ed. see Gibson, Kathleen R.

Petersen, Antje C. The First Berlin Border-Guard Trial. (MacArthur Scholar Series, Occasional Paper: No. 15). 39p. (Orig.). 1992. pap. 3.50 (*1-881157-18-0*) In Ctr Global.

Petersen, Arnold. Capital & Labor. 7th ed. 1975. pap. text 0.50 (*0-935534-06-7*) NY Labor News.

— Daniel De Leon: Social Architect, Vol. 2. 400p. 1953. 2.50 (*0-935534-12-1*) NY Labor News.

— Democracy...Past, Present & Future. 7th ed. 1971. pap. text 0.50 (*0-935534-14-8*) NY Labor News.

— Karl Marx & Marxian Science. 1967. 3.00 (*0-935534-17-2*); pap. 1.00 (*0-935534-18-0*) NY Labor News.

— Reviling of the Great. 112p. 1949. 1.50 (*0-935534-24-5*); pap. 0.75 (*0-935534-25-3*) NY Labor News.

— The Supreme Court. 3rd ed. 1971. pap. text 0.75 (*0-935534-30-X*) NY Labor News.

Petersen, Arona. Food & Folklore of the Virgin Islands. 300p. (Orig.). (YA). (gr. 9-12). 1990. 20.00 (*0-9626577-0-0*) A Petersen.

— Herbs & Proverbs. 1974. write for info. (*0-318-69480-8*) A Petersen.

***Petersen, Bernie.** Discerning the Times: What Time Is It on Israel's Clock? Ball, Jennifer, ed. 98p. 1999. pap. 8.00 (*0-9674022-0-4*) Final Call Pubns.

Petersen, Bill, jt. auth. see Eckert, Amy.

***Petersen, Brad E.** Cooking with Chef Brad Those Wonderful Grains! McKnight, Marianne Wilson, ed. 161p. 1999. pap. 17.95 (*0-9676272-0-6*) M McKnight.

Petersen, Brad L. & Carco, Diane M. The Smart Way to Buy Information Technology: How to Maximize Value & Avoid Costly Pitfalls. LC 97-40153. 304p. 1997. 35.00 (*0-8144-0387-5*) AMACOM.

Petersen, Bruce L. God's Answer for You: Psalms That Speak to Real-Life Needs. 80p. 1994. pap. 7.99 (*0-8341-1493-3*) Beacon Hill.

Petersen, Carol. Between Earth & Heaven. LC 99-198404. 48p. 1998. pap. 12.95 (*1-892668-03-3*) Prospect Pr.

Petersen, Carol A., jt. auth. see Peake, Jacquelyn.

Petersen, Carol M. Bess Streeter Aldrich: All the Dreams Are Real. LC 95-2301. (Illus.). xix, 247p. 1995. text 45.00 (*0-8032-3700-6*) U of Nebr Pr.

Petersen, Carol M., jt. auth. see Aldrich, Bess S.

Petersen, Carol M., ed. & intro. see Aldrich, Bess S.

Petersen, Carolyn C. & Brandt, John C. Hubble Vision: Further Adventures with the Hubble Space Telescope. 2nd rev. ed. LC 98-21341. (Illus.). 320p. (C). 1998. 39.95 (*0-521-59291-7*) Cambridge U Pr.

Petersen, Catherine Fish, jt. auth. see Briggs, Bonnie-Anne.

Petersen, Cathy J., jt. auth. see Thompson, George P.

Petersen, Charles G. Compiler Writing Made Easy. 340p. (C). 1988. pap. text 35.00 (*0-9631838-9-3*) P & M Pub Co.

Petersen, Charles G. & Miller, Nancy E. Move up to Ada. 115p. (C). 1991. pap. text 25.00 (*0-9631838-8-5*) P & M Pub Co.

Petersen, Charlott H. Natufian Chipped Lithic Assemblage from Sunakh Near Petra, Southern Jordan. (Carsten Niebuhr Institute Publications (CNI): No. 18). (Illus.). 100p. 1994. 45.00 (*87-7289-281-1*, Pub. by Mus Tusculanum) Paul & Co Pubs.

Petersen, Charlotte, ed. see Elgart, Robert.

Petersen, Charlotte, ed. see Fuchs, Helmuth.

Petersen, Charlotte, ed. see Marcus, Bernard A.

Petersen, Christian. Bread & the British Economy, 1770-1870. Jenkins, Andrew, ed. 1995. 86.95 (*1-85928-117-6*, Pub. by Scolar Pr) Ashgate Pub Co.

Petersen, Christian, jt. auth. see Toop, Alan.

Petersen, Christine E. Doctor in French Drama: 1700-1775. LC 39-2239. reprint ed. 20.00 (*0-404-04996-6*) AMS Pr.

Petersen, Christine E., jt. auth. see Petersen, David.

Petersen, Connie M., jt. auth. see Kelley.

Petersen, Dan. Analyzing Safety System Effectiveness. 3rd ed. (Industrial Health & Safety Ser.). 271p. 1996. 64.95 (*0-471-28739-3*, VNR) Wiley.

Petersen, Dan. Analyzing Safety Systems Effectiveness. (Industrial Health & Safety Ser.). 288p. 1996. text 51.95 (*0-442-02180-1*, VNR) Wiley.

Petersen, Dan. Human Error Reduction & Safety Management. 3rd ed. (Industrial Health & Safety Ser.). 397p. 1996. 74.95 (*0-471-28740-7*, VNR) Wiley.

— Safety by Objectives: What Gets Measured & Rewarded Gets Done. 2nd ed. 240p. 1995. 74.95 (*0-471-28738-5*, VNR) Wiley.

Petersen, Dan. Safety Management: A Human Approach. 2nd ed. LC 98-26786. 1998. 46.75 (*1-885581-19-X*) ASSE.

— Safety Supervision. 2nd ed. LC 98-49110. 1999. write for info. (*1-885581-22-X*) ASSE.

— Techniques of Safety Management: A Systems Approach. 3rd ed. LC 97-88230. 414p. 1998. 59.95 (*1-885581-20-3*) ASSE.

— What Gets Measured & Rewarded Gets Done. 2nd ed. (Industrial Health & Safety Ser.). 240p. 1996. text 65.95 (*0-442-02179-8*, VNR) Wiley.

Petersen, Daniel, jt. auth. see Brown, Kirk.

Petersen, Daniel C., ed. Readings in Behavioral Issues in Safety. 106p. 1985. 10.00 (*0-939874-63-6*) ASSE.

Petersen, Darla. A Pioneer Poetree Treasury: Generations of Rhyme Through Time. LC 97-92203. x, 246p. (Orig.). 1997. pap. 11.95 (*0-9658926-0-3*) Poet Tree.

Petersen, David. Africa. LC 97-29745. (True Bks.). 48p. (J). 1998. 21.00 (*0-516-20767-9*) Childrens.

— Africa. Taft, James, ed. (True Bks.). (Illus.). 48p. (J). 1998. pap. 6.95 (*0-516-26369-2*) Childrens.

— The Anasazi. LC 91-3036. (New True Books Ser.). 48p. (J). (gr. k-4). 1991. pap. 5.50 (*0-516-41121-7*); lib. bdg. 21.00 (*0-516-01121-9*) Childrens.

— Antarctica. LC 98-25106. (True Bks.). (Illus.). 48p. (J). (gr. 2-4). 1998. 21.00 (*0-516-20770-9*) Childrens.

— Antarctica. (True Bks.). (Illus.). 48p. (J). (gr. 2-4). 1999. pap. text 6.95 (*0-516-26426-5*) Childrens.

— Arches National Park. LC 98-42177. (National Parks Ser.). (Illus.). 48p. (J). (gr. 3-5). 1999. 21.50 (*0-516-20941-8*) Childrens.

***Petersen, David.** Arches National Park. (True Bks.). (J). 2000. pap. text 6.95 (*0-516-26572-5*) Childrens.

Petersen, David. Asia. LC 97-35687. (True Bks.). 48p. (J). 1998. 21.00 (*0-516-20764-4*) Childrens.

— Asia. Taft, James, ed. (True Bks.). (Illus.). 48p. (J). 1998. pap. 6.95 (*0-516-26371-4*) Childrens.

— Audio, Video, & Data Telecommunications. LC 92-9766. 1992. write for info. (*0-07-707427-0*) McGraw.

— Australia: Taft, James, ed. (True Bks.). (Illus.). 48p. (J). 1998. pap. 6.95 (*0-516-26372-2*) Childrens.

— Australia: A True Book. LC 97-33041. 48p. (J). 1998. 21.00 (*0-516-20765-2*) Childrens.

— Bryce Canyon National Park. LC 96-1183. (True Bk.). (Illus.). 48p. (J). 1996. lib. bdg. 21.00 (*0-516-20048-8*) Childrens.

— Bryce Canyon National Park. (True Bks.). 48p. (J). (gr. 3-4). 1997. pap. 6.95 (*0-516-26094-4*) Childrens.

— Chaco Culture National Historical Park. LC 98-42467. (National Parks Ser.). (J). 1999. 21.50 (*0-516-20942-6*) Childrens.

***Petersen, David.** Chaco Culture National Park. (True Bks.). (J). 2000. pap. text 6.95 (*0-516-26757-4*) Childrens.

Petersen, David. Death Valley National Park. LC 96-635. (New True Books Ser.). (Illus.). 48p. (J). (ps-3). 1996. lib. bdg. 21.00 (*0-516-20049-6*) Childrens.

— Death Valley National Park. (True Bks.). 48p. (J). (gr. 3-4). 1997. pap. 6.95 (*0-516-26095-2*) Childrens.

— Denali National Park & Preserve. LC 96-1574. (True Bk.). (Illus.). 48p. (J). 1996. lib. bdg. 21.00 (*0-516-20050-X*) Childrens.

— Denali National Park & Preserve. (True Bks.). 48p. (J). (gr. 3-4). 1997. pap. 6.95 (*0-516-26096-0*) Childrens.

— Dinosaur National Monument. LC 94-35655. (New True Books Ser.). (Illus.). 48p. (J). (gr. k-4). 1995. lib. bdg. 21.00 (*0-516-01074-3*) Childrens.

— Elkheart. LC 98-25871. 240p. 1998. pap. 16.00 (*1-55566-225-0*) Johnson Bks.

— Elkheart: A Personal Tribute to Wapiti & Their World. LC 98-25871. 240p. 1998. 27.50 (*1-55566-224-2*, Sprng Creek Pr) Johnson Bks.

— Europe. LC 97-31009. (True Bks.). 48p. (J). (gr. 3-5). 1998. 21.00 (*0-516-20766-0*) Childrens.

— Europe. (True Bks.). (Illus.). 48p. (J). (gr. 3-5). 1998. pap. 6.95 (*0-516-26375-7*) Childrens.

— Ghost Grizzlies. LC 94-39887. 88p. 1995. 27.50 (*0-8050-3117-0*, J Macrae Bks) H Holt & Co.

— Ghost Grizzlies: Does the Great Bear Still Haunt Colorado? rev. ed. LC 98-2577. 304p. 1998. pap. 16.00 (*1-55566-218-8*) Johnson Bks.

— Grand Canyon National Park. LC 92-11343. (New True Books Ser.). (Illus.). 48p. (J). (gr. 3-5). 1992. lib. bdg. 21.00 (*0-516-02197-4*) Childrens.

***Petersen, David.** Grand Canyon National Park. LC 00-30694. (True Bks.). (Illus.). (J). 2001. write for info. (*0-516-21664-3*) Childrens.

Petersen, David. Great Sand Dunes National Monument. LC 98-42466. (National Parks Ser.). (J). 1999. 21.50 (*0-516-20943-4*) Childrens.

***Petersen, David.** Great Sand Dunes National Monument. (True Bks.). (J). 2000. pap. text 6.95 (*0-516-26763-9*) Childrens.

Petersen, David. Great Smoky Mountains National Park. LC 92-35049. (New True Books Ser.). (Illus.). 48p. (J). (ps-3). 1993. lib. bdg. 21.00 (*0-516-01332-7*) Childrens.

***Petersen, David.** Haleakala National Park. LC 00-30697. (True Bks.). (Illus.). (J). 2001. write for info. (*0-516-21666-X*) Childrens.

— Heartsblood: Hunting, Spirituality & Wildness in America. 256p. 2000. 24.95 (*1-55963-761-7*, Shearwater Bks); write for info. (*1-55963-762-5*) Island Pr.

Petersen, David. A Hunter's Heart. 352p. 1997. pap. 12.95 (*0-8050-5530-4*) H Holt & Co.

— Mesa Verde National Park. LC 91-35275. (New True Books Ser.). (Illus.). 48p. (J). (gr. k-4). 1992. pap. 5.50 (*0-516-41136-5*) Childrens.

— Moose. LC 94-10948. (New True Books Ser.). (Illus.). 48p. (J). (gr. k-4). 1994. pap. 5.50 (*0-516-41069-5*); lib. bdg. 21.00 (*0-516-01069-7*) Childrens.

— Mountain Lions. LC 94-36353. (New True Books Ser.). 48p. (J). (gr. k-4). 1995. lib. bdg. 21.00 (*0-516-01077-8*) Childrens.

— Mountain Lions. (New True Books Ser.). (Illus.). 48p. (J). 1995. pap. 5.50 (*0-516-41077-6*) Childrens.

— The Nearby Faraway: A Personal Journey Through the Heart of the West. LC 97-28206. (Illus.). 240p. 1997. 26.00 (*1-55566-206-4*); pap. 15.00 (*1-55566-187-4*) Johnson Bks.

— North America. LC 98-24337. (True Bks.). 47 p. (J). 1998. 21.00 (*0-516-20768-7*) Childrens.

— North America. (True Bks.). (Illus.). 48p. (J). (gr. 3-5). 1999. pap. text 6.95 (*0-516-26437-0*) Childrens.

— Petrified Forest National Park. LC 96-1181. (True Bk.). (Illus.). 48p. (J). 1996. lib. bdg. 21.00 (*0-516-20052-6*) Childrens.

— Rocky Mountain National Park. LC 93-798. (New True Books Ser.). (Illus.). 48p. (J). (ps-3). 1993. lib. bdg. 21.00 (*0-516-01196-0*) Childrens.

— Saguaro National Park. LC 98-28806. (National Parks Ser.). (J). 1999. 21.50 (*0-516-20944-2*) Childrens.

***Petersen, David.** Saguaro National Park. (True Bks.). (J). 2000. pap. text 6.95 (*0-516-26771-X*) Childrens.

Petersen, David. South America. LC 98-24338. (True Bks.). (Illus.). 47 p. (J). (gr. 2-4). 1998. 21.00 (*0-516-20769-5*) Childrens.

— South America. (True Bks.). (Illus.). 48p. (J). (gr. 2-4). 1999. pap. text 6.95 (*0-516-26440-0*) Childrens.

— True Books: Continents, 7 vols. (J). 1996. 147.00 (*0-516-29755-4*) Childrens Pr.

— Yellowstone National Park. LC 91-37292. (New True Books Ser.). (Illus.). 48p. (J). (ps-3). 1992. lib. bdg. 19.00 (*0-516-01148-0*) Childrens.

***Petersen, David.** Yellowstone National Park. LC 00-31469. (True Bks.). (Illus.). (J). 2001. write for info. (*0-516-21668-6*) Childrens.

Petersen, David. Yosemite National Park. LC 92-39156. (New True Books Ser.). (Illus.). 48p. (J). (ps-3). 1993. lib. bdg. 21.00 (*0-516-01335-1*) Childrens.

***Petersen, David & Petersen, Christine E.** Maps & Globes. LC 00-30716. (True Bks.). (Illus.). (J). 2001. write for info. (*0-516-22044-6*) Childrens.

Petersen, David C. Convention Centers, Stadiums, & Arenas. LC 89-50266. (Illus.). 176p. (Orig.). 1989. reprint ed. pap. 54.60 (*0-608-02953-X*, 206341800006) Bks Demand.

— Sports, Convention, & Entertainment Facilities. LC 95-62037. 331p. 1996. pap. text 59.95 (*0-87420-781-9*, S04) Urban Land.

Petersen, David H. Geologic Map of the Hayes Canyon Quadrangle, Sanpete County, Utah. (Miscellaneous Publication of the Utah Geological Survey Ser.: Vol. 97-3). (Illus.). 18p. 1997. pap. 7.00 (*1-55791-385-4*, MP-97-3) Utah Geological Survey.

Petersen, David L. Haggai & Zechariah 1-8, a Commentary. LC 84-7477. (Old Testament Library). 320p. 1984. 29.95 (*0-664-21830-X*) Westminster John Knox.

— Late Israelite Prophecy: Studies in Deutero-Prophetic Literature & in Chronicles. LC 76-26014. (Society of Biblical Literature, Mongraph Ser.: Vol. 23). 112p. reprint ed. pap. 34.80 (*0-608-08678-9*, 206920100003) Bks Demand.

Petersen, David L. The Roles of Israel's Prophets. (JSOT Supplement Ser.: No. 17). 131p. 1981. pap. 17.95 (*0-905774-32-9*, Pub. by Sheffield Acad) CUP Services.

Petersen, David L. Zechariah 9-14 & Malachi: A Commentary. LC 94-43410. (Old Testament Library). 272p. 1995. 29.00 (*0-664-21298-0*) Westminster John Knox.

Petersen, David L. & Richards, Kent H. Interpreting Hebrew Poetry. LC 92-7934. (Guides to Bibical Scholarship Ser.). 128p. 1992. pap. 14.00 (*0-8006-2625-7*, 1-2625, Fortress Pr) Augsburg Fortress.

Petersen, David M., jt. auth. see Bordner, Diane C.

Petersen, David M., jt. auth. see Thomas, Charles W.

Petersen, Donald J. Folk Art Fish Decoys. (Illus.). 240p. 1996. 59.95 (*0-7643-0053-9*) Schiffer.

***Petersen, Douglas.** No Es Con Ejercito, Ni Con Fuerza. 1999. pap. 8.99 (*0-8297-0345-4*) Vida Pubs.

— Not by Might nor by Power: A Pentecostal Theology of Social Concern in Latin America. 260p. 1996. reprint ed. pap. 20.00 (*1-870345-20-7*, Pub. by Regnum Bks) OM Literature.

Petersen, Douglas, photos by. The Last Light of Day: Landscape of the Delaware River. (Illus.). 48p. 1997. 50.00 (*0-9655747-0-9*) Deerfield Edtns.

Petersen-Dyggve, Holger N. Chansons Francaises du Treizieme Siecle. LC 80-2167. 1981. 29.50 (*0-404-19030-8*) AMS Pr.

— Personnages Historiques Figurant dans la Poesie Lyrique Francaise des XII et XIIIe Siecles. LC 80-2166. 1981. 67.50 (*0-404-19031-6*) AMS Pr.

— Trouveres et Protecteurs De Trouveres Dans les Cours Seigneuriales De France. LC 80-2168. reprint ed. 41.50 (*0-404-19032-4*) AMS Pr.

Petersen, E. L., jt. auth. see Ambroise-Thomas, P.

Petersen, Elise. Tracy's Mess. (Illus.). (J). (ps-2). 1998. pap. 5.95 (*1-58089-003-2*) Charlesbridge Pub.

Petersen, Elizabeth. Maze: How Not to Go into Business. LC 82-62505. 160p. 1983. 14.95 (*0-9610200-0-8*); pap. 9.95 (*0-9610200-1-6*) MEDA Pubns.

***Petersen, Elsa Schepelern.** Sticks & Skewers. LC 99-40074. 64p. (YA). (gr. 11). 2000. write for info. (*0-7370-2034-2*) Time-Life Educ.

Petersen, Emma M. Bible Stories for Young L. D. S. (J). 1995. pap. 9.95 (*0-88494-975-3*) Bookcraft Inc.

— Book of Mormon Stories for Young LDS. 1996. pap. 10.95 (*1-57008-257-X*) Bookcraft Inc.

***Petersen, Erik Nissen.** Rainwater Catchment Systems for Domestic Supply: Designing, Construction & Implementation. (Illus.). 320p. 1999. 25.00 (*1-85339-456-4*) Intermed Tech.

Petersen, Eugene E. Gear Making: Using a Single-Tooth Hob. (Illus.). 128p. 1996. pap. 19.95 (*0-9642614-4-8*) Knoll Pubs.

***Petersen, Eugene E.** Making Gears: By the Single-Toothed Hob Method. (Illus.). 172p. 2000. pap. 15.00 (*0-9642614-5-6*) Knoll Pubs.

Petersen, Eugene E. The Modern Cynic: To Be or Not to Be. LC 94-77719. 112p. 1996. 29.95 (*0-9642614-2-1*) Knoll Pubs.

Petersen, Eugene E. & Bell, Alexis T. Catalyst Deactivation. (Chemical Industries Ser.: Vol. 30). (Illus.). 376p. 1987. text 210.00 (*0-8247-7741-7*) Dekker.

Petersen, Eugene P. Window in the Rock. LC 93-7109. 1993. 22.50 (*0-87770-522-4*); pap. 14.95 (*0-87770-515-1*) Ye Galleon.

Petersen, Eugene T. Mackinac & the Porcelain City. (Illus.). 40p. (Orig.). 1985. pap. 5.00 (*0-911872-53-1*) Mackinac St Hist Pks.

— Mackinac Island: Its History in Pictures. LC 74-17184. (Illus.). 103p. (Orig.). 1973. 18.00 (*0-911872-13-2*) Mackinac St Hist Pks.

Petersen, Eugene T., jt. auth. see Smith, Marian E.

Petersen, Evelyn. Growing Creative Kids. McKinnon, Elizabeth, ed. LC 96-61888. (Seeds for Success Ser.). (Illus.). 96p. (Orig.). 1997. pap. 6.95 (*1-57029-100-4*, 3101) Totline Pubns.

— Growing Happy Kids. Hodges, Susan, ed. LC 96-61889. (Seeds for Success Ser.). (Illus.). 96p. (Orig.). 1997. pap. 6.95 (*1-57029-101-2*, 3102) Totline Pubns.

— Growing Responsible Kids. Gnojewski, Carol, ed. LC 96-61890. (Seeds for Success Ser.). (Illus.). 96p. (Orig.). 1997. pap. 6.95 (*1-57029-102-0*, 3103) Totline Pubns.

— Growing Thinking Kids. Cubley, Kathleen, ed. LC 96-61891. (Seeds for Success Ser.). (Illus.). 96p. (Orig.). 1997. pap. 6.95 (*1-57029-103-9*, 3104) Totline Pubns.

— 1-2-3 Blocks. Bittinger, Gayle, ed. LC 97-62222. (One-Two-Three Ser.). (Illus.). 80p. (J). (ps). 1998. pap. 8.95 (*1-57029-185-3*, 0412) Totline Pubns.

***Petersen, Evelyn.** Parent's Guide to Raising Creative Kids: Practical Advice & Activity Ideas. (Raising... Kids Ser.). (Illus.). 2000. pap. text 3.99 (*1-55254-165-7*) Brighter Vision.

— Parent's Guide to Raising Happy Kids: Practical Advice & Activity Ideas. (Raising... Kids Ser.). (Illus.). 2000. pap. text 3.99 (*1-55254-166-5*) Brighter Vision.

— Parent's Guide to Raising Responsible Kids. (Raising... Kids Ser.). 2000. pap. text 3.99 (*1-55254-167-3*) Brighter Vision.

— Parent's Guide to Raising Thinking Kids. 2000. pap. text 3.99 (*1-55254-168-1*) Brighter Vision.

Petersen, Evelyn. The Practical Guide to Early Childhood Planning Methods & Materials: The What, Why & How of Lesson Plans. 224p. (C). 1995. pap. text 30.00 (*0-205-17404-3*) Allyn.

Petersen, Evelyn & Petersen, J. Allan. For Women Only. 281p. 1982. pap. 5.99 (*0-8423-0897-0*) Tyndale Hse.

***Petersen, Evelyn & Petersen, Karin.** Sams Teach Yourself Today E-Parenting: Using the Internet & Computers to Be a Better Parent. (Teach Yourself Today Ser.). 310p. 2000. pap. 17.99 (*0-672-31818-0*) Sams.

Petersen-Fleming, Judy & Fleming, Bill. Puppy Care & Critters, Too! LC 93-23129. (Illus.). 40p. (J). 1994. 15.00 (*0-688-12563-8*, Wm Morrow); lib. bdg. 14.93 (*0-688-12564-6*, Wm Morrow) Morrow Avon.

— Puppy Training & Critters, Too! LC 95-23031. (Illus.). 39p. (J). (ps-2). 1996. lib. bdg. 15.93 (*0-688-13385-1*, Wm Morrow) Morrow Avon.

Petersen, Florence H. Fisher-Stombaugh: Stombaugh Families & Allied Lineages of Md. & Penna., 1715-1949. (Illus.). 409p. 1997. reprint ed. pap. 62.00 (*0-8328-8570-3*); reprint ed. lib. bdg. 72.00 (*0-8328-8569-X*) Higginson Bk Co.

Petersen, Frank E. & Phelps, J. Alfred. Into the Tiger's Jaw: America's First Black Marine Aviator: The Autobiography of Lt. General Frank E. Petersen. LC 98-26406. (Illus.). 416p. 1998. 24.95 (*0-89141-675-7*, Pub. by Presidio Pr) Natl Bk Netwk.

Petersen, G. W., jt. auth. see Reybold, W. U.

Petersen, Gary W. & Beatty, Marvin T., eds. Planning Future Land Uses. (ASA Special Publications: No. 42). 71p. (C). 1981. pap. 3.85 (*0-89118-067-2*) Am Soc Agron.

Petersen, George. Alesis Adat: The Evolution of a Revolution. LC 98-67692. 1998. pap. 29.95 (*0-87288-686-7*) Intertec Pub.

Petersen, George, ed. see Gibson, David.

Petersen, Glen. High-Impact Sales Force Automation: A Strategic Perspective. (Illus.). 296p. 1997. boxed set 49.95 (*1-57444-093-4*) St Lucie Pr.

Petersen, Glen S. Customer Relationship Management Systems: ROI & Results Measurement. (Illus.). 161p. 1999. pap. 15.00 (*0-9669351-0-1*) Strategic Sales.

Petersen, Gwen. Yellowstone Pioneers: The Story of Hamilton Stores & Yellowstone National Park. Davis, Linda S., ed. LC 85-50965. (Illus.). 120p. 1989. pap. 9.95 (*0-917859-23-5*) Sunrise SBCA.

Petersen, Gwen, et al, eds. Ten Years' Gatherings, Montana Poems & Stories. (Illus.). 192p. (Orig.). 1995. 22.95 (*1-887477-01-2*); pap. 14.95 (*1-887477-02-0*) Ranch Cntry.

Petersen, Gwenn B. The Moon in the Water: Understanding Tanizaki, Kawabata, & Mishima. LC 79-14994. 380p. (C). 1992. reprint ed. pap. text 20.00 (*0-8248-1476-2*) UH Pr.

Petersen, Hanne. Home Knitted Law. Norms & Values in Gendered Rule-Making. (Socio-Legal Studies). (Illus.). 180p. 1996. text 78.95 (*1-85521-837-2*, Pub. by Dartmth Pub) Ashgate Pub Co.

Petersen, Hanne, ed. Love & Law in Europe. 158p. 1998. 76.95 (*1-85521-994-8*, K487.P75L68, Pub. by Ashgate Pub) Ashgate Pub Co.

Petersen, Hanne & Poppel, Birger, eds. Dependency, Autonomy, Sustainability in the Arctic. LC 98-31061. 7p. 1998. text 76.95 (*1-84014-701-6*, Pub. by Ashgate Pub) Ashgate Pub Co.

P

An Asterisk (*) at the beginning of an entry indicates that the title is appearing for the first time.

Petersen, Hanne & Zahle, Henrik, eds. Legal Polycentricity: Consequences of Pluralism in Law. (Illus.). 248p. 1995. text 81.95 (*1-85521-662-0*, Pub. by Dartmth Pub) Ashgate Pub Co.

Petersen, Ingemar S., jt. ed. see Kellaway, Peter.

Petersen, Irene. Great Wire Jewelry: Projects & Techniques. LC 98-40919. (Illus.). 60p. 1999. pap. 14.95 (*1-57990-093-3*, Pub. by Lark Books) Random.

Petersen, J. Allan. El Matrimonio a Prueba de Infidelidad. (Serie Guia de Bolsillo - Pocket Guides Ser.).Tr. of High Fidelity Marriage. (SPA.). 78p. 1987. pap. 2.79 (*0-8423-6513-3*, 498043) Editorial Unilit.

— The Myth of the Greener Grass. rev. ed. 233p. 1984. pap. 9.99 (*0-8423-4651-1*) Tyndale Hse.

Petersen, J. Allan, jt. auth. see Petersen, Evelyn.

Petersen, J. L., jt. ed. see Di Vecchia, P.

***Petersen, James.** The Century of Sex: Playboy's History of the Sexual Revolution, 1900-1999. Heffner, Hugh, ed. LC 99-23668. (Illus.). 560p. 1999. 35.00 (*0-8021-1652-3*, Grove) Grove-Atltic.

Petersen, James B. Archaeological Testing at the Sharrow Site: A Deeply Stratified Early to Late Holocene Cultural Sequence in Central Maine. (Occasional Publications in Maine Archaeology). (Illus.). 165p. (C). 1991. pap. text 15.00 (*0-935447-08-3*) ME Hist Preserv.

Petersen, James B., ed. Ceramic Analysis in the Northeast Part 11: Contribution to Methodology & Culture History. (Occasional Publications in Northeastern Anthropology: No. 9). (Illus.). 159p. 15.00 (*0-318-23458-0*) F Pierce College.

***Petersen, James C.** Stress Management Questionnaire: Thriving, Not Just Surviving, in a World of Stress. 32p. 2000. 14.95 (*0-9701881-0-2*) Assess & Devel.

Petersen, James C., ed. Citizen Participation in Science Policy. LC 84-246. 256p. 1984. pap. 17.95 (*0-87023-434-X*); lib. bdg. 30.00 (*0-87023-433-1*) U of Mass Pr.

Petersen, James F., jt. ed. see Boehm, Richard G.

Petersen, James R. 365 Ways to Improve Your Sex Life: From the Files of the Playboy Advisor. 320p. 1996. pap. 13.95 (*0-452-27576-8*, Plume) Dutton Plume.

Petersen, Jim. Church Without Walls: Moving Beyond Traditional Boundaries. LC 91-67292. 240p. (Orig.). 1991. pap. 12.00 (*0-89109-663-9*) NavPress.

— Lifestyle Discipleship: The Challenge of Following Jesus in Today's World. LC 93-39063. 192p. (Orig.). 1994. pap. 12.00 (*0-89109-775-9*) NavPress.

— Living Proof: Sharing the Gospel Naturally. rev. ed. LC 88-63874. 252p. 1989. pap. 12.00 (*0-89109-561-6*) NavPress.

Petersen, Joan M. The Diaglogues of Gregory the Great in Their Late Antique Cultural Background. xxiv, 227p. pap. text 29.14 (*0-88844-069-3*) Brill Academic Pubs.

Petersen, Joan M., tr. Handmaids of the Lord. (Cistercian Studies: No. 143). 441p. 1996. 49.95 (*0-87907-543-0*); pap. 24.95 (*0-87907-743-3*) Cistercian Pubns.

Petersen, John E., jt. auth. see Twentieth Century Fund, Task Force on Municipal Bo.

Petersen, John L. Out of the Blue: Wild Cards & Other Big Future Surprises. Crockett, Ellen et al, eds. (Orig.). (C). 1997. pap. 13.95 (*0-9659027-2-2*) Arlington Inst.

— Out of the Blue: Wild Cards & Other Big Future Surprises. LC 99-47088. (Orig.). 2000. pap. 16.95 (*1-56833-135-5*) Madison Bks UPA.

***Petersen, John R. & Mohammad, Amin A., eds.** Clinical & Forensic Applications of Capillary Electrophoresis. (Pathology & Laboratory Medicine Ser.). 400p. 2000. 125.00 (*0-89603-645-6*) Humana.

Petersen, John R., jt. ed. see Bissell, Michael G.

Petersen-Jones, Simon M. & Crispin, Sheila M., eds. Manual of Small Animal Ophthalmology. (Illus.). 304p. 1994. pap. text 82.95 (*0-905214-21-8*, Pub. by BSAVA) Iowa St U Pr.

Petersen, Judy, jt. auth. see Lang, Donna.

Petersen, Julie K. Data & Telecommunication Dictionary. LC 98-46077. (Advanced & Emerging Communications Technologies Ser.). (Illus.). 832p. 1999. boxed set 79.95 (*0-8493-9591-7*) CRC Pr.

Petersen, Julius, jt. auth. see Hecker, Max.

Petersen, K., jt. auth. see Lerche, I.

Petersen, Karin & Zwaenepoel, Willy, eds. Proceedings of the 2nd Annual Symposium on Operating Systems Design & Implementation (OSDI '96) 300p. (Orig.). 1996. pap. 27.00 (*1-880446-82-0*) USENIX Assn.

Petersen, Karin, jt. auth. see Petersen, Evelyn.

Petersen, Karl E. Ergodic Theory. (Illus.). 344p. (C). 1990. pap. text 39.95 (*0-521-38997-6*) Cambridge U Pr.

Petersen, Karl E. & Salama, Ibrahim A., eds. Ergodic Theory & Its Connections with Harmonic Analysis: Proceedings of the 1993 Alexandria Conference. (London Mathematical Society Lecture Note Ser.: No. 205). 445p. (C). 1995. pap. text 39.95 (*0-521-45999-0*) Cambridge U Pr.

Petersen, Kate O. On the Sources of the Nonne Prestes Tale. 144p. (C). 1966. lib. bdg. 75.00 (*0-8383-0673-X*) M S G Haskell Hse.

— Sources of the Parson's Tale. LC 72-954. reprint ed. 27.50 (*0-404-04997-4*) AMS Pr.

Petersen, Kathy, ed. Oil Shale: The Environmental Challenges III. (Proceedings of an International Symposium Ser.: No III). (Illus.). 261p. 1983. text 11.00 (*0-918062-54-3*) Colo Sch Mines.

Petersen, Kathy K., jt. ed. see Chappell, Willard R.

Petersen, Keith. Historical Celebrations: A Handbook for Organizers of Diamond Jubilees, Centennials, & Other Community Anniversaries. LC 86-7244. 1986. pap. 14.95 (*0-931406-13-7*) U of Idaho Pr.

Petersen, Keith C. Company Town: Potlatch, Idaho, & the Potlatch Lumber Company. LC 87-14980. (Illus.). 284p. (C). 1987. pap. 15.95 (*0-87422-037-8*) Wash St U Pr.

— Educating in the American West: One Hundred Years at Lewis-Clark State College. LC 93-70922. 394p. 1993. 35.00 (*1-881090-02-7*); pap. 19.95 (*1-881090-01-9*) Confluence Pr.

Petersen, Keith C. & Reed, Mary E. Discovering Washington: A Guide to State & Local History. LC 89-5575. (Illus.). 87p. 1989. pap. 7.50 (*0-87422-059-9*) Wash St U Pr.

Petersen, Kerry, ed. Law & Medicine: A Special Issue of Law in Context. 1994. pap. 19.95 (*1-86324-025-X*, Pub. by LaTrobe Univ) Intl Spec Bk.

Petersen, Kerry, jt. ed. see Freckelton, Ian.

Petersen, Kerry A. Abortion Regimes. (Medico-Legal Issues Ser.). 201p. 1993. 78.95 (*1-85521-159-9*, Pub. by Dartmth Pub) Ashgate Pub Co.

Petersen, Kerry A., ed. Intersections: Women on Law, Medicine & Technology. LC 97-6072. (Medico-Legal Ser.). 256p. 1997. text 78.95 (*1-85521-882-8*, Pub. by Ashgate Pub) Ashgate Pub Co.

Petersen, Kirsten H., ed. Criticism & Ideology: Second African Writers' Conference, Stockholm, 1986. (Scandinavian Institute of African Studies: No. 20). 221p. 1988. 46.50 (*91-7106-276-9*, Pub. by Nordisk Afrikainstitutet) Coronet Bks.

Petersen, Kirsten Holst. Religion, Development & African Identity, No. 17. (Scandinavian Institute of African Studies). 163p. 1987. text 46.00 (*91-7106-263-7*, Pub. by Nordisk Afrikainstitutet) Coronet Bks.

Petersen, Klaus & Hutchinson, Allan C., eds. Interpreting Censorship in Canada. 464p. 1999. text 60.00 (*0-8020-4164-7*); pap. text 29.95 (*0-8020-8026-X*) U of Toronto Pr.

Petersen, Kris & Matthew, Brian. Winning on the Wheel: An Unofficial Guide to Getting on & Winning at Wheel of Fortune. rev. ed. LC 96-80010. vi, 159p. 1997. pap. 19.95 (*0-9653049-1-4*) BK Enterprises.

Petersen, Kristen, ed. see Church, Beverly.

Petersen, Kurt. The Maquiladora Revolution in Guatemala. LC 92-23067. (Occasional Paper Ser.: Vol. 2). xvi, 244p. (Orig.). (C). 1992. pap. text 7.95 (*1-881862-00-3*) O H Schell Yale Law Schl.

Petersen, L. Teacher Resource Kit. 1992. 14.95 (*0-7935-1230-1*, 00860100) H Leonard.

Petersen, LaMar. The Creation of the Book of Morman: A Historical Inquiry. LC 98-11620. 1998. text 16.95 (*1-890686-00-X*) Freethinker.

Petersen, Lance W. The Kenai Peninsula College History. 118p. 1992. pap. 5.00 (*0-9641118-0-2*, KPC Pubs) Kenai Peninsula.

Petersen, Laura M. & Lowry, Thea S., eds. A Man of Letters: Montgomery Remembered. LC 93-71932. 125p. (Orig.). 1993. pap. 15.00 (*0-918704-03-0*) Fels & Firn.

***Petersen, Leiva, et al.** Prosopographia Imperii Romani Saec. I. II. III. Editio altera, Pars VII. Fasciculus 1. 144p. 2000. 61.00 (*3-11-016743-3*) De Gruyter.

Petersen, Lindy. Stop & Think Learning. 1995. pap. 65.00 (*0-86431-173-7*, Pub. by Aust Council Educ Res) St Mut.

Petersen, Lindy & Gannoni, Anne F. Manual for Social Skills Training in Young People with Parent & Teacher Programmes. (C). 1992. 100.00 (*0-86431-116-8*, Pub. by Aust Council Educ Res) St Mut.

— Teachers Manual for Training Social Skills While Managing Student Behaviour. 1992. pap. 120.00 (*0-86431-117-6*, Pub. by Aust Council Educ Res) St Mut.

Petersen-Lowary, Sheila. The 5th Dimension: Channels to a New Reality. 288p. (Orig.). 1997. pap. 13.00 (*0-9655457-0-9*) Theo Press.

Petersen, Marc. This Is My Brother Talking. 36p. 1998. pap. write for info. (*0-9638516-4-0*, Black Dirt) Elgin Comm Coll.

Petersen, Marie, jt. auth. see Mueller-Joseph, Laura.

Petersen, Marilyn D. & White, Diana L., eds. Health Care of the Elderly: An Information Sourcebook. 560p. (C). 1989. text 69.95 (*0-8039-3335-5*) Sage.

— Health Care of the Elderly: An Information Sourcebook. LC 88-6551. (Illus.). 576p. 1989. reprint ed. pap. 178.60 (*0-608-01726-4*, 206238300003) Bks Demand.

Petersen, Marjorie. Red Sky at Night: Circling the Pacific in Stornoway. LC 94-67446. (Illus.). (Orig.). 1994. pap. 12.95 (*0-9642394-1-8*) Paxi Press.

Petersen, Mark D., jt. auth. see Sink, Charles M.

***Petersen, Meg, et al.** Shifts of Vision: An Anthology of Teachers' Writing. 147p. 1999. pap. 9.95 (*0-9666573-3-0*) Plymouth Writers.

Petersen, Morris S., et al. Historical Geology - North America. 2nd ed. 240p. (C). 1980. text. write for info. (*0-697-05062-9*, WCB McGr Hill) McGrw-H Hghr Educ.

Petersen, Morris S., jt. auth. see Rigby, J. Keith.

Petersen, Neal H. American Intelligence Operations, 1775-1990: A Bibliographical Guide. LC 92-16324. (New War - Peace Bibliographical Ser.: Vol. 2). 1992. 49.95 (*0-941690-45-8*) Regina Bks.

Petersen, Neal H., ed. see Dulles, Allen W.

Petersen, Niels E., jt. auth. see Jensen, Finn.

Petersen, Nils H., jt. ed. see Lille, Eva L.

Petersen, P. J. Can You Keep a Secret? LC 97-6148. (Illus.). 80p. (J). (gr. 2-4). 1997. 15.99 (*0-525-45840-9*) NAL.

***Petersen, P. J.** Can You Keep a Secret? (Illus.). 112p. (J). (gr. 2-5). 2000. pap. 3.99 (*0-14-130706-4*, PuffinBks) Peng Put Young Read.

— Can You Keep a Secret? (Illus.). (J). 2000. 9.34 (*0-606-18392-2*) Turtleback.

Petersen, P. J. Freshman Detective. (J). 1992. mass mkt. 3.99 (*0-440-80351-9*) Dell.

— I Hate Camping. (Puffin Chapters Ser.). 1998. 9.09 (*0-606-13504-9*, Pub. by Turtleback) Demco.

— I Hate Company. (Puffin Chapters Ser.). 1998. 9.09 (*0-606-13505-7*, Pub. by Turtleback) Demco.

***Petersen, P. J.** I Hate Weddings. LC 99-48165. (Illus.). (J). 2000. 15.99 (*0-525-46327-5*, Dutton Child) Peng Put Young Read.

Petersen, P. J. I Want Answers & a Parachute. LC 92-38262. (Illus.). 64p. (YA). (gr. 2-6). 1993. mass mkt. 13.00 (*0-671-86577-3*) S&S Bks Yung.

— Liars. LC 91-28490. 176p. (YA). (gr. 7 up). 1992. 15.00 (*0-671-75035-6*) S&S Bks Yung.

— Liars. (J). 1995. 9.30 (*0-606-07786-3*) Turtleback.

***Petersen, P. J.** The Sub. (J). 2000. pap. 3.99 (*0-14-130709-9*, PuffinBks) Peng Put Young Read.

Petersen, P. J. The Sub. (J). 1995. 10.09 (*0-606-08212-3*, Pub. by Turtleback) Demco.

Petersen, Patricia. Magali/Magali: An Aztec Legend about Good Fortune (Una Ieyenja Azteca Sobre La Buena Fortuna) LC 98-14834. (Cuentos en Dos Idiomas (Tales in Two Languages) Ser.). (Illus.). 32p. (J). (gr. 3-6). 1998. 16.95 (*1-56492-250-2*) Laredo.

Petersen, Paul, et al. The Essential Cross-Country Skier: A Step-by-Step Guide. LC 99-23369. (Illus.). 144p. 1999. pap. 15.95 (*0-07-049662-5*) McGraw.

Petersen, Paul, jt. auth. see Hawkins, Jimmy.

Petersen, Paulann. The Animal Bride: Poems by Paulann Petersen. LC 94-34635. 35p. (Orig.). 1994. pap. 7.00 (*0-932264-05-0*) Trask Hse Bks.

— Fabrication. 26p. 1996. 5.00 (*0-614-30124-6*) Skydog OR.

Petersen, Penny A. An Alzheimer's Chronicle: Letters to My Aunt. (Illus.). 224p. (Orig.). 1997. pap. 14.00 (*0-9655969-0-7*) Desert State.

Petersen, Per S., ed. Literary Pedagogics after Deconstruction: Scenarios & Perspectives in the Teaching of English Literature. (The Dolphin Ser.: No. 22). 112p. (C). 1992. pap. 19.95 (*87-7288-372-3*, Pub. by Aarhus Univ Pr) David Brown.

Petersen, Per S. & Westarp, Karl-Heinz, eds. British Drama in the Eighties: Texts & Contexts. (Dolphin Ser.: No. 14). 220p. (Orig.). (C). 1986. pap. 19.95 (*0-614-11379-2*, Pub. by Aarhus Univ Pr) David Brown.

Petersen, Peter. Riemannian Geometry, Vol. 171. LC 97-5786. (Graduate Texts in Mathematics Ser.). 416p. 1997. 49.95 (*0-387-98212-4*) Spr-Verlag.

Petersen, Peter, et al, eds. Buchner-Opern: Georg Buchner in der Musik des 20. Jahrhunderts. (Hamburger Jahrbuch fur Musikwissenschaft Ser.: Bd. 14). (GER., Illus.). 272p. 1997. 63.95 (*3-631-30958-9*) P Lang Pubng.

***Petersen, Peter & Rosing, Helmut.** 50 Jahre Musikwissenschaftliches Institut in Hamburg: Bestandsaufnahme aktuelle Forschung Ausblick. 1999. 79.95 (*3-631-35562-9*) P Lang Pubng.

Petersen, Peter, jt. ed. see Grove, Karsten.

Petersen, Phil. Good If Not Great Living with Lung Disease. 4th ed. 124p. 1999. pap. 14.50 (*0-9621726-4-2*) Raven Pubs.

— Good If Not Great Travel with Oxygen. 3rd rev. ed. Lee, Mary & Paisley, Pam, eds. 64p. (Orig.). 1996. pap. 5.95 (*0-9621726-3-4*) Raven Pubs.

Petersen, Philip R. Arctic Roads & Summer Sun: Business Supplement. rev. ed. LC 89-831737. (Illus.). 108p. 1990. pap. 9.95 (*0-9621726-1-8*) Raven Pubs.

Petersen, P.J. My Worst Friend. LC 98-3219. (J). (gr. 3-4). 1998. 15.99 (*0-525-46028-4*, Dutton Child) Peng Put Young Read.

Petersen, Polly A. Breaking Through... Alternative Pathways to Healing. Thomason, Frank J., ed. (Illus.). 184p. 1997. pap. 18.95 (*0-9655549-1-0*) Table Top.

Petersen Publishing Company Staff, jt. auth. see Hall, Al.

Petersen, R. H. Ramaria, Subgenus Lentoramaria, with Emphasis on North American Taxa. (Bibliotheca Mycologica Ser.: No. 43). 1975. text 40.00 (*3-7682-0961-X*) Lubrecht & Cramer.

Petersen, Randy. The Christian Book of Lists. LC 97-26578. 1997. pap. 10.99 (*0-8423-0365-0*) Tyndale Hse.

— The Complete Book of Bible Puzzles, No. 1. 249p. 1992. pap. 7.99 (*0-8423-1067-3*) Tyndale Hse.

— The Family Book of Bible Fun. 1999. pap. text 9.99 (*0-8423-3151-4*) Tyndale Hse.

— Fear Not! Be Outrageously Courageous Student Journal. (1995 50-Day Spiritual Adventure Ser.). (Illus.). 80p. (Orig.). (YA). (gr. 7-12). 1994. pap. text, student ed. 4.95 (*1-879050-48-X*) Chapel of Air.

— 50 Days to Welcome Christ to Our Church: Youth Journal for the 50-Day Adventure Series. (1991 50-Day Spiritual Adventure Ser.). (Illus.). 64p. (Orig.). (YA). (gr. 7-12). 1990. pap. text, student ed. 3.95 (*1-879050-01-3*) Chapel of Air.

— Getting It Together: How to Energize Your Relationships with Other Believers. (1992 50-Day Spiritual Adventure Ser.). (Illus.). 64p. (Orig.). (YA). (gr. 7-12). 1991. pap. text, student ed. 4.95 (*1-879050-04-8*) Chapel of Air.

Petersen, Randy. I'm So Confused: Following Christ When Life Gets Crazy. Hancock, Jim, ed. (Nineteen Ninety-Six 50-Day Spiritual Adventure Ser.). (Illus.). 80p. (Orig.). (YA). (gr. 7-12). 1995. pap., wbk. ed. 6.00 (*1-879050-71-4*) Chapel of Air.

Petersen, Randy. The Official Frequent Flyer Guidebook. 3rd ed. 495p. (Orig.). 1994. pap. 14.99 (*1-882994-01-9*) AirPress.

— The Official Frequent Flyer Guidebook. 4th ed. 500p. (Orig.). 1995. pap. 14.99 (*1-882994-02-7*) AirPress.

— Survival Skills: Living Strong As a Christian When Times Get Tough. (1993 50-Day Spiritual Adventure Ser.). (Illus.). 64p. (Orig.). (YA). (gr. 7-12). 1992. pap. text, student ed. 4.99 (*1-879050-08-0*) Chapel of Air.

Petersen, Randy & Emmert, Byron. Beyond Your Wildest Dreams: Daring to Risk with God Student Journal. (1994 50-Day Spiritual Adventure Ser.). (Illus.). 80p. (Orig.). (YA). (gr. 7-12). 1993. pap. text, student ed. 4.99 (*1-879050-15-3*) Chapel of Air.

Petersen, Randy & Whiteman, Thomas. Hombres Que Aman Muy Poco.Tr. of Men Who Love Too Little. (SPA.). 192p. 1996. 8.99 (*0-88113-430-9*, B001-4309) Caribe Betania.

— Victim of Love? How You Can Break the Cycle of Bad Relationships. LC 98-12182. 224p. 1998. pap. 13.00 (*1-57683-053-5*) NavPress.

Petersen, Randy, et al. In the House: Turning Your Church Inside Out. (Nineteen Ninety-Seven 50-Day Spiritual Adventure Ser.). (Illus.). 80p. (YA). (gr. 7-12). 1996. pap., student ed., wbk. ed. 6.00 (*1-57849-001-4*) Chapel of Air.

— Power-Up: Kicking Your Faith to a New Level Student Journal. (Nineteen Ninety-Eight Fifty-Day Spiritual Adventure Ser.). 80p. (YA). (gr. 7-12). 1997. wbk. ed. 6.00 (*1-57849-040-5*) Mainstay Church.

Petersen, Randy, et al. The Real Deal: Student Journal. (Nineteen Ninety Nine Fifty-Day Spiritual Adventure Ser.). (Illus.). 80p. (YA). 1998. 7.00 (*1-57849-107-X*) Mainstay Church.

Petersen, Randy, jt. auth. see Novotni, Michele.

Petersen, Randy, jt. auth. see Petersen, William J.

Petersen, Randy, jt. auth. see Whiteman, Thomas.

Petersen, Randy, jt. auth. see Whiteman, Tom.

Petersen, Randy, jt. auth. see Williams, Scott P.

Petersen, Randy, ed. see Spurgeon, Charles H.

Petersen, Ray A. Consumer Health Decisions. (Health Science Ser.). 512p. (C). 1998. pap. 40.00 (*0-86720-936-4*) Jones & Bartlett.

Petersen, Renee, jt. auth. see Petersen, William.

***Petersen, Richard.** Linux. 3rd ed. (Unix Tools Ser.). 900p. 1999. pap. 39.99 (*0-07-212161-0*) Osborne-McGraw.

Petersen, Richard. Linux: The Complete Reference. (Complete Reference Ser.). 816p. 1996. pap. text 39.95 (*0-07-882189-4*) Osborne-McGraw.

— Linux: The Complete Reference. 2nd ed. LC 98-116323. (Complete Reference Ser.). 1008p. 1997. pap. 49.99 (*0-07-882461-3*) Osborne-McGraw.

***Petersen, Richard.** Linux: The Complete Reference. 3rd ed. 929p. 1999. pap. 39.99 (*0-07-212164-5*) Osborne-McGraw.

Petersen, Richard. Linux Programmer's Reference. LC 98-216387. 303p. 1998. pap. 16.99 (*0-07-882587-3*) Osborne-McGraw.

***Petersen, Richard.** Linux Programmer's Reference. 2nd ed. 443p. 1999. pap. 19.99 (*0-07-212355-9*) McGraw.

Petersen, Richard. New Insights to Antiquity: A Drawing Aside of the Veil. LC 97-77780. (Illus.). xiv, 336p. 1998. 27.95 (*0-9662134-1-6*) Engwald & Co.

— On the Irregular Motion of the Moon. 32p. 1999. 3.95 (*0-9662134-2-4*) Engwald & Co.

***Petersen, Richard.** Red Hat Linux: Complete Reference. (Complete Reference Ser.). 2000. pap. 39.99 (*0-07-212537-3*) Osborne-McGraw.

Petersen, Richard G. The Lost Cities of Cibola. 292p. 1980. 5.95 (*0-8199-0790-1*, Frncscn Herld) Franciscan Pr.

Petersen, Richard L. UNIX Clearly Explained. LC 98-15665. (Clearly Explained Ser.). (Illus.). 691p. (C). 1998. pap. text 39.95 (*0-12-552130-8*) Acad Pr.

— UNIX Networking Clearly Explained. (Clearly Explained Ser.). (Illus.). 608p. (C). 1999. pap. 39.95 (*0-12-552145-6*) Morgan Kaufmann.

Petersen-Rigby. Interpreting Earth History. 5th ed. 1993. teacher ed. 22.81 (*0-697-10172-X*) McGraw.

— Interpreting Earth History. 6th ed. LC 98-214486. 240p. 1998. spiral bd. 47.19 (*0-697-28290-2*) McGraw.

Petersen, Robert A. California Tax Handbook: 1996 Edition. rev. ed. Curemmeng, Jose, Jr., ed. 960p. 1995. pap. text 25.95 (*0-7811-0118-2*) Res Inst Am.

Petersen, Robert A. & Curammeng, Jose, Jr. California Tax Handbook, 1995. rev. ed. 944p. 1994. pap. text 24.95 (*0-7811-0093-3*) Res Inst Am.

Petersen, Robert C. Childhood & Adolescent Drug Abuse: A Physicians Guide to Office Practice. rev. ed. LC 87-70131. 55p. 1991. pap. 3.00 (*0-942348-20-6*) Am Council Drug Ed.

Petersen, Robert M. Alleys of the Heart. 130p. 1988. 16.95 (*0-938493-11-6*) Hulogosi Inc.

Petersen, Robert P., jt. ed. see Licata, Salvatore J.

Petersen, Rodney L. & Pater, Calvin Augustine, eds. The Contentious Triangle: Church, State, & University : A Festschrift in Honor of Professor George Huntston Williams. LC 99-17108. 1p. 1999. 45.00 (*0-943549-58-2*) Truman St Univ.

Petersen, Rodney L., ed. Christianity & Civil Society: Theological Education for Public Life. LC 94-43405. (Boston Theological Institute Ser.: Vol. 4). 192p. reprint ed. pap. 59.60 (*0-608-20241-X*, 207150000012) Bks Demand.

Petersen, Roger, jt. auth. see Burr, Carole Reid.

Petersen, Roger, jt. ed. see Bowen, John.

Petersen, Roger G. Agricultural Field Experiments: Design & Analysis. (Books in Soils, Plants & the Environment: Vol. 31). (Illus.). 430p. 1994. text 190.00 (*0-8247-8912-1*) Dekker.

— Design & Analysis of Experiments. (Statistics Ser.: 66). (Illus.). 448p. 1985. text 65.00 (*0-8247-7340-3*) Dekker.

Petersen, Ronald C., jt. ed. see Yanagihara, Takehiko.

Petersen, Ronald H. The Clavarioid Fungi of New Zealand. (Illus.). 170p. 1988. pap. 65.00 (*0-477-02514-5*) Lubrecht & Cramer.

— The Genus Clavulinopsis in North America. (Mycologia Memoirs Ser.: No. 3). (Illus.). 39p. 1968. pap. text 12.50 (*0-945345-38-0*) Lubrecht & Cramer.

Petersen, Ronald H., ed. Evolution in the Higher Basidiomycetes: An International Symposium. LC 73-100410. 592p. reprint ed. pap. 183.60 (*0-608-14035-X*, 202222100025) Bks Demand.

Petersen, Ronald H., jt. auth. see Wise, Kenneth.

Petersen, Sandy & Willis, Lynn. Call of Cthulhu: Horror Roleplaying in the Worlds of H. P. Lovecraft, 1. 5th rev. ed. (Call of Cthulhu Roleplaying Ser.: Vol. 2376). (Illus.). 288p. (C). 1998. pap. 29.95 (*1-56882-134-4*) Chaosium.

Petersen, Sandy, jt. auth. see Brody, Brian.

P

***Petersen-Schepelern, Elsa.** Clay Pot Cooking: From Tandoori to Tagine. LC 99-28216. 64p. (gr. 11). 1999. 15.95 (0-7370-2017-2) T-L Custom Pub.

Petersen-Schepelern, Elsa. Coolers & Summer Cocktails. LC 98-52938. (Illus.). 64p. (gr. 11). 1999. 15.95 (0-7370-2014-8) T-L Custom Pub.

***Petersen-Schepelern, Elsa.** Finger Food. LC 99-26577. (Illus.). 144p. (gr. 11). 1999. 19.95 (0-7370-2022-9) T-L Custom Pub.

— Juices & Tonics. 2000. 12.95 (1-84172-051-8) Ryland Peters & Small.

Petersen-Schepelern, Elsa. Smoothies & Other Blended Drinks. LC 98-52939. (Illus.). 64p. (gr. 11). 1999. 15.95 (0-7370-2015-6) T-L Custom Pub.

***Petersen-Schepelern, Elsa.** Soups: Simple Recipes for All Seasons. LC 99-28217. 64p. (gr. 11). 1999. 15.95 (0-7370-2018-0) T-L Custom Pub.

Petersen-Schepelern, Elsa. Wok: Dishes from China, Japan & Southeast Asia. LC 98-54426. (Illus.). 64p. (gr. 11). 1999. 15.95 (0-7370-2016-4) T-L Custom Pub.

Petersen, Sheila. A Special Way to Care: A Guide for Neighbors, Friends, & Community in their Efforts to Provide Financial & Emotional Support for Terminally & Catastrophically Ill Children. 180p. (Orig.). 1988. pap. write for info. (0-9619785-0-3) Friends Karen.

Petersen, Sherrie, ed. see Eaton, Christopher.

***Petersen, Silke.** Zerstort die Werke der Weiblichkeit: Maria Magdalena, Salome und andere Juengerinnen Jesu in christlich-gnostischen Schriften. (Nag Hammadi & Manichaean Studies: 48). (GER.). 392p. 1999. text 210.00 (90-04-11449-1) Brill Academic Pubs.

Petersen, Steffen B., et al, eds. Carbohydrate Bioengineering: Proceedings of an International Conference, Elsinore, Denmark, 23-26 April, 1995. (Progress in Biotechnology Ser.: Vol. 10). 384p. 1995. 210.50 (0-444-82223-2) Elsevier.

Petersen, Steffen B., jt. ed. see Woolley, Paul.

Petersen, Stephanie, jt. auth. see Parente, Diane.

Petersen, Stephen R. Quantum Practicle Internet. 1997. pap. 7.95 (1-890711-18-7) Empyrean Quest.

***Petersen, Sue.** My Poetry Book. 48p. 1999. pap. 9.95 (0-9660705-6-9) Dykema Pub Co.

Petersen, Suni & Straub, Ronald. School Crisis Survival Guide: Management Techniques & Materials for Counselors & Administrators. 216p. 1991. pap. text 29.95 (0-87628-806-9) Ctr Appl Res.

Petersen, Suni, jt. auth. see Wiggins, Frances K.

Petersen, Svend & Filler, Louis. A Statistical History of the American Presidential Elections: With Supplementary Tables Covering 1968 to 1980. LC 81-6348. 250p. 1981. reprint ed. lib. bdg. 41.50 (0-313-22952-X, PESH, Greenwood Pr) Greenwood.

Petersen, Terri. Low on the Go: Quick Lowfat Recipes for Busy People. 2nd rev. ed. (Illus.). 234p. 1991. pap. 15.95 (0-9639826-0-5) Lean for Life.

Petersen, Theano, ed. 1998 Pacific Northwest Festivals Directory & Resource Guide. 232p. 1997. pap. 14.50 (0-9631954-6-8) NW Folklife.

Petersen, Thor. Using the IBM PC-AT. (Illus.). 144p. 1987. 17.95 (0-13-939471-0) P-H.

Petersen, Toni, ed. Art & Architecture Thesaurus Sourcebook. (Occasional Papers: No. 10). (Illus.). 160p. (Orig.). 1996. pap. 20.00 (0-942740-15-7) Art Libs Soc.

Petersen, Toni & Molholt, Pat, eds. Beyond the Book: Extending MARC for Subject Access. (Professional Librarian Ser.). 230p. 1990. 40.00 (0-8161-1924-4, Hall Reference); 30.00 (0-8161-1925-2, Hall Reference) Macmillan.

***Petersen, Tore T.** The Middle East Between the Great Powers: Anglo-American Conflict & Cooperation, 1952-7. LC 00-26980. 2000. write for info. (0-312-23481-3) St Martin.

Petersen, Troels. Elements of Mathematica Programming. 1996. 45.95 incl. disk (0-387-94590-3) Spr-Verlag.

Petersen, Troels, ed. Elements of Mathematica Programming. 1996. 45.95 incl. disk (0-614-14502-3) Spr-Verlag.

Petersen, Ulrich, jt. auth. see Holland, Heinrich D.

Petersen, Vibeke R. Kursbuch, 1965 to 1975: Social, Political & Literary Perspectives of West Germany. (Illus.). X, 207p. (C). 1988. text 35.00 (0-8204-0737-2) P Lang Pubng.

Petersen, Vinca. No System. 1999. pap. text 19.95 (3-88243-645-X) Steidl.

Petersen, W. The Politics of Population. 1990. 16.50 (0-8446-0845-9) Peter Smith.

Petersen, W., jt. auth. see Buck, Carl D.

Petersen, Wayne R. The Audubon Society Pocket Guide to North American SongBirds & Familiar Backyard Birds: Eastern Region. LC 93-21254. (Audubon Society Pocket Guides Ser.). (Illus.). 1994. pap. 9.00 (0-679-74926-8) Knopf.

Petersen, Wayne R., jt. auth. see Veit, Richard R.

Petersen, William. Ethnicity Counts. LC 96-37513. 482p. 1997. text 49.95 (1-56000-296-4) Transaction Pubs.

— From Birth to Death: A Primer in Demography for the 21st Century. LC 99-56520. 233p. 1999. 39.95 (0-7658-0006-3) Transaction Pubs.

— Malthus. LC 78-31479. 312p. reprint ed. pap. 96.80 (0-7837-2311-3, 205739900004) Bks Demand.

— Malthus: Founder of Modern Demography. LC 98-19058. 332p. 1998. pap. 29.95 (0-7658-0481-6) Transaction Pubs.

— Masonic Quiz. 17.95 (0-685-22032-X) Wehman.

Petersen, William & Petersen, Renee. Dictionary of Demography: Biographies, 2 vols., Set. LC 83-12567. 1365p. 1985. lib. bdg. 195.00 (0-313-21419-0, PDD/) Greenwood.

— Dictionary of Demography: Biographies, 2 vols., Vol. 1. LC 83-12567. xx, 1365p. 1985. lib. bdg. 195.00 (0-313-25137-1, PDD/01) Greenwood.

— Dictionary of Demography: Biographies, 2 vols., Vol. 2. LC 83-12567. xx, 1365p. 1985. lib. bdg. 195.00 (0-313-25138-X, PDD/02) Greenwood.

— Dictionary of Demography: Multilingual Glossary. LC 85-27055. 259p. 1985. lib. bdg. 150.00 (0-313-25139-8, PDG/, Greenwood Pr) Greenwood.

— Dictionary of Demography: Terms, Concepts, & Institutions, 2 vols., Set. LC 83-12571. (Illus.). 1772p. 1986. lib. bdg. 195.00 (0-313-24134-1, PDE/) Greenwood.

— Dictionary of Demography: Terms, Concepts, & Institutions, 2 vols., Vol. 1. LC 83-12571. (Illus.). 1772p. 1986. lib. bdg. 125.00 (0-313-25141-X, PDE/01) Greenwood.

— Dictionary of Demography: Terms, Concepts, & Institutions, 2 vols., Vol. 2. LC 83-12571. (Illus.). 1772p. 1986. lib. bdg. 125.00 (0-313-25142-8, PDE/02) Greenwood.

Petersen, William, et al. Concepts of Ethnicity. (Dimensions of Ethnicity Ser.). 160p. 1982. pap. 13.00 (0-674-15726-5) HUP.

Petersen, William J. O Discipulado de Timoteo. Orig. Title: The Discipling of Timothy. (POR.). 192p. 1986. pap. 5.95 (0-8297-0685-2) Vida Pubs.

— The One Year Book of Psalms. LC 99-38571. 1999. pap. text 14.99 (0-8423-4372-5) Tyndale Hse.

***Petersen, William J.** The One Year Book of Psalms. LC 99-38571. 700p. 1999. 19.99 (0-8423-4373-3) Tyndale Hse.

Petersen, William J. Steamboating on the Upper Mississippi. unabridged ed. (Illus.). 640p. 1995. reprint ed. pap. 15.95 (0-486-28844-7) Dover.

— Those Curious New Cults. LC 72-93700. vii, 214p. 1973. write for info. (0-87983-031-X) NTC Contemp Pub Co.

— 25 Surprising Marriages: Faith-Building Stories from the Lives of Famous Christians. 2nd rev. ed. LC 96-45565. 512p. (Orig.). (gr. 12). 1997. pap. 19.99 (0-8010-5753-1, Husbands & Wive) Baker Bks.

***Petersen, William J. & Petersen, Randy.** 100 Christian Books That Changed the Century. 224p. 2000. pap. 12.99 (0-8007-5735-1) Chosen Bks.

Petersen, William J. & Petersen, Randy. The One Year Book of Hymns. Brown, Robert K. & Norton, Mark R., eds. LC 94-43726. 1995. pap. 14.99 (0-8423-5072-1) Tyndale Hse.

Petersen, William J., ed. see Stalker, James.

Petersen, William L. Tatian's Diatessaron: Its Creation, Dissemination, Significance, & History in Scholarship. LC 94-2883. (Supplements to Vigiliae Christianae Ser.: Vol. 25). 1994. 96.00 (90-04-10034-2) Brill Academic Pubs.

— Tatian's Diatessaron: Its Creation, Dissemination, Significance, & History in Scholarship. LC 94-2883. (Supplements to Vigiliae Christianae Ser.: Vol. 25). xix, 555p. 1994. 164.00 (90-04-09469-5) Brill Academic Pubs.

Petersen, William L., et al, eds. Sayings of Jesus: Canonical & Non-Canonical: Essays in Honour of Tjitze Baarda. LC 97-34258. (Novum Testamentum, Supplements Ser.: No. 89). (Illus.). xxviii, 344p. 1997. 109.50 (90-04-10380-5) Brill Academic Pubs.

Petersens Hot Rod Magazine Staff. 50 Years of the Hot Rod. LC 98-34423. 192p. 1998. 29.95 (0-7603-0575-7) MBI Pubg.

— Hot Rod Magazine: The First 12 Issues. (Illus.). 160p. 1998. pap. 19.95 (0-7603-0638-9) MBI Pubg.

Petersham. The Story of David. (J). 1999. per. 5.99 (0-689-81400-3) S&S Childrens.

— The Story of Ruth & the Story of David. (J). 1999. per. 5.99 (0-689-81399-6) S&S Childrens.

Petersham, Maud & Petersham, Miska. Rooster Crows: A Book of American Rhymes & Jingles. LC 46-446. (Illus.). 64p. (J). (ps-2). 1969. lib. bdg. 16.00 (0-02-773100-6, Mac Bks Young Read) S&S Childrens.

Petersham, Maud Fuller. Rooster Crows: A Book of American Rhymes & Jingles. LC 87-1138. 1987. 12.15 (0-606-03450-1, Pub. by Turtleback) Demco.

Petersham, Miska, jt. auth. see Petersham, Maud.

Petersilia, Joan. Racial Disparities in the Criminal Justice System. LC 83-9777. 128p. 1983. pap. 10.00 (0-8330-0506-5, R-2947-NIC) Rand Corp.

Petersilia, Joan, ed. Community Corrections: Probation, Parole & Intermediate Sanctions. (Readings in Crime & Punishment Ser.). (Illus.). 240p. (C). 1997. pap. text 22.95 (0-19-510543-5) OUP.

— Community Corrections: Probations, Parole & Intermediate Sanctions. (Readings in Crime & Punishment Ser.). (Illus.). 240p. (C). 1997. text 52.00 (0-19-510542-7) OUP.

Petersilia, Joan, et al. Prison Versus Probation in California: Implications for Crime & Offender Recidivism. 63p. 1986. pap. 7.50 (0-8330-0738-6, R-3323-NIJ) Rand Corp.

Petersilia, Joan, jt. auth. see Wilson, James Q.

Petersilia, Joan, jt. ed. see Lane, Jodi.

Petersilia, Joan, jt. ed. see Wilson, James Q.

Petersmann. International Trade Law & the GATT/WTO Dispute Settlement System, Vol. STEL 11. LC 97-30437. 1997. 202.00 (90-411-0684-7) Kluwer Law Intl.

Petersmann, Ernst-Ulrich. The GATT/WTO Dispute Settlement System: International Law, International Organizations & Dispute Settlement, Vol. NLSP 23. LC 96-47563. (Nijhoff Law Specials Ser.). 368p. 1997. 99.00 (90-411-0933-1) Kluwer Law Intl.

— International & European Trade & Environmental Law after the Uruguay Round. (Nijhoff Law Specials Ser.). 1995. 80.00 (90-411-0857-2) Kluwer Law Intl.

Petersmann, Ernst-Ulrich & Hilf, Meinhard, eds. The New GATT Round of Multilateral Trade Negotiations: Legal & Economic Problems. 2nd rev. ed. (Studies in Transnational Economic Law: Vol. V). 648p. 1991. 168.00 (90-6544-518-8) Kluwer Law Intl.

Petersmann, Ernst-Ulrich, jt. ed. see Hilf, Meinhard.

Peterson. Anne of Green Gables. LC 98-27873. (Avonlea Ser.: No. 1). 32p. (YA). (gr. 5-8). 1999. pap. 4.95 (0-06-443535-0) HarpC Child Bks.

— A Biopsychosocial Approach/ Instructor's Resource Kit. 2nd ed. 1997. text 11.00 (0-673-54390-0) Addison-Wesley.

— A Biopsychosocial Approach/Supershell Macintosh. 2nd ed. 1996. text 49.69 (0-673-54382-X) Addison-Wesley.

— Calculus. (C). 2002. mass mkt. 60.00 (0-8273-8072-0) Delmar.

— Calculus with Analytical Geometry. (C). 1988. pap. 28.66 (0-06-045158-0) Addison-Wesley.

— Civil Litigation. LC 98-34334. 438p. 1998. pap. text 75.00 (0-13-787938-5) P-H.

— College Math Through Applications. (TRADE/TECH MATH). (C). 2002. pap. 55.00 (0-8273-8014-3) Delmar.

— College Mathematics Through Applications. LC 98-46896. (Medical Assisting Ser.). 1999. pap. 93.95 (0-7668-0230-2) Delmar.

— A Concise History of Christianity. 2nd ed. (Religion Ser.). 1998. pap. 43.95 (0-534-56079-2) Wadsworth Pub.

— Contemporary Issues in Interpersonal. 5th ed. 1995. pap. text 21.40 (0-536-58885-6) Pearson Custom.

— Conversations in the Rainforest. LC 99-88780. 2000. 65.00 (0-8133-3709-7) HarpC.

***Peterson.** Don't Forget Winona. LC 99-27255. 32p. (J). (ps-2). 2000. lib. bdg. 14.89 (0-06-027198-1) HarpC Child Bks.

Peterson. F G Ferns New. 1999. pap. 18.00 (0-395-97512-3) HM.

— Fabricating Authenticity. 1999. pap. 17.00 (0-226-66285-3) U Ch Pr.

— Field Guide to Birds of the East. large type ed. LC 99-20466. 1999. pap. 24.00 (0-395-96371-0) HM.

— Financial Management & Analysis. 2002. student ed. 14.25 (0-07-049694-3) McGraw.

***Peterson.** Inside IPO's. 2000. 21.95 (0-07-135885-4) McGraw.

Peterson. Intuitive Calculus. (C). 2002. pap. 40.00 (0-8273-8071-2) Delmar.

— Jane Goodall. 2000. 28.00 (0-395-86043-1) HM.

— Job Opportunities in Business, 1997. 4th ed. 344p. 1996. pap. 21.95 (1-56079-646-4) Petersons.

— Job Opportunities in Engineering & Technology, 1997. 4th ed. 384p. 1996. pap. 21.95 (1-56079-647-2) Petersons.

— Job Opportunities in Health Care, 1997. 4th ed. 224p. 1996. pap. 21.95 (1-56079-648-0) Petersons.

— Managerial Economics. 4th ed. (C). 1998. pap. text, student ed. 21.33 (0-13-010296-2) P-H.

— Marketing Action. Date not set. pap. text, teacher ed. write for info. (0-314-36530-3) West Pub.

— Math for Automotive Trade. 3rd ed. 320p. (C). 1995. mass mkt. 43.95 (0-8273-6712-0) Delmar.

— Math for the Automotive Trade. (Trade/Tech Math Ser.). 1983. pap. 16.95 (0-538-33020-1) S-W Pub.

— Math for the Automotive Trade. 2nd ed. (Trade/Tech Math Ser.). 1989. pap., teacher ed. 14.00 (0-8273-3555-5) Delmar.

— Mathematics for the Automotive Trades. 3rd ed. (Trade/Tech Math Ser.). 1996. teacher ed. 15.00 (0-8273-6713-9) Delmar.

***Peterson.** Norton Reader. 10th ed. LC 99-33320. 1999. pap. 26.50 (0-393-97384-0) Norton.

Peterson. Peterson's Guide to MBA Programs, 1997. 1084p. 1996. pap. text 21.95 (1-56079-643-X) Petersons.

— Pollyanna. (J). Date not set. write for info. (0-06-028226-6) HarpC Child Bks.

— Pollyanna. 32p. (J). (gr. k-4). Date not set. pap. 4.95 (0-06-443536-9) HarpC Child Bks.

Peterson. Psychology: A Biopsychosocial Approach. 2nd ed. 1997. 90.66 (0-201-32664-7) P-H.

Peterson. The Psychology of Abnormality. (C). 1995. pap. text 44.50 (0-15-503031-0) Harcourt.

— The Psychology of Abnormality. (C). 1995. pap. text, teacher ed. 35.00 (0-15-503029-9); pap. text, student ed. 25.00 (0-15-503030-2, Pub. by Harcourt Coll Pubs) Harcourt.

— Real-World Research. (C). Date not set. pap. write for info. (0-395-74124-6) HM.

— Real World Research. (C). 1999. pap. text 17.56 (0-395-90126-X) HM.

— Rebecca of Sunnybrook Farm. (Illus.). 32p. (J). (gr. k-4). Date not set. 14.95 (0-06-028225-8) HarpC.

— Rebecca of Sunnybrook Farm. (Illus.). 32p. (J). (gr. k-4). Date not set. pap. 4.95 (0-06-443537-7) HarpC.

— The Role of Work in People's Lives: Applied Career & Vocational Psychology. LC 99-21251. (Counseling Ser.). 630p. 1999. mass mkt. 60.95 (0-534-34688-X) Brooks-Cole.

***Peterson.** Roman Legions Recreated in Color Photographs: Europa Militaria Special #2. 96p. 2000. pap. 23.95 (1-86126-264-7, Pub. by Crolwood) Motorbooks Intl.

Peterson. Social Problems. 1999. pap. text, student ed. 12.00 (0-13-643172-0) P-H.

— Teaching Notes for Technical Math. (C). 2001. 1150.00 (0-8273-9090-4) Thomson Learn.

— Tech Math WI - CALC, IRG. 2nd ed. (Nursing Education Ser.). 320p. 1997. text, teacher ed. 69.95 incl. disk (0-8273-7239-6) Delmar.

***Peterson.** Tech Notes for Tech Calculus with analytic Geometry. (Mechanical Technology Ser.). (C). 2000. pap. 11.50 (0-8273-9089-0) Delmar.

Peterson. Technical Calculus with Analytic Geometry. LC 97-151270. (Trade/Tech Math Ser.). (C). 1997. mass mkt. 79.95 (0-8273-7415-1) Delmar.

— Technical Calculus with Analytic Geometry. (Trade/Tech Math Ser.). 1998. text, teacher ed. 20.00 (0-8273-7416-X); text, student ed. 22.00 (0-8273-7417-8) Delmar.

— Technical Mathematics. 2nd ed. (Trade/Tech Math Ser.). 1997. lab manual ed. 26.50 (0-8273-7238-8) Delmar.

— Technical Mathematics Computer Program. (Physics Ser.). 1994. 10.00 (0-8273-6503-9) Delmar.

— Technical Mathematics with Calculus. 2nd ed. (Trade/Tech Math Ser.). 1997. student ed. 18.95 (0-8273-7237-X) Delmar.

— Technical Mathematics with Calculus CTB. (Physics Ser.). 1994. 49.95 (0-8273-6507-1) Delmar.

***Peterson.** Therapeutic Recreation Program: Principles & Procedures. 3rd ed. LC 99-37469. 370p. 1999. 60.00 (0-205-26520-0) Allyn.

Peterson. Vocational Counseling Models for Diverse. LC 99-28324. (Counseling Ser.). (C). 1999. pap. 45.95 (0-534-34972-2) Brooks-Cole.

— Working with Clay: An Introduction. 192p. (C). 1998. pap. text 37.33 (0-13-099640-8) P-H.

— Write, Edit & Right. LC 98-39803. 384p. 1999. pap. 23.13 (0-07-049885-7) McGraw.

Peterson, ed. Best UMY Programs: 32 Programs for Youth Fellowship. LC 99-162942. 144p. 1997. 15.95 (0-687-72786-3) Abingdon.

— Geology of the Colorado Plateau, No. T130. (IGC Field Trip Guidebooks Ser.). 72p. 1989. 21.00 (0-87590-644-3) Am Geophysical.

***Peterson, ed.** The Norton Reader: An Anthology of Expository Prose. 10th ed. LC 99-33319. 1999. 28.50 (0-393-97383-2) Norton.

Peterson, ed. Point Click & Drag. 4th ed. (C). 1996. text 31.88 (0-673-67646-3) Addison-Wesley.

Peterson & Lewis. Managerial Economics. 4th ed. LC 98-19387. 672p. (C). 1998. 91.93 (0-13-976283-3) P-H.

Peterson & Mountfort, Guy. Birds of Britain & Europe. 1987. 22.95 (0-685-43762-0) Viking Penguin.

Peterson & Nisenholz. Orientation to Counseling. 4th ed. LC 98-12731. 448p. 1998. 71.00 (0-205-27539-7) P-H.

Peterson & Seligson, David. AIDS: Prevention & Treatment. 1991. pap. 29.95 (1-56032-093-1) Hemisp Pub.

Peterson & Wagner. College Math Through Applications: Preliminary Comprehensive Edition. LC 98-140242. (Instructor Material TV Ser.). 928p. 1997. 69.95 (0-7668-0238-8) Delmar.

— College Mathematics Through Applications. LC 98-140242. 448p. 1997. pap. 24.95 (0-7668-0207-8) Delmar.

— College Mathematics Through Applications: Preliminary Edition 2. 2nd ed. 448p. 1997. 24.95 (0-7668-0208-6) Delmar.

***Peterson & Wagner.** Instructor's Guide to Accompany College Mathematics Through Applications. 128p. 1999. teacher ed. 18.95 (0-7668-0157-8) Delmar.

Peterson, et al. Binder Characterization & Evaluation, Vol. 1. 152p. (Orig.). (C). 1994. pap. text 15.00 (0-309-05809-0, SHRP-A-367) SHRP.

Peterson, et al. Birds of Britain & Europe Field Guide. (Illus.). 1993. 35.00 (0-00-219900-9, Pub. by HarpC) Trafalgar.

Peterson, et al. Political Science: An Overview of the Fields. 2nd ed. 304p. (C). 1997. per. 38.95 (0-7872-4179-2, 41417901) Kendall-Hunt.

Peterson, jt. auth. see Ashe, pseud.

Peterson, jt. auth. see Beemer, Rod.

Peterson, jt. auth. see Bronte.

Peterson, jt. auth. see Fabozzi.

Peterson, jt. auth. see Fiorina.

Peterson, ed. see Grant Staff & Wagner.

Peterson, ed. see Harcey, Paul & Edge Ministries Staff.

Peterson, ed. see O'Neil, Dennis.

***Peterson, Jordan B.** Maps of Meaning The Architecture of Belief. LC 98-37486. 1999. 80.00 (0-415-92221-6) Routledge.

Peterson, Jordan B. Maps of Meanings: The Architecture of Belief. LC 98-37486. 1999. pap. 35.00 (0-415-92222-4) Routledge.

Peterson, A. Peterson Psychology Book & Study Guide. 1997. write for info. (0-201-36272-4) Addison-Wesley.

Peterson, A. C., jt. auth. see Brooks-Gunn, J.

Peterson, A. D. The Time Passers. 132p. 1998. pap. 9.95 (0-9646503-3-9) A D Peterson.

Peterson, A. E. & Swan, J. B., eds. Universal Soil Loss Equation: Past, Present & Future. (Special Publications: No. 8). 53p. 1979. pap. 2.00 (0-89118-766-9) Soil Sci Soc Am.

Peterson, Abby. Neo-Sectarianism & Rainbow Coalitions: Youth & the Drama of Immigration in Contemporary Sweden. LC 97-73461. (Research in Ethnic Relations Ser.). 208p. 1997. text 69.95 (1-85972-700-X, Pub. by Ashgate Pub) Ashgate Pub Co.

Peterson, Abby, jt. ed. see Fridlizius, Sandro.

Peterson, Agnes F., compiled by. Western Europe: A Survey of Holdings at the Hoover Institution on War, Revolution & Peace. LC 72-142950. (Library Survey Ser.: No. 1). 60p. 1970. pap. 1.20 (0-8179-5012-5) Hoover Inst Pr.

Peterson, Alan H. The American Focus on Business Management: A Guide for Women (& Men), Vol. 1. (Illus.). 235p. (C). 1990. lib. bdg. 34.95 (1-877858-14-5) Amer Focus Pub.

— The American Focus on Satanic Crime, 1. 134p. 1989. 34.95 (1-877858-00-5) Amer Focus Pub.

— The American Focus on Satanic Crime, 2. 134p. 1989. 49.95 (1-877858-01-3) Amer Focus Pub.

— The American Focus on Satanic Crime Series: Awareness,

An Asterisk (*) at the beginning of an entry indicates that the title is appearing for the first time.

Training, Intervention & Prevention Collection, 23 vols. Marquis, Doc et al, eds. (Illus.). 1996. 1800.00 incl. audio, VHS (*1-877858-20-X*) Amer Focus Pub.

— The Satanism in Prisons Story, Vol. 1. 100p. 1992. pap. 34.95 (*1-877858-22-6*, TSIPT) Amer Focus Pub.

— Secrets of the Illuminati. Marquis, Doc & Nichols, William L., eds. (American Focus on Satanic Crime Ser.: Vol. 5). (Illus.). 390p. 1994. pap. 44.00 (*1-877858-66-8*) Amer Focus Pub.

Peterson, Alan H., ed. The American Focus on Satanic Crime, Vol. 4. 300p. 1992. pap. text 54.95 (*1-877858-10-2*, AFSC4) Amer Focus Pub.

Peterson, Alan H. & Cheney, Victor T. The American Focus on Rape, Vol. 1. (Illus.). 450p. 1992. pap. text 75.00 (*1-877858-25-0*, AFR1) Amer Focus Pub.

Peterson, Alan H. & Kail, Tony. The American Focus on Satanic Crime Vol. 3A: Occult Crime: Analysis & Intervention, 23 vols. (Illus.). 237p. (Orig.). (C). 1996. 39.95 (*1-877858-06-4*, AFSC3A) Amer Focus Pub.

Peterson, Alan H., jt. auth. see Collins, Robert.

Peterson, Alan H., ed. see Caldwell, E. S.

Peterson, Alan H., ed. & illus. see Marquis, Doc.

Peterson, Alan H., ed. & illus. see Willey, Michael R.

Peterson, Alan H., tr. see Cheney, Victor T.

Peterson, Alan W. Truth the Poet Sings. LC 83-51133. 182p. 1984. 3.48 (*0-87159-160-X*) Unity Bks.

Peterson, Allan C., jt. auth. see Ahlbrandt, Calvin D.

Peterson, Allan C., jt. auth. see Kelley, Walter G.

Peterson, Allen D. Our Father's Family. LC 95-68674. 57p. 1995. pap. 7.50 (*0-9646503-0-4*) A D Peterson.

— Our Mother's Family. LC 98-92382. 114p. 1998. pap. 20.00 (*0-9646503-1-2*) A D Peterson.

Peterson, Allen D., ed. see Peterson, Phyllis J.

Peterson, Alma J. Drowning in Debt? Get Out & Stay Out! LC 96-96341. (Illus.). ix, 125p. (Orig.). 1996. pap. 9.50 (*0-9652507-0-9*) AJP Bks.

Peterson, Amy, jt. auth. see Polonsky, William H.

Peterson, Amy A., jt. auth. see Chalmers, Karen Hanson.

Peterson, Amy A., tr. see Wilhelm, James J., ed.

***Peterson, Andrew F.** Dictionary of Islamic Architecture. 352p. 1999. pap. 39.99 (*0-415-21332-0*) Routledge.

Peterson, Andrew F., et al. Computational Methods for Electromagnetics. LC 97-39612. (Illus.). 592p. 1997. 89.95 (*0-7803-1122-1*) Inst Electrical.

— Computational Methods for Electromagnetics. (IREE/OUP Series on Electromagnetic Wave Theory). (Illus.). 592p. 1998. text 175.00 (*0-19-856564-X*) OUP.

***Peterson, Ann Voss.** Inadmissible Passion. (Intrigue Ser.). 2000. mass mkt. 4.25 (*0-373-22579-2*, 1-22579-6) Harlequin Bks.

Peterson, Ann Z., jt. auth. see Rosenberg, Stephen M.

Peterson, Anna L. Martyrdom & the Politics of Religion: Progressive Catholicism in El Salvador's Civil War. LC 96-367. 211p. (C). 1996. text 54.50 (*0-7914-3181-9*); pap. text 17.95 (*0-7914-3182-7*) State U NY Pr.

Peterson, Anne, ed. see American Psychological Association Staff.

Peterson, Art. The Writer's Workout Book: 113 Stretches Toward Better Prose. LC 96-7329. 1996. write for info. (*1-883920-11-6*) Nat Writing Proj.

Peterson, Art, ed. Cityscapes: 8 Views from the Urban Classroom. 176p. (Orig.). (C). 1995. pap. 13.00 (*1-883920-10-8*) Nat Writing Proj.

Peterson, Arthur E., jt. auth. see Edwards, George W.

Peterson, Arthur H., jt. auth. see Krambles, George.

Peterson, Audrey. Dartmoor Burial. Isaacson, Dana, ed. 256p. (Orig.). 1992. mass mkt. 5.50 (*0-671-72970-5*) PB.

— Death Too Soon. Isaacson, Dana, ed. 288p. (Orig.). 1994. mass mkt. 4.99 (*0-671-79509-0*) PB.

— Elegy in a Country Graveyard. Isaacson, Dana, ed. 256p. (Orig.). 1990. pap. 3.95 (*0-671-69356-5*) PB.

— Lament for Christobel. Isaacson, Dana, ed. 224p. (Orig.). 1991. mass mkt. 4.50 (*0-671-72969-1*) PB.

— The Nocturne Murder. 256p. 1988. pap. 5.50 (*0-671-66102-7*) PB.

— Shroud for a Scholar. 1995. mass mkt. 5.50 (*0-671-79510-4*) PB.

Peterson, Axel G. The Training of Elementary & Secondary Teachers in Sweden. LC 70-177151. (Columbia University. Teachers College. Contributions to Education Ser.: No. 575). (C). reprint ed. 37.50 (*0-404-55575-6*) AMS Pr.

***Peterson, B.** Nikon Lenses. 2nd ed. LC 99-38318. (Magic Lantern Guides Ser.). 176p. 2000. pap. 19.95 (*1-883403-63-4*, Silver Pixel Pr) Saunders Photo.

— Nikon System Handbook. 6th ed. LC 99-26695. 176p. 2000. pap. 24.95 (*1-883403-64-2*, Silver Pixel Pr) Saunders Photo.

Peterson, B. M., et al, eds. Emission Lines in Active Galaxies Vol. 113: New Methods & Techniques, Iau Colloquiumisa. LC 96-79362. (ASP Conference Series Proceedings). 534p. 1996. 34.00 (*1-886733-33-3*) Astron Soc Pacific.

Peterson, B. Moose. Nikon Classic Cameras, Vol. 2. (Magic Lantern Guides). (Illus.). 176p. (Orig.). (C). 1998. pap. 19.95 (*1-883403-38-3*, H 192, Silver Pixel Pr) Saunders Photo.

— Nikon F4-F3. LC 95-128067. (Magic Lantern Guides Ser.). (Illus.). 176p. (Orig.). (C). 1998. pap. 19.95 (*1-883403-12-X*, H 130, Silver Pixel Pr) Saunders Photo.

— Nikon Lenses. LC 94-182693. (Magic Lantern Guides Ser.). (Illus.). 176p. (Orig.). (C). 1998. pap. 19.95 (*1-883403-07-3*, H 138, Silver Pixel Pr) Saunders Photo.

— Wildlife Photography: Getting Started in the Field. LC 98-132837. (Illus.). 152p. (C). 1998. pap. 29.95 (*1-883403-27-8*, H 702, Silver Pixel Pr) Saunders Photo.

Peterson, B. Moose & Angel, Heather. Nikon System Handbook. 5th rev. ed. LC 98-28426. (Illus.). 184 p. 1998. pap. 24.95 (*1-883403-50-2*, H 609, Silver Pixel Pr) Saunders Photo.

Peterson, B. Moose & Huber, Michael. Nikon SB-26 Flash System. Riffler-Bonham, Phyllis M., tr. from GER. (Magic Lantern Guides Ser.). (Illus.). 176p. (C). 1998. pap. 19.95 (*1-883403-29-4*, H 140, Silver Pixel Pr) Saunders Photo.

Peterson, B. Moose, jt. auth. see Huber, Michael.

Peterson, B. R. The Complete Waterfouler: A Discourse on Duck Hunting with a Little Goose on the Side. (Illus.). 108p. 1996. pap. 10.99 (*1-55821-391-0*, 13910) Lyons Pr.

— The Original Roadkill Cookbook. 53p. (Orig.). 1987. pap. 4.95 (*0-89815-200-3*) Ten Speed Pr.

Peterson, Baird. XENIX System Services. 1992. pap. write for info. (*0-442-00541-5*, VNR) Wiley.

Peterson, Barbara. Seasons of Life: Self Help Reflections. Halstead, Sharill, ed. (Illus.). 206p. (Orig.). 1995. pap. 10.95 (*0-9650347-0-4*) Caritas Fnd.

Peterson, Barbara Bennett, ed. Notable Women of China: Shang Dynasty to the Early Twentieth Century. LC 99-30322. 432p. 2000. text 74.95 (*0-7656-0504-X*, Sharpe Ref) M E Sharpe.

Peterson, Barbara E. The Bed Rest Survival Guide. LC 98-9587. 176p. 1998. pap. 12.00 (*0-380-79506-X*, Avon Bks) Morrow Avon.

Peterson, Barbara Sturken. Rapid Descent. 1994. 24.50 (*0-671-76069-6*) S&S Trade.

Peterson, Barbara V. & Peterson, Wayne L. Sketches of Florida. (Illus.). 74p. (Orig.). 1996. 29.95 (*0-9651256-1-0*); pap. 14.95 (*0-9651256-0-2*) Peterson Publng.

Peterson Barker, Helen. You Gotta Scratch a Little: To Succeed in Real Estate. 172p. 1997. pap. 14.95 (*1-57502-686-4*, PO1938) Morris Pubng.

Peterson, Barry W. & Richmond, Frances J., eds. Control of Head Movement. (Illus.). 336p. 1988. text 55.00 (*0-19-504499-1*) OUP.

Peterson, Bea. KISS, Keep It Short & Simple Baseball. (Illus.). 170p. (Orig.). 1996. pap. 7.95 (*0-9652921-0-X*) KISS Pub CA.

Peterson, Bernard. The Caravaggio Books. 1997. per. 4.99 (*0-373-26237-X*, 0-26237-8, Wrldwide Lib) Harlequin Bks.

Peterson, Bernard L. The African American Theatre Directory, 1816-1960: A Comprehensive Guide to Early Black Theatre Organizations, Companies, Theatres, & Performing Groups. LC 96-9534. 336p. 1997. lib. bdg. 75.00 (*0-313-29537-9*) Greenwood.

— A Century of Musicals in Black & White: An Encyclopedia of Musical Stage Works by, about, or Involving Black Americans. LC 92-41976. 560p. 1993. lib. bdg. 95.00 (*0-313-26657-3*, PEG, Greenwood Pr) Greenwood.

Peterson, Bernard L., Jr. Contemporary Black American Playwrights & Their Plays: A Biographical Directory & Dramatic Index. LC 87-17814. 651p. 1988. lib. bdg. 79.50 (*0-313-25190-8*, PPL/, Greenwood Pr) Greenwood.

— Early Black American Playwrights & Dramatic Writers: A Biographical Directory & Catalog of Plays, Films & Broadcasting Scripts. LC 90-2961. 328p. 1990. lib. bdg. 75.00 (*0-313-26621-2*, PBW/, Greenwood Pr) Greenwood.

***Peterson, Bernard L., Jr.** Profiles of African American Stage Performers & Theatre People, 1816-1960. LC 99-88456. 400p. 2000. lib. bdg. 95.00 (*0-313-29534-4*, GR9534, Greenwood Pr) Greenwood.

Peterson, Bernard W. Briny to the Blue: Memoirs of World War II, By a Sailor/Marine Fighter Pilot. LC 91-78372. 462p. 1992. 29.95 (*0-9631875-0-3*) Chuckwalla Pub.

— Short Straw: Memoirs of Korea, by a Fighter Pilot/Forward Air Controller. LC 95-83262. (Illus.). 560p. 1996. 29.95 (*0-9631875-3-8*) Chuckwalla Pub.

Peterson, Beth. Myrna Never Sleeps. LC 93-8301. (J). (gr. 2-6). 1995. 13.00 (*0-689-31893-6*) Atheneum Yung Read.

— No Turning Back: Dillon Confronts Death on a Magic Journey. LC 95-30857. 112p. (J). (gr. 5-9). 1996. 14.00 (*0-689-31914-2*) Atheneum Yung Read.

Peterson, Betty B. Your Wedding. 1982. pap. 3.00 (*0-89036-211-4*) Liahona Pub Trust.

Peterson, Bo. Media, Minds & Men: A History of Media in Sweden. (Illus.). 366p. 1988. 71.00 (*91-22-01206-0*) Coronet Bks.

Peterson, Bob. In His Majesty's Service: Christians in Politics. LC 95-47717. 208p. 1995. pap. 11.99 (*1-56384-100-2*) Huntington Hse.

— Out of Body Experiences: How to Have Them & What to Expect. LC 97-176652. 224p. 1997. pap. 11.95 (*1-57174-057-0*) Hampton Roads Pub Co.

— Solve It Yourself Mysteries. (Illus.). 96p. 1998. 5.95 (*0-8069-9427-4*) Sterling.

***Peterson, Bob, ed.** Transforming Teacher Unions: Fighting for Better Schools & Social Justice. LC 99-30500. (Illus.). 142p. 1999. pap. write for info. (*0-942961-24-2*) Rethinking Schls.

Peterson, Bob, jt. auth. see Conrad, Hy.

Peterson, Bob, jt. ed. see Bigelow, Bill.

Peterson, Bobbie. Sweden Visions & Verse of a Land & Its People Collector's Postcard Book. (Collector's Postcard Bks.). (ENG & SWE.). 22p. (Orig.). 1996. pap. 9.95 (*1-881988-22-8*) Paulstad Inc.

Peterson, Bradley M. An Introduction to Active Galactic Nuclei. (Illus.). 254p. (C). 1997. text 74.95 (*0-521-47348-9*); pap. text 28.95 (*0-521-47911-8*) Cambridge U Pr.

Peterson, Brenda. Build Me An Ark. 25.95 (*0-393-05014-9*) Norton.

— Living by Water: New Stories of Nature, Animals & Spirit. 2nd ed. (Illus.). 2000. pap. 13.95 (*0-939165-39-2*) NewSage Press.

Peterson, Brenda. Nature & Other Mothers: Personal Stories of Women & the Body of Earth. 256p. 1995. pap. 12.00 (*0-449-90967-0*) Fawcett.

***Peterson, Brenda.** Singing to the Sound: Visions of Nature, Animals & Spirit. (Illus.). 2000. 21.95 (*0-939165-40-6*); write for info. (*0-939165-41-4*) NewSage Press.

Peterson, Brenda. Sister Stories. 288p. 1997. pap. 12.95 (*0-14-023299-0*) Viking Penguin.

Peterson, Brenda, jt. ed. see Hogan, Linda.

Peterson, Brent D., et al. The Complete Speaker: An Introduction to Public Speaking. 3rd ed. Perlee, Clyde & Simon, eds. 359p. (C). 1992. pap. 31.25 (*0-314-93439-1*) West Pub.

Peterson, Brent D., jt. auth. see Timm, Paul R.

Peterson, Brent O. Popular Narratives & Ethnic Identity: Literature & Community in Die Abendschule. LC 91-55070. (Illus.). 320p. 1992. text 45.00 (*0-8014-2548-4*) Cornell U Pr.

Peterson, Brent T. & Thilgen, Dean R. Stillwater, Minnesota: A Photographic History. (Illus.). 128p. (Orig.). 1992. pap. 16.95 (*0-9634842-0-6*) Valley Hist Pr.

Peterson, Brian. Move over, Girl. LC 98-96364. 316p. 1998. pap. 12.00 (*0-9664587-0-2*) C-Twenty Two.

***Peterson, Brian.** Move over, Girl. LC 99-53711. 288p. 2000. 19.95 (*0-375-50402-8*) Villard Books.

***Peterson, Brian, et al.** John Goodyear: Works from 1950-2000. (Illus.). 48p. 2000. pap. Price not set. (*1-879636-11-5*) J A Michener.

***Peterson, Brian C.** Terrell Davis. LC 00-27463. (NFL Readers Ser.). (gr. 4-7). 2000. write for info. (*0-7894-6377-6*, Pub. by DK Pub Inc); pap. 3.95 (*0-7894-6758-5*) DK Pub Inc.

***Peterson, Brian H.** Intimate Vistas: The Poetic Landscapes of William Langson Lathrop. (Illus.). 150p. 1999. pap. write for info. (*1-879636-10-7*) J A Michener.

Peterson, Brian H. Masterpieces of Photography from the Merrill Lynch Collection. (Illus.). 84p. 1997. pap. write for info. (*1-879636-09-3*) J A Michener.

Peterson, Brian R. Buck Peterson's Guide to Deer Hunting. (Illus.). 158p. 1989. pap. 7.95 (*0-89815-291-7*) Ten Speed Pr.

Peterson, Brice. Camping & Survival: Step-by-Step Guide to Wilderness Skills & Outdoor Living. LC 94-65054. 320p. (Orig.). 1999. 29.95 (*1-884573-00-2*); pap. 19.95 (*1-884573-19-3*) S-By-S Pubns.

— Meat Lovers: Step-by-Step Guide for the Meat Connoisseur. LC 94-65052. 320p. (Orig.). 1998. 29.95 (*1-884573-02-9*); pap. 19.95 (*1-884573-17-7*) S-By-S Pubns.

Peterson, Bryan & DiAMAR Staff. Learning to See Creatively: How to Compose Great Photographs. (Illus.). 144p. 1995. pap. 79.95 incl. cd-rom (*1-886393-02-8*, Amphoto) Watsn-Guptill.

Peterson, Bryan F. Learning to See Creatively. (Illus.). 144p. 1988. pap. 18.95 (*0-8174-4177-8*, Amphoto) Watsn-Guptill.

Peterson, Bryan F. People in Focus: How to Photograph Anyone, Anywhere. (Illus.). 144p. 1993. pap. 22.50 (*0-8174-5388-1*, Amphoto) Watsn-Guptill.

— Understanding Exposure: How to Shoot Great Photographs. (Illus.). 144p. 1990. pap. 22.50 (*0-8174-3712-6*, Amphoto) Watsn-Guptill.

— Using Design Basics to Get Creative Results. (Illus.). 144p. 1996. 29.99 (*0-89134-651-1*, North Lght Bks) F & W Pubns Inc.

Peterson, Bryan F., photos by. Photographing Oregon with Professional Results. LC 84-80434. (Illus.). 96p. (Orig.). 1984. pap. 9.95 (*0-912856-90-4*) Gr Arts Ctr Pub.

Peterson, Buck. The Totalled Roadkill Cookbook. LC 97-176581. 96p. 1996. pap. 5.95 (*0-89087-812-9*) Celestial Arts.

***Peterson, Buck.** Wildlife of the New Millennium: A Field Guide. LC 99-61763. (Illus.). 160p. 1999. pap. 11.95 (*1-56352-546-1*) Longstreet.

Peterson, Buck R. Buck Peterson's Complete Guide to Fishing. (Illus.). 144p. 1991. pap. 8.95 (*0-89815-405-7*) Ten Speed Pr.

Peterson, C., ed. see Craighead, J. J., et al.

Peterson, C., jt. ed. see McCabe, A.

Peterson, C. Arthur. Teacher's Survival Guide. 1985. pap. 10.95 (*0-452-26399-9*, Plume) Dutton Plume.

Peterson, C. D. How to Leave Your Job & Buy a Business of Your Own. 1988. 9.95 incl. audio (*0-07-049648-X*) McGraw.

Peterson, C. D. On Your Own: Discovering Your New Life & Career Beyond the Corporation. LC 96-35572. 303p. 1997. pap. 16.95 (*0-471-14845-8*) Wiley.

Peterson, C. H., jt. auth. see Conlin, Joseph R.

Peterson, Calvin. The Truth Has Been Thrown to the Bribed. 64p. 1988. pap. 5.00 (*0-936978-06-6*) Pheasant Run.

Peterson, Candida D., jt. auth. see Siegal, Michael.

Peterson, Carl. For Anna Akhmatova & Other Poems. LC 77-3193. 50p. 1977. 3.50 (*0-87886-081-9*, Greenfld Rev Pr) Greenfld Rev Lit.

***Peterson, Carl E., et al.** NFPA Fire Prevention Code Handbook. LC 98-65473. x, 614 p. 1998. write for info. (*0-87765-414-X*) Natl Fire Prot.

Peterson, Carl L., Jr. Avoidance & Evasion of Military Service: An American History 1626-1973. LC 97-12202. 224p. 1997. 74.95 (*1-57309-164-2*); pap. 54.95 (*1-57309-163-4*) Intl Scholars.

Peterson, Carl R., jt. auth. see Hill, Philip G.

Peterson, Carla. Reconstructing the Nation: Frances Harper, Charlotte Forten, & the Radical Politics of Periodical Publications. (James Russell Wiggins Lecture in the History of the Book Ser.: Vol. 15). (Illus.). 34p. 1998. pap. 6.50 (*0-944026-90-7*) Am Antiquarian.

Peterson, Carla L. Doers of the Word: African-American Women Speakers & Writers in the North (1830-1880) LC 97-41838. 284p. (C). 1998. pap. text 20.00 (*0-8135-2514-4*) Rutgers U Pr.

Peterson, Carlisle. The Destiny of the Black Race. Cooke, Andrea, ed. 395p. (Orig.). 1994. pap. 14.95 (*1-889448-00-1*, NBNSC 7778) NBN Publishers Group.

Peterson, Carlisle, ed. see Luster, Ivon.

Peterson, Carlisle J. If the Foundations Be Destroyed. LC 98-91107. 200p. 1999. pap. 12.95 (*1-889448-25-7*) NBN Publishers Group.

— Power of Prophetic Synergy. LC 98-91102. 200p. (gr. 8-12). 1999. pap. 12.95 (*1-889448-24-9*) NBN Publishers Group.

***Peterson, Carlisle John.** The Passport: What Really Happened at Calvary. LC 98-91106. 200p. 1999. pap. 39.00 incl. audio (*1-889448-26-5*) NBN Publishers Group.

Peterson, Carol J. Old Stuff. (Illus.). 148p. (Orig.). 1995. pap. write for info. (*1-57579-001-7*) Pine Hill Pr.

Peterson, Carol R. Herbs You Can Master: A Primer for Herbal Enthusiasts. Lilly, Bob & Phillips, Sharon D., eds. LC 93-91797. (Illus.). 228p. (Orig.). 1994. reprint ed. pap. 17.95 (*0-9639620-0-0*, Pub. by Mtn Garden) Partners Pubs Grp.

— More Herbs You Can Master: Twelve Wondrous Plants for Extra Nutrition, Improved Health, Natural Beauty. Chaplin, Connie & Lilly, Bob, eds. LC 99-90021. (Illus.). 255p. 1999. pap. 17.95 (*0-9639620-1-9*) Mtn Garden.

Peterson, Carole & McCabe, Allyssa. Developmental Psycholinguistics: Three Ways of Looking at a Child's Narrative. (Cognition & Language Ser.). 278p. 1983. 59.50 (*0-306-40964-X*, Plenum Trade) Perseus Pubng.

Peterson, Carolyn S. & Fenton, Ann D. Reference Books for Children. 4th ed. LC 92-14234. 414p. 1992. 47.50 (*0-8108-2543-0*) Scarecrow.

— Story Programs: A Source Book of Materials. 2nd rev. ed. Koorey, Stefani, ed. (School Library Media Ser.: No. 10). (Illus.). 272p. 2000. pap. 29.50 (*0-8108-3207-0*) Scarecrow.

Peterson, Carolyn S. & Fenton, Ann D., compiled by. Index to Children's Songs. LC 79-14265. 318p. 1979. 38.00 (*0-8242-0638-X*) Wilson.

Peterson, Carrie. The Secrets of Sebastian Beaumont. (Shadows Ser.). 1993. per. 3.50 (*0-373-27022-4*, 5-27022-8) Silhouette.

Peterson, Carroll V. John Davidson. LC 71-187613. (Twayne's English Authors Ser.). 164p. (C). 1972. lib. bdg. 20.95 (*0-8290-1727-5*) Irvington.

Peterson, Casey, ed. Challenge of Loving: Building Healthy Relationships. 34p. 1986. pap. 2.50 (*0-936098-47-3*) Intl Marriage.

— Grief & Loss: Learning You Are Not Alone. 34p. 1987. pap. 2.50 (*0-936098-56-2*) Intl Marriage.

— Marriage Encounter for Just the Two of You. 50p. 1988. pap. 2.50 (*0-936098-59-7*) Intl Marriage.

Peterson, Cass, jt. auth. see Michalak, Patricia S.

Peterson, Cass, ed. see Sinclair, Ward.

Peterson, Catherine V., jt. auth. see Kielpinski, Penelope.

Peterson, Cecilia & Writers of Saint Louis Staff. 1-888-Cecilia: An Inside Line, Vol. 1. 300p. 1996. 24.95 (*0-9651865-2-0*) Writers St Louis.

Peterson, Charles. Eclectic Pragmatism: Is There a God? LC 98-91707. 400p. 1998. pap. 25.00 (*1-57502-922-7*, PO2544) Morris Pubng.

Peterson, Charles & Blei, Norbert. Charles L. Peterson: Of Time & Place. Quale, Mark E. & Peterson, Susan, eds. (Illus.). 96p. 1994. 135.00 (*0-9643438-0-0*) White Door.

— Charles L. Peterson: Of Time & Place. 2nd ed. Quale, Mark E. & Peterson, Susan, eds. (Illus.). 96p. 1994. pap. text 45.00 (*0-9643438-1-9*) White Door.

Peterson, Charles & Mercer, Lance, photos by. Pearl Jam: Place/Date. (Illus.). 128p. 1998. pap. 19.95 (*0-7893-0269-1*, Pub. by Universe) St Martin.

Peterson, Charles A. How You Can Leave the City Forever. 120p. (Orig.). pap. 10.00 (*0-9614806-0-2*) Peterson Pub CO.

Peterson, Charles C., jt. auth. see Nagy, Kenneth A.

Peterson, Charles E. The Moore House: The Site of Surrender-Yorktown; A National Park Service Historic Structures Report. 116p. 1981. 8.45 (*0-940091-08-9*); pap. 4.20 (*0-940091-07-0*) Natl Parks & Cons.

Peterson, Charles E., intro. The Carpenters' Company 1786 Rule Book. (Illus.). 158p. 1992. reprint ed. 14.95 (*1-879335-28-X*) Astragal Pr.

***Peterson, Charles E. & Stokes, Sally Sims.** Notes on Hampton Mansion. 2nd rev. ed. LC 00-34853. (Illus.). 2000. pap. write for info. (*0-9655233-4-9*) Univ MD Coll Pk.

Peterson, Charles J., jt. ed. see Barber, Dan.

Peterson, Charles M. Diabetes Management in the 1980s: The Role of Home Blood Glucose Monitoring & New Insulin Delivery Systems. LC 82-80561. 328p. 1982. 80.00 (*0-275-91377-5*, C1377, Praeger Pubs) Greenwood.

Peterson, Charles M., et al, eds. Fetal Islet Transplantation: Implications for Diabetes. (Illus.). 260p. 1988. 178.00 (*0-387-96587-4*) Spr-Verlag.

Peterson, Charles M. & Jovanovic-Peterson, Lois. The Diabetes Self-Care Method: The Breakthrough Program of Self-Management That Will Help You Lead a Better, Freer, More Normal Life. rev. ed. (Illus.). 144p. 1990. reprint ed. pap. 12.95 (*0-929923-29-4*) Lowell Hse.

— The Diabetes Self-Care Method: The Breakthrough Program of Self-Management That Will Help You Lead a Better, Freer, More Normal Life. 2nd rev. ed. LC 98-231434. (Illus.). 176p. 1998. pap. 16.00 (*0-7373-0017-5*, 00175W) NTC Contemp Pub Co.

Peterson, Charles M., jt. ed. see Friedman, Eli A.

An Asterisk (*) at the beginning of an entry indicates that the title is appearing for the first time.

Peterson, Charles M., ed. see International Sansum Symposium on Human Fetal Isle.

Peterson, Charles R., jt. auth. see Koch, Edward D.

Peterson, Charles S. Changing Times: A View from Cache Valley, 1890-1915. LC 93-80099. (Faculty Honor Lecture: No. 60). 32p. reprint ed. pap. 30.00 (0-7837-6210-0, 204593400009) Bks Demand.

***Peterson, Cheryl.** Ants. LC 98-46925. (Insects Ser.). (Illus.). 24p. (ps-3). 1999. 13.25 (0-7368-0234-7) Capstone Pr.

Peterson, Cheryl. Bumble Bees. LC 98-49431. (Insects Ser.). 1999. 9.95 (0-7368-0236-3, Pebble Bks) Capstone Pr.

— Dragonflies. LC 98-32304. (Insects Ser.). 1999. write for info. (0-7368-0238-X) Capstone Pr.

— Flies. LC 98-55562. (Insects Ser.). (Illus.). 1999. write for info. (0-7368-0240-1) Capstone Pr.

— Ladybugs. LC 98-43878. (Insects Ser.). 1999. 13.25 (0-7368-0242-8) Capstone Pr.

Peterson, Cheryl & Coughlan, Cheryl. Beetles. Saunders-Smith, Gail, ed. LC 98-52996. (Illus.). 24p. 13.25 (0-7368-0235-5, Pebble Bks) Capstone Pr.

— Crickets. Saunders-Smith, Gail, ed. LC 98-51626. (Illus.). 24p. 13.25 (0-7368-0237-1, Pebble Bks) Capstone Pr.

— Fireflies. Saunders-Smith, Gail, ed. (Illus.). 24p. 13.25 (0-7368-0239-8) Capstone Pr.

— Grasshoppers. Saunders-Smith, Gail, ed. LC 98-52815. (Illus.). 24p. 13.25 (0-7368-0241-X, Pebble Bks) Capstone Pr.

— Misquitoes. Saunders-Smith, Gail, ed. LC 98-43745. (Illus.). 24p. 24.00 (0-7368-0243-6, Pebble Bks) Capstone Pr.

Peterson, Chester, Jr. Hitch up a Computer for Your Farm: The Nuts & Bolts Guide to Getting the Most Use & Value from Your Most Important "Implement" - Your Computer. Kletke, Darrel D. & Reynolds, Ralph, eds. (Agricultural Primer Ser.). (Illus.). 148p. (Orig.). (C). 1996. pap. text 24.95 (0-86691-242-8, FP1O1NC) Deere & Co.

Peterson, Chester. Inside John Deere: A Factory History. LC 98-32353. (ColorTech Ser.). (Illus.). 128p. 1999. 24.95 (0-7603-0441-6) MBI Pubg.

Peterson, Chester, Jr. John Deere New Generation Tractors. LC 98-25570. (Farm Tractor Color History Ser.). (Illus.). 128p. 1998. pap. 21.95 (0-7603-0427-0) MBI Pubg.

Peterson, Chester, Jr. & Beemer, Rod. American Farm Tractors in the 1960s. LC 99-38306. (Illus.). 160p. 1999. text 29.95 (0-7603-0624-9, 129003AP, Pub. by MBI Pubg) Motorbooks Intl.

***Peterson, Chester & Beemer, Rod.** Minneapolis-Moline Farm Tractors. LC 00-28179. (Farm Tractor Histories Ser.). (Illus.). 128p. 2000. 24.95 (0-7603-0625-7, 130117AP, Pub. by MBI Pubg) Motorbooks Intl.

Peterson, Chris. Psychology. 2nd ed. LC 96-24666. 779p. (C). 1997. 84.00 (0-673-52414-0) Addison-Wesley.

Peterson, Chris, ed. The Art of Stained Glass: Designs from 21 Top Glass Artists. (Illus.). 144p. 1998. 29.99 (1-56496-463-9, Quarry Bks) Rockport Pubs.

Peterson, Chris & Pergamit, Gayle. Leaping the Abyss: Putting Group Genius to Work. (Illus.). 290p. (Orig.). 1997. pap. 16.95 (0-9658995-0-0) Knowhere Pr.

Peterson, Chris, jt. auth. see Olsen, Debbie.

Peterson, Chris L. Stress at Work: A Sociological Perspective. LC 98-11799. (Policy, Politics, Health, And Medicine Series). 284p. 1998. 45.00 (0-89503-190-6) Baywood Pub.

***Peterson, Chris L. & Vistnes, Jessica P.** State Differences in Job-Related Health Insurance, 1996. (MEPS Chartbook Ser.: No. 4). 2000. pap. write for info. (1-58763-001-X) Agency Healthcare.

Peterson, Christian A. After the Photo-Secession: American Pictorial Photography 1910-1955. LC 96-39283. (Illus.). 224p. (C). 1997. 45.00 (0-393-04111-5) Norton.

— Alfred Stieglitz's Camera Notes. 208p. 1996. pap. 29.95 (0-393-31126-0) Norton.

***Peterson, Christian A.** Chaining the Sun. 1999. 29.95 (0-8166-3656-7) U of Minn Pr.

Peterson, Christian A. & Minneapolis Institute of Arts. The Poetics of Vision: Photographs from the Collection of Harry M. Drake. LC 97-73720. (Illus.). 1997. write for info. (0-912964-62-6) Minneapolis Inst Arts.

Peterson, Christina. The Women's Migraine Survival Guide: The Complete, Up-to-Date Resource on the Causes of Your Migraine Pain & Treatments for Real Relief. LC 99-27288. 240p. 1999. pap. 12.95 (0-06-095319-5) HarpC.

***Peterson, Christina.** The Women's Migraine Survival Guide: The Most Complete, Up-To-Date Resource on the Causes of Your Migraine Pain, & Treatments for Real Relief. large type ed. LC 00-28816. 308p. 2000. pap. 23.95 (0-7838-9039-7) Mac Lib Ref.

Peterson, Christina & Love, Bertha. Christina Keeps Making a Mess. Cunningham, Ronald & Thomas, N. Charles, eds. LC 96-75163. (Reader Resource Ser.). 70p. (Orig.). 1996. pap. text 6.00 (1-883667-16-X) Christian Meth.

Peterson, Christine E. The Second Malaysian Family Life Survey: User's Guide. LC 93-25706. 1993. pap. 9.00 (0-8330-1357-2, MR-109-NICHNIA) Rand Corp.

Peterson, Christine E. & Campbell, Nancy. The First Malaysian Family Life Survey: Documentation for Subfiles. LC 93-15027. 1993. pap. text 9.00 (0-8330-1355-6, MR-111-NICHD) Rand Corp.

Peterson, Christine E., et al. The Second Malaysian Family Life Survey: Codebook. LC 93-18801. 1993. pap. 9.00 (0-8330-1352-1, MR-108-NICHNIA) Rand Corp.

Peterson, Christine E., jt. auth. see Sine, Jeffrey.

Peterson, Christopher. Personality. 2nd ed. 700p. (C). 1992. text 86.00 (0-15-569600-9) Harcourt Coll Pubs.

— The Psychology of Abnormality. (C). 1995. 3.5 hd 279.50 (0-15-503032-9); 5.25 hd 279.50 (0-15-503033-7) Harcourt Coll Pubs.

— The Psychology of Abnormality. 656p. (C). 1995. text 82.00 (0-15-500092-6, Pub. by Harcourt Coll Pubs) Harcourt.

— The Psychology of Abnormality. (C). 1996. mac hd 279.50 (0-15-503034-5) Harcourt Coll Pubs.

— S/G Psychology. 2nd ed. 400p. (C). 1997. pap. text, student ed. 26.00 (0-673-52546-5) Addison-Wesley.

Peterson, Christopher, et al. Learned Helplessness: A Theory for the Age of Personal Control. (Illus.). 376p. 1995. reprint ed. pap. text 27.50 (0-19-504467-3) OUP.

Peterson, Christopher M., compiled by. Unparalleled Danger Unsurpassed Courage: Recipients of the Indian Order of Merit in the Second World War. 200p. (Orig.). 1997. pap. 19.95 (0-9656205-0-6) C Peterson.

Peterson, Clare G. Perspectives in Surgery. LC 72-115025. 355p. reprint ed. pap. 110.10 (0-608-30536-7, 201457700094) Bks Demand.

Peterson, Clarence S. Known Military Dead During the War of 1812. 74p. 1997. reprint ed. pap. 10.95 (0-8063-4526-8, 9285) Clearfield Co.

Peterson, Clarence Stewart. Known Military Dead During the American Revolutionary War, 1775-1783. 186p. 1999. reprint ed. pap. 21.50 (0-8063-0275-5, 4580, Pub. by Clearfield Co) ACCESS Pubs Network.

Peterson, Clifford. Continuous Quality Assurance: Adapting TQM for Community Colleges. 40p. 1993. pap. 10.00 (0-87117-260-7, 1357) Comm Coll Pr Am Assn Comm Coll.

Peterson Coil, Ann & Hult Crowell, Ann. The Balance Game - A Daybook for Women: Organizing Your Career - Balancing Your Life. (Illus.). 150p. 1999. pap., wbk. ed. 19.95 (1-928977-05-7) People Works.

— Career Portfolio: Personal Career Organizer. (Illus.). 230p. 1999. ring bd. 59.95 (1-928977-02-2) People Works.

***Peterson Coil, Ann & Hult Crowell, Ann.** Career Portfolio: Personal Career Organizer - Executive Style. (Illus.). 230p. 1999. ring bd. 59.95 (1-928977-00-6) People Works.

— So Now What? Career Portfolio to the Rescue. (Illus.). 230p. 1999. mass mkt. 19.95 (1-928977-01-4) People Works.

Peterson Coil, Ann & Hult Crowell, Ann. So Now What? Career Portfolio to the Rescue. (Illus.). 230p. (C). 1999. mass mkt. 19.95 (1-928977-03-0) People Works.

— So Now What? Career Portfolio to the Rescue. gif. ed. (Illus.). 150p. 1999. pap. 29.95 (1-928977-04-9) People Works.

— So Now What? Workbook for the Career Portfolio. (Illus.). 150p. 1999. pap., wbk. ed. 19.95 (1-928977-06-5) People Works.

— So Now What? Career Portfolio to the Rescue: College Edition. gif. ed. (Illus.). 200p. 1999. pap. 29.95 (1-928977-07-3) People Works.

Peterson, Connie M., jt. auth. see Kelley.

Peterson, Cris. Century Farm: One Hundred Years on a Family Farm. LC 98-71792. (Illus.). 32p. (YA). (gr. 3 up). 1999. 16.95 (1-56397-710-9) Boyds Mills Pr.

— Extra Cheese, Please! Mozzarella's Journey from Cow to Pizza. LC 93-70876. (Illus.). 32p. (J). (ps-3). 1994. 15.95 (1-56397-177-1) Boyds Mills Pr.

— Harvest Year. LC 95-80775. (Illus.). 48p. (J). (ps-2). 1996. 15.95 (1-56397-571-8) Boyds Mills Pr.

— Horsepower. LC 96-84679. (Illus.). 32p. (J). (ps-3). 1997. 15.95 (1-56397-626-9) Boyds Mills Pr.

Peterson, Curt, jt. auth. see Dute, Roland.

Peterson, D., jt. auth. see King, T.

Peterson, D. E., jt. ed. see Kassner, M. E.

Peterson, D. J. & Green, Eric. Soviet Environmental Problems. (C). 1996. pap. text 32.50 (0-8133-8194-0) Westview.

Peterson, Dale. The Deluge & the Ark: A Journey into Primate Worlds. 1991. pap. 11.95 (0-380-71199-0, Avon Bks) Morrow Avon.

— Storyville, U. S. A. LC 99-20132. (Illus.). 312p. 1999. 25.95 (0-8203-2151-6) U of Ga Pr.

Peterson, Dale, ed. A Mad People's History of Madness. LC 81-50430. (Contemporary Community Health Ser.). 382p. 1982. pap. 118.50 (0-7837-8541-0, 204935600011) Bks Demand.

***Peterson, Dale & Goodall, Jane.** Visions of Caliban: On Chimpanzees & People. 2000. pap. text 18.95 (0-8203-2206-7) U of Ga Pr.

Peterson, Dale, jt. auth. see Wrangham, Richard.

Peterson, Dale, ed. see Goodall, Jane.

***Peterson, Dallen & Vaughn, Ellen Santilli.** Rags, Riches & Real Success: By Dallen Peterson with Ellen Vaughn. LC 00-32529. 2000. pap. write for info. (0-8423-3956-6) Tyndale Hse.

Peterson, Dan. Human Error Reduction & Safety Management. 3rd ed. (Industrial Health & Safety Ser.). 340p. 1996. text 62.95 (0-442-02183-6, VNR) Wiley.

Peterson, Dan, jt. auth. see Bright, Bill.

Peterson, Daniel. Roman Legions: Recreated in Colour Photographs. (Europa Militaria Ser.: No. 2). (Illus.). 96p. 1992. pap. 19.95 (1-872004-06-7, Pub. by Windrow & Green) Motorbooks Intl.

Peterson, Daniel C. Abraham Divided: An LDS Perspective on the Middle East. 2nd rev. ed. LC 95-40429. 400p. 1995. 16.95 (1-56236-224-0, Pub. by Aspen Bks) Origin Bk Sales.

— The Last Days: Teachings of the Modern Prophets. LC 97-18818. 320p. 1998. 19.95 (1-56236-062-0, Pub. by Aspen Bks) Origin Bk Sales.

Peterson, Dannette, illus. see Murphy, Michael J.

Peterson, Darrell J., jt. auth. see Geltner, Peter B.

***Peterson, David.** Developing Internet Commerce Applications with WebSpace. 512p. 2000. pap. 49,99 (0-471-37642-6) Wiley.

Peterson, David. Developing Smarter Intelligent Agents Using Java. (Illus.). 400p. 1997. pap., pap. text 44.95 incl. cd-rom (0-07-913643-5) McGraw.

— Ecological Scale: Theory & Applications. LC 97-48512. (Complexity in Ecological Systems Ser.). 608p. 1998. 60.00 (0-231-10502-9); pap. 35.00 (0-231-10503-7) Col U Pr.

— Of Wind, Water & Sand: The Natural Bridges Story. (Illus.). 21p. 1990. 3.50 (0-937407-02-X) Canyonlands.

***Peterson, David, ed.** Witness to the World. xvii, 138p. 1999. pap. text 20.00 (0-85364-954-5, Pub. by Paternoster Pub) Eisenbrauns.

Peterson, David & Denney, Dick. The Vox Story: The History of the Vox Amplifier. Marcinello, Angela, ed. (Guitar History Ser.). (Illus.). 150p. pap. 24.95 (0-933224-70-2, T303) Bold Strummer Ltd.

Peterson, David, jt. auth. see Peterson, Joan.

Peterson, David A., et al, eds. Education & Aging. (Illus.). 240p. 1986. text 35.00 (0-13-235698-8) P-H.

Peterson, David A. & Hull, Andrew M. Arizona Rental Rights: A Guide Book for Tenants, Landlords, & Mobile Home Users. LC 93-78484. (Illus.). 96p. (Orig.). 1993. pap. 6.95 (0-935182-63-2) Gem Guides Bk.

***Peterson, David A. & Hull, Andrew M.** Arizona Rental Rights: A Guide Book for Tenants, Landlords & Mobile Home Users. 4th rev. ed. (Illus.). 120p. 2000. pap. 10.95 (1-55838-191-0) R H Pub.

Peterson, David B., et al, eds. Leader As Coach: Strategies for Coaching & Developing Others. LC 98-125168. (Illus.). 140p. 1996. pap. text 19.95 (0-938529-14-5, Pub. by Personnel Decisions) Bookmen Inc.

Peterson, David B. & Hicks, Mary Dee. Development First: Strategies for Self-Development. (Illus.). 90p. 1995. pap. 16.95 (0-938529-13-7, Pub. by Personnel Decisions) Bookmen Inc.

Peterson, David C., jt. auth. see Peterson, Joan.

Peterson, David C., jt. auth. see Peterson, Joan B.

Peterson, David J. Revoking the Moral Order: The Ideology of Positivism & the Vienna Circle. LC 99-13628. 208p. 1999. 50.00 (0-7391-0052-1) Lxngtn Bks.

Peterson, David L. & Johnson, Darryll R., eds. Human Ecology & Climate Change: People & Resources in the Far North. LC 95-19836. 337p. 1995. 74.95 (1-56032-404-X) Taylor & Francis.

Peterson, David R. & Miller, Kathleen N. Mathematics for Business. 2nd ed. 1989. text 40.23 (0-07-049630-7) McGraw.

Peterson, David R. & Schendel, Nancy. An International Accounting Practice Set: The Karissa Jean's Simulation. LC 95-35021. 144p. 1996. pap. 14.95 (0-7890-6021-3) Haworth Pr.

— An International Accounting Practice Set: The Karissa Jean's Simulation. LC 95-35021. (Illus.). 144p. 1996. 39.95 (0-7890-6004-3, Intl Busn Pr) Haworth Pr.

Peterson, David S. Practical Guide to Industrial Metal Cleaning. LC 96-41044. 1997. 49.95 (1-56990-216-X) Hanser-Gardner.

Peterson, David W., jt. auth. see Connolly, Walter B., Jr.

Peterson, Dean F. & Crawford, A. Berry, eds. Values & Choices in the Development of the Colorado River Basin. LC 77-13716. (Illus.). 353p. 1978. pap. 109.50 (0-608-05643-X, 206609700006) Bks Demand.

Peterson, Dean F., jt. ed. see Crawford, A. Berry.

Peterson, Dean R. Hearing Aids New Era. 9.95 (0-89741-005-X) Gila River.

***Peterson, Debra.** Breastfeeding the Adopted Baby. rev. ed. (Illus.). 144p. 1999. pap. 12.95 (0-931722-36-5) Corona Pub.

Peterson, Debra. Things I Couldn't Learn Alone. (Illus.). 122p. 40.00 (0-9637375-1-1) Pringle Pub.

Peterson, Debra A. Playwriting: A Manual for Beginners. 51p. (gr. 10 up). 1999. pap. 9.95 (0-87129-822-8, P85) Dramatic Pub.

Peterson, Dennis. Chiropractic: An Illustrated History. (Illus.). 528p. (C). (gr. 13). 1994. text 73.00 (0-8016-7735-1, 07735) Mosby Inc.

Peterson, Dennis A., et al. An Archeological Survey of the Spiro Vicinity, Le Flore County, Oklahoma. (Archeological Resource Survey Report: No. 37). (Illus.). 87p. (C). 1993. pap. text 3.50 (1-881346-29-3) Univ OK Archeol.

Peterson, Dianna. Brian's Magnificent Medical Alphabet Book. (Illus.). 32p. (J). 1996. pap. write for info. (1-57579-044-0) Pine Hill Pr.

Peterson, Don. Does a Tiger Wear a Necktie? 1969. pap. 5.25 (0-8222-0318-9) Dramatists Play.

— The Masterbook of Portraiture & Studio Management. 5th ed. (Master Ser.: No. 1). (Illus.). 147p. 1989. reprint ed. pap. 29.97 (0-934420-07-6, 1127) Studio Pr NE.

Peterson, Donald. Forms of Representation. 224p. (Orig.). 1994. pap. text 29.95 (1-871516-34-X, Pub. by Intellect) Cromland.

— Wittgenstein's Early Philosophy: Three Sides of the Mirror. 216p. 1990. 40.00 (0-8020-2770-9) U of Toronto Pr.

Peterson, Donald A., ed. Progressive Dies: Principles & Practices of Design & Construction. LC 94-65575. (Illus.). 464p. 1994. 88.00 (0-87263-448-5) SME.

Peterson, Donald I. Relief from Headache. 2nd ed. LC 83-71941. (Illus.). 226p. 1990. pap. 9.95 (0-913657-00-X) D E Donel.

Peterson, Donald R. Educating Professional Psychologists: History & Guiding Conception. LC 97-14077. 281p. 1997. pap. 29.95 (1-55798-420-4, 431-7880) Am Psychol.

Peterson, Donald R., ed. Educating Professional Psychologists. (Rutgers Professional Psychology Review Ser.: Vol. 1). 192p. 1982. text 39.95 (0-87855-449-1) Transaction Pubs.

Peterson, Donald R. & Fishman, Daniel B., eds. Assessment for Decision, Vol. I. (Rutgers Symposia on Applied Psychology Ser.). 463p. (C). 1988. pap. text 20.00 (0-8135-1247-6) Rutgers U Pr.

Peterson, Doris M., jt. auth. see Peterson, John C.

Peterson, Dorothy. Amanda's Birthday. (Amanda Ser.: Vol. 2). (Illus.). 11p. (J). (ps-1). 1997. lib. bdg. 10.95 (1-890547-01-8) Hse Amanda Built.

— My Name Is Amanda. (Amanda Ser.: Vol. 1). (Illus.). 13p. (Orig.). (J). (ps-1). 1996. pap. 8.95 (1-890547-00-X) Hse Amanda Built.

Peterson, Dorothy W. Choices: The Realistic & Moving Story of a Mother's Decision about Abortion. 1988. 9.95 (0-88494-675-4) Bookcraft Inc.

Peterson, Doug. The Bible for Puzzles. LC 97-90314. (Orig.). 1997. pap. 10.95 (0-533-12361-5) Vantage.

— I Never Promised You a Hot Tub. 176p. (Orig.). 1987. pap. 5.95 (0-310-28542-9, 11351P) Zondervan.

— Many Are Called, but Most Leave Their Phone off the Hook. 256p. 1992. pap. 9.99 (0-310-57431-5) Zondervan.

— The Wrong Stuff: How to Have Disastrous Dates & Ridiculous Romances. 144p. 1990. pap. 7.99 (0-310-28721-9) Zondervan.

Peterson, Douglas E., ed. Oral Complications of Cancer Chemotherapy. 1983. lib. bdg. 54.50 (0-89838-563-6) Kluwer Academic.

Peterson, Douglas E., et al, eds. Head & Neck Management of the Cancer Patient. (Developments in Oncology Ser.). 1986. text 226.00 (0-89838-747-7) Kluwer Academic.

Peterson, Douglas L. The English Lyric from Wyatt to Donne. 2nd ed. LC 90-82583. xxxi, 391p. 1990. reprint ed. 42.00 (0-937191-20-5) Mich St U Pr.

— Time, Tide & Tempest: A Study of Shakespeare's Romances. LC 72-94155. 275p. 1973. reprint ed. pap. 85.30 (0-608-03175-5, 206362800007) Bks Demand.

***Peterson, Douglass.** U. S. Lighthouse Service Tenders. (Illus.). 192p. 1999. 39.95 (1-885457-12-X) Eastwind MD.

Peterson, Duncan. Spain on Backroads. (Illus.). 256p. (Orig.). 1994. pap. 14.95 (1-55650-637-6) Hunter NJ.

Peterson, Durby. Puzzles. (Play & Learn Ser.). (Illus.). 48p. (J). (ps-k). 1998. pap. 3.95 (1-57029-232-9, W02311) Totline Pubns.

Peterson, Durby & Warren, Jean. Sing a Song of Animals. (Learn with Piggyback Songs Ser.). (Illus.). 48p. (J). (ps-k). 1998. pap. 3.95 (1-57029-168-3, 3306) Totline Pubns.

— Sing a Song of Colors. (Learn with Piggyback Songs Ser.). (Illus.). 48p. (J). (ps-k). 1998. pap. 3.95 (1-57029-169-1, 3307) Totline Pubns.

— Sing a Song of Nature. (Learn with Piggyback Songs Ser.). (Illus.). 48p. (J). (ps-k). 1998. pap. 3.95 (1-57029-187-X, 3310) Totline Pubns.

— Sing a Song of Shapes. (Learn with Piggyback Songs Ser.). (Illus.). 48p. (J). (ps-k). 1998. pap. 3.95 (1-57029-189-6, 3312) Totline Pubns.

***Peterson, Dwight N.** The Origins of Mark: The Markan Community in Current Debate. 224p. 2000. text 85.00 (90-04-11755-5) Brill Academic Pubs.

Peterson, E. B., et al. Ecology & Management of Sitka Spruce: Emphasizing Its Natural Range in British Columbia. LC 97-222768. (Illus.). 288p. 1997. 75.00 (0-7748-0561-7) U of Wash Pr.

Peterson, E. M., jt. ed. see De La Maza, L. M.

Peterson, E. M., jt. ed. see De la Maza, L. M.

Peterson, E. M., jt. ed. see De la Meza, L. M.

Peterson, Ed Lindley. First to the Flames: The History of Fire Chief Vehicles. LC 99-61453. 240p. 1999. pap. 19.95 (0-87341-674-0) Krause Pubns.

Peterson, Edith. E-Z as A-B-C: A Collection of Columns. 1999. pap. 3.49 (1-928809-02-2) Justwrite.

— E-Z as A-B-C: The Little Instruction Book for People Who Think They Can't. Berger, Tom, ed. 27p. 1999. pap. 3.49 (1-928809-00-6) Justwrite.

— E-Z as A-B-C Enjoying Poetry. 1999. pap. 3.49 (1-928809-01-4) Justwrite.

Peterson, Edward N. The American Occupation of Germany: Retreat to Victory. LC 77-28965. 377p. reprint ed. pap. 116.90 (0-8357-5386-7, 203201800077) Bks Demand.

— An Analytical History of World War II, 1. LC 93-46254. (AUS IX: Vol. 154). X, 470p. (C). 1995. pap. text 29.95 (0-8204-2395-5) P Lang Pubng.

— An Analytical History of World War II, 2. LC 93-46254. (AUS IX: Vol. 155). (C). 1995. pap. text 29.95 (0-8204-2396-3) P Lang Pubng.

— An Analytical History of World War II, 2 vols., Set. LC 93-46254. (AUS IX: Vols. 154 & 155). 470p. (C). 1995. pap. text 59.90 (0-8204-2500-1) P Lang Pubng.

— Russian Commands & German Resistance: The Soviet Occupation, 1945-1949. LC 98-4812. (Studies in Modern European History: Vol. 29). 510p. (C). 1999. text 70.95 (0-8204-3948-7) P Lang Pubng.

Peterson, Elise. Tracy's Mess. (Illus.). 32p. (J). (ps-2). 1996. 15.95 (1-879085-94-1, Whispering Coyote) Charlesbridge Pub.

***Peterson, Elizabeth.** The Mind on Paper. unabridged ed. (Illus.). 20p. 1999. spiral bd. 7.50 (1-929326-41-6) Hal Bar Pubg.

— Roadside Tales. unabridged ed. (Illus.). 20p. 1999. spiral bd. 7.50 (1-929326-40-8) Hal Bar Pubg.

Peterson, Elizabeth A., ed. Freedom Road: Adult Education of African Americans. LC 95-23599. 148p. (Orig.). (C). 1996. 14.50 (0-89464-885-3) Krieger.

Peterson, Elizabeth J. Beginning Math at Home, 4 vols., Set. (Illus.). 75p. (J). (ps-1). 1993. 13.50 (0-938911-01-5) Indiv Ed - Poppy Ln.

— Beginning Reading at Home. (Illus.). 136p. (J). (ps-1). 1992. reprint ed. 35.00 (0-938911-00-7) Indiv Ed - Poppy Ln.

— Christina & the Little Red Bird. (Illus.). 23p. (J). (ps-5). 1999. reprint ed. spiral bd. 5.95 (0-938911-02-3) Indiv Ed - Poppy Ln.

Peterson, Elizabeth J., ed. see Skiff, Andrea.

Peterson, Elmer, jt. ed. see Sanouillet, Michel.

An Asterisk (*) at the beginning of an entry indicates that the title is appearing for the first time.

Peterson, Elmer G. Remembering E. G. Peterson: His Life & Our Story. LC 74-13517. (Illus.). 149p. reprint ed. pap. 46.20 (*0-7837-7066-9*, 204687800004) Bks Demand.

Peterson, Elmer T. Big Dam Foolishness: The Problems of Modern Flood Control & Water Storage. LC 54-10812. 232p. reprint ed. pap. 72.00 (*0-8357-3600-8*, 202270600029) Bks Demand.

— Big Dam Foolishness: Water Conservation in the Future. 1954. 12.95 (*0-8159-5107-8*) Devin.

Peterson, Elsa. Copyright & Permissions: What Every Writer & Editor Should Know. 1996. pap. 5.50 (*1-880407-17-5*) Edit Freelancers.

Peterson, Eobert D. & Wunder, Delores F. Social Problems: Globalization in the 21st Century. 466p. (C). 1998. pap. text 59.00 (*0-13-146895-2*) P-H.

Peterson, Eric. Pride & Prejudice Notes. (Cliffs Notes Ser.). 56p. 1959. pap. 4.95 (*0-8220-1084-4*, Cliff) IDG Bks.

Peterson, Eric, jt. auth. see Gray, John.

Peterson, Eric S. Card Modeling: The Art of Creating Scale Models in Paper. LC 93-72116. (Illus.). 56p. (Orig.). 1994. pap. 14.95 (*0-9637100-0-1*) Caltrop Pub.

Peterson, Erik R., ed. Multinational Corporations. (CSIS Significant Issues Ser.). (C). 1996. pap. text 11.95 (*0-89206-246-0*) Westview.

Peterson, Ernst, jt. auth. see Chaffin, Glenn M., Jr.

Peterson, Esther & Conkling, Winifred. Restless: The Memoirs of Labor & Consumer Advocate Esther Peterson. 193p. 1995. per. 15.00 (*1-886450-02-1*) Caring Pub.

Peterson, Eugene. Five Smooth Stones for Pastoral Work. 251p. 1992. reprint ed. pap. 16.00 (*0-8028-0660-0*) Eerdmans.

— Subversive Spirituality. Lyster, Jim & Sharon, John, eds. 188p. (Orig.). 1994. reprint ed. pap. 17.95 (*1-57383-071-2*) Regent College.

— Wisdom of Each Other. 1997. pap. 8.99 (*0-310-22374-1*) Zondervan.

Peterson, Eugene H. Answering God: The Psalms As Tools for Prayer. 160p. 1991. pap. 12.00 (*0-06-066512-2*, Pub. by Harper SF) HarpC.

— The Contemplative Pastor: Returning to the Art of Spiritual Direction. 179p. 1993. reprint ed. pap. 16.00 (*0-8028-0114-5*) Eerdmans.

— Excellence: Run with the Horses. (Christian Basics Bible Studies). 64p. (Orig.). 1996. pap., wbk. ed. 4.99 (*0-8308-2011-6*, 2011) InterVarsity.

***Peterson, Eugene H.** First & Second Samuel. LC 99-41129. (Westminster Bible Companion Ser.). 303p. 1999. pap. 19.95 (*0-664-25523-X*) Westminster John Knox.

Peterson, Eugene H. Leap Over a Wall: Earthy Spirituality for Everyday ChristiansReflections on the Life of David from. LC 96-25066. 256p. 1998. pap. 13.00 (*0-06-066522-X*, Pub. by Harper SF) HarpC.

— Like Dew Your Youth: Growing up with Your Teenager. 2nd rev. ed. LC 94-25383. 128p. 1994. pap. 10.00 (*0-8028-0116-1*) Eerdmans.

— Living the Message: Daily Reflections with Eugene H. Peterson. 400p. 1996. pap. 13.00 (*0-06-066432-0*, Pub. by Harper SF) HarpC.

— A Long Obedience in the Same Direction. LC 79-2715. 192p. (Orig.). 1980. pap. 11.99 (*0-87784-727-4*, 727) InterVarsity.

***Peterson, Eugene H.** A Long Obedience in the Same Direction: Discipleship in an Instant Society. 128p. 2000. pap. 7.99 (*0-8308-2039-6*) InterVarsity.

— A Long Obedience in the Same Direction: Discipleship in an Instant Society. 20th anniversary ed. 204p. 2000. 16.99 (*0-8308-2277-1*); pap. 11.99 (*0-8308-2257-7*) InterVarsity.

Peterson, Eugene H. The Message: New Testament Psalms & Proverbs. LC 98-35685. 1998. 22.99 (*1-57683-119-1*); pap. 16.99 (*1-57683-120-5*) NavPress.

— The Message: New Testament with Psalms & Proverbs in Contemporary Language. LC 97-194187. 528p. 1997. lthr. 22.00 (*1-57683-022-5*) NavPress.

***Peterson, Eugene H.** The Message Old Testament Prophets. 2000. 21.00 (*1-57683-195-7*) NavPress.

Peterson, Eugene H. The Message Promise Book. LC 97-194439. 144p. (Orig.). 1997. pap. 5.00 (*1-57683-015-2*) NavPress.

— Messages for the Heart: Selected Readings from the Message. 1997. pap. 12.00 incl. audio (*1-57683-038-1*) NavPress.

— Perseverance: A Long Obedience in the Same Direction. (Christian Basics Bible Studies: No. 10). 64p. (Orig.). 1996. pap., wbk. ed. 4.99 (*0-8308-2010-8*, 2010) InterVarsity.

— Praying with Jesus: A Year of Daily Prayers & Reflections on the Words & Actions of Jesus. LC 92-54533. 400p. 1993. pap. 12.00 (*0-06-066566-1*, Pub. by Harper SF) HarpC.

— Praying with Paul: A Year of Daily Prayers & Reflections on the Words of Paul. 400p. 1995. pap. 12.00 (*0-06-066433-9*, Pub. by Harper SF) HarpC.

— Praying with the Psalms: A Year of Daily Prayers & Reflections on the Words of David. LC 92-54532. 400p. 1993. pap. 13.00 (*0-06-066567-X*, Pub. by Harper SF) HarpC.

***Peterson, Eugene H.** The Psalms: An Artist's Impression. (Illus.). 55p. 2000. 19.99 (*0-8308-2289-5*) InterVarsity.

Peterson, Eugene H. Psalms: Prayers of the Heart. (LifeGuide Bible Studies). 64p. (Orig.). 1987. pap., wbk. ed. 4.99 (*0-8308-1034-X*, 1034) InterVarsity.

***Peterson, Eugene H.** Psalms: Prayers of the Heart. 2nd ed. (LifeGuide Bible Studies). 64p. (Orig.). 2000. pap. 4.99 (*0-8308-3034-0*) InterVarsity.

Peterson, Eugene H. Reversed Thunder: The Revelation of John & the Praying Imagination. 224p. 1991. pap. 13.00 (*0-06-066503-3*, Pub. by Harper SF) HarpC.

— Run with the Horses. LC 83-13005. 213p. 1983. pap. 11.99 (*0-87784-905-6*, 905) InterVarsity.

— Sayings of Jesus. LC 99-173775. (Message Ser.). 128p. 1998. 12.00 (*1-57683-104-3*) NavPress.

— Stories of Jesus: From the Text of the Message. 1999. 12.00 (*1-57683-183-3*) NavPress.

— Subversive Spirituality. LC 97-21465. 273p. (Orig.). 1997. pap. 18.00 (*0-8028-4297-6*) Eerdmans.

— Take & Read: Spiritual Reading: An Annotated List. 135p. (Orig.). 1995. pap. text 10.00 (*0-8028-4096-5*) Eerdmans.

— Traveling Light: Modern Meditations on St. Paul's Letter of Freedom. LC 88-11258. 204p. 1988. reprint ed. pap. 15.95 (*0-939443-08-2*) Helmers Howard Pub.

— Under the Unpredictable Plant: An Exploration in Vocational Holiness. 206p. 1994. pap. text 15.00 (*0-8028-0848-4*) Eerdmans.

— Where Your Treasure Is: Psalms That Summon You from Self to Community. 2nd ed. LC 96-31967. 190p. 1993. reprint ed. pap. 13.00 (*0-8028-0115-3*) Eerdmans.

— The Wisdom of Each Other: A Conversation Between Spiritual Friends. LC 96-38906. (Spiritual Directions Ser.). 112p. 1997. 12.99 (*0-310-20198-5*) Zondervan.

— Working the Angles: The Shape of Pastoral Integrity. LC 96-31995. 200p. (Orig.). 1987. pap. 15.00 (*0-8028-0265-6*) Eerdmans.

Peterson, Eugene H., ed. The Message: The New Testament in Contemporary Language. LC 98-10518. 544p. 1998. pap. 5.00 (*1-57683-079-9*) NavPress.

Peterson, Eugene H., jt. auth. see Dawn, Marva J.

Peterson, Eugene H., jt. auth. see Kaai, Anneue.

Peterson, Evangeline, jt. auth. see Lewis, Edna.

Peterson, F. P., jt. auth. see Massey, William S.

Peterson, F. Ross, et al. A History of Cache County. LC 96-60166. (Illus.). write for info. (*0-913738-10-7*) Utah St Hist Soc.

Peterson-Falzone, et al. Cleft Palate Speech. 3rd ed. (Illus.). 432p. (gr. 13). 1999. text 58.00 (*0-8151-3153-4*, 29901) Mosby Inc.

Peterson, Fiona & Whittaker, Claire. Operating Bail - Decision-Making under the Bail Etc. (Scotland) Act 1980. 184p. 1994. pap. 35.00 (*0-11-495173-X*, HM5173X, Pub. by Statnry Office) Bernan Associates.

Peterson-Fleming, Judy & Fleming, Bill. Kitten Training & Critters, Too! LC 95-665. (Illus.). 39p. (J). (ps-2). 1996. 16.00 (*0-688-13386-X*, Wm Morrow) Morrow Avon.

Peterson, Florence. Strikes in the United States. 1988. reprint ed. lib. bdg. 25.00 (*0-7812-0546-8*) Rprt Serv.

— Strikes in the United States, 1880-1936. LC 70-145232. 190p. 1972. reprint ed. 25.00 (*0-403-01148-5*) Scholarly.

***Peterson, Frances L.** The Third Daughter, a Journal. 150p. 2000. pap. 9.95 (*1-891929-38-0*) Four Seasons.

Peterson, Francisca E., tr. see Rape & Abuse Crisis Ctr. Staff.

Peterson, Frank T. Audubon Birds. (Illus.). 1996. pap. 4.95 (*0-89659-091-7*) Abbeville Pr.

Peterson, Franklynn. The Build-It-Yourself Furniture Catalog. LC 76-6567. 1976. pap. 4.95 (*0-13-085902-8*, Reward) P-H.

— How to Fix Damn Near Everything. (Illus.). 480p. 1996. 12.99 (*0-517-66200-0*) Random Hse Value.

Peterson, Franklynn & Kesselman-Turkel, Judi. The Author's Handbook. 248p. 1982. pap. 8.95 (*0-13-053900-7*) P-H.

— The Magazine Writer's Handbook. 263p. 1983. 17.95 (*0-13-543751-2*) P-H.

Peterson, Franklynn, jt. auth. see Kesselman-Turkel, Judi.

Peterson, Fred W. Building Community, Keeping the Faith: German Catholic Vernacular Architecture in a Rural Minnesota Parish. LC 98-38320. (Illus.). 224p. 1998. 39.95 (*0-87351-368-1*, 368-1); pap. 19.95 (*0-87351-369-X*, 369-X) Minn Hist.

— Homes in the Heartland: Balloon Frame Farmhouses of the Upper Midwest, 1850-1920. LC 92-2833. (Rural America Ser.). (Illus.). xii, 300p. 1992. 35.00 (*0-7006-0536-3*) U Pr of KS.

Peterson, Freda C. Over My Dead Body! The Story of Hillside Cemetery, Silverton, Colorado. 2nd abr. ed. LC 96-76377. Orig. Title: The Story of Hillside Cemetery Burials 1872-1988. 154p. 1996. pap. 11.95 (*0-927562-20-0*) Levite Apache.

***Peterson, Freda Carley.** The Story of Hillside Cemetery, Silverton, San Juan County, Colorado. 2nd ed. LC 96-69050. (Illus.). 1998. write for info. (*0-927562-22-7*) Levite Apache.

Peterson, Frederick. Desert Pioneer Doctor. (American Autobiography Ser.). 130p. 1995. reprint ed. lib. bdg. 69.00 (*0-7812-8617-4*) Rprt Serv.

Peterson, G. P. An Introduction to Heat Pipes: Modeling, Testing, & Applications. 368p. 1994. 110.00 (*0-471-30512-X*) Wiley.

Peterson, G. P., jt. ed. see Bayazitoglu, Y.

Peterson, Gail, jt. auth. see Diener, Patricia.

Peterson, Gale R., ed. Understanding Biotechnology Law: Protection, Licensing, & Intellectual Property Policies. LC 93-7101. (Illus.). 496p. 1993. text 195.00 (*0-8247-8935-0*) Dekker.

Peterson, Galen. The Everlasting Tradition: Jewish Customs, Holidays & Historical Events that Reveal Biblical Truth. LC 95-13364. 160p. 1995. pap. 9.99 (*0-8254-3499-8*, 95-049) Kregel.

— Handbook of Bible Festivals: A Celebration Guide for Churches, Families, & Christian Schools. LC 96-41862. (Illus.). 112p. 1997. pap. 12.99 (*0-7847-0595-X*, 03088) Standard Pub.

Peterson, Garneth O., jt. auth. see Frost, Murray.

Peterson, Gary & Byrne, David. Klondike Kalamity. 1978. 5.00 (*0-87129-572-5*, K18) Dramatic Pub.

Peterson, Gary & Nestor, Larry. Stone Soup - Musical. 1983. 4.25 (*0-87129-581-4*, S68) Dramatic Pub.

Peterson, Gary A., et al, eds. Technologies for Sustainable Agriculture in the Tropics. LC 93-21161. (ASA Special Publications: No. 56). 313p. 1993. 30.00 (*0-89118-118-0*) Am Soc Agron.

Peterson, Gary B. & Bennion, Lowell C. Sanpete Scenes: A Guide to Utah's Heart. LC 87-72694. (Illus.). 144p. (Orig.). 1987. pap. 16.95 (*0-9617133-0-5*) Basin-Plateau Pr.

Peterson, Gary J. Ski Bummin' in the Rockies: A Profile of Twenty Western Resorts & the Ski Bum Lifestyle. LC 97-92376. (Illus.). 160p. (Orig.). 1997. mass mkt. 11.50 (*0-9658917-0-4*) Champagne Ent.

Peterson, Gary L., ed. Communicating in Organizations: A Casebook. 2nd ed. LC 99-29088. 198p. (C). 1999. pap. text 32.00 (*0-205-29589-4*, Longwood Div) Allyn.

Peterson, Gary L., ed. see Tesla, Nikola.

Peterson, Gayle. Birthing Normally: A Personal Growth Approach to Childbirth. 2nd ed. (Illus.). 195p. 1991. reprint ed. pap. 17.95 (*0-9625231-1-9*) Shadow & Light.

— An Easier Childbirth: A Mother's Guide for Birthing Normally. 2nd ed. (Illus.). 177p. 1993. reprint ed. pap. 17.95 (*0-9625231-4-3*) Shadow & Light.

***Peterson, Gayle.** Making Healthy Families. 2000. 23.95 (*0-9625231-5-1*) Shadow & Light.

Peterson, Gayle, jt. auth. see Mehl, Lewis E.

Peterson, Gayle H., jt. auth. see Mehl, Lewis E.

Peterson, Geoff. Bad Trades. LC 98-83077. 240p. 2000. pap. 14.95 (*0-88739-246-6*) Creat Arts Bk.

Peterson, Geoffrey. Conscience & Caring. LC 82-7401. (Creative Pastoral Care & Counseling Ser.). 96p. reprint ed. pap. 30.00 (*0-608-17911-6*, 202909600058) Bks Demand.

***Peterson, George.** It Sure Beats Working for a Living (Just Kid-Ing) (Illus.). 280p. 1999. pap. write for info. (*0-7392-0386-X*, PO3607) Morris Pubng.

Peterson, George. Modular Digital Multitracks: The Power User's Guide. 2nd rev. ed. LC 97-73717. 176p. 1998. pap. 29.95 (*0-918371-23-6*, MixBooks) Intertec Pub.

Peterson, George A., jt. auth. see Bender, Roger J.

Peterson, George C. Stuck in the Mud, Vol. 1. (Illus.). 208p. (Orig.). (YA). (gr. 9-12). 1988. pap. write for info. (*0-9621320-0-4*) G Peterson.

Peterson, George E., ed. Big City Politics, Governance, & Fiscal Constraints. (Urban Opportunity Ser.). 294p. (C). 1994. pap. text 29.00 (*0-87766-573-7*); lib. bdg. 64.50 (*0-87766-572-9*) Urban Inst.

Peterson, George E. & Vroman, Wayne, eds. Urban Labor Markets & Job Opportunity. LC 92-10899. (Urban Opportunity Ser.). 342p. (C). 1992. pap. text 31.00 (*0-87766-567-2*) Urban Inst.

Peterson, George E., et al. Corporations as Partners in Strengthening Urban Communities: A Research Report. LC 96-116321. (Report Ser.). 44 p. 1994. write for info. (*0-8237-0526-9*) Conference Bd.

Peterson, George E., jt. ed. see Harrell, Adele V.

Peterson, George H., jt. ed. see McLaren, A. Douglas.

Peterson, George H., jt. ed. see McLaren, Arthur D.

Peterson, George L., et al. Amenity Resource Valuation: Integrating Economics with Other Disciplines. LC 88-50862. 265p. 1988. 27.95 (*0-910251-27-4*) Venture Pub PA.

Peterson, Gerald R., jt. auth. see Hill, Frederick J.

Peterson, Gerald W., jt. auth. see Clapp, Steve.

Peterson, Gerry. "It's 9 O'Clock on Monday Morning... Where Do I Go?" Seminar Edition. 1997. pap. 9.95 (*0-9658437-1-8*) Westco Mktg.

Peterson, Gladys J. Better Photos. LC 94-70903. 96p. 1997. pap. text 15.00 (*1-884752-06-3*, 44248) Cook Min Intl.

— Pieces - The Story of Elgin in a Quilt. (Illus.). 128p. (Orig.). 1988. write for info. (*0-318-64354-5*); pap. 9.95 (*0-685-24078-9*) Amer Healthcare Ctr.

Peterson, Glen. The Power of Words: Literacy & Revolution in South China, 1949-95. LC 97-228623. 352p. 1998. text 75.00 (*0-7748-0611-7*) U of Wash Pr.

Peterson, Glen, et al, eds. Education, Culture & Identity in 20th Century China. (Illus.). 432p. (C). text 55.00 (*0-472-11151-5*, 11151) U of Mich Pr.

Peterson, Glen, jt. auth. see Witherspoon, Gary.

Peterson, Glen D., jt. auth. see Johnson, Graham E.

Peterson, Gordon M. & Graesser, R. F. Calculus. (Quality Paperback Ser.: No. 51). 321p. (Orig.). 1974. reprint ed. pap. 7.95 (*0-8226-0051-X*) Littlefield.

Peterson, Gordon W. Awesome Truth That Makes Sense: It's Time for Clear Thinking. Carraway, W. B., ed. LC 98-74277. 228p. 1999. pap. 12.95 (*0-9633855-4-2*) BAC Pubns.

Peterson, Gregory, tr. see Kora, Takehisa.

***Peterson, Grethe B.** Tanner Lectures on Human Values, Vol. 20. 1999. 30.00 (*0-87480-599-6*) U of Utah Pr.

Peterson, Grethe B., ed. The Tanner Lectures on Human Values. (Tanner Lectures: Vol. 15). 400p. (C). 1994. 30.00 (*0-87480-450-7*) U of Utah Pr.

— The Tanner Lectures on Human Values, Vol. IX: 1988. 320p. 1988. 30.00 (*0-87480-326-8*) U of Utah Pr.

— The Tanner Lectures on Human Values, Vol. X. (Tanner Lectures). 300p. (C). 1989. text 30.00 (*0-87480-318-7*) U of Utah Pr.

— The Tanner Lectures on Human Values, Vol. XI. (Tanner Lectures). 500p. 1990. 30.00 (*0-87480-340-3*) U of Utah Pr.

— The Tanner Lectures on Human Values, Vol. XII. 250p. 1991. 30.00 (*0-87480-350-0*) U of Utah Pr.

— The Tanner Lectures on Human Values, Vol. 13. (Tanner Lectures). 1992. 30.00 (*0-87480-406-X*) U of Utah Pr.

— The Tanner Lectures on Human Values, Vol. 14. (Tanner Lectures). 320p. (C). 1993. text 30.00 (*0-87480-418-3*) U of Utah Pr.

— The Tanner Lectures on Human Values, Vol. 16. 360p. 1995. text 30.00 (*0-87480-476-0*) U of Utah Pr.

— The Tanner Lectures on Human Values, Vol. 17. 320p. (C). 1996. text 30.00 (*0-87480-505-8*) U of Utah Pr.

— The Tanner Lectures on Human Values, Vol. 18. 320p. 1997. 30.00 (*0-87480-543-0*) U of Utah Pr.

— The Tanner Lectures on Human Values, Vol. 19. 1998. 30.00 (*0-87480-564-3*) U of Utah Pr.

***Peterson, Grethe B., ed.** The Tanner Lectures on Human Values 2000, Vol. 21. 384p. 2000. 35.00 (*0-87480-653-4*) U of Utah Pr.

Peterson, H. Craig & Lewis, W. Cris. Managerial Economics. 3rd ed. (Illus.). 688p. (C). 1993. write for info. (*0-318-69915-X*) Macmillan.

Peterson, H. Donl. The Pearl of Great Price: A History & Commentary. LC 87-15672. xiii, 400p. 1987. pap. 14.95 (*0-87579-665-6*) Deseret Bk.

Peterson, H. Donl & Tate, Charles D., eds. The Pearl of Great Price: Revelations from God. (Monograph Ser.: Vol. 14). 1989. 10.95 (*0-88494-683-5*) Bookcraft Inc.

Peterson, Hans-Inge. Tumor Blood Circulation: Angiogenesis, Vascular Morphology & Blood Flow of Experimental & Human Tumors. 240p. 1979. 138.00 (*0-8493-5695-4*, RC255, CRC Reprint) Franklin.

Peterson, Harold A. & Marquardt, Thomas P. Appraisal & Diagnosis of Speech Disorders. 3rd ed. LC 93-33657. 320p. 1994. 78.00 (*0-13-200149-7*) P-H.

Peterson, Harold F. Diplomat of the Americas: A Biography of William I. Buchanan, 1852-1909. LC 76-22652. 458p. (C). 1977. text 32.50 (*0-87395-346-0*) State U NY Pr.

Peterson, Harold I., jt. auth. see Stewart, Watt.

Peterson, Harold L. American Indian Tomahawks. 49.95 (*0-88227-031-1*) Gun Room.

— American Knives. 1980. 24.95 (*0-88227-016-8*) Gun Room.

— The American Sword, Seventeen Seventy-Five to Nineteen Forty-Five. LC 65-25409. (Illus.). 1996. 45.00 (*0-9603094-1-1*) Ray Riling.

— Arms & Armor of the Pilgrims. 1990. reprint ed. 2.00 (*0-940628-04-X*) Pilgrim Soc.

— How Do You Know It's Old? LC 74-13118. (Encore Edition Ser.). (Illus.). 1975. 6.95 (*0-684-15286-X*, Scribners Ref) Mac Lib Ref.

Peterson, Helen S. Oliver Wendell Holmes: Soldier, Lawyer, Supreme Court Justice. LC 78-71848. (Illus.). 91p. 1979. 7.95 (*0-914932-03-9*) Fox Hills Pr.

Peterson, Henry W., jt. auth. see Del Vecchio, Michael J.

Peterson, Hiromi & Omizo, Naomi. Adventures in Japanese: Hiragana & Katakana I with Flashcards. 115p. 1998. pap. text 18.95 (*0-88727-302-5*) Cheng & Tsui.

— Adventures in Japanese. LC 98-72561. 1998. pap. text 29.99 (*0-88727-300-9*); pap. text, wbk. ed. 16.95 (*0-88727-301-7*) Cheng & Tsui.

***Peterson, Hiromi & Omizo, Naomi.** Adventures in Japanese: Level 2. (JPN & ENG., Illus.). (J). 1999. 39.95 (*0-88727-320-3*) Cheng & Tsui.

— Adventures in Japanese: Level 2. (JPN & ENG., Illus.). (J). 1999. 19.95 (*0-88727-321-1*); teacher ed. 49.95 (*0-88727-322-X*) Cheng & Tsui.

Peterson, Hiromi & Omizo, Naomi. Adventures in Japanese Level 1: Teacher's Manual with Language Lab Scripts. 190p. 1998. pap. text, teacher ed. 49.95 (*0-88727-304-1*) Cheng & Tsui.

***Peterson, Hiromi & Omizo, Naomi.** Adventures in Japanese Textbook No. 3: Field Test Edition. (Illus.). 388p. (YA). (gr. 7). 2000. pap. write for info. (*0-88727-385-8*) Cheng & Tsui.

Peterson, Hogan M. Between Species: Women & Animals. 1999. write for info. (*0-449-91038-5*) Fawcett.

Peterson-Hoormon, Janet M., et al. Parish Faith Formation Assessment & Planning Tool. Kaser, Jeffrey, ed. LC 98-33291. 24p. 1998. pap., wbk. ed. 14.95 (*1-58051-057-4*) Sheed & Ward WI.

Peterson, Horace C. & Fite, Gilbert C. Opponents of War, 1917-1918. LC 85-30570. 402p. 1986. reprint ed. lib. bdg. 89.50 (*0-313-25132-0*, FPOP, Greenwood Pr) Greenwood.

Peterson, Houston. Huxley, Prophet of Science. LC 75-30039. reprint ed. 32.50 (*0-404-14040-8*) AMS Pr.

Peterson, Hugh M., jt. auth. see Lewis, Robert T.

Peterson, Ingrid. Clare of Assisi: A Biographical Study. LC 93-24140. 436p. 1993. 25.00 (*0-8199-0964-5*) Franciscan Pr.

Peterson, Ingrid & Miller, Ramona. Praying with Clare of Assisi. Koch, Carl, ed. (Companions for the Journey Ser.). (Illus.). 120p. (Orig.). 1994. pap. 8.95 (*0-88489-333-2*) St Marys.

Peterson, Ingrid, et al. Clarefest Papers. (Clare Centennary Ser.). 285p. 1996. pap. 15.00 (*1-57659-000-3*) Franciscan Inst.

Peterson, Ingrid J. William Nassington: Canon, Mystic, & Poet of the Speculum Vitae. (American University Studies: Theology & Religion: Ser. VII, Vol. 19). X, 199p. 1986. text 34.00 (*0-8204-0322-9*) P Lang Pubng.

Peterson, Irving M. Church Leadership & Interpersonal Relationships: What Church Organizations Might Learn about Dealing with People from Jesus' Dealings with His Disciples. 17p. 1997. pap. 3.95 (*0-943167-26-4*) Faith & Fellowship Pr.

Peterson-Ishaq, Kristin, compiled by. Lake Champlain: Reflections on Our Past - A Bibliography. 90p. (Orig.). 1989. pap. text 9.00 (*0-944277-18-7*, U55) U VT Ctr Rsch VT.

Peterson-Ishaq, Kristin, ed. University of Vermont Graduate Theses on Vermont Topics, 1975-1992. (Ocassional Papers: No. 15). 246p. 1993. pap. text 17.00 (*0-944277-24-1*) U VT Ctr Rsch VT.

Peterson-Ishaq, Kristin, ed. We Vermonters: Perspectives on the Past - A Bibliography. (Illus.). 177p. 1995. pap. text 14.00 (*0-944277-29-2*) U VT Ctr Rsch VT.

Peterson-Ishaq, Kristin, tr. see Idris, Yusuf.

Peterson, Ivars. Fatal Defect. LC 97-105469. 1996. pap. 13.00 (*0-679-74027-9*) McKay.

— Fatal Defect. 1996. pap. 13.00 (*0-614-12620-7*) Vin Bks.

P

— Islands of Truth: A Mathematical Mystery Cruise. LC 89-49501. 325p. (C). 1990. pap. text 21.95 (*0-7167-2113-9*) W H Freeman.
— Islands of Truth: A Mathematical Mystery Cruise. 1991. pap. text 14.95 (*0-7167-2148-1*) W H Freeman.
— The Jungles of Randomness: A Mathematical Safari. LC 97-1275. (Illus.). 256p. 1997. 24.95 (*0-471-16449-6*) Wiley.
***Peterson, Ivars.** The Jungles of Randomness: A Mathematical Safari. 239p. 1998. pap. 14.95 (*0-471-29587-6*) Wiley.
— Math Trek: Adventures in the Mathzone. LC 99-25900. 128p. 1999. pap. 12.95 (*0-471-31570-2*) Wiley.
Peterson, Ivars. The Mathematical Tourist: Snapshots, Vol. 1. LC 98-2697. 266p. 1998. pap. text 14.95 (*0-7167-3250-5*) W H Freeman.
— Newton's Clock: Chaos in the Solar System. LC 93-7176. (Illus.). 317p. 1995. pap. text 15.95 (*0-7167-2724-2*) W H Freeman.
***Peterson, Ivars & Henderson, Nancy.** Math Trek 2: A Mathematical Space Odyssey. 128p. 2000. pap. 12.95 (*0-471-31571-0*) Wiley.
Peterson, J., ed. see Royal Swedish Academy of Sciences Staff.
Peterson, J. A. Your Reactions Are Showing. 1980. pap. 2.50 (*0-8474-0999-6*) Back to Bible.
Peterson, J. E. The Arab Gulf States: Steps Toward Political Participation, 131. LC 87-25836. (Washington Papers: No. 131). 168p. 1988. 49.95 (*0-275-92881-0*, C2881, Praeger Pubs); pap. 13.95 (*0-275-92882-9*, B2882, Praeger Pubs) Greenwood.
— Historical Dictionary of Saudi Arabia. (Asian Historical Dictionaries Ser.: No. 14). (Illus.). 267p. 1993. 40.00 (*0-8108-2780-8*) Scarecrow.
— U. S. - Arab Relations: Security in the Arabian Peninsula & Gulf States, 1974-84, No. 7. 154p. (Orig.). 1985. pap. 8.00 (*0-916729-12-5*) Natl Coun Arab.
Peterson, J. E., jt. ed. see Sindelar, H. Richard.
Peterson, J. L., jt. ed. see DiClemente, R. J.
Peterson, Jack. United States Catholic Elementary Schools & Their Finances, 1989. 66p. (Orig.). 1990. pap. 8.00 (*1-55833-052-6*) Natl Cath Educ.
Peterson, Jack E., ed. Industrial Health. 2nd ed. (Illus.). (C). 1991. text 73.00 (*0-936712-91-0*) Am Conf Govt Indus Hygienist.
Peterson, Jacqueline. Sacred Encounters: Father De Smet & the Indians of the Rocky Mountain West. 1993. 49.95 (*0-8061-2575-6*); pap. 24.95 (*0-8061-2576-4*) U of Okla Pr.
Peterson, James. Dreams of Chaos, Visions of Order: Understanding the American Avant-Garde Cinema. LC 93-25672. (Contemporary Film & Television Ser.). (Illus.). 226p. 1993. pap. 21.95 (*0-8143-2457-6*); text 44.95 (*0-8143-2456-8*) Wayne St U Pr.
— Employee Stock Ownership Plans. 8p. (Orig.). 1978. pap. 8.00 (*0-317-04829-5*) Natl Coun Econ Dev.
— The Enchanted Alphabet. (Illus.). 160p. (Orig.). 1985. pap. 9.95 (*0-85030-765-1*, Pub. by Aqrn Pr) Harper SF.
***Peterson, James.** The Essentials of Cooking. LC 99-32539. (Illus.). 312p. 1999. 40.00 (*1-57965-120-8*, 85120) Artisan.
Peterson, James. Fish & Shellfish: The Cook's Indispensable Companion. LC 95-38375. (Illus.). 456p. 1996. 40.00 (*0-688-12737-1*, Wm Morrow) Morrow Avon.
— More I Could Not Ask: Finding Christ in the Margins: A Priest's Story. 192p. 1998. pap. 12.95 (*0-8245-1772-5*, Crsrd) Crossroad NY.
— Perspectives on Politics: Classic to Contemporary. LC 95-112363. 304p. (C). 1994. pap. text, per. 25.95 (*0-8403-9962-6*) Kendall-Hunt.
— Sauces: Classical & Contemporary Sauce Making. LC 90-39442. (Illus.). 512p. 1991. text 44.95 (*0-442-23773-1*, VNR) Wiley.
— Sauces: Classical & Contemporary Sauce Making. 2nd ed. 624p. 1998. 44.95 (*0-471-29275-3*, VNR) Wiley.
— Sauces: Classical & Contemporary Sauce Making. 2nd rev. ed. LC 97-13433. (Culinary Arts Ser.). (Illus.). 620p. (C). 1998. 44.95 (*0-442-02615-3*, VNR) Wiley.
***Peterson, James.** Splendid Soups: Recipes & Master Techniques for Making the World's Best Soups. rev. ed. (Illus.). 576p. 2000. 45.00 (*0-471-39136-0*) Wiley.
Peterson, James. Vegetables. Schwartz, Justin, ed. (Illus.). 512p. 1998. 35.00 (*0-688-14658-9*, Wm Morrow) Morrow Avon.
Peterson, James, jt. auth. see Bertucci, Bob.
Peterson, James, jt. auth. see Dickerson, Ron.
Peterson, James A. Counseling & Values: A Philosophical Examination. 2nd ed. LC 89-38243. 1989. pap. 21.85 (*0-910328-43-9*) Sulzburger & Graham Pub.
— How to Jump Higher. 144p. 1988. pap. 14.95 (*0-940279-12-6*, 79126H, Mstrs Pr) NTC Contemp Pub Co.
Peterson, James A., ed. Paleotectonics & Sedimentation in the Rocky Mountain Region, United States. LC 86-17467. (American Association of Petroleum Geologists. Memoir Ser.: No. 41). (Illus.). 703p. reprint ed. pap. 200.00 (*0-608-04228-5*, 206498500012) Bks Demand.
Peterson, James A. & Bryant, Cedric X., eds. The StairMaster Fitness Handbook: A User's Guide to Exercise Testing & Prescription. LC 95-70429. (Health, Fitness, & Wellness Ser.). (Illus.). 340p. (Orig.). 1995. pap. 19.95 (*1-57167-024-6*) Sagamore Pub.
Peterson, James A. & Clarke, James W. Geology & Hydrocarbon Habitat of the West Siberian Basin. LC 92-114189. (AAPG Studies in Geology: Vol. 32). (Illus.). 108p. (Orig.). reprint ed. pap. 33.50 (*0-608-08738-6*, 206937700004) Bks Demand.
Peterson, James A. & Hronek, Bruce B. Risk Management: Park, Recreation & Leisure Services. 3rd ed. (Illus.). 196p. 1999. pap. 26.95 (*1-57167-205-2*) Sagamore Pub.
Peterson, James A., et al. Strength Training for Women. LC 94-47646. (Illus.). 168p. 1995. pap. 16.95 (*0-87322-752-2*, PPET0752) Human Kinetics.
— Williston Basin: Anatomy of a Cratonic Oil Province. LC 87-60771. viii, 440p. 1987. write for info. (*0-933979-09-6*) Rocky Mtn Assoc Geol.
Peterson, James A., jt. auth. see Christensen, Dave.
Peterson, James A., jt. auth. see Levra, John.
Peterson, James A., jt. auth. see Marcin, Denny.
Peterson, James A., jt. auth. see Noble, Pete.
Peterson, James A., jt. auth. see Peterson, Susan L.
Peterson, James A., jt. auth. see Reeves, Steve.
Peterson, James A., ed. see American College of Sports Medicine Staff.
Peterson, James B. Ceramic Analysis in the Northeast, No. 9. 1985. 15.00 (*0-318-19888-6*) Fund Anthrop.
Peterson, James B., ed. A Most Indispensable Art: Native Fiber Industries from Eastern North America. LC 95-4405. (Illus.). 232p. 1996. text 45.00 (*0-87049-915-7*) U of Tenn Pr.
Peterson, James E. Otter Creek: The Indian Road. LC 90-82089. (Illus.). 176p. (Orig.). (YA). (gr. 5 up). 1990. pap. 15.00 (*0-914960-83-0*) Academy Bks.
Peterson, James F. & Tuason, Julie A., eds. A Geographic Glimpse of Central Texas & the Borderlands: Images & Encounters. LC 97-101438. (Pathways Ser.: No. 12). (Illus.). 153p. 1995. pap. 12.00 (*1-884136-06-0*) NCFGE.
Peterson, James L. Operating System Concepts. 2nd ed. (C). 1991. pap. text. write for info. (*0-201-50967-9*) Addison-Wesley.
Peterson, James L. & Silberschatz, Abraham. Operating System Concepts. LC 82-22766. (Computer Science Ser.). (Illus.). 576p. 1983. write for info. (*0-201-06097-3*) Addison-Wesley.
— Operating System Concepts. 2nd ed. (Computer Science Ser.). (C). 1985. teacher ed. write for info. (*0-201-06090-6*); text 34.36 (*0-201-06198-8*) Addison-Wesley.
Peterson, James L. & Zill, Nicholas. American Jewish High School Students: A National Profile. LC 84-72249. vi, 32p. (Orig.). 1984. pap. 2.50 (*0-87495-065-1*) Am Jewish Comm.
Peterson, James L., et al. Longitudinal Retirement History Study: Instructor's Manual. (Gerontology Research Toolkit Ser.). 64p. (Orig.). 1994. pap. text, teacher ed. 30.00 (*0-8018-5046-0*) Johns Hopkins.
— Longitudinal Study of Aging: Instructor's Manual. (Gerontology Research Toolkit Ser.). 62p. (Orig.). 1994. pap. text, teacher ed. 30.00 (*0-8018-5044-4*) Johns Hopkins.
— National Long Term Care Survey: Instructor's Manual. (Gerontology Research Toolkit Ser.). 85p. (Orig.). 1994. pap. text, teacher ed. 30.00 (*0-8018-5042-8*) Johns Hopkins.
Peterson, James L., jt. auth. see Silberschatz, Abraham.
Peterson, James M. America Has Problems - Ask Hard Questions. LC 97-223957. 56p. 1997. pap. 8.00 (*0-8059-4034-0*) Dorrance.
Peterson, James R., jt. auth. see Smith, Roland B.
Peterson, Jan. Cathedral Grove: MacMillan Park. 136p. 1996. pap. text 19.95 (*0-88982-160-7*, Pub. by Oolichan Bks) Genl Dist Srvs.
***Peterson, Jan.** Journeys Down The Alberni Canal To Barkley Sound. 1999. pap. 21.95 (*0-88982-178-X*, Pub. by Oolichan Bks) Genl Dist Srvs.
Peterson, Jan. Twin Cities: Alberni-Port Alberni. (Illus.). 389p. 1994. pap. text 19.95 (*0-88982-139-9*, Pub. by Oolichan Bks) Genl Dist Srvs.
Peterson, Jan, ed. see Hurst, Jane.
Peterson, Jane, jt. auth. see Lambert, Judith.
Peterson, Jane, ed. see Abramovitz, Janet.
Peterson, Jane, ed. see Abramovitz, Janet N. & Mattoon, Ashley T.
Peterson, Jane, ed. see French, Hilary.
Peterson, Jane, ed. see Tuxill, John.
Peterson, Jane A., jt. auth. see Kane, Hal.
Peterson, Jane A., ed. see Gardner, Gary & Sampat, Payal.
Peterson, Jane A., ed. see McGinn, Anne P.
Peterson, Jane A., ed. see O'Meara, Molly.
Peterson, Jane A., ed. see Renner, Michael.
Peterson, Jane A., ed. see Tuxill, John.
Peterson, Jane L., et al. Building Skills in High Risk Families: Strategies for the Home-Based Practitioner. LC 96-108848. 265p. 1995. pap. text 29.95 (*0-938510-73-8*, 63-002) Boys Town Pr.
Peterson, Jane T. & Bennett, Suzanne. Women Playwrights of Diversity: A Bio-Bibliographical Sourcebook. LC 96-27388. 416p. 1997. lib. bdg. 79.50 (*0-313-29179-9*, Greenwood Pr) Greenwood.
Peterson, Janet & Rude, Kelli, eds. Peoria - Impressions of 150 Years. limited ed. (Illus.). 180p. 1995. 39.95 (*0-9634793-9-3*) Peoria Jrnl.
Peterson, Janet, jt. auth. see Gaunt, LaRene.
***Peterson, Janice & Lewis, Margaret, eds.** The Elgar Companion to Feminist Economics. LC 99-33956. 832p. 2000. 240.00 (*1-85898-453-X*) E Elgar.
Peterson, Jean. Oneness Remembered - Ultraconsciousness: From: Sananda. Wilkinson, Marilyn J., ed. (Illus.). (Orig.). 1989. pap. 12.00 (*0-685-29784-5*) Meridian Light.
Peterson, Jean S. Talk with Teens about Feelings, Family, Relationships, & the Future: 50 Guided Discussions for School & Counseling Groups. Espeland, Pamela, ed. LC 95-13024. 216p. (Orig.). 1995. pap., teacher ed. 21.95 (*0-915793-88-1*) Free Spirit Pub.
— Talk with Teens about Self & Stress: 50 Guided Discussions for School & Counseling Groups. Espeland, Pamela, ed. LC 93-21514. 192p. (Orig.). 1993. pap. 21.95 (*0-915793-55-5*) Free Spirit Pub.
Peterson, Jeanette F. The Paradise Garden Murals of Malinalco: Utopia & Empire in Sixteenth-Century Mexico. LC 92-7992. (Illus.). 246p. (C). 1993. text 40.00 (*0-292-72750-X*) U of Tex Pr.
— Sacred Gifts: Pre-Columbian Art & Creativity. LC 94-37480. 1994. write for info. (*0-89951-090-6*) Santa Barb Mus Art.
Peterson, Jeanne W. I Have a Sister - My Sister Is Deaf. (Reading Rainbow Bks.). (J). 1984. 11.15 (*0-606-01874-3*, Pub. by Turtleback) Demco.
— I Have a Sister--My Sister Is Deaf. LC 76-24306. (Illus.). 32p. (J). (ps-3). 1977. lib. bdg. 15.89 (*0-06-024702-9*) HarpC Child Bks.
— I Have a Sister--My Sister Is Deaf. LC 76-24306. (Trophy Picture Bk.). (Illus.). 32p. (J). (ps-3). 1984. pap. 5.95 (*0-06-443059-6*, HarpTrophy) HarpC Child Bks.
— I Have a Sister, My Sister Is Deaf. LC 76-24306. (Illus.). (J). (gr. k-3). 1977. 13.95 (*0-06-024701-0*) HarpC Child Bks.
— Sometimes I Dream Horses. LC 83-47710. (Illus.). 32p. (J). (ps-3). 1987. 11.95 (*0-06-024712-6*) HarpC Child Bks.
Peterson, Jeffrey, jt. ed. see Weed, Michael E.
***Peterson, Jesse Lee & Stetson, Brad.** From Rage to Responsibility: Black Conservative Jesse Lee Peterson & America Today. LC 00-20813. 160p. 2000. 19.95 (*1-55778-788-3*) Paragon Hse.
Peterson, Jim. An Afternoon with K. 80p. (Orig.). 1996. pap. 9.95 (*0-9638731-6-4*) Hub City Writers.
Peterson, Jim & Zimmer, Barry R. Birds of the Trans-Pecos. LC 98-25747. (Corrie Herring Hooks Ser.). (Illus.). 184p. 1998. 35.00 (*0-292-76583-5*); pap. 19.95 (*0-292-76584-3*) U of Tex Pr.
Peterson, Joan. Love Has No Fear: One Couple's Search for Healing. rev. ed. LC 97-93355. (Orig.). 1997. pap. 12.95 (*0-9656017-5-7*) Merkaba Pr.
Peterson, Joan & Peterson, David. Eat Smart in Brazil: How to Decipher the Menu, Know the Market Foods & Embark on a Tasting Adventure. LC 94-96252. (Illus.). 168p. (Orig.). 1994. pap. 12.95 (*0-9641168-3-9*) Ginkgo Pr.
Peterson, Joan & Peterson, David C. Eat Smart in Indonesia: How to Decipher the Menu, Know the Market Foods & Embark on a Tasting Adventure. LC 97-92899. (Illus.). 160p. (Orig.). 1997. pap. 12.95 (*0-9641168-1-2*) Ginkgo Pr.
Peterson, Joan & Peterson, Pete. Summertime Recipes. 36p. (Orig.). 1981. pap. 3.25 (*0-940844-02-8*) Wellspring.
Peterson, Joan B. & Peterson, David C. Eat Smart in Poland: How to Decipher the Menu, Know the Market Foods & Embark on a Tasting Adventure. (Eat Smart Ser.). (Illus.). 104p. 2000. pap. 12.95 (*0-9641168-5-5*, Pub. by Ginkgo Pr) Penton Overseas.
Peterson, Joanne. French Cultural Crosswords. (FRE.). 48p. 1996. pap. 21.95 incl. audio (*0-88432-863-5*, SFR310) Audio-Forum.
Peterson, Joe & Peterson, Kay. Encyclopedia for RVers. rev. ed. 230p. 1989. 9.95 (*0-910449-07-4*) RoVers Pubns.
— The New Survival of the RV Snowbird. rev. ed. 256p. 1995. 10.95 (*0-910449-08-2*) RoVers Pubns.
Peterson, Joe, jt. auth. see Peterson, Kay.
***Peterson, John.** Decision-Making in the European Union. LC 99-24109. 336p. 1999. text 55.00 (*0-312-22529-6*) St Martin.
Peterson, John. Europe & America. 2nd ed. 256p. (C). 1996. 85.00 (*0-415-14653-4*); pap. 25.99 (*0-415-13864-7*) Routledge.
— Europe & America in the 1990's: The Prospects for Partnership. 288p. 1993. 95.00 (*1-85278-536-5*) E Elgar.
— Finite Mathematics. LC 73-10457. 1974. 22.95 (*0-8290-2364-X*) Irvington.
— High Technology & the Competition State: An Analysis of the Eureka Initiative. LC 93-811. 272p. (C). 1993. pap. 77.95 (*0-415-09562-X*) Thomson Learn.
***Peterson, John.** Introduction to Scholastic Realism. LC 98-30628. (New Perspectives in Philosophical Scholarship Ser.: Vol. 12). 193p. 1999. text 46.95 (*0-8204-4270-4*, 42704) P Lang Pubng.
Peterson, John. The Littles. (Littles Ser.). (Illus.). 80p. (J). (gr. 1-5). 1993. pap. 2.99 (*0-590-46225-3*) Scholastic Inc.
Peterson, John. The Littles. (Littles Ser.). (Illus.). (J). (gr. 1-5). 1967. 8.70 (*0-606-01054-8*, Pub. by Turtleback) Demco.
— The Littles & the Great Halloween Scare. (Littles Ser.). (Illus.). (J). (gr. 1-5). 1975. 8.70 (*0-606-06541-5*, Pub. by Turtleback) Demco.
Peterson, John. The Littles & the Lost Children. (Littles Ser.). (Illus.). 112p. (J). (gr. 1-5). 1991. pap. 3.50 (*0-590-43026-2*) Scholastic Inc.
— The Littles & the Lost Children. (Littles Ser.). (Illus.). (J). (gr. 1-5). 1991. 8.60 (*0-606-04731-X*, Pub. by Turtleback) Demco.
— The Littles & the Trash Tinies. (Littles Ser.). (Illus.). 80p. (J). (gr. 4-7). 1993. pap. 2.99 (*0-590-46595-3*) Scholastic Inc.
Peterson, John. The Littles & the Trash Tinies. (Littles Ser.). (Illus.). (J). (gr. 1-5). 1977. 8.70 (*0-606-02713-0*, Pub. by Turtleback) Demco.
Peterson, John. The Littles & Their Amazing New Friend. (Littles Ser.). (Illus.). (J). (gr. 1-5). 1999. pap. 3.99 (*0-590-87612-0*) Scholastic Inc.
— The Littles Give a Party. (Littles Ser.). (Illus.). 96p. (J). (gr. 4-7). 1993. pap. 3.50 (*0-590-46597-X*) Scholastic Inc.
Peterson, John. The Littles Give a Party. (Littles Ser.). (Illus.). (J). (gr. 1-5). 1972. 8.70 (*0-606-05435-9*, Pub. by Turtleback) Demco.
Peterson, John. The Littles Go Exploring. (Littles Ser.). (Illus.). 96p. (J). (gr. 1-5). 1993. pap. 3.50 (*0-590-46596-1*) Scholastic Inc.
— The Littles Go Exploring. (Littles Ser.). (Illus.). (J). (gr. 1-5). 1978. 8.60 (*0-606-05436-7*, Pub. by Turtleback) Demco.
— The Littles Go to School. (Littles Ser.). (Illus.). 72p. (J). (gr. 4-7). 1994. pap. 2.99 (*0-590-42129-8*) Scholastic Inc.
Peterson, John. The Littles Go to School. (Littles Ser.). (Illus.). (J). (gr. 1-5). 1983. 8.70 (*0-606-05909-1*, Pub. by Turtleback) Demco.
Peterson, John. The Littles Have a Wedding. (Littles Ser.). (Illus.). 96p. (J). (gr. 1-5). 1993. pap. 2.99 (*0-590-46224-5*) Scholastic Inc.
— The Littles Have a Wedding. (Littles Ser.). (Illus.). (J). (gr. 1-5). 1971. 8.60 (*0-606-05437-5*, Pub. by Turtleback) Demco.
— The Littles Take a Trip. (Littles Ser.). (Illus.). 96p. (J). (gr. 4-7). 1993. pap. 3.50 (*0-590-46222-9*) Scholastic Inc.
Peterson, John. The Littles Take a Trip. (Littles Ser.). (Illus.). (J). (gr. 1-5). 1993. 8.60 (*0-606-12403-9*, Pub. by Turtleback) Demco.
Peterson, John. The Littles to the Rescue. (Littles Ser.). (Illus.). 96p. (J). (gr. 1-5). 1993. pap. 3.50 (*0-590-46223-7*) Scholastic Inc.
— The Littles to the Rescue. (Littles Ser.). (J). 1968. 9.19 (*0-606-02715-7*, Pub. by Turtleback) Demco.
— Technical Mathematics. 2nd ed. LC 95-13517. 928p. 1996. mass mkt. 96.95 (*0-8273-7236-1*) Delmar.
— Technical Mathematics. 2nd ed. 928p. 1997. write for info. (*0-8273-8384-3*) Delmar.
— Technical Mathematics. 2nd ed. 928p. 1997. mass mkt., student ed. 30.25 (*0-8273-8431-9*) Delmar.
— Technical Mathematics with Calculus. 2nd ed. 1376p. 1997. write for info. (*0-8273-8386-X*) Delmar.
— Tom Little's Great Halloween Scare. 80p. (J). (gr. 2-5). 1994. pap. 2.99 (*0-590-42235-9*) Scholastic Inc.
Peterson, John. Yemen, the Search for a Modern State. LC 81-48187. (Illus.). 221p. 1982. reprint ed. pap. 68.60 (*0-608-06186-7*, 206651800008) Bks Demand.
Peterson, John & Bomberg, Elizabeth E. Decision-Making in the European Union LC 99-24109. (European Union Ser.). 1999. pap. 22.95 (*0-312-22521-0*) St Martin.
Peterson, John & Sharp, Margaret. Technology Policy in the European Union. LC 98-4038. (European Union Ser.). 276p. 1998. text 55.00 (*0-312-21641-6*) St Martin.
Peterson, John & Sjursen, Helene. A Common Foreign Policy for Europe? Competing Visions of the CFSP. LC 98-10557. (European Public Policy Ser.). 232p. (C). 1998. 85.00 (*0-415-17071-0*); pap. 27.99 (*0-415-17072-9*) Routledge.
Peterson, John, jt. auth. see Anderson, Edwin.
Peterson, John, jt. auth. see Gayton, Tom.
Peterson, John, jt. ed. see Sindelar, Richard.
Peterson, John A. Utah's Black Hawk War. LC 98-21752. (Illus.). 362p. 1999. 59.95 (*0-87480-583-X*); pap. 19.95 (*0-87480-508-2*) U of Utah Pr.
Peterson, John A., ed. see LeFors, Rufe.
Peterson, John C. Technical Mathematics. LC 92-32234. 846p. 1994. text 49.95 (*0-8273-4575-5*) Delmar.
— Technical Mathematics with Calculus. LC 92-32757. 1342p. 1994. text 54.95 (*0-8273-4577-1*) Delmar.
— Technical Mathematics with Calculus. 2nd ed. LC 95-13516. 1376p. 1996. mass mkt. 102.95 (*0-8273-7243-4*) Delmar.
Peterson, John C. & Herweyer, Alan. Students Solutions Manual to Accompany Technical Mathematics & Technical Mathematics with Calculus. 208p. 1994. pap. 17.00 (*0-8273-6506-3*) Delmar.
— Technical Mathematics & Technical Mathematics with Calculus: Solutions Manual. 647p. 1994. pap. text 31.50 (*0-8273-4582-8*) Delmar.
Peterson, John C. & Peterson, Doris M. Carroll County Indiana Rural Organizations, 1828-1979 Vol. I: History. LC 80-82231. (Illus.). 400p. 1980. 25.00 (*0-9604376-0-6*) J & D Peterson.
Peterson, John C., jt. auth. see Clutter, Martha T.
Peterson, John C., jt. auth. see Dobbs, David E.
Peterson, John L. A Walk in Jerusalem: Stations of the Cross. LC 97-44727. 64p. 1998. pap. 6.95 (*0-8192-1735-2*) Morehouse Pub.
***Peterson, John L. & DiClemente, Ralph J., eds.** Handbook of HIV Prevention. LC 99-53994. (AIDS Prevention & Mental Health Ser.). 337p. 2000. 115.00 (*0-306-46223-0*, Kluwer Plenum) Kluwer Academic.
Peterson, John M., ed. & photos by see Carleton, Geoffrey.
Peterson, Jonathan, jt. auth. see Chiodo, Joe.
Peterson, Joni, jt. auth. see Peterson, Robert B.
Peterson, Joseph. Early Conceptions & Tests of Intelligence. LC 70-98868. 320p. 1970. reprint ed. lib. bdg. 65.00 (*0-8371-2836-6*, PETI, Greenwood Pr) Greenwood.
Peterson, Joseph L., ed. Forensic Science: Scientific Investigation in Criminal Justice. LC 75-11812. (Studies in Criminal Justice: No. 1). 45.00 (*0-404-13139-5*) AMS Pr.
***Peterson, Joyce.** The Secret Garden: Musical Score & Lyrics. 1998. pap. 15.00 (*0-88734-042-3*) Players Pr.
Peterson, Joyce, jt. auth. see Gingerich, Neeltje.
Peterson, Joyce S. American Automobile Workers, 1900-1933. LC 87-1942. (SUNY Series in American Labor History). 231p. (C). 1987. text 21.50 (*0-88706-573-2*) State U NY Pr.
Peterson, Julie P., jt. auth. see Janke, Rebecca A.
Peterson, K., et al, eds. Papers from Twenty-First Regional Meeting of C. L. S., Vol. 1. 438p. (Orig.). 1985. pap. text 8.00 (*0-914203-23-1*) Chicago Ling.
— Papers from Twenty-First Regional Meeting of C. L. S., Vol. 2: Parasession on Causatives & Agentivity. (Orig.). 1985. pap. text 8.00 (*0-914203-24-X*) Chicago Ling.

P

An Asterisk (*) at the beginning of an entry indicates that the title is appearing for the first time.

Peterson, K., et al. Post-Traumatic Stress Disorder: A Clinician's Guide. LC 90-14309. (Stress & Coping Ser.). (Illus.). 276p. (C). 1990. 42.50 (*0-306-43542-X*, Plenum Trade) Perseus Pubng.

Peterson, K. Jean, ed. Health Care for Lesbians & Gay Men: Confronting Homophobia & Heterosexism. LC 96-23147. (Journal of Gay & Lesbian Social Services Ser.: Vol. 5, No. 1). 121p. 1996. pap. 12.95 (*1-56023-079-7*, Harrington Park) Haworth Pr.

— Health Care for Lesbians & Gay Men: Confronting Homophobia & Heterosexism. LC 96-23147. (Journal of Gay & Lesbian Social Services: Vol. 5, No. 1). 121p. 1996. 29.95 (*1-56024-772-X*, Haworth Pastrl) Haworth Pr.

Peterson, Karen E. The Tomorrow Trap: Unlocking the Secrets of the Procrastination-Protection Syndrome. 356p. (Orig.). 1996. pap. 12.95 (*1-55874-417-7*, 4177) Health Comm.

***Peterson, Kathrine P. & Palmer, Fannie R.** Dolls Aren't Just for Kids: The Ultimate Guide for Doll Lovers. DeNault, Cindy, ed. LC 99-73455. (Illus.). 210p. (Orig.). 2000. pap. 15.95 (*0-9666405-8-6*, Pub. by Garrison Oaks) Quality Bks IL.

Peterson, Kathy J. Fish Tales, for Heaven's Sake! The Collected Parables of an Alaskan Harbor. unabridged ed. LC 96-94519. (Illus.). 168p. (Orig.). 1996. pap. 9.95 (*0-9653402-5-2*) Mtn Ministries.

Peterson, Kathy K., ed. Oil Shale: The Environmental Challenges. LC 81-10118. (Proceedings of International Symposium Aug. 11-14, 1980, Vail, Colorado Ser.). (Illus.). 261p. 1981. text 10.00 (*0-918062-43-8*) Colo Sch Mines.

— Oil Shale: The Environmental Challenges II. LC 82-14759. (Illus.). 392p. 1982. 11.00 (*0-918062-51-9*) Colo Sch Mines.

Peterson, Katia, jt. auth. see Canter, Lee.

Peterson, Kay. Home Is Where You Park It. rev. ed. (Illus.). 200p. 1990. reprint ed. pap. 10.95 (*0-910449-00-7*) RoVers Pubns.

Peterson, Kay & Peterson, Joe. Travel While You Work. 160p. 1996. 10.95 (*0-614-30366-4*) RoVers Pubns.

Peterson, Kay, jt. auth. see Peterson, Joe.

***Peterson, Keith.** The Rain. large type ed. 336p. 2000. pap. write for info. (*1-85389-965-8*, Dales) Ulverscroft.

Peterson, Ken M., jt. auth. see Morgan, Karl Z.

Peterson, Kenneth D. Teacher Evaluation: A Comprehensive Guide to New Directions & Practices. (Illus.). 320p. 1995. pap. 34.95 (*0-8039-6244-4*) Corwin Pr.

***Peterson, Kenneth D.** Teacher Evaluation: A Comprehensive Guide to New Directions & Practices. 2nd ed. LC 00-8770. 2000. pap. write for info. (*0-8039-6883-3*) Corwin Pr.

Peterson, Kenneth E. Dollars in Your Pocket: Group Networking Tips That Turn into Sales. LC 98-91203. (Illus.). xii, 160p. 1998. per. 19.95 (*1-891674-15-3*) Letip Ents.

Peterson, Kent D., jt. auth. see Deal, Terrence E.

Peterson, Kent W. Handbook of Occupational Health & Safety Software: Version 10.0. 10th ed. 500p. 1997. pap. 85.00 (*1-885190-04-2*) Amer Col Occ.

***Peterson, Kerstin.** Business Telecom Systems: A Guide to Choosing the Best Technologies & Services. 224p. 1999. pap. 24.95 (*1-57820-041-5*, Pub. by Telecom Bks) Publishers Group.

Peterson, Kevin. Our Spark of Hope. 168p. (Orig.). 1989. 18.00 (*0-944996-05-1*); pap. text 9.95 (*0-944996-04-3*) Carlsons.

Peterson, Kim, ed. see Diamond, Carlin J.

Peterson, Kim, ed. see Ruiz, Shirley.

Peterson, Kim, ed. see Stearn, Marshall B.

Peterson, Kimberly A. Civil Litigation. LC 97-21406. 375p. (C). 1997. 68.00 (*0-13-757840-7*) P-H.

Peterson, Kirk. The Automated Teller Machine As a National Bank under the Federal Law. LC 87-31197. (Legal Research Guides Ser.: Vol. 5). i, 36p. 1987. lib. bdg. 30.00 (*0-89941-587-3*, 305410) W S Hein.

Peterson, Kirk L. & Nicod, Pascal. Cardiac Catheterization. Zorab, Richard, ed. LC 95-3944. (Illus.). 560p. 1996. text 99.00 (*0-7216-3064-2*, W B Saunders Co) Harcrt Hlth Sci Grp.

Peterson, Kirsten H. & Rutherford, Anna, eds. On Shifting Sands: New Art & Literature from South Africa. 180p. (C). 1992. pap. 16.95 (*0-435-08070-9*, 08070) Heinemann.

Peterson, Kirsten H., jt. ed. see Rutherford, Anna.

Peterson, Kirtland C. Mind of the Ninja. (Illus.). 320p. (Orig.). 1986. pap. 18.95 (*0-8092-4951-0*, 495100, Contemporary Bks) NTC Contemp Pub Co.

Peterson, Knut D. The Lost Frontier. LC 79-11657. 1981. 22.95 (*0-87949-172-8*) Ashley Bks.

— When Alaska Was Free. Ashton, Sylvia, ed. LC 77-70299. 1977. 21.95 (*0-87949-081-0*) Ashley Bks.

Peterson, Kolan. Special Effects in Watercolors. (How to Draw & Paint Ser.). (Illus.). 32p. (Orig.). 1989. pap. 6.95 (*0-929261-49-6*, HT207) W Foster Pub.

— Watercolors Step-by-Step. (How to Draw & Paint Ser.). (Illus.). 32p. (Orig.). 1989. pap. 6.95 (*0-929261-47-X*, HT205) W Foster Pub.

Peterson, Kristine. The Strategic Approach to Quality Service in Health Care. (Health Care Administration Ser.). 332p. 71.00 (*0-87189-764-4*) Aspen Pub.

Peterson, L. A., et al. Brain Fuel: The Book That Improves Your Mind As Well As Your Body! 2nd ed. (Illus.). 256p. 1990. reprint ed. pap. 12.95 (*1-878459-01-5*) Total Rsch Pub.

Peterson, L. A., ed. see Wiesend, Rick.

Peterson, L. E., ed. see Armstong, Ray.

***Peterson, L. K. & Cullen, Cheryl.** Global Graphics: Color: Designing with Color for an International Market. (Illus.). 160p. 2000. pap. 40.00 (*1-56496-293-8*) Rockport Pubs.

Peterson, Larry. German Communism, Workers' Protest & Labor Unions: The Politics of the United Front in Rhineland-Westphalia, 1920-1924, Vol. 14. LC 92-41851. (Studies in Social History). 570p. (C). 1993. lib. bdg. 343.00 (*0-7923-2111-1*) Kluwer Academic.

Peterson, Larry, jt. auth. see DePasquale, Dan.

Peterson, Larry, jt. auth. see Gesme, Carole.

Peterson, Larry J. Contemporary Oral & Maxillofacial Surgery. 3rd ed. LC 97-14848. (Illus.). 816p. (C). (gr. 13). 1997. text 69.00 (*0-8151-6699-0*, 25548) Mosby Inc.

Peterson, Larry J., et al. Principles of Oral & Maxillofacial Surgery, 3 vols., Set. (Illus.). 2256p. 1992. text 446.00 (*0-397-51011-X*) Lppncott W & W.

Peterson, Larry L. & Davie, Bruce S. Computer Networks: A Systems Approach. 552p. 1998. text 74.95 (*1-55860-368-9*) Morgan Kaufmann.

***Peterson, Larry L. & Davie, Bruce S.** Computer Networks: A Systems Approach. 2nd ed. LC 99-36400. (Networking Ser.). (Illus.). 600p. 1999. 76.95 (*1-55860-514-2*, Pub. by Morgan Kaufmann) Harcourt.

Peterson, Larry L. & Russell, Charles M. Charles M. Russell, Legacy: Printed & Published Works of Montana's "Cowboy Artist" LC 98-41627. (Illus.). 456p. 1999. 95.00 (*1-56044-683-8*) Falcon Pub Inc.

Peterson, Larry R. Ignatius Donnelly: A Psychohistorical Study in Moral Development Psychology: Dissertations in American Biography. 1981. 27.95 (*0-405-14102-5*) Ayer.

***Peterson, Laura.** Whispers in the Wind: Communications from an Ascended Master. (Illus.). 318p. 1999. pap. 17.95 (*0-9671815-0-X*) Sun Valley Pubs.

***Peterson, Lawrence D., et al.** Farm Publication Editorial poll: Summary Statistics from a Survey of 600 Farmers & Ranchers. 196p. 1999. 495.00 (*0-9675509-0-4*) Peterson Grp.

***Peterson, Lawrence W., Jr.** How to Turn a Dollar a Day into Financial Freedom. 20p. 2000. pap. 7.95 (*0-9700705-0-0*) L W Peterson.

***Peterson, Lee.** San Diego: A Photographic Collection. Lindsay, Lowell, ed. (Illus.). 96p. 2000. 19.95 (*0-932653-28-6*) Sunbelt Pubns.

Peterson, Lee. San Diego (Peterson) LC 91-73732. (Sunbelt Pictoral Bks.). (ENG, ITA, JPN & SPA., Illus.). 80p. 1991. 19.95 (*0-916251-45-4*) Sunbelt Pubns.

Peterson, Lee & Deblieux, Mike. Documenting Employee Discipline. 3rd ed. 170p. 1999. pap. 45.00 (*0-327-00882-2*, 8038111) LEXIS Pub.

— Supervisor's Guide to Documenting Employee Discipline. 4th ed. 70p. 1999. pap. 25.00 (*0-327-00884-9*, 8244711) LEXIS Pub.

Peterson, Lee Allen. Peterson's Edible Wild Plants. 1998. pap. 18.00 (*0-676-57324-X*) Random.

Peterson, Leif E. & Abrahamson, Seymour, eds. Effects of Ionizing Radiation: Atomic Bomb Survivors & Their Children (1945-1995) LC 97-52238. 379p. 1997. 79.95 (*0-309-06402-3*, Joseph Henry Pr) Natl Acad Pr.

Peterson, Lenka & O'Connor, Dan. Kids Take the Stage: Helping Young People Discover the Creative Outlet of Theater. LC 97-43022. (Illus.). 192p. 1997. pap. 19.95 (*0-8230-7742-X*, Back Stage Bks) Watsn-Guptill.

Peterson, Lennart. Post-Apartheid Southern Africa: Economic Challenges & Policies for the Future: Proceedings of the 16th Arne Ryde Symposium, 23-24 August 1996, Lund, Sweden. LC 97-23353. 376p. (C). 1998. 85.00 (*0-415-16184-3*) Routledge.

Peterson, Lennie. Big Picture: A Comic Strip Collection. LC 98-88675. 1999. pap. text 9.95 (*0-8362-7846-1*) Andrews & McMeel.

— Why God Makes Bald Guys. Carle, Cliff, ed. (Illus.). 88p. (Orig.). 1998. pap. 5.95 (*1-57644-043-5*) CCC Pubns.

Peterson, Lennie, jt. auth. see Della Valle, Paula.

Peterson, Leonard. They're All Afraid. (Illus.). 161p. 1981. pap. 8.95 (*0-7725-5032-8*) Genl Dist Srvs.

Peterson, Leroy D., jt. auth. see Harmon, Roy L.

Peterson, Levi S. The Backslider. 2nd ed. LC 90-37395. 368p. 1990. mass mkt. 5.95 (*1-56085-015-9*) Signature Bks.

— Juanita Brooks: Mormon Woman Historian. (Illus.). 528p. (C). 1996. pap. 19.95 (*0-87480-512-0*) U of Utah Pr.

— Juanita Brooks: Mormon Woman Historian. LC 88-17421. (Utah Centennial Ser.: No. 5). 513p. reprint ed. pap. 159.10 (*0-7837-3966-4*, 204379500011) Bks Demand.

Peterson, Linda. Careers Without College: Entertainment. LC 94-6948. 104p. (Orig.). (YA). 1994. pap. 7.95 (*1-56079-352-X*) Petersons.

Peterson, Linda. Emergencies. (Careers Without College Ser.). 1993. 13.15 (*0-606-05185-6*, Pub. by Turtleback) Demco.

Peterson, Linda. Starting Out, Starting Over: Finding the Work That's Waiting for You. LC 95-4177. 208p. (Orig.). 1995. pap. 14.95 (*0-89106-073-1*, 7230, Davies-Black Pub) Consulting Psychol.

— Tx/td,emergencies,careers W/o Coll Series. LC 93-7077. (Tech Prep). 120p. (YA). 1993. pap. 7.95 (*1-56079-252-3*) Petersons.

Peterson, Linda & Hardin, Milton E. Children in Distress: A Guide for Screening Children's Art (Norton Professional Books) LC 97-3930. (Illus.). 144p. 1997. pap. 40.00 (*0-393-70248-0*) Norton.

Peterson, Linda, et al. Telling Without Telling: A Clinical Guide to Screening Children's Art Productions. LC 95-67176. (Illus.). 144p. 1995. pap. 39.95 (*0-9645604-0-2*) Drawing Conclusions.

Peterson, Linda G. & O'Shanick, G. J., eds. Psychiatric Aspects of Trauma. (Advances in Psychosomatic Medicine Ser.: Vol. 16). (Illus.). x, 238p. 1986. 66.75 (*3-8055-4219-4*) S Karger.

Peterson, Linda H. Traditions of Victorian Women's Autobiography: The Poetics & Politics of Life Writing. LC 99-19832. (Victorian Literature & Culture Ser.). (Illus.). 1999. 38.50 (*0-8139-1883-9*) U Pr of Va.

Peterson, Linda H., et al, eds. The Norton Reader: An Anthology of Expository Prose. 9th abr. ed. LC 95-2937. (C). 1995. pap. text 24.50 (*0-393-96827-8*) Norton.

Peterson, Linda H., jt. auth. see Casteras, Susan P.

Peterson, Linda H., ed. see Bronte, Emily Jane.

Peterson, Linda M. Surviving the Heartbreak of Choosing Death for Your Pet: Your Personal Guide for Dealing with Pet Euthanasia. LC 96-94369. 160p. (Orig.). 1997. pap. 12.95 (*0-9652572-2-3*) Greentree Pub PA.

Peterson, Linda M., jt. auth. see Melody, M. E.

Peterson, Linda S. Birth Expectations of U. S. Women: 1973 to 1988. LC 94-33453. (Vital & Health Statistics Ser.: Series 23, No. 17). 1994. write for info. (*0-8406-0501-3*) Natl Ctr Health Stats.

***Peterson, Linda Seigel.** A Squeeze of Lime: Lime Recipes from la Collina Verde along with Treasured Family. LC 99-50929. 208p. 2000. pap. 16.95 (*1-56474-337-3*, Pub. by Fithian Pr) SCB Distributors.

Peterson, Linda W. The Electronic Lifeline: A Media Exploration for Youth. 1990. pap. 3.95 (*0-377-00209-7*) Friendship Pr.

Peterson, Lisa, jt. auth. see Freundlich, Madelyn.

Peterson, Liz. Wind in the Willows (Playscript) (A Musical) (J). 1993. pap. 6.00 (*0-87602-325-1*) Anchorage.

Peterson, Lizette, jt. auth. see Gelfand, Donna M.

Peterson, Lorin. The Brutalitarians & the Bomb. LC 87-83304. (Illus.). 160p. 1988. 9.95 (*0-945690-00-2*) Hillside CA.

Peterson, Lorraine. Anybody Can Be Cool, but Awesome Takes Practice. LC 88-19454. (Devotional for Teens Ser.). (Illus.). 28p. (Orig.). (YA). (gr. 9-12). 1988. pap. 7.99 (*1-55661-040-8*) Bethany Hse.

— Dying of Embarrassment & Living to Tell about It. LC 87-35334. (Devotional Ser.: No. 5). 28p. (Orig.). (YA). (gr. 9-12). 1988. pap. 7.99 (*0-87123-967-1*) Bethany Hse.

— Falling off Cloud Nine & Other High Places. LC 81-38465. (Illus.). 16p. (Orig.). (YA). (gr. 8-12). 1981. pap. 7.99 (*0-87123-167-0*) Bethany Hse.

— How to Get a Life, No Strings Attached! The Power of Grace in a Teen's Life. LC 97-4711. 128p. (YA). (gr. 8-12). 1997. pap. 7.99 (*1-55661-949-9*) Bethany Hse.

— If God Loves Me, Why Can't I Get My Locker Open? LC 80-27014. 16p. (YA). (gr. 6-12). 1980. pap. 7.99 (*0-87123-251-0*) Bethany Hse.

— If God Loves Me, Why Can't I Get My Locker Open? (Devotionals for Teens Ser.). (J). 1983. 13.09 (*0-606-02281-3*, Pub. by Turtleback) Demco.

— If the Devil Made You Do It, You Blew It. 192p. (Orig.). (YA). (gr. 8 up). 1989. pap. 7.99 (*1-55661-052-1*) Bethany Hse.

— If You Really Trust Me, Why Can't I Stay Out Later? 272p. (Orig.). (YA). 1991. pap. 8.99 (*1-55661-212-5*) Bethany Hse.

— Lord, I Haven't Talked to You since the Last Crisis, But . . . The Purpose & Power of Prayer. LC 93-40579. 24p. (YA). (gr. 7-12). 1994. pap. 8.99 (*1-55661-385-7*) Bethany Hse.

— Please Give Me Another Chance, Lord. 16p. (YA). 1995. pap. 7.99 (*1-55661-583-3*) Bethany Hse.

— Radical Advice from the Ultimate Wiseguy. 24p. (Orig.). (YA). (gr. 8-12). 1990. pap. 8.99 (*1-55661-141-2*) Bethany Hse.

— Real Character's in the Making. LC 85-7373. 224p. (YA). (gr. 8-12). 1985. pap. 7.99 (*0-87123-824-1*) Bethany Hse.

— Senor, No Te Hablo Desde la Ultima Crisis, Pero . . .Tr. of Lord, I Haven't Talked to You since the Last Crisis, but.... (SPA.). 256p. 1996. 10.99 (*0-88113-431-7*, B052-4317) Caribe Betania.

— Trying to Get Toothpaste Back into the Tube. 16p. (Orig.). (J). (gr. 7-10). 1993. pap. 7.99 (*1-55661-315-6*) Bethany Hse.

— Why Isn't God Giving Cash Prizes? LC 82-17866. (Devotional for Teens Ser.: No. 3). (Illus.). 176p. (YA). (gr. 8-12). 1982. pap. 7.99 (*0-87123-626-5*) Bethany Hse.

***Peterson, Lyn.** Lyn Peterson's Real Life Decorating. (Illus.). 304p. 2000. pap. 27.95 (*1-58011-028-2*) Creative Homeowner.

Peterson, Lynette. Reading the Landscape. LC 98-115924. (Publications in Geography). xii, 124p. 1996. write for info. (*0-7326-1138-5*) Intl Spec Bk.

Peterson, Lynn, jt. auth. see Haseltine, Beth A.

Peterson, Lynne, jt. auth. see Schiller, Pam.

Peterson, M. International Interest Organizations & the Transmutation of Postwar Society. 740p. (Orig.). 1979. pap. 71.00 (*91-22-00255-3*) Coronet Bks.

Peterson, M. & Winer, W., eds. Wear Control Handbook. 1500p. 95.00 (*0-317-33640-1*, G00169) ASME.

Peterson, M., jt. auth. see Winn, Charles S.

Peterson, M. J. The General Assembly in World Politics. 240p. 1986. text 55.00 (*0-04-327079-4*) Routledge.

Peterson, M. Lewis. Deliver the Message. rev. ed. (Illus.). 70p. (J). (ps-12). 1994. audio 12.00 (*1-885721-02-1*) L P Prods.

— Deliver the Message. unabridged rev. ed. LC 94-96297. (Illus.). 70p. (J). (ps-12). 1994. pap. 27.00 incl. audio (*1-885721-00-5*) L P Prods.

— Poetry Slam. (Illus.). 150p. 1997. pap. 29.95 (*1-885721-03-X*) L P Prods.

Peterson, Mable. No Water: A True, Gripping Story about Demons & Children. 96p. 1987. write for info. (*0-936369-08-6*) Son-Rise Pubns.

Peterson, Mandy. Daniel. LC 97-76769. (Footsteps to Follow Ser.: No. 2). (Illus.). 32p. (J). (gr. k-4). 1997. 14.95 (*0-9657091-2-4*); pap. 9.95 (*0-9657091-3-2*) Christian Soldiers.

Peterson, Marg, ed. Going Places: Workshop Proceedings from the 4th National Rails-to-Trails Conference. (Illus.). 320p. (Orig.). 1993. 19.95 (*0-925794-06-6*) Rails Trails.

Peterson, Margaret. Wallace Stevens & the Idealist Tradition. LC 83-4996. (Studies in Modern Literature: No. 24). 199p. reprint ed. pap. 61.70 (*0-8357-1452-7*, 207051700097) Bks Demand.

Peterson, Margaret S., jt. auth. see Stephenson, D.

Peterson, Marge & Peterson, Rob. Argentina: A Wild West Heritage. 2nd ed. LC 95-49075. (Discovering Our Heritage Ser.). (Illus.). (J). 1996. lib. bdg. 14.95 (*0-382-39287-6*, Dillon Silver Burdett) Silver Burdett Pr.

Peterson, Marie B. Kaleidoscope. 100p. 1990. 14.99 (*0-925037-13-3*) Great Lks Poetry.

Peterson, Marilyn B. Applications in Criminal Analysis: A Sourcebook. LC 94-11219. 336p. 1994. lib. bdg. 85.00 (*0-313-28577-2*, Greenwood Pr) Greenwood.

— Applications in Criminal Analysis: A Sourcebook. LC 94-11219. 336p. 1998. pap. 29.95 (*0-275-96468-X*, Praeger Pubs) Greenwood.

Peterson, Marilyn B., jt. ed. see Andrews, Paul, Jr.

Peterson, Marilyn E. Forshee's Legacy to the Philippines. LC 95-67271. 240p. 1997. pap. 9.99 (*0-933451-32-6*) Prescott Pr.

Peterson, Marilyn R. At Personal Risk: Boundary Violations in Professional-Client Relationships. 200p. (C). 1992. 24.00 (*0-393-70138-7*) Norton.

Peterson, Marilyn S. Eat to Compete: The Guide to Sports Nutrition. 2nd ed. (Illus.). 384p. (C). (gr. 13). 1996. pap. text 33.95 (*0-8151-6786-5*, 26811) Mosby Inc.

— The Role of Mental Health Professionals in the Prevention & Treatment of Child Abuse & Neglect. 73p. (Orig.). (C). 1995. pap. text 35.00 (*0-7881-1664-9*) DIANE Pub.

Peterson, Marion L. HIV-AIDS Resources: The National Directory of Resources on HIV Infection-AIDS. 600p. 1994. pap. text 110.00 (*1-885461-00-3*) National Direct.

— HIV-AIDS Resources the National Directory of Resources on HIV Infection - AIDS. 2nd rev. ed. 650p. pap. text 116.00 (*1-885461-02-X*) National Direct.

— The National Directory of Children, Youth & Families Services. 900p. 1996. pap. text 90.00 (*1-885461-03-8*) National Direct.

— The National Directory of Children, Youth & Families Services. 10th ed. 800p. 1994. pap. text 84.00 (*1-885461-01-1*) National Direct.

— The National Directory of Children, Youth & Families Services. 13th rev. ed. 1997. pap. 96.00 (*1-885461-04-6*) National Direct.

Peterson, Mark. Korean Adoption & Inheritance: Case Studies in the Creation of a Classic Confucian Society. rev. ed. LC 97-145480. (Cornell East Asia Ser.: Vol. 80). 267p. (C). 1996. 23.80 (*1-885445-70-9*, CEAS #80); pap. 14.45 (*1-885445-80-6*, CEAS #80) Cornell East Asia Pgm.

Peterson, Mark, jt. ed. see Kendall, Laurel.

Peterson, Mark A. The Complete Entrepreneur: The Only Book You'll Ever Need to Manage Risk & Build Your Business Wealth. 400p. 1996. pap. 14.95 (*0-8120-9716-5*) Barron.

— Healthy Markets? The New Competition in Medical Care. LC 98-29193. 1998. pap. 22.95 (*0-8223-2138-6*) Duke.

— Healthy Markets? The New Competition in Medical Care. LC 98-29193. 464p. 1999. 64.95 (*0-8223-2236-6*) Duke.

— Legislating Together: The White House & Capitol Hill from Eisenhower to Reagan. 1990. pap. 19.50 (*0-674-52416-0*) HUP.

— Legislating Together: The White House & Capitol Hill from Eisenhower to Reagan. (Illus.). 352p. 1990. 46.50 (*0-674-52415-2*) HUP.

— The Price of Redemption: The Spiritual Economy of Puritan New England. LC 97-33712. 360p. 1997. 45.00 (*0-8047-2912-3*) Stanford U Pr.

Peterson, Mark A., et al. Compensating Permanent Workplace Injuries: A Study of the California System. LC 98-11072. (Illus.). 244p. 1998. pap. 20.00 (*0-8330-2577-5*, MR-920-ICJ) Rand Corp.

Peterson, Mark A., jt. auth. see Chin, Audrey.

Peterson, Mark A., jt. auth. see Rand Corp. Staff.

Peterson, Mark A., jt. auth. see Shanley, Michael G.

Peterson, Mark B., et al. The White Oak Inventory of Large Format Theaters: 1998 Edition. 3rd ed. LC 98-85413. (Illus.). 55p. 1998. spiral bd. 114.95 (*0-9663777-0-2*) White Oak Assocs.

Peterson, Mark F., jt. auth. see Smith, Peter B.

Peterson, Mark L., jt. auth. see Jongsma, Arthur E., Jr.

Peterson, Marlow, jt. auth. see Castle, Larry.

Peterson, Marquita, jt. auth. see Priestley, Lee.

Peterson, Marshall N., ed. The Highland Maya in Fact & Legend: Francisco Ximenez, Fernando Alva de Ixtlilxochitl, & Other Commentators on Indian Origins & Deeds. 120p. 1997. pap. 12.50 (*0-911437-71-1*) Labyrinthos.

Peterson, Martha, jt. auth. see Peterson, Robert.

Peterson, Martha D. The Tides of Loon Island. 171p. Date not set. mass mkt. 4.99 (*1-55197-123-2*) Picasso Publ.

***Peterson, Martin, ed.** Issue 9: European Left. 192p. 1999. pap. 19.50 (*0-85315-878-9*, Pub. by Lawrence & Wishart) NYU Pr.

Peterson, Martin S., jt. ed. see Josephson, Edward S.

Peterson, Marvin W., et al, eds. Black Students on White Campuses: The Impacts of Increased Black Enrollments. (Institute for Social Research Ser.). (Illus.). 400p. (C). 1994. text 62.50 (*0-472-00717-3*) U of Mich Pr.

Peterson, Marvin W., et al, eds. Organization & Governance in Higher Education. 4th ed. (ASHE Reader Ser.). 476p. (C). 1991. pap. text 48.00 (*0-536-57981-4*) Pearson Custom.

P

Peterson, Marvin W., et al. Planning & Management for a Changing Environment: A Handbook on Redesigning Postsecondary Education. LC 96-50208. (Jossey-Bass Higher & Adult Education Ser.). 1997. 55.00 (*0-7879-0849-5*) Jossey-Bass.

Peterson, Mary. Mercy Flights: Stories. LC 84-19490. (Breakthrough Ser.: No. 47). 104p. 1985. pap. 10.95 (*0-8262-0464-3*) U of Mo Pr.

Peterson, Mary, jt. auth. see Simonds, Barbara.

Peterson, Mary E. And I Shall Be Your Ancestor. (Illus.). 48p. (Orig.). 1980. pap. 3.00 (*0-912701-02-1*) Balance Beam Pr.

Peterson, Mary E., ed. The Message in the Mirror. (Illus.). 80p. (Orig.). 1983. pap. 4.70 (*0-912701-00-5*) Balance Beam Pr.

Peterson, Mary J. Universal Bath Planning. (Illus.). 285p. (Orig.). 1996. pap. text 50.00 (*1-887127-01-1*, 5253) Natl Kit Bath.

— Universal Kitchen Planning: Design That Adapts to People. (Illus.). 220p. (Orig.). (C). 1995. pap. text 50.00 (*1-887127-00-3*) Natl Kit Bath.

Peterson, Mary Jo. Accessible Kitchens & Bathrooms by Design: Universal Design Principles in Practice. LC 98-20250. (Illus.). 382p. 1998. 79.95 (*0-07-049980-2*) McGraw.

Peterson, Matthew W., jt. auth. see Shaw, Gordon L.

Peterson, Meg. Complete Autoharp Songbook. (Complete Book). 280p. 1981. pap. 17.95 (*0-87166-769-X*, 93694) Mel Bay.

— The Complete Method for Autoharp or Chromaharp. 1979. pap. 23.95 incl. audio (*0-7866-0920-6*, 93657P) Mel Bay.

— The Complete Method for Autoharp or Chromaharp. 1979. audio 9.98 (*1-56222-593-6*, 93657C) Mel Bay.

— The Complete Method for Autoharp or Chromaharp. 176p. 1979. pap. 17.95 (*0-87166-921-8*, 93657) Mel Bay.

— Country Pickin' for Autoharp. 1993. pap. 23.95 incl. audio (*0-7866-0968-0*, 94060P); audio 9.98 (*1-56222-621-5*, 94060C) Mel Bay.

— Country Pickin' for Autoharp: Complete Book of Traditional & Country Autoharp Picking Styles. 152p. 1986. pap. 17.95 (*1-56222-197-3*, 94060) Mel Bay.

— Hymns for Auto Harp. 56p. 1978. student ed. 7.95 (*0-89228-053-0*) Impact Christian.

— Hymns for Autoharp. 56p. 1978. pap. 7.95 (*0-87166-718-5*, 93617) Mel Bay.

— Let's Play the Autoharp. 40p. 1981. 6.95 (*0-87166-524-7*, 93701) Mel Bay.

— You Can Teach Yourself Autoharp. 18.95 incl. audio (*0-7866-1179-0*, 95024P); audio 9.98 (*0-7866-0018-7*, 95024C) Mel Bay.

— You Can Teach Yourself Autoharp. 96p. 1994. pap. 9.95 (*0-7866-0017-9*, 95024) Mel Bay.

— You Can Teach Yourself Autoharp. 1996. audio compact disk 15.98 (*0-7866-2029-3*, 95024CD) Mel Bay.

***Peterson, Meg.** You Can Teach Yourself Autoharp. 96p. 1998. pap. 17.95 incl. audio compact disk (*0-7866-4665-9*, 95024BCD) Mel Bay.

Peterson, Meg & Fox, Dan. Songs of Christmas for Autoharp. 32p. 1980. pap. 5.95 (*0-87166-618-9*, 93696) Mel Bay.

Peterson, Meg & Pratt, Rosalie. Elementary Music for All Learners. 1981. pap. 14.95 (*0-88284-112-2*, 1974) Alfred Pub.

— Elementary Music for All Learners. 1981. wbk. ed. 4.95 (*0-88284-161-0*, 1975) Alfred Pub.

***Peterson, Melissa.** Charlotte Novel, Vol. 3. (J). (gr. 3-7). 2001. pap. 4.95 (*0-06-440739-X*) HarpC Child Bks.

Peterson, Melissa. The Cocoa Commotion. LC 96-50276. (Carmen Sandiego Mystery Ser.: Vol. 4). (Illus.). 144p. (J). (gr. 3-7). 1997. pap. 4.50 (*0-06-440666-0*, HarpTrophy) HarpC Child Bks.

— The Cocoa Commotion. (Carmen Sandiego Mystery Ser.). (J). (gr. 4-6). 1997. 9.60 (*0-606-11191-3*, Pub. by Turtleback) Demco.

— Hasta La Vista, Blarney. LC 96-29076. (Carmen Sandiego Mystery Ser.: Vol. 2). (Illus.). 144p. (J). (gr. 5-7). 1997. pap. 4.50 (*0-06-440665-2*, HarpTrophy) HarpC Child Bks.

— Hasta La Vista, Blarney. (Carmen Sandiego Mystery Ser.). (J). (gr. 4-6). 1997. 9.60 (*0-606-11189-1*, Pub. by Turtleback) Demco.

***Peterson, Melissa.** Martha Novel, Vol. 4. 304p. (J). (gr. 3-7). 2001. 15.95 (*0-06-027986-9*) HarpC Child Bks.

— Martha Novel, Vol. 4. (J). 2002. lib. bdg. 15.89 (*0-06-028205-3*) HarpC Child Bks.

Peterson, Melissa, ed. see Farha, Gregory R. & Hanna, Michael.

Peterson, Melvin N. David's Star Studded Adventures. (Illus.). 58p. (J). (gr. 1-4). 1988. spiral bd. 48.00 (*0-938880-07-1*) MNP Star.

— Flight Deck Uses for the HP-41C: Celestial Navigation, Vol. 3. 58p. (C). 1984. spiral bd. 48.00 (*0-938880-02-0*) MNP Star.

— Flight Deck Uses for the HP-41C Series, Set, Pts. I & II. (Illus.). 63p. (C). 1989. spiral bd. 177.50 (*0-938880-08-X*) MNP Star.

Peterson, Melvin N., ed. Diversity of Oceanic Life: An Evaluative Review. LC 92-39818. (Significant Issues Ser.: Vol. 14, No. 12). 120p. (gr. 13). 1993. pap. text 9.95 (*0-89206-206-1*) CSIS.

Peterson, Merrill, tr. see Longchenpa.

Peterson, Merrill D. Adams & Jefferson: A Revolutionary Dialogue. LC 76-1145. (Illus.). 160p. 1978. pap. text 16.95 (*0-19-502355-2*) OUP.

— Coming of Age with the "New Republic", 1938-1950. LC 99-44264. 144p. 1999. 27.50 (*0-8262-1257-3*) U of Mo Pr.

— The Great Triumvirate: Webster, Clay, & Calhoun. (Illus.). 591p. 1987. reprint ed. text 35.00 (*0-19-503877-0*) OUP.

— The Great Triumvirate: Webster, Clay, & Calhoun. 582p. 1988. reprint ed. pap. text 17.95 (*0-19-505686-8*) OUP.

— Jefferson & the Revolutionary Mind LC 98-229025. 1995. write for info. (*1-56715-021-7*) Academy Bks.

— The Jefferson Image in the American Mind. LC 98-24052. 560p. 1999. reprint ed. pap. text 19.50 (*0-8139-1851-0*) U Pr of Va.

***Peterson, Merrill D.** Jefferson Memorial: Interpretive Guide to Thomas Jefferson Memorial, District Of Columbia. 48p. 1998. pap. 3.50 (*0-16-061675-1*) USGPO.

Peterson, Merrill D. Jefferson Memorial: Interpretive Guide to Thomas Jefferson Memorial, District of Columbia. LC 97-31440. (Official National Park Handbook Ser.: Vol. 153). (Illus.). 48p. 1998. reprint ed. pap. 3.50 (*0-912627-63-8*) Natl Park Serv.

— Lincoln in American Memory. (Illus.). 496p. 1995. pap. 15.95 (*0-19-509645-2*) OUP.

— Olive Branch & Sword: The Compromise of 1833. LC 81-13739. (Walter Lynwood Fleming Lectures in Southern History Ser.). 144p. 1982. reprint ed. pap. 44.70 (*0-608-00868-0*, 206166000010) Bks Demand.

— Thomas Jefferson & the New Nation: A Biography. LC 70-110394. (Illus.). 1104p. 1986. reprint ed. pap. text 29.95 (*0-19-501909-1*) OUP.

Peterson, Merrill D., ed. Democracy, Liberty & Property: The State Constitutional Conventions of the 1820's. LC 65-23013. (Orig.). 1966. pap. 7.35 (*0-672-60062-5*, AHS43, Bobbs) Macmillan.

— The Political Writings of Thomas Jefferson. (Monticello Monographs). 213p. (Orig.). 1993. pap. 12.95 (*1-882886-01-1*) T J Mem Fnd.

Peterson, Merrill D., intro. Visitors to Monticello. LC 89-5778. (Illus.). 212p. 1989. text 32.50 (*0-8139-1231-8*); pap. text 18.50 (*0-8139-1232-6*) U Pr of Va.

Peterson, Merrill D. & Vaughan, Robert C., eds. The Virginia Statute for Religious Freedom: Its Evolution & Consequences in American History. LC 87-13786. (Cambridge Studies in Religious & American Public Life: 1). (Illus.). 392p. 1988. text 59.95 (*0-521-34329-1*) Cambridge U Pr.

Peterson, Merrill D., ed. see Jefferson, Thomas.

Peterson, Merrill D., ed. see Madison, James.

Peterson, Michael. A Bitter Peace. 1997. per. 6.99 (*0-671-72696-X*) PB.

— God & Evil: An Introduction to the Issues. LC 98-18429. (C). 1998. text 59.00 (*0-8133-2848-9*, Pub. by Westview); pap. text 22.00 (*0-8133-2849-7*, Pub. by Westview) HarpC.

— Straight White Male: Performance Monologues. LC 96-30086. (Performance Studies: Expressive Behavior in Culture). 1997. pap. 18.00 (*0-87805-978-4*) U Pr of Miss.

— A Time of War. 1996. pap., mass mkt. 6.50 (*0-671-56787-X*) PB.

— Vocational Assessment of Special Needs Students for Vocational Education: A State-of-the-Art Review. 1988. 8.00 (*0-318-40005-7*, IN 327) Ctr Educ Trng Employ.

Peterson, Michael, et al, eds. Philosophy of Religion: Selected Readings. (Illus.). 592p. (C). 1996. pap. text 38.95 (*0-19-508909-X*) OUP.

Peterson, Michael & Perlmutt, David. Charlie Two Shoes & the Marines of Love Company. LC 98-30090. 240p. 1998. 28.95 (*1-55750-672-8*) Naval Inst Pr.

***Peterson, Michael, et al.** Philosophy of Religion: Selected Readings. 2nd ed. 656p. (C). 2000. pap. text 39.95 (*0-19-513546-6*) OUP.

Peterson, Michael, et al. Reason & Religious Belief: An Introduction to the Philosophy of Religion. 2nd ed. LC 97-1607. 352p. (C). 1997. text 28.95 (*0-19-511347-0*) OUP.

Peterson, Michael, jt. auth. see Peterson, Walt.

Peterson, Michael E. The Combined Action Platoons: The U. S. Marines Other War in Vietnam. LC 88-34031. 160p. 1989. 57.95 (*0-275-93258-3*, C3258, Praeger Pubs) Greenwood.

— Small Animal Toxicology. (Illus.). 430p. 1999. text. write for info. (*0-7216-7826-2*, W B Saunders Co) Harcrt Hlth Sci Grp.

Peterson, Michael L., ed. The Problem of Evil: Selected Readings. LC 91-50576. (Library of Religious Philosophy: Vol. 8). (C). 1992. pap. text 23.00 (*0-268-01515-5*) U of Notre Dame Pr.

Peterson, Michael P. Interactive & Animated Cartography. LC 94-20878. 464p. (C). 1995. 63.00 (*0-13-079104-0*) P-H.

Peterson, Michael T. DCE Software Developer's Toolkit. (Illus.). 548p. 1997. pap., pap. text 59.95 incl. cd-rom (*0-07-912971-4*) McGraw.

Peterson, Michael T. & Minton, Larry. 3D Studio Max 2 Fundamentals. LC 97-80667. 1997. pap. 39.99 (*1-56205-839-8*) New Riders Pub.

Peterson, Michael Todd. Inside AutoCad 14: Limited Edition. LC 98-84781. 1998. 55.00 (*1-56205-898-3*) New Riders Pub.

Peterson, Mildred J. Family, Love & Work in the Lives of Victorian Gentlewomen. LC 88-45389. (Illus.). 253p. 1989. reprint ed. pap. 78.50 (*0-608-01071-5*, 205937900001) Bks Demand.

***Peterson, Monique.** Santa's Toy Shop. (Walt Disney Classics). (Illus.). 32p. 2000. 14.99 (*0-7868-5313-1*, Pub. by Disney Pr) Time Warner.

— Walt Disney's Mother Goose. (Walt Disney Classics). (Illus.). 32p. 2000. 14.99 (*0-7868-5318-2*, Pub. by Disney Pr) Time Warner.

Peterson, Monique, jt. auth. see Klivans, Richard.

Peterson, Moose. Nikon System Handbook. 164p. 1991. pap. 19.95 (*0-929667-03-4*, 10252) Images NY.

Peterson, N. L. & Harkness, S. D., eds. Radiation Damage in Metals: Papers Presented at a Seminar of the American Society for Metals, Nov. 9-10, 1976. LC 76-25094. 415p. reprint ed. pap. 128.70 (*0-608-30768-8*, 201948500013) Bks Demand.

Peterson, N. V., ed. Health Freedom: Preventive Medicine Can Save Your Life & Fortune. LC 93-74785. 66p. (Orig.). 1994. pap. 9.00 (*1-57000-028-X*) W S Dawson.

— Health Freedom: Preventive Medicine Can Save Your Life & Fortune. abr. ed. LC 93-74785. 66p. (Orig.). 1994. pap. 2.00 (*1-57000-029-8*) W S Dawson.

Peterson, Nadine & Sofie, Barbara N. Singleness: A Guide to Understanding & Satisfaction. LC 87-50532. 184p. (Orig.). 1987. pap. 9.95 (*0-934955-09-3*) Watercress Pr.

Peterson, Nadya. Living Language Russian Conversational Manuel. rev. ed. (RUS.). 1993. pap. 6.00 (*0-517-59054-9*) Liv Lang.

— Living Language Russian Dictionary: Dictionary. rev. ed. (Complete Living Language Course Ser.). (ENG & RUS.). 1993. pap. 5.00 (*0-517-59055-7*) Liv Lang.

Peterson, Nancy. People of the Old Missury: Years of Conflict. LC 89-10723. (Illus.). 192p. (Orig.). 1989. 29.95 (*1-55838-105-8*) R H Pub.

Peterson, Nancy A. People of the Old Missury: Years of Conflict. LC 89-10723. (Illus.). 192p. (Orig.). 1989. pap. 16.95 (*1-55838-106-6*) R H Pub.

Peterson, Nancy J., ed. Toni Morrison: Critical & Theoretical Approaches. LC 97-13838. (Inter-American Dialogue Book Ser.). 304p. 1997. text 48.50 (*0-8018-5701-5*); pap. text 15.95 (*0-8018-5702-3*) Johns Hopkins.

Peterson, Nancy L. Early Intervention for Handicapped & At-Risk Children. LC 86-81467. 580p. 1987. text 58.00 (*0-89108-129-1*) Love Pub Co.

Peterson, Nancy M. People of the Moonshell: A Western River Journal. LC 84-15919. (Illus.). 176p. (Orig.). 1984. pap. 18.95 (*0-939650-42-8*) R H Pub.

— People of the Troubled Water: A Missouri River Journal. LC 88-26418. (Illus.). 176p. (Orig.). 1988. 24.95 (*1-55838-082-5*); pap. 15.95 (*1-55838-083-3*) R H Pub.

Peterson-Nedry, Judy. Oregon Wine Country. LC 97-80275. 1998. pap. text 23.95 (*1-55868-318-6*) Gr Arts Ctr Pub.

Peterson-Nedry, Judy, ed. Regions Northwest: A Wine & Food Yearbook. (Illus.). 102p. (Orig.). 1996. per. 8.95 (*0-9651260-0-5*) Regions NW.

Peterson, Nicholas, ed. see Oldak, Emily.

Peterson, Nicola. Ginkgo & Garlic: Natural Remedies for Respiratory & Circulatory Problems. 128p. 1998. pap. 12.95 (*0-285-63432-1*) IPG Chicago.

Peterson, Nicolas & Sanders, Will, eds. Citizenship & Indigenous Australians: Changing Conceptions & Possibilities. LC 98-10514. (Reshaping Australian Institutions Ser.). (Illus.). 224p. (C). 1998. pap. 24.95 (*0-521-62736-2*); text 64.95 (*0-521-62195-X*) Cambridge U Pr.

Peterson, Nils. The Comedy of Desire. (Illus.). 70p. (Orig.). 1994. pap. 10.00 (*0-9638722-0-6*) Blue Sofa.

Peterson, Norma. Rhonda the Rubber Woman. LC 97-21535. 248p. 1998. 24.00 (*1-57962-003-5*) Permanent Pr.

Peterson, Norma L. Littleton Waller Tazewell. LC 83-3501. 225p. reprint ed. pap. 69.80 (*0-7837-4371-8*, 204408100012) Bks Demand.

— The Presidencies of William Henry Harrison & John Tyler. LC 89-5341. (American Presidency Ser.). xiv, 330p. 1989. 29.95 (*0-7006-0400-6*) U Pr of KS.

Peterson, Norman. Photographic Art: Media & Disclosure. LC 83-18127. (Studies in Photography: No. 4). (Illus.). 147p. reprint ed. pap. 45.60 (*0-8357-1529-9*, 207056900001) Bks Demand.

Peterson, Norman, et al, eds. An Occupational Information System for the 21st Century: The Development of O*NET. LC 98-44293. 336p. 1999. pap. 39.95 (*1-55798-556-1*) Am Psychol.

Peterson, Norman V., ed. Space Rendezvous, Rescue, & Recovery Symposium, Sept. 10-12, 1963, Edwards, CA, 2 Vols, Pt. 1. LC 57-43769. (Advances in the Astronautical Sciences Ser.: Vol. 16). 1028p. 1963. 45.00 (*0-87703-017-0*, Am Astronaut Soc) Univelt Inc.

— Space Rendezvous, Rescue, & Recovery Symposium, Sept. 10-12, 1963, Edwards, CA, 2 Vols, Pt. 2. LC 57-43769. (Advances in the Astronautical Sciences Ser.: Vol. 16). 380p. 1963. 30.00 (*0-87703-018-9*, Am Astronaut Soc) Univelt Inc.

Peterson, O. H. The Electrophysiology of Gland Cells. LC 80-40303. (Physiological Society Monographs: No. 36). 1981. text 157.00 (*0-12-552150-2*) Acad Pr.

Peterson, O. M., jt. ed. see Burgoyne, R. D.

Peterson, Olof, et al, eds. Democracy & Leadership: Report from the Democratic Audit of Sweden 1996. (Center for Business & Policy Studies). 164p. 1997. pap. 52.50 (*91-7150-686-1*, Pub. by Almqvist Wiksell) Coronet Bks.

Peterson, Owen. The Divine Discontent: The Life of Nathan S. S. Beman. LC 85-18765. (Illus.). xvii, 224p. 1985. text 21.95 (*0-86554-170-1*, MUP-H160) Mercer Univ Pr.

Peterson, Owen, jt. auth. see Jeffrey, Robert C.

Peterson, P., jt. auth. see Sims, Jean.

Peterson, P. F., ed. Proceedings of the Second ASME-JSME Joint Conference on Nuclear Engineering, 2 vols. 1993. 200.00 (*0-685-70661-3*, IX0343) ASME.

— Proceedings of the Second ASME-JSME Joint Conference on Nuclear Engineering, Vol. 1. 772p. 1993. write for info. (*0-7918-0636-7*, I0343A) ASME.

— Proceedings of the Second ASME-JSME Joint Conference on Nuclear Engineering, Vol. 2. 916p. 1993. write for info. (*0-7918-0637-5*, I0343B) ASME.

Peterson, P. F. & Kim, J. H., eds. Transient Phenomena in Nuclear Reactor Systems. (HTD Series, Vol. 245: NE: Vol. 11). 148p. 1993. 40.00 (*0-7918-1158-1*, G00802) ASME.

Peterson, P. F., jt. ed. see Cheung, F. B.

Peterson, P. J. Liars. LC 91-28490. 176p. (J). (gr. 5-9). 1995. mass mkt. 3.95 (*0-689-80130-0*) Aladdin.

— Some Days, Other Days. LC 93-3871. (Illus.). 32p. (J). (gr. k-2). 1994. mass mkt. 14.95 (*0-684-19595-X*) S&S Trade.

— White Water. 112p. (J). 1999. pap. 3.99 (*0-440-41552-7*) BDD Bks Young Read.

— White Water. LC 96-10573. 112p. (J). (gr. 3-7). 1997. per. 15.00 (*0-689-80664-7*) S&S Bks Yung.

Peterson, Pamela & Fabozzi, Frank J. Analysis of Financial Statements. (Illus.). 300p. 1999. 55.00 (*1-883249-59-7*) F J Fabozzi.

Peterson, Pamela, jt. auth. see Braham, Jeanne.

Peterson, Pamela P. Financial Management & Analysis. LC 93-33419. (Series in Finance). (C). 1994. text 70.74 (*0-07-049667-6*) McGraw.

— Financial Management & Analysis. 2nd ed. LC 96-54828. (McGraw-Hill Series in Finance). 1997. write for info. (*0-07-049710-9*) McGraw.

Peterson, Pamela P., jt. auth. see Westerman, Marianne.

Peterson, Patricia R. Home Health Care Equipment: A Consumer Guidebook. LC 89-62034. (Illus.). 156p. (Orig.). 1989. 16.95 (*0-944871-34-8*); pap. 9.95 (*0-944871-35-6*) Riegel Pub.

Peterson, Patricia R. Know-It-All: A Resource for Kids & Grown-Ups; A Dictionary of Indispensable Definitions & Facts. (Illus.). 192p. 1997. pap. text 13.95 (*0-673-36377-5*, GoodYrBooks) Addson-Wesley Educ.

Peterson, Patricia W. Changing Times, Changing Tenses: A Review of the English Tense System (Elementary/Intermediate) (Illus.). 155p. 1998. pap. text 15.00 (*0-7881-5977-1*) DIANE Pub.

Peterson, Patrick, ed. see Mortimer, Curtiss.

Peterson, Patti L. & Phillis, John W., eds. Novel Therapies for CNS Injuries: Rationales & Results. 416p. 1995. boxed set 264.95 (*0-8493-7652-1*, 7652) CRC Pr.

Peterson, Paul, et al. Working in Animal Science. Amberson, Max L., ed. (Illus.). (gr. 9-10). 1978. text 19.96 (*0-07-000839-6*) McGraw.

Peterson, Paul, jt. auth. see Koenig, Mark.

Peterson, Paul C., et al. The Feather Mite Family Eustathiidae (Acarina: Sarcoptiformes) (Monograph: No. 21). (Illus.). 143p. 1980. pap. 10.00 (*0-910006-29-6*) Acad Nat Sci Phila.

Peterson, Paul E. City Limits. LC 80-29043. 280p. (C). 1981. pap. text 13.00 (*0-226-66293-4*) U Ch Pr.

— City Limits. LC 80-29043. 280p. (C). 1997. lib. bdg. 33.00 (*0-226-66292-6*) U Ch Pr.

— Law in Arkansas Public Schools. 114p. 1996. pap. text 15.00 (*0-9651331-0-9*) Clearwell Pr.

— Law in Arkansas Public Schools. LC 94-11805. 96p. 1997. pap. 12.95 (*0-944436-21-8*) Pelican.

— Law in Arkansas Public Schools. 3rd ed. 184p. (C). 1998. pap. text 20.00 (*0-9651331-1-7*) Clearwell Pr.

— The Politics of School Reform, 1870-1940. LC 85-1042. x, 256p. 1985. pap. text 14.50 (*0-226-66295-0*) U Ch Pr.

— The Politics of School Reform, 1870-1940. LC 85-1042. x, 242p. 1985. lib. bdg. 27.50 (*0-226-66294-2*) U Ch Pr.

— The Price of Federalism. (Twentieth Century Bks.). 239p. (C). 1995. pap. 16.95 (*0-8157-7023-5*) Brookings.

— The Price of Federalism. LC 95-13773. (Twentieth Century Bks.). 239p. (C). 1995. 38.95 (*0-8157-7024-3*) Brookings.

— School Politics, Chicago Style. LC 76-603. 320p. 1981. pap. text 10.00 (*0-226-66289-6*) U Ch Pr.

— School Politics, Chicago Style. LC 76-603. (Illus.). 1993. lib. bdg. 20.00 (*0-226-66288-8*) U Ch Pr.

Peterson, Paul E., ed. Classifying by Race. LC 95-13494. (Studies in American Politics). 400p. 1996. text 65.00 (*0-691-03796-5*, Pub. by Princeton U Pr) Cal Prin Full Svc.

— Classifying by Race. LC 95-13494. (Studies in American Politics). 400p. 1996. pap. text 20.95 (*0-691-00176-6*, Pub. by Princeton U Pr) Cal Prin Full Svc.

— The New Urban Reality. LC 84-45848. 301p. 1985. 36.95 (*0-8157-7018-9*); pap. 16.95 (*0-8157-7017-0*) Brookings.

— The President, the Congress & the Making of Foreign Policy. LC 94-11855. 312p. 1994. pap. 18.95 (*0-8061-2685-X*) U of Okla Pr.

Peterson, Paul E. & Hassel, Bryan C., eds. Why Not School Choice? LC 98-19747. 428p. 1998. pap. 19.95 (*0-8157-7015-4*); text 49.95 (*0-8157-7016-2*) Brookings.

Peterson, Paul E. & Rom, Mark C. Welfare Magnets: A New Case for a National Standard. 178p. 1990. 32.95 (*0-8157-7022-7*); pap. 12.95 (*0-8157-7021-9*) Brookings.

Peterson, Paul E., et al. When Federalism Works. LC 86-24467. 243p. 1987. 36.95 (*0-8157-7020-0*); pap. 15.95 (*0-8157-7019-7*) Brookings.

Peterson, Paul E., jt. auth. see Fiorina, Morris.

Peterson, Paul E., jt. auth. see Fiorina, Morris P.

Peterson, Paul E., jt. auth. see Greenstone, J. David.

Peterson, Paul E., jt. ed. see Chubb, John E.

Peterson, Paul E., jt. ed. see Jencks, Christopher.

Peterson, Paul E., jt. ed. see Mayer, Susan.

Peterson, Paul M. & Annable, Carol R. Systematics of the Annual Species of Muhlenbergia (Poaceae-Eragrostideae) Anderson, Christiane, ed. (Systematic Botany Monographs: Vol. 31). (Illus.). 109p. 1991. pap. 13.50 (*0-912861-31-2*) Am Soc Plant.

Peterson, Paul M., jt. auth. see Terrell, Edward E.

Peterson, Paula. Coming Home: An Intimate Glance at a Family Camp in the Adirondack North Country. LC 93-14484. 64p. 1993. pap. 9.95 (*0-925168-01-7*) North Country.

— The Oracle of Clarion: Unveiling the Goddess - A Story to Awaken the Heart of Humanity. unabridged ed. 205p. 1996. pap. 12.95 (*0-9653235-0-1*) Rainbow Pyramid.

Peterson, Peggy E., ed. see Peterson, Samantha J.

Peterson, Penelope L., jt. ed. see Neumann, Anna.

An Asterisk (*) at the beginning of an entry indicates that the title is appearing for the first time.

Peterson, Pete. Especially for Seniors: A Collection of Humorous Verse. large type ed. (Illus.). 96p. 1996. per. 7.95 (*1-889103-00-4*) Lead Mine Pr.

Peterson, Pete, ed. They Couldn't Have Won the War Without Us.! Stories of the Merchant Marine - Told by the Men Who Sailed the Ships. LC 97-95109. (Illus.). 185p. 1998. pap. 14.95 (*1-889103-03-9*) Lead Mine Pr.

Peterson, Pete, et al. We're Fighting a War. Be There! LC 96-77439. (Illus.). 160p. (Orig.). 1996. pap. 7.95 (*1-889103-01-2*) Lead Mine Pr.

Peterson, Pete, jt. auth. see Peterson, Joan.

Peterson, Pete, ed. see Oke, Janette.

Peterson, Peter G. Economic Nationalism & International Interdependence: The Global Costs of National Choices. LC HC0106.8.P37. 80p. reprint ed. pap. 30.00 (*0-608-14811-3*, 202590200047) Bks Demand.

— Economic Nationalism & International Interdependence: The Global Costs of National Choices. LC HC0106.8.P37. (Per Jacobsson Lecture Ser.: Vol. 1984). 82p. reprint ed. pap. 30.00 (*0-608-08786-6*, 206942500004) Bks Demand.

— Facing Up. 1993. 22.00 (*0-671-79642-9*) S&S Trade.

***Peterson, Peter G.** Gray Dawn: How the Coming Age Wave Will Transform America - & the World. LC 98-47749. 220p. 1999. 23.00 (*0-8129-3195-5*) Random.

— Gray Dawn: How the Coming Age Wave Will Transform America--And the World. (Illus.). 2000. pap. 14.00 (*0-8129-9069-2*, Times Bks) Crown Pub Group.

Peterson, Peter G. Nacionalismo Economico e Interdependencia Internacional: El Costo Mundial de las Opciones Nacionales. LC HC0106.8.P37. (Conferencia Per Jacobsson de 1984 Ser.). (SPA.). 97p. reprint ed. pap. 30.10 (*0-608-08769-6*, 206940800004) Bks Demand.

— Nationalisme Economique et Independance Internationale: Les Choix Nationaux et Leurs Couts pour l'Economie Mondiale. LC HC0106.8.P37. (Foundation Per Jacobsson Conference de 1984 Ser.). (FRE.). 100p. reprint ed. pap. 31.00 (*0-608-08770-X*, 206940900004) Bks Demand.

Peterson, Phil, ed. see Hoffman, Asa & Donaldson, John.

Peterson, Philip L. Concepts & Language: An Essay in Generative Semantics & the Philosophy of Language. 1973. pap. 40.00 (*90-279-2442-2*) Mouton.

— Fact Proposition Event. LC 97-13664. 1997. text 174.00 (*0-7923-4568-1*) Kluwer Academic.

Peterson, Phillip J., ed. Corrosion of Electronic & Magnetic Materials. LC 91-42686. (Special Technical Publication Ser.: No. 1148). (Illus.). 120p. 1992. text 49.00 (*0-8031-1470-2*, STP1148) ASTM.

Peterson, Phillip K. & Remington, Jack S. In Defense of the Brain: Immunopathogenesis of Infection of the CNS. LC 97-4121. 1997. boxed set 95.00 (*0-86542-555-8*) Blackwell Sci.

***Peterson, Phillip K. & Remington, Jack S.** New Concepts in Immunopathology of CNS Infections. (Illus.). 400p. 2000. 99.95 (*0-632-04528-0*) Blackwell Sci.

Peterson, Phyllis. Assisting the Traumatized Soul: Healing the Wounded Talisman. LC 98-29170. 1998. write for info. (*0-87743-274-0*) Bahai.

Peterson, Phyllis J. The Little Girl in the Woods. Peterson, Allen D., ed. LC 98-92383. (Illus.). 1998. pap. 10.00 (*0-9646503-2-0*) A D Peterson.

Peterson, Phyllis T., jt. auth. see Peterson, Richard D., 2nd.

Peterson, Pipi C. Ready, Set, Organize! Get Your Stuff Together. LC 95-35702. (Illus.). 152p. (Orig.). 1995. pap. 12.95 (*1-57112-072-6*, P072-6) Park Ave.

Peterson, R. The Classical World. (Atlas of Mankind Ser.: Vol. 2). (Illus.). 112p. (C). 1985. 30.00 (*0-941694-15-1*) Cliveden Pr.

— Modern Europe. (Atlas of Mankind Ser.: Vol. 3). (Illus.). 128p. 1987. 30.00 (*0-941694-31-3*) Cliveden Pr.

Peterson, R., ed. The Racial Origins of the Founders of America: Extracted from the Works of Madison Grant & Ales Hrdlicka. (Illus.). 124p. (Orig.). 1995. pap. 15.00 (*1-878465-11-2*) Scott-Townsend Pubs.

Peterson, R., jt. auth. see Sayce, Archibald H.

Peterson, R., ed. see Kingsley, Charles.

Peterson, R. B., et al, eds. Proceedings of the 1995 National Heat Transfer Conference Vol. 2: August 6-9, 1995, Portland, Oregon, Vol. 2. 148p. 1995. 80.00 (*0-7918-1703-2*, H00985) ASME.

Peterson, R. Dean. A Concise History of Christianity. 334p. (C). 1992. pap. 28.50 (*0-534-13278-2*) Wadsworth Pub.

Peterson, R. E. The Theoretical Aspects of Tip Relief. (Technical Papers: Vol. P98). (Illus.). 29p. 1931. pap. text 30.00 (*1-55589-179-9*) AGMA.

Peterson, R. J. & Strottman, D. D., eds. Pion-Nucleus Physics: Future Directions & New Facilities at Lampf. LC 87-72961. (AIP Conference Proceedings Ser.: No. 163). 592p. 1988. lib. bdg. 75.00 (*0-88318-363-3*) Am Inst Physics.

Peterson, R. L., jt. auth. see Nagorsen, D. W.

Peterson, Rai. Writing Teacher's Companion, 001. LC 95-115146. (C). 1994. pap., suppl. ed. 15.16 (*0-395-35033-6*) HM.

Peterson, Ralph. Life in a Crowded Place: Making a Learning Community. LC 92-16468. 142p. (C). 1992. pap. text 19.50 (*0-435-08736-3*, 08736) Heinemann.

Peterson, Ralph L. A Place for Caring & Celebration: The School Media Center. LC 78-31809. (School Media Center: Focus on Trends & Issues Ser.: No. 4). 39p. reprint ed. pap. 30.00 (*0-608-17139-5*, 202735800055) Bks Demand.

***Peterson, Randall W.** Eastern Gulf Coast Directory (Petrochemical Plants) (Illus.). 97p. 2000. pap. 45.00 (*0-9674803-1-0*) Homesite.

Peterson, Randolph L. North American Moose. LC 56-1401. 324p. reprint ed. pap. 100.50 (*0-608-15414-8*, 202934300060) Bks Demand.

Peterson, Ray D., ed. Light Metals 2000. (Illus.). 940p. write for info. (*0-87339-462-3*) Minerals Metals.

Peterson, Raymond H. Accounting for Fixed Assets. (Wiley Institute of Management Accountants Professional Book Ser.). 232p. 1994. 89.95 (*0-471-53703-9*) Wiley.

Peterson, Raymond M. & Cleveland, James O. A Guide for State Planning for the Prevention of Mental Retardation & Related Disabilities. 32p. 1987. write for info. (*1-55672-020-3*) US HHS.

Peterson, Renno L., jt. auth. see Esperti, Robert A.

Peterson, Renno L., jt. ed. see Esperti, Robert A.

Peterson, Richard. Healing the Child Warrior: A Search for Inner Peace. (Illus.). 200p. (Orig.). 1992. pap. 24.95 (*0-9634079-0-2*) R W Peterson.

— Miles to Go, Vol. 1. 1997. mass mkt. 6.50 (*0-312-96275-4*) St Martin.

***Peterson, Richard.** A Trip Through Psychedelica. 2000. pap. write for info. (*1-58235-402-2*) Watermrk Pr.

Peterson, Richard, ed. Teaching Physics Safely: Some Practical Guidelines in Seven Areas of Common Concern in Physics Classrooms. 30p. 1979. 11.00 (*0-917853-87-3*, OP-19) Am Assn Physics.

***Peterson, Richard, et al.** Age & Participation in the Arts. 66p. 2000. pap. 10.95 (*0-929765-87-7*) Seven Locks Pr.

Peterson, Richard, jt. auth. see Cheng, Joseph.

Peterson, Richard, jt. auth. see Kelley, Walter G.

Peterson, Richard, jt. auth. see Schiller, Eric.

Peterson, Richard A. Creating Country Music: Fabricating Authenticity. LC 97-9675. 306p. 1997. 24.95 (*0-226-66284-5*) U Ch Pr.

— The Dynamics of Industrial Society. LC 73-10094. (Studies in Sociology). (C). 1973. pap. text. write for info. (*0-672-61324-7*, Bobbs) Macmillan.

Peterson, Richard A., ed. The Production of Culture. LC 76-41102. (Sage Contemporary Social Science Issues Ser.: No. 33). 144p. 1976. reprint ed. pap. 44.70 (*0-608-01460-5*, 205950400001) Bks Demand.

Peterson, Richard A., et al. Age & Arts Participation with a Focus on the Baby Boom Cohort. LC 96-7841. (National Endowment for the Arts Research Division Report Ser.: No. 34). 142p. 1996. pap. 13.95 (*0-929765-45-1*) Seven Locks Pr.

Peterson, Richard A., jt. auth. see Gouldner, Alvin W.

Peterson, Richard B., ed. Managers & National Culture: A Global Perspective. LC 92-1747. 474p. 1993. 75.00 (*0-89930-602-0*, PMI, Quorum Bks) Greenwood.

Peterson, Richard B. & Tracy, Lane. Systematic Management of Human Resources. LC 78-55826. 1979. text. write for info. (*0-201-05814-6*) Addison-Wesley.

Peterson, Richard B., jt. auth. see Bomers, Gerald B.

Peterson, Richard B., jt. auth. see Lewin, David.

Peterson, Richard D., II. Linn Grove, 1880-1940: A Cultural History of a Small Town in Iowa. LC 98-68557. (Illus.). 410p. 1999. pap. write for info. (*0-941795-03-9*) R D Peterson & Sons.

Peterson, Richard D., ed. ASTD Research Ser., 5 vols. (ASTD Research Ser.). 384p. 11.95 (*0-318-13264-8*); pap. 14.95 (*0-318-13263-X*, PEDPP) Am Soc Train & Devel.

— Studies in Training & Development, No. 1. (ASTD Research Ser.). 196p. pap. 9.50 (*0-318-13283-4*, &ESTP) Am Soc Train & Devel.

Peterson, Richard D., 2nd & Peterson, Phyllis T. A Davies Family History: The Story of the David & Martha Davies Family. LC 94-73835. (Illus.). 273p. (Orig.). 1994. pap. 40.00 (*0-941795-02-0*) R D Peterson & Sons.

Peterson, Richard E. & Uhl, Norman P. Formulating College & University Goals: A Guide for Using the Institutional Goals Inventory. 1988. 8.00 (*0-317-67884-1*) Educ Testing Serv.

Peterson, Richard E., et al. Adult Education & Training in Industrialized Countries. LC 81-84672. 500p. 1981. 47.95 (*0-275-90701-5*, C0701, Praeger Pubs) Greenwood.

— Lifelong Learning in America. LC 79-83576. (Jossey-Bass Series in Higher Education). 552p. reprint ed. pap. 171.20 (*0-7837-2532-9*, 204269100006) Bks Demand.

Peterson, Richard E., jt. ed. see Haynie, W. J., III.

Peterson, Richard F. James Joyce Revisited. (Twayne's English Authors Ser.: No. 490). 170p. (C). 1992. 32.00 (*0-8057-7016-X*) Macmillan.

— William Butler Yeats. (English Authors Ser.). 232p. (C). 1982. 32.00 (*0-8057-6815-7*) Macmillan.

Peterson, Richard F., et al, eds. Work in Progress: Joyce Centenary Essays. LC 82-16943. 192p. 1983. 26.95 (*0-8093-1094-5*) S Ill U Pr.

Peterson, Richard H. The Bonanza Kings: The Social Origins & Business Behavior of Western Mining Entrepreneurs, 1870-1900. LC 91-50311. (Illus.). 208p. 1991. pap. 12.95 (*0-8061-2389-3*) U of Okla Pr.

Peterson, Richard L. Introductory C: Pointers, Functions, & Files. 2nd ed. LC 96-28407. (Illus.). 896p. 1996. pap. text 49.95 (*0-12-552142-1*) Acad Pr.

— The Real Social Security Problem: What Everyone Must Know Before It's Too Late. LC 98-93860. (Illus.). (C). 1998. pap. text 21.95 (*0-9666986-0-6*) Financial Economics.

Peterson, Richard R. Women, Work, & Divorce. LC 88-2133. (SUNY Series in the Sociology of Work). 179p. 1989. text 64.50 (*0-88706-858-8*); pap. text 21.95 (*0-88706-859-6*) State U NY Pr.

Peterson, Richard S. Imitation & Praise in the Poems of Ben Jonson. LC 80-26261. (Illus.). 280p. 1981. 40.00 (*0-300-02586-6*) Yale U Pr.

Peterson, Richard S. & Bartholomew, George A. The Natural History & Behavior of the California Sea Lion. (ASM Special Publications: No. 1). (Illus.). ix, 79p. 1967. 6.00 (*0-943612-00-4*) Am Soc Mammalogists.

Peterson, Richard T. Democratic Philosophy & the Politics of Knowledge. LC 95-23637. 352p. 1996. 60.00 (*0-271-01544-6*); pap. 19.95 (*0-271-01545-4*) Pa St U Pr.

Peterson, Rigby. Interpreting Earth History. 7th ed. 2002. 39.50 (*0-07-235505-0*) McGraw.

Peterson, Rob, jt. auth. see Elliott, Carl W.

Peterson, Rob, jt. auth. see Peterson, Marge.

Peterson, Robert. All the Time in the World. 1996. 20.00 (*1-882413-33-4*); pap. 12.00 (*1-882413-32-6*) Hanging Loose.

— California Tax Handbook: 1994 Edition. rev. ed. Curammeng, Jose, Jr., ed. 928p. 1993. pap. text 25.00 (*0-7811-0080-1*) Res Inst Am.

— Only the Ball Was White. (Illus.). 416p. 1992. pap. 15.95 (*0-19-507637-0*) OUP.

— Only the Ball Was White. LC 98-36777. (Illus.). 416p. 1999. 8.99 (*0-517-20501-7*) Random Hse Value.

— Only the Ball was White. 25.95 (*0-8488-1124-0*) Amereon Ltd.

Peterson, Robert & Licata, Salvatore J., eds. The Gay Past: A Collection of Historical Essays. LC 84-22398. 224p. 1994. pap. text 19.95 (*0-918393-11-6*, Harrington Park) Haworth Pr.

Peterson, Robert & Peterson, Martha. Roaring Lion: Experiencing Victory over Demonic Attack. 1989. pap. 4.95 (*9971-972-80-8*) OMF Bks.

Peterson, Robert & Stradella, Charles. California Tax Handbook: 1993 Edition. rev. ed. 882p. 1992. pap. text 23.00 (*0-7811-0063-1*) Res Inst Am.

Peterson, Robert, jt. auth. see Kerin, Roger.

Peterson, Robert, tr. see Della Casa, Giovanni.

Peterson, Robert A. California Tax Handbook: 1997 Edition. rev. ed. Curemmeng, Jose, Jr., ed. 1000p. 1996. pap. text 28.95 (*0-7811-0148-4*) Res Inst Am.

***Peterson, Robert A.** Calvin & the Atonement. 1999. pap. text 15.99 (*1-85792-377-4*) Christian Focus.

Peterson, Robert A. Hell on Trial: The Case for Eternal Punishment. 270p. (Orig.). 1995. pap. 12.99 (*0-87552-372-2*) P & R Pubng.

— Patriots, Pirates, & Pineys: Sixty Who Shaped New Jersey. LC 98-15153. (Illus.). 154p. 1998. 29.95 (*0-937548-37-5*); pap. 19.95 (*0-937548-39-1*) Plexus Pub.

— Trends in Consumer Behavior Research. LC 76-45657. (American Marketing Association Monograph: No. 6). 46p. reprint ed. pap. 30.00 (*0-608-13402-3*, 202248100027) Bks Demand.

Peterson, Robert A., ed. Electronic Marketing & the Consumer. LC 97-4753. 208p. 1997. 58.00 (*0-7619-1069-7*); pap. 27.95 (*0-7619-1070-0*) Sage.

— The Future of U. S. Retailing: An Agenda for the 21st Century. LC 91-24432. 336p. 1991. 55.00 (*0-89930-679-9*, PFU, Quorum Bks) Greenwood.

Peterson, Robert A., et al. Modern American Capitalism: Understanding Public Attitudes & Perceptions. LC 90-42966. 144p. 1990. 55.00 (*0-89930-625-X*, PMJ/, Quorum Bks) Greenwood.

Peterson, Robert A., jt. auth. see Fudge, Edward W.

Peterson, Robert A., jt. auth. see Kerin, Roger A.

Peterson, Robert A., jt. auth. see Mahajan, Vijay.

Peterson, Robert B. & Peterson, Joni. Rites of Passage: Odyssey of a Grunt. Kirsch, J. Allen, ed. (Illus.). 396p. 1997. 25.00 (*1-878569-48-1*); pap. 14.95 (*1-878569-45-7*) Badger Bks Inc.

Peterson, Robert D., jt. auth. see Cohen, Joel M.

Peterson, Robert D., jt. auth. see Cowen, Joel M.

Peterson, Robert J. A Marriage Service for You. 1977. 5.95 (*0-89536-160-4*) CSS OH.

Peterson, Robert L. Robert Chapman. LC 95-33954. 210p. 1996. text 16.99 (*0-87213-691-4*) Loizeaux.

Peterson, Robert L. & Strauch, Alexander. Agape Leadership: Lessons in Spiritual Leadership from the Life of R. C. Chapman. LC 91-9191. 75p. (Orig.). (C). 1991. pap. 4.99 (*0-936083-05-0*) Lewis-Roth.

Peterson, Robert O. Information Systems Planning. 1990. text 44.95 (*0-07-049649-8*) McGraw.

Peterson, Robert W. The Boy Scouts: An American Adventure. (Illus.). 256p. 1985. pap. 12.95 (*0-685-42998-9*) HM.

— Pigskin: The Early Years of Pro Football. (Illus.). 256p. 1997. pap. 13.95 (*0-19-511913-4*) OUP.

Peterson, Robert W., ed. Agnew: The Coining of a Household Word. LC 70-183844. (Interim History Ser.). 187p. reprint ed. pap. 58.00 (*0-8357-5262-3*, 202289300031) Bks Demand.

Peterson, Roberta. The Elder Filipino. LC 77-83488. (Elder Minority Ser.). 56p. 1978. pap. 9.50 (*0-916304-37-X*) SDSU Press.

Peterson, Robin. Principles of Marketing. (College Outline Ser.). 285p. (C). 1989. pap. text 14.50 (*0-15-601641-9*) Harcourt Coll Pubs.

Peterson, Robin & Phillips, William, eds. Ecology & the Market Place. 1972. 29.50 (*0-8422-5019-0*) Irvington.

Peterson, Robin T., et al. Marketing in Action: An Experiential Approach. (Illus.). 259p. 1978. teacher ed. write for info. (*0-8299-0565-0*) West Pub.

Peterson, Robin T., jt. auth. see Gross, Charles W.

Peterson, Robyn. Training Needs Assessment. 2nd ed. LC 99-218177. 160p. 1998. pap. 25.00 (*0-7494-2568-7*, Kogan Pg Educ) Stylus Pub VA.

Peterson, Robyn G. American Frontier Photography. (Illus.). 36p. 1993. pap. 5.00 (*0-9622038-4-X*) Rockwell NY.

Peterson, Robyn G., ed. see Hollister, Paul.

Peterson, Rodney D. Political Economy & American Capitalism. 240p. (C). 1991. lib. bdg. 80.50 (*0-7923-9142-X*) Kluwer Academic.

Peterson, Rodney L., jt. ed. see Conroy, Donald B.

Peterson, Roger L., et al, eds. The Core Curriculum in Professional Psychology. 179p. 1991. pap. text 29.95 (*1-55798-143-4*) Am Psychol.

Peterson, Roger L., et al. An Introduction to Spread Spectrum Communications. LC 94-27567. 700p. (C). 1995. 105.00 (*0-02-431623-7*, Macmillan Coll) P-H.

Peterson, Roger S., et al. AMA Handbook for Managing Business to Business Marketing Communications. LC 94-14170. (Illus.). 384p. 1996. 39.95 (*0-8442-3595-4*, NTC Business Bks) NTC Contemp Pub Co.

Peterson, Roger T. Eastern Birds. (Peterson Field Guide Ser.). write for info. (*0-614-22107-2*) HM.

— Field Guide to Animal Tracks. (Peterson Field Guide Ser.). (Illus.). 400p. 1998. 27.00 (*0-395-91093-5*, Mariner Bks) HM.

— Field Guide to Animal Tracks. 2nd ed. (Peterson Field Guide Ser.). (Illus.). 400p. 1998. pap. 18.00 (*0-395-91094-3*, Mariner Bks) HM.

— Field Guide to Eastern Birds. 2nd ed. (Peterson Field Guide Ser.). (Illus.). 384p. 1998. 27.00 (*0-395-91175-3*, Mariner Bks) HM.

— A Field Guide to Insects. (Peterson Field Guide Ser.). (Illus.). 416p. 1998. 27.00 (*0-395-91171-0*, Mariner Bks) HM.

— Field Guide to Medicinal Plants. (Peterson Field Guides Ser.). (Illus.). 384p. 1990. pap. 18.00 (*0-395-92066-3*) HM.

— Field Guide to Rocks & Minerals. 6th ed. (Peterson Field Guide Ser.). (Illus.). 416p. 1998. 28.00 (*0-395-91097-8*, Mariner Bks); pap. 18.00 (*0-395-91096-X*, Mariner Bks) HM.

— Field Guide to the Birds. 264p. 1997. 18.95 (*0-395-85493-8*) HM.

— A Field Guide to the Birds. 1996. 18.95 (*0-614-21981-7*) HM.

— A Field Guide to the Butterflies Coloring Book, 001. (Peterson Field Guide Ser.). (Illus.). 64p. 1983. pap. 6.95 (*0-395-34675-4*) HM.

— First Guide to Birds. 2nd ed. (First Guide). (Illus.). 128p. (J). 1998. pap. 5.95 (*0-395-90666-0*, Mariner Bks) HM.

— First Guide to Caterpillers. 2nd ed. (First Guide). (Illus.). 128p. (J). 1998. pap. 5.95 (*0-395-91184-2*, Mariner Bks) HM.

— First Guide to Clouds & Weather. 2nd ed. (First Guide Ser.). (Illus.). 128p. (J). 1998. pap. 5.95 (*0-395-90663-6*, Mariner Bks) HM.

***Peterson, Roger T.** First Guide to Fishes. 2nd ed. (First Guide). (Illus.). 128p. (J). 1998. pap. 5.95 (*0-395-91179-6*, Mariner Bks) HM.

Peterson, Roger T. First Guide to Mammals. 2nd ed. (First Guide). (Illus.). 128p. (J). 1998. pap. 5.95 (*0-395-91181-8*, Mariner Bks) HM.

— First Guide to the Seashore. 2nd ed. (First Guide). (Illus.). 228p. (J). 1998. pap. 5.95 (*0-395-91180-X*, Mariner Bks) HM.

— First Guide to Trees. 2nd ed. (First Guide). (Illus.). 128p. (J). 1998. pap. 5.95 (*0-395-91183-4*, Mariner Bks) HM.

— Penguins. (Illus.). 256p. 1998. pap. 20.00 (*0-395-89897-8*) HM.

— Peterson First Guide to Birds of North America. 1986. 10.05 (*0-606-04504-X*, Pub. by Turtleback) Demco.

— Peterson Flashguides: Atlantic Coastal Birds. (Illus.). 24p. 1996. pap. 7.95 (*0-395-79286-X*) HM.

— Peterson Flashguides: Backyard Birds. (Illus.). 24p. 1996. pap. 7.95 (*0-395-79290-8*) HM.

— Peterson Flashguides: Eastern Mountain Birds. (Illus.). 24p. 1996. pap. 7.95 (*0-395-79288-6*) HM.

— Peterson Flashguides: Hawks. (Illus.). 24p. 1996. pap. 7.95 (*0-395-79291-6*) HM.

— Peterson Flashguides: Pacific Coastal Birds. (Illus.). 24p. 1996. pap. 7.95 (*0-395-79287-8*) HM.

— Peterson Flashguides: Western Mountain Birds. (Illus.). 24p. 1996. pap. 7.95 (*0-395-79289-4*) HM.

— Roadside Wildflowers: Flashguides. (Illus.). 24p. 1997. pap. 7.95 (*0-395-82995-X*) HM.

— Shells. 2nd ed. LC 88-32884. (First Guide). (Illus.). 128p. (J). 1998. pap. 5.95 (*0-395-91182-6*, Mariner Bks) HM.

Peterson, Roger T. The Field Guide Art of Roger Tory Peterson, Vol. 2, Western Birds. LC 92-8460. 356p. 1992. reprint ed. boxed set 150.00 (*0-395-64356-2*) HM.

Peterson, Roger T. Roger Tory Peterson's ABC of Birds: A Book for Little Birdwatchers. LC 95-15540. 32p. (J). (gr. 1-3). 1995. 15.95 (*0-7893-0009-5*, Pub. by Universe) St Martin.

Peterson, Roger T. & Alden, Peter. A Field Guide to Birds Coloring Book, 001. (Illus.). 64p. 1982. pap. 6.95 (*0-395-32521-8*) HM.

Peterson, Roger T. & Peterson, Virginia M. Audubon's Birds of America: The Audubon Society Baby Elephant Folio. (Illus.). 694p. 1993. 100.00 (*0-89660-040-8*, Artabras) Abbeville Pr.

— Audubon's Birds of America: The Audubon Society Baby Elephant Folio. (Tiny Folios Ser.). (Illus.). 436p. 1996. pap. 11.95 (*1-55859-225-3*) Abbeville Pr.

Peterson, Roger T. & Peterson, Virginia Marie. Field Guide to Eastern Birds: A Completely New Guide to All the Birds of Eastern & Central North America. 2nd ed. (Peterson Field Guide Ser.). 384p. 1998. pap. 18.00 (*0-395-91176-1*, Mariner Bks) HM.

Peterson, Roger T. & Tenenbaum, Frances. A Field Guide to Wildflowers Coloring Book, 001. (Illus.). 64p. 1982. pap. 6.95 (*0-395-32522-6*) HM.

Peterson, Roger T., et al. A Field Guide to Forests Coloring Book, 001. (Illus.). 64p. 1983. pap. 6.95 (*0-395-34676-2*) HM.

— A Field Guide to Reptiles & Amphibians Coloring Book, 001. (Illus.). 64p. 1985. pap. 6.95 (*0-395-37704-8*) HM.

— A Field Guide to the Birds of Britain & Europe. 5th ed. LC 93-22426. (Peterson Field Guide Ser.: No. 8). 516p. 1993. pap. 25.00 (*0-395-66922-7*) HM.

Peterson, Roger T., ed. & notes see Roberts, David.

Peterson, Roger Tory. Atlantic Seashore. (Peterson Field Guides Ser.). (Illus.). 1999. pap. 19.00 (*0-618-00209-X*) HM.

P

— Birds of the West Indies. (Peterson Field Guides Ser.). (Illus.). 1999. pap. 22.00 (0-618-00210-3) HM.

— Coral Reefs Caribbean & Florida. (Peterson Field Guides Ser.). (Illus.). 1999. pap. 20.00 (0-618-00211-1) HM.

— Edible Wild Plants. (Peterson Field Guides Ser.). (Illus.). 1999. pap. 19.00 (0-395-92622-X) HM.

***Peterson, Roger Tory.** Mexican Birds. (Peterson Field Guides Ser.). 1999. pap. 21.00 (0-395-97514-X) HM.

Peterson, Roger Tory. Pacific Coast Fishes. (Peterson Field Guides Ser.). (Illus.). 1999. pap. 19.00 (0-618-00212-X) HM.

***Peterson, Roger Tory, et al.** A Field Guide to Feeder Birds, Eastern & Central North America. LC 99-53956. (Peterson Field Guide Ser.). (Illus.). 112p. 2000. pap. 9.95 (0-618-05944-X) HM.

Peterson, Roger W., et al. Caring for Youth in Shelters. 2nd ed. 174p. 1997. pap. text 24.99 (0-938510-99-1, 63-004) Boys Town Pr.

Peterson, Roland. Everyone Is Right. 352p. (Orig.). 1986. pap. 12.95 (0-87516-565-6) DeVorss.

Peterson, Rolf. The Wolves of Isle Royale: A Broken Balance. LC 95-35263. (Illus.). 189p. 1995. 29.50 (1-57223-031-2, 0312) Willow Creek Pr.

Peterson, Ronald C. & Mayo Foundation Staff, eds. The Spectrum of Normal Aging, Mild Cognitive Impairment & Alzheimer's Disease. (Illus.). 300p. 2001. text 55.00 (0-19-512342-5) OUP.

Peterson, Ronald E. A History of Russian Symbolism. LC 90-23250. (Linguistic & Literary Studies in Eastern Europe: Vol. 29). xii, 254p. 1993. 89.00 (90-272-1534-0) J Benjamins Pubng Co.

Peterson, Ronald E., tr. see Borgen, Johan.

Peterson, Rosemary & Felton-Collins, Victoria. The Piaget Handbook for Teachers & Parents: Children in the Age of Discovery, Preschool to 3rd Grade. (Early Childhood Education Ser.). Orig. Title: Piaget: A Handbook for Parents & Teachers in the Age of Discovery. 80p. (C). 1986. pap. text 11.95 (0-8077-2841-1) Tchrs Coll.

Peterson, Rosendo D. Las Novelas de Unamuno. 104p. 1990. 30.00 (0-916379-44-2) Scripta.

Peterson, Roy, jt. auth. see Burke, Stanley.

Peterson, Roy M. The Cults of Campania. LC 23-13673. (American Academy in Rome, Papers & Monographs: Vol. 1). 413p. reprint ed. pap. 128.10 (0-608-16449-6, 202671600051) Bks Demand.

Peterson, Roy Tory. Wild America. LC 97-12874. (Illus.). 448p. 1997. pap. 14.00 (0-395-86497-6) HM.

Peterson, Royal F., tr. see Rosenius, Carl O.

Peterson, Ruby. Fun with Bible Facts. 1974. pap. 3.00 (0-89137-620-8) Quality Pubns.

— More Fun with Bible Facts. 1977. pap. 3.00 (0-89137-617-8) Quality Pubns.

***Peterson, Russell W.** Rebel with a Conscience. LC 99-10337. (Illus.). 403p. 1999. 29.95 (0-87413-681-4) U Delaware Pr.

Peterson, Ruth. Before I Die. 32p. 1987. pap. 0.75 (0-88144-095-7) Christian Pub.

— Dinner at Five. rev. ed. LC 98-65646. (Illus.). 32p. (J). (gr. k-3). 1998. 1.95 (1-891992-00-7) Owls Hse Pr.

Peterson, Ruth, jt. ed. see Hagan, John G.

Peterson, Ruth C. & Thurstone, Louis L. Motion Pictures & the Social Attitudes of Children. LC 76-124031. (Literature of Cinema: Payne Fund Studies of Motion Pictures & Social Values). 1970. reprint ed. 15.95 (0-405-01630-1) Ayer.

Peterson, Samantha J. The Plaid Vest. Peterson, Peggy E., ed. (Illus.). 24p. (Orig.). (J). (gr. k-3). 1996. pap. 5.95 (1-888860-00-6) Plaid Platypus.

Peterson, Samiha S., tr. see Amin, Qasim.

***Peterson, Samuel E.** Tales & Trails: Stories of Atlantic City, South Pass & the Sweetwater. (Illus.). 150p. 1999. pap. 11.95 (0-9658855-3-4) Mortimore Pub.

Peterson, Sandy, ed. see Stafford, Greg.

Peterson, Sarah M. The Book of Names: Over 1000 Biblical, Historical, & Popular Names. LC 97-5537. 288p. 1997. pap. 8.99 (0-8423-0123-2) Tyndale Hse.

***Peterson, Scott.** Batman Beyond: New Hero in Town. (Illus.). 24p. (J). (ps-3). 2000. pap. 3.25 (0-375-80653-9, Pub. by Random Bks Yng Read) Random.

Peterson, Scott. Dragon Flyz Fly Forever: Dragon Flyz Rescue Mission, No. 2. (Dragon Flyz Ser.). (Illus.). 64p. (J). (ps-k). 1997. 4.95 (0-694-01022-7, HarpFestival) HarpC Child Bks.

— Fly the Skies with the Dragon Flyz: Dragonstar Training Manual, No. 1. (Dragon Flyz Ser.). (Illus.). 64p. (J). (ps). 1997. 4.95 (0-694-01021-9, HarpFestival) HarpC Child Bks.

***Peterson, Scott.** Me Against My Brother: At War in Somalia, Sudan & Rwanda. LC 99-56411. (Illus.). 352p. 2000. 27.50 (0-415-92198-8) Routledge.

— Native American Prophecies: History, Wisdom & Startling Predictions. 2nd expanded rev. ed. LC 98-45314. 304p. (Orig.). 1999. pap. 15.95 (1-55778-748-4) Paragon Hse.

— Visual Basic 6 by Example. (By Example Ser.). 550p. 2000. pap. 24.99 (0-7897-2296-8) Que.

Peterson, Scott, jt. auth. see Wald, Mark.

Peterson, Scott, ed. see Canwell, Bruce.

Peterson, Scott, ed. see DeMatteis, J.M.

Peterson, Scott, ed. see Grant, Alan.

Peterson, Scott, ed. see Grell, Mike.

Peterson, Scott K. Plugged In: Electric Riddles. (Illus.). 32p. (J). (gr. 1-4). 1995. pap. 1.98 (0-8225-9700-4) Lerner Pub.

— Wing It: Riddles about Birds. (J). (gr. 1-4). 1991. pap. 3.95 (0-8225-9591-5, First Ave Edns) Lerner Pub.

Peterson, Scott R., jt. auth. see Bednar, Richard L.

Peterson, Shailer A. Preparing to Enter Medical School. 1980. text 14.95 (0-13-697342-6, Spectrum IN) Macmillan Gen Ref.

Peterson, Sharon. Wharfside. DeBarr, Toby, ed. 40p. 1997. pap. 10.00 (1-893409-01-5) LY Prods.

Peterson, Shelley. Dancer. 192p. 1997. pap. 12.95 (0-88984-177-2) Porcup Quill.

Peterson, Sherrie. Help! for Substitutes. (Illus.). 80p. (J). 1985. teacher ed. 3.99 (0-86653-277-3, GA 642) Good Apple.

Peterson, Sherry. The Practical Guide to Quality Assurance. 1990. 39.95 (0-944496-09-1) Precept Pr.

Peterson, Shirley, jt. ed. see Harrison, Elizabeth J.

Peterson, Spiro. Daniel Defoe: A Reference Guide. (Reference Guides to Literature Ser.). 429p. 1987. 55.00 (0-8161-8157-8, Hall Reference) Macmillan.

Peterson Staff. Peterson Flashguides: Birds of the Midwest. (Illus.). 24p. 1997. pap. 8.95 (0-395-86733-9) HM.

— Peterson Flashguides: Freshwater Fish. (Illus.). 24p. 1997. pap. 7.95 (0-395-86713-4) HM.

— Peterson Flashguides: Waterfowl. (Illus.). 24p. 1997. pap. 8.95 (0-395-86734-7) HM.

Peterson, Stephanie. 1 2 3 Boo! LC 97-204212. (Illus.). (J). 1997. write for info. (0-7853-2355-4) Pubns Intl Ltd.

— Scared Silly. LC 97-204233. (Illus.). (J). 1997. write for info. (0-7853-2352-X) Pubns Intl Ltd.

— Teeny Tiny Witch. LC 97-204221. (Illus.). (J). 1997. write for info. (0-7853-2353-8) Pubns Intl Ltd.

Peterson, Stephen, jt. auth. see Somit, Albert.

Peterson, Stephen B., jt. auth. see Cohen, John M.

Peterson, Steve. Breath of Fire II Authorized Game Secrets. 1996. pap. 14.95 (0-7615-0396-X) Prima Pub.

— Empire Vol. 2: The Art of War: The Official Strategy Guide. 1995. pap. 19.95 (0-7615-0207-6) Prima Pub.

Peterson, Steve & Littleton, Mark. Truth about Rock: Shattering the Myth of Harmless Music. LC 97-33957. 21p. 1998. pap. 9.99 (0-7642-2053-5) Bethany Hse.

Peterson, Steve, jt. auth. see Harlick, Bruce.

Peterson, Steven A. Political Behavior: Patterns in Everyday Life. LC 89-27838. (Sage Library of Social Research: Vol. 177). (Illus.). 296p. 1990. reprint ed. pap. 91.80 (0-608-01725-6, 206238200003) Bks Demand.

Peterson, Steven A., ed. Political Behavior: Patterns in Everyday Life. (Library of Social Research: Vol. 177). 296p. (C). 1990. text 59.95 (0-8039-3729-6); pap. text 26.00 (0-8039-3730-X) Sage.

Peterson, Steven A. & Maiden, Robert J. The Public Lives of Rural Older Americans. LC 93-13840. 166p. (Orig.). (C). 1993. pap. text 24.00 (0-8191-9189-2); lib. bdg. 49.50 (0-8191-9188-4) U Pr of Amer.

Peterson, Steven A. & Rasmussen, Thomas H. State & Local Politics. 364p. (C). 1994. pap. 12.95 (0-07-049671-4) McGraw.

Peterson, Steven A. & Somit, Albert. The Political Behavior of Older Americans. LC 94-4762. (Issues in Aging Ser.: Vol. 4). 200p. 1994. text 39.00 (0-8153-1321-7, SS972) Garland.

Peterson, Steven A., jt. auth. see Somit, Albert.

Peterson, Steven A., jt. ed. see Somit, Albert.

Peterson, Steven D. & Tiffany, Paul. Business Plans for Dummies. LC 96-77273. (For Dummies Ser.). (Illus.). 384p. 1997. pap. 19.99 (1-56884-868-4) IDG Bks.

Peterson, Steven L. & Albertson, Timothy E. Neuropharmacology Methods in Epilepsy Research. LC 98-9863. (Methods in Life Science - Cellular & Molecular Neuropharmacology Ser.). 304p. 1998. per. 129.95 (0-8493-3362-8) CRC Pr.

Peterson, Stuart R. Patents, Getting One . . . A Cost Cutting Primer for Inventors. LC 89-81531. (Illus.). 472p. 1990. 43.95 (0-914960-75-X) Academy Bks.

Peterson, Sue H. Swim with Me: A New Fun Approach to Learning to Swim. (Illus.). 24p. (J). (ps-2). 1999. 12.95 (1-883672-94-5) Tricycle Pr.

***Peterson, Susan.** Contemporary Ceramics. (Illus.). 176p. 2000. 35.00 (0-8230-0937-8) Watsn-Guptill.

Peterson, Susan. The Craft & Art of Clay. 2nd ed. LC 96-151781. 1995. pap. text 50.00 (0-13-374463-9) P-H.

***Peterson, Susan.** The Craft & Art of Clay. 3rd ed. (Illus.). 400p. 2000. 65.00 (0-87951-738-7, Pub. by Overlook Pr) Penguin Putnam.

— The Craft & Art of Clay. 3rd ed. (Illus.). 416p. (C). 1999. pap. text 49.33 (0-13-085125-6) P-H.

Peterson, Susan. Craft & the Art of Clay: A Complete Potter's Handbook. 2nd ed. (Illus.). 400p. 1996. 55.00 (0-87951-634-8, Pub. by Overlook Pr) Penguin Putnam.

— Crisis Bargaining & the State: The Domestic Politics of International Conflict. 216p. (C). 1996. text 44.50 (0-472-10628-7, 10628) U of Mich Pr.

— Fun & Educational Places to Go with Kids in Southern California. 4th rev. ed. Orig. Title: Fun & Educational Places to Go with Kids. 650p. (Orig.). 1998. pap. 16.95 (0-9646737-3-8, Pub. by Fun Places) Sunbelt Pubns.

— Fun Places to Go with Kids. 200p. (Orig.). pap. 11.95 (0-9646737-0-3) Fun Places.

— The Living Tradition of Maria Martinez. rev. ed. LC 77-75373. (Illus.). 300p. 1992. pap. 45.00 (0-87011-497-2) Kodansha.

— Lucy M. Lewis: American Indian Potter. (Illus.). 220p. 1984. 65.00 (0-87011-685-1) Kodansha.

— Lucy M. Lewis: American Indian Potter. (Illus.). 220p. 1992. reprint ed. pap. 39.95 (4-7700-1698-0) Kodansha.

— Pottery by American Indian Women: The Legacy of Generations. LC 97-12628. (Illus.). 224p. (J). 2000. 55.00 (0-7892-0353-7, Abbeville Kids) Abbeville Pr.

— Shoji Hamada: A Potter's Way & Work. LC 95-21872. (Illus.). 240p. 1995. pap. 22.95 (0-8348-0345-3) Weatherhill.

***Peterson, Susan.** Smashing Glazes: 50 Artists Share Insights & Recipes. (Illus.). 128p. 2001. 27.99 (1-893164-05-5, Pub. by GUILDcom) F & W Pubns Inc.

Peterson, Susan. Timeline Charts of the Western Church. LC 99-15626. 320p. 1999. pap. 24.99 (0-310-22353-9) Zondervan.

Peterson, Susan, et al. Pottery by American Indian Women: The Legacy of Generations. LC 97-12628. 1997. pap. 37.50 (0-7892-0354-5) Abbeville Pr.

Peterson, Susan, ed. see OnGuard Inc. Staff.

Peterson, Susan, ed. see OnGuard Inc. Staff & Bruegman, Randy R.

Peterson, Susan, ed. see Peterson, Charles & Blei, Norbert.

Peterson, Susan C. & Vaughn-Roberson, Courtney A. Women with Vision: The Presentation Sisters of South Dakota, 1880-1985. LC 87-20451. 334p. 1988. text 29.95 (0-252-01493-6) U of Ill Pr.

Peterson, Susan H. Working in Clay: An Introduction to Ceramics. LC 98-15477. (Illus.). 192p. 1998. 39.95 (0-87951-903-7, Pub. by Overlook Pr) Penguin Putnam.

Peterson, Susan J. Ariel's World: An Exploration of Lake Ontario. (Illus.). 164p. (Orig.). 1995. pap. 11.95 (0-9646149-0-1) Ariel Assocs.

Peterson, Susan K. & Tenenbaum, Henry A. Behavior Management: Strategies & Techniques. LC 86-9113. 84p. (Orig.). (C). 1986. pap. 14.50 (0-8191-5362-1); lib. bdg. 35.50 (0-8191-5361-3) U Pr of Amer.

Peterson, Susan L. At Risk Students: Tools for Teaching in Problem Settings. LC 98-5515. 110p. 1998. 49.95 (1-57309-275-4); pap. 24.95 (1-57309-274-6) Intl Scholars.

— The Changing Meaning of Feminism: Life Cycle & Career Implications from a Sociological Perspective. LC 98-16519. 114p. 1998. 49.95 (1-57309-306-8) Intl Scholars.

— The Educators' Phrase Book: A Complete Reference Guide. LC 97-46965. 120p. 1998. 64.95 (1-57309-242-8); pap. 24.95 (1-57309-241-X) Intl Scholars.

— Feminism: A Research & Content Workbook. 169p. 1998. wbk. ed. 59.95 (1-57309-360-2) Intl Scholars.

***Peterson, Susan L.** Feminist Motivation Therapy. LC 99-12548. 112p. 1999. 39.95 (1-57309-384-X) Intl Scholars.

Peterson, Susan L. Teachers & Technology: Understanding the Teacher's Perspective of Technology. LC 98-50334. 126p. 1999. 64.95 (1-57309-378-5) Intl Scholars.

***Peterson, Susan L.** Why Children Make up Stories. LC 99-10373. 112p. 1999. 39.95 (1-57309-382-3); pap. 24.95 (1-57309-381-5) Intl Scholars.

Peterson, Susan L. & Peterson, James A. Sexy Legs: How to Get Them & How to Keep Them. LC 83-80741. (Orig.). 1984. pap. 6.95 (0-88011-162-3) S&S Trade.

Peterson, Susan Louise. The Changing Meaning of Feminism: Life Cycle & Career Implications from a Sociological Perspective. LC 98-16519. 114p. 1998. pap. 35.00 (1-57309-305-X) Intl Scholars.

— Feminism: A Research & Content Workbook. 169p. 1998. pap., wbk. ed. 39.95 (1-57309-359-9) Intl Scholars.

***Peterson, Susan Louise.** Feminist Motivation Therapy. LC 99-12548. 112p. 1999. pap. 24.95 (1-57309-383-1) Intl Scholars.

Peterson, Susan Louise. The Research Writer's Phrase Book: A Guide to Proposal Writing & Research Phraseology. LC 98-5517. 1998. write for info. (1-57309-277-0) Intl Scholars.

***Peterson, Susan Louise.** The Research Writer's Phrase Book: A Guide to Proposal Writing & Research Phraseology. LC 98-5517. 110p. 1998. pap. 24.95 (1-57309-276-2) Intl Scholars.

— Teachers & Technology: Understanding the Teacher's Perspective of Technology. LC 98-50334. 126p. 1999. pap. 34.95 (1-57309-377-7) Intl Scholars.

Peterson, T., jt. auth. see Pella, J.

Peterson, T. Sarah. Acquired Taste: The French Origins of Modern Cooking. (Illus.). 280p. 1994. text 37.50 (0-8014-3053-4) Cornell U Pr.

Peterson, Tarla R. Sharing the Earth: The Rhetoric of Sustainable Development. LC 97-4737. (Studies in Rhetoric/Communication). 240p. 1997. 29.95 (1-57003-173-8) U of SC Pr.

***Peterson, Teddie.** Talk to Me. 1999. pap. write for info. (1-58235-035-3) Watermrk Pr.

Peterson, Thad D., jt. auth. see Klug, John R.

Peterson, Theodore B. Magazines in the Twentieth Century. 2nd ed. LC 64-18668. (Illus.). 498p. reprint ed. pap. 154.40 (0-8357-6199-1, 203445800090) Bks Demand.

Peterson, Thomas. Doing Something by Doing Nothing. 1985. 6.55 (0-89536-747-5, 5853) CSS OH.

Peterson, Thomas E. Alberto Moravia. 1996. 32.00 (0-8057-8296-6, Twyne) Mac Lib Ref.

— The Ethical Muse of Franco Fortini. LC 96-45637. 208p. 1997. 49.95 (0-8130-1479-4) U Press Fla.

— The Paraphase of an Imaginary Dialogue: The Poetics & Poetry of Pier Pasolini. XVI, 356p. (C). 1994. text 48.95 (0-8204-1529-4) P Lang Pubng.

Peterson, Todd. AutoCAD Secrets. 384p. 1996. pap. 40.00 (1-56205-587-9) New Riders Pub.

Peterson, Tom. Living the Life You Were Meant to Live. LC 97-53278. 256p. 1998. 19.99 (0-7852-7195-3) Nelson.

Peterson, Toni, ed. see Getty Art History Information Program.

Peterson, Tony, ed. see Gomes, Steve.

Peterson, Tracie. Alaska: Four Inspirational Love Stories in America's Final Frontier. 400p. 1998. pap. 4.97 (1-57748-354-5) Barbour Pub.

***Peterson, Tracie.** Colorado Wings. 464p. 2000. pap. 4.97 (1-57748-828-8) Barbour Pub.

Peterson, Tracie. Controlling Interests. LC 98-220285. 256p. (YA). (gr. 10 up). 1998. pap. 8.99 (0-7642-2064-0) Bethany Hse.

— Controlling Interests. large type ed. LC 99-26533. (Christian Mystery Ser.). 407p. 1999. 23.95 (0-7862-1999-8) Thorndike Pr.

— Entangled. LC 96-45849. (Portraits Ser.). 256p. 1997. pap. 8.99 (1-55661-936-7) Bethany Hse.

***Peterson, Tracie.** Entangled. LC 99-46905. 290p. 2000. 23.95 (0-7862-2228-X) Mac Lib Ref.

Peterson, Tracie. Framed. LC 97-33885. (Portraits Ser.). 24p. 1998. pap. 8.99 (1-55661-992-8) Bethany Hse.

***Peterson, Tracie.** Framed. LC 00-32533. 2000. write for info. (0-7862-2696-X) Thorndike Pr.

Peterson, Tracie. Hidden in a Whisper, Vol. 2. LC 99-6413. 304p. 1999. pap. text 9.99 (0-7642-2113-2) Bethany Hse.

— King of Hearts. 1999. pap. 0.99 (1-57748-432-0) Barbour Pub.

— The Shelter of Hope. (Westward Chronicle Ser.). 34p. 1998. pap. 9.99 (0-7642-2112-4) Bethany Hse.

***Peterson, Tracie.** A Slender Thread. LC 99-51016. 320p. 2000. pap. 10.99 (0-7642-2251-1) Bethany Hse.

— Tidings of Peace. 304p. 2000. pap. 9.99 (0-7642-2291-0) Bethany Hse.

— Veiled Reflection. LC 99-6884. (Westward Chronicles Ser.: No. 3). 285p. 2000. pap. 9.99 (0-7642-2114-0) Bethany Hse.

— Westward Chronicles, Vols. 1-3. (Westward Chronicles Ser.). 1999. pap. 29.99 (0-7642-8596-3) Bethany Hse.

Peterson, Tracie & Totman, Lisa. A Celebration of Life. (Illus.). 112p. 1999. 12.99 (1-57748-577-7) Barbour Pub.

Peterson, Tracie, jt. auth. see Pella, Judith.

Peterson, Trudy H. Agricultural Exports, Farm Income, & the Eisenhower Administration. LC 79-15825. 236p. reprint ed. pap. 73.20 (0-8357-3810-8, 203653700003) Bks Demand.

Peterson, V. Spike, ed. Gendered States: Feminist (Re)Visions of International Relations Theory. LC 91-42673. (Gender & Political Theory Ser.). 226p. 1992. pap. text 19.95 (1-55587-328-6) L Rienner.

Peterson, V. Spike & Runyan, Anne Sisson. Global Gender Issues. 2nd ed. LC 98-39827. (Dilemmas in World Politics Ser.). 304p. 1998. pap. text 25.00 (0-8133-6852-9, Pub. by Westview) HarpC.

Peterson, Vern, ed. Cartea Vietii - Romanian Book of Life Vol. 2: English Illustrated. (Book of Life Ser.: Vol. 38). (ENG & RUM., Illus.). 64p. (Orig.). (J). (gr. 1-7). 1997. mass mkt. write for info. (1-890525-00-6) Bk of Hope.

— Russian Book of Life Vol. 2: Youth Version. (Book of Life Ser.: Vol. 39). (ENG & RUS., Illus.). 64p. (Orig.). (YA). (gr. 7 up). 1997. mass mkt. write for info. (1-890525-02-2) Bk of Hope.

— Russian Book of Life Vol. 3: Children's Version. 2nd rev. ed. (Book of Life Ser.: Vol. 40). (ENG & RUS., Illus.). 64p. (J). (gr. 1-7). 1997. mass mkt. write for info. (1-890525-01-4) Bk of Hope.

Peterson, Veronica. Just the Facts: A Pocket Guide to Basic Nursing. 2nd ed. LC 98-23493. 368p. 1998. pap. text. write for info. (0-323-00152-1) Mosby Inc.

Peterson, Vicki. The ABCs of My Feelings: A Journal for Recovering & Discovering Human Beings. (Illus.). 60p. (Orig.). 1991. pap. 14.95 (0-9630195-0-3) Dynamic Des Pr.

Peterson, Vicki, jt. auth. see Spong, Tim.

Peterson, Vince, jt. auth. see Folger, Cleve.

***Peterson, Virginia, ed.** Garbage & Other Pollution: How Do We Live with All the Trash. rev. ed. (Information Plus Compact Ser.). (Illus.). 80p. (YA). 1999. pap. text 15.95 (1-57302-105-9) Info Plus TX.

— Water: The Vital Source. rev. ed. (Information Plus Compact Ser.). (Illus.). 80p. (YA). 1998. pap. text 15.95 (1-57302-107-5) Info Plus TX.

***Peterson, Virginia, et al, eds.** Endangered Species: Quickly Disappearing. 3rd large type rev. ed. (Compact Reference Ser.). (Illus.). 72p. (J). 1999. pap. text 14.95 (1-57302-095-8) Info Plus TX.

Peterson, Virginia, et al, eds. Energy: An Issue of the '90s. 3rd rev. ed. (Information Plus Compact Reference Ser.). (Illus.). 84p. 1998. pap. text 15.95 (1-57302-068-0) Info Plus TX.

— The Environment: Protecting Our Home. 3rd rev. ed. (Information Plus Compact Ser.). (Illus.). 88p. (YA). 1998. pap. text 15.95 (1-57302-080-X) Info Plus TX.

— Gambling: Who Wins? 3rd rev. ed. (Information Plus Compact Reference Ser.). (Illus.). 64p. 1998. pap. text 15.95 (1-57302-069-9) Info Plus TX.

***Peterson, Virginia, et al, eds.** Health: Taking Care of Ourselves. 3rd large type rev. ed. (Compact Reference Ser.). (Illus.). 80p. (gr. 6-9). 1999. pap. text 14.95 (1-57302-094-X) Info Plus TX.

Peterson, Virginia, et al, eds. Minorities: America's Rich Culture. 3rd rev. ed. (Information Plus Compact Reference Ser.). (Illus.). 84p. 1998. pap. text 14.95 (1-57302-070-2) Info Plus TX.

— Nutrition: On the Road to Good Health. 3rd rev. ed. (Information Plus Compact Ser.). (Illus.). 84p. (YA). 1998. pap. text 14.95 (1-57302-081-8) Info Plus TX.

***Peterson, Virginia, et al, eds.** Population: Our Growing Planet. rev. ed. (Information Plus Compact Ser.). (Illus.). 80p. (YA). 1998. pap. text 14.95 (1-57302-104-0) Info Plus TX.

— Recreation: What Do We Do to Have Fun? 3rd large type rev. ed. (Compact Reference Ser.). (Illus.). 60p. 1999. pap. text 14.95 (1-57302-093-1) Info Plus TX.

Peterson, Virginia, et al, eds. Space: New Frontiers. 3rd rev. ed. (Information Plus Compact Ser.). (Illus.). 72p. (J). 1998. pap. text 15.95 (1-57302-082-6) Info Plus TX.

***Peterson, Virginia, et al, eds.** Transportation: Getting from One Place to Another. 3rd large type ed. (Compact Reference Ser.). (Illus.). 80p. 1999. pap. text 15.95 (1-57302-092-3) Info Plus TX.

Peterson, Virginia, et al, eds. Women: New Roles in Society. 3rd rev. ed. (Information Plus Compact Ser.). (Illus.). 84p. (YA). 1998. pap. text 15.95 (1-57302-083-4) Info Plus TX.

Peterson, Virginia M., jt. auth. see Peterson, Roger T.

Peterson, Virginia Marie, jt. illus. see Peterson, Roger T.

Peterson, W., ed. see Quintilianus.

Peterson, W. E. AlmostPerfect: How a Bunch of Regular Guys Built WordPerfect Corporation. LC 93-34366. 240p. 1993. 18.95 (*1-55958-477-7*) Prima Pub.

Peterson, W. H., et al. Peterson. 372p. 1991. reprint ed. pap. 59.00 (*0-8328-2073-3*); reprint ed. lib. bdg. 69.00 (*0-8328-2072-5*) Higginson Bk Co.

Peterson, W. Wesley. Introduction to Economics. 1977. pap. text 36.95 (*0-13-481242-5*) P-H.

Peterson, W. Wesley & Weldon, E. J., Jr. Error-Correcting Codes. 2nd rev. ed. 1972. 69.50 (*0-262-16039-0*) MIT Pr.

Peterson, Wade D. The VME Business Handbook. 4th ed. 375p. Date not set. pap. 53.00 (*1-885731-09-4*) VFEA Int Trade.

— The VMEbus Handbook. 332p. 1993. pap. 53.00 (*1-885731-01-9*) VFEA Int Trade.

Peterson, Wagner. Solutions Manual to Accompany College Mathematics Through Applications. 544p. 1998. 24.95 (*0-7668-0224-8*) Delmar.

Peterson, Wallace. Coming Class War: Power, Conflict, & the Consequences of Middle Class Decline. 1999. pap. 23.95 (*0-7656-0198-2*) M E Sharpe.

Peterson, Wallace C. Income, Employment & Economic Growth: Study Guide. 8th ed. (C). 1996. pap. text, student ed. write for info. (*0-393-96855-3*) Norton.

— Our Overloaded Economy: Inflation, Unemployment, & the Crisis in American Capitalism. LC 81-51288. 256p. reprint ed. pap. 79.40 (*0-608-18131-5*, 203278500081) Bks Demand.

— The Social Security Primer: What Every Citizen Should Know. LC 99-14346. (Illus.). 192p. 1999. text 34.95 (*0-7656-0373-X*) M E Sharpe.

— Transfer Spending, Taxes, & the American Welfare State. (C). 1990. lib. bdg. 91.00 (*0-7923-9077-6*) Kluwer Academic.

Peterson, Wallace C., ed. Market Power & the Economy: Industrial, Corporate, Government & Political Aspects. (C). 1988. lib. bdg. 91.00 (*0-89838-267-X*) Kluwer Academic.

Peterson, Wallace C. & Burgess, Anthony. Silent Depression: Twenty-Five Years of Wage Squeeze & Middle Class Decline. 320p. 1995. pap. 13.95 (*0-393-31282-8*, Norton Paperbks) Norton.

Peterson, Wallace C. & Estenson, Paul S. Income, Employment, & Economic Growth. 8th ed. LC 95-13314. (C). 1996. text 64.00 (*0-393-96854-5*) Norton.

Peterson, Wallace C., jt. auth. see Strobel, Frederick R.

Peterson, Walt. The Baja Adventure Book. 3rd ed. LC 98-8746. (Illus.). 288p. 1998. pap. 19.95 (*0-89997-231-4*) Wilderness Pr.

— Five Thousand Ways to Say No to Your Child. (Illus.). 112p. (Orig.). 1993. pap. 7.95 (*0-9635892-0-2*) Mendocino Coast.

— Lonely Planet Baja California. LC 00-265951. (Diving & Snorkeling Guides Ser.). (Illus.). 128p. 1999. pap. text 16.95 (*0-86442-572-4*) Lonely Planet.

Peterson, Walt & Peterson, Michael. Exploring Baja by R. V. LC 96-14683. (Illus.). 288p. 1996. pap. 19.95 (*0-89997-177-6*) Wilderness Pr.

Peterson, Walter F. An Industrial Heritage: Allis-Chalmers Corporation. LC 76-57456. (Illus.). 448p. 1978. 17.50 (*0-938076-02-7*) Milwaukee Cty Hist Soc.

Peterson, Warren A. & Quadagno, Jill S., eds. Social Bonds in Later Life: Aging & Interdependence. LC 85-1830. (Illus.). 477p. reprint ed. pap. 147.90 (*0-7837-4566-4*, 204409500003) Bks Demand.

Peterson, Wayne, ed. see McAllister, Dawson & Altman, Tim.

Peterson, Wayne L., jt. auth. see Peterson, Barbara V.

Peterson, Wilferd. Art of Living: Thoughts on Meeting the Challenge of Life. 1997. pap. text 7.95 (*0-88486-159-7*, Bristol Park Bks) Arrowood Pr.

— Art of Living: Thoughts on Meeting the Challenge of Life. 1993. 9.98 (*0-88365-831-3*) Galahad Bks.

Peterson, Wilferd A. The Art of Creative Thinking. Olmos, Dan, ed. LC 90-71111. 208p. (Orig.). 1991. pap. 10.00 (*1-56170-004-5*, 131) Hay House.

Peterson, Willard J., et al, eds. The Power of Culture: Studies in Chinese Cultural History. LC 97-178510. 380p. (Orig.). (C). 1997. 44.50 (*962-201-596-4*, Pub. by Chinese Univ) U of Mich Pr.

Peterson, William, ed. Advances in Input-Output Analysis: Technology, Planning & Development. (Illus.). 256p. 1991. text 75.00 (*0-19-506236-1*) OUP.

Peterson, William, jt. ed. see Barker, Terry.

Peterson, William E. Bill. (WPP Bks.). (Illus.). 32p. (J). (gr. k-5). 1995. 5.95 (*1-888078-00-6*) W E Peterson.

— Calculator: And Other Poems by Bill. (WEP Books Ser.). 48p. 1995. 2.75 (*1-888078-02-2*) W E Peterson.

— The Giving Place. (WEP Bks.). 48p. 1995. 2.75 (*1-888078-03-0*) W E Peterson.

— Imagination Paint: And Other Poems by Bill. (WEP Bks.). 48p. 1995. 2.75 (*1-888078-01-4*) W E Peterson.

Peterson, William J., jt. auth. see Eckert, Amy.

Peterson, William J., jt. ed. see Archbold, Lawrence.

Peterson, William N. Mystic Built: Ships & Shipyards of the Mystic River, Connecticut, 1784-1919. (Illus.). xvi, 254p. 1989. 36.00 (*0-913372-51-X*) Mystic Seaport.

Peterson, William N. & Coope, Peter M. Historic Buildings at Mystic Seaport Museum. (Illus.). 136p. 1985. pap. 15.95 (*0-913372-35-8*) Mystic Seaport.

Peterson, William S. A Bibliography of the Kelmscott Press. (Soho Bibliographies Ser.). (Illus.). 210p. 1984. text 74.00 (*0-19-818199-X*) OUP.

— The Kelmscott Press: A History of William Morris's Typographical Adventure. (Illus.). 385p. 1990. 125.00 (*0-520-06138-1*, Pub. by U CA Pr) Cal Prin Full Svc.

Peterson, William S., ed. see Browning, Elizabeth Barrett.

Peterson, Willis. Principles of Economics: Macro. 10th ed. 430p. (C). 1997. text 44.95 (*1-885079-26-5*) Willis Peterson.

— Principles of Economics: Micro. 10th ed. 440p. (C). 1997. text 44.95 (*1-885079-01-X*) Willis Peterson.

Peterson, Willis L. Introduction to Economics. rev. ed. 640p. (C). 1995. pap. text 24.95 (*1-885079-24-9*) Willis Peterson.

— Principles of Economics. 4th ed. (C). 1979. student ed., per. 5.95 (*0-256-02338-7*, Irwn McGrw-H) McGrw-H Hghr Educ.

— Principles of Economics: Macro. 7th ed. (C). 1988. pap. text 33.95 (*0-256-06795-3*, Irwn McGrw-H); student ed. 15.95 (*0-256-07054-7*, Irwn McGrw-H) McGrw-H Hghr Educ.

— Principles of Economics: Macro. 9th ed. (Illus.). 359p. (C). 1994. pap. text 24.95 (*1-885079-25-7*) Willis Peterson.

— Principles of Economics: Macro. 9th ed. (Illus.). 120p. (C). 1994. teacher ed. write for info. (*1-885079-75-3*) Willis Peterson.

— Principles of Economics: Micro. 7th ed. (C). 1988. student ed. 15.95 (*0-256-07055-5*, Irwn McGrw-H) McGrw-H Hghr Educ.

— Principles of Economics: Micro. 9th ed. (Illus.). 303p. (C). 1994. pap. text 24.95 (*1-885079-00-1*) Willis Peterson.

— Principles of Economics: Micro. 9th ed. (Illus.). 120p. 1994. teacher ed. write for info. (*1-885079-50-8*) Willis Peterson.

Peterson, Zelma, ed. see Browder, Anthony T.

***Petersons.** Basic Guidance Set: 4 Volume Set, 2000 Ed., 4. 1999. pap. text 105.80 (*0-7689-0311-4*) Petersons.

— Bricker's International Directory 2000: University-Based Executive Development Programs. 31st ed. 1175p. 1999. 395.00 (*0-7689-0287-8*) Petersons.

— Culinary Schools 2000. 3rd ed. 384p. 1999. pap. text 24.95 (*0-7689-0298-3*) Petersons.

— Distance Learning 2000. 1999. pap. text 26.95 (*0-7689-0257-6*) Petersons.

Petersons. Graduate Studies in Social Sciences & Social Work: The Unique Multimedia Guide to Graduate & 1999. pap. text 24.95 (*0-7689-0210-X*) Petersons.

— Guide to College Visits: How to Make the Most Out of Your Campus Visits. 2nd ed. LC 98-656778. 361p. 1999. pap. 24.95 (*0-7689-0247-9*) Petersons.

***Petersons.** Guide to English Language Programs. 2nd ed. 656p. 1999. pap. text 21.95 (*0-7689-0275-4*) Petersons.

Petersons. Guide to MBA Programs 2000. 5th ed. 1275p. 1999. pap. text 26.95 (*0-7689-0262-2*) Petersons.

***Petersons.** Inside Scoop on College Life: A Guide to Choosing Your Best Place to Live & Learn. 239p. 1999. pap. 16.95 (*0-7689-0325-4*) Petersons.

— International Directory of University-Preparatory Boarding Schools in the United States & Canada. 7th ed. 330p. 1999. pap. text 15.95 (*0-7689-0292-4*) Petersons.

— Internships 2000. 648p. 1999. pap. text 24.95 (*0-7689-0261-4*) Petersons.

— Law Schools 2000: A Comprehensive Guide to All 181 Accredited U.S. Law Schools. 2nd ed. 560p. 1999. pap. text 24.95 (*0-7689-0290-8*) Petersons.

— MBA Distance Learning Programs: The Hottest New Way to Earn a Graduate Business Degree. 2nd ed. 264p. 1999. pap. text 18.95 (*0-7689-0282-7*) Petersons.

— MCAT Success. 4th ed. 364p. 1999. pap. text 16.95 (*0-7689-0297-5*) Petersons.

— Midwest. 15th ed. (Peterson's Colleges in the Midwest Ser.). 139-357p. 1999. pap. 17.95 (*0-7689-0249-5*) Petersons.

— New England. 15th ed. (Peterson's Colleges in New England Ser.). 139-357p. 1999. pap. 17.95 (*0-7689-0252-5*) Petersons.

— New York. 15th ed. (Peterson's Colleges in New York Ser.). 139-357p. 1999. pap. 17.95 (*0-7689-0253-3*) Petersons.

Petersons. Overseas Summer Jobs, 1997. (Orig.). 1997. pap. write for info. (*1-85458-153-8*) Intl School Servs.

— Peterson's Competitive Colleges: Top Colleges & Universities in the US for the World's Best St. 18th ed. 480p. 1999. pap. 18.95 (*0-7689-0213-4*) Petersons.

***Petersons.** Peterson's Guide To Nursing Programs, 5th 1999 Ed. 5th ed. 672p. 1999. pap. 26.95 (*0-7689-0216-9*) Petersons.

— Peterson's Private Secondary Schools 2001. 21st ed. 2000. pap. 29.95 (*0-7689-0569-9*) Petersons.

— Peterson's Regional College Guides 2000. 15th ed. (Peterson's Colleges in the Middle Atlantic States Ser.). 139-357p. 1999. pap. 17.95 (*0-7689-0248-7*) Petersons.

— Scholarships & Loans for Adult Students. 408p. 1999. pap. text 19.95 (*0-7689-0296-7*) Petersons.

— Scholarships for Study in the USA 2000. 2nd ed. 368p. 1999. pap. 21.95 (*0-7689-0266-5*) Petersons.

— South. 15th ed. (Peterson's Colleges in the South Ser.). 139-357p. 1999. pap. 17.95 (*0-7689-0250-9*) Petersons.

— Sports Scholarships & College Athletic Programs. 4th ed. 872p. (C). 1999. pap. 26.95 (*0-7689-0273-8*) Petersons.

— Study Abroad 2000. 7th ed. 1120p. 1999. pap. text 29.95 (*0-7689-0286-X*) Petersons.

— Summer Study Abroad: The Complete Guide to More Than 1,400 Summer Academic & Language Programs. 3rd ed. 622p. 1999. pap. text 29.95 (*0-7689-0299-1*) Petersons.

— Traditional & Specialty Camps. (Summer Fun Ser.). 256p. 1999. pap. 9.95 (*0-7689-0189-8*) Petersons.

Petersons. Undergraduate Study Set: 2000 Ed., 2. 1999. pap. text 51.90 (*0-7689-0319-X*) Petersons.

***Petersons.** U.S. & Canadian Medical Schools: A Comprehensive Guide to All 159 Accredited Medical Schools. 4th ed. 254p. 1999. pap. text 24.95 (*0-7689-0285-1*) Petersons.

— Vocational & Technical Schools: East. 4th ed. 718p. 1999. pap. text 34.95 (*0-7689-0293-2*) Petersons.

— Vocational & Technical Schools: West. 4th ed. 702-718p. 1999. pap. text 34.95 (*0-7689-0294-0*) Petersons.

— West: 2000 Edition. 15th ed. (Peterson's Colleges in the West Ser.: Vol. 2000). 139-357p. 1999. pap. 17.95 (*0-7689-0245-2*) Petersons.

Petersons & Griffith, Susan. Work Your Way Around the World: The Authoritative Guide for the Working Traveler. 9th ed. (Work Your Way Around the World Ser.). (Illus.). 517p. 1999. pap. write for info. (*1-85458-205-4*) Petersons.

Peterson's Guides Staff. ACT Success 2000. 2nd ed. 395p. 1999. pap. 16.95 (*0-7689-0225-8*) Petersons.

— Adventure Holidays 1996: Your Complete Guide to Thousands of Active Vacations Worldwide. 19th rev. ed. (Vacation Work's Ser.). 224p. (Orig.). 1996. pap. 12.95 (*1-85458-140-6*, Pub. by Vac Wrk Pubns) Petersons.

— Basic Guidance: 1999 Editiion. 1998. 103.80 (*0-7689-0120-0*, Petersons Pacesetter) Petersons.

***Peterson's Guides Staff.** Biology, 2000. 352p. 1999. pap. text 16.95 (*0-7689-0368-8*) Petersons.

Peterson's Guides Staff. Bricker's International Directory, 1999: University-Based Executive Development Programs. 29th ed. 1000p. 1998. 395.00 (*0-7689-0047-6*) Petersons.

— Business Majors: 1999 Edition. 15th ed. (Peterson's Job Opportunities For Busines). 360p. 1999. pap. 21.95 (*0-7689-0026-3*) Petersons.

***Peterson's Guides Staff.** Calculus AB/BC, 2000. 352p. 1999. pap. text 16.95 (*0-7689-0369-6*) Petersons.

— Careers Without College, 14 vols. 1997. boxed set 111.30 (*1-56079-575-1*) Petersons.

Peterson's Guides Staff. Christian Colleges & Universities. 6th ed. (Peterson's Guides). 160p. 1998. pap. text 14.95 (*0-7689-0050-6*) Petersons.

— CLEP Success. (Peterson's Test Success Ser.). 512p. 1998. pap. text 16.95 (*0-7689-0023-9*) Petersons.

***Peterson's Guides Staff.** CLEP Success 2000. 2nd ed. 363p. 1999. pap. 16.95 incl. cd-rom (*0-7689-0227-4*) Petersons.

— College & University Almanac 2000. 3rd ed. 512p. 1999. pap. 9.95 (*0-7689-0263-0*) Petersons.

Peterson's Guides Staff. College Money Handbook. 16th ed. 760p. 1998. pap. text 26.95 (*0-7689-0051-4*) Petersons.

***Peterson's Guides Staff.** College Money Handbook 2000. 17th ed. LC 96-643. 890p. 1999. pap. 26.95 (*0-7689-0244-4*) Petersons.

Peterson's Guides Staff. Colleges in New England, 1999: Connecticut, Maine, Massachusetts, New Hampshire, Rhode Island, & Vermont. 15th ed. (Regional College Guides Ser.). 345p. 1998. pap. 17.95 (*0-7689-0032-8*, 870091Q) Petersons.

— Colleges in the Middle Atlantic States: Delaware, District of Columbia, Maryland, New Jersey, Pennsylvania, Virginia & West Virginia. 15th ed. (Regional College Guides Ser.). 345p. 1998. pap. 17.95 (*0-7689-0029-8*, 870093Q) Petersons.

— Colleges in the Midwest: Illinois, Indiana, Iowa, Kansas, Michigan, Minnesota, Missouri, Nebraska, North Dakota, Ohio, Oklahoma, South Dakota, & Wisconsin. 15th ed. (Regional College Guides Ser.). 345p. 1998. pap. 17.95 (*0-7689-0030-1*, 870096Q) Petersons.

— Colleges in the South: Alabama, Arkansas, Florida, Georgia, Kentucky, Louisiana, Mississippi, North Carolina, South Carolina, Tennessee, & Texas. 14th ed. (Regional College Guides Ser.). 345p. 1998. pap. 17.95 (*0-7689-0031-X*, 870098Q) Petersons.

— Competitive Colleges, 1996-1997: Top College for Top Students. 15th ed. 464p. (Orig.). 1996. pap. 16.95 (*1-56079-598-0*) Petersons.

— Core Library Set: 1998 Edition, 15 vols. 1997. pap. text 462.25 (*1-56079-901-3*) Petersons.

— Deluxe Guidance Set: 1998 Edition, 9 vols. 1997. pap. text 210.55 (*1-56079-919-6*) Petersons.

— Directory of College & University Administrators. 12th ed. 1190p. 1998. pap. 49.95 (*0-7689-0130-8*) Petersons.

***Peterson's Guides Staff.** Directory of College & University Administrators: The Complete Guide to Academic & Administration. 13th ed. 1200p. (C). 1999. pap. 49.95 (*0-7689-0264-9*) Petersons.

Peterson's Guides Staff. Distance Learning Programs. 3rd ed. (Peterson's Guides). 636p. 1998. pap. text 26.95 (*0-7689-0129-4*) Petersons.

— Engineering & Computer Science Majors. 20th ed. (Peterson's Job Opportunities for Engineers Ser.). 395p. 1998. pap. text 21.95 (*0-7689-0027-1*) Petersons.

***Peterson's Guides Staff.** English Literature & Composition, 2000. 352p. 1999. pap. text 16.95 (*0-7689-0366-1*) Petersons.

Peterson's Guides Staff. Four-Year Colleges 1999 Everything You Need to Make the Right Choice. 29th ed. 176p. 1998. pap. 24.95 incl. cd-rom (*1-56079-987-0*) Petersons.

***Peterson's Guides Staff.** Four-Year Colleges 2000. 30th ed. (Illus.). 3176p. 1999. pap. 34.95 (*0-7689-0194-4*) Petersons.

Peterson's Guides Staff. GED Success. (Peterson's Test Success Ser.). (Illus.). 549p. 1998. pap. 14.95 (*0-7689-0020-4*) Petersons.

***Peterson's Guides Staff.** GED Success 2000. 2nd ed. 557p. 1999. pap. 16.95 (*0-7689-0226-6*) Petersons.

— GED Success 2001. 3rd ed. 557p. 2000. pap. 16.95 (*0-7689-0408-0*) Petersons.

— GMAT CAT Success 2001. 400p. 2000. pap. 29.95 (*0-7689-0409-9*) Petersons.

— GMAT Success 2000. 4th ed. 229p. 1999. pap. 16.95 incl. cd-rom (*0-7689-0233-9*) Petersons.

Peterson's Guides Staff. The Gold Standard MCAT: For Medical School Admissions. LC 98-49859. 800p. 1999. pap. 44.95 (*0-7689-0192-8*) Petersons.

— Grad Guides Set: 1998 Edition, 6 vols. 1997. pap. text 240.70 (*1-56079-797-5*) Petersons.

— Graduate & Professional Programs Bk. 1: An Overview 1999. 1388p. 1998. 39.95 (*1-56079-941-2*) Petersons.

— Graduate Schools in the U.S. The Unique Multimedia Guide to Graduate & Professional Programs. 1999. pap. text 24.95 (*0-7689-0207-X*) Petersons.

***Peterson's Guides Staff.** Graduate Studies in Arts, Humanities, & Archaeology, 1998. 1999. pap. text 24.95 (*0-7689-0208-8*) Petersons.

Peterson's Guides Staff. Graduate Studies in Biology, Health & Agricultural Sciences. 1999. pap. text 24.95 (*0-7689-0209-6*) Petersons.

— Graduate Studies in Education. 1999. pap. text 24.95 (*0-7689-0206-1*) Petersons.

— Graduate Studies in Engineering, Computer Science & Information Studies. 1999. pap. text 24.95 (*0-7689-0205-3*) Petersons.

— Graduate Studies in Physical Sciences, Mathematics & Environmental Sciences: The Unique Multimedia. 1999. pap. text 24.95 (*0-7689-0204-5*) Petersons.

***Peterson's Guides Staff.** GRE CAT Success 2001. 400p. 2000. pap. 29.95 (*0-7689-0410-2*) Petersons.

Peterson's Guides Staff. GRE Success. (Test Success Ser.). 368p. (Orig.). 1996. pap. 12.95 (*1-56079-686-3*); pap. 24.95 incl. disk (*1-56079-688-X*) Petersons.

***Peterson's Guides Staff.** GRE Success 2000. 4th ed. 365p. 1999. pap. 16.95 incl. cd-rom (*0-7689-0240-1*) Petersons.

— Guide to College Visits: How to Get the Most Out of Your Campus Visits. 448p. 1998. pap. 24.95 incl. cd-rom (*0-7689-0039-5*) Petersons.

Peterson's Guides Staff. Guide to Visual & Performing Arts 2000. 5th ed. (Professional Degree Programs Ser.). 591p. 1999. pap. 26.95 (*0-7689-0255-X*) Petersons.

— Health & Science Majors. 6th ed. (Peterson's Job Opportunities for Health Ser.). 216p. 1998. pap. text 21.95 (*0-7689-0025-5*) Petersons.

— Hidden Job Market: 2000 High-Growth Companies That Are Hiring at Four Times the National Average. 8th ed. 306p. 1998. pap. text 18.95 (*0-7689-0012-3*) Petersons.

— Hidden Job Market 1997. 6th rev. ed. 316p. 1996. pap. 18.95 (*1-56079-644-8*) Petersons.

— Independent Study Catalog: A Guide to over 10,000 Correspondence Courses. 7th rev. ed. 301p. 1998. pap. text 18.95 (*0-7689-0008-5*) Petersons.

***Peterson's Guides Staff.** International Directory of Voluntary Work. 7th ed. 256-528p. 1999. pap. write for info. (*1-85458-237-2*, Pub. by Vac Wrk Pubns) Petersons.

Peterson's Guides Staff. Internships: The Largest Source of Internships Available 1999. 19th ed. (Peterson's Guides). 648p. 1998. pap. text 24.95 (*0-7689-0044-1*) Petersons.

— ISS Directory of Overseas Schools, 1997-1998: The Comprehensive Guide to K-12 American & International Schools Worldwide. 530p. 1998. pap. 34.95 (*0-913663-15-8*) Intl School Servs.

***Peterson's Guides Staff.** Job Opportunities: 1999 Edition. 1998. write for info. (*0-7689-0157-X*) Petersons.

— Jobs Seeker's Almanac. 900p. 1999. pap. 9.95 (*0-7689-0258-4*) Petersons.

— Law Schools 2001. 3rd ed. 560p. 2000. pap. text 24.95 (*0-7689-0437-4*) Petersons.

Peterson's Guides Staff. Learning Programs. (The Summer Fun Ser.). 256p. pap. 9.95 (*0-7689-0188-X*) Petersons.

— Liberal Arts Jobs: Turning Your Learning into Earning Power. 3rd ed. (Peterson's Guides). 240p. 1998. pap. text 14.95 (*0-7689-0148-0*) Petersons.

— Logic & Reading Review for the GRE, GMAT, LSAT, MCAT. LC 99-28088. 288p. 1999. pap. 16.95 (*0-7689-0229-0*) Petersons.

***Peterson's Guides Staff.** LSAT Success 2000. 6th ed. 245p. 1999. pap. 16.95 incl. cd-rom (*0-7689-0224-X*) Petersons.

— LSAT Success 2001. 7th ed. 245p. 2000. pap. 16.95 (*0-7689-0411-0*) Petersons.

Peterson's Guides Staff. MBA Distance Learning Programs: The Best New Way to Earn an MBA 1999. (Peterson's Guides). 240p. 1998. pap. text 18.95 (*0-7689-0125-1*) Petersons.

***Peterson's Guides Staff.** MBA Programs 2001: U.S., Canadian, & International Business Schools 2001. 6th ed. 1275p. 2000. pap. text 29.95 (*0-7689-0441-2*) Petersons.

Peterson's Guides Staff. MCAT Success. LC 96-39646. (Test Success Ser.). 352p. 1996. pap. 12.95 (*1-56079-685-5*); pap. 24.95 incl. disk (*1-56079-689-8*) Petersons.

— MCAT Success 1999. (Peterson's Guides). 356p. 1998. pap. text 16.95 (*0-7689-0149-9*) Petersons.

— Media Companies: 2000 Edition. 324p. 1999. pap. 27.95 (*0-7689-0215-0*) Petersons.

***Peterson's Guides Staff.** Overseas Summer Jobs 2000. 31st ed. 256-528p. 1999. pap. write for info. (*1-85458-229-1*, Pub. by Vac Wrk Pubns) Petersons.

Peterson's Guides Staff. Peterson's Black Colleges & Universities. (Peterson's Guides). 1998. pap. text 12.95 (*0-7689-0145-6*) Petersons.

***Peterson's Guides Staff.** Peterson's CLEP Success 2001. 2nd ed. 363p. 2000. pap. 16.95 (*0-7689-0407-2*) Petersons.

Peterson's Guides Staff. Peterson's College & University Almanac. 2nd ed. 512p. 1998. pap. text 9.95 (*0-7689-0035-2*) Petersons.

— Peterson's Competitive Colleges. 17th ed. 444p. 1998. pap. text 18.95 (*1-56079-988-9*) Petersons.

***Peterson's Guides Staff.** Peterson's Competitive Colleges 2000-2001. 19th ed. 2000. pap. 18.95 (*0-7689-0385-8*) Petersons.

Peterson's Guides Staff. Peterson's Culinary Schools: The Most Comprehensive Guide to U. S. Culinary Schools & Apprenticeship Programs. 300p. 1998. pap. text 21.95 (*1-56079-943-9*) Petersons.

— Peterson's English Learning Programs: A Guide to Short-Term Study Worldwide. 576p. 1998. pap. text 21.95 (*1-56079-999-4*) Petersons.

***Peterson's Guides Staff.** Peterson's Game Plan for Getting into Business Schools. 200p. 2000. pap. 14.95 (*0-7689-0392-0*) Petersons.

— Peterson's Game Plan for Getting into Graduate School. 200p. 2000. pap. 14.95 (*0-7689-0391-2*) Petersons.

— Peterson's Game Plan for Getting into Medical School. LC 99-87860. 2000. pap. 14.95 (*0-7689-0393-9*) Petersons.

Peterson's Guides Staff. Peterson's Graduate & Professional Programs, 1996: An Overview, Bk. 1. 30th ed. 1204p. 1995. pap. 25.95 (*1-56079-501-8*) Petersons.

— Peterson's Graduate Programs in the Humanities, Arts, & Social Sciences 1996, Bk. 2. 30th ed. 1514p. 1995. pap. 34.95 (*1-56079-502-6*) Petersons.

— Peterson's Graduate Programs in the Physical Sciences & Mathematics, 1996, Bk. 4. 30th ed. 818p. 1995. pap. 32.95 (*1-56079-504-2*) Petersons.

— Peterson's Grants for Graduate & Postdoctoral Study. 5th ed. 528p. 1998. pap. text 32.95 (*0-7689-0019-0*) Petersons.

***Peterson's Guides Staff.** Peterson's Guide to College Visits 2001. 3rd ed. 512p. 2000. pap. 24.95 (*0-7689-0400-5*) Petersons.

Peterson's Guides Staff. Peterson's Guide to Colleges for Careers in Allied Health. 1996. pap. 67.80 (*1-56079-531-X*) Intl School Servs.

— Peterson's Guide to Colleges in New England, 1997, 6 vols. 13th rev. ed. (Regional College Guides Ser.). 143p. 1996. pap. 16.95 (*1-56079-623-5*) Petersons.

— Peterson's Guide to Colleges in New York, 1997, 6 vols. 13th ed. (Regional College Guides Ser.). 142p. 1996. pap. 16.95 (*1-56079-622-7*) Petersons.

— Petersons Guide to Colleges in New York, 1999: New York State, Including New York City. 15th ed. (Peterson's Guide to Colleges in New York Ser.). 345p. pap. 17.95 (*0-7689-0033-6*, 870092Q) Petersons.

— Peterson's Guide to Colleges in the Middle Atlantic States, 1996: Delaware, the District of Columbia, Maryland . . . 12th ed. (Regional College Guides Ser.). 218p. (YA). (gr. 11-12). 1995. pap. 14.95 (*1-56079-492-5*, Petersons Pacesetter) Petersons.

— Peterson's Guide to Colleges in the Middle Atlantic States, 1997, 6 vols. 13th ed. (Regional College Guides Ser.). 221p. 1996. pap. 16.95 (*1-56079-626-X*) Petersons.

— Peterson's Guide to Colleges in the Midwest, 1996: Illinois, Indiana, Iowa, Kansas, Michigan... 12th ed. (Regional College Guides Ser.). 345p. (YA). (gr. 11-12). 1995. pap. 14.95 (*1-56079-489-5*) Petersons.

— Peterson's Guide to Colleges in the Midwest, 1997, 6 vols. 13th rev. ed. (Regional College Guides Ser.). 363p. 1996. pap. 16.95 (*1-56079-624-3*) Petersons.

— Peterson's Guide to Colleges in the South, 1996: Alabama, Arkansas, Florida, Georgia, Kentucky... 11th ed. (Regional College Guides Ser.). 288p. (YA). (gr. 11-12). 1995. pap. 14.95 (*1-56079-490-9*) Petersons.

— Peterson's Guide to Colleges in the South, 1997. (Regional College Guides Ser.). 288p. 1996. pap. text 16.95 (*1-56079-625-1*) Petersons.

— Peterson's Guide to Colleges in the South, 1997, 6 vols. 12th rev. ed. (Regional College Guides Ser.). 308p. 1996. pap. 16.95 (*1-56069-625-7*) Petersons.

— Peterson's Guide to Colleges in the West, 1996: Alaska, Arizona, California, Colorado, Hawaii, Idaho... 10th ed. (Regional College Guides Ser.). 195p. (C). 1995. pap. 14.95 (*1-56079-491-7*) Petersons.

— Peterson's Guide to Colleges in the West, 1997, 6 vols. 11th rev. ed. (Regional College Guides Ser.). 195p. 1996. pap. 16.95 (*1-56079-627-8*) Petersons.

— Peterson's Guide to Distance Learning Programs. 2nd rev. ed. Orig. Title: Electronic University. (Illus.). 504p. (Orig.). 1996. pap. 24.95 (*1-56079-664-2*) Petersons.

— Peterson's Guide to Four-Year Colleges, 1997. 27th rev. ed. 3180p. 1996. pap. 24.95 (*1-56079-604-9*) Petersons.

— Peterson's Guide to Medical Schools in the U. S. & Canada: M. D. & M. D. - Ph. D. Programs at Nearly 150 U. S. & Canadian Schools. 2nd ed. Latimer, Jon, ed. 1000p. (C). 1997. pap. 21.95 (*1-56079-631-6*) Petersons.

— Peterson's Guide to New York Colleges, 1996: New York State Including New York City. 12th rev. ed. (Regional College Guides Ser.). 138p. (YA). (gr. 11-12). 1995. pap. 14.95 (*1-56079-487-9*) Petersons.

— Peterson's Guide to Two-Year Colleges, 1996. 26th ed. 752p. (C). 1995. pap. 17.95 (*1-56079-482-8*) Petersons.

— Peterson's Guide to Two-Year Colleges, 1997. 27th rev. ed. (Illus.). 842p. 1996. pap. 21.95 (*1-56079-605-7*) Petersons.

— Peterson's Law Schools, 1998: A Comprehensive Guide to All Accredited U. S. Law Schools. Latimer, Jon, ed. (Peterson's Guide Ser.). 416p. 1997. pap. 24.95 (*1-56079-630-8*) Petersons.

***Peterson's Guides Staff.** Peterson's Math Review for the GRE, GMAT & MCAT. 300p. 2000. pap. 16.95 (*0-7689-0232-0*) Petersons.

— Peterson's MBA Programs: U. S., Canadian & International Business Schools 1999. 5th ed. 1275p. 1998. pap. text 26.95 (*0-7689-0046-8*) Petersons.

Peterson's Guides Staff. Peterson's MCAT Success. (Peterson's Guides Ser.). 356p. 1997. pap. text 14.95 incl. cd-rom (*1-56079-929-3*) Petersons.

— Peterson's Nursing Programs. 4th ed. 632p. 1998. pap. text 26.95 (*1-56079-998-6*) Petersons.

***Peterson's Guides Staff.** Peterson's Nursing Programs 2000-2001. 6th ed. (Nursing Programs Ser.). 672p. 2000. pap. text 26.95 (*0-7689-0396-3*) Petersons.

Peterson's Guides Staff. Peterson's Private Secondary Schools, 1996-97. 17th rev. ed. 1370p. 1996. pap. 29.95 (*1-56079-586-7*) Petersons.

***Peterson's Guides Staff.** Peterson's Private Secondary Schools 2000-2001. 21st ed. 1460p. 2000. pap. 29.95 (*0-7689-0370-X*) Petersons.

— Peterson's PSAT Success 2001. 300p. 2000. pap. 14.95 (*0-7689-0395-5*) Petersons.

Peterson's Guides Staff. Petersons Quick & Concise Guides to Graduate & Professional Degrees Graduate Studies in Engineer. 653p. 1998. pap. 24.95 (*0-7689-0005-0*) Petersons.

— Peterson's Scholarship Almanac: Including the 500 Largest Scholarships to Help Pay for College. (Peterson's Guides). 400p. 1998. pap. text 9.95 (*0-7689-0151-0*) Petersons.

— Peterson's Scholarships for Study in the U. S. A. & Canada. 2nd ed. (Peterson's Guides). 429p. 1998. pap. text 21.95 (*0-7689-0142-1*) Petersons.

— Peterson's Scholarships, Grants & Prizes. 3rd ed. 550p. 1998. pap. text 26.95 (*0-7689-0034-4*) Petersons.

— Peterson's Study Abroad, 1996: Semester, Year Abroad, & Summer Academic Programs. 3rd ed. (Illus.). 1000p. (C). 1995. pap. 26.95 (*1-56079-537-9*) Petersons.

***Peterson's Guides Staff.** Peterson's the Gold Standard MCAT 2000. 2nd ed. 800p. 2000. pap. 44.95 (*0-7689-0493-5*) Petersons.

Peterson's Guides Staff. Peterson's Two-Year Colleges: The Only Guide to More Than 1500 Community & Junior Colleges. 29th ed. 848p. 1998. pap. text 24.95 (*1-56079-993-5*) Petersons.

— Private Secondary Schools. 19th ed. 1408p. 1998. pap. text 29.95 (*1-56079-972-2*) Petersons.

— Private Secondary Schools 1999-2000. 20th ed. 1435p. pap. 29.95 (*0-7689-0186-3*) Petersons.

— Professional Degree Programs in the Visual & Performing Arts 1999. 5th ed. (Peterson's Guides). 591p. 1998. pap. text 26.95 (*0-7689-0112-X*) Petersons.

***Peterson's Guides Staff.** Professional Degree Programs in the Visual & Performing Arts 2001. 6th ed. 603p. 2000. pap. text 26.95 (*0-7689-0442-0*) Petersons.

Peterson's Guides Staff. PSAT/NMSQT Flash. LC 98-5109. 250p. 1998. pap. text 8.95 (*1-56079-989-7*) Petersons.

— Reading Flash. LC 97-27670. (TOEFL Flash Ser.). 176p. 1997. pap. text 8.95 (*1-56079-952-8*) Petersons.

— SAT Success 2000. 6th ed. LC 96-25401. Vol. 2000. (Illus.). 526p. 1999. pap. 16.95 (*0-7689-0234-7*) Petersons.

— Scholarship Almanac 2000. 3rd ed. 400p. 1999. pap. 9.95 (*0-7689-0256-8*) Petersons.

***Peterson's Guides Staff.** Scholarships, Grants & Prizes 2000. 4th ed. 553p. 1999. pap. 26.95 incl. audio compact disk (*0-7689-0239-8*) Petersons.

Peterson's Guides Staff. SSAT/ISEE Success. annuals LC 99-35405. 512p. 1999. pap. 16.95 (*0-7689-0211-8*) Petersons.

***Peterson's Guides Staff.** SSAT/ISEE Success 2001. 2nd ed. 512p. 2000. pap. 156.95 (*0-7689-0414-5*) Petersons.

Peterson's Guides Staff. Study Abroad 1999. 6th ed. (Peterson's Guides). 1008p. 1998. pap. text 29.95 (*1-56079-995-1*) Petersons.

***Peterson's Guides Staff.** Success on the Toeic Test 2nd ed. 1999. pap. text 34.95 (*0-7689-0388-2*) Petersons.

Peterson's Guides Staff. Summer Fun. (Summer Fun Ser.). 256p. 1999. pap. 9.95 (*0-7689-0187-1*) Petersons.

***Peterson's Guides Staff.** Summer Jobs Britain 2000. 31st ed. 528p. 1999. pap. write for info. (*1-85458-232-1*, Pub. by Vac Wrk Pubns) Petersons.

Peterson's Guides Staff. Summer Jobs for Students. 47th ed. (Peterson's Guides Ser.). 372p. 1997. pap. text 16.95 (*1-56079-836-X*) Petersons.

— Summer Jobs for Students: Where the Jobs Are & How to Get Them 1999. 9th ed. (Peterson's Summer Jobs for Students Ser.). 360p. 1998. pap. text 16.95 (*0-7689-0045-X*) Petersons.

— Summer Jobs for Students, 1996 y: Where the Jobs Are & How to Get Them. 45th ed. 360p. (C). 1995. pap. 13.95 (*1-56079-495-X*) Petersons.

***Peterson's Guides Staff.** Summer Jobs for Students 2000: Where the Jobs Are & How to Get Them, 2000. 34th ed. 375p. 1999. pap. 18.95 (*0-7689-0300-9*) Petersons.

Peterson's Guides Staff. Summer Opportunities for Kids & Teenagers, 1997. 14th rev. ed. 1207p. (Orig.). (YA). 1996. pap. 26.95 (*1-56079-587-5*) Petersons.

— Summer Opportunities for Kids & Teenagers 1999. 16th ed. (Peterson's Summer Opportunities for Kids Ser.). 1248p. 1998. pap. text 29.95 (*1-56079-997-8*) Petersons.

— TOEFL Practice Tests. 2nd ed. 318p. 1998. pap. text 29.95 (*0-7689-0015-8*) Petersons.

— TOEFL Practice Tests 2000. 3rd ed. (TOEFL Practice Tests Ser.). 318p. 1999. pap. 16.95 (*0-7689-0235-5*); pap. 29.95 incl. audio (*0-7689-0236-3*) Petersons.

— TOEFL Success. LC 99-192522. 1997. pap. text 14.95 (*1-56079-928-5*) Petersons.

— TOEFL Success. 2nd ed. 580p. 1998. pap. text 29.95 (*0-7689-0017-4*); pap. text 16.95 (*0-7689-0018-2*) Petersons.

— TOEFL Success 2000. 4th ed. (Peterson's TOEFL Success Ser.). 580p. 1999. pap. 16.95 (*0-7689-0237-1*); pap. 29.95 incl. audio (*0-7689-0238-X*) Petersons.

***Peterson's Guides Staff.** Toeic Official Test-Preperation Guide. 512p. 1999. pap. text 29.95 (*0-7689-0476-5*) Petersons.

Peterson's Guides Staff. TOEIC Success. LC 98-23142. 352p. 1998. pap. text 34.95 (*1-56079-991-9*) Petersons.

Petersons Guides Staff. Top Colleges for Science: A Guide to Leading Four-Year Programs in the Biological, Chemical... 650p. 1995. pap. text 24.95 (*1-56079-390-2*) Petersons.

Peterson's Guides Staff. Top 2,500 Employers: 2000 Edition. 734p. 1999. pap. 27.95 (*0-7689-0214-2*) Petersons.

***Peterson's Guides Staff.** Two-Year Colleges 2000. 30th ed. LC 89-646514. 811p. 1999. pap. 24.95 (*0-7689-0195-2*) Petersons.

Peterson's Guides Staff. U. S. & Canadian Medical Schools, 1998. 2nd ed. 240p. 1997. pap. text 24.95 (*1-56079-886-6*) Petersons.

— U. S. & Canadian Medical Schools 1999. 2nd ed. (Peterson's Guides). 254p. 1998. pap. text 24.95 (*0-7689-0150-2*) Petersons.

— Undergraduate Study: 1999 Edition. 1998. 49.90 (*0-7689-0156-1*) Petersons.

***Peterson's Guides Staff.** U.S. History, 2000. 352p. 1999. pap. text 16.95 (*0-7689-0367-X*) Petersons.

Peterson's Guides Staff. Word Flash. LC 97-34268. (TOEFL Flash Ser.). 176p. 1997. pap. text 8.95 (*1-56079-951-X*) Petersons.

Peterson's Guides Staff, ed. Colleges & Universities in the U. S. A. The Complete Guide for International Students. 3rd ed. (Peterson's Guides). 665p. 1998. pap. 24.95 (*0-7689-0139-1*) Petersons.

— Computer Science & Electrical Engineering Programs 1999. 3rd ed. (Peterson's Guides). 776p. 1998. pap. text 26.95 (*0-7689-0147-2*) Petersons.

***Peterson's Guides Staff, ed.** GRE CAT Success 2001. 400p. 2000. pap. 16.95 (*0-7689-0523-0*) Petersons.

Peterson's Guides Staff, ed. Internships, 1997. 17th rev. ed. 528p. 1996. pap. 24.95 (*1-56079-645-6*) Petersons.

— Peterson's College Money Handbook, 1997. 14th rev. ed. 726p. 1996. pap. 26.95 (*1-56079-697-9*) Petersons.

— Peterson's Computer Science & Electrical Engineering Programs. 900p. (Orig.). 1996. pap. 24.95 (*1-56079-663-4*) Petersons.

— Peterson's Guide to Graduate & Professional Programs: An Overview, 1997, Vol. 1. 31st rev. ed. 1264p. 1996. pap. 27.95 (*1-56079-651-0*) Petersons.

— Peterson's Guide to Graduate Programs in Business, Education, Health, Information Studies, Law & Social Work 1997, Vol. 6. 31st rev. ed. 1718p. 1996. pap. 27.95 (*1-56079-656-1*) Petersons.

— Peterson's Guide to Graduate Programs in Engineering & Applied Sciences 1997, Vol. 5. 31st rev. ed. 1567p. 1996. pap. 37.95 (*1-56079-655-3*) Petersons.

— Peterson's Guide to Graduate Programs in the Humanities, Arts & Social Sciences 1997, Vol. 2. 31st rev. ed. 1427p. 1996. pap. 37.95 (*1-56079-652-9*) Petersons.

— Peterson's Guide to Graduate Programs in the Physical Sciences, Mathematics & Agricultural Sciences, Vol. 4. 31st rev. ed. 978p. 1996. pap. 34.95 (*1-56079-654-5*) Petersons.

— Peterson's Guide to Scholarships, Grants & Prizes, 1997. 511p. (Orig.). 1996. pap. 24.95 (*1-56079-696-0*) Petersons.

— Peterson's Learning Adventures Around the World, 1997. 800p. (Orig.). 1996. pap. 24.95 (*1-56079-701-0*) Petersons.

— Peterson's Professional Degree Programs in the Visual & Performing Arts 1997. 3rd rev. ed. 534p. 1996. pap. 24.95 (*1-56079-661-8*) Petersons.

— Peterson's Study Abroad, 1997: Semester, Summer & Year Abroad Academic Programs. 4th rev. ed. 1000p. 1996. pap. 26.95 (*1-56079-659-6*) Petersons.

— Register of Higher Education, 1997: The Who's Who of Higher Education. 10th rev. ed. 1100p. 1996. pap. 49.95 (*1-56079-658-8*) Petersons.

— Summer Jobs for Students, 1997. 46th rev. ed. 360p. 1996. pap. 16.95 (*1-56079-660-X*) Petersons.

— Summer Study Abroad 1999. 5th ed. (Peterson's Guides). 512p. 1998. pap. 29.95 (*0-7689-0152-9*) Petersons.

***Peterson's Guides Staff, ed.** Vocational & Technical Schools Set 2000. (Illus.). 1999. pap. 69.90 (*0-7689-0320-3*) Petersons.

Peterson's Guides Staff, jt. auth. see American Bookworks Staff.

Peterson's Magazine Staff, jt. auth. see Godey's Lady's Book Staff.

Petersons Staff. Colleges in the West: Alaska, Arizona, California, Colorado, Hawaii, Idaho, Montana, Nevada, New Mexico, Oregon, Utah, Washington, & Wyoming. 13th ed. (Regional College Guides Ser.). 345p. 1998. pap. 17.95 (*0-7689-0028-X*, 870100Q) Petersons.

Peterson's Staff. Peterson's Culinary Schools: Where the Art of Cooking Becomes a Career 1999. 2nd ed. 303p. 1998. pap. text 21.95 (*0-7689-0127-8*) Petersons.

Petersons Staff. Peterson's Law Schools. 384p. 1998. pap. text 24.95 incl. cd-rom (*0-7689-0011-5*) Petersons.

— TOEFL Practice Tests. 2nd ed. 318p. 1998. pap. text 16.95 (*0-7689-0016-6*) Petersons.

Peterson's Staff, ed. Peterson's Guide to Graduate Programs in the Biological Sciences, 1997, Vol. 3. 31st rev. ed. 2672p. 1996. pap. 44.95 (*1-56079-653-7*) Petersons.

Petersson, C., jt. ed. see Lattin, A. W.

Petersson, Irmtraud, jt. ed. see Hergenhan, Laurie.

Petersson, O. P., ed. Seminar on Delivery of Child Health Care. (Journal: Paediatrician: Vol. 9, No. 1, 1980). 52p. 1979. pap. 28.75 (*3-8055-0800-X*) S Karger.

Petersson, Torsten. Cicero: A Biography. LC 63-10768. 1920. 30.00 (*0-8196-0119-5*) Biblo.

Petertenen, ed. see Casenotes Publishing Co., Inc. Staff.

Petertic Design Partners Staff, jt. auth. see TNI Stone & Associates Staff.

Petertil Design Partners, jt. illus. see TNT Stone & Associates.

Petertil Design Partners Staff, jt. illus. see TNI Stone & Associates Staff.

Petertil Design Partners Staff, jt. illus. see TNT Stone & Associates Staff.

Petertyl, Mary E. International Adoption Travel Journal. 192p. 1998. 24.00 (*0-9655753-0-6*) Folio One.

— Seeds of Love: For Brothers & Sisters of International Adoption. LC 96-61921. (Illus.). 32p. (J). (ps-4). 1997. 15.95 (*0-9655753-1-4*) Folio One.

Peterzell, Jay. Reagan's Secret Wars. LC 83-226461. 100p. 1984. pap. 3.95 (*0-86566-033-6*) Ctr Natl Security.

Petesch, Donald A. A Spy in the Enemy's Country: The Emergence of Modern Black Literature. LC 88-37391. 299p. 1989. reprint ed. pap. text 13.95 (*0-87745-322-5*) U of Iowa Pr.

Petesch, Natalie L. After the First Death There Is No Other. LC 74-8851. (Iowa Short Fiction Award Ser.). 208p. 1974. pap. 3.25 (*0-87745-064-1*) U of Iowa Pr.

— The Immigrant Train & Other Stories. LC 96-10622. 208p. 1996. pap. 14.95 (*0-8040-0992-9*); text 24.95 (*0-8040-0991-0*) Swallow.

— Justina of Andalusia & Other Stories. LC 90-38575. 120p. 1990. 24.95 (*0-8040-0939-2*) Swallow.

— The Odyssey of Katinou Kalokovich. 199p. (C). 1979. reprint ed. pap. 5.00 (*0-934238-01-4*) Motheroot.

— Wild with All Regret. LC 86-60697. (Illus.). 140p. 1987. 10.95 (*0-930501-06-3*) Swallows Tale Pr.

— Wild with All Regret. 2nd ed. LC 86-60697. (Illus.). 140p. 1987. reprint ed. pap. 10.95 (*0-930501-07-1*) Swallows Tale Pr.

Petesch, Natalie L. M. Duncan's Colony. LC 81-14188. 220p. 1982. 21.95 (*0-8040-0401-3*); pap. 9.95 (*0-8040-0402-1*) Swallow.

— Flowering Mimosa. LC 86-23024. 235p. 1987. 24.95 (*0-8040-0870-1*); pap. 12.95 (*0-8040-0871-X*) Swallow.

Petesch, Patti L. North-South Environmental Strategies, Costs & Bargains. LC 92-15158. (Policy Essay Ser.: No. 5). 124p. (C). 1992. pap. text 13.95 (*1-56517-005-9*) Overseas Dev Council.

Petesch, Patti L. & Williams, Maurice J. Sustaining the Earth: Role of Multilateral Development Institutions. LC 93-5875. (Policy Essay Ser.: No. 9). 112p. (C). 1993. pap. text 13.95 (*1-56517-011-3*) Overseas Dev Council.

Petesch, Patti L., jt. ed. see Narayan, Deepa.

Petev, Valentin. Sozialistisches Zivilrecht. (Sammlung Goeschen Ser.: No. 2851). 246p. (C). 1975. 15.25 (*3-11-004697-0*) De Gruyter.

Petey. The Manor on Cranton-Barry Hill. 136p. 1998. pap. 9.95 (*0-9662636-0-X*) Starr-Vision.

Peth, Howard A. Seven Mysteries . . . Solved!, Vol. 1. (Illus.). 433p. (Orig.). 1988. pap. 14.95 (*0-9618580-0-1*); write for info. (*0-317-68279-2*) Lessons Heaven.

— Seven Mysteries . . . Solved!, Vol. 2. (Illus.). 545p. (Orig.). 1988. pap. 14.95 (*0-9618580-1-X*) Lessons Heaven.

Pethel, James, ed. Come, Thou Almighty King. 72p. 1986. 9.99 (*0-8341-9237-3*, MB-560) Lillenas.

Pethel, Stan. Born a Savior, Born a King, Score. 1997. pap. text 5.95 (*0-7673-3305-5*, Genevox Mus) LifeWay Christian.

Pethel, Stan, contrib. by. Contemporary Piano. 40p. 1988. 9.99 (*0-8341-9178-4*, MB-591) Lillenas.

— God Leads Us Along. 32p. 1984. pap. 8.99 (*0-8341-9748-0*) Nazarene.

Petheram, Harry, jt. auth. see Davis, Mark.

Petheram, Michel, jt. auth. see MacDonald, Barrie I.

Petheram, Michel, tr. see Baczko, Bronislaw.

Petheram, Michel, tr. see Calvet, Louis-Jean.

Petheram, R. J. & Kok, B. Plants of the Kimberley Region of Western Australia. (Illus.). 556p. (Orig.). pap. 34.95 (*0-85564-215-7*, Pub. by Univ of West Aust Pr) Intl Spec Bk.

Petheram, Rosemary. Down under from Devon. (C). 1989. pap. text 70.00 (*1-85821-021-6*, Pub. by Pentland Pr) St Mut.

Petherbridge, Dan. How to Get the Most for Your Money: A Consumer's Guide to Year-Round Savings. 130p. (Orig.). 1990. pap. 9.95 (*0-9625925-0-1*) Sandbridge Pub.

Petherbridge, Deanna. The Quick & the Dead: Artist & Anatomy. LC 99-161893. 120p. 1998. pap. 24.95 (*0-520-21738-1*, Pub. by U CA Pr) Cal Prin Full Svc.

Petherbridge, Robin. Turkey & the Dodecanese Cruising Pilot. (Illus.). 214p. 1985. pap. 32.50 (*0-229-11716-3*, Pub. by Adlard Coles) Sheridan.

Petherick, Simon. The Culture-Vulture's Quotation Book: A Literary Companion. LC 97-66453. (Illus.). 1997. 12.95 (*0-7090-5616-8*) Parkwest Pubns.

— The Eccentric's Quotation Book: A Literary Companion. (Illus.). 1997. 12.95 (*0-7090-5398-3*) Parkwest Pubns.

Pethica, James & Roy, J. C., eds. Henry Stratford Persse's Letters from Galway to America, 1821-1832. LC 98-189080. (Irish Narrative Ser.). (Illus.). 200p. 1998. pap. 15.95 (*1-85918-141-4*, Pub. by Cork Univ) Stylus Pub VA.

Pethica, James, jt. auth. see Yeats, William Butler.

Pethica, James, ed. see Yeats, William Butler.

Pethica, James, ed. & intro. see Gregory, Isabella Augusta.

Pethick, Christopher, jt. auth. see Baym, Gordon.

Pethick, Derek. Vancouver Recalled. (Illus.). 96p. pap. 3.95 (*0-919654-09-6*) Hancock House.

Pethick, John S. An Introduction to Coastal Geomorphology. (Arnold Publications). (Illus.). 272p. 1984. pap. text 39.95 (*0-7131-6391-7*) OUP.

Pethick, Nancy & Norris, Anne. Harnessing Up. (Illus.). 132p. 1990. pap. 21.00 (*0-85131-319-1*, Pub. by J A Allen) St Mut.

Pethig, R. & Schlieper, U., eds. Efficiency, Institutions & Economic Policy. (Illus.). 240p. 1987. 55.00 (*0-387-18450-3*) Spr-Verlag.

Pethig, Ronald. Dielectric & Electronic Properties of Biological Materials. LC 78-13694. (Illus.). 390p. reprint ed. pap. 120.90 (*0-8357-3080-8*, 203933700012) Bks Demand.

Pethig, Rudiger. Valuing the Environment: Methodological & Measurement Issues. LC 93-38948. 376p. (C). 1994. lib. bdg. 204.50 (*0-7923-2602-4*) Kluwer Academic.

P

An Asterisk (*) at the beginning of an entry indicates that the title is appearing for the first time.

Petho, Attila, et al, eds. Computational Number Theory: Proceedings of the Colloquium on Computational Number Theory. xiii, 342p. (C). 1991. lib. bdg. 99.95 (*3-11-012394-0*) De Gruyter.

Pethoe, B., ed. DCR Budapest-Nashville in the Diagnosis & Classification of Functional Psychoses. (Journal: Psychopathology: Vol. 21, Nos. 4-5, 1988). (Illus.). 92p. 1989. pap. 65.25 (*3-8055-4970-9*) S Karger.

Pethrick. Modern Techniques for Polymer Characterization. LC 98-45287. 410p. 1999. 305.00 (*0-471-96097-7*) Wiley.

Pethrick, Richard A. Polymer Yearbook, Vol. 2. xii, 414p. 1985. text 129.00 (*3-7186-0274-1*); pap. text 50.00 (*3-7186-0276-8*) Gordon & Breach.

— Polymer Yearbook, Vol. 5. xii, 466p. 1989. pap. 96.00 (*3-7186-4858-X*); text 291.00 (*3-7186-4857-1*) Gordon & Breach.

— Polymer Yearbook, Vol.6. (Polymer Yearbook Ser.). 373p. 1990. text 351.00 (*3-7186-4997-7*, Harwood Acad Pubs) Gordon & Breach.

— Polymer Yearbook 7, Vol. 7. (Polymer Yearbook Ser.). 384p. 1991. text 462.00 (*3-7186-5075-4*, Harwood Acad Pubs) Gordon & Breach.

— Polymer Yearbook 12. v, 332p. 1995. text 275.00 (*3-7186-5712-0*, Harwood Acad Pubs) Gordon & Breach.

Pethrick, Richard A., ed. Polymer Yearbook, Vol. 3. xiv, 378p. 1986. text 189.00 (*3-7186-0342-X*); pap. text 71.00 (*3-7186-0341-1*) Gordon & Breach.

— Polymer Yearbook, Vol. 4. xii, 410p. 1987. text 231.00 (*3-7186-0406-X*); pap. text 68.00 (*3-7186-0408-6*) Gordon & Breach.

— Polymer Yearbook, Vol. 14. 304p. 1997. text 162.00 (*90-5702-169-2*, Harwood Acad Pubs) Gordon & Breach.

— Polymer Yearbook 8, Vol. 8. 8th ed. 424p. 1991. text 444.00 (*3-7186-5154-8*) Gordon & Breach.

— Polymer Yearbook 11. (Polymer Yearbook Ser.). 428p. 1994. text 303.00 (*3-7186-5481-4*, Harwood Acad Pubs) Gordon & Breach.

— Polymer Yearbook 15. (Polymer Yearbook Ser.: Vol. 15). (Illus.). 352p. 1998. text 162.00 (*90-5702-320-2*, ECU208) Gordon & Breach.

***Pethrick, Richard A., ed.** Polymer Yearbook 16. (Polymer Yearbook Ser.: Vol. 16). 392p. 1999. text 250.00 (*90-5702-473-X*, Harwood Acad Pubs) Gordon & Breach.

Pethrick, Richard A., ed. Polymer Yearbook 10, Vol. 10. (Polymer Yearbook Ser.). 430p. 1993. text 347.00 (*3-7186-5334-6*) Gordon & Breach.

— Polymer Yearbook 13, No. 13. 432p. 1996. text 193.00 (*3-7186-5914-X*, Harwood Acad Pubs) Gordon & Breach.

Pethrick, Richard A., jt. auth. see Richards, R. W.

Pethrick, Richard A., jt. ed. see Elias, Hans-George.

Pethybridge, Roger. One Step Backwards, Two Steps Forward: Soviet Society & Politics in the New Economic Policy. (Illus.). 466p. 1990. text 125.00 (*0-19-821927-X*) OUP.

— Witnesses to the Russian Revolution. (Illus.). 1982. pap. 6.95 (*0-8065-0018-2*, C274, Citadel Pr) Carol Pub Group.

***Petic, Zorika.** Cascadilla Creek. 88p. 2000. pap. 14.95 (*1-882897-54-4*) Lost Coast.

Petich, Edward J. Atlas of Florida Fossil Shells. (Illus.). 408p. 1994. text 60.00 (*1-886094-04-7*) Chicago Spectrum.

Petievich, Gerald. Paramour. large type ed. (General Ser.). 387p. 1992. 20.95 (*0-8161-5376-0*, G K Hall Lrg Type) Mac Lib Ref.

Petig, William E. Literary Antipietism in Germany During the First Half of the Eighteenth Century. LC 83-49223. (Stanford German Studies: Vol. 22). 236p. (Orig.). (C). 1984. pap. text 22.65 (*0-8204-0087-4*) P Lang Pubng.

Petigrew, Mark, jt. auth. see Elliot, David.

Petigru, James L. & Carson, James P. Life, Letters, & Speeches of James Louis Petigru the Union Man of South Carolina. 1977. 24.95 (*0-8369-6969-3*, 7850) Ayer.

Petiot, Georges. Le Robert des Sports: Dictionnaire de la Langue des Sports. (FRE.). 583p. 1990. 69.95 (*0-7859-9226-X*) Fr & Eur.

Petipa, Marius, et al. Six Fairy Variations. Orig. Title: Sleeping Beauty Prologue. (Illus.). 44p. 1961. pap. text 15.00 (*0-932582-66-4*) Dance Notation.

Petit. The French Sampler. (College French Ser.). (C). 1991. 13.95 (*0-8384-2556-9*) Heinle & Heinle.

— Primary Neurologic Care. 2000. text 49.95 (*0-8151-5304-X*, 29742) Mosby Inc.

Petit, ed. see Claudel, Paul.

Petit, ed. see D'Aurevilly.

Petit, Ann. Secrets to Enliven Learning: How to Develop Extraordinary Self-Directed Training Materials. LC 94-65592. 176p. 1994. pap. 29.95 (*0-88390-416-0*, Pfffr & Co) Jossey-Bass.

Petit Bois, G. Tables of Indefinite Integrals. 150p. 1961. pap. text 8.95 (*0-486-60225-7*) Dover.

Petit, Carlos, jt. ed. see Corfis, Ivy A.

Petit, Charles & Savage, William. Dictionnaire Classique Anglais-Francais et Francais-Anglais. (ENG & FRE.). 686p. 1967. pap. 59.95 (*0-8288-6675-9*, M-6444) Fr & Eur.

Petit, Charles E., jt. auth. see Pettifor, Bonnie.

Petit, Chris. The Psalm Killer. 1998. mass mkt. 6.99 (*0-345-42090-X*) Ballantine Pub Grp.

— The Psalm Killer. 1998. mass mkt. 6.99 (*0-449-00289-6*, GM) Fawcett.

— The Psalm Killer. LC 96-39157. 1997. 5.99 (*0-679-45126-9*) Knopf.

Petit, D. B. Street Pizza. Zagury, Carolyn S., ed. LC 96-60787. 288p. 1996. pap. 14.95 (*1-880254-38-7*) Vista.

***Petit, Dan.** Real Visual Basic: A Practical Approach to Enterprise Development in the Corporate World. LC 99-58356. 464p. 1999. pap. 49.95 (*0-201-61604-1*) Addison-Wesley.

Petit, Diane. Goodbye, Charli. LC 97-94020. (Goodbye, Charli Mystery Ser.: Bk. 1). 192p. 1997. 18.95 (*0-8034-9258-8*, Avalon Bks) Bouregy.

***Petit, Diane.** Goodbye, Charli. 4th ed. LC 99-94435. 192p. 1999. 18.95 (*0-8034-9368-1*, Avalon Bks) Bouregy.

Petit, Diane. Goodbye, Charli - Take Two. LC 97-97117. (Goodbye, Charli Mystery Ser.: Bk. 2). 192p. 1998. lib. bdg. 18.95 (*0-8034-9278-2*, Avalon Bks) Bouregy.

— Goodbye Charli - Third Time Lucky. LC 98-96338. 192p. 1998. lib. bdg. 18.95 (*0-8034-9318-5*, Avalon Bks) Bouregy.

— A Savage Ecstasy. Zagury, Carolyn, ed. LC 97-61600. 184p. 1998. pap. 14.95 (*1-880254-48-4*) Vista.

Petit-Dutaillis, Charles E. The Feudal Monarchy in France & England from the Tenth to the Thirteenth Century. LC 80-2011. reprint ed. 64.50 (*0-404-18585-1*) AMS Pr.

Petit, Francis, jt. ed. see Mortreux, Andre.

Petit, Gabriel, et al, eds. Les Allemands et la Science. LC 80-2141. (Develpoment of Science Ser.). (Illus.). 1981. lib. bdg. 38.95 (*0-405-13896-2*) Ayer.

Petit, Gedeon D. Effects of Dissolved Oxygen on Survival & Behavior of Selected Fishes of Western Lake Erie. (Bulletin New Ser.: Vol. 4, No. 4). 1973. pap. text 3.00 (*0-86727-063-2*) Ohio Bio Survey.

Petit, Genevieve. The Seventh Walnut. Herrmann, Dagmar, tr. LC 92-10588. (Illus.). (J). 1992. 13.95 (*0-922984-10-7*) Wellington IL.

Petit, Jack, et al. Building Greener Neighborhoods: Trees As Part of the Plan. LC 95-23613. (Illus.). 140p. 1995. 12.00 (*0-86718-409-4*) Home Builder.

— Building Greener Neighborhoods: Trees as Part of the Plan. 2nd ed. LC 98-35535. 1998. 13.20 (*0-86718-446-9*) Home Builder.

Petit, Jacques, jt. auth. see Claudel, Paul.

Petit, Jacques, ed. see Barbey d'Aurevilly, Jules.

Petit, Jacques, ed. see Claudel, Paul.

Petit, Jacques, ed. see Mauriac, Francois.

Petit, James. Willapa Bay. (Illus.). 22p. (Orig.). 1992. 37.50 (*0-9630863-4-0*); pap. 20.00 (*0-9630863-5-9*) Limner Pr.

— Willapa Bay. deluxe ed. (Illus.). 22p. (Orig.). 1992. 50.00 (*0-9630863-6-7*) Limner Pr.

Petit, Jean Francois Le, see Le Petit, Jean Francois.

Petit-Jean, Michele. Baby Earth. (Illus.). (J). (gr. 1-5). 1995. 13.99 (*0-85953-958-X*) Childs Play.

Petit, John D., Jr., jt. auth. see Lesikar, Raymond Vincent.

Petit, K. Marabout. (FRE.). 480p. 1960. pap. 17.95 (*0-7859-5541-0*, M-6445) Fr & Eur.

Petit, Loretta. Making It Through. (Illus.). 40p. 1996. pap. write for info. (*0-9653573-0-9*) Frstfruit Pubng.

Petit, M., jt. auth. see Giraud, A.

Petit, Marcel, ed. see Barbey d'Aurevilly, Jules.

***Petit, Marianne.** A Find Through Time. Basile, Teresa, ed. LC 00-105146. 216p. 2000. pap. 12.95 (*1-930076-18-5*, New Leaf Books) WigWam Pubng Co.

Petit, Michel. The Emergence of a Global Agricultural Research System: The Role of the Agricultural Research & Extension Group (ESDAR) (Environmentally Sustainable Development Occasional Papers: No. 1). 20p. 1996. pap. 22.00 (*0-8213-3815-3*, 13815) World Bank.

Petit, Pascale. Heart of a Deer. LC 99-217571. 1999. pap. text 17.95 (*1-900564-16-5*) Enitha Pr.

Petit, R. Electromagnetic Theory of Gratings. (Topics in Current Physics Ser.: Vol. 22). (Illus.). 284p. 1980. 79.95 (*0-387-10193-4*) Spr-Verlag.

Petit, R. E., jt. auth. see Jung, P.

Petit, Ronald E. Women & the Career Game: Play to Win!!! (Illus.). 147p. (Orig.). 1982. pap. 7.95 (*0-685-06198-1*) Prof Dev Serv.

Petit-Skinner, Solange. The Nauruans. 2nd ed. LC 96-182615. (Illus.). 315p. 1981. pap. 22.80 (*0-9606272-0-0*) Macduff Pr.

Petit-Skinner, Solange, jt. auth. see Dari, Willie.

Petit, Solange. Les Americains de Paris. (Publications du Censeil International des Sciences Sociales: No. 117). (FRE.). 149p. (Orig.). 1976. pap. text 35.40 (*90-279-7506-X*) Mouton.

Petit, Susan. Michel Tournier's Metaphysical Fictions. LC 91-40887. (Purdue University Monographs in Romance Languages: No. 37). xvi, 224p. 1991. 71.00 (*1-55619-302-5*); pap. 27.95 (*1-55619-303-3*) J Benjamins Pubng Co.

Petit, Susana, tr. see Weninger, Brigitte.

***Petit, Ted L. & Peat, John P.** The Color Encyclopedia of Daylilies. LC 00-26379. (Illus.). 300p. 2000. 49.95 (*0-88192-488-1*) Timber.

Petit, Thomas A. Fundamentals of Management Coordination: Supervisors, Middle Managers, & Executives. LC 74-19474. (Illus.). 525p. reprint ed. pap. 162.80 (*0-7837-3462-X*, 205779000008) Bks Demand.

Petitcolas, Fabien A., jt. ed. see Katzenbeisser, Stefan.

Petite, Mary Deborah. 1836 Facts about the Alamo: And the Texas War for Independence. ("Facts About" History Ser.: Vol. 2). (Illus.). 170p. 1999. pap. 11.95 (*1-882810-35-X*) Savas Pub.

***Petite, Sarah.** Wharves & Breakwaters of Yarmouth County, Nova Scotia. (Illus.). 56p. 1999. pap. 13.50 (*1-896647-13-8*) Genl Dist Srvs.

Petitfils, Pierre. Rimbaud. Sheridan, Alan, tr. from FRE. LC 87-6109. (Illus.). 400p. 1988. text 40.00 (*0-8139-1142-7*) U Pr of Va.

Petitjean, Claude, jt. ed. see Schaller, Lukas A.

Petitjean, Patrick, ed. Science & Empires: Historical Studies about Scientific Development & European Expansion. (Boston Studies in the Philosophy of Science). 428p. (C). 1991. lib. bdg. 175.00 (*0-7923-1518-9*, Pub. by Kluwer Academic) Kluwer Academic.

Petitop, Jean. Naturalizing Phenomenology: Issues in Contemporary Phenomenology & Cognitive Science. LC 99-28716. (Writing Science Ser.). 1999. pap. text 29.95 (*0-8047-3610-3*) Stanford U Pr.

Petitpas, Al, et al. Athlete's Guide to Career Planning. LC 96-46543. (Illus.). 240p. (Orig.). 1997. pap. 17.95 (*0-87322-459-0*, PPET0459) Human Kinetics.

Petitti, Diana B. Meta-Analysis, Decision Analysis & Cost-Effectiveness Analysis: Methods for Quantitative Synthesis in Medicine. 2nd ed. LC 99-13213. (Monographs in Epidemiology & Biostatistics: No. 31). (Illus.). 320p. 1999. text 49.95 (*0-19-513364-1*) OUP.

Petitti, Diana B., jt. ed. see Brownson, Ross C.

Petitti, Richard E. The American Elegy: The Airs & Graces of Corporate Life. (Self Realization Bks.: Bk. IV). (Illus.). 100p. 1986. pap. 10.00 (*0-938582-08-9*) Sensitive Man.

— Brighter Leaves of Grass. (Self Realization Bks.: Bk. VI). (Illus.). 100p. 1986. pap. 10.00 (*0-938582-11-9*) Sensitive Man.

— Executive Notebook: Imbibing the Passion of Adequacy. (Self Realization Bks.: Bk. I). (Illus.). 100p. 1985. pap. 10.00 (*0-938582-05-4*) Sensitive Man.

— Iryit Scarizot Speaks: Alter Egos Are a Dime a Dozen. (Self Realization Bks.: Bk. VII). (Illus.). 100p. 1986. pap. 10.00 (*0-938582-13-5*) Sensitive Man.

— No Time for Me. (Illus.). 150p. 1984. pap. 20.00 (*0-938582-01-1*) Sensitive Man.

— Notions & Reforms: In the Coming of Age. (Self Realization Bks.: Bk. III). (Illus.). 100p. 1986. pap. 10.00 (*0-938582-07-0*) Sensitive Man.

— On an All Time High: A New Wave Collection for Corporate Seminars. (Self Realization Bks.: Bk. XI). (Illus.). 100p. 1988. write for info. (*0-938582-15-1*) Sensitive Man.

— Satan Revisited: The Old New England Blues. (Illus.). 150p. 1985. pap. 20.00 (*0-938582-02-X*) Sensitive Man.

— The Sensitive Man: And It's OK to Be Feminine. (Self Realization Bks.: Bk. II). (Illus.). 150p. 1982. pap. 20.00 (*0-938582-03-8*) Sensitive Man.

— Snake Charmers Are Made, Not Born. (Self Realization Bks.: Bk. V). (Illus.). 100p. 1986. pap. 10.00 (*0-938582-09-7*) Sensitive Man.

— Swelling My Song in Vagabond Shoes: Re-Entering the Corporate Life. (Self Realization Bks.: Bk. IX). (Illus.). 100p. 1986. pap. 10.00 (*0-938582-12-7*) Sensitive Man.

Petiver, James. Papilionum Britanniae Icones. 1984. 95.00 (*0-7855-0668-3*) St Mut.

***Petkanas, Christopher.** At Home in France: Eating & Entertaining with the French. 2000. pap. 21.95 (*0-7538-0708-4*) Phoenix Hse.

Petkeuicius, Jeffrey C. The Unchained Worker: Principles of Ownership in the Workplace. Smart, Dwain, ed. (Illus.). 154p. (Orig.). 1995. pap. 11.95 (*0-9645204-3-5*) Cybernetix.

Petkevich, John M. Sports Illustrated Figure Skating. 1989. pap. 10.95 (*1-56800-070-7*, Pub. by Sports Illus Bks) Natl Bk Netwk.

Petkov, I. Z. & Stoitsov, M. V. Nuclear Density Functional Theory. (Studies in Nuclear Physics: No. 14). (Illus.). 376p. 1991. 79.00 (*0-19-851731-9*) OUP.

Petkov, Kiril. Infidels, Turks, & Women: The South Slavs in the German Mind, ca. 1400-1600. LC 97-6411. (GER., Illus.). 335p. 1997. pap. 57.95 (*3-631-31472-8*) P Lang Pubng.

— Infidels, Turks, & Women: The South Slavs in the German Mind, Ca. 1400-1600. LC 97-6411. (Illus.). 335p. 1997. pap. 57.95 (*0-8204-3259-8*) P Lang Pubng.

Petkov, Nikolay. Systolic Parallel Processing. LC 92-39979. (Advances in Parallel Computing Ser.: Vol. 5). 712p. 1992. 229.25 (*0-444-88769-5*, North Holland) Elsevier.

Petkov, P. P., ed. Mathematical Logic. (Illus.). 420p. (C). 1990. 144.00 (*0-306-43511-X*, Plenum Trade) Perseus Pubng.

Petkov, Petko. The United States & Bulgaria in World War I. 224p. 1991. text 42.00 (*0-88033-203-4*, Pub. by East Eur Monographs) Col U Pr.

Petkov, Steven & Mustazza, Leonard, eds. The Frank Sinatra Reader. (Illus.). 336p. 1995. 35.00 (*0-19-509531-6*) OUP.

— The Frank Sinatra Reader. (Illus.). 336p. 1997. reprint ed. pap. 16.95 (*0-19-511389-6*) OUP.

Petkov, V. & Lazarov, R., eds. Integral Equations & Inverse Problems. LC 90-5575. (Pitman Research Notes in Mathematics Ser.: Vol. 235). 303p. 1991. reprint ed. pap. 94.00 (*0-608-03605-6*, 206442800009) Bks Demand.

Petkovic, Dragutin, jt. auth. see Aigrain, Philippe.

Petkovic, Dusan. Informix-das Relationale Datenbank System. (GER.). (C). 1990. text. write for info. (*0-201-55927-7*) Addison-Wesley.

— Ingres. (C). 1992. text. write for info. (*0-201-57845-X*) Addison-Wesley.

— Mali Leksikon Mikroracunarskih Izraza: Multilingual Computer Dictionary (Serbo-German-English) (CRO, ENG, GER & SER.). 268p. 1990. pap. 95.00 (*0-8288-3924-7*, F101450) Fr & Eur.

— Small Lexicon of Micro-Accounting Terms, English, German & Serbocroatian: Mali Leksikon Mikroracunarskih Izraza. (ENG, GER & SER.). 202p. 1987. 35.00 (*0-8288-0273-4*, F44460) Fr & Eur.

***Petkovic, Dusan.** SQL Server 2000: A Beginner's Guide. (Database Professional's Library). (Illus.). 2000. pap. 39.99 (*0-07-212587-X*) Osborne-McGraw.

— SQL Server 2000 Performance Tuning & Optimization. (Database Professional's Library). 2000. pap. 44.95 (*0-07-212376-1*) Osborne-McGraw.

Petkovic, L. D., ed. see Petkovic, Miodrag S.

Petkovic, M. Iterative Methods for Simultaneous Inclusion of Polynomial Zone. (Lecture Notes in Mathematics Ser.: Vol. 1387). x, 263p. 1989. pap. 37.30 (*0-387-51485-6*) Spr-Verlag.

Petkovic, Miodrag. Mathematics & Chess. LC 97-8398. 1997. pap. 5.95 (*0-486-29432-3*) Dover.

Petkovic, Miodrag S. Complex Interval Arithmetic & Its Applications. Petkovic, L. D., ed. LC 98-227278. (Mathematical Research Ser.). (Illus.). 286p. 1998. 160.00 (*3-527-40134-2*) Wiley.

Petkovich, Anthony. The X Factory: Inside the American Hardcore Film Industry. (Illus.). 196p. (Orig.). 1997. pap. 19.95 (*0-9523288-7-9*, Pub. by Headpress) AK Pr Dist.

Petkovsek, Marko, et al. A=B. LC 95-51210. 224p. (C). 1996. 39.00 (*1-56881-063-6*) AK Peters.

Petkus, Peggy M. Millionaires Row. 1989. mass mkt. 4.50 (*0-8217-2763-X*, Zebra Kensgtn) Kensgtn Pub Corp.

Petley, B. W. The Fundamental Physical Constants & the Frontiers of Medicine. rev. ed. 356p. 1984. 81.00 (*0-85274-427-7*) Taylor & Francis.

Petley, Dexter. Little Nineveh. 232p. (Orig.). 1995. pap. 14.95 (*0-7486-6190-5*, Pub. by Polygon) Subterranean Co.

Petley, H. C. Queen of Slots. 288p. (Orig.). 1990. pap. 4.95 (*0-9625559-0-8*) Gate Pr Pubs.

Petley, Julian, jt. auth. see Barker, Martin.

Petmesidou, Maria & Tsoulouvis, Lefteris. Planning Technological Change & Economic Development in Greece: High Technology & the Microelectronics Industry. (Progress in Planning Ser.: Vol. 33). (Illus.). 88p. 1990. pap. 41.50 (*0-08-040770-6*, Pergamon Pr) Elsevier.

***Peto, Andrea.** Women in Hungarian Politics, 1945-1951. 180p. (C). 2000. 39.95 (*963-9241-01-6*); pap. 21.95 (*963-9241-02-4*) Ctrl Europ Univ.

Peto, Erica, et al. The Tech Team: Student Technology Assistants in the Elementary & Middle School. LC 97-24394. (Professional Growth Ser.). (Illus.). 150p. (Orig.). 1997. pap. 34.95 (*0-938865-60-9*) Linworth Pub.

Peto, Gloria J. & Medve, William J. EMS Driving: The Safe Way. 224p. 1991. pap. text 48.00 (*0-89303-828-8*) P-H.

Peto, Ivan, jt. auth. see Gero, Andras.

Peto, Les. The Dream Lover: Transforming Relationships Through Dreams. LC 90-24119. 192p. 1991. reprint ed. pap. 9.95 (*0-87542-595-X*) Llewellyn Pubns.

Peto, Monica, jt. auth. see Lane, Peter.

Peto, Richard & Hausen, Harald Z., eds. Viral Etiology of Cervical Cancer. LC 86-2227. (Banbury Reports: No. 21). 362p. 1986. text 68.00 (*0-87969-221-9*) Cold Spring Harbor.

Peto, Richard & Schneiderman, Marvin, eds. Quantification of Occupational Cancer. LC 81-10218. (Banbury Reports: Vol. 9). 756p. (C). 1981. 99.00 (*0-87969-208-1*) Cold Spring Harbor.

Peto, Richard, jt. ed. see Zaridze, D.

Peto, S. Morton. Resources & Prospects of America: Ascertained During a Visit to the States in the Autumn of 1865. LC 73-2529. (Big Business; Economic Power in a Free Society Ser.). 1973. reprint ed. 29.95 (*0-405-05108-5*) Ayer.

***Petocz, Agnes.** Freud, Psychoanalysis & Symbolism. LC 98-39047. (Illus.). 296p. (C). 1999. 59.95 (*0-521-59152-X*) Cambridge U Pr.

Petoefi, J. S. & Rieser, H., eds. Studies in Text Grammar. LC 73-75766. (Foundations of Language Supplementary Ser.: No. 19). 370p. 1973. text 162.50 (*90-277-0368-X*) Kluwer Academic.

Petoefi, J. S., jt. ed. see Van Dijk, T. A.

Petofi, Janos S., ed. Text & Discourse Constitution: Empirical Aspects, Theoretical Approaches. (Research in Text Theory Ser.: Vol. 4). 516p. (C). 1987. lib. bdg. 215.40 (*3-11-007566-0*) De Gruyter.

Petofi, Janos S. & Olivi, Terry, eds. Approaches to Poetry: Some Aspects of Textuality, Intertextuality & Intermediality. LC 93-46667. (Research in Text Theory Ser.: No. 20). viii, 300p. (C). 1994. lib. bdg. 149.25 (*3-11-013893-X*) De Gruyter.

***Petofi, Sandor.** John the Valiant. 152p. 1999. pap. 32.00 (*963-13-4740-0*, Pub. by Corvina Bks) St Mut.

Petography. The Quotable Feline. write for info. (*0-679-76585-9*) Fodors Travel.

Petolino, Joseph G., jt. ed. see Collins, Glenn B.

Petonnet, Colette. Those People: The Subculture of a Housing Project. 10. Smidt, Rita, tr. from FRE. LC 72-825. (Contributions in Sociology Ser.: No. 10). 293p. 1973. 59.95 (*0-8371-6393-5*, PTP/, Greenwood Pr) Greenwood.

Petoskey, Eva, ed. see Bainbridge, Delores.

Petot, J. M. Melanie Klein, Vol. 1. Trollope, Christine, tr. from FRE. 324p. 1991. 50.00 (*0-8236-3328-4*) Intl Univs Pr.

— Melanie Klein, Vol. 2. Trollope, Christine, tr. from FRE. 300p. 1991. 50.00 (*0-8236-3329-2*) Intl Univs Pr.

Petovello, Laura R. The Spirit That Moves Us Vol. 1: A Literature-Based Resource Guide, Teaching about Diversity, Prejudice, Human Rights & the Holocaust. rev. ed. 316p. (J). (gr. k-4). 1998. pap. 19.95 (*0-88448-204-9*) Tilbury Hse.

Petr. Future Memories. 1993. pap. 10.00 (*0-9643640-1-8*) Kozina-Lomikar.

Petr, Boldyrev. Uroki Rossii: Dnevnik Rossiiskogo Separatista. LC 92-47060. (RUS.). 248p. (Orig.). 1993. pap. 16.00 (*1-55779-061-2*) Hermitage Pubs.

Petr, Christopher G. Social Work with Children & Their Families: Pragmatic Foundations. LC 97-6222. (Illus.). 336p. (C). 1998. text 49.95 (*0-19-510607-5*) OUP.

P

Petr, J. Weather & Yield. (Developments in Crop Science Ser.: Vol. 20). 288p. 1991. 203.25 (*0-444-98803-3*) Elsevier.

Petr, Mark, jt. auth. see Kimball, Cathy.

Petra Press Staff. Great Heroes of Mythology. LC 97-9045. (Illus.). 176p. 1997. 27.98 (*1-56799-433-4*, MetroBooks) M Friedman Pub Grp Inc.

Petra ten-Doesschate Chu, ed. The Illustrated Bartsch Vol. 121-2, Pt. 2: Dominique Vivant Denon. 346p. 1988. lib. bdg. 149.00 (*0-89835-315-7*) Abaris Bks.

Petra ten-Doesschate Chu, et al, eds. The Illustrated Bartsch Vol. 121-1, Pt. 1: Dominique Vivant Denon. 376p. 1985. lib. bdg. 149.00 (*0-89835-220-7*) Abaris Bks.

Petracca. The Graceful Lie: A Method for Making Fiction. LC 98-7709. 520p. 1998. pap. text 37.00 (*0-13-287418-0*) P-H.

Petracca, Mark P. An Introduction to Political Science. 326p. (C). 1995. text 52.00 (*0-536-59266-7*) Pearson Custom.

Petracca, Michael & Sorapure, Madeleine. Common Culture. 2nd ed. LC 97-28133. 620p. (C). 1997. pap. text 37.60 (*0-13-754888-5*) P-H.

***Petracca, Michael & Sorapure, Madeleine.** Common Culture: Reading & Writing about American Popular Culture. 3rd ed. LC 00-29796. 640p. 2000. pap. 30.00 (*0-13-085098-5*) P-H.

Petracek, Thomas M., jt. auth. see Alvig, Mark R.

Petrachova, V., et al. Vel'ky Slovnik Cudzich Slov (Dictionary of International Words) (SLO.). 1000p. 1997. write for info. (*80-08-02054-7*, Pub. by Slov Pegagog Naklad) IBD Ltd.

Petraglia, Joseph. Reality by Design: Rhetoric, Technology, & the Creation of Authentic Learning Environments. LC 97-28104. (Rhetoric, Knowledge & Society Ser.). 250p. 1997. write for info. (*0-8058-2041-8*) L Erlbaum Assocs.

— Reality by Design: Rhetoric, Technology, & the Creation of Authentic Learning Environments. LC 97-28104. (Rhetoric, Knowledge & Society Ser.). 216p. 1998. pap. 27.50 (*0-8058-2042-6*) L Erlbaum Assocs.

Petraglia, Joseph, ed. Reconceiving Writing, Rethinking Writing Instruction. 288p. (C). 1995. text 59.95 (*0-8058-1691-7*); pap. text 29.95 (*0-8058-1692-5*) L Erlbaum Assocs.

Petraglia, M. D. & Korisettar, Ravi. Early Human Behaviour in the Global Context: The Rise & Diversity of the Lower Paleolithic Period. LC 97-42581. (Illus.). 576p. (C). 1999. 160.00 (*0-415-11763-1*) Routledge.

Petraglia, Patricia P. American Antique Furniture, 1640-1840. LC 94-27973. (Illus.). 176p. 1995. pap. 15.95 (*1-56799-147-5*, Friedman-Fairfax) M Friedman Pub Grp Inc.

Petragnani, Nicola, ed. Tellerium in Organic Synthesis. LC 95-115104. (Best Synthetic Methods Ser.). 248p. 1994. text 77.00 (*0-12-552810-8*) Acad Pr.

Petrak. Victims of Sexual Assault. pap. text 42.00 (*0-471-62691-0*) Wiley.

— Victims of Sexual Assault. 2001. text. write for info. (*0-471-62660-0*) Wiley.

Petrak, Cliff. Complete Guide to Outfield Play. LC 97-32430. (Illus.). 176p. (Orig.). 1998. pap. 20.00 (*1-890450-02-2*) Harding Pr.

Petrak, Joyce. Angels, Guides & Other Spirits. (Illus.). 224p. (Orig.). 1996. pap. 12.95 (*0-9633177-1-7*) Curry-Peterson.

— Bach Flower Remedies - Humor to Remember Them: Or... First, Get the Elephant off Your Foot. 3rd ed. (Illus.). 144p. 1997. pap. 9.95 (*0-9633177-3-3*) Curry-Peterson.

Petrak, Margaret L., ed. Diseases of Cage & Aviary Birds. 2nd ed. LC 81-3792. (Illus.). 720p. reprint ed. pap. 200.00 (*0-8357-7653-0*, 205697900096) Bks Demand.

***Petrakis, Emmanuel, et al, eds.** Environmental Regulation & Market Power: Competition, Time Consistency & International Trade. LC 99-15587. 288p. 2000. 95.00 (*1-85898-889-6*) E Elgar.

Petrakis, Gregory J. Criminal Justice: Contemporary Readings in Current Societal Publishing. (Illus.). 400p. 1999. pap. text 55.00 (*0-8281-1336-X*) Forb Custom Pub.

— Economics: Preparing for the Second Millenium & Beyond. 200p. 1999. pap. text 50.60 (*0-8281-1337-8*) Forb Custom Pub.

— The New Face of Organized Crime. 192p. 1992. per. 34.95 (*0-8403-7411-9*) Kendall-Hunt.

Petrakis, Harry M. Collected Stories. LC 86-20859. 376p. 1987. 29.95 (*0-941702-14-6*); pap. 16.95 (*0-941702-23-5*) Lake View Pr.

— The Founder's Touch: The Life of Paul Galvin of Motorola. 3rd ed. 242p. 1991. reprint ed. 15.00 (*0-89434-119-7*) Motorola Univ.

— The Hour of the Bell. LC 75-40738. 384p. 1984. 19.95 (*0-385-04877-7*) Lake View Pr.

— Reflections: A Writer's Life, a Writer's Work. 252p. (Orig.). 1983. reprint ed. 29.95 (*0-941702-04-9*); reprint ed. pap. 12.95 (*0-941702-05-7*) Lake View Pr.

— Tales of the Heart: Dreams & Memories of a Lifetime. LC 98-49501. 224p. 1999. 25.00 (*1-56663-243-9*, Pub. by I R Dee) Natl Bk Netwk.

Petrakis, Harry Mark. Days of Vengeance: A Novel. LC 98-54198. 288p. 1999. reprint ed. pap. 16.00 (*0-941702-53-7*, 53-7) Lake View Pr.

Petrakis, L., jt. ed. see Cooper, B. R.

Petrakis, Leon & Weiss, F. T., eds. Petroleum in the Marine Environment. LC 79-25524. (ACS Advances in Chemistry Ser.: No. 185). 1980. 60.95 (*0-8412-0475-6*) Am Chemical.

Petrakis, Leonidas & Fraissard, Jacques P., eds. Magnetic Resonance: Introduction, Advanced Topics & Applications to Fossil Energy. 1984. text 326.50 (*90-277-1752-4*) Kluwer Academic.

Petrakis, Leonidas & Weiss, Fred T., eds. Petroleum in the Marine Environment. LC 79-25524. (Advances in Chemistry Ser.: Vol. 185). 382p. 1980. reprint ed. pap. 118.50 (*0-608-03857-1*, 206430400008) Bks Demand.

Petrakis, Leonidas, jt. ed. see Fraissard, Jacques.

Petrakis, Peter. Acquired Immune Deficiency Syndrome & Chemical Dependency. (Illus.). 78p. 1997. reprint ed. pap. text 25.00 (*0-7881-4693-9*) DIANE Pub.

***Petrakos, George.** Integration & Transition in Europe: The Economic Geography of Interaction. LC 99-86053. 256p. 2000. 90.00 (*0-415-21808-X*) Routledge.

Petralia, Joseph F. Flyfishing: First Cast to First Fish. 2nd ed. Comer, John et al, eds. LC 94-65404. (Illus.). 248p. (Orig.). 1997. pap. 16.95 (*0-9605890-9-0*, AB1-3) Sierra Trading.

— Gold! Gold! 110p. 1989. pap. 9.95 (*0-88839-118-8*) Hancock House.

— Gold! Gold! A Beginner's Handbook & Recreational Guide: How & Where to Prospect for Gold. 2nd rev. ed. Applegate, Jill, ed. LC 81-126200. (Illus.). 144p. 1996. reprint ed. pap. 12.95 (*0-9605890-0-7*, AB92) Sierra Trading.

Petralia, Marina. Buenas Noches, Luna: A Study Guide. Friedland, J. & Kessler, R., eds. (Spanish Little Novel-Ties Ser.). (SPA.). (J). (gr. k-2). 1996. pap. text 14.95 (*1-56982-720-6*) Lrn Links.

— Clifford, el Gran Perro Colorado: A Study Guide. Friedland, J. & Kessler, R., eds. (Spanish Little Novel-Ties Ser.). (SPA.). (J). (gr. k-2). 1996. pap. text 14.95 (*1-56982-722-2*) Lrn Links.

— Corduroy: A Study Guide. Friedland, J. & Kessler, R., eds. (Spanish Little Novel-Ties Ser.). (SPA.). (J). (gr. k-2). 1996. pap. text 14.95 (*1-56982-723-0*) Lrn Links.

— El Cuento de Ferdinando: A Study Guide. Friedland, J. & Kessler, R., eds. (Spanish Little Novel-Ties Ser.). (SPA.). (J). (gr. k-2). 1996. pap. text 14.95 (*1-56982-725-7*) Lrn Links.

— Jorge el Curioso: A Study Guide. Friedland, J. & Kessler, R., eds. (Spanish Little Novel-Ties Ser.). (SPA.). (J). (gr. k-2). 1996. pap. text 14.95 (*1-56982-724-9*) Lrn Links.

— Madeline: A Study Guide. Friedland, J. & Kessler, R., eds. (Spanish Little Novel-Ties Ser.). (SPA.). (J). (gr. k-2). 1996. pap. text 14.95 (*1-56982-726-5*) Lrn Links.

— Se Venden Gorras: A Study Guide. Friedland, J. & Kessler, R., eds. (Spanish Little Novel-Ties Ser.). (SPA.). (J). (gr. k-2). 1996. pap. text 14.95 (*1-56982-721-4*) Lrn Links.

— Silbale a Willie: A Study Guide. Friedland, J. & Kessler, R., eds. (Spanish Little Novel-Ties Ser.). (SPA.). (J). (gr. k-2). 1996. pap. text 14.95 (*1-56982-727-3*) Lrn Links.

— Silvestre y la Piedrecita Magica: A Study Guide. Friedland, J. & Kesslere, R., eds. (Spanish Little Novel-Ties Ser.). (SPA.). (J). (gr. k-2). 1996. pap. text 14.95 (*1-56982-728-1*) Lrn Links.

Petran, Tabitha. The Struggle over Lebanon. LC 86-18284. 320p. 1987. 27.50 (*0-85345-651-8*, Pub. by Monthly Rev) NYU Pr.

Petranka, James W. Salamanders of the United States & Canada. LC 97-38094. 587p. 1998. text 60.00 (*1-56098-828-2*) Smithsonian.

Petranker, Jack. Light of Knowledge: Essays on the Interplay of Knowledge, Time, & Space. LC 97-24726. (Perspectives on TSK Ser.). 1997. pap. 16.95 (*0-89800-287-7*) Dharma Pub.

Petranker, Jack, ed. From the Roof of the World: Refugees of Tibet. (Illus.). 292p. (Orig.). (C). 1992. pap. 24.95 (*0-89800-241-9*) Dharma Pub.

***Petrarca, Francesco.** Canzoniere. Nichols, J. G., tr. 220p. 2000. pap. 29.95 (*1-85754-451-X*, Pub. by Carcanet Pr) Paul & Co Pubs.

Petrarca, Francesco. Canzoniere. 1999. pap. 15.95 (*0-14-042249-8*, Viking) Viking Penguin.

— Canzoniere. Musa, Mark, tr. & comment by. Canzoniere, Petrarch, comment. LC 95-35943. (ITA., Illus.). 800p. 1996. text 59.95 (*0-253-33944-8*) Ind U Pr.

— Letters of Old Age: Rerum Senilium Libri, No. I-XVIII, 2 vols. Bernardo, Aldo S. et al, trs. from LAT. 368p. 1992. text 95.00 (*0-8018-4212-3*) Johns Hopkins.

— Letters on Familiar Matters: Rerum Familiarum Libri I-XXIV, 3 vols. Bernardo, Aldo S., tr. from LAT. LC 75-2418. 352p. 1985. text 50.00 (*0-8018-2750-7*); text 50.00 (*0-8018-2902-X*); text 50.00 (*0-8018-2287-4*) Johns Hopkins.

— Letters on Familiar Matters: Rerum Familiarum Libri I-XXIV, 3 vols., Set. Bernardo, Aldo S., tr. from LAT. LC 75-2418. 1985. 135.00 (*0-8018-2768-X*) Johns Hopkins.

— Lord Morley's Tryumphes of Fraunces Petrarcke: The First English Translation of the Trionfi. Carnicelli, D. D., ed. LC 72-164690. 302p. 1971. reprint ed. pap. 93.70 (*0-7837-2312-1*, 205740000004) Bks Demand.

— Love Rimes of Petrarch. Bishop, Morris, tr. from ITA. LC 79-12820. (Illus.). 61p. 1980. reprint ed. lib. bdg. 39.75 (*0-313-22002-6*, PELR, Greenwood Pr) Greenwood.

— Petrarch: The First Modern Scholar & Man of Letters. Robinson, James H., tr. & intro. by. LC 75-127999. (World History Ser.: No. 48). 1970. reprint ed. lib. bdg. 75.00 (*0-8383-1148-2*) M S G Haskell Hse.

— Petrarch's Africa. Bergin, Thomas G. & Wilson, Alice S., trs. LC 77-75380. 311p. reprint ed. pap. 96.50 (*0-8357-8748-6*, 203367000087) Bks Demand.

— Petrarch's Book Without a Name: A Translation of the Liber Sine Nomine. Zacour, Norman P., tr. from LAT. 128p. pap. 8.00 (*0-88844-260-2*) Brill Academic Pubs.

— Petrarch's Bucolicum Carmen. Bergin, Thomas G., tr. & anno. by. LC 73-94049. (ENG & LAT., Illus.). 270p. reprint ed. pap. 83.70 (*0-8357-8749-4*, 203367100087) Bks Demand.

— Petrarch's Lyric Poems: The Rime Sparse & Other Lyrics. Durling, Robert M., ed. 624p. 1976. 46.50 (*0-674-66345-4*) HUP.

— Petrarch's Remedies for Fortune Fair & Foul: A Modern English Translation of "De Remediis Utriusque Fortune," with a Commentary, 5 vols., Set. Rawski, Conrad H., tr. LC 88-46015. (ITA., Illus.). 1991. 198.00 (*0-253-34849-8*) Ind U Pr.

— Physicke Against Fortune. Twyne, Thomas, tr. LC 80-22768. 728p. 1980. reprint ed. 90.00 (*0-8201-1359-X*) Schol Facsimiles.

— The Revolution of Cola di Rienzo. 3rd rev. ed. Musto, Ronald G., ed. LC 86-80577. Orig. Title: Francesco Petrarca & the Revolution of Cola di Rienzo. 224p. 1996. pap. 17.50 (*0-934977-00-3*) Italica Pr.

— Selected Sonnets, Odes & Letters. Bergin, Thomas G., ed. (Crofts Classics). 160p. 1966. pap. text 5.95 (*0-88295-066-5*) Harlan Davidson.

***Petrarca, Francesco.** Selections from the Canzoniere & Other Works. Musa, Mark, ed. (Oxford World's Classics Ser.). 112p. 1999. pap. 8.95 (*0-19-283951-9*) OUP.

Petrarca, Francesco. Songs & Sonnets. Armi, Anna M., tr. LC 75-41212. reprint ed. 67.50 (*0-404-14695-3*) AMS Pr.

Petrarch, Francis. On Solitude. Livernois, Jay, tr. (Dunquin Ser.: Vol. 26). 316p. 2000. pap. 18.00 (*0-88214-228-3*, Pub. by Spring Pubns) Continuum.

Petras. The Only Money Guide You'll Ever Need. 1995. 14.95 (*0-671-75888-8*) S&S Trade.

Petras, James. The Left Strikes Back: Class Conflict in Latin America in the Age of Neoliberalism. LC 98-20772. (Latin American Perspectives Ser.: No. 19). 232p. 1998. text 69.00 (*0-8133-3554-X*, Pub. by Westview) HarpC.

Petras, James & Morley, Morris. Empire or Republic? American Global Power & Domestic Decay. LC 94-17398. 224p. (C). 1994. pap. 18.99 (*0-415-91065-X*, B4481) Routledge.

— Empire or Republic? American Global Power & Domestic Decay. LC 94-17398. 224p. (C). (gr. 13). 1994. 70.00 (*0-415-91064-1*, B4477) Routledge.

Petras, James, jt. auth. see Kurth, James.

Petras, James F. Critical Perspectives on Imperialism & Social Class in the Third World. LC 78-13915. 324p. reprint ed. pap. 100.50 (*0-7837-3901-X*, 204374900010) Bks Demand.

— Politics & Social Structure in Latin America. LC 73-122737. 382p. 1970. reprint ed. pap. 118.50 (*0-7837-9613-7*, 206037000005) Bks Demand.

Petras, James F. & Merino, Hugo Z. Peasants in Revolt: A Chilean Case Study, 1965-1971. Flory, Thomas, tr. LC 72-1578. (Latin American Monographs: No. 28). 168p. reprint ed. pap. 52.10 (*0-8357-7754-5*, 203611200002) Bks Demand.

Petras, James F., jt. auth. see Veltmeyer, Henry.

Petras, Kathryn. Jobs, '98: From Entry-Level to Executive Positions--Leads on More Than 40 Million Jobs. 704p. 1997. pap. 16.00 (*0-684-81826-4*, Fireside) S&S Trade Pap.

— The Premature Menopause Book: When the "Change of Life" Comes Too Early. LC 99-94866. 416p. 1999. pap. 14.00 (*0-380-80541-3*, Avon Bks) Morrow Avon.

— Very Bad Poetry. LC 96-51788. 128p. 1997. pap. 10.00 (*0-679-77622-2*) Random.

Petras, Kathryn & Petras, Ross. Jobs, 1993. 592p. (Orig.). 1992. per. 15.00 (*0-671-76075-0*, Fireside) S&S Trade Pap.

— Mythology. (Fandex Family Field Guide Ser.). (Illus.). 1998. pap. 9.95 (*0-7611-1207-3*) Workman Pub.

— The Only Job Hunting Guide You'll Ever Need: The Most Comprehensive Guide for Job Hunters & Career Switchers. rev. ed. LC 94-47511. 400p. 1995. per. 15.00 (*0-684-80236-8*) S&S Trade.

— Seven Hundred Seventy-Six Stupidest Things. 240p. 1993. pap. 10.00 (*0-385-41928-7*) Doubleday.

— Stupid Celebrities: Over 500 of the Most Idiotic Things Ever Said by Famous People. LC 98-22887. 384p. 1998. 9.95 (*0-8362-6837-7*) Andrews & McMeel.

— Stupid Movie Lines: The 576 Dumbest Things Ever Uttered on the Silver Screen. LC 99-19653. 224p. 1999. pap. 9.95 (*0-375-75330-3*) Villard Books.

Petras, Kathryn & Petras, Ross, eds. The Whole World Book of Quotations: Wisdom from Women & Men Around the Globe Throughout the Centuries. 576p. 1995. 25.00 (*0-201-62258-0*) Addison-Wesley.

Petras, Kathryn, jt. auth. see Petras, Ross.

Petras, Ross & Petras, Kathryn. Jobs, 1990. 320p. 1990. pap. 14.95 (*0-685-31172-4*) P-H.

— The 176 Stupidest Things Ever Done. 208p. 1996. pap. 10.95 (*0-385-48341-4*) Doubleday.

Petras, Ross & Petras, Kathryn. The 776 Even Stupider Things Ever Said. LC 93-44804. 240p. 1994. pap. 11.00 (*0-06-095059-5*, Perennial) HarperTrade.

Petras, Ross & Petras, Kathryn. The 776 Nastiest Things Ever Said. 208p. 1995. pap. 7.95 (*0-06-095060-9*, Perennial) HarperTrade.

— Stupid Sex. LC 98-3266. 208p. 1998. pap. 9.95 (*0-385-48851-3*) Doubleday.

— The Stupidest Things Ever Said by Politicians. 256p. 1999. per. 12.00 (*0-671-04053-7*) S&S Trade.

Petras, Ross, jt. auth. see Petras, Kathryn.

Petras, Ross, jt. ed. see Petras, Kathryn.

Petrascheck, W. E., ed. Ore Mobilization in the Alps & in SE-Europe. (Schriftenreihe der Erdwissenschaftlichen Kommissionen Ser.: Band 6). (ENG & GER.). 106p. 1983. 36.95 (*0-387-86511-X*) Spr-Verlag.

Petrascheck, W. E. & Jankovic, S., eds. Geotectonic Evolution & Metallogeny of the Mediterranean Area & Western Asia: Proceedings of the Final Symposium of IGCP Project 169, Leoben, October, 1984. (Schriftenreihe der Erdwissenschaftlichen Kommissionen Ser.: Band 8). 298p. 1986. 102.95 (*0-387-86527-6*) Spr-Verlag.

***Petraschka, Eveline.** Frankischer Adel und Irische Peregrini im 7, Jahrhundert: Die Vita der Hl. Geretrude von Nivelles - Ein Zeugnis des Hagiographischen Kreises um Den Iren Foillan. (Europaische Hochschulschriften Geschichte und Ihre Hilfswissenschaften Ser.). 174p. 1999. 35.95 (*3-631-34899-1*) P Lang Pubng.

Petrasen, G. I., ed. see Steklov Institute of Mathematics, Academy of Scien.

Petrash, Carol. Earthways: Simple Environmental Activities for Young Children. 206p. 1992. pap. 16.95 (*0-87659-156-X*) Gryphon Hse.

Petrash, G. G., ed. Metal Vapor & Metal Halide Vapor Lasers. (Proceedings of the Lebedev Physics Institute Ser.: Vol. 181). 261p. 1989. text 165.00 (*0-941743-27-6*) Nova Sci Pubs.

— Optics & Lasers. (Proceedings of the Lebedev Physics Institute Ser.: Vol. 211). 247p. 1994. lib. bdg. 165.00 (*1-56072-197-9*) Nova Sci Pubs.

***Petrash, Jack.** Covering Home: Lessons on the Art of Fathering from the Game of Baseball. 2000. 19.95 (*0-87659-217-5*, Robins Ln Pr) Gryphon Hse.

Petrash-Vaughan, M., compiled by. Woods' Illustrated English-Russian/Russian-English Encyclopaedic Reference of Exploration & Production Geophysics - Library Edition. (Illus.). 330p. 1997. 195.00 (*0-9642563-7-1*) Albion Woods.

Petrasovits, G. Proceedings of the Ninth Danube-European Conference on Soil Mechanics & Foundation Engineering: Budapest, Oct. 2-5, 1990. (GER., Illus.). 555p. (C). 1990. 220.00 (*963-05-5898-X*, Pub. by Akade Kiado) St Mut.

— Proceedings of the Sixth Budapest Conference of Soil Mechanics & Foundation Engineering. (ENG & GER.). 640p. (C). 1984. 175.00 (*963-05-3962-4*, Pub. by Akade Kiado) St Mut.

— Soil Mechanics & Foundation Engineering. 640p. (C). 1984. 405.00 (*0-569-08888-7*, Pub. by Collets) St Mut.

Petratca, Francesco. Cancionero, Sonetos y Canciones. Crespo, Angel, tr. & intro. by. (Nueva Austral Ser.: Vol. 42). (SPA.). 1991. pap. text 24.95 (*84-239-1842-4*) Elliots Bks.

Petrazzini, Ben A. Global Telecom Talks: The Trillion Dollar Deal. (Policy Analyses in International Economics Ser.: Vol. 44). (Orig.). 1996. pap. 15.00 (*0-88132-230-X*) Inst Intl Eco.

— The Political Economy of Telecommunications Reform in Developing Countries: Privatization & Liberalization in Comparative Perspective. LC 95-7552. 248p. 1995. 65.00 (*0-275-95294-0*, Praeger Pubs) Greenwood.

Petre, Dede, jt. ed. see Petre, Kelly.

Petre, F. Loraine. Napoleon at Bay, 1814. LC 93-40524. (Illus.). 240p. 1994. 40.00 (*1-85367-163-0*, 5557) Stackpole.

— Napoleon's Conquest of Prussia, 1806. LC 92-41764. 344p. 1993. 40.00 (*1-85367-145-2*, 5561) Stackpole.

— Napoleon's Last Campaign in Germany, 1813. 424p. 1992. 37.50 (*1-85367-121-5*) Stackpole.

Petre, G., et al, eds. Capillarity Today: Proceedings of an Advanced Workshop on Capillarity Held In Memoriam Raymond Defay at Brussels, Belgium, 7-10 May 1990. (Lecture Notes in Physics Ser.: Vol. 386). xi, 384p. 1991. 56.95 (*0-387-54367-8*) Spr-Verlag.

***Petre, Kelly & Petre, Dede, eds.** Our God Is an Awesome God. (Daily Power Ser.: Vol. 11). 153p. 1999. pap. 7.99 (*1-57782-122-X*) Discipleshp.

Petre, M. D., ed. see Gorgolini, Pietro.

Petre, Maude D. & Erb, Peter C. A Week End Book of Thought & Prayer. 220p. 1998. 49.95 (*1-57309-246-0*, Cath Scholar Pr); pap. 29.95 (*1-57309-245-2*, Cath Scholar Pr) Intl Scholars.

Petre, Peter, jt. auth. see Watson, Thomas.

Petre, Peter, ed. see Schwarzkopf, H. Norman.

Petre, Robert, jt. ed. see Schlegel, Eric M.

Petrea, Janice. Just Clowning Around: Sharing God's Love Through Love & Laughter. (Illus.). 96p. (J). (gr. 7-12). 1998. pap. text 10.95 (*1-56309-237-9*, W986101) Womans Mission Union.

Petrecca, Giovanni. Industrial Energy Management: Principles & Applications. LC 92-36761. (International Series in Engineering & Computer Science, VLSI, Computer Architecture, & Digital Screen Processing: Vol. 13). 1992. text 201.50 (*0-7923-9305-8*) Kluwer Academic.

Petree, Arlie. Poems: The Poetry of Arlie Petree. 80p. (Orig.). Date not set. pap. 5.00 (*0-9646344-1-4*) M Padgett.

Petrei, Humberto. Budget & Control: Reforming the Public Sector in Latin America: Guidelines for Reform in Latin America. LC 99-160128. 438p. 1998. 24.95 (*1-886938-41-5*) IADB.

— Presupuesto y Control: Pautas de Reforma para America Latina. (SPA.). 494p. 1997. pap. text 24.95 (*1-886938-28-8*) IADB.

Petrek, Jeanne A., jt. auth. see Robinson, Rebecca Y.

Petrelia, R., jt. ed. see Szalai, A.

Petrella, R., jt. ed. see Kuklinski, Antoni.

Petrelli, M. Italian-English - English-Italian Medical Dictionary. (ENG & ITA.). 737p. 1993. 115.00 (*0-7859-7524-1*, 8871660714); 110.00 (*0-7859-8825-4*) Fr & Eur.

— Italian-English - English-Italian Medical Dictionary. 737p. 1993. 116.00 (*88-7166-071-4*, Pub. by Le Lettere) IBD Ltd.

Petrelli, Maria. Dizionario Medico: Italiano-Inglese/Inglese-Italiano. (ENG & ITA.). 740p. 1992. 135.00 (*0-913298-62-X*) S F Vanni.

Petreman, David A., tr. see Coloane, Francisco.

Petren, Birgitta & Putini, Elisabetta. Why Are You Calling Me A Barbarian? Becker, Mary, tr. from ITA. LC 99-13327. (Illus.). 60p. (YA). (gr. 5 up). 1999. pap. 17.95 (*0-89236-559-5*, Pub. by J P Getty Trust) OUP.

Petrenko, Alexandre A. & Yevtushenko, Nina. Testing of Communicating Systems: Proceedings of the IFIP TC6 11th International Workshop on Testing of Communicating Systems (IWTCS '98), August 31-September 2, 1998, Tomsk, Russia. LC 98-29953. xi, 364 p. 1998. write for info. (*0-7923-8243-9*) Kluwer Academic.

Petrenko, O. K. English - Russian Dictionary of Nuclear Explosions. (ENG & RUS.). 304p. (C). 1977. 19.95 (*0-8285-5300-9*) Firebird NY.

Petrenko, Victor F. & Whitworth, Robert W. Physics of Ice. LC 99-19984. (Illus.). 390p. 1999. text 130.00 (*0-19-851895-1*) OUP.

Petres, J. & Hundeiker, M. Dermatosurgery. 1978. 99.00 (*0-387-90296-1*) Spr-Verlag.

Petreschi, R., jt. auth. see Bovet, D. P.

***Petrescu-Comnene, Nicolae.** Great War & the Romanians: Notes & Documents on World War I. 174p. 2000. 29.95 (*973-9432-16-6*, Pub. by Ctr Romanian Studies) Intl Spec Bk.

Petrescu, M. English & Rumanian Dictionary of Electrical Engineering, Electronic Telecommunication & Cybernetics: Dictionar de Electrotehnica, Electronica, Telecomunicatii, Cibernetica. (ENG & RUM.). 1982. write for info. (*0-8288-0305-6*, M15846) Fr & Eur.

Petreshene, Susan S. Brain Teasers! Over 180 Activities & Worksheets That Make Kids Think. LC 94-11905. (Illus.). 288p. 1994. pap. text 27.95 (*0-87628-123-4*) Ctr Appl Res.

— Mind Joggers! 5 to 15-Minute Activities That Make Kids Think. (Illus.). 224p. 1985. pap. text 27.95 (*0-87628-583-3*) Ctr Appl Res.

Petretschek, Roswitha, ed. see Satchell, Alexis.

***Petretti, Allan.** Classic Coca-Cola Collectibles: Cardboard & Paper Signs. (Illus.). 192p. 2000. 32.95 (*0-87341-893-X*, CCCPS) Krause Pubns.

Petretti, Allan. Petretti's Coca-Cola Collectibles Price Guide: The Encyclopedia of Coca-Cola Collectibles. 10th rev. ed. (Illus.). 648p. 1997. 42.95 (*0-930625-76-5*, Antique Trader) Krause Pubns.

— Petretti's Soda Pop Collectibles Price Guide: The Encyclopedia of Soda-Pop Collectibles. 2nd ed. (Illus.). 384p. 1999. 37.95 (*1-58221-026-8*, Antique Trader); pap. 32.95 (*1-58221-014-4*, Antique Trader) Krause Pubns.

***Petretti, Allan & Beyer, Chris.** Classic Coca-Cola Calendars. (Illus.). 152p. 2000. 32.95 (*1-58221-002-0*, Antique Trader) Krause Pubns.

Petretti, Allan & Beyer, Chris. Classic Coca-Cola Serving Trays. LC 98-70852. (Illus.). 168p. 1998. 32.95 (*0-930625-96-X*, Antique Trader) Krause Pubns.

Petrey, Sandy. History in the Text "Quatrevingt-Treize" & the French Revolution. (Purdue University Monographs in Romance Languages: No 3). viii, 129p. 1980. 35.00 (*90-272-1713-0*) J Benjamins Pubng Co.

— Realism & Revolution: Balzac, Stendahl, Zola & the Performances of History. LC 88-18117. 224p. 1989. text 37.50 (*0-8014-2216-7*) Cornell U Pr.

Petrey, Sandy, intro. The French Revolution, 1789-1989: Two Hundred Years of Rethinking. (Eighteenth Century Ser.). (Illus.). 106p. (C). 1989. 15.95 (*0-89672-198-1*) Tex Tech Univ Pr.

Petrey, Sandy, tr. see Zola, Emile.

Petri. Motivation: Theory & Research. (Psychology Ser.). 1981. mass mkt. 30.50 (*0-534-00936-0*) Brooks-Cole.

— Motivation: Theory & Research. 2nd ed. (Psychology Ser.). 1986. text. write for info. (*0-534-05383-1*) Brooks-Cole.

— Motivation: Theory, Research & Applications. (Adaptable Courseware Ser.). 1996. reprint ed. 15.50 (*0-534-49772-1*) Brooks-Cole.

Petri, Barbara, ed. Kiwi & Emu: An Anthology of Contemporary Poetry by Australian & New Zealand Women. 289p. (C). 1990. 105.00 (*0-947333-05-3*, Pub. by Pascoe Pub) St Mut.

Petri, Catharose De, see Van Rijckenborgh, Jan & De Petri, Catharose.

Petri, Catharose De, see De Petri, Catharose.

Petri, Catharose De, see Van Rijckenborgh, Jan & De Petri, Catharose.

Petri, Catharose De, see De Petri, Catharose.

Petri, Catharose De, see Van Rijckenborgh, Jan & De Petri, Catharose.

Petri, Catharose De, see De Petri, Catharose.

Petri, Fabio, jt. auth. see Mongiovi, Gary.

Petri, Gary. The Proper Care & Feeding of Church Volunteers. LC 97-148992. 72p. 1996. pap. 8.95 (*1-55612-916-5*) Sheed & Ward WI.

Petri, Gary, et al. We Miss You: An Outreach Program for Inactive Catholics, Reproducible. 96p. 1995. pap. 49.95 (*1-55612-613-1*, LL1613) Sheed & Ward WI.

***Petri, Gyorgy.** Eternal Monday. 96p. 2000. pap. 18.95 (*1-85224-504-2*, Pub. by Bloodaxe Bks) Dufour.

Petri, Gyorgy. Night Song of the Personal Shadow: Selected Poems. Wilmer, C. & Gomori, G., trs. from HUN. 80p. (Orig.). 1991. pap. 14.95 (*1-85224-107-1*, Pub. by Bloodaxe Bks) Dufour.

Petri, Herbert L. Motivation: Theory & Research. 2nd ed. 432p. (C). 1985. mass mkt. 40.50 (*0-534-05382-3*) Brooks-Cole.

— Motivation: Theory, Research & Applications. 3rd ed. 434p. (C). 1991. text 46.20 (*0-534-14364-4*) Brooks-Cole.

Petri, Herbert L. Motivation: Theory, Research & Applications. 4th ed. LC 95-22770. 440p. 1995. pap. 87.95 (*0-534-20460-0*) Wadsworth Pub.

Petri, Herbert L. Motivation: Theory, Research, & Applications, Test Items. 4th ed. 1995. mass mkt. write for info. (*0-534-20461-9*) Brooks-Cole.

Petri, Hilda N., ed. see Neihardt, John G.

Petri, Mart & Burkhardt, Gina. CaMaPe: An Organizational & Educational Systems Approach to Secondary School Development. 100p. (Orig.). (C). 1992. pap. text 15.00 (*1-878234-04-8*) Reg Lab Educ IOT NE Isls.

Petri, Peter A. Modeling Japanese-American Trade: A Study of Asymmetric Interdependence. (Economic Studies: No. 156). (Illus.). 232p. 1984. 20.00 (*0-674-57810-4*) HUP.

Petri, Peter A., jt. auth. see Leipziger, Danny M.

Petri, Peter A., jt. ed. see Gerlach, Stefan.

***Petri, Romana.** An Umbrian War. 266p. 2000. write for info. (*1-902881-09-5*, Pub. by Toby Pr Ltd); pap. 15.95 (*1-902881-14-1*, Pub. by Toby Pr Ltd) Toby Pr.

Petric, Vlada. Constructivism in Film: The Man with the Movie Camera. (Studies in Film). (Illus.). 337p. (C). 1993. pap. text 21.95 (*0-521-44387-3*) Cambridge U Pr.

Petricciani, J. C., jt. ed. see Hopps, H. E.

Petricciani, J. C. & Hennessen, W., eds. Cells, Products, Safety. (Developments in Biological Standardization Ser.: Vol. 68). (Illus.). vi, 90p. 1987. pap. 61.00 (*3-8055-4676-9*) S Karger.

***Petrich, Mario & Reilly, Norman R.** Completely Regular Semigroups. LC 97-38037. (Canadian Mathematical Society Ser.). 481p. 1999. 125.00 (*0-471-19571-5*, Wiley-Interscience) Wiley.

Petricic, Dusan. The Enormous Potato. LC 97-930196. 32p. (J). (ps-2). 1998. 14.95 (*1-55074-386-4*, Pub. by Kids Can Pr) Genl Dist Srvs.

Petricioli, Ivo. St. Simeon's Shrine in Zadar, Croatia. 108p. 1983. 30.00 (*0-918660-93-9*) Ragusan Pr.

Petricioli, Marta, ed. Une Occasion Manquee? 1922 (A Missed Opportunity?) La Reconstruction de l'Europe (The Reconstruction of Europe) (FRE.). 512p. 1995. 55.95 (*3-906754-15-4*, Pub. by P Lang) P Lang Pubng.

***Petrick, Jane A.** Beyond Time Management: Life Balancing Connections. 2nd ed. 1998. pap. 19.95 (*0-9664670-1-9*) Informed Dem.

Petrick, Jane A. Making the Connection: Getting Work to Work. LC 98-87262. 79p. 1998. pap. 19.95 (*0-9664670-0-0*) ID Publ.

Petrick, Jane Allen, see Allen Petrick, Jane.

Petrick, Joseph A. & Fur, Dianna. Total Quality in Managing Human Resources. LC 94-46630. (Total Quality Ser.). 388p. 1995. boxed set 54.95 (*1-884015-24-7*) St Lucie Pr.

Petrick, Joseph A. & Quinn, John F. Management Ethics: Integrity at Work. LC 96-51271. (Series on Business Ethics). 384p. 1997. 58.00 (*0-8039-5796-3*); pap. 27.95 (*0-8039-5797-1*) Sage.

Petrick, Joseph A., jt. auth. see Lindsay, William.

Petrick, Neila A. The Christmas Horse. 1998. pap., student ed. 23.95 incl. VHS (*1-880384-25-6*) Coldwater Pr.

— Woman of Texas: The Story of Jane Wilkinson Long. Petrick, Thomas W., ed. (YA). (gr. 7-12). 1997. student ed. 23.95 incl. VHS (*1-880384-11-6*) Coldwater Pr.

— Woman of Texas: The Story of Jane Wilkinson Long. Petrick, Thomas W., ed. 52p. (YA). (gr. 7-12). 1998. student ed. 11.95 (*1-880384-13-2*) Coldwater Pr.

Petrick, Neila Skinner. Jane Long of Texas. 2nd ed. (Illus.). 299p. 23.95 (*0-9642905-0-2*) Prime Time Pr.

Petrick, S. W. Veterinary Eye Surgery. (Illus.). 1983. text 55.00 (*0-409-11265-8*) Buttrwrth-Heinemann.

Petrick-Steward, Elizabeth. Beginning Writers in the Zone of Proximal Development. 288p. 1995. pap. 29.95 (*0-8058-1866-9*); text 75.00 (*0-8058-1302-0*) L Erlbaum Assocs.

Petrick, Thomas W., jt. auth. see Bauld, Jane S.

Petrick, Thomas W., ed. see Petrick, Neila A.

Petrick, Thomas W., ed. see Powell, Mary C.

***Petrick, Tim.** Skiing: Six Ways to Reach Your Skiing Potential. (Illus.). 160p. 2000. pap. 14.95 (*1-892129-81-7*) Total Sprts.

Petrick, Tim. Sports Illustrated Skiing. (Illus.). 1989. pap. 9.95 (*1-56800-028-6*, Pub. by Sports Illus Bks) Natl Bk Netwk.

Petrides. Eastern Trees & Shrubs, 001. 2nd ed. (Peterson Field Guide Ser.). 464p. 1973. pap. 18.00 (*0-395-35370-X*, Peterson Field Guides) HM.

Petrides, Demetri P., jt. auth. see El-Halwagi, Mahmoud M.

Petrides, Faith. The Dance Directory of Ballet Companies. 200p. 1996. per. 39.95 (*1-889836-00-1*) Dance Dir.

Petrides, George A. Peterson First Guide to Trees. LC 92-36586. (Illus.). 128p. (J). 1993. pap. 4.95 (*0-395-65972-8*) HM.

— Peterson First Guide to Trees. (J). 1993. 10.05 (*0-606-05539-8*, Pub. by Turtleback) Demco.

— Trees: Flashguides. (Illus.). 12p. 1996. pap. 8.95 (*0-395-82998-4*) HM.

— Trees of the California Sierra Nevada: A New & Simple Way to Identify & Enjoy Some of the World's Most Beautiful & Impressive Forest Trees in a Mountain Setting of Incomparable Majesty. LC 95-60999. (Backpacker Field Guide Ser.). (Illus.). 80p. (Orig.). 1997. pap. 9.95 (*0-9646674-0-1*) Explr Pr MI.

— Trees of the Pacific Northwest: Including Oregon, Washington, Idaho, NW. Montana, British Columbia, Yukon, & Alaska. LC 96-61922. (Backpacker Field Guide Ser.). (Illus.). 100p. (Orig.). 1998. pap. 12.95 (*0-9646674-1-X*) Explr Pr MI.

***Petrides, George A. & Petrides, Olivia.** Trees of the American Southwest. 112p. 2000. pap. 14.95 (*0-9646674-3-6*, Pub. by Explr Pr MI) IPG Chicago.

Petrides, George A. & Petrides, Olivia. Trees of the Rocky Mountains & Intermountain West. LC 97-61669. (Illus.). 104p. 1998. pap. text 14.95 (*0-9646674-2-8*) Explr Pr MI.

***Petrides, Lisa Ann, ed.** Case Studies on Information Technology in Higher Education: Implications for Policy & Practice. (Illus.). 350p. (C). 2000. pap. 69.95 (*1-878289-74-8*) Idea Group Pub.

Petrides, Olivia, jt. auth. see Petrides, George A.

Petrides, Paul. Suzanne Valadon: The Complete Work. (FRE., Illus.). 370p. 1971. 475.00 (*1-55660-068-2*) A Wofsy Fine Arts.

Petrides, Ted. Greek Dances. rev. ed. (Illus.). 105p. (Orig.). 1993. pap. 10.00 (*960-7269-07-1*, Pub. by Lycabettus Pr) Bosphorus Bks.

***Petridis, Alexis.** Neil Young. Aizlewood, John, ed. (Illus.). 152p. 2000. pap. 13.95 (*1-56025-265-0*, Thunders Mouth) Avalon NY.

Petridis, Dimitris, jt. auth. see Miglierini, Marcel.

Petridis, Vassilios & Kehagias, Athansios. Predictive Modular Neural Networks: Applications to Time Series. LC 98-38777. (International Series in Engineering & Computer Science). 1998. 125.00 (*0-7923-8290-0*) Kluwer Academic.

Petrie. Achieving Academic & Personal Success for Student Athletes. LC 98-46127. (Freshman Orientation/College Success Ser.). 1999. pap. 30.95 (*0-534-54792-3*) Wadsworth Pub.

— Seven Memphite Tomb Chapels Vol. 65: British School of Egyptian Archaeology. 1969. 23.95 (*0-85668-116-4*, Pub. by Aris & Phillips) David Brown.

Petrie & Meldman, Robert E. Federal Taxation Practice & Procedure. 4th ed. 736p. 1992. 55.00 (*0-685-66990-4*, 4727) CCH INC.

***Petrie, A. Roy.** Alexander Graham Bell. (Illus.). 64p. (J). 1999. pap. 6.95 (*1-55041-463-1*) Fitzhenry & W Ltd.

Petrie, Alexander. An Introduction to Roman History, Literature & Antiquities. 3rd ed. LC 78-25840. (Illus.). 160p. 1979. reprint ed. lib. bdg. 38.50 (*0-313-20848-4*, PEIR, Greenwood Pr) Greenwood.

***Petrie, Alistair P.** Releasing Heaven on Earth: God's Principles for Restoring the Land. 288p. 2000. pap. 12.99 (*0-8007-9278-5*) Chosen Bks.

***Petrie, Allyson.** Where Did the Sun Go? Wise, Noreen, ed. (Book-a-Day Collection). (Illus.). 32p. (YA). (ps up). 2000. pap. 5.95 (*1-58584-395-4*) Huckleberry CT.

Petrie, Asenath. Individuality in Pain & Suffering. 2nd ed. LC 77-93608. (Illus.). 1993. reprint ed. pap. text 4.95 (*0-226-66347-7*, P739) U Ch Pr.

— Oasis in Time: Jerusalem. 120p. (Orig.). 1994. pap. text 9.95 (*965-229-109-9*, Pub. by Gefen Pub Hse) Gefen Bks.

***Petrie, Avid & Sabin, Caroline.** Medical Statistics at a Glance. LC 99-47123. (At a Glance Ser.). (Illus.). 136p. (C). 2000. pap. 21.95 (*0-632-05075-6*) Blackwell Sci.

Petrie, Aviva & Watson, Paul. Statistics for Veterinary & Animal Science. LC 99-13540. 254p. 1999. 29.95 (*0-632-05025-X*, Pub. by Blckwell Science) Iowa St U Pr.

Petrie, Barbara. Priscilla Scales & Other Cautionary Tales. (C). 1990. 45.00 (*0-947333-04-5*, Pub. by Pascoe Pub) St Mut.

Petrie, Brian. Puvis de Chavannes. Lee, Simon, ed. LC 97-74710. (Illus.). 192p. 1997. text 86.95 (*1-85928-451-5*, Pub. by Ashgate Pub) Ashgate Pub Co.

Petrie, Bruce L, Jr. Innovations in Ohio Workplace Injury Law: Intentional Torts, VSSR's, Third-Party Liability, Independent Contractors. Qualls, John R., ed. 128p. 1988. text 21.50 (*0-87084-703-1*) Anderson Pub Co.

Petrie, Carol, ed. see National Research Council Staff.

Petrie, Catherine. Hot Rod Harry. LC 81-15549. (Rookie Readers Ser.). (Illus.). 32p. (J). (ps-3). 1982. pap. 4.95 (*0-516-43493-4*); lib. bdg. 17.00 (*0-516-03493-6*) Childrens.

— Joshua James Likes Trucks. LC 81-17076. (Rookie Readers Ser.). (Illus.). 32p. (J). (ps-2). 1982. pap. 4.95 (*0-516-43525-6*) Childrens.

Petrie, Catherine. Joshua James Likes Trucks. rev. ed. LC 98-54222. (Rookie Readers Ser.). 24p. (J). (gr. k-1). 1999. 15.00 (*0-516-21639-2*) Childrens.

***Petrie, Catherine.** Joshua James Likes Trucks. rev. ed. (Rookie Readers Ser.). (J). 2000. pap. text 4.95 (*0-516-27000-1*) Childrens.

Petrie, Charles. Carlton Club. 221p. 1955. 69.50 (*0-614-00061-0*) Elliots Bks.

Petrie, Charles A. Diplomatic History, 1713-1933. LC 83-45834. reprint ed. 35.00 (*0-404-20199-7*) AMS Pr.

Petrie, Charles J., Jr., ed. Enterprise Integration Modeling: Proceedings of the First International Conference. LC 92-29675. (Scientific & Engineering Computation Ser.). (Illus.). 581p. 1992. pap. text 53.00 (*0-262-66080-6*) MIT Pr.

Petrie, Chuck. Just Retrievers. LC 97-33287. (Just Ser.). (Illus.). 146p. 1997. 35.00 (*1-57223-126-2*, 1262) Willow Creek Pr.

***Petrie, Chuck.** Just Retrievers: Half Pint Edition. abr. ed. (Illus.). 96p. 2000. 12.95 (*1-57223-390-7*) Willow Creek Pr

— North America's Greatest Waterfowling Lodges & Outfitters: 250 Prime Destinations in the U. S., Canada & Mexico. (Illus.). 278p. 2000. pap. 19.95 (*1-57223-312-5*) Willow Creek Pr.

Petrie, Chuck, ed. Just Dogs: A Literary & Photographic Tribute to the Great Hunting Breeds. LC 88-50861. (Illus.). 148p. 1988. 35.00 (*1-57223-020-7*, 0207) Willow Creek Pr.

Petrie, Chuck, ed. Windward Crossings: A Treasury of Original Waterfowling Tales. LC 98-27791. (Illus.). 134p. 1998. 35.00 (*1-57223-191-2*) Willow Creek Pr.

Petrie, Chuck, et al. Fishing Wisconsin's Top 50 Muskie Lakes. (Illus.). 1992. 19.95 (*0-939314-52-5*) Fishing Hot.

Petrie, Chuck, ed. see Ford, Corey.

Petrie, Chuck, jt. ed. see Rulseh, Ted.

Petrie, Chuck, ed. & frwd. see Ozoga, John J.

Petrie, Constance C. Tom Petrie's Reminiscences of Early Queensland. (Orig.). pap. 18.95 (*0-7022-2383-2*, Pub. by Univ Queensland Pr) Intl Spec Bk.

Petrie, Dennis W. Ultimately Fiction: Design in Modern American Literary Biography. LC 80-84578. 250p. 1981. 49.95 (*0-911198-62-8*) Purdue U Pr.

Petrie, Dennis W., jt. auth. see Boggs, Joseph M.

Petrie, Donald A. The Prize Game: Lawful Looting on the High Seas in the Days of Fighting Sail. LC 99-11143. 1999. 24.95 (*1-55750-669-8*) Naval Inst Pr.

***Petrie, Doug.** Ring of Fire. (Buffy the Vampire Slayer Ser.). (Illus.). (YA). 2000. pap. 9.95 (*1-56971-482-7*) Dark Horse Comics.

Petrie, Duncan. The British Cinematographer. (Distributed for the British Film Institute Ser.). (Illus.). 176p. 1996. 49.95 (*0-85170-581-2*, Pub. by British Film Inst); pap. 22.50 (*0-85170-582-0*, Pub. by British Film Inst) Ind U Pr.

— Inside Stories. LC 97-123670. 1997. pap. text 16.95 (*0-85170-583-9*) U of Ill Pr.

— New Scholarship from BFI Research. LC 96-139034. 1996. pap. text 19.95 (*0-85170-520-0*, Pub. by British Film Inst) Ind U Pr.

— Television & the Household. LC 95-171595. 1995. pap. text 16.95 (*0-85170-504-9*, Pub. by British Film Inst) Ind U Pr.

Petrie, Duncan, ed. Cinema & the Realms of Enchantment: Lectures, Seminars & Essays by Marina Warner & Others. (Illus.). ix, 140p. 1994. pap. 16.95 (*0-85170-405-0*, Pub. by British Film Inst) Ind U Pr.

— New Questions of British Cinema Vol. 2: Working Papers. (Illus.). 128p. (C). 1993. pap. 16.95 (*0-85170-322-4*, Pub. by British Film Inst) Ind U Pr.

***Petrie, Edward M.** Handbook of Adhesives & Sealants. LC 99-35410. (Illus.). 700p. 1999. 99.95 (*0-07-049888-1*) McGraw-Hill Sch.

Petrie, Ferdinand. The Big Book of Painting Nature in Watercolor. (Illus.). 400p. 1990. pap. 29.95 (*0-8230-0499-6*) Watsn-Guptill.

— Drawing Landscapes in Pencil. (Illus.). 144p. 1992. reprint ed. pap. 16.95 (*0-8230-2646-9*) Watsn-Guptill.

Petrie, Flinders. Historical Scarabs. (Illus.). 1976. pap. 10.00 (*0-89005-122-4*) Ares.

— 3000 Decorative Patterns of the Ancient World for Craftsmen. LC 73-79745. (Illus.). 106p. 1974. reprint ed. 7.95 (*0-486-22986-6*) Dover.

Petrie, G. Tunis-Kairous-An & Carthage. 360p. 1985. 220.00 (*1-85077-067-0*, Pub. by Darf Pubs Ltd) St Mut.

Petrie, George L. Simulation of the Maneuverability of Inland Waterway Tows. LC VM0001.M52. (University of Michigan, Dept. of Naval Architecture & Marine Engineering, Report Ser.: No. 186). 93p. reprint ed. pap. 30.00 (*0-608-12983-6*, 202387100034) Bks Demand.

Petrie, Glen. The Branch-Bearers LC 75-328441. 322p. 1973. write for info. (*0-333-14830-4*) Macmillan.

— The Hampstead Poisonings. 1995. 38.00 (*0-86025-285-X*) Players Pr.

Petrie, Glen. Lucy & the Pirates. (Illus.). 32p. (J). (gr. k-4). 1996. bds. 14.95 (*1-896580-02-5*, Pub. by T1rad Bks) Tricycle Pr.

Petrie, Graham. Seahorse. LC 95-8673. 169p. 1996. 21.00 (*1-56947-077-4*) Soho Press.

— The Siege. LC 95-9076. 195p. 1996. 21.00 (*1-56947-076-6*) Soho Press.

Petrie, Graham & Dwyer, Ruth, eds. Before the Wall Came Down: Soviet & East European Filmakers Working in the West. 254p. (Orig.). (C). 1990. pap. text 26.50 (*0-8191-7859-4*); lib. bdg. 50.00 (*0-8191-7858-6*) U Pr of Amer.

Petrie, Graham, jt. auth. see Johnson, Vida T.

Petrie, Graham, ed. see Sterne, Laurence.

Petrie, Hugh G. The Dilemma of Enquiry & Learning. LC 81-3381. (Chicago Original Paperback Ser.). 1993. pap. text 20.00 (*0-226-66349-3*) U Ch Pr.

— The Dilemma of Enquiry & Learning. LC 81-3391. (Chicago Originals Ser.). (Illus.). 246p. reprint ed. pap. 76.30 (*0-608-09495-1*, 205429600005) Bks Demand.

Petrie, Hugh G., ed. Professionalization, Partnership, & Power: Building Professional Development Schools. LC 94-39617. (SUNY Series, Frontiers in Education). 310p. (C). 1995. text 59.50 (*0-7914-2605-X*); pap. text 19.95 (*0-7914-2606-8*) State U NY Pr.

Petrie, J. C., jt. ed. see Girdwood, Ronald H.

Petrie, J. Howard, jt. auth. see Burton, Paul F.

Petrie, Jennifer, jt. ed. see Barnes, John.

Petrie, Jennifer, tr. see De'Ricci, Catherine.

Petrie, Joanne & Petrie, Ronald G. How to Say Goodbye: Working Through Personal Grief. 2nd rev. ed. (Illus.). 175p. 1998. mass mkt. 14.00 (*1-886153-02-7*) One To Another.

Petrie, John, tr. see Weil, Simone.

Petrie, John N. American Neutrality in the 20th Century: The Impossible Dream. 168p. 1995. per. 6.50 (*0-16-061173-3*) USGPO.

Petrie, John N. American Neutrality in the 20th Century: The Impossible Dream. 155p. (C). 1996. reprint ed. pap. text 35.00 (*0-7881-3682-8*) DIANE Pub.

Petrie, John N., ed. Essays on Strategy, Vol. 11. (Illus.). 403p. (C). 1994. pap. text 50.00 (*0-7881-1426-3*) DIANE Pub.

— Essays on Strategy, Vol. 12. 415p. 1996. pap. text 40.00 (*0-7881-2897-3*) DIANE Pub.

Petrie, Keith J. & Weinman, John, eds. Perceptions of Health & Illness: Current Research & Applications. 320p. 1997. text 68.00 (*90-5702-102-1*, ECU55, Harwood Acad Pubs); pap. text 28.00 (*90-5702-103-X*, ECU20, Harwood Acad Pubs) Gordon & Breach.

Petrie, Lettie A. Adirondack Fairy Tales. LC 96-8038. (J). 1997. pap. 12.50 (*0-925168-53-X*) North Country.

Petrie, Marc. Then All Goes Blue. 71p. 1997. pap. 12.95 (*0-944870-10-4*) Pacific Writers Pr.

Petrie Method Inc., Staff. The Lose Weight Hypnosis Program. 1990. text 49.95 incl. audio (*0-13-540360-X*) P-H.

P

An Asterisk (*) at the beginning of an entry indicates that the title is appearing for the first time.

Petrie, Mildred M. Duck, Duck: The Different Duck. LC 87-80921. (Illus.). 40p. (J). 1987. 12.95 (0-9618241-0-7) Enfield Pubs.

Petrie, Mildred M., ed. The Prima Diner. 2nd ed. (Illus.). 172p. (Orig.). 1984. 7.95 (0-9605844-0-4, TX 727-394) Sarasota Opera.

Petrie, Pat. Communicating with Children & Adults: Interpersonal Skills for Early Years & Playwork. 2nd ed. (Illus.). 170p. 1996. pap. 24.95 (1-56593-821-6, 1614) Singular Publishing.

— Play & Care - Out of School. 252p. 1994. pap. 45.00 (0-11-701844-9, HM18449, Pub. by Statnry Office) Bernan Associates.

Petrie, Paul. Strange Gravity: Songs Physical & Metaphysical. LC 84-50796. (Illus.). 77p. (Orig.). 1984. 10.00 (0-930954-21-1) Tidal Pr.

— Strange Gravity: Songs Physical & Metaphysical. LC 84-50796. (Illus.). 77p. (Orig.). 1984. pap. 5.00 (0-930954-22-X) Tidal Pr.

Petrie, R. H., jt. ed. see Winn, H.

***Petrie, Rhona.** Dead Loss. 160p. 1999. 21.95 (0-7540-8552-X, Black Dagger) Chivers N Amer.

Petrie, Rhona. Thorne in the Flesh. 200p. 1996. 19.50 (0-7451-8678-5, Black Dagger) Chivers N Amer.

Petrie, Robin. Victorian Christmas. 1993. 10.98 incl. audio (1-56222-519-7, 94816C) Mel Bay.

Petrie, Roderic. The Autumn of Saint Francis of Assisi. LC 98-119802. 1997. pap. 6.95 (0-86716-305-4, B3054) St Anthony Mess Pr.

— Brother Leo Remembers Francis. 120p. 1999. pap. text 7.95 (0-86716-365-8) St Anthony Mess Pr.

Petrie, Ronald G., jt. auth. see Petrie, Joanne.

Petrie, Ruth. The Fall of Communism & the Rise of Nationalism. LC 97-185710. (Index Readers Ser.). 1997. 79.95 (0-304-33938-5) Continuum.

— Film & Censorship: The Index Reader. LC 97-160. (Film Studies). 256p. 1997. 75.00 (0-304-33936-9) Continuum.

Petrie, Ruth, ed. The Fall of Communism & the Rise of Nationalism. LC 97-185710. (Index Readers Ser.). 256p. 1997. pap. 27.50 (0-304-33939-3) Continuum.

Petrie, S. E., jt. ed. see Allen, Geoffrey.

Petrie, Sidney & Stone, Robert B. Helping Yourself with Autogenics. LC 82-14488. 205p. 1983. pap. 4.95 (0-13-387399-4, Parker Publishing Co) P-H.

Petrie, Stewart J. Letters & Journal of a Civil War Surgeon. LC 97-75508. 208p. 1998. 21.95 (1-57197-095-9) Pentland Pr.

Petrie, Susan W. Lost & Won. 140p. 1990. 15.95 (0-945942-06-0); pap. 9.95 (0-945942-07-9) Portmanteau Editions.

Petrie, Ted & Randall, John D. Transformation Groups on Manifolds. LC 84-5855. (Monographs & Textbooks in Pure & Applied Mathematics: No. 82). 280p. reprint ed. pap. 86.80 (0-7837-3384-4, 204334200008) Bks Demand.

Petrie, Ted, jt. auth. see Dovermann, Karl H.

Petrie, Trent. Achieving Personal & Academic Success. 1996. pap. text 32.49 (1-56870-255-8) RonJon Pub.

Petrie, W. M. Funeral Furniture & Stone Vessels. (Petrie Egyptian Collection & Excavations). 1937. reprint ed. 49.95 (0-85668-036-2, Pub. by Aris & Phillips) David Brown.

— Historical Scarabs. Obaba, Al I., ed. (Illus.). 100p. 1990. pap. text 8.95 (0-916157-66-0) African Islam Miss Pubns.

— Naukratis I. (IGA VI Ser.: No. 1). (GRE., Illus.). vi, 98p. (C). 1992. text 35.00 (0-89005-508-4) Ares.

— The Religion of Ancient Egypt. (African Heritage Classical Research Studies). 98p. reprint ed. 20.00 (0-938818-38-4) ECA Assoc.

— The Revolutions of Civilization. LC 73-158202. (World History Ser.: No. 48). (C). 1972. reprint ed. lib. bdg. 75.00 (0-8383-1268-3) M S G Haskell Hse.

Petrie, W. M. Flinders. Egyptian Decorative Art. LC 99-42980. 138p. 2000. pap. text 7.95 (0-486-40907-4) Dover.

— Egyptian Tales. LC 99-44537. 192p. 2000. pap. text 6.95 (0-486-40908-2) Dover.

***Petrie, W. M. Flinders.** The Pyramids & Temples of Gizeh. 260p. 2000. text 212.50 (0-7103-0709-8) Col U Pr.

Petrie, William. Guide to Orchids of North America. (Illus.). 128p. 1981. pap. 9.95 (0-88839-089-0) Hancock House.

Petrie, William & Flinders, Matthew. Egyptian Tales, 2 vols. in 1. 1972. 30.95 (0-88143-095-1) Ayer.

Petrie, William F. Ancient Egypt & Ancient Israel. 150p. 1982. pap. 15.00 (0-89005-337-5) Ares.

— Egyptian Tales, 2 vols. in 1. LC 68-56524. (First & Second Ser.). (Illus.). 1969. reprint ed. 30.00 (0-405-08850-7, Pub. by Blom Pubns) Ayer.

— Egyptian Tales, 2 vols., 1 bk., 1. LC 68-56524. (First & Second Ser.). (Illus.). 1972. reprint ed. 18.95 (0-405-08851-5, Pub. by Blom Pubns) Ayer.

— Egyptian Tales, 2 vols., 1 bk., 2. LC 68-56524. (First & Second Ser.). (Illus.). 1972. reprint ed. 19.95 (0-405-08852-3, Pub. by Blom Pubns) Ayer.

— Religion & Conscience in Ancient Egypt. LC 72-83176. 1972. reprint ed. 26.95 (0-405-08854-X) Ayer.

— Ten Years' Digging in Egypt. (Illus.). 201p. 1989. pap. 20.00 (0-89005-107-0) Ares.

Petrie, William L. & Stover, Douglas E. Bibliography of the Frederick Douglass Library at Cedar Hall. (Illus.). 496p. (Orig.). 1995. pap. 30.00 (1-887188-00-2) Silesia Cos.

Petrie, William M. Egyptian Decorative Art. LC 72-8317. (Illus.). 1978. reprint ed. 21.95 (0-405-08849-3, Pub. by Blom Pubns) Ayer.

— A History of Egypt: During the XVIIth & XVIIIth Dynasties, 1896, with Additons to 1904, Vol. 2. 4th ed. LC 73-39204. (Select Bibliographies Reprint Ser.). (Illus.). 1977. reprint ed. 35.95 (0-88143-091-9) Ayer.

— A History of Egypt: From the Earliest Kings to the XVIth Dynasty, Vol. 1. rev. ed. LC 70-39203. (Select Bibliographies Reprint Ser.). (Illus.). 1977. reprint ed. 35.95 (0-88143-090-0) Ayer.

— A History of Egypt: From the XIXth to the XXXth Dynasties, Vol. 3. LC 77-39205. (Select Bibliographies Reprint Ser.). 1977. reprint ed. 39.95 (0-88143-092-7) Ayer.

— Methods & Aims in Archaeology. LC 68-56525. 1972. reprint ed. 18.95 (0-405-08853-1, Pub. by Blom Pubns) Ayer.

— Seventy Years in Archaeology. LC 72-88921. 307p. 1969. reprint ed. lib. bdg. 38.50 (0-8371-2241-4, PESA, Greenwood Pr) Greenwood.

Petrik, James. Descartes' Theory of the Will. LC 91-3485. 1994. text 35.00 (0-89341-678-9, Longwood Academic) Hollowbrook.

***Petrik, James M.** Evil Beyond Belief. LC 00-21347. (Contemporary Perspectives on Philosophy of Religion Ser.). 208p. 2000. text 56.95 (0-7656-0282-2) M E Sharpe.

Petrik, John F. Academic Opportunities: Scholarships, Fellowships, International Study, Undergraduate Research, Post-Baccalaureate Education & Experimental Learning: What They Are, How to Find Them, How to Pursue Them, & What to Do with Them Once You've Got Them. 1997. 30.00 (0-938609-00-9) Graduate Group.

Petrik-Ott, A. J. The Pteridophytes of Kansas, Nebraska, South Dakota & North Dakota, U. S. A. Nova Hedwigia Beiheft, No. 61. 1979. lib. bdg. 80.00 (3-7682-5461-5) Lubrecht & Cramer.

Petrik, Paula. Creating & Designing Multimedia with Director 5.0. LC 97-7763. 522p. (C). 1997. pap. text 63.00 (0-13-528985-8) P-H.

Petrik, Paula, jt. ed. see West, Elliott.

***Petrikin, Chris, et al, eds.** Variety Power Players 2000: Movers & Shakers, Power Brokers & Career Makers in Hollywood. LC 99-46974. 1999. pap. 16.95 (0-399-52569-6, Perigee Bks) Berkley Pub.

Petrikin, Jonathan S., ed. Environmental Justice. LC 94-28350. (At Issue Ser.). 128p. (C). 1994. pap. text 11.20 (1-56510-264-9) Greenhaven.

— Male - Female Roles: Opposing Viewpoints. LC 94-4975. (Opposing Viewpoints Ser.). (Illus.). 312p. (YA). (gr. 10 up). 1995. pap. text 16.20 (1-56510-175-8); lib. bdg. 26.20 (1-56510-174-X) Greenhaven.

Petrikin, Jonathan S., jt. ed. see Cozic, Charles P.

Petrikkos, G. L. & Koenig, W., eds. Meeting the Challenge of Community-Acquired Respiratory Tract Infections: The Role of Cephalosporins. (Journal: Respiration: Vol. 60, Suppl. 1, 1993). (Illus.). vi, 58p. 1993. pap. 28.00 (3-8055-5754-X) S Karger.

***Petrikovsky, Boris M.** Fetal Disorders: A Multidisciplinary Approach. LC 98-6113. 320p. 1998. 110.00 (0-471-19152-3) Wiley.

Petrila, John, jt. auth. see Otto, Randy K.

Petrila, John, jt. ed. see Levin, Bruce L.

Petrilli, Michael J., jt. ed. see Finn, Chestere E., Jr.

Petrilli, Ralph S. Kentucky Family Law with Juvenile Court Practice, 2 vols.. Set. 2nd ed. 1988. 150.00 (0-87084-728-7) Anderson Pub Co.

Petrilli, Susan, ed. see Rossi-Landi, Ferruccio.

Petrilli, Susan, ed. & tr. see Ponzio, Augusto.

Petrilli, Susan, tr. see Deledalle, Gerard.

Petrilli, Susan, tr. see Fano, Giorgio.

Petrillo, Alan M. British Service Rifles & Carbines 1888-1900. LC 94-152823. (British Firearms Ser.: Vol. 4). (Illus.). 72p. (Orig.). 1994. pap. 11.95 (1-880677-05-9) Excalibur AZ.

— Cartridge Carbines of the British Army. LC 99-164908. (British Firearms Ser.: Vol. 7). (Illus.). 72p. 1998. pap. 11.95 (1-880677-13-X) Excalibur AZ.

— The Lee Enfield Number Four Rifles. (British Firearms Ser.: Vol. 1). (Illus.). 64p. (Orig.). 1992. pap. 10.95 (1-880677-00-8) Excalibur AZ.

— The Lee Enfield Number One Rifles. (British Firearms Ser.: Vol. 2). (Illus.). 64p. (Orig.). 1992. pap. 10.95 (1-880677-01-6) Excalibur AZ.

— The Number 5 Jungle Carbine. (British Firearms Ser.: Vol. 5). (Illus.). 32p. (Orig.). 1994. pap. 7.95 (1-880677-06-7) Excalibur AZ.

Petrillo, Anthony J., jt. auth. see Hall, Betty L.

Petrillo, Daniel J. Robert F. Kennedy. (World Leaders Past & Present Ser.). (Illus.). 120p. (Orig.). (YA). (gr. 5 up). 1989. lib. bdg. 19.95 (1-55546-840-3) Chelsea Hse.

***Petrillo, Denny.** Commentary on I & II Timothy & Titus. unabridged ed. 210p. 1998. pap. 9.95 (0-89137-150-8, 71508) Quality Pubns.

Petrillo, F. Charles. Albert Lewis: The Bear Creek Lumber & Ice King - The Bear Creek Ice Company. LC 98-91186. (Illus.). 250p. 1998. pap. 14.95 (1-57502-720-8, PO2023) Morris Pubng.

— Anthracite & Slackwater: The North Branch Canal 1828-1901. LC 86-26872. 1987. 28.75 (0-930973-03-8); pap. 16.25 (0-930973-04-6) H M Historical.

Petrillo, Lisa, jt. auth. see Cantlupe, Joe.

Petrillo, Maureen L. Creating Technology Awareness. Boulais, Katina, ed. (Illus.). 84p. 1994. ring bd. write for info. (0-614-00952-9) E&L Instru.

Petrillo, Michael A., et al. The Law Enforcement Manual. 3rd rev. ed. 341p. 1999. ring bd. 39.95 (1-885682-11-5) Princeton Educ.

Petrillo, Raymond, tr. see Cecchetti, Giovanni.

Petrillo, Robert J. The Complete Arizona Contractors Study Guide-Electrical. 1990. write for info. (0-318-68031-9) ACS Assocs Pub.

Petrillo, Robert J., ed. see Holish, James A.

Petrin, Helene. French - English Vocabulary of Collective Agreements. (ENG & FRE.). 97p. 1991. pap. 29.95 (0-8288-9409-4) Fr & Eur.

Petrin, Helene, ed. Supershell America Past Present. 4th ed. 1997. pap. text 19.33 (0-673-55582-8) P-H.

Petrin, Ronald A. French Canadians in Massachusetts Politics, 1885-1915: Ethnicity & Political Pragmatism. LC 88-64126. 234p. 1990. 40.00 (0-944190-07-3) Balch IES Pr.

Petrin, Tea. Industrial Policy Supporting Economic Transition in Central-Eastern Europe: Lessons from Slovenia. LC 95-76429. (Policy Papers in International Affairs: No. 43). 60p. (Orig.). 1995. pap. text 6.95 (0-87725-543-1) U of Cal IAS.

Petrina, Bernard. Workforce Renewal: Increasing the Quality & Quantity of Work. Carrigan, Chris, ed. LC 93-73205. (Fifty-Minute Ser.). (Illus.). 95p. (Orig.). 1994. pap. 10.95 (1-56052-270-4) Crisp Pubns.

Petrina, Bernard H. How to Sell at a Trade Show. (Orig.). 1990. pap. text 59.95 (0-940799-02-2) Exec Mgmt Renew Prog.

— Motivating People to Care. rev. ed. Ickes, James W., ed. 140p. 1989. pap. text 49.00 (0-940799-01-4) Exec Mgmt Renew Prog.

Petrina, D. Y. Mathematical Foundations of Quantum Statistical Mechanics: Continuous Systems. LC 94-39303. (Mathematics Physics Studies: Vol. 15). 1995. text 250.00 (0-7923-3258-X) Kluwer Academic.

Petrina, D. Y., et al. Mathematical Foundations of Classical Statistical Mechanics, Vol. 6. xviii, 338p. 1989. text 383.00 (2-88124-681-8) Gordon & Breach.

Petrina, John. Art Work: How Produced, How Reproduced. LC 70-107733. (Essay Index Reprint Ser.). 1977. 20.95 (0-8369-1531-3) Ayer.

Petrina, K., tr. see Cercignani, Carlo, et al.

Petrinec, J. N., Jr., ed. Recertification & Stress Classification Issues: Proceedings of the Pressure Vessels & Piping Conference, Minneapolis, MN, 1994. LC 94-71356. (PVP Ser.: Vol. 277). 169p. 1994. pap. 50.00 (0-7918-1350-9) ASME.

Petrinec, John J., Jr., et al, eds. Developments in Pressure Vessels & Piping - 1995. LC 94-71746. (Proceedings of the 1995 ASME/JSME Pressure Vessels & Piping Conference Ser.: PVP-Vol. 301). 260p. 1995. 110.00 (0-7918-1332-0, H00964) ASME.

Petrini, Carlo, jt. ed. see Cernilli, Daniele.

Petrini, Carlo, ed. see Rosso, Gambero.

Petrini, Elisa, ed. see Burnett, Sarah & Octopus, Conran.

Petrini, Joann & March of Dimes Birth Defects Foundation Staff. Birth Defects & Infant Mortality: A National & Regional Profile 1996. LC 96-33556. (Statbook Technical Report Ser.). 1996. write for info. (0-86525-072-3) March of Dimes.

Petrini, John, jt. ed. see Sivak, Michael V., Jr.

Petrini, Julie O. & Robins, Lawrence R. Obtaining, Using & Protecting Trademarks. Hulecki, Anne W., ed. LC 97-70623. 96p. 1997. pap. text 65.00 (1-57589-060-7) Mass CLE.

Petrini, Mark. The Child & the Hero: Coming of Age in Catullus & Vergil. LC 96-25346. 152p. (C). 1997. text 39.50 (0-472-10460-8, 10460) U of Mich Pr.

Petrini, Orlando & Horak, Egon, eds. Taxonomic Monographs of Agaricales. (Bibliotheca Mycologica: Vol. 159). (GER., Illus.). vi, 236p. 1995. 65.00 (3-443-59061-6, Pub. by Gebruder Borntraeger) Balogh.

Petrini, Orlando & Ouellette, Guillemond B., eds. Host Wall Alterations by Parasitic Fungi. LC 94-78283. (Symposium Ser.). (Illus.). viii, 160p. (Orig.). 1994. pap. 39.00 (0-89054-168-X) Am Phytopathol Soc.

Petrini, Orlando, et al. Taxonomic Monographs of Agaricales II. (Bibliotheca Mycologica: Vol. 168). (GER., Illus.). vi, 152p. 1997. 48.00 (3-443-59070-5, Pub. by Gebruder Borntraeger) Balogh.

Petrini, Orlando, ed. see Laursen, Gary A.

Petrini, V. & Save, M., eds. Protection of the Architectural Heritage Against Earthquakes. (CISM International Center for Mechanical Sciences Ser.: Vol. 359). (Illus.). ix, 325p. 1996. pap. 87.00 (3-211-82805-2) Spr-Verlag.

Petrino, Bob & Mouat, Marty. Winning Football with the Option Package Offense. LC 85-21420. 206p. (C). 1985. text 27.95 (0-13-960931-8, Busn) P-H.

Petrino, Elizabeth A. Emily Dickinson & Her Contemporaries: Women's Verse in America, 1820-1885. LC 97-44600. (Illus.). 252p. 1998. pap. 19.95 (0-87451-907-1); text 40.00 (0-87451-838-5) U Pr of New Eng.

Petrinovich, L. Human Evolution, Reproduction & Morality. LC 95-6514. (Illus.). 356p. (C). 1995. text 54.50 (0-306-44939-0, Kluwer Plenum) Kluwer Academic.

***Petrinovich, Lewis.** The Cannibal Within. LC 99-57940. 240p. 2000. pap. text 20.95 (0-202-02048-7); lib. bdg. 41.95 (0-202-02047-9) Aldine de Gruyter.

Petrinovich, Lewis. Human Evolution, Reproduction, & Morality. LC 98-24298. (Illus.). 355p. 1998. pap. text 20.00 (0-262-66143-8, Bradford Bks) MIT Pr.

— Living & Dying Well. (Critical Issues in Social Justice Ser.). (Illus.). 374p. 1996. 54.50 (0-306-45171-9, Kluwer Plenum) Kluwer Academic.

— Living & Dying Well. LC 98-24299. (Illus.). 374p. 1998. pap. text 20.00 (0-262-66142-X, Bradford Bks) MIT Pr.

Petrinovich, Lewis F. Darwinian Dominion: Animal Welfare & Human Interests. LC 98-5036. (Illus.). 448p. 1998. 45.00 (0-262-16178-8, Bradford Bks) MIT Pr.

***Petriska, Thomas W.** The Kingdom of Our Father: Interviews wih Today's Visionaries about the First Person of the Trinity & Their Mystical Experiences with Him. 350p. 1999. pap. 14.95 (1-891903-18-7) St Andrew Prodns.

Petrisko, Thomas W. Call of the Ages. LC 95-69033. 544p. 1995. pap. 11.95 (1-882972-59-7, 3451) Queenship Pub.

***Petrisko, Thomas W.** The Face of the Father: An Exclusive Interview with Barbara Centilli Concerning Her Revelations & Visions of God the Father. (Illus.). 124p. 2000. pap. 8.95 (1-891903-19-5) St Andrew Prodns.

Petrisko, Thomas W. False Prophets of Today: Can Fear & Peace Co-Exist in Our Hearts? 84p. 1997. pap. 4.95 (1-891903-02-0) St Andrew Prodns.

— The Fatima Prophecies: At the Doorstep of the World. (Illus.). 458p. 1998. pap. 14.95 (1-891903-06-3) St Andrew Prodns.

— For the Soul of the Family. LC 96-71244. 336p. (Orig.). 1996. pap. 9.95 (1-882972-90-2, 3452) Queenship Pub.

***Petrisko, Thomas W.** Glory to the Father: A Look at the Mystical Life of Georgette Faniel. (Illus.). 84p. 1999. pap. 6.95 (1-891903-17-9) St Andrew Prodns.

Petrisko, Thomas W. In God's Hands: The Miraculous Story of Little Audrey Santo. (Illus.). 224p. 1997. pap. 12.95 (1-891903-04-7) St Andrew Prodns.

***Petrisko, Thomas W.** Inside Heaven & Hell: What History, Theology & Mystics Tell Us about the After Life. (Illus.). 232p. 2000. pap. 12.95 (1-891903-23-3) St Andrew Prodns.

Petrisko, Thomas W. The Last Crusade. 72p. 1996. pap. 4.95 (1-891903-01-2) St Andrew Prodns.

***Petrisko, Thomas W.** The Miracle of the Illumination of All Consciences. (Illus.). 176p. 2000. pap. 10.95 (1-891903-25-X) St Andrew Prodns.

Petrisko, Thomas W. Mother of the Secret. LC 97-68889. 328p. (Orig.). 1997. pap. text 9.95 (1-57918-003-5, 3453) Queenship Pub.

— Por el Alma de la Familia. Estrada, Rosa M., tr. (SPA., Illus.). 316p. (Orig.). 1997. pap. 9.95 (1-57918-006-X, 3452S) Queenship Pub.

— The Prophecy of Daniel: A Brief Look at How an Ancient Prophecys Fulfillment Is Still Awaited Today. 54p. 1997. pap. 4.95 (1-891903-03-9) St Andrew Prodns.

— St. Joseph & the Triumph of the Saints. (Illus.). 328p. 1998. pap. 10.95 (1-891903-08-X) St Andrew Prodns.

— The Sorrow, the Sacrifice & the Triumph. 320p. 1995. pap. 12.00 (0-684-80388-7, Touchstone) S&S Trade Pap.

— El Sufrimiento, el Sacrificio, el Triunfo los Ojos del Alma. LC 96-197344.Tr. of Sorrow, the Sacrifice, the Triumph. (SPA.). 384p. 1996. per. 12.00 (0-684-81555-9, Libros) S&S Trade Pap.

***Petrison, Lisa A.** Database Marketing Strategy: Course Packet Materials. 216p. 1999. pap. write for info. (1-58692-000-6) Copyright Mgmt.

Petriu, Emil. Instrumentation & Measurement: Technology & Applications. LC 97-44564. (IEEE Technology Update Ser.). 1997. write for info. (0-7803-4268-2) Inst Electrical.

Petriu, Emil, jt. ed. see Archibald, Colin.

Petrivelli, Patricia, jt. auth. see Halliday, Jan.

Petriwsky, Eugene, jt. auth. see Jacobs, Sonia.

Petrizzi, Jennifer A. & Moore, Mordecai. Shalom New York '98: Jewish Programming Guide for Young Adults in Manhattan. Gootnick, Jen, ed. LC 98-147030. (Illus.). (Orig.). 1997. pap. 9.95 (0-9661659-0-X) Shalom Ink.

Petrizzi, Michael J., jt. auth. see Shahady, Edward J.

Petrjanosova. Peniaze - Co S Nimi? (SLO.). 224p. 1996. write for info. (80-08-00992-6, Pub. by Slov Pegagog Naklad) IBD Ltd.

Petro, Beth A. The Book of Kombucha: Unlocking the Secrets of the 2000 Year Old Chinese "Tea Mushroom" LC 95-61972. (Illus.). 160p. (Orig.). 1996. pap. 11.95 (1-56975-049-1) Ulysses Pr.

Petro, Jane A., jt. auth. see Carter, Albert H.

Petro, Jane A., jt. auth. see Carter, Albert Howard.

Petro, Jane A., jt. auth. see Nicosia, Joan E.

Petro, L., ed. see SME Staff.

Petro, Michael T., Jr. How to Protect Yourself, Home & Family from Violent Criminals: A Family Guide for Practical Self-Protection Against Robbers, Burglars, Rapists & Other Violent Criminals. LC 95-92798. 323p. 1996. pap. 24.95 (0-9650411-0-7) Petro Pubns.

— Your Complete Guide to Self-Protection Against Violent Criminals: Protect Yourself, Home & Family Against Robbers, Burglars, Rapists & Other Violent Criminals. LC 95-92799. 293p. 1996. pap. 38.95 (0-9650411-1-5) Petro Pubns.

Petro, Nicolai N. The Rebirth of Russian Democracy: An Interpretation of Political Culture. LC 94-45431. (Illus.). 240p. (C). 1995. text 44.50 (0-674-75001-2) HUP.

— The Rebirth of Russian Democracy: An Interpretation of Political Culture. (Illus.). 240p. 1997. reprint ed. pap. 17.50 (0-674-75002-0) HUP.

Petro, Nicolai N. & Rubinstein, Alvin Z. Russian Foreign Policy. LC 96-16348. 347p. (C). 1997. pap. text 50.00 (0-673-99636-0) Addson-Wesley Educ.

Petro, Pamela. The Newport & Narragansett Bay Book: A Complete Guide with Block Island. 2nd rev. ed. LC 97-32467. (Great Destinations Ser.). (Illus.). 320p. 1998. pap. 17.95 (0-936399-93-7) Berkshire Hse.

Petro, Patrice. Joyless Streets: Women & Melodramatic Representation in Weimar Germany. LC 88-22684. (Illus.). 271p. reprint ed. pap. 84.10 (0-608-09573-7, 205437500006) Bks Demand.

Petro, Patrice, ed. Fugitive Images: From Photography to Video. LC 93-46701. (Theories of Contemporary Culture Ser.). 304p. (C). 1995. 35.00 (0-253-34428-X); pap. 15.95 (0-253-20890-4) Ind U Pr.

Petro, Peter. A History of Slovak Literature. LC 96-154378. 216p. 1995. 55.00 (0-7735-1311-6, Pub. by McG-Queens Univ Pr) CUP Services.

— A History of Slovak Literature. LC PG5401.P481995. 176p. 1997. pap. text 19.95 (0-7735-1402-3, Pub. by McG-Queens Univ Pr) CUP Services.

— Modern Satire: Four Studies. (De Proprietatibus Litterarum, Ser. Minor: No. 27). 162p. 1982. 93.10 (90-279-3180-1) Mouton.

Petro, Peter, tr. see Simecka, Martin M.

Petro, Robert J. & Finch, Theresa A. The Book of Secrets: The Way to Wealth & Success. LC 96-47659. 1997. 18.00 (0-06-251478-4, Pub. by Harper SF); pap. 11.00 (0-06-251497-0) Harper SF.

An Asterisk (*) at the beginning of an entry indicates that the title is appearing for the first time.

Petro, Sandy. Spice up Your Life with Joy. (Women's Inductive Bible Study Ser.). 96p. 1990. pap. text 6.50 (*0-89693-817-4*, 6-1817, Victor Bks) Chariot Victor.

Petro, Sharon. The Tennis Drill Book. LC 84-47518. (Illus.). 128p. (Orig.). 1986. pap. 14.95 (*0-88011-224-7*, PPET0224) Human Kinetics.

Petro, Steve. Fremont Canyon & Dome Rock. (Classic Rock Climbs Ser.: Vol. 19). (Illus.). (Orig.). 1997. pap. 10.95 (*1-57540-044-8*) Falcon Pub Inc.

Petro, Sylvester. The Labor Policy of the Free Society. LC 57-6822. 352p. reprint ed. pap. 109.20 (*0-8357-9524-1*, 201236800081) Bks Demand.

— Power Unlimited: The Corruption of Union Leadership. LC 79-4432. (McClellan Committee Hearings). 323p. 1979. reprint ed. lib. bdg. 35.00 (*0-313-20898-0*, PEPU, Greenwood Pr) Greenwood.

Petrobelli, Pierluigi. Music in the Theater: Essays on Verdi & Other Composers. Parker, Roger, tr. LC 93-3440. (Opera Studies). 208p. (C). 1994. text 45.00 (*0-691-09134-X*, Pub. by Princeton U Pr) Cal Prin Full Svc.

Petrocelli, A. W., ed. see Volnov, Ilya I.

Petrocelli, Daniel M. Triumph of Justice: Closing the Book on the Simpson Saga. LC 98-6251. 304p. 1998. 25.95 (*0-609-60170-9*) Crown Pub Group.

Petrocelli, Richard. Traumatic Brain Injury, 1998 Cumulative Supplement. 120p. 1998. write for info. (*0-327-00847-4*, 66586212) LEXIS Pub.

Petrocelli, Richard W., et al. Traumatic Brain Injury: Evaluation & Litigation. 643p. 1994. 95.00 (*1-55834-172-2*, 65861-10, MICHIE) LEXIS Pub.

Petrocelli, Sam R., jt. ed. see Rand, Gary M.

Petrocelli, William & Repa, Barbara K. Sexual Harassment on the Job: What It Is & How to Stop It. 4th ed. LC 98-24164. 320p. 1999. 18.95 (*0-87337-484-3*) Nolo com.

***Petrocelly, K. L.** Facilities Evaluation Handbook: Safety, Fire Protection & Environmental Compliance. 2nd ed. 1999. 87.00 (*0-13-026220-X*) P-H.

Petrocelly, K. L. Facilities Evaluation Manual: Safety, Fire Protection & Environmental Compliance. (Illus.). 271p. 1991. 74.00 (*0-88173-114-5*, 0286) Fairmont Pr.

— Maintenance Computerization Handbook. LC 92-40191. 186p. 1993. 74.00 (*0-88173-150-1*) Fairmont Pr.

— Physical Plant Operations Handbook. (Illus.). 216p. 1991. 69.00 (*0-88173-054-8*, 0180) Fairmont Pr.

***Petrocelly, K. L. & Thumann, Albert.** Facilities Evaluation Handbook: Safety, Fire Protection & Environmental Compliance. 2nd ed. LC 99-32489. 295p. 1999. 87.00 (*0-88173-322-9*) Fairmont Pr.

Petrocelly, Kenneth L. Before You Build: One Hundred Home-Building Pitfalls to Avoid. (Illus.). 224p. 1991. 25.95 (*0-8306-7712-7*, 3712); pap. 15.95 (*0-8306-3712-5*) McGraw-Hill Prof.

— Before You Build: One Hundred Home Building Pitfalls to Avoid. 1991. 16.95 (*0-07-049662-5*) McGraw.

— Build it Right: Supervising the Construction of Your Home. 208p. 1990. 24.95 (*0-07-156851-4*) McGraw.

— Build it Right Supervising Company. (Illus.). 208p. 1990. 24.95 (*0-8306-7433-0*, 3433); pap. 14.95 (*0-8306-3433-9*) McGraw-Hill Prof.

— Commercial & Institutional Maintenance Management. LC 94-22856. 240p. 1994. 78.00 (*0-88173-184-6*) Fairmont Pr.

— Managing Physical Plant Operations. LC 93-35434. 312p. 1993. 74.00 (*0-88173-160-9*) Fairmont Pr.

— Stationary Engineering Handbook. LC 88-45795. 300p. 1989. text 67.00 (*0-88173-078-5*) Fairmont Pr.

Petrocelly, Kenneth L., jt. auth. see Fairmont Press Staff.

Petrochenko, Nina & Zagorskaia, Aleksandra. English Russian Defining Dictionary of Business. (ENG & RUS.). 112p. (C). 1992. text 100.00 (*0-569-24719-5*, Pub. by Collets) St Mut.

Petrochenko, P. F. Defining Dictionary of Business Commerce & Marketing. 64p. (C). 1992. text 100.00 (*0-569-07110-0*, Pub. by Collets) St Mut.

Petrochenkov, Valerii. Tvorcheskaia Sud'ba Panteleimona Romanova. Krashoshchekova, Elena, ed. LC 88-10990. (Russian Ser.). 208p. (Orig.). 1988. pap. 14.50 (*1-55779-002-7*) Hermitage Pubs.

Petrochenkov, Valery. Osen' Veka. LC 82-84747. (RUS., Illus.). 152p. (Orig.). 1983. 8.00 (*0-911971-00-9*) Effect Pub.

— Sobesednik (Conversationalist) Poems. LC 92-81982. (Illus.). 160p. (Orig.). 1992. pap. 28.00 (*0-911971-77-7*) Effect Pub.

Petrocholis, George A. Foreign Direct Investment & the Development Process: The Case of Greece. (Illus.). 208p. 1989. text 87.95 (*0-566-07108-8*, Pub. by Avebry) Ashgate Pub Co.

Petrocik, John R. Party Coalitions: Realignment & the Decline of the New Deal Party System. LC 80-22212. (Illus.). 224p. reprint ed. pap. 69.50 (*0-608-09496-X*, 205429700005) Bks Demand.

— Party Coalitions: Realignments & the Decline of the New Deal Party System. LC 80-22212. (Illus.). 1993. pap. text 10.00 (*0-226-66378-7*) U Ch Pr.

— Political Parties. (C). 1999. pap. text 36.00 (*0-15-502963-0*, Pub. by Harcourt Coll Pubs) Harcourt.

Petrocokino, Paul. The Heart of It All. 1983. 2.95 (*0-901269-70-0*) Grosvenor USA.

Petrof, Stephen, jt. auth. see Lawless, Gary.

Petroff, Elizabeth. Consolation of the Blessed. (Illus.). 224p. (C). 1980. 12.95 (*0-686-32835-3*) Alta Gaia Bks.

Petroff, Elizabeth A. Body & Soul: Essays on Medieval Women & Mysticism. 256p. (C). 1994. pap. text 21.95 (*0-19-508455-1*) OUP.

Petroff, Elizabeth A., ed. Medieval Women's Visionary Literature. 416p. (Orig.). 1986. pap. text 26.95 (*0-19-503712-X*) OUP.

Petroff, F. & Gijs, M. A. Magnetic Ultra Thin Films, Multilayers & Surfaces: Proceedings of Symposium E of the 1996 E-MRS Spring Conference, Strasbourg, France, June 4-7, 1996. LC 98-149214. 550p. 1997. 327.00 (*0-444-20503-9*) Elsevier.

Petroff, Ivan, et al. Census of the United States: Tenth Decennial Census, 1880: The Newspaper & Periodical Press . . . Alaska: Its Population, Industries, & Resources . . . The Seal Islands of Alaska . . . Ship-Building Industry in the United States . . ., 22 vols., Vol. 8, Series 31. LC 07-18862. (Illus.). 1120p. 1991. reprint ed. lib. bdg. 575.00 incl. fiche (*0-88354-431-8*) N Ross.

Petroff, J. K., jt. ed. see Sheley, Roger L.

Petroff, John N. Handbook of MRP II & JIT: Strategies for Total Manufacturing Control. LC 93-16364. 480p. (C). 1993. text 69.95 (*0-13-374158-3*) P-H.

Petroff, Lillian. Sojourners & Settlers: The Macedonian Community in Toronto in 1940. (Multicultural History Society of Ontario Ser.). (Illus.). 256p. 1995. text 50.00 (*0-8020-0452-0*); pap. text 19.95 (*0-8020-7240-2*) U of Toronto Pr.

Petroff, Pierre M., ed. see Demeester, Piet.

***Petroff, Serge P.** Remembering a Forgotten War: Civil War in Eastern European Russia & Siberia, 1918-1920. 260p. 2000. text 30.00 (*0-88033-458-4*) Col U Pr.

Petrofske, Mary T. Recollections of Caernarvon Township: A Portrait of a Lancaster County Town. LC 93-33392. (Illus.). 304p. 1993. 35.00 (*0-914659-67-7*) Phoenix Pub.

Petroianu, A., jt. auth. see Handschin, E.

Petroleo Internacional Staff. Glossary of the Petroleum Industry. 2nd ed. (ENG & SPA.). 378p. 1982. pap. 95.00 (*0-8288-0706-X*, S 50548) Fr & Eur.

Petroleum Equipment Institute Staff, ed. Petroleum Equipment Institute Safe Practices, a Compilation, 1984-1994. 92p. 1995. pap. 30.00 (*0-9642638-1-5*) Petrol Equip.

— Petroleum Equipment Institute Safety Letters, a Compilation, 1980-1994. 96p. (Orig.). 1995. pap. 30.00 (*0-9642638-0-7*) Petrol Equip.

Petroleum Extension Service Staff. Hydrogen Sulfide in Production Operations. 2nd ed. LC 95-52748. (Oil & Gas Production Ser.). (Illus.). 60p. (Orig.). 1996. pap. text 20.00 (*0-88698-176-X*, 3.30320) PETEX.

Petroleum Industry Symposium Staff. History of the Petroleum Industry Symposium. LC 90-102497. (American Association of Petroleum Geologists Guidebook Ser.). (Illus.). 88p. 1989. reprint ed. pap. 30.00 (*0-608-07371-7*, 206759900009) Bks Demand.

Petroleum Mechanical Engineering Conference & Work. Petroleum Mechanical Engineering Conference & Workshop: Presented at the 1979 Petroleum Mechanical Engineering Conference & Workshop, Tulsa, Oklahoma, October 28-30, 1979. Collier, S. L., ed. LC 79-54866. (Illus.). 120p. reprint ed. pap. 37.20 (*0-8357-2892-7*, 203912800011) Bks Demand.

Petroleum Mechanical Engineering Workshop & Confer. Refinery-Petrochemical Plant Construction & Maintenance, Plant Operation & Control, Noise & Pollution Control in Refiner-Petrochemical Plants: A Workbook for Engineers: Presented at 38th Petroleum Mechanical Engineering Workshop & Conference, September 12-14, 1982, Philadelphia, Pennsylvania. Reagan, J. E., ed. LC 82-228729. (Illus.). 154p. reprint ed. pap. 47.80 (*0-8357-2845-5*, 203908000010) Bks Demand.

Petroleum Products & Lubricants committee D-2. Multi-Cylinder Test Sequences for Evaluating Automotive Engine Oils, Pt. 3: Sequence V-D - STP 315H. LC 83-68369. 146p. 1991. 20.00 (*0-8031-0238-0*, STP315H) ASTM.

Petron, Angela. The Forgotten Duchess. 199p. (C). 1989. text 49.00 (*1-872795-01-3*, Pub. by Pentland Pr) St Mut.

— The Laird's Casket. large type ed. (Linford Romance Library). 1991. pap. 16.99 (*0-7089-6985-2*) Ulverscroft.

— Prelude to Happiness. large type ed. (Linford Romance Library). 288p. 1989. pap. 16.99 (*0-7089-6649-7*, Linford) Ulverscroft.

— Villa of Singing Water. large type ed. (Linford Romance Library). 288p. 1988. pap. 16.99 (*0-7089-6537-7*, Linford) Ulverscroft.

***Petron, Ed.** Linux Essential Reference. (Essential Reference Ser.). 400p. 1999. pap. 37.95 (*0-7357-0852-5*) New Riders Pub.

Petrone. Le Satiricon. (FRE.). 1972. pap. 10.95 (*0-7859-3983-0*) Fr & Eur.

Petrone, Gerard S. Cigar Box Labels: Portraits of Life, Mirrors of History. LC 97-29084. 176p. 1998. 39.95 (*0-7643-0409-7*) Schiffer.

— Judgment at Gallatin: The Trial of Frank James. LC 98-6746. (Illus.). 256p. 1998. 28.95 (*0-89672-398-4*) Tex Tech Univ Pr.

— Tobacco Advertising: The Great Seduction. LC 96-6405. (Illus.). 264p. 1996. write for info. (*0-88740-972-5*) Schiffer.

Petrone, Joseph A. Building the High-Performance Sales Force. 224p. 1994. 26.95 (*0-8144-0219-4*) AMACOM.

***Petrone, Karen.** Life Has Become More Joyous, Comrades: Celebrations in the Time of Stalin. LC 00-23201. (Russian & East European Studies). 2000. pap. write for info. (*0-253-21401-7*) Ind U Pr.

Petrone, Penny. Breaking the Mould: A Memoir. (Prose Ser.: No. 37). (Illus.). 231p. 1995. pap. 15.00 (*1-55071-013-5*) Guernica Editions.

***Petrone, Penny.** Embracing Serafina. (Prose Ser.: No. 56). (Illus.). 650p. 2000. pap. 22.00 (*1-55071-112-1*, Pub. by Guernica Editions) Paul & Co Pubs.

Petrone, Penny. Northern Voices: Inuit Writing in English. (Illus.). 330p. 1988. 27.50 (*0-8020-5772-1*) U of Toronto Pr.

Petrone, Penny, ed. First People, First Voices. 230p. 1985. pap. 20.95 (*0-8020-6562-7*) U of Toronto Pr.

— First People, First Voices. LC 83-227895. (Illus.). 256p. reprint ed. pap. 79.40 (*0-8357-3770-5*, 203649900003) Bks Demand.

— Native Literature in Canada: From the Oral Tradition to the Present. (Illus.). 240p. 1990. pap. text 22.00 (*0-19-540796-2*) OUP.

— Northern Voices: Inuit Writing in English. 332p. 1992. pap. text 19.95 (*0-8020-7717-X*) U of Toronto Pr.

Petrone, Susan, ed. see Iannone, Donald T.

Petrone, Valeria, jt. auth. see Burns, Kate.

Petrone, Valeria, jt. auth. see Jennings, Linda.

Petrone, Valeria, jt. auth. see Levinson, Nancy S.

Petroni, Frank A., et al. Two, Four, Six, Eight, When You Gonna Integrate? 1971. reprint ed. pap. 2.75 (*0-87140-241-6*, Pub. by Liveright) Norton.

***Petroni, Guglielmo.** The World Is a Prison. Shepley, John, tr. from ITA. LC 99-27768. 136p. 1999. 49.95 (*0-8101-6050-1*, Marlboro); pap. 15.95 (*0-8101-6051-X*, Marlboro) Northwestern U Pr.

Petronio, C., jt. auth. see Benedetti, R.

Petronio, Carlo, jt. auth. see Benedetti, R.

Petronio, Sandra, ed. Balancing the Secrets of Private Disclosures. LC 99-11093. (Communication Ser.). 328p. 1999. 69.95 (*0-8058-3114-2*) L Erlbaum Assocs.

Petronio, Sandra, et al. Contemporary Perspectives on Interpersonal Communication. 528p. (C). 1992. text. write for info. (*0-697-13356-7*) Brown & Benchmark.

Petronius. Le Satiricon. 2nd rev. ed. Sage, Evan T. & Gilleland, Brady B., eds. LC 72-87112. (LAT.). (C). 1969. pap. text 14.95 (*0-89197-338-9*) Irvington.

— Saturae. Buecheler, Franz, ed. l, 377p. 1963. write for info. (*3-296-14900-7*) G Olms Pubs.

***Petronius.** The Satyricon. Walsh, P. G., tr. LC 96-40165. (Oxford World's Classics Ser.). 266p. 1999. pap. 9.95 (*0-19-283952-7*) OUP.

— Satyricon. Ruden, Sarah, tr. from LAT. LC 99-55844. 256p. 2000. pap. 9.95 (*0-87220-510-X*); lib. bdg. 34.95 (*0-87220-511-8*) Hackett Pub.

Petronius. The Satyricon, 2 vols., Set. Burmanno, Petro, ed. 1294p. 1974. reprint ed. write for info. (*3-487-05416-7*) G Olms Pubs.

***Petronius.** Satyricon, Vol. 51. 2000. pap. 12.95 (*1-892295-43-1*) Green Integer.

Petronius. The Works of Petronius Arbiter, in Prose & Verse. LC 73-158324. (Augustan Translators Ser.). reprint ed. 55.00 (*0-404-54129-1*) AMS Pr.

Petronno, Gladys G. Medical Psychology of Delusions in Normal & Abnormal Behaviors: Index of New Information & Bibliography. 150p. 1996. 47.50 (*0-7883-0984-6*); pap. 44.50 (*0-7883-0985-4*) ABBE Pubs Assn.

***Petropoulos, Elias.** Songs of the Greek Underworld: A Rebetika Tradition. (Illus.). 140p. 1999. 40.00 (*0-86356-398-8*); pap. 22.95 (*0-86356-368-6*, Pub. by Saqi) Intl Spec Bk.

Petropoulos, J. C. Heat & Lust: Hesiod's Midsummer Festival Scene Revisited. LC 93-47916. (Greek Studies: Interdisciplinary Approaches). 130p. (C). 1994. 47.50 (*0-8476-7901-2*); pap. text 22.95 (*0-8476-7902-0*) Rowman.

Petropoulos, Jonathan. Art As Politics in the Third Reich. LC 98-11738. (Illus.). 464p. 1996. 49.95 (*0-8078-2240-X*) U of NC Pr.

— Art As Politics in the Third Reich. LC 98-11738. (Illus.). 464p. 1999. pap. 19.95 (*0-8078-4809-3*) U of NC Pr.

— The Faustian Bargain: The Art World in Nazi Germany. LC 99-33372. (Illus.). 416p. 2000. 30.00 (*0-19-512964-4*) OUP.

Petropoulou, Zoi. L' Espace Sensoriel Chez Albert Camus. LC 93-36149. (FRE.). 160p. 1993. text 79.95 (*0-7734-9398-0*) E Mellen.

Petropulu, Athina P., jt. auth. see Nikias, Chrysostomos L.

Petros, George, ed. The Exit Collection: Art & Writing from Exit Magazine. LC 97-90729. (Illus.). 384p. 1997. pap. 25.00 (*0-9661340-0-1*) Tacit.

Petros, James K., Jr. & Lacy, William J., eds. Hazardous & Industrial Solid Waste Testing: Fourth Symposium, STP 886. LC 85-28730. (Illus.). 365p. 1986. text 52.00 (*0-8031-0430-8*, STP886) ASTM.

Petros, Nicholas P. I Will Speak for the Children: The Reasons for the Downsizing of American Education Excellence. unabridged ed. LC 97-76286. 320p. 1998. pap. 19.95 (*1-57087-377-1*) Jade Pub Co.

Petrosian, L. Differential Games of Pursuit. LC 93-24420. (Series on Optimization: Vol. 2). 560p. 1993. text 104.00 (*981-02-0979-7*) World Scientific Pub.

Petrosian, Levon T. Ancient Armenian Translations. Maksoudian, Krikor & Kupelian, Nubar, trs. LC 92-39098. (ARM & ENG.). 1992. 10.00 (*0-934728-24-0*) D O A C.

Petrosian, Vahe, jt. ed. see Liang, Edison P.

Petrosino, Barbara A., jt. auth. see Daeffler, Reidun.

Petrosino, Barbara M., ed. Nursing in Hospice & Terminal Care: Research & Practice. LC 86-12015. (Hospice Journal: Vol. 2, No. 1). 138p. 1986. 39.95 (*0-86656-567-1*) Haworth Pr.

***Petrosjan, L. A. & Mazalov, V. V.** Game Theory & Applications, Vol. V. 203p. 2000. lib. bdg. 69.00 (*1-56072-822-1*) Nova Sci Pubs.

Petrosjan, L. A. & Mazalov, V. V., eds. Game Theory & Applications IV. 194p. 1998. 69.00 (*1-56072-629-6*) Nova Sci Pubs.

— Game Theory & Applications III. 221p. 1997. lib. bdg. 95.00 (*1-56072-496-X*) Nova Sci Pubs.

Petrosjan, L. A. & Zakharov, V. V. Mathematical Models in Environmental Policy. LC 98-112188. 207p. 1997. 95.00 (*1-56072-515-X*) Nova Sci Pubs.

Petrosjan, Leon A. & Mazalov, V. V., eds. Game Theory & Applications. 219p. 1995. 85.00 (*1-56072-266-5*) Nova Sci Pubs.

— Game Theory & Applications II. 257p. (C). 1996. lib. bdg. 95.00 (*1-56072-390-4*) Nova Sci Pubs.

Petrosjan, Leon A. & Zenkevich, Nikolay A. Game Theory. LC 98-33547. (Series on Optimization: Vol. 3). 360p. 1996. text 64.00 (*981-02-2396-X*) World Scientific Pub.

Petroske, Kenneth C. Keeping Your Atomic Four Alive. 1998. spiral bd. write for info. (*1-888701-15-3*) Jarrett Pr.

Petroski, Catherine. A Bride's Passage: Susan Hathorn's Year under Sail. LC 96-32145. (Illus.). 304p. 1997. text 42.50 (*1-55553-298-5*); pap. text 16.95 (*1-55553-297-7*) NE U Pr.

— Gravity & Other Stories. LC 81-71003. 120p. (Orig.). 1981. pap. 8.50 (*0-931362-05-9*) Fiction Intl.

***Petroski, Henry.** The Book on the Bookshelf. LC 99-14336. 1999. 26.00 (*0-375-40649-2*) Knopf.

— The Book on the Bookshelf. 2000. pap. 13.00 (*0-375-70639-9*) Vin Bks.

Petroski, Henry. Design Paradigms: Case Histories of Error & Judgment in Engineering. LC 93-32560. (Illus.). 221p. (C). 1994. pap. text 22.95 (*0-521-46649-0*) Cambridge U Pr.

— Engineers of Dreams: Great Bridge Builders & the Spanning of America. 1996. pap. 15.00 (*0-679-76021-0*) Everymns Lib.

— The Evolution of Useful Things. LC 91-39524. (Illus.). 256p. 1992. 24.00 (*0-679-41226-3*) Knopf.

— The Evolution of Useful Things. 1994. pap. 13.00 (*0-679-74039-2*) Vin Bks.

— Invention by Design: How Engineers Get from Thought to Thing. LC 96-19227. (Illus.). 288p. 1996. 24.95 (*0-674-46367-6*) HUP.

— Invention by Design: How Engineers Get from Thought to Thing. (Illus.). 256p. 1998. pap. 12.95 (*0-674-46368-4*) HUP.

— The Pencil: A History of Design & Circumstance. LC 89-45362. 448p. 1992. pap. 20.00 (*0-679-73415-5*) Knopf.

— Remaking the World. 256p. 1999. pap. 13.00 (*0-375-70024-2*) Vin Bks.

— Remaking the World: Adventures in Engineering. LC 97-29328. 256p. 1997. 24.00 (*0-375-40041-9*) Knopf.

— To Engineer Is Human: The Role of Failure in Successful Design. 1992. pap. 13.00 (*0-679-73416-3*) Vin Bks.

Petroski, R. J. & McCormick, S. P. Secondary-Metabolite Biosynthesis & Metabolism. LC 92-49318. (Environmental Science Research Ser.: Vol. 44). (Illus.). 394p. (C). 1992. text 110.00 (*0-306-44309-0*, Kluwer Plenum) Kluwer Academic.

Petroski, Richard J., jt. ed. see Conway, Walter D.

Petroski, Thomas E., jt. auth. see Douchkoff, Wayne L.

Petrosky. Contemporary American Poetry. Date not set. pap. text. write for info. (*0-312-03086-X*) St Martin.

Petrosky, Anthony. Jurgis Petraskas: Poems. LC 82-18003. 70p. 1983. reprint ed. pap. 30.00 (*0-608-00869-9*, 206166100010) Bks Demand.

— Red & Yellow Boat: Poems. LC 93-32204. 64p. 1994. pap. 8.95 (*0-8071-1831-1*); text 15.95 (*0-8071-1830-3*) La State U Pr.

Petrosky, Anthony, ed. see Dobler, Patricia.

Petrosky, Anthony, ed. see Ignatow, David.

Petrosky, Anthony R. & Bartholomae, David, eds. The Teaching of Writing. LC 85-62666. (Eighty-Fifth Yearbook of the National Society for the Study of Education Ser.: Pt. 2). x, 222p. 1997. pap. text 11.95 (*0-226-59949-3*) U Ch Pr.

Petrosky, Anthony R., jt. auth. see Bartholomae, David.

Petrosky, Arlene B. Two Trees. (Illus.). 62p. 1989. 16.95 (*0-9623965-0-8*) ABR Petrosky.

Petrosonne, Pierre W. Crime Analysis--with Medical, Forensic, Political, & Social Involvement: Index of New Information & Research. LC 94-34921. 189p. 1995. 47.50 (*0-7883-0450-X*); pap. 44.50 (*0-7883-0451-8*) ABBE Pubs Assn.

Petrosyan, M. I. Rock Breakage by Blasting. Ghose, A. K., ed. (Illus.). 152p. (C). 1994. text 71.00 (*90-6191-902-9*, Pub. by A A Balkema) Ashgate Pub Co.

Petrotta, Anthony J. Lexus Ludens: Wordplay & the Book of Micah. LC 91-16769. (American University Studies: Theology & Religion: Ser. VII, Vol. 105). 178p. 1991. 36.95 (*0-8204-1539-1*) P Lang Pubng.

Petrou, M., jt. ed. see Perner, P.

***Petrou, Maria & Bosdogianni, Panagiota.** Image Processing: The Fundamentals. LC 99-32327. 354p. 1999. 69.95 (*0-471-99883-4*) Wiley.

Petrouske, Rosalie S. Geisha Box. Bixby, Robert, ed. 35p. 1996. pap. 6.00 (*1-882983-32-7*) March Street Pr.

***Petroutsos, Evangelos.** ASP 3 Developer's Reference. (Illus.). 400p. 2000. pap. text 24.99 (*0-7821-2781-9*) Sybex.

— Mastering Database Programming with Visual Basic 6. 4th ed. 928p. 1999. pap. text 39.99 (*0-7821-2598-0*) Sybex.

Petroutsos, Evangelos. Mastering Visual Basic 5. LC 97-65358. 1104p. 1997. pap. text 49.99 incl. cd-rom (*0-7821-1984-0*) Sybex.

— Mastering Visual Basic 6. 1312p. 1998. pap. text 49.99 incl. cd-rom (*0-7821-2272-8*) Sybex.

***Petroutsos, Evangelos.** Visual Basic for Prgrammer. 2112p. 2000. pap. text 74.98 (*0-7821-2664-2*) Sybex.

Petroutsos, Evangelos. Visual Basic 6 Developer's Handbook. 2nd ed. LC 98-87588. xxxiv, 1504p. 1998. pap. text 49.99 (*0-7821-2283-3*) Sybex.

Petrov, A. A. Einstein Spaces. (C). 1969. 183.00 (*0-08-012315-5*, Pub. by Pergamon Repr) Franklin.

Petrov, A. A., jt. auth. see Marchenko, G. N.

P

Petrov, Aleksei. Medieval Carpathian Rus' The Oldest Documentation about the Carpatho-Rusyn Church & Eparchy. LC 97-61166. 250p. 1998. 35.00 (0-88033-388-X, 491, Pub. by East Eur Monographs) Col U Pr.

Petrov, Alexander. Lady in an Empty Dress: Poems. Burns, R., tr. 38p. 1990. pap. 9.95 (0-948259-90-6, Pub. by Forest Bks) Dufour.

Petrov, Alexander G. The Lyotropic State of Matter: Molecular Physics & Living Matter Physics. 572p. 1999. text 140.00 (90-5699-638-X, ECU124, Harwood Acad Pubs) Gordon & Breach.

Petrov, D. F., ed. Apomixis & Its Role in Evolution & Breeding. Sharma, B. R., tr. from RUS. 275p. (C). 1984. 97.00 (90-6191-437-X, Pub. by A A Balkema) Ashgate Pub Co.

Petrov, Eugene, jt. auth. see Ilf, Ilya.

Petrov, Evgeni I. & Ilf. The Twelve Chairs. Richardson, John H., tr. from RUS. LC 96-29783. (European Classics Ser.). 1997. 17.95 (0-8101-1484-4, Hydra Bks) Northwestern U Pr.

Petrov, Evgenij, jt. auth. see Ilf, Ilja.

Petrov, F. A. & Ianovskii, A. D., compiled by. Napoleon, Sa Famille & Son Entourage: Catalogue des Documents du Musee Historique d'Etat, Moscou.Tr. of Napoleon, His Family & His Entourage: Actalog of the Documents from the State Historial Museum, Moscow. (FRE.). 265p. 1998. lib. bdg. 100.00 (0-88354-229-3) N Ross.

Petrov, I. U., jt. auth. see West, James L. W., III.

Petrov, M. P., et al. Photorefractive Crystals in Coherent Optical Systems. (Optical Sciences Ser.: Vol. 9). (Illus.). 320p. 1991. 101.95 (0-387-52603-X) Spr-Verlag.

Petrov, R. V. Immunology Reviews Vol. 4, Pt. 3: Physico-Chemical Criteria for the Construction of Artificial Immunomodulators & Immunogens on the Basis of Polyelectro, Vol. 4. (Soviet Medical Reviews Ser.: Section D). 116p. 1992. pap. text 137.00 (3-7186-5288-9, Harwood Acad Pubs) Gordon & Breach.

Petrov, R. V., et al. Suppressor B Lymphocytes, 1. Tatarchenko, V. E., tr. from RUS. (Soviet Medical Reviews, Immunology Series Supplement: Vol. 1). xii, 208p. 1988. text 348.00 (3-7186-4800-8) Gordon & Breach.

Petrov, R. V., ed. see Borisova, A. A., et al.

Petrov, R. V., ed. see Khaitov, R. M.

Petrov, R. V., ed. see Khakhalin, L. N.

Petrov, R. V., ed. see Lebedev, K. A., et al.

Petrov, R. V., jt. ed. see Zemskov, V. M.

Petrov, Rem. V., ed. Immunology: Cell Interactions, Myelopeptides Artificial Immunogens. (Soviet Medical Reviews: Section D, Immunology Reviews Ser.: Vol. 1). xviii, 443p. 1987. text 613.00 (3-7186-0315-2) Gordon & Breach.

Petrov, Rem V., et al. Myelopeptides. 200p. 1998. 34.00 (981-02-3507-0) World Scientific Pub.

Petrov-Skitaletz, E. Kronstadt Thesis. 1964. 7.95 (0-8315-0040-9) Speller.

Petrov, V. Thermal Physics Reviews Vol. 4, Pt. 5: Optical & Thermophysical Properties of Semitransparent Materials in the Calculation of Combines Radiation-Cond, Vol. 4. (Soviet Technology Reviews Ser.: Section B). 79p. 1992. pap. text 162.00 (3-7186-5445-8, Harwood Acad Pubs) Gordon & Breach.

— Vasnetsov, Yury. 196p. (C). 1984. 275.00 (0-7855-4506-9, Pub. by Collets) St Mut.

***Petrov, V. A. & Prokudin, A. V., eds.** Elastic & Diffractive Scattering: Proceedings of the International Conference on VIII Blois Workshop. 500p. 2000. 98.00 (981-02-4118-6) World Scientific Pub.

Petrov, V. I. Russian-English Medical Dictionary Phrase Book. 3rd ed. 595p. 1993. 95.00 (0-7859-9075-5) Fr & Eur.

Petrov, V. I., et al. Russian-English Medical Dictionary Phrase-Book. 3rd ed. 596p. (C). 1993. reprint ed. 32.95 (0-8285-5177-4) Firebird NY.

Petrov, V. S. & Tulin, S. A. Russian-Czech Polytechnical Dictionary. (CZE & RUS.). 639p. 1962. 125.00 (0-8288-6813-1, M-9074) Fr & Eur.

Petrov, V. V. Sums of Independent Random Variables. Brown, A. A., tr. LC 75-5766. (Ergebnisse der Mathematik Ser.: Vol. 82). 360p. 1975. text 69.00 (0-387-06635-7) Spr-Verlag.

Petrov, Valentin V. Limit Theorems of Probability Theory. (Oxford Studies in Probability: No. 4). 304p. 1995. text 98.00 (0-19-853499-X) OUP.

Petrov, Viacheslav V. & Svechnikov, Sergei V., eds. International Conference on Optical Storage, Imaging & Transmission of Information, Vol. 3055. LC 97-207735. 332p. 1997. 80.00 (0-8194-2470-6) SPIE.

Petrov, Victor P. Rossiia Na Dal'Nem Vostoke (Russia in a Far East) LC 96-43613. (RUS.). 190p. (Orig.). 1996. pap. 12.00 (1-55779-095-7) Hermitage Pubs.

— Russkie vs. Amerike, XX Vek: Russians in Amerika, XX Century. LC 91-72887. (RUS., Illus.). 240p. (Orig.). 1991. pap. 16.00 (0-911971-67-X) Effect Pub.

Petrov, Vladimir. Escape from the Future: The Incredible Adventures of a Young Russian. LC 73-80380. 470p. reprint ed. pap. 145.70 (0-608-13210-1, 205605100044) Bks Demand.

— Money & Conquest: Allied Occupation Currencies in World War II. LC 66-26685. (Johns Hopkins University Studies in Historical & Political Science: Series 84: No. 2). 282p. reprint ed. pap. 87.50 (0-608-10213-X, 202073200018) Bks Demand.

Petrov, Vladimir, ed. see Borisov, Oleg B. & Koloskov, B. T.

Petrov, Vladimir M., jt. auth. see Golitsyn, German A.

Petrov, Vsevolod. World of Art Nouveau in Russia. (Schools & Movements Ser.). (Illus.). 300p. 1997. 55.00 (1-85995-350-6) Parkstone Pr.

Petrov, Y., jt. auth. see Morozov, Nikita F.

Petrova, A. B. English Self Taught. 8th ed. (ENG & RUS.). 365p. 1992. 29.95 (0-7859-1081-6, 5060029867) Fr & Eur.

Petrova, Ada & Watson, Peter. Death of Hitler: The Full Story with New Evidence from Secret Russian Archives. 192p. 1996. pap. 13.00 (0-393-31543-6) Norton.

Petrova, E. Drawings by Russian Artists: Late 18th Early 19th Centuries. (Illus.). (C). 1983. 330.00 (0-7855-4532-8, Pub. by Collets) St Mut.

— Drawings by Russian Artists: Late 18th-Early 19th Centuries. (Illus.). (C). 1983. text 360.00 (0-7855-5837-3, Pub. by Collets) St Mut.

Petrova, Olga. Black Virgin, & Other Stories. LC 72-128746. (Short Story Index Reprint Ser.). 1977. 17.95 (0-8369-3637-X) Ayer.

Petrova, Sylva & Simpson, Josh. Visionary Landscapes: The Glassworks of Josh Simpson. (Illus.). 40p. 1998. pap. 15.00 (0-9665144-0-8) Bruce Museum.

Petrova, Yevgenia, jt. auth. see Gusyev, Vladimir.

Petrovic, Dusan. SQL Server 7: A Beginner's Guide. LC 99-194896. (SQL Server Professional Library). 1999. pap. text 39.99 (0-07-211891-1) Osborne-McGraw.

Petrovic, Gajo, jt. ed. see Markovic, Mihailo.

Petrovic, Jelena, tr. see Selenic, Slobodan.

Petrovic, W. K., ed. see American Society of Mechanical Engineers Staff.

Petrovic, Z., jt. ed. see Milosavljevic, M.

Petrovich, Janice, jt. auth. see Witt, Sandi.

Petrovich, Michael B. The Emergence of Russian Panslavism, 1856-1870. LC 84-25242. 312p. 1985. reprint ed. lib. bdg. 69.50 (0-313-24742-0, PEER, Greenwood Pr) Greenwood.

Petrovich, Michael B. A History of Modern Serbia, 1804-1918, 2 vols., Set. LC 76-13227. (Illus.). 1976. 49.50 (0-15-140950-1) Harcourt.

Petrovich, Michael B., tr. see Djilas, Milovan.

Petrovich, Peter. Advanced Conversational English. 230p. 1995. pap. text 25.00 (0-9647271-4-5) P Petrovich.

Petrovich, Tija. Lighten Up! Gourmet Recipes for Lowfat Lifestyles. (Illus.). 211p. 1992. spiral bd. 14.95 (0-9630679-0-7) Nutrit Connect.

— Lighten Up! Gourmet Recipes for Lowfat Lifestyles. 240p. 1996. spiral bd. 16.95 (0-7615-0299-8) Prima Pub.

Petrovich, Vesna C. Conaissance et Reve(rie) dans le Discours des Lumieres. (Age of Revolution & Romanticism Ser.: Vol. 15). (FRE.). XII, 222p. (C). 1996. text 47.95 (0-8204-2727-6) P Lang Pubng.

Petrovich, Wayne P. A Fire Investigator's Handbook: Technical Skills for Entering, Documenting & Testifying in a Fire Scene Investigation. LC 97-14973. (Illus.). 344p. 1998. text 69.95 (0-398-06794-5); pap. text 49.95 (0-398-06795-3) C C Thomas.

Petrovich, Z., et al, eds. Carcinoma of the Kidney & Testis, & Rare Urologic Malignancies: Innovations in Management. LC 98-21388. (Medical Radiology Ser.). (Illus.). 400p. 1998. 189.00 (3-540-63215-8) Spr-Verlag.

— Carcinoma of the Prostate: Innovations in Management. LC 95-52110. (Medical Radiology, Diagnostic Imaging & Radiation Oncology Ser.). (Illus.). 400p. 1996. 185.00 (3-540-58749-7) Spr-Verlag.

Petrovich, Z. & Baert, L., eds. Benign Prostatic Hyperplasia: Innovations in the Maanagement. LC 94-527. (Illus.). 384p. 1994. 174.00 (0-387-56628-7) Spr-Verlag.

Petrovich, Zbigniew, et al, eds. Carcinoma of the Bladder: Innovations in Management. LC 97-11285. (Medical Radiology Ser.). (Illus.). 350p. 1997. 160.00 (3-540-60885-0) Spr-Verlag.

Petrovna, Tanya, jt. auth. see Ferry, Steven.

Petrovsij, A. V. Concise Russian Dictionary of Psychology. (RUS.). 431p. 1985. 24.95 (0-8288-2211-5, M15375) Fr & Eur.

Petrovska, Marija. Merope: The Dramatic Impact of a Myth. (American University Studies: Comparative Literature: Ser. III, Vol. 9). 211p. (Orig.). 1984. pap. text 19.00 (0-8204-0084-X) P Lang Pubng.

Petrovskaya, Kyra. Russian Cookbook. LC 92-10473. Orig. Title: Kyra's Secrets of Russian Cooking. 224p. 1992. reprint ed. pap. text 5.95 (0-486-27329-6) Dover.

Petrovskih, B. V. Popular Medical Encyclopedia. (RUS.). 704p. 1984. 85.00 (0-8288-1860-6, M15422) Fr & Eur.

Petrovskij, B. V. Encyclopedic Dictionary of Medical Terms, 2 vols., Set. 1982. 125.00 (0-8288-1859-2, M15410) Fr & Eur.

Petrovsky, A., ed. Concise Psychological Dictionary. 358p. (C). 1987. 60.00 (0-7855-3895-X) St Mut.

Petrovsky, A. V. & Shikhirev, Petr N., eds. A Concise Psychological Dictionary. LC 87-4167. 358p. 1988. 10.95 (0-7178-0657-X) Intl Pubs Co.

Petrovsky, Boris, et al. Resection & Plastic Surgery of Bronchi. Mir Publishers Staff, tr. from RUS. (Illus.). 375p. (C). 1975. 27.95 (0-8464-0790-6) Beekman Pubs.

Petrovsky, I. G. Lectures on Partial Differential Equations. (Illus.). x, 245p. 1992. reprint ed. pap. 9.95 (0-486-66902-5) Dover.

Petrovsky, John & Lozano, Albert. Spanish for Travelers. (Illus.). 137p. 1986. pap. text 59.50 (0-940935-00-7) Vista Press.

Petrovsky, John R., jt. auth. see Lozano, Alberto H.

Petrovsky, Michele. Dynamic HTML in Action. LC 98-111029. 1997. pap. text 29.99 (0-07-882437-0) Osborne-McGraw.

— Linux Quick Reference. 200p. 1999. pap. 9.99 (0-7897-2170-8) Que.

— Microsoft Internet Information Server 4.0 Sourcebook. LC 97-13143. 660p. 1997. pap. 34.99 (0-471-17805-5) Wiley.

***Petrovsky, Michele.** Wine Administrators Handbook. (Administrator's Handbook). 300p. 2000. 24.99 (0-7645-4630-9) IDG Bks.

Petrovsky, Michele J. Implementing CDF Channels. LC 98-2569. (Hands-On Web Development Ser.). 1998. pap. 39.95 (0-07-049887-3) McGraw.

— Optimizing Bandwidth. LC 98-16887. (McGraw Hill Series on Computer Communication). 500p. 1998. pap. 44.95 (0-07-049889-X) McGraw.

Petrow, Stefan. Policing Morals: The Metropolitan Police & the Home Office 1870-1914. (Illus.). 360p. 1994. 65.00 (0-19-820165-6) OUP.

Petrow, Steven, et al, eds. Ending the HIV Epidemic: Community Strategies in Disease Prevention & Health Promotion. LC 90-6384. 140p. 1990. pap. 24.95 (1-56071-030-6) ETR Assocs.

Petrow, Steven, ed. see Weil, Andrew.

Petrowski, Elaine M. Dream Kitchen Planning. 160p. (Orig.). 1996. pap. 12.00 (0-399-51985-8, Perigee Bks) Berkley Pub.

Petrowski, William R. The Kansas Pacific: A Study in Railroad Promotion. Bruchey, Stuart, ed. LC 80-1286. (Railroads Ser.). (Illus.). 1981. lib. bdg. 33.95 (0-405-13758-3) Ayer.

Petrowsky, Marc, jt. ed. see Zellner, William W.

Petrowsky, Matthew & Osborne, John M. Scriptology Vol. 1: Filemaker Pro Demystified. (Illus.). 200p. (C). 1997. pap. 79.95 (0-9660876-0-7) ISO Prods.

Petrozzi, Wayne, ed. Public Policy & Administrative Renewal: Canada & the U. S. 250p. (Orig.). 1996. pap. 21.95 (0-88962-617-0) Mosaic.

Petrozzo, Daniel & Stepper, John C. Successful Reengineering: An In-Depth Guide to Using Information Technology. (General Engineering Ser.). 250p. 1994. text 30.95 (0-442-01722-7, VNR) Wiley.

Petrozzo, Daniel P. The Fast Forward MBA in Technology Management. LC 98-2775. (Fast Forward MBA Ser.). 256p. 1998. pap. 14.95 (0-471-23980-1) Wiley.

Petrozzo, Daniel P. & Stepper, John C. Successful Reengineering. 336p. 1994. 30.95 (0-471-28602-8, VNR) Wiley.

Petru, William C., ed. The Library, an Introduction for Library Assistants. LC 66-29578. 85p. reprint ed. pap. 30.00 (0-8357-2605-3, 201613700098) Bks Demand.

Petru, Zygmunt, et al. From Quantum Mechanics to Technology: Proceedings of the XXXIInd Winter School of Theoretical Physics, Held in Karpacz, Poland, 19-29 February 1996. LC 96-39126. (Lecture Notes in Physics Ser.: Vol. 477). 379p. 1996. 84.00 (3-540-61792-2) Spr-Verlag.

Petrucc, Steven J. Stickers - Action Hero Pictures. (Illus.). (J). (ps-3). 1996. pap. 3.50 (0-486-29342-4, 312272Q) Dover.

— Stickers - Desert Animals. (Illus.). (J). (ps-4). 1996. pap. 1.00 (0-486-29398-X, 255860Q) Dover.

Petruccelli. Applied Statistics for Scientists & Engineers. LC 98-44438. 940p. 1999. 101.33 (0-13-565953-1) P-H.

Petrucci, jt. auth. see Hill.

Petrucci, Armando. Public Lettering: Script, Power, & Culture. Lappin, Linda, tr. (Illus.). 256p. 1993. 37.50 (0-226-66386-8) U Ch Pr.

— Writers & Readers in Medieval Italy: Studies in the History of Written Culture. Radding, Charles M., ed. & tr. by. LC 94-41633. 1995. 32.50 (0-300-06089-0) Yale U Pr.

— Writing the Dead: Death & Writing Strategies in the Western Tradition. Sullivan, Michael, tr. LC 97-28232. (Figurae). (Illus.). 228p. 1997. 35.00 (0-8047-2859-3) Stanford U Pr.

Petrucci, Ottaviano. Canti B Numero Cinquanta. fac. ed. (Monuments of Music & Music Literature in Facsimile, I Ser.: Vol. 23). (FRE & LAT., Illus.). 119p. 1975. lib. bdg. 40.00 (0-8450-2023-4) Broude.

— Canti C No Cento Cinquanta. fac. ed. (Monuments of Music & Music Literature in Facsimile, I Ser.: Vol. 25). (Illus.). 1978. lib. bdg. 60.00 (0-8450-2025-0) Broude.

Petrucci, Ralph H. General Chemistry. 6th ed. 1993. 95.00 (0-02-395082-X) Macmillan.

Petrucci, Ralph H. & Wismer, Robert K. General Chemistry with Qualitative Analysis. Gordon, Peter, ed. (C). 1987. student ed. write for info. (0-318-60808-1) Macmillan.

***Petrucci, Ralph H., et al.** Studying the Kinetics of a Chemical Reaction. (Modular Laboratory in Chemistry Ser.). 16p. (C). 1999. pap. text 1.50 (0-87540-508-8, KINE 508-8) Chem Educ Res.

Petrucci, Ralph H., jt. auth. see Harwood, William N.

Petrucci, Ralph H., jt. auth. see Hill, John W.

Petrucci, Raphael. Chinese Painters. Seaver, Frances, tr. LC 79-102253. (Select Bibliographies Reprint Ser.). 1977. 15.95 (0-8369-5138-7) Ayer.

Petruccio. Aquarium Fish. (Learning about Ser.). (Illus.). 16p. (Orig.). (J). pap. 1.00 (0-486-29527-3) Dover.

— Learning about Cats. (Learning about Bks.). (J). (ps up). 1997. pap. 1.00 (0-614-28720-0) Dover.

Petruccio, J. Medieval Tournament. 1995. pap. text 4.50 (0-486-28721-1) Dover.

Petruccio, J. Moon Exploration Sticker Picture Book. (J). 1995. pap. 3.95 (0-486-28722-X) Dover.

Petruccio, James Steven. Cowboys Stickers. 1998. pap. text 1.00 (0-486-40084-0) Dover.

***Petruccio, Steven James.** Airport Sticker Picture. (Illus.). (J). 1999. pap. 4.50 (0-486-40587-7) Dover.

Petruccio, Steven James. Aquarium Sticker Picture Book. (Sticker Picture Bks.). (J). (ps up). 1998. pap. 4.50 (0-486-29175-8) Dover.

Petruccio, Steven James. Create Your Own Pirate Adventure Sticker Picture. (Illus.). 1995. pap. 4.50 (0-486-28410-7) Dover.

— Desert Life Sticker Activity Book. (J). 1999. pap. 1.00 (0-486-40747-0) Dover.

Petruccio, Steven James. Learning about Cats. (Illus.). 16p. (Orig.). 1997. pap. text 1.00 (0-486-29533-8) Dover.

***Petruccio, Steven James.** Police Station. (Little Activity Bks.). (Illus.). (J). 1999. pap. 1.00 (0-486-40748-9) Dover.

— Pueblo Village Sticker Picture Book. (Illus.). (J). 1995. pap. 4.50 (0-486-28689-4) Dover.

— Rodeo Sticker Picture Book. (Illus.). (J). 1997. pap. 4.50 (0-486-29603-2) Dover.

— Stickers - Pirates. (Illus.). (J). 1998. pap. 1.00 (0-486-40011-5) Dover.

— Super Heroes Sticker Book. (Little Activity Bks.). (Illus.). (J). 1998. pap. 1.00 (0-486-40012-3) Dover.

— Tarzan. (Little Activity Bks.). (Illus.). (J). 1999. pap. 1.00 (0-486-40933-3) Dover.

Petruccio, Steven James. Tropical Fish Stickers. (Illus.). (J). (gr. k-3). 1998. pap. 1.00 (0-486-28110-8) Dover.

Petruccioli, Attilio. Fatehpur Sikri. 55p. 1993. 39.00 (0-685-67847-4, Pub. by Ernst & Sohn) Wiley.

Petruccioli, Attilio, ed. Gardens in the Time of the Great Muslim Empires: Theory & Design. LC 97-7646. (Muqarnas Ser.: No. 7). (Illus.). 200p. 1997. 65.00 (90-04-10723-1, NLG 110) Brill Academic Pubs.

Petruccioli, Sandro. Atoms, Metaphors & Paradoxes: Niels Bohr & the Construction of a New Physics. McGilvray, Ian, tr. from ITA. LC 93-177.Tr. of Atomi, Metafore, Paradossi. 249p. (C). 1994. text 64.95 (0-521-40259-X) Cambridge U Pr.

Petruccione, John, ed. see Halton, Thomas P.

Petrucelle, Don. Poetic Odyssey. 64p. (Orig.). 1996. pap. 9.95 (0-9654297-0-9) D Petrucelle.

Petrucelli, R. Joseph, jt. auth. see Lyons, Albert S.

Petrucelli, Rita. Cher. (Reaching Your Goal Ser.: Set II). (Illus.). 24p. (J). (gr. 1-4). 1989. lib. bdg. 18.60 (0-86592-432-5) Rourke Enter.

— Henry Cisneros. (Biografias de Triunfadores Ser.). 24p. (J). (gr. 1-4). 1994. lib. bdg. 13.95 (0-86593-191-7) Rourke Corp.

— Henry Cisneros. (Reaching Your Goal Ser.: Set II). (Illus.). 23p. (J). (gr. 1-4). 1989. lib. bdg. 18.60 (0-86592-431-7) Rourke Enter.

— Henry Cisneros, Reading Level 2. (Reaching Your Goal Bks.: Set II). (Illus.). 24p. (J). (gr. 1-4). 1989. 10.95 (0-685-58799-1) Rourke Corp.

— Jim Henson, Reading Level 2. (Reaching Your Goal Bks.: Set II). (Illus.). 24p. (J). (gr. 1-4). 1989. lib. bdg. 18.60 (0-86592-426-0) Rourke Enter.

— Loyalty, Reading Level 2. (Learn the Value Ser.: Set II). (Illus.). 32p. (J). (gr. 1-4). 1989. 11.95 (0-685-58786-X) Rourke Corp.

Petrucha, Stefan. Making God. LC 97-77706. 159p. 1998. pap. 12.50 (0-9661593-0-6) Between Lines.

Petrucha, Stefan, et al. The X-Files. (YA). (gr. 10 up). 1996. 19.95 (1-883313-10-4) Topps Comics.

— The X-Files, Vol. II. 180p. (YA). (gr. 10 up). 1997. pap. 19.95 (1-883313-23-6) Topps Comics.

Petruk, William, ed. Waste Characterization & Treatment. LC 98-206261. (Illus.). 168p. 1998. pap. 54.00 (0-87335-158-4, 158-4) SMM&E Inc.

Petruk, William & Rule, Albert R., eds. Process Mineralogy XII: Applications to Environment, Precious Metal, Mineral Beneficiation, Pyrometallurgy, Coal & Refactories. LC 94-75561. (Illus.). 411p. 1994. 10.00 (0-87339-273-6, 2736) Minerals Metals.

Petruk, William, ed. see International Symposium on Applied Mineralogy (198.

Petrukhin, V. P. Construction of Structures on Saline Soils. Mehta, N. K., tr. (Russian Translation Ser.: Vol. 101). (Illus.). 263p. (C). 1993. text 110.00 (90-5410-213-6, Pub. by A A Balkema) Ashgate Pub Co.

Petrulli, Lucia, ed. see Griffin, Julie.

***Petrunak, Stephen.** Infant Holy, 1. 1999. 15.95 (5-550-73193-2) Nairi.

— Sweet Manna, 1. 1999. pap. 10.95 (5-550-07301-3) Nairi.

Petrunis, Sergei. Ieroglify. LC 81-50872. (Russica Poetry Ser.: No. 2). (RUS.). 220p. 1982. pap. 8.95 (0-89830-040-1) Russica Pubs.

Petrunkevitch, Alexander. Amber Spiders in European Collections. (Connecticut Academy of Arts & Sciences Ser., Trans.: Vol. 41). 1958. pap. 100.00 (0-685-22892-4) Elliots Bks.

— Arachnida from Panama. (Connecticut Academy of Arts & Sciences Ser., Trans.: Vol. 27). 1925. pap. 100.00 (0-685-22818-5) Elliots Bks.

— Choice & Responsibility. (Connecticut Academy of Arts & Sciences Ser., Trans.: Vol. 37). 1947. pap. 29.50 (0-685-22909-2) Elliots Bks.

— An Inquiry into the Natural Classification of Spiders, Based on a Study of Their Internal Anatomy. (Connecticut Academy of Arts & Sciences Ser., Trans.: Vol. 31). 1933. pap. 75.00 (0-685-44357-4) Elliots Bks.

— Russia's Contribution to Science. (Connecticut Academy of Arts & Sciences Ser., Trans.: Vol. 23). 1920. pap. 49.50 (0-685-22832-0) Elliots Bks.

— Spiders from the Virgin Islands. (Connecticut Academy of Arts & Sciences Ser., Trans.). 1926. pap. 49.50 (0-685-44361-2) Elliots Bks.

— The Spiders of Porto Rico. (Connecticut Academy of Arts & Sciences Ser., Trans.: Vol. 30, Pt. 1). 1929. pap. 75.00 (0-685-22805-3) Elliots Bks.

— The Spiders of Porto Rico. (Connecticut Academy of Arts & Sciences Ser., Trans.: Vol. 30, Pt. 2). 1930. pap. 75.00 (0-685-22804-5) Elliots Bks.

— The Spiders of Porto Rico. (Connecticut Academy of Arts & Sciences Ser., Trans.: Vol. 31, Pt. 3). 1930. pap. 75.00 (0-685-44359-0) Elliots Bks.

— A Study of Amber Spiders. (CT Academy of Arts & Science Transactions Ser.: Vol. 34). 1942. pap. 100.00 (0-686-51318-5) Elliots Bks.

— A Study of Palaeozoic Arachnida. (Connecticut Academy of Arts & Sciences Ser., Trans.: Vol. 37). 1949. pap. 100.00 (0-685-22904-1) Elliots Bks.

— System Aranearum. (Connecticut Academy of Arts & Sciences Ser., Trans.: Vol. 29). 1928. pap. 75.00 (*0-685-22807-X*) Elliots Bks.

— Tertiary Spiders & Opilionids of North America. (Connecticut Academy of Arts & Sciences Ser., Trans.: Vol. 25). 1922. pap. 75.00 (*0-685-22826-6*) Elliots Bks.

Petrunkevitch, Alexander, et al. Pushkin Centennial Meeting, February 11, 1937: Addresses & Translations of Songs. (Connecticut Academy of Arts & Sciences Ser., Trans.: Vol. 33). 1937. pap. 49.50 (*0-685-22915-7*) Elliots Bks.

Petrus. The New Pearl of Great Price: Treatise Concerning the Treasure & Most Precious Stone of the Philosophers, Vol. 7. LC 74-349. 453p. 1974. reprint ed. 35.95 (*0-405-05911-6*) Ayer.

Petrus, Desiree A. & Warda, Mark. How to Start a Business in Pennsylvania. 2nd ed. LC 99-32840. (Legal Survival Guides Ser.). 256p. 1999. pap. 12.95 (*1-57248-112-9*, Sphinx Pubng) Sourcebks.

Petrus, Klaus. Genese und Analyse: Logik, Rhetorik, und Hermeneutik im 17. und 18. Jahrhundert. (Quellen und Studien Zur Philosophie: Vol. 43). (GER.). viii, 245p. (C). 1997. lib. bdg. 124.45 (*3-11-015394-7*) De Gruyter.

Petrus of Ferrara Bonus. The New Pearl of Great Price. 441p. 1992. reprint ed. pap. 29.95 (*1-56459-142-5*) Kessinger Pub.

Petruschell, Robert L., et al. Overview of the Total Army Design & Cost System. LC 93-19192. 1993. pap. 13.00 (*0-8330-1371-8*, MR-195-A) Rand Corp.

Petrusevski, B. Algae & Particle Removal in Direct Filtration of Biesbosch Water: Influence of Algal Characteristics, Oxidation & Other Pre-Treatment Conditions. (IHE-Thesis Ser.: Vol. 7). (Illus.). 226p. (C). 1996. text 52.00 (*90-5410-407-4*, Pub. by A A Balkema) Ashgate Pub Co.

Petrusewicz, Marta. Latifundium: Moral Economy & Material Life in a European Periphery. Green, Judith C., tr. from ITA. LC 95-52357. 312p. (C). 1996. text 54.50 (*0-472-10342-3*, 10342) U of Mich Pr.

Petrusha, Ron, ed. see Ezzell, Ben.

Petrusha, Ron, ed. see Karp, David.

Petrusha, Ron, ed. see Leonhard, Woody, et al.

Petrusha, Ron, ed. see Lomax, Paul.

Petrusha, Ron, ed. see Powers, Shelley.

Petrusha, Ron, ed. see Roff, Jason T.

Petrusha, Ron, ed. see Roman, Steven.

Petrusha, Ron, ed. see Weissinger, A. Keyton.

Petrusha, Ronald. Inside the Windows 95 Registry: A Guide for Programmers, System Administrators, & Users. Shulmann, Andrew, ed. (Illus.). 300p. (Orig.). 1996. pap. 32.95 (*1-56592-170-4*) Thomson Learn.

Petrusha, Ronald, jt. auth. see Nicita, Michael.

Petrusha, Ronald, ed. see Cohen, Aaron & Woodring, Mike.

Petrusha, Ronald, ed. see Dictor, Evan S.

Petrusha, Ronald, ed. see Lomax, Paul.

Petrusha, Ronald, ed. see Roff, Jason T.

Petrusha, Ronald, ed. see Roman, Steven.

Petrushev, P. P. & Popov, V. A. Rational Approximation of Real Functions: Rational Approximation of Real Functions. (Encyclopedia of Mathematics & Its Applications Ser.: No. 28). (Illus.). 384p. 1988. text 110.00 (*0-521-33107-2*) Cambridge U Pr.

Petrushevskakila, Lkiludmila & Laird, Sally. Immortal Love: Stories. LC 95-187063. 348p. 1995. write for info. (*1-85381-575-6*) Virago.

***Petrushevskaya, Ludmilla.** The Time: Night. 2000. pap. 14.95 (*0-8101-1800-9*) Northwestern U Pr.

Petrushevsky, I. P. Islam in Iran. Evans, Hubert, tr. LC 84-24087. (SUNY Series in Near Eastern Studies). 400p. (C). 1985. text 32.50 (*0-88706-070-6*) State U NY Pr.

Petrusic, Anthony A. Lift up Your Hearts. 300p. 1989. pap. 13.50 (*0-937739-10-3*) Roman IL.

Petrusic, Anthony A. My Daily Prayers & Inspirations - Lift up Your Hearts. Parker, Sue H., ed. (Illus.). 1999. 7.95 (*0-937739-44-8*, 10042) Roman IL.

— My First Communion - Boy Image. 2nd rev. ed. Parker, Sue H., ed. (Illus.). 128p. (J). (gr. 1-3). 1999. 6.00 (*0-937739-35-9*, 10248) Roman IL.

— My First Communion - Boy Image, Padded Cover. 2nd rev. ed. Parker, Sue H., ed. (Illus.). 128p. (J). (gr. 1-3). 1999. 10.00 (*0-937739-37-5*, 10288) Roman IL.

— My First Communion - Faux Mother of Pearl, Grey. 2nd rev. ed. Parker, Sue H., ed. (Illus.). 128p. (J). (gr. 1-3). 1999. 15.00 (*0-937739-41-3*, 10278) Roman IL.

— My First Communion - Faux Mother of Pearl, White. 2nd rev. ed. Parker, Sue H., ed. (Illus.). 128p. (J). (gr. 1-3). 1999. 15.00 (*0-937739-42-1*, 10279) Roman IL.

— My First Communion - Girl Image. 2nd rev. ed. Parker, Sue H., ed. (Illus.). 128p. (J). (gr. 1-3). 1999. 6.00 (*0-937739-36-7*, 10249) Roman IL.

— My First Communion - Girl Image, Padded Cover. 2nd rev. ed. Parker, Sue H., ed. (Illus.). 128p. (J). (gr. 1-3). 1999. 10.00 (*0-937739-38-3*, 10289) Roman IL.

— My First Communion - Symbol Design, Black. 2nd rev. ed. Parker, Sue H., ed. (Illus.). 128p. (J). (gr. 1-3). 1999. 4.50 (*0-937739-39-1*, 10268) Roman IL.

— My First Communion - Symbol Design, White. 2nd rev. ed. Parker, Sue H., ed. (Illus.). 128p. (J). (gr. 1-3). 1999. 4.50 (*0-937739-40-5*, 10269) Roman IL.

— A Prayerful Journey with Mary - Lift up Your Hearts. Parker, Sue H., ed. (Illus.). 1999. 7.95 (*0-937739-43-X*, 10041) Roman IL.

— Prayers for Healing & Strength - Lift up Your Hearts. Parker, Sue H., ed. (Illus.). 1999. 7.95 (*0-937739-45-6*, 10043) Roman IL.

Petruso, Thomas F. Life Made Real: Characterization in the Novel since Proust & Joyce. 232p. (C). 1992. text 42.50 (*0-472-10266-4*, 10266) U of Mich Pr.

Petrusz, Peter, jt. auth. see Bullock, Gillian R.

Petrusz, Peter, ed. see Bullock, Gillian R.

Petrut, Margareta, tr. see Wheelis, Allen.

Petruzella. Programmable Logic Controllers: Activities Manual. 2nd ed. (Illus.). (gr. 6-12). 1999. student ed. 25.00 (*0-02-802662-4*) Glencoe.

Petruzella, Frank. Programmable Logic Controllers. 2nd ed. 1996. 53.50 (*0-02-802661-6*) Glencoe.

Petruzella, Frank D. Automotive Electronic Fundamentals. 432p. 1992. text 44.84 (*0-02-819930-8*) Glencoe.

Petruzella, Frank D. Essentials of Electronics: A Survey. LC 92-32921. 1993. 49.50 (*0-02-800893-6*) Glencoe.

***Petruzella, Frank D.** Essentials of Electronics: A Survey. LC 99-57161. 1999. write for info. (*0-07-821048-8*) McGraw.

Petruzella, Frank D. Industrial Electronic. LC 94-36563. 1994. write for info. (*0-02-801996-2*) Glencoe.

Petruzella, Frank D. Industrial Electronics. 1996. teacher ed. 17.49 (*0-02-801998-9*) Glencoe.

Petruzella, Frank D. Programmable Logic Controllers. 216p. 1989. text 67.12 (*0-07-049687-0*) McGraw.

— Programmable Logic Controllers. 2nd ed. 1997. teacher ed. 15.00 (*0-02-802663-2*) Glencoe.

Petruzzellis, Thomas. The Alarm, Sensor, & Security Circuit Cookbook. LC 93-27562. 1993. 29.95 (*0-8306-4314-1*); pap. 17.95 (*0-8306-4312-5*) McGraw-Hill Prof.

— The Alarm, Sensor & Security Circuit Cookbook. 256p. 1994. 34.95 (*0-07-049706-0*) McGraw.

Petruzzelli, Domenico & Helfferich, Friedrich G., eds. Migration & Fate of Pollutants in Soils & Subsoils. LC 92-45284. (NATO ASI Series G: Ecological Sciences: Vol. 32). 1993. 307.95 (*0-387-56041-6*) Spr-Verlag.

Petruzzellis, Thomas. Optoelectronics, Fiberoptics, & Laser Cookbook. LC 97-423. (Illus.). 300p. 1997. 39.95 (*0-07-049839-3*) McGraw.

— Optoelectronics, Fiberoptics, & Laser Cookbook. LC 97-423. (Illus.). 322p. 1997. pap. 29.95 (*0-07-049840-7*) McGraw.

Petruzzini, Diane M., ed. see Morley, Laurene S.

Petruzzini, Joseph. Shared Expectations. Hankinson, Mari-Lynn, ed. (AT&T Quality Library). (Illus.). 102p. (Orig.). 1994. pap. 24.95 (*0-932764-42-8*) AT&T Customer Info.

Petry, Alice H. Critical Essays on Anne Tyler. (Critical Essays on American Literature Ser.). 250p. 1992. 48.00 (*0-8161-7308-7*, G K Hall & Co) Mac Lib Ref.

— Critical Essays on Kate Chopin. 1996. 49.00 (*0-7838-0032-0*, G K Hall & Co) Mac Lib Ref.

— Fitzgerald's Craft of Short Fiction: The Collected Stories, 1920-1935. LC 91-8642. 256p. 1991. pap. text 19.95 (*0-8173-0547-5*) U of Ala Pr.

— A Genius in His Way: The Art of Cable's Old Creole Days. LC 87-45574. 160p. 1988. 28.50 (*0-8386-3320-X*) Fairleigh Dickinson.

Petry, Ann. Harriet Tubman: Conductor on the Underground Railroad. LC 55-9215. (Trophy Bk.). 256p. (J). (gr. 5 up). 1996. pap. 4.95 (*0-06-446181-5*, HarpTrophy) HarpC Child Bks.

— Harriet Tubman: Conductor on the Underground Railroad. (YA). (gr. 7 up). 1990. pap. 3.99 (*0-614-15695-5*, Archway) PB.

— Harriet Tubman: Conductor on the Underground Railroad. (J). (gr. 7 up). pap. 3.99 (*0-671-73146-7*) S&S Bks Yung.

— Harriet Tubman: Conductor on the Underground Railroad. 1996. 10.05 (*0-606-09390-7*, Pub. by Turtleback) Demco.

***Petry, Ann.** Miss Muriel & Other Stories. LC 99-35548. 304p. 1999. pap. 13.00 (*0-618-00709-1*) HM.

— The Narrows. LC 99-16611. 464p. 1999. pap. 13.00 (*0-618-00710-5*, Mariner Bks) HM.

Petry, Ann. The Street. 436p. 1998. pap. 12.00 (*0-395-90149-9*) HM.

— Tituba of Salem Village. LC 64-20691. (YA). (gr. 7-11). 1964. 14.95 (*0-690-82677-X*) HarpC Child Bks.

— Tituba of Salem Village. LC 64-20691. (Trophy Bk.). 272p. (YA). (gr. 4-7). 1991. pap. 4.95 (*0-06-440403-X*, HarpTrophy) HarpC Child Bks.

Petry, Ann. Tituba of Salem Village. (J). 1991. 10.05 (*0-606-01101-3*, Pub. by Turtleback) Demco.

Petry, Bonnie L., jt. auth. see Shorter, Alan W.

Petry, Bonnie L., jt. auth. see Wilkins, James H.

Petry, Carl F. Protectors & Praetorians? The Last Mamluk Sultans & Egypt's Waning as a Great Power. LC 94-2925. (SUNY Series in Medieval Middle East History). 280p. (C). 1994. text 59.50 (*0-7914-2139-2*); pap. text 19.95 (*0-7914-2140-6*) State U NY Pr.

Petry, Cary F. & Daly, Martin W., eds. Islamic Egypt, 640-1517. LC 98-16515. (Cambridge History of Egypt Ser. : Vol. 1). (Illus.). 672p. (C). 1999. text 120.00 (*0-521-47137-0*) Cambridge U Pr.

***Petry, Dan.** Hangin' Loose, Holdin' Tight: Paul's Epistles, Vol. 4.3. (Generation Why Ser.: Vol. 4, Pt. 3). 45p. (YA). (gr. 9-12). 1998. pap. 14.95 (*0-87303-284-5*) Faith & Life.

***Petry, F., ed.** Cryptosporidiosis & Microsporidiosis. (Contributions to Microbiology Ser.: Vol. 6). (Illus.). viii, 200p. 2000. 174.00 (*3-8055-7050-3*) S Karger.

Petry, Frederick E. Fuzzy Databases: Principles & Applications. (International Series in Intelligent Technologies: Vol. 5). 240p. (C). 1996. text 110.00 (*0-7923-9667-7*) Kluwer Academic.

Petry, Frederick E., jt. auth. see Buckles, Bill P.

Petry, Loren C. A Beachcomber's Botany. LC 68-26716. (Illus.). 160p. 1975. pap. 12.95 (*0-85699-119-8*) Chatham Pr.

Petry, Marvin. Taxation of Intellectual Property: Tax Planning Guide. 1985. ring bd. 235.00 (*0-8205-1688-0*) Bender.

Petry, Michael. A Thing of Beauty Is a Rare Thing. 96p. 1997. pap. 44.95 (*0-471-97684-9*) Wiley.

Petry, Michael, ed. A Thing of Beauty Is . . . (Art & Design Ser.). (Illus.). 96p. (Orig.). 1997. pap. 29.95 (*1-85490-526-0*) Academy Ed UK.

Petry, Michael, ed. see Spinoza, Benedictus De.

Petry, Michael J., ed. G. W. F. Hegel: The Berlin Phenomenology. 320p. 1981. lib. bdg. 104.50 (*90-277-1205-0*, D Reidel) Kluwer Academic.

— Hegel & Newtonianism. LC 93-18478. (Archives Internationales d'Histoire des Idees (International Archives of the History of Ideas) Ser.). 808p. (C). 1993. text 410.50 (*0-7923-2202-9*) Kluwer Academic.

Petry, Michael J., ed. Hegel's Philosophy of Subjective Spirit Vol. 1: Introductions: A German-English Parallel Text Edition. (ENG & GER.). 331p. 1977. lib. bdg. 86.50 (*90-277-0715-4*) Kluwer Academic.

— Hegel's Philosophy of Subjective Spirit Vol. 2: Anthropology: A German-English Parallel Text Edition. (ENG & GER.). 687p. 1977. lib. bdg. 162.50 (*90-277-0716-2*) Kluwer Academic.

— Hegel's Philosophy of Subjective Spirit Vol. 3: Phenomenology & Psychology: A German-English Parallel Edition. (ENG & GER.). 514p. 1977. lib. bdg. 127.50 (*90-277-0717-0*) Kluwer Academic.

***Petry, Mike.** Narratives of Memory & Identity: The Novels of Kazuo Ishiguro. (Aachen British & American Studies). ix, 174p. 1999. pap. 35.95 (*3-631-35360-X*) P Lang Pubng.

— Narratives of Memory & Identity: The Novels of Kazuo Ishiguro. LC 99-38711. (Aachen British & American Studies: Vol. 12). ix, 174p. (C). 1999. pap. text 35.95 (*0-8204-4372-7*) P Lang Pubng.

Petry, Ray C. Francis of Assisi. LC 41-25932. reprint ed. 27.50 (*0-404-05017-4*) AMS Pr.

Petry, Ronald D. Partners in Creation: Stewardship for Pastor & People. fac. ed. LC 79-21770. 126p. 1980. pap. 39.10 (*0-7837-7340-4*, 204729300007) Bks Demand.

Petry, S. & Meyer, G., eds. The Perception of Illusory Contours. (Illus.). 345p. 1987. 214.00 (*0-387-96518-1*) Spr-Verlag.

***Petry, Ulrike.** Kommunikationsbezogene Syntax bei Johann Eberlin von Gunzburg: Zur Funktion Varianter Kompositionstypen in den "Bundesgenossen" (Documenta Linguistica Ser.: Bd. 3). (GER.). xii, 422p. 1999. 80.00 (*3-487-10880-1*, Pub. by G Olms Verlag) Lubrecht & Cramer.

Petryshyn, W. V. Approximation-Solvability of Nonlinear Functional & Differential Equations. (Pure & Applied Mathematics Ser.: Vol. 171). (Illus.). 392p. 1992. text 155.00 (*0-8247-8793-5*) Dekker.

Petryshyn, Wolodymyr V. Generalized Topological Degree & Semilinear Equations. (Tracts in Mathematics Ser.: No. 117). 252p. (C). 1995. text 69.95 (*0-521-44474-8*) Cambridge U Pr.

Petryszyn, Yar, jt. auth. see Cockrum, E. Lendell.

***Pets Part of the Family Firm Staff.** Petspeak: You're Closer Than You Think to a Great Relationship with Your Dog or Cat! LC 00-9290. (Illus.). 496p. 2000. 16.95 (*1-57954-337-5*) Rodale Pr Inc.

Pets: Part of the Family Editors, jt. auth. see Burghoff, Gary.

Pets: Part of the Family Editors, ed. see Murphy, Jana.

Pets: Part of the Family Magazine Editors, jt. auth. see Bricklin, Mark.

***Petsalees-Diomeedees, N. & Harewood, George H.** The Unknown Callas: The Greek Years. LC 00-40155. (Illus.). 2000. write for info. (*1-57467-059-X*, Amadeus Pr) Timber.

Petschauer, Peter. The Education of Women in Eighteenth Century Germany: New Directions from the German Female Perspective. LC 88-26600. (Studies in German Thought & History: Vol. 9). 612p. 1989. lib. bdg. 129.95 (*0-88946-347-6*) E Mellen.

Petschauer, Peter W. Human Space: Personal Rights in a Threatening World. LC 96-20682. 208p. 1997. 59.95 (*0-275-95645-8*, Praeger Pubs) Greenwood.

Petsche, Hellmuth, jt. ed. see Brazier, Mary A.

Petsche, Thomas, ed. Computational Learning Theory & Natural Learning Systems Vol. 3: Making Learning Systems Practical. (Illus.). 437p. 1995. pap. text 47.50 (*0-262-66096-2*, Bradford Bks) MIT Pr.

Petschek, A., et al, eds. Supernovae. (Astronomy & Astrophysics Library). xiii, 293p. 1990. 89.95 (*0-387-97069-X*) Spr-Verlag.

Petschek, Joyce. Beautiful Bargello: 25 Charted Needlepoint & Bargello Designs. LC 97-60006. (Illus.). 160p. 1997. 29.95 (*1-57076-093-4*, Trafalgar Sq Pub) Trafalgar.

— Silver Dreams: A Myth of the Sixth Sense. LC 90-82143. (Illus.). 208p. (YA). (gr. 8-12). 1990. 29.95 (*0-89087-619-3*); pap. 19.95 (*0-89087-620-7*) Celestial Arts.

Petschek, Rodolfo. Kinsey, Photographer: A Half Century of Negatives by Darius & Tabitha May Kinsey, with Contributions by Son & Daughter, Darius, Jr., & Dorothea, Vol. 1. (Illus.). 320p. 1995. 29.98 (*1-884822-22-3*) Blck Dog & Leventhal.

Petschek, Rodolfo, jt. auth. see Bohn, Dave.

Petschel, H. K. Spurious Stamps: A History of U. S. Postal Counterfeits. Wunderly, Kathleen, ed. (Illus.). 274p. 1997. pap. 40.00 (*0-933580-20-7*) Am Philatelic Society.

***Petschniker, Mario.** Kommunikation - Konflikt - Hierarchie: Die Schwierigkeit Im Umgang Mit Indirekter Kommunikation und Nicht Auflosbaren Konflikten In Hierarchischen Betrieben. (GER.). x, 182p. 1999. 37.95 (*3-631-34681-6*) P Lang Pubng.

Petschulat, Neub & Corinna, Joyce. Stroke . . . Now What? 240p. (Orig.). 1991. 17.95 (*0-9631426-0-7*) CAM Pub.

Petschull, Jurgen. With the Wind to the West: The Great Balloon Escape. Searls-Ridge, Courtney, tr. LC 82-106843. 180 p. 1981. write for info. (*0-340-25895-0*) St Martin.

Petsinger, Robert E., ed. see Cryogenic Society of America, LNG Terminals & Safe.

***Petsinis, Tom.** French Mathematician. 2000. pap. text 13.95 (*0-425-17291-0*) Berkley Pub.

Petsinis, Tom. The French Mathematician. LC 98-24076. 400p. 1998. reprint ed. 24.00 (*0-8027-1345-9*) Walker & Co.

Petska-Juliussen, Karen & Juliussen, Egil. Computer Industry Almanac. 8th ed. 1996. 63.00 (*0-942107-08-X*); pap. 53.00 (*0-942107-07-1*) Computer Indus Al.

— Computer Industry Almanac, 1993. 6th ed. (Illus.). 816p. 1993. 55.00 (*0-942107-04-7*); pap. 45.00 (*0-942107-03-9*) Computer Indus Al.

Petska-Juliussen, Karen, jt. auth. see Juliussen, Egil.

Petska, Karen & Juliussen, E. Computer Industry Almanac. 9th ed. 800p. 2000. 70.00 (*0-942107-14-4*) Computer Indus Al.

Petska, Karen & Juliussen, Egil. Computer Industry Almanac. 9th ed. (Illus.). 800p. 2000. pap. 60.00 (*0-942107-11-X*) Computer Indus Al.

Petsky, Michael. Competitive Direct Marketing Strategies: Mergers, Acquisitions & Corporate Development Activities, 1992 Edition. Jones, Melissa D., ed. (Illus.). 232p. 1992. pap. 345.00 (*0-9632267-0-3*) Vos Gruppo & Capell.

— The Direct Marketing Mergers, Acquisitions & Strategic Activities Yearbook. Jones, Melissa D., ed. 1995. pap. 345.00 (*0-9632267-1-1*) Vos Gruppo & Capell.

Petsonik, Judy. Taking Judaism Personally. 1996. 23.00 (*0-02-925098-6*) Free Pr.

— Taking Judaism Personally. 352p. 1996. 24.50 (*0-684-82809-X*) Free Pr.

Petsonk, Judy & Remsen, Jim. The Intermarriage Handbook: A Guide for Jews & Christians. LC 90-19162. 416p. 1991. reprint ed. pap. 14.95 (*0-688-10379-0*, Quil) HarperTrade.

Petsopoulos, Yanni. Kilims: Masterpieces of Turkey. LC 91-52796. (Illus.). 176p. 1991. 50.00 (*0-8478-1417-3*, Pub. by Rizzoli Intl) St Martin.

Petsopoulos, Yanni, ed. Tulips, Arabesques & Turbans: Decorative Arts from the Ottoman Empire. LC 81-20534. (Illus.). 208p. 1982. 75.00 (*0-89659-279-0*) Abbeville Pr.

Pett, Joel W. Rough Sketches: Political Cartoons by Joel Pett, Lexington Herald-Leader. (Illus.). 164p. (Orig.). 1989. pap. write for info. (*0-318-65564-0*) Lex Herald-Leader.

Pett, Marjorie A. Nonparametric Statistics in Health Care Research: Statistics for Small Samples & Unusual Distributions. LC 96-35711. 400p. (C). 1997. 58.00 (*0-8039-7038-2*, 70382); pap. 26.95 (*0-8039-7039-0*, 70390) Sage.

Petta, Paolo, jt. auth. see Trappl, Robert.

Pettas, William. A Sixteenth-Century Spanish Bookstore: The Inventory of Juan de Junta. LC 94-78553. (Transactions Ser.: Vol. 85, Pt. 1). 200p. (C). 1995. pap. 20.00 (*0-87169-851-X*, T851-pew) Am Philos.

Pettas, William A., tr. see Balsamo, Luigi.

Pettavino, Paula J. & Pye, Geralyn. Sport in Cuba: The Diamond in the Rough. LC 93-24372. (Latin American Ser.). 320p. (C). 1994. pap. 19.95 (*0-8229-5512-1*); text 49.95 (*0-8229-3764-6*) U of Pittsburgh Pr.

Pettazzoni, Raffaele. The All Knowing God: Researches into the Early Religion & Culture. Bolle, Kees W., ed. LC 77-79150. (Mythology Ser.). (Illus.). 1978. reprint ed. lib. bdg. 44.95 (*0-405-10559-2*) Ayer.

Pettazzoni, Raffaele & Bolle, Kees W., eds. Miti E. Leggende: Myths & Legends, 4 vols. LC 77-79151. (Mythology Ser.). (ITA.). 1978. reprint ed. lib. bdg. 204.95 (*0-405-10560-6*) Ayer.

Pette, D., ed. Plasticity of Muscle. (C). 1979. 146.15 (*3-11-007961-5*) De Gruyter.

Pette, D., et al. Reviews of Physiology, Biochemistry & Pharmacology, Vol. 116. Blaustein, M. P. et al, eds. (Illus.). 176p. 1990. 97.95 (*0-387-52880-6*) Spr-Verlag.

Pette, Dirk, ed. The Dynamic State of Muscle Fibers: Proceedings of the Int'l Symposium Oct. 1-6, 1989, Konstanz, Fed. Rep. of Germany. (Illus.). xxiv, 729p. (C). 1990. lib. bdg. 288.50 (*3-11-012168-9*) De Gruyter.

Pettegree, Andrew. Emden & the Dutch Revolt: Exile & the Development of Reformed Protestantism. (Illus.). 362p. 1992. text 95.00 (*0-19-822739-6*) OUP.

— Foreign Protestant Communities in Sixteenth-Century London. (Oxford Historical Monographs). (Illus.). 340p. 1987. text 64.00 (*0-19-822938-0*) OUP.

— Marian Protestanism: Six Studies. (St. Andrews Studies in Reformation History). 224p. 1996. 86.95 (*1-85928-176-1*, Pub. by Scolar Pr) Ashgate Pub Co.

***Pettegree, Andrew.** The Reformation World. LC 99-35295. 600p. 2000. 180.00 (*0-415-16357-9*) Routledge.

Pettegree, Andrew, ed. The Early Reformation in Europe. 262p. (C). 1992. text 59.95 (*0-521-39454-6*); pap. text 18.95 (*0-521-39768-5*) Cambridge U Pr.

Pettegree, Andrew, et al, eds. Calvinism in Europe, 1540-1620. LC 93-37383. (Illus.). 295p. (C). 1995. text 59.95 (*0-521-43269-3*) Cambridge U Pr.

Pettegree, Andrew, jt. ed. see Lewis, Gillian.

Pettegrew, J. W., ed. NMR: Principles & Applications to Biomedical Research. (Illus.). 640p. 1989. 132.95 (*0-387-97094-0*) Spr-Verlag.

Pettegrew, Jay W., jt. ed. see Nasrallah, Henry A.

Pettegrew, John, ed. A Pragmatist's Progress? Richard Rorty & American Intellectual History. (American Intellectual Culture Ser.: No. 108). 240p. 2000. pap. 24.95 (*0-8476-9062-8*); text 60.00 (*0-8476-9061-X*) Rowman.

Pettegrew, John, jt. ed. see Keetley, Dawn.

Pettegrove, J., tr. see Cassirer, Ernst.

Pettei, Michael & Levine, Jeremiah. Inflammatory Bowel Disease in Children & Adolescents. (Monographs in Clinical Pediatrics). 257p. 1995. text 50.00 (*3-7186-5656-6*, Harwood Acad Pubs) Gordon & Breach.

P

Pettem, Silvia. Boulder: Evolution of a City. (Illus.). 208p. 1994. 34.95 (*0-87081-350-1*) Univ Pr Colo.

— Chautauqua Centennial (Boulder, Colorado) A Hundred Years of Programs. LC 98-205578. (Illus.). 136p. 1998. pap. 12.00 (*1-891274-00-7*) Book Lode.

— Colorado Traveler: Colorado Mountains & Passes - Day Trips in the Rockies. rev. ed. (American Traveler Ser.: Vol. 13). (Illus.). 48p. 1991. pap. 6.95 (*1-55838-117-1*) R H Pub.

— Excursions from Peak to Peak: Then & Now. LC 97-216335. (Peak to Peak Ser.: No. 1). (Illus.). 136p. (Orig.). 1997. pap. 12.00 (*0-9617799-9-3*) Book Lode.

— Inn & Around Nederland: Accommodations for the Traveler Then & Now. (Peak to Peak Ser.: Vol. 2). (Illus.). 136p. 1998. pap. 10.00 (*1-891274-01-5*) Book Lode.

— The Peaceful Valley Story: Fulfillment of a Dream. LC 94-200416. (Illus.). 64p. (Orig.). 1994. pap. 5.95 (*0-9617799-5-0*) Book Lode.

*__Pettem, Silvia.__ Separate Lives: The Story of Mary Rippon. Long, Elaine, ed. LC 98-93978. (Illus.). 288p. 1999. 29.95 (*1-891274-03-1*); pap. 19.95 (*1-891274-04-X*) Book Lode.

Pettem, Silvia, jt. auth. see Montgomery, Mabel G.

Pettem, Silvia, ed. see Cobb, Harrison S.

Petten, Albert A. Van, see Van Petten, Albert A.

Pettengell, J. M., jt. auth. see Pope, Charles H.

Pettengell, Jim. Rottweiler, New. (Illus.). 224p. 1994. 29.95 (*0-7938-0080-3*, TS202) TFH Pubns.

Pettengill, Marian & Young, Lu A. Nursing Practice - Teaching Roles: Faculty-Clinician; Clinician-Faculty. 150p. (Orig.). 1987. pap. 12.50 (*0-942146-13-1*) Midwest Alliance Nursing.

Pettengill, Marian M., ed. Associate Degree Nursing: Facilitating Competency Development. 1987. write for info. (*0-318-68852-2*) Midwest Alliance Nursing.

Pettengill, Marian M. & Schumann, Pamela A., eds. Substance Abuse: Special Needs of Racial - Ethnic Minorities. 52p. (Orig.). 1992. pap. 7.00 (*0-685-62294-0*) Midwest Alliance Nursing.

Pettengill, Marian M. & Young, Lu A. Society in Transition: Impact on Nursing. 150p. (Orig.). 1987. pap. 12.50 (*0-942146-14-X*) Midwest Alliance Nursing.

Pettengill, Marian M. & Young, Lu Ann, eds. Prospective Payment Reimbursement: The Costs to Nursing. 150p. (Orig.). 1988. pap. 12.50 (*0-942146-16-6*) Midwest Alliance Nursing.

Pettengill, Marian M., ed. see Young, Lu Ann.

Pettengill, Samuel B. & Bartholomew, Paul C. For Americans Only. 192p. 1994. reprint ed. pap. 6.95 (*1-883228-05-0*) Invictus MI.

*__Petter, Constance & Bomberg, Hyman.__ Funics Vol. 1: A Fun Way to Improve Reading, Writing, Spelling & Thinking: Short Vowels. unabridged ed. (J). (gr. k-12). 1999. 8.33 (*1-930676-01-8*) FUNICS.

— Funics Vol. 2: A Fun Way to Improve Reading, Writing, Spelling & Thinking: Long Vowels. (J). (gr. k-12). 1999. 8.33 (*1-930676-02-6*) FUNICS.

— Funics Vol. 3: A Fun Way to Improve Reading, Writing, Spelling & Thinking: More Vowels. (J). (gr. k-12). 2000. 8.33 (*1-930676-03-4*) FUNICS.

Petter, Frank A. Reiki: The Legacy of Dr. Usui. LC 98-67864. (Shangri-La Ser.). (Illus.). 128p. 1999. pap. 12.95 (*0-914955-56-X*) Lotus Pr.

— Reiki Fire: New Information about the Origin of the Reiki Power a Complete Method. LC 97-71444. (Illus.). 144p. (Orig.). 1997. pap. 12.95 (*0-914955-50-0*) Lotus Pr.

Petter, Frank Arjava, jt. auth. see Usui, Mikao.

Petter, H. Lutyens in Italy. (Illus.). 55p. 1992. pap. 13.50 (*0-904152-21-9*, Pub. by British Schl Rome) David Brown.

Petterchak, Janice A. Jack Brickhouse: A Voice for All Seasons. LC 95-43566. (Illus.). 240p. 1996. 19.95 (*0-8092-3207-3*) NTC Contemp Pub Co.

Petterle, Joe. Schools Flunk...Kids Don't. (Orig.). 1992. pap. 15.95 (*1-881805-22-0*) Copernicus Systs.

Petterle, Joseph E. ProActive Discipline: Creating a Schoolwide Behavior Management System That Works. 1994. student ed. 13.00 (*1-881805-25-5*) Copernicus Systs.

Petters. Introduction to Musical Experiences. 1998. 20.50 (*0-07-229817-0*) McGraw.

Petters, A. O., et al. Singularity Theory & Gravitational Lensing: Mathematical Foundations-Physical Applications. (Illus.). 350p. 1997. 69.50 (*0-8176-3668-4*) Birkhauser.

Petters, S. W. Regional Geology of Africa. (Lecture Notes in Earth Sciences Ser.: Vol. 40). (Illus.). xxii, 722p. 1991. 110.00 (*0-387-54528-X*) Spr-Verlag.

Pettersen, Alvyn. Athanasius. LC 96-3570. 224p. (Orig.). 1995. pap. 18.95 (*0-8192-1655-0*) Morehouse Pub.

Pettersen, Carmen L. The Maya of Guatemala: Their Life & Dress. LC 76-42102. (Illus.). 276p. 1977. 60.00 (*0-295-95537-6*) U of Wash Pr.

Petterson, Donald. Inside Sudan: Political Islam, Conflict, & Catastrophe. LC DT157.5.P47 1999. 240p. 1999. 25.00 (*0-8133-3657-0*, Pub. by Westview) HarpC.

Petterson, B. Nervilia (Orchidaceae) De Vogel, E. F., ed. (Orchid Monographs: Vol. 5). (Illus.). v, 90p. 1991. pap. 28.00 (*90-71236-08-0*, Pub. by Rijksherbarium) Balogh.

Petterson, C. B., jt. ed. see Johnson, A. I.

Petterson, J. A. & Kuspit, Donald. Storyteller & Self Revealer. (Illus.). 256p. 1998. pap. 49.95 (*82-03-22272-2*, Pub. by Aschehong) Dist Art Pubs.

*__Petterson, James.__ Postwar Figures of L'Ephemere: Yves Bonnefoy, Louis-Rene de Forets, Jacques Dupin, Andre du Bouchet. LC 00-23107. 248p. 2000. 42.50 (*0-8387-5451-1*) Bucknell U Pr.

Petterson, Jay. Giants, Witches & Dragons Three-D Coloring Book. 32p. (Orig.). (J). 1990. pap. 3.95 (*0-942025-81-4*) Kidsbks.

Petterson, John W. United Methodist Resources Leader. Zinkiewiez, tr. 32p. 1997. pap. 4.95 (*0-687-72797-9*) Abingdon.

Petterson, Kristine. Icky Sticky Foamy Slimy Ooey Gooey Chemistry. (Illus.). (J). (gr. 3-4). 1997. pap. 6.95 (*0-590-36043-4*) Scholastic Inc.

— Stinky Smelly Hold-Your-Nose Science. (Illus.). (J). (gr. 3-7). 1997. pap. 6.95 (*0-590-36046-9*) Scholastic Inc.

Petterson, Lucille, ed. The Door County Letters of Anna & Anders Petterson. (Illus.). 216p. (Orig.). 1997. pap. 12.95 (*0-9659006-0-6*) Ephraim Found.

Petterson, Ole E., tr. see Jones, Michael P.

Petterson, Per. To Siberia. Born, Anne, tr. 256p. 1999. 18.00 (*1-86046-460-2*, Pub. by Harvill Press) FS&G.

Petterson, Steve D. Lost in the Material World: Man's Search for Happiness. Bolinger, Athalie, ed. 215p. (Orig.). 1992. text 17.95 (*1-881353-07-9*); pap. text 12.95 (*1-881353-11-7*) Excaliber Pub.

Petterson, Willy, jt. auth. see Chhabra, Rami.

Petterssen, Sverre, et al. Cloud & Weather Modification: A Group of Field Experiments. (Meteorological Monograph: Vol. 2, No. 11). (Illus.). 111p. 1957. pap. 17.00 (*0-933876-06-8*) Am Meteorological.

Pettersson, H. & Ringertz, Hans. Measurements in Pediatric Radiology. (Illus.). 192p. 1991. 96.95 (*0-387-19665-X*) Spr-Verlag.

Pettersson, Howard. Pelvic Drop Table Adjusting Technique. unabridged ed. LC 98-96782. (Illus.). x, 148p. (C). 1999. pap. text 35.00 (*0-9668191-0-1*) H Pettersson.

*__Pettersson, M., et al, eds.__ Compiling Natural Semantics. LC 99-30642. (Lecture Notes in Computer Science Ser.: Vol. 1549). xvii, 240p. 1999. pap. 52.00 (*3-540-65968-4*) Spr-Verlag.

Pettersson, Max. Complexity & Evolution. (Illus.). 156p. (C). 1996. text 52.95 (*0-521-45400-X*) Cambridge U Pr.

Pettersson, Michael. Cults of Apollo at Sparta: The Hyakinthia, the Gymnopaidai & the Karneia. (Acta Instituti Atheniensis Regni Sueciae Ser.: Sreies 8, XII). (Illus.). 165p. (Orig.). 1992. pap. 43.50 (*91-7916-027-1*, Pub. by P Astroms) Coronet Bks.

Pettersson, Rune. Visual Information. 2nd ed. LC 93-19822. (Illus.). 400p. 1993. 49.95 (*0-87778-262-8*) Educ Tech Pubns.

Pettersson, T. Retention of Religious Experiences. (Illus.). 158p. (Orig.). 1975. pap. text 22.50 (*0-685-13675-2*) Coronet Bks.

Pettersson, Thorleif & Riis, Ole, eds. Scandinavian Values: Religion & Morality in the Nordic Countries. (Psychologia & Sociologia Religionum Ser.: No. 10). 212p. 1994. pap. 38.50 (*91-554-3411-8*) Coronet Bks.

Pettersson, Ulf, jt. ed. see Lindsten, Jan.

Petteruti, Robert E., jt. auth. see Kaplan, Lloyd S.

Pettes, Christy L., jt. auth. see Wanamaker, Boyce P.

Pettes, Dorothy E. Staff & Student Supervision: A Task Centered Approach. 1979. 35.00 (*0-7855-0549-0*, Pub. by Natl Inst Soc Work) St Mut.

*__Pettet, Albert W., Sr.__ The Preacher & His Preaching. LC 99-75572. 256p. 1999. pap. 12.95 (*1-58597-004-2*) Leathers Pub.

Pettet, Ben, ed. Current Legal Problems, 1992 Vol. 45, Pt. 1: Annual Review, Vol. 45, Pt. I. 238p. 1992. pap. text 39.95 (*0-19-825721-X*) OUP.

— Current Legal Problems 1994 Vol. 47, Pt. 1: Annual Review. 248p. 1994. pap. text 29.95 (*0-19-825904-2*) OUP.

Pettet, E. Shakespeare & the Romance Tradition. LC 75-30806. (Studies in Shakespeare: No. 24). 1975. lib. bdg. 75.00 (*0-8383-2081-3*) M S G Haskell Hse.

Pettet, E. C. On the Poetry of Keats. LC 83-45459. reprint ed. 34.50 (*0-404-20200-4*) AMS Pr.

Pettet, Julie, jt. auth. see Warley, Debbie.

Pettet, Simon. Selected Poems. 120p. (Orig.). 1995. pap. 9.95 (*1-883689-30-9*) Talisman Hse.

— Selected Poems, Pettet. 120p. (Orig.). 1995. 29.95 (*1-883689-31-7*) Talisman Hse.

Pettet, Simon, jt. auth. see Burckhardt, Rudy.

Pettet, Simon, ed. see Schuyler, James.

Pettett, George. Charles Crawford Pettett: A Plucky Fellow, Vol. 1. LC 89-92192. (Illus.). 300p. 1989. 14.95 (*0-9624353-0-9*) Lochaber Bks.

— Legends, Plain Truths, & Probabilities: A Crawford/McWilliams Chronicle. LC 97-92617. (Illus.). 316p. 1997. 25.00 (*0-9624353-1-7*) Lochaber Bks.

Petteway, Al. Al Petteway/Midsummer Moon. 80p. 1997. pap. 11.95 (*0-7866-0582-0*, 95552); pap. 26.95 incl. audio compact disk (*0-7866-0584-7*, 95552CDP) Mel Bay.

— Al Petteway/Waters & the Wild. 64p. 1996. pap. 9.95 (*0-7866-0793-9*, 95608) Mel Bay.

— Al Petteway/Waters & the Wild. 64p. 1996. pap. 19.95 incl. audio (*0-7866-0797-1*, 95608P); pap. 24.95 incl. audio compact disk (*0-7866-0796-3*, 95608CDP) Mel Bay.

— Al Petteway/Whispering Stones. 72p. 1995. pap. 19.95 incl. audio (*0-7866-1303-3*, 95381P); pap. 24.95 incl. audio compact disk (*0-7866-1302-5*, 95381CDP) Mel Bay.

— Caledon Wood. 54p. 1999. 9.95 (*0-7866-3274-7*, 96930) Mel Bay.

— Caledon Wood CD Package. 54p. 1999. 24.95 incl. cd-rom (*0-7866-4464-8*, 96930CDP) Mel Bay.

— A Scottish Christmas for Guitar. 48p. 1997. pap. 24.95 incl. audio compact disk (*0-7866-2999-1*, 96783CDP) Mel Bay.

— A Scottish Christmas for Guitar: Intermediate Level. 48p. 1997. pap. 19.95 incl. audio (*0-7866-3001-9*, 96783P); pap. 9.95 (*0-7866-2996-7*, 96783) Mel Bay.

Petteway, Van H. How to Succeed As a Travel Agent. 375p. 1985. 35.00 (*0-9690625-0-8*) Worldwide Travel.

Pettey, George E. The Narcotic Drug Diseases & Allied Ailments: Pathology, Pathogenesis, & Treatment. Grob, Gerald N., ed. LC 80-1246. (Addiction in America Ser.). (Illus.). 1981. reprint ed. lib. bdg. 49.95 (*0-405-13616-1*) Ayer.

Pettey, John C. Nietzsche's Philosophical & Narrative Styles. LC 91-30171. (North American Studies in German Literature: Vol. 10). XV, 215p. (C). 1992. text 42.95 (*0-8204-1550-2*) P Lang Pubng.

Pettey, Richard J. Asherah: Goddess of Israel. LC 90-35025. (American University Studies: Theology & Religion: Ser. VII, Vol. 74). (Illus.). X, 233p. (C). 1991. text 41.95 (*0-8204-1306-2*) P Lang Pubng.

Pettey, Susan. Views of Our Historic District - Galena, Illinois. (Illus.). 72p. (Orig.). 1996. pap. 10.95 (*0-9653052-0-1*) Gear Hse.

Petteys, Chris. Dictionary of Women Artists: An International Dictionary of Women Artists Born Before 1900. LC 84-22511. 872p. 1985. 85.00 (*0-8161-8456-9*, Hall Reference) Macmillan.

Petteys, David. Federal Land Acquisitions Need Better Cost Controls. (Issue Papers: No. 19-93). 2p. 1993. pap. text 8.00 (*1-57655-068-0*) Independ Inst.

— Marine Helo: Helicopter War in Vietnam with the U. S. Marine Corps. (Illus.). 240p. 1995. pap. 20.00 (*0-9671793-0-0*) D M Petteys.

Petti, Anthony, ed. Christmas & Advent. (Chester's Books of Motets: Bk. 6). 1980. pap. 9.95 (*0-685-69006-7*, CH55110) Shawnee Pr.

— Christmas & Advent Book. (Chester's Books of Motets: Bk. 12). 1980. pap. 9.95 (*0-685-69007-5*, CH55262) Shawnee Pr.

— English School. (Chester's Books of Motets: Bk. 2). 1977. pap. 11.95 (*0-685-69039-3*, CH55103) Shawnee Pr.

— English School. (Chester's Books of Motets: Bk. 9). 1977. pap. 11.95 (*0-685-69040-7*) Shawnee Pr.

— Flemish & German Schools. (Chester's Books of Motets: Bk. 11). 1977. pap. 11.95 (*0-685-69045-8*, CH55261) Shawnee Pr.

— Flemish & German Schools. (Chester's Books of Motets: Bk. 15). 1977. pap. 9.95 (*0-685-69046-6*) Shawnee Pr.

— French School. (Chester's Books of Motets: Bk. 8). 1977. pap. 11.95 (*0-685-69065-2*, CH55236) Shawnee Pr.

— Motes for Three Voices. (Chester's Books of Motets: Bk. 7). pap. 9.95 (*0-685-69096-2*, CH55222) Shawnee Pr.

Petti, Michael A., jt. auth. see Poteet, G. Howard.

Petti, Richard J. Introduction to Macsyma. (Math Ser.). 64p. 1997. pap. 18.75 (*0-7637-0505-5*) Jones & Bartlett.

Petti, Theodore A., ed. Childhood Depression. LC 83-58. (Journal of Children in Contemporary Society: Vol. 15, No. 2). 95p. 1983. text 39.95 (*0-917724-95-X*) Haworth Pr.

*__Pettibon, Raymond.__ Raymond Pettibon: The Books, 1978-1998. 2000. 75.00 (*1-891024-17-5*) Dist Art Pubs.

Pettibon, Raymond. Raymond Pettibon: Thinking of You. (Illus.). 112p. 1998. 65.00 (*0-941548-38-4*) Ren Soc U Chi.

Pettibon, Raymond, et al. Raymond Pettibon: A Reader: A Project of the Philadelphia Museum of Art & the Renaissance Society of the University of Chicago. LC 98-38152. 1998. write for info. (*0-87633-145-2*) Phila Mus Art.

Pettibone, Dennis. A Century of Challenge: The Story of Southern College. 356p. (C). 1992. 44.95 (*0-9634258-0-3*) So Coll Seventh Day.

Pettibone, James P. Lodge Goat (1909) 602p. 1999. reprint ed. pap. 39.00 (*0-7661-0750-7*) Kessinger Pub.

Pettibone, James P., jt. auth. see Lesch, Barry M.

Pettibone, Marian H. Additions to the Family Eulepethidae Chamberlin: Polychaeta: Aphroditacea. LC 86-600055. (Smithsonian Contributions to Zoology Ser.: No. 441). 55p. reprint ed. pap. 30.00 (*0-8357-5097-3*, 202936100060) Bks Demand.

— Revision of Some Species Referred to Antinoe, Antinoella, Antinoana, Bylgides, & Harmothoe: Polychaeta: Polynoidae: Harmothinae. LC 93-4229. (Smithsonian Contributions to Zoology Ser.: No. 545). (Illus.). 45p. reprint ed. pap. 30.00 (*0-7837-6292-5*, 204600700010) Bks Demand.

— Revision of the Aphroditoid Polychaetes of the Family Acoetidae Kinberg (Polyodontidae Augener) & Reestablishment of Acoetes Audouin & Milne Edwards, 1832, & Euarche Ehlers, 1887. LC 89-600058. (Smithsonian Contributions to Zoology Ser.: No. 464). 142p. reprint ed. pap. 44.10 (*0-8357-7530-5*, 203624000001) Bks Demand.

Pettie, George. Petite Pallace of Pettie, 2 vols. LC 72-124763. reprint ed. 74.50 (*0-404-05025-5*) AMS Pr.

Pettifer. The Male Image. LC 99-12112. 204p. 1999. text 65.00 (*0-312-22246-7*) St Martin.

*__Pettifer, Adrian.__ English Castles. (Illus.). 384p. 2000. pap. 24.95 (*0-85115-782-3*) Boydell & Brewer.

Pettifer, Adrian. English Castles: A Guide by Counties. (Illus.). 384p. (C). 1996. 45.00 (*0-85115-600-2*) Boydell & Brewer.

*__Pettifer, Adrian.__ Welsh Castles: A Guide by Counties. (Illus.). 208p. 2000. 45.00 (*0-85115-778-5*) Boydell & Brewer.

Pettifer, James. Albania. 2nd ed. (Blue Guide Ser.). (Illus.). 256p. 1996. pap. 19.95 (*0-393-31421-9*, Norton Paperbks) Norton.

— Blue Guide Bulgaria. (Illus.). 224p. 1998. pap. 24.95 (*0-393-31796-X*) Norton.

Pettifer, James. Greeks. 1994. pap. 17.95 (*0-14-015782-4*, Pub. by Pnguin Bks Ltd) Trafalgar.

Pettifer, James, ed. Cockburn in Spain: Despatches from the Spanish Civil War. 208p. (C). 1986. pap. 19.50 (*0-85315-668-9*, Pub. by Lawrence & Wishart) NYU Pr.

Pettifer, James, jt. auth. see Vickers, Miranda.

Pettifor, Bonnie. Reptiles & Amphibians. (Gifted & Talented Ser.). (Illus.). 64p. (J). (gr. 1-2). 1999. pap. 5.95 (*0-7373-0208-9*, Pub. by Lowell Hse) NTC Contemp Pub Co.

*__Pettifor, Bonnie & Petit, Charles E.__ Weeks vs. United States: Illegal Search & Seizure. LC 99-50846. (Landmark Supreme Court Cases Ser.). (Illus.). 128p. (YA). (gr. 6 up). 2000. lib. bdg. 20.95 (*0-7660-1341-3*) Enslow Pubs.

Pettifor, Bonnie, jt. auth. see Bozanksy, Mary K.

Pettifor, D. G. Bonding & Structure of Molecules & Solids. (Illus.). 270p. 1995. pap. text 30.00 (*0-19-851786-6*) OUP.

Pettifor, D. G. & Cottrell, A. H. Electron Theory in Alloy Design. 312p. 1992. 110.00 (*0-901716-17-0*, Pub. by Inst Materials) Ashgate Pub Co.

Pettifor, D. G. & Weaire, D. L., eds. The Recursion Method & Its Applications. (Solid-State Sciences Ser.: Vol. 58). (Illus.). 200p. 1985. 68.95 (*0-387-15173-7*) Spr-Verlag.

Pettifor, D. G., ed. see Hafner, J., et al.

Pettifor, Grace, ed. see Oke, Janette.

*__Pettiford, Candy.__ Mudcloth: Poems from the Fabric of Life. LC 99-90650. 48p. 1999. pap. 10.00 (*1-57921-237-9*) WinePress Pub.

Pettiford, Lloyd & Curley, Melissa. Changing Security Agendas & the Third World. LC 98-30980. 1999. write for info. (*1-85567-538-2*, Pub. by P P Pubs) CRC Pr.

Pettig, Art. Songwriter. LC 97-95014. (Illus.). 146p. 1996. pap. 14.95 (*0-916927-22-9*) Growth Unltd.

Pettigrew. Intergroup Relations. 1998. pap. text. write for info. (*0-7167-2856-7*) W H Freeman.

Pettigrew, Andrew & Whipp, Richard. Managing Change for Competitive Success. 304p. 1993. pap. 31.95 (*0-631-19142-9*) Blackwell Pubs.

Pettigrew, Andrew, et al. Shaping Strategic Change. (Illus.). 336p. (C). 1992. 75.00 (*0-8039-8778-1*); pap. 27.95 (*0-8039-8779-X*) Sage.

Pettigrew, Cinda Wombes. Seeking the White Root: An Australian Story. 1998. pap. text 14.95 (*0-9666739-0-5*) Bald Eagle Pr.

Pettigrew, David. The Snak Posse. Orchanian, Robert, ed. (Illus.). 136p. Date not set. per. 9.95 (*0-9658108-1-X*) HCom.

Pettigrew, David & Raffoul, Francois, eds. Disseminating Lacan. LC 95-40334. (SUNY Series in Contemporary Continental Philosophy). 392p. (C). 1996. text 59.50 (*0-7914-2785-4*); pap. text 19.95 (*0-7914-2786-2*) State U NY Pr.

Pettigrew, David, tr. see Dastur, Francoise.

Pettigrew, David, tr. see Nancy, Jean-Luc & Lacoue-Labarthe, Philippe.

Pettigrew, David, tr. see Nasio, Juan-David.

Pettigrew, David, tr. see Raffoul, Francois.

Pettigrew, David E., tr. see Dastur, Francoise.

Pettigrew, David E., tr. see Raffoul, Francois.

Pettigrew, Eileen. Night Time. (Illus.). 24p. (J). (ps-1). 1992. pap. 4.95 (*1-55037-242-4*, Pub. by Annick); lib. bdg. 14.95 (*1-55037-235-1*, Pub. by Annick) Firefly Bks Ltd.

Pettigrew, G. W. & Moore, G. R. Cytochromes C. (Molecular Biology Ser.). (Illus.). xiv, 282p. 1987. 185.95 (*0-387-17843-0*) Spr-Verlag.

Pettigrew, G. W., jt. auth. see Moore, G. R.

Pettigrew, Jane. Coffee. 1999. pap. text 6.99 (*0-7858-1058-7*) Bk Sales Inc.

— An Edwardian Childhood. 1991. write for info. (*0-316-88865-6*) Little.

— From Grandmother with Love: A Life Recalled for My Grandchild. (Illus.). 64p. 1992. 14.95 (*0-8212-1970-7*, Pub. by Bulfinch Pr) Little.

*__Pettigrew, Jane.__ Juicing It! A Goumet's Guide to Natural Drinks. 2000. pap. 16.95 (*1-85868-866-3*, Pub. by Carlton Bks Ltd) Natl Bk Netwk.

Pettigrew, Jane. The National Trust Book of Tea-Time Recipes. (Illus.). 160p. 1991. 17.95 (*0-7078-0128-1*, Pub. by Natl Trust) Trafalgar.

*__Pettigrew, Jane.__ Souped Up: The Gourmet's Guide. (Illus.). 128p. 2000. pap. 16.95 (*1-84222-005-5*) Carlton Bks Ltd.

— Tea: And Infusions. (Illus.). 96p. 1999. pap. 14.95 (*1-85868-779-9*, Pub. by Carlton Bks Ltd) Natl Bk Netwk.

— Tee. (Evergreens Ser.). 1998. 12.99 (*3-8228-7571-6*) Taschen Amer.

*__Pettigrew, Jane, told to.__ Tea. (Pocket Guide Ser.). (Illus.). 96p. 1999. 6.99 (*0-7858-1057-9*) Bk Sales Inc.

Pettigrew, Jim, jt. auth. see Lathrop, Tad.

Pettigrew, John, ed. see Browning, Robert.

Pettigrew, Joyce, ed. Martyrdom & Political Resistance: Essays from Asia & Europe. (Comparative Asian Studies: Vol. 18). 180p. 1997. pap. 19.50 (*90-5383-501-6*, Pub. by VUB Univ Pr) Paul & Co Pubs.

Pettigrew, Joyce M. The Sikhs of the Punjab: Unheard Voices of the State & Guerrilla Violence. LC 95-13677. (Politics in Contemporary Asia Ser.). (Illus.). 256p. (C). 1995. text 65.00 (*1-85649-355-5*, Pub. by Zed Books) St Martin.

Pettigrew, Judith H. Planned Marketing: The Roadmap to Sales. Voiers, Judith S. et al, eds. 58p. 1989. student ed. 19.95 (*0-9622899-1-4*) Creative Consort Inc.

— Sure I Can Rollerskate on Jell-O! (Illus.). 108p. (Orig.). 1989. pap. 8.95 (*0-9622899-2-2*) Creative Consort Inc.

Pettigrew, Judy. Been There. Done That. Bought the T-Shirt! (Illus.). 136p. (Orig.). 1995. pap. text 8.95 (*0-9622899-3-0*) Creative Consort Inc.

— If I Should Die Before I Wake . . . (Illus.). 128p. 1998. 14.95 (*0-9622899-6-5*) Creative Consort Inc.

Pettigrew, Judy H., jt. auth. see Simpson, Diane.

Pettigrew, M. E., ed. see Casey, Mary.

Pettigrew, M. J., ed. Flow-Induced Vibration. 491p. 1996. pap. text 160.00 (*0-7918-1775-X*, TS283) ASME Pr.

P

An Asterisk (*) at the beginning of an entry indicates that the title is appearing for the first time.

Pettigrew, M. J., et al, eds. Flow Induced Vibration - 1995, Vol. 298. LC 87-72467. (Proceedings of the 1995 ASME/JSME Pressure Vessels & Piping Conference Ser.: PVP-Vol. 298). 188p. 1995. 150.00 (*0-7918-1329-0*, H00961) ASME.

Pettigrew, Mary E., ed. see Henderson, Sharon S.

Pettigrew, Neil. The Stop Motion Filmography: A Critical Guide to over 325 Features using Puppet Animation. LC 98-49799. (Illus.). 878p. 1999. lib. bdg. 110.00 (*0-7864-0446-9*) McFarland & Co.

Pettigrew, R. F. Course of Empire, 2 vols. 1998. lib. bdg. 615.95 (*0-8490-9089-X*) Gordon Pr.

— Imperial Washington, 2 vols. 1998. lib. bdg. 616.99 (*0-8490-9088-1*) Gordon Pr.

Pettigrew, Richard F. Imperial Washington. LC 78-111704. (American Imperialism: Viewpoints of United States Foreign Policy, 1898-1941 Ser.). 1970. reprint ed. 26.95 (*0-405-02044-9*) Ayer.

Pettigrew, Terence. British Film Character Actors: Great Names & Memorable Moments. LC 82-3913. (Illus.). 208p. (C). 1982. text 38.00 (*0-389-20289-4*, N7112) B&N Imports.

Pettigrew, Thomas F. How to Think Like a Social Scientist. LC 95-8952. 208p. (C). 1997. pap. 35.00 (*0-673-99709-X*) Addson-Wesley Educ.

Pettigrew, Thomas F., et al. Prejudice. (Dimensions in Ethnicity Ser.). 128p. 1982. pap. 13.50 (*0-674-70063-5*) HUP.

Pettigrew, Thomas J. Chronicles of the Tombs. LC 68-55555. (Bohn's Antiquarian Library). reprint ed. 46.00 (*0-404-50022-6*) AMS Pr.

— A History of Egyptian Mummies. LC 83-62961. (Classics in Archaeology Ser.). (Illus.). 264p. 1984. reprint ed. 35.00 (*0-915431-00-9*) N American Archives.

Pettigrew, Vera. The Adventures of Henry & Sam & Mr. Fielding. 62p. (J). 1992. pap. 5.95 (*0-947962-18-2*) Dufour.

— Fionuala the Glendalough Goat Goes West. 128p. 1994. pap. 8.95 (*0-947962-85-9*) Dufour.

— Henry & S & Mr. Fielding: Special Agent. 94p. 1992. pap. 6.95 (*0-947962-72-7*) Dufour.

— Where the River Flows: Annamoe Rectory. LC 99-193941. 176p. 1998. pap. 17.95 (*1-901737-12-8*, Pub. by Anvil Books Ltd) Irish Bks Media.

Pettijohn. Sources: Psychology. 2nd ed. 1996. 14.57 (*0-697-34347-2*, WCB McGr Hill) McGrw-H Hghr Educ.

— Sources: Psychology. 3rd ed. 368p. 1999. pap. 20.94 (*0-07-303187-9*) McGraw.

Pettijohn, F. J. Memoirs of an Unrepentant Field Geologist: A Candid Profile of Some Geologists & Their Science, 1921-1981. LC 83-12347. (Illus.). 288p. 1993. pap. 10.95 (*0-226-66405-8*) U Ch Pr.

Pettijohn, F. J., et al. Sand & Sandstone. 2nd ed. (Springer Study Edition Ser.). (Illus.). 500p. 1987. 84.95 (*0-387-96350-2*) Spr-Verlag.

Pettijohn, F. J., jt. auth. see Potter, P. E.

Pettijohn, Terry F. Notable Selections in Social Psychology. 2nd ed. (Sources Ser.). (Illus.). 368p. 1998. pap. text 14.00 (*0-697-39114-0*, Dshkn McG-Hill) McGrw-H Hghr Educ.

— Psychology: A Concise Introduction. 3rd ed. LC 91-77531. (Illus.). 496p. (C). 1992. text 25.95 (*1-56134-063-4*, Dshkn McG-Hill) McGrw-H Hghr Educ.

— Sources: Notable Selections in Psychology. 2nd ed. LC 96-85797. 384p. (C). 1996. text. write for info. (*0-697-34331-6*, WCB McGr Hill) McGrw-H Hghr Educ.

— Study Guide to Accompany Psychology: A Concise Introduction. 3rd ed. LC 92-71288. (Illus.). 254p. (Orig.). (C). 1992. text 16.25 (*1-56134-064-2*, Dshkn McG-Hill) McGrw-H Hghr Educ.

— Working with Psychology: A Concise Introduction. 2nd ed. (C). 1989. per. write for info. (*0-87967-769-4*) Brown & Benchmark.

Pettijohn, Terry F., ed. Sources: Notable Selections in Psychology. LC 93-34527. 384p. (C). 1993. text 14.95 (*1-56134-263-7*, Dshkn McG-Hill) McGrw-H Hghr Educ.

— Sources: Notable Selections in Social Psychology. (Illus.). 336p. (Orig.). (C). 1995. text 14.95 (*1-56134-314-5*, Dshkn McG-Hill) McGrw-H Hghr Educ.

Pettinari, Catherine J. Task Talk & Text in the Operating Room - A Study in Medical Discourse. Freedle, Roy O., ed. LC 88-10396. (Advances in Discourse Processes Ser.: Vol. 33). 192p. 1988. text 78.50 (*0-89391-459-2*) Ablx Pub.

Pettinari, James, jt. auth. see Kasprisin, Ron.

Pettinati, Helen M., ed. Hypnosis & Memory. LC 87-7597. (Clinical & Experimental Hypnosis Ser.). 301p. 1988. lib. bdg. 45.00 (*0-89862-338-3*) Guilford Pubns.

Pettinato, Giovanni. Ebla: A New Look at History. Richardson, C. Faith, tr. LC 90-20907. 303p. 1991. reprint ed. pap. 94.00 (*0-608-03673-0*, 206449900009) Bks Demand.

***Pettine, Eric A.** North Platte Vol. 6, No. 1: River Journal. (Illus.). 48p. 1999. pap. 15.95 (*1-57188-149-2*) F Amato Pubns.

Pettinelli, Vincent D. Human Services Management That Works. unabridged ed. Alloy, Jan L., ed. 101p. 1993. pap. 19.95 (*0-9642598-2-6*) IDS Pubng.

Pettinger, Alasdair, ed. Always Elsewhere: Travels of the Black Atlantic. LC 98-8380. (Black Atlantic Ser.). 320p. 1998. 75.00 (*0-304-70084-3*); pap. 24.95 (*0-304-70085-1*) Continuum.

***Pettinger, Peter.** Bill Evans: How My Heart Sings. LC 97-49991. (Illus.). 320p. 1998. 35.00 (*0-300-07193-0*) Yale U Pr.

Pettinger, Peter. Bill Evans: How My Heart Sings. 320p. 1999. pap. 15.95 (*0-300-08113-8*) Yale U Pr.

Pettinger, R. Managing the Flexible Workforce. 1996. pap. 129.00 (*1-85953-071-0*, Pub. by Tech Comm) St Mut.

Pettinger, R. Measuring Managerial & Business Performance. (Financial Times Management Briefings Ser.). 1997. pap. 89.50 (*0-273-63186-1*, Pub. by F T P-H) Trans-Atl Phila.

Pettinger, R. Measuring Managerial & Business Performance. 1996. pap. 129.00 (*1-85953-067-2*, Pub. by Tech Comm) St Mut.

— Preparing & Handling Industrial Tribunals. 1996. pap. 129.00 (*1-85953-070-2*, Pub. by Tech Comm) St Mut.

Pettinger, Richard. Effective Employee Relations. 1999. pap. text 24.95 (*0-7494-2693-4*) Kogan Page Ltd.

***Pettinger, Richard.** Future of Industrial Relations. 2000. pap. 28.95 (*0-8264-4834-8*) Continuum.

Pettinger, Richard. Introduction to Management. 2nd ed. 440p. (Orig.). 1997. pap. 42.50 (*0-333-68745-0*, Pub. by Macmillan) Trans-Atl Phila.

***Pettinger, Richard.** Investment Appraisal: A Managerial Approach. 2000. text 69.95 (*0-312-23390-6*) St Martin.

Pettinger, Richard. Managing the Flexible Workforce. LC 98-189591. 144p. 1998. 69.95 (*0-304-70108-4*) Continuum.

— Managing the Flexible Workforce. LC 98-189591. 134p. 1998. pap. 21.95 (*0-304-70109-2*) Continuum.

Pettinger, Richard. Managing the Flexible Workforce. (Financial Times Management Briefings Ser.). 1997. pap. 89.50 (*0-273-63183-7*) F T P-H.

— Preparing & Handling Industrial Tribunals. (Financial Times Management Briefings Ser.). 1997. pap. 94.50 (*0-273-63191-8*, Pub. by F T P-H) Trans-Atl Phila.

Pettingill, Amos. The White Flower Farm Garden Book. rev. ed. (Illus.). 376p. 1995. 20.00 (*0-9647440-0-7*) White Flower.

Pettingill, David M., jt. auth. see Coleman, Gerald D.

Pettingill, Marc. Building Sweet Dream: An Ultralight Solo Canoe for Single & Double Paddle. (Illus.). 176p. 1996. pap. 24.95 (*1-888671-03-3*) Tiller.

Pettingill, Olin S., Jr. A Guide to Bird Finding East of the Mississippi. 2nd ed. LC 76-9253. (Illus.). 689p. 1977. text 35.00 (*0-19-502097-9*) OUP.

— A Guide to Bird Finding West of the Mississippi. 2nd ed. LC 80-18666. (Illus.). 725p. 1981. text 35.00 (*0-19-502818-X*) OUP.

— Ornithology at the University of Michigan Biological Station & the Birds of the Region. (Illus.). viii, 118p. 1974. pap. text 5.00 (*0-939294-00-1*, QL-684-M5-P4) Beech Leaf.

— Ornithology in Laboratory & Field. 5th ed. 1985. text 45.00 (*0-12-552455-2*) Acad Pr.

Pettingill, William L. 900 Bible Questions Answered. LC 90-20615. Orig. Title: Bible Questions Answered - Enlarged Edition. 416p. 1991. reprint ed. pap. 19.99 (*0-8254-3541-2*) Kregel.

— 1001 Bible Questions Answered. 496p. 1997. 9.99 (*0-88486-165-1*, Bristol Park Bks) Arrowood Pr.

Pettipas, Katherine. Severing the Ties That Bind: Government Repression of Indigenous Religious Ceremonies on the Prairies. LC 95-157590. (Manitoba Studies in Native History: 7). (Illus.). 336p. 1994. pap. 18.95 (*0-88755-638-8*) U Manitoba Pr.

Pettis, C. R. Public Use of the Forest Preserve. 17p. 1993. reprint ed. lib. bdg. 69.00 (*0-7812-5262-8*) Rprt Serv.

***Pettis, Chuck.** Secrets of Sacred Space: Discover & Create Places of Power. LC 99-41549. (Illus.). 288p. 1999. pap. 19.95 (*1-56718-519-3*) Llewellyn Pubns.

Pettis, Chuck. TechnoBrands: How to Create & Use "Brand Identity" to Market, Advertise & Sell Technology Products. LC 94-31044. (Illus.). 208p. 1994. 26.95 (*0-8144-0243-7*) AMACOM.

Pettis, Joyce. Toward Wholeness in Paule Marshall's Fiction. LC 94-48916. 192p. (C). 1995. text 29.50 (*0-8139-1614-3*) U Pr of Va.

Pettis, Nina, ed. see English, Sarah L.

Pettit. Clinical Lab Techniques. (Agriculture Ser.). 1998. teacher ed. 12.00 (*0-8273-7672-3*) Delmar.

— Clinical Lab Techniques. (Nursing Education Ser.). (C). 2001. pap. 54.00 (*0-8273-7671-5*) Delmar.

***Pettit, Alex.** Selected Works of Eliza Haywood, 3 vols., Pt. I. 2400p. 2000. 395.00 (*1-85196-528-9*, Pub. by Pickering & Chatto) Ashgate Pub Co.

— Selected Works of Eliza Haywood, 3 vols., Pt. II. 2400p. 2001. 395.00 (*1-85196-529-7*, Pub. by Pickering & Chatto) Ashgate Pub Co.

Pettit, Alexander. Illusory Consensus: Bolingbroke & the Polemical Response to Walpole, 1730-1737. LC 96-11942. 256p. 1997. 39.50 (*0-87413-592-3*) U Delaware Pr.

Pettit, Arthur G. Images of the Mexican American in Fiction & Film. Showalter, Dennis E., ed. LC 79-5284. 312p. 1980. 27.95 (*0-89096-095-X*) Tex A&M Univ Pr.

— Mark Twain & the South. LC 73-86405. 240p. 1974. 27.50 (*0-8131-1310-5*) U Pr of Ky.

Pettit, Christopher. Texas Estate Planning & Probate Manual, 2 vols. 1200p. Date not set. ring bd. 350.00 (*1-57823-060-8*) Juris Pubng.

Pettit, D. G., jt. auth. see Patterson, P. G.

Pettit, Dave, jt. auth. see Jaroslovsky, Rich.

Pettit, Eber M. Sketches in the History of the Underground Railroad. LC 73-149875. (Black Heritage Library Collection). 1977. 25.95 (*0-8369-8755-1*) Ayer.

— Sketches in the History of the Underground Railroad. Leone, Paul, ed. (Illus.). 176p. 1999. reprint ed. pap. 12.95 (*0-9658955-3-X*, Pub. by Chautauqua Reg) North Country.

Pettit, Ed. Poder Secreto de las Piramides. (SPA.). 1997. pap. 17.98 (*968-13-1697-5*, Pub. by Edit Diana) Libros Fronteras.

Pettit, Elinor, jt. auth. see Heller, Steven.

Pettit, F. R. Post-Digital Electronics. (Electrical & Electronic Engineering Ser.). 176p. 1982. text 71.95 (*0-470-27334-8*) P-H.

Pettit, F. S., jt. auth. see Blachere, J. R.

Pettit, Florence. Christmas All Around the House: Traditional Decorations You Can Make. LC 75-37876. (Illus.). (J). (gr. 4 up). 1976. 15.95 (*0-690-01013-3*) HarpC Child Bks.

Pettit, G. H., jt. auth. see Waynant, R. W.

Pettit, George R., et al. Anticancer Drugs from Animals, Plants & Microorganisms. LC 93-46997. 688p. 1994. 125.00 (*0-471-03657-9*) Wiley.

Pettit, J. H., et al. Manual of Tropical Dermatology. (Illus.). 270p. 1984. 146.00 (*0-387-90987-7*) Spr-Verlag.

Pettit, Jan. Ute Pass. (Illus.). 64p. (Orig.). 1979. pap. 4.95 (*0-936564-12-1*) Little London.

— Utes: The Mountain People. rev. ed. LC 90-91905. (Illus.). 224p. 1990. pap. 11.95 (*1-55566-065-7*) Johnson Bks.

Pettit, Jane. A Time to Fight Back: True Stories of Wartime Resistance. LC 95-34381. (Illus.). 176p. (J). (gr. 5-9). 1996. 14.95 (*0-395-76504-8*) HM.

Pettit, Jane, jt. auth. see Karlson, David.

Pettit, Jayne. Jane Goodall: Pioneer Researcher. LC 98-26410. (Book Report Biography Ser.). 128p. (YA). (gr. 5-8). 1999. 22.00 (*0-531-11522-4*) Watts.

***Pettit, Jayne.** Martin Luther King, Jr. A Man with a Dream. LC 00-36646. (Book Report Biography Ser.). (Illus.). 2001. write for info. (*0-531-11670-0*) Watts.

Pettit, Jayne. Maya Angelou: Journey of the Heart. 80p. 1998. pap. 4.99 (*0-14-038359-X*, PuffinBks) Peng Put Young Read.

— Maya Angelou: Journey of the Heart. 1998. 9.19 (*0-606-12991-X*, Pub. by Turtleback) Demco.

— Michelangelo: Genius of the Renaissance. LC 97-26724. (Impact Biography Ser.). 112p. (J). (gr. 4-6). 1998. lib. bdg. 22.00 (*0-531-11490-2*) Watts.

— Place to Hide: True Stories of Holocaust Rescues. LC 94-219468. 176p. (J). (gr. 4-7). 1993. pap. 3.50 (*0-590-45353-X*) Scholastic Inc.

— Place to Hide: True Stories of Holocaust Rescues. (Scholastic Biography Ser.). 1993. 9.09 (*0-606-05974-1*, Pub. by Turtleback) Demco.

Pettit, John D., jt. auth. see Lesikar, Raymond Vincent.

***Pettit, John W.** Mipham's Beacon of Certainty: Illuminating the View of Dzogchen, the Great Perfection. LC 99-33810. (Studies in Indian & Tibetan Buddhism: Vol. 2). 576p. 1999. pap. 28.95 (*0-86171-157-2*, Pub. by Wisdom MA) Natl Bk Netwk.

Pettit, Katherine Massucci, see Heller, Dave.

Pettit, Madge. Pioneers & Residents of West Central Alabama Prior to the Civil War. xvi, 337p. (Orig.). 1988. pap. 27.50 (*1-55613-125-9*) Heritage Bk.

Pettit, Marilyn H., jt. auth. see Frusciano, Thomas J.

Pettit, Michael. American Light. LC 83-5773. (Contemporary Poetry Ser.). 80p. (C). 1983. pap. 14.95 (*0-8203-0677-0*) U of Ga Pr.

— Cardinal Points. LC 88-14797. (Iowa Poetry Prize Ser.). 96p. 1988. pap. 11.95 (*0-87745-206-7*) U of Iowa Pr.

Pettit, Michael, ed. The Writing Path 1: Poetry & Prose from Writers' Conferences. 238p. 1995. pap. 15.95 (*0-87745-509-0*) U of Iowa Pr.

— The Writing Path 2: Poetry & Prose from Writers' Conferences. 299p. 1996. pap. 15.95 (*0-87745-548-1*) U of Iowa Pr.

Pettit, Norman, ed. see Edwards, Jonathan.

Pettit, P., ed. see Hookway, Christopher.

Pettit, Paul, jt. auth. see Harris, Nathaniel.

Pettit, Philip. The Common Mind: An Essay on Psychology, Society, & Politics with a New Postscript. LC 97-139739. 400p. 1996. pap. text 29.95 (*0-19-510645-8*) OUP.

— Consequentialism. LC 92-36095. (International Research Library of Philosophy). 490p. 1993. 173.95 (*1-85521-304-4*, Pub. by Dartmth Pub) Ashgate Pub Co.

— Republicanism: A Theory of Freedom & Government. (Oxford Political Theory Ser.). 344p. 2000. pap. text 19.95 (*0-19-829642-8*) OUP.

Pettit, Philip, jt. auth. see Braithwaite, John.

Pettit, Philip, jt. auth. see Kukathas, Chandran.

Pettit, Philip, jt. auth. see MacDonald, Graham.

Pettit, Philip, ed. see Broome, John.

Pettit, Philip, jt. ed. see Goodin, Robert E.

Pettit, R. Richardson, jt. ed. see Horvitz, Paul M.

Pettit, Ray H. ECM & ECCM Techniques for Digital Communications Systems. LC 82-4669. (Systems Engineering Ser.). (Illus.). 178p. 1982. 26.95 (*0-534-97932-7*) Peninsula CA.

Pettit, Rhonda. Joy Harjo. (Western Writers Ser: Vol. 133). pap. 5.95 (*0-88430-132-X*) Boise St U W Writ Ser.

***Pettit, Rhonda S.** A Gendered Collision: Sentimentalism & Modernism in Dorothy Parker's Poetry & Fiction. LC 99-51766. 248p. 2000. 39.50 (*0-8386-3818-X*) Fairleigh Dickinson.

Pettit, Roberta L., et al. Forces & Motion: Teacher's Manual. LC 93-83808. 1993. write for info. (*1-881028-06-2*) Sci for Kids.

Pettit, T. H. Hospital Administration for Veterinary Staff. LC 93-74972. 200p. 1994. pap. text 29.95 (*0-939674-53-X*) Am Vet Pubns.

Pettit, William E. Signature in Blood. LC 95-74596. 256p. 1995. 24.95 (*0-925591-39-4*) Covenant Hse Bks.

Pettitt, C. W., jt. ed. see Nudds, J. R.

Pettitt, Charles, jt. auth. see Orna, Elizabeth.

Pettitt, Charles, jt. auth. see Orna, Wlizabeth.

Pettitt, Deirdre, jt. ed. see Davis, Andrew.

Pettitt, George A. The Quileute of La Push, 1775-1945. fac. ed. Lowie, Robert H., et al, eds. (University of California Publications: No. 14:1). 141p. (C). 1950. reprint ed. pap. 15.63 (*1-55567-134-9*) Coyote Press.

Pettitt, Joe. High Performance Honda Builder's Handbook, Vol. II. 2nd ed. (Illus.). 128p. 1999. pap. 18.95 (*1-884089-38-0*, S-A Design) CarTech.

— High Performance Honda Builder's Handbook: How to Build & Tune High Performance Honda Cars & Engines. (Illus.). 128p. (Orig.). 1996. pap. 18.95 (*1-884089-21-6*, S-A Design) CarTech.

— How to Design & Install High Performance Car Stereo: A Beginner's Guide to High Tech Auto Sound Systems. LC 99-218939. (Illus.). 128p. (Orig.). 1996. pap. 18.95 (*1-884089-17-8*, S-A Design) CarTech.

— Nitrous Oxide Injection Guide: How to Make Maximum Power with Nitrous Oxide Injection. LC 99-218940. (Illus.). 128p. (Orig.). 1998. pap. 18.95 (*1-884089-22-4*, S-A Design) CarTech.

***Pettitt, Joe.** Sport Compact Bolt-On Performance Guide Vol. 1: Import Cars. 160p. 2000. pap. 18.95 (*1-884089-52-6*, Pub. by CarTech) Voyageur Pr.

***Pettitt, Kenneth I.** A Berkeley Antebellum. (Illus.). 200p. 1999. pap. 15.00 (*0-9676781-0-2*) K I Pettitt.

***Pettitt, Lance.** Screening Ireland: Film & Television Representation. LC 99-55157. 2000. write for info. (*0-7190-5269-6*, Pub. by Manchester Univ Pr); pap. write for info. (*0-7190-5270-X*, Pub. by Manchester Univ Pr) St Martin.

Pettitt, Roland A. Exploring the Jemez Country. 2nd rev. ed. LC 90-33924. (Illus.). 112p. 1990. pap. 8.95 (*0-941232-10-7*) Los Alamos Hist Soc.

Pettitt, Stephen. Handel. LC 93-39722. (Compact Companions Ser.). (Illus.). 192p. 1994. 17.50 (*0-671-88790-4*) S&S Trade.

— Opera: A Crash Course. 144p. 1998. 14.95 (*0-8230-0975-0*) Watsn-Guptill.

Pettitt, Stephen, jt. auth. see Brassington, Frances.

Pettitt, Thomas, ed. The Entertainer: In Medieval & Traditional Culture. 148p. 1997. pap. 19.00 (*87-7838-294-7*, Pub. by Odense Univ) Intl Spec Bk.

Pettitt, Wilfrid H. Nine Girls. 101p. (YA). (gr. 10 up). 1942. pap. 5.50 (*0-87129-923-2*, N14) Dramatic Pub.

Pettiway, Leon E. Honey, Honey, Miss Thang: Being Black, Gay, & on the Streets. LC 96-20077. 320p. 1996. 69.95 (*1-56639-497-X*); pap. 22.95 (*1-56639-498-8*) Temple U Pr.

— Workin' It: Women Living Through Drugs & Crime. LC 97-21497. 304p. 1997. 59.95 (*1-56639-579-8*); pap. 19.95 (*1-56639-580-1*) Temple U Pr.

Pettler, Pamela & Heckerling, Amy. The No-Sex Handbook. 1990. mass mkt. 6.95 (*0-446-39054-2*, Pub. by Warner Bks) Little.

Pettman. Moral Claims in World Affairs. (Australian National University Press Ser.). 1996. write for info. (*0-08-033016-5*, Pergamon Pr) Elsevier.

Pettman, Barrie O. Manpower Planning Workbook. 2nd ed. LC 83-18488. 127p. 1984. text 76.95 (*0-566-02468-3*) Ashgate Pub Co.

Pettman, Barrie O., jt. auth. see Dobbins, Richard.

Pettman, Jan. Living in the Margins: Racism, Sexism & Feminism in Australia. 220p. (Orig.). 1992. pap. text 19.95 (*1-86373-005-2*, Pub. by Allen & Unwin Pty) Paul & Co Pubs.

Pettman, Jan J. Worlding Women: Feminist International Politics. 224p. (C). 1996. 85.00 (*0-415-15201-1*); pap. 25.99 (*0-415-15202-X*) Routledge.

***Pettman, Ralph.** Commonsense Constructivism: Or the Making of World Affairs. LC 99-87793. (International Relations in a Constructed World Ser.). (Illus.). 256p. 2000. text 65.95 (*0-7656-0577-5*) M E Sharpe.

— Commonsense Constructivism: Or the Making of World Affairs. (International Relations in a Constructed World Ser.). 256p. 2000. reprint ed. pap. text 25.95 (*0-7656-0578-3*) M E Sharpe.

Pettman, Ralph. International Politics: Balance of Power, Balance of Productivity, Balance of Ideologies. LC 91-2110. 247p. (C). 1991. pap. text 17.95 (*1-55587-281-6*) L Rienner.

— Understanding International Political Economy, with Readings for the Fatigued. 257p. (Orig.). 1996. pap. text 19.95 (*1-55587-677-3*, 87-677-3) L Rienner.

— Understanding International Political Economy, with Readings for the Fatigued. (Orig.). 1996. lib. bdg. 48.00 (*1-55587-666-8*, 87-666-8) L Rienner.

***Pettman, Ralph.** Understanding World Affairs: Beyond Rationalism. LC 00-33298. 2000. write for info. (*0-312-23693-X*) St Martin.

Pettman, William R. The Resources of the United Kingdom: or The Present Distress Considered. LC 68-56563. (Reprints of Economic Classics Ser.). ix, 291p. 1970. reprint ed. 45.00 (*0-678-00661-X*) Kelley.

***Pettnay, Arnold.** Talking Book: The African American Family Book of Record. 650p. 1999. 55.00 (*0-9669759-1-X*, 002) Lola James.

Petto, Andrew J., jt. ed. see Novak, Melinda A.

Pettofrezzo, Anthony J. Matrices & Transformations. 133p. 1978. reprint ed. pap. text 6.95 (*0-486-63634-8*) Dover.

Pettorossi, A., ed. Meta-Programming in Logic: Third International Workshop, META-92, Uppsala, Sweden, June 10-12, 1992: Proceedings. LC 92-41020. (Lecture Notes in Computer Science Ser.: Vol. 649). 1992. 57.95 (*0-387-56282-6*) Spr-Verlag.

Petts, C., jt. ed. see Buttler, H.

Petts, G. & Calow, P. River Flows & Channel Forms. (Illus.). 272p. (Orig.). 1996. pap. text 49.95 (*0-86542-920-0*) Blackwell Sci.

— River Restoration. (Illus.). 240p. (Orig.). 1996. pap. text 49.95 (*0-86542-919-7*) Blackwell Sci.

Petts, G., jt. ed. see Cosgrove, D.

Petts, G. E., jt. auth. see Calow, P.

Petts, G. E., jt. auth. see Carling, Paul A.

Petts, Geoffrey E., jt. ed. see Calow, Peter.

Petts, Geoffrey E., jt. ed. see Gore, James A.

Petts, Geoffrey E., jt. ed. see Gurnell, Angela M.

P

Petts, Judith. Handbook of Environmental Impact Assessment, 2 vols. Incl. Vol. 1. Handbook of Environmental Impact Assessment. LC 98-34000. (Illus.). 1999. 165.00 (*0-632-04772-0*); Vol. 2. Handbook of Environmental Impact Assessment. Wood, Christopher & Therivel, Riki. LC 98-34000. (Illus.). 1999. 165.00 (*0-632-04771-2*); LC 98-34000. (Illus.). 275.00 (*0-632-04773-9*) Blackwell Sci.

Petts, Judith, et al, eds. Risk-Based Contaminated Land Investigation & Assessment. LC 97-7957. 352p. 1997. 100.00 (*0-471-96608-8*) Wiley.

Petts, Judith & Eduljee, Gev. Environmental Impact Assessment for Waste Treatment & Disposal Facilities. 508p. 1994. 170.00 (*0-471-94112-3*) Wiley.

Petts, Kusha. Necklace for a Poor Sod. (C). 1979. 30.00 (*0-85088-435-7*, Pub. by Gomer Pr) St Mut.

Pettus, Alvin M., jt. auth. see Allain, Violet A.

Pettus, Dania, jt. auth. see Lehmann, Peggy.

Pettus, Daniel D., jt. auth. see Pettus, Eloise S.

Pettus, David. Horizontal, Extended-Reach, & Wide-Angle Drilling: An Annotated & Indexed Bibliography. 516p. (Orig.). 1992. 89.00 (*0-89896-441-5*); pap. 50.00 (*0-89896-440-7*) Larksdale.

Pettus, Eloise S. & Pettus, Daniel D. Master Index to More Summaries of Children's Books, 1980-1990. LC 98-11254. 1998. 198.00 (*0-8108-3269-0*) Scarecrow.

— Master Index to Summaries of Children's Books: Title & Subject Indexes, 2 vols. LC 85-1901. 1998. 94.00 (*0-8108-1795-0*) Scarecrow.

Pettus, Louise, ed. see Bodie, Idella F.

Pettus, Sharon W. San Xavier del Bac: An Artist's Portfolio. LC 96-61116. (Illus.). 64p. 1997. 14.95 (*1-887896-04-X*) Treas Chest Bks.

***Pettus, Trent L.** Black Is the Color Left Out of the Rainbow. 32p. 1999. 14.95 (*0-9673829-0-4*) T L P Bk Co.

Pettway, Arnold. African Love Charms: Rythmic Speech & Sweet Song. 133p. 1999. pap. 9.95 (*0-9669759-0-1*) Lola James.

Petty. An Introduction to Molecular Electronics. (Physics Ser.). 1997. pap. 34.50 (*0-340-58009-7*, VNR) Wiley.

— 1997 Year Book of Pulmonary Diseases. (Illus.). 560p. (C). (gr. 13). 1997. text 79.00 (*0-8151-9735-7*, 25022) Mosby Inc.

— Total Joint Replacement. (Illus.). 896p. 1991. text 187.00 (*0-7216-3367-6*, W B Saunders Co) Harcrt Hlth Sci Grp.

***Petty, Barbara.** Thoughts & Memories. 1999. pap. write for info. (*1-58235-347-6*) Watermrk Pr.

***Petty, Bill.** Highways of the Heart. Patton, Claudia, ed. (Illus.). ix, 103p. 2000. pap. 14.00 (*0-9701893-0-3*) CAN-USA.

Petty, Carolyn A. Waterdrum Science: Science Through American Indian Arts & Culture. Duranske, Benjamin, ed. LC 94-78267. (Illus.). 290p. (J). (gr. 4-8). 1994. lib. bdg. 28.50 (*0-9642898-0-6*) Larchmere Ltd.

Petty, Celia, jt. ed. see Bracken, Patrick J.

Petty, Charles E. High Standard Automatic Pistols 1932-1950. 19.95 (*0-88227-029-X*) Gun Room.

Petty, Clayton. The Anesthesia Machine. LC 86-21574. (Illus.). 246p. reprint ed. pap. 76.30 (*0-7837-6809-5*, 204664100003) Bks Demand.

Petty, D. J., jt. auth. see Harrison, D. K.

Petty, Damon H., jt. auth. see Knowles, Harvey C., 3rd.

***Petty, David.** Origami Wreaths & Rings. LC 98-61606. (Illus.). 123p. 1998. pap. 19.95 (*0-9627254-1-2*) Zenagraf.

Petty, Evan R. Martensite: Fundamentals & Technology. LC 70-546066. 217p. reprint ed. pap. 67.30 (*0-608-11413-8*, 200364800038) Bks Demand.

Petty, Fred C. Italian Opera in London, 1760-1800. Buelow, George, ed. LC 79-25564. (Studies in Musicology: No. 16). 441p. 1980. reprint ed. pap. 136.80 (*0-8357-1073-4*, 207022700064) Bks Demand.

Petty, Geoffrey. How to Be a Better Creative Thinker. (How to Be a Better...Ser.). 1997. pap. 15.95 (*0-7494-2167-3*) Kogan Page Ltd.

— Teaching Today: A Practical Guide. 384p. (C). 1993. 42.50 (*0-7487-1697-1*, Pub. by S Thornes Pubs) Trans-Atl Phila.

Petty, Gilbert & Petty, June. A Clean Sweep: A Sailor's Diary in the Pacific World War II. Cornett, June L., ed. (Illus.). 152p. (Orig.). 1988. pap. 9.95 (*0-9620646-0-2*) Petty Pub.

Petty, H. R. Molecular Biology of Membranes: Structure & Function. (Illus.). 424p. (C). 1993. text 69.50 (*0-306-44429-1*, Kluwer Plenum) Kluwer Academic.

Petty Hunter, Carol A., ed. see Posey, Alexander.

***Petty, J. William, et al.** Harvesting Investments in Private Companies. LC 98-73868. 220p. 1999. pap. 39.75 (*1-885065-15-9*) Finan Exec.

Petty, James. Step by Step: Divine Guidance for Ordinary Christians. LC 99-31303. (Resources for Changing Lives Ser.). 1999. pap. 14.99 (*0-87552-603-9*) P & R Pubng.

Petty, James D., jt. auth. see Dempsey, Carla H.

Petty, Jo. An Apple a Day. 1999. 9.95 (*0-7667-2978-8*) Gibson.

— An Apple a Day: Treasured Selections from Apples of Gold. 1979. 8.95 (*0-8378-5025-8*) Gibson.

***Petty, Jo.** Apples of Gold. (Illus.). 2000. 12.99 (*0-7667-6656-X*) Gibson.

Petty, Jo. Apples of Gold. large type ed. 144p. 1985. pap. 9.95 (*0-8027-2502-3*) Walker & Co.

***Petty, Jo.** Apples of Gold: Wings of Silver; Treasures of Silver, 3 bks. in 1. 288p. 1998. 9.99 (*0-88486-218-6*) Arrowood Pr.

Petty, Jo. Jo Petty's Words to Live By: A Treasury of Favorite Sayings. (Illus.). 160p. 1997. pap. text 6.99 (*0-88486-160-0*, Bristol Park Bks) Arrowood Pr.

— Jo Petty's Words to Live By: An Inspirational Book. (Illus.). 160p. 1995. 9.98 (*0-88486-123-6*) Galahad Bks.

— Life's Little Book of Virtues. 160p. 1996. 9.99 (*0-88486-148-1*, Inspirational Pr) Arrowood Pr.

***Petty, Jo.** Wings of Silver. (Illus.). 2000. 12.99 (*0-7667-6657-8*) Gibson.

Petty, Jo. Wings of Silver. large type ed. 128p. 1986. 9.95 (*0-8027-2546-5*) Walker & Co.

Petty, Judson, jt. ed. see Hook, Cass.

Petty, Julian J. The Growth & Distribution of Population in South Carolina. LC 74-34438. (Illus.). 242p. 1975. reprint ed. 30.00 (*0-87152-200-4*) Reprint.

Petty, June, jt. auth. see Petty, Gilbert.

***Petty, Kate.** Amazing Pop-Up Geography Book. (Illus.). 14p. (J). (gr. 3 up). 2000. 22.99 (*0-525-46438-7*, Dutton Child) Peng Put Young Read.

Petty, Kate. The Amazing Pop-Up Multiplication Book. LC 98-208909. (Illus.). 16p. (J). (gr. 2-4). 1998. 19.99 (*0-525-45998-7*, Dutton Child) Peng Put Young Read.

— Baby Animals: Bears. (Illus.). 24p. (J). (ps-3). 1992. pap. 4.95 (*0-8120-4964-0*) Barron.

— Baby Animals: Chimpanzees. (Illus.). 24p. (J). (ps-3). 1992. pap. 3.95 (*0-8120-4965-9*) Barron.

— Baby Animals: Elephants. (Illus.). 24p. (J). (ps-3). 1992. pap. 3.95 (*0-8120-4966-7*) Barron.

— Baby Animals: Kittens. (Illus.). 24p. (J). (ps-3). 1992. pap. 3.95 (*0-8120-4967-5*) Barron.

— Baby Animals: Pandas. (Illus.). 24p. (J). (ps-3). 1992. pap. 3.95 (*0-8120-4968-3*) Barron.

— Baby Animals: Puppies. (Illus.). 24p. (J). (ps-3). 1992. pap. 3.95 (*0-8120-4969-1*) Barron.

— Baby Animals: Seals. (Illus.). 24p. (J). (ps-3). 1992. pap. 3.95 (*0-8120-4970-5*) Barron.

— Baby Animals: Tigers. (Illus.). 24p. (J). (ps-3). 1992. pap. 3.95 (*0-8120-4971-3*) Barron.

— Bears. (Baby Animals Ser.). 1992. 10.15 (*0-606-01601-5*, Pub. by Turtleback) Demco.

— Being Bullied. (Playground Ser.). (Illus.). 24p. (J). (ps-2). 1991. pap. 5.95 (*0-8120-4661-7*) Barron.

— Cats. (First Pets Ser.). (Illus.). 24p. (J). (ps-3). 1993. pap. 4.95 (*0-8120-1485-5*) Barron.

— Chimpanzees. (Baby Animals Ser.). (J). 1990. 9.15 (*0-606-01603-1*, Pub. by Turtleback) Demco.

— Crocodiles Yawn to Keep Cool: And Other Amazing Facts about Crocodiles & Alligators. LC 98-6802. (I Didn't Know That... Ser.). (Illus.). 32p. (J). (gr. 1-3). 1998. 8.95 (*0-7613-0737-0*, Copper Beech Bks); lib. bdg. 20.90 (*0-7613-0818-0*, Copper Beech Bks) Millbrook Pr.

— Dinosaurs Laid Eggs: And Other Amazing Facts about Prehistoric Reptiles. LC 97-8021. (I Didn't Know That... Ser.). (Illus.). 32p. (J). (gr. 1-3). 1997. lib. bdg. 19.90 (*0-7613-0549-1*, Copper Beech Bks) Millbrook Pr.

— Dinosaurs Laid Eggs: And Other Amazing Facts about Prehistoric Reptiles. LC 97-8021. (I Didn't Know That... Ser.). (Illus.). 32p. (J). (gr. 1-3). 1997. 8.95 (*0-7613-0596-3*, Copper Beech Bks) Millbrook Pr.

— Dogs. (First Pets Ser.). (Illus.). 24p. (J). (ps-3). 1993. pap. 4.95 (*0-8120-1484-7*) Barron.

— Ducklings. (Baby Animals Ser.). (Illus.). 24p. (J). (gr. k-3). 1993. pap. 3.95 (*0-8120-1489-8*) Barron.

— Elephants. (Baby Animals Ser.). (J). 1992. 8.90 (*0-606-01604-X*, Pub. by Turtleback) Demco.

— Feeling Left Out. (Playground Ser.). (Illus.). 24p. (J). (ps-2). 1991. pap. 4.95 (*0-8120-4658-7*) Barron.

— Guinea Pigs. LC 94-26050. (First Pets Ser.). (Illus.). 24p. (J). (ps-3). 1995. pap. 4.95 (*0-8120-9080-2*) Barron.

— Hamsters. (First Pets Ser.). (Illus.). 24p. (J). (ps-3). 1993. pap. 4.95 (*0-8120-1472-3*) Barron.

— Into Space. (Around & About Ser.). (Illus.). 32p. (J). (gr. 2-4). 1993. pap. 5.95 (*0-8120-1761-7*) Barron.

— Kangaroos. (Baby Animals Ser.). (Illus.). 24p. (J). (gr. k-3). 1993. pap. 3.95 (*0-8120-1492-8*) Barron.

— Kittens. (Baby Animals Ser.). 1990. 9.15 (*0-606-01605-8*, Pub. by Turtleback) Demco.

— Lions. (Baby Animals Ser.). (Illus.). 24p. (J). (gr. k-3). 1993. pap. 3.95 (*0-8120-1490-1*) Barron.

***Petty, Kate.** Little Rabbit's First Number Book. (Illus.). 30p. (J). 1998. pap. 12.98 (*1-58048-054-3*) Sandvik Pub.

Petty, Kate. Making Friends. LC 91-14193. (Playground Ser.). (Illus.). 24p. (J). (ps-3). 1991. pap. 5.95 (*0-8120-4660-9*) Barron.

— Maps & Journeys. (Around & About Ser.). (Illus.). 32p. (J). (gr. 2-4). 1993. pap. 5.95 (*0-8120-1235-6*) Barron.

— My First Atlas, Vol. 1. LC 90-37926. (Illus.). (J). (ps-8). 1991. 9.95 (*1-55782-361-8*) Little.

— Our Globe, Our World. (Around & About Ser.). (Illus.). 32p. (J). (gr. 2-4). 1993. pap. 5.95 (*0-8120-1236-4*) Barron.

— Pandas. (Baby Animals Ser.). 1992. 9.15 (*0-606-01607-4*, Pub. by Turtleback) Demco.

— People Chase Twisters: And Other Amazing Facts about Violent Weather. LC 97-41607. (I Didn't Know That... Ser.). (Illus.). 32p. (J). (gr. 1-3). 1998. 8.95 (*0-7613-0647-1*, Copper Beech Bks); lib. bdg. 19.90 (*0-7613-0715-X*, Copper Beech Bks) Millbrook Pr.

— Playing the Game. (Playground Ser.). (Illus.). 24p. (J). (ps-2). 1991. pap. 4.95 (*0-8120-4659-5*) Barron.

— Ponies & Foals. (Baby Animals Ser.). (Illus.). 24p. (J). (gr. k-3). 1993. pap. 3.95 (*0-8120-1487-1*) Barron.

— Puppies. (Baby Animals Ser.). 1992. 9.15 (*0-606-01610-4*, Pub. by Turtleback) Demco.

— Rabbits. (First Pets Ser.). (Illus.). 24p. (J). (ps-3). 1993. pap. 4.95 (*0-8120-1473-1*) Barron.

— Rainforests: Around & About. (Around & About Ser.). (Illus.). 32p. (J). (gr. 2-4). 1993. pap. 5.95 (*0-8120-1760-9*) Barron.

— Rosie Plants a Radish. (Lift-the-Flap Nature Bks.). (Illus.). 16p. (J). 1998. 9.95 (*0-8362-5258-6*) Andrews & McMeel.

— Sam Plants a Sunflower. (Illus.). 16p. (J). 1998. 9.95 (*0-8362-5259-4*) Andrews & McMeel.

— Seals. (Baby Animals Ser.). 1992. 9.15 (*0-606-01611-2*, Pub. by Turtleback) Demco.

— Some Planes Hover: And Other Amazing Facts about Flying Machines. LC 97-31923. (I Didn't Know That... Ser.). (Illus.). 32p. (J). (gr. 1-3). 1998. 8.95 (*0-7613-0645-5*, Copper Beech Bks); lib. bdg. 19.90 (*0-7613-0713-3*, Copper Beech Bks) Millbrook Pr.

— Some Trains Run on Water: And Other Amazing Facts about Rail Transport. LC 97-8236. (I Didn't Know That... Ser.). (Illus.). 32p. (J). (gr. 1-3). 1997. 8.95 (*0-7613-0598-X*, Copper Beech Bks) Millbrook Pr.

— Some Trains Run on Water: And Other Amazing Facts about Rail Transport. LC 97-8236. (I Didn't Know That... Ser.). (Illus.). 32p. (J). (gr. 1-3). 1997. lib. bdg. 19.90 (*0-7613-0609-9*, Copper Beech Bks) Millbrook Pr.

— The Sun Is a Star: And Other Amazing Facts about Space. (I Didn't Know That... Ser.). (Illus.). 32p. (J). (gr. 1-3). 1997. 8.95 (*0-7613-0593-9*, Copper Beech Bks); lib. bdg. 19.90 (*0-7613-0567-X*, Copper Beech Bks) Millbrook Pr.

***Petty, Kate.** Tidal Waves Wash Away Cities & Other Facts about Stormy Seas. LC 99-38596. (I Didn't Know That Ser.). (Illus.). 32p. (J). (gr. 1-3). 1999. 21.90 (*0-7613-0922-5*, Copper Beech Bks) Millbrook Pr.

— Tidal Waves Wash Away Cities & Other Facts about Stormy Seas. LC 99-38596. (I Didn't Know That... Ser.). 32p. (J). (gr. 1-3). 1999. 8.95 (*0-7613-0799-0*, Copper Beech Bks) Millbrook Pr.

Petty, Kate. Tigers. (Baby Animals Ser.). 1992. 9.15 (*0-606-01612-0*, Pub. by Turtleback) Demco.

— A Truck Can Be As Big As a House: And Other Amazing Facts about Trucks. LC 98-55543. (I Didn't Know That... Ser.). (Illus.). 32p. (J). 1999. 8.95 (*0-7613-0796-6*, Copper Beech Bks) Millbrook Pr.

***Petty, Kate.** A Truck Can Be as Big as a House: And Other Amazing Facts about Trucks. LC 98-55543. (I Didn't Know That... Ser.). (Illus.). 32p. (J). (gr. 1-3). 1999. lib. bdg. 21.90 (*0-7613-0913-6*, Copper Beech Bks) Millbrook Pr.

Petty, Kate. Whales Sing: And Other Amazing Facts about Sea Mammals. LC 98-6804. (I Didn't Know That... Ser.). (Illus.). 32p. (J). (gr. 1-3). 1998. 8.95 (*0-7613-0738-9*, Copper Beech Bks); lib. bdg. 20.90 (*0-7613-0819-9*, Copper Beech Bks) Millbrook Pr.

— You Can Jump Higher on the Moon: And Other Amazing Facts about Space Exploration. (I Didn't Know That... Ser.). (Illus.). 32p. (J). (gr. 1-3). 1997. 8.95 (*0-7613-0592-0*, Copper Beech Bks); lib. bdg. 19.90 (*0-7613-0564-5*, Copper Beech Bks) Millbrook Pr.

Petty, Kate, jt. auth. see Maizels, Jennie.

Petty, L. Jalik. Black Campus Ministry. 2nd ed. pap. text 4.95 (*0-942428-01-3*) Universal Ministries.

— Reducing Racial Tension in the Schools Through Values Clarification. LC 81-52146. 56p. (Orig.). (C). 1982. pap. 10.00 (*0-942428-00-5*) Universal Ministries.

***Petty, Linda.** Sing Me a Bible Story Vol. 1: User-Friendly Bible Story Lessons & Songs for Church, Home & School - New Testament. (Illus.). 60p. 1999. pap., teacher ed. write for info. incl. audio compact disk (*0-9678739-0-8*); pap., teacher ed. write for info. incl. audio (*0-9678739-1-6*) Shoestring NC.

***Petty, Marsha A.** The Silent Plague - Constipation. (Illus.). 183p. 1999. pap. 12.95 (*0-9671022-0-0*) Mo Better Hlth.

Petty, Mary V. Forgiven: Walking with a Women. (Illus.). 65p. (Orig.). 1997. pap. 12.95 (*0-9655574-0-5*) MVP Bks.

Petty, Michael C. Langmuir-Blodgett Films: An Introduction. (Illus.). 252p. (C). 1996. text 80.00 (*0-521-41396-6*); pap. text 32.95 (*0-521-42450-X*) Cambridge U Pr.

Petty, Michael C., et al. An Introduction to Molecular Electronics. (Illus.). 400p. 1995. pap. text 50.00 (*0-19-521156-1*) OUP.

Petty, Michael W. A Faith That Loves the Earth: The Ecological Theology of Karl Rahner. (Orig.). 1996. pap. text 29.00 (*0-7618-0278-9*) U Pr of Amer.

— A Faith That Loves the Earth: The Ecological Theology of Karl Rahner. 204p. (Orig.). (C). 1996. lib. bdg. 48.00 (*0-7618-0277-0*) U Pr of Amer.

Petty, Michelle. How to Draw Bugs. (Illus.). 32p. (J). (gr. 2-7). 1997. pap. 2.95 (*0-8167-4447-5*) Troll Communs.

— How to Draw Bugs. (How to Draw Ser.). (Illus.). (J). 1997. pap. 2.95 (*0-8167-4322-3*) Troll Communs.

— Let's Go to School. LC 95-20411. (First Start Easy Reader Ser.). (Illus.). 32p. (J). (gr. k-3). 1995. pap. text 2.95 (*0-8167-3853-X*); lib. bdg. 13.05 (*0-8167-3852-1*) Troll Communs.

— Let's Go to School, Big Book ed. 1999. pap. text 16.95 (*0-8167-3955-2*); pap. text 16.95 (*0-8167-3985-4*) Troll Communs.

Petty, Nicola J. & Moore, Ann P. Neuromusculoskeletal Examination & Assessment: A Handbook for Therapists. LC 97-33318. 1998. pap. text 35.00 (*0-443-05980-2*) Church.

Petty, Priscilla H. Under a Lucky Star: The Story of Frederick A. Hauck. LC 86-72173. (Illus.). 180p. 1987. 22.95 (*0-9617747-0-3*) Cin Oral Hist Foun.

Petty, R. E. & Cacioppo, John T. Communication & Persuasion. (Social Psychology Ser.). (Illus.). 220p. 1986. 58.00 (*0-387-96344-8*) Spr-Verlag.

Petty, Richard E. Attitude Strength: Antecedents & Consequences. Krosnick, Jon A., ed. 528p. 1995. pap. 49.95 (*0-8058-1087-0*) L Erlbaum Assocs.

Petty, Richard E., et al, eds. Cognitive Responses in Persuasion. LC 80-26388. 512p. 1981. text 49.95 (*0-89859-025-6*) L Erlbaum Assocs.

Petty, Richard E. & Cacioppo, John T. Attitudes & Persuasion: Classic & Contemporary Approaches. (C). 1996. pap. 29.00 (*0-8133-3005-X*, Pub. by Westview) HarpC.

Petty, Richard E. & Krosnick, Jon A., eds. Attitude Strength: Antecedents & Consequences. 528p. 1995. text 110.00 (*0-8058-1086-2*) L Erlbaum Assocs.

Petty, Richard E., jt. ed. see Cacioppo, John T.

Petty, Robert, et al. Out of the Shadows: Defeating Disabilities. (Illus.). 149p. (Orig.). 1992. pap. text 8.50 (*0-9632731-0-8*) Delano Pr.

Petty, Ross D. The Impact of Advertising Law on Business & Public Policy. LC 92-8403. 248p. 1992. 55.00 (*0-89930-617-9*, PCQ, Quorum Bks) Greenwood.

Petty, Ross E., jt. auth. see Cassidy, James T.

Petty, Sheila, ed. A Call to Action: The Films of Ousmane Sembene. LC 96-28760. 208p. 1996. pap. 20.95 (*0-275-95801-9*, Praeger Pubs) Greenwood.

Petty, Steve. Walk with Jesus: Resources for Holy Week. 48p. 1989. pap. 2.95 (*0-687-44005-X*) Abingdon.

Petty, Thomas L., ed. Chronic Obstructive Pulmonary Disease. 2nd ed. (Lung Biology in Health & Disease Ser.: Vol. 28). (Illus.). 512p. 1985. text 215.00 (*0-8247-7385-3*) Dekker.

Petty, Thomas L. & Nett, Louise M. Enjoying Life with Chronic Obstructive Pulmonary Disease. write for info. (*1-886128-04-9*) Laennec Pub.

Petty, Thomas L., et al. Intensive & Rehabilitative Respiratory Care: A Practical Approach to the Management of Acute & Chronic Respiratory Failure. 3rd ed. LC 81-23630. 478p. reprint ed. pap. 148.20 (*0-7837-2738-0*, 204311800006) Bks Demand.

Petty, Thomas L., jt. auth. see Hodgkin, John E.

Petty, Thomas L., jt. auth. see Scoggin, Charles H.

Petty, Thomas L., jt. ed. see Casaburi, Richard.

Petty, Tom. Tom Petty & the Heartbreakers: Greatest Hits (Guitar) Roed, Tom, ed. (Illus.). 100p. (Orig.). 1994. pap. text 19.95 (*0-89898-766-0*, P1061GTX) Wrner Bros.

— Tom Petty & the Heartbreakers: Greatest Hits (Piano) Roed, Tom, ed. (Illus.). 80p. (Orig.). 1994. pap. text 16.95 (*0-89898-765-2*, P1061SMX) Wrner Bros.

Petty, Vincent. Swedish-English - English-Swedish Standard Dictionary. rev. ed. 804p. 1995. pap. 19.95 (*0-7818-0379-9*) Hippocrene Bks.

Petty, W. Clayton, jt. auth. see Stanley, Theodore H.

Petty, W. Clayton, jt. ed. see Stanley, Theodore H.

Petty, Walter T., et al. Experiences in Language: Tools & Techniques for Language Arts Methods, Examination Copy. 6th ed. (C). 1994. pap. write for info. (*0-205-15895-1*, H5895-1) Allyn.

Petty, William. The Economic Writings of Sir William Petty, 2 vols Hull, Charles H., ed. LC 63-23521. (Reprints of Economic Classics Ser.). xci, 700p. 1986. reprint ed. 65.00 (*0-678-00029-8*) Kelley.

***Petty, William.** Some Cars Swim & other Amazing Facts about Cars. LC 99-39174. 32p. (J). (gr. 1-3). 1999. 21.90 (*0-7613-0921-7*, Copper Beech Bks) Millbrook Pr.

— Some Cars Swim & Other Amazing Facts about Cars. LC 99-39174. (I Didn't Know That... Ser.). 32p. (J). (gr. 1-3). 1999. 8.95 (*0-7613-0798-2*, Copper Beech Bks) Millbrook Pr.

Pettygrove, G. Stuart. How to Perform an Agricultural Experiment. 26p. 1971. 7.25 (*0-86619-039-2*); 7.25 (*0-86619-040-6*) Vols Tech Asst.

Pettygrove, G. Stuart & Asano, Takashi. Irrigation with Reclaimed Municipal Wastewater. (Illus.). 528p. 1985. lib. bdg. 97.50 (*0-87371-061-4*, L061) Lewis Pubs.

Pettyjohn, E. S. & Linden, H. R. Selection of Oils for Carbureted Water Gas, No. 9. iv, 51p. 1952. pap. 25.00 (*1-58222-042-5*) Inst Gas Tech.

Pettyjohn, E. S., jt. auth. see Linden, H. R.

Pettyjohn, Wayne A. Introduction to Artificial Ground Water Recharge. (C). 1989. 90.00 (*81-85046-69-7*, Pub. by Scientific) St Mut.

Pettyjohn, Wayne A., ed. Protection of Public Water Supplies from Ground-Water Contamination. LC 86-31173. (Pollution Technology Review Ser.: No. 141). (Illus.). 177p. 1987. 36.00 (*0-8155-1119-1*) Noyes.

Petuch, Edward. Coastal Paleoceanography of Eastern North America. LC 97-215472. 400p. (C). 1997. per. 70.95 (*0-7872-3719-1*, 41371901) Kendall-Hunt.

Petuch, Edward J. The Edge of the Fossil Sea: Life Along the Shores of Prehistoric Florida. (Illus.). 80p. (Orig.). 1992. pap. 14.00 (*0-9634264-0-0*) B-M Shell Mus.

— Field Guide to the Ecphoras. (Illus.). 1989. 21.50 (*0-938415-03-4*) CERF Inc.

— Neogene History of Tropical American Mollusks. (Illus.). 1988. 64.95 (*0-938415-02-6*) CERF Inc.

— New Caribbean Molluscan Faunas. (Illus.). 1987. 38.50 (*0-938415-01-8*) CERF Inc.

Petuchowski, Elizabeth, tr. see Breuer, Mordechai.

Petuchowski, Jacob J. Freedom of Expression in the Jewish Tradition. 34p. 1984. pap. 2.50 (*0-87495-062-7*) Am Jewish Comm.

Petuchowski, Jakob J. Studies in Modern Theology & Prayer. LC 96-45217. 376p. 1997. 34.95 (*0-8276-0577-3*) JPS Phila.

***Petuchowski, Jakob J.** Theology & Poetry: Studies in the Medieval Piyyut. 160p. 2000. reprint ed. pap. 14.95 (*0-8143-2937-3*) Wayne St U Pr.

Petuchowski, Jakob J. The Theology of Haham David Nieto. 1970. 10.00 (*0-87068-015-3*) Ktav.

Petuchowski, Jakob J., ed. New Perspectives on Abraham Geiger: An HUC-JIR Symposium. LC 75-19131. 64p. reprint ed. pap. 30.00 (*0-7837-3000-4*, 204294100006) Bks Demand.

— When Jews & Christians Meet. LC 87-9981. 160p. 1988. text 18.50 (*0-88706-631-3*) State U NY Pr.

Petukhov, I. M. & Batugina, I. M. Bibliography of Rockbursts 1900-1979, Pt. I. 308p. (C). 1991. text 175.00 (*90-6191-177-X*, Pub. by A A Balkema) Ashgate Pub Co.

Petukhov, I. M., jt. auth. see Batugina, I. M.

An Asterisk (*) at the beginning of an entry indicates that the title is appearing for the first time.

Petulengro, Gipsy. Romany Remedies & Recipes. 62p. 1995. 12.50 (*0-89904-274-0*, Silhouette Imprints); pap. 8.25 (*0-89904-275-9*, Silhouette Imprints) Crumb Elbow Pub.
— Romany Remedies & Recipes. 47p. 1996. reprint ed. spiral bd. 8.50 (*0-7873-0669-X*) Hlth Research.
Petulengro, Gipsy & Starkie, Walter F. Romany Herbal Remedies. 1972. reprint ed. pap. 5.95 (*0-87877-016-X*, H-16) Newcastle Pub.
Petulla, Joseph. Crisis to Wellness: Meditations for a Philosophy of Living. LC 92-74018. (Illus.). 155p. (Orig.). 1993. pap. 9.95 (*0-9628464-2-2*) Cmnty Resc Inst.
— Environmental Protection in the United States. LC 87-60733. 208p. 1987. 18.50 (*0-936434-21-X*); pap. 14.50 (*0-936434-22-8*) SF Study Ctr.
— The Tao Te Ching & the Christian Way. LC 98-35571. (Illus.). 140p. 1998. pap. 12.00 (*1-57075-211-7*) Orbis Bks.
Petursson, G., ed. Maedi-Visna & Related Diseases. (Developments in Veterinary Virology Ser.). (C). 1989. text 191.50 (*0-7923-0481-0*) Kluwer Academic.
Petursson, Hallgrim. The Way of the Cross: Selections from the Poetry of Hallgrim Petursson. Pilcher, Vinn, tr. from ICE. 24p. 1997. pap. 1.75 (*1-891469-00-2*) Repristination.
Petursson, Margeir. Kings Indian Defense Averbakh Variation. 1996. pap. 21.95 (*1-85744-118-4*, Pub. by Cadgn Bks) Macmillan.
Petush, Edward J. & Sargent, Dennis M. Atlas of the Living Olive Shells of the World. (Illus.). 1986. 68.50 (*0-938415-00-X*) CERF Inc.
***Petushkov, Vladimir & Fadeenko, Yury.** Welding Stress Relief by Explosion Treatment. 179p. 1999. 149.95 (*0-9644311-1-4*) Backbone Pubng.
Petviashvili, Vladimir I. Solitary Waves in Plasmas & in the Atmosphere. x, 248p. 1992. text 132.00 (*2-88124-787-3*) Gordon & Breach.
Pety, M. Aquiline, ed. see Jean de la Mote.
Petykiewicz, J. Wave Optics. (C). 1992. text 302.00 (*0-7923-0683-X*) Kluwer Academic.
Petyt, K. M. Dialect & Accent in Industrial West Yorkshire. LC 85-20136. (Varieties of English Around the World General Ser.: 6). viii, 401p. 1985. pap. 87.00 (*90-272-4864-8*) J Benjamins Pubng Co.
Petyt, M., et al, eds. Structural Dynamics: Recent Advances - Proc. of the Fourth Internat. Conf., 15-18 July 1991, Southampton, U. K. 886p. 1991. mass mkt. 199.95 (*1-85166-670-2*) Elsevier.
Petyt, Maurice. Introduction to Finite Element Vibration Analysis. (Illus.). 574p. (C). 1998. pap. text 59.95 (*0-521-63417-2*) Cambridge U Pr.
Petz, D. An Invitation to the Algebra of Canonical Commutation Relations. (Leuven Notes in Mathematical & Theoretical Physics Ser.: No. 2). 200p. (Orig.). 1990. pap. 33.50 (*90-6186-360-0*, Pub. by Leuven Univ) Coronet Bks.
Petz, Denes, jt. auth. see Hiai, Fumio.
Petz, Denes, jt. auth. see Ohya, Masanori.
Petz, Lawrence D., et al, eds. Clinical Practice of Transfusion Medicine. 3rd ed. LC 95-32421. 1115p. 1995. text 165.00 (*0-443-08981-7*) Church.
Petz, Lawrence D. & Garratty, George. Acquired Immune Hemolytic Anemias. LC 79-19235. 478p. reprint ed. pap. 148.20 (*0-7837-3156-6*, 204282900006) Bks Demand.
Petz, Richard. Cry Insanity. Welburn, John, ed. 85p. 1988. pap. write for info. (*0-318-62237-8*) RAPCOM Enter.
Petz, Richard, ed. see Cannon, Frances A.
Petz, Richard A. The Impressionable Years: A Play on Social Issues, No. 1. Cannon, Frances A., ed. LC 84-62640. (Illus.). 40p. 1985. pap. 7.00 (*0-317-00954-0*); 5.00 (*0-317-00955-9*) RAPCOM Enter.
Petz, Rita K., ed. see Cannon, Frances A.
Petz, Wolfgang. Iron-Carbene Complexes. LC 92-46132. (Scripts in Inorganic & Organometallic Chemistry Ser.: Vol. 1). 1993. 54.95 (*0-387-56258-3*) Spr-Verlag.
Petzel, Florence E. Textiles of Ancient Mesopotamia, Persia, & Egypt. LC 87-90471. 226p. 1987. pap. text 14.00 (*0-9618476-0-3*) F E Petzel.
Petzel, Todd E. Financial Futures & Options: A Guide to Markets, Applications, & Strategies. LC 89-3775. 254p. 1989. 65.00 (*0-89930-152-5*, PFF, Quorum Bks) Greenwood.
Petzendorfer, L., ed. Treasury of Authentic Art Nouveau: Alphabets, Decorative Initials, Monograms, Frames & Ornaments. (Lettering, Calligraphy, Typography Ser.). 160p. 1984. reprint ed. pap. 9.95 (*0-486-24653-1*) Dover.
Petzer, J. H. & Hartin, P. J. A South African Perspective on the New Testament: Essays by South African New Testament Scholars Presented to Bruce Manning Metzger During His Vist to South Africa in 1985. (Illus.). xii, 274p. 1986. 73.00 (*90-04-07720-0*) Brill Academic Pubs.
Petzer, J. H., jt. auth. see Hartin, P. J.
Petzer, Leland. A Year in the Cuyamacas. (Illus.). 300p. 1998. pap. 15.00 (*0-938711-52-0*) Tecolote Pubns.
Petzet, Erich & Glauning, Otto. Deutsche Schrifttafeln des IX Bis XVI Jahrhunderts Aus Handschriften der Bayerischen Staatsbibliothek Munchen, 5 pts. in 1. 326p. 1975. reprint ed. write for info. (*3-487-05685-2*) G Olms Pubs.
Petzet, Erich, ed. see Heyse, Paul.
Petzet, Heinrich W. Encounters & Dialogues with Martin Heidegger, 1929-1976. Emad, Parvis & Maly, Kenneth, trs. LC 92-30966. (Illus.). 287p. (C). 1993. 37.95 (*0-226-66441-4*) U Ch Pr.
Petzinger, E., et al, eds. Hepatic Transport of Organic Substances. (Illus.). 420p. 1989. 111.95 (*0-387-50494-X*) Spr-Verlag.
Petzinger, Saori, tr. see Allen, Diane & Frederick, Larry.
Petzinger, Saori, tr. see Black, Susan E.
Petzinger, Saori, tr. see Borgum, Lincoln.
Petzinger, Saori, tr. see Bowman, Lori & Bowman, Carl.
Petzinger, Saori, tr. see Colclazer, Susan.
Petzinger, Saori, tr. see Cook, Kayci.
Petzinger, Saori, tr. see Davies, Denny.
Petzinger, Saori, tr. see Den Dooven, K. C.
Petzinger, Saori, tr. see Dengler, William.
Petzinger, Saori, tr. see Follows, Don S.
Petzinger, Saori, tr. see Gilmore, Jackie.
Petzinger, Saori, tr. see Jackson, Victor L.
Petzinger, Saori, tr. see Mack, James A.
Petzinger, Saori, tr. see Mark, Stephen R.
Petzinger, Saori, tr. see Maxon, James C.
Petzinger, Saori, tr. see McKenzie, Leonard.
Petzinger, Saori, tr. see Nielsen, Cindy.
Petzinger, Saori, tr. see Palmer, John J.
Petzinger, Saori, tr. see Quiring, James P.
Petzinger, Saori, tr. see Rasp, Richard A.
Petzinger, Saori, tr. see Robinson, Sandra C. & Robinson, George B.
Petzinger, Saori, tr. see Rohde, Katherine M.
Petzinger, Saori, tr. see Rudd, Connie.
Petzinger, Saori, tr. see Scharf, Janet.
Petzinger, Saori, tr. see Smith, John L.
Petzinger, Thomas. Hard Landing: The Epic Contest for Power & Profits That Plunged the Airlines into Chaos. LC 97-194593. 594p. 1996. pap. 17.00 (*0-8129-2835-0*, Times Bks) Crown Pub Group.
Petzinger, Thomas, Jr. The New Pioneers: The Men & Women Who Are Transforming the Workplace & Marketplace. LC 98-50132. 304p. 1999. 24.50 (*0-684-84636-5*) S&S Trade.
Petzke, Karl & Slavin, Sara. Espresso: Culture & Cuisine. LC 93-25397. (Illus.). 96p. 1994. pap. 14.95 (*0-8118-0650-2*) Chronicle Bks.
Petzke, Karl, et al. Chocolate: A Sweet Indulgence. LC 96-28605. 1997. 22.95 (*0-8118-1592-7*); pap. 14.95 (*0-8118-1591-9*) Chronicle Bks.
Petzke, Karl, jt. auth. see Slavin, Sara.
Petzold, Andreas. Romanesque Art. LC 94-37842. (The Perspectives Ser.). (Illus.). 176p. 1995. 16.95 (*0-8109-2744-6*, Pub. by Abrams) Time Warner.
— Romanesque Art. 176p. (C). 1995. pap. text 16.40 (*0-13-433517-1*) P-H.
Petzold, Armin. Applied Technical Dictionary: Silicate Technology. (ENG, FRE, GER & SLO.). 268p. (C). 1977. 120.00 (*0-569-08557-8*, Pub. by Collets) St Mut.
***Petzold, Charles.** Code. 400p. 2000. pap. 17.99 (*0-7356-1131-9*) Microsoft.
— Code: The Hidden Language of Computer Hardware & Software. LC 99-40198. 1999. pap. 24.99 (*0-7356-0505-X*) Microsoft.
Petzold, Charles. Programming Windows. 5th ed. LC 98-42529. 1100p. 1998. 59.99 incl. cd-rom (*1-57231-995-X*) Microsoft.
— Programming Windows 95: The Definitive Developer's Guide to the Windows 95 API. 4th ed. 1120p. 1996. pap. 67.95 incl. cd-rom (*1-55615-676-6*) Microsoft.
Petzold, H., jt. auth. see Friedrich, G.
Petzold, Linda R., jt. auth. see Ascher, Uri M.
***Petzold, Michael.** Das Pontifikat Erzbischof Boemunds II von Trier, 1354-1362: Studien zur Reichs, Territorial-Und Verwaltungsgeschichte. (Europaische Hochschulschriften Geschichte und Ihre Hilfswissenschaften Ser.). XXXVIII, 44p. 1999. 67.95 (*3-631-32298-4*) P Lang Pubng.
Petzoldt, Julius, ed. Anzeiger fur Bibliographie und Bibliothekswissenschaft, 6 vols. write for info. incl. fiche (*0-318-71730-1*) G Olms Pubs.
— Anzeiger fur Bibliothekswissenschaft, 3 vols. reprint ed. write for info. incl. fiche (*0-318-71729-8*) G Olms Pubs.
— Anzeiger fur Literature der Bibliothekswissenschaft, 40 vols. write for info. incl. fiche (*0-318-71728-X*) G Olms Pubs.
— Neuer Anzeiger fur Bibliographie und Bibliothekswissenschaft, 31 vols., Set. reprint ed. write for info. incl. fiche (*0-318-71731-X*) G Olms Pubs.
Petzoldt, Leander. Folk Narrative & World View. (Beitrage zur Europaischen Ethnologie und Folklore, Reihe B: Reihe B, Bd. 7). (GER., Illus.). 875p. 1996. 95.95 (*3-631-48698-7*) P Lang Pubng.
Petzoldt, Paul. The Wilderness Handbook. 2nd rev. ed. (Illus.). 1984. pap. 11.95 (*0-393-30171-0*) Norton.
Petzoldt, Paul K. Teton Tales: And Other Petzoldt Anecdotes. LC 95-24428. (Illus.). 224p. 1995. pap. 14.95 (*1-57034-015-3*) Globe Pequot.
Petzoldt, Ruth, et al, eds. Demons: Mediators Between This World & the Other. (Beitrage Zur Europaischen Ethnologie und Folklore, Reihe B: Vol. 8). (Illus.). 176p. 1998. pap. 39.95 (*3-631-33190-8*) P Lang Pubng.
— Mediators Between This World & the Other: Essays on Demonic Beings from the Middle Ages to the Present. LC 98-12436. (Beitrage zur Europaischen Ethnologie und Folklore: Reihe B, Band 8). (GER., Illus.). 176p. (C). 1998. pap. 39.95 (*0-8204-3574-0*) P Lang Pubng.
***Petzow, G.** Metallographic Etching 2nd ed. LC 99-29323. 1999. write for info. (*0-87170-633-4*) ASM.
Petzow, G. & Effenberg, G., eds. Ternary Alloys: A Comprehensive Compendium of Evaluated Constitutional Data & Phase Diagrams, 40 vols. Incl. Vol. 11. Ternary Alloys: A Comprehensive Compendium of Evaluated Constitutional Data & Phase Diagrams, Vol. 11, As-In-Ir to As-Yb-Zn. (Illus.). 586p. 1994. 998.00 (*3-527-29232-2*, Wiley-VCH); write for info. (*0-614-20834-3*, Wiley-VCH) Wiley.
Petzow, G., jt. ed. see Hoffmann, Michael J.
Petzow, Gunter. Metallographic Etching: Metallographic & Ceramographic Methods for Revealing Microstructure. LC 78-8023. 143p. reprint ed. 44.40 (*0-608-17151-4*, 202698700053) Bks Demand.
Petzow, Gunter, jt. ed. see Schneider, Gerold A.
Peucker, Brigitte. Incorporating Images: Film & the Rival Arts. LC 94-18110. 240p. 1995. text 49.50 (*0-691-04098-2*, Pub. by Princeton U Pr); pap. text 17.95 (*0-691-00281-9*, Pub. by Princeton U Pr) Cal Prin Full Svc.
— Lyric Descent in the German Romantic Tradition. LC 86-23393. 242p. reprint ed. pap. 75.10 (*0-7837-4542-7*, 208031700005) Bks Demand.
Peuckert, Detley J. Inside Nazi Germany: Conformity, Opposition, & Racism. LC 86-51431. 288p. (C). 1989. reprint ed. pap. 18.00 (*0-300-04480-1*) Yale U Pr.
— Inside Nazi Germany: Conformity, Opposition, & Racism in Everyday Life. Deveson, Richard, tr. 288p. 1987. 40.00 (*0-300-03863-1*) Yale U Pr.
Peuckert, Will E. Theophrastus Paracelsus. 2nd ed. (GER.). xii, 472p. 1991. reprint ed. write for info. (*3-487-05632-1*) G Olms Pubs.
Peuckert, Will-Erich. Deutscher Volksglaube Im Spatmittelalter. (GER.). 222p. 1978. reprint ed. write for info. (*3-487-06638-6*) G Olms Pubs.
Peugeot, Roger & Carter, Tim. The Home Ranger Helps You Figure It Out! The Home Reference Manual Every Family Needs. LC 98-31727. 356p. 1999. pap. 14.95 (*0-9652080-0-1*) Simplicity Bks.
Peuifoy, Reneau. Overcoming Anxiety: From Short-Time Fixes to Long-Term Recovery. LC 96-29376. 192p. (Orig.). 1997. pap. 12.95 (*0-8050-4789-1*, Owl) H Holt & Co.
Peukert, Detlev J. The Weimar Republic. Deveson, Richard, tr. from GER. 352p. 1992. 28.00 (*0-8090-9674-9*) Hill & Wang.
— Weimar Republic. 216p. 1993. pap. 13.00 (*0-8090-1556-0*) Hill & Wang.
Peukert, Helmut. Science, Action, & Fundamental Theology: Toward a Theology of Communicative Action. Bohman, James, tr. (Studies in Contemporary German Social Thought). 360p. 1984. 42.50 (*0-262-16095-1*) MIT Pr.
Peuquet, Marble. Introductory Reading in Geographic. 1990. pap. 44.95 (*0-85066-857-3*) Taylor & Francis.
Peura, Robin E. & DeBoer, Carolyn J. Story Making: Using Predictable Literature to Develop Communication. LC 94-43564. 1995. pap. 42.00 (*0-930599-33-0*) Thinking Pubns.
Peurifoy. Estimating Construction Costs. 4th ed. 1989. 27.50 (*0-07-049741-9*) McGraw.
Peurifoy, R. L. & Oberlender, Garold D. Formwork for Concrete Structures. 3rd ed. (Construction Engineering Ser.). 352p. 1996. 65.00 (*0-07-049838-5*) McGraw.
Peurifoy, Reneau Z. Anger: Taming the Beast. LC 99-12007. 1999. 21.00 (*1-56836-284-6*) Kodansha.
— Anxiety, Phobias & Panic: A Step-by-Step Program for Regaining Control of Your Life. 384p. 1995. mass mkt. 12.99 (*0-446-67053-7*, Pub. by Warner Bks) Little.
— Anxiety, Phobias & Panic: A Step-by-Step Program for Regaining Control of Your Life. 2nd rev. ed. 304p. 1992. pap. 12.95 (*0-929437-13-6*) Warner Bks.
— Anxiety, Phobias, & Panic: Taking Charge & Conquering Fear. (Orig.). 1988. pap. 12.95 (*0-929437-11-X*) Warner Bks.
Peurifoy, Robert L. & Oberlender, Gary. Estimating Construction Costs. 4th ed. (Construction Engineering & Project Management Ser.). 512p. (C). 1989. 91.88 (*0-07-049740-0*) McGraw.
Peurifoy, Robert L., et al. Construction Planning, Equipment & Methods. 5th ed. LC 95-10819. 688p. (C). 1995. 99.38 (*0-07-049836-9*) McGraw.
***Peurrung, Victoria.** Living with Juvenile Diabetes: A Family Guide. rev. ed. (Illus.). 264p. 2000. pap. 14.95 (*1-57826-057-4*, Pub. by Hatherleigh) Norton.
— My Sugar Babies: Proven Techniques on Controlling Type 1 Diabetes from a Mother's Perspective. (Illus.). 250p. 1999. pap. 15.95 (*1-884707-91-2*) Lifestyles.
Peusch, Leonard. The Three Crosses. 1978. pap. 1.00 (*0-8199-0723-5*, Frncscn Herld) Franciscan Pr.
Peusner, L. The Principles of Network Thermodynamics. xv, 255p. 1987. 19.95 (*0-938876-21-X*) Entropy Ltd.
Peusner, Stella. The Night the Whole Class Slept Over. McDonald, Patricia, ed. 176p. (J). (gr. 3-6). 1992. reprint ed. pap. 3.50 (*0-671-78157-X*, Minstrel Bks) PB.
— Would My Fortune Cookie Lie? (J). (gr. 3-6). 1999. pap. 3.99 (*0-671-00774-2*, Minstrel Bks) PB.
***Peutrell, Ann.** No More Fleas. 1999. 7.95 (*0-7641-5213-0*) Barron.
Peutrell, Jane M. & Mather, Stephen J. Regional Anaesthesia for Babies & Children. (Illus.). 270p. (C). 1997. text 69.50 (*0-19-262425-3*) OUP.
Peutrell, Jane M., jt. auth. see Norton, N. S.
Peva, James R., et al. Essential Case Law for Policing America. LC 92-72183. 400p. (Orig.). 1992. pap. 22.00 (*1-878760-06-8*) Graphics Ltd IN.
Pevac, Irena & Calvert, Joan M. Practicing Recursion in Pascal. 84p. (C). 1996. text 22.80 (*0-536-59300-0*) Pearson Custom.
Pevar, Stephen L. The Rights of Indians & Tribes. 1997. pap. 7.99 (*0-614-28296-9*, PuffinBks) Peng Put Young Read.
— The Rights of Indians & Tribes. LC 97-20124. (Illus.). 224p. (YA). (gr. 7 up). 1997. pap. 8.99 (*0-14-037783-2*, PuffinBks) Peng Put Young Read.
— The Rights of Indians & Tribes: The Basic ACLU Guide to the Indian & Tribal Rights. 2nd rev. ed. (ACLU Handbook Ser.). 335p. 1991. pap. 9.95 (*0-8093-1768-0*) S Ill U Pr.
Pevear, David, jt. auth. see Eslinger, Eric.
Pevear, Richard. Exchanges. 1982. 5.00 (*0-686-34453-7*) S Duyvil.
— Night Talk & Other Poems. LC 77-2533. (Princeton Series of Contemporary Poets). 73p. reprint ed. pap. 30.00 (*0-8357-2778-5*, 203990400014) Bks Demand.
Pevear, Richard, tr. see Bonnefoy, Yves.
Pevear, Richard, tr. see Dostoevsky, Fyodor.
Pevear, Richard, tr. see Dostoyevsky, Fyodor.
Pevear, Richard, tr. see Gogol, Nikolai Vasilevich.
Pevear, Richard, tr. see Kharms, Daniil.
Pevear, Richard, tr. see Marshak, Samuel.
Pevear, Richard, tr. see Savinio, Alberto.
Pevear, Richard, tr. see Sophocles.
Pevear, Richard, tr. see Tolstoy, Leo.
Pevear, Ted. In Light of Reflection. 168p. 1998. pap. 9.95 (*1-890828-06-8*, 06-8, Pub. by Camden Ct) Origin Bk Sales.
***Pevehouse, Dolores.** I, the Christ. 2000. pap. 15.95 (*1-57174-177-1*) N D Walsch.
Peveling, Elisabeth, et al, eds. Progress & Problems in Lichenology in the Eighties: Proceedings of an International Symposium Held at the University of Munster, 16-21.3.1986. (Bibliotheca Lichenologica: Vol. 25). (GER., Illus.). xv, 497p. 1987. pap. 89.00 (*3-443-58004-1*, Pub. by Gebruder Borntraeger) Balogh.
Pevensey Heritage Guides Staff. London. (Illus.). 112p. 1994. pap. 9.95 (*0-907115-78-0*, Pub. by D & C Pub) Sterling.
Pevensey Pr. Staff. Bath. (C). 1987. text 100.00 (*0-907115-31-4*, Pub. by Pevensey); pap. text 40.00 (*0-907115-32-2*, Pub. by Pevensey) St Mut.
— Brighton. (C). 1987. pap. text 35.00 (*0-7855-6013-0*, Pub. by Pevensey) St Mut.
— Bristol. (C). 1987. text 50.00 (*0-907115-35-7*, Pub. by Pevensey) St Mut.
— Cambridge. (C). 1987. text 60.00 (*0-907115-39-X*, Pub. by Pevensey); pap. text 45.00 (*0-907115-40-3*, Pub. by Pevensey) St Mut.
— Cambridge Gardens. (C). 1987. text 65.00 (*0-907115-20-9*, Pub. by Pevensey) St Mut.
— Chester. (C). 1987. text 50.00 (*0-907115-28-4*, Pub. by Pevensey); pap. text 50.00 (*0-907115-29-2*, Pub. by Pevensey) St Mut.
— The City of London. (C). 1987. text 50.00 (*0-907115-17-9*, Pub. by Pevensey); pap. text 40.00 (*0-907115-18-7*, Pub. by Pevensey) St Mut.
— The Cotswolds. (C). 1987. text 45.00 (*0-907115-07-1*, Pub. by Pevensey); pap. text 35.00 (*0-907115-08-X*, Pub. by Pevensey) St Mut.
Pevensey Pr. Staff. Edinburgh. (C). 1987. text 50.00 (*0-907115-23-3*, Pub. by Pevensey) St Mut.
Pevensey Pr. Staff. Historic Cities of England. (Illus.). (C). 1987. text 75.00 (*0-907115-37-3*, Pub. by Pevensey) St Mut.
— London Parks & Gardens. (C). 1987. text 60.00 (*0-907115-30-6*, Pub. by Pevensey) St Mut.
— Oxford Gardens. (C). 1987. text 60.00 (*0-907115-27-6*, Pub. by Pevensey) St Mut.
— Treasures of the Fitzwilliam Museum. (C). 1987. text 60.00 (*0-907115-19-5*, Pub. by Pevensey); pap. text 50.00 (*0-907115-16-0*, Pub. by Pevensey) St Mut.
Pevensey Pr. Staff. York. (C). 1987. text 55.00 (*0-907115-21-7*, Pub. by Pevensey); pap. text 40.00 (*0-907115-22-5*, Pub. by Pevensey) St Mut.
Pevensey Pr. Staff. Yorkshire Moors & Dales. (C). 1987. text 60.00 (*0-907115-33-0*, Pub. by Pevensey); pap. text 40.00 (*0-907115-34-9*, Pub. by Pevensey) St Mut.
Pevere, Geoff. Team Spirit: A Field Guide to Roots Culture. 152p. 1998. pap. 18.95 (*0-385-25808-9*) Bantam.
Peverett, E. J. Fire Insurance Law & Claims. (C). 1982. 190.00 (*0-7855-4169-1*, Pub. by Witherby & Co) St Mut.
Peverill, Jan. Jan Peverill's Inn Places for Bed & Breakfast. 3rd enl. ed. (Illus.). 166p. (Orig.). 1992. pap. 10.95 (*0-9621525-2-8*) Intros Unltd.
— Jan Peverill's Inn Places for Bed & Breakfast, Vol. 2. 2nd ed. (Illus.). 148p. (Orig.). 1990. pap. text 9.95 (*0-9621525-1-X*) Intros Unltd.
— Jan Peverill's Inn Places for Bed & Breakfast in the West. (Illus.). 82p. (Orig.). 1988. pap. 7.95 (*0-9621525-0-1*) Intros Unltd.
Peverill, K. I., et al, eds. Soil Analysis: An Interpretation. (Illus.). 875p. 94.95 (*0-643-06376-5*, Pub. by CSIRO) Accents Pubns.
Pevernage, Andre. Andre Pevernage: The Complete Chansons - Livre Quatrieme des Chansons, 1591 & Other Chansons. Hoekstra, Gerald R., ed. (Recent Researches in Music of the Renaissance Ser.: Vol. RRR63-64). (Illus.). xx, 172p. 1983. pap. 60.00 (*0-89579-190-0*) A-R Eds.
— Andre Pevernage: The Complete Chansons - Livre Troiseme des Chansons, 1590. Hoekstra, Gerald R., ed. (Recent Researches in Music of the Renaissance Ser.: Vol. RRR62) (Illus.). 1983. pap. 40.00 (*0-89579-189-7*) A-R Eds.
— Andre Pevernage: The Complete Chansons: Chansons...Livre Premiere (1589) Hoekstra, Gerald R., ed. (Recent Researches in Music of the Renaissance Ser.: Vol. RRR60). (Illus.). xxiv, 111p. 1983. pap. 45.00 (*0-89579-184-6*) A-R Eds.
— Andre' Pevernage: The Complete Chansons: Livre Second des Chansons (1590) Moekstra, Gerald R., ed. (Recent Researches in Music of the Renaissance Ser.: Vol. RRR61). (Illus.). xvii, 100p. 1983. pap. 40.00 (*0-89579-188-9*) A-R Eds.
Peviani, Nadia, jt. auth. see Tabusso, Guiliana.
***Pevitt, Christine.** The Man Who Would Be King: The Life of Philippe d' Orleans, Regent of France. LC 99-26991. (Illus.). 384p. 1999. reprint ed. pap. 15.00 (*0-688-16983-X*, Wm Morrow) Morrow Avon.

P

Pevitt, Christine. Philippe, Duc D'Orleans: Regent of France. LC 97-27581. 384p. 1997. 30.00 (*0-87113-695-3*, Atlntc Mnthly) Grove-Atltic.

Pevovar, Eddy H. Fundamentals of Colon Hydrotherapy Vol. 1: An Independent Learning Program. (Illus.). 180p. 1997. ring bd. 98.00 (*0-9660627-0-1*) Dotolo Inst.

— Nutrition, the Environment & the Food Chain: Who's Kidding Who . . . ? rev. ed. (Therapeutic Nutrition Ser.). (Illus.). 200p. (Orig.). 1995. pap. text 350.00 (*0-9645077-1-4*, 001-95); lib. bdg. 380.00 (*0-9645077-2-2*, 001-95) Nutr Res Proj.

— Nutrition, the Environment & the Food Chain: Who's Kidding Who . . . ? rev. ed. (Therapeutic Nutrition Ser.: Vol. 1). (Illus.). 200p. (Orig.). 1995. pap. text 350.00 (*0-9645077-0-6*, 001-95) Nutr Res Proj.

Pevsner, Aihud, jt. auth. see Kim, Chung W.

Pevsner, Cher, jt. auth. see Pevsner, Nikolaus.

Pevsner, Niklaus W. Cornwall. text 45.00 (*0-14-071001-9*, Pub. by Pnguin Bks Ltd) Trafalgar.

***Pevsner, Nikolas, et al.** The Penguin Dictionary of Architecture & Landscape Architecture. 5th ed. 656p. 2000. pap. 16.95 (*0-14-051323-X*) Viking Penguin.

Pevsner, Nikolaus. Be - Yorkshire the East Riding. text 65.00 (*0-14-071061-2*, Pub. by Pnguin Bks Ltd) Trafalgar.

— Bedfordshire, Huntingdon Pet. (Illus.). pap. 45.00 (*0-14-071034-5*, Pub. by Pnguin Bks Ltd) Trafalgar.

— Building England Cambridgeshire 1970. rev. ed. (Illus.). 576p. text 50.00 (*0-14-071010-8*, Pub. by Pnguin Bks Ltd) Trafalgar.

— Buildings England Herefordshire 1963. (Illus.). 368p. text 40.00 (*0-14-071025-6*, Pub. by Pnguin Bks Ltd) Trafalgar.

— Buildings England Lancashire North. (Illus.). text 45.00 (*0-14-071036-1*, Pub. by Pnguin Bks Ltd) Trafalgar.

— Buildings England Somerset North & Bristol. text 50.00 (*0-14-071013-2*, Pub. by Pnguin Bks Ltd) Trafalgar.

— Buildings England Sussex 1965. (Illus.). 704p. text 50.00 (*0-14-071028-0*, Pub. by Pnguin Bks Ltd) Trafalgar.

— Buildings England Yorkshire North Riding. (Illus.). text 40.00 (*0-14-071029-9*, Pub. by Pnguin Bks Ltd) Trafalgar.

— Buildings Ireland North West Ulster Country. (Illus.). text 50.00 (*0-14-071081-7*, Pub. by Pnguin Bks Ltd) Trafalgar.

— Buildings of England: City of London. (Illus.). 672p. text 65.00 (*0-14-071092-2*, Pub. by Pnguin Bks Ltd) Trafalgar.

— Buildings of England: London Docklands. (Illus.). 288p. pap. 24.95 (*0-14-071096-5*, Pub. by Pnguin Bks Ltd) Trafalgar.

— Buildings of England: Norwich & Northeast. (Illus.). 800p. text 65.00 (*0-14-071058-2*, Pub. by Pnguin Bks Ltd) Trafalgar.

— Buildings of England Berkshire 1966. (Illus.). text 45.00 (*0-14-071030-2*, Pub. by Pnguin Bks Ltd) Trafalgar.

— Buildings of England, City of London, Churches. 160p. pap. 19.95 (*0-14-071100-7*, Pub. by Pnguin Bks Ltd) Trafalgar.

— Cumberland, Westmorland, 1967. 344p. text 45.00 (*0-14-071033-7*, Pub. by Pnguin Bks Ltd) Trafalgar.

— Englishness of English Art. 1993. pap. 19.95 (*0-14-013738-6*, Pub. by Pnguin Bks Ltd) Trafalgar.

Pevsner, Nikolaus. A History of Building Types. LC 75-4459. (Bollingen Ser.: No. 35). (Illus.). 352p. 1976. pap. text 35.00 (*0-691-01829-4*, Pub. by Princeton U Pr) Cal Prin Full Svc.

— Lexikon der Weltarchitektur. 3rd rev. ed. (GER.). 876p. 1992. pap. 295.00 (*0-8288-1195-4*, M7216) Fr & Eur.

Pevsner, Nikolaus. Northumberland. 600p. text 65.00 (*0-14-071059-0*, Pub. by Pnguin Bks Ltd) Trafalgar.

Pevsner, Nikolaus. The Sources of Modern Architecture & Design. (World of Art Ser.). (Illus.). 216p. 1985. pap. 14.95 (*0-500-20072-6*, Pub. by Thames Hudson) Norton.

Pevsner, Nikolaus. South & West Somerset. text 45.00 (*0-14-071014-0*, Pub. by Pnguin Bks Ltd) Trafalgar.

Pevsner, Nikolaus. Studies in Art, Architecture & Design: Victorian & After. LC 81-48077. (Illus.). 288p. (Orig.). reprint ed. pap. 89.30 (*0-608-07653-8*, 205997100010) Bks Demand.

Pevsner, Nikolaus. Yorkshire West Riding. text 45.00 (*0-14-071017-5*, Pub. by Pnguin Bks Ltd) Trafalgar.

Pevsner, Nikolaus & Cherry. Buildings England Hertfordshire 1977. (Illus.). text 45.00 (*0-14-071007-8*, Pub. by Pnguin Bks Ltd) Trafalgar.

— Buildings England Northamptonshire. rev. ed. (Illus.). text 50.00 (*0-14-071022-1*, Pub. by Pnguin Bks Ltd) Trafalgar.

Pevsner, Nikolaus & Harris. Buildings England Lincolnshire 1964. (Illus.). 880p. text 65.00 (*0-14-071027-2*, Pub. by Pnguin Bks Ltd) Trafalgar.

Pevsner, Nikolaus & Nairn, C. Buildings England Surrey. rev. ed. (Illus.). text 50.00 (*0-14-071021-3*, Pub. by Pnguin Bks Ltd) Trafalgar.

Pevsner, Nikolaus & Pevsner, Cher. Devon. 976p. text 65.00 (*0-14-071050-7*, Pub. by Pnguin Bks Ltd) Trafalgar.

Pevsner, Nikolaus & Radcliff. Buildings England Essex 65. rev. ed. (Illus.). 496p. text 45.00 (*0-14-071011-6*, Pub. by Pnguin Bks Ltd) Trafalgar.

Pevsner, Nikolaus & Sherwood. Buildings England Oxfordshire 1974. (Illus.). 1936p. text 45.00 (*0-14-071045-0*, Pub. by Pnguin Bks Ltd) Trafalgar.

Pevsner, Nikolaus, jt. ed. see Richards, J. M.

Pevsner, Nikolaus C. Buildings England Wiltshire. rev. ed. (Illus.). 672p. pap. 50.00 (*0-14-071026-4*, Pub. by Pnguin Bks Ltd) Trafalgar.

Pevsner, Nikolaus L. Buildings: English Hemisphere: Isle of Wight, 1967. (Illus.). 848p. pap. 50.00 (*0-14-071032-9*, Pub. by Pnguin Bks Ltd) Trafalgar.

Pevsner, Nikolaus N. Buildings England Dorset. (Illus.). pap. 50.00 (*0-14-071044-2*, Pub. by Pnguin Bks Ltd) Trafalgar.

Pevsner, Nikolaus R. Buildings: England-Suffolk. rev. ed. (Illus.). text 50.00 (*0-14-071020-5*, Pub. by Pnguin Bks Ltd) Trafalgar.

Pevsner, Nikolaus S. London North West. (Illus.). 768p. text 65.00 (*0-14-071048-5*, Pub. by Pnguin Bks Ltd) Trafalgar.

Pevsner, Nikolaus W. Buildings England Nottinghamshire. (Illus.). text 50.00 (*0-14-071002-7*, Pub. by Pnguin Bks Ltd) Trafalgar.

— Buildings of England: County Durham. (Illus.). text 50.00 (*0-14-071009-4*, Pub. by Pnguin Bks Ltd) Trafalgar.

Pevsner, Nilkolaus. Diccionario de Arquitectura. 2nd ed. (SPA.). 656p. 1984. 85.00 (*0-7859-5727-8*, 8420652180) Fr & Eur.

Pevsner, Stella. Cute Is a Four-Letter Word. 176p. (J). (gr. 7-9). 1989. per. 2.75 (*0-671-68845-6*, Archway) PB.

— I'm Emma, I'm a Quint. (YA). (gr. 5 up). 1996. per. 3.99 (*0-671-89549-4*) PB.

— I'm Emma, I'm a Quint. (J). 1996. 9.09 (*0-606-11503-X*, Pub. by Turtleback) Demco.

***Pevsner, Stella.** Is Everyone Moonburned but Me? LC 99-36816. (Illus.). 208p. (J). (gr. 4-8). 2000. 15.00 (*0-395-95770-2*, Clarion Bks) HM.

Pevsner, Stella. Jon, Flora, & the Odd-Eyed Cat. 192p. (J). 1997. per. 3.99 (*0-671-56105-7*, Minstrel Bks) PB.

— Jon, Flora, & the Odd-Eyed Cat. (J). 1997. 9.09 (*0-606-11522-6*, Pub. by Turtleback) Demco.

— Would My Fortune Cookie Lie? LC 95-36720. 186p. (J). (gr. 5-9). 1996. 14.95 (*0-395-73082-1*, Clarion Bks) HM.

Pevsner, Stella & Tang, Fay. Sing for Your Father, Su Phan. LC 97-4290. (Illus.). 112p. (J). (gr. 4-6). 1997. 14.00 (*0-395-82267-X*, Clarion Bks) HM.

Pevzner, Leonid Z. Functional Biochemistry of the Neuroglia. Tiplady, Brian, ed. & tr. by. LC 78-26386. (Illus.). 320p. 1979. reprint ed. pap. 99.20 (*0-608-05425-9*, 206589400006) Bks Demand.

***Pevzner, Pavel A.** Computational Molecular Biology: An Algorithmic Approach. (Illus.). 325p. 2000. 44.95 (*0-262-16197-4*) MIT Pr.

Pew, David & Matthews, Jay. Budgeting for Newspapers. rev. ed. (Illus.). 55p. 1989. pap. 49.95 (*1-877888-11-7*) Intl Newspaper.

***Pew, John A.** Instant Java 1.2. 3rd ed. LC 99-462648. 452p. 1998. pap. 34.99 incl. cd-rom (*0-13-010533-3*) P-H.

Pew, Richard W., ed. see National Research Council Staff.

***PEW Staff.** Pew Bible. 1999. 15.99 (*0-529-11019-9*) World Bible.

— Pew Bible. large type ed. 1999. 15.99 (*0-529-11018-0*) World Bible.

Pew, Stephen, jt. auth. see Kline, Kris.

Pew, William H. A Second Chance at Life. 208p. 1993. mass mkt. 4.99 (*1-56399-013-X*) NewLife Pubns.

Pewe, ed. Quaternary Geology & Permafrost along the Richardson & Glenn Highways Between Fairbanks & Anchorage, Alaska. (IGC Field Trip Guidebooks Ser.). 64p. 1989. 21.00 (*0-87590-603-6*, T102) Am Geophysical.

Pewe, Troy L. Permafrost & Its Effect on Life in the North. LC 67-2694. 40p. 1966. reprint ed. pap. 30.00 (*0-608-01832-5*, 206248100003) Bks Demand.

Pewe, Troy L., ed. Desert Dust: Origin, Characteristics, & Effect on Man. LC 81-7031. (Geological Society of America Ser.: Vol. 186). (Illus.). 318p. 1981. reprint ed. pap. 98.60 (*0-608-07721-6*, 206780900010) Bks Demand.

Pewe, Troy L., et al, eds. Eva Interglaciation Forest Bed, Unglaciated East-Central Alaska: Global Warning 125,000 Years Ago, Vol. 319. LC 97-25874. (Special Paper Ser.: No. 319). (Illus.). 1997. pap. 36.00 (*0-8137-2319-1*) Geol Soc.

Pewitt, Lyn. Back Home in Williamson County: Bicentennial Edition. (Illus.). 192p. 1995. pap. 14.95 (*1-881576-60-4*, Hillsboro Pr) Providence Hse.

Pewsey, Lynn. A Taste of Essex: Food & Recipes of Essex Through the Ages. LC 93-40448. 1994. pap. 15.00 (*0-88734-902-1*) Players Pr.

Pexieder, Tomas, ed. Mechanisms of Cardiac Morphogenesis & Teratogenesis. LC 79-65503. (Perspectives in Cardiovascular Research Ser.: No. 5). (Illus.). 528p. 1981. reprint ed. pap. 163.70 (*0-608-00593-2*, 206118000007) Bks Demand.

Pexman, Penny, jt. auth. see Nicol, Adelheid A. M.

Pexton, Pat. Three Ingredient Cookbook. (Illus.). 76p. 1982. spiral bd. 8.00 (*0-9624039-1-1*) DeBry-Pexton.

Peyer, Bernd C. The Tutor'd Mind: Indian Missionary-Writers in Antebellum America. LC 96-51956. (Native Americans of the Northeast Ser.). 432p. 1997. pap. 20.95 (*1-55849-099-X*); text 70.00 (*1-55849-098-1*) U of Mass Pr.

Peyer, Bernd C., ed. The Singing Spirit: Early Short Stories by North American Indians. LC 89-32419. (Sun Tracks Ser.). 175p. 1991. reprint ed. pap. 11.95 (*0-8165-1220-5*) U of Ariz Pr.

Peyer, Tom, jt. auth. see Waid, Mark.

Peyer, Tom, ed. see Gaiman, Neil.

Peyer, Tom, ed. see Rizzuto, Phil.

***Peyerle, Hans G. & Orchard, G. Edward.** Journey to Moscow. LC 98-197749. (Studies on the History of Eastern Europe: Vol. 5). 184p. 1999. 26.95 (*3-8258-3415-8*, Pub. by CE24) Transaction Pubs.

***Peyerwold, David.** Advising & Defending Corporate Directors & Officers - 11/99 Update. LC 98-71495. 192p. 1999. ring bd. 52.00 (*0-7626-0375-5*, BU-32722) Cont Ed Bar-CA.

— Business Buy-Sell Agreements: 3/98 Update. LC 91-72877. 207p. 1998. ring bd. 45.00 (*0-7626-0190-6*, BU-31496) Cont Ed Bar-CA.

— Counseling California Corporations, 5/99 Update. LC 90-80013. 175p. 1999. ring bd. 50.00 (*0-7626-0320-8*, BU-39238) Cont Ed Bar-CA.

***Peyerwold, David, ed.** Business Buy-Sell Agreements, 3/99 Update. LC 91-72877. 212p. 1999. ring bd. 45.00 (*0-7626-0298-8*, BU-31497) Cont Ed Bar-CA.

Peyerwold, David, ed. see Barlow, Wayne E., et al.

Peyerwold, David, ed. see Bonn, John R., et al.

Peyerwold, David, ed. see Brockmeyer, Neal H., et al.

Peyerwold, David, ed. see Burt, Richard G., et al.

Peyerwold, David, ed. see Carrier, George B. & Christopherson, Dean.

Peyerwold, David, ed. see Castro, Leonard E., et al.

Peyerwold, David, ed. see Coleman, Thomas H., et al.

Peyerwold, David, ed. see Derby, Loyd P., et al.

Peyerwold, David, ed. see Dimitriou, Demetrios & Johal, Jack S.

Peyerwold, David, ed. see Edwards, Margaret Hart, et al.

Peyerwold, David, ed. see Friedman, Ellen A. & Given, Bernard R., II.

Peyerwold, David, ed. see Friedman, Ellen A. & Given, Thomas.

Peyerwold, David, ed. see Keligian, David L., et al.

Peyerwold, David, ed. see McBride, Keith W.

Peyerwold, David, ed. see Piels, William B. & Hull, Brian D.

Peyerwold, David, ed. see Roberts, Mary M., et al.

Peyerwold, David, ed. see Schug, Charles.

Peyerwold, David L., ed. see Coleman, Mark J., et al.

Peyman, Gholam A. & Schulman, Joel A. Intravitreal Surgery. 2nd ed. (Illus.). 480p. (C). 1994. pap. text 275.00 (*0-8385-4320-0*, A4320-6, Apple Lange Med) McGraw.

— Vitreous Substitutes. LC 94-39562. 214p. (C). 1995. pap. text 110.00 (*0-8385-9484-0*, A9484-5, Apple Lange Med) McGraw.

Peynado, Celia, tr. see Schubert, Linda.

Peynaud, Emile. Knowing & Making Wine. Spencer, Alan F., tr. LC 84-11936. 416p. 1984. 85.00 (*0-471-88149-X*) Wiley.

— The Taste of Wine: The Art & Science of Wine Appreciation. Schuster, Michael, tr. from FRE. (Illus.). 258p. 1996. reprint ed. 39.95 (*0-932664-64-4*, 940E) Wine Appreciation.

— The Taste of Wine: The Art & Science of Wine Appreciation. 2nd ed. LC 96-24181. 368p. 1996. 69.95 (*0-471-11376-X*) Wiley.

Peyo. The Black Arrow. Decker, Dwight R., tr. from FRE. (Johan & Peewit Ser.: No. 1). (Illus.). 48p. (Orig.). (J). (gr. 2-7). 1996. pap. 8.95 (*1-887911-50-2*) Fantsy Flight.

Peyramaure, Michael. Cleopatra: Reina del Nilo. 1999. pap. text 9.95 (*84-08-02672-0*) Planeta Edit.

Peyrard, M., ed. Nonlinear Excitations in Biomolecules. 424p. 1995. 107.95 (*3-540-59250-4*) Spr-Verlag.

Peyrard, M., jt. ed. see Remoissenet, M.

***Peyrat, Paul.** California Workers' Damages Practice: June 2000 Update. 230p. 2000. 39.00 (*0-7626-0446-8*, WC-30775) Cont Ed Bar-CA.

— California Worker's Damages Practice - 6/99 Update. 226p. 1999. ring bd. 38.00 (*0-7626-0332-1*, WC-30774) Cont Ed Bar-CA.

Peyrat, Paul & Boone, William B. California Tort Guide - 4-97 Update. LC 96-83278. 1997. ring bd. 35.00 (*0-7626-0098-5*, TO-32541) Cont Ed Bar-CA.

— California Tort Guide, 4/99 Update. 3rd ed. LC 96-83278. 504p. 1999. ring bd. 44.00 (*0-7626-0305-4*, TO-32543) Cont Ed Bar-CA.

Peyrat, Paul, jt. auth. see Boone, William B.

Peyrat, Paul, ed. see Boone, William B.

Peyrat, Paul I., ed. see Carlson, Jeffery J.

Peyrat, Paul I., jt. ed. see Compton, Linda.

Peyraud, J., jt. ed. see DeWitt, C.

Peyrazat, Jean E. Les Miserables: Classics of French Literature. (C). 1987. pap. text 14.80 (*0-13-530668-X*) P-H.

Peyre, H. Que Es el Clasicismo. (Breviarios Ser.). (SPA.). pap. 9.99 (*968-16-5019-0*, Pub. by Fondo) Continental Bk.

Peyre, Henri. Historical & Critical Essays. LC 68-12702. 307p. reprint ed. pap. 95.20 (*0-7837-6176-7*, 204589800009) Bks Demand.

Peyre, Henri, et al. The France of Claudel. LC 77-126039. (Review of National Literatures Ser.: Vol. 4, No. 2). 144p. 1974. pap. 4.95 (*0-918680-63-8*) Griffon House.

Peyre, Henri M., ed. Essays in Honor of Albert Feuillerat. LC 75-99633. (Essay Index Reprint Ser.). 1977. 23.95 (*0-8369-1650-6*) Ayer.

Peyrefitte, Roger. Hommage a Arno Breker. deluxe ed. (Illus.). 1990. 600.00 (*0-914301-30-6*, Pub. by Marco) West-Art.

Peyret, R., ed. Handbook of Computational Fluid Mechanics. (Illus.). 480p. 1996. pap. text 125.00 (*0-12-553010-2*) Acad Pr.

Peyret, R., jt. auth. see Taylor, T. D.

Peyret, Raymond. Marthe Robin: The Cross & the Joy. Faulhaber, Clare W., tr. from FRE. LC 83-15591. (Illus.). 135p. 1983. pap. 6.95 (*0-8189-0464-X*) Alba.

***Peyret, Roger, ed.** Handbook of Computational Fluid Mechanics. 350p. 1999. pap. 55.00 (*0-12-532200-3*) Acad Pr.

Peyret, Roger & Taylor, Thomas D. Computational Methods for Fluid Flow. LC 91-142735. (Series in Computational Physics). x, 359p. 1983. write for info. (*3-540-13851-X*) Spr-Verlag.

Peyron, Gabriela, tr. see Cote, Denis.

Peyrous, Pierre. Diccionario de Terminologia Militar Espanol-Frances, 2 vols., Set. (SPA.). 1989. pap. 49.95 (*0-7859-6317-0*, 8478230394) Fr & Eur.

— Diccionario de Terminologia Militar Espanol-Frances, Vol. 1. 2nd ed. (SPA.). 658p. 1991. pap. 29.95 (*0-7859-6318-9*, 8478230408) Fr & Eur.

— Diccionario de Terminologia Militar Espanol-Frances, Vol. 2. 2nd ed. (SPA.). 631p. 1991. pap. 29.95 (*0-7859-6319-7*, 8478230416) Fr & Eur.

— Diccionario de Terminologia Militar Frances-Espanol. (SPA.). 368p. 1976. pap. 49.95 (*0-7859-6044-9*, 8450075289) Fr & Eur.

Peyroux, Earl. Earl Peyroux's "Gourmet Cooking" LC 98-3361. 325p. 1998. 19.95 (*1-56554-323-8*) Pelican.

Peysakhovich, Vladimir. Economics of Automation in the Soviet Machine-Building Industry. Michta, Andrew A., ed. (Illus.). (Orig.). 1987. pap. text 75.00 (*1-55831-054-1*) Delphic Associates.

Peyser Hazouri, Sandra, jt. auth. see Smith McLaughlin, Miriam.

Peyser, Herbert F., jt. auth. see Biancolli, Louis L.

Peyser, James A., ed. Agenda for Leadership. (Pioneer Papers). 182p. (Orig.). 1994. pap. 10.00 (*0-929930-12-6*) Pioneer Inst.

Peyser, Joan. Bernstein: A Biography. rev. ed. LC 98-22551. (Illus.). 510p. 1998. 19.95 (*0-8230-8259-8*, Billboard Bks) Watsn-Guptill.

— The Memory of All That: The Life of George Gershwin. LC 97-49642. 320p. 1998. 18.95 (*0-8230-8332-2*, Billboard Bks) Watsn-Guptill.

— The Music of My Time. (Illus.). 496p. 1995. 35.00 (*0-912483-99-7*) Pro-Am Music.

— To Boulez & Beyond: Music in Europe since the Rite of Spring. LC 99-38536. (Illus.). 382p. 1999. pap. 24.95 (*0-8230-7875-2*, Watson-Guptill Bks) Watsn-Guptill.

***Peyser, Joan, ed.** The Orchestra: Origins & Transformations. LC 00-23681. 672p. 2000. pap. write for info. (*0-8230-8385-3*, Billboard Bks) Watsn-Guptill.

Peyser, Joseph L., ed. Jacques Legardeur de Saint-Pierre: Officer, Gentleman, Entrepreneur. LC 96-19766. (Illus.). 275p. 1996. 39.95 (*0-87013-418-3*, 0-87013-418-3) Mich St U Pr.

Peyser, Joseph L., ed. Letters from New France: The Upper Country, 1686-1783. (Illus.). 264p. 1992. text 34.95 (*0-252-01853-2*) U of Ill Pr.

Peyser, Joseph L., jt. auth. see Edmunds, R. David.

Peyser, Joseph L., jt. auth. see Raymond, Charles D.

Peyser, Sandra & McLaughlin, Miriam. Character Education Activities for K-6 Classrooms. LC 97-76764. (Illus.). 128p. 1997. pap. text 9.95 (*0-932796-85-0*) Ed Media Corp.

Peyser, Sandra, jt. auth. see McLaughlin, Miriam.

Peyser, Thomas. Utopia & Cosmopolis: Globalization in the Era of American Literary Realism. LC 98-5730. (New Americanists Ser.). 1998. 49.95 (*0-8223-2230-7*); pap. 17.95 (*0-8223-2247-1*) Duke.

Peysson-Zeiss, Agnes. Litterature et Architecture: Le Dix-Neuvieme Siecle. LC 98-11247. 168p. 1998. 34.00 (*0-7618-1059-5*) U Pr of Amer.

Peyster, Ann De, see De Peyster, Ann, ed.

Peyster, Robert G. & Hoover, Eric D. Computerized Tomography in Orbital Disease & Neurophthalmology. LC 83-12416. (Illus.). 318p. reprint ed. pap. 98.60 (*0-8357-6314-5*, 203558700096) Bks Demand.

Peyton, A. J. & Walsh, Y. Analog Electronics with Op Amps: A Source Book of Practical Circuits. LC 92-22691. (Illus.). 293p. (C). 1993. text 125.00 (*0-521-33305-9*); pap. text 44.95 (*0-521-33604-X*) Cambridge U Pr.

Peyton, Adella, jt. auth. see Wooton, Andrew.

Peyton, Amaga. Pieces of a Dreamer. 66p. (J). 1999. pap. 12.95 (*1-890667-09-9*, Hand-In-Hand Bks) Introspect Bks.

Peyton, Daniel. Sex & Race Discrimination Law. LC 98-130376. (Blackstone's Employment Law Library). 167p. 1997. pap. 50.00 (*1-85431-641-9*, Pub. by Blackstone Pr) Gaunt.

Peyton, Dennis J. How to Buy Real Estate in Mexico: A Simple Guide to Buying Property in Mexico. LC 94-73098. (Law Mexico Ser.). 440p. (Orig.). 1995. pap. 19.95 (*1-885328-25-7*) Law Mexico.

— How to Buy Real Estate in Mexico: A Simple Guide to Buying Property in Mexico. 2nd rev. ed. (Law Mexico Ser.). 243p. (Orig.). 1997. pap. 24.95 (*1-885328-26-5*) Law Mexico.

Peyton, Elizabeth. Elizabeth Peyton Lives: Forever. 1998. 39.95 (*0-491-58775-9*) Dist Art Pubs.

Peyton, Gary R. & AWWA Research Foundation Staff. Effect of Bicarbonate Alkalinity on Performance of Advanced Oxidation Processes. LC 97-27603. 1997. write for info. (*0-89867-929-X*, 90737) Am Water Wks Assn.

Peyton, Herbert H. Newboy: The Autobiography of Herbert Hill Peyton. LC 97-91993. (Illus.). 240p. 1997. 18.95 (*0-9658277-0-4*) Gate Petrol.

Peyton, J. Lewis. History of Augusta Co., Va. 387p. 1996. reprint ed. lib. bdg. 45.00 (*0-8328-5220-1*) Higginson Bk Co.

— History of Augusta County, Virginia. 420p. 1999. reprint ed. pap. 31.00 (*0-7884-1067-9*, P197) Heritage Bk.

— History of Augusta County, Virginia. 2nd ed. 428p. 1998. pap. 36.00 (*0-8063-4661-2*) Clearfield Co.

***Peyton, J. W. R.** Teaching & Learning in Medical Practice. 256p. 1998. text 55.00 (*1-900887-00-2*, Manticore Europe) Manticore Pubs.

Peyton, Jacob, jt. auth. see Gorrod, J. W.

Peyton, James W. La Cocina de la Frontera: Mexican-American Cooking from the Southwest. LC 93-33788. (Cookbook Ser.). (Illus.). 352p. 1994. pap. 22.50 (*1-878610-34-1*) Red Crane Bks.

— Jim Peyton's New Cooking from Old Mexico. LC 99-38892. (Cookbook Ser.). (Illus.). 1999. 29.95 (*1-878610-70-8*, Pub. by Red Crane Bks) Consort Bk Sales.

P

— El Norte: The Cuisine of Northern Mexico. rev. ed. LC 95-14930. (Cookbook Ser.). (Illus.). 256p. 1995. pap. 22.50 (*1-878610-58-9*) Red Crane Bks.

Peyton, Jeffrey L. Puppetools: Introductory Guide. LC 85-19176. Orig. Title: Puppetry: A Tool for Teaching Puppetry & Creative Learning Techniques. (Illus.). 200p. 1986. pap. text 24.95 (*0-9609506-1-3*) Prescott Durrell & Co.

Peyton, John, jt. auth. see Arnold, Ken.

Peyton, John D. The Leadership Way: Management for the Nineties. 254p. 1991. 24.95 (*0-9628901-5-4*) Davidson Manors.

Peyton, John L. Adventures of My Grandfather. LC 65-27156. 270p. 1972. reprint ed. 18.95 (*0-405-03680-9*) Ayer.

— The Birch: Bright Tree of Life & Legend. LC 94-8264. (Illus.). 96p. (Orig.). 1994. pap. 9.95 (*0-939923-42-4*) M & W Pub Co.

— Bright Beat the Water: Memories of a Wilderness Artist. (Illus.). 250p. (Orig.). 1993. pap. 14.95 (*0-939923-30-0*) M & W Pub Co.

— Faces in the Firelight. (Illus.). viii, 268p. 1992. pap. 14.95 (*0-939923-19-X*) M & W Pub Co.

— The Stone Canoe & Other Stories. LC 89-2294. (Illus.). 175p. 1989. 24.95 (*0-939923-06-8*); pap. 14.95 (*0-939923-07-6*) M & W Pub Co.

— Voices from the Ice. LC 90-13318. (Illus.). 56p. (J). (gr. 5-7). 1990. pap. 9.95 (*0-939923-15-7*) M & W Pub Co.

Peyton-Jones, Christine, ed. see Spyrakos, Constantine C.

Peyton, Joy K., ed. Students & Teachers Writing Together: Perspectives on Journal Writing. LC 89-51728. 154p. 1990. pap. 12.95 (*0-939791-36-6*) Tchrs Eng Spkrs.

Peyton, Joy K. & French, Martha. Making English Accessible: Using Electronic Networks for Interaction in the Classroom. Mahshie, Shawn, ed. (Illus.). 96p. (J). 1996. pap. text, teacher ed. 13.95 (*0-88095-206-7*) Gallaudet U Pre Coll.

Peyton, Joy K. & Reed, Leslee. Dialogue Journal Writing with Nonnative English Speakers: A Handbook for Teachers. LC 89-51727. 124p. 1990. pap. 15.95 (*0-939791-37-4*) Tchrs Eng Spkrs.

***Peyton, Joy K. & Shuy, Roger W.** Language in Action: New Studies of Language in Society: Essays in Honor of Roger W. Shuy. LC 99-51425. 1999. write for info. (*1-57273-274-1*) Hampton Pr NJ.

Peyton, Joy K. & Staton, Jana. Dialogue Journal Writing with Nonnative English Speakers: An Instructional Packet for Teachers & Workshop Leaders. 154p. 1992. pap. 15.95 (*0-939791-39-0*) Tchrs Eng Spkrs.

— Dialogue Journals in the Multilingual Classroom: Building Language Fluency & Writing Skills Through Written Interaction. Farr, Marcia, ed. LC 92-10058. (Writing Research Ser.). 256p. (C). 1990. pap. 39.50 (*0-89391-661-7*); text 73.25 (*0-89391-660-9*) Ablx Pub.

Peyton, Joy K. & Staton, Jana, eds. Writing Our Lives: Reflections on Dialogue Journal Writing with Adults. LC 95-36190. (Language in Education Ser.: No. 77). 1995. write for info. (*0-937354-71-6*) Delta Systems.

Peyton, Joy K., ed. see Rigg, Pat, et al.

***Peyton, K. M.** The Boy Who Wasn't There. 2000. pap. 5.95 (*0-552-52717-3*, Pub. by Transworld Publishers Ltd) Trafalgar.

Peyton, K. M. Darkling. 1989. 16.95 (*0-385-26963-3*) Doubleday.

— Snowfall. LC 98-12213. 352p. (YA). (gr. 5 up). 1998. 16.00 (*0-395-89598-7*) HM.

***Peyton, K. M.** Swallow Summer. (J). 2000. pap. 6.95 (*0-552-52969-9*, Pub. by Transworld Publishers Ltd) Trafalgar.

— Swallow Tale. 2000. pap. 6.95 (*0-552-52807-2*, Pub. by Transworld Publishers Ltd) Trafalgar.

Peyton, K. M. The Team. LC 75-34092. (Illus.). (J). (gr. 6 up). 1967. 12.95 (*0-690-01083-4*) HarpC Child Bks.

Peyton, Kim & Nalco-Exxon Energy Chemicals, L.P. Staff. Fuel Field Manual: Sources & Solutions to Performance Problems. LC 97-16078. (Illus.). 322p. 1997. 69.95 (*0-07-046572-X*) McGraw.

Peyton, Mike. On the Ebb. (Illus.). 96p. 1998. pap. 15.95 (*1-898660-53-0*) Motorbooks Intl.

— Ready About. 96p. (C). 1990. text 59.00 (*0-906754-95-X*, Pub. by Fernhurst Bks) St Mut.

***Peyton, Mike.** Why Do We Do It? (Illus.). 126p. 2000. pap. 15.95 (*1-898660-18-2*, Pub. by Fernhurst Bks) Motorbooks Intl.

Peyton, Patrick. Fr. Peyton's Rosary Prayer Book. 240p. 1991. pap. 7.95 (*1-85390-143-1*, Pub. by Veritas Pubns) St Mut.

Peyton, Paul. People Centered Profit Strategies: 101 Competitive Advantages. LC 99-35939. 260p. 1999. pap. text 18.95 (*1-55571-517-6*) PSI Resch.

Peyton, Richard, ed. Sinister Gambits. 320p. 1993. pap. 18.95 (*1-55082-068-0*, Pub. by Quarry Pr) LPC InBook.

Peyton, W. D. Old Oman. 1983. 30.00 (*0-86685-530-0*) Intl Bk Ctr.

— Old Oman. 2nd ed. (Illus.). 128p. 1983. boxed set 29.95 (*0-905743-34-2*, Pub. by Stacey Intl) Intl Bk Ctr.

Peyton, Wes. San Jose: A Personal View. Muller, Kathleen, ed. (Illus.). 100p. 1989. 12.95 (*0-914139-08-8*) Hist San Jose.

Pezdek, Kathy & Banks, William P., eds. The Recovered Memory/False Memory Debate. (Illus.). 394p. 1996. text 49.95 (*0-12-552975-9*) Acad Pr.

Pezdek, Kathy, jt. auth. see Danks, Joseph H.

Pezdirtz, Richard, jt. auth. see Julien, Fred.

Pezechkian-Weinberg, Pary. Michel Tournier: Marginalite et Creation. (Currents in Comparative Romance Languages & Literatures Ser.: Vol. 48). (ENG & FRE.). XII, 170p. (C). 1998. text 41.95 (*0-8204-3316-0*) P Lang Pubng.

Pezeshki, Charles. Wild to the Last: Environmental Conflict in the Clearwater Country. LC 97-49101. 288p. 1998. pap. 22.95 (*0-87422-159-5*) Wash St U Pr.

Pezeshkzad, Iraj. Asemun Rismun. LC 96-46042. 312p. 1997. pap. 16.00 (*0-936347-79-1*) IBEX.

Pezeshkzad, Iraj. My Uncle Napoleon. Davis, Dick, tr. from PER. LC PK6561.P54 D313 1996. 512p. 1996. 29.95 (*0-934211-48-5*) Mage Pubs Inc.

***Pezeshkzad, Iraj.** My Uncle Napoleon. Davis, Dick, tr. LC PK6561.P54 D313 1996. 512p. 2000. pap. 19.95 (*0-934211-62-0*) Mage Pubs Inc.

Pezim, Michael E. Colon & Rectal Cancer: All You Need to Know to Take an Active Part in Your Treatment. (Illus.). 214p. 1992. pap. 19.95 (*0-9696125-0-8*) ITPG.

Pezinska, Z. & Topulos, A. Polish-English-Russian Data Processing Dictionary. (ENG, POL & RUS.). 119p. 1981. pap. 24.95 (*0-8288-0274-2*, M 9489) Fr & Eur.

Pezman, Steve, jt. ed. see Barrett, Brad.

Pezzano, Chuck, jt. auth. see Weiskopf, Herm.

Pezzenti, John. Alaska: A Photographic Journey Through the Last Wilderness. 256p. 1997. 50.00 (*0-670-87094-3*) Viking Penguin.

***Pezzenti, John.** Bear Book. 2000. write for info. (*0-670-88447-2*) Studio Bks.

***Pezzi, Bryan.** Massachusetts. (American States Ser.). (Illus.). 32p. (J). (gr. 3-7). 2000. write for info. (*1-930954-35-2*) Weigl Pubs.

Pezzi, Kevin. Believe It or Not! True Emergency Room Stories. Lewk, Karla, ed. (Illus.). 186p. 1998. pap. 12.95 (*0-9655606-2-7*) Transcope.

— Fascinating Health Secrets Vol. 1: Intriguing Tips on Medicine, Beauty, Health, Sleep, Nutrition, Weight Loss, Longevity, Exercise, Brainpower, Sexual Attraction, & Sex. Lewk, Karla, ed. (Illus.). 476p. (Orig.). 1996. pap. 19.95 (*0-9655606-0-0*) Transcope.

Pezzini, Wilma. Italy, 1985. Fisher, Robert C., ed. (Fisher Annotated Travel Guides Ser.). 352p. 1984. 12.95 (*0-8116-0065-3*) NAL.

Pezzoli, Keith. Human Settlements & Planning for Ecological Sustainability: The Case of Mexico City. LC 97-39497. (Urban & Industrial Environments Ser.). (Illus.). 459p. 1998. 44.00 (*0-262-16173-7*) MIT Pr.

***Pezzoli, Keith.** Human Settlements & Planning for Ecological Sustainability: The Case of Mexico City. (Illus.). 464p. (C). 2000. reprint ed. pap. 27.95 (*0-262-66114-4*) MIT Pr.

Pezzoni, J. Daniel. The History & Architecture of Lee County, North Carolina. LC 95-37062. 400p. 1995. write for info. (*0-9647954-0-X*) RR Hse Hist Assoc.

Pezzot-Pearce, Terry D., jt. auth. see Pearce, John W.

Pezzullo, Lawrence & Pezzullo, Ralph. At the Fall of Somoza. LC 93-1006. (Latin American Ser.). (Illus.). 328p. (C). 1994. text 34.95 (*0-8229-3756-5*) U of Pittsburgh Pr.

Pezzullo, Mary A. Marketing for Bankers. 2nd ed. (Illus.). 564p. (C). 1988. text 45.00 (*0-89982-354-8*) Am Bankers.

— Marketing for Bankers. 4th ed. (Illus.). 570p. (C). 1993. pap. text 45.00 (*0-89982-317-3*) Am Bankers.

Pezzullo, Mary Ann. Marketing Financial Services. (Illus.). 415p. (C). 1978. 18.00 (*0-89982-062-X*) Am Bankers.

Pezzullo, Ralph, jt. auth. see Pezzullo, Lawrence.

Pezzullo, Thomas R., jt. auth. see Brittingham, Barbara E.

Pezzulo, Ted. April Fish, & the Wooing of Lady Sunday: Two Short Plays. 1975. pap. 5.25 (*0-8222-0062-7*) Dramatists Play.

Pezzuti, Ella, ed. see Stewart, Jeffrey R., Jr., et al.

Pezzuto, A., jt. auth. see Burmester, G. R.

Pfadt, Robert E. Fundamentals of Applied Entomology. 4th ed. 742p. (C). 1985. text 57.00 (*0-02-395490-6*, Macmillan Coll) P-H.

Pfaelzer, Jean. Parlor Radical: Rebecca Harding Davis & the Origins of American Social Realism. 272p. 1996. pap. 19.95 (*0-8229-5654-3*) U of Pittsburgh Pr.

— The Utopian Novel in America, 1886-1896: The Politics of Form. LC 84-40094. 223p. (C). 1984. reprint ed. pap. 14.95 (*0-8229-5413-3*) U of Pittsburgh Pr.

Pfaelzer, Jean, ed. A Rebecca Harding Davis Reader: "Life in the Iron Mills," Selected Fiction, & Essays. 534p. (C). 1995. pap. 24.95 (*0-8229-5569-5*) U of Pittsburgh Pr.

Pfaelzer, Jean, ed. A Rebecca Harding Davis Reader: "Life in the Iron Mills," Selected Fiction, & Essays. LC 95-3296. 534p. 1995. text 35.00 (*0-8229-3887-1*) U of Pittsburgh Pr.

Pfaelzer, Jean, ed. & intro. see Lane, Mary E. Bradley.

Pfaff, Carol W., ed. First & Second Language Acquisition Processes. 288p. (J). 1986. mass mkt. 28.95 (*0-8384-2688-3*, Newbury) Heinle & Heinle.

***Pfaff-Czarnecka, Joanna.** Ethnic Futures: The State & Identity Politics in Asia LC 99-16908. 1999. write for info. (*0-7619-9360-6*) Sage.

Pfaff, D. W. Estrogens & Brain Function: Neural Analysis of a Hormone-Controlled Mammalian Reproductive Behavior. (Illus.). 272p. 1980. 96.95 (*0-387-90487-5*) Spr-Verlag.

Pfaff, D. W., ed. Ethical Questions in Brain & Behavior. (Illus.). 190p. 1983. 82.95 (*0-387-90870-6*) Spr-Verlag.

Pfaff, D. W., jt. ed. see Ganten, D.

Pfaff, Dani B. Broadsides: Indiana, the Early Years Resource Guide. 424p. 1987. ring bd. 8.50 (*1-885323-50-6*) IN Hist Bureau.

Pfaff, Daniel W. Joseph Pulitzer the Second & the Post-Dispatch: A Newspaperman's Life. (Illus.). 448p. 1991. 45.00 (*0-271-00748-6*) Pa St U Pr.

Pfaff, Dieter, jt. auth. see Ordelheide, Dieter.

Pfaff, Donald W. Drive: Neurobiological & Molecular Mechanism of Sexual Motivation. LC 98-43055. 1999. 90.00 (*0-262-16184-2*) MIT Pr.

— Drive: Neurobiological & Molecular Mechanisms of Sexual Motivation. LC 98-43055. (Cellular & Molecular Neuroscience Ser.). (Illus.). 316p. 1999. pap. 45.00 (*0-262-66147-0*, Bradford Bks) MIT Pr.

— Handbook of Genetic Influences on the Nervous System. LC 99-21820. 487p. 1999. boxed set 99.95 (*0-8493-2688-5*) CRC Pr.

Pfaff, Donald W., ed. Taste, Olfaction & the Central Nervous System: A Festschrift in Honor of Carl Pfaffmann. LC 84-43054. 346p. 1985. 29.95 (*0-87470-039-6*) Rockefeller.

Pfaff, Donn, ed. see Cady, Dale R.

Pfaff, Elmer F. Rediscovering Mantua (Portage County, Ohio) (Illus.). 212p. (Orig.). 1985. pap. 10.00 (*0-9615749-0-9*) Mage In Nation.

Pfaff, Eugene E., Jr. & Causey, Michael. Uwharrie. 256p. 1993. 19.95 (*0-936389-30-3*) Tudor Pubs.

Pfaff, Francis. A Cat Named Rush Limbaugh - a Dog Named Howard Stern. LC 97-65942. (Illus.). 80p. (Orig.). 1997. pap. 6.95 (*1-887775-58-7*) Cryptic NY.

Pfaff, Francoise. The Cinema of Ousmane Sembene: A Pioneer of African Film, 79. LC 84-3842. (Contributions in Afro-American & African Studies: No. 79). (Illus.). 207p. 1984. 49.95 (*0-313-24400-6*, PCI/, Greenwood Pr) Greenwood.

— Conversations with Maryse Conde. LC 96-11057. (Illus.). xvi, 189p. 1996. text 45.00 (*0-8032-3713-8*) U of Nebr Pr.

Pfaff, Francoise. Conversations with Maryse Conde. LC 96-11057. (Illus.). xvi, 189p. 1996. pap. 15.00 (*0-8032-8743-7*) U of Nebr Pr.

Pfaff, Francoise. Twenty-Five Black African Filmmakers: A Critical Study, with Fimography & Bio-Bibliography. LC 87-15024. 344p. 1988. lib. bdg. 52.95 (*0-313-24695-5*, PBA/, Greenwood Pr) Greenwood.

Pfaff, Heide-Marie. Die Entwicklung des Restgedankens in Jesaja 1-39. (Europaische Hochschulschriften Ser.: Reihe 23, Bd. 561). (GER., Illus.). 271p. 1996. 51.95 (*3-631-49913-2*) P Lang Pubng.

Pfaff, Henry J. Didactic Verses of an Old-Time Wobbly. 62p. 1983. pap. 5.00 (*0-88286-106-9*) C H Kerr.

Pfaff, Konrad. Salomon Malmon - Hiob der Aufklarung: Mosaiksteine zu Seinem Bildnis. (Philosophische Texte und Studien: Vol. 41). (GER.). viii, 320p. 1995. write for info. (*3-487-10068-1*) G Olms Pubs.

Pfaff, Linda. I Hope They Call Me on a Mission. 24p. (J). 1995. pap. 4.98 (*0-88290-524-4*, 1344) Horizon Utah.

Pfaff, Lucie. The American & German Entrepreneur: Economic & Literary Interplay. (American University Studies: Economics: Ser. XVI, Vol. 4). X, 183p. (C). 1989. text 32.50 (*0-8204-0807-7*) P Lang Pubng.

Pfaff, Lucie, jt. ed. see Geib, Peter J.

Pfaff, Paula, jt. auth. see Meany, Janet.

Pfaff, Phillip. Financial Modeling. 450p. 1989. write for info. (*0-318-63901-7*, H19847) P-H.

Pfaff, Richard W. Liturgical Calenders, Saints, & Services in Medieval England. LC 98-71752. (Variorum Collected Studies Ser.: Vol. 610). 320p. 1998. text 89.95 (*0-86078-677-3*, Pub. by Variorum) Ashgate Pub Co.

— Medieval Latin Liturgy: A Select Bibliography. LC 82-178542. (Toronto Medieval Bibliographies Ser.: No. 9). 151p. reprint ed. pap. 46.90 (*0-608-17999-X*, 202649600049) Bks Demand.

Pfaff, Robert F., et al. Measurement Techniques in Space Plasmas: Fields. LC 98-18385. (Geophysical Monograph Ser.: Vol. 103). 1998. 80.00 (*0-87590-086-0*) Am Geophysical.

— Measurement Techniques in Space Plasmas: Particles. Borovsky, Joseph E. & Young, David T., eds. LC 98-18386. (Geophysical Monographs: Vol. 102). 1998. 90.00 (*0-87590-085-2*) Am Geophysical.

Pfaff, Tim. Hmong in America: Journey from a Secret War. McLeod, Susan, ed. (Illus.). 100p. (Orig.). 1995. pap. 12.95 (*0-9636191-3-6*) Chippewa Val Mus.

— Settlement & Survival: Building Towns in the Chippewa Valley, 1850-1925. McLeod, Susan, ed. LC 94-60673. (Illus.). 120p. (Orig.). 1994. pap. 12.95 (*0-9636191-1-X*) Chippewa Val Mus.

***Pfaff, William.** Barbarian Sentiments. 1999. pap. write for info. (*0-8090-2807-7*) Hill & Wang.

— Barbarian Sentiments: America in the New Century. rev. ed. LC 00-35014. 256p. 2000. pap. 14.00 (*0-8090-2806-9*) Hill & Wang.

Pfaffenberger, B. Publish It on the Web! Windows. 2nd ed. LC 97-18404. (Illus.). 587p. 1997. pap., pap. text 37.95 incl. cd-rom (*0-12-553160-5*) Morgan Kaufmann.

Pfaffenberger, Barbara. Essentials of dBASE VI with Advanced Applications. (C). 1997. pap. 6.00 (*0-06-501138-4*) Addson-Wesley Educ.

— Essentials of DOS. 88p. (C). 1997. pap. 9.00 (*0-06-501135-X*) Addson-Wesley Educ.

— Essentials of Microcomputer Systems. (C). 1997. pap. 8.50 (*0-06-501134-1*) Addson-Wesley Educ.

— Essentials of WordPerfect with Advanced Applications. (C). 1992. pap. 8.50 (*0-06-501136-8*) Addson-Wesley Educ.

Pfaffenberger, Bryan. Adventures in Windows. 176p. 1993. pap. 14.95 (*1-55958-449-1*) Prima Pub.

— Ambulatory Monitoring Markets. (Market Research Reports: No. 441). (Illus.). 120p. 1994. 795.00 (*0-614-09927-7*) Theta Corp.

— Building a Strategic Extranet. LC 97-74803. 432p. 1998. pap. 29.99 (*0-7645-3125-5*) IDG Bks.

— Caste in Tamil Culture: The Religious Foundations of Sudra Domination in Tamil Sri Lanka. LC 82-7321. (Foreign & Comparative Studies Program, South Asian Ser.: No. 7). (Illus.). (Orig.). (C). 1982. pap. 12.00 (*0-915984-84-9*) Syracuse U Foreign Comp.

— Democratizing Information: Online Databases & the Rise of End-User Searching. (Professional Librarian Ser.). 175p. 1989. 40.00 (*0-8161-1860-4*, Hall Reference); 30.00 (*0-8161-1872-8*, Hall Reference) Macmillan.

— Dictionary of Computer Terms. 6th ed. LC 97-80220. (Illus.). 576p. 1997. 10.95 (*0-02-861890-4*) Macmillan.

— Discover the Internet. LC 96-80453. 504p. 1997. pap. 24.99 (*0-7645-4019-X*) IDG Bks.

— Discovering HTML 4. LC 98-3867. (Illus.). 419p. (C). 1998. pap. text 34.95 (*0-12-553167-2*) Acad Pr.

— The Elements of Hypertext Style. LC 96-45092. (Illus.). 297p. 1997. pap. text 24.95 (*0-12-553142-7*) Morgan Kaufmann.

***Pfaffenberger, Bryan.** HTML 4.01 Bible. (Illus.). 900p. 2000. pap. text 39.99 (*0-7645-3473-4*) IDG Bks.

Pfaffenberger, Bryan. I Hate DOS: A Friendly Guide to DOS. 362p. 1993. 16.95 (*1-56529-215-4*) Que.

— Internet in Plain English. 2nd ed. 89p. 1995. pap. 19.95 (*1-55828-439-7*, MIS Pr) IDG Bks.

— Linux Clearly Explained. (Clearly Explained Ser.). 300p. (C). 1999. pap. 44.95 incl. cd-rom (*0-12-553169-9*) Acad Pr.

***Pfaffenberger, Bryan.** Linux Command Instant Reference. 2000. pap. 24.99 (*0-7821-2748-7*) Sybex.

— Linux Networking Clearly Explained. (Clearly Explained Ser.). (Illus.). 400p. 2000. pap. text 44.95 (*0-12-533171-1*) Morgan Kaufmann.

— Mastering Gnome. 800p. 1999. pap. 34.99 (*0-7821-2625-1*) Sybex.

— Mastering KDE. (Mastering Ser.). (Illus.). 704p. 2000. pap. text 34.99 (*0-7821-2629-4*) Sybex.

Pfaffenberger, Bryan. Microcomputer Applications in Qualitative Research. (Qualitative Research Methods Ser.: Vol. 14). 96p. (C). 1988. text 24.00 (*0-8039-3119-0*); pap. text 10.50 (*0-8039-3120-4*) Sage.

— Mosaic User's Guide. LC 94-37780. 1994. pap. 24.95 incl. disk (*1-55828-409-5*, MIS Pr) IDG Bks.

— Netscape Communicator - Windows. (Illus.). 608p. 1997. pap. text 32.95 (*0-12-553164-8*) Morgan Kaufmann.

— Netscape Navigator: Surfing the Web & Exploring the Internet, 2 vols. large type ed. (Illus.). 430p. 107.50 (*0-614-20558-1*, L-03801-00 APHB) Am Printing Hse.

— Netscape Navigator 3.0 (Windows) (Illus.). 464p. 1996. pap., pap. text 29.95 incl. cd-rom (*0-12-553153-2*) Morgan Kaufmann.

— Official Microsoft Internet Explorer Book. LC 96-33397. 348p. 1996. pap. text 24.95 incl. cd-rom (*1-57231-309-9*) Microsoft.

— Official Microsoft Internet Explorer 4.0 Book. LC 97-41707. 350p. 1997. 24.99 (*1-57231-576-8*) Microsoft.

— PCs in Plain English. 89p. 1995. pap. 19.95 (*1-55828-384-6*, MIS Pr) IDG Bks.

— Pocket Internet Directory Dictionary. 400p. 1997. 5.95 (*0-02-861889-0*) Macmillan.

— Protect Your Privacy on the Internet. LC 96-30073. 336p. 1997. pap. 29.99 incl. cd-rom (*0-471-18143-9*) Wiley.

— Publish It on the Web! Macintosh. 2nd ed. LC 97-40600. (Illus.). 568p. 1997. pap., pap. text 37.95 incl. cd-rom (*0-12-553162-1*) Morgan Kaufmann.

— Que's Computer User's Dictionary. 4th ed. 670p. 1993. pap. 12.95 (*1-56529-604-4*) Que.

— Running Microsoft Internet Explorer 5 With CDROM. LC 98-43580. (Running Ser.). (Illus.). 791p. 1999. pap. 3.99 (*1-57231-949-6*) Microsoft.

— The Usenet Book: Finding, Using, & Surviving Newsgroups on the Internet. LC 94-38690. 496p. (C). 1994. pap. 26.95 (*0-201-40978-X*) Addison-Wesley.

— Using Word 5.1 for the Mac. LC 92-63327. (Illus.). 1066p. 1993. 29.95 (*1-56529-143-3*) Que.

— Web Publishing with XML in Six Easy Steps. LC 98-30427. (Illus.). 350p. (C). 1998. pap. text 34.95 (*0-12-553166-4*) Morgan Kaufmann.

***Pfaffenberger, Bryan.** Webster's New World Dictionary of Computer Terms. 8th rev. ed. 2000. pap. text 12.95 (*0-02-863777-1*, Websters New Wrld) Macmillan Gen Ref.

Pfaffenberger, Bryan. World Wide Web Bible. 450p. 1995. pap. 27.95 incl. disk (*1-55828-410-9*, MIS Pr) IDG Bks.

— World Wide Web Bible - Internet Plain English 1-E Package. 1995. pap. 34.99 incl. cd-rom (*1-55828-458-3*) H Holt & Co.

Pfaffenberger, Bryan, compiled by. Webster's New World Dictionary of Computer Terms. 7th ed. LC 98-68180. (Webster's New World Ser.). 580p. 1999. 12.95 (*0-02-862884-5*, Pub. by Macmillan) S&S Trade.

Pfaffenberger, Bryan, ed. Que's Computer Users Dictionary. 5th ed. LC 94-67366. 542p. 1994. 12.99 (*1-56529-881-0*) Que.

Pfaffenberger, Bryan & Gutzman, Alexis D. HTML 4 Bible. (Bible Ser.). 960p. 1998. pap. 49.99 incl. cd-rom (*0-7645-3220-0*) IDG Bks.

Pfaffenberger, Roger C. Statistical Literacy for Business & Economics Casebook. 1996. pap. text. write for info. (*0-201-42177-1*) Addison-Wesley.

Pfaffenberger, Roger C. & Patterson, James H. Statistical Methods: For Business & Economics. 3rd ed. (C). 1987. text 60.95 (*0-256-03664-0*, Irwn McGrw-H) McGrw-H Hghr Educ.

Pfaffenberger, W. E., jt. auth. see Johnsonbaugh, Richard.

Pfaffenbichler, Matthias. Armourers. (Medieval Craftsmen Ser.). (Illus.). 72p. 1992. pap. text 19.95 (*0-8020-7732-3*) U of Toronto Pr.

Pfaffenrath, V., jt. ed. see Lance, J.

Pfaffenroth, S. Faces & Voices: An Intercultural Perspective of the Developing Reader & Writer, Custom Pub. (C). 1992. text 17.25 (*0-07-049702-8*) McGraw.

Pfaffle, A. E. & Nicosia, Sal. Risk Analysis Guide to Insurance & Employee Benefits. LC 77-10973. 71p. reprint ed. pap. 30.00 (*0-608-12445-1*, 205575200036) Bks Demand.

Pfafflin, James R., ed. The Encyclopedia of Environmental Science & Engineering, Vol. 1. 3rd ed. xvi, 649p. 1992. text. write for info. (*2-88124-501-3*) Gordon & Breach.

P

— The Encyclopedia of Environmental Science & Engineering, Vol. 2. 3rd ed. xvi, 586p. 1992. text. write for info. (2-88124-502-1) Gordon & Breach.

Pfafflin, James R. & Zieglar, E. N., eds. The Encyclopedia of Environmental Science & Engineering, 2 vols., Vol. 2. 3rd ed. 1,235p. 1992. text 799.00 (2-88124-504-8) Gordon & Breach.

Pfafflin, James R. & Ziegler, E. N., eds. The Encyclopedia of Environmental Science & Engineering, Vol. 1. 2nd ed. xxiv, 404p. 1983. 310.00 (0-677-06400-4) Gordon & Breach.

— The Encyclopedia of Environmental Science & Engineering, Vol. 2. 2nd ed. xxiv, 408p. 1983. 398.00 (0-677-06410-1) Gordon & Breach.

Pfafflin, James R. & Ziegler, Edward N. Advances in Environmental Science & Engineering, Vol. 3. xiv, 224p. 1980. text 385.00 (0-677-15760-6) Gordon & Breach.

Pfafflin, James R. & Ziegler, Edward N., eds. Advances in Environmental Science & Engineering, Vol. 5. xii, 204p. 1986. text 334.00 (2-88124-184-0) Gordon & Breach.

— Encyclopedia of Environmental Science & Engineering, 2 vols. 4th rev. ed. 1408p. 1998. text 650.00 (90-5699-636-3, ECU500, Harwood Acad Pubs) Gordon & Breach.

— The Encyclopedia of Environmental Science & Engineering, 3 vols., Set. 1350p. 1983. 798.00 (0-677-06430-6) Gordon & Breach.

Pfafflin, James R., et al. Dictionary of Environmental Science & Engineering. 192p. 1996. text 65.00 (90-5699-003-9, ECU54); pap. text 20.00 (90-5699-004-7, ECU25) Gordon & Breach.

***Pfafflin, Margarete, et al.** Comprehensive Care for People with Epilepsy. 2001. write for info. (0-86196-610-4, Pub. by John Libby) Buttrwrth-Heinemann.

Pfahl, John K., jt. auth. see Crary, David T.

Pfahl, P. Blair, Jr., jt. auth. see Pfahl, Peter B.

Pfahl, Peter B. & Pfahl, P. Blair, Jr. The Retail Florist Business. 5th ed. 336p. 1994. 48.75 (0-8134-2967-6) Interstate.

Pfahler, P., jt. ed. see Kastens, U.

***Pfahler, Wilhelm, et al, eds.** Airports & Air Traffic: Regulation, Privatisation & Competition. LC 99-24735. (Illus.). 146p. 1999. 28.95 (0-8204-4327-1) P Lang Pubng.

Pfahler, Wilhelm & Tiedemann, Bernd, eds. Hafen, Transrapid, Telekommunikation - Wachstumsmotoren Fur die Hamburger Metropole? (Illus.). VIII, 229p. 1998. pap. 34.95 (3-631-32159-7) P Lang Pubng.

***Pfahler, Wilhelm, et al.** Wirtschaftsfaktor Bildung und Wissenschaft: Die Regionalwirtschaftliche Bedeutung der Hochschulbildungs- und Wissenschaftseinrichtungen In Bremen. 144p. 1999. 26.95 (3-631-35246-8) P Lang Pubng.

Pfalgerb, Bernhard. Herder Political Lexicon: Herder Lexikon Politik. 4th ed. (GER.). 380p. 1982. 35.00 (0-8288-2257-3, M7450) Fr & Eur.

Pfaller, Alfred, jt. ed. see Gross, Bertram.

Pfaltz, C. R., ed. Neurophysiological & Clinical Aspects of Vestibular Disorders. (Advances in OtoRhinoLaryngology Ser.: Vol. 30). (Illus.). xii, 372p. 1983. 171.50 (3-8055-3607-0) S Karger.

— New Aspects of Cochlear Mechanics & Inner Ear Pathophysiology. (Advances in OtoRhinoLaryngology Ser.: Vol. 44). (Illus.). x, 170p. 1990. 146.25 (3-8055-5020-0) S Karger.

— New Aspects of Fundamental Problems of Larynology & Otology. (Advances in OtoRhinoLaryngology Ser.: Vol. 32). (Illus.). viii, 200p. 1984. 138.50 (3-8055-3701-8) S Karger.

Pfaltz, C. R., et al, eds. Bearing of Basic Research on Clinical Otolaryngology. (Advances in OtoRhinoLaryngology Ser.: Vol. 46). (Illus.). x, 182p. 1991. 161.75 (3-8055-5338-2) S Karger.

Pfaltz, C. R., jt. ed. see Colman, B. H.

Pfaltz, C. R., ed. see International Congress of Radiology in Oto-Rhine-L.

Pfaltz, C. R., ed. see International Otoneurological Symposium Staff.

Pfaltz, C. R., jt. ed. see Jahnke, K.

Pfaltzgraff, Diane K., jt. auth. see Dougherty, James E.

Pfaltzgraff, Robert L., Jr. Energy Issues & Alliance Relationships: The United States, Western Europe & Japan. LC 80-81711. (Special Reports). 71p. 1980. 11.95 (0-89549-021-8) Inst Foreign Policy Anal.

Pfaltzgraff, Robert L. Security in Southeastern Europe & the U. S. - Greek Relationship. Keridis, Dimitris, ed. (Institute for Foreign Policy Anaylsis Ser.). 225p. (Orig.). 1997. pap. 11.95 (1-57488-133-7) Brasseys.

Pfaltzgraff, Robert L., Jr. Security Strategy & Missile Defense. (Institute for Foreign Policy Anaylsis Ser.). 128p. (Orig.). 1995. pap. 11.95 (1-57488-084-5) Brasseys.

Pfaltzgraff, Robert L., Jr., ed. National Security Policy for the 1980's. (Annals of the American Academy of Political & Social Science Ser.: Vol. 457). 250p. 1981. 26.00 (0-8039-1705-8); pap. 17.00 (0-8039-1much-X) Sage.

Pfaltzgraff, Robert L., Jr. & Davis, Jacquelyn K. The Cruise Missile: Bargaining Chip or Defense Bargain? LC 76-51854. (Special Reports). 53p. 1977. 11.95 (0-89549-001-3) Inst Foreign Policy Anal.

Pfaltzgraff, Robert L. & Davis, Jacquelyn K. Japanese-American Relations in a Changing Security Environment. LC 75-37014. (Foreign Policy Papers: Vol. 1, No. 1). 56p. reprint ed. pap. 30.00 (0-7837-1986-8, 204226000002) Bks Demand.

***Pfaltzgraff, Robert L., Jr. & Schultz, Richard H., Jr.** The Role of Naval Forces in 21st Century Operations. LC 99-86769. 2000. 35.00 (1-57488-256-2) Brasseys.

Pfaltzgraff, Robert L., Jr. & Schultz, Richard H., Jr., eds. War in the Information Age: Theory to Practice. (Institute for Foreign Policy Anaylsis Ser.). 320p. 1996. 39.95 (1-57488-104-3) Brasseys.

Pfaltzgraff, Robert L. & Shultz, Richard H. War in the Information Age: New Challenges for U. S. Security Policy. LC 96-22516. (Association of the U. S. Army Book Ser.). 398p. 1997. 39.95 (1-57488-118-3) Brasseys.

Pfaltzgraff, Robert L., et al. The Greens of West Germany: Origins, Strategies & Transatlantic Implications. LC 83-48704. (Special Reports). 105p. 1983. 11.95 (0-89549-056-0) Inst Foreign Policy Anal.

Pfaltzgraff, Robert L., Jr., jt. auth. see Davis, Jacquelyn K.

Pfaltzgraff, Robert L., Jr., jt. auth. see Dougherty, James E.

Pfaltzgraff, Robert L., Jr., jt. auth. see Kintner, William R.

Pfaltzgraff, Robert L., Jr., jt. auth. see Lee, David T.

Pfaltzgraff, Robert L., jt. auth. see Shultz, Richard H., Jr.

Pfaltzgraff, Robert L., Jr., jt. ed. see Keridis, Dimitris.

Pfalzgraf, Beth, jt. auth. see Ewing, Susan A.

Pfalzgraf, Jochen & Wang, Dongming, eds. Automated Practical Reasoning. LC 95-1923. (Texts & Monographs in Symbolic Computation). 232p. 1995. 59.00 (0-387-82600-9) Spr-Verlag.

Pfalzgraft, Beth, jt. auth. see Ewing, Susan A.

Pfalzner, Susanne & Gibbon, Paul. Many-Body Tree Methods in Physics. (Illus.). 177p. (C). 1996. text 54.95 (0-521-49564-4) Cambridge U Pr.

Pfammatter, Ueli. Cuno Brullmann. (Illus.). 128p. 1995. pap. 45.00 (3-7643-5594-8, Pub. by Birkhauser) Princeton Arch.

***Pfammatter, Ulrich.** Making of the Modern Architect & Engineer: Origins & Development of an Occupation. (Illus.). 328p. 2000. pap. 38.00 (3-7643-6217-0) Birkhauser.

Pfan, Judy, jt. auth. see Erting, Lynne.

Pfander, Hanspeter, ed. Key to Carotenoids. 2nd ed. 296p. 1987. 126.50 (0-8176-1860-0) Birkhauser.

Pfandl, Ludwig. Geschichte der Spanischen Nationalliteratur in Ihrer Blutezeit. xiv, 618p. 1967. reprint ed. write for info. (0-318-71638-0) G Olms Pubs.

Pfann, G. Dynamic Modelling of Stochastic Demand for Manufacturing Employment. Beckmann, Martin J. & Krelle, W., eds. (Lecture Notes in Economics & Mathematical Systems Ser.: Vol. 349). (Illus.). iv, 158p. 1990. 31.00 (0-387-52881-4) Spr-Verlag.

Pfanner, Helmut F. Exile in New York: German & Austrian Writers after 1933. LC 83-10465. 253p. reprint ed. pap. 78.50 (0-7837-3664-9, 204353600009) Bks Demand.

Pfanner, Louise. Louise Built House. 1999. text 10.95 (0-312-02015-5) St Martin.

Pfannes, C. & Salamone, Victor A. The Great Admirals of World War II: The Germans, Vol. 2. 1984. mass mkt. 3.25 (0-685-07895-7, Zebra Kensgtn) Kensgtn Pub Corp.

Pfannes, Charles E. & Salamone, Victor A. The Great Admirals of World War II Vol. 1: The Americans. 1983. mass mkt. 3.25 (0-8217-1160-1, Zebra Kensgtn) Kensgtn Pub Corp.

— The Great Commanders of World War II. (Germans Ser.: Vol. 1). (YA). (gr. 7 up). 1981. mass mkt. 2.75 (0-89083-727-9, Zebra Kensgtn) Kensgtn Pub Corp.

— The Great Commanders of World War II Vol. II: The British. (YA). (gr. 7 up). 1981. mass mkt. 2.75 (0-89083-786-4, Zebra Kensgtn) Kensgtn Pub Corp.

Pfannes, Charles E. & Salomone, Victor A. The Great Commanders of World War II. (Americans Ser: Vol. III). 1982. mass mkt. 2.95 (0-89083-923-9, Zebra Kensgtn) Kensgtn Pub Corp.

Pfannkuch, H. O. Elsevier's Dictionary of Environmental Hydrogeology: In English (with Definitions), French & German. (ENG, FRE & GER.). 344p. 1990. 206.25 (0-444-87269-8) Elsevier.

Pfannkuche, Bernd. Parat Dictionary of Ceramics & Earth: English-German, German-English. (ENG & GER.). 555p. 1993. 225.00 (0-7859-6958-6) Fr & Eur.

Pfannl, Beth K., jt. ed. see Hellman, Ronald G.

Pfannmueller, Gustav. Handbuch der Islam-Literatur. (GER.). viii, 436p. (C). 1974. reprint ed. 173.10 (3-11-002488-8) De Gruyter.

***Pfannmuller, Gunter.** In Search of Dignity. (Illus.). 144p. 2000. 45.00 (0-89381-912-3) Aperture.

Pfannsteil, Arthur S. & Schuster, Bernard. Modigliani: A Study of His Sculpture. (Illus.). 101p. 1986. write for info. (0-9616170-0-4) Mega Corp.

Pfanstiehl, John. Automotive Paint Handbook. LC 92-14868. (Illus.). 176p. 1992. pap. 16.95 (1-55788-034-4, HP Books) Berkley Pub.

***Pfanstiehl, John.** Automotive Paint Handbook: Paint Technology for Auto Enthusiasts & Body Shop Professionals. rev. ed. LC 97-45785. (Illus.). 186p. 1998. pap. 17.95 (1-55788-291-6, HP Books) Berkley Pub.

Pfanstiehl, John & Zazarine, Paul. Corvette Weekend Projects. LC 95-30336. 176p. (Orig.). 1995. pap. 17.95 (1-55788-218-5, HP Books) Berkley Pub.

Pfanz, Donald. Richard S. Ewell: A Soldier's Life. LC 97-21473. (Civil War America Ser.). (Illus.). 680p. 1998. 45.00 (0-8078-2389-9) U of NC Pr.

Pfanz, Donald C. The Petersburg Campaign Abraham Lincoln at City Point, March 20-April 9, 1865. (Virginia Civil War Battles & Leaders Ser.). (Illus.). 12.95 (0-930919-76-9) H E Howard.

Pfanz, Harry W. Gettysburg. (Civil War Ser.). 60p. 1994. pap. 4.95 (0-915992-63-9) Eastern National.

— Gettysburg: Culp's Hill & Cemetery Hill. LC 93-3323. (Civil War America Ser.). (Illus.). xx, 508p. (C). 1993. 39.95 (0-8078-2118-7) U of NC Pr.

— Gettysburg - The Second Day. LC 87-5965. (Illus.). 624p. 1998. reprint ed. pap. 19.95 (0-8078-4730-5) U of NC Pr.

— Gettysburg-The Second Day. LC 87-5965. (Illus.). xxii, 602p. 1987. 39.95 (0-8078-1749-X) U of NC Pr.

Pfanzagl, J. Asymptotic Expansions for General Statistical Models. (Lecture Notes in Statistics Ser.: Vol. 31). vii, 505p. 1985. 87.95 (0-387-96221-2) Spr-Verlag.

— Contributions to a General Asymptotic Statistical Theory. (Lecture Notes in Statistics Ser.: Vol. 13). (Illus.). 315p. 1982. 62.95 (0-387-90776-9) Spr-Verlag.

— Estimation in Some Semiparametric Models. (Lecture Notes in Statistics Ser.: Vol. 63). iii, 112p. 1990. 31.95 (0-387-97238-2) Spr-Verlag.

Pfanzagl, Johann. Allgemeine Methodenlehre der Statistik, Pt. 1. 6th ed. (GER.). 254p. 1983. 17.55 (3-11-009674-9) De Gruyter.

— Parametric Statistical Theory. LC 94-21850. xiii, 374p. 1994. text 89.95 (3-11-014030-6); pap. text 59.95 (3-11-013863-8) De Gruyter.

Pfarr, Richard. Mice As a New Pet. 1991. pap. 6.95 (0-86622-530-7, TU022) TFH Pubns.

Pfarrer, Chuck. Virus. (Illus.). 136p. 1995. pap. 16.95 (1-56971-104-6) Dark Horse Comics.

Pfarrer, Chuck, et al. The Thing from Another World & Climate of Fear Collection. (Illus.). 168p. 1993. pap. 15.95 (1-878574-85-X) Dark Horse Comics.

Pfarrer, Don. Guerrilla Persuasion. LC 98-17998. 192p. 1998. pap. 14.00 (0-395-88168-4) HM.

Pfarrer, Donald. Temple & Shipman. LC 98-67764. 272p. 1999. pap. 12.00 (0-9667540-0-X) MS in Bot.

Pfatteicher, Carl F. John Redford: Organist & Almoner of St. Paul's Cathedral in the Reign of Henry VIII. LC 74-24184. reprint ed. 32.50 (0-404-13088-7) AMS Pr.

Pfatteicher, Philip H. Commentary on the Occasional Services. LC 82-48542. 480p. 1983. 37.99 (0-8006-0697-3, 1-697, Fortress Pr) Augsburg Fortress.

— Festivals & Commemorations: Handbook to the Calendar in Lutheran Book of Worship. LC 79-54129. 480p. 1981. 40.99 (0-8066-1757-8, 10-2295, Augsburg) Augsburg Fortress.

— Liturgical Spirituality. LC 97-7376. 302p. (Orig.). 1997. pap. 22.00 (1-56338-194-X) TPI PA.

— School of the Church: Worship & Christian Formation. LC 94-47514. 160p. 1995. pap. 14.00 (1-56338-110-9) TPI PA.

Pfatteicher, Philip H. & Messerli, Carlos R. Manual on the Liturgy: Lutheran Book of Worship. LC 78-68179. 1979. 31.50 (0-8066-1676-8, 3-2015, Augsburg) Augsburg Fortress.

Pfattiecher, Philip H. NSRV Bible. 1998. 15.99 (0-8066-0392-5) Augsburg Fortress.

Pfau, Michael & Parrott, Roxanne. Persuasive Communication Campaigns. 528p. 1995. 73.00 (0-205-13977-9) Allyn.

Pfau, Michael, jt. see Moy, Patricia.

Pfau, Michael W. Debate & Argument: A Systems Approach to Advocacy. LC 87-4859. 349p. 1987. reprint ed. pap. 108.20 (0-7837-8852-5, 204952900001) Bks Demand.

Pfau, Michael W. & Kenski, Henry C. Attack Politics: Strategy & Defense. LC 89-29766. (Praeger Series in Political Communication). 216p. 1990. 47.95 (0-275-93375-X, C3375, Greenwood Pr) Greenwood.

Pfau, Nancy & Seddun, Suzanne. Teaching Basic Skills Through Literature: Math. (Illus.). 144p. 1995. pap., teacher ed. 12.95 (1-55734-790-5) Tchr Create Mat.

Pfau, Richard. No Sacrifice Too Great: The Life of Lewis L. Strauss. LC 84-13153. (Illus.). 326p. reprint ed. pap. 101.10 (0-7837-4368-8, 204407800012) Bks Demand.

***Pfau, Richard H.** Apprenticeship Training: A Guide to This Superb Way for Developing Skilled Personnel. LC 99-97525. (On-the-Job Training Ser.: Vol. 5). iv, 67p. 1999. 16.00 (1-929859-05-8) Workforce Training.

— Briefings: Guidelines for Action. (On-the-Job Training Ser.: Vol. 4). iii, 22p. 1999. 10.00 (1-929859-04-X, OJT-4) Workforce Training.

— Employee Orientation: Guidelines for Action. (On-the-Job Training Ser.: Vol. 2). (Illus.). iv, 51p. 1998. 14.00 (1-929859-02-3, OJT-2) Workforce Training.

— How to Identify the Training Needs of Employees. 3rd ed. (Illus.). iv, 66p. 1997. 16.00 (1-929859-00-7, TNA-1) Workforce Training.

— Job Instruction Training: A Step-by-Step Guide. (On-the-Job Training Ser.: Vol. 3). (Illus.). iv, 23p. 1999. 10.00 (1-929859-03-1, OJT-3) Workforce Training.

— Using Delegation to Train & Develop Employees. (On-the-Job Training Ser.). iii, 31p. 1999. 12.00 (1-929859-06-6, OJT-6) Workforce Training.

— Using Job Rotation to Train & Develop Employees. (On-the-Job Training Ser.: Vol. 1). iv, 28p. 1998. 12.00 (1-929859-01-5, OJT-1) Workforce Training.

Pfau, Thomas. Wordsworth's Profession: Form, Class, & the Logic of Early Romantic Cultural Production. LC 97-2946. 475p. 1997. 49.50 (0-8047-2902-6); pap. write for info. (0-8047-3136-5) Stanford U Pr.

Pfau, Thomas & Gleckner, Robert F. Lessons of Romanticism: A Critical Companion. LC 97-31426. 1998. 22.95 (0-8223-2077-0) Duke.

Pfau, Thomas & Gleckner, Robert F., eds. Lessons of Romanticism: A Critical Companion. LC 97-31426. 475p. 1998. pap. 22.95 (0-8223-2091-6) Duke.

Pfau, Thomas, ed. & tr. see Holderlin, Friedrich.

Pfau, Thomas, ed. & tr. see Schelling, Friedrich Wilhelm Joseph.

Pfau, Werner, jt. auth. see Marx, Siegfried.

Pfautsch, Donna S. Riding the Convection Connection: Teaching Energy: Hot Air Ballons. (Illus.). (Orig.). 1993. pap., teacher ed. 14.99 (0-89824-216-9) Trillium Pr.

Pfautsch, Lloyd. Choral Therapy: Vocal Techniques & Exercises for Church Choirs. LC 93-39299. 96p. (Orig.). 1994. pap. 9.95 (0-687-06510-0) Abingdon.

Pfautsch, Lloyd. The Lord Is My Light. 1.25 (0-687-07135-6) Abingdon.

— Lord Jesus, Think on Me. 1.00 (0-687-06188-1) Abingdon.

Pfautz, Harold W., ed. see Booth, Charles.

Pfefer, Susanna. Faberge Eggs: Masterpieces from Czarist Russia. (Illus.). 128p. 1990. 35.00 (0-88363-090-7) H L Levin.

Pfeffer. Managing with Power. 400p. 1992. 34.95 (0-07-103360-2) McGraw.

— Mechanisms/Interferon Actions, Vol. I. 152p. 1987. 89.00 (0-8493-6146-X, CRC Reprint) Franklin.

— Mechanisms/Interferon Actions, Vol. II. 200p. 1987. 113.00 (0-8493-6147-8, CRC Reprint) Franklin.

— The Riddle Streak. (J). 1995. 14.95 (0-8050-3033-6) H Holt & Co.

Pfeffer, Cynthia R. The Suicidal Child. LC 85-31710. 318p. 1986. lib. bdg. 39.95 (0-89862-664-1) Guilford Pubns.

Pfeffer, Cynthia R., ed. Severe Stress & Mental Disturbance in Children. 697p. 1996. text 72.95 (0-88048-657-0, 8657) Am Psychiatric.

— Suicide among Youth: Perspectives on Risk & Prevention. LC 88-36702. 251p. 1989. reprint ed. pap. 77.90 (0-608-02012-5, 206266800003) Bks Demand.

Pfeffer, Georg & Behera, Deepak K., eds. Contemporary Society: Childhood & Complex Order. LC 96-903270. (Illus.). ix, 452p. 1996. 46.00 (81-86562-06-0, Pub. by Manak Pubns Pvt Ltd) Nataraj Bks.

Pfeffer, Gina. The Follower. 260p. mass mkt. 5.99 (1-896329-39-X) Picasso Publ.

Pfeffer, Glen & Mizel, Mark S., eds. Selected Bibliography of the Foot & Ankle with Commentary. 321p. 1992. pap. 25.00 (0-89203-061-5) Amer Acad Ortho Surg.

Pfeffer, Glenn B. & Frey, Carol C., eds. Current Practice in Foot & Ankle Surgery, Vol. 1. LC 92-49130. (Current Practice in Foot & Ankle Surgery). 304p. 1993. text 55.00 (0-07-049732-X) McGraw-Hill HPD.

— Current Practice in Foot & Ankle Surgery, Vol. 2. (Illus.). 208p. 1994. text 55.00 (0-07-049799-0) McGraw-Hill HPD.

Pfeffer, Glenn B. & Mizel, Mark S. Orthopaedic Knowledge Update: Foot & Ankle. LC 94-77974. (Illus.). 324p. 1994. pap. 115.00 (0-89203-112-3) Amer Acad Ortho Surg.

Pfeffer, Irwin, jt. auth. see Abraham, Henry.

Pfeffer, J. Alan & Cannon, Garland, eds. German Loanwords in English: An Historical Dictionary. 415p. (C). 1994. text 89.95 (0-521-40254-9) Cambridge U Pr.

Pfeffer, Jeffrey. Competitive Advantage through People: Unleashing the Power of the Work Force. LC 93-26599. 288p. 1994. 24.95 (0-8458-4413-X) Harvard Busn.

— Competitive Advantage through People: Unleashing the Power of the Work Force. 304p. (C). 1996. pap. 14.95 (0-87584-717-X) Harvard Busn.

— The Human Equation: Building Profits by Putting People First. LC 97-27510. 368p. 1998. 24.95 (0-87584-841-9) Harvard Busn.

— Managing with Power: Politics & Influence in Organizations. LC 91-26237. 400p. 1992. 24.95 (0-87584-314-X) Harvard Busn.

— Managing with Power: Politics & Influence in Organizations. 400p. 1994. pap. 16.95 (0-87584-440-5) Harvard Busn.

— Managing with Power: Politics & Influence in Organizations. 1993. pap. text 16.95 (0-07-103452-8) McGraw.

— New Directions for Organization Theory: Problems & Prospects. LC 96-33593. (Illus.). 272p. 1997. 38.00 (0-19-511434-5) OUP.

— Organizational Design. Mackenzie, Kenneth D., ed. LC 77-86024. (Organizational Behavior Ser.). (Illus.). (C). 1978. pap. text 15.95 (0-88295-453-9) Harlan Davidson.

— Organizations & Organization Theory. LC 82-10154. 400p. 1986. text 24.95 (0-88730-201-7, HarpBusn) HarpInfo.

— Power in Organizations. LC 80-29883. 391p. 1986. pap. 21.00 (0-88730-199-1, HarpBusn) HarpInfo.

Pfeffer, Jeffrey & Sutton, Robert I. The Knowing-Doing Gap: How Smart Companies Turn Knowledge into Action. LC 99-28307. 256p. 1999. 27.50 (1-57851-124-0) Harvard Busn.

Pfeffer, Jeffrey, jt. auth. see O'Reilly, Charles A., III.

Pfeffer, Jeremy M. & Waldron, Gillian. Psychiatric Differential Diagnosis. LC 86-26356. (Illus.). 192p. (Orig.). (C). 1987. text 40.00 (0-443-03703-5) Church.

Pfeffer, K., et al, eds. Function & Specificity of T Cells: International Workshop Schloss Elmau, Bavaria, FRG, October 14-16, 1990. (Current Topics in Microbiology & Immunology Ser.: Vol. 173). (Illus.). xii, 296p. 1991. 118.00 (0-387-53781-3) Spr-Verlag.

Pfeffer, K. H. International Atlas of Karst Phenomena Sheets 8-12, 1990. (Annals of Geomorphology Ser.: Suppl. 77). (Illus.). 105p. 1990. pap. 54.55 (3-443-21077-5, Pub. by Gebruder Borntraeger) Balogh.

Pfeffer, K. H., ed. Tropical - Subtropical Geomorphology: Research Studies from Coastal Areas to High Mountains. (Zeitschrift fuer Geomorphologie - Annals of Geomorphology Ser.: Supplementband 103). (Illus.). vi, 403p. 1996. pap. 111.00 (3-443-21103-8, Pub. by Gebruder Borntraeger) Balogh.

— Weathering - Erosion - Sedimentation: New Studies in Morphodynamics & Processes. (Zeitschrift fuer Geomorphologie - Annals of Geomorphology Ser.: Supplementband 106). (Illus.). iv, 295p. 1996. pap. 88.00 (3-443-21106-2, Pub. by Gebruder Borntraeger) Balogh.

Pfeffer, K. H., jt. ed. see Fairbridge, R. W.

Pfeffer, L. Religious Freedom. Haiman, Franklyn S., ed. (To Protect These Rights Ser.). 192p. 1991. pap. 12.95 (0-8442-6001-0, Natl Textbk Co) NTC Contemp Pub Co.

P

Pfeffer, Lawrence M., ed. Mechanisims of Interferon Actions, 2 vols., Set. 224p. 1987. 269.90 (*0-8493-6145-1*, QR187) CRC Pr.
— Mechanisims of Interferon Actions, 2 vols., Vol. II: Cellular Effects of Interferons. 224p. 1987. write for info. (*0-318-62189-4*) CRC Pr.
Pfeffer, Leo. The Films of Harrison Ford. rev. ed. (Illus.). 256p. 1999. pap. text 19.95 (*0-8065-1998-3*, Citadel Pr) Carol Pub Group.
— Religion, State & the Burger Court. LC 84-43056. 324p. 1984. 34.95 (*0-87975-275-0*) Prometheus Bks.
Pfeffer, M. Kleines Woerterbuch zur Arbeits und Sozialpolitik. (GER.). 396p. 1972. pap. 14.95 (*0-8288-6403-9*, M-7516) Fr & Eur.
Pfeffer, Naomi. The Stork & the Syringe: A Political History of Reproductive Medicine. LC 93-32897. (Feminist Perspectives Ser.). 244p. 1993. pap. 26.95 (*0-7456-1187-7*) Blackwell Pubs.
Pfeffer, Pamela. The Essential Home Record Book: Ready-to-Use Forms for All Your Personal, Medical, Household & Financial Information. LC 97-158278. 1997. pap. 13.95 (*0-452-27612-8*, Plume) Dutton Plume.
Pfeffer, Paula F. A. Philip Randolph, Pioneer of the Civil Rights Movement. LC 89-38650. (Illus.). 352p. (C). 1996. pap. 15.95 (*0-8071-2075-8*) La State U Pr.
Pfeffer, Philip E. & Gerasimowicz, Walter V., eds. Nuclear Magnetic Resonance in Agriculture. 400p. 1989. lib. bdg. 259.00 (*0-8493-6864-2*, S540) CRC Pr.
Pfeffer, Pierre. Bears, Big & Little. Bogard, Vicki, tr. from FRE. LC 89-8883. (Young Discovery Library). (Illus.). 38p. (J). (gr. k-5). 1989. 5.95 (*0-944589-23-5*, 023) Young Discovery Lib.
— Elephants: Big, Strong & Wise. Matthews, Sarah, tr. from FRE. LC 87-33995. Vol. 4. (Illus.). 38p. (J). (ps-3). 1988. 5.95 (*0-944589-04-9*, 049) Young Discovery Lib.
Pfeffer, Pierre, ed. Predators & Predation: The Struggle for Life in the Animal World. LC 88-3880. (Illus.). 429p. reprint ed. pap. 133.00 (*0-7837-5349-7*, 204509200005) Bks Demand.
Pfeffer, R., jt. ed. see Moser, W. R.
Pfeffer, Rachel. Surviving the Streets: Girls Living on Their Own. rev. ed. LC 96-46547. (Children of Poverty Ser.). (Illus.). 174p. 1997. text 41.00 (*0-8153-2617-3*) Garland.
Pfeffer, Richard M. Understanding Business Contracts in China, Nineteen Forty-Nine to Nineteen Sixty-Three. (East Asia Monographs: Vol. No. 53). 147p. 1973. 20.00 (*0-674-92095-3*) HUP.
Pfeffer, Susan Beth. Beth Makes a Friend. LC 97-27847. (Portraits of Little Women Ser.). (Illus.). 112p. (J). 1998. 9.95 (*0-385-32583-5*) Delacorte.
— Birthday Wishes. 192p. 1999. 9.95 (*0-385-32709-9*) Bantam.
— Devil's Den. LC 97-31172. 115p. (J). (gr. 4-6). 1998. 15.95 (*0-8027-8650-2*) Walker & Co.
***Pfeffer, Susan Beth.** Ghostly Tales: Portraits of Little Women. (Illus.). 2000. 9.95 (*0-385-32741-2*) Delacorte.
Pfeffer, Susan Beth. A Gift for Amy. (Portraits of Little Women Ser.: No. 13). 112p. 1999. 9.95 (*0-385-32671-8*) BDD Bks Young Read.
— A Gift for Jo. LC 98-46261. (Portraits of Little Women Ser.: No. 10). 112p. (J). (gr. 3-7). 1999. 9.95 (*0-385-32668-8*) BDD Bks Young Read.
— A Gift For Meg. 112p. (J). 1999. 9.95 (*0-385-32670-X*) BDD Bks Young Read.
***Pfeffer, Susan Beth.** Justice for Emily. 1998. 9.09 (*0-606-13549-9*, Pub. by Turtleback) Demco.
Pfeffer, Susan Beth. Justice for Emily. 144p. (J). (gr. 3-7). 1998. reprint ed. pap. 3.99 (*0-440-41249-8*, YB BDD) BDD Bks Young Read.
— Kid Power. 128p. (J). (gr. 4-6). 1988. pap. 2.99 (*0-590-42607-9*) Scholastic Inc.
— Kid Power. (J). 1988. 8.09 (*0-606-12143-9*, Pub. by Turtleback) Demco.
— Make Believe. 144p. (J). (gr. 4-7). 1995. 14.95 (*0-8050-1754-2*, Bks Young Read) H Holt & Co.
— Nobody's Daughter. 160p. (J). (gr. 3-7). 1996. pap. 3.99 (*0-440-41160-2*) Dell.
— Nobody's Daughter. LC 94-19681. (J). 1996. 9.09 (*0-606-09698-1*, Pub. by Turtleback) Demco.
***Pfeffer, Susan Beth.** Nobody's Daughter. 154p. (J). (gr. 5-7). 1999. reprint ed. text 15.00 (*0-7881-6627-1*) DIANE Pub.
Pfeffer, Susan Beth. The Pizza Puzzle. 128p. (J). (gr. 3-7). 1997. pap. 3.99 (*0-440-41391-5*) Dell.
— The Pizza Puzzle. 1996. 21.95 (*0-385-31730-1*) Doubleday.
— The Pizza Puzzle. 1997. 9.09 (*0-606-11753-9*, Pub. by Turtleback) Demco.
***Pfeffer, Susan Beth.** The Pizza Puzzle. 119p. (YA). (gr. 7-9). 1999. reprint ed. text 16.00 (*0-7881-6640-9*) DIANE Pub.
— Revenge of the Aztecs: A Story of 1920s Hollywood. (Jamestown's American Portraits Ser.). (Illus.). 144p. (J). 2000. pap. 5.95 (*0-8092-0627-7*, 06277E, Jamestwn Pub) NTC Contemp Pub Co.
Pfeffer, Susan Beth. The Riddle Streak. (Illus.). 64p. (J). (gr. 2-4). 1995. 14.95 (*0-8050-2147-7*, Bks Young Read) H Holt & Co.
— The Riddle Streak. (Illus.). 64p. (J). (gr. k-3). 1995. pap. 4.95 (*0-8050-4260-1*, Redfeather BYR) H Holt & Co.
— Riddle Streak. 1995. 10.15 (*0-606-09790-2*, Pub. by Turtleback) Demco.
— The Ring of Truth. 1994. mass mkt. 4.99 (*0-440-90100-6*) Dell.
— Sara Kate, Super Kid. (J). 1995. 14.95 (*0-8050-3147-2*) H Holt & Co.
— The Trouble with Wishes. LC 95-38200. (Illus.). 64p. (J). (gr. 2-4). 1995. 15.95 (*0-8050-3826-4*, Redfeather BYR) H Holt & Co.
— Twice Taken. (J). 1996. mass mkt. 4.99 (*0-440-91129-X*) BDD Bks Young Read.
— Twice Taken. 208p. (YA). (gr. 7 up). 1996. mass mkt. 4.50 (*0-440-22004-1*, LLL BDD) BDD Bks Young Read.
Pfeffer, Susan Beth. Twice Taken. 1996. 9.09 (*0-606-10001-6*, Pub. by Turtleback) Demco.
— Twice Taken. 199p. (YA). (gr. 6-8). 1999. reprint ed. text 15.00 (*0-7881-6675-1*) DIANE Pub.
Pfeffer, Susan Beth. Twin Surprises. (Redfeather Fiction Ser.). (Illus.). 64p. (J). (gr. 2-4). 1995. 13.95 (*0-8050-1850-6*, Redfeather BYR); pap. 4.95 (*0-8050-2626-6*, Redfeather BYR) H Holt & Co.
— Twin Troubles. (J). 1995. pap. 4.95 (*0-8050-3272-X*) H Holt & Co.
— Twin Troubles. LC 92-5773. (Illus.). (J). 1995. 14.95 (*0-8050-2146-9*, Redfeather BYR) H Holt & Co.
***Pfeffer, Susan Beth.** Who Were They Really? The True Stories Behind Famous Characters. LC 98-47826. 72p. (J). (gr. 4-8). 1999. lib. bdg. 22.40 (*0-7613-0405-3*) Millbrook Pr.
Pfeffer, Susan Beth. The Year without Michael. 176p. (YA). (gr. 7-12). 1988. mass mkt. 4.50 (*0-553-27373-6*, Starfire BDD) BDD Bks Young Read.
Pfeffer, Susan Beth. Year Without Michael. (Bantam Starfire Bks.). (J). 1988. 9.60 (*0-606-03959-7*, Pub. by Turtleback) Demco.
Pfeffer, Susan Beth & Alcott, Louisa May. Beth's Story. LC 97-6146. (Portraits of Little Women Ser.). 112p. (J). (gr. 3-7). 1997. 9.95 (*0-385-32526-6*) Delacorte.
— Christmas Dreams: Portraits of Little Women. LC 98-19845. 192p. (J). (gr. 3-7). 1998. 9.95 (*0-385-32623-8*) Delacorte.
— A Gift for Beth. LC 98-45691. (Portraits of Little Women Ser.: No. 11). 112p. (J). (gr. 3-7). 1999. 9.95 (*0-385-32667-X*) BDD Bks Young Read.
— Jo Makes a Friend. LC 97-49509. (Portraits of Little Women Ser.). (Illus.). 112p. (J). (gr. 3-7). 1998. 9.95 (*0-385-32581-9*, Delacorte Pr Bks) BDD Bks Young Read.
— Portraits of Little Women: Amy's Story. LC 97-6137. 112p. (J). (gr. 3-7). 1997. 9.95 (*0-385-32529-0*) Delacorte.
— Portraits of Little Women: Jo's Story. LC 97-6142. (Portraits of Little Women Ser.). 112p. (J). (gr. 3-5). 1997. 9.95 (*0-385-32523-1*, Delacorte Pr Bks) BDD Bks Young Read.
— Portraits of Little Women: Meg Makes a Friend. LC 97-27855. (Portraits of Little Women Ser.). (Illus.). 112p. (J). 1998. 9.95 (*0-385-32580-0*) Delacorte.
— Portraits of Little Women: Meg's Story. LC 97-6141. 112p. (J). (gr. 3-7). 1997. 9.95 (*0-385-32520-7*) Delacorte.
Pfeffer, Susanna. Quilt Masterpieces, 1. 1998. 14.99 (*1-57866-034-3*) Galahad Bks.
Pfeffer, Washek F. The Riemann Approach to Integration. LC 93-18565. (Cambridge Tracts in Mathematics Ser.: No. 109). 320p. (C). 1994. text 54.95 (*0-521-44035-1*) Cambridge U Pr.
Pfeffer, Washek F., ed. Integrals & Measures. (Pure & Applied Mathematics Ser.: Vol. 42). (Illus.). 280p. 1977. text 135.00 (*0-8247-6530-3*) Dekker.
Pfeffer, Wendy. All about Me: Developing Self Image & Self-Esteem with Hands-On Learning Activities. Minucci, Mary B. & Johansen, Mary L., eds. (Creative Concept Ser.). (Illus.). 48p. 1990. pap. 6.95 (*1-878727-01-X*) First Teacher.
— Arctic Wolves. LC 96-17833. (Creatures in White Ser.). (YA). 1997. 18.95 (*0-382-39486-0*); pap. write for info. (*0-382-39487-9*) Silver.
— Arctic Wolves. LC 96-17834. (Creatures in White Ser.). (Illus.). 32p. (J). (gr. 1-2). 1997. pap. 5.95 (*0-382-39319-8*, Silver Pr NJ); lib. bdg. 15.95 (*0-382-39320-1*, Silver Pr NJ) Silver Burdett Pr.
Pfeffer, Wendy. Dolphin Talk. (J). Date not set. pap. write for info. (*0-06-445210-7*, HarpTrophy) HarpC Child Bks.
— Dolphin Talk. (Illus.). 40p. (J). (gr. k-4). Date not set. 15.95 (*0-06-028801-9*); lib. bdg. 15.89 (*0-06-028802-7*) HarpC Child Bks.
— From Seed to Pumpkin. 40p. (J). (ps-1). 2001. 15.95 (*0-06-028038-7*); pap. 4.95 (*0-06-445190-9*); lib. bdg. 15.89 (*0-06-028039-5*) HarpC Child Bks.
Pfeffer, Wendy. From Tadpole to Frog. LC 93-3135. (Let's-Read-&-Find-Out Science Bks.). (Illus.). 32p. (J). (ps-1). 1994. pap. 4.95 (*0-06-445123-2*, HarpTrophy) HarpC Child Bks.
— From Tadpole to Frog. LC 93-3135. (Let's-Read-&-Find-Out Science Bks.: Stage 1). (Illus.). 32p. (J). (ps-1). 1994. 15.95 (*0-06-023044-4*) HarpC Child Bks.
— From Tadpole to Frog. LC 93-3135. (Let's Read-&-Find-Out Science Ser.). 1994. 10.15 (*0-606-06399-4*, Pub. by Turtleback) Demco.
Pfeffer, Wendy. From Tadpole to Frog Book & Tape. (Let's Read & Find-Out Science Bk.). (Illus.). 32p. (J). (ps-1). 1996. pap. 7.95 incl. audio (*0-694-70046-0*) HarpC.
— Light So Bright. (J). Date not set. pap. write for info. (*0-06-440924-4*, HarpTrophy) HarpC Child Bks.
— Light So Bright. 40p. (J). (ps-1). Date not set. 15.95 (*0-06-029121-4*); lib. bdg. 15.89 (*0-06-029122-2*) HarpC Child Bks.
Pfeffer, Wendy. A Log's Life. LC 95-30020. (Illus.). 32p. (J). (ps-3). 1997. per. 16.00 (*0-689-80636-1*) S&S Childrens.
— Marta's Magnets. LC 94-37223. (Illus.). 32p. (J). (gr. k-2). 1995. pap. 5.95 (*0-382-24932-1*); lib. bdg. 15.95 (*0-382-24930-5*) Silver Burdett Pr.
— Marta's Magnets. LC 94-37223. (Illus.). (J). (gr. 1 up). 1995. 13.95 (*0-382-24931-3*) Silver Burdett Pr.
— Mute Swans. LC 95-52709. (Creatures in White Ser.). (Illus.). 32p. (J). 1996. pap. 5.95 (*0-382-39324-4*, Silver Pr NJ); lib. bdg. 18.95 (*0-382-39325-2*) Silver Burdett Pr.
— Polar Bears. LC 95-25790. (Creatures in White Ser.). (Illus.). 32p. (J). 1996. pap. 5.95 (*0-382-39326-0*); lib. bdg. 14.95 (*0-382-39327-9*) Silver Burdett Pr.
— Popcorn Park Zoo. LC 91-3273. (Illus.). 64p. (J). (gr. 2-5). 1992. 14.95 (*0-671-74587-5*, Julian Messner); pap. 16.95 (*0-671-74589-1*, Julian Messner) Silver Burdett Pr.
— Proverbs in Medieval Occitan Literature. LC 96-15389. 200p. 1997. 49.95 (*0-8130-1480-8*) U Press Fla.
— Snowy Owls. LC 96-16961. (Creatures in White Ser.). (J). 1996. pap. 5.95 (*0-382-39322-8*, Silver Pr NJ); lib. bdg. 15.95 (*0-382-39323-6*, Silver Pr NJ) Silver Burdett Pr.
— Sounds All Around. LC 97-17993. (Let's-Read-&-Find-Out Science Bks.). (Illus.). 32p. (J). (ps-3). 1999. lib. bdg. 15.89 (*0-06-027712-2*) HarpC Child Bks.
— Sounds All Around: Stage 1. LC 97-17993. (Let's-Read-&-Find-Out Science Bks.). (Illus.). 32p. (J). (ps-1). 1999. 15.95 (*0-06-027711-4*) HarpC Child Bks.
— Sounds All Around: Stage 1. LC 97-17993. (Let's-Read-&-Find-Out Science Bks.). (Illus.). 32p. (J). (ps-3). 1999. pap. 4.95 (*0-06-445177-1*, HarpTrophy) HarpC Child Bks.
— What's It Like to Be a Fish? LC 94-6543. (Let's-Read-And-Find-Out Science. Stage 2 Ser.). 1996. 10.15 (*0-606-10055-5*, Pub. by Turtleback) Demco.
— What's It Like to Be a Fish. LC 94-6543. (Trophy Let's-Read-&-Find-Out Bk.). (Illus.). 32p. (J). (ps-1). 1996. pap. 4.95 (*0-06-445151-8*, HarpTrophy) HarpC Child Bks.
— What's It Like to Be a Fish. LC 94-6543. (Let's-Read-&-Find-Out Science Bks.). (Illus.). 32p. (J). (ps-3). 1996. lib. bdg. 15.89 (*0-06-024429-1*) HarpC Child Bks.
— Wiggling Worms at Work. 40p. (J). (gr. k-4). Date not set. lib. bdg. 15.89 (*0-06-028449-8*) HarpC Child Bks.
Pfeffer, Wendy. Wiggling Worms at Work. 40p. (J). (gr. k-4). Date not set. 15.95 (*0-06-028448-X*); pap. 4.95 (*0-06-445199-2*, HarpTrophy) HarpC Child Bks.
Pfeffer, Wendy. The World of Nature. Johansen, Mary L. & Kranyik, Margery A., eds. (Creative Concept Ser.). (Illus.). 48p. 1990. pap. 6.95 (*1-878727-03-6*) First Teacher.
***Pfeffer, Wendy & Lubach, Vanessa.** The Big Flood. LC 00-28381. 2001. lib. bdg. write for info. (*0-7613-1653-1*) Millbrook Pr.
Pfefferblit, Elaine, ed. see Lederer, Richard.
Pfefferblit, Elaine, ed. see Rachlin, Harvey.
Pfefferblit, Elaine, ed. see Thernstrom, Melanie.
Pfefferkorn, Eli, ed. see Nomberg-Przytyk, Sara.
Pfefferkorn, Herman W., jt. ed. see Dutro, J. Thomas, Jr.
Pfefferkorn, Ignaz. Sonora: A Description of the Province. LC 89-5245. (Southwest Center Ser.). 329p. 1990. reprint ed. pap. 15.95 (*0-8165-1144-6*) U of Ariz Pr.
Pfefferle, W. T. New Neighborhoods. (Illus.). 100p. 1998. pap. 15.00 (*1-57502-724-0*, PO2030) Morris Pubng.
— Writing That Matters: A Rhetoric for the New Classroom. LC 98-24399. 363p. 1998. pap. text 35.40 (*0-13-862020-2*) P-H.
Pfeffermann, Guy P. Private Business in Developing Countries: Improved Prospects. (IFC Discussion Paper Ser.: No. 1). 44p. 1988. pap. 22.00 (*0-8213-1130-1*, 11130) World Bank.
Pfeifer. Craniofacial Abnormalities & Clefts of the Lip, Alveolus & Palate. 299.00 (*0-86577-333-5*) Thieme Med Pubs.
— Glory Days. 1985. pap. 3.50 (*0-86683-213-0*); pap. 6.80 (*0-86683-218-1*); pap. 8.95 (*0-86683-223-8*) Harper SF.
Pfeifer. Research in Middle East Economics, Vol. 4. 73.25 (*0-7623-0591-6*) Jai Pr.
Pfeifer, Carl, jt. auth. see Manternach, Janaan.
Pfeifer, Carl J. & Manternach, Janaan. Questions Catechists Ask: And Answers That Really Work. 118p. (Orig.). 1993. pap. 6.95 (*1-55612-620-4*) Sheed & Ward WI.
Pfeifer, Carl J., jt. auth. see Manternach, Janaan.
Pfeifer, Diane. The Angel Cookbook: Heavenly Light Cuisine. Poulton, Gail, ed. LC 94-92351. (Illus.). 160p. (Orig.). 1994. pap. 9.95 (*0-9618306-6-2*) Strawberry GA.
— For Popcorn Lovers Only. Blackmun, Susie & McDonald, Marge, eds. LC 87-90472. (Illus.). 160p. (Orig.). 1987. reprint ed. pap. 9.95 (*0-9618306-0-3*) Strawberry GA.
— Gone with the Grits: Gourmet Cookbook. Poulton, Gail, ed. (Illus.). 160p. (Orig.). 1992. pap. 9.95 (*0-9618306-9-7*) Strawberry GA.
— Marriage Is a For-Better Word. (Illus.). 128p. 1995. pap. 6.95 (*1-887987-00-2*) Strawberry GA.
— Quick Bytes: Computer Lover's Cookbook. LC 93-83442. (Illus.). 160p. 1993. pap. 9.95 (*0-9618306-7-0*) Strawberry GA.
— Stand by Your Pan: Country Music Cookbook. LC 93-92847. (Illus.). 160p. 1994. pap. 9.95 (*0-9618306-3-8*) Strawberry GA.
Pfeifer, Diane, jt. auth. see Justice, Jeff.
Pfeifer, Diane, ed. see Justice, Jeff.
Pfeifer, Gerd P., ed. Technologies for Detection of DNA Damage & Mutations. LC 96-22324. (Illus.). 436p. (C). 1996. text 114.00 (*0-306-45237-5*, Kluwer Plenum) Kluwer Academic.
Pfeifer, Gerhard. Hebraische Wortkonkordanz Zum Amosbuch. (GER.). 86p. 1998. 26.95 (*3-631-31538-4*) P Lang Pubng.
— Die Theologie des Propheten Amos. (GER.). 147p. 1995. 31.95 (*3-631-48459-3*) P Lang Pubng.
***Pfeifer, Hartmut.** Angewandte Pflanzengeographie in Maghrebinischen Oasen unter Besonderer Berucksichtigung der Ackerwildunkraeuter als Agraroekologische Phytoindikatoren (The Problem of Soil Salination of Maghrebian Oases with Special Emphasis on Weed Communities as Index Plants) (Illus.). vlll, 218p. 1999. 73.00 (*3-443-64231-4*, Pub. by Gebruder Borntraeger) Balogh.
***Pfeifer, Heather L.** Race & Crime: An Annotated Bibliography, 8. LC 99-88481. (Bibliographies & Indexes in Ethnic Studies: Vol. 8). 208p. 2000. lib. bdg. write for info. (*0-313-31033-5*, Greenwood Pr) Greenwood.
Pfeifer, Jack A. West from Omaha: A Railroader's Odyssey. Pacific Fast Mail Staff, ed. 207p. 1990. 59.50 (*0-915713-20-9*) Pac Fast Mail.
Pfeifer, Jack A., et al. Journeys Through Western Rail History. LC 70-102682. (Illus.). 168p. 1997. 38.95 (*0-918654-22-X*) CO RR Mus.
Pfeifer, Jane, ed. see Hosmer, Charles B., Jr.
Pfeifer, Janet McGivney, jt. auth. see Cook, Catherine Holloran.
Pfeifer, Jeffrey E., et al, eds. The Ethics of Teaching: Practices & Concerns: A Special Issue of Ethics & Behavior. 78p. pap. 20.00 (*0-8058-9820-4*) L Erlbaum Assocs.
Pfeifer, Karl. Actions & Other Events: The Unifier-Multiplier Controversy. (American University Studies: Philosophy: Ser. V). 210p. (C). 1989. text 24.95 (*0-8204-1044-6*) P Lang Pubng.
Pfeifer, Kathryn B. Henry O. Flipper. (African-American Soldiers Ser.). (Illus.). 80p. (J). (gr. 4-7). 1995. lib. bdg. 17.90 (*0-8050-2351-8*) TFC Bks NY.
— Seven Hundred Sixty-First Tank Battalion. (African-American Soldiers Ser.). (Illus.). 80p. (J). (gr. 4-7). 1995. lib. bdg. 17.90 (*0-8050-3057-3*) TFC Bks NY.
Pfeifer, Ken. Compact Disc Packaging & Graphics: The Best Promotional & Retail Packaging for Compact Discs. (Illus.). 192p. 1992. 39.99 (*1-56496-003-X*, 30397) Rockport Pubs.
Pfeifer, Michael A., jt. auth. see Bowker, John H.
Pfeifer, Patricia. Cook's Cupboard. 276p. 1986. 5.00 (*0-9618855-0-5*) Womans Life Ins.
Pfeifer, Patrick M. Bufotenin (Dimethylserotonin - Mappine) Index of New Information & Medical Research Bible. 160p. 1994. 47.50 (*0-7883-0218-3*); pap. 44.50 (*0-7883-0219-1*) ABBE Pubs Assn.
Pfeifer, Rolf & Scheier, Christian. Understanding Intelligence. LC 98-49138. (Illus.). 700p. 1999. 55.00 (*0-262-16181-8*, Bradford Bks) MIT Pr.
Pfeifer, Rolf, jt. auth. see International Conference on Simulation of Adaptive Behavior Staff.
Pfeifer, Susan K. & Sussman, Marvin B. Families: Intergenerational & Generational Connections. (Marriage & Family Review Ser.: Vol. 16 Nos. 1-4). (Illus.). 174p. 1994. text 59.95 (*0-86656-864-6*) Haworth Pr.
Pfeifer, Walter. The Piano Hammer: A Detailed Investigation into an Important Facet of Piano Mfg. Englehardt, J., tr. from GER. (Illus.). 120p. 1978. pap. 54.95 (*0-933224-33-8*, 1131) Bold Strummer Ltd.
Pfeifer, Wolfgang. Etymologisches Woerterbuch des Deutschen, 2 vols. 2nd ed. (GER.). 1665p. 1993. 225.00 (*0-7859-8262-0*, 3050006269) Fr & Eur.
Pfeiffenberger, Jim. The Complete Guide to Kenai Fjords National Park, Alaska. (Illus.). 144p. (Orig.). 1995. pap. text 11.95 (*0-936425-26-1*) Greatland Graphics.
Pfeiffer. Descriptive Astronomy. (Adaptable Courseware-Hardside Ser.). Date not set. pap. 21.00 (*0-534-16051-4*) Wadsworth Pub.
Pfeiffer. Lost at Sea Leaders Manual. text 17.95 (*0-88390-246-X*) Jossey-Bass.
— LPI Psychometric Properties. 1992. text. write for info. (*0-88390-331-8*, Pfffr & Co) Jossey-Bass.
Pfeiffer. Proposal Writing. LC 99-33817. (Illus.). 335p. 1999. pap. text 34.80 (*0-13-658213-3*) P-H.
***Pfeiffer, ed.** Technical Writing: A Practical Approach. 4th ed. LC 99-24446. (Illus.). 652p. 1999. pap. text 62.00 (*0-13-021372-1*) P-H.
Pfeiffer & Guzzo. Exploring General Chemistry in the Laboratory. 300p. (C). 1998. spiral bd. 27.95 (*0-7872-5162-3*, 41516201) Kendall-Hunt.
Pfeiffer & Mangus. Concepts of Athletic Training. 2nd ed. (Physical Education Ser.). 95p. 1997. pap., teacher ed. 10.00 (*0-7637-0653-1*) Jones & Bartlett.
Pfeiffer & Co Staff. Addressing Sexual Harassment in the Workplace: Trainer's Package. LC 92-93295. 134p. 1992. ring bd. 99.95 (*0-88390-320-2*, Pfffr & Co) Jossey-Bass.
Pfeiffer & Company Staff. Consulting, 1997 Annual, Vol. 2. 1997. pap. text 39.95 (*0-88390-492-6*) Jossey-Bass.
— Deluxe Trainer's Package. (Enneagram Personality Portraits Ser.). 1997. 79.95 (*0-7879-0892-4*, Pfffr & Co) Jossey-Bass.
— Enhancing Professional Relationships Inventory & Profile. (Enneagram Personality Portraits Ser.). 1997. pap. 12.95 (*0-7879-0884-3*, Pfffr & Co) Jossey-Bass.
— Enhancing Team Performance: Participant Workbook. (Enneagram Personality Portraits Ser.). 1997. pap., wbk. ed. 19.95 (*0-7879-0888-6*, Pfffr & Co) Jossey-Bass.
— Enhancing Team Performance: Trainer's Guide. (Enneagram Personality Portraits Ser.). 1997. pap. 24.95 (*0-7879-0887-8*, Pfffr & Co) Jossey-Bass.
— Enneagram Starter Trainer's Package. (Enneagram Personality Portraits Ser.). 1997. 29.95 (*0-7879-0891-6*, Pfffr & Co) Jossey-Bass.
— Improving Problem-Solving Skills. LC 96-71760. (Enneagram Personality Portraits Ser.). 1997. pap. 24.95 (*0-7879-0885-1*, Pfffr & Co) Jossey-Bass.
— Improving Problem Solving Skills. (Enneagram Personality Portraits Ser.). 1997. pap. 19.95 (*0-7879-0886-X*) Jossey-Bass.
— Training, 1997 Annual, Vol. 1. 1997. pap. text 44.95 (*0-88390-491-8*) Jossey-Bass.

P

An Asterisk (*) at the beginning of an entry indicates that the title is appearing for the first time.

Pfeiffer, Baldur E. Die Adventisten Im Nahen Osten, 1878-1939. (Archiv Fur Internationale Adventgeschichte Ser.: Bd. 7). (GER.). vii, 123p. 1996. 32.95 (*3-631-49577-3*) P Lang Pubng.

Pfeiffer, Baldur E., et al, eds. Die Adventisten und Hamburg: Von der Ortsgemeinde zur Internationalen Bewegung. (Archiv Fur Internationale Adventgeschichte Ser.: Bd. 4). (GER.). VII, 161p. 1992. 22.80 (*3-631-44635-7*) P Lang Pubng.

Pfeiffer-Belli, Christian, jt. auth. see Brunner, Gisbert.

Pfeiffer-Belli, Christian, jt. auth. see Brunner, Gisbert L.

Pfeiffer, Bruce B. Frank Lloyd Wright: The Masterworks. Larkin, David, ed. LC 93-10434. (Illus.). 312p. 1993. 75.00 (*0-8478-1715-6*, Pub. by Rizzoli Intl) St Martin.

— Frank Lloyd Wright Drawings: Masterworks from the Frank Lloyd Wright Archives. LC 96-3898. (Illus.). 304p. 1996. pap. 29.98 (*0-8109-8143-2*, Pub. by Abrams) Time Warner.

— Frank Lloyd Wright Master Builder. (Illus.). 240p. 1997. pap. 25.00 (*0-7893-0098-2*, Pub. by Universe) St Martin.

— Treasures of Taliesin: Seventy-Seven Unbuilt Projects. LC 99-32664. (Illus.). 164p. 1999. 50.00 (*0-7649-1041-8*) Pomegranate Calif.

Pfeiffer, Bruce B., ed. Frank Lloyd Wright: The Crowning Decade, 1949-1959. LC 88-63339. 202p. (Orig.). 1991. 24.95 (*0-8093-1540-8*) S Ill U Pr.

Pfeiffer, Bruce B., ed. see Wright, Frank Lloyd.

Pfeiffer, C., et al, eds. Wycliffe Bible Dictionary. 1852p. 1998. 34.95 (*1-56563-362-8*) Hendrickson MA.

Pfeiffer, C. Boyd. Bug Making. (Illus.). 224p. 1995. pap. 14.95 (*1-55821-414-3*) Lyons Pr.

— The Compleat Surfcaster: An American Littoral Society Book. (Illus.). 192p. 1996. pap. 14.95 (*1-55821-052-0*) Lyons Pr.

— The Complete Book of Tackle Making. LC 99-18264. Orig. Title: Modern Tackle Craft. (Illus.). 544p. 1999. reprint ed. pap. 19.95 (*1-55821-721-5*) Lyons Pr.

***Pfeiffer, C. Boyd.** The Field & Stream Baits & Rigs Handbook. LC 98-52123. (Field & Stream Fishing & Hunting Library). (Illus.). 128p. 1999. pap. 9.95 (*1-55821-883-1*) Lyons Pr.

— The Field & Stream Tackle Care & Repair Handbook. rev. ed. LC 98-49147. (Field & Stream Fishing & Hunting Library). 128p. 1999. reprint ed. pap. 9.95 (*1-55821-898-X*) Lyons Pr.

Pfeiffer, C. Boyd. Fly Fishing Bass Basics. LC 96-27608. (Illus.). 192p. 1997. pap. 12.95 (*0-8117-2675-4*) Stackpole.

— Fly Fishing Saltwater Basics. LC 99-14048. (Illus.). 224p. 1999. pap. 12.95 (*0-8117-2763-7*) Stackpole.

— Tackle Care: The Tackle Maintenance Handbook. (Illus.). 160p. (Orig.). 1987. pap. 12.95 (*0-941130-56-8*) Lyons Pr.

Pfeiffer, C. J. Drugs & the Peptic Ulcer, Vol. 1. 224p. 1982. 127.00 (*0-8493-6211-3*, RC821, CRC Reprint) Franklin.

— Drugs & the Peptic Ulcer, Vol. 2. 280p. 1982. 156.00 (*0-8493-6212-1*, CRC Reprint) Franklin.

Pfeiffer, Carl C. Mental & Elemental Nutrients: A Physician's Guide to Nutrition & Health Care. LC 75-19543. 556p. 1976. 27.95 (*0-87983-114-6*, Keats Publng) NTC Contemp Pub Co.

— Nutrition & Mental Illness: An Orthomolecular Approach to Balancing Body Chemistry. 128p. 1988. pap. 12.95 (*0-89281-226-5*, Heal Arts VT) Inner Tradit.

Pfeiffer, Carl J. Cancer of the Esophagus, Vol. I. 176p. 1982. 100.00 (*0-8493-6213-X*, RC280, CRC Reprint) Franklin.

— Cancer of the Esophagus, Vol. II. 280p. 1982. 155.00 (*0-8493-6214-8*, RC280, CRC Reprint) Franklin.

Pfeiffer, Carl J., ed. Animal Models for Intestinal Disease. 320p. 1985. 179.00 (*0-8493-6215-6*, RC860, CRC Reprint) Franklin.

Pfeiffer, Carl J., jt. ed. see Szabo, Sandor.

Pfeiffer, Charles F. Atlas Completo de la Biblia.Tr. of Bakers Bible Atlas. (SPA.). 500p. 1995. 24.99 (*1-56063-670-X*, 498600) Editorial Unilit.

— Baker's Bible Atlas. rev. ed. LC 60-15536. (Illus.). 352p. 1962. 24.99 (*0-8010-6930-0*) Baker Bks.

— Comentario Biblico Moody: Antiguo Testamento.Tr. of Wycliffe Bible Commentary: Old Testament. (SPA.). 912p. 1993. pap. 22.99 (*0-8254-1562-4*, Edit Portavoz) Kregel.

— Comentario Biblico Moody: Antiguo Testamento.Tr. of Wycliffe Bible Commentary: Old Testament. (SPA.). 912p. 1993. 27.99 (*0-8254-1563-2*, Edit Portavoz) Kregel.

— The Epistle to the Hebrews. (Everyman's Bible Commentaries Ser.). pap. 9.99 (*0-8024-2058-3*, 494) Moody.

***Pfeiffer, Charles F.** Wycliffe Dicitonary of Biblical Archaeology. (Illus.). 726p. 2000. 29.95 (*1-56563-562-0*) Hendrickson MA.

Pfeiffer, Charles F., ed. El Comentario Biblico Moody: Antiguo Testamento. (Comentario del Nuevo Testamento Ser.).Tr. of Wycliffe Bible Commentary: Old Testament. (SPA.). 912p. 1993. 27.99 (*0-311-03069-6*) Casa Bautista.

— Diccionario Biblico Arqueologico. Gama, Roberto, tr. from ENG.Tr. of Biblical World a Dictionary of Biblical Archaeology. (SPA.). 768p. 1982. 33.50 (*0-311-03667-8*) Casa Bautista.

Pfeiffer, Charles F. & Harrison, Everett F. Wycliffe Bible Commentary. 39.99 (*0-8024-9695-4*, 331) Moody.

Pfeiffer, Charles R. Hebreos. (Comentario Biblico Portavoz Ser.). Orig. Title: Hebrews. (SPA.). 128p. 1981. pap. 6.99 (*0-8254-1564-0*, Edit Portavoz) Kregel.

Pfeiffer, Christine. Chicago. LC 88-20199. (Downtown America Ser.). (Illus.). 60p. (J). (gr. 3 up). 1988. pap. 7.95 (*0-382-24782-5*, Dillon Silver Burdett); lib. bdg. 13.95 (*0-87518-385-9*, Dillon Silver Burdett) Silver Burdett Pr.

— Germany: A Nation Reunited. 2nd ed. LC 98-5498. (Discovering Our Heritage Ser.). (J). 1998. 23.00 (*0-382-39874-2*, Dillon Silver Burdett) Silver Burdett Pr.

— Poland: Land of Freedom Fighters. LC 90-26093. (Discovering Our Heritage Ser.). (Illus.). 144p. (YA). (gr. 5 up). 1991. lib. bdg. 14.95 (*0-87518-464-2*, Dillon Silver Burdett) Silver Burdett Pr.

Pfeiffer, Chuck. Rebound with Weights. LC 83-70893. (Illus.). 136p. (Orig.). 1983. pap. 6.95 (*0-9611234-0-0*) Beaver Pubns.

Pfeiffer Company Staff. Enhancing Team Performance. 1997. pap. text 6.95 (*0-7879-0890-8*) Jossey-Bass.

— Improving Problem-Solving Skills. 1997. pap. text 6.95 (*0-7879-0889-4*) Jossey-Bass.

Pfeiffer Company Staff, ed. Great Meals of Chicago, Vol. 1. LC 98-104756. (Illus.). 68p. 1997. ring bd. 34.95 incl. cd-rom (*1-890063-01-0*) Pfeiffer St Louis.

Pfeiffer, D. R., et al, eds. Cellular Ca2 Plus Regulation. LC 88-9400. (Advances in Experimental Medicine & Biology Ser.: Vol. 232). (Illus.). 284p. 1988. 79.50 (*0-306-42904-7*, Plenum Trade) Perseus Pubng.

Pfeiffer, David, jt. ed. see Watson, Sara.

Pfeiffer-Dennis, Nancy A. Easy-to-Make Patchwork Skirts. (Illus.). 32p. (Orig.). 1980. pap. 4.50 (*0-486-23888-1*) Dover.

Pfeiffer, E. Chromatography. 1980. pap. 8.00 (*0-938250-21-3*) Bio-Dynamic Farm.

Pfeiffer, E., et al. Alzheimer's Disease: Caregiver Practices, Programs & Community-Based Strategies. LC 89-60347. 103p. 1989. pap. 15.00 (*0-9622070-0-4*) USF SGC.

Pfeiffer, E. E. Weeds & What They Tell. 96p. 1970. pap. 7.50 (*0-938250-04-3*) Bio-Dynamic Farm.

Pfeiffer, Ehrenfried. Bio-Dynamic Gardening & Farming, Vol. 1. 126p. (Orig.). 1983. pap. 10.50 (*0-936132-56-6*) Merc Pr NY.

— Bio-Dynamic Gardening & Farming, 3 vols., Vol. 2. (Illus.). 137p. (Orig.). 1983. pap. 10.50 (*0-936132-60-4*) Merc Pr NY.

— Bio-Dynamic Gardening & Farming, 3 vols., Vol. 3. (Illus.). 131p. (Orig.). 1984. pap. 10.50 (*0-936132-67-1*) Merc Pr NY.

— The Chymical Wedding of Christian Rosenkreutz: A Commentary. 63p. (Orig.). 1984. pap. 7.00 (*0-936132-16-7*) Merc Pr NY.

— Sensitive Crystallization Processes: A Demonstration of the Formative Forces in the Blood. LC 68-31125. 64p. 1975. pap. 16.00 (*0-910142-66-1*) Anthroposophic.

Pfeiffer, Ehrenfried & Riese, Erika. Grow a Garden & Be Self-Sufficient. 2nd ed. Heckel, Alice, tr. from GER. (Illus.). 128p. (Orig.). 1981. pap. 10.00 (*0-936132-37-X*) Merc Pr NY.

***Pfeiffer, Emily.** Sonnets & Songs, 1880. LC 98-28399. 1998. 50.00 (*0-8201-1514-2*) Schol Facsimiles.

***Pfeiffer, Engelbert.** The writer's place: Heimito Von Doderer & the Alsergrund District of Vienna. LC 00-38051. (Studies in Austrian Literature, Culture & Thought). 2000. write for info. (*1-57241-094-9*) Ariadne CA.

Pfeiffer, Enrenfried E., jt. auth. see Bernard, Raymond W.

Pfeiffer, Eric, jt. auth. see Busse, Ewald W.

***Pfeiffer, Erich A.** Talking to Computers. LC 99-64398. 1999. 25.00 (*0-7388-0508-4*); pap. 18.00 (*0-7388-0509-2*) Xlibris Corp.

Pfeiffer, Ernst, ed. see Freud, Sigmund & Andreas-Salome, Lou.

***Pfeiffer, Forsberg.** Ethics on the Job. 2nd ed. LC 99-11359. (Philosophy Ser.). 176p. 1999. pap. text 33.95 (*0-534-57300-2*) Brooks-Cole.

Pfeiffer, Franz. Meister Eckhart. 2 vols. 1977. lib. bdg. 400.00 (*0-8490-2222-3*) Gordon Pr.

— Works of Meister Eckhart. 730p. 1992. reprint ed. pap. 49.95 (*1-56459-274-X*) Kessinger Pub.

***Pfeiffer, Friedrich.** IUTAM Symposium on Multibody Contacts: Proceedings of the IUTAM Symposium Held in Munich, Germany, August 3-7, 1998. LC 99-49943. (Solid Mechanics & Its Applications Ser.). 1999. write for info. (*0-7923-6030-3*) Kluwer Academic.

Pfeiffer, Friedrich & Glocker, Christoph. Multibody Dynamics with Unilateral Contacts. LC 96-12451. (Wiley Series in Nonlinear Science). 336p. 1996. 89.95 (*0-471-15565-9*) Wiley.

Pfeiffer, G. & Wieland, B. Telecommunications in Germany: An Economic Perspective. (Illus.). viii, 199p. 1990. 56.00 (*0-387-52360-X*) Spr-Verlag.

***Pfeiffer, Gabriele C.** Der Mohr im Mor: Interkulturelles Theater in Theorie und Praxis Mit einem Vorwort von Ulf Birbaumer. (Europaische Hochschulschriften Theater-, Film- und Fernsehwissenschaften Ser.). 115p. 1999. 26.95 (*3-631-34368-X*) P Lang Pubng.

Pfeiffer, George & Webster, Judith. The Family Care Healthbook. (Family Care Builder Ser.). (Illus.). 346p. 1999. pap. 22.95 (*1-928679-03-X*) Family Concerns.

Pfeiffer, George J. & Webster, Judith A. WorkCare: A Resource Guide for the Working Person. Piccini, Sara, ed. (Illus.). 398p. 1992. pap. text 19.95 (*0-9634986-0-6*) WorkCare Gp.

Pfeiffer, George J. & Williams, Louise. Taking Care of Today & Tomorrow: A Resource Guide for Health, Aging & Long-Term Care. LC 87-71285. (Illus.). 288p. 1989. pap. 14.95 (*0-9616506-1-3*) Ctr Corporate Hlth.

Pfeiffer, Gladys, jt. auth. see Bendure, Zelma.

Pfeiffer, Gotz, jt. auth. see Geck, Meinolf.

Pfeiffer, Guy O. & Nikel, Casimir M. The Household Environment & Chronic Illness: Guidelines for Constructing & Maintaining a Less Polluted Residence. (Illus.). 208p. 1980. 38.95 (*0-398-03961-5*); pap. 27.95 (*0-398-06322-2*) C C Thomas.

Pfeiffer, H. K. The Diffusion of Electronic Data Interchange. (Contributions to Management Science Ser.). (Illus.). xiv, 257p. 1992. 65.95 (*0-387-91428-5*) Spr-Verlag.

Pfeiffer, Heather D., jt. ed. see Nagle, Timothy E.

Pfeiffer, Herman. For Land's Sake: The Township Plan for Forest Harmony. 200p. 1993. pap. 12.95 (*0-9636194-1-1*) Coyote Pr OR.

Pfeiffer, Hubert, et al. Microscopic Theory of Crystal Growth. (Physical Research Ser.: Vol. II). 400p. 1989. 60.00 (*3-05-500684-4*, Pub. by Akademie Verlag) Wiley.

Pfeiffer, Ida R. The Last Travels of Ida Pfeiffer: Inclusive of a Visit to Madagascar. 1977. text 18.95 (*0-8369-9251-2*, 9104) Ayer.

Pfeiffer, J. William, ed. Annual 1988: Developing Human Resources. LC 86-643030. (Human Resource Development Ser.). (Illus.). 293p. 1987. pap. 44.95 (*0-88390-018-1*, Pfffr & Co); ring bd. 94.95 (*0-88390-017-3*) Jossey-Bass.

— Annual 1987: Developing Human Resources. LC 86-643030. (Human Resource Development Ser.). (Illus.). 294p. 1986. pap. 44.95 (*0-88390-016-5*); ring bd. 94.95 (*0-88390-015-7*) Jossey-Bass.

— The Annual, 1994: Developing Human Resources. LC 86-643030. 320p. 1993. pap. text 44.95 (*0-88390-413-6*, Pfffr & Co); ring bd. 94.95 (*0-88390-412-8*, Pfffr & Co) Jossey-Bass.

— The Annual, 1989: Developing Human Resources. LC 86-643030. (Human Resource Development Ser.). (Illus.). 291p. 1988. pap. 44.95 (*0-88390-020-3*); ring bd. 94.95 (*0-88390-019-X*) Jossey-Bass.

— The Annual, 1990: Developing Human Resources. LC 86-643030. (Human Resource Development Ser.). (Illus.). 294p. 1989. pap. 44.95 (*0-88390-022-X*); ring bd. 94.95 (*0-88390-021-1*) Jossey-Bass.

— The Annual, 1991: Developing Human Resources. LC 86-643030. (Human Resource Development Ser.). (Illus.). 309p. 1991. pap. text 44.95 (*0-88390-289-3*, Pfffr & Co); ring bd. 94.95 (*0-88390-288-5*, Pfffr & Co) Jossey-Bass.

— The Annual, 1992: Developing Human Resources. LC 86-643030. (Human Resource Development Ser.). (Illus.). 294p. 1991. pap. 44.95 (*0-88390-305-9*, Pfffr & Co); ring bd. 94.95 (*0-88390-304-0*, Pfffr & Co) Jossey-Bass.

— The Annual, 1993: Developing Human Resources. LC 86-643030. (Human Resource Development Ser.). (Illus.). 294p. 1992. pap. 44.95 (*0-88390-353-9*, Pfffr & Co); ring bd. 94.95 (*0-88390-352-0*, Pfffr & Co) Jossey-Bass.

— The Encyclopedia of Group Activities: 150 Practical Designs for Successful Facilitating. LC 89-4950. 431p. 1989. ring bd. 99.95 (*0-88390-231-1*, Pfffr & Co) Jossey-Bass.

— The Encyclopedia of Team-Building Activities. LC 90-48873. (Illus.). 316p. 1990. ring bd. 129.00 (*0-88390-257-5*, Pfffr & Co) Jossey-Bass.

— Encyclopedia of Team-Development Activities. LC 90-22868. 348p. 1990. ring bd. 129.95 (*0-88390-258-3*, Pfffr & Co) Jossey-Bass.

Pfeiffer, J. William, intro. Pfeiffer & Company Library Guide - Index, Vol. 28. LC 93-86725. (Illus.). 1994. ring bd. 119.00 (*0-88390-432-2*, Pfffr & Co) Jossey-Bass.

— Pfeiffer & Company Library of Experiential Learning Activities: Communication, Vol. 4. LC 93-86698. (Illus.). 1994. ring bd. 119.00 (*0-88390-388-1*) Jossey-Bass.

— Pfeiffer & Company Library of Experiential Learning Activities: Consulting & Facilitating. LC 93-86708. (Illus.). 1994. ring bd. 119.00 (*0-88390-394-6*, Pfffr & Co) Jossey-Bass.

— Pfeiffer & Company Library of Experiential Learning Activities: Groups, Vol. 10. LC 93-86711. (Illus.). 1994. ring bd. 119.00 (*0-88390-391-1*) Jossey-Bass.

— Pfeiffer & Company Library of Experiential Learning Activities Vol. 1: Individual Development. LC 93-86699. (Illus.). 1994. ring bd. 119.00 (*0-88390-389-X*) Jossey-Bass.

— Pfeiffer & Company Library of Experiential Learning Activities Vol. 11: Teams. LC 93-86710. (Illus.). 1994. ring bd. 119.00 (*0-88390-392-X*) Jossey-Bass.

— Pfeiffer & Company Library of Experiential Learning Activities Vol. 18: Leadership. LC 93-86709. (Illus.). 1994. ring bd. 119.00 (*0-88390-393-8*) Jossey-Bass.

— Pfeiffer & Company Library of Experiential Learning Activities Vol. 21: Training Technologies. LC 93-86700. (Illus.). 1994. ring bd. 119.00 (*0-88390-425-X*, Pfffr & Co) Jossey-Bass.

— Pfeiffer & Company Library of Inventories, Questionnaires, & Surveys: Groups & Teams. LC 93-86704. (Illus.). 1994. ring bd. 119.00 (*0-88390-398-9*, Pfffr & Co) Jossey-Bass.

— Pfeiffer & Company Library of Inventories, Questionnaires, & Surveys Vol. 2: Individual Development. LC 93-86701. (Illus.). 1994. ring bd. 119.00 (*0-88390-396-2*) Jossey-Bass.

— Pfeiffer & Company Library of Inventories, Questionnaires, & Surveys Vol. 5: Communication. LC 93-86702. (Illus.). 1994. ring bd. 119.00 (*0-88390-395-4*) Jossey-Bass.

— Pfeiffer & Company Library of Inventories, Questionnaires, & Surveys Vol. 8: Problem Solving. LC 93-86703. (Illus.). 1994. ring bd. 119.00 (*0-88390-397-0*) Jossey-Bass.

— Pfeiffer & Company Library of Inventories, Questionnaires, & Surveys Vol. 15: Consulting & Facilitating. LC 93-86706. (Illus.). 1994. ring bd. 119.00 (*0-88390-400-4*) Jossey-Bass.

— Pfeiffer & Company Library of Inventories, Questionnaires, & Surveys Vol. 19: Leadership. LC 93-86705. (Illus.). 1994. ring bd. 119.00 (*0-88390-399-7*) Jossey-Bass.

— Pfeiffer & Company Library of Inventories, Questionnaires, & Surveys Vol. 22: Training Technologies. LC 93-86707. (Illus.). 1994. ring bd. 119.00 (*0-88390-426-8*, Pfffr & Co) Jossey-Bass.

— Pfeiffer & Company Library of Presentation & Discussion Resources: Consulting. LC 93-86718. (Illus.). 1994. ring bd. 119.00 (*0-88390-406-3*, Pfffr & Co) Jossey-Bass.

— Pfeiffer & Company Library of Presentation & Discussion Resources Vol. 3: Individual Development. LC 93-86713. (Illus.). 1994. ring bd. 119.00 (*0-88390-402-0*) Jossey-Bass.

— Pfeiffer & Company Library of Presentation & Discussion Resources Vol. 6: Communication. LC 93-86714. (Illus.). 1994. ring bd. 119.00 (*0-88390-401-2*) Jossey-Bass.

— Pfeiffer & Company Library of Presentation & Discussion Resources Vol. 9: Problem Solving. LC 93-86715. (Illus.). 1994. ring bd. 119.00 (*0-88390-403-9*) Jossey-Bass.

— Pfeiffer & Company Library of Presentation & Discussion Resources Vol. 13: Groups & Teams. LC 93-86716. (Illus.). 1994. ring bd. 119.00 (*0-88390-404-7*) Jossey-Bass.

— Pfeiffer & Company Library of Presentation & Discussion Resources Vol. 17: Facilitating. LC 93-86719. (Illus.). 1994. ring bd. 119.00 (*0-88390-407-1*) Jossey-Bass.

— Pfeiffer & Company Library of Presentation & Discussion Resources Vol. 20: Leadership. LC 93-86717. (Illus.). 1994. ring bd. 119.00 (*0-88390-405-5*) Jossey-Bass.

— Pfeiffer & Company Library of Presentation & Discussion Resources Vol. 23: Training Technologies. LC 93-86720. (Illus.). 1994. ring bd. 119.00 (*0-88390-427-6*, Pfffr & Co) Jossey-Bass.

— Pfeiffer & Company Library of Theories & Models Vol. 24: Individual. LC 93-86721. (Illus.). 1994. ring bd. 119.00 (*0-88390-428-4*, Pfffr & Co) Jossey-Bass.

— Pfeiffer & Company Library of Theories & Models Vol. 25: Group. LC 93-86722. (Illus.). 1994. ring bd. 119.00 (*0-88390-429-2*, Pfffr & Co) Jossey-Bass.

— Pfeiffer & Company Library of Theories & Models Vol. 26: Management. LC 93-86723. (Illus.). 1994. ring bd. 119.00 (*0-88390-430-6*, Pfffr & Co) Jossey-Bass.

— Pfeiffer & Company Library of Theories & Models Vol. 27: Organization. LC 93-86724. (Illus.). 1994. ring bd. 119.00 (*0-88390-431-4*, Pfffr & Co) Jossey-Bass.

Pfeiffer, J. William & Ballew, Arlette C. Design Skills in Human Resource Development, Set. LC 87-40536. (Training Technologies Set Ser.). 118p. (Orig.). 1988. pap. text 24.95 (*0-88390-215-X*, Pfffr & Co) Jossey-Bass.

— University Associates Training Technologies, 7 vols., Set. 1988. boxed set 139.00 (*0-88390-286-9*, Pfffr & Co) Jossey-Bass.

Pfeiffer, J. William & Goodstein, Leonard D., eds. Annual for Facilitators, Trainers, & Consultants, 1982. LC 73-92841. (Human Resource Development Ser.). (Illus.). 293p. 1982. pap. 44.95 (*0-88390-006-8*); ring bd. 94.95 (*0-88390-005-X*) Jossey-Bass.

— The Annual, 1984: Developing Human Resources. LC 73-92841. (Illus.). 292p. 1984. pap. 44.95 (*0-88390-010-6*); ring bd. 94.95 (*0-88390-009-2*) Jossey-Bass.

— The Annual, 1986: Developing Human Resources. LC 73-92841. (Human Resource Development Ser.). (Illus.). 294p. 1986. pap. text 44.95 (*0-88390-014-9*); ring bd. 94.95 (*0-88390-013-0*) Jossey-Bass.

Pfeiffer, J. William & Jones, John E., eds. Annual Handbook for Group Facilitators, 1972. LC 73-92841. (Human Resource Development Ser.). (Illus.). 271p. 1972. pap. 44.95 (*0-88390-085-8*, Pfffr & Co); ring bd. 94.95 (*0-88390-072-6*, Pfffr & Co) Jossey-Bass.

— Annual Handbook for Group Facilitators, 1974. LC 73-92841. (Human Resource Development Ser.). (Illus.). 289p. 1974. pap. 44.95 (*0-88390-082-3*, Pfffr & Co); ring bd. 94.95 (*0-88390-074-2*, Pfffr & Co) Jossey-Bass.

— Annual Handbook for Group Facilitators, 1976. LC 73-92841. (Human Resource Development Ser.). (Illus.). 292p. 1976. pap. 44.95 (*0-88390-088-2*, Pfffr & Co); ring bd. 94.95 (*0-88390-087-4*, Pfffr & Co) Jossey-Bass.

— Annual Handbook for Group Facilitators, 1978. LC 73-92841. (Human Resource Development Ser.). (Illus.). 295p. 1978. pap. 44.95 (*0-88390-099-8*, Pfffr & Co); ring bd. 94.95 (*0-88390-098-X*, Pfffr & Co) Jossey-Bass.

— Annual Handbook for Group Facilitators, 1980. LC 73-92841. (Human Resource Development Ser.). (Illus.). 296p. 1980. pap. 44.95 (*0-88390-097-1*, Pfffr & Co); ring bd. 94.95 (*0-88390-096-3*, Pfffr & Co) Jossey-Bass.

— A Handbook of Structured Experiences for Human Relations Training, Set. Incl. Vol. 1. rev. ed. LC 73-92840. 1969. pap. 19.95 (*0-88390-041-6*, Pfffr & Co); Vol. II. rev. ed. LC 73-92840. 1970. pap. 19.95 (*0-88390-042-4*, Pfffr & Co); Vol. III. rev. ed. LC 73-92840. 1971. pap. 19.95 (*0-88390-043-2*, Pfffr & Co); Vol. IV. LC 73-92840. 1973. pap. 19.95 (*0-88390-044-0*, Pfffr & Co); Vol. V. LC 73-92840. 1975. pap. 19.95 (*0-88390-045-9*, Pfffr & Co); Vol. VI. LC 73-92840. 1977. pap. 19.95 (*0-88390-046-7*, Pfffr & Co); Vol. VII. LC 73-92840. 1979. pap. 19.95 (*0-88390-047-5*, Pfffr & Co); Vol. VIII. LC 73-92840. 1981. pap. 19.95 (*0-88390-048-3*, Pfffr & Co); Vol. IX. LC 73-92840. 1983. pap. 19.95 (*0-88390-049-1*, Pfffr & Co); Vol. X. LC 73-92840. 1985. pap. 19.95 (*0-88390-184-6*, Pfffr & Co); LC 73-92840. (Human Resource Development Ser.). 1985. write for info. (*0-88390-040-8*, Pfffr & Co) Jossey-Bass.

Pfeiffer, J. William, jt. ed. see Goodstein, Leonard D.

Pfeiffer, J. William, jt. ed. see Jones, John E.

Pfeiffer, Janet. The Seedling's Journey. 1994. pap. 3.95 (*1-55673-591-X*, 7990, Fairway Pr) CSS OH.

Pfeiffer, John B., ed. Sulfur Removal & Recovery from Industrial Processes. LC 75-11557. (Advances in Chemistry Ser.: No. 139). 1975. 27.95 (*0-8412-0217-6*) Am Chemical.

— Sulfur Removal & Recovery from Industrial Processes.

An Asterisk (*) at the beginning of an entry indicates that the title is appearing for the first time.

LC 75-11557. (Advances in Chemistry Ser.: Vol. 139). 231p. 1975. reprint ed. pap. 71.70 (0-608-03904-7, 206435100008) Bks Demand.

Pfeiffer, Joseph. Give Them a Real Scare This Halloween: A Guide to Scaring Trick-or-Treaters, & Haunting Your House, Yard or Party. Metz, Randolph, ed. LC 97-92452. (Illus.). 123p. 1997. pap. 9.95 (0-9659772-0-X) Chessmore Pub.

***Pfeiffer, Joseph R.** Bereavement Handouts: Reproducible Educational Handouts for Clients. 2nd ed. Usry, J. Kent, ed. 53p. 2000. ring bd. 39.99 (0-9655865-3-7) Landscapes Pub.

Pfeiffer, Joseph R. A Different Season: A Practical Guide for Growth While Grieving a Death. LC 96-80107. (Illus.). xx, 120p. (Orig.). 1997. pap. 10.95 (0-9655865-2-9) Landscapes Pub.

— Educational Bereavement Handouts for Clients. 56p. 1997. 39.99 (0-9655865-1-0) Landscapes Pub.

— Professional Counseling Forms. 2nd rev. ed. 61p. 1996. 54.99 (0-9655865-0-2) Landscapes Pub.

Pfeiffer, Joseph R. & Pfeiffer, Robert J. Billy's Unusual Adventure. large type ed. LC 98-92993. (Illus.). 32p. (J). (gr. k-4). 1998. 11.95 (0-9659772-1-8); pap. 5.95 (0-9659772-2-6) Chessmore Pub.

***Pfeiffer, Joseph R. & Pfeiffer, Robert J.** The One-Legged, Bow-Legged Cricket: A Story in a Story. LC 99-94630. (Illus.). 32p. (J). (gr. k-4). 1999. 14.95 (0-9659772-3-4) Chessmore Pub.

Pfeiffer, Judith & Tenud, Tish. My First Prayers: Play-a-Sound Book. 12p. (J). (ps-k). 1999. 9.99 (0-7847-0890-8, 03750) Standard Pub.

Pfeiffer, Judith M., jt. auth. see Barnes, Robert C.

Pfeiffer, K. Ludwig, jt. ed. see Gumbrecht, Hans U.

Pfeiffer, K. M., jt. auth. see Heim, U.

Pfeiffer, Karl M., jt. auth. see Heim, Urs.

Pfeiffer, Laura B. Uprising of June Twentieth, 1792. LC 78-115360. reprint ed. 29.50 (0-404-05019-0) AMS Pr.

Pfeiffer, Laura S. Hidden Sources: Family History in Unlikely Places. LC 99-55060. 224p. 1998. pap. 29.95 (0-916489-86-8) Ancestry.

Pfeiffer, Lee. The Clint Eastwood Scrapbook: The Ultimate Fan's Guide. LC 97-28530. (Illus.). 240p. 1997. pap. text 19.95 (0-8065-1928-2, Citadel Pr) Carol Pub Group.

— The Incredible World of 007: An Authorized Celebration of James Bond. rev. ed. (Illus.). 240p. 1995. pap. 19.95 (0-8065-1698-4, Citadel Pr) Carol Pub Group.

— The John Wayne Scrapbook. (Citadel Film Ser.). (Illus.). 1989. pap. 18.95 (0-8065-1147-8, Citadel Pr) Carol Pub Group.

— Official Andy Griffith Show Scrapbook. (Illus.). 224p. 1993. pap. 15.95 (0-8065-1449-3, Citadel Pr) Carol Pub Group.

— Official Andy Griffith Show Scrapbook. LC 97-31820. (Illus.). 256p. 1997. pap. text 18.95 (0-8065-1934-7, Citadel Pr) Carol Pub Group.

— True Grits: Recipes Inspired by the Movies of John Wayne. LC 98-4627. (Illus.). 144p. 1998. 15.95 (1-55972-454-4, Birch Ln Pr) Carol Pub Group.

Pfeiffer, Lee & Lewis, Michael. The Films of Harrison Ford. (Illus.). 240p. 1996. pap. 18.95 (0-8065-1658-5, Citadel Pr) Carol Pub Group.

— The Films of Tom Hanks. (Illus.). 224p. 1996. pap. 18.95 (0-8065-1717-4, Citadel Pr) Carol Pub Group.

— True Grits: Recipes Inspired by John Wayne's Movies. LC 98-4627. 1998. write for info. (1-55972-944-9) Carol Pub Group.

— The Ultimate Clint Eastwood Trivia Book. (Illus.). 128p. 1996. pap. 8.95 (0-8065-1789-1, Citadel Pr) Carol Pub Group.

Pfeiffer, Lee & Lisa, Philip. The Films of Sean Connery. LC 92-37561. (Citadel Film Ser.). (Illus.). (Orig.). 1993. pap. 19.95 (0-8065-1391-8) Carol Pub Group.

— Films of Sean Connery. rev. ed. LC 96-35942. (Illus.). 288p. 1996. pap. text 19.95 (0-8065-1837-5, Citadel Pr) Carol Pub Group.

Pfeiffer, Lee, jt. auth. see Lewis, Michael.

Pfeiffer, Lee, jt. auth. see Zmijewsky, Boris.

Pfeiffer, Maureen, ed. see Clark, Madeline A. & Mazza, Virginia S.

Pfeiffer, Maureen, ed. see Drake, Ellen & Drake, Randy.

Pfeiffer, Maureen, ed. see Fordney, Marilyn T. & Diehl, Marcy O.

Pfeiffer, Maureen, ed. see Keegan, Chris & Synder, Katherine.

Pfeiffer, Maureen, ed. see Murphy, Gretchen, et al.

Pfeiffer, Maureen, ed. see Salvo, Susan G.

Pfeiffer, Maureen, ed. see Snyder, Kathy & Keegan, Chris.

Pfeiffer, Michael A. The Uncomplicated Guide to Diabetes Complications. Levin, Marvin E., ed. LC 98-7166. (Illus.). 256p. 1998. pap. 18.95 (0-945448-87-2, 00872Q, Pub. by Am Diabetes) NTC Contemp Pub Co.

Pfeiffer, Michelle. Trust Volition. 256p. (Orig.). 1996. pap. 9.95 (1-57502-333-4, PO1115) Morris Pubng.

Pfeiffer, Mil R., jt. auth. see Austin, Martha R.

Pfeiffer, Patricia. Above All Women. LC 97-60214. 400p. (Orig.). 1997. pap. 14.95 (1-57921-003-1) WinePress Pub.

Pfeiffer, Paul E. Concepts of Probability Theory. 416p. 1978. pap. text 10.95 (0-486-63677-1) Dover.

— Probability for Applications. (Texts in Statistics Ser.). (Illus.). 695p. 1989. 89.95 (0-387-97138-6) Spr-Verlag.

Pfeiffer, Peter, ed. see Lehnert, Herbert.

Pfeiffer, Peter C. & Garcia-Moreno, Laura, eds. Text & Nation: Cross-Disciplinary Essays on National & Cultural Identities. LC 96-18398. (GERM Ser.). xii, 212p. 1996. 60.00 (1-57113-105-1) Camden Hse.

Pfeiffer, Peter C., ed. see Eigler, Friederike U.

Pfeiffer, Philip A. Pensacola's Currency Issuing Banks & Their Bank Notes, 1833-1935. Romond, Marguerite P., ed. LC 75-6130. (Illus.). 1975. pap. 19.95 (0-9601038-1-3) Pfeiffer.

***Pfeiffer, Philip A.** Pensacola's Soda Water Legacy, 1837-1998. Dawkins, Mary M., ed. LC 98-92279. (Illus.). 1998. pap. 19.95 (0-9601038-3-X) Pfeiffer.

Pfeiffer, R. Scott, jt. auth. see McLaughlin, Milbrey.

Pfeiffer, Raymond S. Why Blame the Organization? A Pragmatic Analysis of Collective Moral Responsibility. 178p. (C). 1995. pap. text 22.95 (0-8226-3045-1); lib. bdg. 48.50 (0-8226-3044-3) Littlefield.

Pfeiffer, Raymond S. & Forsberg, Ralph P. Ethics on the Job: Cases & Strategies. 151p. (C). 1992. 22.25 (0-534-19386-2) Wadsworth Pub.

***Pfeiffer, Richard H. Creating Real Relationships: Overcoming the Power of Difference & Shame. 212p. 2000. 34.95 (1-893505-13-8) Growth Publ. Readers learn clearly described relationship skills, which lead to the resolution of differences in needs, thoughts & feelings. This inspiring guide is user-friendly & designed for those who are seeking more meaning & health growth in their relationship. The author explains that creating real relationships can be the most challenging & potentially rewarding of all human endeavors. The book tells how two individuals can develop a relationship that will support, encourage & nuture their real self. People who grew up emotionally healthy families have a head start in learning how to build a real relationship, but the good news according to the author is that everyone can learn these skills. Some of the key skills for building real relationships include: Overcoming the power of difference & letting go of the fantasy that your partner should change to become more like you, Overcoming your own anger & that of your partner, Overcoming the power of shame, Overcoming anxiety because of the potentially damaging effects on the relationship, Overcoming distorted beliefs (especially all or nothing thinking), Learn conflict resolution skills. Available directly from Growth Publishing, NY.**
Publisher Paid Annotation.

Pfeiffer, Richard H. The Real Solution Anger Control Workbook. 129p. 1998. pap. 54.00 (1-893505-00-6) Growth Publ.

— The Real Solution Anxiety - Panic Workbook. 138p. 1998. pap., wbk. ed. 54.00 (1-893505-02-2, 1904) Growth Publ.

— The Real Solution Assertiveness Workbook. 107p. 1998. pap. 49.00 (1-893505-01-4) Growth Publ.

— Real Solution Binge - Compulsive Eating Workbook. 116p. 1998. pap., wbk. ed. 45.00 (1-893505-03-0) Growth Publ.

— Real Solution Relationship Workbook: Skills for the New Millenium. 1999. pap. 45.00 (1-893505-08-1) Growth Publ.

Pfeiffer, Robert J., jt. auth. see Pfeiffer, Joseph R.

Pfeiffer, Ron & Mangus, Brent. Concepts of Athletic Training: Test Bank. (Physical Education Ser.). 56p. 1995. pap. 12.50 (0-86720-493-1) Jones & Bartlett.

Pfeiffer, Ronald & Mangus, Brent. Concepts of Athletic Training. 2nd ed. (Physical Education Ser.). 60p. 1997. pap. 10.00 (0-7637-0655-8) Jones & Bartlett.

Pfeiffer, Ronald P. & Mangus, Brent. Concepts in Athletic Training: Instructor's Manual. (Physical Education Ser.). 96p. 1995. pap. 10.00 (0-86720-949-6) Jones & Bartlett.

Pfeiffer, Ronald P. & Mangus, Brent C. Concepts of Athletic Training. LC 95-1456. 400p. (C). 1995. pap. 43.75 (0-86720-839-2) Jones & Bartlett.

— Concepts of Athletic Training. 2nd ed. LC 97-20506. (Physical Education Ser.). 312p. 1997. pap. 45.75 (0-7637-0235-8) Jones & Bartlett.

Pfeiffer, Rubin. Cuentitos Simpaticos. 192p. 1990. pap. 12.65 (0-8442-7048-2) NTC Contemp Pub Co.

Pfeiffer, Rudolfus, ed. see Callimachus.

Pfeiffer, Rudolph. History of Classical Scholarship: From the Beginning to the End of the Hellenistic Age. 1968. 69.00 (0-19-814342-7) OUP.

Pfeiffer, Rudolph, ed. see Callimachus.

Pfeiffer, S. E. & Barbares, E., eds. Remyelination in the Central Nervous System. (Journal: Developmental Neuroscience: Vol. 11, No. 2, 1989). (Illus.). 72p. 1989. pap. 31.50 (3-8055-5033-2) S Karger.

Pfeiffer Staff. Consulting Annual, 2. 320p. 1997. pap. 44.95 (0-7879-1106-2, Pfffr & Co) Jossey-Bass.

— Consulting Annual, 1998, 2. 320p. 1997. ring bd. 94.95 (0-7879-1105-4, Pfffr & Co) Jossey-Bass.

— 1998 Training Annual. 320p. 1997. pap. 44.95 (0-7879-1104-6, Pfffr & Co) Jossey-Bass.

— 1998 Training Annual, 1. 320p. 1997. 94.95 (0-7879-1103-8, Pfffr & Co) Jossey-Bass.

— Start Your Own Desktop Publishing Business. (Start Your Own Ser.). 240p. 1994. pap. text 12.95 (0-89384-245-1, Pfffr & Co) Jossey-Bass.

— Start Your Own Import-Export Business. (Start Your Own Ser.). 238p. 1994. pap. text 12.95 (0-89384-248-6, Pfffr & Co) Jossey-Bass.

— Start Your Own Mail Order Business. (Start Your Own Ser.). 220p. 1996. pap. text 12.95 (0-89384-243-5, Pfffr & Co) Jossey-Bass.

— Start Your Own Resume Writing Business. (Start Your Own Ser.). 228p. 1996. pap. text 12.95 (0-89384-249-4, Pfffr & Co) Jossey-Bass.

— Start Your Own Secretarial Service Business. (Start Your Own Ser.). 240p. 1996. pap. text 12.95 (0-89384-244-3, Pfffr & Co) Jossey-Bass.

Pfeiffer, Steven E. Neuroscience Approached Through Cell Culture, Vol. I. 256p. 1982. 140.00 (0-8493-6340-3, QP356, CRC Reprint) Franklin.

— Neuroscience Approached Through Cell Culture, Vol. II. 192p. 1983. 114.00 (0-8493-6341-1, QP356, CRC Reprint) Franklin.

Pfeiffer, Steven I., ed. Outcome Assessment in Residential Treatment. LC 96-20075. (Residential Treatment for Children & Youth Ser.: Vol. 13, No. 4). 99p. (C). 1996. 39.95 (1-56024-839-4) Haworth Pr.

***Pfeiffer, Steven I. & Reddy, Linda A., eds.** Inclusion Practices with Special Needs: Education, Training & Application. LC 99-58741. (Special Services in the Schools Monographs). 210p. 1999. pap. text 24.95 (0-7890-0954-4) Haworth Pr.

— Inclusion Practices with Special Needs: Education, Training & Application. LC 99-58741. (Special Services in the Schools Monographs: Vol. 15, Nos. 1-2). 210p. 2000. 39.95 (0-7890-0843-2) Haworth Pr.

Pfeiffer, U. J., jt. ed. see Lewis, F. R.

Pfeiffer, Ulrich, jt. auth. see Hall, Peter Geoffrey.

Pfeiffer, Vera. Positive Thinking: Everything You Have Always Known about Positive Thinking But Were Afraid to Put into Practice. LC 92-26000. 1993. pap. 12.95 (1-85230-079-5, Pub. by Element MA) Penguin Putnam.

Pfeiffer, Walter. Living in Ireland. (Illus.). 96p. 1997. 14.95 (2-08-013585-6, Pub. by Flammarion) Abbeville Pr.

Pfeiffer, William S. Pocket Guide to Technical Writing. LC 97-1404. 170p. 1997. pap. text 14.00 (0-13-242157-7) P-H.

***Pfeiffer, William S.** Pocket Guide to Technical Writing. 2nd ed. LC 00-27689. (Illus.). 240p. 2000. pap. 13.33 (0-13-026102-5) P-H.

***Pfeijffer, Ilja Leonard.** Three Aeginetan Odes of Pindar: A Commentary on Nemean V, Nemean III & Pythian VIII. LC 99-37195. (Mnemosyne, Bibliotheca Classica Batava Ser.). 1999. write for info. (90-04-11381-9) Brill Academic Pubs.

Pfeil. Heidelberg External Fixation. pap. 59.00 (0-86577-756-X) Thieme Med Pubs.

***Pfeil, Brigitte.** Die 'Vision des Tnugdalus' Albers von Windberg: Literatur- und Frommigkeitsgeschichte im Ausgehenden 12, Jahrhundert Mit einer Edition der Lateinischen 'Visio Tnugdali' Aus Clm 22254. (Mikrokosmos. Beitrage zur Literaturwissenschaft und Bedeutungsforschung Ser.). xiii, 376p. 1999. 52.95 (3-631-33817-1) P Lang Pubng.

Pfeil, Don, jt. auth. see Haynes, J. H.

Pfeil, Fred. Another Tale to Tell: Essays on Postmodern Culture. 288p. (C). (gr. 13). 1990. pap. 19.00 (0-86091-992-7, A4301, Pub. by Verso) Norton.

— Goodman 2020. LC 84-43153. 240p. 1986. 5.95 (0-253-32617-6) Ind U Pr.

— Shine On. 1987. pap. 8.00 (0-89924-047-X) SPD-Small Pr Dist.

— What They Tell You to Forget: A Novella & Stories. 277p. 1996. 25.00 (0-916366-49-9) Norton.

— White Guys: Studies in Postmodern Domination & Difference. 240p. 1995. pap. 20.00 (1-85984-032-9, C0538, Pub. by Verso) Norton.

— White Guys: Studies in Postmodern Domination & Difference. 240p. (C). (gr. 13). 1995. 65.00 (1-85984-937-7, C0537, Pub. by Verso) Norton.

Pfeil, W. Protein Stability & Folding: A Collection of Thermodynamic Data. LC 98-13138. (Illus.). 500p. 1998. 250.00 (3-540-63717-6) Spr-Verlag.

Pfeiler, William K. German Literature in Exile: The Concern of the Poets. LC 57-11322. (University of Nebraska Studies: No. 16). 150p. reprint ed. pap. 46.50 (0-608-30817-X, 200287600015) Bks Demand.

Pfeiler, Wolfgang. Intra-German Relations in a Period of East-West Tensions. (CISA Working Papers: No. 50). 42p. (Orig.). 1985. pap. 15.00 (0-86682-063-9) Ctr Intl Relations.

Pfeister, Joseph L. & Pacer, Leonard A. Executive Guide to Federal Income Tax Planning for Life Insurance Companies. LC 81-11413. (Illus.). 303p. 1981. 42.50 (0-942640-01-2) Touche Co.

Pfendler, Jon. Small Figments of Another Time. (Illus.). Date not set. pap. 11.57 (0-9677351-0-6, 1) Dancng Lasagn.

Pfenniger, D., ed. see Burton, W. Butler, et al.

Pfenniger, D., jt. ed. see Gurzadyan, V. G.

Pfennigstorf, Werner. German Insurance Laws: Statutes & Regulations Concerning Insurance Supervision & Insurance Contracts. LC 75-18609. xiii, 235p. 1975. 35.00 (0-910058-73-3, 304830) W S Hein.

Pfennigstorf, Werner & Gifford, Donald G. A Comparative Study of Liability Law & Compensation Schemes in Ten Countries & the United States. 207p. (C). 1991. text 45.00 (1-56594-000-8) Ins Res Coun.

Pfennigstorf, Werner, ed. see American Bar Foundation Staff.

***Pfenning, Frank.** Computation & Deduction. 350p. (C). 2000. Price not set. (0-521-77265-6) Cambridge U Pr.

Pfenning, Frank, ed. Logic Programming & Automated Reasoning: Fifth International Conference, LPAR '94, Kiev, Uraine, July 16-22, 1994. LC 94-21152. (Lecture Notes in Computer Science; Lecture Notes in Artificial Intelligence Ser.). 1994. 55.95 (0-387-58216-9) Spr-Verlag.

— Types in Logic Programming. (Logic Programming Ser.). (Illus.). 380p. 1992. 46.50 (0-262-16131-1) MIT Pr.

Pfenning, Nancy. Chances Are . . . Making Probability & Statistics Fun to Learn & Easy to Teach. 176p. 1997. pap. 24.95 (1-882664-35-3) Prufrock Pr.

Pfenninger, John L. & Fowler, Grant C. Office Procedures for Primary Care. (Illus.). 1200p. (C). (gr. 13). 1994. pap. text 71.95 (0-8016-6384-9, 06384) Mosby Inc.

Pfenninger, Karl H., jt. auth. see Widnell, Christopher C.

Pfenninger, Mary A. Gray Wolf. 209p. 1984. 8.95 (0-89697-235-6) Intl Univ Pr.

Pfenningstorf, Werner, ed. Pollution Insurance: International Survey of Coverages & Exclusions. LC 93-32141. (International Environmental Law & Policy Ser.). 272p. (C). 1993. lib. bdg. 132.50 (1-85333-941-5, Pub. by Graham & Trotman) Kluwer Academic.

Pferdehirt, Julia. Freedom Train North: Stories of the Underground Railroad in Wisconsin. (Illus.). (J). (gr. 3-8). Date not set. pap. 10.00 (0-9664925-0-1) Living History.

Pferdehirt, Julia & Schreiner, Dave. One Nation, Many Peoples: Immigration in the United States. Diprima, Liza, ed. (Illus.). 160p. 1997. teacher ed. 79.95 (1-55933-200-X, 4026GD) Know Unltd.

***Pferdehirt, Julia, et al.** Amy Carmichael: The Hidden Jewel. (Trailblazer Books Curriculum Guides). (Illus.). 24p. 2000. pap. 4.99 (0-7642-2345-3) Bethany Hse.

— David Livingstone: Escape from the Slave Traders. (Trailblazer Books Curriculum Guides). (Illus.). 24p. 2000. pap. 4.99 (0-7642-2346-1) Bethany Hse.

— Hudson Taylor: Shanghaied to China. (Trailblazer Books Curriculum Guides). (Illus.). 24p. 2000. pap. 4.99 (0-7642-2344-5) Bethany Hse.

— Martin Luther: Spy for the Night Riders. (Trailblazer Books Curriculum Guides). (Illus.). 24p. 2000. pap. 4.99 (0-7642-2347-X) Bethany Hse.

Pfetsch, Frank R. West Germany: Internal Structures & External Relations: Foreign Policy of the Federal Republic of Germany. LC 87-29129. 284p. 1988. 65.00 (0-275-92868-3, C2868, Praeger Pubs) Greenwood.

***Pfetsch, Frank R. & Rohloff, Christoph.** National & International Conflicts, 1945-1995: New Empirical & Theoretical Approaches. LC 99-40347. (Advances in International Relations & Politics Ser.). 272p. 2000. 110.00 (0-415-22344-X) Routledge.

Pfetzer, Mark. Within Reach: My Everest Story. LC 98-29215. (Illus.). 224p. (YA). (gr. 7 up). 1998. 16.95 (0-525-46089-6, Dutton Child) Peng Put Young Read.

— Within Reach: My Everest Story. (gr. 7 up). 2000. pap. 6.99 (0-14-130497-9) Viking Penguin.

Pfeuty, Pierre & Toulouse, Gerard. Introduction to the Renormalization Group & to Critical Phenomena. LC 76-26111. 202p. reprint ed. pap. 62.70 (0-608-18638-4, 202428300035) Bks Demand.

Pffeiffer, K. M., jt. auth. see Heim, U.

PFG Staff. Video Detective's Guide to the Top 100 Videos. 1996. pap. text 4.95 (0-9649334-0-3) Palmer Film Group.

Pfiefer, Janet McGinney, jt. auth. see Cook, Catherine Halloran.

Pfieffer, E. E. Using the Bio-Dynamic Compost Preparations & Sprays in Garden, Orchard & Farm. 2nd ed. 64p. (C). 1984. reprint ed. pap. 5.50 (0-938250-26-4) Bio-Dynamic Farm.

***Pfieffer, Lee.** The Essential Bond: The Authorized Guide to the World of 007. (Illus.). 208p. 1999. pap. 23.00 (0-06-107590-6) HarpC.

Pfiefle, Steve. Black Sheep of the Family. (Illus.). 225p. Date not set. per. 12.95 (0-9660809-0-4) Blck Sheep.

Pfiffne. Governance & American Politics. LC 94-75059. (C). 1994. pap. text 38.50 (0-15-501000-X, Pub. by Harcourt Coll Pubs) Harcourt.

***Pfiffner.** Modern Presidency. 3rd ed. 1999. pap. text 21.95 (0-312-20859-6) St Martin.

Pfiffner, George. Earth-Friendly Holidays: How to Make Fabulous Gifts & Decorations from Reusable Objects. LC 95-6584. (Earth-Friendly Ser.). (Illus.). 128p. (J). (gr. 3-7). 1995. pap. 12.95 (0-471-12005-7) Wiley.

— Earth-Friendly Outdoor Fun: How to Make Fabulous Games, Gardens, & Other Projects From Reusable Objects. LC 95-51773. (Illus.). 128p. (J). 1996. pap. 12.95 (0-471-14113-5) Wiley.

— Earth-Friendly Toys: How to Make Fabulous Toys & Games from Reusable Objects. (Illus.). 128p. (J). (gr. 3-7). 1994. pap. 12.95 (0-471-00822-2) Wiley.

— Earth-Friendly Wearables: How to Make Fabulous Clothes & Accessories from Reusable Objects. (Earth-Friendly Ser.). 128p. (J). 1995. pap. 12.95 (0-471-00823-0) Wiley.

Pfiffner, James P. Managerial Presidency. 384p. (C). 1991. pap. text 33.25 (0-534-13194-8) Harcourt.

— The Strategic Presidency: Hitting the Ground Running. 2nd rev. ed. (Studies in Government & Public Policy). 264p. 1996. pap. 15.95 (0-7006-0769-2) U Pr of KS.

— Understanding the Presidency. 2nd ed. LC 99-13191. 488p. (C). 1999. pap. text 47.00 (0-321-04493-2) Addson-Wesley Educ.

Pfiffner, James P., ed. Managerial Presidency. 2nd ed. LC 98-30490. (Joseph V. Hughes, Jr., & Holly O. Hughes Series in the Presidency & Leadership Studies: Vol. 4). 384p. 1999. pap. 16.95 (0-89096-860-8) Tex A&M Univ Pr.

— Managerial Presidency. 2nd rev. ed. LC 98-30490. (Joseph V. Hughes, Jr., & Holly O. Hughes Series in the Presidency & Leadership Studies: Vol. 4). 384p. 1999. 29.95 (0-89096-858-6) Tex A&M Univ Pr.

— The Presidency in Transition. 550p. (Orig.). (C). 1989. 30.00 (0-938204-00-9) Ctr Study Presidency.

***Pfiffner, James P. & Brook, Douglas Alan.** The Future of Merit: 20 Years after the Civil Service Reform Act. LC 00-9187. 2000. pap. 17.95 (0-8018-6465-8) Johns Hopkins.

Pfiffner, James P. & Davidson, Roger H., eds. Understanding Presidency. LC 96-15634. (C). 1997. pap. text 35.63 (0-673-99899-1) Addson-Wesley Educ.

Pfiffner, Linda. All about A. D. H. D. 1996. pap. 16.95 (0-590-25108-2) Scholastic Inc.

P

An Asterisk (*) at the beginning of an entry indicates that the title is appearing for the first time.

Pfiffner, O. A., et al. Deep Structure of the Swiss Alps. LC 96-51014. 460p. 1997. write for info. (3-7643-5254-X) Birkhauser.

Pfiffner, Othmar A. & NRP 20 (Switzerland) Staff. Deep Structure of the Swiss Alps: Results of NRP 20. LC 96-51014. 1996. write for info. (0-8176-5254-X) Birkhauser.

Pfiffuer. Modern Presidency. 2nd ed. LC 97-80009. 256p. 1997. pap. text 21.95 (0-312-17804-2) St Martin.

Pfingsten, Ralph & Downs, Floyd L., eds. Salamanders of Ohio. LC 85-60845. (Bulletin New Ser.: Vol. 7, No. 2). (Illus.). 300p. 1989. pap. text 30.00 (0-86727-099-3) Ohio Bio Survey.

Pfingston, Roger. The Circus of Unreasonable Acts: Poems & Photographs. (Illus.). 44p. (Orig.). 1982. pap. 20.00 (0-9608802-0-8) Years Pr.

— Hazards of Photography. (Chapbook Series I: No. 3). 32p. 1980. pap. 3.00 (1-880649-03-9) Writ Ctr Pr.

— Something Iridescent. LC 85-72587. 98p. (Orig.). 1987. pap. 7.95 (0-935306-37-4) Barnwood Pr.

Pfirrmann, O., et al. Venture Capital & New Technology Based Firms: A U. S.-German Comparison. Fraunhofer Institute for Systems & Innovation Rese, ed. (Technology, Innovation & Policy Ser.: Vol. 4). (Illus.). xii, 153p. 1997. pap. 59.00 (3-7908-0968-3) Spr-Verlag.

Pfirstinger, Rico. Huskies in Action, AKC Rank No. 18. (Illus.). 144p. 1996. 35.95 (0-7938-0056-0, TS234) TFH Pubns.

Pfister, Albrecht. Quadratic Forms with Applications to Algebraic Geometry & Topology. (London Mathematical Society Lecture Note Ser.: No. 217). 187p. (C). 1995. pap. text 39.95 (0-521-46755-1) Cambridge U Pr.

Pfister, D. H., et al. A Bibliography of Taxonomic Literature, 1753-1821. (Mycologia Memoirs Ser.: No. 17). 162p. 1991. pap. text 55.00 (3-443-76007-4, Pub. by Gebruder Borntraeger) Balogh.

Pfister, Fred & Marsh, Jennifer. The Insiders' Guide to Branson & the Ozark Mountains. 3rd rev. ed. (Insiders' Guide Travel Ser.). (Illus.). 350p. Date not set. pap. 14.95 (1-57380-085-6, The Insiders Guide) Falcon Pub Inc.

Pfister, Friedrich. Der Reliquienkult Im Altertum, 2 vols. in 1. (GER.). xii, 686p. (C). 1974. reprint ed. 189.30 (3-11-002453-5) De Gruyter.

***Pfister, Gerhard.** Handkes Mitspieler: Die literarische Kritik zu Der kurze Brief zum langen Abschied, langsame Heimkehr, Das Spiel vom Fragen, Versuch uber die Mudigkeit. 2000. 54.95 (3-906764-78-8, Pub. by P Lang) P Lang Pubng.

Pfister, Gregory F. In Search of Clusters. 2nd ed. LC 98-137730. 608p. (C). 1997. pap. text 44.95 (0-13-899709-8) P-H.

Pfister, Guenter G. Beginning German: A Way to Self-Awareness. (GER., Illus.). 383p. (C). 1989. text 28.80 (0-87563-302-1) Stipes.

Pfister, Guenter G. & Poser, Yvonne. Culture, Proficiency, & Control in Foreign Language Teaching. LC 87-10594. 174p. (Orig.). (C). 1987. pap. text 19.50 (0-8191-6446-1); lib. bdg. 43.50 (0-8191-6445-3) U Pr of Amer.

Pfister, H., jt. ed. see Barbour, J.

Pfister, Herbert, ed. Papilloma Viruses & Human Cancer. 272p. 1990. lib. bdg. 229.00 (0-8493-5860-4, RC268) CRC Pr.

Pfister, Herbert, jt. ed. see Barbour, Julian B.

Pfister, Joel. The Production of Personal Life: Class, Gender & the Psychological in Hawthorne's Fiction. LC 91-16686. 288p. 1991. pap. 15.95 (0-8047-1948-9) Stanford U Pr.

— Staging Depth: The Politics of Psychological Discourse in the Drama of O'Neill. LC 94-26336. (Cultural Studies of the United States). (Illus.). 350p. 1995. pap. text 22.50 (0-8078-4496-9); lib. bdg. 55.00 (0-8078-2186-1) U of NC Pr.

Pfister, Joel & Schnog, Nancy. Inventing the Psychological: Toward a Cultural History of Emotional Life in America. LC 96-23275. 4000p. 1997. 42.00 (0-300-06809-3); pap. 19.00 (0-300-07006-3) Yale U Pr.

Pfister, Joseph, jt. ed. see Hall, Bob.

Pfister, Judith I. & Kneedler, Julia A. A Guide to Lasers in the OR. (Illus.). 1983. write for info. (0-9613138-0-3) ED Inc.

Pfister, Judith I., et al. The Nursing Spectrum of Lasers. (Illus.). 156p. (Orig.). (C). 1988. pap. text 32.50 (0-9622255-0-9) ED Inc.

***Pfister, Marcus.** The Adventures of Rainbow Fish. deluxe ed. (Rainbow Fish Ser.). (Illus.). (J). (ps-3). 2000. boxed set 49.95 (0-7358-1355-8) North-South Bks NYC.

Pfister, Marcus. Arc-en-Ciel et le Petit Poisson Perdu. (Rainbow Fish Ser.). Orig. Title: Regenbogenfisch, Komm Wilf Mir!. (FRE., Illus.). 32p. (J). (ps-3). 1996. 18.95 (3-314-20924-X, Pub. by North-South Bks NYC) Chronicle Bks.

— Arc-en-Ciel, le Plus Beau Poisson des Oceans. (Rainbow Fish Ser.). Orig. Title: Der Regenbogenfisch. (FRE., Illus.). (J). (ps-3). 1995. 18.95 (3-314-20755-7, Pub. by North-South Bks NYC) Chronicle Bks.

— Arcobaleno il Pesciolino Piu Bello di Tutti i Mari. (Rainbow Fish Ser.). Orig. Title: Der Regenbogenfisch. (ITA., Illus.). (J). (ps-3). 1995. 18.95 (88-8203-000-8, Pub. by North-South Bks NYC) Chronicle Bks.

— Arcobaleno, Non Lasciarmi Solo! (Rainbow Fish Ser.). Orig. Title: Regenbogenfisch, Komm Hilf Mir!. (ITA.). (J). (ps-3). 1996. 18.95 (88-8203-041-5, Pub. by North-South Bks NYC) Chronicle Bks.

— The Christmas Star. (JPN., Illus.). (J). (gr. k-3). 1993. 18.95 (4-06-261952-0) North-South Bks NYC.

— The Christmas Star. James, J. Alison, tr. LC 93-15143. (Illus.). 32p. (J). (gr. k-3). 1993. 18.95 (1-55858-203-7); lib. bdg. 18.88 (1-55858-204-5, Pub. by North-South Bks NYC) Chronicle Bks.

— The Christmas Star Mini Book. (Illus.). 32p. (J). (gr. k-3). 1997. 8.95 (1-55858-822-1, Pub. by North-South Bks NYC) Chronicle Bks.

Pfister, Marcus. Cia Ciao, Pit!Tr. of Penguin Pete, Ahoy!. (ITA., Illus.). (J). (gr. k-3). pap. 15.95 (88-8203-142-X, Pub. by North-South Bks NYC) Chronicle Bks.

Pfister, Marcus. Una Cometa a Natale. Crump, Donald J., tr.Tr. of Christmas Star. (ITA.). (J). (gr. k-3). Date not set. 18.95 (88-8203-019-9, Pub. by North-South Bks NYC) Chronicle Bks.

— Dazzle the Dinosaur. James, J. Alison, tr. LC 94-34840. (Illus.). 32p. (J). (gr. k-3). 1994. 18.95 (1-55858-337-8, Pub. by North-South Bks NYC); lib. bdg. 18.88 (1-55858-338-6, Pub. by North-South Bks NYC) Chronicle Bks.

— Dazzle the Dinosaur. (JPN., Illus.). (J). (gr. k-3). 1999. 18.95 (4-06-261958-X, Pub. by North-South Bks NYC) Chronicle Bks.

***Pfister, Marcus.** Dazzle the Dinosaur. (Illus.). 32p. (gr. k-3). 2000. pap. 7.95 (0-7358-1370-1) North-South Bks NYC.

Pfister, Marcus. Destello el Dinosaurio. LC 94-42452.Tr. of Dazzle the Dinosaur. (SPA., Illus.). 32p. (J). (gr. k-3). 1995. lib. bdg. 18.88 (1-55858-388-2, Pub. by North-South Bks NYC) Chronicle Bks.

— Destello el Dinosaurio. LC 94-42452.Tr. of Dazzle the Dinosaur. (SPA., Illus.). 32p. (J). (gr. 2-3). 1995. 18.95 (1-55858-387-4, Pub. by North-South Bks NYC) Chronicle Bks.

***Pfister, Marcus.** Destello el Dinosaurio. Moreno, Jose, tr.Tr. of Dazzle the Dinosaur. (SPA., Illus.). 32p. (gr. k-3). 2000. pap. 7.95 (0-7358-1371-X) North-South Bks NYC.

Pfister, Marcus. Dinodor.Tr. of Dazzle the Dinosaur. (FRE., Illus.). 32p. (J). (gr. k-3). 1996. 18.95 (3-314-20848-0, Pub. by North-South Bks NYC) Chronicle Bks.

— Dinodoro.Tr. of Dazzle the Dinosaur. (ITA., Illus.). 32p. (J). (gr. k-1). 1996. 18.95 (88-8203-037-7, Pub. by North-South Bks NYC) Chronicle Bks.

— La Estrella de Navidad. LC 95-13133. (SPA., Illus.). 32p. (J). (gr. k-3). 1995. 18.95 (1-55858-492-7, Pub. by North-South Bks NYC); lib. bdg. 18.88 (1-55858-493-5, Pub. by North-South Bks NYC) Chronicle Bks.

— Une Etoile, Cette Nuit-La. (FRE., Illus.). (J). (gr. k-3). 1996. 18.95 (3-314-20776-X, Pub. by North-South Bks NYC) Chronicle Bks.

Pfister, Marcus. Fiocco E la Uova Di Pasque.Tr. of Hopper's Easter Surprise. (ITA., Illus.). 32p. (J). (gr. k-3). 15.95 (88-8203-044-X, Pub. by North-South Bks NYC) Chronicle Bks.

Pfister, Marcus. Fiocco, il Coniglietto Delle Nevi. Crump, Donald J., tr.Tr. of Hopper. (ITA., Illus.). 32p. (J). (gr. k-3). 1997. 15.95 (88-8203-021-0, Pub. by North-South Bks NYC) Chronicle Bks.

Pfister, Marcus. Fiocco Trova un Amico.Tr. of Hopper Hunts for Spring. (ITA., Illus.). 32p. (J). (gr. k-3). 15.95 (88-8203-040-7, Pub. by North-South Bks NYC) Chronicle Bks.

— Flocon et Cache-Noisette.Tr. of Hopper's Treetop Adventure. (FRE., Illus.). 15.95 (3-314-21021-3, Pub. by North-South Bks NYC) Chronicle Bks.

Pfister, Marcus. Flocon, le Petit Lapin des Neiges.Tr. of Hopper. (FRE., Illus.). 32p. (J). (gr. k-3). 1996. 15.95 (3-314-20721-2, Pub. by North-South Bks NYC) Chronicle Bks.

— Flocon Trouve un Ami.Tr. of Hopper Hunts for Spring. (FRE., Illus.). 32p. (J). (gr. k-3). 1996. 15.95 (3-314-20754-9, Pub. by North-South Bks NYC) Chronicle Bks.

Pfister, Marcus. Gaia e la Pietra di Fuoco.Tr. of Milo & the Magical Stones. (ITA., Illus.). (J). (gr. k-3). pap. 18.95 (88-8203-046-6, Pub. by North-South Bks NYC) Chronicle Bks.

Pfister, Marcus. Hang on, Hopper! Lanning, Rosemary, tr. LC 94-43635. (Illus.). 32p. (J). (gr. k-3). 1995. 15.95 (1-55858-403-X, Pub. by North-South Bks NYC); lib. bdg. 15.88 (1-55858-404-8, Pub. by North-South Bks NYC) Chronicle Bks.

— Hang on, Hopper! LC 94-43635. (Illus.). 32p. (J). (gr. k-3). 1997. pap. 6.95 (1-55858-771-3, Pub. by North-South Bks NYC) Chronicle Bks.

***Pfister, Marcus.** The Happy Hedgehog. (Illus.). 32p. (J). (gr. k-3). 2000. 15.95 (0-7358-1164-4, Pub. by North-South Bks NYC) Chronicle Bks.

Pfister, Marcus. Hopper. LC 90-47065. (Illus.). 32p. (J). (gr. k-3). 1991. 15.95 (1-55858-106-5, Pub. by North-South Bks NYC) Chronicle Bks.

— Hopper. LC 90-47065. (Illus.). 32p. (J). (gr. k-3). 1994. pap. 6.95 (1-55858-352-1, Pub. by North-South Bks NYC) Chronicle Bks.

***Pfister, Marcus.** Hopper. (Illus.). (J). 2000. 12.95 (0-7358-1348-5) North-South Bks NYC.

Pfister, Marcus. Hopper Board Book. LC 97-42213. 12p. (J). (ps). 1998. bds. 6.95 (1-55858-888-4, Pub. by North-South Bks NYC) Chronicle Bks.

***Pfister, Marcus.** Hopper Board Book Favorites: Hopper, Hopper Hunts for Spring, & Hopper's Easter Surprise, 3 vols. (Illus.). (J). (ps). 2000. 12.95 (0-7358-1347-7, Pub. by North-South Bks NYC) Chronicle Bks.

Pfister, Marcus. Hopper Hunts for Spring. Lanning, Rosemary, tr. LC 91-29671. (Illus.). 32p. (J). (gr. k-3). 1992. 15.95 (1-55858-139-1, Pub. by North-South Bks NYC); lib. bdg. 15.88 (1-55858-147-2, Pub. by North-South Bks NYC) Chronicle Bks.

— Hopper Hunts for Spring. LC 90-47065. (Illus.). 32p. (J). (gr. k-3). 1995. pap. 6.95 (1-55858-416-1, Pub. by North-South Bks NYC) Chronicle Bks.

— Hopper Hunts for Spring. LC 97-42212. (J). (ps). 1998. bds. 6.95 (1-55858-887-6, Pub. by North-South Bks NYC) Chronicle Bks.

— Hopper Hunts for Spring. (J). 1995. 12.15 (0-606-08773-7, Pub. by Turtleback) Demco.

— Hopper's Treetop Adventure. Lanning, Rosemary, tr. LC 96-44946. (Illus.). 32p. (J). (gr. k-3). 1997. 15.95 (1-55858-680-6, Pub. by North-South Bks NYC); lib. bdg. 15.88 (1-55858-681-4, Pub. by North-South Bks NYC) Chronicle Bks.

— How Leo Learned to Be King. LC 97-41779. (Illus.). 32p. (J). (gr. k-3). 1998. 15.95 (1-55858-913-9, Pub. by North-South Bks NYC); lib. bdg. 15.88 (1-55858-914-7, Pub. by North-South Bks NYC) Chronicle Bks.

— Der Kleine Dino.Tr. of Dazzle the Dinosaur. (GER., Illus.). 32p. (J). (gr. k-3). 1996. 18.95 (3-314-00661-6, Pub. by North-South Bks NYC) Chronicle Bks.

***Pfister, Marcus.** Make a Wish, Honey Bear! (Illus.). 32p. (J). (gr. k-3). 1999. lib. bdg. 15.88 (0-7358-1244-6, Pub. by North-South Bks NYC) Chronicle Bks.

— Make a Wish, Honey Bear! Kazeroid, Sibylle, tr. (Illus.). 32p. (J). (ps-k). 1999. 15.95 (0-7358-1243-8, Pub. by North-South Bks NYC) Chronicle Bks.

— Marcus Pfister Favorites Board Book Package: The Rainbow Fish/hopper/penguin Pete. 1999. 14.95 (0-7358-1228-4) North-South Bks NYC.

— Mats und die Wundersteine.Tr. of Milo & the Magical Stones. (GER., Illus.). (J). 1998. 18.95 (3-314-00780-9, Pub. by North-South Bks NYC) Chronicle Bks.

— Milo & the Magical Stones. (Illus.). (J). 1997. 189.50 (1-55858-792-6) North-South Bks NYC.

— Milo & the Magical Stones. (JPN., Illus.). (J). 1998. 18.95 (4-06-261981-4, Pub. by North-South Bks NYC) Chronicle Bks.

Pfister, Marcus. Milo & the Magical Stones: A Book with 2 Endings. Martens, Marianne, tr. LC 97-7543. (Illus.). 32p. (J). (gr. k-3). 1997. 18.95 (1-55858-682-2, Pub. by North-South Bks NYC) Chronicle Bks.

***Pfister, Marcus.** Milo & the Mysterious Island. (Illus.). 32p. (gr. k-3). 2000. 18.95 (0-7358-1352-3) North-South Bks NYC.

Pfister, Marcus. Milo y las Piedras Magicas: Un Libro Con Dos Finales.Tr. of Milo & the Magical Stones: A Book with 2 Endings. (SPA., Illus.). 32p. (J). (gr. k-3). 1997. 18.95 (1-55858-721-7, Pub. by North-South Bks NYC) Chronicle Bks.

Pfister, Marcus. Les Nouveaux Amis de Pit.Tr. of Penguin Pete's New Friends. (FRE., Illus.). 32p. (J). (gr. k-3). 1992. 15.95 (3-314-20632-1, Pub. by North-South Bks NYC) Chronicle Bks.

— Nuovi Amici Per Pit.Tr. of Penguin Pete's New Friends. (ITA., Illus.). (J). (gr. k-3). 1992. 15.95 (88-8203-131-4, Pub. by North-South Bks NYC) Chronicle Bks.

Pfister, Marcus. Ohe Pit! Ohe! (FRE., Illus.). 32p. (J). (gr. k-3). 1996. 15.95 (3-314-20784-0, Pub. by North-South Bks NYC) Chronicle Bks.

— Papa Pit et Tim.Tr. of Penguin Pete & Little Tim. (FRE., Illus.). 32p. (J). (gr. k-3). 1996. 15.95 (3-314-20830-8, Pub. by North-South Bks NYC) Chronicle Bks.

— Papa Pit und Tim.Tr. of Penguin Pete & Little Tim. (GER., Illus.). 32p. (J). (gr. k-3). 1996. 15.95 (3-314-00650-0, Pub. by North-South Bks NYC) Chronicle Bks.

— Penguin Pete. LC 87-1627. (Illus.). 32p. (J). (gr. k-3). 1987. 15.95 (1-55858-018-2, Pub. by North-South Bks NYC); lib. bdg. 15.88 (1-55858-242-8, Pub. by North-South Bks NYC) Chronicle Bks.

— Penguin Pete. LC 87-1627. (Illus.). 32p. (J). (gr. k-3). 1994. pap. 6.95 (1-55858-356-4, Pub. by North-South Bks NYC) Chronicle Bks.

— Penguin Pete. LC 96-44517. (Illus.). 12p. (J). (ps). 1997. bds. 6.95 (1-55858-690-3, Pub. by North-South Bks NYC) Chronicle Bks.

— Penguin Pete, Ahoy! Lanning, Rosemary, tr. LC 93-19921. (Illus.). 32p. (J). (gr. k-3). 1993. 15.95 (1-55858-220-7, Pub. by North-South Bks NYC); lib. bdg. 15.88 (1-55858-221-5, Pub. by North-South Bks NYC) Chronicle Bks.

— Penguin Pete, Ahoy! LC 93-19921. (Illus.). 32p. (J). (gr. k-3). 1998. pap. 6.95 (1-55858-907-4, Pub. by North-South Bks NYC) Chronicle Bks.

— Penguin Pete & Little Tim. Lanning, Rosemary, tr. LC 94-5093. (Illus.). 32p. (J). (gr. k-3). 1994. 15.95 (1-55858-301-7, Pub. by North-South Bks NYC) Chronicle Bks.

— Penguin Pete & Little Tim. LC 94-5093. (Illus.). 32p. (J). (gr. k-3). 1997. pap. 6.95 (1-55858-773-X, Pub. by North-South Bks NYC) Chronicle Bks.

— Penguin Pete & Pat. LC 88-25296. (Illus.). 32p. (J). (gr. k-3). 1989. lib. bdg. 15.88 (1-55858-243-6, Pub. by North-South Bks NYC) Chronicle Bks.

— Penguin Pete & Pat. Bell, Anthea, tr. LC 88-25296. (Illus.). 32p. (J). (gr. k-3). 1989. 15.95 (1-55858-003-4, Pub. by North-South Bks NYC) Chronicle Bks.

— Penguin Pete & Pat. LC 88-25296. (Illus.). 32p. (J). (gr. k-3). 1996. pap. 6.95 (1-55858-618-0, Pub. by North-South Bks NYC) Chronicle Bks.

— Penguin Pete's New Friends. LC 87-72037. (Illus.). 32p. (J). (gr. k-3). 1988. 15.95 (1-55858-025-5, Pub. by North-South Bks NYC); lib. bdg. 15.88 (1-55858-244-4, Pub. by North-South Bks NYC) Chronicle Bks.

— Penguin Pete's New Friends. LC 87-72037. (Illus.). 32p. (J). (gr. k-3). 1995. pap. 6.95 (1-55858-414-5, Pub. by North-South Bks NYC) Chronicle Bks.

— Penguin Pete's New Friends. LC 96-47345. (Illus.). 12p. (J). (ps). 1997. bds. 6.95 (1-55858-691-1, Pub. by North-South Bks NYC) Chronicle Bks.

Pfister, Marcus. Penguin Pete's New Friends. 1995. 11.15 (0-606-08843-1, Pub. by Turtleback) Demco.

Pfister, Marcus. El Pez Arco Iris. LC 94-30500. (Rainbow Fish Ser.). Orig. Title: Der Regenbogenfisch. (SPA., Illus.). 32p. (J). (ps-3). 1994. 18.95 (1-55858-361-0, Pub. by North-South Bks NYC); 25.00 (1-55858-440-4, Pub. by North-South Bks NYC); lib. bdg. 16.88 (1-55858-362-9, Pub. by North-South Bks NYC) Chronicle Bks.

— El Pez Arco Iris. (Rainbow Fish Ser.). Orig. Title: Der Regenbogenfisch. (SPA., Illus.). 12p. (J). (ps-3). 1996. bds. 9.95 (1-55858-559-1, Pub. by North-South Bks NYC) Chronicle Bks.

— El Pez Arco Iris Al Rescate! Gutierrez, Guillermo, tr. from GER. LC 97-42155. (Rainbow Fish Ser.). Orig. Title: Regenbogenfisch, Komm Hilf Mir!. (SPA., Illus.). 32p. (J). (ps-3). 1996. 18.95 (1-55858-558-3, Pub. by North-South Bks NYC) Chronicle Bks.

— El Pez Arco Iris Al Rescate! Gutierrez, Guillermo, tr. from GER. (Rainbow Fish Ser.). Orig. Title: Regenbogenfisch, Komm Hilf Mir!. (SPA., Illus.). 32p. (J). (ps-3). 1997. 25.00 (1-55858-815-9, Pub. by North-South Bks NYC) Chronicle Bks.

— El Pez Arco Iris Al Rescate! (Rainbow Fish Ser.). Orig. Title: Regenbogenfisch, Komm Hilf Mir!. (SPA., Illus.). 12p. (J). (ps-3). 1998. bds. 9.95 (1-55858-885-X, Pub. by North-South Bks NYC) Chronicle Bks.

— El Pez Arco Iris y la Ballena Azul. (Rainbow Fish Ser.). Orig. Title: Regenbogenfisch und Grosser Blauer Wal. (SPA., Illus.). 32p. (J). (ps-3). 1998. 18.95 (0-7358-1002-8, Pub. by North-South Bks NYC) Chronicle Bks.

***Pfister, Marcus.** El Pez Arco Iris y la Ballena Azul. (Rainbow Fish Ser.). Orig. Title: Regenbogenfisch und Grosser Blauer Wal. (SPA., Illus.). 32p. (J). (ps-3). 1999. pap. 25.00 (0-7358-1215-2, Pub. by North-South Bks NYC) Chronicle Bks.

Pfister, Marcus. El Pinguino Pedro. LC 95-36187.Tr. of Penguin Pete. (SPA., Illus.). 32p. (J). (gr. k-3). 1996. 15.95 (1-55858-564-8, Pub. by North-South Bks NYC); pap. 6.95 (1-55858-547-8, Pub. by North-South Bks NYC) Chronicle Bks.

— El Pinguino Pedro.Tr. of Penguin Pete. (SPA., Illus.). 12p. (J). (ps). 1997. bds. 6.95 (1-55858-739-X, Pub. by North-South Bks NYC) Chronicle Bks.

— El Pinguino Pedro, Aprendiz de Marinero. (SPA., Illus.). 32p. (J). (gr. k-3). 1998. 15.95 (1-55858-919-8, Pub. by North-South Bks NYC); pap. 6.95 (1-55858-920-1, Pub. by North-South Bks NYC) Chronicle Bks.

Pfister, Marcus. El Pinguino Pedro y el Pequeno Timoteo. LC 98-19644. (SPA., Illus.). 32p. (J). (gr. k-3). 1996. 15.95 (1-55858-346-7, Pub. by North-South Bks NYC) Chronicle Bks.

Pfister, Marcus. El Pinguino Pedro y el Pequeno Timoteo. (J). (gr. k-3). 1998. pap. 6.95 (1-55858-347-5, Pub. by North-South Bks NYC) Chronicle Bks.

— El Pinguino Pedro y Pat. (SPA., Illus.). 32p. (J). (gr. k-3). 1998. 15.95 (1-55858-886-8, Pub. by North-South Bks NYC); pap. 6.95 (1-55858-892-2, Pub. by North-South Bks NYC) Chronicle Bks.

— El Pinguino Pedro y Sus Nuevos Amigos. (SPA., Illus.). 32p. (J). (gr. k-3). 1996. 15.95 (1-55858-641-5, Pub. by North-South Bks NYC); pap. 6.95 (1-55858-640-7, Pub. by North-South Bks NYC) Chronicle Bks.

— El Pinguino Pedro y Sus Nuevos Amigos. (SPA., Illus.). 12p. (J). (ps). 1997. bds. 6.95 (1-55858-740-3, Pub. by North-South Bks NYC) Chronicle Bks.

— Pit Ahoi!Tr. of Penguin Pete, Ahoy!. (GER., Illus.). 32p. (J). (gr. k-3). 1996. 15.95 (3-314-00600-4, Pub. by North-South Bks NYC) Chronicle Bks.

— Pit et Pat. (FRE., Illus.). 32p. (J). (gr. k-3). 1992. 15.95 (3-314-20657-7, Pub. by North-South Bks NYC) Chronicle Bks.

— Pit il Piccolo Piguino.Tr. of Penguin Pete. (ITA., Illus.). 32p. (J). (gr. k-3). 15.95 (88-8203-030-X, Pub. by North-South Bks NYC) Chronicle Bks.

— Pit, le Petit Pingouin.Tr. of Penguin Pete. (FRE., Illus.). 32p. (J). (gr. k-3). 1996. 15.95 (3-314-20627-5, Pub. by North-South Bks NYC) Chronicle Bks.

— Pit und Pat.Tr. of Penguin Pete & Pat. (GER., Illus.). 32p. (J). (gr. k-3). 1996. 15.95 (3-314-00327-7, Pub. by North-South Bks NYC) Chronicle Bks.

— Pits Neue Freunde.Tr. of Penguin Pete's New Friends. (GER., Illus.). 32p. (J). (gr. k-3). 1996. 15.95 (3-314-00301-3, Pub. by North-South Bks NYC) Chronicle Bks.

Pfister, Marcus. Pits Neue Freunde: German Edition. 1995. 13.95 (3-85825-301-4) Nord-Sud Verlag AG.

Pfister, Marcus. The Rainbow Fish. (Rainbow Fish Ser.). Orig. Title: Der Regenbogenfisch. (JPN., Illus.). (J). (ps-3). 18.95 (4-06-261951-2, Pub. by North-South Bks NYC) Chronicle Bks.

— The Rainbow Fish. James, J. Alison, tr. from GER. LC 91-42158. (Rainbow Fish Ser.). Orig. Title: Der Regenbogenfisch. (Illus.). 32p. (J). (ps-3). 1992. 18.95 (1-55858-009-3, Pub. by North-South Bks NYC); lib. bdg. 18.88 (1-55858-010-7, Pub. by North-South Bks NYC) Chronicle Bks.

— The Rainbow Fish. (Rainbow Fish Ser.). Orig. Title: Der Regenbogenfisch. (Illus.). 12p. (J). (ps-3). 1996. bds. 9.95 (1-55858-536-2, Pub. by North-South Bks NYC) Chronicle Bks.

***Pfister, Marcus.** The Rainbow Fish. (Rainbow Fish Ser.). Orig. Title: Der Regenbogenfisch. (Illus.). (J). (ps-3). 1999. 12.95 incl. audio (0-7358-1233-0, Pub. by North-South Bks NYC); bds. 14.95 (0-7358-1238-1, Pub. by North-South Bks NYC) Chronicle Bks.

— The Rainbow Fish. (Rainbow Fish Ser.). Orig. Title: Der Regenbogenfisch. (Illus.). 32p. (J). (ps-3). 2000. 8.95 (0-7358-1232-2) North-South Bks NYC.

Pfister, Marcus. The Rainbow Fish. (Rainbow Fish Ser.). Orig. Title: Der Regenbogenfisch. (CHI & ENG., Illus.). 32p. (J). (ps-3). 1992. 18.95 (1-57227-027-6); 18.95 (1-57227-028-4); 18.95 (1-57227-029-2); 18.95 (1-57227-030-6); 18.95 (1-57227-031-4); 18.95 (1-57227-032-2) Pan Asian Pubns.

— Rainbow Fish & the Big Blue Whale. James, J. Alison, tr. from GER. LC 98-6894. (Rainbow Fish Ser.). Orig. Title: Regenbogenfisch und Grosser Blauer Wal. (Illus.).

P

An Asterisk (*) at the beginning of an entry indicates that the title is appearing for the first time.

32p. (J). (ps-3). 1998. 18.95 (*0-7358-1009-5*, Pub. by North-South Bks NYC); lib. bdg. 18.88 (*0-7358-1010-9*, Pub. by North-South Bks NYC) Chronicle Bks.

***Pfister, Marcus.** Rainbow Fish & the Big Blue Whale. (Rainbow Fish Ser.). Orig. Title: Regenbogenfisch und Grosser Blauer Wal. (Illus.). 32p. (J). (ps-3). 1999. pap. 25.00 (*0-7358-1214-4*, Pub. by North-South Bks NYC) Chronicle Bks.

— The Rainbow Fish Bath Book. (Rainbow Fish Ser.). (Illus.). 10p. (J). (ps-3). 2000. pap. 6.95 (*0-7358-1299-3*, Pub. by North-South Bks NYC) Chronicle Bks.

Pfister, Marcus. The Rainbow Fish Big Book. (Rainbow Fish Ser.). (Illus.). 32p. (J). (ps-3). 1995. pap. 25.00 (*1-55858-441-2*, Pub. by North-South Bks NYC) Chronicle Bks.

***Pfister, Marcus.** The Rainbow Fish Memory Game. (Rainbow Fish Ser.). (J). (ps-3). 1999. 14.95 (*1-55858-828-0*, Pub. by North-South Bks NYC) Chronicle Bks.

Pfister, Marcus. Rainbow Fish to the Rescue! (Rainbow Fish Ser.). Orig. Title: Regenbogenfisch, Komm Hilf Mir!. (JPN., Illus.). (J). (ps-3). 18.95 (*4-06-261969-5*, Pub. by North-South Bks NYC) Chronicle Bks.

— Rainbow Fish to the Rescue! James, J. Alison, tr. from GER. LC 95-20322. (Rainbow Fish Ser.). Orig. Title: Regenbogenfisch, Komm Hilf Mir!. (Illus.). 32p. (J). (ps-3). 1995. 18.95 (*1-55858-486-2*, Pub. by North-South Bks NYC); lib. bdg. 18.88 (*1-55858-487-0*, Pub. by North-South Bks NYC) Chronicle Bks.

— Rainbow Fish to the Rescue! (Rainbow Fish Ser.). Orig. Title: Regenbogenfisch, Komm Hilf Mir!. (Illus.). 32p. (J). (ps-3). 1997. pap. 25.00 (*1-55858-816-7*, Pub. by North-South Bks NYC) Chronicle Bks.

— Rainbow Fish to the Rescue! James, J. Alison, tr. from GER. LC 97-42317. (Rainbow Fish Ser.). Orig. Title: Regenbogenfisch, Komm Hilf Mir!. (Illus.). (J). (ps-3). 1998. bds. 9.95 (*1-55858-880-9*, Pub. by North-South Bks NYC) Chronicle Bks.

***Pfister, Marcus.** Rainbow Fish to the Rescue! (Rainbow Fish Ser.). Orig. Title: Regenbogenfisch, Komm Hilf Mir!. (Illus.). (J). (ps-3). 2000. 12.95 incl. audio (*0-7358-1289-6*) North-South Bks NYC.

Pfister, Marcus. Rainbow Fish to the Rescue! (Rainbow Fish Ser.). Orig. Title: Regenbogenfisch, Komm Hilf Mir!. (ENG & KOR., Illus.). 32p. (J). (ps-3). 1992. 18.95 (*1-57227-041-1*); 18.95 (*1-57227-042-X*) Pan Asian Pubns.

— Rainbow Fish to the Rescue! (Rainbow Fish Ser.). Orig. Title: Regenbogenfisch, Komm Hilf Mir!. (CHI & ENG., Illus.). 32p. (J). (ps-4). 1992. 18.95 (*1-57227-037-3*); 18.95 (*1-57227-038-1*) Pan Asian Pubns.

— Rainbow Fish to the Rescue! English/Hmong. (Rainbow Fish Ser.). Orig. Title: Regenbogenfisch, Komm Hilf Mir!. (Illus.). 32p. (J). (ps-3). 1992. 18.95 (*1-57227-039-X*) Pan Asian Pubns.

— Rainbow Fish to the Rescue! English/Khmer. (Rainbow Fish Ser.). Orig. Title: Regenbogenfisch, Komm Hilf Mir!. (Illus.). 32p. (J). (ps-3). 1992. 18.95 (*1-57227-040-3*) Pan Asian Pubns.

— The Rainbow Fish Treasury, 2 bks. (Rainbow Fish Ser.). Orig. Title: Der Regenbogenfisch. (Illus.). 32p. (J). (ps-3). 1997. 38.00 (*1-55858-817-5*, Pub. by North-South Bks NYC) Chronicle Bks.

— Der Regenbogenfisch. (Rainbow Fish Ser.). (GER., Illus.). 32p. (J). (ps-3). 1996. 18.95 (*3-314-00581-4*, Pub. by North-South Bks NYC) Chronicle Bks.

— Regenbogenfisch, Komm Hilf Mir! (Rainbow Fish Ser.).Tr. of Rainbow Fish to the Rescue!. (GER., Illus.). 32p. (J). (ps-3). 1995. 18.95 (*3-314-20716-6*, Pub. by North-South Bks NYC) Chronicle Bks.

— Saltarin. (SPA., Illus.). 32p. (J). (gr. k-3). 1996. 15.95 (*1-55858-563-X*, Pub. by North-South Bks NYC); pap. 6.95 (*1-55858-548-6*, Pub. by North-South Bks NYC) Chronicle Bks.

— Saltarin. (SPA., Illus.). 32p. (J). (ps). 1998. bds. 6.95 (*1-55858-890-6*, Pub. by North-South Bks NYC) Chronicle Bks.

— Saltarin y la Primavera. (SPA., Illus.). 32p. (J). (gr. k-3). 1998. 15.95 (*1-55858-877-9*, Pub. by North-South Bks NYC) Chronicle Bks.

***Pfister, Marcus.** Saltarin y la Primavera. (SPA., Illus.). 32p. (J). (gr. k-3). 1998. pap. 6.95 (*1-55858-876-0*, Pub. by North-South Bks NYC) Chronicle Bks.

Pfister, Marcus. Saltarin y la Primavera. (SPA., Illus.). 12p. (J). (ps). 1998. bds. 6.95 (*1-55858-889-2*, Pub. by North-South Bks NYC) Chronicle Bks.

— The Sleepy Owl. (Illus.). 32p. (J). (ps-2). 1998. pap. 6.95 (*1-55858-905-8*, Pub. by North-South Bks NYC) Chronicle Bks.

— Sun & Moon. LC 89-43251. (Illus.). 32p. (J). (gr. k-3). 1998. pap. 6.95 (*1-55858-995-3*, Pub. by North-South Bks NYC) Chronicle Bks.

Pfister, Marcus. Sun & Moon. 32p. (J). (ps-3). 1993. pap. 4.95 (*0-590-44490-5*) Scholastic Inc.

Pfister, Marcus. Sun & Moon. (J). 1990. 10.15 (*0-606-05630-0*, Pub. by Turtleback) Demco.

— Wake up, Santa Claus! LC 96-15964. (Illus.). 32p. (J). (gr. k-3). 1996. 15.95 (*1-55858-605-9*, Pub. by North-South Bks NYC); lib. bdg. 15.88 (*1-55858-606-7*, Pub. by North-South Bks NYC) Chronicle Bks.

— Der Weihnachtsstern.Tr. of Christmas Star. (GER., Illus.). (J). (gr. k-3). 1996. 18.95 (*3-314-00601-2*, Pub. by North-South Bks NYC) Chronicle Bks.

Pfister, Marcus, jt. auth. see Siegenthaler, Kathrin.

Pfister, Michelle M., jt. auth. see Alderman, Eric.

Pfister, Otto, jt. auth. see Grewal, Bieram.

Pfister, Pamela, jt. auth. see Dailey, Barbara Pfister.

Pfister, Patrick. Pilgrimage: Tales from the Open Road. 1999. reprint ed. pap. 14.95 (*0-89733-472-8*) Academy Chi Pubs.

Pfister, Raymond. Soixante Ans de Pentecotisme en Alsace (1930-1990) Une Approche Socio-Historique. (Etudes d'Histoire Interculturelle du Christianisme Ser.: Vol. 93). (FRE.). 238p. 1995. 40.95 (*3-631-48620-0*) P Lang Pubng.

Pfisterer, Bill, ed. see Herbert, Belle.

Pfisterer, Bill, ed. see Herbert, B., et al.

Pfisterer, Bill, ed. see Martin, Richard.

Pfisterer, F., jt. auth. see Bloss, W. H.

Pfisterer, P. Dictionary of Monograms 19th-20th Century, German to English. (ENG & GER.). 1067p. 1995. 950.00 (*0-320-00555-0*) Fr & Eur.

Pfisterer, Paul. Signaturenlexikon/Dictionary of Signatures. 992p. 1998. 325.00 (*3-11-014937-0*) De Gruyter.

Pfisterer, Paul, ed. Monogrammlexikon 2 - Dictionary of Monograms 2: Internationales Verzeichnis der Monogramme Bildender Kuenstler des 19. und 20. Jahrhunderts/International List of Monograms in the Visual Arts of the 19th & 20th Centuries. (ENG & GER.). xx, 1067p. (C). 1998. lib. bdg. 425.35 (*3-11-014300-3*) De Gruyter.

Pfisterer, Susan & Pickett, Carolyn. Playing with Ideas. (Orig.). pap. 29.95 (*0-86819-565-0*, Pub. by Currency Pr) Accents Pubns.

Pfitsch, Patricia C. The Deeper Song. LC 97-23925. 160p. (YA). (gr. 7-12). 1998. 16.00 (*0-689-81183-7*) S&S Childrens.

— Keeper of the Light. LC 96-39745. 137p. (YA). (gr. 5-9). 1997. per. 16.00 (*0-689-81492-5*) S&S Bks Yung.

Pfitzer, Donald W. Hiking Georgia. (Illus.). 304p. 1996. pap. 14.95 (*1-56044-459-2*) Falcon Pub Inc.

***Pfitzer, Donald W.** Hiking Georgia. rev. ed. LC 99-14075. 296p. 1999. pap. 16.95 (*1-56044-717-6*) Falcon Pub Inc.

Pfitzer, Donald W. & Powell, LeRoy. Scenic Driving Georgia. LC 96-2544. (Illus.). 196p. 1996. pap. 14.95 (*1-56044-411-8*) Falcon Pub Inc.

Pfitzer, Gregory M. Samuel Eliot Morison's Historical World: In Quest of a New Parkman. 384p. 1991. text 47.50 (*1-55553-101-6*) NE U Pr.

Pfitzer, Peter & Grundmann, Ekkehard, eds. Current Status of Diagnostic Cytology. (Recent Results in Cancer Research Ser.: Vol. 133). (Illus.). 175p. 1993. write for info. (*3-540-56618-X*) Spr-Verlag.

— Current Status of Diagnostic Cytology. LC 93-11295. (Recent Results in Cancer Research Ser.: Vol. 133). 1993. 93.00 (*0-387-56618-X*) Spr-Verlag.

Pfitzinger, Pete & Douglas, Scott. Road Racing for Serious Runners. (Illus.). 200p. 1998. pap. 16.95 (*0-88011-818-0*, PPFI0818) Human Kinetics.

***Pfitzmann, Andreas, ed.** Information Hiding: Proceedings of the Third International Workshop, IH '99, Dresden, Germany, September 29-October 1, 1999. LC 00-27994. (Lecture Notes in Computer Science Ser.: Vol. 1768). ix, 491p. 2000. pap. 73.00 (*3-540-67182-X*) Spr-Verlag.

Pfitzmann, Birgit. Digital Signature Schemes: General Framework & Fail-Stop Signatures, Vol. 110. LC 96-31539. (Lecture Notes in Computer Science Ser.). 396p. 1996. pap. 59.50 (*3-540-61517-2*) Spr-Verlag.

Pfitzner, C. Barry. Mathematical Fundamentals for Microeconomics. LC 92-72588. 150p. (C). 1992. pap. text 25.95 (*1-878975-13-7*) Blackwell Pubs.

Pfitzner, Victor & Regan, Hilary, eds. The Task of Theology Today: Doctrines & Dogmas. 243p. 1999. pap. 25.00 (*0-8028-4654-8*) Eerdmans.

Pfitzner, Victor C. Hebrews. LC 97-37867. (New Testament Commentaries Ser.). 224p. 1997. pap. 20.95 (*0-687-05724-8*) Abingdon.

Pfizenmaier, Thomas C. The Trinitarian Theology of Dr. Samuel Clarke (1675-1729) Context, Sources, & Controversy. LC 96-45397. (Studies in the History of Christian Thought: Vol. 75). 224p. 1997. 79.50 (*90-04-10719-3*) Brill Academic Pubs.

Pflanze, Otto. Bismarck & the Development of Germany Vol. 1: The Period of Unification, 1815-1871. 2nd ed. LC 89-11004. (Illus.). 548p. reprint ed. pap. 169.90 (*0-608-09103-0*, 206973700001) Bks Demand.

— Bismarck & the Development of Germany Vol. 2: The Period of Consolidation, 1871-1880. LC 89-11004. (Illus.). 572p. reprint ed. pap. 177.40 (*0-608-09104-9*, 206973700002) Bks Demand.

— Bismarck & the Development of Germany Vol. 3: The Period of Fortification, 1880-1898. 2nd ed. LC 89-11004. (Illus.). 486p. reprint ed. pap. 150.70 (*0-608-09105-7*, 206973700003) Bks Demand.

— Bismarck & the Development of Germany, Vol. 1: The Period of Unification, 1815-1871. (Illus.). 1531p. (C). 1990. text 67.50 (*0-691-05587-4*, Pub. by Princeton U Pr) Cal Prin Full Svc.

— Bismarck & the Development of Germany, Vol. 3: The Period of Fortification, 1880-1898. (Illus.). 1531p. (C). 1990. text 67.50 (*0-691-05589-0*, Pub. by Princeton U Pr) Cal Prin Full Svc.

Pflanze, Otto, ed. The Unification of Germany, 1848-1871. LC 78-23470. (European Problem Studies). 128p. 1979. reprint ed. pap. 11.50 (*0-88275-803-9*) Krieger.

Pflanzer. Experimental & Applied Physiology. 6th ed. LC 98-215377. 1998. 43.00 (*0-697-28407-7*, Dshkn McG-Hill) McGrw-H Hghr Educ.

Pflanzer, Richard. Basic Human Physiology: Outlines & Essential Concepts. 342p. (C). 1997. spiral bd. 32.95 (*0-7872-4334-5*, 41433401) Kendall-Hunt.

Pflanzer, Richard G. Basic Human Physiology. (C). Date not set. pap. text, teacher ed., suppl. ed. 42.00 (*0-03-072773-1*); pap. text, student ed. 22.00 (*0-03-072774-X*) Harcourt Coll Pubs.

— Basic Human Physiology. (C). 2000. pap. text 31.00 (*0-03-072776-6*) Harcourt Coll Pubs.

— Experimental & Applied Physiology. 5th ed. 384p. (C). 1994. text 38.00 (*0-697-13786-4*, WCB McGr Hill) McGrw-H Hghr Educ.

— Human Physiology. 288p. (C). 1995. spiral bd. 26.95 (*0-7872-0804-3*) Kendall-Hunt.

Pflaum-Connor, Susanna. The Development of Language & Literacy in Young Children. 3rd ed. 256p. (C). 1990. pap. text 30.75 (*0-675-20447-X*, Merrill Coll) P-H.

Pflaum-Connor, Susanna, ed. Aspects of Reading Education. LC 77-95250. (National Society for the Study of Education Publication Ser.). 234p. 1978. 29.60 (*0-8211-1517-0*) McCutchan.

Pflaum, Hans G. Germany on Film: Theme & Content in the Cinema of the Federal Republic of Germany. Picht, Robert, ed. Helt, Richard C. & Richter, Roland, trs. LC 89-22661. (Contemporary Film & Television Studies & Readers). (Illus.). 158p. reprint ed. pap. 49.00 (*0-608-06272-3*, 206660100008) Bks Demand.

Pflaum, Leanne J., jt. auth. see Reid Rambo, Teresa J.

Pflaum, Rosalynd. Marie Curie & Her Daughter Irene. LC 92-2453. (YA). (gr. 6-9). 1993. lib. bdg. 23.93 (*0-8225-4915-8*, Lerner Publctns) Lerner Pub.

Pflaum, Susanna W., jt. ed. see Pignatelli, Frank.

Pfleeger, Charles P. Security in Computing. 2nd ed. 592p. (C). 1996. 67.00 (*0-13-337486-6*) P-H.

Pfleeger, Janet, jt. auth. see Rosenthal, Neal H.

Pfleeger, Shari L. Software Engineering: Theory & Practice. LC 98-5683. 576p. 1998. 73.00 (*0-13-624842-X*) P-H.

Pfleeger, Shari L. & Straight, David W. Introduction to Discrete Structures. 372p. (C). 1985. reprint ed. pap. text 41.95 (*0-471-80075-9*) Krieger.

Pfleeger, Shari L., jt. auth. see Fenton, Norman E.

Pfleeger, Shari L., jt. ed. see Oman, Paul W.

Pfleger, Carl, ed. see Strauss, Josef.

Pfleger, Deborah B., jt. auth. see Warren, Sandra.

Pfleger, F. L. & Linderman, R. G., eds. Mycorrhizae & Plant Health. LC 93-72994. (APS Symposium Ser.). 360p. 1994. pap. 42.00 (*0-89054-158-2*) Am Phytopathol Soc.

Pfleger, Helmut. Taktik und Witz Im Schach. (Praxis Schach Ser.: Bd. 8). (GER.). 182p. write for info. (*3-283-00252-5*) G Olms Pubs.

***Pfleger, K., et al.** Mass Spectral & Gc Data, 4 vols., Set. 2nd ed. 4700p. 2000. 1350.00 (*3-527-29793-6*) Wiley.

Pfleger, K., et al. Mass Spectral & GC Data, Pt. 4. 2nd ed. 700p. 2000. 325.00 (*3-527-28880-5*) Wiley.

Pfleger, K., et al. Mass Spectral & GC Data of Drugs, Poisons, Pesticides, Pollutants & Their Metabolites, Vol. 1. 2nd rev. ed. 3409p. 1992. 1155.00 (*3-527-26989-4*) Wiley.

Pfleger, Karl. Wrestlers with Christ. Watkin, Edward I., tr. LC 68-16968. (Essay Index Reprint Ser.). 1977. 23.95 (*0-8369-0785-X*) Ayer.

Pfleger, Karl, et al. Mass Spectral & GC Data of Drugs, Poisons, Pesticides, Pollutants & Their Metabolites, Pts. I, II & III. 2nd enl. rev. ed. LC 92-49331. 3000p. 1992. lib. bdg. 825.00 (*0-89573-855-4*, Wiley-VCH) Wiley.

Pfleger, Margot & Fuenzalida, Mizzette, prefs. Multilingual Health Education Resource Guide. 2nd ed. 151p. 1996. pap. text 25.00 (*0-7881-8939-5*) DIANE Pub.

Pfleger, Margot, jt. ed. see Ranard, Donald A.

Pfleger, S., et al, eds. Advances in Human-Computer Interaction: Human Comfort & Security, Vol. XI. LC 95-37102. (Research Reports ESPRIT: Vol. 1). 323p. 1995. 56.00 (*3-540-60145-7*) Spr-Verlag.

— Data Fusion Applications: Workshop Proceedings, Brussels, November 25, 1992. (Research Reports ESPRIT: Vol. 1). 266p. 1993. 45.95 (*0-387-56973-1*) Spr-Verlag.

Pfleger, S. & Lefevre, J. P. Advanced Speech Applications: European Research on Speech Technology. (Project Group Speech Technology Ser.: Vol. 1). 320p. 1996. pap. 55.00 (*0-387-58142-1*) Spr-Verlag.

Pfleger, S., jt. ed. see Varghese, K.

***Pfleger, Susanne.** A Day with Picasso. Wynne, Christopher, tr. (Adventures in Art Ser.). (Illus.). 28p. (YA). (gr. 3-6). 1999. 14.95 (*3-7913-2165-X*, Pub. by Prestel) te Neues.

Pfleger, Susanne. Henri Rousseau: A Jungle Expedition. LC 98-217356. (Illus.). 30p. (J). (gr. 1-6). 1998. 14.95 (*3-7913-1987-6*) te Neues.

Pfleger, T., jt. auth. see Montenbruck, O.

Pfleger, T., jt. auth. see Montenbruck, Oliver.

Pfleider, Eugene P., et al, eds. Surface Mining. LC 68-24169. (Seeley W. Mudd Ser.). (Illus.). 1083p. reprint ed. pap. 200.00 (*0-8357-8338-3*, 203397400087) Bks Demand.

Pfleiderer, A., ed. Ovarialkarzinom. (Journal: Onkologie: Vol. 7, Suppl. 2). 70p. 1984. pap. 17.50 (*3-8055-3922-3*) S Karger.

— Probleme der Krebsnachsorge. (Beitraege Zur Onkologie, Contributions to Oncology Ser.: Band 4). (Illus.). 112p. 1980. pap. 28.75 (*3-8055-1378-X*) S Karger.

Pfleiderer, Glenn M. Softdesk Primer. LC 97-28416. 328p. 1998. pap. text 61.00 (*0-13-617838-3*) P-H.

Pfleiderer, Joanne, jt. auth. see Ponza, Michael.

Pfleiderer, Otto. Lectures on the Influence of the Apostle Paul on the Development of Christianity. Smith, J. Frederick, tr. LC 77-27166. (Hibbert Lectures: 1885). reprint ed. 37.50 (*0-404-60406-4*) AMS Pr.

— Philosophy & Development of Religion, 2 vols., Set. LC 77-27229. (Gifford Lectures: 1894). reprint ed. 84.50 (*0-404-60470-6*) AMS Pr.

Pflieger, Pat. Beverly Cleary. (Twayne's United States Authors Ser.: No. 572). 232p. (C). 1991. 32.00 (*0-8057-7613-3*, Twyne) Mac Lib Ref.

— Reference Guide to Modern Fantasy for Children. LC 83-10692. 690p. 1984. lib. bdg. 85.00 (*0-313-22886-8*, PFC/, Greenwood Pr) Greenwood.

Pflomm, Phyllis N. Chalk in Hand: The Draw & Tell Book. LC 86-15480. (Illus.). 126p. 1986. pap. 17.50 (*0-8108-1921-X*) Scarecrow.

— Puppet Plays Plus: Hand Puppet Plays for Two Puppeteers. LC 94-4875. (Illus.). 253p. 1994. 31.00 (*0-8108-2738-7*) Scarecrow.

Pfloog, Jan. Asi Son los Perritos! (Spanish Translations Picturebacks Ser.). (SPA., Illus.). 32p. (J). (ps-3). 1993. pap. 2.25 (*0-394-85064-5*) Random Bks Yng Read.

— The Kitten Book. (Super Shape Bks.). (Illus.). 24p. (J). (ps-k). 1968. pap. 3.29 (*0-307-10079-0*, 10079) Gldn Bks Pub Co.

— Kittens Are Like That. LC 75-36469. (Pictureback Ser.). (Illus.). 32p. (J). (ps-1). 1976. pap. 3.25 (*0-394-83243-4*, Pub. by Random Bks Yng Read) Random.

— Kittens Are Like That. (Random House Pictureback Ser.). 1976. 8.45 (*0-606-06121-5*, Pub. by Turtleback) Demco.

— The Monkey Book. (Super Shape Bks.). (Illus.). 24p. (J). (ps-k). 1998. pap. 3.29 (*0-307-10347-1*, 10347, Goldn Books) Gldn Bks Pub Co.

— Puppies Are Like That. LC 74-2542. (Pictureback Ser.). (Illus.). 32p. (J). (ps-3). 1975. pap. 3.25 (*0-394-82923-9*, Pub. by Random Bks Yng Read) Random.

Pfloog, Jan. Puppies Are Like That. (Random House Pictureback Ser.). 1975. 8.45 (*0-606-06145-2*, Pub. by Turtleback) Demco.

Pfloog, Jan. The Puppy Book. (Super Shape Bks.). (Illus.). 24p. (J). (ps-k). 1968. pap. 3.29 (*0-307-10078-2*, 10078) Gldn Bks Pub Co.

— The Tiger Book. (Super Shape Bks.). (Illus.). 24p. (J). 1998. pap. 3.29 (*0-307-13024-X*, 13024, Goldn Books) Gldn Bks Pub Co.

Pflueger, Lynda. Dolley Madison: Courageous First Lady. LC 98-5811. (Historical American Biographies Ser.). 128p. (YA). (gr. 6 up). 1999. lib. bdg. 20.95 (*0-7660-1092-9*) Enslow Pubs.

— Jeb Stuart: Confederate Cavalry General. LC 97-4367. (Historical American Biographies Ser.). (Illus.). 128p. (YA). (gr. 6 up). 1998. lib. bdg. 20.95 (*0-7660-1013-9*) Enslow Pubs.

— Mark Twain: Legendary Writer & Humorist. LC 98-31293. (Historical American Biographies Ser.). (Illus.). 128p. (YA). (gr. 6 up). 1999. lib. bdg. 20.95 (*0-7660-1093-7*) Enslow Pubs.

— Mark Twain: Legendary Writer & Humorist. LC 98-31293. (Historical American Biographies Ser.). 1999. write for info. (*0-07-601093-7*) McGraw.

— Stonewall Jackson: Confederate General. LC 96-8827. (Historical American Biographies Ser.). 128p. (YA). (gr. 6 up). 1997. lib. bdg. 20.95 (*0-89490-781-6*) Enslow Pubs.

***Pflueger, Lynda.** Thomas Nast: Political Cartoonist. LC 99-43631. (Historical American Ser.). (Illus.). 128p. (YA). (gr. 6 up). 2000. lib. bdg. 20.95 (*0-7660-1251-4*) Enslow Pubs.

Pflug, Bernd. Education in Ayurveda: A Re-Constructional Analysis. (Illus.). xiii, 213p. (C). 1992. 18.00 (*81-212-0399-6*, Pub. by Gyan Publishing Hse) Nataraj Bks.

Pflug, G. C., et al, eds. Probability & Statistical Inference. 1982. text 171.00 (*90-277-1427-4*) Kluwer Academic.

Pflug, George C. Optimization of Stochastic Models: The Interface Between Simulation & Optimization. LC 96-27381. (Discrete Event Dynamic Systems in Engineering & Computer Science Ser.). 400p. (C). 1996. lib. bdg. 193.50 (*0-7923-9780-0*) Kluwer Academic.

Pflug, I. J. Selected Papers on the Microbiology & Engineering of Sterilization Processes. 5th ed. 298p. (C). 1988. pap. text. write for info. (*0-929340-05-1*) Environ Sterilization Lab.

Pflug, Irving J. Microbiology & Engineering of Sterilization Processes. 8th rev. ed. Orig. Title: A Textbook for an Introductory Course in the Microbiology & Engineering of Sterilization Processes. 526p. (C). 1995. pap. text 65.00 (*0-929340-01-9*) Environ Sterilization Lab.

Pflug, Jackie N. & Kizilos, Peter J. Miles to Go Before I Sleep: My Grateful Journey Back from the Hijacking of EgyptAir Flight 648. 230p. 19.95 (*1-56838-088-7*) Hazelden.

***Pflug, Maja.** Natalia Ginzburg. (Illus.). 2001. pap. 15.95 (*1-900850-22-2*) Arcadia Bks.

Pflug, Melissa A. Ritual & Myth in Odawa Revitalization: Reclaiming a Sovereign Place. LC 97-27798. (Illus.). xvi, 304p. 1998. 28.95 (*0-8061-3007-5*) U of Okla Pr.

Pflug, Peter, jt. auth. see Jarnicki, Marek.

Pflug, Warner W., ed. A Guide to the Archives of Labor History & Urban Affairs. LC 73-6004. 196p. reprint ed. pap. 60.80 (*0-7837-3659-2*, 204353000009) Bks Demand.

Pflugfelder, Gregory M. Cartographies of Desire: Male-Male Sexuality in Japanese Discourse, 1600-1950. LC 98-20632. 357p. 1999. 45.00 (*0-520-20909-5*, Pub. by U CA Pr) Cal Prin Full Svc.

Pflugh-Harttung, Julius Von, see Von Pflugk-Harttung, Julius.

***Pflughoft, Fred.** Wild & Beautiful Yellowstone. 2000. 29.95 (*1-56037-146-3*) Am Wrld Geog.

***Pflughoft, Fred, photos by.** Oregon Wild & Beautiful: Coast. (Illus.). 120p. 2000. 29.95 (*1-56037-152-8*) Am Wrld Geog.

— Oregon Wild & Beautiful: Mountains. (Illus.). 120p. 2000. 29.95 (*1-56037-154-4*) Am Wrld Geog.

Pflughoft, Fred, photos by. Wyoming: Wild & Beautiful. (Illus.). 1999. 29.95 (*1-56037-141-2*) Am Wrld Geog.

***Pflughoft, Fred & Holdsworth, Henry H., photos by.** Grand Teton Wild & Beautiful. (Illus.). 120p. 2000. 29.95 (*1-56037-153-6*) Am Wrld Geog.

Pfluke, Lillian A. Breastfeeding & the Active Woman. 160p. 1995. pap. 11.95 (*1-56796-087-1*) WRS Group.

Pflum, Richard. A Strange Juxtaposition of Parts: Poems by Richard Pflum. 80p. (Orig.). 1995. per. 8.95 (*1-880649-33-0*) Writ Ctr Pr.

Pfnausch, Edward G. Codigo, Comunidad, Ministerio. 170p. 1994. pap. 5.00 (*0-943616-66-2*) Canon Law Soc.

Pfnausch, Edward G., ed. Canon Law Digest 11: Officially Published Documents Affecting the Code of Canon Law 1983-1985. xi, 433p. 1991. 30.00 (*0-943616-50-6*) Canon Law Soc.

P

An Asterisk (*) at the beginning of an entry indicates that the title is appearing for the first time.

— Code, Community, Ministry. 2nd rev. ed. 145p. 1992. pap. 5.00 (0-943616-54-9) Canon Law Soc.

Pfohl, Bruce, et al. Structured Interview for DSM-IV Personality (SIDP-IV) 48p. 1997. pap. text 22.95 (0-88048-937-5, 8937) Am Psychiatric.

Pfohl, Gerhard. Bibliographie der Griechischen Vers-Inschriften. (GER.). 62p. 1964. write for info. (0-318-70446-3); write for info. (0-318-71855-3) G Olms Pubs.

— Bibliographie Der Griechischen Vers-Inschriften. 62p. 1964. write for info. (0-318-70996-1) G Olms Pubs.

Pfohl, Stephen. Death at the Parasite Cafe: Social Science (Fictions) & the Postmodern. Kroker, Arthur & Kroker, Marilouise, eds. (Culture Texts Ser.). 300p. 1992. pap. 14.95 (0-312-07573-1) St Martin.

Pfohl, Stephen J. Images of Deviance & Social Control: A Sociological History. 2nd ed. LC 93-25803. 448p. (C). 1994. 49.69 (0-07-049765-6) McGraw.

Pfordresher, John. A Variorum Edition of Tennyson's Idylls of the King. LC 73-4852. 1088p. 1973. text 122.00 (0-231-03691-4) Col U Pr.

Pfost, Harry, ed. see American Feed Manufacturers Association Staff.

Pfost, Karen S. Psychology of Women. (C). 1995. 33.33 (0-205-15270-8, Macmillan Coll) P-H.

Pfouts, Caroline. Jump Start Your Sales: An Audio Program to Build Sales Skills. 20p. 1988. pap. text 12.00 (0-9663465-1-3) Jasper Pubns.

Pfouts, Chris. True Tales of American Violence. 184p. 1993. text 21.95 (0-87364-742-4) Paladin Pr.

Pfouts, Chris, jt. auth. see MacYoung, Marc A.

Pfoutz, Sara. Missing Person. 1999. pap. 3.95 (0-14-036254-1, Viking) Viking Penguin.

***Pfrang, Elvira.** Towards Liberalisation of the European Electricity Markets: The Directive Concerning Common Rules for an Internal Market in Electricity in the Frame of the Competition & Internal Market Rules of the EC-Treaty. (Schriften zum Staats - und Volkerrecht Ser.: Vol. 80). 138p. (C). 1999. pap. text 31.95 (0-8204-4310-7) P Lang Pubng.

***Pfrengle, Hermann O.** Forget That You Have Been Hitler's Soldiers: A Youth's Service to the Reich. (Illus.). 150p. 2000. 24.95 (1-57249-217-1, Burd St Pr) White Mane Pub.

Pfrimmer, Mildred. Books to Learn & Live by, 5 bks., Set. Incl. Bk. 1. ABCs of Creation. 1977. Bk. 2. ABCs of the Flood. 1977. Bk. 3. Aardvark in the Art. 1977. Bk. 4. Elephant in Eden. 1977. Bk. 5. Tale of the Whale. 1977. (Little Talkers Ser.). (J). (gr. 3-9). 1977. 17.50 (0-685-80546-8) Triumph Pub.

Pfrogner, J. Gruenlandgesellschaften & Grundwasser der Innaue Suedlich Von Rosenheim. (Dissertationes Botanicae Ser.: Vol. 23). (GER., Illus.). 179p. 1973. pap. text 30.00 (3-7682-0921-0) Lubrecht & Cramer.

Pfrommer, Michael. Metalwork from the Hellenized East: The J. Paul Getty Museum. LC 92-34053. (Illus.). 248p. 1993. 75.00 (0-89236-218-9, Pub. by J P Getty Trust) OUP.

Pfrunder, Eric, ed. see Lagerfeld, Karl.

Pfuetze, Paul. Self, Society, Existence: Human Nature & Dialogue in the Thought of George Herbert Mead & Martin Buber. LC 72-11743. 400p. 1973. reprint ed. lib. bdg. 65.00 (0-8371-6708-6, PFSS, Greenwood Pr) Greenwood.

Pfuhl, Erdwin H., Jr. & Henry, Stuart. The Deviance Process. 3rd ed. LC 93-2942. 295p. 1993. pap. text 26.95 (0-202-30470-1); lib. bdg. 49.95 (0-202-30469-8) Aldine de Gruyter.

Pfuhl, Ernst. Masterpieces of Greek Drawing & Painting. Beazley, John D., tr. from GER. LC 79-83879. (Illus.). 1979. reprint ed. lib. bdg. 50.00 (0-87817-250-5) Hacker.

Pfund, P. A., ed. see AIAA-ASME Joint Fluids, Plasma Thermophysics, & Heat Transfer Staff.

Pfund, P. A., ed. see American Society of Mechanical Engineers Staff.

Pfungst, Oskar. Clever Hans (The Horse of Mr. Von Osten) 286p. 90.00 (1-85506-697-1) Thoemmes Pr.

***Pfurtscheller, G. & da Silva, F.H., eds.** Event-Related Desynchronization. LC 99-19484. (Handbook of Electroencephalography & Clinical Neurophysiology, Revised Ser.: Vol. 6). 428p. 1999. 236.00 (0-444-82999-7) Elsevier.

Pfurtscheller, G. & Lopes Da Silva, F. H., eds. Functional Brain Imaging. LC 88-19071. 276p. (C). 1988. text 98.00 (0-920887-28-7) Hogrefe & Huber Pubs.

PGA Staff & Wiren, Gary. The PGA Manual of Golf: The Professional's Way to Play Better Golf. (Illus.). 480p. 1991. 39.95 (0-02-599291-0) Macmillan.

PGE Chef's Night Out Committee. PGE Chef's Night Out Cookbook. Otto, Bridget et al, eds. 95p. (Orig.). 1991. pap. 14.95 (0-9629263-0-2) PGE Chefs.

PGW Staff. Ban Censorship: The Postcard Activist. 1991. pap. 4.95 (1-879096-02-1) Postcard Activist.

— Keep Abortion Safe & Legal: The Postcard Activist. 1991. pap. 4.95 (1-879096-00-5) Postcard Activist.

— No Handguns: The Postcard Activist. 1991. pap. 4.95 (1-879096-01-3) Postcard Activist.

Ph. Nine Fast Profit Angles 90. 1990. pap. text 6.85 (0-13-621137-2) P-H.

— PH Periodic Table. 1997. pap. text 3.00 (0-13-956764-X) P-H.

— Secertary Fast Action Letter #90. 1990. pap. text 6.85 (0-13-796996-1) P-H.

— Small Business Owner Handbook 89. 1988. pap. text 4.95 (0-13-814302-1) P-H.

— What You Must Know Setup. 1987. pap. text 4.95 (0-13-404898-9) P-H.

PH Editorial Staff. Lawyer's Desk Book, 1990-1991 Cumulative Supplement. 168p. 1990. pap. 40.00 (0-13-524208-8) P-H.

— Natural Healing with Aromatherapy. (C). 1996. pap. text 5.95 (0-13-258963-X) P-H.

— Prentice-Hall's Explanation of the Tax Reform Act of 1986: As Passed by the House of Representatives (September 25, 1986) & Sent to the Senate. LC 86-222025. 1986. 12.00 (0-13-695123-6) P-H.

PH Inc. Staff. Motion, Forces & Energy. 2nd ed. 1994. text, student ed. 10.97 (0-13-402041-3) P-H.

— Physical Science Matter: Building Blocks. 2nd ed. text. write for info. (0-13-225418-2) P-H.

Pha, Mac N., ed. see Phach, Nguyen N.

Phaal, R. & Wiesner, C. S. Toughness Requirements for Steels: An International Compendium. (Illus.). 178p. 1993. pap. 185.00 (1-85573-132-0, Pub. by Woodhead Pubng) Am Educ Systs.

Phach, Nguyen N. Vietnam & Meta Revolution. Pha, Mac N., ed.Tr. of Vietnam Va Sieu Cach Menh. (Illus.). 374p. (C). 1992. 50.00 (0-9636159-0-4) Vietnam & Wrld.

Phadke, Anant. Drug Supply & Use: Towards a Rational Policy in India. LC 98-4677. 1998. write for info. (0-7619-9236-7); pap. write for info. (0-7619-9237-5) Sage.

Phadke, Arun G. Handbook of Electrical Engineering Calculations. LC 99-14706. (Electrical Engineering & Electronics Ser.). (Illus.). 336p. 1999. text 135.00 (0-8247-1955-7) Dekker.

Phadke, Madhav S. Quality Engineering Using Robust Design. 250p. 1995. 77.00 (0-13-745167-9) P-H.

Phadke, Uday, et al. Information Engineering: Identification of Influential Technologies, Impact Assessment & Recommendations for Action. (Illus.). 183p. (C). 1997. reprint ed. pap. text 40.00 (0-7881-3821-9) DIANE Pub.

Phadnis, U. & Malani, I. Women of the World: Illusion & Reality. 285p. 1979. 18.95 (0-7069-0489-3) Asia Bk Corp.

Phadnis, Urmila. Domestic Conflicts in South Asia, Vol. 2. 1986. 18.50 (81-7003-071-4, Pub. by S Asia Pubs) S Asia.

— Ethnicity & Nation-Building in South Asia. LC 89-31286. (Illus.). 352p. (C). 1989. 29.95 (0-8039-9607-1) Sage.

Phaedron. Teachings of the Winged Disk. LC 97-147741. (Illus.). 224p. (Orig.). 1997. pap. 14.95 (0-9637498-3-8, Belfry) Toad Hall PA.

Phaf, R. Hans. Learning in Natural & Connectionist Systems: Experiments & a Model. LC 93-47517. 312p. (C). 1994. text 166.50 (0-7923-2685-7) Kluwer Academic.

Phaff, H. J., et al. The Life of Yeasts. 2nd enl. rev. ed. (Illus.). 320p. 1978. 44.00 (0-674-53325-9) HUP.

Phaff, Herman J., ed. A Bibliography of Publications by the Faculty, Staff, & Students of the University of California, 1876-1980, on Grapes, Wines & Related Subjects. (UC Publications in Catalogs & Bibliographies: Vol. 2). 1986. 55.00 (0-520-09702-5, Pub. by U CA Pr) Cal Prin Full Svc.

Phagan, Janice. Communications for Community Associations, GAP #15. 3rd ed. (Illus.). 16p. (C). 1995. pap. 17.50 (0-944715-36-2) CAI.

Phagan, Jesse R. Applied Mathematics. LC 94-30267. 397p. 1997. 38.64 (1-56637-117-1) Goodheart.

— DC/AC Foundations of Electronics. LC 96-22362. (Illus.). 912p. (C). 1996. text 45.28 (1-56637-341-7) Goodheart.

— Mastering Electronics Math. 2nd ed. (Illus.). 352p. 1991. pap. 17.95 (0-8306-3589-0) McGraw-Hill Prof.

Phagan, Jesse R. & Spaulding, William. Learning Electronics: Theory & Experiments with Computer-Aided Instruction for the Commodore 64-128. (Illus.). 380p. 1988. 24.95 (0-8306-7882-4, 2882); pap. 16.95 (0-8306-2882-7) McGraw-Hill Prof.

— Learning Electronics: Theory & Experiments with Computer-Aided Instruction for the Commodore 64-128. (Illus.). 370p. 1988. 24.95 (0-8306-0182-1, 2982); pap. 16.95 (0-8306-2982-3) McGraw-Hill Prof.

— Learning Electronics: Theory & Experiments with Computer-Aided Instruction for the Commodore 64-128. (Illus.). 380p. 1989. 24.95 (0-8306-9082-4, 3082); pap. 16.95 (0-8306-9382-3, 3082) McGraw-Hill Prof.

— Learning Electronics - C-64. 1991. 24.95 (0-8306-6431-9) McGraw-Hill Prof.

— Learning Electronics Theory. 1991. 24.95 (0-8306-6677-X) McGraw-Hill Prof.

Phagan, Mary. The Murder of Little Mary Phagan. (Illus.). 300p. 1988. 21.95 (0-88382-039-7) New Horizon NJ.

Phagan, Patricia, ed. see Eiland, William U. & Pelletier, S. William.

Phagan, Patricia, ed. see Pelletier, S. William.

Phagan, Patricia, ed. see Pelletier, S. William, et al.

Phagan, Patricia Elaine, et al. Images of Women in 17th Century Dutch Art. LC 95-15176. (Illus.). 94p. 1997. pap. 16.00 (0-915977-19-2) Georgia Museum of Art.

Phagan, Patricia Elaine, ed. see Baigell, Matthew, et al.

Phagan, Patricia Elaine, ed. see Brumbaugh, Thomas B. & Ladis, Andrew.

Phagan-Schostok, Patricia A. & Maloney, Karen L. Contemporary Dental Hygiene Practice, Vol. 1. (Illus.). 221p. 1988. pap. text, student ed. 69.00 (0-86715-169-2) Quint Pub Co.

— Contemporary Dental Hygiene Practice, Vol. 2. (Illus.). 120p. 1989. pap. text 38.00 (0-86715-170-6) Quint Pub Co.

Phaidon. Switzerland: Phaidon Cultural Guides. 1985. 15.95 (0-13-879875-3) S&S Trade.

***Phaidon Press Staff.** The American Art Book. LC 99-231734. (Illus.). 512p. 1999. 39.95 (0-7148-3845-4) Phaidon Press.

— Annunciation. 2000. 19.95 (0-7148-3939-6) Phaidon Pr.

— Crucifixion. 2000. 19.95 (0-7148-3941-8) Phaidon Pr.

— Descent from the Cross. 2000. 19.95 (0-7148-3942-6) Phaidon Pr.

— Fresh Cream. (Illus.). 2000. 49.95 (0-7148-3924-8) Phaidon Pr.

— Last Supper. 2000. 19.95 (0-7148-3940-X) Phaidon Pr.

Phaidon Press Staff. The Movie Book. (Illus.). 512p. 1999. 39.95 (0-7148-3847-0) Phaidon Pr.

— The 20th-Century Art Book: Mini Edition. LC 99-231396. (Illus.). 503p. 1999. pap. 9.95 (0-7148-3850-0) Phaidon Press.

Phaidon Press Staff, ed. The Fashion Book. LC 99-171151. (Illus.). 512p. 1998. 39.95 (0-7148-3808-X) Phaidon Pr.

Phaidon Staff. The Art Book. rev. ed. LC 96-137493. (Illus.). (C). 1994. 39.95 (0-7148-2984-6, Pub. by Phaidon Press) Phaidon Pr.

— The Pre-Raphaelite Vision. LC 99-495105. (Miniature Editions Ser.). (Orig.). (C). 1994. pap. 8.95 (0-7148-3252-9, Pub. by Phaidon Press) Phaidon Pr.

***Phair, Charles.** Atlantic Salmon Fishing. (Illus.). 288p. 1999. pap. 27.95 (1-56833-140-1, Pub. by Derrydale Pr) Natl Bk Netwk.

Phair, Charles. Atlantic Salmon Fishing. 219p. 1997. 39.95 (1-887269-03-7) J Culler & Sons.

Phair, John P. & Murphy, Robert L. Contemporary Diagnosis & Management of HIV/AIDS Infections. (Illus.). 175p. (Orig.). (C). 1997. pap. text 29.95 (1-884065-18-X) Assocs in Med.

Phair, Judith & King, Roland. Organizational Charts & Job Descriptions for the Advancement Office. Dorsey, Cathryn, ed. LC 99-183050. 191p. 1998. pap. 42.00 (0-89964-330-2, 28119) Coun Adv & Supp Ed.

Phair, Liz. Whip-Smart. 64p. 1997. otabind 19.95 (0-7935-4579-X) H Leonard.

Phair, Lynne & Good, Valerie. Dementia: A Positive Approach. LC 98-214568. 226p. 1998. 37.95 (1-86156-081-8) Whurr Pub.

Phalen, Carol C., jt. auth. see Wilson, Thomas B.

***Phalen, Diane.** Diane Phalen Quilts: 10 Projects to Celebrate the Seasons. Rymer, Cyndy & Lytle, Joyce, eds. LC 00-8285. (Illus.). 112p. 2000. pap. 25.95 (1-57120-106-8, Pub. by C & T Pub) Watsn-Guptill.

Phalen, Diane. Painting the American Heartland in Watercolor. LC 96-29887. (Illus.). 128p. 1997. pap. 23.99 (0-89134-747-X, North Lght Bks) F & W Pubns Inc.

Phalen, Harold R. History of the Town of Acton, MA. (Illus.). 471p. 1997. reprint ed. lib. bdg. 49.50 (0-8328-5957-5) Higginson Bk Co.

Phalen, Kathleen F. Integrative Medicine: Achieving Wellness Through the Best of Eastern & Western Medical Practices. LC 98-8672. (Illus.). 208p. 1998. 21.95 (1-885203-61-6) Jrny Editions.

— Wellness East & West: Achieving Optimum Health Through Integrative Medicine. 208p. 1999. pap. 16.95 (1-885203-96-9) Jrny Editions.

Phalen, Lane. The Book Lover's Guide to Boston & Cape Cod. (Book Lover's Buide Ser.). 256p. (Orig.). 1992. pap. 14.95 (1-880339-08-0) Brigadoon Bay.

— Book Lover's Guide to Washington, D. C. LC 93-72986. (Book Lover's Guide Ser.). 288p. (Orig.). 1993. pap. 14.95 (1-880339-09-9) Brigadoon Bay.

— The New Book Lover's Guide to Chicagoland: Including Southern Wisconsin. expanded ed. LC 95-79486. (Book Lover's Guide Ser.). 320p. 1995. reprint ed. pap. 14.95 (1-880339-11-0) Brigadoon Bay.

Phalen, Patricia, jt. auth. see Webster, James G.

***Phalen, Richard C.** A Bittersweet Journey: America's Fascination with Baseball. LC 00-25787. 2000. write for info. (0-9653846-1-6) McGregor Pub.

Phalen, Richard C. In Our Time: Rediscovering America, 1940-90's. LC 93-10742. 1993. 29.95 (0-912083-64-6, NO. 64-6) Diamond Communications.

Phalen, Robert F. Inhalation Studies: Foundations & Techniques. 288p. 1984. 163.00 (0-8493-5469-2, RA1270, CRC Reprint) Franklin.

Phalen, Robert F., ed. Methods in Inhalation Toxicology. (Methods in Toxicology Ser.). 176p. 1996. spiral bd. 94.95 (0-8493-3343-1) CRC Pr.

Phalen, Tim. 12-Lead ECG in Acute Myocardial Infarction. (Illus.). 252p. (C). (gr. 13). 1995. pap. text 29.00 (0-8151-6752-0, 25863) Mosby Inc.

Phalgunadi, Gusti P. Indonesian Mahabharata Bhismaparava. 1996. 50.00 (81-86471-05-7, Pub. by Aditya Prakashan) S Asia.

***Phalgunadi, I. G.** Indonesian Ramayan: The Uttarakanda. LC 99-932767. xvi, 240 p. 1999. 115.00 (81-7574-053-1, Pub. by S Asia) S Asia.

Phalgunadi, I. G., tr. The Indonesian Mahabharata, Adiparva: The First Book. (C). 1990. 59.50 (81-85179-50-6, Pub. by Aditya Prakashan) S Asia.

— Indonesian Mahabharata Udyogaparva. (C). 1994. text 58.00 (81-85689-96-2, Pub. by Popular Prakashan) S Asia.

Phalgunadi, I. Gusti Putu, see Putu Phalgunadi, I. Gusti.

Phalle, Niki De Saint, see De Saint Phalle, Niki.

Phalle, Therese De Saint, see De Saint Phalle, Therese.

Phalle, Thibaut D. The Federal Reserve System: An Intentional Mystery. LC 84-15879. 352p. 1984. pap. 19.95 (0-275-91803-3, B1803, Praeger Pubs) Greenwood.

— The Federal Reserve System: An Intentional Mystery. LC 84-15879. 352p. 1985. 69.50 (0-275-90083-5, C0083, Praeger Pubs) Greenwood.

Phaltankar, Kaustubh M. Practical Guide for Implementing Secure Intranets & Extranets. LC 99-45834. (Telecommunications Library). 401p. 1999. 83.00 (0-89006-447-4) Artech Hse.

Pham. Proton & Carbon NMR Spectra of Polymers. 1991. 330.00 (0-8493-7728-5, QC463) CRC Pr.

Pham & Garg. Multithread Program with Win32, 32. 320p. 1998. pap. text 49.99 (0-13-010912-6) P-H.

***Pham, Andrew X.** Catfish & Mandala: A Two-Wheeled Voyage Through the Landscape & Memory of Vietnam. LC 99-22711. 336p. 1999. text 25.00 (0-374-11974-0) FS&G.

— Catfish & Mandala: A Two-Wheeled Voyage Through the Landscape & Memory of Vietnam. 352p. 2000. pap. 14.00 (0-312-26717-7, Picador USA) St Martin.

Pham, Autumn. Vito J. Paratore. (Illus.). 56p. 1999. pap. 8.00 (0-8059-4425-7) Dorrance.

Pham, B. French-English Vocabulary of the Manufacture of Integrated Circuits. (ENG & FRE.). 246p. 1989. 125.00 (0-7859-9270-7) Fr & Eur.

***Pham, Binh, et al, eds.** New Approaches in Medical Image Analysis. 226p. 1999. pap. text 62.00 (0-8194-3229-6) SPIE.

Pham, C. Do, jt. ed. see Otani, I.

Pham, D. T. Robotics & AI: Sensing, Reasoning, Planning, Manipulation, Mobility. (Machine Tools & Manufacture Ser.: Vol. 28). 111p. 1988. 63.00 (0-08-036627-9, Pergamon Pr) Elsevier.

Pham, D. T., ed. Artificial Intelligence in Design. (Artificial Intelligence in Industry Ser.). (Illus.). 520p. 1991. 143.95 (0-387-50634-9) Spr-Verlag.

— Expert Systems in Engineering. (Artificial Intelligence in Industry Ser.). (Illus.). 450p. 1988. 104.00 (0-387-19229-8) Spr-Verlag.

Pham, D. T. & Heginbotham, W. B., eds. Robot Grippers. (International Trends in Manufacturing Technology Ser.). 360p. 1986. 126.95 (0-387-16004-3) Spr-Verlag.

Pham, D. T. & Karaboga, D. Intelligent Optimisation Techniques. LC 98-15571. (Illus.). x, 302p. 2000. pap. 74.95 (1-85233-028-7) Spr-Verlag.

Pham, D. T. & Oztemel, E. Intelligent Quality Systems. LC 96-8205. (Advanced Manufacturing Ser.). 201p. 1996. 89.95 (3-540-76045-8) Spr-Verlag.

Pham, D. T., ed. see Paashuis, Victor.

Pham, David L. Two Hampets in Nam Bo: Memoirs of Life in Vietnam Through Japanese Occupation, the French & American Wars & Communist Rule, 1940-1986. LC 99-54797. (Illus.). 307p. 1999. lib. bdg. 37.50 (0-7864-0646-1) McFarland & Co.

Pham, Duc T. & Xing, Liu. Neural Networks for Identification, Prediction & Control. LC 95-12935. (Illus.). 240p. 1995. 75.95 (3-540-19959-4) Spr-Verlag.

Pham, F. Singualarities des Systemes Differentiels de Gauss-Manin. (Progress in Mathematics Ser.: No. 2). (FRE.). 340p. 1980. 56.50 (0-8176-3002-3) Birkhauser.

Pham, H. & Hamza, M. H., eds. Reliability, Quality Control & Risk Assessment. 224p. 1993. 75.00 (0-88986-181-1, 202) Acta Pr.

— Reliability, Quality Control & Risk Assessment. 135p. 1994. 55.00 (0-88986-208-7, 217) Acta Pr.

Pham, Hoang. Proceedings of the ISSAT International Conference: Reliability & Quality in Design. 436p. (Orig.). (C). 1994. pap. text 60.00 (0-9639998-0-X) ISSAT.

— Software Reliability. LC 99-40446. (Illus.). 250p. 1999. pap. 29.95 incl. disk (981-3083-84-0) Spr-Verlag.

Pham, Hoang, ed. Proceedings of the 3rd ISSAT International Conference: Reliability & Quality in Design. (Orig.). (C). 1997. pap. text 60.00 (0-9639998-2-6) ISSAT.

— Software Reliability & Testing (3-95) LC 95-7582. 144p. 1995. pap. 39.00 (0-8186-6852-0, BP06852) IEEE Comp Soc.

Pham, Hoang & Lu, Ming-Wei, eds. Proceedings of the ISSAT 4th International Conference: Reliability & Quality in Design. 1998. pap. text 60.00 (0-9639998-3-4) ISSAT.

Pham, Hoangmai, et al. Understanding the Second Epidemic: The Status of Research on Women & AIDS in the United States. LC 91-81222. 63p. 1992. 8.00 (1-877966-11-8) Ctr Women Policy.

Pham, John-Peter. A Primer for the Catechism of the Catholic Church. 2nd ed. 112p. Date not set. reprint ed. pap. 4.95 (1-890177-01-6) Midwest Theol.

Pham, John-Peter, ed. The Sacrament of Penance in the Teaching of the Last Five Popes. 64p. (Orig.). 1996. pap. 4.00 (1-890177-02-4) Midwest Theol.

Pham, John-Peter, jt. auth. see Nguydcen, Phanxicco Xavice Vfan Thurcan.

Pham Kim Vinh. The Vietnamese Culture: An Introduction. rev. ed. (Illus.). 314p. 1994. pap. 18.00 (1-882273-25-7) P K Vinh Res.

— White Papers on Today's Vietnam: How the World Can Help the People of Vietnam Reach a Better Life. 164p. (Orig.). 1996. pap. 10.00 (1-882273-28-1) P K Vinh Res.

Pham Kim Vintl. Con Co Hoi Nao Cho Nguo i Quoc Gia - Any Opportunity to the Nationalists. 180p. (Orig.). 1997. pap. 10.00 (1-882273-29-X) P K Vinh Res.

Pham, Mai. The Best of Vietnamese & Thai Cooking: Favorite Recipes from Lemon Grass Restaurant & Cafe. LC 95-5281. (Illus.). 288p. 1995. pap. 19.95 (0-7615-0016-2) Prima Pub.

***Pham, T. N.** Licensed Fuel Facility Status Report: Inventory Difference Data, July 1, 1995-June 30, 1996. 18p. 1998. pap. 2.00 (0-16-062724-9) USGPO.

— Licensed Fuel Facility Status Report: Inventory Difference Data, July 1, 1996-June 30, 1997. 18p. 1998. pap. 2.00 (0-16-062772-9) USGPO.

Pham Van Bich. The Vietnamese Family in Change: The Case of the Red River Delta. 300p. 1998. text 48.00 (0-7007-1105-8, Pub. by Curzon Pr Ltd) UH Pr.

Pham Van Tien. Le Trinh Nu: Tho. LC 95-90282. (VIE.). 80p. 1995. pap. 6.50 (0-9645739-1-1) Van Pham Found.

Pham, X. Y., jt. auth. see Ho-Kim, Q.

Pham Xuam Nam, jt. ed. see Boothroyd, Peter.

***Pham, Xuan Huong Thi.** Mourning in the Ancient Near East & the Hebrew Bible. (Journal for the Study of the Old Testament Supplement Ser.: No. 302). 224p. 2000. 57.50 (1-84127-029-6, Pub. by Sheffield Acad) CUP Services.

An Asterisk (*) at the beginning of an entry indicates that the title is appearing for the first time.

***Phan Boi Chau.** Overturned Chariot: The Autobiography of Phan-Boi-Chau. Wickenden, Nicholas & Sinh, Vinh, trs. from VIE. LC 97-19313. (SHAPS Library of Translations). (Illus.). 288p. 1999. text 28.00 (*0-8248-1875-X*) UH Pr.

Phan Huy Ich, jt. auth. see Dang Tran Con.

Phan, K. H. Electron Microscopy & the Characterization of Keratin Fibres. 1991. pap. 42.00 (*0-7855-2812-1*, Pub. by Textile Inst) St Mut.

***Phan, Long T.** Fire Performance of High Strength Concrete, NIST, Gaithersburg, Maryland, February 13-14, 1997, Proceedings. 174p. 1998. per. 16.00 (*0-16-060861-9*) USGPO.

Phan, Long T. Fujita Tornado Intensity Scale: A Critique Based on Observations of the Jarrell Tornado Of May 27, 1997. 20p. 1998. pap. 3.75 (*0-16-056743-2*) USGPO.

Phan, Long T. & Taylor, Andrew W. State of the Art Report on Seismic Design Requirements for Nonstructural Building Components. (Illus.). 67p. (C). 1998. reprint ed. pap. text 20.00 (*0-7881-4242-9*) DIANE Pub.

Phan, Peter C. Eternity in Time: A Study of Karl Rahner's Eschatology. LC 86-43217. 272p. 1988. 39.50 (*0-941664-83-X*) Susquehanna U Pr.

— Mission & Catechesis: Alexander de Rhodes & Inculturation in the Seventeenth Century Vietnam. LC 97-42447. (Faith & Culture Ser.). 300p. 1998. 50.00 (*1-57075-166-8*) Orbis Bks.

— Responses to 101 Questions on Death & Eternal Life. LC 97-19963. (Responses to 101 Questions Ser.). 144p. (Orig.). 1997. pap. 9.95 (*0-8091-3711-9*, 3711-9) Paulist Pr.

— Social Thought. Halton, Thomas, ed. LC 83-83156. (Message of the Fathers of the Church Ser.: Vol. 20). 268p. 1984. pap. 14.95 (*0-8146-5331-6*) Liturgical Pr.

Phan, Peter C., ed. Christianity & the Wider Ecumenism. (New ERA Bks.). 320p. 1990. 29.95 (*0-89226-074-2*); pap. 14.95 (*0-89226-075-0*) Paragon Hse.

— Church & Theology: Essays in Memory of Carl J. Peter. LC 93-41316. 290p. 1995. 59.95 (*0-8132-0798-3*) Cath U Pr.

— Ethnicity, Nationality, & Religious Experience. (College Theology Society Annual Ser.: Vol. 37). 336p. (C). 1995. pap. text 29.50 (*0-8191-9524-3*); lib. bdg. 62.50 (*0-8191-9509-X*) U Pr of Amer.

***Phan, Peter C., ed.** The Gift of the Church: A Textbook on Ecclesiology. 544p. 2000. 39.95 (*0-8146-5931-4*) Liturgical Pr.

***Phan, Peter C. & Lee, Jung Young, eds.** Journeys at the Margin: Towards an Autobiographical Theology in American-Asian Perspective. LC 98-47088. 178p. 1999. pap. 17.95 (*0-8146-2464-2*) Liturgical Pr.

Phan, Seamus. Service Quality - The Enlightened Approach. (Illus.). 134p. (C). 1994. pap. 18.00 (*981-00-6457-8*) McGallen & Bolden.

Phan, Sem H. & Thrall, Roger S., eds. Pulmonary Fibrosis. LC 94-43568. (Lung Biology in Health & Disease Ser.: Vol. 80). (Illus.). 1008p. 1995. text 275.00 (*0-8247-8851-6*) Dekker.

Phan-Thien, Nhan, jt. auth. see Huilgol, R. R.

Phaneuf, Kaye, ed. see Eddy, Carolyn.

Phang, Andrew B., et al. Cheshire, Fifoot & Furmston's Law of Contract. LC 98-208699. 734p. 1998. write for info. (*0-409-99946-6*) Buttrwrth-Heinemann.

— Cheshire, Fifoot, & Furmston's Law of Contract. LC 98-229794. cxxxiii, 1158 p. 1998. write for info. (*0-409-99945-8*) Buttrwrth-Heinemann.

Phang, V. P. A List of Orchid Hybrids of Singapore & Malaysia, 1960-1980. 92p. (Orig.). 1983. pap. 20.00 (*9971-69-062-4*, Pub. by Sngapore Univ Pr) Coronet Bks.

Phansalkar, S. Making Growth Happen: Learning from Successful First-Generation Entrepreneurs. LC 98-37063. 1998. write for info. (*0-7619-9293-6*); pap. write for info. (*0-7619-9294-4*) Sage.

Phansalkar, S. J. How Not to Ruin Your Small Industry. LC 96-16092. 1996. 35.00 (*0-8039-9323-4*) Sage.

Phansalkar, S. J., jt. auth. see Gulati, V. P.

Phanta, Manny, tr. see Morton, Arthur.

Phantasia, Epiphany. Black Essence. (Illus.). 120p. (Orig.). 1995. pap. 19.95 (*0-9648732-0-6*) Phantasia IN.

Phantha, Manny, tr. see Morton, Arthur.

Phantha, Manny, tr. see Morton, Delma.

Phantha, Manny, tr. see Saul, Barbara.

Phantom Diner. The Best of the Phantom Diner. 184p. (Orig.). 1996. pap. 9.95 (*1-890106-03-8*) WITF.

Pharand, Donat. The Northeast Passage: Arctic Straits. 1984. lib. bdg. 110.00 (*90-247-2979-3*) Kluwer Academic.

Pharand, Donat & Leanza, Umberto, eds. The Continental Shelf & the Exclusive Economic Zone - Le Plateau Continental et la Zone Economique Exclusive: Delimitation & Legal Regime - Delimitation et Regime Juridique. LC 92-37816. (Publications on Ocean Development: Vol. 19). (ENG & FRE.). 1993. lib. bdg. 168.00 (*0-7923-2056-5*) Kluwer Academic.

Pharaoh, Timothy M., jt. auth. see Apel, Dieter.

Phares, jt. auth. see Trull.

Phares, David & Phares, Karen. Fly-Fishing Terms & Tips. (Easy Field Guide Ser.). (Illus.). 32p. (J). 1997. pap. 1.50 (*0-935810-64-1*) R H Pub.

Phares, E. Jerry. Clinical Psychology. 4th ed. 640p. (C). 1992. text 45.00 (*0-534-16830-2*) Brooks-Cole.

— Clinical Psychology: Concepts, Methods & Professions. 3rd ed. 596p. (C). 1988. mass mkt. 42.50 (*0-534-10762-1*) Brooks-Cole.

— Intro to Personality. 4th ed. LC 96-38681. 718p. (C). 1997. 86.00 (*0-673-99456-2*) Addison-Wesley.

— Introduction to Personality. 3rd ed. (C). 1991. text 75.94 (*0-673-46424-5*) Addson-Wesley Educ.

Phares, E. Jerry, ed. Introduction to Personality. 4th ed. (C). 1997. pap. text, student ed. write for info. (*0-673-99457-0*) Addison-Wesley.

Phares, E. Jerry & Trull, Timothy. Clinical Psychology, Concepts, Methods, & Profession. 5th ed. LC 96-33547. (Psychology Ser.). (C). 1996. mass mkt. 80.95 (*0-534-26298-8*) Brooks-Cole.

Phares, E. Jerry & Trull, Timothy J. Clinical Psychology: Concepts, Methods, & Profession, Test Bank. 5th ed. 1997. write for info. (*0-534-34576-X*) Brooks-Cole.

Phares, Jeff. Carving the Human Face: Capturing Character & Expression in Wood. 104p. 1999. pap. 24.95 (*1-56523-102-3*) Fox Chapel Pub.

Phares, Karen, jt. auth. see Phares, David.

Phares, M. I., jt. auth. see Grubb, C. A.

Phares, Ross. Bible in Pocket, Gun in Hand: The Story of Frontier Religion. LC 64-11375. vii, 182p. 1971. pap. 8.95 (*0-8032-5725-2*, Bison Books) U of Nebr Pr.

Phares, Tom K., jt. auth. see Jernstedt, George W.

Phares, Vicky. Fathers & Developmental Psychopathology. LC 95-20363. (Personality Processes Ser.). 405p. 1995. 80.00 (*0-471-59940-9*) Wiley.

— Poppa Psychology: The Role of Fathers in Children's Mental Well Being. LC 98-33614. 168p. 1999. 35.00 (*0-275-96367-5*, Praeger Pubs) Greenwood.

Pharies, David. Bibliography of Latin & Ibero-Romance Suffixation. (Bibliographical Ser.: No. 12). x, 103p. 1994. 20.00 (*1-56954-021-7*) Hispanic Seminary.

Pharies, David A. Charles S. Peirce & the Linguistic Sign. LC 85-11053. (Foundations of Semiotics Ser.: No. 9). vi, 118p. 1985. 39.00 (*90-272-3279-2*) J Benjamins Pubng Co.

Pharis, David B. State Hospital Reform: Why Was It So Hard to Accomplish? LC 98-40711. 300p. 1999. pap. 30.00 (*0-89089-886-3*) Carolina Acad Pr.

Pharis, R. P. & Reid, D. M., eds. Hormonal Regulation of Development III. (Encyclopedia of Plant Physiology Ser.: Vol. 11). (Illus.). 870p. 1985. 310.00 (*0-387-10197-7*) Spr-Verlag.

Pharith, K., jt. auth. see Graybill, E.

Pharmaceutical Society of Great Britain. European Pharmacopoeia, Pt. II-5. 2nd ed. 1983. 191.50 (*0-685-04362-2*, Pub. by Pharmaceutical Pr) Rittenhouse.

Pharmaceutical Society of Japan. Japanese Pharmaceutical Terms, Japanese-English-Japanese. 508p. 1985. 95.00 (*0-8288-1852-5*) Fr & Eur.

Pharmaceuticals & Cosmetics Manufacturing Expo Sta. Pharmaceuticals & Cosmetics Manufacturing Expo: Proceedings of Technical Program May 13-15, 1980, Rosemont, Illinois. LC TP0983.. 318p. reprint ed. pap. 98.60 (*0-608-14598-X*, 202083300019) Bks Demand.

Pharmacists in Ophthalmic Practice, Inc. Staff. Extemporaneous Ophthalmic Preparations. Closson, Richard G. & Reynolds, Lois A., eds. LC 93-72671. (Illus.). 347p. (Orig.). 1993. pap. 37.50 (*0-915486-18-0*) Applied Therapeutics.

Pharmaco Medical Doc., Inc. Staff. Index Guide 11. Anzlowar, Rajka, ed. 1997. 680.00 (*0-913210-18-8*) Pharmaco-Med.

Pharmacology of Thermoregulation symposium Staff. Temperature Regulation & Drug Action: Proceedings of the Pharmacology of Thermoregulation Symposium, 2nd, Paris, 1974. Schonbaum, Edward & Lommax, P., eds. 450p. 1974. 129.75 (*3-8055-1756-4*) S Karger.

Pharmacology of Thermoregulation Symposium Staff, et al. Drugs, Biogenic Amines & Body Temperature: Proceedings of the Pharmacology of Thermoregulation Symposium, 3rd, Banff, Alberta, Sept. 1976. Cooper, K. E., ed. (Illus.). 1977. 101.00 (*3-8055-2395-5*) S Karger.

Pharmex Staff. Pharmex Family Guide to Prescription Drugs. 310p. Date not set. pap. text 5.95 (*0-89529-715-9*, Avery) Penguin Putnam.

Pharoah Games Staff. Pelicar: The Official Game Book. LC 96-204994. (Illus.). 237p. (Orig.). 1996. pap. 25.00 (*0-9653166-0-2*) Ivory & Steel.

Pharoah, Timothy M., jt. auth. see Collins, Michael F.

Pharr, Clyde. Vergil's Aeneid, Bks. 1-6. 518p. 1998. pap. text 24.00 (*0-86516-421-5*) Bolchazy-Carducci.

— Vergil's Aeneid, Bks. 1-6. LC 98-101774. 518p. 1998. reprint ed. 36.00 (*0-86516-433-9*) Bolchazy-Carducci.

Pharr, Clyde & Wright, John. Homeric Greek. rev. ed. LC 84-40698. (Illus.). 416p. 1986. pap. 21.95 (*0-8061-1937-3*) U of Okla Pr.

Pharr, Clyde, tr. see Codex Theodosianus.

***Pharr, Daniel.** Moon Wise: Astrology, Self Understanding & Lunar Energies. 2000. pap. 12.95 (*1-56718-521-5*) Llewellyn Pubns.

Pharr, David. Modern Messages from the Minor Prophets. 1986. pap. 6.95 (*0-89137-330-6*) Quality Pubns.

Pharr, Donald, jt. auth. see Schiffhorst, Gerald J.

Pharr, Mary, jt. auth. see Heldreth, Leonard G.

Pharr, Mary, jt. ed. see Heldreth, Leonard G.

Pharr, Mary O. Woodward's Mill: Its History in Deeds, Stories, Pictures & Memories. 2nd rev. ed. (Illus.). 79p. 1995. pap. 12.00 (*0-614-14824-3*) Gwinnett Hist.

Pharr, Robert D. Giveadamn Brown. LC 96-9577. 224p. 1997. pap. 11.00 (*0-393-31539-8*) Norton.

Pharr, Robert Deane. S. R. O. LC 97-32047. (Old School Bks.). 384p. 1998. pap. 15.00 (*0-393-31706-4*) Norton.

Pharr, Susan J. Losing Face: Status Politics in Japan. 1990. 40.00 (*0-520-06050-4*, Pub. by U CA Pr) Cal Prin Full Svc.

— Losing Face: Status Politics in Japan. 1992. pap. 15.95 (*0-520-08092-0*, Pub. by U CA Pr) Cal Prin Full Svc.

Pharr, Susan J. & Krauss, Ellis S., eds. Media & Politics in Japan. LC 95-8730. 1996. text 50.00 (*0-8248-1698-6*); pap. text 19.95 (*0-8248-1761-3*) UH Pr.

***Pharr, Susan J. & Putnam, Robert D., eds.** Disaffected Democracies: What's Troubling the Trilateral Countries? LC 99-49292. (Illus.). 360p. 2000. 65.00 (*0-691-04923-8*, Pub. by Princeton U Pr); pap. 19.95 (*0-691-04924-6*, Pub. by Princeton U Pr) Cal Prin Full Svc.

Pharr, Suzanne. Homophobia: A Weapon of Sexism. 2nd rev. ed. LC 97-68239. (Illus.). 128p. 1997. pap. 12.00 (*1-890759-01-5*) Chardon Pr.

— In the Time of the Right: Reflections on Liberation. LC 96-84155. 122p. (Orig.). 1996. pap. 10.95 (*0-9620222-8-4*) Chardon Pr.

Pharr, Suzanne, et al. Eyes Right! Challenging the Right Wing Backlash. Berlet, Chip, ed. LC 95-25597. 400p. (C). 1995. pap. 17.00 (*0-89608-523-6*) South End Pr.

Pharr, Virginia & Watson, Janet. Growing in Care of the Earth, Vol. 4. (Life in Abundance Ser.). 96p. 1998. pap. 7.95 (*0-88489-579-3*) St Marys.

Pharrams, Doris & Charles, Anna. All Day...All God. 52p. (Orig.). 1995. pap. 5.95 (*0-9645558-0-8*) Gift of Love.

Phased Array Antenna Symposium (1970: Polytechnic. Phased Array Antennas: Proceedings of the 1970 Phased Array Antenna Symposium. Oliner, Arthur A., ed. LC TK6590.A6P45. (Modern Frontiers in Applied Science Ser.). 393p. reprint ed. pap. 121.90 (*0-608-16258-2*, 202716200054) Bks Demand.

Phatak, Arvind V. International Dimensions Of Management. Ricks, David A., ed. LC 82-17131. (SWC-Management). 160p. (C). 1983. pap. 14.00 (*0-534-01317-1*) PWS Pubs.

— International Dimensions Of Management. 2nd ed. (SWC-Management). 192p. (C). 1988. pap. 14.50 (*0-534-87192-5*, P954) PWS Pubs.

— International Management. (GN - International Business Ser.). 1996. mass mkt. 85.95 (*0-538-85415-4*) S-W Pub.

Phatak, Avind V. International Dimensions of Management. 4th ed. LC 94-21634. (C). 1994. mass mkt. 30.95 (*0-538-84485-X*) S-W Pub.

Phatek, S. & Satpathy, L., eds. High Energy Heavy Ion Collisions & Quark Degrees of Freedom in Nuclei: Proceedings of the Nuclear Workshop of Institute of Physics. 444p. 1987. text 124.00 (*9971-5-0353-0*) World Scientific Pub.

Phaup, Marvin. Assessing the Public Costs & Benefits of Fannie Mae & Freddie Mac. (Illus.). 45p. (Orig.). (C). 1996. pap. text 30.00 (*0-7881-3039-0*) DIANE Pub.

Phay, Robert E. & Ward, Robert M. Local Acts Creating & Providing for North Carolina City School Administrative Units. 423p. (Orig.). (C). 1972. pap. text 4.50 (*1-56011-173-9*, 72.15) Institute Government.

Phay, Wilbert L. John Brown's Family in Red Bluff, 1864-1870. (ANCRR Occasional Publications: No. 12). 66p. 1986. 6.00 (*0-614-05682-9*) Assn NC Records.

Phayer, J. Michael. Protestant & Catholic Women in Nazi Germany. LC 89-16574. (Illus.). 288p. (C). 1990. text 39.95 (*0-8143-2211-5*) Wayne St U Pr.

***Phayer, Michael.** The Catholic Church & the Holocaust, 1930-1965. LC 99-87415. 2000. 29.95 (*0-253-33725-9*) Ind U Pr.

Phayer, Michael & Fleischner, Eva. Cries in the Night: Women Who Challenged the Holocaust. LC 97-24419. (Illus.). 168p. (Orig.). 1997. pap. 15.95 (*1-55612-977-7*, LL1977-7) Sheed & Ward WI.

Phayre, Arthur. The Journal of Arthur Phayre, Envoy to the Court of Ava. 31.00 (*0-19-638075-8*) OUP.

Pheanis, Dd. C., ed. Computers & Their Applications (CATA-94), 7th International Conference March 17-19, 1994, Long Beach, California, U.S.A.: Conference Proceedings March 17-19, 1994 Long Beach, CA. 205p. 1994. write for info. (*1-880843-08-0*) Int Soc Comp App.

Phear, John B. Aryan Village in India & Ceylon. (C). 1995. reprint ed. 26.00 (*81-206-1141-1*, Pub. by Asian Educ Servs) S Asia.

Phears, Bill, jt. auth. see Mann, Hiram.

Phears, William. It's up to Us: A Recipe for Leveling the Playing Field. LC 96-130984. 144p. 1995. pap. 12.95 (*1-878398-39-3*) Blue Note Pubns.

Phears, William D. Ain't, but It Can Be: Persistence & Faith Overcoming Racist-Related Adversities. LC 93-72874. 323p. 1993. pap. 12.95 (*1-878398-37-7*) Blue Note Pubns.

Pheasant, Stephen. Bodyspace: Anthropometry, Ergonomics, & the Design of Work. 2nd ed. LC 97-103991. 256p. 1996. 85.00 (*0-7484-0067-2*, Pub. by Tay Francis Ltd) Taylor & Francis.

— Bodyspace: Anthropometry, Ergonomics & the Design of Work. 2nd ed. LC 97-103991. 256p. 1996. pap. 39.95 (*0-7484-0326-4*, Pub. by Tay Francis Ltd) Taylor & Francis.

Phebus, George, Jr. Alaskan Eskimo Life in the 1890s: As Sketched by Native Artists. 1995. pap. 18.95 (*0-912006-79-X*) U of Alaska Pr.

Pheby, John. Methodology & Economics: A Critical Introduction. LC 90-28626. 145p. (C). (gr. 13). 1991. text 64.95 (*0-87332-851-5*) M E Sharpe.

Pheby, John. Methodology & Economics: A Critical Introduction. LC 90-28626. 145p. (C). (gr. 13). 1991. pap. text 32.95 (*0-87332-852-3*) M E Sharpe.

Pheby, John, ed. J. A. Hobson after 50 Years: Free Thinker of the Social Sciences. LC 93-11883. 1994. text 79.95 (*0-312-10637-8*) St Martin.

— New Directions in Post-Keynesian Economics. (New Directions in Modern Economics Ser.). 288p. 1989. text 100.00 (*1-85278-013-4*) E Elgar.

Pheby, John, tr. see Lang, Ewald.

Pheby, Keith C. Interventions: Displacing the Metaphysical Subject. (Post Modern Positions Ser.: Vol. 3). 136p. (Orig.). (C). 1988. pap. text 9.95 (*0-944624-05-7*); lib. bdg. 18.95 (*0-944624-04-9*) Maisonneuve Pr.

Phegan, Barry. Developing Your Company Culture: The Joy of Leadership. (Illus.). 172p. (Orig.). 1996. pap. 12.95 (*0-9642205-0-4*) Context Pr CA.

Phegan, C. S., jt. auth. see Cavanaugh, S. W.

Pheifer, J. & Cuilleanain, Ni, eds. Noble & Joyous Histories: English Romances, 1375-1650. 1993. 39.50 (*0-7165-2379-5*, Pub. by Irish Acad Pr) Intl Spec Bk.

Phelan, jt. auth. see Cowans.

Phelan, Andrew. Ireland from the Sea. LC 99-175789. 256p. 1999. pap. 15.95 (*0-86327-633-4*, Pub. by Wolfhound Press) Irish Amer Bk.

Phelan, Angela. Kitchens. LC 97-7241. (For Your Home Ser.). (Illus.). 72p. 1997. 24.95 (*1-56799-483-0*, Friedman-Fairfax) M Friedman Pub Grp Inc.

Phelan, Anne, ed. 1995 Guide to Coal Contracts. 690p. (Orig.). 1995. pap. 270.00 (*0-935453-76-8*) Pasha Pubns.

Phelan, Carolyn. Science Books for Young People. 88p. (YA). 1996. pap. text 9.95 (*0-8389-7837-1*) ALA.

Phelan, Charles J. 101 Business Opportunity Scams: How to Recognize & Avoid Rip-Offs. LC 96-75923. 130p. (Orig.). 1996. pap. 19.95 (*0-9652288-1-9*) Manchstr Pub.

Phelan, Chas. Dried Fruit: Its Care, Protection from Worms, Packing, Storing, Etc. (Shorey Lost Arts Ser.). 48p. reprint ed. pap. 10.00 (*0-8466-6049-0*, U49) Shoreys Bkstore.

Phelan, Craig. Divided Loyalties: The Public & Private Life of Labor Leader John Mitchell. LC 93-42744. (SUNY Series in American Labor History). 438p. (C). 1994. text 64.50 (*0-7914-2087-6*); pap. text 21.95 (*0-7914-2088-4*) State U NY Pr.

***Phelan, Craig.** Grand Master Workman: Terence Powderly & The Knights of Labor, 55. LC 99-16145. Vol. 55. 304p. 2000. 65.00 (*0-313-30948-5*) Greenwood.

Phelan, Dennis M., jt. ed. see Klain, Ambrose.

Phelan, Diarmuid R. It's God They Ought to Crucify: Validity & Authority in Law. 96p. 1999. boxed set 24.95 (*1-85182-439-1*, Pub. by Four Cts Pr) Intl Spec Bk.

— It's God We Ought to Crucify. 120p. 1996. 22.00 (*90-802267-4-2*, Pub. by NeXed Edits) Intl Spec Bk.

Phelan, Diarmuid R., jt. auth. see Rudden, Bernard.

Phelan, Donald J. Success, Happiness, Independence: Own Your Own Business. LC 94-79175. 183p. 1995. 19.95 (*0-944435-31-9*) Glenbridge Pub.

Phelan, Dorothy. Traditional Bargello: Stitches, Techniques, & Dozens of Pattern & Project Ideas. (Illus.). 96p. (Orig.). 1991. pap. 15.95 (*0-312-06882-4*) St Martin.

Phelan, Ellen. Joel Shapiro: Painted Wood Sculpture & Drawings. Newman, Amy, ed. LC 95-60651. (Illus.). 59p. (Orig.). 1995. pap. write for info. (*1-878283-49-9*) PaceWildenstein.

Phelan, Gerald B. St. Thomas & Analogy. (Aquinas Lectures). 1941. 15.00 (*0-87462-105-4*) Marquette.

Phelan, Gerald B., tr. see Maritain, Jacques.

Phelan, Gladys, tr. see Fierz-David, Linda.

Phelan, Helene C. The Man Who Owned the Pistols. (Illus.). 336p. (Orig.). 1981. pap. 8.50 (*0-9605836-0-2*) Phelan.

— Who Only Stand & Wait? (Illus.). 406p. (Orig.). 1990. pap. 16.95 (*0-9605836-6-1*) Phelan.

Phelan, Helene C., ed. see Kingman, Eugene C.

Phelan, Helmholtz A. Von, see Von Phelan, Helmholtz A.

Phelan, J. C., jt. ed. see Aneshensel, C. S.

Phelan, J. P., ed. Clough: Selected Poems. LC 94-20379. (Annotated Texts Ser.). 304p. (C). 1995. 85.00 (*0-582-05113-4*, 77035) Addison-Wesley.

— Clough: Selected Poems. LC 94-20379. (Annotated Texts Ser.). 304p. (C). 1996. pap. text 27.50 (*0-582-05112-6*, 77034, Pub. by Addison-Wesley) Longman.

Phelan, J. R. & Chester, Laura. The Money: The Battle for Howard Hughes's Billions. 1997. 23.00 (*0-679-44884-5*) Random.

Phelan, James. Narrative As Rhetoric: Technique, Audiences, Ethics, Ideology. LC 95-50365. (Theory & Interpretation of Narrative Ser.). 237p. (C). 1996. pap. text 14.95 (*0-8142-0689-1*) Ohio St U Pr.

— Reading People, Reading Plots: Character, Progression, & the Interpretation of Narrative. LC 88-20840. 250p. 1997. pap. text 17.00 (*0-226-66692-1*) U Ch Pr.

— Worlds from Words: A Theory of Language in Fiction. LC 80-25844. (Chicago Original Paperback Ser.). xi, 259 p. 1995. pap. text 24.00 (*0-226-66690-5*) U Ch Pr.

— Worlds from Words: A Theory of Language in Fiction. LC 80-25844. 271p. reprint ed. pap. 84.10 (*0-608-09033-6*, 206966800005) Bks Demand.

Phelan, James & Rabinowitz, Peter J., eds. Understanding Narrative. LC 94-5731. (Theory & Interpretation of Narrative Ser.). 287p. 1994. pap. text 18.95 (*0-8142-0634-4*) Ohio St U Pr.

Phelan, James, ed. see Duval, Frank.

Phelan, James, ed. see Twain, Mark, pseud.

Phelan, James R. & Chester, Lewis. The Money: The Battle for Howard Hughes's Millions. 1997. 31.00 (*0-614-28018-4*) Random.

Phelan, Jay, jt. auth. see Burnham, Terry.

Phelan, Jim. The Name's Phelan: The First Part of the Autobiography of Jim Phelan. 298p. 1993. pap. 11.95 (*0-85640-504-3*, Pub. by Blackstaff Pr) Dufour.

Phelan, Joan A., jt. auth. see Ibsen, Olga A.

***Phelan, John E., Jr.** The Church in the Postmodern World. 60p. 2000. mass mkt. 4.99 (*0-87508-479-6*, 479) Chr Lit.

Phelan, John L. The Hispanization of the Philippines: Spanish Aims & Filipino Responses, 1565-1700. LC 59-8602. (Illus.). 240p. reprint ed. pap. 74.40 (*0-7837-1667-2*, 205243800024) Bks Demand.

— The People & the King: The Comunero Revolution in Columbia. LC 76-53654. (Illus.). 331p. reprint ed. pap. 102.70 (*0-608-09920-1*, 206925800003) Bks Demand.

P

Phelan, Joseph F. The Half-Mile Bridge: Lessons of Truth on America's Nonprofit Landscape. LC 96-28821. 1996. pap. text 35.00 (*0-7618-0455-2*); lib. bdg. 62.00 (*0-7618-0454-4*) U Pr of Amer.

Phelan, Laurel. Guinevere: The True Story of One Woman's Quest for Her Past Life Identity & the Healing of Her Eternal Soul. Bestler, Emily, ed. LC 95-38899. 320p. 1996. 22.00 (*0-671-52611-1*, PB Hardcover) PB.

— Guinevere: The True Story of One Woman's Quest for Her Past Life Identity & the Healing of Her Eternal Soul. 1997. per. 14.00 (*0-671-52615-4*) PB.

Phelan, Lisa. Parenting 101. 168p. (Orig.). 1995. pap. 5.95 (*1-56245-188-X*) Great Quotations.

Phelan, Louise, ed. Just Recipes. (Illus.). 312p. 1995. spiral bd. 21.00 (*0-9640488-0-9*) Problems in Ethics.

Phelan, Margaret. Mandy. LC 97-65965. 200p. (Orig.). 1997. pap. 9.95 (*1-57197-060-6*) Pentland Pr.

Phelan, Margaret, ed. Immigration Law Handbook. 537p. 1997. 84.00 (*1-85431-596-X*, Pub. by Blackstone Pr) Gaunt.

Phelan, Marilyn E. The Law of Cultural Property & Natural Heritage: Protection, Transfer & Access. 1998. pap. 95.00 (*0-9643080-1-0*) Kalos Kapp.

— Museum Law: Officers & Counsel. 392p. 1994. pap. 89.00 (*0-9643080-0-2*) Kalos Kapp.

— Nonprofit Enterprise: Law & Taxation, 3 vols. LC 85-7870. 1990. 350.00 (*0-685-10477-X*) West Group.

— Representing Nonprofit Organizations. 1994. 95.00 (*0-318-72537-1*) West Group.

Phelan, Mary K. The Story of the Boston Massacre. LC 75-25961. (Illus.). 160p. (J). (gr. 4-7). 1990. lib. bdg. 13.89 (*0-690-04883-1*) HarpC Child Bks.

— The Story of the Boston Tea Party. LC 72-7554. (Illus.). (J). (gr. 5-9). 1973. 12.95 (*0-690-77653-5*) HarpC Child Bks.

— Waterway West: The Story of the Erie Canal. LC 77-1787. (Illus.). (J). (gr. 5-9). 1977. 12.95 (*0-690-01333-7*) HarpC Child Bks.

Phelan, Michael, et al, eds. Emergency Mental Health Services in the Community. (Studies in Social & Community Psychiatry). (Illus.). 375p. (C). 1995. text 90.00 (*0-521-45251-1*) Cambridge U Pr.

Phelan, Nancy. The Romantic Lives of Louise Mack. 1991. pap. 19.95 (*0-7022-2361-1*, Pub. by Univ Queensland Pr) Intl Spec Bk.

— Setting Out on the Voyage. LC 98-217321. 1998. pap. 19.95 (*0-7022-2996-2*, Pub. by Univ Queensland Pr) Intl Spec Bk.

Phelan, Patricia, ed. High Interest - Easy Reading: An Annotated Booklist for Middle School & Senior High School. 7th ed. 115p. 1996. 11.95 (*0-8141-2098-9*) NCTE.

Phelan, Patricia & Davidson, Ann L. Renegotiating Cultural Diversity in American Schools. LC 93-22720. 272p. (C). 1993. pap. text 18.95 (*0-8077-3287-7*) Tchrs Coll.

Phelan, Patricia, et al. Adolescent Worlds: The Experience of Home, School & Peers. LC 97-37091. 1997. 50.00 (*0-8077-3682-1*); pap. 23.95 (*0-8077-3681-3*) Tchrs Coll.

Phelan, Patricia J., jt. auth. see Davidson, Ann L.

Phelan, Peggy. The Ends of Performance. Lane, Jill, ed. LC 97-33733. 1997. pap. text 19.00 (*0-8147-6647-1*) NYU Pr.

— Mourning Sex: Performing Public Memories. LC 96-9345. 208p. (C). 1997. pap. 20.99 (*0-415-14759-X*) Routledge.

— Mourning Sex: Performing Public Memories. LC 96-9345. (Illus.). 208p. (C). 1997. 85.00 (*0-415-14758-1*) Routledge.

— Unmarked: The Politics of Performance. LC 92-7895. (Illus.). 224p. (C). 1993. pap. 22.99 (*0-415-06822-3*, A9654) Routledge.

Phelan, Peggy, ed. The Ends of Performance. LC 97-33733. 1997. text 55.00 (*0-8147-6646-3*) NYU Pr.

Phelan, Peggy, jt. ed. see Hart, Lynda.

Phelan, Peter & Reynolds, Peter. Argument & Evidence: Critical Analysis for the Social Sciences. LC 95-15784. 272p. (C). (gr. 13). 1996. 75.00 (*0-415-11372-5*) Routledge.

Phelan, Peter D., jt. auth. see Reynolds, Peter.

***Phelan, Regina V.** They Came Around the Horn. LC 99-36653. (Illus.). (J). 1999. write for info. (*0-87062-292-7*, Prosperity Press) A H Clark.

Phelan, Richard M. Fundamentals of Mechanical Design. 3rd ed. LC 79-98487. (C). 1970. text 84.00 (*0-07-049776-1*) McGraw.

Phelan, Robert, ed. see Johnson, Charles & Adelman, Bob.

Phelan, Robin E., jt. auth. see Cowans, Daniel R.

Phelan, Shane. Getting Specific: Postmodern Lesbian Politics. 1994. pap. 17.95 (*0-8166-2110-1*) U of Minn Pr.

— Identity Politics: Lesbian Feminism & the Limits of Community. (Women in the Political Economy Ser.). 256p. (C). 1989. 22.95 (*0-87722-651-2*); pap. 19.95 (*0-87722-902-3*) Temple U Pr.

***Phelan, Shane.** Sexual Strangers: Gays, Lesbians & Dilemmas of Citizenship. (Queer Politics, Queer Theories Ser.). 232p. 2001. 59.50 (*1-56639-827-4*); pap. 18.95 (*1-56639-828-2*) Temple U Pr.

Phelan, Shane, ed. Playing with Fire: Queer Politics, Queer Theories. LC 95-51728. 384p. (C). 1997. 70.00 (*0-415-91416-7*); pap. 18.99 (*0-415-91417-5*) Routledge.

Phelan, Shane, jt. ed. see Blasius, Mark.

***Phelan, Steven.** Strategic Management, 2000. 264p. 2000. write for info. (*1-58692-018-9*) Copyright Mgmt.

Phelan, Susan. Blood Collection: Special Procedures. 1991. 145.00 incl. VHS (*0-89189-309-1*, D47-9-055-VH) Am Soc Clinical.

— Blood Collection: The Pediatric Patient. (NLM Ser.: No. WB382). 1990. 145.00 incl. VHS (*0-89189-302-4*, 47-9-052-VH) Am Soc Clinical.

— Phlebotomy Techniques: A Laboratory Workbook. 1993. wbk. ed. 35.00 (*0-89189-343-1*) Am Soc Clinical.

— Phlebotomy Techniques Curriculum Guide. 1993. 20.00 (*0-89189-359-8*) Am Soc Clinical.

Phelan, Susan E. Phlebotomy Review Guide. LC 98-23247. 1998. 49.00 (*0-89189-433-0*) Am Soc Clinical.

Phelan, Thomas. The Hudson: Mohawk Gateway-An Illustrated History. 192p. 1985. 22.95 (*0-89781-118-6*) Am Historical Pr.

Phelan, Thomas A. Code Name: Octopus. 220p. 2000. pap. 7.99 (*1-889122-49-1*, Pub. by Ariel Starr) ACCESS Pubs Network.

***Phelan, Thomas W.** All about Attention Deficit Disorder. 2nd ed. 2000. pap. 12.95 (*1-889140-11-2*) Child Mgmt.

Phelan, Thomas W. All about Attention Deficit Disorder: Basic Symptoms, Diagnosis & Treatment Children & Adults. rev. ed. (Illus.). 172p. 1993. pap. 12.95 (*0-9633861-1-5*) Child Mgmt.

— All about Attention Deficit Disorder: Symptoms, Diagnosis & Treatment: Children & Adults. 2nd ed. (Illus.). 172p. 1996. reprint ed. pap. 12.95 (*1-889140-00-7*) Child Mgmt.

— 1-2-3 Magia: Disciplina Efectiva para Ninos de 2 a 12. Seijo, Lois, tr.Tr. of One-Two-Three Magic: Effective Discipline for Children 2-12. (ENG & SPA., Illus.). 104p. (Orig.). 1996. pap. 9.95 (*1-889140-02-3*) Child Mgmt.

— 1-2-3 Magic: Effective Discipline for Children 2-12. 2nd rev. ed. (Illus.). 180p. 1996. pap. 12.95 (*0-9633861-9-0*) Child Mgmt.

— One-Two-Three Magic: Training Your Children to Do What You Want! rev. ed. (Illus.). 180p. 1994. pap. 12.95 (*0-9633861-2-3*) Child Mgmt.

— Self-Esteem Revolutions in Children: Understanding & Managing the Critical Transitions in Your Child's Life. (Illus.). 172p. (Orig.). 1996. pap. 12.95 (*1-889140-01-5*) Child Mgmt.

— Surviving Your Adolescents: How to Manage & Let Go of Your 13 to 18 Year Olds. 2nd ed. 1998. pap. 12.95 (*1-889140-08-2*) Child Mgmt.

***Phelan, Tom.** Derrycloney. LC 99-492093. 273p. 1999. pap. 17.95 (*0-86322-253-6*, Pub. by Brandon Bk Pubs) Irish Bks Media.

Phelan, Tom. In the Season of the Daisies. LC 96-25813. 226p. 1996. 22.00 (*1-56858-074-6*) FWEW.

— In the Season of the Daisies. 2nd ed. LC 96-25813. 238p. 1998. reprint ed. pap. 12.95 (*1-56858-108-4*) FWEW.

***Phelan, Tom.** Iscariot. 2nd ed. 279p. 1998. reprint ed. pap. 13.95 (*0-86322-246-3*, Pub. by Brandon Bk Pubs) Irish Bks Media.

Phelan, Virginia. Praying in Your Own Voice...Through Writing. LC 94-78949. 64p. (Orig.). 1994. pap. 3.95 (*0-89243-682-4*) Liguori Pubns.

Phelan, Virginia B. Two Ways of Life & Death. LC 90-3497. (Studies in Comparative Literature). 272p. 1990. reprint ed. 15.00 (*0-8240-0050-1*) Garland.

Phelan, Walter S. The Christmas Hero & Yuletide Tradition in Sir Gawain & the Green Knight. LC 92-28373. (Illus.). 325p. 1992. text 99.95 (*0-7734-9568-1*) E Mellen.

Phelan, Wesley G., jt. auth. see Glitsky, Theodoar.

Phelan, Wynne H., jt. auth. see Neff, Emily Ballew.

***Phelge, James.** Nankering with the Rolling Stones: The Untold Story of the Early Days. LC 99-54413. (Illus.). 305p. 2000. pap. 16.95 (*1-55652-373-4*) A Cappella Bks.

Phelge, James. Phelge's Stones. 350p. 1998. pap. 20.00 (*0-9664338-0-7*) B A Bks.

Phelizon, Jean-Francois. Dictionnaire de l'Economie. 4th ed. (ENG & FRE.). 352p. 1985. pap. 39.95 (*0-7859-7952-2*, 2717810382) Fr & Eur.

Phelon, Donald T. The Tanaiste. 408p. mass mkt. 5.99 (*1-896320-33-3*) Picasso Publ.

Phelon, Mira M., jt. auth. see Phelon, William P.

Phelon, W. P. Our Story of Atlantis. 242p. 1972. 9.95 (*0-932785-36-0*) Philos Pub.

— The Three Sevens: A Story of Ancient Initiation. deluxe ed. 238p. 1977. lthr. 20.00 (*1-891485-10-5*) Philos Pub.

Phelon, William P. & Phelon, Mira M. The Three Sevens: A Story of Ancient Initiation. Clymer, R. Swinburne, ed. 238p. 1977. 9.95 (*0-932785-47-6*) Philos Pub.

***Pheloung, Barbara.** Help Your Class to Learn: Effective Perceptual Movement Programs for Your Classroom. (Illus.). 160p. 1998. pap. 13.95 (*0-646-33096-9*) Pheloung.

Phelphs, Will. The Revolutionary Guide to Visual FoxPro OOP. 600p. 1996. pap. 46.95 incl. cd-rom (*1-874416-40-0*) Wrox Pr Inc.

Phelps. Quick Reference to Nursing Assessment. (Nursing Education Ser.). (C). 1998. pap. text 26.95 (*0-8273-7893-9*) Delmar.

Phelps & Servin. Phelps Family of America & Their English Ancestry, 2 vols. in 1. (Illus.). 1865p. 1989. reprint ed. pap. 259.00 (*0-8328-0963-2*); reprint ed. lib. bdg. 267.00 (*0-8328-0962-4*) Higginson Bk Co.

Phelps & Associates Staff, ed. see Ross, Robert.

Phelps, Albert. Louisiana: A Record of Expansion. LC 72-3748. (American Commonwealths Ser.: No. 18). reprint ed. 42.50 (*0-404-57218-9*) AMS Pr.

Phelps, Amos A. Lectures on Slavery & Its Remedy. LC 70-92438. 1970. reprint ed. 39.00 (*0-403-00182-X*) Scholarly.

Phelps, Arthur J. The Story of Merwin, Hulbert & Company Firearms. LC 91-65703. 226p. 1993. 56.00 (*1-882824-00-8*) Graphic Pubs.

Phelps, Arthur L. Canadian Writers. LC 73-38030. (Essay Index Reprint Ser.). 1977. reprint ed. 16.95 (*0-8369-2617-X*) Ayer.

Phelps, Austin, et al. Hymns & Choirs. LC 78-144671. reprint ed. 32.50 (*0-404-07207-0*) AMS Pr.

Phelps, Brian, jt. auth. see Phelps, Erika.

Phelps-Brown, Henry. The Origins of Trade Union Power. LC 83-1920. 336p. 1983. 39.95 (*0-19-877115-0*) OUP.

— The Origins of Trade Union Power. LC 83-1920. 336p. 1986. pap. 16.95 (*0-19-285156-X*) OUP.

Phelps, Carol A. Three Short Romances. (Illus.). 1977. boxed set 12.00 (*0-87770-195-4*) Ye Galleon.

Phelps, Charles D. & Hansjoerg, E. J., eds. Manual of Common Ophthalmic Surgical Procedures. LC 86-17157. (Illus.). 203p. (Orig.). reprint ed. pap. 63.00 (*0-7837-2557-4*, 204271600006) Bks Demand.

***Phelps, Charles E.** Falstaff & Equity: An Interpretation. xvi, 201p. 1999. reprint ed. 66.00 (*1-56169-561-0*) Gaunt.

Phelps, Charles E. Health Economics. 2nd ed. LC 96-47469. 687p. (C). 1997. 90.00 (*0-673-99398-1*) Addison-Wesley.

Phelps, Charles E., jt. auth. see Kraus, Robert.

Phelps, Christina. The Anglo-American Peace Movement in the Mid-Nineteenth Century. LC 76-37906. (Select Bibliographies Reprint Ser.). 1977. reprint ed. 19.95 (*0-8369-6744-5*) Ayer.

Phelps, Christopher. Young Sidney Hook: Marxist & Pragmatist. LC 97-23738. (Illus.). 280p. 1997. text 35.00 (*0-8014-3328-2*) Cornell U Pr.

Phelps County Genealogical Society Staff. Harry R. McCaw Undertaking Parlor (Records), 1902-1935. 241p. 1989. pap. 60.00 (*1-893474-05-4*) Phelps Cnty Gene.

— Obituaries from the Records of Clarence W. Love Undertaker, 1905-1915. 90p. 1989. pap. 25.00 (*1-893474-06-2*) Phelps Cnty Gene.

— Phelps County Marriage Books One & Two, 2 vols. Date not set. pap. 22.00 (*1-893474-14-3*) Phelps Cnty Gene.

— Phelps County Marriage Sep 4, 1857-Feb 17, 1867, Bk. A. 27p. 1994. pap. 10.00 (*1-893474-15-1*) Phelps Cnty Gene.

— Phelps County Missouri Heritage, Vol. 1. (Illus.). 528p. 1992. 90.00 (*1-893474-01-1*) Phelps Cnty Gene.

— Phelps County Missouri Heritage, Vol. 2. (Illus.). 342p. 1994. 73.50 (*1-893474-02-X*) Phelps Cnty Gene.

— Phelps County Missouri Probate Records Index 1857-1969. 66p. 1997. pap. 30.00 (*1-893474-04-6*) Phelps Cnty Gene.

— Rolla Cemetary: Rolla City Cemetary. 138p. 1995. pap. 40.00 (*1-893474-07-0*) Phelps Cnty Gene.

Phelps, Dale. Chief Rivalries: Your Game-by-Game Guide to the 1998 Season - And the Memories Behind Each Matchup. Dodd, Monroe, ed. (Illus.). 80p. 1998. pap. 12.95 (*0-9604884-7-2*) Kansas Cty Star.

Phelps, Daphne. A House in Sicily. LC 00-502465. (Illus.). 224p. 1999. 25.00 (*0-7867-0656-2*) Carroll & Graf.

***Phelps, Daphne.** A House in Sicily. LC 99-58235. (Basic Ser.). 2000. 29.95 (*0-7862-2383-9*) Thorndike Pr.

— A House in Sicily. (Illus.). 288p. 2000. reprint ed. pap. 12.95 (*0-7867-0794-1*, Pub. by Carroll & Graf) Publishers Group.

Phelps, David, jt. auth. see Rybak, Deborah C.

Phelps, David S., et al. The Prehistory of North Carolina: An Archaeological Symposium. Mathis, Mark A. & Crow, Jeffrey J., eds. (Illus.). xvi, 206p. 1993. reprint ed. pap. 12.00 (*0-86526-225-X*) NC Archives.

Phelps De Cordova, Loretta. Ponce: Rebirth of a Valuable Heritage. 88p. 1991. pap. 19.95 (*0-89825-001-3*) Pub Resces PR.

— Ponce: Rebirth of a Valuable Heritage. deluxe ed. 88p. 1991. 34.95 (*0-89825-002-1*) Pub Resces PR.

— Ponce: Renacimiento De una Valiosa Herencia. Bizjack, Carmen, tr. from ENG. (SPA.). 88p. 1991. pap. 19.95 (*0-89825-003-X*) Pub Resces PR.

— Ponce: Renacimiento De una Valiosa Herencia. deluxe ed. Bizjack, Carmen, tr. from ENG. (SPA.). 88p. 1991. 34.95 (*0-89825-004-8*) Pub Resces PR.

Phelps, Dean. And Now We'll Play a Man's Game: Montana Stories. LC 76-1979. (Illus.). 132p. (Orig.). 1976. pap. 10.95 (*0-914974-10-6*) Holmgangers.

Phelps, Dean. Serum of the Water. LC 78-12785. 1978. pap. 7.95 (*0-914974-17-3*) Holmgangers.

Phelps, Dean. Shoshoni River Witching Hour. 2nd ed. 44p. 1975. pap. 5.00 (*0-914974-04-1*) Holmgangers.

***Phelps, Digger.** Basketball for Dummies. 2nd ed. (For Dummies Ser.). 432p. 2000. pap. 19.99 (*0-7645-5248-1*) IDG Bks.

Phelps, Digger & Walters, John. Basketball for Dummies. LC 97-80304. (For Dummies Ser.). 432p. 1997. pap. 19.99 (*0-7645-5042-X*) IDG Bks.

Phelps, Donald. Reading the Funnies: Looking at Great Cartoonists Throughout the First Half of the Century. (Illus.). 300p. 1999. pap. 19.95 (*1-56097-368-4*) Fantagraph Bks.

Phelps, Donald, ed. Hearing Out James T. Farrell: Selected Lectures. LC 84-52382. 168p. 1985. pap. 10.50 (*0-912292-76-8*) Smith.

Phelps, Donald, ed. see Farrell, James T.

***Phelps, Doug, et al.** 50 Not-So-Simple Things You Can Do to Save the Earth. (Illus.). 160p. 2000. pap. 12.95 (*0-9676618-5-4*) Public Inter Pr CA.

Phelps, E., jt. auth. see Oman, Frydman R.

Phelps, E. R., jt. auth. see Wolfe, John H.

***Phelps, Earl R.** How to Draw Muticulural Supercharacters. LC 00-91052. (Illus.). 96p. (YA). (gr. 4-12). 2000. 18.95 (*1-887627-04-9*) Phelps Pub.

Phelps, Earl R. How to Draw Supercharacters & Supermonsters. LC 98-91317. (Illus.). 88p. 1998. pap. 15.95 (*1-887627-03-0*) Phelps Pub.

— How to Draw Your Own Supercharacters. (J). (gr. 4-12). 1993. pap. 5.95 (*1-887627-00-6*) Phelps Pub.

— How to Draw Your Own Supercharacters, Bk. II. LC 95-92382. (J). (gr. 4-12). 1996. pap. 5.95 (*1-887627-01-4*) Phelps Pub.

— How to Draw Your Own Supermonsters. (J). (gr. 4-12). 1993. pap. 5.95 (*1-887627-02-2*) Phelps Pub.

Phelps, Edmund S. Political Economy: An Introductory Text. (C). 1985. text 48.75 (*0-393-95312-2*) Norton.

— Rewarding Work: How to Restore Participation & Self-Support to Free Enterprise. LC 96-50204. (Illus.). 224p. 1996. 24.95 (*0-674-09495-6*) HUP.

— Rewarding Work: How to Restore Participation & Self-Support to Free Enterprise. 1999. pap. text 14.00 (*0-674-09496-4*) HUP.

— Seven Schools of Macroeconomic Thought: The Arne Ryde Memorial Lectures. (Illus.). 124p. 1990. text 32.00 (*0-19-828333-4*) OUP.

— Structural Slumps: The Modern Equilibrium Theory of Unemployment, Interest & Assets. LC 93-15775. (Illus.). 440p. 1994. 56.00 (*0-674-84373-8*) HUP.

— Structural Slumps: The Modern Equilibrium Theory of Unemployment, Interest & Assets. (Illus.). 440p. 1998. pap. 27.95 (*0-674-84374-6*) HUP.

Phelps, Edmund S., ed. Altruism, Morality, & Economic Theory. LC 74-79448. 242p. 1975. 29.95 (*0-87154-659-0*) Russell Sage.

— The Microeconomic Foundations of Employment & Inflation Theory. (C). 1973. pap. text 21.00 (*0-393-09326-3*) Norton.

— Private Wants & Public Needs. rev. ed. (Problems of Modern Economy Ser.). (Orig.). (C). 1965. pap. text 4.95 (*0-393-09496-0*) Norton.

— Recent Developments in Macroeconomics, 3 vols. (International Library of Critical Writings in Economics: Vol. 13). 1432p. 1991. text 520.00 (*1-85278-297-8*) E Elgar.

Phelps, Elisa, jt. auth. see Nahohai, Milford.

Phelps, Elizabeth S. Chapters from a Life. Baxter, Annette K., ed. LC 79-8822. (Signal Lives Ser.). (Illus.). 1980. reprint ed. lib. bdg. 35.95 (*0-405-12866-5*) Ayer.

— Doctor Zay. LC 87-48. 336p. 1987. reprint ed. pap. 8.95 (*0-935312-72-2*) Feminist Pr.

— A Peep at Number 5: or A Chapter in the Life of a City Pastor. LC 70-164573. (American Fiction Reprint Ser.). 1977. reprint ed. 25.95 (*0-8369-7050-0*) Ayer.

— The Silent Partner. LC 82-25306. 400p. 1983. reprint ed. pap. 12.95 (*0-935312-08-0*) Feminist Pr.

***Phelps, Elizabeth S.** Three Spiritualist Novels. 344p. 2000. 40.00 (*0-252-02597-0*) U of Ill Pr.

Phelps, Elizabeth S., et al. Our Famous Women: An Authorized Record of the Lives & Deeds of Distinguished American Women of Our Times. LC 73-1192. (Essay Index Reprint Ser.). (Illus.). 1977. reprint ed. 38.95 (*0-518-10060-X*) Ayer.

Phelps, Erika & Phelps, Brian. Trampolining. (Skills of the Game Ser.). (Illus.). 112p. 1991. pap. 19.95 (*1-85223-363-X*, Pub. by Crolwood) Trafalgar.

Phelps, Ethel J. The Maid of the North: Feminist Folk Tales from Around the World. LC 80-21500. (Illus.). 192p. 1995. pap. 9.95 (*0-8050-0679-6*, Owl) H Holt & Co.

Phelps, Ethel J. Maid of the North: Feminist Folk Tales from Around the World. 1981. 15.05 (*0-606-01826-3*, Pub. by Turtleback) Demco.

Phelps, Ethel J., ed. Tatterhood & Other Tales. LC 78-9352. (Illus.). 192p. (YA). (gr. 1 up). 1978. pap. 9.95 (*0-912670-50-9*) Feminist Pr.

Phelps, Frederick M., III, ed. MIT Wavelength Tables: Wavelengths by Element, Vol. 2. 816p. 1982. 105.00 (*0-262-16087-0*) MIT Pr.

Phelps, Geneva M. An Annal Begins with Ezekiel & Margaret (Watkins) Phelps. 179p. 1988. 25.75 (*0-9620925-0-9*) G Phelps.

Phelps, Geneva M., contrib. by. Boyles of Michl, Vol. 1. (Illus.). 165p. 1996. spiral bd. 23.00 (*0-614-13001-8*) G Phelps.

Phelps, Gilbert. Russian Novel in English Fiction. LC 79-158907. 1971. reprint ed. 39.00 (*0-403-01301-1*) Scholarly.

— The Winter People. 1993. reprint ed. lib. bdg. 18.95 (*0-89968-410-6*, Lghtyr Pr) Buccaneer Bks.

Phelps, Glenn A. George Washington & American Constitutionalism. LC 92-21824. 238p. 1994. pap. 14.95 (*0-7006-0683-1*) U Pr of KS.

Phelps, H. P. Hamlet from the Actors Standpoint. LC 76-57925. (Studies in Shakespeare: No. 24). 1977. lib. bdg. 75.00 (*0-8383-2171-2*) M S G Haskell Hse.

Phelps, Henry P. Players of a Century: A Record of the Albany Stage. LC 78-91562. 1972. 30.95 (*0-405-08855-8*, Pub. by Blom Pubns) Ayer.

— Players of a Century: A Record of the Albany Stage. 424p. 1993. reprint ed. lib. bdg. 99.00 (*0-7812-5284-9*) Rprt Serv.

Phelps, J. Alfred. Chappie, America's First Black Four-Star General: The Life & Times of Daniel James, Jr. LC 91-43112. (Illus.). 384p. 1992. pap. 9.95 (*0-89141-464-9*) Presidio Pr.

Phelps, J. Alfred, jt. auth. see Petersen, Frank E.

Phelps, James H. The Illinois State Atlas. (Illus.). 117p. (Orig.). 1988. pap. 15.95 (*0-929998-00-6*) Phelps Map.

— The Indiana State Atlas. (Illus.). 118p. (Orig.). 1990. pap. 15.95 (*0-929998-01-4*) Phelps Map.

Phelps, James T., ed. Black & Catholic: The Challenge & Gift of Black Folk: Contributions of African American Experience & World View to Catholic Theology. LC 97-45376. (Studies in Theology). (Orig.). 1995. reprint ed. pap. write for info. (*0-87462-629-3*) Marquette.

***Phelps, Janice.** What Saved Me: A Dozen Ways to Embrace Life. 112p. 2000. pap. 8.95 (*0-9676050-5-9*, Pub. by Lucky Pr) Pathway Bk Serv.

Phelps, Janice, ed. see Davey, Chris.

Phelps, Janice, ed. see Gau-Ghan, David.

Phelps, Janice, ed. see Mantley, John.

Phelps, Janice, ed. see Poscente, Vince.

Phelps, Janice, ed. see Sundt, Peter C.

Phelps, Janice, ed. see Weiner, Mike.

P

An Asterisk (*) at the beginning of an entry indicates that the title is appearing for the first time.

Phelps, Janice K. & Nourse, Alan E. The Hidden Addiction. 250p. 1986. pap. 14.95 (*0-316-70471-7*) Little.

Phelps, Jeana, jt. auth. see Campeau, Frances E.

Phelps, Jennifer, ed. see Chek-Chart Staff.

Phelps, Jo L., ed. see Calkins, Michael.

Phelps, Jocelyn, tr. see Corbin, Alain.

Phelps, Jocelyn, tr. see Pardailhe-Galabrun, Annik.

Phelps, John & Gizzi, Julian. Phelps & Gizzi: VAT for Solicitors. 2nd ed. 94p. 1993. pap. 36.00 (*0-406-02008-6*, U.K., MICHIE) LEXIS Pub.

— Solicitors & VAT. 1986. pap. 30.00 (*0-406-50360-5*, MICHIE) LEXIS Pub.

Phelps, John & Phelps, Ruth. Memories of This Octogenarian. (Illus.). 210p. Date not set. pap. write for info. (*0-9667166-0-4*) R Phelps.

— Memories of This Octogenarian. 2nd ed. (Illus.). 210p. Date not set. write for info. (*0-9667166-1-2*) R Phelps.

Phelps, John W. The Island of Madagascar: A Sketch, Descriptive & Historical. LC 72-4155. (Black Heritage Library Collection). 1977. reprint ed. 19.95 (*0-8369-9102-8*) Ayer.

Phelps, Joseph. More Light, Less Heat: How Dialogue Can Transform Christian Conflict into Growth. LC 98-25321. 176p. 1998. 22.00 (*0-7879-4286-3*) Jossey-Bass.

Phelps, Kay, jt. auth. see Higham, P. E.

Phelps, L. Allen. An Analysis of Fiscal Policy Alternatives for Serving Special Populations in Vocational Education. 45p. 1984. 4.95 (*0-318-22026-1*, IN278) Ctr Educ Trng Employ.

Phelps, LeAdelle, ed. Health-Related Disorders in Children & Adolescents: A Guidebook for Understanding & Educating. LC 98-13919. (School Psychology Ser.). 743p. 1998. 59.95 (*1-55798-485-9*) Am Psychol.

Phelps, Leland R., jt. ed. see Loram, Ian C.

Phelps, Linden, jt. auth. see Hiatt, Beryl.

Phelps, Louise W. Composition As a Human Science: Contributions to the Self-Understanding of a Discipline. (Illus.). 288p. 1991. pap. text 29.95 (*0-19-506782-7*) OUP.

Phelps, Louise W., ed. see Emig, Janet.

Phelps, Lynn. Your Guide to Medical Hypnosis. LC 93-9545. (Focus on Health Ser.). (Illus.). 108p. (Orig.). 1993. pap. 7.95 (*0-944838-28-6*) Med Physics Pub.

Phelps, M. Jeana, jt. auth. see Campeau, Frances E.

Phelps, Michael E., et al, eds. Positron Emission Tomography & Autoradiography: Principles & Applications for the Brain & Heart. LC 85-19602. (Illus.). 704p. 1986. reprint ed. pap. 200.00 (*0-608-07225-7*, 206745000009) Bks Demand.

Phelps, Michael E., jt. ed. see Sorenson, James A.

Phelps, Nicholas A. FDI & the Global Economy: Corporate & Institutional Dynamics of Global-Localization, 22. 1999. pap. text 34.95 (*1-85302-601-8*) Taylor & Francis.

— Multinationals & European Integration: Trade, Investment & Regional Development. LC 97-145347. (Regional Policy & Development Ser.: No. 14). 200p. 1996. pap. 36.95 (*1-85302-353-1*, Pub. by Jessica Kingsley) Taylor & Francis.

Phelps, Orra. When I Was a Girl in the Martin Box. (American Autobiography Ser.). 157p. 1995. reprint ed. lib. bdg. 69.00 (*0-7812-8618-2*) Rprt Serv.

Phelps, Orson Schofield. The High Peaks of Essex: The Adirondack Mountains of Orson Schofield Phelps. 2nd ed. Healy, Bill, ed. LC 92-14117. (Illus.). 114p. 1992. reprint ed. pap. 12.50 (*0-935796-29-0*) Purple Mnt Pr.

Phelps, P. D. & Lloyd, G. A. Diagnostic Imaging of the Ear. 2nd ed. (Illus.). 234p. 1990. 255.00 (*0-387-19570-X*) Spr-Verlag.

Phelps, Patricia H. Beginning to Teach: Strategies for a Successful First Day. LC 98-17911. (Beginning to Teach Booklet Ser.). (Illus.). 16p. 1998. pap. 2.00 (*0-912099-24-0*, 422) Kappa Delta Pi.

Phelps, Paul B. & Brockman, Paul R. Science & Technology Programs in the States, 1992. 96p. 1992. pap. 30.00 (*0-9632443-0-2*) Adv Develop.

Phelps, R. R. Convex Functions, Monotone Operators & Differentiability. (Lecture Notes in Mathematics Ser.: Vol. 1364). 115p. 1989. pap. 18.30 (*0-387-50735-3*) Spr-Verlag.

Phelps, Richard & Scanlon, Pat. Digger Phelps & Notre Dame Basketball. LC 81-43. (Illus.). 216p. 1981. 9.95 (*0-685-03834-3*) P-H.

Phelps, Richard H. History of Newgate of Connecticut, at Simsbury, New East Granby: Its Insurrections & Massacres. LC 74-90189. (Mass Violence in America Ser.). 1969. reprint ed. 24.95 (*0-405-01331-0*) Ayer.

— Newgate of Connecticut: Its Origin & Early History. LC 96-69650. 128p. 1996. 12.95 (*0-89725-271-3*, 1765) Picton Pr.

Phelps, Richard P. Education in States & Nations: Indicators Comparing United States States with Other Industrialized Countries in 1991. 379p. 1996. pap. 23.00 (*0-16-048685-8*) USGPO.

— State Indicators in Education, 1997. 277p. 1997. pap. 20.00 (*0-16-063643-4*) USGPO.

Phelps, Richard P., et al. Education in States & Nations: Indicators Comparing U. S. States with Other Industrialized Countries in 1991. (Illus.). 359p. 1998. reprint ed. pap. text 50.00 (*0-7881-4269-0*) DIANE Pub.

Phelps, Robert. Belles Saisons: A Colette Scrapbook. (Illus.). 304p. 1978. text 15.00 (*0-374-11030-1*) FS&G.

— Guitar Workbook - Learning Guitar Fingerboard Theory. 164p. 1990. pap. 14.95 (*0-87166-862-9*, 94329) Mel Bay.

— Heroes & Orators. 1958. 10.95 (*0-8392-1048-5*) Astor-Honor.

Phelps, Robert G., ed. The Collected Stories of Colette. Ward, Matthew et al, trs. from FRE. LC 83-16449. 605p. 1984. pap. 18.00 (*0-374-51865-3*) FS&G.

Phelps, Robert R. Convex Functions, Monotone Operators, & Differentiability. 2nd ed. LC 93-15613. (Lecture Notes in Mathematics Ser.: Vol. 1364). (Illus.). xii, 117p. 1993. 35.95 (*0-387-56715-1*) Spr-Verlag.

Phelps, Roger P., et al. A Guide to Research in Music Education. 4th ed. LC 92-29643. (Illus.). 385p. 1994. 42.00 (*0-8108-2536-8*) Scarecrow.

Phelps, Rosemary E., jt. auth. see Steward, Robbie.

Phelps, Ruth. The Universe of Numbers. LC 83-51126. 209p. 1984. pap. 12.95 (*0-912057-11-4*, 501920) GLELJ AMORC.

Phelps, Ruth, jt. auth. see Phelps, John.

Phelps, Ruth S. Italian Silhouettes. LC 68-55853. (Essay Index Reprint Ser.). 1977. 19.95 (*0-8369-0786-8*) Ayer.

Phelps, Shannon K. Demon Chaser: Five Mountain Path of the True Warrior Spirit. LC 97-91935. (Illus.). 200p. 1997. mass mkt. 24.95 (*1-891764-00-4*) Tmpl Full Autumn.

Phelps, Shirelle, ed. Contemporary Black Biography, Vol. 12. 275p. 1996. text 60.00 (*0-7876-0100-4*) Gale.

— Contemporary Black Biography: Profiles from the International Black Community, Vol. 13. 275p. 1996. text 60.00 (*0-7876-0101-2*) Gale.

— Contemporary Black Biography: Profiles from the International Black Community, Vol. 15. Vol. 15. 275p. 1997. text 60.00 (*0-7876-0954-4*, 00155983) Gale.

Phelps, Shirleyan B., et al, eds. My Home Is Washington County, North Carolina. LC 98-73085. (Illus.). v, 200p. 1999. 20.00 (*0-9663776-1-3*) Wash Cty NC.

Phelps, Stanlee & Austin, Nancy. The Assertive Woman. 3rd ed. LC 97-2908. 256p. 1997. pap. 14.95 (*1-886230-05-6*) Impact Pubs CA.

Phelps, Stephanie J. & Cochran, Emily B. Guidelines for Administration of Intravenous Medications to Pediatric Patients. 4th ed. 136p. 1993. pap. text 35.00 (*1-879907-28-3*) Am Soc Hlth-Syst.

Phelps, Stephanie J. & Hak, Emily B. Guidelines for Administration of Intravenous Medications to Pediatric Patients. 5th ed. 1996. 50.00 (*1-879907-63-1*) Am Soc Hlth-Syst.

***Phelps, Stephanie J. & Hak, Emily B., eds.** Guidelines for Administration of Intravenous Medications to Pediatric Patients. 6th rev. ed. 2001. pap. text. write for info. (*1-58528-012-7*) Am Soc Hlth-Syst.

Phelps, Stephen F., jt. auth. see Alvermann, Donna E.

Phelps, Steve. All God's Children Got Gum in Their Hair. LC 94-16538. (Illus.). 104p. (Orig.). 1994. pap. 6.99 (*0-8308-1822-7*, 1822) InterVarsity.

Phelps, Stowe C. Edith Catlin Phelps: A Second Look at an Early Provincetown Painter. (Illus.). 72p. 1990. pap. 5.00 (*0-945135-05-X*) Cape Cod Pilgrim.

***Phelps, Stuart.** Three Spiritualist Novels. 344p. 2000. 15.00 (*0-252-06907-2*) U of Ill Pr.

Phelps, Susan. A Guide to Hermit Living . . . Do You Have What It Takes? LC 96-79356. 180p. (Orig.). 1998. 18.95 (*0-9651171-5-4*) Ashton Prods.

— A Lady Without a Latitude. LC 97-72391. 204p. (Orig.). 1997. pap. 14.95 (*0-9651171-3-8*, Lady Line) Ashton Prods.

— When You Lack Latitude . . . LC 96-79355. 160p. 1998. pap. write for info. (*0-9651171-4-6*) Ashton Prods.

— Off the Grid. (Orig.). 2000. pap. write for info. (*0-9651171-8-9*) Ashton Prods.

— Victim of a Drive-By Birth & Other Irreverent Observations. (Orig.). 1999. pap. write for info. (*0-9651171-6-2*) Ashton Prods.

Phelps-Terasaki, Diana, jt. auth. see Phelps, Tricia.

Phelps, Thomas C. & O'Donnell, Peggy. Humanities Programming: A How-to-Do-It Manual for Librarians. (How-to-Do-It Manuals Ser.). 150p. 1996. pap. 45.00 (*1-55570-083-7*) Neal-Schuman.

Phelps, Tony. Poisonous Snakes. LC 81-670067. 1981. 27.50 (*0-7137-0877-8*) Blandford Pr.

Phelps, Tricia & Phelps-Terasaki, Diana. Teaching Written Expression: The Phelps Sentence Guide Program. 112p. 1980. pap. text 15.00 (*0-87879-248-1*); 10.00 (*0-87879-290-2*) Acad Therapy.

***Phelps, Vickie.** 101 Keys for Life: Powerful Thoughts on Christian Living. 40p. 2000. 1.99 (*1-57748-941-1*) Barbour Pub.

Phelps, W. W., tr. see Christophilopoulou, A.

Phelps, William C. The Foreign Expansion of American Banks: American Branch Banking Abroad. Bruchey, Stuart & Bruchey, Eleanor, eds. LC 76-5028. (American Business Abroad Ser.). 1976. reprint ed. 23.95 (*0-405-09295-4*) Ayer.

Phelps, William H., Jr., jt. auth. see De Schauensee, M.

Phelps, William L. Advance of the English Novel. LC 74-145233. 1971. reprint ed. 24.00 (*0-403-01149-3*) Scholarly.

— The Advance of the English Novel. (BCL1-PR English Literature Ser.). 334p. 1992. reprint ed. lib. bdg. 89.00 (*0-7812-7114-2*) Rprt Serv.

— Adventures & Confessions. LC 71-121497. (Essay Index Reprint Ser.). 1977. 19.95 (*0-8369-1771-5*) Ayer.

— Autobiography, with Letters. LC 76-29445. reprint ed. 57.50 (*0-404-15320-8*) AMS Pr.

— Beginnings of the English Romantic Movement: A Study in Eighteenth Century Literature. LC 68-57380. 200p. (C). 1968. reprint ed. 50.00 (*0-87752-084-4*) Gordian.

— Essays on Modern Dramatists. LC 77-105032. (Essay Index Reprint Ser.). 1977. 21.95 (*0-8369-1476-7*) Ayer.

— Robert Browning, How to Know Him. (BCL1-PR English Literature Ser.). 381p. 1992. reprint ed. lib. bdg. 89.00 (*0-7812-7466-4*) Rprt Serv.

— Some Makers of American Literature. LC 70-105033. (Essay Index Reprint Ser.). 1977. 20.95 (*0-8369-1477-5*) Ayer.

— Twentieth Century Theatre: Observations on the Contemporary English & American Stage. LC 67-28764. (Essay Index Reprint Ser.). 1977. 18.95 (*0-8369-0787-6*) Ayer.

Phelps, William L., ed. see Riley, James Whitcomb.

***Phelts, Eddie L.** Let Me Call You Sweethearts: A Thriller with a Touch of Polyamory. 309p. 1999. pap. 16.95 (*0-7414-0227-0*) Buy Books.

Phelts, Marsha D. An American Beach for African Americans. (Illus.). 200p. 1997. 24.95 (*0-8130-1504-9*) U Press Fla.

Pheng. The Role of Construction & Marketing in Economic Development: A Framework for Planning. 1995. pap. 40.00 (*0-85406-676-4*, Pub. by R-I-C-S Bks) St Mut.

Pheng, Vatha, jt. auth. see Adams, W. M.

Pheng, Lee M. Banking Law. xxxii, 334p. 1995. write for info. (*0-409-99757-9*, MICHIE) LEXIS Pub.

Pheng, Low S. Marketing Research in the Global Construction Industry. (Illus.). 138p. (C). 1993. pap. 39.50 (*9971-69-173-6*, Pub. by Sngapore Univ Pr) Coronet Bks.

— Synthesizing Construction & Marketing in Economic Development. 272p. 1995. text 77.95 (*1-85972-219-9*, Pub. by Avebry) Ashgate Pub Co.

— Theory & Practice of Construction Export Marketing. 368p. 1996. 87.95 (*1-85972-304-7*, Pub. by Avebry) Ashgate Pub Co.

Pheng, Low S. & Bee, Tan O. The Global Cement Industry. (Illus.). 124p. (Orig.). 1993. pap. 39.50 (*9971-69-171-X*, Pub. by Sngapore Univ Pr) Coronet Bks.

Phengsy, Novanta, tr. see Marcus, Russell, ed.

Phenix, Bruce, tr. & intro. see Del Granado, Don J.

Phenix, Katharine, et al. On Account of Sex: Annotated Bibliography on the Status of Women in Librarianship, 1982-1986. 152p. 1990. pap. text 10.00 (*0-8389-3375-0*) ALA.

Phenix, Katharine J. Subject Guide to Women of the World. LC 96-14228. 560p. 1996. 79.00 (*0-8108-3190-2*) Scarecrow.

Phenix, Philip H. Man & His Becoming. LC 64-8264. (Brown & Haley Lectures). 125p. reprint ed. pap. 38.80 (*0-608-30587-1*, 205062500087) Bks Demand.

— Religious Concerns in Contemporary Education. LC 59-11329. 118p. reprint ed. 36.60 (*0-8357-9605-1*, 201694900005) Bks Demand.

Phenner, Lee, ed. see Reed, Maxine K. & Reed, Robert M.

Pherigo, George, ed. see Cox, James E.

Pherigo, George, ed. see General Dynamics Convair Div. Staff.

Pherigo, George, ed. see Smilie, Robert W.

Pherigo, Lindsey. The Great Physician: The Healing Stories. LC 90-21917. 144p. 1991. pap. 6.95 (*0-687-15788-9*) Abingdon.

Pherigo, Suzanne, jt. auth. see Mikkelson, Tim.

Phero, J. C., jt. auth. see Dionne, Raymond A.

Pheterson, Gail. The Prostitution Prism. (C). 1995. text 49.50 (*90-5356-185-4*, Pub. by Amsterdam U Pr) U of Mich Pr.

— The Prostitution Prism. (C). 1996. pap. 29.95 (*90-5356-176-5*, Pub. by Amsterdam U Pr) U of Mich Pr.

Pheterson, Gail, ed. A Vindication of the Rights of Whores: The International Movement for Prostitutes' Rights. LC 88-33060. 320p. (Orig.). 1989. pap. 16.95 (*0-931188-73-3*) Seal Pr WA.

Phethean, Jeannette, jt. auth. see Howell, Janel Marie.

Phethean, Richard. The Complete Potter: Throwing. LC 94-12446. (Complete Potter Ser.). (Illus.). 96p. 1994. text 24.95 (*0-8122-3299-2*, Pub. by B T B) U of Pa Pr.

Pheto, Molefe. And Night Fell: Memoirs of a Political Prisoner in South Africa. LC 84-234158. (African Writers Ser.). 218p. (C). 1985. reprint ed. pap. 9.95 (*0-435-90258-X*, 90258) Heinemann.

Phetsadasack, Thomas & Dillman, James R. Land of a Million Elephants. 150p. 1996. pap. 24.95 (*0-9630593-9-4*) Gt Falls North.

Pheysey, Diana C. Organizational Cultures: Types & Transformations. LC 92-30809. 328p. (C). 1996. pap. 25.99 (*0-415-08292-7*, A9685) Thomson Learn.

— Organizational Cultures: Types & Transformations. LC 92-30809. 328p. (C). (gr. 13). 1996. pap. 70.00 (*0-415-08291-9*, A9681) Thomson Learn.

Phi. Choices in Literature G8. 4th ed. 1996. text. write for info. (*0-13-838236-0*, Prentice Hall) P-H.

Phi. World Explorer -The United States & Canada. LC 99-193319. 198p. 1998. text, teacher ed. write for info. (*0-13-433710-7*) P-H.

Phi Delta Kappa Commission for Developing Public C, et al. A Handbook for Developing Public Confidence in Schools. LC 88-61690. 144p. (Orig.). 1988. pap. 11.00 (*0-87367-798-6*) Phi Delta Kappa.

Phi Delta Kappa Commission on Teacher-Faculty Mora, et al. Administrator's Handbook for Improving Faculty Morale. LC 85-61680. 70p. 1985. pap. 8.50 (*0-87367-795-1*) Phi Delta Kappa.

Phialas, Peter G. Shakespeare's Romantic Comedies: The Development of Their Form & Meaning. LC 66-25355. 330p. reprint ed. pap. 102.30 (*0-7837-0316-3*, 204063800018) Bks Demand.

Phibbs, Brendan. Beyond the Boards: ECG Review. LC 96-18845. 280p. 1996. 29.95 (*0-316-70512-8*, Little Brwn Med Div) Lppncott W & W.

— The Human Heart: A Basic Guide to Heart Disease. LC 96-35094. 249p. 1997. pap. text 40.00 (*0-316-70513-6*, Little Brwn Med Div) Lppncott W & W.

Phiddian, Robert. Swift's Parody. (Cambridge Studies in Eighteenth-Century English Literature & Thought Ser.: No. 26). 233p. (C). 1995. text 59.95 (*0-521-47437-X*) Cambridge U Pr.

Phifer, Edward W., Jr. Burke County: A Brief History. (Illus.). viii, 144p. (Orig.). 1979. pap. 6.00 (*0-86526-130-X*) NC Archives.

Phifer, Kate G. Growing up Small: A Handbook for Short People. LC 78-11290. (Illus.). 1979. 9.95 (*0-8397-3136-1*) Eriksson.

— Tall & Small: A Book about Height. LC 86-32401. (Illus.). 96p. (J). (gr. 5 up). 1987. 11.95 (*0-8027-6684-6*); lib. bdg. 12.85 (*0-8027-6685-4*) Walker & Co.

Phifer, Kenneth G. Book of Uncommon Faith. 1991. write for info. (*0-687-60100-2*) Abingdon.

Phifer, Kenneth W. Becoming at Home in the World. 191p. 1992. pap. text 14.95 (*0-9634955-0-X*) Castellio Pr.

Phifer, Martha N. The Colors of Christmas. LC 95-34875. (Illus.). 32p. (Orig.). (J). (ps-3). 1995. pap. 7.99 (*0-8361-9029-7*) Herald Pr.

Phifer, Nan Merrick. Writing for the Workplace. 1998. pap. 14.50 (*0-02-804181-X*) Glencoe.

— Writing Your Life: Developing Skills Through Life Story Writing. 1995. text 9.81 (*0-02-803056-7*) Glencoe.

Phifer, Nan Merrick. Writing Your Life: Developing Skills Through Life Story Writing. 1995. teacher ed. 8.06 (*0-02-803057-5*) Glencoe.

***Phifer, Paul.** College Majors & Careers. 4th ed. LC 99-37769. 250p. 1999. 16.95 (*0-89434-278-9*) Ferguson.

— Great Careers in Two Years: The Associate Degree Option. LC 99-41448. 352p. 1999. pap. 19.95 (*0-89434-285-1*) Ferguson.

Phifer, Ross. Reinsurance Fundamentals: Treaty & Facultative. LC 95-49717. 336p. 1996. 115.00 (*0-471-13452-X*) Wiley.

Phifer, Russell W. From Cradle to Grave-- Laboratory Waste Management: Instructor's Guide LC 97-166754. (Acs Laboratory Safety Ser.). v, 40p. 1997. write for info. (*0-8412-3472-8*) Am Chemical.

Phifer, Russell W. & McTigue, William R., Jr. Handbook of Hazardous Waste Management for Small Quantity Generators. Date not set. write for info. (*0-87371-296-X*, L296) Lewis Pubs.

Phifer, Russell W. & McTigue, William R., Jr. Handbook of Hazardous Waste Management for Small Quantity Generators. (Illus.). 216p. 1988. lib. bdg. 89.95 (*0-87371-102-5*, L102) Lewis Pubs.

Phifer, Sharon. Who Am I? A Search for Identity. 174p. 1997. pap. 8.99 (*1-57502-649-X*, PO1840) Morris Pubng.

Phiffer, Cynthia L. My Body, My Choice. Coy, Stanley C., ed. 40p. (Orig.). (YA). (gr. 7-12). 1994. pap. 2.00 (*1-881459-17-9*) Eagle Pr SC.

Phil, D., jt. auth. see Ramakant, M. A.

Phil, M., jt. auth. see Rose, Jack.

Phil, M., ed. see Nutter, Robert S.

Philabaum, Dabney M. Desert Buddies. (Illus.). 40p. (J). (gr. k-4). 1994. pap. 8.95 (*0-9639215-0-9*) Earth Buddies.

Philabaum, Dabney M. & Alegret, Nancy L. Desert Buddies: Life in a Sunbaked Land. 2nd ed. (Illus.). 40p. (J). (gr. 2-6). 1996. pap. 7.95 (*0-9639215-2-5*) Earth Buddies.

— Ocean Buddies: Life in the Salty Seas. (Illus.). 32p. (Orig.). (J). (gr. 2-6). 1996. pap. 7.95 (*0-9639215-1-7*) Earth Buddies.

Philadelphia Board of Guardians Staff & Massachusetts General Court Staff. Almshouse Experience: Collected Papers. LC 74-137197. (Poverty U. S. A. Historical Record Ser.). 1974. reprint ed. 23.95 (*0-405-03092-4*) Ayer.

Philadelphia Bronze & Brass Staff. Development of Copper-Base Alloys for Use as Dies & Plungers in the Glass & Plastics Industries. 53p. 1963. 7.95 (*0-317-34509-5*, 27) Intl Copper.

Philadelphia Chamber of Commerce Staff. Giant Houseparty Cookbook. 385p. 1981. pap. 10.95 (*0-686-31495-6*) COC.

Philadelphia Child Guidance Center Staff & Maguire, Jack. Your Child's Emotional Health: The Early Years. LC 94-34151. 176p. 1995. 9.95 (*0-02-860001-0*) Macmillan.

***Philadelphia Daily News Staff.** Philadelphia Sports Century. (Illus.). 192p. 2000. 29.95 (*1-58382-059-0*) Sports Pub.

Philadelphia Inquirer Staff. Millennium Philadelphia: The Last 100 Years. LC 99-14970. (Illus.). 256p. 1999. 29.95 (*0-940159-53-8*) Camino Bks.

Philadelphia Inquirer Staff, The, ed. The Inquirer Regional Almanac 1995. rev. ed. 704p. 7.95 (*0-9634709-9-X*) Phila Newspapers.

Philadelphia Institute of Contemporary Art Staff. Group Zero: An American Exhibition. Piene, Otto, ed. LC 68-20081. (Illus.). 1968. reprint ed. 6.00 (*0-405-00389-7*) Ayer.

Philadelphia Institute Staff & Warren, Carl S. Introduction to Corporate Law. 2nd ed. Hannan, ed. 481p. (C). 1991. text 58.25 (*0-314-80907-4*) West Pub.

Philadelphia Institute Staff & Weinstein, Mark. Intro To Civil Litigation 3e. 3rd ed. Hannan, ed. LC 92-42903. (Paralegal). (Illus.). 450p. (C). 1993. mass mkt. 51.00 (*0-314-93380-8*) West Pub.

Philadelphia, Marion, tr. see Jaeger, Roland.

Philadelphia Maritime Museum Staff. George Robert Bonfield: Philadelphia Marine Painter, 1805 to 1898. LC 78-71198. (Illus.). 78p. (Orig.). 1978. pap. text 4.00 (*0-913346-04-7*) Indep Seaport.

— Thomas Birch, 1779-1851: Paintings & Drawings. (Illus.). 64p. 1966. pap. 2.00 (*0-913346-06-3*) Indep Seaport.

Philadelphia Methodist Church (Putnam County, GA) Staff, jt. auth. see Ehrlich, Margaret G.

Philadelphia Museum of Art Staff. Philadelphia: Three Centuries of American Art. LC 76-3170. (Illus.). 666p. 1990. reprint ed. pap. 42.00 (*0-87633-016-2*) Phila Mus Art.

P

An Asterisk (*) at the beginning of an entry indicates that the title is appearing for the first time.

— Philadelphia: Three Centuries of American Art. (Illus.). 666p. 1990. reprint ed. 68.00 (0-87633-113-4) Phila Mus Art.
— Philadelphia Museum of Art: Handbook of the Collections. LC 95-23944. 1995. pap. 16.95 (0-87633-096-0) Phila Mus Art.
— Philadelphia Museum of Art: Handbook of the Collections. (Illus.). 360p. 1995. text 26.95 (0-87633-098-7) Phila Mus Art.
Philadelphia Museum of Art Staff, ed. Paintings from Europe & the Americas in the Philadelphia Museum of Art: A Concise Catalogue. LC 94-23570. (Illus.). 548p. 1994. pap. 30.00 (0-87633-093-6) Phila Mus Art.
— Paintings from Europe & the Americas in the Philadelphia Museum of Art: A Concise Catalogue. LC 94-23570. (Illus.). 548p. (C). 1994. 99.95 (0-8122-7964-6) Phila Mus Art.
Philadelphia Museum of Art Staff & Blum, Dilys. The Fine Art of Textiles: Selections from the Textile Collection of the Philadelphia Museum of Art. LC 97-28336. 1997. 50.00 (0-87633-117-7) Phila Mus Art.
Philadelphia Museum of Art Staff & Blum, Dilys E. The Fine Art of Textiles: Selections from the Textile Collection of the Philadelphia Museum of Art. LC 97-28336. 208p. 1997. pap. 32.00 (0-87633-116-9) Phila Mus Art.
Philadelphia Museum of Art Staff & Winterthur, Henry du Pont Museum Staff, eds. Pennsylvania German Art, 1683-1850. LC 83-18267. (Chicago Visual Library: No. 43). 376p. (C). 1984. lib. bdg. 108.00 incl. fiche (0-226-69535-2) U Ch Pr.
Philadelphia Museum of Art Staff, jt. auth. see Helfand, William H.
Philadelphia Office of Mayor Staff. Record of Indentures (1771-1773) Excerpted from the Pennsylvania-German Society Proceedings & Addresses 16. LC 72-10671. 364p. 1995. reprint ed. pap. 30.00 (0-8063-0540-1) Clearfield Co.
Philadelphia Orchestra Association Staff. The Philadelphia Orchestra: A Century of Music. Ardoin, John, ed. LC 99-10969. (Illus.). 240p. 1999. 75.00 (1-56639-712-X) Temple U Pr.
Philadelphia Orchestra, Contributors & Friends of. Bravo! The Philadelphia Orchestra Cookbook II. (Illus.). 264p. 1996. 19.95 (0-9607586-1-5) W Phila Comm.
Philadelphia Rotary Club Members & Wives. What's Cooking in Philadelphia: A Collection of Favorites Recipes-Cookbook. Brock, Claudie, ed. (Illus.). 224p. 1987. write for info. (0-9619470-0-4) Rotary Club Phila.
Philadelphia Schools Students. From the Young at Heart: A Student Anthology. Goodman, Sharon L., ed. (Illus.). 20p. (Orig.). (J). (gr. 1-8). 1989. pap. write for info. (0-935369-19-8) In Tradition Pub.
Philadelphia Seminar on Christian Origins Staff, tr. see Bauer, Walter.
Philadelphia Women Writer's Group Staff. Every Other Tuesday: Selected Work of the Philadelphia Women Writer's Group. 210p. 1998. pap. 10.00 (1-57502-743-7, PO2065) Morris Pubng.
Philalethes, Eirenaeus. Alchemical Works: Eirenaeus Philalethes Compiled. Broddle, S. Merrow, ed. 570p. 1994. 60.00 (0-9640067-0-7) Cinnabar.
— Collectanea Chemica. 160p. 1992. reprint ed. pap. 11.95 (0-922802-81-5) Kessinger Pub.
— An Open Entrance to the Closed Palace of the King. 1985. reprint ed. pap. 7.95 (0-916411-21-4) Holmes Pub.
— The Secret of the Immortal Liquor Called Alkahest. 1984. reprint ed. pap. 3.95 (0-916411-40-0) Holmes Pub.
Philalethes, Eirenaeus, et al. Collectanea Chemica: Select Treatises of Alchemy & Hermetic Philosophy. Waite, A. E., ed. 1991. reprint ed. pap. 14.95 (1-55818-149-0) Holmes Pub.
Philalethes, Eugenius, pseud. The Fame & Confession of the Fraternity of R: C: Commonly of the Rosie Cross with a Preface Annexed Thereto, & a Short Declaration of Their Physical Work. 190p. 1992. reprint ed. pap. 18.00 (1-56459-257-X) Kessinger Pub.
Philander, S. George. El Nino, la Nina, & the Southern Oscillation. (International Geophysics Ser.). 293p. 1989. text 83.00 (0-12-553235-0) Acad Pr.
— Is the Temperature Rising? The Uncertain Science of Global Warming. LC 97-37613. (Illus.). 258p. 1998. 29.95 (0-691-05775-3, Pub. by Princeton U Pr) Cal Prin Full Svc.
***Philander, S. George.** Is the Temperature Rising? The Uncertain Science of Global Warning. 2000. pap. text 16.95 (0-691-05034-1, Pub. by Princeton U Pr) Cal Prin Full Svc.
Philaret, Bishop. Law of God. 86p. Date not set. pap. 5.50 (1-879038-99-4, 9014) Synaxis Pr.
Philaretos, S. D. The Idea of the Being. Orthodox Christian Educational Society Staff, ed. Cummings, D., tr. 287p. 1963. 14.95 (0-938366-09-2) Orthodox Chr.
Philaretos, Soterios, jt. auth. see Makrakis, Apostolos.
Philaretos, Sotirios D. The Decalogue & the Gospel. Orthodox Christian Educational Society Staff, ed. Cummings, D., tr. 62p. (Orig.). 1957. pap. 2.95 (0-938366-43-2) Orthodox Chr.
Philatethes, Eirenaeus. Secrets Reveal'd: or An Open Entrance to the Shut Palace of the King: A New Edition. Cooper, William, ed. (Alchemical Studies Ser.: No. 8). (Orig.). 1997. pap. 9.95 (1-55818-363-9, Alchemical) Holmes Pub.
Philbeam, Pamela M. Themes in Modern European History, 1780-1830. LC 94-28278. (Themes in Modern European History Ser.). (Illus.). 288p. (C). 1995. pap. 24.99 (0-415-10173-5, C0167) Routledge.
Philbin, Alice. Technical Writing: Method Application & Management. (Technical Communications Ser.). 1989. pap., teacher ed. 10.00 (0-8273-2686-6) Delmar.
Philbin, Alice I. Technical Writing: Method Application & Management. (Technical Communications Ser.). 1988. pap. 35.95 (0-8273-2685-8) Delmar.
Philbin, Marianne, jt. auth. see Lark Books Staff.
Philbin, Marianne, jt. ed. see McLeese, Don.
Philbin, Regis & Gifford, Kathie Lee. Cooking with Regis & Kathie Lee: Quick & Easy Recipes from America's Favorite TV Personality. (Illus.). 272p. (J). 1993. 19.45 (1-56282-930-0, Pub. by Hyperion) Time Warner.
— Cooking with Regis & Kathie Lee: Quick & Easy Recipes from America's Favorite TV Personality. (Illus.). 272p. (YA). 1993. pap. 9.70 (1-56282-752-9, Pub. by Hyperion) Time Warner.
— Entertaining with Regis & Kathie Lee: Year-Round Holiday Recipes, Entertaining Tips, & Party Ideas. Albright, Barbara, ed. (Illus.). 288p. 1998. text 20.00 (0-7881-5739-6) DIANE Pub.
— Entertaining with Regis & Kathie Lee: Year-Round Holiday Recipes, Entertaining Tips, & Party Ideas. (Illus.). 304p. (J). 1995. pap. 9.70 (0-7868-8130-5, Pub. by Hyperion) Time Warner.
— Entertaining with Regis & Kathie Lee: Year-Round Holiday Recipes, Entertaining Tips & Party Ideas. (Illus.). 256p. 1994. 19.95 (0-7868-6067-7, Pub. by Disney Pr) Time Warner.
Philbin, Regis & Zehme, Bill. I'm Only One Man! (Illus.). 304p. 1995. 22.95 (0-7868-6154-1, Pub. by Hyperion) Time Warner.
— I'm Only One Man! (Illus.). 432p. 1996. mass mkt. 5.99 (0-7868-8911-X, Pub. by Hyperion) Time Warner.
— I'm Only One Man! large type ed. LC 95-47562. 1996. 25.95 (1-56895-277-5) Wheeler Pub.
Philbin, Robert A. Doing Science: A Guide for the Perplexed. LC 97-93904. (Illus.). pap. 12.95 (0-9657983-0-5) Inside Out.
Philbin, Stephanie, jt. auth. see Heller, Mark A.
Philbin, Thomas. Plumbing: Installation & Design. 227p. (C). 1988. teacher ed. write for info. (0-15-570676-4); text 53.00 (0-15-570675-6, Pub. by SCP) Harcourt.
Philbin, Tobias R., III. The Lure of Neptune: German-Soviet Naval Collaboration & Ambitions, 1919-1941. LC 94-3207. (Studies in Maritime History). 214p. 1994. text 34.95 (0-87249-992-8) U of SC Pr.
Philbin, Tom. Blink. 1994. mass mkt. 4.50 (0-515-11397-2, Jove) Berkley Pub.
— Cop Speak: The Lingo of Law Enforcement & Crime. LC 95-42354. 240p. 1995. pap. 12.95 (0-471-04304-4) Wiley.
— Costwise Bathroom Remodeling: A Guide to Renovating or Improving Your Bath. LC 91-11573. 204p. 1992. 34.95 (0-471-52895-1); pap. 14.95 (0-471-52896-X) Wiley.
— Everything Home Improvement Book. LC 97-6617. 1997. pap. text 12.95 (1-55850-718-3) Adams Media.
— How to Hire a Home Improvement Contractor Without Getting Chiseled. rev. ed. LC 96-2940. (Illus.). 384p. 1996. pap. 17.95 (0-312-14620-5) St Martin.
— The Illustrated Dictionary of Building Terms. LC 96-35305. (Illus.). 256p. 1996. pap. 24.95 (0-07-049729-X) McGraw.
— The Irish 100: A Ranking of the Most Influential Irish of All Time. LC 98-22700. 383p. 1999. 14.95 (0-8362-6841-5) Andrews & McMeel.
— Knock It down, Break It Up: The Definitive Guide to In-Home Demolition. 224p. (Orig.). 1993. pap. 8.00 (0-380-76850-X, Avon Bks) Morrow Avon.
— Mission Impossible: Ring of Fire. 1996. mass mkt. 5.99 (0-671-00233-3) PB.
— Moving Successfully: Money-Saving, Hassle-Free Moving & Storage. (Illus.). 106p. 1998. reprint ed. pap. text 15.00 (0-7881-5203-3) DIANE Pub.
— Murder, U. S. A. (Illus.). 304p. (Orig.). 1992. mass mkt. 4.99 (0-446-36091-0, Pub. by Warner Bks) Little.
— Painting, Staining & Finishing. LC 96-49071. (Illus.). 317p. 1997. 49.95 (0-07-049730-3); pap. 29.95 (0-07-049731-1) McGraw.
— The Rookie. 1991. mass mkt. 4.50 (0-446-36113-5, Pub. by Warner Bks) Little.
— Tom Philbin's Do-It-Yourself Bargain Book. 256p. (Orig.). 1992. mass mkt. 9.99 (0-446-39339-8, Pub. by Warner Bks) Little.
Philbin, Tom & Ettlinger, Steve R. The Complete, Illustrated Guide to Everything Sold in Hardware Stores. (Illus.). 352p. 1988. text 25.95 (0-02-536310-7) Macmillan.
Philbin, Tom & Sokolin, William. The Complete Wine Investor: Collecting Wines for Pleasure & Profit. LC 98-35912. (Illus.). 288p. 1998. 29.99 (0-7615-1676-X) Prima Pub.
Philbin, Tom, jt. auth. see Dezettel, Louis M.
Philbrick, Allen K. This Human World. rev. ed. (Illus.). 500p. (C). 1986. reprint ed. pap. text 39.95 (1-877751-39-1) Inst Math Geo.
Philbrick, Charles. Nobody Laughs, Nobody Cries. LC 73-93613. (Illus.). 128p. 1976. 15.00 (0-912292-33-4) Smith.
Philbrick, Francis S. The Laws of Indiana Territory, 1801-1809. 741p. 1931. 6.25 (1-885323-45-X) IN Hist Bureau.
Philbrick, Francis S., ed. The Laws of Illinois Territory, 1809 to 1818. LC 50-62758. (Illinois Historical Collections: Vol. 25). 1950. 2.50 (0-912154-11-X) Ill St Hist Lib.
Philbrick, Francis S., tr. see Huebner, Rudolf.
Philbrick, Frederick A. Language & the Law: The Semantics of Forensic English. LC 93-78310. ix, 254p. 1993. reprint ed. 42.00 (0-89941-841-4, 307860) W S Hein.
Philbrick, Harry. Living with Contemporary Art. 66p. 1995. pap. 12.00 (1-888332-00-X) Aldrich Mus.
Philbrick, Harry, text. Robert Gober: The 1996 Larry Aldrich Foundation Award Exhibition. (Illus.). 108p. 1998. pap. 21.00 (1-888332-07-7, 810000) Aldrich Mus.
Philbrick, Harry, jt. text see Princenthal, Nancy.
Philbrick, Helen & Gregg, Richard B. Companion Plants & How to Use Them. rev. ed. 113p. 1990. pap. 7.95 (0-8159-5210-4) Devin.
Philbrick, Helen, jt. auth. see Philbrick, John.
Philbrick, John & Philbrick, Helen. The Bug Book: Harmless Insect Controls. LC 74-75470. (Illus.). 128p. 1983. pap. 7.95 (0-88266-027-6, Garden Way Pub) Storey Bks.
— Gardening for Health & Nutrition: An Introduction to the Method of Biodynamic Gardening. LC 79-150428. (Illus.). 112p. 1995. reprint ed. pap. 9.95 (0-88010-403-1) Anthroposophic.
Philbrick, Marianne, ed. see Cooper, James Fenimore.
Philbrick, Nathaniel. Abram's Eyes. LC 97-76393. 320p. 1998. text 35.00 (0-9638910-8-1) Mill Hill Pr.
— Away Offshore: Nantucket Island & Its People. LC 99-214392. 300p. 1993. text 29.95 (0-9638910-0-6); pap. text 19.95 (0-9638910-1-4) Mill Hill Pr.
***Philbrick, Nathaniel.** In the Heart of the Sea: The Tragedy of the Whaleship Essex. LC 99-53740. (Illus.). 320p. 2000. 24.95 (0-670-89157-6, Viking) Viking Penguin.
Philbrick, Nathaniel. Second Wind: A Sailfish Sailor's Odyssey. LC 97-78241. (Illus.). 256p. 1998. 24.95 (0-940160-77-3) Parnassus Imprints.
Philbrick, Norman, ed. Trumpets Sounding: Propaganda Plays of the American Revolution. 1972. 30.95 (0-405-09803-0) Ayer.
— Trumpets Sounding: Propanda Plays of the American Revolution. LC 77-184007. 1977. reprint ed. lib. bdg. 20.00 (0-405-11192-4, Pub. by Blom Pubns) Ayer.
Philbrick, Rodman. Children of the Wolf. (Werewolf Chronicles Ser.: No. 2). (J). (gr. 3-7). 1996. pap. text 3.99 (0-590-69240-2) Scholastic Inc.
— Children of the Wolf. (Werewolf Chronicles Ser.). 1996. 9.09 (0-606-10034-2, Pub. by Turtleback) Demco.
***Philbrick, Rodman.** Dark Matter: A Novel. LC 00-190993. 2000. 25.00 (0-7388-2172-1) Xlibris Corp.
— Darl Matter: A Novel. LC 00-190993. 2000. pap. 18.00 (0-7388-2173-X) Xlibris Corp.
Philbrick, Rodman. The Fire Pony. LC 95-43330. 192p. (J). (gr. 3-8). 1996. 14.95 (0-590-55251-1, Blue Sky Press) Scholastic Inc.
— The Fire Pony. (J). 1997. pap. text 4.50 (0-590-56862-0) Scholastic Inc.
— The Fire Pony. (Apple Signature Edition Ser.). (J). 1997. 9.60 (0-606-11328-2, Pub. by Turtleback) Demco.
Philbrick, Rodman. Freak the Mighty. 169p. pap. 4.99 (0-8072-1521-X) Listening Lib.
Philbrick, Rodman. Freak the Mighty. LC 93-19913. 176p. (J). (gr. 5-9). 1993. 14.95 (0-590-47412-X) Scholastic Inc.
— Freak the Mighty. LC 93-19913. 176p. (YA). (gr. 7-12). 1995. mass mkt. 3.99 (0-590-47413-8, Point) Scholastic Inc.
— Freak the Mighty. (Illus.). 169p. (YA). (gr. 7-12). 1998. mass mkt. 4.50 (0-590-11022-5) Scholastic Inc.
— Freak the Mighty. (J). 1993. 9.09 (0-606-07540-2, Pub. by Turtleback) Demco.
— Haunting. (House on Cherry Street Ser.). 1995. 8.60 (0-606-07633-6, Pub. by Turtleback) Demco.
— Horror. (House on Cherry Street Ser.). 1995. 8.60 (0-606-07665-4, Pub. by Turtleback) Demco.
— Max the Mighty. (J). 1998. pap. text 47.88 (0-590-65859-X, Blue Sky Press) Scholastic Inc.
— Max the Mighty. LC 97-11762. 176p. (YA). (gr. 7 up). 1998. pap. 3.99 (0-590-57964-9) Scholastic Inc.
— Night Creature. (Werewolf Chronicles Ser.: No. 1). (J). (gr. 4-7). 1996. pap. 3.99 (0-590-68950-9) Scholastic Inc.
***Philbrick, Rodman.** REM World. LC 99-54843. (Illus.). 176p. (J). (gr. 4-7). 2000. 16.95 (0-439-08362-1, Blue Sky Press) Scholastic Inc.
Philbrick, Rodman. The Wereing. (Werewolf Chronicles Ser.: No. 3). (J). (gr. 4-7). 1996. pap. text 3.99 (0-590-69241-0) Scholastic Inc.
— The Wereing. (Werewolf Chronicles Ser.). 1996. 9.09 (0-606-10035-0, Pub. by Turtleback) Demco.
Philbrick, Rodman & Harnett, Lynn. Brain Stealers, Bk. III. LC 97-224458. (Visitors Ser.: Vol. 3). (Illus.). (J). (gr. 4-7). 1997. mass mkt. 3.99 (0-590-97215-4) Scholastic Inc.
— Le Dernier Cauchemar Bk. 3: The Final Nightmare.Tr. of Maison de la Rue du Cerisier: Le Dernier Cauchemar. (FRE.). (YA). mass mkt. 5.99 (0-590-24676-3) Scholastic Inc.
— The Final Nightmare. (House on Cherry Street Ser.: Bk. III). 160p. (J). (gr. 4-6). 1995. pap. 3.50 (0-590-25515-0) Scholastic Inc.
— The Haunting. (House on Cherry Street Ser.: Bk. I). 144p. (J). (gr. 4-6). 1995. pap. 3.50 (0-590-25513-4) Scholastic Inc.
— The Horror. (House on Cherry Street Ser.: Bk. II). 192p. (J). (gr. 4-6). 1995. pap. 3.50 (0-590-25514-2) Scholastic Inc.
— L'Ensorcellement Bk. 1: The Haunting.Tr. of Maison de la Rue du Cerisier: L'Ensorcellement. (FRE.). (YA). mass mkt. 5.99 (0-590-24674-7) Scholastic Inc.
— Strange Invaders, Bk. I. (Visitors Ser.: Vol. 1). 150p. (J). (gr. 3-7). 1997. mass mkt. 3.99 (0-590-97213-8) Scholastic Inc.
— La Terreur Bk. 2: The Horror.Tr. of Maison de la Rue du Cerisier: La Terreur. (FRE.). (YA). mass mkt. 5.99 (0-590-24675-5) Scholastic Inc.
— Things, Bk. II. (Visitors Ser.: Vol. 2). 160p. (J). (gr. 3-7). 1997. mass mkt. 3.99 (0-590-97214-6) Scholastic Inc.
Philbrick, Rodman & Philbrick, W. R. Max the Mighty. LC 97-11762. 166p. (J). (gr. 7-12). 1998. 16.95 (0-590-18892-5, Blue Sky Press) Scholastic Inc.
Philbrick, Rodman, et al. Abduction. 352p. (J). (gr. 6-8). 1998. pap. 4.99 (0-590-34808-6, 893382) Scholastic Inc.
Philbrick, Stephen. No Goodbye. LC 81-615. 84p. (Orig.). 1981. pap. 6.00 (0-912292-68-7) Smith.
— Up to the Elbow. limited ed. LC 97-216198. 25p. 1997. pap. 8.00 (0-938566-76-8) Adastra Pr.
Philbrick, Thomas, ed. see Cooper, James Fenimore.
Philbrick, Thomas, ed. see Dana, Richard Henry.
Philbrick, Thomas L., ed. see Cooper, James Fenimore.
***Philbrick, W. R.** The Last Book in the Universe. LC 99-59878. (Illus.). 192p. (YA). (gr. 5-9). 2001. 16.95 (0-439-08758-9) Scholastic Inc.
Philbrick, W. R., jt. auth. see Philbrick, Rodman.
Philbrook, Carilyn E. Where These Feet Went Since: How Two Families Became One Family. 188p. Date not set. per. write for info. (0-910119-75-9) SOCO Pubns.
Philbrook, W. O., Memorial Symposium Staff. W. O. Philbrook Memorial Symposium Proceedings: Toronto, Ontario, Canada, April 17-20, 1988. LC 88-81558. 291p. 1988. reprint ed. pap. 90.30 (0-608-00469-3, 206128800007) Bks Demand.
Philby, Harris S. Sheba's Daughters. LC 83-45836. reprint ed. 55.00 (0-404-20201-2) AMS Pr.
Philby, Harry. Das Geheimnisvolle Arabien, 2 vols. in 1. (Illus.). 685p. 1985. reprint ed. write for info. (3-487-07684-5) G Olms Pubs.
Philby, Harry S. Arabia of the Wahhabis. LC 73-6297. (Middle East Ser.). 1977. reprint ed. 36.95 (0-405-05355-X) Ayer.
— Sa'udi Arabia. LC 72-4289. (World Affairs Ser.: National & International Viewpoints). (Illus.). 422p. 1978. reprint ed. 26.95 (0-405-04581-6) Ayer.
— Sheba's Daughters. (Illus.). xix, 485p. reprint ed. write for info. (0-318-71552-X) G Olms Pubs.
Philby, J. B. Arabian Highlands. LC 76-10643. (Middle East in the 20th Century Ser.). 1976. reprint ed. lib. bdg. 75.00 (0-306-70765-9) Da Capo.
***Philby, Rufina, et al.** The Private Life of Kim Philby: The Moscow Years. (Illus.). 464p. 2000. 32.00 (0-88064-219-X) Fromm Intl Pub.
Philcox, Phil. How to Earn More Than 30,000 a Year with Your Home Computer. rev. ed. LC 98-52450. (Illus.). 208p. 1999. pap. 12.00 (0-8065-2069-8, Citadel Pr) Carol Pub Group.
Philcox, Phil. How to Earn More Than $25,000 a Year with Your Home Computer: Over 140 Income-Producing Projects. LC 97-1991. (Illus.). 192p. 1997. pap. 10.95 (0-8065-1874-X, Citadel Pr) Carol Pub Group.
Philcox, Phil & Boe, Beverly. Europe--The Two-Wheeled Adventure. LC 77-95255. (Illus.). 1978. pap. 8.95 (0-88435-009-6) Chateau Pub.
— The Sunshine State Almanac & Book of Florida - Related Stuff. LC 98-42751. (Illus.). 400p. 1999. pap. 16.95 (1-56164-178-2) Pineapple Pr.
Philcox, Phil & Boe, Beverly. Toll-Free Travel & Vacation Information Directory. LC 87-32774. 39 p. 1988. write for info. (0-87576-135-6) Pilot Bks.
Philcox, Richard, jt. auth. see Conde, Maryse.
Philcox, Richard, tr. see Conde, Maryse.
Philfer. Book of Uncommon Prayer. 1983. write for info. (0-687-60102-9) Abingdon.
Phili, Ashraf M. Color & Learn Arabic with Us. (Intensive Cassette Ser.). (ARA., Illus.). 56p. (J). (gr. k-6). 1998. pap. 16.00 incl. audio (1-58214-010-3) Mltilingl Bks.
Philibert, J. M., jt. ed. see Manning, Frank.
Philibert, Paul & Kacarcik, Frank. Seeing & Believing: Images of the Christian Faith. 224p. (Orig.). 1995. 49.95 (0-8146-6126-2, Pueblo Bks) Liturgical Pr.
Philibert, Paul, tr. see Rouet, Albert.
Philibosian, Richard, jt. auth. see Imsand, Shirley.
Philidor, Francois-Andre D. Ernelinde: Tragedie Lyrique. Rushton, Julian, ed. LC 92-756279. (French Opera in the 17th & 18th Centuries Ser.: No. 8, Vol. LVI). (Illus.). 1994. lib. bdg. 86.00 (0-945193-23-8) Pendragon NY.
Philip & Meuninck. Cooking with Edible Flowers & Culinary Herbs. 1990. 66.00 (0-939865-13-0) CRC Pr.
Philip, A. B. The Single European Market. (C). 2000. pap. 17.95 (0-582-30491-1) Addison-Wesley.
Philip, A. Davis, ed. The HR Diagram: The 100th. (Symposia of the International Astronomical Union Ser.: No. 80). (Illus.). 1978. pap. text 100.50 (90-277-0906-8); lib. bdg. 146.00 (90-277-0905-X) Kluwer Academic.
Philip, A. G., ed. New Developments in Array Technology & Applications: Proceedings of the 167th Symposium of the International Astronomical Union, Held in the Hague, the Netherlands, August 23-27, 1994. (International Astronomical Union Symposia Ser.). 420p. (C). 1995. pap. text 95.00 (0-7923-3640-2); lib. bdg. 168.00 (0-7923-3639-9) Kluwer Academic.
Philip, A. G., jt. auth. see Grindlay, Jonathan E.
Philip, A. G. Davis, ed. 30 Years of Astronomy at the Van Vlech Observatory: A Meeting in Honor of Arthur R. Upgren. 1997. pap. 30.00 (0-933485-21-2) L Davis Pr.
— X-Ray Symposium, 1981. 76p. 1981. pap. 12.00 (0-9607902-0-9) L Davis Pr.
***Philip, A. G. Davis, et al, eds.** Anni Mirabiles: A Symposium Celebrating the 90th Birthday of Dorrit Hoffleit. (Illus.). 300p. (C). 1999. 35.00 (0-933485-23-9) L Davis Pr.
Philip, A. G. Davis & Hayes, D. S., eds. Astrophysical Parameters for Globular Clusters No. 68: IAU Colloquium. 614p. 1982. 31.00 (0-9607902-2-5); pap. 27.00 (0-9607902-1-7) L Davis Pr.
Philip, A. G. Davis & Upgren, Arthur R. The Nearby Stars & the Stellar Luminosity Function. (IAU Colloquium Ser.: No. 76). 550p. 1983. 32.00 (0-9607902-5-X); pap. 32.00 (0-9607902-4-1) L Davis Pr.

P

An Asterisk (*) at the beginning of an entry indicates that the title is appearing for the first time.

Philip, A. G. Davis, et al. Mm. Series on Fractals Vol. 1: Midgets on the Spike. 160p. 1991. 29.00 (*0-933485-14-X*) L Davis Pr.
— The 3rd Conference on Faint Blue Stars. 1998. 45.00 (*0-933485-22-0*) L Davis Pr.
Philip, A. G. Davis, jt. auth. see Sanduleak, N.
Philip, A. G. Davis, jt. ed. see Straizys, Vytas.
Philip, A. T. & Sivaji Rao, K. H. Indian Government & Politics. 299p. 1981. 19.95 (*0-940500-45-0*, Pub. by Sterling) Asia Bk Corp.
Philip, Alan T., ed. Australian Astronautics Convention Proceedings 1975. (Illus.). 1977. pap. text 18.00 (*0-9596726-1-3*) Univelt Inc.
Philip, Alex J. Dicken's Honeymoon & Where He Spent It. LC 72-6507. (Studies in Dickens: No. 52). 1972. reprint ed. lib. bdg. 49.00 (*0-8383-1619-0*) M S G Haskell Hse.
Philip, Alexander. The Business of Bookbinding, Vol. 14. (History of Bookbinding & Design Ser.). (Illus.). 225p. 1989. text 30.00 (*0-8240-4042-2*) Garland.
Philip, Alexander J. A Dickens Dictionary. (BCL1-PR English Literature Ser.). 375p. 1992. reprint ed. lib. bdg. 89.00 (*0-7812-7514-8*) Rprt Serv.
Philip, Alistair G. Neonatology: A Practical Guide. 4th ed. Fletcher, Judy, ed. LC 95-9516. (Illus.). 400p. 1996. pap. text 50.00 (*0-7216-4776-6*, W B Saunders Co) Harcrt Hlth Sci Grp.
Philip, Andre, jt. ed. see Cole, G. D.
Philip C. Crouse & Associates Staff. Economic Analysis of Horizontal Drilling Investments. fac. ed. LC 90-85985. (Illus.). 118p. pap. 36.60 (*0-7837-7433-8*, 204722800006) Bks Demand.
Philip, Chris. A Bibliography of Firework Books: Works on Recreative Fireworks from the Sixteenth to the Twentieth Century. (Illus.). xxx, 170p. 1988. reprint ed. pap. 19.95 (*0-929931-00-9*) Amer Fireworks.
Philip, Christian, jt. auth. see Barav, Ami.
Philip, Cynthia Owen. How Bar Associations Evaluate Sitting Judges. 62p. 1976. 2.00 (*0-318-14435-2*) IJA NYU.
Philip, Cynthia Owen, et al. Where Do Judges Come From? 132p. 1976. 3.50 (*0-318-14448-4*) IJA NYU.
Philip, Frank. Speech Distinct & Pleasing. 162p. 1991. reprint ed. 69.00 (*0-7812-9302-2*) Rprt Serv.
Philip, Franklin & Lane, Harlan, trs. from FRE. Philosophical Works of Etienne Bonnot, Abbe de Condillac, Vol. II. 192p. 1986. text 49.95 (*0-89859-616-5*) L Erlbaum Assocs.
Philip, Franklin, jt. auth. see Graf, Fritz.
Philip, Franklin, tr. see Compagnon, Antoine.
Philip, Franklin, tr. see Constante, Lena.
Philip, Franklin, tr. see Ferry, Luc.
Philip, Franklin, tr. see Ferry, Luc & Renaut, Alain.
Philip, Franklin, tr. see Graf, Fritz.
Philip, Franklin, tr. see Jacob, Francois.
Philip, Franklin, tr. see Lane, Harlan, ed.
Philip, Franklin, tr. see Louder, Dean R. & Waddell, Eric, eds.
Philip, Franklin, tr. see Phillip, F. & Lane, Harlan.
Philip, Franklin, tr. see Renaut, Alain.
Philip, Franklin, tr. see Walesa, Lech.
Philip, G. The Apostles' Creed. Date not set. pap. 9.99 (*1-871676-38-X*, Pub. by Christian Focus) Spring Arbor Dist.
Philip, George. The Political Economy of International Oil. (Commodities in the International Economy Ser.). 256p. 1994. 60.00 (*0-7486-0490-1*, Pub. by Edinburgh U Pr) Col U Pr.
Philip, George, ed. The Mexican Economy. 256p. 1988. lib. bdg. 57.50 (*0-415-01265-1*) Routledge.
Philip, George D. E. Mexico. 2nd rev. ed. LC 94-182921. (World Bibliographical Ser.). 214p. 1994. lib. bdg. 52.50 (*1-85109-198-X*) ABC-CLIO.
Philip, Hilda, jt. auth. see Conkling, Neil.
Philip, Hugh & Mengersen, Ernest. Insect Pests of the Prairies. (Illus.). 122p. 1989. pap. 15.95 (*0-88864-870-7*) Lone Pine.
Philip, Ian. The Bodleian Library in the Seventeenth & Eighteenth Centuries. (Lyell Lectures). (Illus.). 150p. 1983. text 47.00 (*0-19-822484-2*) OUP.

Philip J., Riley. The Phantom of the Opera: The Original Shooting Script. Conforti, John, ed. LC 90-61040. (Universal Filmscript Series: Classic Horror Films). (Illus.). 1999. pap. text 24.95 (*1-882127-33-1*) Magicimage Filmbooks.
Most people think that they are watching the original Phantom of the Opera on home video or in revival houses. The existing print of the film is actually a silent version of a 1929 dubbed sound reissue, which is missing at least 35 minutes of development scenes, opera scenes, titles & some of the best atmospheric photography & set designs in motion picture history. The present unmasking scene is pale compared to the original. In this comprehensive history of this landmark horror film, author Phil Riley presents the complete, complex production of this amazing film. The 320 page book includes: the complete shooting script, the complete press book, rare behind the scenes photos, & recreations of lost scenes. Contributions by Mary Philbin ("Christine"), cinematographer Charles van Enger, Ray Bradbury, Ron Chaney & more! *Publisher Paid Annotation.*

Philip, James. Growing Christian. 96p. Date not set. 6.99 (*0-906731-98-4*, Pub. by Christian Focus) Spring Arbor Dist.
— Numbers. (Mastering the Old & New Testament Ser.: Vol. 4). 1993. pap. 14.99 (*0-8499-3543-1*) Word Pub.
— Numbers. (Communicator's Commentary Ser.: Vol. 4). 364p. 1997. 22.99 (*0-8499-0409-9*) Word Pub.
Philip, James A. Pythagoras & Early Pythagoreanism. LC 66-9226. (Phoenix Supplementary Ser.: Supplementary Vol. 7). 232p. reprint ed. pap. 72.00 (*0-608-09952-X*, 201434000095) Bks Demand.
Philip, L., jt. auth. see Dhillon, H. S.
Philip, L. F. L. Advances in Coastal & Ocean Engineering, Vol. 1. 328p. 1995. text 86.00 (*981-02-1824-9*) World Scientific Pub.
Philip, Leila. Hidden Dialogue: A Discussion Between Women in Japan & the U. S. 68p. 1992. 12.00 (*0-685-70367-3*) Japan Soc.
Philip Lief Group Inc. Staff. Best Home-Based Franchises. LC 92-13458. 352p. 1992. pap. 15.00 (*0-385-42196-6*) Doubleday.
— Complete Bartender. (J Hook Ser.). 560p. 1990. mass mkt. 6.99 (*0-425-12692-7*) Berkley Pub.
Philip Lief Group Inc. Staff, jt. auth. see Hausman, Carl.
Philip Lief Group Inc. Staff, jt. auth. see Lowe, Carl.
Philip, Loic. Dictionnaire Encyclopedique des Finances Publiques. (FRE.). 1647p. 1991. 225.00 (*0-8288-9494-9*) Fr & Eur.
Philip, M. Nourbese. Frontiers: Essays & Writings on Racism & Culture. 288p. Date not set. per. 15.95 (*0-920544-90-8*, Pub. by Mercury Bk) LPC InBook.
— Genealogy of Resistance: Essays. LC 98-134771. 223p. 1998. pap. text 18.95 (*1-55128-047-7*, Pub. by Mercury Bk) LPC InBook.
— She Tries Her Tongue: Her Silence Softly Breaks. 100p. 1995. pap. 12.95 (*0-921556-03-9*, Pub. by Gynergy-Ragweed) U of Toronto Pr.
Philip, M. S. Measuring Trees & Forests. 2nd ed. 336p. (Orig.). 1994. pap. text 55.00 (*0-85198-883-0*) OUP.
Philip, Marlene N. Harriet's Daughter. (Caribbean Writers Ser.). 150p. (C). 1988. pap. 9.95 (*0-435-98924-3*, 98924) Heinemann.
— Harriet's Daughter, 2 cass. (YA). audio 14.00 (*0-88961-154-8*, Pub. by Womens Pr) LPC InBook.
— Harriet's Daughter. 160p. (YA). reprint ed. pap. 7.95 (*0-88961-134-3*, Pub. by Womens Pr) LPC InBook.
Philip, Marlene Nourbese. Looking for Livingstone: An Odyssey of Silence. 88p. 1995. per. 10.95 (*0-920544-88-6*, Pub. by Mercury Bk) LPC InBook.
Philip, Maxwell. BS 5750/ISO 9000 Made Plain. 248p. 1994. pap. 97.50 (*0-7487-1700-5*, Pub. by S Thornes Pubs) Trans-Atl Phila.
Philip, Maxwell, et al. Emmanuel Appadocca; or, Blighted Life: A Tale of the Boucaneers. Cudjoe, Selwyn R. & Cain, William E., eds. LC 96-47786. 336p. 1997. pap. 19.95 (*1-55849-076-0*); text 60.00 (*1-55849-075-2*) U of Mass Pr.
Philip, Michael S., jt. auth. see Dawkins, H. Colyear.
Philip, Neil. American Fairy Tales: From Rip Van Winkle to the Rootabaga Stories. (J). 17.55 (*0-606-13122-1*, Pub. by Turtleback) Demco.
— Annotated Guides Myths & Legends. LC 98-48836. 128p. 1999. 24.95 (*0-7894-4117-9*) DK Pub Inc.
***Philip, Neil.** Celtic Fairy Tales. LC 98-50081. 144p. 1999. 21.99 (*0-670-88387-5*, Viking) Viking Penguin.
— Mythology. (Eyewitness Books). (J). (gr. 4-7). 2000. 15.95 (*0-7894-6288-5*) DK Pub Inc.
Philip, Neil. Mythology. LC 98-32234. 1999. lib. bdg. 20.99 (*0-375-90135-3*) Knopf.
— The Tale of Sir Gawain. 1997. 14.95 (*0-7188-2670-1*, Lutterworth-Parkwest) Parkwest Pubns.
***Philip, Neil, ed.** American Fairy Tales: From Rip Van Winkle to the Rootabaga Stories. (Illus.). 160p. 2000. text 23.00 (*0-7881-6844-4*) DIANE Pub.
Philip, Neil, ed. In a Sacred Manner I Live: Native American Wisdom. LC 96-6509. (Illus.). 96p. (YA). (gr. 6 up). 1997. 20.00 (*0-395-84981-0*, Pub. by Ticknor & Fields) HM.
***Philip, Neil, ed.** It's a Woman's World: A Century of Women's Voices in Poetry. LC 99-88363. 96p. 2000. 17.99 (*0-525-46328-3*, Dutt) Dutton Plume.
Philip, Neil, ed. The New Oxford Book of Children's Verse. 410p. (J). 1996. 35.00 (*0-19-214247-X*) OUP.
— The New Oxford Book of Children's Verse. (Oxford Books of Verse). 408p. 1998. reprint ed. pap. 18.95 (*0-19-288107-8*) OUP.
— Songs Are Thoughts: Poems of the Inuit. LC 94-27866. (Illus.). 32p. (J). (gr. 1 up). 1995. 15.95 (*0-531-06893-5*) Orchard Bks Watts.
***Philip, Neil, ed.** Stockings of Buttermilk: American Folktales. LC 98-54366. 128p. (J). 1999. 20.00 (*0-395-84980-2*, Pub. by HM) HM.
Philip, Neil, ed. War & the Pity of War. LC 97-32897. 96p. (YA). (gr. 5 up). 1998. 20.00 (*0-395-84982-9*, Pub. by Ticknor & Fields) HM.
***Philip, Neil, ed.** American Fairy Tales: From Rip Van Winkle to the Rootabaga Stories. LC 95-49143. (Illus.). 160p. (J). 1998. pap. 12.45 (*0-7868-1093-9*, Pub. by Hyprn Ppbks) Little.
Philip, Neil & Simborowski, Nicoletta, trs. The Complete Fairy Tales of Charles Perrault. LC 92-17781. (Illus.). 160p. (J). 1993. 24.00 (*0-395-57002-6*, Clarion Bks) HM.
Philip, Neil, ed. see Ness, Caroline.
Philip, Neil, tr. see Andersen, Hans Christian.
Philip, Omana, jt. auth. see Mathew, P. M.
***Philip, Pamela Aroen.** Symbols for Life: Guidance for Creating Peace. Trimble, Sandra, ed. (Illus.). 330p. 2000. pap. 29.95 (*0-9676526-0-X*, Pub. by P A Philip) Blessingway Bks.

Philip, Ralph. World Civilizations: Study Guide, 1. 9th ed. (C). 1997. pap. text, student ed. 17.00 (*0-393-96882-0*) Norton.
— World Civilizations: Study Guide, Vol. 2. 9th ed. (C). 1997. pap. text, student ed. write for info. (*0-393-96883-9*) Norton.
Philip, Robert. Early Recordings & Musical Style: Changing Tastes in Instrumental Performance, 1900-1950. (Illus.). 284p. (C). 1992. text 74.95 (*0-521-23528-6*) Cambridge U Pr.
Philip, T., ed. Computer Applications in Industry & Engineering (CAINE-97), 10th International Conference, December 10-12, 1997, San Antonio, Texas, U.S.A: Conference Proceedings December 10-12, 1997, San Antonio, TX, CAINE-97. LC 98-202323. 207p. 1997. write for info. (*1-880843-22-6*) Int Soc Comp App.
Philip, T. & Distler, A., eds. Hypertension: Mechanisms & Management. 279p. 1980. 62.95 (*0-387-10171-3*) Spr-Verlag.
Philip, Thangam E. Indian Cuisine. 81p. 1985. 8.95 (*0-318-36295-3*) Asia Bk Corp.
— The Thangam Philip Book of Cooking. 122p. 1982. pap. 3.50 (*0-86131-285-6*) Apt Bks.
Philipchal. Invitation to Social Psychology. (C). 1994. pap. text, teacher ed., suppl. ed. 82.00 (*0-15-502464-7*, Pub. by Harcourt Coll Pubs); pap. text, student ed. 28.00 (*0-15-502463-9*) Harcourt Coll Pubs.
— Invitation to Social Psychology. (C). 1994. pap. text, teacher ed. 70.00 (*0-15-502462-0*) Harcourt Coll Pubs.
— Ont's - Invitation To Social Psychology. (C). 1994. pap. text 441.50 (*0-15-502465-5*) Harcourt Coll Pubs.
— Understanding Human Behavior. 8th ed. (C). 1994. pap. text, teacher ed. 35.00 (*0-15-501419-6*); pap. text, student ed. 28.50 (*0-15-501420-X*) Harcourt Coll Pubs.
— Understanding Human Behavior: Test Bank. 8th ed. (C). 1994. pap. text 41.50 (*0-15-501421-8*, Pub. by Harcourt Coll Pubs) Harcourt.
Philipchalk, Ronald P. Psychology & Christianity: An Introduction to Controversial Issues. rev. ed. 258p. (Orig.). (C). 1988. pap. text 22.50 (*0-8191-7124-7*) U Pr of Amer.
Philipchalk, Ronald P. & McConnell, James V. Understanding Human Behavior. 8th ed. (Illus.). 704p. (C). 1994. text 83.50 (*0-15-500991-5*, Pub. by Harcourt Coll Pubs) Harcourt.
Philipchalk, Ronald P., jt. auth. see McConnell, James V.
Philipe, Anne. Ete pres de la Mer. (Folio Ser.: No. 1152). (FRE.). pap. 8.95 (*2-07-037152-2*) Schoenhof.
Philipon, M. M. Conchita: A Mother's Spiritual Diary. Owen, Aloysius, tr. LC 78-1929. 256p. 1978. pap. 14.95 (*0-8189-0578-6*) Alba.
Philipot. Mammography Exam Review. 224p. 1992. pap. text 28.95 (*0-397-55019-7*) Lppncott W & W.
Philipp, B., et al. Polyelectrolytes: Formation, Characterization & Application. LC 94-26915. 1994. 99.50 (*1-56990-127-9*) Hanser-Gardner.
Philipp, Barry S. The Fear Factor: The Core of a Desperate Society. Schmermund, Cathy, ed. LC 98-71730. (Illus.). 354p. 1998. pap. 30.00 (*0-9658057-0-0*) I Corinthians.
— The Fear Factor: The Core of a Desperate Society. 2nd ed. (Illus.). 344p. 1998. pap. text 22.95 (*0-9658057-1-9*) I Corinthians.
Philipp, Cathy. On the Trail: Malibu to Santa Barbara. LC 97-91534. (Illus.). 250p. (Orig.). 1997. pap. 17.95 (*0-9655848-0-1*) C Philipp.
Philipp, Christiane, jt. ed. see Wolfrum, Rudiger.
Philipp, David P., et al, eds. Protection of Aquatic Diversity Theme 3: Proceedings of the World Fisheries Congress, Athens, Greece. 292p. 1996. text 79.00 (*1-886106-11-8*) Science Pubs.
Philipp, E. E., jt. auth. see O'Dowd, M. J.
Philipp, E. E., jt. ed. see O'Dowd, M. J.
Philipp, Emanuel L. Political Reform in Wisconsin: A Historical Review of the Subjects of Primary Election, Taxation & Railway Regulation. Caine, Stanley P. & Wyman, Roger, eds. LC 73-620042. (Illus.). 197p. 1973. reprint ed. 12.00 (*0-87020-123-9*) State Hist Soc Wis.
Philipp, Gudrun. Lehrplanentwicklung im Fach Evangelische Religion in Schleswig-Holstein. (Beitrage zur Erziehungswissenschaft und Biblischen Bildung Ser.: Bd. 2). (GER.). 210p. 1997. 42.95 (*3-631-30922-8*) P Lang Pubng.
Philipp, Kay, jt. compiled by see Henshaw, Wanda.
***Philipp, Klaus J.** Karl Friedrich Schinkel 2 vols. Late Projects. 2000. 240.00 (*3-930698-11-0*) Edition A Menges.
Philipp, Klaus Jan. Um 1800: Architekturtheorie und Architekturkritik in Deutschland Zwischen 1790 und 1810. (GER., Illus.). 280p. 89.00 (*3-930698-76-5*) Edition A Menges.
Philipp, Lillie H. Piano Technique: Tone, Touch, Phrasing & Dynamics. (Illus.). 90p. (J). (gr. 7 up). 1982. reprint ed. pap. 6.95 (*0-486-24272-2*) Dover.
Philipp, Michael. Lappische Schildereyen? (Europaische Hochschulschriften Ser.: Reihe 36, Vol. 178). (Illus.). XII, 402p. 1998. pap. 56.95 (*3-631-33337-4*) P Lang Pubng.
Philipp, Thomas & Haarmann, Ulrich, eds. The Mamluks in Egyptian Politics & Society. LC 97-9821. (Studies in Islamic Civilization). 320p. (C). 1998. text 59.95 (*0-521-59115-5*) Cambridge U Pr.
Philipp, Thomas, ed. & tr. see Zaidan, Jurji.
Philipp, Walter. Mixing Sequences of Random Variables & Probabilistic Number Theory. LC 52-42839. (Memoirs Ser.: No. 1/114). 102p. 1971. pap. 16.00 (*0-8218-1814-7*, MEMO/1/114) Am Math.
Philipp, Walter & Stout, William. Almost Sure Invariance Principles for Partial Sums of Weakly Dependent Random Variables. (Memoirs Ser.: No. 2/161). 140p. 1987. reprint ed. pap. 26.00 (*0-8218-1861-9*, MEMO/2/161) Am Math.

Philippaki-Warburton, Irene, et al, eds. Themes in Greek Linguistics: Papers from the 1st International Conference on Greek Linguistics, Reading, September 1993. LC 94-38050. (Current Issues in Linguistic Theory Ser.: No. 117). xviii, 534p. 1994. 79.00 (*1-55619-571-0*) J Benjamins Pubng Co.
Philippaki-Warburton, Irene, jt. auth. see Joseph, Brian D.
Philippart, David. Prayers of Those Who Mourn. 2nd ed. 64p. (Orig.). 1996. reprint ed. pap. 4.00 (*1-56854-132-5*, MOURNR) Liturgy Tr Pubns.
— Prayers with the Dying. 64p. (Orig.). 1997. pap. 4.00 (*1-56854-115-5*, DYING) Liturgy Tr Pubns.
— Saving Signs, Wondrous Words. LC 96-41455. 140p. (Orig.). 1996. pap. 10.00 (*1-56854-103-1*, SAVING) Liturgy Tr Pubns.
— Serve God with Gladness: A Manual for Servers. Connell, Martin, ed. (Illus.). 106p. (Orig.). 1998. pap., teacher ed. 10.00 (*1-56854-151-1*, SERVER) Liturgy Tr Pubns.
***Philippart, David, ed.** Ash Wednesday. (Liturgy Ser.). (Illus.). 55p. 1999. pap. 10.95 (*0-918208-81-5*) Liturgical Conf.
Philippart, David, ed. Clothed in Glory: Vesting the Church. LC 97-22691. (Illus.). 131p. (Orig.). 1997. pap. 16.00 (*1-56854-187-2*, GLORY) Liturgy Tr Pubns.
— Prayers for Caregivers. (Prayer Book Ser.). 64p. 2000. pap. 4.00 (*1-56854-264-X*, PCARE) Liturgy Tr Pubns.
— Prayers for Later Years. 64p. (Orig.). 1996. pap. 4.00 (*1-56854-146-5*, ELDER) Liturgy Tr Pubns.
— Prayers for Midday. LC 98-89934. (Prayer Book Ser.). 64p. 1999. pap. 4.00 (*1-56854-263-1*, MDAY) Liturgy Tr Pubns.
— Prayers for the Dedication of a Church. LC 97-39787. 84p. 1997. pap. 5.00 (*1-56854-197-X*, CHURCH) Liturgy Tr Pubns.
— Prayers of Those Who Make Music. 2nd rev. ed. 64p. (Orig.). 1996. pap. 4.00 (*1-56854-131-7*, MUSICR) Liturgy Tr Pubns.
Philippart, David, ed. see Buscemi, John.
Philippart, David, ed. see DeSanctis, Michael E.
Philippart, David, ed. see Jones-Frank, Michael.
Philippart, David, jt. ed. see Luty, Kathy.
Philippart, David, ed. see Overbeck, T. Jerome.
Philippart, David, ed. see Ryan, Thomas.
Philippart, David, ed. see Smith, Peter E.
Philippart, David, ed. see Sovik, Edward A.
Philippart, David, ed. see Stroik, Christopher V.
Philippatos, George C. Financial Management: Theory & Techniques. LC 72-83249. 661p. (C). 1973. text 36.95 (*0-8162-6736-7*) Holden-Day.
Philippatos, George C. & Sihler, William W. Financial Management: Intermediate Text & Cases. 2nd ed. 600p. 1991. write for info. (*0-318-66340-6*, H24409); write for info. (*0-318-66341-4*, H27014) P-H.
Philippe, Anne. Un Ete pres de la Mer. (FRE.). 1979. pap. 10.95 (*0-7859-4123-1*) Fr & Eur.
— Les Resonances de l'Amour. (FRE.). 1985. pap. 8.95 (*0-7859-4223-8*) Fr & Eur.
Philippe, Anne & Weelen, Guy. Arpad Szenes. (Grandes Monografias). (SPA., Illus.). 340p. 1993. 300.00 (*84-343-0663-8*) Elliots Bks.
Philippe, Charles-Louis. La Mere et l'Enfant-Le Pere Perdrix. (FRE.). 1983. pap. 13.95 (*0-7859-4194-0*) Fr & Eur.
Philippe De Remi. Roman de la Manekine par Philippe de Reimes. LC 74-174193. (Bannatyne Club, Edinburgh. Publications: No. 68). reprint ed. 47.50 (*0-404-52788-4*) AMS Pr.
— The Romance of Blonde of Oxford & Jehan of Dammartin. Le-Roux De Lincy, M., ed. (Camden Society, London. Publications, First Ser.: No. 72). reprint ed. 55.00 (*0-404-50172-9*) AMS Pr.
Philippe, Jean-Baptiste. Free Mulatto. LC 98-16087. 298p. 1996. reprint ed. pap. text 15.95 (*0-911565-15-9*) Calaloux Pubns.
Philippe, Jorge & Quintanilla, Jaime. El Vendedor Efectivo de Bienes Raices.Tr. of Successful Real Estate Sales. 192p. 1998. 21.95 (*0-7931-3009-3*) Dearborn.
***Philippe Op, Marie Dominique.** Retracing Reality: A Philosophical Itinerary. Peridans, Dominique F., tr. 192p. 1999. 39.95 (*0-567-08664-X*) T&T Clark Pubs.
Philippe, Pierre P. & Spiteri, Laurence J. The Virgin Mary & the Priesthood. LC 93-6682.Tr. of Vergine Marie e il sacerdozio. (ENG.). 158p. (Orig.). 1993. pap. 9.95 (*0-8189-0668-5*) Alba.
Philippi, Charles, tr. see De Vogue, Adalbert.
Philippi, Charles, tr. see Vogue, Adalbert de.
Philippi, Donald L. Songs of Gods, Songs of Humans: The Epic Tradition of the Ainu. LC 78-18002. (Illus.). 426p. reprint ed. pap. 132.10 (*0-8357-3704-7*, 203642900003) Bks Demand.
Philippi, Donald L., tr. Kojiki. 1982. pap. 44.50 (*0-86008-320-9*, Pub. by U of Tokyo) Col U Pr.
— Norito: A Translation of the Ancient Japanese Ritual Prayers. 95p. (C). 1998. pap. text 15.00 (*0-7881-5459-1*) DIANE Pub.
— Songs of Gods, Songs of Humans: The Epic Tradition of the Ainu. 432p. 1995. 55.00 (*0-86008-235-0*, Pub. by U of Tokyo) Col U Pr.
Philippi, Jorie. Literacy at Work: The Workbook for Program Developers. 1991. mass mkt. 200.00 (*0-13-528837-1*) P-H.
Philippi, Nancy S. Floodplain Management. 1996. text 69.95 (*0-12-554010-8*) Acad Pr.
— Floodplain Management: Ecologic & Economic Perspectives. LC 96-20763. (Environmental Intelligence Unit Ser.). 138p. 1996. 79.00 (*1-57059-364-7*) Landes Bioscience.
Philippi, Nancy S., jt. auth. see Hey, Donald.

Philippides, Dia M. Census of Modern Greek Literature: Check-List of English-Language Sources Useful in the Study of Modern Greek Literature (1824-1987) (MSGA Occasional Papers: No. 2). xviii, 248p. (Orig.). (C). 1990. reprint ed. pap. write for info. (*0-912105-01-1*) Modern Greek Studies Assn.

— The Iambic Trimeter of Euripides. rev. ed. Connor, W. R., ed. LC 80-2663. 1981. lib. bdg. 35.95 (*0-405-14048-7*) Ayer.

***Philippides, Dimitris.** Greek Design & Decoration: Three Centuries of Architectural Style. (Illus.). 285p. 2000. 65.00 (*0-8109-6690-5*, Pub. by Abrams) Time Warner.

Philippides, Marios. Constantine Eleventh Dragas Palaeologus: A Biography of the Last Greek Emperor. (Hellenism: Ancient, Mediaeval, Modern Ser.: No. 17). 600p. (C). 1993. text 85.00 (*0-89241-522-3*) Caratzas.

— Emperors, Patriarchs & Sultans: Short Chronicle of the Sixteenth Century. Vaporis, Nomikos M., ed. LC 85-30184. (Archbishop Iacovos Library of Ecclesiastical & Historical Sources: No. 13). 192p. (C). 1990. 14.95 (*0-917653-15-7*, Pub. by Hellenic Coll Pr); pap. 14.95 (*0-917653-16-5*, Pub. by Hellenic Coll Pr) BookWorld.

Philippides, Marios, tr. Byzantium, Europe & the Early Ottoman Sultans, 1373-1513: An Anonymous Greek Chronicle of the Seventeenth Century (Codex Barberinus Graecus III) (Late Byzantine & Ottoman Studies: No. 4). viii, 229p. 1990. text 50.00 (*0-89241-430-8*) Caratzas.

Philippides, Marios, ed. & tr. see Nestor-Iskander.

Philippides, Mary Z., jt. auth. see Moore, Mary B.

Philippine Center for Investigative Journalism Staff, jt. auth. see Dadnguilan, Marilen J.

Philippines Commonwealth Constitution 1972 Staff, ed. see Malcolm, George A.

Philippoff, Jennifer, jt. auth. see Maurer-Mathison, Diane V.

Philippon, Daniel J., jt. auth. see Branch, Michael P.

Philippon, Patrice, ed. Approximations Diophantiennes et Nombres Transcendants: Diophantine Approximations & Transcendental Numbers. x, 310p. (C). 1992. lib. bdg. 159.95 (*3-11-013486-1*) De Gruyter.

Philippot, Jean R. & Schuber, Francis, eds. Liposomes As Tools in Basic Research & Industry. 286p. 1994. boxed set 246.95 (*0-8493-4569-3*, 4569) CRC Pr.

Philippot, Patrick. Turbo Pascal: Procedures & Functions for IBM PCs & Compatibles. Beeson, David & Keith, Seth, eds. LC 87-18797. 204p. reprint ed. pap. 63.30 (*0-7837-0114-4*, 204039100016) Bks Demand.

Philippot, Pierre, et al, eds. The Social Context of Nonverbal Behavior. LC 98-11637. (Studies in Emotion & Social Interaction). (Illus.). 432p. (C). 1999. text 64.95 (*0-521-58371-3*); pap. text 24.95 (*0-521-58666-6*) Cambridge U Pr.

Philippou, A. N., et al, eds. Applications of Fibonacci Numbers. (C). 1988. text 156.00 (*90-277-2673-6*) Kluwer Academic.

Philipps, Christopher, tr. see Mauries, Patrick.

***Philipps, Gordian.** Das Konzept der Organisationsentwicklung: Ansatze und Kritik Sowie Konsequenzen Fur die Ausgestaltung Von Oe-Prozessen In der Praxis. (GER.). 310p. 1999. 56.95 (*3-631-34616-6*) P Lang Pubng.

***Philipps, Helen.** New Cross Stitch Sampler Book: 25 Fabulous Samples & 72 Projects to Stitch from Them. (Illus.). 2000. 24.95 (*0-7153-0797-5*) D & C Pub.

Philipps, John. Die Deutschen Am Schwarzeen Meer Zwischen Bug & Dnjester. (Illus.). 1999. pap. 20.00 (*1-891193-04-X*) ND State Univ.

— The Tragedy of the Soviet Germans. LC 83-61289. (Illus.). 190p. (Orig.). 1983. pap. 6.50 (*0-9611412-0-4*) John Philipps.

Philippsborn, H. E. Dictionary of Industrial Technology, English, German & Portuguese. (ENG, GER & POR.). 943p. 1994. 495.00 (*0-7859-9381-9*) Fr & Eur.

***Philippsborn, H. E.** Elsevier's Dictionary of Cosmetic Science. LC 00-37197. (FRE & POR., Illus.). 2000. write for info. (*0-444-50171-1*) Elsevier.

Philippsborn, H. E., compiled by. Elsevier's Dictionary of Industrial Technology. LC 94-1644. (ENG, GER & POR.). 952p. 1994. 324.25 (*0-444-89945-6*) Elsevier.

Philippson, Robert. Studien Zur Epikur und Den Epikureern. Classen, C. Joachim, ed. (Olms GW Studien: Bd. 17). (GER.). vi, 354p. 1983. write for info. (*3-487-07380-3*) G Olms Pubs.

Philippus De Thame. Knights Hospitallers in England: Being the Report of Prior Phillip De Thame to the Grand Master Elyan De Villanova for A. D. 1338. Larking, Lambert B., ed. (Camden Society, London. Publications, First Ser.: No. 65). reprint ed. 75.00 (*0-404-50165-6*) AMS Pr.

Philippus, M. J., jt. auth. see Wallace, B. D.

Philips. Beechcraft: Pursuit of Perfection. (Illus.). 92p. 1992. 24.95 (*0-911139-11-7*) Flying Bks.

***Philips.** Family World Atlas. (Illus.). 56p. 2000. 9.95 (*0-540-07697-X*) Sterling.

Philips, jt. auth. see Fess, Elaine.

Philips, Betty J. & Ruscello, Dennis M. Differential Diagnosis in Speech-Language Pathology. LC 97-34816. 360p. 1997. text 47.50 (*0-7506-9675-3*) Buttrwrth-Heinemann.

Philips, C. H. Beyond the Ivory Tower: An Autobiography. LC 96-107687. 1995. text 45.00 (*1-86064-016-8*) St Martin.

— Correspondence David Scott, Director & Chairman of the East India Company Relating to Indian Affairs, 1787-1805, Vol. I. (Camden Third Ser.). 63.00 (*0-86193-075-4*) David Brown.

— Correspondence David Scott, Director & Chairman of the East Indian Company Relating to Indian Affairs, 1787-1805, Vol. II. (Camden Third Ser.). 63.00 (*0-86193-076-2*) David Brown.

— Handbook of Oriental History. (RHS Guides & Handbooks Ser.: No. 6). 273p. 17.50 (*0-901050-16-4*) David Brown.

Philips, C. H., ed. see University of London, Dept. of Oriental & African.

Philips, Carey, jt. ed. see Yates, Katherine.

Philips, Catherine A., tr. see Ugarte, Manuel.

Philips, Chris, jt. auth. see Lee, Peter.

Philips, Curt. Love's Journey. LC 84-70262. (Illus.). 139p. (Orig.). (C). 1984. pap. text 6.95 (*0-918899-00-1*) Dragonscales & Mane Pub.

Philips, D. Z. Wittgenstein & Religion, Vol. 1. 1994. pap. 20.95 (*0-312-12300-0*) St Martin.

Philips, Dan, ed. see Thompson, Larry.

Philips, Dana. Blacksmith's Tale, or Once Upon a Flower. LC 98-50321. (J). 2000. 24.95 (*1-889274-07-0*) Posterity Press.

Philips, Dave. Nature Mazes. (Illus.). 48p. 1998. pap. text 2.95 (*0-486-40401-3*) Dover.

Philips, David. Legendary Connecticut. LC 92-24532. (Illus.). 303p. 1992. pap. 15.95 (*1-880684-05-5*) Curbstone.

Philips, David & Davies, Susanne, eds. A Nation of Rogues? Crime, Law & Punishment in Colonial Australia. 224p. 1994. pap. 24.95 (*0-522-84601-7*, Pub. by Melbourne Univ Pr) Paul & Co Pubs.

Philips, David & Storch, Robert D. Policing Provincial England, 1829-1856: The Politics of Reform. LC 98-26883. 1999. 75.00 (*0-7185-0112-8*) Bks Intl VA.

Philips, Deborah & Haywood, Ian. Brave New Causes: Women in British Postwar Fictions. LC 97-16934. 224p. 1998. 75.00 (*0-7185-0058-X*); pap. 24.95 (*0-7185-0059-8*) Bks Intl VA.

Philips, Deborah, et al. Writing Well: Creative Writing & Mental Health. LC 98-41232. 1998. 29.95 (*1-85302-650-6*) Jessica Kingsley.

Philips, Dewi Z. Through a Darkening Glass: Philosophy, Literature & Cultural Change. LC 81-40456. 206p. 1982. reprint ed. pap. 63.90 (*0-608-00888-5*, 206168200010) Bks Demand.

Philips, E. Lakin. Permissiveness in Child Rearing & Education - A Failed Doctrine? New Trends for the 1990s. LC 92-35833. 134p. (C). 1993. text 42.50 (*0-8191-8978-2*) U Pr of Amer.

Philips, Edward H. Cessna: A Masters Expression. LC 85-81741. (Illus.). 152p. 1985. 29.95 (*0-911139-04-4*) Flying Bks.

— Travel Air: Wings over the Prairie. (Illus.). 128p. 1994. reprint ed. pap. 21.95 (*0-911139-17-6*) Flying Bks.

Philips, Elizabeth. Beyond My Keeping. 80p. 1995. pap. 8.95 (*1-55050-077-5*, Pub. by Coteau) Genl Dist Srvs.

Philips, Elizabeth D., et al. Intermediate Algebra: Applications & Problem Solving. 2nd ed. LC 93-4030. 672p. (C). 1997. 86.00 (*0-06-045220-X*) Addson-Wesley Educ.

— Intermediate Algebra: Applications & Problem Solving. 2nd ed. LC 93-4030. 208p. (C). 1997. pap., student ed. 22.00 (*0-06-501927-X*) Addson-Wesley Educ.

Philips, Frederick. Forty-Five Years with Philips. 1980. 4.95 (*0-7137-0931-6*) Grosvenor USA.

Philips, G. Freedom Through Obedience. 7.99 (*0-906731-90-9*, Pub. by Christian Focus) Spring Arbor Dist.

Philips, Gary W., jt. auth. see Johnson, Eugene G.

Philips, George O. Philips Family Record, 1978. (Illus.). 520p. (Orig.). 1979. pap. 17.50 (*0-940846-00-4*) Hastings Bks.

Philips, Georges & Buncher, Lyn. Gold Counselling: A Practical Psychology with NLP. 221p. 1997. pap. 24.95 (*1-899836-06-3*, Pub. by Crown Hse) Empowerment Tech.

***Philips, Georges & Buncher, Lyn.** GOLD Counselling: A Structured Psychotherapeutic Approach to the Mapping & Re-Aligning of Belief Systems. 284p. 1999. pap. 24.95 (*1-899836-33-0*, Pub. by Crown Hse) LPC Group.

***Philips, Georges & Watts, Terence.** Rapid Cognitive Therapy: The Professional Therapists' Guide to Rapid Change Work, Vol. 1. 246p. 1999. pap. 34.95 (*1-899836-37-3*, Pub. by Crown Hse) LPC Group.

***Philips, Gretchen, et al.** The Quizm Message: Trash Landing. (Illus.). 36p. (J). (gr. k-2). 1999. 11.99 (*0-9671611-0-X*) KRW Intl.

— The Quizm Message: Trash Landing, 1, 1. (Illus.). 36p. (J). (gr. k-2). 1999. pap. 7.99 (*0-9671611-1-8*) KRW Intl.

Philips, H. Clare & Rachman, Stanley J. The Psychological Management of Chronic Pain, 2 vols. 2nd ed. Incl. Psychological Management of Chronic Pain: A Treatment Manual. 2nd ed. (Illus.). 304p. 1996. 42.95 (*0-8261-6111-1*); Psychological Management of Chronic Pain: Patient Manual. 2nd ed. (Illus.). 80p. 1996. teacher ed. 14.95 (*0-8261-6112-X*); (Behavior Therapy & Behavioral Medicine Ser.). 1996. 52.00 (*0-8261-6113-8*, P4821) Springer Pub.

Philips, Henry Gerard. The Making of a Professional: Manton S. Eddy, U.S.A, 185. LC 99-15456. 185. 280p. 2000. 65.00 (*0-313-31183-8*, Greenwood Pr) Greenwood.

Philips IMS Staff. The CD-I Design Handbook. LC 92-15877. 224p. (C). 1992. pap. text 24.95 (*0-201-62749-3*) Addison-Wesley.

— The CD-I Production Handbook. LC 92-15878. 224p. (C). 1992. pap. text 24.95 (*0-201-62750-7*) Addison-Wesley.

***Philips, Ingram.** Beyond Sundown. LC 99-91657. 275p. 2000. 25.00 (*0-7388-1158-0*); pap. 18.00 (*0-7388-1159-9*) Xlibris Corp.

Philips, Ivor R. An Engineer's C++ Primer. (C). 1997. pap. text. write for info. (*0-201-87725-2*) Addison-Wesley.

Philips, J. G., tr. see Eitel, Wilhelm.

***Philips, Jane H.** Gloria Estefan. (Women of Achievement Ser.). 2000. 19.95 (*0-7910-5883-2*) Chelsea Hse.

— Gloria Estefan. (Women of Achievement Ser.). (Illus.). 2001. pap. 9.95 (*0-7910-5884-0*) Chelsea Hse.

Philips, Jeanette, jt. auth. see Orell, Svante R.

Philips, Jeremy & Hooke, James. The Sports of Debating: Winning Skills & Strategies. 176p. 1998. pap. 19.95 (*0-86840-664-3*, Pub. by New South Wales Univ Pr) Intl Spec Bk.

Philips, Jim. The Great Alliance: Economic Recovery & the Problems of Power, 1945-1951. LC 95-38684. 176p. 1996. 54.95 (*0-7453-1038-9*, Pub. by Pluto GBR); pap. 19.95 (*0-7453-1037-0*, Pub. by Pluto GBR) Stylus Pub VA.

Philips, John. People of the Bible. LC 98-37055. 432p. 1999. 8.99 (*0-517-20421-5*) Random Hse Value.

***Philips, John.** SAP Production Planning & Materials Management: An End-User Guide to the SAP R/3 Modules. 2000. pap. text. write for info. (*0-07-212259-5*) McGrw-H Intl.

Philips, John E., jt. ed. see Miura, Toru.

Philips, Judson. Death Is a Dirty Trick. large type ed. (Linford Mystery Library). 352p. 1997. pap. 16.99 (*0-7089-5159-7*) Ulverscroft.

— Escape a Killer. large type ed. (Linford Mystery Library). 336p. 1997. pap. 16.99 (*0-7089-5104-X*, Linford) Ulverscroft.

— Five Roads to Death. large type ed. (Linford Mystery Library.). 384p. 1997. pap. 16.99 (*0-7089-5171-6*) Ulverscroft.

— The Larkspur Conspiracy. large type ed. (Linford Mystery Library). 320p. 1998. pap. 17.99 (*0-7089-5219-4*, Linford) Ulverscroft.

Philips, Julia, jt. auth. see Philips, Matthew.

Philips, Katherine. Poems by the Most Deservedly Admired Mrs. Katherine Phillips: The Matchless Orinda. LC 92-1093. (Scholars' Facsimiles & Reprints Ser.). 200p. 1992. reprint ed. 50.00 (*0-8201-1462-6*) Schol Facsimiles.

Philips, Laura, jt. auth. see Lerner, Mark.

Philips, Leslie N., ed. Design with Advanced Composite Materials. (Illus.). 384p. (C). 1989. 67.95 (*0-85072-238-1*, Pub. by Gower) Ashgate Pub Co.

***Philips Maps Publishing Staff.** World Atlas & Gazetteer: In Association with the Royal Geographical Society. (Illus.). 188p. 2000. 29.95 (*0-540-07709-7*) Philips Maps.

Philips, Mary E., jt. auth. see Brown, Carol E.

Philips, Matthew & Philips, Julia. Witches of Oz. 1994. pap. 19.95 (*1-898307-18-0*, Pub. by Capall Bann Pubng) Holmes Pub.

Philips, Michael. Between Universalism & Skepticism: Ethics As Social Artifact. 224p. 1994. text 55.00 (*0-19-508646-5*) OUP.

Philips, Michael, ed. Philosophy & Science Fiction. LC 83-62874. 400p. 1984. pap. 24.95 (*0-87975-248-3*) Prometheus Bks.

Philips, Neil. A Braid of Lives: Growing up Native American. (Illus.). 96p. (gr. 8-12). 2000. 20.00 (*0-395-64528-X*) HM.

***Philips, Neil.** Mythology. LC 98-32234. 60p. (YA). (gr. 5-9). 1999. 19.00 (*0-375-80135-9*) Knopf.

Philips, Paul. Time-Space Transcendence. LC 84-71711. 72p. (Orig.). 1984. pap. 8.95 (*0-930149-00-9*) AAP Calif.

— Transpersonal Psychology for Daily Life. LC 80-66662. (Illus.). 98p. (Orig.). 1984. pap. 8.95 (*0-930149-01-7*) AAP Calif.

Philips, Peter, jt. ed. see Mangum, Garth L.

Philips, Robert. History Teaching, Nationhood & the State: A Study in Educational Politics. LC 99-207617. 196p. 1998. 75.00 (*0-304-70298-6*); pap. 24.95 (*0-304-70299-4*) Continuum.

Philips, Roger A. Guide to Software Export: A Handbook for International Software Sales. LC 97-14967. 228p. (C). 1998. 49.95 (*0-7890-0143-8*, Intl Busn Pr) Haworth Pr.

***Philips, Ronald J.** Made Kindred by the Spirit. 2000. pap. 12.99 (*0-87148-609-1*) Pathway Pr.

Philips, Ronald J., jt. auth. see Mercer, James L.

Philips, Rosemarie, jt. auth. see Tucker, Stuart K.

***Philips, Skin.** Skateboard Roadmap. 1999. pap. text 16.95 (*1-85868-803-5*, Pub. by Carlton Bks Ltd) Natl Bk Netwk.

Philips, Steve, ed. see Ukeni, Stanley.

Philips, Susan U. Ideology in the Language of Judges: How Judges Practice Law, Politics & Courtroom Control. LC 97-48671. (Oxford Studies in Anthropological Linguistics). 224p. 1998. text 65.00 (*0-19-511340-3*) OUP.

— Ideology in the Language of Judges: How Judges Practice Law, Politics & Courtroom Control. LC 97-48671. (Oxford Studies in Anthropological Linguistics: No. 17). 224p. 1998. pap. 35.00 (*0-19-511341-1*) OUP.

— The Invisible Culture: Communication in Classroom & Community on the Warm Springs Indian Reservation. rev. ed. 147p. (C). 1993. reprint ed. pap. text 11.50 (*0-88133-694-7*) Waveland Pr.

Philips, Susan U., et al, eds. Language, Gender, & Sex in Comparative Perspective. (Studies in the Social & Cultural Foundations of Language: No. 4). (Illus.). 350p. 1987. pap. text 24.95 (*0-521-33807-7*) Cambridge U Pr.

Philips, Sylvia. Management Skills for Senior Coordinators in the Primary School. LC 99-183112. (Subject Leaders Handbks.). 238p. 1998. pap. 23.95 (*0-7507-0697-X*, Falmer Pr) Taylor & Francis.

***Philips, Tom.** Africa: The Art of the Continent. (Illus.). 1999. 49.95 (*3-7913-2004-1*, Pub. by Prestel) te Neues.

Philips, Tracy. Affirmations for Twenty Somethings: Keeping the Old Chin up in the Face of Utter Disaster. LC 97-141670. 96p. 1996. pap. 7.95 (*0-930753-21-6*) Spect Ln Pr.

Philips University Graduate Seminary Staff, jt. auth. see Hamburger, Roberta.

Philips, V. A., jt. auth. see Moiser, C. H.

Philips, William. St. Stephen's Green: Generous Lovers. 112p. 1980. 23.95 (*0-85105-367-X*, Pub. by Smyth) Dufour.

Philipsborn, K. L. Von, see Hochleitner, R. H.

Philipsborn's. Fasions of the Early Twenties: The 1921 Philipsborn's Catalog. unabridged ed. LC 96-27377. (Illus.). 288p. reprint ed. pap. 18.95 (*0-486-29385-8*) Dover.

***Philipse, Herman.** Heidegger's Philosophy of Being: A Critical Interpretation. 555p. 1999. pap. 200.00 (*81-208-1684-6*, Pub. by Motilal Bnarsidass) St Mut.

— Heidegger's Philosophy of Being: A Critical Interpretation. LC 98-34876. 1998. 60.00 (*0-691-00117-0*, Pub. by Princeton U Pr); pap. 29.95 (*0-691-00119-7*, Pub. by Princeton U Pr) Cal Prin Full Svc.

Philipsen, Dirk. We Were the People: Voices from East Germany's Revolutionary Autumn of 1989. LC 92-12762. 432p. 1992. pap. 19.95 (*0-8223-1294-8*); text 59.95 (*0-8223-1282-4*) Duke.

Philipsen, Gerry. Speaking Culturally: Explorations in Social Communication. LC 91-33107. (SUNY Series, Human Communication Processes). 154p. (C). 1992. pap. text 18.95 (*0-7914-1164-8*) State U NY Pr.

Philipsen, Gerry & Albrecht, Terrance L., eds. Developing Communication Theories. LC 96-10632. (SUNY Series, Human Communication Processes). 196p. (C). 1997. text 67.50 (*0-7914-3159-2*); pap. text 20.95 (*0-7914-3160-6*) State U NY Pr.

Philipsen, Hans Peter, jt. auth. see Reichart, Peter A.

Philipsen, Maike. Values Spoken & Values Lived: The Cultural Consequences of a School Closing. LC 98-53139. (Understanding Education & Policy Ser.). 192p. (C). 1998. text 42.50 (*1-57273-208-3*); pap. text 20.95 (*1-57273-209-1*) Hampton Pr NJ.

Philipson, David. The Jew in English Fiction. LC 76-30568. (English Literature Ser.: No. 33). 1977. lib. bdg. 57.00 (*0-8383-2150-X*) M S G Haskell Hse.

— Old European Jewries. LC 74-178586. reprint ed. 41.50 (*0-404-56663-4*) AMS Pr.

Philipson, David, et al. Studies in Jewish Literature Issued in Honor of Professor Kaufmann Kohler, Ph.D. Katz, Steven, ed. LC 79-7167. (Jewish Philosophy, Mysticism & History of Ideas Ser.). 1980. reprint ed. lib. bdg. 29.95 (*0-405-12283-7*) Ayer.

Philipson, David, ed. see Wise, Isaac.

Philipson, Ilene J. On the Shoulders of Women: The Feminization of Psychotherapy. LC 93-25404. 177p. 1993. lib. bdg. 24.95 (*0-89862-017-1*) Guilford Pubns.

Philipson, Ilene J., jt. ed. see Hansen, Karen V.

Philipson, L., et al. The Molecular Biology of Adenoviruses. LC 75-6658. (Virology Monographs: Vol. 14). (Illus.). iv, 115p. 1975. 47.00 (*0-387-81284-9*) Spr-Verlag.

Philipson, L., jt. auth. see Lonberg-Holm, K.

Philipson, Lorrin & Willis, H. Lee. Understanding Electric Utilities & De-Regulation. LC 98-38126. (Power Engineering Ser.). (Illus.). 384p. 1998. text 145.00 (*0-8247-1920-4*) Dekker.

Philipson, Morris, ed. see Barzun, Jacques.

***Philipson, Morris H.** A Man in Charge: A Novel. LC 00-37790. (Phoenix Fiction Ser.). 2000. pap. write for info. (*0-226-66751-0*) U Ch Pr.

Philipson, Morris H. Outline of a Jungian Aesthetics. LC 63-15299. 224p. reprint ed. pap. 69.50 (*0-608-11192-9*, 200688400060) Bks Demand.

— Outline of Jungian Aesthetics. 1991. pap. 18.95 (*0-938434-88-8*) Sigo Pr.

***Philipson, Morris H.** Secret Understandings: A Novel. LC 00-39223. (Phoenix Fiction Ser.). 2000. pap. write for info. (*0-226-66752-9*) U Ch Pr.

— Somebody Else's Life: A Novel. LC 99-59838. 2000. pap. 13.00 (*0-226-66750-2*) U Ch Pr.

— Wallpaper Fox. LC 99-87635. 2000. pap. 12.00 (*0-226-66748-0*) U Ch Pr.

***Philipson, Robert.** The Identity Question: Blacks & Jews in Europe & America. LC 00-35196. 225p. 2000. pap. 18.00 (*1-57806-293-4*); lib. bdg. 45.00 (*1-57806-292-6*) U Pr of Miss.

***Philipson, Sandra.** Annie Loses Her Leg but Finds Her Way. (Illus.). 38p. (J). (gr. 1-6). 1999. 17.95 (*1-929821-00-X*) Chagrin River.

— Max's Wild Goose Chase. (Illus.). (J). (gr. k-4). 1999. 17.95 (*1-929821-01-8*) Chagrin River.

Philipson, Sten M. A Metaphysics for Theology: A Study of Some Problems in the Later Philosophy of Alfred North Whitehead & Its Applications to Issues in Contemporary Theology. (Studia Doctrinae Christianae Upsaliensia: No. 22). 174p. (Orig.). 1982. pap. 31.00 (*91-554-1246-7*, Pub. by Uppsala Univ Acta Univ Uppsaliensis) Coronet Bks.

***Philipson, Tomas J.** Data Markets. 1999. 38.00 (*0-226-66742-1*) U Ch Pr.

Philipson, Tomas J. & Posner, Richard A. Private Choices & Public Health: The AIDS Epidemic in an Economic Perspective. LC 93-17417. (Illus.). 272p. 1993. 37.95 (*0-674-70738-9*) HUP.

Philipson, Trevor. Carriage by Air. 1994. boxed set 209.00 (*0-406-02136-8*, UK, MICHIE) LEXIS Pub.

Philipson, U. N. Political Slang, 1750 to 1850. (Lund Studies in English: Vol. 9). 1974. reprint ed. pap. 45.00 (*0-8115-0552-9*) Periodicals Srv.

Philipson, Warren R. The Manual of Photographic Interpretation. 2nd ed. (Illus.). 700p. 1997. 124.00 (*1-57083-039-8*, 4725) ASP & RS.

Phillabaum, Stephen D. Employee-Employer Rights: The Complete Guide for the Washington Work Force. 2nd ed. (Legal Ser.). 112p. 1992. pap. 8.95 (*0-88908-749-0*) Self-Counsel Pr.

An Asterisk (*) at the beginning of an entry indicates that the title is appearing for the first time.

Phillander, Anthony S. There's a Sparrow in My Heart. LC 98-85819. 112p. 1998. text 14.95 (*1-56167-434-6*) Noble Hse MD.

Phillay, M. Abithana Kosha: The Tamil Classical Dictionary. (ENG & TAM.). 1985. 29.95 (*0-8288-1723-5*, M14481) Fr & Eur.

Phileo, Joanne, et al, eds. Cultural Competence in Substance Abuse Prevention. LC 97-6111. 224p. (Orig.). (C). 1997. pap. text 29.95 (*0-87101-278-2*, 2782) Natl Assn Soc Wkrs.

Philliber, William W., et al, eds. The Invisible Minority: Urban Appalachians. fac. ed. LC 79-4008. 205p. 1994. pap. 63.60 (*0-7837-7597-0*, 204735000007) Bks Demand.

Philliber, William W. & Obermiller, Phillip J., eds. Too Few Tomorrows: Urban Appalachians in the 1980's. LC 86-28816. 170p. (Orig.). 1987. pap. 8.95 (*0-913239-47-X*) Appalach Consortium.

Philliber, William W., jt. auth. see Vannoy-Hiller, Dana.

Philliber, William W., jt. ed. see Obermiller, Phillip J.

***Phillies, George D.** Elementary Lectures in Statistical Mechanics. Birman, J. L. et al, eds. LC 99-42810. (Graduate Texts in Contemporary Physics Ser.). (Illus.). 400p. 1999. 69.95 (*0-387-98918-8*) Spr-Verlag.

Phillimore, Jane. Katherine Mansfield. (Life & Works Ser.: Set II). (Illus.). 112p. (YA). (gr. 7 up). 1990. lib. bdg. 18.95 (*0-86593-020-1*) Rourke Corp.

Phillimore, Jane, et al. Life & Works, 6 bks., Set. (Illus.). 672p. (YA). (gr. 7 up). 1990. lib. bdg. 89.70 (*0-685-36350-3*) Rourke Corp.

Phillimore, John G. Introduction to the Study & History of the Roman Law. xvi, 320p. 1996. reprint ed. 45.00 (*0-8377-2558-5*, Rothman) W S Hein.

— Private Law among the Romans from the Pandects. xv, 423p. 1994. reprint ed. 57.50 (*0-8377-2550-X*, Rothman) W S Hein.

Phillimore, Polly. Netherlands. (Essential Guides Ser.). (Illus.). 128p. 1994. pap. 7.95 (*0-8442-8924-8*, 89248, Passprt Bks) NTC Contemp Pub Co.

Phillimore, Robert. Commentaries upon International Law, 3 vols. 1985. reprint ed. 165.00 (*0-8377-1018-9*, Rothman) W S Hein.

— Principal Ecclesiastical Judgments Delivered in the Court of Arches 1867 to 1875. xiii, 420p. 1981. reprint ed. 46.00 (*0-8377-2504-6*, Rothman) W S Hein.

Phillimore, W. P. Holbrow. Some Account of the Family of Holbrow, Anciently of Kingscote, Uley & Leonard Stanley in Gloucestershire. (Illus.). 45p. 1997. reprint ed. pap. 9.00 (*0-8328-9176-2*); reprint ed. lib. bdg. 19.00 (*0-8328-9175-4*) Higginson Bk Co.

Phillimore, W. P., ed. A Calendar of Wills Relating to the Counties of Northampton & Rutland. (British Record Society Index Library: Vols. 1,2 & 3). 1972. reprint ed. 80.00 (*0-8115-1452-8*) Periodicals Srv.

— Calendars of Wills & Administrations in the Consistory Court of the Bishop of Lichfield & Coventry, 1516-1652. (British Record Society Index Library: Vol. 7). 1972. reprint ed. pap. 65.00 (*0-8115-1454-4*) Periodicals Srv.

— An Index to Bills of Privy Signet, Commonly Called Signet Bills: 1584 -1596 & 1603-1624. (British Record Society Index Library Ser.: Vols. 4, 5 & 6). 1969. 80.00 (*0-8115-1453-6*) Periodicals Srv.

— Index to Wills Proved & Administrations Granted in the Court of the Archdeacon of Berkshire: 1508-1652. (British Record Society Index Library: Vols. 8, 9 & 10). 1969. reprint ed. 90.00 (*0-8115-1455-2*) Periodicals Srv.

— Placita Coram Domino Rege Apud Westmonasterium de Termino Sancte Trinitatis Anno Regni Regis Edwardii Filii Regis Henrici Vicesimo Quinto: The Pleas of the Count of Kings Bench, Trinity Team, 25 Edward I, 1297. (British Record Society Index Library: Vol. 19). 1974. reprint ed. pap. 36.00 (*0-8115-1464-1*) Periodicals Srv.

Phillimore, W. P. & Duncan, Leland L., eds. A Calendar of Wills Proved in the Consistory Court of the Bishop of Gloucester, 1541-1650. (British Record Society Index Library: Vol. 12). 1972. reprint ed. pap. 36.00 (*0-8115-1457-9*) Periodicals Srv.

Phillimore, W. P. & Fry, George S., eds. Abstracts of Inquisitiones Post Mortem for Gloucestershire Returned into the Court of Chancery During the Stuart Period, Pt. III: Miscellaneous Series, 13-18 Charles I, 1637-1642. (British Record Society Index Library: Vol. 13). 1972. reprint ed. pap. 25.00 (*0-8115-1458-7*) Periodicals Srv.

Phillimore, W. P., jt. ed. see Fry, Edward A.

Phillimore, William P. Fillmore: Memorials of the Family of Fynmore, with Notes on the Origin of Fynmore, Finnimore, Phillimore, Fillmore, Etc., & Particulars of Some of Those Surnames from the Year 1208 to (1886) (Illus.). 77p. 1997. reprint ed. pap. 15.00 (*0-8328-8554-1*); reprint ed. lib. bdg. 25.00 (*0-8328-8553-3*) Higginson Bk Co.

Phillimore, William P. & Thrift, Gertrude, eds. Indexes to Irish Wills, 5 vols. in 1. 827p. 1997. reprint ed. 50.00 (*0-8063-0440-5*) Genealog Pub.

Phillip, jt. auth. see Sturges.

Phillip, Dave. Sea Life Mazes. (Illus.). (J). (ps-3). 1997. mass mkt. 1.00 (*0-486-29422-6*) Dover.

Phillip, F. & Lane, Harlan. Philosophical Works of Etienne Bonnot, Abbe de Condillac, Vol. 1. Philip, Franklin, tr. 448p. (C). 1982. text 89.95 (*0-89859-181-3*) L Erlbaum Assocs.

Phillip, Franklin, ed. see Walesa, Lech.

Phillip, J. Christian Warfare & Armour. Date not set. pap. 5.99 (*1-871676-12-6*, Pub. by Christian Focus) Spring Arbor Dist.

— Up Against It. 1995. 8.50 (*1-871676-54-1*, Pub. by Christian Focus) Spring Arbor Dist.

Phillip, Jay-Michael, II. The Black Man's Problem Is His Own. Stafford, Marina, ed. 225p. (Orig.). 1994. pap. 11.95 (*1-884500-00-5*) Dynamic Key.

***Phillip, John & Carroll.** Mayo Clinic W/S Cookbook (gr. 11). 1999. pap. 18.95 (*0-7370-2035-0*) T-L Custom Pub.

Phillip, Laurie A. The Traffic Accident Manual: The Only Step-by-Step How-To Book That You Absolutely Need, but . . . Hope You'll Never Use. viii, 205p. 1997. pap. 29.95 (*0-9661481-1-8*) Right Direct.

Phillip, W., tr. see De Veer, Gerrit.

Phillip, Z. A Skeptic's Guide to the Twelve Steps. 242p. (Orig.). 1990. pap. 11.00 (*0-89486-722-9*, 5130A) Hazelden.

Phillipe, Esther. God's Back Pocket. (Family Missionary Ser.). (Illus.). 124p. (Orig.). 1988. pap. 5.99 (*0-89827-054-5*, BKC00) Wesleyan Pub Hse.

Phillipo, Stephanie, ed. see Bryan, L. A. & Bryan, E. A.

Phillipo, Stephanie, ed. see Bryan, Luis A. & Bryan, Eric A.

Phillipp, Isidor, ed. French Piano Music: An Anthology. (Anthology of French Piano Music Ser.). 188p. 1977. pap. 9.95 (*0-486-23381-2*) Dover.

***Phillippe, Esther.** The Ants Will Carry the Elephant. (Illus.). 24p. (J). (gr. 1-3). 2000. pap. text 3.99 (*0-89827-211-4*) Wesleyan Pub Hse.

Phillippe, William R. Bible Stories You Never Heard Before. LC 87-11618. ix, 155p. (Orig.). 1989. pap. 9.95 (*0-940473-06-2*) Wm Caxton.

***Phillippe, William R.** A Stewardship Scrapbook. LC 98-47900. 120p. 1999. pap. 14.95 (*0-664-50044-7*) Geneva Press.

Phillippi, Wendell C. Dear Ike. 274p. 1991. 15.75 (*0-9630859-0-5*); pap. 10.50 (*0-9630859-1-3*) Two-Star.

Phillippo, James M. Jamaica: Its Past & Present State. LC 79-157374. (Black Heritage Library Collection). 1977. 41.95 (*0-8369-8812-4*) Ayer.

— Jamaica: Its Past & Present State. LC 70-109998. (Illus.). 1970. reprint ed. 23.75 (*0-8371-4132-X*, PIA&) Greenwood.

Phillippo, S., ed. see Sallebray.

Phillippou, Margaret J. Transcendental Dancing. 1982. pap. 3.00 (*0-941500-29-2*) Sharing Co.

***Phillipps, Anthea.** Kinabalu Sabah: Malaysian Borneo. (Globetrotter Visitor's Guides Ser.). 2000. pap. 14.95 (*1-85974-405-2*) New5 Holland.

Phillipps, Anthea & Lamb, Anthony. Pitcher - Plants of Borneo. (Illus.). x, 171p. 1996. 42.00 (*983-812-009-X*, Pub. by Royal Botnic Grdns) Balogh.

Phillipps, Calvin C. & McFadden, David A. Investigating the Fireground. LC 86-4379. (Illus.). 296p. 1986. reprint ed. text 25.00 (*0-912212-14-4*) Fire Eng.

— Investigating the Fireground. 2nd rev. ed. Feldman, Diane & Dittmer, Mary-Jane, eds. LC 96-11790. (C). 49.85 (*0-912212-50-0*) Fire Eng.

Phillipps, Evelyn M. The Venetian School of Painting. LC 70-37907. (Select Bibliographies Reprint Ser.). 1977. reprint ed. 24.95 (*0-8369-6745-3*) Ayer.

Phillipps, K. C. The Language of Thackeray. (C). 1978. text 26.50 (*0-233-96917-9*) Westview.

Phillipps, Karen, jt. auth. see He, Fen-qi.

Phillipps, Marilyn. First Aid for a Wounded Marriage. 32p. 1986. pap. text. write for info. (*1-884794-00-9*) Eden Pubng.

— El Reporte de Quien Creeras? O'Hara, Carol, tr. 60p. (Orig.). 1995. pap. text, teacher ed. write for info. (*1-884794-20-3*) Eden Pubng.

— Standing Day by Day. 1994. write for info. (*1-884794-13-0*) Eden Pubng.

— Together Day by Day. 1995. pap. text. write for info. (*1-884794-16-5*) Eden Pubng.

— Whose Report Will You Believe? 60p. 1993. pap. text. write for info. (*1-884794-04-1*) Eden Pubng.

Phillipps, Marilyn, jt. auth. see Phillipps, Mike.

Phillipps, Mike & Phillipps, Marilyn. Casado por Uida. (SPA.). 208p. 1986. pap. text. write for info. (*1-884794-05-X*) Eden Pubng.

— Casado por Vida Manual de Liderato. (SPA.). 320p. 1986. pap. text. write for info. (*1-884794-06-8*) Eden Pubng.

— Elaman Liitto, Couples. 195p. 1995. pap. text. write for info. (*1-884794-14-9*) Eden Pubng.

— Elaman Liitto, Leaders. 320p. 1995. pap. text. write for info. (*1-884794-15-7*) Eden Pubng.

— Gifta for Livet Ledarhandbok. Smedberg, Jan-Olaf, tr. from ENG. (SWE.). 322p. (Orig.). 1994. pap. write for info. (*1-884794-08-4*) Eden Pubng.

— Leaders of Leaders Int'l. 100p. (Orig.). 1994. pap. text. write for info. (*1-884794-11-4*) Eden Pubng.

— Leader's of Leader's USA. 100p. 1994. pap. text. write for info. (*1-884794-10-6*) Eden Pubng.

— Manual de Lideres de Lideres. (SPA.). 100p. 1995. pap. text. write for info. (*1-884794-17-3*) Eden Pubng.

— Married for Life: Couple's Manual. 208p. 1983. pap. text. write for info. (*1-884794-02-5*) Eden Pubng.

— Married for Life: Couple's Manual. 195p. 1995. pap. text. write for info. (*1-884794-19-X*) Eden Pubng.

— Married for Life: Leader's Manual. 320p. 1983. pap. text. write for info. (*1-884794-01-7*) Eden Pubng.

— Married for Life: Leader's Manual. Bren, Valentina, tr. (RUS.). 320p. 1992. pap. text, teacher ed. write for info. (*1-884794-25-4*) Eden Pubng.

— Married for Life: Leader's Manual. 320p. 1995. pap. text. write for info. (*1-884794-18-1*) Eden Pubng.

— Married for Life, Couples. (TAG.). 195p. (Orig.). 1995. pap. text. write for info. (*1-884794-12-2*) Eden Pubng.

— Married for Life, Couples. Bren, Valentina, tr. (RUS.). 195p. (Orig.). 1995. pap. text. write for info. (*1-884794-24-6*) Eden Pubng.

— Married for Life Leder Hanbog. Thorslund, Lena, tr. from ENG. (DAN.). 322p. (Orig.). 1994. pap. write for info. (*1-884794-07-6*) Eden Pubng.

Phillipps, S. M. Famous Cases of Circumstantial Evidence, 2 vols. in 1. 1979. reprint ed. 55.00 (*0-8377-1002-2*, Rothman) W S Hein.

Phillippy, Patricia B. Love's Remedies: Recantation & Renaissance Lyric Poetry. LC 94-21457. 1995. 39.50 (*0-8387-5263-2*) Bucknell U Pr.

Phillips. Advanced Lotus 1-2-3/R2.4 for Business. (New Perspectives Ser.). 704p. pap. write for info. incl. disk (*1-56527-062-2*) Course Tech.

— Biomechanical Measurement. 1997. pap. text. write for info. (*0-7216-4473-2*, W B Saunders Co) Harcrt Hlth Sci Grp.

— Communicating Employee Benefits. 496p. (Orig.). 1995. 165.00 (*1-56706-093-5*, CEMB) Aspen Pub.

— Computational Numerical Methods. (Computers & Their Applications Ser.). 1986. text 59.95 (*0-470-20336-6*) P-H.

— Cottagers Handbook. pap. 19.95 (*0-13-181306-4*) P-H.

— Cpse Developmental Writing Lm. 1997. pap. text 15.74 (*0-07-221386-8*) McGraw.

***Phillips.** DOS: Comprehensive Enhanced. (New Perspectives Ser.). (C). 2000. text 36.00 (*0-619-01976-X*) Course Tech.

— Effective Web Site Architecture. (C). 1999. pap. text. write for info. (*0-201-60447-7*) Addison-Wesley.

Phillips. Ensuring Image Quality Student Workbook. 96p. (C). (gr. 13). 1987. pap. text, wbk. ed. 17.95 (*0-8016-3906-9*, 03906) Mosby Inc.

— Epistemological. (Educational Psychology Ser.: Vol. 29, No. 1). 1994. 20.00 (*0-8058-9976-6*) L Erlbaum Assocs.

— Exhibiting Authenticity. LC 97-12648. 1998. 74.95 (*0-7190-4796-X*, Pub. by Manchester Univ Pr); pap. 24.95 (*0-7190-4797-8*, Pub. by Manchester Univ Pr) St Martin.

— Extra-Sensory Perception of Quarks. 1994. 15.00 (*0-8356-0227-3*, Quest) Theos Pub Hse.

— Family-Centered Maternity-Newborn Care. 4th ed. (Illus.). 96p. (C). (gr. 13). 1996. teacher ed., spiral bd. write for info. (*0-8151-6793-8*, 25334) Mosby Inc.

— First Crusade: Origins & Impact. LC 96-52877. 256p. 1997. pap. 27.95 (*0-7190-5174-6*) St Martin.

— From Obscurity Bright Dawn: How Nyasaland Became Malawi, an Insider's Account. 191p. 1998. text 39.50 (*1-86064-248-9*, Pub. by I B T) St Martin.

— Future of Labor Management Cooperative Programs. LC 94-239664. 156p. 1994. pap. 35.00 (*0-8080-0019-5*, BLS-3327) CCH INC.

— A Guide to Sensitivity Testing - Report of the Working Party on Antibiotic Sensitivity Testing of the British Society for Ant. 1999. write for info. (*0-12-553890-1*) Acad Pr.

— Healing Moves with Power Therapies. 35.00 (*0-393-70326-6*) Norton.

— The Heart of the Earth. 1968. 33.75 (*0-685-64773-0*) Jones & Bartlett.

— Introduction to Film. 1999. pap. text 10.00 (*0-312-19606-7*) St Martin.

— Introduction to Film, Vol. 1. LC 98-87541. 1999. pap. text 41.95 (*0-312-17818-2*) St Martin.

— Invention of Religion. 1999. text. write for info. (*0-312-17541-8*) St Martin.

— Jesus & the Kingdom. 1986. pap. text. write for info. (*0-582-20293-0*, Pub. by Addison-Wesley) Longman.

***Phillips.** LIT Environment. 216p. 2001. 74.95 (*0-7506-4889-9*, Architectural Pr) Buttrwrth-Heinemann.

Phillips. Locksmithing. LC 99-34586. 544p. 1999. pap. 34.95 (*0-07-134436-5*) McGraw.

Phillips. Long Preparation Course Toefl Test with Answers. 1997. 27.19 (*0-201-31521-1*) Addison-Wesley.

— Nineteenth Century Markets. 68.95 (*1-85928-058-7*) Ashgate Pub Co.

Phillips. Notting Hill in the 60s. (C). 1991. pap. 25.00 (*0-85315-751-0*, Pub. by Lawrence & Wishart) NYU Pr.

***Phillips.** NP on MS Windows 2000 for Power Users. (New Perspectives Ser.). (C). 2000. pap. 48.95 (*0-619-01935-2*) Course Tech.

— People Capability Maturity Model. 448p. (C). 1999. text. write for info. (*0-201-60445-0*) Addison-Wesley.

Phillips. Physics of the Stars. 2nd ed. LC 99-20530. 262p. (C). 1999. 145.00 (*0-471-98797-2*) Wiley.

***Phillips.** Physics of the Stars. 2nd ed. LC 99-20530. 262p. (C). 1999. pap. 65.00 (*0-471-98798-0*) Wiley.

— Rise Europe Middle Ages: New Subtitle. 160p. 2000. write for info. (*0-8133-1577-8*, Pub. by Westview) HarpC.

Phillips. Sex & Architecture. 2000. text 39.95 (*0-312-19178-2*) St Martin.

— Study Guide Prentice Hall Fedrl Taxatn 1997:Individ. 1996. pap. text, student ed. 33.00 (*0-13-240052-9*) P-H.

***Phillips.** Understanding Marketing: A European Casebook. LC 99-59517. 232p. 2000. pap. 34.95 (*0-471-86093-X*) Wiley.

Phillips. Urban Social Work. (C). 2000. text 34.67 (*0-205-29019-1*, Longwood Div) Allyn.

— World Philosophy of Religion. (C). 1995. text 59.00 (*0-15-501753-5*, Pub. by Harcourt Coll Pubs) Harcourt.

— World Womens Studies. 2001. pap. 15.31 (*0-07-092047-8*) McGraw.

— Young Medieval Women. LC 98-48753. (Illus.). 224p. 1999. text 35.00 (*0-312-22130-4*) St Martin.

Phillips, ed. Annual Report of the Secretary of State to the Governor of Ohio: Jail Reports 1854 & 1855. 138p. 1983. reprint ed. pap. 12.00 (*1-55613-103-8*) Heritage Bk.

Phillips & Adams. The Year Book of Chiropractic, 1996. (Illus.). 464p. (gr. 13). 1996. text 69.95 (*0-8151-6736-9*, 21966) Mosby Inc.

Phillips & Axelrod. Encyclopedia of the American West, Vol. 4. 1996. 100.00 (*0-02-897499-9*) Macmillan.

Phillips & Pryor. Products Liability, 1996, Vol. 3. 2nd ed. 736p. 1997. text 80.00 (*1-55834-578-7*, 60818-11, MICHIE) LEXIS Pub.

Phillips, et al. Clinical Chiropractic Care No. 1: Clinical Care. 400p. 1994. pap. 45.00 (*0-8016-6822-0*) Mosby Inc.

— Tort Law, Cases, Materials & Problems: 1991 Edition. 1991. write for info. (*0-87473-720-6*, 12626-10, MICHIE) LEXIS Pub.

— Tort Law Cases Materials & Problems, 1997. 2nd ed. LC 97-74186. 1492p. 1997. text 56.00 (*1-55834-599-X*, 12626-11, MICHIE) LEXIS Pub.

Phillips, jt. auth. see Brathwaite.

Phillips, jt. auth. see Denning.

Phillips, jt. auth. see Stahl, Barbara.

Phillips, Donna P. Heritage Hunting. LC 98-204423. 287 p. 1998. 23.00 (*0-7884-0880-1*) Heritage Bk.

Phillips, R. M. MultiBody System SIMulation No. 7: Numerical Methods, Algorithms & Software. Griebel, M. et al, eds. LC 99-30072. xv, 251p. 1999. pap. 82.00 (*3-540-65662-6*) Spr-Verlag.

***Phillips, Wilbur H.** Oberlin Colony (Oltio) The Story of a Century. (Illus.). 328p. 2000. pap. 24.86 (*0-7884-1491-7*, 1491) Heritage Bk.

Phillips, A. How to Grow Old Without Aging. 1995. pap. 8.00 (*0-927936-30-5*) Vincom Pubng Co.

Phillips, A. A. Henry Lawson. (Twayne's World Authors Ser.). (C). 1972. lib. bdg. 20.95 (*0-8057-2512-1*) Irvington.

***Phillips, A. W. H. & Leeson, Robert, eds.** Collected Works in Contemporary Perspective. LC 99-11998. (Illus.). 536p. (C). 2000. 80.00 (*0-521-57135-9*) Cambridge U Pr.

Phillips, Adam. The Beast in the Nursery: On Curiosity & Other Appetites. LC 97-19575. 165p. 1998. 21.00 (*0-375-40049-4*) Pantheon.

— The Beast in the Nursery: On Curiosity & Other Appetites. 1999. pap. 12.00 (*0-375-70047-1*) Vin Bks.

***Phillips, Adam.** Darwin's Worms: On Life Stories & Death Stories. 2000. pap. 13.00 (*0-465-05676-8*, Pub. by Basic); text 20.00 (*0-465-05675-X*, Pub. by Basic) HarpC.

Phillips, Adam. Monogamy. LC 96-27857. 1997. 1.99 (*0-679-44264-2*) Pantheon.

— Monogamy. 1999. pap. 11.00 (*0-679-77617-6*) Vin Bks.

— On Flirtation. LC 94-18821. 256p. 1994. text 19.95 (*0-674-63437-3*, PHIFLI) HUP.

— On Flirtation. 256p. 1996. pap. 14.00 (*0-674-63440-3*) HUP.

— On Kissing, Tickling, & Being Bored: Psychoanalytic Essays on the Unexamined Life. 152p. 1994. pap. text 12.95 (*0-674-63463-2*, PHIKAX) HUP.

— On Kissing, Tickling & Being Bored: Psychoanalytic Essays on the Unexamined Life. LC 92-20662. 152p. 1993. text 19.95 (*0-674-63462-4*) HUP.

***Phillips, Adam.** Promises, Promises: Writing On Psychoanalysis And Literature. 280p. 2000. 26.00 (*0-465-05677-6*, Pub. by Basic) HarpC.

Phillips, Adam. Terrors & Experts. LC 95-38506. 128p. 1996. 19.95 (*0-674-87479-X*) HUP.

— Terrors & Experts. 128p. 1997. pap. text 12.00 (*0-674-87480-3*) HUP.

— Winnicott. LC 88-28390. 176p. 1989. reprint ed. 31.95 (*0-674-95360-6*); reprint ed. pap. 15.95 (*0-674-95361-4*) HUP.

Phillips, Adam, jt. auth. see Eigen, Michael.

Phillips, Adam, ed. & intro. see Burke, Edmund.

Phillips, Adam, ed. & intro. see Pater, Walter.

Phillips, Alan, pseud. Jazz Improvisation & Harmony. 4th ed. 96p. 1989. reprint ed. pap. text 10.00 (*0-7692-0094-X*, TMF0135) Wrner Bros.

***Phillips, Alexander & Fattaruso, Paul.** In War, My Uncle: A Selection of Poems. 71p. 1999. pap. 10.00 (*0-9670924-0-X*, Bazarov Pr) Max Graphics.

Phillips, Alfred. Phillips: Professional Ethics for Scottish Solicitors. 232p. 1990. pap. 40.00 (*0-406-12890-1*, MICHIE) LEXIS Pub.

Phillips, Allan R. The Known Birds of North & Middle America, Distributions & Variation, Migrations, Changes, Hybrids, Etc., Pt. I. (Illus.). 320p. 1986. 60.00 (*0-9617402-0-5*) A R Phillips.

— The Known Birds of North & Middle America, Distributions & Variation, Migrations, Changes, Hybrids, Etc., Pt. 2: Bombycillidae; Sylviidae to Sturnidae; Vireonidae. (Illus.). ii, 249p. 1991. lib. bdg. 64.00 (*0-9617402-1-3*) A R Phillips.

Phillips, Allan R., et al. The Birds of Arizona. LC 64-17265. (Illus.). 292p. reprint ed. pap. 90.60 (*0-7837-1910-8*, 204211400001) Bks Demand.

Phillips, Allan R., jt. auth. see Monson, Gale.

Phillips, Allen, ed. see Greenhaw, Wayne.

Phillips, Allyn E. The Development of a Practical Thermal Rating Method for Enclosed Gear Drives. (Technical Papers: Vol. 96FTM9). (Illus.). 8p. 1996. pap. text 30.00 (*1-55589-676-6*) AGMA.

Phillips, Almarin, ed. Perspectives on Antitrust Policy. LC 64-19822. 466p. 1965. reprint ed. pap. 144.50 (*0-7837-9419-3*, 206016000004) Bks Demand.

— Promoting Competition in Regulated Markets. LC 74-277. (Studies in the Regulation of Economic Activity). 411p. reprint ed. pap. 127.50 (*0-608-17115-8*, 202774100056) Bks Demand.

Phillips, Almarin, et al. Biz Jets: Technology & Market Structure in the Corporate Jet Aircraft Industry. LC 93-42692. (Economics of Science, Technology & Innovation Ser.). 288p. (C). 1994. lib. bdg. 136.00 (*0-7923-2660-1*) Kluwer Academic.

Phillips, Althea, jt. auth. see Maccalous, Sarah.

Phillips, Amy. Lewis-Gale Medical Center. Harholdt, Phyllis & Nelson, Rodney, eds. (Illus.). 250p. (C). 1993. 50.00 (*0-929690-21-4*) Herit Pubs AZ.

Phillips, Amy, ed. see Finnerty, Margaret.

P

An Asterisk (*) at the beginning of an entry indicates that the title is appearing for the first time.

Phillips, Amy L., ed. Playing for Keeps Vol. 2: Supporting Children's Play. LC 96-35870. (Topics in Early Childhood Education Ser.). 192p. (Orig.). (C). 1996. pap. 14.95 (1-884834-29-9) Redleaf Pr.

Phillips, Andrew. The Rebirth of England & English: The Vision of William Barnes. 160p. 1997. pap. 18.95 (1-898281-17-3, Pub. by Anglo-Saxon Bks) Paul & Co Pubs.

Phillips, Andrew, jt. auth. see Van Dulken, Stephen.

Phillips, Andrew F. Medical Negligence Law: Seeking a Balance. LC 96-32164. (Medico-Legal Issues Ser.). (Illus.). 248p. 1997. text 82.95 (1-85521-643-4, Pub. by Dartmth Pub) Ashgate Pub Co.

Phillips, Andy & Dunayevskaya, Raya. The Coal Miner's General Strike of Nineteen Forty-Nine to Fifty & the Birth of Marxist-Humanism in the United States. (Illus.). 50p. 1984. pap. 2.00 (0-914441-21-3) News & Letters.

Phillips, Angela. Discrimination. LC 92-39446. (Past & Present Ser.). (Illus.). 48p. (YA). (gr. 6 up). 1993. lib. bdg. 20.00 (0-02-786881-8, Mac Bks Young Read) S&S Childrens.

— The Trouble with Boys: A Wise & Sympathetic Guide to the Risky Business of Raising Sons. 304p. 1995. pap. 14.00 (0-465-08735-3, Pub. by Basic) HarpC.

— Until They Are Five: A Parent's Guide. 208p. 1989. pap. text 12.50 (0-04-440361-5) NYU Pr.

Phillips, Angela, et al. Your Body, Your Baby, Your Life. 1993. pap. 11.50 (0-86358-006-8, Pub. by Rivers Oram) NYU Pr.

Phillips-Angeles, Ellen, jt. auth. see Jolley, Sandra.

Phillips, Anita. A Defense of Masochism. LC 98-30136. 224p. 1998. text 22.95 (0-312-19258-4) St Martin.

Phillips, Ann. Understanding Woodturning. LC 98-113517. (Illus.). 160p. 1997. pap. text 17.95 (1-86108-034-4, Pub. by Guild Master) Sterling.

Phillips, Ann & Phillips, Terry. Business Objectives. 2nd ed. 94p. 1996. pap. text, teacher ed. 7.50 (0-19-451393-9) OUP.

Phillips, Ann, jt. ed. see Goldberg, Merryl R.

***Phillips, Ann L.** Power & Influence after the Cold War: Germany in East-Central Europe. 272p. 2000. pap. 26.95 (0-8476-9523-9); text 69.00 (0-8476-9522-0) Rowman.

Phillips, Ann L. Soviet Policy Toward East Germany Reconsidered: The Postwar Decade, 142. LC 85-17729. (Contributions in Political Science Ser.: No. 142). (Illus.). 274p. 1986. 55.00 (0-313-24671-8, PSP/, Greenwood Pr) Greenwood.

Phillips, Anne. Democracy & Difference. 176p. 1993. 35.00 (0-271-01096-7); pap. 17.95 (0-271-01097-5) Pa St U Pr.

— Engendering Democracy. 200p. 1991. 40.00 (0-271-00783-4); pap. 18.95 (0-271-00784-2) Pa St U Pr.

— A Keyhole View: Like Waves on the Shore, Their Dreams Go On & On. 278p. 1999. pap. 6.50 (0-9665475-0-0) Open Pr Pubs.

— The Politics of Presence. (Oxford Political Theory Ser.). 220p. 1998. pap. text 19.95 (0-19-829415-8) OUP.

— The Politics of Presence: Democracy & Group Representation. (Oxford Political Theory Ser.). 220p. 1995. text 38.00 (0-19-827942-6) OUP.

Phillips, Anne. Roses for Sarah. 183p. mass mkt. 4.99 (1-55197-125-9) Picasso Publ.

Phillips, Anne. Which Equalities Matter? LC 99-16943. 160p. (C). 1999. 59.95 (0-7456-2108-2, Pub. by Polity Pr); pap. 24.95 (0-7456-2109-0, Pub. by Polity Pr) Blackwell Pubs.

Phillips, Anne, ed. Feminism & Equality. (Readings in Social & Political Theory Ser.). 224p. (C). 1987. pap. text 18.50 (0-8147-6605-6) NYU Pr.

— Feminism & Politics. (Oxford Readings in Feminism Ser.). 480p. 1998. text 65.00 (0-19-878206-3); pap. text 19.95 (0-19-878205-5) OUP.

Phillips, Anne, jt. ed. see Barrett, Michele.

Phillips, Anne, jt. ed. see Eiselein, Gregory K.

Phillips, Anne D. & Sotiriou, Peter E. Steps to Reading Proficiency. 2nd ed. 359p. (C). 1987. pap. write for info. (0-534-06966-5) Wadsworth Pub.

— Steps to Reading Proficiency. 3rd ed. 340p. (C). 1991. mass mkt. 21.75 (0-534-16518-4) Wadsworth Pub.

— Steps to Reading Proficiency. 4th ed. LC 95-23159. (C). 1995. pap. 27.50 (0-534-26412-3) Wadsworth Pub.

Phillips, Anne W. A Basket Full of Surprises: Big Book. large type ed. (Little Books & Big Bks.). (Illus.). 8p. (J). (ps-1). 1998. pap. text 19.89 (0-8215-0851-2) Sadlier.

— Harry's Hat: Big Book. large type ed. (Little Books & Big Bks.). (Illus.). 8p. (J). (ps-1). 1998. pap. text 19.89 (0-8215-0845-8) Sadlier.

— Show & Tell: Big Book. large type ed. (Little Books & Big Bks.). (Illus.). 8p. (J). (ps-1). 1998. pap. text 19.89 (0-8215-0844-X) Sadlier.

— When Mr. Quinn Snored: Big Book. large type ed. (Little Books & Big Bks.). (Illus.). 8p. (J). (ps-1). 1998. pap. text 19.89 (0-8215-0872-5) Sadlier.

***Phillips, Annelise Tracey.** Family Working Rights: A Practical Guide. (Legal Guidance Ser.). 300p. 2000. pap. 50.00 (0-11-702391-4, Pub. by Statnry Office) Balogh.

Phillips, Annelise Tracey, jt. auth. see Rankin, Claire.

Phillips, Anthony. Lower Than the Angels. 68p. 1996. pap. 8.95 (1-85311-136-8, 846, Pub. by Canterbury Press Norwich) Morehouse Pub.

— The Passion of God. 86p. (Orig.). 1995. pap. 9.95 (1-85311-101-5, 852, Pub. by Canterbury Press Norwich) Morehouse Pub.

Phillips, Anthony, et al. Antiquity Revisited: English & French Silver-Gilt from the Collection of Audrey Love. LC 98-104225. vi, 150 p. 1997. write for info. (0-903432-50-1) CMW Ltd.

— Basic Accounting for Lawyers. 4th ed. 268p. 1988. text 28.00 (0-8318-0467-X, B467) Am Law Inst.

Phillips, Anthony V. & Stone, David A. A Topological Chern-Weil Theory. LC 93-25081. (Memoirs of the American Mathematical Society Ser.: No. 504). 79p. 1993. pap. 28.00 (0-8218-2566-6, MEMO/105/504) Am Math.

Phillips, Anthony V., jt. ed. see Goldberg, Lisa R.

Phillips, Antonia, jt. auth. see Castro, Isabel C.

Phillips, Arthur. Survey of African Marriage & Family Life. LC 74-15079. reprint ed. 67.50 (0-404-12128-4) AMS Pr.

Phillips, Arthur & Morris, Henry I. Marriage Laws in Africa. LC 75-28914. 239p. reprint ed. pap. 74.10 (0-8357-3028-X, 205711500010) Bks Demand.

Phillips, Arthur & Phillips, Barbara. High Country Wildflowers. (Illus.). 32p. 1987. 4.95 (0-89734-061-2, PL58-3) Mus Northern Ariz.

Phillips, Arthur H. Handbook of Computer-Aided Composition. LC 80-16031. (Books in Library & Information Science: Vol. 31). (Illus.). 456p. reprint ed. pap. 141.40 (0-608-08973-7, 206960800005) Bks Demand.

Phillips, Arthur M., 3rd. Grand Canyon Wildflowers. rev. ed. Priehs, T. J., ed. LC 79-54236. (Illus.). 145p. 1995. pap. 10.95 (0-938216-01-5) GCA.

Phillips, Arthur S. The Borden Murder Mystery. (Illus.). 40p. 1986. 20.00 (0-9614811-1-0) King Philip Pub.

Phillips, Aubrey. Atmospheric Landscapes in Watercolor. (Illus.). 32p. 1990. pap. 4.95 (0-85532-655-7, 655-7, Pub. by Srch Pr) A Schwartz & Co.

— Painting with Pastels. LC 94-9024. (Illus.). 126p. 1994. pap. text 12.95 (0-486-28159-0) Dover.

— Sky & Water in Pastel. (Leisure Arts Ser.: No. 21). (Illus.). 32p. (Orig.). pap. 4.95 (0-85532-531-3, 531-3, Pub. by Srch Pr) A Schwartz & Co.

Phillips, B. The Complete Book of Locks & Locksmithing. 4th ed. (Illus.). 483p. 1995. pap. 24.95 (0-07-049866-0) McGraw.

Phillips, B. A. Goodbye, Friends: Stories by B. A. Phillips. LC 92-43030. 163p. 1993. 15.95 (1-882593-01-4) Bridge Wrks.

Phillips, Barbara, et al. Monitoring the Effects of Recreational Use on Colorado River Beaches in Grand Canyon National Park. (Bulletin Ser.: No. 55). (Illus.). 230p. (Orig.). 1986. pap. 14.95 (0-89734-057-4) Mus Northern Ariz.

Phillips, Barbara, jt. auth. see Morton, Rosemary.

Phillips, Barbara, jt. auth. see Phillips, Arthur.

Phillips, Barbara, ed. see Maginnis, John.

Phillips, Barbara, jt. ed. see Ring, Francis J.

Phillips, Barbara A. Finding Common Ground: A Field Guide to Mediation. LC 94-75151. 224p. (Orig.). 1994. pap. 16.95 (0-9633919-7-6) Hells Canyon.

Phillips, Barbara G., et al. Annotated Checklist of Vascular Plants of Grand Canyon National Park 1986. (Monographs: No. 7). (Illus.). 80p. 1987. pap. 15.00 (0-938216-30-9) GCA.

***Phillips, Barry & Phillips, Shelley.** Wondrous Love. 80p. 1999. pap. 32.95 incl. audio compact disk (0-7866-3641-6, 96467CDP) Mel Bay.

— Wondrous Love: Beginning Level. 80p. 1999. pap. 12.95 (0-7866-2596-1, 96467) Mel Bay.

***Phillips, Barry & Phillips, Shelly.** Wondrous Love. 80p. 1999. pap. 22.95 incl. audio (0-7866-3643-2, 96467P) Mel Bay.

Phillips, Barty. Carpet Style. (Illus.). 160p. 1997. 19.98 (0-7858-0816-7) Bk Sales Inc.

— Decorating: Technique & Style. LC 98-49708. 232p. 1999. 24.98 (1-57145-176-5, Thunder Bay) Advantage Pubs.

— Home Design Guide. LC 97-53195. 1998. pap. 30.00 (1-57959-008-X, SOMA) BB&T Inc.

***Phillips, Barty.** Home Office Planner: Hundreds of Great Ideas for Your New Office. 2001. 24.95 (0-8118-2942-1) Chronicle Bks.

Phillips, Barty. How to Clean Absolutely Everything. 192p. (Orig.). 1995. mass mkt. 4.99 (0-380-77736-3, Avon Bks) Morrow Avon.

— Tapestry. 240p. 1999. pap. 29.95 (0-7148-3862-4) Phaidon Pr.

Phillips, Barty. Tapestry. LC 96-109539. (Illus.). 240p. (C). 1994. text 55.00 (0-7148-2920-X, Pub. by Phaidon Press) Phaidon Pr.

***Phillips, Becky.** Beanie Mania II: A Comprehensive Collector's Guide. 1998. pap. 24.95 (0-9659036-1-3) Dinomates.

Phillips, Becky. Beanie Mania II: A Comprehensive Collector's Guide. deluxe ed. 1998. 49.95 (0-9659036-2-1) Dinomates.

— Beanie Mania International. LC 98-93024. 1998. pap. 9.95 (0-9659036-3-X); pap. 9.95 (0-9659036-4-8) Dinomates.

Phillips, Becky & Estenssoro, Becky. Beanie Mania: A Comprehensive Collector's Guide. LC 97-92285. (Illus.). 125p. (YA). (gr. 3 up). 1997. pap. 24.95 (0-9659036-0-5) Dinomates.

Phillips, Beeman N. Educational & Psychological Perspectives on Stress in Students, Teachers, & Parents. LC 92-75446. 1993. lib. bdg. 29.95 (0-88422-122-9) Clinical Psych.

— School Psychology at a Turning Point: Ensuring a Bright Future for the Profession. LC 89-27510. (Social & Behavioral Sciences Ser.). 324p. 1990. text 39.95 (1-55542-195-4) Jossey-Bass.

— School Stress & Anxiety. LC 77-21658. 165p. 1978. 32.95 (0-87705-324-3, Kluwer Acad Hman Sci) Kluwer Academic.

Phillips, Benny & Phillips, Sheree. Walking with the Wise: God's Plan for Parents & Teens. Somerville, Greg, ed. 176p. (Orig.). (YA). (gr. 7-12). 1994. pap. 8.99 (1-881039-04-8) PDI Ministries.

Phillips, Benny, jt. auth. see Phillips, David.

Phillips, Bernard, ed. & intro. see Suzuki, D. T.

Phillips, Betty L. Provencal Interiors: French Country Style in America. LC 98-17493. (Illus.). 150p. 1998. 39.95 (0-87905-848-X) Gibbs Smith Pub.

***Phillips, Betty Lou.** French by Design. (Illus.). 176p. 2000. 39.95 (0-87905-972-9) Gibbs Smith Pub.

Phillips, Bill. Body for Life: 12 Weeks to Mental & Physical Strength. Date not set. pap. 13.50 (0-06-093157-4) HarpC.

***Phillips, Bill.** Body for Life Success Journal: A 12-Week Workout Guide to Eternal Fitness. 256p. 2001. pap. 18.00 (0-06-095698-4, Perennial) HarperTrade.

Phillips, Bill. Home Mechanix Guide to Security: Protecting Your Home, Car, & Family. LC 93-10303. 240p. 1993. pap. 16.95 (0-471-58893-8) Wiley.

***Phillips, Bill.** Nutrition for Life. 2000. 26.00 (0-06-019768-4) HarpC.

Phillips, Bill. Professional Locksmithing Techniques. (Illus.). 400p. 1991. pap. 25.95 (0-8306-3523-8) McGraw-Hill Prof.

— Professional Locksmithing Techniques. 2nd ed. 426p. 1996. pap. 36.95 (0-07-049867-9) McGraw.

Phillips, Bill & D'Orso, Michael. Body-for-Life: 12 Weeks to Mental & Physical Strength. LC 99-26145. (Illus.). 201p. 1999. 26.00 (0-06-019339-5) HarpC.

***Phillips, Bill & D'Orso, Michael.** Body For Life: 12 Weeks to Mental & Physical StrengthPhillips,&Bill. Set. abr. ed. 1999. audio 18.00 (0-694-52148-5) HarperAudio.

Phillips, Bill, jt. auth. see Roper, C. A.

Phillips, Billie R., jt. auth. see Baker, Rance G.

Phillips, Bob. The All-New Clean Joke Book. LC 90-36617. 192p. 1990. mass mkt. 3.99 (0-89081-830-4) Harvest Hse.

— Awesome Animal Jokes for Kids. LC 98-167107. (YA). (gr. 8-12). 1998. mass mkt. 3.99 (1-56507-791-1) Harvest Hse.

— The Awesome Book of Bible Trivia. 1994. pap. 9.99 (1-56507-294-4) Harvest Hse.

— Awesome Good Clean Jokes for Kids. LC 92-12109. 207p. (J). (gr. 4-7). 1996. mass mkt. 3.99 (1-56507-062-3) Harvest Hse.

— Best Ever Book of Good Clean Jokes. 1998. 9.99 (1-57866-012-2) Galahad Bks.

— The Best of the Good Clean Jokes. LC 89-32386. 301p. (YA). (gr. 5 up). 1989. mass mkt. 4.99 (0-89081-769-3) Harvest Hse.

— Bob Phillips' Encyclopedia of Good Clean Jokes. (Illus.). 385p. (Orig.). 1992. pap. 9.99 (0-89081-947-5) Harvest Hse.

— 52 More Offbeat Texas Stops: Traveling with Bob Phillips, Texas Country Reporter. LC 97-91943. (Illus.). 160p. 1997. pap. 13.95 (0-9636541-5-2) Phillips Prods.

— Fifty-Two Offbeat Texas Stops: Traveling with Bob Phillips, Texas Country Reporter. LC 93-92751. (Illus.). 144p. 1993. pap. 10.95 (0-9636541-1-X) Phillips Prods.

— Good Clean Jokes for Kids. (J). 1991. mass mkt. 3.99 (0-89081-902-5) Harvest Hse.

— Goofy Good Clean Jokes for Kids! LC 94-14563. 176p. (J). (gr. 5-7). 1997. mass mkt. 3.99 (1-56507-491-2) Harvest Hse.

— How Can I Be Sure? Questions to Ask Before You Get Married. rev. ed. 156p. 1999. pap. 8.99 (0-7369-0038-1) Harvest Hse.

— Jest Another Good Clean Joke Book. LC 96-167930. 1996. mass mkt. 4.99 (1-56507-450-5) Harvest Hse.

***Phillips, Bob.** The Joke Book. 176p. 2001. mass mkt. 3.99 (0-7369-0307-0) Harvest Hse.

Phillips, Bob. KC8 Burma: CBI Air Warning Team, 1942-1945. (Illus.). 194p. (Orig.). 1992. pap. 18.95 (0-89745-145-7) Sunflower U Pr.

— More Awesome Good Clean Jokes for Kids. LC 94-29224. (J). 1995. mass mkt. 3.99 (1-56507-270-7) Harvest Hse.

— Over the Hill & on a Roll: Laugh Lines for the Better Half of Life. LC 99-224098. 250p. 1999. mass mkt. 4.99 (0-7369-0002-0) Harvest Hse.

— Phillip's Book of Great Thoughts & Funny Sayings. LC 92-37072. 345p. 1993. 9.99 (0-8423-5035-7) Tyndale Hse.

— Redi-Reference. 1975. mass mkt. 3.99 (0-89081-043-5) Harvest Hse.

— Redi-Reference Daily Bible Reading Plan. 1992. mass mkt. 3.99 (0-89081-997-1) Harvest Hse.

***Phillips, Bob.** Super-Duper Good Clean Jokes for Kids. 176p. (J). (gr. 4-7). 2000. mass mkt. 3.99 (0-7369-0308-9) Harvest Hse.

— Texas Country Reporter: A Backroads Companion. (Illus.). 160p. 2000. 29.95 (0-7627-0715-1); pap. 19.95 (0-7627-0714-3) Globe Pequot.

Phillips, Bob. Totally Cool Clean Jokes for Kids. LC 97-194958. 200p. (YA). (gr. 5-12). 1997. mass mkt. 3.99 (1-56507-571-4) Harvest Hse.

— Ultimate Good Clean Jokes for Kids. (J). 1993. mass mkt. 4.99 (1-56507-085-2) Harvest Hse.

— The World's All-Time Best Collection of Good Clean Jokes. LC 96-77054. 352p. 1996. 9.98 (0-88365-967-0) Galahad Bks.

— The World's Best Collection of Great Games. LC 99-185646. 220p. 1998. pap. 7.99 (1-56507-973-6) Harvest Hse.

— World's Greatest Collection of Clean Jokes. LC 99-186748. 176p. 1998. mass mkt. 3.99 (1-56507-987-6) Harvest Hse.

— The World's Greatest Collection of Knock Knock Jokes. 112p. 1995. mass mkt. 1.99 (1-55748-650-6) Barbour Pub.

***Phillips, Bob.** The World's Greatest Knock-Knock Jokes for Kids. 224p. 2000. mass mkt. 4.99 (0-7369-0273-2) Harvest Hse.

Phillips, Bob. World's Most Crazy, Wacky & Goofy Good Clean Jokes for Kids. 1999. 7.99 (1-57866-046-7) Galahad Bks.

Phillips, Bob & Russo, Steve. Squeaky Clean Jokes for Kids. LC 97-226709. 176p. (J). (gr. 3-7). 1997. mass mkt. 3.99 (1-56507-719-9) Harvest Hse.

Phillips, Bob, jt. auth. see Dabczynski, Andrew.

Phillips, Bob, jt. auth. see Dabczynski, Andrew H.

Phillips, Bob, jt. auth. see Jones, Charlie T.

Phillips, Bob, jt. auth. see LaHaye, Tim F.

Phillips, Bob, ed. see Dockery, Wallene T.

Phillips, Bonnie. Clean Dirty Jokes. 40p. (Orig.). 1995. pap. 10.00 (0-938041-66-5) Arc Pr AR.

Phillips, Bonnie D. Business Communication. 2nd ed. LC 82-73090. (Illus.). 272p. 1983. teacher ed. 14.95 (0-8273-2191-0); text 45.95 (0-8273-2188-0) Delmar.

Phillips, Bradley R. & Helmick, Kyle L. The History of Atlas, W. V. & Vicinity, Upshur County, 1700's-1984. (Illus.). 160p. (Orig.). 1984. pap. text 8.95 (0-9613513-0-6) K L Helmick.

Phillips, Brenda. The World of Dogs: Flatcoated Retrievers. (Illus.). 288p. 1997. 44.95 (1-85279-018-0, GB-006) TFH Pubns.

Phillips, Brenda D., ed. see Slaton, Russell.

Phillips, Brian D. Global Production & Domestic Decay: Plant Closings in the U. S. rev. ed. LC 98-29072. (Studies on Industrial Productivity). (Illus.). 224p. 1998. 62.00 (0-8153-3196-7) Garland.

Phillips, Bruce F., jt. ed. see Cobb, J. Stanley.

Phillips, C. Wadi al Qawr, Fashgha Vol. 1: The Excavation of a Prehistoric Burial Structure in Ras Al Khaimah. (Illus.). 32p. 1987. pap. 8.00 (0-614-21842-X) David Brown.

Phillips, C., jt. auth. see Baxter, R. E.

Phillips, C., jt. ed. see Freeman, L.

Phillips, C. A. Functional Electrical Rehabilitation: Technological Restoration after Spinal Cord Injury. (Illus.). 240p. 1991. 145.00 (0-387-97459-8) Spr-Verlag.

Phillips, C. A., ed. Effective Upper & Lower Extremity Prostheses: A Special Issue of the Journal Automedica. 276p. 1989. pap. text 875.00 (0-677-25830-5) Gordon & Breach.

Phillips, C. A., et al. Banking & the Business Cycle: A Study of the Great Depression in the United States. LC 70-172226. (Right Wing Individualist Tradition in America Ser.). 1976. reprint ed. 24.95 (0-405-00435-4) Ayer.

Phillips, C. Abbott, Jr., tr. see Calamandrei, Piero, Jr.

Phillips, C. B. & Smith, J. H. Lancashire & Cheshire from AD 1540. LC 92-23399. (Regional History of England Ser.). 1994. pap. text. write for info. (0-582-49249-1) Longman.

Phillips, C. J. America's Funniest Bathroom Graffiti, Vol. 3. rev. ed. (Illus.). 110p. 1998. pap. 19.95 (0-9621639-8-8) Grand Natl Pr.

— America's Funniest Raunchy Bathroom Graffiti, Vol. I. (Illus.). 120p. 1998. spiral bd. 7.95 (0-9621639-2-9) Grand Natl Pr.

— The Best Tobacco Cartoons of All Time. Hemeon, Brad, ed. (Illus.). 80p. 1992. pap. 5.95 (0-9621639-9-6) Grand Natl Pr.

— The Official Book of Excuses & Related Reasons. Gurian, Philip, ed. (Illus.). 64p. (Orig.). 1989. pap., per. 4.95 (0-9621639-0-2) Grand Natl Pr.

Phillips, C. J., ed. Progress in Dairy Science. (A CAB International Publication). (Illus.). 416p. 1996. text 110.00 (0-85198-974-8) OUP.

***Phillips, C. J. C.** Principles of Cattle Production. (CABI Publishing Ser.). 2000. write for info. (0-85199-438-5) OUP.

***Phillips, Cabell B. H.** From the Crash to the Blitz, 1929-1939. LC 99-16824. (Illus.). 596p. 2000. pap. 22.00 (0-8232-2000-1, Pub. by Fordham) BookMasters.

Phillips, Calvin, jt. auth. see McFadden, David A.

Phillips, Carl. Cortege. LC 95-77948. 96p. (Orig.). 1995. pap. 12.95 (1-55597-230-6) Graywolf.

— Cortege: A Poem. (Illus.). 10p. (Orig.). 1994. pap. 3.00 (1-884235-00-X) Helicon Nine Eds.

— From the Devotions. LC 97-70218. 81p. 1998. pap. 12.95 (1-55597-263-2) Graywolf.

— In the Blood. (Samuel French Morse Poetry Prize Ser.). 69p. 1992. pap. text 11.95 (1-55553-135-0) NE U Pr.

***Phillips, Carl.** Pastoral. 80p. 2000. pap. 14.00 (1-55597-298-5, Pub. by Graywolf) SPD-Small Pr Dist.

Phillips, Carla R. Ciudad Real, 1500-1750: Growth, Crisis & Readjustment in the Spanish Economy. LC 78-9293. (Illus.). 208p. 1979. 29.00 (0-674-13285-8) HUP.

— Six Galleons for the King of Spain: Imperial Defense in the Early Seventeenth Century. LC 86-45444. (Softshell Bks.). (Illus.). 332p. 1992. pap. text 29.95 (0-8018-4513-0) Johns Hopkins.

Phillips, Carla R. & Phillips, William D., Jr. Spain's Golden Fleece: Wool Production & the Wool Trade from the Middle Ages to the Nineteenth Century. LC 96-47945. 464p. 1997. text 49.95 (0-8018-5518-7) Johns Hopkins.

Phillips, Carla R., jt. auth. see Phillips, William D., Jr.

Phillips, Carla R., ed. see Axtell, James.

Phillips, Carla R., ed. see Kupperman, Karen O.

Phillips, Carla R., ed. see Phillips, William D., Jr.

Phillips, Carla R., ed. see Ronda, James P.

Phillips, Carla R., tr. see Perez-Mallaina, Pablo E.

Phillips, Carly. Brazen: Blaze. (Temptation Ser.: No. 736). 1999. per. 3.75 (0-373-25836-4, 1-25836-7, Harlequin) Harlequin Bks.

***Phillips, Carly.** Simply Sinful. (Temptation Ser.: Vol. 775). 2000. per. 3.99 (0-373-25875-5) Harlequin Bks.

Phillips, Carol. The Household Inventory Guide: Ideas & Lists for Stocking, Restocking, & Taking Stock of Your Home. LC 92-74281. (Illus.). 107p. (Orig.). 1995. pap. 9.95 (0-9634495-0-8) IPP Pr.

— Milady/Salon Ovation's in the Bag: Selling in the Salon. LC 94-6811. (Career Development Ser.). 320p. 1994. pap. 34.95 (1-56253-236-7) Thomson Learn.

P

An Asterisk (*) at the beginning of an entry indicates that the title is appearing for the first time.

Phillips, Carol B., ed. Essentials for Child Development Associates. LC 91-71482. (Illus.). 500p. (Orig.). 1991. pap. text 30.00 (*1-879891-00-X*) Council Early Child.
— Field Advisor's Guide to Essentials for Child Development Associates. LC 91-71483. (Illus.). 125p. (Orig.). 1991. pap. text 15.00 (*1-879891-01-8*) Council Early Child.
— Seminar Instructor's Guide to Essentials for Child Development Associates. (Illus.). 135p. (Orig.). 1991. pap. text 12.50 (*1-879891-02-6*) Council Early Child.
Phillips, Carol B. & Derman-Sparks, Louise. Teaching/Learning Anti-Racism: A Developmental Approach. LC 97-18761. 192p. (Orig.). 1997. 40.00 (*0-8077-3638-4*); pap. 17.95 (*0-8077-3637-6*) Tchrs Coll.
Phillips, Carol J., et al. The Advanced Team Guide: Tools, Techniques & Tips for Experienced Teams. Uhlfelder, Helene, ed. (Illus.). 420p. (Orig.). 1996. student ed., spiral bd. 49.95 (*0-9629679-4-7*) Miller Howard Cnslt.
Phillips, Carole. The New Money Workbook for Women. LC 87-27657. 160p. (Orig.). 1988. pap. 9.95 (*0-931790-82-4*) Brick Hse Pub.
Phillips, Caroline. The Religious Quest in the Poetry of T. S. Eliot, Vol. 14. LC 94-38440. (Studies in Art & Religious Interpretation). 112p. 1995. text 59.95 (*0-7734-9152-X*) E Mellen.
***Phillips, Caroline.** Waihou Journeys. (Illus.). 200p. 2000. pap. 35.00 (*1-86940-227-8*, Pub. by Auckland Univ) Paul & Co Pubs.
***Phillips, Caryl.** The Atlantic Sound. 304p. 2000. 26.00 (*0-375-40110-5*, Pub. by Knopf) Random House.
Phillips, Caryl. Cambridge: A Novel. LC 92-56359. 1993. pap. 12.00 (*0-679-73689-1*) Random.
— Crossing the River. 1995. pap. 12.00 (*0-679-75794-5*) Vin Bks.
***Phillips, Caryl.** The European Tribe. LC 99-48045. 160p. 2000. pap. 12.00 (*0-375-70704-2*) Vin Bks.
Phillips, Caryl. The European Tribe. 135p. 1993. reprint ed. pap. 10.95 (*0-571-19803-1*) Faber & Faber.
— The Final Passage. LC 95-14370. 1995. pap. 10.00 (*0-679-75931-X*) Vin Bks.
— Higher Ground: A Novel in Three Parts. LC 95-14371. 1995. pap. 12.00 (*0-679-76376-7*) Vin Bks.
— The Nature of Blood. LC 96-49641. 1997. 23.00 (*0-679-45470-5*) Knopf.
— The Nature of Blood. LC 96-49641. 1998. pap. 12.00 (*0-679-77675-3*) Random.
— The Right Set: A Tennis Anthology. LC 99-17240. 364p. 1999. pap. 14.00 (*0-375-70646-1*, Vin) Random.
— Speak Fiction & Poetry! The Best of BOMB Magazine's Interviews with Writers. LC 99-458417. 270p. 1998. text 49.95 (*90-5701-271-5*) Gordon & Breach.
— A State of Independence. LC 94-31112. 1995. pap. 10.00 (*0-679-75930-1*) Vin Bks.
Phillips, Caryl, ed. Extravagant Strangers: A Literature of Belonging. LC 98-29751. 352p. 1998. pap. 14.00 (*0-679-78154-4*) Random.
Phillips, Cath. River's Edge. 1998. pap. text 12.95 (*1-875243-25-9*, Pub. by Blackwattle) LPC InBook.
Phillips, Catherine. Robert Bridges: A Biography. (Illus.). 392p. 1992. 65.00 (*0-19-212251-7*) OUP.
Phillips, Catherine, ed. Gerard Manley Hopkins. LC 85-21405. (Authors Ser.). (Illus.). 470p. 1987. pap. text 23.95 (*0-19-281386-2*) OUP.
Phillips, Catherine, ed. see Yeats, William Butler.
Phillips, Catherine, ed. & intro. see Hopkins, Gerard Manley.
Phillips, Catherine, ed. & intro. see Smith, A. J.
Phillips, Catherine A., tr. see Basch, Victor.
Phillips, Catherine A., tr. see Grousset, Rene.
Phillips, Catherine A., tr. see Moulin-Eckart, Richard D.
Phillips, Catherine A., tr. see Specht, Richard.
Phillips, Catherine C. Jessie Benton Fremont: A Woman Who Made History. LC 94-43803. (Illus.). xvii, 361p. 1995. pap. 15.00 (*0-8032-8740-2*, Bison Books) U of Nebr Pr.
Phillips, Cecelia. The Best Chicken Recipes. 51p. (Orig.). 1990. pap. 6.95 (*0-9618870-0-1*) L C Ellsworth.
— Natural Solutions: A Guide to a Better Complexion. 30p. (Orig.). 1989. pap. 6.95 (*0-9618870-1-X*) L C Ellsworth.
— Weight Loss Made Easy: Hundreds of Tips for a Weight Loss Life-Style. LC 88-91234. 150p. (Orig.). 1993. write for info. (*0-9618870-3-6*); pap. 14.95 (*0-9618870-2-8*) L C Ellsworth.
Phillips, Cecil E. Cromwell's Captains. LC 73-37908. (Select Bibliographies Reprint Ser.). 1977. reprint ed. 27.95 (*0-8369-6746-1*) Ayer.
Phillips, Celeste R. Family Centered Maternity & Newborn Care: A Basic Text. 4th ed. (Illus.). 464p. (C). (gr. 13). 1995. pap. text 34.95 (*0-8151-6794-6*, 25335) Mosby Inc.
Phillips, Ceri. Economic Evaluation & Health Promotion. LC 96-80385. 144p. 1997. text 61.95 (*1-85972-487-6*, Pub. by Avebry) Ashgate Pub Co.
***Phillips, Chandler Allen.** Human Factors Engineering. LC 99-48715. 564p. 1999. text 102.95 (*0-471-24089-3*) Wiley.
Phillips, Charles. Another Look at Sex: The Biblical Perspective. 1995. mass mkt. 5.99 (*1-56229-421-0*) Pneuma Life Pub.
— Archie: His First Fifty Years. (Illus.). 128p. 1993. 15.98 (*0-89660-035-1*, Artabras) Abbeville Pr.
***Phillips, Charles.** Building ASP Solutions. (Application Development Reference Ser.). (Illus.). 2000. pap. 39.99 (*0-07-212300-1*) McGrw-H Intl.
Phillips, Charles. Shenfield to Southend Line. (C). 1985. 39.00 (*0-85361-308-7*) St Mut.
***Phillips, Charles & Axelrod, Alan.** Cops, Crooks & Criminologists: An International Biographical Dictionary of Law Enforcement. 2nd ed. (Illus.). 2000. pap. 18.95 (*0-8160-4076-1*, Checkmark) Facts on File.
Phillips, Charles & Axelrod, Alan. My Brother's Face: Portraits of the Civil War. LC 92-13958. (Illus.). 1993. 27.50 (*0-8118-0386-4*) Chronicle Bks.
Phillips, Charles, jt. auth. see Axelrod, Alan.
Phillips, Charles, tr. see Paterson, Janet M.
Phillips, Charles A. To Grow Spiritually. 312p. 1989. 9.95 (*0-685-26989-2*) C A Phillips.
Phillips, Charles D., jt. ed. see Whitaker, Gordon P.
Phillips, Charles F., Jr. The Regulation of Public Utilities: Theory & Practice. 3rd ed. 1025p. 1993. 50.00i (*0-910325-45-6*) Public Util.
Phillips, Charles H. The History of the Colored Methodist Episcopal Church in America: Comprising Its Organization, Subsequent Developments & Present Status. LC 73-38459. (Religion in America, Ser. 2). 252p. 1974. reprint ed. 19.95 (*0-405-04080-6*) Ayer.
Phillips, Charles J. Paderewski: The Story of a Modern Immortal. LC 77-17399. (Music Reprint Ser.). (Illus.). 1978. reprint ed. lib. bdg. 55.00 (*0-306-77534-4*) Da Capo.
Phillips, Charles L. Basic Life Support: Skills Manual. LC 77-8351. 1977. pap. 14.95 (*0-87618-883-8*) P-H.
— Basic Life Support Skills. 2nd ed. (Illus.). 224p. 1986. pap. text 30.00 (*0-89303-253-0*) P-H.
— Paramedic Skills Manual. 2nd ed. 256p. 1989. pap. write for info. (*0-318-65460-1*) P-H.
Phillips, Charles L. Rain of Fire: B-29s over Japan, 1945. LC 95-78454. (Illus.). 208p. (Orig.). 1995. pap. 19.95 (*0-9647577-0-2*) B-Nijuku Pubng.
Phillips, Charles L. Signals, Systems & Transforms. 2nd ed. LC 98-25861. 688p. 1998. 100.00 (*0-13-095322-9*) P-H.
— Specimens of Irish Eloquence. 1977. text 22.95 (*0-8369-8171-5*, 8311) Ayer.
Phillips, Charles L. & Harbor, Royce D. Feedback Control Systems. 4th ed. LC 99-24770. 658p. 1999. 100.00 (*0-13-949090-6*) P-H.
Phillips, Charles L. & Nagle, Troy. Digital Control System Analysis & Design. 3rd ed. LC 94-3482. 704p. (C). 1994. 105.00 (*0-13-309832-X*) P-H.
Phillips, Charles O. Practical Spread Spectrum: Frequency Hopping, Bk. II. 187p. 1994. pap. 48.80 (*0-89412-224-X*) Aegean Park Pr.
— Practical Spread Spectrum Bk. IV: Detection, Recognition & Recording of Spread Spectrum Signals. 154p. 1993. pap. 48.80 (*0-89412-220-7*) Aegean Park Pr.
Phillips, Charles P. Law of Copyright in Works & Literature & Art & in the Application of Designs: With the Statutes Relating Thereto. xvi, 261,cxiiip. 1989. reprint ed. 42.50 (*0-8377-1055-3*, Rothman) W S Hein.
***Phillips, Charles S.** Construction Contract Administration. LC 99-43494. 1999. pap. write for info. (*0-87335-191-6*) SMM&E Inc.
Phillips, Charles S. Secrets of Successful Public Relations. LC 85-6426. 315p. 1985. 49.95 (*0-317-39230-1*) P-H.
Phillips, Cherie. Alsharqi Dance, Vol. 1. LC 87-92039. (Hip Movements Ser.: Vol. 1, No. 1). (Illus.). 250p. (Orig.). 1987. spiral bd. write for info. (*0-9616287-2-3*) IntelSpectrum.
— Stick Exercises. LC 86-62541. (Illus.). 281p. 1989. pap. write for info. (*0-9616287-0-7*) IntelSpectrum.
— Stoic Encheiridion. 89p. 1997. write for info. (*0-9616287-5-8*) IntelSpectrum.
Phillips, Cheryl. 1001 Craft Verses. (Illus.). 96p. 1996. write for info. (*0-614-13950-3*) Landmark Pubs Inc.
Phillips, Chester A. Bank Credit. Bruchey, Stuart, ed. LC 80-1165. (Rise of Commercial Banking Ser.). (Illus.). 1981. reprint ed. lib. bdg. 38.95 (*0-405-13675-7*) Ayer.
Phillips, Chris, et al. International Marketing Strategy. LC 94-43121. 250p. (C). 1995. pap. text, teacher ed. 49.95 (*0-415-12498-0*) Thomson Learn.
— International Marketing Strategy: Analysis, Development & Implementation. (Bus Press-New). 450p. 1994. pap. 34.95 (*1-86152-220-7*) Thomson Learn.
Phillips, Christopher. Damned Yankee: The Life of General Nathaniel Lyon. LC 89-20470. (Illus.). 368p. 1996. pap. 12.95 (*0-8071-2103-7*) La State U Pr.
— Damned Yankee: The Life of General Nathaniel Lyon. Foley, William E., ed. (Missouri Biography Ser.). (Illus.). 321p. 1990. 29.95 (*0-8262-0731-6*) U of Mo Pr.
— Freedom's Port: The African American Community of Baltimore, 1790-1860. LC 96-45818. 376p. 1997. text 60.00 (*0-252-02315-3*); pap. text 21.95 (*0-252-06618-9*) U of Ill Pr.
***Phillips, Christopher.** Missouri's Confederate: Claiborne Fox Jackson & the Creation of Southern Identity. LC 00-21061. (Missouri Biography Ser.). (Illus.). 360p. 2000. 29.95 (*0-8262-1272-7*) U of Mo Pr.
Phillips, Christopher. Photography in the Modern Era: European Documents & Critical Writings, 1913-1940. (Illus.). 368p. 1989. pap. 19.95 (*0-89381-407-5*) Aperture.
***Phillips, Christopher.** Socrates Cafe: Tales of the Examined Life. 224p. 2000. 23.95 (*0-393-04956-6*) Norton.
Phillips, Christopher, ed. Photography in the Modern Era: European Documents & Critical Writings, 1913-1940. (Illus.). 368p. 1989. 60.00 (*0-89381-406-7*) Aperture.
Phillips, Christopher, et al, texts. Voices. (Illus.). 168p. 1999. pap. 40.00 (*90-73362-39-3*, 915005) Witte De With CFCA.
Phillips, Christopher, jt. auth. see Hambourg, Maria Morris.
Phillips, Cindy & Williams, Levi. A Positive Steps Approach: A Parent's Guide to Teaching Youth to Be Responsible for Today! Ford, June, ed. LC 93-48830. 240p. (Orig.). 1994. pap. 9.95 (*1-56530-124-2*) Summit TX.
Phillips, Claire. Black Market Babies. LC 98-92898. 182p. 1998. pap. 10.00 (*0-9664488-0-4*) Elevnth Hr Pr.
Phillips, Clare. Jewelry: From Antiquity to the Present. LC 95-60284. (World of Art Ser.). (Illus.). 216p. (Orig.). 1996. pap. 14.95 (*0-500-20287-7*, Pub. by Thames Hudson) Norton.
— Jewels & Jewelry. LC 99-67588. (Illus.). 160p. 2000. write for info. (*0-8230-2584-5*) Watsn-Guptill.
Phillips, Claude. Emotion in Art. LC 68-29238. (Essay Index Reprint Ser.). 1977. 23.95 (*0-8369-0788-4*) Ayer.
— Fifty Years of Public School Teaching. (American Autobiography Ser.). 145p. 1995. reprint ed. lib. bdg. 69.00 (*0-7812-8619-0*) Rprt Serv.
Phillips, Claude S. The Development of Nigerian Foreign Policy. LC 64-13703. (Northwestern University African Studies Ser.: No. 13). 166p. reprint ed. pap. 51.50 (*0-608-11808-7*, 201530500001) Bks Demand.
Phillips, Claudia, ed. Studies in Public Administration: The Berkeley-Hong Kong Project, 1988-1989. (C). 1992. pap. text 20.00 (*1-880963-00-0*) U of Cal HK Proj.
Phillips, Claudia, et al, eds. Studies in Public Administration: The Berkeley-Hong Kong Project, 1989-1990. LC 93-24207. 1993. write for info. (*1-880963-01-9*) U of Cal HK Proj.
Phillips, Clifford E. China Beckons: An Insight to the Culture & National Language. 324p. 1993. pap. 39.95 incl. audio (*0-88864-240-7*, C19041) Audio-Forum.
Phillips, Clifton J. Indiana in Transition, 1880-1920. (History of Indiana Ser.: Vol. 4). (Illus.). xiv, 674p. 1968. 17.50 (*0-87195-092-8*) Ind Hist Soc.
Phillips, Clive. Cattle Behavior. (Illus.). 224p. 1993. text 34.95 (*0-85236-251-X*, Pub. by Farming Pr) Diamond Farm Bk.
Phillips, Clyde. Blindsided: A Mystery. LC 99-44732. 320p. 2000. 24.00 (*0-688-17154-0*, Wm Morrow) Morrow Avon.
— Fall from Grace: A Noir Thriller. LC 97-36057. 320p. 1998. 24.00 (*0-688-15744-0*, Wm Morrow) Morrow Avon.
— Fall from Grace: A Noir Thriller. 437p. 1999. reprint ed. mass mkt. 6.50 (*0-671-03428-6*) PB.
Phillips, Colette & Langhart, Janet. 21 Steps for Women to Win: A Guide for Women Who Want to Succeed As Entrepreneurs & Managers. (Illus.). 54p. 1998. pap. 7.95 (*0-9668068-0-8*) C Phillips Commns.
Phillips Collection Staff. A Collection in the Making. LC 76-10817. 69p. 1976. lib. bdg. 54.00 incl. fiche (*0-226-69538-7*) U Ch Pr.
— Jacob Lawrence. (Migration Ser.). 174p. 1993. 40.00 (*0-9636129-0-5*) Rappahnck Pr.
— Jacob Lawrence. (Migration Ser.). (Illus.). 174p. 1993. pap. 25.00 (*0-9636129-1-3*) Rappahnck Pr.
— The Phillips Collection: A Summary Catalogue. Passantino, Erika D., ed. LC 85-9575. 300p. 1985. pap. 20.00 (*0-943044-05-7*) Phillips Coll.
Phillips, Connie, ed. see Food & Nutrition Group Staff.
Phillips, Craig, abr. Wondrous Love Organ. 1997. pap. 12.95 (*0-634-00341-0*) H Leonard.
Phillips, Cynthia, jt. auth. see Jones, Iris.
Phillips, D. The Longman TOEFL Preparation Program: (Longman Preparation Course for the TOEFL) 1989. pap. text 8.50 (*0-8013-0212-9*, 75870) Longman.
— Mazes. 1994. pap. text 1.00 (*0-486-27859-X*) Dover.
— Pract Test Cassette. 1988. audio 37.95 (*0-8013-0032-0*, 75697) Longman.
Phillips, D. & Desrochers, P., eds. Multimedia Communications: Proceedings of Multimedia Communications Conference, 13-16 April 1993, Banff, Canada. LC 93-78137. 658p. (gr. 12). 1993. 98.00 (*90-5199-132-0*, Pub. by IOS Pr) IOS Press.
Phillips, D. & Grice, R. Laser Chemistry in the U. K., Vol. 9, Nos. 4-6. Letokhov, V. S. et al, eds. (Laser Chemistry Ser.). 314p. 1988. pap. text 453.00 (*3-7186-4869-5*) Gordon & Breach.
Phillips, D., jt. auth. see Thomas, F. J.
Phillips, D. A. Subsea Production Systems - Can Engineering Reduce Pipeline Costs? (C). 1989. 100.00 (*0-89771-731-7*, Pub. by Lorne & MacLean Marine) St Mut.
***Phillips, D. C.** Constructivism in Education. (National Society for the Study of Education Publication Ser.). 320p. 2000. 30.00 (*0-226-60170-6*) U Ch Pr.
— The Expanded Social Scientist's Bestiary: A Guide to Fabled Threats to & Defenses of, Naturalistic Social Science. LC 00-28412. 272p. 2000. pap. 23.95 (*0-8476-9891-2*) Rowman.
— The Expanded Social Scientist's Bestiary: A Guide to Fabled Threats to, & Defenses of, Naturalistic Social Science. 272p. 2000. 69.00 (*0-8476-9890-4*) Rowman.
Phillips, D. C. The Social Scientist's Bestiary: A Guide to Fabled Threats to, & Defences of, Naturalistic Social Science. LC 92-21654. 280p. 1992. 42.95 (*0-08-040254-2*, Pergamon Press) Buttrwrth-Heinemann.
***Phillips, D. C. & Burbules, Nicholas C.** Postpositivism & Educational Research. LC 99-49770. (Philosophy, Theory, & Educational Research Ser.). 150p. 2000. text 15.95 (*0-8476-9121-7*) Rowman.
— Postpositivism & Educational Research. LC 99-49770. (Illus.). 150p. 2000. pap. 15.95 (*0-8476-9122-5*) Rowman.
Phillips, D. C. & Soltis, Jonas F. Perspective on Learning. 3rd rev. ed. LC 98-20832. (Thinking about Education Ser.). 128p. 1998. pap. 15.95 (*0-8077-3703-8*) Tchrs Coll.
— Perspectives on Learning. 2nd ed. (Thinking about Education Ser.). 128p. (Orig.). (C). 1991. pap. text 11.95 (*0-8077-3116-1*) Tchrs Coll.
Phillips, D. C., jt. auth. see Cleverley, John F.
Phillips, D. C., jt. auth. see McLaughlin, Milbrey W.
Phillips, D. C., ed. see Bragg, Lawrence.
Phillips, D. C., jt. ed. see McLaughlin, Milbrey W.
Phillips, D. E. Modern Eletronics & Communications. 132p. (C). 1986. 180.00 (*0-948691-12-3*, Pub. by Witherby & Co) St Mut.
Phillips, D. H., et al, eds. Postlabelling Methods for the Detection of DNA Adducts. (IARC Scientific Publications: No. 124). (Illus.). 404p. 1993. pap. text 85.00 (*92-832-2124-9*) OUP.
Phillips, D. H. & Venitt, S., eds. Environmental Mutagenesis: Current Methods for Detecting Mutagens in the Environment. LC 96-140584. (Human Molecular Genetics Ser.). 350p. 1996. 149.50 (*1-872748-19-8*, Pub. by Bios Sci) Coronet Bks.
***Phillips, D. Michael.** Fall of Freedom. LC 98-75192. 164p. 1998. pap. 16.95 (*0-9656929-1-4*) InfoNovels.
Phillips, D. Z. Faith after Foundationalism. 275p. 1988. text 49.95 (*0-415-00333-4*) Routledge.
— From Fantasy to Faith: The Philosophy of Religion & Twentieth-Century Literature. 224p. 1991. text 45.00 (*0-312-05300-2*) St Martin.
— Introducing Philosophy: The Challenge of Scepticism. 224p. (C). 1996. 53.95 (*0-631-20040-1*); pap. 24.95 (*0-631-20041-X*) Blackwell Pubs.
— J. R. Jones. 121p. 1996. pap. 12.95 (*0-7083-1300-0*, Pub. by Univ Wales Pr) Paul & Co Pubs.
***Phillips, D. Z.** Kant & Kierkegaard on Religion. LC 99-86014. 2000. text 65.00 (*0-312-23234-9*) St Martin.
Phillips, D. Z. Philosophy's Cool Place LC 98-50653. 1999. 32.50 (*0-8014-3600-1*) Cornell U Pr.
— R. S. Thomas: Poet of the Hidden God. LC 85-31998. (Princeton Theological Monographs: No. 2). 192p. (Orig.). 1986. pap. 15.00 (*0-915138-83-2*) Pickwick.
— Recovering Religious Concepts: Closing Epistemic Divides. LC 99-30116. (Swansea Studies in Philosophy). 272p. 1999. text 59.95 (*0-312-22704-3*) St Martin.
Phillips, D. Z., ed. Interventions in Ethics. LC 91-19790. (SUNY Series in Ethical Theory). 300p. (C). 1992. pap. text 19.95 (*0-7914-0996-1*) State U NY Pr.
— Religion & Morality. LC 95-17961. (Claremont Studies in the Philosophy of Religion). 304p. 1996. text 49.95 (*0-312-12868-1*) St Martin.
— Wittgenstein & the Possibility of Discourse: Rush Rhees. LC 97-25416. (Illus.). 316p. (C). 1998. text 59.95 (*0-521-62261-1*) Cambridge U Pr.
Phillips, D. Z. & Tessin, Timothy. Religion & Hume's Legacy. LC 99-21892. (Claremont Studies in the Philosophy of Religion). 1999. text 65.00 (*0-312-22526-1*) St Martin.
Phillips, D. Z. & Tessin, Timothy, eds. Religion Without Transcendence? LC 97-13671. (Claremont Studies in the Philosophy of Religion). 292p. 1997. text 65.00 (*0-312-17630-9*) St Martin.
Phillips, D. Z., ed. see Rhees, Rush.
Phillips, Dale E. Let Me Introduce You to My Father: A Study on the Nature of God. 120p. 1992. pap. 6.50 (*0-9633335-1-8*) Dryden Pubs.
***Phillips, Dale R.** My People's Waltz: Stories. 2000. pap. 13.00 (*0-380-73336-6*) Morrow Avon.
Phillips, Dale R. My People's Waltz: Stories. LC 98-37090. 192p. 1999. 22.95 (*0-393-04715-6*) Norton.
Phillips, Daniel L. Griswold - A History: Being a History of the Town of Griswold, from the Earliest Times to the Entrance of Our Country in the World War in 1917. (Illus.). 456p. 1995. reprint ed. lib. bdg. 49.00 (*0-8328-4981-2*) Higginson Bk Co.
Phillips, Daphne. The Great Road to Bath. 192p. 1987. 30.00 (*0-905392-26-4*) St Mut.
— Reading Old & New. 96p. 1987. pap. 35.00 (*0-905392-73-6*) St Mut.
— Reminiscences of Reading. 128p. 1987. 35.00 (*0-905392-39-6*) St Mut.
Phillips, Darlene S., et al. Kentucky Insurance Law. xvi, 340p. 1992. pap. 45.00 (*1-58757-001-7*, AM-11) Univ of KY.
Phillips, Dave. Animal Mazes. (Illus.). 48p. (J). 1998. pap. 2.95 (*0-486-26707-5*) Dover.
Phillips, Dave. Celtic Mazes. 48p. pap. 2.95 (*0-486-40154-5*) Dover.
Phillips, Dave. Egyptian Mazes. (Illus.). 48p. (Orig.). 1997. pap. text 2.95 (*0-486-29658-X*) Dover.
— Endangered Animal Mazes. (Illus.). pap. 2.95 (*0-486-29147-2*) Dover.
— Graphic & Op-Art Mazes. (Illus.). 1976. pap. 3.95 (*0-486-23373-1*) Dover.
***Phillips, Dave.** Linux Music & Sound. LC 99-42680. (Illus.). 350p. 2000. 39.95 (*1-886411-34-4*) No Starch Pr.
Phillips, Dave. Mind-Boggling Mazes: Forty Graphic & Three-D Labyrinths. (Illus.). 1979. pap. 3.95 (*0-486-23798-2*) Dover.
— Monster Mazes. 48p. 1989. pap. 2.95 (*0-486-26005-4*) Dover.
— Mother Goose Mazes. LC 92-17679. (J). 1992. pap. 2.95 (*0-486-27319-9*) Dover.
— Mystifying Mazes. 48p. 1984. pap. 3.50 (*0-486-24722-8*) Dover.
— Pirate Treasure Mazes. 48p. pap. 2.95 (*0-486-27049-1*) Dover.
— Scary Mazes. LC 93-18312. 1993. 2.95 (*0-486-27608-2*) Dover.
— Space Age Mazes. (J). (gr. 2 up). 1988. pap. 2.95 (*0-486-25659-6*) Dover.
— Sports Mazes. (Illus.). (J). pap. 1.00 (*0-486-28277-5*) Dover.
— Storybook Mazes. (Illus.). 62p. 1978. pap. 2.95 (*0-486-23628-5*) Dover.
— Trip to Mars Maze. 1999. pap. text 3.95 (*0-486-40841-8*) Dover.
— Wonders of the Word Mazes. (Illus.). pap. 2.95 (*0-486-28786-6*) Dover.
— The World's Most Difficult Maze, Vol. 181. 1981. pap. 4.95 (*0-486-23970-5*) Dover.

P

Phillips, Dave. Hidden Treasure Maze Book. (Puzzles, Amusements, Recreations Ser.). 48p. (Orig.). (J). (gr. 2 up). 1984. pap. 2.95 (*0-486-24566-7*) Dover.

Phillips, David. Accessibility & Utilization: Geographical Perspectives on Health Care Delivery. 220p. (C). 1984. pap. 90.00 (*0-06-318276-9*) St Mut.

— Chronicles of the Civil War: An Illustrated History of the War Between the States. (Illus.). 1999. 29.98 (*1-56799-728-7*) M Friedman Pub Grp Inc.

Phillips, David. Chronicles on the Civil Wars An Illustrated History of War Between the States. 1999. 29.98 (*1-56799-823-2*) M Friedman Pub Grp Inc.

— Controlling Iodine Deficiency Disorders in Developing Countries, No. 5. (Practical Health Guide Ser.). (Illus.). 40p. (C). 1989. pap. 7.95 (*0-85598-107-5*, Pub. by Oxfam Pub) Stylus Pub VA.

— Eating Out in Glasgow 1994. 112p. (C). 1993. pap. write for info. (*1-874640-45-9*, Pub. by Argyll Pubng) St Mut.

— Health & Health Care 3rd World. 1990. pap. 55.95 (*0-582-01418-2*, Drumbeat) Longman.

— Light up Your Life. Balkwill, Fran, ed. (Making Sense of Science Ser.). (Illus.). 32p. (J). 1997. pap. 12.00 (*1-85578-090-9*, Pub. by Portland Pr Ltd) Ashgate Pub Co.

— Maps of the Civil War: The Roads They Took. (Illus.). 160p. 1998. 24.98 (*1-56799-586-1*, MetroBooks) M Friedman Pub Grp Inc.

— Soldier's Story: The Double Life of a Confederate Spy. LC 97-12842. (Civil War Chronicles Ser.). 1997. 15.98 (*1-56799-425-3*, MetroBooks) M Friedman Pub Grp Inc.

Phillips, David, ed. American Motor Sports. (Illus.). 192p. 1997. 19.98 (*0-7858-0716-0*) Bk Sales Inc.

— Education in Germany: Tradition & Reform in Historical Context. LC 94-44701. (International Developments in School Reform Ser.). 240p. (C). (gr. 13). 1995. 100.00 (*0-415-11397-0*) Routledge.

— Polymer Photophysics: Luminescence, Energy Migration & Molecular Motion in Synthetic Polymers. 250p. (C). 1985. text 79.95 (*0-412-16510-4*, NO. 9309) Chapman & Hall.

Phillips, David & Atkinson, George H., eds. Time-Resolved Laser Raman Spectroscopy. viii, 180p. 1987. text 182.00 (*3-7186-0343-8*) Gordon & Breach.

Phillips, David & Berman, Yitzhak. Human Services in the Age of New Technology: Harmonizing Social Work & Computerization. (European Centre Vienna Ser.). 168p. 1995. pap. 41.95 (*1-85972-128-1*, Pub. by Avebry) Ashgate Pub Co.

Phillips, David & Filmer-Sankey, Caroline. Diversification in Modern Language Teaching: Choice & the National Curriculum. LC 92-15265. 208p. 1992. pap. write for info. (*0-415-07201-8*) Routledge.

Phillips, David & Phillips, Benny. Motorsports America, 1996-97: The Men & Machines of American Motorsport, 3 vols. (Annual Ser.). (Illus.). 192p. 1997. 29.90 (*0-929323-15-7*) Autosport Intl.

Phillips, David & Wolfkiel, Bill. Estate Planning Made Easy: Your Step-by-Step Guide to Protecting Your Family. 2nd ed. LC 97-42129. 248p. 1998. pap. 21.95 (*0-7931-2712-2*, 5608-8102) Dearborn.

Phillips, David A. Careers in Secret Operations: How to Be a Federal Intelligence Officer. 93p. 1975. pap. 24.95 (*0-313-27011-2*, P7011, Greenwood Pr) Greenwood.

Phillips, David A., Jr. Effects of Inundation on Cultural Resources in Painted Rock Reservoir, Arizona, 2 pts. Incl. Pt. 2. Effects of Inundation on Cultural Resources in Painted Rock Reservoir, Arizona: An Assessment. Rozen, Kenneth C. (Illus.). 27p. 1982. 7.95 (*1-889747-22-X*); Pt. 1. (Illus.). 115p. 1982. (*1-889747-21-1*); 1982. pap. write for info. (*1-889747-23-8*) Ariz St Mus.

Phillips, David A. The Minimax Diet & Nutrition Book: Maximum Nutrition, Minimum Calories. LC 88-6937. 160p. (Orig.). 1988. pap. 8.95 (*0-88007-165-6*) Woodbridge Pr.

— My Secret Wars Scrapbook: Adventures in Combat, Covert Action & Espionage Operations. 260p. 1988. pap. 15.00 (*0-317-90861-8*) Stone Trail Pr.

— Writing for Pleasure & Profit in Retirement. (Self Confidence - Self Competence Ser.). 52p. (Orig.). 1985. pap. 6.95 (*0-932123-01-5*) Stone Trail Pr.

Phillips, David A., ed. see Johnson, William R.

Phillips, David C. Collected Works, 22 vols., Set. 1988. reprint ed. lib. bdg. 2054.00 (*0-7812-1320-7*) Rprt Serv.

— The Conflict. (Collected Works of David G. Phillips). 1988. reprint ed. lib. bdg. 79.00 (*0-7812-1341-X*) Rprt Serv.

— The Cost. (Collected Works of David G. Phillips). 1988. reprint ed. lib. bdg. 79.00 (*0-7812-1326-6*) Rprt Serv.

— Degarmo's Wife & Other Stories. (Collected Works of David G. Phillips). 1988. reprint ed. lib. bdg. 59.00 (*0-7812-1345-2*) Rprt Serv.

— The Fashionable Adventure of Joshua Craig. (Collected Works of David G. Phillips). 1988. reprint ed. lib. bdg. 59.00 (*0-7812-1337-1*) Rprt Serv.

— George Helm. (Collected Works of David G. Phillips). 1988. reprint ed. lib. bdg. 59.00 (*0-7812-1344-4*) Rprt Serv.

— Golden Fleece. (Collected Works of David G. Phillips). 1988. reprint ed. lib. bdg. 59.00 (*0-7812-1324-X*) Rprt Serv.

— The Grain of Dust. (Collected Works of David G. Phillips). 1988. reprint ed. lib. bdg. 79.00 (*0-7812-1342-8*) Rprt Serv.

— The Great God Success. (Collected Works of David G. Phillips). 1988. reprint ed. lib. bdg. 79.00 (*0-7812-1321-5*) Rprt Serv.

— Her Serene Highness. (Collected Works of David G. Phillips). 1988. reprint ed. lib. bdg. 79.00 (*0-7812-1322-3*) Rprt Serv.

— The Hungry Heart. (Collected Works of David G. Phillips). 1988. reprint ed. lib. bdg. 79.00 (*0-317-90729-8*) Rprt Serv.

— The Husband's Story. (Collected Works of David G. Phillips). 1988. reprint ed. lib. bdg. 79.00 (*0-7812-1339-8*) Rprt Serv.

— Light Fingered Gentry. (Collected Works of David G. Phillips). 1988. reprint ed. lib. bdg. 59.00 (*0-7812-1334-7*) Rprt Serv.

— The Master-Rogue. (Collected Works of David G. Phillips). 1988. reprint ed. lib. bdg. 59.00 (*0-7812-1325-8*) Rprt Serv.

— The Mother-Light. (Collected Works of David G. Phillips). 1988. reprint ed. lib. bdg. 59.00 (*0-7812-1327-4*) Rprt Serv.

— Old Wives for New. (Collected Works of David G. Phillips). 1988. reprint ed. lib. bdg. 59.00 (*0-7812-1335-5*) Rprt Serv.

— The Plum Tree. (Collected Works of David G. Phillips). 1988. reprint ed. lib. bdg. 59.00 (*0-7812-1328-2*) Rprt Serv.

— The Price She Paid. (Collected Works of David G. Phillips). 1988. reprint ed. lib. bdg. 59.00 (*0-7812-1343-6*) Rprt Serv.

— The Reign of Guilt. (Collected Works of David G. Phillips). 1988. reprint ed. lib. bdg. 59.00 (*0-7812-1329-0*) Rprt Serv.

— The Second Generation. (Collected Works of David G. Phillips). 1988. reprint ed. lib. bdg. 59.00 (*0-7812-1333-9*) Rprt Serv.

— White Magic. (Collected Works of David G. Phillips). 1988. reprint ed. lib. bdg. 79.00 (*0-7812-1340-1*) Rprt Serv.

— Worth of a Woman. (Collected Works of David G. Phillips). 1988. reprint ed. lib. bdg. 79.00 (*0-7812-1336-3*) Rprt Serv.

Phillips, David G. American Stampless Cover Catalog: Standard Reference Catalog of American Postal History, 3 vols. 5th rev. ed. 454p. 1997. 50.00 (*1-877998-10-9*) D G Phillips.

Phillips, David G. The Collected Works of David G. Phillips, 11 vols., Set. Incl. Degarmo's Wife & Other Stories. 1913. reprint ed. 26.00 Fashionable Adventures of Joshua Craig. 1972. reprint ed. 39.00 (*0-403-03157-5*); George Helm. 1912. reprint ed. 29.00 (*0-403-02999-6*); Grain of Dust. 1911. reprint ed. 39.00 Hungry Heart. 1909. reprint ed. 40.00 Husband's Story. 1910. reprint ed. 38.00 Old Wives for New. 1908. reprint ed. 39.00 Price She Paid. 1912. reprint ed. 39.00 (*0-403-02960-0*); Susan Lenox: Her Fall & Rise., 2 vols. 1917. reprint ed. 79.00 Worth of a Woman. 1908. reprint ed. 39.00 785.00 (*0-686-01741-2*) Somerset Pub.

— The Conflict. (American Author Ser.). 1981. reprint ed. lib. bdg. 49.00 (*0-686-71911-5*) Scholarly.

— The Cost. (American Author Ser.). reprint ed. lib. bdg. 69.00 (*0-685-47615-4*) Scholarly.

— The Deluge. LC 70-104541. (Illus.). 482p. reprint ed. lib. bdg. 18.50 (*0-8398-1563-8*) Irvington.

— The Deluge. (Illus.). 482p. (C). 1986. reprint ed. pap. text 7.95 (*0-8290-1913-8*) Irvington.

— The Deluge. 1988. reprint ed. lib. bdg. 75.00 (*0-7812-1331-2*) Rprt Serv.

— The Deluge. (American Author Ser.). 1981. reprint ed. lib. bdg. 69.00 (*0-685-47616-2*) Scholarly.

— Fashionable Adventures of Joshua Craig. 25.95 (*0-8488-1125-9*) Amereon Ltd.

— Federal-State Relations & the Control of Atomic Energy. Bruchey, Stuart, ed. LC 78-22706. (Energy in the American Economy Ser.). 1979. lib. bdg. 18.95 (*0-405-12008-7*) Ayer.

— The Fortune Hunter. (American Author Ser.). 1981. reprint ed. lib. bdg. 69.00 (*0-686-71917-4*) Scholarly.

— Golden Fleece. (American Author Ser.). 1981. reprint ed. lib. bdg. 59.00 (*0-686-71920-4*) Scholarly.

— The Great God Success. (Americans in Fiction Ser.). reprint ed. pap. text 6.95 (*0-89197-777-5*); reprint ed. lib. bdg. 20.00 (*0-8398-1564-6*) Irvington.

— The Great God Success. (American Author Ser.). 1981. reprint ed. lib. bdg. 49.00 (*0-686-71921-2*) Scholarly.

— Her Serene Highness. (American Author Ser.). 1981. reprint ed. lib. bdg. 69.00 (*0-686-71923-9*) Scholarly.

— Light-Fingered Gentry. (American Author Ser.). 1981. reprint ed. lib. bdg. 69.00 (*0-686-71929-8*) Scholarly.

— The Master-Rogue. (American Author Ser.). 1981. reprint ed. lib. bdg. 69.00 (*0-686-71931-X*) Scholarly.

— The Master Rogue: The Confessions of Croesus. LC 68-23724. (Americans in Fiction Ser.). (Illus.). reprint ed. pap. text 10.95 (*0-89197-841-0*); reprint ed. lib. bdg. 21.00 (*0-8398-1565-4*) Irvington.

— The Mother-Light. (American Author Ser.). 1981. reprint ed. lib. bdg. 69.00 (*0-686-71935-2*) Scholarly.

— The Plum Tree. LC 68-57547. (Muckrakers Ser.). (Illus.). 389p. reprint ed. lib. bdg. 20.50 (*0-8398-1566-2*) Irvington.

— The Plum Tree. (Muckrakers Ser.). (Illus.), 389p. (C). 1986. reprint ed. pap. text 9.95 (*0-8290-1884-0*) Irvington.

— The Plum Tree. (American Author Ser.). 1981. reprint ed. lib. bdg. 49.00 (*0-686-71938-7*) Scholarly.

— The Reign of Guilt. (American Author Ser.). 1981. reprint ed. lib. bdg. 49.00 (*0-686-71939-5*) Scholarly.

— The Second Generation. (American Author Ser.). 1981. reprint ed. lib. bdg. 49.00 (*0-686-71943-3*) Scholarly.

— The Social Secretary. (Illus.). 1972. reprint ed. lib. bdg. 32.00 (*0-8422-8169-X*) Irvington.

— The Social Secretary. (Illus.). 1982. reprint ed. pap. text 5.95 (*0-8290-1160-9*) Irvington.

— Susan Lenox: Her Fall & Rise. large type ed. LC 99-31950. 650p. 1999. 29.95 (*1-56000-479-7*) Transaction Pubs.

— Susan Lenox: Her Fall & Rise, 2 vols. in 1. LC 70-121842. (Illus.). reprint ed. 35.00 (*0-404-05029-8*) AMS Pr.

— Susan Lenox: Her Fall & Rise, 2 vols., Set. LC 68-57548. (Muckrakers Ser.). 1076p. reprint ed. lib. bdg. 19.00 (*0-8398-1568-9*) Irvington.

— Susan Lenox: Her Fall & Rise, 2 vols., Set. (Muckrakers Ser.). 1076p. 1986. reprint ed. pap. text 12.50 (*0-8290-2038-1*) Irvington.

— Susan Lenox: Her Fall & Rise, 2 vols., Set. (Collected Works of David G. Phillips). 1988. reprint ed. lib. bdg. 99.00 (*0-7812-1346-0*) Rprt Serv.

— White Magic. (American Author Ser.). 1981. reprint ed. lib. bdg. 49.00 (*0-686-71946-8*) Scholarly.

— A Woman Ventures. LC 78-104543. (Illus.). 337p. reprint ed. lib. bdg. 30.50 (*0-8398-1569-7*) Irvington.

— A Woman Ventures. (Illus.). 337p. (C). 1986. reprint ed. pap. text 6.95 (*0-8290-1958-8*) Irvington.

— A Woman Ventures. (American Author Ser.). 1981. reprint ed. lib. bdg. 49.00 (*0-686-71947-6*) Scholarly.

Phillips, David G., jt. ed. see Alperin, Richard M.

***Phillips, David Graham.** Susan Lenox Vol. 2: Her Fall & Rise. 470p. 2000. text 34.95 (*1-56000-448-7*) Transaction Pubs.

***Phillips, David H.** Environmental Mutagenesis. (Human Molecular Genetics Ser.). 402p. 1999. 110.00 (*0-12-220432-8*) Acad Pr.

Phillips, David L. Daring Raiders. LC 97-30541. (Civil War Chronicles Ser.). (Illus.). 128p. (YA). (gr. 6-12). 1999. 12.98 (*1-56799-553-5*) M Friedman Pub Grp Inc.

— War Diaries: The 1861 Kanawha Valley Campaigns. (Illus.). 479p. (C). 1990. 40.00 (*0-9628218-0-2*) Gauley Mount Pr.

Phillips, David L., ed. War Stories: Civil War in West Virginia. (Illus.). 490p. (C). 1991. 30.00 (*0-9628218-1-0*) Gauley Mount Pr.

Phillips, David L., jt. auth. see Lucy, William H.

***Phillips, David R.** Ageing in the Asia-Pacific Region: Issues, Policies & Future Trends. LC 99-87586. 2000. write for info. (*0-415-22018-1*) Routledge.

Phillips, David R., ed. Aging in East & Southeast Asia. (Research Studies in Gerontology). 224p. 1992. text 59.95 (*0-340-54367-1*, A9633, Pub. by E A) Routldge.

Phillips, David R. & Verhasselt, Yola, eds. Health & Development. LC 93-13465. (Illus.). 304p. (C). 1994. pap. 27.99 (*0-415-08529-2*) Routledge.

Phillips, David R. & Yeh, Anthony G., eds. New Towns in East & South-East Asia. (Illus.). 268p. 1987. 36.00 (*0-19-584087-9*) OUP.

Phillips, Dawn & Edwards, Judith. Five Steps to the Great Commission. 56p. 1996. pap. text 5.95 (*1-56309-164-X*, W963102) Womans Mission Union.

Phillips, Debbie. Hairdos in a Hurry. (Illus.). 32p. (Orig.). 1992. pap. 3.99 (*1-56722-004-5*) Word Aflame.

Phillips, Debora & Bernstein, Fred. How to Give Your Child a Great Self-Image: Proven Techniques to Build Confidence from Infancy to Adolescence. 272p. 1991. pap. 13.95 (*0-452-26589-4*, Plume) Dutton Plume.

Phillips, Debora & Judd, Robert. How to Fall Out of Love. 192p. 1985. mass mkt. 5.99 (*0-446-31408-0*, Pub. by Warner Bks) Little.

Phillips, Deborah. Introductory Course for the TOEFL Test: User's Guide. 96p. 1996. pap. text 11.59 (*0-201-89898-5*) Addison-Wesley.

— Longman Introductory Course for the TOEFL Test. LC 96-1447. 1996. pap. text 21.00 (*0-201-89899-3*, Pub. by Addison-Wesley) Longman.

— Longman Preparation Course for the TOEFL Test. (C). 1999. pap. text 46.60 (*0-201-37908-2*) Addison-Wesley.

— Longman Preparation Course for the TOEFL Test: CBE: Companion to Skills & Strategies, Vol. V. (Longman Preparation Course for the TEOFL Ser.). 1999. 46.60 (*0-201-52077-X*) Addison-Wesley.

***Phillips, Deborah.** Longman Preparations Course for the TOEFL Test--CBT Volume. LC 98-43066. 1998. pap. text. write for info. (*0-201-60437-X*) Addison-Wesley.

Phillips, Deborah. Longman TOEFL Preparation Course User Guide. 2nd ed. 1995. pap. text 11.58 (*0-201-84678-0*) Addison-Wesley.

— Preparation Course for the TOEFL Test Vol. A: Skills & Strategies. 2nd ed. LC 95-31469. 432p. 1995. pap. text, student ed. 25.36 (*0-201-84676-4*) Addison-Wesley.

— Preparation Course for the TOEFL Test Vol. B: Practice Tests. 2nd ed. LC 95-31469. 1995. pap. text, student ed. 19.85 (*0-201-84961-5*) Longman.

Phillips, Deborah & Crowell, Nancy A., eds. Cultural Diversity & Early Education: Report of a Workshop. 44p. (C). 1998. reprint ed. pap. text 20.00 (*0-7881-4871-0*) DIANE Pub.

Phillips, Deborah, ed. see National Research Council Staff & Institute of Medicine Staff.

Phillips, Deborah A., ed. Child Care for Low-Income Families: Summary of Two Workshops. (Illus.). 63p. (C). 1998. pap. text 25.00 (*0-7881-4870-2*) DIANE Pub.

— Quality in Child Care: What Does Research Tell Us? LC 87-62195. 130p. 1987. pap. text 6.00 (*0-935989-08-0*, NAEYC #140) Natl Assn Child Ed.

Phillips, Deborah A., ed. see National Research Council, Roundtable on Head Star & Institute of Medicine Staff.

Phillips, Deborah A., ed. see National Research Council Staff.

Phillips, Deborah A., jt. ed. see Shonkoff, Jack P.

***Phillips, Debra.** Kiss or Keep. unabridged ed. 295p. (Orig.). 1999. pap. 8.95 (*1-885478-96-8*, Pub. by Genesis Press) BookWorld.

Phillips, Denis C. Holistic Thought in Social Science. LC 76-7688. x, 149p. 1976. pap. 11.95 (*0-8047-1015-5*) Stanford U Pr.

***Phillips, Denise Michelle.** Poems, Essays, & Short Stories for Sharing: Portraits of a Writer's Soul! 163p. 2000. pap. text 16.00 (*1-55605-300-2*) Wyndham Hall.

Phillips, Dennis. Arena. (New American Poetry Ser.: No. 10). 176p. (Orig.). 1991. pap. 10.95 (*1-55713-127-9*) Sun & Moon CA.

— Credence. LC 96-31637. (New American Poetry Ser.: No. 23). 80p. 1996. pap. 10.95 (*1-55713-259-3*) Sun & Moon CA.

— The Hero Is Nothing. 88p. (Orig.). 1985. pap. 8.00 (*0-9614385-0-9*) Kajun Pr.

— Revenge Incorporated. large type ed. (Linford Mystery Library). 400p. 1998. pap. 17.99 (*0-7089-5225-9*, Linford) Ulverscroft.

— Twenty Questions. 47p. (Orig.). 1992. pap. 5.95 (*0-9629903-0-2*) Jahbone Pr.

— A World. (New American Poetry Ser.: No. 3). 103p. 1989. pap. 9.95 (*1-55713-072-8*) Sun & Moon CA.

Phillips, Dennis & Wallace, Les. Influence in the Workplace: Maximizing Personal Empowerment. 132p. 1995. pap. text 16.95 (*0-8403-7594-8*) Kendall-Hunt.

Phillips, Dennis, ed. see Joyce, James.

Phillips, Dennis H. Living with Huntington's Disease: A Book for Patients & Families. LC 81-16492. 251p. reprint ed. pap. 77.90 (*0-7837-2645-7*, 204299900006) Bks Demand.

Phillips, Dennis J. Teaching, Coaching, & Learning Tennis: An Annotated Bibliography. LC 89-10534. 190p. 1989. 20.50 (*0-8108-2254-7*) Scarecrow.

— The Tennis Sourcebook. LC 95-3842. 548p. 1995. 84.00 (*0-8108-3001-9*) Scarecrow.

Phillips, Derek. Lighting Historic Buildings. LC 96-29853. (Illus.). 224p. 1997. 79.95 (*0-07-049864-4*) McGraw.

— Lighting Historic Buildings: A Prospectus. LC 96-51636. 216p. 1997. text 69.95 (*0-7506-3342-5*) Buttrwrth-Heinemann.

***Phillips, Derek.** Lighting Modern Buildings. 216p. 2000. 79.95 (*0-7506-4082-0*, Architectural Pr) Buttrwrth-Heinemann.

Phillips, Derek L. Abandoning Method: Sociological Studies in Methodology. LC 72-13598. (Jossey-Bass Behavioral Science Ser.). 218p. 1973. reprint ed. pap. 67.60 (*0-8357-5003-5*, 202776500056) Bks Demand.

— Looking Backward: A Critical Appraisal of Communitarian Thought. 258p. (C). 1993. pap. text 17.95 (*0-691-04484-8*, Pub. by Princeton U Pr) Cal Prin Full Svc.

— Looking Backward: A Critical Appraisal of Communitarian Thought. LC 92-36381. 280p. (C). 1993. text 42.50 (*0-691-07425-9*, Pub. by Princeton U Pr) Cal Prin Full Svc.

— Toward a Just Social Order. LC 85-43303. 471p. 1986. reprint ed. pap. 146.10 (*0-608-04648-5*, 206533400003) Bks Demand.

Phillips, Derek M., ed. Histones & Nucleohistones. LC 71-161306. 319p. reprint ed. pap. 98.90 (*0-608-16604-9*, 202629900049) Bks Demand.

Phillips, Diane. It's a Wrap: Great Meals in Small Packages. LC 97-17024. 224p. 1997. pap. 14.95 (*0-312-16873-X*) St Martin.

— Keys to Successful Baking, Vol. 6. (Illus.). (Orig.). 1984. pap., per. 3.95 (*0-942320-11-5*) Am Cooking.

— The Perfect Basket: Make Your Own Special Occasion Baskets. LC 94-6974. 115p. 1994. 15.00 (*0-688-13031-3*, Hearst) Hearst Commns.

— The Perfect Mix: Bread, soup, dessert, & other homemade mixes from your kitchen. LC 92-41328. 1993. 15.00 (*0-688-12104-7*, Hearst) Hearst Commns.

***Phillips, Diane.** Pot Pies: Comfort Food under Cover. LC 99-36312. (Illus.). 224p. 2000. 24.95 (*0-385-49458-0*) Doubleday.

Phillips, Diane, jt. auth. see Cameron, Nonnie.

Phillips, Diane H. & Krasny, Marianne E. Field Guides Made Easy: Experience 4-H Natural Resources. (Four-H Ser.). (Illus.). 20p. (YA). (gr. 7-12). 1991. pap. 2.50 (*1-57753-197-3*, 147L5-21) Corn Coop Ext.

Phillips, Dianna. A Dog Owner's Guide to the Chow Chow. (Illus.). 95p. 1995. 10.95 (*1-56465-151-7*, 16046) Tetra Pr.

***Phillips, Doc'.** Internal Principles. LC 99-91174. 1999. 25.00 (*0-7388-0652-8*); pap. 18.00 (*0-7388-0653-6*) Xlibris Corp.

Phillips, Don. Alone with God. 40p. 1990. 9.99 (*0-8341-9179-2*, MB-619) Lillenas.

— A Selected Bibliography of Music Librarianship. LC ML0111.P5. (Illinois University Graduate School of Library Science Occasional Papers: No.113). 48p. reprint ed. pap. 30.00 (*0-608-11016-7*, 200725700064) Bks Demand.

***Phillips, Don.** The Technology of Fly Rods. 116p. 2000. 34.95 (*1-57188-191-3*, TFRH) F Amato Pubns.

— The Technology of Fly Rods: An In-Depth Look at the Design of the Modern Fly Rod, History & It's Role in Fly Fishing. 116p. 2000. pap. 19.95 (*1-57188-190-5*, TFR) F Amato Pubns.

Phillips, Don, contrib. by. Devotional Piano. 36p. 1987. 9.99 (*0-8341-9121-0*, MB-577) Lillenas.

Phillips, Donald E. Human Communication Behavior & Information Processing: An Interdisciplinary Sourcebook. LC 91-37399. 960p. 1992. text 40.00 (*0-8240-3531-3*, SS620) Garland.

— Karl Barth's Philosophy of Communication. (Philosophische Texte und Studien: No. 2). 416p. 1981. text 37.70 (*3-487-07154-1*) G Olms Pubs.

***Phillips, Donald G.** Germany & the Transnational Building Blocks for Post-National Community. LC 00-25467. 256p. 2000. 65.00 (*0-275-96490-6*, C6490) Greenwood.

— Post-National Patriotism & the Feasibility of Post-National Community in United Germany. LC 00-35972. 2000. write for info. (*0-275-97049-3*) Greenwood.

P

An Asterisk (*) at the beginning of an entry indicates that the title is appearing for the first time.

***Phillips, Donald T.** A Diamond in Spring. LC 99-6522. 343p. 1999. 14.95 (*1-56530-303-2*) Summit TX.

Phillips, Donald T. The Founding Fathers on Leadership: Classic Teamwork in Changing Times. 272p. 1998. mass mkt. 14.00 (*0-446-67425-7*, Pub. by Warner Bks) Little.

***Phillips, Donald T.** The Founding Fathers on Leadership: Classic Teamwork in Changing Times. 264p. 2000. reprint ed. 22.00 (*0-7881-9334-1*) DIANE Pub.

— Lincoln on Leadership: Executive Strategies for Tough Times. 208p. 1993. reprint ed. mass mkt. 13.95 (*0-446-39459-9*, Pub. by Warner Bks) Little.

Phillips, Donald T. Lincoln Stories for Leaders. LC 96-51265. 128p. 1997. pap. 12.99 (*1-56530-242-7*, Pub. by Summit TX) BookWorld.

— Martin Luther King, Jr. on Leadership: Inspiration & Wisdom for Challenging Times. LC 98-3795. 272p. 1999. 22.00 (*0-446-52367-4*, Pub. by Warner Bks) Little.

— Martin Luther King, Jr., on Leadership: Inspiration & Wisdom for Challenging Times. 384p. 2000. mass mkt. 13.95 (*0-446-67546-6*, Pub. by Warner Bks) Little.

Phillips, Donald T., jt. auth. see Brinker, Norman.

Phillips, Donald T., jt. auth. see Krzyzewski, Mike.

Phillips, Donna-Lee, ed. Eros & Photography. LC 77-81897. (Illus.). 1980. pap. 500.00 (*0-917986-02-4*) NFS Pr.

***Phillips, Doyle, ed.** Howard County, Texas Historic Photographs: Bascom A. Reagan, 1886-1977. (Illus.). 60p. 1999. pap. 16.95 (*1-929540-01-9*) D Phillips.

— A Howard County, Texas Primer: A Subjective Survey of Notable People, Places, Events & Historical Occurrences. (Illus.). 60p. 1999. pap. 14.95 (*1-929540-02-7*) D Phillips.

Phillips, Duane. Berlin. (Architecture Guides Ser.). (Illus.). 320p. 1998. pap. 5.95 (*3-89508-634-7*, 520201) Konemann.

Phillips, Duncan, ed. Art & Understanding, Nos. 1 & 2. LC 68-9235. (Contemporary Art Ser.). (Illus.). 1968. reprint ed. 20.95 (*0-405-00713-2*) Ayer.

Phillips, Dwayne. Image Processing in C: Analyzing & Enhanding Digital Images. (Illus.). 724p. 1997. pap. 39.95 incl. disk (*0-87930-443-X*) C M P Books.

— Software Project Management: Basics That Work at Work. LC 97-32260. 1998. write for info. (*0-8186-8300-7*, IEEE Inst Elec) IEEE Comp Soc.

Phillips, Dwayne R. Guilt of a Rapist. LC 96-90650. 104p. 1998. pap. 10.95 (*0-533-12122-1*) Vantage.

Phillips, E. & Sneddon, Ian N. Some Topics in Complex Analysis. (International Series of Monographs on Pure & Applied Mathematics: Vol. 86). 69.00 (*0-08-011421-0*, Pub. by Pergamon Repr) Franklin.

Phillips, E. Barbara. City Lights: Urban-Suburban Life in a Global Society. 2nd ed. (Illus.). 624p. (C). 1996. pap. text 49.95 (*0-19-505689-2*) OUP.

Phillips, E. D. Aspects of Greek Medicine. LC 86-72186. 240p. 1987. text 32.95 (*0-914783-18-1*) Charles.

Phillips, E. F. Beekeeping as a Hobby. (Shorey Lost Arts Ser.). 40p. reprint ed. pap. 10.00 (*0-8466-6039-3*, U39) Shoreys Bkstore.

Phillips, E. J. Corpus Signorium Imperii Romani: Hadrian's Wall, East of North Tyne, Vol. I, Fsc. I. (British Academy Ser.). (Illus.). 1977. 69.00 (*0-19-725954-5*) OUP.

Phillips, E. J., jt. auth. see Coulston, J. C.

Phillips, E. L., et al. Intelligence & Personality Factors Associated with Poliomyelitis Among School Age Children. (SRCD M Ser.: Vol. 12, No. 2). 1947. pap. 25.00 (*0-527-01541-5*) Periodicals Srv.

Phillips, E. Lakin. Permissiveness in Child Rearing & Education - A Failed Doctrine? New Trends for the 1990s. LC 92-35833. 134p. (C). 1993. pap. text 21.50 (*0-8191-8979-0*) U Pr of Amer.

— Psychotherapy Revised: New Frontiers in Research & Practice. 264p. (C). 1985. text 49.95 (*0-89859-571-1*) L Erlbaum Assocs.

Phillips, Earl H., jt. ed. see Eui-Young Yu.

Phillips, Earl H., jt. ed. see Yu, Eui-Young.

Phillips, Ed. Crisis in the Atmosphere: The Greenhouse Factor. (Illus.). (Orig.). 1990. pap. 6.95 (*0-9625245-0-6*) D B Clark & Co Pub.

Phillips, Edgar G. Functions of a Complex Variable: With Applications. LC QA0331.P45. (Longman Mathematical Texts Ser.). 154p. reprint ed. pap. 47.80 (*0-608-30870-6*, 201356200087) Bks Demand.

Phillips, Edward. Briefcase on Law of Evidence. (Briefcase Ser.). 161p. 1996. pap. 20.00 (*1-85941-244-0*, Pub. by Cavendish Pubng) Gaunt.

— The New World of English Words: or A General Dictionary. (Anglistica & Americana Ser.: No. 48). 358p. 1969. reprint ed. 76.70 (*0-685-66500-3*, 05102596) G Olms Pubs.

— The New World of English Words: or A Gereral Dictionary Containing the Interpretation of Such Hard Words As Are Derived from Other Languages. (Anglistica & Americana Ser.: No. 48). 358p. 1969. reprint ed. lib. bdg. 132.50 (*3-487-02596-5*) G Olms Pubs.

— Sunday's Child. (Stonewall Inn Editions Ser.). 240p. 1988. pap. 7.95 (*0-312-02294-8*) St Martin.

— Theatrum Poetarum: or a Compleat Collection of the Poets, Especially the Most Eminent, of All Ages. (Anglistica & Americana Ser.: No. 61). 453p. 1970. reprint ed. 76.70 (*0-685-66501-1*, 05102475) G Olms Pubs.

— The World's Best After-Dinner Jokes. 90p. 1998. pap. 6.95 (*0-00-637960-5*, Pub. by HarpC) Trafalgar.

— The World's Best Boss Jokes. 96p. 1998. pap. 6.95 (*0-00-638241-X*, Pub. by HarpC) Trafalgar.

— The World's Best Football Jokes. 96p. 1998. pap. 6.95 (*0-00-637962-1*, Pub. by HarpC) Trafalgar.

— The World's Best Rugby Jokes. 96p. 1998. pap. 6.95 (*0-00-638866-3*, Pub. by HarpC) Trafalgar.

— The World's Best Sailing Jokes. 96p. 1998. mass mkt. 6.95 (*0-00-638712-8*, Pub. by HarpC) Trafalgar.

Phillips, Edward, jt. auth. see Hopkins, Cathy.

Phillips, Edward D. Roosevelt's Children. LC 96-909799. (Orig.). 1997. pap. 14.95 (*0-533-12168-X*) Vantage.

Phillips, Edward H. The Lower Shenandoah Valley in the Civil War: The Impact of War upon the Civilian Population & upon Civil Institutions. (Virginia Civil War Battles & Leaders Ser.). (Illus.). 224p. 1993. 19.95 (*1-56190-042-7*) H E Howard.

***Phillips, Edward H.** Mystery Ship! A History of the Travel Air Type R Monoplanes. LC 99-40372. (Historic Aircraft Ser.). 1999. 29.95 (*0-911139-29-X*) Flying Bks.

Phillips, Edward H. Piper Airplanes: A Legend Aloft. 1993. 29.95 (*0-911139-14-1*) Flying Bks.

— The Staggerwing Story: A History of the Beechcraft Model 17. LC 96-61501. ii, 148 p. 1996. 24.95 (*0-911139-27-3*) Flying Bks.

Phillips, Edward H. & Rosenthal, Raul J., eds. Operative Strategies in Laparoscopic Surgery. 1995. write for info. (*0-387-59214-8*) Spr-Verlag.

— Operative Strategies in Laparoscopic Surgery. 288p. 1995. 110.00 (*3-540-59214-8*) Spr-Verlag.

Phillips, Edward J. The Founding of Russia's Navy: Peter the Greatand the Azov Fleet, 1688-1714, 159. LC 94-46941. (Contributions in Military Studies Ser.: No. 159). 232p. 1995. 59.95 (*0-313-29520-4*, Greenwood Pr) Greenwood.

— Manufacturing Plant Layout: Fundamentals & Fine Points of Optimum Facility Design. LC 97-65261. (Illus.). 259p. 1997. 59.00 (*0-87263-484-1*, 2570) SME.

***Phillips, Edward R.** Gabriele Faure: A Guide to Research. LC 99-45622. (Composer Resource Manuals: No. 49). 464p. 1999. 95.00 (*0-8240-7073-9*) Garland.

Phillips, Eileen, ed. The Left & the Erotic. (C). 1983. pap. 18.50 (*0-85315-583-6*, Pub. by Lawrence & Wishart) NYU Pr.

Phillips, Eileen, et al. Creative Mathematics. LC 96-47925. (Illus.). 192p. (C). 1997. 85.00 (*0-415-16462-1*) Routledge.

— Creative Mathematics. LC 96-47925. (Illus.). 192p. (C). 1997. pap. 20.99 (*0-415-16463-X*) Routledge.

Phillips, Elaine M., jt. auth. see Thompson, Chantal P.

Phillips, Eleanor. Chung, the China Gold, & Me. 150p. (Orig.). (J). (gr. 6-10). 1990. pap. 7.95 (*0-9624210-0-6*) Laurelwood Pr.

Phillips, Elizabeth. Crimes of Passion No. 9. 1997. per. 5.99 (*0-671-00949-4*) PB.

— Emily Dickinson: Personae & Performance. 1997. pap. text 19.95 (*0-271-01645-0*) Pa St U Pr.

Phillips, Elizabeth, et al. Patterns & Functions. Curcio, Frances R., ed. LC 91-18820. (Curriculum & Evaluation Standards for School Mathematics Addenda Ser.: Grades 5-8). (Illus.). 72p. 1991. pap. 15.95 (*0-87353-324-0*) NCTM.

Phillips, Elizabeth, jt. auth. see Fortlage, Kate.

Phillips, Elizabeth, jt. ed. see Harris, R. Cole.

Phillips, Elizabeth C. Monarch Notes on Faulkner's Absalom, Absalom. (Orig.). (C). 3.95 (*0-671-00664-9*, Arco) Macmillan Gen Ref.

Phillips, Elizabeth D., ed. see Lappan, Glenda, et al.

Phillips, Elizabeth V., ed. see Butler, Henry.

Phillips, Ellen. Shocked, Appalled, & Dismayed! How to Write Letters of Complaint That Get Results. LC 98-13819. 320p. 1999. pap. 12.00 (*0-375-70120-6*) Vin Bks.

— The Tale-Teller Tells All. 1990. write for info. (*0-9628226-0-4*) Cricket Papers Pr.

Phillips, Ellen & Burrell, C. Colston. Rodale's Illustrated Encyclopedia of Perennials. LC 92-30109. 533p. 1993. text 27.95 (*0-87596-570-9*, 01-690-0) Rodale Pr Inc.

— Rodale's Illustrated Encyclopedia of Perennials. (Illus.). 544p. 1999. pap. 19.95 (*0-87596-999-2*) Rodale Pr Inc.

Phillips, Ellen Blue, jt. auth. see Foreman, Laura.

Phillips, Elwood. Florida Retirees' Handbook: Answers to Your Legal & Financial Questions. 3rd ed. 230p. (Orig.). 1995. pap. write for info. (*1-56164-065-4*) Pineapple Pr.

Phillips, Emily. Decorative Accents for the Garden. LC 95-45969. (Illus.). 144p. 1996. 24.95 (*0-8069-6122-8*) Sterling.

— Decorative Accents for the Garden. 1999. pap. text 14.95 (*0-8069-6123-6*) Sterling.

Phillips, Erin. Research for Romance. (First Love Ser.). 186p. (YA). (gr. 7 up). 1996. pap. 49.95 (*0-671-53396-7*) PB.

Phillips, Estelle M. & Pugh, D. S. How to Get a Phd: A Handbook for Students & Their Supervisors. 2nd ed. LC 93-32693. 1994. 29.95 (*0-335-19214-9*) OpUniv Pr.

***Phillips, Estelle M. & Pugh, Derek S.** How to Get a Phd: A Handbook for Students & Their Supervisors. 3rd ed. LC 99-16163. 256p. 2000. pap. 24.95 (*0-335-20550-X*) Taylor & Francis.

Phillips, Esther R., ed. An Introduction to Analysis & Integration Theory. 480p. 1984. reprint ed. pap. 14.95 (*0-486-64747-1*) Dover.

— Studies in the History of Mathematics. LC 87-60581. (Studies in Mathematics: Vol. 26). 320p. 1987. text 5.00 (*0-88385-128-8*, MAS-26) Math Assn.

Phillips, Ethan & Birnes, William J. Star Trek Cookbook. LC 99-194424. 320p. 1999. per. 20.00 (*0-671-00022-5*, Pocket Books) PB.

Phillips, Ewing L. Counseling & Psychotherapy: A Behavioral Approach. LC 77-1771. (Wiley Series on Personality Processes). 303p. reprint ed. pap. 94.00 (*0-608-30404-2*, 201985000014) Bks Demand.

Phillips, Faye. Congressional Papers Management: Collecting, Appraising, Arranging & Describing Documentation of United States Senators, Representatives, Related Individuals & Organizations. LC 96-13036. (Illus.). 208p. 1996. lib. bdg. 38.50 (*0-7864-0242-3*) McFarland & Co.

— Local History Collections in Libraries. xii, 164p. 1995. lib. bdg. 34.00 (*1-56308-141-5*) Libs Unl.

Phillips, Frances. The Celebrated Running Horse Messenger. (Illus.). 48p. 1979. 5.00 (*0-932716-08-3*) Kelsey St Pr.

— For a Living. 1981. pap. 7.00 (*0-914610-26-0*) Hanging Loose.

— Up at Two. 1991. 15.00 (*0-914610-90-2*); pap. 9.00 (*0-914610-89-9*) Hanging Loose.

Phillips, Francine, jt. auth. see Bennett, Jeffrey P.

Phillips, Francine, jt. auth. see Hedgecock, Roger.

Phillips, Francis R. Bishop Beck & English Education, 1949-1959. (Studies in Education: Vol. 14). 304p. 1990. write for info. (*0-88946-796-X*) E Mellen.

— Creating an Education System for England & Wales. LC 92-12724. (Welsh Studies: Vol. 8). 212p. 1992. lib. bdg. 89.95 (*0-7734-9528-2*) E Mellen.

Phillips, Frank. The Justified Walk. LC 94-61687. 224p. 1995. per. 8.95 (*1-57258-023-2*) Teach Servs.

Phillips, Fred. Washington Closing Officer's Guide. 2nd ed. LC 98-67064. 651p. 1998. ring bd. 120.00 (*0-327-00207-7*, 80298-11) LEXIS Pub.

Phillips, Fred B. Closing Officer's Guide: Washington, 1983-1993. 550p. Date not set. ring bd. 95.00 (*0-409-20149-9*, 80298-10, MICHIE) LEXIS Pub.

Phillips, Fred M. Desert People & Mountain Men: Exploration of the Great Basin, 1824-1865. LC 77-23351. (Illus.). 1977. pap. 6.25 (*0-912494-25-5*) Commun Print.

Phillips, Fred Y., ed. Systems & Management Science by Extremal Methods: Research Honoring Abraham Charnes at Age 70. 608p. (C). 1992. lib. bdg. 265.00 (*0-7923-9139-X*) Kluwer Academic.

— Thinkwork: Working, Learning, & Managing in a Computer-Interactive Society. LC 91-47085. 300p. 1992. 55.00 (*0-275-93964-2*, C3964, Praeger Pubs) Greenwood.

Phillips, Fred Y., et al. United States & Japan: Shared Progress in Technology Management. 429p. 1993. pap. 25.00 (*1-887406-03-4*) ICTwo Inst.

Phillips, Fred Y., jt. auth. see Desai, Chirag.

Phillips, G. Ceramic Packaging of Electronic Circuits. 1992. text. write for info. (*0-442-00665-9*, VNR) Wiley.

Phillips, G. A. & Maddock, R. T. The Growth of the British Economy, 1918-1968. LC 74-162518. No. 8. 188p. 1973. write for info. (*0-04-330233-5*) Allen & Unwin Pty.

Phillips, G. Briggs & Miller, William S., eds. Industrial Sterilization: International Symposium. LC 72-97473. (Illus.). x, 430p. 1973. text 49.95 (*0-8223-0299-3*) Duke.

Phillips, G. C., jt. ed. see Gamborg, O. L.

Phillips, G. C., ed. see International Conference on Fast Neutron Physics S.

***Phillips, G. M.** Two Millennia of Mathematics: From Archimedes to Gauss. LC 00-23807. (CMS Advanced Books in Mathematics). (Illus.). 240p. (C). 2000. text 49.95 (*0-387-95022-2*) Spr-Verlag.

Phillips, G. M. & Taylor, P. J. Theory & Applications of Numerical Analysis. 2nd ed. (Illus.). 464p. 1996. pap. text 39.95 (*0-12-553560-0*) Acad Pr.

Phillips, G. O. Advances in Tissue Banking, Vol. 3. (Advances in Tissue Banking Ser.). 350p. 1999. 68.00 (*981-02-3872-X*) World Scientific Pub.

Phillips, G. O., et al, eds. Gums & Stabilizers for the Food Industry: Interactions of Hydrocolloids. (Illus.). 420p. 1982. 170.00 (*0-08-026843-9*, Pergamon Pr) Elsevier.

Phillips, G. O., et al. Advances in Tissue Banking, Vol. 1. LC 97-37807. 340p. 1997. 82.00 (*981-02-3190-3*) World Scientific Pub.

— Advances in Tissue Banking, Vol. 2. 300p. 1998. 68.00 (*981-02-3534-8*) World Scientific Pub.

***Phillips, G. O., et al.** Advances in Tissue Banking, Vol. 4. 350p. 2000. 84.00 (*981-02-4287-5*) World Scientific Pub.

Phillips, G. O., jt. auth. see Williams, P. A.

Phillips, G. O., jt. ed. see Williams, P. A.

Phillips, G. R. & Hunt, L. J. Writing Essays & Dissertations: A Guide to the Preparation of Written Assignments in Colleges & Universities. pap. 6.95 (*0-85564-118-5*, Pub. by Univ of West Aust Pr) Intl Spec Bk.

Phillips, G. Robert. Historical Highlights of Charleston: An Overview of the City's 300 Year Past. 56p. 1992. spiral bd. 5.95 (*0-9633815-0-4*) P & R Enter.

Phillips, Garry D., jt. ed. see Cousins, Michael J.

Phillips, Gary. Bad Night Is Falling. LC 97-34988. 320p. 1998. pap. 21.95 (*0-425-16302-4*) Berkley Pub.

— Commodore 64 Expansion Guide. LC 84-23999. (Illus.). 277p. 1985. pap. 16.60 (*0-8306-1961-5*, 1961) McGraw-Hill Prof.

— The Desecrator. (Illus.). 48p. 1999. 35.00 (*1-892011-04-2*); 70.00 (*1-892011-05-0*) ASAP Pub.

— The Jook: A Crime Novel. LC 99-65030. 222p. 1999. pap. 12.95 (*1-893329-04-6*) Really Great Bks.

***Phillips, Gary.** Only the Wicked. 352p. 2000. 24.95 (*1-885173-64-4*, Pub. by Write Way) Midpt Trade.

Phillips, Gary. Perdition, U. S. A. 272p. 1997. mass mkt. 5.99 (*0-425-15900-0*, Prime Crime) Berkley Pub.

— Perdition, U. S. A. LC 93-61105. 260p. 1994. pap. 13.00 (*0-9639050-6-6*, Pub. by Blue Heron OR) Consort Bk Sales.

— Violent Spring. LC 93-61105. 275p. 1994. pap. 9.00 (*1-883303-13-3*, West Coast Crime) Blue Heron OR.

— Violent Spring. 27p. 1997. reprint ed. mass mkt. 5.99 (*0-425-15625-7*, Prime Crime) Berkley Pub.

Phillips, Gary, ed. Reference Encyclopedia for the IBM Personal Computer, 2 vols. 1984. 69.95 (*0-317-03007-8*) P-H.

Phillips, Gary, tr. see Entrevernes Group Staff.

Phillips, Gary L., et al. Fishes of the Minnesota Region. 1982. pap. 16.95 (*0-8166-0982-9*) U of Minn Pr.

Phillips, Gay, et al. Managing Aggressive Behavior: Participant Manual. 2nd ed. (Illus.). 110p. 1997. student ed., wbk. ed. 10.95 (*1-878848-19-4*) Natl Res Ctr.

— Managing Aggressive Behavior: Trainer's Guide. 2nd ed. 262p. 1997. teacher ed., ring bd. 100.00 (*1-878848-18-6*, 200C) Natl Res Ctr.

— Managing Aggressive Behavior: Trainer's Guide & Participant Manual. 2nd ed. (Illus.). 372p. 1997. teacher ed., student ed., ring bd. 110.95 (*1-878848-17-8*, 200) Natl Res Ctr.

Phillips, Gay, ed. see Marshall, John A.

Phillips, Gene D. Conrad & Cinema: The Art of Adaptation. 2nd ed. (Arts Interpretandi Ser.: Vol. 4). (Illus.). 218p. (C). 1997. pap. text 32.95 (*0-8204-3915-0*) P Lang Pubng.

***Phillips, Gene D.** Creatures of Darkness: Raymond Chandler, Detective Fiction & Film Noir. LC 00-28306. (Illus.). 352p. 2000. 27.50 (*0-8131-2174-4*) U Pr of Ky.

Phillips, Gene D. Exiles in Hollywood: Major European Film Directors in America. LC 97-41009. (Illus.). 256p. 1998. 42.50 (*0-934223-49-1*) Lehigh Univ Pr.

— The Films of Tennessee Williams. LC 76-50204. (Illus.). 336p. 1980. 40.00 (*0-87982-025-X*) Art Alliance.

— Graham Greene: The Films of His Fiction. LC 73-85352. (Studies in Culture & Communication). 222p. reprint ed. pap. 68.90 (*0-608-14836-9*, 202605600048) Bks Demand.

— Major Film Directors of the American & British Cinema. LC 88-46163. (Illus.). 288p. 1990. 49.50 (*0-934223-08-4*) Lehigh Univ Pr.

— Major Film Directors of the American & British Cinema. rev. ed. LC 98-31914. 320p. 1999. 46.50 (*0-934223-59-9*) Lehigh Univ Pr.

***Phillips, Gene D., ed.** Stanley Kubrick: Interviews. (Conversations with Filmmakers Ser.). (Illus.). 192p. 2001. pap. 18.00 (*1-57806-297-7*); lib. bdg. 45.00 (*1-57806-296-9*) U Pr of Miss.

Phillips, Geoff. Electronics Toolkit. 2nd ed. 177p. 1999. pap. text 29.95 (*0-7506-3790-0*, Newnes) Buttrwrth-Heinemann.

Phillips, George. Black Tickets. 288p. 1979. pap. 11.95 (*0-385-28088-2*, Delta Trade) Dell.

Phillips, George H. The Enduring Struggle: Indians in California History. Hundley, Norris, Jr. & Sanutz, John A., eds. (Golden State Ser.). (Illus.). 104p. 1996. reprint ed. pap. 12.00 (*0-614-14686-0*) MTL.

— Indians & Indian Agents: The Origins of the Reservation System in California, 1849-1852. LC 96-31860. 256p. 1997. 27.95 (*0-8061-2904-2*) U of Okla Pr.

— Indians & Intruders in Central California, 1769-1849. LC 92-54134. (Civilization of the American Indian Ser.: Vol. 207). 1993. 27.95 (*0-8061-2446-6*) U of Okla Pr.

Phillips, Gerald & Zolten, Jerry. Speaking to Audience: Practical Method, Preparation & Performance. 368p. (C). 1994. text 57.00 (*0-536-58677-2*) Pearson Custom.

Phillips, Gerald M. Communication Incompetencies: A Theory of Training Oral Performance Behavior. 360p. (C). 1991. 36.95 (*0-8093-1459-2*) S Ill U Pr.

Phillips, Gerald M. & Dervin, Brenda, eds. Teaching How to Work in Groups. LC 90-867. (Communication & Information Science Ser.). 272p. (C). 1990. pap. 39.50 (*0-89391-730-3*); text 73.25 (*0-89391-690-0*) Ablx Pub.

Phillips, Gerald M. & Wood, Julia T., eds. Emergent Issues in Human Decision Making. LC 84-1323. 192p. 1984. 21.95 (*0-8093-1151-8*) S Ill U Pr.

— Speech Communication: Essays to Commemorate the 75th Anniversary of the Speech Communication Association. LC 89-5875. 256p. (C). 1990. text 31.95 (*0-8093-1520-3*) S Ill U Pr.

Phillips, Gerald M., et al. Development of Oral Communication in the Classroom. LC 71-77821. (C). 1970. text. write for info. (*0-672-60857-X*, Bobbs) Macmillan.

— Speaking in Public & Private. 384p. (Orig.). (C). 1985. teacher ed. write for info. (*0-672-61613-0*); pap. text. write for info. (*0-672-61612-2*); student ed. write for info. (*0-672-61622-X*) Macmillan.

— Survival in the Academy: A Guide for Beginning Academics. LC 93-44472. (Hampton Press - SCA Applied Communication Ser.). 288p. 1994. pap. text 26.50 (*1-881303-69-1*) Hampton Pr NJ.

Phillips, Gerald M., jt. auth. see Werman, Robert.

Phillips, Gerald M., jt. auth. see Wyatt, Nancy.

Phillips, Gerald M., ed. see Berge, Zane & Collins, Mauri.

Phillips, Gerald M., ed. see Jones, J. Alfred, et al.

***Phillips, Gervase.** The Anglo-Scots Wars, 1513-1550: A Military History. LC 99-30714. (Warfare in History Ser.: Vol. 7). (Illus.). 352p. 1999. 75.00 (*0-85115-746-7*) Boydell & Brewer.

Phillips, Gina. First Facts about Giant Sea Creatures. (First Facts about Ser.). (Illus.). 24p. (J). 1991. 2.98 (*1-56156-084-7*) Kidsbks.

— First Facts about Giant Sea Creatures. (First Facts about Ser.). (Illus.). 24p. (J). 1992. pap. 2.50 (*1-56156-156-8*) Kidsbks.

— First Facts about Prehistoric Animals. (First Facts about Ser.). (Illus.). 24p. (J). 1991. 2.98 (*1-56156-083-9*) Kidsbks.

— First Facts about Prehistoric Animals. (First Facts about Ser.). (Illus.). 24p. (J). 1992. pap. 2.50 (*1-56156-157-6*) Kidsbks.

— First Facts about Snakes & Reptiles. (First Facts about Ser.). (Illus.). 24p. (Orig.). (J). 1991. pap. 2.50 (*1-56156-037-5*) Kidsbks.

— First Facts about Snakes & Reptiles. (First Facts about Ser.). (Illus.). 24p. (Orig.). (J). 1991. write for info. (*1-56156-060-X*) Kidsbks.

— First Facts about Wild Animals. (First Facts about Ser.). (Illus.). 24p. (Orig.). (J). 1991. pap. 2.50 (*1-56156-038-3*) Kidsbks.

P

An Asterisk (*) at the beginning of an entry indicates that the title is appearing for the first time.

— First Facts about Wild Animals. (First Facts about Ser.). (Illus.). 24p. (Orig.). (J). 1991. write for info. (*1-56156-061-8*) Kidsbks.

Phillips, Gina, ed. Three Minute Aesop's Fables. (Three Minute Bks.). (Illus.). 24p. (J). 1991. 2.98 (*1-56156-088-X*) Kidsbks.

— Three Minute Bedtime Stories. (Three Minute Bks.). (Illus.). 24p. (J). 1991. 2.98 (*1-56156-087-1*) Kidsbks.

Phillips, Glen. Allison Engine Mustang Walk Around. LC 98-164594. (Walk Around Ser.: Vol. 13). (Illus.). 80p. 1998. pap. 14.95 (*0-89747-386-8*, 5513) Squad Sig Pubns.

Phillips, Glen & Hjermstad, Kevin. Building the P-40 Warhawk: A Modeler's Guide to Building Projects. unabridged ed. LC 97-152899. (Illus.). 88p. (Orig.). 1997. pap. 15.95 (*0-89024-565-7*, 12181, Kalmbach Books) Kalmbach.

Phillips, Glen, jt. auth. see Hjermstadt, Kevin.

Phillips, Glen C. Lombton: An Illustrated History of the County. (Illus.). 128p. 1999. pap. 22.95 (*0-921818-20-3*) I G Pub.

Phillips, Glenn O., jt. auth. see Chapelle, Suzanne E.

Phillips, Gloria A., jt. auth. see Solomon, Eldra P.

***Phillips, Glyn & Williams, Peter.** Handbook of Hydrocolloids. 472p. 2000. text 270.00 (*1-85573-501-6*, Pub. by Woodhead Pubng) Am Educ Systs.

Phillips, Glyn O., et al, eds. Gums & Stabilisers for the Food Industry, Vol. 8. (Illus.). 470p. 1997. text 135.00 (*0-19-963627-3*) OUP.

— Gums & Stabilisers for the Food Industry No. 7. (Illus.). 448p. 1995. text 120.00 (*0-19-963465-3*) OUP.

Phillips, Glyn O., et al, eds. Gums & Stabilizers for the Food Industry, Vol. 6. (Illus.). 588p. 1992. text 120.00 (*0-19-963284-7*) OUP.

***Phillips, Glyn O. & Williams, Peter A.** Handbook of Hydrocolloids. LC 00-30421. 2000. write for info. (*0-8493-0850-X*) CRC Pr.

Phillips, Glyn O., jt. auth. see Hongu, Tatsuya.

Phillips, Gordon. Take It Personally: On the Art & Process of Personal Acting. 250p. 1999. pap. 15.95 (*1-55783-390-7*) Applause Theatre Bk Pubs.

Phillips, Gordon & Whiteside, Noel. Casual Labour: The Unemployment Question in the Port Transport Industry, 1880-1970. (Illus.). 1985. 49.00 (*0-19-822777-9*) OUP.

Phillips, Gordon M. Increased Debt & Product Market Competition: An Empirical Analysis. (Illus.). 60p. (Orig.). (C). 1993. pap. text 20.00 (*1-56806-914-6*) DIANE Pub.

Phillips, Gordon M. & Weiner, Robert. Trading Performance in Forward Markets: Information versus Normal Backwardation. (Illus.). 44p. (Orig.). (C). 1993. pap. text 20.00 (*1-56806-913-8*) DIANE Pub.

Phillips, Graham. The Search for the Grail. LC 96-101732. (Illus.). 182p. 1996. 24.95 (*0-7126-7533-7*, Pub. by CEN3) Trafalgar.

Phillips, Graham & Keatman, Martin. King Arthur: The True Story. (Illus.). 221p. 1994. pap. 9.95 (*0-09-929681-0*, Pub. by Arrow Bks) Trafalgar.

Phillips, Greer L. & Washlick, John R. NAFTA Text: Including Supplemental Agreements. Schwartz, Maureen, ed. LC 94-186661. 824p. (Orig.). 1994. pap. 39.50 (*0-8080-0006-3*) CCH INC.

Phillips, Greg & Johnston, Gail. Think Light! Breaking Free from the Diet Prison. 4th ed. 126p. 1989. reprint ed. pap. 6.95 (*0-9625095-1-5*) Speaking Fitness.

Phillips, Gregory D. The Diehards: Aristocratic Society & Politics in Edwardian England. LC 78-16949. (Historical Studies: No. 96). 248p. 1979. 20.00 (*0-674-20555-3*) HUP.

Phillips, Harold L. Living with Christ. (Eagle Bible Ser.). 1989. pap. 0.99 (*0-87162-500-8*, D9152) Warner Pr.

Phillips, Harry. Microsoft Windows 95 - Advanced, Incl. instr. resource kit, online comp., files. (New Perspectives Ser.). (Illus.). 480p. 1996. pap. 48.95 (*0-7600-3572-5*) Course Tech.

— New Perspectives on Microsoft Windows 95: Advanced. 480p. 1996. teacher ed. 40.00 (*0-7600-3933-X*) Course Tech.

P

— Phillips: Brief History of the Phillips Family, Beginning with the Emigration from Wales & a Detailed Genealogy of the Descendants of John & Benjamin Philips, Pioneer Citizens of Wilson Co. TN. (Illus.). 261p. 1994. reprint ed. pap. 42.00 (*0-8328-4371-7*); reprint ed. lib. bdg. 52.00 (*0-8328-4370-9*) Higginson Bk Co.

Phillips, Harry I. The Making (And Occasional Unraveling) of a Sports Car Buff. Thurber, Bruce, ed. (Illus.). 132p. (Orig.). 1991. pap. 6.00 (*0-9629911-0-4*) H I Phillips.

Phillips, Harry L. Comprehensive DOS 5.0/6.0/6.2 with Windows 3.1. (New Perspectives Ser.). 608p. (C). 1994. pap. 31.50 (*1-56527-150-5*) Course Tech.

— Comprehensive DOS 5.0/6.0/6.2 with Windows 3.1. 608p. (C). 1994. teacher ed. 18.50 (*1-56527-203-X*) Course Tech.

— DBase Version 5 for Windows - Illustrated, Incl. instr. resource kit, test bank, transparency. (Illustrated Ser.). (Illus.). 216p. 1995. text, mass mkt. 20.95 incl. 3.5 ld (*0-7600-3283-1*) Course Tech.

Phillips, Harry R. Growing & Propagating Wild Flowers. Moore, J. Kenneth & Bell, C. Ritchie, eds. LC 84-25734. (Illus.). 341p. 1985. pap. 19.95 (*0-8078-4131-5*) U of NC Pr.

Phillips, Harvey, jt. auth. see Winkle, William.

Phillips, Hattie M. The Animal Picnic. (Illus.). 32p. (J). (ps-6). 1997. 14.95 (*0-9659978-0-4*) H M Phillips.

Phillips, Heather, jt. auth. see Drew, Rosa.

***Phillips, Helen.** An Introduction to the Canterbury Tales: Fiction, Writing, Context. LC 99-22268. 2000. pap. 18.95 (*0-312-22740-X*); text 59.95 (*0-312-22739-6*) St Martin.

Phillips, Helen, tr. see Galilea, Segundo.

Phillips, Henry. American Paper Currency: Series One, Historical Sketches of the Paper Currency of the American Colonies Prior to the Adoption of the Federal Constitution: Series Two, Continental Paper Money, 2 Vols. in 1. LC 68-18223. (Library of Money & Banking History). 1972. reprint ed. lib. bdg. 65.00 (*0-678-00787-X*) Kelley.

— Church & Culture in Seventeenth-Century France. 340p. (C). 1997. text 59.95 (*0-521-57023-9*) Cambridge U Pr.

— The Theatre & Its Critics in Seventeenth-Century France. (Oxford Modern Languages & Literature Monographs). 1980. 36.00 (*0-19-815535-2*) OUP.

Phillips, Henry, Jr., jt. auth. see Chase, Alston H.

Phillips, Henry, Jr., jt. ed. see Chase, Alston H.

Phillips, Henry A. Photodrama. LC 70-124032. (Literature of Cinema, Ser. 1). 1970. reprint ed. 12.95 (*0-405-01632-8*) Ayer.

Phillips, Henry G. Sedjenane: The Pay-Off Battle. (Illus.). 150p. (Orig.). 1993. pap. 11.25 (*0-9637444-0-2*) H G Phillips.

Phillips, Herbert E., jt. auth. see Frankfurter, George M.

Phillips, Herbert M. Basic Education-a World Challenge: Measures & Innovations for Children & Youth in Developing Countries. LC 74-6995. 270p. reprint ed. pap. 83.70 (*0-8357-5978-4*, 202240500026) Bks Demand.

Phillips, Hollibert E. Vicissitudes of the I: An Introduction to the Philosophy of the Mind. LC 94-4967. 176p. 1994. pap. text 28.20 (*0-13-108721-5*) P-H.

Phillips, Horace. Envoy Extraordinary. (Illus.). 224p. 1995. text 45.00 (*1-85043-964-8*, Pub. by I B T) St Martin.

Phillips, Howard. Moscow's Challenge to U. S. Vital Interests in Southern Africa. 204p. (Orig.). 1987. pap. 5.95 (*0-940355-01-9*) Policy Analysis.

— The Next Four Years: A Vision of Victory. 190p. 1992. pap. 10.00 (*0-9633469-3-8*) Policy Analysis.

Phillips, Howard, jt. auth. see Brandes, Donna.

Phillips, Hubert C. My Best Puzzles in Logic & Reasoning. 81st ed. (Orig.). 1961. pap. 4.95 (*0-486-20119-8*) Dover.

— My Best Puzzles in Mathematics. (Orig.). 1961. pap. 4.95 (*0-486-20091-4*) Dover.

Phillips, Ian R. & Shephard, Elizabeth A. Cytochrome P450 Protocols. LC 98-5208. (Methods in Molecular Biology Ser.: Vol. 107). (Illus.). 496p. 1998. 89.50 (*0-89603-519-0*) Humana.

Phillips, J. Licensing Law Guide. 286p. 1994. pap. text 55.00 (*0-406-02878-8*, UK, MICHIE) LEXIS Pub.

Phillips, J. A., et al, eds. Planets Around Pulsars. (ASP Conference Series Proceedings: Vol. 36). 391p. 1993. 34.00 (*0-937707-55-4*) Astron Soc Pacific.

Phillips, J. B. The New Testament in Modern English. 1995. 14.98 (*0-88486-127-9*) Galahad Bks.

— The Price of Success: An Autobiography. LC 84-23472. 222p. (Orig.). 1985. pap. 8.99 (*0-87788-659-8*, H Shaw Pubs) Waterbrook Pr.

— The Ring of Truth: A Translator's Testimony. LC 77-80627. 124p. 1977. pap. 7.99 (*0-87788-724-1*, H Shaw Pubs) Waterbrook Pr.

— Your God Is Here & Now. 130p. 1998. pap. 9.99 (*0-86347-218-4*, Pub. by Eagle Bks) Sourcebks.

— Your God Is Too Small. 1997. per. 5.00 (*0-684-84696-9*) S&S Trade.

Phillips, J. F. Town & Village in the Nineteenth Century. (C). 1983. text 45.00 (*0-7855-3202-1*, Pub. by Univ Nottingham) St Mut.

Phillips, J. F. Town & Village in 19th Century Nottingham & Nottinghamshire Villages. 1972. pap. 21.00 (*0-902031-27-9*, Pub. by Continuing Education Pr) St Mut.

Phillips, J. H. C. I. I. Interruption Insurance, No. 260. (C). 1981. suppl. ed. 230.00 (*0-7855-4291-4*, Pub. by Witherby & Co) St Mut.

— The Trial of Ned Kelly. xiii, 135p. 1987. 19.50 (*0-455-20759-3*, Pub. by LawBk Co) Gaunt.

Phillips, J. H., ed. Reliability & Risk in Pressure Vessels & Piping. (PVP Ser.: Vol. 251). 172p. 1993. 45.00 (*0-7918-0978-1*, H00810) ASME.

Phillips, J. H. & Bowen, J. K. Forensic Science & the Expert Witness. rev. ed. x, 139p. 1989. 32.50 (*0-455-20958-8*, Pub. by LawBk Co) Gaunt.

Phillips, J. J. Mojo Hand: An Orphic Tale. LC 85-71335. 200p. 1985. reprint ed. pap. 6.95 (*0-933944-12-8*) City Miner Bks.

Phillips, J. L. & Bar-Yosef, O., eds. The Prehistory of the Levant: A Reader. (Illus.). 490p. (C). 1999. write for info. (*0-306-46077-7*, Kluwer Plenum) Kluwer Academic.

— The Prehistory of the Levant: A Reader. (Illus.). 490p. (C). 1999. pap. write for info. (*0-306-46078-5*, Plenum Trade) Perseus Pubng.

Phillips, J. M. D. H. Lawrence: An Annotated Bibliography. 1992. lib. bdg. 250.00 (*0-8490-1372-0*) Gordon Pr.

Phillips, J. R. The Medieval Expansion of Europe. 2nd ed. LC 99-179710. (Illus.). 342p. 1998. pap. text 24.95 (*0-19-820740-9*) OUP.

Phillips, J. S. Tax Treaty Networks, 1988-1989. xxii, 712p. 1988. text 229.00 (*2-88316-000-7*) Gordon & Breach.

Phillips, Jack. Freedom in Machinery Vol.2: Screw Theory Exemplified. (Illus.). 265p. (C). 1990. text 109.95 (*0-521-25442-6*) Cambridge U Pr.

— Return on Investment in Training & Performance Improvement Programs. LC 97-12089. (Improving Human Performance Ser.). (Illus.). 320p. 1997. pap. 34.95 (*0-88415-492-0*, 5492) Gulf Pub.

Phillips, Jack J. Accountability in Human Resource Management. LC 95-42091. (Improving Human Performance Ser.). 342p. 1995. 34.95 (*0-88415-396-7*, 5396) Gulf Pub.

— Handbook of Training Evaluation & Measurement Methods. 328p. 1990. pap. 79.95 (*0-8464-1369-8*) Beekman Pubs.

— Handbook of Training Evaluation & Measurement Methods. 2nd ed. LC 91-12239. (Building Blocks of Human Potential Ser.). (Illus.). 429p. 1991. reprint ed. pap. 133.00 (*0-608-07289-3*, 206751700009) Bks Demand.

— Handbook of Training Evaluation & Measurement Methods. 3rd ed. LC 97-16782. (Improving Human Performance Ser.). (Illus.). 422p. 1997. 55.00 (*0-88415-387-8*, 5387) Gulf Pub.

— Handbook of Training Evaluation & Measurement Methods: Instructor's Guide. 3rd ed. 204p. 1997. teacher ed. 20.00 (*0-88415-398-3*, 5398) Gulf Pub.

— HRD Trends Worldwide: Shared Solutions to Compete in a Global Economy. LC 98-51367. (Improving Human Performance Ser.). 400p. 1999. 39.95 (*0-88415-356-8*, 5356) Gulf Pub.

— Improving Supervisors' Effectiveness. LC 84-43032. (Jossey-Bass Management Ser.). (Illus.). 443p. reprint ed. pap. 137.40 (*0-7837-6524-X*, 204563600007) Bks Demand.

— Recruiting, Training, & Retaining New Employees: Managing the Transition from College to Work. LC 86-46332. 346p. reprint ed. pap. 107.30 (*0-7837-6520-7*, 204563200007) Bks Demand.

Phillips, Jack J., ed. Measuring Return on Investment. LC 94-78503. (In Action Ser.: Vol. 2). 282p. 1997. pap. 50.00 (*1-56286-065-8*) Am Soc Train & Devel.

Phillips, Jack J., ed. Measuring Return on Investment. LC 94-78503. (In Action Ser.). 271p. 1994. pap. 50.00 (*1-56286-008-9*) Am Soc Train & Devel.

Phillips, Jack J., et al, eds. Creating the Learning Organization. LC 96-83346. (In Action Ser.). 285p. 1996. pap. 50.00 (*1-56286-052-6*) Am Soc Train & Devel.

— In Action Vol. 2: Developing High-Performance Work Teams. LC 97-78237. 266p. 1999. pap. 50.00 (*1-56286-113-1*) Am Soc Train & Devel.

***Phillips, Jack J. & Ashby, Franklin C., eds.** In Action: Effective Leadership Programs. LC 99-73473. 255p. 1999. pap. 50.00 (*1-56286-119-0*) Am Soc Train & Devel.

Phillips, Jack J. & Ford, Donald J., eds. Designing Training Programs. LC 96-85648. (In Action Ser.). 340p. 1996. pap. 50.00 (*1-56286-057-7*) Am Soc Train & Devel.

***Phillips, Jack J. & Hite, James A., Jr., eds.** Implementing HRD Technology. LC 99-73472. (In Action Ser.). 302p. 1999. pap. 50.00 (*1-56286-127-1*) Am Soc Train & Devel.

***Phillips, Jack J. & Hodges, Toni K., eds.** Measuring Learning & Performance. LC 99-72120. (In Action Ser.). 320p. 1999. pap. 50.00 (*1-56286-123-9*) Am Soc Train & Devel.

Phillips, Jack J. & Holton, Elwood F., eds. Conducting Needs Assessment. LC 95-76269. (In Action Ser.). 311p. 1995. pap. 50.00 (*1-56286-017-8*) Am Soc Train & Devel.

— Leading Organizational Change. LC 97-74235. (In Action Ser.). 260p. 1997. pap. 50.00 (*1-56286-064-X*) Am Soc Train & Devel.

Phillips, Jack J., jt. auth. see Fitz-Enz, Jac.

Phillips, Jack J., ed. see American Society for Training and Development Staff.

Phillips, Jack J., jt. ed. see Broad, Mary L.

Phillips, Jack J., jt. ed. see Rothwell, William J.

***Phillips, James.** Tolerance in the State of Jefferson: A Short History. 1999. pap. text 13.95 (*1-883991-35-8*) WhiteCloub Pubg.

Phillips, James, tr. see Esteban, Claude.

Phillips, James C. Covalent Bonding in Crystals, Molecules & Polymers. LC 74-104037. (Chicago Lectures in Physics Ser.). (C). 1995. pap. text 15.00 (*0-226-66770-7*) U Ch Pr.

Phillips, James D. Salem in the Eighteenth Century. LC 37-36381. (Illus.). 533p. 1969. reprint ed. 30.00 (*0-88389-017-8*, PEMP160, Essx Institute) Peabody Essex Mus.

Phillips, James F. & Ross, John A., eds. Family Planning Programmes & Fertility. (International Studies in Demography). 352p. 1992. 85.00 (*0-19-828385-7*) OUP.

Phillips, James M. From the Rising of the Sun: Christians & Society in Contemporary Japan. LC 80-24609. (American Society of Missiology Ser.: No. 3). 320p. (Orig.). reprint ed. pap. 99.20 (*0-8357-2687-8*, 204022300015) Bks Demand.

***Phillips, James M.** Representational Strategies in Les Miserables & Selected Drawings by Victor Hugo: An Intermedial Comparison. LC 98-53629. (Currents in Comparative Romance Languages & Literatures Ser.: Vol. 86). 176p. (C). 1999. text 44.95 (*0-8204-4441-3*) P Lang Pubng.

Phillips, James M. & Coote, Robert T., eds. Towards the 21st Century in Christian Mission. viii, 376p. (Orig.). 1993. pap. 28.00 (*0-8028-0638-4*) Eerdmans.

Phillips, James W. Printing & Bookselling in Dublin, 1670-1800: A Bibliographical Enquiry. (Illus.). 256p. 1997. 65.00 (*0-7165-2680-8*, Pub. by Irish Acad Pr) Intl Spec Bk.

Phillips, James W. Printing & Bookselling in Dublin, 1670-1800: A Bibliographical Enquiry. LC 95-170922. (Illus.). 368p. 1998. 59.50 (*0-7165-2580-1*, Pub. by Irish Acad Pr) Intl Spec Bk.

— Washington State Place Names. rev. ed. LC 73-159435. (Illus.). 186p. 1971. pap. 12.95 (*0-295-95498-1*) U of Wash Pr.

***Phillips, Jan.** God Is at Eye Level: Photography as a Healing Art. LC 99-45606. (Illus.). 160p. 2000. pap. 21.95 (*0-8356-0785-2*, Quest) Theos Pub Hse.

Phillips, Jan. Making Peace: One Woman's Journey Around The World. 1990. pap. 12.95 (*0-377-00200-3*) Friendship Pr.

— Marry Your Muse: Making a Lasting Commitment to Your Creativity. LC 97-19472. (Illus.). 320p. 1997. pap. 18.00 (*0-8356-0759-3*, Quest) Theos Pub Hse.

— Whole Numbers & Money. (Smart Solutions Ser.). 1995. pap. 9.64 (*1-56420-118-X*) New Readers.

***Phillips, Jan, et al.** A Waist is a Terrible Thing to Mind: A Wake up Call. 2000. pap. 16.95 (*0-9679576-0-5*) Breakthru Pr.

Phillips, Jane. The Magic Daughter: A Memoir of Living with Multiple Personality Disorder. 238p. 1999. reprint ed. text 23.00 (*0-7881-5682-9*) DIANE Pub.

Phillips, Jane E., tr. & anno. see Erasmus, Desiderius.

Phillips, Janet, ed. see Beckwith, Alice.

Phillips, Janine. My Secret Diary. 160p. 1982. 10.95 (*0-317-54333-4*) Dufour.

Phillips, Jayne Anne. Fast Lanes. 148p. 1988. pap. 5.95 (*0-671-64014-3*, WSP) PB.

— Fast Lanes. (Illus.). 56p. 1984. pap. 12.00 (*0-931428-17-3*) Vehicle Edns.

***Phillips, Jayne Anne.** Fast Lanes. LC 99-57850. (Contemporaries Ser.). 192p. 1999. pap. 11.00 (*0-375-70284-9*) Vin Bks.

— Machine Dreams. LC 99-18315. 352p. 1999. pap. 14.00 (*0-375-70525-2*) Vin Bks.

Phillips, Jayne Anne. Machine Dreams. Rosenman, Jane, ed. LC 91-2014. 400p. 1999. reprint ed. pap. 14.00 (*0-671-74235-3*, WSP) PB.

***Phillips, Jayne Anne.** MotherKind: A Novel. LC 99-49256. 295p. 2000. 24.00 (*0-375-40194-6*) Knopf.

Phillips, Jayne Anne. Shelter. 336p. 1995. pap. 11.95 (*0-385-31389-6*, Delta Trade) Dell.

— Shelter. 288p. 1994. write for info. (*0-7710-6997-9*) McClelland & Stewart.

Phillips, Jean. Pasaporte Al Exito. 2nd ed. (Illus.). 232p. reprint ed. pap. text 21.95 (*0-945933-02-9*) Intechnos.

Phillips, Jean A. For Better Reading: Lots You Need to Know about Short Vowels. (Illus.). 56p. 1981. pap. write for info. (*0-911305-00-9*) P Friends Co Inc.

— For Better Reading: Lots You Need to Know about Vowels. (Illus.). 58p. 1983. pap. 5.98 (*0-911305-01-7*) P Friends Co Inc.

Phillips, Jeanne. Monkey Mountain Madness. LC 95-49114. (Living the West Ser.). 172p. (C). 1996. 14.95 (*0-89301-192-4*) U of Idaho Pr.

Phillips, Jeff, ed. see Takakjian, Portia.

Phillips, Jeffery D. Quantitative Analysis in Financial Markets: Collected Papers of the New York University Mathematics. LC 99-44136. 367p. 1999. 86.00 (*981-02-3788-X*); pap. text 48.00 (*981-02-3789-8*) World Scientific Pub.

— Quarry. 1998. 24.95 (*1-891128-54-X*) Chapel & Croft.

Phillips, Jeffery D. & Brown, Gail. Quick Gifts & Decor. LC 98-65709. (Illus.). 144p. 1998. pap. 19.95 (*0-8487-1679-5*, 108603) Oxmoor Hse.

Phillips, Jeffery D. & Nichols, A. Question of Life, A Scribe of the Kingdom, 2 vols. 1990. pap. 70.00 (*0-7220-7120-5*) St Mut.

Phillips, Jeffrey A., ed. see Heinz, John.

Phillips, Jeffrey D., jt. auth. see Bhikkhu, Ajahn Sumano.

Phillips, Jeffrey D., jt. auth. see Phillips, Susan W.

Phillips, Jen. The NAG Library: A Beginner's Guide. (Illus.). 252p. 1987. text 35.00 (*0-19-853263-6*) OUP.

Phillips, Jennie. I Am Responsible. Eldredge, A., ed. 32p. 1994. pap. 6.00 (*1-885857-03-9*) Four Wnds Pubng.

— Mama Come Home. 60p. 1996. pap. 8.00 (*1-885857-18-7*) Four Wnds Pubng.

***Phillips, Jennifer.** Terra Cognita Guide to Germany. 2000. write for info. (*0-609-60556-9*) Liv Lang.

— Terra Cognita Guide to Mexico. 2000. write for info. (*0-609-60557-7*) Liv Lang.

***Phillips, Jennifer M.** Preaching Creation: Throughout the Church Year. LC 99-49302. 250p. 2000. pap. 16.95 (*1-56101-174-6*) Cowley Pubns.

Phillips, Jenny. Pressure Sores. LC 97-17573. (Access to Clinical Education Ser.). 1997. text 65.00 (*0-443-05532-7*) Church.

— Symbol, Myth, & Rhetoric: The Politics of Culture in an Armenian-American Population. LC 87-45788. (Immigrant Communities & Ethnic Minorities in the U. S. & Canada Ser.: No. 23). 1989. 47.50 (*0-404-19433-8*) AMS Pr.

Phillips, Jeremy. An Introduction to Intellectual Property Law. 2nd rev. ed. 325p. 1990. pap. 42.00 (*0-406-51240-X*, U.K., MICHIE) LEXIS Pub.

***Phillips, Jeremy, ed.** Employees' Inventions. 2nd ed. 300p. 2000. 104.00 (*1-902558-28-6*, Pub. by Palladian Law) Gaunt.

Phillips, Jeremy, ed. The Inventor's Guide: What to Do, Where to Go. 125p. 1997. pap. 26.95 (*0-566-07994-1*, Pub. by Gower) Ashgate Pub Co.

Phillips, Jeremy & Hooke, James. The Debating Book. LC 95-115776. 120p. 1994. pap. 17.95 (*0-86840-325-3*, Pub. by New South Wales Univ Pr) Intl Spec Bk.

Phillips, Jeremy, et al. Whale on Copyright. 5th ed. LC 99-159273. (British Tax Library Ser.). xiii, 185 p. 1997. write for info. (*0-421-59380-6*) Sweet & Maxwell.

Phillips, Jerry J. Products Liability: Cases, Materials, Problems, 1994. 1994. text 54.00 (*1-55834-136-6*) Bender.

Phillips, Jerry J. Products Liability in a Nutshell. 4th ed. LC 93-1654. (NutShell Ser.). 322p. (C). 1993. pap. text 16.00 (*0-314-02252-X*) West Pub.

— Products Liability in a Nutshell. 5th ed. (Paralegal). 300p. 1998. pap. text 15.00 (*0-314-22585-4*) West Pub.

Phillips, Jerry J. & Pryor, Robert E. Products Liability, Vol. 1. 3rd ed. LC 98-88875. 550p. 1998. 240.00 (*0-327-00746-X*, 6081612) LEXIS Pub.

— Products Liability, 1998 Cumulative Supplement & 1998 Supplement, 2 vols., Set. 2nd ed. 150p. 1998. pap., suppl. ed. write for info. (*0-327-00747-8*, 6082315) LEXIS Pub.

An Asterisk (*) at the beginning of an entry indicates that the title is appearing for the first time.

— Products Liability, 1998 Cumulative Supplement, Vol. 2. 2nd ed. 150p. 1998. pap., suppl. ed. write for info. (*0-327-00748-6*, 6082515) LEXIS Pub.

— Products Liability, 1998 Supplement, Vol. 3. 2nd ed. 150p. 1998. pap., suppl. ed. write for info. (*0-327-00749-4*, 6082615) LEXIS Pub.

Phillips, Jerry J., et al. Products Liability, 1993, 3 vols., Vol. 1. 2nd ed. 519p. 1993. text 240.00 (*1-55834-109-9*, 60816-11, MICHIE) LEXIS Pub.

Phillips, Jerry J., jt. auth. see Cartwright, Robert E.

Phillips, Jerry J., jt. auth. see Christie, George C.

Phillips, Jill. Annus Mirabilis: A Bibliography of Medieval Times. (Bibliographies for Librarians Ser.). 1980. lib. bdg. 250.00 (*0-8490-1398-4*) Gordon Pr.

— George Bernard Shaw: A Bibliography. 1975. lib. bdg. 250.00 (*0-87968-335-X*) Gordon Pr.

— Occult Bibliography. 1975. lib. bdg. 250.00 (*0-8490-0748-8*) Gordon Pr.

Phillips, Jill & Phillips, Leona. D. W. Griffith & His Films. 490p. 1975. lib. bdg. 250.00 (*0-87968-334-1*) Gordon Pr.

Phillips, Jill, jt. auth. see Phillips, Leona.

Phillips, Jill M. Archaeology of the Collective East: Greece, Asia Minor, Egypt, Lebanon, Mesopatamia, Syria, Palestine, an Annotated Bibliography. 1977. lib. bdg. 250.00 (*0-8490-1362-3*) Gordon Pr.

— Birthday Secrets, 1 vol. 480p. 1999. mass mkt. 6.99 (*0-451-19922-7*) NAL.

— Birthday Secrets. 480p. 1999. mass mkt. 6.99 (*0-7853-3926-4*) Pubns Intl Ltd.

***Phillips, Jill M.** Birthday Secrets: What the Heavens Reveal About You & Your Birthday. LC 99-179295. 400 p. 1998. write for info. (*0-7853-3007-0*) Pubns Intl Ltd.

Phillips, Jill M. The Darkling Plain: A Bibliography of Books about World War I. (Bibliographies for Librarians Ser.). 1980. lib. bdg. 250.00 (*0-8490-3207-5*) Gordon Pr.

— The Fate Weaver. 256p. 1992. 17.95 (*1-55972-102-2*, Birch Ln Pr) Carol Pub Group.

— The Rain Maiden. 570p. 1987. 16.95 (*0-8065-1008-0*, Citadel Pr) Carol Pub Group.

— The Second World War in History, Biography, Diary, Poetry, Literature, & Film: A Bibliography. 1983. lib. bdg. 250.00 (*0-8490-3231-8*) Gordon Pr.

— T. E. Lawrence: A Portrait in Paradox Controversy & Caricature in the Biographies of T. E. Lawrence. 600p. 1975. 250.00 (*0-8490-1172-8*) Gordon Pr.

— Walford's Oak. 386p. 1990. 18.95 (*0-8065-1159-1*, Citadel Pr) Carol Pub Group.

Phillips, Jim. The Devil's Bodyguard. LC 83-61388. (Illus.). 350p. 1986. 19.95 (*0-932572-12-X*) Phillips Pubns.

— History of the American Bladesmiths Society. 2nd ed. 32p. 3.00 (*0-932572-14-6*) Phillips Pubns.

Phillips, Jim, et al, eds. Crime & Criminal Justice: Essays in the History of Canadian Law, Vol. 5. (Osgoode Society for Canadian Legal History Ser.). 584p. 1994. text 70.00 (*0-8020-0633-7*) U of Toronto Pr.

— Essays in the History of Canadian Law Vol. 5: Crime & Criminal Justice. 584p. 1994. pap. text 45.00 (*0-8020-7587-8*) U of Toronto Pr.

Phillips, Jim, ed. see Andrews, John C.

Phillips, Jim, ed. see Beard, Ross E.

Phillips, Jim, jt. ed. see Girard, Philip.

Phillips, Jim, ed. see Mason, Peter.

Phillips, Jim, ed. see White, William.

Phillips, Jim, ed. see Yeaton, Kelly, et al.

Phillips, Jim M., ed. see Doyle, Charles H. & Stuart, Terrell.

Phillips, Jo. Exploring Triangles: Paper-Folding Geometry. LC 74-14862. (Young Math Ser.). (Illus.). 40p. (J). (gr. k-3). 1975. lib. bdg. 12.89 (*0-690-00645-4*) HarpC Child Bks.

— Right Angles: Paper-Folding Geometry. LC 72-171007. (Young Math Ser.). (Illus.). (J). (gr. 1-4). 1972. lib. bdg. 11.89 (*0-690-60917-5*) HarpC Child Bks.

Phillips, Joan. Lucky Bear. LC 85-14467. (Step into Reading Ser.: A Step 1 Book). (Illus.). 32p. (J). (ps-1). 1986. pap. 3.99 (*0-394-87987-2*, Pub. by Random Bks Yng Read) Random.

— Lucky Bear. (Step into Reading Ser.: A Step 1 Book). (J). (ps-1). 1986. 9.19 (*0-606-12406-3*, Pub. by Turtleback) Demco.

— My New Boy. LC 85-30129. (Step into Reading Ser.: A Step 1 Book). (Illus.). 32p. (J). (ps-1). 1986. pap. 3.99 (*0-394-88277-6*, Pub. by Random Bks Yng Read) Random.

— My New Boy. (Step into Reading Ser.: A Step 1 Book). (J). (ps-1). 1986. 9.19 (*0-606-12443-8*, Pub. by Turtleback) Demco.

— My New Boy. 93rd ed. (Step into Reading Ser.: A Step 1 Book). (J). (ps-1). 1993. pap. text 10.80 (*0-15-300313-8*, Harcourt Child Bks) Harcourt.

— Peek-a-Boo! I See You! (So Tall Board Bks.). (Illus.). 18p. (J). (ps). 1983. bds. 4.99 (*0-448-03092-6*, G & D) Peng Put Young Read.

— Tiger Is a Scaredy Cat. LC 85-19673. (Step into Reading Ser.: A Step 1 Book). (Illus.). 32p. (J). (ps-1). 1986. pap. 3.99 (*0-394-88056-0*, Pub. by Random Bks Yng Read) Random.

Phillips, Joan. Tiger Is a Scaredy Cat. (Step into Reading Ser.: A Step 1 Book). (J). (ps-1). 1986. 9.19 (*0-606-12542-6*, Pub. by Turtleback) Demco.

***Phillips, Joan & Simms, Debbie.** Elements of Art Therapy. 2001. pap. 29.95 (*1-885473-44-3*) Wood N Barnes.

Phillips, Joan, jt. auth. see Masse, Sydna.

Phillips, Joan, jt. auth. see Vives, Miguel.

Phillips, Joan N., ed. see Nash, Ralph C., Jr. & Schooner, Steven L.

Phillips, Joan Nelson, jt. auth. see Tobin, Patricia.

Phillips, Joann. Let's Go to the Tackle Store & Fondle the Plugs. 1994. pap. text 8.95 (*0-913507-58-X*) New Forums.

Phillips, JoAnn. The Run According to Hawkeye. (Illus.). 24p. (Orig.). (J). 1993. pap. 9.95 (*0-9638403-0-4*) Cherokee Strip.

Phillips, Joann, ed. see Zerler, Kathryn S.

Phillips, Joanna, compiled by. Into the Eighties with Alaskan Environmental Impact Statements: Bibliography. (Elmer E. Rasmuson Library Occasional Papers: No. 11). 234p. (Orig.). 1985. pap. text 12.50 (*0-937592-06-4*) U Alaska Rasmuson Lib.

Phillips, John. Bible Explorer's Guide. LC 86-18565. 272p. 1987. pap., student ed. 14.99 (*0-87213-682-5*) Loizeaux.

— Carew Manor: A Short Guide. (C). 1985. pap. 30.00 (*0-907335-21-7*, Pub. by Sutton Libs & Arts) St Mut.

***Phillips, John.** Contested Knowledge: A Guide to Critical Theory. LC 00-33416. 2000. write for info. (*1-85649-558-2*, Pub. by Zed Books) St Martin.

Phillips, John. Deer & Fixings. 188p. 1991. pap. 12.00 (*0-937866-23-7*) Atlantic Pub Co.

— Exploring Acts. LC 91-21850. 528p. 1991. reprint ed. 29.99 (*0-87213-668-X*) Loizeaux.

— Exploring Ephesians. LC 93-6579. 212p. 1993. 19.99 (*0-87213-650-7*) Loizeaux.

— Exploring Genesis. LC 92-31406. 380p. 1992. reprint ed. 24.99 (*0-87213-659-0*) Loizeaux.

— Exploring Hebrews. LC 91-44909. 204p. 1992. reprint ed. 19.99 (*0-87213-671-X*) Loizeaux.

— Exploring Philippians. LC 95-23853. 188p. 1996. 19.99 (*0-87213-580-2*) Loizeaux.

— Exploring Proverbs, Vol. 1. LC 94-23095. (Exploring Ser.). (Illus.). 2p. 1996. 32.99 (*0-87213-577-2*) Loizeaux.

— Exploring Proverbs, Vol. 2. LC 94-23095. (Exploring Ser.). (Illus.). 2p. 1996. 32.99 (*0-87213-578-0*) Loizeaux.

— Exploring Revelation. LC 91-18869. 265p. 1991. reprint ed. 21.99 (*0-87213-672-8*) Loizeaux.

— Exploring Romans. LC 91-35605. 286p. 1992. reprint ed. 21.99 (*0-87213-669-8*) Loizeaux.

— Exploring the Future: A Comprehensive Guide to Bible Prophecy. LC 91-39048. (Illus.). 413p. 1992. pap. 15.99 (*0-87213-625-6*) Loizeaux.

— Exploring the Gospels: John. LC 88-13345. (Illus.). 425p. 1989. 26.99 (*0-87213-658-2*) Loizeaux.

— Exploring the Gospels: Matthew. LC 99-25232. (Exploring Ser.). 1999. 29.99 (*0-87213-654-X*) Loizeaux.

— Exploring the Minor Prophets. LC 98-20660. (Exploring Ser.). (Illus.). 1998. 24.99 (*0-87213-656-6*) Loizeaux.

Phillips, John. Exploring the Psalms, 2 vols., Set. LC 88-12938. 2p. 1988. 69.98 (*0-87213-653-1*) Loizeaux.

Phillips, John. Exploring the Psalms, Vol. 1. LC 88-12938. Vol. 1. 1988. 34.99 (*0-87213-678-7*) Loizeaux.

— Exploring the Psalms, Vol. 2. LC 88-12938. 1988. 34.99 (*0-87213-679-5*) Loizeaux.

— Exploring the Scriptures. LC 92-46619. 256p. 1993. pap., student ed. 14.99 (*0-87213-673-6*) Loizeaux.

— Exploring the Song of Solomon. LC 84-7881. 157p. (C). 1984. pap. 8.99 (*0-87213-683-3*) Loizeaux.

— Exploring the World of the Jew. LC 92-18121. (Illus.). 256p. 1993. pap. 14.99 (*0-87213-674-4*) Loizeaux.

— Fish & Fixings. 210p. 1991. pap. 12.00 (*0-937866-29-6*) Atlantic Pub Co.

***Phillips, John.** Forbidden Fictions: Pornography & Censorship in Twentieth-Century French Literature. LC 98-45087. 224p. 1999. 59.95 (*0-7453-1222-5*, Pub. by Pluto GBR); pap. 19.95 (*0-7453-1217-9*, Pub. by Pluto GBR) Stylus Pub VA.

Phillips, John. Free Spirit in a Troubled World: A Photoreporter for Life, 1936-1959. (Illus.). 304p. 1996. 39.95 (*3-931141-20-9*, 610171, Pub. by Scalo Pubs) Dist Art Pubs.

— How to Live Forever. (Teach Yourself the Bible Ser.). 1980. pap. 5.99 (*0-8024-3700-1*) Moody.

— Introducing People of the Bible, Vol. 1. LC 91-39819. Vol. 1. 192p. 1992. pap. 8.99 (*0-87213-627-2*) Loizeaux.

— Introducing People of the Bible, Vol. 2. Vol. 2. 137p. 1993. pap. 8.99 (*0-87213-628-0*) Loizeaux.

— Introducing People of the Bible, Vol. 3. Vol. 3. 1995. pap., student ed. 8.99 (*0-87213-629-9*) Loizeaux.

— Introducing People of the Bible, 4 vols., Vol. 4. Vol. 4. 1998. pap. 8.99 (*0-87213-626-4*) Loizeaux.

***Phillips, John.** John Phillips. Gerhart, Klaus, ed. (Photorotic Ser.: Vol. 2). (Illus.). 72p. 2000. 24.95 (*1-890377-17-1*) Pohlmann Pr.

Phillips, John. John Phillips Personal History. 1995. 29.95 (*0-614-96883-6*) DAP Assocs.

— Life on Earth: Its Origin & Succession. Gould, Stephen Jay, ed. LC 79-8343. (History of Paleontology Ser.). 1980. reprint ed. lib. bdg. 23.95 (*0-405-12733-2*) Ayer.

— The Masters' Secrets of Catfishing. LC 93-79799. (Illus.). 160p. (Orig.). 1993. pap. text 9.95 (*0-936513-44-6*) Larsens Outdoor.

— The Masters' Secrets of Deer Hunting. LC 91-90327. (Deer Hunting Library). 160p. (Orig.). 1991. pap. 11.95 (*0-936513-14-4*) Larsens Outdoor.

— Memoirs of William Smith. Albritton, Claude C., Jr., ed. LC 77-6535. (History of Geology Ser.). (Illus.). 1978. reprint ed. lib. bdg. 18.95 (*0-405-10455-3*) Ayer.

— Mid-Atlantic Winter Sports & Ski America: Complete Guide to Winter Sports Throughout the Mid-Atlantic Region. (Illus.). 284p. 2000. pap. text 19.95 (*1-882997-08-5*, Pub. by Beachway Pr) Globe Pequot.

— Nathalie Sarraute Vol. 13: Metaphor, Fairy-Tale & the Feminine of the Text. LC 93-40239. (Writing about Women Ser.). XIII, 284p. (C). 1995. text 50.95 (*0-8204-2366-1*) P Lang Pubng.

— One Hundred Outlines from the Old Testament. LC 94-16340. 100p. 1994. pap., student ed. 7.99 (*0-87213-575-6*) Loizeaux.

— One Hundred Sermon Outlines from the New Testament. LC 94-16339. 112p. 1994. pap. 7.99 (*0-87213-576-4*) Loizeaux.

— Only One Life: The Biography of Stephen F. Olford. LC 94-43087. 352p. 1995. 22.99 (*0-87213-676-0*) Loizeaux.

— Poet & Pilot: Antoine de Saint-Exupery. (Illus.). 1994. 40.00 (*1-881616-23-1*, Pub. by Scalo Pubs) Dist Art Pubs.

— Protecting Designs - Law & Litigation. 425p. 1994. 110.00 (*0-455-21275-9*, Pub. by LawBk Co) Gaunt.

***Phillips, John.** Sap Finance & Controlling. 512p. 1999. pap. 39.99 (*0-07-135638-X*) McGraw-Hill HPD.

Phillips, John. The Science of Deer Hunting. LC 92-71317. (Deer Hunting Library). (Illus.). 160p. (Orig.). 1992. pap. 9.95 (*0-936513-22-5*) Larsens Outdoor.

— Sermon Outlines from Exodus: Alliterated Outline for the Entire Book. 1998. pap. 7.99 (*0-87213-573-X*) Loizeaux.

— Sermon Outlines from Jeremiah: Alliterated Outline for the Entire Book. 1998. pap. 7.99 (*0-87213-574-8*) Loizeaux.

— Sermon Outlines on the Psalms: Pastoral Aids. 1995. pap. 7.99 (*0-87213-677-9*) Loizeaux.

— Turkey Hunting Tactics. LC 88-63557. (Hunter's Information Ser.). 183p. 1989. write for info. (*0-914697-19-6*) N Amer Outdoor Grp.

Phillips, John & O'Donovan, James. The Modern Contract of Guarantee. 3rd ed. 850p. 1996. 156.00 (*0-455-21435-2*, Pub. by LawBk Co) Gaunt.

Phillips, John & Stonebridge, Lyndsey. Reading Melanie Klein. LC 97-47651. (Illus.). 280p. (C). 1998. 85.00 (*0-415-16236-X*); pap. 25.99 (*0-415-16237-8*) Routledge.

Phillips, John & Vines, Jerry. Exploring the Book of Daniel. LC 90-31819. 289p. 1990. 21.99 (*0-87213-988-3*) Loizeaux.

Phillips, John, et al. The Last Edwardians: An Illustrated History of Violet Trefusis & Alice Keppel. LC 85-71852. (Illus.). 93p. (Orig.). 1985. pap. 10.00 (*0-934552-44-4*) Boston Athenaeum.

Phillips, John, jt. auth. see Ironside, H. A.

Phillips, John, jt. auth. see Jullian, Philippe.

Phillips, John, jt. auth. see McDermott, James.

Phillips, John, tr. see Torwesten, Hans.

Phillips, John A. Electoral Behavior in Unreformed England: Plumpers, Splitters, & Straights. LC 82-47608. 375p. reprint ed. pap. 116.30 (*0-7837-6772-2*, 204660200003) Bks Demand.

— The Great Reform Bill in the Boroughs: English Electoral Behaviour, 1818-1841. 352p. 1992. 75.00 (*0-19-820296-2*) OUP.

— Personal Wireless Comunication with DECT & PWT: Wireless Communications Engineering. LC 98-30072. 1998. 93.00 (*0-89006-872-0*) Artech Hse.

Phillips, John B. The New Testament in Modern English. rev. ed. 576p. 1972. 14.95 (*0-02-596970-6*) Macmillan.

Phillips, John B., Jr. Tennessee Employment Law. 2nd ed. 1992. ring bd. 89.00 (*0-925773-13-1*) M Lee Smith.

Phillips, John C. American Game Mammals & Birds: A Catalogue of Books. Sterling, Keir B., ed. LC 77-83129. (Biologists & Their World Ser.). (Illus.). 1978. reprint ed. lib. bdg. 54.95 (*0-405-10744-7*) Ayer.

— A Natural History of the Ducks, 2 vols., 1. 1920p. 1986. reprint ed. 50.00 (*0-486-25141-1*) Dover.

— A Natural History of the Ducks, 2 vols., 2. 1920p. 1986. reprint ed. 50.00 (*0-486-25142-X*) Dover.

— Sociology of Sport. LC 92-22181. 364p. 1992. pap. text 41.00 (*0-205-13983-3*) Allyn.

Phillips, John D., Jr. Employment Law Desk Book for Tennessee Employers. 1989. ring bd. 87.00 (*0-925773-03-4*) M Lee Smith.

Phillips, John E. Bass Fishing Central Alabama: You Can Find & Catch More & Bigger Bass in Central Alabama Lakes. Ellington, Coke, ed. (Illus.). 160p. (Orig.). 1994. pap. 15.00 (*1-882616-05-7*) Advertiser.

— The Masters' Secrets of Bowhunting Deer: Secret Tactics from Master Bowmen. LC 93-78226. (Illus.). 160p. (Orig.). 1993. pap. text 9.95 (*0-936513-34-9*) Larsens Outdoor.

— The Masters' Secrets of Crappie Fishing. LC 92-74324. (Fishing Library). (Illus.). 160p. (Orig.). (C). 1992. pap. text 9.95 (*0-936513-29-2*) Larsens Outdoor.

— The Masters' Secrets of Turkey Hunting. LC 91-76443. (Turkey Hunting Ser.). (Illus.). 160p. (Orig.). 1991. pap. 11.95 (*0-936513-18-7*) Larsens Outdoor.

— Monster Bucks, How to Take: Secrets to Finding Trophy Deer. LC 94-72944. 160p. (Orig.). 1995. pap. 11.95 (*0-936513-46-2*) Larsens Outdoor.

Phillips, John H. Prac Quantitative Doppler, 001. (Illus.). 152p. 1991. boxed set 99.95 (*0-8493-4921-4*, RC683) CRC Pr.

Phillips, John L. The Bends: Compressed Air in the History of Science, Diving, & Engineering. LC 97-35206. 272p. 1998. 30.00 (*0-300-07125-6*) Yale U Pr.

— How to Think about Statistics. 5th ed. (Series of Books in Psychology). 192p. (C). 1995. pap. text 16.95 (*0-7167-2822-2*) W H Freeman.

— How to Think about Statistics. 6th ed. LC 99-34901. 1999. pap. text 16.95 (*0-7167-3654-3*) W H Freeman.

Phillips, John L., Jr. Piaget's Theory: A Primer. LC 80-20800. (Psychology Ser.). (Illus.). (C). 1981. pap. text 11.20 (*0-7167-1236-9*) W H Freeman.

Phillips, John M. & Parker, Barbara N., eds. The Discoveries of Waldron Phoenix Belknap, Jr. Concerning the Influence of the English Mezzotint on Colonial Painting. LC 55-14827. (Illus.). 47p. 1955. reprint ed. pap. 30.00 (*0-7837-4177-4*, 205902600012) Bks Demand.

Phillips, John N. Running with Bonnie & Clyde: The Ten Fast Years of Ralph Fults. LC 95-42771. (Illus.). 416p. 1996. 27.95 (*0-8061-2810-0*) U of Okla Pr.

Phillips, John P., et al, eds. Organic Electronic Spectral Data. (Organic Electronic Spectral Data Ser.: Vol. 30). 929p. 1994. 275.00 (*0-471-10971-1*) Wiley.

— Organic Electronic Spectral Data, Vol. 5: 1960-61. LC 60-16428. 1029p. pap. 200.00 (*0-608-11732-3*, 200636100058) Bks Demand.

— Organic Electronic Spectral Data, Vol. 6: 1962-63. LC 60-16428. 1340p. reprint ed. pap. 200.00 (*0-608-11733-1*, 200636100059) Bks Demand.

— Organic Electronic Spectral Data, Vol. 9: 1967. LC 60-16428. 976p. reprint ed. pap. 200.00 (*0-608-11734-X*, 200636100060) Bks Demand.

— Organic Electronic Spectral Data, Vol. 25. 1020p. 1989. 325.00 (*0-471-51505-1*) Wiley.

— Organic Electronic Spectral Data, Vol. 26. 932p. 1990. 385.00 (*0-471-51941-3*) Wiley.

— Organic Electronic Spectral Data, Vol. 31. LC 60-16428. 887p. 1995. 235.00 (*0-471-14093-7*) Wiley.

Phillips, John P., et al. Organic Electronic Spectral Data, 1985, Vol. 27. 944p. 1991. 385.00 (*0-471-55553-3*) Wiley.

Phillips, John P., ed. see Feuer, Henry, et al.

Phillips, John P., jt. ed. see Kessler, M. F.

Phillips, John R., ed. see Gray, Robert D., et al.

Phillips, John S. Tax Treaty Networks, 1991. 2nd ed. xvii, 882p. 1991. text 355.00 (*2-88316-003-1*) Gordon & Breach.

***Phillips, John T., II.** George Washington's Rules of Civility: Complete with the Original French Text & New French-to-English Translations. 2nd rev. unabridged large type ed. Conway, Moncure D., tr. (Compleat George Washington Ser.). (FRE.). 128p. 2000. lthr. 24.95 (*0-9656758-8-2*) Goose Creek.

Phillips, John T., II. The Historian's Guide to Loudoun County, Virginia Vol. I: Colonial Laws of Virginia & County Court Orders, 1757-1766. (Illus.). 618p. 1996. lib. bdg. 44.95 (*0-9656758-0-7*) Goose Creek.

***Phillips, John T.** Software Directory for Records Management Systems. 10th ed. 294p. 1999. pap. 68.00 (*0-933887-84-1*) ARMA Intl.

Phillips, John T., II, ed. The Bulletin of the Historical Society of Loudoun County, Virginia, 1957-1976. 2nd annot. rev. ed. (Illus.). xx, 332p. 1998. reprint ed. lib. bdg. 24.95 (*0-9656758-3-1*) Goose Creek.

Phillips, John T., II, et al. The Bulletin of the Historical Society of Loudoun County, Virginia, 1997. annot. ed. (Bulletin of Historical Society . . . Ser.). (Illus.). vi, 74p. 1997. pap. 10.00 (*0-9656758-4-X*) Goose Creek.

Phillips, John T., II, ed. see Castillo Parker, Tamarra C. & Schaefer, Mary.

Phillips, John T., II, ed. & illus. see Green, Carolyn.

Phillips, John T., II, ed. & illus. see Ramsay, David.

Phillips, John W. Descendants of Reuben Phillips. 419p. 1996. pap. 54.00 (*0-7884-0390-7*, P334) Heritage Bk.

***Phillips, John W.** Sign of the Cross. LC 99-89656. (Illus.). 272p. 2000. 19.95 (*0-664-22196-3*, Pub. by Westminster John Knox) Presbyterian Pub.

Phillips, Johnthan P. Defenders of the Holy Land: Relations Between the Latin East & the West, 1119-1187. LC 95-43444. (Illus.). 326p. (C). 1996. text 70.00 (*0-19-820540-6*) OUP.

***Phillips, Jonathan.** Conquest of Lisbon (De Expugnatione Lyxbonesi) (POR & ENG.). 2000. 45.00 (*0-231-12122-9*) Col U Pr.

— Conquest of Lisbon (De Expugnations Lyxbonesi) (POR & ENG.). 2000. pap. text 15.50 (*0-231-12123-7*) Col U Pr.

***Phillips, Jonathan, et al.** The Biology of Disease. 2nd ed. LC 00-41405. (Illus.). 2001. write for info. (*0-632-05404-2*) Blackwell Sci.

Phillips, Jonathan D. Earth Surface Systems: Order, Complexity & Scale. LC 98-21952. (Natural Environment Ser.). 320p. 1999. 74.95 (*1-55786-934-0*) Blackwell Pubs.

Phillips, Jonathon, et al, eds. The Biology of Disease. LC 94-46340. 250p. 1995. 34.95 (*0-632-03855-1*) Blackwell Sci.

Phillips-Jones, Linda. The New Mentors & Proteges: How to Succeed with the New Mentoring Partnerships. rev. ed. LC 93-84972. 184p. 1997. pap. 10.00 (*1-890608-00-9*) Coalition Cnsling.

Phillips, Joseph. MCSE Training: Windows 98. LC 98-88580. (Training Guides). 1998. 49.99 (*1-56205-890-8*) New Riders Pub.

— MCSE Training Guide Windows 95. 2nd ed. (MCSE Training Guides). 700p. 1998. 49.99 (*1-56205-880-0*) New Riders Pub.

— Operation Elbow Room. 240p. (Orig.). 1995. pap. 11.95 (*1-56474-138-9*) Fithian Pr.

Phillips, Joseph C. Portrait in Reflections. LC 97-66321. 96p. (Orig.). 1997. pap. 14.95 (*1-883122-11-2*) Pearce Pub.

Phillips, Joseph D. Little Business in the American Economy, Volume 42. LC 81-4217. (Illinois Studies in the Social Sciences: Vol. 42). (Illus.). 135p. 1981. reprint ed. lib. bdg. 59.50 (*0-313-23055-2*, PHLB, Greenwood Pr) Greenwood.

Phillips, Joseph D., jt. ed. see Schiller, Herbert I.

Phillips, Joy. The Rooster Crowed Early: In the Ozarks. (Illus.). ix, 66p. (Orig.). (YA). (gr. 6 up). 1997. pap. 6.00 (*0-9621669-5-2*) Lil Red Hen OK.

Phillips, Joyce B. & Phillips, Paul G. The Brainerd Journal: A Mission to the Cherokees, 1817-1823. LC 98-4021. (Indians of the Southeast Ser.). xix, 584p. 1999. text 60.00 (*0-8032-3718-9*) U of Nebr Pr.

Phillips, Juanita. Mandy Miami & the Miracle Motel No. 2. (Newspaper Kids Ser.). 1998. pap. text 5.95 (*0-207-19152-2*) HarpC.

— Newspaper Kids. (Illus.). (J). 1998. pap. 5.95 (*0-207-19160-3*) HarpC.

***Phillips, Juanita.** Newspaper Kids #4. 1999. pap. 5.95 (*0-207-19052-6*) Collins Angus & Robertson Pubs.

P

An Asterisk (*) at the beginning of an entry indicates that the title is appearing for the first time.

Phillips, Juanita. Pegleg Paddy's Puppy Factory No. 2. (Newspaper Kids Ser.). 1998. pap. text 5.95 (*0-207-19051-8*) HarpC.

Phillips, Judith. Natural by Design: Beauty & Balance in Southwest Gardens. (Illus.). 208p. 1995. 45.00 (*0-89013-276-3*); pap. 35.00 (*0-89013-277-1*) Museum NM Pr.

— New Mexico Gardener's Guide: The What, Where, When, How & Why of Gardening in New Mexico. (Illus.). 400p. 1998. pap. 19.95 (*1-888608-55-2*) Cool Springs Pr.

— Plants for Natural Gardens: Southwestern Native & Adaptive Trees, Shrubs, Wildflowers & Grasses. (Illus.). 160p. 1995. pap. 27.50 (*0-89013-281-X*) Museum NM Pr.

— Southwestern Landscaping with Native Plants. (Illus.). 160p. 1987. pap. 24.95 (*0-89013-166-X*) Museum NM Pr.

Phillips, Judith, ed. Working Carers: International Perspectives on Work & Care of Older People. LC 95-80345. 176p. 1996. 77.95 (*1-85628-675-4*, Pub. by Avebry) Ashgate Pub Co.

Phillips, Judith & Penhale, Bridget, eds. Evaluating Care Management for Older People. LC 95-32046. 250p. 1995. pap. 29.95 (*1-85302-317-5*, Pub. by Jessica Kingsley) Taylor & Francis.

Phillips, Judy, jt. auth. see Phillips, Michael.

Phillips, Judy, jt. auth. see Phillips, Michael R.

***Phillips, Julia.** Driving under the Affluence. 321p. 1999. reprint ed. text 24.00 (*0-7881-6724-3*) DIANE Pub.

Phillips, Julia. You'll Never Eat Lunch in This Town Again. 656p. 1992. mass mkt. 7.99 (*0-451-17072-5*, Sig Classics) NAL.

Phillips, Julie A., ed. see Phillips, Trevor M.

Phillips, June, et al. Five C's. LC 99-187474. (C). 1998. pap. text, wbk. ed. 9.50 (*0-8384-7686-4*) Heinle & Heinle.

Phillips, June K., ed. Reflecting on Proficiency from the Classroom Perspective. (Reports of the Northeast Conference on the Teaching of Foreign Languages). 222p. 1993. pap. 14.21 (*0-8442-9271-0*) NE Conf Teach Foreign.

Phillips, June K., et al. Chez Vous, Chez Nous: Language in Action: First Year. 608p. (C). 1988. pap., lab manual ed. 12.95 (*0-685-18204-5*) McGraw.

— Quoi de Neuf? Language in Action: A Beginning Course. (C). 1988. pap. text, lab manual ed. 19.00 (*0-07-553810-5*) McGraw.

Phillips, K. J. Dying Gods in Twentieth-Century Fiction. LC 88-48036. 256p. 1990. 37.50 (*0-8387-5161-X*) Bucknell U Pr.

Phillips, Kate. White Rabbit. 224p. 1997. reprint ed. pap. 12.50 (*0-06-097719-1*, Perennial) HarperTrade.

Phillips, Katharine. Broken Mirror: Understanding & Treating Body Dysmorphic Disorder. 368p. 1996. 25.00 (*0-19-508317-2*) OUP.

Phillips, Katharine A. The Broken Mirror: Understanding & Treating Body Dysmorphic Disorder. (Illus.). 368p. 1998. reprint ed. pap. 15.95 (*0-19-512126-0*) OUP.

Phillips, Kathleen. The Power of Health Care Teams: Strategies for Success. Joint Commission on Accreditation of Healthcare Organizations, ed. & illus. by. LC 96-77364. 201p. 1997. pap. 50.00 (*0-86688-473-4*, HCT-100) Joint Comm Hlthcare.

Phillips, Kathleen C. How to Write a Story. LC 95-2073. (Speak Out, Write On! Ser.). (Illus.). 96p. (YA). (gr. 7-12). 1995. lib. bdg. 24.00 (*0-531-11239-X*) Watts.

— How to Write a Story. LC 95-2073. (Speak Out, Write On! Ser.). (Illus.). (YA). (gr. 7-12). 1996. pap. 7.95 (*0-531-15787-3*) Watts.

Phillips, Kathleen C., jt. auth. see Steiner, Barbara.

Phillips, Kathryn. Paradise by Design. LC 97-18172. 265p. 1998. 25.00 (*0-86547-519-9*) N Point Pr.

— Tracking the Vanishing Frogs: An Ecological Mystery. (Illus.). 256p. 1995. pap. 13.95 (*0-14-024646-0*, Penguin Bks) Viking Penguin.

***Phillips, Kathy.** Vogue Beauty. (Illus.). 2000. 35.00 (*1-84222-050-0*) Carlton Bks Ltd.

— Vogue Book of Blondes. (Illus.). 160p. 2000. 24.95 (*0-670-89259-9*, Viking) Viking Penguin.

Phillips, Kathy, jt. auth. see Stewart, Mary.

Phillips, Kathy J. Virginia Woolf Against Empire. LC 93-43714. (Illus.). 307p. 1994. reprint ed. pap. 95.20 (*0-608-07784-4*, 206787200010) Bks Demand.

Phillips, Kay & Rejai, Mostafa. Loyalists & Revolutionaries: Political Leaders Compared. LC 87-27888. (Illus.). 203192p. 1988. 49.95 (*0-275-92915-9*, C2915, Praeger Pubs) Greenwood.

Phillips, Kay, jt. auth. see Rejai, M.

Phillips, Kay, jt. auth. see Rejai, Mostafa.

Phillips, Keith. Out of Ashes. (Illus.). 196p. (Orig.). 1996. 12.00 (*0-9655553-0-5*) World Impact.

— Texas Hunting & Fishing Leases. 1996. pap. text 9.95 (*1-888103-00-0*) Trophy Pubng.

Phillips, Keith, jt. auth. see Pitts, Marian.

Phillips, Ken. Koalas: Australia's Ancient Ones. LC 94-14093. 1994. 27.50 (*0-671-79777-8*) S&S Trade.

Phillips, Kenneth H. Basic Techniques of Conducting. LC 96-16707. (Illus.). 256p. (C). 1997. pap. 41.95 (*0-19-509937-0*) OUP.

Phillips, Kenneth H. Teaching Kids to Sing. (Illus.). 392p. 1992. 39.00 (*0-02-871795-3*, Schirmer Books) Mac Lib Ref.

Phillips, Kenneth J. Guide to the Sun. (Illus.). 400p. (C). 1995. pap. text 19.95 (*0-521-39788-X*) Cambridge U Pr.

Phillips, Keri & Shaw, Patricia. A Consultancy Approach for Trainers. LC 89-5156. 1989. write for info. (*0-88390-234-6*) U Pr of Amer.

— A Consultancy Approach for Trainers & Developers. 2nd ed. LC 97-28406. 250p. 1998. 74.95 (*0-566-07937-2*, Pub. by Gower) Ashgate Pub Co.

Phillips, Kevin. Arrogant Capital: The Acclaimed Indictment of Washington Gridlock. LC 97-121223. 320p. 1995. pap. 12.95 (*0-316-70602-7*) Little.

Phillips, Kevin, jt. auth. see Willocks, James.

Phillips, Kevin P. The Cousin's Wars: Religion, Politics & the Triumph of Anglo-America. Date not set. pap. 16.50 (*0-465-01370-8*, Pub. by Basic) HarpC.

— The Cousins' Wars: Religion, Politics, & the Triumph of Anglo-America. LC 98-49935. (Illus.). 707p. 1998. 35.00 (*0-465-01369-4*, Pub. by Basic) HarpC.

Phillips, Kim T. William Duane, Radical Journalist in the Age of Jefferson. (Outstanding Studies in Early American History). 681p. 1989. reprint ed. 35.00 (*0-8240-6193-4*) Garland.

***Phillips, Kimberley L.** Alabama North. LC 98-58128. (Illus.). 400p. 1999. 59.95 (*0-252-02477-X*) U of Ill Pr.

Phillips, Kimberley L. Alabamanorth: African-American Migrants, Community & Working-Class Activism in Cleveland, 1915-45. LC 98-58128. (The Working Class in American History Ser.). 400p. 1999. pap. 21.95 (*0-252-06793-2*) U of Ill Pr.

Phillips, Kimberly. Purpose Lies Within. 240p. 1998. pap. 15.95 (*0-9667913-0-4*) Messenger.

Phillips, Kimberly, ed. see Swanson, Johnny.

***Phillips, Kimberly S.** Purpose Lies Within: A Motivational Book for the Heart & Soul. 80p. 2000. pap. 9.95 (*0-9667913-1-2*, 500) Messenger Publ.

Phillips, Kristy S. & Wilde, Kathleen B. Superhighway to Wealth: Making Money on the Net. 207p. 1995. pap. text 19.95 (*0-9649424-0-2*) Info Directions.

— Superhighway to Wealth: Making Money on the Net. 2nd rev. ed. Phillips, Lee R., ed. (Illus.). 247p. 1996. pap. 12.95 (*0-9649424-1-0*) Info Directions.

Phillips, Kristy S., jt. auth. see Phillips, Lee R.

Phillips, Kyle, tr. see Artusi, Pellegrino.

Phillips, Kyle M., Jr. In the Hills of Tuscany: Recent Excavations at the Etruscan Site of Poggio Civitate (Murlo, Siena) (Illus.). xxiv, 136p. 1993. pap. 18.95 (*0-934718-96-2*) U Museum Pubns.

Phillips, Kyle M., Jr., jt. auth. see Ashmead, Ann H.

Phillips, L. The Envoi Messages. 1985. pap. 6.95 (*0-88145-031-6*) Broadway Play.

Phillips, L., jt. auth. see Emsley, James W.

Phillips, L. C. Bloodlines. LC 79-153403. 91p. 1971. 21.95 (*0-912282-02-9*) Pulse-Finger.

— Disco Candy & Other Stories. LC 78-72027. 210p. 1979. 24.95 (*0-912282-07-X*) Pulse-Finger.

— Sistine Cartoons. 2nd ed. LC 68-59442. 84p. 1970. 21.95 (*0-912282-00-2*) Pulse-Finger.

— Twelve Muscle Tones. 104p. 1980. 21.95 (*0-912282-08-8*) Pulse-Finger.

***Phillips, L. Edward & Phillips, Sara Webb.** In Spirit & Truth: Toward a New Understanding of Worship in the UMC. LC 00-102007. 96p. 2000. pap. 13.95 (*0-88177-278-X*, DR278) Discipleship Res.

Phillips, L. K. Aviation for the Private Pilot. 1975. lib. bdg. 250.00 (*0-87968-686-3*) Gordon Pr.

Phillips, L. M. In the Desert - The Hiterland of Algiers. 352p. 1985. 240.00 (*1-85077-072-7*, Pub. by Darf Pubs Ltd) St Mut.

Phillips, L. N., ed. Design with Advanced Composite Materials. (Illus.). 360p. 1990. 94.95 (*0-387-51800-2*, 3659) Spr-Verlag.

Phillips, Lance. Yonder Comes the Train. 1993. 24.98 (*0-88365-715-5*) Galahad Bks.

Phillips, Lance G., et al. Structure-Function Properties of Food Proteins. (Food Science & Technology International Ser.). (Illus.). 271p. 1994. text 73.00 (*0-12-554360-3*) Acad Pr.

Phillips, Larry W. Covering the Second Coming. Kirsey, J. Allen, ed. 224p. (Orig.). 1996. pap. 12.95 (*1-878569-34-1*) Badger Bks Inc.

***Phillips, Larry W.** Ernest Hemingway on Writing. (Illus.). (J). 1999. 17.35 (*0-606-18623-9*) Turtleback.

Phillips, Larry W. Madison Retro. Balousek, Marv, ed. 222p. (Orig.). 1994. pap. 12.95 (*1-878569-22-8*) Badger Bks Inc.

— Zen & the Art of Poker: Timeless Secrets to Transform Your Game. LC 99-32700. 208p. 1999. pap. 12.95 (*0-452-28126-1*, Plume) Dutton Plume.

Phillips, Larry W., ed. see Hemingway, Ernest.

***Phillips, Laura.** Bride's Best Man. (Bouquet Ser.: Vol. 54). 2000. mass mkt. 3.99 (*0-8217-6650-3*, Zebra Kensgtn) Kensgtn Pub Corp.

***Phillips, Laura A.** Bolsheviks & the Bottle: Drink & Worker Culture in St. Petersburg, 1900-1929. LC 99-87014. (Illus.). 250p. 2000. 38.00 (*0-87580-264-8*, 264-8) N Ill U Pr.

Phillips, Laura W. & Thompson, Deborah. Transylvania: The Architectural History of A Mountain County. LC 98-86439. 1998. 39.95 (*0-943335-10-8*) Marblehead Pub.

***Phillips, Laurel & Stahl, Barbara.** Parenting, SportsMom Style: Real-Life Solutions for Surviving Youth Sports. Meyer, Barb, ed. (Illus.). 186p. 2000. pap. 16.95 (*0-9659445-5-7*, Pub. by Three Hund Seven Bks) BookWorld.

Phillips, Laurel, jt. auth. see Stahl, Barbara.

Phillips, Lauren. In the Name of the Patient: Consumer Advocacy in Health Care. 100p. (Orig.). 1995. pap. 45.00 (*0-87258-679-0*, 157800) Am Hospital.

***Phillips, Laurence.** Paris Scene: 1998 to 1999 Edition. (Illus.). 1999. pap. 12.95 (*1-902644-02-6*) Prowler Pr.

Phillips, Laurence. Paris Scene, 1995-1996. (Illus.). 208p. (Orig.). 1995. pap. 10.95 (*0-85449-220-8*, Pub. by Gay Mens Pr) LPC InBook.

***Phillips, Lavearne.** Consonant Blends & Digraphs Coloring Book. 16p. (J). (gr. 1-3). 1999. pap. 4.00 (*1-930058-03-9*) Lave Phillips.

— Easy to Read Short Poems Coloring Book. (Illus.). 23p. (J). (gr. k-2). 1998. pap. 4.00 (*1-930058-00-4*) Lave Phillips.

— Learning to Count 1 2 3 Coloring Book. 12p. (J). (ps-1). 1999. pap. 3.00 (*1-930058-02-0*) Lave Phillips.

— Now Let's Say Alphabet Coloring Book. (Illus.). 15p. (J). (ps-1). 1998. pap. 3.00 (*1-930058-01-2*) Lave Phillips.

Phillips, Lawrence. French Entree: Paris, No. 11. 1993. pap. 11.95 (*1-870948-81-5*, Pub. by Quiller Pr) St Mut.

— French Entree Eleven Paris. 1993. pap. 29.95 (*1-870948-83-1*, Pub. by Quiller Pr) St Mut.

— 1998 Year Book of Chiropractic. (Illus.). 448p. (C). (gr. 13). 1997. text 73.00 (*0-8151-6737-7*, 21967) Mosby Inc.

Phillips, Lawrence E. American La France 700 1945-1952 Series Photo Archive. LC 98-71289. (Illus.). 128p. 1998. pap. 29.95 (*1-882256-90-5*, AL-001) Iconografix.

— American LaFrance 900 Series 1958-1964 Photo Archive. (Illus.). 128p. 1999. pap. 29.95 (*1-58388-002-X*, Pub. by Iconografix) Motorbooks Intl.

— American LaFrance 700 & 800 Series 1953-1958 Photo Archive. LC 98-75267. (Photo Archives Ser.). (Illus.). 128p. 1999. pap. 29.95 (*1-882256-91-3*) Iconografix.

***Phillips, Lawrence E.** American LaFrance 700 Series, 1945-1952. (Photo Archives Ser.: Vol. 2). (Illus.). 128p. 2000. pap. 29.95 (*1-58388-025-9*, 130633AE, Pub. by Iconografix) Motorbooks Intl.

***Phillips, Lee.** Fury at Sweetwater Pass. large type ed. 264p. 2000. pap. 18.99 (*0-7089-5625-4*, Linford) Ulverscroft.

— The Lone Rider. 280p. 2000. 18.99 (*0-7089-5685-8*) Ulverscroft.

***Phillips, Lee Ann & Darnell, Rick.** Using HTML 4.0. 4th ed. LC 97-80845. (Using... Ser.). 704p. 1998. pap. text 29.99 (*0-7897-1562-7*) Que.

***Phillips, Lee Anne.** Practical HTML 4. 850p. 1999. pap. 29.99 (*0-7897-2148-1*) S&S Trade.

Phillips, Lee R. & Phillips, Kristy S. Protecting Your Financial Future: The Inside Story on Wills, Living Trusts, Probate, Estate Taxes, & Asset Protection. 3rd rev. ed. LC 98-67786. 364p. 1999. 24.95 (*0-9648965-2-4*) LegaLees.

— Trust Me! The Truth about Living Revocable Trusts: Use Living Trusts: Leave Nothing to Chance. (Illus.). 337p. 1995. 24.95 (*0-9648965-0-8*) LegaLees.

Phillips, Lee R., ed. see Hamblin, David & Speirs, Ron.

Phillips, Lee R., ed. see Phillips, Kristy S. & Wilde, Kathleen B.

Phillips, Leilani. Science of Me. 1998. pap. write for info. (*1-57553-969-1*) Watermrk Pr.

Phillips, Leo A., ed. Viruses Associated with Human Cancer. LC 82-25240. (Illus.). 668p. reprint ed. pap. 200.00 (*0-7837-3354-2*, 204331200008) Bks Demand.

Phillips, Leona. A Christmas Bibliography. 1977. lib. bdg. 250.00 (*0-8490-1363-1*) Gordon Pr.

— Colonial Days & the Revolutionary War: An Annotated Bibliography. 1976. lib. bdg. 250.00 (*0-87968-337-6*) Gordon Pr.

— Hitler: An Annotated Bibliography. 1976. lib. bdg. 250.00 (*0-8490-1355-0*) Gordon Pr.

Phillips, Leona & Phillips, Jill. Chinese History: An Annotated Bibliography. 1978. lib. bdg. 250.00 (*0-8490-1391-7*) Gordon Pr.

— Film Appreciation: An Outline & Study Guide for Colleges & Universities. 1978. lib. bdg. 250.00 (*0-8490-1390-9*) Gordon Pr.

Phillips, Leona, jt. auth. see Phillips, Jill.

Phillips, Leona R. Martin Luther & the Reformation: An Annotated Bibliography. 1985. lib. bdg. 250.00 (*0-8490-3242-3*) Gordon Pr.

— Silent Cinema: An Annotated Critical Bibliography. 1977. lib. bdg. 250.00 (*0-8490-1368-2*) Gordon Pr.

Phillips, Leona Rasmussen. Edgar Allan Poe: An Annotated Bibliography. LC 78-6783. (Bibliographies for Librarians Ser.). 139 p. 1978. write for info. (*0-8490-1392-5*) Gordon Pr.

Phillips, Leonard E. Parks: Design & Management. LC 95-37116. (Illus.). 229p. 1996. 64.95 (*0-07-049871-7*) McGraw.

Phillips, Leonard E., Jr. Urban Trees: A Guide for Selection, Maintenance, & Master Planning. LC 92-43723. 1993. pap. 37.00 (*0-07-049835-0*) McGraw.

Phillips, Leroy, jt. auth. see Curriden, Mark.

Phillips, Leslie, et al. Basic Debate. 4th ed. LC 96-273. 1996. 29.26 (*0-8442-5981-0*) NTC Contemp Pub Co.

Phillips, Leyson K. Airlines of the World. 1979. lib. bdg. 250.00 (*0-8490-1359-3*) Gordon Pr.

Phillips, Lincoln. Soccer Goalkeeping: The First Line of Attack, the Last Line of Defense. (Illus.). 160p. (Orig.). 1996. pap. 12.95 (*1-57028-077-0*, 80770H, Mstrs Pr) NTC Contemp Pub Co.

Phillips, Linda. Concise Guide to Executive Etiquette. 224p. 1990. pap. 10.95 (*0-385-24766-4*) Doubleday.

***Phillips, Linda.** Puppies are for Life. 408p. 2000. 31.99 (*0-7089-4233-4*) Ulverscroft.

Phillips, Linda M., jt. ed. see Norris, Stephen P.

Phillips, Lionel. All That Glittered: Selected Correspondence of Lionel Phillips, 1890-1924. Fraser, Maryna & Jeeves, Alan, eds. (Illus.). 1978. text 31.00 (*0-19-570100-3*) OUP.

Phillips, Lisa. The American Century: Art & Culture, 1950-2000. LC 99-24969. (Illus.). 408p. 1999. 60.00 (*0-393-04815-2*) Norton.

— Beat Culture & the New America, 1950-1965. 1995. 35.00 (*0-87427-098-7*) Whitney Mus.

— Photoplay: Works from the Chase Manhattan Collection. Russell, Emily, ed. Guibert, Rita & Landers, Clifford, trs. (Illus.). 200p. 1992. 42.00 (*0-9635340-1-7*); pap. text 28.50 (*0-9635340-0-9*) Chase Manhattan.

Phillips, Lisa & Neri, Louise. 1997 Biennial Exhibition: Whitney Museum of Art. (Illus.). 256p. 1997. pap. 39.95 (*0-8109-6825-8*) Whitney Mus.

Phillips, Lisa, jt. auth. see Schimmel, Paul.

Phillips, Llad & Votey, Harold L. The Economics of Crime Control. LC 81-13588. (Sage Library of Social Research: No. 132). (Illus.). 312p. reprint ed. pap. 96.80 (*0-8357-4845-6*, 203777600009) Bks Demand.

Phillips, Lloyd. Fire from the Sky: Essays on the Apocalypse. LC 96-61943. 192p. (Orig.). 1997. pap. 9.95 (*1-883893-99-2*) WinePress Pub.

Phillips, Lois. Lieder Line by Line No. 2: And Word for Word. 2nd rev. ed. 444p. 1996. pap. text 32.00 (*0-19-879017-1*) OUP.

Phillips, Lois B. Wildlife Woodcraft, Vol. 1. LC 78-5267. (Illus.). 64p. 1978. pap. 5.95 (*0-87961-066-2*) Naturegraph.

Phillips, Lois I. Crumbs from My Master's Table. 124p. 1998. pap. write for info. (*1-57502-899-9*, PO2468) Morris Pubng.

Phillips, Lorene, ed. see Brent, Vickie.

Phillips, Lori, jt. auth. see Mack, Stevie.

Phillips, Louis. Alligator Wrestling & You: An Impractical Guide to an Impossible Sport. 96p. (Orig.). (J). (gr. 7-12). 1992. pap. 3.50 (*0-380-76303-6*, Avon Bks) Morrow Avon.

— Ask Me Anything about Baseball. LC 94-31034. 96p. (Orig.). 1995. pap. 3.99 (*0-380-78029-1*, Avon Bks) Morrow Avon.

— Ask Me Anything about Dinosaurs. LC 96-48486. 128p. (J). 1997. pap. 3.99 (*0-380-78552-8*, Avon Bks) Morrow Avon.

Phillips, Louis. Ask Me Anything about Dinosaurs. 1997. 9.09 (*0-606-11061-5*, Pub. by Turtleback) Demco.

Phillips, Louis. Ask Me Anything about Monsters. LC 96-31433. (J). (gr. 3-7). 1997. pap. 4.50 (*0-380-78551-X*, Avon Bks) Morrow Avon.

Phillips, Louis. Ask Me Anything about Monsters. 1997. 9.60 (*0-606-10743-6*, Pub. by Turtleback) Demco.

— Ask Me Anything about the Presidents. 144p. (YA). 1992. mass mkt. 4.50 (*0-380-76426-1*, Avon Bks) Morrow Avon.

— Ask Me Anything about the Presidents. (J). 1992. 9.60 (*0-606-05731-5*, Pub. by Turtleback) Demco.

Phillips, Louis. Bulkington. (Hollow Spring Poetry Ser.). (Illus.). 32p. (Orig.). 1982. pap. 4.00 (*0-936198-08-7*) Hollow Spring Pr.

***Phillips, Louis.** Chicken Run/Cracked Up: The Chicken Run Joke Book. (Illus.). (J). 2000. pap. 3.99 (*0-14-130876-1*, Puffin-Dream) Peng Put Young Read.

Phillips, Louis. The Continuing Education Guide: The CEU & Other Professional Development Criteria. 160p. (C). 1996. pap. text, per. 24.95 (*0-8403-9351-2*) Kendall-Hunt.

— A Dream of Countries Where No One Dare Live: Stories. LC 93-24851. 160p. (Orig.). 1993. 19.95 (*0-87074-349-X*); pap. 9.95 (*0-87074-365-1*) SMU Press.

***Phillips, Louis.** Haunted House Jokes. 1999. pap. 3.99 (*0-14-130650-5*, PuffinBks) Peng Put Young Read.

Phillips, Louis. Hot Corner: Baseball Stories & Writing. unabridged ed. 160p. 1996. 21.95 (*0-942979-35-4*, 942979); pap. 11.95 (*0-942979-36-2*, 942979) Livingston U Pr.

— How to Tell if Your Parents Are Aliens. 80p. (J). 1994. pap. 3.50 (*0-380-77387-2*, Avon Bks) Morrow Avon.

— Monster Riddles. LC 96-47722. (Viking Easy-To-Read Ser.). (Illus.). 32p. (J). (gr. 1-4). 1998. pap. 3.99 (*0-14-038790-0*) Viking Penguin.

— Random House Treasury of Best-Loved Poem. 1996. pap. write for info. (*0-679-77703-2*) Random Ref & Info.

— Random House Treasury of Best Loved Poems. 2nd ed. LC 95-14513. 352p. 1995. pap. 10.00 (*0-679-76315-5*) Random Ref & Info.

— Random House Treasury of Humorous Verse. LC 99-11295. 1999. pap. 10.00 (*0-375-70588-0*) Random Ref & Info.

— Random House Treasury of Light Verse. 1996. pap. write for info. (*0-679-77704-0*) Random Ref & Info.

— School Daze: Jokes Your Teacher Will Hate. 1996. 9.19 (*0-606-09822-4*, Pub. by Turtleback) Demco.

— Simply Monsters. LC 96-47722. (Illus.). 32p. (ps-3). 1998. 13.89 (*0-670-87459-0*) Viking Penguin.

— Singer in the White Pajamas. 29p. 1991. pap. 3.50 (*0-87129-090-1*, S97) Dramatic Pub.

***Phillips, Louis.** Treasury of Humorous Quotations. 256p. 1999. pap. 7.95 (*0-375-70706-9*) Random Ref & Info.

Phillips, Louis. Two Hundred Sixty-Three Brain Busters: Just How Smart Are You, Anyway? LC 85-40446. (Novels Ser.). (Illus.). 87p. (J). (gr. 4-7). 1985. pap. 4.99 (*0-14-031875-5*, PuffinBks) Peng Put Young Read.

Phillips, Louis. Wackysauraus, Dinosaur Jokes. (Puffin Chapters Ser.). (J). 1997. 9.19 (*0-606-12042-4*, Pub. by Turtleback) Demco.

Phillips, Louis. Wackysaurus: Dinosaur Jokes. (Illus.). 64p. (J). (gr. 2-5). 1997. pap. 3.99 (*0-14-038648-3*) Viking Penguin.

Phillips, Louis & Holmes, Burnham. The Complete Book of Sports Nicknames. LC 98-38168. (Illus.). 352p. 1998. pap. 12.95 (*1-58063-037-5*) Renaissance.

— TV Almanac. LC 94-14094. (Illus.). 256p. 1994. per. 10.00 (*0-671-88798-X*) Macmillan.

Phillips, Louis, jt. auth. see Cole, William.

Phillips, Louis, jt. auth. see Howe, James.

Phillips, Louise. The First Leaf of Fall, Vol. 500. LC 96-60940. (Illus.). 40p. (Orig.) (J). (ps-3). 1996. pap. 6.95 (*1-883650-36-4*) Windswept Hse.

— The First Sunbeam of Summer, Vol. 500. LC 96-60939. (Illus.). 40p. (Orig.). (J). (ps-3). 1996. pap. 6.95 (*1-883650-35-6*) Windswept Hse.

— The First Tulip of Spring. LC 95-60704. (Illus.). 40p. (J). (ps up). 1995. pap. 6.95 (*1-883650-22-4*) Windswept Hse.

An Asterisk (*) at the beginning of an entry indicates that the title is appearing for the first time.

— Moving On! A Journey Through Sexual Assault. 1996. pap. text 14.95 (*1-86351-156-3*, Pub. by Sally Milner) Seven Hills Bk.
— We Are the Children of the Forest. Weinberger, Jane, ed. (Illus.). 48p. (J). (ps-4). 1997. 15.95 (*1-883650-42-9*) Windswept Hse.
Phillips, Louise, jt. auth. see Silver, Patricia.
Phillips, Louise S. The First Snowflake of Winter. LC 87-62210. (Illus.). 40p. (J). (ps up). 1996. pap. 6.95 (*0-932433-37-5*) Windswept Hse.
Phillips, Lucinda M., ed. see Tamayo, Reve, et al.
Phillips, Lynn. The Girls Report: What We Know & Need to Know about Growing up Female. National Council for Research on Women Staff, ed. 121p. 1998. pap. 20.00 (*1-880547-24-4*) Nat Coun Res Wom.
Phillips, Lynn, et al. Spinal Cord Injury: A Guide for Patient & Family. 320p. 1987. text 18.00 (*0-88167-274-2*); pap. text 18.00 (*0-88167-275-0*) Lppncott W & W.
— Spinal Cord Injury: A Guide for Patient & Family. LC 84-42866. (Illus.). 319p. reprint ed. pap. 98.90 (*0-608-09632-6*, 205440800007) Bks Demand.
Phillips, Lynn D. Manual of I. V. Therapeutics. 2nd ed. LC 96-40183. (Illus.). 644p. (C). 1997. pap. text 29.95 (*0-8036-0131-X*) Davis Co.
Phillips, Lynn D. & Kuhn, Marrily K. Manual of IV Medications. LC 95-21517. 700p. 1996. spiral bd. 29.95 (*0-316-70601-9*, Little Brwn Med Div) Lppncott W & W.
Phillips, Lynn D. & Kuhn, Merrily A. Manual of IV Medications. 2nd ed. LC 98-2987. 816p. 1998. spiral bd. 29.95 (*0-7817-1546-6*) Lppncott W & W.
Phillips, Lynn M. Flirting with Danger: Young Women's Reflections on Sexuality & Domination. 256p. 1999. text 55.00 (*0-8147-6657-9*); pap. text 19.00 (*0-8147-6658-7*) NYU Pr.
Phillips, Lynne, et al, eds. The Third Wave of Modernization in Latin America: Cultural Perspectives on Neoliberalism. LC 97-22853. (Jaguar Books on Latin America: No. 16). 226p. (C). 1997. 55.00 (*0-8420-2606-1*, SR Bks); pap. 18.95 (*0-8420-2608-8*, SR Bks) Scholarly Res Inc.
Phillips, Lynne, jt. ed. see Ilcan, Suzan.
Phillips, M. & Tomkinson, W. S. English Women in Life & Letters. LC 72-151974. (Illus.). 1972. reprint ed. 23.95 (*0-405-08856-6*) Ayer.
Phillips, M., jt. auth. see Dye, C.
Phillips, M. H., ed. Physical Aspects of Stereotactic Radiosurgery. (Illus.). 312p. (C). 1993. text 75.00 (*0-306-44535-2*, Kluwer Plenum) Kluwer Academic.
Phillips, M. J., jt. auth. see Ansell, J. I.
Phillips, M. J., jt. auth. see MacDonald, George.
Phillips, M. James. The Liver: An Atlas & Text of Ultrastructural Pathology. LC 87-43075. (Illus.). 600p. 1987. reprint ed. pap. 186.00 (*0-608-05874-2*, 205984100007) Bks Demand.
Phillips, M. T. & Sechzer, J. A. Animal Research & Ethical Conflict. (Illus.). 250p. 1989. 124.00 (*0-387-96935-7*, 2512) Spr-Verlag.
Phillips, Maberly, jt. auth. see Avery, Graham.
Phillips, Maggie & Frederick, Claire. Healing the Divided Self: Clinical & Ericksonian Hypnotherapy for Post-Traumatic & Dissociative Conditions. 384p. 1995. 40.00 (*0-393-70184-0*) Norton.
Phillips, Maggie, jt. auth. see Sturkie, Joan.
Phillips, Marcia & Porter, John, eds. Advances in Powder Metallurgy & Particulate Materials, 1995, 3 vols., Set. (Illus.). 2300p. (C). 1995. 560.00 (*1-878954-56-3*) Metal Powder.
Phillips, Marcus & Long, Sandra. Indian Folklore Atlas of Hot Springs National Park. (Illus.). 195p. (Orig.). 1994. pap. 25.00 (*0-929604-76-8*) Arkansas Ancestors.
Phillips, Margaret E. Letters to Barbara Bush. 152p. (Orig.). 1992. pap. 9.95 (*0-943487-38-2*) Sevgo Pr.
***Phillips, Margaret I.** The Governors of Tennessee. 2nd ed. LC 00-35960. 2000. pap. write for info. (*1-56554-826-4*) Pelican.
Phillips, Margaret M. Willingly to School. (C). 1989. text 35.00 (*0-948929-23-5*) St Mut.
Phillips, Margaret M., tr. see Erasmus, Desiderius.
Phillips, Maria C., tr. see Maccaferri, Elena.
Phillips, Marilyn, jt. auth. see Phillips, Mike.
Phillips, Marion. Colonial Autocracy: New South Wales under Governor Macquarie, 1810-1821. 336p. 1971. reprint ed. 35.00 (*0-7146-2658-9*, Pub. by F Cass Pubs) Intl Spec Bk.
Phillips, Marjorie. Duncan Phillips & His Collection. (Illus.). 1982. 35.00 (*0-393-01608-0*) Norton.
— Duncan Phillips & His Collection. (Illus.). 1982. pap. 18.95 (*0-393-30041-2*) Norton.
— Marjorie Phillips & Her Paintings. Partridge, Sylvia, ed. (Illus.). 1985. 35.00 (*0-393-02290-0*) Norton.
Phillips, Marjorie & Phillips, Robert. The Pioneer Squire Barker Family. rev. ed. LC 96-78966. (Illus.). vi, 70p. (Orig.). 1996. pap. write for info. (*0-9655473-0-2*) HARP Ent.
Phillips, Mark. Francesco Guicciardini: The Historian's Craft. LC 76-56341. 208p. reprint ed. pap. 64.50 (*0-608-17079-8*, 202643900049) Bks Demand.
— The Memoir of Marco Parenti: A Life in Medici Florence. LC 87-45533. 298p. 1987. reprint ed. pap. 92.40 (*0-608-07138-2*, 206736400009) Bks Demand.
***Phillips, Mark.** Society & Sentiment: Genres of Historical Writing in Britain, 1740-1820. LC 99-48753. 369p. 2000. 55.00 (*0-691-03179-7*, Pub. by Princeton U Pr) Cal Prin Full Svc.
Phillips, Mark. Trike Flyer's Manual, Vol. 1. (Illus.). iv, 42p. 1997. pap. text 11.95 (*0-9658271-1-9*) US Ultralight.
Phillips, Mark, ed. The Best of Quiet Riot (Guitar - Vocal) (Illus.). 63p. (Orig.). 1990. pap. text 12.95 (*0-89524-381-4*) Cherry Lane.
— Boston - Third Stage: Guitar Edition. (Illus.). 80p. (Orig.). 1990. pap. text 19.95 (*0-89524-334-2*) Cherry Lane.
— Faster Pussycat (Guitar - Vocal) (Illus.). 53p. (Orig.). 1990. pap. text 19.95 (*0-89524-399-7*) Cherry Lane.
— Guns n' Roses - Appetite for Destruction: Bass Guitar. (Illus.). (Orig.). 1990. pap. text 19.95 (*0-89524-416-0*, Pub. by Cherry Lane) H Leonard.
— Guns n' Roses - Appetite for Destruction: Guitar - Vocal. (Illus.). (Orig.). 1990. pap. text 14.95 (*0-89524-564-7*); pap. text 22.95 (*0-89524-386-5*, Pub. by Cherry Lane) H Leonard.
— Guns n' Roses - The Spaghetti Incident? 1994. pap. 22.95 (*0-89524-826-3*) Cherry Lane.
— Heavy Metal Ballads: Guitar - Vocal. (Illus.). 94p. (Orig.). 1990. pap. text 14.95 (*0-89524-446-2*) Cherry Lane.
— Heavy Metal Guitar, Vol. 3. (Illus.). 111p. (Orig.). 1990. pap. text 14.95 (*0-89524-389-X*) Cherry Lane.
— Heavy Metal in the Hot One Hundred: Guitar - Vocal. (Illus.). 126p. (Orig.). 1990. pap. text 14.95 (*0-89524-521-3*, Pub. by Cherry Lane) H Leonard.
— Heavy Metal Mixed Bag: Guitar Edition. (Illus.). 118p. (Orig.). 1990. pap. text 16.95 (*0-89524-470-5*) Cherry Lane.
— Hot Metal: Guitar Vocal. (Illus.). 126p. (Orig.). 1990. pap. text 14.95 (*0-89524-412-8*) Cherry Lane.
— Hot Metal (Guitar - Vocal), Vol. II. (Illus.). 111p. (Orig.). 1990. pap. text 14.95 (*0-89524-439-X*) Cherry Lane.
— Lita - Lita Ford (Guitar - Vocal) (Illus.). 51p. (Orig.). 1990. pap. text 19.95 (*0-89524-394-6*) Cherry Lane.
— The Love Songs of John Denver (Piano - Vocal) (Illus.). 79p. (Orig.). 1990. pap. text 9.95 (*0-89524-378-4*) Cherry Lane.
— Metallica - Master of Puppets: Guitar - Vocal. (Illus.). (Orig.). 1990. pap. text 19.95 (*0-89524-565-5*); pap. text 19.95 (*0-89524-358-X*, Pub. by Cherry Lane) H Leonard.
— Metallica - Master of Puppets (Bass Guitar) (Illus.). 55p. (Orig.). 1990. pap. text 19.95 (*0-89524-408-X*, Pub. by Cherry Lane) H Leonard.
— Metallica Riff by Riff: Guitar. 1994. pap. 17.95 (*0-89524-840-9*, Pub. by Cherry Lane) H Leonard.
— The Music of Richard Marx: Easy Guitar. (Illus.). 52p. (Orig.). 1990. pap. text 10.95 (*0-89524-500-0*) Cherry Lane.
— Overkill - The Years of Decay. (Play-It-Like-It-Is Guitar Ser.). pap. 19.95 (*0-89524-553-1*); pap. 14.95 (*0-89524-597-3*) Cherry Lane.
— Richard Daniels - Be Dangerous on Rock Guitar. (Illus.). 146p. (Orig.). 1990. pap. text 18.95 (*0-89524-314-8*, Pub. by Cherry Lane) H Leonard.
— Rock Guitar. (Illus.). 93p. (Orig.). 1990. pap. text 10.95 (*0-89524-371-7*) Cherry Lane.
— Tesla - Mechanical Resonance: Bass Guitar. (Illus.). 71p. (Orig.). 1990. pap. text 14.95 (*0-89524-429-2*) Cherry Lane.
— Tesla - Mechanical Resonance: Guitar - Vocal. (Illus.). 70p. (Orig.). 1990. pap. text 19.95 (*0-89524-393-8*) Cherry Lane.
— Van Halen Live - Right Here, Right Now. 1994. pap. 29.95 (*0-89524-787-9*) Cherry Lane.
Phillips, Mark, et al, eds. America Takes Note: Official Menc Songbook: Piano - Vocal. (Illus.). 112p. (Orig.). (YA). 1988. pap. text 14.95 (*0-89524-369-5*) Cherry Lane.
Phillips, Mark & Aledort, Andy, eds. Heavy Metal Guitar, Vol. 2. (Illus.). 118p. (Orig.). 1990. pap. text 14.95 (*0-89524-356-3*) Cherry Lane.
Phillips, Mark & Chappell, Jon. Guitar for Dummies. LC MT580.P45 1998. (For Dummies Ser.). 384p. 1998. pap. 24.99 incl. audio compact disk (*0-7645-5106-X*) IDG Bks.
— Piano for Dummies: A Reference for the Rest of Us! (For Dummies Ser.). 368p. 1998. pap. 24.99 incl. audio compact disk (*0-7645-5105-1*) IDG Bks.
Phillips, Mark & Garcia, Frank. Science Fiction Television Series: Episode Guides, Histories, & Casts & Credits for 62 Prime Time Shows, 1959-1989. LC 95-47667. (Illus.). 703p. 1996. lib. bdg. 85.00 (*0-7864-0041-2*) McFarland & Co.
Phillips, Mark & Marshall, Wolf, eds. Ozzy Osbourne - Randy Rhoads Tribute: Guitar - Vocal. (Illus.). 127p. (Orig.). 1990. pap. text 22.95 (*0-89524-347-4*, Pub. by Cherry Lane) H Leonard.
Phillips, Mark & Okun, Milton, eds. Bruce Hornsby & the Range - Scenes from the Southside (Piano - Vocal) (Illus.). 63p. (Orig.). 1990. pap. text 12.95 (*0-89524-385-7*) Cherry Lane.
Phillips, Mark, jt. auth. see O'Brien, Cathy.
Phillips, Mark, ed. see Burgie, Irving.
Phillips, Mark, jt. ed. see Chappell, Jon.
Phillips, Mark, ed. see Guns N' Roses.
***Phillips, Mark A.** Secrets & Lies: My Journey to Enlightenment. 272p. 1999. pap. 12.95 (*0-9674433-7-7*) Wadena Hse.
Phillips, Mark M., jt. ed. see Blanco, Victor M.
Phillips, Marshall, et al, eds. The Impact of Chemistry on Biotechnology: Multidisciplinary Discussions. LC 87-30751. (Symposium Ser.: No. 362). (Illus.). xiii, 398p. 1987. 87.95 (*0-8412-1446-8*) Am Chemical.
— The Impact of Chemistry on Biotechnology: Multidisciplinary Discussions. LC 87-30751. (ACS Symposium Ser.: Vol. 362). 429p. 1988. reprint ed. pap. 133.00 (*0-608-03884-9*, 206433100008) Bks Demand.
Phillips, Marshall, jt. ed. see Jorgenson, James W.
Phillips, Martin A. The Official National Table Hockey League Handbook, Vol. 1. Phillips, Zoe A., ed. LC 89-91696. (Illus.). 66p. (Orig.). (YA). (gr. 12). 1989. write for info. (*0-9623588-0-0*); pap. write for info. (*0-9623588-1-9*) Gnu Wine Pr.
Phillips, Marty J. The Edge: A Novel of Living on It. 432p. 1996. 12.95 (*0-89754-099-9*) Dan River Pr.
Phillips, Marvin. Never Lick a Frozen Flagpole! More! Humorous Insights That Motivate & Encourage. LC 98-56642. (Illus.). 224p. 1999. pap. 10.99 (*1-58229-009-1*) Howard Pub LA.
— Never Lick a Moving Blender! Humorous Insights That Motivate & Encourage. gif. ed. (Illus.). 215p. 1996. pap. 10.99 (*1-878990-58-6*) Howard Pub LA.
Phillips, Mary. Learn, Grow & Change: Creating Openness to Change & Inclusive Community Involvement. (Changing The Paradigm Organizational Effectiveness Ser.: Vol. 5). 30p. 1996. pap. write for info. (*1-58534-014-6*) Points of Light.
— U-DECIDE Cards. 1998. boxed set 9.95 (*0-9667464-0-6*) Yellow Brick Pubg.
Phillips, Mary, jt. auth. see MacKenzie, Judith-Anne.
Phillips, Mary W. Creative Knitting. LC 72-110061. 1986. pap. 16.00 (*0-932394-06-X*) Dos Tejedoras.
— Knitting Counterpanes: Traditional Coverlet Patterns for Contemporary Knitters. Timmons, Christine, ed. LC 88-51354. (Illus.). 192p. 1989. pap. 19.95 (*0-918804-98-1*, 070068) Taunton.
Phillips-Matz, Mary J. Rosa Ponselle: American Diva. LC 97-19825. (Illus.). 320p. 1997. text 29.95 (*1-55553-317-5*) NE U Pr.
— Verdi: A Biography. (Illus.). 972p. 1996. reprint ed. pap. text 22.50 (*0-19-816600-1*) OUP.
***Phillips-Matz, Mary Jane.** Leonard Warren: American Baritone. LC 99-40444. (Opera Biography Ser.: Vol. 13). (Illus.). 478p. 2000. 39.95 (*1-57467-053-0*, Amadeus Pr) Timber.
Phillips, Maureen M., jt. auth. see Miller, Jeffrey M.
Phillips, Maurice E. Guide to the Manuscript Collections in the Academy of Natural Sciences of Philadelphia. (Special Publication: No. 5). (Illus.). 553p. 1963. lib. bdg. 10.00 (*0-910006-33-4*) Acad Nat Sci Phila.
Phillips, Maurice E., ed. Minutes & Correspondence of the Academy of Natural Sciences of Philadelphia: 1812-1924, Microfilm Publication Guide. (Special Publication: No. 7). 92p. (Orig.). 1967. pap. 5.00 (*0-910006-35-0*) Acad Nat Sci Phila.
Phillips, Maverick. Come West with Me: Trivia, Truth & Spoof. unabridged ed. (Illus.). viii, 87p. (Orig.). 1996. pap. 14.00 (*0-9655773-0-9*, 1) M E Phillips.
Phillips, Max. A.M. A Novel. 1999. write for info. (*0-316-70604-3*) Little.
Phillips, Maya. Emotional Excellence: A Course in Self-Mastery. LC 97-26611. (Illus.). 224p. 1997. 24.95 (*1-86204-112-1*, Pub. by Element MA) Penguin Putnam.
— Emotional Excellence: A Practical Guide to Self-Discovery. (Illus.). 224p. 1999. pap. 16.95 (*1-86204-374-4*, Pub. by Element MA) Penguin Putnam.
Phillips, Maya & Comfort, Max. The A to Zen of Life Maintenance: Mapping the Emotional Mind. LC 96-897. 160p. 1996. pap. 12.95 (*1-85230-810-9*, Pub. by Element MA) Penguin Putnam.
Phillips, McCandlish. The Bible, the Supernatural & the Jew. 368p. 1995. pap. 11.99 (*0-88965-115-9*, Pub. by Horizon Books) Chr Pubns.
Phillips-McClenahan, Sallie. Touchstones. LC 82-11454. (Illus.). 300p. (Orig.). 1982. pap. 8.95 (*0-87233-066-4*) Bauhan.
Phillips, Megen, ed. see Whitney, Lyman.
Phillips, Melanie, jt. auth. see Dawson, John.
Phillips, Melba, ed. The Life & Times of Modern Physics: History of Physics II. LC 92-12669. (Readings from Physics Today Ser.: No. 4). 1992. 44.95 (*0-88318-846-5*) Spr-Verlag.
— On Teaching Physics. 192p. 1980. per. 24.00 (*0-917853-77-6*, OP-17) Am Assn Physics.
— Physics History from AAPT Journals. 240p. 1985. per. 23.00 (*0-917853-14-8*, OP-54) Am Assn Physics.
Phillips, Melba & Weart, Spencer R., intros. History of Physics. LC 85-70236. (Readings from Physics Today Ser.). (Illus.). 384p. (Orig.). 1987. pap. 49.95 (*0-88318-468-0*, R-315.1) Spr-Verlag.
Phillips, Melicia, jt. auth. see Waltuck, David.
Phillips, Melicia, jt. auth. see Waltuck, David.
Phillips, Meredith, jt. ed. see Jencks, Christopher.
Phillips, Mervyn. Wales: Nation & Region. 1997. pap. 23.95 (*0-8464-4594-8*) Beekman Pubs.
— Wales: Nation & Region. 1997. pap. 30.00 (*1-85902-423-8*, Pub. by Gomer Pr) St Mut.
Phillips, Michael. Alternative Man: Poems & Stories by Michael Phillips. 1995. pap. 8.95 (*0-9636829-5-4*) Mother Road.
***Phillips, Michael.** An Ancient Strife. LC 00-8584. (Caledonia Ser.). 544p. 2000. 19.99 (*0-7642-2354-2*); pap. 13.99 (*0-7642-2218-X*) Bethany Hse.
Phillips, Michael. The Apple Grower: A Guide for the Organic Orchardist. LC 98-3631. (Illus.). 300p. 1998. pap. 35.00 (*1-890132-04-7*) Chelsea Green Pub.
— Braxtons of Miracle Springs. LC 96-25227. (Journals of Corrie & Christopher). 272p. 1996. pap. 9.99 (*1-55661-635-X*) Bethany Hse.
— Caledonia: An Epic Novel of Scotland. 512p. 1996. 19.99 (*0-345-39564-6*, Moorings) Ballantine Pub Grp.
— Dawn of Liberty. LC 95-14556. (Secret of the Rose Ser.: Vol. 4). 605p. 1995. pap. 11.99 (*0-8423-5958-3*) Tyndale Hse.
— Disarming Anti-Japanese Prejudice: A Guide for Japanese Businesses. LC 97-146608. 204p. (Orig.). 1996. pap. 25.00 (*0-931425-31-X*) Clear Glass.
— Discourses: More Readings for Thinkers on Airplanes. Speer, Tom, ed. LC 89-92418. (Illus.). 142p. (Orig.). 1990. pap. 10.00 (*0-931425-19-0*) Clear Glass.
— The Eleventh Hour. LC 93-4858. (Secret of the Rose Ser.: Vol. 1). 504p. 1993. pap. 7.99 (*0-8423-3933-7*) Tyndale Hse.
— Escape to Freedom. LC 94-23235. (The Secret of the Rose Ser.: No. 3). 487p. 1994. pap. 11.99 (*0-8423-5942-7*) Tyndale Hse.
— The Garden at the Edge of Beyond. 16p. 1998. text 11.99 (*0-7642-2042-X*) Bethany Hse.
— Gods of Commerce: How Business Really Works. 128p. (Orig.). 1997. pap. 45.00 (*0-931425-03-4*) Clear Glass.
— Grayfox. 34p. 1993. pap. 9.99 (*1-55661-368-7*) Bethany Hse.
— Grayfox. 34p. 1997. text 14.99 (*1-55661-950-2*) Bethany Hse.
***Phillips, Michael.** Heathersleigh Homecoming. 3. LC 99-6750. (Secrets of Heathersleigh Hall Ser.). 432p. 1999. pap. 12.99 (*0-7642-2045-4*) Bethany Hse.
— Heathersleigh Homecoming. 3. LC 99-6750. (Secrets of Heathersleigh Hall Ser.). 432p. 1999. 17.99 (*0-7642-2237-6*) Bethany Hse.
Phillips, Michael. Home for My Heart. LC 94-4893. (Journals of Corrie Belle Hollister: Vol. 8). 32p. 1994. pap. 9.99 (*1-55661-440-3*) Bethany Hse.
— Into the Long Dark Night. (Journals of Corrie Belle Hollister: Vol. 6). 34p. (Orig.). 1992. pap. 9.99 (*1-55661-300-8*) Bethany Hse.
— Land of the Brave & the Free. (Corrie Belle Hollister Ser.: Vol. 7). 32p. (Orig.). (J). 1993. pap. 9.99 (*1-55661-308-3*) Bethany Hse.
— Legend of the Celtic Stone. LC 99-6432. (Caledonia Ser.). 576p. 1999. pap. 13.99 (*0-7642-2217-1*) Bethany Hse.
***Phillips, Michael.** Legend of the Celtic Stone. No. 1. 576p. 1999. 19.99 (*0-7642-2250-3*) Bethany Hse.
Phillips, Michael. Mental Snacks: Readings for Thinkers on Airplanes. 2nd ed. LC 87-72261. (Illus.). 152p. 1988. pap. 10.00 (*0-931425-12-3*) Clear Glass.
— A New Beginning. LC 96-45914. (Journals of Corrie & Christopher: No. 2). 24p. 1997. pap. 9.99 (*1-55661-933-2*) Bethany Hse.
— On the Trail of the Truth. large type ed. 450p. 1995. 21.95 (*0-7838-1490-9*, G K Hall Lrg Type) Mac Lib Ref.
— On the Trail of Truth No. 3: The Journal of Corrie Belle Hollister. 32p. (Orig.). 1991. pap. 9.99 (*1-55661-106-4*) Bethany Hse.
— A Place in the Sun: The Journals of Corrie Belle Hollister, Bk. 4. large type ed. 448p. 1996. 23.95 (*0-7838-1702-9*, G K Hall Lrg Type) Mac Lib Ref.
— A Rift in Time. LC 97-24138. (Secret of the Rose Ser.). 1997. 12.99 (*0-8423-5525-1*) Tyndale Hse.
— A Rift in Time. 2000. 12.99 (*0-8423-5500-6*) Tyndale Hse.
— A Rose Remembered. LC 94-4351. (Secret of the Rose Ser.: Vol. 2). 576p. 1994. pap. 11.99 (*0-8423-5929-X*) Tyndale Hse.
***Phillips, Michael.** Secrets of Heatherleigh Hall Mix. 1999. pap. text 38.99 (*0-7642-8555-6*) Bethany Hse.
Phillips, Michael. The Seven Laws of Money. LC 99-203290. 128p. 1997. pap. 10.95 (*1-57062-277-9*, Pub. by Shambhala Pubns) Random.
— Stonewycke Legacy, 3 vols. in 1. 720p. 1997. 12.99 (*0-88486-169-4*, Bristol Park Bks) Arrowood Pr.
— The Stonewycke Trilogy, 3 vols. in 1. 640p. 1996. 12.98 (*0-88486-133-3*) Arrowood Pr.
— To Be a Father Like the Father: Modeling the Fatherly Attributes of God. LC 91-76511. 309p. 1996. pap. 10.99 (*0-87509-475-9*) Chr Pubns.
— Wayward Winds. LC 99-6577. (Secrets of Heathersleigh Hall Ser.). 432p. 1999. pap. 12.99 (*0-7642-2044-6*); text 16.99 (*0-7642-2082-9*) Bethany Hse.
— Wild Grows the Heather in Devon. LC 97-33862. (Secrets of Heathersleigh Hall Ser.). 448p. 1998. pap. 12.99 (*0-7642-2043-8*) Bethany Hse.
***Phillips, Michael.** William Blake: The Creation of the Songs from Manuscript to Illuminated Painting. (Illus.). 160p. 2000. 55.00 (*0-691-05720-6*); pap. 29.95 (*0-691-05721-4*) Princeton U Pr.
Phillips, Michael & Campbell, Catherine. Simple Living Investments: For True Security & Adventure in Old Age. rev. ed. LC 84-71943. 72p. 1988. pap. 6.00 (*0-931425-00-X*) Clear Glass.
Phillips, Michael & Pella, Judith. The Crown & the Crucible. (Russians Ser.: Bk. 1). 416p. (Orig.). 1991. pap. 10.99 (*1-55661-172-2*) Bethany Hse.
— Daughter of Grace. (Journals of Corrie Belle Hollister: Bk. 2). 34p. 1990. pap. 9.99 (*1-55661-105-6*) Bethany Hse.
— Daughter of Grace. large type ed. 376p. 1995. 21.95 (*0-7838-1179-9*, G K Hall Lrg Type) Mac Lib Ref.
— A House Divided. (Russians Ser.: Vol. 2). 352p. (Orig.). 1992. pap. 10.99 (*1-55661-173-0*) Bethany Hse.
— My Father's World. (Journals of Corrie Belle Hollister: No. 1). 288p. 1990. pap. 9.99 (*1-55661-104-8*) Bethany Hse.
— My Father's World. large type ed. LC 94-14261. 366p. 1994. lib. bdg. 20.95 (*0-8161-5994-7*, G K Hall Lrg Type) Mac Lib Ref.
— A Place in the Sun. LC 91-4987. (Journals of Corrie Belle Hollister: Bk. 4). 34p. (Orig.). 1991. pap. 9.99 (*1-55661-222-2*) Bethany Hse.
— Sea to Shining Sea. (Journals of Corrie Belle Hollister: Vol. 5). 32p. (Orig.). (J). 1992. pap. 9.99 (*1-55661-227-3*) Bethany Hse.
***Phillips, Michael & Pella, Judith.** The Stonewycke Legacy. 624p. 2000. pap. 12.99 (*0-7642-2377-1*) Bethany Hse.
Phillips, Michael & Pella, Judith. Travail & Triumph. (Russians Ser.: Vol. 3). 4p. (Orig.). 1992. pap. 10.99 (*1-55661-174-9*) Bethany Hse.
Phillips, Michael & Phillips, Judy. Good Things to Remember. 176p. (Orig.). 1993. pap. 5.99 (*1-55661-337-7*) Bethany Hse.
Phillips, Michael & Rasberry, Salli. Marketing Without Advertising. 2nd rev. ed. LC 96-50111. (Illus.). 240p. 1997. pap. 19.00 (*0-87337-369-3*) Nolo com.
Phillips, Michael, et al. Business Law & the Regulatory Environment. 9th ed. 336p. (C). 1994. text, student ed., wbk. ed. 26.87 (*0-256-17738-4*, Irwn McGrw-H) McGrw-H Hghr Educ.

An Asterisk (*) at the beginning of an entry indicates that the title is appearing for the first time.

— Business Law & the Regulatory Environment: Concepts & Cases. 8th ed. 832p. 1993. text 41.95 (*0-7863-0038-8*, Irwn McGrw-H) McGrw-H Hghr Educ.
— Business Law & the Regulatory Environment - College of Charleston: Concepts & Cases. 8th ed. (C). 1992. text 38.95 (*0-256-12138-9*, Irwn McGrw-H) McGrw-H Hghr Educ.
Phillips, Michael, jt. auth. see Callenbach, A. Ernest.
Phillips, Michael, jt. auth. see MacDonald, George.
Phillips, Michael, ed. see Connor, Ralph.
Phillips, Michael, ed. see MacDonald, George.
Phillips, Michael, tr. see Sa'edi, Gholamboseyn.
Phillips, Michael D., ed. Belize: Selected Proceedings from the Second Interdisciplinary Conference. 216p. (C). 1996. lib. bdg. 39.50 (*0-7618-0246-0*) U Pr of Amer.
Phillips, Michael E., jt. auth. see Ohanian, Thomas A.
Phillips, Michael J. The Dilemmas of Individualism: Status, Liberty, & American Constitutional Law, 67. LC 82-15580. (Contributions in American Studies: No. 67). 226p. 1983. 59.95 (*0-313-23690-9*, PSF/, Greenwood Pr) Greenwood.
— Dreamgirls. (Poetry Ser.). (Illus.). 80p. (Orig.). 1989. pap. 7.00 (*0-918342-27-9*) Cambric.
— Ethics & Manipulation in Advertising: Answering a Flawed Indictment. LC 96-40911. 224p. 1997. 55.00 (*1-56720-063-X*, Quorum Bks) Greenwood.
***Phillips, Michael J.** The Lochner Court, Myth & Reality: Substantive Due Process from the 1890s to the 1930s. LC 00-29848. 264p. 2000. 64.00 (*0-275-96930-4*, Praeger Pubs) Greenwood.
Phillips, Michael J. Selected Concrete Poems. (Cambric Poetry Ser.). 108p. (Orig.). 1986. pap. 11.95 (*0-918342-25-2*) Cambric.
— Superbeuts. 64p. (Orig.). 1983. pap. 5.00 (*0-918342-19-8*) Cambric.
Phillips, Michael J., jt. auth. see Fisher, Bruce D.
Phillips, Michael K. & Smith, Douglas W. The Wolves of Yellowstone. LC 96-14286. (Illus.). 112p. 1996. 12.95 (*0-89658-330-9*) Voyageur Pr.
— The Wolves of Yellowstone. (Illus.). 128p. 1998. pap. 19.95 (*0-89658-391-0*) Voyageur Pr.
Phillips, Michael R. Flight from Stonewycke. (Stonewycke Trilogy Ser.). 288p. 1994. mass mkt. 5.99 (*1-55661-453-5*) Bethany Hse.
— Garden at the Edge of Beyond. LC 98-51857. 1999. 24.95 (*0-7838-8515-6*) Macmillan Gen Ref.
***Phillips, Michael R.** Hidden in Time, 6. LC 98-48042. (Secret of the Rose Ser.). 2000. pap. text 12.99 (*0-8423-5501-4*) Tyndale Hse.
Phillips, Michael R. Mercy & Eagleflight. LC 96-9793. 1996. pap. 10.99 (*0-8423-3920-5*) Tyndale Hse.
Phillips, Michael R. & Pella, Judith. Shadows over Stonewycke. LC 88-10332. (Stonewycke Legacy Fiction Ser.: Vol. 2). 4p. (Orig.). 1988. pap. 9.99 (*0-87123-901-9*) Bethany Hse.
— Shadows over Stonewycke. (Stonewycke Legacy Ser.: Bk. 2). 464p. (Orig.). 1995. mass mkt. 6.99 (*1-55661-632-5*) Bethany Hse.
***Phillips, Michael R. & Pella, Judith.** The Stonewycke Trilogy. LC 99-50411. (Illus.). 630p. 1999. pap. 12.99 (*0-7642-2324-0*) Bethany Hse.
Phillips, Michael R. & Pella, Judith. Treasure of Stonewycke. (Stonewycke Legacy Ser.). 4p. (Orig.). 1988. pap. 9.99 (*0-87123-902-7*) Bethany Hse.
Phillips, Michael R. & Phillips, Judy. Best Friends for Life. LC 96-45910. 24p. 1997. pap. 9.99 (*1-55661-943-X*) Bethany Hse.
Phillips, Michael R., jt. auth. see MacDonald, George.
Phillips, Michael R., jt. auth. see Wright, Harold Bell.
Phillips, Michael R., ed. see Connor, Ralph.
Phillips, Michael R., ed. see MacDonald, George.
Phillips, Michael R., ed. see Wright, Harold Bell.
Phillips, Mike. The Coat Holder. LC 84-24251. 1986. 13.95 (*0-87949-248-1*) Ashley Bks.
— Control Through Planned Budgeting: An Alternative Approach to Inventory Control & Ordering Procedures in the Christian Bookstore. 1978. pap. 12.95 (*0-940652-01-3*) Sunrise Bks.
— Image to Die For: A Sam Dean Mystery. LC 96-47575. 1997. 22.95 (*0-312-15147-0*) St Martin.
— A Vision for the Church. 110p. 1981. pap. 3.95 (*0-940652-02-1*) Sunrise Bks.
***Phillips, Mike.** Windrush. 1998. 35.00 (*0-00-255909-9*, Pub. by HarpC) Trafalgar.
Phillips, Mike & Phillips, Marilyn. Gifta for Livet. Smedberg, Jan-Olaf, tr. from ENG. (SWE.). 195p. (Orig.). 1994. pap. text. write for info. (*1-884794-09-2*) Eden Pubng.
Phillips, Mike, ed. see MacDonald, George.
Phillips, Mildred. And the Cow Said Moo! LC 99-14356. (Illus.). 24p. (J). (ps-3). 2000. lib. bdg. 15.89 (*0-688-16803-5*, Grenwillow Bks) HarpC Child Bks.
***Phillips, Mildred.** And the Cow Said Moo! LC 99-14356. (Illus.). 24p. (J). (ps-3). 2000. 15.95 (*0-688-16802-7*, Grenwillow Bks) HarpC Child Bks.
Phillips, Mildred. The Sign in Mendel's Window. (Aladdin Picture Bks.). 1996. 11.19 (*0-606-11842-X*, Pub. by Turtleback) Demco.
— The Sign Is Mendel's Window. (Illus.). 32p. (J). (gr. k-3). 1996. per. 5.99 (*0-689-80979-4*) S&S Childrens.
Phillips-Miles, K. Dictionary of Finance English-Spanish. (ENG & SPA.). 162p. 1994. pap. 25.00 (*1-897762-05-4*, Pub. by AMCD) IBD Ltd.
Phillips, Mobi Warren, ed. see Underwood, Paula.
***Phillips, Murray.** From Sidelines to Centre Field: A History of Sports Coaching in Australia. (Illus.). 192p. 2000. pap. 29.95 (*0-86840-410-1*, Pub. by NSW U Pr) Intl Spec Bk.
Phillips, Myfawny, jt. auth. see Lorimer, James.
Phillips, Myfawny, jt. auth. see Lorimer, Jmaes.
***Phillips, Myrna.** Forgiveness Who Needs It? 2000. pap. text 5.99 (*0-8272-9044-6*) Chalice Pr.
Phillips, N. C. Equivariant K-Theory & Freeness of Group Actions on C Algebras. (Lecture Notes in Mathematics Ser.: Vol. 1274). viii, 371p. 1987. 52.95 (*0-387-18277-2*) Spr-Verlag.
Phillips, N. Christopher, jt. auth. see Lin, Huaxin.
Phillips, Nancy. Johnny Appleseed. (Literature Unit Ser.). (Illus.). 48p. 1995. pap., teacher ed. 7.95 (*1-55734-536-8*) Tchr Create Mat.
Phillips, Nancy, ed. see Miller, O. Victor.
Phillips, Nancy H. Choosing Schools & Child Care Options: Answering Parents' Questions. LC 94-19163. (Illus.). 112p. (C). 1994. 36.95 (*0-398-05923-3*); pap. 24.95 (*0-398-05969-1*) C C Thomas.
— Mallwalker Wisdom: It's Good for Your Heart. LC 97-94494. 240p. 1997. pap. 7.95 (*0-9660466-1-7*) A&R Assocs.
Phillips, Nancy Hopkins, see Hopkins, Margaret L.
Phillips, Nancy Hopkins, see Lail Hopkins, Margaret & Hopkins Phillips, Nancy.
Phillips, Nancy O., compiled by. Town Records of Derby, 1655-1710. 496p. 1997. reprint ed. lib. bdg. 52.50 (*0-8328-5635-5*) Higginson Bk Co.
Phillips, Nancy O., ed. see Parsons, Richard & Brooks, Neal A.
Phillips, Nancy V., et al. Network Models in Optimization & Their Applications in Practice. LC 91-41110. (Wiley-Interscience Series in Discrete Mathematics & Optimization). 304p. 1992. 109.95 (*0-471-57138-5*) Wiley.
***Phillips, Nicky.** E-motional Business. 300p. 2000. pap. text 24.00 (*0-273-65019-X*) Financial Times VA.
Phillips, Nicola. Motivating for Change: Coaching & Motivating Your Team. (Institute of Management Ser.). 250p. 1995. pap. 48.50 (*0-273-61176-3*, Pub. by Pitman Pub) Trans-Atl Phila.
— Reality Hacking: Unusual Ideas & Provocations for Reinventing Your Work, 1. 1999. pap. text 16.95 (*1-900961-10-5*) Capstone Pub NH.
— Smart Things to Know About Influencing. 1999. pap. text 16.95 (*1-84112-065-0*) Capstone Pub NH.
Phillips, Norma. Adventures of a "Wild" Plants Woman: In Pursuit of Native Plant Preservation. LC 88-51160. (Illus.). 236p. (Orig.). (C). 1988. pap. text 12.95 (*0-9622758-1-6*) Little Bridge.
— Let's Get to Work: A Collection of Ideas & Proposals. 25p. (Orig.). 1996. mass mkt. 3.00 (*0-9622758-2-4*) Little Bridge.
— The Root Book: How to Plant Wildflowers. LC 83-91289. (Illus.). 118p. (Orig.). (C). 1983. spiral bd. 9.50 (*0-9622758-0-8*) Little Bridge.
Phillips, Norma K. & Straussner, Shulamith L., eds. Children in the Urban Environment: Linking Social Policy & Clinical Practice. LC 96-23906. (Illus.). 258p. (Orig.). 1996. text 60.95 (*0-398-06707-4*); pap. text 46.95 (*0-398-06708-2*) C C Thomas.
Phillips, O. M. Flow & Reactions in Permeable Rocks. (Illus.). 295p. (C). 1991. text 74.95 (*0-521-38098-7*) Cambridge U Pr.
Phillips, O. M. & Hasselmann, Klaus, eds. Wave Dynamics & Radio Probing of the Ocean Surface. 687p. 1986. 135.00 (*0-306-41992-0*, Plenum Trade) Perseus Pubng.
Phillips, O. S. Isaac Nathan: Jewish Musician & Friend of Byron. 1976. lib. bdg. 34.95 (*0-8490-2078-6*) Gordon Pr.
Phillips, O. Virginia. Ashes to Life. Snell, Mikki, ed. (Illus.). 103p. (Orig.). 1994. lib. bdg. 14.95 (*0-9641507-0-0*) Fmily Connect.
— Sure You Fit In. (Illus.). 200p. 1998. 15.00 (*0-9641507-1-9*) Fmily Connect.
Phillips, Oliver. The God of a Second Chance. 90p. (Orig.). 1996. pap. 9.95 (*1-57502-281-8*, P0984) Morris Pubng.
Phillips, Osborne, jt. auth. see Denning, Melita.
Phillips, Owen, jt. auth. see Maurice, Charles S.
Phillips, P. & Moutinho, L. Strategic Planning Systems in Hospitality & Tourism. LC 98-22772. (CAB International Publication Ser.). 250p. 1998. text 70.00 (*0-85199-286-2*) OUP.
Phillips, P. Lee. A List of Books, Magazine Articles & Maps Relating to Central America. 109p. 1984. reprint ed. pap. 12.50 (*0-913129-11-9*) La Tienda.
— Maps & Views of Washington & District of Columbia. 2nd ed. LC 97-119747. (Illus.). 87p. 1996. reprint ed. text, lib. bdg. 45.00 (*0-9649000-2-5*, T Nova Pr) G B Manasek.
— Notes on the Life & Works of Bernard Romans. Ware, John, ed. LC 74-20757. (Floridiana Facsimile & Reprint Ser.). (Illus.). 138p. 1975. reprint ed. 19.95 (*0-8130-0413-6*) U Press Fla.
Phillips, Paige. A Stranger's Wife. (Intrigue Ser.: No. 508). 1999. per. 3.99 (*0-373-22508-3*, 1-22508-5) Harlequin Bks.
— The Tender Hours. (Intrigue Ser.). 1996. per. 3.75 (*0-373-22372-2*, 1-22372-6) Harlequin Bks.
Phillips, Pamela I. When the Moon Peeps In. (J). 1994. 7.95 (*0-533-10982-5*) Vantage.
Phillips, Pamela M. Fashion Promotion: Sales & Advertising Behind the Selling. 2nd rev. ed. LC 95-36919. Orig. Title: Fashion Sales Promotion. 225p. 1995. 42.80 (*0-13-362799-3*) P-H.
***Phillips, Pat.** Invitation to Danger. large type ed. LC 00-23443. 174p. 2000. 19.95 (*0-7862-2592-0*) Thorndike Pr.
Phillips, Pat. Love Waits at Penrhyn. large type ed. LC 97-36278. (Candlelights Ser.). 217p. 1997. lib. bdg. 18.95 (*0-7862-1240-3*) Thorndike Pr.
— Mediterranean Adventure. LC 98-31302. 200p. 1999. write for info. (*0-7540-3628-6*) Chivers N Amer.
— Mediterranean Adventure. large type ed. LC 98-31302. 1999. 30.00 (*0-7838-0414-8*, G K Hall Lrg Type) Mac Lib Ref.
— Memories of Mama. 50p. 1998. pap. text 12.00 (*1-889745-04-9*) Triangle Publctns.
Phillips, Patricia. Fabulous Fry Pan Favorites. (Illus.). 160p. 1984. 21.99 (*0-9654108-1-1*) Ntl Presto Ind.
— The Rose of Ravenscrag. 368p. (Orig.). 1996. pap. text 4.99 (*0-8439-3905-2*) Dorchester Pub Co.
***Phillips, Patricia.** The Sword & the Flame. 320p. 2000. mass mkt. 4.99 (*0-8439-4726-8*, Leisure Bks) Dorchester Pub Co.
Phillips, Patricia, ed. City Speculations. LC 97-208521. (Illus.). 112p. (Orig.). 1997. pap. 17.95 (*1-56898-077-9*) Princeton Arch.
Phillips, Patricia & Mair, George. Divorce: A Guide for Women: What Every Woman Needs to Know about Getting a Fair Divorce Even When She Thinks She Doesn't Need to Know It. LC 95-5872. 1995. pap. 15.00 (*0-671-50057-0*) Macmillan.
— Divorce: A Woman's Guide to Getting A Fair Share. LC 95-5872. 256p. 1995. 15.95 (*0-02-860344-3*, Arc) IDG Bks.
— Know Your Rights: Legal Handbook for Women. LC 96-79996. 272p. 1997. 16.95 (*0-02-861696-0*, Arc) IDG Bks.
Phillips, Patricia A. Something in Common. 460p. 1999. pap. 14.95 (*1-881524-46-9*) Milligan Bks.
Phillips, Patricia C. Jackie Ferrara: Traversing Space. Nesbitt, Perry L., ed. & intro. by. (Illus.). 6p. (Orig.). 1993. pap. 20.00 (*0-941972-13-5*) Freedman.
Phillips, Patricia P. Greenup County, Kentucky: Naturalizations, Rev. War Pensions, Lunacy Inquests, 1804-1902. 182p. (Orig.). 1995. pap. text 17.00 (*0-7884-0243-9*) Heritage Bk.
— Greenup County, Kentucky Will Abstracts, 1822-1860. LC 99-187300. 320p. 1999. pap. 28.00 (*0-7884-1071-7*, P333) Heritage Bk.
Phillips, Patricia S. Life in Illisconsin, 1927-1951. (Illus.). 224p. (Orig.). 1995. pap. 9.95 (*0-9647032-0-3*) Whispering Pn.
Phillips, Patrick L. Developing with Recreational Amenities: Golf, Tennis, Skiing, & Marinas. LC 86-61896. 257p. 1986. pap. 56.95 (*0-87420-664-2*, D44) Urban Land.
Phillips, Paul, jt. auth. see Ferfila, Bogomil.
Phillips, Paul G., jt. auth. see Phillips, Joyce B.
Phillips, Paul J., jt. auth. see Boyd, Richard H.
Phillips, Paul S., et al. The Stenter's Notebook. (Illus.). 226p. (C). Date not set. pap. text 39.95 (*1-890114-06-5*) Physicians Pr.
Phillips, Paul T. A Kingdom on Earth: Anglo-American Social Christianity, 1880-1940. LC 95-14590. 328p. 1996. 65.00 (*0-271-01497-0*); pap. 18.95 (*0-271-01580-2*) Pa St U Pr.
***Phillips, Peggy.** A Golden Sorrow. LC 99-91578. 2000. 25.00 (*0-7388-0900-4*); pap. 18.00 (*0-7388-0901-2*) Xlibris Corp.
Phillips, Peggy. Two Women under Water. LC 97-34610. (Illus.). 224p. (Orig.). 1998. pap. 12.95 (*1-56474-239-3*) Fithian Pr.
Phillips, Peggy A. Modern France: Theories & Realities of Urban Planning. LC 86-28225. (Illus.). 262p. (Orig.). 1987. pap. text 25.50 (*0-8191-6038-5*) U Pr of Amer.
— Republican France: Divided Loyalties, 325. LC 92-45075. (Contributions in Political Science Ser.: No. 325). 208p. 1993. 52.95 (*0-313-27503-3*, PCJ, Greenwood Pr) Greenwood.
Phillips, Penny, ed. see Giles, Doug.
Phillips, Percival. Red Dragon & the Black Shirts: How Italy Found Her Soul, the True Story of the Fascisti Movement. 1982. lib. bdg. 69.95 (*0-87700-349-1*) Revisionist Pr.
Phillips, Peter & Censored, Project. Censored 1997: The News That Didn't Make the News - the Year's Top 25 Censored News Stories. (Illus.). 384p. 1997. pap. 16.95 (*1-888363-41-X*) Seven Stories.
***Phillips, Peter & Project Censored Staff.** Censored 2000: The News That Didn't Make the News. (Illus.). 352p. 2000. pap. 17.95 (*1-58322-023-2*) Seven Stories.
Phillips, Peter & Project Censored Staff. Censored, 1999: The News That Didn't Make the News. (Illus.). 100p. 1999. pap. 18.95 (*1-888363-79-7*, Pub. by Seven Stories) Publishers Group.
Phillips, Peter & Project Command Staff. Censored, 1998: The News That Didn't Make the News. (Illus.). 368p. 1998. pap. 16.95 (*1-888363-64-9*) Seven Stories.
Phillips, Peter, jt. ed. see Richner, Hans.
Phillips, Peter C., ed. Models, Methods, & Applications of Econometrics: Essays in Honor of A. R. Bergstrom. LC 92-27177. 1992. 87.95 (*1-55786-110-2*) Blackwell Pubs.
Phillips, Peter H. The Rhythm Book: Studies in Rhythmic Reading & Principles. unabridged ed. LC 95-17333. (Illus.). 208p. 1995. reprint ed. pap. text 10.95 (*0-486-28693-2*) Dover.
Phillips, Peter W. Wheat, Europe & the GATT: A Political Economy Analysis. LC 90-37799. 272p. 1990. text 49.95 (*0-312-05038-0*) St Martin.
Phillips, Phil. Angels, Angels, Angels - Embraced by the Light...or...Embraced by the Darkness? LC 94-67444. 320p. 1995. pap. 10.95 (*0-914984-65-9*) Starburst.
— Dinosaurs: The Bible, Barney & Beyond. LC 94-66616. 200p. 1995. pap. 9.95 (*0-914984-59-4*) Starburst.
— Halloween & Satanism. LC 87-91287. 208p. 1987. pap. 9.95 (*0-914984-11-X*) Starburst.
— Horror & Violence: The Deadly Duo in the Media. LC 88-60884. 256p. 1988. pap. 9.95 (*0-914984-16-0*) Starburst.
— The Truth about Power Rangers. LC 95-69506. 96p. (Orig.). 1995. pap. 6.95 (*0-914984-67-5*) Starburst.
— Turmoil in the Toybox. LC 86-60428. 208p. 1986. pap. 9.95 (*0-914984-04-7*) Starburst.
Phillips, Philip. Condensed Matter Physics: With Applocations to Many-Body Theory & Interacting Electron System. 400p. Date not set. text 55.00 (*0-7382-0067-0*, Pub. by Perseus Pubng) HarpC.
Phillips, Philip & Brown, James A. Pre-Columbian Shell Engravings from the Craig Mound at Spiro, Oklahoma, Pt. 1, Vols. I-III. limited ed. LC 78-56050. (Illus.). 530p. 1978. pap. 35.00 (*0-87365-795-0*) Peabody Harvard.
— Pre-Columbian Shell Engravings from the Craig Mound at Spiro, Oklahoma, Pt. 2, Vols. IV-VI. limited ed. LC 78-56050. (Illus.). 596p. 1984. pap. 35.00 (*0-87365-802-7*) Peabody Harvard.
Phillips, Philip, et al. Pre-Columbian Shell Engravings from the Craig Mound at Spiro, Oklahoma, 6 vols. limited ed. LC 74-77557. (Illus.). 1990. 360.00 (*0-87365-777-2*) Peabody Harvard.
Phillips, Philip, jt. auth. see Brain, Jeffrey P.
Phillips, Philip, jt. auth. see Willey, Gordon R.
***Phillips, Philip B., Jr.** Rascal & Me. LC 99-91017. 1999. 25.00 (*0-7388-0582-3*); pap. 18.00 (*0-7388-0583-1*) Xlibris Corp.
***Phillips, Philip Edward.** John Milton's Epic Invocations: Converting the Muse. LC 98-20805. (Renaissance & Baroque Ser.: No. 26). 176p. 2000. text 44.95 (*0-8204-4119-8*) P Lang Pubng.
Phillips, Philip L. A List of Books, Magazine Articles & Maps Relating to Brazil. (Brazil Ser.). 1979. lib. bdg. 44.95 (*0-8490-2962-7*) Gordon Pr.
— A List of Geographical Atlases in the Library of Congress, 4 vols., Set. 3673p. 1995. reprint ed. 35.00 (*1-888262-82-6*) Martino Pubng.
— Maps & Atlases of the World War I Period: A List of Atlases & Maps Applicable to the World War. 207p. 1995. reprint ed. lib. bdg. 45.00 (*0-9649000-0-9*, T Nova Pr) G B Manasek.
***Phillips, Philip Lee, ed.** Phillips' Maps & Atlases of World War I. (C). 2000. reprint ed. 25.00 (*0-7881-9419-4*) DIANE Pub.
***Phillips, Philip Lee, ed.** The Lowery Collection - A Descriptive List of Maps of the Spanish Possessions... of the United States. 567p. 1999. reprint ed. 75.00 (*1-57898-163-8*) Martino Pubng.
***Phillips, Phoebe.** My Favorite Hanukkah Book. LC 98-60693. (Read Aloud Ser.). (Illus.). 20p. (J). (ps-3). 1998. bds. 9.98 (*0-7651-0804-6*) Smithmark.
— My Very Own Halloween Box, 4 bks. LC 98-183739. (Carry Cases Ser.). (Illus.). 10p. (J). (ps-3). 1998. bds. 7.98 (*0-7651-0802-X*) Smithmark.
Phillips, P.J., jt. auth. see Bowyer, Kevin.
Phillips Production, Inc., Staff. Texas Country Reporter Cookbook. 256p. 1990. pap. 13.95 (*0-940672-54-5*) Shearer Pub.
Phillips Publishing Staff. The Cellular Marketplace. LC 84-247991. 475p. 1984. 97.00 (*0-934960-22-4*) Phillips Business.
Phillips-Pulverman, Dian & Lloyd, Peter. Los Angeles. (Architecture Guides Ser.). (Illus.). 320p. 1997. pap. 5.95 (*3-89508-285-6*, 520195) Konemann.
***Phillips, Quitman Eugene.** Practices of Painting in Japan, 1475-1500. (Illus.). 259p. 2000. 49.50 (*0-8047-3446-1*) Stanford U Pr.
Phillips, R. Blue Baby Book. 1997. 12.95 (*1-56799-519-5*, Friedman-Fairfax) M Friedman Pub Grp Inc.
— Yellow Baby Book. 1997. 12.95 (*1-56799-517-9*, Friedman-Fairfax) M Friedman Pub Grp Inc.
Phillips, R. & Lunniss, P., eds. Anal Fistula: Surgical Evaluation & Management. (Illus.). 204p. 1995. text 65.00 (*0-412-54430-X*, Pub. by E A) OUP.
Phillips, R. & Rix, Martyn. Perfect Plants for Your Garden. (Illus.). 320p. 1996. pap. write for info. (*0-333-65341-6*) Humanities.
Phillips, R. C. Cauthorn: Record of the Cauthorn Family. Luxford, Lucy A., ed. (Illus.). 59p. 1997. reprint ed. pap. 12.00 (*0-8328-7898-7*); reprint ed. lib. bdg. 22.00 (*0-8328-7897-9*) Higginson Bk Co.
Phillips, R. Cody. A Guide to U. S. Army Museums. (Illus.). 118p. 1997. reprint ed. pap. text 25.00 (*0-7881-4671-8*) DIANE Pub.
Phillips, R. Cody. United States Army Museums. 128p. 1992. per. 6.50 (*0-16-061303-5*) USGPO.
Phillips, R. D. & Gillis, M. F., eds. Biological Effects of Extremely Low Frequency Electromagnetic Fields: Proceedings. LC 79-607778. (DOE Symposium Ser.). 593p. 1979. pap. 22.50 (*0-87079-118-4*, CONF-781016); fiche 9.00 (*0-87079-148-6*, CONF-781016) DOE.
Phillips, R. Dixon & Finley. Protein Quality & the Effects of Processing. (Food Science & Technology Ser.: Vol. 29). (Illus.). 416p. 1988. text 145.00 (*0-8247-7984-3*) Dekker.
Phillips, R. Hart. Cuba: Island of Paradox. (Illus.). 1960. 23.95 (*0-8392-1019-1*); pap. 8.95 (*0-8392-5012-6*) Astor-Honor.
— Cuban Dilemma. 1962. 19.95 (*0-8392-1018-3*) Astor-Honor.
***Phillips, R. Milchele.** CompuServe 2000 for Dummies. (For Dummies Ser.). (Illus.). 360p. 2000. pap. 19.99 (*0-7645-0677-3*) IDG Bks.
Phillips, R. S., jt. auth. see Hille, Einar.
Phillips, R. T. Coherent Optical Interactions in Semiconductors. (NATO ASI Ser.: Vol. 330). (Illus.). 382p. (C). 1994. text 120.00 (*0-306-44737-1*, Kluwer Plenum) Kluwer Academic.
***Phillips, Rachael.** Frederick Douglass. (Heroes of the Faith Ser.). 208p. (J). 2000. pap. 3.97 (*1-57748-668-4*) Barbour Pub.
— Frederick Douglass: Abolitionist & Reformer. LC 00-32534. 2000. write for info. (*0-7862-2720-6*) Thorndike Pr.
Phillips, Rachel, tr. see Paz, Octavio.
Phillips, Raelene. Freedom in White Mittens. 186p. (Orig.). 1987. pap. 5.99 (*0-934998-28-0*) Evangel Indiana.

P

An Asterisk (*) at the beginning of an entry indicates that the title is appearing for the first time.

Phillips, Raelene. Freedom's Tremendous Cost. 155p. 1993. pap. 5.99 (*0-934998-47-7*) Evangel Indiana.

Phillips, Ralph L., et al. A Handbook for Raising Small Numbers of Sheep. LC 84-72384. (Illus.). 56p. 1985. pap. 5.00 (*0-931876-68-0*, 21389) ANR Pubns CA.

Phillips, Ralph S., jt. ed. see Lax, Peter D.

Phillips, Ralph W. Jottings & Images. 129p. 1992. 16.00 (*0-9613620-2-2*) McClain.

— Letters from China & India & Other Barnyard Rememberances. 1990. 22.50 (*0-9613620-1-4*) McClain.

— The World Was My Barnyard. (Illus.). 250p. 1984. reprint ed. 15.95 (*0-9613620-0-6*) McClain.

Phillips, Ralph W. & Moore, B. Keith. Elements of Dental Materials: For Dental Hygienists & Dental Assistants. 5th ed. LC 93-12562. (Illus.). 352p. 1993. pap. text 36.95 (*0-7216-4298-5*, W B Saunders Co) Harcrt Hlth Sci Grp.

***Phillips, Randy.** Peace in the Midst of the Storm, 2 vols. 1999. pap. 16.97 (*5-550-10701-5*) Nairi.

Phillips, Raphael T. Roots of Strategy: A Collection of Classics. LC 82-11890. 448p. 1982. reprint ed. lib. bdg. 48.50 (*0-313-23657-7*, PHRS, Greenwood Pr) Greenwood.

Phillips, Ray. Edison's Kinetoscope & Its Films: A History to 1896, 65. LC 97-12290. (Contributions to the Study of Popular Culture: Vol. 65). 192p. 1997. 67.95 (*0-313-30508-0*, Greenwood Pr) Greenwood.

Phillips, Ray E. The Bantu in the City. LC 74-15080. reprint ed. 59.50 (*0-404-12129-2*) AMS Pr.

Phillips, Raymond C., Jr. Struthers Burt. LC 82-74090. (Western Writers Ser.: No. 56). (Illus.). 48p. (Orig.). 1983. pap. 4.95 (*0-88430-030-7*) Boise St U W Writ Ser.

Phillips, Raymond E. & Feeney, Mary K. The Cardiac Rhythms: A Systematic Approach to Interpretation. 3rd ed. (Illus.). 608p. 1990. pap. text 42.00 (*0-7216-2427-8*, W B Saunders Co) Harcrt Hlth Sci Grp.

Phillips, Rena & McWilliam, Emma. After Adoption: Working with Adoptive Families. 226p. 1996. pap. 75.00 (*1-873868-27-8*) BAAF.

Phillips, Rene F. Encyclopedic Guide for Professionals in Elementary Education. 556p. (Orig.). (C). 1986. pap. text 42.00 (*0-8191-5170-X*) U Pr of Amer.

***Phillips, Renee.** GraphicIdea Promotion: Making the Sale with Great Graphics, (Graphic Idea Resource Ser.). (Illus.). 96p. 2000. pap. text 17.99 (*1-56496-666-6*) Rockport Pubs.

Phillips, Renee. New York Contemporary Art Galleries: The Complete Annual Guide. 3rd rev. ed. 264p. 1998. mass mkt. 18.95 (*0-9646358-4-4*) Manhattan Arts Intl.

— New York Contemporary Art Galleries: The Complete Annual Guide 2000 Edition. 4th rev. ed. 264p. 2000. pap. 18.95 (*0-9646358-9-5*) Manhattan Arts Intl.

— New York Fine Arts Resources. 264p. 1999. pap. 18.95 (*0-9646358-0-1*) Manhattan Arts Intl.

— Presentation Power Tools for Fine Artists. 100p. 1998. pap. 18.95 (*0-9646358-5-2*) Manhattan Arts Intl.

— Success Now! for Artists: A Motivational Guide for the Artrepreneur. LC 97-75488. 200p. 1997. pap. 18.95 (*0-9646358-6-0*) Manhattan Arts Intl.

Phillips, Renee, ed. New York Contemporary Art Galleries: The Complete Annual Guide, Vol. 2. 2nd rev. ed. 252p. 1997. pap. 18.95 (*0-9646358-3-6*) Manhattan Arts Intl.

Phillips, Renee, ed. New York Contemporary Art Galleries: The Complete Annual Guide. 254p. 1995. pap. 16.95 (*0-9646358-2-8*) Manhattan Arts Intl.

Phillips, Richard. Managing for Greater Returns. 1962. 11.95 (*0-686-00369-1*) AG Pr.

— Mapping Men & Empire: A Geography of Adventure. LC 96-10899. (Illus.). 224p. (C). 1996. 85.00 (*0-415-13771-3*); pap. 25.99 (*0-415-13772-1*) Routledge.

— Numbers: Facts, Figures & Fiction. (Illus.). 96p. (C). 1994. 22.95 (*0-521-46481-1*) Cambridge U Pr.

***Phillips, Richard, et al, eds.** De-Centering Sexualities: Politics & Representations Beyond the Metropolis. (Critical Geographies Ser.). 312p. 2000. pap. 29.99 (*0-415-19466-0*) Routledge.

Phillips, Richard, et al. Auto Industries of Europe, United States & Japan. LC 82-13856. (Economist Intelligence Ser.). 352p. 1982. 32.00 (*0-685-42673-4*, HarpBusn) HarpInfo.

Phillips, Richard, ed. see ACA Public Information Committee, 1990-1992 Staff.

Phillips, Richard, ed. see Hunter, Warren.

Phillips, Richard, tr. & photos by see Symonds, Peter.

Phillips, Richard D. The Heart of an Executive: Lesson on Leadership from the Life of King David. 288p. 2000. pap. 11.95 (*0-385-49233-2*) Doubleday.

— The Heart of an Executive: Lessons on Leadership from the Life of King David. LC 98-21259. 288p. 1999. 21.00 (*0-385-49232-4*) Doubleday.

Phillips, Richard D., jt. auth. see DeVries, John A.

Phillips, Richard H. Bindweed. Fuller, Jean O., ed. (Illus.). 100p. (Orig.). 1988. pap. 7.95 (*0-317-92520-2*) Ganders Knob.

— Building Big Is Beautiful. 3rd rev. ed. (Illus.). 146p. 1985. pap. 11.95 (*0-934575-00-2*) Vip Pubs.

Phillips, Richard L. & McConnell, Charles R. The Effective Corrections Manager: Maximizing Staff Performance in Demanding Times. LC 96-3789. 480p. 1996. 39.00 (*0-8342-0812-1*) Aspen Pub.

***Phillips, Richard L. & Roberts, John W.** Quick Reference to Correctional Administration. LC 99-45037. 257p. 1999. pap. 45.00 (*0-8342-1756-2*) Aspen Pub.

Phillips, Richard M., jt. auth. see Adelman, Roger M.

Phillips, Richard T. China since 1911. LC 95-24654. 288p. 1996. text 49.95 (*0-312-12941-6*) St Martin.

Phillips, Rick. Healing Communication: A Psychospiritual Approach. (Illus.). 192p. (Orig.). 1996. pap. 12.00 (*0-9653059-0-2*) Deva Pubng.

— Windows to the Soul: Healing the Emotional Body. 5th rev. ed. LC 98-231368. 200p. 1998. pap. 12.00 (*0-9653059-1-0*) Deva Pubng.

Phillips, Rob, jt. auth. see Phillips, Robert.

Phillips, Robert. Breakdown Lane: Poems. LC 93-43813. (Johns Hopkins Poetry & Fiction Ser.). 1994. 30.00 (*0-8018-4854-7*); pap. 12.95 (*0-8018-4855-5*) Johns Hopkins.

***Phillips, Robert.** Classics Illustrated: Where Bach Meets Rock. (Guitar Presents Ser.). 1999. pap. 9.95 (*1-57560-220-2*, Pub. by Cherry Lane) H Leonard.

Phillips, Robert. Denton Welch. LC 73-16129. (Twayne's English Authors Ser.). 190p. (C). 1974. lib. bdg. 20.95 (*0-8057-1567-3*) Irvington.

— Public Landing Revisited. 208p. 1992. 19.95 (*0-934257-78-7*) Story Line.

***Phillips, Robert.** Spinach Days. LC 99-57067. 2000. 19.95 (*0-8018-6451-8*) Johns Hopkins.

Phillips, Robert. Themes & Variations for Classic Guitar. 208p. 1996. pap. 24.95 (*0-7866-0394-1*, MB95421) Mel Bay.

Phillips, Robert, ed. An Omnibus of Twentieth Century Ghost Stories. 384p. 1991. pap. 11.95 (*0-88184-780-1*) Carroll & Graf.

— Nightshade: 20th Century Ghost Stories. 496p. 1999. 25.00 (*0-7867-0614-7*) Carroll & Graf.

***Phillips, Robert, ed.** Nightshade: 20th Century Ghost Stories. 496p. 2000. reprint ed. pap. 14.00 (*0-7867-0808-5*, Pub. by Carroll & Graf) Publishers Group.

***Phillips, Robert & Motta, Glenda.** Coping with Endometriosis: A Practical Guide to Understanding, Treating & Living with Chronic Endometriosis. 224p. 2000. pap. 14.95 (*1-58333-074-7*, Avery) Penguin Putnam.

Phillips, Robert & Phillips, Rob. Practical Ways to Improve Your Communication. 38p. pap. text 49.50 incl. audio (*0-88432-182-7*, S08100) Audio-Forum.

Phillips, Robert, jt. auth. see Arthur, James.

Phillips, Robert, jt. auth. see McKnight, Thomas W.

Phillips, Robert, jt. auth. see Phillips, Marjorie.

Phillips, Robert, ed. see Goyen, William.

Phillips, Robert B. One of God's Children: In the Toe River Valley. LC 83-70886. (Illus.). 176p. (YA). (gr. 9-12). 1983. 7.00 (*0-9620577-0-3*) R B Phillips Pub.

— Through My Picture Window. LC 88-90639. (Illus.). 256p. (YA). (gr. 9-12). 1988. 9.95 (*0-9620577-1-1*) R B Phillips Pub.

Phillips, Robert F. To Save Bastogne. rev. unabridged ed. LC 96-84715. (Illus.). 280p. 1996. pap. 14.95 (*0-9653229-0-4*) Borodino Bks.

Phillips, Robert H., Jr. Accounting with New Views: Educational Version. 264p. (Orig.). (C). 1989. pap. text 39.95 (*0-8162-6739-1*) Holden-Day.

Phillips, Robert H. Control Your Pain! 169 Painless Strategies for Taking Charge of Your Body. (Strategy Guidebooks Ser.). 52p. 1996. pap. 6.95 (*1-888614-00-5*) Balance Enter.

***Phillips, Robert H.** Coping with Diabetes: Sound, Compassionate Advice to Alleviate the Challenges of Type I & Type II Diabetes. 304p. 2000. pap. 14.95 (*0-89529-923-2*, Avery) Penguin Putnam.

Phillips, Robert H. Coping with Lupus: A Guide to Living with Lupus for You & Your Family. 2nd ed. LC 90-1270. 288p. pap. 12.95 (*0-89529-475-3*, Avery) Penguin Putnam.

Phillips, Robert H. Coping with Mitral Valve Prolapse: A Guide to Living with MVP for You & Your Family. LC 91-46165. 271p. 1993. pap. 9.95 (*0-89529-514-8*, Avery) Penguin Putnam.

Phillips, Robert H. Coping with Rheumatoid Arthritis: A Guide to Living with Arthritis for You & Your Family. LC 88-3450. 272p. 1988. pap. 9.95 (*0-89529-371-4*, Avery) Penguin Putnam.

***Phillips, Robert H.** A Peek Through the Curtain: A Trilogy. LC 98-91131. 564p. 2000. 24.95 (*0-533-13063-8*) Vantage.

Phillips, Robert H. Reduce Your Test Anxiety! 128 Strategies to Help You Make the Grade. (Strategy Guidebooks Ser.). 52p. (YA). 1996. pap. 6.95 (*1-888614-01-3*) Balance Enter.

Phillips, Robert H. & Goldstein, Paula. Coping with Breast Cancer: A Practical Guide to Understanding, Treating & Living with Breast Cancer. LC 98-20436. 272p. 1998. pap. 13.95 (*0-89529-858-9*, Avery) Penguin Putnam.

Phillips, Robert H., jt. auth. see Glanz, Larry.

Phillips, Robert H., jt. auth. see Krumholz, Harlan M.

Phillips, Robert H., jt. auth. see Lahita, Robert G.

Phillips, Robert H., jt. auth. see McKnight, Thomas W.

Phillips, Robert L., Jr. Shelby Foote: Novelist & Historian. LC 91-26636. 1992. text 35.00 (*0-87805-531-2*) U Pr of Miss.

Phillips, Robert L. & Cady, Duane L. Humanitarian Intervention: Just War vs. Pacifism. (Point/Counterpoint Ser.). 112p. 1995. lib. bdg. 42.50 (*0-8476-8141-6*) Rowman.

— Humanitarian Intervention: Just War vs. Pacifism. (Point/Counterpoint Ser.). 112p. (C). 1995. pap. text 16.95 (*0-8476-8142-4*) Rowman.

Phillips, Robert L. & Hunt, James G., eds. Strategic Leadership: A Multiorganizational-Level Perspective. LC 92-8383. 352p. 1992. 59.95 (*0-89930-756-6*, PSJ, Quorum Bks) Greenwood.

Phillips, Robert M., ed. High Energy Density Microwaves. (AIP Conference Proceedings Ser.: Vol. 474). (Illus.). 22p. 1999. 135.00 incl. cd-rom (*1-56396-796-0*) Am Inst Physics.

Phillips, Robert W. Roy Rogers: A Biography, Radio History, Television Career Chronicle, Discography, Filmography, Comicography, Merchandising & Advertising History, Collectibles Description, Bibliography & Index. LC 94-31152. (Illus.). 446p. 1995. lib. bdg. 65.00 (*0-89950-937-1*) McFarland & Co.

Phillips, Robin. The Developer's Handbook to Interactive Multimedia: A Practical Guide for Education Applications. 224p. 1997. pap. 35.00 (*0-7494-2121-5*, Kogan Pg Educ) Stylus Pub VA.

Phillips, Robin, ed. Colorectal Surgery. (Companion Guide to Specialist Surgical Practice Ser.: Vol. 4). (Illus.). 380p. 1997. text 89.00 (*0-7020-2143-1*, Pub. by W B Saunders) Saunders.

Phillips, Robin K., ed. see Thomson, James P.

***Phillips, Rod.** "Forest Beatniks" & "Urban Thoreaus" Gary Snyder, Jack Kerouac, Lew Welch & Michael McClure. LC 98-30527. (Modern American Literature Ser.: Vol. 22). 184p. (C). 2000. 45.95 (*0-8204-4159-7*) P Lang Pubng.

Phillips, Roderick. Society, State & Nation. LC 95-24431. 537p. (C). 1995. pap. text 45.80 (*0-13-103821-4*) P-H.

— Untying the Knot: A Short History of Divorce. (Canto Book Ser.). 277p. (C). 1991. pap. 11.95 (*0-521-42370-8*) Cambridge U Pr.

Phillips, Rodney, jt. auth. see Clay, Steven.

***Phillips, Roger.** Climbers. (Book of... Garden Plants Ser.). 2000. pap. 8.99 (*0-375-75441-5*) Random.

— Hiking & Angling in McCall, Idaho: A Guide to 32 Trails, 20 Lakes & Eight Rivers & Streams. 2000. pap. 12.95 (*0-9700520-0-6*) Lizard Prints.

Phillips, Roger. Mushrooms: The Photographic Guide to Identify Common & Important Mushrooms. 159p. 1986. pap. text 18.00 (*0-241-11756-9*) Lubrecht & Cramer.

— Mushrooms & Other Fungi of Great Britain & Europe. (Illus.). 288p. (Orig.). 1981. pap. 47.50 (*0-330-26441-9*, Pub. by Pan) Trans-Atl Phila.

— Mushrooms of North America: The Most Comprehensive Mushroom Guide Ever. 1991. pap. 29.95 (*0-316-70613-2*) Little.

***Phillips, Roger.** Plants for Pots & Patios. (Book of... Garden Plants Ser.). 2000. pap. 8.99 (*0-375-75443-1*) Random.

— Plants for Shade. (Book of... Garden Plants Ser.). (Illus.). 2000. pap. 8.99 (*0-375-75444-X*) Random.

Phillips, Roger. The Random House Book of Shrubs. (Illus.). 288p. 1989. pap. 27.50 (*0-679-72345-5*) Vin Bks.

— Random House Book of Trees of North America & Europe. (Illus.). 224p. 1978. pap. 27.50 (*0-394-73541-2*) Random.

***Phillips, Roger.** Summer Annuals. (Book of... Garden Plants Ser.). 2000. pap. 8.99 (*0-375-75442-3*) Random.

Phillips, Roger, et al, eds. Child Therapy Today, Vol. 2. 277p. 1996. 36.95 (*1-882732-50-2*) Childswork.

Phillips, Roger & Rix, Martyn. The Best Scented Plants & How to Grow Them. (Pan Garden Plants Ser.). (Illus.). 96p. 1998. pap. 12.95 (*0-330-35550-3*, Pub. by Pan) Trans-Atl Phila.

— Climbers for Walls & Arbors & How to Grow Them. (Pan Garden Plants Ser.). (Illus.). 96p. 1998. pap. 12.95 (*0-330-35549-X*, Pub. by Pan) Trans-Atl Phila.

— Herbs for Cooking & How to Grow Them. (Pan Garden Plants Ser.). (Illus.). 96p. 1998. pap. 12.95 (*0-330-35546-5*, Pub. by Pan) Trans-Atl Phila.

— Plants for Pots & Patios & How to Grow Them. (Pan Garden Plants Ser.). (Illus.). 96p. 1998. pap. 12.95 (*0-330-35547-3*, Pub. by Pan) Trans-Atl Phila.

— Plants for Shade & How to Grow Them. (Pan Garden Plants Ser.). (Illus.). 96p. 1998. pap. 12.95 (*0-330-35548-1*, Pub. by Pan) Trans-Atl Phila.

— Salad Plants for Your Garden & How to Grow Them. (Pan Garden Plants Ser.). (Illus.). 96p. 1998. pap. 12.95 (*0-330-35551-1*, Pub. by Pan) Trans-Atl Phila.

— Summer Annuals & How to Grow Them. (Pan Garden Plants Ser.). (Illus.). 96p. 1998. pap. 12.95 (*0-330-31174-3*, Pub. by Pan) Trans-Atl Phila.

— Traditional Old Roses & How to Grow Them. (Pan Garden Plants Ser.). (Illus.). 96p. 1998. pap. 12.95 (*0-330-35552-X*, Pub. by Pan) Trans-Atl Phila.

Phillips, Roger & Rix, Martyn E. A Guide to the Freshwater Fish of Britain, Ireland & Europe. (Illus.). 144p. (Orig.). 1985. pap. 27.50 (*0-330-28690-0*, Pub. by Pan) Trans-Atl Phila.

— The Random House Book of Perennials, 2 vols. 1991. 25.00 (*0-685-74390-X*) Random.

— Roses. LC 87-43216. (Illus.). 224p. 1988. pap. 27.50 (*0-394-75867-6*) Random.

Phillips, Roger, jt. auth. see Stuebner, Stephen.

Phillips, Roger W. A Concise Russian Review Grammar with Exercises. LC 73-15260. (ENG & RUS.). 126p. reprint ed. pap. 39.10 (*0-7837-4386-6*, 204412600012) Bks Demand.

***Phillips, Ron.** Awakened by the Spirit. LC 99-39350. 192p. 1999. pap. 12.99 (*0-7852-6901-0*) Nelson.

— Beginning Java Design & Development. 600p. 2000. pap. 49.99 (*1-86100-378-1*) Wrox Pr Inc.

Phillips, Ron. The Risk Business. (C). 1989. 35.00 (*1-871058-05-8*, Pub. by Dragonheart Pr) St Mut.

— Vanquishing the Enemy: Triumphant in the Battles of Life. LC 96-71988. 218p. 1997. pap. 9.99 (*0-87148-872-8*) Pathway Pr.

Phillips, Ron, jt. auth. see Wittich, John.

Phillips, Ron, ed. see Broach-Sowels, Holly.

Phillips, Ronald C. & Menez, Ernani G. Seagrasses. LC 87-23245. (Smithsonian Contributions to the Marine Sciences Ser.: No. 34). (Illus.). 110p. reprint ed. pap. 34.10 (*0-8357-8316-2*, 203407700087) Bks Demand.

Phillips, Ronald L. & Vasil, Indra K., eds. DNA-Based Markers in Plants. LC 93-49927. (Advances in Cellular & Molecular Biology of Plants Ser.: Vol. 1). 380p. (C). 1994. text 255.50 (*0-7923-2714-4*) Kluwer Academic.

Phillips, Ronald L., jt. auth. see Andrews, Larry C.

Phillips, Ronnie J. The Chicago Plan & New Deal Banking Reform. LC 94-17713. 244p. (gr. 13). 1994. 75.95 (*1-56324-469-1*) M E Sharpe.

— The Chicago Plan & the New Deal Banking Reform. LC 94-17713. 244p. (gr. 13). 1994. pap. 35.95 (*1-56324-470-5*) M E Sharpe.

— Economic Mavericks: The Texas Institutionalists. LC 95-40572. (Political Economy & Public Policy Ser.: Vol. 9). 193p. 1995. 78.50 (*1-55938-467-0*) Jai Pr.

— Narrow Banking Reconsidered: The Functional Approach to Financial Reform. (Public Policy Brief Ser.: Vol. 17). 52p. (Orig.). 1995. pap. 3.00 (*0-941276-05-8*) J Levy.

Phillips, Ruth, jt. auth. see Berlo, Janet Catherine.

Phillips, Ruth B. Representing Woman: Sande Masquerades of the Mende of Sierra Leone. (Illus.). 200p. 1995. 50.00 (*0-930741-44-7*) UCLA Fowler Mus.

— Trading Identities: The Souvenir in Native North American Art from the Northeast, 1700-1900. LC 98-11511. (Illus.). 352p. 1999. 75.00 (*0-295-97751-5*); pap. write for info. (*0-295-97648-9*) U of Wash Pr.

— Unpacking Culture: Art & Commodity in Colonial & Postcolonial Worlds. LC 98-38035. 435p. 1999. 50.00 (*0-520-20796-3*, Pub. by U CA Pr); pap. 19.95 (*0-520-20797-1*, Pub. by U CA Pr) Cal Prin Full Svc.

Phillips, S. Flora of Tropical East Africa: Eriocaulaceae. Polhill, R. M., ed. 44p. 1997. pap. 10.50 (*90-6191-377-2*, Pub. by A A Balkema) Ashgate Pub Co.

Phillips, S., jt. auth. see Franklin, A.

Phillips, S. F. & Wingate, D. L., eds. Functional Disorders of the Gut. (Illus.). 384p. 1995. write for info. (*0-443-05420-7*) Church.

Phillips, S. Michael & Escobar, Mario R., eds. The Reticuloendothelial System: A Comprehensive Treatise & Hypersensitivity, Vol. 9. LC 79-25933. (Illus.). 512p. (C). 1986. text 150.00 (*0-306-42305-7*, Kluwer Plenum) Kluwer Academic.

Phillips, Samantha. Blonde Ambition. LC 96-209254. 252p. 1997. pap. 17.95 (*0-7126-7614-7*, Pub. by CEN3) Trafalgar.

Phillips, Samantha, jt. auth. see Gray, Heather.

Phillips, Sandra. Matt Phillips: The Graphic Work. 1976. pap. 7.50 (*0-686-24037-5*) Bellevue Pr.

***Phillips, Sandra B.** Photography of John Gutmann: Culture Shock. (Illus.). 144p. 2000. 35.00 (*1-85894-097-4*) Merrell Holberton.

Phillips, Sandra S. Police Pictures: The Photograph As Evidence. LC 97-14539. (Illus.). 144p. 1997. 24.95 (*0-8118-1984-1*) Chronicle Bks.

Phillips, Sara Webb, jt. auth. see Phillips, L. Edward.

Phillips, Sarah. The Healthy Oven Baking Book. LC 98-35411. 288p. 1999. 17.95 (*0-385-49281-2*) Doubleday.

— Young Learners. Maley, Alan, ed. (Illus.). 188p. 1994. pap. text 13.95 (*0-19-437195-6*) OUP.

Phillips, Sarah H. & Williams, Mary H. The Secret Ingredient. (Illus.). 179p. 1987. 10.00 (*0-9619306-0-8*) Secret Ingrediants.

Phillips, Scarlett L. & Meador, Kristen A., eds. Here Is Your Indiana Government. 316p. 1995. pap. text 10.00 (*1-883698-08-1*) IN Chamber Comm.

***Phillips, Scott.** The Ice Harvest. 2000. 19.95 (*0-345-44018-8*) Ballantine Pub Grp.

Phillips, Semira A. Mahaska County (Iowa), A Story of the Early Days. 383p. 1993. reprint ed. lib. bdg. 42.00 (*0-8328-3520-X*) Higginson Bk Co.

Phillips, Sharon D., ed. see Peterson, Carol R.

Phillips, Sheena, jt. auth. see Tsipis, Kosta.

Phillips, Sheila, et al, eds. Qualitative Research in Pharmacy Practice. (Cardiff Papers in Qualitative Research). 224p. 1996. 72.95 (*1-85972-211-3*, Pub. by Avebry) Ashgate Pub Co.

Phillips, Shelley, jt. auth. see Phillips, Barry.

Phillips, Shelly, jt. auth. see Phillips, Barry.

Phillips, Sheree, jt. auth. see Phillips, Benny.

Phillips, Sherry, ed. see Thoreau, Henry David.

Phillips, Shively W., jt. auth. see Achen, Christopher H.

Phillips, Sidney. Around the World in 80 Dames. LC 97-61890. iv, 293p. 1997. pap. 9.95 (*1-891213-00-8*) H A Schroeder.

Phillips, Sidney, et al, eds. Gastrointestinal Motility Disorders for the Clinician: Practical Guidelines for Patient Care. (Illus.). v, 25p. 1998. pap. text 24.95 (*0-934205-13-2*) Academy Prof Inform.

Phillips, Sidney F., et al, eds. The Large Intestine: Physiology, Pathophysiology & Disease. LC 91-14685. (Illus.). 923p. reprint ed. pap. 200.00 (*0-608-09726-8*, 206989300007) Bks Demand.

Phillips, Sidney F., et al. The Large Intestine: Physiology, Pathophysiology, & Diseases. (Illus.). 928p. 1991. text 223.00 (*0-88167-777-9*) Lppncott W & W.

Phillips, Sidney L., jt. ed. see Perry, Dale L.

Phillips Simpson, Peter L. A Philosophical Commentary on the Politics of Aristotle. LC 97-16515. 512p. (C). (gr. 13). 1998. 55.00 (*0-8078-2380-5*) U of NC Pr.

Phillips Simpson, Peter L., tr. & intro. see Aristotle.

Phillips, Sky. Secret Mission to Melbourne: November, 1941. (Illus.). 296p. (Orig.). 1992. pap. 18.95 (*0-89745-148-1*) Sunflower U Pr.

***Phillips, Sonia.** Girl in the Yellow Dress. large type ed. LC 99-44279. 1999. pap. 22.95 (*0-7838-8776-0*, G K Hall & Co) Mac Lib Ref.

Phillips, Stacy. The Art of Hawaiian Steel Guitar. 160p. 1991. spiral bd. 17.95 (*1-56222-103-5*, 94383) Mel Bay.

— The Art of Hawaiian Steel Guitar. 1993. audio 9.98 (*1-56222-877-3*, 94383C) Mel Bay.

Phillips, Stacy. Art of Hawaiian Steel Guitar. 160p. 1991. spiral bd. 23.95 incl. audio (*0-7866-1022-0*, 94383P) Mel Bay.

Phillips, Stacy. Beginning Dobro. (Illus.). 56p. pap. 5.95 (*0-8256-1123-7*, AM67497) Music Sales.

P

— Beginning Fiddle. (Illus.). 64p. 1990. pap. 5.95 (0-8256-2541-6, AM71275) Music Sales.

Phillips, Stacy. Beginning Fiddle Solos. 48p. 1996. pap. 17.95 incl. audio compact disk (0-7866-0707-6, 95590BCD) Mel Bay.

Phillips, Stacy. Complete Country Fiddler. 1992. audio 9.98 (1-56222-438-7, 94696C) Mel Bay.

***Phillips, Stacy.** Complete Country Fiddler. 152p. 1999. spiral bd. 22.95 incl. audio compact disk (0-7866-5128-8, 94696BCD) Mel Bay.

— Complete Dobro Player. 248p. 1996. pap. 25.00 (0-7866-0113-2, 95271); spiral bd. 48.95 incl. audio compact disk (0-7866-1248-7, 95271CDP) Mel Bay.

Phillips, Stacy. Contest Fiddling. 1983. pap. 36.95 (0-7866-0952-4, 93940P) Mel Bay.

— Contest Fiddling. 176p. 1983. spiral bd. 19.95 (1-56222-144-2, 93940); audio 19.95 (1-56222-611-8, 93940C) Mel Bay.

— The Dobro Book. (Illus.). 96p. 1977. pap. 17.95 (0-8256-0183-5, OK63289, Oak) Music Sales.

— The Dobro Case Chord Book. (Illus.). 40p. pap. 5.95 (0-8256-1124-5, AM67158) Music Sales.

— The Fiddle Case Tunebook: British Isles. LC 66-19062. (Illus.). 52p. (Orig.). 1967. pap. 5.95 (0-8256-2545-9, AM71317, Oak) Music Sales.

— Fiddle Case Tunebook: Old-Time Southern. (Illus.). 48p. 1989. pap. 5.95 (0-8256-2544-0, AM71309) Music Sales.

— The Great Dobro Sessions. 116p. 1996. spiral bd. 17.95 (0-7866-2081-1, MB95771) Mel Bay.

— Hot Licks for Bluegrass Fiddle. (Illus.). 144p. 1984. pap. 21.95 (0-8256-0289-0, OK64378, Oak) Music Sales.

— Klezmer Collection for B Instruments. 192p. 1998. pap. 22.95 (0-7866-3089-2, 96844) Mel Bay.

Phillips, Stacy. Klezmer Collections for C Instruments. 192p. 1996. pap. 22.95 (0-7866-0841-2, 95540) Mel Bay.

Phillips, Stacy. Phillips Collection, Vol. 1. 1994. pap. 29.95 (1-56222-582-0, 94711) Mel Bay.

— Phillips Collection, Vol. 2. 392p. 1995. spiral bd. 29.95 (1-56222-914-1, 95078) Mel Bay.

Phillips, Stacy. Skip, Hop & Wobble - Dobro Edition. 72p. 1997. pap. 24.95 incl. audio (0-7866-3098-1, 95765CDP) Mel Bay.

— Twin Fiddling. 148p. 1996. pap. 22.95 incl. audio compact disk (0-7866-0476-X, 45458BCD) Mel Bay.

Phillips, Stacy & Kosek, Kenny. Bluegrass Fiddle Styles. (Illus.). 112p. pap. 17.95 (0-8256-0185-1, OK63487, Oak) Music Sales.

Phillips, Stacy, jt. auth. see O'Connor, Mark.

Phillips, Stacy, tr. see Douglas, Jerry, et al.

Phillips, Stella. Dear Brother, Here Departed. large type ed. (Linford Mystery Library). 1990. pap. 16.99 (0-7089-6847-3) Ulverscroft.

— Death in Arcady. large type ed. (Linford Mystery Library). 331p. 1988. pap. 16.99 (0-7089-6571-7, Linford) Ulverscroft.

— Death in Sheep's Clothing. large type ed. (Linford Mystery Library). 1990. pap. 16.99 (0-7089-6838-4) Ulverscroft.

— Down to Death. large type ed. (Linford Mystery Library). 320p. 1988. pap. 16.99 (0-7089-6515-6) Ulverscroft.

— The Hidden Wrath. large type ed. (Linford Mystery Library). 304p. 1988. pap. 16.99 (0-7089-6623-3, Linford) Ulverscroft.

— Yet She Must Die. large type ed. (Linford Mystery Library). 352p. 1993. pap. 16.99 (0-7089-7343-4, Linford) Ulverscroft.

Phillips, Stephen & Luehrs, John. Rural Hospitals in Evolution: State Policy Issues & Initiatives. Glass, Karen, ed. 40p. (Orig.). 1989. pap. text 20.00 (1-55877-067-4) Natl Governor.

Phillips, Stephen, jt. auth. see Bonevac, Daniel.

Phillips, Stephen B. Twentieth-Century Still-Life Paintings from the Phillips Collection. Hirzy, Ellen, ed. LC 97-14554. (Illus.). 128p. 1997. pap. 18.95 (0-943044-22-7) Phillips Coll.

***Phillips, Stephen Bennett, et al.** Degas to Matisse: Impressionist & Modernist Masterworks. (Illus.). 120p. 2000. write for info. (1-85894-117-2, Pub. by Merrell Holberton) Rizzoli Intl.

Phillips, Stephen H., jt. ed. see Kane, Robert.

Phillips, Stephen J., ed. Jane's High-Speed Marine Transportation, 98-99. 486p. 1998. 380.00 (0-7106-1796-8, VM) Janes Info Group.

***Phillips, Sterling.** Poems from the Schoolhouse. iii, 37p. 2000. pap. 9.95 (0-9700467-1-5) Pollyanna Pr.

— Whispers. iii, 61p. 2000. pap. 15.95 (0-9700467-0-7) Pollyanna Pr.

Phillips, Steve. Evaluation: Library Training Guide. 64p. 1993. pap. 35.00 (1-85604-079-8, LAP0798, Pub. by Library Association) Bernan Associates.

— Positively Pregnant. Carle, Cliff, ed. 1995. pap. text 4.99 (0-918259-81-9) CCC Pubns.

— Surface Tension: Poems. LC 95-53754. (Illus.). 64p. 1996. 14.95 (0-7734-2680-9, Mellen Poetry Pr) E Mellen.

Phillips, Steve, jt. auth. see Elledge, Robin L.

Phillips, Steve, jt. auth. see Harshman, Carl L.

Phillips, Steven. No Heroes, No Villains: The Story of a Murder. 1978. pap. 11.00 (0-394-72531-X) Vin Bks.

Phillips, Steven J. Old-House Dictionary: An Illustrated Guide to American Domestic Architecture (1600-1940) LC 96-23062. (Illus.). 240p. 1995. reprint ed. pap. 16.95 (0-471-14407-X) Wiley.

Phillips, Steven L. & Elledge, Robin L. The Team-Building Source Book. LC 89-5094. 208p. 1989. ring bd. 99.95 (0-88390-232-X, Pfffr & Co) Jossey-Bass.

Phillips, Steven R. Creating Effective Relationships: A Basic Guide to Relationship Awareness theory. LC 90-64345. 129 p. 1996. write for info. (0-9628732-0-9) Prsnl Strengths.

Phillips, Steven R., jt. auth. see Bergquist, William H.

P

Phillips, Sue. Complete Step-by-Step Book of Gardening: How to Create & Sustain a Beautiful Garden. (Illus.). 400p. 1997. 29.95 (1-55110-499-7) Whitecap Bks.

— Container Gardening Encyclopedia: Creative Gardening in Pots, Tubs, Troughs & Baskets. 1998. 24.99 (1-85833-385-7) Quadrillion Pubng.

— Gardeners' World Book of Bulbs. (Illus.). 112p. 1992. pap. 14.95 (0-563-36099-2, BBC-Parkwest) Parkwest Pubns.

— Healing Stones. (Illus.). 1998. pap. 19.95 (1-86163-034-4, Pub. by Capall Bann Pubng) Holmes Pub.

Phillips, Susan. The Lessons of Love. (Serenade Serenata Ser.: No. 35). 1986. pap. 1.49 (0-310-47232-6, 15569P) Zondervan.

— Wallbangin' Graffiti & Gangs in L. A. LC 98-31899. (Illus.). 336p. 1999. pap. 25.00 (0-226-66772-3); lib. bdg. 73.00 (0-226-66771-5) U Ch Pr.

***Phillips, Susan Elizabeth.** Dream a Little Dream. 400p. 1998. mass mkt. 6.99 (0-380-79447-0, Avon Bks) Morrow Avon.

Phillips, Susan Elizabeth. Dream & Little Dream. large type ed. LC 98-18674. 541p. 1998. 28.95 (0-7838-0183-1, G K Hall & Co) Mac Lib Ref.

— Fancy Pants. 497p. 1991. reprint ed. per. 6.99 (0-671-74715-0) PB.

***Phillips, Susan Elizabeth.** First Lady. LC 99-95329. 384p. 2000. mass mkt. 6.99 (0-380-80807-2, Avon Bks) Morrow Avon.

— First Lady. LC 00-39856. 2000. write for info. (1-56895-891-9) Wheeler Pub.

Phillips, Susan Elizabeth. Heaven, Texas: Where Even a Angel Can Raise a Little Hell... LC 94-96284. 371p. 1995. mass mkt. 6.99 (0-380-77684-7, Avon Bks) Morrow Avon.

***Phillips, Susan Elizabeth.** Heaven, Texas: Where Even a Angel Can Raise a Little Hell... LC 98-47825. 1998. write for info. (1-56895-699-1) Wheeler Pub.

Phillips, Susan Elizabeth. Honey Moon. Zion, Claire, ed. 440p. (Orig.). 1993. mass mkt. 6.50 (0-671-73593-4) PB.

— Hot Shot. Zion, Claire, ed. 490p. 1991. mass mkt. 6.99 (0-671-65831-X) PB.

Phillips, Susan Elizabeth. It Had to Be You. 376p. 1994. mass mkt. 6.99 (0-380-77683-9, Avon Bks) Morrow Avon.

Phillips, Susan Elizabeth. Kiss an Angel. 373p. 1996. mass mkt. 6.50 (0-380-78233-2) Morrow Avon.

— Lady Be Good. LC 98-93457. 384p. 1999. mass mkt. 6.99 (0-380-79448-9, Avon Bks) Morrow Avon.

***Phillips, Susan Elizabeth.** Lady Be Good. 2001. write for info. (0-380-97572-6) Morrow Avon.

— Lady Be Good. large type ed. LC 99-22159. (Large Print Book Ser.). 1999. write for info. (1-56895-733-5) Wheeler Pub.

Phillips, Susan Elizabeth. Nobody's Baby but Mine. LC 96-96877. 376p. 1997. mass mkt. 6.99 (0-380-78234-0, Avon Bks) Morrow Avon.

— Nobody's Baby but Mine. large type ed. LC 97-6785. (Core Ser.). 501p. 1997. lib. bdg. 27.95 (0-7838-8197-5, G K Hall Lrg Type) Mac Lib Ref.

Phillips, Susan S. & Benner, Patricia, eds. The Crisis of Care: Affirming & Restoring Caring Practices in the Helping Professions. 208p. 1996. pap. 14.95 (0-87840-599-2) Georgetown U Pr.

Phillips, Susan W. & Phillips, Jeffrey D. Quick Drug Reference for the Optometrist. 260p. 1998. spiral bd. 34.00 (1-890018-27-9) Anadem Pubng.

Phillips, Sylvia. California Arbitrator & Mediator Reviews. 653p. 1997. pap. 125.00 (1-58012-012-1) James Pub Santa Ana.

Phillips, Sylvia, ed. see Marazon, Renee A.

Phillips, T. J. Dance of the Mongoose. 288p. 1995. pap. 19.95 (0-425-14786-X, Prime Crime); pap. 9.00 (0-425-14921-8, Prime Crime) Berkley Pub.

— Woman in the Dark. (Joe Wilder Mystery Ser.). 208p. 1997. reprint ed. mass mkt. 5.99 (0-425-16110-2, Prime Crime) Berkley Pub.

— Woman in the Dark: A Joe Wilder Mystery. LC 96-31437. 288p. 1997. pap. 21.95 (0-425-15312-6, Prime Crime) Berkley Pub.

Phillips, T. S. Dance of the Mongoose. 288p. 1996. mass mkt. 5.99 (0-425-15623-0, Prime Crime) Berkley Pub.

Phillips, Terry, jt. auth. see Phillips, Ann.

Phillips, Terry M., ed. Analytical Techniques in Immunochemistry. (Illus.). 364p. 1991. text 195.00 (0-8247-8477-4) Dekker.

***Phillips, Terry M. & Dickens, Benjamin F.** Affinity & Immunoaffinity Purification Techniques. LC 00-21411. (Biotechniques Molecular Laboratory Methods Ser.). 2000. write for info. (1-881299-22-8) Eaton Pub Co.

Phillips, Terry M., jt. auth. see Friedlander, Mark P.

Phillips, Theodore & Sandberg, Teena D. Creative Movement Activities for Preschoolers: Perceptual & Tactile Approach. (Illus.). 177p. (Orig.). (C). 1994. pap. text 17.95 (0-89641-272-5) American Pr.

Phillips, Theodore L., jt. auth. see Leibel, Steven A.

Phillips, Theodore L. & Wara, William, eds. Radiation Oncology, 1987. LC 87-654098. 183p. 1987. reprint ed. pap. 56.80 (0-608-00405-7, 206111900002) Bks Demand.

Phillips, Theodore L., jt. ed. see Pistenmaa, David A.

Phillips, Thomas. The Welsh Revival: Its Origins & Development. 147p. 1995. pap. 8.50 (0-85151-685-8) Banner of Truth.

Phillips, Thomas, ed. see Vegetius Renatus, Flavia.

Phillips, Thomas Bruce, jt. auth. see Reynolds, Annie.

Phillips, Thomas G., ed. Advanced Technology MMW, Radio & Terahertz Telescopes. LC 98-227282. (Proceedings of SPIE Ser.: Vol. 3357). 802p. 1998. 124.00 (0-8194-2804-3) SPIE.

Phillips, Thomas H. The Bitterweed Path: A Rediscovered Novel. (Chapel Hill Bks.). 336p. 1996. pap. 17.95 (0-8078-4595-7) U of NC Pr.

— The Loved & the Unloved. LC 97-42205. 260p. 1998. pap. 17.00 (1-57806-056-7, Banner Bk) U Pr of Miss.

***Phillips, Thomas Hal.** Kangaroo Hollow. LC 99-54642. 317p. 2000. reprint ed. pap. 18.00 (1-57806-260-8) U Pr of Miss.

Phillips, Thomas R., ed. Roots of Strategy: The Five Greatest Military Classics of All Time-Complete in One Volume. LC 84-26826. 448p. 1985. pap. 14.95 (0-8117-2194-9) Stackpole.

Phillips, Tim. Keeping Your Job in the Digital Age: How to Stop Worrying & Learn to Love Your Computer. 1998. pap. text 14.95 (0-906097-15-0, Pub. by Bowerdean Pub) Capital VA.

Phillips, Timothy R. Between the Fog & the Freight Train. (Illus.). iv, 75p. 1997. pap. 9.25 (0-9660055-2-X, Wannabe) Twaanevie Poetry.

— Six Feet under, Twelve Feet High: How to Fight Post-Mortem Depression. iv, 50p. 1994. 20.00 (0-9660055-1-1, Blue Forrest) Twaanevie Poetry.

Phillips, Timothy R. & Okholm, Dennis L., eds. Christian Apologetics in the Postmodern World. LC 95-1682. 227p. (Orig.). 1995. pap. 15.99 (0-8308-1860-X, 1860) InterVarsity.

— The Nature of Confession: Evangelicals & Postliberals in Conversation. LC 96-13028. 300p. (Orig.). 1996. pap. 16.99 (0-8308-1869-3, 1869) InterVarsity.

Phillips, Todd & McMaster, Darren. Y2K: How to Protect Your Family in the Quiet Crisis. 128p. 1998. pap. 14.95 (0-9667797-0-3) Safe Two Thous.

Phillips, Tom. Hument. 3rd ed. LC 97-60273. 1998. pap. 24.95 (0-500-28028-2, Pub. by Thames Hudson) Norton.

— The Humument: A Treated Victorian Novel. 3rd rev. ed. LC 97-60273. (Illus.). 384p. 1997. pap. 24.95 (0-500-97455-1, Pub. by Thames Hudson) Norton.

— Music in Art: Through the Ages. LC 98-186539. (Illus.). 128p. 1997. 39.95 (3-7913-1864-0, Pub. by Prestel) te Neues.

***Phillips, Tom.** The Postcard Century. LC 00-10117. (Illus.). 2000p. 2000. pap. 29.95 (0-500-97590-6, Pub. by Thames Hudson) Norton.

Phillips, Tom. The World at Your Door: Reaching International Students in Your Home, Church & School. LC 97-21028. 24p. 1997. pap. 9.99 (1-55661-964-2) Bethany Hse.

Phillips, Tom, ed. Africa: The Art of a Continent. LC 97-229396. (Illus.). 620p. 1995. 95.00 (3-7913-1603-6, Pub. by Prestel) te Neues.

Phillips, Tom, frwd. Tom Phillips: Selections from the Ruth & Marvin Sackner Archive of Concrete & Visual Poetry. LC 90-63612. (Illus.). 28p. (Orig.). 1990. pap. 4.95 (0-88259-961-5) NCMA.

Phillips, Tom & Whalin, W. T. Rekindle the Fire: An Interactive Guide to Spiritual Revival That Begins with You. 1999. pap. 14.99 (0-8024-5248-5) Moody.

Phillips, Tom, ed. see Ryle, John C.

Phillips, Toni & Simonich, Juanita. Quilt-a-Saurus. (Illus.). 36p. (Orig.). 1993. 9.95 (0-9638806-0-8) Fabric Express.

Phillips, Toni, jt. auth. see Simonich, Junanita.

Phillips, Tori. Fool's Paradise (March Madness) (Historical Ser.). 1996. per. 4.50 (0-373-28907-3, 1-28907-3) Harlequin Bks.

***Phillips, Tori.** Halloween Knight. (Historical Ser.: Vol. 527). 2000. mass mkt. 4.99 (0-373-29127-2, 1-29127-7) Harlequin Bks.

Phillips, Tori. Lady of the Knight. (Historical Ser.). 1999. per. 4.99 (0-373-29076-4, 1-29076-6) Harlequin Bks.

— Midsummer's Knight. (Historical Ser.). 304p. 1998. mass mkt. 4.99 (0-373-29015-2, 1-29015-4) Harlequin Bks.

— Silent Knight. 1996. per. 4.99 (0-373-28943-X, 1-28943-8) Harlequin Bks.

— Three Dog Knight: The Cavendish Chronicles. 1998. per. 4.99 (0-373-29038-1, 1-29038-6) Harlequin Bks.

Phillips, Trevor M. Cast of Millions. Young, Paul J., Jr., ed. 1985. write for info. (0-9622708-7-3) Zubra Pub.

— Divine Footprints. Phillips, Julie A. & Young, Paul J., eds. (Illus.). 926p. 1990. 47.95 (0-9622708-5-7); pap. 27.95 (0-9622708-4-9) Zubra Pub.

— Lose Weight Religiously. 128p. 1990. pap. write for info. (0-9622708-3-0) Zubra Pub.

— A New Breeze Is Blowing. (Illus.). 232p. (Orig.). 1989. text 23.96 (0-9622708-0-6) Zubra Pub.

— Supercrats. 454p. 1989. write for info. (0-9622708-1-4) Zubra Pub.

— Supercrats. 2nd ed. Phillips, Julie A., ed. 486p. 1989. write for info. (0-9622708-2-2) Zubra Pub.

Phillips, Trevor M., ed. see Young, Paul J., Jr.

Phillips, U. B. Correspondence of Robert Toombs, Alexander H. Stephens, & Howell Cobb. LC 68-54846. (American Scene Ser.). 1970. reprint ed. lib. bdg. 95.00 (0-306-71191-5) Da Capo.

Phillips, Ulrich B. American Negro Slavery. 1990. 36.75 (0-8446-1348-7) Peter Smith.

— American Negro Slavery. (History - United States Ser.). 529p. 1992. reprint ed. lib. bdg. 99.00 (0-7812-6155-4) Rprt Serv.

— American Negro Slavery: A Survey of the Supply, Employment, & Control of Negro Labor As Determined by the Plantation Regime. LC 66-31730. (Illus.). xxvi, 530p. 1966. pap. text 24.95 (0-8071-0109-5) La State U Pr.

— Georgia & State Rights. LC 83-19635. (Reprints of Scholarly Excellence Ser.). 224p. 1984. text 14.95 (0-86554-103-5, MUP\H095) Mercer Univ Pr.

— The Slave Economy of the Old South: Selected Essays in Economic & Social History. fac. ed. Genovese, Eugene D., ed. LC 68-21806. 318p. 1968. reprint ed. pap. 98.60 (0-7837-7814-7, 204757000007) Bks Demand.

Phillips, Ulrich B., ed. see Commons, John R., et al.

Phillips, Ursula, tr. see Maczak, Antoni.

Phillips, Ursula, tr. see Mysliwski, Wieslaw.

Phillips, Utah. The Old Guy Poems. 31p. (Orig.). 1988. pap. 6.00 (0-9621041-0-8) Brownell Library Pr.

Phillips, V. N. Between the States: Bristol Tennessee/ Virginia: During the Civil War. (Illus.). 191p. 1997. 24.95 (1-57072-068-1) Overmountain Pr.

— The Book of Kings: The King Family's Contribution to the History of Bristol, Tennessee - Virginia. (Illus.). 343p. 1999. 29.95 (1-57072-083-5) Overmountain Pr.

— Bristol, Tennessee - Virginia: A History, 1852-1900. (Illus.). 492p. 1992. 27.95 (0-932807-63-1) Overmountain Pr.

Phillips, Vicki. Empowering Discipline: An Approach Which Works with at Risk Students. LC 99-90159. 116p. 1999. pap. 17.95 (0-9628482-9-8) Prsnl Dev.

— Personal Development: A One Semester Curriculum Designed to Develop Respect, Reponsibility, & Resiliency in At-Risk Adolescents, Preview Packet. rev. ed. 1991. 15.00 (0-9628482-7-1) Prsnl Dev.

— Personal Development: A One Semester Curriculum Designed to Develop Respect, Responsibility, & Resiliency in At-Risk Adolescents, Group & Individualized Version. rev. ed. 1991. 595.00 (0-9628482-6-3) Prsnl Dev.

— Personal Development: A One Semester Curriculum Designed to Develop Respect, Responsibility, & Resiliency in At-Risk Adolescents, Group Version. rev. ed. 1991. 375.00 (0-9628482-4-7) Prsnl Dev.

— Personal Development: A One Semester Curriculum Designed to Develop Respect, Responsibility, Resiliency in At-Risk Adolescents, Individualized Version. rev. ed. 1991. 350.00 (0-9628482-5-5) Prsnl Dev.

— Turning Them Around: Developing Motivation, Responsibility, & Self-Discipline in At-Risk Youth. (Illus.). 296p. (Orig.). 1996. pap. 49.95 (0-9628482-8-X) Prsnl Dev.

Phillips, Vicki & McCullough, Laura. Student/Staff Support Teams: SST Program Kit, 3 vols., Set. (Illus.). 390p. 1993. pap. text 145.00 (0-944584-74-8, 42KIT) Sopris.

— Student/Staff Support Teams (SST) Administrator Handbook. (Illus.). 78p. 1993. pap. text 16.50 (0-944584-61-6, 42AH) Sopris.

— Student/Staff Support Teams (SST) Team Member Implementation Guide. (Illus.). 86p. 1993. pap. text 16.50 (0-944584-60-8, 42TG) Sopris.

— Student/Staff Support Teams (SST) Trainer Manual. (Illus.). 226p. 1993. pap. text, teacher ed. 125.00 (0-944584-68-3, 42TM) Sopris.

***Phillips, Vicky.** Never Too Late to Learn: The Adult Student's Guide to College. 304p. 2000. pap. 13.95 (0-375-75478-4, Pub. by PRP NY) Random.

Phillips, Vicky & Yager, Cindy. Writer's Guide to Internet Resources. LC 97-70667. 272p. 1998. pap. 15.95 (0-02-861882-3, 847812, Arc) IDG Bks.

Phillips, Victor D., jt. auth. see Takahashi, Patrick K.

Phillips, Vivian A. The Biblical Alphabets Book. (Illus.). 32p. (Orig.). (J). Date not set. pap. text. write for info. (1-888413-01-8) Seasoning Quilting.

— Biblical Plays. (Illus.). 37p. (Orig.). Date not set. pap. text. write for info. (1-888413-06-9) Seasoning Quilting.

— Education: Show & Tell. (Illus.). 10p. (Orig.). (J). Date not set. pap. text. write for info. (1-888413-05-0) Seasoning Quilting.

— Intrique Math. (Illus.). 16p. (Orig.). (YA). Date not set. pap. text. write for info. (1-888413-04-2) Seasoning Quilting.

— Jesus Christ Is My Lover. (Illus.). Date not set. pap. write for info. (1-888413-08-5) Seasoning Quilting.

— My Dog & His Bone, Vol. I. (Illus.). 15p. (J). Date not set. pap. text. write for info. (1-888413-03-4) Seasoning Quilting.

— My Dog & His Bone, Vol. II. (Illus.). 14p. (J). Date not set. text. write for info. (1-888413-07-7) Seasoning Quilting.

— My Dog & His Bone, Vol. III. (Illus.). Date not set. pap. text. write for info. (1-888413-11-5) Seasoning Quilting.

— Show & Tell: Education. (Illus.). 10p. (Orig.). (J). Date not set. pap. write for info. (1-888413-00-X) Seasoning Quilting.

— Swan. (Illus.). 20p. (Orig.). (J). Date not set. pap. text. write for info. (1-888413-02-6) Seasoning Quilting.

Phillips, W., et al, eds. Laser Manipulation of Atoms & Ions: Proceedings of the Intl. School of Physics "Enrico Fermi", Course CXVIII, July 9-19, 1991. LC 92-47136. 798p. 1993. 300.00 (0-444-89993-6, North Holland) Elsevier.

Phillips, W. A., ed. Amorphous Solids. (Topics in Current Physics Ser.: Vol. 24). (Illus.). 167p. 1981. 64.95 (0-387-10330-9) Spr-Verlag.

Phillips, W. A., tr. see Gratz, Gustav & Schuller, Richard.

Phillips, W. Andrew, jt. auth. see Sproull, Robert L.

Phillips, W. Gary & Brown, William E. Making Sense of Your World: A Biblical Worldview. 291p. (C). 1996. pap. text 15.50 (1-879215-32-2) Sheffield WI.

Phillips, W. R., jt. auth. see Grant, I. S.

Phillips, W. S. Social Stratification & Mobility in Urban India. 1990. 23.00 (81-7033-084-X, Pub. by Rawat Pubns) S Asia.

— Street Children in India. (C). 1994. 22.50 (81-7033-188-9, Pub. by Rawat Pubns) S Asia.

Phillips, Wade G. Constitutional Law: An Outline of the Law & Practice of the Constitution, Including English Local Government, the Constitutional Relations of the British Empire & the Church of England. xxii, 476p. 1999. reprint ed. 150.00 (1-56169-501-7) Gaunt.

Phillips, Wade H. The Church of God: History & Prophecy. (Systematic Ecclesiology Ser.). 120p. (Orig.). 1990. pap. 6.95 (0-934942-82-X, 2442) White Wing Pub.

— God, the Church & Revelation. 376p. (Orig.). 1986. pap. 8.95 (0-934942-60-9, 4048) White Wing Pub.

An Asterisk (*) at the beginning of an entry indicates that the title is appearing for the first time.

Phillips, Wally. The Wally Phillips People Book. LC 79-88664. (Illus.). 252p. 1979. 7.95 (*0-89803-012-9*) Jameson Bks.

***Phillips, Walt.** Eccentric Stew. Metzger, Joyce, ed. (Illus.). 52p. 1999. pap. 7.95 (*1-878116-90-8*) JVC Bks.

Phillips, Walter R. Family Farmer & Individual Adjustment of Debts Chapters 12 & 13: The Bankruptcy Code. 1987. write for info. (*0-318-66758-4*) Harrison Co GA.

— Reorganizations under Chapter 11 of the Bankruptcy Code. 1980. write for info. (*0-318-66759-2*) Harrison Co GA.

Phillips, Wanda C. Daily Grams: Guided Review Aiding Mastery Skills. 190p. (J). (gr. 6 up). 1987. pap. text 18.95 (*0-936981-05-9*) ISHA Enterprises.

— Daily Grams: Guided Review Aiding Mastery Skills for 3rd & 4th Grades. 190p. (J). (gr. 3-4). 1989. pap. text 18.95 (*0-936981-07-5*) ISHA Enterprises.

— Daily Grams: Guided Review Aiding Mastery Skills for 4th & 5th Grades. 190p. (J). (gr. 4-5). 1987. pap. text 18.95 (*0-936981-06-7*) ISHA Enterprises.

— Daily Grams: Guided Review Aiding Mastery Skills for 5th & 6th Grades. 190p. (YA). (gr. 6 up). 1992. pap. text, teacher ed. 18.95 (*0-936981-10-5*) ISHA Enterprises.

— Daily Guided Teaching & Review Aiding Mastery Skills for 2nd & 3rd Grades. 190p. 1991. pap. text, teacher ed. 18.95 (*0-936981-09-1*) ISHA Enterprises.

***Phillips, Wanda C.** Easy Grammar: Grades 3 & 4. (J). (gr. 3-4). 1998. pap. text 24.95 (*0-936981-17-2*) ISHA Enterprises.

Phillips, Wanda C. Easy Grammar: Grades 4 & 5. 521p. (J). (gr. 4-5). 1996. pap. text 24.95 (*0-936981-15-6*) ISHA Enterprises.

— Easy Grammar: Grades 5 & 6. 626p. (Orig.). (J). (gr. 5-6). 1994. pap. text, teacher ed. 26.95 (*0-936981-11-3*) ISHA Enterprises.

— Easy Grammar: Workbook 45. 252p. (J). (gr. 4-5). 1996. pap. text, wbk. ed. 13.95 (*0-936981-16-4*) ISHA Enterprises.

— Easy Grammar Plus. 663p. (YA). (gr. 6 up). 1995. pap. text 28.95 (*0-936981-13-X*) ISHA Enterprises.

— Easy Grammar Plus Workbook. 347p. (J). (gr. 6 up). 1985. pap. text, wbk. ed. 13.95 (*0-936981-14-8*) ISHA Enterprises.

— Easy Grammar Workbook 56. 346p. (J). (gr. 5-6). 1994. pap. text, wbk. ed. 13.95 (*0-936981-12-1*) ISHA Enterprises.

***Phillips, Wanda C.** Easy Grammar Workbook 34. 234p. (J). (gr. 3-4). 1998. pap. text, wbk. ed. 13.95 (*0-936981-18-0*) ISHA Enterprises.

Phillips, Wanda C. Easy Writing: Teaching Students How to Write Complex Sentence Structures. 469p. (Orig.). (J). (gr. 4-12). 1990. pap. text 20.95 (*0-936981-08-3*) ISHA Enterprises.

— My Mother Doesn't Like to Cook. (Illus.). 28p. (Orig.). (J). (gr. 1-5). 1935. pap. 6.95 (*0-936981-20-2*) ISHA Enterprises.

Phillips, Wayne. Central Rocky Mountain Wildflowers: Including Yellowstone & Grand Teton National Parks. LC 98-46909. (Illus.). 272p. 1999. pap. 19.95 (*1-56044-729-X*) Falcon Pub Inc.

Phillips, Wendel. Oman a History. 246p. 1971. 16.00 (*0-86685-024-4*, LDL0244, Pub. by Librairie du Liban) Intl Bk Ctr.

— Unknown Oman. (Arab Background Ser.). 319p. 1972. 16.00 (*0-86685-025-2*, LDL0252, Pub. by Librairie du Liban) Intl Bk Ctr.

Phillips, Wendell. Review of Lysander Spooner's Essay on the Unconstitutionality of Slavery. LC 76-82220. (Anti-Slavery Crusade in America Ser.). 1970. reprint ed. 11.95 (*0-405-00648-9*) Ayer.

— Speeches, Lectures & Letters, Second Series. LC 79-82210. (Anti-Slavery Crusade in America Ser.). 1970. reprint ed. 41.95 (*0-405-00649-7*) Ayer.

Phillips, Wilbur C. Adventuring for Democracy. LC 74-3216. (Children & Youth Ser.). 380p. 1974. reprint ed. 33.95 (*0-405-05994-9*) Ayer.

Phillips, Will. Every Dreamer's Handbook. 1996. pap. 12.00 (*1-57566-048-2*) Kensgtn Pub Corp.

Phillips, Willard. A Manual of Political Economy: With Particular Reference to the Institutions, Resources & Condition of the U. S. LC 65-26373. (Reprints of Economic Classics Ser.). 278p. 1968. reprint ed. 45.00 (*0-678-00278-9*) Kelley.

— Propositions Concerning Protection & Free Trade. LC 67-29515. (Reprints of Economic Classics Ser.). xv, 233p. 1968. reprint ed. 39.50 (*0-678-00369-6*) Kelley.

Phillips, Willard & Sewell, Samuel E., notes. Summary of the Law of Bills of Exchange, Cash Bills, & Promissory Notes: With Notes & References to American Decisions. 4th ed. xii, 426p. 1994. reprint ed. 55.00 (*0-8377-1976-3*, Rothman) W S Hein.

***Phillips, William.** An Affair in Madison. LC 99-65236. 144p. 2000. pap. 12.95 (*1-58501-053-7*, Pub. by CeShore Pubg) Natl Bk Netwk.

Phillips, William, ed. Sixty Years of Great Fiction from Partisan Review. LC 96-50882. 425p. 1997. 24.95 (*0-9644377-5-9*); pap. 14.95 (*0-9644377-4-0*) Partisan Rev Pr.

Phillips, William, jt. ed. see Kurzweil, Edith.

Phillips, William, jt. ed. see Peterson, Robin.

Phillips, William B. Pastoral Transitions: From Endings to New Beginnings. LC 88-71755. 77p. 1988. reprint ed. pap. 9.95 (*1-56699-029-7*, AL108) Alban Inst.

Phillips, William D., Jr. Before 1492: Christopher Columbus's Formative Years. Phillips, Carla R. & Weber, David J., eds. LC 92-81880. (Essays on the Columbian Encounter Ser.). (Illus.). 64p. (Orig.). (C). 1992. pap. 7.00 (*0-87229-065-4*) Am Hist Assn.

— Enrique IV & the Crisis of Fifteenth-Century Castile, 1425-1480. LC 77-89931. 1978. pap. 12.00 (*0-910956-63-4*) Medieval Acad.

Phillips, William D. Slavery from Roman Times to the Early Transatlantic Trade. LC 84-10470. 299p. 1985. reprint ed. pap. 92.70 (*0-608-00794-3*, 205934300010) Bks Demand.

Phillips, William D., Jr. & Phillips, Carla R. The Worlds of Christopher Columbus. (Illus.). 336p. (C). 1991. text 16.95 (*0-521-35097-2*) Cambridge U Pr.

— The Worlds of Christopher Columbus. (Illus.). 336p. (C). 1993. pap. 16.95 (*0-521-44652-X*) Cambridge U Pr.

Phillips, William D., Jr., jt. auth. see Phillips, Carla R.

Phillips, William D., jt. ed. see Prentiss, Mara G.

Phillips, William H. St. John Hankin: Edwardian Mephistopheles. LC 77-89783. 150p. 1979. 24.50 (*0-8386-2155-4*) Fairleigh Dickinson.

— Writing Short Scripts. LC 89-21961. (Illus.). 240p. (C). 1990. text 35.00 (*0-8156-2485-9*); pap. text 17.95 (*0-8156-2486-7*) Syracuse U Pr.

— Writing Short Scripts. 2nd ed. LC 98-53790. 256p. 1999. pap. 19.95 (*0-8156-2802-1*) Syracuse U Pr.

Phillips, William J. Carols, Their Origin, Music, & Connection with Mystery-Plays: A Greenwood Archival Edition. LC 75-109821. (Illus.). 134p. 1971. reprint ed. lib. bdg. 45.50 (*0-8371-4312-8*, PHCA, Greenwood Pr) Greenwood.

— An Introduction to Mineralogy for Geologists. LC 79-42898. (Illus.). 374p. reprint ed. pap. 116.00 (*0-8357-2955-9*, 203921100011) Bks Demand.

Phillips, William L. & Gendle, Edward J. Building Services Management. 152p. 1994. pap. 25.00 (*0-944352-10-3*) Cleaning Cons.

Phillips, William M., Jr. An Unillustrious Alliance: The African American & Jewish American Communities, 146. LC 91-17126. (Contributions in Afro-American & African Studies: No. 146). 176p. 1991. 52.95 (*0-313-27776-1*, PUL, Greenwood Pr) Greenwood.

Phillips, William R. The Conquest of Kansas, by Missouri & Her Allies. LC 76-161271. (Black Heritage Library Collection). 1977. reprint ed. 31.95 (*0-8369-8830-2*) Ayer.

— The Holocaust. (Illus.). 28p. (YA). 1992. student ed. 39.00 (*1-56696-000-2*) Jackdaw.

— Night of the Silver Stars: The Battle of Lang Vei. LC 97-29824. (Special Warfare Ser.). (Illus.). 208p. 1997. 29.95 (*1-55750-691-4*) Naval Inst Pr.

— An Outline of Mineralogy & Geology: Intended for the Use of Those Who May Desire to Become Acquainted with the Elements of Those Sciences. Albritton, Claude C., Jr., ed. LC 77-6536. (History of Geology Ser.). (Illus.). 1978. reprint ed. lib. bdg. 19.95 (*0-405-10456-1*) Ayer.

Phillips, William R. & Rosenberg, Janet, eds. Changing Patterns of Law: The Courts & the Handicapped: An Original Anthology. LC 79-6009. (Physically Handicapped in Society Ser.). 1980. lib. bdg. 44.95 (*0-405-13101-1*) Ayer.

— Cleveland Symposium on Behavioral Research in Rehabilitation. rev. ed. LC 79-6898. (Physically Handicapped in Society Ser.). 1980. reprint ed. lib. bdg. 25.95 (*0-405-13110-0*) Ayer.

— Education & Occupations of Cripples: Juveniles & Adults. LC 79-6924. (Physically Handicapped in Society Ser.). 1980. reprint ed. lib. bdg. 19.95 (*0-405-13131-3*) Ayer.

— The Origins of Modern Treatment & the Education of Physically Handicapped Children: An Original Anthology. LC 79-6010. (Physically Handicapped in Society Ser.). 1980. lib. bdg. 44.95 (*0-405-13102-X*) Ayer.

— Physically Handicapped in Society Series, 39 bks. 1980. lib. bdg. 965.00 (*0-405-13100-3*) Ayer.

— Social Scientists & the Physically Handicapped: An Original Anthology. LC 79-6011. (Physically Handicapped in Society Ser.). 1980. lib. bdg. 35.95 (*0-405-13103-8*) Ayer.

Phillips, William R., jt. auth. see Conybeare, W. D.

Phillips, William R., ed. see Anderson, Roy N.

Phillips, William R., ed. see Axford, Wendy A. & McMurtrie, Douglas C.

Phillips, William R., ed. see Barton, George E.

Phillips, William R., ed. see Berkowitz, Edward D.

Phillips, William R., ed. see Carling, Finn & Haecker, Theodor.

Phillips, William R., ed. see Charity Organisation Society Staff.

Phillips, William R., ed. see Eisenson, Jon, et al.

Phillips, William R., ed. see Giralestone, Gathrone R.

Phillips, William R., ed. see Graham, Earl C. & Mullen, Marjorie.

Phillips, William R., ed. see Hathaway, Katharine B.

Phillips, William R., ed. see Hinshaw, David.

Phillips, William R., ed. see Hoyer, Louis & Hay, Charles K.

Phillips, William R., ed. see Hunt, Agnes.

Phillips, William R., ed. see Kenny, Elizabeth & Ostenso, Martha.

Phillips, William R., ed. see Kessler, Henry H.

Phillips, William R., ed. see Landis, Carney & Bolles, M. Marjorie.

Phillips, William R., ed. see Leavitt, Moses A.

Phillips, William R., ed. see Macdonald, Mary E.

Phillips, William R., ed. see Mallinson, Vernon.

Phillips, William R., ed. see Mawson, Thomas.

Phillips, William R., ed. see McMurtrie, Douglas C.

Phillips, William R., ed. see Obermann, C. Esco.

Phillips, William R., ed. see Orr, H. Winnett.

Phillips, William R., ed. see Sullivan, Oscar M. & Snortum, Kenneth O.

Phillips, William R., ed. see Tracy, Susan R.

Phillips, William R., ed. see Watson, Frederick.

Phillips, William R., ed. see Wright, Henry C.

Phillips, William R., ed. see Wurtz, Hans.

Phillips, William R., ed. see Ziegler, Carlos R.

Phillips, William S. The Art of William S. Phillips: The Glory of Flight. LC 94-15294. 172p. 1994. 45.00 (*0-86713-022-9*, 88083) Greenwich Wrkshop.

Phillips, Zoe A., ed. see Phillips, Martin A.

***Phillipson, Chris.** Family & Community Life of Older People. 256p. 2000. pap. 25.99 (*0-415-20531-X*) Routledge.

— Reconstructing Old Age: New Agendas in Social Theory & Practice. LC 98-61237. 192p. 1998. 69.00 (*0-8039-7988-6*) Sage.

Phillipson, Chris, et al, eds. Dependency & Interdependency in Old Age. 300p. 1986. 45.00 (*0-7099-3987-6*, Pub. by C Helm) Routldge.

Phillipson, Chris, jt. auth. see Laczko, Frank.

Phillipson, Chris, jt. auth. see Walker, Alan.

Phillipson, Coleman. The International Law & Custom of Ancient Greece & Rome, Vol. 1. Vlastos, Gregory, ed. LC 78-19383. (Morals & Law in Ancient Greece Ser.). 1979. reprint ed. lib. bdg. 44.95 (*0-405-11565-2*) Ayer.

— Three Criminal Law Reformers: Beccaria, Bentham, Romilly. LC 77-17157. (Criminology, Law Enforcement, & Social Problems Ser.: No. 113). 1970. reprint ed. 27.00 (*0-87585-113-4*); reprint ed. pap. 15.00 (*0-87585-904-6*) Patterson Smith.

Phillipson, D. W. Ancient Ethiopia: Aksum, Its Antecedents & Successors LC 98-153695. 176 p. 1998. write for info. (*0-7141-2539-3*) British Mus Pr.

— The Later Prehistory of Eastern & Southern Africa. (Illus.). 323p. 1978. 49.50 (*0-8419-0347-6*, Africana) Holmes & Meier.

— The Prehistory of Eastern Zambia. (Illus.). 230p. 1977. pap. 28.50 (*1-872566-03-0*, Pub. by Brit Inst Estrn Africa) David Brown.

Phillipson, David. Band of Brothers: Boy Seamen in the Royal Navy, 1800-1956. (Illus.). 160p. 1997. 24.95 (*1-55750-099-1*) Naval Inst Pr.

— Roll on the Rodney. 1999. 31.95 (*0-7509-1968-X*) Sutton Pub Ltd.

Phillipson, David & Grossman, Louis, eds. Selected Writings of Isaac Mayer Wise. LC 71-83433. (Religion in America, Ser. 1). 1975. reprint ed. 31.95 (*0-405-00258-0*) Ayer.

Phillipson, David W. African Archaeology. 2nd ed. LC 92-35021. (Cambridge World Archaeology Ser.). (Illus.). 284p. (C). 1994. text 59.95 (*0-521-44103-X*); pap. text 21.95 (*0-521-44658-9*) Cambridge U Pr.

Phillipson, Gavin, jt. auth. see Fenwick, Helen.

Phillipson, Ian. Do Your Own P. R. Getting the Right Publicity for Your Organisation. 128p. 1995. pap. 19.95 (*1-85703-145-8*, Pub. by How To Bks) Trans-Atl Phila.

— How to Market Yourself: A Practical Guide to Winning at Work. (Illus.). 144p. 1995. pap. 19.95 (*1-85703-160-1*, Pub. by How To Bks) Trans-Atl Phila.

— How to Start Word Processing: A Step-by-Step Guide for Beginners. 128p. 1995. pap. 19.95 (*1-85703-156-3*, Pub. by How To Bks) Trans-Atl Phila.

— How to Work from Home: A Practical Handbook for the Independent Professional. 2nd ed. 176p. 1995. pap. 19.95 (*1-85703-158-X*, Pub. by How To Bks) Trans-Atl Phila.

Phillipson, J. D. & Zenk, M. H., eds. Indole & Biogenetically Related Alkaloids. (Annual Proceedings of the Phytochemical Society of Europe: No. 17). 1981. text 209.00 (*0-12-554450-2*) Acad Pr.

Phillipson, Julia, jt. auth. see Foster, Gayle.

Phillipson, Julia, jt. ed. see Foster, Gayle.

Phillipson, Laurel. The Stone Age of the Upper Zambezi Valley. 1978. pap. 12.00 (*1-872566-07-3*, Pub. by Brit Inst Estrn Africa) David Brown.

Phillipson, Michael. In Modernity's Wake. 176p. 1989. pap. 9.95 (*0-415-03232-6*, A3636) Routledge.

— Painting, Language & Modernity. 256p. 1985. pap. 35.00 (*0-7102-0480-9*, Routledge Thoemms) Routledge.

Phillipson, N. T. & Mitchison, Rosalind, eds. Scotland in the Age of Improvement: Essays in Scottish History in the Eighteenth Century. LC 97-178968. 270p. 1997. reprint ed. pap. text 25.00 (*0-7486-0876-1*, DA760, Pub. by Edinburgh U Pr) Col U Pr.

Phillipson, Nicholas & Skinner, Quentin, eds. Political Discourse in Early Modern Britain. (Ideas in Context Ser.: No. 24). 460p. (C). 1993. text 69.95 (*0-521-39242-X*) Cambridge U Pr.

Phillipson, R. Linguistic Imperialism. (Illus.). 374p. 1992. pap. text 21.95 (*0-19-437146-8*) OUP.

Phillipson, Robert, et al, eds. Foreign - Second Language Pedagogy Research: A Commemorative Volume for Claus Faerch. (Multilingual Matters Ser.: No. 64). 360p. 1991. 39.95 (*1-85359-085-1*, Pub. by Multilingual Matters); pap. 39.95 (*1-85359-084-3*, Pub. by Multilingual Matters) Taylor & Francis.

Phillipson, Robert, jt. auth. see Faerch, Claus.

Phillipson, Robert, jt. auth. see Skutnabb-Kangas, Tove.

Phillipson, William M. Life & Voyages of Wm. M. Phillipson. LC 71-99667. (Select Bibliographies Reprint Ser.). 1977. 20.95 (*0-8369-5096-8*) Ayer.

Phillipws, Earl H. & Eui-Young Yu, eds. Religions in Korea: Beliefs & Cultural Values. 127p. 1982. pap. 17.95 (*0-8420-2225-2*) Scholarly Res Inc.

Phillipy, Ruby. An Apronful of Memories. 90p. (Orig.). 1996. pap. write for info. (*0-9644370-5-8*) Dryden Publ.

— Through My Glasses: Reflections on This & That in Essays & Stories. (Illus.). 55p. (Orig.). 1996. pap. 10.95 (*0-9644370-6-6*) Dryden Publ.

Phillis, J. W., jt. ed. see Kerkut, G. A.

Phillis, John W. Adenosine & Adenine Nucleotides as Regulators of Cellular Function. (Illus.). 408p. 1991. lib. bdg. 250.00 (*0-8493-6928-2*, QP625) CRC Pr.

— The Regulation of Cerebral Blood Flow. 448p. 1993. lib. bdg. 225.00 (*0-8493-5096-4*, QP108) CRC Pr.

Phillis, John W., jt. ed. see Peterson, Patti L.

***Phillis, Randy.** Kismet, Colorado. LC 00-32441. (Illus.). 2000. pap. write for info. (*0-7734-1268-9*) E Mellen.

Phillis, Randy, jt. ed. see Learst, Allen.

Phillis, Susan, jt. ed. see Jenkins, Betty L.

Phillott, D. C. English-Hindustani Vocabulary for Higher Standard & Frequency. 1985. 35.00 (*0-8288-1746-4*, M9945) Fr & Eur.

Phillott, D. C. & Harcourt, E. S., trs. from PER. Falconry - Two Treatises. 1968. text 45.00 (*0-685-57148-3*) Falcon Head Pr.

Phillpot, Clive. Fluxus: Selections from the Gilbert & Lila Silverman Collection. (Illus.). 64p. (Orig.). 1989. pap. 9.95 (*0-87070-311-0*, Pub. by Mus of Modern Art) Abrams.

— Fluxus: Silverman Co. (Illus.). 64p. 1990. pap. 9.95 (*0-8109-6033-8*, Pub. by Abrams) Time Warner.

— Ray Johnson. Longhauser, Elsa, ed. LC 91-73923. (Illus.). 30p. 1991. pap. 25.00 (*1-58442-025-1*) Galleries at Moore.

Phillpot, Clive, jt. auth. see Lauf, Cornelia.

Phillpot, Clive, jt. auth. see Medvedow, Jill.

Phillpot, S. R., et al, eds. Microscopic Simulation of Interfacial Phenomena in Solids & Liquids Vol. 492: Materials Research Society Symposium Proceedings. LC 98-15404. 410p. 1998. text 77.00 (*1-55899-397-5*) Materials Res.

Phillpott, Pat. Small-Scale Weaving. 32p. 1989. pap. write for info. (*0-85532-452-X*, Pub. by Srch Pr) St Mut.

Phillpotts, Adelaide E. Lodgers in London. LC 74-150483. (Short Story Index Reprint Ser.). 1977. reprint ed. 20.95 (*0-8369-3824-0*) Ayer.

Phillpotts, Bertha S. Edda & Saga. 1977. lib. bdg. 59.95 (*0-8490-1752-1*) Gordon Pr.

Phillpotts, Eden. Black, White & Brindled. LC 77-142272. (Short Story Index Reprint Ser.). 1977. 21.95 (*0-8369-3756-2*) Ayer.

— Chronicles of St. Tid. LC 78-132124. (Short Story Index Reprint Ser.). 1977. 20.95 (*0-8369-3681-7*) Ayer.

— A Deal with the Devil. Reginald, R. & Menville, Douglas A., eds. LC 75-46300. (Supernatural & Occult Fiction Ser.). 1976. reprint ed. lib. bdg. 18.95 (*0-405-08160-X*) Ayer.

— Folk Afield. LC 76-128747. (Short Story Index Reprint Ser.). 1977. 20.95 (*0-8369-3638-8*) Ayer.

— Human Boy. LC 70-170592. (Short Story Index Reprint Ser.). 1977. reprint ed. 20.95 (*0-8369-4021-0*) Ayer.

— Human Boy & the War. LC 70-128748. (Short Story Index Reprint Ser.). 1977. 19.95 (*0-8369-3639-6*) Ayer.

— Peacock House, & Other Mysteries. LC 73-128749. (Short Story Index Reprint Ser.). 1977. 19.95 (*0-8369-3640-X*) Ayer.

Phillpotts, Eden. The Red Redmaynes. (Illus.). 384p. (C). 1982. reprint ed. pap. 6.95 (*0-486-24255-2*) Dover.

Phillpotts, Eden. The Torch, & Other Tales. LC 71-144167. (Short Story Index Reprint Ser.). 1977. reprint ed. 19.95 (*0-8369-3782-1*) Ayer.

— Up Hill, Down Dale: A Volume of Short Stories. 2nd ed. LC 79-150558. (Short Story Index Reprint Ser.). 1977. reprint ed. 20.95 (*0-8369-3855-0*) Ayer.

***Phillpotts, Karl.** The Testimony of His Imperial Majesty, Emperor Haile Selassie I: Defender of the Faith. 168p. 1999. pap. 15.00 (*0-9609684-1-5*) Zewd Pubs.

Phillps, G. C., jt. ed. see Gamborg, O. L.

Phillps, Shawn D., jt. auth. see Shenker, Nancy.

Phillus, J. W., jt. ed. see Kerkut, G. A.

Philo. Philonis Alexandrini in Flaccum. Connor, W. R., ed. LC 78-18570. (Greek Texts & Commentaries Ser.). 1979. reprint ed. lib. bdg. 25.95 (*0-405-11414-1*) Ayer.

***Philo, Chris & Wilbert, Chris.** Animal Spaces, Beastly Places: New Geographies of Human-Animal Relations. LC 99-89955. (Critical Geographies Ser.). 2000. pap. write for info. (*0-415-19847-X*) Routledge.

Philo, Greg. Glasgow Media Group Reader Vol. 2: Industry, Economy, War & Politics. (Communication & Society Ser.). 304p. (C). 1995. pap. 22.95 (*0-415-12262-7*) Routledge.

Philo, Greg, ed. Glasgow Media Readers Vol. 2: Industry, Economy, War & Politics. (Communication & Society Ser.). 240p. (C). 1995. text 65.00 (*0-415-12261-9*) Routledge.

— Media Mental Distress. LC 96-9069. (Illus.). 135p. (C). 1997. pap. 21.20 (*0-582-29219-0*) Longman.

Philo, Harry M. Lawyers Desk Reference, 3 vols. 8th ed. (Tort Personal Injury Law Ser.). 1993. 345.00 (*0-685-68852-6*) West Group.

— Lawyers Desk Reference, 3 vols., Set. 8th ed. LC 65-12985. 1993. 365.00 (*0-685-59885-3*) West Group.

— Trial Handbook for Michigan Lawyers. 2nd ed. LC 87-82165. 369p. 1993. suppl. ed. 55.00 (*0-317-03182-1*) West Group.

— Trial Handbook for Michigan Lawyers. 3rd ed. LC 95-80184. 1270p. 1995. text 125.00 (*0-7620-0006-6*) West Group.

***Philo, M.** Antique Style: Ideas & Techniques for Ageing Furniture & Accessories. (Illus.). 144p. 2000. 27.95 (*1-85410-656-2*, Pub. by Aurum Pr) London Brdge.

Philo, Maggie. The Decoupage Collection. LC 97-75703. (Illus.). 144p. 1998. 29.95 (*0-8478-2094-7*, Pub. by Rizzoli Intl) St Martin.

***Philo, Maggie.** Discover Decoupage: 40 Original Projects to Build Your Papercraft Skills. 112p. 1999. pap. text 14.95 (*0-600-59949-3*) Hamlyn Publishing Group Ltd.

Philo, Maggie. Paint Effects. (The Inspirations Ser.). (Illus.). 96p. 1998. 12.95 (*1-85967-602-2*, Lorenz Bks) Anness Pub.

***Philo, Maggie.** The Stencil Collection: Traditional Borders. 2000. pap. 14.95 (*1-85391-882-2*, Pub. by Merehurst Ltd) Tuttle Pubng.

P

Philo, Maggie & Lovric, Michelle. Victorian Cats: Decoupage Book with 10 Projects. (Illus.). 48p. 1997. 22.50 (*1-85410-462-4*, Pub. by Aurum Pr) London Brdge.

Philo, Ron, jt. auth. see Clayton, Martin.

Philodemos of Garada. Uber die Gedichte, Funftes Buch. xi, 178p. 1973. write for info. (*3-296-14930-9*) G Olms Pubs.

Philodemus. Philodemus on Piety Pt. 1: Critical Text with Commentary, Pt. 1. Obbink, Dirk, ed. & tr. by. (Illus.). 688p. 1997. text 145.00 (*0-19-815008-3*) OUP.

***Philodemus.** Philodemus: On Poems Bk. 1: Edited with Introduction, Translation, & Commentary. Janko, Richard, ed. LC 99-88853. 700p. 2000. text 130.00 (*0-19-815041-5*) OUP.

Philodemus of Garada. The Rhetorica of Philodemus. Hubbell, Harry M., tr. (Connecticut Academy of Arts & Sciences Ser., Trans.: Vol. 23). 1920. pap. 75.00 (*0-685-22831-2*) Elliots Bks.

Philogene, Gina. From Black to African American: A New Social Representation. LC 99-21594. 256p. 1999. 69.50 (*0-275-96284-9*) Greenwood.

Philombe, Rene. Tales from Cameroon. Bjornson, Richard, tr. from FRE. LC 84-50629. (Illus.). 136p. (C). 1984. 12.00 (*0-89410-314-8*, Three Contnts) L Rienner.

***Philomel Books Staff.** The Philomel Anthology of Humorous Verse. LC 99-89398. (Illus.). (J). 2001. write for info. (*0-399-23567-1*, Philomel) Peng Put Young Read.

Philomene, Marie. The New Year's Poetry Party at the Imperial Court: Two Decades in Postwar Years, 1960-1979. (Illus.). 250p. 1983. 39.95 (*4-590-00653-7*, Pub. by Hokuseido Pr) Book East.

Philomusus, S. Mr. Law's Unlawfulness of the Stage Entertainment Examin'd. (English Stage Ser.: Vol. 50). 1977. lib. bdg. 55.00 (*0-8240-0633-X*) Garland.

Philon, Helen. Early Islamic Ceramics: Catalogue of Islamic Art in the Benaki Museum, Vol. 1. (Illus.). 376p. 1980. 120.00 (*0-85667-098-7*) Sothebys Pubns.

Philoponus & Simplicius. On Aristotle's "Physics 5-8", with On Aristotle on the Void. Lettinck, Paul & Urmson, J. O., trs. LC 93-31609. (Ancient Commentators on Aristotle Ser.). 288p. 1994. text 49.95 (*0-8014-3005-4*) Cornell U Pr.

— Place, Void, & Eternity. Furley, David & Wildberg, Christian, trs. from GRE. (Ancient Commentators on Aristotle Ser.). 160p. 1991. text 49.95 (*0-8014-2634-0*) Cornell U Pr.

Philoponus, Ioannes. De Aeternitate Mundi Contra Proclum. Rabe, Hugo, ed. xiii, 699p. 1984. reprint ed. write for info. incl. 3.5 hd (*3-487-00420-8*) G Olms Pubs.

Philoponus, John. On Aristotle on the Intellect (De Anima 3. 408) Charlton, William, tr. from GRE. LC 91-8806. (Ancient Commentators on Aristotle Ser.). 180p. 1991. text 55.00 (*0-8014-2681-2*) Cornell U Pr.

— On Aristotle's "Physics 3" Edwards, M. J., tr. (Ancient Commentators on Aristotle Ser.). 1994. text 47.50 (*0-8014-3089-5*) Cornell U Pr.

— On Aristotle's "Physics 2" Lacey, A. R., tr. (Ancient Commentators on Aristotle Ser.). 1993. text 45.00 (*0-8014-2815-7*) Cornell U Pr.

***Philoponus, John, et al.** On Aristotle's "On the Soul 3.9-13" LC 99-88450. (Ancient Commentators on Aristotle Ser.). 2000. write for info. (*0-8014-3795-4*) Cornell U Pr.

Philosophy of Science Association Staff. Boston Studies in the Philosophy of Science, Vol. 20: Proceedings of the Philosophy of Science Association, Biennial Meeting, 1972. Schaffner, Kenneth F. & Cohen, R. S., eds. LC 72-624169. (Synthese Library: Vol. 64). 454p. 1974. pap. text 91.00 (*90-277-0409-0*, D Reidel); lib. bdg. 141.50 (*90-277-0408-2*, D Reidel) Kluwer Academic.

— Boston Studies in the Philosophy of Science, Vol 8: Proceedings of the Philosophy of Science Association, Biennial Meeting, 1970. Buck, R. Creighton & Cohen, R. S., eds. LC 73-20858. (Synthese Library: No. 39). 615p. 1971. pap. text 78.50 (*90-277-0309-4*); lib. bdg. 171.00 (*90-277-0187-3*) Kluwer Academic.

— PSA 1974: Proceedings of the Philosophy of Science Association, Biennial Meeting, 1974. Michalos, Alex C. & Cohen, R. S., eds. (Synthese Library: No. 91). 747p. 1976. pap. text 148.50 (*90-277-0648-4*, D Reidel); lib. bdg. 187.00 (*90-277-0647-6*, D Reidel) Kluwer Academic.

Philostratus, Flavius. Life of Apollonius of Tyana. Epistles of Apollonius & the Treatise of Eusebius, 2 vols., 1. (Loeb Classical Library: No. 16-17). 610p. 1912. text 18.95 (*0-674-99018-8*) HUP.

— Life of Apollonius of Tyana. Epistles of Apollonius & the Treatise of Eusebius, 2 vols., 2. (Loeb Classical Library: No. 16-17). 630p. 1912. text 18.95 (*0-674-99019-6*) HUP.

— Lives of the Sophists. (Loeb Classical Library: No. 134). 19.95 (*0-674-99149-4*) HUP.

— Opera, 2 vols. in 1. Kayser, C. L., ed. lxxxviii, 964p. 1985. reprint ed. write for info. (*3-487-00626-X*) G Olms Pubs.

— Vitae Sophistarum. xlii, 416p. 1971. reprint ed. write for info. (*3-487-04155-3*) G Olms Pubs.

Philostratus The Elder. Imagines, Bks. 1 & 2. (Loeb Classical Library: No. 256). 19.95 (*0-674-99282-2*) HUP.

Philotus. Ane Verie Excellent & Delectabill Tratise. Intitulit Philotus Quhairin We May Persave the Greit Inconveineences That Fallis Out in the Marriage Betwene Age & Youth. LC 75-26325. (English Experience Ser.: No. 121). 48p. 1969. reprint ed. 15.00 (*90-221-0121-5*) Walter J Johnson.

Philp & Horn. Plants Are Alive. (Illus.). (Orig.). 1989. pap. text 16.95 (*1-877991-14-7*, AP4286) Flinn Scientific.

Philp, jt. auth. see Claeys.

***Philp, Dawn N. & Walz, Deborah L.** Pocket Guide to I. V. Drugs. LC 99-52578. 2000. otabind. write for info. (*1-58255-044-1*) Springhouse Corp.

Philp, Geoffrey. Florida Bound. 64p. 1998. pap. 12.95 (*0-948833-82-3*, Pub. by Peepal Tree Pr) Paul & Co Pubs.

— Hurricane Center. 67p. 1998. pap. 12.95 (*1-900715-23-6*, Pub. by Peepal Tree Pr) Paul & Co Pubs.

— Uncle Obadiah & the Alien. 160p. 1997. pap. 12.95 (*1-900715-01-5*, Pub. by Peepal Tree Pr) Paul & Co Pubs.

Philp, Howard L. Freud & Religious Belief. LC 72-12635. 140p. 1974. reprint ed. lib. bdg. 38.50 (*0-8371-6682-9*, PHFR, Greenwood Pr) Greenwood.

Philp, J. R., jt. auth. see Morgan, John.

Philp, J. R., jt. auth. see Morgan, John S.

Philp, Kenneth R. John Collier's Crusade for Indian Reform, 1920-1954. LC 76-4427. (Illus.). 320p. reprint ed. pap. 99.20 (*0-7837-1911-6*, 204211500001) Bks Demand.

— Termination Revisited: American Indians on the Trail to Self-Determination, 1933-1953. LC 98-39667. (Illus.). 1999. text 50.00 (*0-8032-3723-5*) U of Nebr Pr.

Philp, Kenneth R., ed. Indian Self Rule: First Hand Accounts of Indian-White Relations from Roosevelt to Reagan. LC 94-36862. 343p. 1995. pap. text 19.95 (*0-87421-180-8*) Utah St U Pr.

Philp, Mark. Godwin's Political Justice. LC 86-47538. 288p. 1986. 45.00 (*0-8014-1908-5*) Cornell U Pr.

Philp, Mark, et al, eds. The Collected Novels & Memoirs of William Godwin, 8 vols. (Pickering Masters Ser.). 1992. 730.00 (*1-85196-007-4*, Pub. by Pickering & Chatto) Ashgate Pub Co.

— The Political & Philosophical Writings of William Godwin, 7 vols. LC 99-58650. (Pickering Masters Ser.). 1993. 635.00 (*1-85196-026-0*, Pub. by Pickering & Chatto) Ashgate Pub Co.

Philp, Mark, ed. & intro. see Paine, Thomas.

Philp, Peter. Journey with the Poor. 144p. 1991. reprint ed. pap. 8.95 (*0-85924-562-4*) Harper SF.

Philp, Richard B. Environmental Hazards & Human Health. 320p. 1995. lib. bdg. 85.00 (*1-56670-133-3*, L1133) Lewis Pubs.

Philp, Richard B., ed. Mathematical Models in Microbial Population Dynamics. 288p. 1981. 164.00 (*0-8493-6110-9*, RM340, CRC Reprint) Franklin.

Philp, Stephanie, ed. see Miller, Margaret J.

Philp, T. Improve Your Decision Making Skills. 104p. 1984. pap. text 14.95 (*0-07-084766-5*) McGraw.

Philp, Tom. Appraising Performance for Results. 2nd ed. 144p. 1990. pap. text 9.95 (*0-07-707334-7*) McGraw.

Philpin, C. H., jt. ed. see Aston, T. H.

Philpin, John. Dreams in the Key of Blue. 2000. mass mkt. 6.50 (*0-553-58006-X*) Bantam Dell.

— Stalemate. 384p. 1997. mass mkt. 6.50 (*0-553-56999-6*) Bantam.

Philpin, John & Sierra, Patricia. The Prettiest Feathers. 336p. 1997. mass mkt. 5.50 (*0-553-57555-4*) Bantam.

— Tunnel of Night. 384p. 1999. mass mkt. 6.50 (*0-553-57954-1*) Bantam.

Philpot, Carol L., et al. Bridging Separate Gender Worlds: Why Men & Women Clash & How Therapists Can Bring Them Together. LC 96-41554. 410p. 1997. text 29.95 (*1-55798-381-X*) Am Psychol.

***Philpot, Don.** Barbados. (Visitors Guides Ser.). (Illus.). 96p. 2000. pap. 10.95 (*1-901522-32-6*, Pub. by Landmark Pub) Hunter NJ.

Philpot, Ed, jt. auth. see Philpot, Jan.

Philpot, Gloria & Gunn, Mildred, eds. Sunday Morning Atlanta, Preaching: Sermons, Afro American, Atlanta. 72p. (Orig.). 1994. pap. write for info. (*0-9621362-1-2*) T E Balls Pubns.

Philpot, Graham. Where Is Zak? (Illus.). 16p. (J). (ps-3). 1999. 12.99 (*0-7636-0892-0*) Candlewick Pr.

Philpot, Graham, jt. auth. see Philpot, Lorna.

Philpot, J. H. The Sacred Tree: The Tree in Religion & Myth. 1977. lib. bdg. 250.00 (*0-8490-2553-2*) Gordon Pr.

— The Seceders. 1970. pap. 4.50 (*0-85151-132-5*) Banner of Truth.

Philpot, Jan & Philpot, Ed. Partners in Learning & Growing: Linking the Home, School, & Community Through Curriculum-Based Programs. Britt, Leslie, ed. (Illus.). 80p. (Orig.). 1994. pap. text 9.95 (*0-86530-298-7*, 270-8) Incentive Pubns.

Philpot, Jan G. Bibliotherapy for Classroom Use. Britt, Leslie, ed. LC 96-78571. (Illus.). 80p. (J). (gr. 4-8). 1997. pap. text 9.95 (*0-86530-353-3*, 349-9) Incentive Pubns.

— Book-a-Brations: Activities, Special Events & More to Promote a Love of Literature. Sharpe, Sally D., ed. (Illus.). 80p. (Orig.). (J). (gr. k-6). 1990. pap. text 9.95 (*0-86530-073-9*, 168-0) Incentive Pubns.

— Book-a-Tivities! High-Interest Activities to Turn Students into Booklovers. Keeling, Jan, ed. (Illus.). 80p. (Orig.). (J). (gr. 1-6). 1993. pap. text, teacher ed. 9.95 (*0-86530-248-0*, 197-3) Incentive Pubns.

— Class Act Awards & Motivators: To Encourage School Spirit, Self-Esteem, & Attendance. Keeling, Jan, ed. (Illus.). 80p. (Orig.). 1993. teacher ed. 9.95 (*0-86530-214-6*, 197-5) Incentive Pubns.

— Once upon a Tradition: Using Traditional Literature to Develop Reading, Writing, Thinking, & Research Skills. Keeling, Jan, ed. (Illus.). 80p. (Orig.). (J). (gr. k-4). 1993. pap. text 9.95 (*0-86530-286-3*, 270-5) Incentive Pubns.

— Readers' Clubhouse: Organized Reading Programs with a Purpose. Binkley, Margaret, ed. (Illus.). 80p. (Orig.). (J). (gr. k-6). 1991. pap. text 9.95 (*0-86530-204-9*, IP 192-7) Incentive Pubns.

— Scissor-Tales for Any Day: Storytelling Cutups, Activities, & Extensions. Britt, Leslie, ed. (Illus.). 80p. (Orig.). (J). (gr. k-4). 1994. pap. text 9.95 (*0-86530-285-5*, 64-X) Incentive Pubns.

— Scissor-Tales for Special Days: Storytelling Cutups, Activities, & Extensions. Keeling, Jan, ed. (Illus.). 80p. (Orig.). (J). (gr. k-4). 1994. pap. text 9.95 (*0-86530-284-7*, 64-1) Incentive Pubns.

— Year of the Reader! Creative Activities to Promote Reading Excitement. Keeling, Jan, ed. (Illus.). 96p. (Orig.). (J). (gr. 3-6). 1993. pap. text, teacher ed. 10.95 (*0-86530-247-2*, 196-9) Incentive Pubns.

Philpot, Lorna & Philpot, Graham. Anthony Ant's Treasure Hunt. LC 95-73107. 1996. 14.99 (*0-679-88219-7*) McKay.

Philpot, Terry & Douglas, Anthony. Caring & Coping: A Guide to Social Services. LC 97-32824. 272p. (C). 1998. 80.00 (*0-415-16032-4*) Routledge.

Philpot, Terry, jt. ed. see Hanvey, Chris.

Philpot, Terry, jt. ed. see Ward, Linda.

Philpot, Tery & Douglas, Anthony. Caring & Coping: A Guide to Social Services. LC 97-32824. 272p. (C). 1998. pap. 24.99 (*0-415-16033-2*) Routledge.

Philpot, Tracy. Incorrect Distances: Poems by Tracy Philpot. LC 97-18687. 1998. pap. 15.95 (*0-8203-1957-0*) U of Ga Pr.

Philpot, William M., ed. Best Black Sermons. LC 72-75358. 96p. 1972. pap. 12.00 (*0-8170-0533-1*) Judson.

Philpott. Handbook of Hospital Infection. 1994. pap. text 41.00 (*0-7020-1658-6*, W B Saunders Co) Harcrt Hlth Sci Grp.

— The Slum & the Ghetto. (Adaptable Courseware-Softside Ser.). Date not set. pap. 24.75 (*0-534-15922-2*) Wadsworth Pub.

Philpott, A. B., jt. ed. see Anderson, E. J.

Philpott, Adrian. Witnessing Justice in Queensland. 154p. (C). 1990. pap. text 48.00 (*0-646-03848-6*, Pub. by Boolarong Pubns) St Mut.

Philpott, Bryan. German Bombers over England. 1986. pap. 7.95 (*1-85260-154-X*) HarpC.

Philpott, Bryan. Making Model Aircraft. 1990. pap. 12.95 (*1-85260-192-2*, Pub. by P Stephens) Haynes Manuals.

Philpott, D. R., jt. auth. see Barnard, R. H.

Philpott, Don. Antigua & Barbuda. (Landmark Visitors Guides Ser.). (Illus.). 160p. 1999. pap. 9.95 (*1-901522-02-4*) Hunter NJ.

— Barbados. (Caribbean Sunseekers Ser.). (Illus.). 160p. 1996. pap. 10.95 (*0-8442-4931-9*) NTC Contemp Pub Co.

— Bermuda. (Landmark Visitors Guides Ser.). (Illus.). 160p. 1999. pap. 13.95 (*1-901522-07-5*) Hunter NJ.

***Philpott, Don.** Cayman Islands. (Visitors Guides Ser.). (Illus.). 96p. 2000. pap. 10.95 (*1-901522-33-4*, Pub. by Landmark Pub) Hunter NJ.

Philpott, Don. Cayman Islands. (Caribbean Sunseekers Ser.). (Illus.). 160p. 1996. pap. 10.95 (*0-8442-4933-5*, Passprt Bks) NTC Contemp Pub Co.

— Dominican Republic. (Landmark Visitors Guides Ser.). (Illus.). 160p. 1999. pap. 13.95 (*1-901522-08-3*) Hunter NJ.

— Florida Keys. (Caribbean Sunseekers Ser.). (Illus.). 160p. 1996. pap. 10.95 (*0-8442-4937-8*, Passprt Bks) NTC Contemp Pub Co.

***Philpott, Don.** Jamaica. (Visitors Guides Ser.). (Illus.). 96p. 2000. pap. 10.95 (*1-901522-31-8*, Pub. by Landmark Pub) Hunter NJ.

Philpott, Don. Jamaica. (Caribbean Sunseekers Ser.). (Illus.). 256p. 1996. pap. 14.95 (*0-8442-4938-6*, Passprt Bks) NTC Contemp Pub Co.

— Puerto Rico. (Caribbean Sunseekers Ser.). (Illus.). 256p. 1996. pap. 14.95 (*0-8442-4940-8*, Passprt Bks) NTC Contemp Pub Co.

— St. Lucia: Caribbean Sunseekers. (Caribbean Sunseekers Ser.). (Illus.). 160p. (Orig.). 1996. pap. 10.95 (*0-8442-4927-0*, Passprt Bks) NTC Contemp Pub Co.

— St. Vincent & Grenadines: Caribbean Sunseekers. (Caribbean Sunseekers Ser.). (Illus.). 160p. (Orig.). 1996. pap. 10.95 (*0-8442-4928-9*, 49289, Passprt Bks) NTC Contemp Pub Co.

— The Virgin Islands. (Landmark Visitors Guides Ser.). (Illus.). 256p. 1999. pap. 15.95 (*1-901522-03-2*) Hunter NJ.

Philpott, Donna, jt. ed. see Delbert.

Philpott, Jane, jt. auth. see Crellin, J. K.

Philpott, Jane, jt. auth. see Crellin, John K.

Philpott, John. The National Minimum Wage. (Issues Ser.: No. 13). 1996. pap. 60.00 (*0-85292-663-4*, Pub. by IPM Hse) St Mut.

Philpott, John, ed. Working for Full Employment. LC 96-5645. 264p. (C). 1997. 85.00 (*0-415-14347-0*) Routledge.

Philpott, John, ed. Working for Full Employment. 264p. (C). 1997. pap. 29.99 (*0-415-14348-9*) Routledge.

***Philpott, John E.** Gourmet Meals That Will Melt in Your Mouth: The Dental Transition Cookbook. 128p. 1999. pap. 12.95 (*0-931571-14-6*) RP Pubng.

Philpott-Jones, Pamela & McClure, Paul L. Woodworking for the Serious Beginner. (Illus.). 176p. (Orig.). 1995. pap. 19.95 (*0-9643999-2-X*, 9992X) Cambium Pr.

Philpott, Kent. Are You Really Born Again. 1998. pap. text 10.99 (*0-85234-405-8*) P & R Pubng.

Philpott, Peter. The Art of Wrist Spin Bowling. (Illus.). 1997. pap. 24.95 (*1-86126-063-6*, Pub. by Crolwood) Trafalgar.

***Philpott, Simon.** Rethinking Indonesia: Postcolonial Theory, Authoritainism & Identity. LC 00-42069. 2000. write for info. (*0-312-23642-5*) St Martin.

Philpott, Stuart B. West Indian Migration: The Montserrat Case. LC 74-165105. (London School of Economics: No. 47). x, 210p. 1973. write for info. (*0-391-00287-2*) Humanities.

Philpott, V. Know How Book of Puppets. 13.96 (*0-88110-494-9*) EDC.

***Philpott, William.** Brain Allergies: The Psychonutrient & Magnetic Connections. LC 99-55470. (Illus.). 256p. 2000. pap. 14.95 (*0-658-00398-4*, 003984, Keats Publng) NTC Contemp Pub Co.

Philpott, William H. & Kalita, Dwight K. Brain Allergies. 235p. (Orig.). 1987. pap. 14.95 (*0-87983-426-9*, Keats Publng) NTC Contemp Pub Co.

Philpott, William H. & Taplin, Sharon. The BioMagnetic Handbook. 97p. 1989. 17.95 (*0-9636964-0-8*) Enviro-Tech.

Philpotts, Anthony R. Petrography of Igneous & Metamorphic Rocks. 178p. (C). 1988. pap. text 41.00 (*0-13-662313-1*) P-H.

Philpotts, Kaui. Floral Traditions at the Honolulu Academy of Arts. rev. ed. (Illus.). 88p. (Orig.). 1995. 29.95 (*0-937426-35-0*); pap. 19.95 (*0-937426-31-8*) Honolulu Arts.

— Great Chefs of Hawaii. Miller, Carolyn, ed. (Illus.). 247p. 1996. 29.95 (*0-929714-73-3*); pap. 24.95 (*0-929714-72-5*) Great Chefs TV.

— Hawaiian Country Tables: Vintage Recipes for Today's Cook. (Illus.). 144p. 1998. pap. 19.95 (*1-57306-076-3*) Bess Pr.

Philps, J. W. The Functional Foot Orthosis. (Illus.). 180p. 1990. pap. text 35.00 (*0-443-04058-3*) Church.

— The Functional Foot Orthosis. 2nd ed. 1995. text 42.00 (*0-443-04991-2*) Church.

Phil's Photo Staff, ed. A Typeface Sourcebook: Homage to the Alphabet. rev. ed. 565p. 1990. pap. 39.99 (*0-935603-47-6*, 30254) Rockport Pubs.

Philsbury. Green Giant, Making Meals Easy. 75th anniversary ed. 96p. 1999. pap. 14.95 (*0-86573-169-1*) Creat Pub Intl.

Philyaw, Chuck & Lippincott, David. The PC Technical Source-Book, 1988. Kleine, Marty, ed. (Illus.). 95p. 1996. pap. 9.95 (*1-882069-54-4*) Industrial Computer Source.

Philyaw, Jessica & Dellwo, Lisa. Romantic North Carolina: More Than 300 Things to Do for Southern Lovers. LC 99-34406. 160p. 1999. pap. 10.95 (*1-892514-14-1*) Hill St Pr.

Phimister, Euan. Savings & Investment in Farm Household: Analysis Using Life Cycles Models. 100p. 1993. 61.95 (*1-85628-596-0*, Pub. by Avebry) Ashgate Pub Co.

***Phin, John.** Practical Information for Cabinet-Makers & Furniture Men. 130p. 2000. pap. 15.95 (*1-892836-09-2*, Pub. by Cambium Pr) IPG Chicago.

***Phinezy, Ophelia Paschell.** Reading & Writing. 14p. 2000. pap. 695.00 (*0-923242-98-8*) Sparrowgrass Poetry.

Phini, Reuven, jt. auth. see Zaarur, Eliahu.

***Phinn, Gervase.** The Other Side of the Dale. large type unabridged ed. 310p. 2000. pap. 19.95 (*0-7531-5079-4*, 150794, Pub. by ISIS Lrg Prnt) ISIS Pub.

***Phinnemore, David.** Association: Stepping-Stone or Alternative to EU Membership? (Contemporary European Studies: No. 6). 166p. 1999. pap. 16.95 (*1-84127-000-8*, Pub. by Sheffield Acad) CUP Services.

Phinnemore, David, jt. auth. see Light, Duncan.

Phinney, ed. Cambridge Latin Course, Unit 1: Worksheet Masters, North American. 3rd ed. (School Classics Project Ser.). 1996. spiral bd. 38.95 (*0-521-45846-3*) Cambridge U Pr.

Phinney, Archie. Nez Perce Texts. LC 73-82344. (Columbia University. Contributions to Anthropology Ser.: Vol. 25). reprint ed. 49.50 (*0-404-50575-9*) AMS Pr.

Phinney, Davis & Carpenter, Connie. Training for Cycling: The Ultimate Guide to Improved Performance. (Illus.). 256p. (Orig.). 1992. pap. 13.95 (*0-399-51731-6*, Perigee Bks) Berkley Pub.

***Phinney, Dennis.** Simplus Code Finder. 3rd ed. 1999. pap. 74.95 (*1-55701-336-5*) BNI Pubns.

Phinney, Donna J. & Halstead, Judy. Introduction to Dental Assisting. LC 98-55682. (Dental Assisting Procedures Ser.). 787p. (C). 1999. pap. 56.95 (*0-8273-9073-4*) Delmar.

Phinney, E., jt. auth. see Spooner, A.

Phinney, Ed. Cambridge Latin Course, Unit I. 3rd ed. LC 87-10281. 232p. 1988. text 22.95 (*0-521-34379-8*) Cambridge U Pr.

— Cambridge Latin Course Unit 1. 3rd ed. 128p. (C). 1988. pap. text, teacher ed. 16.95 (*0-521-34853-6*) Cambridge U Pr.

— Cambridge Latin Course, Unit 2. 3rd ed. 128p. (C). 1988. pap. text, teacher ed. 17.95 (*0-521-34855-2*) Cambridge U Pr.

— Cambridge Latin Course, Unit 2: North American Edition. 224p. 1988. text 24.95 (*0-521-34381-X*) Cambridge U Pr.

— Cambridge Latin Course, Unit 3: Student's Book for Stages 21-34. 352p. 1990. text, student ed. 34.95 (*0-521-34382-8*) Cambridge U Pr.

— Cambridge Latin Course, Unit 4: North American. 3rd ed. 112p. (C). 1992. pap. text, student ed. 10.95 (*0-521-34860-9*) Cambridge U Pr.

Phinney, Ed, ed. Cambridge Latin Course, Unit 4: North America. 3rd ed. 416p. 1991. text 44.95 (*0-521-34380-1*) Cambridge U Pr.

— The History of the American Classical League, 1919-1994. 317p. (Orig.). 1994. pap., per. 40.00 (*0-939507-47-1*) Amer Classical.

Phinney, Ed, jt. auth. see Griffin, M. R.

Phinney, Ed, ed. see Morwood, James & Warman, Mark.

***Phinney, Halstead.** Dental Drug Reference. LC 99-30080. 600p. (C). 1999. pap. 26.50 (*0-7668-0115-2*) Delmar.

Phinney, Jean S. & Rotheram, Mary. Children's Ethnic Socialization. Society for Research in Child Development Staff, ed. (Focus Editions Ser.: Vol. 81). 400p. (Orig.). 1986. text 59.95 (*0-8039-2815-7*); pap. text 26.00 (*0-8039-2816-5*) Sage.

An Asterisk (*) at the beginning of an entry indicates that the title is appearing for the first time.

Phinney, Joanna, jt. auth. see Dodge, Diane T.
Phinney, Lucy. Yesterday's Schools Vol. 1: Public Elementary Education in Prince William County, Virginia 1869-1969. (Illus.). 220p. 1993. 20.00 (*0-9612862-9-6*) R E F Typesetting Pub.
Phinney, M. A. Allen: A Brief History of Lewis Allen of Fisher's Island & New London, CT, & His Descendants, from 1699-1954. 207p. 1991. reprint ed. pap. 34.50 (*0-8328-1804-6*); reprint ed. lib. bdg. 44.50 (*0-8328-1803-8*) Higginson Bk Co.
— Isham Genealogy: A Brief History of Jirah Isham. 179p. 1991. reprint ed. pap. 27.00 (*0-8328-2155-1*); reprint ed. lib. bdg. 37.00 (*0-8328-2154-3*) Higginson Bk Co.
Phinney, Margaret Y. Baba Yaga: A Russian Folktale. LC 95-5430. (Illus.). 40p. (J). (gr. 1-5). 1995. lib. bdg. 13.95 (*1-57255-004-X*) Mondo Pubng.
— Exploring Land Habitats. LC 94-14058. (Illus.). 24p. (Orig.). (J). (gr. 1-5). 1994. pap. 4.95 (*1-879531-38-0*); lib. bdg. 9.95 (*1-879531-48-8*) Mondo Pubng.
— Exploring Underground Habitats. LC 97-20291. (Exploring Ser.). (Illus.). 24p. (J). (gr. 1-5). 1999. pap. 4.95 (*1-57255-161-5*) Mondo Pubng.
— Reading with the Troubled Reader. LC 88-11211. (Illus.). 138p. (C). 1988. pap. text 20.00 (*0-435-08480-1*, 08480) Heinemann.
— Reading with the Troubled Reader. pap. 16.95 (*0-590-71881-9*) Scholastic Inc.
— We're off to Thunder Mountain. LC 95-8418. (Illus.). 16p. (J). (ps-3). 1995. pap. 3.95 (*1-57255-031-7*) Mondo Pubng.
— Will You Play with Us? LC 95-17747. (Illus.). 8p. (J). (ps-1). 1995. pap. 2.95 (*1-57255-036-8*) Mondo Pubng.
Phinney, Marianne. Process Your Thoughts. (College ESL Ser.). (J). 1994. pap. 23.95 (*0-8384-5289-2*) Heinle & Heinle.
Phinney, Richard & Whitley, Scott. Links of Heaven: A Complete Guide to Golf Journeys in Ireland. LC 95-81020. (Great Golf Journeys Ser.). (Illus.). 306p. (Orig.). 1996. pap. 19.95 (*1-888132-02-7*) Baltray Bks.
Phinney, Robert A., ed. The History of the Earth's Crust: A Symposium. LC 68-20875. 254p. 1968. reprint ed. pap. 78.80 (*0-608-02919-X*, 206398300008) Bks Demand.
Phinney, William R., et al, eds. Thomas Ware, a Spectator at the Christmas Conference: A Miscellany on Thomas Ware & the Christmas Conference. LC 84-70457. (Illus.). 320p. (Orig.). 1984. reprint ed. 8.95 (*0-914960-48-2*) Academy Bks.
Phint, Anthoney, ed. see Fowler, Sharon H.
Phippen, George. The Life of a Cowboy. LC 70-101102. (Illus.). 104p. reprint ed. pap. 32.30 (*0-8357-9622-1*, 201935200011) Bks Demand.
Phippen, Mark L. & Wells, Maryann P. Patient Care During Operative & Invasive Procedures. Connor, Maura, ed. LC 98-43363. (Illus.). 860p. 1999. text 69.00 (*0-7216-7292-2*) Church.
Phippen, Mark L. & Wells, Maryann P., eds. Perioperative Nursing: Principles & Practice. LC 92-24341. (Illus.). 1088p. 1993. text 66.00 (*0-7216-7233-7*, W B Saunders Co) Harcrt Hlth Sci Grp.
Phippen, Mark L., et al. Review of Perioperative Nursing. Connor, Maura, ed. LC 96-16726. 300p. 1999. pap. text 29.95 (*0-7216-3413-3*, W B Saunders Co) Harcrt Hlth Sci Grp.
Phippen, Sanford. Kitchen Boy. 380p. (Orig.). 1996. pap. 13.95 (*0-942396-77-4*) Blackberry ME.
— The Messiah in the Memorial Gym: And Other Writings, 1973-1998. 445p. 1999. pap. 16.95 (*0-942396-81-2*) Blackberry ME.
— People Trying to Be Good. 3rd ed. Hunting, Constance, ed. 150p. 1991. pap. 8.95 (*0-913006-40-8*) Puckerbrush.
— The Police Know Everything: And Other Maine Stories. Hunting, Constance, ed. 149p. (Orig.). 1982. pap. 8.95 (*0-913006-27-0*) Puckerbrush.
Phippen, Sanford, ed. High Clouds Soaring, Storms Driving Low: The Letters of Ruth Moore. (Illus.). 560p. 1993. pap. 16.95 (*0-942396-66-9*) Blackberry ME.
Phippen, Sanford, et al, eds. The Best Maine Stories. LC 94-5391. 320p. (Orig.). 1994. pap. 12.95 (*0-89272-351-3*) Down East.
Phipps. Engineered Masonry. (C). 1997. text. write for info. (*0-582-21985-X*, Pub. by Addison-Wesley) Longman.
***Phipps & Fairmont, Press.** Fundmentals of Electrical Control. 2nd ed. LC 98-47049. 232p. 1999. 84.00 (*0-13-012699-3*) P-H.
Phipps & Simmons. Understanding Customers 1998-99. 200p. pap. text. write for info. (*0-7506-4037-5*) Buttrwrth-Heinemann.
***Phipps, Alison M.** Acting Identities: An Investigation into South West German Naturtheater. (European University Studies Ser.: Vol. 1748). xii, 226p. 2000. pap. 37.95 (*0-8204-4362-X*) P Lang Pubng.
— Acting Identities: An Investigation into South West German Naturtheater, 1748. (Illus.). 226p. 2000. 37.95 (*3-631-35142-9*) P Lang Pubng.
Phipps, Beckey, ed. see Singh, Swayam P.
Phipps, Bonnie. Beginning Autoharp. 1983. pap. 9.95 (*0-88284-260-9*, 2222) Alfred Pub.
— Singing with Young Children. (Illus.). 64p. 1991. pap. 17.95 incl. audio (*0-88284-492-X*, 3558) Alfred Pub.
Phipps, Brian. The Catamaran Book. (Illus.). 128p. 1998. pap. 19.95 (*1-898660-44-1*) Motorbooks Intl.
— The Catamaran Book. 2nd ed. (C). 1993. text 59.00 (*0-906754-86-0*, Pub. by Fernhurst Bks) St Mut.
Phipps, C. & Hawthorne, Philip. Piano Classics (Blue) (Learn to Play Ser.). (Illus.). 128p. (J). (gr. 4-7). 1994. pap. 17.95 (*0-7460-1967-X*, Usborne) EDC.
Phipps, Clarence A. Fundamentals of Electrical Control. LC 95-19042. 207p. 1995. 79.00 (*0-88173-217-6*) Fairmont Pr.
— Fundementals of Electrical Control. 2nd ed. LC 98-47049. 212p. 1998. 84.00 (*0-88173-312-1*) Fairmont Pr.
— Variable Speed Drive Fundamentals. LC 93-50689. 1994. 75.00 (*0-88173-191-9*) Fairmont Pr.
— Variable Speed Drive Fundamentals. 2nd ed. LC 96-52187. 213p. 1997. 79.00 (*0-88173-258-3*) Fairmont Pr.
— Variable Speed Drive Fundamentals. 3rd ed. LC 98-48642. 212p. 1998. 84.00 (*0-88173-310-5*) Fairmont Pr.
— Variable Speed Drive Fundamentals. 3rd ed. 224p. 1999. 84.00 (*0-13-021649-6*) P-H.
Phipps, Claude R., ed. High-Power Laser Ablation. LC 98-227298. (Proceedings of SPIE Ser.: Vol. 3343). 1092p. 1998. 158.00 (*0-8194-2790-X*) SPIE.
***Phipps, Claude R. & Niino, Masayuki, eds.** High-Power Laser Ablation II. 2000. pap. text 120.00 (*0-8194-3483-3*) SPIE.
Phipps, D. A. Metals & Metabolism, No. 26. (Oxford Chemistry Ser.). (Illus.). 1978. pap. 12.50 (*0-19-855413-3*) OUP.
Phipps, David, jt. auth. see Blunsden, John.
Phipps, Frances. Let Me Be Los: A Code Book for Finnegans Wake. Quasha, George, ed. LC 87-6451. (Illus.). 211p. (C). 1987. reprint ed. pap. 16.95 (*0-88268-042-0*) Station Hill Pr.
— Let Me Be LOS: Codebook for Finnegans Wake. (Illus.). 1987. 43.50 (*0-9606540-5-4*) Classic Nonfic.
***Phipps, Grace M.** Doctor Gregory on Call. large type ed. 288p. 1999. pap. 20.99 (*1-85389-937-2*, Dales) Ulverscroft.
Phipps, Graeme, jt. auth. see Stanbury, Peter.
Phipps, Jeffrey H. Laparoscopic Hysterectomy & Oopherectomy: A Practical Manual & Colour Atlas. LC 93-7324. (Illus.). 120p. 1993. text 110.00 (*0-443-04929-7*) Church.
Phipps, Joe. Summer Stock: Behind the Scenes with LBJ in '48. LC 92-13118. (Illus.). 338p. 1992. 27.95 (*0-87565-107-0*) Tex Christian.
Phipps, John. John Phipps: Citizen - Soldier. Wheaton, Grace, ed. (Illus.). 304p. 1998. 18.00 (*0-9655389-1-5*) G Wheaton.
Phipps, Kelly L. Celestial Renaissance Vol. 1: A Revolution of Astrology: Forging New Pathways Through Awareness. (Illus.). vi, 320p. 1997. pap. 29.95 (*1-891313-11-8*) Astrofantasy.
Phipps, L. B., jt. auth. see Janosik, E. H.
Phipps, Larry W. How to Improve Your Financial Health...Made Easy! 3rd ed. 99p. 1996. pap., wbk. ed. 16.45 (*0-9651253-0-0*) LWP Enter.
Phipps, Linda. Eras of Elegance: Fashionable Clothing 1850-1935. (Illus.). 111p. 1995. pap. 33.00 (*0-912823-54-2*, BT-154, Pub. by Gold Horse) Dollmasters.
Phipps, Lloyd J. & Miller, Glen M. AgriScience Mechanics. LC 97-70235. (Illus.). 672p. 1998. 74.95 (*0-8134-3088-7*, 3088); teacher ed. 9.95 (*0-8134-3089-5*, 3089) Interstate.
— AgriScience Mechanics Activity Manual. (Illus.). 1998. teacher ed. 14.95 (*0-8134-3156-5*, 3156); student ed. 19.95 (*0-8134-3155-7*, 3155) Interstate.
***Phipps, Marilene.** Crossroads & Unholy Water. LC 99-38613. (Crab Orchard Award Series in Poetry). 2000. pap. 11.95 (*0-8093-2306-0*) S Ill U Pr.
Phipps, Marlynn, et al. Feed a Family of Four for as Low as 10 Dollars Per Week: And Enjoy a Nibble of Independence. 162p. 1992. pap. 15.99 (*0-9631522-0-3*) Phipps AZ.
***Phipps, Patricia.** My Grandma Always Told Me. 176p. 1999. pap. 15.25 (*0-9671542-0-0*) Five Dreams Pubns.
Phipps, Paula, ed. see Burkle, Frank.
Phipps, Paula, ed. see Marshak, David.
Phipps, Phyllis. The Relationship Revolution: A Baby Boomers Guide to Finding Love. 1993. pap. 10.95 (*0-9638341-9-3*) Summer Hill.
Phipps, R. H., jt. ed. see Pollmer, W. G.
Phipps, Ramsay W. The Armies of the First French Republic & the Rise of the Marshals of Napoleon I, 5 vols., Set. LC 79-23801. (Illus.). 1980. reprint ed. lib. bdg. 295.00 (*0-313-22208-8*, PHAR) Greenwood.
— The Armies of the First French Republic & the Rise of the Marshals of Napoleon I, 5 vols., Vol. 1. LC 79-23801. (Illus.). 1980. reprint ed. lib. bdg. 65.00 (*0-313-22209-6*, PHAR01) Greenwood.
— The Armies of the First French Republic & the Rise of the Marshals of Napoleon I, 5 vols., Vol. 2. LC 79-23801. (Illus.). 1980. reprint ed. lib. bdg. 65.00 (*0-313-22210-X*, PHAR02) Greenwood.
— The Armies of the First French Republic & the Rise of the Marshals of Napoleon I, 5 vols., Vol. 3. LC 79-23801. (Illus.). 1980. reprint ed. lib. bdg. 65.00 (*0-313-22211-8*, PHAR03) Greenwood.
— The Armies of the First French Republic & the Rise of the Marshals of Napoleon I, 5 vols., Vol. 4. LC 79-23801. (Illus.). 1980. reprint ed. lib. bdg. 65.00 (*0-313-22212-6*, PHAR04) Greenwood.
— The Armies of the First French Republic & the Rise of the Marshals of Napoleon I, 5 vols., Vol. 5. LC 79-23801. (Illus.). 1980. reprint ed. lib. bdg. 65.00 (*0-313-22213-4*, PHAR05) Greenwood.
Phipps, Richard P. Pulmonary Fibroblast Heterogeneity. 352p. 1992. 194.00 (*0-8493-6038-2*, RC776, CRC Reprint) Franklin.
Phipps, Ronald A. & Sumler, David. The Maryland Interactive Distance Learning Network. 1994. 10.00 (*0-614-13559-1*) SHEEO.
Phipps, Rosemary. Start a Successful Business: A Practical Guide to Starting Your Own Business. (Illus.). 1996. pap. 10.95 (*0-563-36962-0*, BBC-Parkwest) Parkwest Pubns.
— Understanding Customers Workbook: Revision Tips, Exam Hints, Model Answers. 240p. 1996. pap. text 28.95 (*0-7506-1996-1*) Buttrwrth-Heinemann.
Phipps, Rosemary, jt. auth. see Simmons, Craig J.
Phipps, Shirley. Santa Fe & Beyond. LC 93-84179. 1993. 9.95 (*0-916809-61-7*) Scott Pubns MI.
— A Touch of Santa Fe. LC 90-60514. 52p. (Orig.). 1990. pap. 9.95 (*0-916809-41-2*) Scott Pubns MI.
Phipps, Stephanie, ed. see Whitney, Harold C.
Phipps, Thomas E., Jr. Heretical Verities: Mathematical Themes in Physical Description. (Illus.). 632p. 1987. 39.95 (*0-9606540-2-X*) Classic Nonfic.
Phipps, Tim T., et al, eds. Agriculture & the Environment. LC 87-43010. 316p. reprint ed. pap. 98.00 (*0-8357-3282-7*, 203950500013) Bks Demand.
Phipps, William E. Assertive Biblical Women, 128. LC 92-3026. (Contributions in Women's Studies: No. 128). 184p. 1992. 49.95 (*0-313-28498-9*, PAP/, Greenwood Pr) Greenwood.
— Cremation Concerns. (Illus.). 114p. (C). 1989. text 36.95 (*0-398-05532-7*) C C Thomas.
— Death: Confronting the Reality. LC 86-45405. 204p. (Orig.). 1987. pap. 16.95 (*0-8042-0487-X*) Westminster John Knox.
— Genesis & Gender: Biblical Myths of Sexuality & Their Cultural Impact. LC 88-27509. 141p. 1989. 47.95 (*0-275-93200-1*, C3200, Praeger Pubs) Greenwood.
— Muhammad & Jesus: A Comparison of the Prophets & Their Teachings. LC 75-29600. 256p. 1996. 27.50 (*0-8264-0914-8*) Continuum.
***Phipps, William E.** Muhammad & Jesus: A Comparison of the Prophets & Their Teachings. 320p. 1999. pap. 19.95 (*0-8264-1207-6*) Continuum.
Phipps, William E. The Sexuality of Jesus. LC 96-30147. 264p. (Orig.). 1996. pap. 16.95 (*0-8298-1144-3*) Pilgrim OH.
— The Wisdom & Wit of Rabbi Jesus. LC 93-19528. 272p. (Orig.). 1993. pap. 22.95 (*0-664-25232-X*) Westminster John Knox.
Phipps, Wilma J., et al. Medical-Surgical Nursing: Concepts, & Clinical Practice. 5th ed. (Illus.). student ed. write for info. (*0-8016-8131-6*) Mosby Inc.
***Phipps, Wilma J., et al.** Medical-Surgical Nursing: Concepts & Clinical Practice, Includes Testbank. 6th ed. (Illus.). 2336p. 1998. teacher ed. write for info. (*0-323-00527-6*) Mosby Inc.
— Medical-Surgical Nursing: Concepts & Clinical Practice: Text-Skidmore Drug Guide Package. 6th ed. (Illus.). 2336p. 1998. write for info. (*0-323-00740-6*) Mosby Inc.
Phipson, Emma. The Animal-Lore of Shakespeare's Time. 1976. lib. bdg. 59.95 (*0-8490-1432-8*) Gordon Pr.
— Animal-Lore of Shakespeare's Time. LC 79-174197. reprint ed. 52.50 (*0-404-05044-1*) AMS Pr.
Phiri, Kings M. Democratisation in Malawi a Stocktaking. Ross, Kenneth R., ed. LC 99-889491. (Illus.). 398p. 1998. pap. 54.95 (*99908-16-06-9*) Intl Scholars.
Phish, jt. auth. see Gehr, Richard.
Phish Merchandising Incorporated Staff. Show. 1998. write for info. (*0-316-70537-3*) Little.
Phister, Montgomery, Jr. Data Processing Technology & Economics. 1979. 75.00 (*0-917640-04-7*) Santa Monica Pub.
— Data Processing Technology & Economics. 2nd ed. LC 79-25052. (Illus.). 720p. 1979. pap. 50.00 (*0-917640-05-5*) Santa Monica Pub.
— Data Processing Technology & Economics: 1975-1978 Supplement. LC 79-25052. (Illus.). 1979. pap. 10.00 (*0-917640-03-9*) Santa Monica Pub.
— Logical Design of Digital Computers. LC 58-6082. 424p. reprint ed. pap. 131.50 (*0-608-10265-2*, 201648200004) Bks Demand.
Phisterer, Frederick. Statistical Record of the Armies of the United States: A Treasury of Information about the U. S. Civil War. fac. ed. Kallmann, John D., ed. & intro. by. 343p. 1996. 29.95 (*0-9650926-1-5*, L-1002) J Kallmann.
Phitsanoukanh, Bounta, tr. see Hutchinson, Hanna.
Phizacklea, Annie & Wolkowitz, Carol. Homeworking Women: Gender, Race & Class at Work. 160p. 1995. text 69.95 (*0-8039-8873-7*); pap. text 26.95 (*0-8039-8874-5*) Sage.
Phizacklea, Annie, jt. auth. see Westwood, Sallie.
Phlegar, Janet & Kaufman, Jill. Effective Professional Development: A Guide for Youth Apprenticeship & Work-Based Learning Programs. 56p. 1992. pap. 10.00 (*1-887410-73-2*) Jobs for Future.
Phlegar, Phyllis. Love Online: A Practical Guide to Digital Dating. 192p. (C). 1995. pap. text 9.95 (*0-201-40965-8*) Addison-Wesley.
— Love Online: A Practical Guide to Digital Dating. 192p. (C). 1995. pap. 119.40 (*0-201-41038-9*) Addison-Wesley.
Phleger, Frederick B. Red Tag Comes Back. LC 61-11452. (I Can Read Science Bks.). (Illus.). 64p. (J). (ps-3). 1961. lib. bdg. 13.89 (*0-06-024706-1*) HarpC Child Bks.
Phleger, Marjorie. Pilot Down, Presumed Dead. LC 63-16244. (Trophy Bk.). 224p. (J). (gr. 4-7). 1975. pap. 5.95 (*0-06-440067-0*, HarpTrophy) HarpC Child Bks.
Phleger, Marjorie. Pilot Down, Presumed Dead. 206p. (J). (gr. 5-6). pap. 5.95 (*0-8072-1426-4*) Listening Lib.
Phleger, Marjorie. Pilot Down, Presumed Dead. 1963. 9.60 (*0-606-03888-4*, Pub. by Turtleback) Demco.
Phlegming, I. M. Last of the Secret Agents. 230p. (Orig.). 1986. pap. 7.95 (*0-9614706-0-7*) Thalia Bks.
Phleps, Herman. The Craft of Log Building. MacGregor, Roger, tr. from GER. (Illus.). 336p. 1942. pap. 19.95 (*0-9691019-1-0*, Pub. by LVTL) Veritas Tools.
Philps, Louis. Competition Policy: A Game-Theoretic Perspective. (Illus.). 288p. (C). 1995. pap. text 20.95 (*0-521-49871-6*) Cambridge U Pr.
— The Economics of Imperfect Information. (Illus.). 304p. 1989. text 85.00 (*0-521-30920-4*); pap. text 25.95 (*0-521-31381-3*) Cambridge U Pr.
Phlips, Louis, ed. Applied Industrial Economics. LC 97-25537. 416p. (C). 1998. 85.00 (*0-521-62054-6*); pap. 29.95 (*0-521-62954-3*) Cambridge U Pr.
— Commodity, Futures & Financial Markets. (Advanced Studies in Theoretical & Applied Econometrics). (C). 1990. lib. bdg. 171.00 (*0-7923-1043-8*) Kluwer Academic.
Phlips, Louis & Taylor, Lester D., eds. Aggregation, Consumption & Trade: Essays in Honor of H.S. Houthakker. LC 92-33114. (Advanced Studies in Theoretical & Applied Econometrics: Vol. 27). (C). 1992. lib. bdg. 138.00 (*0-7923-2001-8*) Kluwer Academic.
Phlipt-Scroggins. Lippincott's Computed Tomography Review. 288p. 1995. pap. text 26.95 (*0-397-55157-6*) Lppncott W & W.
Phllips, Michael R., ed. see Wright, Harold Bell.
Pho, Hai B. Vietnamese Public Management in Transition: South Vietnam Public Administration, 1955-1975. LC 89-14648. (Illus.). 210p. (C). 1990. lib. bdg. 42.50 (*0-8191-7517-X*) U Pr of Amer.
Phoa, Wesley. Advanced Fixed Income Analytics. (Illus.). 229p. 1998. 65.00 (*1-883249-34-1*) F J Fabozzi.
***Phoca , Sophia.** Introducing Postfeminism. 176p. 1999. pap. 10.95 (*1-84046-010-5*, TOTM) Topaz Maps.
Phoenix, ed. see Thompson, Diana L.
Phoenix, Ann, et al, eds. Motherhood: Meanings, Practices, & Ideologies. (Gender & Psychology Ser.). (Illus.). 256p. 1991. 45.00 (*0-8039-8313-1*); pap. 14.99 (*0-8039-8314-X*) Sage.
Phoenix, Ann, jt. auth. see Tizard, Barbara.
Phoenix, Ann, jt. ed. see Bhavnani, Kum-Kum.
Phoenix Art Museum Staff. Copper As Canvas: Two Centuries of Masterpiece Paintings on Copper, 1525-1775. LC 98-25798. (Illus.). 368p. 1999. pap. 27.50 (*0-19-512397-2*); text 49.95 (*0-19-512396-4*) OUP.
— The Popular West: American Illustrators, 1900-1940. (Illus.). 55p. (Orig.). 1982. pap. 8.00 (*0-910407-08-8*) Phoenix Art.
Phoenix Art Museum Staff & Eden Siu-Hung Yu. The Modern Spirit in Chinese Painting: Selections from the Jeannette Shambaugh Elliott Collection. Brown, Claudia & Ju-hsi Chou, eds. LC 85-72990. (Illus.). (Orig.). 1985. pap. 15.00 (*0-910407-17-7*) Phoenix Art.
Phoenix, Arthur T. Touched by the Jacksons. LC 98-90321. 264p. (Orig.). 1998. pap. 15.95 (*0-9663719-0-9*) Spirit Publ.
Phoenix Arts Commission. Public Art Works: The Arizona Models. LC 93-6893. 1992. spiral bd. 20.00 (*0-9611710-7-3*) Western States.
Phoenix, Charles, jt. auth. see Basten, Fred E.
***Phoenix, Charlotte Y. & Bain-Pew, Gilda.** The S. A. F. E. College Planning Guide for Students Grades 9 - 12: What You Need to Know about Selecting, Applyingto, Financing & Excelling in College. viii, 116p. (YA). (gr. 9-12). 1999. pap. 12.95 (*0-9671869-0-0*, 99001) Lenroc.
Phoenix, Clay. Cancer: Memories in Ink & Other Poems. (Illus.). 38p. 1987. pap. 5.00 (*0-9619448-0-3*) Consultantswest Inc.
Phoenix, David. Introductory Mathematics for the Life Sciences. LC 97-209947. (Modules in Life Science Ser.). 256p. 1997. pap. 24.95 (*0-7484-0428-7*, Pub. by Tay Francis Ltd) Taylor & Francis.
Phoenix, David, ed. Protein Targeting & Translocation. (Portland Press Research Monograph Ser.: No. 12). (Illus.). 304p. 1998. text 127.50 (*1-85578-121-2*, Pub. by Portland Pr Ltd) Ashgate Pub Co.
***Phoenix, David A.** Protein Targeting & Translocation LC 99-189360. (Portland Press Research Monographs). xii, 292p. 1998. 85.00 (*0-691-00901-5*, Pub. by Princeton U Pr) Cal Prin Full Svc.
Phoenix, E. Chilton, jt. auth. see Link, Paul.
Phoenix, Eamonn, ed. A Century of Northern Life: The Irish News & 100 Years of Ulster History. (Illus.). 232p. (Orig.). 1995. pap. 22.95 (*0-901905-70-4*, Pub. by Ulster Hist Fnd) Irish Bks Media.
***Phoenix Mapping Service Staff.** Phoenix Valley of the Sun Street Guide. 124p. 1999. pap. 3.95 (*1-887749-17-9*) Wide World Maps.
Phoenix Publishing Staff. Book of Shadows. 272p. 14.95 (*0-919345-66-2*) Phoenix WA.
Phoenix Publishing Systems, Inc. Surviving Day One with Windows 95. 91p. 1995. 12.99 (*0-7897-0581-8*) Que.
Phoenix Publishing Systems Staff. Surviving Day 1 with Windows 95. (Illus.). 96p. (Orig.). 1995. pap. 99.90 (*0-7897-0579-6*) Que.
— Surviving Day 1 with Windows NT Workstation 4.0. LC 96-70549. 96p. 1996. 12.99 (*0-7897-0995-3*) Que.
Phoenix, Rodney. Stewart's Clinical Removable Partial Prosthodontics. 3rd rev. ed. (Illus.). 700p. Date not set. 85.00 (*1-891949-02-0*) Med Dent Media.
Phoenix, S. Whitney. The Whitney Family of Connecticut, 3 vols. 2740p. 1989. reprint ed. 269.95 (*0-945433-16-6*) Herit Quest.
Phoenix Staff. The Rape of Emergency Medicine. 288p. (Orig.). 1992. pap. 19.95 (*0-9632237-1-2*) Phoenix.
Phoenix Technologies Staff. ABIOS for IBM PS-2 Computers & Compatibles: The Complete Guide to ROM-Based System Software for OS-2. 688p. (C). 1989. pap. text 26.95 (*0-201-51805-8*) Addison-Wesley.
— CBIOS for IBM PS-2 Computers & Compatibles: The Complete Guide to ROM-Based System Software for DOS. 592p. 1989. pap. text 26.95 (*0-201-51804-X*) Addison-Wesley.
Phoenix Technologies Staff. System BIOS for IBM PCs, Compatibles & EISA Computers: The Complete Guide to ROM-Based System Software. 2nd ed. (Illus.). 624p. 1991. pap. 34.95 (*0-201-57760-7*) Addison-Wesley.
Phoggeler, Otto. The Paths of Heidegger's Life & Thought. LC 99-10396. 1999. write for info. (*1-57392-503-9*, Humanity Bks) Prometheus Bks.
Pholer, Rolf J. Continuity & Change in Christian Doctrine: A Study of the Problem of Doctrinal Development. 156p. 1999. 31.95 (*3-631-33201-7*) P Lang Pubng.

P

Phondke, G. P., jt. auth. see Pakrashi, S. C.

Phong, Dang & Beresford, Melanie. Authority Relations & Economic Decision-Making in Vietnam: An Historical Perspective. LC 98-211646. 128p. 1998. 45.00 (*87-87062-65-8*, Pub. by NIAS) Paul & Co Pubs.

Phong, Duong H., ed. Mirror Symmetry III: Conference Proceedings on Complex Geometry & Mirror Symmetry, 1996. LC 98-37643. (IP Studies in Advanced Mathematics: Vol. 10). 312p. 1999. 42.00 (*0-8218-1193-2*) Am Math.

Phongpaichit, Pasuk. Corruption & Democracy in Thailand. 212p. 1998. pap. text 12.95 (*974-7100-31-2*) U of Wash Pr.

— From Peasant Girls to Bangkok Masseuses. (Women, Work & Development Ser.: No. 2). ix, 80p. 1992. pap. 13.50 (*92-2-103013-X*) Intl Labour Office.

Phongpaichit, Pasuk. Thailand: Economy & Politics. (Illus.). 466p. pap. text. write for info. (*983-56-0024-4*) OUP.

***Phongpaichit, Pasuk & Piriyarangsan, Sungsidh.** Guns, Girls, Gambling, Ganja: Thailand's Illegal Economy & Public Policy. LC 98-943683. (Illus.). 284p. 1999. pap. 17.50 (*974-7100-75-4*) U of Wash Pr.

Phongpaichit, Pasuk, et al. Challenging Social Exclusion: Rights & Livelihood in Thailand. LC 97-145297. x, 122p. 1996. pap. 18.00 (*92-9014-538-2*) Intl Labour Office.

— Thailand's Boom & Bust. rev. ed. LC 98-949323. 372p. 1998. pap. 17.50 (*974-7100-57-6*) U of Wash Pr.

Phoon, Colin K. & Stanger, Paul. Guide to Pediatric Cardiovascular Physical Examination. LC 98-5745. 192p. 1998. pap. text 34.50 (*0-7817-1042-1*) Lppncott W & W.

Phoon, Wai-On & Chen, P. C. Textbook of Community Medicine in South-East Asia. LC 84-5073. (Wiley-Medical Publication). (Illus.). 629p. reprint ed. pap. 195.00 (*0-7837-1878-0*, 204207900001) Bks Demand.

Phornirunlit, Supon. Best of International Self-Promotion. (Illus.). 192p. 1993. 45.00 (*0-942604-32-6*) Madison Square.

— International Logos & Trademarks II, No. II. 196p. 1993. 45.00 (*0-942604-26-1*) Madison Square.

— International Women in Design. (Illus.). 198p. 2000. 39.95 (*0-942604-30-X*, Pub. by Madison Square) BHB Intl.

— The Newest Logo from California, Vol. 3. 3rd ed. (Illus.). 2192p. 1997. 37.50 (*0-942604-58-X*) Madison Square.

Phornirunlit, Supon, ed. Innovative Low-Budget Design. (Illus.). 224p. 1996. 44.95 (*0-942604-48-2*) Madison Square.

Phornirunlit, Supon, ed. The Right Portfolio for the Right Job. (Illus.). 192p. 1994. 45.00 (*0-942604-36-9*) Madison Square.

Photiades, V. Renoir: Nudes. (Rhythem & Color One Ser.). 1970. 9.95 (*0-8288-9503-1*) Fr & Eur.

Photiadis, John D., ed. Religion in Appalachia. 1979. 10.75 (*0-686-26337-5*) W Va U Ctr Exten.

Photiadis, John D. & Schwarzweller, Harry K. Change in Rural Appalachia: Implications for Action Programs. 284p. 1971. text 41.95 (*0-8122-7618-3*) U of Pa Pr.

Photiou, Paul. My Conversion to Christ. Orthodox Christian Educational Society Staff, ed. (GRE.). (Orig.). 1970. reprint ed. 2.00 (*0-938366-41-6*) Orthodox Chr.

Photius, Patriarcha C. Epistolae. 851p. 1978. reprint ed. write for info. (*3-487-06675-0*) G Olms Pubs.

— On the Mystagogy of the Holy Spirit LC 83-60028. 213p. 1983. write for info. (*0-943670-00-4*) Studion Pubs Inc.

Photo Disk Inc. Staff. PhotoDisc Starter Kit 98.1. (Illus.). 253p. 1998. pap. 19.95 (*0-9665538-0-2*) PhotoDisc Inc.

Photography Sesquicentennial Project Staff, jt. contrib. by see Finkel, Kenneth.

***Photomaps, Inc. Staff.** Photomaps: Crow Wing County. (Illus.). 80p. 1999. pap. write for info. (*0-9661599-2-6*, 99-1) Evergrn Pr.

Photoplay Research Society Staff. Opportunities in the Motion Picture Industry & How to Qualify for Positions in Its Many Branches. LC 73-124033. (Literature of Cinema, Ser. 1). 1970. reprint ed. 12.95 (*0-405-01633-6*) Ayer.

PhotoTherapy Centre Staff, jt. auth. see Weiser, Judy.

Phototype Composing Limited Staff, jt. auth. see Winter, Stephen.

Photz, Walter & Schroeder, W. Andreas. Coherent Control in Atoms, Molecules, & Semiconductors: Proceedings of an International Workshop Held in Chicago, USA, 19-22 May 1998. LC 99-13937. 1999. write for info. (*0-7923-5649-7*) Kluwer Academic.

Phoutrides, Aristides, jt. tr. see Brown, Demetra V.

PHP Institute, Inc. Staff, ed. Japan: A Business Traveler's Handbook. (Illus.). 192p. 1996. pap. 12.95 (*4-569-54867-9*, Pub. by PHP Kenkyujo) Weatherhill.

Phpn Edit. Dollar Saving Answer Business Career. 1987. pap. text 4.95 (*0-13-217563-0*) P-H.

Phram, Thri Hoaai. The Crystal Messenger. LC 98-119283. 146 p. 1997. write for info. (*1-877133-40-X*) Univ Otago Pr.

Phred, S. J. The Guide to Success in College. 2nd rev. ed. 80p. 1996. pap. 10.00 (*0-9648102-0-4*) College CT.

Phrihoda, Deborah. Mommy, Why Are They Holding Hands? 1998. pap. 6.99 (*0-9663380-0-6*) Cutting PA.

Phrynichos, Arabius. The New Phrynichus Being a Revised Text of the Ecloga of the Grammarian Phrynichus. xi, 539p. 1968. reprint ed. 83.20 (*0-685-66502-X*, 05101885) G Olms Pubs.

— The New Phrynichus Being a Revised Text of the Ecloga of the Grammarian Phrynichus. xi, 539p. 1968. reprint ed. write for info. (*0-318-70998-8*) G Olms Pubs.

Phua, K. H., et al. Optimization Techniques & Applications: International Conference, 2 vols., Set. 1200p. 1992. text 190.00 (*981-02-1062-0*) World Scientific Pub.

Phua, K. K., et al, eds. High Temperature Superconductivity & Other Related Topics: First Asia-Pacific Conference on Condensed Matter Physics. (Progress in High Temperature Superconductivity Ser.: Vol. 12). 328p. 1989. pap. 55.00 (*9971-5-0706-4*); text 125.00 (*9971-5-0671-8*) World Scientific Pub.

Phua, K. K. & Yamaguchi, Y., eds. International Conference on High Energy Physics, 25th. 1576p. (C). 1991. pap. 87.00 (*981-00-2433-9*); text 273.00 (*981-00-2434-7*) World Scientific Pub.

Phukan, Arvind, ed. Frost in Geotechnical Engineering: Proceedings of the 2nd International Symposium on Frost in Geotechnical Engineering, Anchorage, U. S. A. 28 June - 1 July 1993. (Illus.). 199p. (C). 1993. text 104.00 (*90-5410-319-1*, Pub. by A A Balkema) Ashgate Pub Co.

Phukan, Umananda. Agricultural Development in Assam, 1950-85. 1990. 21.50 (*81-7099-202-8*, Pub. by Mittal Pubs Dist) S Asia.

Phul, Raj K. Landmarks of World Civilization. 390p. 1986. 39.95 (*0-318-36971-0*) Asia Bk Corp.

Phulpin, Thierry, jt. ed. see Guyot, Gerard.

Phuong, Mai. Behind the Bamboo Hedges. (Illus.). 344p. (Orig.). 1996. pap. 10.00 (*1-889880-00-0*) Nguoi Dan.

Phuq, K. K., et al, eds. Singapore Super Computing Conference, '90. 500p. (C). 1991. text 104.00 (*981-02-0700-X*) World Scientific Pub.

PhVogel, J., jt. auth. see Hutchison, J.

Phy, Allene S. Presenting Norma Klein. (United States Authors Ser.). 176p. 1988. 20.95 (*0-8057-8205-2*, TUSAS 538, Twyne) Mac Lib Ref.

Phychological Harcourt Staff. MAT 7 English Pretest. 1993. 24.00 (*0-15-831407-7*) Harcourt.

Phye, Gary D., ed. Handbook of Academic Learning. LC 96-8681. (Educational Psychology Ser.). (Illus.). 607p. 1996. text 79.95 (*0-12-554255-0*) Morgan Kaufmann.

— Handbook of Academic Learning: The Construction of Knowledge. LC 96-8681. (Educational Psychology Ser.). (Illus.). 607p. 1996. pap. text 49.95 (*0-12-554256-9*) Morgan Kaufmann.

— Handbook of Classroom Assessment: Learning, Achievement, & Adjustment. LC 96-41805. (Educational Psychology Ser.). (Illus.). 545p. 1996. text 79.95 (*0-12-554155-4*); pap. text 49.95 (*0-12-554156-2*) Morgan Kaufmann.

Phye, Gary D., jt. auth. see Klauer, Karl J.

Phylos. Dweller on Two Planets. 1952. pap. 13.50 (*0-87505-088-3*) Borden.

***Phylos, Orpheus & Essene, Virginia.** Earth the Cosmos & You: Revelations by Archangel Michael. (Illus.). 240p. 1999. pap. 14.95 (*0-937147-31-1*, Pub. by SEE Pub Co) Bookpeople.

Phylos the Thibetan. A Dweller on Two Planets: The Dividing of the Way. 423p. 1964. reprint ed. pap. 25.00 (*0-7873-0670-3*) Hlth Research.

— A Dweller on Two Planets or the Dividing of the Way (1920) 423p. 1996. reprint ed. pap. 24.95 (*1-56459-715-6*) Kessinger Pub.

— Earth Dweller Returns. 1940. pap. 13.50 (*0-87505-089-1*) Borden.

— Habitante de Dos Planetas. Garces, Soledad, tr. from ENG. (SPA.). 438p. 1992. pap. write for info. (*1-883482-06-2*) Edic Gran Dir.

Phylos The Thibetan. Habitante de Dos Planetas. 438p. 1992. pap. write for info. (*0-318-71306-3*) Edic Gran Dir.

Phylotus. Esoteric Masonry: The Storehouse Unlocked. 77p. 1996. reprint ed. spiral bd. 10.00 (*0-7873-0673-8*) Hlth Research.

— Esoteric Masonry or the Storehouse Unlocked. 80p. 1992. reprint ed. pap. 9.95 (*1-56459-190-5*) Kessinger Pub.

— Private Lessons: Interpreting the Inner Meaning of Masonry. 78p. 1996. reprint ed. pap. 8.95 (*1-56459-845-4*) Kessinger Pub.

— Private Lessons Interpreting the Inner Meaning of Masonry & the Bible. 78p. 1996. reprint ed. spiral bd. 10.00 (*0-7873-0671-1*) Hlth Research.

— That Man up North. 50p. 1998. reprint ed. pap. 12.95 (*0-7661-0121-5*) Kessinger Pub.

Phyne, John. Disputed Waters: Rural Social Change & Conflicts Associated with the Irish Salmon Farming Industry, 1987-1995. LC HD9469.S23I737 1999. (Illus.). 274p. (C). 1999. text 69.95 (*1-84014-876-4*, Pub. by Ashgate Pub) Ashgate Pub Co.

Physical Best (Program) Staff & American Alliance for Health, Physical Education, Recreation & Dance Staff. Physical Best Activity Guide for Secondary Level. LC 98-40311. 240p. 1999. 24.00 (*0-88011-971-3*) Human Kinetics.

Physical Science for Nonscience Students Project S. An Approach to Physical Science: Physical Science for Nonscience Students. Strassenburg, Arnold A., ed. LC 74-1024. (Illus.). 432p. 1974. reprint ed. pap. 134.00 (*0-7837-3463-8*, 205779100008) Bks Demand.

Physicians Desk Reference. PDR Guide to Over-the-Counter. LC 97-97165. 1998. mass mkt. 6.99 (*0-345-41716-X*, Ballantine Epiphany) Ballantine Pub Grp.

Physicians' Desk Reference Staff. Family Guide to Common Ail. 1999. mass mkt. 6.99 (*0-345-41715-1*) Ballantine Pub Grp.

***Physicians' Desk Reference Staff.** The PDR Family Guide to Natural Medicines & Healing Therapies. 752p. 2000. mass mkt. 7.99 (*0-345-43377-7*, Ballantine) Ballantine Pub Grp.

Physicians' Desk Reference Staff. The PDR Family Guide to Natural Medicines & Healing Therapies. LC 99-13367. 576p. 1999. pap. 23.00 (*0-609-80071-X*) Crown Pub Group.

Take advantage of all your health options & reap the rewards of better health with this unique consumer's guide to affordable, effective healthcare alternatives. From age-old secrets of harmony, balance & well-being to the very latest nutritional discoveries, readers will find dozens of alternative treatments discussed in this one home handbook. Here are all the latest findings on acupuncture & acupressure, aromatherapy, chiropractic adjustments, environmental medicine, naturopathic medicine, tai chi, yoga & more. Available now. *Publisher Paid Annotation.*

***Physicians' Desk Reference Staff.** The PDR Family Guide to Prescription Drugs No. 5, Vol. 1. 7th ed. 1999. pap. 23.00 (*0-609-80491-X*, Three Riv Pr) Crown Pub Group.

Physicians' Desk Reference Staff, ed. The PDR Pocket Guide to Prescription Drugs. 3rd rev. ed. (Illus.). 1480p. 1998. per. 6.99 (*0-671-02585-6*) PB.

Physicians for Human Rights - Asia Watch Staff. Thailand - Bloody May: Excessive Use of Lethal Force in Bangkok. 50p. 1992. pap. 7.00 (*1-879707-11-X*) Phy Human Rights.

Physicians for Human Rights Staff. Bloody Sunday: Trauma in Tbilisi. (Illus.). 70p. 1990. pap. 6.00 (*0-614-14417-5*) Phy Human Rights.

— The Casualties of Conflict: Medical Care & Human Rights in the West Bank & Gaza Strip. 46p. 1988. pap. 6.00 (*0-614-14421-3*) Phy Human Rights.

— Commercial Sexual Exploitation of Women & Children in Cambodia: Personal Narratives/A Psychological Perspective. 31p. (Orig.). 1996. pap. 3.00 (*1-879707-22-5*) Phy Human Rights.

— El Salvador: Health Care Under Seige. (Illus.). 73p. 1990. pap. 6.00 (*0-614-14418-3*) Phy Human Rights.

— Health Care in Detention: A Study of Israel's Treatment of Palestinians. 46p. 1990. pap. 6.00 (*0-614-14422-1*) Phy Human Rights.

— Health Conditions in Haiti's Prisons. 40p. 1992. pap. text 3.00 (*1-879707-08-X*) Phy Human Rights.

— Hidden Enemies: Land Mines in Northern Somalia. (Illus.). ii, 51p. 1992. pap. 7.00 (*1-879707-12-8*) Phy Human Rights.

— Human Rights on Hold: A Report on Emergency Measures & Access to Health Care in the Occupied Territories. LC 93-83144. 87p. 1992. pap. 10.00 (*1-879707-09-8*) Phy Human Rights.

Physicians For Human Rights Staff. Israel & the Occupied Territories: "Shaking As a Form of Torture", Death in Custody of 'Abd al-Samad Harat. LC 96-194726. 30p. 1995. pap. 3.00 (*1-879707-19-5*) Phy Human Rights.

Physicians for Human Rights Staff. Liberia: Anguish in a Divided Land. 12p. 1991. pap. 2.50 (*0-614-14424-8*) Phy Human Rights.

— Panama, 1987: Health Consequences of Police & Military Actions. 73p. 1988. pap. 6.00 (*0-614-14419-1*) Phy Human Rights.

— The Suppression of a People: Torture & Imprisonment in Tibet. (Illus.). 62p. 1989. pap. 6.00 (*0-614-14416-7*) Phy Human Rights.

— Torture in Turkey & Its Unwilling Accomplices: The Scope of State Persecution & the Coercion of Physicians. (Illus.). 288p. (Orig.). 1996. pap. text 10.00 (*1-879707-21-7*) Phy Human Rights.

— United States: Cruel & Inhuman Treatment: The Use of Four-Point Restraint in the Onondaga County Public Safety Building. LC 93-84902. (Illus.). 67p. 1993. pap. 7.00 (*1-879707-16-0*) Phy Human Rights.

— War Crimes in the Balkans: Medicine under Siege in the Former Yugoslavia 1991-1995. LC 96-67670. 100p. 1996. pap. text 10.00 (*1-879707-20-9*) Phy Human Rights.

— Winds of Death: Iraq's Use of Poison Gas Against Its Kurdish Population. 39p. 1989. pap. 6.00 (*0-614-14420-5*) Phy Human Rights.

Physicians for Human Rights Staff & Africa Watch Staff. Somalia: No Mercy in Mogadishu: The Human Cost of the Conflict & the Struggle for Relief. (Illus.). 30p. 1992. pap. 7.00 (*1-879707-07-1*) Phy Human Rights.

Physicians for Human Rights Staff & American Refugee Committee. Health Conditions in Cambodia's Prisons. 91p. 1995. pap. 7.00 (*1-879707-18-7*) Phy Human Rights.

Physicians for Human Rights Staff & Asia Watch Staff. The Crackdown in Kashmir: Torture of Detainees & Assaults on the Medical Community. (Illus.). 50p. 1993. pap. text 7.00 (*1-879707-14-4*) Phy Human Rights.

Physicians for Human Rights Staff & Cohen, Barend. Yugoslavia: Mistreatment of Ethnic Albanians: A Case Study. 30p. 1991. pap. text 3.00 (*1-879707-03-9*) Phy Human Rights.

Physicians for Human Rights Staff, et al. United States - Breach of Trust: Physician Participation in Executions in the United States. 80p. (Orig.). 1994. pap. 7.00 (*1-56432-125-8*) Hum Rts Watch.

Physicians for Human Rights Staff, jt. auth. see Americas Watch Staff.

Physicians for Human Rights Staff, jt. auth. see Human Rights Watch Americas Staff.

Physicians for Human Rights Staff, jt. auth. see Human Rights Watch Arms Project Staff.

Physicians for Human Rights Staff, jt. auth. see Human Rights Watch Asia Staff.

Physicians Genrx Staff. 1997 Physicians' GenRx. 7th rev. ed. LC 99-33332. (Illus.). 880p. (C). (gr. 13). 1999. text 64.95 (*0-8151-9017-4*, 31745) Mosby Inc.

Physicians GenRx Staff Corporation. Physicians GenRx 1997 Book Update, No. 1. rev. ed. 1997. write for info. (*0-8151-7222-2*) Mosby Inc.

— Physicians GenRx 1997 Book Update, No. 2. 2nd rev. ed. 1997. write for info. (*0-8151-7223-0*) Mosby Inc.

Physics & Engineering Communities Database Staff. Temperature Measurements: Technology & Standards. 1996. 85.00 (*0-614-18489-4*, 135P26) Info Gatekeepers.

Physics Education Group Staff, jt. auth. see McDermott, Lillian C.

Physiologus. Icelandic Physiologus. Hermannsson, Halldor, ed. (Islandica Ser.: Vol. 27). 1938. 25.00 (*0-527-00357-3*) Periodicals Srv.

Physiology & Pharmacology of Vascular Neuroeffecto. Vascular Neuroeffector Systems, Physiology & Pharmacology: Proceedings of the Symposium, Interlaken, 1969. Bevan, J. A. et al, eds. (Illus.). viii, 350p. 1971. 62.75 (*3-8055-1184-1*) S Karger.

Phythian-Adams, Charles. Land of the Cumbrians: A Study in British Provincial Origins, AD 400-1120. (Illus.). 224p. 1996. 78.95 (*1-85928-327-6*, Pub. by Scolar Pr) Ashgate Pub Co.

Phythian-Adams, Charles, ed. Societies, Cultures & Kinships, 1580-1850: Cultural Provinces & English Local History. 230p. 1996. pap. 33.95 (*0-7185-0052-0*) Bks Intl VA.

Phythian-Adams, Charles, intro. Societies, Cultures, & Kinship, 1580-1850: Cultural Provinces & English Local History. LC 92-36511. (Illus.). 240p. 1993. 65.00 (*0-7185-1453-X*) St Martin.

Phythian, B. A. A Concise Dictionary of Confusables: All Those Impossible Words You Never Get Right. LC 90-35359. 198p. 1990. pap. 10.95 (*0-471-52880-3*) Wiley.

Phythian, B. A., ed. Concise Dictionary of Correct English. 166p. 1979. 19.50 (*0-8476-6212-8*) Rowman.

Phythian, Mark. Arming Iraq: How the U. S. & Britain Secretly Built Saddam's War Machine. (Northeastern Series in Transnational Crime). (Illus.). 320p. 1996. text 35.00 (*1-55553-285-3*) NE U Pr.

***Phythian, Mark.** The Politics of British Arms Sales since 1964: To Secure Our Rightful Share. LC 00-21988. 2000. pap. write for info. (*0-7190-5907-0*, Pub. by Manchester Univ Pr) St Martin.

— The Politics of British Arms Sales Since 1964: To Secure Our Rights. text. write for info. (*0-7190-5196-7*, Pub. by Manchester Univ Pr) St Martin.

Phytochemical Society of North America Symposium S. Recent Advances in Phytochemistry, Vol. 2: Proceedings of the 7th Annual Symposium of. Seikel, Margaret K., ed. LC 67-26242. 187p. reprint ed. pap. 58.00 (*0-608-12388-9*, 205568900002) Bks Demand.

Phytochemical Society of North America Symposium S, et al, eds. Symposia, Vols. 5 & 6. Incl. Vol. 5. Structural & Functional Aspects of Phytochemistry. 1972. 67.00 (*0-12-612405-1*); Vol. 6. Terpenoids: Structure, Biogenesis, Distribution. 1973. 51.00 (*0-12-612406-X*); write for info. (*0-318-50372-7*) Acad Pr.

Pi, Chung-Ron. Expression of Culture in Economic Development. 112p. 1996. 58.95 (*1-85972-359-4*, Pub. by Avebry) Ashgate Pub Co.

Pi, Douglas, jt. auth. see Prince, Francie.

Pi-Kwang Tsung & Hong-Yen Hsu. Allergies & Chinese Herbal Medicine. (Educational Series on Chinese Medicine: No. 3). 40p. (Orig.). (C). 1987. pap. text 5.95 (*0-941942-26-0*) Orient Heal Arts.

Pi-Kwang Tsung & Hong-yen Hsu. Arthritis & Chinese Herbal Medicine. 32p. 1987. pap. 4.95 (*0-941942-25-2*) Orient Heal Arts.

Pi, S. Y., jt. auth. see Abbott, L.

Pi Sigma Alpha Committee on Publications. Major Problems in State Constitutional Revision. Graves, W. Brooke, ed. LC 78-779. 306p. 1978. reprint ed. lib. bdg. 59.75 (*0-313-20266-4*, PSAM, Greenwood Pr) Greenwood.

Pi-Sunyer, Xavier F., jt. ed. see Allison, David B.

Pi, Ying-Hsien, jt. auth. see Jo, Yung-Hwan.

Pia, jt. auth. see Midgley.

Pia, ed. see Leautaud, Paul.

Pia, ed. see Maupassant, Guy de.

Pia, Albert. A Doll's House. 47p. 1972. pap. 3.50 (*0-87129-102-9*, D19) Dramatic Pub.

Pia, H. W., et al, eds. Spontaneous Intracerebral Haematomas: Advances in Diagnosis & Therapy. (Illus.). 500p. 1981. 158.00 (*0-387-10146-2*) Spr-Verlag.

Pia-Hall, Annette. 101 Fabulous Dairy-Free Desserts Everyone Will Love: For the Lactose-Intolerant, the Dairy-Allergic, & their Friends & Families. (Illus.). 256p. 1998. pap. 14.95 (*1-58177-018-9*) Barrytown Ltd.

Pia, Julius. Kohlensaeure und Kalk. Einfuhrung in das Verstandnis Ihres Verhaltens in Den Binnengewassern. (Binnengewaesser Ser.: Band XIII). (GER., Illus.). vii, 183p. 1933. 26.00 (*3-510-40713-X*, Pub. by E Schweizerbartsche) Balogh.

Pia, Leslie, jt. auth. see Gallagher, Gerry.

Pia, Leslie, jt. auth. see Johnson, Donald-Brian.

Pia, Renato. Airplanes: A Troubador Color & Story Album. (Troubador Color & Story Ser.). 32p. (J). (gr. 1-7). 1998. pap. 5.99 (*0-8431-7855-8*) Putnam Pub Group.

— Trains: A Troubador Color & Story Album. (Troubador Color & Story Ser.). (Illus.). 32p. (J). (gr. 1-7). 1998. pap. 5.99 (*0-8431-7854-X*) Putnam Pub Group.

***Pia, Simon.** Edinburgh: A Cultural & Literary Companion. (Illus.). 2000. pap. 15.00 (*1-56656-362-3*) Interlink Pub.

Pia, Simon. Pat Stanton: The Quiet Man. 128p. (C). 1996. 45.00 (*0-85976-288-2*, Pub. by J Donald) St Mut.

***PIA Staff.** 1999 PIA Ratios: All Printers by Product Specialty. (PIA Ratios Ser.: Vol. 3). (Illus.). 80p. (C). 1999. pap. text 199.00 (*0-88362-269-6*, 00FM99003) GATFPress.

— 1999 PIA Ratios: All Printers by Sales Volume & Geographic Areas. (PIA Ratios Ser.: Vol. 2). (Illus.). 80p. (Orig.). (C). 1999. pap. text 199.00 (*0-88362-268-8*, 00FM99002) GATFPress.

An Asterisk (*) at the beginning of an entry indicates that the title is appearing for the first time.

— 1999 PIA Ratios: Binders' Ratios. (PIA Ratios Ser.: Vol. 11). (Illus.). 80p. (C). 1999. pap. text 199.00 (*0-88362-277-7*, 00FM99011) GATFPress.

— 1999 PIA Ratios: Book Manufacturer's Ratios. (PIA Ratios Ser.: Vol. 8). (Illus.). 80p. (C). 1999. pap. text 199.00 (*0-88362-274-2*, 00FM99008) GATFPress.

— 1999 PIA Ratios: Business Forms Ratios. (PIA Ratios Ser.: Vol. 14). (Illus.). 80p. (C). 1999. pap. text 199.00 (*0-88362-280-7*, 00FM99014) GATFPress.

— 1999 PIA Ratios: Combination Offset-Sheetfed/Web. (PIA Ratios Ser.: Vol. 7). (Illus.). 80p. (C). 1999. pap. text 199.00 (*0-88362-273-4*, 00FM99007) GATFPress.

— 1999 PIA Ratios: Commercial & Advertising Printers. (PIA Ratios Ser.: Vol. 17). (Illus.). 80p. (C). 1999. pap. text 199.00 (*0-88362-283-1*, 00FM99017) GATFPress.

— 1999 PIA Ratios: Digital Printers' Ratios. (PIA Ratios Ser.: Vol. 16). (Illus.). 80p. (C). 1999. pap. text 199.00 (*0-88362-282-3*, 00FM99016) GATFPress.

— 1999 PIA Ratios: Label Printers' Ratios. (PIA Ratios Ser.: Vol. 15). (Illus.). 80p. (C). 1999. pap. text 199.00 (*0-88362-281-5*, 00FM99015) GATFPress.

— 1999 PIA Ratios: Managament Guide to PIA Ratios. (PIA Ratios Ser.: Vol. 1). (Illus.). 80p. (C). 1999. pap. text 199.00 (*0-88362-267-X*, 00FM990001) GATFPress.

— 1999 PIA Ratios: Prepress Specialists' Ratios. (PIA Ratios Ser.: Vol. 10). (Illus.). 80p. (C). 1999. pap. text 199.00 (*0-88362-276-9*, 00FM99010) GATFPress.

— 1999 PIA Ratios: Printers with Sales over $10,000,000. (PIA Ratios Ser.: Vol. 9). (Illus.). 80p. (C). 1999. pap. text 199.00 (*0-88362-275-0*, 00FM99009) GATFPress.

— 1999 PIA Ratios: Printers with Sales under $1,500,000. (PIA Ratios Ser.: Vol. 12). (Illus.). 80p. (C). 1999. pap. text 199.00 (*0-88362-278-5*, 00FM99012) GATFPress.

— 1999 PIA Ratios: Quick Printers' Ratios. (PIA Ratios Ser.: Vol. 13). (Illus.). 80p. (C). 1999. pap. text 199.00 (*0-88362-279-3*, 00FM99013) GATFPress.

— 1999 PIA Ratios: Sheetfed Printers by Size & Geographic Area. (PIA Ratios Ser.: Vol. 4). (Illus.). 80p. (C). 1999. pap. text 199.00 (*0-88362-270-X*, 00FM99004) GATFPress.

— 1999 PIA Ratios: Web Offset Printers, Heatset. (PIA Ratios Ser.: Vol. 5). (Illus.). 80p. (C). 1999. pap. text 199.00 (*0-88362-271-8*, 00FM99005) GATFPress.

— 1999 PIA Ratios: Web Offset Printers, Non-Heatset, Vol. 6. (PIA Ratios Ser.: Vol. 6). (Illus.). 80p. (C). 1999. pap. text 199.00 (*0-88362-272-6*, 00FM99006) GATFPress.

— PIA Productivity Benchmarks: Sheetfed Printers' Production Characteristics. (Illus.). 50p. 2000. pap. text 129.00 (*0-88362-310-2*) GATFPress.

— PIA Survey of Printing Management & Administrative Compensation: 1999-2000 Edition. 145p. (C). 2000. pap. text 250.00 (*0-88362-296-3*) GATFPress.

— PIA Survey of Sales Compensation: 1999-2000 Edition. 222p. (C). 2000. pap. text 250.00 (*0-88362-295-5*) GATFPress.

— PIA Technology Benchmarks: Printes' Awareness, Use & Assessment of New Graphic Communications Technology, 1999 Edition. (Illus.). 56p. (C). 1999. pap. text 129.00 (*0-88362-263-7*) GATFPress.

— 2000 PIA Ratios: All Printers by Product Specialty. (PIA Ratios Ser.: Vol. 3). (Illus.). 80p. (C). 2000. pap. text 199.00 (*0-88362-317-X*) GATFPress.

— 2000 PIA Ratios: All Printers by Sales Volume & Geographic Areas. (PIA Ratios Ser.: Vol. 2). (Illus.). 80p. (C). 2000. pap. text 199.00 (*0-88362-316-1*) GATFPress.

— 2000 PIA Ratios: Binders' Ratios. (PIA Ratios Ser.: Vol. 11). (Illus.). 80p. (C). 2000. pap. text 199.00 (*0-88362-325-0*) GATFPress.

— 2000 PIA Ratios: Book Manufacturers' Ratios. (PIA Ratios Ser.: Vol. 8). 80p. (C). 2000. pap. text 199.00 (*0-88362-322-6*) GATFPress.

— 2000 PIA Ratios: Business Forms Ratios. (PIA Ratios Ser.: Vol. 14). (Illus.). 80p. (C). 2000. pap. text 199.00 (*0-88362-328-5*) GATFPress.

— 2000 PIA Ratios: Combination Offset - Sheetfed/Web. (PIA Ratios Ser.: Vol. 7). (Illus.). 80p. (C). 2000. pap. text 199.00 (*0-88362-321-8*) GATFPress.

— 2000 PIA Ratios: Commercial & Advertising Printers. (PIA Ratios Ser.: Vol. 17). (Illus.). 80p. (C). 2000. pap. text 199.00 (*0-88362-331-5*) GATFPress.

— 2000 PIA Ratios: Digital Printers' Ratios. (PIA Ratios Ser.: Vol. 16). (Illus.). 80p. (C). 2000. pap. text 199.00 (*0-88362-330-7*) GATFPress.

— 2000 PIA Ratios: In-Plant Printers. (PIA Ratios Ser.: Vol. 18). (Illus.). 80p. (C). 2000. pap. 199.00 (*0-88362-332-3*) GATFPress.

— 2000 PIA Ratios: Label Printers' Ratios. (PIA Ratios Ser.: Vol. 15). (Illus.). 80p. (C). 2000. pap. text 199.00 (*0-88362-329-3*) GATFPress.

— 2000 PIA Ratios: Management Guide to PIA Ratios. (PIA Ratios Ser.: Vol. 1). (Illus.). 80p. (C). 2000. pap. text 199.00 (*0-88362-315-3*) GATFPress.

— 2000 PIA Ratios: Prepress Specialists' Ratios. (PIA Ratios Ser.: Vol. 10). (Illus.). 80p. (C). 2000. pap. text 199.00 (*0-88362-324-2*) GATFPress.

— 2000 PIA Ratios: Printers with Sales Over $10,000,000. (PIA Ratios Ser.: Vol. 9). 80p. (C). 2000. pap. text 199.00 (*0-88362-323-4*) GATFPress.

— 2000 PIA Ratios: Printers with Sales Under $1,500,000. (PIA Ratios Ser.: Vol. 12). (Illus.). 80p. (C). 2000. pap. text 199.00 (*0-88362-326-9*) GATFPress.

— 2000 PIA Ratios: Quick Printers' Ratios. (PIA Ratios Ser.: Vol. 13). (Illus.). 80p. (C). 2000. pap. text 199.00 (*0-88362-327-7*) GATFPress.

— 2000 PIA Ratios: Sheetfed Printers by Size & Geographic Area. (Illus.). 80p. (C). 2000. pap. text 199.00 (*0-88362-318-8*) GATFPress.

— 2000 PIA Ratios: Web Offset Printers, Heatset. (PIA Ratios Ser.: Vol. 5). (Illus.). 80p. (C). 2000. pap. text 199.00 (*0-88362-319-6*) GATFPress.

— 2000 PIA Ratios: Web Offset Printers, Non-Heatset. (PIA Ratios Ser.: Vol. 6). (Illus.). 80p. (C). 2000. pap. text 199.00 (*0-88362-320-X*) GATFPress.

Pia-Terry, Carole D., jt. auth. see Olson, Richard P.

Piacente, Adam J. Computer-Assisted Legal Research Unplugged: The User-Friendly Guide to Lexis-Nexis & Westlaw. (Illus.). 476p. 1997. pap. 60.00 (*0-9662482-0-1*) Montag Multimedia.

— Computer-Assisted Legal Research Unplugged: The User-Friendly Guide to Lexis-Nexis & Westlaw. 2nd rev. ed. (CALR Unplugged Ser.). (Illus.). 497p. (C). 1999. pap. 75.00 (*0-9662482-1-X*) Montag Multimedia.

***Piacente, Adam J.** The KeyCite Report: An Interactive Guide to Westlaw's New Citation Service. (Illus.). 27p. 1999. pap. 15.00 (*0-9662482-6-0*) Montag Multimedia.

Piacente, Adam J. Lexis-Nexis 7.X Unplugged: The User-Friendly Guide to Lexis-Nexis Version 7.X. (CALR Unplugged Ser.). (Illus.). (C). 1999. pap. 60.00 (*0-9662482-2-8*) Montag Multimedia.

***Piacente, Adam J.** Lexis.com Unplugged: The User-Friendly Guide to Lexis.com. (Illus.). 246p. (C). 1999. pap. 60.00 (*0-9662482-4-4*) Montag Multimedia.

Piacente, Adam J. Westlaw 6.X Unplugged: The User-Friendly Guide to Westlaw Version 6.X. (CALR Unplugged Ser.). (Illus.). (C). 1999. pap. 60.00 (*0-9662482-3-6*) Montag Multimedia.

— Westlaw.com Unplugged: The User-Friendly Guide to Westlaw on the Internet. (C). Date not set. write for info. (*0-9662482-5-2*) Montag Multimedia.

Piacente, Steve & Keeler, Todd. The Almanac of the Unelected: Staff of the U. S. Congress, 1999. 11th ed. (Illus.). 691p. 1999. 169.00 (*1-886222-15-0*, BPD2150) Bernan Pr.

Piacentini, Ernesto. Immaculate Conception: Panorama of the Marian Doctrine of Maximilian Kolbe. Kos, Donald, tr. from ITA. 64p. (Orig.). 1975. pap. 2.00 (*0-913382-04-3*, 105-3) Marytown Pr.

Piacentini, G. M. & Strickland, E., eds. Topics in Computational Algebra. (C). 1990. text 155.50 (*0-7923-1117-5*) Kluwer Academic.

Piacentino, Edward J. T. S. Stribling: Pioneer Realist in Modern Southern Literature. 194p. (Orig.). (C). 1988. pap. text 20.00 (*0-8191-6720-7*) U Pr of Amer.

Piacere, Diana & Piacere, Nicholas. Lovemaking: A No-Nonsense Practical Solution. 64p. 1992. pap. 9.95 (*0-9640117-0-0*) InFour Grp.

Piacere, Nicholas, jt. auth. see Piacere, Diana.

Piaf, Edith. My Life. Crosland, Margaret, tr. from FRE. (Illus.). 144p. 1990. 30.00 (*0-7206-0797-3*, Pub. by P Owen Ltd) Dufour.

Piaget, Gerald W. & Binkley, Barbara. Overcoming Your Barriers. 236p. 1985. 14.95 (*0-8290-0438-6*) Irvington.

Piaget, Gerald W. & Binkley, Barbara M. Overcoming Your Barriers: A Guide to Personal Reprogramming. 14.95 (*0-88282-005-2*) New Horizon NJ.

Piaget, J., jt. auth. see Beth, E. W.

Piaget, Jean. Adaptation & Intelligence: Organic Selection & Phenocopy. Eames, Steward, tr. LC 79-25592. vi, 124p. (C). 1980. 11.00 (*0-226-66777-4*) U Ch Pr.

— Adaptation & Intelligence: Organic Selection & Phenocopy. Eames, Steward, tr. LC 79-25592. vi, 124p. (C). 1997. pap. text 8.95 (*0-226-66778-2*) U Ch Pr.

— Adaptation & Intelligence: Organic Selection & Phenocopy. Eames, Stewart, tr. LC 79-25592. 130p. reprint ed. pap. 40.30 (*0-608-09497-8*, 205429800005) Bks Demand.

— Biology & Knowledge: An Essay on the Relations Between Organic Regulations & Cognitive Processes. LC 70-157421. (C). 1971. lib. bdg. 19.00 (*0-226-66775-8*) U Ch Pr.

— The Child's Conception of the World. (Quality Paperback Ser.: No. 213). 398p. 1983. reprint ed. pap. 14.95 (*0-8226-0213-X*) Littlefield.

— Le Comportement: Moteur de l'Evolution. (FRE.). 1976. pap. 10.95 (*0-7859-2846-4*) Fr & Eur.

— The Equilibration of Cognitive Structures: The Central Problem of Intellectual Development. Brown, Terence A. & Thampy, Kishore J., trs. (Illus.). 178p. 1998. lib. bdg. 30.00 (*0-226-66781-2*) U Ch Pr.

— Experiments in Contradiction. Coltman, Derek, tr. LC 80-14248. 328p. reprint ed. pap. 101.70 (*0-608-09498-6*, 205429900005) Bks Demand.

— Genetic Epistemology. Duckworth, Eleanor, tr. 1971. reprint ed. pap. 5.95 (*0-393-00596-8*) Norton.

— Jean Piaget, 9 vols. Incl. Vol. 4. Child's Conception of Numbers. 264p. (C). 1998. 110.00 (*0-415-16888-0*); LC 98-196306. 2864p. (C). 1998. 770.00 (*0-415-16886-4*) Routledge.

— Logique & Connaissance Scientifique. (Methodique Ser.). 1360p. 55.95 (*0-686-56429-4*) Fr & Eur.

— Logique et Connaissance Scientifique. (FRE.). 1364p. 1973. lib. bdg. 130.00 (*0-7859-3776-5*, 2070104133) Fr & Eur.

— The Moral Judgment of the Child. Gabain, Marjorie, tr. 416p. 1965. pap. 17.95 (*0-02-925240-7*) Free Pr.

— The Moral Judgment of the Child. 416p. 1997. per. 15.00 (*0-684-83330-1*) Free Pr.

— Origins of Intelligence in Children. 418p. (Orig.). 1974. pap. 27.95 (*0-8236-8207-2*, 23900) Intl Univs Pr.

— Piaget Sampler: An Introduction to Jean Piaget Through His Own Words. Campbell, Sarah F., ed. LC 75-34129. 168p. reprint ed. pap. 52.10 (*0-608-30711-4*, 202059400018) Bks Demand.

— Psychologie. (FRE.). 1987. lib. bdg. 165.00 (*0-7859-3854-0*) Fr & Eur.

— Psychologie et Pedagogie. (FRE.). 1988. pap. 12.95 (*0-7859-2814-6*) Fr & Eur.

— Six Etudes de Psychologie. (FRE.). 1987. pap. 12.95 (*0-7859-2805-7*) Fr & Eur.

Piaget, Jean. Six Psychological Studies. Elkind, David, ed. Tenzer, Anita, tr. (Orig.). 1968. pap. 10.00 (*0-394-70462-2*) Vin Bks.

Piaget, Jean. Sociological Studies. Smith, Leslie, ed. LC 94-27215. 368p. (C). (gr. 13). 1995. 75.00 (*0-415-10780-6*, B4388) Routledge.

— Success & Understanding. LC 78-16435. (Illus.). 248p. 1978. 28.00 (*0-674-85387-3*) HUP.

Piaget, Jean, ed. Intelligence & Affectivity: Their Relationship During Child Development. Brown, T. A. & Kaegi, C. E., trs. (Illus.). 1981. text 8.00 (*0-8243-2901-5*) Annual Reviews.

Piaget, Jean & Garcia, Rolando, eds. Toward a Logic of Meanings. Easley, Jack & Davidson, Phil, trs. 200p. 1991. text 39.95 (*0-8058-0301-7*) L Erlbaum Assocs.

Piaget, Jean & Garcia, Rolando V. Psychogenesis & the History of Science. Feider, Helga, tr. from FRE. (Illus.). 336p. 1989. text 64.50 (*0-231-05992-2*) Col U Pr.

Piaget, Jean & Inhelder, Barbel. Psychology of the Child. Weaver, Helen, tr. LC 73-78449. 192p. 1972. pap. 17.00 (*0-465-09500-3*, Pub. by Basic) HarpC.

***Piaget, Jean & Valsiner, Jane.** The Child's Conception of Physical Causality. 307p. 2000. pap. 29.95 (*0-7658-0641-X*) Transaction Pubs.

Piaget, Jean, et al. Epistemology & Psychology of Functions. Castellanos, Javier & Anderson, Vivian, trs. (Synthese Library: No. 83). 219p. 1977. lib. bdg. 112.00 (*90-277-0804-5*, D Reidel) Kluwer Academic.

— Experiments in Contradiction. Coltman, Derek, tr. LC 80-14248. 256p. 1995. lib. bdg. 31.50 (*0-226-66779-0*) U Ch Pr.

— Morphisms & Categories: Comparing & Transforming. Brown, Terrance, tr. from FRE. 248p. 1992. text 49.95 (*0-8058-0300-9*) L Erlbaum Assocs.

Piaget, Jean, Foundation Archives, Geneva Staff. Phylogeny & Ontogeny. (Human Development Ser.: Vol. 27, No. 5). (Illus.). vi, 134p. 1984. pap. 34.00 (*3-8055-3904-5*) S Karger.

Piaggi, Anna. Anna Piaggi's Fashion Algebra. Treves, Cecilia, tr. from ITA. LC 98-60494. (Illus.). 326p. 1998. 60.00 (*0-500-01876-6*, Pub. by Thames Hudson) Norton.

Pialat, M. New Larousse of Scrabble & Word Games: Nouveau Larousse du Scrabble, Dictionnaire des Jeux de Letters. (FRE.). 830p. 1981. pap. 31.95 (*0-8288-2345-6*, M14461) Fr & Eur.

— Nouveau Larousse du Scrabble. (FRE.). 880p. 1981. 52.50 (*0-8288-2344-8*, F82270) Fr & Eur.

Pialorsi, Frank, ed. Teaching the Bilingual: New Methods & Old Traditions. LC 73-87717. 263p. 1974. pap. 81.60 (*0-608-05638-3*, 206609200006) Bks Demand.

Pialorsi, Frank, jt. auth. see Dunkel, Patricia.

***Piamenta, M.** Jewish Life in Arabic Language & Jerusalem Arabic in Communal Perspective: A Lexico-Semantic Study. LC 00-20629. (Studies in Semitic Languages & Linguistics Ser.). 2000. write for info. (*90-04-11762-8*) Brill Academic Pubs.

Piamenta, Moshe. A Dictionary of Post-Classical Yemeni Arabic, Vol. I. LC 90-2137. (ARA & ENG.). xxiv, 274p. 1990. 132.50 (*90-04-09261-7*) Brill Academic Pubs.

— A Dictionary of Post-Classical Yemeni Arabic, Vol. 2. LC 90-2137. (ARA & ENG.). 275-541p. 1991. 132.50 (*90-04-09293-5*) Brill Academic Pubs.

Pian, R. Da, see Pasqualin, A., ed.

Pian, R. Da, see Pasqualin, A. & Da Pian, R., eds.

Pian, R. Da, see Pasqualin, A., ed.

Pian, Rulan C. A Syllabus for Mandarin Primer. LC PL1125.E6P5. (Illus.). 118p. reprint ed. pap. 36.60 (*0-7837-4178-2*, 205902700012) Bks Demand.

Pian, Shuch J. Dr. Pian's Talks of Herbal Cure. (CHI.). 228p. 1997. pap. 15.00 (*1-890474-01-0*) Nrth Amer Chinese Wrters.

Piana, Paul. Big Walls. LC 97-7405. (Illus.). 224p. 1998. 35.00 (*0-87156-960-4*, Pub. by Sierra) Random.

— Great Rock Hits of Hueco Tanks: A Climbers Guide. LC 92-19455. (Illus.). 48p. (Orig.). 1992. pap. 6.95 (*1-879415-03-8*) Mtn n Air Bks.

Pianca, Marina. El Teatro de Nuestra America: Un Proyecto Continental, 1959-1989. (Series Towards a Social History of Hispanic & Luso-Brazilian Literatures). 408p. (Orig.). (C). 1990. pap. 14.95 (*1-877660-05-1*) IFTSOIL.

Piancastelli, M. N., jt. auth. see De Crescenzi, M.

Pianesi, Fabio, jt. auth. see Giorgi, Alessandra.

***Pianetta, Piero, et al, eds.** Synchrotron Radiation Instrumentation: SRI99: Eleventh U. S. National Conference. LC 00-103465. (AIP Conference Proceedings Ser.: Vol. 521). (Illus.). xiv, 487p. 2000. 145.00 (*1-56396-941-6*) Am Inst Physics.

Pianfetti, Alice T., jt. auth. see Ismail, Mohamed I.

Piani, Andrea L. & Schoenborn, Charlotte A. Health Promotion & Disease Prevention, United States, 1990. LC 92-48186. (Vital & Health Statistics Ser.: No. 185). 1992. write for info. (*0-8406-0474-2*) Natl Ctr Health Stats.

Piani, Giovanni A. Giovanni Antonio Piani: Sonatas for Violin Solo & Violoncello with Cembalo. Jackson, Barbara G., ed. (Recent Researches in Music of the Baroque Era Ser.: Vol. RRB20). (Illus.). xii, 122p. 1975. pap. 45.00 (*0-89579-058-0*, RRB20) A-R Eds.

***Piani, Judith A. & Bookin-Weiner, Hedy.** Trait Secrets: Winning Together When You Don't Think Alike. LC 00-104922. (Illus.). 176p. 2000. pap. 19.95 (*0-9701272-0-0*) Teric Pub.

Pianin, Eric, jt. auth. see Hager, George.

Pianka, Eric R. Ecology & Natural History of Desert Lizards: Analyses of the Ecological Niche & Community Structure. LC 85-19097. (Illus.). 229p. 1986. reprint ed. pap. 71.00 (*0-7837-8179-2*, 204788400008) Bks Demand.

— Evolutionary Ecology. 6th ed. LC 99-48042. 512p. (C). 1999. 73.00 (*0-321-04288-3*) Addson-Wesley Educ.

— The Lizard Man Speaks. LC 93-38067. (Corrie Herring Hooks Ser.: No. 26). (Illus.). 224p. (C). 1994. 24.95 (*0-292-76552-5*) U of Tex Pr.

Pianka, Eric R., jt. ed. see Vitt, Laurie J.

Pianka, Phyllis T. The Thackery Jewels: Amethyst; Emerald; Topaz. LC 95-4596. (Regency Romance Ser.). 664p. 1994. per. 5.99 (*0-373-31216-4*, 1-31216-4) Harlequin Bks.

Pianka, Phyllis Taylor. How to Write Romances. rev. ed. LC 98-23353. (Howdunit Ser.). 192p. 1998. pap. 14.99 (*0-89879-867-1*, Wrtrs Digest Bks) F & W Pubns Inc.

Pianko, Howard, jt. auth. see Samuels, David G.

Piankoff, A. & Rambova, N., eds. The Tomb of Ramesses VI, 2 vols., Vol. 1 - Texts. LC 54-5646. (Bollingen Ser.: No. 40). 583p. 1954. reprint ed. pap. 180.80 (*0-608-08509-X*, 205134800097) Bks Demand.

— The Tomb of Ramesses VI, 2 vols., Vol. 2 - Plates. LC 54-5646. (Bollingen Ser.: No. 40). 212p. 1954. reprint ed. pap. 65.80 (*0-608-08510-3*, 205134800098) Bks Demand.

Piano, Mariann, jt. ed. see Kleinpell, Ruth M.

Piano, Renzo. Renzo Piano: Logbook. LC 97-5774. (Illus.). 272p. 1997. pap. 29.95 (*1-885254-65-2*, Pub. by Monacelli Pr) Penguin Putnam.

Piano Teacher Staff. Selections from the Piano Teacher, 1958-1963: A Collection of Articles from the Piano Teacher's First Five Years. Savler, Roberta, ed. LC 64-57578. 136p. reprint ed. pap. 42.20 (*0-608-10966-5*, 200532700052) Bks Demand.

Piano Teachers Congress Members. Technical Control for the Modern Pianist: Finger Exercises Used by Members of the Piano Teachers Congress of N.Y., Inc. De Vito, Albert, ed. LC 78-95128. 1978. pap. 9.95 (*0-934286-11-6*) Kenyon.

Pianta, Mario, jt. auth. see Archibugi, Daniele.

Pianta, Robert C. Enhancing Relationships Between Children & Teachers. LC 98-42492. (School Psychology Book Ser.). 207p. 1998. text 34.95 (*1-55798-542-1*, 431-613A) Am Psychol.

— High Risk Children. 198p. (C). 1996. 65.00 (*0-415-91621-6*); pap. 18.99 (*0-415-91622-4*) Routledge.

Pianta, Robert C., ed. Beyond the Parent: The Role of Other Adults in Children's Lives. LC 85-644581. (New Directions for Child Development Ser.: No. CD57). 110p. 1992. pap. 25.00 (*1-55542-732-4*) Jossey-Bass.

Pianta, Robert C., et al. The Transition to Kindergarten. LC 99-28677. 1999. pap. text 36.00 (*1-55766-399-8*) P H Brookes.

Piantadosi, Roger. Escape Plans: Quick Getaways Within Easy Reach of Washington. Epstein, Noel, ed. (Illus.). 213p. 1998. pap. 9.95 (*0-9625971-6-3*) Washington Post.

Piantadosi, Steven. Clinical Trials: A Methodologic Perspective. LC 96-46311. (Probability & Mathematics Ser.). 624p. 1997. 89.95 (*0-471-16393-7*) Wiley.

Piantanida, Kevin, ed. Poetic Classics of 1997. LC 97-65159. 300p. (Orig.). 1997. pap. 32.00 (*0-9656699-0-4*) Delta Pubns NJ.

Piantanida, Maria. Quick Reference Systems for Physical Assessment. rev. ed. (Illus.). 19p. 1997. ring bd. 18.99 (*0-9670164-0-1*, Pub. by Jalor Med) Millenium Mktg.

— Quiet Water. 144p. 1999. pap. 11.99 (*1-57532-129-7*) Press-Tige Pub.

— Quilts: An American Heritage, 1. 1998. 12.98 (*1-57717-091-1*) Todtri Prods.

— Quite Vacation. 27p. 1998. 6.00 (*0-937013-83-8*) Potes Poets.

Piantanida, Maria & Garman, Noreen. The Qualitative Dissertation: A Guide for Students & Faculty. LC 98-58139. (One-Off Ser.). (Illus.). 368p. 1999. 74.95 (*0-8039-6688-1*) Corwin Pr.

***Piantanida, Maria & Odesser-Torpey, Marilyn.** Quick Escapes: Philadelphia: Twenty-Four Weekend Get-a-Ways from the City of Brotherly Love. LC 99-15495. (Quick Escapes Ser.). (Illus.). 288p. 1999. pap. text 14.95 (*0-7627-0444-6*) Globe Pequot.

Piantanida, Maria, et al. The Qualitative Dissertation: A Guide for Students & Faculty. LC 98-58139. (1-Off Ser.). (Illus.). 368p. 1999. pap. 34.95 (*0-8039-6689-X*) Corwin Pr.

Pianu, G., jt. compiled by see Torelli, M.

Pianzola, Arturo, jt. auth. see Moody, Robert V.

***Piaquadio, Gilbert J.** How to Claim Your Money. (Illus.). 55p. 1998. pap. 19.95 (*0-9673581-0-8*) A&A Detective.

Piar, Carlos R. Jesus & Liberation: A Critical Analysis of the Christology of Latin American Liberation Theology. LC 93-6958. (AUS VII: Vol. 148). 178p. (C). 1995. pap. text 32.95 (*0-8204-2098-0*) P Lang Pubng.

Piard, Christian, jt. auth. see Piard, Joelle.

Piard, Joelle & Piard, Christian. Dictionnaire Quartet-Systems du Macintosh. (FRE.). 1990. write for info. (*0-7859-8247-7*, 2-908796-00-7) Fr & Eur.

Piarist Fathers Staff. Constitutions of the Order of the Pious Schools. Cudinach, Salvidor, ed. & tr. by. from LAT. LC 85-60915.Tr. of Constitutiones Ordinis Scholarum Piarum. 110p. write for info. (*0-9614908-0-2*) Piarist Father.

Piascik. Applied Calculus for Business. 1992. mass mkt. 15.50 (*0-314-00396-7*) Wadsworth Pub.

— Excel Manual for Finite Mathematics. LC 99-52210. (Math Ser.). 135p. 1999. pap. text 20.95 (*0-534-37057-8*) Brooks-Cole.

***Piascik.** Mathematics with Excel. 2001. pap. 15.00 (*0-534-37059-4*) Thomson Learn.

Piascik, Chester. Applications for Finite Mathematics. Date not set. pap. text, student ed. write for info. (*0-314-00833-0*) West Pub.

— Applications in Mathematical Statistics. Date not set. pap. text, suppl. ed. write for info. (*0-314-01336-9*) West Pub.

P

— Applied Mathematics for Business & the Social & Natural Sciences. Pullins, ed. 966p. (C). 1992. text 69.75 (*0-314-83981-X*) West Pub.
— Calculus with Applications. Date not set. pap. text, teacher ed. write for info. (*0-314-02186-8*) West Pub.
— Calculus with Applications: Test Bank. Date not set. pap. text, suppl. ed. write for info. (*0-314-02188-4*) West Pub.
Piascik, Robert S., et al, eds. Elevated Temperature Effects on Fatigue & Fracture, Vol. 129. 2nd ed. LC 96-52047. (STP 1297 Ser.). (Illus.). 240p. 1997. text 83.00 (*0-8031-2413-9*, STP1297) ASTM.
— Fatigue & Fracture Mechanics, Vol. 27. 2nd ed. (STP Ser.: No. 1296). (Illus.). 650p. 1997. text 187.00 (*0-8031-2412-0*, STP1296) ASTM.
Piascik, Robert S., jt. ed. see Newman, James C., Jr.
Piasecki, Anthony A. Estimation of Demand for Emergency Medical Services. (Special Project Reports). 202p. 1986. pap. 8.00 (*0-89940-854-0*) LBJ Sch Pub Aff.
Piasecki, Bruce W. Corporate Environmental Strategy: The Avalanche of Change since Bhopal. 180p. 1995. 24.95 (*0-471-10627-5*) Wiley.
Piasecki, Bruce W., ed. Toxic Waste: New Strategies for Controlling Toxic Contamination. LC 83-24510. (Quorum Ser.). (Illus.). 239p. 1984. 59.95 (*0-89930-056-1*, PIT/, Quorum Bks) Greenwood.
Piasecki, Bruce W. & Davis, Gary A. America's Future in Toxic Waste Management: Lesson from Europe. LC 87-2559. 339p. 1987. 72.95 (*0-89930-113-4*, PMA/, Quorum Bks) Greenwood.
Piasecki, Bruce W., et al. Environmental Management & Business Strategy: Leadership Skills for the 21st Century. LC 98-28233. 368p. 1998. pap. 61.95 (*0-471-16972-2*) Wiley.
Piasecki, Jerry. The Adventures of Na Uh & Na Huh: The Super Rockin' Rollin' Roller Coaster Ride & No Ordinary Sandwich, Vol. 1. unabridged ed. LC 97-69414. (Illus.). 24p. (J). (gr. k-3). 1997. pap. 12.00 incl. audio (*0-9659936-0-4*, CTR-02) Cantoo Recs.
— Laura for Dessert. (Orig.). (J). 1995. 8.60 (*0-606-07776-6*) Turtleback.
— What is the Teacher's Toupee Doing in the Fish Tank? 1994. 8.60 (*0-606-08365-0*, Pub. by Turtleback) Demco.
***Piasecki, Melissa.** Nicotine in Psychiatry: Psychopathology & Emerging Therapeutics. LC 99-40827. (Clinical Practice Ser.). 2000. 40.00 (*0-88048-797-6*) Am Psychiatric.
Piasek, Martin. Chinese-German Dictionary: Woerterbuch Chinesisch-Deutsch. 6th ed. (CHI & GER.). 336p. 1986. 69.95 (*0-8288-1008-7*, M7320) Fr & Eur.
***Piasetsky, Lome & World Book, Inc. Staff.** Fur Seals & Other Pinnipeds. LC 00-21633. (Animals of the World Ser.). (Illus.). 64p. (J). (gr. 1-4). 2000. write for info. (*0-7166-1202-X*) World Bk.
Piat, Jean. Dictionnaire Francais-Langue d'Oc. (FRE.). 1000p. 75.00 (*0-7859-0723-8*, M-6451) Fr & Eur.
Piat, L. Dictionary French to Occitan, 2 vols. (FRE & PRO.). 1112p. 1997. 195.00 (*0-320-00475-9*) Fr & Eur.
Piat, Stephane-Joseph. Celine: Sister & Witness of St. Therese of the Child Jesus. Carmelite Sisters of the Eucharist of Colchester,, tr. LC 97-70157. 1997. pap. text 12.95 (*0-89870-602-5*) Ignatius Pr.
— The Story of a Family: The Home of the Little Flower. LC 93-61562. (Illus.). 421p. 1994. pap. 18.50 (*0-89555-502-6*) TAN Bks Pubs.
Piatagorsky, Alexandre. Element Classics: Bhagavadgita. LC 96-6607. (Element Classics of World Spirtuality Ser.). 144p. 1997. pap. 14.95 (*1-85230-917-2*, Pub. by Element MA) Penguin Putnam.
Piatak, Jean & Avrashov, Regina. Russian Songs & Arias: Phonetic Readings, Word-by-Word Translations, & a Concise Guide to Russian Diction. (ENG & RUS.). 206p. (Orig.). 1991. pap. 37.95 (*1-877761-52-4*) Pst.
Piatelli-Palmarini, Massimo. Inevitable Illusions: How Mistakes of Reason Rule Our Minds. LC 94-12759. 256p. 1996. pap. 16.95 (*0-471-15962-X*) Wiley.
Piatetski-Shapiro, Ilya. Complex Representations of GL (2,K) for Finite Fields K. LC 82-24484. (Contemporary Mathematics Ser.: Vol. 16). 71p. 1983. pap. 22.00 (*0-8218-5019-5*, CONM/16) Am Math.
Piatetski-Shapiro, Ilya & Gelbart, Stephen S., eds. The Schur Lectures (1992) (Israel Mathematical Conference Proceedings Ser.: Vol. 8). 236p. 1995. pap. 52.00 (*0-614-08385-0*, IMCP/8) Am Math.
Piatetsky-Shapiro, Gregory, ed. Knowledge Discovery in Databases: Papers from the 1993 Workshop. (Technical Reports). (Illus.). 336p. 1994. spiral bd. 30.00 (*0-929280-49-0*) AAAI Pr.
Piatigorsky, Alexander. Who's Afraid of Freemasons? 380p. 1996. 40.00 (*1-86046-029-1*) Harvill Press.
— Who's Afraid of Freemasons? The Phenomenon of Freemasonry. 416p. 2000. pap. 16.00 (*1-86046-265-0*, Pub. by Harvill Press) FS&G.
***Piatigorsky, Anton.** Easy Lenny & the Great Western Ascension. 96p. 2000. pap. 14.95 (*0-88754-588-2*) Theatre Comm.
Piatkus Books Staff, jt. auth. see Dela, Helena.
***Piatonni, Gary.** Batforum. (Squares Ser.: Vol. 2). 20p. 1999. pap. 15.00 (*1-888636-15-7*) Sara Ranchouse.
Piatos, Emmanuel. Solo in an Instant. (Illus.). 24p. (Orig.). (C). pap. 6.95 (*1-56516-033-9*) H Leonard.
Piatt, Bill. Black & Brown in America: The Case for Cooperation. LC 96-45863. 1997. text 22.50 (*0-8147-6645-5*) NYU Pr.
— Immigration Law: Cases & Materials, 1994 Edition. 462p. 1994. text 44.00 (*1-55834-152-8*, 12725-10, MICHIE) LEXIS Pub.
Piatt, Emma C. History of Piatt County, Illinois. (Illus.). 643p. 1994. reprint ed. lib. bdg. 65.50 (*0-8328-3985-X*) Higginson Bk Co.
***Piatt, Norma.** Effective Direct & Cross Examination - 11/99 Update. LC 86-70031. 420p. 1999. ring bd. 48.00 (*0-7626-0369-0*, CP-32335) Cont Ed Bar-CA.
Piatt, Norma, jt. auth. see Sorgen, Michael S.
Piatt, Norma, ed. see Adams, Jean M., et al.
Piatt, Norma, ed. see Avery, Luther J., et al.
Piatt, Norma, ed. see Bader, Elizabeth E.
Piatt, Norma, ed. see Lombardi, Ralph A.
Piatt, Norma, ed. see Pearl, Richard M.
Piatt, Norma, ed. see Pickus, Bob.
Piatt, Norma, ed. see Preston, Frank E.
Piatt, Norma, ed. see Ruud, Anita E.
Piatt, Norma, ed. see Sorgen, Michael S.
Piatt, Norma, ed. see Tidus, Jeffrey A.
Piattelli, Massimo P. Inevitable Illusions: How Mistakes of Reason Rule Our Minds. LC 94-12759. 256p. 1994. 27.95 (*0-471-58126-7*) Wiley.
Piattelli-Palmarini, Massimo, ed. Language & Learning: The Debate Between Jean Piaget & Noam Chomsky. 445p. 1984. pap. 18.50 (*0-674-50941-2*) HUP.
Piatti, Alberto, et al. Planning of Geothermal District Heating Systems. LC 92-26787. (C). 1992. text 185.00 (*0-7923-1968-0*) Kluwer Academic.
Piatti, James. Firehouse Memorabilia: Identification & Price Guide. rev. ed. viii, 272p. 1994. reprint ed. pap. 12.00 (*0-380-77092-X*, Avon Bks) Morrow Avon.
***Piattini, Mario.** Advanced Databases: Technology & Design. (Illus.). 443p. 2000. 85.00 (*0-89006-395-8*) Artech Hse.
— Auditing Information Systems. (Illus.). 350p. 2000. pap. write for info. (*1-878289-75-6*) Idea Group Pub.
Piau, J. M. & Agassant, J. F. Rheology for Polymer Melt Processing. LC 96-31377. (Rheological Ser.: Vol. 5). 434p. 1996. 240.75 (*0-444-82236-4*) Elsevier.
Piauton, Marilyn. How to Eat Out in France: How to Understand the Menu & Make Yourself Understood. (Illus.). 208p. pap. 6.95 (*88-7301-098-9*, Pub. by Gremese Intl) Natl Bk Netwk.
Piazza. Multiple Forms of Literacy: Teaching Literacy & the Arts. LC 98-33602. 244p. (C). 1998. pap. text 30.00 (*0-13-095503-5*) P-H.
Piazza, A. Anthony. Sue, Settle or Be Silent? 1994. pap. 18.95 (*0-9635237-0-8*) P M C & B.
Piazza, Donna P., ed. When Love Is Not Enough: The Management of Covert Dynamics in Organizations That Treat Children & Adolescents. LC 95-44786. (Residential Treatment for Children & Youth Ser.: Vol. 13, No. 1). 105p. (C). 1996. 29.95 (*1-56024-778-9*) Haworth Pr.
— When Love Is Not Enough: The Management of Covert Dynamics in Organizations That Treat Children & Adolescents. LC 95-44786. (Residential Treatment for Children & Youth Ser.: Vol. 13, No. 1). 105p. (C). 1997. pap. 14.95 (*0-7890-0223-X*) Haworth Pr.
Piazza, G. J., ed. Lipoxygenase & Lipoxygenase Pathway Enzymes. 248p. 1996. 85.00 (*0-935315-74-8*) Am Oil Chemists.
Piazza, Gail, jt. auth. see McKay, Hilary.
Piazza, Jane. Working Together in Troubled Times: Community-Based Therapies. LC 97-1465. 250p. 1997. 49.50 (*0-7618-0694-6*); pap. 29.50 (*0-7618-0695-4*) U Pr of Amer.
Piazza, Linda. Call of the Deep. 160p. (Orig.). 1994. pap. 3.50 (*0-380-77330-9*, Avon Bks) Morrow Avon.
— Evil in the Attic. 156p. (Orig.). (YA). (gr. 8 up). 1995. mass mkt. 3.99 (*0-380-77576-X*, Avon Bks) Morrow Avon.
Piazza, Louise D., ed. see Martin, Charles.
Piazza, Michael S. Growth or Death. 2nd ed. 130p. 1996. pap. 7.95 (*1-887129-03-0*) Sources of Hope.
Piazza, Michael S. Holy Homosexuals: The Truth about Being Gay or Lesbian & Christian. rev. ed. LC 98-130222. xii, 207 p. 1997. pap. 14.00 (*1-887129-04-9*) Sources of Hope.
Piazza, Michael S. Mourning to Morning. 80p. 1996. pap. 9.95 (*1-887129-01-4*) Sources of Hope.
— Rainbow Family Values. 240p. (Orig.). 1996. pap. 14.95 (*1-887129-02-2*) Sources of Hope.
Piazza, Paul. Christopher Isherwood: Myth & Anti-Myth. LC 77-14271. 1978. text 46.50 (*0-231-04118-7*) Col U Pr.
Piazza, Robert, jt. auth. see Buzzell, Judith B.
Piazza, Thomas, jt. auth. see Sniderman, Paul M.
Piazza, Tom. Blues & Trouble. 192p. 1996. 21.95 (*0-312-13934-9*) St Martin.
— Blues & Trouble. 192p. 1997. pap. 11.95 (*0-312-16788-1*) St Martin.
— Blues up & Down: Jazz in Our Time. LC 97-21944. 208p. 1997. text 21.95 (*0-312-16789-X*) St Martin.
— The Guide to Classic Recorded Jazz. LC 94-36373. 410p. (Orig.). 1995. pap. 22.95 (*0-87745-489-2*) U of Iowa Pr.
— Pantheon Great Jazz. 1991. pap. 14.95 (*0-679-40187-3*) McKay.
— True Adventures with the King of Bluegrass. LC 99-6762. (Country Music Foundation Press Ser.). (Illus.). 112p. 1999. 17.95 (*0-8265-1360-3*) Vanderbilt U Pr.
Piazza, Tom, ed. Setting the Tempo: Fifty Years of Great Jazz Liner Notes. 256p. 1996. pap. 14.00 (*0-385-48000-8*, Anchor NY) Doubleday.
***Piazzesi, Elizabetta.** Pizza & Neopolitan Cookery. 1999. pap. text 20.95 (*88-8029-898-4*) Bonechi.
Pibiri, Giovanni. Maddalena Licheri: Italian Essays. 126p. 1986. pap. 15.00 (*0-89304-579-9*) Cross-Cultrl NY.
Piboubes, Raoul. Dictionary Ocean: English, French, German, Spanish. (ENG, FRE, GER & SPA.). 761p. 1989. write for info. (*0-7859-4578-4*) Fr & Eur.
Pibouleau, R., jt. auth. see Kleczkowski, B. M.
Piburn, Gregg. Beyond Chaos: One Man's Journey Alongside His Chronically Ill Wife. LC 98-31883. 320p. 1999. pap. 14.95 (*0-912423-20-X*) Arthritis Found.
Piburn, Bill. Complete Book of Fiddle Tunes for Acoustic Guitar. (Complete Bks.). 220p. 1995. pap. 25.00 (*0-7866-0492-1*, MB95471) Mel Bay.
***Piburn, Bill.** French Music for Guitar. 120p. 1999. pap. 24.95 incl. audio compact disk (*0-7866-3824-9*, 97064BCD) Mel Bay.
Piburn, Michael D., et al. Constructing Science in Middle & Secondary School Classrooms. LC 96-15754. 428p. 1996. 69.00 (*0-205-16588-5*) Allyn.
Piburn, Michael D., jt. auth. see Baker, Dale R.
Piburn, Sidney D., ed. & compiled by see Dalai Lama XIV, et al.
Pica. Experiences in Movement with Music, Activities & Theory IG. 32p. 1995. teacher ed. 14.95 (*0-8273-6479-2*) Delmar.
***Pica, Karen.** Chinua Achebe's Things Fall Apart. LC 98-66037. (MaxNotes Ser.). 1999. pap. 3.95 (*0-87891-233-9*) Res & Educ.
Pica, Karen. Maxnotes: Sula. LC 98-66564. v, 111 p. 1999. pap. 3.95 (*0-87891-229-0*) Res & Educ.
***Pica, Nicola.** 120 Competitive Games & Exercises. (Illus.). 245p. 1999. pap. 14.95 (*1-890946-29-X*) Reedswain.
Pica, Rae. Experiences in Movement with Music, Activitie & Theory. LC 94-33269. (Illus.). 416p. (C). 1995. mass mkt. 26.25 (*0-8273-6478-4*) Delmar.
***Pica, Rae.** Experiences in Movement with Music, Activities, & Theory. 2nd ed. LC 98-55061. 384p. 1999. pap. 38.95 (*0-7668-0358-9*) Delmar.
Pica, Rae. Moving & Learning Across the Curriculum: 315 Activities & Games to Make Learning Fun. abr. rev. ed. LC 98-4893. 288p. (C). 1998. text 34.95 (*0-8273-8537-4*) Delmar.
Pica, Teresa & Barnes, Gregory A. Teaching Matters. (J). 1990. mass mkt. 26.95 (*0-8384-2788-X*) Heinle & Heinle.
***Picabia, Francis.** I Am a Beautiful Monster: Selected Writings of Francis Picabia. Lowenthal, Marc, tr. from FRE. (Illus.). 256p. 2000. pap. 15.95 (*1-878972-33-2*, Pub. by Exact Change) Consort Bk Sales.
Picabia, Francis. Who Knows. Hall, Remy, tr. from FRE. 168p. (Orig.). 1987. pap. 5.95 (*0-937815-04-7*) Hanuman Bks.
— Yes No. Hall, Remy, tr. from FRE. 57p. (Orig.). 1990. pap. 5.95 (*0-937815-41-1*) Hanuman Bks.
Picander. The Coffee Cantata. Hess, Harvey, tr. (GER.). 24p. 1986. pap. 3.00 (*0-931909-05-8*) Malama Arts.
Picano. Ecocardiography in Ischemic Heart Disease. (Illus.). 170p. 1996. write for info. (*88-299-1228-X*, Pub. by Piccin Nuova) Gordon & Breach.
Picano, Felice. Ambidextrous. 1995. mass mkt. 6.95 (*1-56333-275-2*, Hard Candy) Masquerade.
— Best Gay Erotica 1999. (Lesbian Erotica Ser.). 200p. 1999. pap. text 14.95 (*1-57344-048-5*) Cleis Pr.
***Picano, Felice.** The Book of Lies: A Novel. LC 99-38406. 424p. 1999. 24.95 (*1-55583-541-4*, Pub. by Alyson Pubns) Consort Bk Sales.
— The Book of Lies: A Novel. 432p. 2000. reprint ed. pap. 14.95 (*1-55583-592-9*, Pub. by Alyson Pubns) Consort Bk Sales.
Picano, Felice. Dryland's End. 1995. pap. 12.95 (*1-56333-279-5*, R Kasak Bks) Masquerade.
— A House on the Ocean, a House on the Bay: A Memoir. 256p. 1998. pap. 14.95 (*0-571-19936-4*) Faber & Faber.
— Late in Season. 1997. pap. 12.95 (*0-312-15564-6*) St Martin.
— Like People in History. 528p. 1996. pap. 12.95 (*0-14-024525-1*, Penguin Bks) Viking Penguin.
— Looking Glass Lives: A Novel. LC 98-21812. (Illus.). 240p. 1998. pap. 12.95 (*1-55583-481-7*) Alyson Pubns.
— The Lure. 1996. reprint ed. mass mkt. 6.95 (*1-56333-398-8*, Hard Candy) Masquerade.
— Men Who Loved Me. 1994. mass mkt. 6.95 (*1-56333-274-4*, Hard Candy) Masquerade.
***Picano, Felice.** The New York Years: Stories. LC 99-89539. 232p. 2000. pap. 12.95 (*1-55583-522-8*, Pub. by Alyson Pubns) Consort Bk Sales.
Picano, Felice. To the Seventh Power. 320p. 1990. mass mkt. 4.50 (*0-380-70276-2*, Avon Bks) Morrow Avon.
Picano, Felice, jt. auth. see Silverstein, Charles.
Picarazzi, Teresa, ed. & tr. see Spadoni, Nevio.
Picarazzi, Teresa L., ed. see Goldoni, Carlo & Martinelli, Gabrieli M.
Picard. Theory & Media Economics. (MacEachran Lectures: Vol. 8, No. 2). 1995. pap. 20.00 (*0-8058-9944-8*) L Erlbaum Assocs.
Picard, ed. see Prevost, Abbe.
Picard, Barbara L. French Legends, Tales & Fairy Stories. (Oxford Myths & Legends Ser.). (J). 1992. 18.05 (*0-606-05300-X*, Pub. by Turtleback) Demco.
— Iliad & Odyssey of Homer. 1991. pap. 4.95 (*0-671-08155-1*) S&S Trade.
— The Iliad of Homer. (Oxford Myths & Legends Ser.). (Illus.). 224p. (YA). (gr. 5-12). 1991. pap. 12.95 (*0-19-274147-0*) OUP.
— The Midsummer Bride. (Illus.). 32p. (J). 1999. 16.95 (*0-19-279879-0*) OUP.
— The Odyssey of Homer. (Oxford Myths & Legends Ser.). (Illus.). 284p. (YA). (gr. 5-12). 1991. pap. 12.95 (*0-19-274146-2*) OUP.
— Selected Fairy Tales. LC 96-102081. (Illus.). 208p. (YA). (gr. 7 up). 1995. pap. 12.95 (*0-19-274162-4*) OUP.
Picard, Barbara L., as told by. Tales of the Norse Gods. LC 94-241159. (Myths & Legends Ser.). (Illus.). 176p. (YA). (gr. 5-12). 1994. pap. 12.95 (*0-19-274167-5*) OUP.
Picard, Caroline L. First You Buy a Roux. 28p. (Orig.). 1991. pap. 4.95 (*0-9614228-6-6*) Juliahouse Pubs.
Picard, Dennis D. Out of the Crackerbarrel: 150 Years of Recipes & Remembrances. Nano, Gail, ed. 108p. 1998. pap. write for info. (*1-57502-879-4*, PO2395) Morris Pubng.
Picard, Didier, ed. Nuclear Receptor Superfamily. 2nd ed. LC 99-24782. (Practical Approach Ser.: 207). (Illus.). 304p. 1999. pap. text 55.00 (*0-19-963742-3*) OUP.
— Nuclear Receptors: A Practical Approach. 2nd ed. LC 99-24782. (The Practical Approach Ser.: No. 207). (Illus.). 304p. 1999. text 110.00 (*0-19-963743-1*) OUP.
Picard, E. Rafaela. Danger: Drugs & Your Parents. LC 96-40329. (Drug Awareness Library). (J). (gr. k-4). 1997. lib. bdg. 15.93 (*0-8239-5050-6*, PowerKids) Rosen Group.
— Danger & Drugs in Your Neighborhood. LC 96-37654. (Drug Awareness Library). (J). (gr. k-4). 1997. lib. bdg. 15.93 (*0-8239-5051-4*, PowerKids) Rosen Group.
Picard, E. Rafarela. Danger: Drugs & Your Friends. LC 96-39267. (Drug Awareness Library). (J). (gr. k-4). 1997. lib. bdg. 15.93 (*0-8239-5049-2*, PowerKids) Rosen Group.
Picard, Emile & Simart, G. Theorie des Fonctions Algebriques de Deux Variables Independantes, 2 vols. in 1. LC 67-31156. 1971. 49.50 (*0-8284-0248-5*) Chelsea Pub.
Picard, Fred A., jt. ed. see Billigmeier, Robert H.
Picard, G. S., jt. ed. see Sequeira, Cesar A.
Picard, J. M. & De Pontfarcy, Y. The Vision of Tnugdal. (Illus.). 192p. 1989. 35.00 (*1-85182-039-6*, Pub. by Four Cts Pr) Intl Spec Bk.
Picard, Jacques, ed. see Racine, Jean.
Picard, Jean-Michel, ed. Aquitaine & Ireland in the Middle Ages. 272p. 1994. 45.00 (*1-85182-135-X*, Pub. by Four Cts Pr) Intl Spec Bk.
Picard, Jean-Michel & De Pontfarcy, Y. The Vision of Tnugdal. 160p. 1990. 35.00 (*1-85182-038-8*, Pub. by Four Cts Pr) Intl Spec Bk.
***Picard, Jeanine.** Helias: Le Cheval d'Orgueil. 80p. 1999. pap. 35.00 (*0-85261-658-9*, Pub. by U of Glasgow) St Mut.
Picard, Jeanine, jt. auth. see Garnier, Mike.
Picard, Jim, et al. The CEO/Board Bond: Strengthening Credit Union Leadership. 72p. (Orig.). 1995. pap. 59.00 (*1-889394-11-4*) Credit Union Execs.
Picard, John & Picard, Ruth. Chevron & Nueva Cadiz Beads. (Beads from the West African Trade Ser.: Vol. VII). (Illus.). 128p. 1993. 35.00 (*0-9622884-2-X*) Picard African.
— Millefiori Beads from the West African Trade. (Beads from the West African Trade Ser.: Vol. VI). (Illus.). 88p. (Orig.). 1991. pap. 25.00 (*0-9622884-1-1*) Picard African.
— Russian Blues, Faceted & Fancy Beads from the West African Trade, Vol. V. (Beads from the West African Trade Ser.). (Illus.). 44p. (Orig.). 1989. pap. 15.00 (*0-9622884-0-3*) Picard African.
Picard, L. A., jt. ed. see Garrity, M.
***Picard, Liza.** Restoration London: Engaging Anecdotes & Tantalizing Trivia from the Most Magnificent & Renowned City of Europe. 352p. 2000. pap. 14.00 (*0-380-73236-X*, Avon Bks) Morrow Avon.
Picard, Liza. Restoration London: From Poverty to Pets, from Medicine to Magic, from Slang to Sex, from Wallpaper to Women's Rights. LC 98-12925. 330p. 1998. text 27.50 (*0-312-18659-2*) St Martin.
Picard, Louis A. & Zariski, Raphael, eds. Subnational Politics in the 1980s: Organization, Reorganization & Economic Development. LC 86-20479. 276p. 1986. 65.00 (*0-275-92314-2*, C2314, Praeger Pubs) Greenwood.
***Picard, Lynne.** The Elephant's Rope & the Untethered Spirit: A Remarkable True Story of Healing & Hope. LC 99-66909. 150p. 2000. 19.95 (*1-885003-25-0*, Pub. by R D Reed Pubs) Midpt Trade.
Picard, Marc. Principles & Methods in Historical Phonology: From Proto-Algonkian to Arapaho. 208p. 1994. 65.00 (*0-7735-1171-7*, Pub. by McG-Queens Univ Pr) CUP Services.
Picard, Max. The Flight from God. Kuschnitzky, Marianne & Cameron, J. M., trs. LC 89-38837. 185p. 1989. reprint ed. pap. 9.95 (*0-89526-752-7*) Regnery Pub.
Picard, Michel & Wood, Robert E., eds. Tourism, Ethnicity & the State in Asian & Pacific Societies. LC 96-53034. (Illus.). 1997. text 47.00 (*0-8248-1863-6*); pap. text 22.95 (*0-8248-1911-X*) UH Pr.
Picard, Paula, jt. auth. see Miquel, Pierre.
Picard, Phillipe, jt. auth. see Aubin, Michel.
Picard, Pierre. Wages & Unemployment: A Study in Non-Walrasian Macroeconomics. LC 92-19475. (Illus.). 275p. (C). 1993. text 59.95 (*0-521-35057-3*) Cambridge U Pr.
Picard, R. French Dishes, Easy & Delicious. pap. 11.95 (*0-87557-101-8*) Saphrograph.
Picard, Raymond. New Criticism or New Fraud. Towne, Frank, tr. LC 70-5767. 63p. reprint ed. pap. 30.00 (*0-608-18355-5*, 203303600083) Bks Demand.
Picard, Robert G. Media Economics: Concepts & Issues. (CommText Ser.: Vol. 22). 160p. (C). 1989. text 42.00 (*0-8039-3501-3*); pap. text 18.95 (*0-8039-3502-1*) Sage.
— The Press & the Decline of Democracy: The Democratic Socialist Response in Public Policy, 4. LC 85-5585. (Contributions to the Study of Mass Media & Communications Ser.: No. 4). (Illus.). 176p. 1985. 49.95 (*0-313-24915-6*, PPD/) Greenwood.
— The Ravens of Odin: The Press in the Nordic Nations. LC 87-22750. (Illus.). 171p. 1988. reprint ed. pap. 53.10 (*0-608-00047-7*, 206081300006) Bks Demand.
Picard, Robert G., et al, eds. Press Concentration & Monopoly: New Perspectives on Newspaper Ownership & Operation. LC 87-33328. (Communication & Information Science Ser.). 256p. 1988. text 73.25 (*0-89391-464-9*) Ablx Pub.
Picard, Robert G. & Brody, Jeffrey. The Insider's Guide to the Newspaper Publishing Industry. LC 96-19616. 224p. (C). 1996. pap. text, suppl. ed. 26.00 (*0-205-16145-6*) Allyn.

Picard, Robert G., jt. auth. see Busterna, John C.

Picard, Rosalind W. Affective Computing. LC 97-33285. (Illus.). 304p. 1997. 29.95 (*0-262-16170-2*) MIT Pr.

***Picard, Rosalind W.** Affective Computing. (Illus.). 304p. (C). 2000. pap. 19.95 (*0-262-66115-2*) MIT Pr.

Picard, Ruth, jt. auth. see Picard, John.

Picarda, Hubert A. The Law Relating to Receivers, Managers, & Administrators. 2nd ed. 854p. 1990. boxed set 236.00 (*0-406-10501-4*, U.K., MICHIE) LEXIS Pub.

Picardat, Robert, jt. auth. see Tolf, Robert.

***Picardello, M. & Woess, W., eds.** Random Walks & Discrete Potential Theory. (Symposia Mathematica 39 Ser.). (Illus.). 371p. 2000. 69.95 (*0-521-77312-1*) Cambridge U Pr.

Picardello, M. A., ed. Harmonic Analysis & Discrete Potential Theory. (Illus.). 312p. (C). 1992. text 114.00 (*0-306-44225-6*, Kluwer Plenum) Kluwer Academic.

Picardello, M. A., jt. auth. see Figa-Talamanca, Alessandro.

Picardi, Patti, ed. see Gertsch, Karin M.

Picardi, Patti, ed. see Gomes, Alan W.

***Picardie, Ruth.** Before I Say Goodbye. 128p. 1998. pap. 12.95 (*0-14-027630-0*, Pub. by Pnguin Bks Ltd) Trafalgar.

— Before I Say Goodbye: Recollections & Observations from One Woman's Final Year. LC 00-29582. 128p. 2000. pap. 13.00 (*0-8050-6612-8*, Owl) H Holt & Co.

Picardo, Cheyenne, ed. see Agnos, Peter.

Picardo, Eddie. Tales of a Tail Gunner: A Memoir of Seattle & World War II. LC 96-77149. 254p. 1996. pap. 14.95 (*1-883697-33-6*) Hara Pub.

Picardo, Hector, tr. Amo los Montes: Black & White Nellie Edge I Can Read & Sing Big Book. (SPA., Illus.). 8p. (J). (ps-2). 1996. pap. text 20.00 (*0-922053-43-X*, 01-43) N Edge Res.

Picardt, C. R., ed. Graves' Ophthalmopathy. (Developments in Ophthalmology Ser.: Vol. 20). (Illus.). 230p. 1989. 169.75 (*3-8055-5040-5*) S Karger.

***Picardy, Allan.** Psychosis God, Pt. 1. 1999. pap. write for info. (*1-57553-997-7*) Watermrk Pr.

— Psychosis God, Pt. 2. 1999. pap. write for info. (*1-57553-998-5*) Watermrk Pr.

Picare, jt. auth. see Evangelista.

***Picarello, Robert.** Rulers of the Ring: Wrestling's Hottest Superstars. (Illus.). 2000. pap. 10.95 (*0-425-17780-7*) Berkley Pub.

Picariello, Gloria, ed. see Osterman, Helen.

Picariello, Gloria, ed. see Sanchez, Diana V.

Picarski, Ron. Friendly Foods. (Illus.). 258p. (Orig.). 1991. pap. 16.95 (*0-89815-377-8*) Ten Speed Pr.

Picart, Caroline. Resentment & "The Feminine" in Nietzche's Politico-Aesthetics. LC 98-39331. 1999. 45.00 (*0-271-01888-7*); pap. 17.95 (*0-271-01889-5*) Pa St U Pr.

Picas, ed. see Cota-Robles, Patricia D.

***Picasso, Pablo.** Art Mini-Picasso. (Illus.). 96p. 2000. pap. text 4.95 (*3-8290-2978-0*) Konemann.

Picasso, Pablo. The Artist & His Model: One Hundred Eighty Drawings. LC 93-37470. (Illus.). 192p. 1993. pap. 12.95 (*0-486-27877-8*) Dover.

— Designs for "The Three-Cornered Hat" (Le Tricorn) Migel, Parmenia, ed. (Illus.). 48p. 1978. pap. 7.95 (*0-486-23709-5*) Dover.

— Drawings of Picasso. Longstreet, Stephen, ed. (Master Draughtsman Ser.). (Illus.). (Orig.). 1974. pap. 4.95 (*0-87505-179-0*) Borden.

***Picasso, Pablo.** Pablo Picasso: The Appeal of Surface. (Illus.). 2000. pap. 45.00 (*3-7757-0858-8*) Gerd Hatje.

— Picasso. (Illus.). 2000. pap. 1.00 (*0-486-41076-5*) Dover.

— Picasso: Artist of the Century. LC 99-209122. (ENG & DUT.). 143p. 1999. pap. write for info. (*90-400-9357-1*) Waandrs.

Picasso, Pablo. Picasso: Drawings, 1966-1967. (FRE., Illus.). 74p. 1968. pap. 25.00 (*1-55660-273-1*) A Wofsy Fine Arts.

— Picasso: Drawings, 1969-1971. (FRE., Illus.). 110p. 1971. pap. 30.00 (*1-55660-274-X*) A Wofsy Fine Arts.

— Picasso: Last Etchings, 1968-72. (FRE., Illus.). 216p. 1973. pap. 40.00 (*1-55660-266-9*) A Wofsy Fine Arts.

— Picasso: Painter & Sculptor in Clay. LC 98-73227. (Illus.). 264p. 1999. 60.00 (*0-8109-4353-0*, Pub. by Abrams) Time Warner.

— Picasso Line Drawings & Prints. (Art Library). (Illus.). 48p. (Orig.). 1982. pap. 4.95 (*0-486-24196-3*) Dover.

— Picasso Lithographs: 61 Works. (Art Library). (Illus.). 64p. (Orig.). 1980. pap. 3.95 (*0-486-23949-7*) Dover.

— Picasso Postcard Book. 1997. pap. 5.99 (*3-8228-7917-7*) Taschen Amer.

— Picasso's One-Liners. LC 97-3776. (Illus.). 80p. 1997. 14.95 (*1-885183-78-X*) Artisan.

Picasso, Pablo, et al. Picasso--The Early Years, 1892-1906. LC 96-49663. (Illus.). 1997. 60.00 (*0-89468-268-7*) Natl Gallery Art.

***Picasso Project Staff.** The Fifties Pt. I: 1950-1954. (Picasso's Paintings, Watercolors, Drawings & Sculpture Ser.). (Illus.). 248p. 2000. 150.00 (*1-55660-301-0*) A Wofsy Fine Arts.

— The Fifties Pt. II: 1955-1959. (Picasso's Paintings, Watercolors, Drawings & Sculpture Ser.). (Illus.). 248p. 2000. 150.00 (*1-55660-302-9*) A Wofsy Fine Arts.

— The Final Years, 1970-1973. (Picasso's Paintings, Watercolors, Drawings & Sculpture Ser.). (Illus.). 248p. 2001. 150.00 (*1-55660-305-3*) A Wofsy Fine Arts.

Picasso Project Staff. Picasso's Paintings, Watercolors, Drawings & Sculpture: Surrealism, 1930-1936. (Illus.). 336p. 1997. 150.00 (*1-55660-234-0*) A Wofsy Fine Arts.

— Picasso's Paintings, Watercolors, Drawings & Sculpture - A Comprehensive Illustrated Catalogue: From Cubism to Neoclassicism, 1917-1919. (Illus.). 320p. 1995. 150.00 (*1-55660-230-8*) A Wofsy Fine Arts.

— Picasso's Paintings, Watercolors, Drawings & Sculpture - A Comprehensive Illustrated Catalogue: Liberation & Post-War Years, 1944-1949. (Illus.). 288p. 1999. 150.00 (*1-55660-237-5*) A Wofsy Fine Arts.

— Picasso's Paintings, Watercolors, Drawings & Sculpture - A Comprehensive Illustrated Catalogue: Nazi Occupation, 1940-1944. (Illus.). 400p. 1999. 150.00 (*1-55660-236-7*) A Wofsy Fine Arts.

— Picasso's Paintings, Watercolors, Drawings & Sculpture - A Comprehensive Illustrated Catalogue: Neoclassicism I, 1920-21. (Illus.). 304p. 1995. 150.00 (*1-55660-231-6*) A Wofsy Fine Arts.

— Picasso's Paintings, Watercolors, Drawings & Sculpture - A Comprehensive Illustrated Catalogue: Neoclassicism II, 1922-1924. (Illus.). 288p. 1996. 150.00 (*1-55660-232-4*) A Wofsy Fine Arts.

— Picasso's Paintings, Watercolors, Drawings & Sculpture - A Comprehensive Illustrated Catalogue: Spanish Civil War, 1937-1939. (Illus.). 288p. 1997. 150.00 (*1-55660-262-6*) A Wofsy Fine Arts.

— Picasso's Paintings, Watercolors, Drawings & Sculpture - A Comprehensive Illustrated Catalogue: Toward Surrealism, 1925-1929. (Illus.). 288p. 1996. 150.00 (*1-55660-233-2*) A Wofsy Fine Arts.

***Picasso Project Staff.** The Sixties Pt. I: 1960-1965. (Picasso's Paintings, Watercolors, Drawings & Sculpture Ser.). (Illus.). 248p. 2000. 150.00 (*1-55660-303-7*) A Wofsy Fine Arts.

— The Sixties Pt. II: 1965-1969. (Picasso's Paintings, Watercolors, Drawings & Sculpture Ser.). (Illus.). 248p. 2000. 150.00 (*1-55660-304-5*) A Wofsy Fine Arts.

Picasso Project Staff, et al. Picasso's Paintings, Watercolors, Drawings & Sculpture - A Comprehensive Illustrated Catalogue: Europe at War, 1939-1940. (Illus.). 233p. 1998. 150.00 (*1-55660-235-9*) A Wofsy Fine Arts.

Picasso, Sydney, jt. auth. see Baudez, Claude-Francois.

***Picaud, Raphael.** Fitnessology by Raphael. (Illus.). 159p. 1999. pap. 20.00 (*0-9675507-0-X*) Fitnessology.

— Fitnessology Daily Fitness Journal. 159p. 1999. 15.99 (*0-9675507-2-6*) Fitnessology.

Picavet, Francois J. Essais sur l'Histoire General et Comparee des Theologies et des Philosophes Medievales. (FRE.). viii, 415p. reprint ed. write for info. (*0-318-71388-8*) G Olms Pubs.

— Les Idealogues: Scientific, Philosophical, & Religious Theories in France Since 1789. LC 74-25774. (European Sociology Ser.). 646p. 1975. reprint ed. 53.95 (*0-405-06528-0*) Ayer.

— Les Ideologues. xiii, 628p. 1972. reprint ed. write for info. (*3-487-04397-1*) G Olms Pubs.

Picayune Staff. Picayune Creole Cookbook. (Cookbook Ser.). 1971. pap. 9.95 (*0-486-22678-6*) Dover.

Picazo, Gloria. Riera I Arago. (Great Monographs). (Illus.). 464p. 1993. 300.00 (*84-343-0729-4*) Elliots Bks.

Picazo, J., ed. Glucagon in Acute Medicine: Pharmacological, Clinical, & Therapeutic Implications. LC 93-24960. 1993. text 58.00 (*0-7923-8832-1*) Kluwer Academic.

— Glucagon in Gastroenterology & Hepatology: Pharmacological, Clinical & Therapeutic Implications. 160p. 1982. text 101.50 (*0-85200-447-8*) Kluwer Academic.

— Glucagon in Nineteen Eighty-Seven: Gastrointestinal & Hepatobiliary Physiology, Diagnosis & Treatment. (C). 1987. lib. bdg. 124.00 (*0-7462-0055-2*, Pub. by Kluwer Academic) Kluwer Academic.

***Picbon, Jacinto O. & Fedorchek, Robert M.** Sweet & Delectable: A Novel. LC 99-55809. (Illus.). 312p. 2000. write for info. (*0-8387-5456-2*) Bucknell U Pr.

Piccaluga, Andrea, jt. auth. see Lopez, Roberto E.

***Piccaluga, G., et al, eds.** Sol-Gel Preparations & Characterization of Metal-Silica & Metal Oxide-Silica Nanocomposites. (Materials Science Foundations Ser.: Vol. 13). (Illus.). 56p. (C). 2000. text 48.00 (*0-87849-856-7*, Pub. by Trans T Pub) Enfield Pubs NH.

***Piccard, Bertrand & Jones, Brian.** Around the World in 20 Days: The Story of Our Adventure History-Making Balloon Flight. (Illus.). 320p. 2000. pap. text 14.95 (*0-471-39537-4*) Wiley.

— Around the World in 20 Days: The Story of Our History-Making Balloon Fight. LC 99-46233. (Illus.). 320p. 1999. text 24.95 (*0-471-37820-8*) Wiley.

Piccard, George. Liquid Conspiracy: LSD, JFK, the CIA, Area 51 & UFOs. 256p. 1999. pap. 14.95 (*0-932813-57-7*) Adventures Unltd.

Picchi, Blaise. The Five Weeks of Giuseppe Zangara: The Man Who Would Assassinate FDR. LC 98-11938. (Illus.). 272p. 1998. 26.95 (*0-89733-443-4*) Academy Chi Pubs.

***Picchi, Debra.** The Bakairi Indians of Brazil: Politics, Ecology & Change. 217p. (C). 2000. pap. 13.95 (*1-57766-121-4*) Waveland Pr.

Picchi, F., ed. Economics & Business: Dizionario Enciclopedico Economico Inglese Italiano. 2nd ed. (ENG & ITA.). 1350p. 1990. 135.00 (*0-913298-37-9*) S F Vanni.

Picchi, Fernando. Dictionary of Economics & Business & of Modern Language: English-Italian--Italian-English. (ENG & ITA.). 1792p. 100.00 (*0-7859-8874-2*) Fr & Eur.

— English & Italian Encyclopedic Economic & Commercial Dictionary, 2 vols., Set. 2nd ed. (ENG & ITA.). 1325p. 1990. 175.00 (*0-8288-0107-X*, F16130) Fr & Eur.

— Italian-English - English-Italian Financial & Commercial Encyclopedia Dictionary. 2nd ed. 1594p. 1990. 131.00 (*88-08-06862-5*, Pub. by Zanichelli) IBD Ltd.

— A Practical Guide for Mariners English-Italian. (ENG & ITA.). 319p. 1980. pap. 29.95 (*0-8288-4713-4*, M9193) Fr & Eur.

Picchi, Fernando, jt. auth. see Bernabo, M.

Picchio, Antonella. Social Reproduction: The Political Economy of the Labour Market. 205p. (C). 1992. text 54.95 (*0-521-41872-0*) Cambridge U Pr.

Picchio, Riccardo. Studies on the Literary Tradition of Medieval Orthodox Slavdom. Goldblatt, Harvey, ed. (Renovatio Ser.: No. 2). (Illus.). 480p. 2001. text 50.00 (*0-916458-33-4*) Harvard Ukrainian.

Picchio, Riccardo & Goldblatt, Harvey, eds. Aspects of the Slavic Language Question: Church Slavonic-South Slavic-West Slavic,, Vol. 1. (Yale Russian & East European Publications: No. 4a). 416p. 1984. 35.00 (*0-936586-03-6*, Pub. by Yale Russian) Slavica.

— Aspects of the Slavic Language Question: East Slavic, Vol. II. (Yale Russian & East European Publications: No. 4b). 367p. 1984. 35.00 (*0-936586-04-4*, Pub. by Yale Russian) Slavica.

Picchione, John & Smith, Lawrence R., eds. Twentieth-Century Italian Poetry: An Anthology. (Italian Linguistics & Language Pedagogy Ser.). 480p. 1992. pap. text 35.00 (*0-8020-7368-9*) U of Toronto Pr.

Picchione, Nick, ed. see Dome Financial Services Staff.

Picchioni, Tony. Emotional Intelligence: Psychology. 1998. text 7.94 (*1-56870-319-8*) RonJon Pub.

— Love Maps: A Guide & Discussion Workbook. 1998. text, wbk. ed. 7.94 (*1-56870-318-X*) RonJon Pub.

Picci, G., jt. ed. see Gilliam, S.

Picci, Giorgio & Gilliam, D. S. Dynamical Systems, Control, Coding, Computer Vision: New Trends, Interfaces, & Interplay LC 99-18063. (Progress in Systems & Control Theory Ser.). 1999. write for info. (*0-8176-6060-7*) Birkhauser.

Picci, Giorgio, jt. ed. see Bittanti, Sergio.

Piccialli, Aldo, jt. ed. see De Poli, Giovanni.

Picciani, Ron, jt. auth. see Ginter, Steven J.

***Picciano, Anthony G.** Distance Learning: Making Connections Across Virtual Space & Time. LC 99-89132. 288p. 2000. pap. 43.00 (*0-13-080900-4*, Merrill Coll) P-H.

Picciano, Anthony G. Educational Leadership & Planning for Technology. 2nd ed. LC 96-52859. 323p. 1997. pap. text 57.00 (*0-13-262122-3*) P-H.

Picciano, Mary F. & Lonnerdal, Bo. Mechanisms Regulating Lactation & Infant Nutrient Utilization. (Contemporary Issues in Clinical Nutrition Ser.). 480p. 1992. 395.00 (*0-471-56134-7*) Wiley.

Picciarelli, Patrick, jt. auth. see Wagner, James J.

Piccigallo, B., jt. auth. see Bassani, R.

Piccini, Sara, ed. see Pfeiffer, George J. & Webster, Judith A.

Piccinini, Livio C., et al. Ordinary Differential Equations in R to the Nth Power. (Applied Mathematical Sciences Ser.: Vol. 39). 386p. 1984. 79.95 (*0-387-90723-8*) Spr-Verlag.

Piccinini, R., ed. Groups of Self-Equivalences & Related Topics: Proceedings of a Conference Held in Montreal, Canada, August 8-12 1988. (Lecture Notes in Mathematics Ser.: Vol. 1425). v, 214p. 1990. 38.95 (*0-387-52658-7*) Spr-Verlag.

Piccinini, R. & Sjerve, D., eds. Conference on Algebraic Topology in Honor of Peter Hilton. LC 84-24518. (Contemporary Mathematics Ser.: Vol. 37). 161p. 1985. pap. 30.00 (*0-8218-5036-9*, CONM/37) Am Math.

Piccinini, Renzo, jt. auth. see Fritsch, Rudolf.

Piccinni, Niccolo. Atys, Tragedie Lyrique. Rushton, Julian, ed. LC 91-757502. (French Opera in the 17th & 18th Centuries Ser.: No. 7, Vol. LXV). (Illus.). 1991. lib. bdg. 85.00 (*0-945193-21-1*) Pendragon NY.

Piccioli, Emma, et al, eds. Writing in Psychoanalysis: A Clinical Synthesis. 144p. 1997. pap. 24.95 (*0-88163-239-2*) Analytic Pr.

Piccione, Anthony. For the Kingdom. (American Poets Continuum Ser.: No. 32). 80p. 1995. 20.00 (*1-880238-22-5*); pap. 12.50 (*1-880238-23-3*) BOA Edns.

Piccione, Sandi. Polar Sun. LC 79-4685. 1979. pap. 4.00 (*0-918366-12-7*) Slow Loris.

Piccioni, M., ed. Diccionario de Alimentacion Animal. (SPA.). 820p. 1970. 85.00 (*0-7859-0586-3*, S-36852) Fr & Eur.

Picciolo, tr. see Nejar, Carlos.

Picciotto, Elliot De, see De Picciotto, Elliot.

***Picciotto, Henri.** Geometry Labs. (Illus.). 264p. (YA). (gr. 8-11). 1999. pap. 19.95 (*1-55953-361-7*, 53361) Key Curr Pr.

Picciotto, Linda. Learning Together: A Whole Year in a Primary Classroom. pap. 12.00 (*0-590-74712-6*) Scholastic Inc.

Picciotto, Linda P. Managing an Integrated Language Arts Classroom: Practical Strategies for Record Keeping... 1996. pap. text 9.95 (*0-590-24543-0*) Scholastic Inc.

Picciotto, Linda Pierce. Evaluation: Team Effort. 1993. pap. 10.95 (*0-590-73091-6*) Scholastic Inc.

Picciotto, Madeleine. Critical Thinking: A Casebook. LC 99-31465. (Illus.). 200p. 1999. pap. text 15.80 (*0-13-040025-4*) P-H.

Picciotto, Robert. Putting Institutional Economics to Work: From Participation to Governance. LC 95-40233. (Discussion Paper Ser.: No. 304). 30p. 1995. pap. 22.00 (*0-8213-3458-1*) World Bank.

Picciotto, Robert & Rist, Ray C., eds. Evaluation & Development: Proceedings of the 1994 World Bank Conference. LC 95-25563. (World Bank Operations Evaluation Study Ser.). 288p. 1995. pap. 22.00 (*0-8213-3466-2*) World Bank.

***Picciotto, Robert & Van Wicklin, Warren, eds.** Involuntary Resettlement: Comparative Perspectives. LC 99-87303. (Series on Evaluation & Development: Vol. 2). 360p. 2000. 39.95 (*0-7658-0018-7*); pap. 24.95 (*0-7658-0683-5*) Transaction Pubs.

Picciotto, Robert & Wiesner, Eduardo, eds. Evaluation & Development: The Institutional Dimension. LC 98-9641. (World Bank Evaluation & Development Ser.). 320p. 1998. text 34.95 (*1-56000-370-7*) Transaction Pubs.

— Evaluation & Development: The Institutional Dimesion. LC 98-9641. (World Bank Series on Evaluation & Development). 300p. 1998. pap. 22.95 (*0-7658-0423-9*, 31650) Transaction Pubs.

Picciotto, Robert, tr. see Goldemberg, Isaac.

Picciotto, Robert S., jt. auth. see Goldemberg, Isaac.

Picciotto, Sol. International Business Taxation: A Study in the Internationalization of Business Regulation. LC 91-47952. 416p. 1992. 69.50 (*0-89930-777-9*, PIX, Quorum Bks) Greenwood.

Picciotto, Sol & Mayne, Ruth, eds. Regulating International Business: Beyond Liberalization. LC 99-15309. 277p. 1999. text 79.95 (*0-312-22587-3*) St Martin.

Piccirelli, R. A., ed. see American Institute of Physics.

***Piccirilli, Richard S.** Mental Math Kids Can't Resist! Tips, Short-Cut Strategies & 60 Fun Practice Pages That Reinforce. (Illus.). (J). 2000. pap. 11.95 (*0-439-18605-6*) Scholastic Inc.

Piccirilli, Tom. The Dead Past. 212p. 1997. 21.95 (*1-885173-28-8*) Write Way.

— The Dead Past. large type ed. LC 98-56659. 258p. 1999. 25.95 (*0-7862-1833-9*) Mac Lib Ref.

***Piccirilli, Tom.** The Dead Past, Vol. 1. 208p. 1999. reprint ed. pap. 5.99 (*0-425-16696-1*, Prime Crime) Berkley Pub.

— The Deceased. 352p. 2000. pap. 5.50 (*0-8439-4752-7*, Leisure Bks) Dorchester Pub Co.

— Deep into That Darkness Peering. 562p. 1999. 45.00 (*0-9658135-5-X*) Terminal Fright.

— Hexes. 368p. 1999. mass mkt. 5.50 (*0-8439-4483-8*, Leisure Bks) Dorchester Pub Co.

Piccirilli, Tom. Pentacle. (Illus.). 156p. (Orig.). pap. 5.99 (*0-9640168-2-6*) Pirate Writings.

— Shards. 214p. 1996. 20.95 (*1-885173-23-7*) Write Way.

— Shards. 1997. mass mkt. 5.95 (*1-885173-41-5*) Write Way.

***Piccirilli, Tom.** Sorrow's Crown. 1999. mass mkt. 5.99 (*0-425-17028-4*, Prime Crime) Berkley Pub.

Piccirilli, Tom. Sorrow's Crown. 240p. 1999. 21.95 (*1-885173-53-9*) Write Way.

Piccirilli, Tom, et al. Endings: Four Stories, Sixteen Endings. (Illus.). 48p. (Orig.). pap. 3.00 (*0-9640168-3-4*) Pirate Writings.

Piccirilli, Tom, jt. ed. see McFadden, Edward J.

Piccirillo, Albert C. The German V STOL Fighter Program: A Quest for Survivability in a Theater Nuclear Environment. LC 97-15441. 75p. 1997. pap. 30.00 (*1-56347-247-3*) AIAA.

Piccirillo, Albert C. & Aronstein, David C. The Lightweight Fighter Program: A Successful Approach to Fighter Technology Transition. 59p. 1997. pap. 30.00 (*1-56347-193-0*) AIAA.

Piccirillo, Albert C., jt. auth. see Aronstein, David C.

Piccirillo, Ann & Harris, Ruth. Thighs to Die For. LC 97-2162. (Illus.). 96p. 1997. pap. 14.95 (*0-7611-0556-5*, 10556) Workman Pub.

Picco, Elizabeth R. Baby Basics: Children's Activities in How Life Begins. LC 92-20519. (Illus.). 1992. 14.95 (*1-56071-126-4*) ETR Assocs.

Picco, Giandomenico. Man Without a Gun: One Diplomat's Secret Struggle to Free the Hostages, Fight Terrorism, & End a War. (Illus.). 352p. 1999. 27.50 (*0-8129-2910-1*, Times Bks) Crown Pub Group.

Picco, Pierre, jt. auth. see Bovier, Anton.

Piccola, Michael D. Intrepid's Odyssey: The Deception That Haunts the Intrepid Museum. LC 94-92135. (Illus.). 390p. (Orig.). 1994. pap. text 16.95 (*0-9641022-0-X*) Odyssey Pubng.

Piccola, Richard, jt. auth. see Buttram, Harold.

Piccoli, Sean. Jimi Hendrix. LC 95-38704. (Illus.). 124p. (YA). (gr. 4-7). 1996. lib. bdg. 19.95 (*0-7910-2042-8*) Chelsea Hse.

Piccoli, Terese S., ed. see League of Women Voters of Pennsylvania Education F.

Piccolino, F. C., jt. ed. see Zingirian, M.

Piccolo, Alessandro, ed. Humic Substances in Terrestrial Ecosystems. LC 96-18554. 688p. 1996. 305.75 (*0-444-81516-3*) Elsevier.

Piccolo, Jack. Timing Is Everything: The Complete Timing Guide to Cooking. LC 99-36295. 416p. 2000. pap. 16.95 (*0-609-80207-0*, Three Riv Pr) Crown Pub Group.

Piccolo, Lucio. Collected Poems of Lucio Piccolo. Swann, Brian & Feldman, Ruth, eds. LC 74-37576. 215p. reprint ed. pap. 66.70 (*0-7837-1407-6*, 204176100023) Bks Demand.

Piccolo, Rina. The Trouble with Men: A Wickedly Funny Analysis of Male Behavior, Vol. 1. LC 95-79165. (Illus.). 136p. (Orig.). 1995. pap. 9.95 (*0-9648010-9-4*) Hypertext Pub.

Piccolomini, Anneas Sylvis. The Two Lovers: The Goodly History of Lady Lucrece & Her Lover Eurialus. O'Brien, Emily & Bartlett, Kenneth R., eds. (Publications of the Barnabe Riche Society : No. 7). 225p. 1997. text 12.00 (*1-895537-36-3*, Pub. by Dovehouse) Sterling.

Piccolomini, Manfredi. The Brutus Revival: Parricide & Tyrannicide During the Renaissance. LC 89-78134. (Illus.). 200p. (C). 1991. 26.95 (*0-8093-1649-8*) S Ill U Pr.

Piccolpasso, Cipriano. The Three Books of the Potter's Art. 1980. 239.95 (*0-85967-452-5*, Pub. by Scolar Pr) Ashgate Pub Co.

Piccone, Anthony. Seeing It Was So. (American Poets Continuum Ser.: No. 12). 67p. 1986. 18.00 (*0-918526-50-7*); pap. 10.00 (*0-918526-51-5*) BOA Edns.

Piccone, Paul, ed. see International Telos Conference Staff.

Piccone, Paul, tr. see Paci, Enzo.

Picconi, Marcello. Dictionnaire des Aliments pour les Animaux. (FRE.). 620p. 1965. 65.00 (*0-8288-6741-0*, M-6452) Fr & Eur.

P

Picconi, Mario J., et al. Business Statistics: Elements & Application. (C). 1997. pap. 15.00 (*0-06-500723-9*) Addson-Wesley Educ.
— Business Statistics: Elements & Application, Minitab Manual IBM. (C). 1997. pap. 28.00 (*0-06-501667-X*) Addson-Wesley Educ.
— Business Statistics: Elements & Applications. LC 92-16383. 951p. (C). 1997. 114.00 (*0-06-500174-5*) Addson-Wesley Educ.
Picerno, Richard A. Medieval Spanish Ejempla: A Study of Selected Tales from Calila y Dimna, El Libro de los Enganos de las Mujeres & the Libro de los Exemplos por ABC. LC 88-81376. (Coleccion Textos). (ENG & SPA.). 55p. (Orig.). 1988. pap. 10.00 (*0-89729-492-0*) Ediciones.
Picerno, Vincent J. Dictionary of Musical Terms. LC 76-14903. (Studies in Music: No. 42). (C). 1976. lib. bdg. 75.00 (*0-8383-2119-4*) M S G Haskell Hse.
Pices, Charles A. Du, see Du Pices, Charles A.
Pichal, M. & Sifner, O., eds. Properties of Water & Steam: Proceedings of the 11th International Conference. 704p. 1990. 220.00 (*1-56032-042-7*) Hemisp Pub.
Pichanick, Valerie. Harriet Martineau: The Woman & Her Work, Eighteen Hundred & Two to Eighteen Seventy-Six. (Women & Culture Ser.). 312p. 1980. text 44.50 (*0-472-10002-5*, 10002) U of Mich Pr.
***Pichard, C., et al, eds.** From Nutrition Support to Pharmacologic Nutrition in the ICU: Nutrition in the ICU. (Update in Intensive Care & Emergency Medicine: 34). 440p. 2000. 175.00 (*3-540-64087-8*) Spr-Verlag.
Pichard, G. Wolinski. Paulette, Tome I. 1981. pap. 11.95 (*0-7859-4140-1*) Fr & Eur.
— Paulette, Tome II. (FRE.). 1981. pap. 11.95 (*0-7859-4155-X*, 2070373061) Fr & Eur.
Pichard, Georges. Carmen. 64p. 1995. pap. 10.95 (*1-56163-123-X*, Eurotica) NBM.
— Marie-Gabrielle. 136p. 1995. pap. 15.95 (*1-56163-138-8*, Eurotica) NBM.
Pichard, Georges & Von Sacher-Masoch, Leopold. The Countess in Red. LeClerc, Jacinthe, tr. from FRE. 48p. 1994. pap. 9.95 (*1-56163-098-5*, Eurotica) NBM.
Pichard, J. Brent. Winning with Words: Secrets of a Successful Job Interview & a Successful Career. 10th rev. ed. Robinson, Ann M., ed. (Illus.). iv, 40p. (YA). (gr. 9 up). 1997. pap. 10.00 (*0-9637351-0-1*) FL Retail Fed.
— Winning with Words: Secrets of the Job Interview. 2nd ed. 77p. (C). 1983. pap. 4.95 (*0-9612312-1-1*) Magister Inc.
Pichard, Pierre. Inventory of Monuments at Pagan Sites, Vol. 1. LC 93-228386. (Illus.). 432p. (C). 1995. 130.00 (*1-870838-01-7*, Pub. by Kiscadale) Weatherhill.
— Inventory of Monuments at Pagan Sites, Vol. 2. LC 93-228386. (Illus.). 432p. (C). 1995. 130.00 (*1-870838-16-5*, Pub. by Kiscadale) Weatherhill.
— Inventory of Monuments at Pagan Sites, Vol. 2, 256-552. LC 93-228386. 424p. 1993. pap. 135.00 (*92-3-102836-7*, U8367, Pub. by UNESCO) Bernan Associates.
— Inventory of Monuments at Pagan Sites, Vol. 3. LC 93-228386. (Illus.). 432p. (C). 1995. 130.00 (*1-870838-31-9*, Pub. by Kiscadale) Weatherhill.
— Inventory of Monuments at Pagan Sites, Vol. 4. (Illus.). 432p. 1995. 130.00 (*1-870838-86-6*, Pub. by Kiscadale) Weatherhill.
— Inventory of Monuments at Pagan Sites Vol. 1: Monuments, 1-255. LC 93-228386. 409p. 1993. pap. 150.00 (*92-3-102795-6*, U7956, Pub. by UNESCO) Bernan Associates.
— Inventory of Monuments at Pagan Sites Vol. 5: Monuments, 1137-1439. 424p. 1995. pap. text 160.00 (*92-3-103128-7*, U2287, Pub. by UNESCO) Bernan Associates.
— Inventory of Monuments at Pagan Sites Vol. 6: Monuments, 1440-1736. 424p. 1998. pap. 160.00 (*92-3-103223-2*, U3223, Pub. by UNESCO) Bernan Associates.
Pichardo, Hector, tr. Un Elefante Se Balanceaba: Black & White Nellie Edge I Can Read & Sing Big Books. (Illus.). (J). (ps-2). 1996. 20.00 (*0-922053-45-6*) N Edge Res.
— Entre Mas Nos Reunimos: Black & White Nellie Edge I Can Read & Sing Big Book. (Illus.). (J). (ps-2). 1996. 20.00 (*0-922053-44-8*) N Edge Res.
— Las Mananitas: Black & White Nellie Edge I Can Read & Sing Big Books. (Illus.). (J). (ps-2). 1996. 20.00 (*0-922053-40-5*) N Edge Res.
— Mi Rancho: Black & White Nellie Edge I Can Read & Sing Big Book. (Illus.). (J). (ps-2). 1996. 20.00 (*0-922053-39-1*) N Edge Res.
— Los Pollitos: Black & White Nellie Edge I Can Read & Sing Book. (Illus.). (J). (ps-2). 1996. 20.00 (*0-922053-42-1*) N Edge Res.
Pichardo, Hector, tr. see Ledbetter, H. & Lomax, John A.
Pichaske, David. Rehearsals Against Retirement. 70p. 1996. pap. 5.95 (*0-944024-33-5*) Spoon Riv Poetry.
Pichaske, David R. A Generation in Motion. 248p. 1989. 15.95 (*0-944024-12-2*); pap. 10.95 (*0-944024-16-5*) Ellis Pr.
— The Jubilee Diary: April 10, 1980-April 19, 1981. (Illus.). 240p. (Orig.). 1982. pap. 5.95 (*0-933180-42-X*) Ellis Pr.
— The Poetry of Rock: The Golden Years. 192p. (Orig.). 1981. pap. 5.95 (*0-933180-17-9*) Ellis Pr.
— Poland in Transition, 1989-1991. (Illus.). 256p. (Orig.). 1994. pap. 11.95 (*0-944024-27-0*) Ellis Pr.
— Polarities. (Illus.). 28p. (Orig.). 1997. pap. 9.95 (*0-944024-34-3*) Spoon Riv Poetry.
— Salem-Peoria, 1883-1982. (Illus.). 256p. (Orig.). 1982. pap. 6.95 (*0-933180-40-3*) Ellis Pr.
— Visiting the Father. 1987. 2.50 (*0-941127-02-8*) Dacotah Terr Pr.
— Writing Sense: A Handbook of Composition. LC 74-15134. (C). 1975. pap. text 10.95 (*0-02-925170-2*) Free Pr.
Pichaske, David R., ed. Gates: Poems on the Restoration of Jubilee College. 26p. 1986. pap. 3.00 (*0-933180-93-4*) Spoon Riv Poetry.
— Late Harvest: Rural American Writing by Edward Abbey, Wendell Berry, Carolyn Chute, Annie Dillard, William Gass, Garrison Keillor, Bobbie Ann Mason, Wallace Stegner & Others. 452p. 1994. pap. 18.95 (*1-56924-867-2*) Marlowe & Co.
***Pichaske, David R. & Amato, Joseph, eds.** Southwest Minnesota: The Land & the People. (Illus.). 116p. 1999. pap. 15.00 (*0-9614119-8-8*, Pub. by Crossings Pr) Plains Press.
Pichaske, David R., jt. ed. see Groen, Gerrit.
Piche, Denise, jt. ed. see Dagenais, Huguette.
Piche, Michel, ed. Advances in Optical Beam Characterization & Measurements, Vol. 3418. 1998. 48.00 (*0-8194-2872-8*) SPIE.
Piche, Thomas, Jr. & Golden, Thelma. Carrie Mae Weems: Recent Work, 1992-1998. (Illus.). 152p. 1999. pap. 35.00 (*0-8076-1449-1*) Braziller.
Piche, Thomas, Jr., jt. auth. see Perrault, John.
Piche, Thomas E. Art Nouveau Glass & Pottery. Meyer, Faith, ed. (Illus.). 16p. (Orig.). 1982. pap. text 4.00 (*0-932660-06-1*) U of NI Dept Art.
Piche, Thomas E., et al. Fiction, Function, Figuration: The Twenty-Ninth Ceramic National. Herbert, Linda M., ed. 80p. 1993. pap. text 18.00 (*0-914407-17-1*) Everson Mus.
***Piche, Thomas E., Jr., et al.** Marc Leuthold. (Illus.). 36p. 1999. pap. 9.95 (*0-914407-21-X*) Everson Mus.
Piche, Thomas E., ed. see Doroshenko, Peter.
Piche, Thomas E., ed. see Doroshenko, Peter & Druckrey, Timothy.
Piche, Thomas E., Jr., ed. see Greengold, Jane.
Piche, Thomas E., Jr., ed. see Kingsley, April.
Piche, Thomas E., Jr., ed. see McEvilley, Thomas.
Piche, Thomas E., ed. see Nahas, Dominique & Perreault, John.
Piche, Thomas E., Jr., ed. see Perry, Barbara.
Piche, Thomas E., ed. see Perry, Barbara, et al.
Piche, Thomas E., Jr., ed. see Sandys, Edwina & Morton, James P.
Pichelmaier, H. & Schildberg, F. W., eds. Thoracic Surgery. (Illus.). 480p. 1989. 477.00 (*0-387-18464-3*) Spr-Verlag.
Picherit, Jean-Louis, ed. from FRO. The Journey of Charlemagne. LC 84-52505. 138p. 1985. 12.95 (*0-917786-46-7*) Summa Pubns.
***Pichette, Marise.** Show & Tell Food. (Illus.). 12p. 2000. bds. 4.95 (*2-922148-83-1*) Presses Avent.
***Pichette, Marise & Rousseau, Serge.** Show & Tell Animals. (Illus.). 12p. 2000. bds. 4.95 (*2-922148-80-7*) Presses Avent.
— Show & Tell at Home. (Illus.). 12p. 2000. bds. 4.95 (*2-922148-82-3*) Presses Avent.
— Show & Tell Nature. (Illus.). 12p. 2000. bds. 4.95 (*2-922148-81-5*) Presses Avent.
Pichevin, M. F., et al. Studies on the Self & Social Cognition. 344p. 1993. text 109.00 (*981-02-1237-2*) World Scientific Pub.
Pichler, F. R. A. Process in Cybernetics & Systems Research, Vol. 7. 1981. 80.00 (*0-07-049847-4*) McGraw.
Pichler, Franz & Diaz, R. Moreno, eds. Computer Aided Systems Theory - EUROCAST '97: Proceedings, a Selection of Papers from the Sixth International Workshop on Computer Aided Systems Theory, Las Palmas de Gran Canaria, Spain, February 24-28, 1997, Vol. 133. LC 97-39197. (Lecture Notes in Computer Science Ser.: Vol. 1333). xi, 626p. 1997. pap. 89.00 (*3-540-63811-3*) Spr-Verlag.
Pichler, Franz R., ed. Advances in Crypotology - Eurocrypt '85. (Lecture Notes in Computer Science Ser.: Vol. 219). ix, 218p. 1986. 36.00 (*0-387-16468-5*) Spr-Verlag.
— Eurocast Nineteen Eighty-Nine. (Lecture Notes in Computer Science Ser.: Vol. 410). vii, 427p. 1990. 44.95 (*0-387-52215-8*) Spr-Verlag.
Pichler, Franz R. & Diaz, R. Moreno, eds. Computer Aided Systems Theory, EUROCAST '91: A Selection of Papers from the Second International Workshop on Computer Aided Systems Theory, Krems, Austria, April 15-19, 1991: Proceedings. LC 92-9634. (Lecture Notes in Computer Science Ser.: Vol. 585). x, 761p. 1992. 111.95 (*0-387-55354-1*) Spr-Verlag.
Pichler, Franz R. & Schwartzel, Heinz, eds. Computer Aided Systems Theory: Methods in Modelling: Computer Aided Systems Theory for the Design of Intelligent Machines. LC 92-8524. (Illus.). 392p. 1992. 126.95 (*0-387-55405-X*) Spr-Verlag.
Pichler, Hans. Italienische Vulkan-Gebiete III Lipari, Vulcano, Stromboli, Tyrrhenisches Meer. 2nd ed. (Sammlung Geologischer Fuehrer Ser.: Band 69). (GER., Illus.). xix, 272p. 1990. spiral bd. 29.00 (*3-443-15052-7*, Pub. by Gebruder Borntraeger) Balogh.
— Italienische Vulkangebiete Vol. IV: Aetna und Sizilien. (Sammlung Geologischer Fuehrer Ser.: Band 76). (GER., Illus.). xiv, 326p. 1984. spiral bd. 35.00 (*3-443-15037-3*, Pub. by Gebruder Borntraeger) Balogh.
— Italienische Vulkangebiete V. Mte. Vulture, Aeolische Inseln II (Saline, Filicudi, Alicudi, Panarea), Mti. Iblei, Capo Passero, Ustica, Pantelleria und Linosa. (Sammlung Geologischer Fuehrer Ser.: Band 83). (GER., Illus.). x, 271p. 1989. spiral bd. 32.00 (*3-443-15050-0*, Pub. by Gebruder Borntraeger) Balogh.
Pichler, P., jt. ed. see Ryssel, H.
Pichler, Tibor & Gasparikova, Jana. Interests & Values: The Spirit of Venture in a Time of Change. LC 99-17721. (Cultural Heritage & Contemporary Change Series IVA: Vol. 11). 1999. 17.50 (*1-56518-125-5*) Coun Res Values.
Pichler, Tibor & Gasparikova, Jana, eds. Language, Values, & the Slovak Nation. LC 93-11884. (Cultural Heritage & Contemporary Change Series IVA: Vol. 5). 1993. 45.00 (*1-56518-036-4*); 17.50 (*1-56518-037-2*) Coun Res Values.
***Pichler, Tony & Broslavick, Chris, compiled by.** Reaching Out: 20 Ways for Teens to Serve Origins. (Youth Ministry Resource Library). 96p. 2000. pap. 19.95 (*0-937997-77-3*, 3215) Hi-Time Pflaum.
Pichler, W. J., et al, eds. Progress in Allergy & Clinical Immunology Vol. 1: Montreux. LC 89-1678. 580p. 1989. 48.00 (*0-920887-45-7*) Hogrefe & Huber Pubs.
Pichler, W. J., jt. ed. see Stadler, B. M.
Pichlmayr, ed. Aurelii Victoris. (LAT.). 1993. reprint ed. pap. 44.50 (*3-8154-1108-4*, T1108, Pub. by B G Teubner) U of Mich Pr.
Pichney, Carole. How to Serve a Proper Victorian Tea: Using Antique China & Silver to Bring the Past to the Present. LC 96-97051. 98p. (Orig.). 1996. pap. 11.95 (*1-57502-306-7*, P1052) Morris Pubng.
Pichois, ed. see Colette, Sidonie-Gabrielle.
Pichois, Claude, jt. auth. see Baudelaire, Charles.
Pichois, Claude, ed. see Baudelaire, Charles.
Pichois, Claude, ed. see Colette, Sidonie-Gabrielle.
Pichois, Raymond, ed. see Baudelaire, Charles.
Pichon, Francisco J., et al, eds. Traditional & Modern Natural Resource Management in Latin America. LC 99-6638. (Pitt Latin American Ser.). 320p. (C). 1999. pap. 19.95 (*0-8229-5703-5*); text 45.00 (*0-8229-4103-1*) U of Pittsburgh Pr.
Pichon, Jacqueline, jt. auth. see Wagner, Rene-Louis.
Pichon, Joelle. The Sea Lion. (Animal Close-Ups Ser.).Tr. of Otarie, Espiegle Sirene. 1997. 12.15 (*0-606-13764-5*, Pub. by Turtleback) Demco.
— The Sea Lion: Ocean Diver. LC 96-17855. (Animal Close-ups Ser.). (Illus.). 28p. (J). (ps-3). 1997. pap. 6.95 (*0-88106-438-6*) Charlesbridge Pub.
Pichon, Liz. Hot Dogs & Cool Cats. (Illus.). 32p. (Orig.). (J). (ps-3). 1996. pap. 2.95 (*0-8167-4067-4*) Troll Communs.
Pichon, Liz. Twilight Verses, Moonlight Rhymes. LC 98-31491. 64p. (J). (ps-k). 1999. 16.99 (*0-8066-3885-0*, 9-3885, Augsburg) Augsburg Fortress.
Pichon, Rene. Index Verborum Amatoriorum. iv, 229p. 1991. reprint ed. write for info. (*3-487-01411-4*) G Olms Pubs.
Pichon, Y., ed. Comparative Molecular Neurobiology. LC 92-49315. (Experientia Supplementa Ser.: No. 63). ix, 433p. 1992. write for info. (*3-7643-2785-5*); 174.50 (*0-8176-2785-5*) Birkhauser.
Pichot, Andre. La Naissance de la Science: Grece Presocratique, Vol. 2. (FRE.). 1991. pap. 26.95 (*0-7859-3972-5*) Fr & Eur.
— La Naissance de la Science: Mesopotamie, Egypte, Vol. 1. (FRE.). 1991. pap. 22.95 (*0-7859-3971-7*) Fr & Eur.
Pichot, P. & Olivier-Martin, R., eds. Psychological Measurements in Psychopharmacology. (Modern Problems of Pharmacopsychiatry Ser.: Vol. 7). (Illus.). 1974. 85.25 (*3-8055-1630-4*) S Karger.
Pichot, Pierre. Compressor Application Engineering Vol. 1: Compression Equipment. Miller, Ryle & Miller, Ethel B., trs. from FRE. LC 86-7587. 271p. reprint ed. pap. 84.10 (*0-608-00827-3*, 206161600001) Bks Demand.
— Compressor Application Engineering Vol. 2: Drivers for Rotating Equipment. Miller, Ryle & Miller, Ethel B., trs. from FRE. LC 86-7587. 260p. pap. 80.60 (*0-608-05052-0*, 206161600002) Bks Demand.
Pichot, Sylvie, tr. see Graham, Michelle.
Pichowiak, Siegfried, jt. auth. see Damm, Klaus-Werner.
Picht, Robert, ed. see Pflaum, Hans G.
***Pichtel, John.** Fundamentals of Site Remediation: For Metal & Hydrocarbon Contaminated Soils. LC 99-88790. 350p. 2000. pap. 69.00 (*0-86587-689-4*, 689) Gov Insts.
Pichugina, Valentina. Otglagol"nye Sushchestvitel"nye s Suffiksom -k(a) v Russkom Iazyke XI-XVII Vekov. LC 95-35739. (RUS.). 174p. (Orig.). 1995. pap. 17.50 (*1-55779-085-X*) Hermitage Pubs.
Pici, Nick, jt. auth. see Macklin, F. Anthony.
Picinbono, Bernard, jt. ed. see Longo, G.
Picinelli, Filippo. Mundus Symbolicus, 2 vols. in 1. (GER.). 1276p. 1979. reprint ed. write for info. (*3-487-05790-5*); reprint ed. write for info. (*3-487-05970-3*) G Olms Pubs.
Picirilli, Richard. Mental Math: Computation Activities for Anytime. 1994. pap. text 12.95 (*0-590-49796-0*) Scholastic Inc.
Picirilli, Robert E. The Book of Romans. 324p. (C). 1975. 9.95 (*0-89265-026-5*) Randall Hse.
— The Book of Romans, 3 vols., 1. 1974. pap. 5.95 (*0-89265-015-X*) Randall Hse.
— The Book of Romans, 3 vols., 2. 1974. pap. 5.95 (*0-89265-016-8*) Randall Hse.
— The Book of Romans, 3 vols., 3. 1974. pap. 5.95 (*0-89265-017-6*) Randall Hse.
— Church Government & Ordinances. 1973. pap. 1.95 (*0-89265-102-4*) Randall Hse.
— Fundamentals of the Faith. 30p. 1973. pap. 1.95 (*0-89265-106-7*) Randall Hse.
— The Gifts of the Spirit. 1980. pap. 1.95 (*0-89265-065-6*) Randall Hse.
— Paul the Apostle. pap. 12.99 (*0-8024-6325-8*, 245) Moody.
— Pauline Writings Notes. 1967. pap. 4.95 (*0-89265-001-X*) Randall Hse.
— Perseverance. 28p. 1973. pap. 0.95 (*0-89265-108-3*) Randall Hse.
— What the Bible Says about Tongues. 1981. pap. 0.95 (*0-89265-071-0*) Randall Hse.
Picirilli, Robert E. & Harrison, H. D., eds. Randall House Bible Commentary Series, 6 vols. 1989. write for info. (*0-89265-115-6*) Randall Hse.
Picirilli, Robert E., jt. auth. see Hampton, Ralph, Jr.
Pick. Arts Administration. 2nd ed. 192p. (C). 1995. pap. 34.99 (*0-419-18970-X*, E & FN Spon) Routledge.
***Pick.** Mexico Megacity. 1999. pap. 40.00 (*0-8133-3754-2*, Pub. by Westview) HarpC.
Pick, A. D. Minnesota Symposia on Child Psychology, Vol. 6. Masten, Ann, ed. 1973. 36.00 (*0-89859-397-2*) L Erlbaum Assocs.
— Minnesota Symposia on Child Psychology, Vol. 7. Masten, Ann, ed. 1974. 36.00 (*0-89859-398-0*) L Erlbaum Assocs.
— Minnesota Symposia on Child Psychology, Vol. 8. Masten, Ann, ed. 1975. 36.00 (*0-89859-399-9*) L Erlbaum Assocs.
— Minnesota Symposia on Child Psychology, Vol. 9. Masten, Ann, ed. 1976. 36.00 (*0-89859-400-6*) L Erlbaum Assocs.
— Minnesota Symposia on Child Psychology, Vol. 10. Masten, Ann, ed. 1977. 36.00 (*0-89859-401-4*) L Erlbaum Assocs.
Pick, A. D., ed. Perception & Its Development: A Tribute to Eleanor J. Gibson. 272p. 1979. text 49.95 (*0-89859-409-X*) L Erlbaum Assocs.
Pick, A. I. Plasma Cell Dyscrasias. (Journal: Acta Haematologica: Vol. 68, No. 3). (Illus.). vi, 96p. 1982. pap. 51.50 (*3-8055-3549-X*) S Karger.
Pick, Albert. Standard Catalog of World Paper Money: General Issues, Vol. II. 8th ed. LC 97-173008. (Illus.). 1072p. 1997. 55.00 (*0-87341-469-1*) Krause Pubns.
— Standard Catalog of World Paper Money, Specialized Issues, Vol. 1. 8th ed. Shafer, Neil & Bruce, Colin R., 2nd, eds. LC 83-83100. (Illus.). 1184p. 1999. pap. 60.00 (*0-87341-648-1*) Krause Pubns.
Pick, Alfred & Langendorf, Richard. Interpretation of Complex Arrhythmias. LC 79-10741. (Illus.). 598p. 1979. reprint ed. pap. 185.40 (*0-7837-1493-9*, 205718900023) Bks Demand.
Pick, Anne D., jt. auth. see Gibson, Eleanor J.
Pick, Bernard. The Cabala: Its Influence on Judaism & Christianity. 1991. lib. bdg. 75.00 (*0-8490-4257-7*) Gordon Pr.
— The Cabala: Its Influence on Judaism & Christianity. 115p. 1993. pap. 9.00 (*0-89540-287-4*, SB-287) Sun Pub.
Pick, Christopher. Exploring Rural England & Wales. (Illus.). 182p. 1993. pap. 12.95 (*0-8442-9464-0*, 94640, Passprt Bks) NTC Contemp Pub Co.
— Undersea. (Young Scientist Ser.). (Illus.). 32p. (J). (gr. 4-8). 1976. pap. 6.95 (*0-86020-092-2*); lib. bdg. 14.95 (*0-88110-437-X*) EDC.
***Pick, Daniel.** Svengali's Web: The Alien Enchanter in Modern Culture. LC 99-59164. (Illus.). 268p. 2000. 29.95 (*0-300-08204-5*) Yale U Pr.
Pick, Daniel. War Machine: The Rationalization of Slaughter in the Modern Age. LC 92-44183. (Illus.). 288p. (C). 1993. 40.00 (*0-300-05417-3*) Yale U Pr.
— War Machine: The Rationalization of Slaughter in the Modern Age. 1996. pap. text 18.00 (*0-300-06719-4*) Yale U Pr.
Pick, Daniel, ed. see Kinsey, Jean.
Pick, Doris J. & Hadley, Michelle. Am I Hiring the Right Nanny? With This Hiring Guide You Will Know! 1998. pap. 19.95 (*0-9664259-0-1*) Innov Personnel.
Pick, Doris J., et al. GuidePak: A Computerized Career Planning Guide Including Your Occupational Interests, Psychological Assessment & Personality Traits. rev. ed. 101p. 1991. pap. 89.00 (*1-879858-00-2*) Behaviordyne.
Pick, E., tr. see Escarpit, Robert.
Pick, Frederick W. The Baltic Nations: Estonia, Latvia, & Lithuania. LC 83-45837. reprint ed. 32.50 (*0-404-20202-0*) AMS Pr.
Pick, H. L., Jr. & Saltzman, E., eds. Modes of Perceiving & Processing Information. 240p. 1978. text 49.95 (*0-89859-354-9*) L Erlbaum Assocs.
***Pick, Hella.** The Guilty Victims: Austria after the Holocaust. 2000. text 35.00 (*1-86064-618-2*, Pub. by I B T) St Martin.
Pick, Hella. Simon Wiesenthal: A Life in Search of Justice. LC 96-11808. (Illus.). 384p. 1996. 35.00 (*1-55553-273-X*) NE U Pr.
Pick, Herbert L., Jr., et al, eds. Cognition: Conceptual & Methodological Issues. (Illus.). 374p. 1992. text 39.95 (*1-55798-165-5*) Am Psychol.
Pick, Herbert L. & Acredolo, Linda, eds. Spatial Orientation: Theory, Research, & Application. 398p. 1983. 85.00 (*0-306-41255-1*, Plenum Trade) Perseus Pubng.
Pick, Herbert L., Jr., jt. ed. see Walk, Richard D.
Pick, J. B., et al. The Strange Genius of David Lindsay: An Appreciation. LC 70-543746. viii, 183 p. 1970. write for info. (*0-212-98361-X*) A C Blk.
Pick, James B. & Butler, Edgar W. Mexico Megacity. LC 96-38152. (C). 1997. text 95.00 (*0-8133-8983-6*, Pub. by Westview) HarpC.
Pick, James B., jt. auth. see Butler, Edgar W.
Pick, John. Gerard Manley Hopkins: Priest & Poet. LC 78-14838. 169p. 1978. reprint ed. lib. bdg. 38.50 (*0-313-20589-2*, PIGH, Greenwood Pr) Greenwood.
***Pick, John & Anderson, Malcolm.** Building Jerusalem: Art, Industry & the British Millennium. 303p. 1999. text 38.00 (*90-5702-434-9*, Harwood Acad Pubs) Gordon & Breach.
Pick, Joseph R. VHDL: Techniques, Experiments & Caveats. (Illus.). 382p. 1995. 55.00 (*0-07-049906-3*) McGraw.
Pick, Liza, et al, trs. International Tapestry Network. (Illus.). 64p. (Orig.). (C). 1992. pap. 17.00 (*0-9625772-1-9*) ITNET.
Pick, M. & Machado, M. E., eds. Fundamental Problems in Solar Activity: Proceedings of Symposium E3 of the COSPAR 29th Plenary Meeting Held in Washington, D. C., U. S. A., 28 August-5 September, 1992. (Advances in Space Research Ser.: Vol. 13). 470p. 1993. pap. 190.25 (*0-08-042339-6*, Pergamon Pr) Elsevier.
Pick, M., jt. ed. see Trottet, G.

An Asterisk (*) at the beginning of an entry indicates that the title is appearing for the first time.

Pick, Marc G. Cranial Sutures: Analysis, Morphology & Manipulative Strategies. LC 98-74358. (Illus.). 469p. (C). 1999. 80.00 (0-939616-29-7) Eastland.
Pick, Otto, jt. auth. see Busch, Marie.
Pick, Richard. Complete Richard Pick School of Guitar. 280p. 1992. pap. 29.95 (0-7866-0006-3, 95059) Mel Bay.
— Diatonic & Chromatic Scales/Classic Guitar. 20p. 1996. pap. 4.95 (0-7866-0406-9, 95429) Mel Bay.
— Masterpieces for 2 Guitars. 68p. 1996. pap. 9.95 (0-7866-0405-0, 95428) Mel Bay.
Pick, Richard. School of Guitar: The Guitar in Pedagogy, Practice, Performance, 2 vols., Set. LC 92-14177. 1992. pap. 25.00 (0-936186-73-9) Edit Orphee.
Pick, Robert M., jt. ed. see Miserendino, Leo J.
***Pick, Scott.** Scenic Driving British Columbia. (Illus.). 216p. 2000. pap. 16.95 (1-56044-958-6) Falcon Pub Inc.
Pick, Zuzana M. The New Latin American Cinema: A Continental Project. Schatz, Thomas G., ed. LC 93-73. (Film Studies). 264p. (C). 1993. text 37.50 (0-292-76545-2) U of Tex Pr.
Pickands, Marcia. Psychic Abilities: How to Train & Use Them. LC 99-22982. 45p. 1999. pap. 9.95 (1-57863-111-4) Weiser.
Pickands, Marcia L. The Psychic Self-Defense Personal Training Manual. LC 96-40272. (Illus.). 128p. (Orig.). 1997. pap. 9.95 (1-57863-004-5) Weiser.
Pickar. Dosage Calculations. 6th ed. LC 98-32460. (Nursing Education Ser.). 400p. (C). 1999. pap. 42.95 (0-7668-0504-2) Delmar.
— Dosage Calculations Ratio & Proportion: A Ratio-Proportion Approach. LC 98-3830. 368p. (C). 1998. pap. 39.95 (0-7668-0630-8) Delmar.
***Pickar.** Dosage Calculations Ratio & Proportion: Instructor's Manual. 192p. 1999. teacher ed. 12.00 (0-7668-0645-6) Delmar.
Pickar, Arnold D. Preparing for General Physics: Math Skill Drills & Other Useful Help: Calculus Version. LC 92-41812. 188p. (C). 1993. pap. text 19.80 (0-201-53802-4) Addison-Wesley.
Pickar, Gertrud B. Ambivalence Transcended: A Study of the Writings of Annette von Droste-Hulshoff. LC 97-9879. (GERM Ser.). 330p. 1997. 75.00 (1-57113-141-8) Camden Hse.
Pickar, Gloria D. Dosage Calculations. 2nd ed. LC 82-71146. (Illus.). 128p. (C). 1987. reprint ed. disk 160.00 (0-8273-2778-1) Delmar.
— Dosage Calculations. 4th ed. LC 92-23154. 1993. pap. 27.20 (0-8273-4982-3) Delmar.
— Dosage Calculations. 4th ed. 153p. 1993. teacher ed. 14.00 (0-8273-5741-9) Delmar.
— Dosage Calculations. 5th ed. (Nursing Education Ser.). 176p. 1996. teacher ed. 14.95 (0-8273-6781-3) Delmar.
Pickar, Roger L. Marketing for Design Firms in the 1990s. 112p. (Orig.). 1991. pap. 20.00 (1-55835-037-3) AIA Press.
Pickard, Bertram. Peacemakers' Dilemma. (C). 1936. pap. 4.00 (0-87574-016-2) Pendle Hill.
Pickard, Brent K., ed. Skier's Guide to North America. LC 88-50618. (Illus.). 256p. (Orig.). 1988. pap. 11.95 (0-944982-01-8) Wise Guide Pub.
Pickard-Cambridge, Arthur W. Demosthenes & the Last Days of Greek Freedom, 384-322 B.C. LC 73-14463. (Heroes of the Nations Ser.). reprint ed. 45.00 (0-404-58281-8) AMS Pr.
Pickard-Cambridge, Arthur W., jt. auth. see Lewis, David M.
Pickard, Cynthia. The World in an Olive Leaf. 48p. (Orig.). 1985. 25.00 (0-931757-26-6); pap. 15.00 (0-931757-27-4) Pterodactyl Pr.
Pickard, George L. Descriptive Physical Oceanography: An Introduction. 5th ed. 336p. 1990. pap. text 39.95 (0-7506-2759-X) Buttrwrth-Heinemann.
Pickard, George L., jt. auth. see Pond, S.
Pickard, George L., jt. ed. see Emery, W. J.
Pickard, J. D., et al, eds. Neuroendocrinological Aspects of Neurosurgery. (Acta Neurochirugica - Supplementum Ser.: Supplement 47). (Illus.). 130p. 1990. 114.95 (0-387-82160-0) Spr-Verlag.
— Neurosurgical Aspects of Epilepsy: Proceedings of the 4th Advanced Seminar in Neurosurgical Research of the European Association of Neurosurgical Societies, May 17-18, 1989, Bressco die Teolo, Padova, Italy. (Acta Neurochirugica - Supplementum Ser.: No. 50). (Illus.). viii, 144p. 1990. 128.00 (0-387-82227-5) Spr-Verlag.
Pickard, James. North American Shortwave Frequency Guide, Vol. 3. rev. ed. (Illus.). 208p. 1996. pap. 19.95 (0-917963-09-1) Artsci Inc.
***Pickard, Jerry.** Scanner Modification & Antennas. 176p. 1999. pap. 20.00 (1-58160-041-0) Paladin Pr.
Pickard, Jerry. Scanner Modification & Antennas: Everything You Ever Wanted to Know but Were Afraid to Ask. LC 95-81303. (Illus.). 164p. (Orig.). 1998. pap. 22.95 (1-56866-120-7) Index Pub Grp.
Pickard, John B., ed. see Whittier, John Greenleaf.
Pickard, Kate E. The Kidnapped & the Ransomed: The Narrative of Peter & Vina Still after Forty Years of Slavery. LC 95-30735. (Illus.). xv, 409p. 1995. pap. 15.00 (0-8032-9233-3, Bison Books) U of Nebr Pr.
Pickard, Laurens R. Decision Making in Cardiothoracic Surgery. 208p. 1989. text 120.00 (0-7216-1168-0, W B Saunders Co) Harcrt Hlth Sci Grp.
***Pickard, Laurie.** Family Business: United We Stand - Divided We Fall: Is Working with Relatives Working for You? 1999. pap. 19.00 (0-9666978-0-4) Avant-Courier Pr.
Pickard, Liz, et al. Voices from the Landwash: West Moon; The End of the Road; The Only Living Father; Tomorrow Will Be Sunday; Woman in a Monkey Cage; Flux. Lynde, Denyse, ed. (Orig.). 1997. pap. 29.95 (0-88754-527-0) Theatre Comm.
Pickard, Mary A. Feasting Naturally: From Your Own Recipes. LC 80-68229. 155p. 1980. spiral bd. 7.95 (0-934474-18-4) Cookbook Pubs.
— Feasting Naturally with Our Friends. LC 82-60390. 164p. 1982. spiral bd. 7.95 (0-934474-24-9) Cookbook Pubs.
— Feasting...Naturally. LC 79-64450. 159p. 1979. pap., spiral bd. 7.95 (0-934474-05-2) Cookbook Pubs.
Pickard, Michael. The Gerfnit Chronicles. LC 98-86691. 325p. 1998. 25.00 (0-7388-0065-1); pap. 15.00 (0-7388-0066-X) Xlibris Corp.
***Pickard, Nancy.** The Blue Corn Murders: A Eugenia Potter Mystery. large type ed. LC 98-48269. 356p. 1999. write for info. (0-7540-3688-X, G K Hall Audio) Chivers N Amer.
— The Blue Corn Murders: A Eugenia Potter Mystery. large type ed. LC 98-48269. 353p. 1999. 28.95 (0-7838-8479-6) Macmillan Gen Ref.
Pickard, Nancy. Bum Steer. Marrow, Linda, ed. 288p. 1991. reprint ed. mass mkt. 5.99 (0-671-68042-0) PB.
— But I Wouldn't Want to Die There: A Jenny Cain Mystery. large type ed. LC 93-33294. 305p. 1993. lib. bdg. 20.95 (0-7862-0080-4) Thorndike Pr.
— But I Wouldn't Want to Die There: A Jenny Cain Mystery. Marrow, Linda, ed. 272p. 1994. reprint ed. mass mkt. 5.50 (0-671-72331-6, Pocket Star Bks) PB.
— Confession. 1995. mass mkt. 5.99 (0-671-78262-2, PB Trade Paper) PB.
— Confession: A Jenny Cain Mystery. large type ed. LC 94-37389. 570p. 1995. 23.95 (0-7862-0344-7) Thorndike Pr.
— Dead Crazy. Marrow, Linda, ed. 1989. mass mkt. 4.99 (0-671-73430-X) PB.
— The First Lady Murders. 1999. mass mkt. 6.99 (0-671-01444-7) S&S Trade.
— Generous Death. 1987. mass mkt. 5.50 (0-671-73264-1) S&S Trade.
***Pickard, Nancy.** Generous Death. large type ed. LC 99-20969. (Mystery Ser.). 1999. 25.95 (1-57490-207-5, Beeler LP Bks) T T Beeler.
Pickard, Nancy. I. O. U. Marrow, Linda, ed. 240p. 1992. per. 4.99 (0-671-68043-9) PB.
— I. O. U. large type ed. LC 91-24262. 408p. 1991. reprint ed. lib. bdg. 21.95 (1-56054-248-9) Thorndike Pr.
— Marriage Is Murder. Marrow, Linda, ed. 1988. mass mkt. 5.50 (0-671-73428-8) PB.
— No Body. 1987. per. 5.99 (0-671-73429-6) PB.
— Say No to Murder. Marrow, Linda, ed. 1988. mass mkt. 5.50 (0-671-73431-8) PB.
***Pickard, Nancy.** Say No to Murder: A Jenny Cain Mystery. LC 98-46683. 1999. 20.95 (0-7862-1703-0, Five Star MI) Mac Lib Ref.
— Storm Warnings. LC 98-56117. 1999. 21.95 (0-7862-1811-8) Thorndike Pr.
Pickard, Nancy. The Twenty-Seven Ingredient Chili con Carne Murders: A Eugenia Potter Mystery. 288p. 1994. mass mkt. 5.99 (0-440-21641-9) Dell.
— The Twenty Seven Ingredient Chili con Carne Murders: Based on Characters & a Story Created by Virginia Rich. large type ed. LC 93-46336. 399p. 1993. reprint ed. lib. bdg. 21.95 (1-56054-636-0) Thorndike Pr.
— Twilight. 1996. mass mkt. 5.99 (0-671-78290-8) PB.
***Pickard, Nancy.** The Whole Truth. LC 99-46816. 272p. 2000. 22.95 (0-671-88795-5, PB Hardcover) PB.
— The Whole Truth. large type ed. LC 00-23474. (Basic Ser.). 378p. 2000. write for info. (0-7862-2577-7) Thorndike Pr.
***Pickard, Nancy, ed.** Mom, Apple Pie & Murder: A Collection of New Mysteries for Mother's Day. 320p. 1999. pap. 13.00 (0-425-16890-5, Prime Crime) Berkley Pub.
— Mom, Apple Pie & Murder: A Collection of New Mysteries for Mother's Day. 2000. mass mkt. 5.99 (0-425-17410-7) Berkley Pub.
Pickard, Nancy, et al, eds. Malice Domestic Vol. 3: An Anthology of Original Traditional Mystery Stories. 288p. 1994. mass mkt. 4.99 (0-671-73828-3) PB.
Pickard, Nancy & Virginia, Rich. The Blue Corn Murders. (Eugenia Potter Mysteries Ser.). 336p. 1999. mass mkt. 5.99 (0-440-21765-2) Dell.
Pickard, R. D. Conservation Built Environment. (C). 1996. pap. text. write for info. (0-582-22818-2, Pub. by Addison-Wesley) Longman.
***Pickard, Robert.** Management of Historic Centres. LC 00-44058. (Conservation of the European Built Heritage Ser.). (Illus.). 2000. pap. write for info. (0-419-23290-7, E & FN Spon) Routledge.
— Policy & Law in Heritage Conservation. LC 00-44057. (Conservation of the European Built Heritage Ser.). 2000. pap. write for info. (0-419-23280-X, E & FN Spon) Routledge.
Pickard, Roy. Frank Sinatra at the Movies. (Illus.). 190p. 14.95 (0-7090-6101-3, Pub. by R Hale Ltd) Seven Hills Bk.
Pickard, Roy. James Stewart: The Hollywood Years. large type ed. (Charnwood Large Print Ser.). (Illus.). 304p. 1995. 27.99 (0-7089-8725-7, Charnwood) Ulverscroft.
— The Oscar Stars from A to Z. (Illus.). 448p. 1998. pap. 19.95 (0-7472-7690-0, Pub. by Headline Bk Pub) Trafalgar.
Pickard, Samuel T. Hawthorne's First Diary. LC 72-285. (Studies in Hawthorne: No. 15). 1972. reprint ed. lib. bdg. 75.00 (0-8383-1408-2) M S G Haskell Hse.
— Life & Letters of John Greenleaf Whittier. (BCL1-PS American Literature Ser.). 804p. 1992. reprint ed. lib. bdg. 119.00 (0-7812-6903-2) Rprt Serv.
— Life & Letters of John Greenleaf Whittier, 2 vols., Set. LC 68-24941. (American Biography Ser.: No. 32). 1969. reprint ed. lib. bdg. 150.00 (0-8383-0191-6) M S G Haskell Hse.
— Whittier-Land: A Handbook of North Essex. LC 73-7511. (American Literature Ser.: No. 49). 1973. reprint ed. lib. bdg. 75.00 (0-8383-1698-0) M S G Haskell Hse.
Pickard, Sid. Chess Games of Adolph Anderssen: Master of Attack. 1997. pap. text 24.95 (1-886846-03-0) Pickard & Son.
— Hastings 1895, Grand International Chess Congress: The Centennial Edition. 259p. 1995. pap. 18.95 (1-886846-01-4) Pickard & Son.
— Scotch 4 . . . QH4: The Steinitz Variation. 103p. 1995. pap. 14.95 (1-886846-02-2) Pickard & Son.
Pickard, Sid, ed. The Puzzle King: Sam Loyd's Chess Problems & Selected Mathematical Puzzles. 240p. 1996. pap. 22.95 (1-886846-05-7) Pickard & Son.
***Pickard, Stephen L.** Liberating Evangelism: Gospel Theology & the Dynamics of Communication. LC 99-26134. (CMMC Ser.). 120p. 1999. pap. 10.00 (1-56338-279-2) TPI PA.
Pickard, Susan. Living on the Frontline. 334p. 1995. 79.95 (1-85972-168-0, Pub. by Avebry) Ashgate Pub Co.
Pickard, Tom. Tiepin Eros: New & Selected Poems. LC 94-146173. 160p. 1994. pap. 16.95 (1-85224-130-6, Pub. by Bloodaxe Bks) Dufour.
Pickard, Wayland. Complete Singers Guide: To Becoming a Working Professional. (Illus.). 180p. (Orig.). (C). 1989. 24.95 (0-685-26328-2); pap. text 24.95 (0-685-26329-0) Pickard Pub.
— Complete Singers Guide to Becoming a Working Professional. 2nd rev. unabridged ed. (Illus.). 200p. pap. 24.95 (0-9623458-0-6) Vocal Power.
Pickard, William M. Offer Them Christ. LC 98-65599. 128p. 1998. pap. 14.95 (1-57736-090-7) Providence Hse.
***Pickarski, Ron.** The As You Like It Cookbook: Imaginative Gourmet Dishes with Exciting Vegetarian Options. 2001. pap. 16.95 (0-7570-0013-4) Square One.
Pickarski, Ron. Eco-Cuisine. (Illus.). 288p. 1995. pap. 19.95 (0-89815-635-1) Ten Speed Pr.
Pickart, Andrea J. & Sawyer, John O. Ecology & Restoration of Northern California Coastal Dunes. (Illus.). 172p. 1998. pap. 24.95 (0-943460-38-7) Calif Native.
Pickart, Joan E. Angels & Elves (Man of the Month, Baby Bet) 1995. per. 3.25 (0-373-05961-2, 1-05961-7) Silhouette.
— Apache Dream Bride. (Desire Ser.). 1996. per. 3.50 (0-373-75999-1, 1-75999-2) Silhouette.
— Experiencia Prematrimonial: Texas Glory. (Silhouette Deseo Ser.: Vol. 241).Tr. of Experience Before Marriage. (SPA.). 1998. per. 3.50 (0-373-35241-7, 1-35241-8) Harlequin Bks.
— Family Secrets. 368p. (Orig.). 1989. mass mkt. 3.95 (0-445-20877-5, Pub. by Warner Bks) Little.
— The Father of Her Child (The Baby Bet) 1996. per. 3.99 (0-373-24025-2, 1-24025-8) Silhouette.
— Friends, Lovers...& Babies! 1996. per. 3.99 (0-373-24011-2, 1-24011-8) Silhouette.
— Friends, Lovers...& Babies! large type ed. (Silhouette Romance Ser.). 1998. 20.95 (0-373-59857-2) Thorndike Pr.
— Gauntlet Run. (Family Continuity Program Ser.: No. 11). 1999. mass mkt. 4.50 (0-373-82159-X, 1-82159-4) Harlequin Bks.
— El Juego del Escondite. (Deseo Ser.). 1996. per. 3.50 (0-373-35151-8, 1-35151-9) Harlequin Bks.
— Just My Joe. (Desire Ser.: No. 1202). 1999. per. 3.75 (0-373-76202-X, 1-76202-0) Harlequin Bks.
— Luna de Pasion: Texas Moon. (Deseo Ser.: Vol. 115).Tr. of Passion Moon. (SPA.). 1998. per. 3.50 (0-373-35245-X, 1-35245-9) Harlequin Bks.
— The Magic of the Moon. large type ed. (Nightingale Series Large Print Bks.). 211p. 1992. pap. 14.95 (0-8161-5301-9, G K Hall Lrg Type) Mac Lib Ref.
— The Rancher & the Amnesiac Bride: Follow That Baby! (Special Edition Ser.: No. 1204). 1998. per. 4.25 (0-373-24204-2, 1-24204-9) Harlequin Bks.
***Pickart, Joan E.** Solo Amigos. (Deseo Ser.: No. 184).Tr. of Only Friends. (SPA.). 1999. per. 3.50 (0-373-35314-6, 1-35314-3) Harlequin Bks.
Pickart, Joan E. Taming Tall, Dark Brandon: The Bachelor Bet. (Desire Ser.: No. 1223). 1999. per. 3.75 (0-373-76223-2, 1-76223-6) Silhouette.
— Texas Baby: That's My Baby! (Special Edition Ser.: No. 1141). 1997. per. 3.99 (0-373-24141-0, 1-24141-3) Harlequin Bks.
— Texas Dawn. (Family Men Ser.). 1997. per. 3.99 (0-373-24100-3, 1-24100-9) Silhouette.
— Texas Glory. 1997. per. 3.50 (0-373-76088-4, 1-76088-3) Silhouette.
— Texas Moon. (Desire Ser.). 1997. per. 3.50 (0-373-76051-5, 1-76051-1) Silhouette.
— Tucker Boone. (Loveswept Ser.: No. 285). 192p. 1988. pap. 2.50 (0-318-32847-X) Bantam.
— Wife Most Wanted. 1998. per. 4.25 (0-373-24160-7, 1-24160-3) Silhouette.
***Pickart, Joan Elliott.** Baby: MacAllister-Made. (Desire Ser.: Bk. 1326). 2000. mass mkt. 3.99 (0-373-76326-3, 1-76326-7) Silhouette.
— The Baby Bet: His Secret Son. mass mkt. 5.99 (0-373-48409-7, 1-48409-6) Harlequin Bks.
Pickart, Joan Elliott. Father of Her Child. 1999. 21.95 (0-373-59603-0) Silhouette.
***Pickart, Joan Elliott.** Man... Mercenary... Monarch. (Special Edition Ser.: Vol. 130). 248p. 2000. per. 4.50 (0-373-24303-0) Silhouette.
— Mas Que un Recuerdo (More Than a Memory) Taming Tall, Dark Brandon. (Deseo Ser.: No. 195). (SPA.). 2000. per. 3.50 (0-373-35325-1, 1-35325-9) Silhouette.
Pickart, Joan Elliott. The Most Eligible M. D. The Bachelor Bet. (Special Edition Ser.). 1999. per. 4.25 (0-373-24262-X, 1-24262-7) Silhouette.
***Pickart, Joan Elliott.** To a MacAllister Born: The Baby Bet. (Special Edition Ser.: Bk. 1329). 2000. per. 4.50 (0-373-24329-4, 1-24329-4) Silhouette.
Pickart, Joan Elliott, jt. auth. see James, B. J.
Pickavat, Rairden, et al. Using WordPerfect 6: Special Edition. (Using... Ser.). (Illus.). 1196p. (Orig.). 1993. 29.95 (1-56529-077-1) Que.
Picke, Frank N., ed. see Benton, Gregor.
Pickel, Andreas, jt. auth. see Wiesenthal, Helmut.
Pickel, Birgit. Ethnicity & Identity in the Former Colored Areas in the Western Cape/South Africa: A Case Study in Mitchells Plain, Paarl & Piketberg. 136p. 1997. pap. text 19.95 (3-8258-3418-2, Pub. by CE24) Transaction Pubs.
Pickelhaupt, Bill. Shanghaied in San Francisco: Politics & Personalities. LC 96-96781. (Illus.). 270p. 1996. 29.95 (0-9647312-1-5); pap. 17.95 (0-9647312-2-3) Flyblister Pr.
Pickelhaupt, William R. Club Rowing on San Francisco Bay, 1869-1939, Featuring the South End Rowing Club. (Illus.). 132p. (Orig.). 1995. pap. 12.95 (0-9647312-0-7) Flyblister Pr.
***Pickell, Daniel & Daniel, D. M.** Extension Courses for Trading Commodities. (Traders Masterclass Ser.). (Illus.). 350p. 2000. 65.00 (0-273-64976-0, Pub. by F T P H) Trans-Atl Phila.
Pickell, David. Underwater Indonesia: A Guide to the World's Best Diving. 1993. pap. 15.95 (0-8442-9908-1, Passprt Bks) NTC Contemp Pub Co.
Pickell, David & Cooper, Mike, eds. Sulawesi: The Celebes. 2nd ed. 290p. 1995. pap. 19.95 (962-593-005-1) Periplus.
Pickell, David & Siagian, Wally. Diving Bali: A Guide to the World's Greatest Diving. (Action Guide Ser.). (Illus.). 224p. 2000. pap. 24.95 (962-593-323-9) Tuttle Pubng.
Pickell, David, ed. see Eiseman, Fred B., Jr.
Pickell, David, ed. see Muller, Kal.
Pickell, Garfield C., jt. auth. see Barrows, Howard S.
Pickell, Mark B., ed. Pipeline Infrastructure: Proceedings of the International Conference, San Antonio, Texas, August 16-17, 1993. LC 93-21532. 720p. 1993. 63.00 (0-87262-923-6) Am Soc Civil Eng.
— Pipelines in Adverse Environments II. 748p. 1983. 64.00 (0-87262-385-8) Am Soc Civil Eng.
***Pickell, Orren T.** Luxury Homes & Lifestyles: Elements for the New Millennium. 1999. per. 39.95 (0-9642057-4-2) Ashley Group.
Pickell, Paul, ed. Michigan Manufacturers Directory. rev. ed. Orig. Title: Directory of Michigan Manufacturers. 964p. 1999. 157.00 (0-936526-37-8) Pick Pub MI.
Pickell, William, ed. see Clausen, Barry & Pomeroy, Dana R.
Pickels, Dwayne E. Ancient & Annual Customs. LC 97-28788. (Looking into the Past). (Illus.). 64p. (YA). (gr. 5 up). 1999. lib. bdg. 16.95 (0-7910-4682-6) Chelsea Hse.
— Ancient Warriors. LC 98-29900. (Cultures, Customs & Traditions Ser.). (Illus.). 64p. 1998. 19.95 (0-7910-5166-8) Chelsea Hse.
***Pickels, Dwayne E.** Psychological Testing & What Those Tests Mean: Am I Okay? LC 99-30473. (Encyclopedia of Psychological Disorders Ser.). (Illus.). 144p. 1999. 24.95 (0-7910-5319-9) Chelsea Hse.
Pickels, Dwayne E. Roman Mythological Gods & Goddesses. LC 98-29113. (Cultures, Customs & Traditions Ser.). (Illus.). 64p. 1998. 16.95 (0-7910-5164-1) Chelsea Hse.
***Pickels, Dwayne E.** Shania Twain. LC 00-23680. (Overcoming Adversity Ser.). (Illus.). (YA). 2000. pap. write for info. (0-7910-5902-2) Chelsea Hse.
Picken, Andrew. The Sectarian: Or, the Church & the Meeting-House, 3 vols., 2 bks., 2. LC 79-8189. reprint ed. write for info. (0-404-62096-5) AMS Pr.
Picken, Fiona M., jt. auth. see Matthews, David A.
Picken, J. R. Creator, Protector, Destroyer: Discover That You Are God. LC 96-36849. (Illus.). 176p. 1997. pap. 12.95 (1-56718-522-3) Llewellyn Pubns.
Picken, Joseph C. & Dess, Gregory G. Mission Critical: The 7 Strategic Traps That Derail Even the Smartest Companies. LC 96-23782. 300p. 1996. text 29.95 (0-7863-0969-5, Irwn Prfssnl) McGraw-Hill Prof.
Picken, Joseph C., jt. auth. see Dess, Gregory G.
Picken, Laurence, ed. Musica Asiatica, No. 4. 280p. 1984. pap. text 80.00 (0-521-27837-6) Cambridge U Pr.
Picken, Laurence & Nickson, Noel. Music from the Tang Court 6. 308p. (C). 1997. text 85.00 (0-521-62100-3) Cambridge U Pr.
***Picken, Laurence E. R. & Nickson, Noel J., eds.** Music from the Tang Court 7: Some Ancient Connections Explored. (Illus.). 320p. (C). 2000. 89.95 (0-521-78084-5) Cambridge U Pr.
Picken, Mary B. A Dictionary of Costume & Fashion: Historic & Modern. unabridged ed. LC 98-30715. (Illus.). 446p. 1999. pap. 14.95 (0-486-40294-0) Dover.
— Old-Fashioned Ribbon Trimmings & Flowers. abr. ed. LC 93-2506. Orig. Title: Ribbon Trimmings & Flowers: Instruction Paper with Examination Questions. (Illus.). 48p. 1993. reprint ed. pap. 3.50 (0-486-27521-3) Dover.
Picken, Peter, ed. The Concert Performer Series: Bach - Prelude in C Major. 3p. 1999. pap. text 6.95 (0-8256-1731-6, AM948630) Music Sales.
— The Concert Performer Series: Bach - Two-Part Invention. 3p. 1999. pap. 6.95 (0-8256-1732-4, AM948640) Music Sales.
— The Concert Performer Series: Beethoven - Fur Elise. (Illus.). 3p. 1999. pap. text 6.95 (0-8256-1733-2, AM948657) Music Sales.
— The Concert Performer Series: Beethoven - Moonlight Sonata. (Illus.). 3p. 1999. pap. text 6.95 (0-8256-1734-0, AM948662) Music Sales.

P

An Asterisk (*) at the beginning of an entry indicates that the title is appearing for the first time.

— The Concert Performer Series: Brahms - Waltz in A Flat (Op 39, No. 15) 3p. 1999. pap. text 6.95 (0-8256-1738-3, AM948706) Music Sales.
— The Concert Performer Series: Chopin - Two Preludes (Op 28, Nos. 7 & 20) (Illus.). 3p. 1999. pap. text 6.95 (0-8256-1735-9, AM948673) Music Sales.
— The Concert Performer Series: Debussy - Clair de Lune. (Illus.). 3p. 1999. pap. 6.95 (0-8256-1736-7, AM948684) Music Sales.
— The Concert Performer Series: Elgar - Pomp & Circumstance. (Illus.). 3p. 1999. pap. text 6.95 (0-8256-1737-5, AM948695) Music Sales.
— The Concert Performer Series: MacDowell - To a Wild Rose. 3p. 1999. pap. text 6.95 (0-8256-1739-1, AM948717) Music Sales.
— The Concert Performer Series: Satie - Trois Gymnopedies. 3p. 1999. pap. text 6.95 (0-8256-1740-5, AM948728) Music Sales.
— The Concert Performer Series: Schubert - Moment Musicale. (Illus.). 3p. 1999. pap. text 6.95 (0-8256-1741-3, AM948139) Music Sales.
— The Concert Performer Series: Shumann - The Happy Farmer. 3p. 1999. pap. text 6.95 (0-8256-1742-1, AM948740) Music Sales.
Picken, Stuart D. B. Essentials of Shinto: An Analytical Guide to Principal Teachings. LC 93-40619. 440p. 1994. lib. bdg. 99.50 (0-313-26431-7, Greenwood Pr) Greenwood.
Pickenhagen, W., tr. see Ohloff, Gunther.
Pickenpaugh, Roger. Rescue by Rail: Troop Transfer & the Civil War in the West, 1863. LC 97-32444. (Illus.). 216p. 1998. 27.95 (0-8032-3720-0) U of Nebr Pr.
***Pickens.** Second Chances. (Signet Regency Romance Ser.). 224p. 2000. mass mkt. 4.99 (0-451-19821-2, Sig) NAL.
Pickens, Andrea. Code of Honor. (Signet Regency Romance Ser.). 224p. 1998. mass mkt. 4.99 (0-451-19546-9, Sig) NAL.
— Hired Hero. 224p. 1999. mass mkt. 4.99 (0-451-19692-9) NAL.
***Pickens, Andrea.** Lady of Letters. 2000. mass mkt. 4.99 (0-451-20170-1, Sig) NAL.
— Major's Mistake. (Regency Romance Ser.). 2000. mass mkt. 4.99 (0-451-20096-9) Signet.
Pickens, Buford, notes. The Missions of Northern Sonora: A 1935 Field Documentation Relating Piman Indians to the Material Culture of the Hispanic Southwest. LC 92-30728. (Southwest Center Ser.). (Illus.). 198p. (Orig.). 1993. pap. 15.95 (0-8165-1356-2); lib. bdg. 31.95 (0-8165-1342-2) U of Ariz Pr.
Pickens, Donald K. Eugenics & the Progressives. LC 68-28769. 272p. 1968. reprint ed. pap. 84.40 (0-608-01828-7, 206247700003) Bks Demand.
Pickens, Elaine E. Learn WordPerfect 5.1 Plus in a Day. (Popular Applications Ser.). 172p. (Orig.). 1995. pap. 15.95 incl. disk (1-55622-449-4) Wordware Pub.
— Learn WordPerfect Presentations in a Day. LC 93-45585. (Popular Applications Ser.). 136p. 1994. pap. 15.95 incl. disk (1-55622-362-5) Wordware Pub.
Pickens, J. W. Wizard's Compendium, Vol. 1. 1996. 25.00 (0-7869-0436-4, Pub. by TSR Inc) Random.
Pickens, James B. Arte de Cerrar un Trato. 1997. pap. text 13.98 (84-253-2481-5) Grijalbo Edit.
Pickens, James B., jt. auth. see Mitchell, John E.
Pickens, James W. The Art of Closing Any Deal. abr. ed. 1991. pap. 15.95 incl. audio (1-55927-163-9) Audio Renaissance.
Pickens, James W. The Art of Closing Any Deal: How to Be a Master Closer in Everything You Do. 1991. mass mkt. 14.99 (0-446-39098-4, Pub. by Warner Bks) Little.
— The Closers. (Illus.). 1988. reprint ed. pap. 19.95 (0-9620915-7-X) Cobra Pub.
Pickens, Jim. The Closers: Sales Closer's Bible. 2nd ed. Gay, Ben, III, ed. LC 87-81170. 320p. 1989. reprint ed. pap. 24.95 (0-942645-00-6) Hampton Books.
— The Closers: Sales Closer's Bible, 15 cass., Set. 2nd ed. Gay, Ben, III, ed. LC 87-81170. 1988. reprint ed. audio 99.95 (0-942645-01-4) Hampton Books.
Pickens, Jon. Priest's Spell. (AD&D Accessory Ser.). 1999. 24.95 (0-7869-1359-2, Pub. by TSR Inc) Random.
***Pickens, Jon.** Priest's Spell Compendium, Vol. 3. (AD & D Accessory Ser.). 288p. 2000. pap. 24.95 (0-7869-1611-7) TSR Inc.
Pickens, Jon. Wizard's Spell Compendium: Volume 2, Vol. 2. Middleton, Mark, ed. 1997. 24.95 (0-7869-0664-2, Pub. by TSR Inc) Random.
Pickens, Judy, ed. see Mittelstrass, Muriel.
Pickens, Kel, jt. auth. see Meyer, Carolyn.
Pickens, L. Self-Awareness & Drug Abuse & Drug Control. Zak, Therese A., ed. (Lifeworks Ser.). (Illus.). 128p. 1981. text 13.96 (0-07-049910-1) McGraw.
Pickens, R. Dan. Freddy the Flea. (Illus.). (J). (gr. 2-8). 1997. 20.00 (0-944551-15-7) Sundance Pr TX.
Pickens, Raymond, jt. auth. see Kanack, Alice K.
Pickens, Ricky. Chinese Ring Daggers: The Ultimate Close-Quarter Weapons. (Illus.). 104p. 1987. pap. 12.00 (0-87364-444-1) Paladin Pr.
Pickens, Roy, jt. ed. see Glantz, Meyer.
Pickens, Rupert T. The Welsh Knight: Paradoxicality in Chretien's Erec et Enide. LC 76-47499. (French Forum Monographs: No. 6). 163p. (Orig.). 1977. pap. 10.95 (0-917058-05-4) French Forum.
Pickens, Rupert T., ed. Chretien de Troyes: The Story of the Grail or Perceval (Li Contesd del Graal) Kibler, William W., tr. LC 90-3025. (Library of Medieval Literature: Vol. 62A). 576p. 1990. text 20.00 (0-8240-4599-8) Garland.
— The Sower & His Seed: Essays on Chretien de Troyes. LC 82-84402. (French Forum Monographs: No. 44). 164p. (Orig.). 1983. pap. 12.95 (0-917058-43-7) French Forum.
— Studies in Honor of Hans-Erich Keller: Medieval French & Occitan Literature & Romance Linguistics. LC 93-12695. (Studies in Medieval Culture). 1993. pap. 25.00 (1-879288-22-2); boxed set 45.00 (1-879288-21-4) Medieval Inst.
Pickens, Rupert T., jt. auth. see Rudel, Jaufre.
***Pickens, T. Boone.** The Luckiest Guy in the World. LC 00-31192. 2000. write for info. (1-58798-019-3) Beard Bks.
Pickens, William. American Aesop: Negro & Other Humor. LC 76-99888. reprint ed. 34.00 (0-404-00206-4) AMS Pr.
— New Negro, His Political, Civil & Mental Status & Related Essays. LC 72-95399. reprint ed. 21.50 (0-404-00271-4) AMS Pr.
— The Vengeance of the Gods: And Three Other Stories of Real American Color Line Life. LC 72-4612. (Black Heritage Library Collection). 1977. reprint ed. 21.95 (0-8369-9120-6) Ayer.
— The Vengeance of the Gods & Three Other Stories of Real American Color Line Life. LC 73-18564. reprint ed. 24.50 (0-404-11376-1) AMS Pr.
Pickens, William J., jt. auth. see Johnson, Ira J.
Picker, jt. auth. see Bernstein.
Picker, Fred. The Zone VI Workshop. (Illus.). 128p. 1978. 13.95 (0-8174-0574-7, Amphoto) Watsn-Guptill.
Picker, Martin, ed. The Motet Books of Andrea Antico. LC 85-754400. (Monuments of Renaissance Music Ser.: Vol. III). (Illus.). 456p. (C). 1987. lib. bdg. 120.00 (0-226-66796-0) U Ch Pr.
Picker, Rolf. Europaisches Wahrungssystem/ECU. (GER.). 227p. 1987. write for info. (3-487-07922-4) G Olms Pubs.
Pickerell, Cheryl, jt. auth. see Pickerell, Jim.
Pickerell, Jim & Pickerell, Cheryl. Negotiating Stock Photo Prices, 1997. 4th ed. 272p. 1997. pap. 30.00 (1-886469-04-0) Stock Connect.
Pickeri. The Use of Forensic Anthro. LC 97-187767. 192p. 1996. boxed set 74.95 (0-8493-8111-8) CRC Pr.
Pickering. History Experience & Culture Studies. LC 96-51470. 288p. 1997. text 55.00 (0-312-17345-8) St Martin.
Pickering, Danby & Finch, Henry. Law: or A Discourse Thereof: To Which Are Now Added, Notes & References & a Table to the Chapters, 4 bks. (Illus.). 528p. 1969. reprint ed. 22.50 (0-8377-2125-3, Rothman) W S Hein.
Pickering, A. D., ed. Stress & Fish. LC 81-67907. 1981. text 104.00 (0-12-554550-9) Acad Pr.
Pickering, A. D., et al, eds. Fish Stress & Health in Aquaculture. LC 96-44740. (Society for Experimental Biology Seminar Ser.: No. 62). (Illus.). 286p. (C). 1997. text 95.00 (0-521-55518-3) Cambridge U Pr.
Pickering, Alan D., jt. ed. see Black, Kenneth D.
Pickering, Andrew. Constructing Quarks: A Sociological History of Particle Physics. LC 84-235. xii, 480p. 1986. pap. text 26.00 (0-226-66799-5) U Ch Pr.
— Constructing Quarks: A Sociological History of Particle Physics. LC 84-235. xii, 468p. 1995. lib. bdg. 42.50 (0-226-66798-7) U Ch Pr.
***Pickering, Andrew.** Lancastrians to Tudors: England 1450-1509. (Perspectives in History Ser.). 160p. (C). 2000. pap. 12.95 (0-521-55746-1) Cambridge U Pr.
Pickering, Andrew. The Mangle of Practice: Time, Agency & Science. LC 94-44546. 296p. 1995. pap. text 17.95 (0-226-66803-7); lib. bdg. 45.00 (0-226-66802-9) U Ch Pr.
— Science as Practice & Culture. (Illus.). 482p. 1992. pap. text 24.95 (0-226-66801-0) U Ch Pr.
— Science as Practice & Culture. (Illus.). 482p. 1998. lib. bdg. 75.00 (0-226-66800-2) U Ch Pr.
Pickering, B. T., et al, eds. Neurosecretion: Cellular Aspects of the Production & Release of Neuropeptides. LC 88-12440. (Illus.). 282p. 1988. 75.00 (0-306-42919-5, Plenum Trade) Perseus Pubng.
Pickering, Brooke, et al. Moroccan Carpets. (Illus.). 160p. 1998. 75.00 (1-85669-146-2) L King Pubng.
Pickering, C. A. & Jones, W. P. Health & Hygienic Humidification. (C). 1986. pap. 120.00 (0-86022-104-0, Pub. by Build Servs Info Assn) St Mut.
Pickering, C. M. Chronological History of Plants (Man's Records) 1222p. (C). 1986. reprint ed. pap. 1250.00 (81-7089-042-X, Pub. by Intl Bk Distr) St Mut.
***Pickering, Chris.** E-Business Success Strategies: Achieving Business & IT Alignment. LC 99-88568. (Illus.). 220p. 2000. pap. 295.00 (1-56607-081-3) Comput Tech Res.
Pickering, Cindy. A Study Guide for Orientation & Terminology. 3rd ed. Adams, Barbara, ed. 76p. 1998. pap. text, student ed., wbk. ed. 17.00 (0-87939-151-0, 36250) IFSTA.
***Pickering, Cindy.** Study Guide for the 6th Edition of Fire & Emergency Services Instructor. 116p. 2000. pap. write for info. (0-87939-172-3) IFSTA.
Pickering, Cindy, jt. auth. see Hilley, Robert.
Pickering, Cindy, jt. auth. see Joerschke, John.
Pickering, Cindy, ed. see Joerschke, John.
Pickering, David. Cassell Companion to 20th-Century Music. 416p. 1998. pap. 19.95 (0-304-35099-0) Sterling.
— Cassell Dicationary of Witchcraft. (Illus.). 320p. 1998. pap. 16.95 (0-304-35098-2) Continuum.
— The Cassell Dictionary of Abbreviations. 352p. 1998. pap. 14.95 (0-304-35033-8) Sterling.
— Cassell Soccer Companion. 1998. pap. text 14.95 (0-304-34930-5) Continuum.
***Pickering, David.** The Dictionary of Folklore. 320p. 1999. 29.95 (0-304-34786-8) Continuum.
— Dictionary of Folklore. (Illus.). 2000. 40.00 (0-8160-4250-0) Facts on File.
— The Ultimate Star Wars Episode I Sticker Book. (Star Wars Ser.). (Illus.). 8p. (J). (gr. 3-7). 1999. pap. 6.95 (0-7894-3964-6) DK Pub Inc.
Pickering, David, ed. International Dictionary of Theatre Vol. 3: Actors, Directors, & Designers, Vol. 3. (Illus.). 830p. 1995. 140.00 (1-55862-097-4, 200108) St James Pr.
***Pickering, David & Falls, Judy.** Brush Men & Vigilantes: Civil War Dissent in Texas. LC 99-45093. (Sam Rayburn Series on Rural Life). (Illus.). 240p. 2000. 24.95 (0-89096-923-X) Tex A&M Univ Pr.
Pickering, David F., et al. Utility Mapping & Record Keeping for Infrastructure. LC 93-10646. (Urban Management Program Ser.: No. 10). 86p. 1993. pap. 22.00 (0-8213-2426-8, 12426) World Bank.
Pickering, Deborah. Putting Process into Practice. 241p. (C). 1991. pap. text 35.40 (0-673-38066-1) Addson-Wesley Educ.
Pickering, Debra J., jt. auth. see Marzano, Robert J.
Pickering, Des. Resources for People with Special Needs, 1994. 247p. 1995. pap. 80.00 (0-909184-43-7, Pub. by Deakin Univ) St Mut.
Pickering, Ernest. El Espiritu del Dios Vivo. Meyer, Richard, ed. (Adult Sunday School Ser.). (SPA.). 97p. 1991. 4.40 (1-879892-05-7) Editorial Bautista.
Pickering, Ernest D. Biblical Separation: The Struggle for a Pure Church. LC 78-26840. 259p. 1979. reprint ed. pap. 9.99 (0-87227-069-6, RBP5075) Reg Baptist.
— Charismatic Confusion. 23p. 1980. reprint ed. pap. 2.99 (0-87227-196-X, RBP5089) Reg Baptist.
— For the Hurting Pastor: And Those Who Hurt Him. LC 87-20622. 47p. (Orig.). 1987. reprint ed. pap. 4.99 (0-87227-121-8, RBP5148) Reg Baptist.
Pickering, F. B., ed. see American Society for Metals Staff.
Pickering, Fran. The Element Illustrated Encyclopedia of Animals in Nature, Myth & Spirit. (Illus.). 160p. (YA). (gr. 5 up). 1999. text 21.95 (1-901881-84-9, Pub. by Element MA) Penguin Putnam.
Pickering, Frederick P. Essays on Medieval German Literature & Iconography. LC 78-73815. (Anglica Germanica Ser.: No. 2). 240p. reprint ed. pap. 68.40 (0-608-15764-3, 2031707) Bks Demand.
Pickering, George. The Law & Theory of Trademarks. 256p. 1998. 70.00 (1-901362-64-7, Pub. by Hart Pub) Northwestern U Pr.
Pickering, George, et al. JavaScript How To. 650p. 1996. 44.99 (1-57169-047-6) Sams.
Pickering, Glenn. Being a Gentle-Man. 177p. 1997. reprint ed. pap. 19.95 (0-9656780-0-8, Gentle-Man Ntwrk) Helping Ourselves.
Pickering, Henry, ed. Chief Men among the Brethren. LC 96-13526. (Powerscourt Classic Library). 405p. 1995. text 18.99 (0-87213-798-8) Loizeaux.
***Pickering-Iazzi, Robin.** I Like Chocolate. LC 00-20921. (Good Food Ser.). (Illus.). 24p. (J). (ps-3). 2000. pap. 4.95 (0-516-23008-5) Childrens.
Pickering-Iazzi, Robin. Politics of the Visible: Writing Women, Culture, & Fascism. 240p. (C). 1997. pap. 21.95 (0-8166-2923-4); text 54.95 (0-8166-2922-6) U of Minn Pr.
Pickering-Iazzi, Robin, ed. Mothers of Invention: Women, Italian Fascism, & Culture. 280p. 1995. pap. 19.95 (0-8166-2651-0); text 49.95 (0-8166-2650-2) U of Minn Pr.
Pickering-Iazzi, Robin, ed. Unspeakable Women: Selected Short Stories Written by Italian Women During Fascism. LC 93-13534. 140p. 1993. 35.00 (1-55861-062-6); pap. 14.95 (1-55861-063-4) Feminist Pr.
Pickering-Iazzi, Robin & Baldassaro, Lawrence. In Terza Pagina. LC 88-12834. (ITA.). 224p. (C). 1989. pap. text 40.00 (0-03-013687-3) Harcourt Coll Pubs.
Pickering, J. B., jt. auth. see Rosner, B. S.
Pickering, J. F. Resale Price Maintenance in Practice. LC 66-78485. 236p. 1966. 35.00 (0-678-06025-8) Kelley.
Pickering, J. F. & Cockerill, T. A., eds. The Economic Management of the Firm. LC 84-11098. (Illus.). 432p. 1984. 57.00 (0-389-20495-1, N8058) B&N Imports.
Pickering, James H. Fiction 50: An Introduction to the Short Story. (Illus.). 736p. (C). 1992. pap. text 26.80 (0-02-395555-4, Macmillan Coll) P-H.
— Fiction Fifty: An Introduction to the Short Story. abr. ed. (Illus.). 736p. (C). 1992. teacher ed. write for info. (0-318-69333-X) Macmillan.
***Pickering, James H.** Fiction 100: An Anthology of Short Stories. 8th ed. 1999. pap. 50.00 (0-13-780305-2) P-H.
— Fiction 100: An Anthology of Short Stories. 9th ed. LC 99-89572. 2001. write for info. (0-13-014321-9) P-H.
— Fiction 100: An Anthology of Short Stories. 9th ed. 1500p. 2000. pap. 44.00 (0-13-014328-6) Prntice Hall Bks.
— Mr. Stanley of Estes Park. LC 00-40051. 2000. pap. write for info. (1-886727-05-8) Stanley Mus.
— "This Blue Hollow" Estes Park, The Early Years, 1859-1915. LC 99-41476. 360p. 1999. 29.95 (0-87081-528-8) Univ Pr Colo.
Pickering, James H., ed. Fiction 100: An Anthology of Short Stories with Reader's Guide. 8th ed. LC 97-15407. 1506p. (C). 1997. pap. 51.00 (0-13-755092-8) P-H.
Pickering, James H. & Hoeper, Jeffrey D., compiled by. Literature. 5th ed. LC 96-7112. 1951p. 1996. pap. text 57.00 (0-13-226770-5) P-H.
Pickering, James H., ed. see Cooper, James Fenimore.
Pickering, Jean, jt. ed. see Kehde, Suzanne.
Pickering, Jeffrey. Britain's Withdrawal from East of Suez: The Politics of Retrenchment. LC 98-4957. (Contemporary History in Context Ser.). 231p. 1998. text. write for info. (0-312-21436-7) St Martin.
Pickering, Jim. Soldier of the Sixth. 200p. (C). 1989. text 60.00 (1-85821-010-0, Pub. by Pentland Pr) St Mut.
Pickering, John. The Drummer's Cook Book. 80p. 1972. pap. 9.95 (0-87166-826-2, 93301) Mel Bay.
— The Interlude of Vice. LC 73-133720. (Tudor Facsimile Texts. Old English Plays Ser.: No. 37). reprint ed. 59.50 (0-404-53337-X) AMS Pr.
— Routes of the Valkyries. 94p. (C). 1987. 49.00 (0-902633-43-0, Pub. by Picton) St Mut.
— Studio-Jazz Drum Cookbook. 96p. 1979. pap. 11.95 (0-87166-682-0, 93625) Mel Bay.
— Working Man's Political Economy, Founded upon the Principle of Immutable Justice & the Inalienable Rights of Man: Designed for the Promotion of National Reform. LC 79-156421. (American Labor Ser., No. 2). 1977. reprint ed. 21.95 (0-405-02940-3) Ayer.
Pickering, John, ed. The Authority of Experience: Readings on Buddhism & Psychology. LC 97-128167. (Curzon Studies in Asian Philosophy). 260p. (C). 1998. text 42.00 (0-7007-0450-7, Pub. by Curzon Pr Ltd); pap. text 22.95 (0-7007-0455-8, Pub. by Curzon Pr Ltd) UH Pr.
Pickering, John & Skinner, Martin. From Sentience to Symbols: Readings on Consciousness. 331p. 1991. text 60.00 (0-8020-2795-4); pap. text 18.95 (0-8020-6856-1) U of Toronto Pr.
Pickering, Julie, tr. see Chong-jun, Yi.
Pickering, Julie, tr. see Sun-Won, Hwang.
Pickering, Julie, tr. see Sun-won, Hwang.
Pickering, K. T. & Owen, Lewis A. An Introduction to Global Environmental Issues. 2nd ed. LC 96-42364. (Illus.). 576p. (C). 1997. 110.00 (0-415-14098-6) Routledge.
Pickering, K. T., et al. Deep Marine Environments: Clastic Sedimentation & Tectonics. (Illus.). 352p. 1989. 130.00 (0-04-551122-5) Routledge.
— Deep Marine Environments: Clastic Sedimentation & Tectonics. (Illus.). 352p. 1990. pap. 91.50 (0-04-445201-2) Thomson Learn.
Pickering, K. T., jt. ed. see Whateley, M. K.
***Pickering, Kathleen Ann.** Echoes of Love. 1999. 6.99 (1-57343-015-3) LionHearted.
— Lakota Culture, World Economy. LC 00-23482. (Illus.). 224p. 2000. text 39.95 (0-8032-3690-5) U of Nebr Pr.
Pickering, Ken. Beowulf: A Rock Musical. (Illus.). 42p. (Orig.). (YA). (gr. 7 up). 1986. pap. 4.50 (0-88680-248-2) I E Clark.
— Ring of Lead: A Play in One Act. 10p. (J). 1997. pap. 2.50 (0-88680-445-0) I E Clark.
— Snow White & the Seven Dwarfs (a Play in Eleven Scenes) A Musical Play for Children of All Ages. (Illus.). 38p. (J). 1996. pap. 4.50 (0-88680-425-6) I E Clark.
Pickering, Ken, et al. The Inside Story: An Ecological Warning. 24p. (J). 1992. pap. 4.00 (0-88680-371-3) I E Clark.
Pickering, Ken, jt. auth. see Sunderland, Margot.
Pickering, Kenneth. Drama Improvised: A Source Book for Teachers & Therapists. 2nd ed. LC 97-18164. 1997. pap. write for info. (0-87830-066-X) Routledge.
— Drama Improvised: Source Book for Teachers & Therapists. 2nd ed. LC 97-18164. 112p. 1997. pap. 13.99 (0-415-91968-1) Routledge.
Pickering, Kenneth, jt. auth. see Herzog, Michael.
Pickering, Kenneth, jt. auth. see Sugano, Douglas.
Pickering, Kevin T. & Owen, Lewis A. An Introduction to Global Environmental Issues. 2nd ed. (Illus.). 576p. (C). 1997. pap. 29.99 (0-415-14099-4) Routledge.
Pickering, Leslie. The Liberal: Lord Byron, Leigh Hunt & the Liberal. LC 68-763. (Studies in Byron: No. 5). 1972. lib. bdg. 75.00 (0-8383-0609-8) M S G Haskell Hse.
Pickering, Lulu, et al. Resource Informagen: Biotechnology Information Resource, 3 vols. Incl. Companies Vol. 1: United States A-H. Pickering, Marjorie. LC 97-77401. 1998. 375.00 (1-891537-00-8); Companies Vol. 2: United States I-Z. Pickering, Marorie. LC 97-77401. 1998. 375.00 (1-891537-01-6); Index Vol. 3: United States. Pickering, Marorie. LC 97-77401. 1998. 225.00 (1-891537-02-4); LC 97-77401. 975.00 (1-891537-03-2) Informagen.
Pickering, Marianne. Lessons for Life: Education & Learning. Steinhorn, Beth, ed. LC 94-47413. (Our Human Family Ser.). (Illus.). 80p. (YA). (gr. 7 up). 1995. lib. bdg. 22.45 (1-56711-127-0) Blackbirch.
Pickering, Marisue, jt. ed. see Crago, Martha B.
Pickering, Martin & Ross, Michael. Pedigrees of Leading Winners, 1981-1984. 198p. 1990. 120.00 (0-85131-413-9, Pub. by J A Allen) St Mut.
— Pedigrees of Leading Winners, 1981-1984. 194p. 1986. 65.00 (0-8131-1601-5) U Pr of Ky.
Pickering, Martin, jt. ed. see Garrod, Simon.
Pickering, Mary. Auguste Comte: An Intellectual Biography, Vol. 1. LC 92-44510. 790p. (C). 1993. text 54.95 (0-521-43405-X) Cambridge U Pr.
Pickering, Mary, ed. see Emery, Bruce.
***Pickering, Mel.** Picture Reference Atlas. (Illus.). 2000. pap. 7.95 (1-58728-651-3) Two Can Pub.
Pickering, Mel, jt. auth. see Solway, Andrew.
Pickering, Mel, jt. illus. see Quigley, Sebastian.
Pickering, Michael & Green, Tony. Everyday Culture: Popular Song & the Vernacular Milieu. (Popular Music in Britain Ser.). 244p. 1988. 123.00 (0-335-15289-9) OpUniv Pr.
Pickering, Michael, et al. Researching Communications: A Practical Guide to Methods in Media & Cultural Analysis. LC 98-44900. (Arnold Publications). (Illus.). 448p. 1999. pap. text 24.95 (0-340-59685-6) OUP.
Pickering, Michael G. Woman's Self-Defense. LC 78-22054. (Illus.). 144p. 1979. pap. 5.95 (0-89037-166-0) Anderson World.
Pickering, Neil, jt. ed. see Evans, Donald.
Pickering, O. S., ed. Individuality & Achievement in Middle English Poetry. LC 96-44578. 240p. 1997. 75.00 (0-85991-424-0) Boydell & Brewer.
Pickering, O. S. & O'Mara, V. M., eds. The Index of Middle English Prose: Handlist XIII: Lambeth Palace Library, Vol. 13. LC 99-20119. (Index of Middle English Prose Ser.: Vol. 0267-2472). 192p. 1999. 60.00 (0-85991-547-6) Boydell & Brewer.

P

An Asterisk (*) at the beginning of an entry indicates that the title is appearing for the first time.

Pickering, O. S. & Powell, Susan. The Index of Middle English Prose Handlist VI: Manuscripts Containing Middle English Prose in Yorkshire Libraries & Archives. 99p. 1989. 55.00 (*0-85991-276-0*) Boydell & Brewer.

Pickering, Paul A. Chartism & Chartists in Manchester & Salford. LC 95-8228. 1995. text 69.95 (*0-312-12727-8*) St Martin.

***Pickering, Paul A. & Tyrell, Alex.** The People's Bread: A History of the Anti-Corn Law League. LC 00-24647. 2000. write for info. (*0-7185-0218-3*, Pub. by Leicester U Pr) Cassell & Continuum.

Pickering, Robert. Lautreamont: Image, Theme & Self-Identity. 88p. 1993. 39.00 (*0-85261-289-3*, Pub. by Univ of Glasgow) St Mut.

Pickering, Robert B. The People. LC 95-3046. (Prehistoric North America Ser.). (Illus.). 48p. (J). (gr. 2-4). 1996. lib. bdg. 21.90 (*1-56294-550-5*) Millbrook Pr.

— Seeing the White Buffalo. LC 97-7411. (Illus.). 160p. 1997. pap. 16.95 (*1-55566-182-3*) Johnson Bks.

***Pickering, Robin.** I Like Bagels. (Welcome Bks.). (Illus.). (J). 2000. 13.50 (*0-516-23081-6*) Childrens.

— I Like Bagels. LC 00-24371. (Good Food Ser.). (Illus.). 24p. (J). (ps-2). 2000. pap. write for info. (*0-516-23006-9*) Childrens.

— I Like Cheese. (Welcome Bks.). (Illus.). (J). 2000. 13.50 (*0-516-23082-4*) Childrens.

— I Like Cheese. LC 00-24372. (Good Food Ser.). (Illus.). 24p. (J). (ps-2). 2000. pap. write for info. (*0-516-23007-7*) Childrens.

— I Like Chocolate. (Welcome Bks.). (Illus.). (J). 2000. 13.50 (*0-516-23083-2*) Childrens.

— I Like Corn. (Welcome Bks.). (Illus.). (J). 2000. 13.50 (*0-516-23084-0*) Childrens.

— I Like Corn. LC 00-24373. (Good Food Ser.). (Illus.). 24p. (J). (ps-2). 2000. pap. write for info. (*0-516-23009-3*) Childrens.

— I Like Ice Cream. (Welcome Bks.). (Illus.). (J). 2000. 13.50 (*0-516-23085-9*) Childrens.

— I Like Ice Cream. LC 00-24374. (Good Food Ser.). (Illus.). 24p. (J). (ps-2). 2000. pap. write for info. (*0-516-23010-7*) Childrens.

— I Like Oranges. LC 00-24620. (Good Food Ser.). (Illus.). 24p. (J). (ps-3). 2000. pap. 4.95 (*0-516-23011-5*) Childrens.

— I Like Oranges. (Welcome Bks.). (Illus.). (J). 2000. 13.50 (*0-516-23086-7*) Childrens.

Pickering, Sam. Deprived of Unhappiness: Essays. LC 98-24080. 176p. 1998. 24.95 (*0-8214-1234-5*) Ohio U Pr.

— A Little Fling & Other Essays. LC 99-6208. 196p. 1999. 26.00 (*1-57233-062-7*, Pub. by U of Tenn Pr) U Ch Pr.

— Living to Prowl. LC 97-18691. 192p. 1998. 24.95 (*0-8203-1940-6*) U of Ga Pr.

— Trespassing. 14.95 (*1-875560-30-0*, Pub. by Univ of West Aust Pr) Intl Spec Bk.

Pickering, Samuel. The Moral Tradition in English Fiction, 1785-1850. LC 74-12540. 194p. reprint ed. pap. 60.20 (*0-7837-0380-5*, 204070000018) Bks Demand.

Pickering, Samuel F. The Blue Caterpillar & Other Essays. LC 96-33049. 229p. 1997. 24.95 (*0-8130-1482-4*) U Press Fla.

— A Continuing Education. LC 85-40492. 176p. Date not set. reprint ed. pap. 54.60 (*0-608-20689-X*, 207179700002) Bks Demand.

— John Locke & Children's Books in Eighteenth-Century England. fac. ed. LC 80-24899. (Illus.). 300p. pap. 93.00 (*0-7837-7359-5*, 204716800005) Bks Demand.

Pickering, Samuel F., Jr. Let It Ride. 192p. (C). 1991. 24.95 (*0-8262-0801-0*) U of Mo Pr.

— Let It Ride. 192p. 1992. reprint ed. pap. 14.95 (*0-8262-0869-X*) U of Mo Pr.

— May Days. LC 87-34292. 208p. 1988. reprint ed. pap. 14.95 (*0-87745-522-8*) U of Iowa Pr.

— Still Life. LC 89-28605. 240p. 1990. pap. 17.95 (*0-87451-561-0*) U Pr of New Eng.

Pickering, Samuel F. Trespassing. LC 93-38325. 262p. reprint ed. pap. 81.30 (*0-608-09092-1*, 206972600005) Bks Demand.

Pickering, Samuel F., Jr. Walkabout Year: Twelve Months in Australia. (Illus.). 344p. (Orig.). (C). 1995. pap. 19.95 (*0-8262-1043-0*) U of Mo Pr.

Pickering, Sharon & Thompson, Jeanette. Promoting Positive Practice in Nursing Older People. (Illus.). 315p. 1998. pap. write for info. (*0-7020-2080-X*) Bailliere Tindall.

Pickering, Susan E., jt. auth. see Ackerman, Robert J.

Pickering, Thomas. Good News about High Blood Pressure. 1997. per. 12.00 (*0-684-83211-9*, Fireside) S&S Trade Pap.

— Good News about High Blood Pressure: Everything You Need to Know to Take Control of Hypertension...& Your Life. 352p. 1996. 22.50 (*0-684-81396-3*) S&S Trade.

Pickering, W. A. Pioneering in Formosa. 1993. reprint ed. 35.00 (*957-638-163-0*) Oriental Bk Store.

Pickering, W. F. Modern Analytical Chemistry. LC 77-138500. 634p. (C). reprint ed. 196.60 (*0-8357-9087-8*, 205500800007) Bks Demand.

Pickering, W. R., ed. Information Sources in Pharmaceuticals. (Guides to Information Sources Ser.). 528p. 1990. lib. bdg. 100.00 (*0-408-02518-2*) Bowker-Saur.

Pickering, W. R., jt. auth. see Landreau, Anthony N.

Pickering, W. S. Durkheim's Sociology of Religion: Themes & Theories. 576p. 1984. 65.00 (*0-7100-9218-9*, Routledge Thoemms) Routledge.

Pickering, W. S., jt. ed. see Walford, Geoffrey.

Pickering, W. S. F. Durkheim & Representations LC 99-24304. (Studies in Social & Political Thought). 1999. text. write for info. (*0-415-19090-8*) Routledge.

***Pickering, W. S. F.** Emile Durkheim: Critical Assessments. LC 00-42477. 2000. write for info. (*0-415-20560-3*) Routledge.

Pickering, W. S. F., ed. see Durkheim, Emile.

Pickering, William. Anglo-Catholicism. 320p. 1989. 59.95 (*0-415-01343-7*, A3475) Routledge.

— Annual Message of the Governor of Washington Territory, Delivered December 17th, 1862. 12p. 1972. pap. 2.95 (*0-87770-098-2*) Ye Galleon.

Pickering, William F. Pollution Evaluation: The Quantitative Aspects. LC 77-12910. (Environmental Science & Technology Ser.: Vol. 2). (Illus.). 207p. reprint ed. pap. 64.20 (*0-608-08974-5*, 206960900005) Bks Demand.

Pickering, William S. & Martins, Hermino, eds. Debating Durkheim. LC 93-46095. 288p. (C). (gr. 13). 1994. 90.00 (*0-415-07720-6*, B3473) Routledge.

Pickersgill, B. & Lock, M. J. Advances in Legume Systematics Pt. 8: Legumes of Economic Importance. viii, 142p. 1996. pap. 24.00 (*1-900347-08-3*, Pub. by Royal Botanic Grdns) Balogh.

Pickersgill, David. The 1998 Competition Act Explained. LC 99-210002. (Point of Law Ser.). 1999. 50.00 (*0-11-702683-2*, Pub. by Statnry Office) Balogh.

Pickersgill, David & Stanton, Tony. Making Sense of NHS Complaints & Disciplinary Procedures. LC 97-1119. 1997. write for info. (*1-85775-163-9*, Radcliffe Med Pr) Scovill Paterson.

Pickersgill, Frank. Making of a Secret Agent. Ford, George H., ed. (Illus.). 274p. 1978. mass mkt. 5.95 (*0-88780-123-4*, Pub. by Formac Publ Co) Formac Dist Ltd.

Pickersgill, Harold E., jt. ed. see Wall, John P.

Pickersgill, J. W. My Years with Louis St. Laurent: A Political Memoir. LC 75-24675. (Illus.). 352p. reprint ed. pap. 109.20 (*0-8357-8239-5*, 203400800088) Bks Demand.

— The Road Back: By a Liberal in Opposition. 255p. 1986. text 30.00 (*0-8020-2598-6*) U of Toronto Pr.

Pickersgill, J. W. & Forster, Donald F., eds. The Mackenzie King Record, 1945-1946, Vol. 3. 424p. 1970. text 75.00 (*0-8020-1713-4*) U of Toronto Pr.

— The Mackenzie King Record, 1947-48, Vol. 4. 338p. 1990. text 75.00 (*0-8020-1714-2*) U of Toronto Pr.

Pickert, Diane. I Don't Like Turkey Noodle Soup. (Illus.). 28p. (J). 1998. pap. 6.95 (*1-885206-63-1*) Cader Pubng.

Pickert, G. Projektive Ebenen. 2nd ed. LC 75-9953. (Grundlehren der Mathematischen Wissenschaften Ser.: Vol. 80). (Illus.). 371p. 1975. 108.95 (*0-387-07280-2*) Spr-Verlag.

Pickert, Perry L. Intelligence for Multilateral Decision & Action. Swenson, Russell G., ed. LC 97-72395. (Illus.). 600p. 1997. pap. 85.00 (*0-9656195-0-8*, PB98-101983INF) Joint Military.

Pickert, Sarah M. Preparing for a Global Community: Achieving an International Perspective in Higher Education. Fife, Jonathan D., ed. LC 92-85442. (ASHE-ERIC Higher Education Reports: No. 92-2). 94p. 1992. 24.00 (*1-878380-15-X*) GWU Grad Schl E&HD.

Picket, William. The Generic Pizza Tastes Great. 1993. pap. text 23.00 (*0-685-70618-4*) P-H.

Pickett. The Acoustics of Speech Communication: Fundamentals, Speech Perception Theory & Technology. LC 98-38945. 404p. 1998. 64.00 (*0-205-19887-2*) Allyn.

— At Home in Two Lands. 246p. (J). 1991. mass mkt. 15.00 (*0-8384-3019-8*) Heinle & Heinle.

— Salsa. 1999. pap. text, wbk. ed. 13.33 (*0-13-020430-7*) P-H.

— Salsa Is Hot Student. LC 98-49581. 192p. 1999. pap. text 20.40 (*0-13-020436-6*) P-H.

Pickett, jt. auth. see Lynch.

Pickett, Adrian. Hybrid Wheat. Results & Problems. 1993. 57.00 (*3-8263-2696-2*, Pub. by Blckwell Wissenschafts) Balogh.

Pickett, Albert J. History of Alabama: And Incidentally of Georgia & Mississippi from the Earliest Period. 2nd ed. 822p. 1997. reprint ed. lib. bdg. 90.00 (*0-8328-6591-5*) Higginson Bk Co.

— History of Alabama, & Incidentally of Georgia & Mississippi, from the Earliest Period, 2 vols. LC 76-146410. (First American Frontier Ser.). (Illus.). 1971. reprint ed. 58.95 (*0-405-02872-5*) Ayer.

***Pickett, Albert J.** McGillivray & McIntosh Traders: On the Old Southwest Frontier, 1716-1815. 450p. 2000. pap. 23.95 (*1-57966-025-8*, Black Belt) Black Belt Communs.

— Pickett's History of Alabama: And Incidentally of Georgia & Mississippi from the Earliest. (Illus.). 686p. 1999. pap. 23.95 (*1-880216-67-1*, Black Belt) Black Belt Communs.

***Pickett, Albert James.** History of Alabama: And Incidentally of Georgia & Mississippi, from the Earliest Period. 773p. 2000. reprint ed. pap. 55.00 (*0-8063-4989-1*, Pub. by Clearfield Co) ACCESS Pubs Network.

Pickett, Anna L. & Gerlach, Kent, eds. Supervising Paraeducators in School Settings: A Team Approach. LC 96-46625. 254p. 1997. pap. text 29.00 (*0-89079-713-7*) PRO-ED.

Pickett, Anola. Old Enough for Magic. LC 88-30320. (I Can Read Bks.). (Illus.). 64p. (J). (ps-3). 1989. 13.00 (*0-06-024731-2*) HarpC Child Bks.

***Pickett, Bertha.** Songs of Praise. 2000. write for info. (*1-58235-498-7*) Watermrk Pr.

Pickett, Beth. 50 Nifty Things to Do after School. LC 95-22227. (Illus.). 64p. (J). 1995. pap. 5.95 (*1-56565-276-2*) Lowell Hse.

— Shark Attack Almanac. LC 96-42324. (Illus.). (J). 1997. pap. 5.99 (*0-679-87769-X*, Pub. by Random Bks Yng Read) Random.

Pickett, Beth Kneeland. 50 Nifty Super Things to do After School. LC 98-66658. (Fifty Nifty Super Ser.). (Illus.). 80p. (J). (gr. 3-7). 1998. pap. 6.95 (*1-56565-686-5*, 06865W, Pub. by Lowell Hse Juvenile) NTC Contemp Pub Co.

Pickett, Bob, jt. auth. see Allman, Sheldon.

Pickett, Bob, jt. auth. see Brown, J. D.

Pickett, Brian. The Heart of Love: Prayers of German Women Mystics. 132p. (C). 1996. pap. 39.95 (*0-85439-366-8*, Pub. by St Paul Pubns) St Mut.

Pickett, Carolyn, jt. auth. see Pfisterer, Susan.

Pickett, Cecil, ed. see Shakespeare, William.

Pickett, Charles H. Enhancing Biological Control: Habitat Management to Promote Natural Enemies of Agricultural Pest. LC 95-48418. 1998. 50.00 (*0-520-21362-9*, Pub. by U CA Pr) Cal Prin Full Svc.

Pickett, Christine, ed. see Wright, J. Allen.

Pickett, Christopher M. Patent Law Index. LC 97-154257. (Orig.). 1997. pap. 75.00 (*1-57018-033-4*, 1033) BNA Books.

Pickett, Debra, jt. auth. see Byham, William.

Pickett, Debra, jt. auth. see Byham, William C.

***Pickett, Deitra D.** My Child's Medical Journal. rev. ed. Orig. Title: Innocence...a Child's Medical Portfolio. 2000. spiral bd. write for info. (*0-9655577-1-5*) Princess Pubns.

Pickett, Douglas. Early Persian Tilework: The Medieval Flowering of Kashi. LC 88-46224. (Illus.). 248p. 1997. 95.00 (*0-8386-3365-X*) Fairleigh Dickinson.

Pickett, Elizabeth, ed. see Wood, Francis E.

Pickett, Elizabeth, ed. see Wood, Francis Eugene.

Pickett, Evelyne, jt. ed. see Schwantes, Carlos A.

***Pickett, Fuchsia.** Deborah: Empowered by the Spirit to Fulfill God's Purposes. LC 98-94938. (SpiritLed Woman Bible Study Ser.). 96p. 1999. pap. 6.99 (*0-88419-586-4*) Creation House.

— Esther: Unfolding God's Plan to Redeem His Bride. LC 98-94936. (SpiritLed Woman Bible Study Ser.). 96p. 1999. pap. 6.99 (*0-88419-584-8*) Creation House.

Pickett, Fuchsia. For Such a Time as This: A Prophetic View of the Church in Esther. 1997. pap. 9.99 (*0-88419-520-1*) Creation House.

— How to Search the Scriptures. LC 98-53968. 1999. pap. 12.99 (*0-88419-587-2*) Creation House.

— The Next Move of God. pap. 9.99 (*0-88419-384-5*) Creation House.

— Presenting the Holy Spirit. (Orig.). 1997. 15.99 (*0-88419-518-X*) Creation House.

— The Prophetic Romance. 154p. (Orig.). 1996. pap. 10.99 (*0-88419-423-X*) Creation House.

— Receiving Divine Revelation. LC 96-85037. 180p. 1999. pap. 10.99 (*0-88419-441-8*) Dake Pub.

Pickett, Fuchsia. Revelacion Divina. (SPA.). 1996. pap. 8.99 (*0-88419-551-1*) Casa Creacion.

— Ruth: The Bridegroom's Love for the Church Revealed. LC 98-94937. (SpiritLed Woman Bible Study Ser.). 96p. 1999. pap. 6.99 (*0-88419-585-6*) Creation House.

— Worship Him! Discover the Thrill of Pure Spiritual Worship. LC 99-58696. 208p. 2000. pap. 12.99 (*0-88419-723-9*) Creation House.

Pickett, Fuchsia T. Stones of Remembrance: How Twelve Visitations of the Holy Spirit One Woman's Life. LC 98-9320. 168p. 1998. pap. 12.99 (*0-88419-538-4*) Creation House.

Pickett, Fuschia, et al. Spirit-Led Reader. LC 98-41148. 1998. 9.99 (*0-88419-595-3*) Creation House.

Pickett, George. The Heart of a Soldier: The Intimate Letters of General George Pickett, CSA to His Wife. 2nd ed. Pickett, LaSalle C., ed. (Illus.). 215p. 1996. reprint ed. pap. 12.95 (*1-879664-24-0*) Stan Clark Military.

"The letters composing this book begin in 1861, when the then Captain George Pickett resigned his commission in the United States Army & threw in his lot with the Southern cause. They continue through the war & at the end a few undated ones give glimpses of events & vicissitudes through later years...General Pickett commanded a division of the Confederate Army & his name stands out in the history of the Civil War because of the brilliant charge he made during the Battle of Gettysburg, which failed after his division was almost wiped out. After the battle General Pickett wrote to his wife that if his expected support had come, the South would have won the battle, & the Confederate Army would have been in Washington within a few days...The half dozen letters dealing with the Battle of Gettysburg are the most interesting & important section of the volume. General & Mrs. Pickett were married during the war, & his letters both during their courtship & after their marriage showed him to have been an ardent & devoted lover & husband, for nothing seems to have been deleted from even their most intimate passages."--New York Times Book Review.
Publisher Paid Annotation.

Pickett, George & Pickett, Terry W. Opportunities in Public Health Careers. 160p. 1992. text 13.95 (*0-8442-6011-8*, VGM Career) NTC Contemp Pub Co.

— Opportunities in Public Health Careers. 160p. 1993. pap. 10.95 (*0-8442-6012-6*, VGM Career) NTC Contemp Pub Co.

Pickett, George E. Soldier of the South: General Pickett's War Letters to His Wife. Inman, Arthur C., ed. LC 78-160986. (Select Bibliographies Reprint Ser.). 1977. reprint ed. 25.95 (*0-8369-5854-3*) Ayer.

— Soldier of the South: General Pickett's War Letters to His Wife. (American Biography Ser.). 157p. 1991. reprint ed. lib. bdg. 59.00 (*0-7812-8313-2*) Rprt Serv.

Pickett, George E. & Pickett, Terry W. Public Health. 2nd ed. (Opportunities In . . . Ser.). (Illus.). 160p. pap. 11.95 (*0-8442-4416-3*, 44163, VGM Career) NTC Contemp Pub Co.

Pickett-Heaps, Jeremy D. & Pickett-Heaps, Julianne. Living Cells: Structure, Diversity, & Evolution. (Illus.). 1994. pap., teacher ed. write for info. (*0-87893-653-X*) Sinauer Assocs.

Pickett-Heaps, Julianne, jt. auth. see Pickett-Heaps, Jeremy D.

Pickett, Helen R. Rejoice Together. 1995. pap. 9.00 (*1-55896-298-0*, Skinner Hse Bks) Unitarian Univ.

Pickett, J. The Choice of Technology in Developing Countries. 1978. pap. 40.00 (*0-08-023006-7*, Pergamon Pr) Elsevier.

Pickett, James & Singer, Hans W., eds. Towards Economic Recovery in Sub-Saharan Africa. 288p. (C). (gr. 13). 1990. text 99.95 (*0-415-05409-5*, A4706) Routledge.

Pickett, Jeanne. Indian Art Designs. rev. ed. 80p. 1994. pap. text 4.95 (*0-916809-73-0*) Scott Pubns MI.

Pickett Jones, James. Black Jack: John A. Logan & Southern Illinois in the Civil War Era. LC 94-42300. (Shawnee Classics Ser.). (C). 1995. pap. 14.95 (*0-8093-2002-9*) S Ill U Pr.

— Black Jack: John A. Logan & Southern Illinois in the Civil War Era. LC 94-42300. (Shawnee Classics Ser.). 360p. (C). 1995. reprint ed. 31.95 (*0-8093-2001-0*) S Ill U Pr.

Pickett, Keri. Love in the 90s, B. B. & Jo: The Story of a Lifelong Love, a Granddaughter's Portrait. (Illus.). 112p. 1995. 14.95 (*0-446-52032-2*, Pub. by Warner Bks) Little.

***Pickett, Keri, photos by.** Faeries: Visions, Voices & Pretty Dresses. (Illus.). 128p. 2000. 40.00 (*0-89381-896-8*) Aperture.

***Pickett, Kim.** Overview of Ocular Surgery & Surgical Counseling. LC 98-46244. (Basic Bookshelf for Eyecare Professionals Ser.). 128p. 1999. pap. 30.00 (*1-55642-332-2*, 63322) SLACK Inc.

Pickett, LaSalle. Across My Path. LC 74-128287. (Essay Index Reprint Ser.). 1977. 19.95 (*0-8369-1841-X*) Ayer.

Pickett, LaSalle C., ed. see Pickett, George.

Pickett, Liam E. Organising Development Through Participation Co-Operative Organisation & Services for Land Settlement. 176p. 1988. lib. bdg. 57.50 (*0-7099-5607-X*, Pub. by C Helm) Routldge.

Pickett, Mike. Explosives Identification Guide. LC 98-24768. 80p. (C). 1998. pap. 14.95 (*0-7668-0490-9*) Delmar.

Pickett, Nell A. & Laster, Ann A. Technical English: Writing, Reading & Speaking. 5th ed. 757p. (C). 1988. pap. 35.33 (*0-06-045204-8*) Addson-Wesley Educ.

— Technical English Writing. 7th ed. 704p. (C). 1997. pap. text 70.00 (*0-673-99794-4*) Addson-Wesley Educ.

Pickett, Nell A., jt. auth. see Laster, Ann A.

Pickett, Nell Alan & Laster, Ann A. Technical English. 6th ed. (C). 1997. 58.00 (*0-06-500278-4*) Addson-Wesley Educ.

***Pickett, Nell Ann, et al.** Technical English: Writing, Reading & Speaking. 8th ed. LC 00-33182. 2000. write for info. (*0-8130-1798-X*) U Press Fla.

Pickett, O. Gordon. The Coming Star-Shift & Many Prophecies of Bible & Pyramid Fulfilled. 584p. 1981. pap. 65.00 (*0-89540-087-1*, SB-087) Sun Pub.

Pickett, Raymond. The Cross in Corinth: The Social Significance of the Death of Jesus. LC 97-203338. (JSNTS Ser.: Vol. 143). 230p. 1997. 70.00 (*1-85075-663-5*, Pub. by Sheffield Acad) CUP Services.

Pickett, Robert S. House of Refuge: Origins of Juvenile Reform in New York State 1815-1857. LC 69-19745. (New York State Study Ser.). 239p. reprint ed. pap. 74.10 (*0-608-15211-0*, 202740500055) Bks Demand.

Pickett, Robert T. Feedback Control Systems for Technicians. (Illus.). 272p. 1988. text 51.00 (*0-13-313933-6*) P-H.

Pickett, Spencer. The Internal Audit Handbook. LC 96-42896. 656p. 1997. 137.95 (*0-471-96911-7*) Wiley.

Pickett, Steward T. & White, P. S., eds. Ecology of Natural Disturbances & Patch Dynamics. 472p. (C). 1986. pap. text 58.00 (*0-12-554521-5*) Acad Pr.

— Natural Disturbance: The Patch Dynamics Perspective. (C). 1985. text 55.00 (*0-12-554520-7*) Acad Pr.

Pickett, Steward T., et al. Ecological Understanding: The Nature of Theory & the Theory of Nature. (Illus.). 206p. 1994. text 62.00 (*0-12-554720-X*) Acad Pr.

Pickett, Steward T., jt. ed. see McDonnell, Mark J.

Pickett, Sue. Little Dog Scooter. 21p. (J). (gr. 4). 1992. pap. text. write for info. (*0-9633197-0-1*) Instant Heirloom.

Pickett, Suzanne. Hot Dogs for Thanksgiving: A Memoir. LC 98-122748. 1998. pap. 16.95 (*1-881320-76-6*, Black Belt) Black Belt Communs.

Pickett, Terry H. Inventing Nations: Justifications of Authority in the Modern World, 56. LC 95-42920. (Contributions in Philosophy Ser.: Vol. 56). 168p. 1996. 55.00 (*0-313-29891-2*, Greenwood Pr) Greenwood.

Pickett, Terry W., jt. auth. see Pickett, George.

Pickett, Terry W., jt. auth. see Pickett, George E.

Pickett, Velma B., jt. auth. see Elson, Benjamin F.

Pickett, Vera. Can God Deliver? LC 92-96905. 52p. 1998. 10.95 (*0-533-10450-5*) Vantage.

Pickett, William. The Chicken Smells Good. 2nd ed. LC 96-37552. (Illus.). 208p. 1997. pap. text 20.40 (*0-13-576216-2*) P-H.

— Dwight David Eisenhower, an American Power. Kraut,

P

Alan M. & Wakelyn, Jon L., eds. (American Biographical History Ser.). (Illus.). 144p. (C). 1995. pap. text 12.95 (*0-88295-918-2*) Harlan Davidson.
— Leaders of the Americas Bk. I: Short Biographies & Dialogues. 192p. 1994. pap. text 22.33 (*0-13-102484-1*) P-H.
***Pickett, William B.** Eisenhower Decides to Run: Presidential Politics & Cold War Strategy. LC 00-31534. 288p. 2000. 27.50 (*1-56663-325-7*, Pub. by I R Dee) Natl Bk Netwk.
Pickett, William B. Homer E. Capehart: A Senator's Life, 1897-1979. (Illus.). xv, 243p. 1990. 19.95 (*0-87195-054-5*) Ind Hist Soc.
Pickett, William P. Far from Home: Reading & Word Study. 2nd ed. LC 93-25537. 192p. (J). 1993. mass mkt. 20.95 (*0-8384-4852-6*) Heinle & Heinle.
— Far from Home: Reading & Word Study Instructor's Manual. 2nd ed. (College ESL Ser.). (J). 1996. mass mkt., teacher ed. 7.95 (*0-8384-4853-4*) Heinle & Heinle.
— Pizza Tastes Great. 1995. pap. text, wbk. ed. 13.60 (*0-13-102492-2*) P-H.
— The Pizza Tastes Great: Dialogues & Stories. (Illus.). 176p. (C). 1987. pap. text 22.27 (*0-13-677626-4*) P-H.
Pickett, Winston, jt. auth. see Melton, Louisa.
Pickford, Brett, ed. see Goode, Sue.
Pickford, Cedric E., ed. Gyron le Courtoys c. 1501. 522p. 1970. 90.00 (*0-85991-152-7*) Boydell & Brewer.
— Merlin, 1498. (French Arthurian Romances Ser.). 1975. 133.95 (*0-85967-196-8*, Pub. by Scolar Pr) Ashgate Pub Co.
Pickford, Grace E. Contributions to a Study of South African Microchaetinae (Annedida: Oligochaeta) (Connecticut Academy of Arts & Sciences Ser., Trans.: Vol. 46). 1975. pap. 29.50 (*0-685-22881-9*) Elliots Bks.
— Studies on the Digestive Enzymes of Spiders. (Connecticut Academy of Arts & Sciences Ser., Trans.: Vol. 35). 1942. pap. 49.50 (*0-685-22911-4*) Elliots Bks.
Pickford, Grace E., et al. Studies on the Blood Serum of the Euryhaline Cyprinodont Fish, Fundulus Heteroclitus, Adapted to Fresh or to Salt Water. (Connecticut Academy of Arts & Sciences Ser., Trans.: Vol. 43). 1969. pap. 39.50 (*0-685-22887-8*) Elliots Bks.
Pickford, Henry W., tr. see Adorno, Theodor W.
Pickford, Ian. Antique Silver. LC 99-229016. (Illus.). 180p. 1997. 25.00 (*1-85149-244-5*) Antique Collect.
— Pocket Edition Jackson's Hallmarks of England, Scotland & Ireland. 172p. 1991. 25.00 (*1-85149-128-7*) Antique Collect.
Pickford, Ian, ed. Jackson's Silver & Gold Marks of England, Scotland & Ireland. (Illus.). 766p. 1989. 99.50 (*0-907462-63-4*) Antique Collect.
— Pocket Edition Jackson's Hallmarks of England, Scotland & Ireland. (Illus.). 172p. 1993. 14.50 (*1-85149-169-4*) Antique Collect.
Pickford, J. Analysis of Water Surge. x, 204p. 1969. text 274.00 (*0-677-61670-8*) Gordon & Breach.
Pickford, Joel. California Light: The Watercolors of Rollin Pickford. LC 98-66409. (Illus.). 350p. 1998. 55.00 (*0-912201-32-0*) CSU Pr Fresno.
Pickford, John. Low-Cost Sanitation: A Survey of Practical Experience. 176p. 1995. pap. 19.50 (*1-85339-233-2*, Pub. by Intermed Tech) Stylus Pub VA.
— The Safegarde from Ship-Wracke: or Heaven's Haven. LC 76-370280. (English Recusant Literature, 1558-1640 Ser.). 285p. 1975. write for info. (*0-85967-271-9*) Scolar Pr.
Pickford, John, ed. Reaching the Unreached: Challenges for the 21st Century. 192p. 1998. pap. 37.95 (*1-85339-412-2*, Pub. by Intermed Tech) Stylus Pub VA.
Pickford, John, et al, eds. Sustainability of Water & Sanitation Systems. 168p. (Orig.). 1996. pap. 30.00 (*1-85339-339-8*, Pub. by Intermed Tech) Stylus Pub VA.
Pickford, Louise. Book of Vegetarian Cooking. (Illus.). 120p. 1993. pap. 12.00 (*1-55788-076-X*, HP Books) Berkley Pub.
— How to See Mental Images. 1997. 20.00 (*0-913412-74-0*) Brandon Hse.
— The Inspired Vegetarian. LC 92-9094. (Illus.). 144p. 1992. 12.50 (*1-55670-230-2*) Stewart Tabori & Chang.
— Picnics. 112p. 1996. write for info. (*1-57215-191-9*) World Pubns.
***Pickford, Louise.** Tapas: 100 Recipes for Irresistible Appetizers & Snacks. (Illus.). 2000. pap. 14.95 (*0-600-60097-1*) P HM.
— 30 Minute Entertaining. LC 00-44372. 2000. pap. write for info. (*1-57145-677-5*, Laurel Glen Pub) Advantage Pubns.
Pickford, Martin. Louis S. B. Leakey: Beyond the Evidence. LC 98-147155. (Illus.). 187p. 1998. pap. 25.00 (*1-85756-396-4*, Pub. by Janus Pubng) Paul & Co Pubs.
Pickford, Nigel. The Atlas of Shipwrecks & Treasure. LC 93-48856. 1994. 29.95 (*1-56458-599-9*) DK Pub Inc.
— Lost Treasure Ships of the Twentieth Century. LC 99-14514. (Illus.). 192p. 1999. 40.00 (*0-7922-7472-5*) Natl Geog.
Pickford, Peter. Wilderness Dawning. 160p. (C). 1988. 170.00 (*1-85368-001-X*, Pub. by New5 Holland) St Mut.
Pickford, Susan. Barron & Lyla: An Anti-Drug Play for Little Folks. (Illus.). 38p. (J). (gr. 3-7). 1991. pap. 3.25 (*0-88680-356-X*) I E Clark.
Pickford, Susan B. Antonio's la Amistad. (Illus.). 100p. (Orig.). (J). (gr. 7-9). 1997. pap. 6.95 (*1-889664-08-1*) SBP.
— The Drama of La Amistad. (J). (gr. 5-9). 1998. pap. 10.00 (*1-57960-034-4*) Disc Enter Ltd.
— Expectations: The Life of Phillis Wheatley. 18p. (J). (gr. 5-9). pap., wbk. ed. 10.00 (*1-878668-67-6*) Disc Enter Ltd.
— The Fairy Houses of Monhegan Island. (Illus.). 8p. (Orig.). (J). (ps-6). 1995. pap. 5.95 (*1-889664-01-4*) SBP.
— The History of the Chelmsford Carlisle Cranberry Bog. (Illus.). ii, 54p. (Orig.). 1991. pap. 6.95 (*1-889664-00-6*) SBP.
— Libby: The Black Duck of Wadleigh Pond. LC 96-92539. (Illus.). 32p. (Orig.). (J). (gr. k-6). 1996. pap. 6.95 (*1-889664-03-0*) SBP.
— Marching Through Time: A Play about Turns-of-Centuries. (J). (gr. 5-9). 1996. pap., wbk. ed. 10.00 (*1-878668-57-9*) Disc Enter Ltd.
— The Ram of Manana. (Illus.). 8p. (Orig.). (J). (ps-6). 1996. pap. 6.95 (*1-889664-02-2*) SBP.
— Roxy's Gift. (Illus.). 16p. (Orig.). (YA). (gr. 4-8). 1999. pap. 6.95 (*1-889664-06-5*) SBP.
— Zic-Zac & the Crocodile. LC 96-92540. (Illus.). 16p. (Orig.). (J). (gr. k-6). 1997. pap. 6.95 (*1-889664-04-9*) SBP.
Pickford, Susan T. It's up to You, Griffin! (Illus.). 32p. (J). (gr. k-4). 1993. 10.95 (*0-87033-446-8*, Tidewtr Pubs) Cornell Maritime.
Pickhardt, Carl E. Case of the Scary Divorce: A Jackson Skye Mystery. (Jackson Skye Mystery Ser.). 1997. pap. text 12.95 (*1-55798-457-3*) Am Psychol.
***Pickhardt, Carl E.** Keys to Developing Your Child's Self-Esteem. LC 99-56439. (Parenting Keys Ser.). (Illus.). 208p. 2000. pap. 6.95 (*0-7641-0847-6*) Barron.
Pickhardt, Carl E. Keys to Parenting the Only Child. LC 97-18747. (Parenting Keys Ser.). 176p. 1997. pap. text 6.95 (*0-8120-9769-6*) Barron.
— Keys to Raising a Drug-Free Child. LC 99-23278. (Parenting Keys Ser.). 208p. 1999. pap. text 6.95 (*0-7641-0848-4*) Barron.
— Keys to Single Parenting. LC 95-20820. (Parenting Keys Ser.). 192p. 1996. pap. 6.95 (*0-8120-9331-3*) Barron.
— Keys to Successful Stepfathering. LC 96-21074. (Barron's Parenting Keys Ser.). x, 182p. 1997. pap. 6.95 (*0-8120-9715-7*) Barron.
— Parenting the Adolescent. (Illus.). 200p. (Orig.). 1987. pap. 12.95 (*0-938934-16-3*) LCN.
Pickholz, Marvin G. Securities Crimes, 1 vol. LC 93-14817. (Securities Law Ser.). 1993. ring bd. 145.00 (*0-87632-971-7*) West Group.
Pickin, Chrissie & St. Leger, Selwyn. Assessing Health Need Using the Life Cycle Framework. LC 92-18760. 192p. 1992. 123.00 (*0-335-15743-2*); pap. 34.95 (*0-335-15742-4*) OpUniv Pr.
Pickinpaugh, Donald D. & Pickinpaugh, Sherri. Fidelity Select Money: The Complete Investor's Guide to Track & Improve Fidelity Select Mutual Fund Performance. LC 97-15099. (Illus.). 105p. (Orig.). 1998. pap. 22.95 (*1-882360-00-1*) ATL Pr Sci.
— Fidelity Select Money: The Complete Investor's Guide to Track & Improve Fidelity Select Mutual Fund Performance. LC 97-15099. (Illus.). 150p. (Orig.). 1998. 44.95 (*1-882360-01-X*) ATL Pr Sci.
Pickinpaugh, Sherri, jt. auth. see Pickinpaugh, Donald D.
Pickle, Hal B. & Abrahamson, Royce L. Small Business Management. LC 86-19198. (Wiley Series in Management). (Illus.). 649p. reprint ed. pap. 200.00 (*0-7837-3507-3*, 205784000008) Bks Demand.
Pickle, Hal B. & Arahamson, Royce L. Small Business Management. 5th ed. LC 89-36239. 736p. 1990. text 77.95 (*0-471-50071-2*) Wiley.
Pickle, Jake & Pickle, Peggy. Jake. LC 96-10090. (Illus.). 272p. 1997. 22.95 (*0-292-76572-X*) U of Tex Pr.
Pickle, Julianne M. One Hundred Percent Vegetarian: Eating Naturally from Your Grocery Store. LC 90-92224. 120p. (Orig.). 1990. pap., spiral bd. 6.95 (*0-9627645-0-7*) Pickle Pub Co.
Pickle, Linda S. Contented Among Strangers: Rural German-Speaking Women & Their Families in the Nineteenth-Century Midwest. Daniels, Roger et al, eds. LC 95-9849. (Statue of Liberty-Ellis Island Centennial Ser.). (Illus.). 360p. (C). 1995. text 49.95 (*0-252-02182-7*) U of Ill Pr.
Pickle, Peggy, jt. auth. see Pickle, Jake.
Pickleman, Jack, ed. Problems in General Surgery. LC 81-22702. (Reviewing Surgical Topics Ser.). 382p. (C). 1982. 75.00 (*0-306-40765-5*, Kluwer Plenum) Kluwer Academic.
Pickles. Physiotherapy with Older People. 1995. pap. text 62.00 (*0-7020-1931-3*, W B Saunders Co) Harcrt Hlth Sci Grp.
Pickles & Lafferty. Accountancy Questions & Key. pap. 19.95 (*0-8464-4452-6*) Beekman Pubs.
*** Pickles, Angelica.** How to Be a Princess. (Rugrats Ser.). (gr. k-3). 2000. pap. 9.99 (*0-689-83481-0*, Simon Spot) Litle Simon.
Pickles, David, jt. auth. see Kleindl, Micheal.
Pickles, Dorothy M. The Fifth French Republic. LC 75-32461. 222p. 1976. reprint ed. lib. bdg. 38.50 (*0-8371-8544-0*, PIFF, Greenwood Pr) Greenwood.
Pickles, J. & Smith, Adrian. Theorising Transition: The Political Economy of Transition in Post-Communist Countries. LC 97-30851. (Illus.). 544p. (C). 1998. 90.00 (*0-415-16266-1*); pap. 32.99 (*0-415-16267-X*) Routledge.
Pickles, J., jt. ed. see Dunstan, F.
Pickles, J. A. & Dawson, J. L., eds. Concordance to John Gower's Confessio Amantis. 1987. 265.00 (*0-85991-245-0*) Boydell & Brewer.
Pickles, J. D., ed. see Shepherd, G. T.
Pickles, James O. An Introduction to the Physiology of Hearing. 2nd ed. 367p. 1988. pap. text 54.95 (*0-12-554754-4*) Acad Pr.
Pickles, John, ed. Ground Truth: The Social Implications of Geographic Information Systems. LC 94-31711. (Mappings). 248p. 1994. pap. text 21.95 (*0-89862-295-6*, 2295); lib. bdg. 40.00 (*0-89862-294-8*) Guilford Pubns.
Pickles, Pilla A.C. Managing the Curriculum for Children with Severe Motor Difficulties: A Practical Approach. 1998. 29.95 (*1-85346-511-9*) Taylor & Francis.
***Pickles, Sheila.** The Complete Victorian Treasury. (Illus.). 192p. 1999. 24.95 (*1-86205-250-6*, Pub. by Pavilion Bks Ltd) Trafalgar.
Pickles, Sheila. The Language of Herbs: Scented by Penhaligon's. (Illus.). 96p. 1997. 22.95 (*1-85793-663-9*, Pub. by Pavilion Bks Ltd) Trafalgar.
Pickles, Sydney. Metallurgical Changes in Late Bronze Age Cyprus. 40p. 1988. pap. 8.00 (*0-614-21834-9*) David Brown.
Pickles, Tim. Malta, 1565. (Campaign Ser.: No. 50). (Illus.). 96p. 1998. pap. 16.95 (*1-85532-603-5*, Pub. by Ospry) Stackpole.
— New Orleans, 1815. (Campaign Ser.). (Illus.). 96p. 1994. pap. 14.95 (*1-85532-360-5*, 9527, Pub. by Ospry) Stackpole.
— Tool Kit for Trainers: A Compendium of Techniques for Trainers & Group Workers. LC 96-26045. 214p. (Orig.). 1996. pap. 27.95 (*1-55561-112-5*) Fisher Bks.
Pickles, W., tr. see Blum, Leon.
Pickman, Alan J. The Handbook of Outplacement Counseling. 176p. 1994. 39.95 (*0-8058-1647-X*); pap. 19.95 (*0-8058-1648-8*) L Erlbaum Assocs.
— Special Challenges in Career Management: The Counselor's Perspective. LC 96-18079. 264p. 1996. 49.95 (*0-8058-1856-1*); pap. 26.00 (*0-8058-1857-X*) L Erlbaum Assocs.
Pickman, James, et al. Producing Lower Income Housing: Local Initiatives. LC 86-26424. 389p. reprint ed. pap. 120.60 (*0-7837-4608-3*, 204432700002) Bks Demand.
Pickney, Gloria J. The Sunday Outing. LC 93-25383. (Illus.). (J). (gr. k-4). 1994. 14.99 (*0-8037-1198-0*, Dial Yng Read) Peng Put Young Read.
Pickover, Cliff. The Science of Aliens. (Illus.). 368p. 2000. pap. 12.00 (*0-465-07315-8*, Pub. by Basic) HarpC.
Pickover, Clifford. Black Holes: A Traveler's Guide. 224p. 1998. pap. 16.95 (*0-471-19704-1*) Wiley.
***Pickover, Clifford.** Cryptorunes: Codes & Secret Writing. LC Z103.P5 2000. 2000. pap. 13.95 (*0-7649-1251-8*) Pomegranate Calif.
Pickover, Clifford A. Black Holes: A Traveler's Guide. LC 95-41336. (Illus.). 224p. 1996. 24.95 (*0-471-12580-6*) Wiley.
— Chaos & Fractals: A Computer Graphical Journey: Ten Year Compilation of Advanced Research. LC 98-38378. 452p. 1998. 184.00 (*0-444-50002-2*) Elsevier.
— Computers & the Imagination: Visual Adventures Beyond the Edge. (Illus.). 444p. 1992. pap. 19.95 (*0-312-08343-2*) St Martin.
— Fractal Horizons: The Future Uses of Fractals. 256p. 1996. text 35.00 (*0-312-12599-2*) St Martin.
***Pickover, Clifford A.** The Girl Who Gave Birth to Rabbits: A True Medical Mystery. LC 99-56193. 260p. 2000. pap. 18.95 (*1-57392-794-5*) Prometheus Bks.
Pickover, Clifford A. Key to Infinity. LC 94-45541. 352p. 1995. 24.95 (*0-471-11857-5*) Wiley.
— Keys to Infinity. (Illus.). 208p. 1997. pap. 16.95 (*0-471-19334-8*) Wiley.
— The Loom of God: Mathematical Tapestries at the Edge of Time. LC 96-45675. (Illus.). 292p. (C). 1997. 29.95 (*0-306-45411-4*, Plenum Trade) Perseus Pubng.
— The Pattern Book: Recipes for Beauty. 250p. 1995. text 59.00 (*981-02-1426-X*) World Scientific Pub.
— Science of Aliens. LC 99-182126. 224p. 2000. 21.00 (*0-465-07314-X*, Pub. by Basic) HarpC.
— Strange Brains & Genius: The Secret Lives of Eccentric Scientists & Madmen. LC 98-10232. (Illus.). 340p. (C). 1998. 28.95 (*0-306-45784-9*, Plenum Trade) Perseus Pubng.
***Pickover, Clifford A.** Strange Brains & Genius: The Secret Lives of Eccentric Scientists & Madmen. LC 99-20675. (Illus.). 352p. 1999. reprint ed. pap. 14.00 (*0-688-16894-9*, Quil) HarperTrade.
— Surfing Through Hyperspace: Understanding Higher Universes in Six Easy Lessons. LC 98-48660. (Illus.). 272p. 1999. 25.00 (*0-19-513006-5*) OUP.
Pickover, Clifford A. Time: A Traveler's Guide. (Illus.). 304p. 1998. 25.00 (*0-19-512042-6*) OUP.
— Time: A Traveller's Guide. (Illus.). 304p. 1999. pap. 15.95 (*0-19-513096-0*) OUP.
— The Visual Display of Biological Information. 300p. 1995. text 74.00 (*981-02-1427-8*) World Scientific Pub.
***Pickover, Clifford A.** Wonders of Numbers: Brain-Crushing Adventures in Math, Mind, & Meaning. LC 99-27044. 352p. 2000. 27.50 (*0-19-513342-0*) OUP.
Pickover, Clifford A., ed. Future Health: Computers & Medicine in the 21st Century. LC 95-34799. (Illus.). 256p. 1995. text 25.95 (*0-312-12602-6*) St Martin.
Pickover, Clifford A. & Tewksbury, Stuart K., eds. Frontiers of Scientific Visualization. LC 93-11136. 284p. 1994. pap. 44.95 (*0-471-30972-9*) Wiley.
Pickover, Clifford A., jt. auth. see Anthony, Piers.
Pickover, Clifford A., jt. ed. see Hargittai, Istvan.
Pickover, Clifford A., jt. ed. see Tewksbury, Stuart K.
Pickow, Jonathan. Christmas Songs for Children. (Illus.). 56p. 1988. pap. 7.95 (*0-8256-1121-0*, AM67117) Music Sales.
Pickow, Peter. Beginning Bass Scales. (Illus.). 48p. 1992. pap. 5.95 (*0-8256-1342-6*, AM87482) Music Sales.
— Hammered Dulcimer. 1979. pap. 19.95 (*0-8256-0174-6*, OK63552, Oak) Music Sales.
— Manual de Accordes Para Guitarra. (SPA.). 48p. 1997. pap. 5.95 (*0-8256-1540-2*, AM 91802) Music Sales.
— The Original Guitar Case Chord Book. 48p. pap. 5.95 (*0-8256-2367-7*, AM35841) Music Sales.
— The Original Guitar Case Scale Book. (Illus.). 48p. 1996. pap. 4.95 (*0-8256-2588-2*, AM 76217) Music Sales.
— The Penny Whistle Primer. 1982. pap. 5.95 (*0-8256-0268-8*, AM34877, Oak) Music Sales.
— Play Guitar Today! pap. 16.95 incl. audio compact disk (*0-8256-1427-9*, AM92242) Omnibus NY.
Pickow, Peter. Play Pennywhistle Now! The Fun & Easy Way to Play Pennywhistle. (Illus.). 52p. 1989. pap. 16.95 (*0-8256-1779-0*, Amsco Music) Music Sales.
— Silver Anniversary Guitar Case Chord Book. 1999. pap. text 7.95 (*0-8256-1728-6*) Music Sales.
Pickow, Peter. Step One: Playing Bass Guitar. 1997. pap. 7.95 incl. audio compact disk (*0-8256-1592-5*) Omnibus NY.
— Step One: Playing Bass Scales. pap. 7.95 incl. audio compact disk (*0-8256-1593-3*) Omnibus NY.
— Step One: Playing Guitar Scales. pap. 7.95 incl. audio compact disk (*0-8256-1590-9*) Omnibus NY.
— You Can Play Bass Guitar. (Illus.). 64p. 1998. pap. 17.95 (*0-8256-1655-7*, AM945703) Music Sales.
***Pickow, Peter, ed.** De Falla: Ritual Fire Dance. (Concert Performer Ser.). 4p. 1999. pap. text 6.95 incl. cd-rom (*0-8256-1752-9*, AM949850) Music Sales.
Pickow, Peter, ed. The Easiest Guitar Case Chord Book. (Illus.). 55p. 1999. pap. text 5.95 (*0-8256-1696-4*, AM948750) Music Sales.
— Guitar Chord Songbook: Christmas Songs & Carols. LC 99-193011. 48p. 1998. pap. 5.95 (*0-7119-7072-6*, AM951016) Omnibus NY.
***Pickow, Peter, ed.** Joplin: Maple Leaf Rag. (Concert Performer Ser.). 4p. 1999. pap. text 6.95 incl. cd-rom (*0-8256-1747-2*, AM949806) Music Sales.
— Joplin: The Entertainer. (Concert Performer Ser.). 4p. 1999. pap. text 6.95 incl. cd-rom (*0-8256-1748-0*, AM949817) Music Sales.
— Mozart: Alla Turca. (Concert Performer Ser.). 4p. 1999. pap. text 6.95 incl. cd-rom (*0-8256-1749-9*, AM949828) Music Sales.
— Mozart: Sonata K. 545. (Concert Performer Ser.). 4p. 1999. pap. text 6.95 incl. cd-rom (*0-8256-1750-2*, AM949837) Music Sales.
— Palchalbel: Canon in D. (Concert Performer Ser.). 4p. 1999. pap. text 6.95 incl. cd-rom (*0-8256-1751-0*, AM949840) Music Sales.
Pickow, Peter, ed. The 6 Chord Songbook: Christmas Songs & Carols. 48p. 1998. pap. text 7.95 (*0-7119-7073-4*, AM951027) Omnibus NY.
Pickow, Peter & Shulman, Jason. Facil Clasicos a Modernos.Tr. of Easy Classics to Moderns. (SPA.). 1997. 12.95 (*0-8256-1472-4*) Omnibus NY.
Pickow, Peter & Shulman, Jason A. Como Tocar la Armonica de Bolsillo. (SPA.). 64p. 1997. pap. 5.95 (*0-8256-1444-9*, AM 92239) Music Sales.
— Step One: Playing Harmonica. 1997. pap. 7.95 incl. audio compact disk (*0-8256-1594-1*) Omnibus NY.
Pickow, Peter, jt. auth. see Appleby, Amy.
Pickow, Peter, jt. auth. see Bell, Joe "Cool Papa".
Pickow, Peter, jt. auth. see Shulman, Jason.
Pickow, Peter, ed. see Sales Corporation Music Staff.
Pickrahn, H., jt. auth. see Held, P.
***Pickrell, Doug.** Invariant Measures for Unitary Groups Associated to KAC-Moody LIE Algebras. LC 00-36256. 2000. write for info. (*0-8218-2068-0*) Am Math.
Pickrell, Jesse. Group Health Insurance. 2nd ed. (C). 1961. 10.50 (*0-256-00671-7*, Irwn McGrw-H) McGrw-H Hghr Educ.
Pickrell, John A., ed. Lung Connective Tissue: Location, Metabolism, & Response to Injury. 224p. 1981. 98.95 (*0-8493-5749-7*, RC756) CRC Pr.
Pickrell, Martha M. Dr. Miles: The Life of Dr. Franklin L. Miles (1845-1929) LC 97-77133. 120p. 1998. pap. 12.00 (*1-57860-023-5*) Guild Pr IN.
— Emma Speaks Out: Life & Writings of Emma Molloy (1839-1907) LC 99-71526. (Indiana Women Who Made a Difference Ser.: Vol. II). 162p. 1999. 24.95 (*1-57860-073-1*) Guild Pr IN.
Pickrell, Melvin H. & Siegmund, Vera T. My Ukrainian Footprints. (Illus.). 232p. 1995. 24.95 (*0-9655652-0-3*) M H Pickrell.
***Pickren, Charles.** Memories of an Old Mountain Man. 200p. 2000. pap. 19.95 (*0-938041-76-2*) Arc Pr AR.
Pickron, John E., tr. see Goedan, Juergen C.
Pickslay, Pat, jt. auth. see Coombs, Ted.
Pickstock, Catherine. After Writing: On the Liturgical Consummation of Philosophy. LC 97-8844. (Challenges in Contemporary Theology Ser.: Vol. 1). 256p. (C). 1997. text 68.95 (*0-631-20671-X*); pap. text 31.95 (*0-631-20672-8*) Blackwell Pubs.
— Ascending Numbers: Augustine's de Musica & the Western Tradition. (Radical Traditions Ser.). 208p. 2000. text 45.00 (*0-8133-6700-X*) Westview.
Pickthal, M. M. Cultural Side of Islam. 202p. 1990. 14.95 (*81-7151-094-9*) Asia Bk Corp.
— The Holy Quran. 810p. 1990. pap. 22.95 (*81-7151-026-4*) Asia Bk Corp.
— The Meaning of the Glorious Quran. 810p. 1995. 14.95 (*81-7151-106-6*) Asia Bk Corp.
— Sadhus of India. 258p. 19.95 (*0-318-37160-X*) Asia Bk Corp.
Pickthall. The Meaning of the Glorious Quran. 1982. pap. 5.95 (*1-56744-133-5*) Kazi Pubns.
Pickthall, M. Cultural Side of Islam. 1990. 12.75 (*0-935782-66-4*) Kazi Pubns.
— The Holy Qur'an Translation. 1990. text 25.00 (*81-7101-105-5*, 35) Tahrike Tarsile Quran.
Pickthall, M., ed. Holy Quran. 1983. reprint ed. 18.50 (*0-8364-0989-2*, Pub. by R Taj Co) S Asia.
Pickthall, M. M. The Meaning of the Glorious Quran: Text & Explanatory Translation. rev. ed. El-Ashi, Arafat K., ed. & rev. by. LC 94-24009. 744p. (Orig.). 1996. pap. 12.00 (*0-915957-22-1*) amana pubns.
— The Meaning of the Holy Quran. 464p. 1992. 12.95 (*81-85274-00-2*) Asia Bk Corp.
Pickthall, M. M., ed. Holy Quran with English Translation. 1976. reprint ed. 19.50 (*0-8364-0415-7*) S Asia.

An Asterisk (*) at the beginning of an entry indicates that the title is appearing for the first time.

Pickthall, M. M., tr. see Ghazi, Abidullah & Quraishi-Ahmed, Huda, eds.

***Pickthall, M. Marmaduke, tr.** Juz' Four: Lantana Luah Birra: A Textbook for the Classroon. LC 98-88207. 9p. (YA). (gr. 10-12). 1999. pap. text 6.00 (1-56316-121-4) Iqra Intl Ed Fdtn.

Pickthall, M. Marmaduke, tr. see Ghazi, Abidullah & Quraishi-Ahmed, Huda, eds.

Pickthall, Mardaduke, tr. Holy Quran. 1986. reprint ed. 20.00 (0-8364-1623-6, Pub. by Rajesh) S Asia.

Pickthall, Marjorie. The Worker in Sandalwood. unabridged ed. (Illus.). 32p. (J). (gr. k up). 1991. 13.95 (1-895555-10-8) STDK.

Pickthall, Marmaduke. Glorious Quran: The Arabic Test & English Rendering. 800p. 1983. pap. 14.95 (0-933511-24-8) Kazi Pubns.

Pickthall, Marmaduke, ed. The Glorious Koran. 1696p. 1976. text 59.95 (0-04-297036-9) Routledge.

Pickthall, Marmaduke, tr. Holy Quran Al-Karim. deluxe ed. 280p. (C). 1997. 29.95 (1-871031-68-0) Kazi Pubns.

— The Koran. LC 92-52928. 544p. 1992. 22.00 (0-679-41736-2) Everymns Lib.

— The Meaning of the Glorious Quran. 464p. 1997. pap. 8.95 (1-879402-51-3) Tahrike Tarsile Quran.

***Pickthall, Marmaduke W.** The Life of the Prophet Muhammad: A Brief History. LC 98-35847. 1998. 9.95 (0-915957-86-8) amana pubns.

Pickthall, Mohammad M. Glorious Quran: The Arabic Test & English Rendering. 1993. 25.75 (1-56744-044-4) Kazi Pubns.

Pickthall, Mohammed M. The Meaning of the Holy Quran. (C). 1995. 10.00 (81-7476-005-9, Pub. by UBS Pubs Dist) S Asia.

Pickthall, Mohammed M., tr. The Quran with Transliteration. (ARA & ENG.). 608p. 1997. 25.00 (1-879402-52-1) Tahrike Tarsile Quran.

Pickthall, Muhammad M. The Glorious Qur'an: Arabic & English. LC 92-64030. (ENG & ARA.). 768p. 1997. pap. 8.95 (1-879402-16-5) Tahrike Tarsile Quran.

Pickthall, Muhammad M., tr. The Glorious Koran. 767p. 1983. 20.00 (0-940368-30-7, 2) Tahrike Tarsile Quran.

— The Glorious Quran. xxxiv, 605p. 1994. 14.95 (0-9638962-0-2) Crescent NY.

— The Glorious Quran. LC 92-64030. 768p. pap. text 8.95 (0-940368-95-1) Tahrike Tarsile Quran.

Pickthall, Muhammad M., tr. see Ghazi, Abidullah.

Pickthorn, William E., compiled by. Ministers Manual Ser., 3 vols., Set. Incl. Vol. 1. Services for Special Occasions. LC 65-13222. 132p. 1965. 7.99 (0-88243-547-7, 02-0547); Vol. 2. Services for Weddings & Funerals. LC 65-13222. 130p. 1965. 7.99 (0-88243-548-5, 02-0548); Vol. 3. Services for Ministers & Workers. LC 65-13222. 134p. 1965. 7.99 (0-88243-549-3, 02-0549); LC 65-13222. 1965. 22.99 (0-88243-544-2, 02-0544) Gospel Pub.

Pickup, F., jt. auth. see Parker, M. A.

Pickup, Gregory. The Trouble with Bubbles. LC 97-177252. (Illus.). 64p. (Orig.). 1996. pap. 9.95 (0-9641715-7-0) Airplane Bks.

Pickup, Ian. Dictionary of Sports, French-English/English-French. (ENG & FRE.). 287p. 1995. 65.00 (0-7859-9897-7) Fr & Eur.

— French-English - English-French Dictionary of Sports. 287p. 1995. pap. 46.00 (2-7298-9502-7) IBD Ltd.

Pickup, J. C. Biotechnology of Insulin Therapy. (Frontiers in Pharmacology & Therapeutics Ser.). (Illus.). 200p. 1991. 125.00 (0-632-03038-0) Blackwell Sci.

Pickup, J. C. & Williams, G. Textbook of Diabetes Slide Atlas. (Illus.). 20p. 1993. 99.95 (0-632-03569-2) Blackwell Sci.

Pickup, J. C., jt. auth. see Williams, G.

Pickup, John C. & Williams, Gareth. Textbook of Diabetes. 2nd ed. LC 96-25940. (Illus.). 1600p. 1997. 295.00 (0-632-03802-0) Blackwell Sci.

Pickup, John C., jt. auth. see Williams, Gareth.

Pickup, L., jt. auth. see Banister, D.

Pickup, Laurie, et al. Bus Deregulation in the Metropolitan Areas. Kenny, Francesca, ed. (Oxford Studies in Transport). 264p. 1991. text 80.95 (1-85628-198-1, Pub. by Avebry) Ashgate Pub Co.

***Pickup, Michael.** The Adventures of Bhakta Musika & the Lion. (Illus.). 40p. (J). (ps-5). 1998. pap. 4.95 (81-87216-03-4) Torchlght Pub.

— The Adventures of Bhakta Musika & the Terrible Snake. (Illus.). 38p. (J). (ps-5). 1998. pap. 4.95 (81-87216-08-5) Torchlght Pub.

Pickup, Paul. Intranets: Best Practice in Planning, Implementation & Use. LC 99-488662. 128p. 1998. pap. 135.00 (1-85835-511-7, Indust Soc) Stylus Pub VA.

Pickup, Ronald, ed. see Morgan, Tom.

Pickup, Sharon L. Overseas Presence: More Data & Analysis Needed to Determine Whether Cost-Effective Alternatives Exist. (Illus.). 56p. (C). 1997. pap. text 25.00 (0-7881-4738-2) DIANE Pub.

***Pickus, Bob.** California Criminal Law Forms Manual. LC 94-69730. 168p. 1999. ring bd. 46.00 (0-7626-0340-2, CR-32152) Cont Ed Bar-CA.

— California Liability Insurance Practice: Claims & Litigation - 8/99 Update, 2 vols. Piatt, Norma, ed. LC 90-84639. 399p. 1999. ring bd. 68.00 (0-7626-0353-4, CP-39268) Cont Ed Bar-CA.

— California Marital Settlement & Other Family Law Agreements - 6-99 Update. 2nd ed. LC 97-32962. 200p. 1999. ring bd. 52.00 (0-7626-0350-X, FA-32962) Cont Ed Bar-CA.

— California Marital Settlement & Other Family Law Agreements - 6/98 Update. 2nd ed. LC 97-68155. 238p. 1998. ring bd. 50.00 (0-7626-0243-0, FA-32961) Cont Ed Bar-CA.

Pickus, Bob. California Marital Termination Agreements: June 1994 Update. LC 88-70540. 366p. 1994. 45.00 (0-88124-779-0, FA-30876) Cont Ed Bar-CA.

— Divorce & Family Law in California: A Guide for the General Public. 141p. (Orig.). 1991. pap. 8.95 (0-9630684-0-7) B Pickus.

— Fee Agreement Forms Manual: January 1993 Update. LC 88-63608. 172p. 1993. ring bd. 25.00 (0-88124-585-2, MI-30442) Cont Ed Bar-CA.

— Fee Agreement Forms Manual: May 1994 Update. LC 88-63608. 126p. 1994. 30.00 (0-88124-757-X, MI-30443) Cont Ed Bar-CA.

Pickus, Bob. Fee Agreement Forms Manual: 6/96 Update. LC 88-63608. 86p. 1996. ring bd. 36.00 (0-7626-0003-9, MI-30444) Cont Ed Bar-CA.

— Fee Agreement Forms Manual - 6/98 Update. LC 88-63608. 109p. 1998. ring bd. 40.00 (0-7626-0246-5, MI-30445) Cont Ed Bar-CA.

***Pickus, Bob, ed.** Fee Agreement Forms Manual, 6/99 Update. 86p. 1999. ring bd. 40.00 (0-7626-0339-9, MI-30446) Cont Ed Bar-CA.

Pickus, Bob & Sanders, Carol S. Fee Agreement Forms Manual: December 1991 Update. LC 88-63608. 74p. 1991. ring bd. 20.00 (0-88124-455-4, MI-30441) Cont Ed Bar-CA.

Pickus, Bob, ed. see Blair, Sandra, et al.

Pickus, Bob, ed. see Harris, Anne.

Pickus, Bob, ed. see Markun, Rachael, et al.

Pickus, Bob, ed. see Walker, Robert L.

***Pickus, David.** Dying with an Enlightening Fall: Poland in the Eyes of German Intellectuals, 1764-1800. LC 00-40195. 2000. write for info. (0-7391-0153-6) Lxngtn Bks.

Pickus, Keith. Constructing Modern Identities: Jewish University Sudents in Germany, 1815-1914. LC 99-11845. 224p. 1999. 29.95 (0-8143-2787-7) Wayne St U Pr.

Pickus, Noah M., ed. Immigration & Citizenship in the Twenty-First Century. 272p. 1998. 63.00 (0-8476-9220-5); pap. 23.95 (0-8476-9221-3) Rowman.

Pickuth, D. Essentials of Ultrasonography: A Practical Guide. (Illus.). 150p. 1995. 81.95 (3-540-58973-2) Spr-Verlag.

Pickvance, C. G. & Preteceille, Edmond. State & Locality: A Comparative Perspective on State Restructuring. 224p. 1991. text 39.00 (0-86187-983-X, Pub. by P P Pubs) Cassell & Continuum.

Pickvance, C. G., jt. ed. see Gottdiener, M.

Pickvance, Chris G., jt. ed. see Gottdiener, M.

***Pickvance, Else.** Themes for a Hundred Days. 1999. pap. 21.00 (1-85072-172-6, Pub. by W Sessions) St Mut.

Pickvance, Katy. Environmental Movements in Eastern Europe: A Comparative Study of Hungary & Russia. 208p. 1998. 69.00 (0-8133-3518-3, Pub. by Westview) HarpC.

Pickvance, Ronald. Vincent Van Gogh: Irises. (Getty Museum Studies on Art). pap. write for info. (0-89236-226-X, J P Getty Museum) J P Getty Trust.

Pickvet, Mark. Collecting Glassware. (Instant Expert Ser.). 130p. (Orig.). 1996. pap. 14.00 (1-887110-05-4) Allian Pubng.

— The Definitive Guide to Shot Glasses. (Illus.). 228p. 1993. pap. 19.95 (0-915410-90-7) Antique Pubns.

— The Encyclopedia of Shot Glasses. LC 99-163010. (Illus.). 336p. 1998. pap. 29.95 (1-57080-042-1) Antique Pubns.

***Pickvet, Mark.** The Official Price Guide to Glassware. 3rd ed. 800p. 2000. pap. 17.00 (0-676-60188-X) Ballantine Pub Grp.

Pickwell, George V., jt. auth. see Culotta, Wendy A.

Pickworth, J., jt. auth. see Pickworth, R.

Pickworth, R. & Pickworth, J. Passing HSC Legal Studies. 120p. 1991. pap. 30.00 (0-409-30194-9, Austral, MICHIE) LEXIS Pub.

Picle, Eli. Guide to Sabbath Observance. 179p. 1997. 15.95 (1-56871-131-X) Targum Pr.

Picler, F. & Diaz, R. Moreno, eds. Computer Aided Systems Theory - EUROCAST '93: A Selection of Papers from the Third International Workshop on Computer Aided Systems Theory, Las Palmas, Spain, February 1993: Proceedings. LC 93-44606. (Lecture Notes in Computer Science Ser.: Vol. 763). 1994. 65.95 (0-387-57601-0) Spr-Verlag.

Pico Della Mirandola, Giovanni. On the Dignity of Man. Wallis, Charles G. et al, trs. LC 65-26540. 1965. pap. 7.00 (0-672-60483-3, LLA227) Macmillan.

— Oracion Acerca de la Dignidad del Hombre. (SPA.). 38p. 1986. pap. 1.50 (0-8477-0730-X) U of PR Pr.

— Oration on the Dignity of Man. Caponigri, A. Robert, tr. 72p. 1996. pap. 8.95 (0-89526-713-6, Gateway Editions) Regnery Pub.

— Pico Della Mirandola: Of Being & Unity. Hamm, Victor M., tr. (Medieval Philosophical Texts in Translation Ser.). 1943. pap. 10.00 (0-87462-203-4) Marquette.

Pico Della Mirandola, Giovanni & Pico, Gian F. Opera Omnia, 2 vols., Set. xxvi, 2301p. 1969. reprint ed. write for info. (0-318-71271-7); reprint ed. write for info. (0-318-71605-4) G Olms Pubs.

Pico, Fernando. Al Filo del Poder: Subalternos y Dominantes en Pueto Rico, 1739-1910. (Caribbean Collection). (SPA.). 1993. pap. 11.95 (0-8477-0180-8) U of PR Pr.

— Amargo Cafe. LC 81-69788. (Coleccion Semilla). 162p. 1981. pap. 7.95 (0-940238-49-7) Ediciones Huracan.

— Contra la Corriente. (SPA.). 190p. (Orig.). 1996. pap. 9.25 (0-929157-31-1) Ediciones Huracan.

— El Dia Menos Pensado: Historia de los Presidiarios en Puerto Rico 1793-1993. (SPA.). 198p. 1994. pap. text 10.50 (0-929157-27-3) Ediciones Huracan.

— Don Quijote En Motora y Otras Andanzas. (SPA., Illus.). 120p. (Orig.). 1993. pap. 7.50 (0-929157-24-9) Ediciones Huracan.

— Los Gallos Peleados. LC 83-83055. (Coleccion Semilla). (SPA.). 179p. 1983. pap. 6.95 (0-940238-71-3) Ediciones Huracan.

— Historia General de Puerto Rico. LC 86-80150. (Huracan Academia Ser.). (SPA.). 300p. 1986. pap. 12.25 (0-940238-86-1) Ediciones Huracan.

— Mil Ochocientos Noventa y Ocho: La Guerra Despues de la Guerra. LC 87-80624. (Coleccion Semilla). (SPA.). 215p. 1987. pap. 8.50 (0-940238-25-X) Ediciones Huracan.

— La Peineta Colorado (The Red Shell-Comb) (SPA., Illus.). 48p. (YA). (gr. 3 up). 1999. pap. 7.95 (980-257-174-1, Pub. by Ediciones Ekare) Kane-Miller Bk.

— The Red Comb. Palacios, Argentina, tr. from SPA. LC 94-9832. (Illus.). 48p. (J). (gr. k-4). 1995. pap. 4.95 (0-8167-3540-9, Troll Medallion) Troll Communs.

— The Red Comb. 1994. 10.40 (0-606-08064-3) Turtleback.

— Vivir en Caimito. LC 88-83372. 185p. 1989. pap. 7.25 (0-940238-74-8) Ediciones Huracan.

Pico, Fernando & Izcoa, Carmen R. Puerto Rico, Tierra Adentro y Mar Afuera: Historia y Cultura de los Puertorriquenos. LC 91-71358. (SPA.). 304p. (J). (gr. 7). 1991. text 24.95 (0-929157-12-5) Ediciones Huracan.

Pico, Fernando & Ordonez, Maria A. Peineta Colorada. (SPA.). 49p. 1991. 10.50 (980-257-098-2) Ediciones Huracan.

Pico, Fernando, et al. Las Vallas Rotas. LC 82-83477. (Nave y el Puerto Ser.). (SPA.). 238p. 1982. pap. text 7.50 (0-940238-69-1) Ediciones Huracan.

Pico, Gian F., jt. auth. see Pico Della Mirandola, Giovanni.

Pico, Isabel, ed. Album de la Familia. (Illus.). 45p. 1989. pap. 5.75 (0-8477-2473-5) U of PR Pr.

Pico, Isabel & Alegria, Idsa. El Texto Libre de Prejuicios Sexuales y Raciales: Guia para la Preparacion de Materiales de Ensenanza. (SPA.). 56p. 1989. pap. 6.50 (0-8477-2470-0) U of PR Pr.

Pico, Isabel, et al. Machismo y Educacion en Puerto Rico. (SPA.). 135p. 1989. pap. 6.25 (0-8477-2466-2) U of PR Pr.

Pico, Juan H., jt. auth. see Sobrino, Jon.

Pico, Larry. Will God Enjoy Your Videotape??? LC 95-92556. 92p. 1995. pap. 7.95 (0-7880-0642-8, Fairway Pr) CSS OH.

Picoche, J. Robert Dictionary Etymologique du Francais. (FRE.). 619p. 1997. 69.95 (0-320-00495-3) Fr & Eur.

Picoche, Jacqueline. Dictionnaire Etymologique du Francais. (FRE.). 740p. 1994. 34.95 (0-7859-9204-9) Fr & Eur.

— Dictionnaire Etymologique du Francais. rev. ed. (FRE.). 620p. 1992. 110.00 (0-7859-9188-3) Fr & Eur.

Picon, ed. see Bernanos, Georges, et al.

Picon, Alice, ed. PAIS Foreign Language Index, 1990, Vol. 20. 660p. 1990. lib. bdg. 495.00 (1-877874-05-1) Pub Aff Info.

Picon, Carlos A., et al. Greek Vases in the San Antonio Museum of Art. Shapiro, H. Alan et al, eds. LC 95-73323. (Illus.). 287p. (Orig.). 1996. pap. 39.95 (1-883502-04-7) San Ant Mus Art.

Picon, G. Panorama de la Nouvelle Litterature Francaise. (FRE.). 1988. pap. 24.95 (0-7859-2939-8) Fr & Eur.

Picon, Geotan. Panorama Mysli Wspolczesnych. 713p. 1960. 9.00 (0-940962-20-9) Polish Inst Art & Sci.

Picon, Leon, tr. see Inoue, Yasushi.

Picon-Salas, Mariano. A Cultural History of Spanish America: From Conquest to Independence. Leonard, Irving A., tr. from SPA. LC 82-951. 192p. 1982. reprint ed. lib. bdg. 38.50 (0-313-23454-X, PSCH, Greenwood Pr) Greenwood.

— De la Conquista a la Independencia (From the Conquest to Independence) (SPA.). 261p. 1994. pap. 8.99 (968-16-0075-4, Pub. by Fondo) Continental Bk.

Picone, Michael D. Anglicisms, Neologisms & Dynamic French. LC 96-38628. (Linguisticae Investigationes Supplementa Ser.: No. 18). xii, 462p. 1996. lib. bdg. 99.00 (1-55619-258-4) J Benjamins Pubng Co.

Picornell, Miguel, ed. Measured Performance of Shallow Foundations. (Sessions Proceedings Ser.). 116p. 1988. 17.00 (0-87262-643-1) Am Soc Civil Eng.

Picot, A. & Schlicht, E., eds. Firms, Markets, & Contracts: Contributions to Neoinstitutional Economics. viii, 298p. 1996. pap. 78.00 (3-7908-0947-0) Spr-Verlag.

Picot, Andre, ed. see Prokopetz, Andrew T.

Picot, C. E., jt. ed. see Baumgartner, A.

Picot, Derek. Hotel Reservations: Calamaties & Hospitality Hiccups from the World's Hotels. (Illus.). 203p. 1995. pap. 12.95 (0-86051-930-9, Robson-Parkwest) Parkwest Pubns.

Picot, Dreek. Hotel Reservations: Calamities & Hospitality Hiccups from the World's Hotels. (Illus.). 203p. 1995. pap. 23.95 (0-86051-825-6, Robson-Parkwest) Parkwest Pubns.

Picot, Edward. Outcasts from Eden: Ideas of Landscape in British Poetry since 1945. LC 96-224899. 322p. 1997. 39.95 (0-85323-531-7, Pub. by Liverpool Univ Pr); pap. 24.95 (0-85323-541-4, Pub. by Liverpool Univ Pr) Intl Spec Bk.

Picot, Gerhard. Mergers & Acquisitions in Germany. LC 98-43288. 1998. 90.00 (1-57823-059-4) Juris Pubng.

Picot, J. J. Forestry Pesticide Aerial Spraying: Spray Droplet Generation, Dispersion, & Deposition. LC 96-37439. (Environmental Science & Technology Library). 228p. (C). 1997. text 113.50 (0-7923-4371-9) Kluwer Academic.

Picot, Jean-Paul & Tobias, Doris. La Bonne Soupe Cookbook. LC 96-17765. 1996. 25.00 (0-02-860994-8) Macmillan.

Picot, Marjorie N., ed. see Stephens, Joyce L.

Picot, Pierrick. Getting by in French: A Quick Beginner's Course for Tourists & Business People. (Get by In...Ser.). (ENG & FRE.). 1996. pap. 18.95 incl. audio (0-8120-8440-3) Barron.

Picott, J. Rupert. A Quarter Century of the Black Experience in Elementary & Secondary Education, 1950-1975. (YA). 1990. 9.95 (0-87498-087-9) Assoc Pubs DC.

Picott, J. Rupert, ed. Walter Washington. (YA). 1990. 5.95 (0-87498-094-1) Assoc Pubs DC.

Picott, R. & Ridley, W. N. History of the Restitution Fund Commission of the Episcopal Diocese of Pennsylvania, a Challenge. (YA). 1990. 15.95 (0-87498-091-7) Assoc Pubs DC.

Picou, Gary. The GPS Resource Guide: The Ultimate How-To Consumer Guide to GPS Satellite Aero-Navigation. (Illus.). 300p. 1999. pap. 29.95 (1-886743-16-9) Kindrd Sprt Pr.

Picou, J. Steven, et al. Exxon Valdez Disaster. 2nd ed. LC 99-180964. 354p. (C). 1999. per. 45.95 (0-7872-5685-4, 41568501) Kendall-Hunt.

Picoulin, Cathy. Fight Alzheimer's Naturally. LC 97-41569. 192p. 1999. pap. 14.00 (0-7615-1261-6) Prima Pub.

Picoult, Jodi. Harvesting the Heart. LC 93-7190. 416p. 1993. pap. 11.00 (0-685-64794-3, Viking) Viking Penguin.

— Harvesting the Heart. 464p. 1995. pap. 13.95 (0-14-023027-0, Penguin Bks) Viking Penguin.

***Picoult, Jodi.** Keeping Faith: A Novel. 432p. 2000. pap. 13.00 (0-688-17774-3, Perennial) HarperTrade.

Picoult, Jodi. Keeping Faith: A Novel. LC 98-43953. 432p. 1999. 24.00 (0-688-16825-6, Wm Morrow) Morrow Avon.

Picoult, Jodi. Mercy. large type ed. LC 96-43978. (Core Ser.). 662p. 1997. lib. bdg. 26.95 (0-7838-2003-8, G K Hall Lrg Type) Mac Lib Ref.

Picoult, Jodi. The Pact: A Love Story. LC 97-36432. 384p. 1998. 24.00 (0-688-15812-9, Wm Morrow) Morrow Avon.

***Picoult, Jodi.** The Pact: A Love Story. LC 97-36432. 400p. 1999. reprint ed. pap. 13.00 (0-688-17052-8, Wm Morrow) Morrow Avon.

Picoult, Jodi. Picture Perfect. 432p. 1996. reprint ed. mass mkt. 6.50 (0-425-15411-4) Berkley Pub.

***Picoult, Jodi.** Plain Truth. LC 99-462185. 416p. 2000. 24.95 (0-671-77612-6, PB Hardcover) PB.

Picouly, Daniel. Le Champ de Personne. large type ed. 528p. 1996. pap. 25.99 (2-84011-149-7) Ulverscroft.

Picozzi, Michele. Controlling Herpes Naturally: A Holistic Approach to Prevention & Treatment. LC 97-68478. (Illus.). 115p. 1998. pap. 12.95 (0-9658600-0-0) Southpaw Pr.

— Pocket Guide to Hatha Yoga. LC 98-5022. (Crossing Press Pocket Ser.). (Illus.). 112p. 1998. pap. 6.95 (0-89594-911-3) Crossing Pr.

Picq. Lucy & Her Times. 1996. write for info. (0-8050-5284-4) H Holt & Co.

Picq, Jean-Yves. The Case of Kaspar Mayer. Feingold, Michael, tr. from FRE. 60p. 1995. pap. 8.95 (0-913745-45-6) Ubu Repertory.

Picquet, Raymond, jt. auth. see Shanty, Frank.

Picquet, D. Cheryn, ed. Computer Law & Software Protection: A Bibliography of Crime, Liability, Abuse, & Security, 1984 Through 1992. LC 92-56631. 253p. 1993. pap. 47.50 (0-89950-840-5) McFarland & Co.

Picquet, Louisa, et al. Collected Black Women's Narratives. (Schomburg Library of Nineteenth-Century Black Women Writers). 384p. 1988. text 38.00 (0-19-505260-9) OUP.

Picqueur, L., ed. High Pressure Technology, 1998: Proceedings, ASME/JSME Joint Pressure Vessels & Piping Conference (1998, San Diego, CA) LC 98-213937. 371. 157p. 1998. pap. 80.00 (0-7918-1867-5) ASME.

Picraux, S. T., et al, eds. Surface Alloying by Ion, Electron & Laser Beams: Papers Presented at the 1985 ASM Materials Science Seminar Held October 12-13, 1985, Toronto, Ontario, Canada. LC 86-71028. (Illus.). 429p. 1987. reprint ed. pap. 133.00 (0-608-02649-2, 206330800004) Bks Demand.

Pictet, Francois J. Traite Elementaire De Paleontologie Histoire Naturelle Des Animaux Fossiles Consideres Ans Leur S Rapports Zoologiques et Geologiques, 4 vols. Gould, Stephen Jay, ed. LC 79-8344. (History of Paleontology Ser.). (FRE., Illus.). 1980. reprint ed. lib. bdg. 191.95 (0-405-12734-0) Ayer.

— Traite Elementaire De Paleontologie Histoire Naturelle Des Animaux Fossiles Consideres Ans Leur S Rapports Zoologiques et Geologiques, 4 vols., Vol. 1. Gould, Stephen Jay, ed. LC 79-8344. (History of Paleontology Ser.). (FRE., Illus.). 1980. reprint ed. lib. bdg. 47.95 (0-405-12735-9) Ayer.

— Traite Elementaire De Paleontologie Histoire Naturelle Des Animaux Fossiles Consideres Ans Leur S Rapports Zoologiques et Geologiques, 4 vols., Vol. 2. Gould, Stephen Jay, ed. LC 79-8344. (History of Paleontology Ser.). (FRE., Illus.). 1980. reprint ed. lib. bdg. 47.95 (0-405-12736-7) Ayer.

— Traite Elementaire De Paleontologie Histoire Naturelle Des Animaux Fossiles Consideres Ans Leur S Rapports Zoologiques et Geologiques, 4 vols., Vol. 3. Gould, Stephen Jay, ed. LC 79-8344. (History of Paleontology Ser.). (FRE., Illus.). 1980. reprint ed. lib. bdg. 47.95 (0-405-12737-5) Ayer.

— Traite Elementaire De Paleontologie Histoire Naturelle Des Animaux Fossiles Consideres Ans Leur S Rapports Zoologiques et Geologiques, 4 vols., Vol. 4. Gould, Stephen Jay, ed. LC 79-8344. (History of Paleontology Ser.). (FRE., Illus.). 1980. reprint ed. lib. bdg. 47.95 (0-405-12738-3) Ayer.

Picthal, M. M. Quranic Advices - Arabic Text with Translation. 154p. 1989. 8.95 (81-7151-024-8) Asia Bk Corp.

Piction Pub. Chippenham Ltd. Staff, ed. Half Penny Green: Postcards from Barnes & Mortlake. 96p. 1993. pap. 35.00 (0-948251-78-6, Pub. by Picton) St Mut.

P

Picto, A. & Grenouillet, P. Safety in the Chemistry & Biochemistry Laboratory. 336p. 1994. 79.95 (*0-471-18556-6*, Wiley-VCH) Wiley.

Picton, Bernard. A Field Guide to the Shallow Water: Echinoderms of the British Isles. (Illus.). 96p. (C). 1995. pap. 48.00 (*0-907151-88-4*, Pub. by IMMEL Pubng) St Mut.

Picton, Bernard & Morrow, Christine. A Field Guide to the Nudibranchs of the British Isles. (Illus.). 128p. 1994. pap. 48.00 (*1-898162-05-0*, Pub. by IMMEL Pubng) St Mut.

— A Field Guide to the Shallow-Water Nudibranchs of the British Isles. 128p. (C). 1990. pap. 125.00 (*0-7855-7120-5*, Pub. by IMMEL Pubng) St Mut.

Picton, Bernard, jt. auth. see Erwin, David.

***Picton, David & Broderick, Amanda, eds.** Integrated Marketing Communications. 576p. (Orig.). 2000. pap. 62.50 (*0-273-62513-6*) F T P H.

Picton, Howard, ed. see Steffan, Joseph M.

Picton, Howard J. The Life & Works of Joseph Anton Steffan (1726-1797) With Special Reference to His Keyboard Concertos, 2 vols., Set. rev. ed. LC 89-23792. (Outstanding Dissertations in Music from British Universities Ser.). 788p. 1990. text 10.00 (*0-8240-2345-5*) Garland.

Picton, John. The Art of African Textiles: Technology, Tradition & Lurex. 1999. 45.00 (*0-85331-796-8*) Lund Humphries.

Picton, John, et al, eds. The Art of African Textiles: Technology, Tradition & Lurex. (Illus.). 144p. 1996. pap. 35.00 (*0-85331-682-1*, Pub. by Lund Humphries) Antique Collect.

***Picton, Margaret.** Book of Magical Herbs. 128p. 2000. 16.95 (*0-7641-5224-6*) Barron.

Picton, Paul. The Gardeners Guide to Growing Asters. LC 99-17620. (Gardener's Guide Ser.). (Illus.). 160p. 1999. 29.95 (*0-88192-473-3*) Timber.

Picton Press Staff, ed. Index to Georgia Drew Merrill's History of Carroll County, N. H. LC 99-475189. 92p. 1997. pap. 12.50 (*0-89725-335-3*, 1860) Picton Pr.

Picton Publishing (Chippenham) Ltd. Staff. An Anthology of Poems. (C). 1987. 50.00 (*0-948251-21-2*, Pub. by Picton) St Mut.

— The Army in India & Its Evolution: Including an Account of the Establishment of the Royal Air Force in India. 253p. 1992. 85.00 (*0-948251-68-9*, Pub. by Picton) St Mut.

— The Art Gallery & Other Poems. (C). 1987. 50.00 (*0-7855-5327-4*, Pub. by Picton) St Mut.

— Beyond the Art Gallery. (C). 1987. 50.00 (*0-948251-08-5*, Pub. by Picton) St Mut.

— Bombs & Booby Traps: World War II Bomb Clearance. Hunt, James, ed. 148p. (C). 1990. pap. 45.00 (*0-948251-19-0*, Pub. by Picton) St Mut.

— British & Indian Armies in the East Indies, 1685-1935. (C). 1987. 125.00 (*0-7855-5335-5*, Pub. by Picton) St Mut.

— British & Indian Armies in the East Indies, 1685-1935. deluxe ed. (C). 1987. 475.00 (*0-7855-5336-3*, Pub. by Picton) St Mut.

— Cautionary Tales & Other Verses. (C). 1987. 50.00 (*0-948251-20-4*, Pub. by Picton) St Mut.

— Devizes in Focus: A Town in Photographic Profile. (Illus.). (C). 1987. 85.00 (*0-948251-48-4*, Pub. by Picton); pap. 45.00 (*0-948251-47-6*, Pub. by Picton) St Mut.

— 47th Sikhs War Record: The Great War 1914-1918. 321p. 1992. 120.00 (*0-948251-61-1*, Pub. by Picton) St Mut.

— Gainst All Disaster: The Edward & Albert Medal Conversions to the George Cross. (C). 1987. 75.00 (*0-7855-5330-4*, Pub. by Picton) St Mut.

— Gannet. (FAA Ser.). (C). 1987. 45.00 (*0-948251-46-8*, Pub. by Picton) St Mut.

— Make Your Bets: How to Win at Gambling. (C). 1987. pap. 22.00 (*0-948251-49-2*, Pub. by Picton) St Mut.

— Operation Nestegg: The Liberation of Jersey, 1945. (C). 1987. 20.00 (*0-948251-26-3*, Pub. by Picton) St Mut.

— Operation Skua. (FAA Ser.). (C). 1987. 39.00 (*0-7855-5334-7*, Pub. by Picton) St Mut.

— Poems Humorous & Inconsequential. (C). 1987. 35.00 (*0-948251-30-1*, Pub. by Picton) St Mut.

— Poems Pensive & Peculiar. (C). 1987. 40.00 (*0-7855-5326-6*, Pub. by Picton) St Mut.

— The Pomprey Train: The Portsmouth Line Explored. (C). 1987. 30.00 (*0-948251-45-X*, Pub. by Picton) St Mut.

— Putting the Record Straight: World Helicopter Speed Record. (C). 1987. 22.00 (*0-948251-38-7*, Pub. by Picton) St Mut.

— Royal Flying Corps: (Military Wing) Honours & Awards. (C). 1987. 75.00 (*0-7855-5328-2*, Pub. by Picton) St Mut.

— Satellite TV Installation Guide. (C). 1987. 60.00 (*0-7855-5324-X*, Pub. by Picton) St Mut.

— Scimitar. (FAA Ser.). (C). 1987. 50.00 (*0-948251-39-5*, Pub. by Picton) St Mut.

— Simkin's Soldiers, Vol. 1. (C). 1987. 60.00 (*0-7855-5333-9*, Pub. by Picton) St Mut.

— Socialist International at Gunpoint: Did the CIA Murder Olaf Palme? (C). 1987. 65.00 (*0-948251-40-9*, Pub. by Picton) St Mut.

— Stamps of Alderney. (C). 1987. 50.00 (*0-948251-33-6*, Pub. by Picton) St Mut.

— Supplement to the Falkland Islands Catalogue, 1988. (C). 1987. 75.00 (*0-7855-5325-8*, Pub. by Picton) St Mut.

— Terriers in the Trenches: The Post Office Rifles at War, 1914-1918. (C). 1987. 65.00 (*0-7855-5331-2*, Pub. by Picton) St Mut.

— The 28th Light Cavalry in Persia, & Russian Turkestan 1915-1920. Vloth, G. & Kreger, R. A., eds. 203p. (C). 1990. 105.00 (*0-948251-35-2*, Pub. by Picton) St Mut.

Picton Publishing (Chippenham) Ltd. Staff, ed. Prince of Wales Own, the Scinde Horse: A Regimental History. (C). 1987. 150.00 (*0-7855-5332-0*, Pub. by Picton) St Mut.

— Unarmed into Battle: The Story of the Air Observation Post by Major General H. J. Parham CB, CBE, DSO, & E.M.G. Belfield, MA. 1990. reprint ed. pap. 39.00 (*0-948251-14-X*, Pub. by Picton) St Mut.

Picton Publishing (Chippenham) Ltd. Staff, jt. auth. see Glendinning, D.

Picton Publishing (Chippenham) Ltd. Staff, jt. auth. see Kincaid-Smith.

Picton Publishing (Chippenham) Ltd. Staff, jt. auth. see Perkins, Roger.

Picton Publishing Staff. Angus' Mull. rev. ed. 1987. 30.00 (*0-7855-2185-2*, Pub. by Picton) St Mut.

— The Army of India Medal Roll, 1799-1826. 123p. (C). 1987. 120.00 (*0-7855-2228-X*, Pub. by Picton) St Mut.

— The Artwork Interviews. (C). 1987. 35.00 (*0-7855-2177-1*, Pub. by Picton) St Mut.

— Ben Nevis & Its Observatory. (Illus.). (C). 1987. 45.00 (*0-7855-2204-2*, Pub. by Picton) St Mut.

— The Celtic-Rangers Joke Book. (Illus.). (C). 1987. 9.00 (*0-7855-2203-4*, Pub. by Picton) St Mut.

— The Crinan Canal. (Illus.). 40p. 1987. 45.00 (*0-7855-2183-6*, Pub. by Picton) St Mut.

— Geoff. (C). 1987. 35.00 (*0-7855-2176-3*, Pub. by Picton) St Mut.

— Glasgow, London: A Traveller's Guide. (C). 1987. 45.00 (*0-7855-2179-8*, Pub. by Picton) St Mut.

— The Highland Line. (Illus.). 118p. (C). 1987. 22.00 (*0-7855-2190-9*, Pub. by Picton) St Mut.

— HMS Invincible: The Falklands Deployment, 1982. 78p. (C). 1987. 91.00 (*0-7855-2166-6*, Pub. by Picton) St Mut.

— Honours & Awards Indian Army, August 1914-August 1921. 302p. (C). 1987. 65.00 (*0-7855-2232-8*, Pub. by Picton) St Mut.

— Jamie Fleeman's Country Cookbook. (Illus.). (C). 1987. 30.00 (*0-7855-2188-7*, Pub. by Picton) St Mut.

— Kilmartin. 1987. 30.00 (*0-7855-2184-4*, Pub. by Picton) St Mut.

— The Lochaber Narrow Gauge Railway. (Illus.). (C). 1987. 30.00 (*0-7855-2194-1*, Pub. by Picton) St Mut.

— Mallaig Line Steam. (Illus.). (C). 1987. 22.00 (*0-7855-2192-5*, Pub. by Picton) St Mut.

— Natural History of Loch Lomond. 1987. 30.00 (*0-7855-2181-X*, Pub. by Picton) St Mut.

— The Old Firm Guide. (C). 1987. 25.00 (*0-7855-2202-6*, Pub. by Picton) St Mut.

— Old Nooks of Stirling. (Illus.). (C). 1987. 25.00 (*0-7855-2207-7*, Pub. by Picton) St Mut.

— The Public Enquiry. (C). 1987. 25.00 (*0-7855-2180-1*, Pub. by Picton) St Mut.

— The Punjab Campaign: Casualty Roll, 1849. 76p. (C). 1987. 105.00 (*0-7855-2227-1*, Pub. by Picton) St Mut.

— The Road to the Road to the Isles. (C). 1987. 25.00 (*0-7855-2200-X*, Pub. by Picton) St Mut.

— Robert Burns. 240p. (C). 1987. 35.00 (*0-7855-2198-4*, Pub. by Picton) St Mut.

— Robert Burns. limited ed. 240p. (C). 1987. 333.00 (*0-7855-2199-2*, Pub. by Picton) St Mut.

— Scotland's Distilleries. (Illus.). (C). 1987. 45.00 (*0-7855-2210-7*, Pub. by Picton) St Mut.

— Scotland's Malt Whiskies. (C). 1987. 25.00 (*0-7855-2212-3*, Pub. by Picton) St Mut.

— Scotland's Threatened Lines. (C). 1987. 28.00 (*0-7855-2189-5*, Pub. by Picton) St Mut.

— Scottish Farm Animals. (C). 1987. 22.00 (*0-7855-2201-8*, Pub. by Picton) St Mut.

— Steam Lines. 1987. 30.00 (*0-7855-2182-8*, Pub. by Picton) St Mut.

— Supplement to the Half-Yearly Army List for the Period Ending 31st December, 1924: War Services of Officers on Retired Pay, Etc. 703p. (C). 1987. 245.00 (*0-7855-2225-5*, Pub. by Picton) St Mut.

— Tales of the Tay. (Illus.). 1987. 40.00 (*0-7855-2187-9*, Pub. by Picton) St Mut.

— Tree Life of Argyll. 1987. 25.00 (*0-7855-2186-0*, Pub. by Picton) St Mut.

— W. D. & H. O. Wills Roll of Honour & War Service Roll, 1914-1918. 46p. (C). 1987. pap. 56.00 (*0-948251-28-X*, Pub. by Picton) St Mut.

— West Highland Steam. (C). 1987. 32.00 (*0-7855-2178-X*, Pub. by Picton) St Mut.

Picton Publishing Staff, ed. The Army of the Sutlej: Casualty Roll, 1845-46. 50p. (C). 1987. 110.00 (*0-7855-2223-9*, Pub. by Picton) St Mut.

— Casualties Sustained by the British Army in the Korean War, 1950-1953. 85p. (C). 1987. 105.00 (*0-7855-2231-X*, Pub. by Picton) St Mut.

— It's Angus Again. (C). 1987. 30.00 (*0-7855-2196-8*, Pub. by Picton) St Mut.

— The South African War Casualty Rolls: Natal Field Force, 20th October, 1899-26th October, 1900. 237p. (C). 1987. 133.00 (*0-7855-2213-1*, Pub. by Picton) St Mut.

Picton Publishing Staff & Barnard, Alfred. The Whiskey Distillers of Scotland, 1887. (Illus.). 160p. (C). 1987. reprint ed. 60.00 (*0-7855-2211-5*, Pub. by Picton) St Mut.

Picton Publishing Staff & Keegan, Alan. Scotch in Miniature. rev. ed. (Illus.). (C). 1987. 30.00 (*0-7855-2209-3*, Pub. by Picton) St Mut.

Picton Publishing Staff & MacBrayne. Summer Tours in Scotland. (C). 1987. reprint ed. 18.00 (*0-7855-2205-0*, Pub. by Picton) St Mut.

Picton Publishing Staff & MacIntyre, Angus. Angus MacIntyre's Ceilidii Collection. (C). 1987. 22.00 (*0-7855-2197-6*, Pub. by Picton) St Mut.

Picton Publishing Staff & Weir, Tom. The Oban Line. (Illus.). (C). 1987. 22.00 (*0-7855-2191-7*, Pub. by Picton) St Mut.

Picton, T. W., ed. Human Event-Related Potentials: Handbook of Electroencephalography & Clinical Neurophysiology. 542p. 1988. 329.25 (*0-444-80929-5*) Elsevier.

Picton, Tom. Old Gotham Theatricals: Selections from a Series, "Reminiscences of a Man about Town" Slout, William L., ed. LC 95-20579. (Clipper Studies in the Theater: No. 12). x, 170p. 1995. pap. 21.00 (*0-89370-462-8*) Millefleurs.

Pictor, Mike. Conversations with Christ. 73p. (Orig.). 1984. pap. 6.95 (*0-942494-84-9*) Coleman Pub.

Pictor, Philip, jt. auth. see Johnson, Jeffrey.

Pictor Publ. Chippenham Ltd. Staff. Emperor's Chambermaids: The Story of the 14-20th King's Hussars by Lt. Col. L. Boats DSO. (Illus.). 518p. (C). 1990. 60.00 (*0-7063-1001-2*, Pub. by Picton) St Mut.

Picture Primal. Lecture Lab: Image & Text Management Made Easy. 1998. 89.95 (*0-7484-0855-X*) Taylor & Francis.

Picucci, Michael. Complete Recovery: An Expanded Model of Community Healing. 1996. 23.95 (*0-9650380-1-7*) Mombaccus Pubng.

— The Journey Toward Complete Recovery: Reclaiming Our Emotional, Spiritual & Sexual Wholeness. LC 98-7069. 244p. 1998. pap. 16.95 (*1-55643-286-0*) North Atlantic.

Picus, Larry, jt. auth. see Selvin, Molly.

***Picus, Lawrence O.** Resource Allocation. (J). (gr. k-12). 2000. write for info. (*0-86552-147-6*) U of Oreg ERIC.

Picus, Lawrence O. & Wattenbarger, James L. Where Does the Money Go? Resource Allocation in Elementary & Secondary Schools. (Yearbook of the American Education Finance Association Ser.). (Illus.). 296p. 1995. 54.95 (*0-8039-6162-6*) Corwin Pr.

Picus, Lawrence O., jt. auth. see Odden, Allan R.

Picut, Catherine A., jt. auth. see Lewis, Robert M.

Pidal, Menendez. Flor Nueva de Romances Viejos. 33rd ed. 264p. 1991. pap. 12.95 (*0-7859-5190-3*) Fr & Eur.

Pidal, Ramon M. Historia de Espana Vol. 10: Los Comienzos de la Reconquista (711-1038) De Urbal, F. J. & Balbas, L. T., eds. (SPA.). 660p. 1992. 195.00 (*0-7859-0515-4*, 8423948080) Fr & Eur.

— Historia de Espana Vol. 12: Los Reinos Cristianos en los Siglos XI y XII: Vol. I, Economias, Sociedades, Instituciones. Carles, M. & Pastor, Reyna, eds. (FRE.). 478p. 1992. 195.00 (*0-7859-0516-2*, 8423948129) Fr & Eur.

— Historia de Espana Vol. 36: La Epoca del Romanticismo (1808-1874): Las Letras, las Artes, la Vida Cotidiana. Zavala, Iris M. et al, eds. (SPA.). 780p. 1992. 195.00 (*0-7859-0539-1*, 8423949931) Fr & Eur.

Pidal, Ramon M., jt. auth. see Gallego Morell, Antonio.

Pidcock, David M. Satanic Voices: A Surfeit of Blasphemy Including the Rushdie Report. 1992. pap. text 14.95 (*1-871012-03-1*, Pub. by Mustaquim-Islamic) Intl Spec Bk.

Pidcoke, Heather F., ed. & tr. see Ruaro, Luir J.

***Pidd, Michael.** Computer Simulation in Management Science. 4th ed. LC 97-30971. 298p. 1998. pap. 54.99 (*0-471-97931-7*) Wiley.

Pidd, Michael. Tools for Thinking: Modelling in Management Science. LC 96-32158. 360p. 1997. 67.95 (*0-471-96455-7*) Wiley.

Piddington, H. An English Index to the Plants of India. 243p. 1980. 15.00 (*0-88065-174-1*) Scholarly Pubns.

Piddington, J. H. Cosmic Electrodynamics. 2nd ed. LC 77-22303. 376p. 1981. lib. bdg. 39.50 (*0-88275-587-0*) Krieger.

Piddington, Ralph, ed. see Williamson, Robert W.

Piddocke, Stuart. Teachers in Trouble: An Exploration of the Normative Character in Teaching. LC 98-116763. (Illus.). 352p. 1997. text 45.00 (*0-8020-2979-5*); pap. text 18.95 (*0-8020-7436-7*) U of Toronto Pr.

Piderit, John J. The Ethical Foundations of Economics. LC 92-41288. (Illus.). 360p. 1993. reprint ed. pap. 111.60 (*0-608-03977-2*, 205965900011) Bks Demand.

Pidgeon, C. Tutorials for the Biomedical Sciences: Animations, Simulations, & Calculations. 328p. 1996. pap. 95.00 (*0-471-18637-6*, Wiley-VCH) Wiley.

Pidgeon, C., ed. Advanced Tutorials for the Biomedical Sciences: Animations, Simulations & Calculations Using Mathematica. 304p. 1996. pap. 95.00 (*0-471-18646-5*, Wiley-VCH) Wiley.

Pidgeon, Charles, ed. Advanced Tutorials for the Biomedical Sciences: Animations, Simulations, & Calculations Using Mathematica. LC 96-1059. (Illus.). 304p. 1996. pap. 79.95 incl. 3.5 ld, mac hd (*1-56081-950-2*, Wiley-VCH) Wiley.

— Tutorials for the Biomedical Sciences: Animations, Simulations, & Calculations Using Mathematica. LC 95-25624. (Illus.). xxviii, 300p. 1996. pap. 79.95 incl. disk (*1-56081-928-6*, Wiley-VCH) Wiley.

Pidgeon, Harry. Around the World Single-Handed: The Cruise of the Islander. (Illus.). 272p. 1989. pap. 7.95 (*0-486-25946-3*) Dover.

Pidgeon, Jean. See What's in the Sea. (Sticker Stories Ser.). (Illus.). 16p. (J). 1997. pap. text 4.95 (*0-448-41724-3*, G & D) Peng Put Young Read.

Pidgeon, Mary. Woman: Her Purpose, Position & Power. 1998. pap. 10.99 (*1-56043-330-2*, Treasure Hse) Destiny Image.

Pidgeon, Mary E. Women in the Economy of the United States of America. LC 75-8784. (FDR & the Era of the New Deal Ser.). 1975. reprint ed. lib. bdg. 29.50 (*0-306-70731-4*) Da Capo.

Pidgeon, Mary J. We've Come a Long Way, Baby! LC 94-223360. 192p. 1994. pap. 9.99 (*0-89274-725-0*, HH-725) Harrison Hse.

Pidgeon, Monica, jt. ed. see McCorquodale, D.

Pidgeon, Nick F., jt. auth. see Turner, Barry A.

Pidgeon, Sue, jt. ed. see Barrs, Myra.

***Pidgeon, Trevor.** Boom Ravine. 1998. pap. 16.95 (*0-85052-612-4*, Pub. by Leo Cooper) Trans-Atl Phila.

Pidgeon, Walter P. The Universal Benefits of Volunteering: A Practical Workbook for Nonprofit Organizations, Volunteers, & Corporations. LC 97-42939. 319p. 1997. text 39.95 incl. disk (*0-471-18505-1*) Wiley.

Pidgie, Sere W. The Gathering at Charlie's. Rietveld, Jeffrey & Champlin, Allen R., Sr., eds. LC 94-93917. 262p. (Orig.). (YA). (gr. 12). 1993. pap. 7.00 (*0-9628802-2-1*) DeChamp CA.

— Sam Sleuth Snooper Dog. Edwards, Beryl, ed. 450p. (YA). (gr. 12). 1993. pap. 7.00 (*0-9628802-5-6*) DeChamp CA.

Pidgin, Charles F. & Taylor, J. M. The Chronicles of Quincy Adams Sawyer, Detective. LC 75-32774. (Literature of Mystery & Detection Ser.). (Illus.). 1976. reprint ed. 28.95 (*0-405-07893-5*) Ayer.

Pidgora, V. O., jt. auth. see Belichko, Iu. V.

Pidhiryanka, Maria. The Joys of Winter. (UKR., Illus.). 34p. (J). (gr. k-5). 1994. 10.00 (*0-9603782-1-9*) Chwyli Dnistra.

Pidna, Leslie A., jt. auth. see Johnson, Donald B.

Pidoux, Blaise, ed. Eustache du Caurroy, OEuvres Completes. (Gesamtausgaben-Collected Works: Vol. IX, Pt. 1). (ENG, FRE & GER.). 130p. 1976. lib. bdg. 4.00 (*0-912024-70-4*) Inst Mediaeval Mus.

Pidoux, Pierre, ed. see Goudimel.

Pie & Neudeck Staff. Solid State DEV 4 Volume Set. 1983. pap. 31.00 (*0-201-05287-3*) Addison-Wesley.

P.I.E. Books Editorial Staff. Advertising Flyer Graphics. (Illus.). 224p. 1997. 89.95 (*4-89444-026-1*, Pub. by AG Pubs) Bks Nippan.

— Brochure Design Forum, Vol. 3. LC 97-203348. (Illus.). 208p. 1997. 79.95 (*4-89444-034-2*, Pub. by PIE Bks) Bks Nippan.

— Corporate Profile Graphics, Vol. 2. LC 96-124906. (Illus.). 224p. 1997. 65.00 (*4-89444-041-5*, Pub. by Pie Bks) Bks Nippan.

Pie Books Editorial Staff. New Typographics, Vol. 2. 59.95 (*4-89444-056-3*, Pub. by Pie Bks) Bks Nippan.

— Timing Zero. (Illus.). 80p. 1997. pap. 12.95 (*4-89444-044-X*, Pub. by PIE Bks) Bks Nippan.

P.I.E. Books Editorial Staff, ed. Artifile Vol. 5: The Production Index, Vol. 5. (Illus.). 224p. 1996. 69.95 (*4-89444-017-2*, Pub. by PIE Bks) Bks Nippan.

— Company Brochure Collection, Vol. 2. LC 96-471155. (Illus.). 224p. 1996. 85.00 (*4-89444-003-2*, Pub. by PIE Bks) Bks Nippan.

***Pie Books Editorial Staff, ed.** Corporate Profile Graphics, Vol. 3. (Illus.). 224p. 1999. 65.00 (*4-89444-087-3*, Pub. by Pie Bks) Bks Nippan.

— Diagram Graphics Vol. 3: The World's Best Graphs, Charts, Maps & Technical Illustrations. (Illus.). 224p. 1999. 75.00 (*4-89444-120-9*, Pub. by Pie Bks) Bks Nippan.

— Direct Mail & Announcement Collection. (Illus.). 224p. 1999. pap. 39.95 (*4-89444-009-1*, Pub. by Pie Bks) Bks Nippan.

— Effective Sales Catalog Design. (Illus.). 224p. 1999. (*4-89444-098-9*, Pub. by Pie Bks) Bks Nippan.

— Flyer & Leaflet Collection. (Illus.). 224p. 1999. pap. 39.95 (*4-89444-109-8*, Pub. by Pie Bks) Bks Nippan.

— Graphic Beat Vol. 2: The Softmix. (Illus.). 224p. pap. (*4-89444-072-5*, Pub. by Pie Bks) Bks Nippan.

— New Business Card Graphics, Vol. 2. (Illus.). 224p. 1999. 65.00 (*4-89444-117-9*, Pub. by Pie Bks) Bks Nippan.

— New CD Jacket Collection. (Illus.). 180p. Date not set. pap. 69.96 (*4-89444-084-9*, Pub. by Pie Bks) Bks Nippan.

— New Postcard Graphics. (Illus.). 224p. 1999. pap. 89.95 (*4-89444-110-1*, Pub. by Pie Bks) Bks Nippan.

Pie Books Editorial Staff, ed. Sensual Images. (Illus.). 208p. pap. 29.95 (*4-938586-57-6*, Pub. by Pie Bks) Bks Nippan.

***Pie Books Editorial Staff, ed.** Sign Graphics: Cool Edition. (Illus.). 224p. 1999. 69.95 (*4-89444-111-X*, Pub. by Pie Bks) Bks Nippan.

— Sign Graphics: Hot Edition. (Illus.). 224p. 1999. 69.95 (*4-89444-103-9*, Pub. by Pie Bks) Bks Nippan.

— Successful Direct Mail Design, Vol. 2. 224p. 1999. 75.00 (*4-89444-114-4*, Pub. by Pie Bks) Bks Nippan.

— Tokyo Typedirectors Club Annual '99. (Illus.). 224p. 1999. pap. 89.95 (*4-89444-115-2*, Pub. by Pie Bks) Bks Nippan.

Pie Books Staff. C. D. Jacket Collection. LC 95-166182. (Illus.). 224p. 1994. reprint ed. pap. 49.95 (*4-938586-55-X*, Pub. by PIE Bks) Bks Nippan.

— Direct Mail Graphics. (Illus.). 224p. 1994. 79.95 (*4-938586-60-6*, Pub. by PIE Bks) Bks Nippan.

— Fashion & Cosmetic Graphics. (Illus.). 224p. 1994. 69.95 (*4-938586-50-9*, Pub. by PIE Bks) Bks Nippan.

Pie Editorial Staff. Labels & Tags, Vol. 3. 69.95 (*4-89444-074-1*, Pub. by Pie Bks) Bks Nippan.

Pie Editorial Staff, ed. Magazine Advertising Graphics. 1998. 69.95 (*4-89444-082-2*, Pub. by Pie Bks) Bks Nippan.

— New Logos & Trademark Design. 1998. 69.95 (*4-89444-081-4*, Pub. by Pie Bks) Bks Nippan.

— One & Two Color Graphics, Vol. 2. 1998. 69.95 (*4-89444-093-8*, Pub. by Pie Bks) Bks Nippan.

***Piebnkowski, Jan.** Bel & Bub & the Black Hole. LC 00-26179. (Illus.). (J). (ps-k). 2000. 9.95 (*0-7894-6528-0*) DK Pub Inc.

Piece O'Cake Designs Staff. Stars in the Garden: Fresh Flowers in Applique. White, Janet, ed. LC 98-10349. (Piece O Cake Designs Ser.). (Illus.). 48p. 1998. pap. 18.95 (*1-56477-223-3*, B335, That Patchwrk Pl) Martingale & Co.

An Asterisk (*) at the beginning of an entry indicates that the title is appearing for the first time.

***Piechocinski, Elizabeth C.** The Old Burying Ground: Colonial Park Cemetery, Savannah Georgia, 1750-1853. (Illus.). 1999. pap. 18.00 (*1-891495-09-7*) Oglethorpe Pr.

— The Old Burying Ground: Colonial Park Cemetery, Savannah Georgia, 1750-1853. unabridged ed. (Illus.). 23.50 (*1-891495-08-9*) Oglethorpe Pr.

Pieck, Cecilia, tr. see Murail, Marie-Aude.

Pieck, Werner. Algerien - Die Wiedergewonnene Wurde. (Historische Texte und Studien Ser.: Bd. 8). (GER.). xii, 208p. 1987. write for info. (*3-487-07834-1*) G Olms Pubs.

Pieczenik, Steve. State of Emergency. 1999. mass mkt. 6.99 (*0-515-12525-3*, Jove) Berkley Pub.

— State of Emergency. 1999. reprint ed. mass mkt. 6.99 (*0-515-12444-3*, Jove) Berkley Pub.

Pieczenik, Steve, jt. auth. see Clancy, Tom.

Pieczenik, Steve, jt. creator see Clancy, Tom.

Pieczenik, Steve R. Blood Heat. 352p. 1988. 17.95 (*0-15-113216-X*) Harcourt.

— Blood Heat. 1989. mass mkt. 4.95 (*0-446-35673-5*, Pub. by Warner Bks) Little.

— My Life Is Great, Why Do I Feel So Awful? Successful Women, Hidden Passions. LC 89-39118. 1990. 18.45 (*0-446-51458-6*) Warner Bks.

— Pax Pacifica. 1995. write for info. (*0-446-51818-2*) Warner Bks.

Pieczenik, Steve R., jt. auth. see Clancy, Tom.

Pieczenik, Steve R., jt. creator see Clancy, Tom.

Pieczka, Magda, jt. auth. see L'Etang, Jacquie.

Pieczynska, E., jt. ed. see Hillbricht-Ilkowska, A.

Piedad, Floyd, jt. auth. see Hawkins, Michael.

Piedade, M. E. Energetics of Stable Molecules & Reactive Intermediates LC 99-25677. (NATO Science Ser.). 1999. write for info. (*0-7923-5740-X*) Kluwer Academic.

Piedmont, Donlan. Peanut Soup & Spoonbread: An Informal History of Hotel Roanoke. Virginia Tech Real Estate Foundation Staff, ed. LC 94-44863. 1994. 19.95 (*0-9617635-1-5*) VA Tech Found.

Piedmont-Palladino, Susan & Branch, Mark A. Devil's Workshop: 25 Years of Jersey Devil Architecture. LC 97-23411. (Illus.). 144p. (Orig.). 1997. pap. 29.95 (*1-56898-113-9*) Princeton Arch.

Piedmont Peace Project Staff, jt. ed. see Arnow, Pat.

Piedmont, R. L. The Revised NEO Personal Inventory: Clinical & Research Applications. (Plenum Series in Social-Clinical Psychology). (Illus.). 275p. (C). 1998. text 65.00 (*0-306-45943-4*, Kluwer Plenum) Kluwer Academic.

Piedmont, Ralph L., jt. auth. see Mostofsky, David I.

Piednoir, Christian, jt. photos by see Paule, Marie.

Piedra, Joaquin E. Sangre Bajo Las Banderas (de Rusia Vino el Martillo - y la Hoz de Mi Garganta) LC 85-81209. (Coleccion Espejo de Paciencia). (SPA.). 101p. (Orig.). 1986. pap. 9.95 (*0-89729-382-7*) Ediciones.

Piegl, Les, ed. Fundamental Developments in Computer-Aided Geometric Modelling. (Illus.). 432p. 1993. text 71.00 (*0-12-554765-X*) Acad Pr.

Piegl, Les & Tiller, Wayne. The Nurbs Book. LC 95-32273. (Monographs in Visual Communication). 1995. write for info. (*3-540-55069-0*) Spr-Verlag.

Piegl, Les A. & Tiller, Wayne. The Nurbs Book. 2nd ed. LC 96-48140. (Monographs in Visual Communication). (Illus.). 650p. 1997. pap. 54.95 (*3-540-61545-8*) Spr-Verlag.

Piehl, Frank. The Caxton Club 1895-1995: Celebrating a Century of the Book in Chicago. (Illus.). 224p. 1995. 75.00 (*0-940550-09-1*, 41478) Oak Knoll.

Piehl, Hauptmann. The German Fallschirmjager in World War II. LC 96-70649. (Illus.). 96p. 1997. 24.95 (*0-7643-0230-2*) Schiffer.

Piehler, G. Kurt. Remembering War the American Way. LC 94-10755. (Illus.). 248p. 1995. text 34.95 (*1-56098-461-9*) Smithsonian.

Piehler, G. Kurt, jt. auth. see Chambers, John W.

***Piehler, Glenn R.** Exit Here for Fish! Enjoying & Conserving New Jersey's Recreational Fisheries. LC 99-53440. (Illus.). 256p. 2000. pap. 22.00 (*0-8135-2785-6*); text 52.00 (*0-8135-2784-8*) Rutgers U Pr.

Piek, Jan P. Motor Behavior & Human Skill: A Multidisciplinary Approach. LC 97-40755. (Illus.). 448p. 1998. text 49.00 (*0-88011-675-7*, BPIE0675) Human Kinetics.

Piek, Jan P., jt. ed. see Glencross, Denis J.

Piekalkiewicz, Janusz. The Battle for Cassino. LC 80-51757. 224p. 1980. 16.95 (*0-672-52667-0*, Bobbs) Macmillan.

— BMW Motorcycles in World War II. LC 91-60854. (Illus.). 192p. 1991. 29.95 (*0-88740-306-9*) Schiffer.

— The Cavalry of World War II. LC 80-5800. (Illus.). 256p. (C). 1980. 25.00 (*0-8128-2749-X*, Scrbrough Hse) Madison Bks UPA.

— The German 88 Gun in Combat: The Scourge of Allied Armor. Force, Edward, tr. from GER. LC 91-62737. (Illus.). 192p. 1992. 29.95 (*0-88740-341-7*) Schiffer.

— Rommel & the Secret War in North Africa, 1941-1943: Secret Intelligence in the North African Campaign. Clemens, Fred, tr. from GER. LC 91-62740. (Illus.). 240p. 1992. 29.95 (*0-88740-340-9*) Schiffer.

Piekalkiewicz, Jaroslaw & Bede, Barry. Public Opinion Polling in Czechoslovakia, 1968-1969: Results & Analysis of Surveys Conducted During the Dubcek Era. LC 70-176398. (Special Studies in International Politics & Government). 1972. 32.50 (*0-275-28631-2*) Irvington.

Piekalkiewicz, Jaroslaw & Hamilton, Christopher, eds. Public Bureaucracies Between Reform & Resistance: Legacies, Trends & Effects in China, the U. S. S. R., Poland & Yugoslavia. LC 90-20250. 256p. 1991. 19.50 (*0-85496-295-6*) Berg Pubs.

Piekalkiewicz, Jaroslaw & Penn, Alfred W. Politics of Ideocracy. LC 94-8841. 274p. (C). 1995. text 49.50 (*0-7914-2297-6*); pap. text 16.95 (*0-7914-2298-4*) State U NY Pr.

Piekarski, Alexander Z., ed. see Schneersohn, Dovber.

Piekarski, Chana T., ed. Shlichus - Outreach Insights: A Panorama of Programs & Projects. (Illus.). 480p. 1996. 25.00 (*0-8266-0397-1*, Neshei Chabad) Kehot Pubn Soc.

Piekarski, Vicki, ed. Westward the Women: An Anthology of Western Stories by Women. LC 87-34238. 186p. 1988. reprint ed. pap. 11.95 (*0-8263-1063-X*) U of NM Pr.

Piekarski, Vicki, jt. ed. see Tuska, Jon.

Pieke, Frank N. The Ordinary & the Extraordinary: An Anthropological Study of Chinese Reform & the 1989 People's Movement in. LC 95-35861. 280p. (C). 1996. 110.00 (*0-7103-0540-0*, Pub. by Kegan Paul Intl) Col U Pr.

***Piekutowski, Lynna.** Remembering the Boys: A Collection of Letters, a Gathering of Memories. LC 00-38459. (Illus.). 2000. write for info. (*0-87338-677-9*) Kent St U Pr.

Piel. You, Me & Technology. (Tech & Industrial Education Ser.). 1989. pap., teacher ed. 8.00 (*0-8273-3406-0*) Delmar.

Piel Cook, Ellen. Psychological Androgyny. (General Psychology Ser.: No. 133). 256p. 1985. pap. text 25.00 (*0-08-031612-3*, Pergamon Pr) Elsevier.

Piel, Gerard. Only One World. 3rd ed. (C). 1992. 8.00 (*0-7167-2323-9*) W H Freeman.

Piel, Robert J. & Van Der Linden, Paul C. Become an Officer in Law Enforcement: Getting the Edge. (Illus.). 132p. 1996. pap. text 14.95 (*0-89262-495-7*) Career Pub.

***Piel, Stobie.** Blue-Eyed Bandit. (Timeswept Ser.). 368p. 2000. mass mkt. 5.50 (*0-505-52394-9*, Love Spell) Dorchester Pub Co.

Piel, Stobie. A Brighter Dawn. 1997. mass mkt. 5.50 (*0-7860-0403-7*, Pinncle Kensgtn) Kensgtn Pub Corp.

Piel, Stobie. The Dawn Star. 400p. (Orig.). 1996. mass mkt. 5.99 (*0-505-52148-2*) Dorchester Pub Co.

Piel, Stobie. Flights of Angels. 352p. 1996. mass mkt. 4.99 (*0-7860-0349-9*, Pinncle Kensgtn) Kensgtn Pub Corp.

***Piel, Stobie.** Free Falling. 368p. 1999. mass mkt. 5.99 (*0-505-52329-9*, Pub. by Dorchester Pub Co) CMG.

Piel, Stobie. The Midnight Moon. 368p. 1998. mass mkt. 5.50 (*0-505-52268-3*, Love Spell) Dorchester Pub Co.

— Molly in the Middle. 400p. (Orig.). 1997. mass mkt. 5.99 (*0-505-52193-8*) Dorchester Pub Co.

— A Patriot's Heart. 384p. 1998. mass mkt. 5.50 (*0-7860-0472-X*, Pinncle Kensgtn) Kensgtn Pub Corp.

— Rebel Wind. 416p. 1995. mass mkt. 4.99 (*0-8217-0110-X*, Zebra Kensgtn) Kensgtn Pub Corp.

— The White Sun. 368p. 1999. mass mkt. 5.50 (*0-505-52292-6*, Love Spell) Dorchester Pub Co.

Piel, Stobie, et al. Scottish Magic. LC 96-80349. 288p. 1997. 21.95 (*1-57566-182-9*, Knsington) Kensgtn Pub Corp.

— Scottish Magic: Lily/Isbel/Faerie Princess/Beneath the Midnight Sky. 320p. 1998. mass mkt. 5.99 (*1-57566-278-7*, Knsington) Kensgtn Pub Corp.

— Trick or Treat. 400p. (Orig.). 1997. mass mkt. 5.99 (*0-505-52220-9*, Love Spell) Dorchester Pub Co.

Piela, Catherine, jt. auth. see Saunders, Robin.

Piela, Suzane. You Are So Beautiful Without Your Hair: A Daughter's Journey with the Death of Her Parents. LC 99-21686. 336p. 2000. pap. 16.95 (*1-885394-37-3*, Pub. by Bluestar Communs) ACCESS Pubs Network.

Piele, Phillip K., jt. auth. see Farquhar, Robin H.

Pielenz Hampton, Mary. Coffee, Cookies, & Inspiration: Heartwarming Moments with God: A Collection of Devotions & Recipes. (Illus.). 96p. 1998. 15.99 (*0-310-97205-1*, Zondervan Gifts) Zondervan.

Pielenz, Mary. Tea & Inspiration. 96p. 1995. 15.99 (*0-7852-7704-8*, J Thoma Bks) Nelson.

***Pielin, Don, et al.** American Dimestore Toy Soldiers & Figures. LC 00-9479. (Illus.). 2000. write for info. (*0-7643-1189-1*) Schiffer.

Pielke, R. A., ed. see Beniston, M.

Pielke, Robert G. Critiquing Moral Arguments. 56p. (C). 1992. text 29.50 (*0-8191-8642-2*); pap. text 12.00 (*0-8191-8643-0*) U Pr of Amer.

— You Say You Want a Revolution: Rock Music in American Culture. LC 85-25940. 270p. 1986. pap. text 25.95 (*0-8304-1201-8*) Burnham Inc.

Pielke, Roger A. Hurricanes: Their Nature & Impacts on Society. LC 97-11316. 298p. 1998. 90.00 (*0-471-97354-8*) Wiley.

***Pielke, Roger A.** Storms, 2 vols. LC 98-48488. 1999. 275.00 (*0-415-17239-X*) Routledge.

Pielke, Roger A., ed. U. S. National Report to International Union of Geodesy & Geophysics, 1991-1994, 2 vols. 1432p. 1995. text 75.00 (*0-87590-863-2*) Am Geophysical.

Pielke, Roger A. & Pearce, Robert P. Mesoscale Modeling of the Atmosphere. LC 95-191502. (Meteorological Monograph: Vol. 25, No. 47). 1994. 65.00 (*1-878220-15-2*) Am Meteorological.

Pielke, Roger A., jt. auth. see Cotton, William R.

Pieller, Evelyne. Tango. Giammanco-Frongia, Rosanna M., tr. from SPA. LC 97-165189. (Illus.). 110p. 1997. 35.00 (*1-55670-597-2*) Stewart Tabori & Chang.

Pielmeier, HeidiMarie & Schirner, Markus. Illustrated Tarot Spreads: 78 New Layouts for Personal Discovery. (Illus.). 96p. 1999. pap. 12.95 (*0-8069-6345-X*) Sterling.

Pielmeier, John. Haunted Lives: Three Related Short Plays. 1984. pap. 5.25 (*0-8222-0503-3*) Dramatists Play.

— Impassioned Embraces. 1989. pap. 5.25 (*0-8222-0556-4*) Dramatists Play.

***Pielmeier, John.** Voices in the Dark. 98p. 1999. pap. 6.95 (*0-88145-154-1*) Broadway Play.

Pielou, E. C. After the Ice Age: The Return of Life to Glaciated North America. LC 90-11024. (Illus.). 384p. 1991. 29.95 (*0-226-66811-8*) U Ch Pr.

— After the Ice Age: The Return of Life to Glaciated North America. LC 90-11024. (Illus.). x, 376p. 1992. pap. 18.00 (*0-226-66812-6*) U Ch Pr.

— Biogeography. LC 92-7291. 366p. (C). 1992. reprint ed. lib. bdg. 49.95 (*0-89464-739-3*) Krieger.

— Ecological Diversity. LC 75-9663. 173p. reprint ed. pap. 53.70 (*0-608-15369-9*, 205634900060) Bks Demand.

— Fresh Water. LC 97-51562. (Illus.). 288p. 1998. 24.00 (*0-226-66815-0*) U Ch Pr.

— Fresh Water. LC 97-51562. 275p. 2000. pap. 14.00 (*0-226-66816-9*) U Ch Pr.

— The Interpretation of Ecological Data: A Primer on Classification & Ordination. LC 84-7284. 288p. 1984. 99.00 (*0-471-88950-4*) Wiley.

— A Naturalist's Guide to the Arctic. LC 94-2555. 344p. 1994. lib. bdg. 57.00 (*0-226-66813-4*) U Ch Pr.

— A Naturalist's Guide to the Arctic. LC 94-2555. 344p. 1994. pap. 20.00 (*0-226-66814-2*) U Ch Pr.

— Population & Community Ecology: Principles & Methods. LC 72-86334. (Illus.). viii, 429p. 1974. text 225.00 (*0-677-03580-2*) Gordon & Breach.

— The World of Northern Evergreens. (Illus.). 200p. 1988. text 42.50 (*0-8014-2116-0*); pap. text 15.95 (*0-8014-9424-9*) Cornell U Pr.

Pielow, Dorothee. Die Quellen der Weisheit die Arabische Magie im Spiegel des Usul Al-Hikma Von Ahmad Ibn Ali Al-Buni. (GER.). viii, 210p. 1995. 58.00 (*3-487-09983-7*) G Olms Pubs.

Piels, William B. & Hull, Brian D. Sales & Leases in California Commercial Law Practice: 7/96 Update. Peyerwold, David, ed. LC 93-70675. 330p. 1996. ring bd. 34.00 (*0-7626-0022-5*, BU-32072) Cont Ed Bar-CA.

Piemonte, G., et al, eds. Developments in Analytical Methods in Pharmaceutical, Biomedical, & Forensic Sciences. LC 87-7180. 340p. 1988. 85.00 (*0-306-42695-1*, Plenum Trade) Perseus Pubng.

***Piemonte, Raffaele & Jamison, Scott.** Developing Applications with Outlook 2000, CDO, Exchange & Visual Basic. LC 99-43582. (Illus.). 704p. (C). 1999. pap. text 54.95 (*0-201-61575-4*) Addison-Wesley.

Piemontes, Grayce. Classic Shirley Temple-Paperdolls, Vol. 181. (J). 1989. pap. 4.95 (*0-486-25193-4*) Dover.

Piemontese, Allesio. The Thyrde & Last Parte of the Secretes of Maister Alexis of Piemont. Warde, W., tr. LC 77-6844. (English Experience Ser.: No. 840). 1977. reprint ed. lib. bdg. 20.00 (*90-221-0840-6*) Walter J Johnson.

***Pien, Homer H., ed.** Battlefield Biomedical Technologies. 128p. 1999. pap. text 50.00 (*0-8194-3186-9*) SPIE.

Pienaar, G. J., jt. auth. see Van Der Walt, A. J.

Pienaar, Kristo, jt. auth. see Johnson-Barker, Carole.

Pienaar, W. Negotiation: Theories, Strategies & Skills. 2nd ed. LC 96-220533. 272p. 1996. pap. 40.00 (*0-7021-3578-X*, Pub. by Juta & Co) Gaunt.

Pienaar, Wynand & Spoelstra, Manie. Negotiation: Theories, Strategies & Skills. rev. ed. 258p. 1994. reprint ed. text 39.60 (*0-7021-2485-0*, Pub. by Juta & Co) Intl Spec Bk.

Pienciak, Richard T. Mama's Boy. 1997. mass mkt. 6.99 (*0-451-40748-2*, Onyx) NAL.

***Piene, Otto.** Otto Piene: Retrospektive 1952, 1996. (Illus.). 208p. 2000. 65.00 (*3-87909-468-3*, Pub. by Wienand) Nazraeli Press.

Piene, Otto & Goldring, Elizabeth, eds. Centerbeam. (Illus.). 131p. (Orig.). 1980. pap. text 17.50 (*0-262-66047-4*) MIT Pr.

Piene, Otto & Mack, Heinz. Zero. 1973. 30.00 (*0-262-16041-2*) MIT Pr.

Piene, Otto, ed. see Philadelphia Institute of Contemporary Art Staff.

Pienemann, Manfred. Language Processing & Second Language Development: Processability Theory. LC 98-23896. (Studies in Bilingualism: Vol. 15). xviii, 367p. 1998. 69.00 (*1-55619-549-4*) J Benjamins Pubng Co.

Pienemann, Manfred, jt. ed. see Hyltenstam, Kenneth.

Piening, Christopher. Global Europe: The E. U. in World Affairs. LC 97-43. 1997. 49.95 (*1-55587-694-3*); pap. 19.95 (*1-55587-700-1*) L Rienner.

Pienkos, Angela. The Imperfect Autocrat: Grand Duke Constantine Pavlovich & the Polish Congress Kingdom. 185p. 1987. text 47.50 (*0-88033-113-5*, 217, Pub. by East Eur Monographs) Col U Pr.

Pienkos, Donald E. One Hundred Years Young: A History of the Polish Falcons of America, 1887-1987. (East European Monographs: No. 231). 348p. 1987. text 79.50 (*0-88033-128-3*, Pub. by East Eur Monographs) Col U Pr.

— PNA: A Centennial History of the Polish National Alliance of the U. S. A. 485p. 1984. text 72.00 (*0-88033-060-0*, Pub. by East Eur Monographs) Col U Pr.

— Polish American Eff Pol, No. 311. 400p. 1992. text 75.50 (*0-88033-208-5*, Pub. by East Eur Monographs) Col U Pr.

Pienkowski. ABC Board Book. (Illus.). 16p. (J). 1998. 4.99 (*0-689-82095-X*) S&S Childrens.

— 1-2-3 Board Book. (Illus.). 16p. (J). 1998. 4.99 (*0-689-82096-8*) S&S Childrens.

— Shapes Board Book. (Illus.). 16p. (J). (ps). 1998. 4.99 (*0-689-82097-6*) S&S Childrens.

— Zoo Board Book. (Illus.). 16p. (J). (ps). 1998. 4.99 (*0-689-82098-4*) S&S Childrens.

Pienkowski, Jan. Animals. 8p. (J). (ps-k). 1995. 4.50 (*0-689-80434-2*) Atheneum Yung Read.

***Pienkowski, Jan.** Baby Bird. (Illus.). (ps-3). 2000. write for info. (*0-7894-6526-4*, Pub. by DK Pub Inc) Pub Resources Inc.

— Bel & Bub & the Bad Snowball. LC 00-24508. (Illus.). (J). (ps-3). 2000. 9.95 (*0-7894-6529-9*) DK Pub Inc.

— Bel & Bub & the Big Brown Box. LC 00-24509. (Illus.). 995p. (J). (ps-3). 2000. 9.95 (*0-7894-6527-2*) DK Pub Inc.

— Botticelli's Bed & Breakfast. (Illus.). 8p. (J). (gr. 3-5). 2000. 23.00 (*0-7881-9364-3*) DIANE Pub.

Pienkowski, Jan. Botticelli's Bed & Breakfast. (J). 1997. 23.00 (*0-684-83523-1*) S&S Trade.

— Colors. (Nursery Board Bks.). (Illus.). 14p. (J). (ps). 1989. 3.50 (*0-671-68134-6*) Litle Simon.

— Dinnertime. (Pienkowski Mini Pop-Up Ser.). (Illus.). 10p. (J). (ps-3). 1991. pap. 6.99 (*0-8431-2963-8*, Price Stern) Peng Put Young Read.

— Door Bell. (Illus.). 5p. (J). (ps up). 1993. (*1-888443-37-5*) Can Manda Gp.

— Faces. (Nursery Board Bks.). (Illus.). 24p. (J). (ps). 1991. 2.95 (*0-671-72846-6*) Litle Simon.

— Ferme. (Folio Ser.). (FRE.). (J). 5.95 (*2-07-056307-3*) Schoenhof.

— Food. (Nursery Board Bks.). (Illus.). 24p. (J). (ps). 1991. 2.95 (*0-671-72845-8*) Litle Simon.

— Friends. 8p. (J). (ps up). 1995. 4.50 (*0-689-80433-4*) Atheneum Yung Read.

— Fun. 8p. (J). (ps-k). 1995. 4.50 (*0-689-80432-6*) Atheneum Yung Read.

— Good Night: A Pop-Up Lullaby. LC 98-86853. (Illus.). 12p. (J). (ps). 1999. 14.99 (*0-7636-0763-0*) Candlewick Pr.

— Good Night, Moo! (Introducing Furrytails Ser.). (Illus.). 8p. (J). (ps). 1995. pap. 19.99 (*0-525-45355-5*, Dutton Child) Peng Put Young Read.

— Homes. (Nursery Board Bks.). (Illus.). 14p. (J). (ps). 1990. pap. 2.95 (*0-671-70478-8*) Litle Simon.

— Jan Pienkowski's Sea. (Animal Action Pops Ser.). (Illus.). 12p. (J). (gr. 2 up). 1998. 4.95 (*1-58117-019-X*, Piggy Toes Pr) Intervisual Bks.

— Little Monsters. (Pienkowski Mini Pop-Up Ser.). (Illus.). 10p. (J). (ps up). 1991. 6.99 (*0-8431-2964-6*, Price Stern) Peng Put Young Read.

— One Two Three. (Nursery Board Bks.). (Illus.). 14p. (J). (ps). 1989. 2.95 (*0-671-68136-2*) S&S Trade.

— Play. 8p. (J). (ps-k). 1995. 4.50 (*0-689-80431-8*) Atheneum Yung Read.

— Shapes. (Nursery Board Bks.). (Illus.). (J). (ps). 1989. 2.95 (*0-671-68135-4*) Litle Simon.

— Sizes. (Nursery Board Bks.). (Illus.). 24p. (J). (ps). 1991. 2.95 (*0-671-72844-X*) Litle Simon.

— Small Talk. (Pienkowski Mini Pop-Up Ser.). (Illus.). 10p. (J). (ps up). 1991. 4.95 (*0-8431-2966-2*, Price Stern) Peng Put Young Read.

— Stop Go. (Illus.). 24p. (J). (ps). 1992. 2.95 (*0-671-74519-0*) Litle Simon.

— Time. LC 82-42884. (Nursery Board Bks.). (Illus.). 24p. (J). (ps-k). 1991. pap. 2.95 (*0-671-72847-4*) Litle Simon.

— Wheels. (Illus.). 24p. (J). (ps). 1992. pap. 2.95 (*0-671-74517-4*) Litle Simon.

— Yes No. (Illus.). 24p. (J). (ps). 1992. 2.95 (*0-671-74520-4*) Litle Simon.

Pienkowski, Jan. Jan Pienkowski's Farm: Pop-Up. (Animal Action Pops Ser.). 12p. (J). (gr. 2 up). 1998. 4.95 (*1-58117-021-1*, Piggy Toes Pr) Intervisual Bks.

— Jan Pienkowski's Jungle. (Animal Action Pops Ser.). 12p. (J). (gr. 2 up). 1998. 4.95 (*1-58117-020-3*, Piggy Toes Pr) Intervisual Bks.

— Jan Pienkowski's Pets: Pop-Up. (Animal Action Pops Ser.). 12p. (J). (gr. 2 up). 1998. 4.95 (*1-58117-022-X*, Piggy Toes Pr) Intervisual Bks.

Pienkowski, Jan, jt. auth. see Nicoll, Helen.

Pienn, Rochelle T. The Claws in the Eiderdown. 82p. 1998. mass mkt. 12.00 (*0-9652018-2-1*) Bloody Someday.

Pienta, Kenneth J., ed. Diagnostic Advances: Molecular Medicine in the Diagnosis & Prognosis of Genito-Urinary Malignancies. LC 96-30169. (Cancer Treatment & Research Ser.). 280p. (C). 1996. text 260.00 (*0-7923-4164-3*) Kluwer Academic.

Pienta, P., et al, eds. ATCC Bacteria & Bacteriophages. 19th ed. 804p. 1996. pap. text. write for info. (*0-930009-59-2*) ATCC.

***Pientka, Cheryl.** Frommer's Paris from $80 a Day 2001. (Illus.). 2000. pap. 14.99 (*0-7645-6163-4*) IDG Bks.

Piepenbring, Meike. Smut Fungi (Ustilaginales & Tilletiales) in Costa Rica. LC 96-172358. (Nova Hedwigia, Beihefte/Supplementary Issues Ser.: Beih 113). (Illus.). 155p. 1996. pap., suppl. ed. 77.00 (*3-443-51035-3*, Pub. by Gebruder Borntraeger) Balogh.

Piepenbrink, Arthur. In the Image of God. LC 92-31645. (Illus.). 96p. 1993. pap. 9.95 (*0-942963-28-8*) Distinctive Pub.

***Piepenbrink, Fredric E.** How to Interpret the Bible. 1999. 37.99 (*0-8100-0911-0*) Northwest Pub.

Piepenbrink, Linda, ed. Christmas Country Style. LC 91-62465. 100p. 1991. 14.95 (*0-89821-096-8*, 6596) Reiman Pubns.

— Sweet & Scrumptious Chocolate. LC 92-63183. 52p. 1993. 4.95 (*0-89821-102-6*, 11655) Reiman Pubns.

Piepenburg, Matthew. Time & the Maiden. LC 97-72256. 256p. 1997. pap. 15.95 (*1-882897-15-3*) Lost Coast.

Piepenburg, Robert. Raku Pottery. rev. ed. (Illus.). 160p. 1994. pap. 26.95 (*0-9628481-1-5*) Pebble Pr.

— Raku Pottery. 4th rev. ed. LC 98-65060. (Illus.). 160p. 1998. pap. 26.95 (*0-9628481-5-8*) Pebble Pr.

— The Spirit of Clay. LC 94-66588. (Illus.). 448p. (Orig.). 1996. pap. text 39.95 (*0-9628481-2-3*) Pebble Pr.

— The Spirit of Clay: A Classic Guide to Ceramics. 2nd rev. ed. LC 98-65059. (Illus.). 448p. 1998. pap. 39.95 (*0-9628481-4-X*) Pebble Pr.

— Treasures of the Creative Spirit: An Artist's Understanding of Human Creativity. LC 97-75480. (Illus.). 166p. 1998. pap. 12.95 (*0-9628481-3-1*) Pebble Pr.

Piepenburg, Roy L. Celestine: A Trilogy. LC 98-183429. 1997. write for info. (*0-9682699-0-7*) EHP.

P

An Asterisk (*) at the beginning of an entry indicates that the title is appearing for the first time.

***Piepenburg, Scott.** Easy Marc: Incorporating Format Integration. 3rd ed. 215p. 1999. pap. 28.00 (*0-9652126-0-2*) Hi Willow.

***Pieper, Adi.** The Easy Guide to Solar Electric: For Home Power Systems. Johnson, Barbara, ed. (Illus.). 212p. 1999. pap. 14.95 (*0-9671891-0-1*) A D I Solar.

Pieper, August. Isaiah II. 1980. 38.99 (*0-8100-0109-8*, 15N0357) Northwest Pub.

Pieper, Bill. So Trust Me. LC 99-61368. 160p. 2000. pap. 13.95 (*0-88739-267-9*) Creat Arts Bk.

***Pieper, Donald.** Large Catechism Pt. II: Bible Study. 1999. 37.99 (*0-8100-0812-2*) Northwest Pub.

Pieper, Donald J. Large Catechism Pt. 1: Bible Study. 1998. 37.99 (*0-8100-0811-4*, 22N0886) Northwest Pub.

Pieper, Edgart, tr. see Sydnor, Caroline.

Pieper, Eleonore F. Imitation Is Criticism: Dante Gabriel Rossetti und William Blake. (Europaische Hochschulschriften, Reihe 14: No. 330). (GER., Illus.). 428p. 1997. 63.95 (*3-631-31899-5*) P Lang Pubng.

Pieper, Francis. Christian Dogmatics, 4 vols., 1. Engelder, Theodore et al, trs. 577p. 1957. 29.00 (*0-570-06712-X*, 15-1001) Concordia.

— Christian Dogmatics, 4 vols., 2. Engelder, Theodore et al, trs. 577p. 1957. 29.00 (*0-570-06713-8*, 15-1002) Concordia.

— Christian Dogmatics, 4 vols., 3. Engelder, Theodore et al, trs. 555p. 1957. 29.00 (*0-570-06714-6*, 15-1003) Concordia.

— Christian Dogmatics, 4 Vols., Set. Engelder, Theodore et al, trs. 1957. 111.99 (*0-570-06715-4*, 15-1852) Concordia.

— Christian Dogmatics, 4 Vols, Vol. 4. Engelder, Theodore et al, trs. 1957. 35.00 (*0-570-06711-1*, 15-1000) Concordia.

— What Is Christianity? And Other Essays. Mueller, John T., tr. from GER. 290p. 1997. reprint ed. 25.00 (*1-891469-20-7*) Repristination.

Pieper, Irene T. My Culinary Journey. (Illus.). 168p. 1993. 19.93 (*0-9638234-0-X*) I K Pieper.

Pieper, Jan. Pienza: Der Entwurf Einer Humanistischen Weltsicht. (GER., Illus.). 632p. 1997. 240.00 (*3-930698-06-4*) Edition A Menges.

— Pienza: Il Progetto Di una Visione Umanistica del Mondo. (Illus.). 632p. 2000. 216.00 (*3-930698-07-2*) Edition A Menges.

Pieper, Jeanne. The Catholic Woman: Difficult Choices in a Modern World. 272p. 1994. pap. 13.95 (*1-56565-157-X*) Lowell Hse.

— A Special Place for Santa: A Legend for Our Time. (Illus.). 32p. (J). (gr. 1-4). 1991. 8.95 (*0-9616286-1-8*) Roman IL.

Pieper, Josef. Abuse of Language, Abuse of Power. Krauth, Lothar, tr. from GER. LC 90-85240. 54p. (Orig.). 1992. pap. 5.95 (*0-89870-362-X*) Ignatius Pr.

— Belief & Faith: A Philosophical Tract. Winston, Richard & Winston, Clara, trs. from GER. LC 75-31841. 106p. 1975. reprint ed. lib. bdg. 39.75 (*0-8371-8490-8*, PIBF, Greenwood Pr) Greenwood.

— A Brief Reader on the Virtues of the Human Heart. Krauth, Lothar, tr. from GER. LC 90-81767. 54p. 1991. pap. 5.95 (*0-89870-303-4*) Ignatius Pr.

***Pieper, Josef.** Death & Immortality. unabridged ed. Winston, Richard & Winston, Clara, trs. from GER. LC 99-48135. Orig. Title: Tod und Unsterblich Keit. 144p. (C). 2000. reprint ed. pap. text 11.00 (*1-890318-18-3*, Pub. by St Augustines Pr) Chicago Distribution Ctr.

Pieper, Josef. Divine Madness: Plato's Case Against Secular Humanism. LC 95-75667. 60p. (Orig.). 1995. pap. 5.95 (*0-89870-557-6*) Ignatius Pr.

— End of Time: St. Peter & the Primacy of Rome in Scripture & the Early Church. LC 98-74070. 1999. pap. text 11.95 (*0-89870-726-9*) Ignatius Pr.

***Pieper, Josef.** Enthusiasm & Divine Madness: On the Platonic Dialogue Phaedrus. unabridged ed. Winston, Richard & Winston, Clara, trs. from GER. Orig. Title: Begeisterung und Gottlicher Wahnsiun. 125p. 2000. reprint ed. pap. text 11.00 (*1-890318-23-X*, Pub. by St Augustines Pr) Chicago Distribution Ctr.

Pieper, Josef. Faith, Hope, Love. LC 96-78013. 1997. pap. text 17.95 (*0-89870-623-8*) Ignatius Pr.

— Four Cardinal Virtues. LC 65-14713. 1966. pap. 10.50 (*0-268-00103-0*) U of Notre Dame Pr.

— Guide to Thomas Aquinas. LC 90-86251. 192p. 1991. reprint ed. pap. 14.95 (*0-89870-319-0*) Ignatius Pr.

— Happiness & Contemplation. Winston, Richard & Winston, Clara, trs. from GER. 126p. 1998. 19.00 (*1-890318-30-2*); pap. text 11.00 (*1-890318-31-0*) St Augustines Pr.

— Hope & History. LC 93-78535. 112p. (Orig.). 1994. pap. 9.95 (*0-89870-465-0*) Ignatius Pr.

— In Defense of Philosophy. Krauth, Lothar, tr. from GER. LC 91-76072. 128p. (Orig.). 1992. pap. 9.95 (*0-89870-397-2*) Ignatius Pr.

— In Search of the Sacred: Contributions to an Answer. Krauth, Lothar, tr. from GER. LC 90-81770. 136p. (Orig.). 1991. pap. 9.95 (*0-89870-301-8*) Ignatius Pr.

***Pieper, Josef.** In Tune with the World: A Theory of Festivity. Winston, Richard & Winston, Clara, trs. from GER. LC 99-14341. 114p. 1999. reprint ed. pap. text 11.00 (*1-890318-33-7*) St Augustines Pr.

Pieper, Josef. Josef Pieper: An Anthology. LC 88-83748. 255p. (Orig.). 1989. pap. 14.95 (*0-89870-226-7*) Ignatius Pr.

— Leisure: The Basis of Culture. Dru, Alexander, tr. from GER. LC 98-40641. Orig. Title: Musse und Kult - Was Heisst Philosophieren?. 158p. 1999. 17.00 (*0-86597-210-9*) Liberty Fund.

— Leisure, the Basis of Culture (Musse und Kult & Was Heisst Philesephieren) Malsbary, Gerald, tr. from GER. LC 98-15340. 176p. 1998. pap. text 12.00 (*1-890318-35-3*) St Augustines Pr.

— Living the Truth. Krauth, Lothar & Lange, Stella, trs. from GER. LC 89-84891.Tr. of Reality of the Good. 190p. (Orig.). 1989. reprint ed. pap. text 14.95 (*0-89870-261-5*) Ignatius Pr.

— Only the Lover Sings: Art & Contemplation. Krauth, Lothar, tr. from GER. LC 90-81771. 76p. (Orig.). 1990. pap. 6.95 (*0-89870-302-6*) Ignatius Pr.

— Problems of Modern Faith: Essays & Addresses. Van Heurck, Jan, tr. 307p. 1983. 7.49 (*0-8199-0856-8*, Frncscn Herld) Franciscan Pr.

— The Silence of St. Thomas. Murray, John & O'Connor, Daniel, trs. from GER. LC 99-14342. 128p. 1999. pap. text 11.00 (*1-890318-78-7*) St Augustines Pr.

Pieper, Kalle. Sango. LC 99-169485. 1998. 44.95 (*3-925443-83-5*) Janvid Pubs.

***Pieper, Keith.** Internet Data Market: An Overview of the Players & Opportunity. 78p. 1999. pap. 690.00 (*1-929504-03-9*) Innovative Ventures.

— Interstitial Advertising: Insights into Effective Implementation. 2nd rev. ed. (Illus.). 67p. 1999. pap. 690.00 (*1-929504-02-0*) Innovative Ventures.

Pieper, Martha H. & Pieper, William J. Intrapsychic Humanism: An Introduction to a Comprehensive Psychology & Philosophy of Mind. 402p. 1990. 47.50 (*0-9624919-0-X*) Falcon Two Pr.

Pieper, Martha Heineman & Pieper, William J. Smart Love: The Compassionate Alternative to Discipline That Will Make You a Better Parent & Your Child a Better Person. LC 98-32053. 288p. 1999. 22.95 (*1-55832-142-X*) Harvard Common Pr.

Pieper, Norbert H. Arbeitsmarktpolitik in Deutschland und Japan im Vergleich. (Arbeit - Technik - Organisation - Soziales Ser.: Bd. 2). (GER., Illus.). 198p. 1996. pap. 42.95 (*3-631-49449-1*) P Lang Pubng.

***Pieper, Richard, et al.** Ithaca Then & Now. rev. ed. 128p. 2000. 39.95 (*0-935526-88-9*) McBooks Pr.

Pieper, Richard, jt. auth. see Hesch, Merrill.

Pieper, Richard R. TeamPower. LC 88-92255. 70p. (Orig.). (C). 1989. pap. 30.00 (*0-9621149-0-1*) PPC Inc.

Pieper, Rudiger. Lexikon Management. (GER.). 418p. 1992. 105.00 (*0-7859-8338-4*, 3409132147) Fr & Eur.

Pieper, Rudiger, ed. Human Resource Management: An International Comparison. (Studies in Organization: No. 26). (Illus.). xii, 285p. (C). 1990. lib. bdg. 54.95 (*3-11-012573-0*) De Gruyter.

Pieper, Thomas I. & Gidney, James B. Fort Laurens, 1778-79: The Revolutionary War in Ohio. LC 75-44712. (Illus.). 128p. 1980. pap. 8.50 (*0-87338-240-4*) Kent St U Pr.

Pieper, Ursula & Stickel, Gerhard. Studia Linguistica Diachronica et Synchronica. 988p. 1985. text 292.30 (*3-11-009664-1*) Mouton.

Pieper, Vicki, ed. see Diaz, Marino.

Pieper, William J., jt. auth. see Pieper, Martha H.

Pieper, William J., jt. auth. see Pieper, Martha Heineman.

Piepho, Lee, tr. see Mantuanus, Baptista.

Piepke, Susan L., tr. see Buchner, Luise.

Piepkorn, Arthur C. The Church: Selected Writings of Arthur Carl Piepkorn. Plekon, Michael P. & Wiecher, William S., eds. 304p. (Orig.). (C). 1993. pap. text 12.00 (*0-9633142-2-X*) Am Luth Pub Bur.

— Profiles in Belief: The Religious Bodies of the United States & Canada, Vols. 3 & 4. Incl. Vol. 3. Holiness & Pentecostal Bodies. 1990. Vol. 4. Evangelical, Fundamental, & Other Christian Bodies. 1990. LC 89-45748. 1990. 24.95 (*0-06-066581-5*) Harper SF.

Piepkorn, Arthur C., jt. auth. see Mayer, F. E.

Pieprzyk, Josef & Sadeghiyan, Babak. Design of Hashing Algorithms. LC 93-41251. 1994. 43.00 (*0-387-57500-6*) Spr-Verlag.

Pieprzyk, Josef & Seberry, Jennifer. Information Security & Privacy: First Australian Conference, ACISP '96, Wollongong, NSW, Australia, June 24-26, 1996: Proceedings. LC 96-48646. (Lecture Notes in Computer Science Ser.: Vol. 1172). 333p. 1996. text 56.00 (*3-540-61991-7*) Spr-Verlag.

Pieprzyk, Josef, ed. see Fourth International Conference on the Theory & Ap.

Pier, A., ed. see Goetz, Friedrich, et al.

Pier, Arthur S. & Forbes, W. Cameron. American Apostles to the Philippines. LC 74-160926. (Biography Index Reprint Ser.). 1977. reprint ed. 20.95 (*0-8369-8089-1*) Ayer.

Pier Brodie, Julie, compiled by. Making a Difference: Lessons from Teach for America Classrooms, Vol. 1. LC 97-212062. (Illus.). 1997. write for info. (*0-7622-0594-6*) Creative Pubns.

Pier, J. P., jt. ed. see Eymard, P.

Pier, Jean-Paul. Amenable Banach Algebras. 1988. pap. text. write for info. (*0-582-01480-8*, Pub. by Addison-Wesley) Longman.

Pieragostini. Britain, Aden & South Arabia. 1991. text 55.00 (*0-312-05723-7*) St Martin.

Pierangelo, Roger. The Special Education Teacher's Book of Lists. LC 95-36912. 363p. 1995. pap. text 29.95 (*0-87628-876-X*) Ctr Appl Res.

— The Special Education Teacher's Book of Lists. 380p. 1997. pap. text 29.50 (*0-87628-578-7*) Ctr Appl Res.

— A Survival Kit for the Special Education Teacher. LC 93-44763. 320p. 1994. spiral bd. 29.95 (*0-87628-870-0*) Ctr Appl Res.

Pierangelo, Roger & Crane, Rochelle. Complete Guide to Special Education Transition Services: Ready-to-Use Help & Materials for Successful Transitions from School to Adulthood. LC 97-26606. 272p. 1997. pap. text 29.95 (*0-87628-274-5*) Ctr Appl Res.

***Pierangelo, Roger & Crane, Rochelle.** The Special Education Yellow Pages. LC 99-18774. 214p. 2000. 27.33 (*0-13-020309-2*) P-H.

Pierangelo, Roger & Giuliani, George A. Special Educator's Complete Guide to 109 Diagnostic Tests: Review of Evaluation Measures, How to Interpret Test Scores, Incorporate Results in Reports & IEP's, & Remediate Specific Disabilities. LC 97-46821. 1998. pap. 29.95 (*0-87628-893-X*) Ctr Appl Res.

Pierangelo, Roger & Jacoby, Robert. Parents' Complete Special Education Guide: Tips, Techniques & Materials for Helping Your... 336p. (C). 1996. pap. text 27.95 (*0-87628-614-7*) P-H.

Pierannunz, Carol, jt. auth. see Fleischmann, Arnold.

Pierard, John. Bruce Coville's Book of Ghosts II: More Tales to Haunt You. 1998. 9.09 (*0-606-11169-7*, Pub. by Turtleback) Demco.

— Bruce Coville's Book of Magic: Tales to Cast a Spell on You. 1996. 9.09 (*0-606-09108-4*, Pub. by Turtleback) Demco.

— Bruce Coville's Book of Nightmares: Tales to Make You Scream. 1995. 9.09 (*0-606-07322-1*, Pub. by Turtleback) Demco.

Pierard, John. Bruce Coville's Book of Spine Tinglers: Tales to Make You Shiver. 1996. 9.09 (*0-606-09110-6*, Pub. by Turtleback) Demco.

Pierard, Richard, et al. Two Kingdoms: The Church & Culture Through the Ages. 689p. 35.99 (*0-8024-8590-1*, 306) Moody.

Pierard, Richard V., jt. auth. see Linder, Robert D.

Pierard, Richard V., ed. see Swoboda, Jorg.

Pieraut-Le Bonniec, Gilberte & Dolitsky, Marlene, eds. Language Bases . . . Discourse Bases: Some Aspects of Contemporary French-Language Psycholinguistics Research. LC 91-6685. (Pragmatics & Beyond New Ser.: No. 17). vi, 342p. 1991. 59.00 (*1-55619-283-5*) J Benjamins Pubng Co.

Pierce. Genetics. 2000. pap. text. write for info. (*1-57259-160-9*) W H Freeman.

— Introduction to Technology. 2nd ed. Date not set. write for info. (*0-314-06809-0*) West Pub.

— Introduction to Technology. 11th ed. (TP-Technology Education Ser.). 1993. pap. 49.95 (*0-314-00033-X*) S-W Pub.

— Introduction to Technology. 11th ed. (Tp - Technology Education (K-12)). (C). 1992. pap. 49.50 (*0-314-00032-1*) West Pub.

— Operational Math for Business. (Math). 1981. student ed. 7.50 (*0-534-00962-X*) Brooks-Cole.

— Operational Math For Business. (Math). 1980. 19.75 (*0-534-00789-9*) Brooks-Cole.

— Operational Math for Business. 2nd ed. (Mathematics Ser.). 1983. student ed. 8.25 (*0-534-01953-6*) Brooks-Cole.

— Swallow Right. 1993. 35.00 (*0-7616-7186-2*) Commun Skill.

— Technology in News. Date not set. pap. text. write for info. (*0-314-06018-9*) West Pub.

Pierce & Karwatka. Introduction to Technology. (Illus.). (YA). (gr. 6-12). 1999. student ed. 36.70 (*0-02-831275-9*) Glencoe.

Pierce & Moss. Economics: Study Guide. (C). 1985. pap. text 12.00 (*0-201-08046-X*) Addison-Wesley.

Pierce, jt. auth. see Dunham.

Pierce, jt. auth. see Guthrie.

Pierce, jt. auth. see Vandeveer.

Pierce, A. & Pierce, R. Expressive Movement: Posture & Action in Daily Life, Sports, & the Performing Arts. (Illus.). 236p. (C). 1989. 19.95 (*0-306-43269-2*, Plen Insight) Perseus Pubng.

Pierce, Alan. Cheung Chau Dog Fancier's Society. 232p. 1999. pap. 14.00 (*962-7160-38-5*) Weatherhill.

Pierce, Alan & Karwatka, Dennis. Introduction to Technology. annot. ed. 1999. teacher ed. 49.50 (*0-02-831276-7*) Glencoe.

Pierce, Alexandra. Spanning: Essays on Music Theory, Performance, & Movement. 139p. 1983. pap. 16.00 (*1-879970-01-5*) Ctr Balance Pr.

Pierce, Alexandra & Pierce, Roger. Generous Movement: A Practical Guide to Balance in Action. (Illus.). 171p. (Orig.). 1991. pap. 18.00 (*1-879970-00-7*) Ctr Balance Pr.

Pierce, Allan D. Acoustics: An Introduction to Its Physical Principles & Applications. LC 89-80362. 678p. 1989. 39.00 (*0-88318-612-8*) Acoustical Soc Am.

Pierce, Allan D., jt. ed. see Thurston, Robert N.

Pierce, Alycon T. Selected Final Pension Payment Vouchers, 1818-1864: Alabama: Decatur - Huntsville - Mobile - Tuscaloosa. 113p. 1997. pap. 13.50 (*1-888265-13-2*) Willow Bend.

Pierce, Alycon Trubey, see Trubey Pierce, Alycon.

Pierce, Amy E. Language Acquisition & Syntactic Theory: A Comparative Analysis of French & English Child Grammars. 184p. (C). 1992. text 125.00 (*0-7923-1553-7*) Kluwer Academic.

Pierce, Ann C., jt. ed. see Scoggins, J. F.

Pierce, Ann C., ed. see Sherkyen, Anne H.

Pierce, Anne M. So Many Gifts, Miniature edition. (Illus.). 32p. (J). (gr. k-6). 1994. 7.95 (*0-9623937-2-X*) Forword MN.

— So Many Gifts: A Story by Anne Marie Pierce. unabridged ed. Lindquist, Tom, ed. (Illus.). 32p. (J). (gr. k-6). 1993. reprint ed. 25.00 incl. audio (*0-9623937-0-3*) Forword MN.

Pierce, Anne W. Galaxy Girls Wonder Women: Short Stories. LC 93-8411. (Winner of the 1993 Willa Cather Fiction Prize Ser.). 1993. pap. 12.95 (*0-9627460-9-6*) Helicon Nine Eds.

***Pierce, Anne Whitney.** Rain Line. LC 99-41911. (Hardscrabble Bks.). 371p. 2000. 24.95 (*1-58465-021-4*) U Pr of New Eng.

Pierce, AnneMarie. Pieces of Me. (Illus.). (J). (gr. 1-9). write for info. (*0-9623937-3-8*) Forword MN.

Pierce, Annette. Rachel's Hope. LC 96-158213. 1996. pap. 10.95 (*1-55503-923-5*, 01112309) Covenant Comms.

Pierce, Arthur & Swarthout, Douglas. Jean Arthur: A Bio-Bibliography, 15. LC 90-3316. (Bio-Bibliographies in the Performing Arts Ser.: No. 15). 288p. 1990. lib. bdg. 45.00 (*0-313-26699-9*, PJA/, Greenwood Pr) Greenwood.

Pierce, Arthur, jt. auth. see Billips, Connie J.

Pierce, Arthur, ed. see Wager, Daniel E.

Pierce, Arthur D. Smugglers Woods. 322p. (C). 1984. reprint ed. pap. 14.95 (*0-8135-0444-9*) Rutgers U Pr.

Pierce Atwood Environmental Department Staff, et al. Maine Environmental & Land Use Statutes Deskbook, 1994. 670p. 1994. 67.50 (*1-56257-346-2*, MICHIE) LEXIS Pub.

— Maine Environmental & Land Use Statutes Deskbook, 1995. Ahrens, Philip F., ed. 670p. 1994. pap. 70.00 (*0-88063-755-2*, MICHIE) LEXIS Pub.

Pierce, B. Patchouli Quintet. 1995. pap. text 20.00 (*0-7935-4823-3*, 00000542) H Leonard.

Pierce-Baker, Charlotte. Surviving the Silence: Black Women's Stories of Rape. LC 98-14518. 288p. 1998. 23.95 (*0-393-04661-3*) Norton.

***Pierce-Baker, Charlotte.** Surviving the Silence: Black Women's Stories of Rape. (Illus.). 288p. 2000. pap. text 13.95 (*0-393-32045-6*) Norton.

***Pierce, Barbara.** Desperate Game. 2000. mass mkt. 4.99 (*0-8217-6479-9*, Zebra Kensgtn) Kensgtn Pub Corp.

Pierce, Barbara, ed. The World under My Fingers: Personal Reflections on Braille. large type ed. (Illus.). 150p. 1995. pap. 1.00 (*1-885218-01-X*) Natl Fed Blind.

Pierce, Benjamin A. Family Genetic Sourcebook. LC 89-24884. 340p. 1990. pap. 14.95 (*0-471-61709-1*) Wiley.

Pierce, Benjamin C. Basic Category Theory for Computer Science. 128p. 1991. pap. text 21.00 (*0-262-66071-7*) MIT Pr.

Pierce, Bern D., ed. History of Trempealeau County, Wisconsin. (Illus.). 922p. 1993. reprint ed. lib. bdg. 92.00 (*0-8328-3509-9*) Higginson Bk Co.

Pierce, Bessie L. Civic Attitudes in American School Textbooks. LC 76-165727. (American Education, Ser, No. 2). 1972. reprint ed. 18.95 (*0-405-03716-3*) Ayer.

***Pierce, Bill.** Western Trilogy. 2000. 21.95 (*1-56311-532-8*) Turner Pub KY.

***Pierce, Billie, et al.** Osborne's NetWare 5 Administration Answers! Tech Support. (Answers! Ser.). (Illus.). 490p. 1998. pap. 29.99 (*0-07-211885-7*) Osborne-McGraw.

Pierce, Bob & Ashley, Larry, eds. Pierce Piano Atlas. 10th enl. rev. ed. LC 65-2545. (Illus.). 448p. 1997. 38.95 (*0-614-30059-2*); pap. 28.95 (*0-911138-02-1*) Pierce Piano.

Pierce, Brenda H. Creative Art Picture Starters: General Subjects - Level I. (Illus.). 32p. 1988. teacher ed. 3.95 (*0-922694-02-8*) Moons Creat Prods.

— Creative Art Picture Starters: General Subjects - Level II. (Illus.). 32p. (J). (gr. 4-6). 1988. teacher ed. 3.95 (*0-922694-03-6*) Moons Creat Prods.

— Creative Art Picture Starters: Landscapes - Level I. (Illus.). 32p. 1988. teacher ed. 3.95 (*0-922694-00-1*) Moons Creat Prods.

— Creative Art Picture Starters: Landscapes - Level II. (Illus.). 32p. 1988. teacher ed. 3.95 (*0-922694-01-X*) Moons Creat Prods.

Pierce, Burton & LeBuffe, Michael. Exercises for the Microbiology Laboratory. 2nd ed. (Illus.). 176p. 1998. pap. text 13.95 (*0-89582-462-0*) Morton Pub.

Pierce, Burton, jt. auth. see Leboffe, Michael.

Pierce, Burton, jt. auth. see LeBuffe, Michael.

Pierce, Burton W. Our Glorious Tomorrow. 207p. (Orig.). 1991. pap. 9.95 (*0-9628973-0-2*) Daybreak Pubs.

Pierce, Carl, ed. see Elmore, Tim & Higgins, Rebecca.

Pierce, Carl H. New Harlen, Part & Present: The Story of an Amazing Civil Wrong, Now at Last Righted. (Illus.). 332p. 1997. reprint ed. lib. bdg. 39.50 (*0-8328-6153-7*) Higginson Bk Co.

Pierce, Carl W., et al, eds. IR Genes: Past, Present & Future. LC 82-4291. (Experimental Biology & Medicine Ser.: Vol. 4). (Illus.). 621p. 1983. 99.50 (*0-89603-050-4*) Humana.

Pierce, Carol, et al. A Male - Female Continuum: Paths to Colleagueship. 2nd ed. LC 88-92431. (Illus.). 82p. 1998. pap. 14.00 (*0-929767-02-0*) New Dynam Pubns.

Pierce, Carol, jt. auth. see Wishik, Heather.

***Pierce, Carol J.** Local People in Logged Forests: Perspectives on Sustainability & Human Well-Being. 2000. 50.00 (*1-891853-05-8*); pap. 25.95 (*1-891853-06-6*) Resources Future.

Pierce, Carol J. The Power Equity Group: A Guide for Understanding Equity & Acknowledging Diversity. 180p. 1998. pap. 24.00 (*0-929767-05-5*) New Dynam Pubns.

Pierce, Carolyn B. Shadows of Love. LC 85-90440. (Illus.). 75p. 1985. 6.95 (*0-9615667-0-1*) Starlight Pubns.

Pierce, Catherine D. Christmas Thief. (Illus.). (Orig.). (J). (ps). 1988. pap. text 4.50 (*0-9621397-0-X*) C D Pierce.

Pierce, Catherine S., jt. auth. see Cuca, Roberto.

Pierce, Cecil E. Fifty Years a Planemaker & User. LC 92-60195. (Illus.). 80p. 1992. pap. 18.00 (*0-9628001-2-0*) Monmouth Pr.

— The Precision Handcutting of Dovetails: With a Sequence to the Author's Fifty Years a Planemaker & User. (Illus.). 56p. 1995. 18.00 (*0-9628001-4-7*) Monmouth Pr.

Pierce, Charles. Beach House Cooking: Good Food for the Great Outdoors. LC 98-29714. (Williams-Sonoma Outdoors Ser.). (Illus.). 108p. (YA). (gr. 7). 1999. pap. 14.95 (*0-7370-2009-1*) T-L Custom Pub.

— Collected Papers. (Notable American Authors Ser.). 1999. reprint ed. lib. bdg. 125.00 (*0-7812-8738-3*) Rprt Serv.

P

An Asterisk (*) at the beginning of an entry indicates that the title is appearing for the first time.

— Comfort Classics: Burgers. LC 96-86720. (Comfort Classics Ser.). (Illus.). 80p. 1997. 14.95 (0-8362-2786-7) Andrews & McMeel.

***Pierce, Charles.** In the Country of My Disease, 1 vol. LC 99-20358. 224p. 2000. 25.00 (0-679-45291-5) Random.

— The New Settlement Cookbook: The First Classic Collection of American Ethnic Recipes. rev. ed. (Illus.). 832p. 1997. 12.98 (0-7651-9310-8) Smithmark.

Pierce, Charles. Photometric Researches. (Notable American Authors Ser.). 1999. reprint ed. lib. bdg. 125.00 (0-7812-8737-5) Rprt Serv.

— Southern Light Cooking: Easy, Healthy, Low-Calorie Recipes from BBQ to Bourbon Peach Shortcake. 192p. 1993. pap. 15.95 (0-399-51808-8, Perigee Bks) Berkley Pub.

Pierce, Charles E., Jr., frwd. Illuminated Manuscripts: Treasures of the Pierpont Morgan Library. LC 96-43628. (Tiny Folio Ser.). (Illus.). 288p. 1998. bds. 11.95 (0-7892-0216-6) Abbeville Pr.

Pierce, Charles L., ed. The New Settlement Cookbook: The First Collection of American Ethnic Recipes. rev. ed. (Illus.). 640p. 1991. 25.00 (0-671-69336-0) S&S Trade.

Pierce, Charles R., Jr. The Religious Life of Samuel Johnson. LC 82-13938. 184p. (C). 1982. lib. bdg. 32.00 (0-208-01992-8, Archon Bks) Shoe String.

Pierce, Charles W. Pioneer Life in Southeast Florida. Curl, Donald W., ed. LC 70-122290. 1981. 19.95 (0-87024-304-7) U of Miami Pr.

Pierce, Chester M., ed. Capital Punishment in the United States. LC 76-5828. (Studies in Modern Society: Political & Social Issues: No. 10). lib. bdg. 59.50 (0-404-10325-1) AMS Pr.

— Television & Education. LC 77-94473. (Sage Contemporary Social Science Issues Ser.: No. 44). 104p. reprint ed. pap. 32.30 (0-608-10124-9, 202194000026) Bks Demand.

Pierce, Chonda. Chonda Pierce on Her Soapbox. LC 99-39362. 192p. 1999. pap. 12.99 (0-310-22579-5) Zondervan.

— It's Always Darkest Before the Fun Comes Up. LC 98-34522. 176p. 1998. pap. 12.99 (0-310-22567-1) Zondervan.

— Second Row, Piano Side: With Humor, Heartache, & Hope: Chonda Pierce Tells Her Story. LC 96-11035. 120p. (Orig.). 1996. pap. 9.99 (0-8341-1589-1) Beacon Hill.

Pierce, Christina, jt. ed. see Wekesser, Carol.

Pierce, Christine. How to Solve: The Lockheed Case. (Original Papers: No. 5). 50p. (Orig.). 1986. pap. 4.00 (0-912051-11-6) Soc Phil Pol.

Pierce, Christine & VanDeVeer, Donald. People, Penguins, & Plastic Trees: Basic Issues in Environmental Ethics. 2nd ed. LC 94-13151. 485p. 1994. pap. 56.95 (0-534-17922-3) Wadsworth Pub.

Pierce, Christine, jt. auth. see VanDeVeer, Donald.

Pierce, Chuck D. Receiving the Word of the Lord: Bringing Life to Your Prophetic Word. unabridged ed. Wagner Sytsema, Rebecca, ed. 48p. 1999. pap. 6.00 (0-9667481-2-3) Wagner Inst Pubns.

***Pierce, Chuck D. & Sytsema, Rebecca Wagner.** The Future War of the Church. 2000. pap. 9.99 (0-8307-2517-2, Regal Bks) Gospel Lght.

Pierce, Chuck D. & Sytsema, Rebecca Wagner. Possessing Your Inheritance: Moving Forward in God's Covenant Plan for Your Life. LC 98-56162. 216p. (Orig.). 1999. pap. 10.99 (0-8307-2357-9, Renew) Gospel Lght.

Pierce, Clayton C. Classical Ciphers. LC 98-92259. Orig. Title: Hobby Cryptography. (Illus.). 108p. 1999. lib. bdg. 29.95 (0-9601564-2-9); per. 9.95 (0-9601564-5-3); ring bd. 14.95 (0-9601564-6-1) C C Pierce.

— CryptoPrivacy: A Cryptographer's Manual on Classic Ciphers. 3rd rev. ed. LC 89-91620. (Illus.). 128p. 1994. lib. bdg. 19.95i (0-9601564-9-6) C C Pierce.

***Pierce, Clinton.** Sams Teach Yourself Perl in 24 Hours. (Teach Yourself... in 24 Hours Ser.). (Illus.). 1999. pap. 24.99 (0-672-31773-7) Sams.

Pierce, Constance. Hope Mills. 311p. 1998. pap. 14.50 (1-888889-11-X) Pushcart Pr.

— Hope Mills. 320p. 1999. reprint ed. pap. 12.50 (0-380-73219-X) Morrow Avon.

— When Things Get Back to Normal. LC 86-27870. 256p. 1987. 15.95 (0-932511-00-7); pap. 7.95 (0-932511-01-5) Fiction Coll.

Pierce, Constance, jt. ed. see Sloan, Kay.

Pierce, Dale. Wild West Characters. LC 91-2039. (Illus.). 144p. (Orig.). 1991. pap. 6.95 (0-914846-53-1) Golden West Pub.

***Pierce, Daniel S.** The Great Smokies: From Natural Habitat to National Park. LC 99-50464. (Illus.). 280p. 2000. 40.00 (1-57233-076-7, Pub. by U of Tenn Pr) U Ch Pr.

— The Great Smokies: From Natural Habitat to National Park. LC 99-50464. (Illus.). 280p. 2000. pap. 18.95 (1-57233-079-1, Pub. by U of Tenn Pr) U Ch Pr.

Pierce, David. The Beast. (J). 1996. pap. 4.75 (0-553-54238-9) BDD Bks Young Read.

— James Joyce's Ireland. (Illus.). 256p. (C). 1992. 40.00 (0-300-05055-0) Yale U Pr.

— Yeats's Worlds: Ireland, England & the Poetic Imagination. LC 95-2457. (Illus.). 346p. 1995. 45.00 (0-300-06323-7) Yale U Pr.

Pierce, David, jt. ed. see Atwell, Robert.

Pierce, David E. Kansas Oil & Gas Handbook, Vol. I. LC 88-82765. 1986. 100.00 (0-942357-07-8) KS Bar.

— Kansas Oil & Gas Handbook, Vol. II. LC 88-82765. 400p. 1989. 115.00 (0-942357-24-8) KS Bar.

Pierce, David F. World Air Cargo Forecast (1994) (Illus.). 74p. (Orig.). (C). 1994. pap. text 65.00 (0-7881-1198-1) DIANE Pub.

***Pierce, David F.** World Air Cargo Forecast, 1998-1999. (Illus.). 68p. (C). 1999. pap. text 30.00 (0-7881-7580-7) DIANE Pub.

Pierce, David G. & Tysome, Peter J. Monetary Economics. 2nd ed. 320p. 1984. pap. 34.95 (0-408-70953-7) Buttrwrth-Heinemann.

Pierce, David M. Angels in Heaven. 208p. 1993. mass mkt. 4.99 (0-446-40163-3, Pub. by Warner Bks) Little.

— Build Me a Castle. 1995. write for info. (0-89296-485-5) Mysterious Pr.

— Write Me a Letter. 272p. 1993. 18.95 (0-89296-484-7) Mysterious Pr.

Pierce, David R., Jr. Project Scheduling Management Construction. 3rd rev. ed. LC 99-162329. Orig. Title: Project Planning & Control. 250p. 1998. 64.95 (0-87629-533-2, 67247A) R S Means.

Pierce, Deirdre, jt. auth. see Altobello, Patricia.

Pierce, Don. Beading on a Loom. LC 99-14771. 1999. pap. 21.95 (1-883010-63-2, Pub. by Interweave) IPG Chicago.

Pierce, Donald. Process Safety Pocket Guide, 10 copies. Franklin, Catherine et al, eds. (Illus.). 84p. (Orig.). 1993. pap. text 41.80 (0-931690-56-0) Genium Pub.

Pierce, Donald & Wright, Edward B. Mathematics for Life: Preliminary. 552p. (C). 1997. pap. text 44.00 (0-13-493859-3) P-H.

Pierce, Donna & Weigle, Marta. Spanish New Mexico: The Spanish Colonial Arts Society Collection, 2 vols., Set. (Spanish New Mexico Ser.). (Illus.). 312p. (Orig.). 1996. pap. 60.00 (0-89013-311-5) Museum NM Pr.

Pierce, Dorothy H. Inspections & Reflections. LC 98-71558. v, 43p. 1998. pap. write for info. (0-9663193-1-1) D H Pierce.

— Surviving the Workplace. LC 98-74876. Orig. Title: Secrets Told - Power over Power Play. v, 53p. 1998. pap. write for info. (0-9663193-2-X) D H Pierce.

Pierce, Edward L. Memoir & Letters of Charles Sumner, 4 vols., Set. LC 78-82211. (Anti-Slavery Crusade in America Ser.). 1970. reprint ed. 88.95 (0-405-00650-0) Ayer.

— Memoir & Letters of Charles Sumner, 4 Vols., Set. (Black Heritage Library Collection). 1977. reprint ed. 96.95 (0-8369-8641-5) Ayer.

— Memoir & Letters of Charles Sumner, 4 vols., Vol. 1. LC 78-82211. (Anti-Slavery Crusade in America Ser.). 1970. reprint ed. 23.95 (0-405-00675-6) Ayer.

— Memoir & Letters of Charles Sumner, 4 vols., Vol. 2. LC 78-82211. (Anti-Slavery Crusade in America Ser.). 1970. reprint ed. 23.95 (0-405-00676-4) Ayer.

— Memoir & Letters of Charles Sumner, 4 vols., Vol. 3. LC 78-82211. (Anti-Slavery Crusade in America Ser.). 1970. reprint ed. 23.95 (0-405-00677-2) Ayer.

— Memoir & Letters of Charles Sumner, 4 vols., Vol. 4. LC 78-82211. (Anti-Slavery Crusade in America Ser.). 1970. reprint ed. 23.95 (0-405-00678-0) Ayer.

Pierce, Elwood W. My Life & Times. LC 90-91579. 389p. 1990. 19.50 (0-9626545-0-7) Power Pub Co.

Pierce, F. B. Pierce Genealogy, Being the Record of the Posterity of Thomas Pierce, an Early Inhabitant of Charlestown. Pierce, F. C., ed. (Illus.). 369p. 1989. reprint ed. pap. 66.00 (0-8328-0965-9); reprint ed. lib. bdg. 74.00 (0-8328-0964-0) Higginson Bk Co.

Pierce, F. C. Batchelder, Batcheller: Descendants of Rev. Stephen Bachilar of England, a Leading Non-Conformist Who Settled in the Town of New Hampton, N. H., & Joseph, Henry, Joshua, & John Batcheller of Essex Co., Mass. (Illus.). 623p. 1988. reprint ed. pap. 93.50 (0-8328-0207-7); reprint ed. lib. bdg. 103.50 (0-8328-0206-9) Higginson Bk Co.

— The Descendants of John Whitney, Who Came from London, England to Watertown, Massachusetts, in 1635. (Illus.). 692p. 1989. reprint ed. pap. 85.00 (0-8328-1261-7); reprint ed. lib. bdg. 95.00 (0-8328-1260-9) Higginson Bk Co.

— Field Genealogy: Being the Record of All of the Field Family in America Whose Ancestors Were in This Country, 2 vols., Set. (Illus.). 1196p. 1989. reprint ed. pap. 179.00 (0-8328-0545-9); reprint ed. lib. bdg. 189.00 (0-8328-0544-0) Higginson Bk Co.

— Fiske & Fish Family: The Descendants of Symond Fiske, Lord of the Manor of Studhaugh, Suffolk County, England, from the Time of Henry IV to Date, Including All American Members of the Family. (Illus.). 660p. 1989. reprint ed. pap. 82.00 (0-8328-0549-1); reprint ed. lib. bdg. 92.00 (0-8328-0548-3) Higginson Bk Co.

— Foster Genealogy: A Record of the Posterity of Reginald Foster, Early Inhabitant of Ipswich & All Other American Fosters. (Illus.). 1081p. 1989. reprint ed. pap. 135.00 (0-8328-0551-3); reprint ed. lib. bdg. 145.00 (0-8328-0550-5) Higginson Bk Co.

— Pierce Genealogy, Being the Record of the Posterity of Captain Michael, John, & Captain William Pierce, Who Came to This County England, No. IV. 441p. 1989. reprint ed. pap. 66.00 (0-8328-0967-5); reprint ed. lib. bdg. 74.00 (0-8328-0966-7) Higginson Bk Co.

Pierce, F. C., ed. see Pierce, F. B.

Pierce, F. David. Managing Change for Safety & Health Professionals: A Six Step Process. LC 96-37927. 208p. 1997. 59.00 (0-86587-563-4) Gov Insts.

Pierce, F. David. Project Management for Environmental, Health & Safety Professionals: 18 Steps to Success. LC 97-37709. (Illus.). 264p. 1998. text 69.00 (0-86587-598-7, 598) Gov Insts.

— Shifting Safety & Health Paradigms. 239p. 1996. text 59.00 (0-86587-527-8) Gov Insts.

— Total Quality for Safety & Health Professionals. LC 95-8268. 229p. 1995. 59.00 (0-86587-462-X) Gov Insts.

Pierce, F. E., ed. see Blake, William.

Pierce, F. J. The State of Site Specific Management for Agriculture. Sadler, E. J., ed. LC 97-71149. 430p. 1997. 38.00 (0-89118-134-2) Am Soc Agron.

Pierce, F. J., ed. Soil Management for Sustainability. (Illus.). 178p. (Orig.). (C). 1991. pap. text 18.00 (0-935734-23-6) Soil & Water Conserv.

Pierce, Frances L., ed. see Sherman, Betty G.

Pierce, Francis & Frye, Wilbur W., eds. Advances in Soil & Water Conservation. LC 97-51557. (Illus.). 300p. 1998. ring bd. 59.95 (1-57504-083-2) CRC Pr.

Pierce, Francis J., jt. auth. see Schabenberger, Oliver.

Pierce, Frank H. A Boy's Eye View of World War II. (Illus.). 133p. 1998. pap. 15.00 (0-7884-0886-0, P320) Heritage Bk.

Pierce, Frank H., 3rd. The Tagebuch of Ernst Silge U. S. N. LC 96-75428. (Illus.). (Orig.). 1996. pap. 25.00 (0-7884-0489-X, P316) Heritage Bk.

Pierce, Franklin. Federal Usurpation. xx, 437p. 1980. reprint ed. 45.00 (0-8377-1007-3, Rothman) W S Hein.

Pierce, Frederick C. History of Grafton, Worcester Co., Mass., from Early Settlement by the Indians in 1647 to 1879, Including Genealogies of 79 Old Families. 623p. 1989. reprint ed. lib. bdg. 68.00 (0-8328-0827-X, MA0053) Higginson Bk Co.

Pierce, Frederick E. Currents & Eddies in the English Romantic Generation. LC 68-56470. 1972. reprint ed. 26.95 (0-405-08857-4) Ayer.

Pierce, G., ed. Developments in Industrial Microbiology Vol. 27: Symposia of the 42nd General Meeting 1985 Boston MA. (Illus.). 183p. 1987. text 110.00 (0-444-80870-1) Lubrecht & Cramer.

— Developments in Industrial Microbiology Vol. 28: Proceedings of Symposium Held August 1986. (Illus.). 181p. 1987. text 120.00 (0-945345-16-X) Lubrecht & Cramer.

— Developments in Industrial Microbiology Vol. 29: Symposium of the 44th General Meeting 1987. (Illus.). 318p. 1988. text 156.00 (0-945345-17-8) Lubrecht & Cramer.

Pierce, G. A. & Wheeler, W. A. Dickens Dictionary: A Key to the Plots-Characters in the Tales of Charles Dickens. rev. ed. 1914. 45.00 (0-527-71200-0) Periodicals Srv.

Pierce, Gail. Gourmet Meat-Less Entrees for a Month. (Illus.). 36p. (Orig.). 1983. pap. 5.95 (0-9607436-1-8) Sea-Wind Pr.

— The New Age Brown Rice Cookbook. LC 81-84830. (Illus.). 172p. (Orig.). 1982. pap. 9.95 (0-9607436-0-X) Sea-Wind Pr.

Pierce, Gary J., jt. auth. see Zander, Richard H.

Pierce, Gilbert A. The Congressman. (Notable American Authors Ser.). 1999. reprint ed. lib. bdg. 125.00 (0-7812-8745-6) Rprt Serv.

— A Dangerous Woman. (Notable American Authors Ser.). 1999. reprint ed. lib. bdg. 125.00 (0-7812-8747-2) Rprt Serv.

— The Dickens Dictionary. LC 72-3189. (Studies in Dickens: No. 52). 1972. reprint ed. lib. bdg. 75.00 (0-8383-1526-7) M S G Haskell Hse.

— The Dickens Dictionary. (Notable American Authors Ser.). 1999. reprint ed. lib. bdg. 125.00 (0-7812-8744-8) Rprt Serv.

— One Hundred Wives. (Notable American Authors Ser.). 1999. reprint ed. lib. bdg. 125.00 (0-7812-8746-4) Rprt Serv.

Pierce, Gladys C. Grandmother's Christmas Stories. LC 97-91297. (J). 1998. pap. 6.95 (0-533-12620-7) Vantage.

Pierce, Glen A., ed. see Johns, Helen & Leadley, Robert.

Pierce, Glen Palen, jt. auth. see Frassica, Pietro.

Pierce, Glenn F., jt. auth. see Ziegler, Thomas R.

Pierce, Glenn P. Manzoni & the Aesthetics of the Lombard Seicento: Art Assimilated into the Narrative of I Promessi Sposi. LC 97-40777. (Illus.). 256p. 1998. 42.50 (0-8387-5367-1) Bucknell U Pr.

Pierce, Gloria. Peripheral Visions. LC 82-80581. (Illus.). 64p. (Orig.). 1982. pap. 4.95 (0-943148-00-6) Nikki Pr.

Pierce, Grant M. Molecular & Cellular Effects of Nutrition on Disease Process. LC 98-3954. (Developments in Molecular & Cellular Biochemistry Ser.). 237p. 1998. write for info. (0-7923-8171-8) Kluwer Academic.

Pierce, Grant N., et al. Heart Dysfunction in Diabetes. 256p. 1988. 146.00 (0-8493-6887-1, RC682, CRC Reprint) Franklin.

Pierce, Grant N., ed. see Claycomb, William C.

Pierce, Gregory F. Activism That Makes Sense: Congregations & Community Organization. LC 83-82016. 148p. 1984. reprint ed. pap. 9.95 (0-914070-53-3, 111) ACTA Pubns.

— Perspectives on Marriage: Catholic Wedding Ceremony Edition. 88p. 1992. student ed. 4.95 (0-915388-37-5, 153) ACTA Pubns.

Pierce, Gregory F., ed. Of Human Hands: A Reader in the Spirituality of Work. LC 90-44647. (Christian at Work in the World Ser.). 128p. 1991. pap. 8.95 (0-87946-057-1, 120) ACTA Pubns.

Pierce, Gregory F. & Artz, Thomas R. Spiritual Bouquets: Priceless Gifts for Special Occasions. 64p. 1998. pap. 4.95 (0-87946-183-7, 277) ACTA Pubns.

Pierce, Gregory F., jt. auth. see Konieczny, Stanley.

Pierce, Gregory R., et al, eds. Cognitive Interference: Theories, Methods, & Findings. (Personality & Clinical Psychology Ser.). 448p. 1995. text 49.95 (0-8058-1624-0) L Erlbaum Assocs.

— Sourcebook of Social Support & Personality. LC 97-17811. (Series in Social/Clinical Psychology). (Illus.). 522p. (C). 1997. 85.00 (0-306-45535-8, Plenum Trade) Perseus Pubng.

Pierce, Gwendolyn. Exploration into the Applicability of a Psychological Technique for Anthropological Research. 144p. 1973. pap. 4.95 (0-913244-02-3) Hapi Pr.

Pierce, H. A. Preliminary Bibliography of the Geology & Mineral Deposits of Nicaragua. 34p. (Orig.). (C). 1993. pap. text 25.00 (1-56806-360-1) DIANE Pub.

Pierce, Hazel B. A Literary Symbiosis: Science Fiction-Fantasy Mystery, 6. LC 82-1710. (Contributions to the Study of Science Fiction & Fantasy Ser.: No. 6). 255p. 1983. 49.95 (0-313-23065-X, PLS/, Greenwood Pr) Greenwood.

Pierce, Henry B., jt. auth. see Durant, Samuel W.

Pierce, Herman & Spencer, Thel. Sheriff Takes the Stand. LC 92-19120. (Illus.). 192p. 1992. 14.95 (0-87714-173-8) Denlingers.

Pierce-Higgins, Lucinda, ed. Do It Yourself Decorating. LC 96-5011. (Illus.). 224p. 1996. 24.98 (1-57145-111-0, Thunder Bay) Advantage Pubs.

Pierce, Ian. The Holistic Approach to Cancer. 152p. (Orig.). pap. 14.95 (0-8464-4225-6) Beekman Pubs.

— One Man's Odyssey. 296p. (Orig.). pap. 20.95 (0-8464-4263-9) Beekman Pubs.

Pierce, J. A. Negro Business & Business Education: Their Present & Prospective Development. LC 95-625. (Plenum Studies in Work & Industry). (Illus.). 368p. (C). 1995. 49.50 (0-306-45073-9, Plenum Trade) Perseus Pubng.

Pierce, J. Calvin. The Sorceress of Ambermere. 256p. (Orig.). 1993. mass mkt. 4.99 (0-441-33741-4) Ace Bks.

— Wizard of Abermere. 1993. mass mkt. 4.99 (0-441-01959-5) Ace Bks.

Pierce, J. D. Guide to Owning an American Pit Bull Terrier. (Guide to Owning Ser.). (Illus.). 64p. Date not set. pap. 6.95 (0-7938-1866-4, RE-316) TFH Pubns.

Pierce, J. F. Singularity Theory, Rod Theory & Symmetry-Breaking Loads. (Lecture Notes in Mathematics Ser.: Vol. 1377). iv, 177p. 1989. 32.95 (0-387-51304-3) Spr-Verlag.

Pierce, J. F. & Paulus, T. J. Applied Electronics. rev. ed. (Illus.). 702p. (C). 1992. reprint ed. text 121.00 (1-878907-42-5) TechBooks.

Pierce, J. Kingston. America's Historic Trails with Tom Bodett. LC 97-7090. (Illus.). 272p. (Orig.). 1997. pap. 19.95 (0-912333-00-6) BB&T Inc.

— San Francisco, You're History! A Chronicle of the People Who Helped Create California's Wildest City. (Illus.). 304p. (Orig.). 1995. pap. 14.95 (1-57061-007-X) Sasquatch Bks.

Pierce, J. P. Killer Monologues: Highly Actable Monologues & Performance Tips to Give You an Almost Unfair Advantage in the Auditioning Game. LC 98-96377. 128p. 1998. pap. 14.95 (1-892553-00-7); pap. 39.95 (1-892553-02-3) Impct Flms.

Pierce, J. R. The Beginnings of Satellite Communications. (Illus.). 1968. 20.00 (0-911302-05-0) San Francisco Pr.

— An Introduction to Information Theory: Symbols, Signals & Noise. 2nd rev. ed. 320p. 1980. reprint ed. pap. 8.95 (0-486-24061-4) Dover.

Pierce, J. R. & Posner, E. C. Introduction to Communication Science & Systems. LC 80-14877. (Applications of Communications Theory Ser.). (Illus.). 406p. (C). 1980. 79.50 (0-306-40492-3, Plenum Trade) Perseus Pubng.

Pierce, J. T. The Food Resource. LC 96-960211. xx, 334p. 1990. pap. 25.95 (0-582-30537-3, Pub. by Addison-Wesley) Longman.

Pierce, James. From Abacus to Zeus: A Handbook of Art History. 5th rev. ed. LC 97-223256. 213p. (C). 1997. pap. text 20.40 (0-13-783028-9) P-H.

***Pierce, James.** From Abacus to Zeus: Handbook of Art History. 6th ed. 224p. 2001. pap. text 18.67 (0-13-019728-9, Prentice Hall) P-H.

Pierce, James. How to Stay Focused on God's Vision for Your Life. 15p. 1994. student ed. 5.00 (1-886880-00-X) Life Changers.

Pierce, James & Pierce, Stacia. Ministers in Training Manual. 60p. 1996. wbk. ed. 39.95 (1-886880-11-5) Life Changers.

Pierce, James A., jt. auth. see Anzaldua, Mike M., Jr.

Pierce, James B. Heart Healthy Magnesium: Your Nutritional Key to Cardiovascular Wellness. LC 94-805. (Illus.). 192p. pap. 12.95 (0-89529-579-2, Avery) Penguin Putnam.

Pierce, James L. The Future of Banking. (Twentieth Century Fund Reports). 192p. (C). 1991. 40.00 (0-300-05058-5) Yale U Pr.

Pierce, James L., jt. auth. see Hester, Donald D.

***Pierce, Jan.** World Chamber of Commerce Directory 2000. 2000. pap. 50.00 (0-943581-13-3) WWCCD.

***Pierce, Jan, ed.** World Chamber of Commerce Directory. 400p. 1999. pap. 35.00 (0-943581-12-5) WWCCD.

Pierce, Jan & Parish, Pat. Rosson House: The Story of A Historic Phoenix Landmark. LC 99-159188. 20p. 1996. write for info. (0-929526-50-3) Double B Pubns.

***Pierce, Jean.** Diving & Snorkeling Cayman Islands. (Illus.). 144p. 1999. pap. 16.95 (0-86442-770-0) Lonely Planet.

Pierce, Jeffrey L. Go Tell the Mountain: The Lyrics & Writings of Jeffrey Lee Pierce. (Illus.). 128p. 1998. pap. text 15.00 (1-880985-60-8) Two Thirteen Sixty-one.

Pierce, Jennifer E. Breakin' into Nashville. LC 97-44501. 352p. 1998. pap. 16.95 (1-56833-110-X) Madison Bks UPA.

***Pierce, Jennifer E.** Off the Record: Country Music's Top Label Executives Tell Their Stories. LC 99-50264. 2000. 26.95 (1-56833-148-7) Madison Bks UPA.

Pierce, Jennifer E. Playin' Around: The Lives & Careers of Famous Session Musicians. LC 97-45588. 368p. 1998. 49.50 (0-8108-3434-0) Scarecrow.

Pierce, Jennifer L. Gender Trials: Emotional Lives in Contemporary Law Firms. LC 94-24940. 276p. 1996. 50.00 (0-520-20107-8, Pub. by U CA Pr); pap. 18.95 (0-520-20108-6, Pub. by U CA Pr) Cal Prin Full Svc.

Pierce, Jessica. Lost. 1999. mass mkt. 3.50 (0-8217-5056-9) NAL.

— Overboard. 144p. 1999. mass mkt. 3.50 (0-8217-5121-2) NAL.

— Paintball Warrior. (Spider's Child Ser.: Vol. 4). 144p. 1999. mass mkt. 3.50 (0-8217-4917-X, Zebra Kensgtn) Kensgtn Pub Corp.

— Puzzle. (Spider's Child Ser.: No. 5). 144p. 1999. mass mkt. 3.50 (0-8217-4985-4, Pinncle Kensgtn) Kensgtn Pub Corp.

P

***Pierce, Joan B.** Medicine Man. 124p. (YA). (gr. 5-8). 2000. pap. 9.99 (*0-88092-069-6*, 0696, Kav Bks) Royal Fireworks.

***Pierce, Joanne M. & Downey, Michael.** Source & Summit: Commemorating the Life & Legacy of Josef A. Jungmann. LC 99-20800. 1999. pap. text 24.95 (*0-8146-2461-8*) Liturgical Pr.

Pierce, Joe E. Because of August. LC 81-81920. 200p. (Orig.). 1981. pap. 6.95 (*0-913244-54-6*) Hapi Pr.

— Big Bang? Baloney! LC 91-74062. 137p. (Orig.). 1991. pap. 8.50 (*0-913244-27-9*) Hapi Pr.

— The Bitter Winds. LC 77-71932. 184p. 1977. 6.95 (*0-913244-12-0*) Hapi Pr.

— The Curse of Life. 185p. 1980. pap. 6.95 (*0-913244-24-4*) Hapi Pr.

— The Development of a Linguistic System in English Speaking American Children, Vol. 2. LC 77-91612. 125p. (Orig.). 1982. pap. 6.95 (*0-913244-56-2*) Hapi Pr.

— Fairy Princess. LC 82-83473. 125p. (Orig.). 1982. pap. 6.95 (*0-913244-58-9*) Hapi Pr.

— How English Really Works. LC 79-202. (Illus.). 1979. pap. 12.95 (*0-913244-18-X*) Hapi Pr.

— Language: Learning or Acquisition. 55p. (Orig.). 1987. pap. 6.95 (*0-913244-70-8*) Hapi Pr.

— Language & Dialect Distance in a Space of N-Dimensions. 73p. (Orig.). 1983. pap. 5.95 (*0-685-26996-5*) Hapi Pr.

— Life in a Turkish Village. Spindler, Louise S. & Spindler, George D., eds. (Case Studies in Cultural Anthropology). (Illus.). 1983. reprint ed. pap. text 7.95 (*0-8290-0278-2*) Irvington.

— The Nature of Natural Languages. 163p. 1979. pap. 7.95 (*0-913244-20-1*) Hapi Pr.

— A Practical Guide to the Structure of English for the English Teacher. LC 87-80359. 100p. (Orig.). 1987. pap. 7.50 (*0-913244-67-8*) Hapi Pr.

— Red Runs the Earth. 2nd ed. LC 70-93459. 1977. pap. 5.95 (*0-913244-06-6*) Hapi Pr.

— The Sapien Homo. LC 78-71820. 1978. pap. 7.95 (*0-913244-01-5*) Hapi Pr.

— Shades of Minos. 139p. 1973. pap. 6.95 (*0-913244-04-X*) Hapi Pr.

— Some Vital Statistics on English Grammar. 600p. 1991. lib. bdg. 40.00 (*0-913244-26-0*) Hapi Pr.

— Terrorism, the Middle East & You. 132p. 1986. pap. 5.50 (*0-913244-65-1*) Hapi Pr.

— A Theory of Language, Culture & Human Behavior. 160p. 1972. 9.95 (*0-913244-03-1*) Hapi Pr.

— Thorns, Thistles & Chrome. 160p. 1984. pap. 6.95 (*0-913244-63-5*) Hapi Pr.

— Why Terrorism? 160p. (Orig.). 1991. pap. 8.50 (*0-913244-25-2*) Hapi Pr.

Pierce, Joe E. & Hanna, Ingrid V. The Development of a Phonological System in English Speaking American Children. (Illus.). 120p. 1972. pap. 6.95 (*0-913244-09-0*) Hapi Pr.

Pierce, Joe E., jt. auth. see Hanna, Inga.

Pierce, John & Barnsely, Roland. Easy Lifelong Gardening: A Practical Guide for Seniors. 256p. 1993. pap. 15.95 (*0-943955-72-6*, Trafalgar Sq Pub) Trafalgar.

Pierce, John, ed. see Opie, Amelia.

Pierce, John B. Flexible Design: Revisionary Poetics in Blake's Vala or The Four Zoas. (Illus.). 232p. 1998. text 65.00 (*0-7735-1682-4*, Pub. by McG-Queens Univ Pr) CUP Services.

Pierce, John C. River Earth: A Personal Map. LC 99-17125. (Northwest Voices Essay Ser.). 208p. 1999. pap. 14.95 (*0-87422-177-3*) Wash St U Pr.

— River Earth: A Personal Map. LC 99-17125. (Northwest Voices Essay Ser.). (Illus.). 208p. 1999. 30.00 (*0-87422-176-5*) Wash St U Pr.

Pierce, John C., et al. Citizens, Political Communication & Interest Groups: Environmental Organizations in Canada & the United States. LC 92-15686. (Praeger Series in Political Communication). 256p. 1992. 55.00 (*0-275-93579-5*, C3579, Praeger Pubs) Greenwood.

***Pierce, John C., et al.** Political Culture & Public Policy in Canada & the United States: Only a Border Apart? LC 99-47699. (Canadian Studies: Vol. 22). 428p. 2000. text 109.95 (*0-7734-7897-3*) E Mellen.

Pierce, John E. Development of Comprehensive Insurance for the Household. (C). 1958. 11.50 (*0-256-00673-3*, Irwn McGrw-H) McGrw-H Hghr Educ.

Pierce, John G., jt. auth. see Conolly, Brian.

Pierce, John H. Home Solar Gardening: Solar Greenhouses for Your Home, Backyard or Apartment. (Illus.). 164p. 1981. pap. 12.95 (*1-55013-381-0*) Firefly Bks Ltd.

Pierce, John J. Foundations of Science Fiction: A Study in Imagination & Evolution, 25. LC 86-22810. (Contributions to the Study of Science Fiction & Fantasy Ser.: No. 25). 305p. 1987. 59.95 (*0-313-25455-9*, PFS/, Greenwood Pr) Greenwood.

— Great Themes of Science Fiction: A Study in Imagination & Evolution, 29. LC 87-8475. (Contributions to the Study of Science Fiction & Fantasy Ser.: No. 29). 265p. 1987. 65.00 (*0-313-25456-7*, PTS/, Greenwood Pr) Greenwood.

— Odd Genre: A Study in Imagination & Evolution, 60. LC 93-29100. (Contributions to the Study of Science Fiction & Fantasy Ser.: No. 60). 240p. 1994. 62.95 (*0-313-26897-5*, Greenwood Pr) Greenwood.

— When World Views Collide: A Study in Imagination & Evolution, 37. LC 88-7708. (Contributions to the Study of Science Fiction & Fantasy Ser.). 255p. 1989. 59.95 (*0-313-25457-5*, PWH, Greenwood Pr) Greenwood.

Pierce, John R. & Posner, Edward C. Introduction to Communication Science & Systems. 406p. 1980. teacher ed. write for info. (*0-318-55324-4*, Plenum Trade) Perseus Pubng.

Pierce, John R., ed. see International Symposium on Visual Science Staff.

Pierce, John R., jt. ed. see Mathews, Max V.

Pierce, John T., Sr. Historical Tracts of the Town of Portsmouth, Rhode Island. LC 91-77837. 120p. (Orig.). 1991. pap. 19.95 (*0-9631722-0-4*) Hamilton Print.

Pierce-Johnson, Joy, ed. see Singeltary, Theresa, et al.

***Pierce, Jon L.** The Manager's Bookshelf. 5th ed. 2000. teacher ed. write for info. (*0-321-03061-3*) S&S Trade.

Pierce, Jon L. The Manager's Bookshelf: A Mosaic of Contemporary Views. 5th ed. LC 99-43083. 374p. (C). 1999. pap. 46.67 (*0-321-01714-5*) Addison-Wesley.

***Pierce, Jon L. & Newstrom, John W.** Leaders & the Leadership Process: Readings, Self-assesments & Applications. 2nd ed. LC 99-34640. 400p. 1999. pap. 53.44 (*0-07-231122-3*) McGraw.

Pierce, Jon L. & Newstrom, John W. Leaders & the Leadership Process: Readings, Self-Assessments, & Applications. LC 94-16990. 331p. (C). 1994. text 56.25 (*0-256-16311-1*, Irwn McGrw-H) McGrw-H Hghr Educ.

— The Manager's Bookshelf. 3rd ed. 416p. (C). 1997. pap. 36.00 (*0-06-500707-7*) Addson-Wesley Educ.

Pierce, Jon R. Living with Parkinson's Disease: Don't Rush Me! I'm Coping As Fast As I Can. LC 89-63189. 176p. (Orig.). 1989. pap. text. write for info. (*0-9630559-0-9*) J R Pierce.

Pierce, Joshua M. Ride Guide New Jersey Mountain Biking. LC 97-61517. (Illus.). 136p. (Orig.). 1997. pap. 14.95 (*0-933855-13-3*) Anacus Pr.

Pierce, Josiah. History of the Town of Gorham. (Illus.). 239p. 1997. reprint ed. lib. bdg. 29.50 (*0-8328-5845-5*) Higginson Bk Co.

— History of the Town of Gorham (ME) 240p. 1985. reprint ed. pap. 25.00 (*0-935207-22-8*) Danbury Hse Bks.

Pierce, Jotham D., Jr. Construction Contracts & Litigation, 1989. (Real Estate Law & Practice Course Handbook Ser.). 869p. 1989. pap. 17.50 (*0-685-69399-6*) PLI.

Pierce, Judith, jt. auth. see Saurman, Judith.

Pierce, Julia. A Child Was Chosen. (Family Missionary Ser.). (Illus.). 76p. (J). (gr. 4-7). 1984. pap. 5.99 (*0-89827-023-5*, BKA00) Wesleyan Pub Hse.

***Pierce, Julian R.** Speak Rwanda. LC 99-22079. 304p. 1999. text 23.00 (*0-312-20367-5*, Picador USA) St Martin.

— Speak Rwanda. 2000. pap. 13.00 (*0-312-27679-6*, Picador USA) St Martin.

Pierce, Karen F., jt. auth. see Deacy, Susan.

Pierce, Kathryn & Gilles, Carol, eds. Cycles of Meaning: Exploring the Potential of Talk in Learning Communities. LC 93-5968. (Illus.). 352p. (C). 1993. pap. text 29.50 (*0-435-08797-5*, 08797) Heinemann.

***Pierce, Kathryn M., ed.** Adventuring with Books: A Booklist for Pre-K-Grade 6. 12th ed. 632p. 2000. pap. 32.95 (*0-8141-0077-5*) NCTE.

Pierce, Kathryn M., jt. ed. see Short, Kathy G.

Pierce, Kathy & Rowland, Lori. Guiding Your Catholic Preschooler. 78p. 1992. pap. 4.95 (*0-9638235-0-7*) Pierce Pubng.

Pierce, Ken, jt. auth. see Good, John.

Pierce, Kent A., jt. auth. see Pavkov, Thomas W.

Pierce, Kerry. Chairs. LC 97-22144. (Illus.). 144p. 1997. 19.95 (*0-8069-9466-5*) Sterling.

— Making Shaker Woodenware. LC 98-39310. (Illus.). 128p. 1998. pap. 17.95 (*0-8069-3178-7*) Sterling.

— Small-Production Woodworking for the Home Shop. LC 97-49056. (Illus.). 128p. 1998. pap. 23.99 (*1-55870-462-0*, Popular Woodwking Bks) F & W Pubns Inc.

— The Woodworker's Visual Guide to Pricing Your Work. LC 99-21733. (Illus.). 128p. 1999. pap. 21.99 (*1-55870-507-4*, 70443, Popular Woodwking Bks) F & W Pubns Inc.

Pierce, Kim, jt. auth. see Gollman, Barbara.

Pierce, L. D. The Dreamer. (J). (gr. 7). 1996. mass mkt. 3.99 (*0-380-78062-3*, Avon Bks) Morrow Avon.

— Human Prey. 176p. (YA). (gr. 7 up). 1996. pap. 3.99 (*0-380-78274-X*, Avon Bks) Morrow Avon.

Pierce, L. Jack. General Biology 1407: Lecture & Laboratory Manual. 324p. (C). 1998. spiral bd. 38.95 (*0-7872-5180-1*, 41518004) Kendall-Hunt.

***Pierce, La'Trice.** Recipes from the Mathaland Africa. (International Gourmet Ser.). 124p. 1999. pap. 15.95 (*0-932045-32-4*, Pub. by Dace Pub) ACCESS Pubs Network.

Pierce, Lawrence. Freshman Legislator: Problems & Opportunities. 2nd ed. (Illus.). 112p. 1972. pap. 2.00 (*0-8323-0210-4*) Binford Mort.

Pierce, Linda, jt. auth. see Alfino, Mark.

Pierce, Linda, ed. see Saphire, Rick.

Pierce, Linda, ed. see Washburn, Beverly & Saphire, Rick.

Pierce, Linda Breen. Choosing Simplicity: Real People Finding Peace & Fulfillment in a Complex World. LC 99-63503. 348p. 2000. pap. 16.95 (*0-9672067-1-5*) Gallagher Pr.

Pierce, Linda C., ed. see American Institute of Certified Public Accountants.

Pierce, LuAnn. Growing up Sane: (In Uncertain Times) LC 96-95232. 160p. 1997. pap. 14.95 (*0-9648972-2-9*) OnQ.

Pierce, Luther C. Be Thou My Vision. LC 97-92939. 232p. (Orig.). 1997. pap. 17.95 (*0-9656620-0-4*) Birch Hill.

— Christmas Giving: Daily Advent Devotions for Christian Families. 32p. 1997. pap. 2.50 (*0-9656620-1-2*) Birch Hill.

— The Servant Book. LC 98-93316. 132p. 1998. pap. 10.95 (*0-9656620-2-0*) Birch Hill.

***Pierce, Luther C.** Taylor & Brittany Discover Christmas. (Illus.). 44p. (J). (gr. 4-6). 1999. pap. 5.00 (*0-9656620-3-9*) Birch Hill.

Pierce, Lynelle N. Guide to Mechanical Ventilation & Intensive Respiratory Care. (Illus.). 400p. 1995. pap. text, spiral bd. 28.00 (*0-7216-6478-4*, W B Saunders Co) Harcrt Hlth Sci Grp.

Pierce, Margret. Most Wanted. 1996. mass mkt. 5.50 (*0-312-95759-9*, Pub. by Tor Bks) St Martin.

Pierce, Marjorie. East of the Gabilans. LC 76-56566. 194p. 1981. reprint ed. pap. 14.95 (*0-934136-11-4*) Good Life.

Pierce, Mark. Storytelling Tips & Tales. (Illus.). 144p. 1998. pap. 12.95 (*0-673-36386-4*) Addson-Wesley Educ.

Pierce, Mark, jt. auth. see Musnick, David.

***Pierce, Mark C.** Why Just Cook It? Make It Fool Proof: Recipes for Professional Results with the Shake of a Jar. Bell, Carol, ed. (Make It Fool Proof Ser.). 96p. (Orig.). 1999. pap. 9.95 (*0-9673060-0-0*, Pub. by In Great Taste Pubg) Herveys Bklink.

— Why Just Cook It? Make It Fool Proof (The Spice Set) Recipes for Professional Results with the Shake of a Jar. Bell, Carol, ed. (Make It Fool Proof Ser.: Vol. II). 96p. 1999. pap. 32.95 (*0-9673060-1-9*, Pub. by In Great Taste Pubg) Herveys Bklink.

Pierce, Mark F. & Carnovale, Richard L. Comprehensive Review for the Radiology Registry: A Centralized Resource. LC 97-42655. (Illus.). 323p. 1998. pap. 29.95 (*0-683-30145-4*) Lppncott W & W.

Pierce, Mary Ellen. Critical Thinking. 1988. 4.95 (*1-55708-223-5*, MCR325) McDonald Pub Co.

— Interpretation. 1989. 4.95 (*1-55708-215-4*, MCR326) McDonald Pub Co.

— More Vocabulary Expanders. 1987. 4.95 (*1-55708-371-1*, MCR360) McDonald Pub Co.

— Nouns. 1992. 4.95 (*1-55708-221-9*, MCR315) McDonald Pub Co.

— Verbs. 1987. 4.95 (*1-55708-222-7*, R316) McDonald Pub Co.

Pierce, Mary Ellen, ed. Capitali. & Punct. 1988. 4.95 (*1-55708-200-6*, MCR321) McDonald Pub Co.

— Skills for Life - Voc.-Re. 1987. 4.95 (*1-55708-205-7*, R377) McDonald Pub Co.

— Word Play. 1988. 4.95 (*1-55708-202-2*, R323) McDonald Pub Co.

Pierce, Mary F., ed. Town of Weston, Massachusetts: Births, Deaths & Marriages, 1707-1850. 649p. 1993. reprint ed. lib. bdg. 66.00 (*0-8328-3145-X*) Higginson Bk Co.

Pierce, Matthew D. State Initiatives to Establish Basic Health Insurance Plans. (Working Paper Ser.: No. 61). 23p. 1992. pap. 5.50 (*0-89940-543-6*) LBJ Sch Pub Aff.

Pierce, Meredith A. Dark Moon. 256p. (YA). (gr. 7 up). 1992. 15.95 (*0-685-59346-0*, Joy St Bks) Little.

— A Gathering of Gargoyles. (Illus.). 272p. (J). 1985. reprint ed. pap. 2.95 (*0-8125-4902-3*, Pub. by Tor Bks) St Martin.

***Pierce, Meredith A.** Gathering of Gargoyles, Vol. 2. (Darkangel Trilogy Ser.). 1998. 11.10 (*0-606-13415-8*, Pub. by Turtleback) Demco.

Pierce, Meredith Ann. The Darkangel, 3 vols., Vol. 1. LC 97-21253. 304p. (YA). 1998. pap. 6.00 (*0-15-201768-2*) Harcourt.

— The Darkangel, Vol. 1. (Darkangel Trilogy Ser.). 1998. 11.10 (*0-606-13316-X*, Pub. by Turtleback) Demco.

— A Gathering of Gargoyles, 3 vols., Vol. 2. LC 97-32517. 352p. (YA). 1998. pap. 6.00 (*0-15-201801-8*) Harcourt.

— The Pearl of the Soul of the World Vol. III: The Darkangel Trilogy. LC 98-35707. (Darkangel Trilogy Ser.). 320p. (YA). 1999. pap. 6.00 (*0-15-201800-X*) Harcourt.

— The Woman Who Loved Reindeer. 256p. (J). (gr. 7-12). 2000. pap. 6.00 (*0-15-201799-2*) Harcourt.

Pierce, Michael. Meet the Cookie Man: The Lattice Inn Bed & Breakfast. 138p. 1996. pap. 10.00 (*1-56383-070-1*) G & R Pub.

Pierce, Michael D. The Most Promising Young Officer: A Life of Ranald Slidell Mackenzie. LC 92-32281. 1993. 24.95 (*0-8061-2494-6*) U of Okla Pr.

***Pierce, Michelle B.** Nutrition Support to Elderly Women: Influence on Diet Quality. LC 99-55080. (Studies on the Elderly in America). 2000. write for info. (*0-8153-3812-0*) Garland.

Pierce, Mike. Adopt-a-Puppet. 38p. 1996. pap. 8.00 (*1-58302-008-X*) One Way St.

Pierce, N. F., jt. ed. see Kuwahara, S.

Pierce, Neal R. The Creative Partnership: State Power & Local Initiative. 1978. 1.00 (*1-55614-031-2*) U of SD Gov Res Bur.

— The Great Plains States of America. 1973. 15.95 (*0-393-05349-0*) Norton.

— The Mountain States of America: People, Politics & Power in the Eight Rocky Mountain States. (Illus.). 320p. 1971. 15.95 (*0-393-05255-9*) Norton.

— The New England States: People, Politics & Power in the Six New England States. (Illus.). 1976. 15.95 (*0-393-05558-2*) Norton.

Pierce-Norton, MaryJane. Come! Follow Me! (Great Big Bks.). (Illus.). 16p. (J). (gr. k-3). 1996. pap. 14.95 (*0-687-06678-6*) Abingdon.

Pierce, Olive. No Easy Roses: A Look at the Lives of City Teenagers. (Illus.). 94p. 1986. pap. write for info. (*0-9617101-0-1*) Olive Pierce.

— Up River: The Story of a Maine Fishing Community. LC 95-47137. (Illus.). 131p. 1996. pap. 19.95 (*0-87451-756-7*) U Pr of New Eng.

Pierce, Ovid W. Old Man's Gold, & Other Stories. LC 75-19101. 80p. reprint ed. pap. 30.00 (*0-8357-3876-0*, 203660800004) Bks Demand.

Pierce, Paul. Freedmen's Bureau: A Chapter in the History of Reconstruction. LC 68-24993. (American History & Americana Ser.: No. 47). 1969. reprint ed. lib. bdg. 75.00 (*0-8383-0229-7*) M S G Haskell Hse.

Pierce, Paulette. Noncapitalist Development: Struggle to Nationalize the Guyanese Sugar Industry. LC 84-17882. 220p. (C). 1984. 42.00 (*0-86598-118-3*) Rowman.

Pierce, Pauline. Egg Painting & Decorating: 305 Fantastic & Fun Patterns for the Whole Family. LC 97-15267. (Illus.). 96p. 1997. 10.95 (*0-8069-9895-4*) Sterling.

— Egg Painting & Decorating Book & Kit. 1997. 19.95 (*0-8069-1337-1*, Chapelle) Sterling.

Pierce, Percy E. & Marcus, Robert T. Color & Appearance. (Illus.). 44p. 1994. pap. 30.00 (*0-934010-17-X*) Fed Soc Coat Tech.

Pierce, Percy E. & Schoff, Clifford K. Coating Film Defects. (Illus.). 25p. 1994. pap. 30.00 (*0-934010-14-5*) Fed Soc Coat Tech.

Pierce, Peter. Australian Melodramas: Thomas Keneally's Fiction. LC 95-193653. (Studies in Australian Literature). 222p. 1995. pap. 14.95 (*0-7022-2813-3*, Pub. by Univ Queensland Pr) Intl Spec Bk.

— The Country of Lost Children: An Australian Anxiety. LC 99-11495. (Illus.). 240p. (C). 1999. 54.95 (*0-521-59440-5*); pap. 19.95 (*0-521-59499-5*) Cambridge U Pr.

Pierce, Peter, ed. The Oxford Literary Guide to Australia. (Illus.). 360p. 1988. text 62.00 (*0-19-554592-3*) OUP.

— The Oxford Literary Guide to Australia. 2nd ed. (Illus.). 516p. 1993. reprint ed. pap. text 35.00 (*0-19-553447-6*) OUP.

Pierce, Peter, jt. ed. see Wallace-Crabbe, Chris.

Pierce, Phyllis S., ed. The Irwin Investor's Handbook, 1996. 15th ed. 232p. 1996. pap. 27.50 (*0-7863-0975-X*, Irwn Prfssnl) McGraw-Hill Prof.

Pierce-Picciotto, Linda. Student-Led Parent Conferences. LC 97-112694. 73p. 1997. pap. text 10.95 (*0-590-89649-0*) Scholastic Inc.

Pierce, R., jt. auth. see Pierce, A.

Pierce, R. A., tr. see Fedorova, Svetlana G.

Pierce, R. A., tr. see Khlebnikov, Kirill T.

Pierce, R. S. Compact Zero-Dimensional Metric Spaces of Finite Type. LC 72-11822. (Memoirs Ser.: No. 1/130). 64p. 1972. pap. 16.00 (*0-8218-1830-9*, MEMO/1/130) Am Math.

Pierce, R. S., jt. auth. see Beaumont, Ross A.

Pierce, R. W. & Hart, G. F. Phytoplankton of the Gulf of Mexico: Taxonomy of Calcareous Nannoplankton. (Geoscience & Man Ser.: Vol. 20). (Illus.). 106p. 1979. pap. 12.00 (*0-938909-19-3*) Geosci Pubns LSU.

Pierce, Renae, jt. auth. see Ling, Lincoln.

Pierce, Richard, jt. auth. see MacDonald, Charles.

Pierce, Richard, jt. auth. see Macdonald, Charles.

Pierce, Richard A. Alaskan Shipping, 1867-1878: Arrivals & Departures at the Port of Sitka. (Alaska History Ser.: Vol. 1). (Illus.). 1972. pap. 3.95 (*0-919642-86-1*) Limestone Pr.

— Builders of Alaska: The Russian Governors, 1818-1867. LC 96-3165. (Alaska History Ser.: No. 28). (Illus.). 53p. 1985. 11.00 (*0-919642-07-1*) Limestone Pr.

— Russian America, 1741-1867: A Biographical Dictionary. (Alaska History Ser.: No. 33). (Illus.). 1990. 45.00 (*0-919642-45-4*) Limestone Pr.

— Russia's Hawaiian Adventure, 1815 to 1817. (Alaska History Ser.: No. 8). (Illus.). 1976. pap. 18.00 (*0-919642-69-1*) Limestone Pr.

— Soviet Central Asia, a Bibliography, 1558-1966, 3 pts. 1966. pap. 15.00 (*0-919642-94-2*) Limestone Pr.

Pierce, Richard A., ed. The Journals of Iakov Netsvetov: The Yukon Years, 1845-1863. Black, Lydia T., tr. from RUS. (Alaska History Ser.: No. 26). 514p. 1984. 32.00 (*0-919642-01-2*) Limestone Pr.

— The Lovtsov Atlas of the North Pacific Ocean, Compiled at Bol'sheretsk, Kamchatka, in 1782. Black, Lydia T., tr. from RUS. LC 96-30697. (Alaska History Ser.: No. 38). (Illus.). 62p. 1991. pap. 12.50 (*0-919642-38-1*) Limestone Pr.

— The Round-the-World Voyage of Hieromonk Gideon, 1803-1809. Black, Lydia T., tr. from RUS. (Alaska History Ser.: No. 32). (Illus.). 1989. 29.00 (*0-919642-20-9*) Limestone Pr.

Pierce, Richard A., tr. from RUS. Russian-American Company Correspondence: Communications Sent, 1818. (Alaska History Ser.: No. 25). (Illus.). 1984. 30.00 (*0-919642-02-0*) Limestone Pr.

Pierce, Richard A. & Black, Michael H. Life-Span Development: A Diversity Reader. 368p. (C). 1993. per. 18.95 (*0-8403-8565-X*) Kendall-Hunt.

Pierce, Richard A., ed. see Adams, George R.

Pierce, Richard A., ed. see Alekseev, Aleksandr I.

Pierce, Richard A., ed. see Belcher, Edward & Simpkinson, F. G.

Pierce, Richard A., ed. see Gutman, A. Ya.

Pierce, Richard A., ed. see Huggins, Eli L.

Pierce, Richard A., ed. see Ivashintsov, Nikolai A.

Pierce, Richard A., ed. see Kordan, Bohdan S. & Luciuk, Lubomyr Y.

Pierce, Richard A., ed. see Luciuk, Lubomyr Y. & Kordan, Bohdan S.

Pierce, Richard A., ed. see Luetke, Frederick.

Pierce, Richard A., ed. see Shelikhov, Grigorii I.

Pierce, Richard A., ed. see Tikhmenev, Petr A.

Pierce, Richard A., ed. see Veniaminov, Ivan.

Pierce, Richard A., ed. see Von Langsdorff, Georg H.

Pierce, Richard A., ed. & tr. see Teben'kov, Mikhail D.

Pierce, Richard A., tr. see Bolkhovitinov, Nikolai N.

Pierce, Richard D., ed. Records of the 1st Church in Salem, Massachusetts, 1629-1736. LC 73-93302. 1974. 30.00 (*0-88389-050-X*, PEMP177, Essx Institute) Peabody Essex Mus.

Pierce, Richard J. Economic Regulation: Cases & Materials. LC 93-38939. 410p. 1994. 54.95 (*0-87084-275-7*) Anderson Pub Co.

Pierce, Richard J. & Gellhorn, Ernest. Regulated Industries in a Nutshell. 3rd ed. LC 94-8849. (Nutshell Ser.). 374p. (C). 1994. pap. 19.95 (*0-314-03660-1*) West Pub.

Pierce, Richard J., Jr., et al. Administrative Law & Process. 2nd ed. (University Textbook Ser.). 600p. 1992. text 35.95 (*0-88277-968-0*) Foundation Pr.

***Pierce, Richard LaMonte.** One Acts: A Collection of One Act Plays. 199p. 1999. pap. text 12.95 (*1-889534-36-6*) Jay St Pubs.

An Asterisk (*) at the beginning of an entry indicates that the title is appearing for the first time.

Pierce, Richard S. Associative Algebras. (Graduate Texts in Mathematics Ser.: Vol. 88). 416p. 1997. 59.00 (*0-387-90693-2*) Spr-Verlag.

— Introduction to the Theory of Abstract Algebras. LC 68-16477. 1968. 39.50 (*0-03-056010-1*) Irvington.

— Modules over Commutative Regular Rings. LC 52-42839. (Memoirs Ser.: No. 1/70). 112p. 1977. reprint ed. pap. 21.00 (*0-8218-1270-X*, MEMO/1/70) Am Math.

— Translation Lattices. LC 52-42839. (Memoirs Ser.: No. 1/32). 66p. 1983. reprint ed. pap. 22.00 (*0-8218-1232-7*, MEMO 1/32) Am Math.

Pierce, Richard S., jt. auth. see Beaumont, Ross A.

Pierce, Robert. I Can Draw That! Easy Animals & Monsters. (Books & Stuff Ser.). (Illus.). 32p. (Orig.). (J). (ps-3). 1997. pap. 6.95 (*0-448-41600-X*, G & D) Peng Put Young Read.

— I Can Draw That, Too! (Books & Stuff Ser.). 32p. 1999. pap. 7.99 (*0-448-42030-9*, G & D) Peng Put Young Read.

Pierce, Robert, et al. Emotional Expression in Psychotherapy. LC 83-5604. 356p. 1983. 29.95 (*0-89876-015-1*) Gardner Pr.

Pierce, Robert N. A Sacred Trust: Nelson Poynter & the St. Petersburg Times. (Illus.). 408p. 1993. 39.95 (*0-8130-1234-1*) U Press Fla.

***Pierce, Roberta B.** Speech-Language Pathologist's Guide to Home Health Care. (Illus.). 1999. pap. 59.95 (*0-12-554830-3*) Acad Pr.

Pierce, Robyn, ed. Research on Mature-Age Students Returning to Study Mathematics at Tertiary Level. 67p. 1993. pap. 65.00 (*0-7300-2057-6*, Pub. by Deakin Univ) St Mut.

Pierce, Robyn, jt. ed. see Martin, Peter J.

Pierce, Roger, jt. auth. see Pierce, Alexandra.

Pierce, Ronald K. What Are We Trying to Teach Them Anyway? A Father's Focus on School Reform. LC 92-21143. 176p. 1993. 19.95 (*1-55815-239-3*) ICS Pr.

Pierce, Roxanne H., jt. auth. see Heide, Florence P.

Pierce, Roy. Choosing the Chief: Presidential Elections in France & the United States. 320p. 1995. text 49.50 (*0-472-10559-0*, 10559) U of Mich Pr.

— Choosing the Chief: Presidential Elections in France & the United States. 320p. (C). 1998. pap. text 24.95 (*0-472-08474-7*, 08474) U of Mich Pr.

Pierce, Roy, jt. auth. see Converse, Philip E.

Pierce-Ruhland, Koehlinger Mari. Luminescent Banner Designs. 96p. 1998. pap. 9.99 (*0-570-05341-2*) Concordia.

Pierce, S. G. Limpy's Homemade Sausage: For the Hunter & the Homemaker. (Illus.). 82p. 1998. pap. 15.95 (*1-57188-170-0*) F Amato Pubns.

Pierce, S. K. & Maugel, T. K. Illustrated Invertebrate Anatomy: A Laboratory Guide. (Illus.). 320p. (C). 1989. reprint ed. pap. text 39.95 (*0-19-504077-5*) OUP.

Pierce, Sally. Whipple & Black: Commercial Photographers in Boston. (Illus.). 132p. 1987. 45.00 (*0-934552-49-5*); pap. 18.00 (*0-934552-50-9*) Boston Athenaeum.

Pierce, Sally & Slautterback, Catherina. Boston Lithography, 1825-1880: The Boston Athenaeum Collection. LC 91-73405. (Illus.). 204p. 1991. 48.00 (*0-934552-57-6*) Boston Athenaeum.

Pierce, Sally & Smith, Temple D. Citizens in Conflict: Prints & Photographs of the American Civil War. LC 81-70895. (Illus.). 50p. (Orig.). 1981. pap. 7.50 (*0-934552-38-X*) Boston Athenaeum.

Pierce, Sally, et al. Early American Lithography: Images to 1830 LC 97-70985. 87p. 1997. write for info. (*0-934552-64-9*) Boston Athenaeum.

Pierce, Sarah H. Turning Points. (Illus.). 128p. (Orig.). 1996. pap. 11.95 (*0-9645451-6-0*, Swann Pubns) F Swann Pubns.

Pierce, Sherri. Expressions in Glass. (Illus.). 51p. 1994. pap. 12.95 (*0-936459-26-3*) Stained Glass.

Pierce, Sophia B. Key to Love. LC 99-220258. (Charming Petite Ser.). 1998. 4.95 (*0-88088-826-1*) Peter Pauper.

Pierce, Stacia. Hospitality & Greeters Training Manual. 15p. 1994. student ed. 5.00 (*1-886880-02-6*) Life Changers.

— How to Develop a Successful Women's Ministry. 40p. 1994. student ed. 10.00 (*1-886880-04-2*) Life Changers.

— How to Develop Your Own Personal Growth Program. 10p. 1998. pap., wbk. ed. 10.00 (*1-886880-17-4*) Life Changers.

— How to Provide Standout Service. 13p. pap., wbk. ed. 10.00 (*1-886880-15-8*) Life Changers.

— How to Set Goals & Achieve Them. 1997. pap., wbk. ed. 10.00 (*1-886880-14-X*) Life Changers.

— The Image Workshop. 26p. 1994. student ed. 15.00 (*1-886880-01-8*) Life Changers.

— Motivated Women. 15p. 1994. student ed. 10.00 (*1-886880-03-4*) Life Changers.

— The Success Secrets of a Reader. 112p. 1999. pap. 9.00 (*1-886880-24-7*) Life Changers.

— Time Management Strategies of Very Successful People. 11p. 1997. pap., wbk. ed. 10.00 (*1-886880-16-6*) Life Changers.

— 25 Ways Moms Can Raise Extraordinary Children. 194p. 1999. pap. 12.00 (*1-886880-22-0*) Life Changers.

— 25 Ways Women Can Motivate Themselves. 240p. 1998. 12.00 (*1-886880-19-0*) Life Changers.

***Pierce, Stacia.** The Women's Portfolio. 200p. 2000. 149.00 (*1-886880-26-3*) Life Changers.

Pierce, Stacia, jt. auth. see Pierce, James.

Pierce, Steven R. & Macpherson, Colin. Blood Group Systems: Duffy, Kidd & Lutheran. LC 88-19267. 151p. 1988. 25.00 (*0-915355-55-8*) Am Assn Blood.

Pierce, Steven R., jt. ed. see Vengelen-Tyler, Virginia.

Pierce, Sue & Suit, Verna. Art Quilts: Playing with a Full Deck. LC 94-36681. (Illus.). 152p. (Orig.). 1995. pap. 25.00 (*0-87654-300-X*) Pomegranate Calif.

Pierce, Susan. This Is Me - U. S. Memories to Gather & Keep. Finkbeiner, Gloria, ed. (Illus.). 82p. 1995. 36.00 (*1-930218-00-1*) Adopt Option.

Pierce, Susan & Schick-Jacobowitz, Jean. You're My Friend Be Claus. (Charming Petites Ser.). (Illus.). 64p. 1996. 4.95 (*0-88088-803-2*) Peter Pauper.

Pierce, Susan K., jt. auth. see Humphreys, Robert E.

Pierce, Sydney J., ed. Weeding & Maintenance of Reference Collections. LC 90-30910. (Reference Librarian Ser.: No. 29). 183p. 1990. text 49.95 (*1-56024-001-6*) Haworth Pr.

— Weeding & Maintenance of Reference Collections. LC 90-30910. (Reference Librarian Ser.: No. 29). (Illus.). 183p. (C). 1995. reprint ed. pap. text 19.95 (*1-56024-976-5*) Haworth Pr.

Pierce, T. Burton. Ministerial Ethics: A Guide for Spirit-Filled Leaders. Horton, Stanley M., ed. LC 96-3636. 288p. 1996. 19.95 (*0-88243-320-2*) Gospel Pub.

***Pierce, Tamora.** Alanna: The First Adventure. (J). (gr. 5 up). 1999. 19.00 (*0-8446-7002-2*) Peter Smith.

Pierce, Tamora. Alanna: The First Adventure. (Song of the Lioness Ser.). (YA). (gr. 5 up). 1997. pap. 4.99 (*0-614-28945-9*) Random Bks Yng Read.

— Briar's Book. LC 98-26148. (Circle of Magic Ser.: Vol. 4). 272p. (YA). (gr. 6-12). 1999. 15.95 (*0-590-55359-3*) Scholastic Inc.

***Pierce, Tamora.** Briar's Book, # 4. (Circle of Magic Ser.: Vol. 4). (Illus.). 272p. (J). (gr. 6-12). 2000. mass mkt. 4.99 (*0-590-55411-5*) Scholastic Inc.

— Daja's Book. LC 97-44825. (Circle of Magic Ser.: Bk. 3). 224p. (YA). (gr. 6-12). 1998. 15.95 (*0-590-55358-5*, Pub. by Scholastic) Scholastic Inc.

— Daja's Book, # 3. (Circle of Magic Ser.: Vol. 3). (Illus.). 240p. (J). (gr. 6-12). 2000. mass mkt. 4.99 (*0-590-55410-7*) Scholastic Inc.

Pierce, Tamora. The Emperor Mage. LC 96-42022. (Immortals Ser.: Vol. 3). 294p. (YA). (gr. 7-12). 1997. pap. 4.99 (*0-679-88290-1*, Pub. by Random Bks Yng Read) Random.

***Pierce, Tamora.** Emperor Mage. (Illus.). 1999. pap. 12.25 (*0-613-01855-9*) Econo-Clad Bks.

Pierce, Tamora. First Test. LC 98-30903. (Protector of the Small Ser.). (Illus.). 224p. (J). (gr. 5). 2000. pap. 4.99 (*0-679-88917-5*, Pub. by Random Bks Yng Read) Random.

— First Test, 1. LC 98-30903. 216p. (YA). (gr. 5-9). 1999. 16.00 (*0-679-88914-0*, Pub. by Random Bks Yng Read) Random.

***Pierce, Tamora.** In the Hand of the Goddess. (J). (gr. 5 up). 1999. 19.00 (*0-8446-7003-0*) Peter Smith.

Pierce, Tamora. In the Hand of the Goddess. (Song of the Lioness Ser.). (YA). (gr. 5 up). 1997. pap. 4.99 (*0-614-28946-7*) Random Bks Yng Read.

— In the Hand of the Goddess. LC 84-2946. (Song of the Lioness Ser.: Vol. 2). 209p. (J). (gr. 4-7). 1990. reprint ed. mass mkt. 4.99 (*0-679-80111-1*, Pub. by Random Bks Yng Read) Random.

— Lioness Rampant. (Song of the Lioness Ser.). (YA). (gr. 5 up). 1997. pap. 4.99 (*0-614-28947-5*) Random Bks Yng Read.

***Pierce, Tamora.** Magic Steps. LC 99-31943. (Circle Opens Ser.: Vol. 1). (Illus.). 288p. (J). (gr. 4-7). 2000. 16.95 (*0-590-39588-2*, Scholastic Ref) Scholastic Inc.

Pierce, Tamora. Page. LC 99-89894. (Protector of the Small Ser.: No. 2). 240p. (J). (gr. 5-9). 2000. 16.00 (*0-679-88915-9*, Pub. by Random Bks Yng Read) Random.

— Page. LC 99-89894. (Protector of the Small Ser.: No. 2). (Illus.). 240p. (J). (gr. 5-9). 2000. lib. bdg. 17.99 (*0-679-98915-3*, Pub. by Random Bks Yng Read) Random.

— Protector of the Small, Vol. 1. LC 98-30903. (J). 1999. lib. bdg. 17.99 (*0-679-98914-5*) Random.

— Protector of the Small, Vol. 3. (J). 2001. lib. bdg. 17.99 (*0-679-98916-1*) Random.

— The Realms of the Gods. LC 96-45006. 288p. (J). 1998. pap. 4.99 (*0-679-88291-X*, Pub. by Random Bks Yng Read) Random.

— The Realms of the Gods. 224p. (J). (gr. 5 up). 1996. 17.00 (*0-689-31990-8*) S&S Bks Yung.

— Sandry's Book. LC 95-39540. (Circle of Magic Ser.: No. 1). 256p. (J). (gr. 6-12). 1997. 15.95 (*0-590-55356-9*) Scholastic Inc.

***Pierce, Tamora.** Sandry's Book. (Circle of Magic Ser.: Vol. 1). 252p. (YA). (gr. 6-12). 1999. pap. 4.99 (*0-590-55408-5*) Scholastic Inc.

Pierce, Tamora. Tris's Book. LC 97-8521. (Circle of Magic Ser.). 251p. (J). (gr. 5-10). 1998. 15.95 (*0-590-55357-7*) Scholastic Inc.

***Pierce, Tamora.** Tris's Book. Vol. 2. 251p. (YA). (gr. 6-12). 1999. pap. 4.99 (*0-590-55409-3*) Scholastic Inc.

Pierce, Tamora. Wild Magic. LC 96-42023. (Immortals Ser.: Vol. 1). 299p. (YA). (gr. 7-12). 1997. pap. 4.99 (*0-679-88288-X*, Pub. by Random Bks Yng Read) Random.

— Wild Magic. large type ed. LC 93-8427. (Immortals Ser.). (J). 1993. pap. 15.95 (*1-56054-796-0*) Thorndike Pr.

— Wild Magic: The Immortals. LC 91-43909. 208p. (YA). (gr. 5 up). 1992. 17.00 (*0-689-31761-1*) Atheneum Yung Read.

— Wolf-Speaker. LC 93-21909. (Immortals Ser.). 192p. (J). (gr. 5 up). 1994. 16.00 (*0-689-31833-2*) Atheneum Yung Read.

— Wolf-Speaker. (Immortals Ser.). (YA). (gr. 7 up). 1997. pap. 4.99 (*0-614-28949-1*) Random Bks Yng Read.

— Wolf-Speaker. LC 96-42024. (Immortals Ser.: Vol. 2). 281p. (YA). (gr. 7-12). 1997. pap. 4.99 (*0-679-88289-8*, Pub. by Random Bks Yng Read) Random.

— The Woman Who Rides Like a Man. (Song of the Lioness Ser.). (YA). (gr. 5 up). 1997. pap. 4.99 (*0-614-28948-3*) Random Bks Yng Read.

— The Woman Who Rides Like a Man. LC 85-20054. (Song of the Lioness Ser.: Vol. 3). 228p. (J). (gr. 4-7). 1990. reprint ed. pap. 4.99 (*0-679-80112-X*, Pub. by Knopf Bks Yng Read) Random.

Pierce, Thomas H. & Hohne, Bruce A., eds. Artificial Intelligence Applications in Chemistry. LC 86-3315. (ACS Symposium Ser.: Vol. 306). 410p. 1986. reprint ed. pap. 127.10 (*0-608-03512-2*, 206423100008) Bks Demand.

Pierce, Thomas H., jt. ed. see Hohne, Bruce A.

Pierce, Timothy J., ed. see CGI Staff.

Pierce, Tony, tr. see Froman, Bernard.

Pierce, Vivienne, ed. Pastoral Responses to Older Adults & Their Families: An Annotated Bibliography, 15. LC 91-43560. (Bibliographies & Indexes in Gerontology Ser.: No. 15). 288p. 1992. lib. bdg. 59.95 (*0-313-28039-8*, SXD/, Greenwood Pr) Greenwood.

Pierce, W. D., jt. auth. see Epling, W. Frank.

Pierce, W. David & Epling, W. Frank. Behavior Analysis & Learning. 2nd ed. LC 98-10083. 444p. (C). 1998. 59.00 (*0-13-080743-5*) P-H.

Pierce, W. David, jt. ed. see Epling, W. Frank.

Pierce, W. MacBeth. Old Hancock County Families: Containing Genealogies of Families Resident in Hancock County in 1933, Whose Ancestors of Their Surnames Settled in the Town in or Before 1790. (Illus.). 133p. 1997. reprint ed. pap. 18.50 (*0-8328-5852-8*) Higginson Bk Co.

Pierce, W. S. Furnishing the Library Interior. (Books in Library & Information Science: Vol. 29). (Illus.). 304p. 1980. text 137.50 (*0-8247-6900-7*) Dekker.

Pierce, Walter M. Oregon Cattleman, Governor, Congressman: Memoirs & Times of Walter M. Pierce. Bone, Arthur H., ed. LC 80-81718. (Illus.). 528p. 1981. pap. 14.95 (*0-87595-098-1*) Oregon Hist.

Pierce, William, jt. auth. see Adamec, Christine A.

Pierce, William L. Gun Control in Germany 1928-1945: Attitude of the Hitler Government Towards the Private Ownership of Firearms. (ENG & GER., Illus.). 48p. (Orig.). 1996. pap. 4.95 (*0-937944-07-6*) Natl Vanguard.

Pierce, William L., jt. auth. see Adamec, Christine A.

Pierce, William L., jt. auth. see Macdonald, Andrew.

***Pierce/University of Minnesota Staff.** Management. 2001. pap. 60.00 (*0-324-04958-7*) Thomson Learn.

Pierceall, Gregory M. An Illustrated Guide to Landscape Design, Construction, & Management. LC 97-73995. (Illus.). 614p. 1998. 74.95 (*0-8134-3019-4*); text, teacher ed. 14.95 (*0-8134-3020-8*) Interstate.

— Residential Landscapes: Graphics, Planning & Design. (Illus.). 468p. (C). 1994. reprint ed. text 57.95 (*0-88133-788-9*) Waveland Pr.

— Sitescapes. 272p. (C). 1990. text 65.20 (*0-13-812066-8*) P-H.

Piercey. Reading Actv Content Area. 3rd ed. 1995. text. write for info. (*0-205-10490-8*) Allyn.

Piercey, Bertha E. A Widow's Story. LC 92-23311. (Orig.). 1993. pap. 8.95 (*0-9627635-4-3*) Brandylane.

Piercy & Barclay Designers, Inc. Staff. Designer Duplex Home Plans. (Illus.). 24p. 1985. 8.95 (*0-929939-08-5*) Piercy Barclay.

— Designer Home Plans, Vol. 4. (Illus.). 63p. 1982. 12.95 (*0-929939-02-6*) Piercy Barclay.

— Designer Home Plans, Vol. 5. (Illus.). 63p. 1985. 12.95 (*0-929939-03-4*) Piercy Barclay.

— Designer Home Plans, Vol. 6. (Illus.). 64p. 1990. pap. text 12.95 (*0-929939-04-2*) Piercy Barclay.

— Designer Leisure Home Plans. (Illus.). 1985. 8.95 (*0-929939-07-7*) Piercy Barclay.

— Designers Book of Home Plans, Vol. 2. (Illus.). 48p. 1976. 12.95 (*0-929939-00-X*) Piercy Barclay.

— Designers Book of Home Plans, Vol. 3. 2nd ed. (Illus.). 1990. 12.95 (*0-929939-09-3*) Piercy Barclay.

— Designers Book of Home Plans: Executive Homes. 4th ed. (Illus.). 64p. 1991. 12.95 (*0-929939-12-3*) Piercy Barclay.

— Designers Book of Home Plans: Narrow Lot Homes. 3rd ed. (Illus.). 64p. 1991. 12.95 (*0-929939-11-5*) Piercy Barclay.

Piercy, Caroline B. & Tolve, Arthur P. The Shaker Cookbook: Recipes & Lore from the Valley of God's Pleasure. rev. ed. (Illus.). 192p. 1984. pap. 14.95 (*0-911861-02-5*) Gabriels Horn.

Piercy, Day, Jr. Day's Creating Your Life Notebook. 89p. (Orig.). 1996. pap., spiral bd. 12.95 (*0-9651903-0-7*) Createnet.

Piercy, Day. Day's Strategic Planning Manual for Non-Profit Organizations. 177p. (Orig.). 1996. pap., spiral bd. 38.00 (*0-9651903-1-5*) Createnet.

— Day's Tools for Groups: Increase Your Skills in Working with People - Build the Effectiveness of Your Team, Work Group, or Committee. 79p. (Orig.). 1996. pap., spiral bd. 22.00 (*0-9651903-2-3*) Createnet.

Piercy, Fred P., ed. Family Therapy Education & Supervision. LC 85-21958. (Journal of Psychotherapy & the Family: Vol. 1, No. 4). 145p. 1986. text 4.95 (*0-86656-510-8*); pap. text 19.95 (*0-86656-511-6*) Haworth Pr.

Piercy, Fred P., et al. Family Therapy Sourcebook. 2nd ed. 475p. 1996. pap. text 27.00 (*1-57230-151-1*, 0151); lib. bdg. 44.95 (*1-57230-150-3*, 0150) Guilford Pubns.

Piercy, Frederick. Route from Liverpool to Great Salt Lake Valley James, Linforth, ed. LC 98-9656. (Illus.). 120p. 1998. reprint ed. 29.95 (*1-55709-468-3*) Applewood.

Piercy, Frederick & James, Linforth, eds. Route from Liverpool to Great Salt Lake Valley. limited ed. (Illus.). 120p. 1998. reprint ed. boxed set 300.00 (*1-55709-467-5*) Applewood.

Piercy, James E., jt. auth. see Forbes, J. Benjamin.

Piercy, Josephine. Studies in Literary Types in Seventeenth Century America. (BCL1-PS American Literature Ser.). 360p. 1993. reprint ed. lib. bdg. 89.00 (*0-7812-6573-8*) Rprt Serv.

Piercy, LaRue W. Big Island History Makers: Remarkable Historical Characters Who Shaped Events on the Island of Hawaii - Explorers, Hawaiian Royalty, Western Adventurers, Missionaries. 48p. 1990. pap. 3.95 (*1-56647-063-3*) Mutual Pub HI.

Piercy, Larue W. Hawaii: Truth Stranger Than Fiction. 128p. 1994. pap. 6.95 (*1-56647-062-5*) Mutual Pub HI.

Piercy, LaRue W. Hawaii Island Leaders. pap. 3.95 (*0-681-02763-0*) Booklines Hawaii.

Piercy, Larue W. Hawaii This & That. 60p. 1994. pap. 4.95 (*1-56647-064-1*) Mutual Pub HI.

Piercy, LaRue W. Hawaii's Missionary Saga. 232p. 1992. pap. 16.95 (*0-935180-05-2*) Mutual Pub HI.

Piercy, Marge. The Art of Blessing the Day: Poems with a Jewish Theme. LC 98-14207. 208p. 1999. 23.00 (*0-375-40477-5*) Knopf.

***Piercy, Marge.** The Art of Blessing the Day: Poems with a Jewish Theme. 192p. 2000. pap. 16.00 (*0-375-70431-0*) Knopf.

Piercy, Marge. Available Light. LC 87-40490. 144p. 1988. pap. 15.00 (*0-394-75691-6*) Knopf.

— Braided Lives. 1997. pap. 12.00 (*0-449-00091-5*) Fawcett.

— Braided Lives. LC 81-16695. 441p. 1982. 25.00 (*0-671-43834-4*) Ultramarine Pub.

— Circles on the Water: Selected Poems of Marge Piercy. 320p. 1982. pap. 19.00 (*0-394-70779-6*) Knopf.

Piercy, Marge. City of Darkness, City of Light. 1997. pap. 12.00 (*0-449-91275-2*) Fawcett.

Piercy, Marge. City of Light. 1996. 24.00 (*0-614-20638-3*, Columbine) Fawcett.

— Early Grrrl: The Early Poems of Marge Piercy. LC 98-25157. 160p. (Orig.). 1999. pap. 15.00 (*0-9654578-6-9*, Pub. by Leapfrog Pr) Consort Bk Sales.

— Early Ripening. 1987. pap. 14.95 (*0-86358-141-2*, Pub. by Pandora) Harper SF.

— The Earth Shines Secretly: A Book of Days. LC 89-52050. (Illus.). 96p. 1990. 15.95 (*0-944072-10-0*) Zoland Bks.

— Fly Away Home. 432p. 1985. mass mkt. 5.95 (*0-449-20691-2*, Crest) Fawcett.

— Gone to Soldiers. 800p. 1988. mass mkt. 6.99 (*0-449-21557-1*, Crest) Fawcett.

— He, She & It. 448p. 1993. mass mkt. 5.99 (*0-449-22060-5*) Fawcett.

— The Longings of Women. 448p. 1995. mass mkt. 6.99 (*0-449-22349-3*, Crest) Fawcett.

— The Longings of Women. large type ed. LC 94-18341. 752p. 1994. lib. bdg. 25.95 (*0-8161-7457-1*, G K Hall Lrg Type) Mac Lib Ref.

— Mars & Her Children. 1992. pap. 15.00 (*0-679-73877-0*) Knopf.

— The Moon Is Always Female. LC 79-21866. 133p. 1980. pap. 15.00 (*0-394-73859-4*) Knopf.

— My Mother's Body. Nicholas, Nancy, ed. LC 84-48661. 160p. 1985. pap. 14.00 (*0-394-72945-5*) Knopf.

— Parti-Colored Blocks for a Quilt: Poets on Poetry. 336p. 1982. pap. 13.95 (*0-472-06338-3*, 06338) U of Mich Pr.

— Small Changes. 544p. 1985. mass mkt. 6.99 (*0-449-21083-9*, Crest) Fawcett.

— Stone, Paper, Knife. LC 82-48050. 125p. 1983. pap. 15.00 (*0-394-71219-6*) Knopf.

— Three Women. LC 99-13324. 320p. 1999. 25.00 (*0-688-17106-0*, Wm Morrow) Morrow Avon.

***Piercy, Marge.** Three Women. 384p. 2000. mass mkt. 6.99 (*0-06-101467-2*, HarpTorch) Morrow Avon.

Piercy, Marge. What Are Big Girls Made Of? 1997. 25.00 (*0-614-29416-9*); pap. 15.00 (*0-614-29417-7*) Knopf.

— What "R" Big Girls Made Of. LC 96-29207. 160p. 1997. 25.00 (*0-679-45065-3*); pap. 15.00 (*0-679-76594-8*) McKay.

— Woman on the Edge of Time. 384p. 1985. mass mkt. 6.99 (*0-449-21082-0*) Fawcett.

— A Woman on the Edge of Time. 1997. pap. 12.00 (*0-449-00094-X*) Fawcett.

Piercy, Marge & Wood, Ira. Storm Tide. LC 97-48414. 304p. 1998. 25.00 (*0-449-00166-0*) Fawcett.

— Storm Tide. 1999. pap. 25.00 (*0-449-00157-1*) Fawcett.

***Piercy, Nigel.** Market-Led Strategic Change. 2000. pap. 37.95 (*0-7506-4382-X*) Buttrwrth-Heinemann.

Piercy, Nigel. Market-Led Strategic Change: Making Marketing Happen in Your Organization. LC 92-250048. (Marketing Ser.). (Illus.). 416p. 1992. reprint ed. pap. 129.00 (*0-608-07432-2*, 206765900009) Bks Demand.

— Market-Led Strategic Change: Transforming the Process of Going to Market. 2nd ed. LC 98-135256. (Marketing Ser.). 480p. 1998. pap. text 42.95 (*0-7506-3285-2*) Buttrwrth-Heinemann.

— Marketing Organisation: An Analysis of Information Processing, Power & Politics. (Illus.). 224p. 1985. text 34.95 (*0-04-658245-2*) Routledge.

Piercy, Nigel F. Tales from the Marketplace: Stories of Revolution, Reinvention. 256p. 2000. pap. text 49.95 (*0-7506-4265-3*) Buttrwrth-Heinemann.

Piercy, Patricia A. The Great Encounter: A Special Meeting Before Columbus. (Illus.). 47p. (J). (gr. 1-7). 1991. pap. 6.95 (*0-913543-26-8*) African Am Imag.

***Piercy, Robert.** Celebrating Our Faith. (Illus.). 1999. 24.95 (*5-550-72342-5*); 18.95 (*5-550-72343-3*) Nairi.

Piercy, Robert, jt. auth. see Haas, David.

Piercy, Robert, jt. auth. see Mazar, Peter.

Piercy, Robert W. Walking by Faith: Liturgy & Ritual Book LC 99-166227. 150p. 1998. write for info. (*0-15-950532-1*) Harcourt.

— When Children Gather, 2 vols. 1998. 24.95 (*0-15-950642-5*, Harcourt Child Bks) Harcourt.

***Piercy, Robert W.** When Children Gather: 20 Eucharistic Liturgies for the School Year. 1998. pap. 19.95 (*0-15-950609-3*) Harcourt.

P

An Asterisk (*) at the beginning of an entry indicates that the title is appearing for the first time.

Piercy, Robert W. When We Gather, 2 vols. 1998. 19.95 (*0-15-950643-3*, Harcourt Child Bks) Harcourt.

Piercy, Robert W. & Bross, Jean E. Confirmation: Anointed & Sealed with the Spirit: Rituals & Retreats, Vol. 4. DeVries, Dirk, ed. LC 98-104211. (Illus.). 112p. 1997. 9.95 (*1-889108-32-4*) Liv Good News.

Piercy, Robert W. & William, Vivian E., compiled by. When Children Gather: Full Score. 104p. 1997. spiral bd. 19.95 (*1-57999-014-2*, G-4806FS) GIA Pubns.

Piercy, Robert W. & Williams, Vivian E. When Children Gather: 20 Eucharistic Liturgies for the School Year. LC 97-38192. 1997. pap. 19.95 (*1-57999-013-4*) GIA Pubns.

— When Children Gather: 20 Prayer Services for the Liturgical Year. (Illus.). 125p. 1997. 19.95 (*1-57999-030-4*, G-4807) GIA Pubns.

Piercy, Robert W. & Williams, Vivian E., compiled by. When Children Gather: Student Melody Book. 30p. 1997. pap. 1.50 (*1-57999-015-0*, G-4806P) GIA Pubns.

Piercy, Robert W., jt. auth. see Baltikas, Linda B.

Piercy, William C., jt. ed. see Wace, Henry.

Pierdes, G. Philippou. Tetralogy of Time: Stories of Cyprus: Nostos Books on Modern Greek History & Culture. Stavrou, Theofanis G., ed. Martin, Donald E. & Stavrou, Soterios G., trs. LC 98-67496. (GRE.). 288p. 1998. 30.00 (*0-932963-09-9*) Nostos Bks.

Pierfrancesco, jt. auth. see Tosi.

Pieri, Christian, et al. Land Quality Indicators. LC 95-44781. (Discussion Paper Ser.: Vol. 315). 74p. 1996. pap. 22.00 (*0-8213-3511-1*) World Bank.

***Pieri, Joe.** Tales of the Savoy: Stories from a Glasgow Cafe. 192p. 2000. pap. 15.00 (*1-897784-94-5*, Pub. by N Wilson Pubng) Interlink Pub.

Pierick, Jean, ed. see Zinnen, Tom & Voichick, Jane.

Pierik, Perry. Hungary, 1944-1945 - The Forgotten Tragedy: Germany's Final Offensives During World War II. 304p. 1998. pap. 25.95 (*90-75323-10-7*) Intl Spec Bk.

Pierik, R. L. In Vitro Culture of Higher Plants. (C). 1987. pap. text 100.50 (*90-247-3531-9*); lib. bdg. 204.50 (*90-247-3530-0*) Kluwer Academic.

— In Vitro Culture of Higher Plants. LC 98-31690. 1998. write for info. (*0-7923-5267-X*) Kluwer Academic.

Pierik, R. L. & Prakash, J., eds. Horticulture - New Technologies & Applications: Proceedings of the International Seminar on New Frontiers in Horticulture. (Current Plant Science & Biotechnology in Agriculture Ser.). 428p. 1991. lib. bdg. 145.00 (*0-7923-1279-1*) Kluwer Academic.

Pierik, T., jt. auth. see Prakash, J.

Pierini, Adrian-Martin, ed. see International Congress of Pediatric Dermatology St.

Pierini, Pascal, tr. see St. John of the Cross.

Pierini, Stephen, jt. auth. see Eddleston, Michael.

Pieris, Aloysius. Asian Theology of Liberation. 1997. pap. 24.95 (*0-567-29158-8*, Pub. by T & T Clark) Bks Intl VA.

— Fire & Water: Basic Issues in Asian Buddhism & Christianity. LC 96-9441. (Faith Meets Faith Ser.). 250p. (Orig.). 1996. pap. 20.00 (*1-57075-055-6*) Orbis Bks.

***Pieris, Indrani.** Disease, Treatment, & Health Behaviour in Sri Lanka. LC 99-939177. 1999. write for info. (*0-19-564470-0*) OUP.

Pieris, P. E. Ceylon & the Hollanders, 1658-1796. 3rd ed. LC 99-932490. viii, 122 p. 1999. (*81-206-1343-0*) Asian Educ Servs.

— Prince Vijaya Pala of Ceylon, 1634-1654. 1995. 8.50 (*0-614-18150-X*, Pub. by Asian Educ Servs) S Asia.

Pieris, P. E., jt. auth. see Ribeiro, Jodao.

Pieris, Ralph. Asian Development Styles. LC 77-74486. 1977. 7.50 (*0-88386-831-8*) S Asia.

Pierloot, R. A., ed. Recent Research in Psychosomatics. (Psychotherapy & Psychosomatics Ser.: Vol. 18, No. 1-6). (Illus.). viii, 376p. 1971. reprint ed. 99.25 (*3-8055-1219-8*) S Karger.

Pierman, Carol J. The Age of Krypton. LC 88-70389. (Poetry Ser.). 1989. pap. 11.95 (*0-88748-075-6*) Carnegie-Mellon.

Piermattei, D. L. An Atlas of Surgical Approaches to the Bones & Joints of the Dog & Cat. 3rd ed. (Illus.). 336p. 1992. text 61.00 (*0-7216-1012-9*, W B Saunders Co) Harcrt Hlth Sci Grp.

Piermattei, Donald L. & Flo, Gretchen L. Handbook of Small Animal Orthopedics & Fracture Repair. 3rd ed. Kersey, Ray, ed. LC 96-39430. (Illus.). 736p. 1997. pap. text 60.00 (*0-7216-5689-7*, W B Saunders Co) Harcrt Hlth Sci Grp.

Piero D. Francesca. De Prospetiva Pingendi, Facsimile of Parma, Biblioteca Palatina, MS 1576. (Documents of Art & Architectural History Ser.: Series II, Vol. 2). (LAT., Illus.). 420p. 1994. lib. bdg. 125.00 (*0-89371-201-9*) Broude Intl Edns.

Piero, G. Del, see Del Piero, G., ed.

Piero, Ulisse Del, see Del Piero, Ulisse.

Piero, W. S. Di, see Di Piero, W. S.

Piero, W. S. Do, see Do Piero, W. S.

Pieron, Henri. Thought & the Brain. LC 73-2981. (Classics in Psychology Ser.). 1980. reprint ed. 25.95 (*0-405-05153-0*) Ayer.

— Vocabulaire de la Psychologie. 8th ed. (FRE.). 608p. 1990. 115.00 (*0-7859-4835-X*) Fr & Eur.

Pieron, Maurice, ed. see Olympic Scientific Congress (1984: Eugene, OR) Sta.

Pieroni, G. G., ed. Issues on Machine Vision. (Illus.). vi, 339p. 1989. 85.95 (*0-387-82148-1*) Spr-Verlag.

Pieroni, Robert E. Appelton & Lange Review of Internal Medicine. 3rd ed. 200p. 1999. pap. text 19.95 (*0-8385-0216-4*, A0216-0) Appleton & Lange.

Pierot, Suzanne. The Ivy Book: The Growing & Care of Ivy. (Illus.). 183p. (Orig.). 1995. pap. 12.95 (*1-887738-00-2*) Grdn By The Stream.

Pieroth, Doris Hinson. Their Day in the Sun: Women of the 1932 Olympics. (Samuel & Althea Stroum Bks.). (Illus.). 208p. 1996. pap. 16.95 (*0-295-97554-7*) U of Wash Pr.

Pieroth, Gerhard, jt. auth. see Schneider, Petra.

***Pierotti, Jane.** Supercharged Living: A Woman's Guide to Plugging into the Power of God. LC 99-24531. (SpiritLed Woman Bible Study Ser.). 264p. 1999. pap. 12.99 (*0-88419-600-3*) Creation House.

Pierotti, N. J. Almost Inkfish. 105p. 1993. pap. 10.00 (*0-9638096-0-1*) Inkfish Pr.

Pieroway, Phyllis. Memories of Sandy Point, St. George's Bay, Newfoundland. (Illus.). 96p. 1996. pap. 11.25 (*0-921411-33-2*) Genl Dist Srvs.

Pierpaoli, Paul G., Jr. Truman & Korea: The Political Culture of the Early Cold War. LC 98-33326. 280p. 1999. 32.50 (*0-8262-1206-9*) U of Mo Pr.

Pierpaoli, Walter. The Melatonin Miracle: Nature's Age-Reversing, Disease-Fighting, Sex-Enhancing Hormone. 1996. mass mkt. 6.99 (*0-671-53435-1*) PB.

Pierpoint, Bonnie. Auburn. (Images of America Ser.). 128p. 1996. pap. 16.99 (*0-7524-0249-8*) Arcadia Publng.

Pierpoint, Richard J. Cam Bridges. (Cambridge Town, Gown & County Ser.: Vol. 3). (Illus.). 40p. 1976. pap. 5.95 (*0-902675-63-X*) Oleander Pr.

Pierpoint, Robert C., jt. ed. see Kihlstedt, Andrea.

Pierpont, S., jt. auth. see Robb, D. A.

***Pierpont, Claudia Roth.** Passionate Minds: Women Rewriting the World. LC 99-33349. (Illus.). 320p. 2000. 26.95 (*0-679-43106-3*) Knopf.

Pierpont, John. Anti-Slavery Poems. LC 71-104544. reprint ed. lib. bdg. 40.50 (*0-8398-1570-0*) Irvington.

Pierpont, Mary E., ed. Genetics of Cardiovascular Disease. 1986. text 254.00 (*0-89838-790-6*) Kluwer Academic.

Pierpont, Morgan. Histoire Naturelle des Indes: The Drake Manuscript in the Pierpont Morgan Library. LC 96-28780. (FRE.). 288p. 1996. 59.95 (*0-393-03994-3*) Norton.

Pierpont Morgan Library Curators Staff. Major Acquisitions of the Pierpont Morgan Library, 1924-1974, 4 vols. Incl. Vol. 1. Autograph Letters & Manuscripts. 1974. (*0-87598-043-0*); (Illus.). 1974. Set pap. (*0-686-86598-7*) Pierpont Morgan.

Pierpont Morgan Library Staff, et al. From Mantegna to Picasso: Drawings from the Thaw Collection at the Pierpont Morgan Library, New York. LC 96-9895. 1996. write for info. (*0-87598-116-X*) Pierpont Morgan.

Pierpont Morgan Library Staff, jt. auth. see Braun, Emily.

Pierpont Morgan Library Staff, jt. auth. see Schmitz, Barbara.

Pierpont Publishing, Inc. Staff, ed. see Calandro, Ed.

Pierpont, William. What You Can Do about Allergy. 6p. 1996. reprint ed. spiral bd. 8.00 (*0-7873-1107-3*) Hlth Research.

Pierpont, William G., ed. The New Testament in the Original Greek: According to the Byzantine-Majority Textform. LC 91-60094. (ENG & GEC.). 576p. 1991. pap. 24.95 (*0-9626544-3-4*) Original Word.

— The New Testament in the Original Greek: According to the Byzantine-Majority Textform. deluxe limited ed. LC 91-60094. (ENG & GEC.). 576p. 1991. 74.95 (*0-9626544-2-6*) Original Word.

Pierquin, Bernard & Marinello, Ginette, eds. A Practical Manual of Brachytherapy. Wilson, Frank et al, trs. from FRE. LC 96-49909.Tr. of Manuel Pratique de Curietherapie. (Illus.). 300p. 1997. text 109.95 (*0-944838-73-1*) Med Physics Pub.

Pierradrd, Pierre. Larousse des Prenoms et des Saints. (FRE.). 256p. 1976. 42.50 (*0-8288-5725-3*, M6454) Fr & Eur.

Pierrakos, Eva. Creating Union: The Pathwork of Relationship. Saly, Judith, ed. LC 93-86256. (Pathwork Ser.). xvii, 189p. (Orig.). 1993. pap. 14.95 (*0-9614777-3-3*) Pathwork Pr.

— Guide Lectures for Self-Transformation. Saly, Judith, ed. LC 85-134343. 203p. (Orig.). 1985. pap. 12.00 (*0-9614777-1-7*) Pathwork Pr.

— Surrender to God Within: Pathwork at the Soul Level. Thesenga, Donovan, ed. & intro. by. x, 204p. (Orig.). 1997. pap. 14.95 (*0-9614777-5-X*) Pathwork Pr.

Pierrakos, Eva & Thesenga, Donovan. Fear No Evil: The Pathwork Method of Transforming the Lower Self. LC 93-84262. (Pathwork Ser.). xviii, 270p. 1993. pap. 15.95 (*0-9614777-2-5*) Pathwork Pr.

Pierrakos, Eve. Pathwork of Self Transformation. 288p. 1990. pap. 12.95 (*0-553-34896-5*) Bantam.

Pierrakos, John. Eros, Love & Sexuality: The Forces That Unify Man & Woman. LC 97-28378. 144p. 1997. 17.95 (*0-940795-05-1*) LifeRhythm.

Pierrakos, John C. Core Energetics: Developing the Capacity to Love & Heal. (Illus.). 302p. 1990. pap. 20.00 (*0-940795-08-6*) LifeRhythm.

Pierrard, Pierre. Larousse Dictionnaire des Prenoms et des Saints. (FRE.). 224p. 1987. pap. 19.95 (*0-7859-1254-1*, 2037300174) Fr & Eur.

Pierre, Alain C. Introduction to Sol-Gel Processing. LC 98-4679. (Kluwer International Series in Sol-Gel Processing). 1998. 145.00 (*0-7923-8121-1*) Kluwer Academic.

Pierre, Andrew J. The Global Politics of Arms Sales. LC 81-15895. (Illus.). 372p. 1982. reprint ed. pap. 115.40 (*0-7837-9420-7*, 206016100004) Bks Demand.

Pierre, Andrew J., ed. Cascade of Arms: Controlling Conventional Weapons Proliferation in the 1990s. LC 97-33822. 466p. (C). 1997. 42.95 (*0-8157-7064-2*); pap. 19.95 (*0-8157-7063-4*) Brookings.

Pierre, Andrew J. & Quandt, William B. The Algerian Crisis: Policy Options for the West. 65p. 1996. pap. 7.95 (*0-87003-106-6*) Carnegie Endow.

Pierre, Andrew J. & Trenlin, Dmitri, eds. Russia in the World Arms Trade. LC 97-31844. (Carnegie Endowment for International Peace Bks.). 132p. 1997. pap. 12.95 (*0-87003-083-3*) Brookings.

Pierre, Arnauld. Frank Kupka: In White & Black. LC 98-200942. (Illus.). 62p. 1997. pap. 34.95 (*0-85323-772-7*, Pub. by Liverpool Univ Pr) Intl Spec Bk.

Pierre, B., ed. see Barlow, M. T. & Nualart, D.

Pierre, Bernard & Pierre, Genevieve. Medical Dictionary for Tropical Regions: Dictionnaire Medical pour les Regions. 2nd ed. (FRE.). 850p. 1988. pap. 75.00 (*0-8288-1823-1*) Fr & Eur.

Pierre, Brian St., see St. Pierre, Brian.

Pierre, Brian St., see Herbert, Malcolm.

Pierre, C. & Maurande, G. French-English - English-French Vocabulary of Ecology. 94p. 1989. pap. 28.00 (*2-85608-036-7*, Pub. by La Maison Du Dict) IBD Ltd.

Pierre, C. & Perkins, N. C., eds. Structural Dynamics of Large Scale & Complex Systems. LC 93-72635. (DE Ser.: Vol. 59). 160p. 1993. 55.00 (*0-7918-1176-X*, G00820) ASME.

Pierre, Chantal & Pierre, Maurande. Lexique de l'Ecologie, Anglais-Francais, Francais-Anglais. (ENG & FRE.). 1989. pap. 49.95 (*0-7859-3918-0*) Fr & Eur.

Pierre, Cyrille & Laplace, Theodore. Voyage Autour du Monde par les Mers de Pinde et de Chine, Tome 1. (FRE., Illus.). 602p. 1998. reprint ed. pap. 240.00 (*1-85297-001-4*, Pub. by Archival Facs) St Mut.

Pierre, D. St., see Keers, C. & St. Pierre, D.

Pierre, Dominique La, see Collins, Larry & La Pierre, Dominique.

Pierre, Donald A. Optimization Theory with Applications. 640p. 1998. reprint ed. pap. 16.95 (*0-486-65205-X*) Dover.

Pierre du Moulin the Elder. The Anatomy of Arminianisme. LC 76-57380. (English Experience Ser.: No. 797). 1977. reprint ed. lib. bdg. 65.00 (*90-221-0797-3*) Walter J Johnson.

Pierre, Edwards R. Welding Processes & Power Sources. 3rd ed. (Student Study Guide Ser.). (Illus.). 416p. (C). 1985. text. write for info. (*0-8087-3369-9*); student ed. write for info. (*0-8087-3370-2*) Pearson Custom.

Pierre, Genevieve, jt. auth. see Pierre, Bernard.

***Pierre, Gerard J.** The Last Captured. LC 99-93576. 2000. pap. 11.95 (*0-533-13071-9*) Vantage.

***Pierre, Jon.** Partnerships Urban Governance. LC 97-49943. 206p. 1998. text 59.95 (*0-333-68939-9*, Pub. by Macmillan) St Martin.

Pierre, Jon, ed. Bureaucracy in the Modern State: An Introduction to Comparative Public Administration. LC 94-6261. 240p. 1995. 95.00 (*1-85278-725-2*) E Elgar.

— Debating Governance: Authenticity, Steering, & Democracy. LC 99-48959. 272p. 2000. 60.00 (*0-19-829514-6*) OUP.

— Debating Governance: Authenticity, Steering, & Democracy. LC 99-48959. 272p. 2000. pap. 24.95 (*0-19-829772-6*) OUP.

Pierre, Jon, ed. Urban & Regional Policy. LC 94-22993. (International Library of Comparative Public Policy: Vol. 2). 688p. 1995. 270.00 (*1-85278-909-3*) E Elgar.

***Pierre, Jon & Peters, B. Guy.** Governance, Politics & the State. LC 99-56510. 2000. write for info. (*0-312-23176-8*); pap. write for info. (*0-312-23177-6*) St Martin.

Pierre, Jon, jt. ed. see King, Desmond S.

Pierre, Jose, ed. Investigating Sex: Surrealist Discussions, 1928-32. Imrie, Malcolm, tr. (Illus.). 220p. (C). (gr. 13). 1994. pap. 18.00 (*0-86091-603-0*, B3643, Pub. by Verso) Norton.

Pierre, Joseph. The Descendants of Thomas Pier: A Record of the Descendants of Thomas Pier, a Late 17th Century Inhabitant of Lyme, CT. (Illus.). 319p. (Orig.). 1995. pap. text 24.50 (*0-7884-0266-8*) Heritage Bk.

***Pierre, L. & Kropf, T., eds.** Correct Hardware Design & Verification Methods: Proceedings of the 10th IFIP WG10.5 Advanced Research Working Conference, CHARME'99, Bad Herrenalb, Germany, September 27-29, 1999. LC 99-51458. (Lecture Notes in Computer Science Ser.: Vol. 1703). xi, 366p. 1999. pap. 62.00 (*3-540-66559-5*) Spr-Verlag.

Pierre, L., jt. ed. see Milne, G. J.

Pierre, M. Dictionnaire de l'Histoire de la France. (FRE.). 1998. reprint ed. 55.00 (*0-320-00226-8*) Fr & Eur.

Pierre, Maurande, jt. auth. see Pierre, Chantal.

Pierre, Melvin, Sr. How to Get Visa & Mastercards...Even Though You May Have Previously Been Turned Down. 1986. pap. 5.00 (*0-318-36086-1*) RMP Finan Consul.

Pierre, Melvin. How to Manage Your Family Budget During These Troubled Times. rev. ed. 1978. pap. 5.00 (*0-931664-00-4*) RMP Finan Consul.

Pierre, Michel. Atlas of the Medieval World: In Europe (IV-XV Century) (Atlas Ser.). 64p. (J). 1999. 19.95 (*0-87226-530-7*, 65307B, P Bedrick Books) NTC Contemp Pub Co.

— The Atlas of the 20th Century. LC 99-58525. (Atlas Ser.). (Illus.). 64p. (YA). (gr. 5 up). 2000. 19.95 (*0-87226-291-X*, P Bedrick Books) NTC Contemp Pub Co.

Pierre, Michel De Saint, see De Saint Pierre, Michel.

Pierre-Michel, V. Dictionary of the History of France. (FRE.). 464p. 1991. 49.95 (*0-8288-6924-3*, 2203156031) Fr & Eur.

Pierre, Stephanie S. Elmo's Valentine. LC 98-101151. (J). 1997. 3.99 (*0-679-88899-3*, Pub. by Random Bks Yng Read) Random.

Pierre, Ulwyn L. The Myth of Black Corporate Mobility. LC 98-42967. (Studies in African American History & Culture). 1998. 60.00 (*0-8153-3138-X*) Garland.

***Pierre, Wendy J.** Moon Flower. LC 99-94918. 2000. pap. 7.95 (*0-533-13220-7*) Vantage.

Pierrehumbert, Janet & Beckman, Mary E. Japanese Tone Structure. (Linguistic Inquiry Monographs). 280p. (Orig.). 1988. 33.00 (*0-262-16109-5*) MIT Pr.

Pierrehumbert, Janet, jt. ed. see Broe, Michael.

Pierret, Antonio P. & Perez, Antonio C. Antonio Perez Pierret: Obra Po Etica. LC 98-11359. xxiv, 194 p. 1998. pap. write for info. (*0-8477-0318-5*) U of PR Pr.

Pierret, Janine, jt. auth. see Herzlich, Claudine.

Pierret, Paul. Recueil d'Inscriptions Inedites du Musee Egyptien du Louvre. ix, 320p. 1978. reprint ed. write for info. (*3-487-06534-7*) G Olms Pubs.

Pierret, Robert F. Advanced Semiconductor Fundamentals: Solutions Manual. (Modular Series on Solid State Devices: Vol. VI). 1987. pap., student ed. 6.33 (*0-201-05339-X*) Addison-Wesley.

Pierret, Robert F. Dispositivos de Efecto de Campo. (SPA.). 208p. (C). 1994. pap. text 12.66 (*0-201-60141-9*) Addison-Wesley.

— Field Effect Devices. LC 81-15035. (Modular Series on Solid State Devices: No. 4). (Illus.). 116p. 1983. pap. write for info. (*0-201-05323-3*) Addison-Wesley.

— Fundamentos de Semiconductores. (SPA.). 160p. (C). 1994. pap. text 12.33 (*0-201-60144-3*) Addison-Wesley.

— Semiconductor Device Fundamentals. Harutunian, Katherine, ed. LC 95-17387. 800p. (C). 1995. 105.00 (*0-201-54393-1*) Addison-Wesley.

— Semiconductor Fundamentals. 2nd ed. (Modular Series on Solid State Devices). (Illus.). 160p. (C). 1988. pap. text 22.40 (*0-201-12295-2*) Addison-Wesley.

Pierret, Robert F. & Neudeck, Gerold W. Advanced Semiconductor Fundamentals, Vol. 6. LC 86-20593. (Modular Series on Solid State Devices: Vol. 6). (Illus.). 160p. (C). 1987. pap. 22.40 (*0-201-05338-1*) Addison-Wesley.

Pierret, Robert F. & Neudeck, Gerold W. S/M All Four Vol Modular, Vol. I. LC 81-14978. (Electrical Engineering Ser.). (Illus.). 1983. pap. text, teacher ed. 2.00 (*0-201-05324-1*) Addison-Wesley.

Pierro, Albino. Selected Poems. Bonaffini, Luigi, tr. from ITA. (Essential Poets Ser.: Vol. 85). 144p. 2000. pap. 13.00 (*1-55071-078-8*) Guernica Editions.

Pierron, Agnes. Dictionnaire de Citations sur les Personnages Celebres. (FRE.). 600p. 1995. 110.00 (*0-7859-9896-9*) Fr & Eur.

***Pierros, Filippos, et al.** Bridges & Barriers: The European Union's Mediterranean Policy, 1961-1998. 340p. 1999. text 87.95 (*1-84014-447-5*, Pub. by Ashgate Pub) Ashgate Pub Co.

Pierrot, ed. see Balzac, Honore de.

Pierrot, Jean. The Decadent Imagination, Eighteen Eighty to Nineteen Hundred. Coltman, Derek, tr. LC 81-4828. 304p. (C). 1992. lib. bdg. 25.00 (*0-226-66822-3*) U Ch Pr.

— The Decadent Imagination, Eighteen Eighty to Nineteen Hundred. Coltman, Derek, tr. from FRE. LC 81-4828. viii, 310p. (C). 1984. reprint ed. pap. text 12.50 (*0-226-66823-1*) U Ch Pr.

Pierrot, Lane, et al. A Look at Tomorrow's Tactical Air Forces. (Illus.). 89p. (C). 1997. pap. text 30.00 (*0-7881-4298-4*) DIANE Pub.

Piers, Balaikie. The Political Economy of Soil Erosion in Developing Countries. 1985. pap. text 30.95 (*0-582-30089-4*) Addison-Wesley.

Piers, Frank. Orchids of East Africa. 304p. (C). 1984. 80.00 (*0-7855-3284-6*, Pub. by Scientific) St Mut.

— Orchids of East Africa. 2nd rev. ed. (Illus.). 1984. pap. 50.00 (*3-7682-0569-X*) Lubrecht & Cramer.

Piers, Helen. Is There Room on the Bus? (Illus.). 36p. (J). (ps-1). 1996. pap. text 7.99 (*0-7112-0951-0*) F Lincoln.

Piers, Helen. Is There Room on the Bus? LC 95-19631. (Illus.). 36p. (J). (ps-2). 1996. 14.00 (*0-689-80610-8*) S&S Bks Yung.

— Taking Care of Your Cat. (Young Pet Owner's Guides Ser.). (Illus.). 32p. (YA). (gr. 3 up). 1992. pap. 4.95 (*0-8120-4873-3*) Barron.

— Taking Care of Your Cat. (Young Pet Owner's Guide Ser.). (J). 1992. 10.15 (*0-606-01648-1*, Pub. by Turtleback) Demco.

— Taking Care of Your Dog. (Young Pet Owner's Guides Ser.). (Illus.). 32p. (J). (gr. 3 up). 1992. pap. 4.95 (*0-8120-4874-1*) Barron.

— Taking Care of Your Dog. (Young Pet Owner's Guide Ser.). (J). 1992. 10.15 (*0-606-01649-X*, Pub. by Turtleback) Demco.

— Taking Care of Your Gerbils. Vriends, Matthew M., ed. LC 92-26959. (Young Pet Owner's Guides Ser.). (Illus.). 32p. (J). 1993. pap. 4.95 (*0-8120-1369-7*) Barron.

— Taking Care of Your Gerbils. (Young Pet Owner's Guide Ser.). (J). 1993. 10.15 (*0-606-05659-9*, Pub. by Turtleback) Demco.

— Taking Care of Your Goldfish. Vriends, Matthew M., ed. LC 92-32170. (Young Pet Owner's Guides Ser.). (Illus.). 32p. (J). (gr. 3 up). 1993. pap. 4.95 (*0-8120-1368-9*) Barron.

— Taking Care of Your Goldfish. (Young Pet Owner's Guide Ser.). (J). 1993. 10.15 (*0-606-05660-2*, Pub. by Turtleback) Demco.

— Taking Care of Your Guinea Pig. (Young Pet Owner's Guides Ser.). (Illus.). 32p. (J). (gr. 3 up). 1993. pap. 4.95 (*0-8120-1367-0*) Barron.

Piers, Helen. Taking Care of Your Guinea Pigs. (Young Pet Owner's Guide Ser.). (J). 1993. 10.15 (*0-606-06046-4*, Pub. by Turtleback) Demco.

Piers, Helen. Taking Care of Your Hamster. (Young Pet Owner's Guides Ser.). (Illus.). 32p. (J). (gr. 3 up). 1992. pap. 5.95 (*0-8120-4695-1*) Barron.

— Taking Care of Your Hamster. (Young Pet Owner's Guide Ser.). (J). 1992. 11.15 (*0-606-01650-3*, Pub. by Turtleback) Demco.

P

— Taking Care of Your Parakeet. (Young Pet Owner's Guides Ser.). (Illus.). 32p. (J). (gr. 3 up). 1993. pap. 4.95 (*0-8120-1370-0*) Barron.

— Taking Care of Your Parakeet. (J). 1993. 9.90 (*0-606-06047-2*, Pub. by Turtleback) Demco.

— Taking Care of Your Rabbit. (Young Pet Owner's Guides Ser.). (Illus.). 32p. (J). (gr. 3 up). 1992. pap. 5.95 (*0-8120-4697-8*) Barron.

Piers, Helen. Taking Care of Your Rabbit. (Young Pet Owner's Guide Ser.). (J). 1992. 11.15 (*0-606-01651-1*, Pub. by Turtleback) Demco.

Piers, Helen. Who's in My Bed? Guess Who's under the Flaps. LC 98-37017. (Illus.). 24p. (J). (ps-k). 1999. 15.95 (*0-7614-5046-7*, Cav Child Bks) Marshall Cavendish.

Piersall, Jim & Hirshberg, Al. Fear Strikes Out: The Jim Piersall Story. LC 98-49645. 221p. 1999. pap. 12.95 (*0-8032-8761-5*, Bison Books) U of Nebr Pr.

Piersanti, Jay. Otto Cartoons. LC 93-80698. (Illus.). 96p. 1994. pap. 5.95 (*0-87341-296-6*, OS01) Krause Pubns.

Pierse, D., ed. see Ophthalmic Microsurgery Study Group Symposium Staf.

Pierse, Robert. Pierse: The Law of Road Traffic in the Republic of Ireland. 1989. boxed set 73.00 (*1-85475-055-0*, MICHIE) LEXIS Pub.

Piersel. Photomath. (J). (gr. 3-9). teacher ed. 0.29 (*0-87783-201-3*); pap. 1.99 (*0-87783-076-2*) Oddo.

— Photophonics I. (Illus.). (J). (gr. 1-5). 1968. teacher ed. 0.29 (*0-685-03702-9*); pap. 1.99 (*0-87783-073-8*) Oddo.

— Photophonics II. (Illus.). (J). (gr. 1-5). 1968. teacher ed. 0.29 (*0-685-03703-7*); pap. 2.39 (*0-87783-074-6*) Oddo.

Piersen, William D. Black Legacy: America's Hidden Heritage. LC 92-41003. 280p. (C). 1993. pap. 17.95 (*0-87023-859-0*) U of Mass Pr.

— Black Yankees: The Development of an Afro-American Subculture in Eighteenth-Century New England. LC 87-13862. 256p. (Orig.). (C). 1988. pap. 17.95 (*0-87023-587-7*) U of Mass Pr.

— From Africa to America: African American History, 1600-1790. LC 95-32327. (Twayne's African American History Ser.). 1996. 33.00 (*0-8057-3902-5*, Twyne) Mac Lib Ref.

— From Africa to America: African American History, 1600-1790. LC 95-32327. (Twayne's African American History Ser.). 1997. pap. 19.00 (*0-8057-3903-3*, Twyne) Mac Lib Ref.

Pierskalla, Carol S. & Heald, Jane D. Help for Families of the Aging: Caregivers Can Express Love & Set Limits, Leader's Manual. 2nd enl. rev. ed. (Illus.). 224p. 1988. 39.95 (*0-9619558-0-5*) Support Source.

— Help for Families of the Aging: Caregivers Can Express Love & Set Limits, Participant's Wkbk. enl. rev. ed. (Illus.). 80p. 1988. student ed. 11.95 (*0-9619558-1-3*) Support Source.

Piersma, Mary L., jt. auth. see Allen, Diane D.

Piersol, Allan G., jt. auth. see Bendat, Julius S.

***Piersol, Catherine Verrier & Ehrlich, Phyllis L., eds.** Home Health Practice: A Guide for the Occupational Therapist. 2000. 51.50 (*1-883315-50-6*) Imaginart Intl.

Piersol, Daniel. Echoes in the Silence: Benjamin Levy Drawings. LC 98-66147. (Illus.). 64p. 1998. 18.95 (*0-89494-067-8*); pap. 14.95 (*0-89494-066-X*) New Orleans Mus Art.

— Walter Rutkowski Drawings. (Illus.). 36p. 1997. pap. 12.95 (*0-89494-065-1*) New Orleans Mus Art.

Piersol, Mary B. Van Every - Records of the Van Every Family, United Empire Loyalists, N. Y. State, 1653-1784, Canada, 1784-1947. 131p. 1995. reprint ed. pap. 24.50 (*0-8328-4566-3*); reprint ed. lib. bdg. 34.50 (*0-8328-4565-5*) Higginson Bk Co.

Pierson. Florida. (Discover America Ser.). 1984. 6.99 (*0-8442-7475-5*) NTC Contemp Pub Co.

— Greeley Longmont. pap. text 2.95 (*0-914449-52-4*) Pierson Graph.

— Practical Manual of Mechanical Ventilation. 1998. pap. text 27.95 (*0-7216-6072-X*, P1231, W B Saunders Co) Harcrt Hlth Sci Grp.

Pierson & Mayer, J. P. La Photographie Consideree Comme Art et Comme Industrie. Bunnell, Peter C. & Sobieszek, Robert A., eds. LC 76-24666. (Sources of Modern Photography Ser.). (FRE.). 1979. reprint ed. lib. bdg. 18.95 (*0-405-09643-7*) Ayer.

Pierson, jt. auth. see Bitter.

Pierson, A. T. Acts of the Holy Spirit. 127p. 1980. pap. 8.99 (*0-87509-659-X*) Chr Pubns.

***Pierson, A. T.** George Muller. (Classic Biographies Ser.). (Illus.). 330p. 1999. pap. 14.99 (*1-84030-058-2*) Emerald House Group Inc.

— George Muller of Bristol: His Life of Prayer & Faith. LC 99-57660. 2000. pap. 15.99 (*0-8254-3464-5*) Kregel.

Pierson, A. T. The Heart of the Gospel: Sermons on the Life-Changing Power of the Good News. LC 95-38172. 688p. 1996. pap. 24.99 (*0-8254-3462-9*, Kregel Class) Kregel.

— Traditions of Freemasonry & Its Coincidences with the Ancient Mysteries. 384p. 1996. reprint ed. pap. 27.00 (*1-56459-534-X*) Kessinger Pub.

— World's Guide to Understanding the Bible. 349p. 1994. 14.99 (*0-529-10336-2*, WGB) World Publng.

***Pierson, Arthur T.** George Muller of Bristol. 462p. 1999. pap. 28.00 (*1-57910-241-7*) Wipf & Stock.

Pierson, Arthur T. Knowing the Scriptures. (Bible Study Ser: Pulpit Legends Collections). 350p. 1994. 14.99 (*0-89957-203-0*) AMG Pubs.

Pierson, Carlos C., tr. see Tidwell, J. B.

Pierson, Caryl. Moving with Math Extensions: Grade 1 Student Book. (Illus.). 80p. (J). (gr. 1). 1998. pap. text 5.95 (*1-891192-14-0*) Math Teachers Pr.

— Moving with Math Extensions: Grade 1 Teachers Manual. (Illus.). 228p. 1998. pap. text, teacher ed. 59.95 (*1-891192-23-X*) Math Teachers Pr.

— Moving with Math Extensions: Grade 2 Student Book. (Illus.). 80p. (J). (gr. 2). 1998. pap. text 5.95 (*1-891192-15-9*) Math Teachers Pr.

— Moving with Math Extensions: Grade 2 Teachers Manual. (Illus.). 230p. 1998. pap. text, teacher ed. 59.95 (*1-891192-24-8*) Math Teachers Pr.

— Moving with Math Extensions: Grade 4 Student Book. (Illus.). 80p. (J). (gr. 4). 1998. pap. text 5.95 (*1-891192-17-5*) Math Teachers Pr.

— Moving with Math Extensions: Grade 4 Teachers Manual. (Illus.). 230p. 1998. pap. text, teacher ed. 59.95 (*1-891192-26-4*) Math Teachers Pr.

— Moving with Math Extensions: Grade 5 Student Book. (Illus.). 80p. (J). (gr. 5). 1998. pap. text 5.95 (*1-891192-18-3*) Math Teachers Pr.

— Moving with Math Extensions: Grade 5 Teachers Manual. (Illus.). 230p. 1998. pap. text, teacher ed. 59.95 (*1-891192-27-2*) Math Teachers Pr.

— Moving with Math Extensions: Grade 6 Student Book. (Illus.). 80p. (J). (gr. 6). 1998. pap. text 5.95 (*1-891192-19-1*) Math Teachers Pr.

— Moving with Math Extensions: Grade 6 Teachers Manual. (Illus.). 230p. 1998. pap., teacher ed. 59.95 (*1-891192-28-0*) Math Teachers Pr.

— Moving with Math Extensions: Grade 7 Student Book. (Illus.). 96p. (J). (gr. 7). 1998. pap. text 6.95 (*1-891192-20-5*) Math Teachers Pr.

— Moving with Math Extensions: Grade 7 Teachers Manual. (Illus.). 280p. 1998. pap. text, teacher ed. 69.95 (*1-891192-29-9*) Math Teachers Pr.

— Moving with Math Extensions: Grade 8 Student Book. (Illus.). 96p. (J). (gr. 8). 1998. pap. text 6.95 (*1-891192-21-3*) Math Teachers Pr.

— Moving with Math Extensions: Grade 8 Teachers Manual. (Illus.). 280p. 1998. pap. text, teacher ed. 69.95 (*1-891192-30-2*) Math Teachers Pr.

— Moving with Math Extensions: Kindergarten Student Book. (Illus.). 64p. (J). (gr. k). 1998. pap. text 4.95 (*1-891192-13-2*) Math Teachers Pr.

— Moving with Math Extensions: Kindergarten Teacher Manual. (Illus.). 200p. 1998. pap. text, teacher ed. 49.95 (*1-891192-22-1*) Math Teachers Pr.

Pierson, Caryl K. Math Teachers Press: Using Models to Learn Addition & Subtraction Facts. rev. ed. 52p. (J). (gr. 1-2). 1991. pap. 4.95 (*0-933383-10-X*) Math Teachers Pr.

— Math Teachers Press: Using Models to Learn Multiplication & Division Facts. rev. ed. (Illus.). 52p. 1991. pap. 4.95 (*0-933383-11-8*) Math Teachers Pr.

— Moving with Math: AI Numeration. rev. ed. (Illus.). 80p. (J). (gr. k-2). 1993. pap. 5.95 (*0-933383-58-4*) Math Teachers Pr.

— Moving with Math: AI Numeration Teacher Guide. rev. ed. 28p. 1993. pap., teacher ed. 5.95 (*0-933383-57-6*) Math Teachers Pr.

— Moving with Math: AII Addition & Subtraction. rev. ed. (Illus.). 80p. (J). (gr. k-2). 1993. pap. 5.95 (*0-933383-60-6*) Math Teachers Pr.

— Moving with Math: AII Addition & Subtraction Teacher Guide. rev. ed. 37p. 1993. pap., teacher ed. 7.95 (*0-933383-59-2*) Math Teachers Pr.

— Moving with Math: AIII Fractions, Geometry & Measurement. rev. ed. (Illus.). 80p. (J). (gr. k-2). 1993. pap. 5.95 (*0-933383-62-2*) Math Teachers Pr.

— Moving with Math: AIII Fractions, Geometry & Measurement Teacher Guide. rev. ed. 32p. 1993. pap., teacher ed. 7.95 (*0-933383-61-4*) Math Teachers Pr.

— Moving with Math: BI Numeration, Addition & Subtraction Teacher Guide. rev. ed. 39p. 1993. pap., teacher ed. 8.95 (*0-933383-54-1*) Math Teachers Pr.

— Moving with Math: BI Numeration, Addition, Subtraction. rev. ed. (Illus.). 80p. (J). (gr. 3-4). 1993. pap. 5.95 (*0-933383-07-X*) Math Teachers Pr.

— Moving with Math: BII Multiplication & Division. rev. ed. (Illus.). 80p. (J). (gr. 3-4). 1993. pap. 5.95 (*0-933383-49-5*) Math Teachers Pr.

— Moving with Math: BII Multiplication & Division Teacher Guide. rev. ed. 39p. 1993. pap., teacher ed. 7.95 (*0-933383-55-X*) Math Teachers Pr.

— Moving with Math: BIII Fractions, Geometry & Measurement. rev. ed. (Illus.). 80p. (J). (gr. 3-4). 1996. pap. 5.95 (*0-933383-48-7*) Math Teachers Pr.

— Moving with Math: BIII Fractions, Geometry & Measurement Teacher Guide. rev. ed. (Illus.). 35p. 1993. pap., teacher ed. 8.95 (*0-933383-56-8*) Math Teachers Pr.

— Moving with Math: CI Numeration & Problem Solving with Whole Numbers. rev. ed. (Illus.). 80p. (J). (gr. 5-6). 1995. pap. 5.95 (*0-933383-89-4*) Math Teachers Pr.

— Moving with Math: CIII Geometry & Measurement. 72p. (J). (gr. 5-6). 1993. pap. 5.95 (*0-933383-15-0*) Math Teachers Pr.

— Moving with Math: CIII Geometry, Measurement & Problem Solving Teacher Guide. rev. ed. 40p. 1993. pap., teacher ed. 8.95 (*0-933383-70-3*) Math Teachers Pr.

— Moving with Math: DI Numeration & Problem Solving with Whole Numbers Teacher Guide. rev. ed. 35p. 1990. pap., teacher ed. 8.95 (*0-933383-37-1*) Math Teachers Pr.

— Moving with Math: DII Problem Solving with Fractions & Decimals Teacher Guide. rev. ed. 48p. 1990. pap., teacher ed. 9.95 (*0-933383-38-X*) Math Teachers Pr.

— Moving with Math: DIII Problem Solving with Percent Teacher Guide. rev. ed. 37p. 1995. pap., teacher ed. 8.95 (*0-933383-39-8*) Math Teachers Pr.

— Moving with Math: DIV Geometry & Measurement Teacher Guide. rev. ed. 51p. 1995. pap., teacher ed. 9.95 (*0-933383-40-1*) Math Teachers Pr.

— Moving with Math: DV Algebra & Computer Teacher Guide. rev. ed. 47p. 1990. pap., teacher ed. 7.95 (*0-933383-41-X*) Math Teachers Pr.

— Moving with Math: Grade 2 Teachers Resource Manual. rev. ed. (Illus.). 1998. pap., teacher ed. 120.00 (*0-933383-98-3*) Math Teachers Pr.

— Moving with Math: Grades 5 & 6 Skill Builders Using Action Math. rev. ed. (Illus.). 208p. (J). (gr. 5-6). 1995. pap. 29.95 (*0-933383-86-X*) Math Teachers Pr.

— Moving with Math: Level A Secondary Workbook. rev. ed. (Illus.). 126p. (YA). (gr. 7-12). 1999. pap., wbk. ed. 7.95 (*1-891192-62-0*) Math Teachers Pr.

— Moving with Math: Level A Workbook Teacher Guide. rev. ed. 44p. 1995. pap., teacher ed., wbk. ed. 14.95 (*0-933383-91-6*) Math Teachers Pr.

— Moving with Math: Level B Math Capsules Diagnostic Tests & Daily Reviews. rev. ed. (J). (gr. 3-4). 1994. pap. 19.95 (*0-933383-06-1*) Math Teachers Pr.

— Moving with Math: Level C Math Capsules Diagnostic Tests & Daily Reviews. rev. ed. (J). (gr. 5-6). 1994. pap. 19.95 (*0-933383-50-9*) Math Teachers Pr.

— Moving with Math: Level D Math Capsules Diagnostic Tests & Daily Reviews. (YA). (gr. 7-8). 1994. pap. 19.95 (*0-933383-17-7*) Math Teachers Pr.

— Moving with Math: Math Capsules Diagnostic Tests & Daily Reviews - Level A. rev. ed. (J). (gr. 1-2). 1994. pap. 19.95 (*0-933383-01-0*) Math Teachers Pr.

— Moving with Math Extensions: Grade 1 Student Book. Solberg, David W., ed. Garcia, Carmen & McGuinnes, Annelise, trs. (SPA.). 80p. (J). (gr. 1). 2000. pap. 6.95 (*1-891192-69-8*) Math Teachers Pr.

— Moving with Math Extensions: Grade 2 Student Book. Solberg, David W., ed. Garcia, Carmen & McGuinnes, Annelise, trs. (SPA.). 80p. (J). (gr. 2). 2000. pap. 6.95 (*1-891192-70-1*) Math Teachers Pr.

— Moving with Math Extensions: Grade 3 Student Book. Solberg, David W., ed. Garcia, Carmen & McGuinnes, Annelise, trs. (SPA.). 80p. (J). (gr. 3). 2000. pap. 6.95 (*1-891192-71-X*) Math Teachers Pr.

— Moving with Math Extensions: Grade 4 Student Book. Solberg, David W., ed. Garcia, Carmen & McGuinnes, Annelise, trs. (SPA.). 80p. (J). (gr. 4). 2000. pap. 6.95 (*1-891192-72-8*) Math Teachers Pr.

— Moving with Math Extensions: Kindergarten Student Book. Solberg, David W., ed. Garcia, Carmen & McGuinnes, Annelise, trs. (SPA.). 64p. (J). (gr. k). 2000. pap. 5.95 (*1-891192-68-X*) Math Teachers Pr.

— Moving with Math Extensions: Moviendose Con Matematicas Grade 1 Resource Pack. Solberg, David W., ed. Garcia, Carmen & McGuinnes, Annelise, trs. (SPA.). (J). (gr. 1). 2000. pap. 19.95 (*1-891192-74-4*) Math Teachers Pr.

— Moving with Math Extensions: Moviendose Con Matematicas Grade 2 Resource Pack. Solberg, David W., ed. Garcia, Carmen & McGuinnes, Annelise, trs. (SPA.). (J). (gr. 2). 2000. pap. 19.95 (*1-891192-75-2*) Math Teachers Pr.

— Moving with Math Extensions: Moviendose Con Matematicas Grade 3 Resource Pack. Solberg, David W., ed. Garcia, Carmen & McGuinnes, Annelise, trs. (SPA.). (J). (gr. 3). 2000. pap. 19.95 (*1-891192-76-0*) Math Teachers Pr.

— Moving with Math Extensions: Moviendose Con Matematicas Grade 4 Resource Pack. Solberg, David W., ed. Garcia, Carmen & McGuinnes, Annelise, trs. (SPA.). (J). (gr. 4). 2000. pap. 19.95 (*1-891192-77-9*) Math Teachers Pr.

— Moving with Math Extensions: Moviendose Con Matematicas Kindergarten Resource Pack. Solberg, David W., ed. Garcia, Carmen & McGuinnes, Annelise, trs. (SPA.). (J). (gr. k). 2000. pap. 19.95 (*1-891192-73-6*) Math Teachers Pr.

Pierson, Caryl K. & DeVoss, Vicki. Moving with Math: CI Numeration & Problem Solving with Whole Numbers Teacher Guide. rev. ed. (Illus.). 80p. 1995. pap., teacher ed. 9.95 (*0-933383-90-8*) Math Teachers Pr.

— Moving with Math: CII Fractions, Decimals & Percent. rev. ed. (Illus.). 100p. (J). (gr. 5-6). 1995. pap. 6.95 (*0-933383-51-7*) Math Teachers Pr.

— Moving with Math: CII Fractions, Decimals & Percent Teacher Guide. rev. ed. (Illus.). 100p. 1995. pap., teacher ed. 9.95 (*0-933383-53-3*) Math Teachers Pr.

— Moving with Math: DI Numeration & Problem Solving with Whole Numbers. rev. ed. (Illus.). 72p. (YA). (gr. 7-8). 1994. pap. 5.95 (*0-933383-18-5*) Math Teachers Pr.

— Moving with Math: DII Fractions & Decimals. rev. ed. 104p. (YA). (gr. 7-8). 1994. pap. 6.95 (*0-933383-19-3*) Math Teachers Pr.

— Moving with Math: DIII Problem Solving with Percent. rev. ed. (Illus.). 72p. (YA). (gr. 7-8). 1993. pap. 5.95 (*0-933383-65-7*) Math Teachers Pr.

— Moving with Math: DIV Geometry & Measurement. rev. ed. (Illus.). 100p. (YA). (gr. 7-8). 1994. pap. 6.95 (*0-933383-46-0*) Math Teachers Pr.

Pierson, Caryl K. & DeVoss, Vicki. Moving with Math: DV Algebra & Computer. rev. ed. (Illus.). 80p. (YA). (gr. 7-8). 1990. pap. 5.95 (*0-933383-22-3*) Math Teachers Pr.

— Moving with Math: Grades 7 & 8 Skill Builders. rev. ed. (Illus.). 208p. (YA). (gr. 7-8). 1994. pap. 29.95 (*0-933383-29-0*) Math Teachers Pr.

Pierson, Caryl K. & Heimkes, Judy. Moving with Math: Grades 3 & 4 Skill Builders Using Action Math. rev. ed. (Illus.). 192p. (J). (gr. 3-4). 1993. pap. 29.95 (*0-933383-52-5*) Math Teachers Pr.

Pierson, Caryl K. & Whisnant, Susie. Moving with Math: Grade 1 Activity Book. rev. ed. Solberg, David W., ed. (Illus.). 256p. (J). (gr. 1). 1997. pap. 15.95 (*0-933383-93-2*) Math Teachers Pr.

— Moving with Math: Grade 1 Teachers Resource Manual. rev. ed. Solberg, David W., ed. (Illus.). 410p. 1997. pap., teacher ed. 120.00 (*0-933383-94-0*) Math Teachers Pr.

— Moving with Math: Grade 2 Activity Book. rev. ed. Solberg, David W., ed. (Illus.). 240p. (J). (gr. 2). 1998. pap. 15.95 (*0-933383-97-5*) Math Teachers Pr.

— Moving with Math: Kindergarten Teachers Resource Manual. rev. ed. 2000. pap., teacher ed. 79.95 (*1-891192-58-2*) Math Teachers Pr.

— Moving with Math: Moviendose Con Matematicas Grade 1. Solberg, David W., ed. (SPA., Illus.). (J). (gr. 1). 2000. pap. 180.00 (*0-933383-95-9*) Math Teachers Pr.

— Moving with Math: Moviendose Con Matematicas Grade 2. rev. ed. Solberg, David W., ed. (SPA., Illus.). (J). (gr. 2). 1998. pap. 180.00 (*0-933383-99-1*) Math Teachers Pr.

— Moving with Math: Moviendose Con Matematicas Kindergarten. rev. ed. (SPA., Illus.). (J). (gr. k). 2000. pap. 120.00 (*1-891192-59-0*) Math Teachers Pr.

Pierson, Caryl K., et al. Moving with Math: Grades 1 & 2 Skill Builders. rev. ed. (Illus.). 176p. (J). (gr. 1-2). 1994. pap. 29.95 (*0-933383-23-1*) Math Teachers Pr.

***Pierson, Caryl K., et al.** Moving with Math: Kindergarten Student Activity Book. rev. ed. (Illus.). 176p. (J). (gr. k). 2000. pap. 11.95 (*1-891192-12-4*) Math Teachers Pr.

Pierson, Caryle. Moving with Math Extensions: Grade 3 Student Book. (Illus.). 80p. (J). (gr. 3). 1998. pap. text 5.95 (*1-891192-16-7*) Math Teachers Pr.

— Moving with Math Extensions: Grade 3 Teachers Manual. (Illus.). 230p. 1998. pap. text, teacher ed. 59.95 (*1-891192-25-6*) Math Teachers Pr.

Pierson, Chris. Dezra's Quest. (DragonLance Bridges of Time Ser.). 1999. pap. 5.99 (*0-7869-1368-1*, Pub. by TSR Inc) Random.

***Pierson, Chris.** Politics at the Edge. 330p. 2000. text 75.00 (*0-312-23137-7*) St Martin.

Pierson, Chris. Spirit of the Wind. (DragonLance Bridges of Time Ser.). 1998. pap. 5.99 (*0-7869-1174-3*, Pub. by TSR Inc) Random.

Pierson, Christopher. Beyond the Welfare State? The New Political Economy of Welfare. 260p. 1991. pap. 18.95 (*0-271-00821-0*); text 35.00 (*0-271-00820-2*) Pa St U Pr.

— Beyond the Welfare State? The New Political Economy of Welfare. 2nd ed. LC 98-16948. 1998. 45.00 (*0-271-01860-7*) Pa St U Pr.

— Beyond the Welfare State: The New Political Economy of Welfare. 2nd ed. LC 98-16948. 234p. 1998. pap. 19.95 (*0-271-01861-5*) Pa St U Pr.

— The Modern State. LC 96-10759. (Key Ideas Ser.). 224p. (C). 1996. 80.00 (*0-415-14413-2*); pap. 22.99 (*0-415-07452-5*) Routledge.

— Socialism After Communism: The New Market Socialism. LC 94-47518. 260p. 1995. pap. 18.95 (*0-271-01479-2*) Pa St U Pr.

— Socialism After Communism: The New Market Socialism. LC 94-47518. 260p. 1995. 50.00 (*0-271-01478-4*) Pa St U Pr.

***Pierson, Christopher & Castles, Francis G., eds.** The Welfare State Reader. 320p. 1999. 64.95 (*0-7456-2252-6*); pap. text 32.95 (*0-7456-2253-4*) Blackwell Pubs.

Pierson, David J. & Kacmarek, Robert M., eds. Foundations of Respiratory Care. LC 92-17459. (Illus.). 1045p. (C). 1992. text 117.00 (*0-443-08509-9*) Church.

Pierson, David J., jt. auth. see Kacmarek, Robert.

Pierson, David L. History of the Oranges to 1921, Reviewing the Rise, Development & Progress of an Influential Community, 3 vols. (Illus.). 1749p. 1997. reprint ed. lib. bdg. 77.50 (*0-8328-6068-9*) Higginson Bk Co.

***Pierson, David S.** Tuskers: An Armor Battalion in the Gulf War. (Illus.). 232p. 1999. 27.95 (*0-9648793-5-2*) Darlington Prods.

Pierson, Don, jt. auth. see Ditka, Mike.

Pierson, Edna C. The Witch of Turner's Bald. (Illus.). 1971. 5.00 (*0-686-05889-5*) Puddingstone.

Pierson, Elizabeth C., et al. A Birder's Guide to Maine. 2nd rev. ed. LC 96-5728. (Illus.). 400p. (Orig.). 1996. pap., otabind 23.95 (*0-89272-365-3*) Down East.

***Pierson, Eric.** 2000 Wiley Family Law Update. 440p. 1999. pap. text 160.00 (*0-7355-1315-5*, Aspen Law & Bus) Aspen Pub.

*** Pierson Esq., Eric.** 2000 Wiley Expert Witness Update, 1. 384p. 1999. pap. text 165.00 (*0-7355-1293-0*) Panel Pubs.

Pierson, Frank C. The Minimum Level of Unemployment & Public Policy. LC 80-26536. 194p. 1980. pap. text 12.00 (*0-911558-75-6*) W E Upjohn.

Pierson, Frank M. Principles & Techniques of Patient Care. 2nd ed. Kuhn, Shirley, ed. LC 98-5492. (Illus.). 384p. (C). 1998. pap. text 39.95 (*0-7216-7524-7*, W B Saunders Co) Harcrt Hlth Sci Grp.

***Pierson, Gary C. & Fulkerson, Sam R.** Age Discrimination in the Workplace. 130p. 1999. pap. 25.00 (*0-939900-90-4*) Soc Human Resc Mgmt.

Pierson, George W. The Founding of Yale. Vol. 5. 275p. (C). 1988. 47.00 (*0-300-04252-3*) Yale U Pr.

— Tocqueville in America. LC 96-27754. 852p. 1996. reprint ed. pap. text 24.95 (*0-8018-5506-3*) Johns Hopkins.

Pierson, Hamilton W. Jefferson at Monticello: The Private Life of Thomas Jefferson. LC 71-154161. (Select Bibliographies Reprint Ser.). 1977. reprint ed. 24.95 (*0-8369-5777-6*) Ayer.

— A Letter to Hon. Charles Sumner. LC 78-38018. (Black Heritage Library Collection). reprint ed. 12.50 (*0-8369-8985-6*) Ayer.

Pierson, Herbert, jt. auth. see Giles, Howard.

Pierson, Herbert, jt. ed. see Bornstein, Marc H.

Pierson, Herbert, jt. ed. see Ekbatani, Glayol.

Pierson, Hugh O. Handbook of Carbon, Graphite, Diamond, & Fullerenes: Properties, Processing, & Applications. LC 93-29744. (Illus.). 405p. 1994. 145.00 (*0-8155-1339-9*) Noyes.

P

— Handbook of Chemical Vapor Deposition. LC 91-46658. (Illus.). 436p. 1992. 98.00 (*0-8155-1300-3*) Noyes.

— Handbook of Chemical Vapor Deposition 2nd ed. LC 99-26065. 482p. 1999. 139.00 (*0-8155-1432-8*) Noyes.

— Handbook of Refractory Carbides & Nitrides: Properties, Characteristics, Processing, & Applications. 340p. 1996. 139.00 (*0-8155-1392-5*) Noyes.

Pierson, J. K., jt. auth. see Zwass, Vladimir.

Pierson, Jack. All of a Sudden. (Illus.). 192p. 1995. 75.00 (*1-881616-55-X*, pwerHse Bks) pwerHse Cultrl.

— Lonely Life. (Illus.). 144p. 1997. 39.95 (*3-908162-61-0*) Dist Art Pubs.

***Pierson, Jack, photos by.** Jack Pierson. 144p. 2000. 75.00 (*0-944092-78-0*) Twin Palms Pub.

Pierson, James O. No Disabled Souls: How to Welcome People with Disabilities into Your Life & Your Church. Hayes, Theresa C., ed. LC 98-9994. (Illus.). 160p. 1998. pap. 9.99 (*0-7847-0768-5*, 11-03140) Standard Pub.

Pierson, Jane & Mintz, Joshua. Assessment of the Chief Executive No. 120: A Tool for Boards & Chief Executives of Nonprofit Organizations. rev. ed. 53p. 1995. pap. 52.00 (*0-925299-47-2*) Natl Ctr Nonprofit.

Pierson, Jennifer, jt. auth. see Pierson, Richard E.

Pierson, Jim. Dark Shadows Resurrected. 176p. 1993. pap. 15.95 (*0-938817-23-X*) Pomegranate Pr.

— Dark Shadows Resurrected. (Illus.). 176p. 1993. 24.95 (*0-938817-24-8*) Pomegranate Pr.

— Just Like Everybody Else. (Illus.). 32p. (J). (ps-3). 1993. 5.99 (*0-87403-842-1*, 03661) Standard Pub.

Pierson, Jim, jt. auth. see Scott, Kathryn L.

Pierson, Jim, jt. auth. see Scott, Kathryn Leigh.

Pierson, Jim, ed. see Scott, Kathryn L. & Jackson, Kate.

Pierson, Johann. Moeris Atticista: Lexicon Atticum, 2 vols., Set. 1969. reprint ed. write for info. (*0-318-72055-8*) G Olms Pubs.

***Pierson, John, ed.** Patek Philippe Geneve: 1920-1965 Material Catalog. (Illus.). 40p. 1999. reprint ed. pap. 9.95 (*0-9631669-2-1*) Clockwks Pr.

Pierson, John & Smith, Kevin. Spike, Mike, Slackers & Dykes: A Guided Tour Across a Decade of American Independent Cinema. LC 97-123253. (Illus.). 384p. (J). 1997. pap. 12.45 (*0-7868-8222-0*, Pub. by Hyperion) Time Warner.

Pierson, John D. Tokutomi Soho, 1863-1957: A Journalist for Modern Japan. LC 79-3226. 464p. 1980. reprint ed. pap. 143.90 (*0-7837-9421-5*, 206016200004) Bks Demand.

Pierson, John H. Full Employment. 1941. 59.50 (*0-686-83556-5*) Elliots Bks.

— Full Employment: Why We Need It, How to Guarantee It - One Man's Journey. LC 96-8688. 111p. 1996. 21.95 (*1-57392-072-X*) Prometheus Bks.

Pierson, John R. Clock Repair: Part-Time Hours, Full-Time Pay. LC 91-78023. 160p. 1992. 24.95 (*0-9631669-6-4*); pap. 19.95 (*0-9631669-5-6*) Clockwks Pr.

— Clock Repair, Part-Time Hours, Full-Time Pay. 2nd rev. ed. LC 98-34619. (Illus.). 200p. 1998. pap. 24.95 (*0-9631669-9-9*) Clockwks Pr.

— Clock Repair, Part-Time Pay: Part-Time Hours, Full-Time Pay. 2nd rev. ed. LC 98-34619. (Illus.). 200p. 1998. pap. 19.95 (*0-9631669-8-0*) Clockwks Pr.

Pierson, John R., frwd. The Keystone Watch Co. Material Catalog. (Illus.). 84p. 1998. reprint ed. pap. 12.95 (*0-9631669-0-5*) Clockwks Pr.

Pierson, Judith. The Always Moon. LC 98-11363. (Illus.). 24p. (J). (gr. k-2). 1998. 13.95 (*1-890326-17-8*) First Story Pr.

— Moving Women Up: A Manual for Breaking down Barriers. LC 83-60668. 201p. reprint ed. pap. 62.40 (*0-7837-6539-8*, 204567600007) Bks Demand.

Pierson, Karen M. A Tale of Two Worcesters: Paths to Prosperity in Worcester, England & Worcester, Massachusetts. (Illus.). 288p. 1998. pap. 19.95 (*1-873827-20-2*, Pub. by Logaston Pr) St Mut.

Pierson, Linda L., ed. Through Children's Eyes: Poetry from Art. (Illus.). 77p. 1998. pap. text. write for info. (*1-882710-01-0*) USU N E H Mus.

Pierson, Lorette. Washington, D. C. Ulysses Travel Guide. (Ulysses Travel Guide Ser.). (Illus.). 272p. pap. 13.95 (*2-89464-172-9*) Ulysses Travel.

***Pierson, Marion John Bennett.** Louisiana Soldiers in the War of 1812. 126p. 1999. pap. 22.50 (*0-8063-4912-3*) Clearfield Co.

Pierson, Melissa H. The Perfect Vehicle: What It Is about Motorcycles. (Illus.). 240p. 1998. pap. 13.00 (*0-393-31809-5*) Norton.

***Pierson, Melissa Holbrook.** Dark Horses & Black Beauties: Animals, Women, a Passion. 192p. 2000. 22.95 (*0-393-04947-7*) Norton.

Pierson, Melissa Holbrook, jt. ed. see Sante, Luc.

Pierson, Merle D. & Corlett, Donald A., Jr., eds. HACCP: Principles & Applications. 230p. 1992. text 54.95 (*0-442-00989-5*) Chapman & Hall.

Pierson, Merle D. & Stern, Norman J. Foodborne Microorganisms & Their Toxins (IFT) LC 99-49286. (IFT Basic Symposium Ser.: Vol. 1). (Illus.). 488p. 1986. text 99.75 (*0-8247-7607-0*) Dekker.

Pierson, Michael & Springer, Stephen. Cooperative Education Handbook. 74p. 1990. pap. 17.95 (*0-945483-02-3*) E Bowers Pub.

Pierson, Michael J. & Dorsey, Oscar L. Portfolio Development for Career Planning. 116p. 1987. pap. text 19.95 (*0-912855-71-1*) E Bowers Pub.

Pierson, Paul. Dismantling the Welfare State? Reagan, Thatcher & the Politics of Retrenchment. (Cambridge Studies in Comparative Politics). (Illus.). 223p. 1995. pap. text 18.95 (*0-521-55570-1*) Cambridge U Pr.

— European Social Policy: Between Fragmentation & Integration. Leibfried, Stephan, ed. (Integrating National Economies: Promise & Pitfalls Ser.). 492p. (C). 1995. 52.95 (*0-8157-5248-2*); pap. 24.95 (*0-8157-5247-4*) Brookings.

***Pierson, Paul, ed.** The New Politics of the Welfare State. 342p. 2000. pap. 19.95 (*0-19-829756-4*) OUP.

Pierson, Peter. Commander of the Armada: A Life of the Seventh Duke of Medina Sidonia, 1549-1615. LC 89-5258. 312p. (C). 1989. 40.00 (*0-300-04408-9*) Yale U Pr.

— The History of Spain. LC 98-22901. (Histories of the Modern Nations Ser.). 248p. 1999. 35.00 (*0-313-30272-3*, Greenwood Pr) Greenwood.

Pierson, R. H. Guide to Spanish Idioms. (ENG & SPA.). 174p. 1980. pap. 6.95 (*0-8288-2329-4*, S 31738) Fr & Eur.

Pierson, Raymond H. Guide to Spanish Idioms: Guia de Modismos Espanoles. (ENG & SPA., Illus.). 184p. 1995. pap. 6.95 (*0-8442-7325-2*, 73252, Natl Textbk Co) NTC Contemp Pub Co.

Pierson, Richard E. & Pierson, Jennifer. Pierson Millenium. LC 98-107759. viii, 332p. 1997. pap. 34.50 (*0-7884-0742-2*, P319) Heritage Bk.

Pierson, Richard N., ed. Quantitative Nuclear Cardiology. LC 74-20990. (Illus.). 299p. reprint ed. pap. 92.70 (*0-608-30260-0*, 201258200082) Bks Demand.

Pierson, Robert W., Jr., jt. ed. see Tourbier, Joachim T.

Pierson, Ruth & Vik, Susan. Making Sense in English. Sands-Boehmer, Kathleen, ed. 304p. (Orig.). (C). 1987. pap. text 24.91 (*0-201-14585-5*) Addison-Wesley.

Pierson, Ruth R., et al, eds. Women & Peace: Theoretical, Historical & Practical Perspectives. LC 87-6778. 249p. 1987. 45.00 (*0-7099-4068-8*, Pub. by C Helm) Routldge.

Pierson, Ruth R. & Chaudhuri, Nupur, eds. Nation, Empire, Colony: Historicizing Gender & Race. LC 98-19966. (Illus.). 288p. 1998. 29.95 (*0-253-33398-9*); pap. 14.95 (*0-253-21191-3*) Ind U Pr.

Pierson, Ruth R. & Cohen, Marjorie G. Canadian Women's Issues Vol. II: Bold Visions, Vol. II. 500p. 39.95 (*1-55028-429-0*, Pub. by J Lorimer); pap. 27.95 (*1-55028-428-2*, Pub. by J Lorimer) Formac Dist Ltd.

Pierson, Stanley. British Socialists: The Journey from Fantasy to Politics. LC 78-25820. 415p. 1979. reprint ed. pap. 128.70 (*0-7837-1720-2*, 205724900024) Bks Demand.

— Marxist Intellectuals & the Working-Class Mentality in Germany, 1887-1912. LC 92-41089. 344p. 1993. text 49.95 (*0-674-55123-0*) HUP.

Pierson, Stephanie. Vegetables Rock! A Complete Guide for Teenage Vegetarians. LC 98-29570. (Illus.). 240p. 1999. pap. 12.95 (*0-553-37924-0*) Bantam.

Pierson, Vernon, et al. California Evidence Pocketbook. 2nd ed. 156p. 1996. 17.75 (*1-889110-04-3*) CA District Attys.

Pierson, William H., Jr. American Buildings & Their Architects Vol. 1: The Colonial & Neo-Classical Styles. (Illus.). 541p. 1986. pap. 19.95 (*0-19-504216-6*) OUP.

— American Buildings & Their Architects Vol. 2: Technology & the Picturesque, the Corporate & the Early Gothic Styles, Vol 2. (Illus.). 528p. 1986. pap. 16.95 (*0-19-504217-4*) OUP.

Pierson, William W., jt. ed. see Foerster, Norman.

Pierson, William W., Jr., ed. see Malone, Bartlett Y.

Pierssene. Environmental Interpretation. 224p. 1997. write for info. (*0-419-21940-4*, E & FN Spon) Routledge.

Pierzchala, Edmund. Field-Programmable Analog Arrays. LC 98-35330. 169p. 1998. write for info. (*0-7923-8232-3*) Kluwer Academic.

***Pierzynowski, S. G. & Zabielski, R.** Biology of the Pancreas in Growing Animals. LC 99-34045. 476p. 1999. 182.50 (*0-444-50217-3*) Elsevier.

***Pierzynski, Gary M., et al.** Soils & Environmental Quality. LC 99-57039. 800p. 1999. 64.95 (*0-8493-0022-3*) CRC Pr.

Pierzynski, Gary M., et al. Soils & Environmental Quality. 336p. (C). 1993. boxed set 85.00 (*0-87371-680-9*, L680) Lewis Pubs.

Pies, Cheri. Considering Parenthood: A Handbook for Lesbians. LC 88-29463. 304p. (Orig.). 1988. pap. 12.95 (*0-933216-17-3*) Spinsters Ink.

Pies, Ronald. Lean Soil. limited ed. 28p. 1985. pap. 7.95 (*0-944754-07-4*) Pudding Hse Pubns.

Pies, Ronald M. Riding down Dark. Page, Carolyn, ed. & illus. by. Butters, Nancy, illus. (Chapbook Ser.). 32p. (Orig.). 1992. pap. 6.00 (*1-879205-31-9*) Nightshade Pr.

Pies, Ronald W. Clinical Manual of Psychiatric Diagnosis & Treatment: A Biopsychosocial Approach. 544p. 1994. spiral bd. 51.95 (*0-88048-534-5*, 8534) Am Psychiatric.

— A Consumer's Guide to Choosing the Right Therapist. LC 96-12685. 240p. 1997. pap. 35.00 (*1-56821-861-3*) Aronson.

***Pies, Ronald W.** The Ethics of the Sages: An Interfaith Commentary on Pirkei Avot. LC 99-25806. 232p. 1999. 30.00 (*0-7657-6103-3*) Aronson.

Pies, Ronald W. Handbook of Essential Psychopharmacology. 416p. 1998. 42.95 (*0-88048-765-8*, 8765) Am Psychiatric.

Piesarskas, B. Lithuanian-English Dictionary. (ENG & LIT.). 511p. 1991. 39.95 (*0-8288-4015-6*, F109070) Fr & Eur.

Piesarskas, Bronius & Svecevicius, Bronius. Lithuanian Dictionary: English-Lithuanian, Lithuanian-English. LC 95-18213. (ENG & LIT.). 848p. (C). (gr. 13). 1995. pap. 32.99 (*0-415-12857-9*) Routledge.

Piesiewicz, Krzysztof, jt. auth. see Kieslowski, Krzysztof.

Piesinger, Gregory H. Nuclear Radiation: What It Is, How to Detect It, How to Protect Yourself from It. LC 80-24001. (Illus.). 127p. (Orig.). (C). 1980. pap. 9.95 (*0-937224-00-6*) Dyco Inc.

Piesman, Marissa. Unorthodox Practices. 224p. 1989. mass mkt. 4.99 (*0-671-67315-7*) PB.

***Piesner, Michael B., et al.** Maine, New Hampshire, Rhode Island & Vermont Limited Liability Company: Forms & Practice Manual, 2 vols. LC 99-37730. 938p. 1999. ring bd. 295.00 (*1-57400-042-X*) Data Trace Pubng.

Piesold, David D. Civil Engineering Practice: Engineering Success by Analysis of Failure. 340p. 1991. 52.00 (*0-07-707239-1*) McGraw.

Pieson, Ruth R., et al. Canadian Women's Issues Vol. I: Strong Voices. LC 94-133038. 460p. pap. 27.95 (*1-55028-415-0*, Pub. by J Lorimer) Formac Dist Ltd.

— Canadian Women's Issues Vol. I: Strong Voices, Vol. 1: Strong Voices. LC 94-133038. (Illus.). 460p. 39.95 (*1-55028-414-2*, Pub. by J Lorimer) Formac Dist Ltd.

Piesse, J., jt. auth. see Ward, Charles W.

Piesse, Jenifer. Efficiency Issues in Transitional Economies: An Application to Hungary. LC 98-74444. 242p. 1999. text 65.95 (*1-84014-979-5*) Ashgate Pub Co.

Piessens, R., et al. Quadpack: A Subroutine Package for Automatic Integration. (Computational Mathematics Ser.: Vol. 1). (Illus.). 301p. 1983. 79.95 (*0-387-12553-1*) Spr-Verlag.

Piest, Oskar, ed. Mill: Utilitarianism. 88p. (C). 1957. pap. text 5.20 (*0-02-395670-4*, Macmillan Coll) P-H.

Piest, Oskar, ed. see Cornford, Francis M.

Pieston, Mark. California Mission Cookery. (Border Bks.). (Illus.). 220p. 1993. pap. 15.95 (*0-9623865-5-3*) Out West Pub.

Piet, John H. A Path Through the Bible. LC 81-2258. 318p. reprint ed. pap. 98.60 (*0-7837-2633-3*, 204298300006) Bks Demand.

Piet-Pelon, Nancy J. & Hornby, Barbara. Women Overseas: A Practical Guide. 168p. (C). 1986. pap. 40.00 (*0-7855-6848-4*, Pub. by IPM Hse) St Mut.

— Women Overseas: A Practical Guide. 168p. (C). 1986. 75.00 (*0-85292-375-9*) St Mut.

— Women's Guide to Overseas Living. 2nd rev. ed. LC 92-40422. 210p. 1992. reprint ed. pap. 15.95 (*1-877864-05-6*) Intercult Pr.

Pietarinen, Fred. With Wine & Songs & Strange People Rushing Thru Me. (Illus.). 40p. (Orig.). 1983. pap. text 2.50 (*1-879594-07-2*) Androgyne Bks.

Pieter, Dariane, ed. It's Her Voice That Haunts Me Now: Poems from the Literary Review. 160p. 1998. pap. 17.95 (*1-86066-092-4*, Pub. by R Cohen Bks) Trafalgar.

Pieter van Dijk, Meine & Rabellotti, Roberta, eds. Enterprise Clusters & Networks in Developing Countries. LC 96-48445. (EADI Ser.: No. 20). (Illus.). 304p. (Orig.). (C). 1997. pap. 32.50 (*0-7146-4333-5*, Pub. by F Cass Pubs) Intl Spec Bk.

Pieter, Willey. Scientific Coaching for Olympic Taekwondo. 1997. pap. text 17.95 (*3-89124-389-8*) Meyer & Meyer.

Pieters, A. Stephen. I'm Still Dancing! A Gay Man's Health Experience. 96p. 1991. pap. 8.95 (*1-888493-04-6*) Chi Rho Pr.

Pieters, Aleida J. Dutch Settlement in Michigan. (Illus.). 207p. 1997. reprint ed. lib. bdg. 29.00 (*0-8328-6758-6*) Higginson Bk Co.

Pieters, C. M. & Englert, P. A., eds. Remote Geochemical Analysis: Elemental & Mineralogical Composition. LC 92-42655. (Topics in Remote Sensing Ser.: No. 4). (Illus.). 618p. (C). 1993. text 39.95 (*0-521-40281-6*) Cambridge U Pr.

Pieters, D. Introduction into the Basic Principles of Social Security. LC 93-42438. 1993. write for info. (*90-6544-787-3*) Kluwer Law Intl.

— Social Security Law in the Fifteen Member State of the European Union. LC 99-199158. 288p. 1997. 98.00 (*90-6215-590-1*) Gaunt.

***Pieters, Danny, ed.** International Impact upon Social Security. (European Institute of Social Security Yearbook Ser.: Vol. 3). 232p. 1999. text 90.00 (*90-411-1272-3*) Kluwer Law Intl.

— Social Protection of the Next Generation in Europe: EISS Yearbook, 1997. (European Institute of Social Security Yearbook Ser.: Vol. 2). 340p. 1998. 95.00 (*90-411-0572-7*) Kluwer Law Intl.

Pieters, Danny, ed. Social Security in Europe: Miscellanea of the Erasmus Programme of Studies Relating to Social Security in the European Communities. 295p. 1991. pap. 93.00 (*90-6215-284-8*, Pub. by Maklu Uitgev) Gaunt.

Pieters, Danny, et al. Introduction into the Social Security Law of the Member States of the European Community. 2nd ed. 239p. 1993. pap. 63.00 (*90-6215-361-5*, Pub. by Maklu Uitgev) Gaunt.

Pieters, Eli. Female Disorders & Symptoms. 1984. 2.95 (*0-8062-1671-9*) Eli Mail.

Pieters, Eli, ed. Healing Herbs. 1978. 5.95 (*0-8062-1493-7*) Eli Mail.

***Pieters, Gerald R. & Young, Doyle W.** The Ever Changing Organization: Creating the Capacity for Continuous Change, Learning & Improvement. LC 99-30449. (Illus.). 296p. 1999. boxed set 34.95 (*1-57444-262-7*) St Lucie Pr.

Pieters, J. M., et al, eds. Learning Environments. (Recent Research in Psychology Ser.). ix, 364p. 1990. pap. 41.00 (*0-387-52903-9*) Spr-Verlag.

Pieters, J. M., et al. Research on Computer-Based Instruction. 176p. 1990. pap. 36.00 (*90-265-1109-4*) Swets.

Pieters, Jurgen, ed. Critical Self-Fashioning: Stephen Greenblatt & the New Historicism. LC 98-56000. 240p. (C). 1999. pap. text 39.95 (*0-8204-3640-2*) P Lang Pubng.

***Pieters, Philip C., et al.** Venous Catheters: A Practical Manual. (Illus.). 304p. 2000. pap. 39.00 (*0-86577-921-X*) Thieme Med Pubs.

Pieters, R., et al, eds. Drug Resistance in Leukemia & Lymphoma, Vol. 2. 2nd ed. (Advances in Blood Disorders Ser.). 504p. 1997. text 98.00 (*3-7186-5934-4*, Harwood Acad Pubs) Gordon & Breach.

Pieters, Richard S. & Rising, Gerald F. Statistics: A Guide to Political & Social Issues. LC 76-50852. 1977. reprint ed. pap. text 8.95 (*0-8162-8574-8*) Holden-Day.

Pieters, Richard S. & Rising, Gerald R. Statistics: A Guide to Biological & Health Sciences. LC 76-50856. 1977. reprint ed. pap. text 8.95 (*0-8162-8564-0*) Holden-Day.

Pieters, Richard S., jt. auth. see Lux, J. Richard.

Pieters, Walter. Above Flanders' Fields: A Complete History of the Belgian Air Force in World War I. 160p. 1998. 27.95 (*1-898697-83-3*, Pub. by Grub St) Seven Hills Bk.

Pieterse, Cosmo & Munro, Donald, eds. Protest & Conflict in African Literature. LC 77-80856. 127p. 1970. pap. 15.00 (*0-8419-0005-1*, Africana) Holmes & Meier.

Pieterse, Cosmo, jt. ed. see House, Amelia B.

Pieterse, Herman, et al, eds. International Medical Device Clinical Investigations: A Practical Approach. LC 97-26007. (Illus.). 550p. 1997. 219.00 (*1-57491-054-X*) Interpharm.

Pieterse, Hermann, et al, eds. International Medical Device Clinical Investigations: A Practical Approach. 2nd ed. LC 99-19067. 562p. 1998. text 219.00 (*1-57491-085-X*) Interpharm.

Pieterse, Jan & Parekh, Bhikhu, eds. The Decolonization of the Imagination: Culture, Knowledge & Power. LC 95-13685. (Illus.). 256p. (C). 1995. text 65.00 (*1-85649-279-6*, Pub. by Zed Books) St Martin.

Pieterse, Jan N. Emancipations, Modern & Postmodern. (Illus.). 328p. (C). 1992. 69.96 (*0-8039-8777-3*); pap. 24.95 (*0-8039-8781-1*) Sage.

— Empire & Emancipation: Power & Liberation on a World Scale. LC 88-25302. 436p. 1989. 75.00 (*0-275-92529-3*, C2529, Praeger Pubs) Greenwood.

— White on Black: Images of Africa & Blacks in Western Popular Culture. LC 91-41603. 259p. (C). 1992. 45.00 (*0-300-05020-8*) Yale U Pr.

— White on Black: Images of Africa & Blacks in Western Popular Culture. (Illus.). 242p. 1995. pap. 25.00 (*0-300-06311-3*) Yale U Pr.

Pieterse, Jan N., ed. Christianity & Hegemony: Christianity & Politics on the Frontiers of Social Change. 336p. 1992. 19.50 (*0-85496-749-4*) Berg Pubs.

Pieterse, Jan N. & Institute of Social Studies Staff (Netherlands). World Orders in the Making: Humanitarian Intervention & Beyond. LC 98-17283. 1998. text 69.95 (*0-312-21548-7*) St Martin.

***Pietersen, Lloyd, ed.** The Mark of the Spirit? A Charismatic Critique of the Toronto Blessing. x, 121p. 1998. reprint ed. pap. 12.99 (*0-85364-861-1*, Pub. by Paternoster Pub) OM Literature.

Pietersma, Albert. Translation Manual for "a New English Translation of the Septuagint" (NETS) 60p. 1996. ring bd. 15.00 (*0-9653269-0-X*) Uncial Bks.

Pietersma, Albert, tr. from GEC. The Apocryphon of Jannes & Jambres the Magicians: Papyrus Chester Beatty XVI (with New Editions of Papyrus Vindobonensis Greek Inv. 29456-29828 Verso & British Library Cotton Tiberius B. v f. 87) LC 94-4473. (Religions in the Graeco-Roman World Ser.: Vol. 119). (ENG, GEC & LAT.). 1994. 120.00 (*90-04-09938-7*) Brill Academic Pubs.

Pietersma, Henry. Phenomenological Epistemology. LC 99-20502. 224p. 2000. text 45.00 (*0-19-513190-8*) OUP.

Pietersma, Henry, ed. Merleau-Ponty: Critical Essays. LC 89-38160. (Current Continental Research Ser.: No. 553). 300p. (Orig.). (C). 1990. pap. text 25.50 (*0-8191-7589-7*); lib. bdg. 49.00 (*0-8191-7588-9*) U Pr of Amer.

Pietil-Ainen, Pekka, jt. auth. see Chakraborty, Tapash.

Pietila, Hilkka & Vickers, Jeanne. Making Women Matter: The Role of the United Nations. 3rd ed. (Illus.). 224p. 1996. text 19.95 (*1-85649-458-6*) Zed Books.

Pietilainen, P., jt. auth. see Chakraborty, Tapash.

Pietkiewicz, Karen. A Lucky Strike for God: And Other Stories. 144p. 1995. pap. 14.95 (*0-88962-588-3*) Mosaic.

Pietra, Charles, jt. auth. see Folts, Scott.

Pietra, Charles, jt. auth. see Rosen, Gary.

Pietra, Francesco. A Secret Life: Natural Products & Marine Life. 300p. 1990. 109.50 (*0-8176-2346-9*) Birkhauser.

Pietra, G. G., ed. Pathology of the Lung. (Journal: Applied Pathology: Vol. 4, No. 3, 1986). (Illus.). 96p. 1987. pap. 40.00 (*3-8055-4573-8*) S Karger.

Pietra, Giuseppe G., jt. auth. see Brooks, John S.

Pietralla, M., ed. Permanent & Transient Networks. (Progress in Colloid & Polymer Science Ser.: Vol. 75). 205p. 1988. 107.00 (*0-387-91310-6*) Spr-Verlag.

Pietralla, M., jt. ed. see Kilian, H. G.

Pietralunga, Mario, tr. see Lajolo, Davide.

Pietralunga, Mark. Beppe Fenoglio & English Literature: A Study of the Writer As Translator. LC 86-19300. (University of California Publications in Entomology: No. 118). 255p. 1987. pap. 79.10 (*0-7837-7497-4*, 204921900010) Bks Demand.

Pietralunga, Mark, tr. see Lajolo, Davide.

Pietrange, Carlo. Paintings in the Vatican. LC 96-86159. (Illus.). 608p. 1996. 135.00 (*0-8212-2316-X*, Pub. by Bulfinch Pr) Little.

Pietrantonj, E. D. Ineffective Erythropoiesis: A Probability Phenomenon. 1987. pap. text 16.00 (*1-57235-059-8*) Piccin Nuova.

***Pietrapiana.** Tomasa the Cow. LC 98-47010.Tr. of Vaca Tomasa. (SPA., Illus.). 32p. (J). (ps-3). 1999. 14.95 (*1-55885-284-0*, Pinata Bks) Arte Publico.

Pietrek, Matt. Windows 95 System Programming Secrets. 816p. 1995. pap. 49.99 (*1-56884-318-6*) IDG Bks.

Pietrewicz, Alexandra T., jt. ed. see Johnston, Timothy D.

Pietri, Arturo U. La Invencion de America Mestiza (The Invention of the Mestee America) (SPA.). 762p. 1996. 46.99 (*968-16-4904-4*, Pub. by Fondo) Continental Bk.

Pietri, Arturo Uslar, see Uslar Pietri, Arturo.

P

An Asterisk (*) at the beginning of an entry indicates that the title is appearing for the first time.

P

— Down & Out in the United States: An Inside Look at the Out of the Labor Force Population. (Public Policy Brief Ser.: Vol. 54). 48p. 1999. pap. write for info. (0-941276-75-9) J Levy.

Pigeon, R., jt. auth. see Gallagher, C.

Pigeon, Robert F., ed. see AEC Technical Information Center Staff.

Pigeon, Robert L., jt. ed. see Burke, Michael E.

Pigford. Expert Systems for Business. 2nd ed. (Introduction to Computing Ser.). (C). 1995. pap., mass mkt. 42.95 incl. 3.5 ld (0-87709-512-4) Course Tech.

***Pigford.** Interviewing Success. 2000. pap. 18.75 (0-7668-2235-4) Delmar.

Pigford & Baur, Gregory R. Expert Systems for Business: Concepts & Applications. 448p. (C). 1990. mass mkt. 35.00 (0-87835-439-5) Course Tech.

Pigford, J. N., jt. auth. see Hartmann-Petersen, P.

Pigg, Janice S., et al. Rheumatology Nursing: A Problem-Oriented Approach. LC 84-19551. 462p. 1989. text 39.95 (0-8273-4333-7) Delmar.

Piggford, George, jt. auth. see Martin, Robert K.

Piggin, C. & Lack, S. Research & Development Prospects for Faba Bean. 1994. pap. 45.00 (1-86320-118-1, Pub. by ACIAR) St Mut.

Piggin, Stuart. Evangelical Christianity in Australia: Spirit, Word, & World. (Illus.). 304p. (C). 1996. pap. text 42.00 (0-19-553538-3) OUP.

Piggin, Stuart & Lee, Henry. The Mt. Kembla Disaster. (Illus.). 372p. 1993. text 49.95 (0-19-553419-0) OUP.

Pigging Products & Services Association Staff. Introduction to Pipeline Pigging. 128p. 1995. 34.00 (0-88415-405-X, 5405) Gulf Pub.

Piggins, Carol A., jt. auth. see Thurman, Anne H.

Piggly Wiggly Carolina Company Staff. By Special Request. 1993. write for info. (0-9637716-0-4) Piggly Wiggly.

***Piggot, Carolyn S.** Business Planning for Healthcare Management. 2nd ed. (Illus.). 192p. 2000. pap. text. write for info. (0-335-20647-6, Pub. by OpUniv Pr) Taylor & Francis.

Piggot, Jan. Turner's Vignettes. (Illus.). 128p. 1994. pap. 40.00 (1-85437-132-0) U of Wash Pr.

Piggot, Joan R. The Emergence of Japanese Kingship. LC 97-11323. (Illus.). 424p. 1997. 49.50 (0-8047-2832-1) Stanford U Pr.

Piggot, Patrick J., et al, eds. Regulation of Bacterial Differentiation. LC 93-29794. (Illus.). 300p. (C). 1993. text 72.00 (1-55581-066-7) ASM Pr.

***Piggott.** Original Triumph TR4/4A/5/6. 128p. 2000. 35.95 (1-901432-04-1, Pub. by MBI Pubg) Motorbooks Intl.

***Piggott, Bill.** Original Triumph TR7 & TR8. (Illus.). 96p. 2000. 35.95 (0-7603-0972-8, 130765AP, Pub. by MBI Pubg) Motorbooks Intl.

— Triumph: The Sporting Cars. (Illus.). 160p. 2000. 24.95 (0-7509-2280-X) Sutton Publng.

Piggott, Derek. Beginning Gliding. (Illus.). 224p. 2000. pap. 15.95 (0-7136-5799-5, Pub. by A & C Blk) Midpt Trade.

— Beginning Gliding. 2nd ed. (Illus.). 208p. 1998. pap. 24.95 (0-7136-4285-8, Pub. by A & C Blk) Midpt Trade.

***Piggott, Derek.** Beginning Gliding. 3rd ed. 2000. pap. 24.95 (0-7136-4155-X) A & C Blk.

Piggott, Derek. Gliding: A Handbook on Soaring Flight. 5th ed. LC 87-11459. 276p. 1987. pap. 46.00 (0-389-20748-9, N8304) B&N Imports.

— Gliding Safety. 2nd ed. 1998. pap. text. write for info. (0-7136-4853-8) Lubrecht & Cramer.

— Going Solo: A Simple Guide to Soaring. (Illus.). 112p. 1978. pap. 17.50 (0-06-495571-0, N6638) B&N Imports.

— Understanding Flying Weather. 2nd.ed. (Illus.). 96p. 1998. pap. 15.95 (0-7136-4346-3, Pub. by A & C Blk) Midpt Trade.

— Understanding Gliding. 3rd ed. (Illus.). 256p. pap. 25.95 (0-7136-4343-9, Pub. by A & C Blk) Midpt Trade.

Piggott, Derek, ed. Gliding: A Handbook On Soaring Flight. 7th ed. LC 97-183763. (Illus.). 316p. (Orig.). 1997. pap. text 27.95 (0-9605676-4-X) Knauff.

Piggott, J. & Whalley, John, eds. Applied General Equilibrium. (Studies in Empirical Economics). (Illus.). 160p. 1991. 35.00 (0-387-91397-1) Spr-Verlag.

Piggott, J. R. & Paterson, A., eds. Distilled Beverage Flavour: Recent Developments. 2nd ed. LC 88-35234. (Ellis Horwood Series in Food Science & Technology). 352p. 1989. 260.00 (3-527-26887-1, Wiley-VCH) Wiley.

Piggott, J. R., jt. auth. see Paterson, A.

Piggott, John. International Trade Policy & the Pacific Rim. LC 98-25637. Vol. 120. 464p. 1999. text 79.95 (0-312-21801-X) St Martin.

Piggott, Judith & Cook, Mark. International Business Economics: A European Perspective. 2nd ed. LC 98-20729. 1998. pap. write for info. (0-582-30580-2) Longman.

Piggott, Judith & Cook, Mark, eds. International Business Economics: A European Perspective. 402p. (C). 1992. pap. text 26.95 (0-582-05876-7, 76770, Pub. by Addison-Wesley) Longman.

***Piggott, Lester.** Lester Piggott Autobiography. 2000. pap. 10.95 (0-552-14153-4, Pub. by Transworld Publishers Ltd) Trafalgar.

Piggott, Margaret H. Discover Southeast Alaska with Pack & Paddle. 2nd ed. LC 90-36104. (Illus.). 240p. 1990. pap. 12.95 (0-89886-242-6) Mountaineers.

Piggott, Mary. A Topography of Cataloguing: Showing the Most Important Landmarks, Communications & Perilous Places. LC 88-14961. 297p. reprint ed. pap. 92.10 (0-608-08890-0, 206952700004) Bks Demand.

Piggott, Mattie G., et al. From Dear Friends to Marriage: The Letters of Mattie Piggott & Robert Trumbull, 1902-1908. O'Neil, Anelle T., ed. LC 97-21545. (Illus.). xvi, 354p. 1997. lib. bdg. 85.00 (0-911459-27-8) Wedgestone Pr.

Piggott, Michael R. Load-Bearing Composite Materials. 1980. text 134.00 (0-08-024230-8, Pub. by Pergamon Repr) Franklin.

Piggott, R. R., et al. Food Price Policy in Indonesia. 189p. 1993. pap. 114.00 (1-86320-094-0, Pub. by ACIAR) St Mut.

Piggott, Stephen. Cics: A Practical Guide to System Fine Turning. (J. Ranade IBM Ser.). 352p. 1989. text 44.95 (0-07-050054-1) McGraw.

Piggott, Stuart. Antiquity Depicted: Aspects of Archaeological Illustration. (Ancient Peoples & Places Ser.: Vol. 10). (Illus.). 64p. 1979. 9.95 (0-500-55010-7, Pub. by Thames Hudson) Norton.

— The Druids. LC 84-51870. (Ancient Peoples & Places Ser.). (Illus.). (C). 1985. pap. 15.95 (0-500-27363-4, Pub. by Thames Hudson) Norton.

— Prehistoric India to 1000 B.C. LC 83-45838. reprint ed. 28.00 (0-404-20203-9) AMS Pr.

— Scotland Before History. 1990. 14.00 (0-7486-6067-4, Pub. by Polygon) Subterranean Co.

Piggott, Stuart, ed. The Agrarian History of England & Wales, Vol. 1, Pt. 1: Prehistory. LC 66-19763. (Agrarian History of England & Wales Ser.). 448p. 1981. text 130.00 (0-521-08741-4) Cambridge U Pr.

— The Prehistoric Peoples of Scotland. LC 80-27371. (Studies in Ancient History & Archaeology). (Illus.). 165p. 1981. reprint ed. lib. bdg. 59.50 (0-313-22916-3, PIPR, Greenwood Pr) Greenwood.

Piggott, Stuart & Daniel, Glyn E. A Picture Book of Ancient British Art. LC 53-3905. (Illus.). 85p. reprint ed. pap. 25.00 (0-608-11301-8, 2051470) Bks Demand.

Piggott, Stuart, et al. France Before the Romans LC 74-189866. 233p. 1974. write for info. (0-500-05017-1) Thames Hudson.

Piggott, Vincent C., ed. see Perry, Martin.

Piggott, W. R., jt. ed. see Rawer, Karl.

Piggy, Toes Press. Hurray for Hands! 1999. pap. text. write for info. (1-58117-045-9, Piggy Toes Pr) Intervisual Bks.

***Piggy Toes Press Staff.** Baby Tweety's Bedtime. (Lovable Huggable Baby Looney Tunes Cloth Bks.). (Illus.). 6p. (J). 2000. 14.95 (1-58117-077-7, Piggy Toes Pr) Intervisual Bks.

— Fun with Numbers: One to Ten. (Illus.). 10p. (J). 2000. bds. 16.95 (1-58117-080-7, Piggy Toes Pr) Intervisual Bks.

— Safari School Bus. (Illus.). (J). Date not set. 15.95 (1-58117-081-5, Piggy Toes Pr) Intervisual Bks.

***Piggy Toes Press Staff, ed.** Farm Faces. (Illus.). (J). 2000. 14.95 (1-888443-51-0, Piggy Toes Pr) Intervisual Bks.

— Zoo Faces. (Illus.). (J). 2000. 14.95 (1-888443-52-9, Piggy Toes Pr) Intervisual Bks.

Piggytoes Press Staff. Christmas Toys: With Antique Changing Pictures. (Ernest Nister's Mini Christmas Books Ser.). 1997. 4.95 (1-888443-33-2, Piggy Toes Pr) Intervisual Bks.

— Santa's Surprise: With Antique Changing Pictures. (Ernest Nister's Mini Christmas Books Ser.). 1997. 4.95 (1-888443-34-0, Piggy Toes Pr) Intervisual Bks.

— Snowy Days: With Antique Changing Pictures. (Ernest Nister's Mini Christmas Books Ser.). 1997. 4.95 (1-888443-35-9, Piggy Toes Pr) Intervisual Bks.

— Yuletide Delights: With Antique Changing Pictures. (Ernest Nister's Mini Christmas Books Ser.). 1997. 4.95 (1-888443-32-4, Piggy Toes Pr) Intervisual Bks.

Pighetti, Toni. The Children's Organizer: A Calendar System of Daily Tasks for Children. (Illus.). 32p. (Orig.). (J). (gr. k-8). 1983. pap. 7.95 (0-913005-03-7) TAM Assoc.

— Nitty Gritty Bare Bones Method of Housekeeping. (Illus.). 26p. (Orig.). 1985. pap. 6.95 (0-913005-05-3) TAM Assoc.

— Stop the Vacuum! I Want to Get Off. 110p. 1987. pap. 6.95 (0-913005-06-1) TAM Assoc.

***Piglia, Ricardo.** The Absent City. Waisman, Sergio, tr. LC 00-29392. 136p. 2000. lib. bdg. 45.95 (0-8223-2557-8) Duke.

— The Absent City. Waisman, Sergio, tr. & intro. by. LC 00-29392. 136p. 2000. pap. 15.95 (0-8223-2586-1) Duke.

Piglia, Ricardo. Artificial Respiration. Balderston, Daniel, tr. LC 93-29571. (Latin America in Translation - En Traduccion - Em Traducao Ser.). 240p. 1994. text 39.95 (0-8223-1426-6); pap. text 15.95 (0-8223-1414-2) Duke.

— Assumed Name. Miller, Yvette E., ed. Waisman, Sergio, tr. from SPA. LC 95-22340. (Discoveries Ser.). (SPA.). 160p. 1995. pap. 15.95 (0-935480-71-4) Lat Am Lit Rev Pr.

Pigliaru, Francesco, jt. ed. see Adams, John.

***Pigliucci, Massimo.** Tales of the Rational: Skeptical Essays about Nature & Science. (Illus.). 278p. 2000. pap. 17.00 (1-887392-11-4, Freethought Pr) Atl Freethought Soc.

Pigliucci, Massimo, jt. auth. see Schlichting, Carl D.

Pigman, C. W., III. Grief & English Renaissance Elegy. 192p. 1985. text 80.00 (0-521-26871-0) Cambridge U Pr.

Pignacca, Brizio, text. Alfa Romeo Giulia GT. (Cars That Made History Ser.). (Illus.). 84p. 1994. 24.95 (88-7911-055-1, Pub. by Giorgio Nada Editore) Howell Pr VA.

Pignarre, Robert, jt. auth. see De La Bruyere, Jean.

Pignataro, M., et al. Stability, Bifurcation & Postcritical Behaviour of Structures. (Developments in Civil Engineering Ser.: Vol. 39). 358p. 1991. 153.75 (0-444-88140-9) Elsevier.

Pignatelli, Frank & Pflaum, Susanna W., eds. Celebrating Diverse Voices: Progressive Education & Equity. LC 92-30439. 272p. 1992. pap. 27.95 (0-8039-6039-5) Corwin Pr.

— Experiencing Diversity: Toward Educational Equity. LC 94-7438. 232p. 1994. pap. 27.95 (0-8039-6143-X) Corwin Pr.

Pignatti, Teresio, ed. Venice: A Guide to Paintings in Original Settings. (Illus.). 160p. 1996. pap. 19.95 (88-86502-07-9, Pub. by Canal & Stamperia) Antique Collect.

Pignatti, Terisio. Canaletto: Selected Drawings. LC 74-104778. (Illus.). 200p. 1970. boxed set 160.00 (0-271-00105-4) A Wofsy Fine Arts.

— Tiepolo in Venice: A Guide to Paintings in Original Settings. (Illus.). 160p. (Orig.). 1996. pap. 19.95 (88-86502-18-4, Pub. by Canal & Stamperia) Antique Collect.

Pignatti, Terisio & Pedrocco, Filippo. Giorgione. LC 99-14405. (Illus.). 248p. 1999. 75.00 (0-8478-2202-8, Pub. by Rizzoli Intl) St Martin.

Pignede, Bernard. The Gurungs. 1993. 325.00 (0-7855-0228-9, Pub. by Ratna Pustak Bhandar) St Mut.

Pignolet De Monteclair, Michel. Michel Pignolet de Monteclair: Cantatas for One & Two Voices. Anthony, James R. & Akmajian, Diran, eds. (Recent Researches in Music of the Baroque Era Ser.: Vol. RRB29-30). (Illus.). xxvi, 169p. 1978. pap. 60.00 (0-89579-106-4, RRB29-30) A-R Eds.

Pignolet, Louis M., ed. Homogeneous Catalysis with Metal Phosphine Complexes. LC 83-17609. (Modern Inorganic Chemistry Ser.). 506p. 1983. 120.00 (0-306-41211-X, Plenum Trade) Perseus Pubng.

Pigom, Catherine, jt. auth. see Fabyankovic, Janet.

Pigors, Faith, jt. auth. see Pigors, Paul.

Pigors, Paul & Pigors, Faith. The Pigors Incident Process of Case Study. LC 79-23530. (Instructional Design Library). 128p. 1980. 27.95 (0-87778-149-4) Educ Tech Pubns.

Pigoski, Thomas M. Life Cycle Strategies: Software Support on the Front Line. 107p. 1994. pap. 45.00 (1-884521-03-7) Software Maint.

— Practical Software Maintenance: Best Practices for Managing Your Software Investment. LC 96-25884. 384p. 1996. 59.99 (0-471-17001-1) Wiley.

Pigot, Bill. Original Triumph TR2/3/3A: The Restorers Guide to All Sidescreen Models Including the Francorchamps, Italia & TR3B Versions. (Illus.). 128p. 1998. 35.95 (1-901432-03-3, Bay View Bks) MBI Pubg.

***Pigot, John.** Hilda Rix Nicholas: Her Life & Art. (Miegunyah Press Ser.: Vol. 30). (Illus.). 400p. 2000. 75.00 (0-522-84890-7, Pub. by Melbourne Univ Pr) Paul & Co Pubs.

Pigott, Charlie & Vallely, Fintan. Blooming Meadows: The World of Irish Traditional Musicians. LC 98-231202. (Illus.). 272p. 1998. 26.95 (1-86059-067-5, Pub. by Town Hse) Roberts Rinehart.

Pigott, Francis, ed. Free Fall to-? (C). 1989. text 30.00 (0-902662-01-5, Pub. by R K Pubns) St Mut.

Pigott, George M. & Tucker, Barbee W. Seafood: Effects of Technology on Nutrition. (Food Science & Technology Ser.: Vol. 39). (Illus.). 384p. 1990. text 155.00 (0-8247-7922-3) Dekker.

Pigott, Grenville. A Manual of Scandinavian Mythology: Containing a Popular Account of the Two Eddas & of the Religion of Odin. Bolle, Kees W., ed. LC 77-79152. (Mythology Ser.). 1978. reprint ed. lib. bdg. 30.95 (0-405-10561-4) Ayer.

Pigott, Rod & Power, Christine, eds. Adhesion Molecules Facts Book. (Facts Book Ser.). (Illus.). 190p. 1993. pap. text 48.00 (0-12-555180-0) Acad Pr.

Pigott, Stephen J. My Banking Workbook. (Illus.). 80p. 1999. pap. text, wbk. ed. 14.95 (0-9672932-2-7) S J Pubg Inc.

— My Budget Workbook. (Illus.). 80p. 1999. pap. text, wbk. ed. 14.95 (0-9672932-1-9) S J Pubg Inc.

— You, Your Kids, Their Finances: Teach Your Children Finances. (Illus.). 270p. 1999. pap. 29.95 (0-9672932-0-0) S J Pubg Inc.

Pigott, Stuart. The Wine Atlas of Germany: And Traveller's Guide to the Vineyards. (Illus.). 232p. 1995. 45.00 (1-85732-625-3, Pub. by Reed Illust Books) Antique Collect.

Pigott, Stuart, jt. auth. see Anderson, Burton.

Pigott, Stuart, jt. auth. see Johnson, Hugh.

Pigott, Teresa, ed. see Schemmel, Todd.

***Pigou, A. C.** A. C. Pigou: Collected Economic Writings, 14 vols. 4500p. 2000. lib. bdg. write for info. (0-333-77848-0) Macmillan.

Pigou, A. C. Protective & Preferential Import Duties: London School of Economics. (LSE Scarce Tracts in Economics Ser.). 132p. (C). 1997. 60.00 (0-415-14391-8) Routledge.

Pigou, A. C., ed. see Marshall, Alfred.

Pigou, Arthur C. Aspects of British Economic History. 251p. 1971. reprint ed. 32.50 (0-7146-2630-9, Pub. by F Cass Pubs) Intl Spec Bk.

— The Economics of Welfare. 4th ed. LC 75-41213. reprint ed. 110.00 (0-404-14583-3) AMS Pr.

— Essays in Applied Economics. 199p. 1965. reprint ed. 32.50 (0-7146-1240-5, BHA-01240, Pub. by F Cass Pubs) Intl Spec Bk.

— Income: An Introduction to Economics. LC 78-21487. 120p. 1979. reprint ed. lib. bdg. 45.00 (0-313-20665-1, PIIN, Greenwood Pr) Greenwood.

— Income Revisited, Being a Sequel to Income, an Introduction to Economics. LC 78-20835. viii, 86p. 1956. reprint ed. lib. bdg. 25.00 (0-678-07010-5) Kelley.

— Industrial Fluctuations, Nineteen Twenty-Nine. 2nd ed. 425p. 1968. reprint ed. 45.00 (0-7146-2185-4, BHA-02185, Pub. by F Cass Pubs) Intl Spec Bk.

— Lapses from Full Employment. LC 76-52488. (Reprints of Economic Classics Ser.). viii, 72p. 1978. reprint ed. lib. bdg. 19.50 (0-678-01226-1) Kelley.

— Riddle of the Tariff. LC 74-1328. (Reprints of Economic Classics Ser.). xi, 107p. 1975. reprint ed. 25.00 (0-678-01227-X) Kelley.

— A Study in Public Finance. 3rd rev. ed. xviii, 285p. 1975. reprint ed. lib. bdg. 39.50 (0-678-07009-1) Kelley.

Pigozzi, D. L., jt. auth. see Blok, W. J.

Pigozzi, Don, jt. auth. see Blok, W. J.

Pigram, J. J. & Jenkins, John. Outdoor Recreation Management. LC 98-48278. 1999. 100.00 (0-415-15999-7) Routledge.

Pigram, J. J., jt. auth. see Wahab, Salah.

Pigram, Ron. Discovering Walks in the Chilterns. 1989. pap. 25.00 (0-85263-991-0, Pub. by Shire Pubns) St Mut.

Piguet, Charles & Sentis, Michel. The World at the Turning. Hamilton, Ailsa, tr. from FRE. 132p. 1989. reprint ed. pap. 8.95 (0-901269-68-9) Grosvenor USA.

Piguet, Jacqueline. For the Love of Tomorrow: The Story of Irene Laure. Sciortino, Joanna, tr. from FRE. (Illus.). 144p. (Orig.). 1985. pap. 5.00 (0-901269-93-X) Grosvenor USA.

Piguet, Olivier & Sorella, Silvio P. Algebraic Renormalization: Perturbative Renormalization, Symmetries & Anomalies. LC 95-15984. (Lecture Notes in Physics: New Series M, Monographs: Vol. 28). 144p. 1995. 49.95 (3-540-59115-X) Spr-Verlag.

Pihel, K. & Pikamae, A. Finnish-Estonian Dictionary: Soome-Eesti Sonaraamat. (EST & FIN.). 686p. 1986. 95.00 (0-8288-1690-5, M2825) Fr & Eur.

Pihera, Larry. The Making of a Winner: The Porsche 917. LC 72-7354. 183p. 1972. write for info. (0-397-00807-4, Lippnctt) Lppncott W & W.

Pihl, Lisa. Signe Toksvig's Irish Diaries, 1926-1937. LC 94-165375. 450p. 1994. 39.95 (1-874675-26-0) Dufour.

Pihl, Marshall R. The Korean Singer of Tales. LC 93-39953. (Harvard-Yenching Institute Monographs: No. 37). 350p. 1994. text 38.00 (0-674-50564-6) HUP.

— Korean Word Book. LC 93-73161. (ENG & KOR., Illus.). 112p. (J). (gr. k-6). 1993. 19.95 (1-880188-53-8); pap. 11.95 (1-880188-52-X) Bess Pr.

Pihl, Marshall R. Korean Word Book. LC 93-73161. (Rainbow International Word Book Ser.). (ENG & KOR., Illus.). 112p. (J). (gr. k-6). 1993. pap. 19.95 incl. audio (1-880188-72-4) Bess Pr.

Pihl, Marshall R., et al, eds. Land of Exile: Contemporary Korean Fiction. Fulton, Ju-Chan et al, trs. from KOR. LC 93-25238. (Illus.). 304p. (gr. 13). 1993. pap. text 24.95 (1-56324-195-1, East Gate Bk) M E Sharpe.

Pihl, Marshall R., et al, eds. Land of Exile: Contemporary Korean Fiction. Fulton, Bruce et al, trs. from KOR. LC 93-25238. (Illus.). 304p. (C). (gr. 13). 1993. text 65.95 (1-56324-194-3, East Gate Bk) M E Sharpe.

Pihlaja, K. & Kleinpeter, E. Carbon-13 NMR Chemical Shifts in Structural & Stereochemical Analysis. (Methods in Stereochemical Analysis Ser.). 394p. 1994. 125.00 (0-471-18546-9) Wiley.

Pihlaja, Kalevi & Kleinpeter, Erich. Carbon-13 NMR Chemical Shifts in Structural & Stereochemical Analysis. LC 94-5420. (Methods in Stereochemical Analysis Ser.). 1994. 85.00 (0-89573-332-3, Wiley-VCH) Wiley.

Pihlstrom, Sami. Pragmatism & Philosophical Anthropology: Understanding Our Human Life in a Human World. (American University Studies: Vol. 186, No. V). XV, 287p. (C). 1998. text 47.95 (0-8204-4076-0) P Lang Pubng.

Piho, Virve. Iztapalapan Durante la Conquista. (SPA., Illus.). 270p. 1996. pap. 20.00 (968-29-5245-X, IN77, Pub. by Dir Gen Pubicaiones) UPLAAP.

***Pihun, Peter J.** Available to a Warm Heart. 100p. 2000. pap. 10.95 (0-7414-0304-8) Buy Books.

Piiper, J., et al, eds. Oxygen Transport to Tissue, No. XII. LC 90-7835. (Advances in Experimental Medicine & Biology Ser.: Vol. 277). (Illus.). 930p. 1990. 175.00 (0-306-43682-5, Plenum Trade) Perseus Pubng.

Piiper, J. & Scheid, P., eds. Gas Exchange Function of Normal & Diseased Lungs. (Progress in Respiratory Research Ser.: Vol. 16). (Illus.). xvi, 320p. 1981. 172.25 (3-8055-1638-X) S Karger.

Piiper, J., jt. ed. see Meyer, M.

Piirainen, Ilpo T. Das Stadtrechtsbuch Von Sillein: Einleitung Edition und Glossar. (Quellen und Forschungen zur Sprach und Kulturgeschichte der Germanischen Voelker: No. 46). (C). 1972. 109.25 (3-11-003543-X) De Gruyter.

Piirainen, Timo. Towards a New Social Order in Russia: Transforming Structures & Everyday Life. LC 96-32176. (Illus.). 272p. 1997. text 72.95 (1-85521-690-6, Pub. by Dartmth Pub) Ashgate Pub Co.

Piirainen, Timo, ed. Change & Continuity in Eastern Europe. 256p. 1994. 77.95 (1-85521-499-7, Pub. by Dartmth Pub) Ashgate Pub Co.

Piirma, Irja, ed. Polymeric Surfactants. (Surfactant Science Ser.: Vol. 42). (Illus.). 302p. 1992. text 185.00 (0-8247-8608-4) Dekker.

***Piirto, Douglas D.** Environmental Impact Analysis Study Guide. 250p. (C). 1999. per. 39.95 (0-7872-6020-7, 41602001) Kendall-Hunt.

Piirto, Douglas D. Forestry Study Guide. 440p. 1992. per. 33.95 (0-8403-8159-X) Kendall-Hunt.

Piirto, Jane. A Location in the Upper Peninsula: Poems, Stories, Essays. (Illus.). 234p. (Orig.). 1994. pap. text 13.95 (0-9632975-4-6) Sampo Pub.

— My Teeming Brain: Creativity in Creative Writers. (Perspectives on Creativity Ser.). 256p. 1999. text 52.50 (1-57273-275-X); pap. text 21.95 (1-57273-276-8) Hampton Pr NJ.

***Piirto, Jane.** Talented Children & Adults: Their Development & Education. 2nd ed. LC 98-21644. 648p. (C). 1998. pap. text 74.00 (0-13-096146-9, Merrill Coll) P-H.

Piirto, Jane. Understanding Those Who Create. 2nd rev. ed. LC 98-11314. (Illus.). 444p. 1998. pap. 27.00 (0-910707-27-8) Gifted Psych Pr.

P

An Asterisk (*) at the beginning of an entry indicates that the title is appearing for the first time.

Piirto, Rebecca. Beyond Mind Games: The Marketing Power of Psychographics. LC 91-58121. 263p. (C). 1991. 34.50 (*0-936889-08-X*) American Demo.
— Beyond Mind Games: The Marketing Power of Psychographics. LC 91-58121. 263p. (C). 1992. pap. 29.95 (*0-936889-10-1*) American Demo.
— Beyond Mind Games: The Marketing Power of Psychographics. abr. ed. (Maro Business Reviews Ser.). 52p. 1993. pap. 7.95 (*0-9627362-1-X*); audio 19.95 (*0-9627362-2-8*) Maro Comns.
Piirto, Rebecca, jt. auth. see Francese, Peter.
Piispanen-Krabbe, Tuula, ed. see Brake, Terence & Walker, Danielle M.
Pijanowska, Stanislawa. Przerwany Bieg. (POL.). 1000p. (Orig.). 1988. pap. 18.95 (*0-930401-16-6*) Artex Pub.
Pijanowski, Kate. The Solomon Decision Whose Child Is This? An Adoption Dialogue. LC 88-71629. 234p. (Orig.). 1989. pap. 9.95 (*0-934896-48-8*) Adopt Aware Pr.
Pijanowski, Kathy, ed. see Kehret, Peg.
Pijanowski, Kathy, ed. see Litherland, Janet.
Pijanowski, Kathy, ed. see Novelly, Maria C.
Pijanowski, Kathy, ed. see Toomey, Susie K.
Pijawka, David & Mushkatel, Alvin H., eds. Nuclear Waste Policy: Siting the High-Level Nuclear Waste Repository. (Orig.). 1991. pap. 15.00 (*0-944285-27-9*) Pol Studies.
Pijawka, K. David & Shetter, Kim. The Environment Comes Home: Arizona Public Service Environmental Showcase Home. (Illus.). 140p. (Orig.). 1995. pap. 12.95 (*1-884320-13-9*) ASU Herberger Ctr.
Pijco, A. B., ed. Application of Non Linear Analysis to Structural Problems. (PVP Ser.: Vol. 76). 141p. 1983. pap. text 30.00 (*0-317-02552-X*, H00262) ASME.
Pijet, André. Hansel & Gretel. (Pocketaudio Ser.). 48p. (J). (gr. k-3). 9.95 incl. audio (*2-921997-81-9*, Pub. by Coffragants) Penton Overseas.
— Jack & the Beanstalk. (Classic Stories Ser.). (J). 9.95 incl. audio (*2-921997-82-7*, Pub. by Coffragants) Penton Overseas.
— The Little Mermaid. (Classic Stories Ser.). 48p. (J). 9.95 incl. audio (*2-89517-048-7*, Pub. by Coffragants) Penton Overseas.
— Snow White. (Pocketaudio Ser.). (J). (ps-2). 2000. boxed set 9.95 incl. audio (*2-921997-87-8*, Pub. by Coffragants) Penton Overseas.
Pijis, Nico H. & De Bruyne, Bernard. Coronary Pressure. LC 97-26047. (Developments in Cardiovascular Medicine Ser.: No. 195). 368p. 1997. text 167.00 (*0-7923-4672-6*) Kluwer Academic.
Pijl, Kees Van Der, see Van Der Pijl, Kees.
Pijl, Kees Van der, see Van der Pijl, Kees.
Pijl, S. J., et al. Inclusive Education: A Global Agenda. LC 96-26329. 200p. (C). 1996. 80.00 (*0-415-14748-4*); pap. 25.99 (*0-415-14749-2*) Routledge.
Pijls, Nico H. Maximal Myocardial Perfusion As a Measure of the Functional Significance of Coronary Artery Disease: From a Pathoanatomic to a Pathophysiologic Interpretation of the Coronary Arteriogram. (Developments in Cardiovascular Medicine Ser.). 208p. 1991. text 137.50 (*0-7923-1430-1*) Kluwer Academic.
***Pijls, Nico H. J. & De Bruyne, Bernard.** Coronary Pressure. 2nd ed. LC 99-89548. 423p. 2000. 150.00 (*0-7923-6170-9*) Kluwer Academic.
Pijnappel, Johan, ed. Fluxus. (Art & Design Ser.: No. 28). (Illus.). 96p. (Orig.). 1993. pap. 26.95 (*1-85490-194-X*, Pub. by Wiley) Wiley.
Pijoan de Van Etten, Teresa. Spanish-American Folktales. (Illus.). 128p. (Orig.). 1990. pap. 14.95 (*0-87483-155-5*) August Hse.
Pijoan, Jose. Arte Barbaro y Preromanico: Desde el Siglo IV Hasta el Ano 1000. (Summa Artis Ser.: Vol. 8). 600p. 1989. 295.00 (*84-239-5208-8*) Elliots Bks.
— El Arte Barroco en Francia, Italia y Aemania, Siglos XVII y XVIII. (Summa Artis Ser.: Vol. 16). 600p. 1989. 295.00 (*84-239-5216-9*) Elliots Bks.
— Arte Cristiano Primitivo. Arte Bizantino: Hasta el Saqueo de Constantinopla por los Cruzados el Ano 1204. (Summa Artis Ser.: Vol. 7). 600p. 1989. 295.00 (*84-239-5207-X*) Elliots Bks.
— Arte de los Pueblos Aborigenes. (Summa Artis Ser.: Vol. 1). 600p. 1989. 295.00 (*84-239-5201-0*) Elliots Bks.
— Arte del Asia Occidental, Sumeria, Babilonia, Asiria, Hititia, Fenicia, Persia, Partia, Sasania, Escitia. (Summa Artis Ser.: Vol. 2). 600p. 1989. 295.00 (*84-239-5202-9*) Elliots Bks.
— Arte del Periodo Humanistico: Trecento y Cuatrocento. (Summa Artis Ser.: Vol. 13). 600p. 1989. 295.00 (*84-239-5213-4*) Elliots Bks.
— El Arte del Renacimiento en el Centro y Norte de Europe. (Summa Artis Ser.: Vol. 15). 600p. 1989. 295.00 (*84-239-5215-0*) Elliots Bks.
— El Arte Egipcio: Hasta la Conquista Romana. (Summa Artis Ser.: Vol. 3). 600p. 1989. 295.00 (*84-239-5203-7*) Elliots Bks.
— Arte Gotico de la Europa Occidental: Siglos XIII, XIV y XV. (Summa Artis Ser.: Vol. 11). 600p. 1989. 295.00 (*84-239-5211-8*) Elliots Bks.
— El Arte Griego: Hasta la Toma de Corinto por los Romanos (146 a. de J. C.) (Summa Artis Ser.: Vol. 4). 600p. 1989. 295.00 (*84-239-5204-5*) Elliots Bks.
— Arte Islamico. (Summa Artis Ser.: Vol. 12). 600p. 1989. 295.00 (*84-239-5212-6*) Elliots Bks.
— Arte Precolombino, Mexicano y Maya. (Summa Artis Ser.: Vol. 10). 600p. 1989. 295.00 (*84-239-5210-X*) Elliots Bks.
— El Arte Prehistorico Europeo. (Summa Artis Ser.: Vol. 6). 600p. 1989. 295.00 (*84-239-5206-1*) Elliots Bks.
— Arte Romanico: Siglos XI y XII. (Summa Artis Ser.: Vol. 9). 5p. 1989. 295.00 (*84-239-5209-6*) Elliots Bks.
— El Arte Romano: Hasta la Muerte de Diocleciano: Arte Etrusco y Arte Helenistico Despues de la Toma de Corinto. (Summa Artis Ser.: Vol. 5). 600p. 1989. 295.00 (*84-239-5205-3*) Elliots Bks.
— Renacimiento Romano y Veneciano: Siglo XVI. (Summa Artis Ser.: Vol. 14). 600p. 1989. 295.00 (*84-239-5214-2*) Elliots Bks.
Pijoan, Jose, ed. Summa Artis, 39 vols., Set. (SPA.). 19200p. 1989. 1150.00 (*84-239-5200-2*) Elliots Bks.
Pijoan, Jose, et al. Arte Europeo de los Siglos XIX y XX. (Summa Artis Ser.: Vol. 23). 600p. 1989. 295.00 (*84-239-5223-1*) Elliots Bks.
Pijoan, Teresa. La Cuentista: Traditional Tales in Spanish & English. Zimmerman, Nancy, tr. LC 93-38779. (Illus.). 272p. 1994. pap. 13.95 (*1-878610-42-2*) Red Crane Bks.
— Listen, a Story Comes: Escuchaque, Viene un Cuento. Franco, Sharon, ed. & tr. by. from SPA. LC 96-33039. (ENG & SPA., Illus.). 192p. (Orig.). 1996. pap. 14.95 (*1-878610-59-7*) Red Crane Bks.
***Pijoan, Teresa.** Pueblo Indian Wisdom: Native American Legends & Mythology. (Illus.). 117p. 2000. pap. 10.95 (*0-86534-319-5*) Sunstone Pr.
Pijoan, Teresa. Stories from a Dark & Evil World. LC 99-23217. (Bilingual Ser.).Tr. of Cuentos del Mundo Malevolo. 229p. 1999. pap. text 14.95 (*1-878610-71-6*, Pub. by Red Crane Bks) Consort Bk Sales.
— White Wolf Woman: And Other Native American Transformation Myths. 160p. 1992. pap. 11.95 (*0-87483-200-4*) August Hse.
Pijper, J. R. De, see De Pijper, J. R.
Pijpers, Alfred, ed. The European Community at the Crossroads: Major Issues & Priorities for the EC Presidency. 336p. (C). 1992. lib. bdg. 141.50 (*0-7923-1470-0*) Kluwer Academic.
Pijpers, Alfred, jt. ed. see Edwards, Geoffrey.
Pijpers, F. P., et al, eds. Score'96: Solar Convection & Oscillations & Their Relationship. LC 97-45519. (Astrophysics & Space Science Library: No. 225). 315p. 1997. 142.00 (*0-7923-4852-4*) Kluwer Academic.
Pijuan, Hernandez. Hernandez, Pijuan: Dibuixos 1989-1990. Goerg, Charles & Queralt, Rosa, eds. (SPA., Illus.). 124p. 1993. 69.50 (*84-343-0325-6*) Elliots Bks.
Pika, Joseph A. & Watson, Richard A. The Presidential Contest. 5th ed. LC 95-25241. 218p. (YA). (gr. 11). 1995. pap. text 20.95 (*0-87187-837-2*) Congr Quarterly.
Pika, Joseph A., jt. auth. see Thomas, Norman C.
Pikaev, Aleksei K. Pulse Radiolysis of Water & Aqueous Solutions. Hart, Edwin J., ed. LC 66-14343. (Illus.). 311p. reprint ed. pap. 96.50 (*0-608-30102-7*, 205522600011) Bks Demand.
Pikaev, Alexei K., jt. auth. see Woods, Robert J.
Pikale, P. Non-Residents: Taxation & Investment in India. 2nd ed. (C). 1989. 350.00 (*0-7855-4725-8*) St Mut.
Pikamae, A., jt. auth. see Pihel, K.
Pikas, Anatol. Abstraction & Concept Formation: An Interpretative Investigation into a Group of Psychological Frames of Reference. Tomkinson, Neil, tr. LC 66-3915. 177p. reprint ed. pap. 54.90 (*0-8357-5023-X*, 200297300017) Bks Demand.
***Pikayev, Alexander A.** Neotraditionalism in the Russian North: Indigenous Peoples & the Legacy of Perestroika. LC 99-26273. Vol. 6. (Illus.). 200p. 1999. pap. text 30.00 (*0-295-97829-5*) U of Wash Pr.
Pikayev, Alexander A., et al. Russia, the U. S. & the Missile Technology Control Regime. LC U162.A3 no. 317. (Adelphi Papers: No. 317). (Illus.). 96p. 1998. pap. text 28.95 (*0-19-922365-3*) OUP.
Pikcunas, Diane, et al. George Mason & the Legacy of Constitutional Liberty: An Examination of the Influence of George Mason on the American Bill of Rights. Horrell, Joseph & Senese, Donald J., eds. (Illus.). 192p. (Orig.). 1989. write for info. (*0-9623905-0-X*); pap. write for info. (*0-9623905-1-8*) Fairfax Cty Hist Com.
Pikcunas, Diane D. Nations at the Crossroads: Unification Policies for Germany, Korea & China. LC 92-47227. (Journal of Social, Political & Economic Studies: No. 22). 96p. (C). 1993. pap. text 10.00 (*0-930690-51-6*) Coun Soc Econ.
Pikcunas, Diane P., jt. auth. see Senese, Donald J.
Pike. Health Promotion for All. 1995. pap. text 19.95 (*0-443-05089-9*, W B Saunders Co) Harcrt Hlth Sci Grp.
— Tall Trees, Tough Men. 1999. reprint ed. pap. 13.95 (*0-393-31917-2*) Norton.
Pike & Fischer. Administrative Law Decisions, Set, Nos. 1-5. LC 51-28517. (Consolidated Digest Ser.: No. 2). 1980. suppl. ed. 250.00 (*1-57588-226-4*, 200910) W S Hein.
— Radio Regulation Vols. 1 & 2: Consolidated Digest. LC 70-5088. 1969. 130.00 (*1-57588-434-8*, 200980) W S Hein.
— Radio Regulations First Series, 1948-1963. LC 48-2103. 1980. reprint ed. lib. bdg. 1325.00 (*0-89941-207-6*, 200920) W S Hein.
— Radio Regulations Second Series, 1963-1993, 73 vols. LC 70-24229. 1963. lib. bdg. 5695.00 (*0-89941-208-4*, 200930) W S Hein.
Pike & Fischer, eds. Communications Regulation, 6 vols. 1997. reprint ed. 1500.00 (*1-57588-459-3*, 202050) W S Hein.
Pike & Wilkins, A. A Comprehensive English Oriya Dictionary. (ORI & ENG.). 1988. reprint ed. 30.00 (*81-206-0383-4*, Pub. by Asian Educ Servs) S Asia.
Pike & Wilkins, N. Comprehensive English & Oriya Dictionary. 688p. 1988. 49.95 (*0-8288-8472-2*) Fr & Eur.
Pike, et al. Administrative Law Decisions Second Series, 1952-1989, Set, Vols. 1-67. rev. ed. LC 51-28517. 1978. reprint ed. lib. bdg. 3750.00 (*0-89941-205-X*, 200900) W S Hein.
— Administrative Law Decisions Third Series: 1989-1944, Set, Vols. 1-7. 1989. 660.00 (*0-89941-757-4*, 201990) W S Hein.
— Catching the Tune. Armstrong, ed. LC 84-4845. (Illus.). 68p. (Orig.). 1984. pap. 7.50 (*0-943924-08-1*) Mus Stony Brook.
Pike & Fischer, Inc. Staff. Shipping Regulation: Cases, Vols. 1-26, 1961-1995. LC 61-31808. 1978. reprint ed. 1925.00 (*0-89941-206-8*, 200950) W S Hein.
Pike & Fischer, Inc. Staff, ed. Uniform Commercial Code: State Variations Service, 3 vols. LC 82-9735. 1992. 425.00 (*0-317-12222-3*) West Group.
— Uniform Commercial Code Case Digest & Code Service, 33 vols. LC 70-126080. 1992. 1850.00 (*0-317-11804-8*) West Group.
— Uniform Commercial Code Reporting, 1965-1983, 63 vols. 2650.00 (*0-318-42414-2*) West Group.
Pike & Fischer, Inc. Staff, ed. see Fischer.
Pike, Aebulon M. The Journals of Zebulon Montgomery Pike: With Letters & Related Documents, 2 vols., Set. (American Biography Ser.). 1991. reprint ed. lib. bdg. 148.00 (*0-7812-8315-9*) Rprt Serv.
— Southwestern Expedition of Zebulon M. Pike. (American Biography Ser.). 239p. 1991. reprint ed. lib. bdg. 69.00 (*0-7812-8316-7*) Rprt Serv.
Pike, Albert. The Book of the Lodge: Pike's Blue Lodge Degrees. 404p. 1993. reprint ed. pap. 45.00 (*1-56459-308-8*) Kessinger Pub.
— The Book of the Words. 180p. 1992. reprint ed. pap. 24.95 (*1-56459-161-1*) Kessinger Pub.
— Esoteric Work of the 1-3 Degree According to the Ancient & Accepted Scottish Rite. 50p. 1996. reprint ed. pap. 14.95 (*1-56459-992-2*) Kessinger Pub.
— The Evil Consequences of Schisms & Disputes for Power in Masonry & of Jealousies & Dissensions Between Masonic Rites. 70p. 1997. reprint ed. pap. 12.95 (*0-7661-0107-X*) Kessinger Pub.
— Ex Corde Locutiones: Words from the Heart Spoken of His Dead Brethren. 363p. 1993. reprint ed. pap. 29.95 (*1-56459-350-9*) Kessinger Pub.
— Hymns to God & Other Poems. 100p. 1998. reprint ed. pap. 17.95 (*0-7661-0379-X*) Kessinger Pub.
— Indo-Aryan Deities & Worship As Contained in the Rig-Veda. 659p. 1992. reprint ed. pap. 70.00 (*1-56459-183-2*) Kessinger Pub.
— Irano-Aryan Faith & Doctrine As Contained in the Zend-Avesta. 700p. 1992. reprint ed. pap. 70.00 (*1-56459-181-6*) Kessinger Pub.
— Lecture on Masonic Symbolism & a Second Lecture on Symbolism on the Omkara & Other Ineffable Words. 500p. 1992. reprint ed. pap. 45.00 (*1-56459-162-X*) Kessinger Pub.
— Lectures of the Arya. 340p. 1992. reprint ed. pap. 45.00 (*1-56459-182-4*) Kessinger Pub.
— The Legenda of the Ancient & Accepted Scottish Rite of Freemasonry. 436p. 1993. reprint ed. pap. 45.00 (*1-56459-309-6*) Kessinger Pub.
— The Liturgy of the Ancient & Accepted Scottish Rite of Freemasonry. 680p. 1993. reprint ed. pap. 45.00 (*1-56459-310-X*) Kessinger Pub.
— Liturgy of the Blue Degrees of the Ancient & Accepted Scottish Rite of Freemasonry for the Southern Jurisdiction. 227p. 1993. reprint ed. pap. 24.95 (*1-56459-323-1*) Kessinger Pub.
— Magnum Opus: or The Great Work: The Complete Ritual Work of Scottish Rite Freemasonry. 650p. 1992. reprint ed. pap. 45.00 (*1-56459-245-6*) Kessinger Pub.
— Masonic Baptism: Reception of a Louveteau & Adoption. 221p. 1993. reprint ed. pap. 24.95 (*1-56459-348-7*) Kessinger Pub.
— Masonry of Adoption: Albert Pike's Masonic Rituals for Women. 220p. 1992. reprint ed. pap. 19.95 (*1-56459-286-3*) Kessinger Pub.
— The Meaning of Masonry. 66p. 1992. reprint ed. pap. 12.95 (*1-56459-050-X*) Kessinger Pub.
— Morals & Dogma of the Ancient & Accepted Scottish Rite of Freemasonry. (Illus.). 878p. 1992. reprint ed. pap. 45.00 (*1-56459-275-8*) Kessinger Pub.
— Morals & Dogma of the Ancient & Accepted Scottish Rite of Freemasonry. (Notable American Authors Ser.). 1999. reprint ed. lib. bdg. 125.00 (*0-7812-8749-9*) Rprt Serv.
— Old Cahier of the 33 Degree. 50p. 1996. reprint ed. pap. 12.95 (*1-56459-995-7*) Kessinger Pub.
— The Point Within a Circle: A System of Masonry Veiled in Allegory & Illustrated by Symbols. (Illus.). 1994. pap. 3.95 (*1-55818-305-1*, Sure Fire) Holmes Pub.
— Prose Sketches & Poems: Written in the Western Country. Weber, David J., ed. LC 86-29994. (Southwest Landmark Ser.: No. 6). (Illus.). 336p. 1987. reprint ed. 27.50 (*0-89096-305-3*) Tex A&M Univ Pr.
— Prose Sketches & Poems: Written in the Western Country. Weber, David J., ed. LC 86-29994. (Southwest Landmark Ser.: No. 6). (Illus.). 336p. 1987. reprint ed. pap. 15.95 (*0-89096-323-1*) Tex A&M Univ Pr.
— Prose Sketches & Poems Written in the Western Country. (Notable American Authors Ser.). 1999. reprint ed. lib. bdg. 125.00 (*0-7812-8748-0*) Rprt Serv.
***Pike, Albert.** Pythagoras & Hermes. (Illus.). 1999. pap. 5.95 (*1-55818-466-X*) Holmes Pub.
Pike, Albert. Reprints of Old Rituals. 76p. 1996. reprint ed. pap. 24.95 (*1-56459-983-3*) Kessinger Pub.
Pike, Albert, ed. 1886 Bulletin of the Supreme Council of France. rev. ed. 94p. 1995. reprint ed. pap. text 15.00 (*1-887560-15-7*) M Poll Pub.
Pike, Allen R. The Family of John Pike of Newbury, Massachusetts, 1635-1995. LC 96-67647. (Illus.). 896p. 1995. 59.50 (*0-89725-262-4*, 1748, Penobscot Pr) Picton Pr.
Pike, Anne A. Climbing to the Top. LC 96-70176. (Illus.). 320p. 1996. write for info. (*0-9653914-0-X*) F S Pike Elect.
Pike, B. A. Campion's Career a Study of the Novels of Margery Allingham. LC 86-72912. 253p. 1987. 27.95 (*0-87972-379-3*) Bowling Green Univ Popular Press.
Pike, B. A., jt. auth. see Cooper, John.
Pike-Bakey, Meredith, jt. auth. see Laurie, Laurie.
Pike-Baky. Tapestry Writing. LC 99-89165. (C). 2000. pap., student ed. 25.95 (*0-8384-0038-8*) Heinle & Heinle.
— Tapestry Writing. 2nd ed. (C). 2000. pap., teacher ed. 14.00 (*0-8384-0036-1*) Heinle & Heinle.
Pike-Baky, Meredith. Tapestry Writing: Level 1. LC 99-57626. (C). 2000. pap. text 25.95 (*0-8384-0033-7*) Heinle & Heinle.
Pike-Baky, Meredith, jt. auth. see Blass, Laurie.
Pike-Baky, Meredith, jt. auth. see Lass, Laure.
Pike, Barry A., jt. auth. see Cooper, John.
Pike, Benjamin, Jr. Pike's Illustrated Descriptive Catalogue of Optical, Mathematical, & Philosophical Instruments. (Illus.). 755p. 1993. reprint ed. 125.00 (*0-930405-54-4*) Norman SF.
Pike, Bill. Motorboating: A Complete Guide. LC 95-12176. 176p. 1995. pap. 17.95 (*1-56799-206-4*, Friedman-Fairfax) M Friedman Pub Grp Inc.
Pike, Bob. High-Impact Presentations. Kirchner, Dave, ed. LC 97-75605. (AMI How-to Ser.). 90p. 1995. per. 12.95 (*1-884926-35-5*, PIKES) Amer Media.
— 101 Games for Trainers. 1998. pap. text 21.95 (*0-943210-41-0*) Lakewood Pubns.
Pike, Bob, ed. Dreams Vol. I: Working Words of Wit & Wisdom. 96p. 12.95 (*0-7879-5120-X*, Pfffr & Co) Jossey-Bass.
***Pike, Bob & Busse, Chris.** 101 Games for Trainers: A Collection of the best Activities from Creative Training Techniques, 1 Vol. (Illus.). 108p. 1998. pap. 21.95 (*0-943210-38-0*) Lakewood Pubns.
Pike, Bob, jt. auth. see Solem, Lynn.
Pike, Bonnie. Three Brass Monkeys. LC 88-9331. 96p. (Orig.). 1988. pap. 7.95 (*0-932419-11-9*) Cherokee.
Pike, Brian, tr. see Quetel, Claude.
Pike, Burton. The Image of the City in Modern Literature. LC 81-47149. (Princeton Essays in Literature Ser.). 183p. reprint ed. pap. 56.80 (*0-8357-6152-5*, 203429200089) Bks Demand.
Pike, Burton, ed. see Mann, Thomas.
Pike, Burton, ed. see Musil, Robert.
Pike, Burton, ed. & tr. see Musil, Robert.
Pike, Burton, tr. see Musil, Robert.
Pike, Chester. I Refuse to be A Loser: You Too Can be A Winner. LC 99-168278. 224 p. 1998. write for info. (*1-55630-846-9*) Brentwood Comm.
Pike, Christopher, jt. auth. see Oltion, Jerry.
Pike, Christopher, pseud. Aliens in the Sky. (Spooksville Ser.). (J). (gr. 4-6). 1996. pap. 3.99 (*0-671-53728-8*, Pocket Books) PB.
Pike, Christopher, pseud. Aliens in the Sky. (Spooksville Ser.). (J). (gr. 4-6). 1996. 9.09 (*0-606-08614-5*, Pub. by Turtleback) Demco.
Pike, Christopher, pseud. The Ancient Evil. MacDonald, Patricia, ed. (Chain Letter Ser.: No. 2). 240p. (Orig.). (YA). (gr. 9 up). 1992. mass mkt. 4.50 (*0-671-74506-9*, Archway) PB.
— Attack of the Killer Crabs. (Spooksville Ser.). (J). (gr. 4-6). 1997. per. 3.99 (*0-671-00266-X*) PB.
— Attack of the Killer Crabs. (Spooksville Ser.). (J). (gr. 4-6). 1997. 9.09 (*0-606-12818-2*, Pub. by Turtleback) Demco.
— Blind Mirror. 22.95 (*0-312-85895-7*, Pub. by Tor Bks) St Martin.
— Bury Me Deep. MacDonald, Patricia, ed. 224p. (YA). (gr. 8 up). 1991. mass mkt. 3.99 (*0-671-69057-4*, Archway) PB.
Pike, Christopher, pseud. Bury Me Deep. Date not set. 9.09 (*0-606-04882-0*, Pub. by Turtleback) Demco.
Pike, Christopher, pseud. Chain Letter. 192p. (J). (gr. 7 up). 1986. mass mkt. 3.99 (*0-380-89968-X*, Avon Bks) Morrow Avon.
Pike, Christopher, pseud. Chain Letter. (J). 1986. 9.09 (*0-606-02005-5*, Pub. by Turtleback) Demco.
Pike, Christopher, pseud. Chain Letter 2: The Ancient Evil. (J). 1992. 9.09 (*0-606-02549-9*, Pub. by Turtleback) Demco.
— Christopher Pike, 5 vols. 1989. pap., boxed set 11.80 (*0-671-92249-1*) PB.
— Christopher Pike. (YA). (gr. 8 up). 1998. pap. 4.50 (*0-671-55062-4*, Archway) PB.
— Christopher Pike, 4 vols. (YA). 1990. pap., boxed set 11.80 (*0-671-96377-5*) S&S Trade.
— Christopher Pike's Tales of Terror. (J). 1997. 9.60 (*0-606-12658-9*, Pub. by Turtleback) Demco.
— Christopher Pike's Tales of Terror, No. 1. (J). (gr. 8 up). 1996. 14.00 (*0-671-55079-9*, Archway) PB.
— Christopher Pike's Tales of Terror, No. 1. (YA). (gr. 8 up). 1997. mass mkt. 4.50 (*0-671-55074-8*) PB.
— Christopher Pike's Tales of Terror, No. 2. (J). (gr. 8 up). 1996. 14.00 (*0-671-55082-9*, Archway) PB.
— Christopher Pike's Tales of Terror, No. 2. (J). (gr. 8 up). 1998. per. 4.50 (*0-671-55076-4*, Archway) PB.
— Christopher Pike's Tales of Terror, No. 3. (J). (gr. 8 up). 1999. per. 4.99 (*0-671-55077-2*, Archway) PB.
— Christopher Pike's Tales of Terror No. 2. 1998. 9.60 (*0-606-13275-9*, Pub. by Turtleback) Demco.
— The Cold One. 416p. 1995. mass mkt. write for info. (*0-614-05506-7*); mass mkt. 5.99 (*0-8125-1245-6*, Pub. by Tor Bks) St Martin.
— The Cold People. (Spooksville Ser.). (J). (gr. 4-6). 1996. pap. 3.99 (*0-671-55064-0*, Minstrel Bks) PB.
— The Cold People. (Spooksville Ser.). (J). (gr. 4-6). 1996. 9.09 (*0-606-09884-4*, Pub. by Turtleback) Demco.
— Creature in the Teacher. (Spooksville Ser.). (J). (gr. 4-6). 1996. per. 3.99 (*0-671-00261-9*) PB.
— Creature in the Teacher. (Spooksville Ser.). (J). (gr. 4-6). 1996. 9.09 (*0-606-10940-4*, Pub. by Turtleback) Demco.
— Creatures of Forever. (Last Vampire Ser.: No. 6). (YA). (gr. 9 up). 1996. pap. 3.99 (*0-671-55052-7*) PB.

P

An Asterisk (*) at the beginning of an entry indicates that the title is appearing for the first time.

— The Creepy Creature. (Spooksville Ser.). (J). (gr. 4-6). 1998. per. 3.99 (0-671-00270-8) PB.
— The Creepy Creature. (Spooksville Ser.). (J). (gr. 4-6). 1998. 9.09 (0-606-13798-X, Pub. by Turtleback) Demco.
— The Dance. (Final Friends Ser.: No. 2). (YA). (gr. 8 up). 1991. pap. 3.90 (0-671-73679-5, Archway) PB.
Pike, Christopher, pseud. The Dance. (Final Friends Ser.). (J). 1988. 9.09 (0-606-04120-6, Pub. by Turtleback) Demco.
Pike, Christopher, pseud. The Dance Final. (Friends Ser.: No. 2). (J). 1998. per. 3.99 (0-671-01928-7) PB.
— The Dangerous Quest. (Spooksville Ser.). (J). (gr. 4-6). 1998. per. 3.99 (0-671-00268-6) PB.
— The Dangerous Quest. (Spooksville Ser.). (J). (gr. 4-6). 1998. 9.09 (0-606-13037-3, Pub. by Turtleback) Demco.
— The Dark Corner. (Spooksville Ser.). (J). (gr. 4-6). 1996. pap. 3.99 (0-671-55066-7, Minstrel Bks) PB.
— The Dark Corner. (Spooksville Ser.). (J). (gr. 4-6). 1996. 9.09 (0-606-09886-0, Pub. by Turtleback) Demco.
Pike, Christopher, pseud. The Deadly Past. (Spooksville Ser.). (J). (gr. 4-6). 1996. per. 3.99 (0-671-55072-1) PB.
Pike, Christopher, pseud. The Deadly Past. (Spooksville Ser.). (J). (gr. 4-6). 1996. 9.09 (0-606-11876-4, Pub. by Turtleback) Demco.
— Die Softly. MacDonald, Patricia, ed. 224p. (J). (gr. 9 up). 1991. mass mkt. 3.99 (0-671-69056-6, Archway) PB.
Pike, Christopher, pseud. Die Softly. 1991. 9.09 (0-606-04907-X, Pub. by Turtleback) Demco.
Pike, Christopher, pseud. The Eternal Enemy. MacDonald, Patricia, ed. 224p. (J). (gr. 9 up). 1993. mass mkt. 3.99 (0-671-74509-3) PB.
— The Eternal Enemy. (J). 1999. per. 4.50 (0-671-02038-2) PB.
— The Eternal Enemy. (J). 1993. 9.09 (0-606-05268-2, Pub. by Turtleback) Demco.
— The Evil House. (Spooksville Ser.). 144p. (J). (gr. 4-6). 1997. per. 3.99 (0-671-00262-7) PB.
— The Evil House. LC 49-244320. (Spooksville Ser.). (J). (gr. 4-6). 1997. 9.09 (0-606-10941-2, Pub. by Turtleback) Demco.
— Evil Thirst. (Last Vampire Ser.: No. 5). 224p. (J). 1996. per. 4.50 (0-671-55050-0, Archway) PB.
— Evil Thirst. (Last Vampire Ser.). (J). 1996. 9.09 (0-606-10250-7, Pub. by Turtleback) Demco.
— Execution of Innocence. 224p. (YA). (gr. 9 up). 1997. per. 4.50 (0-671-55055-1, PB Trade Paper) PB.
— Execution of Innocence. (J). 1997. 9.60 (0-606-11304-5, Pub. by Turtleback) Demco.
— Fall into Darkness. 224p. (YA). (gr. 8 up). 1991. pap. 3.99 (0-671-73684-1, Archway) PB.
— Fall Into Darkness. 1990. 9.09 (0-606-01003-3, Pub. by Turtleback) Demco.
— Gimme a Kiss. 160p. (YA). (gr. 8 up). 1991. mass mkt. 4.50 (0-671-73682-5, Archway) PB.
— Gimme a Kiss. (J). 1988. 9.60 (0-606-03792-6, Pub. by Turtleback) Demco.
— Graduation. (Final Friends Ser.). (J). 1998. per. 4.50 (0-671-01927-9, Archway) PB.
— Graduation. (Final Friends Ser.). (J). 1989. 9.09 (0-606-04121-4, Pub. by Turtleback) Demco.
— Graduation, 3. (Final Friends Ser.). 1998. 9.60 (0-606-13383-6, Pub. by Turtleback) Demco.
***Pike, Christopher, pseud.** Grave. (Illus.). (J). 1999. 10.34 (0-606-17950-X) Turtleback.
Pike, Christopher, pseud. The Haunted Cave. (Spooksville Ser.). (J). (gr. 4-6). 1995. pap. 3.50 (0-671-53727-X) PB.
Pike, Christopher, pseud. The Haunted Cave. (Spooksville Ser.). (J). (gr. 4-6). 1995. 8.60 (0-606-08613-7, Pub. by Turtleback) Demco.
Pike, Christopher, pseud. The Hidden Beast. (Spooksville Ser.). (J). (gr. 4-6). 1996. per. 3.99 (0-671-55073-X) PB.
— The Hidden Beast. (Spooksville Ser.). (J). (gr. 4-6). 1996. 9.09 (0-606-10939-0, Pub. by Turtleback) Demco.
— The Hollow Skull. (J). 1998. per. 4.50 (0-671-55059-4) S&S Trade.
— The Hollow Skull. 1998. 9.60 (0-606-12965-0, Pub. by Turtleback) Demco.
— The Howling Ghost. LC 95-232287. (Spooksville Ser.). (J). (gr. 4-6). 1995. pap. 3.50 (0-671-53726-1) PB.
Pike, Christopher, pseud. The Howling Ghost. (Spooksville Ser.). (J). (gr. 4-6). 1995. 8.60 (0-606-08612-9, Pub. by Turtleback) Demco.
Pike, Christopher, pseud. The Immortal. MacDonald, Patricia, ed. 256p. (J). (gr. 9 up). 1993. mass mkt. 3.99 (0-671-74510-7, Archway) PB.
Pike, Christopher, pseud. The Immortal. (J). 1993. 9.09 (0-606-05373-5, Pub. by Turtleback) Demco.
Pike, Christopher, pseud. The Immortal. large type ed. LC 93-32608. (Teen Scene Ser.). 241p. (YA). (gr. 9-12). 1993. lib. bdg. 15.95 (0-7862-0071-5) Thorndike Pr.
— Invasion of the No-Ones. (Spooksville Ser.). (J). (gr. 4-6). 1997. pap. 3.99 (0-671-00263-5) PB.
— Invasion of the No-Ones. (Spooksville Ser.). (J). (gr. 4-6). 1997. 9.09 (0-606-11877-2, Pub. by Turtleback) Demco.
— The Last Act. (YA). (gr. 8 up). 1991. mass mkt. 3.99 (0-671-73683-3, Archway) PB.
Pike, Christopher, pseud. The Last Act. 1988. 9.09 (0-606-03841-8, Pub. by Turtleback) Demco.
Pike, Christopher, pseud. The Last Story. MacDonald, Patricia, ed. No. 3. 224p. (YA). (gr. 9 up). 1995. mass mkt. 3.99 (0-671-87267-2, Archway) PB.
— The Last Story. (Remember Me Ser.). (J). 1995. 9.09 (0-606-08069-4, Pub. by Turtleback) Demco.
— The Last Vampire. MacDonald, Patricia, ed. (YA). (gr. 9 up). 1994. 14.00 (0-671-87256-7, Archway); per. 3.99 (0-671-87264-8, Archway) PB.
Pike, Christopher, pseud. The Last Vampire. 1994. 9.09 (0-606-06522-9, Pub. by Turtleback) Demco.
Pike, Christopher, pseud. The Last Vampire: Collector's Edition, Vol. 2. (Last Vampire Ser.: No. 2). (J). (gr. 9 up). 1998. pap. 6.99 (0-671-02290-3, Archway) PB.
— The Last Vampire Collector's Edition. (Last Vampire Ser.: No. 1, Vols. 1-3). (J). (gr. 9 up). 1998. per. 6.99 (0-671-02060-9, Archway) PB.
— The Last Vampire, Four: Phantom. 1996. 9.09 (0-606-09529-2, Pub. by Turtleback) Demco.
— The Last Vampire, Four: The Phantom. LC 95-81220. (YA). (gr. 9 up). 1996. 14.00 (0-671-55049-7) PB.
— The Last Vampire, Two: Black Blood. MacDonald, Patricia, ed. (Last Vampire Ser.: No. 2). 208p. (YA). (gr. 9 up). 1994. per. 3.99 (0-671-87266-4, Archway) PB.
Pike, Christopher, pseud. The Last Vampire, Two: Black Blood. 1994. 9.09 (0-606-07022-2, Pub. by Turtleback) Demco.
Pike, Christopher, pseud. The Listeners. 352p. (Orig.). 1995. mass mkt. 5.99 (0-8125-5039-0, Pub. by Tor Bks) St Martin.
— The Little People. (Spooksville Ser.). 128p. (J). (gr. 4-6). 1996. per. 3.99 (0-671-55067-5, Minstrel Bks) PB.
— The Little People. (Spooksville Ser.). (J). (gr. 4-6). 1996. 9.09 (0-606-09887-9, Pub. by Turtleback) Demco.
— The Living Dead. (Spooksville Ser.). (J). (gr. 4-6). 1998. per. 3.99 (0-671-00269-4) PB.
— The Living Dead. (Spooksville Ser.). (J). (gr. 4-6). 1998. 9.09 (0-606-13797-1, Pub. by Turtleback) Demco.
— The Lost Mind. 213p. (J). (gr. 6-10). 1995. 14.00 (0-671-87261-3, Archway) PB.
— The Lost Mind. 256p. (YA). (gr. 9 up). 1995. per. 3.99 (0-671-87269-9, Archway) PB.
— The Lost Mind. 1995. 9.09 (0-606-07809-6, Pub. by Turtleback) Demco.
— Magic Fire. (YA). 1999. per. 4.50 (0-671-02057-9, Archway) PB.
— Magic Fire. 1998. 9.60 (0-606-13588-X, Pub. by Turtleback) Demco.
— Master of Murder. MacDonald, Pat, ed. (YA). (gr. 9 up). 1999. mass mkt. 3.99 (0-671-69059-0, Archway) PB.
— Master of Murder. 1992. 9.09 (0-606-02089-6, Pub. by Turtleback) Demco.
— The Midnight Club. MacDonald, Patricia, ed. LC 93-20917. 224p. (J). 1994. mass mkt. 3.99 (0-671-87263-X, Archway) PB.
— The Midnight Club. MacDonald, Patricia, ed. LC 93-20917. 256p. (YA). (gr. 9 up). 1994. 14.00 (0-671-87255-9, Archway) PB.
— The Midnight Club. (J). 1994. 9.09 (0-606-05925-3, Pub. by Turtleback) Demco.
— Monster. MacDonald, Pat, ed. 256p. (YA). (gr. 9 up). 1992. mass mkt. 3.99 (0-671-74507-7, Archway) PB.
Pike, Christopher, pseud. Monster. (J). 1992. 9.09 (0-606-02203-1, Pub. by Turtleback) Demco.
Pike, Christopher, pseud. Night of the Vampire. (Spooksville Ser.). (J). (gr. 4-6). 1997. per. 3.99 (0-671-00267-8) PB.
— Night of the Vampire. (Spooksville Ser.). (J). (gr. 4-6). 1997. 9.09 (0-606-13036-5, Pub. by Turtleback) Demco.
— The Party. (Final Friends Ser.: No. 1). (YA). (gr. 8 up). 1991. mass mkt. 3.99 (0-671-73678-7, Archway) PB.
— The Party. (Final Friends Ser.). (J). 1997. per. 3.99 (0-671-01926-0, Archway) PB.
— The Party. (Final Friends Ser.). (J). 1988. 9.09 (0-606-04122-2, Pub. by Turtleback) Demco.
— The Phantom: The Last Vampire. (YA). (gr. 9 up). 1996. mass mkt. 3.99 (0-671-55030-6) PB.
— Phone Fear. (Spooksville Ser.). (J). (gr. 4-6). 1998. per. 3.99 (0-671-00271-6, Pocket Books) PB.
— Phone Fear. (Spooksville Ser.). (J). (gr. 4-6). 1998. 9.09 (0-606-13799-8, Pub. by Turtleback) Demco.
— Red Dice. (Last Vampire Ser.). 1995. 9.09 (0-606-07775-8, Pub. by Turtleback) Demco.
— Red Dice, No. 3. (Last Vampire Ser.: Vol. 3). 208p. (YA). (gr. 9 up). 1995. mass mkt. 3.99 (0-671-87268-0, Archway) PB.
— Remember Me. MacDonald, Pat, ed. 224p. (YA). (gr. 8 up). 1990. per. 3.99 (0-671-73685-X, Archway) PB.
Pike, Christopher, pseud. Remember Me. (J). 1989. 9.09 (0-606-04306-3, Pub. by Turtleback) Demco.
Pike, Christopher, pseud. Remember Me, Three: The Last Story. MacDonald, Patricia, ed. No. 3. (gr. 9 up). 1995. 14.00 (0-671-87259-1, Archway) PB.
Pike, Christopher, pseud. Remember Me Two: The Return. 1994. 9.09 (0-606-06693-4, Pub. by Turtleback) Demco.
Pike, Christopher, pseud. The Return. MacDonald, Patricia, ed. (Remember Me Two Ser.). 224p. (YA). (gr. 9 up). 1994. per. 3.99 (0-671-87265-6, Archway) PB.
— Road to Nowhere. MacDonald, Pat, ed. 224p. (YA). (gr. 9 up). 1993. mass mkt. 3.99 (0-671-74508-5, Archway) PB.
— Road to Nowhere. (J). 1993. 9.09 (0-606-02876-5, Pub. by Turtleback) Demco.
— Sati. 1991. mass mkt. 4.99 (0-8125-1035-6, Pub. by Tor Bks) St Martin.
— Scavenger Hunt. (YA). (gr. 9 up). 1990. mass mkt. 3.99 (0-671-73686-8, Archway) PB.
Pike, Christopher, pseud. Scavenger Hunt. (J). 1989. 9.09 (0-606-04315-2, Pub. by Turtleback) Demco.
Pike, Christopher, pseud. The Season of Passage. 480p. 1993. mass mkt. 4.99 (0-8125-1048-8, Pub. by Tor Bks) St Martin.
— The Secret Path. (Spooksville Ser.). (J). (gr. 4-6). 1995. mass mkt. 3.50 (0-671-53725-3) PB.
Pike, Christopher, pseud. The Secret Path. (Spooksville Ser.). (J). (gr. 4-6). 1995. 8.60 (0-606-08611-0, Pub. by Turtleback) Demco.
Pike, Christopher, pseud. See You Later. (J). 1998. per. 4.50 (0-671-02025-0) PB.
— See You Later. (J). 1990. 9.60 (0-606-04535-X, Pub. by Turtleback) Demco.
— See You Later. MacDonald, Patricia, ed. 240p. (YA). (gr. 8 up). 1991. reprint ed. pap. 3.99 (0-671-74390-2, Archway) PB.
— Slumber Party. 176p. (Orig.). (J). (gr. 7-9). 1985. pap. 3.50 (0-590-43014-9) Scholastic Inc.
— Spellbound. (YA). (gr. 8 up). 1990. mass mkt. 3.99 (0-671-73681-7, Archway) PB.
— Spellbound. (YA). 1988. 9.09 (0-606-03927-9, Pub. by Turtleback) Demco.
— Spooksville Seires Boxed Set: The Howling Ghosts; The Haunted Cave; Aliens in the Sky; The Cold People, 4 vols., Set. (Spooksville Ser.). (J). (gr. 4-6). 1996. per., boxed set 14.98 (0-671-85164-0) PB.
Pike, Christopher, pseud. Spooksville Series Boxed Set: The Witch's Revenge; The Dark Corner; The Little People; The Wishing Star, 4 vols., Set. (Spooksville Ser.). (J). (gr. 4-6). 1997. boxed set 15.96 (0-671-87829-8) PB.
Pike, Christopher, pseud. Star Group. 1997. 14.00 (0-671-55058-6, Archway) PB.
— Star Group. (YA). 1997. pap. 3.99 (0-671-55057-8, Archway) PB.
Pike, Christopher, pseud. Star Group. 1997. 9.09 (0-606-11882-9, Pub. by Turtleback) Demco.
Pike, Christopher, pseud. The Starlight Crystal. (YA). (gr. 9 up). 1996. mass mkt. 3.99 (0-671-55028-4, Archway) PB.
— The Starlight Crystal. (YA). (gr. 9 up). 1996. 14.00 (0-671-55029-2, Archway) PB.
— The Starlight Crystal. 1996. 9.09 (0-606-09894-1, Pub. by Turtleback) Demco.
— The Tachyon Web. 208p. (YA). (gr. 9 up). 1997. per. 3.99 (0-671-69060-4) PB.
Pike, Christopher, pseud. The Tachyon Web. (J). 1997. 9.09 (0-606-11964-7, Pub. by Turtleback) Demco.
Pike, Christopher, pseud. The Thing in the Closet. (Spooksville Ser.). (J). (gr. 4-6). 1997. per. 3.99 (0-671-00265-1) PB.
— The Thing in the Closet. (Spooksville Ser.). (J). (gr. 4-6). 1997. 9.09 (0-606-11879-9, Pub. by Turtleback) Demco.
— Time Terror. (Spooksville Ser.). (J). (gr. 4-6). 1997. per. 3.99 (0-671-00264-3) PB.
— Time Terror. (Spooksville Ser.). (J). (gr. 4-6). 1997. 9.09 (0-606-11878-0, Pub. by Turtleback) Demco.
— The Visitor. (J). 1995. mass mkt. 3.99 (0-671-87270-2, Archway) PB.
Pike, Christopher, pseud. The Visitor. 1995. 9.09 (0-606-08656-0, Pub. by Turtleback) Demco.
Pike, Christopher, pseud. Weekend. (J). 1986. pap. 2.75 (0-590-42968-X) Scholastic Inc.
— Weekend. 240p. (YA). (gr. 7 up). 1986. pap. 3.50 (0-590-44256-2) Scholastic Inc.
— Weekend. (Point Ser.). 1986. 10.09 (0-606-01207-9, Pub. by Turtleback) Demco.
— Whisper of Death. MacDonald, Patricia, ed. 256p. (YA). (gr. 9 up). 1991. mass mkt. 3.99 (0-671-69058-2, Archway) PB.
Pike, Christopher, pseud. Whisper of Death. 1991. 9.09 (0-606-00826-8, Pub. by Turtleback) Demco.
Pike, Christopher, pseud. The Wicked Cat. (Spooksville Ser.). (J). (gr. 4-6). 1996. per. 3.99 (0-671-55069-1) PB.
— The Wicked Cat. (Spooksville Ser.). (J). (gr. 4-6). 1996. 9.09 (0-606-10305-8, Pub. by Turtleback) Demco.
— The Wicked Heart. (YA). (gr. 9 up). 1993. pap. 4.50 (0-671-02039-0, Archway) PB.
— The Wicked Heart. MacDonald, Patricia, ed. 224p. (YA). (gr. 9 up). 1993. mass mkt. 3.99 (0-671-74511-5, Archway) PB.
— The Wicked Heart. 1993. 9.09 (0-606-06100-2, Pub. by Turtleback) Demco.
— The Wishing Stone. (Spooksville Ser.). 144p. (J). (gr. 4-6). 1996. per. 3.99 (0-671-55068-3, Minstrel Bks) PB.
— The Wishing Stone. (Spooksville Ser.). (J). (gr. 4-6). 1996. 9.09 (0-606-10306-6, Pub. by Turtleback) Demco.
Pike, Christopher, pseud. Witch. MacDonald, Patricia, ed. 240p. (Orig.). (YA). (gr. 8 up). 1990. per. 3.99 (0-671-69055-8, Archway) PB.
— The Witch's Gift. (Spooksville Ser.). (J). (gr. 4-6). 1999. pap. 3.99 (0-671-00272-4, Minstrel Bks) PB.
Pike, Christopher, pseud. The Witch's Revenge. (Spooksville Ser.). (J). (gr. 4-6). 1996. pap. 3.99 (0-671-55065-9, Minstrel Bks) PB.
— The Witch's Revenge. (Spooksville Ser.). (J). (gr. 4-6). 1996. 9.09 (0-606-09885-2, Pub. by Turtleback) Demco.
Pike, Christopher, pseud & Smith, Sinclair. Thirteen: 13 Tales of Horror. Pines, Tonya, ed. 343p. (YA). (gr. 7-12). 1991. mass mkt. 4.99 (0-590-45256-8, Point) Scholastic Inc.
Pike, Clarence E. Around the World in 80 Years. LC 97-69385. 144p. 1998. 17.95 (1-887750-76-2) Rutledge Bks.
Pike County Historical Society Staff. History & Families: Pike County, Indiana 1816-1987. LC 87-51612. 236p. 1987. 52.50 (0-938021-57-5) Turner Pub KY.
Pike, D., ed. see Ledbetter, H. & Lomax, John A.
Pike, Dag. Fast Boat Navigation. (Illus.). 176p. 1990. 25.00 (0-229-11859-3) Sheridan.
— Fishing Boats & Their Equipment. 1978. 50.00 (0-7855-6924-3) St Mut.
— Fishing Boats & Their Equipment. 3rd ed. (Illus.). 200p. 1992. pap. 44.95 (0-85238-190-5) Blackwell Sci.
— Inflatables. (Illus.). 192p. 1994. pap. 30.00 (0-7136-3881-8) Sheridan.
Pike, Dave. Bonsai: Step by Step to Growing Success. (Illus.). 128p. 1990. pap. 17.95 (1-85223-128-9, Pub. by Cro1wood) Trafalgar.
— Indoor Bonsai: A Beginner's Step-By-Step Guide. 1992. pap. 17.95 (1-85223-254-4, Pub. by Cro1wood) Trafalgar.
Pike, David. German Writers in Soviet Exile, 1933-1945. LC 81-10394. xv, 448p. (C). 1982. 49.95 (0-8078-1492-X) U of NC Pr.
— Lukacs & Brecht. LC 84-17406. xviii, 337p. 1985. text 55.00 (0-8078-1640-X) U of NC Pr.
Pike, David L. Passage Through Hell: Modern Descents, Medieval Underworlds. LC 96-18284. (Illus.). 280p. 1996. text 37.50 (0-8014-3163-8) Cornell U Pr.
Pike, David W. In the Service of Stalin: The Spanish Communists in Exile, 1939-1945. LC 92-42791. (Illus.). 474p. (C). 1993. text 59.00 (0-19-820315-2) OUP.
Pike, David W. The Opening of the Second World War. LC 90-15503. (American University Studies: History: Ser. IX, Vol. 105). (Illus.). XL, 387p. (C). 1991. text 62.95 (0-8204-1524-3) P Lang Pubng.
— The Politics of Culture in Soviet-Occupied Germany, 1945-1949. 700p. (C). 1993. 59.50 (0-8047-2093-2) Stanford U Pr.
Pike, Derek J., tr. see Neuilly, Michele.
Pike, Diane K. Life Is Victorious: How to Grow Through Grief. LC 76-17328. (Illus.). 209p. 1982. 11.95 (0-916192-20-2) L P Pubns.
— My Journey into Self Phase One. LC 79-12179. 161p. 1979. pap. 9.95 (0-916192-13-X) L P Pubns.
— The Process of Awakening: An Overview, Vol. 1. LC 85-8083. (Illus.). 75p. (Orig.). 1985. pap. 9.95 (0-916192-29-6) L P Pubns.
Pike, Diane K., jt. auth. see Lorrance, Arleen.
Pike, Donald G. & Muench, David. Anasazi: Ancient People of the Rock. LC 73-90795. (Images of America Ser.). 192p. 1986. pap. 18.00 (0-517-52690-5) Harmony Bks.
Pike, Douglas. Australian Dictionary of Biography, 4 vols. Incl. Vol. 1. 1788-1850, A-H. 581p. 1968. reprint ed. 59.95 (0-522-83516-3); Vol. 2. 1788-1850, I-Z. 634p. 1967. 59.95 (0-522-83705-0); Vol. 3. 1851-1890, A-C. 516p. 1974. 59.95 (0-522-83909-6); Vol. 4. 1851-1890, D-J. 1972. 59.95 (0-522-84034-5); write for info. (0-318-53676-5) Intl Spec Bk.
— PAVN: People's Army of Vietnam. 408p. 1986. 46.00 (0-08-033614-0, Pergamon Pr) Elsevier.
Pike, Douglas, ed. The Bunker Papers: Reports to the President from Vietnam, 1967-1973, 3 vols. (Indochina Research Monographs). 902p. 1990. pap. 35.00 (1-55729-019-9) IEAS.
Pike, E. R. & Abbiss, J. B., eds. Light Scattering & Photon Correlation Spectroscopy: Proceedings of the NATO Advanced Research Workshop, Krakow, Poland, August 26-30, 1996. LC 97-33973. (NATO ASI Ser.). 488p. 1997. text 251.00 (0-7923-4736-6) Kluwer Academic.
Pike, E. R. & Lugiato, L. A., eds. Chaos, Noise & Fractals. (Malvern Physics Ser.). (Illus.). 614p. 1987. 110.00 (0-85274-364-5) IOP Pub.
Pike, E. R. & Sarkar, Sarben. The Quantum Theory of Radiation. (International Series of Monographs on Physics: No. 86). (Illus.). 354p. 1996. text 105.00 (0-19-852032-8) OUP.
Pike, E. R. & Sarker, S., eds. Quantum Measurement & Chaos. LC 87-18934. (NATO ASI Series B, Physics: Vol. 161). (Illus.). 304p. 1987. 79.50 (0-306-42669-2, Plenum Trade) Perseus Pubng.
Pike, E. R., jt. ed. see Bertero, M.
Pike, E. R., jt. ed. see Tombesi, P.
Pike, Earl A. Protection Against Bombs & Incendiaries: For Business, Industrial & Educational Institutions. (Illus.). 92p. 1973. 20.95 (0-398-02517-7) C C Thomas.
Pike, Earl C. We Are All Living with AIDS: How You Can Set Policies & Guidelines for the Workplace. 416p. 1993. pap. 14.95 (0-925190-68-3) Fairview Press.
Pike, Edgar R. Dicc. de Religiones. (SPA.). 23.99 (968-16-2373-8, Pub. by Fondo) Continental Bk.
Pike, Elizabeth H. Family & Society in the Works of Elizabeth Gaskell, Vol. 174. LC 93-35970. (American University Studies: Series IV). VIII, 166p. (C). 1995. text 39.95 (0-8204-2241-X) P Lang Pubng.
Pike, Eunice V. Dictation Exercises in Phonetics. 188p. 1963. pap. 9.00 (0-88312-900-0) S I L Intl.
— Ken Pike: Scholar & Christian. LC 81-51058. (Illus.). 270p. (Orig.). 1981. pap. 5.00 (0-88312-920-5) S I L Intl.
— The Last Five Feet. LC 93-87633. 129p. (Orig.). 1994. pap. 8.00 (0-88312-709-1) S I L Intl.
— Sarah's Life. LC 93-85571. xi, 53p. 1993. pap. 4.95 (0-88312-618-4) S I L Intl.
— An Uttermost Part. 2nd rev. ed. LC 91-75053. 274p. 1991. pap. 8.00 (0-88312-810-1) S I L Intl.
Pike, Evelyn, jt. auth. see Pike, Kenneth.
Pike, Frank & Dunn, Thomas G. The Playwright's Handbook. rev. ed. LC 85-318. 272p. 1996. pap. 13.95 (0-452-27588-1, Plume) Dutton Plume.
— Scenes & Monologues from the New American Theater. 304p. 1988. mass mkt. 6.99 (0-451-62547-1, Ment) NAL.
Pike, Frederick B. FDR's Good Neighbor Policy: Sixty Years of Generally Gentle Chaos. LC 94-29811. (Illus.). 416p. 1995. 34.95 (0-292-76557-6) U of Tex Pr.
Pike, Fredrick B. The Politics of the Miraculous in Peru: Haya de la Torre & the Spiritualist Tradition. LC 85-1162. (Illus.). 409p. 1986. reprint ed. pap. 126.80 (0-608-08000-4, 206796500012) Bks Demand.
— The United States & Latin America: Myths & Stereotypes of Civilization & Nature. LC 91-42454. (Illus.). 464p. 1992. pap. 19.95 (0-292-78524-0); text 40.00 (0-292-78523-2) U of Tex Pr.
— The United States & the Andean Republics: Peru, Bolivia & Ecuador. (American Foreign Policy Library). (Illus.). 493p. 1977. 66.50 (0-674-92300-6) HUP.
Pike, Fredrick B., jt. ed. see Falcoff, Mark.
Pike, G. & Selby, David. Global Teacher, Global Learner. (Illus.). 312p. 1988. pap. text 42.00 (0-340-40261-X, Pub. by Hodder & Stought Ltd) Lubrecht & Cramer.

An Asterisk (*) at the beginning of an entry indicates that the title is appearing for the first time.

Pike, G. Holden. The Life & Work of Charles Haddon Spurgeon. 608p. 1992. reprint ed. 69.99 (*0-85151-622-X*) Banner of Truth.

Pike, Garnet E. Receiving the Promise of the Father: How to Be Baptized in the Holy Spirit. LC 97-76041. 117p. 1997. pap. 7.95 (*0-911866-39-6*) LifeSprings Res.

Pike, Geoff. Henry Golightly: A Novel of the Sea. LC 75-318041. xiii, 225 p. (J). 1974. write for info. (*0-207-13206-2*, Pub. by Angus & Roberts) HarpC.

Pike, Geoff & Pike, Phyllis. Ch'i: The Power Within: Chi Kung Breathing Exercises for Health, Relaxation & Energy. 272p. 1996. pap. 16.95 (*0-8048-3099-1*) Tuttle Pubng.

***Pike, George Leon, Sr.** The Revelation of Jesus Christ. LC 99-65129. 472p. 1999. write for info. (*0-9673516-0-X*) Jesus Christs.

Pike, Gordon, contrib. by. National Space Engineering Symposium, 9th, 1994: Satellite Communications. (National Conference Proceedings 94 Ser.: Vol. 7). (Illus.). 230p. 1994. pap. 38.50 (*0-85825-605-3*, Pub. by Inst Engrs Aust-EA Bks) Accents Pubns.

Pike, Gregory. Sports Massage for Peak Performance. LC 97-5528. 224p. 1997. pap. 20.00 (*0-06-095167-2*, Perennial) HarperTrade.

Pike, Gustavus D. Jubilee Singers, & Their Campaign for Twenty Thousand Dollars. LC 72-1692. reprint ed. 36.50 (*0-404-08329-3*) AMS Pr.

— The Singing Campaign for Ten Thousand Pounds. rev. ed. LC 75-164392. (Black Heritage Library Collection). 1977. reprint ed. 29.95 (*0-8369-8851-5*) Ayer.

Pike, Helen-Chantal. Asbury Park. LC 97-183786. (Images of America Ser.). 1997. pap. 16.99 (*0-7524-0538-1*) Arcadia Publng.

— West Long Branch. (Images of America Ser.). 1999. pap. 16.99 (*0-7524-0472-5*) Arcadia Publng.

Pike, Helen-Chantal & Vogel, Glenn D. Eatontown & Fort Monmouth. LC 95-237526. (Images of America Ser.). 1999. pap. 16.99 (*0-7524-0250-1*) Arcadia Publng.

Pike, J. G. A Guide for Young Disciples. 364p. (YA). (gr. 5 up). 1996. 29.95 (*1-57358-037-6*) Soli Deo Gloria.

— Persuasives to Early Piety. 362p. (YA). (gr. 5-11). 1996. 29.95 (*1-57358-036-8*) Soli Deo Gloria.

Pike, James. Scout & Ranger. LC 74-39282. (American Scene Ser.). (Illus.). 164p. 1972. reprint ed. lib. bdg. 25.00 (*0-306-70458-7*) Da Capo.

— Scout & Ranger: Being the Personal Adventures of James Pike of the Texas Rangers in 1859-60. (American Biography Ser.). 164p. 1991. reprint ed. lib. bdg. 59.00 (*0-7812-8314-0*) Rprt Serv.

Pike, James A. Beyond the Law: The Religious & Ethical Meaning of the Lawyer's Vocation. LC 73-10754. 102p. 1973. reprint ed. lib. bdg. 35.00 (*0-8371-7021-4*, PIBL, Greenwood Pr) Greenwood.

Pike, Jeff. The Death of Rock & Roll: Untimely Demises, Morbid Preoccupations, & Forecasts of Doom in Rock Music. 250p. (Orig.). 1993. pap. 14.95 (*0-571-19808-2*) Faber & Faber.

Pike, Jeffrey A. Automotive Safety, Injury, Testing, & Regulation. 184p. 1996. 59.00 (*1-56091-873-X*, R-171) Soc Auto Engineers.

***Pike, Jennifer.** A Safe Place: A Journal for Women with Breast Cancer. rev. ed. LC 98-32412. 216p. 1999. reprint ed. spiral bd. 22.95 (*0-8118-2267-2*) Chronicle Bks.

Pike, John. John Pike Paints Watercolors. 2nd ed. (Illus.). 160p. 1997. reprint ed. spiral bd. 29.95 (*0-9661553-0-0*) J Pike Art.

Pike, John & Barnes, Richard. TQM in Action: A Practical Approach to Continuous Performance Improvement. LC 93-34332. 1993. write for info. (*0-412-48790-X*) Chapman & Hall.

Pike, John E. & Morton, Douglas R., Jr., eds. Chemistry of the Prostaglandins & Leukotrienes. LC 84-42772. (Advances in Prostaglandin, Thromboxane & Leukotriene Research Ser.: No. 14). (Illus.). 456p. 1985. reprint ed. pap. 141.40 (*0-7837-9636-6*, 206038900005) Bks Demand.

Pike, Jonathan E. From Aristotle to Marx: Aristotelianism in Marxist Social Ontology. LC 98-74935. (Avebury Series in Philosophy). 204p. 1999. text 65.95 (*1-84014-309-6*, Pub. by Ashgate Pub) Ashgate Pub Co.

Pike, Joseph B. Classical Studies & Sketches. LC 67-23259. (Essay Index Reprint Ser.). 1977. 16.95 (*0-8369-0790-6*) Ayer.

Pike, Kathy. Books Don't Have to Be Flat! 96p. (J). 1998. pap. text 12.95 (*0-590-12049-2*) Scholastic Inc.

***Pike, Kathy, et al.** Teaching Kids to Care & Cooperate. (Illus.). 96p. (J). 2000. pap. 11.95 (*0-439-09849-1*) Scholastic Inc.

Pike, Kenneth & Pike, Evelyn. Text & Tagmeme. 144p. 1983. text 73.25 (*0-89391-210-7*) Ablx Pub.

Pike, Kenneth L. Conceptos Linguisticos: Una Introduccion a la Tagmemica. Hemingway, Thomas & Langan, Katherine, trs. LC 94-65901. (SPA.). 190p. 1996. pap. 17.50 (*0-88312-710-5*) S I L Intl.

— The Intonation of American English. 1. LC 78-27696. (University of Michigan Publications, Linguistics: No. 1). (Illus.). 203p. 1979. reprint ed. lib. bdg. 35.00 (*0-313-20910-3*, PIIA, Greenwood Pr) Greenwood.

— Language in Relation to a Unified Theory of the Structure of Human Behavior. (Janua Linguarum, Ser. Major: No. 24). 1967. text 118.50 (*90-279-1869-4*) Mouton.

— Linguistic Concepts: An Introduction to Tagmemics. LC 81-19814. (Illus.). 162p. 1982. reprint ed. pap. 50.30 (*0-7837-6889-3*, 204671900003) Bks Demand.

— Phonetics: A Critical Analysis of Phonetic Theory & a Technic for the Practical Description of Sounds. 192p. 1943. pap. text 19.95 (*0-472-08733-9*, 08733) U of Mich Pr.

— Tagmemics, Discourse & Verbal Art. LC 81-9541. (Michigan Studies in the Humanities: No. 3). (C). 1981. pap. 6.00 (*0-936534-02-8*) Mich Studies Human.

— Talk, Thought, & Thing: The Emic Road Toward Conscious Knowledge. LC 92-82114. xii, 85p. 1993. pap. 5.00 (*0-88312-610-9*) S I L Intl.

— With Heart & Mind: A Personal Synthesis of Scholarship & Devotion. LC 96-15101. 1996. pap. write for info. (*1-887493-06-9*) Adult Lrng Systs.

Pike, Kenneth L. & Pike, Stephen B. Songs of Fun & Faith by "Fish & Chip" LC 79-115755. (Edward Sapir Monographs in Language, Culture & Cognition: No. 1). (Illus.). viii, 48p. (Orig.). 1977. pap. 10.00 (*0-933104-00-6*) Jupiter Pr.

Pike, Kenneth L., et al. The Mystery of Culture Contacts, Historical Reconstruction & Text Analysis: An Emic Approach. Jankowsky, Kurt R., ed. LC 95-14739. 120p. 1995. 29.95 (*0-87840-295-0*) Georgetown U Pr.

Pike, Kenneth L., jt. ed. see Brend, Ruth M.

Pike, Kermit J. A Guide to the Manuscripts & Archives of the Western Reserve Historical Society. 425p. 1972. 20.00 (*0-911704-08-6*) Western Res.

— A Guide to the Shaker Manuscripts in the Library of the Western Reserve Historical Society, with Inventory of Its Shaker Photographs. 159p. 1974. pap. 10.00 (*0-911704-10-8*) Western Res.

Pike, Kermit J., compiled by. A Guide to the Major Manuscript Collections Accessioned & Processed by the Library of the Western Reserve Historical Society since 1970. 91p. 1987. pap. 9.95 (*0-911704-33-7*) Western Res.

Pike, Larry. Killer Instinct. 480p. 1993. mass mkt. 4.50 (*1-55817-749-3*, Pinncle Kensgtn) Kensgtn Pub Corp.

Pike, Lawrence. Pierced by Sound: Stories, Sketches & Poems. 2nd rev. ed. 83p. 1994. pap. 9.95 (*1-56439-042-X*) Ridgeway.

Pike, Linda J., ed. Administrative Science Quarterly: Cumulative Index, 1956-1985, Vols. 1-30. LC 88-9295. 330p. 1988. 143.50 (*0-89232-731-6*) Jai Pr.

Pike, Lionel. Beethoven, Sibelius & "The Profound Logic" Studies in Symphonic Analysis. (Illus.). 240p. (C). 1978. text 56.00 (*0-485-11178-0*, Pub. by Athlone Pr) Humanities.

— Hexachords in Late-Renaissance Music. LC 97-20327. (Illus.). 280p. Date not set. text 86.95 (*1-85928-455-8*, Pub. by Scolar Pr) Ashgate Pub Co.

Pike, Louise. Southern Echoes. LC 72-1519. (Black Heritage Library Collection). 1977. reprint ed. 15.95 (*0-8369-9046-3*) Ayer.

Pike, Luke O. A History of Crime in England, 2 vols., Set. Reams, Bernard D., ed. LC 10-19490. (Historical Reprints in Jurisprudence Ser.). 1983. reprint ed. lib. bdg. 110.00 (*0-89941-256-4*, 303170) W S Hein.

— History of Crime in England, Illustrating the Changes of the Laws in the Progress of Civilization, 2 Vols, Set. LC 68-55779. (Criminology, Law Enforcement, & Social Problems Ser.: No. 19). 1968. 50.00 (*0-87585-019-7*) Patterson Smith.

Pike, Luke O., jt. ed. see Horwood, Alfred J.

Pike, Maggie, et al. Parent-Child Retreats: Spiritual Experiences for Children Ages 3-6 & Their Parents. Coffey, Kathy & DeVries, Dirk, eds. LC 97-217782. (Illus.). 224p. 1997. pap. 14.95 (*1-889108-16-2*) Liv Good News.

Pike, Malcolm C., et al, eds. Hormones & Breast Cancer. LC 80-28015. (Banbury Report: No. 8). 503p. reprint ed. pap. 156.00 (*0-7837-1999-X*, 204227300002) Bks Demand.

Pike, Margaret M. & Wheeler, Sara R. Goodbye My Child: A Handbook for Parents Whose Child Dies. (Illus.). 64p. (Orig.). 1992. pap. 5.95 (*1-56123-052-9*, GMCC) Centering Corp.

Pike, Mary A. Special Edition Using the Internet with Windows 95. LC 95-72572. (Illus.). 1300p. (Orig.). 1996. 49.99 (*0-7897-0646-6*) Que.

Pike, Mary A., et al. Special Edition Using the Internet. 3rd ed. LC 96-69965. 1187p. 1996. 49.99 (*0-7897-0846-9*) Que.

Pike, Mary H. Ida May: A Story of Things Actual & Possible, by Mary Langdon. LC 72-6534. (Black Heritage Library Collection). 1977. reprint ed. 39.95 (*0-8369-9171-0*) Ayer.

Pike-Nase, Christal A., jt. auth. see Hollings, Robert L.

Pike, Nelson. Mystic Union: An Essay in the Phenomenology of Mysticism. LC 91-55553. (Cornell Studies in the Philosophy of Religion). (Illus.). 240p. 1992. text 39.95 (*0-8014-2684-7*) Cornell U Pr.

— Mystic Union: An Essay in the Phenomonology of Mysticism. (Cornell Studies in the Philosophy of Religion). (Illus.). 240p. 1994. pap. text 15.95 (*0-8014-9969-0*) Cornell U Pr.

Pike, Nicholas. Sub-Tropical Rambles in the Land of the Aphanapteryx: Personal Experiences, Adventures & Wanderings in & Around the Island of Mauritus. LC 72-4081. (Black Heritage Library Collection). 1977. reprint ed. 44.95 (*0-8369-9103-6*) Ayer.

Pike, Norman. The Peach Tree. (Illus.). 36p. (J). (ps up). 1984. 12.95 (*0-88045-014-2*) Stemmer Hse.

Pike, P. G. BEMS Performance Testing. 117p. (C). 1994. pap. 100.00 (*0-86022-359-0*, Pub. by Build Servs Info Assn) St Mut.

***Pike, P. G.** Guidance & the Standard Specification for Electronic Security Systems. 1998. pap. 100.00 (*0-86022-501-1*, Pub. by Build Servs Info Assn) St Mut.

Pike, P. G. Improved Fresh Air Control. (C). 1994. pap. 60.00 (*0-86022-364-7*, Pub. by Build Servs Info Assn) St Mut.

Pike, P. G. Weather Data. 1994. pap. 240.00 (*0-86022-405-8*, Pub. by Build Servs Info Assn) St Mut.

Pike, P. G. & Pennycook, K. A. Commissioning of BEMS Code of Practice. 86p. 1992. pap. 80.00 (*0-86022-275-6*, Pub. by Build Servs Info Assn) St Mut.

— Installation, Commissioning & Maintenance of Fire & Security Systems Pt. 2: Fire Detection Systems. (C). 1992. pap. 260.00 (*0-86022-311-6*, Pub. by Build Servs Info Assn) St Mut.

— Installation, Commissioning & Maintenance of Fire & Security Systems Pt. 3: Security Detection Systems. (C). 1992. 160.00 (*0-7855-2667-6*, Pub. by Build Servs Info Assn) St Mut.

— Installation, Commissioning & Maintenance of Fire & Security Systems Pt. 3: Security Detection Systems. 1992. pap. 260.00 (*0-86022-312-4*, Pub. by Build Servs Info Assn) St Mut.

Pike, P. G., jt. auth. see BSRIA Staff.

Pike, Phyllis, jt. auth. see Pike, Geoff.

Pike, R. William. Facing Substance Abuse: Discussion-Starting Skits for Teenagers. LC 96-19835. (Acting It Out Ser.). 192p. (Orig.). 1996. pap. text 19.95 (*0-89390-374-4*) Resource Pubns.

— Facing Violence: Discussion-Starting Skits for Teenagers. LC 95-4932. 192p. (J). 1995. pap. 19.95 (*0-89390-344-2*) Resource Pubns.

— Stop, Look, Listen Up! And Other Dramas for Confronting Social Issues in Elementary Schools. LC 93-1816. 128p. (Orig.). (C). 1993. pap., teacher ed. 14.95 (*0-89390-267-5*) Resource Pubns.

Pike, Raymond F., jt. auth. see Fung, Rosaline L.

Pike, Richard. Corporate Finance & Investment: Decisions & Strategies. 3rd ed. LC 98-50422. 1998. 55.01 (*0-13-081270-6*) P-H.

Pike, Richard J., et al, eds. Advances in Geomorphometry: Proceedings of the Walter F. Wood Memorial Symposium, 3rd International Conference on Geomorphology, McMaster University, Hamilton, Ontario, Canada, August 23-28, 1993. (Zeitschrift fuer Geomorphologie - Annals of Geomorphology Ser.: Supplementband 101). (Illus.). vi, 238p. 1995. pap. 82.00 (*3-443-21101-1*, Pub. by Gebruder Borntraeger) Balogh.

Pike, Rob, jt. auth. see Kernighan, Brian W.

Pike, Robert. Creative Training Techniques Handbook. 175p. 1989. 45.50 (*0-943210-06-2*) Lakewood Pubns.

— Spiked Boots: Sketches of the North Country. LC 99-38141. 288p. 1999. pap. 14.95 (*0-88150-436-X*, Pub. by Countryman) Norton.

Pike, Robert, jt. auth. see Kernighan, Brian W.

***Pike, Robert E.** Tall Trees, Tough Men. 2000. 25.50 (*0-8446-7131-2*) Peter Smith.

Pike, Robert W. Checker Power: A Game of Problem Solving. LC 97-7136. (J). 1997. pap. 6.95 (*1-57091-153-3*) Charlesbridge Pub.

Pike, Robert W. Checker Problem Solving: Teacher Guide. (Illus.). 1997. pap., teacher ed. 12.95 (*1-57091-156-8*) Charlesbridge Pub.

Pike, Robert W. Creating Training Techniques Handbook: Tips, Tactics & How-To's from Delivering Effective Training. 2nd ed. (Illus.). 197p. 1994. 49.95 (*0-943210-33-X*) Lakewood Pubns.

***Pike, Robert W.** 101 Checker Puzzles. LC 00-28503. (Illus.). 2000. 7.95 (*0-8069-6080-9*) Sterling.

Pike, Robert W. Play Winning Checkers Official American Mensa Game Book. LC 98-48172. 1999. pap. text 7.95 (*0-8069-3794-7*) Sterling.

— Winning Checkers for Kids of All Ages. (Illus.). 64p. (Orig.). (J). (gr. 3-8). 1993. pap. 15.00 incl. VHS (*0-9635300-0-3*) C&M Pub MA.

Pike, Robert W. & Arch, Dave. Dealing with Difficult Participants: 127 Practical Strategies for Minimizing Resistance & Maximizing Results in Your Presentations. LC 97-21160. 1997. 24.95 (*0-7879-1116-X*) Jossey-Bass.

***Pike, Robert W. & Solem, Lynn.** 50 Creative Training Openers & Energizers: Innovative Ways to Start Your Training with a Bang! LC 99-54008. 2000. 34.95 (*0-7879-5303-2*) Jossey-Bass.

Pike, Roberta. Habitat Conservation Plans, 1984-1994. LC 95-41169. (CPL Bibliographies Ser.: Vol. 327). 90p. 1995. 10.00 (*0-86602-327-5*, Sage Prdcls Pr) Sage.

Pike, Royston. The Encyclopaedia of Religion & Religions Vol. II: Contains Letters J-Z. 222p. 1990. pap. text 27.00 (*0-916157-77-6*) African Islam Miss Pubns.

— The Encyclopaedia of Religion & Religions, Vol. I: Contains Letters A-J. 222p. 1990. pap. text 27.00 (*0-916157-76-8*) African Islam Miss Pubns.

— Round the Year with the World's Religions. (Illus.). 208p. 1993. reprint ed. lib. bdg. 40.00 (*1-55888-996-5*) Omnigraphics Inc.

Pike, Royston E., ed. Human Documents of the Industrial Revolution in Britain. 368p. 1966. pap. text 15.95 (*0-04-942060-7*) Routledge.

Pike, Ruth. Penal Servitude in Early Modern Spain. LC 82-70551. 223p. 1983. reprint ed. pap. 69.20 (*0-7837-9793-1*, 206052200005) Bks Demand.

***Pike, Sarah M.** Earthly Bodies, Magical Selves: Contemporary Pagans & the Search for Community. (Illus.). 315p. 2001. 50.00 (*0-520-22030-7*); pap. 19.95 (*0-520-22086-2*) U CA Pr.

Pike, Stephen B., jt. auth. see Pike, Kenneth L.

***Pike, Tom.** Rethink, Retool, Results. 237p. 1999. pap. text 20.20 (*0-536-02239-9*) Pearson Custom.

— Y2K: Coming Crisis - A Personal Survival Manual. 60p. 1999. pap. 7.45 (*0-536-02238-0*) Pearson Custom.

Pike, V. W., jt. ed. see Stocklin, G.

Pike, Wilbur L. Leading the Transition: Management's Role in Creating a Team-Based Culture. LC 94-44928. 116p. 1995. 28.00 (*0-527-76247-4*) Productivity Inc.

***Pike, William H.** Why Stocks Go up & down. 3rd ed. LC 98-92062. viii, 328p. 1999. write for info. (*0-9666775-0-1*) B Pike Bks.

Pike, Zebulon M. The Expeditions of Zebulon Montgomery Pike, 1. 1088p. 1987. reprint ed. pap. 12.95 (*0-486-25254-X*) Dover.

— The Expeditions of Zebulon Montgomery Pike, 2. 1088p. 1987. reprint ed. pap. 12.95 (*0-486-25255-8*) Dover.

— Zebulon Pike's Arkansas Journal. Hart, Stephen H. & Hulbert, Archer B., eds. LC 72-138172. (Illus.). 200p. 1972. reprint ed. lib. bdg. 38.50 (*0-8371-5629-7*, PIAJ, Greenwood Pr) Greenwood.

Pikebaky. Word Strands 1, No. 1. (College ESL Ser.). 140p. (J). 1996. mass mkt. 20.95 (*0-8384-6068-2*) Heinle & Heinle.

— Word Strands 2, No. 2. (College ESL Ser.). 140p. (J). 1996. pap. 20.95 (*0-8384-6074-7*) Heinle & Heinle.

Pikelner, S. B., jt. auth. see Kaplan, Samuil A.

Piker, Sasha, ed. see Wien, Zentrum.

Piker, Steven. A Peasant Community in Changing Thailand. (Anthropological Research Papers: No. 30). (Illus.). ix, 157p. 1983. pap. 15.00 (*0-685-73906-6*) AZ Univ ARP.

Pikes, Noah. Dark Voices: The Genesis of the Roy Hart Theatre. (Africa Ser.: Vol. 1). 155p. 2000. pap. 19.00 (*1-882670-19-1*, Pub. by Spring Jrnl) Continuum.

Pikin, S. A. Structural Transformations in Liquid Crystals. Alferieff, Michael, tr. from RUS. xii, 423p. 1991. text 450.00 (*2-88124-296-0*) Gordon & Breach.

Pikin, S. A., et al. Polarization Properties of Liquid Crystals, Vol. 11. (Soviet Scientific Reviews Ser.: Vol. 11, Pt. 3). ii, 100p. 1989. pap. text 107.00 (*3-7186-4904-7*) Gordon & Breach.

Pikitch, E. K., et al, eds. Global Trends: Fisheries Management. LC 97-72126. (Symposium Ser.: Vol. 20). 352p. 1997. pap. text 65.00 (*1-888569-03-4*, 540.20P) Am Fisheries Soc.

Pikl, Barbara H., ed. see Massachusetts General Hospital Department of Nursi.

Pikoff, Howard B. Treatment Effectiveness Handbook: A Reference Guide to the Key Research Reviews in Mental Health & Substance Abuse. LC 96-84425. 192p. 1996. 65.00 (*0-9640981-0-5*) Data for Decisions.

Pikouch, Natalia. Diablos.Tr. of Devils. (SPA., Illus.). 82p. (J). (gr. 4-6). 1994. 14.99 (*958-07-0315-9*, Pub. by Santillana) T R Bks.

Pikoulakis, Emmanuel. International Macroeconomics. LC 95-5716. 1995. pap. 24.95 (*0-312-12659-X*) St Martin.

Pikoulis, John. Alun Lewis: A Life. rev. ed. (Illus.). 290p. 1991. pap. 24.00 (*1-85411-018-7*, Pub. by Seren Bks) Dufour.

Pikoulis, John, jt. auth. see Roberts, Lynette.

Pikul, David T. & Plante, Ellen M. Collectible Enameled Ware: American & European. LC 97-80466. (Illus.). 160p. 1998. 34.95 (*0-7643-0456-9*) Schiffer.

Pikul, David T., jt. auth. see Plante, Ellen M.

Pikulik, Ivan I. & Leger, Francois, eds. Secherie d'Une Machine a Papier - Etude et Depannage. Bonin, P. & Lavoie, P., trs. LC 98-1829. (ENG & FRE., Illus.). 170p. 1997. pap. 22.44 (*1-896742-20-3*) Pulp & Paper.

Pikunas, Justin. Manual for the Pikunas Graphoscopic Scale. 3rd ed. LC 81-43841. (Illus.). 70p. (Orig.). 1982. 16.50 (*0-8191-2351-X*) U Pr of Amer.

Pikus, Grigori I., jt. auth. see Ivchenko, E. L.

Pikus, P. E. & Ivchenko, E. L. Superlattices & Other Heterostructures: Symmetry & Optical Phenomena. LC 94-3452. (Springer Series in Solid-State Sciences: Vol. 110). 1995. 107.95 (*0-387-58197-9*) Spr-Verlag.

Pil, Teresita V. Philippine Folk Fiction & Tales. 1977. pap. 7.50 (*971-10-0300-7*, Pub. by New Day Pub) Cellar.

Pila of Hawaii. Secrets & Mysteries of Hawaii. 244p. 1995. pap. 10.95 (*1-55874-362-6*, 3626) Health Comm.

Pilachowski, Mel. Purchasing Performance Measurements: A Roadmap for Excellence. LC 95-49424. (Illus.). 100p. (Orig.). 1996. pap. text 14.95 (*0-945456-21-2*) PT Pubns.

Pilachowski, Mel, jt. auth. see Grieco, Peter L., Jr.

Piland, Neill F. Physician Profiling: A Source Book for Health Care Administrators. LC 99-11319. (Jossey-Bass Health Ser.). 1999. 42.95 (*0-7879-4601-X*) Jossey-Bass.

***Piland, Neill F. & Glass, Kathryn P., eds.** Chart of Accounts for Health Care Organizations. 347p. 1999. pap. 74.00 incl. disk (*1-56829-023-3*) Med Group Mgmt.

Piland, Sherry. Women Artists: An Historical, Contemporary, & Feminist Bibliography. 2nd ed. LC 93-27248. (Illus.). 497p. 1994. 65.00 (*0-8108-2559-7*) Scarecrow.

Pilapil & Studva. Programmed Instruction: Radiation Therapy. (gr. 13). 1980. 11.00 (*0-89352-099-3*) Mosby Inc.

Pilapil, Vicente R. Alfonso XIII. LC 78-77035. (Twayne's Rulers & Statesmen of the World Ser.). 242p. (C). 1969. lib. bdg. 20.95 (*0-8290-1749-6*) Irvington.

Pilar Arguelles, Maria Del, see Del Pilar Arguelles, Maria.

Pilar, Arlene. Reading Books for Social Studies: A Study Guide. Friedland, Joyce & Kessler, Rikki, eds. (Primary Ser.). (J). (gr. 1-3). 1991. pap. text 20.95 (*0-88122-692-0*) Lrn Links.

Pilar, Jacquelin. Turning Point: Ara F. Normart, Jr., Watercolorist Designer of the Inner Dome of the Great Rotunda, Church of the Holy Sepulcher, Jerusalem. Linxwiler, Julie, ed. 12p. 1998. pap. 7.50 (*0-932325-37-8*) Fresno Arts Mus.

Pilar, Jacquelin, ed. & pref. see Henderson, Maren.

Pilarczyk, Daniel E. Our Priests: Who They Are & What They Do. LC 81-85454. (Illus.). 48p. (Orig.). (YA). 1995. pap. 1.50 (*0-87973-661-5*, 661) Our Sunday Visitor.

Pilarczyk, Daniel E. Believing Catholic. rev. ed. Orig. Title: 'We Believe'. 96p. 1999. pap. text 6.95 (*0-86716-386-0*, B3860) St Anthony Mess Pr.

— Bringing Forth Justice: Basics for Just Christians. 73p. 1999. pap. 5.95 (*0-86716-382-8*) St Anthony Mess Pr.

— Catholic Guide to Confession. 32p. 1990. pap. text 1.50 (*0-87973-166-4*) Our Sunday Visitor.

P

— Lenten Lunches: Reflections on the Weekday Readings for Lent & Easter Week. LC 95-222975. 112p. 1995. pap. 7.95 (*0-86716-243-0*) St Anthony Mess Pr.
— The Parish: Where God's People Live. LC 91-42032. 88p. 1992. pap. 4.95 (*0-8091-3299-0*) Paulist Pr.
— Practicing Catholic. 88p. 1998. pap. text 6.95 (*0-86716-361-5*) St Anthony Mess Pr.
— Thinking Catholic. LC 98-120184. 104p. 1997. pap. text 6.95 (*0-86716-327-5*) St Anthony Mess Pr.
— Twelve Tough Issues: What the Church Teaches & Why. 83p. (Orig.). 1989. pap. 4.95 (*0-86716-104-3*) St Anthony Mess Pr.
Pilarczyk, K. W., ed. Coastal Protection: Proceedings of a Short Course, Delft University of Technology, 30 June-1 July 1990. (Illus.). 550p. (C). 1990. text 136.00 (*90-6191-127-3*, Pub. by A A Balkema) Ashgate Pub Co.
— Dikes & Revetments: Design, Maintenance & Safety Assessment. (Illus.). 582p. (C). 1998. text 132.00 (*90-5410-455-4*) Ashgate Pub Co.
Pilarczyk, K. W. & Zeidler, Ryszard B. Offshore Breakwaters & Shore Evolution Control. LC 99-227568. (Illus.). 570p. (C). 1996. text 181.00 (*90-5410-627-1*, Pub. by A A Balkema) Ashgate Pub Co.
***Pilarczyk, Krystian W.** Geosynthetics & Geosystems in Hydraulic & Coastal Engineering. (Illus.). 936p. (C). 1999. text 155.00 (*90-5809-302-6*, Pub. by A A Balkema) Ashgate Pub Co.
Pilardeau, P. Dictionnaire Encyclopedie Pediatric en Medecine du Sport. (FRE.). 1998. 110.00 (*0-320-00392-2*) Fr & Eur.
Pilardi, Jo-Ann. Simone de Beauvoir Writing the Self: Philosophy Becomes Autobiography. LC 97-44836. 152p. 1999. pap. 15.95 (*0-275-96334-9*, Praeger Pubs) Greenwood.
— Simone de Beauvoir Writing the Self: Philosophy Becomes Autobiography, 60. LC 97-44836. (Contributions in Philosophy Ser.: Vol. 60). 152p. 1999. 49.95 (*0-313-30253-7*, Greenwood Pr) Greenwood.
Pilaroscia, Jill. Colors for Living: Kitchens. Ragan, Sandra, ed. 128p. 1995. 24.99 (*1-56496-102-8*) Rockport Pubs.
— Colors for Living: Kitchens. (Colors for Living Ser.). (Illus.). 128p. 1998. pap. 19.99 (*1-56496-551-1*) Rockport Pubs.
***Pilarski, Mark.** Deal Me In. 1999. pap. 14.95 (*0-9653214-2-8*) Winners Pubng.
Pilarski, Michael, ed. Restoration Forestry: An International Guide to Sustainable Forestry Practices. (Illus.). 528p. (Orig.). (C). 1994. pap. 26.95 (*1-882308-51-4*) Kivaki Pr.
Pilarski, Slawomir & Kameda, Tiko. A Probabilistic Analysis of Test-Response Compaction. LC 94-27227. 112p. 1995. pap. 25.00 (*0-8186-6532-7*, BP06532) IEEE Comp Soc.
Pilat, Bianca, jt. auth. see Anselmino, Luciano.
Pilat, Dirk. The Economics of Rapid Growth: The Experience of Japan & Korea. LC 94-12017. 352p. 1994. 95.00 (*1-85278-762-7*) E Elgar.
Pilat, Joseph F., ed. The Nonproliferation Predicament. 150p. (C). 1985. 32.95 (*0-88738-047-6*) Transaction Pubs.
Pilat, Mary. Adolescent Parenthood & Education: Exploring Alternative Programs. Michigan State University Staff, ed. LC 96-35890. (MSU Series on Children, Youth & Families: Vol. 2). (Illus.). 264p. 1997. text 50.00 (*0-8153-1884-7*, SS1004) Garland.
Pilates, Joseph H. Your Health. Robbins, Judd, ed. LC 98-223207. 63p. 1998. pap. 19.95 (*0-9614937-8-X*) Present Dynam.
***Pilates, Joseph H. & Miller, John.** The Complete Writings of Joseph H. Pilates: "Return to Life Through Contrology" & " Your Health" - The Authorized Edition. Gallagher, Sean P., ed. & compiled by by. (Illus.). 128p. 2000. 19.95 (*1-891696-15-7*, Pub. by BainBridgeBooks) Trans-Atl Phila.
***Pilates, Joseph H. & Miller, William J.** A Pilates' Primer: The Millennium Edition: Return to Life Through Contrology & Your Health. (Illus.). 2000. reprint ed. 15.95 (*1-928564-00-3*) Present Dynam.
Pilates, Joseph H. & Miller, William J. Pilates' Return to Life Through Contrology. Robbins, Judd, ed. Orig. Title: Return to Life Through Contrology. 93p. 1998. pap. 29.95 (*0-9614937-9-8*) Present Dynam.
***Pilato, Denise E.** The Retrieval of a Legacy: Nineteenth-century American Women Inventors. LC 99-55017. 232p. 2000. 69.95 (*0-275-96600-3*, Praeger Pubs) Greenwood.
***Pilato, Grace.** Cooking with Grace. 2000. text 29.95 (*0-312-26138-1*) St Martin.
Pilato, Herbie J. Bewitched Forever: The Immortal Companion to Television's Most Magical Supernatural Situation Comedy. LC 96-51199. Orig. Title: Bewitched. (Illus.). 312p. 1996. pap. 15.99 (*1-56530-225-7*) Summit TX.
— Kung Fu Book of Caine. 192p. 1993. pap. 16.95 (*0-8048-1826-6*) Tuttle Pubng.
— The Kung Fu Book of Wisdom: Sage Advice from the Original Television Series. (Illus.). 160p. 1995. 14.95 (*0-8048-3044-4*) Tuttle Pubng.
Pilato, Louis A. & Michno, Michael J. Advanced Composite Materials. LC 94-10694. 1994. write for info. (*3-540-57563-4*) Spr-Verlag.
— Advanced Composite Materials. LC 94-10694. 1994. 111.95 (*0-387-57563-4*) Spr-Verlag.
Pilato, Louis A., jt. auth. see Knop, A.
Pilato, Louis A., jt. ed. see Christiansen, Alfred W.
Pilavakis, Andreas J. UNIX Workshop. 1989. 32.00 (*0-8493-7104-X*, QA76) CRC Pr.
Pilbeam. Mechanical Ventilation: Physiological & Clinical Applications. 3rd ed. LC 97-40495. (Illus.). 460p. (C). (gr. 13). 1998. pap. text 43.00 (*0-8151-2600-X*, 31083) Mosby Inc.
— Negotiating. 1992. pap. text. write for info. (*0-582-06443-0*, Pub. by Addison-Wesley) Longman.
Pilbeam, Cairo. McPherson's Respiratory Care Equipment. 6th ed. LC 98-55692. (Illus.). 787p. (gr. 13). 1999. text 55.00 (*0-8151-2148-2*, 30759) Mosby Inc.
Pilbeam, D. J., jt. ed. see Mengel, K.
Pilbeam, David, et al, eds. The Cambridge Encyclopedia of Human Evolution. (Illus.). 520p. (C). 1994. pap. text 39.95 (*0-521-46786-1*) Cambridge U Pr.
Pilbeam, David, ed. see Bar-Yosef, Ofer.
Pilbeam, John. Gymnocalycium: A Collector's Guide. (Illus.). 176p. (C). 1995. text 76.00 (*90-5410-192-X*, Pub. by A A Balkema) Ashgate Pub Co.
Pilbeam, Mavis. Japan. (Focus On Ser.). (Illus.). 32p. (J). (gr. 4-8). 1992. write for info. (*0-237-51661-6*) EVN1 UK.
— Japan under the Shoguns, 1185-1868. LC 98-29665. (Looking Back Ser.). 64p. (J). 1999. 25.69 (*0-8172-5434-X*); 25.69 (*0-8172-5431-5*) Raintree Steck-V.
***Pilbeam, Pamela M.** The Constitutional Monarchy in France, 1814-1848. LC 99-45367. (Seminar Studies In History). 140p. 1999. pap. 12.66 (*0-582-31210-8*) Longman.
Pilbeam, Pamela M. The Middle Classes in Europe, 1789-1914: France, Germany, Italy & Russia. LC 89-13220. 328p. (C). 1990. text 49.95 (*0-925065-29-3*); pap. text 25.95 (*0-925065-26-9*) Lyceum IL.
— Republicanism in Nineteenth-Century France, 1814-1871. LC 94-30651. (European Studies). 1995. text 55.00 (*0-312-12420-1*) St Martin.
Pilbrow, Giles. The Chock-a-Block Book. (Illus.). 32p. (J). 1995. (*0-19-279955-X*) OUP.
Pilbrow, Richard. Stage Lighting Design: The Art - The Craft - The Life. LC 92-26071. (Illus.). 528p. 1997. pap. text 34.95 (*0-89676-235-1*) QSMG Ltd.
***Pilcer, Sonia.** The Holocaust Kid: Stories. 192p. 2001. 22.95 (*0-89255-261-1*, Pub. by Persea Bks) Norton.
Pilch, Ernst, ed. see Sophocles.
Pilch, Herbert. Empirical Linguistics. 1978. pap. 6.95 (*3-7720-1090-3*) Adlers Foreign Bks.
Pilch, John. Healing in the New Testament: Insights from Medical & Mediterranean Anthropology. LC 99-33004. 1999. pap. 18.00 (*0-8006-3178-1*, Fortress Pr) Augsburg Fortress.
***Pilch, John J.** Choosing a Bible Translation. 24p. 2000. pap. 1.95 (*0-8146-2581-9*) Liturgical Pr.
Pilch, John J. The Cultural Dictionary of the Bible. LC 98-7101. (Illus.). 209p. 1999. pap. 17.95 (*0-8146-2527-4*) Liturgical Pr.
— Cultural World of Jesus: Sunday by Sunday, Cycle A: Matthew. 184p. (Orig.). 1995. pap. 11.95 (*0-8146-2286-0*, Liturg Pr Bks) Liturgical Pr.
— The Cultural World of Jesus: Sunday by Sunday, Cycle B: Mark. 184p. (Orig.). 1996. pap. 11.95 (*0-8146-2287-9*, Liturg Pr Bks) Liturgical Pr.
— The Cultural World of Jesus: Sunday by Sunday, Cycle C: Luke. 184p. (Orig.). 1997. pap. text 11.95 (*0-8146-2288-7*, Liturg Pr Bks) Liturgical Pr.
— Introducing the Cultural Context of the Old Testament. 1991. pap. 14.95 (*0-8091-3271-0*) Paulist Pr.
Pilch, John J. & Karris, Robert J. Galatians & Romans, No. 6. (Collegeville Bible Commentary - New Testament Ser.). 80p. (C). 1983. pap. 4.95 (*0-8146-1306-3*) Liturgical Pr.
Pilch, John J. & Malina, Bruce J. Handbook of Biblical Social Values. LC 98-11537. 224p. 1998. 19.95 (*1-56563-355-5*) Hendrickson MA.
Pilch, John J., jt. auth. see Malina, Bruce J.
***Pilch, M. M.** Assessment of the DCH Issue for Plants with Ice Condenser Containments. 392p. 2000. per. 36.00 (*0-16-059226-7*) USGPO.
— Resolution of the Direct Containment Heating Issue for Combustion Engineering Plants & Babcock & Wilcox Plants. 336p. 1998. per. 27.00 (*0-16-062976-4*) USGPO.
Pilch, Michael, jt. auth. see Reddin, Mike.
Pilchen, Ira, jt. ed. see Goldschmidt, Jona.
Pilcher. Title to Come. mass mkt. write for info. (*0-312-97312-8*) St Martin.
Pilcher, Dan. Learning How to Compete: Workforce Skills & State Development Policies. LC 95-623346. (Investing in People Ser.). 40p. 15.00 (*1-55516-349-1*, 3126) Natl Conf State Legis.
Pilcher, Donald M. Data Analysis for Helping Professions: A Practical Guide. LC 89-28109. (Sage Sourcebooks for the Human Services Ser.: Vol. 10). 259p. 1990. reprint ed. pap. 80.30 (*0-608-02984-X*, 205962400006) Bks Demand.
Pilcher, Donald M., ed. Data Analysis for the Helping Professions: A Practical Guide. (Sourcebooks for the Human Services Ser.: Vol. 10). 264p. (C). 1990. text 56.00 (*0-8039-3724-5*); pap. text 26.00 (*0-8039-3061-5*) Sage.
Pilcher, Edith. The Constables: First Family of the Adirondacks. LC 92-8393. (Illus.). xiv, 160p. 1992. 32.50 (*0-925168-05-X*); pap. 24.95 (*0-925168-04-1*) North Country.
— Up the Lake Road: The First Hundred Years of the Adirondack Mountain Reserve 1887-1987. (Illus.). 208p. 1987. 35.00 (*0-9618456-0-0*); pap. 17.50 (*0-9618456-1-9*) Adk Mtn Reserve.
Pilcher, J. E., jt. ed. see Fabjan, C. W.
Pilcher, Jane. Age & Generation in Modern Britain. (Oxford Modern Britain Ser.). (Illus.). 176p. 1995. text 42.00 (*0-19-827961-2*) OUP.
Pilcher, Jane. Age & Generation in Modern Britain. (Illus.). 176p. 1995. pap. text 19.00 (*0-19-827962-0*) OUP.
— Women in Contemporary Britain: An Introduction. LC 99-11392. 1999. write for info. (*0-415-18273-5*) Routledge.
Pilcher, Jane. Women in Contemporary Britain: An Introduction. LC 99-11392. 1999. pap. write for info. (*0-415-18274-3*) Routledge.
— Women of Their Time: Generation, Gender Issues & Feminism. LC 98-73398. (Cardiff Papers in Qualitative Research). 154p. 1998. text 61.95 (*1-84014-197-2*, Pub. by Ashgate Pub) Ashgate Pub Co.
Pilcher, Jane & Coffey, Amanda, eds. Gender & Qualitative Research. LC 96-84602. (Cardiff Papers in Qualitative Research). 174p. 1996. 72.95 (*1-85972-199-0*, Pub. by Avebry) Ashgate Pub Co.
Pilcher, Jane & Wagg, Stephen. Thatcher's Children? Politics, Childhood, & Society in the 1980s & 1990s. (World of Childhood & Adolescence Ser.). 240p. 1996. 89.95 (*0-7507-0461-6*, Falmer Pr); pap. 29.95 (*0-7507-0462-4*, Falmer Pr) Taylor & Francis.
***Pilcher, Jeffrey M.** Cantinflas & the Chaos of Mexican Modernity. 2000. 55.00 (*0-8420-2769-6*); pap. 19.95 (*0-8420-2771-8*) Scholarly Res Inc.
Pilcher, Jeffrey M. Que Vivan los Tamales! Food & the Making of Mexican Identity. LC 97-46508. (Dialogos Ser.). 243p. 1998. pap. 16.95 (*0-8263-1873-8*) U of NM Pr.
Pilcher, Jeremy, jt. auth. see Etherington-Smith, Meredith.
Pilcher, Jobeth. Pocket Guide to Neonatal EKG Interpretation. LC 97-26769. (Illus.). 53p. 1998. spiral bd. 17.95 (*1-887571-02-7*) NICU Ink.
Pilcher, Larry L. Hospital Philanthropy: The Impact of the Tax Reform Act of 1986, Government Regulations, & Healthcare Trends. LC 92-40119. (Non-profit Institutions in America Ser.). 168p. 1993. text 10.00 (*0-8153-0910-4*) Garland.
Pilcher, M. C. Campbell. 444p. 1991. reprint ed. pap. 68.50 (*0-8328-2044-X*); reprint ed. lib. bdg. 78.50 (*0-8328-2043-1*) Higginson Bk Co.
Pilcher, Paul, jt. auth. see Boffey, Barnes.
Pilcher, Richard B. Alchemists in Art & Literature. (Illus.). 54p. 1996. reprint ed. pap. 12.00 (*1-56459-598-6*) Kessinger Pub.
Pilcher, Robin. An Ocean Apart. LC 98-11664. 470p. 1998. text 24.95 (*0-312-19995-3*, Thomas Dunne) St Martin.
— An Ocean Apart: A Novel. LC 99-19828. 1999. 29.95 (*0-7862-1911-4*) Mac Lib Ref.
— An Ocean Apart: A Novel. 512p. 1999. pap. 6.99 (*0-312-97184-2*, St Martins Paperbacks) St Martin.
Pilcher, Rosamunde. Another View. 272p. 1989. mass mkt. 5.50 (*0-440-20251-5*) Dell.
— Another View. 1997. mass mkt. 5.99 (*0-312-96131-6*) St Martin.
— The Blue Bedroom. 1991. mass mkt. 5.99 (*0-312-92628-6*, Pub. by Tor Bks) St Martin.
— The Blue Bedroom & Other Stories. large type ed. LC 90-48877. 367p. 1991. reprint ed. 23.95 (*1-56054-094-X*) Thorndike Pr.
— The Carousel. 1991. mass mkt. 3.25 (*0-312-92629-4*) St Martin.
— The Carousel. large type ed. LC 91-31107. 233p. 1992. reprint ed. lib. bdg. 19.95 (*1-56054-148-2*) Thorndike Pr.
— Christmas with Rosamunde Pilcher. Bublitz, Siv, ed. LC 98-31054. 144p. 1999. text 25.00 (*0-312-19247-9*) St Martin.
— Coming Home. 752p. 1995. 35.00 (*0-7710-7011-X*) McCland & Stewart.
— Coming Home. LC 95-21656. 736p. 1995. 25.95 (*0-312-13451-7*) St Martin.
— Coming Home. 1995. mass mkt. 25.95 (*0-312-95848-X*) St Martin.
— Coming Home. 977p. 1996. mass mkt. 7.99 (*0-312-95812-9*) St Martin.
— Coming Home. large type ed. LC 95-30747. 1236p. 1995. 29.95 (*0-7862-0531-8*) Thorndike Pr.
— The Day of the Storm. 272p. 1989. mass mkt. 5.50 (*0-440-20253-1*) Dell.
— The Day of the Storm. 1997. mass mkt. 5.99 (*0-312-96130-8*) St Martin.
— The Empty House. 1996. mass mkt. 5.99 (*0-312-96127-8*) St Martin.
— The Empty House. large type ed. LC 92-12558. 248p. 1992. reprint ed. 21.95 (*1-56054-149-0*) Thorndike Pr.
— The End of Summer. 1997. mass mkt. 5.99 (*0-312-96128-6*) St Martin.
— The End of Summer. large type ed. 211p. 1991. reprint ed. lib. bdg. 19.95 (*1-56054-153-9*) Thorndike Pr.
— Flowers in the Rain: And Other Stories. 1992. mass mkt. 4.50 (*0-312-92774-6*) St Martin.
— Love Stories. 1996. mass mkt. 5.99 (*0-312-95756-4*, Pub. by Tor Bks) St Martin.
— A New Collection of Three Complete Novels. LC 96-27249. 624p. 1997. 13.99 (*0-517-18237-8*) Wings Bks.
— Rosamunde Pilcher, 3 vols., Set. 1991. pap. 19.97 (*0-312-92620-0*) St Martin.
— Rosamunde Pilcher, 3 vols., Set. 1992. pap. 20.97 (*0-312-92893-9*) St Martin.
— September. 1991. mass mkt. 7.99 (*0-312-92480-1*) St Martin.
— September. large type ed. LC 90-11097. 874p. 1991. pap. 17.95 (*1-56054-089-3*) Thorndike Pr.
— The Shell Seekers. large type ed. LC 88-14756. 909p. 1991. reprint ed. lib. bdg. 15.95 (*0-89621-166-5*) Thorndike Pr.
— The Shell Seekers. 592p. 1989. reprint ed. mass mkt. 7.50 (*0-440-20204-3*) Dell.
— The Shell Seekers. 10th ed. LC 97-18535. 560p. 1997. 25.00 (*0-312-17023-8*, Thomas Dunne) St Martin.
— The Shell Seekers, Vol. 1. annot. ed. 582p. 1997. mass mkt. 7.99 (*0-312-96132-4*) St Martin.
— Sleeping Tiger. 288p. 1989. mass mkt. 5.50 (*0-440-20247-7*) Dell.
— Sleeping Tiger. 3rd ed. 288p. 1996. mass mkt. 5.99 (*0-312-96125-1*) St Martin.
— Snow in April. 256p. 1989. mass mkt. 5.50 (*0-440-20248-5*) Dell.
— Three Complete Novels. 736p. 1995. 13.99 (*0-517-12190-5*) Wings Bks.
— Three Complete Novels: The Empty House, The Day of the Storm, Under Gemini. LC 99-18818. 1999. 10.99 (*0-517-20583-1*) Random Hse Value.
— Under Gemini. 1996. mass mkt. 5.99 (*0-312-96124-3*) St Martin.
— Voices in Summer. 1990. mass mkt. 5.99 (*0-312-92527-1*) St Martin.
— Voices in Summer. large type ed. LC 92-6493. 396p. 1992. reprint ed. lib. bdg. 19.95 (*1-56054-150-4*) Thorndike Pr.
— Wild Mountain Thyme. 1996. mass mkt. 5.99 (*0-312-96123-5*) St Martin.
— Wild Mountain Thyme. 304p. 1989. reprint ed. mass mkt. 5.50 (*0-440-20250-7*) Dell.
Pilcher, Rosamunde. Winter Solstice. 464p. 2000. 27.95 (*0-312-24426-6*, Thomas Dunne) St Martin.
***Pilcher, Rosamunde.** Winter Solstice. LC 00-37437. 2000. write for info. (*0-7862-2646-3*) Thorndike Pr.
Pilcher, Roy. Principles of Construction Management. 3rd ed. (International Series in Civil Engineering). (C). 1992. text 59.74 (*0-07-707236-7*) McGraw.
Pilcher, V. E. Early Science & the First Century of Physics at Union College, 1795-1895. LC 94-92379. (Illus.). 114p. 1994. 25.00 (*0-9643133-0-8*) V E Pilcher.
Pilcher, Vinn, tr. see Petursson, Hallgrim.
Pilcher, William W. Urban Anthropology: A Research Bibliography, Nos. 944-945. 1975. 10.50 (*0-686-20380-1*, Sage Prdcls Pr) Sage.
Pilchick, Terry. Jai Bhim! Dispatches from a Peaceful Revolution. 256p. 1996. pap. 12.95 (*0-938077-15-5*) Parallax Pr.
Pilcox Cons Svc Staff & Bach, C. Ions for Breathing: Control Air Electrical Climate for Health. LC 67-27480. 1967. 52.00 (*0-08-012463-1*, Pub. by Pergamon Repr) Franklin.
Pilditch. Communication by Design: A Study in Corporate Identity. 1970. 19.50 (*0-07-094214-5*) McGraw.
Pilditch, Jan, ed. The Critical Response to Katherine Mansfield, 21. LC 95-23548. (Critical Responses in Arts & Letters Ser.: No. 21). 288p. 1996. lib. bdg. 59.95 (*0-313-29064-4*, Greenwood Pr) Greenwood.
***Pile.** History of Interior Design. 400p. 2000. write for info. (*0-471-35666-2*) Wiley.
Pile, Frederick D. Better Than Riches. 116p. (C). 1989. text 65.00 (*1-85821-005-4*, Pub. by Pentland Pr) St Mut.
Pile, John. Color in Interior Design. (Illus.). 320p. 1996. pap. text 49.95 (*0-07-050166-1*) McGraw.
— Color in Interior Design. LC 96-47590. (Illus.). 320p. 1997. 64.95 (*0-07-050165-3*) McGraw.
— Dictionary of Twentieth Century Design. (Illus.). 320p. 1990. 35.00 (*0-8160-1811-1*) Facts on File.
— Dictionary of Twentieth Century Design. LC 93-39780. (Illus.). 320p. 1994. reprint ed. pap. 18.95 (*0-306-80569-3*) Da Capo.
Pile, John. Perspective for Interior Designers. (Illus.). 160p. 1989. pap. 22.50 (*0-8230-4008-9*, Whitney Lib) Watsn-Guptill.
Pile, John F. Interior Design. 2nd ed. LC 94-6342. (Illus.). 584p. 1995. 65.00 (*0-8109-3463-9*, Pub. by Abrams) Time Warner.
— Interior Design. 2nd ed. (C). 1995. pap. text 72.00 (*0-13-149733-2*) P-H.
Pile, Kathryne E., jt. auth. see Johnson, David E.
Pile, Naomi. Art Experiences for Young Children. (Illus.). 112p. (C). 1991. reprint ed. pap. text 16.50 (*0-87411-444-6*) Copley Pub.
Pile, Robert. Country Club. 128p. 1998. pap. 13.00 (*0-8059-4513-X*) Dorrance.
Pile, Robert B. Top Entrepreneurs & Their Businesses. LC 92-38267. (Profiles Ser.). (Illus.). 160p. (YA). (gr. 5-12). 1999. lib. bdg. 18.95 (*1-881508-04-8*) Oliver Pr MN.
— Women Business Leaders. LC 94-46814. (Profiles Ser.). (Illus.). 160p. (YA). (gr. 5-12). 1995. lib. bdg. 18.95 (*1-881508-24-2*) Oliver Pr MN.
Pile, Shirley, jt. auth. see Hinton, Virginia.
Pile-Spellman, John, jt. auth. see Taveras, Juan M.
Pile, Stephen. The Private Farmer: Transformation & Ligitimation in Advanced Capitalist Agriculture. (Illus.). 218p. 1990. text 66.95 (*1-85521-003-7*, Pub. by Dartmth Pub) Ashgate Pub Co.
Pile, Steve. The Body & the City: Psychoanalysis, Space, & Subjectivity. LC 95-46814. (Illus.). 288p. (C). 1996. 85.00 (*0-415-06649-2*); pap. 27.99 (*0-415-14192-3*) Routledge.
***Pile, Steve.** Unruly Cities? Order/Disorder. (Understanding Cities Ser.). 368p. 2000. pap. 27.99 (*0-415-20074-1*) Routledge.
Pile, Steve, ed. Geographies of Resistance. LC 97-186948. (Illus.). 336p. (C). 1997. 85.00 (*0-415-15496-0*); pap. 25.99 (*0-415-15497-9*) Routledge.
Pile, Steve & Keith, Michael, eds. Place & the Politics of Identity. LC 93-9979. 240p. (C). 1993. pap. 25.99 (*0-415-09009-1*, A9827) Routledge.
***Pile, Steve & Thrift, N. J.** City A-Z: Urban Fragments. LC 99-53842. 352p. 2000. pap. write for info. (*0-415-20728-2*) Routledge.
Pile, Steve & Thrift, Nigel, eds. Mapping the Subject: Geographies of Cultural Transformation. LC 94-23747. (Illus.). 512p. (C). 1995. pap. 27.99 (*0-415-10226-X*) Routledge.
— Mapping the Subject: Geographies of Cultural Transformation. LC 94-23747. (Illus.). 512p. (C). (gr. 13). 1995. 90.00 (*0-415-10225-1*) Routledge.
Pile, Steve, jt. auth. see Nast, Heidi J.

P

An Asterisk (*) at the beginning of an entry indicates that the title is appearing for the first time.

Pile, Virginia. Cedarsong. O'Dell, Mary, ed. 50p. 1998. pap. 8.00 (*1-891703-00-5*) Green Rvr Writers.

Pile, William. Going for the Gold in Discipleship. 100p. (Orig.). 1989. pap. 5.95 (*0-940999-41-2*, C-2153) Star Bible.

Pilegaard, M. Medical Dictionary Danish-English - English-Danish. (DAN & ENG.). 913p. 1994. 140.00 (*87-12-02240-3*, Pub. by GAD) IBD Ltd.

***Pilegard, Virginia Walton & Debon, Nicolas.** The Warlord's Puzzle. LC 99-54656. (Illus.). 32p. (J). (ps-3). 2000. 14.95 (*1-56554-495-1*) Pelican.

Pileggi-Gabbamonte, Anne J. Cinderella in Rhyme. 32p. (J). (gr. k-6). 1999. pap. 10.00 (*0-8059-4686-1*) Dorrance.

Pileggi, Nicholas. Casino. (Orig.). 1995. mass mkt. 6.99 (*0-671-00160-4*) PB.

***Pileggi, Nicholas.** Casino. (Orig.). 1999. pap. 9.98 (*0-671-04450-8*) PB.

Pileggi, Nicholas. Casino: Love & Honor in Las Vegas. 368p. 1996. per. 6.99 (*0-671-66570-7*) PB.

— Wise Guy - Good Fellas. 1990. mass mkt. 6.99 (*0-671-72322-7*) PB.

Pileggi, Nicholas & Scorsese, Martin. Casino. (Illus.). 150p. (Orig.). 1996. pap. 15.00 (*0-571-17992-4*) Faber & Faber.

Pileggi, Nicholas, ed. see Ragano, Frank & Raab, Selwyn.

Pilenky, Philip, jt. auth. see Evans, Donald.

Piles, Roger D. Abrege de la Vie des Peintres. 540p. 1969. reprint ed. write for info. (*0-318-71940-1*) G Olms Pubs.

Pilet. Influenza. (Comparative Immunology, Microbiology Ser.). 1981. pap. 39.00 (*0-08-026842-0*, Pergamon Pr) Elsevier.

— Lymphocytes in Comparative Immunology. (Comparative Immunology, Microbiology Ser.). 1981. pap. 24.00 (*0-08-026841-2*, Pergamon Pr) Elsevier.

Pilevsky, Philip. Captive Continent: The Stockholm Syndrome in European-Soviet Relations. LC 88-26573. 170p. 1989. 47.95 (*0-275-93064-5*, C3064, Praeger Pubs) Greenwood.

Pilger, A. & Roesler, A., eds. Afar Depression of Ethiopia. (Geology Bks.: No. 14). xix, 416p. 1974. pap. 80.00 (*3-510-65069-7*, Pub. by E Schweizerbartsche) Balogh.

Pilger, Andreas & Roesler, Artur, eds. Afar Between Continental & Oceanic Rifting. (Geology Bks.: No. 16). (Illus.). xiv, 216p. (Orig.). 1974. pap. text 53.00 (*3-510-65070-0*, Pub. by E Schweizerbartsche) Balogh.

Pilger, John. Hidden Agendas. 416p. 1999. pap. 18.95 (*1-56584-520-X*, Pub. by New Press NY) Norton.

Pilger, Mary A. Multicultural Projects Index: Things to Make & Do to Celebrate Festivals, Cultures, & Holidays Around the World. 2nd ed. LC 98-4445. 300p. 1998. 49.00 (*1-56308-524-0*) Libs Unl.

— Science Experiments Index for Young People. 2nd ed. 400p. 1996. lib. bdg. 62.00 (*1-56308-341-8*) Libs Unl.

***Pilgreen, Janice.** The SSR Handbook: How to Organize & Manage a Sustained Silent Reading Program. LC 99-87986. 2000. 15.00 (*0-86709-462-1*, Pub. by Boynton Cook Pubs) Heinemann.

Pilgrim, Adrian. Outline of Manx Language & Literature. 1985. pap. 9.95 (*0-89979-064-X*) British Am Bks.

Pilgrim, Anne, jt. auth. see Langton, Mandy.

Pilgrim, Aubrey. Build Your Own IBM Compatible & Save a Bundle. 224p. (Orig.). 1987. 22.95 (*0-8306-0231-3*, 2831); pap. 16.95 (*0-8306-2831-2*) McGraw-Hill Prof.

— Build Your Own LAN & Save a Bundle. LC 92-5692. (Illus.). 256p. 1992. pap. 21.95 (*0-8306-4089-4*, 4210, Windcrest) TAB Bks.

— Build Your Own LAN & Save a Bundle. 2nd ed. 1992. 21.95 (*0-07-050108-4*) McGraw.

Pilgrim, Aubrey. Build Your Own Multimedia with CD-ROM. 2nd ed. LC 95-39482. (Illus.). 371p. 1995. pap., pap. text 39.95 incl. cd-rom (*0-07-912226-4*) McGraw.

Pilgrim, Aubrey. Build Your Own Pentium Class Processor. LC 96-18005. (Illus.). 400p. 1996. 34.95 (*0-07-050186-6*) McGraw.

— Build Your Own Pentium Pro Processor PC. (Illus.). 334p. 1996. pap. 21.95 (*0-07-050187-4*) McGraw.

— Build Your Own Pentium Processor PC. 2nd ed. LC 95-32910. (Illus.). 396p. 1995. pap. 21.95 (*0-07-050184-X*) McGraw.

— Build Your Own Pentium II PC. LC 98-9670. 500p. 1998. pap. 29.95 (*0-07-050239-0*) McGraw.

— Build Your Own 486-486DX. 3rd ed. LC 95-23677. (Illus.). 256p. 1995. 34.95 (*0-07-050181-5*); pap. 21.95 (*0-07-050182-3*) McGraw.

— Build Your Own 486SX & Save a Bundle. 2nd ed. (Illus.). 256p. 1992. 29.95 (*0-8306-4217-X*, 4270, Windcrest) TAB Bks.

— Build Your Own 80286 IBM Compatible & Save a Bundle. (Illus.). 208p. 1988. 24.95 (*0-8306-0331-X*) McGraw-Hill Prof.

— Build Your Own 80386 IBM Compatible & Save a Bundle. (Illus.). 224p. 1988. 24.95 (*0-8306-9131-6*, 3131); pap. 17.95 (*0-8306-3131-3*, 3131) McGraw-Hill Prof.

***Pilgrim, Aubrey.** A Revolutionary Approach to Prostate Cancer. rev. ed. LC 99-64526. (Illus.). 120p. 2000. pap. 19.95 (*1-58501-015-4*, Pub. by CeShore Pubg) Natl Bk Netwk.

Pilgrim, Aubrey. A Revolutionary Approach to Prostate Cancer: Alternatives to Standard Treatment Options, Doctors & Survivors Share Their Stories. LC 98-101691. (Illus.). 328p. 1998. pap. 18.95 (*1-56315-086-7*) SterlingHse.

— Upgrade & Repair Your Pc. LC 97-41388. 1997. write for info. (*0-07-050237-4*) McGraw.

— Upgrade or Repair Your PC: Save a Bundle. LC 97-41388. (McGraw Hill Save a Bundle Ser.). 688p. 1997. pap., pap. text 34.95 incl. cd-rom (*0-07-913668-0*) McGraw.

— Upgrade or Repair Your PC & Save a Bundle. LC 97-41388. (Illus.). 640p. 1997. 54.95 incl. cd-rom (*0-07-913667-2*) McGraw.

— Upgrade Your IBM Compatible & Save a Bundle. (Illus.). 240p. 1990. 26.95 (*0-8306-8468-9*, 3468, Windcrest) TAB Bks.

***Pilgrim, Buddy.** Seven Steps to Unlimited Success: Timeless Principals for Unleashing Your Full Potential. 2000. pap. 12.99 (*1-57794-189-6*) Harrison Hse.

Pilgrim, Constance. Dear Jane. 192p. (C). 1989. text 59.00 (*1-872795-25-0*, Pub. by Pentland Pr) St Mut.

— This Is Illyria, Lady. 179p. (C). 1989. text 59.00 (*1-872795-21-8*, Pub. by Pentland Pr) St Mut.

Pilgrim, David. Psychotherapy & Society. 170p. 1997. 69.95 (*0-8039-7504-X*); pap. 23.95 (*0-8039-7505-8*) Sage.

***Pilgrim, David.** Sociology of Mental Health & Illness. 2nd ed. LC 98-44939. 1999. 29.95 (*0-335-20347-7*) Taylor & Francis.

Pilgrim, David, ed. On Being Black - An In-Group Analysis: Essays in Honor of W. E. B. Du Bois. LC 85-52309. 187p. 1986. 30.00 (*0-932269-75-3*) Wyndham Hall.

— W. E. B. Du Bois in Memoriam: A Centennial Celebration of His Collegiate Education. LC 90-50113. (Illus.). 150p. (C). 1990. text 34.95 (*0-685-35412-1*); pap. text 16.00 (*1-55605-150-6*) Wyndham Hall.

Pilgrim, David & Rogers, Anne. A Sociology of Mental Health & Illness. LC 98-44939. 1999. 95.00 (*0-335-20348-5*) OpUniv Pr.

Pilgrim, Donna, jt. auth. see Munger, Prudence.

Pilgrim, G. E. New Siwalik Primates: Their Bearing on the Question of Evolution of Man & the Anthropoidea. LC 77-86436. (India Geological Survey: Records of the Geological Survey of India Ser.: Vol. 45). reprint ed. 15.00 (*0-404-16675-X*) AMS Pr.

Pilgrim, Judith & Pilgrim, Larry. Biology Laboratory Manual for Majors. 232p. (C). 1996. ring bd. 29.95 (*0-7872-2539-8*) Kendall-Hunt.

Pilgrim, Larry, jt. auth. see Pilgrim, Judith.

Pilgrim, Mary D. It's Showtime! How to Sell & Showcase Your Home. 85p. 1998. pap. 11.95 (*0-9660107-8-7*) Home Pub.

Pilgrim, Millie W. All Kneel down & Pray. 186p. 1998. mass mkt. 10.95 (*0-9613184-3-0*) H & M Ent.

— Jason's Adventures with the Tuskegee Airmen. rev. ed. (Illus.). 54p. (J). (gr. 3 up). 1992. teacher ed. 2.00 (*0-685-60295-8*); pap. text 8.00 (*0-685-60294-X*, 133-720) H & M Ent.

Pilgrim, Peace. Pasos Hacia la Paz Interior: Sugestiones Para el Uso de Principios. Zanelli, Clandio, tr. from ENG. (Peace Pilgrim Ser.).Tr. of Steps Towards Inner Peace. (SPA., Illus.). 64p. (Orig.). 1987. pap. 5.00 (*0-943734-09-6*) Ocean Tree Bks.

— Peace Pilgrim: Her Life & Work in Her Own Words. LC 82-18854. (Illus.). 214p. 1991. 14.95 (*0-943734-20-7*) Ocean Tree Bks.

— Peace Pilgrim: Her Life & Work in Her Own Words. Rush, Ann et al, eds. LC 82-18854. (Illus.). 224p. 1994. pap. 12.00 (*0-943734-29-0*) Ocean Tree Bks.

— Peace Pilgrim's Wisdom: A Very Simple Guide. Canfield, Cheryl, ed. LC 95-41443. 224p. 1996. pap. 14.00 (*1-884997-11-2*) Blue Dove Pr.

— Peace Pilgrim's Wisdom: A Very Simple Guide. (Illus.). 224p. 1996. per. 14.00 (*0-943734-30-4*) Ocean Tree Bks.

— Steps Toward Inner Peace. (Keepsake Editions Ser.). 64p. 1993. per. 8.00 (*0-943734-24-X*) Ocean Tree Bks.

Pilgrim Press Staff. Day to Remember My Baptism Book. 1983. pap. 5.95 (*0-8298-0647-4*) Pilgrim OH.

— Renderings by Pilgrim. (Illus.). 160p. 1998. pap. 14.95 (*0-9666078-0-5*) Pilgrim Press.

Pilgrim, Richard B. Buddhism & the Arts of Japan. LC 98-15070. 1998. 14.50 (*0-231-11347-1*) Col U Pr.

Pilgrim, Richard B., jt. auth. see Ellwood, Robert S., Jr.

Pilgrim, Robert. Our Puppy's Baby Book: Pink for Girl Dogs. (Illus.). 32p. 1961. per. 11.95 (*0-87605-773-3*) Howell Bks.

— Our Puppy's Baby Book (BLUE) Blue for Boy Dogs. (Illus.). 32p. 1961. per. 11.95 (*0-87605-772-5*) Howell Bks.

Pilgrim, Susan. Living InSync: Creating Your Life with Balance & Purpose. 320p. (Orig.). 1995. pap. 9.95 (*1-55874-340-5*, 3405) Health Comm.

***Pilgrim, Thomas.** They Came Together in Bethlehem: Messages for the Advent/Christmas Season. LC 99-37625. 78p. 1999. pap. 8.50 (*0-7880-1512-5*) CSS OH.

Pilgrim, Thomas A. Behold the Man: Sermons & Object Lessons for Lent & Easter. LC 95-36214. 92p. (Orig.). 1996. pap. 10.95 (*0-7880-0711-4*) CSS OH.

— The Man from Galilee: Sermons & Orders of Worship for Lent & Easter. LC 97-26626. 94p. 1997. pap. 9.50 (*0-7880-1131-6*) CSS OH.

— The Roads Jesus Traveled. 1991. pap. 9.50 (*1-55673-383-6*, 9201) CSS OH.

Pilgrim, Tim A. Nothing Ventured, Nothing Gained: The Seattle JOA & Newspaper Preservation. LC 97-15997. (Illus.). 288p. 1997. pap. 39.50 (*1-56750-050-1*); text 78.50 (*0-89391-886-5*) Ablx Pub.

Pilgrim, Tom. Man from Galilee: Sermons & Orders for Lent & Easter. 1997. pap. text 9.50 (*0-7880-1134-0*) CSS OH.

— The Master Has Come. (Orig.). 1989. pap. 4.95 (*1-55673-102-7*, 9813) CSS OH.

Pilgrim, Walter E. Uneasy Neighbors: Church & State in the New Testament. LC 98-50385. (Overtures to Biblical Theology Ser.). xiv, 224p. 1999. pap. 20.00 (*0-8006-3113-7*, 1-3113, Fortress Pr) Augsburg Fortress.

***Piliar, Russell.** The Place Between "Amen" 2000. pap. 8.99 (*1-930027-06-0*, Pub. by Insght Pub) BookWorld.

Piliavin, Jane A. & Callero, Peter L. Giving Blood: The Development of an Altruistic Identity. LC 90-15650. (Series in Contemporary Medicine & Public Health). (Illus.). 320p. 1991. text 50.00 (*0-8018-4152-6*) Johns Hopkins.

Piliavin, Michael A. & Margaryan, Alfred. Germanate Glasses: Structure, Spectroscopy & Properties. LC 93-13302. 1993. 10.00 (*0-89006-506-3*) Artech Hse.

***Pilibosian, Helene.** At Quarter Past Reality: New & Selected Poems. LC 98-91396. vi, 96p. 1998. per. 11.50 (*1-929966-03-2*) Ohan.

— Carvings from an Heirloom: Oral History Poems. LC 83-138464. vi, 64p. 1983. per. 4.95 (*1-929966-00-8*) Ohan.

Pilibosian, Helene, jt. auth. see Pilibosian, Khachadoor.

Pilibosian, Helene, ed. see Sarkissian, Hovhannes H., et al.

Pilibosian, Helene, ed. see Topalian, Naomi G.

Pilibosian, Khachadoor & Pilibosian, Helene. They Called Me Mustafa: Memoir of an Immigrant. (Illus.). vi, 84p. 1992. per. 9.00 (*1-929966-01-6*) Ohan.

— They Called Me Mustafa: Memoir of an Immigrant. Sarkissian, Hagop, tr. from ARM. LC 99-70203. (Illus.). 167p. 1999. per. 16.00 (*1-929966-04-0*) Ohan.

Pilides, Despina. Handmade Burnished Wares of the Late Bronze Age in Cyprus. (Studies in Mediterranean Archaeology: Vol. CV). (Illus.). 233p. (Orig.). 1994. pap. 78.00 (*91-7081-074-5*, Pub. by P Astroms) Coronet Bks.

Piliero, Christopher. Sharpshooters. 427p. mass mkt. 5.99 (*1-55197-297-2*) Picasso Publ.

Pilington. Beyond the Mother Country. 1990. text 59.50 (*1-85043-113-2*, Pub. by I B T) St Martin.

Pilinszky, Janos, et al. The Desert of Love. 80p. 1989. 21.95 (*0-85646-177-6*, Pub. by Anvil Press); pap. 14.95 (*0-85646-178-4*, Pub. by Anvil Press) Dufour.

Pilipenko, A. T., jt. auth. see Samchuk, A. I.

Pilipovic, Dragana. Energy Risk: Valuing & Managing Energy Derivatives. LC 97-26541. (Illus.). 308p. 1997. 60.00 (*0-7863-1231-9*, Irwn Prfssnl) McGraw-Hill Prof.

Pilipp, Frank. New Critical Perspectives on Martin Walser. LC 94-1979. (GERM Ser.). xii, 196p. 1994. 60.00 (*1-879751-67-4*) Camden Hse.

— The Novels of Martin Walser: A Critical Introduction. (GERM Ser.: Vol. 64). (Illus.). xii, 196p. 1991. 60.00 (*0-938100-98-X*) Camden Hse.

Pilipp, Frank, ed. The Legacy of Kafka in Contemporary Austrian Literature. LC 97-9314. (Studies in Austrian Literature, Culture, & Thought). 231p. 1997. 29.50 (*1-57241-044-2*) Ariadne CA.

Pilipski, Mark. Les Belles Lettres Ser. I: Poems of Love. LC 92-62379. 50p. 1993. pap. 4.95 (*1-882965-00-0*) Markov Pr.

— Les Belles Lettres Ser. II: The Marriage of Mark & Marianne. LC 92-62382. 50p. 1993. pap. 4.95 (*1-882965-01-9*) Markov Pr.

— Les Belles Lettres Ser. III: The Vision. LC 92-62391. 50p. 1993. pap. 4.95 (*1-882965-02-7*) Markov Pr.

— Les Belles Lettres Ser. IV: Four Roles for Three Characters. LC 92-62380. 50p. (J). (gr. k-8). 1993. pap. 4.95 (*1-882965-03-5*) Markov Pr.

Pilisuk, Marc & Parks, Susan H. The Healing Web: Social Networks & Human Survival. LC 85-26290. (Illus.). 256p. 1986. pap. text 19.95 (*0-87451-470-3*) U Pr of New Eng.

Pilisuk, Marc & Pilisuk, Phyllis, eds. How We Lost the War on Poverty. LC 72-91471. 300p. 1973. 32.95 (*0-87855-079-8*); pap. 19.95 (*0-87855-574-9*) Transaction Pubs.

— Poor Americans: How the White Poor Live. 192p. 1971. reprint ed. pap. text 18.95 (*0-87855-569-2*) Transaction Pubs.

Pilisuk, Phyllis, jt. ed. see Pilisuk, Marc.

Pilitowski, Thomas. How Can I Invest in Rare Coins? 1997. pap. 2.50 (*0-915513-87-0*) Ctr Futures Ed.

Pilitsis, George, ed. Greek Proverbs & Other Popular Sayings. 144p. (Orig.). 1997. pap. 9.95 (*1-885778-23-6*) Seaburn.

Pilitsis, George, tr. see Pagoulatou, Regina.

Pilitsis, George, tr. see Ritsos, Yannis.

Piljac, Pamela A. The Bride to Bride Book. rev. ed. (Illus.). 160p. 1990. pap. 9.95 (*0-913339-08-3*) Bryce-Waterton Pubns.

— The Bride to Bride Book: A Complete Wedding Planner for the Bride. (Illus.). 160p. (Orig.). 1996. pap. text 11.95 (*1-55652-270-3*) Chicago Review.

— The Bride's Money Book: How to Have a Champagne Wedding on a Ginger-Ale Budget. LC 95-25464. 112p. (Orig.). 1996. pap. 11.95 (*1-55652-261-4*) Chicago Review.

— The Bride's Thank You Guide. LC 87-24917. 96p. 1993. pap. 5.95 (*1-55652-200-2*) Chicago Review.

— The Bride's Thank You Guide: Thank You Writing Made Easy. LC 87-24917. (Illus.). 96p. 1988. pap. 4.95 (*0-913339-06-7*) Bryce-Waterton Pubns.

— Newlywed: A Survival Guide to the First Years of Marriage. LC 85-21288. (Illus.). 256p. (Orig.). 1985. pap. 8.95 (*0-913339-02-4*) Bryce-Waterton Pubns.

— You Can Go Home Again: The Career Woman's Guide to Leaving the Work Force. (Illus.). (Orig.). 1985. pap. 9.95 (*0-913339-03-2*) Bryce-Waterton Pubns.

Piljac, Pamela A. & Piljac, Thomas M. Mackinac Island: Historic Frontier, Vacation Resort, Timeless Wonderland. LC 88-4962. (Illus.). 320p. (Orig.). 1988. pap. 9.95 (*0-913339-07-5*) Bryce-Waterton Pubns.

— Mackinac Island: Historic Frontier, Vacation Resort, Timeless Wonderland. (Illus.). 320p. (Orig.). 1996. pap. 14.95 (*1-55652-305-X*) Chicago Review.

Piljac, Thomas M. The Groom to Groom Book. rev. ed. (Illus.). 112p. 1990. pap. 9.95 (*0-913339-09-1*) Bryce-Waterton Pubns.

Piljac, Thomas M., jt. auth. see Piljac, Pamela A.

Pilkey. Thin-Walled Beams. text. write for info. (*0-471-38152-7*) Wiley.

Pilkey, Dav. The Adventures of Captain Underpants: An Epic Novel. LC 96-37544. (Illus.). 128p. (J). (gr. 2-5). 1997. 16.95 (*0-590-84627-2*); pap. 3.99 (*0-590-84628-0*) Scholastic Inc.

— Captain Underpants & the Attack of the Talking Toilets. LC 98-27382. (Captain Underpants Ser.). (Illus.). 144p. (J). (gr. 2-5). 1999. 16.95 (*0-590-63136-5*, Blue Sky Press); pap. 3.99 (*0-590-63427-5*, Blue Sky Press) Scholastic Inc.

***Pilkey, Dav.** Captain Underpants & the Attack of the Talking Toilets. (Captain Underpants Ser.). (Illus.). (J). (gr. 2-5). 1999. 9.34 (*0-606-15830-8*) Turtleback.

— Captain Underpants & the Invasion of the Incredibly Naughty Cafeteria Ladies from Outer Space: (And the Subsequent Assault of the Equally Evil Lunchroom Zombie Nerds) LC 98-56107. (Captain Underpants Ser.). (Illus.). 134p. (J). (gr. 2-5). 1999. 16.95 (*0-439-04995-4*, Pub. by Scholastic Inc); pap. 3.99 (*0-439-04996-2*, Blue Sky Press) Scholastic Inc.

— Captain Underpants & the Perilous Plot of Professor Poopypants. LC 99-54825. (Captain Underpants Ser.). (Illus.). 160p. (J). (gr. 2-5). 2000. 16.95 (*0-439-04997-0*, Blue Sky Press); pap. 3.99 (*0-439-04998-9*, Blue Sky Press) Scholastic Inc.

Pilkey, Dav. Dog Breath! The Horrible Terrible Trouble with Hally Tosis. LC 93-43405. (Illus.). 32p. (J). (ps-3). 1994. 12.95 (*0-590-47466-9*, Blue Sky Press) Scholastic Inc.

— Dogzilla. LC 92-37906. (Illus.). 32p. (J). (ps-3). 1993. 12.00 (*0-15-223944-8*); pap. 7.00 (*0-15-223945-6*) Harcourt.

— Dragon Gets By. LC 90-46027. (Illus.). 48p. (J). (ps-3). 1996. pap. 5.95 (*0-531-07081-6*) Orchard Bks Watts.

— Dragon's Fat Cat. LC 91-16369. (Illus.). 48p. (J). (gr. 1-3). 1992. 15.95 (*0-531-05982-0*) Orchard Bks Watts.

— Dragon's Fat Cat. LC 91-16369. (Illus.). 48p. (J). (gr. 1-3). 1996. pap. 5.95 (*0-531-07068-9*) Orchard Bks Watts.

— Dragon's Fat Cat: Dragon's Fourth Tale. 1995. 10.15 (*0-606-08730-3*, Pub. by Turtleback) Demco.

— Dragon's Halloween. LC 91-21107. (Illus.). 48p. (J). (gr. 1-3). 1993. 15.95 (*0-531-05990-1*) Orchard Bks Watts.

— Dragon's Halloween. LC 91-21107. (Illus.). 48p. (J). (ps-3). 1996. pap. 5.95 (*0-531-07069-7*) Orchard Bks Watts.

— Dragon's Halloween: Dragon's Fifth Tale. (Dragon Tales Ser.). 1995. 10.15 (*0-606-09209-9*, Pub. by Turtleback) Demco.

— Dragon's Merry Christmas. LC 91-1996. (Illus.). 48p. (J). (gr. 1-3). 1991. lib. bdg. 16.99 (*0-531-08557-0*) Orchard Bks Watts.

— Dragon's Merry Christmas. LC 91-1996. (Illus.). 48p. (J). (ps-3). 1991. 15.95 (*0-531-05957-X*) Orchard Bks Watts.

— Dragon's Merry Christmas. LC 91-1996. (Illus.). 48p. (J). (ps-3). 1994. pap. 5.95 (*0-531-07055-7*) Orchard Bks Watts.

— Dragon's Merry Christmas: Dragon's Third Tale. (Dragon Tales Ser.). 1994. 10.15 (*0-606-09210-2*, Pub. by Turtleback) Demco.

— A Friend for Dragon. LC 90-45219. (Illus.). 48p. (J). (gr. 1-3). 1991. 14.95 (*0-531-05934-0*) Orchard Bks Watts.

— A Friend for Dragon. LC 90-45219. (Illus.). 48p. (J). (gr. 1-3). 1994. pap. 4.95 (*0-531-07054-9*) Orchard Bks Watts.

— A Friend for Dragon: Dragon's First Tale. 1994. 10.15 (*0-606-08746-X*, Pub. by Turtleback) Demco.

— God Bless the Gargoyles. LC 95-2467. (Illus.). 40p. (J). 1996. 15.00 (*0-15-200248-0*, Harcourt Child Bks) Harcourt.

— God Bless the Gargoyles. 36p. (C). 1999. pap. 6.00 (*0-15-202104-3*, Voyager Bks) Harcourt.

— The Hallo-Wiener. LC 94-40949. (Illus.). 32p. (J). (ps-3). 1995. 12.95 (*0-590-41703-7*, Blue Sky Press) Scholastic Inc.

— Hallo-Wiener, 1 vol. (Illus.). 32p. (J). (ps-2). 1999. pap. text 5.99 (*0-439-07946-2*) Scholastic Inc.

— Hallytosis (Dog Breath) El Horrible Problema de un Perro (The Horrible Trouble with Hally Tosis) 1997. 15.95 (*84-261-2948-X*) Lectorum Pubns.

— Kat Kong. LC 92-14483. (Illus.). 32p. (J). (ps-3). 1993. 10.95 (*0-15-242036-3*); pap. 7.00 (*0-15-242037-1*) Harcourt.

— The Moonglow Roll-O-Rama. LC 94-24846. (Illus.). 32p. (J). (ps-3). 1995. 15.95 (*0-531-06876-5*); lib. bdg. 16.99 (*0-531-08726-3*) Orchard Bks Watts.

***Pilkey, Dav.** La Navidad de Dragon. (SPA., Illus.). 48p. (J). (gr. 1-3). 1999. pap. 6.95 (*980-257-217-9*, Pub. by Ediciones Ekare) Kane-Miller Bk.

Pilkey, Dav. The Paperboy. LC 95-30641. (Illus.). 32p. (J). (ps-5). 1996. 14.95 (*0-531-09506-1*); lib. bdg. 15.99 (*0-531-08856-1*) Orchard Bks Watts.

— The Paperboy. LC 95-30641. (Illus.). 32p. (J). (ps-5). 1999. pap. 5.95 (*0-531-07139-1*) Orchard Bks Watts.

— Ricky Ricotta's Giant Robot: An Epic Novel. LC 99-26548. (Illus.). 112p. (J). (ps-3). 2000. 16.95 (*0-590-30719-3*, Blue Sky Press) Scholastic Inc.

***Pilkey, Dav.** Ricky Ricotta's Giant Robot: An Epic Novel. (Secrets of Droon Ser.). (Illus.). 112p. (J). (ps-3). 2000. pap. 3.99 (*0-590-30720-7*, Blue Sky Press) Scholastic Inc.

— Ricky Ricotta's Giant Robot vs. the Mutant Mosquitoes from Mercury. (Illus.). 2000. pap. text 95.76 (*0-439-21522-6*) Scholastic Inc.

— Ricky Ricotta's Giant Robot vs. the Mutant Mosquitos from Mercury. (Illus.). 128p. (J). (gr. 1-5). 2000. pap. 3.99 (*0-590-30722-3*, Blue Sky Press) Scholastic Inc.

— Ricky Ricotta's Giant Robot vs. the Mutant Mosquitos from Mercury: An Adventure Novel. LC 99-67469. (Illus.). 128p. (J). (ps up). 2000. 16.95 (*0-590-30721-5*, Blue Sky Press) Scholastic Inc.

— Silly Gooses. (Illus.). 40p. (J). (ps-3). 2000. pap. 5.99 (0-590-95735-X) Scholastic Inc.

Pilkey, Dav. The Silly Gooses Build a House. LC 96-52435. (Illus.). (J). Date not set. 13.95 (0-590-94741-9, Blue Sky Press) Scholastic Inc.

— 'Twas the Night Before Christmas: The Wrath of Mrs. Claus. LC 97-33134. (J). 1999. write for info. (0-590-12073-5, Blue Sky Press) Scholastic Inc.

— 'Twas the Night Before Thanksgiving. LC 89-48941. (Illus.). 32p. (J). (ps-2). 1990. 15.95 (0-531-05905-7) Orchard Bks Watts.

— When Cats Dream. LC 91-31355. (Illus.). 32p. (J). (ps-2). 1992. 15.95 (0-531-05997-9) Orchard Bks Watts.

— When Cats Dream. LC 91-31355. (Illus.). 32p. (J). (ps-3). 1992. lib. bdg. 16.99 (0-531-08597-X) Orchard Bks Watts.

— When Cats Dream. LC 91-31355. (Illus.). 32p. (J). (ps-2). 1996. pap. 5.95 (0-531-07075-1) Orchard Bks Watts.

— World War Won. LC 87-2711. (Books for Students by Students Ser.). (Illus.). 32p. (J). (gr. 1 up). 1987. lib. bdg. 15.95 (0-933849-22-2) Landmark Edns.

Pilkey, Dav & Denim, Sue. Ready, Set, Go! LC 96-52916. 40p. (J). (ps-3). 1998. 13.95 (0-590-94733-8) HarpC Child Bks.

***Pilkey, Dave.** Captain Underpants & the Perilous Plot of Professor Poopypants. (Captain Underpants Ser.). (Illus.). (J). 2000. 9.34 (0-606-18526-7) Turtleback.

Pilkey, John. Think Again: Poems, 1981-97. 1997. pap. write for info. (1-57553-689-7) Watermrk Pr.

Pilkey, O. H., et al, eds. Coastal Land Loss. (Short Course Ser.: Vol. 2). 73p. 1989. 13.00 (0-87590-701-6) Am Geophysical.

Pilkey, Orrin H. The North Carolina Shore & Its Barrier Islands: Restless Ribbons of Sand. LC 98-4578. (Living with the Shore Ser.). 1998. 54.95 (0-8223-2208-0); pap. 18.95 (0-8223-2224-2) Duke.

Pilkey, Orrin H. & Dixon, Katharine L. The Corps & the Shore. 256p. 1998. pap. 16.95 (1-55963-439-1) Island Pr.

Pilkey, Orrin H. & Dixon, Katherine L. The Corps & the Shore. 256p. (C). 1996. text 25.00 (1-55963-438-3) Island Pr.

Pilkey, Orrin H., Jr., et al. From Currituck to Calabash: Living with North Carolina's Barrier Islands. LC 80-42835. (Living with the Shore Ser.). (Illus.). xi, 258p. 1982. reprint ed. pap. 17.95 (0-8223-0548-8) Duke.

Pilkey, Orrin H., et al. Living with the East Florida Shore. LC 84-10297. (Living with the Shore Ser.). 275p. 1984. pap. 17.95 (0-8223-0515-1); text 49.95 (0-8223-0514-3) Duke.

Pilkey, Orrin H., Jr., jt. auth. see Kaufman, Wallace.

Pilkey, Orrin H., jt. auth. see Pilkey, Walter D.

Pilkey, Orrin H., Jr., ed. see Bush, David M., et al.

Pilkey, Orrin H., jt. ed. see Doyle, Larry J.

Pilkey, W., et al, eds. Structural Mechanics Computer Programs: Surveys, Assessments, & Availability. LC 74-8300. 1118p. reprint ed. pap. 200.00 (0-608-13372-8, 205572800034) Bks Demand.

Pilkey, W., jt. ed. see Perrone, Nicholas.

Pilkey, W. D. & Cohen, R., eds. System Identification of Vibrating Structures: Mathematical Models from Test Data Presented at 1972 Winter Annual Meeting of the American Society of Mechanical Engineers. LC 72-92594. (Illus.). 206p. reprint ed. pap. 63.90 (0-608-30322-4, 201947300012) Bks Demand.

Pilkey, Walter D. Formulas for Stress, Strain & Structural Matrices. 1488p. 1994. 175.00 (0-471-52746-7) Wiley.

Pilkey, Walter D. & Pilkey, Orrin H. Mechanics of Solids. LC 85-46011. 464p. (C). 1986. reprint ed. text 48.50 (0-89874-917-4) Krieger.

Pilkey, Walter D. & Wunderlich, Walter. Mechanics of Structures: Variational & Computational Methods. 880p. 1993. boxed set 104.95 (0-8493-4435-2, 4435) CRC Pr.

Pilkey, Walter D., et al. Peterson's Stress Concentration Factors. 2nd ed. LC 96-27514. 544p. 1997. 125.00 (0-471-53849-3) Wiley.

Pilkey, Walter D., jt. auth. see Haviland, John K.

Pilkington. The British Constitution: A Student's Companion. LC 99-232875. 224p. 1999. pap. 19.95 (0-7190-5303-X) St Martin.

***Pilkington.** The British Constitution: A Student's Companion. LC 99-232875. 224p. 1999. text 64.95 (0-7190-5302-1) St Martin.

Pilkington. Issues British Politics. LC 97-47643. 288p. 1998. pap. 19.95 (0-312-21382-4); text 55.00 (0-312-21381-6) St Martin.

— Representative Democracy Britain Today. LC 96-34391. (Politics Today Ser.). 1997. 59.95 (0-7190-4817-6, Pub. by Manchester Univ Pr); pap. 19.95 (0-7190-4818-4, Pub. by Manchester Univ Pr) St Martin.

Pilkington, A., ed. Apollinaire: Alcools. (Bristol French Texts Ser.). (FRE.). 200p. 1993. pap. 18.95 (1-85399-373-5, Pub. by Brist Class Pr) Focus Pub-R Pullins.

Pilkington, Ace G. Screening Shakespeare from Richard II to Henry V. LC 90-50310. 216p. 1991. 39.50 (0-87413-412-9) U Delaware Pr.

***Pilkington, Adrian.** Poetic Effects: A Relevance Theory Perspective. LC 99-88714. (Pragmatics & Beyond New Ser.: Vol. 75). xii, 209p. 2000. 65.00 (1-55619-922-8); pap. 34.95 (1-55619-923-6) J Benjamins Pubng Co.

Pilkington, Anthony E. Bergson & His Influence: A Reassessment. LC 75-22555. 261p. reprint ed. pap. 74.40 (0-8357-7137-7, 2031708) Bks Demand.

Pilkington, C. M. Teach Yourself Judaism. (Illus.). 256p. 1995. pap., student ed. 11.95 (0-8442-3748-5, Teach Yrslf) NTC Contemp Pub Co.

Pilkington, Colin. Britain in the European Union Today. LC 95-4958. (Politics Today Ser.). 256p. 1995. text 19.95 (0-7190-4562-2) Manchester Univ Pr.

***Pilkington, Colin.** Civil Service in Britain Today. 2000. text 59.95 (0-7190-5223-8, Pub. by Manchester Univ Pr) St Martin.

Pilkington, Doris. Caprice: A Stockman's Daughter. (Orig.). 1991. pap. 12.95 (0-7022-2400-6, Pub. by Univ Queensland Pr) Intl Spec Bk.

Pilkington, Doris & Garimara, Nugi. Follow the Rabbit-Proof Fence. 140p. 1996. pap. 14.95 (0-7022-2709-9, Pub. by Univ Queensland Pr) Intl Spec Bk.

Pilkington, Hilary. Migration, Displacement & Identity in Post-Soviet Russia. LC 97-20608. 264p. (C). 1998. 90.00 (0-415-15824-9); pap. 29.99 (0-415-15825-7) Routledge.

— Russia's Youth & Its Culture: A Nation's Constructors & Constructed. LC 93-26766. 320p. (C). 1994. pap. 29.99 (0-415-09044-X) Routledge.

Pilkington, Hilary, ed. Gender, Generation & Identity in Contemporary Russia. 320p. (C). 1996. 90.00 (0-415-13543-5) Routledge.

— Gender, Generationn & Identity in Contemporary Russia. 320p. (C). 1996. pap. 29.99 (0-415-13544-3) Routledge.

Pilkington, Hilary, tr. see Wolf, Christa.

Pilkington, J. M. His Will Also. (C). 1989. pap. 29.00 (0-7223-2299-2, Pub. by A H S Ltd) St Mut.

Pilkington, John, Jr. Francis Marion Crawford. LC 64-20717. (Twayne's United States Authors Ser.). 1964. pap. 3.95 (0-8290-0004-6); lib. bdg. 20.95 (0-89197-763-5) Irvington.

— Henry Blake Fuller. LC 69-18504. (Twayne's United States Authors Ser.). 1970. pap. text 9.95 (0-8290-0005-4); lib. bdg. 20.95 (0-8057-0300-4) Irvington.

Pilkington, John D., jt. ed. see McCarthy, Dennis D.

Pilkington, Kevin. Spare Change. Iddings, Kathleen, ed. LC 97-72360. (National Poetry Book Ser.: Vol. 2). (Illus.). 80p. (Orig.). 1997. per. 10.00 (0-931721-14-8) La Jolla Poets.

Pilkington, Laetitia V. The Celebrated Mrs. Pilkington's Jests: or The Cabinet of Wit & Humor. LC 73-37707. reprint ed. 42.50 (0-404-56775-4) AMS Pr.

— Memoirs of Laetitia Pilkington. Elias, A. C., Jr., ed. LC 94-40317. 1997. 95.00 (0-8203-1719-5) U of Ga Pr.

— Memoirs with Anecdotes of Dean Swift, 1748-1754. LC 75-1027. (Swiftiana Ser.). 1975. write for info. (0-8240-1278-X) Garland.

Pilkington, Roger. History & Legends of the European Waterways. (Illus.). 331p. 1998. 52.50 (1-85776-219-3, Pub. by Book Guild Ltd) Trans-Atl Phila.

— I Sailed on the Mayflower: The True Story of a Pilgrim Youngster. 1990. 12.95 (0-533-08820-8) Vantage.

— Small Boat in the Midi. 210p. (C). 1989. 125.00 (0-907864-44-9, Pub. by Laurie Norie & Wilson Ltd) St Mut.

— View from the Shore: Recollections from an Author & Scientist. 286p. 1995. 42.50 (1-85776-017-4, Pub. by Book Guild Ltd) Trans-Atl Phila.

Pilkington, Theo, et al. High Performance Computing in Biomedical Research. 544p. 1992. boxed set 125.00 (0-8493-4474-3, R853) CRC Pr.

Pilkington, Tom. State of Mind: Texas Literature & Culture. LC 98-22261. (Tarleton State University Southwestern Studies in the Humanities: No. 10). 224p. 1999. 24.95 (0-89096-839-X) Tex A&M Univ Pr.

Pilkington, Tom, ed. Careless Weeds: Six Texas Novellas. LC 92-53613. (Southwest Life & Letters Ser.). 352p. 1993. pap. 14.95 (0-87074-339-2) SMU Press.

— Careless Weeds: Six Texas Novellas. LC 92-53613. (Southwest Life & Letters Ser.). 352p. 1993. text 35.00 (0-87074-338-4) SMU Press.

Pilkington, Tom, jt. ed. see Clifford, Craig E.

Pilkington, Tom, jt. ed. see Clifford, Craig.

Pilkington, William T. Imagining Texas: The Literature of the Lone Star State. (Texas History Ser.). (Illus.). 37p. 1981. pap. text 8.95 (0-89641-095-1) American Pr.

***Pilkinton, Colin.** Civil Service in Britain Today. 2000. pap. 19.95 (0-7190-5224-6, Pub. by Manchester Univ Pr) St Martin.

Pilkis, S. J., ed. Fructose-2,6-Bisphosphate: The Unique Sugar Diphosphate. 288p. 1990. lib. bdg. 179.00 (0-8493-4795-5, QP702) CRC Pr.

Pilko Associates Staff, jt. auth. see Arthur Andersen & Co. Staff.

Pill Enterprises Staff, ed. see Furlong, Marjorie & Pill, Virginia.

Pill, Virginia, jt. auth. see Furlong, Marjorie.

Pilla, Daniel J. Forty-One Ways to Lick the IRS with a Postage Stamp. 15.95 (0-685-68185-8) Winning St Paul.

— Forty-One Ways to Lick the IRS with a Postage Stamp. Engstrom, David M., ed. LC 90-71404. 224p. 1990. pap. 15.95 (0-9617124-8-1) Winning St Paul.

— How to Double Your Tax Refund: A Simple Guide to Managing Your Taxes & Getting Free Money. Engstrom, Paul L., ed. 192p. 1999. pap. 15.95 (1-884367-04-6) Winning St Paul.

— How to Fire the IRS: A Plan to Eliminate the Income Tax & the IRS. Engstrom, David M., ed. LC 93-94197. 256p. (Orig.). 1993. pap. 12.95 (1-884367-00-3) Winning St Paul.

— How to Get Tax Amnesty: A Guide to the Forgiveness of IRS Debt. LC 92-96839. 224p. (Orig.). 1992. pap. 12.95 (0-9617124-9-X) Winning St Paul.

— IRS, Taxes & the Beast. Engstrom, Paul L., ed. 224p. 1996. pap. 15.95 (1-884367-01-1) Winning St Paul.

— Taxpayers' Ultimate Defense Manual: Nine Devastating Weapons Against I.R.S. Abuse. Engstrom, David M., ed. 224p. (Orig.). 1989. 39.95 (0-9617124-7-3) Winning St Paul.

Pilla, I. P. Law of Torts. (C). 1991. 90.00 (0-89771-793-7, Pub. by Eastern Book) St Mut.

Pillage, Lawrence T. Electronic Circuit & System Simulation Methods. LC 94-24429. 1994. 55.00 (0-07-050169-6) McGraw.

Pillai, C. N., ed. see Editions Technip Staff.

Pillai, C. S. Giopinadha. Sahajayoga & Other Meditations. 1987. 8.95 (0-318-37038-7) Asia Bk Corp.

Pillai, C. S. Giopinadha & Scheer, Georg. Zoologica Band XLIII, Heft 126: Report on the Stony Corals from the Maldive Archipelago, Results of the Xarifa Expedition 1957/58 of the International Institute for Submarine Research, Vaduz, Liechtenstein. (Publications in Zoology). (Illus.). iv, 83p. 1976. pap. 109.00 (3-510-55010-2) Balogh.

Pillai, C. S. Giopinadha, see Scheer, Georg & Giopinadha Pillai, C. S.

Pillai, C. S. Giopinadha, jt. auth. see Scheer, Georg.

Pillai, G. Narayana. Social Background of Political Leadership in India. 1984. 18.50 (0-8364-1060-2, Pub. by Uppal Pub Hse) S Asia.

Pillai, Jaya K. Women & Empowerment. LC 95-910279. viii, 171p. 1995. 19.00 (81-212-0512-3, Pub. by Gyan Publishing Hse) Nataraj Bks.

Pillai, K. C. Light Through an Eastern Window. 1963. pap. 6.95 (0-8315-0057-3) Speller.

— Orientalisms of the Bible, Vol. 2. 1974. 4.95 (0-912178-04-3) Mor-Mac.

Pillai, K. N. Double Jeopardy Protection: A Comparative Overview. (C). 1988. 35.00 (81-7099-058-0, Pub. by Mittal Pubs Dist) S Asia.

Pillai, L. D. Indian Chronology (Solar, Lunar & Planetary) 1989. reprint ed. 26.50 (81-206-0250-1, Pub. by Asian Educ Servs) S Asia.

Pillai, M., jt. auth. see James, D. K.

Pillai, M. N., tr. see Sarukhanyan, E. I.

Pillai, M. S. Ravana King of Lanka. (C). 1993. reprint ed. 10.00 (81-206-0547-0, Pub. by Asian Educ Servs) S Asia.

— Tamil Literature. (C). 1995. 24.00 (81-206-0955-7, Pub. by Asian Educ Servs) S Asia.

Pillai, Mary, jt. auth. see James, D. K.

Pillai, Mary, jt. auth. see James, David.

Pillai, P. Mohanan, jt. auth. see Subrahmanian, K. K.

Pillai, P. S. Jurisprudence & Legal Theory. 1986. 65.00 (0-7855-1477-5) St Mut.

— Principles of Law of Tort. 1986. 70.00 (0-7855-1476-7) St Mut.

Pillai, P. S., ed. Law of Tort. (C). 1991. 90.00 (0-89771-797-X, Pub. by Eastern Book) St Mut.

Pillai, Philip N. Sourcebook of Singapore & Malaysian Company Law. 1386p. 1986. 277.00 (0-409-99511-8, MICHIE) LEXIS Pub.

Pillai, R. N. Veerabrahmam: India's Nostradamus Saint. (C). 1991. 19.50 (81-7017-279-9, Pub. by Abhinav) S Asia.

***Pillai, Ravi & Wright, John E. C., eds.** Surgery for Ischaemic Heart Disease. LC 98-49159. (Illus.). 320p. 1999. text 149.50 (0-19-262466-0) OUP.

Pillai, S. Lymphocyte Development: Cell Election Events & Signals During Immune Ontogeny. (Illus.). 350p. 1997. 74.50 (0-8176-3853-9) Birkhauser.

Pillai, S. D. Slums & Urbanization. (C). 1990. 45.00 (81-7154-259-X, Pub. by Popular Prakashan) S Asia.

Pillai, S. Devadas. Indian Sociology Through Ghurye: A Dictionary. (C). 1997. 42.00 (81-7154-807-5, Pub. by Popular Prakashan) S Asia.

Pillai, S. O. Problems & Solutions in Solid State Physics. 1994. write for info. (81-224-0658-0, Pub. by Wiley Estrn) Franklin.

— Solid State Physics: Structure & Electron Related Properties. 1994. write for info. (81-224-0643-2, Pub. by Wiley Estrn) Franklin.

Pillai, Sivaraja. The Chronology of the Early Tamils. (Illus.). 284p. 1986. 22.00 (0-8364-1713-5, Pub. by Manohar) S Asia.

Pillai, Suresh D. Microbial Pathogens Within Aquifers: Principles & Protocols. LC 97-47086. (Environmental Intelligence Unit Ser.). 1998. 129.00 (1-57059-520-8) Landes Bioscience.

Pillai, Suresh D., ed. Microbial Pathogens Within Aquifers: Principles & Protocols. LC 97-47086. (Environmental Intelligence Unit Ser.). 150p. 1998. 129.00 (3-540-63891-1) Spr-Verlag.

Pillai, T. Sivasankara. Scavenger's Son. (Asian Writers Ser.). 124p. 1994. pap. 9.95 (0-435-95082-7, 95082) Heinemann.

Pillai, U. S. Array Signal Processing. (Illus.). xi, 221p. 1989. 49.50 (0-318-41905-X) Spr-Verlag.

Pillai, V. C. The Origins of the Indo-European Races & Peoples, 2 vols. 1990. reprint ed. 110.00 (81-85326-25-8, Pub. by Vintage) S Asia.

Pillai, Velumni A., jt. auth. see Fleming, Darrin W.

Pillai, Vijayan K., et al, eds. Developing Areas: A Book of Readings & Research. 544p. 1995. 59.50 (0-85496-741-9, Pub. by Berg Pubs); pap. 19.50 (1-85973-002-7, Pub. by Berg Pubs) NYU Pr.

Pillai, Vijayan K. & Wang, Guang-zhen. Women's Reproductive Rights in Developing Countries. LC 99-72243. 7p. 1999. 61.95 (1-84014-908-6, Pub. by Ashgate Pub) Ashgate Pub Co.

Pillai, Vijayan K., jt. auth. see Barton, Thomas R.

Pillai, Vinod, jt. ed. see Shah, D. O.

Pillai Viswanatha, V. Dictionary of Tamil & English. (ENG & TAM.). 732p. 1908. 45.95 (0-7859-9811-X) Fr & Eur.

Pillans, Brian, jt. auth. see Bourne, Nicholas.

Pillant, Christopher. Gem & Mineral Collection: Hold the Treasures of the Earth in the Palm of Your Hand. (Illus.). 1998. pap. 19.95 (0-8069-9764-8) Sterling.

Pillar, Arlene. Folk Tales: A Study Guide. Friedland, J. & Kessler, R., eds. (Novel-Ties Ser.). 1988. pap. text, student ed. 15.95 (0-88122-867-2) Lrn Links.

Pillar, Laurence. Essential Cardiac Technology. 260p. 1996. text 33.00 (3-7186-5896-8, Harwood Acad Pubs); pap. text 18.00 (3-7186-5897-6, Harwood Acad Pubs) Gordon & Breach.

Pillar, Marjorie. Join the Band! LC 90-23261. (Illus.). 32p. (J). (gr. 1-3). 1992. 15.00 (0-06-021834-7); lib. bdg. 14.89 (0-06-021829-0) HarpC Child Bks.

— Pizza Man. LC 89-35526. (Illus.). 40p. (J). (gr. k-3). 1990. 11.95 (0-690-04836-X); lib. bdg. 11.89 (0-690-04838-6) HarpC Child Bks.

Pillarella, Debi & Roberts, Scott O. Fitness Stepping. LC 96-1625. (Fitness Spectrum Ser.). 168p. (Orig.). 1996. pap. 14.95 (0-87322-835-9, PPIL0835) Human Kinetics.

Pillari. Human Behavior in the Social Environment. 2nd ed. LC 97-26560. 350p. 1997. pap. 45.95 (0-534-35028-3) Brooks-Cole.

Pillari, Vimala. Family Myths in Therapy. LC 93-74374. 206p. 1994. pap. 40.00 (1-56821-198-8) Aronson.

— Human Behavior in the Social Environment. LC 88-14539. 352p. (Orig.). (C). 1988. mass mkt. 24.25 (0-534-09060-5) Brooks-Cole.

— Models of Family Therapy. (C). 2000. 55.33 (0-205-26217-1, Macmillan Coll) P-H.

— Shadows of Pain: Intimacy & Sexual Problems in Family Life. LC 96-14384. 248p. 1997. pap. 50.00 (0-7657-0009-3) Aronson.

— Social Work Practice. (C). 2000. 53.33 (0-205-26486-7, Macmillan Coll) P-H.

Pillari, Vimala & Newsome, Moses. Human Behavior in the Social Environment: Families, Groups, Organizations, & Communities. LC 97-26559. 1997. pap. 37.95 (0-534-35029-1) Brooks-Cole.

Pillay. Tamil - English Dictionary. (ENG & TAM.). 731p. 1988. 19.95 (0-7859-7525-X, 8120604377) Fr & Eur.

Pillay, Anand. Geometric Stability Theory. (Oxford Logic Guides Ser.: No. 32). (Illus.). 372p. 1996. text 120.00 (0-19-853437-X) OUP.

— An Introduction to Stability Theory. (Oxford Logic Guides Ser.). 1983. 42.50 (0-19-853196-9) OUP.

***Pillay, K. K. S. & Kim, K. C., eds.** Plutonium Futures - The Science: Topical Conference on Plutonium & Actinides. LC 00-104645. (AIP Conference Proceedings Ser.: Vol. 532). (Illus.). xviii, 439p. 2000. 115.00 (1-56396-948-3) Am Inst Physics.

Pillay, P. K., et al, eds. Towards Minimally Invasive Neurosurgery. (Journal Ser.: Vol. 64, No. 2, 1995). (Illus.). 44p. 1995. pap. 21.75 (3-8055-6269-1) S Karger.

Pillay, T. V. Aquaculture: Principles & Practices. 1998. 115.00 (0-8464-4367-8) Beekman Pubs.

— Aquaculture: Principles & Practices. (Illus.). 575p. (C). 1990. text 115.00 (0-85238-168-9) Blackwell Sci.

Pillay, T. V. R. Aquaculture Development: Progress & Prospects. 182p. 1994. text 69.95 (0-470-23432-6) Halsted Pr.

***Pillay, Veerasamy K.** Pathoghomonic Signs. 2000. pap. 9.00 (0-8059-4973-9) Dorrance.

Pillement, Georges, et al. Encyclopedie de l'Impressionnisme. (FRE.). 288p. 1976. 59.95 (0-8288-5681-8, M6515) Fr & Eur.

***Pillemer, David B.** Momentous Events, Vivid Memories. 256p. 2000. pap. 17.95 (0-674-00418-3) HUP.

Pillemer, David B., jt. auth. see Light, Richard J.

Pillemer, David H. Momentous Events, Vivid Memories. LC 97-47043. (Illus.). 256p. 1998. 35.00 (0-674-58205-5) HUP.

***Pillemer, Karl.** Social Integration in the Second Half of Life. (Illus.). 304p. 2000. 48.00 (0-8018-6453-4); pap. 24.95 (0-8018-6454-2) Johns Hopkins.

Pillemer, Karl & Johnson, Philip T. Leading the Way: Practical Management Skills for the Long-Term Care Nurse. Schumacher, Martin, ed. 50p. 1997. 10.95 (0-9653629-1-4) Frontline Pub.

***Pillemer, Karl, et al.** The Nursing Assistant's Survival Guide: Tips & Techniques for the Most Important Job in America. (Illus.). 100p. 1999. 11.95 (0-9653629-2-2) Frontline Pub.

Pillemer, Karl, et al. Project EASE. 36p. 1993. 18.00 (1-57753-104-3, 321 EASE) Corn Coop Ext.

Pillemer, Karl A. Solving the Frontline Crisis in Long-Term Care Vol. 1: A Practical Guide to Finding & Keeping Quality Nursing Assistants. Hoffman, Richard & Schumacher, Martin, eds. 124p. (Orig.). 1996. pap. 39.00 (0-9653629-0-6) Frontline Pub.

Pillemer, Karl A. & Wolf, Rosalie S., eds. Elder Abuse: Conflict in the Family. LC 86-14014. 381p. 1986. 37.95 (0-86569-133-9, Auburn Hse); pap. 22.95 (0-86569-134-7, Auburn Hse) Greenwood.

Pillemer, Karl A., jt. ed. see McCartney, Kathleen.

Pillemer, Karl A., tr. see Gehlen, Arnold.

Pillemer, Stanley R., ed. Neuroscience & Endocrinology of Fibromyalgia: 2nd National Institutes of Health Fibromyalgia Conference. LC 98-37606. (Journal of Musculoskeletal Pain Ser.: Vol. 6, No. 3). 110p. 1998. 39.95 (0-7890-0683-9) Haworth Pr.

Pillemer, Stanley R., ed. The Fibromyalgia Syndrome: Current Research & Future Directions in Epidemiology, Pathogenesis & Treatment. LC 94-35454. (Illus.). 200p. 1994. lib. bdg. 39.95 (1-56024-714-2, Hawrth Medical) Haworth Pr.

Piller, Charles. The Fail-Safe Society: Community Defiance & the End of American Technological Optimism. LC 92-24104. 1993. reprint ed. 15.95 (0-520-08202-8, Pub. by U CA Pr) Cal Prin Full Svc.

***Pillersdorf, Gary B., et al.** New York Motor Vehicle Accidents. 1999. write for info. (1-58012-050-4) James Pub Santa Ana.

Pillet, Christophe, jt. text see Cassagnau, Pascale.

Pillet, Roger A. Foreign-Language Study. LC 73-84194. 1993. lib. bdg. 15.00 (0-226-66826-6) U Ch Pr.

Pillet, Roger A., jt. auth. see Dunkel, Harold B.

P

An Asterisk (*) at the beginning of an entry indicates that the title is appearing for the first time.

Pilley, Christopher. Adult Education, Community Development & Older People: Releasing the Resource. (Council of Europe Ser.). 70p. 1990. pap. text 27.95 (*0-304-32271-7*) Continuum.

Pilley, H. Robert & Pilley, Lois V. GPS-Based Airport Operations: Requirements, Analysis & Algorithms. LC 94-69078. (Engineering Source Book Ser.: Vol. I). (Illus.). 400p. (Orig.). 1994. pap. 150.00 incl. disk (*0-9643568-0-5*) DSDC.

Pilley, Lois V., jt. auth. see Pilley, H. Robert.

Pillick, Aleta M., ed. see Ervin, Thomas J.

Pillider, Sarah, jt. auth. see Rose, John.

***Pilliner, Sarah.** Care of the Older Horse. (Allen Photographic Guides Ser.). (Illus.). 24p. 2000. pap. 10.95 (*0-85131-734-0*, Pub. by J A Allen) Trafalgar.

Pilliner, Sarah. Getting Horses Fit: Improve Your Horse's Performance. 2nd ed. 256p. 1993. pap. 29.95 (*0-632-03476-9*) Blackwell Sci.

— Horse Nutrition & Feeding. 1992. pap. 32.95 (*0-632-03239-1*) Blackwell Sci.

***Pilliner, Sarah.** Horse Nutrition & Feeding 2nd ed. LC 99-32651. 1999. write for info. (*0-632-05016-0*) Blackwell Sci.

Pilliner, Sarah. Practical Feeding of Horses & Ponies. LC 97-27543. 1998. pap. 29.95 (*0-632-04828-X*) Blackwell Sci.

Pilliner, Sarah & Davies, Zoe. Equine Science, Health & Performance: The Essentials. LC 96-11750. 240p. 1996. pap. 29.95 (*0-632-03913-2*) Blackwell Sci.

***Pilliner, Sarah & Davies, Zoe.** Getting Horses Fit: Improve Your Horse's Performance. 3rd ed. LC 00-29789. (Illus.). 2000. write for info. (*0-632-04811-5*) Blackwell Sci.

Pilliner, Sarah, jt. auth. see Houghton-Brown, Jeremy.

Pilling. Donkeys Day out. 1993. pap. 8.95 (*0-7459-2254-6*, Pub. by Lion Pubng) Trafalgar.

Pilling. The Professional Liability of Architects. 224p. 1998. pap. 59.50 (*0-419-17900-3*) Thomson Learn.

Pilling. Something to do with Love. 1997. pap. 10.95 (*0-7459-3115-4*, Pub. by Lion Pubng) Trafalgar.

Pilling, Ann. The Big Pink. large type ed. 382p. (J). 1989. 18.95 (*0-7451-0959-4*, G K Hall Lrg Type) Mac Lib Ref.

— Considering Helen. large type ed. 1993. 39.95 (*0-7066-1026-1*, Pub. by Remploy Pr) St Mut.

***Pilling, Ann.** The Kingfisher Treasury of Bible Stories, Poems & Prayers for Bedtime. (Illus.). 96p. (J). 2000. 18.95 (*0-7534-5329-0*) LKC.

— Who Laid the Cornerstone of the World: Great Stories from the Bible. (Illus.). 48p. (J). (ps-3). 2000. 15.95 (*0-8294-1485-1*) Loyola Pr.

Pilling, Arnold R. Aborigine Culture History: A Survey of Publications, 1954-1957. LC 61-12268. (Wayne State University Studies: No. 11: Anthropology). 229p. reprint ed. pap. 71.00 (*0-8357-5013-2*, 202765100055) Bks Demand.

Pilling, Claudia. Otto Ludwig: Das Literarische und Musikalische Werk Mit Einer Vollstandigen Otto-Ludwig-Bibliographie. 567p. 1998. 79.95 (*3-631-33149-5*) P Lang Pubng.

Pilling, Donald L. Competition in Defense Procurement. 80p. 1989. pap. 8.95 (*0-8157-7081-2*) Brookings.

Pilling, Doria & Watson, Graham, eds. Evaluating Quality in Services for Disabled & Older People. LC 95-7249. (Disability & Rehabilitation Ser.: Vol. 7). 1995. 29.95 (*1-85302-289-6*) Taylor & Francis.

Pilling, Doria, jt. auth. see National Children's Bureau Staff.

Pilling, Geoff, jt. auth. see Lea, John.

Pilling, James C. Bibliographies of the Languages of the North American Indians, 9 pts. in 3 vols. LC 76-174200. reprint ed. 125.00 (*0-404-07390-5*) AMS Pr.

— Bibliography of the Algonquian Languages. (Bureau of American Ethnology Bulletins Ser.). 614p. 1995. lib. bdg. 149.00 (*0-7812-4013-1*) Rprt Serv.

— Bibliography of the Algonquian Languages, 2 pts. 1988. reprint ed. lib. bdg. 75.00 (*0-7812-0312-0*) Rprt Serv.

— Bibliography of the Athapascan Languages. (Bureau of American Ethnology Bulletins Ser.). 125p. 1995. lib. bdg. 79.00 (*0-7812-4014-X*) Rprt Serv.

— Bibliography of the Chinookan Languages, Including the Chinook Jargon. (Bureau of American Ethnology Bulletins Ser.). 81p. 1995. lib. bdg. 79.00 (*0-7812-4015-8*) Rprt Serv.

— Bibliography of the Eskimo Languages. (Bureau of American Ethnology Bulletins Ser.). 161p. 1995. lib. bdg. 79.00 (*0-7812-4001-8*) Rprt Serv.

— Bibliography of the Iroquoian Languages. (Bureau of American Ethnology Bulletins Ser.). 208p. 1995. lib. bdg. 89.00 (*0-7812-4006-9*) Rprt Serv.

— Bibliography of the Muskhogean Languages. (Bureau of American Ethnology Bulletins Ser.). 114p. 1995. lib. bdg. 79.00 (*0-7812-4009-3*) Rprt Serv.

— Bibliography of the Salishan Languages. (Bureau of American Ethnology Bulletins Ser.). 86p. 1995. lib. bdg. 79.00 (*0-7812-4016-6*) Rprt Serv.

— Bibliography of the Siouan Language. (Bureau of American Ethnology Bulletins Ser.). 87p. 1995. lib. bdg. 79.00 (*0-7812-4005-0*) Rprt Serv.

— Bibliography of the Wakashan Languages. (Bureau of American Ethnology Bulletins Ser.). 70p. 1995. lib. bdg. 79.00 (*0-7812-4019-0*) Rprt Serv.

Pilling, Jayne, ed. A Reader in Animation Studies. 1998. pap. 24.95 (*1-86462-000-5*) Ind U Pr.

Pilling, John. Beckett Before Godot. LC 97-6870. 292p. (C). 1998. text 59.95 (*0-521-46496-X*) Cambridge U Pr.

— Phase Diagrams & Microstructures: A Computer Aided Learning Guide. 100p. 1992. 192.00 (*0-901716-11-1*, Pub. by Inst Materials) Ashgate Pub Co.

Pilling, John, ed. The Cambridge Companion to Beckett. LC 92-47287. (Cambridge Companions to Literature Ser.). (Illus.). 273p. (C). 1994. pap. text 19.95 (*0-521-42413-5*) Cambridge U Pr.

Pilling, John & Ridley, Norman. Superplasticity in Crystalline Solids. 214p. 1989. pap. text 36.00 (*0-901462-56-X*, Pub. by Inst Materials) Ashgate Pub Co.

Pilling, M. J. Low-Temperature Combustion & Autoignition. LC 97-44671. (Comprehensive Chemical Kinetics Ser.). 818p. 1997. 462.50 (*0-444-82485-5*) Elsevier.

Pilling, Marilyn Gear. My Nose Is a Gherkin Pickle Gone Wrong. LC 97-151273. 192p. 1996. pap. text 16.95 (*0-920953-96-4*) Stoddart Publ.

Pilling, Michael J. & Seakins, Paul W. Reaction Kinetics. 2nd ed. (Illus.). 318p. (C). 1996. pap. text 38.95 (*0-19-855527-X*) OUP.

***Pilling, Ron.** Annapolis a Portrait. Miller, Roger, ed. & photos by by. (Illus.). 168p. 2000. 39.95 (*0-911897-47-X*) Image Ltd.

Pilling, Simon, jt. auth. see Nicol, David.

Pilling, Stella, jt. ed. see Woodward, Hazel.

***Pilliod, Elizabeth.** Pontormos Diary. 1999. 32.00 (*0-226-66827-4*); pap. 20.00 (*0-226-66828-2*) U Ch Pr.

Pillion, jt. auth. see Pootler.

Pillips, W. R., jt. auth. see Grant, I. S.

Pillitteri, Adele. Child Health Nursing: Care of the Child & Family LC 98-51353. 1999. write for info. (*0-7817-1624-1*) Lppncott W & W.

— Maternal & Child Health Nursing: Care of the Childbearing & Childrearing Family. 2nd ed. LC 94-16338. 1,936p. 1994. text 72.95 (*0-397-55113-4*) Lppncott W & W.

— Maternal & Child Health Nursing: Care of the Childbearing & Childrearing Family. 3rd ed. LC 98-22348. 1775p. 1998. text 73.95 (*0-7817-1547-4*) Lppncott W & W.

— Pocket Guide for Maternal & Child Health Nursing. 816p. 1995. pap. text 19.95 (*0-397-55114-2*) Lppncott W & W.

Pillitteri, Joseph. Life Pulse. 1989. mass mkt. 3.95 (*1-55817-280-7*, Pinncle Kensgtn) Kensgtn Pub Corp.

***Pillitz, Christopher, photos by.** In the Flesh: The Body Cult in Brazil. (Illus.). 2000. 75.00 (*3-908163-24-2*, Pub. by Edit Stemmle) Abbeville Pr.

Pillman, Naka. African Diary: The Day-by-Day Account of an Incredible Adventure. LC 89-42868. 304p. 1990. 18.95 (*0-937552-31-3*) Quail Ridge.

Pillman, Naka, ed. Camel Crochet. 32p. 1990. pap. 9.95 (*0-944351-03-4*) N S D Products.

Pillo, G. Di, see Di Pillo, G.

Pilloud, Claude, et al, eds. Commentaire des Protocoles Additionnels du 8 Juin 1977 aux Conventions de Geneve du 12 Aout 1949. 1986. lib. bdg. 320.00 (*90-247-3403-7*) Kluwer Academic.

Pillow Gee, Marth, ed. Things to Make & Do for Lent & Easter: Creative Activities for Children's Ministry. unabridged ed. LC 97-37088. (Things to Make & Do Ser.). (Illus.). 98p. (J). (gr. k-5). 1998. pap. 12.95 (*1-57895-016-3*, Bridge Res) Curriculm Presbytrn KY.

— Things to Make & Do for Pentecost: Creative Activities for Children's Ministry. unabridged ed. LC 97-35299. (Things to Make & Do Ser.). (Illus.). 98p. (J). (gr. k-5). 1998. pap. 12.95 (*1-57895-017-1*, Bridge Res) Curriculm Presbytrn KY.

Pillow Gee, Martha, ed. Things to Make & Do/Advent-Christmas. unabridged ed. LC 97-17816. (Things to Make & Do Ser.: Vol. 1). (Illus.). 96p. (Orig.). (J). (gr. k-4). 1997. pap. 12.95 (*1-57895-015-5*, Bridge Res) Curriculm Presbytrn KY.

***Pillow, Kirk.** Sublime Understanding: Aesthetic Reflection in Kant & Hegel. LC 00-21975. (Studies in Contemporary German Social Thought). 386p. (C). 2000. 37.95 (*0-262-16192-3*) MIT Pr.

Pillow, Martha, ed. see Dare, Alice.

Pillow, Wanda S., jt. ed. see St. Pierre, Elizabeth.

Pillsbury. Operative Challenges in Head & Neck Surgery. 1991. write for info. (*0-8151-6707-5*) Mosby Inc.

***Pillsbury Company.** Pillsbury Complete Cookbook: Recipes from America's Most Trusted Kitchens. Rosener, Maureen, ed. LC 99-46945. (Illus.). 544p. 2000. 26.95 (*0-609-60284-5*) C Potter.

Pillsbury Company Staff. A Book for a Cook. LC 94-1089. 128p. 1994. reprint ed. 12.95 (*1-55709-225-7*) Applewood.

— A Little Book for a Little Cook. 32p. (J). 1992. 14.95 (*1-55709-172-2*) Applewood.

— Pillsbury: Best Desserts. LC 98-9183. (Illus.). 352p. 1998. 24.95 (*0-609-60285-3*) C Potter.

— Pillsbury: Fast & Healthy Cookbook. LC 97-23960. 352p. 1998. 24.95 (*0-609-60085-0*) C Potter.

— Pillsbury Best Cookies Cookbook: Favorite Recipes from America's Most-Trusted Kitchens. LC 97-1773. 1997. 19.95 (*0-609-60084-2*) C Potter.

— Pillsbury, Best Muffins & Quick Breads Cookbook: Favorite Recipes from America's Most-Trusted Kitchens. LC 98-38176. (Pillsbury Ser.). (Illus.). 239p. 1999. 19.95 (*0-609-60283-7*) Crown Pub Group.

— Pillsbury Chicken Cookbook. LC 97-184242. 1997. 19.95 (*0-517-70880-9*) C Potter.

— Pillsbury Kitchens' Family Cookbook. write for info. (*0-318-58126-4*) S&S Trade.

— Pillsbury One Dish Meals: More than 300 Recipes for Crock-Pot Dishes, Casseroles, Stir-Fries & More. LC 99-14444. 336p. 1999. 24.95 (*0-609-60282-9*) Crown.

Pillsbury Company Staff, ed. The Best of Classic Cookbooks: 350 Recipes from 20 Years of Pillsbury's Best-Selling Cooking Magazine. LC 98-28784. (Illus.). 352p. 1998. 24.95 (*0-609-60279-9*) Crown.

— Pillsbury: Best of the Bake-Off Cookbook. LC 96-221257. 1996. 24.95 (*0-517-70574-5*) Random.

Pillsbury Company Staff, jt. auth. see Creative Publishing International Staff.

Pillsbury, Edmund P. & Richards, Louise E. The Graphic Art of Federico Barocci. 1978. pap. 6.00 (*0-89467-004-2*) Yale Art Gallery.

Pillsbury, Edmund P., jt. auth. see Riely, John.

Pillsbury, Harold, jt. auth. see Weissler, Mark.

Pillsbury, Harold C., jt. ed. see Carrasco, Vincent N.

Pillsbury, Linda G. Survival Tips for Working Moms: Two Hundred Ninety-Seven Real Tips from Real Moms. LC 93-87732. (Illus.). 192p. (Orig.). 1994. pap. 10.95 (*0-9622036-5-3*) Prsptive Pub.

***Pillsbury, Michael.** China Debates the Future Security Environment LC 99-26623. 1999. write for info. (*1-57906-024-2*) Natl Defense.

— Chinese Views of Future Warfare. 471p. 1998. per. 22.00 (*0-16-061222-5*) USGPO.

Pillsbury, Michael, ed. Chinese Views of Future Warfare. (Illus.). 421p. (C). 1997. pap. text 40.00 (*0-7881-4668-8*) DIANE Pub.

— Chinese Views of Future Warfare. rev. ed. LC 98-40459. (Illus.). 471p. 1998. pap., per. 22.00 (*1-57906-016-1*) Natl Defense.

Pillsbury, Norman H., et al, eds. Proceedings of a Symposium on Oak Woodlands: Ecology, Management, & Urban Interface Issues. (Illus.). 738p. (C). 1999. reprint ed. pap. text 75.00 (*0-7881-7674-9*) DIANE Pub.

Pillsbury, Parker. Acts of the Anti-Slavery Apostles. LC 76-82212. (Anti-Slavery Crusade in America Ser.). 1970. reprint ed. 43.95 (*0-405-00651-9*) Ayer.

— Acts of the Anti-Slavery Apostles. LC 70-92758. 503p. 1969. reprint ed. lib. bdg. 69.50 (*0-8371-2183-3*, PIA&) Greenwood.

Pillsbury, Richard. No Foreign Food: The American Diet in Time & Place. LC 97-47342. (Geographies of Imagination Ser.). 272p. (C). 1998. pap. text 23.00 (*0-8133-2739-3*, Pub. by Westview) HarpC.

Pillsbury, Samuel H. The Invasion of Planet Wampetter. LC 95-8432. (Illus.). 144p. (J). (gr. 3-8). 1995. 15.00 (*0-9622036-6-1*) Prsptive Pub.

Pillsbury, Samuel H. Judging Evil: Rethinking the Law of Murder & Manslaughter. pap. text 20.00 (*0-8147-6680-3*) NYU Pr.

Pillsbury, Samuel H. Judging Evil: Rethinking the Law of Murder & Manslaughter. LC 98-28137. 256p. 1998. text 50.00 (*0-8147-6665-X*) NYU Pr.

Pillsbury, Walter B. Attention. LC 73-2982. (Classics in Psychology Ser.). 1980. reprint ed. 28.95 (*0-405-05154-9*) Ayer.

***Pillunat, L. E., ed.** Current Concepts on Ocular Blood Flow in Glaucoma. 274p. 1999. 75.00 (*90-6299-173-4*) Kugler Pubns.

Pilnyak, Boris. Mahogany & Other Stories. Reck, Vera T. & Green, Michael, trs. (RUS.). 302p. 1993. pap. 16.95 (*0-87501-104-7*) Ardis Pubs.

— The Naked Year. Tulloch, Alexander R., tr. from RUS. 207p. 1975. pap. 10.95 (*0-88233-078-0*) Ardis Pubs.

— The Naked Year. LC 70-174201. reprint ed. 34.50 (*0-404-06778-6*) AMS Pr.

— Volga Falls to the Caspian Sea. LC 71-110428. reprint ed. 37.50 (*0-404-05047-6*) AMS Pr.

Pilon, Charles D. Bridging the Gap: Twenty Years after the War in Vietnam. Pilon, Linda M., ed. LC 96-92168. (Illus.). 201p. (Orig.). 1996. pap. 10.95 (*1-889052-03-5*) Quail Publns.

Pilon, Frederick. Essay on the Character of Hamlet. 2nd ed. LC 73-174202. reprint ed. 29.50 (*0-404-05048-4*) AMS Pr.

Pilon, J., jt. auth. see Larouche, L.

Pilon, Jean-Luc, jt. ed. see Morrison, David A.

Pilon, Juliana G. The Bloody Flag: Post-Communist Nationalism in Eastern Europe: Spotlight on Romania. 280p. (C). 1992. 34.95 (*1-56000-062-7*); pap. 19.95 (*1-56000-620-X*) Transaction Pubs.

— Notes from the Other Side of Night. LC 94-7701. 1994. reprint ed. pap. text 14.95 (*0-8191-9510-3*) U Pr of Amer.

Pilon, Juliana G. & Bennett, Ralph K. The U. N. Assessing Soviet Abuses. (C). 1990. 45.00 (*0-907967-90-6*, Pub. by Inst Euro Def & Strat) St Mut.

***Pilon, Karen.** Ludlow. (Images of America Ser.). 128p. 1999. pap. 18.99 (*0-7385-0224-3*) Arcadia Publng.

Pilon, Linda M., ed. see Pilon, Charles D.

Pilon, Pierre & Burmeister, Steve, eds. Chemistry- & Biology-Based Technologies for Contraband Detection, Vol. 2937. LC 96-69887. 278p. 1997. 66.00 (*0-8194-2339-4*) SPIE.

Pilon, Roger. Politics & Law of Term Limits. LC 94-35217. 152p. 1994. 19.95 (*1-882577-12-4*); pap. 10.95 (*1-882577-13-2*) Cato Inst.

***Pilon, Roger, pref.** The Declaration of Independence & the Constitution of the United States. 58p. 2000. pap. 4.95 (*1-882577-98-1*) Cato Inst.

Pilot Books Staff. Free U. S. Tourist Attractions, 1998/1999 Edition: A Directory of Free Family Entertainment in Every State of the Union. rev. ed. LC 77-3251. 224p. 1998. pap. 12.95 (*0-87576-204-2*) Pilot Bks.

— The 1999 Zip/Area Code Directory: The Quick, Easy Way to Locate Area Codes for All U. S. Postal Zip Codes... Without Operator Assistance. rev. ed. (Where to Find What You Want to Know Ser.). 80p. 1999. pap. 9.95 (*0-87576-254-9*) Pilot Bks.

***Pilot Books Staff.** Zip/Area Code Directory 2000: The Quick, Easy Way to Locate Area Codes for All U. S. Postal Zip Codes Without Operator Assistance! 2000. reprint ed. pap. text 9.95 (*0-87576-226-3*, Pub. by Pilot Bks) Midpt Trade.

Pilot, Kevin. Credit Approved. 144p. 1992. pap. 6.95 (*1-55850-111-8*) Adams Media.

Pilot, Michael, jt. auth. see Rosenthal, Neal H.

Pilot, Patricia L. Theron Came Later. 210p. 1984. 7.45 (*0-89697-137-6*) Intl Univ Pr.

Pilot-Raichoor, Christiane, jt. auth. see Hockings, Paul.

Pilot Staff. National Directory of Budget Motels, 1998-1999 Edition. 22nd rev. ed. (Well-Prepared Traveler Ser.). 346p. 1998. pap. 12.95 (*0-87576-221-2*) Pilot Bks.

Pilot Study on Database Interfaces Committee, ed. see National Research Council Staff.

Pilotta, Joseph, jt. auth. see Mickunas, Algis.

Pilotta, Joseph J. & Mickunas, Algis. Science of Communication: Its Phenomenological Foundation. (Communication Textbook Series, General Communication Theory & Methodology Subser.). 200p. 1990. text 49.95 (*0-8058-0401-3*) L Erlbaum Assocs.

Pilotta, Joseph J., jt. ed. see Golden, James L.

Piloty, R., et al. CONLAN Report. (Lecture Notes in Computer Science Ser.: Vol. 151). 174p. 1983. 24.00 (*0-387-12275-3*) Spr-Verlag.

Pilous, V. & Stransky, K. Structural Stability of Deposits & Welded Joints in Power Engineering. 200p. 1995. pap. 74.00 (*1-898326-08-8*, Pub. by CISP) Balogh.

Pilowsky, Daniel J., jt. ed. see Chambers, William.

Pilowsky, Issy. Abnormal Illness Behaviour. LC 96-38645. 278p. 1997. 83.95 (*0-471-96573-1*) Wiley.

Pilpay, T. The Fables of Pilpay. 220p. 1987. 78.00 (*1-85077-144-8*, Pub. by Darf Pubs Ltd) St Mut.

Pilsbry, H. A., et al. Land Snails from Hawaii, Christmas Island & Samoa. (BMB Ser.: Vol. 47). 1969. reprint ed. pap. 25.00 (*0-527-02153-9*) Periodicals Srv.

Pilsbry, Henry A. Land Mollusca of North America: North of Mexico, Vol. 1, Pts. 1 & 2. (Monograph Ser.: No. 3). (Illus.). 992p. (Orig.). 1939. reprint ed. pap. 70.00 (*0-910006-11-3*) Acad Nat Sci Phila.

— Land Mollusca of North America: North of Mexico, Vol. 2, Pts. 1 & 2. (Illus.). (Orig.). write for info. (*0-685-08428-0*) Acad Nat Sci Phila.

— Land Mollusca of North America: North of Mexico, Vol. 2, Pts. 1 & 2. (Monograph Ser.: No. 3). (Illus.). 1112p. (Orig.). 1946. reprint ed. pap. 70.00 (*0-910006-12-1*) Acad Nat Sci Phila.

Pilsbury, D. B. & Getchell, E. A. The Pillsbury Family; Being a History of William & Dorothy Pillsbury (or Pilsbery) of Newbury in New England, & Their Descendants to the Eleventh Generation. (Illus.). 336p. 1989. reprint ed. pap. 40.25 (*0-8328-0969-1*); reprint ed. lib. bdg. 48.25 (*0-8328-0968-3*) Higginson Bk Co.

Pilson, Betty A., jt. auth. see Baughan, Barbara C.

Pilson, Michael E. Introduction to the Chemistry of the Sea. LC 97-35215. 431p. (C). 1998. 84.00 (*0-13-258971-0*) P-H.

Pilsudska, Alexandra. Pilsudski: A Biography by His Wife. LC 76-135829. (Eastern Europe Collection). 1971. reprint ed. 24.95 (*0-405-02771-0*) Ayer.

Pilsudski Institute of America Staff. Poland in the British Parliament: Documentary Material Relating to the Cause of Poland During World War Two, 3 vols., 2. Jedrzejewicz, Waclaw, ed. 1834p. write for info. (*0-940962-26-8*) Polish Inst Art & Sci.

— Poland in the British Parliament: Documentary Material Relating to the Cause of Poland During World War Two, 3 vols., 3. Jedrzejewicz, Waclaw, ed. 1834p. write for info. (*0-940962-27-6*) Polish Inst Art & Sci.

Pilsudski, Jozef. Joseph Pilsudski: The Memories of a Polish Revolutionary & Soldier. Gillie, D. R., ed. LC 70-101275. reprint ed. 42.50 (*0-404-05049-2*) AMS Pr.

Piltch, Benjamin & Smergut, Peter. Class Trips. (Skyview Ser.). 64p. (J). (gr. 4-8). 1983. 6.95 (*0-934618-00-3*) Learning Well.

— Money Matters. (Skyview Ser.). 64p. (YA). (gr. 7-12). 1983. 6.95 (*0-934618-03-8*) Learning Well.

Piltch, Benjamin, ed. see Funes, Marilyn & Lazarus, Alan.

Piltch, Benjamin, ed. see Kaufman, Tanya & Wishny, Judith.

Piltz, Elisabeth. The Von Post Collection of Cypriote Late Byzantine Glazed Pottery. (Studies in Mediterranean Archaeology: Vol. CXIX). (Illus.). 94p. (Orig.). 1996. pap. 45.00 (*91-7081-160-1*, Pub. by P Astroms) Coronet Bks.

Piltz, Elisabeth, ed. Byzantium & Islam in Scandinavia: Acts of a Symposium at Uppsala University June 15-16 1996. (Studies in Mediterranean Archaeology: Vol. CXXVI). (GER, FRE & ENG.). 138p. 1998. pap. 65.00 (*91-7081-151-2*) P Astroms.

Piltz, Elisabeth & Astrom, Paul, eds. Kairos: Studies in Art History & Literature. (Studies in Mediterranean Archaeology & Literature Pocket Bk.: No. 147). (Illus.). 189p. 1998. pap. 49.50 (*91-7081-180-6*, Pub. by P Astroms) Coronet Bks.

Piltz, Rick. Our Changing Planet: The FY 1999 U. S. Global Change Research Program. (Illus.). 130p. (C). 1999. pap. text 35.00 (*0-7881-7589-0*) DIANE Pub.

Pilu, G., jt. ed. see Wladimiroff, Juri W.

***Pilu, Gianluigi & Nicolaides, Kypros H., eds.** Diagnosis of Fetal Abnormalities: The 18-23-Week Scan. LC 99-42950. (Diploma in Fetal Medicine Ser.: Vol. 1). (Illus.). 150p. 1999. 55.00 (*1-85070-492-9*) Prthnon Pub.

Piluek, K., jt. auth. see Siemonsma, J. S.

Piluso, V., jt. auth. see Mazzolani, F. M.

Piluso, Vincenzo, jt. auth. see Faella, Ciro.

Pilutik, Anastasia D., jt. auth. see Seco, Nina S.

Pilyugin, S. Y. Introduction to Structurally Stable Systems of Differential Equations. 200p. 1992. 86.00 (*0-8176-2574-7*) Birkhauser.

Pilyugin, Sergei Y. The Space of Dynamical Systems with the C POS-Topology. LC 94-887. (Lecture Notes in Mathematics Ser.: Vol. 1571). (Illus.). x, 188p. 1994. 34.95 (*0-387-57702-5*) Spr-Verlag.

P

***Pilyugin, Sergei Yu.** Shadowing in Dynamical Systems. Dold, A. et al, eds. LC 99-38998. (Lecture Notes in Mathematics Ser.: Vol. 1706). xvii, 271p. 1999. pap. 49.00 (*3-540-66299-5*) Spr-Verlag.

Pilz, David & Molina, Randy, eds. Managing Forest Ecosystems to Conserve Fungus Diversity & Sustain Wild Mushroom Harvests. 104p. (C). 1998. pap. text 35.00 (*0-7881-4343-3*) DIANE Pub.

Pilz, G., jt. auth. see Lidl, Rudolf.

Pilz, Gunter, jt. auth. see Lidl, Rudolf.

***Pilz, Wolfgang.** Widerstand: Konstruktion Eines Begriffes Fur die Improvisatorische Musiktherapie Nach Nordoff/Robbins Mit Psychiatrischen Patienten. (Europaische Hochschulschriften Ser.). X, 278p. 1999. 48.95 (*3-631-34877-0*) P Lang Pubng.

Pilzer, Karl. The Treasure of the Tear. (Illus.). 40p. (J). Date not set. pap. write for info. (*0-936015-51-9*) Pocahontas Pr.

Pilzer, Paul Z. God Wants You to Be Rich. 288p. 1997. per. 12.00 (*0-684-82532-5*) S&S Trade Pap.

— God Wants You to Be Rich: The Theology of Economics. LC 95-20457. 288p. 1995. 22.50 (*0-684-80767-X*) Simon & Schuster.

— Unlimited Wealth. abr. ed. 1991. 11.00 incl. audio (*0-679-40227-6*) Knopf.

Pim, Alan. Financial & Economic History of the African Tropical Territories. 1970. reprint ed. 25.00 (*0-87266-046-X*) Argosy.

Pim, Bedford. Negro & Jamaica. LC 72-157375. (Black Heritage Library Collection). 1977. 15.95 (*0-8369-8813-2*) Ayer.

Pim, Ralph L. Winning Basketball: Techniques & Drills for Playing Better Basketball. (Illus.). 192p. 1994. pap. 12.95 (*0-8092-3553-6*, 355360, Contemporary Bks) NTC Contemp Pub Co.

Pimenov, G. S., jt. auth. see Novichkov, N. N.

Pimenov, M. G. & Leonov, M. V. The Genera of the Umbelliferae. viii, 156p. 1993. pap. 24.00 (*0-947643-58-3*, Pub. by Royal Botnic Grdns) Balogh.

Pimenoz & Novichkov, N. N. English-Russian Military Dictionary of Radioelectronics, Laser & Infrared Engineering. (ENG & RUS.). 1984. 125.00 (*0-8288-3971-9*, F37440) Fr & Eur.

Pimenta, Wendy, ed. see LeBell, Gene.

Pimental-Habib, Richard L. Empowering the Tribe: A Positive Guide to Gay & Lesbian Self-Esteem. 266p. 1999. pap. 12.00 (*1-57566-424-0*) Kensgtn Pub Corp.

Pimental, Ken & Teixeira, Kevin. Virtual Reality: Through the New Looking Glass. 2nd ed. LC 94-3440. 1994. 36.95 (*0-07-050167-X*, Windcrest) TAB Bks.

Pimentel. Handbook of Growth Factors, 3 Vols. 1994. 628.80 (*0-8493-2508-0*) CRC Pr.

Pimentel, Alejandro, ed. see Averill, Diane & Bajema, Edith.

Pimentel, Alejandro, ed. see Douma, J.

Pimentel, Alejandro, ed. see Ridderbos, Herman.

Pimentel, Alejandro, ed. see Rudie, Carol Veldman.

Pimentel, Alejandro, ed. see Stott, John.

Pimentel, Alejandro, ed. see Vander Griend, Donna.

Pimentel, Benjamin. Rebolusyon: A Generation of Struggle in the Philippines. 365p. 1991. 26.00 (*0-85345-822-7*, Pub. by Monthly Rev); pap. 15.00 (*0-85345-823-5*, Pub. by Monthly Rev) NYU Pr.

Pimentel, D., jt. auth. see Paoletti, M. G.

Pimentel, David. Handbook of Energy Utilization in Agriculture. 496p. 1980. ring bd. 134.00 (*0-8493-2661-3*, S494, CRC Reprint) Franklin.

— Techniques for Reducing Pesticide Use: Economic & Environmental Benefits. LC 96-27169. 456p. 1997. 135.00 (*0-471-96838-2*) Wiley.

Pimentel, David, ed. Handbook of Pest Management in Agriculture, I. 2nd ed. 784p. 1990. lib. bdg. 325.00 (*0-8493-3844-1*, SB950) CRC Pr.

— Handbook of Pest Management in Agriculture, II. 2nd ed. 784p. 1990. lib. bdg. 325.00 (*0-8493-3845-X*, SB950) CRC Pr.

— Handbook of Pest Management in Agriculture, III. 2nd ed. 768p. 1990. lib. bdg. 325.00 (*0-8493-3846-8*, SB950) CRC Pr.

— Handbook of Pest Management in Agriculture, Vol. 1. 296p. 1981. 333.00 (*0-8493-3841-7*, SB950) CRC Pr.

— Handbook of Pest Management in Agriculture, Vol. 2. 336p. 1981. 282.00 (*0-8493-3842-5*) CRC Pr.

— Handbook of Pest Management in Agriculture, Vol. 3. 672p. 1981. 364.00 (*0-8493-3843-3*) CRC Pr.

***Pimentel, David, et al, eds.** Ecological Integrity: Integrating Environment, Conservation & Health. 375p. 2000. 70.00 (*1-55963-807-9*); pap. 35.00 (*1-55963-808-7*) Island Pr.

Pimentel, David & Pimentel, Marcia H., eds. Food, Energy & Society. 2nd rev. ed. 392p. 1996. 39.95 (*0-87081-386-2*) Univ Pr Colo.

Pimentel, David, jt. ed. see Kidd, Charles V.

Pimentel, David, jt. ed. see Sheets, T. J.

Pimentel, Enrique. Handbook of Growth Factors, 1. LC 93-40108. 384p. 1994. boxed set 146.95 (*0-8493-2505-6*) CRC Pr.

— Handbook of Growth Factors, Vol. 3. LC 93-40108. 384p. 1994. boxed set 146.95 (*0-8493-2507-2*) CRC Pr.

— Handbook of Growth Factors, Vol. II: Peptide Growth Factors, Vol. 2. 384p. 1994. boxed set 146.95 (*0-8493-2506-4*, 2506) CRC Pr.

— Hormones, Growth Factors & Oncogenes. 256p. 1987. lib. bdg. 239.00 (*0-8493-5346-7*, QP571) CRC Pr.

— Oncogenes. LC 85-28085. 224p. 1986. 125.00 (*0-8493-6566-X*, RC268, CRC Reprint) Franklin.

— Oncogenes, Vol. 1. 2nd ed. LC 85-28085. 528p. 1989. 206.00 (*0-8493-6505-8*, RC268) Franklin.

Pimentel, Enrique, ed. Oncogenes, Vol. II. 2nd ed. 448p. 1989. 234.00 (*0-8493-6506-6*, RC268, CRC Reprint) Franklin.

Pimentel, George C., ed. Chemistry: An Experimental Science. LC 63-18323. (Chemical Education Material Study Ser.). (Illus.). 466p. (C). 1963. pap. text, student ed. 5.60 (*0-7167-0002-6*) W H Freeman.

Pimentel, George C. & Coonrod, Janice A. Opportunities in Chemistry: Today & Tomorrow. National Research Council Staff, ed. 256p. (Orig.). (C). 1987. pap. text 10.00 (*0-309-03742-5*) Natl Acad Pr.

Pimentel, George C. & Sprately, Richard D. Chemical Bonding Clarified Through Quantum Mechanics. LC 71-75914. 1969. 22.95 (*0-8162-6781-2*) Holden-Day.

Pimentel, George C. & Spratley, Richard D. Understanding Chemical Thermodynamics. LC 69-13419. (Illus.). (C). 1969. pap. text 22.00 (*0-8162-6791-X*) Holden-Day.

— Understanding Chemistry. LC 70-142944. (C). 1971. 38.00 (*0-8162-6761-8*) Holden-Day.

Pimentel, Luz A. Metaphoric Narration: The Paranarrative Dimension of a la Recherche du Temps Perdu. (Romance Ser.). 168p. 1990. text 45.00 (*0-8020-2735-0*) U of Toronto Pr.

Pimentel, Marcia H., jt. ed. see Pimentel, David.

Pimentel, Ricardo. House with Two Doors. LC 97-9912. 176p. 1997. pap. 14.00 (*0-927534-67-3*) Biling Rev-Pr.

Pimentel, Richard. Developing Jobs for Persons with Disabilities. (C). 1984. 79.00 (*0-942071-06-9*) M Wright & Assocs.

— The Return to Work Process: A Case Management Approach. 1996. text 29.95 (*0-942071-33-6*) M Wright & Assocs.

Pimentel, Richard, et al. The Americans with Disabilities Act: A Comprehensive Guide to Title I. 374p. (C). 1992. text 125.00 (*0-942071-17-4*) M Wright & Assocs.

— The Americans with Disabilities Act: Making the ADA Work for You. 2nd ed. 142p. 1992. 39.50 (*0-685-56811-3*, PB14) Soc Human Resc Mgmt.

— The Job Placement - ADA Connection: Limiting Liabilities & Maximizing Opportunities for Training & Placement of Persons with Disabilities. Wright, Anita L., ed. 63p. (Orig.). 1993. pap. 24.95 (*0-942071-27-1*, 242B) M Wright & Assocs.

— Job Placement for the Industrially Injured Worker. 95p. (C). 1988. student ed. 28.50 (*0-942071-04-2*) M Wright & Assocs.

— Performance Based Placement Manual. rev. ed. 52p. 1987. reprint ed. student ed. 19.50 (*0-942071-01-8*) M Wright & Assocs.

— What Managers & Supervisors Need to Know about the ADA: Trainer's Guide. 113p. (C). 1992. 395.00 (*0-942071-18-2*) M Wright & Assocs.

— The Workers' Compensation-ADA Connection: Supervisory Tools for Workers' Compensation Cost Containment That Reduce ADA Liability. Wright, Anita L., ed. LC 93-12743. 55p. (Orig.). (C). 1993. pap. text 29.50 (*0-942071-24-7*) M Wright & Assocs.

Pimentel, Richard, jt. auth. see Bissonnette, Denise.

Pimentel, Richard K., et al. The Taking Control Process: Beyond Light Duty. Wexler, Barbara & Wright, Anita L., eds. 135p. (C). 1995. 89.00 (*0-942071-31-X*) M Wright & Assocs.

Pimentel, Susan, jt. auth. see Doyle, Denis P.

Pimentel, Wayne. Dogtown & Ditches: Life on the Westside. LC 87-82867. 134p. 1987. pap. 18.95 (*0-944707-00-9*) Loose Change.

Pimlott, Ben. Labour & the Left in the 1930's. (Illus.). 272p. 1986. reprint ed. pap. text 18.95 (*0-04-941016-4*) Routledge.

— The Queen: A Biography of Elizabeth II. LC 97-21270. 672p. 1997. 30.00 (*0-471-19431-X*) Wiley.

— The Queen: A Biography of Elizabeth II. 672p. 1998. pap. 18.95 (*0-471-28330-4*) Wiley.

Pimlott, Ben, jt. ed. see MacGregor, Susanne.

Pimlott, J. A. The Englishman's Holiday: A Social History LC 75-16045. (Flare Books Ser.). 318 p. 1976. write for info. (*0-8002-0159-0*) Intl Pubns Serv.

Pimlott, John. Luftwaffe: The Illustrated History of the German Air Force in WW II. LC 98-2581. (Illus.). 176p. 1998. 24.95 (*0-7603-0516-1*) MBI Pubg.

— The Military Quiz Book. 128p. 1993. pap. 9.95 (*1-85367-151-7*, 5425) Stackpole.

— SS: Hell on the Eastern Front: The Waffen-SS War in Russia 1941-45. LC 98-15423. (Illus.). 192p. 1998. 24.95 (*0-7603-0538-2*) MBI Pubg.

Pimlott, John, ed. Rommel: In His Own Words. (Illus.). 192p. 1994. 29.95 (*1-85367-185-1*, 5439) Stackpole.

Pimlott, John & Bullock, Alan, contrib. by. The Historical Atlas of World War II. LC 94-39820. (Reference Bks.). 223p. 1995. 45.00 (*0-8050-3929-5*) H Holt & Co.

Pimlott, John, jt. ed. see Crenshaw, Martha.

Pimlott, John, jt. ed. see Holmes, Richard.

Pimm, David. Speaking Mathematically: Communications in Mathematics Classrooms. 240p. 1989. 44.95 (*0-7102-1133-3*, 11333, Routledge Thoemms) Routledge.

— Symbols & Meanings in School Mathematics. LC 94-39323. (Illus.). 240p. (C). 1995. pap. 22.99 (*0-415-11385-7*, C0464) Routledge.

Pimm, June B. & Feist, Joseph R. Psychological Risks of Coronary Bypass Surgery. 226p. 1984. 59.50 (*0-306-41586-0*, Plenum Trade) Perseus Pubng.

Pimm, Malcolm V., jt. auth. see Perkins, Alan C.

***Pimm, Paul.** Living with Cerebral Palsy. LC 99-27202. 32p. 1999. lib. bdg. 22.83 (*0-8172-5744-6*) Raintree Steck-V.

Pimm, Stuart L. The Balance of Nature? Ecological Issues in the Conservation of Species & Communities. LC 91-3089. (Illus.). 448p. 1991. pap. text 27.50 (*0-226-66830-4*) U Ch Pr.

— The Balance of Nature? Ecological Issues in the Conservation of Species & Communities. LC 91-3089. (Illus.). 464p. 1993. lib. bdg. 62.00 (*0-226-66829-0*) U Ch Pr.

Pimpinelli, Alberto & Villain, Jacques. Physics of Crystal Growth. (Collection Alea - Saclay Ser.: Vol. 4). (Illus.). 398p. (C). 1999. text 90.00 (*0-521-55198-6*); pap. text 44.95 (*0-521-55855-7*) Cambridge U Pr.

Pimple, Kenneth D., et al, eds. Ethical Issues in the Use of Animals in Research: A Special Issue of Ethics & Behavior, Vol. 7, No. 2. 100p. 1997. pap. 20.00 (*0-8058-9860-3*) L Erlbaum Assocs.

Pimsler, Steven, jt. auth. see Yamada, Yoshimitsu.

Pimsleur. Counterparts. 2nd ed. (College ESL Ser.). (J). 1994. text, suppl. ed. 7.95 (*0-8384-5008-3*) Heinle & Heinle.

— Encounters. 3rd ed. (C). 1986. pap. text, teacher ed. 3.00 (*0-15-522601-0*) Harcourt Coll Pubs.

***Pimsleur.** Romanian. 2000. text 95.00 (*0-671-31529-3*) S&S Trade.

Pimsleur, Beverly. Counterparts. 2nd ed. LC 94-22498. (College ESL Ser.). 173p. (J). 1994. mass mkt. 26.95 (*0-8384-5006-7*) Heinle & Heinle.

Pimsleur, Beverly, jt. auth. see Pimsleur, Paul.

***Pimsleur International.** English As a Second Language: Russian Basic. unabridged ed. (RUS.). 1999. audio 29.95 (*0-671-31573-0*) S&S Audio.

— Portuguese (Brazilian) Basic. unabridged ed. (POR.). 1998. audio 29.95 (*0-671-31578-1*) S&S Audio.

Pimsleur International Staff. Pimsleur Hebrew, Set. unabridged ed. (HEB.). 1997. audio 295.00 (*0-671-57932-0*) S&S Audio.

— Pimsleur Ojibwe, Set. unabridged ed. (OJI.). 1997. audio 295.00 (*0-671-57941-X*) S&S Audio.

— Pimsleur Spanish III, Set. unabridged ed. (SPA.). 1997. audio 295.00 (*0-671-57952-5*) S&S Audio.

***Pimsleur International Staff, ed.** Hindi. 1999. 95.00 (*0-671-04472-9*) S&S Trade.

***Pimsleur Language Method Staff.** Danish. 1999. 95.00 (*0-671-04397-8*) S&S Trade.

Pimsleur Language Method Staff. Norwegian. 1999. 95.00 (*0-671-04398-6*) S&S Trade.

***Pimsleur Language Programs Staff.** French. 2000. text 29.95 (*0-671-31576-5*); text 295.00 (*0-671-31600-1*) S&S Trade.

— German. 2000. text 29.95 (*0-671-31577-3*); text 295.00 (*0-671-31601-X*) S&S Trade.

— Italian. 2000. text 29.95 (*0-671-31568-4*); text 295.00 (*0-671-31602-8*) S&S Trade.

— Japanese. 2000. text 29.95 (*0-671-31649-4*); text 295.00 (*0-671-31604-4*) S&S Trade.

— Russian. 2000. text 29.95 (*0-671-31646-X*); text 295.00 (*0-671-31603-6*) S&S Trade.

Pimsleur, Meira G., ed. Copyright Society of the U. S. A. Bulletin: Cumulative Index, Vols. 1-20, 1953-1973. LC 74-25274. x, 229p. 1975. text 32.50 (*0-8377-0421-9*, Rothman) W S Hein.

Pimsleur, Paul. Albanian: Short Course, Set. 1994th ed. (Pimsleur Language Learning Ser.). 1994. pap., student ed. 149.95 incl. audio SyberVision.

— Ukranian, Set. 1993rd ed. (Pimsleur Language Learning Ser.). 1993. pap., student ed. 345.00 incl. audio SyberVision.

Pimsleur, Paul & Pimsleur, Beverly. C'Est la Vie. 5th ed. (FRE.). 225p. (C). 1992. pap. text 36.50 (*0-03-055813-1*) Harcourt Coll Pubs.

Pimsleur, Paul, et al. Encounters: An ESL Reader. 3rd ed. 192p. (C). 1986. pap. text 20.50 (*0-15-522600-2*) Harcourt Coll Pubs.

— SOL Y SOMBRA 3E. 3rd ed. (SPA., Illus.). 224p. (C). 1983. pap. text 36.00 (*0-15-582413-9*) Harcourt Coll Pubs.

Pimsleur, Paul, ed. see International Congress of Applied Linguistics Staf.

***Pimsleur, X.** Croatian. 1999. 95.00 (*0-671-58189-9*) S&S Trade.

— English: English For Japanese Speakers. 2nd ed. 1999. 295.00 (*0-671-58114-7*) S&S Trade.

Pin Calmon, Paulo Du, see Galbraith, James K. & Du Pin Calmon, Paulo.

Pin, Emile J. & Turndorf, Jamie. The Pleasure of Your Company: A Socio-Psychological Analysis of Modern Sociability. 288p. 1985. 59.95 (*0-275-91755-X*, C1755, Praeger Pubs) Greenwood.

Pin, Hired, ed. see Lee, Brenda.

Pin, J. E. Varieties of Formal Languages. (Foundations of Computer Science Ser.). (Illus.). 148p. (C). 1986. 65.00 (*0-306-42294-8*, Plenum Trade) Perseus Pubng.

Pin, J. E., ed. Formal Properties of Finite Automata & Applications. (Lecture Notes in Computer Science Ser.: Vol. 386). viii, 260p. 1989. 37.00 (*0-387-51631-X*) Spr-Verlag.

Pin Xin. Collection of Bin Xin's Prose, 2 vols. (CHI.). pap. 29.95 (*7-5339-0621-7*, Pub. by China Intl Bk) Distribks Inc.

Pina-Cabral, Joao De, see De Pina-Cabral, Joao, ed.

Pina da Silva, F. A., jt. ed. see Montalvao e Silva, J. M.

Pina, Frank. A Passion for Life. LC 97-154589. 144p. (Orig.). 1996. pap. 9.95 (*1-883893-38-0*) WinePress Pub.

Pina, H. & Brebbia, C. A., eds. Boundary Element Technology VIII. 400p. 1993. 137.00 (*1-85312-249-1*) Computational Mech MA.

Pina, H. & Brebbia, Carlos A., eds. Boundary Element Technology VIII. LC 93-71016. (BETECH Ser.: Vol. 8). 383p. 1993. 137.00 (*1-56252-173-X*, 2491) Computational Mech MA.

Pina, Ileana L., jt. ed. see Balady, Gary J.

Pina, Kenneth R. & Pines, Wayne L., eds. A Practical Guide to Food & Drug Law & Regulation. LC 98-203165. 354p. (C). 1998. pap. 129.00 (*1-885259-55-7*) Food & Drug Law.

Pina, Larry. Mac Classic & SE Repair & Upgrade Secrets. (Illus.). 296p. (C). 1995. pap. text 28.00 (*1-56609-022-9*) Peachpit Pr.

— Mac Printer Secrets. 1990. 34.95 (*0-672-48463-3*, Bobbs) Macmillan.

Pina, Leslie. Alexander Girard Designs for Herman Miller. LC 98-14505. 192p. 1998. 49.95 (*0-7643-0605-7*) Schiffer.

***Pina, Leslie.** Blenko: Fifties & Sixties Glass. (Illus.). 208p. 2000. 39.95 (*0-7643-1135-2*) Schiffer.

— Blenko Glass: 1962-1971. (Illus.). 160p. 1999. 29.95 (*0-7643-1026-7*) Schiffer.

— Crackle Glass in Color: Depression to Seventies. (Illus.). 176p. 2000. 29.95 (*0-7643-1136-0*) Schiffer.

— Depression Glass by Duncan. LC 99-62080. (Illus.). 176p. 1999. 29.95 (*0-7643-0928-5*) Schiffer.

— Fifties Furniture. 2nd rev. ed. LC 99-59904. (Illus.). 240p. 2000. 39.95 (*0-7643-0985-4*) Schiffer.

— Fifties Glass. 2nd rev. ed. (Illus.). 224p. 2000. 49.95 (*0-7643-0986-2*) Schiffer.

Pina, Leslie. Fostoria American Line 2056. LC 99-60263. (Illus.). 160p. 1999. 29.95 (*0-7643-0829-7*) Schiffer.

— Herman Miller 1940 Catalog & Supplement: Gilbert Rohde Modern Furniture Design. LC 98-86919. (Illus.). 144p. 1999. reprint ed. 39.95 (*0-7643-0705-3*) Schiffer.

***Pina, Leslie, pref.** Dunbar: Fine Furniture of the 1950's. (Illus.). 232p. 1999. 39.95 (*0-7643-1053-4*) Schiffer.

Pina, Leslie, pref. The Herman Miller Collection: The 1955-1956 Catalog. LC 97-80057. (Illus.). 168p. 1998. 39.95 (*0-7643-0440-2*) Schiffer.

— Herman Miller 1939 Catalog: Gilbert Rohde Modern Design. LC 97-81387. 112p. 1998. 39.95 (*0-7643-0501-8*) Schiffer.

Pina, Leslie & Friedland, Shirley. Wearable Art Accessories & Jewelry, 1900-2000. (Illus.). 184p. 1999. 39.95 (*0-7643-0971-4*) Schiffer.

Pina, Leslie & Johnson, Donald-Brian. The Chase Catalogs 1934 & 1935. LC 98-85652. 112p. 1998. pap. 24.95 (*0-7643-0631-6*) Schiffer.

Pina, Leslie & Korosec, Constance. Fashion Fabrics, 1960s. LC 98-84472. 176p. 1998. pap. 29.95 (*0-7643-0584-0*) Schiffer.

— The Synthetic '70s. LC 98-87850. (Illus.). 112p. (Orig.). 1999. pap. 24.95 (*0-7643-0717-7*) Schiffer.

Pina, Leslie & Ockner, Paula. Depression Era Art Deco Glass. LC 98-87982. (Illus.). 160p. 1999. 24.95 (*0-7643-0718-5*) Schiffer.

Pina, Leslie, et al. Beads in Fashion 1900-2000. LC 98-89925. (Illus.). 192p. 1999. 39.95 (*0-7643-0792-4*) Schiffer.

Pina, Leslie, jt. auth. see Brian-Johnson, Donald.

Pina, Leslie, jt. auth. see Friedland, Shirley.

Pina, Leslie, jt. auth. see Johnson, Donald Brian.

Pina, Leslie, jt. auth. see Jupp, Ken.

Pina, Leslie, jt. auth. see Korosec, Constance.

Pina, Leslie A. Circa Fifties Glass from Europe & America. LC 96-45938. 216p. 1997. 49.95 (*0-7643-0229-9*) Schiffer.

— Classic Herman Miller. LC 97-41179. 1998. 49.95 (*0-7643-0471-2*) Schiffer.

— Fifties & Sixties Glass, Ceramic & Enamel Ware: Designed & Signed by George Briard, Sascha Brastoff, Bellaire, Higgins... LC 95-26284. 192p. 1996. 29.95 (*0-88740-935-0*) Schiffer.

— Fifties Furniture. LC 96-22060. (Illus.). 256p. 1996. 39.95 (*0-7643-0152-7*) Schiffer.

— Fifties Glass. LC 93-85078. (Illus.). 224p. 1993. 49.95 (*0-88740-548-7*) Schiffer.

— Fostoria Designer George Sakier. LC 95-37083. (Schiffer Book for Collectors Ser.). 176p. (YA). (gr. 10). 1996. 29.95 (*0-88740-858-3*) Schiffer.

— Furniture 2000: Modern Classics & New Designs in Production. 4th ed. LC 98-11507. 208p. 1998. write for info. (*0-7643-0496-8*) Schiffer.

— Herman Miller, Interior Views. LC 97-51772. 224p. 1998. 49.95 (*0-7643-0503-4*) Schiffer.

— Louis Rorimer: A Man of Style. LC 90-34121. (Illus.). 158p. 1990. 25.00 (*0-87338-418-0*) Kent St U Pr.

— Popular '50s & '60s Glass: Color along the River. LC 95-11909. (Books for Collectors Ser.). (Illus.). 176p. 1995. 29.95 (*0-88740-829-X*) Schiffer.

— Pottery, Modern Wares, 1920-1960. LC 94-66781. (Illus.). 240p. 1994. 49.95 (*0-88740-692-0*) Schiffer.

Pina, Leslie A., jt. auth. see Ockner, Paula.

Pina, Leslie A., jt. auth. see Wasserstrom, Donna.

Pina, Ravi. Cracker Jack Collectibles: With Price Guide. LC 95-19727. (Illus.). 112p. (Orig.). 1995. pap. 19.95 (*0-88740-847-8*) Schiffer.

Pina, Roman. Historia Arqueologica y Arte Pre-Hispanico (Archeologic History & Pre-Hispanic Art) (SPA.). 216p. 1972. pap. 10.99 (*968-16-2376-2*, Pub. by Fondo) Continental Bk.

Pina Rosales, Gerardo. La Obra Narrativa de Segundo Serrano Poncela: Cronica Del Desarraigo, Vol. 1. LC 98-53356. (Spanish Studies: No. 1). 186p. 1999. text 79.95 (*0-7734-8162-1*) E Mellen.

Pina, Terri de la, see Chin-Lee, Cynthia & de la Pina, Terri.

Pinalie, Pierre. Dictionnaire Elementaire Francais-Creole. (FRE.). 237p. 1992. 59.95 (*0-8288-9493-0*) Fr & Eur.

***Pinalt, Lewis.** Consulting Demons: Inside the Unscrupulous World of Global Corporate Consulting. LC 99-48468. 304p. 2000. 26.00 (*0-06-661997-1*) HarpC.

Pinamontu, John P. The Immaculate Heart of Mary: From the Original Italian "Considerations" 144p. 1995. pap. 8.95 (*1-887548-00-9*) St Michael NC.

Pinano, et al. Managerial Cost Accounting: Planning & Control (Study Guide) 3rd ed. 1996. pap., student ed. 28.95 (*0-87393-246-3*) Dame Pubns.

Pinano, jt. auth. see Aiken, Susan Hardy.

Pinansky, Robert. After Life, What? A Post-Death Quest. 105p. (Orig.). 1995. pap. 11.95 (*1-885395-12-4*) Book Tree.

An Asterisk (*) at the beginning of an entry indicates that the title is appearing for the first time.

Pinar, Coleen. Melody, Rhythm, Songs & Games: A Multi-Developmental Approach. (Illus.). 1996. teacher ed., spiral bd. 20.95 (*1-881641-54-6*) Pencil Point.

***Pinar, Coleen.** Let's Sing about Math: Teacher Planner. (Illus.). 4p. 1998. teacher ed., spiral bd. 20.95 (*1-881641-70-8*) Pencil Point.

Pinar, M., jt. auth. see Meng, U. C.

Pinar, William. Curriculum: Toward New Identities. LC 97-37890. (Critical Education Practice Ser.). 432p. 1998. pap. text 25.95 (*0-8153-2522-3*) Garland.

Pinar, William & Hillis, Vikki, eds. The Lure of the Transcendent: Collected Essays by Dwayne E. Huebner. LC 98-35222. (Studies in Curriculum Theory Ser.). 496p. 1999. 89.95 (*0-8058-2533-9*); pap. 36.00 (*0-8058-2534-7*) L Erlbaum Assocs.

Pinar, William F. Autobiography, Politics, & Sexuality: Essays in Curriculum Theory, 1972-1992. LC 94-132. (Counterpoints Studies in the Postmodern Theory of Education: Vol. 2). X, 278p. (Orig.). (C). 1995. pap. text 24.95 (*0-8204-1849-8*) P Lang Pubng.

— Curriculum: Toward New Identities. Kincheloe, Joe, ed. LC 97-37890. (Critical Education Practice Ser.: 12). 432p. 1998. text 70.00 (*0-8153-2550-9*) Garland.

— Passionate Mind of Maxine Greene: I Am....Not Yet" LC 98-230641. 268p. 1998. 77.00 (*0-7507-0812-3*) Taylor & Francis.

— Passionate Mind Of Maxine Greene: "i Am....not Yet" LC 98-230641. 1998. pap. text 29.95 (*0-7507-0878-6*) Taylor & Francis.

***Pinar, William F., ed.** Contemporary Curriculum Discourses: Twenty Years of JCT. LC 99-21198. (Counterpoints: Vol. 70). XXX, 578p. (C). 1999. pap. text 39.95 (*0-8204-3882-0*) P Lang Pubng.

Pinar, William F., ed. Teaching Positions Knowledge of Bodies: Queer Theory in Education. LC 98-25271. (Studies in Curriculum Theory Ser.). 300p. 1998. write for info. (*0-8058-2864-8*); pap. write for info. (*0-8058-2921-0*) L Erlbaum Assocs.

Pinar, William F., et al. Understanding Curriculum: An Introduction to the Study of Historical & Contemporary Curriculum Discourses. LC 94-44009. (Counterpoints Studies in the Postmodern Theory of Education Ser.: Vol. 17). XVIII, 1144p. (C). 1995. pap. 49.95 (*0-8204-2601-6*) P Lang Pubng.

Pinar, William F., jt. ed. see Castenell, Louis A., Jr.

Pinar, William F., jt. ed. see Kincheloe, Joe L.

Pinar, William F., jt. ed. see Reynolds, William.

Pinard, Adrien. The Conservation of Conservation: The Child's Acquisition of a Fundamental Concept. Feider, Helga, tr. LC 80-26339. (Chicago Original Paperback Ser.). 212p. (C). 1992. pap. text 15.00 (*0-226-66834-7*) U Ch Pr.

— The Conservation of Conservation: The Child's Acquisition of a Fundamental Concept. Feider, Helga, tr. LC 80-26339. 211p. reprint ed. pap. 65.50 (*0-608-09034-4*, 206966900005) Bks Demand.

Pinard, Adrien, jt. auth. see Laurendeau, Monique.

***Pinard, Georges-Franck & Pagani, Linda, eds.** Clinical Assessment of Dangerousness: Empirical Contributions. (Illus.). 300p. (C). 2000. Price not set. (*0-521-64123-3*) Cambridge U Pr.

***Pinard, Katherine.** Word 97 The Lazy Way. 304p. 1999. pap. text 12.95 (*0-02-863015-7*) Macmillan.

Pinard, Maurice. The Rise of a Third Party: A Study in Crisis Politics. enl. ed. LC 75-329930. 331p. reprint ed. pap. 102.70 (*0-7837-1146-8*, 204167500022) Bks Demand.

***Pinard, Nancy.** Shadow Dancing. 265p. 1998. pap. 17.95 (*1-58444-003-1*, Looking Glass Pr) DiscUs Bks.

— Shadow Dancing. 224p. 2000. pap. write for info. (*1-58444-074-0*) DiscUs Bks.

Pinard, Nicole, jt. auth. see Swanson, Marie L.

Pinard, Nicole Jones. Microsoft Publisher 2000 - Illustrated Essentials. (Illus.). 88p. per. 10.95 (*0-7600-6146-7*, Pub. by Course Tech) Thomson Learn.

Pinardo, Mario, jt. auth. see Newell, Michael.

Pinaud, Henri, jt. ed. see Kester, Gerard.

Pinaula, Juan. Poetic Messages to My Students & Other Poems. 1998. pap. write for info. (*1-57553-865-2*) Watermrk Pr.

Pinault. Horse of Karbala. 1999. text. write for info. (*0-312-21637-8*) St Martin.

Pinault, Alain, jt. auth. see Chiche, Gerard.

Pinault, David. The Shiites: Ritual & Popular Piety in a Muslim Community. 224p. 1993. pap. 17.95 (*0-312-10024-8*) St Martin.

— Story-Telling Techniques in the Arabian Nights. LC 91-28023. (Journal of Arabic Literature Supplements Ser.: No. 15). 292p. 1992. 87.50 (*90-04-09530-6*) Brill Academic Pubs.

Pinault, Jody R. Hippocratic Lives & Legends. LC 91-43634. (Studies in Ancient Medicine: No. 4). x, 160p. 1992. 74.50 (*90-04-09574-8*) Brill Academic Pubs.

Pinay, Maurice. The Plot Against the Catholic Church: Communism, Free Masonry & the Jewish Fifth Column in the Clergy. 1979. lib. bdg. 69.95 (*0-8490-2984-8*) Gordon Pr.

***Pinberhughes, John.** The Family of the Spirit Cookbook. 2001. 20.00 (*0-06-095809-X*) HarpC.

Pincas, Stephane. Versailles: The History of the Gardens & Their Sculpture. LC 96-60114. (Illus.). 280p. 1996. 75.00 (*0-500-01701-8*, Pub. by Thames Hudson) Norton.

Pincetl, Stephanie Sabine. Transforming California: A Political History of Land Use & Development. LC 99-11398. (Illus.). 372p. 1999. 45.00 (*0-8018-6110-1*) Johns Hopkins.

Pinch. Votive Offerings to Hathor. (Griffith Institute Ser.). (Illus.). 512p. 1994. 91.50 (*0-900416-54-8*, Pub. by Aris & Phillips) David Brown.

Pinch, Adela. Strange Fits of Passion: Epistemologies of Emotion, Hume to Austen. LC 95-52593. (C). 1996. pap. write for info. (*0-8047-2549-7*); text. write for info. (*0-8047-2548-9*) Stanford U Pr.

— Strange Fits of Passion: Epistemologies of Emotion, Hume to Austen. 1999. pap. text 18.95 (*0-8047-3656-1*) Stanford U Pr.

Pinch, Alan, ed. & tr. see Tolstoy, Leo.

Pinch, Dorothy H. Happy Horsemanship. 192p. 1985. per. 10.00 (*0-671-76321-0*) S&S Trade.

Pinch, Dorothy Henderson. Happy Horsemanship. LC 98-34253. (Illus.). 192p. (J). 1998. per. 11.00 (*0-684-85215-2*, Fireside) S&S Trade Pap.

Pinch, Enid R. Optimal Control & the Calculus of Variations. (Illus.). 242p. (C). 1995. pap. text 39.95 (*0-19-851489-1*) OUP.

***Pinch, Geraldine.** Handbook of Egyptian Mythology. 2002. lib. bdg. 55.00 (*1-57607-242-8*) ABC-CLIO.

Pinch, Geraldine. Magic in Ancient Egypt. (Illus.). 192p. (Orig.). 1995. pap. 19.95 (*0-292-76559-2*) U of Tex Pr.

Pinch, Richard. Computational Number Theory. (London Mathematical Society Student Texts Ser.: Vol. 36). 250p. (C). 1999. text 59.95 (*0-521-45248-1*); pap. text 22.95 (*0-521-45887-0*) Cambridge U Pr.

Pinch, Steven. Worlds of Welfare: Understanding the Changing Geographies of Social Welfare Provision. LC 96-7594. (Illus.). 176p. (C). 1997. 75.00 (*0-415-11188-9*); pap. 24.99 (*0-415-11189-7*) Routledge.

Pinch, Trevor. Confronting Nature. 1986. lib. bdg. 162.50 (*90-277-2224-2*) Kluwer Academic.

Pinch, Trevor, jt. auth. see Collins, Harry.

Pinch, Trevor, jt. auth. see Collins, Harry M.

Pinch, William R. Peasants & Monks in British India. LC 95-18661. 264p. (C). 1996. 55.00 (*0-520-20060-8*, Pub. by U CA Pr) Cal Prin Full Svc.

— Peasants & Monks in British India. LC 95-18661. (Illus.). 264p. 1996. pap. 24.95 (*0-520-20061-6*, Pub. by U CA Pr) Cal Prin Full Svc.

Pinchback, jt. ed. see Casper.

Pinchbeck, Ivy. Women Workers & the Industrial Revolution, 1750-1850. 2nd rev. ed. 342p. 1969. 45.00 (*0-7146-1351-7*, Pub. by F Cass Pubs) Intl Spec Bk.

Pinchdeck, Daniel, ed. see Berman, David, et al.

Pinchdeck, Daniel, ed. see Gaitskill, Mary, et al.

Pinchdeck, Daniel, ed. see Lewinsky, Monica S., et al.

Pinchdeck, Daniel, ed. see Shapiro, Harvey, et al.

Pinchdeck, Daniel, ed. see Wallace, David Foster, et al.

Pinchera, A. & Vanhaelst, L., eds. Autoimmunity & Endocrine Diseases. (Journal: Hormone Research Ser.: Vol. 16, No. 5). (Illus.). 84p. 1982. pap. 35.75 (*3-8055-3658-5*) S Karger.

Pinchera, A., et al. Thyroid Autoimmunity. LC 87-29258. (Illus.). 654p. 1987. 120.00 (*0-306-42762-1*, Plenum Trade) Perseus Pubng.

Pinchera, Aldo, et al. Endocrinology & Metabolism. (Clinical Medicine Ser.). (Illus.). 891p. 1999. pap. text 75.00 (*0-07-709520-0*) McGraw-Hill HPD.

Pincherle, Alberto, see Moravia, Alberto, pseud.

Pincherle, Marc. Corelli: His Life & His Music. LC 79-9155. (Music Reprint Ser.). 1979. reprint ed. lib. bdg. 32.50 (*0-306-79576-0*) Da Capo.

Pinches, Charles R. & McDaniel, Jay B., eds. Good News for Animals? Christian Approaches to Animal Well-Being. LC 92-41682. (Ecology & Justice Ser.). 270p. reprint ed. pap. 83.70 (*0-608-20259-2*, 207151800012) Bks Demand.

Pinches, Charles & McDaniel, Jay B. Good News for Animals? Contemporary Christian Approaches to Animal Well-Being. LC 92-41682. (Ecology & Justice Ser.). 250p. 1993. 40.00 (*0-88344-866-1*) Orbis Bks.

Pinches, Charles, jt. auth. see Hauerwas, Stanley.

Pinches, George E. Essentials of Financial Management. 4th ed. 944p. (C). 1997. pap. 74.00 (*0-06-500072-2*) Addson-Wesley Educ.

— Essentials of Financial Management. 5th ed. Date not set. teacher ed. write for info. (*0-673-55400-7*) Addson-Wesley Educ.

— Essentials of Financial Management. 5th ed. (C). 1997. 92.00 (*0-673-99029-X*) Addson-Wesley Educ.

— Essentials of Financial Management: Using Financial & Business Calculators. 5th ed. 704p. (C). 1995. text 50.00 (*0-673-98205-X*) Addson-Wesley Educ.

— Financial Management. (C). 1994. pap. 65.00 (*0-06-501369-7*) Addson-Wesley Educ.

Pinches, George E., ed. Finacial Management. 2nd ed. (C). 1998. text. write for info. (*0-321-01448-0*); pap. text, student ed. write for info. (*0-321-01449-9*) Addson-Wesley Educ.

Pinches, George E., jt. auth. see Gordon, Lawrence.

***Pinches, Michael.** Culture & Privilege in Capitalist Asia. LC 99-212899. (New Rich in Asia Ser.). 1999. pap. 32.99 (*0-415-19764-3*) Routledge.

***Pinches, Michael & Asia Research Centre.** Culture & Privilege in Capitalist Asia. LC 99-212899. 1999. write for info. (*0-415-19763-5*) Routledge.

Pinches, Michael & Lakha, Salim, eds. Wage Labor & Social Change: The Proletariat in Asia & the Pacific. 283p. (Orig.). 1992. pap. 17.50 (*971-10-0453-4*, Pub. by New Day Pub) Cellar.

Pinches, Michael, jt. auth. see Callear, Brian.

Pinches, Theophilus G., et al. Late Babylonian Astronomical & Related Texts Copied by J. Schaumberger. Sachs, A. J. & Schaumberger, J., eds. LC 56-1209. (Brown University Studies: No. 18). 326p. reprint ed. pap. 101.10 (*0-608-10243-1*, 200466800045) Bks Demand.

Pinchin, Calvin. Issues in Philosophy. (C). 1989. text 50.00 (*0-389-20870-1*, N 8428) B&N Imports.

Pinchin, Doug. The Beatrix Potter & Bunnykins Price Guide. 2nd ed. (Illus.). 88p. 1998. pap. 19.95 (*1-870703-13-8*, Pub. by Francis Jos Pubns) Krause Pubns.

Pinchin, Jane L. Alexandria Still: Forster, Durrell & Cavafy. LC 76-6996. (Princeton Essays in Literature Ser.). 261p. 1977. reprint ed. pap. 81.00 (*0-608-02549-6*, 206319300004) Bks Demand.

Pinchin, Nick, jt. auth. see Tzimas, Nick.

Pinchin, Tony, jt. auth. see Withers, Margaret.

Pinching, A. J., et al, eds. AIDS & HIV Infection - The Wider Perspective. (Illus.). 234p. 1988. text. write for info. (*0-443-03978-X*) Church.

Pinchock, George, ed. see Rudolph, Thomas & Richmond, Floyd.

Pinchon, Edgcumb. Viva Villa: A Recovery of the Real Pancho Villa, Peon, Bandit, Soldier, Patriot. LC 70-111729. (American Imperialism: Viewpoints of United States Foreign Policy, 1898-1941 Ser.). 1980. reprint ed. 26.95 (*0-405-02045-7*) Ayer.

Pinchon, Edgcumb, jt. auth. see De Lara, L. Gutierrez.

Pinchon, Edgcumb, jt. auth. see Gutierrez De Lara, L.

Pinchon, Jean-Francois, ed. Rob Mallet-Stevens: Architecture, Furniture, Interior Design. LC 89-12971. (Illus.). 136p. 1991. 40.00 (*0-262-16116-8*) MIT Pr.

Pinchot, Amos R. History of the Progressive Party, 1912-1916. Hooker, Helene M., ed. LC 77-26637. 305p. 1978. reprint ed. lib. bdg. 38.50 (*0-313-20074-2*, PIHP, Greenwood Pr) Greenwood.

Pinchot, Elizabeth, jt. auth. see Pinchot, Gifford.

Pinchot, Gifford. Adirondack Spruce, A Study of the Forest in Ne-Ha-Sa-Ne Park. LC 77-125756. (American Environmental Studies). 1974. reprint ed. 17.95 (*0-405-02682-X*) Ayer.

— Biltmore Forest. LC 70-125757. (American Environmental Studies). 1974. reprint ed. 16.95 (*0-405-02683-8*) Ayer.

***Pinchot, Gifford.** Breaking New Ground. LC 98-12418. (Illus.). 546p. 1998. reprint ed. pap. 25.00 (*1-55963-670-X*) Island Pr.

Pinchot, Gifford. Fishing Talk. (Illus.). 288p. 1993. reprint ed. pap. 14.95 (*0-8117-2512-X*) Stackpole.

***Pinchot, Gifford.** Intrapreneuring: Why You Don't Have to Leave the Corporation to Become an Entrepreneur. 2nd ed. LC HB615.P46 2000. 380p. 2000. reprint ed. pap. 17.95 (*1-57675-082-5*) Berrett-Koehler.

Pinchot, Gifford. The Use of the National Forests. 42p. 1999. 4.95 (*0-944091-08-3*) Intaglio Pr.

Pinchot, Gifford & Pellman, Ron. Intrapreneuring in Action: A Handbook for Business Innovation. LC 99-47667. 120p. 1999. pap. text 14.95 (*1-57675-061-2*) Berrett-Koehler.

Pinchot, Gifford & Pinchot, Elizabeth. The End of Bureaucracy & the Rise of the Intelligent Organization. LC 93-40302. (Illus.). 399p. 1994. 24.95 (*1-881052-34-6*) Berrett-Koehler.

— The Intelligent Organization: Engaging the Talent & Initiative of Everyone in the Workplace. LC 93-40302. Orig. Title: The End of Bureaucracy & the Risk of the Intelligent Organization. (Illus.). 420p. 1996. pap. 19.95 (*1-881052-98-2*) Berrett-Koehler.

Pinchot, Reuven. Chanukah: A Lesson in Religious Freedom. Friedman, Yosef B., ed. (Illus.). 56p. (Orig.). 1985. pap. 3.00 (*0-8266-0377-7*, Merkos LInyonei Chinuch) Kehot Pubn Soc.

Pinchover, Yehuda, jt. auth. see Lin, Vladimir.

Pinchuck, Tony. The Rough Guide to Zimbabwe & Botswana. 3rd ed. 480p. 1996. pap. 18.95 (*1-85828-186-5*, Penguin Bks) Viking Penguin.

Pinchuck, Tony, jt. auth. see Clark, Richard.

***Pinchuk, Alexei I. & Paul, A. J.** Zooplankton of the Okhotsk Sea: A Review of Russian Studies. (Illus.). 62p. 2000. pap. 10.00 (*1-56612-064-0*) AK Sea Grant CP.

Pincione, Guido, jt. auth. see Spector, Horacio.

Pinciroli, Francesco, jt. ed. see Meester, Greert T.

***Pinciss, G. M.** Forbidden Matter: Religion in the Drama of Shakespeare & His Contemporaries. LC 99-38700. 144p. 2000. 31.50 (*0-87413-706-3*) U Delaware Pr.

Pinciss, Gerald M. & Lockyer, Roger, eds. Shakespeare's World: Background Readings in the English Renaissance. 220p. 1989. reprint ed. pap. text 24.50 (*0-8264-0451-0*) F Ungar Bks.

Pinckaers, Julius C. From Privacy Toward a New Intellectual Property Right in Persona. LC 96-53637. (Information Law Ser.). 1997. pap. 114.50 (*90-411-0355-4*) Kluwer Law Intl.

Pinckaers, Servais. Pursuit of Happiness - God's Way: Living the Beatitudes. Noble, Mary T., tr. from FRE. LC 97-19086. Orig. Title: La Quete du Bonheur. 216p. (Orig.). 1998. mass mkt. 5.95 (*0-8189-0797-5*) Alba.

— The Sources of Christian Ethics. Noble, Mary T., tr. LC 94-28663. Orig. Title: Sources de la Morale Chretienne. 489p. 1995. 44.95 (*0-8132-0834-3*) Cath U Pr.

— The Sources of Christian Ethics. 3rd ed. Noble, Mary T., tr. from FRE. LC 94-28663. Orig. Title: Sources de la Morale Chretienne. 489p. 1995. pap. 24.95 (*0-8132-0818-1*) Cath U Pr.

Pinckernelle, Erdewin, tr. German General Rules of Marine Insurance (ADS) 5th ed. 77p. (C). 1990. pap. 20.00 (*3-11-012666-4*) De Gruyter.

Pinckey-Harris, Claudette. Monroe Pinckey, My Father. 135p. (Orig.). 1995. pap. 12.95 (*0-910671-14-1*) Path Pr Chicago.

Pinckley, Diana, et al. New Orleans: River Region Renaissance. LC 96-39345. 288p. 1996. 45.00 (*1-885352-46-8*); write for info. (*1-885352-47-6*) Community Comm.

Pinckney, Callan. Callanetics: Ten Years Younger in Ten Hours. 208p. 1987. pap. 12.50 (*0-380-70261-4*, Avon Bks) Morrow Avon.

— Callanetics Countdown: Thirty Days to a Beautiful Body. 192p. 1991. pap. 12.00 (*0-380-71453-1*, Avon Bks) Morrow Avon.

— Callanetics Fit Forever. 240p. 1997. pap. 13.00 (*0-399-52263-8*, Perigee Bks) Berkley Pub.

— Callanetics for Your Back. 192p. 1990. pap. 11.95 (*0-380-70506-0*, Avon Bks) Morrow Avon.

Pinckney, Cathey & Pinckney, Edward R. Do-It-Yourself Medical Testing: 240 Tests You Can Perform at Home. 3rd ed. LC 88-37412. (Illus.). 396p. 1989. reprint ed. pap. 122.80 (*0-7837-9920-9*, 206064700006) Bks Demand.

Pinckney, Darryl. High Cotton. LC 91-23158. 320p. 1992. text 21.00 (*0-374-16998-5*) FS&G.

***Pinckney, Darryl.** Sold & Gone: African American Literature & U. S. Society. 320p. 2000. text 26.00 (*0-374-28188-2*) FS&G.

Pinckney, Diana. White Linen. 48p. 1998. pap. 9.95 (*1-879205-75-0*) Nightshade Pr.

Pinckney, Edward R., jt. auth. see Pinckney, Cathey.

Pinckney, Eliza L. The Letterbook of Eliza Lucas Pinckney, 1739-1762. rev. ed. Zahniser, Marvin R., ed. LC 96-51677. (Illus.). 230p. 1977. reprint ed. pap. 16.95 (*1-57003-186-X*) U of SC Pr.

Pinckney, Francis M. Products Comaparison Manual for Trademark Users: 1998 Cumulative Supplement. LC 86-9732. 584p. 1998. pap., suppl. ed. 85.00 (*0-87179-501-9*, 9813-PR8) BNA Books.

Pinckney, Jerry. The Tales of Uncle Remus: The Adventures of Brer Rabbit, Vol. I. LC 85-20449. (J). (ps up). 1987. 19.99 (*0-8037-0271-X*, Dial Yng Read) Peng Put Young Read.

Pinckney, Neal. Healthy Heart Handbook. pap. 15.95 (*0-9643880-0-6*) Healing Heart.

— Healthy Heart Handbook. 306p. 1996. pap. 11.95 (*1-55874-384-7*, 3847) Health Comm.

Pinckney, Roger. Blue Roots: African-American Folk Magic of the Gullah People. LC 98-27091. (Illus.). 192p. 1998. pap. 12.95 (*1-56718-524-X*) Llewellyn Pubns.

***Pinckney, Sarah N., ed.** Bonaventure Cemetery, Savannah, Georgia, Sections A-H. (Illus.). 528p. 2000. 37.00 (*0-9679652-0-9*) Bonaventure Hist.

Pincoe, Ruth. Glenn Gould: Descriptive Catalogue of the Glenn Gould Papers. (FRE., Illus.). 318p. (Orig.). 1992. pap. 51.95 (*0-660-57327-X*, Pub. by Canadian Govt Pub) Accents Pubns.

Pincoffs, Edmund L., ed. see Conference on the Concept of Academic Freedom Staf.

Pincombe, Michael. The Plays of John Lyly: Eros & Eliza. LC 95-47235. 224p. 1997. text 79.95 (*0-7190-3858-8*) Manchester Univ Pr.

Pincon, Jacinto O. Moral Divorce & Other Stories. Fedorchek, Robert M., tr. LC 94-28807. 1995. 35.00 (*0-8387-5299-3*) Bucknell U Pr.

Pincu, Gloria. How to Improve Your Business Reading Skills: Read with Added Confidence, Speed, Comprehension, & Recall. (Illus.). 102p. 1997. pap., wbk. ed. 19.95 (*0-9658173-1-8*) BLS Pub.

Pincus. Core Concepts Accou. Information Theme. 6th ed. 1997. 31.50 (*0-07-027627-7*); 31.00 (*0-07-027629-3*); 23.00 (*0-07-027675-7*) McGraw.

— Core Concepts Accou. Information Theme. 6th ed. 1997. 23.50 (*0-07-027631-5*) McGraw.

— England's Glorious Revolution. 2000. pap. text 10.95 (*0-312-16714-8*) St Martin.

— Perspectives in Business Ethics. 2nd ed. 2001. 50.00 (*0-07-231405-2*) McGraw.

Pincus, Alexis G. Combustion Melting in the Glass Industry. LC 78-55358. (Processing in the Glass Industry Ser.). 300p. 1980. 29.95 (*0-911993-11-8*) Ashlee Pub Co.

— Melting Furnace Design in the Glass Industry. LC 78-55352. (Processing in the Glass Industry Ser.). 269p. 1980. 24.95 (*0-911993-08-8*) Ashlee Pub Co.

— Melting Furnace Operation in the Glass Industry. LC 77-55374. (Processing in the Glass Industry Ser.). 250p. 1980. 24.95 (*0-911993-10-X*) Ashlee Pub Co.

— Refractories in the Glass Industry. LC 78-55364. (Provessing in the Glass Industry Ser.). 280p. 1980. 24.95 (*0-911993-09-6*) Ashlee Pub Co.

Pincus, Alexis G., ed. Forming in the Glass Industry Pt. I: Forming Machines & Methods, Set. (Processing in the Glass Industry Ser.). (Illus.). 248p. 1983. text 69.95 (*0-911993-03-7*) Ashlee Pub Co.

— Forming in the Glass Industry Pt. II: Accessories to Glass Forming, Set. LC 83-70120. (Processing in the Glass Industry Ser.). (Illus.). 254p. 1983. text 69.95 (*0-911993-05-3*) Ashlee Pub Co.

Pincus, Alexis G. & Chang, S. H. Joining in the Glass Industry. LC 83-73581. (Processing in the Glass Industry Ser.). (Illus.). 282p. 1985. 34.95 (*0-911993-16-9*) Ashlee Pub Co.

— Secondary Manufacturing in the Glass Industry. LC 78-55369. (Processing in the Glass Industry Ser.). 314p. 1978. 34.95 (*0-911993-14-2*) Ashlee Pub Co.

Pincus, Alexis G. & Chang, Shung-Huei, eds. Decorating in the Glass Industry. 2nd ed. LC 84-73283. (Processing in the Glass Industry Ser.). (Illus.). 1985. 39.95 (*0-911993-23-1*) Ashlee Pub Co.

Pincus, Alexis G. & Davies, David H. Batching in the Glass Industry. LC 81-67427. (Processing in the Glass Industry Ser.). 217p. 1981. 24.95 (*0-911993-07-X*) Ashlee Pub Co.

Pincus, Alexis G. & Davies, David H., eds. Raw Materials in the Glass Industry: Minor Ingredients, 2 pts. LC 83-70137. (Processing in the Glass Industry Ser.). (Illus.). 454p. 1983. text 29.95 (*0-911993-02-9*) Ashlee Pub Co.

— Raw Materials in the Glass Industry Pt. I: Major Ingredients. LC 83-70137. (Processing in the Glass Industry Ser.). (Illus.). 254p. 1983. text 29.95 (*0-911993-00-2*) Ashlee Pub Co.

Pincus, Alexis G. & Holmes, Thomas R., eds. Annealing & Strengthening in the Glass Industry. 2nd ed. LC 87-70822. (Processing in the Glass Industry Ser.). (Illus.). 1988. text 39.95 (*0-911993-24-X*) Ashlee Pub Co.

P

An Asterisk (*) at the beginning of an entry indicates that the title is appearing for the first time.

Pincus, Andrew L. Tanglewood: The Clash Between Tradition & Change. LC 98-9605. (Illus.). 192p. 1998. 26.95 (1-55553-346-9) NE U Pr.

***Pincus, Arthur.** Official Illustrated NHL History: From the Original Six to a Global Game. 1999. pap. 36.95 (1-57243-344-2) Triumph Bks.

Pincus, Debbie. Feeling Good about Others: Activities to Encourage Positive Interaction. (Illus.). 96p. 1994. 11.99 (0-86653-794-5, GA1488) Good Apple.

— Feeling Good about Yourself. (Illus.). 96p. (J). (gr. 3-8). 1990. 11.99 (0-86653-516-0, GA 1139) Good Apple.

— How I Learned to Control My Temper. (Illus.). 68p. (J). (gr. 1-6). 1995. pap. 17.95 (1-882732-28-6) Childswork.

— Interactions. 96p. (J). (gr. 4-9). 1988. student ed. 11.99 (0-86653-448-2, GA1057) Good Apple.

— Manners Matter. (Illus.). 112p. (J). (gr. 3-7). 1992. student ed. 12.99 (0-86653-688-4, 1422) Good Apple.

— Sharing. (Illus.). 80p. (J). (gr. 4-8). 1983. student ed. 10.99 (0-86653-117-3, GA 468) Good Apple.

Pincus, Debbie & Ward, Richard J. Citizenship. 112p. (J). (gr. 4-9). 1991. 12.99 (0-86653-608-6, GA 1327) Good Apple.

Pincus, Debra. The Tombs of the Doges of Venice. LC 98-43281. (Illus.). 350p. 1999. 80.00 (0-521-59354-9) Cambridge U Pr.

Pincus, Edward, jt. auth. see Ascher, Steven.

Pincus, Elizabeth. The Hangdog Hustle. LC 94-37956. (Neil Fury Ser.). 205p. (Orig.). 1995. pap. 9.95 (1-883523-05-2) Spinsters Ink.

— The Solitary Twist. LC 93-84274. (Neil Fury Ser.). 225p. (Orig.). 1993. pap. 9.95 (0-933216-93-9) Spinsters Ink.

— The Two Bit Tango. LC 92-17511. (Neil Fury Ser.). (Illus.). 193p. (Orig.). 1992. pap. 9.95 (0-933216-88-2) Spinsters Ink.

Pincus, Fred L. & Archer, Elayne. Bridges to Opportunity. 56p. 1989. pap. 2.00 (0-685-59931-0) Acad Educ Dev.

Pincus, Fred L. & Ehrlich, Howard J., eds. Race & Ethnic Conflict: Contending Views on Prejudice, Discrimination & Ethnoviolence. 2nd ed. LC 98-28116. 480p. 1998. 33.00 (0-8133-3498-5, Pub. by Westview) HarpC.

Pincus, Gregory, jt. ed. see Laurentian Hormone Conferences Staff.

Pincus, Harold A., et al, eds. Ethics in Psychiatric Research: A Resource Manual on Human Subjects Research. LC 98-17948. 334p. 1999. 79.00 (0-89042-281-8, 2281) Am Psychiatric.

Pincus, Harold A. & Pardes, Herbert, eds. The Integration of Neuroscience & Psychiatry. LC 85-11270. (Clinical Insights Ser.). 106p. reprint ed. pap. 32.90 (0-8357-7827-4, 203620000002) Bks Demand.

Pincus, Harold A., ed. see American Psychiatric Association Office of Researc.

Pincus, Harriet, ed. see Grimm, Jacob W. & Grimm, Wilhelm K.

Pincus, Howard J. & Hoskins, Earl R., eds. Measurement of Rock Properties at Elevated Pressures & Temperatures-STP 869. LC 84-24558. (Illus.). 162p. 1985. text 30.00 (0-8031-0237-2, STP869) ASTM.

Pincus, J. David & DeBonis, J. Nicholas. Top Dog: A Different Kind of Book about Becoming an Excellent Leader. LC 94-217. 384p. 1996. pap. 14.95 (0-07-050188-2) McGraw.

Pincus, Jack. J. S. Bach in Tablature. 48p. 1997. pap. 14.95 incl. audio compact disk (0-7866-2877-4, 94581BCD) Mel Bay.

Pincus, Joel D. & Zhou, Shaojie. Principal Currents for a Pair of Unitary Operators. LC 94-4146. (Memoirs of the American Mathematical Society Ser.: No. 522). 103p. 1994. pap. 32.00 (0-8218-2609-3, MEMO/109/522) Am Math.

Pincus, John A. Economic Aid & International Cost Sharing. LC 65-19539. 240p. reprint ed. pap. 74.40 (0-608-10694-1, 202073300018) Bks Demand.

Pincus, Jonathan. Class, Power, & Agrarian Change: Land & Labour in Rural West Java. (Studies in the Economies of East & Southeast Asia). 256p. 1996. text 85.00 (0-312-15827-0) St Martin.

Pincus, Jonathan H. & Tucker, Gary J. Behavioral Neurology. 3rd ed. (Illus.). 320p. 1985. pap. text 21.95 (0-19-503555-0) OUP.

***Pincus, Karen.** Core Concepts of Accounting Information 1999-2000: Theme 1. 8th ed. 648p. (C). 1999. pap. 38.44 (0-07-232192-X) McGrw-H Hghr Educ.

— Core Concepts Of Accounting Information 1999-2000: Theme 2. 8th ed. 408p. (C). 1999. pap. 31.25 (0-07-232194-6) McGrw-H Hghr Educ.

— Core Concepts Of Accounting Information 1999-2000: Theme 3. 8th ed. 512p. (C). 1999. pap. 39.69 (0-07-232196-2) McGrw-H Hghr Educ.

— Core Concepts Of Accounting Information 1999-2000: Theme 4. 8th ed. 288p. (C). 1999. pap. 31.25 (0-07-232198-9) McGrw-H Hghr Educ.

Pincus, Laura & Moore, Arva. We'll Be There: History of Greater Miami & Keys Chapter of American Red Cross. 80p. 1997. pap. write for info. (0-9629402-6-7) Centennial Pr.

Pincus, Laura, jt. auth. see Alexander-Bennett, Dawn.

Pincus, Laura B. Perspectives in Business Ethics. LC 97-22530. 1997. 71.00 (0-256-23317-9, Irwn Prfssnl) McGraw-Hill Prof.

Pincus, Laura B., jt. auth. see Bennett-Alexander, Dawn.

Pincus, Laura B., jt. auth. see Bennett-Alexander, Dawn D.

Pincus, Laura B., jt. auth. see McAdams, Tony.

Pincus, Lee. The Songwriters' Success Manual. LC 77-352498. (Illus.). 1976. pap. 9.95 (0-918318-01-7) Music Pr.

Pincus, Leo I. Practical Boiler Water Treatment: Including Air-Conditioning Systems. LC 80-29604. 284p. 1981. reprint ed. lib. bdg. 33.50 (0-89874-255-2) Krieger.

Pincus, Leslie. Authenticating Culture in Imperial Japan: Kuki Shuzo & the Rise of National Aesthetics. LC 95-12978. (Twentieth-Century Japan: The Emergence of a World Power Ser.: Vol. 5). (Illus.). 285p. (C). 1996. 48.00 (0-520-20134-5, Pub. by U CA Pr) Cal Prin Full Svc.

***Pincus, Marilyn.** Business Success: Interview Strategies That Lead to Job Offers. LC 98-45626. (Barron's Business Success Ser.). (Illus.). 142p. 1999. pap. 6.95 (0-7641-0684-8) Barron.

Pincus, Marilyn. Everyday Business Etiquette. LC 96-18528. 224p. 1996. pap. 12.95 (0-8120-9517-0) Barron.

— Projecting a Positive Image. (Barron's Business Success Ser.). 112p. 1993. pap. 4.95 (0-8120-1455-3) Barron.

Pincus, Marilyn, jt. auth. see Doty, Dorothy I.

Pincus, Marilyn, jt. auth. see Miller, Robert F.

Pincus, Robert, et al. Jud Fine: February 1985. Starrels, Josine I. & Lewis, Helen N., eds. LC 85-50180. (Illus.). 52p. (Orig.). 1985. pap. 7.50 (0-936429-04-6) LA Municipal Art.

Pincus, Robert L. On a Scale That Competes with the World: The Art of Edward & Nancy Reddin Kienholz. (Illus.). 135p. 1990. 60.00 (0-520-06730-4, Pub. by U CA Pr) Cal Prin Full Svc.

— On a Scale That Competes with the World: The Art of Edward & Nancy Reddin Kienholz. (Illus.). 135p. (C). 1994. pap. 34.95 (0-520-08446-2, Pub. by U CA Pr) Cal Prin Full Svc.

Pincus, Stanley. Respiratory Therapist Manual. LC 74-79838. (Allied Health Ser.). 1975. pap. 7.05 (0-672-61389-1, Bobbs) Macmillan.

Pincus, Steven C. Protestantism & Patriotism: Ideologies & the Making of English Foreign Policy, 1650-1668. (Cambridge Studies in Early Modern British History). 518p. (C). 1996. text 74.95 (0-521-43487-4) Cambridge U Pr.

Pincus, T. H. On the Offensive: Wall Street's Socially Incorrect Humor--A Treasury of the Unprintable 100. LC 98-90312. 1999. 16.95 (0-533-12763-7) Vantage.

Pincus, Theodore & Henkel, Gretchen. Your Guide to Living Well with Rheumatoid Arthritis. 1999. pap. 14.95 (0-912423-21-8) Arthritis Found.

Pincus, Theodore, jt. ed. see Wolfe, Frederick.

Pincus, William H. The Problems of Gauguin's Therapist: Language, Madness & Therapy. 134p. 1994. 66.95 (1-85628-374-7, Pub. by Avebry) Ashgate Pub Co.

Pincus-Witten, Robert. Entries (Maximalism) (Illus.). 250p. 1983. pap. 14.95 (0-915570-20-3) Oolp Pr.

— Eye to Eye: Twenty Years of Art Criticism. Kuspit, Donald, ed. LC 83-24121. (Contemporary American Art Critics Ser.: No. 4). 248p. 1984. reprint ed. pap. 76.90 (0-8357-1534-5, 207075000004) Bks Demand.

— Jedd Garet. (Illus.). 162p. 1984. 45.00 (0-942642-12-0) Twelvetrees Pr.

— Postminimalism: American Art of the Decade. LC 77-77010. (Illus.). 1981. pap. text 25.00 (0-915570-07-6) Oolp Pr.

— Postminimalism into Maximalism: American Art, 1966-1986. LC 86-24925. (Studies in the Fine Arts: Criticism: No. 22). 445p. reprint ed. pap. 138.00 (0-8357-1763-1, 207064800012) Bks Demand.

Pincus-Witten, Robert & Zimmerman, Elyn. Elyn Zimmerman. (Illus.). 70p. (Orig.). 1996. pap. 30.00 (1-880154-07-2) Gagosian Gallery.

Pincus-Witten, Robert, ed. see Fuchs, R. H.

Pincus-Witten, Robert, ed. see Nittve, Lars.

Pinczes, Elinor. Arctic Fives Arrive. LC 95-3693. (Illus.). 32p. (J). (ps-3). 1996. 14.95 (0-395-73577-7) HM.

Pinczes, Elinor J. One Hundred Hungry Ants. (Illus.). 32p. (J). (gr. k-3). 1993. 16.00 (0-395-63116-5) HM.

***Pinczes, Elinor J.** One Hundred Hungry Ants. LC 91-45415. (Illus.). 32p. (J). (ps-3). 1999. pap. 5.95 (0-395-97123-3, Sandpiper) HM.

Pinczes, Elinor J. A Remainder of One. LC 94-5446. (Illus.). 32p. (J). (gr. 1-4). 1995. 15.00 (0-395-69455-8) HM.

Pinczuk, Aron, jt. ed. see Lockwood, David J.

Pinczuk, Aron, jt. ed. see Sarma, Sankar D.

Pinczuk, Jane. Michele, the Nursing Toddler: A Story about Sharing Love. LC 98-67505. (Illus.). (J). (gr. 1-5). 1998. 14.95 (0-912500-40-9, 253) La Leche.

Pindado, Juan J. Texto Hibrido: Entre Ficcion e Informacion Periodismo o Literatura? iii, 149p. Date not set. 69.95 (1-882528-26-3) Scripta.

Pindar. The Isthmian Odes of Pindar. 194p. 1998. reprint ed. lib. bdg. 79.00 (0-7812-7718-3) Rprt Serv.

— Pindar: The Olympian & Pythain Odes. 1998. reprint ed. lib. bdg. 79.00 (0-7812-4796-9) Rprt Serv.

Pindar, Peter. Carmina Cum Fragmentis. 2nd ed. Bowra, C. Maurice, ed. (Oxford Classical Texts Ser.). 302p. 1935. text 28.00 (0-19-814539-X) OUP.

— Isthmian Odes of Pindar. 1988. reprint ed. lib. bdg. 59.00 (0-317-90885-5) Rprt Serv.

— Isthmian Odes of Pindar. Bury, John B., ed. 1892. reprint ed. 49.00 (0-403-00333-4) Scholarly.

— Nemean Odes of Pindar. 1890. reprint ed. 19.00 (0-403-00332-6) Scholarly.

— Odes & Fragments. (Loeb Classical Library: No. 56). 682p. 1915. 19.95 (0-674-99062-5) HUP.

— The Odes of Pindar. Bowra, C. M., tr. & intro. by. 256p. 1982. pap. 11.95 (0-14-044209-X, Penguin Classics) Viking Penguin.

— The Odes of Pindar. 2nd ed. Lattimore, Richmond, tr. from GRE. LC 75-22336. 184p. 1976. reprint ed. pap. 8.00 (0-226-66845-2, P33) U Ch Pr.

— The Olympian & Pythian Odes. Connor, W. R., ed. LC 78-18577. (Greek Texts & Commentaries Ser.). (Illus.). 1979. reprint ed. lib. bdg. 41.95 (0-405-11420-6) Ayer.

— Pindar: Selected Odes. Instone, Stephen, ed. & tr. by. from GRE. (Classical Texts Ser.). (Illus.). 200p. 1996. 59.99 (0-85668-668-9, Pub. by Aris & Phillips); pap. text 28.00 (0-85668-669-7, Pub. by Aris & Phillips) David Brown.

— Pindar, the Olympian & Pythian Odes. Gildersleeve, Basil L., ed. 1885. 59.00 (0-403-00331-8) Scholarly.

— Pindar's Odes. Swanson, Roy A., tr. from GRE. 416p. reprint ed. pap. 15.95 (0-8290-0332-0) Irvington.

— Victory Odes: Olympians 2, 7 & 11; Nemean 4; Isthmians 3, 4 & 7. Willcock, Malcolm M., ed. (Cambridge Greek & Latin Classics Ser.). 189p. (C). 1995. text 60.00 (0-521-43055-0) Cambridge U Pr.

— Victory Odes: Olympians 2, 7 & 11; Nemean 4; Isthmians 3, 4 & 7. Willcock, Malcolm M., ed. (Cambridge Greek & Latin Classics Ser.). 189p. (C). 1995. pap. text 22.95 (0-521-43636-2) Cambridge U Pr.

Pindar Press Staff. The Official Sports Guide of the Centennial Olympic Games: Atlanta, 1996. (Illus.). 128p. 1996. pap. 10.95 (0-918223-93-8) Pindar Pr.

Pindborg, J. J. & Wahi, P. N. Histological Typing of Cancer & Precancer of the Oral Mucosa. 2nd ed. LC 97-8019. (International Histological Classification of Tumors Ser.). 1997. pap. write for info. (3-540-61848-1) Spr-Verlag.

Pindborg, Jens J., et al. Histological Typing of Odontogenic Tumours. 2nd ed. Sobin, Leslie H., ed. (WHO International Histological Classification of Tumours Ser.). (Illus.). 100p. 1997. reprint ed. 59.95 (0-387-54142-X) Spr-Verlag.

Pindborg, Jens Jrgen. Atlas Diseases of Oral Mucosa. 5th ed. (C). 1992. text 155.00 (0-7216-4988-2) Harcourt.

***Pindell, James L. & Drake, Charles, eds.** Paleogeographic Evolution & Non-Glacial Eustacy: Northern South America. (Special Publications: Vol. 58). (Illus.). 443p. 1998. 119.00 (1-56576-041-7) SEPM.

Pindell, Terry. Good Place to Live. 88p. 1995. 27.50 (0-8050-2352-6) H Holt & Co.

— A Good Place to Live: America's Last Migration. 432p. 1997. pap. 14.95 (0-8050-5024-8) H Holt & Co.

— Last Train to Toronto: A Canadian Rail Odyssey. 400p. 1995. pap. 15.95 (0-8050-2358-5, Owl) H Holt & Co.

— Making Tracks: An American Rail Odyssey. (Illus.). 88p. 1995. pap. 14.95 (0-8050-1740-2, Owl) H Holt & Co.

— Yesterday's Train: A Rail Odyssey Through Mexican History. 400p. 1998. pap. text 15.95 (0-8050-5598-3) H Holt & Co.

Pinder, Angi. Beazley's Design & Detail of the Space Between Buildings. (Illus.). 304p. (C). 1990. 80.00 (0-419-13620-7, E & FN Spon) Routledge.

Pinder-Cracraft, Caroline, tr. see Rathenau, Walter.

Pinder, Craig C. Work Motivation in Organizational Behavior. LC 97-30764. (C). 1997. text 74.00 (0-02-395622-4) Macmillan Gen Ref.

Pinder, Craig C. & Moore, Larry F., eds. Middle Range Theory & the Study of Organizatons. 1980. lib. bdg. 118.50 (0-89838-021-9) Kluwer Academic.

Pinder, David. The New Europe: Economy, Society & Environment. LC 97-31195. 504p. 1998. pap. 49.95 (0-471-97123-5) Wiley.

Pinder, David A., jt. auth. see Hoyle, Brian S.

Pinder, David A., jt. ed. see Hoyle, Brian S.

Pinder, Eric. Life at the Top: Tales, Truths, & Trusted Recipes from the Mount Washington Observatory. LC 97-11519. (Illus.). 160p. (Orig.). 1997. pap. 14.95 (0-89272-396-3) Down East.

***Pinder, Eric.** Tying down the Wind: Adventures in the Worst Weather on Earth. (Illus.). 272p. 2000. 24.95 (1-58542-060-3, Tarcher Putnam) Putnam Pub Group.

Pinder, G. E. Zimbabwe Sales Tax & Stamp Duties Legislation. ring bd. write for info. (0-7021-3161-X, R220,00, Pub. by Juta & Co) Gaunt.

Pinder, G. F., ed. Flow Through Porous Media. (Progress in Engineering Ser.). 125p. 1983. pap. 46.00 (0-931215-37-4) Computational Mech MA.

Pinder, George F., jt. auth. see Lapidus, Leon.

Pinder, John. Altiero Spinelli & The British Federalists: Writings by Beveridge, Robbins & Spinelli. 130p. 1999. 30.00 (0-901573-58-2, Kogan Pg Educ) Stylus Pub VA.

— The Building of the European Union. 3rd ed. 308p. 1999. pap. text 16.95 (0-19-289315-7) OUP.

— European Community: The Building of a Union. 2nd ed. 288p. 1995. pap. text 19.95 (0-19-289265-7) OUP.

***Pinder, John.** Foundations of Democracy in the European Union: From the Genesis of Parliamentary Democracy to the European Parliament LC 98-55306. 1999. text 68.00 (0-312-22296-3) St Martin.

Pinder, John, et al. Monitoring & Controlling the International Transfer of Technology. (Illus.). 90p. 1998. pap. text 15.00 (0-8330-2635-6, MR-979-OSTP) Rand Corp.

Pinder, John, ed. see Duff, Andrew, et al.

Pinder, L. C. A Key to the Adult Males of the British Chironomidae (Diptera) 1978. 39.00 (0-900386-32-0) St Mut.

Pinder, Margaret E., tr. see Burkert, Walter.

***Pinder, Polly.** Handmade Cards. (Illus.). 2000. pap. 11.95 (0-85532-887-8) Srch Pr.

Pinder, Polly. How to Make Mobiles: Many Creative Step-by-Step Projects - Chimes, Birds, Fish, Lanterns, Figures, Flowers, Leaves, Seeds. (Illus.). 64p. (Orig.). 1997. pap. 15.95 (0-85532-814-2, Pub. by Srch Pr) A Schwartz & Co.

— How to Make Paper Candle-Shades. 48p. 1997. pap. 11.95 (0-85532-781-2, Pub. by Srch Pr) A Schwartz & Co.

— Polly Pinder's Papercrafts Book. (Illus.). 128p. 1994. pap. 19.95 (0-85532-661-1, 661-1, Pub. by Srch Pr) A Schwartz & Co.

— Scented Herb Papers: How to Use Natural Scents & Colours in Hand-Made Recycled & Plant Papers. (Illus.). 64p. 1995. pap. 14.95 (0-85532-789-8, 7898X, Pub. by Srch Pr) A Schwartz & Co.

Pinder, Richard. Mobilizing Human Resources. 1995. pap. 7.95 (1-56229-415-6) Pneuma Life Pub.

***Pinder, Richard.** Redeemed & Justified. 1999. 4.99 (1-56229-128-9) Pneuma Life Pub.

Pindera, J. T. & Pindera, M. J. Isodyne Stress Analysis. (C). 1989. text 223.00 (0-7923-0269-9) Kluwer Academic.

***Pindera, Jerzy-Tadeusz.** Techniques of Tomographic Isodyne Stress Analysis. LC 00-31323. (Solid Mechanics & Its Applications Ser.). 2000. write for info. (0-7923-6388-4) Kluwer Academic.

Pindera, M. J., jt. auth. see Pindera, J. T.

Pinderhughes, Dianne M. Race & Ethnicity in Chicago Politics: A Reexamination of Pluralist Theory. LC 86-19297. 339p. reprint ed. pap. 105.10 (0-8357-3297-5, 203952000013) Bks Demand.

Pinderhughes, Dianne M., jt. auth. see Hopps.

Pinderhughes, Elaine. Understanding Race, Ethnicity, & Power: The Key to Efficacy in Clinical Practice. 256p. 1989. 35.00 (0-02-925341-1) Free Pr.

Pinderhughes, Elaine, jt. auth. see Hopps, June G.

Pinderhughes, Howard. Race in the Hood: Conflict & Violence among Urban Youth. LC 97-13526. 1997. pap. 17.95 (0-8166-2919-6); text 44.95 (0-8166-2918-8) U of Minn Pr.

Pinderhughes, John. Family of the Spirit Cookbook. LC 94-25187. (Illus.). 320p. 1994. pap. 14.95 (1-56743-064-3, Amistad) HarperTrade.

— Family of the Spirit Cookbook. 1997. 24.95 (1-56743-071-6, Amistad) HarperTrade.

Pinderhughes, John, photos by. The Golden Rule. LC 98-65996. (Large-Size Photo Board Bks.). 12p. (J). (ps-k). 1999. mass mkt. 4.99 (0-7681-0105-0, McClanahan Book) Learn Horizon.

— Hurt No Living Thing. LC 98-65997. 12p. (J). (ps-k). 1999. mass mkt. 4.99 (0-7681-0104-2, McClanahan Book) Learn Horizon.

Pinderhughes, Raquel, jt. ed. see Moore, Joan.

Pinders, Jerzy T., ed. Modeling Problems in Crack Tip Mechanics. 1984. text 173.50 (90-247-3067-8) Kluwer Academic.

Pindroh, Robert A. Employee Services: A Strategic Component of Business. 1996. pap. 15.95 (1-57167-045-9) Sagamore Pub.

Pindsdorf, Marion K. Communicating When Your Company Is under Siege. 2nd rev. ed. LC 98-38612. xv, 190p. 1999. 32.00 (0-8232-1783-3); pap. 19.00 (0-8232-1784-1) Fordham.

Pindyck. Microeconomics. 4th ed. 1997. pap. text, student ed. 23.00 (0-13-849472-X) P-H.

Pindyck, Robert S. Econometric Models & Economic Forecasts. 3rd ed. (C). 1991. text 91.00 (0-07-050098-3) McGraw.

— Optimal Planning for Economic Stabilization. (Contributions to Economic Analysis Ser.: Vol. 81). 168p. 1983. 59.00 (0-7204-3183-2, North Holland) Elsevier.

— The Structure of World Energy Demand. (Illus.). 308p. 1979. 35.00 (0-262-16074-9) MIT Pr.

Pindyck, Robert S. & Rubinfeld, Daniel L. Econometric Models & Economic Forecasts. 4th ed. LC 97-10357. (C). 1997. text 68.00 (0-07-050208-0) McGraw.

***Pindyck, Robert S. & Rubinfeld, Daniel L.** Microeconomics. 5th ed. 704p. 2000. write for info. (0-13-016583-2) P-H.

Pindyck, Robert S. & Rubinfield, Daniel L. Econometric Models & Economic Forecasts. 4th ed. 1997. text 86.88 (0-07-913292-8) McGraw.

— Microeconomics. 4th ed. LC 97-6658. 726p. 1997. 91.33 (0-13-272923-7) P-H.

Pindyck, Robert S., jt. auth. see Dixit, Avinash K.

Pindyke, Robert S., ed. The Structure of Energy Markets. (Advances in the Economics of Energy & Resources Ser.: Vol. 1). 310p. 1979. 73.25 (0-89232-078-8) Jai Pr.

Pindyke, Robert S., jt. ed. see Moroney, John R.

Pindzola, M. S., jt. ed. see Boyle, James J.

Pindzola, Rebekah H., jt. auth. see Haynes, William O.

Pine. Essential Logic. LC 95-77264. (C). 1995. pap. text 44.50 (0-15-502496-5, Pub. by Harcourt Coll Pubs) Harcourt.

— Essential Logic. 3rd ed. (C). 1995. pap. text, teacher ed. 45.00 (0-15-503250-X) Harcourt Coll Pubs.

Pine & Hartman. Readings for Astronomy. (Adaptable Courseware Ser.). 1994. mass mkt. 33.95 (0-534-32035-X) Wadsworth Pub.

Pine & Morrison. Zap Instructor's Manual. (Physics Ser.). 48p. Date not set. pap., teacher ed. 12.50 (0-86720-519-9) Jones & Bartlett.

Pine, Ana, jt. auth. see Carbone, Joyce.

Pine, B. Joseph, II. Mass Customization: The New Frontier in Business Competition. LC 92-17506. 368p. 1999. 32.50 (0-87584-372-7) Harvard Busn.

— Mass Customization: The New Frontier in Business Competition. 368p. 1999. pap. 16.95 (0-87584-946-6) Harvard Busn.

— Mass Customization: The New Frontier in Business Competition. 380p. 1992. 32.50 (0-07-103385-8) McGraw.

Pine, B. Joseph, II & Gilmore, James H. The Experience Economy: Work Is Theatre & Every Business a Stage. LC 98-33202. 336p. 1999. 24.95 (0-87584-819-2) Harvard Busn.

Pine, B. Joseph, II, jt. auth. see Gilmore, James H.

Pine, Barbara A., et al, eds. Together Again: Family Reunification in Foster Care. 1993. pap. 21.95 (0-87868-525-1) Child Welfare.

Pine, Charles. C: A Programming Workshop. LC 85-63275. 302p. (Orig.). (C). 1986. teacher ed. write for info. (0-938188-45-3); pap. text 29.95 (0-938188-35-6) Mitchell Pub.

An Asterisk (*) at the beginning of an entry indicates that the title is appearing for the first time.

— The C Workshop. 1992. write for info. (*0-917419-13-8*) Wordcraft.

Pine-Coffin, R. S., tr. & intro. see Augustine, Saint.

Pine, Cynthia M. Community Oral Health. LC 97-108396. 288p. 1996. pap. text 69.50 (*0-7236-1095-9*, RK52, Pub. by John Wright) Buttrwrth-Heinemann.

Pine, David J. Three Hundred Sixty-Five Good Health Hints. LC 94-16934. 192p. (Orig.). 1994. pap. 5.95 (*1-56170-099-1*, 162) Hay House.

Pine, Eli S. How to Enjoy Calculus: With Computer Applications. 5th rev. ed. LC 83-60717. (Illus.). 160p. (Orig.). (C). 1975. reprint ed. pap. 14.95 (*0-917208-02-1*) Eli Pine.

Pine, Frances & Bridger, Susan. Surviving Post-Socialism: Local Strategies & Regional Responses. LC 97-8843. 240p. (C). 1997. 85.00 (*0-415-15850-8*) Routledge.

Pine, Fred. Developmental Theory & Clinical Process. LC 84-20841. 272p. 1987. pap. 17.00 (*0-300-04002-4*, Y-661) Yale U Pr.

— Diversity & Direction in Psychoanalytic Technique. LC 97-37013. 224p. 1997. 25.00 (*0-300-07344-5*) Yale U Pr.

— Drive, Ego, Object, & Self: A Synthesis for Clinical Work. LC 89-43168. 288p. 1990. 38.00 (*0-465-01722-3*, Pub. by Basic) HarpC.

Pine, Gerald J., jt. auth. see Boy, Angelo V.

Pine, Jerry, et al. Zap! Electrical Circuits & Fields, No. 2. LC 95-18694. (Physics Ser.). 128p. 1996. spiral bd. 30.00 (*0-86720-482-6*) Jones & Bartlett.

Pine, Joan, jt. ed. see Geehr, Edward C.

Pine, John C. Block Island. 18p. (Orig.). 1982. pap. 2.50 (*0-943430-01-1*) Moveable Feast Pr.

— Chinese Camp & Other California Poems. 28p. (Orig.). 1982. pap. 2.50 (*0-943430-00-3*) Moveable Feast Pr.

— Chinese Camp & Other California Poems: Poems. LC 85-22079. 64p. (Orig.). 1985. pap. 6.95 (*0-86534-078-1*) Sunstone Pr.

— Cliff Walk. LC 84-61838. 96p. 1985. 12.50 (*0-943430-02-X*); pap. 6.95 (*0-943430-03-8*) Moveable Feast Pr.

— The Last Liberty Ship. 32p. (Orig.). 1997. pap. 7.50 (*0-943430-05-4*) Moveable Feast Pr.

— Silhouettes at Eventide. 32p. (Orig.). 1989. pap. 4.50 (*0-943430-04-6*) Moveable Feast Pr.

Pine, Joseph B., jt. auth. see Anderson, David M.

***Pine, Joslyn T.** Wit & Wisdom of the American Presidents: A Book of Quotations. LC 00-31693. (Thrift Editions Ser.). 2000. pap. write for info. (*0-486-41427-2*) Dover.

Pine, Julia. Ontario's Amazing Museums. (Illus.). 290p. 1994. pap. 14.95 (*1-55022-208-2*, Pub. by ECW) Genl Dist Srvs.

Pine, L. A., jt. ed. see Lovink, H. J.

Pine, Lisa. Nazi Family Policy, 1933-1945. LC 98-116485. 1997. 60.00 (*1-85973-902-4*, Pub. by Berg Pubs); pap. 18.50 (*1-85973-907-5*, Pub. by Berg Pubs) NYU Pr.

Pine, Nicholas. Boy Crazy. (Terror Academy Ser.: No. 15). 192p. (Orig.). (YA). 1995. mass mkt. 3.99 (*0-425-14727-4*) Berkley Pub.

— Breaking Up. abr. ed. (Terror Academy Ser.: No. 12). 192p. (YA). 1994. mass mkt. 3.50 (*0-425-14398-8*) Berkley Pub.

— The Prom. (Terror Academy Ser.: No. 9). 192p. (Orig.). (YA). 1994. mass mkt. 3.99 (*0-425-14153-5*) Berkley Pub.

— School Spirit. (Terror Academy Ser.: No. 14). 192p. (Orig.). (YA). 1995. mass mkt. 3.99 (*0-425-14644-8*) Berkley Pub.

— Sixteen Candles. (Terror Academy Ser.: No. 3). 192p. (Orig.). (YA). 1993. mass mkt. 3.50 (*0-425-13841-0*) Berkley Pub.

— Spring Break. (Terror Academy Ser.: No. 4). 208p. (Orig.). (YA). 1993. mass mkt. 3.50 (*0-425-13969-7*) Berkley Pub.

— Stalker. (Terror Academy Ser.: No. 2). 192p. (Orig.). (J). 1993. mass mkt. 3.50 (*0-425-13814-3*) Berkley Pub.

— Summer School. (Terror Academy Ser.: No. 11). 192p. (Orig.). (YA). (gr. 4 up). 1994. mass mkt. 3.50 (*0-425-14338-4*) Berkley Pub.

— Terror Academy, Box set. (Terror Academy Ser.). (YA). 1994. pap. 14.00 (*0-425-14597-2*) Berkley Pub.

Pine, Nicholas J. Goss & Other Crested China. (Album Ser.: No. 120). (Illus.). 32p. 1999. pap. 4.75 (*0-85263-662-8*, Pub. by Shire Pubns) Parkwest Pubns.

Pine, Phil. Master the SAT & PSAT. 2000th ed. (Arco Preparation for the SAT & PSAT Ser.). (Illus.). 717p. 1999. pap. 12.95 (*0-02-863214-1*, Arc) IDG Bks.

***Pine, Phil.** SAT & PSAT, 2000 Edition, with CD. 2000th ed. (Arco Preparation for the SAT & PSAT Ser.). (Illus.). 717p. 1999. pap. 14.95 incl. cd-rom (*0-02-863215-X*, Arc) IDG Bks.

Pine, Rachel N., ed. see Goldstein, Anne T.

Pine, Rachel N., ed. see Mertus, Julie A.

Pine, Randall, et al. Transit Scheduling: Basic & Advanced Manuals. LC 98-60091. (TCRP Report Ser.). 148p. 1998. pap. write for info. (*0-309-06262-4*) Natl Acad Pr.

Pine, Ray, jt. auth. see Go, Frank M.

Pine, Red. The Zen Teachings of Bodhidharma. LC 89-9229. (Bilingual Edition Ser.). 126p. 1989. pap. 11.00 (*0-86547-399-4*) N Point Pr.

Pine, Red & O'Connor, Mike, eds. The Clouds Should Know Me by Now: Buddhist Poet Monks of China. LC 98-17768. (Illus.). 224p. 1998. pap. 15.95 (*0-86171-143-2*) Wisdom MA.

Pine, Red, tr. see Cold Mountain Staff.

Pine, Red, tr. see Po-jen, Sung.

Pine, Red, jt. tr. see Porter, Bill.

Pine, Red, tr. see Shan, Han.

***Pine, Richard.** The Diviner: The Art of Brian Friel. 2nd ed. LC 99-198203. 352p. 1999. pap. 29.95 (*1-900621-23-1*, Pub. by Univ Coll Dublin Pr) Dufour.

Pine, Richard. Oscar Wilde. 2nd ed. (Gill's Irish Lives Ser.). (Illus.). 151p. 1998. reprint ed. pap. 13.95 (*0-7171-2690-0*, Pub. by Gill & MacMill) Irish Bks Media.

Pine, Richard & Cave, Richard. The Dublin Gate Theatre 1928-1978. (Theatre in Focus Ser.). (Illus.). 124p. 1984. pap. write for info. incl. sl. (*0-85964-156-2*) Chadwyck-Healey.

Pine, Richard, ed. see Kennelly, Brendan.

Pine, Stanley H. Organic Chemistry. 5th ed. (C). 1987. pap. text, student ed. write for info. (*0-07-050119-X*) McGraw.

Pine, Ted, jt. auth. see Schwerin, Julie B.

Pine, Ted A., ed. see Schwerin, Julie B.

Pine, Theodore A., jt. auth. see Schwerin, Julie B.

Pine Tree Legal Assistance, Inc. Staff. Do Your Own Divorce in Maine. (Illus.). 216p. 1991. reprint ed. pap. 16.50 (*0-9610570-0-9*) Bks by Village.

Pine, Vanderlyn R. Death's Critical Issues: Reflections in Studying Death. (Death, Value & Meaning Ser.). Date not set. text 42.95 (*0-89503-135-3*) Baywood Pub.

Pine, Wilfred H. Natural Resources Economics. 1977. pap. 4.00 (*0-686-00368-3*) AG Pr.

Pineau, A. Osium, ed. see International Union of Theoretical & Applied Mecha & Zaoui, A.

Pineau des Forets, Guillaume, jt. ed. see Combes, Francoise.

***Pineau, Gisele.** The Drifting of Spirits. Dash, Michael, tr. 2000. pap. 12.95 (*0-7043-8101-X*, Pub. by Quartet) Interlink Pub.

Pineau, Jean. Mariage, Separation, Divorce: L'Etat du Droit au Quebec. 2nd rev. ed. LC 77-565419. (FRE.). 314p. 1978. reprint ed. pap. 97.40 (*0-7837-6947-4*, 204677600003) Bks Demand.

Pineau, Roger, tr. see Ito, Masanori.

Pinecrest, Richard F. Animal Social Behavior: Index of New Information with Authors, Subjects & Bibliography. rev. ed. 173p. 1995. 47.50 (*0-7883-0716-9*); pap. 44.50 (*0-7883-0717-7*) ABBE Pubs Assn.

Pineda, Ana M., jt. ed. see Schreiter, Robert.

Pineda de Gyvez, Jose. Integrated Circuit Defect-Sensitivity: Theory & Computational Models. LC 92-35547. (International Series in Engineering & Computer Science, VLSI, Computer Architecture, & Digital Screen Processing: Vol. 208). 192p. (C). 1992. text 116.50 (*0-7923-9306-6*) Kluwer Academic.

Pineda, Leonardo A., jt. auth. see Davidson, Alma M.

Pineda, M. H. & Dooley, M. P. McDonald's Veterinary Endocrinology & Reproduction. 5th ed. LC 98-9931. 1999. write for info. (*0-683-06920-9*) Lppncott W & W.

Pineda-Ofreneo, Rosalinda. The Philippine Debt & Poverty. 120p. (C). 1991. text 80.00 (*0-85598-049-4*, Pub. by Oxfam Pubns); pap. text 28.00 (*0-85598-050-8*, Pub. by Oxfam Pubns) St Mut.

Pineda Ofreneo, Rosalinda. The Philippines: Debt & Poverty. (Trade, Aid & Debt Ser.). (Illus.). 120p. (C). 1991. pap. 11.95 (*0-85598-150-4*, Pub. by Oxfam Pub) Stylus Pub VA.

Pineda, Roberto & Alzate, Beatriz, eds. Pasado y Presente Del Amazonas: Su Historia Economica y Social. (Memorias del VI Congreso de Antropologia en Colombia Ser.). (SPA.). 180p. 1993. pap. 10.00 (*958-95572-1-X*, UA003) UPLAAP.

Pineda, Sysy, tr. see Brown, J. Aaron, ed.

Pineda y Ramirez, Antonio de. The Guam Diary of Naturalist Antonio de Pineda y Ramirez, 1792. Driver, Marjorie G., ed. Mallada, Victor F., tr. from SPA. (Illus.). viii, 85p. (Orig.). (C). 1990. pap. 5.00 (*1-878453-01-7*) Univ Guam MAR Ctr.

Pinedo, H. M., et al, eds. Cancer Chemotherapy & Biological Response Modifiers. 732p. 1994. 324.25 (*0-444-82056-6*) Elsevier.

— Cancer Chemotherapy & Biological Response Modifiers. (Cancer Chemotherapy Annual Ser.: Vol. 17). 768p. 1997. 185.00 (*0-444-82671-8*, North Holland) Elsevier.

— Cancer Chemotherapy & Biological Response Modifiers: Annual 14, Vol. 14. 698p. 1993. 320.50 (*0-444-81509-0*) Elsevier.

— Cancer Chemotherapy & Biological Response Modifiers: Annual 16, Vol. 16. 704p. 1995. 305.75 (*0-444-82326-3*) Elsevier.

Pinedo, H. M. & Schornagel, J. H., eds. Platinum & Other Metal Coordination Compounds in Cancer Chemotherapy 2: Proceeding of the 7th International Symposium Held in Amsterdam, The Netherlands, March 1-4, 1995, Vol. 2. (Illus.). 368p. 1996. 102.00 (*0-306-45287-1*, Kluwer Plenum) Kluwer Academic.

Pinedo, Herbert M., et al, eds. Soft Tissue Sarcomas: New Developments in the Multidisciplinary Approach to Treatment. (C). 1991. text 159.50 (*0-7923-1139-6*) Kluwer Academic.

Pinedo, Herbert M. & Giaccone, Giuseppe, eds. Drug Resistance in the Treatment of Cancer. (Cancer Ser.). (Illus.). 340p. (C). 1998. text 95.00 (*0-521-47321-7*) Cambridge U Pr.

Pinedo, Herbert M. & Verweij, Jaap, eds. Treatment of Soft Tissue Sarcomas. (Cancer Treatment & Research Ser.). (C). 1988. text 114.00 (*0-89838-391-9*) Kluwer Academic.

Pinedo, Herbert M., jt. auth. see Potmesil, Milan.

Pinedo, Isabel C. Recreational Terror: Women & the Pleasures of Horror Film Viewing. LC 97-8033. (SUNY Series, Interruptions). 177p. (C). 1997. text 44.50 (*0-7914-3441-9*); pap. text 14.95 (*0-7914-3442-7*) State U NY Pr.

Pinedo, L. F., jt. ed. see Henriques, J. M.

Pinedo, Michael. Scheduling: Theory, Algorithms & Systems. LC 94-8256. (International Industrial & Systems Engineering Ser.). 416p. 1994. 95.00 (*0-13-706757-7*) P-H.

Pinedo, Michael & Chao, Xiuli. Operations Scheduling with Applications in Manufacturing & Services. LC 98-18851. 1998. 64.50 (*0-07-289779-1*) McGraw.

Pinegar, Ed. Communication with God, Companions & with Investigators. (Especially for Missionaries Ser.: No. 2). Date not set. pap. 3.95 (*1-57734-140-6*, 01113119) Covenant Comms.

— Teaching by the Spirit with the Power of God. (Especially for Missionaries Ser.: No. 3). Date not set. pap. 3.95 (*1-57734-141-4*, 01113127) Covenant Comms.

— Your Capacity & Potential As a Missionary. (Especially for Missionaries Ser.: No. 4). Date not set. pap. 3.95 (*1-57734-142-2*, 01113135) Covenant Comms.

Pinegar, Ed J. Fatherhood. pap. 11.98 (*1-55517-269-5*) CFI Dist.

— The Mighty Change. pap. 11.98 (*1-55517-275-X*) CFI Dist.

— The Power of the Word. pap. 12.98 (*1-55517-281-4*) CFI Dist.

Pinegar, Ed J. Preparing for Your Mission. 109p. (YA). (gr. 12 up). 1992. pap. 7.95 (*0-87579-646-X*) Deseret Bk.

Pinegar, Ed J. Steps to Spirituality. pap. 12.98 (*1-55517-284-9*) CFI Dist.

— You, Your Family & the Scriptures. pap. 13.98 (*1-55517-270-9*) CFI Dist.

Pinegar, Ed J. & Pinegar, Patricia. Preparing for Your Mission. pap. 14.95 (*1-55517-347-0*) CFI Dist.

Pinegar, Ed J., jt. auth. see Cannon, Elaine.

Pinegar, Ed J., jt. auth. see Pinegar, Patricia.

Pinegar, Patricia & Pinegar, Ed J. Missionary Dialogues. pap. 10.95 (*1-55517-317-9*) CFI Dist.

Pinegar, Patricia, jt. auth. see Pinegar, Ed J.

Pinegar, Pit M. Nine Years Between Two Poems. 1996. pap. 5.00 (*0-916897-23-0*) Andrew Mtn Pr.

— The Possibilities of Empty Space: Poems. LC 97-19113. 1997. pap. 12.95 (*0-916897-29-X*) Andrew Mtn Pr.

***Pineiro.** Shutdown. 320p. 2000. 24.95 (*0-312-86909-6*) Tor Bks.

Pineiro, R. J. Breakthrough. LC 97-11946. 384p. 1997. text 23.95 (*0-312-85983-X*) St Martin.

— Breakthrough. 1999. mass mkt. 6.99 (*0-8125-4390-4*, Pub. by Tor Bks) St Martin.

— Exposure. 1998. mass mkt. 6.99 (*0-8125-4389-0*, Pub. by Forge NYC) St Martin.

— 01-01-00: A Novel of the Millennium. LC 99-24573. 1999. 24.95 (*0-312-87058-2*, Pub. by Forge NYC) St Martin.

***Pineiro, R. J.** 01-01-00: The Novel of the Millennium. 416p. 1999. mass mkt. 6.99 (*0-8125-6871-0*, Pub. by Tor Bks) St Martin.

Pineiro, R. J. Retribution. 1996. pap. 6.99 (*0-614-98102-6*) Tor Bks.

— Retribution, Vol. 1. 1996. mass mkt. 6.99 (*0-8125-4463-3*, Pub. by Tor Bks) St Martin.

— Retribution, Vol. 1. 2nd ed. 1995. 23.95 (*0-614-06177-6*) Forge NYC.

***Pineiro, R. J.** Shutdown. 2001. mass mkt. write for info. (*0-8125-7504-0*) Tor Bks.

Pineiro, R. J. Ultimatum. 416p. 1995. 5.99 (*0-8125-2400-4*, Pub. by Tor Bks) St Martin.

***Pineiro, R. J.** Y2K. 1999. mass mkt. 6.99 (*0-8125-6867-2*, Pub. by Tor Bks) St Martin.

Pinel. Introduction to Psychology. 1995. pap. text, student ed. write for info. (*0-205-13842-X*) Allyn.

Pinel, J., ed. Medicaments Essentiels. Guide Pratique d'Utilisation pour l'Emploi et la Gestion de Medicaments et Materiel Medical Dans les Dispensaires, les Centres Medicaux et les Camps de Refugies. A l'Usage des Medecins, Infirmier(e) s et Auxiliaries de Sante. (Medecins Sans Frontieres - Hatier Ser.). (FRE.). 255p. 1991. pap. 26.95 (*2-218-02650-3*) Schoenhof.

Pinel, Jane. The Picnic Basket. LC 83-90332. (Illus.). 96p. 1983. pap. 5.00 (*0-915909-00-6*) Ruggles Pub.

Pinel, John P. Biopsychology. 608p. 1989. text 50.00 (*0-205-12052-0*, H20522) Allyn.

— Colorful Introduction to the Anatomy of the Human Brain: A Brain a Psychology Coloring Book. 226p. 1997. pap. text 19.00 (*0-205-16299-1*) P-H.

***Pinel, John P. J.** Biopsychology. 4th ed. LC 99-25001. 564p. (C). 1999. 83.00 (*0-205-28992-4*) Allyn.

Pinel, Philippe. The Clinical Training of Doctors: An Essay 1793. Weiner, Dora B., ed. LC 80-14500. (Henry E. Sigerist Supplements to the Bulletin of the History of Medicine, New Ser.: No. 3). 112p. reprint ed. pap. 34.80 (*0-608-15189-0*, 202737800055) Bks Demand.

— Traite Medico-Philosophique sur l'Alienation Mentale. 2nd ed. LC 75-16727. (Classics in Psychiatry Ser.). (FRE.). 1976. reprint ed. 46.95 (*0-405-07450-6*) Ayer.

Pinel, Stephen L. Old Organs of Princeton: Being an Historical Chronology & Description of All the Known Pipe Organs Installed in the Town of Princeton, New Jersey, from 1760 to 1925, Including Photographs & Stoplists When Available, as Well as Accounts from Newspapers, Church Records, Histories, & Diaries. LC 89-62170. 146p. 1989. 29.95 (*0-9610092-2-5*) Boston Organ Club.

Pinelli, Giuseppe, jt. ed. see Di Pasquale, Giuseppe.

Pinelli, P. Brain Control of Behaviour: An Analysis of Verbal Delayed Reactions & Their Impairment in Mental Disorders. LC 96-43505. (Illus.). xii, 342p. 1997. 299.25 (*3-8055-6305-1*) S Karger.

Pinelli, Thomas E., et al. Knowledge Diffusion in the U. S. Aerospace Industry. LC 97-25175. (Information Management, Policy & Services Ser.). (Illus.). 350p. 1998. pap. 85.00 (*1-56750-226-1*); text 157.00 (*1-56750-225-3*) Ablx Pub.

Pinello, Daniel R. The Impact of Judicial-Selection Method on State-Supreme Court Policy: Innovation, Reaction & Atrophy, 80. LC 95-16269. (Contributions in Legal Studies: Vol. 80). 248p. 1995. 59.95 (*0-313-29243-4*, Greenwood Pr) Greenwood.

Pinelo, Antonio De Leon, see De Leon Pinelo, Antonio.

Pineo, Graham F., jt. auth. see Hull, Russell.

Pineo, Ronn, ed. see Baer, James A.

Pineo, Ronn F. Social & Economic Reform in Ecuador: Life & Work in Guayaquil. LC 95-45919. (Illus.). 256p. (C). 1996. 49.95 (*0-8130-1437-9*) U Press Fla.

Pinera, Angel. Los Cubanos. 1978. pap. 4.50 (*84-400-4714-2*) Ediciones.

Pinera, David. American & English Influence on the Early Development of Ensenada, Baja California & Mexico. LC 96-110851. 162p. 1995. text 12.50 (*0-925613-13-4*) SDSU Inst Reg Studies.

Pinera, David & Zepeda, Jorge M., eds. Baja California 1901-1905: Considerations & Data for Its Demographic History. 334p. 1994. text 15.00 (*968-7826-11-8*) SDSU Inst Reg Studies.

Pinera, Humberto, et al. Proceso del las Ideas Politicas en Cuba. (SPA.). 132p. (Orig.). 1988. pap. 15.00 (*0-89729-489-0*, Pub. by Laurenty Pub Inc) Ediciones.

Pinera-Llera, Humberto. Introduccion e Historia de la Filosofia. 3rd ed. LC 89-65885. (Coleccion Textos). (SPA., Illus.). 348p. 1980. reprint ed. pap. 12.95 (*0-89729-254-5*) Ediciones.

Pinera, Virgilio. Cold Tales. Schafer, Mark, tr. from SPA. LC 88-80807. 256p. 1988. pap. 15.00 (*0-941419-80-0*, Eridanos Library) Marsilio Pubs.

— Cold Tales. 1988. pap. text 15.00 (*0-941419-19-3*, Eridanos Library) Marsilio Pubs.

— Rene's Flesh. Schafer, Mark, tr. LC 89-83811. 256p. 1992. pap. 12.95 (*1-56886-017-X*, Eridanos Library) Marsilio Pubs.

Pinera, Virgilio & Gonzales-Cruz, Luis F. Una Caja de Zapatos Vacia. LC 86-80352. (Coleccion Teatro). (SPA.). 83p. (Orig.). 1986. pap. 7.95 (*0-89729-390-8*) Ediciones.

Pineri, Michel & Eisenberg, Adi, eds. Structure & Properties of Ionomers. 1987. text 278.50 (*90-277-2458-X*) Kluwer Academic.

Pinero, Arthur W. The Collected Letters of Sir Arthur Pinero. Wearing, J. P., ed. LC 74-76742. 314p. reprint ed. pap. 97.40 (*0-608-15962-X*, 203324500084) Bks Demand.

— The Second Mrs. Tanqueray. Landes, William-Alan, ed. LC 96-37918. 70p. (Orig.). 1997. pap. 7.00 (*0-88734-719-3*) Players Pr.

— Social Plays, 4 vols. (BCL1-PR English Literature Ser.). 1992. reprint ed. lib. bdg. 300.00 (*0-7812-7618-7*) Rprt Serv.

— Social Plays, 4 vols., Set. Hamilton, Clayton, ed. LC 79-18169. reprint ed. 325.00 (*0-404-05080-8*) AMS Pr.

— Trelawny of the "Wells" & Other Plays. Bratton, Jacky, ed. & intro. by. (World's Classics Ser.). 360p. 1995. pap. 11.95 (*0-19-282568-2*) OUP.

— Trelawny of the "Wells" & Other Plays: The Magistrated; TheSchoolmistress; The Second Mrs. Tanqueray. Bratton, Jacky, ed. & intro. by. (World's Classics Ser.). 354p. 1995. text 59.00 (*0-19-812148-2*) OUP.

— Two Plays: Dr. Harmer's Holidays & Child Man. (BCL1-PR English Literature Ser.). 245p. 1992. reprint ed. lib. bdg. 79.00 (*0-7812-7619-5*) Rprt Serv.

Pinero, Daniel. De las Bacterias Al Hombre: La Evolucion. (Ciencia para Todos Ser.). (SPA.). pap. 6.99 (*968-16-2540-4*, Pub. by Fondo) Continental Bk.

Pinero, Eugenio. The Town of San Felipe & Colonial Cacao Economics. LC 94-71251. (Transactions Ser.: Vol. 84, Pt. 3). (Illus.). 190p. (C). 1994. pap. 15.00 (*0-87169-843-9*, T843-pie) Am Philos.

Pinero, Miguel. Outrageous One Act Plays. LC 86-71600. 160p. 1986. pap. 9.50 (*0-934770-68-9*, Pub. by Arte Publico) Empire Pub Srvs.

— Short Eyes. 128p. 1975. pap. 10.00 (*0-374-52147-6*) FS&G.

— The Sun Always Shines for the Cool. LC 83-72582. 128p. (C). 1984. pap. 11.00 (*0-934770-25-5*, Pub. by Arte Publico) Empire Pub Srvs.

Pines. Experiencing Social Psychology. 4th ed. 2001. 26.25 (*0-07-231684-5*) McGraw.

— Money Coach. 5th ed. 148p. (C). 1997. pap. text. write for info. (*0-201-31613-7*) Addison-Wesley.

— Social Psychology. 3rd ed. 1993. teacher ed. 28.12 (*0-07-040774-6*) McGraw.

Pines, Alexander, jt. ed. see Bell, Alexis T.

Pines, Ayala M. Couple Burnout. 277p. 1996. pap. 19.99 (*0-415-91632-1*) Routledge.

— Couple Burnout. 277p. (C). 1996. 70.00 (*0-415-91631-3*) Routledge.

***Pines, Ayala M.** Falling in Love: Why We Choose the Lovers We Choose. LC 99-22987. 1999. 24.95 (*0-415-92046-9*) Routledge.

Pines, Ayala M. Romantic Jealousy: Causes Symptoms Cures. 2nd ed. LC 97-44734. 320p. (Orig.). (C). (gr. 13). 1998. pap. 17.99 (*0-415-92010-8*) Routledge.

Pines, Ayala M. & Maslach, Christina. Experiencing Social Psychology: Readings & Projects. 3rd ed. LC 92-11918. (Series in Social Psychology). 352p. (C). 1993. pap. 33.75 (*0-07-040773-8*) McGraw.

***Pines, Ayala Malach.** Falling in Love: Why We Choose the Lovers We Choose. 2000. reprint ed. pap. 17.95 (*0-415-92919-9*) Routledge.

Pines, Burton Y. & Lamer, Timothy W. Out of Focus: Network Television & the American Economy. LC 93-46426. 384p. 1994. 24.00 (*0-89526-490-0*) Regnery Pub.

Pines, Christopher L. Ideology & False Consciousness: Marx & His Historical Progenitors. LC 92-15168. (SUNY Series in the Philosophy of the Social Sciences). 242p. (C). 1993. text 57.50 (*0-7914-1431-0*); pap. text 18.95 (*0-7914-1432-9*) State U NY Pr.

Pines, David. Elementary Excitations in Solids. LC 99-60034. 320p. 1999. pap. text 35.00 (*0-7382-0115-4*, Pub. by Perseus Pubng) HarpC.

P

An Asterisk (*) at the beginning of an entry indicates that the title is appearing for the first time.

— Emerging Syntheses in Science-on Demand. 1997. pap. write for info. (*0-201-31601-3*) Addison-Wesley.
— The Many-Body Problems. LC 97-43363. 1997. 39.00 (*0-201-32834-8*) Addison-Wesley.
Pines, David, ed. Emerging Syntheses. 1987. 39.95 (*0-317-66911-7*, 15677); pap. 19.95 (*0-317-66912-5*, 15686) Addison-Wesley.
— Emerging Syntheses in Science. (Santa Fe Institute Ser.: Vol. I). 256p. (C). 1988. pap. 33.00 (*0-201-15686-5*); text 30.87 (*0-201-15677-6*) Addison-Wesley.
Pines, David, et al, eds. Topics in Public Economics: Theoretical & Applied Analysis. LC 96-20417. (Illus.). 368p. (C). 1997. text 64.95 (*0-521-56136-1*) Cambridge U Pr.
Pines, David & Nozieres, Philippe. Theory of Quantum Liquids Vol. I: Normal Fermi Liquids. LC 88-24104. (Classics Ser.). (Illus.). 384p. (C). 1989. 49.95 (*0-201-09429-0*) Addison-Wesley.
— Theory of Quantum Liquids Vol. I: Normal Fermi Liquids. LC 88-24104. (Illus.). (C). 1994. pap. 50.00 (*0-201-40774-4*) Addison-Wesley.
Pines, David & Stevens, Benjamin H. Mathematical Programming & Competitive Equilibrium in the Location of Agricultural Production. (Discussion Papers: No. 23). 1968. pap. 10.00 (*1-55869-073-5*) Regional Sci Res Inst.
Pines, David, jt. auth. see Nozieres, Philippe.
Pines, David, jt. auth. see Papageorgiou, Yorgos Y.
Pines, David, jt. ed. see Ventura, Joseph.
Pines, Derek A. International Culinary Dictionary. 160p. 1997. pap. 10.95 (*1-873475-63-2*, Pub. by Summers) Howell Pr VA.
Pines, Dinora. A Woman's Unconscious Use of Her Body. 256p. 1994. 32.00 (*0-300-05960-4*) Yale U Pr.
Pines, Eunice & Sabo, Eleanor, eds. Barnum Memorial Cemetery. 2nd ed. (Illus.). 72p. 1987. reprint ed. pap. 8.00 (*0-940133-04-0*) Kinseeker Pubns.
Pines, Jim, ed. Black & White in Colour: Black People in British Television since 1936. (Illus.). 256p. 1992. 55.00 (*0-85170-328-3*, Pub. by British Film Inst); pap. 22.95 (*0-85170-329-1*, Pub. by British Film Inst) Ind U Pr.
Pines, Jim & Willemen, Paul, eds. Questions of Third Cinema. (Illus.). 256p. 1990. 29.95 (*0-85170-262-7*, Pub. by British Film Inst); pap. 14.95 (*0-85170-230-9*, Pub. by British Film Inst) Ind U Pr.
Pines, Malcolm. Circular Reflections: Selected Papers of Malcolm Pines. LC 98-150914. (International Library of Group Analysis). 325p. 1998. 85.00 (*1-85302-493-7*, Pub. by Jessica Kingsley); pap. 29.95 (*1-85302-492-9*, Pub. by Jessica Kingsley) Taylor & Francis.
Pines, Malcolm, ed. Bion & Group Psychotherapy. (International Library of Group Psychotherapy & Group Process Ser.). 336p. 1985. 49.95 (*0-7100-9949-5*, 99495, Routledge Thoemms) Routledge.
Pines, Malcolm & Rafaelsen, Lise, eds. The Individual & the Group: Boundaries & Interrelations, 2 vols., Set. LC 81-17924. 1982. 145.00 (*0-685-04077-1*, Plenum Trade) Perseus Pubng.
— The Individual & the Group: Boundaries & Interrelations, 2 vols., Vol. 1: Theory. LC 81-17924. 378p. 1982. 65.00 (*0-306-40837-6*, Plenum Trade) Perseus Pubng.
— The Individual & the Group: Boundaries & Interrelations, 2 vols., Vol. 2: Practice. LC 81-17924. 700p. 1982. 95.00 (*0-306-40838-4*, Plenum Trade) Perseus Pubng.
Pines, Malcolm, jt. ed. see Harwood, Irene.
Pines, Malcolm, jt. ed. see Schermer, Victor L.
Pines, Marion W., jt. auth. see Packer, Arnold H.
Pines, Maya. Inside the Cell. (Illus.). 62p. (C). 1993. pap. text 20.00 (*1-56806-208-7*) DIANE Pub.
***Pines, Mindy.** Microsoft: Simple Projects (Intermediate) with CD-ROM. 96p. 2000. pap. 18.95 incl. cd-rom (*1-57690-728-7*) Tchr Create Mat.
Pines, Paul. Hotel Madden Poems. (Illus.). 54p. (Orig.). (C). 1991. pap. 6.00 (*0-936556-25-0*) Contact Two.
— Onion. LC 72-83855. (Illus.). 72p. 1972. pap. 3.00 (*0-913142-00-X*) Mulch Pr.
Pines, Philip A., ed. see Slobody, Evelyn & Slobody, Lawrence B.
Pines, Shlomo. Studies in Arabic Versions of Greek Texts & in Medieval Science. (Collected Works of Shlomo Pines: Vol. 2). ix, 468p. 1986. lib. bdg. 95.50 (*965-223-626-8*) Brill Academic Pubs.
Pines, Shlomo, jt. ed. see Yovel, Y.
Pines, Shlomo, tr. see Maimonides.
Pines, Shlomo, tr. & intro. see Maimonides.
Pines, Susan, ed. see Czerlinsky, Thomas & Chandler, Shirley K.
Pines, Susan, ed. see Farr, J. Michael.
Pines, Susan, ed. see Farr, J Michael & Christophersen, Susan.
Pines, Susan, ed. see Farr, J. Michael & Christophersen, Susan.
Pines, Tonya, ed. see Pike, Christopher, pseud & Smith, Sinclair.
Pines, Wayne L., jt. ed. see Pina, Kenneth R.
Pineshi, jt. auth. see Treves.
***Pinet, Andre.** 15 Days of Prayer with Johannes Tauler. 128p. 2000. pap. 7.95 (*0-7648-0653-X*) Liguori Pubns.
Pinet, Andre, jt. auth. see Vrai, Suzanne.
Pinet, B. & Bois, C. Potential of Deep Seismic Profiling for Hydrocarbon Exploration: 5th IFP Exploration & Production Research Conference, Arles, 1989. (Illus.). 502p. (C). 1990. 615.00 (*2-7108-0590-1*, Pub. by Edits Technip) Enfield Pubs NH.
Pinet, Celine & Devlin, Kimberly, eds. Threads: Insights by Women Architects. (Publications in Architecture & Urban Planning: No. R91-1). (Illus.). 53p. 1991. per. 15.00 (*0-938744-73-9*) U of Wis Ctr Arch-Urban.
Pinet, G., contrib. by. Is the Law Fair to the Disabled? A European Survey. (WHO Regional Publications: No. 29). xiii, 354p. 1990. pap. text 45.00 (*92-890-1120-3*, 1310029) World Health.
Pinet, Helene. Rodin: The Hand of Genius. Palmer, Caroline, tr. (Discoveries Ser.). (Illus.). 144p. 1992. pap. 12.95 (*0-8109-2888-4*, Pub. by Abrams) Time Warner.
Pinet, Michele. Be Your Own Rock & Mineral Expert. Greenbaum, Fay, tr. from FRE. LC 96-27611. (Illus.). 40p. (J). 1997. 14.95 (*0-8069-9580-7*) Sterling.
Pinet, Paul B. Invitation to Oceanography. (Earth Science Ser.). 54p. (C). 1996. pap. text, teacher ed. 10.00 (*0-314-08933-0*) Jones & Bartlett.
Pinet, Paul R. Invitation to Oceanography. (Earth Science Ser.). 227p. 1996. pap. 17.50 (*0-314-08967-5*) Jones & Bartlett.
— Invitation to Oceanography. LC 95-30442. (Earth Science Ser.). 300p. (C). 1996. pap. text 51.25 (*0-314-06339-0*) Jones & Bartlett.
***Pinet, Paul R.** Invitation to Oceanography. 2nd ed. LC 99-40851. 1999. write for info. (*0-7637-0914-X*) Jones & Bartlett.
Pinet, Paul R. Invitation to Oceanography: Test Bank. (Earth Science Ser.). 196p. 1996. pap. 10.00 (*0-314-08756-7*) Jones & Bartlett.
— Invitation to Oceanography: WWW Edition. (Earth Science Ser.). 1997. pap. 51.25 (*0-7637-0614-0*) Jones & Bartlett.
— Oceanography: Introduction to Planet Oceanus. Pullins, ed. (Earth Science Ser.). 572p. (C). 1992. 51.25 (*0-314-77008-9*) Jones & Bartlett.
— Study Guide for Oceanography. (Earth Science Ser.). 185p. 1992. pap. 10.00 (*0-314-00053-4*); pap., teacher ed. 10.00 (*0-314-00016-X*) Jones & Bartlett.
Pinette, Matthieu, jt. auth. see Musbee de Picardie Staff.
Pineus, Kaj. Ship's Value. 2nd ed. 1986. 85.00 (*1-85044-062-X*) LLP.
Piney, M., et al, eds. Controlling Airborne Contaminants in the Workplace: Technical Guide, No. 7. 173p. (C). 1994. pap. 150.00 (*0-905927-42-7*, Pub. by H&H Sci Cnslts) St Mut.
Pinfield, Lawrence T. The Operation of Internal Labor Markets: Staffing Practices & Vacancy Chains. LC 96-34163. (Plenum Studies in Work & Industry). (Illus.). 372p. (C). 1995. 52.50 (*0-306-45046-1*, Kluwer Plenum) Kluwer Academic.
Pinfield, N. Indian Sub-Continent: India, Pakistan & Bangladesh. 1992. pap. text 14.04 (*0-582-20661-8*) Longman.
Pinfold, John R. Tibet. LC 92-122704. (World Bibliographical Ser.). 188p. 1991. lib. bdg. 66.00 (*1-85109-158-0*) ABC-CLIO.
Pinfold, Mike, jt. auth. see Crowther, Bruce.
Pinfold, P., jt. ed. see Sahoo, M.
Pinfold, Wallace, jt. auth. see Hazard, Edith.
Pinfold, Wallace G. A Closer Shave: Man's Daily Search for Perfection. LC 98-51400. (Illus.). 160p. 1999. 16.95 (*1-57965-136-4*, 85136) Artisan.
Ping, April G., ed. see Eames, David.
Ping, C., ed. Chinese Therapeutical Tuina. (Traditional Chinese Medicine Ser.: No. 7). (YA). (gr. 12). Date not set. 70.00 (*90-5199-259-9*) IOS Press.
Ping, C. & Guili, Z., eds. Chinese Herbs & Compatibility. LC 95-8092. (Traditional Chinese Medicine Ser.: Vol. 4). 600p. (YA). (gr. 12). Date not set. 90.00 (*90-5199-244-0*, 244-0) IOS Press.
Ping, Charles J. Ohio University in Perspective II: The Annual Convocation Addresses of President Charles J. Ping, 1985-1993. LC 94-9002. 285p. 1994. 24.95 (*0-8214-1101-2*) Ohio U Pr.
Ping Chen & Chinian, Lin, eds. Well-Known Formulas & Modified Applications. LC 96-78114. (Traditional Chinese Medicine Ser.: Vol. 5). 250p. Date not set. 83.00 (*90-5199-302-1*, 302-1) IOS Press.
Ping Chen & Hongwen, Xu, eds. Diagnostic Methods & Syndrome Identification. LC 96-78111. (Traditional Chinese Medicine Ser.: Vol. 3). 450p. Date not set. 77.00 (*90-5199-297-1*, 297-1) IOS Press.
Ping-Chun Hsiung. Living Rooms As Factories: Class, Gender, & the Satellite Factory System in Taiwan. (Illus.). (Orig.). (C). 1996. pap. text 22.95 (*1-56639-390-6*); lib. bdg. 69.95 (*1-56639-389-2*) Temple U Pr.
Ping-Gam, Go. What Character is That: An Easy-Access Dictionary of 5,000 Chinese Characters. 2nd ed. LC 98-101103. 1997. pap. text 18.95 (*0-9623113-5-9*) Simplex Pubns.
Ping, Jiao, jt. auth. see Minick, Scott.
Ping, Margaret. Looking Back - Moving Forward: History of the Billings YWCA, 1907-1988. Schaffer, Rachel, ed. (Orig.). 1991. pap. write for info. (*0-9629912-0-1*) M Ping.
Ping-Robbins, Nancy R. & Marco, Guy, eds. Scott Joplin: A Guide to Research. LC 98-10988. (Composer Resource Manuals Ser.: Vol. 7). 426p. 1998. 76.00 (*0-8240-8399-7*) Garland.
Ping, Shen & Sim, Cheung Y. Splendid China: Shenzhen Miniature Scenic Spot. (Illus.). 120p. 1994. pap. 16.95 (*0-8351-2535-1*) China Bks.
***Ping, Wang.** Aching for Beauty: Footbinding in China. 2000. 27.95 (*0-8166-3605-2*) U of Minn Pr.
Ping, Wang. American Visa. LC 94-12599. 172p. (Orig.). 1994. pap. 11.95 (*1-56689-025-X*) Coffee Hse.
— Of Flesh & Spirit. LC 97-43199. 90p. 1998. pap. 12.95 (*1-56689-068-3*) Coffee Hse.
Ping, Wang & Franca, Jose E. Multirate Switched-Capacitor Circuits for 2-D Signal Processing. Vol. 427. LC 97-40162. (Kluwer International Series in Engineering & Computer Science). 124p. 1998. text 104.50 (*0-7923-8051-7*) Kluwer Academic.
Pingali, P. L., et al. Asian Rice Bowls: The Returning Crisis? LC 96-48886. (A CAB International Publication). 352p. 1997. text 100.00 (*0-85199-162-9*) OUP.
Pingali, Prabhu, et al. Agricultural Mechanization & the Evolution of Farming Systems in Sub-Saharan Africa. LC 86-27523. (Illus.). 224p. reprint ed. pap. 69.50 (*0-608-06103-4*, 206643500008) Bks Demand.
Pingali, Prabhu L., ed. see Roger, Pierre A.
Pingatore, Diane R. A Reader's Guide to Short Stories of Eudora Welty. LC 95-31368. 1996. 50.00 (*0-8161-7371-0*, G K Hall & Co) Mac Lib Ref.
Pingatore, Gene, jt. auth. see Mayer, John.
Pingaud, Bernard. L' Amour Triste. (FRE.). 1973. pap. 8.95 (*0-7859-4020-0*) Fr & Eur.
Pingborn, R. N., et al. Damage Assessment, Reliability & Life Prediction of Power Plant Components: Presented at the 1990 Pressure Vessels & Piping Conference, Nashville, Tennessee, June 17-21, 1990 / LC 90-55370. 1990. write for info. (*0-7918-0504-2*) ASME Pr.
Pingel, D. Kent & Briggs, Jennifer. Nolan Ryan: The Authorized Pictorial History. LC 91-58019. (Illus.). 1991. write for info. (*0-9626219-8-6*) Summit TX.
Pingel, Lee Ann, jt. auth. see Chittick, William O.
Pingel, Volker. Die Vorgeschichtlichen Goldfund der Iberischen Halbinsel: Eine Archaeologische Unterschung zur Auswertung der Spektralanalysen. (Madrider Forschungen Ser.: Bd. 17). (GER., Illus.). xxi, 321p. (C). 1992. lib. bdg. 270.80 (*3-11-012337-1*) De Gruyter.
Pingenot, Ben E. Siringo. LC 88-29511. (Centennial Series of the Association of Former Students: No. 31). (Illus.). 268p. 1989. 29.50 (*0-89096-381-9*) Tex A&M Univ Pr.
Pingeot, Anne. The Musee D'Orsay: Sculpture. (Illus.). 128p. 1999. 30.00 (*1-85759-200-X*) Scala Books.
Pinger. Dream Catcher. 48p. 1998. spiral bd. 7.81 (*0-07-292784-4*) McGraw.
— Drugs. 4th ed. 2002. 32.18 (*0-07-231986-0*) McGraw.
— Leaving Home. 48p. 1998. spiral bd. 7.81 (*0-07-292781-X*) McGraw.
— Shattered Lives. 48p. 1998. spiral bd. 7.81 (*0-07-292783-6*) McGraw.
— A Stranger in a Strange Land. 48p. 1998. spiral bd. 7.81 (*0-07-292782-8*) McGraw.
Pinger, Robert R., jt. auth. see McKenzie, James F.
Pingert, Patti, jt. auth. see Zander, Amy K.
Pinget, Robert. Abel & Bela. Wright, Barbara, tr. LC 87-42246. (French Ser.). 48p. 1987. 4.00 (*0-87376-052-2*) Red Dust.
— The Apocrypha. Wright, Barbara, tr. LC 86-61607. (French Ser.). 143p. 1987. 12.95 (*0-87376-050-6*) Red Dust.
— Baga. Stevenson, John, tr. from FRE. 144p. (Orig.). 1985. reprint ed. pap. 9.95 (*0-7145-0099-2*) Riverrun NY.
— Be Brave. Wright, Barbara, tr. from FRE. (French Ser.). 32p. 1994. pap. 6.95 (*0-87376-075-1*) Red Dust.
— Between Fantoine & Agapa. Wright, Barbara, tr. LC 82-60911. (French Ser.). (Illus.). 83p. 1983. 8.95 (*0-87376-040-9*) Red Dust.
— A Bizarre Will. Wright, Barbara, tr. (French Ser.). 150p. 1989. 10.95 (*0-87376-065-4*) Red Dust.
— Cette Voix. (FRE.). 232p. 1991. pap. 24.95 (*0-7859-1503-6*, 2707300470) Fr & Eur.
— The Enemy. Wright, Barbara, tr. LC 91-62212. (French Ser.). 89p. 1992. 12.95 (*0-87376-071-9*) Red Dust.
— Fable. Wright, Barbara, tr. from FRE. LC 80-50203. (French Ser.). 1980. 6.95 (*0-87376-036-0*) Red Dust.
— Graal Flibuste. (FRE.). 240p. 1989. pap. 19.95 (*0-7859-1518-4*, 2707304905) Fr & Eur.
— Identite: Avec: Abel et Bela. (FRE.). 127p. 1992. pap. 16.95 (*0-7859-1517-6*, 2707303593) Fr & Eur.
Pinget, Robert. L' Inquisitoire. (FRE.). 512p. 1986. pap. 16.95 (*0-7859-1519-2*, 2707310700) Fr & Eur.
Pinget, Robert. The Inquisitory. Watson, Donald, tr. from FRE. 399p. (Orig.). 1982. pap. 12.95 (*0-7145-3911-2*) Riverrun NY.
— Le Libera. (FRE.). 224p. 1984. pap. 24.95 (*0-7859-1516-8*, 2707303488) Fr & Eur.
— The Libera Me Domine. Wright, Barbara, tr. from FRE. LC 78-53831. (New French Writing Ser.). 1979. 10.50 (*0-87376-025-5*) Red Dust.
— Mahu: or The Material. Sheridan-Smith, Alan, tr. from FRE. 144p. (Orig.). (C). 1985. pap. 8.95 (*0-7145-0354-1*) Riverrun NY.
— Monsieur Songe. Wright, Barbara, tr. LC 88-61955. (French Ser.). 200p. 1989. 10.95 (*0-87376-060-3*) Red Dust.
— Paralchimie: Avec: Architruc, l'Hypothese, Nuit. 2nd ed. (FRE.). 96p. 1990. pap. 17.95 (*0-7859-1520-6*, 2707313289) Fr & Eur.
— Passacaglia. Wright, Barbara, tr. from FRE. LC 78-53832. (French Ser.). 1979. 6.95 (*0-87376-033-6*) Red Dust.
— Passacaille. (FRE.). 136p. 1969. pap. 17.95 (*0-7859-1508-7*, 2707300861) Fr & Eur.
— Quelqu'un. (FRE.). 264p. 1965. pap. 18.95 (*0-7859-1609-1*, 270730347X) Fr & Eur.
— Le Renard et la Boussole. 2nd ed. (FRE.). 245p. 1971. pap. 13.95 (*0-7859-1515-X*, 2707303453) Fr & Eur.
— Someone. Wright, Barbara, tr. from FRE. LC 83-63101. (French Ser.). 253p. (C). 1984. 12.95 (*0-87376-043-3*) Red Dust.
— That Voice. Wright, Barbara, tr. LC 82-60910. (French Ser.). 114p. 1983. 10.95 (*0-87376-041-7*) Red Dust.
— Theo or the New Era. Wright, Barbara, tr. from FRE. (French Ser.). 32p. 1994. pap. 6.95 (*0-87376-079-4*) Red Dust.
***Pinget, Robert.** Traces of Ink. Wright, Barbara, tr. from FRE. (French Ser.). Orig. Title: Taches d'Encre. 69p. 2000. pap. 8.95 (*0-87376-089-1*) Red Dust.
Pinggera, W., jt. auth. see Wick, M.
Pingle. Rethinking Developmental State. LC 98-54383. 1999. text 49.95 (*0-312-21995-4*) St Martin.
***Pingo, Roy.** Simply Sauces. LC 99-95698. 80p. 1999. pap. 12.95 (*0-9675458-0-3*) R Pingo.
Pingree, ed. Hephaestionis Thebani, Vol. I. (GRE.). 1973. 69.50 (*3-322-00210-1*, T1366, Pub. by B G Teubner) U of Mich Pr.
— Hephaestionis Thebani, Vol. II. (GRE.). 1974. 79.50 (*3-322-00212-8*, T1367, Pub. by B G Teubner) U of Mich Pr.
— Vettii Valentis Antiocheni. (GRE.). 1986. 125.00 (*3-322-00275-6*, T1878, Pub. by B G Teubner) U of Mich Pr.
Pingree, jt. ed. see Boer.
Pingree, Amanda, tr. see De Senarclens, Pierre.
Pingree, Amanda, tr. see Duclos, Denis.
Pingree, Chellie. North Island Designs Five: A Scrapbook of Sweaters from a Maine Island. LC 92-72725. (Illus.). 96p. 1993. pap. 17.95 (*0-89272-329-7*) Down East.
— North Island Designs Four: Sixteen New Patterns from Talented Maine Designers. LC 93-150314. (Illus.). 96p. 1992. pap. 17.95 (*0-89272-318-1*) Down East.
Pingree, Chellie & Anderson, Debby. Maine Island Classics: Living & Knitting on a Maine Island. (Illus.). 80p. 1992. pap. 15.95 (*0-89272-315-7*) Down East.
— Maine Island Kids: Sweaters & Stories from Offshore. (Illus.). 80p. (Orig.). 1992. pap. 15.95 (*0-89272-316-5*) Down East.
Pingree, D. & Reiner, Erica. Babylonian Planetary Omens Pt. 1: The Venus Tablet. (Bibliotheca Mesopotamica Ser.: Vol. 2-1). 65p. (C). 1975. pap. text 20.00 (*0-89003-010-3*) Undena Pubns.
Pingree, D., jt. auth. see Reiner, Erica.
Pingree, David. The Astronomical Works of Gregory Chioniades Vol. 1, Pt. 1: The Zij Al-Ala Text, Translation, Commentary. (Corpus des Astronomes Byzantins Ser.: Vol. II). 412p. (C). 1985. pap. 80.00 (*90-70265-65-6*, Pub. by Gieben) J Benjamins Pubng Co.
— The Astronomical Works of Gregory Chioniades Vol. 1, Pt. 2: The Zii Al-Ala Tables. (Corpus des Astronomes Byzantins Ser.: Vol. II). 235p. (C). 1986. pap. 100.00 (*90-70265-50-8*, Pub. by Gieben) J Benjamins Pubng Co.
— Census of the Exact Sciences in Sanskrit, Series A, Vol. 3. LC 75-46233. (Memoirs Ser.: Vol. 111). 208p. 1976. pap. 20.00 (*0-87169-111-6*, M111-pid) Am Philos.
— Census of the Exact Sciences in Sanskrit, Series A, Vol. 4. LC 80-68492. (Memoirs Ser.: Vol. 146). 447p. 1981. pap. 30.00 (*0-87169-146-9*, M146-pid) Am Philos.
— Census of the Exact Sciences in Sanskrit, Series A, Vols. 1 & 2. LC 70-115882. (Memoirs Ser.: Vol. 81 & 86). 1970. pap. 20.00 (*0-87169-081-0*, M081-086) Am Philos.
— Census of the Exact Sciences in Sanskrit Ser. A, Vol. 5. LC 94-72374. (Memoirs Ser.: Vol. 213). 756p. (C). 1994. pap. 45.00 (*0-87169-213-9*, M213-pid) Am Philos.
Pingree, DAvid. Descriptive Catalogue of Sanskirt & Other Indian Manuscripts of the Chandra Shum Shere Collection in the Bodleian Library, Pt. I. Katz, Jonathan, ed. 200p. 1984. pap. 45.00 (*0-19-817368-7*) OUP.
Pingree, David, tr. The Yavanajataka of Sphujidhvaja, 2 vols., Set. (Harvard Oriental Ser: No. 48). 1024p. 1978. 90.00 (*0-674-96373-3*) HUP.
Pingree, David, jt. auth. see Goldstein, Bernard R.
Pingree, David, jt. auth. see Hunger, Hermann.
Pingree, David, jt. auth. see Kennedy, Edward S.
Pingree, David, ed. see Hashimi, Ali Ibn Sulayman al.
Pingree, David E. Census of the Exact Sciences in Sanskrit, Vol. 3. LC 70-115882. (Memoirs of the American Philosophical Society Ser.: Vol. 111). 214p. 1970. reprint ed. pap. 66.40 (*0-7837-0541-7*, 204086900019) Bks Demand.
— Eastern Astrolabes. Chandler, Bruce, ed. (Historic Scientific Instruments of the Adler Planetarium Ser.: Vol. 2). (Illus.). Date not set. write for info. (*1-891220-02-0*) Adler Planetarium.
Pingree, Suzanne, jt. auth. see Cantor, Muriel G.
Pingry, Julie. Practical Machine Vision. 140p. student ed. 77.00 (*0-943779-00-6*) Cutter Information.
Pingry, Patricia. Joseph's Story. LC 97-41530. (Illus.). (J). (gr. 1-3). 1997. 16.95 (*0-8249-4092-X*, Candy Cane Pr) Ideals.
— The Natural Beauty of America. (Illus.). 160p. 1995. pap. 12.95 (*0-8249-4076-8*) Ideals.
***Pingry, Patricia.** The Story of America's Birthday. LC 99-59544. (Illus.). (J). 1999. 6.95 (*0-8249-4170-5*, Candy Cane Pr) Ideals.
— The Story of Baby Moses. LC 00-23739. (Illus.). (J). 2000. write for info. (*0-8249-4180-2*, Candy Cane Pr) Ideals.
Pingry, Patricia. The Story of Christmas. LC 97-41532. (Illus.). 26p. (J). 1997. bds. 6.95 (*0-8249-4091-1*, Candy Cane Pr) Ideals.
— Story of Daniel. LC 99-12932. 1999. bds. 6.95 (*0-8249-4163-2*) Ideals.
— Story of Daniel & the Lions. (Story of...Ser.). (Illus.). 24p. (Orig.). (J). (ps-2). 1988. pap. 3.95 (*0-8249-8179-0*, Ideals Child) Hambleton-Hill.
— Story of David & the Slingshot. (Story of...Ser.). (Illus.). 24p. (J). (ps-2). 1988. pap. 3.95 (*0-8249-8180-4*, Ideals Child) Hambleton-Hill.
— The Story of Esther. (Story of...Ser.). (Illus.). 24p. (J). (ps-2). 1990. pap. 3.95 (*0-8249-8420-X*, Ideals Child) Hambleton-Hill.
— The Story of Jonah. LC 97-32399. (Illus.). 26p. (J). 1998. bds. 6.95 (*0-8249-4094-6*, Candy Cane Pr) Ideals.
— The Story of Jonah & the Big Fish. (Story of...Ser.). (Illus.). 24p. (Orig.). (J). (ps-2). 1988. pap. 3.95 (*0-8249-8181-2*, Ideals Child) Hambleton-Hill.
— Story of Joseph. LC 98-43290. 1999. bds. 6.95 (*0-8249-4152-7*, Candy Cane Pr) Ideals.

— The Story of Joseph & a Dream Come True. (Story of...Ser.). (Illus.). 24p. (Orig.). (J). (ps-2). 1988. pap. 3.95 (*0-8249-8182-0*, Ideals Child) Hambleton-Hill.

***Pingry, Patricia.** Story of Joshua. LC 98-43295. 1999. bds. 6.95 (*0-8249-4153-5*, Candy Cane Pr) Ideals.

Pingry, Patricia. The Story of Joshua & the Bugles of Jericho. (Story of...Ser.). (Illus.). 24p. (Orig.). (J). (ps-2). 1988. pap. 3.95 (*0-8249-8178-2*, Ideals Child) Hambleton-Hill.

— The Story of Moses & the Ten Commandments. (Story of...Ser.). (Illus.). 24p. (J). (ps-2). 1990. pap. 3.95 (*0-8249-8418-8*, Ideals Child) Hambleton-Hill.

— The Story of Noah. LC 97-32415. (Illus.). (J). 1997. bds. 6.95 (*0-8249-4095-4*, Candy Cane Pr) Ideals.

— The Story of Noah & the Rainbow. (Story of...Ser.). (Illus.). 24p. (J). (ps-2). 1988. pap. 3.95 (*0-8249-8176-6*, Ideals Child) Hambleton-Hill.

— The Story of Samson & His Great Strength. (Story of...Ser.). (Illus.). 24p. (Orig.). (J). (ps-2). 1994. pap. 3.95 (*0-8249-8655-5*, Ideals Child) Hambleton-Hill.

— The Story of the Garden of Eden. (Story of...Ser.). (Illus.). 24p. (Orig.). (J). (ps-2). 1994. pap. 3.95 (*0-8249-8654-7*, Ideals Child) Hambleton-Hill.

— Story of the Ten Commandments. LC 99-12933. (J). (ps-1). 1999. bds. 6.95 (*0-8249-4165-9*) Ideals.

***Pingry, Patricia & Britt, Stephanie.** The Story of George Washington. LC 00-27568. (Illus.). 2000. write for info. (*0-8249-4188-8*, Candy Cane Pr) Ideals.

***Pingry, Patricia & Hinke, George.** Jolly Old Santa Claus: The Ideals Classic. LC 00-24080. (J). 2000. pap. write for info. (*0-8249-4182-9*, Candy Cane Pr) Ideals.

***Pingry, Patricia & Venturi-Pickett, Stacy.** The Story of Mary. LC 00-23720. 2000. write for info. (*0-8249-4183-7*, Candy Cane Pr) Ideals.

Pingry, Patricia, ed. see Irving, Washington.

Pingry, Patricia A. He Touched Them. (Illus.). 160p. 1997. 24.95 (*0-8249-4083-0*, Ideals TN) Ideals.

***Pingry, Patricia A.** La Historia de la Pascua.Tr. of Story of Easter. (SPA., Illus.). 26p. (J). (ps-k). 2000. 6.95 (*0-8249-4185-3*) Ideals.

Pingry, Patricia A. The Ideals Treasury of Best Loved Poems. LC 97-18918. 1997. 24.95 (*0-8249-4088-1*, Ideals TN) Ideals.

***Pingry, Patricia A.** Story of David. LC 99-89402. 2000. 6.95 (*0-8249-4171-3*) Ideals.

Pingry, Patricia A. The Story of Easter. LC 97-41531. (Illus.). 26p. (J). 1998. bds. 6.95 (*0-8249-4090-3*, Candy Cane Pr) Ideals.

Pinguet, Maurice. Voluntary Death in Japan. Morris, Rosemary, tr. from FRE. (Illus.). 360p. 1993. 34.95 (*0-7456-0870-1*) Blackwell Pubs.

Pingwa, Jia. Heavenly Rain. 416p. 1996. pap. 12.95 (*0-8351-3182-3*) China Bks.

— Turbulence. Novel. Goldblatt, Howard, tr. from CHI. LC 91-9890. 592p. 1991. 22.95 (*0-8071-1687-4*) La State U Pr.

Pingying Hsieh. Girl Rebel: The Autobiography of Hsieh Pingying with Extracts from Her "New War Diaries" Lin, Adet & Lin, Anor, trs. from CHI. LC 74-34583. (China in the 20th Century Ser.). (Illus.). xviii, 270p. 1975. reprint ed. lib. bdg. 32.50 (*0-306-70691-1*) Da Capo.

Pinhas, Alan R., jt. auth. see Kegley, Susan.

Pinheiro, Aileen F., compiled by. The Heritage of Balowin Park. (Illus.). 272p. 1981. 10.55 (*0-9607306-0-5*) Hist Soc Baldwin Pk.

Pinheiro, C. U. & Balick, M. J. Brazilian Palms: Notes on Their Uses, & Vernacular Names & Added Illustrations, Contributions from The New York Botanical Garden, Vol. 17. LC 87-12201. (Illus.). 64p. 1987. pap. 7.45 (*0-89327-317-1*) NY Botanical.

Pinheiro, Edwin J. Introduction to Multimedia Featuring Windows Applications. LC 95-23941. (C). 1995. 43.95 (*0-534-26634-7*) Wadsworth Pub.

***Pinheiro, Jose C. & Bates, Douglas M.** Mixed Effects Models in S & S-Plus. LC 99-53566. (Statistics & Computing Ser.). (Illus.). 552p. 2000. 69.95 (*0-387-98957-9*) Spr-Verlag.

Pinheiro, Leonardo, jt. auth. see Jones, Robyn.

Pinheiro, Patricia M., jt. auth. see Fryer, Peter.

Pinhey, E. C. Moths of Southern Africa. (Illus.). 347p. 1993. 140.00 (*90-6191-078-1*, Pub. by A A Balkema) Ashgate Pub Co.

Pinho, Mario V. Volver Al Ser: Un Acercamiento a la Poetica de Octavio Paz. (Wor(l)ds of Change Ser.: Vol. 5). (SPA.). 133p. (C). 1997. text 36.95 (*0-8204-2458-7*) P Lang Pubng.

***Pini, Gian A.** Tectonosomes & Olistostromes in the Argille Scagliose of the Northern Apennines, Italy. LC 99-32430. (Special Paper Ser.). 70p. 1999. write for info. (*0-8137-2335-3*) Geol Soc.

Pini, Richard. Against the Wind. 288p. 1992. mass mkt. 4.99 (*0-8125-2274-5*, Pub. by Tor Bks) St Martin.

— Captives of Blue Mountain, 3. (Elfquest Reader's Collection: Vol. 3). 1999. pap. text 11.95 (*0-936861-57-6*, Pub. by Warp Graphics) Midpt Trade.

— Dark Hours: Blood of Ten Chiefs. (Elfquest Ser.: Vol. 5). 1993. pap. text 7.99 (*0-8125-2341-5*) Tor Bks.

— Elfquest: Against the Wind, Vol. 4. 1990. pap. 7.95 (*0-8125-4906-6*) Tor Bks.

— Elfquest: Winds of Change, Vol. 3. 1989. pap. 7.95 (*0-8125-4905-8*) Tor Bks.

— Elfquest: Wolfsong, Vol. 2. 1989. mass mkt. 4.50 (*0-8125-0377-5*, Pub. by Tor Bks) St Martin.

— Quest's End, 4. (Elfquest Reader's Collection: Vol. 4). 1999. pap. text 11.95 (*0-936861-58-4*, Pub. by Warp Graphics) Midpt Trade.

— Secret of Two-Edge, 1, 6. (Elfquest Reader's Collection: Vol. 6). 1999. pap. text 11.95 (*0-936861-60-6*, Pub. by Warp Graphics) Midpt Trade.

— Seige at Blue Mountain, 1, 5. (Elfquest Reader's Collection: Vol. 5). 1999. pap. text 11.95 (*0-936861-59-2*, Pub. by Warp Graphics) Midpt Trade.

Pini, Richard, ed. Big Elfquest Gatherum. (Illus.). 244p. 1994. 19.95 (*0-936861-13-4*) Warp Graphics.

— Dark Hours. (Blood of Ten Chiefs Ser.: No. 5). 320p. 1994. mass mkt. 4.99 (*0-8125-2342-3*, Pub. by Tor Bks) St Martin.

Pini, Richard, et al, eds. Elfquest: Blood of Ten Chiefs, Vol. 1. 320p. (Orig.). 1986. pap. 6.95 (*0-8125-3041-1*) Tor Bks.

— Elfquest: Blood of Ten Chiefs, Vol. 1. (Orig.). 1987. pap. 3.50 (*0-8125-3043-8*) Tor Bks.

— Elfquest: Wolfsong, Vol. 2. 320p. 1988. pap. 7.95 (*0-8125-3037-3*) Tor Bks.

***Pini, Richard & Blair, Barry.** Dream's End. (Elfquest Reader's Collection: Vol. 15A). (Illus.). 208p. (YA). (gr. 5 up). 2001. pap. 12.95 (*0-936861-65-7*, Pub. by Warp Graphics) Midpt Trade.

***Pini, Richard & Murphy, Vickie.** Wave Dancers. (Elfquest Reader's Collection: Vol. 16). (Illus.). (YA). 2000. pap. 11.95 (*0-936861-71-1*, Pub. by Warp Graphics) Midpt Trade.

Pini, Richard, jt. auth. see Pini, Wendy.

Pini, Richard, jt. ed. see Pini, Wendy.

Pini, Wendy. Ascent. (Elfquest Reader's Collection: Vol. 12). 1999. pap. 12.95 (*0-936861-43-6*, Pub. by Warp Graphics) Midpt Trade.

— Beauty & the Beast: Night of Beauty, Bk. 2. 1990. pap. 5.95 (*0-915419-75-0*) First Classics.

— Beauty & the Beast: Portrait of Love. 1989. pap. 5.95 (*0-915419-50-5*) First Classics.

— Blood of Ten Chiefs, Vol. 9. 1999. pap. 12.95 (*0-936861-68-1*) Berkeley Pr.

— The Cry from Beyond, 7. (Elfquest Reader's Collection). 1999. pap. 11.95 (*0-936861-61-4*, Pub. by Warp Graphics) Midpt Trade.

— Dreamtime. (Elfquest Reader's Collection: Vol. 8-A). (Illus.). 176p. (YA). 1998. pap. 11.95 (*0-936861-52-5*, Pub. by Warp Graphics) Midpt Trade.

— Fire & Flight. (Elfquest Reader's Collection: Vol. 1). 1999. pap. text 11.95 (*0-936861-55-X*, Pub. by Warp Graphics) Midpt Trade.

— Forbidden Grove. (Elfquest Reader's Collection: Vol. 2). 1999. pap. text 11.95 (*0-936861-56-8*, Pub. by Warp Graphics) Midpt Trade.

— Forevergreen, 15. (Elfquest Reader's Collection: Vol. 15). 1999. pap. 12.95 (*0-936861-64-9*, Pub. by Warp Graphics) Midpt Trade.

— A Gift of Her Own: An Elfquest Story. (Illus.). 48p. (J). (gr. k-3). 1995. 16.95 (*0-936861-38-X*, Pub. by Warp Graphics) Midpt Trade.

— Huntress, 12. (Elfquest Reader's Collection: Vol. 11-A). 1999. pap. 11.95 (*0-936861-46-0*, Pub. by Warp Graphics) Midpt Trade.

— Jink, (Elfquest Reader's Collection: Vol. 14). 1999. pap. text 11.95 (*0-936861-48-7*, Pub. by Warp Graphics) Midpt Trade.

— Kings of the Broken Wheel, 8. (Elfquest Reader's Collection: Vol. 8). 1999. pap. text 11.95 (*0-936861-62-2*, Pub. by Warp Graphics) Midpt Trade.

— Legacy. (Elfquest Reader's Collection: Vol. 11). (Illus.). 1998. pap. text 11.95 (*0-936861-45-2*, Pub. by Warp Graphics) Midpt Trade.

— Mindcoil. (Elfquest Reader's Collection: Vol. 14-A). 1999. pap. 11.95 (*0-936861-50-9*, Pub. by Warp Graphics) Midpt Trade.

— Quest Begins. (Elfquest Ser.). 1997. mass mkt. 5.99 (*0-441-00418-0*) Ace Bks.

— Reunion, 12. (Elfquest Reader's Collection: Vol. 12-A). 1999. pap. 12.95 (*0-936861-44-4*, Pub. by Warp Graphics) Midpt Trade.

— Shards. (Elfquest Reader's Collection: Vol. 10). (Illus.). 1998. pap. text 13.95 (*0-936861-42-8*, Pub. by Warp Graphics) Midpt Trade.

Pini, Wendy & Pini, Richard. Captives of Blue Mountain. LC 97-133592. 272p. (Orig.). 1997. pap. 12.00 (*0-441-00403-2*) Ace Bks.

— Captives of Blue Mountain. (Elfquest Ser.: No. 3). 240p. (Orig.). 1997. mass mkt. 5.99 (*0-441-00492-X*) Ace Bks.

— Elfquest: The Hidden Years. (Illus.). 160p. 1992. 19.95 (*0-936861-30-4*, Pub. by Warp Graphics) Midpt Trade.

— Elfquest No. 2: The Quest Begins. 272p. (Orig.). 1996. pap. 11.00 (*0-441-00294-3*) Ace Bks.

— Elfquest Novel - Journey to Sorrow's End. 320p. 1993. mass mkt. 5.99 (*0-441-18371-9*) Ace Bks.

— Wolfrider. (Elfquest Reader's Collection: Vol. 9A). (Illus.). 176p. (YA). 1999. pap. 11.95 (*0-936861-67-3*, Pub. by Warp Graphics) Midpt Trade.

***Pini, Wendy & Pini, Richard.** Worldpool. (Elfquest Reader's Collection). (Illus.). 192p. (YA). 2000. pap. 12.95 (*0-936861-73-8*, Pub. by Warp Graphics) Midpt Trade.

Pini, Wendy & Pini, Richard, eds. Elfquest: Bedtime Stories. (Illus.). 128p. 1994. 19.95 (*0-936861-37-1*, Pub. by Warp Graphics) Midpt Trade.

— Elfquest: New Blood. (Illus.). 176p. 1993. 19.95 (*0-936861-31-2*, Pub. by Warp Graphics) Midpt Trade.

***Pini, Wendy, et al.** Kahvi. (Elfquest Reader's Collection: Vol. 9C). (Illus.). 272p. (YA). (gr. 5 up). 2000. pap. 13.95 (*0-936861-74-6*, Pub. by Warp Graphics) Midpt Trade.

— Rogue's Curse. (Elfquest Reader's Collection: Vol. 9). (Illus.). 272p. (YA). 2000. pap. 13.95 (*0-936861-72-X*, Pub. by Warp Graphics) Midpt Trade.

— Shadowstalker. (Elfquest Reader's Collection: Vol. 11C). (Illus.). 176p. (YA). (gr. 5 up). 2000. pap. 12.95 (*0-936861-75-4*, Pub. by Warp Graphics) Midpt Trade.

Pini, Wendy, ed. see Auklandus, Joellyn.

Piniarski, William J. Launching Onto the Web: A Small Business View. (Illus.). 258p. 1998. pap. 19.95 (*1-892614-13-8*) Briarwood VA.

Piniella, J. F., jt. ed. see Jeffrey, G. A.

Pinilla, Luis D. Bernal, see Bernal Pinilla, Luis D.

Pininska, Mary. Little Polish Cookbook. (Illus.). 60p. 1992. 7.95 (*0-8118-0262-0*) Chronicle Bks.

Pininska, Mary, jt. auth. see Lussiana, Bernard.

Pinion, F. B. A D. H. Lawrence Companion: Life, Thought & Works. LC 78-12348. (Illus.). 316p. 1979. text 45.00 (*0-06-495574-5*, N6849) B&N Imports.

Pinion, F. B., ed. A George Eliot Companion: Literary Achievement & Modern Significance. LC 81-8044. (Companion Ser.). 290p. 1981. 59.50 (*0-389-20208-8*, N6990) B&N Imports.

Pinion, F. B., ed. see Hardy, Thomas.

Pinion, Frank B. A Wordsworth Chronology. 160p. 1988. 40.00 (*0-8161-8950-1*, Hall Reference) Macmillan.

Pinizzotto, Russell F. Surfing the Waves of Musical Acoustics. (Orig.). (C). 1995. pap. 28.14 (*1-56870-178-0*) RonJon Pub.

Pink, A. W. Life of Faith. 8.50 (*1-85792-047-3*, Pub. by Christian Focus) Spring Arbor Dist.

— The Seven Sayings of the Saviour on the Cross. 8.50 (*1-85792-059-7*, Pub. by Christian Focus) Spring Arbor Dist.

***Pink, A. W.** La Soberania de Dios: Quien Tiene el Control? abr. ed. Montgomery, Thomas & Negrete, Omar Ibanez, trs. Orig. Title: The Sovereignty of God. (SPA.). 74p. 1999. pap. 1.68 (*1-928980-04-X*) Pub Faro.

Pink, Ar. Life of Faith. 1994. pap. 9.99 (*1-85792-271-9*, Pub. by Christian Focus) Spring Arbor Dist.

***Pink, Arthur W.** Ability of God: Prayers of the Apostle Paul. 2000. write for info. (*0-8024-6573-0*) Moody.

Pink, Arthur W. The Antichrist. LC 87-29898. 320p. 1988. pap. 13.99 (*0-8254-3539-0*, Kregel Class) Kregel.

— Los Atributos de Dios. 132p. 1997. reprint ed. 4.99 (*0-85151-540-1*) Banner of Truth.

— The Attributes of God. 96p. (YA). (gr. 10). 1977. pap. 7.99 (*0-8010-6989-0*) Baker Bks.

— The Beatitudes & the Lord's Prayer. 144p. (YA). (gr. 10). 1995. reprint ed. pap. 8.99 (*0-8010-7142-9*) Baker Bks.

Pink, Arthur W., II. Camino a la Oracion Ferviente. (SPA.). 10.95 (*1-55883-112-6*, 6784-1601) Libros Desafio.

Pink, Arthur W. Comfort for Christians. 96p. (YA). (gr. 10). 1989. pap. 6.99 (*0-8010-7109-7*) Baker Bks.

— The Divine Inspiration of the Bible. 112p. (Orig.). (gr. 10). 1996. reprint ed. pap. 8.99 (*0-8010-7005-8*) Baker Bks.

— Eternal Security. 136p. (gr. 10). 1996. reprint ed. pap. 9.99 (*0-8010-6985-8*) Baker Bks.

— An Exposition of the Sermon on the Mount. 456p. (gr. 10). 1982. pap. 18.99 (*0-8010-7075-9*) Baker Bks.

— Exposition on the Gospel of John, 4 vols. 1160p. 1968. 49.99 (*0-310-31180-2*, 10566) Zondervan.

— Gleanings from Elisha. (Gleanings Ser.). 288p. 1972. pap. 19.99 (*0-8024-3000-7*) Moody.

— Gleanings from Paul. (Gleanings Ser.). pap. 21.99 (*0-8024-3005-8*, 370) Moody.

— Gleanings in Exodus. (Gleanings Ser.). 1964. pap. 19.99 (*0-8024-3001-5*) Moody.

— Gleanings in Genesis. (Gleanings Ser.). pap. 19.99 (*0-8024-3002-3*, 372) Moody.

— Gleanings in Joshua. (Gleanings Ser.). pap. 21.99 (*0-8024-3004-X*, 373) Moody.

— A Guide to Fervent Prayer. White, Donald, ed. 224p. (YA). (gr. 10). 1995. reprint ed. pap. 9.99 (*0-8010-7141-0*) Baker Bks.

— Letters of A. W. Pink. 1978. pap. 4.99 (*0-85151-262-3*) Banner of Truth.

— The Life of David. 768p. (YA). (gr. 10). 1998. reprint ed. pap. 24.99 (*0-8010-7061-9*) Baker Bks.

— The Life of Elijah. 313p. 1991. reprint ed. pap. 6.99 (*0-85151-041-8*) Banner of Truth.

— The Nature of God. 347p. 1999. pap. 21.99 (*0-8024-6571-4*) Moody.

***Pink, Arthur W.** Our Accountability to God. 478p. 1999. pap. 21.99 (*0-8024-6572-2*) Moody.

Pink, Arthur W. Practical Christianity. 232p. (gr. 10). 1995. pap. 9.99 (*0-8010-6990-4*) Baker Bks.

— Profiting from the Word. 1977. pap. 5.99 (*0-85151-032-9*) Banner of Truth.

— Repentance. unabridged ed. 31p. 1996. reprint ed. pap. 1.50 (*1-58339-167-3*, E4) Triangle Press.

— The Seven Sayings of the Saviour on the Cross. LC 58-59715. 144p. (gr. 10). 1984. pap. 8.99 (*0-8010-7084-8*) Baker Bks.

— La Soberania de Dios. 3rd ed. Blanch, Jose M., tr. from ENG.Tr. of Sovereignty of God. (SPA.). 215p. (Orig.). 1995. reprint ed. pap. 5.99 (*0-85151-416-2*) Banner of Truth.

— The Sovereignty of God. 272p. (gr. 10). 1984. pap. 12.99 (*0-8010-7088-0*) Baker Bks.

— The Sovereignty of God. 1976. pap. 5.99 (*0-85151-133-3*) Banner of Truth.

— The Ten Commandments. 80p. (YA). (gr. 10). 1995. reprint ed. pap. 7.99 (*0-8010-7140-2*) Baker Bks.

— La Vida de Elias. (SPA.). 360p. 1992. reprint ed. pap. 10.99 (*0-85151-424-3*) Banner of Truth.

Pink, Brenda. Beatitudes: Godly Attitudes for Every Day Living. 1991. pap. text 3.99 (*0-529-10030-4*) World Publng.

Pink, Brenda, jt. auth. see Pink, Michael.

Pink, David. Door to the River. 27p. 1997. 3.50 (*0-941127-21-4*) Dacotah Terr Pr.

Pink Floyd. The Dark Side of the Moon. (Illus.). 72p. 1997. pap. 21.95 (*0-8256-1078-8*, AM64171) Omnibus NY.

— Pink Floyd: The Division Bell. 1996. pap. 29.95 (*0-8256-1409-0*, AM 92188) Music Sales.

Pink, Louis H. Gaynor, the Tammany Mayor Who Swallowed the Tiger: Lawyer, Judge, Philosopher. LC 77-124251. (Select Bibliographies Reprint Ser.). 1977. reprint ed. 20.95 (*0-8369-5439-4*) Ayer.

— The New Day in Housing. LC 73-11941. (Metropolitan America Ser.). (Illus.). 262p. 1974. reprint ed. 18.95 (*0-405-05410-6*) Ayer.

Pink, Marilyn M., ed. see Jobe, Frank W.

Pink, Matthew. Paterson's Licensing Acts, 1994. 102nd ed. 1900p. 1994. 253.00 (*0-406-02653-X*, MICHIE) LEXIS Pub.

Pink, Michael. His Little Instruction Book. 160p. (Orig.). 1995. pap. 5.99 (*0-529-10393-1*, HLIB) World Publng.

— Promises Worth Keeping. 160p. (Orig.). 1996. pap. 5.99 (*0-529-10630-2*, PROM1) World Publng.

Pink, Michael, ed. The Words in Red. pap. 3.99 (*0-529-10009-6*, WR1) World Publng.

Pink, Michael & Pink, Brenda. Grace for Grief. LC 95-61694. 224p. 1995. 8.99 (*0-529-10479-2*, GFG1); 12.99 (*0-529-10484-9*, GFG2) World Publng.

Pink, Sarah. Women & Bullfighting. LC 98-185397. 1997. 55.00 (*1-85973-956-3*, Pub. by Berg Pubs); pap. 19.50 (*1-85973-961-X*, Pub. by Berg Pubs) NYU Pr.

***Pink, Steven.** High Speed Rowers & Firewalls. (C). 2000. text. write for info. (*0-201-59610-5*) Addison-Wesley.

Pink, Thomas. The Psychology of Freedom. 294p. (C). 1996. text 52.95 (*0-521-55504-3*) Cambridge U Pr.

Pink, Tom. Wingshooter's Guide to Michigan: Upland Birds & Waterfowl. (Illus.). 300p. (Orig.). 2000. pap. 26.95 (*1-885106-57-2*) Wild Adven Pr.

Pink, William, jt. auth. see Noblit, George W.

Pink, William, ed. see Corbett, H. Dickson & Wilson, Bruce L.

Pink, William, ed. see Fox, Thomas.

Pink, William T., et al, eds. Effective Staff Development for School Change. (Interpretive Perspectives on Education & Policy Ser.). 320p. (C). 1992. pap. 39.50 (*0-89391-938-1*); text 73.25 (*0-89391-832-6*) Ablx Pub.

Pink, William T., ed. see Corson, David.

Pink, William T., ed. see Kanpol, Barry.

Pink, William T., ed. see Miron, Louis.

Pink, William T., jt. ed. see Noblit, George W.

Pink, William T., ed. see Tesconi, Charles A.

Pinkal, Manfred. Logic & Lexicon: The Semantics of the Indefinite. LC 95-3466. (Studies in Linguistics & Philosophy: Vol. 56). 380p. (C). 1995. lib. bdg. 129.00 (*0-7923-3387-X*, Pub. by Kluwer Academic) Kluwer Academic.

Pinkard, Bruce. The Nude: Creative Photography Workshop. LC 99-14005. (Illus.). 192p. 1999. pap. 29.95 (*1-883403-60-X*, Pub. by Saunders Photo) Sterling.

***Pinkard, Terry.** Hegel: A Biography. LC 99-34812. (Illus.). 816p. 2000. 39.95 (*0-521-49679-9*) Cambridge U Pr.

Pinkard, Terry. Hegel's Phenomenology: The Sociality of Reason. 463p. 1996. pap. text 25.95 (*0-521-56834-X*) Cambridge U Pr.

Pinkard, Terry, jt. ed. see Englehardt, H. Tristram, Jr.

Pinkard, Terry P., jt. ed. see Beauchamp, Thomas L.

Pinkas, Lilly. Fairchild Tropical Garden. LC 96-69024. (Illus.). 60p. 1996. write for info. (*0-9652810-0-0*) Photo Images.

— Guide to the Gardens of Florida. LC 98-30009. 1998. 14.95 (*1-56164-169-3*) Pineapple Pr.

***Pinkas, Lilly.** Guide to the Gardens of Georgia. LC 99-53479. (Illus.). 160p. 2000. pap. 14.95 (*1-56164-198-7*) Pineapple Pr.

Pinkau, K. & Sprecher, eds. Umweltstandards: Grundlagen, Tatsachen und Bewertungen Am Beispiel Des Strahlenrisikos. (Akademie der Wissenschaften zu Berlin, Forschungsbericht Ser.: No. 2). (GER.). xv, 494p. (C). 1992. lib. bdg. 75.40 (*3-11-013450-0*) De Gruyter.

Pinkau, K., ed. see NATO Advanced Study Institute Staff.

Pinkau, Klaus & Renn, Ortwin, eds. Environmental Standards Scientific Foundations & Rational Procedures of Regulation with Emphasis on Radiological Risk Management. Jaeger, G. & Kais-Heinrich, Sonja, trs. from GER. LC 97-50116. 432p. 1998. lib. bdg. 150.00 (*0-7923-8109-2*) Kluwer Academic.

Pinkel, Benjamin. Consciousness, Matter & Energy: The Emergence of Mind in Nature. LC 92-1575. 221p. 1992. 20.00 (*0-9635403-0-0*) Turover Pr.

— The Existential Adventure: The Roles of Science & Belief. LC 75-36964. 156p. 1976. pap. 12.50 (*0-87516-210-X*) DeVorss.

Pinkel, Daniel, jt. ed. see Andreeff, Michael.

Pinkel, Sheila & Chang, Kou. Kou Chang's Story. (Artists' Books Ser.). (Illus.). 128p. (Orig.). 1992. pap. 16.00 (*0-89822-103-X*) Visual Studies.

Pinkele, Carl F. & Louthan, William C., eds. Discretion, Justice, & Democracy: A Public Policy Perspective. LC 84-22509. (Illus.). 147p. 1985. reprint ed. pap. 45.60 (*0-608-00097-3*, 206086200006) Bks Demand.

Pinkele, Carl F. & Pollis, Adamantia, eds. The Contemporary Mediterranean World. LC 82-16658. 369p. 1983. 65.00 (*0-275-91058-X*, C1058, Praeger Pubs) Greenwood.

Pinkele, Carl F., jt. auth. see Ginsburgs, George.

Pinkele, Carl F., jt. auth. see Musto, Stefan A.

Pinkelman, Jim. Background Notes, Czechoslovakia: 1990, Feb. 8p. 1990. pap. 3.00 (*0-16-021120-4*) USGPO.

— Background Notes, Laos: 1991, Mar. 4p. 1991. pap. 1.25 (*0-16-033304-0*) USGPO.

Pinker, Steven. How the Mind Works. LC 97-1855. (Illus.). 672p. 1999. pap. 17.00 (*0-393-31848-6*, Norton Paperbks) Norton.

— Language & Mind. (Science Masters Ser.). 176p. 2000. pap. write for info. (*0-465-07270-4*) Basic.

— The Language Instinct: How the Mind Creates Language. LC 94-39138. 496p. 1995. pap. 15.00 (*0-06-097651-9*, Perennial) HarperTrade.

***Pinker, Steven.** The Language Instinct: How the Mind Creates Language. 496p. 2000. pap. 15.00 (*0-06-095833-2*, Perennial) HarperTrade.

Pinker, Steven. Language Learnability & Language Development. (Cognitive Science Ser.: No. 7). 456p. 1987. pap. 16.95 (*0-674-51055-0*) HUP.

— Language Learnability & Language Development. 480p. 1996. pap. 20.95 (*0-674-51053-4*) HUP.

Pinker, Steven. Words & Rules: The Ingredients of Language. LC 99-43013. (Science Masters Ser.). (Illus.). 368p. 1999. 26.00 (*0-465-07269-0*, Pub. by Basic) HarpC.

***Pinker, Steven.** Words & Rules: The Ingredients of Language. 356p. 2000. pap. 14.00 (*0-06-095840-5*) HarpC.

Pinker, Steven & Mehler, Jacques A., eds. Connections & Symbols. (Cognition Special Issue Ser.). 255p. (Orig.). 1988. pap. text 18.50 (*0-262-66064-4*, Bradford Bks) MIT Pr.

Pinker, Steven & Mehler, Jacques A., eds. Learnability & Cognition: The Acquisition of Argument Structure. (Illus.). 427p. 1991. pap. text 39.95 (*0-262-66073-3*, Bradford Bks) MIT Pr.

Pinkert, Carl A., ed. Transgenic Animal Technology: A Laboratory Handbook. (Illus.). 364p. 1994. pap. 45.00 (*0-12-557165-8*) Acad Pr.

Pinkerton, A. Molly Maguires & the Detectives. LC 72-2092. (American History & Americana Ser.: No. 47). 1972. lib. bdg. 75.00 (*0-8383-1289-6*) M S G Haskell Hse.

Pinkerton, A. Alan, tr. see Schwarzenbach, Dieter.

Pinkerton, Allan. Criminal Reminiscences & Detective Sketches. LC 70-109632. (Select Bibliographies Reprint Ser.). 1977. 30.95 (*0-8369-5241-3*) Ayer.

— Criminal Reminiscences & Detective Sketches. 1972. reprint ed. 28.00 (*0-8422-8104-5*) Irvington.

— The Expressman & the Detective. LC 75-32775. (Literature of Mystery & Detection Ser.). (Illus.). 1976. reprint ed. 24.95 (*0-405-07894-3*) Ayer.

— Professional Thieves & the Detective. LC 73-156031. reprint ed. 72.50 (*0-404-09133-4*) AMS Pr.

— The Spy of the Rebellion: Being a True History of the Spy System of the United States Army During the Late Rebellion, Revealing Many Secrets of the War Hitherto Not Made Public. LC 89-33081. 680p. 1989. reprint ed. pap. 200.00 (*0-608-02670-0*, 206332300004) Bks Demand.

— Strikers, Communists, Tramps & Detectives. LC 79-90190. (Mass Violence in America Ser.). 1977. reprint ed. 32.95 (*0-405-01332-9*) Ayer.

— Thirty Years a Detective: A Thorough & Comprehensive Expose of Criminal Practices of All Grades & Classes. (Criminology, Law Enforcement, & Social Problems Ser.: No. 154). (Illus.). 1975. reprint ed. 28.00 (*0-87585-154-1*) Patterson Smith.

Pinkerton, Barbara. Good Blood, Bad Blood. LC 98-67001. 156p. 1998. pap. 13.95 (*0-9657993-3-6*) mwynhad.

Pinkerton, C. R. & Plowman, P. N. Pediatric Oncology: Clinical Practice & Controversies. 2nd ed. 799p. 1997. text 135.00 (*0-412-63080-X*, Pub. by E A) OUP.

Pinkerton, C. R., jt. ed. see Plowman, P. N.

Pinkerton, Charlene. Halloween Favorites in Plastic. LC 97-80850. 112p. 1998. pap. 19.95 (*0-7643-0509-3*) Schiffer.

— Holiday Plastic Novelties: The Styrene Toys. LC 98-89602. (Illus.). 160p. 1999. pap. 24.95 (*0-7643-0781-9*) Schiffer.

Pinkerton, Edward C. Word for Word. LC 77-20391. xxxii, 423p. 1982. 39.95 (*0-930454-06-5*) Verbatim Bks.

Pinkerton, Elaine. Santa Fe on Foot: Running, Walking & Bicycling Adventures in the City Different. rev. ed. Polese, Richard L., ed. LC 86-60510. (Adventure Roads Travel Ser.: No. 1). (Illus.). 143p. 1994. pap. 9.95 (*0-943734-25-8*) Ocean Tree Bks.

— The Santa Fe Trail by Bicycle: A Historic Adventure. (Illus.). 176p. 1993. pap. 12.95 (*1-878610-24-4*) Red Crane Bks.

Pinkerton, Elizabeth, jt. auth. see Tsukamoto, Mary.

Pinkerton, James P. What Comes Next? The End of Big Government - & the New Paradigm Ahead. LC 95-18432. 356p. (J). 1995. 24.45 (*0-7868-6105-3*, Pub. by Hyperion) Time Warner.

Pinkerton, James R., jt. auth. see Hassinger, Edward W.

Pinkerton, Joan T. Knights of the Broadax: The Story of the Wyoming Tie Hacks. LC 79-57239. 198p. 1981. reprint ed. pap. 61.40 (*0-608-00726-9*, 206150100009) Bks Demand.

Pinkerton, John. In Care at Home: Parenting, the State & Civil Society. 180p. 1994. 66.95 (*1-85628-536-7*, Pub. by Avebry) Ashgate Pub Co.

Pinkerton, John, ed. Ancient Scottish Poems, Never Before in Print, 2 vols. LC 77-144530. reprint ed. 35.00 (*0-404-08677-2*) AMS Pr.

— Scotish Poems, 3 vols., Set. LC 70-144531. reprint ed. 165.00 (*0-404-08680-2*) AMS Pr.

— Select Scottish Ballads, 2 vols. 2nd enl. ed. LC 72-144529. reprint ed. 20.00 (*0-404-08674-8*) AMS Pr.

Pinkerton, John & McCrea, Ross, eds. Meeting the Challenge? LC 98-46652. 150p. (C). 1999. text 56.95 (*1-84014-328-2*, HV751.N67P55, Pub. by Ashgate Pub) Ashgate Pub Co.

Pinkerton, John, jt. auth. see Iwaniec, Dorota.

Pinkerton, Judith. Sound of Healing: Create Your Own Music Program for Better Health. 1996. pap. 16.00 (*1-887110-00-3*) Allian Pubng.

Pinkerton, Lee. The Many Faces of Michael Jackson. LC 98-178581. (Illus.). 62p. 1997. pap. text 16.95 (*0-7119-6783-0*, 02100023, Pub. by Ozone Bks) Omnibus NY.

Pinkerton, Linda F. The Writer's Law Primer. 224p. 1990. pap. 12.95 (*1-55821-085-7*) Lyons Pr.

Pinkerton, Mitzi. 101 Reasons It's Great to Be a Woman. 128p. 1999. pap. 6.95 (*1-84024-097-0*, Pub. by Summers) Seven Hills Bk.

Pinkerton, P., tr. see Puccini, Giacomo.

Pinkerton, P. H. & Reis, M. D., eds. Genetic Markers of Haematological Malignancy: Journal: Tumor Biology 1990, Vol 2, Suppl. 1. (Illus.). iv, 94p. 1990. pap. 30.50 (*3-8055-5312-9*) S Karger.

Pinkerton, Percy, tr. see Artsybashev, Mikhail P.

Pinkerton, Percy, tr. see Shakespeare, William, et al.

Pinkerton, Philip. Childhood Disorder: A Psychosomatic Approach. LC 74-18488. (Illus.). 192p. 1975. text 46.00 (*0-231-03955-7*) Col U Pr.

Pinkerton, Richard L., jt. auth. see Burt, David N.

Pinkerton, Robert. Russia: or Miscellaneous Observations on the Past & Present State of That Country & Its Inhabitants. LC 74-115579. (Russia Observed, Series I). 1970. reprint ed. 28.95 (*0-405-03058-4*) Ayer.

Pinkerton, Robert, tr. see Metropolitan Philaret of Moscow Staff.

Pinkerton, Scott. Mariposa Courthouse: "A Shrine to Justice" (Illus.). 112p. 1989. pap. 5.95 (*0-685-29449-8*) Mariposa Heritage Pr.

Pinkerton, Sharon. German Wirehaired Pointers Today. (Illus.). 160p. 1994. 25.95 (*0-87605-182-4*) Howell Bks.

Pinkerton, Steven D., jt. auth. see Abramson, Paul R.

Pinkerton, Steven D., jt. ed. see Abramson, Paul R.

Pinkerton, SueEllen & Schroeder, Patricia. Commitment to Excellence: Developing a Professional Nursing Staff. 304p. (C). 1988. 69.00 (*0-87189-882-9*, 89882) Aspen Pub.

Pinkerton, William A. Train Robberies, Train Robbers, & the Holdup Men. LC 74-15748. (Popular Culture in America Ser.). (Illus.). 88p. 1980. reprint ed. 15.95 (*0-405-06383-0*) Ayer.

Pinkett, Harold T. Gifford Pinchot: Private & Public Forester. LC 74-76830. 180p. reprint ed. pap. 55.80 (*0-608-13875-4*, 202023400016) Bks Demand.

Pinkevich, A. & Amelin, B. Diccionario Espanol-Ruso de le Prospeccion y Refinacion del Petroleo. Dobriansky, A. F., ed. (RUS & SPA.). 424p. 1966. 39.95 (*0-8288-6705-4*, S-37368) Fr & Eur.

Pinkguni, Manolito. Piranhas. LC 98-23989. (Fish Ser.). (Illus.). 64p. (YA). (gr. 3 up). 1999. lib. bdg. 17.95 (*0-7910-5093-9*) Chelsea Hse.

— Piranhas, Keeping & Breeding Them in Captivity: Keeping & Breeding Them in Captivity. (Illus.). 64p. 1996. pap. 6.95 (*0-7938-0363-2*, RE614) TFH Pubns.

Pinkham, J. R., et al. Pediatric Dentistry: Infancy Through Adolescence. 3rd ed. Fletcher, Judy, ed. LC 99-24326. (Illus.). 670p. (C). 1999. text. write for info. (*0-7216-8238-3*, W B Saunders Co) Harcrt Hlth Sci Grp.

Pinkham, James R., et al, eds. Pediatric Dentistry: Infancy Through Adolescence. 2nd ed. LC 92-49086. (Illus.). 576p. 1993. text 70.00 (*0-7216-4695-6*, W B Saunders Co) Harcrt Hlth Sci Grp.

Pinkham, Joan, jt. auth. see Press, Margaret.

Pinkham, Joan, tr. see Cesaire, Aime.

Pinkham, Joan, tr. see Nizan, Paul.

Pinkham, Joan, tr. see Troyat, Henri.

Pinkham, Julia. The BirdAlphabet Encyclopedia Coloring Book. (Illus.). 1996. pap. 6.95 (*0-88045-137-8*) Stemmer Hse.

— The Insect Alphabet Encyclopedia. 2nd ed. (NaturEncyclopedia Ser.). (Illus.). 48p. (J). (ps-3). 1995. pap. 6.95 (*0-88045-134-3*, Intl Design) Stemmer Hse.

— The Polar Seas Encyclopedia Coloring Book. (NaturEncyclopedia Ser.). (Illus.). 48p. (Orig.). 1996. pap. 6.95 (*0-88045-120-3*) Stemmer Hse.

— The Rainforest Encyclopedia Coloring Book. (NaturEncyclopedia Ser.). (Illus.). 48p. (J). (gr. 1-6). 1998. pap. 6.95 (*0-88045-142-4*) Stemmer Hse.

Pinkham, Linda, ed. see Bond, Ronald L.

Pinkham, Linda, ed. see Low, Robert J.

Pinkham, Linda, ed. see Powers, Dennis M.

Pinkham, Mark A. The Return of the Serpents of Wisdom. (Illus.). 366p. 1997. pap. 16.95 (*0-932813-51-8*) Adventures Unltd.

***Pinkham, Mark Amaru.** Conversations with the Goddess. 246p. 2000. 14.95 (*0-932813-81-X*, Pub. by Adventures Unltd) SCB Distributors.

Pinkham, Mary. Best of Helpful Hints. 1986. mass mkt. 5.95 (*0-446-38391-0*, Pub. by Warner Bks) Little.

Pinkham, Mary E. Mary Ellen's Best of Helpful Hints, Bk. II. (Illus.). 144p. (Orig.). 1981. 4.50 (*0-941298-00-0*) M E Pinkham.

— Mary Ellen's Best of Helpful Hints Library. 1981. pap. 12.50 (*0-941298-03-5*) M E Pinkham.

— Mary Ellen's Best of Helpful Kitchen Hints. (Illus.). 144p. (Orig.). 1980. pap. 4.50 (*0-941298-01-9*) M E Pinkham.

— Mary Ellen's Giant Book of Helpful Hints, 3 bks. in 1. LC 93-38935. 416p. 1994. 9.99 (*0-517-10179-3*) Random Hse Value.

— Mary Ellen's Greatest Hints. 352p. 1990. mass mkt. 5.99 (*0-449-21714-0*, Crest) Fawcett.

— Mary Ellen's Wow! Ideas That Really Work. 150p. 1992. 6.95 (*0-9631933-0-9*) M Ellen Bks.

Pinkham, Mary Ellen. Mary Ellen's Best of Helpful Hints, Bk. Two. LC 81-10376. (Illus.). 144p. 1989. mass mkt. 6.95 (*0-446-38644-8*, Pub. by Warner Bks) Little.

— Mary Ellen's Best of Helpful Kitchen Hints. (Illus.). (Orig.). 1980. mass mkt. 4.50 (*0-446-97212-6*, Pub. by Warner Bks) Little.

— Mary Ellen's Clean House. 1994. pap. 14.00 (*0-517-88185-3*) Crown Pub Group.

Pinkham, Myra, jt. ed. see LaRue, Gloria T.

Pinkham, Peter. The Hidden Mountain. 233p. 1998. pap. 12.95 (*0-9662661-0-2*, MFDC Pr) Merriman Forest.

Pinkhassov, Gueorgui. Sightwalk. (Illus.). 40p. 1998. 49.95 (*0-7148-3809-8*) Phaidon Pr.

Pinkleton, Bruce E., jt. auth. see Austin, Erica Weintraub.

***Pinkley, Diane.** Letters to Parents - ESL. (Illus.). 1999. pap. 11.95 (*0-673-59232-4*, GoodYrBooks) Addson-Wesley Educ.

Pinkley, Diane, jt. auth. see Purpura, James E.

***Pinkley, Robin & Northcraft, Gregory B.** Get Paid What Youre Worth: Expert Negotiators Guide To Salary & Compensation. LC 99-56770. 240p. 2000. text 23.95 (*0-312-24254-9*) St Martin.

Pinkman, John A. In the Legion of the Vanguard. (Illus.). 240p. 1999. pap. 15.95 (*1-85635-233-1*) Irish Bks Media.

Pinknett, Lynn. The Templar Revelation: Secret Guardians of the True Identity of Christ. (Illus.). 432p. 1998. per. 15.00 (*0-684-84891-0*) S&S Trade.

Pinkney. Dear Benjamin Banneker. LC 93-31162. (Illus.). 32p. (J). (gr. 1-5). 1998. pap. 6.00 (*0-15-201892-1*) Harcourt.

Pinkney. Raymond Williams. 76.95 (*1-85928-221-0*) Ashgate Pub Co.

Pinkney. Solo Girl Club. (J). 1997. pap. 3.95 (*0-7868-1276-1*, Pub. by Hyperion) Little.

Pinkney, jt. auth. see De Bertier de Sauvigny, Guillaume.

***Pinkney, Alphonso.** Black Americans. 5th ed. LC 99-19865. 274p. (C). 1999. pap. text 30.67 (*0-13-082577-8*) P-H.

Pinkney, Alphonso. The Committed: White Activists in the Civil Rights Movement. 1968. 19.95 (*0-8084-0084-3*) NCUP.

— Lest We Forget: Howard Beach & Other Racial Atrocities. 300p. (Orig.). (C). 1993. pap. 14.95 (*0-88378-088-7*) Third World.

— The Myth of Black Progress. LC 84-1912. 208p. 1986. pap. text 17.95 (*0-521-31047-4*) Cambridge U Pr.

Pinkney, Alphonso & Woock, Roger R. Poverty & Politics in Harlem. 1970. 19.95 (*0-8084-0249-8*); pap. 15.95 (*0-8084-0250-1*) NCUP.

Pinkney, Andrea. Duke Ellington: The Piano & His Orchestra. 32p. (J). Date not set. pap. 5.99 (*0-7868-1420-9*, Pub. by Hyperion) Little.

Pinkney, Andrea. Ella Fitzgerald. 32p. (J). 2001. 15.99 (*0-7868-0568-4*) Little.

— I Smell Honey. LC 96-75236. (Illus.). 16p. (J). 1997. pap. 4.95 (*0-15-200640-0*, Red Wagon Bks) Harcourt.

***Pinkney, Andrea.** Let It Shine: Stories of Black Women Freedom Fighters. (Illus.). 2000. 32.83 (*0-7398-3073-2*) Raintree Steck-V.

Pinkney, Andrea. Pretty Brown Face. LC 96-75235. (Illus.). 16p. (J). (ps). 1997. pap. 4.95 (*0-15-200643-5*, Red Wagon Bks) Harcourt.

— Shake Shake Shake. LC 96-75237. (Illus.). 16p. (J). 1997. pap. 4.95 (*0-15-200632-X*) Harcourt.

— Watch Me Dance. LC 96-75238. (Illus.). 16p. (J). 1997. pap. 4.95 (*0-15-200631-1*) Harcourt.

Pinkney, Andrea D. Bill Pickett: Rodeo-Ridin' Cowboy. LC 95-35920. (Illus.). 32p. (J). (gr. k-4). 1996. 16.00 (*0-15-200100-X*, Gulliver Bks) Harcourt.

— Bill Pickett: Rodeo-Ridin' Cowboy. (Illus.). (J). (gr. 4-8). 1996. 16.00 (*0-614-25372-1*) Harcourt.

— Bill Pickett: Rodeo-Ridin' Cowboy. (Illus.). 32p. (J). (ps-3). 1999. reprint ed. pap. 6.00 (*0-15-202103-5*, Voyager Bks) Harcourt.

— Dear Benjamin Banneker. LC 93-31162. (Illus.). 32p. (J). (gr. 1-5). 1994. 16.00 (*0-15-200417-3*, Gulliver Bks) Harcourt.

— Dear Benjamin Banneker. 1998. 11.20 (*0-606-13324-0*, Pub. by Turtleback) Demco.

— Duke Ellington. LC 96-46031. (Illus.). 32p. (J). (ps-3). 1998. lib. bdg. 16.49 (*0-7868-2150-7*, Pub. by Hyprn Child) Little.

— Duke Ellington: The Piano Prince & His Orchestra. LC 96-46031. (Illus.). 32p. (J). (ps-3). 1998. 15.95 (*0-7868-0178-6*, Pub. by Hyprn Child) Time Warner.

— Solo Girl. LC 96-49502. Vol. 1. (Illus.). 64p. (J). (gr. 2-4). 1997. lib. bdg. 14.49 (*0-7868-2265-1*, Pub. by Hyprn Child) Little.

— Solo Girl. LC 96-49502. (Chapters Ser.: Vol. 1). (Illus.). 64p. (J). (gr. 2-4). 1997. pap. 3.95 (*0-7868-1216-8*, Pub. by Hyprn Ppbks) Little.

Pinkney, Andrea Davis. Alvin Ailey. LC 92-54865. (Illus.). 32p. (J). (ps-3). 1993. 13.45 (*1-56282-413-9*, Pub. by Hyprn Child) Time Warner.

— Alvin Ailey. LC 92-54865. (Illus.). 32p. (J). (ps-4). 1995. pap. 4.95 (*0-7868-1077-7*, Pub. by Hyprn Ppbks) Little.

Pinkney, Andrea Davis. Alvin Ailey. LC 92-54865. 1995. 10.15 (*0-606-08982-9*, Pub. by Turtleback) Demco.

Pinkney, Andrea Davis. Hold Fast to Dreams. LC 94-32909. (Illus.). 112p. (YA). (gr. 5 up). 1995. 16.00 (*0-688-12832-7*, Wm Morrow) Morrow Avon.

— Hold Fast to Dreams. LC 96-1985. 1996. 9.60 (*0-606-11469-6*, Pub. by Turtleback) Demco.

— Raven in a Dove House. LC 97-36180. 208p. (J). (gr. 6). 1998. 16.00 (*0-15-201461-6*, Harcourt Child Bks) Harcourt.

— Raven in a Dove House. LC 98-42721. 224p. (J). (gr. 6-12). 1999. pap. text 6.99 (*0-7868-1349-0*, Pub. by Hyprn Child) Time Warner.

— Seven Candles for Kwanzaa. LC 92-3698. (Illus.). 32p. (J). (gr. k up). 1993. 15.99 (*0-8037-1292-8*, Dial Yng Read) Peng Put Young Read.

— Seven Candles for Kwanzaa. (Illus.). 32p. (J). (ps-2). 1998. pap. 5.99 (*0-14-056428-4*, PuffinBks) Peng Put Young Read.

— Silent Thunder. LC 98-32071. (Illus.). 208p. (YA). (gr. 4-7). 1999. lib. bdg. 16.49 (*0-7868-2388-7*, Pub. by Hyprn Child) Little.

— Silent Thunder: A Civil War Story. LC 98-32071. (Illus.). 208p. (YA). (gr. 4-7). 1999. 15.99 (*0-7868-0439-4*, Pub. by Hyprn Child) Time Warner.

***Pinkney, Andrea Davis.** Sleeping Cutie. 2002. write for info. (*0-15-202544-8*) Harcourt.

***Pinkney, Andrea Davis & Alcorn, Stephen.** Let It Shine: The Stories of Ten Black Women Freedom Fighters. LC 99-42806. (Illus.). 128p. (J). (ps up). 2000. 20.00 (*0-15-201005-X*, Harcourt Child Bks) Harcourt.

***Pinkney, Andrea Davis & Pinkney, J. Brian.** Belly-Hum Christmas LC 99-6346. (J). 2001. write for info. (*0-15-201918-9*) Harcourt.

Pinkney, Brian. The Adventures of Sparrow Boy. LC 96-19028. (Illus.). 40p. (J). (ps-4). 1997. 16.00 (*0-689-81071-7*) S&S Bks Yung.

***Pinkney, Brian.** The Adventures of Sparrowboy. (Illus.). 40p. (J). (gr. k-4). 2000. per. 5.99 (*0-689-83534-5*) Aladdin.

— Benjamin & the Shrinking Book. (J). 2001. 15.95 (*0-688-17476-0*, Grenwillow Bks); lib. bdg. 15.89 (*0-688-17477-9*, Grenwillow Bks) HarpC Child Bks.

Pinkney, Brian. Cosmo & the Robot. LC 99-32209. (Illus.). 32p. (J). (ps-3). 2000. 15.95 (*0-688-15940-0*, Grenwillow Bks); 15.89 (*0-688-15941-9*, Grenwillow Bks) HarpC Child Bks.

— Jojo's Flying Side Kick. LC 94-24318. (Illus.). 32p. (J). (ps-3). 1998. per. 5.99 (*0-689-82192-1*) Aladdin.

— Jojo's Flying Side Kick. (J). 1995. 14.00 (*0-671-88111-6*) S&S Bks Yung.

— Max Found Two Sticks. (J). 1997. mass mkt. 5.99 (*0-689-81593-X*) Aladdin.

— Max Found Two Sticks. LC 93-12525. (Illus.). 40p. (J). (ps-3). 1994. pap. 16.00 (*0-671-78776-4*) S&S Bks Yung.

— Max Found Two Sticks. 1997. 11.19 (*0-606-11605-2*, Pub. by Turtleback) Demco.

Pinkney, David H. Decisive Years in France, 1840-1847. LC 85-43304. 248p. reprint ed. pap. 76.90 (*0-7837-1425-4*, 204178000023) Bks Demand.

— The French Revolution of 1830. Halsey, F. D., tr. LC 72-39051. 407p. reprint ed. 126.20 (*0-8357-9498-9*, 201487500093) Bks Demand.

Pinkney, David H., jt. auth. see De Bertier De Sauvigny, Guillaume.

Pinkney, Debbie, jt. illus. see McCafferty, Catherine.

Pinkney, Edward C. Poems. LC 72-4970. (Romantic Tradition in American Literature Ser.). 76p. 1972. reprint ed. 21.95 (*0-405-04640-5*) Ayer.

Pinkney, Gloria J. Back Home. LC 91-22610. (Illus.). 40p. (J). (ps-3). 1992. 16.99 (*0-8037-1168-9*, Dial Yng Read) Peng Put Young Read.

Pinkney, Gloria Jean. Back Home. (Illus.). 40p. (J). (ps-3). 1999. pap. 5.99 (*0-14-056547-7*, PuffinBks) Peng Put Young Read.

Pinkney, J. Brian, jt. illus. see Pinkney, Andrea Davis.

***Pinkney, Jerry.** Aesop's Fables. (Illus.). (J). 2000. 19.95 (*1-58717-000-0*) SeaStar.

— Strange Animals of the Sea. 10p. 1991. 15.50 (*0-87044-686-X*, Pub. by Natl Geog) S&S Trade.

Pinkney, Jerry. The Adventures of Spider: West African Folk Tales. LC 92-444. 58p. (J). (gr. k-3). 1992. pap. 7.95 (*0-316-05107-1*) Little.

— Los Huevos Hablantes - The Talking Egg. LC 95-22751. (SPA.). 32p. (J). (ps-3). 1996. 16.99 (*0-8037-1991-4*, Dial Yng Read) Peng Put Young Read.

— The Last Tales of Uncle Remus. LC 93-7531. (J). (ps-4). 1994. 18.99 (*0-8037-1303-7*, Dial Yng Read) Peng Put Young Read.

— More Tales of Uncle Remus: Further Adventures of Brer Rabbit, His Friends, Enemies & Others. LC 86-32890. 160p. (J). (gr. 2 up). 1988. 18.99 (*0-8037-0419-4*, Dial Yng Read) Peng Put Young Read.

— Rabbit Makes a Monkey of Lion: A Swahili Tale. 32p. (J). (ps-3). 1993. pap. 5.99 (*0-14-054593-X*, PuffinBks) Peng Put Young Read.

— Read-to-Me: Recommended Literature for Children Ages Two Through Seven. 144p. (Orig.). (C). 1996. pap. text 30.00 (*0-7881-2723-3*) DIANE Pub.

***Pinkney, Jerry.** The Ugly Duckling. LC 98-23604. Orig. Title: Grimme aelling. 48p. (J). 1999. 15.89 (*0-688-15933-8*, Wm Morrow) Morrow Avon.

Pinkney, Jerry, jt. auth. see Gibson, Barbara.

Pinkney, Nancy W. Jojo's Flying Side Kick. LC 94-24318. (Illus.). 32p. (J). (ps-3). 1995. 15.00 (*0-689-80283-8*) S&S Bks Yung.

Pinkney, Nathaniel. Conversation Games: Vol. I-People Times. 87p. (Orig.). (J). (ps-6). 1978. pap. 15.00 (*0-939632-17-9*) ILM.

— Conversation Games: Vol. II-Experiences. 87p. (Orig.). (J). (ps-6). 1978. pap. 15.00 (*0-939632-20-9*) ILM.

Pinkney, Robert. Democracy in the Third World. LC 93-16049. (Issues in Third World Politics Ser.). 182p. (C). 1994. pap. text 18.95 (*1-55587-454-1*) L Rienner.

— Democracy in the Third World. Randall, Vicky, ed. (Issues in Third World Politics Ser.). 192p. 1993. 9.00 (*0-335-15705-X*); pap. 2.00 (*0-335-15704-1*) OpUniv Pr.

— Right-Wing Military Government. (Twayne's Themes in Right-Wing Ideology & Politics Ser.: No. 3). 256p. (C). 1990. 30.95 (*0-8057-9554-5*, Twyne); pap. 16.95 (*0-8057-9555-3*, Twyne) Mac Lib Ref.

***Pinkney, Sandra L.** Shades of Black: A Celebration of Our Children. LC 99-86593. (Illus.). 40p. (J). (ps-2). 2000. write for info. (*0-439-14892-8*) Scholastic Inc.

Pinkney, Tony. D. H. Lawrence & Modernism. LC 90-70151. 190p. (C). 1990. pap. text 14.95 (*0-87745-295-4*) U of Iowa Pr.

— Raymond Williams: Postmodernist Novelist. 144p. 1991. 35.00 (*1-85411-047-0*, Pub. by Seren Bks); pap. 15.95 (*1-85411-048-9*, Pub. by Seren Bks) Dufour.

Pinkney, William, Jr. Life of William Pinkney. LC 75-75276. (Law, Politics & History Ser.). 1969. reprint ed. lib. bdg. 49.50 (*0-306-71307-1*) Da Capo.

Pinkoski, Jim. Discovered: Sodom & Gomorrah. (Illus.). 24p. (Orig.). 1992. 2.95 (*0-945383-40-1*) Teach Servs.

— Discovered: True! The Genesis Story of Creation. (Illus.). 32p. (Orig.). 1992. 2.95 (*0-945383-39-8*) Teach Servs.

An Asterisk (*) at the beginning of an entry indicates that the title is appearing for the first time.

P

Pinney, et al. Decision Support Software (DSS)-2.6a Version. 1997. pap. 29.95 (*0-87393-716-3*) Dame Pubns.
— Quantitive Methods for Management with Decisions Support Software (DSS) Textbook/Workbook with 2.6 Version Disk. rev. ed. LC 97-67112. 1998. wbk. ed. 97.95 incl. disk (*0-87393-691-4*) Dame Pubns.
***Pinney, Chris.** Boxers. (Complete Pet Owner's Manual Ser.). (Illus.). 2000. pap. text 6.95 (*0-7641-1051-9*) Barron.
Pinney, Chris. Vizslas: A Complete Pet Owners Manual. LC 98-18036. (Barron's Complete Pet Owner's Manuals). (Illus.). 96p. 1998. pap. 6.95 (*0-7641-0321-0*) Barron.
***Pinney, Chris C.** The Complete Home Veterinary Guide. 2nd ed. LC 99-58867. (Illus.). 896p. 2000. 29.95 (*0-07-135186-8*) McGraw-Hill Prof.
— Dachshunds: Everything about Purchase, Care, Nutrition, Behavior & Training. 2nd ed. LC 00-23598. (Complete Pet Owner's Manual Ser.). (Illus.). 64p. 2000. 6.95 (*0-7641-1247-3*) Barron.
Pinney, Chris C. German Shorthaired Pointers. LC 97-44383. (Barron's Complete Pet Owner's Manuals). (Illus.). 1998. pap. 6.95 (*0-7641-0316-4*) Barron.
Pinney, Christopher. Camera Indica: The Social Life of Indian Photographs. LC 97-23831. 192p. 1998. lib. bdg. 55.00 (*0-226-66865-7*); lib. bdg. 29.00 (*0-226-66866-5*) U Ch Pr.
Pinney, Christopher C. Caring for Your Older Cat. LC 95-25360. (Barron's Educational Ser.). 1996. pap. 10.95 (*0-8120-9148-5*) Barron.
— Caring for Your Older Dog. LC 95-6756. (Illus.). 192p. 1995. pap. 10.95 (*0-8120-9149-3*) Barron.
— Guide to Home Pet Grooming. 144p. 1990. pap. 9.95 (*0-8120-4298-0*) Barron.
— Illustrated Veterinary Guide for Dogs, Cats, Birds, & Exotic Pets. (Illus.). 1995. pap. 21.95 (*0-07-050179-3*) McGraw-Hill Prof.
— Illustrated Veterinary Guide for Dogs, Cats, Birds & Exotic Pets. 512p. 1992. 29.95 (*0-8306-1986-0*) McGraw-Hill Prof.
Pinney, Edward C. Orthopaedic Nursing. 6th ed. (Illus.). 368p. 1983. text 22.00 (*0-7216-0933-3*, W B Saunders Co) Harcrt Hlth Sci Grp.
Pinney, Edward L., Jr. A First Group Psychotherapy Book. LC 95-17203. 224p. 1995. pap. 40.00 (*1-56821-617-3*) Aronson.
Pinney, Estelle R. A Net Full of Honey. (YA). 1996. pap. 12.95 (*0-7022-2744-7*, Pub. by Univ Queensland Pr) Intl Spec Bk.
Pinney, Geoff, jt. auth. see Tarring, Trevor.
Pinney, John & Pinney, Robert D. Beginning in the Nursery Business. 70p. 1985. pap. 4.95 (*1-887632-54-9*) Amer Nurseryman Pub.
Pinney, Peter. The Barbarians: A Soldier's New Guinea Diary. (Orig.). 1989. pap. 16.95 (*0-7022-2158-9*, Pub. by Univ Queensland Pr) Intl Spec Bk.
— The Glass Cannon: A Bougainville Diary, 1944-45. 1991. pap. 16.95 (*0-7022-2329-8*, Pub. by Univ Queensland Pr) Intl Spec Bk.
— Signaller Johnston's Secret War: New Guinea, 1943-45. LC 98-217355. 1998. reprint ed. pap. 18.95 (*0-7022-2993-8*, Pub. by Univ Queensland Pr) Intl Spec Bk.
Pinney, R. Pythons. LC 97-38570. (Complete Pet Owner's Manual Ser.). (Illus.). 120p. 1997. pap. 6.95 (*0-8120-9365-8*) Barron.
Pinney, Robert D., jt. auth. see Pinney, John.
Pinney, Susanna, ed. I'll Stand by You: Selected Letters of Sylvia Townsend Warner & Valentine Ackland. LC 99-206601. 392p. 1999. pap. 24.95 (*0-7126-7371-7*, Pub. by Pimlico) Trafalgar.
Pinney, Thomas. A History of Wine in America: From the Beginnings to Prohibition. 1989. 55.00 (*0-520-06224-8*, Pub. by U CA Pr) Cal Prin Full Svc.
— A Short Handbook & Style Sheet. 58p. (Orig.). (C). 1977. pap. text 19.50 (*0-15-580925-3*, Pub. by Harcourt Coll Pubs) Harcourt.
Pinney, Thomas, ed. see Kipling, Rudyard.
Pinney, Tom, ed. see Rosano, Dick.
Pinney, William E. & McWilliams, Donald B. Management Science: An Introduction to Quantitative Analysis for Management. 2nd ed. (Illus.). xvii, 620p. 1987. 29.95 (*0-06-350589-4*) Valian Assocs.
Pinnick, Alfred W., jt. auth. see Middlebrook, Stanley M.
Pinnick, Shirley, jt. auth. see Elmusa, Mary.
Pinnie, Lawrence J. The Passing of Spanish Traditionalism: Deprivation, Transformation, Credence. LC 95-90395. (Illus.). xvii, 198p. (Orig.). 1996. pap. 13.95 (*0-9655698-0-2*) L J Pinnie.
Pinniger, R. S., ed. see Jones, Bruce V. & British Small Animal Veterinary Association Staff.
Pinnington, Adrian, ed. see Dickens, Charles.
***Pinnington, Ashly & Edwards, Tony.** Introduction to Human Resource Management. LC 99-58574. 2000. write for info. (*0-19-877543-1*) OUP.
Pinnix, Marshall H. Insurance in the United States: A Handbook for Professionals. (DYP Textbook Ser.). 307p. 1993. pap. 125.00 (*1-870255-66-6*) LLP.
Pinnock. Peripheral Nerve Blockade. 1996. text 55.00 (*0-443-05064-3*, W B Saunders Co) Harcrt Hlth Sci Grp.
Pinnock, Clark. Biblical Revelation: The Foundation of Christian Theology. 256p. 1992. reprint ed. pap. 20.50 (*1-57383-002-X*) Regent College.
— The Scripture Principle. 250p. 1992. reprint ed. pap. 20.50 (*1-57383-000-3*) Regent College.
Pinnock, Clark, et al. The Openness of God: A Biblical Challenge to the Traditional Understanding of God. LC 94-3575. 192p. (Orig.). 1994. pap. 12.99 (*0-8308-1852-9*, 1852) InterVarsity.
***Pinnock, Clark H.** Biblical Revelation: The Foundation of Christian Theology. 256p. 1998. pap. 23.00 (*1-57910-126-7*) Wipf & Stock.
Pinnock, Clark H. Flame of Love: A Theology of the Holy Spirit. LC 96-19407. 292p. 1996. 24.99 (*0-8308-1879-0*, 1879) InterVarsity.
***Pinnock, Clark H.** Flame of Love: A Theology of the Holy Spirit. 1999. pap. 14.99 (*0-8308-1590-2*) InterVarsity.
Pinnock, Clark H. Reason Enough: A Case for the Christian Faith. 126p. 1997. pap. 14.00 (*1-57910-046-5*) Wipf & Stock.
— The Scripture Principle. 272p. 1998. pap. 23.00 (*1-57910-108-9*) Wipf & Stock.
— Three Keys to Spiritual Renewal: A Challenge to the Church. 108p. 1998. pap. 14.00 (*1-57910-101-1*) Wipf & Stock.
***Pinnock, Clark H.** Tracking the Maze: Finding Our Way Through Modern Theology from an Evangelical Perspective. 240p. 1998. pap. 22.00 (*1-57910-117-8*) Wipf & Stock.
Pinnock, Clark H. Truth on Fire: The Message of Galatians. 94p. 1998. pap. 12.00 (*1-57910-103-8*) Wipf & Stock.
— A Wideness in God's Mercy: The Finality of Jesus Christ in a World of Religions. 218p. 1997. pap. 18.00 (*1-57910-059-7*) Wipf & Stock.
Pinnock, Clark H., ed. The Grace of God & the Will of Man. LC 95-44772. 32p. (Orig.). 1995. reprint ed. pap. 11.99 (*1-55661-691-0*, Hampshire MN) Bethany Hse.
***Pinnock, Clark H., ed.** Grace Unlimited. 264p. 1999. pap. 23.00 (*1-57910-237-9*) Wipf & Stock.
Pinnock, Clark H. & Brow, Robert C. Unbounded Love: A Good News Theology for the 21st Century. LC 94-26381. 192p. 1994. pap. 12.99 (*0-8308-1853-7*, 1853) InterVarsity.
Pinnock, Clark H. & Brown, Delwin. Theological Crossfire: An Evangelical/Liberal Dialogue. 262p. 1998. pap. 23.00 (*1-57910-105-4*) Wipf & Stock.
Pinnock, Clark H., et al. Freedom, Justice & Hope: Toward a Strategy for the Poor & the Oppressed. LC 87-72955. (Turning Point Christian Worldview Ser.). 1988. pap. 13.99 (*0-89107-478-3*) Crossway Bks.
Pinnock, Clark H., jt. ed. see Cobb, John B., Jr.
Pinnock, Colin A. & Haden, Robert M. MCQ Tutor in Anaesthesia: Clinical Practice. 304p. (Orig.). 1993. pap. text 27.95 (*0-443-04610-7*) Church.
Pinnock, Colin A. & Jones, Robert P. MCQ Tutor in Anaesthesia Pt. 1: FRCA. LC 93-29089. 1993. write for info. (*0-443-04963-7*) Church.
— MCQ Tutor in Basic Sciences for Anaesthesia. 240p. (Orig.). 1993. pap. text 27.95 (*0-443-04611-5*) Church.
***Pinnock, Hugh W.** Finding Biblical Hebrew & Other Ancient Literary Forms in the Book of Mormon. LC 99-11006. 1999. write for info. (*0-934893-38-1*) Res Press UT.
Pinnock, J., jt. auth. see Bindloss, H.
Pinnock, Jill, jt. ed. see McLoughlin, William.
Pinnock, Tom. The Male Homemaker's Handbook. unabridged ed. Richmond, Dick, ed. LC 96-61715. 108p. 1997. pap. 10.00 (*1-882467-15-9*) Wildstone Media.
— You Can Be Rich by Thursday: The Secrets of Making a Fortune in Multi-Level Marketing. LC 96-61714. 125p. (Orig.). 1997. pap. 12.00 (*1-882467-14-0*) Wildstone Media.
Pinnow, Hermann. History of Germany. Brailsford, Mabel R., tr. from GER. LC 74-130563. (Select Bibliographies Reprint Ser.). 1977. reprint ed. 25.95 (*0-8369-5536-6*) Ayer.
Pinnow, Marilyn. Romancing the Mountain: Two Tales of Marin Trails. 224p. (Orig.). 1994. pap. 12.00 (*0-9643293-0-1*) F I D Ent.
Pino, David. The Clarinet & Clarinet Playing. unabridged ed. LC 98-44312. (Illus.). 320p. 1998. pap. 9.95 (*0-486-40270-3*) Dover.
Pino, Edward C. Remaking Our Schools: What Has Gone Wrong & New Ways to Fix It. 200p. (Orig.). (C). 1993. lib. bdg. 19.95 (*1-883732-01-8*) I G S.
Pino, G. Del, see Del Pino, G., ed.
Pino, Julio C. Family & Favela: The Reproduction of Poverty in Rio de Janeiro, 10. LC 96-47433. (Contributions in Latin American Studies: Vol. 10). 216p. 1997. 55.00 (*0-313-30362-2*, Greenwood Pr) Greenwood.
Pino, Laurence J. The Business Success Start-up Kit, 8 bklts., Set. 1990. 99.95 (*1-56354-000-2*) Open U FL.
— Cash in on Cash Flow. LC 98-11150. 256p. (YA). 1998. 25.00 (*0-684-84862-7*) S&S Trade.
— The Desktop Lawyer, 2 vols., Set. 1991. ring bd. 495.00 (*1-56354-003-7*) Open U FL.
— The Desktop Lawyer Software. 300p. 1991. 139.95 incl. disk (*1-56354-004-5*) Open U FL.
— Double Your Income with Your Own Home Business. 1991. write for info. (*0-318-68778-X*) Open U FL.
— Finding Your Niche: A Handbook for Entrepreneurs. 224p. (Orig.). 1994. pap. 9.00 (*0-425-14148-9*) Berkley Pub.
— How to Choose & Use a Lawyer. 1991. write for info. (*0-318-68777-1*) Open U FL.
— How to Incorporate in Any State Without a Lawyer. 1991. write for info. (*0-318-68779-8*) Open U FL.
— Money Makers of America. 1991. student ed. 99.95 incl. audio (*1-56354-002-9*) Open U FL.
— What You Need to Know about Business Law. 1991. write for info. (*0-318-68780-1*) Open U FL.
Pino, Ondina, jt. auth. see Yenes, Martha.
Pino, Pedro L. The Life & Times of a Vietnam Vet: A Collection of War Poems. LC 96-85361. (Illus.). 56p. (Orig.). 1996. pap. 5.95 (*0-9646450-3-3*) DeeMar Commun.
Pino, Piero, jt. ed. see Wender, Irving.
Pino, Raul F. El Canto del Angel. unabridged ed. (SPA., Illus.). 241p. 1995. 19.95 (*0-9652492-0-4*) Desdin Pub.
Pino, Robert. Corporate Aikido: Unleash the Potential Within Your Company to Neutralize Competition. (Illus.). 192p. 1998. 19.95 (*0-07-050240-4*) McGraw.
Pino, Salvador Rodriguez del, see Rodriguez del Pino, Salvador, ed.
Pino, Yolanda Ortiz y, see Ortiz y Pino, Yolanda.
Pinol, Jean-Luc & Menjot, Denis. Water & European Cities from the Middle Ages to the Nineteenth Century. LC 98-49692. (Historical Urban Studies). 140p. 1999. text 59.95 (*1-85928-205-9*) Ashgate Pub Co.
***Pinol, Roser.** Creating Costumes. LC 00-8070. (Illus.). 32p. 2000. 18.95 (*1-56711-438-5*) Blackbirch.
Pinola, Rudy. Other Times & Other Places. 116p. 1999. pap. 8.75 (*1-883428-03-3*) Econ Res Srv.
***Pinola, Rudy.** Social Security: Issues, Problems & Myths. 70p. 1999. per. write for info. (*1-883428-04-1*) Econ Res Srv.
Pinola, Rudy & Rahgozar, Reza. Applied Regression & Time Series Analysis. 210p. (C). 1997. text 20.95 (*1-883428-02-5*) Econ Res Srv.
Pinola, Rudy, jt. auth. see Sher, William.
Pinon, Christopher, jt. ed. see Kanazawa, Makoto.
Pinon, Christopher J., ed. see Johnson, Karen E.
Pinon, Christopher J., jt. ed. see Kanazawa, Makoto.
Pinon, Nelida. The Republic of Dreams: A Novel. Lane, Helen, tr. from SPA. (Texas Pan American Ser.). 669p. 1991. reprint ed. pap. 17.95 (*0-292-77050-2*) U of Tex Pr.
Pinon, Pierre. Istanbul, Rassenga 72. 1998. pap. 35.00 (*88-85322-35-2*) Birkhauser.
***Pinon, Ramon.** Biology of Human Reproduction. (Illus.). 432p. 2000. text. write for info. (*1-891389-12-2*) Univ Sci Bks.
Pinoni, Francesca, jt. auth. see Cetojevic, Igor.
Pinos, Carme. Carme Pinos: Projects. (Illus.). 220p. 1999. pap. 27.00 (*84-89698-48-1*) Actar.
Pinot-Correia. Ovary of Eve. (Illus.). 396p. 1998. pap. 17.50 (*0-226-66954-8*) U Ch Pr.
Pinot, H. M. Fahnestock Genealogy: Ancestors & Descendants of Johann Diedrich Fahnestock. (Illus.). 442p. 1991. reprint ed. pap. 67.50 (*0-8328-1706-6*); reprint ed. lib. bdg. 77.50 (*0-8328-1705-8*) Higginson Bk Co.
Pinot, Pierre, jt. auth. see Auge-Laribe, Michel.
Pinsdorf, Marion K. German-Speaking Entrepreneurs: Builders of Business in Brazil. (American University Studies: Economics: Ser. XVI, Vol. 6). IV, 411p. (C). 1990. text 77.95 (*0-8204-1099-3*) P Lang Pubng.
Pinsent, Gordon. By the Way. (Illus.). 272p. 1992. 26.95 (*0-7737-2647-0*) Genl Dist Srvs.
Pinsent, John. Greek Mythology: The Library of the World's Myths & Legends. LC 83-71479. (Illus.). 144p. 1990. pap. 10.95 (*0-87226-299-5*, P Bedrick Books) NTC Contemp Pub Co.
Pinsent, Lynsy, contrib. by. Face Painting. (Crafts for Children Ser.). (Illus.). 32p. (YA). (gr. 3 up). 1997. pap. 4.95 (*1-56010-211-X*, CC01) W Foster Pub.
Pinsent, P. J. & Fuller, C. J. Outline of Clinical Diagnosis in the Horse. 2nd ed. LC 96-52363. (Illus.). 202p. 1997. pap. 41.95 (*0-632-04136-6*) Blackwell Sci.
Pinsent, Pat. Children's Literature & the Politics of Equality. (Roehampton Teaching Studies Ser.). 160p. 1997. pap. 24.95 (*1-85346-425-2*, Pub. by David Fulton) Taylor & Francis.
— Children's Literature & the Politics of Equality. LC 97-17342. (Language & Literacy Ser.). 188p. 1997. write for info. (*0-8077-3680-5*) Tchrs Coll.
Pinsent, Pat, ed. Language Culture & Young Children: Developing English in the Multi-Ethnic Nursery & Infant School. 144p. 1992. pap. 24.95 (*1-85346-184-9*, Pub. by David Fulton) Taylor & Francis.
— The Power of the Page: Children's Books & Their Readers. 144p. 1993. pap. 27.50 (*1-85346-234-9*, Pub. by David Fulton) Taylor & Francis.
Pinske, J. Orchideen Fuer zu Hause. (GER., Illus.). 127p. 1984. pap. text 15.00 (*3-405-12923-0*) Lubrecht & Cramer.
Pinsker, Ann, jt. auth. see Pinsker, Sanford.
Pinsker, Harold M. & Willis, William D., Jr., eds. Information Processing in the Nervous System. LC 78-68641. 378p. 1980. reprint ed. pap. 117.20 (*0-608-00385-9*, 206109900007) Bks Demand.
Pinsker, Henry. A Primer of Supportive Psychotherapy. LC 97-41400. 312p. 1997. 49.95 (*0-88163-274-0*) Analytic Pr.
Pinsker, Lev S. Road to Freedom. LC 70-162734. 142p. 1975. reprint ed. lib. bdg. 49.50 (*0-8371-6195-9*, PIRF, Greenwood Pr) Greenwood.
Pinsker, Richard. Getting Hired: A Guide for Managers & Professionals. Reider, Andrea, ed. LC 93-73202. (Illus.). 86p. (Orig.). 1994. pap. 10.95 (*1-56052-252-6*) Crisp Pubns.
Pinsker, Richard J. Hiring Winners. 160p. 1991. 19.95 (*0-8144-5051-2*, 040547) AMACOM.
Pinsker, S. Jewish American Fiction. (Twayne's United States Authors Ser.). 200p. 1992. 28.95 (*0-8057-3959-9*) Macmillan.
Pinsker, Sanford. Bearing the Bad News: Contemporary American Literature & Culture. LC 90-35570. 195p. 1990. text 25.95 (*0-87745-292-X*) U of Iowa Pr.
Pinsker, Sanford. Between Two Worlds: The American Novel in the 1960s. LC 79-64168. x, 139p. 1980. 29.00 (*0-87875-169-6*) Whitston Pub.
Pinsker, Sanford. The Catcher in the Rye: Innocence under Pressure. 128p. 1993. 25.95 (*0-8057-7978-7*, Twyne) Mac Lib Ref.
— The Catcher in the Rye: Innocence under Pressure. LC 92-31048. (Masterwork Studies: No. 114). 107p. 1993. pap. 18.00 (*0-8057-8028-9*, Twyne); lib. bdg. 21.95 (*0-8057-8365-2*, Twyne) Mac Lib Ref.
— Oedipus Meets the Press, & Other Tragi-Comedies of Our Time. LC 95-511. 64p. 1996. pap. 14.95 (*0-7734-2741-4*, Mellen Poetry Pr) E Mellen.
— The Schlemiel As Metaphor: Studies in Yiddish & American Jewish Fiction. enl. rev. ed. 216p. (C). 1991. 31.95 (*0-8093-1581-5*) S Ill U Pr.
— The Uncompromising Fictions of Cynthia Ozick. LC 86-30788. 128p. 1987. pap. 12.95 (*0-8262-0635-2*) U of Mo Pr.
Pinsker, Sanford. Worrying about Race, 1985-1995: Reflections During a Troubled Time. LC 95-62173. viii, 144p. 1996. 39.00 (*0-87875-474-1*) Whitston Pub.
Pinsker, Sanford & Fischel, Jack R., eds. America & the Holocaust, Vol. I. (Holocaust Studies Annual). 200p. (C). 1984. lib. bdg. 15.00 (*0-913283-02-9*) Penkevill.
— Holocaust Studies Annual 1990. LC 88-648983. 176p. 1990. text 10.00 (*0-8240-6987-0*) Garland.
— Holocaust Studies Annual, 1991: General Essays. LC 88-648983. 176p. 1992. text 10.00 (*0-8153-0393-9*, SS787) Garland.
— Literature, the Arts, & the Holocaust, Vol. III. (Holocaust Studies Annual). (Illus.). 288p. (C). 1987. lib. bdg. 30.00 (*0-913283-21-5*) Penkevill.
Pinsker, Sanford & Pinsker, Ann. Understanding the Catcher in the Rye: A Student Casebook to Issues, Sources & Historical Documents. LC 98-55339. (Literature in Context Ser.). 200p. 1999. 39.95 (*0-313-30200-6*) Greenwood.
Pinsker, Sanford, jt. ed. see Fischel, Jack R.
Pinsker, Z. G. Dynamical Scattering of X-Rays in Crystals. (Solid-State Sciences Ser.: Vol. 3). (Illus.). 1978. 63.95 (*0-387-08564-5*) Spr-Verlag.
Pinskey, Raleigh. 101 Ways to Promote Yourself: Tricks Of The Trade For Taking Charge Of Your Own Success. LC 96-95160. 352p. 1997. mass mkt. 6.99 (*0-380-78508-0*, Avon Bks) Morrow Avon.
***Pinskey, Raleigh.** 101 Ways to Promote Yourself: Tricks Of The Trade For Taking Charge Of Your Own Success. LC 99-96994. 416p. 1999. pap. 12.50 (*0-380-81054-9*, Avon Bks) Morrow Avon.
Pinskey, Raleigh. The Zen of Hype: An Insider's Guide to the Publicity Game. 208p. (Orig.). 1991. pap. 10.95 (*0-8065-1239-3*, Citadel Pr) Carol Pub Group.
Pinski, David. Temptations: A Book of Short Stories. Goldberg, Isaac, tr. from YID. LC 74-163045. (Short Story Index Reprint Ser.). 1977. reprint ed. 23.95 (*0-8369-3959-X*) Ayer.
— Three Plays. Goldberg, Isaac, tr. from YID. LC 74-29513. (Modern Jewish Experience Ser.). 1975. reprint ed. 23.95 (*0-405-06739-9*) Ayer.
***Pinsky.** Introduction to Fourier Analysis. 2001. pap. 60.00 (*0-534-37660-6*) Thomson Learn.
Pinsky, Bruce, jt. auth. see Leinward, Allen.
Pinsky, Laura & Douglas, Paul H. The Essential AIDS Fact Book: Newly Revised & Updated. rev. ed. 144p. 1996. per. 7.00 (*0-671-55287-2*) S&S Trade.
Pinsky, Laura, et al. Essential HIV Treatment Fact Book. Centrello, Gina, ed. 464p. 1992. per. 14.00 (*0-671-72528-9*) PB.
Pinsky, Leonard. Genetic Disorders of Human Sexual Development. LC 98-42996. (Illus.). 432p. 1999. text 85.00 (*0-19-510907-4*) OUP.
Pinsky, M., jt. auth. see Durrett, R.
Pinsky, M. R., et al, eds. The Splanchnic Circulation: No Longer a Silent Partner, No. 23. LC 95-37674. (Update in Intensive Care & Emergency Medicine Ser.: Vol. 23). 192p. 1995. 123.00 (*3-540-59198-2*) Spr-Verlag.
Pinsky, M. R., jt. ed. see Park, G. R.
Pinsky, Mark, et al. Video Display Terminals: Health & Safety Update, 1983. (Excerpts from Microwave News Ser.). 29p. 1984. pap. 10.00 (*0-9610580-1-3*) Microwave.
Pinsky, Mark, jt. ed. see Green, Mark.
Pinsky, Mark A. Diffusion Processes & Related Problems in Analysis. 600p. 1991. 69.00 (*0-8176-3516-5*) Birkhauser.
— Lecture Notes on Random Evolution. 150p. (C). 1991. text 36.00 (*981-02-0559-7*) World Scientific Pub.
— Partial Differential Equations & Boundary Value Problems with Applications. 2nd ed. 488p. (C). 1991. text 86.50 (*0-07-050128-9*) McGraw.
— Partial Differential Equations & Boundary-Value Problems with Applications. 3rd ed. LC 97-36120. 544p. 1997. 82.81 (*0-07-050227-7*) McGraw.
— Stochastic Analysis & Applications. (Advances in Probability & Related Topics Ser.: Vol. 7). (Illus.). 472p. 1984. text 167.50 (*0-8247-1906-9*) Dekker.
Pinsky, Mark A. & Wihstutz, V., eds. Diffusion Processes & Related Problems in Analysis, Vol. II: Stochastic Flows. (Progress in Probability Ser.: Vol. 27). ix, 346p. 1991. 80.50 (*0-8176-3543-2*) Birkhauser.
Pinsky, Maxine A. Marx Toys: Robots, Space & Comic Characters. (Illus.). 176p. (YA). (gr. 10-13). 1995. 39.95 (*0-88740-936-9*) Schiffer.
Pinsky, Michael R. Applied Bedside Cardiovascular Physiology. LC 96-53123. (Update in Intensive Care & Emergency Medicine Ser.). 1997. pap. 133.00 (*3-540-62411-2*) Spr-Verlag.
***Pinsky, Michael R., et al, eds.** Coronary Circulation & Myocardial Ischemia. LC 00-21646. (Update in Intensive Care & Emergency Medicine Ser.). (Illus.). 190p. 2000. 109.00 (*3-540-62584-4*) Spr-Verlag.
Pinsky, Michael R., et al, eds. The Pulmonary Circulation: Moving from Passive to Active Control. (Illus.). 275p. 1996. text 78.95 (*0-7020-2201-2*, Pub. by W B Saunders) Saunders.
Pinsky, Michael R. & Dhainaut, Jean-Francois A. Pathophysiologic Foundations of Critical Care. LC 92-15867. (Illus.). 1008p. 1993. 125.00 (*0-683-06888-1*) Lppncott W & W.
Pinsky, Robert. An Explanation of America. LC 79-83974. (Contemporary Poets Ser.). 80p. 1979. pap. 9.95 (*0-691-01360-8*, Pub. by Princeton U Pr) Cal Prin Full Svc.

P

An Asterisk (*) at the beginning of an entry indicates that the title is appearing for the first time.

— The Figured Wheel: New & Collected Poems, 1966-1996. LC 95-47617. 300p. 1996. text 30.00 (0-374-15493-7) FS&G.
— The Figured Wheel: New & Collected Poems, 1966-1996. 320p. 1997. pap. text 15.00 (0-374-52506-4, Noonday) FS&G.
— History of My Heart. LC 99-178792. 64p. 1998. pap. 12.00 (0-374-52530-7) FS&G.
— History of My Heart. (American Poetry Ser.: Vol. 30). 51p. 1985. pap. 7.50 (0-88001-048-7) HarpC.
— The Inferno of Dante. LC 93-40169. (Illus.). 355p. 1996. pap. 8.00 (0-374-52452-1, Noonday) FS&G.
Pinsky, Robert. Inferno of Dante - Reader's Guide. 1997. pap. write for info. (0-374-94113-0) FS&G.
— Jersey Rain. LC 99-44209. 80p. 2000. 21.00 (0-374-17887-9) FS&G.
Pinsky, Robert. Poetry And The World. 11th ed. LC 88-4411. 1992. pap. 10.95 (0-88001-217-X) HarpC.
— Poetry of the World. 256p. (C). 2000. pap. 10.95 (0-88001-216-1) HarpC.
— Sadness & Happiness: Poems. LC 75-3486. (Contemporary Poets Ser.). 740p. 1975. pap. 9.95 (0-691-01322-5, 358, Pub. by Princeton U Pr) Cal Prin Full Svc.
— The Situation of Poetry: Contemporary Poetry & Its Traditions. LC 76-3015. (Essays in Literature Ser.). 200p. 1976. pap. 14.95 (0-691-01352-7, Pub. by Princeton U Pr) Cal Prin Full Svc.
— The Sounds of Poetry: A Brief Guide. LC 98-18873. 129p. 1998. 16.00 (0-374-26695-6) FS&G.
***Pinsky, Robert.** The Sounds of Poetry: A Brief Guide. 144p. 1999. pap. 11.00 (0-374-52617-6) FS&G.
Pinsky, Robert. The Want Bone. 1991. pap. 12.00 (0-88001-251-X) HarpC.
Pinsky, Robert, ed. The Handbook of Heartbreak: 101 Poems of Lost Love & Sorrow. LC 98-34190. 176p. 1998. 18.00 (0-688-16286-X, Wm Morrow) Morrow Avon.
Pinsky, Robert & Dietz, Maggie, eds. America's Favorite Poems: 200 Poems from the Favorite Poem Project with Comments by the Pople Who Chose Them. LC 99-31979. 288p. 1999. text 25.00 (0-393-04820-9) Norton.
Pinsky, Robert, tr. see Alighieri, Dante.
Pinsky, Robert, tr. see Dante Alighieri.
Pinsky, Ross G. Positive Harmonic Functions & Diffusion. (Studies in Advanced Mathematics: No. 45). 490p. (C). 1995. text 80.00 (0-521-47014-5) Cambridge U Pr.
Pinsky, Susan, jt. auth. see Starkman, David.
Pinsky, William, jt. ed. see Ransom, Scott B.
***Pinsler, Jeffrey.** Civil Practice in Singapore & Malaysia LC 98-474029. 1998. write for info. (0-409-99998-9) Buttrwrth-Heinemann.
Pinsler, Jeffrey. Civil Practice in Singapore & Malaysia, 2 vols. rev. ed. LC 98-474029. 1996. ring bd. write for info. (0-409-99759-5, MICHIE) LEXIS Pub.
Pinsof, William M. Integrative Problem-Centered Therapy: A Synthesis of Biological, Individual & Family Therapies. (Illus.). 304p. 1995. 37.00 (0-465-03328-8, Pub. by Basic) HarpC.
Pinsof, William M., jt. ed. see Greenberg, Leslie S.
Pinson, jt. auth. see Bangs.
Pinson, jt. auth. see Brooks.
Pinson, Arie. Heart Cell in Culture, Vol. I. 208p. 1987. 117.00 (0-8493-4697-5, CRC Reprint) Franklin.
— Heart Cell in Culture, Vol. II. 184p. 1987. 105.00 (0-8493-4698-3, CRC Reprint) Franklin.
— Heart Cell in Culture, Vol. III. 160p. 1987. 93.00 (0-8493-4699-1, CRC Reprint) Franklin.
Pinson, Arie, ed. The Heart Cell in Culture, 3 vols., Set. 1987. 393.00 (0-8493-4696-7, QP114) CRC Pr.
Pinson, Dar. Sticks 'n' Bones 'n' Chewing Gum: Creating Gifts from Finder's Art. 43p. 1993. spiral bd. 14.95 (1-886724-00-8) Pinson Pr.
Pinson, DovBer. Inner Rhythms: The Kabbalah of Music. LC 99-25253. 232 p. 2000. 25.00 (0-7657-6098-3) Aronson.
— Reincarnation & Judaism: The Journey of the Soul. LC 98-42260. 216p. 1999. 30.00 (0-7657-6064-9) Aronson.
Pinson, G. S., et al. The Decortication of Tropical Oilseeds & Edible Nuts. 1991. pap. 25.00 (0-85954-290-4, Pub. by Nat Res Inst) St Mut.
Pinson, Hermine. ASHE. limited ed. Whitebird, J., ed. (New Texas Poetry Sampler Ser.). 28p. (Orig.). 1992. pap. 10.00 (0-930324-23-4) Wings Pr.
— Mama Yetta & Other Poems. viii, 54p. 1999. pap. 12.00 (0-930324-39-0) Wings Pr.
Pinson, James L., jt. auth. see Brooks, Brian S.
Pinson, Koppel S. Modern Germany: Its History & Civilization. 2nd ed. (Illus.). 682p. (C). 1989. reprint ed. pap. text 29.95 (0-88133-434-0) Waveland Pr.
Pinson, Koppel S., tr. see Lichtenberger, Henri.
Pinson, Lewis, jt. auth. see Wiener, Richard.
Pinson, Lewis J. Electro-Optics. LC 85-5397. 282p. 1985. text 56.95 (0-471-88142-2) Krieger.
Pinson, Lewis J., jt. auth. see Wiener, Richard S.
Pinson, Lewis J., ed. see Wiener, Richard S.
Pinson, Linda. Anatomia De un Plan De Negocio. 1997. pap. text 19.95 (0-944205-30-5) Out Your Mind.
— Anatomy of a Business Plan: A Step-by-Step Guide to Starting Smart, Building the Business & Securing your Companies Future. 4th ed. LC 99-26126. 272p. 1999. pap. 21.95 (1-57410-127-7) Dearborn.
***Pinson, Linda.** Keeping the Books. 5th ed. 2000. pap. 22.95 (1-57410-140-4) Dearborn.
Pinson, Linda & Jinnett, Jerry. Business Plans for Small Companies: UK & European Edition. 260p. 1998. pap. 80.00 (0-85297-484-1, Pub. by Chartered Bank) St Mut.
— Keeping the Books: Basic Recordkeeping & Accounting for the Small Business. 4th ed. LC 97-52382. 224p. 1998. pap. text 22.95 (1-57410-107-2) Dearborn.
— Steps to Small Business Start-Up. 4th ed. LC 99-42096. 256p. 2000. pap. 22.95 (1-57410-132-3, 61003604) Dearborn.
— 20 Pasos para Desarrollar Tu Negocio.Tr. of Steps to Small Business Start Up. (SPA.). 320p. 1998. pap. text 19.95 (0-7931-2905-2) Dearborn.
Pinson, Linda & Jinnett, Jerry A. Keeping the Books: Basic Recordkeeping & Accounting for the Small Business. 2nd rev. ed. 208p. 1993. pap. 19.95 (0-936894-47-4) Dearborn.
— Keeping the Books: Basic Recordkeeping & Accounting for the Small Business. 3rd ed. 208p. 1996. pap. 22.95 (1-57410-028-9, 6100-3202) Dearborn.
— Steps to Small Business Start-Up: Everything You Need to Know to Turn Your Ideas into... 2nd ed. 256p. 1996. pap. 22.95 (1-57410-038-6, 61003602) Dearborn.
— Target Marketing for the Small Business: Researching, Reaching & Retaining Your Target Market. LC 93-9086. 176p. 1993. pap. 19.95 (0-936894-51-2, 6100-3701) Dearborn.
— Target Marketing for the Small Business: Researching, Reaching & Retaining Your Target Market. 2nd ed. 176p. 1996. pap. 22.95 (1-57410-027-0, 6100-3702) Dearborn.
Pinson, Mark, ed. The Muslims of Bosnia - Herzegovina: Their Historic Development from the Middle Ages to the Dissolution of Yugoslavia. rev. ed. (C). 1996. reprint ed. pap. 14.95 (0-932885-12-8) Harvard CMES.
Pinson, Mary E. You're an Orphan, Molly Brown. 128p. (J). (gr. 5-7). 1998. pap. 8.95 (1-57168-263-5, Eakin Pr) Sunbelt Media.
Pinson, Peter. Emanuel Raft: Painting-Jewellery-Sculpture-Printmaking. LC 97-183464. (Illus.). 176p. 1997. text 65.00 (90-5703-521-9) Gordon & Breach.
— Rod Milgate. LC 96-147633. (Illus.). 168p. 1996. text 45.00 (976-641-065-8, ECU58, Harwood Acad Pubs) Gordon & Breach.
***Pinson, Richard D.** Self Health: The Perfect Health Plan. LC 99-96631. (Illus.). X,335p. 1999. 19.95 (0-9671059-1-9) Well Being.
Pinson, Richard D. Self Health: The Perfect Health Plan. limited ed. LC 99-93863. (Illus.). vi, 322p. 1999. pap. 19.95 (0-9671059-0-0) Well Being.
Pinson, Rosemary & Pinson, Tony. Travel Organizer & Journal, Vol. 1. (Illus.). 140p. 1998. mass mkt. write for info. (0-9667918-0-0) ROAM-TO.
Pinson, Stephen, contrib. by. Prints of the Fort Worth Circle, 1940-1960. (Illus.). 45p. 1992. pap. 10.00 (0-935213-22-8) J S Blanton Mus.
Pinson, Tony, jt. auth. see Pinson, Rosemary.
Pinson, William W. In White & Black: A Story. LC 72-1560. (Black Heritage Library Collection). 1977. reprint ed. 32.95 (0-8369-9047-1) Ayer.
Pinsonneault, Susan, ed. see Carella, C. J.
Pinsonneault, Susan, ed. see Dale, Malcolm & Thomas, Klaude.
Pinsonneault, Susan, ed. see Hite, Kenneth, et al.
Pinsonneault, Susan, ed. see Masters, Phil.
Pinsonneault, Susan, ed. see Maykrantz, Scott Paul.
Pinsonneault, Susan, ed. see Pulver, David.
Pinsonneault, Susan, ed. see Thibault, Daniel U. & Ross, S. John.
Pinstrup-Andersen, Per. Macroeconomic Policy Reforms, Poverty, & Nutrition: Analytical Methodologies. (Monographs). (C). 1990. pap. text 12.00 (1-56401-003-1) Cornell Food.
Pinstrup-Andersen, Per, ed. The Political Economy of Food & Nutrition Policies. LC 92-25287. (International Food Policy Research Institute Ser.). 352p. 1993. text 38.50 (0-8018-4480-0) Johns Hopkins.
Pinstrup-Anderson, Per. Agricultural Research & Technology in Economic Development. LC 81-14297. (Illus.). 304p. (C). 1982. text 39.95 (0-582-46048-4) Longman.
Pinstrup-Anderson, Per, ed. Food Subsidies in Developing Countries: Costs, Benefits & Policy Options. LC 88-1709. 416p. 1988. text 39.50 (0-8018-3632-8) Johns Hopkins.
Pint, Ellen M. & Schmidt, Rachel. Financial Condition of U. S. Military Aircraft Prime Contractors. LC 93-42657. 1994. pap. text 9.00 (0-8330-1494-3, MR-372-AF) Rand Corp.
Pint, Ellen M., et al. Strategic Sourcing: Theory & Evidence from Economics & Business Management. LC 97-29454. (Project Air Force Ser.). (Illus.). 86p. 1997. pap. 13.00 (0-8330-2533-3, MR-865-AF) Rand Corp.
***Pintabona, Don, et al.** The Tribeca Grill Cookbook. LC 00-26931. (Illus.). 208p. 2000. 35.00 (0-375-50435-4) Villard Books.
Pintarich, Paul. Boys up North: Dick Erath & the Early Oregon Winemakers. 1998. pap. text 14.95 (0-9656082-6-3) Wyatt Grp.
— History by the Glass: Portland's Past & Present Saloons, Bars & Taverns. (Illus.). 128p. (Orig.). 1996. pap. 12.95 (0-9643408-2-8) Bianco Pub.
Pintaud, Jean-Christophe, jt. auth. see Hodel, Donald R.
Pintauro, Joe. Beside Herself. 1990. pap. 6.95 (0-88145-084-7) Broadway Play.
— Raft of the Medusa. 1992. pap. 5.25 (0-8222-1314-1) Dramatists Play.
— Reindeer Soup. 1996. pap. 5.25 (0-8222-1533-0) Dramatists Play.
— Snow Orchid. LC 97-162423. 1997. pap. 5.25 (0-8222-1546-2) Dramatists Play.
Pintauro, Joe & Matthiessen, Peter. Men's Lives. 1994. pap. 5.25 (0-8222-1381-8) Dramatists Play.
Pintauro, Joseph. Cacciatore: Three Short Plays. 1980. pap. 5.25 (0-8222-0172-0) Dramatists Play.
— Metropolitan Operas by Joe Pintauro: 27 Short Plays. LC 97-162422. 1996. pap. 9.75 (0-8222-1508-X) Dramatists Play.
Pintauro, Joseph, et al. By the Sea By the Sea By the Beautiful Sea. 1997. pap. 5.25 (0-8222-1507-1) Dramatists Play.
Pintchman, Tracy. The Rise of the Goddess in the Hindu Tradition. LC 93-40617. (FRE.). 288p. (C). 1994. pap. text 21.95 (0-7914-2112-0) State U NY Pr.
Pintchovski, F. S., jt. ed. see Cale, T. S.
Pintel, Gerald, jt. auth. see Diamond, Jay.
Pintelon, R., jt. auth. see Schoukens, J.
Pintens, Walter, ed. Family & Succession Law. (International Encyclopaedia of Laws Ser.). 1997. spiral bd. 270.00 (90-6544-888-8) Kluwer Academic.
Pinter, C. C. A Book of Abstract Algebra. 2nd ed. 384p. (C). 1989. 69.69 (0-07-050138-6) McGraw.
Pinter, H. African Grey Parrots As a Hobby. (Illus.). 96p. 1994. pap. 8.95 (0-7938-0093-5, TT036) TFH Pubns.
Pinter, Harold. Ashes to Ashes. LC 97-1598. 96p. (Orig.). 1997. pap. 12.00 (0-8021-3510-2, Grove) Grove-Atltic.
— Betrayal. 1980. pap. 3.25 (0-8222-0109-7) Dramatists Play.
— Betrayal. LC 78-65251. 144p. 1988. pap. 11.00 (0-8021-3080-1, Grove) Grove-Atltic.
— The Birthday Party & the Room. LC 61-11770. (Illus.). 128p. 1989. pap. 10.00 (0-8021-5114-0, Grove) Grove-Atltic.
— The Caretaker. 1962. pap. 5.25 (0-8222-0184-4) Dramatists Play.
— The Caretaker & the Dumbwaiter. LC 61-10903. (Illus.). 128p. 1991. pap. 11.00 (0-8021-5087-X, Grove) Grove-Atltic.
***Pinter, Harold.** Celebration & the Room. LC 99-87478. 176p. 2000. pap. 13.00 (0-8021-3708-3, Pub. by Grove-Atltic) Publishers Group.
Pinter, Harold. Collected Poems & Prose. LC 95-35957. 112p. 1995. pap. 11.00 (0-8021-3434-3, Grove) Grove-Atltic.
— Complete Works, Vol. 1. LC 90-13933. 256p. 1990. pap. 12.00 (0-8021-5096-9, Grove) Grove-Atltic.
— Complete Works, Vol. 2. LC 90-13933. 256p. 1990. pap. 13.00 (0-8021-3237-5, Grove) Grove-Atltic.
— Complete Works, Vol. 3. LC 90-13933. 256p. 1990. pap. 12.00 (0-8021-5049-7, Grove) Grove-Atltic.
— The Dwarfs. LC 90-44459. 192p. 1991. pap. 11.95 (0-8021-3266-9, Grove) Grove-Atltic.
— Dwarfs & Eight Review Sketches. 1965. pap. 5.25 (0-8222-0344-8) Dramatists Play.
***Pinter, Harold.** Dwarfs & Nine Revue Sketches. 1999. pap. 5.95 (0-8222-1733-3) Dramatists Play.
Pinter, Harold. The Homecoming. LC 66-28734. 96p. 1989. pap. 10.00 (0-8021-5105-1, Grove) Grove-Atltic.
— The Hothouse. 1980. pap. 5.25 (0-8222-0535-1) Dramatists Play.
— The Hothouse. 160p. 1999. reprint ed. pap. 12.00 (0-8021-3643-5, Grove) Grove-Atltic.
— I Know the Place. (C). 1990. 150.00 (0-906887-02-X, Pub. by Greville Pr) St Mut.
— The Lover. 1965. pap. 3.25 (0-8222-0704-4) Dramatists Play.
— Moonlight. 1995. pap. 5.25 (0-8222-1481-4) Dramatists Play.
— Moonlight: A Play. LC 94-76461. 112p. 1994. pap. 12.00 (0-8021-3393-2, Grove) Grove-Atltic.
— Mountain Language. 1988. pap. 5.25 (0-8222-0777-X) Dramatists Play.
— Mountain Language. LC 88-35782. 48p. 1989. pap. 7.95 (0-8021-3168-9, Grove) Grove-Atltic.
— The New World Order: Manuscript Edition. 1992. pap. 2.50 (0-8222-1449-0) Dramatists Play.
— No Man's Land. LC 75-13555. 96p. 1975. pap. 9.95 (0-8021-5187-6, Grove) Grove-Atltic.
— Old Times. LC 72-182581. 80p. 1989. pap. 7.95 (0-8021-5029-2, Grove) Grove-Atltic.
— One for the Road: A Play. LC 86-4662. (Illus.). 80p. 1986. pap. 7.95 (0-8021-5188-4, Grove) Grove-Atltic.
— Other Places: Three Plays; A Kind of Alaska; Victoria Station; Family Voices. LC 82-24185. 96p. 1983. pap. 6.95 (0-8021-5189-2, Grove) Grove-Atltic.
— Other Places: Three Short Plays. 1984. pap. 5.25 (0-8222-0866-0) Dramatists Play.
— Party Time & the New World Order. LC 93-28859. 80p. 1993. pap. 11.00 (0-8021-3352-5, Grove) Grove-Atltic.
— Tea Party & The Basement: Two Plays. 1969. pap. 5.25 (0-8222-1115-7) Dramatists Play.
— Three Plays. Incl. Collection. 1962. pap. Dwarfs. 1962. Slight Ache. 1962. pap. 1962. Set pap. 4.95 (0-394-17240-X, E350) Grove-Atltic.
— Various Voices: Prose, Poetry, Politics, 1948-1998. LC 98-53371. 224p. 1999. 23.00 (0-8021-1643-4, Grove) Grove-Atltic.
Pinter, Harold, et al, eds. 99 Poems in Translation. 160p. 1997. reprint ed. pap. 11.00 (0-8021-3489-0, Grove) Grove-Atltic.
Pinter, Harold, et al, selected by. One Hundred Poems by One Hundred Poets. LC 87-206. 192p. 1995. pap. 12.00 (0-8021-3279-0, Grove) Grove-Atltic.
***Pinter, Harold, et al.** The Proust Screenplay: A la Recherche du Temps Perdu. 192p. 1999. pap. 14.00 (0-8021-3646-X, Grove) Grove-Atltic.
Pinter, Harold, ed. see Ali, Tariq.
Pinter, Helmut. Amazon Parrots in Your Home. (Illus.). 160p. 1988. lib. bdg. 17.95 (0-86622-901-9, TS-115) TFH Pubns.
— Labyrinth Fish. (Illus.). 176p. 1986. 18.95 (0-8120-5635-3) Barron.
— The Proper Care of Cockatoos. (TW Ser.). (Illus.). 256p. 1993. text 16.95 (0-86622-387-8, TW-126) TFH Pubns.
Pinter, Istvan. Hungarian Anti-Fascism & Resistance, 1941-1945. 234p. (C). 1986. 60.00 (963-05-4025-8, Pub. by Akade Kiado) St Mut.
Pinter, Janos D. Global Optimization in Action: Continuous & Lipschitz Optimization: Algorithms, Implementations & Applications. LC 95-35543. (Nonconvex Optimization & Its Applications Ser.: No. 6). 508p. (C). 1995. text 217.50 (0-7923-3757-3) Kluwer Academic.
Pinter-Lucke, Claudia & Shabell, Barbara. Preparation for Calculus. 196p. (C). 1996. pap. text, per. 23.95 (0-7872-2699-8) Kendall-Hunt.
Pinter, Neil. The Eternal Question...Does God Exist? New Powerful Evidence - Scientific, Historical, Mathematical. LC 91-67660. (Illus.). 246p. (Orig.). 1994. pap. 12.95 (0-9633317-2-8) Westhaven Pub.
Pinter, Nicholas, jt. auth. see Keller, Edward A.
Pinter, Robert B. & Nabet, Bahram. Nonlinear Vision. 576p. 1992. 99.95 (0-8493-4292-9, QP475) CRC Pr.
Pinter, Robert B., jt. auth. see Nabet, Bahram.
***Pinter, Ron Y., et al, eds.** Next Generation Information Technologies & Systems: 4th International Workshop, NGITS'99, Zikhron-Yaakov, Israel, July 5-7, 1999, Proceedings. LC 99-33674. (Lecture Notes in Computer Science Ser.: Vol. 1649). ix, 327p. 1999. pap. 56.00 (3-540-66225-1) Spr-Verlag.
Pinter, Tamas & Kaiser, Anna. The Churches of Budapest. (Pocket Guide Ser.). 140p. 1990. pap. 21.00 (963-13-3825-8, Pub. by Corvina Bks) St Mut.
Pinthus, Kurt, ed. Menschheitsdammerung: Dawn of Humanity. Ratych, Joanna M. et al, trs. LC 93-2165. (GERM Ser.). 410p. 1994. 90.00 (1-879751-48-8) Camden Hse.
Pinti, Daniel J., ed. Writing after Chaucer: Essential Readings in Chaucer & the Fifteenth Century. LC 97-38558. (Basic Readings in Chaucer & His Time Ser.: Vol. 1). 293p. 1998. reprint ed. text 70.00 (0-8153-2651-3, H2040) Garland.
Pintner, Walter. The Future of Russia in Historical Perspective. (CIR Working PaperS: No. 9). 1995. pap. 15.00 (0-86682-100-7) Ctr Intl Relations.
***Pinto.** Chosen. 1999. write for info. (0-8125-7931-3) Tor Bks.
***Pinto, Antonio Costa.** The Blue Shirts: Portuguese Fascism in Interwar Europe. 320p. 2000. text 34.50 (0-88033-982-9) Col U Pr.
Pinto, Arthur R. & Branson, Douglas M. Understanding Corporate Law. LC 99-19941. (Casebook Skills Ser.). 1999. 30.00 (0-8205-3098-0) Bender.
Pinto, Arthur R. & Visentini, Gustavo, eds. The Legal Basis of Corporate Governance in Publicly Held Corporations: A Comparative Approach. LC 98-309995. (Studies in Comparative Corporate & Financial Law). 328p. 1998. 116.00 (90-411-9663-3) Kluwer Academic.
Pinto, Brian, jt. auth. see Glen, Jack D.
Pinto, Celsa. Trade & Finance in Portuguese India. (C). 1994. text 40.00 (81-7022-507-8, Pub. by Concept) S Asia.
Pinto, Constancio & Jardine, Matthew. East Timor's Unfinished Struggle: Inside the Timorese Resistance. LC 96-40951. (Illus.). 289p. 1997. 40.00 (0-89608-542-2); pap. 16.00 (0-89608-541-4) South End Pr.
Pinto-Correia, Clara. Ovary of Eve: Egg & Sperm & Preformation. LC 97-14011. 396p. 1997. 29.95 (0-226-66952-1) U Ch Pr.
***Pinto-Correia, Clara.** Return of the Crazy Bird: How the Dodo Manages to Never Really Die. 228p. 1999. 28.00 (0-387-98876-9) Spr-Verlag.
Pinto da Cunha, A., ed. Scale Effects in Rock Masses: Proceedings of the First International Workshop, Loen, 7 - 8 June 1990. (Illus.). 352p. (C). 1990. text 105.00 (90-6191-126-5, Pub. by A A Balkema) Ashgate Pub Co.
Pinto de Matos, Maria A. Chinese Export Porcelain: From the Museum of Anastacio Goncalves Lisbon. (Illus.). 288p. 1996. 90.00 (0-85667-448-6, Pub. by P Wilson) Scala Books.
Pinto, Desiderio. Piri Muridi Relationship: Study of the Nizamuddin Dargah. (C). 1995. 38.00 (81-7304-111-3, Pub. by Manohar) S Asia.
Pinto-Duschinsky, Michael. British Political Finance, Eighteen Thirty to Nineteen Eighty. LC 81-7963. (AEI Studies: No. 330). (Illus.). 368p. reprint ed. pap. 114.10 (0-8357-4441-8, 203727500008) Bks Demand.
Pinto, E., jt. ed. see Seco, Pedro S.
Pinto, Fernao Mendes. The Travels of Mendes Pinto. Catz, Rebecca D., ed. & tr. by. LC 88-39778. (Illus.). 752p. 1989. 60.00 (0-226-66951-3) U Ch Pr.
Pinto-Ferreira, Carlos, jt. ed. see Mamede, Nuno J.
***Pinto, Gabrielle & Feldman, Murray.** Homeopathy for Children: A Parent's Guide to the Treatment of Common Childhood Illnesses. 2000. pap. 19.95 (0-85207-337-2, Pub. by C W Daniel) Natl Bk Netwk.
***Pinto, George Frederick.** George Frederick Pinto: Three Sonatas for Pianoforte with Violin. Perry, Linda W., ed. (Recent Researches in Music of the 19th & Early 20th Centuries Ser.: No. RRN27). (Illus.). xiii, 108p. 1999. pap. 45.00 (0-89579-430-6) A-R Eds.
Pinto, James V., jt. auth. see Eggert, James.
Pinto, Jeffrey K. Power & Politics in Project Management. (Illus.). 160p. (Orig.). 1996. pap. 32.95 (1-880410-43-5) Proj Mgmt Inst.
Pinto, Jeffrey K., ed. The Project Management Institute Project Management Handbook. LC 98-12381. (Business & Management Ser.). 544p. 1998. 74.95 (0-7879-4013-5) Jossey-Bass.
Pinto, Jeffrey K. & Kharbanda, O. P. Successful Project Managers: Leading Your Team to Success. 421p. 1995. pap. 49.95 (0-471-29403-9) Wiley.
Pinto, Jeffrey K. & Kharbanda, O. P. What Made Gertie Gallop. (Industrial Engineering Ser.). 336p. 1996. text 36.95 (0-442-02158-5, VNR) Wiley.
***Pinto, Jeffrey K. & Millet, Ido.** Successful Information System Implementation: The Human Side. 2nd ed. LC 99-38110. 300p. 1999. pap. 32.95 (1-880410-66-4) Proj Mgmt Inst.

P

An Asterisk (*) at the beginning of an entry indicates that the title is appearing for the first time.

Pinto, Jeffrey K. & Trailer, Jeffrey W., eds. Essentials of Project Control. LC 99-41753. (Editors' Choice Ser.). (Illus.). 165p. 1999. pap. 32.95 (*1-880410-64-8*) Proj Mgmt Inst.

— Leadership Skills for Project Managers. LC 98-12191. (Editor's Choice Ser.: No. 1). (Illus.). 131p. 1998. pap. 32.95 (*1-880410-49-4*) Proj Mgmt Inst.

Pinto, Jeffrey K., et al. Project Leadership: From Theory to Practice. 300p. 1998. pap. 39.95 (*1-880410-10-9*) Proj Mgmt Inst.

Pinto, Jeffrey K., jt. auth. see Kharbanda, O. P.

Pinto, Jeffrey K., jt. auth. see Obermeyer, Nancy J.

Pinto, John. John Pinto's Little Green Book of Ophthalmology: Strategies, Tips & Pearls to Help You Grow & Manage a Practice of Distinction. 138p. 1997. pap. write for info. (*1-929196-05-9*) Am Opthlmc Admin.

Pinto, John A., jt. auth. see Kieven, Elisabeth.

Pinto, John A., jt. auth. see MacDonald, William L.

Pinto, John B. Marketing an Orthopedic Practice. 160p. (Orig.). 1991. pap. 19.95 (*1-879952-02-5*) Inst Spine.

***Pinto, John Brigham & Walker, Allan.** Ten Eyecare Practices: Benchmark for Success. 98p. 1998. pap. write for info. (*1-929196-06-7*) Am Opthlmc Admin.

Pinto, John D. Behavior & Taxonomy of the Epicauta Maculata Group (Coleoptera, Meloidae) LC 79-27381. (University of California Publications in Social Welfare: No. 89). (Illus.). 117p. reprint ed. pap. 36.30 (*0-8357-7107-5*, 203158400075) Bks Demand.

— The Taxonomy of North American Epicauta: Coleoptera: Meloidae: With a Revision of the Nominate Subgenus & a Survey of Courtship Behavior. (Publications in Entomology: Vol. 110). 448p. (C). 1991. pap. 55.00 (*0-520-09764-5*, Pub. by U CA Pr) Cal Prin Full Svc.

Pinto, Julio C. The Reading of Time: A Semantic-Semiotic Approach. (Approaches to Semiotics Ser.: No. 82). x, 162p. (C). 1989. lib. bdg. 79.25 (*0-89925-354-7*) Mouton.

Pinto, Lawrence, jt. auth. see Wood, Eugene.

***Pinto, Lina K.** The Angel & the Detective. 150p. 1999. pap. 10.00 (*0-9676613-0-7*) Big Purr Pr.

Pinto-Lopez, J. Polyporaceae, Contribuicao Rara a Sua Bio-Taxonomia (Broteriana 8) (Illus.). 1968. reprint ed. pap. 48.00 (*3-7682-0555-X*) Lubrecht & Cramer.

Pinto, Macia, jt. auth. see Villanueva, Paulina.

Pinto, Magdalena G., ed. Historias Intimas: Conversaciones con diez Escritoras Latinoamericans. (SPA.). 286p. 1988. pap. 17.00 (*0-910061-35-1*) Ediciones Norte.

Pinto, Magdalena G., tr. see Garcia Pinto, Magdalena.

Pinto, Magdalena Garcia, see Garcia Pinto, Magdalena.

Pinto, Maria & Llanos, Hector. Las Industrias Liticas de San Agustin. (Illus.). 130p. 1997. pap. 9.50 (*1-877812-56-0*) UPLAAP.

Pinto, Matthew J. Did Adam & Eve Have Belly Buttons? And 199 Other Questions from Catholic Teenagers. 272p. (YA). 1998. pap. 11.99 (*0-9659228-0-4*) Ascensn Pr.

Pinto, O. Scenas Infantis: Memories of Childhood: Five Pieces for the Piano. 16p. 1986. pap. 7.95 (*0-7935-0585-2*, 50327100) H Leonard.

Pinto, P. S. Seco e, see Seco e Pinto, P. S., ed.

Pinto, Patrick R. & Walker, James W. A Study of Professional Training & Development Roles & Competencies. 124p. pap. 9.00 (*0-318-13285-0*, PWBCP) Am Soc Train & Devel.

Pinto, Pedro S. Seco e, see Seco e Pinto, Pedro S., ed.

***Pinto, Ricardo.** The Chosen. 2001. pap. 14.95 (*0-312-87566-5*) St Martin.

— The Chosen: Book One of the Stone Dance of the Chameleon Trilogy. LC 99-88106. Vol. 1. 512p. 2000. 24.95 (*0-312-87208-9*, Pub. by Tor Bks) St Martin.

— Standing Dead. 2000. pap. write for info. (*0-312-87565-7*) St Martin.

— Stone Dance of the Chameleon 2. 2001. text. write for info. (*0-312-87209-7*) St Martin.

Pinto, Ricardo R. Estate Action Initiative: A Study of Council Housing Renewal, Management & Effectiveness. 304p. 1993. 72.95 (*1-85628-358-5*, Pub. by Avebry) Ashgate Pub Co.

Pinto, Ricardo R., ed. Developments in Housing Management & Ownership. LC 94-43135. 1995. text 79.95 (*0-7190-3713-1*, Pub. by Manchester Univ Pr) St Martin.

Pinto, Robert. Basic Estate Planning. (Illus.). 200p. 1992. pap. 35.00 (*0-685-14622-7*) NJ Inst CLE.

Pinto, Robert C., jt. ed. see Hansen, Hans V.

Pinto, Roger. Aspects de l'Evolution Gouvernementale de l'Indochine Francaise. LC 77-179234. reprint ed. 34.50 (*0-404-54861-X*) AMS Pr.

Pinto, Rogerio F. Projectizing the Governance Approach to Civil Service Reform: An Environmental Assessment for Preparing a Sectoral Adjustment Loan in the Gambia. LC 94-28328. (World Discussion Papers Africa Technical Department: 252). 120p. 1994. pap. 22.00 (*0-8213-2966-9*) World Bank.

Pinto, Rogerio F. & Mrope, Angelous J. Assessing Sector Institutions: Lessons of Experience from Zambia's Education Sector, Vol. 297. LC 95-36808. (World Bank Discussion Papers). 152p. 1995. pap. 22.00 (*0-8213-3430-1*) World Bank.

Pinto, Santan. Discernment in Your Life. 96p. pap. 10.00 (*1-888080-00-0*) ABCD Prnting.

— Discipleship: Your Way of Life. 66p. 1995. pap. 10.00 (*1-888080-01-9*) ABCD Prnting.

— Prayer in Your Life. 63p. 1995. pap. 10.00 (*1-888080-02-7*) ABCD Prnting.

Pinto, Sousa, jt. auth. see Hoskins.

Pinto, Vivian De Sola. Rochester: Portrait of a Restoration Poet. LC 73-175707. (Select Bibliographies Reprint Ser.). 1977. reprint ed. 23.95 (*0-8369-6622-8*) Ayer.

Pinto, Vivian de Sola. Sir Charles Sedley, 1639-1701: A Study in the Life & Literature of the Restoration. LC 76-85904. reprint ed. 49.50 (*0-404-05056-5*) AMS Pr.

Pinto, Vivian De Sola, ed. The Divine Vision. LC 68-24905. (Studies in Blake: No. 3). 1973. reprint ed. lib. bdg. 75.00 (*0-8383-0790-6*) M S G Haskell Hse.

— English Biography in the Seventeenth Century. LC 72-101833. (Biography Index Reprint Ser.). 1977. 23.95 (*0-8369-8007-7*) Ayer.

Pinto, Vivian De Sola, see De Sola Pinto, Vivian.

Pintoff, Ernest. Animation 101. LC 98-11981. 1999. 16.95 (*0-941188-68-X*) M Wiese.

— The Complete Guide to American Film Schools & Cinema & Television Courses. LC 93-30073. 624p. 1994. pap. 17.95 (*0-14-017226-2*, Penguin Bks) Viking Penguin.

— Directing 101. LC 97-51540. 216p. 1999. 16.95 (*0-941188-67-1*) M Wiese.

Pinton, Giorgio A., tr. see Vico, Giambattista.

Pintor, C., ed. see New, Maria I.

Pintor Genaro, Mercedes. Eduardo Mallea, Novelista. LC 76-6545. (Coleccion Mente y Palabra). (SPA.). 277p. 1976. 5.00 (*0-8477-0524-2*); pap. text 4.00 (*0-8477-0525-0*) U of PR Pr.

Pintozzi, Colleen, jt. auth. see Pintozzi, Frank.

Pintozzi, Frank & Pintozzi, Colleen. Passing the Florida High School Competency Test. (Illus.). 200p. (Orig.). (YA). (gr. 11-12). 1996. pap. text 15.00 (*0-89892-141-4*) Contemp Pub Co of Raleigh.

— Passing the Georgia High School Graduation Test. (Illus.). 260p. (Orig.). (YA). (gr. 11-12). 1995. pap. text, student ed. 15.00 (*0-89892-130-9*) Contemp Pub Co of Raleigh.

Pintozzi, Frank & Valeri-Gold, Maria. Taking Charge of Your Reading. LC 99-52260. 414p. (C). 2000. pap. text 44.00 (*0-321-01209-7*) Longman.

Pintozzi, Frank, et al. Passing the College Placement Examination. 2nd ed. 262p. (C). 1990. pap. text 29.95 (*0-89892-086-8*) Contemp Pub Co of Raleigh.

Pintrich, Paul R., ed. Current Issues in Research on Self-Regulated Learning: A Discussion with Commentaries. 58p. 1995. pap. 20.00 (*0-8058-9931-6*) L Erlbaum Assocs.

Pintrich, Paul R., et al, eds. Student Motivation, Cognition, & Learning: Essays in Honor of Wilbert J. McKeachie. 400p. 1994. text 79.95 (*0-8058-1376-4*) L Erlbaum Assocs.

Pintrich, Paul R. & Schunk, Dale H. Motivation in Education. 434p. 1995. pap. text, student ed. 48.00 (*0-02-395621-6*, Macmillan Coll) P-H.

Pintrich, Paul R., jt. ed. see Maehr, Martin L.

Pintur, David A. Finite Element Beginnings. 200p. 1994. 109.00 (*0-8176-3752-4*) Birkhauser.

— Finite Element Beginnings. (Illus.). 200p. 1994. 49.50 (*0-8176-3751-6*) Birkhauser.

Pintus, Lorraine. Diapers, Pacifiers, & Other Holy Things. 192p. 1996. 9.99 (*0-7814-0246-8*) Lion USA.

Pintus, Lorraine, jt. auth. see Dillow, Linda.

Pintz, William S. Ok Tedi: Evolution of a Third World Mining Project. 206p. 1984. 34.00 (*0-685-50784-X*) EW Ctr HI.

Pintzuk, Edward C. Reds, Racial Justice, & Civil Liberties: Michigan Communists During the Cold War. LC 97-34855. 232p. 1997. 39.95 (*0-930656-70-9*); pap. 14.95 (*0-930656-71-7*) MEP Pubns.

Pintzuk, Susan. Phrase Structures in Competition: Variation & Change in Old English Word Order. LC 98-51954. (Outstanding Dissertations in Linguistics Ser.). 285p. 1999. 63.00 (*0-8153-3269-6*) Garland.

Pinus, A. G. Boolean Constructions in Universal Algebras. LC 92-44823. (Mathematics & Its Applications Ser.: Vol. 242). 1993. text 214.50 (*0-7923-2117-0*) Kluwer Academic.

Pinus, Lee. The Songwriters' Success Manual. 2nd ed. LC 78-60263. 1978. pap. 9.95 (*0-918318-02-5*) Music Pr.

Pinxten, Rik. When the Day Breaks: Essays in Anthropology & Philosophy. LC 98-5436. 226p. (C). 1997. pap. text 40.95 (*0-8204-3514-7*) P Lang Pubng.

Pinxten, Rik, ed. Universalism Versus Relativism in Language & Thought: Proceedings of a Colloquium on the Sapir-Whorf Hypothesis. (Contributions to the Sociology of Language Ser.: No. 11). 1977. text 63.10 (*90-279-7791-7*) Mouton.

Pinxten, Rik, et al. Anthropology of Space: Explorations into the Natural Philosophy & Semantics of the Navajo. LC 82-23703. 252p. reprint ed. pap. 78.20 (*0-7837-3005-5*, 204293600006) Bks Demand.

Pinxten, Rik, jt. ed. see Callebaut, Werner.

Pinyan, Pamela, jt. auth. see Friendlander, Eva.

Pinyopusarerk, K. Styrax Tonkinensis: Taxonomy, Ecology, Silviculture & Uses. 1994. pap. 51.00 (*1-86320-130-0*, Pub. by ACIAR) St Mut.

***Pinz, Shelley.** Echoes of Angels. (Illus.). 2000. pap. write for info. (*0-9700251-2-2*) S Pinz Music.

Pinza, Ezio & Magidoff, Robert. Ezio Pinza: An Autobiography. Farkas, Andrew, ed. LC 76-29962. (Opera Biographies Ser.). (Illus.). 1977. reprint ed. lib. bdg. 30.95 (*0-405-09702-6*) Ayer.

Pinzer, Maimie. The Maimie Papers: Letters from an Ex-Prostitute. Davidson, Sue & Rosen, Ruth C., eds. LC 77-21693. 528p. 1997. pap. text 19.95 (*1-55861-143-6*) Feminist Pr.

Pinzke. Foundations of Earth Science. 1996. pap. text, student ed. 30.20 (*0-13-229733-7*) P-H.

Pinzon, Diego R., et al. La Dimension Internacional de los Derechos Humanos: Guia para la Aplicacion de Normas Internacionales en el Derecho Interno. (SPA.). 620p. 1999. pap. text 24.95 (*1-886938-57-1*) IADB.

Pinzon, Eduardo. En Nombre de Dios Pedimos Posada: Nueve Noches de Esperanza Antes de Navidad. LC 95-76473. (SPA.). 128p. (Orig.). 1995. pap. 6.95 (*0-89243-643-3*) Liguori Pubns.

Pinzon, Renee, jt. auth. see Pinzon, Scott.

Pinzon, Scott. Splendini of the Apes. 208p. 1984. pap. 5.95 (*0-310-45611-8*, 18356P) Zondervan.

Pinzon, Scott & Pinzon, Renee. Knights of Evermore. 201p. 1994. pap. 5.99 (*0-934998-56-6*) Evangel Indiana.

***Pinzon-Umana, Eduardo.** En Nombre de Dios Pedimos Posada: Nueve Noches de Esperanza Antes de Navidad. (SPA., Illus.). 48p. 1999. pap. 1.95 (*0-7648-0403-0*, Libros Liguori) Liguori Pubns.

Pio, Damasco. Encuentros Con Angeles. (SPA.). 1997. pap. text 7.98 (*968-403-856-9*) Selector.

Pio, Padre. The Agony of Jesus. 40p. 1992. pap. 2.00 (*0-89555-097-0*) TAN Bks Pubs.

— Meditation Prayer on Mary Immaculate. (Illus.). 28p. 1992. pap. 1.50 (*0-89555-099-7*) TAN Bks Pubs.

***Piola, Giorgio.** Formula 1 '99 Technical Analysis. (Illus.). 96p. 2000. 29.95 (*88-7911-216-3*, 130635AE, Pub. by Giorgio Nada Editore) Motorbooks Intl.

Pioli, Richard. Stung by Salt & War: Creative Texts of the Italian Avant-Gardist F.T. Marinetti. (Reading Plus Ser.: Vol. 2). VIII, 187p. (C). 1987. text 31.50 (*0-8204-0381-4*) P Lang Pubng.

Piombino, Nick. Boundary of Blur. LC 92-63355. (Roof Bks.: No. 6). 122p. (Orig.). 1993. pap. 13.95 (*0-937804-50-9*) Segue NYC.

— Poems. 88p. (Orig.). 1988. pap. 8.95 (*1-55713-011-6*) Sun & Moon CA.

— Theoretical Objects. (Green Integer Bks.: No. 34). 176p. 1999. pap. text 10.95 (*1-892295-23-7*, Pub. by Green Integer) Consort Bk Sales.

Piomelli, Daniele. Arachidonic Acid in Cell Signaling. LC 96-35506. (Molecular Biology Intelligence Unit Ser.). 189p. 1996. 99.00 (*1-57059-394-9*) Landes Bioscience.

Piomelli, U., jt. ed. see Ragab, S. A.

Pion, jt. auth. see Kittleson.

Pion-Berlin, David. Through Corridors of Power: Institutions & Civil-Military Relations in Argentina. LC 96-48046. 1997. 45.00 (*0-271-01705-8*) Pa St U Pr.

— Through Corridors of Power: Institutions & Civil-Military Relations In Argentina. LC 96-48046. 1997. pap. 17.95 (*0-271-01706-6*) Pa St U Pr.

Pion, Paul, jt. auth. see Spadafori, Gina.

Pioneer. Frederick Banting. (J). 1995. lib. bdg. 13.95 (*0-8050-2335-6*) H Holt & Co.

Pioneer Historical Society Staff. Telfair County, Georgia. (Illus.). 574p. 1988. 70.00 (*0-88107-114-5*) Curtis Media.

Pioneer Institute for Public Policy Research Staff. Bay State Auto Rates: What Are the Driving Forces?: Edited Remarks. (Dialogue Ser.: No. 2). 25p. (Orig.). 1990. pap. 5.00 (*0-929930-04-5*) Pioneer Inst.

***Pioneer Museum Staff.** Ambush, Arson & Murder on the Nacimiento. Blythe, Hy & Root, Elizabeth, eds. LC 99-41829. (Illus.). 1999. pap. 14.95 (*1-929117-00-0*) BlueOak.

Pioneer Press, ed. see Daniel, Larry J. & Gunter, Riley W.

Pioneer Press Staff, ed. see Reese, Michael, II.

Pioneer Press Staff, ed. see Schreier, Konrad F., Jr.

Pioneers Club of Birmingham Staff. Early Days in Birmingham. 1968. 5.95 (*0-87651-006-3*); pap. 9.95 (*0-87651-007-1*) Southern U Pr.

Pionke, Harry B., jt. ed. see Krueger, Charles R.

Piontac, Nechemiah. The Arizal: The Life & Times of Rabbi Yitzchak Luria. Weinbach, Shaindel, tr. from HEB. (ArtScroll Youth Ser.). (Illus.). 288p. (J). (gr. 5-12). 1988. 12.95 (*0-89906-835-9*); pap. 9.95 (*0-89906-836-7*) Mesorah Pubns.

Piontek, Heinz. Alive or Dead. Exner, Richard, tr. from GER. LC 72-77917. (German Ser.: Vol. 4). 64p. 1975. pap. 10.00 (*0-87775-089-0*) Unicorn Pr.

— Selected Poems. Osers, Ewald, tr. from GER. LC 93-71942. 80p. 1994. pap. 14.95 (*1-85610-033-2*, Pub. by Forest Bks) Dufour.

Piontek, Sherry, jt. auth. see Garlock, Kristen L.

***Piontek, Slawomir.** Der Mythos Von Der Osterreichischen Identitat: Uberlegungen Zu Aspekten Der Wirklichkeitsmythisierung In Romanen Von Albert Paris Gutersloh, Heimito Von Doderer Und Herbert Eisenreich. 250p. 1999. 45.95 (*3-631-33437-0*) P Lang Pubng.

Piontelli, Alessandra. From Fetus to Child: An Observational & Psychoanalytic Study. LC 91-5236. (New Library of Psychoanalysis). 320p. (C). 1992. pap. 29.99 (*0-415-07437-1*, A7373, Pub. by Tavistock) Routldge.

Piore, Emanuel. Science & Academic Life in Transition. 96p. (C). 1990. 29.95 (*0-88738-337-8*) Transaction Pubs.

Piore, Michael J. Beyond Individualism. LC 94-34909. 223p. 1995. 22.95 (*0-674-06897-1*, PIOBEY) HUP.

— Birds of Passage: Migrant Labor & Industrial Societies. LC 78-12067. 239p. reprint ed. pap. 68.20 (*0-8357-7272-1*, 2024518) Bks Demand.

Piore, Michael J. Unemployment & Inflation: Institutional & Structuralist Views: A Reader in Labor Economics. LC 79-55274. 300p. (gr. 13). 1980. pap. text 32.95 (*0-87332-165-0*) M E Sharpe.

Piore, Michael J. & Sabel, Charles F. The Second Industrial Divide: Possibilities for Prosperity. LC 83-46080. 366p. 1986. pap. 22.00 (*0-465-07561-4*, Pub. by Basic) HarpC.

Piore, Michael J., jt. auth. see Berger, Suzanne.

Piore, Michael J., jt. auth. see Doeringer, Peter B.

Piore, Nancy K. Lightning: The Poetry of Rene Char. LC 80-22001. (Illus.). 153p. 1981. text 30.00 (*0-930350-08-1*) NE U Pr.

Pioro, I. L., et al. Industrial Two-Phase Thermosyphons & Their Industrial Applications. LC 96-39875. 300p. 1996. 97.50 (*1-56700-064-9*) Begell Hse.

Pioro, I. L., jt. auth. see Pioro, L. S.

Pioro, L. S. & Pioro, I. L. Two-Phase Industrial Thermosyphons. 200p. 1991. 75.00 (*0-89116-765-X*) CRC Pr.

***Piostone, Joseph D.** Donnie Brasco: Mobbed Up. 2000. mass mkt. 6.99 (*0-451-40910-8*, Onyx) NAL.

Piot, Charles. Remotely Global: Village Modernity in West Africa. LC 99-11071. 184p. 1999. pap. text 15.00 (*0-226-66969-6*) U Ch Pr.

***Piot, Charles.** Remotely Global: Village Modernity in West Africa. LC 99-11071. 184p. 1999. lib. bdg. 28.00 (*0-226-66968-8*) U Ch Pr.

***Piot, Joseph L.** Concentric Circles. LC 99-91018. 1999. 25.00 (*0-7388-0584-X*); pap. 18.00 (*0-7388-0585-8*) Xlibris Corp.

Piot, M., jt. auth. see Flahault, D.

Piot, P., et al. AIDS in Africa: A Manual for Physicians. (ENG & FRE., Illus.). viii, 125p. 1992. pap. text 16.00 (*92-4-154435-X*, 1150381) World Health.

***Piotet, Denis.** Droit Cantonal Complementaire. LC 99-206659. (Traite de Droit Prive Suisse Ser.). xxii, 494 p. 1998. write for info. (*2-8271-0813-5*, Pub. by Ed Univ Fri) Eisenbrauns.

Piotet, Francoise. Policies on Health & Safety in 13 Countries of the European Union Vol. II: The European Situation. 102p. 1996. pap. 18.00 (*92-827-6642-X*, SY94-96-938-ENC, Pub. by Comm Europ Commun) Bernan Associates.

Piotrkowski, Chaya S. Work & the Family System: A Naturalistic Study of Working-Class & Lower-Middle-Class Families. LC 79-7478. (Illus.). 1979. 19.95 (*0-02-925340-3*) Free Pr.

Piotrovsky, Boris B. Hermitage. (Illus.). 391p. (C). 1989. text 400.00 (*0-569-09215-9*, Pub. by Collets) St Mut.

Piotrovsky, Boris B., et al. Scythian Art. (Illus.). 312p. 1990. text 50.00 (*0-7148-2442-9*) Phaidon Pr.

***Piotrovsky, Mikhail.** Earthly Beauty, Heavenly Art: Art of Islam. (Illus.). 312p. 2000. 50.00 (*0-85331-806-9*, Pub. by Lund Humphries) Antique Collect.

Piotrovsky, Mikhail B. Treasures of the Hermitage. LC 96-13374. (Tiny Folio Ser.). (Illus.). 288p. 1996. pap. 11.95 (*0-7892-0104-6*) Abbeville Pr.

Piotrovsky, Mikhail B., intro. Great Art Treasures of the Hermitage Museum, St. Petersburg, 2 vols. LC 94-8939. (Illus.). 1520p. 1994. 195.00 (*0-8109-3428-0*, Pub. by Abrams) Time Warner.

Piotrovsky, T. Scythian Art. (C). 1990. 250.00 (*0-7855-4483-6*, Pub. by Collets) St Mut.

Piotrow, Phyllis T. World Population: The Present & Future Crisis. LC 80-69582. (Headline Ser.: No. 251). (Illus.). 80p. (Orig.). (C). 1980. pap. 5.95 (*0-87124-064-5*) Foreign Policy.

Piotrow, Phyllis T., et al. Family Planning Communication: State of the Art. LC 94-78725. 175p. 1995. write for info. (*1-885960-00-X*) JHU Sch Hygiene.

— Health Communication: Lessons from Family Planning & Reproductive Health. LC 97-19235. 328p. 1997. 62.95 (*0-275-95577-X*, Praeger Pubs); pap. 25.95 (*0-275-95578-8*, Praeger Pubs) Greenwood.

Piotrowki, Tadeusz & Saloni, Zygmunt. Nowy Slownik Angielsko-Polsk & Polsko-Angielski. 688p. 1995. pap. 24.00 (*0-614-25053-6*) Szwede Slavic.

Piotrowska, Irena G. Art of Poland. LC 75-179736. (Biography Index Reprint Ser.). 1977. reprint ed. 38.95 (*0-8369-8104-9*) Ayer.

Piotrowska, Maria. Learning Translation--Learning the Impossible? A Course of Translation from English into Polish LC 97-193576. (ENG & POL.). 125p. 1997. write for info. (*83-7052-965-8*, Pub. by Universitas) IBD Ltd.

Piotrowska, Maria, tr. see Bigon, Maria, et al.

Piotrowski, Christine M. Interior Design Management: A Handbook for Owners & Managers. 352p. 1992. text 54.95 (*0-442-00760-4*, VNR) Wiley.

Piotrowski, Christine M. Interior Design Management Han. 360p. 1992. 54.95 (*0-471-28431-9*, VNR) Wiley.

Piotrowski, Christine M. Professional Practice for Interior Design. 2nd ed. (Illus.). 448p. 1994. text 52.95 (*0-442-01684-0*, VNR) Wiley.

— Professional Practice for Interior Designers. 2nd ed. (Interior Design Ser.). 448p. 1994. 64.95 (*0-471-28597-8*, VNR) Wiley.

Piotrowski, Christine M. & Rogers, Elizabeth A. Designing Commercial Interiors. LC 98-29967. 344p. 1998. 59.95 (*0-471-17103-4*) Wiley.

Piotrowski, Harry, jt. auth. see McWilliams, Wayne C.

Piotrowski, John. Shaft Alignment Handbook. 2nd ed, (Mechanical Engineering Ser.: Vol. 98). (Illus.). 592p. 1995. text 99.75 (*0-8247-9666-7*) Dekker.

Piotrowski, Judith. Coordinating Art Across the Primary School. LC 98-231807. (Subject Leaders Handbks.). 10p. 1998. pap. 23.95 (*0-7507-0695-3*, Falmer Pr) Taylor & Francis.

— Expressive Arts in the Primary School. (Special Needs in the Primary School Ser.). (Illus.). 128p. 1996. 70.00 (*0-304-33418-9*); pap. 25.95 (*0-304-33419-7*) Continuum.

***Piotrowski, Karen A.** Maternity Nursing. 5th ed. (Illus.). 224p. 1998. student ed. write for info. (*0-323-00216-1*) Mosby Inc.

Piotrowski, Karen A., jt. auth. see Rollant, Paulette D.

Piotrowski, Maryann V. Effective Business Writing: Strategies, Suggestions & Examples, a Guide for Those Who Write on the Job. 2nd rev. ed. LC 95-46256. 160p. 1996. pap. 12.00 (*0-06-273381-8*) HarpC.

Piotrowski, R. G., et al. Oil & Gas Developments in Pennsylvania in 1978. (Progress Reports: No. 192). (Illus.). 61p. 1984. reprint ed. pap. 3.45 (*0-8182-0040-5*) Commonweal PA.

Piotrowski, Remigiusz & Pan Instytut Geografii Staff, contrib. by. Atlas Rzeczycospolitej Polskiej - Atlas of the Republic of Poland, 2 pts. (Illus.). 1996. ring bd. 185.00 (*83-86339-00-4*) Szwede Slavic.

Piotrowski, Roman. Cartels & Trusts: Their Origin & Historical Development, from the Economic & Legal Aspects. LC 78-14461. 376p. 1978. reprint ed. lib. bdg. 45.00 (*0-87991-951-5*) Porcupine Pr.

An Asterisk (*) at the beginning of an entry indicates that the title is appearing for the first time.

Piotrowski, Susan, jt. auth. see Capel, Susan Anne.
Piotrowski, Tadeusz. Poland's Holocaust: Ethnic Strife, Collaboration with Occupying Forces & Genocide in the Second Republic, 1918-1947. LC 97-26233. (Illus.). 451p. 1997. boxed set 55.00 (*0-7864-0371-3*) McFarland & Co.
— Polish/English-English/Polish Dictionary. (ENG & POL.). 790p. 1997. 49.95 (*0-7859-9645-1*) Fr & Eur.
— Vengeance of the Swallows: Memoir of a Polish Family's Ordeal under Soviet Aggression, Ukrainian Ethnic Cleansing & Nazi Enslavement, & Their Emigration to America. LC 94-24862. (Illus.). 229p. 1995. lib. bdg. 29.95 (*0-7864-0001-3*) McFarland & Co.
***Piotrowski, Tadeusz, ed.** Genocide & Rescue in Wolyn: Recollections of the Ukrainian Nationalist Ethnic Cleansing Campaign Against the Poles During World War II. LC 99-88668. (Illus.). 331p. 2000. 45.00 (*0-7864-0773-5*) McFarland & Co.
Piotrowski, Z. A. Perceptanalysis. 523p. 1957. text 49.95 (*0-8058-0102-2*) L Erlbaum Assocs.
Piotrowski, Zygmunt a. & Biele, Albert M. Dreams: A Key to Self-Knowledge. 200p. 1986. text 39.95 (*0-89859-691-2*) L Erlbaum Assocs.
Piott, Steven L. The Anti-Monopoly Persuasion: Popular Resistance to the Rise of Big Business in the Midwest, 60. LC 84-15964. (Contributions in Economics & Economic History Ser.: No. 60). 194p. 1985. 49.95 (*0-313-24545-2*, PAN/) Greenwood.
— Holy Joe: Joseph W. Folk & the Missouri Idea. LC 97-18907. (Biography Ser.). (Illus.). 224p. 1997. 34.95 (*0-8262-1130-5*) U of Mo Pr.
Piotti, Vittorio, jt. auth. see Pugh, Harry F.
Pioud, G., jt. auth. see Lofmarker, R.
Pious, ed. The Harper Collins Annual: American Politics. 2nd ed. (C). 1998. text. write for info. (*0-321-01007-8*) Addson-Wesley Educ.
Pious, Richard M. Crisis of Authority. 1996. 25.00 (*0-02-924995-3*) Free Pr.
— Crisis of Authority. 2002. 25.00 (*0-684-82808-1*) Free Pr.
Pious, Richard M. The Presidency. LC 95-12298. 464p. (C). 1995. pap. text 44.00 (*0-02-395792-1*, Macmillan Coll) P-H.
Pious, Richard M. The Presidency, Incl. Test Bank. (C). 1997. pap., teacher ed. write for info. (*0-205-26702-5*, T6702-9) Allyn.
— Young Oxford Companion to Governments of the World: A Student Companion, 2 vols., Set. LC 95-36684. (Illus.). 848p. (J). (gr. 5-8). 1998. 130.00 (*0-19-508486-1*) OUP.
— The Young Oxford Companion to the Presidency of the United States. LC 93-19908. (Illus.). 304p. (YA). (gr. 7 up). 1994. text 40.00 (*0-19-507799-7*) OUP.
***Pious, Richard M. & Ritchie, Donald A.** The Oxford Guide to the United States Government. Patrick, John J., ed. 640p. 2001. 35.00 (*0-19-514273-X*) OUP.
Pious, Richard M., et al. The Young Oxford Companion to the U. S. Government, 3 vols., Set. (Illus.). 912p. (YA). (gr. 7 up). 1995. lib. bdg. 120.00 (*0-19-509737-8*) OUP.
Piovano, Barbara. Parallel Psychotherapy with Children & Parents. LC 97-18427. 240p. 1998. 45.00 (*0-7657-0126-X*) Aronson.
Piovesana, Gino K. Recent Japanese Philosophical Thought, 1862-1994: A Survey. 3rd rev. ed. (Japan Library). 320p. (C). 1997. text 49.00 (*1-873410-65-4*, Pub. by Curzon Pr Ltd) UH Pr.
Piozzi, Hester Lynch. Anecdotes of Samuel Johnson. Roberts, S. C., ed. LC 75-99668. (Select Bibliographies Reprint Ser.). 1980. 25.48 (*0-8369-5097-6*) Ayer.
— Anecdotes of the Late Samuel Johnson. (BCL1-PR English Literature Ser.). 205p. 1992. reprint ed. lib. bdg. 79.00 (*0-7812-7367-6*) Rprt Serv.
— Anecdotes of the Late Samuel Johnson, L.D: During the Last Twenty Years of His Life. Roberts, S. C., ed. LC 70-95109. 205p. 1971. reprint ed. lib. bdg. 59.50 (*0-8371-3138-3*, PIAN, Greenwood Pr) Greenwood.
— Autobiography, Letters, & Literary Remains of Mrs. Piozzi (Thrale), 2 vols. LC 70-178349. reprint ed. 115.00 (*0-404-56776-2*) AMS Pr.
— French Journals of Mrs. Thrale & Doctor Johnson. LC 72-1263. (English Literature Ser.: No. 33). 274p. 1972. reprint ed. lib. bdg. 75.00 (*0-8383-1430-9*) M S G Haskell Hse.
— The Piozzi Letters: Correspondence of Hester Lynch Piozzi, 1784-1821 (Formerly Mrs. Thrale), Vol. 2: 1792-1798. Bloom, Edward A. & Bloom, Lillian D., eds. LC 87-40231. (Illus.). 592p. 1991. 75.00 (*0-87413-360-2*) U Delaware Pr.
— The Piozzi Letters Vol. 5, 1811-1816: Correspondence of Hester Lynch Piozzi, 1784-1821 (Formerly Mrs. Thrale) Bloom, Edward A. et al, eds. LC 87-40231. (Illus.). 608p. 1999. 69.50 (*0-87413-394-7*) U Delaware Pr.
Pip, Eva. A Bird Must Fly. LC 96-61940. 400p. (Orig.). 1997. pap. 9.95 (*1-883893-98-4*) WinePress Pub.
Pipa, Arshi. Albanian Stalinism: Ideo-Political Aspects. (East European Monographs: No. 287). 240p. 1990. text 46.50 (*0-88033-184-4*, Pub. by East Eur Monographs) Col U Pr.
— Contemporary Albanian Literature. 224p. 1991. text 42.00 (*0-88033-202-6*, Pub. by East Eur Monographs) Col U Pr.
— Montale & Dante. LC 68-31650. (Minnesota Monographs in the Humanities: Vol. 4). 227p. reprint ed. pap. 70.40 (*0-608-15975-1*, 203328300084) Bks Demand.
— The Politics of Language in Socialist Albania. 283p. 1989. text 61.00 (*0-88033-168-2*, Pub. by East Eur Monographs) Col U Pr.
Pipa, Jo. Lord's Day. 1996. pap. 9.99 (*1-85792-201-8*, Pub. by Christian Focus) Spring Arbor Dist.
Pipa, Joseph A. Leader's Guide for T. Norton Sterrett's "How to Understand Your Bible" A Teaching Manual for Use in Adult Study Groups. (Orig.). 1977. pap. 3.95 (*0-934688-06-0*) Great Comm Pubns.
— The Root & Branch. 140p. Date not set. pap. write for info. (*1-871676-16-9*, Pub. by Christian Focus) Spring Arbor Dist.
Piparo, C. A. Brett Favre: Quarterback Dreams. (All-Star Bks.). (Illus.). 32p. (J). (ps-3). 1998. pap. 3.95 (*1-58260-000-7*) Infnty Plus One.
***Piparo, C. A.** Mark McGuire: Home Run King. (All-Star Bks.). (Illus.). 32p. (J). (ps-3). 1999. pap. 3.95 (*1-58260-017-1*, Pub. by Infnty Plus One) Assoc Pubs Grp.
Piparo, C. A. Reggie White: Minister of Defense. (All-Star Bks.). 32p. (J). (gr. k-3). 1998. pap. 3.95 (*1-58260-001-5*) Infnty Plus One.
***Piparo, C. A.** Sammy Sosa: Slammin' Sammy. (All-Star Bks.). (Illus.). 32p. (J). (gr. k-3). 1999. pap. 3.95 (*1-58260-018-X*, Pub. by Infnty Plus One) Assoc Pubs Grp.
Pipe, David & Rapley, Linda. Ocular Anatomy & Histology. (C). 1989. 130.00 (*0-900099-19-4*, Pub. by Assn Brit Dispen Opticians) St Mut.
Pipe, G. Russell, ed. The ISDN Workshop: INTUG Proceedings. 123p. 1985. pap. write for info. (*0-89006-183-1*) Artech Hse.
Pipe, G. Russell, et al, eds. Assessing Data Privacy in the 1990's & Beyond. (CSIS International Communications Reports). 45p. 1997. pap. 18.95 (*0-89206-343-2*) CSIS.
Pipe, Jim. Aliens. (Illus.). 40p. (J). (gr. 4-6). 1995. lib. bdg. 23.90 (*0-7613-0540-8*, Copper Beech Bks) Millbrook Pr.
— Aliens. (Illus.). 40p. (J). (gr. 4-6). 1996. pap. 6.95 (*0-7613-0515-7*, Copper Beech Bks) Millbrook Pr.
Pipe, Jim. Aliens. LC 96-24574. (J). 1996. 12.15 (*0-606-08977-2*, Pub. by Turtleback) Demco.
Pipe, Jim. Bugs & Creepy Crawlies. LC 97-51776. (Giant Book of... Ser.). (Illus.). 32p. (J). (gr. 2 up). 1998. lib. bdg. 24.90 (*0-7613-0716-8*, Copper Beech Bks) Millbrook Pr.
— Bugs & Creepy Crawlies. LC 97-51776. (Giant Book of... Ser.). (Illus.). 32p. (YA). 1998. 17.95 (*0-7613-0648-X*, Copper Beech Bks) Millbrook Pr.
— Creatures of the Night. LC 98-21355. (Giant Book of... Ser.). (Illus.). 32p. (J). (gr. 2 up). 1998. 17.95 (*0-7613-0777-X*, Copper Beech Bks); lib. bdg. 25.90 (*0-7613-0858-X*, Copper Beech Bks) Millbrook Pr.
— Dracula. LC 95-13148. (In the Footsteps of...Ser.). (Illus.). 40p. (J). (gr. 4-6). 1995. lib. bdg. 21.90 (*1-56294-646-3*, Copper Beech Bks) Millbrook Pr.
— Dracula. LC 95-13148. (In the Footsteps Of--Ser.). 1995. 12.15 (*0-606-09460-1*, Pub. by Turtleback) Demco.
***Pipe, Jim.** The Jungle. LC 98-53240. (Giant Book of... Ser.). (Illus.). 32p. (J). 1999. 17.95 (*0-7613-0792-3*, Copper Beech Bks) Millbrook Pr.
Pipe, Jim. The Jungle. LC 98-53240. (Giant Book of . . . Ser.). (Illus.). 32p. (YA). (gr. 2 up). 1999. lib. bdg. 25.90 (*0-7613-0907-1*, Copper Beech Bks) Millbrook Pr.
— Medieval Castle. LC 96-12638. (Mystery History Ser.). (Illus.). 32p. (J). (gr. 4-6). 1996. 9.95 (*0-7613-0501-7*, Copper Beech Bks); lib. bdg. 23.90 (*0-7613-0495-9*, Copper Beech Bks) Millbrook Pr.
— Pharaoh's Tomb. LC 96-50172. (Mystery History Ser.). (Illus.). 32p. (YA). (gr. 3 up). 1997. lib. bdg. 23.90 (*0-7613-0600-5*, Copper Beech Bks) Millbrook Pr.
— Pharaoh's Tomb. LC 96-50172. (Mystery History Ser.). (Illus.). 32p. (J). (gr. 3 up). 1997. 9.95 (*0-7613-0591-2*, Copper Beech Bks) Millbrook Pr.
***Pipe, Jim.** Read about Ancient Greece. (Read about Ser.). (Illus.). 32p. (J). (gr. 2-4). 2000. 17.90 (*0-7613-1169-6*, Copper Beech Bks) Millbrook Pr.
— Sharks & Other Scary Predators. LC 98-49738. (Giant Book of... Ser.). (Illus.). 32p. 1999. 17.95 (*0-7613-0793-1*, Copper Beech Bks) Millbrook Pr.
Pipe, Jim. Sharks & Other Scary Predators. LC 98-49738. (Giant Book of... Ser.). (Illus.). 32p. (YA). (gr. 2 up). 1999. lib. bdg. 25.90 (*0-7613-0908-X*, Copper Beech Bks) Millbrook Pr.
— Snakes & Slithery Creatures. LC 97-51780. (Giant Book of... Ser.). (Illus.). 32p. (J). (gr. 3-5). 1998. 17.95 (*0-7613-0729-X*, Copper Beech Bks); lib. bdg. 25.90 (*0-7613-0804-0*, Copper Beech Bks) Millbrook Pr.
— T. Rex & Deadly Dinosaurs. LC 98-21353. (Giant Book of... Ser.). (Illus.). 32p. (J). (gr. 2 up). 1998. 17.95 (*0-7613-0776-1*, Copper Beech Bks); lib. bdg. 25.90 (*0-7613-0857-1*, Copper Beech Bks) Millbrook Pr.
— Trojan Horse. LC 97-10021. (Illus.). (J). (gr. 3-5). 1997. 9.95 (*0-7613-0626-9*, Copper Beech Bks) Millbrook Pr.
— Trojan Horse. LC 97-10021. (Mystery History of a--Ser.). (Illus.). 32p. (J). (gr. 4-6). 1997. lib. bdg. 23.90 (*0-7613-0614-5*, Copper Beech Bks) Millbrook Pr.
— The Werewolf. (In the Footsteps of... Ser.). (Illus.). 40p. (J). (gr. 4-6). 1996. lib. bdg. 21.90 (*0-7613-0450-9*, Copper Beech Bks) Millbrook Pr.
— The Werewolf. LC 95-39830. (In the Footsteps Of--Ser.). 1996. 12.15 (*0-606-09463-6*, Pub. by Turtleback) Demco.
— Witches. LC 97-7460. (Illus.). 40p. (J). (gr. 4-6). 1997. lib. bdg. 22.40 (*0-7613-0607-2*, Copper Beech Bks) Millbrook Pr.
Pipe, John H., jt. auth. see Revoir, Trudie W.
Pipe, M. E. & Seymour, Fred. Psychology & Family Law: A New Zealand Perspective. LC 98-168648. 176p. 1997. pap. 39.95 (*1-877133-22-1*, Pub. by Univ Otago Pr) Intl Spec Bk.
Pipe, Peter, jt. auth. see Mager, Robert F.
Pipe, Rhona. One Christmas Night. Smith, Julie, ed. (Illus.). 24p. (J). (ps-3). 1994. 4.99 (*0-7814-1511-X*, Chariot Bks); 4.99 (*0-7814-1510-1*, Chariot Bks) Chariot Victor.
***Pipe, Rhona.** Where Is Noah? (Illus.). (J). 1998. 7.99 (*1-85608-171-0*) Hunt GBR.
Pipe, Rhona & Round, Graham. The Big Book of Bible People. LC 96-394. (Illus.). 64p. (J). (gr. k-4). 1996. 9.99 (*0-7852-7893-1*) Tommy Nelson.
Pipeline Supervisory & Control Systems Workshop St. Pipeline Supervisory & Control Systems Workshop: Presented at the 5th Annual Energy-Sources Technology Conference, New Orleans, Louisiana, March 8-10, 1982. Seiders, E. J., ed. LC 82-70514. 96p. reprint ed. pap. 30.00 (*0-8357-8750-8*, 203365300087) Bks Demand.
Piper. Fishing in New Mexico. LC 88-33746. (Coyote Bks.). (Illus.). 298p. 1989. pap. 14.95 (*0-8263-1138-5*) U of NM Pr.
— Stories from Ugidali: Cherokee Story Teller. 1981. pap. 3.95 (*0-89992-078-0*) Coun India Ed.
Piper, et al. Personal Shorthand for the Executive Secretary: Syllabus. 211p. 1977. pap. text 14.95 (*0-89420-030-5*, 217150) Natl Book.
— Waste Reduction: Policy & Practice. 1990. pap. 39.95 (*1-55840-272-1*) Exec Ent Pubns.
Piper & Marbury Law Firm Staff. Maryland Environmental Law Handbook. 3rd rev. ed. LC 98-170180. (State Environmental Law Ser.). 258p. 1997. pap. text 89.00 (*0-86587-555-3*) Gov Insts.
Piper & Marbury Law Firm Staff, jt. auth. see Waste Management, Inc. Staff.
Piper, A. J., jt. auth. see Ker, Neil R.
Piper, A. J., ed. see Beadle, Richard.
Piper, A. J., ed. see Offler, H. S.
Piper, Adrian. Out of Order, Out of Sight, 2 vols. Incl. Vol. 1. Selected Writings in Meta-Art 1968-1992. LC 95-24490. (Illus.). 320p. 1996. 50.00 (*0-262-16155-9*); Vol. 2. Selected Writings in Art Criticism 1967-1992. (Illus.). 320p. 1996. 50.00 (*0-262-16156-7*); 1996. 90.00 (*0-262-16163-X*) MIT Pr.
— Out of Order, Out of Sight: Selected Writings, Vol. 1. (Illus.). 1999. pap. text 25.00 (*0-262-66152-7*) MIT Pr.
— Out of Order, Out of Sight: Selected Writings, Vol. 2. (Illus.). 1999. pap. text 25.00 (*0-262-66153-5*) MIT Pr.
— Out of Order, Out of Sight: Selected Writings, Vols. 1 & 2. (Illus.). 1999. pap. text 45.00 (*0-262-66154-3*) MIT Pr.
Piper, B. Diet & Nutrition: A Guide for Students & Practitioners. (Illus.). 438p. (Orig.). (C). 1996. pap. text 39.95 (*1-56593-424-5*, 1091) Singular Publishing.
Piper, Beverly. Quick & Easy Healthy Cookery. (Illus.). 136p. (Orig.). 1993. pap. 9.95 (*0-563-36339-8*, BBC-Parkwest) Parkwest Pubns.
Piper, Boni & Balswick, Judith K. Then They Leave Home: Parenting after the Kids Grow Up. LC 97-12915. 204p. 1997. pap. 10.99 (*0-8308-1964-9*, 1964) InterVarsity.
Piper, Boni, jt. auth. see Balswick, Judith.
Piper, Buddy, jt. auth. see Darnell, Jeanie.
Piper, Christina. The Unheard Music: Photographs, 1991-1997. Maryansky, Glenn & Brownell, Sara, eds. (Illus.). 160p. (Orig.). 1997. pap. 9.00 (*0-9657534-0-9*) P A Kane.
Piper, Christine & Sclater, Shelley D. Undercurrents of Divorce. LC 98-74640. (Socio-Legal Studies). 7p. 1999. text 70.95 (*1-84014-733-4*) Ashgate Pub Co.
Piper, Christine, jt. auth. see King, Michael.
***Piper, Colin.** Rhyme & Reason. 1999. pap. write for info. (*1-58235-331-X*) Watermrk Pr.
Piper, D., jt. auth. see Powell, L.
Piper, D. Z., jt. ed. see Bischoff, J. L.
Piper, David. The Companion Guide to London. 7th rev. ed. LC 92-52545. (Illus.). 528p. 1996. pap. 24.95 (*1-900639-06-8*) Boydell & Brewer.
— The English Face. Rogers, Malcolm, ed. (Illus.). 272p. 1992. 85.00 (*1-85514-008-X*, Pub. by Natl Port Gall); pap. 49.50 (*1-85514-009-8*, Pub. by Natl Port Gall) Antique Collect.
— Language Theories & Educational Practice. LC 92-28795. 472p. 1992. 109.95 (*0-7734-9864-8*) E Mellen.
Piper, David, intro. Michael Ayrton: Exhibition Catalogue. (Illus.). 16p. 1973. pap. 1.00 (*0-911209-01-8*) Palmer Mus Art.
Piper, David, ed. see Meredith, Fred.
Piper, David N. Is Higher Education Fair? SRHE Annual Conference Papers, 1981. 194p. 1981. 38.00 (*0-900868-82-1*) OpUniv Pr.
Piper, David W. Are Professors Professional? The Organisation of University Examinations. LC 93-38452. (Higher Education Policy Ser.: No. 25). 252p. 1994. 59.95 (*1-85302-540-2*) Taylor & Francis.
Piper, David W., jt. ed. see Acker, Sandra.
Piper, Dean J. Is He Coming Soon? A Reader's Guide to the Book of Revelation. LC 98-44911. 102p. 1999. pap. 9.95 (*0-7880-1336-X*) CSS OH.
Piper, Deb. Jake's the Name: Sixth Grade's the Game. (Orig.). (J). (gr. 3-6). 1996. pap. 9.99 (*0-88092-135-8*) Royal Fireworks.
Piper Deschenes, Elizabeth, et al. Chronic Juvenile Offenders: Final Results from the Skillman Aftercare Experiment. LC 93-40155. 1993. pap. text 13.00 (*0-8330-1477-3*, MR-220-SKF) Rand Corp.
Piper, Don C. The International Law of the Great Lakes: A Study of Canadian-United States Co-operation. LC 66-29860. (Duke University, Commonwealth-Studies Center, Publication Ser.: No. 30). 179p. reprint ed. pap. 55.50 (*0-608-11976-8*, 202343400033) Bks Demand.
Piper, Don C. & Terchek, Ronald J., eds. Interaction: Foreign Policy & Public Policy. LC 83-8810. (AEI Studies: No. 381). (Illus.). 255p. pap. 79.10 (*0-8357-4493-0*, 203734600008) Bks Demand.
Piper, Douglas W., jt. ed. see Powell, Lawrie W.
***Piper, Eloise.** Batik: For Artists & Quilters. (Illus.). 2000. 29.99 (*0-9666383-4-4*, Pub. by Design Books) F & W Pubns Inc.
— Sewing & Sculpting Dolls: Easy-to-Make Dolls from Fabric, Modeling Paste & Polymer Clay. LC 96-46185. (Illus.). 128p. 1997. pap. 21.95 (*0-8019-8872-1*) Krause Pubns.
Piper, Eloise & Dilligan, Mary. Creating & Crafting Dolls: Patterns, Techniques & Inspiration for Making Cloth Dolls. LC 93-45404. (Craft Kaleidoscope Ser.). (Illus.). 113p. 1994. pap. 19.95 (*0-8019-8524-2*) Krause Pubns.
Piper, Ernest. Alaska Sportfishing. Rennick, Penny, ed. LC 97-38049. (Alaska Geographic Guides Ser.). (Illus.). 160p. 1997. pap. 17.95 (*1-56661-037-0*) Alaska Geog Soc.
Piper, Evelyn. Bunny Lake Is Missing. large type ed. LC 92-28645. (Nightingale Ser.). 320p. 1993. pap. 15.95 (*0-8161-5634-4*, G K Hall Lrg Type) Mac Lib Ref.
— The Lady & Her Doctor. 320p. 1986. reprint ed. pap. 6.00 (*0-89733-194-X*) Academy Chi Pubs.
Piper, F. C., jt. auth. see Beker, Henry J.
***Piper, H. Beam.** The Complete Fuzzy. LC 99-160215. 448p. 1998. pap. 14.00 (*0-441-00581-0*) Ace Bks.
Piper, H. Beam. Murder in the Gunroom. 272p. 1993. reprint ed. pap. 20.00 (*1-882968-02-6*) Old Earth Bks.
Piper, H. W. The Singing of Mount Abora: Coleridge's Use of Biblical Imagery & Natural Symbolism in Poetry & Philosophy. LC 86-45480. 128p. 1987. 28.50 (*0-8386-3295-5*) Fairleigh Dickinson.
Piper, Hans M., ed. Cell Culture Techniques in Heart & Vessel Research. (Illus.). 375p. 1990. 115.00 (*0-387-51934-3*) Spr-Verlag.
— Pathophysiology of Severe Ischemic Myocardial Injury. 440p. 1990. text 294.00 (*0-7923-0459-4*) Kluwer Academic.
Piper, Hans M. & Isenberg, Gerrit, eds. Isolated Adult Cardiomyocytes, 2 vols., Vol. 1. 336p. 1989. boxed set 217.00 (*0-8493-4741-6*, QP114) CRC Pr.
— Isolated Adult Cardiomyocytes, 2 vols., Vol. II. 304p. 1989. boxed set 230.00 (*0-8493-4742-4*) CRC Pr.
Piper, Hans M. & Preuse, Claus J., eds. Ischemia-Reperfusion in Cardiac Surgery. LC 93-16723. (Developments in Cardiovascular Medicine Ser.: Vol. 142). 1993. text 264.50 (*0-7923-2241-X*) Kluwer Academic.
Piper, Henry D. Fitzgerald's Great Gatsby: The Novel, the Critics, the Background. (Research Anthologies Ser.). (Illus.). 235p. (Orig.). (C). 1970. pap. text 28.20 (*0-02-395710-7*, Macmillan Coll) P-H.
Piper, J., jt. ed. see Lundsteen, C.
Piper, J. D. Palaeomagnetic Database. LC 87-34995. 304p. 1991. 360.00 (*0-471-93255-8*) Wiley.
Piper, J. Richard. Ideologies & Institutions: American Conservative & Liberal Governance Prescriptions since 1933. LC 96-51886. 416p. 1997. pap. 29.95 (*0-8476-8459-8*); text 78.00 (*0-8476-8458-X*) Rowman.
Piper, Jacqueline M. Rice in South-East Asia: Cultures & Landscapes. (Images of Asia Ser.). (Illus.). 108p. 1994. text 17.95 (*967-65-3038-7*) OUP.
Piper, James E. Handbook of Facility Management: Tools & Techniques, Formulas & Tables. LC 94-33199. 704p. (C). 1995. text 79.95 (*0-13-554296-0*) P-H.
— Operations & Maintenance Manual for Energy Management. LC 98-47335. 368p. (C). 1999. text 73.95 (*0-7656-0050-1*, Sharpe Prof) M E Sharpe.
Piper, Joanne. Filing: Syllabus. 2nd ed. 1979. pap. text 10.95 (*0-89420-037-2*, 327007); audio 105.25 (*0-89420-146-8*, 106000) Natl Book.
Piper, Joanne. Vowel Sounds & Silent Letters. (J). 1975. audio 22.45 (*0-89420-196-4*, 240000) Natl Book.
Piper, Joanne. Vowel Sounds & Silent Letters: Syllabus. 1975. pap. text 6.45 (*0-89420-023-2*, 240008) Natl Book.
Piper, Joanne & Yerian, C. Theodore. Personal Shorthand: Syllabus. 2nd ed. 1975. pap. text 16.95 (*0-89420-083-6*, 217000) Natl Book.
— Personal Shorthand: Teacher's Manual & Key to Syllabus. 1975. teacher ed. 5.95 (*0-89420-094-1*, 217007) Natl Book.
Piper, John. Desiring God: Meditations of a Christian Hedonist. 358p. 1996. pap. 12.99 (*0-88070-869-7*, Multnomah Bks) Multnomah Pubs.
— Future Grace: The Purifying Power of Living by Faith. 448p. 1998. pap. text 14.99 (*1-57673-337-8*) Multnomah Pubs.
— God's Passion for His Glory: Living the Vision of Jonathon Edwards. LC 98-19029. 1998. 17.99 (*1-58134-007-9*) Crossway Bks.
— Godward Life: Savoring the Supremacy of God in All of Life. LC 97-19035. 336p. 1997. 16.99 (*1-57673-183-9*, Multnomah Bks) Multnomah Pubs.
— A Godward Life Vol. 2: Savoring the Supremacy of God in All of Life. 350p. 1999. 16.99 (*1-57673-405-6*) Multnomah Pubs.
— A Hunger for God: Desiring God Through Fasting & Prayer. LC 97-15577. 244p. 1997. pap. 12.99 (*0-89107-966-1*) Crossway Bks.
— Innkeeper. LC 98-36322. (Illus.). 32p. 1998. 9.99 (*1-58134-027-3*) Crossway Bks.
— The Justification of God: An Exegetical & Theological Study of Romans 9: 1-23. 2nd ed. LC 82-74139. 256p. 1993. pap. 16.99 (*0-8010-7079-1*) Baker Bks.
***Piper, John.** The Legacy of Sovereign Joy: God's Triumphant Grace in the Lives of Augustine, Luther, & Calvin. (Swans Are Not Silent Ser.: Vol. 1). 176p. 2000. 17.99 (*1-58134-173-3*) Crossway Bks.
Piper, John. Let the Nations Be Glad! The Supremacy of God in Missions. LC 93-14327. 240p. 1993. pap. 12.99 (*0-8010-7124-0*) Baker Bks.
***Piper, John.** The Pleasures of God: Meditation on God's Delight in Being God. 400p. 2000. pap. 14.99 (*1-57673-665-2*, Pub. by Multnomah Pubs) GL Services.
Piper, John. The Supremacy of God in Preaching. LC 90-34898. 128p. (Orig.). 1990. pap. 7.99 (*0-8010-7112-7*) Baker Bks.
— The Way to Trade: Find Your Own Path to a Successful Trading Personality. (Illus.). 293p. 2000. 45.00 (*0-273-63754-1*) F T P H.

P

An Asterisk (*) at the beginning of an entry indicates that the title is appearing for the first time.

— What's the Difference? Manhood & Womanhood According to the Bible. LC 90-80358. 64p. (YA). 1990. pap. 4.99 (*0-89107-562-3*) Crossway Bks.

Piper, John, et al, eds. Recovering Biblical Manhood & Womanhood: A Response to Evangelical Feminism. LC 90-20258. 576p. 1991. pap. 22.00 (*0-89107-586-0*) Crossway Bks.

Piper, John, frwd. John Piper's Stowe. (Illus.). (C). 1989. 950.00 (*0-903696-25-8*, Pub. by Hurtwood Pr Ltd) St Mut.

***Piper, John F., Jr.** Robert E. Speer: Prophet of the American Church. (Illus.). 448p. 2000. 29.95 (*0-664-50132-X*) Geneva Press.

Piper, John T., ed. see American Bar Association, Section of Taxation Staf.

Piper, Jon K., jt. auth. see Soule, Judith D.

***Piper, June-el, ed.** El Camino Real de Tierra Adentro. (Cultural Resources Ser.: No. 13). (Illus.). xiii, 364p. 1999. pap. 12.00 (*1-878178-14-8*) Bureau of Land Mgmt NM.

Piper, June-el, ed. Dine Baa Hane Bi Naaltsoos: Collected Papers from the Seventh Through Tenth Navajo Studies. (Illus.). xi, 245p. 1999. pap. 25.00 (*0-9639162-2-X*) Navajo Nation.

— Papers from the Third, Fourth & Sixth Navajo Studies Conferences. 1993. pap. 25.00 (*0-9639162-0-3*) Navajo Nation.

Piper, June-el, jt. ed. see Jacobson, LouAnn.

Piper, June-el, ed. see Staski, Edward.

Piper, Kevin. Riders in the Chariot. LC 97-198634. (Review Ser.). 152p. 1997. write for info. (*0-86431-188-5*) St Mut.

Piper, L. J. Contractors' All Risks & Public Liability Insurance. 80p. 1981. pap. 95.00 (*0-948691-03-4*, Pub. by Witherby & Co) St Mut.

Piper, Lanny, et al. How to Conduct Victimization Surveys: A Workbook. (Illus.). 250p. 1997. pap. text 45.00 (*0-7881-4708-0*) DIANE Pub.

Piper, Laurie & Ruvinsky, Anatoly, eds. The Genetics of Sheep. LC 97-14632. 626p. (C). 1997. text 175.00 (*0-85199-200-5*) OUP.

Piper, Linda J. The Spartan Twilight. (Illus.). xx, 244p. 1986. lib. bdg. 60.00 (*0-89241-378-6*) Caratzas.

Piper, Mandy Erylene. The Talented One-Hundredth: Issues in Ethenicity & Education. (Institutional Structures of Feeling Ser.). 2000. text 34.95 (*0-8133-1587-5*) Westview.

Piper, Margo. Jill Came Tumbling After: One Caregiver's Journey to Acceptance. LC TX4-312-248. (Illus.). 141p. (Orig.). 1996. pap. 12.95 (*0-9641216-1-1*) RitAmelia Pr.

— Staying on Top: A Survival Handbook for the Ages of Our Lives. LC 91-17592. 80p. 1991. pap. 9.95 (*0-942963-14-8*) Distinctive Pub.

***Piper, Margo.** View from the Edge of over the Hill: Reflections from Here. 144p. 2000. pap. text 9.95 (*0-9641216-5-4*) RitAmelia Pr.

Piper, Mark, tr. see Decroux, Etienne.

Piper, Martha C. & Darrah, Johanna. Alberta Infant Motor Scale (AIMS) (Illus.). 1994. 25.00 (*0-7216-4721-9*, W B Saunders Co) Harcrt Hlth Sci Grp.

— Motor Assessment of the Developing Infant. LC 93-24914. (Illus.). 224p. 1994. text 46.00 (*0-7216-4307-8*, W B Saunders Co) Harcrt Hlth Sci Grp.

Piper, Mel L. Adventures of One. (Illus.). 24p. (Orig.). (J). (gr. 1-6). 1996. pap. 3.95 (*1-881477-50-9*) Piper Hse.

— Cain & Abel. 48p. 1987. pap. 2.95 (*0-88144-103-1*) Christian Pub.

— Enoch Leaps into Eternity. Mackall, Phyllis, ed. (Heroes of Faith Ser.). (Illus.). 65p. (Orig.). 1994. pap. 4.95 (*1-881477-02-9*) Piper Hse.

— The Humanity of Jesus. (Illus.). 112p. 1995. pap. 6.95 (*1-881477-77-0*) Piper Hse.

— Jacob & Esau: The Truth Unfolded. (Heroes of Faith Ser.). 80p. 1992. pap. 4.95 (*1-881477-01-0*) Piper Hse.

— Poems of the Kingdom. 16p. (Orig.). (YA). (gr. 7 up). 1996. pap. 2.95 (*1-881477-51-7*) Piper Hse.

Piper, Michael C. Final Judgment: The Missing Link in the JFK Assassination Conspiracy. 4th rev. ed. LC 98-92562. (Illus.). 672p. 1998. pap. 25.00 (*0-935036-51-7*) Liberty Lobby.

***Piper, Molly.** ET My Bat. 56p. (J). 1999. pap. 7.95 (*1-891360-04-3*) Little Deer.

Piper, Molly. The Magic Crayon. (Illus.). 32p. (J). (gr. k-5). 1997. pap. 5.95 (*1-891360-00-0*) Little Deer.

— Rosey & Amanda. (Illus.). (J). (gr. k-6). Date not set. pap. 7.95 (*1-891360-01-9*) Little Deer.

— Skatepark Scrapbook. 42p. (J). (gr. 4-12). 1998. pap. 5.95 (*1-891360-03-5*) Little Deer.

Piper, Nicola. Racism, Nationalism & Citizenship: Ethnic Minorities in Britain & Germany. LC 98-70151. (Research in Ethnic Relations Ser.). 286p. 1998. text 67.95 (*1-84014-537-4*, Pub. by Ashgate Pub) Ashgate Pub Co.

Piper, Pat, jt. auth. see King, Larry.

Piper, Patricia L., et al. Manual on KF: The Library of Congress Classification Schedule for Law of the United States. LC 72-86471. (AALL Publications Ser.: No. 11). viii, 135p. 1972. 25.00 (*0-8377-0109-0*, Rothman) W S Hein.

Piper, Paul, ed. Die Geistliche Dichtung des Mittelalters, 2 vols. in 1. vi, 699p. 1985. reprint ed. write for info. (*3-283-07723-1*) G Olms Pubs.

Piper, Priscilla J. SRS-A & Leukotrienes: Proceedings of the Annual Symposium of the Institute of Basic Medical Sciences, Royal College of Surgeons of England, 24th September 1980. LC 80-41758. (Prostaglandins Research Studies Ser.: No. 1). (Illus.). 296p. reprint ed. pap. 91.80 (*0-8357-3549-4*, 203423200089) Bks Demand.

Piper, Priscilla J., ed. The Leukotrienes: Their Biological Significance: a Biological Council Symposium. LC 86-6643. 235p. 1986. reprint ed. pap. 72.90 (*0-608-00424-3*, 206113900007) Bks Demand.

Piper, Priscilla J., jt. ed. see Costello, John F.

Piper, Priscilla J., ed. see Royal College of Surgeons of England, Institute of.

Piper Pub. Co. Editorial Staff, ed. Kitchen Gourmet (Twin Cities) LC 79-87647. (Illus.). 1979. 10.00 (*0-87832-044-X*) Piper.

Piper, R. G. & Schramm, H. L., Jr., eds. Uses & Effects of Cultured Fishes in Aquatic Ecosystems. LC 95-60393. (Symposium Ser.: No. 15). 608p. 1995. 58.00 (*0-913235-91-1*, 540.15C) Am Fisheries Soc.

Piper, R. K. The Jefferson Square Business Association Area: Profiles & Prospects. (Illus.). 15p. (Orig.). 1983. pap. 1.50 (*1-55719-009-7*) U NE CPAR.

— Kellom Heights Stage II: Trends & Conditions Impacting Commercial & Office Space Development. 49p. (Orig.). 1983. pap. 3.50 (*1-55719-010-0*) U NE CPAR.

— Neighborhood & Community Histories: Their Value & Suggestions for Their Preparation. 33p. (Orig.). 1983. pap. 2.50 (*1-55719-031-3*) U NE CPAR.

— Re-Use of the Muse Theater: A Study of Consumer Preferences. 20p. (Orig.). 1986. pap. 2.00 (*1-55719-089-5*) U NE CPAR.

Piper, R. K., et al. Legal Aid Clients with General Assistance Problems: A Study of Housing Conditions. 14p. (Orig.). 1984. pap. 1.50 (*1-55719-077-1*) U NE CPAR.

Piper, R. K., jt. auth. see Ruff, Jack J.

Piper, Ralph E. Point of No Return: An Aviator's Story. LC 89-27919. (Illus.). 222p. 1990. 34.95 (*0-8138-0158-3*) Iowa St U Pr.

Piper, Robert G., et al. Fish Hatchery Management. 517p. 1982. pap. 51.00 (*0-913235-03-2*, 550.03) Am Fisheries Soc.

***Piper, Robert J.** Architecture Careers. rev. ed. (Opportunities in . . . Ser.). 2000. 14.95 (*0-658-00474-3*, VGM Career) NTC Contemp Pub Co.

***Piper, Robert J. & Rush, Richard D.** Opportunities in Architectural Careers. rev. ed. LC 00-39270. (VGM Opportunities Ser.). 2000. pap. write for info. (*0-658-00475-1*) NTC Contemp Pub Co.

Piper, Robert J. & Rush, Richard D. Opportunities in Architecture Careers. LC 92-20018. (Opportunities In . . . Ser.). 160p. pap. 12.95 (*0-8442-4039-7*, 297OIARC, VGM Career) NTC Contemp Pub Co.

— Opportunities in Architecture Careers. LC 92-20018. (Opportunities in...Ser.). 160p. 1994. 14.95 (*0-8442-4038-9*, VGM Career) NTC Contemp Pub Co.

Piper, Ronald A. The Gospel Behind the Gospels: Current Studies on Q. LC 94-23349. (Supplements to Novum Testamentum Ser.: 75). xi, 411p. 1994. 149.50 (*90-04-09737-6*) Brill Academic Pubs.

***Piper, Susie S.** Perceptions. (J). 1999. pap. 6.00 (*0-9618280-3-X*) S S Piper.

Piper, Susie S. Season of Inspiration One. (Orig.). 1985. pap. write for info. (*0-9618280-1-3*) S S Piper.

— Seasons of Inspiration Two. (Orig.). 1986. pap. 3.50 (*0-9618280-2-1*) S S Piper.

— Squibbles & Quotes. (Orig.). 1983. pap. write for info. (*0-9618280-0-5*) S S Piper.

Piper, Terry. And Then There Were Two: Children & Second Language Learning. 109p. 1993. pap. text 16.00 (*0-88751-060-4*, 00745) Heinemann.

— Language & Learning: The Home & School Years. 2nd ed. LC 97-29947. 355p. (gr. 1). 1998. pap. text 53.00 (*0-13-863903-5*, Merrill Coll) P-H.

Piper, Thomas R., et al. Can Ethics Be Taught? Perspectives, Challenges, & Approaches at the Harvard Business School. LC 92-27077. 208p. 1993. 24.95 (*0-87584-400-6*) Harvard Busn.

Piper, Walter N. Regulation of Heme Biosynth by Drugs, Hormones & Toxicants. 1994. 139.95 (*0-8493-6834-0*) CRC Pr.

Piper, Watty. The Easy-to-Read-Little Engine That Could. (All Aboard Bks.). (Illus.). 32p. (J). (ps-3). 1986. pap. 2.99 (*0-448-19078-8*, Plat & Munk) Peng Put Young Read.

— The Little Engine That Could. (Illus.). 40p. (J). (ps-k). 1997. 3.97 (*1-57748-081-3*) Barbour Pub.

Piper, Watty. The Little Engine That Could. 37p. (J). (gr. k-1). pap. 7.99 (*0-8072-1262-8*) Listening Lib.

Piper, Watty. The Little Engine That Could. (Illus.). 48p. (J). 1930. 6.99 (*0-448-40520-2*, Plat & Munk) Peng Put Young Read.

— The Little Engine That Could. LC 99-44044. (Pop-up Bks.). (Illus.). 12p. (J). (ps up). 1984. 10.99 (*0-448-18963-1*, Philomel) Peng Put Young Read.

— The Little Engine That Could. (Illus.). 10p. (J). (ps-3). 1991. 5.99 (*0-448-40101-0*, Plat & Munk) Peng Put Young Read.

***Piper, Watty.** The Little Engine That Could. (Illus.). 40p. (J). (ps-3). 1999. pap. 19.99 (*0-698-11856-1*, PapStar) Peng Put Young Read.

Piper, Watty. Little Engine that Could. (Illus.). 12p. (J). 1998. pap. 5.99 (*0-525-46075-6*, Dutton Child) Peng Put Young Read.

— The Little Engine That Could. 40p. (J). 1981. reprint ed. lib. bdg. 15.95 (*0-89966-366-4*); reprint ed. lib. bdg. 10.95 (*0-89967-040-7*, Harmony Rain) Buccaneer Bks.

— The Little Engine that Could: A Storybook & Windup Train. (Illus.). (J). (ps-2). 1998. pap. 18.99 (*0-525-46029-2*, Dutton Child) Peng Put Young Read.

***Piper, Watty.** Little Engine That Could: Giant Lift-&-Learn Book. (Illus.). 12p. (J). (ps-3). 2000. 9.99 (*0-448-42400-2*, Planet Dexter) Peng Put Young Read.

Piper, Watty. The Little Engine That Could: Miniature Edition. (Illus.). 48p. (J). 1990. 4.99 (*0-448-40071-5*, Plat & Munk) Peng Put Young Read.

— The Little Engine That Could: Sixtieth Anniversary Edition. 60th anniversary ed. (Illus.). 48p. (J). 1990. 16.99 (*0-448-40041-3*, Plat & Munk) Peng Put Young Read.

***Piper, Watty.** Little Engine That Could - ABC Time. (Illus.). 32p. (J). (ps-3). 2000. pap. 3.49 (*0-448-42166-6*, G & D) Peng Put Young Read.

Piper, Watty. The Little Engine That Could & the Snowy, Blowy Christmas. LC 97-47358. (All Aboard Bks.). (Illus.). 24p. (J). (ps-3). 1998. bds. 2.95 (*0-448-41850-9*, G & D) Peng Put Young Read.

— The Little Engine That Could Let's Count 123. LC 90-83240. (Illus.). 24p. (J). (ps-1). 1991. 12.95 (*0-448-40131-2*, Plat & Munk) Peng Put Young Read.

— La Pequena Locomotora Que Si Pudo (The Little Engine That Could) Ada, Alma F., tr. (SPA., Illus.). 48p. (J). (ps-6). 1992. 7.99 (*0-448-41096-6*, Plat & Munk) Peng Put Young Read.

Piper, Watty, retold by. The Little Engine That Could. (Comes to Life Bks.). 16p. (J). (ps-2). 1993. 18.99 (*1-883366-15-1*) YES Ent.

Piper, William, ed. see Swift, Jonathan.

Piper, William B. Common Courtesy in Eighteenth-Century English Literature. LC 97-10684. 200p. 1997. 34.50 (*0-87413-645-8*) U Delaware Pr.

Piper, William E., et al. Adaptation to Loss Through Short-Term Group Psychotherapy. LC 92-1424. 219p. 1992. lib. bdg. 40.00 (*0-89862-796-6*) Guilford Pubns.

Piper, William E., et al. Time-Limited Day Treatment for Personality Disorders: Integration of Research & Practice in a Group Program. LC 96-20928. 360p. 1996. 29.95 (*1-55798-370-4*) Am Psychol.

Piper, William E., jt. ed. see McCallum, Mary.

Piperno, Dolores R. Phytolith Analysis: An Archaeological & Geological Perspective. 280p. 1987. text 89.95 (*0-12-557175-5*) Acad Pr.

Piperno, Dolores R. & Pearsall, Deborah M. The Origins & Development of Agriculture in the Lowland Neotropics of Latin America. LC 98-84003. (Illus.). 400p. 1998. boxed set 99.00 (*0-12-557180-1*) Morgan Kaufmann.

— The Silica Bodies of Tropical American Grasses: Morphology, Taxonomy & Implications for Grass Systematics & Fossil Phytolith Identification. LC 97-22711. (Smithsonian Contributions to Botany Ser.: Vol. 85). (Illus.). 44p. reprint ed. pap. 30.00 (*0-608-10421-3*, 206994200008) Bks Demand.

Piperno, Dolores R., jt. auth. see Kealhofer, Lisa.

Pipes. Hidden Hand. 1998. pap. 16.95 (*0-312-17688-0*) St Martin.

— How Nations Learn. 21.00 (*0-02-925385-3*) CDG Bks.

— Russia under the Old Regime. 1984. 21.75 (*0-684-14826-9*) S&S Trade.

Pipes, Alan. Drawing for 3-Dimensional Design. 224p. (C). 1991. text. write for info. (*0-697-13945-X*) Brown & Benchmark.

— Production for Graphic Designers. 2nd ed. LC 97-19717. (Illus.). 224p. 1998. 45.00 (*0-87951-815-4*, Pub. by Overlook Pr) Penguin Putnam.

— Production for Graphic Designers. 2nd ed. 240p. (C). 1997. pap. text 53.33 (*0-13-642380-9*) P-H.

Pipes, Daniel. Conspiracy: The Power of the Paranoid Style in History. LC 97-20949. 256p. 1997. 24.50 (*0-684-83131-7*) Free Pr.

— Damascus Courts the West: Syrian Politics, 1989-1991. LC 91-30228. (Policy Papers: No. 26). 84p. 1991. pap. 8.00 (*0-944029-13-2*) Wash Inst NEP.

— Hidden Hand. LC 96-18729. 432p. 1996. text 49.95 (*0-312-16254-5*) St Martin.

— The Long Shadow: Culture & Politics in the Middle East. 320p. 1988. pap. 39.95 (*0-88738-220-7*) Transaction Pubs.

— The Long Shadow: Culture & Politics in the Middle East. 320p. (C). 1990. pap. 24.95 (*0-88738-849-3*) Transaction Pubs.

— The Rushdie Affair: The Novel, the Ayatollah, & the West. 224p. 1990. 18.95 (*1-55972-025-5*, Birch Ln Pr) Carol Pub Group.

— Slave Soldiers & Islam: The Genesis of a Military System. LC 80-23969. 276p. reprint ed. pap. 85.60 (*0-7837-2990-1*, 204319300006) Bks Demand.

— Syria Beyond the Peace Process. LC 95-39452. (Policy Papers: No. 40). 127p. 1996. pap. 8.00 (*0-944029-64-7*) Wash Inst NEP.

Pipes, Daniel, ed. Sandstorm: Middle East Conflicts & America. LC 92-29688. 422p. (Orig.). (C). 1993. pap. text 24.50 (*0-8191-8894-8*); lib. bdg. 71.50 (*0-8191-8893-X*) U Pr of Amer.

Pipes, Douglas, jt. auth. see White, Bonnie M.

Pipes, Jerry & Hamner, Curt. People Sharing Jesus Leader's Guide. LC 95-16643. 1995. pap., teacher ed. 10.99 (*0-7852-7682-3*) Nelson.

Pipes, L. Douglas & Gagen, William E., Jr. California Criminal Discovery. 1995. 90.00 (*0-8321-0038-2*, 68615, MICHIE) LEXIS Pub.

— California Criminal Discovery. 1995. im. lthr. write for info. (*0-327-00062-7*) LEXIS Pub.

***Pipes, L. Douglas & Gagen, William E., Jr.** California Criminal Discovery, 1999 Edition. 200p. 1999. 128.00 (*0-327-04953-7*, 6861511) LEXIS Pub.

Pipes, Louis A. & Hovanessian, Shahen A. Matrix-Computer Methods in Engineering. LC 77-23111. 346p. 1978. reprint ed. 34.50 (*0-88275-591-9*) Krieger.

Pipes, Mary. Understanding Abortion. pap. 16.95 (*0-7043-4480-7*, Pub. by Womens Press) Trafalgar.

Pipes, Nancy A. The Pocket Guide to Business Writing. (Illus.). 150p. (Orig.). 1990. pap. write for info. (*0-923768-03-3*) Tekne Pr.

Pipes, R. B., ed. Nondestructive Evaluation & Flaw Criticality for Composite Materials - STP 696. 364p. 1979. 34.50 (*0-8031-0527-4*, STP696) ASTM.

Pipes, R. Byron & Blake, Robert A., Jr. Delaware Composites Design Encyclopedia Vol. 6: Test Methods. LC 89-51098. 1990. lib. bdg. 116.95 (*0-87762-704-5*) Technomic.

Pipes, R. Byron & Lagneborg, Rune, eds. Materials Futures: Strategies & Opportunities. (MFSO Conference Proceedings Ser.). 1988. text 17.50 (*1-55899-000-3*) Materials Res.

Pipes, R. Byron, jt. auth. see Carlsson, Leif A.

Pipes, Randolph B. & Davenport, Donna S. Introduction to Psychotherapy: Common Clinical Wisdom. 2nd ed. LC 98-22426. 400p. (C). 1998. 75.00 (*0-205-29252-6*, Longwood Div) Allyn.

Pipes, Richard. A Concise History of the Russian Revolution. LC 97-119600. 1996. pap. 16.00 (*0-679-74544-0*) Knopf.

— A Concise History of the Russian Revolution. pap. 16.00 (*0-614-26955-5*) Vin Bks.

— Formation of the Soviet Union: Communism & Nationalism, 1917-1923. rev. ed. LC 97-226712. 400p. 1997. pap. text 17.95 (*0-674-30951-0*) HUP.

— Legalised Lawlessness: Soviet Revolutionary Justice. (C). 1990. 50.00 (*0-907967-73-6*, Pub. by Inst Euro Def & Strat) St Mut.

— Property & Freedom. LC 98-41728. 384p. 1999. 30.00 (*0-375-40498-8*) Knopf.

***Pipes, Richard.** Property & Freedom. 352p. 2000. pap. 15.00 (*0-375-70447-7*) Vin Bks.

Pipes, Richard. Russia under Bolshevik Regime. 1995. pap. 19.00 (*0-679-76184-5*) Vin Bks.

— Russia under the Old Regime. LC 97-140963. 384p. 1997. pap. 12.95 (*0-14-024768-8*) Viking Penguin.

— Social Democracy & the St. Petersburg Labor Movement, 1885-97. 2nd ed. LC 85-27842. xviii, 107p. (C). 1985. 20.00 (*1-884445-13-6*) C Schlacks Pub.

— Three Why's of the Russian Revolution. LC 96-46857. 1997. pap. 11.00 (*0-679-77646-X*) Random.

— The Unknown Lenin: From the Secret Archive. LC 96-8415. (Illus.). 216p. 1999. pap. text 15.95 (*0-300-07662-2*) Yale U Pr.

Pipes, Richard, ed. The Unknown Lenin: From the Secret Archive. (Illus.). 204p. Date not set. 27.50 (*0-614-22118-8*) Yale U Pr.

Pipes, Richard, ed. see Conference on the Russian Revolution Staff, et al.

Pipes, Richard, ed. see Lenin, Vladimir Il'ich.

Pipes, Richard E. Formation of the Soviet Union: Communism & Nationalism, 1917-1923. rev. ed. LC 64-21284. (Russian Research Center Studies: No. 13). (Illus.). 377p. 1964. 43.00 (*0-674-30950-2*) HUP.

— The Russian Revolution. LC 91-50008. 976p. 1991. pap. 25.00 (*0-679-73660-3*) Vin Bks.

— Struve: Liberal on the Left, 1870-1905. (Russian Research Center Studies: No. 64). (Illus.). 429p. 1970. 46.50 (*0-674-84595-1*) HUP.

— Struve: Liberal on the Right, 1905-1944. LC 79-16145. (Russian Research Center Studies: No. 80). (Illus.). 536p. 1980. 47.50 (*0-674-84600-1*) HUP.

Pipes, Rose. Coasts & Shores. LC 97-46755. (World Habitats Ser.). 32 p. (J). 1999. 22.83 (*0-8172-5008-5*) Raintree Steck-V.

— Forests & Woodlands. LC 97-46517. (World Habitats Ser.). (J). 1999. 22.83 (*0-8172-5007-7*) Raintree Steck-V.

— Grasslands. LC 97-9073. (World Habitats Ser.). (J). 1998. lib. bdg. 22.83 (*0-8172-5005-0*) Raintree Steck-V.

— Hot Deserts. LC 97-9071. (World Habitats Ser.). (J). 1998. lib. bdg. 22.83 (*0-8172-5004-2*) Raintree Steck-V.

— Islands. LC 97-46757. (World Habitats Ser.). 32 p. (J). 1999. 22.83 (*0-8172-5009-3*) Raintree Steck-V.

— Mountains & Volcanoes. LC 97-5986. (World Habitats Ser.). (J). 1998. lib. bdg. 22.78 (*0-8172-5006-9*) Raintree Steck-V.

— Rain Forests. LC 97-9070. (World Habitats Ser.). (J). 1998. 22.83 (*0-8172-5003-4*) Raintree Steck-V.

— Rivers & Lakes. LC 97-9069. (World Habitats Ser.). (J). 1998. lib. bdg. 22.83 (*0-8172-5002-6*) Raintree Steck-V.

— Tundra & Cold Deserts. LC 97-46756. (World Habitats Ser.). 32 p. (J). 1999. 22.83 (*0-8172-5010-7*) Raintree Steck-V.

— Wetlands. LC 97-9072. (World Habitats Ser.). (J). 1998. lib. bdg. 22.83 (*0-8172-5001-8*) Raintree Steck-V.

— World Habitats. (World Habitats Ser.). 1998. 159.80 (*0-8172-5012-3*) Raintree Steck-V.

Pipes, Wesley O. Bacterial Indicators of Pollution. 184p. 1982. 109.00 (*0-8493-5970-8*, QR48, CRC Reprint) Franklin.

Pipes, William H. Say Amen, Brother! Old-Time Negro Preaching: A Study in American Frustration. LC 91-19572. (African American Life Ser.). 230p. 1992. pap. 16.95 (*0-8143-2384-7*) Wayne St U Pr.

Pipes, William H. Say Amen, Brother! Old-Time Negro Preaching: A Study in American Frustration. LC 91-19572. (African American Life Ser.). 230p. 1992. 29.95 (*0-8143-2383-9*) Wayne St U Pr.

Pipes, William H. Say Amen, Brother! Old-Time Negro Preaching: A Study in American Frustration. LC 73-111585. 210p. 1970. reprint ed. lib. bdg. 35.00 (*0-8371-4611-9*, PSA&) Greenwood.

***Pipher, Mary.** Another Country: Navigating the Emotional Terrain of Our Elders. LC 98-31877. 328p. 2000. pap. 13.95 (*1-57322-784-6*, Riverhd Trade) Berkley Pub.

Pipher, Mary. Another Country: Navigating the Emotional Terrain of Our Elders. LC 98-31877. 328p. 1999. 24.95 (*1-57322-129-5*, Riverhead Books) Putnam Pub Group.

***Pipher, Mary.** Another Country: Navigating the Emotional Terrain of Our Elders. large type ed. 1999. 24.95 (*1-56895-828-5*) Wheeler Pub.

An Asterisk (*) at the beginning of an entry indicates that the title is appearing for the first time.

Pipher, Mary. Hunger Pains: The Modern Woman's Tragic Quest for Thinness. 1997. pap. 10.00 (0-345-41393-8) Ballantine Pub Grp.

*Pipher, Mary. Reviving Ophelia. 1999. pap. 14.00 (0-345-91549-6) Ballantine Pub Grp.

Pipher, Mary. Reviving Ophelia: Saving the Selves of Adolescent Girls. 345p. 1995. pap. 12.50 (0-345-39282-5) Ballantine Pub Grp.

— Reviving Ophelia: Saving the Selves of Adolescent Girls. 1998. mass mkt. write for info. (0-345-41878-6) Ballantine Pub Grp.

— Reviving Ophelia: Saving the Selves of Adolescent Girls. 320p. 1994. 24.95 (0-399-13944-3, Grosset-Putnam) Putnam Pub Group.

*Pipher, Mary. The Shelter of Each Other. 1999. pap. 12.95 (0-345-91551-8) Ballantine Pub Grp.

Pipher, Mary. The Shelter of Each Other: Rebuilding Our Families. 282p. 1997. pap. 12.95 (0-345-40603-6) Ballantine Pub Grp.

Pipics, Zoltan. Woerterbuch des Bibliothekars in 22 Sprachen: Librarian's Practical Dictionary in 22 Languages. 6th rev. ed. 385p. 1974. 295.00 (0-8288-6227-3, M-7540) Fr & Eur.

Pipikwass. When No One Was Looking. 50p. (Orig.). 1990. pap. 7.00 (0-9621498-4-5, Robin Hood) R Hood Little.

Pipili, Maria. Laconian Iconography of the Sixth Century BC. (Illus.). 124p. 1987. pap. 39.95 (0-947816-12-7, Pub. by Oxford Univ Comm Arch) David Brown.

*Pipino, Mary Frances. "I Have Found My Voice" The Italian-American Woman Writer. LC 97-49386. (Currents in Comparative Romance Languages & Literatures Ser.: Vol. 71). 200p. 2000. text 46.95 (0-8204-3965-7) P Lang Pubng.

Pipitone, David A., ed. Safe Storage of Laboratory Chemicals. 2nd ed. LC 90-12949. 320p. 1991. 135.00 (0-471-51581-7) Wiley.

Pipitone, Phyllis L. The Inner World of Dreams. 141p. 1996. pap. text 9.95 (0-912057-98-X, 500079) GLELJ AMORC.

*Pipkin. Oceanography. 3rd ed. 2000. pap. text, lab manual ed. write for info. (0-7167-3742-6) W H Freeman.

Pipkin, A. C. A Course on Integral Equations. (Texts in Applied Mathematics Ser.: Vol. 9). (Illus.). xiii, 268p. 1991. 52.95 (0-387-97557-8) Spr-Verlag.

— Lectures on Viscoelasticity Theory. 2nd ed. (Applied Mathematical Sciences Ser.: Vol. 7). (Illus.). viii, 188p. 1986. 65.95 (0-387-96345-6) Spr-Verlag.

Pipkin, Bernard & Cummings, David. Environmental Geology: Practical Exercises. (Illus.). 240p. (C). 1983. pap. 26.95 (0-89863-058-4) Star Pub CA.

Pipkin, Bernard & Proctor, Richard, eds. Engineering Geology Practice in Southern California. LC 92-29101. (Illus.). 1992. lib. bdg. 79.95 (0-89863-171-8) Star Pub CA.

Pipkin, Bernard W. Geology & Environment. 2nd ed. LC 96-34500. 1996. 51.00 (0-314-09239-0) West Pub.

— Geology & the Environment. LC 93-40808. 450p. (C). 1994. pap. text 53.25 (0-314-02834-X) West Pub.

— Geology & the Environment. 2nd ed. (Earth Science Ser.). 1997. mass mkt., student ed. 16.75 (0-314-20936-0) West Pub.

*Pipkin, Bernard W. Geology & the Environment. 3rd ed. (Earth Science Ser.). 2000. 49.00 (0-534-51383-2) Wadsworth Pub.

Pipkin, Bernard W. Geology & the Environment with Infotrac. 2nd ed. (Earth Science Ser.). 1997. 51.00 incl. cd-rom (0-534-54099-6) Wadsworth Pub.

— Lab Exercises in Oceanography. 2nd ed. (C). 1987. pap. text. write for info. (0-7167-1917-7) W H Freeman.

*Pipkin, Bernard W. & Trent, D. D. Geology & the Environment. 3rd ed. (Earth Science Ser.). 2000. pap. 49.00 (0-534-37797-1) Brooks-Cole.

Pipkin, Bernard W. & Trent, D. D. Geology & the Environment. 3rd ed. (Earth Science Ser.). 2000. pap., student ed. 19.25 (0-534-37515-4) Brooks-Cole.

Pipkin, Bernard W., et al. Laboratory Exercises in Oceanography. 2nd ed. (Illus.). (C). 1987. teacher ed. 4.80 (0-7167-1845-6) W H Freeman.

Pipkin, Brian. Unwelcome Love. large type ed. (Ulverscroft Large Print Ser.). 608p. 1997. 27.99 (0-7089-3852-3) Ulverscroft.

Pipkin, Donald L. Halting the Hacker: A Guide to Computer Security. LC 96-46381. 224p. (C). 1996. pap. text 44.95 (0-13-243718-X) P-H.

*Pipkin, Donald L. Information Security: Protecting the Global Enterprise. 364p. (C). 2000. pap. text 39.99 (0-13-017323-1) P-H.

Pipkin, George. Pete Aguereberry: Death Valley Prospector. LC 81-84564. (Illus.). 1982. 10.95 (0-930704-11-8) Sagebrush Pr.

Pipkin, H. Wayne, compiled by. A Zwingli Bibliography. LC 73-153549. (Bibliographia Tripotamopolitana Ser.: No. 7). 1972. 7.00 (0-931222-06-0) Pitts Theolog.

Pipkin, H. Wayne, ed. Essays in Anabaptist Theology. (Text Reader Ser.: No. 5). 271p. (Orig.). 1994. pap. 15.00 (0-936273-21-6) Inst Mennonite.

— Seek Peace & Pursue It: Proceedings from the 1988 International Baptist Peace Conference. 222p. (Orig.). 1989. pap. 15.00 (0-9622896-0-4) Baptist Peace.

Pipkin, H. Wayne & Yoder, John H., eds. Balthasar Hubmaier. LC 88-28425. (Classics of the Radical Reformation Ser.: Vol. 5). 496p. 1989. 49.99 (0-8361-3103-7) Herald Pr.

Pipkin, H. Wayne, jt. ed. see Furchs, E. J.

Pipkin, H. Wayne, ed. see Shenk, Wilbert R.

Pipkin, J. J. The Story of a Rising Race. LC 70-173609. (Black Heritage Library Collection). 1977. reprint ed. 38.95 (0-8369-8901-5) Ayer.

Pipkin, James, jt. auth. see Jackson-Stops, Gervase.

Pipkin, Patsy. Years, Fears & Running Gears: Essays on Life. Jackson, Tommy, ed. (Illus.). vii, 132p. 1998. pap. 12.95 (0-9663368-0-1) Searcy Newspapers.

Pipkin, Turk. Be a Clown: The Complete Guide to Instant Clowning. LC 88-51585. (Illus.). 104p. 1989. pap. 9.95 (0-89480-347-6, 1347) Workman Pub.

*Pipkin, Turk. When Angels Sing. LC 99-28804. 128p. 1999. 14.95 (1-56512-252-6) Algonquin Bks.

Pipkin, Turk. The Winner's Guide to the Texas Lottery. (Illus.). 128p. (Orig.). 1992. pap. 4.95 (1-881484-03-3) Softshoe Pub.

Pipkin, Wayne H., jr. Huldrych Zwingli-Writings in Search of True Religion Vol. 2: Reformation, Pastoral & Eucharistic Writings. LC 84-25454. (Pittsburgh Theological Monographs: No. 13). 1984. pap. 25.00 (0-915138-59-X) Pickwick.

Piplani, Lalit K. Systems Acquisition Manager's Guide for the Use of Models & Simulations: Report of the DSMC 1993-1994 Military Research Fellows. 212p. 1994. per. 15.00 (0-16-045161-2) USGPO.

Pipoly, J. J. A Systematic Revision of the Genus Cybianthus Subgenus Grammadenia (Myrsinaceae) LC 87-11221. (Memoirs Ser.: Vol. 43). (Illus.). 76p. 1987. pap. 17.50 (0-89327-314-7) NY Botanical.

Piponnier, Fran C. & Mane, Perrine. Dress in the Middle Ages. Beamish, Caroline, tr. from FRE. LC 96-29994. 208p. 1997. 25.00 (0-300-06906-5) Yale U Pr.

*Piponnier, Francoise & Mane, Perrine. Dress in the Middle Ages. (Illus.). 176p. 2000. pap. 15.00 (0-300-08691-1) Yale U Pr.

Pippa, Arshi & Repishti, Sami, eds. Studies on Kosova. 279p. 1984. text 64.50 (0-88033-047-3, Pub. by East Eur Monographs) Col U Pr.

Pippa, Norris. Electoral Change in Britain: Since 1945. LC 96-24899. (Making Contemporary Britain Ser.). (Illus.). 256p. (C). 1996. text 66.95 (0-631-16715-3) Blackwell Pubs.

Pippa Sales Staff. Improve Your Squash Game: 101 Drills, Coaching Tips & Resources. LC 95-70403. (Illus.). 96p. (Orig.). 1996. pap. 13.95 (1-884633-03-X) Ixia Pubns.

Pippard, A. B. Reconciling Physics with Reality: An Inaugural Lecture. LC 70-187082. 40p. reprint ed. pap. 25.00 (0-608-30936-2, 2051384) Bks Demand.

Pippard, John & Ellam, Les. Electroconvulsive Treatment in Great Britain, 1980: A Report to the Royal College of Psychiatrists. LC RC0485.. 172p. reprint ed. pap. 53.40 (0-608-15849-6, 203146100074) Bks Demand.

Pippen, Delois B. The Manager Who Became a Superstar: The Story of Scottie Pippen. 78p. 1994. 10.95 (0-533-10730-X) Vantage.

— The Right Career. LC 97-90838. 1998. pap. 10.95 (0-533-12492-1) Vantage.

Pippen, Joseph F., Jr. Ask an Attorney All about Florida Law. LC 95-26816. 268p. (Orig.). 1999. pap. 17.95 (0-935343-76-8) Peartree.

*Pippen, Kitty. Quilting with Japanese Fabrics. (Illus.). 80p. 2000. pap. write for info. (1-56477-297-7, B429, Pub. by Martingale & Co) F & W Pubns Inc.

*Pippen, Scottie. Out of the Shadows 2001. mass mkt. write for info. (0-7868-8982-9) Disney Pr.

— Out of the Shadows. 256p. 2000. 22.95 (0-7868-6618-7, Pub. by Disney Pr) Time Warner.

Pippen, Scottie & Brown, Greg. Reach Higher. LC 97-3307. (Illus.). 40p. (J). (gr. 2-6). 1997. 14.95 (0-87833-981-7) Taylor Pub.

Pippenger, C. E., et al, eds. Antiepileptic Drugs: Quantitative Analysis & Interpretation. fac. ed. LC 76-58055. 383p. pap. 118.80 (0-7837-7503-2, 204700300005) Bks Demand.

Pippenger, J. J., jt. auth. see Mitchell, Richard J.

Pippenger, John E., jt. auth. see Pease, Dudley A.

Pippenger, John H. & Hicks, Tyler Gregory. Industrial Hydraulics. 3rd ed. (Illus.). 1979. text 102.50 (0-07-050140-8) McGraw.

Pippenger, John J. Fluid Power: The Hidden Giant. (Global Series in Fluid Power). (Illus.). 503p. 1994. 100.00 (0-929276-02-7) Amalgam Pub Co.

— Hydraulic Cartridge Valve Technology. (Global Series in Fluid Power). (Illus.). 347p. 1990. text 84.95 (0-929276-01-9) Amalgam Pub Co.

— Hydraulic Valves & Controls: Selection & Application. LC 83-20980. (Fluid Power & Control Ser.: Vol. 4). (Illus.). 268p. reprint ed. pap. 83.10 (0-608-08975-3, 206961000005) Bks Demand.

— Zero Downtime Hydraulics. (Global Series in Fluid Power). (Illus.). 85p. (C). 1989. text 24.95 (0-929276-00-0) Amalgam Pub Co.

Pippenger, John J. & Gordon, Greg P. Basics for the Fluid Power Mechanic. (Illus.). 238p. 1994. 48.00 (0-929276-04-3); pap., teacher ed. 6.00 (0-929276-05-1) Amalgam Pub Co.

Pippenger, John J. & Lansky, Z. J. Zero Downtime Pneumatics. (Global Series in Fluid Power). (Illus.). 256p. 1994. 48.00 (0-929276-03-5) Amalgam Pub Co.

Pippenger, John J., jt. auth. see Mitchell, Richard J.

Pippenger, Nicholas. Theories of Computability. LC 98-3161. (Illus.). 261p. (C). 1997. text 47.95 (0-521-55380-6) Cambridge U Pr.

Pippenger, Wesley E., ed. Marriage Notices from Richmond, Virginia, Newspapers, 1841-1853. 360p. 1997. pap. 25.00 (1-888192-02-X) VA Geneal Soc.

*Pippert, Rebecca. Evangelism. (LifeGuide Bible Studies). 2000. pap. 4.99 (0-8308-3050-2) InterVarsity.

Pippert, Rebecca M. A Heart Like His: The Shaping of Character in the Choices of Life. LC 96-1852. 256p. 1996. 19.99 (0-89107-769-3) Crossway Bks.

— Out of the Saltshaker: Evangelism As a Way of Life. LC 79-1995. 192p. 1979. reprint ed. pap. 10.99 (0-87784-735-5, 735) InterVarsity.

Pippert, Rebecca M., jt. auth. see Siemens, Ruth.

*Pippert, Rebecca Manley. Out of the Saltshaker: Evangelism As a Way of Life. 1999. pap. 7.99 (0-8308-2234-8) InterVarsity.

— Out of the Saltshaker: Evangelism As a Way of Life (Anniversary Edition) 20th ed. LC 99-30885. 1999. 16.99 (0-8308-2233-X) InterVarsity.

— Out of the Saltshaker: Evangelism As a Way of Life, 20th Anniversary Edition. 20th ed. LC 99-30885. 1999. pap. 11.99 (0-8308-2220-8) InterVarsity.

Pippert, Wesley G. An Ethics of News: A Reporter's Search for Truth. LC 88-24700. 170p. (Orig.). reprint ed. pap. 52.70 (0-608-08049-7, 206901400002) Bks Demand.

*Pippin, Aleta & Mulhearn, Robyn. Yikes!! My Butt's Falling: Humorous "Tails" of Aging Baby Boomers. 2nd rev. ed. LC 99-94066. (Illus.). 160p. 2000. pap. 14.95 (0-9660546-3-6) Inner Sources.

Pippin, Aleta, jt. auth. see Mulhearn, Robyn.

Pippin, James A. Developing Casework Skills. LC 80-18799. (Human Services Guides Ser.: Vol. 15). 149p. 1980. pap. 18.95 (0-8039-1503-9) Sage.

— Developing Casework Skills. LC 80-18799. (Sage Human Services Guides Ser.: No. 15). 159p. 1980. reprint ed. pap. 49.30 (0-7837-9907-1, 206063300006) Bks Demand.

Pippin, Karma, jt. auth. see Windle, John.

Pippin, Kathryn. The Devil's Justice. 280p. (Orig.). 1999. pap. write for info. (0-9654213-3-3) Cheston on Wye.

— Poor Little Butterflies. 280p. (Orig.). 1999. pap. write for info. (0-9654213-2-5) Cheston on Wye.

— Wind in the Cane. 200p. (Orig.). 1998. pap. write for info. (0-9654213-1-7) Cheston on Wye.

Pippin, Kathryn A. The Devil's Crossroads. 280p. (Orig.). 1997. pap. 5.99 (0-9654213-0-9) Cheston on Wye.

Pippin, Lonnie C. The Prehistory & Paleoecology of Guadalupe Ruin, New Mexico. (Anthropological Papers: No. 112). (Illus.). 272p. (Orig.). 1987. pap. text 25.00 (0-87480-281-4) U of Utah Pr.

Pippin, Michael J. Retirement Plans: A Users Guide for Employees & Retirees. LC 94-69148. 192p. 1995. pap. 12.95 (0-9644272-0-6) Pension Srv Design.

Pippin, Robert, et al. Marcuse: Critical Theory & the Promise of Utopia. LC 87-20002. 288p. 1987. 59.95 (0-89789-106-6, Bergin & Garvey); pap. 24.95 (0-89789-107-4, Bergin & Garvey) Greenwood.

*Pippin, Robert B. Henry James & Modern Moral Life. LC 99-23183. 272p. (C). 1999. 49.95 (0-521-65230-8) Cambridge U Pr.

Pippin, Robert B. Idealism As Modernism: Hegelian Variations. LC 96-8627. (Modern European Philosophy Ser.). 480p. (C). 1997. text 59.95 (0-521-56025-X); pap. text 21.95 (0-521-56873-0) Cambridge U Pr.

— Modernism as a Philosophical Problem: On the Dissatisfactions of European High Culture. 2nd ed. LC 99-17513. 320p. 1999. pap. text 26.95 (0-631-21414-3) Blackwell Pubs.

— Modernism as a Philosophical Problem: On the Dissatisfactions of European High Culture. 2nd ed. LC 99-17513. 320p. (C). 1999. text 59.95 (0-631-21413-5) Blackwell Pubs.

Pippin, Robert S. Hegel's Idealism: The Satisfactions of Self-Consciousness. 344p. (C). 1989. pap. text 26.95 (0-521-37923-7) Cambridge U Pr.

Pippin, Tina. Apocalyptic Bodies: The Biblical End of the World in Text & Image. LC 98-25925. 1998. pap. 24.99 (0-415-18249-2) Routledge.

— Apocalyptic Bodies: The Biblical End of the World in Text & Image. LC 98-25925. 1999. 75.00 (0-415-18248-4) Routledge.

Pippin, Tina, jt. auth. see Aichele, George.

Pippin, Tina, jt. ed. see Aichele, George.

Pipping, Knut. Land Holding in the Usangu Plain. (Research Report Ser.: No. 33). 122p. 1976. write for info. (91-7106-097-9, Pub. by Nordic Africa) Transaction Pubs.

Pipping van Hulten, Ida. An Episode of Colonial History: The German Press in Tanzania. (Research Report Ser.: No. 22). 47p. 1974. write for info. (91-7106-077-4, Pub. by Nordic Africa) Transaction Pubs.

Pippinger, Wesley E. District of Columbia Marriage Licenses: Register 2, 1858-1870. 494p. 1996. pap. 32.00 (1-888265-17-5) Willow Bend.

Piprek, J. Large German-Polish Dictionary: Grosswoerterbuch Deutsch-Polnisch, 2 vols. 6th ed. (GER & POL.). 2116p. 1984. 150.00 (0-8288-0484-2, F33210) Fr & Eur.

— Large Polish-German Dictionary: Grosswoerterbuch Polnisch-Deutsch, 2 vols. 5th ed. (GER & POL.). 2100p. 1984. 125.00 (0-8288-0485-0, M9128) Fr & Eur.

Pirell, Collin & Boyd, Ashley. Diving in Thailand. (Illus.). 192p. 1994. pap. 22.50 (0-7818-0315-2) Hippocrene Bks.

Pique, Antoni M. The 5th Annual Malofiej 1997 Infographics Awards Vol. 5: Malofiej Infographic Awards. (ENG & SPA., Illus.). 80p. (Orig.). 1998. 30.00 (1-878107-08-9) Soc News Design.

Pique, Chantal, jt. auth. see Pique, Gil.

*Pique, Francesca, et al. Palace Sculptures of Abomey: History Told on Walls. LC 99-31042. (Conservation & Cultural Heritage Ser.). (Illus.). 120p. 1999. pap. 24.95 (0-89236-569-2, Pub. by J P Getty Trust) OUP.

Pique, Gil & Pique, Chantal. Papillote Fish, Secrets of Papillote Cooking Vol. 5: No Mess Gourmet Cooking en Papillote. (Illus.). 112p. 1994. text. write for info. (0-9633688-5-0) Papillote.

— Papillote Meat, Secret of Papillote Cooking Vol. 2: No Mess Gourmet Cooking en Papillote. (Illus.). 112p. 1994. text. write for info. (0-9633688-4-2) Papillote.

— Papillote Poultry, Secret of Papillote Cooking Vol. 3: No Mess Gourmet Cooking en Papillote. (Illus.). 112p. 1994. text. write for info. (0-9633688-3-4) Papillote.

— Papillote Vegetable, Secret of Papillote Cooking Vol. 4: No Mess Gourmet Cooking en Papillote. (Illus.). 112p. 1994. text. write for info. (0-9633688-2-6) Papillote.

— Papillotes: Secret of Papillote Cooking. (Illus.). 120p. 1993. reprint ed. pap. 15.00 (0-9633688-1-8) Papillote.

— Secret of Papillote Cooking No. 1: No Mess Gourmet Cooking. (Illus.). 112p. text 19.95 (0-9633688-7-7) Papillote.

*Piquemal, Michel. The Panda. LC 00-26186. (My Animal Library). (Illus.). (J). 2000. 6.95 (0-7892-0664-1) Abbeville Pr.

*Piqueras, J., et al, eds. Optical Microstructural Characterization of Semiconductors Vol. 588: Materials Research Society Symposium Proceedings. LC 00-28177. 333p. 2000. text 90.00 (1-55899-496-3) Materials Res.

Piquero & Mazerolle. Crime Over the Life Course. (Criminal Justice Ser.). 2000. pap. 42.00 (0-534-57492-0) Wadsworth Pub.

Piquero, Alex, jt. auth. see Alpert, Geoffry.

Piquet, Jean. Turbulent Flows: Models & Physics. LC 98-53261. (Illus.). xii, 763p. 1999. 199.00 (3-540-65411-9) Spr-Verlag.

Piquet, O. & Sibold, K. Renormalized Supersymmetry: The Perturbation Theory of N-1 Supersymmetric Theories in Flat Space-Time. (Progress in Physics Ser.: Vol. 12). 368p. 1986. 76.50 (0-8176-3346-4) Birkhauser.

Pira, Edward S. Guide to Golf Course Irrigation System Design & Drainage. LC 98-128801. (Illus.). 435p. (C). 1997. text 69.95 (1-57504-030-1, Ann Arbor Press) Sleepng Bear.

Pira International Staff. Adhesives in Recycling Seminar: Proceedings. 99p. 1996. pap. 150.00 (1-85802-189-8, Pub. by Pira Internatl) Bks Intl VA.

— Asian Paper Markets. 1998. 760.00 (1-85802-224-X) Pira Pub.

— Directory of Paper Merchants in Western Europe. 196p. 1997. pap. 560.00 (1-85802-177-4, Pub. by Pira Internatl) Bks Intl VA.

— International Pulp & Paper Sourcebook. 293p. 1998. pap. 240.00 (1-85802-164-2, Pub. by Pira Internatl) Bks Intl VA.

— International Refining Conference: Proceedings. 150p. 1997. pap. 150.00 (1-85802-203-7, Pub. by Pira Internatl) Bks Intl VA.

— Use of Minerals in Papermaking. 200p. 1997. pap. 150.00 (1-85802-212-6, Pub. by Pira Internatl) Bks Intl VA.

Pira Staff. Advertising in a Multimedia Age. 1998. 80.00 (1-85802-159-6, Pub. by Pira Pub) Bks Intl VA.

— Book Production Control. LC 96-160489. 1998. 30.00 (1-85802-108-1, Pub. by Pira Pub) Bks Intl VA.

— CD-ROM for Publishers. 1998. 90.00 (1-85802-111-1, Pub. by Pira Pub) Bks Intl VA.

— CD-ROM Marketing for Publishers. 1998. 90.00 (1-85802-178-2, Pub. by Pira Pub) Bks Intl VA.

— Collage with Photoshop. 1998. 65.00 (1-85713-056-1, Pub. by Pira Pub) Bks Intl VA.

— Colour Control in Lithography. 1993. 70.00 (1-85802-036-0, Pub. by Pira Pub) Bks Intl VA.

— Colour Management-Graphic Arts-Pub. 1998. 110.00 (1-85802-156-1, Pub. by Pira Pub) Bks Intl VA.

— Colour Reproduction Digital Age. 2nd ed. 1998. 90.00 (1-85802-217-7, Pub. by Pira Pub) Bks Intl VA.

— Creative Duotone Effects. 1998. 50.00 (1-85713-055-3, Pub. by Pira Pub) Bks Intl VA.

— Effective Copywriting for Publishers. 1998. 55.00 (1-85802-200-2, Pub. by Pira Pub) Bks Intl VA.

— Effective Editor's Handbook. 1998. 30.00 (1-85802-186-3, Pub. by Pira Pub) Bks Intl VA.

— EP, Multimedia & Communications GS. 1998. 40.00 (1-85802-113-8, Pub. by Pira Pub) Bks Intl VA.

— Finishing for the Customer. 1998. 100.00 (1-85802-032-8, Pub. by Pira Pub) Bks Intl VA.

— First Steps in Design. 1998. 65.00 (1-85802-162-6, Pub. by Pira Pub) Bks Intl VA.

— Flexography - Visual Aid Kit. 1998. 95.00 (1-85802-058-1, Pub. by Pira Pub) Bks Intl VA.

— Getting the Measure of Your Business. 1998. 105.00 (0-85168-168-9, Pub. by Pira Pub) Bks Intl VA.

— Gravure - Visual Aid Kit. 1998. 95.00 (1-85802-059-X, Pub. by Pira Pub) Bks Intl VA.

— HTML Desktop Guide. 1998. 15.00 (1-85802-205-3, Pub. by Pira Pub) Bks Intl VA.

— Intro to Printing Process - Visual G. 1998. 15.00 (1-85802-080-8, Pub. by Pira Pub) Bks Intl VA.

— Introduction to Offset Lithography. 1998. 15.00 (1-85802-101-4, Pub. by Pira Pub) Bks Intl VA.

— Introduction to Printing Processes. 1998. 95.00 (1-85802-050-6, Pub. by Pira Pub) Bks Intl VA.

— Introduction to Typography. 1998. 55.00 (1-85802-199-5, Pub. by Pira Pub) Bks Intl VA.

— Introduction to Web Printing. 1998. 55.00 (1-85802-076-X, Pub. by Pira Pub) Bks Intl VA.

— Letterpress - Visual Aid Kit. 1998. 95.00 (1-85802-057-3, Pub. by Pira Pub) Bks Intl VA.

— Managing Change in the Printing & Publishing Industry. LC 95-232937. 1998. 135.00 (1-85802-083-2, Pub. by Pira Pub) Bks Intl VA.

— Modelling Drainage-Wire Section. 1998. 110.00 (1-85802-196-0, Pub. by Pira Pub) Bks Intl VA.

— Offset Lithography - Visual Aid Kit. 1998. 95.00 (1-85802-056-5, Pub. by Pira Pub) Bks Intl VA.

— Personnel Management for Printers. 1998. 70.00 (1-85802-098-0, Pub. by Pira Pub) Bks Intl VA.

— Pocket Print Production Guide. Date not set. 15.00 (1-85713-005-7, Pub. by Pira Pub) Bks Intl VA.

— Print & Production Manual. 1998. 200.00 (1-85802-238-X, Pub. by Pira Pub) Bks Intl VA.

— Print Estimators: The Handbook. 1998. 86.00 (0-85168-202-2, Pub. by Pira Pub) Bks Intl VA.

P

— Print Management. 1998. 70.00 (*1-85802-021-2*, Pub. by Pira Pub) Bks Intl VA.
— Print Order Processing. 1998. 80.00 (*0-85168-197-2*, Pub. by Pira Pub) Bks Intl VA.
— Printer & the Environment. 1998. 35.00 (*0-85168-188-3*, Pub. by Pira Pub) Bks Intl VA.
— Printers' Guide to Copyright. 1998. 25.00 (*0-85168-195-6*, Pub. by Pira Pub) Bks Intl VA.
— Printing Inks. 1998. 70.00 (*1-85802-027-1*, Pub. by Pira Pub) Bks Intl VA.
— Printing Materials: Science & Tech. 1999. 90.00 (*1-85802-150-2*, Pub. by Pira Pub) Bks Intl VA.
— Professional Print Buying. 1998. 80.00 (*1-85802-137-5*, Pub. by Pira Pub) Bks Intl VA.
— Screen Printing. 2nd ed. 1998. 110.00 (*1-85802-249-5*, Pub. by Pira Pub) Bks Intl VA.
— Specifying Printing & Materials Fr. Pr. 1998. 55.00 (*1-85802-104-9*, Pub. by Pira Pub) Bks Intl VA.
— Standard Folding Impositions. 1998. 25.00 (*0-85168-191-3*, Pub. by Pira Pub) Bks Intl VA.
— Stochastic Screening. 1998. 120.00 (*1-85802-126-X*, Pub. by Pira Pub) Bks Intl VA.
— Subscription Marketing. 1998. 55.00 (*1-85802-208-8*, Pub. by Pira Pub) Bks Intl VA.
— Troubleshooting for Printers. 2nd ed. 1998. 25.00 (*0-85168-189-1*, Pub. by Pira Pub) Bks Intl VA.
— Understanding Digital Colour. 1998. pap. 80.00 (*1-85713-002-2*, Pub. by Pira Pub) Bks Intl VA.
— Wet End Chemistry Conference '97. 1997. write for info. (*1-85802-231-2*, Pub. by Pira Pub) Bks Intl VA.

Pirages, Dennis. Global Technopolitics. 2nd ed. (Political Science Ser.). 1997. pap. 23.95 (*0-534-51380-8*) Wadsworth Pub.

Pirages, Dennis C., ed. Building Sustainable Societies: A Blueprint for a Post-Industrial World. LC 95-40079. 372p. (C). (gr. 13). 1996. text 64.95 (*1-56324-738-0*); pap. text 32.95 (*1-56324-739-9*) M E Sharpe.

Piraino, Anthony. A Psychological Study of Tolstoy's Anna Karenina. LC 93-29917. 172p. 1993. pap. 24.95 (*0-7734-1943-8*) E Mellen.

Piraino, Thomas A. Antitrust Aspects of Joint Ventures. (Corporate Practice Ser.: No. 66). 1996. 95.00 (*1-55871-324-7*) BNA.

Pirajno, F. Hydrothermal Mineral Deposits: Principles & Fundamental Concepts for the Exploration Geologist. (Illus.). 728p. 1992. 205.95 (*0-387-52517-3*) Spr-Verlag.

Piran, Niva, et al. Preventing Eating Disorders: A Handbook of Interventions & Special Challenges. LC 99-21923. 347p. 1999. 54.95 (*0-87630-968-6*) Brunner-Mazel.

Piran, T., et al, eds. Supernovae: Sixth Jerusalem Winter School for Theoretical Physics. 344p. (C). 1990. text 74.00 (*9971-5-0963-6*); pap. text 36.00 (*9971-5-0964-4*) World Scientific Pub.

Piran, T., jt. ed. see Weinberg, S.

Piran, Tsvi. Eighth Marcel Grossman Meeting: On Recent Developments in Theoretical & Experimental General R, 2 vol. 1900p. 1999. 178.00 (*981-02-3793-6*) World Scientific Pub.

Pirandello, Luigi. Better Think Twice about It: And Twelve Other Stories. (Short Story Index Reprint Ser.). 1977. reprint ed. 29.95 (*0-8369-4269-8*) Ayer.
— Eleven Short Stories - Undici Novelle: A Dual-Language Book. Appelbaum, Stanley, tr. (ENG & ITA.). 208p. (Orig.). 1994. pap. 8.95 (*0-486-28091-8*) Dover.

***Pirandello, Luigi.** Henry IV. Landes, William-Alan, ed. LC 99-51857. 55p. 1999. pap. 7.00 (*0-88734-839-4*) Players Pr.
— Her Husband. King, Martha & Witt, Mary Ann Frese, trs. LC 00-30868. 264p. 2000. 24.95 (*0-8223-2600-0*) Duke.

Pirandello, Luigi. The Late Mattia Pascal. Weaver, William, tr. from ITA. LC 87-83302. 262p. 1988. reprint ed. pap. 12.00 (*0-941419-09-6*, Eridanos Library) Marsilio Pubs.
— The Late Mattia Pascal. 2nd ed. Simborowski, Nicobella, ed. (Dedalus European Classic Ser.). 251p. 1999. reprint ed. pap. 8.99 (*0-946626-18-9*, Pub. by Dedalus) Hippocrene Bks.

***Pirandello, Luigi.** Luigi Pirandelio, 1867-1936 Vol. I: His Plays in Sicilian. Privitera, Joseph F., tr. LC 98-24056. (Studies in Italian Literature: Vol. 5a & 5b). 272p. 1998. text 89.95 (*0-7734-8337-3*) E Mellen.
— Luigi Pirandelio, 1867-1936 Vol. II: His Plays in Sicilian. Privitera, Joseph F., tr. LC 98-24056. (Studies in Italian Literature: Vol. 5a & 5b). 284p. 1998. text 89.95 (*0-7734-8339-X*) E Mellen.
— Naked. 96p. 1998. pap. 14.95 (*1-85459-339-0*) Theatre Comm.

Pirandello, Luigi. Naked Masks. 1957. pap. 13.95 (*0-452-01082-9*, Mer) NAL.
— Novelle per un Anno: An Anthology. McCormick, C. A., ed. (Italian Texts Ser.). (ITA.). 240p. (C). 1988. pap. 19.95 (*0-7190-0469-1*, Pub. by Manchester Univ Pr) St Martin.
— The Oil Jar & Other Stories. unabridged ed. Appelbaum, Stanley, tr. (Thrift Editions Ser.). (Illus.). 96p. 1995. pap. text 1.00 (*0-486-28459-X*) Dover.
— On Humor. LC 74-4281. (University of North Carolina Studies in Comparative Literature: No. 58). 166p. 1974. reprint ed. pap. 51.50 (*0-7837-9034-1*, 204978500003) Bks Demand.
— Piradello: Plays. Bentley, Eric, tr. from ITA. LC 97-44195. (European Drama Classics Ser.). 200p. 1998. 16.95 (*0-8101-1652-9*) Northwestern U Pr.
— Pirandello: Three Plays. 1999. pap. write for info. (*0-14-044646-X*) Viking Penguin.
— Pirandello's Love Letters to Marta Abba. Ortolani, Benito, ed. & tr. by. from ENG. LC 93-38617. (ITA.). 440p. 1994. text 39.50 (*0-691-03499-0*, Pub. by Princeton U Pr) Cal Prin Full Svc.
— Right You Are, If You Think You Are. Appelbaum, Stanley, tr. LC 96-36041. (Illus.). 64p. 1997. reprint ed. pap. text 1.50 (*0-486-29576-1*) Dover.
— The Rules of the Game. Hare, David, tr. & adapted by by. 96p. 1995. pap. 12.95 (*0-948230-61-4*, Pub. by Absolute Classics) Theatre Comm.
— Shoot! The Notebooks of Serafino Gubbio. 2nd ed. Simborowski, Nicoletta, ed. Scott-Moncrieff, C. K., tr. from ITA. (Nobel Prize Winner Ser.). 334p. 1997. reprint ed. pap. 12.99 (*0-946626-58-8*, Pub. by Dedalus) Subterranean Co.
— Six Characters in Search of an Author. LC 97-24711. (Plays for Performance Ser.). 112p. 1998. pap. 7.95 (*0-929587-58-8*, EL406, Pub. by I R Dee); lib. bdg. 15.95 (*0-929587-62-6*, EL406, Pub. by I R Dee) Natl Bk Netwk.
— Six Characters in Search of an Author. Bentley, Eric, tr. from ITA. LC 97-39835. 96p. 1998. mass mkt. 5.95 (*0-451-52688-0*) NAL.
— Six Characters in Search of an Author. unabridged ed. Storer, Edward, tr. LC 97-33362. (Illus.). 64p. 1998. pap. 1.50 (*0-486-29992-9*) Dover.
— Six Characters in Search of an Author & Other Plays. Musa, Mark, tr. 224p. 1996. pap. 11.95 (*0-14-018922-X*) Viking Penguin.
— Six Personnages en Quete d'Auteur, la Volupte de l'Honneur. (FRE.). 1978. pap. 10.95 (*0-7859-4105-3*) Fr & Eur.
— The Sounds of the Girgenti Dialect, & Their Development. Bussino, Giovanni R., tr. from ITA. & intro. by. LC 92-21618. (American University Studies: Linguistics: Ser. XIII, Vol. 18). (Illus.). XXIV, 194p. (C). 1992. text 45.95 (*0-8204-1457-3*) P Lang Pubng.
— Tales of Madness: A Selection from Luigi Pirandello's Short Stories for a Year. Bussino, Giovanni R., tr. (ITA.). 1984. 17.95 (*0-937832-26-X*) Dante U Am.
— Tales of Suicide: A Selection from Luigi Pirandello's Short Stories for a Year. Bussino, Giovanni R., tr. & intro. by. 1988. 14.95 (*0-937832-31-6*) Dante U Am.
— Theatre Complet, Vol. 1. 1536p. 45.00 (*0-686-56547-9*) Fr & Eur.
— Theatre Complet, Vol. 1. deluxe ed. Bouissy, Andre, ed. (FRE.). 1536p. 1977. 120.00 (*0-7859-3832-X*, 2070108791) Fr & Eur.
— Theatre Complet, Vol. 2. Bouissy, Andre, ed. (FRE.). 1985. lib. bdg. 150.00 (*0-7859-3869-9*) Fr & Eur.
— Three Plays. Firth, Felicity, ed. (Italian Texts Ser.). (ITA.). 308p. (C). 1988. text 19.95 (*0-7190-0346-6*, Pub. by Manchester Univ Pr) St Martin.
— Tonight We Improvise: And, "Leonora, addio!" Sbrocchi, Leonard G. & Campbell, J. Douglas, trs. from ITA. (Biblioteca di Quaderni d'Italianistica Ser.: Vol. 3). (Illus.). 122p. (Orig.). 1987. pap. 10.00 (*0-9691979-2-6*, Pub. by Can Soc Ital Stu) Speedimpex.
— Vetir Ceux Qui Sont Nus, Comme Avant, Mieux Qu'Avant. (FRE.). 1982. pap. 10.95 (*0-7859-4176-2*) Fr & Eur.

Piranesi, Giovanni B. Differentes Vues de Quelques Restes...de l'Ancienne Ville de Pesto. (Illus.). 25p. 1973. 95.00 (*1-55660-198-0*) A Wofsy Fine Arts.
— Giovanni Battista Piranesi: Drawings in the Pierpont Morgan Library. Stampfle, Felice, ed. 1978. pap. 9.95 (*0-486-23714-1*) Dover.
— The Prisons (Le Carceri) The Complete First & Second States. LC 72-92762. (Illus.). 63p. 1974. reprint ed. pap. 12.95 (*0-486-21540-7*) Dover.

Piranesi, Giovanni B. & Levit, Herschel. Views of Rome Then & Now. (Illus.). 109p. (Orig.). 1976. pap. 14.95 (*0-486-23339-1*) Dover.

Pirani, Alex, ed. The Absent Mother: Restoring the Goddess of Judaism & Christianity. 256p. (Orig.). 1991. pap. 14.95 (*1-85274-099-X*, Pub. by Mandala) IBD Ltd.

Pirani, C. L., ed. Ultrastructural Pathology of the Kidney. (Journal: Applied Pathology: Vol. 5, No. 2, 1987). (Illus.). 68p. 1987. pap. 39.25 (*3-8055-4634-3*) S Karger.

Pirani, F. What's the Big Idea? Nuclear Power. (Illus.). (J). 1997. mass mkt. 8.95 (*0-340-69339-8*, Pub. by Hodder & Stought Ltd) Trafalgar.

Pirani, Felix. Introducing the Universe. (Illus.). 176p. 1994. pap. text 9.95 (*1-874166-06-4*, Pub. by Totem Bks) Natl Bk Netwk.
— Rosalie, Sylvia & Melanie. (I Love to Read Collection). (Illus.). 48p. (J). (ps-3). 1993. lib. bdg. 12.79 (*0-89565-888-7*) Childs World.
— Triplets. 1999. pap. 3.95 (*0-14-054267-1*) NAL.

Pirani, Felix A., et al. Local Jet Bundle Formulation of Backlund Transformations. (Mathematical Physics Studies: No. 1). 1979. pap. text 70.50 (*90-277-1036-8*) Kluwer Academic.

Pirani, G., et al, eds. Advanced Algorithms & Architectures for Speech Understanding. (Research Reports ESPRIT, Project 26 SIP: Vol. 1). xiv, 274p. 1990. 35.00 (*0-387-53402-4*) Spr-Verlag.

Piranio, Josie. I Have Come to Give You Life: A Training Course on Catholic Evangelization. 112p. (Orig.). 1996. pap. 8.95 (*1-883520-11-8*) Jeremiah Pr.

***Pirardello, Luigo.** Luigo Pirardello from Novelle. Falyhera, Maurizio & Giocometti, Cristina, eds. 1999. 29.95 incl. audio compact disk (*1-58214-121-5*) Mltilingl Bks.

Piraro, Dan. Best of Bizarro Vol. II, Vol. II. (Illus.). 144p. 1994. pap. 9.95 (*0-8118-0771-1*) Chronicle Bks.
— The Best of Bizzaro. (Illus.). 144p. 1992. pap. 9.95 (*0-8118-0276-0*) Chronicle Bks.
— Bizarro. (Illus.). 104p. (Orig.). 1986. pap. 5.95 (*0-87701-402-7*) Chronicle Bks.
— Bizarro among the Savages: A Relatively Famous Guy's Experiences on the Road with & in the Homes of Strangers. LC 96-33267. (Illus.). 272p. 1997. 16.95 (*0-8362-2173-7*) Andrews & McMeel.
— Bizarro Number 10, No. 10. (Illus.). 112p. (Orig.). 1996. pap. 7.95 (*0-8362-2235-0*) Andrews & McMeel.
— Bizarro Number 9, No. 9. (Illus.). 112p. (Orig.). 1995. pap. 6.95 (*0-8362-0430-1*) Andrews & McMeel.
— Glasnost Bizarro. 104p. 1990. pap. 5.95 (*0-87701-693-3*) Chronicle Bks.
— Mondo Bizarro. (Illus.). 104p. 1989. pap. 5.95 (*0-87701-711-5*) Chronicle Bks.
— Post-Modern Bizarro. (Illus.). 96p. (Orig.). 1991. pap. 6.95 (*0-87701-854-5*) Chronicle Bks.
— Sumo Bizarro. (Illus.). 96p. (Orig.). 1990. pap. 5.95 (*0-87701-774-3*) Chronicle Bks.
— Too Bizarro. (Illus.). 104p. 1988. pap. 5.95 (*0-87701-536-8*) Chronicle Bks.

Pirault, J. P., jt. auth. see Collings, Nick.

Piraux, B., et al. Super-Intense Laser-Atom Physics. (NATO ASI Ser.: Vol. 316). (Illus.). 518p. (C). 1994. text 135.00 (*0-306-44587-5*, Kluwer Plenum) Kluwer Academic.

Piraux, H. English-French Dictionary of Electronic, Electrotechnical & Data-Processing Terms. 6th ed. (ENG & FRE.). 402p. 1995. 150.00 (*0-7859-9758-X*) Fr & Eur.

Piraux, Henri. Diccionario General de Acustica y Electro Acustica. (SPA.). 374p. 1967. 29.95 (*0-8288-6672-4*, S-50237) Fr & Eur.
— Dictionaire Francais-Anglais d'Electro-Technique et d'Electronique. (FRE.). 75.00 (*0-685-36687-1*) Fr & Eur.
— Dictionary of Electrical Engineering, Electronics & Related Applications: Dictionnaire de l'Electrotechnique, l'Electronique & Applications Connexes. (FRE & GER.). 272p. 1983. 75.00 (*0-8288-0923-2*, M6455) Fr & Eur.
— Dizionario Inglese-Italiano dei Termini Relativi all'Elettronica: all'Elettrotecnica e Alle Applicazioni Connesse: English-Italian Dictionary of Terms Relative to Electronics, Electrical Engineering & Related Applications. (ENG & ITA.). 534p. 1977. pap. 59.95 (*0-8288-5463-7*, M9195) Fr & Eur.
— English - French Dictionary of Electronics & Related Terms. 16th ed. (ENG & FRE.). 401p. 1992. reprint ed. pap. 125.00 (*0-7859-4630-6*) Fr & Eur.
— English- French Dictionary of Electrotechnic Electronics & Allied Fields. 11th ed. (ENG & FRE.). 218p. 1988. 69.00 (*2-212-00870-8*) IBD Ltd.
— French-English Dictionary of Electrical Engineering & Related Terms (Dictionnaire Francais-Anglais des Termes Relatifs a l'Electrotechnique) 11th rev. ed. 218p. 1988. 110.00 (*0-7859-4629-2*) Fr & Eur.

Pirazizy, A. A. Mountain Environment: Understanding the Change. (Illus.). x, 194p. 1993. 25.00 (*81-7024-563-X*, Pub. by Ashish Pub Hse) Nataraj Bks.

Pirazzoli. Sea Level Changes: The Last 20,000 Years. LC 96-25986. (Coastal Morphology & Research Ser.). 224p. 1996. pap. 54.95 (*0-471-96913-3*) Wiley.

Pirazzoli, P. A. & Pluet, J. World Atlas of Holocene Sea-Level Changes. (Oceanography Ser.: Vol. 58). 300p. 1991. 155.00 (*0-444-89086-6*) Elsevier.

Pirbazari, Massoud & Devinny, Joseph S., eds. Environmental Engineering. 810p. 1984. 10.00 (*0-87262-405-6*) Am Soc Civil Eng.

Pirbhai, Imtiaz A., jt. auth. see Hatley, Derek J.

Pirchner, Franz. Population Genetics in Animal Breeding. 2nd ed. Frape, D. L., tr. from GER. LC 83-2164. 424p. 1983. 95.00 (*0-306-41201-2*, Plenum Trade) Perseus Pubng.

Pirckheimer, Willibald. Opera Politica, Historica, Philologica et Epistolica. Goldast, Melchior, ed. (GER.). 406p. 1969. reprint ed. write for info. (*0-318-70502-8*); reprint ed. write for info. (*0-318-71272-5*) G Olms Pubs.

Pirece, Christine. How to Solve the Lockheed Case. (Studies in Social Philosophy & Policy). 49p. 1986. pap. 14.95 (*0-88738-660-1*) Transaction Pubs.

Pirelli Company Staff. The Pirelli Calendar. LC 98-67172. (Illus.). 396p. 2000. 70.00 (*0-8478-2150-1*, Pub. by Rizzoli Intl) St Martin.

Pirello, Christa. Cooking the Whole Foods Way: Your Complete Everyday Guide to Healthy Delicious Eating with 500 Recipes, Menus, Meal Planning Techniques. LC 96-23176. (Illus.). 524p. 1997. pap. 18.00 (*1-55788-262-2*, HP Books) Berkley Pub.

***Pirello, Christina.** Cook Your Way to the Life You Want. LC 99-42896. (Illus.). 336p. 1999. 24.95 (*1-55788-321-1*, HP Books) Berkley Pub.

Pirenne, Henri. Belgian Democracy: Its Early History. LC 73-120219. reprint ed. 42.50 (*0-404-05057-3*) AMS Pr.
— Bibliographiie de l'Histoire de Belgique. viii, 440p. 1979. reprint ed. lib. bdg. 63.70 (*3-487-06722-6*) G Olms Pubs.
— Economic & Social History of Medieval Europe. Clegg, I. E., tr. LC 37-28587. 252p. 1956. pap. 13.00 (*0-15-627533-3*, Harvest Bks) Harcourt.
— Medieval Cities: Their Origins & the Revival of Trade. Halsey, Frank D., tr. 272p. (C). 1952. pap. text 14.95 (*0-691-00760-8*, Pub. by Princeton U Pr) Cal Prin Full Svc.

Pires, A., et al. Computational Physics & Cellular Automata: Workshop. 208p. 1990. text 130.00 (*981-02-0074-9*) World Scientific Pub.

Pires, Deborah S., jt. auth. see Malkemes, Fred.

Pires, Fernando T. Fazendas: The Great Houses & Plantations of Brazil. Rabassa, Gregory, tr. from POR. LC 95-24443. (Illus.). 204p. 1995. 67.50 (*1-55859-876-6*) Abbeville Pr.
— Fazendas: The Great Houses & Plantations of Brazil. (POR., Illus.). 204p. 1996. 67.50 (*0-7892-0064-3*) Abbeville Pr.

Pires, Manuel. International Juridical Double Taxation of Income. (Series on International Taxation: Vol. 11). 336p. 1990. 100.00 (*90-6544-426-2*) Kluwer Law Intl.

Piret, P. Convolutional Codes: An Algebraic Approach. 360p. 1988. 47.50 (*0-262-16110-9*) MIT Pr.

Pirgl, Les. Book of Nurbs, Vol. 1. (Monographs in Visual Communication). 600p. 1995. 89.00 (*0-387-55069-0*) Spr-Verlag.

Pirgo, Helm M. Virgin Mary, Queen of Poland: Historical Essay. 33p. 1966. pap. 2.50 (*0-940962-44-6*) Polish Inst Art & Sci.

Piri, Erkki, ed. see Vilkama, Kirsti.

Pirich, Andrew R. & Boncek, Raymond K., eds. Photonic Processing Technology & Applications. LC 98-111053. 26p. 1997. pap. 59.00 (*0-8194-2490-0*) SPIE.

Pirich, Andrew R. & Parker, Michael A., eds. Photonic Processing Technology & Applications II. LC 98-227292. (Proceedings of SPIE Ser.: Vol. 3384). 220p. 1998. 59.00 (*0-8194-2833-7*) SPIE.

Pirich, Andrew R. & SPIE Staff. Photonic Component Engineering & Applications: 8-9 April, 1996, Orlando, Florida. LC 95-73019. (Proceedings Ser.). ix, 230p. 1996. pap. write for info. (*0-8194-2130-8*) SPIE.

***Pirich, Andrew R. & Taylor, Edward W., eds.** Enabling Photonic Technologies for Aerospace Applications. 230p. 1999. pap. text 72.00 (*0-8194-3188-5*) SPIE.

Pirich, Andrew R., jt. ed. see Hotaling, Steven P.

Pirideola, Michael S., jt. ed. see Oks, Eugene.

Pirie, Alex, jt. auth. see Herman, Hollis.

***Pirie, Andrew.** Alternative Dispute Resolution: Skills, Science & the Law. (Essentials of Canadian Law Ser.). 2000. pap. 35.95 (*1-55221-006-5*, Pub. by Irwin Law) Gaunt.

Pirie, Bruce. Reshaping High School English. LC 97-15512. 116p. (Orig.). (YA). (gr. 8-12). 1997. 14.95 (*0-8141-5668-1*) NCTE.

Pirie, D. B. How to Write Critical Essays: Guide for Students of Literature. 160p. (C). 1985. pap. 18.99 (*0-415-04533-9*) Routledge.

Pirie, David. Shelley. (Open Guides to Literature Ser.). 128p. 1988. 96.50 (*0-335-15091-8*); pap. 27.99 (*0-335-15082-9*) OpUniv Pr.

Pirie, David, jt. ed. see Empson, William.

Pirie, David B. How to Write Critical Essays: A Guide for Students of Literature. 136p. (C). 1985. pap. 12.95 (*0-416-34290-6*, 4146) Routledge.

Pirie, David B., ed. The Romantic Period, Vol. 5. LC 94-198829. (Penguin History of Literature Ser.: Vol. 5). 448p. 1994. pap. 18.99 (*0-14-017755-8*, Penguin Bks) Viking Penguin.

Pirie, Donald, ed. from POL. Young Poets of a New Poland: Anthology. (Illus.). 280p. 1994. pap. 24.00 (*1-85610-010-3*, Pub. by Forest Bks) Dufour.

Pirie, E. J. Sylloge of Coins of the British Isles Vol. 21: Coins in Yorkshire Collections. 1975. 19.98 (*0-19-725939-1*) David Brown.

***Pirie, Gayle & Clark, John.** Country Egg, City Egg: New Egg Classics. LC 99-56347. (Illus.). 128p. 2000. 15.95 (*1-57965-151-8*, 85151) Artisan.

Pirie, Inez. Coping with Caregiving: A Common Sense Approach to Home Care. McBride, Geraldine, ed. 224p. (Orig.). 1996. pap., per. 14.95 (*0-9650215-0-5*) Ruhl Pr.

Pirie, James W. Books for Junior College Libraries: A Selected List of Approximately 19,700 Titles. LC 76-82133. 464p. reprint ed. pap. 143.90 (*0-8357-7345-0*, 202394200034) Bks Demand.

Pirie, Lynne & Reynolds, Bill. Getting Built. (Illus.). 224p. (Orig.). 1985. mass mkt. 12.50 (*0-446-38289-2*, Pub. by Warner Bks) Little.

Pirie, M., ed. Elgin International. (Illus.). 70p. 1986. 18.50 (*0-08-032459-2*, Pub. by Aberdeen U Pr); pap. 7.75 (*0-08-032452-5*, Pub. by Aberdeen U Pr) Macmillan.

Pirie, Madsen. The Book of the Fallacy: A Training Manual for Intellectual Subversives. (Illus.). 192p. 1985. 19.95 (*0-7102-0521-X*, Routledge Thoemms) Routledge.

Pirie, Madsen, jt. auth. see Butler, Eamonn.

Pirie, Marcia. Travellers on a Trade Wind. LC 98-214721. (Illus.). 344p. 1998. pap. 16.50 (*1-57409-065-8*) Sheridan.

Pirie, Mark, ed. The Next Wave. LC 98-228811. 280p. 1998. pap. 24.95 (*1-877133-44-2*, Pub. by Univ Otago Pr) Intl Spec Bk.

Pirie, N. W. Leaf Protein & Its Biproducts in Human & Animal Nutrition. 224p. 1987. text 59.95 (*0-521-33030-0*) Cambridge U Pr.

Pirie, Norman W., jt. ed. see Clark, Frederick L.

Pirie, Peter J. Twentieth Century British Music: A Collector's Guide. (Front Music Publications: No. 2). 20p. (Orig.). 1980. pap. 6.50 (*0-934082-02-2*) Theodore Front.

Pirie, R. Gordon. Oceanography: Contemporary Readings in Ocean Sciences. 3rd ed. LC 95-3650. (Illus.). 448p. 1996. pap. text 44.95 (*0-19-508768-2*, GC26) OUP.

***Pirie, Reg.** Your Own Consulting Business: From Starting to Marketing. 184p. 1998. pap. write for info. (*0-9698196-1-7*) IIP.

Pirillo, Chris. Poor Richard's Email Publishing: Newsletters, Bulletins, Discussion Groups & Other Powerful... LC 98-96891. (Poor Richard's Ser.). (Illus.). 352p. 1999. pap. 29.95 (*0-9661032-5-4*) Top Floor Pub.

Pirillo, Rose M. Decision Making & Problem Solving: The Process Approach. rev. ed. (Illus.). 1987. teacher ed. 14.95 (*1-55631-003-X*) Chron Guide.

***Piringer, Otto G.** Plastic Food Packaging Materials: Barrier Function, Mass Transport, Quality Assurance, Legislation. 606p. 2000. 245.00 (*3-527-28868-6*) Wiley.

Piriou, Jean-Pierre, jt. auth. see Walz, Joel.

Piriyarangsan, Sungsidh, jt. auth. see Phongpaichit, Pasuk.

Pirke, K. M., et al, eds. The Psychobiology of Bulimia Nervosa. (Illus.). 120p. 1988. pap. 53.00 (*0-387-18670-0*) Spr-Verlag.

Pirker-Mosher, Gordana, jt. auth. see Pavicic, Liliana.

Pirkey, Louis T. & Practising Law Institute Staff. Understanding the Intellectual Property License. LC 98-113241. (Patents, Copyrights, Trademarks, & Literary Property Course Handbook Ser.). 800p. 1997. 129.00 (*0-87224-382-6*) PLI.

An Asterisk (*) at the beginning of an entry indicates that the title is appearing for the first time.

Pirkl & Babic. Guidelines & Strategies for Designing Transgenerational Products. 1988. pap. 19.95 (*0-87411-230-3*); 9.95 (*0-87411-270-2*) Copley Pub.

Pirkl, James J. Transgenerational Design: Products for an Aging Population. (Design & Graphic Design Ser.). 260p. 1994. 64.95 (*0-471-28469-6*, VNR) Wiley.

Pirkl, James J. Transgenerational Design: Products for an Aging Population. LC 93-9870. (Illus.). 260p. 1994. text 56.95 (*0-442-01065-6*, VNR) Wiley.

Pirkle, Arthur. Winchester Lever Action Repeating Rifles Vol. I: The Models of 1866, 1873, & 1876. (For Collectors Only Ser.). (Illus.). 202p. 1995. pap. 19.95 (*1-882391-05-5*) N Cape Pubns.

— Winchester Lever Action Repeating Rifles Vol. 2: The Models of 1886 & 1892. (For Collectors Only Ser.). (Illus.). 125p. (Orig.). 1996. pap. 19.95 (*1-882391-13-6*) N Cape Pubns.

— Winchester Lever Action Repeating Rifles Vol. 3: The Models of 1894 & 1895. (For Collectors Only Ser.: Vol. 3). (Illus.). 200p. 1998. pap. 19.95 (*1-882391-11-X*) N Cape Pubns.

Pirkle, Estus W. Percy Ray - A Ray for God. (Illus.). 624p. 1998. 26.00 (*0-9663391-0-X*) E Pirkle.

Pirkle, Hubert. Hemostasis & Animal Venoms. Markland, Francis S., Jr., ed. (Hematology Ser.: Vol. 7). (Illus.). 658p. 1988. text 275.00 (*0-8247-7806-5*) Dekker.

Pirkle, John. Oiler Blues: The Story of Pro Football's Most Frustrating Team. LC 99-72809. (Illus.). 368p. 1999. 24.95 (*1-891422-00-6*); pap. 19.95 (*1-891422-01-4*) Sportline Pub.

***Pirmantgen, Tad A.** Ports of Call: A Young Man's Odyssey on the Great Lakes Freighters. (Illus.). 176p. 2000. pap. 13.95 (*1-882376-76-5*, Pub. by Thunder Bay Pr) Partners Pubs Grp.

Pirmell, Charles. The Trashing of America. 1975. 7.00 (*0-686-11117-6*); pap. 3.50 (*0-686-11118-4*) Kulchur Foun.

Pirner, Connie White. Even Little Kids Get Diabetes. Tucker, Kathy, ed. LC 90-12738. (Illus.). 24p. (J). (ps-2). 1990. lib. bdg. 13.95 (*0-8075-2158-2*) A Whitman.

— Even Little Kids Get Diabetes. (Albert Whitman Prairie Book Ser.). (J). (ps-1). 1994. pap. 5.95 (*0-8075-2159-0*) A Whitman.

— Even Little Kids Get Diabetes. LC 90-12738. 1991. 10.15 (*0-606-06364-1*, Pub. by Turtleback) Demco.

Pirner, Hans P. Die Organisation von Vertraulichkeit: Eine Empirische Analyse der Compliance-Systeme Deutscher Universalbanken. (GER., Illus.). 252p. 1996. 44.95 (*3-631-30771-3*) P Lang Pubng.

Pirnie, Bruce. Analysis of Special Operations Forces in Decision Aids: Recommendations. LC 94-3128. 1994. pap. text 13.00 (*0-8330-1510-9*, MR-243-SOCOM) Rand Corp.

— An Objectives-Based Approach to Military Campaign Analysis. LC 96-14140. (Illus.). 141p. (Orig.). 1996. pap. text 15.00 (*0-8330-2397-7*, MR-656-JS) Rand Corp.

***Pirnie, Bruce R.** Civilians & Soldiers: Achieving Better Coordination. LC 98-52863. (Illus.). 146p. 1998. pap. 15.00 (*0-8330-2691-7*, MR-1026-SRF) Rand Corp.

Pirnie, Bruce R. & Francisco, Corazon M. Assessing Requirements for Peacekeeping, Humanitarian Assistance, & Disaster Relief. LC 98-13469. (Illus.). 143p. 1998. pap. 15.00 (*0-8330-2594-5*, MR-951-OSD) Rand Corp.

Pirnie, Bruce R., et al. Soldiers for Peace: An Operational Typology. LC 96-2897. (Illus.). 114p. 1996. pap. 15.00 (*0-8330-2396-9*, MR-582-OSD) Rand Corp.

— Soldiers for Peace: Critical Operational Issues. LC 96-22855. (Illus.). 167p. 1996. pap. 15.00 (*0-8330-2412-4*, MR-583-OSD) Rand Corp.

Pirnot, Thomas. Mathematics All Around. 736p. (C). 2000. text. write for info. (*0-201-30815-0*) Addison-Wesley.

Piro, Stephanie H. Blank Tapes, Boots & Salads. 64p. 1992. pap. 4.95 (*1-880053-01-2*) Pge One Pubs.

Piro, Timothy J. The Political Economy of Market Reform in Jordan. LC 98-24370. 152p. 1998. 54.00 (*0-8476-8881-X*); pap. 19.95 (*0-8476-8882-8*) Rowman.

Pirocacos, Elly. False Belief & the Meno Paradox. LC 98-73400. (Avebury Series in Philosophy). 1p. 1998. text 63.95 (*1-84014-852-7*, Pub. by Ashgate Pub) Ashgate Pub Co.

Piroch, Sigrid S. Design Challenges: Monograph One. LC 91-72743. (Illus.). 169p. (Orig.). 1991. pap., spiral bd. 24.95 (*0-9630006-0-8*) Design Orig.

Pirodda, E., ed. Neurophysiology of the Vestibular System. (Advances in OtoRhinoLaryngology Ser.: Vol. 41). (Illus.). xii, 244p. 1988. 148.75 (*3-8055-4766-8*) S Karger.

Pirog, Gerald. Aleksandr Blok's Ital'janskie Stixi: Confrontation & Disillusionment. (Illus.). 203p. (Orig.). 1983. pap. 19.95 (*0-89357-095-8*) Slavica.

Pirog-Good, Maureen A. & Stets, Jan E., eds. Violence in Dating Relationships: Emerging Social Issues. LC 88-31894. 302p. 1989. 57.95 (*0-275-93004-1*, C3004, Praeger Pubs); pap. 22.95 (*0-275-93353-9*, B3353, Praeger Pubs) Greenwood.

Pirog, John, jt. auth. see Robinson, Susan B.

Pirog, John E. The Practical Application of Meridian-Style Acupuncture. LC 95-69801. (Illus.). 392p. (Orig.). 1996. pap. 70.00 (*1-881896-13-7*) Pacific View Pr.

Pirogov, Nikolai I. Questions of Life: Diary of an Old Physician. LC 89-24332. (Resources in Medical History Ser.). (Illus.). xxii, 480p. 1992. 29.95 (*0-88135-061-3*, Sci Hist) Watson Pub Intl.

Pirogova, L. I. Aspectual Usage in Modern Russian. 320p. (C). 1988. 50.00 (*0-7855-4227-2*, Pub. by Collets) St Mut.

— Complete Handbook of Russian Verbs. (RUS & ENG., Illus.). 320p. (Orig.). 1994. pap. 17.95 (*0-8442-4270-5*, 42705, Natl Textbk Co) NTC Contemp Pub Co.

— Conjugation of Russian Verbs. 320p. (C). 1988. 75.00 (*0-7855-5356-8*, Pub. by Collets) St Mut.

— Conjugation of Russian Verbs. 319p. 1988. text 10.95 (*0-8285-4944-3*) Firebird NY.

Pirok, Kenneth R. Commercial Loan Analysis: Principles & Techniques for Credit Analysts & Lenders. 150p. 1994. per. 45.00 (*1-55738-716-8*, Irwn Prfssnl) McGraw-Hill Prof.

— The Lender's Toolkit: The Pocket Guide to the Essential Formulas, Ratios & Tables. 150p. (C). 1995. text 24.95 (*1-55738-756-7*, Irwn Prfssnl) McGraw-Hill Prof.

— Managing Credit Department Functions: A Manager's Guide to Improving Loan Analysis, Documentation & Reporting. 225p. (C). 1995. text 50.00 (*1-55738-755-9*, Irwn Prfssnl) McGraw-Hill Prof.

Pirok, Kenneth R. & Glantz, Morton. Commercial Loan Analysis & Loan Risk Management. 1994. text 95.00 (*1-55738-729-X*, Irwn Prfssnl) McGraw-Hill Prof.

***Pirola, Teresa.** 100 Inspiring Stories: Finding Love & Laughter, Hope & Healing, Forgiveness & Faith. LC 98-61013. 128p. 1999. pap. 9.95 (*0-89622-942-4*) Twenty-Third.

Pirolo, Neal. Serving As Senders: How to Care for Your Missionaries While They Are Preparing to Go, While They Are on the Field, When They Return Home. 207p. (Orig.). 1991. pap. 7.95 (*1-880185-00-8*) Emmaus Rd Intl.

— Sirviendo Alenviar Obreros: Como Apoyar a Sus Misioneros Mientras Se Preparan para Salir, Mientras Estan en el Campo, Cuardo Regresan a Casa. Lopez, Manuel & Lopez, Ruth, trs. (SPA.). 206p. (Orig.). 1996. pap. 7.95 (*1-880185-05-9*) Emmaus Rd Intl.

— Sirviendo Como Enviadores - Serving As Senders. (SPA.). 180p. 1995. write for info. (*1-56063-720-X*) Editorial Unilit.

Pirolo, Neal & Pirolo, Yvonne. Prepare for Battle! Basic Training in Spiritual Warfare. 250p. (Orig.). 1997. pap. 8.95 (*1-880185-06-7*) Emmaus Rd Intl.

Pirolo, Yvonne, jt. auth. see Pirolo, Neal.

Piron, Claude. Gerda Malaperis! Vortlisto - Wordlist. (ENG & ESP.). 26p. (YA). 1998. reprint ed. pap. text 3.75 (*1-882251-05-9*) Eldonejo Bero.

Pirone, James & Sweeney, Paula. Jake Montana: A Matter of Destiny. 124p. (Orig.). (YA). 1993. pap. 9.99 (*0-88092-072-6*) Royal Fireworks.

— Jake Montana: Mystery at Deep Ravine. Kemnitz, Myrna, ed. LC 97-216199. (Jake Montana Ser.: Bk. 2). (Orig.). (YA). (gr. 7 up). 1996. pap. 9.99 (*0-88092-295-8*) Royal Fireworks.

— Mystery at Monster Lake. (Jake Montana Ser.: Bk. 3). (YA). (gr. 6 up). 2000. pap. 9.99 (*0-88092-407-1*, 2958) Royal Fireworks.

Pirone, James, jt. auth. see Sweeney, Paula.

***Pirone, Jon.** Internet Law: The Most up to Date Handbook of Important Answers to Issues Facing Every Entrepreneur, Lawyer, & Anyone with a Website. (Inside the Minds Ser.). 224p. 2000. pap. 27.95 (*1-58762-006-5*) ebrandedbooks.com.

Pirone, P. P., tr. see Fontana, Felice.

Pirone, Pascal P. Diseases & Pests of Ornamental Plants. 5th ed. 584p. 1978. 110.00 (*0-471-07249-4*) Wiley.

Pirone, Pascal P., et al. Tree Maintenance. 6th ed. (Illus.). 528p. (C). 1988. text 49.95 (*0-19-504370-7*) OUP.

Pirone, T. P. & Shaw, J. G., eds. Viral Genes & Plant Pathogenesis. (Illus.). xvi, 215p. 1990. 79.95 (*0-387-97313-3*) Spr-Verlag.

Pironio, Eduardo. Joyful in Hope. (C). 1988. 39.00 (*0-85439-156-8*, Pub. by St Paul Pubns) St Mut.

— We Wish to See Jesus. 214p. 1982. pap. 10.50 (*0-8189-0392-9*) Alba.

Pironio, Eduardo, ed. We Wish to See Jesus. (C). 1988. 39.00 (*0-85439-198-3*, Pub. by St Paul Pubns) St Mut.

Pironneau, O. Optimal Shape Design for Elliptic Systems. (Computational Physics Ser.). (Illus.). 190p. 1983. 75.95 (*0-387-12069-6*) Spr-Verlag.

Pironneau, Olivier, jt. auth. see Lucquin, B.

Pirot, Christian. Impressions des Bords de Creuse. (Livres Gourmands et Beaux Livres Collection). (FRE., Illus.). 200p. 1995. pap. 89.95 (*2-86808-040-5*) Intl Scholars.

***Pirotin, Debra.** No Naughty Cats: The First Guide to Intelligent Cat Training. 2000. 7.99 (*0-517-16200-8*) Random Hse Value.

Pirotta, Saviour. Deep in the Rain Forest. (J). (gr. 2-5). 1998. 63.92 (*0-8172-5136-7*) Raintree Steck-V.

Pirotta, Saviour. Fossils & Bones. LC 96-31734. (Remarkable World Ser.). (Illus.). 48p. (J). (gr. 4-8). 1997. lib. bdg. 24.26 (*0-8172-4542-1*) Raintree Steck-V.

— Italy. LC 98-46691. 32p. (J). 1999. lib. bdg. 22.83 (*0-8172-5760-8*) Raintree Steck-V.

Pirotta, Saviour. Italy. (Food & Festivals Ser.). 32p. (J). (gr. 2-5). 1999. pap. 6.95 (*0-7398-0958-X*) Raintree Steck-V.

— Jerusalem. LC 92-30130. (Holy Cities Ser.). (Illus.). 48p. (YA). (gr. 5 up). 1993. lib. bdg. 13.95 (*0-87518-569-X*, Dillon Silver Burdett) Silver Burdett Pr.

— Joy to the World: Christmas Stories from Around the Globe. LC 97-47366. (Illus.). 48p. (J). (gr. 3-4). 1998. 15.95 (*0-06-027902-8*) HarpC.

— Monsters of the Deep. (Remarkable World Ser.). (Illus.). 48p. (YA). (gr. 3-8). 1995. lib. bdg. 24.26 (*1-56847-367-2*) Raintree Steck-V.

— People in the Rain Forest. LC 97-48525. (Deep in the Rain Forest Ser.). 1999. write for info. (*0-7502-2197-6*) Raintree Steck-V.

— People in the Rain Forest. LC 97-48525. (Deep in the Rain Forest Ser.). 32p. (J). 1999. 22.83 (*0-8172-5137-5*) Raintree Steck-V.

***Pirotta, Saviour.** People in the Rain Forest. 1999. pap. text 5.95 (*0-8172-8111-8*) Raintree Steck-V.

Pirotta, Saviour. Pirates & Treasure. LC 94-48746. (Remarkable World Ser.). (Illus.). 48p. (YA). (gr. 3-8). lib. bdg. 24.26 (*1-56847-366-4*) Raintree Steck-V.

— Pirates & Treasure: The Remarkable World. 1997. 24.25 (*0-8172-4820-X*) Raintree Steck-V.

— Predators in the Rain Forest. (Deep in the Rain Forest Ser.). (Illus.). 32p. (J). (gr. 2-5). 1998. pap. 5.95 (*0-8172-8113-4*) Raintree Steck-V.

— Predators in the Rain Forest. LC 98-4588. (Deep in the Rain Forest Ser.). (J). 1999. 22.83 (*0-8172-5132-4*) Raintree Steck-V.

— Rivers in the Rain Forest. (Deep in the Rain Forest Ser.). (Illus.). 32p. (J). (gr. 2-5). 1998. pap. 5.95 (*0-8172-8114-2*) Raintree Steck-V.

— Rivers in the Rain Forest. LC 98-4587. (Deep in the Rain Forest Ser.). (J). 1999. 22.83 (*0-8172-5138-3*) Raintree Steck-V.

— Rome. LC 92-19685. (Holy Cities Ser.). (Illus.). 48p. (YA). (gr. 5 up). 1993. lib. bdg. 13.95 (*0-87518-570-3*, Dillon Silver Burdett) Silver Burdett Pr.

***Pirotta, Saviour.** Stories from China. LC 99-47865. (Illus.). (J). 2000. write for info. (*0-7398-2034-6*) Raintree Steck-V.

— Stories from China. (Illus.). 48p. (ps-3). 2000. lib. bdg. 25.69 (*0-7398-1337-4*) Raintree Steck-V.

— Stories from the Amazon. (Multicultural Stories Ser.). 2000. pap. text 7.95 (*0-7398-1818-X*) Raintree Steck-V.

Pirotta, Saviour. Trees & Plants in the Rain Forest. (Deep in the Rain Forest Ser.). (Illus.). 32p. (J). (gr. 2-5). 1998. pap. 5.95 (*0-8172-8112-6*) Raintree Steck-V.

— Trees & Plants in the Rain Forest. LC 97-43891. (Deep in the Rain Forest Ser.). (J). 1999. write for info. (*0-7502-2198-4*) Raintree Steck-V.

— Trees & Plants in the Rain Forest. LC 97-43891. (Deep in the Rain Forest Ser.). (Illus.). 32p. (J). (gr. 2-4). 1999. 22.83 (*0-8172-5134-0*) Raintree Steck-V.

— Turtle Bay. LC 96-31676. (Illus.). (J). (ps-3). 1997. 15.00 (*0-374-37888-6*) FS&G.

***Pirotta, Saviour & Cann, Helen.** Christian Festival Tales. LC 00-36936. (Festival Tales Ser.). (Illus.). 2000. write for info. (*0-7398-2732-4*) Raintree Steck-V.

***Pirotta, Saviour & Gryspeerdt, Becky.** Stories from the Amazon. LC 99-32788. (Multicultural Stories Ser.). 48p. (J). 2000. 25.69 (*0-7398-1332-3*) Raintree Steck-V.

***Pirotta, Saviour & Kelly, Anne M.** Jewish Festival Tales. LC 00-36938. (Illus.). (J). 2000. write for info. (*0-7398-2733-2*) Raintree Steck-V.

Pirotte, A., et al, eds. Advances in Database Technology - EDBT '92. (Lecture Notes in Computer Science Ser.: Vol. 580). 551p. 1992. 82.95 (*0-387-55270-7*) Spr-Verlag.

***Pirotte, Claire, et al, contrib. by.** Responding to Emergencies or Fostering Development? The Dilemmas of Humanitarian Aid. LC 99-52393. 183p. 1999. 65.00 (*1-85649-754-2*); pap. text 25.00 (*1-85649-755-0*) Zed Books.

Pirotte, Jean & Derroitte, Henri, eds. Churches & Health Care in the Third World. LC 91-9389. (SCM Ser.: No. 5). (ENG & FRE.). xxvi, 176p. 1991. 75.00 (*90-04-09470-9*) Brill Academic Pubs.

Pirotton, S., jt. auth. see Boeynaems, J. M.

Pirouet, Edmund. Heard Melodies Are Sweet: A History of the London Philharmonic Orchestra. (Illus.). 277p. 1998. 32.50 (*1-85776-381-5*, Pub. by Book Guild Ltd) Trans-Atl Phila.

Pirouet, M. Louise. Historical Dictionary of Uganda. LC 94-20483. (African Historical Dictionaries Ser.: No. 64). 1995. 66.00 (*0-8108-2920-7*) Scarecrow.

Pirouz, Raymond. Click Here. LC 97-27394. 255p. 1997. pap. 45.00 (*1-56205-792-8*) New Riders Pub.

— HTML Web Magic. 2nd ed. LC 98-85794. 1998. pap. 39.99 (*1-56830-475-7*) Hayden.

— Illustrator 8 Magic. LC 98-86036. (Illus.). 275p. 1999. 29.99 (*1-56205-952-1*) New Riders Pub.

Piroyan, Wallace. Love Is Forever. 143p. (Orig.). 1983. pap. 2.50 (*0-9613129-1-2*) Chiwaukee Pub Co.

Pirozhkova, A. N. At His Side: The Last Years of Isaac Babel. Frydman, Anne & Busch, Robert L., trs. from RUS. LC 96-33283. (Illus.). 175p. 1996. 22.00 (*1-883642-37-X*) Steerforth Pr.

— At His Side: The Last Years of Isaac Babel. Busch, Robert L. & Frydman, Anne, trs. from RUS. LC 96-33283. (Illus.). 171p. 1998. reprint ed. pap. 14.00 (*1-883642-98-1*) Steerforth Pr.

Pirozynski, K. A. & Hawksworth, David L., eds. The Coevolution of Fungi with Plants & Animals. 490p. 1988. text 77.00 (*0-12-557365-0*) Acad Pr.

Pirozzi, Richard. Critical Reading, Bk. 2. 384p. (C). 2000. pap. text 43.00 (*0-321-00331-4*) Addison-Wesley.

***Pirozzi, Richard.** Critical Reading, Critical Thinking. 1999. teacher ed., suppl. ed. 26.00 (*0-321-04456-8*) Longman.

Pirozzi, Richard. Strategies for Reading & Study Skills. LC 94-67318. 336p. pap., student ed. 23.00 (*0-8442-5823-7*) NTC Contemp Pub Co.

— Strategies for Reading & Study Skills. annot. ed. 1995. pap., teacher ed. 27.99 (*0-8442-5824-5*) NTC Contemp Pub Co.

Pirozzolo, Dick, jt. auth. see Corzine, Linda.

Pirozzolo, Fran, jt. auth. see McLean, Jim.

Pirozzolo, Fran, jt. auth. see Snead, Sam.

Pirozzolo, Francis J., jt. ed. see Maletta, Gabe J.

Pirquet, Clemens. Volksgesundheit Im Krieg, 2 vols. (Wirtschafts-Und Sozialgeschichte des Weltkrieges (Osterreichische Und Ungarische Serie)). (GER.). 1926. 235.00 (*0-317-27641-7*) Elliots Bks.

Pirrie, Jill, ed. Apple Fire: The Halesworth Middle School Anthology. 128p. 1993. pap. 16.95 (*1-85224-206-X*, Pub. by Bloodaxe Bks) Dufour.

Pirrie, S. R., et al, eds. Iran U. S. Claims: Tribunal Reports, 27 vols. (C). 1993. text 368.00 (*0-7855-7117-5*, Pub. by Grotius Pubns Ltd) St Mut.

Pirrie, S. R. & Arnold, J. S., eds. Iran-U. S. Claims Tribunal Reports, Vol. 9. 1994. text 150.00 (*0-521-46443-9*) Cambridge U Pr.

— Iran-U. S. Claims Tribunal Reports, Vol. 13. 1994. text 150.00 (*0-521-46447-1*) Cambridge U Pr.

— Iran-U. S. Claims Tribunal Reports, Vols. 1-7. (C). 1992. text 310.00 (*0-7855-0124-X*, Pub. by Grotius Pubns Ltd) St Mut.

Pirro, Andre. Johann Sebastian Bach: The Organist & His Works for the Organ. Goodrich, Wallace, tr. from FRE. LC 74-24185. reprint ed. 29.50 (*0-404-13089-5*) AMS Pr.

Pirro, Ellen B., jt. ed. see Zeff, Eleanor E.

***Pirro, Robert.** Hannah Arendt & the Politics of Tragedy. LC 00-36159. 250p. 2000. 38.00 (*0-87580-268-0*) N Ill U Pr.

Pirronello, V., jt. ed. see Greenberg, J. M.

Pirrong, S. Craig. Grain Futures Contracts: An Economic Appraisal. LC 92-44334. 1993. lib. bdg. 104.50 (*0-7923-9327-9*) Kluwer Academic.

Pirrong, Stephen C. The Economics, Law, & Public Policy of Market Power Manipulation. LC 96-26901. 272p. (C). 1996. lib. bdg. 121.00 (*0-7923-9762-2*) Kluwer Academic.

Pirrotta, Nino. Don Giovanni's Progress: A Rake Goes to the Opera. Saunders, Harris, tr. from ITA. (Illus.). 208p. 1994. pap. 17.00 (*0-941419-94-0*) Marsilio Pubs.

— Music & Culture in Italy from the Middle Ages to the Baroque: A Collection of Essays. LC 83-12827. (Studies in the History of Music: No. 1). 501p. reprint ed. pap. 155.40 (*0-7837-2313-X*, 205740100004) Bks Demand.

— Paolo Tenorista in a New Fragment of the Italian Ars Nova. (Illus.). 83p. 1961. 22.50 (*0-934082-07-3*, M61-2053) Theodore Front.

Pirrung, Michael C. & Morehead, Andrew T. The Total Synthesis of Natural Products Vol. 10: Acyclic & Monocyclic. (Total Synthesis of Natural Products Ser.). 192p. 1997. 74.95 (*0-471-59679-5*) Wiley.

Pirrwitz, D., jt. auth. see Palz, Wolfgang.

Pirsch, John D. Transplantation Drug Manual. 3rd ed. Simmons, William & Sollinger, Hans, eds. LC 99-28833. (Vademecum Ser.). 15p. 1999. 45.00 (*1-57059-593-3*) Landes Bioscience.

Pirsch, P. Architectures for Digital Signal Processing. LC 98-10613. 432p. 1998. 95.00 (*0-471-97145-6*) Wiley.

Pirsch, P., ed. VLSI Implementations for Image Communications. LC 93-30175. (Advances in Image Communication Ser.: Vol. 2). 412p. 1993. 184.00 (*0-444-88790-3*) Elsevier.

Pirsein, Robert W. The Voice of America. Sterling, Christopher H., ed. LC 78-21733. (Dissertations in Broadcasting Ser.). 1980. lib. bdg. 44.95 (*0-405-11770-1*) Ayer.

Pirsig. Pirsig on Minnesota Pleading, 1998 Cumulative Supplement. 1998. pap. text 80.00 (*0-327-00137-2*, 81883-14) LEXIS Pub.

Pirsig, Maynard E. Pirsig on Minnesota Pleading, 2 vols. 5th ed. 1987. 175.00 (*0-327-00994-2*, 81880, MICHIE); boxed set 175.00 (*0-86678-554-X*, 81880, MICHIE) LEXIS Pub.

— Pirsig on Minnesota Pleading, 2 vols. 5th ed. 960p. 1992. suppl. ed. 60.00 (*1-56257-835-9*, MICHIE) LEXIS Pub.

— Pirsig on Minnesota Pleading, 1999 Cumulative Supplement. 400p. 1999. pap. write for info. (*0-327-01363-X*, 8188315) LEXIS Pub.

Pirsig, Maynard E. & Kirwin, Kenneth F. Professional Responsibility: Cases & Materials. LC 84-7566. 107p. 1986. pap. text, teacher ed. write for info. (*0-314-98583-2*) West Pub.

— Professional Responsibility: Cases & Materials. 4th ed. LC 84-7566. 603p. (C). 1984. reprint ed. 45.50 (*0-314-83001-4*) West Pub.

***Pirsig, Robert.** Zen & the Art of Motorcycle Maintenance: An Inquiry Into Values. 448p. 2000. pap. 13.00 (*0-06-095832-4*) HarpC.

Pirsig, Robert M. Lila: An Inquiry into Morals. 480p. 1992. mass mkt. 7.99 (*0-553-29961-1*) Bantam.

— Zen & the Art of Motorcycle Maintenance: An Inquiry into Values. 410p. 1984. mass mkt. 7.99 (*0-553-27747-2*, Bantam Classics) Bantam.

***Pirsig, Robert M.** Zen & the Art of Motorcycle Maintenance: An Inquiry into Values. LC 73-12275. 432p. 1999. 25.00 (*0-688-00230-7*, Wm Morrow) Morrow Avon.

— Zen & the Art of Motorcycle Maintenance: An Inquiry into Values. LC 99-221640. 448p. 1999. pap. 13.00 (*0-688-17166-4*, Wm Morrow) Morrow Avon.

— Zen & the Art of Motorcycle Maintenance: An Inquiry into Values. 1974. 13.09 (*0-606-03960-0*, Pub. by Turtleback) Demco.

Pirsig, Robert M. Zen & the Art of Motorcycle Maintenance: An Inquiry into Values, Set. unabridged ed. 1999. 49.95 incl. audio (*1-55927-556-1*) Audio Renaissance.

— Zen & the Art of Motorcycle Maintenance: An Inquiry into Values, Set abr. ed. 1996. audio 24.95 (*1-55927-378-X*, 693879, Pub. by Audio Renaissance) Lndmrk Audiobks.

Pirson, A., ed. General Index. (New Encyclopedia of Plant Physiology Ser.: Vol. 20). 320p. 1993. 238.95 (*0-387-18162-8*) Spr-Verlag.

Pirson, Sylvain J. Geologic Well Log Analysis. 3rd ed. LC 82-24218. 496p. 1983. reprint ed. pap. 153.80 (*0-608-01342-0*, 206208500001) Bks Demand.

***Pirsos, Rena.** Your Paycheck Factbook: 2000 Edition. 5th rev. ed. 70p. 2000. 9.95 (*1-930471-09-2*, 12000) American Payroll.

Pirt, S. John. Control of Foam Formation & Antifoam Action in Aerated Systems. (C). 1992. 75.00 (*1-874685-00-2*, Pub. by Pirtferm Ltd) St Mut.

— The Penicillin Fermentation: A Model for Secondary Metabolite Production. (C). 1993. 75.00 (*1-874685-10-X*, Pub. by Pirtferm Ltd) St Mut.

— Stoichiometry & Kinetics of Microbial Growth. (C). 1994. 75.00 (*1-874685-20-7*, Pub. by Pirtferm Ltd) St Mut.

P

— Total Biocombustion of Sewage Sludge by the Bicycle Process. (C). 1993. 80.00 (*1-874685-05-3*, Pub. by Pirtferm Ltd) St Mut.

Pirt, S. John, ed. Product Formation in Cultures of Microbes & the Microbial Growth Process. (C). 1994. 75.00 (*1-874685-15-0*, Pub. by Pirtferm Ltd) St Mut.

Pirtle, Caleb. Dying Man's Bluff. 1996. mass mkt. 5.99 (*1-57297-181-9*) Blvd Books.

Pirtle, Caleb, III, et al, eds. Texas: Generations of Harvest. 96p. write for info. (*1-879234-11-4*) Herit Pub TX.

Pirtle, Caleb, III & Dobbs, Frank Q. Jokers Are Wild. (Gambler Ser.: No. 1). 432p. (Orig.). 1996. mass mkt. 5.99 (*1-57297-053-7*) Blvd Books.

Pirtle, Caleb & Dobbs, Frank Q. Kenny Rogers' the Gambler: Dead Man's Hand. (Gambler Ser.: Vol. 2). 1996. mass mkt. 5.99 (*1-57297-093-6*) Blvd Books.

Pirtle, Caleb, 3rd, jt. ed. see Lively, Ken.

***Pirtle, Carol.** Escape Betwixt Two Suns: A True Tale of the Underground Railroad in Illinois. 2000. 39.95 (*0-8093-2300-1*); pap. 16.95 (*0-8093-2301-X*) S Ill U Pr.

Pirtle, Carol. Where Illinois Began: A Pictorial History of Randolph County. LC 95-11610. (Illus.). 1995. write for info. (*0-89865-939-6*) Donning Co.

Pirtle-Frazer, Beth E., ed. see Hughes, Lisa R.

Pirtle, Henry. The Lost Word of Freemasonry. 240p. 1993. reprint ed. pap. 19.95 (*1-56459-320-7*) Kessinger Pub.

Pirtle, Rebecca B., ed. see Mehrhoff, Charlie.

Pirtle, Sarah. Discovery Time for Cooperation & Conflict Resolution. (Illus.). 167p. 1998. pap. 20.00 (*1-891955-09-8*) Creative Resp.

— Linking Up! Using Music, Movement, & Language Arts to Promote Caring, Cooperation, & Communication. Roerden, Laura P., ed. (Illus.). 309p. 1998. pap. 29.00 incl. audio compact disk (*0-942349-10-5*) Eductrs Soc Respons.

Pirtle, Thomas R. History of the Dairy Industry. LC 72-89079. (Rural America Ser.). 1973. reprint ed. 42.00 (*0-8420-1494-2*) Scholarly Res Inc.

Pirumov, U. G. & Roslyakov, G. S. Gas Flow in Nozzles. (Chemical Physics Ser.: Vol. 29). (Illus.). 436p. 1986. 117.95 (*0-387-12413-6*) Spr-Verlag.

Pirumova, Olga. Moscow. (Great Cities Ser.). (Illus.). 96p. 1996. 20.00 (*1-85995-194-5*) Parkstone Pr.

Pirus, jt. auth. see Mezzo.

Pirz, Therese S. Kids Stuff - Italian: Easy Italian Phrases to Teach Your Kids. LC 97-77713. (Bilingual Kids Ser.). (ENG & ITA., Illus.). 150p. 1997. pap. 14.95 (*0-9606140-8-7*) Chou-Chou.

***Pirz, Therese S.** Kids' Stuff Spanish: Easy Spanish Phrases to Teach your Kids (And Yourself) LC 99-94904. (Bilingual Kids Ser.: Vol. 2). (Illus.). 168p. (J). (gr. k-8). 1999. pap. 16.95 (*0-9606140-2-8*) Chou-Chou.

Pirz, Therese S. & Hobson, Mark. Kids' Stuff German: Easy German Phrases to Teach Your Kids (And Yourself) LC 99-94906. (Bilingual Kids Ser.: Vol. 3). (ENG & GER., Illus.). 172p. (J). (ps-8). 1999. pap. 16.95 (*0-9606140-4-4*) Chou-Chou.

***Pirzada, Sayyid A. S.** The Politics of the Jamiat-i-ulema-i-islam Pakistan; 1971-1977. 345p. 2000. text 26.00 (*0-19-579302-1*) OUP.

Pisa, Maria G., jt. auth. see Russel, K. W.

Pisacane, Vincent L. & Moore, Robert C., eds. Fundamentals of Space Systems. LC 92-9490. (Johns Hopkins Applied Physics Laboratory Series in Science & Engineering). (Illus.). 784p. 1994. text 90.00 (*0-19-507497-1*) OUP.

Pisacreta, Sharon. Magic & Moonlight, 1. (Love Spell Ser.). 368p. 1999. mass mkt. 5.50 (*0-8439-4541-9*) Dorchester Pub Co.

***Pisan, Christine.** Book of the City of Ladies. 352p. 2000. pap. 12.95 (*0-14-044689-3*, Penguin Classics) Viking Penguin.

Pisan, Christine De, see De Pisan, Christine.

Pisani, Assunta. European Defence, vol. 2. (Contemporary European Affairs Ser.). 190p. 1990. pap. 13.00 (*0-08-040246-1*, Pergamon Pr) Elsevier.

Pisani, Assunta, ed. Euro-Librarianship: Shared Resources, Shared Responsibilities. LC 91-38269. (Collection Management Ser.: Vol. 15, Nos. 1-4). 578p. 1992. lib. bdg. 169.95 (*1-56024-266-3*, Harrington Park) Haworth Pr.

Pisani, C. Quantum-Mechanical Ab-Initio Calculation of the Properties of Crystalline Materials: Proceedings of the IV School of Computational Chemistry of the Italian Chemical Society, Vol. 67. LC 96-36109. 336p. 1996. 71.00 (*3-540-61645-4*) Spr-Verlag.

Pisani, C., et al. Hartree-Fock Ab Initio Treatment of Crystalline Systems. (Lecture Notes in Chemistry Ser.: Vol. 48). 193p. 1988. 45.95 (*0-387-19317-0*) Spr-Verlag.

Pisani, Donald J. To Reclaim a Divided West: Water, Law, & Public Policy, 1848-1902. LC 92-14161. (Histories of the American Frontier Ser.). (Illus.). 509p. 1992. reprint ed. pap. 157.80 (*0-608-07869-7*, 205405200011) Bks Demand.

— Water, Land, & Law in the West: The Limits of Public Policy, 1850-1920. LC 96-14093. (Development of Western Resources Ser.). 248p. 1996. 29.95 (*0-7006-0795-1*) U Pr of KS.

Pisani, Edgard, ed. Health & Social Welfare. (Journal of Contemporary European Affairs Ser.: No. 2). 182p. 1990. pap. 13.00 (*0-08-040234-8*, 2701; 2902; 3002, Pergamon Pr) Elsevier.

— Politics & Religion. (Contemporary European Affairs Ser.: No. 2). 204p. 1990. pap. 12.50 (*0-08-040794-3*, Pergamon Pr) Elsevier.

Pisani, Edgard, et al, eds. Educating Europe. (Contemporary European Affairs Ser.: No. 3). 202p. 1991. pap. 14.50 (*0-08-041390-0*, Pergamon Pr) Elsevier.

— Europe: Two Perspectives. (Journal of Contemporary European Affairs Ser.: No. 2). 176p. 1990. pap. 13.00 (*0-08-040490-1*, Pergamon Pr) Elsevier.

— European Immigration Policy. (Contemporary European Affairs Ser.: No. 3). 200p. 1991. pap. 15.00 (*0-08-041388-9*, Pergamon Pr) Elsevier.

— The Gulf Crisis. (Contemporary European Affairs Ser.: No. 4). 192p. 1991. pap. 16.25 (*0-08-041391-9*, Pergamon Pr) Elsevier.

Pisani, Edgard, ed. see Bell, David S. & Gaffney, John.

Pisani, Mario, intro. Architecture Studio. LC 99-495106. (Master Architect Ser.). (Illus.). 256p. 1996. 59.95 (*1-875498-39-7*) AIA Press.

Pisani, Mary A. Services for the Seriously Mentally Ill in Texas: Facts & Issues. 39p. (Orig.). 1988. pap. 1.00 (*0-915757-11-7*) League Women Voters TX.

Pisani, Sallie. The CIA & the Marshall Plan. LC 91-16840. x, 190p. 1991. 25.00 (*0-7006-0502-9*) U Pr of KS.

Pisano. Manufacturing Renaissance. 1995. 29.95 (*0-07-103620-2*) McGraw.

Pisano, A. P., et al, eds. Micromechanical Systems, 1993. LC 93-73713. 107p. 1993. pap. 40.00 (*0-7918-1000-3*) ASME.

Pisano, Albert P., jt. ed. see Muller, Richard S.

Pisano, Beverly. Afghan Hounds. (Illus.). 157p. 1980. 9.95 (*0-87666-682-9*, KW-077) TFH Pubns.

— Beagles. 1998. pap. 9.95 (*0-7938-2301-3*, KW-0802) TFH Pubns.

— Boxers: AKC Rank No. 13. (Illus.). 1997. pap. 9.95 (*0-7938-2306-4*, KW-041S) TFH Pubns.

— Brittanys. (Illus.). 1996. pap. 9.95 (*0-7938-2354-4*, KW092S) TFH Pubns.

— Chihuahuas, AKC Rank No. 15. (KW Dog Ser.). (Illus.). 1996. pap. 9.95 (*0-7938-2362-5*, KW087S) TFH Pubns.

— Chow Chows, AKC Rank No. 17. (KW Dog Ser.). (Illus.). 1995. pap. 9.95 (*0-7938-2355-2*, KW089S) TFH Pubns.

— Dalmatians. (Illus.). 1997. pap. 9.95 (*0-7938-2365-X*, KW-090S) TFH Pubns.

— English Setters. 1997. pap. text 9.95 (*0-7938-2310-2*, KW-102S) TFH Pubns.

— Irish Wolfhounds. (Illus.). (Orig.). 1996. pap. 9.95 (*0-7938-2372-2*, KW108S) TFH Pubns.

— Miniature Schnauzers. 1998. pap. text 9.95 (*0-7938-2336-6*) TFH Pubns.

— Old English Sheepdogs. (Illus.). 1996. pap. 9.95 (*0-7938-2367-6*, KW-093S) TFH Pubns.

— Pekingese. (Illus.). 1997. pap. 9.95 (*0-7938-2399-4*, KW-095S) TFH Pubns.

— Pomeranians. (Illus.). 1997. pap. 9.95 (*0-7938-2322-6*, KW-091S) TFH Pubns.

— Shetland Sheepdogs. (Illus.). 224p. 1994. 9.95 (*0-7938-1183-X*, KW079) TFH Pubns.

— Shetland Sheepdogs, AKC Rank No. 13. (KW Dog Ser.). (Illus.). 224p. 1996. pap. 9.95 (*0-7938-2357-9*, KW079S) TFH Pubns.

— Siberian Huskies: AKC Rank #17. (Illus.). 1997. pap. 9.95 (*0-7938-2327-7*, KW-068S) TFH Pubns.

Pisano, Dominick, jt. auth. see Hardesty, Von.

Pisano, Dominick A. To Fill the Skies with Pilots: The Civilian Pilot Training Program, 1939-46. LC 92-29061. (Illus.). 224p. 1993. text 34.95 (*0-252-01994-6*) U of Ill Pr.

***Pisano, Doug.** Mass. Pharm. Laws & Regulations for Law 351. (C). 1999. pap. text 22.54 (*1-56870-368-6*) RonJon Pub.

— The Massachusetts Pharmacy Law Review. 1998. pap. text 19.68 (*1-56870-342-2*) RonJon Pub.

Pisano, Gary P. The Development Factory: Unlocking the Potential Of Process Innovation. LC 96-4073. 304p. 1996. 35.00 (*0-87584-650-5*) Harvard Busn.

Pisano, Gary P. & Hayes, Robert H., eds. Manufacturing Renaissance: A Harvard Business Review Book. LC 94-43320. (Business Review Bk.). 384p. 1995. 29.95 (*0-87584-610-6*) Harvard Busn.

Pisano, Jane G. Los Angeles, 2000. (Urban Studies: No. 8). 48p. (Orig.). 1988. pap. 6.00 (*0-913749-10-9*) U MD Urban Stud.

Pisano, Janice A. Miniature Schnauzer. (Illus.). 224p. 1995. 9.95 (*0-7938-1184-8*, KW042) TFH Pubns.

Pisano, Lewis, ed. Air & Space History: An Annotated Bibliography. LC 88-342. 571p. 1988. text 30.00 (*0-8240-8543-4*, H00834) Garland.

Pisano, Mary B. Going to New Orleans to Visit Weezie Anna. LC 93-34203. (Illus.). 24p. (J). 1994. 8.95 (*0-937552-52-6*) Quail Ridge.

Pisano, Ronald G. An American Place. LC 81-81364. (Illus.). 40p. (Orig.). (C). 1981. pap. 5.00 (*0-943526-28-0*) Parrish Art.

— A Leading Spirit in American Art: William Merritt Chase, 1849-1916. LC 83-82428. (Illus.). 204p. 1983. 25.00 (*0-935558-14-4*) Henry Art.

— The Long Island Landscape, 1914-1946: The Transitional Years. LC 82-81697. (Illus.). 40p. (Orig.). 1982. pap. 4.00 (*0-943526-35-3*) Parrish Art.

***Pisano, Ronald G.** Tile Club: And the Aesthetic Movement in America. LC 99-28099. 112p. 1999. 29.95 (*0-8109-3894-4*, Pub. by Abrams) Time Warner.

Pisano, Ronald G. William Merritt Chase: Master of American Impressionism. (Illus.). 5p. 1994. pap. write for info. (*0-945936-10-9*) Spanierman Gallery.

— William Merritt Chase (1849-1916) (Illus.). 25p. (Orig.). (C). 1976. pap. 5.00 (*0-943526-43-4*) Parrish Art.

— William Merritt Chase in the Company of Friends. LC 79-87491. (Illus.). 70p. 1979. 4.00 (*0-943526-06-X*) Parrish Art.

Pisano, Ronald G., intro. American Paintings from the Parrish Art Museum. LC 82-61450. (Illus.). 54p. (Orig.). (C). 1982. pap. 10.00 (*0-943526-27-2*) Parrish Art.

— 17 Abstract Artists of East Hampton: The Pollock Years, 1946-56. LC 80-81980. (Illus.). 32p. (Orig.). 1980. pap. text 4.00 (*0-943526-40-X*) Parrish Art.

Pisano, Ronald G. & Longwell, Alicia G. Photographs from the William Merritt Chase Archives. LC 92-85286. (Illus.). 118p. 1992. pap. 18.00 (*0-943526-22-1*) Parrish Art.

Pisano, Ronald G. & Rood, Beverly. The Art Students League: Selections from the Permanent Collection. (Illus.). 110p. 1987. 20.00 (*0-934483-09-4*) Gal Assn NY.

Pisano, Ronald G., jt. auth. see Weber, Bruce.

Pisano, Stephen, jt. ed. see Norton, Gerard J.

Pisano, Vittorfranco S. The Dynamics of Subversion & Violence in Contemporary Italy. (Publication Ser.: No. 355). 224p. (C). 1987. pap. text 14.95 (*0-8179-8552-2*) Hoover Inst Pr.

Pisano, Vivian M., jt. auth. see Mackay, Nancy.

Pisano, Vivian M., jt. ed. see Guerena, Salvador.

Pisarenkova, Lubov. Food & Gossip in the Moscow Circus. Klopfer, Fred, ed. (Illus.). 97p. 1994. pap. 9.95 (*0-9638715-1-X*) Vanatech Systs.

Pisarev, Alexei, jt. auth. see Kostrovitskaya, Vera S.

Pisar'kova, Liubov' F. Izdaniia Gubernskikh Uchenykh Akhivnykh Komissii, 1884-1923 - Index to the Publications of the Russian Provincial Archeographic Commissions, 1884-1923, 5 vols., II. Shmidt, Sigurd O., ed. LC 92-60510. (RUS.). vi, 133p. 1994. lib. bdg. 100.00 (*0-88354-360-5*) N Ross.

— Izdaniia Gubernskikh Uchenykh Akhivnykh Komissii, 1884-1923 - Index to the Publications of the Russian Provincial Archeographic Commissions, 1884-1923, 5 vols., III. Shmidt, Sigurd O., ed. LC 92-60510. (RUS.). viii, 155p. 1995. lib. bdg. 100.00 (*0-88354-361-3*) N Ross.

— Izdaniia Gubernskikh Uchenykh Akhivnykh Komissii, 1884-1923 - Index to the Publications of the Russian Provincial Archeographic Commissions, 1884-1923, 5 vols., IV. Shmidt, Sigurd O., ed. LC 92-60510. (RUS.). 160p. 1999. lib. bdg. 100.00 (*0-88354-362-1*) N Ross.

— Izdaniia Gubernskikh Uchenykh Akhivnykh Komissii, 1884-1923 - Index to the Publications of the Russian Provincial Archeographic Commissions, 1884-1923, 5 vols., V. Shmidt, Sigurd O., ed. LC 92-60510. (RUS.). 160p. 1999. lib. bdg. 100.00 (*0-88354-363-X*) N Ross.

— Izdaniia Gubernskikh Uchenykh Akhivnykh Komissii, 1884-1923 - Index to the Publications of the Russian Provincial Archeographic Commissions, 1884-1923, 5 vols., Vol. 1. Shmidt, Sigurd O., ed. LC 92-60510. (RUS.). xx, 139p. 1994. lib. bdg. 100.00 (*0-88354-359-1*) N Ross.

Pisarowicz, James, ed. Proceedings Death Valley Conference on History & Prehistory, 3rd. LC 91-74081. (Death Valley History Conference Ser.). (Illus.). 260p. (Orig.). (C). 1992. pap. 10.95 (*1-878900-26-9*) DVNH Assn.

Pisarra, Drew. Publick Spanking. (Illus.). 75p. (Orig.). 1996. pap. 8.95 (*1-882550-16-1*) Quiet Lion Pr.

Pisarski, Cathryn & Smith, Phil, contrib. by. Robin Hood: A Full Length Play. (Illus.). 28p. (J). (gr. 1 up). 1988. pap. 3.50 (*0-88680-308-X*) I E Clark.

Pisarski, R. D., jt. auth. see Gocksch, A.

Pisarski, Robert D., jt. ed. see Muller, Berndt.

Pisaturn, Angela. A Gift for Abigail. 54p. (J). 1998. pap. write for info. (*1-57502-940-5*, P02580) Morris Pubng.

Piscataway Conoy Confereracy & Subtribes, Inc. Sta. A Piscataway Story: The Legend of Kittimuquinn. Seib-Toup, Rebecca, ed. (Illus.). 96p. (J). (gr. 4-6). 1994. 10.00 (*0-945253-09-5*) Thornsbury Bailey Brown.

Piscatella, Bernie, jt. auth. see Piscatella, Joseph C.

Piscatella, Joseph. Choices for a Healthy Heart. LC 86-40199. (Illus.). 592p. (Orig.). 1987. pap. 16.95 (*0-89480-138-4*, 1138) Workman Pub.

Piscatella, Joseph C. Fat-Proof Your Child. LC 97-9065. (Illus.). 512p. 1997. pap. 15.95 (*1-56305-150-8*, 3150) Workman Pub.

— Joseph C. Piscatella's Don't Eat Your Heart Out Cookbook. rev. ed. LC 94-32730. (Illus.). 704p. 1994. pap. 17.95 (*1-56305-558-9*) Workman Pub.

— Joseph C. Piscatella's Everyday Guide to Low-Fat Restaurant Foods. LC 97-45608. 400p. 1998. 7.95 (*0-7611-0950-1*) Workman Pub.

Piscatella, Joseph C. & Piscatella, Bernie. Joseph C. Piscatella's Controlling Your Fat Tooth. rev. ed. LC 90-50361. (Illus.). 544p. 1991. pap. 15.95 (*0-89480-431-6*, 1431) Workman Pub.

Piscatori, James P. Transnational Religion & Fading States. Rudolph, Susanne H., ed. LC 96-35187. (C). 1996. pap. 75.00 (*0-8133-2767-9*, Pub. by Westview) HarpC.

Piscatori, James P. & Harris, George S., eds. Law, Personalities, & Politics of the Middle East: Essays in Honor of Majid Khadduri. (Illus.). 270p. (C). 1987. text 60.00 (*0-916808-32-7*) Westview.

Piscatori, James P., jt. auth. see Eickelman, Dale F.

Piscatori, James P., jt. auth. see Marty, Martin E.

Piscatori, James P., jt. ed. see Eickelman, Dale F.

Piscatori, James P., jt. ed. see Rudolph, Susanne H.

Pischel, Barbara. Radegunde: Zur Europaischen Volkskunde. (Illus.). 224p. 1997. 44.95 (*3-631-43603-3*) P Lang Pubng.

Pischel, Dohrmann K. Dohrmann Kaspar Pischel, M. D. American Links with Germanic Ophthalmology, Retinal Detachment Surgery, San Francisco. (Ophthalmology Oral History Ser.). (Illus.). xxii, 142p. (Orig.). (C). 1988. pap. 35.00 (*0-926866-00-1*) FAAO.

Pischinger, Alfred. Matrix & Matrix Regulation: Basis for a Holistic Theory in Medicine. Heine, Hartmut, ed. Mac Lean, Norman, tr. from GER. (Illus.). 221p. (C). 1991. text 39.95 (*2-8043-4000-7*, Pub. by Edits Haug Intl) Medicina Bio.

Pischke, Linda & Langmade, Calvin. In the Care of Strangers. LC 99-192035. 133p. 1998. pap. 19.50 (*0-929442-37-7*, 2146PP) Prof Prnting & Pub.

Pischke, Linda, jt. auth. see Gardner, Michelle.

Pischke, Sibyl J. Ashes of Roses & War. 900p. 1996. pap. 18.95 (*0-9608532-3-5*) S J Pischke.

— The Legend of Mammy Jane. 3rd ed. 405p. 1994. pap. 14.95 (*0-9608532-2-7*) S J Pischke.

— Matches at Midnight. (Illus.). 365p. (Orig.). 1987. pap. 4.95 (*0-9608532-1-9*) S J Pischke.

— Sibyl's Legend of Mammy Jane. 1981. 14.95 (*0-9608532-0-0*) S J Pischke.

Pischna, J. Little Pischna: 48 Practice Pieces for the Piano. 40p. 1986. pap. 3.95 (*0-7935-5312-1*) H Leonard.

Piscicelli, U. Respiratory Autogenic Training & Obstetric Psychoprophylaxis. 292p. 1987. pap. text 25.00 (*1-57235-026-1*) Piccin Nuova.

Piscicelli, U. Respiratory Autogenic Training & Obstetric Psychoprophylaxis. 292p. 1987. text 28.00 (*88-299-0242-X*, Pub. by Piccin Nuova) Gordon & Breach.

Pisciotta, Alexander W. Benevolent Repression: Social Control & the American Reformatory-Prison Movement. LC 93-41515. (Illus.). 197p. (C). 1994. text 47.50 (*0-8147-6623-4*) NYU Pr.

— Benevolent Repression: Social Control & the American Reformatory-Prison Movement. (Illus.). 197p. (C). 1996. pap. text 19.50 (*0-8147-6638-2*) NYU Pr.

Piscitelli, Kathryn S., jt. auth. see Gibson, Paul C.

Piscitelli, Kathryn S., ed. see Fox, John C.

Piscitelli, Nicola. Diccionario Atlas de Anatomia Humana. 2nd ed. (SPA., Illus.). 256p. 1980. pap. 29.95 (*0-7859-5106-7*) Fr & Eur.

Piscitelli, Stephen. I Don't Need This Stuff! (Or Do I?) LC 96-77281. 192p. (C). 1997. pap. text 29.50 (*0-15-504059-6*) Harcourt Coll Pubs.

***Piscitelli, Stephen C. & Rodvold, Keith A., eds.** Drug Interactions in Infectious Diseases. (Infectious Disease Ser.). 385p. 2000. 99.50 (*0-89603-750-9*) Humana.

Piscitello, David M. & Chapin, A. Lyman. Open Systems Networking, TCP - IP & OSI. 624p. 1993. 59.95 (*0-201-56334-7*) Addison-Wesley.

Piscitello, E. Scott & Bogach, V. Susan. Financial Incentives for Renewable Energy Development: Proceedings of an International Workshop, February 17-21, 1997, Amsterdam, the Netherlands. LC 98-27530. (Discussion Paper Ser.: No. 391). 55p. 1998. pap. 22.00 (*0-8213-4283-5*, 14283) World Bank.

Piscol, K., et al, eds. Neurosurgical Standards, Cerebral Aneurysms, Malignant Gliomas. (Advances in Neurosurgery Ser.: Vol. 20). (Illus.). 360p. 1992. pap. 79.00 (*0-387-54838-6*) Spr-Verlag.

Piscop. Cryptic Crosswords for Beginners. LC 98-216269. (Illus.). 96p. 1999. pap. 6.95 (*0-8069-7751-5*) Sterling.

Piscopo, Joe. The Piscopo Tapes. 1987. pap. 5.95 (*0-317-56817-5*) PB.

Piscopo, Maria. The Photographer's Guide to Marketing & Self-Promotion. 2nd ed. LC 95-75285. (Illus.). 176p. 1995. pap. 18.95 (*1-880559-24-2*) Allworth Pr.

Piscoya, Francisco M. Estructuras Algebraicas VI: Formas Cuadraticas. Organization of American States General Secretaria, ed. (Mathematics Ser.: Monograph No. 23). (SPA.). 98p. (C). 1981. pap. 3.50 (*0-8270-1359-0*) OAS.

Pise, Charles C. Father Rowland: A North American Tale. 1978. 18.95 (*0-405-10847-8*, 11850) Ayer.

Pisemskii, Aleksei F. One Thousand Souls. Litvinov, Ivy, tr. 1970. reprint ed. lib. bdg. 75.00 (*0-8371-2239-2*, PIOS, Greenwood Pr) Greenwood.

Pisetsky, David S. & Trien, Susan F. The Duke University Medical Center Book of Arthritis. 416p. 1995. pap. 12.95 (*0-449-90887-9*) Fawcett.

Pishdad, A. Alan, ed. Hazardous Waste Sites in the U. S. 175p. 1981. pap. 46.00 (*0-08-026274-0*, Pergamon Pr) Elsevier.

Pishko, Charles, ed. see Knight, David W., Sr.

Pisier, Gilles. Factorization of Linear Operators & Geometry of Banach Spaces. LC 85-18605. (CBMS Regional Conference Series in Mathematics: No. 60). 154p. 1986. reprint ed. pap. 25.00 (*0-8218-0710-2*, CBMS/60) Am Math.

— The Operator Hilbert Space OH, Complex Interpolation, & Tensor Norms, Vol. 122, No. 585. LC 96-13644. (Memoirs of the American Mathematical Society Ser.). 103p. 1996. pap. 36.00 (*0-8218-0474-X*, MEMO/122/585) Am Math.

— Similarity Problems & Completely Bounded Maps. LC 95-44959. (Lecture Notes in Mathematics Ser.: No. 1618). 156p. 1995. 38.95 (*3-540-60322-0*) Spr-Verlag.

— The Volume of Convex Bodies & Banach Space Geometry. (Tracts in Mathematics Ser.: No. 94). 266p. 1999. pap. 29.95 (*0-521-66635-X*) Cambridge U Pr.

Pisier, Gilles, jt. auth. see Marcus, Michael B.

Piske, Thorsten. Basic Structures German Bk. 1: A Textbook for the Learnables. Winitz, Harris, ed. (GER., Illus.). 132p. (YA). (gr. 7 up). 1997. pap. 45.00 (*1-887371-27-3*) Intl Linguistics.

Piske, Thorsten, et al. Wetter. (German Language Ser.). (GER., Illus.). 42p. (YA). (gr. 7 up). 1993. pap. 25.00 (*0-939990-86-5*) Intl Linguistics.

Piske, Thorsten, tr. see Hanneman, Melitta & Winitz, Harris.

Piskin, Erhan & Hoffman, Allan S., eds. Polymeric Biomaterials. 1986. text 175.00 (*90-247-3303-0*) Kluwer Academic.

Piskulich, John P. Collective Bargaining in State & Local Government. LC 91-28142. 144p. 1992. 47.95 (*0-275-94043-8*, C4043, Praeger Pubs) Greenwood.

Piskunov, Nikolai. Differential & Integral Calculus. 896p. 1965. text 480.00 (*0-677-20600-3*) Gordon & Breach.

Piskurich, George M. ASTD Handbook of Training Design & Delivery. 2nd ed. LC 99-49214. (ASTD Trainer's Sourcebook Series). 640p. 1999. 79.95 (*0-07-134310-5*) McGraw.

P

An Asterisk (*) at the beginning of an entry indicates that the title is appearing for the first time.

— An Organizational Guide to Telecommuting: Setting up & Running a Successful Telecommuter Program LC 98-70650. 175 p. 1998. write for info. (*1-56286-086-0*) Am Soc Train & Devel.

***Piskurich, George M.** Rapid Instructional Design: Learning ID Fast & Right. 240p. 2000. pap. 44.95 (*0-7879-4721-0*, Pfffr & Co) Jossey-Bass.

Piskurich, George M. Self-Directed Learning: A Practical Guide to Design, Development & Implementation. LC 93-12369. (Management Ser.). 379p. 1993. text 39.95 (*1-55542-532-1*) Jossey-Bass.

Piskurich, George M., ed. The ASTD Handbook of Instructional Technology. LC 92-23142. 1992. 69.50 (*0-07-001531-7*) Am Soc Train & Devel.

Pislaru, Sorin V. New Aspects of Thrombolytic Therapy for Acute Myocardial Infarction. (Acta Biomedica Lovaniensia Ser.). (Illus.). 126p. 1998. pap. 45.00 (*90-6186-888-2*, Pub. by Leuven Univ) Coronet Bks.

Pismen, Leonid M. Vortices in Nonlinear Fields. LC 99-219978. (International Series of Monographs on Physics: 100). (Illus.). 306p. 1999. text 105.00 (*0-19-850167-6*) OUP.

Pison, Gilles, jt. ed. see Bledsoe, Caroline.

Pison, Gilles, ed. see National Research Council Staff.

Pisoni, David B., jt. ed. see Chin, Steven B.

***Pisoni, Susan.** Hello Sunshine. (Illus.). 42p. 2000. pap. 10.95 (*1-57377-106-6*, 0-1988-4-02350-0) Easl Pubns.

— A Snowman's Smile Vol. II: The Garden Variety. (Illus.). 32p. 1999. pap. 10.95 (*1-57377-075-2*) Easl Pubns.

Pissard, Hippolyte. La Guerre Sainte en Pays Chretien. LC 78-63357. (Crusades & Military Orders Ser.: Second Series). reprint ed. 47.50 (*0-404-17027-7*) AMS Pr.

***Pissarides, Christopher.** Equilibrium Unemployment Theory. 2nd ed. LC 99-41746. (Illus.). 399p. 2000. 35.00 (*0-262-16187-7*) MIT Pr.

Pissarro. Monet & Mediterranean. 1999. pap. 29.95 (*0-912804-33-5*) St Martin.

***Pissarro, Camille.** Camille Pissarro. (Illus.). 224p. 2000. 40.00 (*3-7757-0861-8*) Gerd Hatje.

Pissarro, Camille. Letters to His Son Lucien. Rewald, John, ed. Abel, Lionel, tr. from FRE. LC 94-49368. (Illus.). 431p. 1995. reprint ed. pap. 15.95 (*0-306-80631-2*) Da Capo.

Pissarro, Camille, et al, eds. Letters to His Son Lucien. 3rd enl. rev. ed. (Illus.). 399p. 37.50 (*0-911858-22-9*) Appel.

Pissarro, Joachim. Camille Pissarro. LC 93-12280. (Illus.). 312p. 1993. 75.00 (*0-8109-3724-7*, Pub. by Abrams) Time Warner.

Pissarro, Joachim & Kimbell Art Museum Staff. Monet & the Mediterranean. LC 96-35758. (Illus.). 92p. 1997. 45.00 (*0-8478-1783-0*, Pub. by Rizzoli Intl) St Martin.

***Pissarro, Joachim, et al.** Robert Indiana: Retrospective 1958-1998. LC 99-234685. (Illus.). 328p. 2000. pap. 60.00 (*2-9512920-0-7*) U of Wash Pr.

Pissarro, Joachim, jt. auth. see Brettell, Richard R.

Pissarro, Ludovic-Rodo. Pissarro's Art & Oeuvre: A Catalogue Raisonne, 2 vols. (FRE., Illus.). 1989. reprint ed. 295.00 (*1-55660-027-5*) A Wofsy Fine Arts.

Pissin, Raimund. Almanache der Romantik. xii, 450p. 1970. reprint ed. write for info. (*0-318-71856-1*) G Olms Pubs.

Pissiotis, C., jt. ed. see Androulakis, G.

Pistelli, ed. Iamblichi: In Nicomachi Arithmeticam Introductionem. rev. ed. (GRE.). 1975. pap. 33.50 (*3-519-01444-0*, T1444, Pub. by B G Teubner) U of Mich Pr.

— Iamblichi: Protrepticus. (GRE.). 1996. reprint ed. pap. 43.50 (*3-519-11442-9*, T1442, Pub. by B G Teubner) U of Mich Pr.

Pistenmaa, David A. & Phillips, Theodore L., eds. Radiation Oncology Annual, 1983. LC 84-644857. (Illus.). 287p. 1984. reprint ed. pap. 89.00 (*0-7837-9534-3*, 206028300005) Bks Demand.

Pisters, Peter W., jt. auth. see Brennan, Murray F.

Pisto, John. Monterey's Cookin' Pisto Style: From Sicily to Monterey. (Illus.). 110p. (Orig.). 1994. pap. 12.95 (*0-9640828-0-2*) Pistos Kitchen.

Pistoia, G., ed. Lithium Batteries: New Materials, Development & Perspectives. LC 93-42028. (Industrial Chemistry Library: Vol. 5). 494p. 1993. 295.25 (*0-444-89957-X*) Elsevier.

***Pistoia, Marco, et al.** Java 2 Network Security. 2nd ed. LC 99-41138. 713p. 1999. pap. text 49.99 (*0-13-015592-6*) P-H.

Pistole, Larry M. & Sylvia, Stephen W. The Pictorial History of the Flying Tigers. LC 81-84192. (Illus.). 261p. 1981. 29.95 (*0-943522-05-6*) North South Trader.

Pistolese, Clifford. Nerves of Steel: Mastering Your Emotions to Beat the Market. 225p. 1992. 22.95 (*1-55738-467-3*, Irwn Prfssnl) McGraw-Hill Prof.

— Using Technical Analysis: A Step-by-Step Guide to Understanding & Applying Stock Market Charting Techniques. rev. ed. LC 94-156782. 240p. (C). 1994. per. 24.95 (*1-55738-527-0*, Irwn Prfssnl) McGraw-Hill Prof.

***Pistolesi, Roseanna.** How to Draw Christmas. 32p. (J). (gr. 2-7). 1999. pap. 2.95 (*0-8167-6344-5*) Troll Communs.

— Let's Celebrate Christmas: A Book of Drawing Fun. (J). 1988. 7.15 (*0-606-03601-6*, Pub. by Turtleback) Demco.

Pistolesi, Roseanna. Let's Celebrate Halloween: A Book of Drawing Fun. (J). 1968. 7.15 (*0-606-03602-4*, Pub. by Turtleback) Demco.

Pistoleta. Der Trobador Pistoleta. LC 80-2184. reprint ed. 27.00 (*0-404-19013-8*) AMS Pr.

Pistolis, Donna R. Hit List: Frequently Challenged Books for Children. LC 96-5759. 150p. 1996. pap. 22.00 (*0-8389-3458-7*) ALA.

Pistolis, Donna R., jt. auth. see Monks, Merri M.

Piston, W. Duo for Viola & Violoncello. 16p. 1994. pap. text 8.95 (*0-7935-4048-8*, 50482308) H Leonard.

— Incredible Flutist: Study Score Suite from the Ballet. 96p. 1989. pap. 25.00 (*0-7935-0490-2*, 50488405) H Leonard.

— Souvenir Flute Viola Harp. 8p. 1991. pap. 6.95 (*0-7935-0954-8*) H Leonard.

— Three Pieces for Flute, Clarinet & Bassoon 1926. 1986. pap. text 18.50 (*0-7935-2205-6*) H Leonard.

Piston, Walter. Counterpoint. (Illus.). (C). 1947. 32.00 (*0-393-09728-5*) Norton.

— Orchestration. (Illus.). (C). 1955. text 43.75 (*0-393-09740-4*) Norton.

— Principles of Harmonic Analysis. 1933. pap. 19.95 (*0-911318-05-4*) E C Schirmer.

Piston, Walter, et al. Harmony. 500p. (C). 1987. pap. text, teacher ed. write for info. (*0-393-95681-4*) Norton.

— Harmony. 5th ed. 500p. (C). 1987. text 54.25 (*0-393-95480-3*) Norton.

— Harmony: Workbook. 5th ed. 500p. (C). 1987. pap., student ed. 23.75 (*0-393-95484-6*) Norton.

Piston, William G. Carter's Raid: An Episode of the Civil War in East Tennessee. (Illus.). 92p. (Orig.). 1989. pap. 8.95 (*0-932807-42-9*) Overmountain Pr.

— Lee's Tarnished Lieutenant: James Longstreet & His Place in Southern History. LC 86-16025. (Brown Thrasher Bks.). 264p. 1990. pap. 15.95 (*0-8203-1229-0*) U of Ga Pr.

Piston, William Garrett & Hatcher, Richard W., III. Wilson's Creek: The Second Battle of the Civil War & the Men Who Fought It. LC 99-23239. (Illus.). 464p. 2000. 37.50 (*0-8078-2515-8*) U of NC Pr.

Pistone, Joseph D. Donnie Brasco: Deep Cover. 368p. 1999. mass mkt. 6.99 (*0-451-40881-0*, Onyx) NAL.

Pistone, Joseph D. & Woodley, Richard. Donnie Brasco. 416p. 1997. mass mkt. 6.99 (*0-451-19257-5*, Sig) NAL.

***Pistone, Peter.** Official Nascar Craftsman Series Handbook. 2000. pap. write for info. (*0-06-107331-8*, HarpEntertain) Morrow Avon.

Pistor, Katharina & Wellons, Philip A. The Role of Law & Legal Institutions in Asian Economic Development, 1960-1995. LC 98-54397. (Illus.). 306p. 1999. pap. text 39.95 (*0-19-590983-6*) OUP.

Pistor, Katharina, jt. auth. see Sachs, Jeffrey.

***Pistorious, Robin.** Scientists, Plants & Politics: A History of the Plant Genetic Resources Movement. 134p. (C). 1999. reprint ed. pap. text 35.00 (*0-7881-7525-4*) DIANE Pub.

Pistorius, Alan. Everything You Need to Know about Birding & Backyard Attraction. LC 98-17820. (Illus.). 275p. 1998. pap. 20.00 (*0-395-89274-0*) HM.

Pistorius, Alan & Gartlein, Delight. The Pember Museum of Natural History. (Illus.). 96p. (Orig.). 1986. pap. 9.95 (*0-9616427-0-X*) Pember Lib Mus.

Pistorius, Alan, jt. ed. see Eriksson, Paul S.

***Pistorius, Christel.** Restoring Teddy Bears & Stuffed Animals. (Illus.). 2000. 29.95 (*0-942620-34-8*) Portfolio Pr.

Pistorius, Christel & Pistorius, Rolf. Steiff: Sensational Teddy Bears, Animals & Dolls. (Illus.). 160p. 1991. 39.95 (*0-87588-356-7*) Hobby Hse.

Pistorius, Christel, jt. auth. see Pistorius, Rolf.

Pistorius, D. Pollak on Jurisdiction. 231p. 1993. write for info. (*0-7021-2953-4*, Pub. by Juta & Co) Gaunt.

***Pistorius, R. & Van Wijk, J.** The Exploitation of Plant Genetic Information: Political Strategies in Crop Development. LC 99-16220. (Biotechnology in Agriculture Ser.: Vol. 22). 250p. 2000. text 75.00 (*0-85199-363-X*) OUP.

Pistorius, Rolf & Pistorius, Christel. Die Schonsten Teddys und Tiere von Steiff. 2nd ed. (GER., Illus.). 160p. (C). 1993. 67.00 (*3-8170-1008-7*, Pub. by Knstvrlag Weingrtn) Intl Bk Import.

— Teddys Traumwelt: So Leben Alte Steiff-Teddybaren. (GER., Illus.). 128p. (C). 1993. 67.00 (*3-8170-1011-7*, Pub. by Knstvrlag Weingrtn) Intl Bk Import.

Pistorius, Rolf, jt. auth. see Pistorius, Christel.

Pistotnik, Bradley. Divorce War! Fifty Strategies Every Woman Needs to Know to Win. 288p. 1996. pap. 12.00 (*1-55850-600-4*) Adams Media.

Piszczek, K. & Niziol, J. Random Vibration of Mechanical Systems. LC 85-16338. (Mechanical Engineering Ser.). 343p. 1986. text 129.00 (*0-470-20247-5*) P-H.

Piszkiewicz, Dennis. From Nazi Test Pilot to Hitler's Bunker: The Fantastic Flights of Hanna Reitsch. LC 97-11458. 168p. 1997. 22.95 (*0-275-95456-0*, Praeger Pubs) Greenwood.

— The Nazi Rocketeers: Dreams of Space & Crimes of War. LC 95-10102. 288p. 1995. 24.95 (*0-275-95217-7*, Praeger Pubs) Greenwood.

— Wernher Von Braun: The Man Who Sold the Moon. LC 98-14481. (Illus.). 288p. 1998. 27.95 (*0-275-96217-2*, Pub. by Greenwood) Natl Bk Netwk.

Piszkiewicz, Leonard, ed. see Rustad, Roland.

Pita Andrade, Jose M., ed. see National Gallery of Art Staff.

Pita, Beatrice, ed. see Ruiz de Burton, Maria A.

Pita, Dianne D. Addictions Counseling: A Practical Guide to Counseling People with Chemical & Other Addictions. 144p. 1994. pap. 14.95 (*0-8245-1386-X*) Crossroad NY.

Pita, Edward G. Air Conditioning Principles & Systems. 3rd ed. LC 97-20014. 512p. (C). 1997. 88.00 (*0-13-505306-4*) P-H.

— Refrigeration Principles & Systems: An Energy Approach. LC 91-14219. 1991. 32.95 (*0-912524-61-8*) Busn News.

— Refrigeration Principles & Systems: An Energy Approach. 2nd ed. LC 83-21780. 116p. (C). 1989. pap. text 13.50 (*0-471-89758-2*) P-H.

Pita, Juana R. Florencia Nuestra. Editorial Arcos, Inc., Staff, ed. (Arcos Poetica Ser.: No. 3). (SPA., Illus.). 82p. (Orig.). 1992. lib. bdg. 8.00 (*0-937509-07-8*) Edit Arcos.

— Sorbos de Luz (Sips of Light) De Salvatierra, Mario, tr. (Eboli Poetry Ser.). (ENG & SPA., Illus.). 64p. (Orig.). 1990. pap. write for info. (*0-932367-09-7*) Ed El Gato Tuerto.

Pita, Juana R., ed. see Ruiz, Enrique L.

Pitacco, E., jt. auth. see Haberman, Steven.

Pitambar Publ. Co. Private Ltd. Bharat Junior English-Bangla Dictionary. 120p. 1997. 200.00 (*81-86378-21-9*) Pitambar Pub.

Pitambar Publ. Co. Private Ltd. Staff. This Is India. 174p. 1997. 300.00 (*81-209-0837-6*, Pub. by Pitambar Pub); pap. 80.00 (*81-209-0838-4*, Pub. by Pitambar Pub) St Mut.

Pitambar Publ. Staff. Ambar Number Book. 64p. 1997. pap. 24.00 (*81-209-0577-6*, Pub. by Pitambar Pub) St Mut.

— Ambar Nursery Rhymes. (Illus.). (J). (ps). 1997. pap. 20.00 (*81-209-0515-6*, Pub. by Pitambar Pub) St Mut.

— Ambar Table Book. 1997. pap. 20.00 (*81-209-0679-9*, Pub. by Pitambar Pub) St Mut.

— Bharat Junior English Assamese Dictionary. 120p. 1998. pap. 75.00 (*81-86378-22-7*, Pub. by Pitambar Pub) St Mut.

— Bharat Junior English-Bangla Dictionary. 120p. 1998. pap. 75.00 (*81-86378-12-X*, Pub. by Pitambar Pub) St Mut.

— Bharat Junior English Dictionary. 104p. 1998. 150.00 (*81-86378-05-7*, Pub. by Pitambar Pub); pap. 60.00 (*81-86378-06-5*, Pub. by Pitambar Pub); pap. 75.00 (*81-86378-07-3*, Pub. by Pitambar Pub) St Mut.

— Bharat Junior English-Hindi Dictionary. 120p. 1998. 200.00 (*81-86378-02-2*, Pub. by Pitambar Pub); pap. 60.00 (*81-86378-03-0*, Pub. by Pitambar Pub); pap. 75.00 (*81-86378-04-9*, Pub. by Pitambar Pub) St Mut.

— Bharat Junior English-Punjabi Dictionary. 120p. 1998. pap. 50.00 (*81-86378-09-X*, Pub. by Pitambar Pub) St Mut.

— Bharat Junior English-Tamil Dictionary. 120p. 1998. pap. 50.00 (*81-86378-18-9*, Pub. by Pitambar Pub) St Mut.

Pitanguy, I. Aesthetic Plastic Surgery of Head & Body. (Illus.). 425p. 1981. 719.00 (*0-387-08706-0*) Spr-Verlag.

Pitard, Francis F. Pierre Gy's Sampling Theory & Sampling Practice. 2nd ed. 528p. 1993. boxed set 131.95 (*0-8493-8917-8*, TN560) CRC Pr.

— Pierre Gy's Sampling Theory & Sampling Practice, 2 Vols., Vol. I. 208p. 1989. lib. bdg. 177.00 (*0-8493-6658-5*, TN560) CRC Pr.

— Pierre Gy's Sampling Theory & Sampling Practice, 2 Vols., Vol. II. 288p. 1989. lib. bdg. 217.00 (*0-8493-6659-3*, TN560) CRC Pr.

Pitard, Wayne T. Ancient Damascus: A Historical Study of the Syrian City-State from Earliest Times until Its Fall to the Assyrians in 732 B.C. LC 86-24360. ix, 230p. 1987. reprint ed. text 34.50 (*0-931464-29-3*) Eisenbrauns.

Pitarresi, James M., jt. auth. see Shames, Irving H.

Pitas, Ioannis. Digital Image Processing Algorithms. 1993. write for info. (*0-318-70002-6*) P-H.

***Pitas, Ioannis.** Digital Image Processing Algorithms & Applications. LC 99-56959. 419p. 2000. 89.95 (*0-471-37739-2*) Wiley.

— Image/Video Processing. text. write for info. (*0-471-37735-X*) Wiley.

Pitas, Ioannis, ed. Parallel Algorithms for Digital Image Processing, Computer Vision & Neural Networks. LC 00-92. (Parallel Computing Ser.). 410p. 1993. 100.00 (*0-471-93566-2*) Wiley.

Pitas, Ioannis & Venetsanopoulos, Anastasios N. Nonlinear Digital Filters: Principles & Applications. (C). 1990. text 132.50 (*0-7923-9049-0*) Kluwer Academic.

Pitas, Ioannis, jt. auth. see Nikolaidis, Nikos.

***Pitasky, Vicki M.** The Complete OSEP Handbook. LC 00-39125. (Illus.). 2000. write for info. (*1-57834-016-0*) LRP Pubns.

Pitasky, Vicki M. School Law Handbook. LC 98-17016. 1998. write for info. (*1-57834-009-8*) LRP Pubns.

Pitblado, John R. The North Mkata Plain, Tanzania: A Study of Land Capability & Land Tenure. LC HD0987.Z63P5. (University of Toronto, Department of Geography Research Publications: No. 16). (Illus.). 192p. reprint ed. pap. 59.60 (*0-608-18012-2*, 202649700049) Bks Demand.

Pitblado, Robin, et al. Risk Assessment & Management Handbook: For Environmental, Health, & Safety Professionals. 688p. 1995. 99.00 (*0-07-035987-3*) McGraw.

Pitblado, Robin, jt. ed. see Turney, Robin.

Pitcairn, D. M. & Flahault, D. M., eds. Medical Assistant: An Intermediate Level of Health Care Personnel. (Public Health Papers: No. 60). 1974. pap. text 10.00 (*92-4-130060-4*, 1110060) World Health.

Pitcairn, Feodor U. & Humann, Paul. Cayman: Underwater Paradise. Pitcairn, Kirstin, ed. LC 79-84293. (Illus.). (Orig.). 1979. 21.95 (*0-9602530-0-9*); pap. 14.95 (*0-685-04291-X*) Reef Dwellers.

Pitcairn, Harold F. & Odhner, Hugo L., eds. A Concordance of Selected Subjects Treated of in the Rational Psychology of Emanuel Swedenborg. 337p. 1960. 6.50 (*0-915221-11-X*) Swedenborg Sci Assn.

Pitcairn, Kirstin, ed. see Pitcairn, Feodor U. & Humann, Paul.

***Pitcairn-Knowles, Richard.** The Edwardian Eye of Andrew Pitcairn-Knowles: A Photographic Collection. (Illus.). 96p. 2000. 47.50 (*1-85776-427-7*, Pub. by Book Guild Ltd) Trans-Atl Phila.

Pitcairn, Richard H. & Pitcairn, Susan H. Dr. Pitcairn's Complete Guide to Natural Health for Dogs & Cats. rev. ed. (Illus.). 383p. 1995. pap. 16.95 (*0-87596-243-2*) Rodale Pr Inc.

Pitcairn, Robert. Ancient Criminal Trials in Scotland, 3 pts. in 4 vols. LC 71-174207. (Maitland Club, Glasgow, Publications: No. 19). reprint ed. 205.00 (*0-404-52748-5*) AMS Pr.

Pitcairn, Robert, ed. Chronicon Coenobit Sanctae Crucis Edinburgensis. LC 75-169478. (Bannatyne Club, Edinburgh. Publications: No. 20). reprint ed. 34.50 (*0-404-52724-8*) AMS Pr.

Pitcairn, Robert, ed. see Bannatyne, Richard.

Pitcairn, Susan H., jt. auth. see Pitcairn, Richard H.

Pitcairn, Theodore. The Beginning & Development of Doctrine in the New Church. 64p. 1968. pap. 3.25 (*1-883270-09-X*) Swedenborg Assn.

— The Bible, or Word of God, Uncovered & Explained: After the Revelation Given Through Emanuel Swedenborg. 96p. 1964. pap. 3.75 (*1-883270-08-1*) Swedenborg Assn.

— My Lord & My God: Essays on Modern Religion, the Bible, & Emanuel Swedenborg. (Illus.). 312p. 1967. 7.50 (*1-883270-03-0*); pap. 5.00 (*1-883270-04-9*) Swedenborg Assn.

— The Ten Commandments: A Series of Sermons. 70p. 1964. pap. 3.75 (*1-883270-05-7*) Swedenborg Assn.

Pitcairne, Archibald. The Assembly. Tobin, Terence, ed. LC 74-171849. 120p. 1972. 36.95 (*0-911198-30-X*) Purdue U Pr.

— Babell. LC 75-174208. (Maitland Club, Glasgow. Publications: No. 6). reprint ed. 32.50 (*0-404-52931-3*) AMS Pr.

Pitch, Anthony S. The Burning of Washington: The British Invasion of 1814. LC 98-13805. (Illus.). 289p. 1998. 32.95 (*1-55750-692-2*) Naval Inst Pr.

***Pitch, Anthony S.** The Burning of Washington: The British Invasion of 1814. 2000. reprint ed. pap. 17.95 (*1-55750-425-3*) Naval Inst Pr.

Pitch, Anthony S. Congressional Chronicles: Amusing & Amazing Anecdotes of the U. S. Congress & Its Members. LC 90-91538. (Illus.). 200p. (Orig.). 1990. pap. 4.95 (*0-931719-07-0*) Mino Pubns.

— Exclusively First Ladies Trivia. LC 85-60254. 176p. (Orig.). 1994. pap. 4.95 (*0-931719-03-8*) Mino Pubns.

— Exclusively Presidential Trivia. annuals LC 84-62716. 176p. (Orig.). 1996. pap. 4.95 (*0-931719-01-1*) Mino Pubns.

— Exclusively Washington Trivia. annuals LC 84-62046. 176p. (Orig.). 1996. pap. 4.95 (*0-931719-00-3*) Mino Pubns.

— Exclusively White House Trivia. LC 98-65048. 176p. 1998. pap. 4.95 (*0-931719-10-0*) Mino Pubns.

— A Walk in the Past - Georgetown. (Walk in the Past Ser.: Vol. 1). (Illus.). 64p. (Orig.). 1997. pap. 5.95 (*0-931719-09-7*) Mino Pubns.

— Washington, D. C. Sightseers' Guide. annuals LC 86-70380. (Illus.). 128p. (Orig.). 1998. pap. 5.95 (*0-931719-04-6*) Mino Pubns.

Pitch, Richard J., jt. auth. see Howell, Mary C.

Pitch, Tamar. Limited Responsibilities. Lea, John, tr. 256p. (C). 1995. pap. 25.99 (*0-415-08654-X*, B4217) Routledge.

Pitchaiah, P. Sankara. Ground Water. 1994. pap. 190.00 (*0-614-11799-2*, Pub. by Scientific Pubs) St Mut.

Pitcher, Arthur. Memoirs of Peter. 1981. 4.95 (*0-86544-015-8*) Salv Army Suppl South.

Pitcher, Arthur R. Christmas Remembered. 1985. pap. 5.95 (*0-86544-029-8*) Salv Army Suppl South.

— Holiness in the Traffic. 125p. (Orig.). 1987. pap. 4.95 (*0-86544-046-8*) Salv Army Suppl South.

— People of My Pilgrimage. 1989. 8.95 (*0-86544-052-2*) Salv Army Suppl South.

***Pitcher, Caroline.** Are You Spring? LC 99-49804. (Share-a-Story Ser.). (Illus.). 32p. (J). (ps-3). 2000. 5.95 (*0-7894-5614-1*, D K Ink) DK Pub Inc.

— Are You Spring? (Share-a-Story Ser.). 2000. 9.95 (*0-7894-6350-4*) DK Pub Inc.

— Mariana & the Merchild: A Folk Tale from Chile. LC 99-39926. (Illus.). 32p. (J). (ps-7). 2000. 17.00 (*0-8028-5204-1*, Eerdmans Bks) Eerdmans.

— The Snow Whale. (Illus.). (J). 1999. pap. text 7.99 (*0-7112-1093-4*) F Lincoln.

Pitcher, Caroline. The Time of the Lion. LC 97-50366. (Illus.). 32p. (J). (ps-5). 1998. 15.95 (*1-885223-83-8*) Beyond Words Pub.

Pitcher, Diana. Tokoloshi: African Folktales Retold. LC 93-26253. (Illus.). 64p. (J). (gr. 4 up). 1993. reprint ed. pap. 8.95 (*1-883672-03-1*) Tricycle Pr.

Pitcher, Don. Moon Handbooks: Washington: Including Seattle, Mount Rainier & Olympic National Park. 6th rev. ed. Vol. 6. (Illus.). 840p. 1999. pap. 19.95 (*1-56691-148-6*, Moon Handbks) Avalon Travel.

***Pitcher, Don.** Moon Handbooks: Wyoming: Including Yellowstone & Grand Teton National Parks. 4th rev. ed. (Illus.). 620p. 2000. pap. 17.95 (*1-56691-204-0*, Moon Handbks) Avalon Travel.

— Moon Handbooks: Yellowstone - Grand Teton. (Illus.). 240p. 2000. pap. 14.95 (*1-56691-199-0*, Moon Handbks) Avalon Travel.

Pitcher, Don & Castleman, Deke. Moon Handbooks: Alaska-Yukon. 6th ed. (Illus.). 540p. 1997. pap. 17.95 (*1-56691-089-7*, Moon Handbks) Avalon Travel.

Pitcher, E. J. Science & Engineering on Supercomputers: Fifth International Symposium October 22-24, 1990, London, England. ix, 628p. 1990. 223.95 (*0-387-53226-9*) Spr-Verlag.

***Pitcher, E. W.** The Lady's Monthly Museum, 1798-1806: An Annotated Index of Signatures & Ascriptions. LC 99-55512. (Studies in British & American Magazines : Vol. 2). 356p. 2000. 99.95 (*0-7734-7836-1*) E Mellen.

Pitcher, E. W., jt. auth. see Murphy, Graham J.

***Pitcher, Edward W.** An Anthology of the Short Story in 18th & 19th Century America Vol. 1. LC 99-53207. (Studies in British & American Magazines : Vol. 5). 404p. 2000. 109.95 (*0-7734-7842-6*) E Mellen.

— The British Magazine, January 1760-December 1767: An Annotated Index of Signatures, Ascriptions, Subjects &

P

Titles of Literary Prose. LC 00-20030. (Studies in British & American Magazines : Vol. 8). 202p. Date not set. text 89.95 (*0-7734-7791-8*) E Mellen.

— Facts & Fictions Vol. 1: Discoveries in Periodicals, 1720-1820. LC 99-52636. (Studies in British & American Magazines : Vol. 7). 600p. 2000. 119.95 (*0-7734-7846-9*) E Mellen.

Pitcher, Edward W. Fiction in American Magazines Before 1800: An Annotated Catalogue. LC 93-60539. 321p. 1993. 42.50 (*0-912756-27-6*) Union Coll.

***Pitcher, Edward W. R.** An Anthology of the Short Story in 18th & 19th Century America Vol. 2. LC 99-53207. (Studies in British & American Magazines : Vol. 6). 420p. 2000. 109.95 (*0-7734-7844-2*) E Mellen.

— The Literary Prose of Westminster Magazine (1773-1785) An Annotated Index under Contributors' Names, Pseudonymous Signature & Ascriptions. LC 99-53208. (Studies in British & American Magazines). 316p. 2000. 99.95 (*0-7734-7834-5*) E Mellen.

***Pitcher, Edward William.** The New York Weekly Museum: An Annotated Index of the Literary Prose, 1800-1811. LC 99-55511. (Studies in British & American Magazines : Vol. 4). (Illus.). 496p. 2000. text 109.95 (*0-7734-7840-X*) E Mellen.

Pitcher, Emma B. Of Woods & Other Things. Evans, Monica A. & Noble, Valerie A., eds. (Illus.). 256p. (Orig.). 1996. pap. 10.95 (*0-939294-18-4*) Beech Leaf.

Pitcher, Eric J., ed. Science & Engineering on Supercomputers. LC 90-84073. 628p. 1990. 212.00 (*0-945824-99-8*) Computational Mech MA.

Pitcher, Evelyn G. & Schultz, Lynn H. Boys & Girls at Play: The Development of Sex Roles. 220p. 1983. 55.00 (*0-275-91059-8*, C1059, Praeger Pubs) Greenwood.

— Boys & Girls at Play: The Development of Sex Roles. LC 82-16579. 219p. 1985. pap. 14.95 (*0-89789-055-8*, Bergin & Garvey) Greenwood.

Pitcher, Evelyn G., et al. Helping Young Children Learn. 5th ed. LC 88-80961. 352p. (C). 1990. pap. text 62.00 (*0-675-21054-2*, Merrill Coll) P-H.

Pitcher, Everett. A History of the Second Fifty Years, American Mathematical Society, 1939-1988. LC 88-22318. (Centennial Publications: Vol. I). 360p. 1988. text 50.00 (*0-8218-0125-2*, HMPITCHER) Am Math.

Pitcher, Gayle D. & Poland, Scott. Crisis Intervention in the Schools. LC 92-1417. (School Practitioner Ser.). 246p. 1992. lib. bdg. 32.00 (*0-89862-364-2*) Guilford Pubns.

Pitcher, George. The Dogs Who Came to Stay. (Illus.). 184p. 1996. pap. 8.95 (*0-452-27553-9*, W Abrahams Bks) Dutton Plume.

Pitcher, George, ed. A Theory of Perceptions. LC 73-120759. 250p. reprint ed. pap. 77.50 (*0-608-11353-0*, 201139900075) Bks Demand.

Pitcher, H. J., ed. Gogol: The Tale of How Ivan Ivanovich Quarrelled with Ivan Nikiforovich (Povest' o Tom, Kak Possorilsya Ivan Ivanovich s Ivanom Nikiforovichem) (Bristol Russian Texts Ser.). (RUS.). (C). 1991. reprint ed. pap. 18.95 (*1-85399-261-5*, Pub. by Brist Class Pr) Focus Pub-R Pullins.

Pitcher, Harvey, tr. see Chekhov, Anton.

Pitcher, James. Rip Van Winkle in Verse. 33p. pap. 6.95 (*0-941567-40-0*) J C & A L Fawcett.

Pitcher, James S. Sourdough Jim Pitcher: The Autobiography of a Pioneer Alaskan. LC 85-22857. (Northern History Library). (Illus.). 64p. (Orig.). 1985. pap. 6.95 (*0-88240-308-7*, Alaska NW Bks) Gr Arts Ctr Pub.

Pitcher, John, ed. Medieval & Renaissance Drama in England, Vol. 11. 400p. 1999. 72.50 (*0-8386-3805-8*) Fairleigh Dickinson.

***Pitcher, John, et al, eds.** Medieval & Renaissance Drama in England, Vol. 12. (Illus.). 392p. 1999. 72.50 (*0-8386-3836-8*) Fairleigh Dickinson.

Pitcher, John & Cerasano, Susan, eds. Medieval & Renaissance Drama in England, Vol. 9. 280p. 1997. 72.50 (*0-8386-3703-5*) Fairleigh Dickinson.

— Medieval & Renaissance Drama in England, Vol. 10. (Illus.). 400p. 1998. 72.50 (*0-8386-3770-1*) Fairleigh Dickinson.

Pitcher, John, ed. see Daniel, Samuel.

Pitcher, M. A. Management Accounting for the Lending Banker. 176p. 1979. 55.00 (*0-85297-050-1*, Pub. by Chartered Bank); pap. 44.00 (*0-85297-047-1*, Pub. by Chartered Bank) St Mut.

Pitcher, M. Anne. Politics in the Portuguese Empire: The State, Industry, & Cotton, 1926-1974. LC 92-41457. (Illus.). 344p. (C). 1993. text 75.00 (*0-19-827373-8*, Clarendon Pr) OUP.

Pitcher, Max G., ed. see International Symposium on Arctic Geology Staff.

Pitcher, Patricia. The Drama of Leadership: Introducing Artists, Craftsmen & Technocrats & Their Starring Roles in Business's Epic Power Struggles. LC 96-26887. 268p. 1996. 27.50 (*0-471-14843-1*) Wiley.

Pitcher, Seymour M., et al, eds. Two Creative Traditions in English Poetry. LC 72-450. (Granger Index Reprint Ser.). 1977. reprint ed. 23.95 (*0-8369-6367-9*) Ayer.

Pitcher, T. J., ed. Behaviour of Teleost Fishes. 2nd ed. (Fish & Fisheries Ser.). (Illus.). 576p. (C). 1992. text 125.00 (*0-412-42930-6*, A9620) Chapman & Hall.

Pitcher, Terry, jt. auth. see Kalinich, David B.

Pitcher, Tony J., ed. The Behavior of Teleost Fishes. LC 85-19887. (Illus.). 554p. reprint ed. pap. 171.80 (*0-7837-1107-7*, 204163700021) Bks Demand.

Pitcher, Tony J., et al, eds. Reinventing Fisheries Management. LC 98-70426. (Fish & Fisheries Ser.). 646p. 1999. 288.00 (*0-412-83410-3*) Kluwer Academic.

Pitcher, W. Alvin, jt. ed. see Amjad-Ali, Charles.

Pitcher, W. R. Imaging America: Anecdote, Tale, & Short Story in the Eighteenth Century. write for info. (*0-912756-29-2*) Union Coll.

Pitcher, W. R. & Gado, Frank, eds. First Person: Conversations on Writers & Writing. 266p. (C). 1995. text 29.95 (*0-912756-03-9*) Union Coll.

Pitcher, Wayne H., Jr. Immobilized Enzymes for Food Processing. LC 79-25738. 232p. 1980. 132.00 (*0-8493-5345-9*, TP456, CRC Reprint) Franklin.

Pitchers, Alrah L. The Christology of Hans Kung: A Critical Examination. LC 97-20815. (European University Studies: Series 23, Vol. 602). 254p. (C). 1997. 41.95 (*0-8204-3415-9*, Pub. by P Lang) P Lang Pubng.

— The Christology of Hans Kung: A Critical Examination. (European University Studies, Series 23: Vol. 602). (GER.). 254p. 1997. 41.95 (*3-906756-32-7*, Pub. by P Lang) P Lang Pubng.

Pitchford, E. D., ed. Law of Tort. 490p. 1996. pap. 125.00 (*0-7510-0689-0*, Pub. by HLT Pubns) St Mut.

— Tort Cases. 344p. 1996. pap. 125.00 (*0-7510-0656-4*, Pub. by HLT Pubns) St Mut.

Pitchford, Gene. Young Folks' Hawaiian Time. (Illus.). (J). (ps). 1965. pap. 3.00 (*0-87505-275-4*) Borden.

Pitchford, John. The Current Account & Foreign Debt. LC 94-46487. 208p. (C). (gr. 13). 1995. 90.00 (*0-415-09401-1*) Routledge.

Pitchford, Kenneth, tr. see Rilke, Rainer Maria.

Pitchford, L. C., et al, eds. Swarm Studies & Inelastic Electron-Molecule Collisions. (Illus.). xi, 403p. 1986. 131.95 (*0-387-96402-9*) Spr-Verlag.

Pitchford, Paul. Healing with Whole Foods: Oriental Traditions & Modern Nutrition. 2nd rev. ed. LC 93-87. (Illus.). 705p. (C). 1996. 60.00 (*1-55643-221-6*); pap. 32.50 (*1-55643-220-8*) North Atlantic.

Pitchford, Polly & Quigley, Delia. Cookin' Healthy with One Foot Out the Door: Quick Meals for Fast Times. LC 93-43471. 160p. 1994. 8.95 (*0-913990-86-8*) Book Pub Co.

Pitchford, Polly, jt. auth. see Quigley, Delia.

Pitchford, Ruth, jt. auth. see Essex, Martin.

Pitchfork, E. D., ed. Tort. 248p. (C). 1990. pap. 60.00 (*1-85352-765-3*, Pub. by HLT Pubns) St Mut.

Pitchfork, Graham. The Men Behind the Medals: The Actions of 21 Aviators During World War Two. (Illus.). 224p. 1998. 49.95 (*0-85052-586-1*, Pub. by Leo Cooper) Trans-Atl Phila.

Pitchkites, Ed. 60 Years with the Feathered Shaft. LC 99-173107. 185 p. 1997. write for info. (*0-9634527-2-X*) C D Hay.

Pite, Ralph. The Circle of Our Vision: Dante's Presence in English Romantic Poetry. (Illus.). 282p. 1994. text 49.95 (*0-19-811294-7*) OUP.

Pitej, Leona, ed. Teaching More Than English: Using TESL/TEFL on the Mission Field at Home & Abroad. 96p. (Orig.). 1996. pap. 8.00 (*0-614-25194-X*) Berry Pub Srv.

***Pitelis, Christos & Sugden, Roger, eds.** Nature of the Transnational Firm. 2nd ed. LC 99-53474. 240p. (C). 2000. text 100.00 (*0-415-16787-6*) Routledge.

Pitelis, Christos N. Market & Non-Market Hierarchies: Theory of Institutional Failure. LC 93-16051. 258p. 1993. reprint ed. pap. 29.95 (*0-631-19061-9*) Blackwell Pubs.

Pitelis, Christos N., ed. Surveys in Transaction Costs, Markets & Hierarchies. LC 92-30554. 1993. pap. 31.95 (*0-631-18898-3*) Blackwell Pubs.

***Pitelis, Christos N. & Sugden, Roger.** The Nature of the Transnational Firm. 2nd ed. LC 99-53474. 240p. 2000. pap. 32.99 (*0-415-16788-4*) Routledge.

Piterbarg, Leonid I. & Ostrovskii, Alexander G. Advection & Diffusion in Random Media: Implications for Sea Surface Temperature Anomalies. LC 97-6181. 1997. text 174.00 (*0-7923-4450-2*) Kluwer Academic.

Piterbarg, Vladimir I. Asymptotic Methods in the Theory of Gaussian Processes & Fields. LC 95-20514. (Translations of Mathematical Monographs: Vol. 148). 206p. 1995. text 99.00 (*0-8218-0423-5*, MMONO/148) Am Math.

Piterman, Mark A., tr. see Nigmatulin, R. I.

Piterman, Mark A., tr. see Polyanin, Andrei D. & Dilman, Victor V.

Piterski, Brahm & Piterski, Paul. Like a Fish on a Bike! large type ed. LC 97-611122. (Illus.). 32p. (J). (gr. 2-5). 1999. 14.95 (*0-9658435-0-5*) Verdant Pub.

Piterski, Paul, jt. auth. see Piterski, Brahm.

Pitfield, D. E., jt. ed. see Button, K. J.

Pitfield, M. Developing International Managers. 1996. pap. 129.00 (*1-85953-047-8*, Pub. by Tech Comm) St Mut.

Pitfield, Michael. Developing International Managers. (Financial Times Management Briefings Ser.). 1997. pap. 89.50 (*0-273-63174-8*) F T P-H.

Pitfield, Michael & Donnelly, Robert. How to Take Exams. 112p. (C). 1980. 60.00 (*0-85292-262-0*, Pub. by IPM Hse) St Mut.

Pitfield, P. & Donnelly, D. How to Take Exams. 112p. (C). 1980. 90.00 (*0-7855-5653-2*, Pub. by Inst Pur & Supply) St Mut.

***Pither, Donald E.** Reliant Sportscars. (Illus.). 160p. 2000. 24.95 (*0-7509-2388-1*) Sutton Publng.

Pithers, William, et al. From Trauma to Understanding: A Guide for Parents of Children with Sexual Behavior Problems. Bear, Euan & Knopp, Fay H., eds. 32p. 1993. pap. text 5.00 (*1-884444-07-5*) Safer Soc.

Pithisaria, M. K., jt. ed. see Chaturvedi, K.

Pithisaria, V., jt. auth. see Chaturvedi, T. N.

***Pithouse, Andrew.** Social Work; The Social Organization of an Invisible Trade. (Cadiff Papers in Qualitative Research). 200p. 1998. text 59.95 (*1-84014-367-3*) Ashgate Pub Co.

Pithouse, Andrew, et al, eds. Family Support & Family Centre Services: Issues, Research & Evaluation in U. K., U. S. A. & Hong Kong. LC 97-78098. 211p. 1998. text 63.95 (*1-85972-109-5*, Pub. by Ashgate Pub) Ashgate Pub Co.

Pithouse, Andrew, jt. auth. see Levi, Michael.

***Pitino, Rick & Reynolds, Bill.** Lead to Succeed: 10 Traits of Great Leadership in Business & Life. 288p. 2000. 26.00 (*0-7679-0341-2*) Broadway BDD.

Pitino, Rick & Reynolds, Bill. Success Is a Choice: Ten Steps to Overachieving in Business & Life. LC 97-2298. 288p. 1997. 27.50 (*0-553-06668-4*) Bantam.

— Success Is a Choice: Ten Steps to Overachieving in Business & Life. 288p. 1998. pap. 14.95 (*0-7679-0132-0*) Broadway BDD.

Pitino, Rick & Weiss, Dick. Full Court Pressure: A Year in Kentucky Basketball. (Illus.). 336p. (YA). 1993. pap. 10.45 (*1-56282-753-7*, Pub. by Hyperion) Time Warner.

Pitisaria, C. Chaturvediand. Income Tax Law, 6 vols. (C). 1990. 210.00 (*0-89771-275-7*) St Mut.

Pitkanen, Allan M., tr. see Paulaharju, Samuli.

Pitkanen, Matti A. & Harkonen, Reijo. The Grandchildren of the Vikings. LC 94-38679. (Children of the World Ser.).Tr. of Viikinkien Jalkelaiset. (J). 1995. lib. bdg. 21.27 (*0-87614-889-5*, Carolrhoda) Lerner Pub.

Pitkanen, Pirkko. Platonische Philosophie des Guten Lebens und Moderne Orientierungslosigkeit. Schroder, Hartmut, ed. (Scandinavian University Studies in the Humanities & Social Sciences: Bd. 11). (GER.). 140p. 1996. 32.95 (*3-631-31051-X*) P Lang Pubng.

Pitkethly, Alan S., jt. auth. see Fernie, John.

Pitkin. Attack of the Blob: Hannah Arendt's Concept of the Social. LC 98-13333. 1998. 30.00 (*0-226-66990-4*) U Ch Pr.

Pitkin, Barbara. What Pure Eyes Could See: Calvin's Doctrine of Faith in its Exegetical Context. LC 98-28136. (Oxford Studies in Historical Theology). 272p. 1999. text 55.00 (*0-19-512828-1*) OUP.

Pitkin, David J. Saratoga County Ghosts. LC 98-92859. (Illus.). 214p. 1998. pap. 13.95 (*0-9663925-0-7*, one) Aurora Publns.

***Pitkin, David J.** Spiritual Numerology: Caring for Number One. LC 99-96347. (Illus.). 149p. 2000. pap. 14.95 (*0-9663925-1-5*, Pub. by Aurora Publns) ACCESS Pubs Network.

Pitkin, Donald S. The House That Giacomo Built: History of an Italian Family, 1898-1978. (Dowling Scholarly Reprint Ser.). 307p. 1998. reprint ed. pap. text 24.00 (*1-883058-70-8*) Global Pubns.

Pitkin, Gary M., ed. Cost-Effective Technical Services: How to Track, Manage, & Justify Internal Operations. 325p. (Orig.). 1989. pap. text 45.00 (*1-55570-041-1*) Neal-Schuman.

— The Impact of Emerging Technologies on Reference Service & Bibliographic Instruction, 87. LC 95-3802. (Contributions in Librarianship & Information Science Ser.: No. 87). 192p. 1995. 52.95 (*0-313-29365-1*, Greenwood Pr) Greenwood.

— The National Electronic Library: A Guide to the Future for Library Managers. LC 95-40028. (Greenwood Library Management Collection). 208p. 1996. lib. bdg. 57.95 (*0-313-29613-8*, Greenwood Pr) Greenwood.

Pitkin, Hanna F. The Concept of Representation. 1967. pap. 16.95 (*0-520-02156-8*, Pub. by U CA Pr) Cal Prin Full Svc.

Pitkin, Hanna Fenichel. Fortune is a Woman: Gender & Politics in the Thought of Nicollo Machiavelli. LC 99-28728. 1999. pap. text 16.00 (*0-226-66992-0*) U Ch Pr.

Pitkin, Hanna R. Wittgenstein & Justice: The Significance of Ludwig Wittgenstein for Social & Political Thought. 1972. reprint ed. 50.00 (*0-520-05471-7*, Pub. by U CA Pr); reprint ed. pap. 17.95 (*0-520-02329-3*, Pub. by U CA Pr) Cal Prin Full Svc.

Pitkin, Harvey. Wintu Dictionary. LC 85-14859. (University of California Publications in Entomology: No. 95). 943p. 1985. pap. 200.00 (*0-7837-7499-0*, 204922100010) Bks Demand.

— Wintu Grammar. LC 84-16268. (University of California Publications in Linguistics: No. 94). 326p. 1984. pap. 101.10 (*0-7837-7498-2*, 204922000010) Bks Demand.

Pitkin, Julia M. Specialties of the House: A Country Inn & Bed & Breakfast Cookbook. LC 96-18008. (Illus.). 624p. 1996. 27.95 (*1-888952-00-8*, Cumberland Hearthside) Cumberland Hse.

Pitkin, Julia M., ed. Great Chefs - Great Chocolate: Spectacular Desserts from America's Great Chefs. LC 98-28033. (Illus.). 240p. 1998. 24.95 (*1-888952-83-0*) Cumberland Hse.

***Pitkin, Julia M., ed.** Great Chefs of the Caribbean: Signature Recipes from the Islands. LC 99-50054. (Hearthside Ser.: Vol. 3). (Illus.). 240p. 1999. 22.95 (*1-58182-019-4*) Cumberland Hse.

Pitkin, Julia M., et al. Bless This Food: Four Seasons of Menus, Recipes, & Table Graces. LC 96-42173. (Illus.). 240p. 1996. 18.95 (*1-888952-05-9*, Cumberland Hearthside) Cumberland Hse.

Pitkin, Julia M., ed. see Clark, Jim & Beck, Kenneth.

Pitkin, Julie M., ed. see Maynard, Kitty & Maynard, Lucian.

Pitkin, Linda. Under Northern Seas. 1998. 45.00 (*1-55192-104-9*) Raincoast Bk.

Pitkin, Olive. My Garden & I. 160p. 1992. 19.95 (*1-55821-180-2*) Lyons Pr.

— There & Then: A Vermont Childhood. 160p. (Orig.). 1997. pap. 10.95 (*1-56474-198-2*) Fithian Pr.

Pitkin, Thomas M. The Black Hand: A Chapter in Ethnic Crime. 274p. 1977. pap. 16.50 (*0-8226-0333-0*) St Aedans Pr & Bk.

Pitkin, Timothy. Political & Civil History of the United States of America from the Year 1763 to the Close of the Administration of President Washington in March, 1797, 2 vols. LC 79-109613. (Era of the American Revolution Ser.). 1970. reprint ed. lib. bdg. 135.00 (*0-306-71908-8*) Da Capo.

Pitkin, Walter B. Life Begins at Forty. 1994. lib. bdg. 24.95 (*1-56849-381-9*) Buccaneer Bks.

Pitkin, William H. & Smith, Lawrence J. Qualifications for the Priesthood in the Liberal Catholic Church. rev. ed. 13p. 1994. pap. 2.25 (*0-918980-15-1*) St Alban Pr.

Pitkin, William H., ed. see Sheehan, Edmund W.

Pitluga, Phyllis, ed. Our Solar System & It's Planets. (Powertools for Kids Ser.: No. 12). (Illus.). 4p. (J). (gr. 3-7). 1998. pap., wbk. ed. 4.95 (*1-58220-011-4*, 32502, PowerTools for Kids) Navigator.

***Pitman.** An Autobiography. 1999. pap. 12.95 (*0-553-50491-6*, Pub. by Transworld Publishers Ltd) Trafalgar.

Pitman. Teach Yourself Typing. (Illus.). 240p. 1995. pap. 7.95 (*0-8442-3944-5*, Teach Yrslf) NTC Contemp Pub Co.

Pitman, jt. auth. see Newman, Jack.

Pitman, A. J., jt. ed. see Henderson-Sellers, A.

Pitman, Ben. Business Process Reengineering Plain & Simple: Planning to Successfully Achieve Dramatic... LC 96-222983. 1996. pap. text 24.95 (*0-87425-308-X*) HRD Press.

Pitman, Bonnie. Museums, Magic & Children: Youth Education in Museums. Kendall, Aubyn & Bannerman, Carol, eds. (Illus.). 262p. (Orig.). 1982. pap. 21.00 (*0-944040-13-6*) AST Ctrs.

Pitman, Bonnie, ed. Presence of Mind: Museums & the Spirit of Learning. LC 98-53146. 250p. 1999. pap. 40.00 (*0-931201-58-6*) Am Assn Mus.

Pitman, Brian. Fencing: Techniques of Foil, Epee & Sabre. (Illus.). 144p. 1989. 39.95 (*1-85223-152-1*) Crolwood.

Pitman, C. B., tr. see Bonvalot, Gabriel.

Pitman, C. B., tr. see Orleans, Henri P.

Pitman, C. E. Pitman: History & Pedigree of the Family Pitman of Dunchideock, Exeter, & Collaterals, & of the Pitmans of Alphington, Norfolk & Edinburgh. (Illus.). 181p. 1992. reprint ed. pap. 27.50 (*0-8328-2707-X*); reprint ed. lib. bdg. 37.50 (*0-8328-2706-1*) Higginson Bk Co.

Pitman, Dianne W. Bazille: Purity, Pose & Painting in the 1860s. LC 96-49128. 1998. 65.00 (*0-271-01700-7*) Pa St U Pr.

Pitman, E. J. Some Basic Theory for Statistical Inference. LC 78-11921. (Monographs on Statistics & Applied Probability). 105p. (gr. 13). 1979. lib. bdg. 69.95 (*0-412-21720-1*, 6221) Chapman & Hall.

Pitman, E. R. Ann H. Judson of Burma. 1988. pap. 5.99 (*0-87508-601-2*) Chr Lit.

Pitman, Elizabeth. This Won't Change Your Life (But It Might Help!) 140p. 1990. pap. 24.95 (*1-873150-00-8*, Pub. by Multilingual Matters) Taylor & Francis.

Pitman, Emma R. Elizabeth Fry. LC 69-14036. 269p. 1969. reprint ed. lib. bdg. 38.50 (*0-8371-1005-X*, PIEF, Greenwood Pr) Greenwood.

Pitman, Gerald H. Liposuction & Aesthetic Surgery. LC 92-532. (Illus.). 478p. 1992. 200.00 (*0-942219-18-X*); 245.00 incl. VHS (*1-57626-041-0*, QMP) Quality Med Pub.

— Tumescent Technique. (Illus.). 19p. 1995. pap. 85.00 (*0-942219-95-3*) Quality Med Pub.

Pitman, Jim. Probability. LC 92-39051. (Texts in Statistics Ser.). 596p. 1997. 58.95 (*0-387-97974-3*) Spr-Verlag.

Pitman, John. Breechloading Carbines of the United States Civil War Period, Vol. 1. LC 87-70171. (Illus.). 94p. 1987. 29.95 (*0-939683-00-8*) Thomas Publications.

— The Pitman Notes on U. S. Martial Small Arms & Ammunition, 1776-1933: Miscellaneous Notes, Vol. 5. (Illus.). 212p. (C). 1993. text 29.95 (*0-939631-35-0*) Thomas Publications.

— The Pitman Notes on U. S. Martial Small Arms & Ammunition, 1776-1933: U. S. Magazine Rifles & Carbines, Cal. 30, Vol. 4. (Illus.). 194p. (C). 1992. text 29.95 (*0-939631-34-2*) Thomas Publications.

— The Pitman Notes on U. S. Martial Small Arms & Ammunition, 1776-1933 Vol. 2: Revolvers & Automatic Pistols. (Illus.). 192p. (C). 1991. text 29.95 (*0-939631-32-6*) Thomas Publications.

— The Pitman Notes on U. S. Martial Small Arms & Ammunition, 1776-1933 Vol. 3: U. S. Breech-Loading Rifles & Carbines, Cal. 45. (Illus.). 192p. 1991. 29.95 (*0-939631-33-4*) Thomas Publications.

Pitman, John, ed. see Lightfoot, John.

Pitman, John C., jt. auth. see Roueche, John E.

Pitman, Karen T., et al. The Parapharyngeal Space: Diagnosist & Management of Commonly Encountered Entities. 3rd ed. LC RC280.P4P56 1998. (Self-Instructional Package Ser.). (Illus.). 67p. 1999. pap. text 25.00 (*1-56772-070-6*, 5506115) AAO-HNS.

***Pitman, Lesley.** Moscow. 1999. lib. bdg. 63.00 (*1-85109-270-6*) ABC-CLIO.

Pitman, Lesley. Russia/USSR, Vol. 6. 2nd rev. ed. (World Bibliographical Ser.). 414p. 1994. lib. bdg. 86.50 (*1-85109-221-8*) ABC-CLIO.

Pitman, Martha B. & Szyfelbein, Wanda M. Fine Needle Aspiration Biopsy of the Liver. LC 94-15909. (Illus.). 123p. 1994. text 110.00 (*0-7506-9463-7*) Buttrwrth-Heinemann.

Pitman, Martha Bishop, jt. auth. see Centeno, Barbara A.

Pitman, Mary A. & Zorn, Debbie, eds. Caring As Tenacity: Stories of Urban School Survival. LC 99-51612. (Understanding Education & Policy Ser.). 192p. (C). 1999. 39.50 (*1-57273-210-5*) Hampton Pr NJ.

— Caring As Tenacity: Stories of Urban School Survival. LC 99-51612. (Understanding Education & Policy Ser.). 192p. (C). 1999. pap. 17.95 (*1-57273-211-3*) Hampton Pr NJ.

Pitman, Mary A., et al. Culture Acquisition: A Holistic Approach to Human Learning. LC 88-27507. 252p. 1989. 62.95 (*0-275-93031-9*, C3031, Praeger Pubs) Greenwood.

P

An Asterisk (*) at the beginning of an entry indicates that the title is appearing for the first time.

— Culture Acquisition: A Holistic Approach to Human Learning. LC 88-27507. (Illus.). 252p. 1989. lib. bdg. 42.95 (*0-318-41925-4*, C3031, Greenwood Pr) Greenwood.

Pitman, Norah, jt. auth. see Palmer, Eve.

Pitman, Paul M., III, ed. Turkey: A Country Study. 4th ed. LC 88-8844. (Area Handbook Ser.). (Illus.). 498p. 1996. text 24.00 (*0-16-001710-6*, S/N008020013943) USGPO.

Pitman Publishing Ltd Staff, ed. Pitman New Era Shorthand Pocket Dictionary. 2nd ed. 221p. 1985. pap. text 24.50 (*0-582-29890-3*, Pub. by Pitman Pub) Trans-Atl Phila.

Pitman Publishing Ltd. Staff, ed. Pitman New Era Shorthand Workbook: Lessons 13-20. 1988. pap. text, student ed. 19.95 (*0-273-02903-7*, Pub. by Pitman Pub) Trans-Atl Phila.

Pitman Publishing Staff. Directory of Financial Sites on the Internet. (Financial Times Management Ser.). 1997. pap. 249.00 (*0-273-63060-1*) F T P H.

Pitman Publishing Staff, ed. Pitman New Era Shorthand: Anniversary Edition Workbooks, Vol. 1. 192p. 1988. pap., student ed. 19.95 (*0-582-28863-0*, Pub. by Pitman Pub) Trans-Atl Phila.

— Pitman 2000 Shorthand Pocket Dictionary. 2nd ed. 221p. 1996. pap. 24.50 (*0-582-28722-7*, Pub. by Addison-Wesley) Trans-Atl Phila.

Pitman, Ralph. Children of Alcoholics in Schools. 1990. 9.00 (*1-881678-43-1*) CSEE.

Pitman, Randy. The Video Librarian's Guide to Collection Development & Management. LC 92-15104. (Professional Librarian Ser.). 280p. 1992. 40.00 (*0-8161-1978-3*, Hall Reference); 25.00 (*0-8161-1979-1*, Hall Reference) Macmillan.

Pitman, Randy & Swanson, Elliott. Video Movies: A Core Collection for Libraries. LC 89-48387. 266p. 1990. lib. bdg. 45.00 (*0-87436-577-5*) ABC-CLIO.

Pitman, Richard. Blood Ties. large type ed. (Magna Large Print Ser.). 481p. 1997. 27.99 (*0-7505-1179-6*, Pub. by Mgna Lrg Print) Ulverscroft.

— Warned Off. large type ed. (Ulverscroft). 512p. 1994. 27.99 (*0-7089-3048-4*) Ulverscroft.

Pitman, Richard & McNally, John. The Hunted. large type ed. (Magna Large Print Ser.). 1994. 27.99 (*0-7505-0725-X*) Ulverscroft.

Pitman, Rod. Reel Extra Money: The Background Actor's Handbook. (Orig.). pap. write for info. (*0-9642118-6-6*) Cascade Press.

***Pitman, Sally, et al.** Medical Transcription: Fundamentals & Practice. 2nd ed. LC 99-36720. 494p. 1999. pap. 47.00 (*0-13-013833-9*) P-H.

Pitman, Sally C., ed. Laboratory/Pathology Words & Phrases. 2nd rev. ed. 648p. (Orig.). 1996. pap. 37.00 (*0-934385-66-1*) Hlth Prof Inst.

Pitman, Sally C., intro. The Empty Laugh Book. (Orig.). 1981. pap. text 15.00 (*0-935229-07-8*) Am Assoc Med.

Pitman, Sally C., ed. see Pyle, Vera.

***Pitman, Teresa & Kaufman, Miriam.** The Overweight Child: Promoting Fitness & Self-Esteem. (Issues in Parenting Ser.). 192p. 2000. pap. 14.95 (*1-55209-474-X*) Firefly Bks Ltd.

Pitman, Vicki. Herbal Medicine: The Use of Herbs for Health & Healing. LC 94-23421. (Health Essentials Ser.). 128p. 1995. pap. 9.95 (*1-85230-591-6*, Pub. by Element MA) Penguin Putnam.

***Pitman, Vicki.** Herbal Remedies: An Introductory Guide to Herbs for Health & Well-Being. (New Perspectives (Element) Ser.). (Illus.). 128p. 2000. pap. 9.95 (*1-86204-767-7*, Pub. by Onewrld Pubns) Penguin Putnam.

Pitman, Vicki, et al. Reflexology: A Practical Approach. (Illus.). 288p. (Orig.). 1998. pap. 38.50 (*0-7487-2867-8*, Pub. by S Thornes Pubs) Trans-Atl Phila.

Pitman, Walter & Ryan, William. Noah's Flood: The New Scientific Discoveries about the Event That Changed History. LC 98-45384. (Illus.). 320p. 1999. 24.50 (*0-684-81052-2*) S&S Trade.

Pitman, Walter C., jt. auth. see Ryan, William B. F.

Pitman, Walter C., III, jt. ed. see Talwani, Manik.

Pitman, Walter G. The Baptists & Public Affairs in the Province of Canada: 1840-1867. Gaustad, Edwin S., ed. LC 79-52576. (Baptist Tradition Ser.). 1980. lib. bdg. 23.95 (*0-405-12444-9*) Ayer.

Pitner, E. Maximilian's Lieutenant: A Personal History of the Mexican Campaign, 1864-67. LC 92-44670. 206p. 1994. 18.95 (*0-8263-1425-2*) U of NM Pr.

Pitner, Erin C. Stones & Roses. 80p. (Orig.). 1993. pap. 5.95 (*0-9637559-0-0*) Chamisa.

***Pitney, John J.** The Art of Political Warfare. LC 00-26710. 256p. 2000. 24.95 (*0-8061-3263-9*) U of Okla Pr.

Pitney, John J., Jr., jt. auth. see Bessette, Joseph M.

Pitney, John J., Jr., jt. auth. see Connelly, William F., Jr.

Pitney, William A., jt. auth. see Cartwright, Lorin A.

Pitocchelli. Biostatistics. Date not set. pap. text, teacher ed. write for info. (*0-471-17079-8*) Wiley.

Piton, Camille. The Civil Costumes of France of Thirteenth & Fourteenth Century. (Illus.). 380p. 1986. reprint ed. pap. text 35.00 (*0-87556-387-2*) Saifer.

Pitone, Louise. Absence & Lateness: How to Reduce It, How to Control It. rev. ed. 1986. ring bd. 29.95 (*1-55645-515-1*, 515) Busn Legal Reports.

— The BLR Encyclopedia of Prewritten Personnel Letters. rev. ed. 436p. 1988. ring bd. 99.95 (*1-55645-527-5*, 527) Busn Legal Reports.

***Pitoni, Valeria D.** Bridging the Gap: A Writer's Guide to Transitions, Connective Phrases, & Speech References. LC 00-90268. 79p. 2000. pap. 11.95 (*0-9678709-1-7*) Serendipity Pubng.

Pitoniak, Scott. The Buffalo Bills Official All-New Trivia Book II. (Illus.). 112p. (Orig.). 1992. pap. 8.95 (*0-312-08151-0*) St Martin.

— Playing Write Field: Selected Works by Scott Pitoniak. 150p. (Orig.). 1997. pap. 10.95 (*0-9659348-0-2*) S Pitoniak.

Pitoniak, Scott, jt. auth. see Mandelaro, Jim.

Pitorri, Peter. Counterespionage for American Business. LC 98-9708. 130p. 1998. pap. 26.95 (*0-7506-7044-4*) Buttrwrth-Heinemann.

***Pitot, Genevieve.** Tha Mauritian Shekel: The Story of Jewish Detainees in Mauritius, 1940-1945. 272p. 2000. pap. 28.00 (*0-7425-0855-2*) Rowman.

Pitot, Henry C. Fundamentals of Oncology. 3rd rev. ed. (Illus.). 544p. 1985. text 49.75 (*0-8247-7457-4*) Dekker.

Pitot, James. Observations on the Colony of Louisiana from 1796 to 1802. LC 79-14897. 231p. reprint ed. pap. 71.70 (*0-7837-8695-6*, 204944100011) Bks Demand.

Pitou, Spire. The Paris Opera: An Encyclopedia of Operas, Ballets, Composers & Performers, Genesis & Glory, 1671-1715. LC 82-21140. 364p. 1983. lib. bdg. 59.95 (*0-313-21420-4*, PFO/, Greenwood Pr) Greenwood.

— The Paris Opera: An Encyclopedia of Operas, Ballets, Composers & Performers, Genesis & Glory, 1671-1715. LC 82-21140. 619p. 1985. lib. bdg. 115.00 (*0-313-24394-8*, POR/, Greenwood Pr) Greenwood.

— The Paris Opera: An Encyclopedia of Operas, Ballets, Composers & Performers, Genesis & Glory, 1671-1715. LC 87-21140. 1608p. 1990. lib. bdg. 185.00 (*0-313-26218-7*, PGH, Greenwood Pr) Greenwood.

— The Paris Opera: An Encyclopedia of Operas, Ballets, Composers, & Performers; Growth & Grandeur, 1815-1914; A-L, Vol. 1. LC 82-21140. 816p. 1990. lib. bdg. 185.00 (*0-313-27782-6*, PGH01, Greenwood Pr) Greenwood.

— The Paris Opera: An Encyclopedia of Operas, Ballets, Composers, & Performers; Growth & Grandeur, 1815-1914; A-L, Vol. 2. LC 82-21140. 768p. 1990. lib. bdg. 185.00 (*0-313-27783-4*, Greenwood Pr) Greenwood.

Pitoura, Evaggelia & Samaras, George. Data Management for Mobile Computing. LC 97-31841. (The Kluwer International Series on Advances in Database Systems: No. 10). 168p. 1997. text 107.50 (*0-7923-8053-3*, D Reidel) Kluwer Academic.

Pitowsky, I., ed. Quantum Probability - Quantum Logic. (Lecture Notes in Physics Ser.: Vol. 321). ix, 209p. 1989. 36.95 (*0-387-50679-9*) Spr-Verlag.

Pitrat, J., ed. An Artificial Approach to Understanding Natural Language. 162p. 1988. 35.00 (*0-87683-945-6*, PR-4) Soc Computer Sim.

Pitre. Financial Accounting: The Business Cycle Approach. rev. ed. LC 98-74481. 1999. 64.95 (*0-87393-837-2*) Dame Pubns.

Pitre & Malone. A Merchandising Practice Set in Financial Accounting: Creative Thoughts, Inc. 1994. pap. 15.95 (*0-87393-360-5*) Dame Pubns.

Pitre, David W. To Martin Luther King, with Love: A Southern Quaker's Tribute. LC 84-60119. 1984. pap. 1.00 (*0-87574-254-8*) Pendle Hill.

***Pitre, Frank M.** California Personal Injury Proof: June 2000 Update. Compton, Linda, ed. LC 71-630382. 200p. 2000. 45.00 (*0-7626-0448-4*, TO-30564) Cont Ed Bar-CA.

— California Personal Injury Proof - 6/99 Update. Compton, Linda A., ed. LC 71-630682. 186p. 1999. ring bd. 44.00 (*0-7626-0341-0*, TO-30563) Cont Ed Bar-CA.

Pitre, Giuseppe. Grammatica Siciliana del Dialetto E Delle Parlate. Wentrup, Christian F., ed. (ITA.). 92p. (Orig.). 1995. pap. 22.00 (*0-913298-73-5*) S F Vanni.

— Sicilian Folk Medicine. (Illus.). 320p. 1971. 48.50 (*0-87291-013-X*) Coronado Pr.

Pitre, Glen & Benoit, Michelle. Country Roads of Louisiana. LC 95-9758. (Country Roads of... Ser.). (Illus.). 184p. (Orig.). 1995. pap. 10.95 (*1-56626-138-4*, 61384, Cntry Rds Pr) NTC Contemp Pub Co.

Pitre, Glen & Benoit, Michelle. Country Roads of Louisiana. (Country Roads Ser.). 200p. (Orig.). 1996. pap. 10.95 (*1-56626-169-4*, Cntry Rds Pr) NTC Contemp Pub Co.

— Great River. LC 93-22333. (Illus.). 224p. 1993. pap. 12.95 (*0-88289-783-7*) Pelican.

Pitre, John. The Art & Works of a Visionary. limited ed. (Illus.). 150p. 1996. 59.95 (*0-9648183-0-2*) Pitre Fine Arts.

Pitre, Marianne R., jt. auth. see Anderson, Anne S.

Pitre, Merlene. Through Many Dangers, Toils & Snares: Black Leadership in Texas, 1870-1890. rev. ed. LC 98-100506. (Illus.). 300p. 1997. reprint ed. pap. 19.95 (*1-57168-165-5*, 165-5, Eakin Pr) Sunbelt Media.

Pitre, Merline. In Struggle Against Jim Crow: Lulu B. White & the NAACP, 1900-1957. LC 98-42050. (Centennial Series of the Association of Former Students, Texas A&M University: No. 81). (Illus.). 200p. 1999. 29.95 (*0-89096-869-1*) Tex A&M Univ Pr.

Pitre, Verne. Grandma Was a Sailmaker: Tales of the Cajun Wetlands. (Illus.). 160p. (Orig.). (YA). (gr. 7 up). 1991. pap. 6.00 (*0-9621725-6-1*) Blue Heron LA.

Pitroda, Sam. Exploding Freedom: Roots in Technology. (C). 1993. 18.00 (*81-7023-270-8*, Pub. by Allied Pubs) S Asia.

Pitrone, Jean M. Jean Hoxie: The Robin Hood of Tennis. LC 85-70768. 130p. 1985. 11.95 (*0-910977-01-1*) Avenue Pub.

Pitrone, Jean M. & Nosis, George J. Tangled Web: Legacy of Auto Pioneer, John F. Dodge. 336p. 1989. 19.95 (*0-910977-05-4*) Avenue Pub.

***Pitrone, Jeanne Maddern.** Take It from the Big Mouth: The Life of Martha Raye. LC 98-49383. (Illus.). 248p. 1999. 25.00 (*0-8131-2110-8*) U Pr of Ky.

Pitsch, Peter K. The Innovation Age: A New Perspective on the Telecom Revolution. LC 97-116788. 150p. (Orig.). 1996. pap. text 12.95 (*1-55813-059-4*) Hudson Instit IN.

Pitschas, Rainer. Policies on Labour Relations & Social Dialogue in European Countries: The Portuguese & German Cases. LC 98-177126. 176 p. 1997. write for info. (*3-7890-4982-4*) Nomos Verlags.

Pitscher, Benedikt M. & Prucha, Ingmar R. Dynamic Nonlinear Econometric Models: Asymptotic Theory. LC 97-19176. xii, 312p. 1997. 95.00 (*3-540-62857-6*) Spr-Verlag.

Pitschmann, Louis A. Scholars' Guide to Washington, D. C., for Northwest European Studies: Belgium, Denmark, Finland, Great Britain, Greenland, Iceland, Ireland, Luxembourg, the Netherlands, Norway, & Sweden. David, Zdenek V., ed. LC 84-600036. 452p. 1991. 29.95 (*0-87474-754-6*); pap. text 15.00 (*0-87474-753-8*) W Wilson Ctr Pr.

Pitseolak, Peter. Peter Pitseolak, 1902-1973: Inuit Historian of Seekooseelak: Photographs & Drawings from Cape Dorset, Baffin Island. Bellman, David, ed. 1980. pap. 29.95 (*0-7735-0400-1*, Pub. by McG-Queens Univ Pr) CUP Services.

Pitseolak, Peter & Eber, Dorothy H. People from Our Side: A Life Story with Photographs & Oral Biography. Hanson, Ann, tr. (Illus.). 160p. 1993. 60.00 (*0-7735-0996-8*, Pub. by McG-Queens Univ Pr); pap. 24.95 (*0-7735-1118-0*, Pub. by McG-Queens Univ Pr) CUP Services.

Pitsikalis, M., et al. Blockcopolymers/Polyelectrolytes/ Biodegradation. LC 98-139496. (Advances in Polymer Science Ser.: Vol. 135). (Illus.). 242p. 1997. 159.00 (*3-540-63156-9*) Spr-Verlag.

Pitskhelauri, G. Z. The Longliving of Soviet Georgia. Lesnoff-Caravaglia, Gari, tr. from RUS. LC 81-4176. (Illus.). 158p. 1982. 30.95 (*0-89885-073-8*, Kluwer Acad Hman Sci) Kluwer Academic.

Pitson, Len, photos by. Dylan Thomas & His World. (Illus.). 150p. 1995. 19.95 (*1-85772-159-4*) Intl Spec Bk.

Pitspopany Press Staff. Jewish Kids: Activity Book. (Illus.). 32p. 1998. pap. text 5.95 (*0-943706-43-2*) Pitspopany.

Pitstow, Margaret. The Hand of Destiny. (Rainbow Romances Ser.). 160p. 1993. 14.95 (*0-7090-4897-1*) Parkwest Pubns.

— The Hand of Destiny. large type ed. (Romance Ser.). 1994. pap. 16.99 (*0-7089-7617-4*, Linford) Ulverscroft.

Pitsula, James M. & Rasmusse, Ken. Privatizing a Province: The New Right. 294p. 1990. pap. 14.95 (*0-921586-09-4*, Pub. by New Star Bks) Genl Dist Srvs.

Pitsvada, Bernard T. The Senate, Treaties & National Security, 1945-1974. 252p. (C). 1991. pap. text 29.50 (*0-8191-8199-4*); lib. bdg. 52.50 (*0-8191-8198-6*) U Pr of Amer.

***Pitt.** Fungi & Food Spoilage. 593p. 1998. 159.00 (*0-8342-1306-0*) Aspen Pub.

Pitt, Bertram. Clinical Trials in Cardiology. 1997. text 90.00 (*0-7020-2156-3*) Bailliere Tindall.

Pitt, Brice. Making the Most of Middle Age. large type ed. 119p. 1991. 17.95 (*1-85089-170-2*, Pub. by ISIS Lrg Prnt) Transaction Pubs.

— Psychogeriatrics: An Introduction to the Psychiatry of Old Age. 2nd ed. (Illus.). 224p. 1982. pap. text 24.00 (*0-443-01598-8*) Church.

Pitt-Brook. Rehabilitation of Movement. 1997. pap. text 69.00 (*0-7020-2157-1*, W B Saunders Co) Harcrt Hlth Sci Grp.

Pitt, D. C., ed. Deforestation: Social Dynamics in Watersheds & Mountain Ecocystems. 224p. 1988. lib. bdg. 55.00 (*0-415-00456-X*) Routledge.

Pitt, D. H., et al, eds. Category Theory & Computer Science. (Lecture Notes in Computer Science Ser.: Vol. 389). vi, 365p. 1989. 43.00 (*0-387-51662-X*, 3506) Spr-Verlag.

Pitt, D. H., et al. Category Theory & Computer Science. (Lecture Notes in Computer Science Ser.: Vol. 283). v, 300p. 1987. 39.00 (*0-387-18508-9*) Spr-Verlag.

Pitt, Dale, jt. auth. see Pitt, Leonard.

Pitt, David. Biosphere & Noosphere Reader: Global Environment, Society & Change. LC 98-42866. 1999. pap. 29.99 (*0-415-16645-4*) Routledge.

Pitt, David, et al, eds. Category Theory & Computer Science: 6th International Conference, CTCS '95, Cambridge, United Kingdom, August 7-11, 1995, Proceedings, Vol. VII. (Lecture Notes in Computer Science Ser.: Vol. 953). 252p. 1995. 49.00 (*3-540-60164-3*) Spr-Verlag.

Pitt, David & Thompson, Gordon, eds. Nuclear Free Zones. 160p. 1987. lib. bdg. 55.00 (*0-7099-4076-9*, Pub. by C Helm) Routldge.

Pitt, David, jt. ed. see Briceno, Salvano.

Pitt, David C. Using Historical Sources in Anthropology & Sociology. (George & Louise Spindler Case Studies in Cultural Anthropology). 92p. (C). reprint ed. pap. write for info. (*0-8290-0587-0*) Irvington.

Pitt, David C., ed. Development from Below: Anthropologists & Development Situations. (World Anthropology Ser.). x, 278p. 1976. 36.95 (*90-279-7869-7*) Mouton.

— The Future of the Environment: The Social Dimensions of Conservation & Ecological Alternatives. LC 88-4402. (European Year of the Environment Ser.). 224p. reprint ed. pap. 69.50 (*0-608-20371-8*, 207162400002) Bks Demand.

Pitt, David G. E. J. Pratt: The Master Years 1927-1964. (Illus.). 576p. 1987. 40.00 (*0-8020-5753-5*) U of Toronto Pr.

— E. J. Pratt: The Truant Years Eighteen Eighty-Two to Nineteen Twenty-Seven. (Illus.). 448p. 1984. 30.00 (*0-8020-5660-1*); pap. 17.95 (*0-8020-6563-5*) U of Toronto Pr.

Pitt, David G. E. J. Pratt, the Truant Years, 1882-1927. LC 85-114711. xix, 414 p. 1984. write for info. (*0-920502-37-7*) Jesperson Pr.

Pitt, Esmond & McNiff, Kathy. Java Technology's Remote Method Invocation: Programmer's Guide & Class Reference. 1966. pap. text 39.95 (*0-201-70043-3*) Addison-Wesley.

Pitt, Estella, ed. see Bynum, Doris.

Pitt, Estella M. Partakers (with Christ) (Illus.). 53p. (Orig.). 1995. pap. text 4.95 (*0-9642764-1-0*) E Pitt.

— A Restoring God. 40p. 1994. pap. 4.95 (*0-9642764-0-2*) E Pitt.

— When You've Been There. 68p. (Orig.). 1996. pap. 5.95 (*0-9642764-2-9*) E Pitt.

Pitt, Estella M., ed. see Fozard, Nora.

Pitt, Eva, jt. auth. see Pitt, Martin J.

Pitt, G. D., jt. auth. see Parker, H.

Pitt, G. J. & Milward, G. R., eds. Coal & Modern Coal Processing: An Introduction. 1979. text 73.00 (*0-12-557850-4*) Acad Pr.

Pitt, Gwyneth. Butterworths Commercial & Consumer Law Handbook. 2nd ed. 1995. pap. write for info. (*0-406-05223-9*, BCLH2, MICHIE) LEXIS Pub.

— Butterworths Commercial Law Handbook. 490p. 1989. pap. 50.00 (*0-406-54722-X*, UK, MICHIE) LEXIS Pub.

Pitt, H. G. Abraham Lincoln. (New Pocket Biographies Ser.). (Illus.). 128p. 1998. pap. 9.95 (*0-7509-1511-0*, Pub. by Sutton Pub Ltd) Bks Intl VA.

Pitt, H. R. Measure & Integration for Use. (Institute of Mathematics & Its Applications Conference Series, New Ser.). 150p. 1985. text 29.95 (*0-19-853608-9*) OUP.

Pitt, Harvey L., et al, eds. Twenty-Third Annual Institute on Securities Regulation Transcript - The SEC in a New Environment - Securitization - Troubled Companies - Sharehold Activism Enforcement. 350p. 1992. 105.00 (*0-685-69368-6*) PLI.

Pitt, Harvey L., et al. The Evolving Financial Services Industry. 1985. 75.00 (*0-317-29383-4*, #H44003) Harcourt.

— The Law of Financial Services, 8 vols. 9530p. 1988. ring bd. 695.00 (*0-13-099276-3*) Aspen Law.

— The Law of Financial Services, 6 vols. 5000p. 1988. write for info. (*0-318-65468-7*, H44003) P-H.

Pitt, Harvey L., jt. auth. see Block, Dennis J.

Pitt, Harvey L., jt. auth. see Greene, Edward F.

Pitt, Harvey L., jt. auth. see Levine, Theodore A.

Pitt, Henry A., et al. Hepatic & Pancreatic Disease: The Team Approach to Management. LC 94-46416. 528p. 1995. text 99.95 (*0-316-70915-8*, Little Brwn Med Div) Lppncott W & W.

Pitt, Hester. So Dearly Loved, So Much Admired: Letters to Hester Pitt, Lady Chatham from Her Relations & Friends, 1744-1801. Birdwood, Vere, ed. xxxii, 362p. 1994. 50.00 (*0-11-887546-9*, Pub. by Statnry Office) Balogh.

***Pitt, Ingrid.** Ingrid Pitt Bedside Companion for Ghosthunters. 1999. pap. text 19.95 (*0-7134-8444-6*) B T B.

Pitt, Ingrid. The Ingrid Pitt Bedside Companion for Vampire Lovers. (Illus.). 192p. 1998. pap. text 19.95 (*0-7134-8277-X*, Pub. by B T B) Branford.

Pitt, Ivan L. & Norsworthy, J. R. Economics of the U. S. Commercial Airline Industry: Productivity, Technology & Deregulation. LC 99-20658. (Transportation Research, Economics & Policy Ser.). xiv, 190p. 1999. 115.00 (*0-7923-8505-5*) Kluwer Academic.

Pitt, J. C., ed. The Philosophy of Wilfrid Sellars: Queries & Extensions. (Philosophical Studies in Philosophy: No. 12). 313p. 1978. text 106.00 (*90-277-0903-3*, D Reidel) Kluwer Academic.

***Pitt, John.** U. S. A. by Rail. 3rd ed. LC 98-46480. (Bradt Rail Guides Ser.). (Illus.). 368p. 1999. pap. text 17.95 (*1-898323-83-6*, Pub. by Bradt Pubns) Globe Pequot.

Pitt, John I., jt. ed. see Samson, Robert A.

Pitt, Joseph C. Galileo, Human Knowledge & the Book of Nature: Method Replaces Metaphysics. (Western Ontario Ser.). 216p. (C). 1992. lib. bdg. 141.50 (*0-7923-1510-3*, Pub. by Kluwer Academic) Kluwer Academic.

— Pictures, Images & Conceptual Change: An Analysis of Wilfrid Sellars' Philosophy of Science. (Synthese Library: No. 151). 175p. 1981. pap. text 51.50 (*90-277-1277-8*) Kluwer Academic.

— Pictures, Images & Conceptual Change: Wilfrid Sellars & the Philosophy of Science. 175p. 1981. lib. bdg. 78.00 (*90-277-1276-X*, D Reidel) Kluwer Academic.

— Theories of Explanation. (Illus.). 234p. 1988. pap. text 21.95 (*0-19-504971-3*) OUP.

— Thinking about Technology: Foundations of the Philosophy of Technology. LC 99-42441. (Illus.). 192p. (C). 1999. pap. text 21.95 (*1-889119-12-1*, Chatham House Pub) Seven Bridges.

Pitt, Joseph C., ed. Change & Progress in Modern Science. (University of Western Ontario Series in Philosophy of Science: No. 27). 408p. 1984. text 179.50 (*90-277-1898-9*) Kluwer Academic.

— New Directions in the Philosophy of Technology. (Philosophy & Technology Ser.: Vol. 11). 234p. (C). 1995. text 107.00 (*0-7923-3661-5*) Kluwer Academic.

— Philosophy in Economics. 217p. 1981. text 94.00 (*90-277-1210-7*, D Reidel) Kluwer Academic.

Pitt, Joseph C. & Pera, Marcello, eds. Rational Changes in Science. 240p. (C). 1987. text 152.50 (*90-277-2417-2*, D Reidel) Kluwer Academic.

Pitt, Joseph C., jt. ed. see Butts, Robert E.

Pitt, Joseph C., jt. ed. see Byrne, Edmund F.

Pitt, Joseph C., jt. ed. see Johnson, Deborah.

Pitt, K., jt. auth. see Haskard, M. R.

***Pitt, Kathleen & Pitt, Michael D.** Three Seasons in the Wind: 950 Kilometres by Canoe down Northern Canada's Thelon River. 2nd rev. ed. 145p. 1999. pap. 16.95 (*0-9686581-0-5*) H2 Hse Pubns.

Pitt, Kathleen, jt. auth. see Pitt, Michael D.

Pitt-Kethley, Fiona. Double Act. LC 97-147007. 50p. 1997. pap. 14.95 (*1-900850-00-1*) Dufour.

P

An Asterisk (*) at the beginning of an entry indicates that the title is appearing for the first time.

— The Misfortunes of Nigel. 176p. 1991. 29.95 (0-7206-0830-9, Pub. by P Owen Ltd) Dufour.
— Too Hot to Handle. 136p. 1992. 32.00 (0-7206-0875-9, Pub. by P Owen Ltd) Dufour.
Pitt, Leonard. California Controversies. 2nd ed. 48p. 1990. pap. text, student ed. Price not set. (0-88295-893-3) Harlan Davidson.
— The Decline of the Californios: A Social History of the Spanish-Speaking Californians, 1846-1890. 1966. pap. 15.95 (0-520-01637-8) U CA Pr.
***Pitt, Leonard.** The Decline of the Californios: A Social History of the Spanish-Speaking Californians, 1846-1890. LC 99-229612. 340p. 1999. pap. 15.95 (0-520-21958-9, Pub. by U CA Pr) Cal Prin Full Svc.
Pitt, Leonard. Documenting America Vol. 1: A Reader in United States History: Colonial Times to 1877. 320p. 1993. per. 62.95 (0-8403-5245-X) Kendall-Hunt.
— Study Guide for We Americans, Vol. I. 3rd ed. 112p. 1989. per. 28.95 (0-8403-5628-5) Kendall-Hunt.
— Study Guide for We Americans, Vol. II. 3rd ed. 160p. 1989. per. 31.95 (0-8403-5629-3) Kendall-Hunt.
Pitt, Leonard, ed. California Controversies: Major Issues in the History of the State. 2nd ed. (Illus.). 384p. 1990. pap. text 18.95 (0-88295-879-8) Harlan Davidson.
Pitt, Leonard & Pitt, Dale. Los Angeles A to Z: An Encyclopedia of the City & County. LC 96-50261. (Illus.). 600p. 1997. 39.95 (0-520-20274-0, Pub. by U CA Pr) Cal Prin Full Svc.
— Los Angeles A to Z: An Encyclopedia of the City & County. LC 96-50261. (Illus.). 600p. 2000. pap. 24.95 (0-520-20530-8, Pub. by U CA Pr) Cal Prin Full Svc.
Pitt, Leonard, jt. ed. see Haussler, David.
Pitt, Leyland F. Marketing for Managers: A Practical Approach. LC 98-178282. 288p. 1998. pap. 32.00 (0-7021-4222-0, Pub. by Juta & Co) Intl Spec Bk.
Pitt, Leyland F. & Bromfield, Derek. The Marketing Decision Maker: From MKIS to MDSS. 2nd rev. ed. (Illus.). 209p. (C). pap. text 37.00 (0-7021-3042-7, Pub. by Juta & Co) Intl Spec Bk.
Pitt, Mark. Women's Schooling, the Selectivity of Fertility, & Child Mortality in Sub-Saharan Africa. (World Bank Living Standards Measurement Series Paper: No. 119). 64p. 1995. pap. 22.00 (0-8213-3332-1, 13332) World Bank.
Pitt, Mark M. & Khandker, Shahidur R. Household & Intrahousehold Impacts of the Grammeen Bank & Similar Targeted Credit Programs in Bangladesh, Vol. 320. LC 96-6828. (World Bank Discussion Papers: No. 320). 120p. 1996. pap. 22.00 (0-8213-3594-4, 13594) World Bank.
Pitt, Martin J. & Pitt, Eva. Handbook of Laboratory Waste Disposal: A Practical Manual. LC 85-7615. (Chemical Science Ser.). 360p. 1985. text 124.00 (0-470-20202-5) P-H.
Pitt, Martyn, jt. auth. see Baden-Fuller, Charles.
Pitt, Martyn, jt. ed. see Baden-Fuller, Charles.
***Pitt, Matthew.** Apache Helicopter: The AH-64. (High Interest Bks.). (Illus.). (J). 2000. 19.00 (0-516-23336-X) Childrens.
— Apache Helicopter: The AH-64. LC 00-24369. (High Interest Bks.). (Illus.). 48p. (J). (gr. 4-7). 2000. pap. write for info. (0-516-23536-2) Childrens.
— Tomahawk Cruise Missile. (High Interest Bks.). (Illus.). (J). 2000. 19.00 (0-516-23343-2) Childrens.
— Tomahawk Cruise Missile. LC 00-24375. (High Interest Bks.). (Illus.). 48p. (J). (gr. 4-7). 2000. pap. write for info. (0-516-23543-5) Childrens.
Pitt, Michael D. & Pitt, Kathleen. Three Seasons in the Wind. 156p. 1999. 14.92 (1-55212-229-8) Trafford Pub.
Pitt, Michael D., jt. auth. see Pitt, Kathleen.
Pitt, Nick. The Prince & the Prophet: The Rise of Naseem Hamed. LC 98-54243. (Illus.). 256p. 1999. pap. 16.00 (1-56858-130-0) FWEW.
Pitt, R. E. Silage & Hay Preservation. (Illus.). 54p. 1990. pap. text 8.00 (0-935817-47-6, 5) NRAES.
Pitt-Rivers. Love of Food, Love of God. 300p. (C). 2000. lib. bdg. 34.95 (0-226-67005-8) U Ch Pr.
Pitt-Rivers, Augustus H. Antique Works of Art from Benin. LC 68-9011. (Illus.). 1971. 50.00 (0-87817-017-0) Hacker.
— Antique Works of Art from Benin, West Africa. LC 74-138344. (Black Heritage Library Collection). 1977. 23.95 (0-8369-8736-5) Ayer.
— The Evolution of Culture, & Other Essays. Myres, John L., ed. LC 76-44719. reprint ed. 62.50 (0-404-15858-7) AMS Pr.
— Excavations in Cranborne Chase: Near Rushmore, on the Borders of Dorset & Wilts: 1880-1896, 4 vols., Set. LC 77-86426. reprint ed. 315.00 (0-404-16640-7) AMS Pr.
Pitt-Rivers, Julian A. The Fate of Shechem or The Politics of Sex: Essays in the Anthropology of the Mediterranean. LC 76-27913. (Cambridge Studies in Social Anthropology: No. 19). 207p. reprint ed. pap. 59.00 (0-608-15765-1, 2031710) Bks Demand.
— People of the Sierra. 2nd ed. LC 70-153710. 260p. 1996. pap. text 12.00 (0-226-67010-4, P55) U Ch Pr.
Pitt-Rivers, Rosalind & Trotter, W. R., eds. The Thyroid Gland, 2 vols., I. LC 64-9966. (Illus.). 337p. 1964. reprint ed. pap. 104.50 (0-608-08508-1, 202571400002) Bks Demand.
— The Thyroid Gland, 2 vols., II. LC 64-9966. (Illus.). 456p. 1964. reprint ed. pap. 141.40 (0-608-08507-3, 202571400001) Bks Demand.
Pitt, Robert, et al. Groundwater Contamination from Stormwater Infiltration. 250p. (C). 1996. ring bd. 54.95 (1-57504-015-8) CRC Pr.
— Investigation of Inappropriate Pollutant Entries into Storm Drainage Systems: A User's Guide. (Illus.). 87p. (Orig.). 1994. pap. text 30.00 (0-7881-1359-3) DIANE Pub.
— Potential Groundwater Contamination from Intentional & Nonintentional Stormwater Infiltration. (Illus.). 120p. (Orig.). (C). 1994. pap. text 40.00 (0-7881-1059-4) DIANE Pub.
Pitt, Robert E. & Girts, Michelle A. Stormwater Quality Management. 1998. 69.95 (1-56670-143-0) Lewis Pubs.
Pitt, Valeria. Enciclopedia Juvenil de la Ciencia. (SPA.). 260p. (J). 1975. 95.00 (0-8288-5870-5, S26475) Fr & Eur.
Pitt, Valerie. Tennyson Laureate. LC PR5588.P5. 304p. reprint ed. pap. 94.30 (0-8357-4166-4, 203694000007) Bks Demand.
Pitt, Valerie, ed. see Eiler, Andrew.
Pitta, Robert. U. N. Forces, 1948-1994. (Elite Ser.). (Illus.). 64p. 1994. pap. 12.95 (1-85532-454-7, 9469, Pub. by Osprey) Stackpole.
Pitta, Robert & Fannell, Jeff. South African Special Forces. (Elite Ser.: No. 47). (Illus.). 64p. pap. 12.95 (1-85532-295-1, 9462, Pub. by Osprey) Stackpole.
Pittam, Jeffery. Voice in Social Interaction: An Interdisciplinary Approach to Vocal Communication. (Language & Language Behaviors Ser.: Vol. 5). 200p. 1994. 48.00 (0-8039-5750-5); pap. 22.95 (0-8039-5751-3) Sage.
Pittam, Jeffery & Gallois, Cynthia, eds. Mentoring & Nurturing Communication in Health Contexts: A Special Issue of "Health Communication" 1998. pap. write for info. (0-8058-9821-2) L Erlbaum Assocs.
Pittano, Giuseppe. Phraseological Synonym & Antonym Dictionary of Equivalences, Analogous & Contrary Terms: Sinonimi e Contrari Dizionario Fraseologico delle Parole Equivalenti Analoghe e Contrarie. (ITA.). 864p. 1987. lib. bdg. 95.00 (0-8288-3337-0, F120160); lib. bdg. 85.00 (0-685-59882-X) Fr & Eur.
Pittano, Giuseppe & Fatta, Frase. Capo Ha: Dizionario Dei Modi di Dire, Proverbi e Locuzioni. (ITA.). 352p. 1993. 75.00 (0-8288-9428-0) Fr & Eur.
Pittard, Kay & Mitchell, Robert W. Comparative Morphology of the Life Stages of Cryptocellus Pelaezi (Arachnida, Ricinulie) (Graduate Studies: No. 1). (Illus.). 77p. (Orig.). 1972. pap. 4.00 (0-89672-008-X) Tex Tech Univ Pr.
Pittard, Lynne. More Magic Methods in Oil with Lynne Pittard: Thirteen New Paintings Illustrated in Four Stages, in Full Color. (Illus.). 72p. (Orig.). 1984. pap. 14.95 (0-943295-05-X) Graphics Plus FL.
— Paint with Pittard: 13 New Paintings with Lynne Pittard in Four Stages & Full Color. (Illus.). 72p. (Orig.). 1985. pap. 14.95 (0-943295-06-8) Graphics Plus FL.
— Paint with Pittard III: 12 New Paintings by Lynne Pittard in Four Stages & Full Color. (Illus.). 72p. (Orig.). 1989. pap. 14.95 (0-943295-10-6) Graphics Plus FL.
Pittard, Suzan Z., ed. see Zedick, Mary P.
Pittaro, John. Cuentos Faciles de Hoy y de Ayer. 1973. pap. text 7.95 (0-88334-059-3, 76059) Longman.
Pittas-Hershbach, Mary. Time & Space in Euripides & Racine: The Hippolytos of Euripides & Racine's Phedre. LC 89-29820. (American University Studies: Comparative Literature: Ser. III, Vol. 32). (Illus.). XVIII, 344p. (C). 1991. text 53.95 (0-8204-1182-5) P Lang Pubng.
Pittas, Peggy A. Blow Your Little Tin Whistle: A Biography of Richard Clarke Sommerville. LC 92-11142. 258p. (Orig.). (C). 1992. pap. text 29.00 (0-8191-8745-3); lib. bdg. 57.50 (0-8191-8744-5) U Pr of Amer.
Pittau, Joseph. Political Thought in Early Meiji Japan, 1868-1889. LC 65-22065. (Harvard East Asian Ser.: No. 24). 261p. reprint ed. pap. 81.00 (0-608-10278-4, 200378100033) Bks Demand.
Pittaway, A. R. Arthropods of Medical & Veterinary Importance: A Checklist of Preferred Names & Allied Terms. 192p. 1991. pap. 59.95 (0-8288-7365-8, 851987419) Fr & Eur.
Pittaway, A. R., compiled by. Arthropods of Medical & Veterinary Importance: A Checklist of Preferred Names & Allied Terms. 160p. 1991. pap. text 45.00 (0-85198-741-9) OUP.
Pittaway, David & Hammerton, Alastair. Pittaway & Hamerton: Professional Negligence Cases. 1997. write for info. (0-406-08191-3, PHPNC, MICHIE) LEXIS Pub.
Pittaway, Donald. Endometriosis: A Problem-Oriented Approach. 380p. 1997. text 80.00 (0-7817-0299-2) Lppncott W & W.
***Pittel, Jamie.** Sweet Sixteen: Marisa, No. 5. LC 00-100191. (Sweet Sixteen Ser.: No. 5). 240p. (YA). (gr. 12 up). 2000. pap. 5.95 (0-06-440816-7, HarpTrophy) HarpC Child Bks.
***Pittelli, Jan.** Bridge over Troubled Bidding. (Illus.). 175p. 1999. pap. 34.50 (0-9643958-1-9) Assoctd W Palm Bch.
— Bridge over Troubled Bidding. (Illus.). 189p. 2000. pap. 34.50 (0-9643958-7-8) Assoctd W Palm Bch.
— Bridge Over Troubled Bidding. iii, 189p. 2000. pap. 34.50 (0-9702770-0-8) J Pittelli.
Pittelman, Susan D. Semantic Feature Analysis: Classroom Application. 66p. 1991. pap. 8.95 (0-87207-235-5) Intl Reading.
Pittelman, Susan D., jt. auth. see Heimlich, Joan E.
Pittendrigh. Circadian Oscillation & Organization in Nervous. 1976. pap. text 8.95 (0-262-66024-5) MIT Pr.
***Pittenger, A. O.** An Introduction to Quantum Computing Algorithms. LC 99-47513. (Illus.). 136p. 1999. 42.95 (0-8176-4127-0, Pub. by Birkhauser) Spr-Verlag.
***Pittenger, Arthur O.** An Introduction to Quantum Computing Algorithms. LC 99-47513. (Progress in Computer Science & Applied Logic Ser.). 1999. write for info. (3-7643-4127-0) Birkhauser.
Pittenger, Candace. Ribbons of Wisdom: How to Communicate with Our Elderly. (Illus.). 80p. 1997. pap. 10.95 (0-9662089-0-0, Pub. by C Pittenger) Origin Bk Sales.
***Pittenger, David J.** Fundamentals of Behavioral Research Methods. (C). 2000. pap., student ed. 47.81 (0-07-233310-3) McGrw-H Hghr Educ.
— Fundamentals of Behavioral Statistics. 9th ed. 350p. (C). 1999. pap., student ed. 25.63 (0-07-232406-6) McGrw-H Hghr Educ.
Pittenger, David J., jt. auth. see Allen, Joseph D.
Pittenger, David J., jt. auth. see Runyon, Richard P.
Pittenger, John, jt. ed. see Valenti, S. Stavros.
Pittenger, Mark. American Socialists & Evolutionary Thought, 1870-1920. LC 92-28041. (History of American Thought & Culture Ser.). 320p. (Orig.). (C). 1993. 60.00 (0-299-13600-0); pap. 24.95 (0-299-13604-3) U of Wis Pr.
Pittenger, Michael A., jt. auth. see Wolfe, Donald J., Jr.
Pittenger, Norman. After Death-Life in God. 96p. 1982. 6.95 (0-8164-0108-X) Harper SF.
Pittenger, Norman. Our Lady: The Mother of Jesus in Christian Faith & Devotion. 1996. pap. text 16.00 (0-334-02627-X) TPI PA.
Pittenger, Owen E. & Gooding, C. Thomas. Learning Theories in Educational Practice: An Integration of Psychological Theory & Educational Philosophy. LC 79-140553. 228p. (C). reprint ed. 70.70 (0-8357-9922-0, 205174700005) Bks Demand.
Pittenger, Peggy. Reschooling the Thoroughbred: How to Buy & Retrain a Racehorse. LC 97-2696. 1997. pap. 23.95 (0-939481-49-9) Half Halt Pr.
Pittenger, W. Norman. Richard the Lion-Hearted, the Crusader King. LC 72-98670. (Immortals of History Ser.). 149p. 1970. write for info. (0-531-00945-9) Watts.
Pittenger, William. Daring & Suffering: A History of the Andrews Railroad Raid. 3rd ed. LC 99-16377. 480p. 1999. pap. 18.95 (1-58182-034-8, Cumberland Hearthside) Cumberland Hse.
Pittenger, William N. Catholic Faith in a Process Perspective. LC 81-9615. 160p. (Orig.). reprint ed. pap. 49.60 (0-8357-8825-3, 203356000086) Bks Demand.
— Christian Faith & the Question of History. LC 73-79353. 159p. reprint ed. pap. 49.30 (0-608-16421-6, 202691000053) Bks Demand.
Pitter. Introducing Microsoft Office. 1994. 33.50 (0-07-052068-2) McGraw.
— Using Lotus 1-2-3 DOS 3.1. 1993. teacher ed. 20.62 (0-07-050297-8) McGraw.
— Using Microsft Excel 4.0. 1993. pap., teacher ed. 13.43 (0-07-050300-1) McGraw.
Pitter, Keiko. Every Student's Guide to the World Wide Web: With Internet Explorer. LC 96-77644. (C). 1999. pap. text 23.03 (0-07-052491-2) McGraw.
— Introducing Microsoft Excel 5.0 for Windows. LC 93-78721. (C). 1994. text 11.25 (0-07-051596-4) McGraw.
— Introducing Microsoft Excel 4.0 for Windows. 125p. (C). 1993. pap. text 16.75 (0-07-051576-X) McGraw.
— Introducing Microsoft Excel 4.0 for Windows. 100p. (C). 1993. pap. text 15.00 (0-07-051586-7) McGraw.
— Introducing Microsoft Word 6.0 for Windows. LC 94-77137. (C). 1994. pap. text 11.25 (0-07-051767-3) McGraw.
— Introducing the PC & Windows 3.1. 150p. (C). 1993. pap. text 11.95 (0-07-051584-0) McGraw.
— Introducing WordPerfect for Windows. 150p. (C). 1993. pap. text 15.00 (0-07-051588-3) McGraw.
— Introducing WordPerfect 6.0 for Windows. (C). 1994. pap. text 10.74 (0-07-051597-2) McGraw.
— Using Lotus 1-2-3, 2.2 for the IBM Pc. 3rd ed. (C). 1990. text 37.75 (0-07-050258-7) McGraw.
— Using Microcomputers: An Apple Lab Manual. 237p. 1984. pap. text 17.95 (0-938188-21-6) Mitchell Pub.
Pitter, Keiko, ed. Biodegradability of Organic Substances in Aquatic Environ. 320p. 1990. 179.00 (0-8493-5131-6, QH530, CRC Reprint) Franklin.
Pitter, Keiko & Amato, Sara. Every Student's Guide to the Internet: Macintosh Version. Text Plus Internet Yellow Pages. (C). 1995. pap. text 26.50 (0-07-912201-9) McGraw.
Pitter, Keiko & Minato, Robert. Every Student's Guide to the World Wide Web. LC 95-81012. 150p. (C). 1996. pap. text 15.25 (0-07-052232-4) McGraw.
— Every Student's Guide to the World Wide Web. Text with Amato: Every Student's Guide to the Internet, Windows Version 1.0. (C). 1995. pap. text, student ed. 15.74 (0-07-844942-1) McGraw.
Pitter, Keiko & Pitter, Richard. Using Microcomputers: An IBM PC Lab Manual. 280p. 1984. pap. text 17.95 (0-938188-22-4) Mitchell Pub.
— Using Microcomputers: An IBM-PC Lab Manual. 2nd ed. 256p. (Orig.). (C). 1986. pap. text 19.95 (0-938188-38-0) Mitchell Pub.
Pitter, Keiko & Trainor, Timothy N. Introducing Microsoft Works 3.0 for Windows. LC 93-78719. (C). 1994. text 19.74 (0-07-051595-6) McGraw.
Pitter, Keiko, et al. Every Student's Guide to the Internet. 1994. pap. text. write for info. (0-07-912113-6) McGraw.
— Every Student's Guide to the Internet. large type ed. 202p. 50.50 (0-614-20557-3, L-53353-00 APHB) Am Printing Hse.
— Every Student's Guide to the Internet: Macintosh Version. (C). 1995. pap. text 14.25 (0-07-052109-3) McGraw.
— Every Student's Guide to the Internet: Unix Version. 2nd ed. (C). 1996. pap. text 14.25 (0-07-052416-5) McGraw.
— Every Student's Guide to the Internet: Windows Version. (C). 1995. pap. text 14.25 (0-07-052107-7) McGraw.
— Every Student's Guide to the Internet: Windows Version. (C). 1995. pap. text 26.00 (0-07-912264-7) McGraw.
Pitter, Richard, jt. auth. see Pitter, Keiko.
Pitter, Ruth. Collected Poems. 299p. 1990. pap. 22.00 (1-870612-06-X, Pub. by Enitha Pr) Dufour.
— Collected Poems. (Illus.). 306p. 1996. pap. 19.95 (1-870612-14-0, Pub. by Enitha Pr) Dufour.
— Collected Poems (1990) 1990. 38.00 (1-870612-11-6, Pub. by Enitha Pr) Dufour.
***Pitteri, M. & Zanzotto, G.** Continuum Models for Twinning in Crystals. 304p. 1999. 99.95 (0-8493-0327-3, Chap & Hall CRC) CRC Pr.
Pittford, Thomas R., jt. auth. see Rstavik, Dag.
Pittham, Keith S. Rehabilitation: Index of Modern Information with Bibliography. LC 88-47796. 150p. (Orig.). 1988. 47.50 (0-88164-884-1); pap. 44.50 (0-88164-885-X) ABBE Pubs Assn.
Pitti, Mary J. & Meier, Traci. Problem-Solving Picture Cards: Daily Living Situations for Adults with Disabilities. 13p. 1992. pap., student ed. 72.50 (0-7616-7798-4) Commun Skill.
Pittier de Fabrega, Henri. Ethnographic & Linguistic Notes on the Paez Indians of Tierra Adentro, Cauca, Colombia. LC 08-3129. (American Anthropological Association Memoirs Ser.). 1907. 25.00 (0-527-00504-5) Periodicals Srv.
***Pittiglio, C. L.** Standard Review Plan for Evaluating Nuclear Power Reactor License Termination Plans: Final Report. 28p. 2000. pap. 3.25 (0-16-059236-4) USGPO.
Pittiglio, D. Harmening, jt. auth. see Isbister, James.
Pittilo, R. M. & Machin, S. J. Platelet-Vessel Wall Interaction. (Bloomsbury Series in Clinical Science). (Illus.). 195p. 1988. 103.00 (0-387-17488-5) Spr-Verlag.
Pittinger, Charles B., ed. James Taylor Gwathmey - American Pioneer Anesthesiologist. LC 88-51678. 630p. (C). 1989. 55.00 (0-9623307-0-1) Anesthesia Pr.
Pittinger, Jill, tr. see Fritz, Volkmar.
Pittingill, jt. compiled by see Mitchell.
Pittinsky, Todd L., jt. auth. see Levine, James A.
Pittion-Rossillon, Lynn Palm, see Savoie, Jane.
Pittis, Arthur. Pedagogical Theatre. Mitchell, David, ed. 173p. 1997. pap. 15.00 (1-888365-02-1) Assn Waldorf Schls.
Pittis, Donald & Henders, Susan J., eds. Macao: Mysterious Decay & Romance. (Illus.). 284p. 1998. pap. text 32.00 (0-19-590569-5) OUP.
Pittis, Margaret B. Pittis Genealogy: The Pittis Family in England & America, 464 Years, 16 Generations, 1480-1944, with Allied Families. (Illus.). 315p. 1996. reprint ed. pap. 49.50 (0-8328-5254-6); reprint ed. lib. bdg. 59.50 (0-8328-5253-8) Higginson Bk Co.
Pittman, jt. auth. see Conrath.
Pittman, Allan, jt. auth. see Smith, Robert W.
Pittman, Allen, jt. auth. see Smith, Robert W.
Pittman, Anne. Tennis. (Sport for Life Ser.). (C). 1988. pap. text 10.50 (0-673-18346-7) Addson-Wesley Educ.
Pittman, April C., jt. auth. see Briggs, Martha W.
Pittman, Avril. From Ostpolitik to Reunification: West German-Soviet Political Relations since 1974. (Cambridge Russian, Soviet & Post-Soviet Studies: No. 85). (Illus.). 246p. (C). 1992. text 74.95 (0-521-40166-6) Cambridge U Pr.
***Pittman, Bill.** Courage to Change. 1998. 12.95 (1-56838-245-6) Hazelden.
— Drop the Rock. 1992. pap. text 10.00 (1-56838-504-8) Hazelden.
Pittman, Bill. Practice These Principles. LC 99-188657. 1997. pap. 9.95 (1-56838-150-6, 1059 A) Hazelden.
Pittman, Bill. Roots of AA: AA the Way It Began. 1989. pap. 12.00 (1-56838-505-6) Hazelden.
Pittman, Bill. Stepping Stones to Recovery. LC 87-73389. 308p. pap. 8.95 (0-934125-04-X) Hazelden.
***Pittman, Bill.** Stepping Stones to Recovery. 2000. pap. text 12.00 (1-56838-508-0) Hazelden.
— 12 Step Prayer Book. (Lakeside Meditation Ser.). 1999. pap. 9.00 (1-56838-376-2) Hazelden.
Pittman, Bill. The 12 Step Prayer Book: A Collection of Favorite 12 Step Prayers & Inspirational Readings. 128p. (Orig.). pap. 5.95 (0-934125-11-2) Hazelden.
Pittman, Bill, intro. Easy Does It: A Book of Daily 12 Step Meditations. 400p. (Orig.). pap. 8.95 (0-934125-12-0) Hazelden.
***Pittman, Bill & McElrath, Damian.** Harry Tiebout: The Collected Writings. LC 99-36844. 160p. 1999. pap. text 12.00 (1-56838-345-2) Hazelden.
Pittman, Bill, jt. auth. see Bishop, Charlie, Jr.
Pittman, Blair. Texas Caves. LC 98-27196. (Louise Lindsey Merrick Natural Environment Ser.). (Illus.). 1999. 34.95 (0-89096-849-7) Tex A&M Univ Pr.
***Pittman, Blair.** Texas Caves. LC 98-27196. (Louise Lindsey Merrick Natural Environment Ser.). 144p. 2000. pap. 19.95 (0-89096-899-3) Tex A&M Univ Pr.
Pittman, Blair, photos by. The Natural World of the Texas Big Thicket. LC 78-6369. (Louise Lindsey Merrick Texas Environement Ser.: No. 2). (Illus.). 100p. 1978. reprint ed. 24.95 (0-89096-061-5) Tex A&M Univ Pr.
— The Natural World of the Texas Big Thicket. LC 78-6369. (Louise Lindsey Merrick Texas Environement Ser.: No. 2). (Illus.). 100p. 1986. reprint ed. pap. 17.95 (0-89096-303-7) Tex A&M Univ Pr.
Pittman-Brown, Sandra. Life As I See It. 64p. 2000. pap. 8.00 (0-8059-4800-7) Dorrance.
Pittman, C. U., Jr., et al. Metal-Containing Polymeric Materials. (Illus.). 528p. (C). 1996. text 135.00 (0-306-45295-2, Kluwer Plenum) Kluwer Academic.
Pittman, David J. & White, Helene R. Society, Culture, & Drinking Patterns Reexamined. 824p. 1991. pap. 34.95 (0-911290-22-2) Rutgers Ctr Alcohol.
Pittman, Don A., et al, eds. Ministry & Theology in Global Perspective: Contemporary Challenges for the Church. 542p. (Orig.). 1996. pap. 35.00 (0-8028-0844-1) Eerdmans.
Pittman, Douglas R. Principles for Living on the Edge. ix, 131p. 1997. 25.00 (1-890225-00-2) Quantum Hse Pubg.
— Principles for Living on the Edge. LC 97-65265. ix, 146p. 1997. pap. 14.95 (1-890225-02-9) Quantum Hse Pubg.

Pittman, E. D. & Lewan, M. D., eds. Organic Acids in Geological Processes. LC 94-3819. 1994. 111.95 (*0-387-56953-7*) Spr-Verlag.

Pittman, Eddie P., Jr. Words Chiseled from Rock. LC 87-61254. (Illus.). 80p. (Orig.). 1987. pap. 10.00 (*0-9618791-0-6*) Pub Press.

Pittman, Edward H., jt. ed. see Houseknecht, David W.

Pittman, Frank. Grow Up! How Taking Responsibility Can Make You a Happy Adult. 1999. pap. 14.00 (*1-58238-040-6*, Whitman Coin) St Martin.

— Private Lies: Infidelity & the Betrayal of Intimacy. 312p. 1998. reprint ed. lib. bdg. 30.00 (*0-7351-0025-X*) Replica Bks.

— Private Lies, Infidelity & the Betrayal of Intimacy. 1990. pap. 14.95 (*0-393-30707-7*) Norton.

Pittman, Frank S. Grow Up! How Taking Responsibility Can Make You a Happy Adult. unabridged ed. LC 97-52576. 304p. 1998. text 23.95 (*0-307-44064-8*, Whitman Coin) St Martin.

Pittman, Frank S., III. Turning Points: Treating Families in Transition & Crisis. (Professional Bks.). 1987. 34.95 (*0-393-70040-2*) Norton.

Pittman, H. C. Inside the Third House: A Fifty Year Frolic Through Texas Politics. LC 92-30776. 256p. 1992. 24.95 (*0-89015-879-7*) Sunbelt Media.

Pittman, Helena C. The Angel Tree. LC 97-26667. (Illus.). 32p. (J). (gr. k-3). 1998. 15.99 (*0-8037-1939-6*, Dial Yng Read) Peng Put Young Read.

— Counting Jennie. (J). (ps-3). 1994. lib. bdg. 19.93 (*0-87614-745-7*, Carolrhoda) Lerner Pub.

— A Grain Of Rice. 80p. (J). 1995. pap. 3.99 (*0-440-41301-X*) BDD Bks Young Read.

— Grain of Rice. 1996. 9.19 (*0-606-00485-8*, Pub. by Turtleback) Demco.

— Martha & the Nightbird. (J). (ps-3). 1986. 10.95 (*0-89845-491-3*, Caedmon) HarperAudio.

— The Moon's Party. LC 92-40866. (J). 1994. 15.95 (*0-399-22541-2*, G P Putnam) Peng Put Young Read.

— Still Life Stew. LC 97-25646. (Illus.). 32p. (J). (gr. k-4). 1998. lib. bdg. 16.49 (*0-7868-2206-6*, Pub. by Hyprn Child) Little.

— Still Life Stew. LC 97-25646. (Illus.). 32p. (J). (gr. k-4). 1998. 15.95 (*0-7868-0251-0*, Pub. by Hyprn Child) Time Warner.

— Sunrise. LC 97-2925. (Illus.). 32p. (J). (ps-1). 1998. 12.00 (*0-15-201684-8*) Harcourt.

— Uncle Phil's Diner. LC 96-44326. (Illus.). 32p. (J). (ps-2). 1997. 14.95 (*1-57505-083-8*, Carolrhoda) Lerner Pub.

***Pittman, Helena Clare.** Snowman's Path. (Illus.). 32p. (J). (ps-3). 2000. 15.99 (*0-8037-2170-6*) Peng Put Young Read.

Pittman, Holly. Art of the Bronze Age: Southeastern Iran, Western Central Asia, & the Indus Valley. Ekman, Joanna, ed. LC 84-728. 100p. 1984. pap. 4.95 (*0-87099-365-8*, 0-8109-6446-5) Metro Mus Art.

Pittman, J. F., et al, eds. Numerical Analysis of Forming Processes. LC 83-21600. (Wiley Series in Numerical Methods in Engineering). 462p. reprint ed. pap. 143.30 (*0-7837-4012-3*, 204384200011) Bks Demand.

Pittman, John. Africa Calling: Isolate the Racists! the Liberation Struggle in Southern Africa. 32p. 1973. pap. 0.60 (*0-87898-107-1*) New Outlook.

Pittman, John P., ed. African-American Perspectives & Philosophical Traditions. 312p. (C). 1996. 70.00 (*0-415-91639-9*); pap. 19.99 (*0-415-91640-2*) Routledge.

Pittman Learning Staff. Black Sunday. pap. text 1.65 (*0-8224-2916-0*) Fearon Teacher Aids.

— Health & Safety: Young Child. pap. 7.00 (*0-8224-5410-6*) Pittman Pub.

Pittman-Lindeman, Mary, jt. ed. see Corless, Inge B.

Pittman, Mary A., jt. frwd. see Fox, Daniel M.

Pittman, Nancy P. From the Land. LC 88-25551. (Conservation Classics Ser.). (Illus.). 473p. 1988. pap. 25.00 (*0-933280-65-3*) Island Pr.

Pittman, Philip M. The Present State of the European Settlements on the Mississippi: With a Geographical Description of That River Illustrated by Plans & Draughts. LC 73-2821. (Floridiana Facsimile & Reprint Ser.). (Illus.). 156p. 1973. reprint ed. 16.95 (*0-8130-0368-7*) U Press Fla.

Pittman, Philip M., ed. see Sellman, John J.

Pittman, Phillip M., jt. ed. see Watson, Jeanie.

Pittman£ittman, Helena Clare. The Gift of the Willows. 32p. (J). (gr. 1-4). 1999. pap. 7.95 (*0-930545-19-2*) Maple Hill Pr.

Pittman, Rachel N. The Wedding of G. Washington Bear. (Illus.). 42p. (Orig.). (J). (ps-5). 1986. pap. 6.95 (*0-9615382-1-X*) Pittman Pub.

Pittman, Rebecca. Mississippi River. unabridged ed. (Illus.). 128p. 1996. pap. 15.95 (*0-934520-96-8*, PPB 0006) Cartwheel Co.

Pittman, Riitta H. The Writer's Divided Self in Bulgakov's The Master & Margarita. LC 91-2123. 224p. 1991. text 49.95 (*0-312-06148-X*) St Martin.

Pittman, Ruth. Roadside History of California. Greer, Dan, ed. LC 95-2918. (Roadside History Ser.). (Illus.). 430p. 1995. 30.00 (*0-87842-317-6*); pap. 18.00 (*0-87842-318-4*) Mountain Pr.

Pittman, Sandra. Lord, Let Me Prove That Winning the Lottery Won't Spoil Me! (Illus.). 144p. (Orig.). 1992. pap. 9.95 (*0-940873-92-3*) AKG.

— With Tongue in Cheek. LC 86-72589. (Illus.). 128p. (Orig.). 1986. pap. 6.95 (*0-940873-86-9*) AKG.

Pittman, Steve. The Case for an Illinois Coal Severance Tax. (Illus.). (Orig.). 1984. pap. text 2.00 (*0-943724-08-2*) Illinois South.

Pittman, Steven G. The Marital Check-up. 26p. 1994. wbk. ed. 149.95 incl. audio (*0-9670678-0-4*) S G Pittman.

Pittman, Thane S., jt. ed. see Boggiano, Ann K.

Pittman, Thomas & Peters, James. The Art of Compiler Design: Theory & Practice. 368p. (C). 1991. text 48.80 (*0-13-048190-4*) P-H.

Pittman, Von V. Surviving Graduate School Part Time. LC 97-4584. (Graduate Survival Skills Ser.: Vol. 1). 169p. 1997. 42.00 (*0-7619-0439-5*); pap. 19.95 (*0-7619-0440-9*) Sage.

Pittman, Von V., jt. ed. see Duning, Becky S.

Pittman, Walter E., Jr. Navalist & Progressive: The Life of Richmond P. Hobson. 235p. 1981. pap. text 37.95 (*0-89126-100-1*) MA-AH Pub.

Pittner, Ludwig. Algebraic Foundations of Non-Commutative Differential Geometry & Quantum Groups. (Lecture Notes in Physics Ser.: Vol. 39). 469p. 1995. 79.95 (*3-540-60587-8*) Spr-Verlag.

Pittner, Ludwig, jt. ed. see Grosse, Harald.

Pittner, Ludwig, jt. ed. see Mitter, H.

Pittock. Jacobitism. LC 97-49335. 176p. 1998. text 45.00 (*0-312-21306-9*) St Martin.

Pittock, A. B., et al. Environmental Consequences of Nuclear War, 2E, Vol. 1, Physical & Atmospheric Effects, Vol. 1, Physical and Atmospheric Effects. 2nd ed. LC 89-22712. (Scientific Committee on Problems of the Environment Ser.: No. 28). 428p. 1989. pap. 155.00 (*0-471-92469-5*) Wiley.

Pittock, Joan, jt. auth. see Carter, Jennifer E.

***Pittock, Joan H.** Henry Birkhead, Founder of the Oxford Chair of Poetry: Poetry & the Redemption of History. LC 98-50511. (Illus.). 1999. write for info. (*0-88946-927-X*) E Mellen.

Pittock, Joan H. Henry Birkhead, Founder of the Oxford Chair of Poetry (1617-1697) Vol. 39: Poetry & the Redemption of History. LC 98-50511. (Studies in British Literature: Vol. 39). 188p. 1999. lib. bdg. 79.95 (*0-7734-8212-1*) E Mellen.

Pittock, Joan H. & Wear, Andrew, eds. Interpretation & Cultural History. 320p. 1991. text 49.95 (*0-312-05360-6*) St Martin.

Pittock, Murray G. Investing & Resisting Britain: Cultural Identities in Britain & Ireland, 1685-1789. LC 96-41005. 176p. 1997. text 49.95 (*0-312-16576-5*) St Martin.

— The Myth of the Jacobite Clans. 240p. 1996. pap. 25.00 (*0-7486-0715-3*, Pub. by Edinburgh U Pr) Col U Pr.

— Poetry & Jacobite Politics in Eighteenth-Century Britain & Ireland. LC 93-42500. (Studies in Eighteenth-Century English Literature & Thought: No. 23). 270p. (C). 1995. text 69.95 (*0-521-41092-4*) Cambridge U Pr.

***Pittock, Murray G. H.** Celtic Idenity & the British Image. (Illus.). 224p. 2000. pap. 19.95 (*0-7190-5826-0*) Manchester Univ Pr.

— Celtic Identity & the British Image. (Illus.). 224p. 2000. text 74.95 (*0-7190-5266-1*) Manchester Univ Pr.

Pitton, Debra E. Stories of Student Teaching: A Case Approach to the Student Teaching Experience. LC 96-49892. 166p. 1997. pap. text 28.00 (*0-13-437310-3*, Merrill Coll) P-H.

Pittoni, Mario. Brief Writing & Argumentation. 3rd ed. (University Textbook Ser.). 217p. 1991. reprint ed. pap. text 12.95 (*0-88277-415-8*) Foundation Pr.

Pittrof, Kurt. Dominik Biemann: Boemischer Glasgraweur des Biedermeier. (GER., Illus.). 184p. 75.00 (*3-925369-31-7*, Pub. by Arnoldsche Art Pubs) Antique Collect.

Pitts. Accounting & Finance for Mangers. 2nd ed. (C). 1999. pap. text 45.00 (*0-536-02117-1*) Pearson Custom.

— Strategic Management. Date not set. pap. text, teacher ed. write for info. (*0-314-08285-9*) West Pub.

Pitts, et al. Academic Writing: A Brief Guide. 192p. (C). 1992. pap. text 23.95 (*0-8403-8158-1*) Kendall-Hunt.

Pitts, A. & Dybjer, P., eds. Semantics & Logics of Computation. LC 96-50390. (Publications of the Newton Institute: No. 14). 373p. (C). 1997. text 57.95 (*0-521-58057-9*) Cambridge U Pr.

Pitts, Alice & Champ, Minnie. Collin County, Texas. (Illus.). 397p. 1994. 61.00 (*0-88107-246-X*) Curtis Media.

Pitts, Alice, jt. ed. see Cross, Pamela.

Pitts, Andrew M., jt. ed. see Gordon, Andrew D.

Pitts, Audre. Let Me Keep Laughter. 112p. 1985. pap. 7.99 (*0-8341-1090-3*) Beacon Hill.

— Music Keeps on Playing. 96p. (Orig.). 1988. pap. 7.99 (*0-8341-1250-7*) Beacon Hill.

Pitts, Barbara, jt. auth. see Basadur, Min.

Pitts, Beverley J. The Process of Media Writing. LC 96-22525. 325p. 1996. pap. text 48.00 (*0-205-15636-3*) Allyn.

Pitts, Beverley J., et al. The Process of Media Writing. (C). 1996. pap. text, teacher ed. write for info. (*0-205-26344-5*, T6344-0) Allyn.

Pitts, Brenda G., ed. Case Studies in Sport Marketing. LC 98-71809. 203p. (C). 1998. text 31.00 (*1-885693-13-3*) Fit Info Tech.

Pitts, Brenda G. & Stotlar, David K. Fundamentals of Sport Marketing. LC 95-61902. 304p. 1996. text 39.00 (*1-885693-02-8*) Fit Info Tech.

Pitts, Callista. Gettysburg Addresses. (Illus.). 70p. Date not set. 13.95 (*1-57747-057-5*) Thomas Publications.

Pitts, Colin. Motivating Your Organization: Achieving Business Success Through Reward & Recognition. LC 95-1427. (Quality in Action Ser.). 1995. 22.95 (*0-07-707967-1*) McGraw.

Pitts, David. How in the World Do I Get along With My Parents? 40p. 1982. pap. 0.95 (*0-88144-046-9*) Christian Pub.

Pitts, David, et al. Red Hat Linux Unleashed. 2nd ed. 1019p. 1997. 39.99 (*0-672-31173-9*) Sams.

Pitts, David L. Songs about God & His Son. 85p. 1995. 3.95 (*0-9649138-0-1*) Passwrd Pubng.

Pitts, Donald G. & Kleinstein, Robert N. Environmental Vision: Interactions of the Eye, Vision & the Environment. (Illus.). 422p. 1993. text 94.50 (*0-7506-9051-8*) Buttrwrth-Heinemann.

Pitts, Donald R. & Sissom, Leighton E. Schaum's Outline of Heat Transfer. 2nd ed. LC 98-21008. 384p. (C). 1998. pap. 14.95 (*0-07-050207-2*) McGraw.

***Pitts, Emma T.** People & Programs That Make a Difference in a Multicultural Society: Volunteerism in America. LC 99-27737. 200p. 1999. text 79.95 (*0-7734-7945-5*) E Mellen.

Pitts, Emma T., jt. ed. see Duhon-Sells, Rose M.

Pitts, George. Obsessions: Tony Ward. (Illus.). 132p. 1998. 70.00 (*3-908162-99-8*) Abbeville Pr.

Pitts, Gertrude & Scott, Anne. George Sampson Brite. LC 94-42140. (African American Women Writers, 1910-1940 Ser.). 1996. 25.00 (*0-8161-1634-2*, G K Hall & Co) Mac Lib Ref.

Pitts, J. M. & Schormans, J. A. Introduction to ATM Design & Performance: With Applications Analysis Software. 2nd ed. LC 96-5966. 206p. 1996. text 82.95 incl. disk (*0-471-96340-2*) Wiley.

Pitts, J. Martin, contrib. by. Gymnopaediae. 112p. 1993. pap. text 130.00 (*0-907664-22-9*, Pub. by Old Stiles) St Mut.

Pitts, Jack B. P-47 Pilot: Scared, Bored, & Deadly. (Illus.). xviii, 250p. 1997. pap. 13.95 (*0-9656793-0-6*) Pitts Enterprises.

Pitts, James M., ed. The Way of Faith: Words of Admonition & Encouragement for the Journey Based on the Letter to the Hebrews. 176p. (Orig.). 1985. pap. 8.95 (*0-913029-10-6*) Stevens Bk Pr.

Pitts, Jennifer, ed. & tr. see DeTocqueville, Alexis.

Pitts, John. A Manual of Geology for Civil Engineers. 228p. 1985. text 48.00 (*9971-978-05-9*); pap. text 23.00 (*9971-978-12-1*) World Scientific Pub.

— The Politics of Juvenile Crime. (Contemporary Criminology Ser.: Vol. 2). 192p. (C). 1988. text 69.95 (*0-8039-8132-5*); pap. text 16.50 (*0-8039-8133-3*) Sage.

Pitts, John, jt. ed. see Gupta, Avijit.

Pitts, John D. & Finbow, Malcolm E., eds. The Functional Integration of Cells in Animal Tissues. LC 81-10213. (British Society for Cell Biology Symposium Ser.: No. 5). (Illus.). 360p. 1982. text 120.00 (*0-521-24199-5*) Cambridge U Pr.

Pitts, Jonathan, jt. auth. see Herzog, Whitey.

Pitts, Judy M., jt. auth. see Stripling, Barbara K.

***Pitts, Kathy Roots.** The Efficiency Handbook: The Levelheaded & Aggressive Control of Personal Excess, Blind Confusion, & Emotional Extortion. (Illus.). 168p. 2000. pap. write for info. (*0-9702081-0-3*) Wolf River.

Pitts, Lee. Back Door People. (Illus.). 112p. 1998. pap. 11.95 (*0-9666334-0-7*) Lee Pitts.

***Pitts, Lei.** Strategic Management. 2nd ed. LC 99-27657. (SWC-Management Ser.). 494p. 1999. pap. 50.95 (*0-324-00699-3*) Thomson Learn.

Pitts, Leonard, Jr. Becoming Dad: Black Men & the Journey to Fatherhood. LC 99-60103. (Illus.). 263p. 1999. 22.00 (*1-56352-501-1*) Longstreet.

Pitts, Lulie. History of Gordon County Georgia. (Illus.). 480p. 1997. reprint ed. lib. bdg. 52.00 (*0-8328-7065-X*) Higginson Bk Co.

Pitts, M. E., jt. auth. see Hannan, N. M.

Pitts, Mabel, jt. auth. see Ard, Linda.

Pitts, Marian & Phillips, Keith. The Psychology of Health: An Introduction. 2nd ed. LC 97-40283. (Illus.). 432p. (C). 1998. 85.00 (*0-415-15023-X*); pap. 27.99 (*0-415-15024-8*) Routledge.

Pitts, Mark & Fabozzi, Frank J. Interest Rate Futures & Options. 350p. 1987. 65.00 (*0-917253-95-7*, Irwn Prfssnl) McGraw-Hill Prof.

Pitts, Marty, ed. see Martinetti, Ron & Hansen, Vagn.

Pitts, Mary. Hyde Park, Massachusetts This Modern Cannan. (Illus.). 91p. (Orig.). 1988. pap. 12.00 (*0-913553-06-9*) Albert Hse Pub.

Pitts, Mary E. Theodore Dwight Weld - This Was a Man! 30p. 1987. pap. 8.00 (*0-913553-05-0*) Albert Hse Pub.

— Toward a Dialogue of Understandings: Loren Eiseley & the Critique of Science. LC 94-46994. 352p. 1995. 47.50 (*0-934223-37-8*) Lehigh Univ Pr.

***Pitts, Michael & Howard, Hilary, eds.** Stones Cookbook: Vegetarian Recipes from Stones Restaurant. (Illus.). 224p. 1999. pap. 22.95 (*0-09-186548-4*, Pub. by Ebury Pr) Trafalgar.

Pitts, Michael & Roberts, Mark. Fairweather Eden: Life Half a Million Years Ago As Revealed by the Excavations at Boxgrove. LC 98-9734. (Illus.). 352p. 1998. 28.00 (*0-88064-194-0*) Fromm Intl Pub.

***Pitts, Michael & Roberts, Mark.** Fairweather Eden: Life Half a Million Years Ago As Revealed by the Excavations at Boxgrove. (Illus.). 368p. 2000. pap. 17.00 (*0-88064-247-5*) Fromm Intl Pub.

***Pitts, Michael R.** Charles Bronson: The 94 Films & the 82 Television Appearances. LC 99-31430. (Illus.). 376p. 1999. lib. bdg. 45.00 (*0-7864-0601-1*) McFarland & Co.

Pitts, Michael R. Famous Movie Detectives, No. II. LC 90-9083. (Illus.). 357p. 1991. 50.00 (*0-8108-2345-4*) Scarecrow.

***Pitts, Michael R.** Famous Movie Detectives III. 352p. 2000. 59.50 (*0-8108-3690-4*) Scarecrow.

Pitts, Michael R. Kate Smith: A Bio-Bibliography. 2. LC 87-25154. (Bio-Bibliographies in the Performing Arts Ser.: No. 2). 276p. 1988. lib. bdg. 45.00 (*0-313-25541-5*, PKS/, Greenwood Pr) Greenwood.

— Poverty Row Studios, 1929-1940: An Illustrated History of 53 Independent Film Companies, with a Filmography for Each. LC 96-22311. (Illus.). 542p. 1997. lib. bdg. 75.00 (*0-7864-0168-0*) McFarland & Co.

— Radio Soundtracks: A Reference Guide. 2nd ed. LC 85-30409. 349p. 1986. 34.50 (*0-8108-1875-2*) Scarecrow.

— Western Movies: A TV & Video Guide to 4200 Genre Films. LC 85-31014. (Illus.). 635p. 1997. pap. 25.00 (*0-7864-0421-3*) McFarland & Co.

Pitts, Michael R., jt. auth. see Campbell, Richard H.

Pitts, Michael R., jt. auth. see Parish, James R.

Pitts, Michael S. Breaking the Assignment of Spiritual Assassins. 2nd ed. 82p. 1994. reprint ed. pap. 7.00 (*0-9633583-1-6*) Present Trth.

— Breaking Ungodly Soul Ties. LC 99-188239. (Orig.). 1997. reprint ed. pap. 7.00 (*0-9633583-3-2*) Present Trth.

— Living on the Edge: Spiritual Help for the Soul under attack. 57p. (Orig.). 1994. reprint ed. pap. 7.00 (*0-9633583-2-4*) Present Trth.

— Making the Holy Spirit Your Partner: Discovering His Plan, Purpose, & Power. 71p. 1992. pap. 7.00 (*0-9633583-0-8*) Present Trth.

— Some Shall Soar! Not Everyone Is Called to be Average! LC 99-188198. 127 p. 1991. write for info. (*0-927936-14-3*) Vincom Pubng Co.

— Some Shall Soar: Not Everyone Is Called to be Average. 127p. (Orig.). 1991. reprint ed. pap. 7.00 (*0-9633583-4-0*) Present Trth.

Pitts, Natanya, jt. auth. see LeVitus, Bob.

Pitts, Natanya, jt. auth. see Sybex, Inc. Staff.

Pitts, Nolan T. The Message, the Mess, the Mileage. LC 94-77544. 96p. (Orig.). 1994. pap. 5.95 (*1-883928-08-7*) Longwood.

— Sweet & Sour Grapes. 144p. 1999. pap. 8.95 (*1-883928-33-8*) Longwood.

Pitts, Paul. Crossroads. LC 94-94084. 1994. 9.09 (*0-606-06297-1*, Pub. by Turtleback) Demco.

Pitts, Paul. For a Good Time, Don't Call Claudia. 128p. (J). (gr. 7 up). 1986. pap. 2.50 (*0-380-75117-8*, Avon Bks) Morrow Avon.

Pitts, Paul. Racing the Sun. 160p. (J). (gr. 4-7). 1988. mass mkt. 4.50 (*0-380-75496-7*, Avon Bks) Morrow Avon.

Pitts, Paul. Racing the Sun. 1988. 9.60 (*0-606-03897-3*, Pub. by Turtleback) Demco.

— The Shadowman's Way. 128p. (Orig.). (J). (gr. 5). 1992. pap. 3.99 (*0-380-76210-2*, Avon Bks) Morrow Avon.

— Shadowman's Way. 1992. 9.09 (*0-606-00294-4*, Pub. by Turtleback) Demco.

Pitts, Ralph A., jt. auth. see Jenkins, A. Felton, Jr.

Pitts, Robert A. & Lei, David. Strategic Management: Building & Sustaining Competitive Advantage. LC 95-32131. 450p. (C). 1995. mass mkt. 36.50 (*0-314-06113-4*) West Pub.

Pitts, Robert A. & Snow, Charles C. Strategies for Competitive Success. LC 85-10483. 76p. 1986. pap. 33.95 (*0-471-81656-6*) Wiley.

Pitts, Robert E., jt. ed. see Woodside, Arch G.

Pitts, Sadie T. Sparkle. 1989. pap. 5.95 (*0-913543-12-8*) African Am Imag.

Pitts, Senetta, ed. see Koger, Dorothy P.

Pitts, Terence. Contemporary Photography in Mexico. (Illus.). 16p. 1978. pap. 3.50 (*0-938262-00-9*) Ctr Creat Photog.

— Edward Weston, 1886-1958. Heiting, Manfred, ed. (Illus.). 251p. 1999. 39.99 (*3-8228-7180-X*) Taschen Amer.

— Four Spanish Photographers. (Illus.). 24p. (Orig.). 1988. pap. 8.00 (*0-938262-18-1*) Ctr Creat Photog.

Pitts, Terence, contrib. by. Arizona Photographers: The Snell & Wilmer Collection. (Illus.). 80p. (Orig.). 1990. pap. 15.00 (*0-938262-19-X*) Ctr Creat Photog.

Pitts, Terence, intro. A Portrait Is Not a Likeness. (Illus.). 48p. 1991. pap. 14.00 (*0-938262-22-X*) Ctr Creat Photog.

Pitts, Terence & Codrescu, Andrei. Points of Entry: Reframing America. large type ed. (Illus.). 144p. (Orig.). (C). 1995. pap. write for info. (*0-933286-70-8*) Frnds Photography.

Pitts, Terence, et al. Edward Weston: Color Photography. (Illus.). 64p. 1986. 15.00 (*0-938262-14-9*); pap. 8.95 (*0-938262-15-7*) Ctr Creat Photog.

Pitts, Terence, jt. contrib. by see Codrescu, Andrei.

Pitts, Teresa A. The Music of a Poet's Heart. (Illus.). 147p. (Orig.). (YA). (gr. 7 up). 1987. pap. 10.00 (*0-9618600-0-6*) T A Pitts.

— Where Freedom Begins. (Illus.). 27p. (Orig.). (J). (gr. 5 up). 1990. pap. 10.00 (*0-9618600-1-4*) T A Pitts.

Pitts, Teresa A., ed. see Lothario.

Pitts, Vincent J. The Man Who Sacked Rome: Charles de Bourbon, Constable of France, 1490-1527. LC 93-18629. (American University Studies: Vol. 142). (Illus.). X, 614p. 1994. 89.95 (*0-8204-2456-0*) P Lang Pubng.

Pitts, Vincent J., jt. auth. see Montpensier, Anne-Marie-Louise d'Orleans.

Pitts, Walter C., jt. auth. see Lund, Adrienne F.

Pitts, Walter F. Old Ship of Zion: The Afro-Baptist Ritual in the African Diaspora. (Religion in America Ser.). 216p. 1996. reprint ed. pap. 19.95 (*0-19-511145-1*) OUP.

Pitts, William E. My Personal Health History. 95p. 1999. 19.95 (*0-9671388-0-9*) Bea Pubg.

Pitts, William W. Commanding WordStar Professional Release 4.0. (Illus.). 310p. 1988. pap. 16.95 (*0-8306-2983-1*, 2983P) McGraw-Hill Prof.

***Pittsburg Community Staff.** Three Rivers Renaissance Cookbook, Vol. IV. Child Health Volunteers Staff, ed. (Illus.). 250p. 2000. spiral bd. (*0-9607634-3-0*) T Rivers Cookbook.

Pittsburgh Cornin Europe N.V. Staff, ed. Foamglas Industrial Insulation Handbook. 512p. 1992. 590.00 (*2-930049-00-6*, Pub. by Edits Technip) Enfield Pubs NH.

Pittsburgh Post-Gazette Staff. Mario Lemieux: Best There Ever Was. (Illus.). 160p. 1997. 24.95 (*1-57028-161-0*, Mstrs Pr) NTC Contemp Pub Co.

Pittson, Todd, jt. auth. see Gradnitzer, Louisa.

Pittwood, tr. see Martignoni, M. & Schonenberger.

P

Pitty, Alistair F., ed. Geomorphology: Themes & Trends. LC 84-24436. (Illus.). 286p. 1985. 53.00 (*0-389-20537-0*, BNB-08099) B&N Imports.

Pitucco, Anthony P. & Agut, Shawn. The Restaurant at the Beginning of the Universe: Exploring the Wonderment of the World Through Physics. LC 96-28581. vi, 152 p. 1996. teacher ed. 32.00 (*1-56976-056-X*) Zephyr Pr AZ.

Pityana, Barney, et al, eds. Bounds of Possibility: The Legacy of Steve Biko & Black Consciousness. 288p. (C). 1991. pap. 17.50 (*1-85649-048-3*, Pub. by Zed Books); text 49.95 (*1-85649-047-5*, Pub. by Zed Books) St Martin.

Pityn, P. J., jt. auth. see Fraser, T. M.

Pitz, Gordon F. & McKillip, Jack. Decision Analysis for Program Evaluators. LC 84-6934. (Contemporary Evaluation Research Ser.: No. 7). 311p. 1984. reprint ed. pap. 96.50 (*0-608-01124-X*, 205942800001) Bks Demand.

Pitz, Henry C. Drawing Outdoors. unabridged ed. LC 95-7137. (Illus.). 144p. 1995. reprint ed. pap. text 8.95 (*0-486-28679-7*) Dover.

Pitz, Henry C., ed. & intro. see Remington, Frederic.

***Pitz, Jane.** Table, Bread & Cup. 64p. 2000. pap. 10.95 (*0-9700709-0-X*) Notr Dam Ctr Pas.

Pitz, Mary E. Careers in Government. LC 93-47955. (Illus.). 160p. 1994. pap. 13.95 (*0-8442-4195-4*) NTC Contemp Pub Co.

— Careers in Government. LC 93-47955. (VGM Professional Careers Ser.). (Illus.). 160p. 1995. 17.95 (*0-8442-4194-6*) NTC Contemp Pub Co.

— Careers in Government. 2nd ed. LC 99-19944. (VGM Professional Careers Ser.). 224p. 1999. 17.95 (*0-8442-2066-3*, 20663, VGM Career); pap. 13.95 (*0-8442-2067-1*, 20671, VGM Career) NTC Contemp Pub Co.

Pitzele, Peter. Scripture Windows: Toward a Practice of Bibliodrama. 1998. pap. 16.95 (*1-881283-27-5*) Alef Design.

Pitzele, Sefra. We Are Not Alone: Learning to Live with Chronic Illness. LC 84-16378. (Illus.). 320p. 1985. pap. 14.95 (*0-918351-01-4*) Thompson Co Inc.

Pitzele, Sefra K. Kind Words for Caring People: Affirmations for Caregivers. 365p. (Orig.). 1992. pap. 7.95 (*1-55874-210-7*) Health Comm.

— One More Day: Daily Meditations for the Chronically Ill. large type ed. (Large Print Inspirational Ser.). (Orig.). 1989. pap. 12.95 (*0-8027-2638-0*) Walker & Co.

— We Are Not Alone: Learning to Live with Chronic Illness. LC 86-40200. (Illus.). 336p. 1986. pap. 10.95 (*0-89480-139-2*, 1139) Workman Pub.

***Pitzele, Sefra Kobrin.** Finding the Joy in Today: Practical Readings for Living with Chronic Illness. LC 99-37665. 400p. 1999. pap. text 12.00 (*1-56838-348-7*) Hazelden.

Pitzen, Howard. Rodeo Road Code. 160p. 1998. pap. 11.95 (*0-9664225-0-3*) Stampede Pr.

Pitzer, David. Inside AutoCAD Release 13C4 for Windows 95, Windows NT, & Windows 3.11. 1092p. 1996. pap. text 49.99 incl. cd-rom (*1-56205-645-X*) New Riders Pub.

Pitzer, Donald E., ed. America's Communal Utopias. LC 96-10889. 592p. (C). (gr. 13). 1997. 60.00 (*0-8078-2299-X*); pap. 24.95 (*0-8078-4609-0*) U of NC Pr.

Pitzer, George C. Suggestion in the Cure of Diseases & the Correction of Vices. 1991. lib. bdg. 79.95 (*0-8490-4493-6*) Gordon Pr.

— Suggestion in the Cure of Diseases & the Correction of Vices. 80p. 1996. reprint ed. spiral bd. 12.00 (*0-7873-1093-X*) Hlth Research.

— Suggestion in the Cure of Diseases & the Correction of Vices (1899) 84p. 1996. reprint ed. pap. 11.95 (*1-56459-831-4*) Kessinger Pub.

Pitzer, Gloria. The Copycat Cook Book. 13th ed. (Secret Recipes Bks.). (Illus.). 60p. 1998. reprint ed. pap. 9.75 (*1-886138-04-4*) G Pitzers.

***Pitzer, Gloria.** The Great Imitator's Cookbook. 50p. 1999. pap. 9.75 (*1-886138-10-9*) G Pitzers.

Pitzer, Gloria. Restaurant Recipe Secrets: And Other Classified Information for Imitating Famous Food at Home. 5th rev. ed. (Secret Recipes Bks.). (Illus.). 60p. 1999. pap. 9.75 (*1-886138-09-5*) G Pitzers.

— Secret Fast Food Recipes, Bk. 6. 20th ed. (Secret Recipes Bks.). Orig. Title: Fast Food Recipes. (Illus.). 60p. 1998. reprint ed. pap. 9.75 (*1-886138-03-6*) G Pitzers.

— Secret Fast Food Recipes: The Fast Food Cookbook. rev. ed. (Illus.). 120p. 1995. reprint ed. pap. 8.75 (*1-886161-38-0*) G Pitzers.

— Secret Make Alike Recipes. 8th rev. ed. (Secret Recipes Bks.). Orig. Title: Make Alike Recipes Book. (Illus.). 60p. 1999. pap. 9.75 (*1-886138-02-8*) G Pitzers.

— That's the Flavor Recipes: Selections from Books 1 Through 5: 1979-1981. 3rd ed. (Secret Recipes Bks.). 60p. 1999. reprint ed. pap. 9.75 (*1-886138-11-7*) G Pitzers.

— 3-in-1 Book of Less Fat & Sugar & Breads. (Illus.). 60p. 1997. pap. 8.75 (*0-614-28387-6*) G Pitzers.

Pitzer, Kenneth S. Activity Coefficients in Electrolyte Solutions. 2nd ed. (Illus.). 536p. 1991. 249.95 (*0-8493-5415-3*, QD565) CRC Pr.

— Molecular Structure & Statistical Thermodynamics. (Twentieth Century Chemistry Ser.). 536p. 1993. text 83.00 (*981-02-1439-1*) World Scientific Pub.

Pitzer, Mary R. Wild Game Cookbook. (Illus.). ix, 54p. (Orig.). 1993. pap. 5.50 (*0-9650698-0-X*) M R Pitzer.

Pitzer, Paul C. Grand Coulee: Harnessing a Dream. LC 94-27155. (Illus.). 512p. 1994. pap. 24.95 (*0-87422-110-2*) Wash St U Pr.

— Grand Coulee: Harnessing a Dream. LC 94-27155. (Illus.). 512p. 1994. 42.00 (*0-87422-113-7*) Wash St U Pr.

Pitzer, S. Baking with Sourdough. 1983. pap. 2.95 (*0-88266-225-2*, Storey Pub) Storey Bks.

— Buying an Old House. 1983. pap. 2.95 (*0-88266-328-3*, Storey Pub) Storey Bks.

— Cooking with Dried Beans. 1983. pap. 2.95 (*0-88266-291-0*, Storey Pub) Storey Bks.

Pitzer, Sara. Dixie: A Traveler's Guide. LC 96-11670. (Discover Historic America Ser.). (Illus.). 384p. (Orig.). 1996. pap. 15.95 (*1-56440-648-2*) Globe Pequot.

— Growing & Using Oregano. LC 96-22504. (Storey Publishing Bulletin Ser.). 1996. pap. 2.95 (*0-88266-526-X*, Storey Pub) Storey Bks.

— The More Than Chicken Cookbook. LC 83-48975. (Illus.). 160p. (Orig.). 1984. pap. 9.95 (*0-88266-368-2*, Garden Way Pub) Storey Bks.

***Pitzer, Sara.** North Carolina: A Guide to Unique Places. 5th ed. (Off the Beaten Path Ser.). (Illus.). 2000. pap. 12.95 (*0-7627-0818-2*) Globe Pequot.

Pitzer, Sara. North Carolina: Off the Beaten Path: A Guide to Unique Places. 4th ed. LC 98-35319. (Off the Beaten Path Ser.). (Illus.). 288p. 1998. pap. 12.95 (*0-7627-0272-9*) Globe Pequot.

— Simply Strawberries: A Cookbook. Mason, Jill, ed. LC 84-28790. (Illus.). 128p. 1985. pap. 6.95 (*0-88266-382-8*, Garden Way Pub) Storey Bks.

— Simply Strawberries: A Cookbook. Mason, Jill, ed. LC 84-28790. (Illus.). 128p. 1985. 13.95 (*0-88266-383-6*, Garden Way Pub) Storey Bks.

Pitzer, Sara, jt. auth. see Cline, Don.

Pitzer, Sara, ed. see Bledsoe, Jerry.

Pitzl. Annual Editions: Geography, 97-98. 12th ed. 256p. (C). 1996. text. write for info. (*0-697-37271-5*, WCB McGr Hill) McGrw-H Hghr Educ.

— Geography. 9th ed. 1994. 12.74 (*1-56134-275-0*) McGraw.

— Geography. 10th ed. 1995. 12.74 (*1-56134-356-0*) McGraw.

— Geography 1996/97. 11th annot. ed. 1996. teacher ed. (*0-697-31587-8*, WCB McGr Hill) McGrw-H Hghr Educ.

Pitzl, Gerald R. Geography: 1996-1997. annuals 11th ed. 256p. (C). 1996. text. write for info. (*0-697-31586-X*) Brown & Benchmark.

— Geography, 98-99. 13th ed. (Annual Ser.). (Illus.). 240p. 1998. pap. text 12.25 (*0-697-39188-4*, Dshkn McG-Hill) McGrw-H Hghr Educ.

— The Northern Territories Controversy: A Four-Decade Stalemate Between Japan & Russia. (Pew Case Studies in International Affairs). 50p. (C). 1994. pap. text 3.50 (*1-56927-364-2*, GU Schl Foreign) Geo U Inst Dplmcy.

***Piumelli, Frederick A. & Schmidt, David A.** Power Collecting: Automation for Effective Asset Management. LC 97-34854. 352p. 1998. 74.95 (*0-471-18043-2*) Wiley.

Piumini, Roberto. The Store. LC 92-72120. (Illus.). 14p. (J). (ps). 1993. bds. 4.50 (*1-56397-203-4*) Boyds Mills Pr.

***Piumini, Roberto.** There Is a Book. 2000. pap. text 15.95 (*0-8050-6206-8*) St Martin.

Piunovskiy, A. B. Optimal Control of Random Sequences in Problems with Constraints. LC 97-16602. 1997. text 197.50 (*0-7923-4571-1*) Kluwer Academic.

Pius, Basil K. & Kison, Joann. Agatha Christie, the Unknown Assyrian & Baklava. unabridged ed. (Illus.). 133p. 1993. pap. 8.00 (*0-9638003-4-5*) Tri-C Printing.

***Pius X.** Ad Diem Illum Laetissimum: On the Jubilee of the Immaculate Conception. 23p. 1999. reprint ed. pap. 2.95 (*0-935952-73-X*) Angelus Pr.

***Pius XII, pseud.** "Divini Redemptoris" On Atheistic Communism. 50p. 1998. pap. 4.25 (*0-935952-65-9*) Angelus Pr.

— E Supremi Apostolatus: On the Restoration of All Things in Christ. 17p. 1998. reprint ed. pap. 2.95 (*0-935952-59-4*) Angelus Pr.

— "Humani Generis" On Evolution & Other Modern Errors. 24p. 1998. pap. 1.95 (*0-935952-45-4*) Angelus Pr.

— "Mortalium Animos" On Fostering True Religious Unity. 16p. 1998. reprint ed. pap. 1.95 (*0-935952-46-2*) Angelus Pr.

— On the Christian Eduction of Youth: Divini Illius Magistri. 58p. 2000. pap. 4.25 (*1-892331-03-9*) Angelus Pr.

Pius XII, pseud. On the Mystical Body of Christ & Our Union in It with Christ: Mystici Corporis. 73p. pap. 2.50 (*0-8198-4739-9*) Pauline Bks.

— Pius XII: Selected Encyclicals & Addresses. vi, 387p. 1995. text 21.95 (*0-912141-19-0*) Roman Cath Bks.

— The Sacred Liturgy: Mediator Dei. 80p. pap. 2.50 (*0-8198-6924-4*) Pauline Bks.

Pius XI, pseud. Atheistic Communism: Divini Redemptoris. 50p. pap. 1.75 (*0-8198-0749-4*) Pauline Bks.

— Essays in History, Written Between the Years 1896-1912. LC 67-26771. (Essay Index Reprint Ser.). 1977. 19.95 (*0-8369-0791-4*) Ayer.

— On Christian Marriage: Casti Connubii. 72p. pap. 3.75 (*0-8198-1488-1*) Pauline Bks.

— On Social Reconstruction: Quadragesimo Anno. 75p. pap. 1.25 (*0-8198-6926-0*) Pauline Bks.

Pius, X, pseud. On the Doctrine of the Modernists: Pascendi Dominici: Syllabus Condemning the Errors of the Modernists: Lamentabili Sane. 77p. pap. 2.50 (*0-8198-0248-4*) Pauline Bks.

— Our Apostolic Mandate: Letter to the French Archbishops & Bishops on the "Sillon" Dupont, Yves, tr. from FRE.Tr. of Notre Charge Apostolique. 58p. 1998. pap. 4.45 (*0-935952-49-7*) Angelus Pr.

Pius, V, pseud. The Traditional Latin Roman Catholic Mass. De Pauw, Gommar A., tr. from LAT. (Illus.). 98p. (Orig.). 1989. ring bd. 10.00 (*0-685-25984-6*) CTM Pubns.

— The Traditional Latin Roman Catholic Mass for the Faithful Departed. De Pauw, Gommar A., tr. from LAT. & illus. by. 78p. 1989. ring bd. 20.00 (*0-685-25985-4*) CTM Pubns.

***Piux IX.** Quanta Cura & the Syllabus of Errors Condemning Current Errors. 28p. 1998. reprint ed. pap. 3.45 (*0-935952-63-2*) Angelus Pr.

— Qui Pluribus: On Faith & Religion. O'Cleirigh, Padraig M., tr. 22p. 1998. reprint ed. pap. 3.25 (*0-935952-61-6*) Angelus Pr.

Piva, R., jt. ed. see Morino, L.

Pival, Jean G., jt. auth. see Adelstein, Michael E.

***Pivano, Fernanda.** Charles Bukowski: Laughing with the Gods. Waldron, Daniel, ed. Viciani, Simona, tr. LC 99-88647. (Illus.). 160p. 2000. pap. 14.95 (*0-941543-26-9*, Pub. by Sun Dog Pr) SPD-Small Pr Dist.

Pivar, Corinne E. California Real Estate. 10th ed. LC 96-3012. 368p. (C). 1996. pap. text 55.00 (*0-13-578626-6*) P-H.

Pivar, David J. Purity Crusade: Sexual Morality & Social Control, 1868-1900, 23. LC 70-179650. (Contributions in American History Ser.: No. 23). 308p. 1973. 38.50 (*0-8371-6319-6*, PPC/, Greenwood Pr) Greenwood.

Pivar, Stuart. The Barye Bronzes: A Catalogue Raisonne. 2nd ed. (Illus.). 308p. 1990. reprint ed. 89.50 (*1-85149-142-2*) Antique Collect.

Pivar, William H. The Big Book of Real Estate Ads: 1001 Ads That Sell. LC 97-136620. 1997. pap. text 41.95 incl. disk (*0-7931-2473-5*, 1926-1102) Dearborn.

— California Real Estate License Preparation Text. 6th rev. ed. (Illus.). 320p. (C). 1984. student ed. 17.95 (*0-685-08873-1*) P-H.

***Pivar, William H.** Real Estate Exam Guide: Designed for ASI Sales & Broker Exams. 6th ed. LC 00-32331. 2000. write for info. (*0-7931-3655-5*, Real Estate Ed) Dearborn.

Pivar, William H. Real Estate Exam Guide for ASI. 5th ed. LC 97-10587. 271p. 1997. pap. text 27.95 (*0-7931-2527-8*, 1970-0605, Real Estate Ed) Dearborn.

— Real Estate Investing from A to Z. 2nd rev. ed. LC 96-48061. 264p. 1997. text 19.95 (*0-7863-1214-9*, Irwn Prfssnl) McGraw-Hill Prof.

***Pivar, William H. & Bruss, Robert.** California Real Estate Law. 4th ed. LC 99-45983. 2000. 47.95 (*0-7931-3637-7*, Real Estate Ed) Dearborn.

Pivar, William H. & Harian, Donald L. Real Estate Ethics Good Ethics = Good Business. 3rd ed. 192p. 1995. pap. 16.95 (*0-7931-1236-2*, 1966-0103, Pub. by R-I-C-S Bks) St Mut.

***Pivar, William H. & McKenzie, Dennis J.** California Real Estate License Preparation. 11th ed. LC 00-22541. (Illus.). 400p. 2000. pap. 29.33 (*0-13-085956-7*) P-H.

Pivar, William H. Power Real Estate Letters. 3rd ed. LC 97-121392. 1997. pap. text 39.95 incl. disk (*0-7931-2474-3*, 1926-0303) Dearborn.

Pivato, Joseph. The Anthology of Italian-Canadian Writing. LC 98-73309. (Prose Ser.: Vol. 52). 388p. 1998. pap. 18.00 (*1-55071-069-9*) Guernica Editions.

— Echo: Essays on Other Literatures. 272p. 1994. pap. 15.00 (*1-55071-004-4*) Guernica Editions.

***Pivato, Joseph, ed.** Caterina Edwards. (Writers Ser.: No. 2). 128p. 2000. pap. 8.00 (*1-55071-114-8*) Guernica Editions.

Pivato, Joseph, ed. Contrasts: Comparative Essays on Italian-Canadian Writing. 258p. 1991. pap. 13.00 (*0-920717-35-7*) SPD-Small Pr Dist.

Pivcevic, Edo. Change & Selves. 160p. 1990. text 45.00 (*0-19-824249-2*) OUP.

— What Is Truth? (Avebury Series in Philosophy). 224p. 1997. text 64.95 (*1-85972-701-8*, Pub. by Ashgate Pub) Ashgate Pub Co.

Piven, Frances F. The Breaking of the American Social Compact. 464p. 1997. 27.50 (*1-56584-391-6*, Pub. by New Press NY) Norton.

— The Poor Peoples' Movements. rev. ed. 1999. pap. 0.00 (*0-375-70647-X*) Knopf.

Piven, Frances F. & Cloward, Richard A. The Breaking of the American Social Compact. 464p. 1998. pap. 17.95 (*1-56584-476-9*, Pub. by New Press NY) Norton.

— Poor People's Movements: Why They Succeed, How They Fail. LC 78-54652. 1979. pap. 7.96 (*0-394-72697-9*) Vin Bks.

Piven, Frances F. & Cloward, Richard A., eds. Regulating the Poor: The Functions of Public Welfare. LC 93-17460. 1993. pap. 15.00 (*0-679-74516-5*) Vin Bks.

***Piven, Frances Fox & Cloward, Richard A.** Why Americans Still Don't Vote: And Why Politicians Want It That Way. rev. ed. LC 00-39770. 336p. 2000. pap. 18.00 (*0-8070-0449-9*) Beacon Pr.

***Piven, Joshua, ed.** The Joy of Friendship: A Treasury of Quotations. (Illus.). 120p. 2000. 4.95 (*1-930408-02-1*) Lawrnce Teach.

***Piven, Joshua, et al.** Worst-Case Scenario Survival Handbook: How to Escape from Quicksand, Wrestle an Alligator, Break Down a Door, Land a Plane... (Illus.). 192p. 1999. pap. 14.95 (*0-8118-2555-8*) Chronicle Bks.

Piver, M. Steven. Manual Gyn-Onc ISE. 1989. 15.95 (*0-316-70937-9*, Little Brwn Med Div) Lppncott W & W.

— Myths & Facts about Ovarian Cancer. 1997. pap. text 9.95 (*0-9641823-5-1*) PRR.

Piver, M. Steven, ed. Handbook of Gynecologic Oncology. 2nd rev. ed. LC 95-331. 450p. 1995. pap. text 37.00 (*0-316-70939-5*, Little Brwn Med Div) Lppncott W & W.

***Piver, M. Steven & Eltabbakh, Gamal.** Myths & Facts about Ovarian Cancer: What You Need to Know. 2nd ed. LC 00-132234. (Illus.). 64p. 2000. pap. 9.95 (*1-891483-07-2*) PRR.

Piver, M. Steven, jt. auth. see Wilder, Gene.

***Piver, Susan.** The Hard Questions: 100 Essential Questions to Ask the One You Love. LC 99-88430. 2000. pap. 9.95 (*1-58542-004-2*, Tarcher Putnam) Putnam Pub Group.

Pivert, Francois. Schism or Not? The Episcopal Consecrations of Archbishop Marcel Lefebore. 50p. 1995. pap. text 4.45 (*0-935952-54-3*) Angelus Pr.

Pivevic, Edo. The Concept of Reality. (Modern Revivals in Philosophy Ser.). 312p. 1993. 56.95 (*0-7512-0273-8*, Pub. by Gregg Revivals) Ashgate Pub Co.

Pivin, Jean L. Augustt Cornelius Yao Azaglo: Photographs From the Ivory Coast. 1997. pap. text 18.00 (*2-909571-18-1*) Dist Art Pubs.

— Ousamne Sow: Sculptures. (Illus.). 184p. 1996. 69.95 (*2-909571-14-9*, Pub. by Revue Noire) Dist Art Pubs.

Pivka, Otto Von, see Von Pivka, Otto.

Pivnichny, John. Ladder Crystal Filters. (Illus.). 136p. 1999. mass mkt. 14.95 (*1-891237-20-9*, MFJ-3509) MFJ Ent.

Pivnicny. Analytical Methods/T. Q. M. in Health Care. (Health Services Administration Ser.). 1998. pap. 34.95 (*0-8273-7381-3*) Delmar.

***Pivot, Monique.** The Perfect Life of Lovers. (Illus.). 120p. 2000. 24.95 (*0-7641-5315-3*) Barron.

Pivot Point Staff. Designing Hair Additions Course Book. (Cosmetology Ser.). Date not set. pap. 36.95 (*5-272-52124-2*, VNR) Wiley.

Pivovarnick, John. America Online 6 in 1. 1997. pap. text 29.99 incl. cd-rom (*0-7897-1425-6*) Que.

— The Complete Idiot's Guide to America Online. 350p. 1999. 16.99 (*0-7897-2111-2*) Que.

— The Complete Idiot's Guide to America Online. 2nd ed. (Illus.). 328p. 1995. 19.99 (*1-56761-597-X*, Alpha Ref) Macmillan Gen Ref.

— The Complete Idiot's Guide to CD-ROM. 2nd ed. (Illus.). 327p. (Orig.). 1995. 21.99 (*1-56761-606-2*, Alpha Ref) Macmillan Gen Ref.

— The Complete Idiot's Guide to the Mac. 2nd ed. 344p. 1994. 16.95 (*1-56761-534-1*, Alpha Ref) Macmillan Gen Ref.

— Netscape Navigator 3 Complete Handbook. LC 96-69520. 312p. 1996. per. 24.99 (*0-7615-0852-X*) Prima Pub.

— This MAC Mine. LC 92-10937. 144p. 1992. pap. text 19.95 (*0-201-63206-3*) Addison-Wesley.

Pivovarnick, John & Que Staff. The Complete Idiot's Guide to the Microsoft Network. LC 95-71745. (Illus.). 341p. (Orig.). 1995. 19.99 (*0-7897-0603-2*) Que.

Pivovarov, Ju L. & Potylitsin, A. P., eds. Radiation of Relativistic Electrons in Periodic Structures: Proceedings of Second International Symposium (RREPS-95) (Illus.). 210p. (Orig.). 1996. pap. text 148.00 (*1-898326-38-X*, Pub. by CISP) Balogh.

Piwonka, J. Forging Ahead in Life: How to Chart Your Life, Your Physical, Intellectual & Mental Self. 1991. lib. bdg. 69.95 (*0-8490-4178-3*) Gordon Pr.

Piwonka, James M. The Secret of Facial Rejuvenation. 15p. 1994. reprint ed. spiral bd. 8.00 (*0-7873-1052-2*) Hlth Research.

— You Can Help Yourself to Beauty. 31p. 1994. reprint ed. spiral bd. 8.50 (*0-7873-1166-9*) Hlth Research.

Piwonka, Ruth & Blackburn, Roderic H. A Visible Heritage: Columbia County, New York: A History in Art & Architecture. 2nd ed. LC 96-20746. (Illus.). 160p. 1996. reprint ed. 35.95 (*1-883789-10-9*) Blk Dome Pr.

Piwonka, T. S., ed. see International Conference on Modeling of Casting &.

Piwonski, Shirley, jt. auth. see Marer, Sharon.

Pix, Mary. Inhumane Cardinal. LC 84-5358. 264p. 1984. reprint ed. 50.00 (*0-8201-1396-4*) Schol Facsimiles.

Pixar Animation Studios Staff, jt. auth. see Disney Enterprises, Inc. Staff.

Pixen, Francis F., ed. Labor Parties in Postindustrial Societies. (Europe & the International Order Ser.). 304p. (C). 1992. text 56.95 (*0-19-520926-5*); pap. text 23.95 (*0-19-520927-3*) OUP.

***Pixis, Christian.** World Design: The Best in Classic & Contemporary Furniture, Fashion, Graphics & More. Polster, Bernd, ed. (Illus.). 432p. 2000. 40.00 (*0-8118-2624-4*) Chronicle Bks.

Pixler, Mark, ed. see Kieft, Gary.

Pixley, Alden F., jt. auth. see Kaarli, Kalle.

Pixley, Aristene. Vermont Country Cooking. 1979. reprint ed. pap. 3.50 (*0-486-23803-2*) Dover.

Pixley, Colleen. Domestic Violence: Cracking the Code of Silence. rev. ed. 2000. pap. 0.50 (*0-89230-250-X*) Do It Now.

Pixley, Francis W. Auditors: Their Duties & Responsibilities Under the Joint-Stock Companies Acts & the Friendly Societies & Industrial & Provident Societies Acts. LC 75-18480. (History of Accounting Ser.). (Illus.). 1978. reprint ed. 20.95 (*0-405-07562-6*) Ayer.

— The Profession of a Chartered Accountant & Other Lectures: Delivered to the Institute of Chartered Accountants in England & Wales. Brief, Richard P., ed. LC 77-87285. (Development of Contemporary Accounting Thought Ser.). 1978. reprint ed. lib. bdg. 26.95 (*0-405-10913-X*) Ayer.

Pixley, Frank, jt. auth. see Read, Opie.

Pixley, George V., jt. auth. see Boff, Clodovis.

Pixley, Jocelyn. Citizenship & Employment: Investigating Post-Industrial Options. LC 92-19634. (Illus.). 347p. (C). 1993. text 64.95 (*0-521-41793-7*) Cambridge U Pr.

Pixley, Jocelyn, jt. auth. see Bittman, Michael.

Pixley, Jorge. Biblical Israel: A People's History. LC 92-38146. 176p. (Orig.). 1993. pap. 16.00 (*0-8006-2551-X*, 1-2551, Fortress Pr) Augsburg Fortress.

Pixley, Jorge & Boff, Clodovis. The Bible, the Church & the Poor. 288p. 1994. pap. 30.00 (*0-86012-165-8*, Pub. by Srch Pr) St Mut.

Pixner, Bargil. With Jesus Through Galilee According to the Fifth Gospel. LC 95-50709. (Illus.). 136p. 1996. pap. 24.95 (*0-8146-2427-8*) Liturgical Pr.

***Pixter, Paul.** Hiking Trails of Southwestern Colorado. 3rd rev. ed. LC 00-36604. 256p. 2000. pap. 18.95 (*0-87108-911-4*) Pruett.

***Pixton, Bob.** Warrington Railways. (Transport Ser.). 1999. pap. 18.99 (*0-7524-0750-3*) Arcadia Publng.

— Widnes & St. Helens Railways. (Transport Ser.). 1999. pap. 18.99 (*0-7524-0751-1*) Arcadia Publng.

P

An Asterisk (*) at the beginning of an entry indicates that the title is appearing for the first time.

Pixton, Paul B. The German Episcopacy & the Implementation of the Decrees of the Fourth Lateran Council, 1216-1245: Watchmen on the Tower. LC 94-44944. (Studies in the History of Christian Thought: Vol. 64). 1994. 167.50 (*90-04-10262-0*) Brill Academic Pubs.

Piyasena, S. & Parmanand. Chandrika & the Electoral Revolution in Sri Lanka. LC 95-900411. (C). 1995. 27.00 (*81-7013-136-7*, Pub. by Navarang) S Asia.

Piza Lopez, Eugenia & March, Candida. Gender Considerations in Economic Enterprises. (Oxfam Research Discussion Papers). 40p. (C). 1991. pap. 9.95 (*0-85598-189-X*, Pub. by Oxfam Pub) Stylus Pub VA.

Piza Lopez, Eugenia, jt. auth. see El Bushra, Judy.

Pizam, Abraham & Gu, Zheng. Journal of Travel Research Index, 1986-1988 Vols. 25 & 26, 2 vols., Set. 39p. (Orig.). 1989. pap. 18.00 (*0-89478-012-3*) U CO Busn Res Div.

***Pizam, Abraham & Mansfeld, Yoel, eds.** Consumer Behavior in Travel & Tourism. LC 99-17251. (Illus.). 530p. 1999. pap. 49.95 (*0-7890-0611-1*) Haworth Pr.

Pizam, Abraham & Mansfeld, Yoel, eds. Consumer Behavior in Travel & Tourism. LC 99-17251. (Illus.). 530p. 1999. lib. bdg. 69.95 (*0-7890-0610-3*) Haworth Pr.

Pizam, Abraham & Mansfield, Yoel. Tourism, Crime & International Security Issues. LC 95-20449. 330p. 1996. 130.00 (*0-471-96107-8*) Wiley.

Pizam, Abraham, jt. auth. see Gu, Zheng.

Pizam, Abraham, jt. auth. see Jones, Peter.

Pizam, Abraham, jt. ed. see Jones, Peter.

Pizan, Christine De, see De Pizan, Christine.

Pizanias, Caterina & Frideres, James S., eds. Freedom Within the Margins: The Politics of Exclusion. 276p. (Orig.). 1995. pap. text. write for info. (*1-55059-127-4*) Detselig Ents.

Pizante, Raymond. Lost Twin, 3. (Longman Originals Ser.). 1995. pap. text 5.51 (*0-582-08142-4*) Addison-Wesley.

Pizarro, Fernando P. New Reflections on Terrorism & Terrorism in America: International Connections. Serio, Joseph & Samaniego, George, trs. from SPA.Tr. of Nuevas Reflexiones Respecto Al Terrorismo Y el Terrorismo En America (Conexiones Internacionales). (Illus.). 66p. (C). 1989. pap. 7.95 (*0-942511-09-3*) OICJ.

Pizarro, Haydee. The Genus Characiopsis Borzi (Mischococcales, Tribophyceae) Taxonomy, Biogeography & Ecology. (Bibliotheca Phycologica Ser.: Vol. 98). (Illus.). 145p. 1995. 45.00 (*3-443-60025-5*, Pub. by Gebruder Borntraeger) Balogh.

Pizarro, Joanne A. Coming Home. LC 96-95150. 1997. 29.95 (*0-9655184-1-8*) Igloo Pub.

Pizarro, Joaquin M. A Rhetoric of the Scene: Dramatic Narrative in the Early Middle Ages. 280p. 1989. text 40.00 (*0-8020-5754-3*) U of Toronto Pr.

— Writing Ravenna: The Liber Pontificalis of Andreas Agnellus. LC 95-8303. (Recentiores Later Latin Texts & Contexts Ser.). 224p. 1995. text 44.50 (*0-472-10606-6*, 10606) U of Mich Pr.

Pizarro, Jose L. I Like the Way I Am Right Now: A 5th Grade Student Writes About His Feelings for His Class, His Teacher, His Family & His Future. (Illus.). 1974. pap. 0.50 (*0-918374-08-1*) City Coll Wk.

Pizarro, Kris Ann, jt. auth. see Tingley, Joseph V.

***Pizer, Abigail.** It's a Perfect Night. (Illus.). 32p. (J). 2000. pap. 7.99 (*0-333-63755-0*) Mcm Child Bks.

Pizer, Carol H., jt. auth. see Nevinskas, Nancy A.

Pizer, Donald. American Expatriate Writing & the Paris Moment: Modernism & Place. (Illus.). 168p. 1997. pap. text 14.95 (*0-8071-2220-3*) La State U Pr.

— Critical Essays on Stephen Crane's "The Red Badge of Courage" Nagel, James, ed. (Critical Essays on American Literature Ser.). 264p. (C). 1990. 48.00 (*0-8161-8898-X*, G K Hall & Co) Mac Lib Ref.

— Documents of American Realism & Naturalism. LC 97-20787. 672p. 1998. 59.95 (*0-8093-2096-7*) S Ill U Pr.

— Dos Passos' U. S. A. A Critical Study. LC 87-27905. 222p. reprint ed. pap. 68.90 (*0-8357-2570-7*, 204026200015) Bks Demand.

— The Novels of Frank Norris. LC 72-6785. (Studies in Fiction: No. 34). 1972. reprint ed. lib. bdg. 75.00 (*0-8383-1666-2*) M S G Haskell Hse.

— The Novels of Theodore Dreiser: A Critical Study. LC 75-20769. 394p. reprint ed. pap. 122.20 (*0-8357-6536-9*, 203589800097) Bks Demand.

— Realism & Naturalism in 19th-Century American Literature. rev. ed. LC 83-20406. 176p. 1984. 21.95 (*0-8093-1125-9*) S Ill U Pr.

— Theodore Dreiser: A Primary Bibliography & Reference Guide. (Reference Guides to Literature Ser.). 450p. 1991. 80.00 (*0-8161-8976-5*, Hall Reference) Macmillan.

— The Theory & Practice of American Literary Naturalism: Selected Essays & Reviews. LC 92-23398. 272p. (C). 1993. 36.95 (*0-8093-1847-4*) S Ill U Pr.

— Twentieth-Century American Literary Naturalism: An Interpretation. LC 81-5606. (Crosscurrents-Modern Critiques, New Ser.). 187p. 1982. 21.95 (*0-8093-1027-9*) S Ill U Pr.

Pizer, Donald, ed. The Cambridge Companion to American Realism & Naturalism: From Howells to London. (Cambridge Companions to Literature Ser.). 304p. (C). 1995. text 64.95 (*0-521-43300-2*); pap. text 19.95 (*0-521-43876-4*) Cambridge U Pr.

— New Essays on "Sister Carrie" (American Novel Ser.). 137p. (C). 1991. text 32.95 (*0-521-38278-5*); pap. text 14.95 (*0-521-38714-0*) Cambridge U Pr.

Pizer, Donald, ed. see Crane, Stephen.

Pizer, Donald, ed. see Dos Passos, John.

Pizer, Donald, ed. see Dreiser, Theodore.

Pizer, Donald, ed. see Garland, Hamlin.

Pizer, Donald, jt. ed. see Harbert, Earl.

Pizer, Donald, ed. see London, Jack.

Pizer, Donald, ed. see Norris, Frank.

Pizer, H. F., jt. auth. see Massachusetts General Hospital Organ Transplant Staff.

Pizer, Harry & Sloan, Stephen. Corporate Aviation Security: The Next Frontier in Aerospace Operations. LC 92-54135. (Illus.). 176p. 1992. 50.00 (*0-8061-2470-9*) U of Okla Pr.

Pizer, John. Toward a Theory of Radical Origin: Essays on Modern German Thought. LC 94-45932. (Modern German Culture & Literature Ser.). xi, 215p. 1995. text 50.00 (*0-8032-3711-1*) U of Nebr Pr.

Pizer, John D. Ego - Alter Ego: Double & As Other in the Age of German Poetic Realism. LC 97-30010. (Studies in the Germanic Languages & Literatures). 176p. 1998. lib. bdg. 37.50 (*0-8078-8120-1*) U of NC Pr.

Pizer, Laurence R. Plymouth in the Nineteenth Century. (Pilgrim Society Notes Ser.: No. 31). 1983. 2.00 (*0-940628-48-1*) Pilgrim Soc.

Pizer, Russell A. Administering the Elementary Band: Teaching Beginning Instrumentalists & Developing a Band Support Program. LC 72-155291. 227p. 1971. write for info. (*0-13-004994-8*) PH School.

Pizer, Stuart A. Building Bridges: The Negotiation of Paradox in Psychoanalysis. LC 98-19362. (Relational Perspectives Ser.: No. 11). 248p. 1998. 39.95 (*0-88163-170-1*) Analytic Pr.

Pizey, J. S. Synthetic Reagents: Chloramine-T; Hydrogen Peroxide; Polyphosphoric Acid, Vol. 6. (Synthetic Reagents Ser.). 160p. 1985. 111.00 (*0-470-20152-5*) P-H.

— Synthetic Reagents: Dimethylformamide: Lithium Aluminum Hybride: Mercuric Oxide: Thionyl Chloride, Vols. 1-2. LC 73-14417. (Synthetic Reagents Ser.). 353p. 1974. reprint ed. text 119.00 (*0-470-69104-2*) P-H.

— Synthetic Reagents: Dimethylformamide: Lithium Aluminum Hybride: Mercuric Oxide: Thionyl Chloride, Vols. 1-2. LC 73-14417. (Synthetic Reagents Ser.). 353p. 1974. reprint ed. text 121.95 (*0-470-69107-7*) P-H.

Pizey, J. S., ed. Synthetic Reagents: Synthetic Reagents. Diborane; 2, 3-Dichloro-5, 6-Dicyanobenzoquinone (DDQ): Iodine: Lead Tetra-Acetate. Vol. 3, Vol. 3. LC 73-14417. (Synthetic Reagents Ser.). 447p. 1977. reprint ed. text 129.00 (*0-470-99118-6*) P-H.

Pizika, Steven. Corporate Mentality: The Galaxy Was Threatened with a Hostile Takeover! 1999. mass mkt. 6.99 (*0-671-57811-1*) Baen Bks.

Piziks. In the Company of Mind. 1998. mass mkt. 6.99 (*0-671-57776-X*) S&S Trade.

Pizor, Faith K. & Comp, T. Allan. The Man in the Moone: An Anthology of Antique Science Fiction & Fantasy. LC 72-190276. xx, 230p. (J). 1971. write for info. (*0-283-97815-5*, Pub. by S1 & J) Trafalgar.

Pizurki, H., jt. auth. see Mangay-Maglacas, A.

Pizurki, H., jt. auth. see Mejia, A.

Pizurki, H., jt. auth. see Turnbull, L. M.

Pizz Staff, jt. auth. see Zone, Ray.

Pizzano. Michael Harrington. 1999. write for info. (*0-201-62293-9*) Addison-Wesley.

Pizzarelli, Alan. Zenryu & Other Works, 1974. (Xtras Ser.: No. 2). (Illus.). 36p. (Orig.). 1975. pap. 2.00 (*0-89120-001-0*) From Here.

***Pizzarelli, Bucky.** Romance of the Chordal Guitar Sound. 20p. 1998. pap. 14.95 (*0-7866-3471-5*, 95105BCD) Mel Bay.

Pizzarelli, Francesco, jt. ed. see Maggiore, Quirino.

Pizzarello, Donald J., ed. Radiation Biology. 312p. 1982. 139.95 (*0-8493-6011-0*, QP82, CRC Reprint) Franklin.

Pizzarello, Donald J., jt. auth. see Cooper, Jay S.

Pizzato, Mark. Edges of Loss: From Modern Drama to Postmodern Theory. LC 98-8955. (Theater--Theory/Text/Performance Ser.). 240p. (C). 1998. text 39.50 (*0-472-10914-6*, 10914) U of Mich Pr.

Pizzatto, Giuseppe. Euro 5: Woerterbuch Italien-Franzoesich-Englisch-Deutsch-Spanisch. (FRE, GER & ITA.). 511p. 1990. 39.95 (*0-7859-8539-5*, 3889750419) Fr & Eur.

Pizzey, Alan. Finance & Accounting for Non-Specialists. 320p. 1998. pap. 44.50 (*0-273-63020-2*, Pub. by Pitman Pub) Trans-Atl Phila.

Pizzey, Erin & Shapiro, Jeff. Prone to Violence LC 98-168194. 252p. 1982. write for info. (*0-600-20551-7*) P HM.

Pizzey, Graham. A Field Guide to the Birds of Australia. LC 80-8588. (Illus.). 432p. 1980. pap. 35.00 (*0-691-08483-1*, Pub. by Princeton U Pr) Cal Prin Full Svc.

Pizzi. Trials Without Truth. pap. text 18.00 (*0-8147-6650-1*) NYU Pr.

Pizzi, A., jt. auth. see Mittal, K. L.

Pizzi, Antonio. Advanced Wood Adhesives Technology. LC 94-21042. (Illus.). 304p. 1994. text 135.00 (*0-8247-9266-1*) Dekker.

— Wood Adhesives: Chemistry & Technology, Vol. 2. (Illus.). 424p. 1989. text 195.00 (*0-8247-8052-3*) Dekker.

— Wood Adhesives Vol. 1: Chemistry & Technology. (Illus.). 384p. 1983. text 185.00 (*0-8247-1579-9*) Dekker.

Pizzi, Antonio & Mittal, K. L. Handbook of Adhesive Technology. LC 94-4800. (Illus.). 696p. 1994. text 225.00 (*0-8247-8974-1*) Dekker.

Pizzi, Emilio. Mario Botta. 3rd expanded ed. (Illus.). 256p. 1998. pap. 29.95 (*3-7643-5438-0*) Birkhauser.

— Mario Botta: The Complete Works, 3 vols. (Illus.). 800p. 1997. 250.00 (*3-7643-5767-3*, Pub. by Birkhauser) Princeton Arch.

— Mario Botta Vol. 1: The Complete Works, 1960-1985. (Mario Botta Ser.). (Illus.). 256p. 1993. 98.00 (*3-7643-5530-1*, Pub. by Birkhauser) Princeton Arch.

— Mario Botta Vol. 2: The Complete Works, 1985-1990. 280p. 1994. 98.00 (*3-7643-5538-7*, Pub. by Birkhauser) Princeton Arch.

— Mario Botta Vol. 3: The Complete Works, 1990-1997. LC 94-200100. (Illus.). 256p. 1997. 98.00 (*3-7643-5541-7*, Pub. by Birkhauser) Princeton Arch.

***Pizzi, Emilio.** Renzo Piano Studio. (Illus.). 256p. 2000. pap. 29.95 (*3-7643-6118-2*, Pub. by Birkhauser) Princeton Arch.

Pizzi, J. R., jt. ed. see Guinet, D.

Pizzi, Michael, jt. ed. see Johnson, Jerry A.

Pizzi, William T. Trials Without Truth: Why Our System of Criminal Trials Has Become an Expensive Failure & What We Need to Do to Rebuild It. LC 98-25530. 272p. 1999. 27.95 (*0-8147-6649-8*) NYU Pr.

Pizzichil, W. Low Cycle & Static Bending Strength of Carburized & High Hardness Through Hardened Gear Teeth. (Nineteen Ninety-One Fall Technical Meeting Ser.: Vol. 91FTM7). (Illus.). 13p. 1991. pap. text 30.00 (*1-55589-604-9*) AGMA.

Pizzigati, G. A. & Drago, Raymond J. Some Progress in the Accurate Evaluation of Tooth Root & Fillet Stresses in Lightweight, Thin-Rimmed Gears. (Technical Papers: Vol. P229.21). (Illus.). 12p. 1980. pap. text 30.00 (*1-55589-288-4*) AGMA.

Pizzigati, Sam. The Maximum Wage: A Common-Sense Prescription for Revitalizing America by Taxing the Very Rich. LC 91-33410. (Illus.). 144p. (Orig.). 1992. pap. 11.95 (*0-945257-45-7*) Apex Pr.

Pizzigati, Sam & Solowey, Fred J., eds. The New Labor Press: Journalism for a Changing Union Movement. LC 92-10352. (Illus.). 256p. (Orig.). 1992. text 42.50 (*0-87546-189-1*, ILR Press); pap. text 17.95 (*0-87546-190-5*, ILR Press) Cornell U Pr.

Pizzimenti, David M. Tongues: Scriptural Answers to Common Objections. 112p. 1996. pap. 7.99 (*1-880089-99-8*, AP-999, Pub. by Albury Pub) Appalach Bk Dist.

Pizzimenti, John J. Evolution of the Prairie Dog Genus Cynomys. (Occasional Papers: No. 39). 73p. 1975. pap. 1.00 (*0-317-04900-3*) U KS Nat Hist Mus.

Pizzimenti, Mark. Victor Padrini: A Novel of the United States Air Force Academy. 128p. 1998. pap. 13.95 (*0-9666635-0-0*) Acedia Pr.

Pizzini, S., ed. Defects in Electronic Ceramics. (Materials Science Forum Ser.: Vol. 116). 260p. 1993. text 100.00 (*0-87849-653-X*, Pub. by Trans T Pub) Enfield Pubs NH.

Pizzini, S., et al, eds. Polycrystalline Semiconductors IV: Physics, Chemistry & Technology. (Solid State Phenomena Ser.: Vols. 51 & 52). 656p. 1996. 200.00 (*3-908450-19-5*, Pub. by Scitec Pubns) Enfield Pubs NH.

Pizzo, Albert. Doc Pizzo's Nutrition Handbook. 102p. (J). 1980. pap. 4.95 (*0-939126-14-1*) Back Bay Bks.

***Pizzo, Christopher.** Marry Me! Three Professional Men Reveal How to Get Mr. Right to Pop the Question. 256p. 2000. 22.95 (*0-06-019539-8*, Cliff Street) HarperTrade.

Pizzo, Joan. Pelican Bill. (Tales of the Back Bay Ser.). (Illus.). (J). (gr. k-6). 1990. lib. bdg. 11.95 (*0-939126-10-9*) Back Bay Bks.

Pizzo, Joan E. Amy Avocet. LC 83-70739. (Tales of the Back Bay Ser.). (Illus.). (J). (gr. k-6). 1983. 8.95 (*0-939126-06-0*) Back Bay Bks.

— Little Crumb: Tales of the Back Bay. (Illus.). 35p. (Orig.). (J). (gr. k-6). 1980. teacher ed. 8.95 (*0-939126-03-6*); pap. 7.95 (*0-939126-01-X*); lib. bdg. 10.95 (*0-939126-00-1*) Back Bay Bks.

— Little Crumb Fun Book. (Illus.). 32p. (Orig.). (J). (gr. k-6). 1983. pap. 3.95 (*0-939126-04-4*) Back Bay Bks.

— Nutrition Handbook Teacher's Manual. 28p. 1983. pap. 5.95 (*0-939126-15-X*) Back Bay Bks.

Pizzo, Joe, jt. auth. see Moore, Greg.

Pizzo, P., et al. Lessons Learned: Provision of Technical Assistance to States. Beatty, Noelle, ed. 90p. (Orig.). 1993. pap. 9.00 (*0-943657-29-6*) ZERO TO THREE.

Pizzo, Philip A. & Poplack, David G. Principles & Practice of Pediatric Oncology. 3rd ed. LC 96-41637. 1200p. 1996. text 205.00 (*0-397-51561-8*) Lppncott W & W.

Pizzo, Philip A. & Wilfert, Catherine M. Pediatric AIDS: The Challenge of HIV Infection in Infants, Children & Adolescents. 2nd ed. (Illus.). 1088p. 1994. 99.00 (*0-683-06895-4*) Lppncott W & W.

Pizzo, Philip A. & Wilfert, Catherine M., eds. Pediatric AIDS: The Challenge of HIV Infection in Infants, Children & Adolescents. 3rd ed. LC 98-6398. 849p. 1998. 99.00 (*0-683-30399-6*) Lppncott W & W.

Pizzo, Stephen & Muolo, Paul. Profiting from the Bank & S&L Crisis: How Anyone Can Find Bargains at America's Greatest Garage Sale. LC 92-53369. 256p. 1993. 23.00 (*0-88730-596-2*, HarpBusn) HarpInfo.

Pizzo, Stephen P., jt. auth. see Cotchett, Joseph W.

Pizzo, Wilson Del, see Fox, James M. & Del Pizzo, Wilson, eds.

Pizzolato, Susan & Withiam, Scott, eds. The Onset Review, Vol. 3, No. 1. 72p. 1998. pap. 10.00 (*0-9654360-1-2*) Word Studio.

***Pizzoni, Filippo.** The Garden: A History in Landscape & Art. (Illus.). 264p. 1999. 50.00 (*0-8478-2218-4*, Pub. by Rizzoli Intl) St Martin.

Pizzorno, Alessandro, jt. auth. see Crouch, Colin.

Pizzorno, Alessandro, jt. ed. see Crouch, Colin.

Pizzorno, Joseph E. Natural Medicine & Medicare: How to Solve the Medicare Crisis & Improve Our Health Care. 1997. pap. text 16.00 (*1-880831-18-X*) Aletheia Pr.

— Total Wellness: Improve Your Health by Understanding the Body's Healing System. 432p. 1997. per. 18.00 (*0-7615-1094-X*) Prima Pub.

— Total Wellness: Improve Your Health by Understanding the Body's Healing System. LC 96-224. (Illus.). 432p. 1996. boxed set 22.95 (*0-7615-0433-8*) Prima Pub.

Pizzorno, Joseph E., ed. Natural Medicine. (C). Date not set. text 195.00 Church.

Pizzorno, Joseph E., et al. A Textbook of Natural Medicine, 2 vols., Set, Vols. 1-2. rev. ed. (Illus.). 1230p. (C). 1993. ring bd. 295.00 (*0-9618764-0-9*, K03V2) John Bastyr.

— A Textbook of Natural Medicine, 2 vols., Vol. 1. rev. ed. (Illus.). 750p. (C). 1993. write for info. (*0-9618764-1-7*) John Bastyr.

— A Textbook of Natural Medicine, 2 vols., Vol. 2. rev. ed. (Illus.). 400p. (C). 1993. write for info. (*0-9618764-2-5*) John Bastyr.

Pizzorno, Joseph E., jt. auth. see Murray, Michael.

Pizzorno, Lara. The New Complete Book of Bread Machine Baking. LC 97-29131. 224p. 2000. pap. 12.95 (*0-7615-1125-3*) Prima Pub.

Pizzorusso, Alessandro, ed. Developing Trends of Parliamentarism: XIVth International Congress of Comparative Law, Athens, August 1994; General & National Reports. 1995. lib. bdg. 94.50 (*90-411-0148-9*) Kluwer Academic.

— Italian Studies in Law Vol. II: A Review of Legal Problems. 264p. (C). 1994. lib. bdg. 98.00 (*0-7923-2483-8*) Kluwer Academic.

— Italian Studies in Law, 1991 Vol. I: A Review of Legal Problems. 184p. (C). 1992. lib. bdg. 103.50 (*0-7923-1564-2*) Kluwer Academic.

***Pizzuti, Marge.** Dog Tails. LC 00-190862. 178p. 2000. 25.00 (*0-7388-2046-6*); pap. 18.00 (*0-7388-2047-4*) Xlibris Corp.

Pizzuti, Sally. Say Uncle & Aunt. large type ed. LC 98-44513. (Christian Fiction Ser.). 1999. 22.95 (*0-7862-1707-3*) Thorndike Pr.

Pizzuti, Suzy. Raising Cain... And His Sisters. LC 99-10755. (Halo Hattie's Boarding House Ser.: Vol. 2). 256p. 1999. pap. 6.95 (*1-57856-141-8*) Waterbrook Pr.

***Pizzuti, Suzy.** Raising Cain... And His Sisters. large type ed. LC 00-24258. (Christian Fiction Ser.). 307p. 2000. 24.95 (*0-7862-2533-5*) Thorndike Pr.

— Say Uncle... And Aunt. (Halo Hattie's Boarding House Ser.: No. 1). 256p. 1998. pap. 6.95 (*1-57856-044-6*) Waterbrook Pr.

Pizzutillo, Peter D., ed. Pediatric Orthopedics in Primary Practice. LC 96-20621. (Illus.). 369p. 1996. text 65.00 (*0-07-050252-8*) McGraw-Hill HPD.

Pizzuto, J. J., et al. Fabric Science Swatch Kit, Gray. 7th rev. ed. 100p. 1998. ring bd. 32.00 (*1-56367-161-1*) Fairchild.

Pjerrou, Joe. Go Ask the Owl. Jacobsen, Steven, ed. & illus. by. 40p. 1990. pap. 6.50 (*0-685-47506-9*) Guerilla Poetics.

PKF Consulting Staff. Hotel Development. 200p. 1996. pap. 59.95 (*0-87420-798-3*, H06) Urban Land.

PKM Publications Staff. Visitor's Guide to Florida's Suncoast. 396p. 1993. pap. 17.95 (*0-9633219-0-0*) PKM Pubns.

P.Koss, Joseph, Jr., ed. see Allan, Francis C. & Goddard, Carl J.

PKR Foundation Scientific Advisors Staff. Q & A on PKD, Vol. 3. rev. ed. Grantham, Jared J. et al, eds. 96p. (C). 1995. pap. 15.00 (*0-9614567-2-8*) PKR Foundation.

Pla Dalmau, Jose M. Enciclopedia Autodidactica. (SPA.). 1556p. 1965. 59.95 (*0-8288-6746-1*, S-11964) Fr & Eur.

— Enciclopedia Autodidactica. 4th ed. (SPA.). 1060p. 1987. 69.95 (*0-7859-5049-4*) Fr & Eur.

Plaa, Gabriel L. & Hewitt, William R. Toxicology of the Liver. 2nd ed. LC 97-22577. 456p. 1997. boxed set 135.00 (*1-56032-719-7*) Hemisp Pub.

— Toxicology of the Liver. 2nd ed. (Target Organ Toxicology Ser.). 500p. 1993. text 121.00 (*0-88167-886-4*) Lppncott W & W.

Plaat, Otto. Ordinary Differential Equations. LC 70-156869. 350p. 1971. 33.95 (*0-8162-6844-4*) Holden-Day.

Plaatje, Sol T. Native Life in South Africa: Before & since the European War & the Boer Rebellion. LC 90-24402. (Ravan Writers Ser.). 450p. 1996. pap. 14.95 (*0-86975-466-1*, Pub. by Ravan Pr) Ohio U Pr.

Plaatje, Solomon T. Mafeking Diary. Comaroff, John, ed. LC 89-22784. (Illus.). 190p. 1990. pap. 12.95 (*0-8214-0945-X*); text 24.95 (*0-8214-0944-1*) Ohio U Pr.

— Native Life in South Africa: Before & since the European War & the Boer Rebellion. LC 90-24402. 450p. (Orig.). (C). 1991. pap. text 13.95 (*0-8214-0986-7*, Pub. by Ravan Pr) Ohio U Pr.

— Native Life in South Africa, Before & since the European War & the Boer Rebellion. 2nd ed. LC 76-78585. (Illus.). 352p. 1970. lib. bdg. 35.00 (*0-8371-1420-9*, PLN&) Greenwood.

— Sol T. Plaatje: Select Writing. Willan, Brian, ed. LC 97-145451. 480p. (Orig.). 1997. pap. text 29.95 (*0-8214-1186-1*) Ohio U Pr.

Plaats, G. J. Van Der, see Van Der Plaats, G. J.

Placcius, Vicentius. Theatrum Anonymorum et Pseudonymorum Ex Symbolis et Collatione Virorum Per Europam Doctissimorum Ac Celeberrimorum Post Syntagma Dudum Editum, 2 vols. reprint ed. write for info. (*0-318-71941-X*) G Olms Pubs.

Place, Allen R., jt. ed. see Robb, Frank T.

Place, C. H., jt. auth. see Arrowsmith, D. K.

Place, C. M., jt. auth. see Arrowsmith, D. K.

Place, Chuck. Ancient Walls: Indian Ruins of the Southwest. LC 91-58636. (Illus.). 112p. (Orig.). 1992. 34.95 (*1-55591-125-0*); pap. 19.95 (*1-55591-126-9*) Fulcrum Pub.

— Los Angeles. LC 96-20832. (California Sights & Scenes Ser.). 64p. 1997. 14.95 (*0-88415-834-9*, 5834) Gulf Pub.

— San Diego. LC 96-23766. (California Sights & Scenes Ser.). 64p. 1997. 14.95 (*0-88415-835-7*, 5835) Gulf Pub.

Place, Edwin B., ed. see Tourney, Gautier de.

Place, Edwin B., tr. see De Segura, Juan.

Place, Enoch H. & Wentworth, William E. Journal of Enoch Hayes Place. LC 98-33719. 1998. 125.00 (*0-88082-080-2*) New Eng Hist.

P

An Asterisk (*) at the beginning of an entry indicates that the title is appearing for the first time.

Place, Francis. Illustrations & Proofs of the Principle of Population: Being the First Work on Population in the English Language Recommending Birth Control. LC 67-16338. (Reprints of Economic Classics Ser.). 1967. reprint ed. 49.50 (*0-678-00210-X*) Kelley.

Place, Francois. The Last Giants. Rodarmor, William, tr. from FRE. (Illus.). 78p. 1993. 15.95 (*0-87923-990-5*) Godine.

***Place, Francois.** Los Ultimos Gigantes. (Illus.). 78p. (J). (gr. 3). 1999. 15.95 (*980-257-235-7*, Pub. by Ediciones Ekare) Kane-Miller Bk.

Place, Georges, et al. Bibliographie des Auteurs Modernes de Langue Francaise, 1801-1972: Montfort, Montherlant, Vol. 20. (FRE.). 299p. 1973. 150.00 (*0-7859-5387-6*) Fr & Eur.

Place, Irene M. Opportunities in Business Management. (Illus.). 150p. 1985. 13.95 (*0-8442-6185-8*, VGM Career) NTC Contemp Pub Co.

— Opportunities in Business Management. (Illus.). 150p. 1988. pap. 10.95 (*0-8442-6186-6*, VGM Career) NTC Contemp Pub Co.

— Opportunities in Business Management Careers. rev. ed. LC 90-50738. (Opportunities In . . . Ser.). 160p. (YA). (gr. 7 up). pap. 12.95 (*0-8442-8160-3*, 297OIBUM, VGM Career) NTC Contemp Pub Co.

— Opportunities in Business Management Careers. rev. ed. LC 90-50738. (Opportunities in...Ser.). 160p. (YA). (gr. 7 up). 1994. 14.95 (*0-8442-8158-1*, VGM Career) NTC Contemp Pub Co.

— Women in Management. (Illus.). 160p. 1986. pap. 10.95 (*0-8442-6650-7*, VGM Career) NTC Contemp Pub Co.

Place, Irene M. & Baratz, Lewis. Opportunities in Business Management Careers. rev. ed. LC 97-21307. (Opportunities in...Ser.). 160p. 1997. pap. 11.95 (*0-8442-2326-3*, 23263) NTC Contemp Pub Co.

— Opportunities in Business Management Careers. rev. ed. LC 97-21307. (Opportunities in...Ser.). (Illus.). 160p. 1997. 14.95 (*0-8442-2325-5*, 23255) NTC Contemp Pub Co.

Place, J. A. The Non-Western Films of John Ford. (Illus.). 1979. pap. 9.95 (*0-8065-0779-9*, Citadel Pr) Carol Pub Group.

— The Western Films of John Ford. (Illus.). 226p. 1974. text 12.00 (*0-8065-0445-5*, Citadel Pr) Carol Pub Group.

— The Western Films of John Ford. 1977. pap. 9.95 (*0-8065-0594-X*, Citadel Pr) Carol Pub Group.

Place, Lew, ed. see Cooper, James Fenimore.

Place, Maurice, jt. auth. see Elliott, Julian.

Place, Patricia A., jt. auth. see Hanft, Barbara E.

Place, Robet M., jt. auth. see Guiley, Rosemary E.

Place, Robin. Bodies from the Past. (Digging up the Past Ser.). (Illus.). 48p. (J). (gr. 5-6). 1995. lib. bdg. 24.26 (*1-56847-397-4*) Raintree Steck-V.

— Excavating People: Archaeology in Britain. (Illus.). 32p. (C). 1992. write for info. (*0-521-36224-5*) Cambridge U Pr.

Place, Stan C. The Art & Science of Professional Makeup. (SKIN). (Illus.). 324p. 1990. pap. 31.95 (*0-87350-361-9*) Thomson Learn.

Place, Susan E., et al, eds. Tropical Rainforests: Latin American Nature & Society in Transition. LC 93-4335. (Jaguar Books on Latin America: No. 2). (Illus.). 222p. (C). 1993. text 55.00 (*0-8420-2423-9*) Scholarly Res Inc.

Place, T. Alan, et al, eds. Computer-Aided Microscopy & Metallography: Proceedings of the Twenty-Second Annual Technical Meeting of the International Metallographic Society. LC 90-84729. (Microstructural Science Ser.: No. 18). (Illus.). 547p. 1990. reprint ed. pap. 169.60 (*0-608-02653-0*, 206331300004) Bks Demand.

***Place, Timothy Harrison.** Military Training in the British Army, 1940-1944: From Dunkirk to D-Day. LC 00-31480. (Military History & Policy Ser.). (Illus.). 2000. write for info. (*0-7146-5037-4*, Pub. by F Cass Pubs) Intl Spec Bk.

***Place, Viana L.** Desserts & Sweet Snacks: Rustic, Italian-Style Treats. Schwartz, Justin, ed. LC 97-44586. (Illus.). 144p. 1998. 23.00 (*0-688-14139-0*, Wm Morrow) Morrow Avon.

Placek, Joseph A., jt. auth. see Mandich, D. R.

Placek, Tomasz. Mathematical Intuitionism & Intersubjectivity: A Critical Exposition of Arguments for Intuitionism. LC 99-18111. (Synthese Library). 1999. write for info. (*0-7923-5630-6*) Kluwer Academic.

Placencia, Porrero I. The European Context for Assistive Technology-TIDE 95. LC 95-75770. 1995. 93.00 (*0-614-06284-5*) IOS Press.

Placenicia, Jose F., et al. Business Owner's Guide to Accounting & Bookkeeping. 2nd ed. LC 97-37067. (Successful Business Library). (Illus.). 172p. (Orig.). 1997. pap. 19.95 (*1-55571-381-5*, Oasis Pr) PSI Resch.

Plach, Thomas A. The Creative Use of Music in Group Therapy. 2nd ed. 84p. 1996. 31.95 (*0-398-06585-3*); pap. 20.95 (*0-398-06586-1*) C C Thomas.

— Residential Treatment & the Sexually Abused Child. LC 93-7334. 170p. 1993. pap. 28.95 (*0-398-06324-9*) C C Thomas.

— Residential Treatment & the Sexually Abused Child. LC 93-7334. 170p. (C). 1993. text 40.95 (*0-398-05864-4*) C C Thomas.

Placher, William C. The Domestication of Transcendence: How Modern Thinking about God Went Wrong. LC 95-46686. 320p. (Orig.). 1996. pap. 24.95 (*0-664-25635-X*) Westminster John Knox.

— A History of Christian Theology: An Introduction. LC 83-16778. 324p. (C). 1983. pap. 24.95 (*0-664-24496-3*) Westminster John Knox.

— Narratives of a Vulnerable God: Christ, Theology, & Scripture. LC 93-47618. 192p. (Orig.). 1994. pap. 17.95 (*0-664-25534-5*) Westminster John Knox.

— Readings in the History of Christian Theology Vol. I: From Its Beginnings to the Eve of the Reformation, Vol. 1. LC 87-29540. 204p. (Orig.). 1988. pap. 24.95 (*0-664-24057-7*) Westminster John Knox.

— Readings in the History of Christian Theology Vol. II: From the Reformation to the Present, Vol. 2. LC 87-29540. 216p. (Orig.). 1988. pap. 24.95 (*0-664-24058-5*) Westminster John Knox.

— Unapologetic Theology: A Christian Voice in a Pluralistic Conversation. LC 88-27706. 178p. 1989. pap. 19.95 (*0-664-25064-5*) Westminster John Knox.

Placher, William C. & Willis-Watkins, David. Belonging to God: A Commentary on "A Brief Statement of Faith" 224p. (Orig.). 1992. pap. 13.95 (*0-664-25296-6*) Westminster John Knox.

Placher, William C., ed. see Frei, Hans W.

Placher, William C., jt. ed. see Thiemann, Ronald F.

Plachno, Jackie, ed. The Steam Locomotive Directory of North America, Vol. 1. LC 87-30098. (Illus.). 192p. 1988. pap. 25.00 (*0-933449-04-6*) Transport Trails.

— The Steam Locomotive Directory of North America, Vol. 2. LC 87-30098. (Illus.). 176p. 1988. pap. 25.00 (*0-933449-05-4*) Transport Trails.

Plachno, Jackie, ed. see Plachno, Larry.

Plachno, Joe, ed. see Hinton, Howard J.

Plachno, Larry. Beginner's Guide to Converted Coaches. (Illus.). 120p. 1992. reprint ed. pap. 15.00 (*0-933449-13-5*) Transport Trails.

— The Longest Interurban Charter. Bronsky, Eric, ed. LC 88-24784. (Illus.). 96p. 1988. pap. 16.00 (*0-933449-08-9*) Transport Trails.

— Modern Intercity Coaches: A Review of Over-the-Road Coaches & Manufacturers Active in the United States & Canada from 1953 to 1993. LC 97-6485. 1997. 62.00 (*0-933449-27-5*) Transport Trails.

— Sunset Lines: The Story of the Chicago Aurora & Elgin Railroad, Number 1, Trackage. Bronsky, Eric, ed. (Illus.). 160p. 1987. 36.00 (*0-933449-02-X*) Transport Trails.

— Sunset Lines - The Story of the Chicago Aurora & Elgin Railroad: History. LC 86-30751. (Sunset Lines Ser.). (Illus.). 352p. 1990. text 64.00 (*0-933449-10-0*) Transport Trails.

— Used Intercity Bus Pricing, 1978-1986. Plachno, Jackie, ed. LC 87-19189. (Illus.). 40p. 1987. pap. 20.00 (*0-933449-03-8*) Transportation.

Plachno, Larry, ed. see Bruns, James H.

Plachno, Larry, ed. see Insull, Samuel.

Plachno, Larry, ed. see Van Horn, Martin K. & Williams, Robert L.

Plachy, Roger J. & Plachy, Sandra J. Building a Fair Pay Program. 2nd ed. LC 98-20006. 336p. 1998. 65.00 (*0-8144-7965-0*) AMACOM.

— More Results Oriented Job Descriptions. LC 97-35903. 320p. 1997. spiral bd. 65.00 (*0-8144-7961-8*) AMACOM.

— Results-Oriented Job Descriptions: More Than 225 Models to Use or Adapt - with Guidelines for Creating Your Own. LC 93-6946. 300p. 1993. spiral bd. 65.00 (*0-8144-7806-9*) AMACOM.

Plachy, Sandra J., jt. auth. see Plachy, Roger J.

Plachy, Sylvia. Signs & Relics. (Illus.). 224p. 1999. text 50.00 (*1-58093-057-3*, Pub. by Monacelli Pr) Penguin Putnam.

— Unguided Tour. 1990. 60.00 (*0-89381-393-1*) Aperture.

Plachy, Sylvia, photos by. The Horse: The Most Abused Domestic Animal. unabridged ed. (Illus.). 1998. 14.99 (*0-9663411-0-4*) G Bunting.

— Unguided Tour. (Illus.). 144p. 1991. pap. 44.95 (*0-89381-431-8*) Aperture.

Placidi, G. F., et al, eds. Recurrent Mood Disorders: New Perspectives in Therapy. LC 92-48355. 1993. 178.00 (*3-540-54046-6*); 143.00 (*0-387-54046-6*) Spr-Verlag.

Placius, Lactantius & Statius, P. Papinius. In Statii Thebaida Commentum: Testimonia, Indices, Vol. 2. Sweeney, Robert D., ed. (Illus.). 128p. (C). text 49.50 (*3-519-01824-1*) U of Mich Pr.

Plackett, Robert L. Principles of Regression Analysis. LC 60-50875. 184p. reprint ed. pap. 57.10 (*0-608-10285-7*, 205161300097) Bks Demand.

Plackett, Robert L., ed. see Pearson, Egon Sharpe.

Placksin, Sally. Mothering the New Mother - Women's Feelings & Needs after Childbirth: A Support & Resource Guide. 2nd rev. ed. LC 98-9194. 420p. 2000. pap. 16.95 (*1-55704-317-5*) Newmarket.

Placzek & Giral, Angela. Avery's Choice: Five Centuries of Great Architectural Book. LC 97-3066. 1997. 185.00 (*0-7838-1597-2*, G K Hall & Co) Mac Lib Ref.

Placzek, Adolf K., ed. Macmillan Encyclopedia of Architects, Vol. 1. 1982. 110.00 (*0-02-925010-2*) Mac Lib Ref.

PLAE, Inc. Staff. Universal Access to Outdoor Recreation: A Design Guide. LC 93-92806. (Illus.). 254p. 1993. pap. 44.95 (*0-944661-25-4*) MIG Comns.

— Universal Access to Outdoor Recreation: A Pocket Guide. (Illus.). 64p. (Orig.). 1994. pap. text 9.95 (*0-944661-28-9*) MIG Comns.

Plaep, David R. Beholders of the Rising Sun: Stories of the First Christmas. LC 97-61002. 64p. 1997. pap. 11.95 (*1-57921-039-2*, Pub. by WinePress Pub) BookWorld.

Plaetzer, Ross F., ed. Lincoln for the Defense: The Only Known Transcript of an Abraham Lincoln Criminal Jury Trial. 198p. 1994. pap. 15.95 (*0-9641176-0-6*) High Hse Pr.

Plaff, Paula, jt. auth. see Meany, Janet.

Plafker, George & Berg, H. C., eds. The Geology of Alaska. (DNAG, Geology of North America Ser.: Vol. G1). (Illus.). 1994. 67.50 (*0-8137-5219-1*) Geol Soc.

Plag, Ingo. Morphological Productivity: Structural Constraints in English Derivation. LC 98-51325. 240p. 1999. 124.00 (*3-11-015833-7*) De Gruyter.

Plageman, Karen. Good, Hearty Soups. LC 78-70972. (Illus.). 1979. pap. 2.95 (*0-915942-12-7*) SF Design.

— Great Casseroles! LC 80-80567. (Illus.). 1980. pap. 2.95 (*0-915942-14-3*) SF Design.

— Slow-Crock Cookery. LC 74-24590. (Illus.). 1974. pap. 2.95 (*0-915942-02-X*) SF Design.

Plageman, Karen, jt. auth. see Herbert.

Plagemann, Catherine. Fine Preserving: Jams & Jellies, Pickles & Relishes, Conserves & Chutneys & Brandied Fruits for City & Country Cooks. rev. ed. Fisher, M. F. K., tr. (Illus.). 144p. 1986. reprint ed. 17.95 (*0-943186-35-8*); reprint ed. pap. 9.95 (*0-943186-31-5*) Aris Bks.

Plagemann, Thomas & Goebel, Vera. Interactive Distributed Multimedia Systems & Telecommunication Applications: 5th International Workshop, IDMS'98 Oslo, Norway, September 8-11, 1998, Proceedings, Vol. 148. Goos, G. et al, eds. LC 98-38785. (Lecture Notes in Computer Science Ser.: Vol. 1483). xv, 326p. 1998. pap. 55.00 (*3-540-64955-7*) Spr-Verlag.

Plagens, Peter. DeWain Valentine. 24p. 1975. 7.00 (*0-686-99813-8*) Mus Contemp Art.

— Moonlight Blues: An Artist's Art Criticism. LC 86-11335. (Contemporary American Art Critics Ser.: No. 9). 355p. reprint ed. pap. 110.10 (*0-8357-1753-4*, 207061200005) Bks Demand.

***Plagens, Peter.** Sunshine Muse. LC 99-46117. 225p. 2000. 19.95 (*0-520-22392-6*, Pub. by U CA Pr) Cal Prin Full Svc.

— Time for Robo. 303p. 1999. 24.95 (*0-930773-54-3*) Black Heron Pr.

***Plagens, Peter & Guenther, Bruce.** Tony DeLap. LC 00-37467. (Illus.). 128p. 2001. 45.00 (*1-55595-200-3*, Pub. by Hudson Hills) Natl Bk Netwk.

— Tony DeLap. Neff, Terry A., ed. (Illus.). 2000. pap. 29.95 (*0-917493-31-1*, Pub. by Orange Cnty Mus) Hudson Hills.

Plahacek, Thomas J. Blueberry Castle. 125p. 2000. pap. 11.99 (*1-57532-250-1*) Press-Tige Pub.

Plaice, John, jt. auth. see Krief, Phillipe.

Plaice, Neville, tr. see Bloch, Ernst.

Plaice, Neville, tr. see Bloch, Ernst, et al.

Plaice, Stephen, tr. & intro. see Bloch, Ernst, et al, eds.

***Plaid.** Glass Art: The Easy Way to a Stained Glass Look. (Illus.). 2000. pap. 14.95 (*0-8069-8225-X*) Sterling.

— One Stroke Painting Course. (Illus.). 2000. pap. 14.95 (*0-8069-1975-2*) Sterling.

Plaid. Paint Techniques for Home Decorating: Walls, Furniture & Floors. LC 97-35572. (Plaid Enterprises Ser.). (Illus.). 128p. 1998. 27.95 (*0-8069-0551-4*) Sterling.

— Paint Techniques for Home Decorating: Walls, Furniture & Floors. 1999. pap. text 14.95 (*0-8069-7783-3*) Sterling.

— Painted Birdhouses. LC 98-14776. (Illus.). 128p. 1998. 24.95 (*0-8069-1345-2*, Chapelle) Sterling.

— Painted Birdhouses. 1999. 14.95 (*0-8069-1877-2*) Sterling.

***Plaid Enterprises Staff.** Fresh & Fabulous Painted Furniture. LC 99-55370. (Illus.). 2000. 27.95 (*0-8069-7793-0*) Sterling.

Plaid Enterprises Staff. Glass Art: The Easy Way to a Stained Glass Look. LC 98-3573. (Illus.). 128p. 1998. 27.95 (*0-8069-8173-3*) Sterling.

***Plaid Enterprises Staff.** Painted Pots. (Illus.). 128p. 1999. pap. 14.95 (*0-8069-8201-2*, Chapelle) Sterling.

Plaid Enterprises Staff. Painting Floorcloths. LC 99-21383. (Illus.). 128p. 1999. 24.95 (*0-8069-6521-5*) Sterling.

Plaidy, Jean, pseud. The Bastard King. 24.95 (*0-8488-0605-0*) Amereon Ltd.

— Gay Lord Robert. large type ed. (Shadows of the Crown Ser.). 1974. 27.99 (*0-85456-608-2*) Ulverscroft.

— A Health Unto His Majesty. 253p. reprint ed. lib. bdg. 23.95 (*0-88411-894-0*) Amereon Ltd.

***Plaidy, Jean, pseud.** Katherine, the Virgin Widow. large type unabridged ed. 2000. 25.95 (*0-7531-5564-8*, 155648, Pub. by ISIS Lrg Prnt) ISIS Pub.

— The Lion of Justice. Date not set. lib. bdg. 23.95 (*0-8488-2157-2*) Amereon Ltd.

— Milady Charlotte. large type ed. 368p. 2000. write for info. (*0-7089-4186-9*) Ulverscroft.

Plaidy, Jean, pseud. The Passionate Enemies. 24.95 (*0-8488-0606-9*) Amereon Ltd.

— The Plantagenet Prelude. 24.95 (*0-8488-0607-7*) Amereon Ltd.

— The Princess of Celle. 27.95 (*0-8488-0608-5*) Amereon Ltd.

— The Princess of Celle. large type ed. (Shadows of the Crown Ser.). 1974. 27.99 (*0-85456-594-9*) Ulverscroft.

— The Queen & Lord M. large type ed. (Shadows of the Crown Ser.). 1975. 27.99 (*0-85456-600-7*) Ulverscroft.

— The Queen & Lord M. 268p. reprint ed. lib. bdg. 22.95 (*0-88411-895-9*) Amereon Ltd.

— Queen in Waiting. 26.95 (*0-8488-0609-3*) Amereon Ltd.

— The Reluctant Queen: The Story of Anne of York. large type ed. LC 94-919. 468p. 1994. lib. bdg. 22.95 (*0-8161-7426-1*, G K Hall Lrg Type) Mac Lib Ref.

— The Rose Without a Thorn. large type ed. 1994. 23.95 (*1-56895-161-2*) Wheeler Pub.

— St. Thomas's Eve. 22.95 (*0-8488-0610-7*) Amereon Ltd.

— The Third George. large type ed. (Shadows of the Crown Ser.). 1974. 27.99 (*0-85456-596-5*) Ulverscroft.

— El Trono Codiclado. 1999. pap. text 11.95 (*84-08-02242-3*) Planeta Edit.

— The Widow of Windsor. large type ed. (Shadows of the Crown Ser.). 1975. 15.95 (*0-85456-602-3*) Ulverscroft.

Plail, William, jt. ed. see McDonald, William C.

***Plain, Belva.** After the Fire. LC 00-23258. 352p. 2000. 25.95 (*0-385-33470-2*) Delacorte.

— After the Fire. large type ed. LC 99-89000. 432p. 2000. 25.95 (*0-375-40976-9*) Random Hse Lrg Prnt.

Plain, Belva. Blessings. 400p. 1990. reprint ed. mass mkt. 7.50 (*0-440-20652-9*) Dell.

— The Carousel. 448p. 1996. mass mkt. 7.50 (*0-440-21684-2*) Dell.

— The Carousel. 1995. mass mkt. 6.99 (*0-440-29540-8*) Doubleday.

— The Carousel. large type ed. LC 95-2475. 436p. 1995. lib. bdg. 26.95 (*0-7838-1116-0*, G K Hall Lrg Type) Mac Lib Ref.

— The Carousel. large type ed. LC 95-2475. 436p. 1996. pap. 18.95 (*0-7838-1117-9*, G K Hall Lrg Type) Mac Lib Ref.

— Crescent City. 528p. 1987. mass mkt. 7.50 (*0-440-11549-3*) Dell.

— Daybreak. 448p. 1989. mass mkt. 7.50 (*0-440-21681-8*) Dell.

— Eden Burning. 480p. 1987. mass mkt. 7.50 (*0-440-12135-3*) Dell.

— Evergreen. 704p. 1987. mass mkt. 7.50 (*0-440-13278-9*) Dell.

— Evergreen. 598p. 1991. reprint ed. lib. bdg. 38.95 (*0-89966-813-5*) Buccaneer Bks.

— Evergreen: A Novel. 1978. 15.95 (*0-440-02661-X*) Dell.

— Evergreen Saga, 3 vols. 1990. boxed set 16.50 (*0-440-36011-0*) Dell.

***Plain, Belva.** Fortune's Hand. LC 99-17794. 356p. 1999. 25.95 (*0-385-31692-5*) Delacorte.

— Fortune's Hand. 1999. mass mkt. 7.99 (*0-440-29575-0*) Dell.

— Fortune's Hand. 448p. 2000. mass mkt. 7.99 (*0-440-22641-4*) Dell.

— Fortune's Hand. (Illus.). (J). 2000. 13.34 (*0-606-18103-2*) Turtleback.

— Fortune's Hand. large type ed. LC 99-27637. 519p. 1999. pap. 28.95 (*0-7862-2013-9*) Mac Lib Ref.

Plain, Belva. Fortune's Hand. large type ed. LC 99-27637. 1999. 30.95 (*0-7862-2012-0*) Thorndike Pr.

— The Golden Cup. 608p. 1987. mass mkt. 7.50 (*0-440-13091-3*) Dell.

— Harvest. 432p. 1991. mass mkt. 7.50 (*0-440-20891-2*) Dell.

— Homecoming. LC 97-23880. 224p. 1997. 16.95 (*0-385-31980-0*) Delacorte.

— Homecoming. 304p. 1998. mass mkt. 6.99 (*0-440-22527-2*) Dell.

— Homecoming. large type ed. LC 97-43156. 2001. pap. 24.95 (*0-7862-1294-2*) Thorndike Pr.

— Legacy of Silence. 432p. 1999. mass mkt. 7.99 (*0-440-22640-6*) Dell.

— Legacy of Silence. LC 98-23619. 1998. 28.95 (*0-7862-1511-9*) Thorndike Pr.

— Legacy of Silence. large type ed. LC 98-23619. 1998. pap. 26.95 (*0-7862-1512-7*) Thorndike Pr.

— Legacy of Silence: Belva Plain. LC 98-2934. 352p. 1998. 24.95 (*0-385-31689-5*) Doubleday.

— Promises. 464p. 1997. mass mkt. 7.50 (*0-440-21687-7*) Dell.

— Promises. 1996. pap. 6.99 (*0-440-29544-0*) Doubleday.

— Promises. large type ed. LC 96-20236. 1996. lib. bdg. 27.95 (*0-7838-1842-4*, G K Hall Lrg Type) Mac Lib Ref.

— Promises. large type ed. LC 96-20236. 1997. pap. 25.95 (*0-7838-1841-6*, G K Hall Lrg Type) Mac Lib Ref.

— Random Winds. 528p. 1982. mass mkt. 7.50 (*0-440-17562-3*) Dell.

— Secrecy. large type ed. LC 97-28019. (Basic Ser.). 495p. 1997. lib. bdg. 28.95 (*0-7862-1219-5*) Thorndike Pr.

— Secrecy. large type ed. LC 97-28019. 1999. pap. 26.95 (*0-7862-1220-9*) Thorndike Pr.

— Secrecy. 432p. 1998. reprint ed. mass mkt. 7.50 (*0-440-22511-6*, Dell Trade Pbks) Dell.

— Tapestry. 560p. 1989. mass mkt. 7.50 (*0-440-20271-X*) Dell.

— Treasures. 528p. 1993. mass mkt. 7.50 (*0-440-21400-9*) Dell.

— Treasures. large type ed. LC 93-1991. 1993. pap. 19.95 (*0-8161-5803-7*, G K Hall Lrg Type) Mac Lib Ref.

— Whispers. 480p. 1994. mass mkt. 7.50 (*0-440-21674-5*) Dell.

— Whispers. large type ed. 1994. 90.95 (*0-7862-9990-8*, G K Hall Lrg Type) Mac Lib Ref.

Plain, Deborah & Dixon, James, eds. Farming & Birds in Europe: The Common Agricultural Policy & It's Implications for Bird Conservation. 96th ed. (Illus.). 452p. 1996. text 99.95 (*0-12-544280-7*) Acad Pr.

Plain English Campaign Staff. Language on Trial: The Plain English Guide to Legal Writing. (Illus.). 90p. 1996. pap. 7.95 (*1-86105-006-2*, Robson-Parkwest) Parkwest Pubns.

Plain, Gill. Women's Fiction of the Second World War. LC 96-26694. 240p. 1996. pap. 19.95 (*0-312-16414-9*); text 59.95 (*0-312-16413-0*) St Martin.

Plain, Marilyn V. Howard Hanson: A Comprehensive Catalog of the Manuscripts. LC 97-60600. xii, 157p. (Orig.). 1997. pap. 19.95 (*0-614-30244-7*) Eastman Sch Music.

Plain, Nancy. Frederic Remington: Artist of the American West. LC 98-23900. (People in Focus Ser.). 1999. write for info. (*0-382-39769-X*, Dillon Silver Burdett); pap. write for info. (*0-382-39768-1*, Dillon Silver Burdett) Silver Burdett Pr.

— Leonardo Da Vinci. LC 97-46943. (Biographies Ser.). (J). 1999. write for info. (*0-7614-0790-1*) Benchmark Books.

— Mary Cassatt, the Life of an Artist. LC 93-46578. (People in Focus Ser.). 112p. (J). (gr. 5). 1994. pap. 7.95 (*0-382-24720-5*); text, lib. bdg. write for info. (*0-87518-597-5*, Dillon Silver Burdett) Silver Burdett Pr.

An Asterisk (*) at the beginning of an entry indicates that the title is appearing for the first time.

Plaines, Judy A. Patient Education for the Ill & the Well: Index of New Information. 160p. 1997. 47.50 (*0-7883-1774-1*); pap. 44.50 (*0-7883-1775-X*) ABBE Pubs Assn.

Plains Genealogical Society Staff. Kimball County, Nebraska. (Illus.). 924p. 1988. 65.00 (*0-88107-113-7*) Curtis Media.

Plainview Writers Guild Staff, contrib. by. S-t-r-e-t-c-h-i-n-g. 66p. 1998. pap. 10.00 (*1-887150-17-X*) Millennia Bks.

Plaisance, George. Dictionnaire des Forets. 5th ed. (FRE.). 1975. pap. 49.95 (*0-8288-5851-9*, M6457) Fr & Eur.

— Lexique Pedologique Trilingue. (FRE.). 355p. 1958. pap. 39.95 (*0-8288-6851-4*, M-6458) Fr & Eur.

Plaismond, Marcus. Haitian Days: Ti Djo Remembers. (J). (gr. k-2). 1993. pap. 8.95 incl. audio (*0-7608-0488-5*); pap. 4.95 (*1-56801-360-4*) Sundance Pub.

— Haitian Days: Ti Djo Remembers, Big bk. (J). (gr. k-2). 1993. pap. 17.95 (*1-56801-362-0*) Sundance Pub.

Plaison, ed. Map Projection: Theory & Applications. 384p. 1990. lib. bdg. 139.00 (*0-8493-6888-X*, GA110) CRC Pr.

***Plaisted.** Efficiency of Theorem Proving. LC 98-129040. (C). 1999. pap. text 36.00 (*3-528-05574-X*) Harcourt.

Plaisted, Caroline. I'm in the Wedding, Too: A Complete Guide for Flower Girls & Junior Bridesmaids. LC 96-9122. (Illus.). 64p. 1997. 14.99 (*0-525-45752-6*) NAL.

***Plaisted, Caroline.** Love Lines: Every Girls Guide to First Love. (J). 2000. pap. text 5.95 (*1-902618-77-7*, Pub. by Element Childrns) Penguin Putnam.

— Totally Secret: Every Girl's Guide to Keeping & Sharing Secrets. 2000. pap. 4.95 (*1-902618-08-4*) Element Childrns.

Plaisted, Caroline. A Treasury of Ballet Stories. LC 97-32276. (J). (gr. 1-5). 1998. 6.95 (*0-7534-5147-6*) LKC.

Plaisted, Jon. Sam's Valley Serenade. 80p. (Orig.). 1992. pap. 5.95 (*0-9634702-0-5*) Goodwin Coffin Pubs.

Plaister, Elisabeth, tr. see Del Paso, Fernando.

***Plaistow Historical Society Staff.** Plaistow. (Images of America Ser.). 128p. 1999. pap. 18.99 (*0-7385-0071-2*) Arcadia Publng.

Plaistowe, F. G., jt. ed. see Thompson, J.

Plaitakis, Andreas, ed. Cerebellar Degenerations: Clinical Neurobiology. (Foundations of Neurological Surgery Ser.). 528p. (C). 1992. text 326.50 (*0-7923-1490-5*) Kluwer Academic.

Plaitakis, Andreas, jt. ed. see Duvoisin, Roger C.

Plaja, Guillermo Diaz, see Mosquera, Cristobal.

Plakans, Andrejs. Historical Dictionary of Latvia. LC 96-49234. (European Historical Dictionaries Ser.: No. 19). (Illus.). 216p. 1997. 34.50 (*0-8108-3292-5*) Scarecrow.

— The Latvians: A Short History. (Publication Ser.: No. 422). (Illus.). 257p. (C). 1995. 39.95 (*0-8179-9301-0*); pap. 24.95 (*0-8179-9302-9*) Hoover Inst Pr.

Plakans, Andrejs. Social History Land Reform. text. write for info. (*0-312-23298-5*) St Martin.

Plake, Barbara S. & Impara, James C., eds. Supplement to the Thirteenth Mental Measurements Yearbook. (Mental Measurements Yearbks.). 300p. 1999. pap. text 65.00 (*0-910674-46-9*) Buros Inst Mental.

Plake, Barbara S., jt. ed. see Impara, James C.

Plake, James Michael, ed. see Heatherley, E. X.

Plake, Jennifer, ed. see Heatherley, E. X.

Plakida, N. M. High-Temperature Superconductivity: Experiment & Theory. LC 94-21156. (Lecture Notes in Computer Science Ser.). 1994. 64.95 (*0-387-57072-1*) Spr-Verlag.

***Plakidas, John D.** Identification of North American Porricondyline Larvae (Diptera: Cecidomgiidae) large type ed. LC 99-71503. (Illus.). 129p. 1999. pap. text 25.00 (*1-929094-00-0*) Loyal Field Pubg.

Plakides, Antonios G. Strawberry Diseases. LC 64-21596. (Louisiana State University Studies Biological Science Ser.: No. 5). 207p. reprint ed. pap. 64.20 (*0-608-14361-8*, 201956600013) Bks Demand.

Plaks. World Literature. 1993. text 105.00 (*0-03-075204-3*) Holt R&W.

Plaks, Andrew H. Archetype & Allegory in the Dream of the Red Chamber. LC 75-3469. (Illus.). 280p. reprint ed. pap. 86.80 (*0-8357-7893-2*, 203631200002) Bks Demand.

— The Four Masterworks of the Ming Novel = Ssu ta ch'i-shu. LC 87-45534. (Illus.). 608p. reprint ed. pap. 188.50 (*0-608-09570-2*, 205437200006) Bks Demand.

Plaks, Andrew H., ed. Chinese Narrative: Critical & Theoretical Essays. LC 76-45907. 378p. reprint ed. pap. 117.20 (*0-7837-6774-9*, 204660400003) Bks Demand.

Plaks, T. M. Piecewise Regular Arrays: Application-Specific Computations. (Parallel Processing Ser.: Vol. 1). 260p. 1998. text 45.00 (*90-5699-173-6*, ECU64, Harwood Acad Pubs) Gordon & Breach.

Plaksin, I. N., ed. Flotation Properties of Rare Metal Minerals. LC 67-16333. (Illus.). 91p. 1967. 19.25 (*0-911184-05-8*) Primary.

Plambeck, Herb. Iowa's Heritage of Pioneer Family Farms: Family Owned Farms Settled from 1834 to 1864. 360p. (Orig.). 1996. pap. text. write for info. (*1-888223-05-7*) Sigler Print.

— The Way It Was. 300p. (Orig.). 1993. pap. 12.95 (*0-9635812-2-8*) Sigler Print.

Plambeck, James A. Electroanalytical Chemistry: Basic Principles & Applications. LC 82-2803. (Wiley-Interscience Publications). 426p. 1982. reprint ed. pap. 132.10 (*0-7837-2406-3*, 204009100006) Bks Demand.

Plamenac, Dragan, intro. Dijon: Bibliotheque Publique, Ms. 517. (Veroffentlichungen Mittelalterlicher Musikhandschriften - Publications of Mediaeval Musical Manuscripts Ser.). 1972. 127.00 (*0-912024-12-7*) Inst Mediaeval Mus.

Plamenac, Dragan, ed. see Ockeghem, Johannes.

Plamenevskii, B. A. Algebras of Pseudodifferential Operators. (C). 1989. text 223.00 (*0-7923-0231-1*) Kluwer Academic.

PLamenevsky, Boris A., jt. auth. see Nazarov, S. A.

Plamondon. Progress in Automatic Signature Verification. 180p. 1994. text 74.00 (*981-02-1852-4*) World Scientific Pub.

Plamondon, Ann L. Whitehead's Organic Philosophy of Science. LC 78-7350. 174p. (C). 1979. text 29.50 (*0-87395-387-8*) State U NY Pr.

***Plamondon, Martin.** Lewis & Clark Trail Maps Vol. I: A Cartographic Reconstruction. (Illus.). 176p. 2000. 65.00 (*0-87422-232-X*); pap. 45.00 (*0-87422-233-8*) Wash St U Pr.

Plamondon, R., et al, eds. Computer Recognition & Human Production of Handwriting. 408p. 1989. text 81.00 (*9971-5-0665-3*) World Scientific Pub.

— Pattern Recognition: Architectures, Algorithms & Applications. 396p. (C). 1991. text 104.00 (*981-02-0604-6*) World Scientific Pub.

Plamondon, R. & Leedham, G. Computer Processing of Handwriting. 424p. 1990. pap. 37.00 (*981-02-0520-1*); text 113.00 (*981-02-0408-6*) World Scientific Pub.

Plan Carpini, Giovanni Di, see Di Plan Carpini, Giovanni.

***PLAN International Staff.** Whose Habitat? Children Build Their Future. (Illus.). 57p. 1999. pap. write for info. (*1-902280-03-2*) PLAN Intl.

Planadeball, Marta J., jt. auth. see La Verne, Walker.

Planadeball, Marta J., jt. auth. see Walker, La Verne.

***Planalp, Sally.** Communicating Emotion: Social, Moral & Cultural Processes. LC 98-49524. (Studies in Emotion & Social Interaction). 312p. (C). 1999. 59.95 (*0-521-55315-6*); pap. 24.95 (*0-521-55741-0*) Cambridge U Pr.

***Planat, Michel.** Noise, Oscillators & Algebraic Randomness: From Noise in Communication Systems to Number Theory: Lectures of a School Held in Chapelle des Bois, France, April 5-10, 1999. LC 00-32966. (Lecture Notes in Physics). 2000. write for info. (*3-540-67572-8*) Spr-Verlag.

Planchart, Alejandro, jt. ed. see Boe, John.

Planchart, Alejandro E. The Repertory of Tropes at Winchester, 2 vols., Vol. 1. LC 76-3033. 407p. reprint ed. pap. 126.20 (*0-8357-3430-7*, 203968800001) Bks Demand.

— The Repertory of Tropes at Winchester, 2 vols., Vol. 2. LC 76-3033. 408p. reprint ed. pap. 126.50 (*0-8357-3431-5*, 203968800002) Bks Demand.

Planche, Bernard. Living on a Tropical Island. Matthews, Sarah, tr. from FRE. LC 87-34592. (Illus.). 38p. (J). (gr. k-5). 1988. 5.95 (*0-944589-13-8*, 138) Young Discovery Lib.

— Living with the Eskimos. Matthews, Sarah, tr. from FRE. LC 87-31805. (Illus.). 38p. (J). (gr. k-5). 1988. 5.95 (*0-944589-12-X*, 12X) Young Discovery Lib.

Planche, James R. Recollections & Reflections. LC 78-17733. (Music Reprint Ser.). (Illus.). 1978. reprint ed. lib. bdg. 65.00 (*0-306-79501-9*) Da Capo.

Plancher, Luisa M. The Angel of the Lord. (Illus.). 500p. 1998. pap. 39.95 (*0-9664198-0-4*) New Day Phnx.

Planck, Annika, tr. see Lundkvist, Artur.

Planck, Charles R. The Changing Status of German Reunification in Western Diplomacy, 1955-1966. LC 67-22894. (Washington Center of Foreign Policy Research. Studies in International Affairs: No. 4). 73p. reprint ed. pap. 30.00 (*0-608-13621-2*, 202074200018) Bks Demand.

Planck, H. I., et al, eds. Degradation Phenomena on Polymeric Biomaterials: Proceedings of the 4th International ITV Conference on Biomaterials, Denkendorf, September 3-5, 1991. LC 92-14876. (Illus.). x, 197p. 1992. 118.95 (*0-387-55548-X*) Spr-Verlag.

Planck, H. I., et al. Medical Textiles for Implantation: Proceedings of the 3rd International ITV Conference on Biomaterials, Stuttgart, June 14-16, 1989. (Illus.). 368p. 1991. 118.95 (*0-387-52741-9*) Spr-Verlag.

Planck, Julius W. Von, see Von Planck, Julius W.

Planck, Kristi, tr. see Branner, Hans Christian.

Planck, Max. Eight Lectures on Theoretical Physics. Wills, A. P., tr. LC 98-10716. (Illus.). 160p. 1997. reprint ed. pap. text 6.95 (*0-486-69730-4*) Dover.

— A Survey of Physical Theory. LC 93-6110. 128p. 1994. reprint ed. pap. text 7.95 (*0-486-67867-9*) Dover.

Planck, Max. The Theory of Heat Radiation - Waermestrahlung. Masius, Morton, tr. (History of Modern Physics & Astronomy Ser.: No. 11). (Illus.). 224p. 1989. 59.95 (*0-88318-597-0*) Spr-Verlag.

Planck, Max. Treatise on Thermodynamics. 297p. 1990. pap. 9.95 (*0-486-66371-X*) Dover.

— Where Is Science Going? Murphy, James, tr. from GER. LC 80-84974. 224p. 1981. reprint ed. 26.00 (*0-918024-21-8*); reprint ed. pap. 14.00 (*0-918024-22-6*) Ox Bow.

Planck, Max. Yearbook of United Nations Law 1998, Vol. 2. text 159.00 (*90-411-9665-X*) Kluwer Law Intl.

Planck, Max K. Scientific Autobiography & Other Papers. Gaynor, Frank, tr. LC 68-23319. 192p. 1968. reprint ed. lib. bdg. 35.00 (*0-8371-0194-8*, PLAP, Greenwood Pr) Greenwood.

— Where Is Science Going? Murphy, James, tr. LC 75-41215. reprint ed. 18.50 (*0-404-14696-1*) AMS Pr.

Planck, Max, Society for the Advancement of Scienc. B Boron Compounds Vol. II: Boron & Oxygen. 8th ed. (Gmelin Handbuch der Anorganischen Chemie Ser.: Suppl. 4). (Illus.). xvi, 297p. 1993. 1295.00 (*0-387-93673-4*) Spr-Verlag.

— Borverbindungen-Boron Compounds. (Gmelin Handbuch der Anorganischen Chemie Ser.: Vol. 23, Pt. 5). (Illus.). 277p. 1975. 400.00 (*0-387-93292-5*) Spr-Verlag.

— Boverbindungen-Boron Compounds. (Gmelin Handbuch der Anorganischen Chemie Ser.: Vol. 22, Pt. 4). (Illus.). 360p. 1975. 535.00 (*0-387-93289-5*) Spr-Verlag.

— Manganese Pt. C: The Compounds: Section 2, Manganate Compounds with Metals, from Li to U. (Gmelin Handbuch der Anorganischen Chemie Ser.). (Illus.). 302p. 1975. 445.00 (*0-387-93287-9*) Spr-Verlag.

— Nickel-Organische Verbibdunger Register - Organical Compounds Index for Pts. 1 & 2 of the Gmelin Handbuch, Vol. 18. 129p. 1975. 130.00 (*0-387-93296-8*) Spr-Verlag.

— Organonickel Compounds. (Gmelin Handbuch der Anorganischen Chemie Ser.: Vol. 16, Pt. 1). (Illus.). 419p. 1975. 630.00 (*0-387-93294-1*) Spr-Verlag.

— Organotin Compounds. 8th ed. (Gmelin Handbuch der Anorganischen Chemie Ser.: Vol. 26, Pt. 1). 182p. 1975. 290.00 (*0-387-93291-7*) Spr-Verlag.

— Perfluorhalogenorano-Verbindungen der Haupt Gruppenelemente-Perfluorohalogenorgano-Compounds of Main Group Elements. (Gmelin Handbuch der Anorganischen Chemie Ser.: Vol. 24, Pt. 3). 233p. 1975. 315.00 (*0-387-93293-3*) Spr-Verlag.

— Register-Index for the Gmelin Handbuch Dev Anorganischen Chemie. (Gmelin Handbuch der Anorganischen Chemie Ser.: Vol. 1, Ac-Au). 254p. 1975. 270.00 (*0-387-93295-X*) Spr-Verlag.

— Tin, Pt. C. (Gmelin Handbuch der Anorganischen Chemie Ser.). (Illus.). 206p. 1975. 330.00 (*0-387-93284-4*) Spr-Verlag.

— Transurane-Transuranium Elements. (Gmelin Handbuch der Anorganischen Chemie Ser.: Vol. 20d, Pt. 2). (Illus.). 278p. 1975. 425.00 (*0-387-93288-7*) Spr-Verlag.

— Uranium, Pt. C, Section 3. (Illus.). 360p. 1975. 540.00 (*0-387-93290-9*) Spr-Verlag.

Planck, Max, Society for the Advancement of Scienc, et al. Oxygen: Walter Desalting. (Gmelin Handbuch der Anorganischen Chemie Ser.). (Illus.). 339p. 1974. 565.00 (*0-387-93280-1*) Spr-Verlag.

Planck, Max Society for the Advancement of Science. Th Thorium: Compounds with Si, P, As, Sb, Bi, & Ge. (Gmelin Handbuch der Anorganischen Chemie Ser.). (Illus.). xxiii, 301p. 1993. 1310.00 (*0-387-93675-0*) Spr-Verlag.

Plancke, Chantal van der, see Van der Plancke, Chantal.

Plander, I. Artificial Intelligence Information-Control Systems of Robots '94. 432p. 1994. text 109.00 (*981-02-1877-X*) World Scientific Pub.

Plander, Ivan, ed. Artificial Intelligence & Information-Control Systems of Robots: Proceedings of the 7th International Conference Slovakia 10-14 September, 1997. 400p. 1997. 84.00 (*981-02-3235-7*) World Scientific Pub.

Plane & Pilot Magazine Staff. Plane & Pilot International Aircraft Directory. 1995. pap. 24.95 (*0-07-050305-2*) McGraw-Hill Prof.

***Plane, Ann Marie.** Colonial Intimacies: Indian Marriage in Early New England. 2000. 39.95 (*0-8014-3291-X*); pap. write for info. (*0-8014-8363-8*) Cornell U Pr.

Plane, David A. & Rogerson, Peter A. The Geographical Analysis of Population with Applications to Planning & Business. 417p. 1994. text 81.95 (*0-471-51014-9*) Wiley.

Plane, Donald R. & Crummer, Roy E. Quantitative Tools for Decision Support Using IFPS-Optimum. LC 84-24368. 400p. (C). 1986. pap. text 45.25 (*0-201-05844-8*) Addison-Wesley.

Planel, Philippe G., jt. auth. see Stone, Peter G.

Planel, Philippe G., tr. see Rouland, Norbert.

Planells, M. Dictionary of the Secrets of Ibiza: Diccionario de Secretos de Ibiza. (ENG & SPA.). 345p. 1982. pap. 16.95 (*0-8288-1463-5*, S39884) Fr & Eur.

***Planells, Pere, photos by.** Mediterranean Lifestyle. (Illus.). 192p. 2000. pap. 29.95 (*0-8230-3042-3*) Watsn-Guptill.

Planer, F. E. Superstition. LC 88-43038. 385p. 1988. pap. 22.95 (*0-87975-494-X*) Prometheus Bks.

Planes, Kindersley. Planes. LC 91-25688. (Eye Openers Ser.). (Illus.). 24p. (J). (ps-k). 1992. mass mkt. 8.99 (*0-689-71564-1*) Aladdin.

Planet Design Company Staff. Redefining Design. 1998. pap. text 45.00 (*1-56830-447-1*) Hayden.

Planet Dexter Editors. Bathroom Reader for Kids. LC 97-165045. 80p. 1996. pap. 8.95 (*0-201-95990-9*) Addison-Wesley.

— Calculator Mania. 2nd rev. ed. 64p. (J). (gr. 3-7). 1996. pap. 12.99 (*0-201-59047-6*) Addison-Wesley.

— The Hairy Book: The (Uncut) Truth about the Weirdness of Hair. LC 97-126149. 64p. (J). (gr. 3-8). 1996. pap. 12.99 (*0-201-91442-5*) Addison-Wesley.

— Instant Creature: The Swimming Critters from Way Back Then. LC 96-144225. 1995. pap. 14.99 (*0-201-48387-4*) Addison-Wesley.

— Lefty: A Handbook for Left-Handed Kids, 7 vols. (J). 1997. pap. 54.75 (*0-201-30439-2*) Addison-Wesley.

— Shake, Rattle & Roll. 2nd rev. ed. (Illus.). 32p. 1997. spiral bd. 11.99 (*0-201-15436-6*) Addison-Wesley.

— Whaddaya Doin' in There? A Bathroom Companion (For Kids) (J). (gr. 4-8). Date not set. 10.00 (*0-614-19318-4*) Addison-Wesley.

Planet Dexter Staff. Going, Going, Gone! This Book Disappears! 64p. (J). 1998. pap. 12.99 (*0-448-44076-8*) Putnam Pub Group.

***Planet Dexter Staff.** It's not Just Tissues. (Illus.). 48p. (YA). (gr. 3 up). 1999. pap. 5.95 (*0-448-44078-4*, Planet Dexter) Peng Put Young Read.

Planet Dexter Staff. This Book Really Sucks. LC 99-27095. (Illus.). 80p. (J). (gr. 3-7). 1998. mass mkt. 12.99 (*0-448-44075-X*) Putnam Pub Group.

— Whaddaya Doin' in There: A Bathroom Companion for Kids. (Planet Dexter Ser.). (Illus.). 128p. (J). (gr. 3-7). 1999. pap. text 4.99 (*0-448-44082-2*, G & D) Peng Put Young Read.

Planeta-Agostini. Illustrated Encyclopedia of Cooking, 8 vols., Set. (SPA., Illus.). 1987. 595.00 (*0-8288-7574-X*, 8439501234) Fr & Eur.

— Mil Ano de Poesia Espanola. 1998. pap. 44.95 (*84-08-01733-0*) Planeta.

***Planeta Editorial Staff.** La Busqueda de Dios. 1999. 24.95 (*84-08-01778-0*) Planeta Edit.

— Llame al Cielo y No Me Oyo. (SPA.). 1999. pap. 9.95 (*84-239-7063-9*) Espasa Calpe.

***Planeta Publishers Staff.** Abuso Sexual en la Infancia: Victimas y Agresores. (SPA.). 208p. 2000. pap. 15.95 (*84-344-7469-7*) Planeta Edit.

— Codigos Eticos de Publicidad y Marketing. (SPA.). 160p. 2000. pap. 13.95 (*84-344-1279-9*) Planeta Edit.

— Crisis del Antiguo Regimen y Revolucion Liberal en Espana. (SPA.). 224p. 2000. pap. 16.95 (*84-344-2856-3*) Planeta Edit.

— El Lugar Vacio. 2000. pap. 13.95 (*84-239-8840-6*) Espasa Calpe.

Planeta Staff. Clasicos del Arte: Classics of Art. 1989. write for info. (*0-7859-5232-2*) Fr & Eur.

***Planeta Staff.** Comidas de Negocios. (SPA.). 168p. 2000. pap. 16.95 (*84-08-03399-9*) Planeta Edit.

Planeta Staff. Diccionario Bompiano de Autores Literarios, Vol. 2. (SPA.). 616p. 1987. 29.95 (*0-7859-6005-8*, 8439506457) Fr & Eur.

— Diccionario Bompiano de Autores Literarios, Vol. 3. (SPA.). 632p. 1988. 29.95 (*0-7859-6006-6*, 8439506465) Fr & Eur.

— Diccionario Bompiano de Autores Literarios, Vol. 4. (SPA.). 632p. 1988. 29.95 (*0-7859-6007-4*, 8439506473) Fr & Eur.

— Diccionario Bompiano de Autores Literarios, Vol. 5. (SPA.). 640p. 1988. 29.95 (*0-7859-6008-2*, 8439506481) Fr & Eur.

— Diccionario Larousse de Historia Univeral, Vol. 1. (SPA.). 680p. 1988. 29.95 (*0-7859-6019-8*, 8439507690) Fr & Eur.

— Diccionario Larousse de Historia Univeral, Vol. 2. (SPA.). 760p. 1988. 29.95 (*0-7859-6003-1*, 8439407704) Fr & Eur.

— Diccionario Larousse de Historia Univeral, Vol. 3. (SPA.). 776p. 1988. 29.95 (*0-7859-6020-1*, 8439507712) Fr & Eur.

— Diccionario Larousse de Historia Univeral, Vol 5. (SPA.). 832p. 1988. 29.95 (*0-7859-6022-8*, 8439509731) Fr & Eur.

— Diccionario Larousse de la Pintura, 6 vols. (SPA.). 1988. write for info. (*0-7859-6023-6*, 8439509766) Fr & Eur.

— Diccionario Larousse de la Pintura, Vol. 1. (SPA.). 368p. 1989. 16.95 (*0-7859-6024-4*, 8439509774) Fr & Eur.

— Diccionario Larousse de la Pintura, Vol. 2. (SPA.). 376p. 1989. 16.95 (*0-7859-6025-2*, 8439509782) Fr & Eur.

— Diccionario Larousse de la Pintura, Vol. 3. (SPA.). 360p. 1989. 16.95 (*0-7859-6026-0*, 8439509790) Fr & Eur.

— Diccionario Larousse de la Pintura, Vol. 4. (SPA.). 368p. 1989. 16.95 (*0-7859-6027-9*, 8439509804) Fr & Eur.

— Diccionario Larousse de la Pintura, Vol. 5. (SPA.). 328p. 1989. 16.95 (*0-7859-6028-7*, 8439509812) Fr & Eur.

— Diccionario Larousse de la Pintura, Vol. 6. (SPA.). 344p. 1989. 16.95 (*0-7859-6029-5*, 8439509820) Fr & Eur.

— Diccionario UNESCO de Ciencias Sociales, Vol. 1. (SPA.). 624p. 1987. 29.95 (*0-7859-6009-0*, 8439506619) Fr & Eur.

— Diccionario UNESCO de Ciencias Sociales, Vol. 2. (SPA.). 592p. 1988. 29.95 (*0-7859-6010-4*, 8439506627) Fr & Eur.

— Diccionario UNESCO de Ciencias Sociales, Vol. 3. (SPA.). 616p. 1988. 29.95 (*0-7859-6011-2*, 8439506635) Fr & Eur.

— Diccionario UNESCO de Ciencias Sociales, Vol. 4. (SPA.). 568p. 1988. 29.95 (*0-7859-6012-0*, 8439506643) Fr & Eur.

— Enciclopedia Planeta de las Ciencias Ocultas y Parapsicologia: Planeta Encyclopedia of Occult Sciences & Parapsychology, 8 vols., Set. (SPA.). 300p. 1978. 250.00 (*0-8288-5228-6*, S50576) Fr & Eur.

— Gran Atlas de Espana: Large Atlas of Spain, 7 vols. (Illus.). 1991. 795.00 (*0-7859-5229-2*) Fr & Eur.

— Historia de Espana. (SPA.). 1991. 1495.00 (*0-7859-5230-6*) Fr & Eur.

— Historia Universal del Arte, 10 vols. 1992. write for info. (*0-7859-5227-6*) Fr & Eur.

— Illustrated Encyclopedia of Cooking, 8 vols., Set. (SPA., Illus.). 1986. 595.00 (*0-8288-8229-0*, 8439501218) Fr & Eur.

— Mamiferos. 1998. 109.95 (*84-88720-30-0*) Planeta.

— El Mundo de los Animales: The World of Animals. 1990. write for info. (*0-7859-5228-4*) Fr & Eur.

— Practical Encyclopedia of Pedagogy, 6 vols., Set. (SPA.). 695.00 (*0-8288-8254-1*) Fr & Eur.

— Las Travesuras Ratitas Verdes. 1998. 84.95 (*84-395-5386-2*) Planeta.

— Tu Cocina. 1998. 79.95 (*84-88720-31-9*) Planeta.

Plangiere. Grimoirium Verum. 100p. 1997. 40.00 (*1-879000-03-2*); pap. 12.95 (*1-879000-02-4*); lib. bdg. 95.00 (*1-879000-04-0*) Trident Pr WA.

***PlanGraphics, Inc. Staff.** GIS Database Concepts: A Tutorial. (Quick Study Ser.: Vol. 1). (Illus.). 27p. 1999. pap. 19.00 (*0-916848-09-4*) Urban & Regional Information Systems.

Planhol, Xavier De, see De Planhol, Xavier.

P

An Asterisk (*) at the beginning of an entry indicates that the title is appearing for the first time.

Planinc, Zdravko. Plato's Political Philosophy: Prudence in the Republic & the Laws. 328p. (C). 1991. text 37.50 (*0-8262-0798-7*) U of Mo Pr.

Planisek, Sandra, jt. auth. see Crum, Howard.

Planitz, Hans Von der, see Von der Planitz, Hans.

***Plank.** 60 Minute Investmnt Plan. 1999. text 20.00 (*0-7352-0070-X*) P-H.

***Plank, Angelika.** Akademischer und Schulischer Elementarzeichenunterricht Im 18 Jahrhundert. (GER., Illus.). 358p. 1999. 52.00 (*3-631-33885-6*) P Lang Pubng.

Plank, Anna. Harrap's Polish Phrase Book. 1991. pap. 4.00 (*0-13-382649-X*) P-H.

Plank, Bryan. 60-Minute Investment Planner. (Illus.). 288p. (C). 1999. text 34.95 (*0-13-631656-5*) P-H.

Plank, David N. The Means of Our Salvation: Public Education in Brazil, 1930-1995. 208p. (C). 1996. pap. 69.00 (*0-8133-8982-8*, Pub. by Westview) HarpC.

Plank, David N. & Ginsberg, Rick, eds. Southern Cities, Southern Schools: Public Education in the Urban South, 38. LC 89-49230. (Contributions to the Study of Education Ser.: No. 38). 296p. 1990. 57.95 (*0-313-26297-7*, GIB/, Greenwood Pr) Greenwood.

Plank, David N., jt. ed. see Ginsberg, Rick.

Plank, Donald M. Xanta Vele's Dream Numbers Winners Book. Boone, Edgar S., ed. (Illus.). 81p. (Orig.). 1992. 3.95 (*1-881938-02-6*) Economy Pubns.

Plank, Frans, ed. Double Case: Agreement by Suffixaufnahme. (Illus.). 520p. 1995. text 85.00 (*0-19-508775-5*) OUP.

— Paradigms: The Economy of Inflection. LC 91-33626. (Empirical Approaches to Language Typology Ser.: No. 9). x, 317p. (C). 1991. lib. bdg. 136.95 (*3-11-012761-X*) Mouton.

— Relational Typology. (Trends in Linguistics, Studies & Monographs: No. 28). xii, 443p. 1985. 161.55 (*0-89925-086-6*) Mouton.

***Plank, Geoffrey.** An Unsettled Conquest: The British Campaign Against the People of Acadia. 2000. 29.95 (*0-8122-3571-1*) U of Pa Pr.

Plank, Harry, tr. see Smith, Frank K.

Plank, Karl. Mother of the Wire Fence: Inside & Outside the Holocaust. 192p. (Orig.). 1994. pap. 19.95 (*0-664-25219-2*) Westminster John Knox.

Plank, Lois R., jt. ed. see Plank, Tom M.

Plank, Marlin E. Lumber Recovery from Ponderosa Pine in the Black Hills, South Dakota. (Illus.). 24p. 1998. reprint ed. pap. 3.40 (*0-89904-519-7*, Ecosytems Resrch) Crumb Elbow Pub.

Plank, Richard E., jt. auth. see Johnson, William C.

Plank, Robert. George Orwell's Guide Through Hell: A Psychological Study of 1984. rev. ed. LC 94-30950. (Milford Ser.: Vol. 41). 136p. 1994. pap. 19.00 (*0-89370-413-X*) Millefleurs.

Plank, Roger, jt. auth. see Bell, Trevor.

Plank, Shawn, jt. auth. see Knudsen, Mark.

Plank, Shawn, jt. auth. see Knudsen, Mark A.

***Plank, Stephen B.** Finding One's Place: Teaching Styles & Peer Relations in Diverse Classrooms. LC 00-41776. (Sociology of Education Ser.). 2000. write for info. (*0-8077-3989-8*) Tchrs Coll.

Plank, Steven. The Way to Heavens Door: An Introduction to Liturgical Process & Musical Style. LC 94-34082. (Studies in Liturgical Musicology: No. 2). 183p. 1994. 32.00 (*0-8108-2953-3*) Scarecrow.

Plank, Tom M. Accounting Deskbook, 2000 Supplement Ed. 1999. pap. text 39.95 (*0-13-012414-1*, Prentice Hall) P-H.

Plank, Tom M. & Plank, Lois R., eds. Encyclopedia of Accounting Systems. 2nd ed. LC 93-23812. 640p. (C). 1994. text 110.00 (*0-13-276817-8*) Prntice Hall Bks.

Plank, Tom M., jt. auth. see Blensly, Douglas L.

Plank, William. Gulag Sixty-Five: A Humanist Looks at Aging. (American University Studies Anthropology & Sociology: Ser. XI, Vol. 25). VIII, 205p. (C). 1989. text 35.30 (*0-8204-0784-4*) P Lang Pubng.

— Sartre & Surrealism. LC 81-431. (Studies in the Fine Arts - Art Theory). 110p. reprint ed. pap. 34.10 (*0-8357-1175-7*, 207025300065) Bks Demand.

***Plankinton, John C.** Crossword Proper Name Finder. (Illus.). 2000. pap. 13.95 (*0-88739-318-7*) Creat Arts Bk.

Plann, Susan. Relative Clauses in Spanish Without Overt Antecedents & Related Constructions. LC 78-68838. (University of California Publications in Linguistics: No. 93). 208p. 1980. pap. 64.50 (*0-7837-8420-1*, 204922200010) Bks Demand.

Plann, Susan J. Silent Minority: Deaf Education in Spain, 1550-1835. LC 96-10171. (Illus.). 343p. 1997. 40.00 (*0-520-20471-9*, Pub. by U CA Pr) Cal Prin Full Svc.

Planned Parenthood Federation of America, Inc. Sta. A Tradition of Choice: Planned Parenthood at 75. LC 91-75358. (Illus.). 108p. 1991. 19.95 (*0-934586-71-3*) Plan Parent.

Planned Parenthood Federation Staff. All about Birth Control. LC 98-13643. 352p. 1998. pap. 12.00 (*0-517-88506-9*) Random Hse Value.

Planned Pottery Staff. Brick Oven Baking with Planned Pottery Bakeware, Vol. 1. rev. ed. (Illus.). 1988. pap. 6.00 (*0-9620282-0-7*) Planned Pottery.

Planner, John. Astro Agenda Daily Planner. 1999. 14.95 (*1-56931-355-5*) Viz Commns Inc.

— Llewellyn's Astrological Pocket Planner: Daily Ephemeris & Aspectarian 2000-2001. 176p. 1999. pap. 6.95 (*1-56718-956-3*) Llewellyn Pubns.

Planner, John, intro. MECH '91 Australia: Engineering for a Competitive World, Conference 5: Cost Effective Bulk Materials Handling. (Illus.). 107p. (Orig.). 1991. pap. 38.50 (*0-85825-529-4*, Pub. by Inst Engrs Aust-EA Bks) Accents Pubns.

Planning Commission Staff. Nehru & Planning in India: Proceedings of the National Seminar on Pandit Jawaharlal Nehru. (C). 1989. 28.00 (*0-8364-2865-X*, Pub. by Manohar) S Asia.

Plano, J. P. & Olton, Roy. Dictionary of International Relations: Diccionario de Relaciones Internacionales. (ENG & SPA.). 465p. 1980. pap. 14.95 (*0-8288-2270-0*) Fr & Eur.

Plano, Jack C. & Greenberg, Milton. The American Political Dictionary. 10th ed. LC 96-78286. 720p. (C). 1996. pap. text 35.50 (*0-03-017317-5*, Pub. by Harcourt Coll Pubs) Harcourt.

Plano, Jack C. & Olton, Roy. The International Relations Dictionary. 4th ed. LC 87-26943. (Clio Dictionaries in Political Science Ser.). 446p. 1988. pap. text 24.75 (*0-87436-478-7*); lib. bdg. 56.50 (*0-87436-477-9*) ABC-CLIO.

Plano, Jack C., jt. auth. see Chandler, Ralph C.

Plano, Jack C., jt. auth. see Riggs, Robert E.

Plano, Jack C., jt. ed. see Rossi, Ernest E.

Plans, Miriam L. Antique Trader's Cashing in Your Collectibles: How to Identify, Value, & Sell Your Treasures. (Illus.). 160p. 1999. pap. 16.95 (*1-58221-003-9*, Antique Trader) Krause Pubns.

— Caring for Your Antiques & Collectibles. LC 97-76817. (Illus.). vi, 208p. 1997. pap. 15.95 (*0-930625-88-9*, AT5889) Krause Pubns.

Plans Sanz De Bremond, Jose M. Diccionario Practico: Asesor de la Propiedad & Copropiedad Inmobiliaria. (SPA.). 392p. 1975. pap. 24.95 (*0-7859-0649-5*, S50138) Fr & Eur.

Plans y de Gabriel Sanz de Bremond, Fructuoso Staf. Diccionario Ortografico Mikron. 51st ed. (SPA.). 640p. 1978. 9.95 (*0-8288-5147-6*, S50033) Fr & Eur.

Plansquaert, P. & Haggar, R. Legumes in Farming Systems. (Developments in Plant & Soil Sciences Ser.). (C). 1989. text 101.50 (*0-7923-0134-X*) Kluwer Academic.

***Plant & Melvin.** Maine Central in Color, Vol. 2. (Illus.). 128p. 1999. 54.95 (*1-58248-030-3*) Morning NJ.

Plant, et al. Maryland Estate Planning, Will Drafting & Estate Administration Forms, 2 vols. 2nd ed. 1995. ring bd. 229.00 (*0-327-03917-5*, 81584-10, MICHIE) LEXIS Pub.

— Maryland Estate Planning, Will Drafting & Estate Administration Forms, Issue 3. 1998. ring bd. 229.00 (*0-327-00144-5*, 81587-14) LEXIS Pub.

Plant, jt. auth. see University of Wisconsin Staff.

Plant, A. MacDonough. Maryland Estate Planning, Will Drafting & Estate Administration Forms. 220p. 1993. spiral bd. 159.00 incl. disk (*0-87189-280-4*, MICHIE) LEXIS Pub.

Plant, Al. Petagwana to Pele: The Story of Great Lakes Prehistoric & Historic Sites & Their People (Point Edward to Point Pelee) 3rd ed. (Illus.). 116p. (YA). (gr. 7 up). 1995. pap. 12.95 (*0-913611-06-9*) W E C Plant.

— Wahiawa Town. (Hawaii Mini History Ser.). (Illus.). 36p. (Orig.). 1995. pap. 3.95 (*0-913611-04-2*) W E C Plant.

Plant, Al & Plant, Julie. Gourmet Odyssey: Cooking in a Tiny Kitchen from Michigan to Molokai. (Illus.). 192p. 1994. 16.95 (*0-913611-05-0*) W E C Plant.

Plant, Albin M. Maryland Estate Planning, Will Drafting & Estate Administration Forms. 220p. 1993. ring bd., suppl. ed. 79.00 incl. disk (*1-56257-795-6*, MICHIE) LEXIS Pub.

Plant, Andrew. Drawing Is Easy. LC 93-16116. (Illus.). (J). 1994. pap. write for info. (*0-383-03692-5*) SRA McGraw.

Plant, Arnold, ed. Some Modern Business Problems: A Series of Studies. LC 67-23260. (Essay Index Reprint Ser.). 1977. 23.95 (*0-8369-0792-2*) Ayer.

Plant Breeding Symposium Staff. Plant Breeding: A Symposium, Iowa State University, 1965. Frey, Kenneth J., ed. LC 66-21642. 438p. reprint ed. pap. 135.80 (*0-608-14570-X*, 202493200040) Bks Demand.

— Plant Breeding II. Frey, Kenneth J., ed. LC 80-28879. (Illus.). 507p. 1981. reprint ed. pap. 157.20 (*0-608-00051-5*, 206081700006) Bks Demand.

***Plant Breeding Symposium Staff, et al.** Concepts & Breeding of Heterosis in Crop Plants: Proceedings of the Plant Breeding Symposium Sponsored by the Crop Science Society of America & the American Society of Horticultural Science, 3 November 1996, in Indianapolis, Indiana. LC 98-71578. (CSSA Special Publication). 127p. 1998. 24.00 (*0-89118-546-1*) Soil Sci Soc Am.

Plant, Brian D., jt. auth. see Plant, Jeremy F.

***Plant, Charles, ed.** Blackstone's Civil Practice 2000. 2954p. 2000. 178.50 (*1-84174-000-4*, Pub. by Blackstone Pr) Gaunt.

Plant, Christopher, jt. auth. see Plant, Judith.

Plant, Darrel. Flash! Creative Web Animation. LC 98-134179. 320p. 1997. pap. 29.95 incl. cd-rom (*0-201-69666-5*) Peachpit Pr.

— Flash 3! Creative Web Animation. 2nd ed. LC 99-234107. 352p. 1998. pap. text 29.99 (*0-201-35368-7*) Peachpit Pr.

***Plant, Darrel.** Short Order Macromedia Flash X. (Illus.). 256p. 2000. pap. text 19.99 (*0-7897-2358-1*) Hayden.

— Special Edition Using Macromedia Flash X. (Illus.). 800p. 2000. pap. 39.99 (*0-7897-2444-8*) Que.

Plant, David, jt. auth. see Ross, Alec.

Plant, David W., et al, eds. Patenting of Life Forms. LC 82-4191. (Banbury Report: No. 10). 351p. reprint ed. pap. 108.90 (*0-7837-2001-7*, 204227500002) Bks Demand.

Plant, Deborah G. Every Tub Must Sit on Its Own Bottom: The Philosophy & Politics of Zora Neale Hurston. LC 94-47523. 224p. 1995. 25.95 (*0-252-02183-5*) U of Ill Pr.

Plant, Elton M. Radio's First Broadcaster. (Illus.). 105p. 1989. pap. 9.95 (*0-913611-03-4*) W E C Plant.

Plant, Geoff. Analytika: Analytical Testing & Training Lists. 400p. 1994. ring bd. 110.00 (*1-56593-677-9*, 1332); ring bd. 135.00 incl. disk (*1-56593-678-7*, 1334) Singular Publishing.

Plant, Geoff, ed. see Spens, Karl-Grik.

Plant, Glen, ed. Environmental Protection & the Law of War. 302p. 1992. text 69.00 (*1-85293-234-1*) St Martin.

Plant, J. A., jt. ed. see Hale, M.

Plant, Jeffrey G., jt. auth. see Plant, Jeremy F.

Plant, Jeremy. Boston & Maine in Color. LC 96-78482. (Illus.). 128p. 1997. 49.95 (*1-878887-74-2*) Morning NJ.

***Plant, Jeremy.** Railroads in Pennsylvania. (Illus.). 40p. 2000. pap. 20.00 (*1-58036-144-7*) Penn State Data Ctr.

Plant, Jeremy. Transportation & Population Change. Shoop, Diane, ed. (Illus.). 44p. 1999. pap. 20.00 (*1-58036-133-1*) Penn State Data Ctr.

Plant, Jeremy F. Maine Central in Color, Vol. 1. (Illus.). 128p. 1998. 49.95 (*1-878887-96-3*) Morning NJ.

— Reading Company in Color, Vol. 1. LC 98-65131. (Illus.). 128p. 1998. 49.95 (*1-878887-95-5*) Morning NJ.

— RS3 Vol. 4: Classic Locomotives. (Illus.). 160p. 1998. 39.95 (*1-882608-20-8*) H & M Prods.

Plant, Jeremy F. & MacNamara, Thomas J. New Haven Trackside withThomas J. Mcnamara. LC 98-65133. 127 p. 1998. write for info. (*1-878887-98-X*) Morning NJ.

Plant, Jeremy F. & Melvin, George F. Maine Central in Color. LC 98-65132. (Illus.). 1998. write for info. (*1-878887-97-1*) Morning NJ.

Plant, Jeremy F. & Plant, Brian D. Trackside East of the Hudson with William J. McChesney. LC 98-138282. (Illus.). 128p. 1998. 49.95 (*1-878887-89-0*) Morning NJ.

Plant, Jeremy F. & Plant, Jeffrey G. Delaware & Hudson In Color, Vol. 2. LC 92-80546. (Illus.). 128p. 1993. 49.95 (*1-878887-27-0*) Morning NJ.

Plant, Jeremy F. & Steinbrenner, Richard T. Lehigh Valley-3 in Color. LC 99-186852. (Illus.). 128p. 1999. 49.95 (*1-58248-013-3*) Morning NJ.

***Plant, Jeremy F. & Yanosey, Robert J.** Pennsylvania - Standard RR of World. (Illus.). 128p. 1999. 54.95 (*1-58248-017-6*) Morning NJ.

Plant, Jeremy F., jt. auth. see Arnold, David S.

Plant, John B. Some Iterative Solutions in Optimal Control. 1968. 20.00 (*0-262-16020-X*) MIT Pr.

Plant, Judith & Plant, Christopher. Green Business: Hope or Hoax?: Toward an Authentic Strategy for Restoring the Earth. (New Catalyst Bioregional Ser.). 144p. 1991. pap. 9.95 (*0-86571-196-8*) New Soc Pubs.

— Turtle Talk: Voices for a Sustainable Future. (New Catalyst Bioregional Ser.). (Illus.). 144p. (Orig.). 1990. pap. 9.95 (*0-86571-186-0*) New Soc Pubs.

Plant, Julie, jt. auth. see Plant, Al.

Plant, K. P., ed. Ashover Light Railway. 92p. (C). 1985. 39.00 (*0-85361-350-8*) St Mut.

Plant, Kathryn, jt. auth. see Collinson, Diana.

Plant, Ken. Bed & Breakfast Directory. 1998. pap. text 14.95 (*0-9522807-5-2*, Pub. by KGP Publ) Seven Hills Bk.

— Great British Bed & Breakfast. 1998. pap. text 14.95 (*0-9522807-4-4*, Pub. by KGP Publ) Seven Hills Bk.

Plant, Ken. The Jewish Contribution in the 20th Century. 34.95 (*0-9523751-1-7*, Pub. by Polo Pubg) Seven Hills Bk.

Plant, Ken, ed. see KGP Publishing Staff.

Plant, M. Alcohol-Related Problems in High Risk Groups. (Euro Reports & Studies Ser.: No. 109). 122p. 1989. pap. text 11.00 (*92-890-1275-7*) World Health.

— Microelectronics A to Z. Date not set. pap. text 4.95 (*0-582-89285-6*) Addison-Wesley.

— Microelectronics Dictionary. Date not set. pap. text. write for info. (*0-582-89200-7*, Pub. by Addison-Wesley) Longman.

— Spanish-English Dictionary of Microelectronics. (ENG & SPA.). 227p. 1987. 49.95 (*0-8288-7252-X*, S30009) Fr & Eur.

— Spanish-English Dictionary of Microelectronics with an English-Spanish Vocabulary. (ENG & SPA.). 227p. 1987. pap. 30.50 (*84-283-1559-0*, Pub. by Paraninfo) IBD Ltd.

Plant, Martin A., et al, eds. Alcohol: Minimizing the Harm. 220p. (C). 1997. 55.00 (*1-85343-348-9*, Pub. by Free Assoc Bks); pap. 22.00 (*1-85343-349-7*, Pub. by Free Assoc Bks) NYU Pr.

— Alcohol & Drugs. 1991. text 68.00 (*0-7486-0113-9*, Pub. by Edinburgh U Pr) Col U Pr.

— Economics & Alcohol. 302p. 1983. 32.50 (*0-89876-089-5*) Gardner Pr.

Plant, Martin A., et al. Alcohol: Minimising the Harm. 300p. pap. 25.00 (*1-85343-359-4*) Free Assoc Bks.

— Alcohol: Minimising the Harm. LC 97-192285. 300p. 1997. 55.00 (*1-85343-358-6*, Pub. by Free Assoc Bks) Intl Spec Bk.

Plant, Mike. Iron Will: The Triathlete's Ultimate Challenge. 2nd ed. LC 99-37778. (Illus.). 1999. pap. 19.95 (*1-884737-67-6*) VeloPress.

Plant-Moeller, Jean, ed. Proceedings of the Twelfth National Convention of the Registry of Interpreters for the Deaf. 224p. (Orig.). (C). 1992. pap. 3.50 (*0-916883-11-6*) RID Pubns.

Plant, Moira. Women & Alcohol. LC 98-112692. 1997. 49.50 (*1-85343-363-2*, Pub. by Free Assoc Bks); pap. 22.50 (*1-85343-364-0*, Pub. by Free Assoc Bks) NYU Pr.

— Women, Drinking & Pregnancy. 208p. 1985. 45.00 (*0-422-78610-1*, 9483, Pub. by Tavistock) Routldge.

Plant, Nancy K., jt. auth. see Jarecke, George W.

Plant, Oliver. Woodturning: Step-by-Step Techniques. (Illus.). 128p. 1994. pap. 29.95 (*1-85223-759-7*, Pub. by Crolwood) Trafalgar.

Plant, Raymond. Modern Political Thought: An Introduction to Political Philosophy. 352p. 1991. pap. 28.95 (*0-631-14224-X*) Blackwell Pubs.

Plant, Raymond, jt. auth. see Hoover, Kenneth.

Plant, Raymond, jt. ed. see Blackburn, Robert.

Plant, Richard. The Pink Triangle: The Nazi War Against Homosexuals. LC 86-346. 272p. 1995. pap. 11.95 (*0-8050-0600-1*) H Holt & Co.

Plant, Richard, et al. Three Novellas. LC 97-37355. (Texas Review Southern & Southwestern Breakthrough Ser.). 160p. (Orig.). 1997. pap. 10.00 (*1-881515-10-9*) TX Review Pr.

Plant, Richard, jt. auth. see Ball, John.

Plant, Richard, jt. ed. see Saddlemyer, Ann.

Plant, Richard M. Formulae for the Mariner. 2nd ed. LC 86-47710. (Illus.). 118p. 1986. pap. text 12.50 (*0-87033-361-5*) Cornell Maritime.

***Plant, Robert.** E-Commerce: Formulation of Strategy. 295p. 2000. pap. 29.00 (*0-13-019844-7*, Prentice Hall) P-H.

Plant, Robert. Industries in Trouble. vi, 178p. (Orig.). 1981. 27.00 (*92-2-102678-7*); pap. 18.00 (*92-2-102679-5*) Intl Labour Office.

Plant, Robert & Antoniou, Grigoris, eds. Verification & Validation of Knowledge-Based Systems. (Technical Reports: No. WS-97-01). 70p. 1997. spiral bd. 25.00 (*1-57735-028-6*) AAAI Pr.

***Plant, Ruth.** Beyond the Nursery Window. large type ed. (Illus.). 272p. 1999. 31.99 (*0-7089-4068-4*) Ulverscroft.

Plant, Ruth. Nanny & I. large type ed. (Ulverscroft Large Print Ser.). (Illus.). 368p. 1998. 29.99 (*0-7089-3919-8*) Ulverscroft.

Plant, Sadie. The Most Radical Gesture: The Situationist International in the Postmodern Age. LC 91-32553. 240p. (Orig.). (C). 1992. pap. 22.99 (*0-415-06222-5*, A6857) Routledge.

***Plant, Sadie.** Writing on Drugs. 272p. 2000. 24.00 (*0-374-29334-1*) FS&G.

Plant, Sadie. Zero & Ones. 1998. mass mkt. write for info. (*0-385-48270-1*) Doubleday.

Plant, Stephen. Simone Weil. Vardy, Peter, ed. LC 96-52490. (Great Christian Thinkers Ser.). 112p. 1997. reprint ed. pap. 9.00 (*0-7648-0116-3*, Liguori Triumph) Liguori Pubns.

Plant, Sue, ed. From Needs to Practice: Effective Sex Education Training & Support. LC 98-134336. 48p. 1996. pap. 22.50 (*1-874579-90-3*, Pub. by Natl Childrens Bur) Paul & Co Pubs.

Plant, T. M. & Lee, P. A., eds. The Neurobiology of Puberty. 368p. 1995. 79.95 (*1-898099-06-5*) Blackwell Sci.

Plant, W. D., jt. auth. see Tomson, C. R.

Plant, W. Gunther, et al. The Haftarah Commentary. Sperling, S. David, ed. LC 96-5140. (ENG & HEB.). 928p. 1996. 40.00 (*0-8074-0551-5*, 381603) UAHC.

Planta, Balthasar. How to Select a Bow for the Violin Family of Instruments. 32p. 1981. pap. 12.95 (*0-933224-31-1*, T022) Bold Strummer Ltd.

Planta, Robert Von, see Von Planta, Robert.

Plantagenet Somerset Fry Staff. Castles of Britain & Ireland. LC 97-202490. (Illus.). 312p. 1997. 39.95 (*0-7892-0278-6*) Abbeville Pr.

Plantamura, Carol. The Opera Lover's Guide to Europe. (Illus.). 352p. 1996. pap. text 21.95 (*0-8065-1842-1*, Citadel Pr) Carol Pub Group.

— Woman Composers. (Illus.). 48p. 1988. pap. 3.95 (*0-88388-110-1*) Bellerophon Bks.

Plante. Clinical Psychology: A Bio-Psycho-Social Approach. (Psychology Ser.). Date not set. mass mkt. 50.95 (*0-534-34348-1*) Brooks-Cole.

Plante & Beeson. Communcation & Communation Disorders: A Clinical Introduction. 321p. 1998. pap. 58.00 (*0-205-28320-9*) Allyn.

Plante, Clare la, see La Plante, Clare.

Plante, David. The Age of Terror. 240p. 1998. text 24.95 (*0-312-19824-8*) St Martin.

***Plante, David.** The Age of Terror: Novel. 240p. 1999. pap. 13.95 (*0-312-25366-4*) St Martin.

Plante, Edmund. Alone in the House. 176p. (Orig.). (J). (gr. 5). 1991. pap. 3.50 (*0-380-76424-5*, Avon Bks) Morrow Avon.

— Last Date. 176p. (Orig.). (YA). (gr. 5 up). 1993. pap. 3.50 (*0-380-77154-3*, Avon Bks) Morrow Avon.

Plante, Ellen M. The American Kitchen: 1700 to the Present: From Hearth to Highrise. LC 94-33235. 352p. 1995. 29.95 (*0-8160-3038-3*) Facts on File.

— The Country Home. LC 98-13418. (Illus.). 176p. 1998. 24.98 (*1-56799-528-4*, MetroBooks) M Friedman Pub Grp Inc.

— Country Victorian. LC 97-7239. (Architecture & Design Library Ser.). (Illus.). 96p. 1997. write for info. (*1-56799-453-9*, Friedman-Fairfax) M Friedman Pub Grp Inc.

— Formal Victorian. LC 96-214. (Architecture & Design Library Ser.: No. 2). 1996. 17.95 (*1-56799-257-9*, Friedman-Fairfax) M Friedman Pub Grp Inc.

***Plante, Ellen M.** Home Magazine: Outdoor Living with Style. LC 99-13365. (Illus.). 144p. 1999. text 25.00 (*1-56799-736-8*) M Friedman Pub Grp Inc.

Plante, Ellen M. Live-in Kitchens. LC 99-18452. (For Your Home Ser.). 1999. pap. text 12.95 (*1-56799-719-8*, Friedman-Fairfax) M Friedman Pub Grp Inc.

***Plante, Ellen M.** Natural Color Palettes. LC 99-49515. (For Your Home Ser.). (Illus.). 72p. 2000. write for info. (*1-56799-918-2*, Friedman-Fairfax) M Friedman Pub Grp Inc.

Plante, Ellen M. The Traditional Home. LC 98-13400. (Illus.). 176p. 2000. 40.00 (*1-56799-477-6*, MetroBooks) M Friedman Pub Grp Inc.

— Victorian Home. (Illus.). 176p. 1998. 17.98 (*0-7624-0390-X*, Courage) Running Pr.

***Plante, Ellen M.** Victorian Home: The Grandeur & Comfort of the Victorian Era, in Households Past & Present. (Illus.). 2000. 19.98 (*0-7624-0915-0*, Courage) Running Pr.

Plante, Ellen M. Women at Home in Victorian America: A Social History. LC 97-11457. 1997. 29.95 (*0-8160-3392-7*) Facts on File.
***Plante, Ellen M. & Pikul, David T.** Enameled Kitchenware: American & European. (Illus.). 176p. 1999. 34.95 (*0-7643-1022-4*) Schiffer.
Plante, Ellen M., jt. auth. see Pikul, David T.
Plante, Jacques. On Goaltending: Fundamentals of Netminding by the Master of the Game. 2nd ed. (Illus.). 144p. 1997. pap. 15.99 (*1-55207-003-4*, Pub. by R Davies Pub) Genl Dist Srvs.
***Plante, Jean-Francois.** Oils & Vinegars. (Illus.). 224p. 2000. pap. 19.95 (*1-55209-437-5*) Firefly Bks Ltd.
Plante, Julian G. Austrian Monasteries, Part 1: Gottweig, Heiligenkreuz, Herzogenburg,...Seitenstetten, & Wilhering. (Checklists of Manuscripts Microfilmed for the Hill Monastic Manuscript Library Ser.: Vol. I). iv, 52p. (Orig.). 1967. pap. 10.00 (*0-940250-26-8*) Hill Monastic.
— Austrian Monasteries, Part 2: Admont, Altenburg,..."Osterreichische Nationalbibliothek, Universitatsbibliothek, Wilten, Zwettl. (Checklists of Manuscripts Microfilmed for the Hill Monastic Manuscript Library Ser.: Vol. I). viii, 296p. 1974. pap. 20.00 (*0-940250-27-6*) Hill Monastic.
Plante, Julian G., ed. Translatio Studii: Manuscript & Library Studies Honoring Oliver L. Kapsner, OSB. LC 73-76553. (GER & SPA.). xii, 288p. 1972. 20.00 (*0-940250-75-6*) Hill Monastic.
***Plante, Kelly Gregson.** Isabelle. LC 99-91686. 532p. 1999. 25.00 (*0-7388-0722-2*); pap. 18.00 (*0-7388-0723-0*) Xlibris Corp.
Plante, Michael, et al. Deborah Kass: The Warhol Project. (Illus.). 92p. 1999. 35.00 (*0-9668595-0-2*, Pub. by Newcomb Art) Dist Art Pubs.
Plante, Patricia R. Art of Decision Making: Issues & Cases in Higher Education. (ACE-Oryx Series on Higher Education). 224p. 1987. 27.95 (*0-02-924550-8*) Free Pr.
— The Art of Decision Making: Issues & Cases in Higher Education. LC 86-28443. (American Council on Education/Macmillan Series on Higher Education). 217p. reprint ed. pap. 67.30 (*0-608-20857-4*, 207195600003) Bks Demand.
Plante, Patricia R. & Caret, Robert L. Myths & Realities of Academic Administration. (ACE-Oryx Series on Higher Education). 160p. 1990. 27.95 (*0-02-897335-6*) Oryx Pr.
Plante, Patty. The Believer's Heart. (Joy for Jesus Ser.). 110p. Date not set. teacher ed., spiral bd. 14.95 (*1-889723-04-5*) Family Harvest.
— Joy for Jesus, 3 vols. 236p. 1991. teacher ed., spiral bd. 37.00 (*1-889723-00-2*) Family Harvest.
— Joy for Jesus, Bk. 1. 81p. 1989. teacher ed., spiral bd. 14.95 (*1-889723-01-0*) Family Harvest.
— Joy for Jesus, Bk. 2. 87p. 1990. teacher ed., spiral bd. 14.95 (*1-889723-02-9*) Family Harvest.
— Joy for Jesus, Bk. 3. 68p. 1991. teacher ed., spiral bd. 14.95 (*1-889723-03-7*) Family Harvest.
Plante, Raymond. Camera, Cinema, Tralala. (Novels in the Roman Jeunesse Ser.). (FRE., Illus.). 96p. (J). (gr. 4-7). 1989. pap. 8.95 (*2-89021-094-4*, Pub. by La Courte Ech) Firefly Bks Ltd.
— Marylou on Stage. (Early Readers Ser.). (Illus.). 62p. (J). (gr. 1-4). 1999. mass mkt. 3.99 (*0-88780-480-2*) Formac Publ Co.
— Un Monsieur Nomme Piquet Qui Adorait les Animaux. (Il Etait une Fois... Ser.: Vol. 4). (FRE., Illus.). 24p. (J). 1996. pap. write for info. (*2-89021-271-8*, Pub. by La Courte Ech) Firefly Bks Ltd.
— Le Roi de Rien. (Novels in the Roman Jeunesse Ser.). (FRE.). 96p. (J). (gr. 4-7). 1988. pap. 8.95 (*2-89021-081-2*, Pub. by La Courte Ech) Firefly Bks Ltd.
— Veloville. (Novels in the Premier Roman Ser.). (FRE.). 64p. (J). (gr. 2-5). 1989. pap. 7.95 (*2-89021-100-2*, Pub. by La Courte Ech) Firefly Bks Ltd.
Plante, Royal La, see La Plante, Royal.
Plante, Thomas. Snow Birds & Other Birds. 90p. 1997. 20.00 (*1-890193-02-X*) Red Dragonfly.
***Plante, Thomas G.** Contemporary Clinical Psychology. LC 98-20474. 440p. 1998. text 80.95 (*0-471-31626-1*) Wiley.
Plante, Thomas G., ed. Bless Me Father for I Have Sinned: Perspectives on Sexual Abuse Committed by Roman Catholic Priests. LC 98-56635. 200p. 1999. 59.95 (*0-275-96386-1*, C6386, Praeger Pubs) Greenwood.
Plante, Tom. My Back Yardstick. 56p. 1998. pap. 4.95 (*0-9647373-2-9*) Marimbo Commun.
Plantenga, Bart. Wiggling Wishbone: Stories of Patasexual Speculation. 160p. Date not set. 7.00 (*1-57027-009-0*) Autonomedia.
Plantenga, Janneke, jt. auth. see Dijkstra, Geske.
Plantenga, Janneke, jt. ed. see Dijkstra, Geske.
Plantigna, Theodore. How Memory Shapes Narratives: A Philosophical Essay on Redeeming the Past. LC 92-24382. 200p. 1992. text 79.95 (*0-7734-9575-4*) E Mellen.
Planting, Scott, jt. auth. see Pappas, Anthony.
Plantinga, Alvin. The Analytic Theist: An Alvin Plantinga Reader. Sennett, James F., ed. LC 98-18063. 387p. 1998. pap. 30.00 (*0-8028-4229-1*) Eerdmans.
— Does God Have a Nature? LC 80-6585. (Aquinas Lectures). 1980. pap. 15.00 (*0-87462-145-3*) Marquette.
— God & Other Minds: A Study of the Rational Justification of Belief in God. 288p. 1990. pap. text 15.95 (*0-8014-9735-3*) Cornell U Pr.
— God, Freedom, & Evil. 1989. pap. 10.00 (*0-8028-1731-9*) Eerdmans.
— The Nature of Necessity. (Clarendon Library of Logic & Philosophy). 268p. 1979. pap. text 26.00 (*0-19-824414-2*) OUP.
— Warrant: The Current Debate. LC 92-13183. 240p. 1993. pap. text 26.00 (*0-19-507862-4*) OUP.
— Warrant & Christian Belief. LC 98-54362. 528p. 2000. pap. 24.95 (*0-19-513193-2*); text 60.00 (*0-19-513192-4*) OUP.
— Warrant & Proper Function. LC 92-408. 272p. 1993. pap. 19.95 (*0-685-56686-2*) OUP.
— Warrant & Proper Function. LC 92-408. 256p. 1993. text 65.00 (*0-19-507863-2*); pap. text 24.95 (*0-19-507864-0*) OUP.
Plantinga, Alvin & Wolterstorff, Nicholas, eds. Faith & Rationality: Reason & Belief in God. LC 83-14843. 336p. (C). 1984. pap. text 17.50 (*0-268-00965-1*) U of Notre Dame Pr.
Plantinga, Carl R. Rhetoric & Representation in Nonfiction Film. (Studies in Film). 265p. (C). 1997. text 59.95 (*0-521-57326-2*) Cambridge U Pr.
Plantinga, Carl R. & Smith, Greg M. Passionate Views; Film Cognition & Emotion. LC 98-43308. 1999. 49.95 (*0-8018-6010-5*) Johns Hopkins.
— Passionate Views: Film Cognition & Emotion. LC 98-43308. (Illus.). 312p. 1999. pap. 17.95 (*0-8018-6011-3*) Johns Hopkins.
Plantinga, Cornelius. Not The Way It's Supposed to Be: A Breviary of Sin. 216p. 1996. pap. 16.00 (*0-8028-4218-6*) Eerdmans.
Plantinga, Cornelius, Jr., jt. ed. see Long, Thomas G.
Plantinga, Leon. Beethoven's Concertos: History, Style, Performance. LC 98-22552. 384p. 1999. 49.95 (*0-393-04691-5*) Norton.
— Clementi: His Life & Music. LC 84-1797. (Music Reprint Ser.). 360p. 1985. reprint ed. lib. bdg. 42.50 (*0-306-76198-X*) Da Capo.
— Romantic Music. LC 83-42653. (Introduction to Music History Ser.). (Illus.). (C). 1985. text 47.25 (*0-393-95196-0*) Norton.
Plantinga, Leon, ed. Anthology of Romantic Music. LC 83-42652. (Introduction to Music History Ser.). (Illus.). (C). 1985. pap. text. write for info. (*0-393-95211-8*) Norton.
***Plantinga, Richard J.** Christianity & Plurality: Classic & Contemporary Readings. LC 98-52528. 400p. 1999. pap. 32.95 (*0-631-20915-8*) Blackwell Pubs.
***Plantinga, Richard J., ed.** Christianity & Plurality: Classic & Contemporary Readings. 400p. 1999. 59.95 (*0-631-20914-X*) Blackwell Pubs.
Plantinga, Theodore. Historical Understanding in the Thought of Wilhelm Dilthey. LC 92-45581. (Studies in the History of Philosophy: Vol. 31). 216p. 1993. text 89.95 (*0-7734-9240-2*) E Mellen.
— Historical Understanding in the Thought of Wilhelm Dilthey. LC 79-19240. 215p. reprint ed. pap. 66.70 (*0-8357-6401-X*, 203575900096) Bks Demand.
— Learning to Live with Evil. LC 81-22041. 163p. reprint ed. pap. 50.60 (*0-608-14508-4*, 202533900043) Bks Demand.
— Public Knowledge & Christian Education. LC 87-35552. (Studies in Religious Education: Vol. 1). 136p. 1988. 69.95 (*0-88946-477-4*) E Mellen.
— Reading the Bible As History. 110p. (Orig.). 1980. pap. 4.25 (*0-919532-58-6*) Dordt Coll Pr.
— Seeking Our Brothers in the Light: A Plea for Reformed Ecumenicity. 142p. (Orig.). 1992. pap. 4.50 (*0-921100-48-5*) Inhtce Pubns.
— Wait for the Lord: Meditations on the Christian Life. 137p. (Orig.). 1981. pap. 5.75 (*0-932914-12-8*) Dordt Coll Pr.
Plantinga, Theodore, tr. see Boer, Theodore De.
Plantinga, Theodore, tr. see Bouma, Hendrik.
Plantinga, Theodore, tr. see Knepper, J. A.
Plantinga, Theodore, tr. see Los, D.
Plantinga, Theodore, tr. see Van der Waal, Cornelis.
Plantinga, Theodore, tr. see Van't Veer, M. B.
Plantinga, Theodore, tr. see Veldkamp, Herman.
Plantinga, Theodore, tr. see Wagner, Gerrit A.
Plantinga, Theodore, tr. & intro. see Deddens, Karel.
Plantinga, Theodore, tr. & intro. see Van Reest, Rudolf.
Plantos, Ted. At Home on Earth. (Illus.). 36p. (J). (ps up). 1996. pap. 6.00 (*0-88753-232-2*) Black Moss.
— Heather Hits Her First Home Run. (Illus.). 24p. (J). (ps-4). 1989. pap. 4.95 (*0-88753-185-7*) Black Moss.
Plantos, Ted, ed. Not to Rest in Silence: A Celebration of People's Poetry. LC 96-13124. 30p. (Orig.). 1996. pap. 5.00 (*1-884206-00-X*) Unfinish Monumnt.
Plants, Forrest M. A Loving Community. (Eagle Bible Ser.). 1989. pap. 0.99 (*0-87162-551-2*, D9153) Warner Pr.
Plants, Raymond. Ciclo Villa. (Coleccion Rosa Ser.). (SPA., Illus.). 60p. (J). (gr. 5 up). 1994. pap. 5.95 (*958-07-0067-2*) Firefly Bks Ltd.
Plantu. Ouverture en Bemol. (FRE.). 174p. 1991. pap. 15.95 (*0-7859-4365-X*, 2070383857) Fr & Eur.
Planty-Bonjour, G. Les Categories du Materialisme Dialectique: L'Ontologie Sovietique Contemporaine. (Sovietica Ser.: No. 21). (FRE.). 206p. 1965. lib. bdg. 71.50 (*90-277-0063-X*) Kluwer Academic.
— The Categories of Dialectical Materialism: Contemporary Soviet Ontology. (Sovietica Ser.: No. 24). (Illus.). 182p. 1967. lib. bdg. 130.50 (*90-277-0064-8*) Kluwer Academic.
— Hegel et la Pensee Philosophique en Russie, 1830-1914. (International Archives of the History of Ideas Ser.: No. 64). 351p. 1974. lib. bdg. 126.50 (*90-247-1576-8*, Pub. by M Nijhoff) Kluwer Academic.
Planty, Earl, jt. auth. see Meellone, Michael A.
Planty, Earl, jt. auth. see Mellone, Michael.
Planty, Earl, jt. auth. see Mellone, Michael A.
Plantz. ACLS Pearls of Wisdom. (Pearls of Wisdom Ser.). 1999. pap. 12.00 (*1-58409-004-9*) Boston Medical.
Plantz, et al. Medical Student USMLE Pts. II & III: Pearls of Wisdom. 1998. pap. 32.00 (*1-890369-10-1*) Boston Medical.
Plantz, Scott H. Emergency Medicine Pearls of Wisdom. 4th ed. 1997. pap. text 84.00 (*1-890369-00-4*) Boston Medical.
— Getting into Medical School Today. 4th ed. LC 97-81127. 176p. 1998. pap. text 14.95 (*0-02-862500-5*, Arc) IDG Bks.
Plantz, Scott H. & Acosta, Antonio. Getting into Medical School Today. 3rd ed. 688p. 1996. 12.95 (*0-02-861064-4*, Arco) Macmillan Gen Ref.
Plantz, Scott H. & Adler, Jonathan N. Emergency Medicine. LC 97-21471. (National Medical Series for Independent Study). 780p. 1997. pap. 30.00 (*0-683-18107-6*) Lppncott W & W.
— Emergency Medicine Clinical Manual. LC 98-42719. (National Medical Series for Independent Study). 600p. 1997. write for info. (*0-683-30349-X*) Lppncott W & W.
Plantz, Scott H., jt. ed. see Cole, Jesse A.
Plantzos, Dimitris. Hellenistic Engraved Gems. LC 97-39161. (Oxford Monographs on Classical Archaeology). (Illus.). 260p. 1999. text 145.00 (*0-19-815037-7*) OUP.
Planyavsky, Alfred. The Baroque Double Bass Violone. Barket, James, tr. LC 98-7957. (Illus.). xvi, 196p. 1998. 55.00 (*0-8108-3448-0*) Scarecrow.
***Planz, Allen.** Dune Heath. 118p. 1998. pap. 15.00 (*1-886435-06-5*) Canios Edit.
Planz, Allen, ed. see Moran, Daniel T.
Plarr, Victor. In the Dorian Mood, 1896. LC 93-41355. (Decadents, Symbolists, Anti-Decadents Ser.). 1994. 48.00 (*1-85477-154-X*) Continuum.
Plas, Jeanne M. Person-Centered Leadership: An American Approach to Participatory Management. 240p. (C). 1996. 52.00 (*0-8039-5598-7*) Sage.
Plas, Jeanne M., jt. auth. see Arnold, William W.
Plas, Jim. Teach Yourself Windows NT Workstation 5.0 in 24 Hours. 400p. 1999. 19.99 (*0-672-31225-5*) Sams.
Plas, L. H. Van der, see Lambers, H. & Van der Plas, L. H., eds.
Plas, Rob Van Der, see Van Der Plas, Rob.
Plas, Rob Van Der, see Norcliffe, Glen & Van Der Plas, Rob, eds.
Plas, Rob Van Der, see Van Der Plas, Rob.
Plas, Robert Van der, see Van der Plas, Robert.
Plas, Robert Van der, see Langley, Jim.
***Plasa, Carl.** Textual Politics from Slavery to Postcolonialism: Race & Identification. LC 99-50362. 2000. pap. 18.95 (*0-312-23004-4*); text 59.95 (*0-312-23003-6*) St Martin.
Plasa, Carl. Toni Morrison, Beloved. LC 98-39506. (Columbia Critical Guides Ser.). 167p. 1998. 39.50 (*0-231-11526-1*); pap. 14.50 (*0-231-11527-X*) Col U Pr.
Plasa, Carl & Ring, Betty J., eds. The Discourse of Slavery: Aphra Behn to Toni Morrison. LC 93-27522. (Illus.). 224p. (C). 1994. pap. 25.99 (*0-415-08152-1*) Routledge.
Plasberg, jt. ed. see Simbeck.
Plasberg-Ax, ed. Ciceronis, M. Tulli Fascicule 45: De Natura Deorum. (LAT.). 1987. reprint ed. 26.95 (*3-519-01221-9*, T1221, Pub. by B G Teubner) U of Mich Pr.
Plasberg, O., ed. see Cicero, Marcus Tullius.
Plaschke, Bill, jt. auth. see Knox, Chuck.
Plaschke, Bill, jt. auth. see Williams, Dick.
Plascik, Chester. Applied Calculus Business & Social Natural Sciences. Pullins, ed. (Math). 604p. (C). 1992. pap. 68.75 (*0-314-91851-5*) West Pub.
Plascott, Roy. Kent Rambles. 64p. 1987. 35.00 (*0-905392-76-0*) St Mut.
Plascov, Avi, ed. Modernization, Political Development & Stability. LC 80-28387. (Security in the Persian Gulf Ser.: Vol. 3). 192p. 1982. pap. text 19.50 (*0-86598-046-2*) Rowman.
***Plasencia, Emma, intro.** Air Pollution Research, 1989-1996: Short Summaries of Research Studies Funded by the Air Resources Board. 141p. (C). 2000. reprint ed. pap. text 30.00 (*0-7881-8944-1*) DIANE Pub.
Plasencia, Jorge R. Pinceladas Criollas. LC 87-83348. (Coleccion Caniqui). (SPA.). 88p. (Orig.). 1988. pap. 9.95 (*0-89729-472-6*) Ediciones.
Plasencia, Madeline. The Right to Privacy & the Constitution, 3 vols. Finkelman, Paul, ed. LC 99-39710. (Controversies in Constitutional Law Ser.). 1125p. 1999. text 225.00 (*0-8153-3144-4*) Garland.
Plasger, U. Dictionary Terminologie Musicale: French/German/French. (FRE & GER.). 289p. 1995. 275.00 (*0-320-00558-5*) Fr & Eur.
Plasil, Ellen. Therapist. 1988. pap. 3.95 (*0-317-65539-6*) St Martin.
Plasil, Frantisek & Jeffery, Keith G., eds. SOFSEM'97 - Theory & Pactice of Informatics: Proceedings, 24th Seminar on Current Trends in Theory & Practice of Informatics, Milovy, Czech Republic, November 22-29, 1997. LC 97-39202. (Lecture Notes in Computer Science Ser.: Vol. 1338). xiv, 571p. (C). 1997. pap. 79.00 (*3-540-63774-5*) Spr-Verlag.
Plasker, James R., ed. U. S. National Report to FIG, 1990. (Surveying & Land Information Systems Journal Ser.: Vol. 50, No. 2). 124p. 1990. 20.00 (*0-614-06107-5*, SM502) Am Congrs Survey.
Plasketes, George. Images of Elvis Presley in American Culture, 1977-1997: The Mystery Terrain. LC 96-32995. (Illus.). 334p. 1997. 39.95 (*1-56024-910-2*); pap. 24.95 (*1-56023-861-5*, Harrington Park) Haworth Pr.
Plasketes, George, jt. auth. see Denisoff, R. Serge.
***Plaskett, James.** Sicilian: Openings 2 F4. 1999. pap. text 15.95 (*0-7134-8589-2*) B T B.
— Sicilian Grand Prix Attack. 2000. pap. 19.95 (*1-85744-291-1*, Pub. by Everyman Chess) Globe Pequot.
Plaskett, James. Sicilian Tamanov. 1997. pap. 19.95 (*1-901259-01-3*) Macmillan.
Plaskett, L. G. The Health & Medical Use of Aloe Vera. LC 96-32704. 1996. write for info. (*0-943685-21-4*) Biosocial.
Plaskett, Norman. The Ancient Egyptian Oracle: The Cards of Ra-Maat. (Illus.). 1999. pap. 26.95 (*1-885203-75-6*) Tuttle Pubng.
Plaskin, Glenn. The Turning Point: Pivotal Moments in the Lives of Celebrities. (Illus.). 208p. 1992. 18.95 (*1-55972-138-3*, Birch Ln Pr) Carol Pub Group.
Plaskota, Leszek. Noisy Information & Computational Complexity. 319p. (C). 1996. text 64.95 (*0-521-55368-7*) Cambridge U Pr.
Plaskow, Judith. Sex, Sin & Grace: Women's Experience & the Theologies of Reinhold Niebuhr & Paul Tillich. LC 79-5434. 1980. pap. text 21.00 (*0-8191-0882-0*) U Pr of Amer.
— Standing Again at Sinai: Judaism from a Feminist Perspective. LC 89-45559. 304p. 1991. reprint ed. pap. 17.00 (*0-06-066684-6*, Pub. by Harper SF) HarpC.
— Women & Religion. Arnold, Joan & Romero, Joan A., eds. LC 74-83126. (American Academy of Religion. Aids for the Study of Religion Ser.). 216p. reprint ed. 67.00 (*0-8357-9581-0*, 201755700007) Bks Demand.
Plaskow, Judith & Christ, Carol P., eds. Weaving the Visions: New Patterns in Feminist Spirituality. LC 88-45697. 368p. 1989. pap. 18.00 (*0-06-061383-1*, Pub. by Harper SF) HarpC.
Plaskow, Judith, jt. auth. see Christ, Carol P.
Plaskowski, A., et al. Imaging Industrial Flows: Applications in Electrical Process Tomography. (Illus.). 228p. 1995. 137.00 (*0-7503-0296-8*) IOP Pub.
Plaskowski, A., jt. auth. see Beck, M. S.
Plasman, Daniel. Lovely Are the Messengers. LC 98-61617. 203p. 1998. pap. 12.95 (*1-881636-36-4*) Windsor Hse Pub Grp.
Plasmans, Joseph E., ed. Econometric Modelling in Theory & Practice. 225p. 1982. lib. bdg. 155.50 (*90-247-2553-4*) Kluwer Academic.
Plasmeijer, Rinus, jt. ed. see Hartel, Pieter H.
Plass, Adrian. The Horizontal Epistles of Andromeda Veal. (Illus.). 144p. (J). 1989. pap. 7.95 (*0-310-55831-X*, 19098P) Zondervan.
— Learning to Fly: A Shared Journey. (Illus.). 59p. 1996. reprint ed. 25.00 (*1-900507-14-5*, Pub. by Solway) OM Literature.
— The Sacred Diary of Adrian Plass (Age 373-4) 144p. 1990. pap. 6.99 (*0-310-51201-8*) Zondervan.
***Plass, Adrian.** Words from the Cross. (Illus.). 28p. 1998. pap. text 30.00 (*1-900507-37-4*, Pub. by Solway) Eisenbrauns.
Plass, Ewald. What Luther Says: A Practical-in-Home Anthology for the Active Christian. 1696p. 1987. 43.00 (*0-570-04240-2*, 15-1232) Concordia.
Plass, Paul. The Game of Death in Ancient Rome: Arena Sport & Political Suicide. LC 94-40884. (Studies in Classics). 296p. (C). 1995. lib. bdg. 40.00 (*0-299-14570-0*) U of Wis Pr.
— The Game of Death in Ancient Rome: Arena Sport & Political Suicide. 1999. pap. text 17.95 (*0-299-14574-3*) U of Wis Pr.
— Wit & the Writing of History: The Rhetoric of Historiography in Imperial Rome. LC 88-40193. 204p. (C). 1988. pap. text 18.95 (*0-299-11804-5*) U of Wis Pr.
Plass, Richard M., jt. auth. see Reep, Marianna L.
Plass, Richard M., ed. see Kranepool, Harry A.
Plassard, Marie-France, ed. Guidelines for Subject Authority & Reference Entries. (UBCIM Publications). 625p. 1993. 35.00 (*3-598-11180-0*) K G Saur Verlag.
— ISBD (PM) International Standard Bibliographic Description for Printed Music. 2nd rev. ed. 73p. 1991. lib. bdg. 36.00 (*3-598-10985-7*) K G Saur Verlag.
— UNIMARC Manual: Bibliographic Format. (UBCIM Publications). 100p. 1994. 35.00 (*3-598-11211-4*) K G Saur Verlag.
Plassche, Rudy J. Van de, see Van de Plassche, Rudy J.
Plassche, Rudy J. Van De, see Van De Plassche, Rudy J.
Plassche, Rudy J. Van de, see Huijsing, Johan H. & Van de Plassche, Rudy J.
Plasser, Fritz & Pribersky, Andreas, eds. Political Culture in East Central Europe. 242p. 1996. 69.95 (*1-85972-259-8*, Pub. by Avebry) Ashgate Pub Co.
Plasser, Fritz, et al. Democratic Consolidation in East-Central Europe. LC 98-13607. 255p. 1998. text 65.00 (*0-312-21495-2*) St Martin.
Plassmann, R., ed. Factitious Disease. Vol. 62, Nos. 1-2, 1994. (Illus.). 140p. 1994. pap. 87.00 (*3-8055-6013-3*) S Karger.
Plassmann, Reinhard, jt. ed. see Olbrich, Dieter.
Plaster. Soil Science. 1997. pap. text, teacher ed. 12.75 (*0-8273-8228-6*) Delmar.
Plaster, David R. Ordinances: What Are They? 1985. pap. 7.99 (*0-88469-164-0*) BMH Bks.
Plaster, Edward. Soils: Science & Management. LC 85-4486. 352p. (C). 1985. text 41.95 (*0-8273-2406-5*) Delmar.
— Soils: Science & Management. LC 85-4486. 352p. (C). 1985. teacher ed. 12.00 (*0-8273-2407-3*) Delmar.
Plaster, Edward F. Soil Science & Management. 3rd ed. (Agriculture Ser.). 1997. mass mkt., lab manual ed. 16.00 (*0-8273-7864-5*) Delmar.
Plaster, Edward J. Soil Science & Management. 2nd ed. 1991. pap., teacher ed. 12.75 (*0-8273-4051-6*); mass mkt. 44.75 (*0-8273-4050-8*) Delmar.
— Soil Science & Management. 3rd ed. LC 96-8875. (Agriculture Ser.). 416p. 1996. pap. 78.95 (*0-8273-7293-0*) Delmar.
— Soil Science & Management. 3rd ed. (Agriculture Ser.). 1997. teacher ed. 13.95 (*0-8273-7294-9*) Delmar.
Plaster, H. J. Blast Cleaning & Allied Processes, 2 vols., Set. 826p. (C). 1989. 370.00 (*0-901994-03-0*, Pub. by Fuel Metallurgical Jrnl) St Mut.

P

Plaster, John. Sog: The Secret Wars of America's Commandos in Vietnam. 384p. 1998. mass mkt. 6.99 (*0-451-19508-6*, Sig) NAL.

Plaster, John L. SOG: A Photo History of the Secret Wars. (Illus.). 496p. 79.95 (*1-58160-058-5*) Paladin Pr.

Plaster, John L. Sog: The Secret Wars of America's Commandos in Vietnam. LC 96-34557. 1997. 25.00 (*0-684-81105-7*) S&S Trade.

— Ultimate Sniper: An Advanced Training Manual for Military & Police Snipers. (Illus.). 464p. 1993. pap. 42.95 (*0-87364-704-1*) Paladin Pr.

Plasterer, Nicholas N. Assignment Jonesville: A News Reporting Workbook. 2nd ed. xii, 210p. (C). 1971. pap. text 16.95 (*0-8071-0037-4*) La State U Pr.

Plastic Design Library Staff, jt. ed. see Woishnis, William A.

Plastics Committee D-20, ed. Bibliography on Size Exclusion Chromatography (Gel Permeation Chromatography) - AMD 40-S3. LC 85-6242. (Atomic & Molecular Data Series AMD-S3). 298p. 1985. pap. text 29.00 (*0-8031-0439-1*, \) ASTM.

Plastics Design Library Staff. Chemical Resistance: Thermoplastics, Thermosets, Thermoplastic Elastomers, Rubbers, Vol. 3. (PDL Handbook Ser.). 850p. 2000. 285.00 (*1-884207-83-9*) William Andrew.

— Chemical Resistance Vol. I: Thermoplastics, Vol. 1. 2nd ed. (PDL Handbook Ser.). 1100p. 1994. text 285.00 (*1-884207-12-X*, 6531U) William Andrew.

— Chemical Resistance Vol. II: Elastomers, Thermosets, & Rubbers, Vol. 2. 2nd ed. LC 94-65726. (PDL Handbook Ser.). 977p. 1994. text 285.00 (*1-884207-13-8*, 6533U) William Andrew.

— Effect of Creep, Vol. I. 425p. 1991. write for info. (*1-884207-04-9*) William Andrew.

— Effect of Creep, Vol. II. 100p. 1991. write for info. (*1-884207-05-7*) William Andrew.

— Effect of Creep & Other Time Related Factors on Plastics & Elastomers, 2 vols., Set. (PDL Handbook Ser.). 528p. 1991. spiral bd. 285.00 (*1-884207-03-0*) William Andrew.

— Effect of Sterilization Methods on Plastics & Elastomers. (PDL Handbook Ser.). 470p. 1994. text 285.00 (*1-884207-10-3*) William Andrew.

— Effect of Temperature, Vol. I. 380p. 1990. write for info. (*1-884207-07-3*) William Andrew.

— Effect of Temperature, Vol. II. 100p. 1990. write for info. (*1-884207-08-1*) William Andrew.

— Effect of Temperature & Other Factors on Plastics & Elastomers, 2 vols., Set. (PDL Handbook Ser.). 474p. 1991. spiral bd. 285.00 (*1-884207-06-5*) William Andrew.

— Effect of UV Light & Weather on Plastics & Elastomers. (PDL Handbook Ser.). 481p. 1994. text 285.00 (*1-884207-11-1*) William Andrew.

— Fatigue & Tribological Properties of Plastics & Elastomers. LC 94-66603. (PDL Handbook Ser.). 549p. 1995. text 285.00 (*1-884207-15-4*) William Andrew.

— Handbook of Plastics Joinings: A Practical Guide. LC 97-65526. (PDL Handbook Ser.). 600p. 1997. 285.00 (*1-884207-17-0*) William Andrew.

— Permeability & Other Film Properties of Plastics & Elastomers. (PDL Handbook Ser.). 716p. 1995. text 285.00 (*1-884207-14-6*) William Andrew.

Plastics Education Foundation Staff. Curriculum Guide for Plastics Education. LC 77-4080. 1977. pap. write for info. (*0-672-97113-5*) Macmillan.

Plastics Institute of America Staff. FoodPlas VIII-91: Proceedings of the Annual FoodPlas Conference, 8th. 1991. pap. 29.95 (*0-87762-866-1*) Technomic.

Plastino, Ben J. Coming of Age: Idaho Falls & the Idaho National Engineering Laboratory. Graves, Diane P., ed. LC 98-72266. 132p. 1998. pap. 7.95 (*0-9664842-0-7*) Diane P Graves.

Plastino, Janice G., jt. auth. see Penrod, James.

***Plastock, R. A.** Schaum's Outline of Computer Graphics. 2nd ed. 352p. 2000. 16.95 (*0-07-135781-5*, Schaums Outlne) McGraw-Hill Prof.

Plastock, R. A. & Kalley, G. Schaum's Outline of Computer Graphics. (Schaum's Outline Ser.). 288p. (C). 1986. pap. 14.95 (*0-07-050326-5*) McGraw.

Plastow. Church Life Sketches & Skits. 1995. pap. 24.95 (*1-57320-039-5*) PraiseGathering.

— Proverbs & Be-Act-itudes. 1995. pap. 24.95 (*1-57320-040-9*) PraiseGathering.

— Sunday Morning Sketches & Skits. 1995. pap. 24.95 (*1-57320-042-5*) PraiseGathering.

— Tough Topics: Skits. 1995. pap. 24.95 (*1-57320-044-1*) PraiseGathering.

Plastow, Jane, jt. ed. see Boon, Richard.

Plastow, John. Teen Life 1: Skits. 1995. pap. 24.95 (*1-57320-045-X*) PraiseGathering.

— Teen Life 2: Skits. 1995. pap. 24.95 (*1-57320-046-8*) PraiseGathering.

Plastow, John R. Football, Pizza & Success! 130p. (Orig.). 1987. pap. 5.95 (*0-937382-03-5*) Rhinos Pr.

Plastow, Michael. Exploring Kanto: Weekend Pilgrimages from Tokyo. (Illus.). 256p. (Orig.). 1996. pap. 19.95 (*0-8348-0332-1*) Weatherhill.

— Exploring Kiryu, Ashio & Nikko: Mountain Walks in the Land of Shodo Shonin. (Exploring Japan Ser.). (Illus.). 272p. (Orig.). (C). 1992. pap. 19.95 (*0-8348-0242-2*) Weatherhill.

Plastrik, Peter, jt. auth. see Osborne, David.

Plastrik, Peter, jt. auth. see Sykes, Gary.

Plat, Hugh. Floures of Philosophie. LC 81-21324. 312p. 1982. reprint ed. 50.00 (*0-8201-1374-3*) Schol Facsimiles.

Plat, R. Gravitational & Centrifugal Oil-Water Separators with Plate Pack Internals. 172p. (Orig.). 1994. pap. 52.50 (*90-6275-985-8*, Pub. by Delft U Pr) Coronet Bks.

Plata, Maria C. Justice for Whom? 1997. pap. write for info. (*1-86106-111-0*, Pub. by Minerva Pr) Unity Dist.

Plata, Maximino, jt. auth. see Elliot, Norbert.

Plata, Sababu N., ed. see Robinson, Helen.

Plata, Sababu N., ed. see Spencer-Strachan, Louise.

Plata, Sababu N., ed. see Wilson, Ames N.

Plata, Sababu N., ed. see Wilson, Amos N.

Platania, Jon & Lee, Joe. Jung for Beginners. (for Beginners Ser.). (Illus.). 176p. 1997. 11.00 (*0-86316-184-7*) Writers & Readers.

Plataniotis, K., jt. auth. see Venetsanoupoulos, A.

Platanov, K. K. Concise Dictionary of the System of Psychological Understanding. 2nd ed. (RUS.). 174p. 1984. 12.95 (*0-8288-2212-3*, M15380) Fr & Eur.

Plate, Erich J. Aerodynamic Characteristics of Atmospheric Boundary Layers. LC 70-611329. (AEC Critical Review Ser.). 190p. 1971. pap. 12.75 (*0-87079-132-X*, TID-25465); fiche 9.00 (*0-87079-133-8*, TID-25465) DOE.

— Buoyant Convection in Geophysical Flows. LC 98-24600. (NATO ASI Series). 491p. 1998. write for info. (*0-7923-5176-2*) Kluwer Academic.

Plate, Erich J., jt. ed. see Duckstein, Lucien.

Plate, Kenneth H. Management Personnel in Libraries. 1970. 7.95 (*0-685-03095-4*) Am Faculty Pr.

Plate, N. A. Liquid-Crystal Polymers. (Specialty Polymers Ser.). (Illus.). 448p. (C). 1992. text 120.00 (*0-306-44219-1*, Kluwer Plenum) Kluwer Academic.

Plate, N. A. & Shibaev, V. P. Comb-Shaped Polymers & Liquid Crystals. Cowie, J. M., ed. Schnur, S. L., tr. from RUS. LC 87-18518. (Specialty Polymers Ser.). (Illus.). 428p. (C). 1987. text 150.00 (*0-306-42723-0*, Kluwer Plenum) Kluwer Academic.

Plate, Nicolai A., et al. Macromolecular Reactions: Peculiarities, Theory & Experimental Approaches. LC 94-30634. 450p. 1995. 345.00 (*0-471-94392-4*) Wiley.

Plate, Peter. Black Wheel of Anger: Three Novels. 192p. (Orig.). 1990. pap. 14.95 (*0-7486-6037-2*, Pub. by Polygon) Subterranean Co.

— Darkness Throws down the Sun. 1991. pap. 12.95 (*0-7486-6117-4*, Pub. by Edinburgh U Pr) Col U Pr.

— Joaquin (in the Fog) (Autofiction Ser.). 70p. (Orig.). (C). 1988. pap. 7.00 (*1-878124-01-3*) Flatland.

— One Foot off the Gutter. 200p. (Orig.). 1995. pap. 13.00 (*1-884615-11-2*) Incommcdo San Diego.

— Police & Thieves: A Novel. LC 98-55232. 192p. 1999. text 20.00 (*1-888363-95-9*, Pub. by Seven Stories) Publishers Group.

— Romance of the American Living Room. 192p. (Orig.). 1994. pap. 14.95 (*0-7486-6166-2*, Pub. by Polygon) Subterranean Co.

— Snitch Factory. 175p. (Orig.). 1996. pap. 13.00 (*1-888277-02-5*) Incommcdo San Diego.

***Plate, S. Brent & Jasper, David, eds.** Imag(in)ing Otherness: Filmic Visions of Living Together. LC 99-45495. (American Academy of Religion Cultural Criticism Ser.). (Illus.). 230p. 1999. pap. 29.95 (*0-7885-0593-9*, 010707) OUP.

Plateaux, L., jt. auth. see Montenat, C.

Platek, R. Small Area Statistics: An International Symposium. Singh, M. P. et al, eds. 294p. (C). 1987. reprint ed. text 47.95 (*0-471-84456-X*) Krieger.

***Platen, Angelika, photos by.** Angelika Platen - Artists: No Photos Please. (Illus.). 1999. 50.00 (*3-908161-55-X*) Abbeville Pr.

Platen, Eckhard, jt. auth. see Kloeden, Peter E.

Plater. Environmental Law 95-96. Date not set. pap. text, teacher ed. write for info. (*0-314-07624-7*) West Pub.

Plater, Alan. The Beiderbecke Connection. 2nd large type ed. 273p. 1993. 22.95 (*1-85695-360-2*, Pub. by ISIS Lrg Prnt) Transaction Pubs.

***Plater, Alan.** Close the Coalhouse Door. rev. ed. 1999. pap. 18.95 (*1-85224-489-5*) Bloodaxe Bks.

***Plater, Inge.** Green Turtle. (Illus.). 32p. (gr. 1-3). 2000. 16.00 (*0-207-19690-7*) HarpC.

Plater, Michael A. African American Entrepreneurship in Richmond, 1890-1940: The Story of R. C. Scott. LC 96-3464. (Garland Studies in Entrepreneurship). 250p. 1996. text 54.00 (*0-8153-2673-4*) Garland.

Plater, Ormonde. Deacons in the Liturgy. LC 91-39693. 80p. (Orig.). 1992. pap. 8.95 (*0-8192-1585-6*) Morehouse Pub.

— Intercession: A Practical & Theological Guide. xx, 138p. 1995. pap. 11.95 (*1-56101-115-0*) Cowley Pubns.

— Many Servants: An Introduction to Deacons. LC 91-622. 218p. (Orig.). 1991. pap. 13.95 (*1-56101-043-X*) Cowley Pubns.

Plater, William M. The Grim Phoenix: Reconstructing Thomas Pynchon. LC 77-12833. 288p. reprint ed. pap. 89.30 (*0-608-18258-3*, 205671500081) Bks Demand.

Plater-Zyberk, Elizabeth, et al. Black & White No. 3: A Journal of Architecture & Ideas. Penabad, Carie & Cure, Adib, eds. (Illus.). 52p. (Orig.). (C). 1996. pap. 10.00 (*0-9652301-8-X*) X Press FL.

Plater, Zygmunt J. Environmental Law & Policy: Nature, Law, & Society. 2nd ed. LC 98-202339. (American Casebook Ser.). xlii, 1238p. 1998. 46.50 (*0-314-21135-7*) West Pub.

Plater, Zygmunt J. & Abrams, Robert H. Environmental Law & Policy: Nature, Law & Society As a First Course, Supplementary Manual for Teaching. Goldfarb, William, ed. (American Casebook Ser.). 247p. 1992. reprint ed. pap. text write for info. (*0-314-01382-2*) West Pub.

Plater, Zygmunt J., et al. Environmental Law & Policy: Nature, Law & Society a Coursebook on Nature, Law & Society, Cases, Materials & Text. (American Casebook Ser.). 1039p. (C). 1991. reprint ed. text 51.00 (*0-314-00341-X*) West Pub.

— Environmental Law & Policy: Nature, Law & Society, Teacher's Manual to Accompany. (American Casebook Ser.). 353p. (C). 1992. pap. text, teacher ed. write for info. (*0-314-00583-8*) West Pub.

— Environmental Law & Policy & Society: Nature, Law & Society, 1994 Supplement. (American Casebook Ser.). 1039p. (C). 1994. suppl. ed. 16.50 (*0-314-04693-3*) West Pub.

Platero, Paul, jt. ed. see Fernald, Theodore B.

Platford, Gary, jt. auth. see Bayne, Allan P.

Plath, Anthony D., jt. auth. see Nunnally, Bennie.

Plath, Anthony D., jt. auth. see Nunnally, Bennie, Jr.

Plath, David W. The After Hours: Modern Japan & the Search for Enjoyment. LC 83-22869. 222p. 1984. reprint ed. lib. bdg. 55.00 (*0-313-24297-6*, PLAF, Greenwood Pr) Greenwood.

— Long Engagements: Maturity in Modern Japan. 248p. 1980. pap. 12.95 (*0-8047-1176-3*) Stanford U Pr.

Plath, David W., ed. Work & Lifecourse in Japan. LC 82-10481. (Illus.). 267p. (C). 1984. pap. text 21.95 (*0-87395-705-9*) State U NY Pr.

***Plath, Gloria.** Feathers of My Wings. 1999. pap. write for info. (*1-58235-397-2*) Watermrk Pr.

Plath, Iona. Decorative Arts of Sweden. (Illus.). 218p. 1965. pap. 9.95 (*0-486-21478-8*) Dover.

Plath, James, ed. Conversations with John Updike. LC 94-44741. (Literary Conversations Ser.). 308p. 1994. pap. 17.00 (*0-87805-700-5*) U Pr of Miss.

Plath, James & Simons, Frank D. Remembering Ernest Hemingway. LC 99-27999. 11p. 1999. 19.95 (*0-9641735-5-7*, Pub. by Ketch & Yawl); pap. 12.95 (*0-9641735-6-5*, Pub. by Ketch & Yawl) KWIB.

Plath, Roger, et al. Guyana Election Assistance Project: Final Report, October 1990-November 1992. viii, 194p. 1992. pap. text 22.00 (*1-879720-41-8*) Intl Fndt Elect.

Plath, Roger H. Honduras: Electoral Training Project, September to December 1993. iv, 58p. 1994. pap. text 8.00 (*1-879720-43-4*) Intl Fndt Elect.

Plath, Sylvia. Ariel. 1999. reprint ed. 21.95 (*1-56849-723-7*) Buccaneer Bks.

— Ariel: Perennial Classics Edition. LC 98-56144. 128p. 1999. pap. 11.00 (*0-06-093172-8*) HarpC.

— The Bed Book. LC 76-3825. (Illus.). 40p. (J). (ps-3). 1976. 12.95 (*0-06-024746-0*) HarpC Child Bks.

***Plath, Sylvia.** The Bed Book. (J). 1999. write for info. (*0-316-71228-0*) Little.

Plath, Sylvia. The Bell Jar. (Illus.). 224p. 1978. mass mkt. 7.50 (*0-553-27835-5*, Bantam Classics) Bantam.

***Plath, Sylvia.** The Bell Jar. LC 98-27309. 1998. 17.00 (*0-375-40463-5*) Everymns Lib.

Plath, Sylvia. The Bell Jar. 1972. 11.09 (*0-606-02294-5*, Pub. by Turtleback) Demco.

— The Bell Jar. large type ed. LC 96-43537. (Perennial Ser.). 313p. 1996. 22.95 (*0-7838-1987-0*) Thorndike Pr.

— The Bell Jar. 300p. 1991. reprint ed. lib. bdg. 27.95 (*0-89966-815-1*) Buccaneer Bks.

— The Bell Jar. 20th anniversary ed. 320p. 1996. 20.00 (*0-06-017490-0*) HarpC.

— The Bell Jar: A Novel. 288p. 2000. pap. 13.00 (*0-06-093018-7*, Perennial) HarperTrade.

— Colleced Poems Reissue. LC 75-25075. Vol. 900. 352p. 1992. pap. 17.50 (*0-06-090900-5*, CN 900, Perennial) HarperTrade.

— Collected Poems. 1998. reprint ed. 39.95 (*1-56849-703-2*) Buccaneer Bks.

— The Colossus. 1991. reprint ed. lib. bdg. 29.95 (*1-56849-040-2*) Buccaneer Bks.

— The Colossus & Other Poems. 84p. 1968. pap. 9.00 (*0-394-70466-5*) Vin Bks.

— The Colossus & Other Poems. LC 98-160899. 1998. pap. 12.00 (*0-375-70446-9*) Vin Bks.

— Crossing the Water. LC 71-138756. 64p. 1980. pap. 10.00 (*0-06-090789-4*, CN 789, Perennial) HarperTrade.

Plath, Sylvia. Johnny Panic & the Bible of Dreams. 1994. lib. bdg. 37.95 (*1-56849-385-1*) Buccaneer Bks.

— Johnny Panic & the Bible of Dreams: Short Stories, Prose & Diary Excerpts. 336p. 2000. pap. 14.00 (*0-06-095529-5*, Perennial) HarperTrade.

Plath, Sylvia. The Journals of Sylvia Plath. McCullough, Frances, ed. LC 98-15790. 384p. 1998. pap. 12.95 (*0-385-49391-6*) Doubleday.

— Letters Home: Correspondence, 1950-1963. LC 91-58567. (Illus.). 512p. 1992. reprint ed. pap. 17.00 (*0-06-097491-5*, Perennial) HarperTrade.

***Plath, Sylvia.** Plath: Poems. LC 98-23336. 1998. 12.50 (*0-375-40464-3*) Everymns Lib.

Plath, Tony & Nunnally, Bennie, eds. Cases in Finance. LC 94-27736. 400p. (C). 1994. text 25.75 (*0-256-12338-1*, Irwn McGrw-H) McGrw-H Hghr Educ.

Platiere, Marie J. Roland De La, see Roland De La Platiere, Marie J.

***Platinum Media Inc. Staff.** Modeling & Talent World Book. Huhn, Laura & Dillon, Michael, eds. 320p. 1999. per. 44.95 (*0-9670588-0-5*) Platinum Media.

Platinum Press Staff. Dates to Remember. 128p. 1996. 5.95 (*1-879582-22-8*) Platinum Pr.

— Journal. 128p. 1996. 5.95 (*1-879582-23-6*) Platinum Pr.

— Telephone Address Books. 128p. 1996. 5.95 (*1-879582-24-4*) Platinum Pr.

— U. S. Army Survival Manual. 416p. 1997. 29.95 (*1-879582-00-7*) Platinum Pr.

Platizky, Roger S. A Blueprint of His Dissent: Madness & Method in Tennyson's Poetry. LC 87-46433. 144p. 1989. 28.50 (*0-8387-5151-2*) Bucknell U Pr.

***Platka-Bird, Lorraine.** The Just-in-Case Food Pantry: A Common-Sense Guide for Y2K or Any Other Emergency. (Illus.). 56p. 1999. 7.50 (*0-912986-33-6*) Am Media.

Platke, Marilee J. The Elementary School Play. 64p. 1981. 10.00 (*0-87879-906-0*) Acad Therapy.

Platko, Elizabeth, jt. auth. see Starbuck, Marjorie.

Platnauer, M., ed. Aristophanes: Peace. (Bristol Greek Texts Ser.). (GRE.). 202p. 1981. reprint ed. pap. text 27.95 (*0-86292-001-9*, Pub. by Brist Class Pr) Focus Pub-R Pullins.

Platnauer, Maurice, tr. Poems, 2 vols., 1. (Loeb Classical Library: No. 135, 136). 420p. 1922. 18.95 (*0-674-99150-8*) HUP.

— Poems, 2 vols., 2. (Loeb Classical Library: No. 135, 136). 420p. 1922. 18.95 (*0-674-99151-6*) HUP.

Platner, Ernst. Antropologic Fuer Aerzte und Weltweise: Erster Theil. (GER.). xxxviii, 300p. 1998. reprint ed. write for info. (*3-487-10586-1*) G Olms Pubs.

Platnick, A. Joseph. Index to the Code of Jewish Law. 233p. 1989. text 19.95 (*0-9626361-0-X*) A J Platnick.

Platnick, Norman I. Advances in Spider Taxonomy 1988-1991: With Synonymies & Transfers 1940-1980. Merrett, P., ed. 864p. 1993. text 75.00 (*0-913424-10-2*) Am Mus Natl Hist.

Platnick, Norman I. & Funk, Vicki A., eds. Advances in Cladistics Vol. 2: Proceedings of the Second Meeting of the Willi Hennig Society. 288p. 1983. text 71.50 (*0-231-05646-X*) Col U Pr.

Plato. Anonymer Kommentar Zu Platons Theaetet. (GER.). xxxvii, 62p. 1905. write for info. (*0-318-70540-0*) G Olms Pubs.

— Apologia de Socrates. Criton. Carta VII. Lopez Castellon, Enrique, ed. & tr. by. (Nueva Austral Ser.: Vol. 164). (SPA.). 1991. pap. text 24.95 (*84-239-1964-1*) Elliots Bks.

— The Apologia of Plato. Riddell, James, ed. (GER.). 244p. 1974. reprint ed. 50.70 (*3-487-05225-3*) G Olms Pubs.

— The Apology of Plato: With a Revised Text & English Notes, & a Digest of Platonic Idioms. LC 72-9300. (Philosophy of Plato & Aristotle Ser.). (ENG & GRE.). 1977. reprint ed. 19.95 (*0-405-04855-6*) Ayer.

— Apology of Socrates & Crito. Dyer, Louis, ed. (College Classical Ser.). 246p. (C). 1992. reprint ed. pap. 17.50 (*0-89241-345-X*); reprint ed. lib. bdg. 32.50 (*0-89241-000-0*) Caratzas.

— The Apology of Socrates & The Crito. rev. ed. Ash, A. S., ed. Jowett, Benjamin, tr. from GRE. LC 86-64057. (Humanist Classics Ser.). 48p. 1990. pap. 6.95 (*0-942208-05-6*) Bandanna Bks.

— The Being of the Beautiful: Plato's Theaetetus, Sophist, & Statesman. LC 83-18318. (Illus.). 592p. reprint ed. pap. 183.60 (*0-608-09500-1*, 205430100005) Bks Demand.

— Charmides. West, Thomas G. & West, Grace S., eds. & trs. by. from GRE. LC 85-24934. (HPC Classics Ser.). 60p. (Orig.). (C). 1986. pap. text 5.95 (*0-87220-010-8*); lib. bdg. 24.95 (*0-87220-011-6*) Hackett Pub.

— Complete Works. Cooper, John M., ed. LC 96-53280. 1848p. 1997. lib. bdg. 45.00 (*0-87220-349-2*) Hackett Pub.

— Concordantiae in Platonis Opera Omnia Pt. 1: Euthyphro. Siviero, Mauro, ed. (Alpha-Omega, Reihe A Ser.: Bd. CX). (GER.). 180p. 1990. write for info. incl. 3.5 hd (*3-487-09360-X*) G Olms Pubs.

— Cratylus. Reeve, C. D., tr. from GRE. LC 98-37806. (Classics Ser.). 290p. (C). 1998. pap. 12.95 (*0-87220-416-2*); lib. bdg. 29.95 (*0-87220-417-0*) Hackett Pub.

— Defence of Socrates: Euthyphro, Crito. Gallop, David, ed. & tr. by. (Oxford World's Classics Ser.). 160p. 1999. pap. 9.95 (*0-19-283864-4*) OUP.

— Dialogos (Gorgias - Fedon - el Banquete) Roig de Lluis, Luis, tr. (Nueva Austral Ser.: Vol. 22). (SPA.). 1991. pap. text 24.95 (*84-239-1822-X*) Elliots Bks.

— The Dialogues of Plato. Kaplan, Justin E., ed. Jowett, Benjamin E., tr. 400p. (C). 1984. mass mkt. 5.99 (*0-671-52524-7*, WSP) PB.

— Early Socratic Dialogues. Saunders, Trevor J., ed. 400p. 1987. pap. 12.95 (*0-14-044447-5*, Penguin Classics) Viking Penguin.

— Euthydemus. Sprague, Rosamond K., tr. LC 65-26539. (Orig.). 1965. pap. 2.30 (*0-672-60478-7*, LLA222, Bobbs) Macmillan.

— Euthydemus. Sprague, Rosamond K., tr. from GRE. LC 93-14427. (Hackett Classics Ser.). 96p. (Orig.). (C). 1993. reprint ed. pap. text 5.95 (*0-87220-234-8*); reprint ed. lib. bdg. 24.95 (*0-87220-235-6*) Hackett Pub.

— The Euthydemus of Plato. LC 72-9288. (Philosophy of Plato & Aristotle Ser.). (ENG & GRE.). 1977. reprint ed. 22.95 (*0-405-04838-6*) Ayer.

— Euthyphro. Burnet, John, ed. 228p. 1977. pap. text 23.00 (*0-19-814015-0*) OUP.

— Euthyphro, Apology & Crito. Stawell, Florence M., tr. LC 73-174210. (Temple Greek & Latin Classics: No. 2). reprint ed. 29.50 (*0-404-07902-4*) AMS Pr.

— Euthyphro, Apology & Crito: With the Death Scene from Phaedo. Church, F. J. & Cummings, R. D., trs. (gr. 9). 1956. pap. 3.50 (*0-672-60166-4*, LLA4) Macmillan.

— Euthyphro, Crito, Apology, & Symposium. LC 53-8797. 142p. 1953. reprint ed. pap. 9.95 (*0-89526-916-3*) Regnery Pub.

— Five Dialogues: Apology, Crito, Euthyphro, Meno & Phaedo. Grube, G. M., tr. from GRE. LC 81-82275. (HPC Classics Ser.). 168p. (C). 1981. text 27.95 (*0-915145-23-5*); pap. text 5.95 (*0-915145-22-7*) Hackett Pub.

— Gorgias. Nichols, James H., Jr., tr. & intro. by. LC 98-26833. (Agora Editions Ser.). 320p. 1998. pap. text 9.95 (*0-8014-8527-4*) Cornell U Pr.

Plato. Gorgias. Irwin, Terence H., tr. from GRE. (Clarendon Plato Ser.). 280p. 1980. pap. text 35.00 (*0-19-872091-2*) OUP.

Plato. Gorgias. Zeyl, Donald J., ed. & tr. by. from GRE. LC 86-14946. (HPC Classics Ser.). 132p. (C). 1986. pap. text 5.95 (*0-87220-016-7*) Hackett Pub.

— Gorgias: A Revised Text. Dodds, E. R., ed. (Illus.). 414p. 1990. reprint ed. pap. text 34.00 (*0-19-814495-4*) OUP.

An Asterisk (*) at the beginning of an entry indicates that the title is appearing for the first time.

— Gorgias: And, Phaedrus. Nichols, James H., Jr., tr. & intro. by. LC 98-26830. (Agora Editions Ser.). 144p. 1998. 45.00 (*0-8014-3530-7*) Cornell U Pr.

— Gorgias: And, Phaedrus. Waterfield, Robin, ed. (Oxford World's Classics Ser.). 214p. 1998. pap. 7.95 (*0-19-283630-7*) OUP.

— Gorgias: Translated (from the ancient Greek) Hamilton, Walter, tr. & intro. by. (Classics Ser.). 160p. 1960. pap. 8.95 (*0-14-044094-1*, Penguin Classics) Viking Penguin.

— The Gorgias of Plato. LC 72-9308. (Philosophy of Plato & Aristotle Ser.). (ENG & GRE.). 1980. reprint ed. 28.95 (*0-405-04867-X*) Ayer.

— Hippias Major. LC 81-7027. (HPC Classics Ser.). 232p. (C). 1982. 34.95 (*0-915145-25-1*) Hackett Pub.

— The Hippias Major Attributed to Plato. LC 75-13284. (History of Ideas in Ancient Greece Ser.). (ENG & GRE.). 1978. reprint ed. 21.95 (*0-405-07326-7*) Ayer.

— Ion & Hippias Major: Two Comic Diaglogues. Woodruff, Paul, tr. from GRE. LC 83-269. (HPC Classics Ser.). 93p. (C). 1983. lib. bdg. 27.95 (*0-915145-76-6*) Hackett Pub.

— Ion & Hippias Major: Two Comic Dialogues. Woodruff, Paul, tr. from GRE. LC 83-269. (HPC Classics Ser.). 93p. (C). 1983. pap. text 6.95 (*0-915145-77-4*) Hackett Pub.

— Laches & Charmides. Sprague, Rosamond K., tr. from GRE. & intro. by. LC 92-6207. 112p. (C). 1992. reprint ed. pap. text 6.95 (*0-87220-134-1*); reprint ed. lib. bdg. 24.95 (*0-87220-135-X*) Hackett Pub.

— The Last Days of Socrates. Tredennick, Hugh & Tarrant, Harold, trs. 256p. 1993. pap. 11.95 (*0-14-044582-X*, Penguin Classics) Viking Penguin.

***Plato.** Laws. Jowett, Benjamin, tr. LC 99-87820. (Great Books in Philosophy Ser.). 305p. 2000. pap. 9.95 (*1-57392-799-6*) Prometheus Bks.

Plato. Laws. Saunders, Trevor J., tr. from GRE. & intro. by. (Classics Ser.). 558p. 1970. pap. 11.95 (*0-14-044222-7*, Penguin Classics) Viking Penguin.

— The Laws of Plato. Pangle, Thomas L., tr. & notes by. xiv, 576p. 1988. pap. text 22.50 (*0-226-67110-0*) U Ch Pr.

— The Laws of Plato, 2 vols. LC 75-13285. (History of Ideas in Ancient Greece Ser.). 1979. reprint ed. 82.95 (*0-405-07327-5*) Ayer.

— Libro Llamado Fedron: Plato's Phaedo. Round, Nicholas G., ed. (Textos B Ser.: No. 39). (SPA.). 406p. 1993. 75.00 (*1-85566-024-5*) Boydell & Brewer.

— Meno. Sharples, R. W., ed. 1985. 49.00 (*0-86516-089-9*) Bolchazy-Carducci.

— Meno: Text & Critical Essays. Brown, Malcolm, ed. Guthrie, William K., tr. from GRE. LC 78-162302. (Text & Commentary Ser.). (C). 1971. pap. 6.00 (*0-672-61123-6*, TC10, Bobbs) Macmillan.

— Oeuvres. (Vol. 1). (FRE.). 1940. lib. bdg. 95.00 (*0-8288-3572-1*, F17630) Fr & Eur.

— Oeuvres. (Vol. 2). (FRE.). 1977. lib. bdg. 110.00 (*0-8288-3573-X*, F17180) Fr & Eur.

— Oeuvres Completes: Hippias, Protagoras, l'Apologie de Socrates, Criton, Le Banquet, Phedon, La Republique etc., Vol. 1. 1472p. 39.95 (*0-686-56548-7*) Fr & Eur.

— Oeuvres Completes: Theetete, Parmenide, Critias, les Lois, etc., Vol. 2. 1676p. 42.95 (*0-686-56549-5*) Fr & Eur.

— On Homosexuality: Lysis, Phaedrus & Symposium. Jowett, Benjamin & O'Connor, Eugene, trs. LC 90-63048. (Great Books in Philosophy). 157p. (Orig.). (C). 1991. pap. 6.95 (*0-87975-632-2*) Prometheus Bks.

— Parmenides. Gill, Mary L. & Ryan, Paul, trs. LC 95-48981. 144p. 1996. pap. text 9.95 (*0-87220-328-X*); lib. bdg. 32.95 (*0-87220-329-8*) Hackett Pub.

— Phaedo. Hackforth, R., ed. 200p. (C). 1972. pap. 15.95 (*0-521-09702-9*) Cambridge U Pr.

— Phaedo. Gallop, David, tr. & notes by. (Clarendon Plato Ser). 254p. 1977. pap. text 24.95 (*0-19-872049-1*) OUP.

***Plato.** Phaedo. Gallop, David, ed. (Oxford World's Classics Ser.). 136p. 1999. pap. 8.95 (*0-19-283953-5*) OUP.

Plato. Phaedo. Burnet, John, ed. 218p. 1979. reprint ed. pap. text 19.95 (*0-19-814014-2*) OUP.

— The Phaedo of Plato. LC 72-9280. (Philosophy of Plato & Aristotle Ser.). 1977. reprint ed. 22.95 (*0-405-04831-9*) Ayer.

— Phaedrus. Nehamas, Alexander & Woodruff, Paul, trs. from GRE. LC 94-46613. (HPC Classics Ser.). 240p. (C). 1995. text 27.95 (*0-87220-221-6*); pap. text 6.95 (*0-87220-220-8*) Hackett Pub.

— Phaedrus. Hackforth, R., ed. 172p. (C). 1972. pap. text 15.95 (*0-521-09703-7*) Cambridge U Pr.

***Plato.** Phaedrus. Nichols, James H., Jr., tr. & intro. by. LC 98-27372. (Agora Editions Ser.). 224p. 1998. pap. text 9.95 (*0-8014-8532-0*) Cornell U Pr.

Plato. Phaedrus, & The Seventh & Eighth Letters. Hamilton, Walter, tr. & intro. by. (Classics Ser.). 160p. (Orig.). 1973. pap. 13.99 (*0-14-044275-8*, Penguin Classics) Viking Penguin.

— Philebus. Frede, Dorothea, tr. & intro. by. LC 93-587. 150p. 1993. pap. text 9.95 (*0-87220-170-8*); lib. bdg. 32.95 (*0-87220-171-6*) Hackett Pub.

— Philebus. Waterfield, Robin A., tr. from GRE. LC 83-164424. 160p. 1983. pap. 9.95 (*0-14-044395-9*, Penguin Classics) Viking Penguin.

— The Philebus of Plato. Bury, Robert G., ed. LC 72-9284. (Philosophy of Plato & Aristotle Ser.). (ENG & GRE.). 1977. reprint ed. 25.95 (*0-405-04834-3*) Ayer.

— Plato: Apology. rev. ed. (ENG & GRE.). viii, 127p. 1997. pap. text 15.00 (*0-86516-348-0*) Bolchazy-Carducci.

— Plato: Apology of Socrates. Stokes, M. C., ed. & tr. by. (Classical Texts Ser.). 1997. 59.99 (*0-85668-371-X*, Pub. by Aris & Phillips); pap. 28.00 (*0-85668-372-8*, Pub. by Aris & Phillips) David Brown.

— Plato: Meno. Sharples, R. W., ed. (Classical Texts Ser.). 1985. 59.99 (*0-85668-248-9*, Pub. by Aris & Phillips); pap. 28.00 (*0-85668-249-7*, Pub. by Aris & Phillips) David Brown.

— Plato: Phaedrus. Rowe, C. J., ed. (Classical Texts Ser.). 1986. 59.99 (*0-85668-313-2*, Pub. by Aris & Phillips); pap. 28.00 (*0-85668-314-0*, Pub. by Aris & Phillips) David Brown.

— Plato: Statesman. Rowe, C. J., ed. & tr. by. from GRE. (Classical Texts Ser.). 256p. 1995. 59.99 (*0-85668-612-3*, Pub. by Aris & Phillips); pap. 28.00 (*0-85668-613-1*, Pub. by Aris & Phillips) David Brown.

— Plato: The Martyrdom of Socrates. Doherty, F., ed. (Bristol Greek Texts Ser.). (GRE.). 112p. 1981. reprint ed. 16.95 (*0-906515-96-3*, Pub. by Brist Class Pr) Focus Pub-R Pullins.

— Plato V: Republic. Halliwell, ed. 1992. pap. 28.00 (*0-85668-536-4*, Pub. by Aris & Phillips) David Brown.

— Plato X: Republic. Halliwell, S., ed. (Classical Texts Ser.). 1986. 59.99 (*0-85668-405-8*, Pub. by Aris & Phillips) David Brown.

— Plato X: Republic. Halliwell, F. S., ed. (Classical Texts Ser.). 1986. pap. 28.00 (*0-85668-406-6*, Pub. by Aris & Phillips) David Brown.

***Plato.** Plato, Clitophon. Slings, S. R., ed. LC 98-52085. (Cambridge Classical Texts & Commentaries Ser.: No. 37). 364p. (C). 1999. 69.95 (*0-521-62368-5*) Cambridge U Pr.

Plato. Plato on Poetry. Murray, Penelope, ed. (Greek & Latin Classics Ser.). 260p. (C). 1996. text 64.95 (*0-521-34182-5*) Cambridge U Pr.

— Plato on Rhetoric & Language: Four Key Dialogues. LC 98-46510. 300p. 1998. pap. write for info. (*1-880393-33-6*) L Erlbaum Assocs.

— The Plato Reader. Chappell, Tim, ed. & tr. by. 320p. 1996. pap. 24.50 (*0-7486-0788-9*, Pub. by Edinburgh U Pr) Col U Pr.

Plato. Plato Reader, . Levinson, Ronald B., ed. (YA). (gr. 9 up). 1967. pap. 13.96 (*0-395-05197-5*, RivEd) HM.

— Plato the Apology. abr. ed. Jowett, Benjamin E., tr. LC 78-752121. 1972. audio 22.00 (*0-694-50405-X*, SWC 2050, Caedmon) HarperAudio.

Plato. The Platonic Epistles. Harward, J., tr. LC 75-13287. (History of Ideas in Ancient Greece Ser.). 1979. reprint ed. 26.95 (*0-405-07330-5*) Ayer.

— Platonis Opera. 2nd ed. Duke, E. A. et al, eds. (Classical Texts Ser.). 604p. 1995. text 36.00 (*0-19-814569-1*) OUP.

— Plato's Apology of Socrates: An Interpretation, with a New Translation. LC 78-11532. 240p. 1979. text 37.50 (*0-8014-1127-0*) Cornell U Pr.

— Plato's Dialogue of the Immortality of the Soul. LC 73-161797. (Augustan Translators Ser.). reprint ed. 49.50 (*0-404-54134-8*) AMS Pr.

— Plato's Euthyphro. LC 75-13272. (History of Ideas in Ancient Greece Ser.). (ENG & GRE.). 1978. reprint ed. 16.95 (*0-405-07313-5*) Ayer.

— Plato's Euthyphro, Apology & Crito, Set. unabridged ed. (Theater of the Mind Ser.). 69p. 1995. pap. 12.50 incl. audio (*1-887250-05-0*) Agora Pubns.

— Plato's Euthyphro, Apology of Socrates & Crito. Burnet, John, ed. LC 76-29434. reprint ed. 45.00 (*0-404-15322-4*) AMS Pr.

— Plato's Gorgias. unabridged ed. (Theater of the Mind Ser.). 114p. (C). 1994. pap. 12.50 incl. audio (*1-887250-01-8*) Agora Pubns.

— Plato's Ion & Meno. unabridged ed. Jowett, Benjamin, tr. (Theater of the Mind Ser.). (Illus.). 77p. (gr. 7 up). 1998. pap. 12.50 incl. audio (*1-887250-10-7*) Agora Pubns.

— Plato's Meno. 2nd ed. Grube, G. M., tr. from GRE. LC 76-40412. (HPC Classics Ser.). 48p. (C). 1980. pap. 3.95 (*0-915144-24-7*) Hackett Pub.

— Plato's Parmenides. rev. ed. Allen, R. E., tr. from GEC. & comment by. LC 97-128617. (Dialogues of Plato Ser.: Vol. 4). 384p. 1997. 45.00 (*0-300-06616-3*) Yale U Pr.

— Plato's Phaedo. Grube, G. M., tr. LC 76-49565. (HPC Classics Ser.). 72p. (C). 1980. pap. 4.25 (*0-915144-18-2*) Hackett Pub.

— Plato's Protagoras: A Socratic Commentary. Hubbard, B. A., ed. LC 83-18122. xvi, 172p. 1993. pap. text 11.95 (*0-226-67036-8*) U Ch Pr.

— Plato's Republic, Bks. 1 & 2. unabridged ed. (Theater of the Mind Ser.). 102p. (YA). (gr. 7 up). 1997. pap. 12.50 incl. audio (*1-887250-07-7*) Agora Pubns.

— Plato's Republic Vol. 2: The Greek Text, Volume II; Essays. Jowett, Benjamin E. & Campbell, Lewis, eds. LC 72-9295. (Philosophy of Plato & Aristotle Ser.). (GRE.). 1974. reprint ed. 37.95 (*0-405-04846-7*) Ayer.

— Plato's Republic for Readers: A Constitution. Blair, George A., tr. LC 98-10666. 440p. (C). 1998. pap. 36.50 (*0-7618-1044-7*) U Pr of Amer.

— Plato's Sophist. Cobb, William S., tr. 144p. (C). 1990. pap. text 14.95 (*0-8476-7653-6*) Rowman.

— Plato's Sophist. Cobb, William S., tr. & intro. by. 144p. (C). 1990. text 55.00 (*0-8476-7652-8*) Rowman.

— Plato's Statesman. Skemp, J. B., tr. LC 92-26568. 136p. (C). 1992. reprint ed. 29.95 (*0-87220-139-2*); reprint ed. pap. 7.95 (*0-87220-138-4*) Hackett Pub.

— The Portable Plato. Buchanan, Scott, ed. (Portable Library: No. 40). 696p. 1977. pap. 15.95 (*0-14-015040-4*, Penguin Bks) Viking Penguin.

— Protagoras. Taylor, C. C., tr. (The World's Classics Ser.). 122p. 1996. pap. 8.95 (*0-19-282330-2*) OUP.

— Protagoras. Lombardo, Stanley & Bell, Karen, trs. from GRE. LC 91-28322. (HPC Classics Ser.). 112p. (C). 1992. pap. text 6.95 (*0-87220-094-9*); lib. bdg. 27.95 (*0-87220-095-7*) Hackett Pub.

— Protagoras. (College Classical Ser.). ix, 232p. (C). 1984. reprint ed. pap. text 17.50 (*0-89241-387-5*) Caratzas.

— Protagoras. 2nd rev. ed. Taylor, C. C., tr. & notes by. (Clarendon Plato Ser.). 266p. 1992. pap. text 35.00 (*0-19-823934-3*) OUP.

— Protagoras & Meno. Guthrie, W. K., tr. & intro. by. (Classics Ser.). 160p. 1957. pap. 9.95 (*0-14-044068-2*, Penguin Classics) Viking Penguin.

— Protagoras, Philebus, & Gorgias. Jowett, Benjamin, tr. (Great Books in Philosophy). 213p. 1996. pap. 7.95 (*1-57392-062-2*) Prometheus Bks.

***Plato.** The Republic. Ferrari, G.R.F., ed. Griffith, Tom, tr. (Cambridge Texts in the History of Political Thought Ser.). 432p. 2000. write for info. (*0-521-48173-2*) Cambridge U Pr.

Plato. The Republic. Larson, Raymond, ed. & tr. by. LC 77-86034. (Crofts Classics). 336p. (C). 1979. pap. text 9.95 (*0-88295-118-1*) Harlan Davidson.

— The Republic. Jowett, Benjamin E., tr. 1955. pap. 6.95 (*0-394-70128-3*) Vin Bks.

— The Republic. Jowett, Benjamin, tr. LC 86-70379. (Great Books in Philosophy). 401p. 1986. pap. 9.95 (*0-87975-345-5*) Prometheus Bks.

— Republic. (Classics of World Literature Ser.). 1998. pap. 5.95 (*1-85326-483-0*, 4830WW, Pub. by Wrdsworth Edits) NTC Contemp Pub Co.

— Republic. Waterfield, Robin, tr. & intro. by. (Oxford World's Classics Ser.). (Illus.). 548p. 1998. reprint ed. pap. 7.95 (*0-19-283370-7*) OUP.

***Plato.** The Republic. rev. ed. Lee, Desmond, tr. & intro. by. (Classics Ser.). 472p. (YA). (gr. 9 up). 1998. pap. 5.33 (*0-14-044048-8*) Addson-Wesley Educ.

Plato. Republic. 2nd ed. Grube, G. M., tr. from GRE. LC 92-21578. 320p. (C). 1992. pap. text 6.95 (*0-87220-136-8*); lib. bdg. 34.95 (*0-87220-137-6*) Hackett Pub.

— The Republic, 2 vols., Vols. V & VI. write for info. (*0-318-53175-5*) HUP.

— The Republic & Other Works. Jowett, Benjamin E., tr. 560p. 1960. pap. 8.95 (*0-385-09497-3*, C12, Anchor NY) Doubleday.

— The Republic of Plato. Cornford, Francis M., ed. 396p. 1951. pap. text 11.95 (*0-19-500364-0*) OUP.

— The Republic of Plato. 2nd ed. Bloom, Allan, tr. LC 68-54141. 512p. 1991. pap. 18.00 (*0-465-06934-7*, Pub. by Basic) HarpC.

— The Roots of Political Philosophy: Ten Forgotten Socratic Dialogues translated, with interpretive studies. Pangle, Thomas L., ed. LC 87-47550. 424p. (C). 1987. pap. text 18.95 (*0-8014-9465-6*) Cornell U Pr.

— Selected Dialogues of Plato. 288p. 1999. 19.95 (*0-679-60228-3*) Modern Lib NY.

— Sophist. White, Nicholas, tr. from GRE. & intro. by. (Hackett Classics Ser.). 128p. (Orig.). (C). 1993. pap. text 9.95 (*0-87220-202-X*); lib. bdg. 28.95 (*0-87220-203-8*) Hackett Pub.

— The Sophistes & Politicus of Plato. LC 72-9286. (Philosophy of Plato & Aristotle Ser.). 1977. reprint ed. 40.95 (*0-405-04836-X*) Ayer.

— Statesman. Annas, Julia & Waterfield, Robin, eds. (Cambridge Texts in the History of Political Thought Ser.). 121p. (C). 1995. text 49.95 (*0-521-44262-1*) Cambridge U Pr.

— Statesman. Ostwald, Martin, ed. Skemp, B. J., tr. LC 57-14633. 1957. pap. 3.95 (*0-672-60230-X*, LLA57, Bobbs) Macmillan.

— Statesman. rev. ed. Rowe, Christopher, tr. from GEC. LC 99-30085. 128p. (C). 1999. pap. text, student ed. 7.95 (*0-87220-462-6*) Hackett Pub.

— Statesman. rev. ed. Rowe, Christopher, tr. from GEC. & intro. by. LC 99-30085. 128p. (C). 1999. lib. bdg., student ed. 29.95 (*0-87220-463-4*) Hackett Pub.

— Statesman & Philebus. Warmington, E. H., ed. (Loeb Classical Library: No. 164). (ENG & GRE.). 15.50 (*0-674-99182-6*) HUP.

— Symposium. Dover, Kenneth J., ed. LC 78-67430. (Cambridge Greek & Latin Classics Ser.). 196p. 1980. pap. text 22.95 (*0-521-29523-8*) Cambridge U Pr.

— Symposium. Woodruff, Paul, tr. from GRE. LC 89-30960. (HPC Classics Ser.). 110p. (C). 1989. pap. 6.95 (*0-87220-076-0*); lib. bdg. 27.95 (*0-87220-077-9*) Hackett Pub.

— Symposium. Waterfield, Robin, tr. & intro. by. (Oxford World's Classics Ser.). 160p. 1998. pap. 7.95 (*0-19-283427-4*) OUP.

***Plato.** The Symposium. Gill, Christopher, tr. from GRE. & intro. by. LC 99-462573. 144p. 1999. pap. 8.95 (*0-14-044616-8*, Penguin Classics) Viking Penguin.

Plato. Symposium & Death of Socrates. (Classics of World Literature Ser.). 1998. pap. 5.95 (*1-85326-479-2*, 4792WW, Pub. by Wrdsworth Edits) NTC Contemp Pub Co.

— Symposium & Phaedrus. 96p. 1993. reprint ed. pap. text 1.50 (*0-486-27798-4*) Dover.

— The Symposium & the Phaedo. Larson, Raymond, ed. & tr. by. LC 79-55931. (Crofts Classics). 144p. (C). 1980. pap. text 4.95 (*0-88295-122-X*) Harlan Davidson.

— The Symposium & the Phaedrus: Plato's Erotic Dialogues. LC 92-35391. (SUNY Series in Ancient Greek Philosophy). 214p. (C). 1993. pap. text 14.95 (*0-7914-1618-6*) State U NY Pr.

— Symposium of Plato. Jowett, Benjamin, tr. 1996. pap. 5.95 (*0-8283-1456-X*, 17) Branden Bks.

— The Symposium of Plato. Brentlinger, John A., ed. Groden, Suzy Q., tr. LC 79-103478. (Illus.). 144p. (C). 1970. pap. 13.95 (*0-87023-076-X*) U of Mass Pr.

— Theaetetus. Levett, M. J., tr. from GRE. LC 92-28261. 128p. (C). 1992. 27.95 (*0-87220-159-7*); pap. 7.95 (*0-87220-158-9*) Hackett Pub.

— Theaetetus. Waterfield, Robin A., ed. 256p. 1987. pap. 10.95 (*0-14-044450-5*, Penguin Classics) Viking Penguin.

— The Theaetetus of Plato. LC 72-9287. (Philosophy of Plato & Aristotle Ser.). 1977. reprint ed. 21.95 (*0-405-04837-8*) Ayer.

***Plato.** Timaeus. Zeyl, Donald J., tr. LC 99-59574. 160p. (C). 2000. pap. 10.95 (*0-87220-446-4*); lib. bdg. 29.95 (*0-87220-447-2*) Hackett Pub.

Plato. Timaeus & Critias. Lee, Desmond, tr. & intro. by. (Classics Ser.). 176p. 1972. pap. 9.95 (*0-14-044261-8*, Penguin Classics) Viking Penguin.

— Timaeus, Critias, Cleitophon, Menexenus, Epistolae, Vol. IX. (Loeb Classical Library: No. 234). 644p. 1929. text 19.95 (*0-674-99257-1*) HUP.

— The Timaeus of Plato. vii, 358p. write for info. (*0-318-71000-5*) G Olms Pubs.

— The Timaeus of Plato. (GER.). vii, 358p. 1988. write for info. (*0-318-70539-7*) G Olms Pubs.

— The Timaeus of Plato. Archer-Hind, Richard D., ed. LC 72-9281. (Philosophy of Plato & Aristotle Ser.). (ENG & GRE.). 1977. reprint ed. 32.95 (*0-405-04832-7*) Ayer.

— The Tragedy & Comedy of Life: Plato's Philebus. Benardete, Seth G., tr. LC 92-44620. (Illus.). 264p. (C). 1993. 37.50 (*0-226-04239-1*) U Ch Pr.

— The Trial & Death of Socrates: Four Dialogues. (Thrift Editions Ser.). 128p. 1992. reprint ed. pap. 1.00 (*0-486-27066-1*) Dover.

— The Trial & Death of Socrates: Plato's Euthyphro, Apology, Crito, & death scene from Phaedo. Grube, G. M., tr. from GRE. LC 75-33058. (HPC Classics Ser.). 64p. (C). 1980. pap. 3.95 (*0-915144-15-8*) Hackett Pub.

— Works of Plato. Edman, Irwin, ed. Jowett, Benjamin E., tr. 577p. (C). 1965. pap. 7.50 (*0-07-553651-X*, T71) McGraw.

— Works of Plato, 5 vols. LC 78-16080. reprint ed. 380.00 (*0-404-16360-2*) AMS Pr.

***Plato & Jowett, Benjamin.** The Republic. LC 99-56941. (Thrift Editions Ser.). 2000. pap. 2.50 (*0-486-41121-4*) Dover.

***Plato & Nussbaum, Martha.** The Republic. Ferrari, G.R.F., ed. Griffith, Tom, tr. (Cambridge Texts in the History of Political Thought Ser.). 432p. 2000. pap. 27.95 (*0-521-48443-X*) Cambridge U Pr.

***Plato & Scolnicov, Samuel.** Plato's Parmenides. LC 00-21808. 2001. write for info. (*0-520-22403-5*) U CA Pr.

Plato & Sigler, Julius A. Education: Ends & Means. 2nd ed. LC 96-25023. (Lynchburg College Symposium Readings Ser.). 1996. pap. text 26.50 (*0-7618-0452-8*) U Pr of Amer.

Plato & Strycker, Emile de. Plato's Apology of Socrates: A Literary & Philosophical Study with a Running Commentary. LC 94-20723. (Mnemosyne, Bibliotheca Classica Batava, Supplementum: Vol. 137). xvii, 405p. 1994. 135.50 (*90-04-10103-9*) Brill Academic Pubs.

Plato & Thompson, W. H. The Phaedrus of Plato. LC 72-9307. (Philosophy of Plato & Aristotle Ser.). (ENG & GRE.). 1977. reprint ed. 18.95 (*0-405-04866-1*) Ayer.

***Plato, et al.** Plato's Symposium. LC 00-32593. 2000. pap. write for info. (*0-226-04275-8*) U Ch Pr.

Plato, jt. auth. see Biffle, Christopher.

Plato, jt. auth. see Sayre, Kenneth M.

Plato, Ann. Essays. (Schomburg Library of Nineteenth-Century Black Women Writers). 177p. 1988. text 35.00 (*0-19-505247-1*) OUP.

Plato Center Grade School Third Graders. Stone Age Soccer. (WeWrite Kids! Ser.: No. 8). (Illus.). 23p. (J). (ps-3). 1994. pap. 3.95 (*1-884987-28-1*) WeWrite.

Plato, Chris C., et al. Dermatoglyphics: Science in Transition. (Birth Defects: Original Article Ser.: No. 1903). 348p. 1991. 465.00 (*0-471-56104-5*, Wiley-Liss) Wiley.

Plato, Chris C., jt. ed. see Durham, Norris M.

Plato, Chris C., jt. ed. see Wertelecki, Wladimir.

Platon. Orthodox Doctrine of the Apostolic Eastern Church. 1973. 5.00 (*0-89981-066-7*) Eastern Orthodox.

— Orthodox Doctrine of the Apostolic Eastern Church: A Compendium of Christian Theology. LC 70-81772. reprint ed. 42.50 (*0-404-05058-1*) AMS Pr.

— Present State of the Greek Church in Russia. LC 75-131031. reprint ed. 49.50 (*0-404-05059-X*) AMS Pr.

— Rules for a Pious Life. 1994. pap. 0.50 (*0-89981-153-1*) Eastern Orthodox.

Platon, Lefteris & Pararas, Yannis. Pedestalled Offering Tables in the Aegean World. (Studies in Mediterranean Archaeology & Literature: No. 106). (Illus.). 76p. (Orig.). 1991. pap. 29.50 (*91-7081-046-X*, Pub. by P Astroms) Coronet Bks.

Platon, Nicholas. Zakros: The Discovery of a Lost Palace of Ancient Crete. 345p. 1985. reprint ed. pap. 98.00 (*90-256-0865-5*, Pub. by AM Hakkert) BookLink Distributors.

Platon, Schema-Monk. Blessed Paisius Velichkovsky Vol. 1: The Man Behind the Philokalia. 2nd ed. St. Herman of Alaska Brotherhood Staff, ed. Rose, Seraphim, tr. from RUS. & intro. by. LC 76-12010. (Illus.). 299p. 1994. pap. 17.00 (*0-938635-13-1*) St Herman Pr.

***Platonas, Paula.** A Book of Shadows. LC 00-190420. 2000. 25.00 (*0-7388-1675-2*); pap. 18.00 (*0-7388-1676-0*) Xlibris Corp.

Platonov, Andrei. The Foundation Pit. 192p. 1997. pap. text 14.00 (*1-86046-050-X*) Harvill Press.

— The Foundation Pit. Ginsburg, Mirra, tr. from RUS. & intro. by. (European Classics Ser.). 156p. 1994. pap. 12.95 (*0-8101-1145-4*) Northwestern U Pr.

— The Return. Livingstone, Angela & Chandler, Robert, trs. 256p. 1999. pap. 14.00 (*1-86046-516-1*, Pub. by Harvill Press) HarpC.

***Platonov, Andrei, et al.** The Fierce & Beautiful World. Barnes, Joseph, tr. LC 99-46036. 288p. 2000. pap. 12.95 (*0-940322-33-1*) NY Rev Bks.

P

Platonov, Sergei F. Time of Troubles: A Historical Study of the Internal Crisis & Social Struggles in Sixteenth & Seventeenth-Century Muscovy. Alexander, John T., tr. LC 79-97029. xviii, 198p. (C). 1970. pap. 9.95 (*0-7006-0062-0*) U Pr of KS.

Platonov, Sergei F. & Wieczynski, Joseph L. Ivan the Terrible. reprint ed. pap. 16.00 (*0-87569-054-8*) Academic Intl.

Platonov, Vladimir & Rapinchuk, Andrei. Algebraic Groups & Number Theory. Rowen, Rachel, tr. LC 92-35876. (Pure & Applied Mathematics Ser.: Vol. 139). (ENG & RUS., Illus.). 614p. 1993. text 117.00 (*0-12-558180-7*) Acad Pr.

Platou, Dode. Chas H. Reinike: Louisiana Watercolors from 1935-1952. McCaffrey, Rosanne, ed. (Illus.). 16p. 1981. pap. 5.50 (*0-917860-07-1*) Historic New Orleans.

Platova, Valentina & Gregg, Sue. How Do You Like It? Recipes for Russian & American Appetites. (RUS., Illus.). 30p. 1996. pap. 5.00 (*1-878272-11-X*) S Gregg Cookbks.

Platova, Valentina, jt. auth. see Gregg, Sue.

Platova, Victoria. Neiarkaia Zhizn' Sani Kornilova: Stories. LC 90-25013. (RUS.). 115p. (Orig.). 1991. pap. 7.50 (*1-55779-031-0*) Hermitage Pubs.

***Platsky, Scott.** CoursewareWizard. (Illus.). (YA). 2000. pap. write for info. (*0-7423-0432-9*, COURSE990CLS) ComputerPREP.

***Platsky, Scott, et al, eds.** A+ Certification: PC Hardware. (Illus.). (YA). 1999. pap., teacher ed. write for info. (*0-7423-0386-1*, APCHC8042WI); pap., student ed. write for info. (*0-7423-0383-7*, APCHC8042WL) ComputerPREP.

— A+ Certification: PC Operating Systems, 2 vols. (Illus.). 1999. pap., student ed. write for info. (*0-7423-0382-9*) ComputerPREP.

— A+ Certification Vol. 1: PC Hardware. (Illus.). (YA). 1999. pap., teacher ed. write for info. (*0-7423-0387-X*, APCHC2001WI); pap., student ed. write for info. (*0-7423-0384-5*, APCHC2001WL) ComputerPREP.

— A+ Certification Vol. 1: PC Operating Systems. (Illus.). (C). 1999. pap., student ed. write for info. (*0-7423-0389-6*) ComputerPREP.

— A+ Certification Vol. 2: PC Hardware. (Illus.). (YA). 1999. pap., teacher ed. write for info. (*0-7423-0388-8*, APCHC2002WI); pap., student ed. write for info. (*0-7423-0385-3*, APCHC2002WL) ComputerPREP.

— A+ Certification Vol. 2: PC Operating Systems. (Illus.). (C). 1999. pap., student ed. write for info. (*0-7423-0390-X*) ComputerPREP.

***Platsky, Scott & Desek, Shannon, eds.** A+ Certification: PC Operating Systems, 2 vols. (Illus.). 400p. 1999. pap., teacher ed. write for info. (*0-7423-0391-8*, APOSC8042WI) ComputerPREP.

— A+ Certification Vol. 1: PC Operating Systems. (Illus.). 200p. 1999. pap., teacher ed. write for info. (*0-7423-0392-6*, APOSC2001WI) ComputerPREP.

— A+ Certification Vol. 2: PC Operating Systems. (Illus.). 1999. pap., teacher ed. write for info. (*0-7423-0393-4*, APOSC2002WI) ComputerPREP.

Platt. Fleetwood Mac: Brit Blues. 400p. 1999. 27.00 (*0-02-864894-3*) Mac Lib Ref.

— Great Rebuildings of Tudor & St: Revolutions in Architectural Taste. LC 94-32050. 1994. 65.00 (*1-85728-315-5*, Pub. by UCL Pr Ltd); pap. 21.95 (*1-85728-316-3*, Pub. by UCL Pr Ltd) Taylor & Francis.

Platt. Medieval England. 2nd ed. (Illus.). 312p. (C). 1995. pap. 29.99 (*0-415-12913-3*) Routledge.

Platt. Police Guide to the Young Offender's Act. 224p. 1991. pap. 27.00 (*0-409-89340-4*, MICHIE) LEXIS Pub.

— Test Bank T/a Intro to Computer Science. (C). 1994. pap. text 6.00 (*0-03-097241-8*) Harcourt Coll Pubs.

— Young Offenders Law in Canada. 352p. 1990. 87.00 (*0-409-80990-X*, MICHIE) LEXIS Pub.

Platt, A. M., et al, eds. Nuclear Fact Book. xvi, 176p. 1985. text 82.00 (*3-7186-0273-3*) Gordon & Breach.

Platt, A. M., jt. ed. see Tedder, P. William.

Platt, Adam & Carter, Nicola. Making Health Care Equipment: Ideas for Local Design & Production. (Illus.). 96p. 1990. pap. 15.00 (*1-85339-067-4*, Pub. by Intermed Tech) Stylus Pub VA.

Platt, Alan. Arms Control & Confidence Building in the Middle East. LC 92-18784. 1992. pap. text 13.95 (*1-878379-18-6*) US Inst Peace.

Platt, Alan, jt. auth. see Bowie, Christopher J.

Platt, Anne E. Infecting Ourselves: How Environmental & Social Disruptions Trigger Disease. 70p. (Orig.). 1996. pap. 5.00 (*1-878071-31-9*) Worldwatch Inst.

Platt, Anthony M. The Child Savers. LC 69-14827. (Phoenix Ser.). 270p. 1977. reprint ed. pap. text 16.00 (*0-226-67072-4*, P462) U Ch Pr.

— E. Franklin Frazier Reconsidered. LC 90-36223. (Illus.). 310p. (C). 1991. text 35.00 (*0-8135-1631-5*) Rutgers U Pr.

Platt, Arthur. Nine Essays. LC 68-16969. (Essay Index Reprint Ser.). 1977. reprint ed. 19.95 (*0-8369-0793-0*) Ayer.

Platt, Billy. Only English? Law & Language Policy in The United States. LC 89-24968. 199p. 1993. reprint ed. pap. 8.95 (*0-8263-1373-6*) U of NM Pr.

Platt, Brenda. Creating Wealth from Everyday Items. (Illus.). 47p. 1997. pap. text 15.00 (*0-917582-90-X*) Inst Local Self Re.

— Waste Prevention, Recycling & Composting Options: Lessons from 30 Communities. (Illus.). 168p. (C). 1999. reprint ed. pap. text 30.00 (*0-7881-4350-6*) DIANE Pub.

— Weaving Textile Reuse into Waste Reduction. LC 97-3520. 1997. 15.00 (*0-917582-93-4*) Inst Local Self Re.

Platt, Brenda & Hyde, Jennifer. Plug into Electronics Reuse. LC 97-97. 1997. pap. 15.00 (*0-917582-92-6*) Inst Local Self Re.

Platt, Brenda A. Minimizing Waste, Maximizing Recycling. 34p. 1994. 6.00 (*0-614-18036-8*) Inst Local Self Re.

Platt, Brenda A. & Seldman, Neil. Garbage in Europe: Technologies, Economics & Trends. LC 88-671. (Illus.). 260p. 1988. per. 25.00 (*0-917582-42-X*) Inst Local Self Re.

Platt, Brenda A. & Zachary, Jill. Co-Collection of Recyclables & Mixed Waste: Problems & Opportunities. LC 92-34141. 60p. 1992. pap. text 15.00 (*0-917582-26-8*) Inst Local Self Re.

Platt, Brenda A., et al. Directory of Waste Utilization Technologies in Europe & the United States. LC 88-28436. 225p. 1989. pap. text 25.00 (*0-917582-41-1*) Inst Local Self Re.

— In-Depth Studies of Recycling & Composting Programs, Vols. I-III: Designs, Costs, Results, 3 vols., Set. LC 92-9856. (Illus.). (Orig.). 1992. pap. text 45.00 (*0-917582-32-2*) Inst Local Self Re.

— In-Depth Studies of Recycling & Composting Programs, Vols. I-III: Designs, Costs, Results, 3 vols., Vol. I: Rural Communities. LC 92-9856. (Illus.). 127p. (Orig.). 1992. pap. text 18.00 (*0-917582-31-4*) Inst Local Self Re.

— In-Depth Studies of Recycling & Composting Programs, Vols. I-III: Designs, Costs, Results, 3 vols., Vol. II: Suburbs & Small Cities. LC 92-9856. (Illus.). 202p. (Orig.). 1992. pap. text 18.00 (*0-917582-30-6*) Inst Local Self Re.

— In-Depth Studies of Recycling & Composting Programs, Vols. I-III: Designs, Costs, Results, 3 vols., Vol. III: Urban Areas. LC 92-9856. (Illus.). 207p. (Orig.). 1992. pap. text 18.00 (*0-917582-29-2*) Inst Local Self Re.

— Pitfalls & Promise of Resource Recovery in Union County, New Jersey. rev. ed. LC 89-7632. 200p. 1989. pap. text 20.00 (*0-917582-36-5*) Inst Local Self Re.

— Recycling Means Business in Baltimore, D. C., & Richmond. 86p. 1995. 12.00 (*0-614-18039-2*) Inst Local Self Re.

Platt, Brenda A., jt. auth. see Morris, David.

Platt, Cameron & Wright, John. Treasure Islands: The Fascinating World of Pirates, Buried Treasure, & Fortune Hunters. LC 94-34454. (Illus.). 224p. 1995. pap. 15.95 (*1-55591-190-0*) Fulcrum Pub.

Platt, Carolyn, ed. see Bockhoff, Esther & Fleming, Nancy I.

Platt, Carolyn V. & Meszaros, Gary. Creatures of Change: An Album of Ohio Animals. LC 97-34531. (Illus.). 294p. 1998. 60.00 (*0-87338-585-3*) Kent St U Pr.

Platt, Charles. Anarchy Online: Anarchy Online. LC 96-39918. 384p. 1997. pap. 14.00 (*0-06-100990-3*, HarperPrism) HarpC.

— Artificial Intelligence in Action: Commodore 64. 1985. pap. 12.99 (*0-89824-119-7*) Trillium Pr.

— Free Zone. 1989. pap. 3.50 (*0-380-75411-8*, Avon Bks) Morrow Avon.

— The Gas. 160p. (Orig.). 1968. pap. 11.95 (*0-86130-023-8*, Pub. by Savoy Bks) AK Pr Dist.

Platt, Charles, Jr. Platt Genealogy in America, from the Arrival of Richard Platt in New Haven, Conn., in 1638. (Illus.). 453p. 1993. reprint ed. pap. 71.00 (*0-8328-3573-0*); reprint ed. lib. bdg. 81.00 (*0-8328-3572-2*) Higginson Bk Co.

Platt, Charles. Protektor. 1996. mass mkt. 5.99 (*0-380-78431-9*, Avon Bks) Morrow Avon.

— The Silicon Man. LC 97-19832. (Cortext: Science Fiction That Changed the World Ser.). 327p. 1997. pap. 12.95 (*1-888869-14-3*) Wired Bks.

— The Silicon Man. LC 93-60317. 232p. 1993. reprint ed. 19.95 (*0-9623712-7-0*) Tafford Pub.

— Who Writes Science Fiction? 400p. (Orig.). 1981. pap. 3.95 (*0-86130-048-3*, Pub. by Savoy Bks) AK Pr Dist.

Platt, Charles A. Italian Gardens. LC 92-33622. (Illus.). 170p. 1993. reprint ed. 34.95 (*0-88192-273-0*) Sagapr.

Platt, Chris. Willow King. LC 97-27846. (J). (gr. 5 up). 1998. 15.00 (*0-679-88655-9*, Pub. by Random Bks Yng Read); lib. bdg. 16.99 (*0-679-98655-3*, Pub. by Random Bks Yng Read) Random.

— Willow King. LC 97-27846. 193p. (J). 1999. pap. 4.99 (*0-679-88656-7*, Pub. by Random Bks Yng Read) Random.

***Platt, Chris.** Willow King: Race the Wind, Vol. 2. 208p. (J). 2000. lib. bdg. 16.99 (*0-679-98657-X*, Pub. by Random Bks Yng Read) Random.

Platt, Chris. Willow King - Race No. 2, Vol. 2. 208p. (J). 2000. 15.00 (*0-679-88657-5*) Random.

— Willow King Sequel. 1998. pap. 4.99 (*0-679-88658-3*) Random Bks Yng Read.

Platt, Colin. The Architecture of Medieval Britain: A Social History. (Illus.). 352p. (C). 1991. 60.00 (*0-300-04953-6*) Yale U Pr.

— King Death: The Black Death & Its Aftermath in Late-Medieval England. (Illus.). 224p. 1996. text 55.00 (*0-8020-0930-1*); pap. text 18.95 (*0-8020-7900-8*) U of Toronto Pr.

— Medieval England: A Social History & Archaeology from the Conquest to 1600 A. D. LC 94-42748. 256p. 1989. pap. text 17.95 (*0-415-00278-8*) Routledge.

— The Monastic Grange in Medieval England: A Reassessment. LC 74-417643. 272p. 1969. write for info. (*0-333-09356-9*) Macmillan.

— The Monastic Grange in Medieval England: A Reassessment. LC 73-80106. 280p. reprint ed. pap. 86.80 (*0-7837-0463-1*, 204078600018) Bks Demand.

Platt, Constance A., jt. auth. see Hoffman, Stephanie B.

Platt, D., ed. Gerontology. (Illus.). 336p. 1990. 94.95 (*0-387-51544-5*) Spr-Verlag.

Platt, D. C., ed. Business Imperialism, Eighteen Forty to Nineteen Thirty: An Inquiry Based on British Experience in Latin America. (Illus.). 1978. 69.00 (*0-19-828271-0*) OUP.

Platt, David. Celluloid Power: Social Film Criticism from the Birth of a Nation to Judgement at Nuremberg. LC 91-35568. (Illus.). 700p. 1992. 85.00 (*0-8108-2442-6*) Scarecrow.

— Essence of Com with Activex: Programmers Workbook. 3rd ed. 368p. (C). 2000. pap. 44.99 (*0-13-016581-6*) S&S Trade.

— Intimations of Divinity. (American University Studies: Philosophy: Ser. V, Vol. 72). VIII, 248p. (C). 1988. text 35.95 (*0-8204-0856-5*) P Lang Pubng.

Platt, David C., jt. auth. see Shaffer, Dale.

Platt, David C., jt. auth. see Shaffer, Dale O.

Platt, David D., contrib. by. Sustaining Island Communities: The Story of the Economy & Life of Maine's Year-Round Islands. (Illus.). 98p. 1997. pap. 9.95 (*0-942719-22-0*) Island Inst.

***Platt, David D., ed.** Island Journal: An Annual Publication of the Islant Institute, Vol. 17. (Island Journals: Vol. 17). (Illus.). 92p. (C). 2000. pap. 14.95 (*0-942719-25-5*, Pub. by Island Inst) Magazines Inc.

Platt, David D., ed. Island Journal Vol. XV: An Annual Publication of the Island Institute. (Illus.). 96p. 1998. pap. 7.95 (*0-942719-20-4*) Island Inst.

— Island Journal Vol. XVI: An Annual Publication of the Island Institute. (Illus.). 96p. 1999. pap. 9.95 (*0-942719-24-7*) Island Inst.

— Penobscot, the Forest, River & Bay. (Illus.). 200p. (Orig.). 1997. reprint ed. pap. 16.95 (*0-942719-16-6*) Island Inst.

— Rim of the Gulf: Restoring Estuaries in the Gulf of Maine. (Illus.). 1998. pap. 19.95 (*0-942719-21-2*) Island Inst.

Platt, David D., jt. ed. see Conkling, Philip W.

Platt, David S. The Essence of COM with ActiveX: A Programer's Workbook. 2nd ed. LC 97-35515. 592p. (C). 1997. pap. 49.95 incl. cd-rom (*0-13-079989-0*) P-H.

— The Gift of Contingency. LC 91-8283. (American University Studies: Philosophy: Ser. V, Vol. 120). XII, 210p. 1991. 38.95 (*0-8204-1543-X*) P Lang Pubng.

***Platt, David S.** Understanding Com+ rev. ed. 256p. 2001. pap. 24.99 (*0-7356-1136-X*) Microsoft.

Platt, David W. & Conkling, Philip W., eds. Island Journal, Vol. XIV. annuals (Illus.). 96p. (Orig.). 1997. pap. 7.95 (*0-942719-17-4*) Island Inst.

***Platt, Dayna & Shrock, Carissa.** Creating a More Tolerant World: Teaching Young Students in Grades 2-4 about Racism. (Illus.). 16p. (J). (gr. 2-4). 2000. pap. write for info. (*1-57543-082-7*) Mar Co Prods.

Platt, Dendy & Shemmings, David, eds. Making Inquiries into Alleged Child Abuse & Neglect: Partnership with Families. 302p. 1998. pap. 54.95 (*0-471-97222-3*) Wiley.

Platt, Donald. Fresh Peaches, Fireworks, & Guns. LC 93-40660. 88p. (Orig.). 1994. pap. 13.95 (*1-55753-048-3*) Purdue U Pr.

***Platt, Donald.** Leap Second at the Turn of the Millennium. 30p. 1999. 25.00 (*0-9621526-1-7*) Ctr Bk Arts.

Platt, Donald M. & DeSantis, Carl. Vitamin Enriched: A Mega Prescription for Wealth & Health by Carl DeSantis Founder of Rexall Sundown, Inc. LC 98-90144. (Illus.). 320p. 1998. 22.00 (*1-890819-03-4*) TransMedia FL.

— Vitamin Enriched: A Mega Prescription for Wealth & Health by Carl DeSantis Founder of Rexall Sundown, Inc. (Illus.). 320p. 1999. pap. 14.00 (*1-890819-04-2*) TransMedia FL.

Platt, Dora B. The Miracle on Harding Road. (Illus.). 136p. 1989. lib. bdg. write for info. (*0-9623777-0-8*) Saint Thomas Hospital.

Platt, Eddie, jt. auth. see Vogt, Elizabeth.

Platt, Edmund. History of Poughkeepsie, 1683-1905. 328p. 1987. reprint ed. lib. bdg. 25.00 (*0-932334-83-0*, NY14011) Hrt of the Lakes.

Platt, Eleanor S. Wreaths, Arrangements & Basket Decorations: Using Flowers, Foliage, Herbs & Grasses to Make Colorful Crafts. (Illus.). 176p. 1994. 24.95 (*0-87596-587-3*) Rodale Pr Inc.

Platt, Elizabeth. Scenes from Day Care: How Teachers Teach & What Children Learn. LC 91-31286. (Early Childhood Education Ser.: No. 35). 128p. (C). 1992. pap. text 16.95 (*0-8077-3131-5*) Tchrs Coll.

Platt, Ellen J. & Simoni, Christopher. Author's Guide to Legal Periodicals. Date not set. write for info. (*1-57588-001-6*, 309040) W S Hein.

Platt, Ellen Spector. How to Profit from Flower & Herb Crafts. LC 96-12968. (Illus.). 224p. 1996. pap. 14.95 (*0-8117-2448-4*) Stackpole.

— Lavender; How to Grow & Use the Fragrant Herb, 1. LC 98-41973. 1999. pap. text 19.95 (*0-8117-2849-8*) Kitch Keepsakes.

— Natural Crafts from America's Backyards: Decorate Your Home with Wreaths, Arrangements & Wall Decorations Gathered from Nature's Harvest. LC 96-53570. (Illus.). 224p. 1997. text 27.95 (*0-87596-763-9*) Rodale Pr Inc.

— Ultimate Wreath Book. 1998. pap. 20.00 (*0-87596-978-X*) Rodale Pr Inc.

— The Ultimate Wreath Book: Hundreds of Beautiful Wreaths to Make from Natural Materials. (Illus.). 246p. 1995. text 27.95 (*0-87596-720-5*) Rodale Pr Inc.

Platt, F. DeWitt, jt. auth. see Matthews, Roy T.

Platt, F. DeWitt, jt. ed. see Matthews, Roy T.

Platt, Frederic W. Conversation Failure: Case Studies in Doctor-Patient Communication. LC 92-15049. 1992. 16.95 (*0-943685-16-8*) Biosocial.

— Conversation Repair. LC 95-835. 1995. 24.95 (*0-316-71082-2*, Little Brwn Med Div) Lppncott W & W.

***Platt, Frederic W. & Gordon, Geoffrey H.** Field Guide to the Difficult Patient Interview. LC 99-19265. 201p. 1999. 29.95 (*0-7817-2044-3*) Lppncott W & W.

Platt, Frederic W., jt. auth. see Markoff, Mortimer.

Platt, Frederick. America's Gilded Age. 25.00 (*0-8453-1322-3*, Cornwall Bks) Assoc Univ Prs.

Platt, G. L. Platt Lineage: A Genealogical Research & Record. (Illus.). 398p. 1989. reprint ed. pap. 60.00 (*0-8328-0973-X*); reprint ed. lib. bdg. 68.00 (*0-8328-0972-1*) Higginson Bk Co.

Platt, Geoffrey. A Writer's Journey. LC 90-82233. 258p. (C). 1991. pap. text 35.96 (*0-669-20298-3*) HM Trade Div.

— A Writer's Journey. 2nd ed. (C). 1995. text, teacher ed. 37.16 (*0-669-35143-1*); pap. text 35.96 (*0-669-35142-3*) HM Trade Div.

— A Writer's Journey with "Newsweek" 2nd ed. (C). 1995. text 42.76 (*0-669-39522-6*) HM Trade Div.

Platt, George. George Platt Lynes: Portrait, 1927-1955. Woody, Jack, ed. (Illus.). 144p. 1994. 65.00 (*0-944092-27-6*) Twin Palms Pub.

Platt, George M. South Dakota's 1965 Legislative Session. 1965. 1.00 (*1-55614-004-5*) U of SD Gov Res Bur.

Platt, George M., jt. auth. see Clem, Alan L.

Platt, Gerald, ed. see Harris, Anthony.

Platt, Gerald, ed. see Mortimer, Jeylan T., et al.

Platt, Gerald, ed. see Suttles, Gerald & Zald, Mayer N.

Platt, Gerald M. & Gordon, Chad, eds. Self, Collective Behavior & Society Vol. 12: Essays Honoring the Contributions of Ralph H. Turner. LC 94-3519. (Contemporary Studies in Sociology: Vol. 12). 413p. 1994. 78.50 (*1-55938-755-6*) Jai Pr.

Platt, Gerald M., jt. auth. see Parsons, Talcott.

Platt, Gertrude, ed. see Platt, John M. & Kirson, Ian J.

Platt, Gillian. Suite for Five Viols. (Charney Manor Ser.: No. 7). i, 15p. 1994. pap. text 10.00 (*1-56571-083-5*, CM007) PRB Prods.

Platt, Harlan D. The First Junk Bond: A Story of Corporate Boom & Bust. LC 93-17066. 224p. (gr. 13). 1994. text 76.95 (*1-56324-275-3*) M E Sharpe.

Platt, Harlan D. The First Junk Bond: A Story of Corporate Boom & Bust. LC 93-17066. 224p. (gr. 13). 1994. pap. text 35.95 (*1-56324-276-1*) M E Sharpe.

Platt, Harlan D. Principles of Corporate Renewal. LC 97-38129. (Illus.). 440p. (C). 1998. text 57.50 (*0-472-10838-7*, 10838) U of Mich Pr.

Platt, Harold, jt. ed. see Adams, Rosemary K.

Platt, Harold L. The Electric City: Energy & the Growth of the Chicago Area, 1880-1930. LC 90-38285. (Illus.). 423p. 1991. 39.95 (*0-226-67075-9*) U Ch Pr.

Platt, Harvey J. Your Living Trust & Estate Plan: How to Maximize Your Family's Assets & Protect Your Loved Ones. LC 95-75284. 256p. 1995. pap. 14.95 (*1-880559-25-0*) Allworth Pr.

— Your Living Trust & Estate Plan: How to Maximize Your Family's Assets & Protect Your Loved Ones. 2nd ed. LC 98-72768. 292p. 1999. pap. text 14.95 (*1-58115-019-9*) Allworth Pr.

Platt, Heinrich, ed. Intertextuality. (Research in Text Theory Ser.: Vol. 15). viii, 268p. (C). 1991. lib. bdg. 101.45 (*3-11-011637-5*) Mouton.

Platt, Helen Spector. Ultimate Wreath Book. 1998. pap. 20.00 (*0-676-57329-0*) Random.

Platt, Hugh. A New, Cheape & Delicate Fire of Cole-Balles. LC 72-7838. (English Experience Ser.: No. 550). 32p. 1972. reprint ed. 15.00 (*90-221-0550-4*) Walter J Johnson.

Platt, Isaac H. Bacon Cryptograms in Shake-Speare & Other Studies. 134p. 1996. reprint ed. pap. 17.95 (*1-56459-538-2*) Kessinger Pub.

Platt, Janan, jt. auth. see Mack, Stephen.

Platt, Janet V., et al. Actividades Diarias Despues de Tu Reemplazo Total de Rodilla. Irizarry, Dyhalma, tr. (Illus.). (C). 1993. pap. text. write for info. (*1-56900-005-0*) Am Occup Therapy.

— Daily Activities after Your Total Knee Replacement. (Illus.). 28p. (C). 1992. pap. text 6.00 (*0-910317-80-1*) Am Occup Therapy.

Platt, Jean S. Ribbons. (Illus.). 96p. (Orig.). 1992. pap. text 11.95 (*0-9634688-0-4*) Persona Pr PA.

Platt, Jeffrey L. Xenotransplantation from Basic Research to Clinical Application. 2000. 139.00 (*0-8493-4892-7*) CRC Pr.

***Platt, Jeffrey L., ed.** Xenotransplantation. 400p. 2000. 89.95 (*1-55581-167-1*) ASM Pr.

Platt, Jennifer. A History of Sociological Research Methods in America, 1920-1960. (Ideas in Context Ser.: No. 40). 372p. (C). 1999. pap. text 22.95 (*0-521-64649-9*) Cambridge U Pr.

Platt, Jennifer & Olson, Judy. Teaching Adolescents with Mild Disabilities. (Special Education Ser.). 448p. (C). 1996. 61.95 (*0-534-21006-6*) Brooks-Cole.

Platt, Jennifer M. A History of Sociological Research Methods in America, 1920-1960. (Ideas in Context Ser.: No. 40). 349p. (C). 1996. text 64.95 (*0-521-44173-0*) Cambridge U Pr.

Platt, Jerome J. Cocaine Addiction: Theory, Research & Treatment. LC 96-37435. 448p. 1997. 52.00 (*0-674-13632-2*) HUP.

***Platt, Jerome J.** Cocaine Addiction: Theory, Research & Treatment. 2000. pap. text 24.95 (*0-674-00178-8*) HUP.

Platt, Jerome J. Heroin Addiction, 3 vols., Set. 1074p. 1995. 99.95 (*0-89464-923-X*) Krieger.

— Heroin Addiction: Theory, Research & Treatment, Vol. 1. 2nd ed. LC 88-13253. 464p. (C). 1989. reprint ed. lib. bdg. 46.50 (*0-89464-325-8*) Krieger.

— Heroin Addiction Vol. 2: Theory, Research & Treatment: The Addict, the Treatment Process, & Social Control. LC 83-19584. 288p. (C). 1995. 37.50 (*0-89464-267-7*) Krieger.

Platt, Jerome J., et al, eds. The Effectiveness of Drug Abuse Treatment: Dutch & American Perspectives. 344p. 1990. 55.00 (*0-89464-266-9*) Krieger.

Platt, Jerome J., jt. ed. see Buhringer, Gerhard.

Platt, John, et al. The New Englishes. 190p. 1984. pap. 12.95 (*0-7102-0194-X*, Routledge Thoemms) Routledge.

An Asterisk (*) at the beginning of an entry indicates that the title is appearing for the first time.

— Singapore & Malaysia. (Varieties of English Around the World General Ser.: T4). iv, 138p. 1983. pap. 32.00 (*90-272-4712-9*) J Benjamins Pubng Co.

Platt, John, jt. auth. see Mitchell, Mitch.

Platt, John, jt. auth. see Owens, Dan.

Platt, John A. London's Rock Routes LC 86-136225. 180 p. 1985. write for info. (*0-947795-70-7*) Fourth Estate.

— Whispers from Old Genesee & Echoes of the Salmon River. (Illus.). 184p. 1975. 16.95 (*0-87770-143-1*) Ye Galleon.

Platt, John A., et al. Yardbirds. LC 84-150093. 160 p. 1983. write for info. (*0-283-98982-3*, Pub. by S1 & J) Trafalgar.

Platt, John D. Global History of Philosophy, Vol. 1. 1977. 16.00 (*81-208-0158-X*, Pub. by Motilal Bnarsidass) S Asia.

— Jeremiah Wadsworth, Federalist Entrepreneur. 1981. 27.95 (*0-405-14103-3*) Ayer.

Platt, John M. & Kirson, Ian J. Infant Sleep. Platt, Gertrude & Smith, Troy M., eds. (Illus.). 40p. 1995. 5.00 (*0-9624446-2-6*) Dynamic Training.

Platt, John P. The Petrology, Structure, & Geologic History of the Catalina Schist Terrain, Southern California. LC 74-22941. (University of California Publications in Social Welfare: Vol. 112). (Illus.). 141p. reprint ed. pap. 43.80 (*0-608-18017-3*, 201496200093) Bks Demand.

Platt, John R., ed. New Views of the Nature of Man. LC 65-24980. 1994. lib. bdg. 10.00 (*0-226-67080-5*) U Ch Pr.

— New Views of the Nature of Man. LC 65-24980. (C). 1993. reprint ed. pap. text 1.95 (*0-226-67081-3*, P389) U Ch Pr.

Platt, John T., jt. auth. see Ho Mian-Lian.

Platt, Joseph. Harvey Mudd College: The First Twenty Years. LC 94-7452. (Illus.). 224p. 1994. 28.95 (*1-56474-097-8*); pap. 16.95 (*1-56474-100-1*) Fithian Pr.

Platt, Kevin M. History in a Grotesque Key: Russian Literature & the Idea of Revolution. LC 96-43067. 1997. 45.00 (*0-8047-2834-8*) Stanford U Pr.

Platt, Kin. The Ape Inside Me. LC 79-2402. (Lippincott Page-Turner Ser.). (YA). (gr. 7 up). 1979. lib. bdg. 11.89 (*0-397-31863-4*) HarpC Child Bks.

— Big Max. LC 65-14488. (I Can Read Bks.). (Illus.). 64p. (J). (ps-3). 1965. lib. bdg. 15.89 (*0-06-024751-7*) HarpC Child Bks.

— Big Max. LC 65-14488. (I Can Read Bks.). (Illus.). 64p. (J). (ps-3). 1978. pap. 3.75 (*0-06-444006-0*, HarpTrophy) HarpC Child Bks.

— Big Max. (I Can Read Bks.). (Illus.). (J). (gr. 1-3). 1965. 8.95 (*0-606-01486-1*, Pub. by Turtleback) Demco.

Platt, Kin. Big Max Book & Tape. unabridged ed. (I Can Read Bks.). (Illus.). 64p. (J). (gr. k-3). 1991. 8.95 incl. audio (*1-55994-496-X*, TBC 496X) HarperAudio.

Platt, Kin. Big Max in the Mystery of the Missing Moose. LC 76-58727. (I Can Read Mystery Bks.). (Illus.). 64p. (J). (ps-3). 1983. pap. 3.50 (*0-06-444044-3*, HarpTrophy) HarpC Child Bks.

— Brogg's Brain. LC 79-9622. 128p. (J). (gr. 6 up). 1981. 12.95 (*0-397-31945-2*); lib. bdg. 11.89 (*0-397-31946-0*) HarpC Child Bks.

— Crocker. LC 82-48456. (Lippincott Page-Turner Ser.). 128p. (YA). (gr. 7 up). 1983. 11.95 (*0-397-32025-6*); lib. bdg. 11.89 (*0-397-32026-4*) HarpC Child Bks.

— Flames Going Out. 144p. (gr. 10 up). 1980. 8.95 (*0-416-30621-7*, NO. 0150) Routledge.

Platt, Kin, ed. see London, Jack.

Platt, Kin, ed. see Stevenson, Robert Louis.

***Platt, L. Steven & Ventrell-Monsees, Cathy.** Age Discrimination. 2000. write for info. (*1-58012-058-X*) James Pub Santa Ana.

***Platt, Larry.** Keepin' It Real: A Turbulent Season at the Crossroads with the NBA. LC 99-12059. 320p. 1998. 24.00 (*0-380-97714-1*, Avon Bks) Morrow Avon.

Platt, Larry, jt. auth. see Negroni, Andrea L.

Platt, Larry A. & Persico, V. Richard, Jr. Grief in Cross-Cultural Perspective: A Casebook. LC 91-25907. 446p. 1992. text 25.00 (*0-8240-4565-3*, 557) Garland.

Platt, Laurence E. & Schulman, Phillip L. A Practical Guide to the Real Estate Settlement Procedures Act. 624p. 1995. pap. 175.00 (*0-7913-2202-5*) Warren Gorham & Lamont.

Platt, LaVonne G. Bela Banerjee: Bringing Health to India's Villages. LC 87-51688. (Illus.). xi, 178p. (Orig.). 1988. pap. 11.95 (*0-945530-00-5*) Wordsworth KS.

Bela Banerjee was a remarkable Indian nurse who spent her life serving the poor in India. This book describes her work in Quacker, Gandhian & other indigenous & international development projects. it shows how her training of young village women to be health workers led to higher health standards & a greater acceptance of women as village leaders. It also tells of her early life as the youngest daughter of a widowed mother & later experiences that enlarged her circle of relationships to friends throughout the world. Weaving together research, interviews & experiences while traveling with Bela Banerjee, the author brings alive the people & places important to the life of this extraordinary woman whose deep sense of identification with the poor gave direction to her life. The book is illustrated with photographs & a map of India indicating places where Bela Banerjee lived & worked. Several RabindranathTagore poems that she found meaningful are included in the book.

In memory of Bela Banerjee: A Coda to Her Biography (ISBN 0-945530-17-x, 1996) also written by Platt & published by Wordsworth following Banerjee's death, is available as a companion piece to the biography. *Publisher Paid Annotation.*

— In Memory of Bela Banerjee: A Coda to Her Biography. (Illus.). 40p. (Orig.). 1996. pap. 2.95 (*0-945530-17-X*) Wordsworth KS.

Platt, Lawrence D., ed. Genetic Disorders & Pregnancy Outcome. LC 96-39335. 156p. 1997. text 85.00 (*1-85070-721-9*) Prthnon Pub.

Platt, Lawrence D., jt. auth. see Evans, Mark I.

Platt, Lyman D. Census Records for Latin America & the Hispanic United States. LC 97-78047. 198p. 1998. pap. 19.95 (*0-8063-1555-5*, 103010) Genealog Pub.

Platt, Lyman D. Hispanic Surnames & Family History. 349p. 1996. pap. 19.95 (*0-8063-1480-X*) Genealog Pub.

Platt, Lyman De, see De Platt, Lyman.

Platt, M. P., ed. see Little, R. A.

Platt, Marc. Lungbarrow. (New Adventures Ser.). 256p. 1997. mass mkt. 5.95 (*0-426-20502-2*, Pub. by Virgin Bks) London Brdge.

Platt, Michael P. Freedom over Servitude: Montaigne, la Boetie & On Voluntary Servitude, 64. Schaefer, David L., ed. LC 98-14238. (Contributions in Philosophy Ser.: Vol. 64). 264p. 1998. 59.95 (*0-313-30527-7*, Greenwood Pr) Greenwood.

Platt, Naomi D. Word Processing & Desktop Publishing Applications. 2nd ed. LC 93-8600. 1994. write for info. (*0-02-801021-3*) Glencoe.

Platt, Nicholas, jt. auth. see Undeland, Charles.

Platt, Norman, tr. see Mozart, Wolfgang Amadeus.

Platt, Pamela. Pig with a View. (Illus.). 80p. (J). (gr. 2-6). 1995. pap. 9.95 (*0-7022-2589-4*, Pub. by Univ Queensland Pr) Intl Spec Bk.

— Rock & Roll Rainforest. LC 97-121969. 110p. (J). 1996. pap. 10.95 (*0-7022-2773-0*, Pub. by Univ Queensland Pr) Intl Spec Bk.

Platt, Peter G. Reason Diminished: Shakespeare & the Marvelous. LC 96-31074. xviii, 273p. 1997. text 50.00 (*0-8032-3714-6*) U of Nebr Pr.

— Wonders, Marvels, & Monsters in Early Modern Culture. LC 99-11686. (Illus.). 344p. 2000. 49.50 (*0-87413-678-4*) U Delaware Pr.

Platt, Peter G. & Saunders, W. L. A Guide to Book Lists & Bibliographies for the Use of Schools. 3rd rev. ed. LC 76-513871. vi, 41 p. 1969. write for info. (*0-900641-02-9*) School Library Assn.

— A Guide to Book Lists & Bibliographies for the Use of Schools 4th ed. LC 75-326662. (School Library Association Book Lists). vi, 32 p. 1975. write for info. (*0-900641-23-1*) School Library Assn.

***Platt, Philip W.** Gentle Eminence: A Life of Cardinal Flahiff. 1999. 34.95 (*0-7735-1846-0*) McG-Queens Univ Pr.

Platt, Polly. French or Foe? Getting the Most Out of Living & Working in France. (Illus.). 254p. (Orig.). 1995. reprint ed. pap. 14.95 (*0-9646684-0-8*) Cultural Crossing.

***Platt, Polly.** Savoir Flair! 101 Tips for Enjoying France & the French. 304p. 2000. pap. 16.95 (*0-9646684-1-6*) Culture Crossings.

Platt, Priscilla. When Kids Get into Trouble: A Guide for Parents & Children, Teachers & Professionals, Including the Young Offenders Act. 208p. 1987. pap. 14.95 (*0-7737-5104-1*) Genl Dist Srvs.

Platt, Randall Beth. The Cornerstone. LC 98-7943. 224p. 1998. 21.95 (*0-945774-40-0*) Catbird Pr.

***Platt, Randall Beth.** The 1898 Base-Ball Fe-As-Ko. LC 99-53066. 304p. 2000. 24.00 (*0-945774-47-8*) Catbird Pr.

Platt, Randall Beth. The Four Arrows Fe-As-Ko. LC 90-28802. 225p. 1991. 17.95 (*0-945774-14-1*, PS3566.L29386) Catbird Pr.

— Honor Bright. 240p. (YA). 1998. mass mkt. 4.50 (*0-440-21987-6*, LLL BDD) BDD Bks Young Read.

— Honor Bright. 1998. 9.60 (*0-606-13486-7*, Pub. by Turtleback) Demco.

***Platt, Randall Beth.** The Likes of Me. LC 99-33284. 256p. (J). (gr. 4-8). 2000. 15.95 (*0-385-32692-0*) Delacorte.

Platt, Randall Beth. The Royalscope Fe-As-Ko. LC 96-54506. 288p. 1997. 21.95 (*0-945774-35-4*, PS3566.L293R68) Catbird Pr.

Platt, Richard. Cross Sections: Man-of-War. LC 92-21227. (Illus.). 32p. (J). (gr. 3 up). 1993. 16.95 (*1-56458-321-X*) DK Pub Inc.

— Disaster! Catastrophes That Shook the World. LC 97-15423. (Illus.). 32p. (J). (gr. 5-9). 15.95 (*0-7894-2034-1*) DK Pub Inc.

***Platt, Richard.** DK Space Explorer Atlas. LC 99-28593. 32p. 1999. 14.95 (*0-7894-4284-1*) DK Pub Inc.

Platt, Richard. Eyewitness: Corsarios y Piratas. (Eyewitness Books). (SPA.). 1996. 19.95 (*84-372-3804-8*) Santillana.

***Platt, Richard.** Film. (Eyewitness Books). (Illus.). (gr. 4-7). 2000. 19.99 (*0-7894-6583-3*) DK Pub Inc.

— Film. (Eyewitness Books). (J). (gr. 4-7). 2000. 15.95 (*0-7894-5587-0*) DK Pub Inc.

Platt, Richard. Film. LC 91-53133. (Eyewitness Books). (Illus.). 64p. (J). (gr. 5 up). 1992. 19.00 (*0-679-81679-8*, Pub. by Knopf Bks Yng Read) Random.

— In the Beginning: The Nearly Complete History of Almost Everything. LC 95-2427. (Illus.). 72p. (J). (gr. 5-8). 1995. 19.95 (*0-7894-0206-8*, 5-70619) DK Pub Inc.

— Inventions Explained: A Beginner's Guide to Technological Breakthroughs, 6. LC 97-11969. (Your World Explained Ser.). (Illus.). 72p. (J). 1997. 18.95 (*0-8050-4876-6*) H Holt & Co.

***Platt, Richard.** Julius Caesar: The Founder of the Roman Empire. LC 00-23668. (Discoveries Ser.). 2000. write for info. (*0-7894-6504-3*) DK Pub Inc.

— Firate. (Eyewitness Books). (Illus.). (J). (gr. 4-7). 2000. 19.99 (*0-7894-6608-2*) DK Pub Inc.

— Firate. (Eyewitness Books). (Illus.). (J). (gr. 4-7). 2000. 15.95 (*0-7894-6024-6*) DK Pub Inc.

— Firate. (Illus.). (J). 1995. 19.00 (*0-679-87255-8*) Knopf.

— Flants Bite Back! LC 99-20403. (Eyewitness Readers). 48p. (J). (gr. 2-3). 1999. 12.95 (*0-7894-4755-X*); pap. text 3.95 (*0-7894-4754-1*) DK Pub Inc.

— Fop-up 3-D Time Scape. (Illus.). (YA). (gr. 3 up). 1999. 19.95 (*0-7894-4716-9*) DK Pub Inc.

— Shipwreck. (Eyewitness Books). (Illus.). (J). (gr. 4-7). 2000. 19.99 (*0-7894-6621-X*) DK Pub Inc.

— Shipwreck. (Eyewitness Books). (J). (gr. 4-7). 2000. 15.95 (*0-7894-5884-5*) DK Pub Inc.

Platt, Richard. The Smithsonian Visual Timeline of Inventions. LC 94-21429. (Illus.). 64p. (J). (gr. 3 up). 1994. 16.95 (*1-56458-675-8*) DK Pub Inc.

***Platt, Richard.** Spies! (Dorling Kindersley Readers). (Illus.). (J). (gr. 2-3). 1999. 12.95 (*0-7894-5712-1*, D K Ink) DK Pub Inc.

— Spies! (Dorling Kindersley Readers). (Illus.). (J). (gr. 2-3). 2000. pap. 3.95 (*0-7894-5713-X*, D K Ink) DK Pub Inc.

— Spy. (Eyewitness Books). (Illus.). (J). (gr. 4-7). 2000. 19.99 (*0-7894-6616-3*) DK Pub Inc.

— Spy. (Eyewitness Books). (J). (gr. 4-7). 2000. 15.95 (*0-7894-5852-7*) DK Pub Inc.

— Spy. LC 96-11003. (Eyewitness Books). (J). 1996. 19.00 (*0-679-88122-0*); lib. bdg. 20.99 (*0-679-98122-5*) Knopf.

Platt, Richard. Stephen Biesty's Incredible Body. LC 98-16806. 32p. (J). (gr. 4 up). 1998. 19.95 (*0-7894-3424-5*) DK Pub Inc.

— Stephen Biesty's Incredible Everything. LC 97-75426. (Illus.). 32p. (YA). (gr. 5 up). 1997. 19.95 (*0-7894-2049-X*) DK Pub Inc.

— Stephen Biesty's Incredible Explosions. (Illus.). 32p. (J). 1996. 19.95 (*0-7894-1024-9*) DK Pub Inc.

— Stephen Bietsy's Incredible Cross-Sections. LC 91-27439. (Illus.). 48p. (J). 1992. 22.00 (*0-679-81411-6*, Pub. by Knopf Bks Yng Read) Random.

Platt, Richard, et al, photos by. Shipwreck. LC 97-9278. (Eyewitness Books). (Illus.). 64p. (J). (gr. 5-9). 1997. 19.00 (*0-679-88562-5*) Knopf.

Platt, Richard & Biesty, Stephen. Castle. (Illus.). 32p. (J). 21.95 (*0-590-24346-2*) Scholastic Inc.

— Man-of-War. (Illus.). (J). 21.95 (*0-590-74610-3*) Scholastic Inc.

— Stephen Biesty's Incredible Cross-Sections Book. (Illus.). (J). text 24.95 (*0-590-73870-4*) Scholastic Inc.

Platt, Richard, jt. auth. see Biesty, Stephen.

Platt, Richard, jt. auth. see Delf, Brian.

Platt, Rickard. Castle Diary: The Journal of Tobias Burgess, Page. LC 98-42779. (Illus.). 64p. (J). (gr. 4-8). 1999. 19.99 (*0-7636-0489-5*) Candlewick Pr.

Platt, Roger, jt. auth. see Biesty, Stephen.

Platt, Ron. Cannibal Eyes. LC 91-51145. (Illus.). 24p. (Orig.). 1992. pap. 7.00 (*0-938437-40-2*) MIT List Visual Arts.

— Jno Cook: Radically Recycled Cameras. LC 89-64406. (Illus.). 8p. 1990. pap. 3.50 (*0-938437-30-5*) MIT List Visual Arts.

— Maria Fernanda Cardoso. (Illus.). 32p. (Orig.). 1994. pap. 5.00 (*0-938437-46-1*) MIT List Visual Arts.

Platt, Ron, et al. Next of Kin: Looking at the Great Apes. unabridged ed. (Illus.). 48p. (Orig.). 1995. pap. 12.00 (*0-938437-50-X*) MIT List Visual Arts.

— Warren Neidich: Historical In(ter) vention. LC 91-14972. (Illus.). 16p. 1991. pap. 5.00 (*0-938437-38-0*) MIT List Visual Arts.

Platt, Rorin M. Virginia in Foreign Affairs, 1933-1941. 270p. (C). 1991. lib. bdg. 47.50 (*0-8191-7803-9*) U Pr of Amer.

Platt, Rutherford. One Thousand-One Questions Answered about Trees. (Illus.). 352p. 1992. reprint ed. pap. 8.95 (*0-486-27038-6*) Dover.

Platt, Rutherford H. Disasters & Democracy: The Politics of Extreme Natural Events. LC 99-18910. (Illus.). 335p. (C). 1999. pap. 35.00 (*1-55963-696-3*) Island Pr.

— Land Use & Society: Geography, Law & Public Policy. rev. ed. LC 95-39226. 425p. 1995. pap. text 32.00 (*1-55963-435-9*) Island Pr.

— Open Land in Urban Illinois: Roles of the Citizen Advocate. LC 78-146641. 132p. 1971. pap. 15.00 (*0-87580-506-X*) N Ill U Pr.

— The Open Space Decision Process: Spatial Allocation of Costs & Benefits. LC 72-85930. (University of Chicago, Department of Geography, Research Paper Ser.: No. 142). 204p. 1972. reprint ed. pap. 63.30 (*0-608-02270-5*, 206291100004) Bks Demand.

Platt, Rutherford H., ed. The Forgotten Books of Eden. (Illus.). 300p. 1996. reprint ed. pap. 24.95 (*1-56459-636-2*) Kessinger Pub.

— Regional Management of Metropolitan Floodplains. (Program on Environment & Behavior Monograph Ser.: No. 45). 334p. (C). 1987. pap. 20.00 (*0-685-28119-1*) Natural Hazards.

Platt, Rutherford H., et al, eds. Cities on the Beach: Management Issues of Developed Coastal Barriers. LC 86-25051. (Research Papers: No. 224). 324p. 1987. pap. text 14.50 (*0-89065-128-0*) U Ch Pr.

— The Ecological City: Preserving & Restoring Urban Biodiversity. LC 93-26506. (Illus.). 304p. 1994. 45.00 (*0-87023-883-3*); pap. 18.95 (*0-87023-884-1*) U of Mass Pr.

Platt, Rutherford H. & Macinko, George, eds. Beyond the Urban Fringe: Land Use Issues of Nonmetropolitan America. LC 83-3518. 432p. reprint ed. pap. 134.00 (*0-7837-2926-X*, 205752800006) Bks Demand.

Platt, Rutherford H., et al. Coastal Erosion: Has Retreat Sounded? LC 92-34852. (Program on Environment & Behavior Monograph Ser.: No. 53). 1992. 20.00 (*1-877943-07-X*) Natural Hazards.

Platt, Rutherford Hayes & Brett, J. Alden. The Lost Books of the Bible & the Forgotten Books of Eden. 1974. pap. 17.95 (*0-452-00944-8*) NAL.

Platt, Shay. Lambency Letters: Radiant Thoughts to Warm Your Heart. (Illus.). 242p. 1997. pap. text 12.95 (*1-884416-26-8*) A Press.

Platt, Stephen, jt. ed. see Watson, Jonathan.

Platt, Stephen D., et al. Teams: A Game to Develop Group Skills. 1988. 148.95 (*0-566-02735-6*, Pub. by Gower) Ashgate Pub Co.

Platt, Stephen D., jt. auth. see Maris, Ronald W.

Platt, Stephen D., jt. auth. see Watson, Jonathan.

***Platt, Susan N.** Art & Politics in the 1930s: Americanism, Marxism & Modernism. 1999. text 38.00 (*1-877675-29-6*) Midmarch Arts.

— Art & Politics in the 1930s: Americanism, Marxism & Modernism. LC 98-66819. (Art History Ser.). (Illus.). 320p. 1999. pap. 27.00 (*1-877675-28-8*) Midmarch Arts.

Platt, Susan N. Modernism in the Nineteen Twenties: Interpretations of Modern Art in New York from Expressionism to Constructivism. LC 85-1070. (Studies in the Fine Arts: Criticism: No. 17). 203p. reprint ed. pap. 63.00 (*0-8357-1661-9*, 207059700004) Bks Demand.

Platt, Suzy, ed. Respectfully Quoted: A Dictionary of Quotations from the Library of Congress. LC 91-45490. 546p. 1992. 47.95 (*0-87187-687-6*) Congr Quarterly.

Platt, Thomas C. The Autobiography of Thomas Collier Platt. LC 73-19172. (Politics & People Ser.). (Illus.). 580p. 1974. reprint ed. 44.95 (*0-405-05894-2*) Ayer.

— The Autobiography of Thomas Collier Platt. (American Biography Ser.). 556p. 1991. reprint ed. lib. bdg. 129.00 (*0-7812-8317-5*) Rprt Serv.

Platt, Thomas C., ed. see Orr & Reno P. A. Staff.

Platt, Tony & Takagi, Paul, eds. Punishment & Penal Discipline: Essays on the Prison & the Prisoner's Movement. 2nd ed. LC 79-90275. (Illus.). (Orig.). 1982. pap. 10.95 (*0-935206-00-0*) Soc Justice.

Platt, W. R. Color Atlas of Hematology: Atlas de Hematologia en Color. 645p. 1982. 175.00 (*0-8288-1873-8*) Fr & Eur.

Platt, Wendy, ed. Fort Ross Cookbook: Recipes of Fort Ross & Russia. (Illus.). 93p. (Orig.). 1994. pap. text 10.00 (*0-9617973-4-7*) Ft Ross Interpret.

Plattard, Jean. Life of Francois Rabelais. Roache, L. D., tr. 308p. 1968. reprint ed. 35.00 (*0-7146-2077-7*, BHA-02077, Pub. by F Cass Pubs) Intl Spec Bk.

Plattard, Jean, ed. see D'Aubigne, Agrippa.

Plattard, Jean, ed. see Rabelais, Francois.

Platte, Curtis R., III, ed. see Weatherford, John R.

Platteau, Jean-Phillipe, jt. auth. see Baland, Jean-Marie.

Platteel, Andre & Rohde, Carl C. Symbol Soup. LC 99-70823. (Illus.). 272p. (Orig.). 1999. pap. 85.00 (*0-500-28127-0*, Pub. by Thames Hudson) Norton.

Platten, David. Michel Tournier & the Metaphor of Fiction. LC 98-27468. 256p. 1999. text 49.95 (*0-312-21810-9*) St Martin.

***Platten, David, ed.** Djian: 37.2 le Matin. 96p. 1999. pap. 35.00 (*0-85261-368-7*, Pub. by U of Glasgow) St Mut.

Platten, J. K. & Legros, J. C. Convection in Liquids. (Illus.). 700p. 1983. 151.95 (*0-387-12637-6*) Spr-Verlag.

Platten, Stephen & Pattison, George. Spirit & Tradition: An Essay on Change. 184p. (Orig.). 1997. pap. 23.95 (*1-85311-130-9*, 858, Pub. by Canterbury Press Norwich) Morehouse Pub.

***Platter, Amanda.** Scarring Rituals: Poems. (Pocket Scriptures Ser.: Vol. 7). (Illus.). 2000. pap. 10.00 (*0-9679678-0-5*) Chrch Head Pr.

Platter, John. John Platter's South African Wine Guide, 1995. (Illus.). 324p. 1995. 13.95 (*1-85732-613-X*, Pub. by Reed Illust Books) Antique Collect.

— South African Wine Guide, 1996. 315p. 1996. 13.95 (*1-85732-815-9*, Pub. by Reed Illust Books) Antique Collect.

Plattes, Gabriel. A Discovery of Infinite Treasure, Hidden Since the Worlde's Beginning. LC 74-80202. (English Experience Ser.: No. 682). 96p. 1974. reprint ed. 20.00 (*90-221-0682-9*) Walter J Johnson.

Platti, Giovanni B. Giovanni Benedetto Platti: Two Keyboard Concertos. Freeman, Daniel E., ed. (Recent Researches in Music of the Classic Era Ser.: Vol. RRC37). (Illus.). xiv, 85p. 1991. pap. 35.00 (*0-89579-260-5*) A-R Eds.

Plattner, Andy. Winter Money: Stories by Andy Plattner. LC 97-12248. (Flannery O'Connor Award for Short Fiction Ser.). 184p. 1997. 22.95 (*0-8203-1958-9*) U of Ga Pr.

Plattner, B. Datenkommunikation und Elektronische Post. 2nd ed. (GER.). (C). 1990. text. write for info. (*0-201-55912-9*) Addison-Wesley.

Plattner, Bernard, ed. Broadband Communications: Networks, Services, Applications, Future Directions: Proceedings of the 1996 International Zurich Seminar on Digital Communications, Held February 21-23, 1996, Zurich, Switzerland. (Lecture Notes in Computer Science Ser.: Vol. 1044). xiv, 359p. 1996. pap. 62.00 (*3-540-60895-8*) Spr-Verlag.

***Plattner, Hasso.** Anticipating Change: Secrets Behind the SAP Empire. 312p. 2000. 29.99 (*0-7615-2913-6*) Prima Pub.

Plattner, Helmut, ed. Electron Microscopy of Subcellular Dynamics. 368p. 1989. lib. bdg. 249.00 (*0-8493-6079-X*, QH212) CRC Pr.

Plattner, Helmut, et al, eds. Advances in Cell & Molecular Biology of Membranes & Organelles Vol. 2, Pts. A & B: Membrane Transport in Protozoa, Set. 483p. 1993. 257.00 (*1-55938-628-2*) Jai Pr.

P

***Plattner, Marc F. & Smolar, Aleksander.** Power, Globalization & Democracy. LC 00-33040. (Journal of Democracy Book Ser.). 180p. 2000. 16.95 (*0-8018-6568-9*) Johns Hopkins.

Plattner, Marc F., jt. ed. see Diamond, Larry J.

Plattner, Marc F., jt. ed. see Diamond, Larry.

Plattner, Robert D. & Klein, Mark S. New York City Tax Handbook, 1998. rev. ed. 212p. 1997. pap. text 45.00 (*0-7811-0186-7*) Res Inst Am.

— New York City Tax Handbook, 1999. rev. ed. 234p. 1998. pap. text 35.75 (*0-7811-0198-0*) Res Inst Am.

— New York State Tax Handbook, 1998. rev. ed. 336p. 1997. pap. text 45.00 (*0-7811-0185-9*) Res Inst Am.

— New York State Tax Handbook, 1999. rev. ed. Jenis, Richard E., ed. 386p. 1998. pap. text 35.75 (*0-7811-0197-2*) Res Inst Am.

Plattner, Sandra S. Connecting Around the World. (J). (ps-k). 1991. pap. 9.99 (*0-86653-978-6*) Fearon Teacher Aids.

— Connecting with Holidays. (J). (ps-k). 1991. pap. 9.99 (*0-8224-1634-4*) Fearon Teacher Aids.

— Connecting with My Community. (J). (ps-k). 1991. pap. 9.99 (*0-8224-3912-3*) Fearon Teacher Aids.

— Connecting with Myself. (J). (ps-k). 1991. pap. 9.99 (*0-86653-986-7*) Fearon Teacher Aids.

— Connecting with Nature. (J). (ps-k). 1991. pap. 9.99 (*0-86653-976-X*) Fearon Teacher Aids.

— Connecting with the Seasons. (J). (ps-k). 1991. pap. 9.99 (*0-86653-977-8*) Fearon Teacher Aids.

— Explore, Discover, Connect! Set, 6 bks., Set. (J). 54.99 (*1-56417-744-0*, FE0024) Fearon Teacher Aids.

Plattner, Steven, jt. ed. see Schulz, Constance B.

Plattner, Steven W. Roy Stryker: U. S. A., 1943-1950, The Standard Oil (New Jersey) Photography Project. (Illus.). 144p. 1983. 27.95 (*0-292-77028-6*) U of Tex Pr.

Plattner, Stuart. High Art Down Home: An Economic Ethnography of a Local Art Market. LC 96-14864. (Illus.). 312p. 1996. 29.95 (*0-226-67082-1*) U Ch Pr.

— High Art Down Home: An Economic Ethnography of a Local Art Market. LC 96-14864. (Illus.). 250p. 1998. pap. text 16.00 (*0-226-67084-8*) U Ch Pr.

Plattner, Stuart, ed. Economic Anthropology. LC 89-4547. 504p. 1989. 57.50 (*0-8047-1645-5*); pap. 19.95 (*0-8047-1752-4*) Stanford U Pr.

— Markets & Marketing: Proceedings of the 1984 Meeting of the Society for Economic Development. (Monographs in Economic Anthropology: No. 4). (Illus.). 438p. 1985. pap. text 37.00 (*0-8191-4605-6*); lib. bdg. 55.00 (*0-8191-4604-8*) U Pr of Amer.

***Platto, Charles.** Economic Consequences of Litigation Worldwide. LC 98-46646. 1998. 150.00 (*90-411-1095-X*) Kluwer Law Intl.

Platto, Charles. Enforcement of Foreign Judgments. (C). 1989. lib. bdg. 155.50 (*1-85333-315-8*, Pub. by Graham & Trotman) Kluwer Academic.

Platto, Charles, ed. Civil Appeal Procedures Worldwide. LC 92-18821. (International Bar Association Ser.). 448p. (C). 1992. lib. bdg. 194.00 (*1-85333-725-0*, Pub. by Graham & Trotman) Kluwer Academic.

— Obtaining Evidence in Another Jurisdiction in Business Disputes. 2nd ed. (International Bar Association Ser.). 208p. (C). 1993. lib. bdg. 114.00 (*1-85333-758-7*, Pub. by Graham & Trotman) Kluwer Academic.

— Pre-Trial & Pre-Hearing Procedures Worldwide. (C). 1990. lib. bdg. 181.50 (*1-85333-458-8*, Pub. by Graham & Trotman) Kluwer Academic.

— Trials & Court Procedures Worldwide. (International Bar Association Ser.). 480p. (C). 1991. lib. bdg. 200.00 (*1-85333-608-4*, Pub. by Graham & Trotman) Kluwer Academic.

Platto, Charles & Horton, William G., eds. Enforcement of Foreign Judgments Worldwide. 2nd ed. LC 93-29171. (International Bar Association Ser.). 1993. lib. bdg. 133.50 (*1-85333-757-9*, Pub. by Graham & Trotman) Kluwer Academic.

Platts, David E. Playful Self-Discovery: A Findhorn Foundation Approach to Building Trust in Groups. (Guidebooks for Growth Together). 128p. (Orig.). 1996. pap. 10.95 (*1-899171-06-1*, Pub. by Findhorn Pr) Words Distrib.

Platts, David E., ed. Divinely Ordinary, Divinely Human: Celebrating the Life & Work of Eileen Caddy. (Illus.). 136p. 1999. 19.95 (*1-899171-87-8*) Findhorn Pr.

Platts, David E., ed. International Psychosynthesis Directory. 4th rev. ed. 120p. 1994. pap. 10.00 (*0-9524004-0-5*, Pub. by Platts Pub Co) Synthesis Dist.

Platts, David E., jt. auth. see Caddy, Eileen.

Platts, David E., ed. see Caddy, Eileen.

Platts, Dennis R., jt. ed. see Boulous, Edward N.

Platts, Geoffrey. Trek! Man Alone in the Arizona Wild. Grenard, Jack, ed. (Illus.). 208p. (Orig.). 1991. pap. 10.50 (*0-9631487-0-2*) Carefree Comm.

Platts, J. & St. Aubyn, J. D., eds. Uninterruptible Power Supplies. (Power Ser.: No. 14). 168p. 1992. text 70.00 (*0-86341-263-7*, PO014) INSPEC Inc.

Platts, James. Jesus: The Petulant Archangel. 104p. 1999. pap. 9.50 (*0-8059-4603-9*) Dorrance.

Platts, John T. Dictionary of Urdu, Classical Hindi & English. (ENG, HIN & URD.). 1987. 95.00 (*0-8288-1745-6*, F29960) Fr & Eur.

— Dictionary of Urdu, Classical Hindi & English. 2nd ed. (ENG & URD.). (C). 1988. 56.00 (*0-8364-2410-7*) S Asia.

— The Grammar of the Hindustani or Urdu Language. (ENG & HIN.). 1992. reprint ed. 49.95 (*0-8288-8473-0*) Fr & Eur.

— The Grammar of the Hindustani or Urdu Language. 1990. reprint ed. 27.00 (*0-685-48703-2*, Pub. by M Manoharial) S Asia.

Platts, Linda E., ed. see Lippke Fretwell, Holly.

Platts, Mark. Ways of Meaning: An Introduction to a Philosophy of Language. 2nd ed. LC 96-45206. (Illus.). 326p. 1997. pap. text 26.50 (*0-262-66107-1*) MIT Pr.

Platts-Mills, Thomas. Asthma: Causes & Mechanisms. LC 99-17632. (Indoor Air Research Ser.). 256p. 1999. boxed set 69.95 (*1-56670-373-5*) Lewis Pubs.

***Platts, Mitchell.** Illustrated History of Golf. (Illus.). 256p. 2000. 19.99 (*0-517-16177-X*) Random Hse Value.

Plattus, Alan J., et al. Koetter Kim & Associates: Place Time. LC 97-11847. (Illus.). 224p. 1997. 60.00 (*0-8478-2050-5*, Pub. by Rizzoli Intl) St Martin.

Platvoet, J. G. Comparing Religions: A Limitative Approach. (Religion & Reason Ser.: No. 24). xiv, 350p. 1982. 75.40 (*90-279-3170-4*) Mouton.

***Platvoet, Jan & Molendijk, Arie L.** The Pragmatics of Defining Religion: Contexts, Concepts & Contests. LC 99-33639. (Studies in the History of Religions). 496p. 1999. 118.00 (*90-04-11544-7*) Brill Academic Pubs.

Platvoet, Jan & Van der Toorn, Karel, eds. Pluralism & Identity: Studies in Ritual Behavior. LC 95-16624. (Studies in the History of Religions: Vol. 67). vi, 376p. 1995. 119.00 (*90-04-10373-2*) Brill Academic Pubs.

***Platz, Ann.** The Best Is Yet to Come: Celebrating the Second Half of Life. LC 99-85699. 250p. 2000. pap. 10.99 (*0-7369-0230-9*) Harvest Hse.

***Platz, Ann & Wales, Susan.** The Pleasure of Your Company: Simple Ideas for Enjoyable Entertaining. LC 99-18437. (Illus.). 112p. 1999. 14.99 (*0-7369-0111-6*) Harvest Hse.

— Social Graces: Manners, Conversation & Charm for Today. LC 99-18851. (Illus.). 112p. 1999. 14.99 (*0-7369-0112-4*) Harvest Hse.

Platz, Ann, jt. auth. see Wales, Susan.

Platz-Horster, Gertrud. Nil und Euthenia. (Winckelmannsprogramm der Archaologischen Gesellschaft zu Berlin Ser.: No. 133). (GER.). 47p. (C). 1992. pap. text 29.25 (*3-11-013779-8*) De Gruyter.

Platz, Joseph, tr. see Nimzowitsch, Aron.

Platz, M. S. Kinetics & Spectroscopy of Carbenes & Biradicals. LC 89-29219. (Illus.). 388p. (C). 1990. text 110.00 (*0-306-43282-X*, Kluwer Plenum) Kluwer Academic.

Platz, Theodore A., Jr. Banking. deluxe ed. (Barron's Business Library). 320p. 1991. pap. 18.95 (*0-8120-4542-4*) Barron.

***Platz, Theodore A. & Fitch, Thomas P.** Business Banking. 2nd ed. LC 00-34287. 2001. write for info. (*0-7641-1398-4*) Barron.

Platz, Valerie A., jt. ed. see Kratz, Charles E.

Platzack, Christer, jt. auth. see Holmberg, Anders.

Platzer, B., et al. Thermophysical Properties of Refrigerants. (Illus.). 464p. 1990. 316.95 (*0-387-16112-0*) Spr-Verlag.

Platzer, Hans-Wolfgang, jt. auth. see Lecher, Wolfgang.

Platzer, Hans-Wolfgang, jt. auth. see Lecher, Wolfgang.

Platzer, Michaela, et al. California Cybercities: California's Hottest High-Technology Metropolitan Areas. LC 99-166907. (Illus.). 50p. 1998. pap. 90.00 (*0-928391-03-5*) American Electronics Association.

— Cyber Education: U. S. Education & the High-Technology Workforce, a National & State-by-State Perspective. (Illus.). 123p. 1999. pap. 190.00 (*0-928391-04-3*) American Electronics Association.

— Cybernation: The Importance of the High-Technology Industry to the American Economy. (Illus.). 145p. 1997. spiral bd. 190.00 (*0-928391-00-0*) American Electronics Association.

***Platzer, Michaela, et al.** Cybernation 2.0: The U.S. High-Tech Industry & World Markets. (Illus.). 111p. 2000. spiral bd. 190.00 (*0-928391-07-8*) American Electronics Association.

Platzer, Michaela D. & Novak, Christopher. Cyberstates: A State-by-State Overview of the High-Technology Industry. (Illus.). 115p. 1997. spiral bd. 190.00 (*0-928391-01-9*) American Electronics Association.

Platzer, Michaela D., et al. Cyberstates Update: A State-by-State Overview of the High-Technology Industry. (Illus.). 86p. 1998. spiral bd. 190.00 (*0-928391-02-7*) American Electronics Association.

— Cyberstates 3.0: A State-by-State Overview of the High-Technology Industry. 106p. 1999. pap. 190.00 (*0-928391-05-1*) American Electronics Association.

Platzer, Norbert A., ed. Copolymers, Polyblends, & Composites. LC 75-17726. (Advances in Chemistry Ser.: Vol. 142). 502p. 1975. reprint ed. pap. 155.70 (*0-608-03905-5*, 206435200008) Bks Demand.

— Polymerization Kinetics & Technology: A Symposium Co-Sponsored by the Division of Industrial & Engineering Chemistry & the Division of Polymer Chemistry at the 163rd Meeting of the American Chemical Society, Boston, MA, April 10-14, 1972. LC 73-91733. (Advances in Chemistry Ser.: No. 128). (Illus.). 304p. 1973. reprint ed. pap. 94.30 (*0-608-06777-6*, 206697400009) Bks Demand.

— Polymerization Reactions & New Polymers: A Symposium Co-Sponsored by the Division of Industrial & Engineering Chemistry & the Division of Polymer Chemistry at the 163rd Meeting of the American Chemical Society, Boston, MA, April 10-14, 1972. LC 73-91734. (Advances in Chemistry Ser.: No. 129). (Illus.). 302p. 1973. reprint ed. pap. 93.70 (*0-608-06774-1*, 206697100009) Bks Demand.

Platzer, Steven, tr. see Horio, Teruhisa.

Platzer, W., ed. European Anatomical Congress, 7th, Insbruck, September 1984: Abstracts. (Journal: Acta Anatomica: Vol. 120, No. 1-2). 92p. 1984. pap. 33.25 (*3-8055-3955-X*) S Karger.

Platzer, Werner, et al. Color Atlas & Textbook of Human Anatomy: Locomotor System, Vol. I. 4th ed. (Illus.). 440p. 1992. pap. 28.50 (*0-86577-423-4*) Thieme Med Pubs.

Platzer, Werner, ed. see Pernkopf, Eduard.

Platzes, Monika, jt. ed. see Blanco, Evangeline.

***Platzker, David & Wyckoff, Elizabeth.** Hard Pressed: 600 Years of Prints & Process. (Illus.). 128p. 2000. 45.00 (*1-55595-192-9*, Pub. by Hudson Hills); write for info. (*1-55595-193-7*) Hudson Hills.

Platzker, David, jt. auth. see Axsom, Richard H.

Platzky, Laurine & Walker, Cherryl. The Surplus People: Forced Removals in South Africa. LC 82-95958. 250p. 1985. pap. text 16.95 (*0-86975-255-3*, Pub. by Ravan Pr) Ohio U Pr.

Platzman, George W. A Catalogue of Early Printed Editions of the Works of Fredric Chopin in the University of Chicago Library. LC 97-28000. (Illus.). 1998. pap. 30.00 (*0-943056-24-1*) Univ Chi Lib.

Platzmann, Julius. Vezeichniss Einer Auswahl Amerikanischer Grammatiken. 1977. reprint ed. 23.95 (*0-518-19010-2*) Ayer.

Platzner, Gloria, jt. auth. see Harris, Stephen L.

Platzner, I. Application of Stable Isotopes. text. write for info. (*0-471-49051-2*) Wiley.

Platzner, I. Modern Isotope Radio Mass Spectrometry. LC 97-7329. (Chemical Analysis Ser.). 530p. 1997. 305.00 (*0-471-97416-1*) Wiley.

Platzner, Robert L. The Metaphysical Novel in England: The Romantic Phase. Varma, Devendra P., ed. LC 79-8468. (Gothic Studies & Dissertations). 1980. lib. bdg. 36.95 (*0-405-12656-5*) Ayer.

— Mishnah: The Oral Law. 64p. 1995. pap., teacher ed. 6.95 (*0-87441-390-7*) Behrman.

Platzner, Robert L. & Harris, Stephen L. Touchstones: Classic Texts in the Humanities. 600p. (C). 1991. pap. text 32.50 (*0-03-047504-X*) Harcourt Coll Pubs.

Platzner, Robert L., jt. auth. see Gersh, Harry.

Platzoder & Verlaan. The Baltic Sea: New Developments in National Politics & International Cooperation. LC 96-49309. 1997. 146.00 (*90-411-0357-0*) Kluwer Law Intl.

Platzoder, Renate. 3rd United Nations Conference on the Law of the Sea: Documents of the Geneva Session 1975. xiv, 322p. 1975. pap. 29.95 (*3-7875-2127-5*) W S Hein.

Platzoder, Renate, jt. auth. see Von Welck, Stephan.

Plauche. Surgical Obstetrics. 1991. text 115.00 (*0-7216-3049-9*, W B Saunders Co) Harcrt Hlth Sci Grp.

Plaud, Joseph J. & Eifert, Georg H., eds. From Behavior Theory to Behavior Therapy. LC 97-23806. 352p. (C). 1998. 55.00 (*0-205-17477-9*) Allyn.

Plauger, P. J. The Draft Standard C++ Library. LC 94-36379. 590p. 1994. pap. 62.00 (*0-13-117003-1*) P-H.

— Programming on Purpose: Essays on Programming Design. LC 92-45905. (Illus.). 256p. (C). 1993. pap. text 24.80 (*0-13-721374-3*) P-H.

— Standard C Library. 512p. (C). 1991. pap. 63.00 (*0-13-131509-9*) P-H.

Plauger, P. J., et al. Standard Template Library: A Definitive Approach to C++ Programming Using STL. 600p. (C). 2002. pap. 38.00 (*0-13-437633-1*) P-H.

Plauger, P. J., jt. auth. see Kernighan, Brian W.

Plauger, P. L., jt. auth. see Kernighan, Brian W.

Plaugher, Gregory, ed. Textbook of Clinical Chiropractic. LC 92-5613. (Illus.). 526p. 1993. 89.00 (*0-683-06897-0*) Lppncott W & W.

Plaugher, Gregory, jt. auth. see Anrig, Claudia.

Plaugher, Gregory, jt. auth. see Anrig, Claudia A.

Plaul, Heiner, ed. see May, Karl.

Plaumann, Peter, jt. ed. see Strambach, Karl.

Plaut, David, jt. auth. see Running Press Staff.

Plaut, Elizabeth S. The Guggenheim Wormser Family: A Genealogical 300-Year Memoir. LC 96-32992. 1996. 49.50 (*0-88125-572-6*) Ktav.

Plaut, Eric A. Grand Opera: Mirror of the Western Mind. LC 93-8351. (Illus.). 336p. 1993. 28.50 (*1-56663-034-7*) I R Dee.

Plaut, Eric A., ed. & tr. see Marx, Karl.

Plaut, Gunther. The Magen David: How the Six-Pointed Star Became the Emblem of the Jewish People. (Illus.). 114p. 1990. 22.50 (*0-910250-16-2*) Bnai Brith Intl.

Plaut, H. Japanese Conversation - Grammar with Numerous Reading Lessons & Dialogues, 2 vols., Set. 1991. lib. bdg. 98.95 (*0-8490-4512-6*) Gordon Pr.

Plaut, James S., ed. Sources of Modern Painting. LC 79-91372. (Contemporary Art Ser.). 1970. reprint ed. 19.95 (*0-405-00734-5*) Ayer.

Plaut, Joshua E. Greek Jewry in the Twentieth Century, 1913-1983: Patterns of Jewish Survival in the Greek Provinces Before & after the Holocaust. LC 92-52718. (Illus.). 224p. 1996. 38.50 (*0-8386-3463-X*) Fairleigh Dickinson.

Plaut, L., ed. see International Astronomical Union Staff.

Plaut, Mary, ed. see Michael, Christine.

Plaut, Steven E. Import Dependence & Economic Vulnerability. Altman, Edward I. & Walter, Ingo I., eds. LC 83-48090. (Contemporary Studies in Economic & Financial Analysis: Vol. 43). 139p. 1983. 78.50 (*0-89232-392-2*) Jai Pr.

Plaut, Thomas. An Econometric Analysis of Regional Wastepaper Markets. (Discussion Papers: No. 104). 1978. pap. 10.00 (*1-55869-030-1*) Regional Sci Res Inst.

— The Effects of Urbanization on the Loss of Farmland at the Rural-Urban Fringe: A National & Regional Perspective. (Discussion Papers: No. 94). 1976. pap. 10.00 (*1-55869-034-4*) Regional Sci Res Inst.

***Plaut, Thomas.** People, Politics & Economic Life: Exploring Appalachia with Quantitative Methods. 2nd ed. 164p. (C). 1999. spiral bd. 34.95 (*0-7872-6419-9*, 41641901) Kendall-Hunt.

Plaut, Thomas. The Real Property Tax, Differential Assessment, & the Loss of Farmland on the Rural-Urban Fringe. (Discussion Papers: No. 97). 1977. pap. 10.00 (*1-55869-104-9*) Regional Sci Res Inst.

Plaut, Thomas & Steiker, Gene. Characteristics of Wastepaper Markets & Trends in Scrap Paper Recycling, Prices, Demand & Availability: A National & Regional Overview. (Discussion Papers: No. 103). 1978. pap. 10.00 (*1-55869-012-3*) Regional Sci Res Inst.

Plaut, Thomas, jt. auth. see Coughlin, Robert E.

Plaut, Thomas F. El Asma En Un Minuto: Lo Que Usted Necesita Saber. 3rd rev. ed. DiStilio, Veronica et al, trs. LC 97-46567. (SPA., Illus.). 48p. 1998. pap. 5.00 (*0-914625-19-5*) Pedipress.

— Children with Asthma: A Manual for Parents. 2nd rev. ed. LC 98-19135. (Illus.). xxi, 276p. 1998. pap. 10.00 (*0-914625-21-7*) Pedipress.

— One Minute Asthma: What You Need to Know. 4th ed. Jones, Teresa B., ed. LC 98-25976. (Illus.). 56p. 1998. 5.00 (*0-914625-20-9*) Pedipress.

Plaut, Thomas F. & Jones, Teresa B. Dr. Tom Plaut's Asthma Guide for People of All Ages. LC 99-46826. (Illus.). 304p. 1999. pap. 25.00 (*0-914625-22-5*) Pedipress.

Plaut, W. Gunther. Asylum: A Moral Dilemma. LC 95-3330. 192p. 1995. 59.95 (*0-275-95195-2*, Praeger Pubs); pap. 17.95 (*0-275-95196-0*, Praeger Pubs) Greenwood.

— The Magen David: How the Six-Pointed Star Became the Emblem of the Jewish People. (Illus.). 114p. 1990. pap. 12.95 (*0-910250-17-0*) Bnai Brith Intl.

— The Man Who Would Be Messiah: A Biographical Novel. 258p. 1990. pap. 12.95 (*0-88962-400-3*) Mosaic.

— More Unfinished Business. LC 98-106746. (Illus.). 376p. 1997. text 35.00 (*0-8020-0888-7*) U of Toronto Pr.

***Plaut, W. Gunther.** The Price & Privilege of Growing Old. LC 99-33766. (Illus.). 152p. 2000. 22.95 (*0-88123-080-4*, Pub. by Central Conf); pap. 14.95 (*0-88123-081-2*, Pub. by Central Conf) Natl Bk Netwk.

Plaut, W. Gunther. Teshuvot for the 1990s: Reform Judaisms Answers to Today's Dilemmas. 1996. pap. text 15.00 (*0-88123-071-5*) Central Conf.

Plaut, W. Gunther, ed. The Torah: A Modern Commentary (English Opening) 1824p. 1981. 45.00 (*0-8074-0055-6*, 381600) UAHC.

— The Torah: A Modern Commentary (Hebrew Opening) 1824p. 1981. 45.00 (*0-8074-0165-X*, 381590) UAHC.

— The Torah: A Modern Commentary (Pulpit Edition) large type ed. 1824p. 1981. 100.00 (*0-8074-0286-9*, 381597) UAHC.

***Plaut, W. Gunther & Meyer, Michael.** The Reform Judaism Reader: North American Documents. (YA). 2000. 14.95 (*0-8074-0732-1*) UAHC.

Plaut, W. Gunther, jt. auth. see Stern, Chaim.

Plaute. Oeuvres Completes. (FRE.). 1971. lib. bdg. 95.00 (*0-8288-3574-8*, F40040) Fr & Eur.

Plaute & Terence. Oeuvres Completes. 1512p. 41.50 (*0-686-56550-9*) Fr & Eur.

***Plautus.** Amphitruo. Christenson, David M., ed. (Cambridge Greek & Latin Classics Ser.). 350p. (C). 2000. 64.95 (*0-521-45401-8*) Cambridge U Pr.

— Amphitruo. Christenson, David M., ed. (Cambridge Greek & Latin Classics Ser.). 350p. (C). 2000. pap. 24.95 (*0-521-45997-4*) Cambridge U Pr.

Plautus. Amphitryon: Index Verborum, Lexiques Inersese, Releves Lexicaux et Grammaticaux. Maniet, Albert & Paquot, Annette, eds. (GER.). vii, 217p. 1970. write for info. (*0-318-70439-0*) G Olms Pubs.

— Ausgewahlte Komodien, 3 vols. Lorenz, August O., ed. 1981. write for info. (*0-318-71196-6*) G Olms Pubs.

— Ausgewahlte Komodien, 3 vols., Set. Lorenz, August O., ed. 1981. write for info. (*0-318-71195-8*) G Olms Pubs.

— The Captivi of Plautus. Connor, W. R. & Lindsey, Wallace M., eds. LC 78-67134. (Latin Texts & Commentaries Ser.). (ENG & LAT.). 1979. reprint ed. lib. bdg. 30.95 (*0-405-11608-X*) Ayer.

— Comoediae, 2 vols. Leo, Friedrich, ed. 1958. 3.5 hd. write for info. (*0-318-71198-2*); 3.5 hd. write for info. (*0-318-71199-0*) G Olms Pubs.

— Comoediae, 2 vols., Set. Leo, Friedrich, ed. 1958. 3.5 hd. write for info. (*0-318-71197-4*) G Olms Pubs.

— Lexique Inverse: Listes Grammaticales, Releves Divers. Maniet, Albert, ed. (GER.). viii, 201p. 1969. write for info. (*0-318-70440-4*) G Olms Pubs.

— Menaechmi. Gratwick, A. S., ed. LC 92-17790. (Greek & Latin Classics Ser.). 286p. (C). 1993. text 65.00 (*0-521-34162-0*); pap. text 24.95 (*0-521-34970-2*) Cambridge U Pr.

— Plaute, Amphitryon. Index Verborum, Lexiques Inverses, Releves Lexicaux et Grammaticaux. Maniet, Albert & Paquot, Annette, eds. vii, 217p. 1970. write for info. (*0-318-71200-8*) G Olms Pubs.

— Plaute, Lexique Inverse: Listes Grammaticales. Releves Divers. Maniet, Albert, ed. viii, 201p. 1969. write for info. (*0-318-71201-6*) G Olms Pubs.

— Plauti Truculentus, 2 vols. Connor, W. R., ed. LC 78-67132. (Latin Texts & Commentaries Ser.). (LAT.). 1979. reprint ed. lib. bdg. 28.95 (*0-405-11602-0*) Ayer.

— Plautus: Bacchides. Barsby, J., ed. (Classical Texts Ser.). 1986. pap. 28.00 (*0-85668-227-6*, Pub. by Aris & Phillips) David Brown.

— The Rope & Other Plays. Watling, E. F., tr. Incl. Amphitryon. 1964. pap. Ghost. 1964. pap. Three-Dollar Day. 1964. pap. (Classics Ser.). 288p. 1964. Set pap. 10.95 (*0-14-044136-0*, Penguin Classics) Viking Penguin.

— Rudens. Fay, H. C., ed. & intro. by. (College Classical Ser.). v, 221p. (C). 1983. reprint ed. pap. text 17.50 (*0-89241-386-7*) Caratzas.

— Stichus, Vol. V. (Loeb Classical Library: No. 328). 15.50 (*0-674-99362-4*) HUP.

— T. Macci Plauti Aulularia: With Critical & Exegetical Notes & an Introduction. Connor, W. R., ed. LC 78-67156. (Latin Texts & Commentaries Ser.). (ENG & LAT.). 1979. reprint ed. lib. bdg. 19.95 (*0-405-11623-3*) Ayer.

An Asterisk (*) at the beginning of an entry indicates that the title is appearing for the first time.

— T. Macci Plauti Epidicus. Connor, W. R., ed. (Latin Texts & Commentaries Ser.). (ENG & LAT.). 1979. reprint ed. lib. bdg. 37.95 (*0-405-11600-4*) Ayer.

— T. Macci Plauti Pseudolus. Connor, W. R., ed. LC 78-11622. (Latin Texts & Commentaries Ser.). (ENG & LAT.). 1979. reprint ed. lib. bdg. 15.95 (*0-405-11622-5*) Ayer.

— T. Macci Plauti Rudens. Connor, W. R. & Sonnenschein, Edward A., eds. LC 78-67153. (Latin Texts & Commentaries Ser.). (ENG & LAT.). 1979. reprint ed. lib. bdg. 25.95 (*0-405-11620-9*) Ayer.

Plautus & Terence. Five Comedies: Bacchides, Menaechmi, Miles Gloriosus, Hecyra, & Adelphoe. Berg, Deena & Parker, Douglass, trs. from LAT. LC 98-50732. (HPC Classics Ser.). 352p. (C). 1999. pap. 12.95 (*0-87220-362-X*) Hackett Pub.

***Plautus & Terence.** Five Comedies: Bacchides, Menaechmi, Miles Gloriosus, Hecyra, & Adelphoe. Berg, Deena & Parker, Douglass, trs. from LAT. LC 98-50732. (HPC Classics Ser.). 352p. (C). 1999. lib. bdg. 37.95 (*0-87220-363-8*) Hackett Pub.

Plautus, jt. auth. see Aristophanes.

Plautus, J. A. Plautus: Bacchides. Barsby, J., ed. (Classical Texts Ser.). 1986. 59.99 (*0-85668-226-8*, Pub. by Aris & Phillips) David Brown.

Plautus, Titus Maccius. Fabularum Reliquiae Ambrosianae. Studemund, Guilelmus, ed. (GER.). xxxii, 524p. 1972. reprint ed. write for info. (*3-487-04334-3*) G Olms Pubs.

***Plautus, Titus Maccius.** Four Comedies: The Braggart Soldier The Brothers Menaechmus, The Haunted House, The Pot of Gold. Segal, Erich, tr. from LAT. & intro. by. LC 95-44849. (Oxford World's Classics Ser.). 288p. 1998. pap. 8.95 (*0-19-283896-2*) OUP.

Plautus, Titus Maccius. Menaechmi. rev. ed. Hammond, Mason & Moseley, Nicholas, eds. 140p. 1961. 22.50 (*0-674-56725-0*) HUP.

— Miles Gloriosus. 2nd rev. ed. Hammond, Mason et al, eds. LC 73-122213. 140p. 1963. 24.45 (*0-674-57436-2*) HUP.

— Plauti Mercator, 2 vols. Connor, W. R., ed. LC 78-67131. (Latin Texts & Commentaries Ser.). (ENG & LAT.). 1979. reprint ed. lib. bdg. 25.95 (*0-405-11601-2*) Ayer.

— Three Comedies: Miles Gloriosus - Pseudolus - Rudens. LC 90-41383. (Masters of Latin Literature Ser.). 320p. 1991. text 42.50 (*0-8014-2355-4*); pap. text 14.95 (*0-8014-9594-6*) Cornell U Pr.

Plautz, Elizabeth, jt. auth. see Garcia, Gillian G.

Plautz, Penny. Wellness Works!, Vol. 1. 1998. ring bd., wbk. ed. 20.00 (*0-9660408-0-5*) Words With.

Plavchan, Ronald J. A History of Anheuser-Busch, 1852 - 1933. LC 75-41779. (Companies & Men: Business Enterprises in America Ser.). 1980. 32.11 (*0-405-08094-8*) Ayer.

Plavec, Mirek J., ed. see International Astronomical Union Staff.

Plavec, Robert L., tr. see Kuriyama, Noriko & Donnellan, Patrick E.

Plavsic, Branko M., et al. Gastrointestinal Radiology: A Concise Text. 640p. 1991. 89.01 (*0-08-040685-8*, Pub. by PPI) McGraw.

Plawin, Paul. Careers for Travel Buffs & Other Restless Types. (VGM Careers for You Ser.). (Illus.). 144p. 1995. 14.95 (*0-8442-8109-3*, 81093, VGM Career); pap. 9.95 (*0-8442-8127-1*, 81271, VGM Career) NTC Contemp Pub Co.

Plawin, Paul, ed. The Official Guide to the Perkins Act of 1998. 200p. (Orig.). 1998. pap. 34.95 (*0-89514-003-9*) ACTE.

Plawrence, David. Statistics Using the TI-85. (Skill & Practice Masters Using the TI-85 Ser.). Date not set. pap. 12.95 (*1-881641-38-4*) Pencil Point.

***Plax, Julie Anne.** Watteau & the Cultural Politics of Eighteenth-Century France. (Illus.). 336p. (C). 2000. text 80.00 (*0-521-64268-X*) Cambridge U Pr.

Plax, Timothy G., jt. auth. see Kearney, Patricia.

***Plaxco, Kelli.** Thematic Unit Clothing: Primary. (Illus.). 80p. 1999. pap., teacher ed. 9.95 (*1-57690-379-6*, TCM 2379) Tchr Create Mat.

Plaxton, Elizabeth, jt. auth. see Plaxton, John.

Plaxton, Elmer H., ed. North American Terrestrial Orchids: Symposium II - Proceedings & Lectures. LC 82-62805. (Illus.). 144p. 1983. pap. 17.95 (*0-9610332-0-7*) Mich Orchid Soc.

***Plaxton, John & Plaxton, Elizabeth.** Mexico & Central America by Campervan: Travel Adventure Guide. (Illus.). 1998. pap. 24.95 (*1-895907-87-X*) ITMP Pub.

— RVing into Canada's Arctic. rev. ed. 2000. pap. 19.95 (*0-9680314-2-0*) Travel n Write.

Play, Frederic Le, see Le Play, Frederic.

Playboy Enterprises, Inc. Staff. The Playboy Interview: The Best of 3 Decades, 1962-1992. (Illus.). (Orig.). 24.95 (*0-87223-909-8*); pap. 9.95 (*0-87223-908-X*) Playboy Ent.

— Playboy Presents: Dian Parkinson. (Illus.). 96p. (Orig.). 1993. pap. 5.95 (*0-87223-913-6*) Playboy Ent.

— Playboy Presents International Playmates. (Playboy Presents Ser.). (Illus.). 112p. (Orig.). 1992. pap. 5.95 (*0-87223-900-4*, Playboy Pr) Playboy Ent.

— Playboy Presents Playboy's Playmate Review. (Playboy Presents Ser.). (Illus.). 112p. (Orig.). 1992. pap. 5.95 (*0-87223-903-9*, Playboy Pr) Playboy Ent.

— Playboy's Bathing Beauties. (Illus.). 112p. (Orig.). 1992. pap. 5.95 (*0-87223-902-0*, Playboy Pr) Playboy Ent.

— Playboy's Career Girls. (Illus.). 112p. (Orig.). 1992. pap. 5.95 (*0-87223-905-5*, Playboy Pr) Playboy Ent.

— Playboy's Girls of Summer, '92. (Illus.). 112p. (Orig.). 1992. pap. 5.95 (*0-87223-904-7*, Playboy Pr) Playboy Ent.

— Playboy's Girls of the World. (Illus.). 112p. (Orig.). 1992. pap. 5.95 (*0-87223-906-3*, Playboy Pr) Playboy Ent.

— Playboy's Nudes. (Illus.). 112p. (Orig.). 1992. pap. 5.95 (*0-87223-907-1*, Playboy Pr) Playboy Ent.

— Playboy's Sisters. (Illus.). 112p. (Orig.). 1992. pap. 5.95 (*0-87223-901-2*, Playboy Pr) Playboy Ent.

***Player, Corrie Lynn.** So Your Teen Knows All the Answers... LC 99-26714. 1999. pap. 13.95 (*1-57734-532-0*, 01114271) Covenant Comms.

Player, Elaine, jt. auth. see Genders, Elaine.

***Player, Gary.** Complete Golfer's Handbook. (Illus.). 2000. 24.95 (*1-58574-029-2*) Lyons Pr.

Player, Gary. Fit for Golf: One hundred exercises that will improve your game-Whatever your age, whatever your handicap. LC 94-10738. 176p. 1995. pap. 15.00 (*0-671-89994-5*) S&S Trade.

Player, Gary & Tolhurst, Desmond. Golf Begins at Fifty: Playing the Lifetime Game Better Than Ever. 256p. 1989. pap. 14.00 (*0-671-68319-5*, Fireside) S&S Trade Pap.

Player, Ian. Zulu Wilderness: Shadow & Soul. (Illus.). 320p. 1998. pap. 21.95 (*1-55591-363-6*) Fulcrum Pub.

Player, Ian, intro. South African Passage: Diaries of the Wilderness Leadership School. LC 86-25752. 208p. 1987. 13.95 (*1-55591-009-2*) Fulcrum Pub.

Player, Jay & Player, Margaret, compiled by. Index to the Ninth Federal Census, 1870, Grand Traverse County, Michigan. 104p. 1989. pap. 9.00 (*0-9622372-3-X*) Grand Traverse.

Player, Jay, jt. compiled by see Player, Margaret.

Player, Lesley. Start a Craft: Decoupage. 1996. 8.98 (*0-7858-0572-9*) Bk Sales Inc.

Player, Mack A. Federal Law of Employment Discrimination in a Nutshell. 3rd ed. (Nutshell Ser.). 338p. (C). 1992. reprint ed. pap. text 15.00 (*0-314-00128-X*) West Pub.

— Federal Law of Employment Discrimination in a Nutshell. 4th ed. LC 99-175472. (Paralegal). 356 p. 1999. 15.00 (*0-314-21168-3*) West Pub.

— Hornbook on Employment Discrimination Law. (Hornbook Ser.). 708p. (C). 1988. 38.50 (*0-314-58916-3*) West Pub.

Player, Mack A., et al. Cases & Materials on Employment Discrimination Law. 2nd ed. LC 95-16452. (American Casebook Ser.). 799p. (C). 1995. 57.50 (*0-314-06393-5*) West Pub.

— Cases & Materials on Employment Discrimination Law: 1995 Statutory Supplement. 2nd ed. (American Casebook Ser.). 152p. 1995. pap., suppl. ed. 20.00 (*0-314-07604-2*) West Pub.

— Employment Discrimination: Third Edition, Cases & Materials. (American Casebook Ser.). 827p. 1990. text 46.00 (*0-314-73435-X*) West Pub.

— Employment Discrimination Law, Cases & Materials, 1992 Supplement to Accompany. (American Casebook Ser.). 240p. (C). 1992. pap. text 11.00 (*0-314-01212-5*) West Pub.

— Employment Discrimination, Teacher's Manual to Accompany Cases & Materials On. (American Casebook Ser.). 300p. 1990. pap. text. write for info. (*0-314-79654-1*) West Pub.

— Teacher's Manual to Accompany Employment Discrimination Law, Cases & Materials. 2nd ed. (American Casebook Ser.). 370p. 1997. pap. text. write for info. (*0-314-22697-4*) West Pub.

Player, Margaret & Player, Jay, compiled by. Cemetery Records of Evergreen & Sparling, Paradise Township, Grand Traverse County, Michigan. (Illus.). 184p. (Orig.). 1993. pap. 17.00 (*0-614-30155-6*) Grand Traverse.

— Index to the Ninth Federal Census, 1870, Leelanau County, Michigan. 101p. 1990. pap. 9.00 (*0-9622372-6-4*) Grand Traverse.

Player, Margaret, jt. compiled by see Player, Jay.

Player, Robert. Let's Talk of Graves, of Worms, of Epitaphs. 1996. 19.50 (*0-7451-8690-4*, Black Dagger) Chivers N Amer.

— Oh! Where Are Bloody Mary's Earrings? A Mystery Story at the Court of Queen Victoria. LC 74-194032. (Illus.). 228 p. (J). 1972. write for info. (*0-575-01429-6*) V Gollancz.

Player, Stephen. Celtic Myths. LC 97-32853. (Myths of the World Ser.). 96p. (YA). (gr. 3-7). 1998. 22.50 (*0-87226-561-7*, 65617B, P Bedrick Books) NTC Contemp Pub Co.

Player, Steve. Cornerstones of Decision Making: Profiles of Enterprise ABM. LC 98-40951. (Illus.). 280p. 1998. 24.95 (*1-886939-29-2*, Pub. by OakHill Pr VA) ACCESS Pubs Network.

— Win: Lotto & Daily Numbers Playing Techniques. LC 88-81912. (LOMAP Ser.: Vol. 7). (Illus.). 108p. 1988. pap. 9.95 (*0-936181-17-6*) Intergalactic NJ.

***Player, Steve & De Lacerda, Roberto S.** Arthur Andersen's Global Lessons in Activity-Based Management. LC 99-30532. 268p. 1999. 29.95 (*0-471-36288-3*) Wiley.

Player, Steve & Keys, David. Activity-Based Management: Arthur Andersen's Lessons from the ABM Battlefield. LC 98-42305. (Cost Management Ser.). (Illus.). 268p. (C). 1999. 29.95 (*0-471-31288-6*) Wiley.

Player, Theresa J., et al. California Trial Techniques. 814p. 1995. spiral bd. 105.00 (*1-55943-115-6*, MICHIE) LEXIS Pub.

— California Trial Techniques, No. 1. 1993. suppl. ed. 45.00 (*1-55943-174-1*, MICHIE) LEXIS Pub.

Player's Club Staff & Axelrod, Alan. Complete Idiot's Guide to Mixing Drinks. LC 97-73154. 384p. 1997. 16.95 (*0-02-861941-2*) Macmillan Gen Ref.

Playfair. Medical Immunology for Students. 1995. pap. text 26.95 (*0-443-05000-7*, W B Saunders Co) Harcrt Hlth Sci Grp.

Playfair, Emma, ed. International Law & the Administration of Occupied Territories: Two Decades of Israeli Occupation of the West Bank Gaza Strip. (Illus.). 572p. 1992. text 150.00 (*0-19-825297-8*) OUP.

Playfair, George M. The Cities & Towns of China: A Geographical Dictionary. 1976. lib. bdg. 59.95 (*0-8490-1635-5*) Gordon Pr.

Playfair, Helen. A Kiss to Remember. 416p. 1993. mass mkt. 4.50 (*0-8217-4129-2*, Zebra Kensgtn) Kensgtn Pub Corp.

— A Kiss to Remember. large type ed. LC 93-5223. 415p. 1993. reprint ed. lib. bdg. 16.95 (*0-7862-0011-1*) Thorndike Pr.

Playfair, J. H., et al. General Pathology, Microbiology, & Immunolgy for Health Care Students. LC 97-49686. 1997. pap. text 24.95 (*0-443-05722-2*) Church.

Playfair, John H. Immunology at a Glance. 6th ed. LC 95-40124. (Illus.). 96p. 1996. pap. 21.95 (*0-86542-677-5*) Blackwell Sci.

***Playfair, John H.** Immunology at a Glance. 7th ed. (At a Glance Ser.). (Illus.). 96p. (C). 2000. pap. 25.95 (*0-632-05406-9*) Blackwell Sci.

Playfair, John H. Infection & Immunity. (Illus.). 160p. 1995. text 39.50 (*0-19-854926-1*); pap. text 21.50 (*0-19-854925-3*) OUP.

Playfair, Nigel R. Story of the Lyric Theatre, Hammersmith. LC 77-84524. (Illus.). 1972. 24.95 (*0-405-08858-2*) Ayer.

Playfair, Robert L. The Scourge of Christendom: Annals of British Relations with Algiers Prior to the French Conquest. LC 72-3987. (Black Heritage Library Collection). 1977. reprint ed. 35.95 (*0-8369-9104-4*) Ayer.

***Playfair, Robert Lambert.** A Bibliography of Algeria from the Expedition of Charles V in 1541 to 1887. fac. ed. (Illus.). 304p. 2000. 70.00 (*1-57898-229-4*) Martino Pubng.

Playfoot, Jane, jt. ed. see Gonzalez, Jose L.

Playford, John. English Dancing Master: Or, Plaine & Easie Rules for the Dancing of Country Dances, with the Tune to Each Dance. (Illus.). 120p. 1984. reprint ed. pap. 17.95 (*0-903102-80-3*, Pub. by Dance Bks) Princeton Bk Co.

Playford, John & Purcell, Henry. An Introduction to the Skill of Musick. LC 67-27551. (Music Reprint Ser.). 282p. 1972. reprint ed. lib. bdg. 39.50 (*0-306-70937-6*) Da Capo.

Playford, Phillip. A Carpet of Silver: The Wreck of the Zuytdorp. LC 97-120219. 272p. 1996. 45.00 (*1-875560-73-4*, Pub. by Univ of West Aust Pr); pap. 34.95 (*1-875560-85-8*, Pub. by Univ of West Aust Pr) Intl Spec Bk.

Playgirl Editors. 50 Playgirl Fantasies. 2nd ed. 1998. reprint ed. mass mkt. 6.95 (*1-56333-648-0*) Masquerade.

Playko, Marsha A., jt. auth. see Daresh, John C.

Playland Staff. Peapod Dollhouse Text. (J). 0.00 (*0-698-13003-0*) Putnam Pub Group.

— Playland Bunnies Book. (J). 13.95 (*0-698-12069-8*) Putnam Pub Group.

— Playland Night Before Xmas Book. (J). 13.95 (*0-698-13034-0*) Putnam Pub Group.

— Playland Three Pigs Book. (J). 13.95 (*0-698-12073-6*) Putnam Pub Group.

Playle, Richard C., jt. ed. see Portner, H. O.

Playskool Books Staff. Baby Faces. 7p. (J). 1998. 6.99 (*0-525-45545-0*, Dutton Child) Peng Put Young Read.

— Mister Potato Head & the Mixed-up Groceries, 1. (J). (ps-2). 1999. 2.99 (*0-525-46194-9*, Dutton Child) Peng Put Young Read.

— Mister Potato Head Makes His Lunch, 1 vol. (YA). (ps up). 1999. pap. 5.99 (*0-525-46190-6*, Dutton Child) Peng Put Young Read.

— Mister Potato Head: Space Spud! With Stickers, 1. (J). (ps-2). 1999. 4.99 (*0-525-46193-0*, Dutton Child) Peng Put Young Read.

— Mister Potato Head's Busy Beach Day: Sticker Storybooks, 1 vol. (J). (ps-2). 1999. 4.99 (*0-525-46192-2*, Dutton Child) Peng Put Young Read.

— Mister Potato Head's Missing Sock, 1. (J). (ps-2). 1999. 2.99 (*0-525-46195-7*, Dutton Child) Peng Put Young Read.

— Mrs. Potato Head Chooses Her Shoes, 1 vol. (ps). 1999. pap. 5.99 (*0-525-46191-4*, Dutton Child) Peng Put Young Read.

— My Giant Preschool Lift-the-Flap Book: With Sixty Five Fun Flaps to Open! (Illus.). 10p. (J). (ps up). 1999. 9.99 (*0-525-46196-5*) Penguin Putnam.

— My Nose, My Toes! (Illus.). 24p. 1995. 5.99 (*0-525-45472-1*, Dutton Child) Peng Put Young Read.

Playskool Staff. In the Playgym. (J). 1999. 5.99 (*0-525-45622-8*) NAL.

— Mi Gran Libro de Palabras.Tr. of My Play-Doh Book of Words. (SPA.). 5p. (J). (ps). 1997. pap. 9.99 (*0-525-45813-1*, Dutton Child) Peng Put Young Read.

Playskool, Staff. Mr. Potato's Neighborhood. (J). 1999. 9.99 (*0-525-45810-7*) NAL.

Playskool Staff. My First Clock. (Illus.). 6p. (J). 1997. 11.99 (*0-525-45772-0*) NAL.

— On the Playground. (J). 1999. 5.99 (*0-525-45623-6*) NAL.

— Our Wedding. (J). 1999. pap. 9.99 (*0-525-45782-8*) NAL.

— See My Giant Activity. 1996. pap. 25.00 (*0-525-45725-9*, Dutton Child) Peng Put Young Read.

— Teen Books, No. 2. (J). 1999. pap. 3.99 (*0-525-45819-0*) NAL.

— Teeny Books, No. 1. (J). 1999. pap. 3.99 (*0-525-45818-2*) NAL.

— Teeny Books, No. 3. (J). 1999. pap. 4.99 (*0-525-45820-4*) NAL.

— Teeny Books, No. 4. 1999. pap. 4.99 (*0-525-45821-2*) Viking Penguin.

Playwright, Young. Inside Out-Upside Down. 40p. 1986. pap. 5.50 (*0-87129-153-3*, I43) Dramatic Pub.

Playwrights Canada Press Staff. Another Perfect Piece. LC 96-133732. 232p. 1997. pap. text 21.99 (*0-88754-518-1*) Playwrights.

— Four New Comedies: The Late Blumer, Cakewalk, Monkeyshines, Would You Like A Cup Of Tea? 364p. 1987. pap. 17.95 (*0-88754-427-4*) Theatre Comm.

— Perfect Piece. LC 91-175301. 276p. 1997. pap. text 16.95 (*0-88754-498-3*) Theatre Comm.

— Taking the Stage. LC 94-225160. 266p. 1997. pap. text 19.95 (*0-88754-530-0*) Theatre Comm.

— You're Making a Scene. 316p. 1997. pap. text 19.95 (*0-88754-489-4*) Theatre Comm.

***Plaza & Janes Editor Staff.** Cronica del Siglo XX. 2000. 59.00 (*0-553-06110-0*) Bantam.

Plaza & Janes Staff. Gran Diccionario Enciclopedico, 20 vols. 7th ed. (SPA.). 3896p. 1991. 3500.00 (*0-7859-5057-5*) Fr & Eur.

Plaza, A. Diccionario de las Americas. (SPA.). 1216p. 1991. 125.00 (*0-7859-5684-0*, 8401601657) Fr & Eur.

— Diccionario Enciclopedico, 6 vols. (SPA.). 3796p. 1991. 895.00 (*0-7859-5686-7*, 8401607256) Fr & Eur.

— Gran Diccionario Enciclopedico, Vol. 1. (SPA.). 416p. 1991. 175.00 (*0-7859-5687-5*, 8401612012) Fr & Eur.

— Gran Diccionario Enciclopedico, Vol. 2. (SPA.). 416p. 1991. 175.00 (*0-7859-5688-3*, 8401612020) Fr & Eur.

— Gran Diccionario Enciclopedico, Vol. 3. (SPA.). 416p. 1991. 175.00 (*0-7859-5689-1*, 8401612039) Fr & Eur.

— Gran Diccionario Enciclopedico, Vol. 4. (SPA.). 416p. 1991. 175.00 (*0-7859-5690-5*, 8401612047) Fr & Eur.

— Gran Diccionario Enciclopedico, Vol. 5. (SPA.). 416p. 1991. 175.00 (*0-7859-5691-3*, 8401612055) Fr & Eur.

— Gran Diccionario Enciclopedico, Vol. 6. (SPA.). 416p. 1991. 175.00 (*0-7859-5692-1*, 8401612063) Fr & Eur.

— Gran Diccionario Enciclopedico, Vol. 8. 416p. 1991. 175.00 (*0-7859-6443-6*) Fr & Eur.

— Gran Diccionario Enciclopedico, Vol. 9. (SPA.). 416p. 1991. 175.00 (*0-7859-5694-8*, 8401612098) Fr & Eur.

— Gran Diccionario Enciclopedico, Vol. 10. (SPA.). 416p. 1991. 175.00 (*0-7859-5695-6*, 8401612101) Fr & Eur.

— Gran Diccionario Enciclopedico, Vol. 11. 416p. 1991. 175.00 (*0-7859-6444-4*) Fr & Eur.

— Gran Diccionario Enciclopedico, Vol. 12. (SPA.). 416p. 1991. 175.00 (*0-7859-5696-4*, 8401612128) Fr & Eur.

— Gran Diccionario Enciclopedico, Vol. 13. (SPA.). 416p. 1991. 175.00 (*0-7859-5697-2*, 8401612136) Fr & Eur.

— Gran Diccionario Enciclopedico, Vol. 14. (SPA.). 416p. 1991. 175.00 (*0-7859-5698-0*, 8401612144) Fr & Eur.

— Gran Diccionario Enciclopedico, Vol. 15. (SPA.). 416p. 1991. 175.00 (*0-7859-5699-9*, 8401612152) Fr & Eur.

— Gran Diccionario Enciclopedico, Vol. 16. (SPA.). 416p. 1991. 175.00 (*0-7859-5700-6*, 8401612160) Fr & Eur.

— Gran Diccionario Enciclopedico, Vol. 17. (SPA.). 416p. 1991. 175.00 (*0-7859-5701-4*, 8401612179) Fr & Eur.

— Gran Diccionario Enciclopedico, Vol. 18. (SPA.). 416p. 1991. 175.00 (*0-7859-5702-2*, 8401612187) Fr & Eur.

— Gran Diccionario Enciclopedico, Vol. 19. (SPA.). 416p. 1991. 175.00 (*0-7859-5703-0*, 8401612195) Fr & Eur.

— Gran Diccionario Enciclopedico, Vol. 20. (SPA.). 416p. 1991. 175.00 (*0-7859-5704-9*, 8401612209) Fr & Eur.

Plaza, Enric, et al, eds. Knowledge Acquisition, Modeling & Management: 10th European Workshop, EKAW '97, Sant Feliu de Guixols, Catalonia, Spain, October 15-18, 1997 : Proceedings. LC 97-38161. (Lecture Notes in Computer Science Ser.: Vol. 1319). xi, 389p. 1997. pap. 59.00 (*3-540-63592-0*) Spr-Verlag.

Plaza, Enric, jt. auth. see Leake, David B.

Plaza, Enric, jt. auth. see Lopez de Mantaras, Ramon.

Plaza, Fuensanta. Clint Eastwood: Malpaso. LC 91-71749. (Illus.). 256p. (Orig.). 1991. pap. 24.95 (*0-9629481-9-5*) Ex Libris CA.

Plaza, Jan, jt. auth. see Calmet, Jacques.

Plaza Janes Staff. Diccionario Manual Auxiliar Basico. 2nd ed. (SPA.). 432p. 1991. write for info. (*0-7859-5091-5*) Fr & Eur.

— Family Larousse Dictionary, English-Spanish, Vol. 2. (ENG & SPA.). 62p. 1991. pap. 39.95 (*0-7859-5707-3*, 8401614082) Fr & Eur.

— Family Larousse Dictionary, Spanish-English, Vol. 1. (ENG & SPA.). 66p. 1991. pap. 39.95 (*0-7859-5706-5*, 8401614074) Fr & Eur.

Plaza, Lasso G. Problems of Democracy in Latin America. LC 81-36. (Weil Lectures on American Citizenship). 88p. 1981. reprint ed. lib. bdg. 55.00 (*0-313-22877-9*, PLPD, Greenwood Pr) Greenwood.

Plazaola, Luis T. Cine Sudamericano: Diccionario de Directores. (UPREX, Teatro y Cine Ser.: No. 72). 373p. 1985. pap. 6.00 (*0-8477-0072-0*) U of PR Pr.

— Cine y Mujer en America Latina. 304p. 1992. pap. 17.50 (*0-8477-2507-3*) U of PR Pr.

— Divas. (Aqui y Ahora Ser.). 108p. 1997. pap. 6.95 (*0-8477-0310-X*) U of PR Pr.

— South American Cinema: A Dictionary of Film Makers. 236p. 1989. pap. 10.95 (*0-8477-2011-X*) U of PR Pr.

Plazas, Christian. Inside Internet Information Server. 700p. 1997. pap. text 49.99 (*1-56205-743-X*) New Riders Pub.

Plazas, Clemencia, et al. La Sociedad Hidraulica Zenu: Estudio Arqueologico de 2.000 Anos de Historia en las Llanuras del Caribe Colombiano. (SPA., Illus.). 308p. (Orig.). (C). 1993. pap. 22.00 (*958-9028-92-6*, BR034, Pub. by Banco de la Repub) UPLAAP.

Plaziat, Jean-Claude, jt. auth. see Freytet, Pierre.

Plazy, Gilles. In the Footsteps of Van Gogh. LC 98-18837. (Illus.). 168p. 1998. 29.95 (*0-670-88250-X*) Viking Penguin.

— A Weekend with Rousseau. LC 93-12187. (Illus.). 64p. (J). 1993. 19.95 (*0-8478-1717-2*, Pub. by Rizzoli Intl) St Martin.

Plazyk, Judy, jt. auth. see Groeber, Joan F.

Plea. Passive & Low Energy Alternatives, 3 vols., Vols. 1-3. 1985. 259.00 (*0-08-032541-6*, Pergamon Pr) Elsevier.

Plead, Jane. Worlds Apart. 150p. 1995. 19.95 (*0-9646885-0-6*) Manoa Valley.

Pleadwell, F. L., ed. see Drake, Joseph R.

P

An Asterisk (*) at the beginning of an entry indicates that the title is appearing for the first time.

Pleas, Keith. Visual Basic Programming Pearls. 352p. (C). 1997. pap. text 34.95 (*0-201-56070-4*) Addison-Wesley.

Pleasance, Simon, tr. see Fumagalli, Beonio-Brocchiery.

Pleasant, Barbara. Alabama Gardener's Almanac. 64p. 1992. pap. 5.95 (*0-9633210-0-5*) Southern Ground.

— Controlling Garden Weeds. LC 97-11508. 1997. 2.95 (*0-88266-719-X*, A171) Storey Bks.

— Easy Garden Projects for All Seasons. LC 96-37972. (Illus.). 184p. (Orig.). 1997. pap. 15.95 (*0-87833-922-1*) Taylor Pub.

— The Gardener's Bug Book: Earth-Safe Insect Control. Stell, Liz & Balmuth, Deborah, eds. LC 93-36907. (Illus.). 160p. 1994. pap. 12.95 (*0-88266-609-6*, Garden Way Pub) Storey Bks.

— The Gardener's Guide to Plant Diseases: Earth-Safe Remedies. LC 94-34067. (Illus.). 192p. 1995. 16.95 (*0-88266-297-X*, Storey Pub); pap. 12.95 (*0-88266-274-0*) Storey Bks.

— Gardener's Weed Book. 1996. 18.95 (*0-88266-942-7*, Storey Pub) Storey Bks.

— The Gardener's Weed Book: Earth-Safe Controls. Lappies, Pamela, ed. (Illus.). 144p. (Orig.). 1996. pap. 12.95 (*0-88266-921-4*, 921-4, Storey Pub) Storey Bks.

— Warm-Climate Gardening: Tips - Techniques - Plans - Projects for Humid or Dry Conditions. Steege, Gwen, ed. LC 92-54255. (Illus.). 208p. 1993. 21.95 (*0-88266-819-6*, Garden Way Pub) Storey Bks.

Pleasant, Barbara, et al. Container Gardens. LC 99-484107. (Illus.). 1997. write for info. (*0-914697-97-8*) N Amer Outdoor Grp.

Pleasant Company Staff. Addy's Craft Book: A Look at Crafts from the Past with Projects You Can Make Today. LC 94-26045. (American Girls Collection). (Illus.). 48p. (YA). (gr. 2 up). 1994. pap. text 5.95 (*1-56247-124-4*) Pleasant Co.

***Pleasant Company Staff.** Addy's Craft Book: A Look at Crafts from the Past with Projects You Can Make Today. (American Girls Collection). (Illus.). (YA). (gr. 2 up). 1998. 11.40 (*0-606-18351-5*) Turtleback.

Pleasant Company Staff. Addy's Theater Kit. LC 94-28339. (American Girls Collection). 48p. (Orig.). (J). (gr. 2 up). 1994. pap. text 5.95 (*1-56247-125-2*) Pleasant Co.

— American Girl: Trading Card Album. (J). (gr. 4-8). 1995. pap. text 14.95 (*1-56247-266-6*) Pleasant Co.

— Birthday Cards for Girls to Make. (Illus.). 28p. (Orig.). (J). (gr. 3-6). 1995. pap. text 9.95 (*1-56247-233-X*) Pleasant Co.

***Pleasant Company Staff.** Birthday Memory Book. (American Girl Backpack Bks.). (Illus.). 32p. (YA). (gr. 3). 2000. pap. 1.95 (*1-58485-068-X*) Pleasant Co.

— Boo! (American Girl Backpack Bks.). (Illus.). (J). 1999. pap. text 1.95 (*1-56247-799-4*) Pleasant Co.

— Charactective Postcard Books: 25 Colorful Post Cards, 4 Pictures of Each Character. (Illus.). 1998. 5.95 (*1-56247-680-7*) Pleasant Co.

Pleasant Company Staff. Felicity's Theater Kit. LC 94-28340. (American Girls Collection). (Illus.). 48p. (Orig.). (J). (gr. 2 up). 1994. pap. 5.95 (*1-56247-122-8*) Pleasant Co.

— Games & Giggles: Just for Girls. LC 95-10868. (American Girl Library Ser.). (Illus.). 96p. (Orig.). (J). (gr. 3-6). 1995. pap. text 5.95 (*1-56247-232-1*, Amer Girl Library) Pleasant Co.

***Pleasant Company Staff.** Go Team! Cheers & Chants. 1999. pap. 1.95 (*1-56247-798-6*) Pleasant Co.

— Great Gifts: For Girls to Make & Give. 1999. pap. 1.95 (*1-56247-796-X*) Pleasant Co.

Pleasant Company Staff. Hand Book. (gr. 9-12). 1999. pap. text 1.95 (*1-56247-742-0*) Pleasant Co.

— Kirsten's Theater Kit. LC 94-16811. (American Girls Collection). (Illus.). 48p. (Orig.). (YA). (gr. 2 up). 1994. pap. 5.95 (*1-56247-113-9*) Pleasant Co.

— Little Book of Buzzwords. 1999. pap. text 1.95 (*1-56247-727-7*) Pleasant Co.

***Pleasant Company Staff.** Little Book of Notes. 1999. pap. text 1.95 (*1-56247-797-8*) Pleasant Co.

Pleasant Company Staff. A Map of Addy's World. (American Girls Collection). (YA). (gr. 2 up). 1996. 5.95 (*1-56247-493-6*) Pleasant Co.

Pleasant Company Staff. A Map of Felicity's World. (American Girls Collection). (YA). (gr. 2 up). 1996. 5.95 (*1-56247-491-X*) Pleasant Co.

Pleasant Company Staff. A Map of Kirsten's World. (American Girls Collection). (YA). (gr. 2 up). 1996. 5.95 (*1-56247-492-8*) Pleasant Co.

— A Map of Molly's World. (American Girls Collection). (YA). (gr. 2 up). 1996. 5.95 (*1-56247-495-2*) Pleasant Co.

— A Map of Samantha's World. (American Girls Collection). (YA). (gr. 2 up). 1996. 5.95 (*1-56247-494-4*) Pleasant Co.

— Meet the American Girls, 6 bks., Set. (American Girls Collection). (J). 1997. pap. text, boxed set 34.95 (*1-56247-542-8*) Pleasant Co.

Pleasant Company Staff. Molly's Paper Dolls. (American Girls Collection). 24p. (YA). (gr. 2 up). 1992. pap. text 5.95 (*1-56247-057-4*) Pleasant Co.

Pleasant Company Staff. Molly's Theater Kit. LC 94-234172. (American Girls Collection). (Illus.). 48p. (Orig.). (J). (gr. 3-7). 1994. pap. 5.95 (*1-56247-119-8*) Pleasant Co.

— My Trip to Felicity's Williamsburg: An American Girl's Journal. (Illus.). 14p. (J). (gr. 2-5). 1991. 1.00 (*1-56247-029-9*) Pleasant Co.

— Pin Pals. (gr. 9-12). 1999. pap. text 1.95 (*1-56247-740-4*) Pleasant Co.

***Pleasant Company Staff.** Pop! A Popcorn Party. 1999. pap. text 1.95 (*1-56247-778-1*) Pleasant Co.

Pleasant Company Staff. Rockin' Sock Hop Party Guide. LC 98-7393. (J). 1998. write for info. (*1-56247-699-8*) Pleasant Co.

Pleasant Company Staff. Samantha's Paper Dolls. (American Girls Collection). (Illus.). 24p. (YA). (gr. 2 up). 1992. pap. 5.95 Pleasant Co.

Pleasant Company Staff. Samantha's Stationery Set. (J). (gr. 3-7). 1996. pap. text 9.95 (*1-56247-489-8*) Pleasant Co.

— Samantha's Theater Kit. LC 94-234178. (American Girls Collection). (Illus.). 48p. (Orig.). (YA). (gr. 2 up). 1994. pap. text 5.95 (*1-56247-116-3*) Pleasant Co.

— Say Cheese. (gr. 4-7). 1998. pap. text 1.95 (*1-56247-734-X*) Pleasant Co.

***Pleasant Company Staff.** Secrets on 26th Street. LC 99-29899. (American Girl History Mysteries Ser.). 160p. (J). (gr. 5-9). 1999. 7.96 (*1-56247-816-8*) Pleasant Co.

Pleasant Company Staff. Secrets on 26th Street. LC 99-29899. 1999. pap. text 4.76 (*1-56247-760-9*) Pleasant Co.

— Sip & Slurp. (gr. 9-12). 1999. pap. text 1.95 (*1-56247-744-7*) Pleasant Co.

— Splash! 1999. pap. text 1.95 (*1-56247-737-4*) Pleasant Co.

***Pleasant Company Staff.** Stable Stories: True Stories from American Girls. LC 00-20718. (J). 2000. write for info. (*1-58485-039-6*) Pleasant Co.

— Tricky Doodles. (American Girl Backpack Bks.: Vol. 33). (Illus.). 32p. (J). (gr. 3-7). 2000. pap. 1.95 (*1-58485-070-1*) Pleasant Co.

Pleasant Company Staff. Truly Tropical Party Guide. LC 98-7394. (J). 1998. write for info. (*1-56247-701-3*) Pleasant Co.

***Pleasant Company Staff.** Welcome to Josefina's World, 1824. LC 99-26634. (American Girls Collection). (Illus.). 64p. (YA). (gr. 2 up). 1999. 14.95 (*1-56247-769-2*) Pleasant Co.

— Wig Out. (American Girl Backpack Bks.). (Illus.). 32p. (YA). (gr. 3-7). 2000. pap. 1.95 (*1-58485-125-2*) Pleasant Co.

Pleasant Company Staff. You're It! Great Games for Girls. 1999. pap. text 1.95 (*1-56247-731-5*) Pleasant Co.

Pleasant Company Staff, ed. Addy's Paper Dolls. (American Girls Collection). (Illus.). 24p. (Orig.). (YA). (gr. 2 up). 1994. pap. 5.95 (*1-56247-126-0*) Pleasant Co.

— Addy's Pastimes, 4 bks. (American Girls Collection). (Illus.). 168p. (YA). (gr. 2 up). 1995. boxed set 22.95 (*1-56247-261-5*) Pleasant Co.

— Beautiful Barrettes: Dazzling Designs to Create. (American Girl Library Ser.). 1999. pap. text 1.95 (*1-56247-733-1*) Pleasant Co.

— Daisy Crazy. (American Girl Library Ser.). 1999. pap. text 1.95 (*1-56247-743-9*) Pleasant Co.

— 50 Best Babysitting Tips. (American Girl Library Ser.). 1999. pap. text 1.95 (*1-56247-725-0*) Pleasant Co.

— Heart Art. (American Girl Library Ser.). 1999. pap. 1.95 (*1-56247-741-2*) Pleasant Co.

— Help Wanted: Fashion Designer. (American Girl Library Ser.). 1999. pap. 1.95 (*1-56247-739-0*) Pleasant Co.

— Homesick Blues? Here's What to Do! (American Girl Library Ser.). 1999. pap. 1.95 (*1-56247-726-9*) Pleasant Co.

— I.O.U. Love Gift Coupons from Me to You. (American Girl Library Ser.). 1999. pap. 1.95 (*1-56247-732-3*) Pleasant Co.

— Just Giggles. (American Girl Library Ser.). 1999. pap. 1.95 (*1-56247-729-3*) Pleasant Co.

— Kirsten's Pastimes, 4 bks., Set. (American Girls Collection). (Illus.). 168p. (YA). (gr. 2 up). 1995. boxed set 22.95 (*1-56247-260-7*) Pleasant Co.

— Miles of Smiles! Backseat Games. (American Girl Library Ser.). 1999. pap. 1.95 (*1-56247-728-5*) Pleasant Co.

— Molly's Pastimes, 4 bks., Set. (American Girls Collection). (Illus.). 168p. (J). (gr. 3-7). 1995. text, boxed set 22.95 (*1-56247-263-1*) Pleasant Co.

— Samantha's Pastimes, 4 bks., Set. (American Girls Collection). (Illus.). 168p. (Orig.). (YA). (gr. 2 up). 1995. pap. text, boxed set 22.95 (*1-56247-262-3*) Pleasant Co.

Pleasant Company Staff, et al. Meet the American Girls, 5 bks., Set. (American Girls Collection). (Illus.). (J). (gr. 2-5). 1993. pap., boxed set 28.95 (*1-56247-096-5*) Pleasant Co.

Pleasant Company Staff, jt. auth. see Tripp, Valerie.

Pleasant, Hazen H. A History of Crawford County, Indiana. (Illus.). 644p. 1992. reprint ed. lib. bdg. 65.00 (*0-8328-2544-1*) Higginson Bk Co.

Pleasant, James W. Doctor Jim's Odyssey. LC 94-60592. 138p. 1994. pap. 8.00 (*0-912400-14-5*) Western Res Pr.

Pleasant, Judith. My Spirit Helpers. LC 98-93410. 136p. 1998. pap. text 12.95 (*0-9666446-0-3*) BootSun Pub.

***Pleasant Publishers Staff.** American Girl Planner: Blue. (YA). (gr. 4-7). 2000. pap. 11.95 (*1-58485-155-4*) Pleasant Co.

— American Girl Planner: Lavender. (YA). (gr. 4-7). 2000. pap. 11.95 (*1-58485-154-6*) Pleasant Co.

— American Girl Planner: Purple. (J). (gr. 4-7). 2000. 11.95 (*1-58485-156-2*) Pleasant Co.

— Bitty Bites. (American Girl Backpack Bks.: Vol. 35). (Illus.). 32p. (YA). (gr. 3). 2000. 1.95 (*1-58485-126-0*) Pleasant Co.

— Can You Do It? (American Girl Backpack Bks.: Vol. 27). (Illus.). 32p. (YA). (gr. 3). 2000. 1.95 (*1-58485-064-7*) Pleasant Co.

— Cute Cupcakes. (American Girl Backpack Bks.: Vol. 29). (Illus.). 32p. (YA). (gr. 3). 2000. 1.95 (*1-58485-066-3*) Pleasant Co.

— 103 Purfect Pet Names. (American Girl Backpack Bks.: Vol. 26). (Illus.). 32p. (J). (ps-3). 2000. 1.95 (*1-58485-063-9*) Pleasant Co.

Pleasants County Library Board Staff, ed. West Virginia... That's the Story. LC 95-71839. 184p. 1995. pap. 10.00 (0-87012-552-4) McClain.

A project to make West Virginia & its history more interesting & more colorful for people of all ages through stories. *Publisher Paid Annotation.*

Pleasants, Craig. The Three Little Pigs: As It Was Originally Passed into English Folklore in 1620. LC 95-170315. (Illus.). 16p. (Orig.). (J). (gr. 3 up). 1994. pap. 5.00 (*0-9638129-2-0*) Gates of Heck.

Pleasants, Henry, ed. The Music Criticism of Hugo Wolf. LC 77-11092. 291p. 1979. 39.50 (*0-8419-0331-X*) Holmes & Meier.

Pleasants, Henry, ed. see Hanslick, Eduard.

Pleasants, Henry, ed. see Spohr, Louis.

Pleasants, Henry, ed. see Wieck, Friedrich.

Pleasants, Henry, tr. see Spohr, Louis.

Pleasants, J. Hall. Curzon Family of New York & Baltimore, & Their English Descents. 75p. 1997. reprint ed. pap. 15.00 (*0-8328-8182-1*); reprint ed. lib. bdg. 25.00 (*0-8328-8181-3*) Higginson Bk Co.

Pleasants, Jacob H. Four Late Eighteenth Century Anglo-American Landscape Painters. LC 78-128288. (Essay Index Reprint Ser.). 1977. 20.95 (*0-8369-1894-0*) Ayer.

***Pleasants, Julian M.** Buncombe Bob: The Life & Times of Robert Rice Reynolds. (James Sprunt Studies in History & Political Science). (Illus.). 420p. 2000. 34.95 (*0-8078-5064-0*) U of NC Pr.

Pleasants, Julian M. & Burns, Augustus M., III. Frank Porter Graham & the 1950 Senate Race in North Carolina. LC 90-50011. (Fred W. Morrison Series in Southern Studies). (Illus.). xviii, 356p. (C). 1990. text 39.95 (*0-8078-1933-6*) U of NC Pr.

Pleasants, Mary M. Which One? & Other Ante Bellum Days. LC 72-4620. (Black Heritage Library Collection). 1977. reprint ed. 19.95 (*0-8369-9121-4*) Ayer.

***Pleasants, Nigel.** Wittgenstein & the Idea of Critical Social Theory: Giddens, Habermas & Bhaskar. LC 99-22356. (Studies in Social & Political Thought). 1999. text. write for info. (*0-415-18953-5*) Routledge.

Pleasants, Samuel A. Fernando Wood of New York. LC 48-7608. (Columbia University. Studies in the Social Sciences: No. 536). reprint ed. 20.00 (*0-404-51536-3*) AMS Pr.

Pleasants, William J. Twice Across the Plains to California, 1849-1856. 74p. 1981. 16.95 (*0-87770-259-4*) Ye Galleon.

Please, Stanley. Sector Adjustment Lending & the Inter-American Development Bank. 28p. 1989. pap. text 8.00 (*0-940602-29-6*) IADB.

Please Touch Museum Staff. Please Touch Cookbook. Brook, Bonnie, ed. (Illus.). 64p. (J). (ps-2). 1990. lib. bdg. 7.95 (*0-671-70558-X*) S&S Bks Yung.

Pleasure, David E., jt. ed. see Rosenberg, Roger N.

Pleasure, Mose, Jr. & Lofton, Fred C., eds. Living in Hell: The Dilemma of African-American Survival. LC 95-12479. 224p. 1995. pap. 12.99 (*0-310-49781-7*) Zondervan.

Pleau, Jean-Christian. Bernanos: La Part Obscure. (Currents in Comparative Romance Languages & Literature Ser.: 56). (FRE.). 129p. (C). 1998. text 36.95 (*0-8204-3753-0*) P Lang Pubng.

Pleau, R., jt. auth. see Pigeon, M.

Pleban, Patricia L. Scruffy's Pawsitive Mission: A Tail of a Dog & Her Master Attacking Panic. (Illus.). 149p. 1999. pap. 12.95 (*1-58446-003-2*, Legacy OH) Temple Pubg.

Plebanek, B., tr. see Lipska, Ewa.

Plebani, M. & Di Mario, F. Gastric Secretion. (Advances in Gastroenterology Ser.: No. 5). 160p. 1992. text 32.00 (*1-57235-021-0*) Piccin Nuova.

Plebanski, J., jt. auth. see Infeld, Leopold.

Plechanoff, George. The Bourgeois Revolution. 3rd ed. Kuhn, Henry, tr. 1968. pap. text 0.50 (*0-935534-05-9*) NY Labor News.

Plechner, Alfred J. & Zucker, Martin. Pet Allergies: Remedies for an Epidemic. LC 85-51341. 130p. (Orig.). 1986. pap. 6.95 (*0-9615452-0-8*) Very Healthy Ent.

***Pleck, Elizabeth H.** Celebrating the Family: Ethnicity, Consumer Culture & Family Rituals. LC 99-45200. 2000. 55.00 (*0-674-00230-X*); pap. text 22.95 (*0-674-00279-2*) HUP.

Pleck, Elizabeth H., et al. The Legacies Book: A Companion Volume to the Audiocourse. 288p. (Orig.). 1987. pap. 25.00 (*0-89776-206-1*) Jennings & Keefe.

Pleck, Elizabeth H., jt. auth. see Cott, Nancy F.

Pleck, Joseph H. Working Wives, Working Husbands. LC 85-11974. (New Perspectives on Family Ser.). 168p. 1985. reprint ed. pap. 52.10 (*0-608-01525-3*, 205956900002) Bks Demand.

Pleck, M. H., et al. Problems in Engineering Graphics. (Engineering Graphics Ser.: No. 88). (Illus.). 91p. (C). 1989. pap. text 15.80 (*0-87563-413-3*) Stipes.

— Problems in Engineering Graphics, No. 87. (Engineering Graphics Ser.: Vol. 87). 90p. (C). 1987. pap. text, student ed. 15.80 (*0-87563-292-0*) Stipes.

Plecnik, Jose & Gooding, Mel. National & University Library, Ljubljana. (Architecture in Detail Ser.). (Illus.). 1997. pap. 29.95 (*0-7148-2938-2*, Pub. by Phaidon Press) Phaidon Pr.

Pledge, H. T. Science since 1500: A Short History of Mathematics, Physics, Chemistry, Biology. 1990. 16.50 (*0-8446-0850-5*) Peter Smith.

Pledge, Robert. Strange Friends. (Illus.). 240p. 1998. 45.00 (*3-908161-40-1*) Abbeville Pr.

Pledge, Thomas A. Saudi Aramco & Its People: A History of Training. Dialdin, Ali M. & Tahlawi, Muhammad A., eds. LC 97-62572. (Illus.). 304p. 1998. 30.00 (*0-9601164-4-3*) Saudi Arab Oil Co.

Pledger, Florence M. Pledger Family History. 176p. 1991. 29.95 (*0-942407-13-X*) Father & Son.

Pledger, Maurice. An Adventure with Billy Bunny. (Illus.). 20p. (J). (ps). 1995. pap. 14.98 (*1-881445-47-X*) Sandvik Pub.

— An Adventure with Billy Bunny: A Peek & Find Book, 8 vols. (Peek & Find Ser.). (Illus.). 9p. (J). (ps-3). 1996. 10.95 (*1-57145-069-6*, Silver Dolph) Advantage Pubs.

— An Adventure with Bobby Bear: A Peek & Find Book, 8 vols. (Peek & Find Ser.). (Illus.). 9p. (J). (ps-k). 1996. 10.95 (*1-57145-070-X*, Silver Dolph) Advantage Pubs.

— An Adventure with Charlie Chick: A Peek & Find Book, 8 vols. (Peek & Find Ser.). (Illus.). 9p. (J). (ps-3). 1996. 10.95 (*1-57145-071-8*, Silver Dolph) Advantage Pubs.

— An Adventure with Morris Mouse: A Peek & Find Book, 8 vols. (Peek & Find Ser.). (Illus.). 9p. (J). (ps-3). 1996. 10.95 (*1-57145-072-6*, Silver Dolph) Advantage Pubs.

— Adventure with Olivia Owl: A Peek & Find Book, 8 vols. (Peek & Find Ser.). 9p. (J). (ps-3). 1998. 10.95 (*1-57145-076-9*, Silver Dolph) Advantage Pubs.

— Adventure with Oscar Otter: A Peek & Find Book, 8 vols. (Peek & Find Ser.). 9p. (J). (ps-3). 1998. 10.95 (*1-57145-078-5*, Silver Dolph) Advantage Pubs.

— Adventure with Polly Polar Bear: A Peek & Find Book, 8 vols. (Peek & Find Ser.). (Illus.). 9p. (J). (ps-3). 1997. 10.95 (*1-57145-077-7*, Silver Dolph) Advantage Pubs.

— An Adventure with Winnie Wolf: A Peek & Find Book, 8 vols. (Peek & Find Ser.). (Illus.). 9p. (J). (ps-3). 1997. 10.95 (*1-57145-075-0*, Silver Dolph) Advantage Pubs.

***Pledger, Maurice.** Billy Bunny's 123. (Illus.). 8p. (J). 2000. 6.95 (*1-57145-408-X*, Silver Dolph) Advantage Pubs.

— Bobby Bear's ABC. (Illus.). 8p. (J). 2000. 6.95 (*1-57145-409-8*, Silver Dolph) Advantage Pubs.

Pledger, Maurice. Bobby Bears Sticker Stories. (Maurice Pledger Sticker Stories Ser.). (Illus.). 96p. (J). (ps). 1999. pap. 10.95 (*1-57145-384-9*, Silver Dolph) Advantage Pubs.

— By the Seashore: A Touch-&-Feel Adventure, 4 vols. (Nature Trail Ser.). (Illus.). 8p. (J). (ps-3). 1998. 12.95 (*1-57145-322-9*, Silver Dolph) Advantage Pubs.

— In the Forest: A Touch-&-Feel Adventure, 4 vols. (Nature Trail Ser.). (Illus.). 8p. (J). (ps-3). 1998. 12.95 (*1-57145-321-0*, Silver Dolph) Advantage Pubs.

— In the Rain Forest: A Touch-&-Feel Adventure. (Nature Trail Ser.: Vol. 4). (Illus.). 16p. (J). (ps-1). 1999. 12.95 (*1-57145-352-0*, Silver Dolph) Advantage Pubs.

— On the Mountain: A Touch-&-Feel Adventure. (Nature Trails Ser.: Vol. 3). (Illus.). 16p. (J). (ps-1). 1999. 12.95 (*1-57145-353-9*, Silver Dolph) Advantage Pubs.

— Oscar Otters Sticker Stories. (Illus.). 96p. (J). (ps). 1999. pap. 10.95 (*1-57145-385-7*, Silver Dolph) Advantage Pubs.

***Pledger, Maurice.** Billy Bunny's Sticker Book. 96p. (J). (ps-1). 2000. pap. 10.95 (*1-57145-441-1*, Silver Dolph) Advantage Pubs.

Plee, H. D. Karate: Beginner to Black Belt. (Illus.). 1967. 19.95 (*0-685-05344-X*) Wehman.

— Karate by Pictures. 19.95 (*0-685-22004-4*) Wehman.

Pleeter, Saul. Economics in the News. 3rd ed. (C). 1996. pap. text. write for info. (*0-201-60992-4*) Addison-Wesley.

Pleeter, Saul & Way, Philip K. Economics in the News. (Illus.). 320p. (C). 1990. pap. text 13.95 (*0-201-50924-5*) Addison-Wesley.

***Plegan, S.** Developing Your Company Culture. 1998. pap. 88.00 (*81-86982-17-5*, Pub. by Business Pubns) St Mut.

Pleger, Wolfgang H. Schleiermacher's Philosophie. (GER.). x, 207p. (C). 1988. lib. bdg. 26.15 (*3-11-011706-1*) De Gruyter.

Pleh, C. S., jt. auth. see Kardos, L.

Pleh, Csaba, jt. ed. see Harlig, Jeffrey.

Plehinger, Russell. Marathon Flyers & the Flights to Nowhere. (Illus.). 192p. 1989. 27.00 (*0-8187-0112-9*) Harlo Press.

Plehve, Igor R. Kolb: A German Colony on the Volga. 1992. pap. 20.00 (*0-614-23857-9*) Am Hist Soc Ger.

Pleijel, Agneta. The Dog Star. 120p. 1992. 29.95 (*0-7206-0844-9*, Pub. by P Owen Ltd) Dufour.

— Eyes from a Dream: Poems. Born, Anne, tr. from SWE. LC 91-72164. (Illus.). 49p. (Orig.). 1991. pap. 16.95 (*1-85610-015-4*, Pub. by Forest Bks) Dufour.

Pleijel, F. & Dales, R. P. Polychaetes: British Phyllodocoideans, Typhloscolecoideans & Tomopteroideans. (Synopses of the British Fauna Ser.: No. 45). (Illus.). 210p. 1991. pap. 65.00 (*90-73348-12-9*, Pub. by Backhuys Pubs) Balogh.

Pleil, Nadine M. Free from Bondage: After Forty Years in Bruderhof Communities on Three Continents. Huntington, Gertrude E., ed. LC 94-72099. (Women from Utopia Ser.). (Illus.). 350p. (Orig.). 1994. pap. 17.00 (*1-882260-07-4*) Carrier Pigeon.

Pleiman, H., Jr. You Be Hoobee. LC 94-240407. (Illus.). 45p. (J). (gr. 1 up). 1994. 24.95 (*0-9621755-1-X*) Metahomin Pub.

Pleiman, H., Jr. You Be Hoobee. (Illus.). 45p. (J). (gr. 1 up). 1994. pap. 17.95 (*0-9621755-2-8*) Metahomin Pub.

Pleiman, Herbert P., Jr. Itch of an Islander. unabridged ed. LC 98-14741. 428p. 1998. pap. 19.95 (*0-9621755-3-6*) Metahomin Pub.

Plein, L. Christopher, jt. auth. see Hahm, Sung D.

***Pleiner, Christoph M.** Du Utest Mit Mir Das Feuerfeste Lied: Eros Und Intertexualitat Bei Claire Und Iwan Goll. (Illus.). 346p. 1999. 51.95 (*3-631-34409-0*) P Lang Pubng.

Pleiner, Radomir. The Celtic Sword. (Illus.). 212p. (C). 1993. text 105.00 (*0-19-813411-8*) OUP.

Pleines, Juergen Eckardt. Aesthetik und Vernunftkritik. (Studien Zur Kunstgeschichte Ser.: Bd. 51). (GER.). viii, 334p. 1989. write for info. (*3-487-09134-8*) G Olms Pubs.

P

An Asterisk (*) at the beginning of an entry indicates that the title is appearing for the first time.

Pleines, Jurgen-Eckardt. Begreifendes Denken: Vier Studien Zu Hegel. (Philosophische Texte und Studien: Vol. 21). (GER.). ii, 330p. 1990. write for info. (*3-487-09231-X*) G Olms Pubs.
— Hegels Theorie der Bildung. (Philosophische Texte und Studien: Vol. 8). (GER.). 361p. 1983. write for info. (*3-487-07433-8*) G Olms Pubs.
— Hegels Theorie der Bildung. (Philosophische Texte und Studien: Vol. 9). (GER.). xxxvi, 350p. 1986. write for info. (*3-487-07734-5*) G Olms Pubs.
— Studien Zur Ethik. (Philosophische Texte und Studien: Vol. 27). (GER.). iv, 431p. 1992. write for info. (*3-487-09452-5*) G Olms Pubs.
Pleins, J. David. The Psalms: Songs of Tragedy, Hope, & Justice. LC 93-17541. (Bible & Liberation Ser.). 160p. (Orig.). 1993. pap. 15.00 (*0-88344-928-5*) Orbis Bks.
***Pleins, John D.** Social Visions of the Hebrew Bible: A Theological Introduction. (Illus.). 624p. 2000. pap. 34.95 (*0-664-22175-0*) Westminster John Knox.
Pleit-Kuiper, Angie, tr. see Van der Hart, Onno.
Pleket, H. W. & Stroud, R. S., eds. SEG, 1983: Supplementum Epigraphicum Graecum. xx, 532p. (C). 1986. 130.00 (*90-70265-57-5*, Pub. by Gieben) J Benjamins Pubng Co.
Plekhanov, George V. Fundamental Problems of Marxism. Katzer, Julius, tr. from RUS. (ENG.). 1962. pap. 14.95 (*0-8464-0435-4*) Beekman Pubs.
— Fundamental Problems of Marxism. rev. ed. LC 69-20358. 160p. 1992. pap. 6.95 (*0-7178-0073-3*) Intl Pubs Co.
***Plekhanov, Vladimir, ed.** Isotope Effects in Solid State Physics. (Semiconductors & Semimetals Ser.: Vol. 68). 192p. 2000. 165.00 (*0-12-752177-1*) Acad Pr.
Plekhov, A. Dictionary of Military Terms. 336p. (C). 1988. 125.00 (*0-7855-5063-1*, Pub. by Collets) St Mut.
Plekker, Robert J. Divorce & the Christian: What the Bible Teaches. 2nd rev. ed. LC 97-76461. 168p. 1997. reprint ed. 24.95 (*0-9660565-0-7*, 101) Joint Heirs.
— Who Is Jesus Christ? & What Is Christianity? (Illus.). 284p. (Orig.). (YA). (gr. 6 up). 1998. pap. 19.95 (*0-9660565-1-5*) Joint Heirs.
Plekon, Michael P., ed. see Piepkorn, Arthur C.
Pleming, L. Triumph of Job. 1978. 7.95 (*0-933062-00-1*) R H Sommer.
Plemmons, Fred M. Had She Not Been a Wolf He Would Have Married Her. 160p. 1997. pap. 7.95 (*1-57502-642-2*, PO 1821) Morris Pubng.
Plemmons, Patrick & Myers, David. Personal Computer Buyer's Guide. 184p. (Orig.). pap. 12.95 (*0-685-08848-0*) Random.
Plemmons, Richard J., jt. ed. see Meyer, Carl D.
Plemmons, Robert J., jt. auth. see Berman, Abraham.
Plender, John. A Stake in the Future: The Stakeholding Solution. LC 97-6369. (Illus.). 224p. 1997. 25.00 (*1-85788-175-3*) Nicholas Brealey.
— That's the Way the Money Goes: The Financial Institutions & the Nation's Savings LC 88-175190. 224p. 1982. write for info. (*0-233-97398-2*) Andre Deutsch.
Plender, Richard. International Migration Law. 1988. lib. bdg. 174.50 (*90-247-3604-8*) Kluwer Academic.
Plender, Richard, ed. Basic Documents on International Migration Law. 2nd ed. LC 96-8150. 1997. 250.00 (*90-411-0252-3*) Kluwer Law Intl.
— Legal History & Comparative Law: Essays in Honour of Albert Kiralfy. 239p. 1990. text 40.00 (*0-7146-3397-6*, Pub. by F Cass Pubs) Intl Spec Bk.
Plenderleith, John, jt. auth. see Whyte, Ian.
Plenderleith, P., jt. ed. see Whyte, W.
Plendl, jt. auth. see Lind.
***Plenert.** Finite Capacity Scheduling. LC 99-44971. 251p. 2000. 55.00 (*0-471-35264-0*) Wiley.
***Plenert, Gerhard J.** International Operations Management. 2000. Price not set. (*87-16-13492-3*, Pub. by Copenhagen Busn Schl) Bks Intl VA.
Plenert, Gerhard J. The Plant Operations Handbook: A Tactical Guide to Everyday Management. 528p. 1992. 75.00 (*1-55623-707-3*, Irwn Prfssnl) McGraw-Hill Prof.
Plenert, Gerhard J. & Hibino, Shozo. Making Innovation Happen: Concept Management Through Integration. LC 97-37096. 200p. 1997. lib. bdg. 39.95 (*1-57444-090-X*) St Lucie Pr.
Plenge, Jane T. Social Studies. 1997. 4.95 (*1-55708-576-5*, J803) McDonald Pub Co.
Plenk, Agnes M. Helping Young Children at Risk: A Psychoeducational Approach. LC 93-20303. 232p. 1993. 59.95 (*0-275-94591-X*, C4591, Praeger Pubs); pap. 22.95 (*0-275-94592-8*, Praeger Pubs) Greenwood.
Plenk, Anton. The Obersalzberg & the Third Reich. (Illus.). 87p. 1982. pap. 20.00 (*3-922590-13-6*) Johnson Ref Bks.
Plenk, Bruce & Aldous, Kathy. Utah Consumer Law Manual. 3rd rev. ed. (Utah Legal Services Manuals). 240p. 1992. ring bd. 175.00 (*1-891414-01-1*) Utah Legal.
Plenk, Bruce, et al. Utah Landlord Tenant Manual: A Tenant Perspective. (Utah Legal Services Manuals). 1997. ring bd. 175.00 incl. disk (*1-891414-00-3*) Utah Legal.
Plenk, H. Osteolathyrismus: Quantitativ-Morphologische Untersuchungen der Experimentellen Skeletterkrankungen bei der Ratte. Wolf-Heidegger, G., ed. (Bibliotheca Anatomica Ser.: No. 14). (Illus.). 104p. 1976. 41.75 (*3-8055-2306-8*) S Karger.
Plenn. El Arbol de la Violeta. 1964. 6.95 (*0-87751-015-6*) E Torres & Sons.
— La Cancion Verde. 1956. 6.95 (*0-87751-014-8*) E Torres & Sons.
Plenn, Doris T. The Green Song. large type ed. (Illus.). 1994. 29.50 (*0-614-09805-X*, L-34103-00) Am Printing Hse.
Plenty International Staff & Haren, Charles T., eds. Recipes from the Global Kitchen: A Collection of Vegetarian Recipes. LC 95-14033. 122p. (Orig.). 1995. pap. 11.95 (*1-57067-006-4*) Book Pub Co.
Plenzdorf, U., et al. The New Sufferings of Young W. And Other Stories from the German Democratic Republic. Hornigk, Therese & Stephan, Alexander, eds. LC 96-53312. (The German Library). 348p. 1997. pap. 19.95 (*0-8264-0952-0*) Continuum.
Plenzdorf, Ulrich. The New Sufferings of Young W. Wilcox, Kenneth P., tr. 84p. 1996. reprint ed. pap. text 7.50 (*0-88133-891-5*) Waveland Pr.
Plesa Eyk. Enciclopedia de Nuestro Mundo. (SPA.). 98p. 1979. pap. 19.95 (*0-8288-4739-8*, S50442) Fr & Eur.
Plesch, P. H. High Vacuum Techniques for Chemical Synthesis & Measurement. (Illus.). 184p. (C). 1989. text 85.00 (*0-521-25756-5*) Cambridge U Pr.
Pleschtschejew, S. Ubersicht des Russischen Reichs Nach Seiner Gegenwartigen Neu Eingerichteten Verfassung Aufgesetzt Von Sergei Pleschtschejew, Seekapitan und Ritter des Heiligen Georgen-Ordens. (GER.). iv, 220p. 1992. write for info. (*3-487-09614-5*) G Olms Pubs.
Plescia, Joseph. The Bill of Rights & Roman Law: A Comparative Study. 118p. (Orig.). 1995. 69.95 (*1-57292-005-X*); pap. 49.95 (*1-57292-004-1*) Austin & Winfield.
— The Oath & Perjury in Ancient Greece. LC 73-13540. 124p. reprint ed. pap. 38.50 (*0-7837-4903-1*, 204456800004) Bks Demand.
Plesea, Gabriel. Bitter Be Thy Bread. LC 89-92290. 307p. (Orig.). 1989. pap. 7.00 (*0-9624498-0-6*) G Plesea.
Plesent, Stanley. Preparing Matrimonial Agreements. (Basic Practice Skills Ser.). 237p. 1989. text 15.00 (*0-87224-001-0*, Q1-3003) PLI.
***Pleshakov.** Tsushima. 2000. 35.00 (*0-465-05791-8*, Pub. by Basic) HarpC.
Pleshakov, Constantine, jt. auth. see Zubok, Vladislav.
Pleshakov, Constantine V., jt. auth. see Perry, John C.
Pleshakova, T., jt. ed. see Maslova, N.
Pleshanova, I. & Likhachova, Liudmila. Old Russian Decorative & Applied Art. (Illus.). 224p. (C). 1985. text 330.00 (*0-7855-5873-X*, Pub. by Collets) St Mut.
Pleshoyano, Dan V. Colonel Nicolae Plesoianu & the National Regeneration Movement in Walachia. 200p. 1991. text 37.50 (*0-88033-207-7*, Pub. by East Eur Monographs) Col U Pr.
Pleska, Cathy, ed. see Kleeman, Sydney M.
Plesken, W. & Nebe, G. Finite Rational Matrix Groups. LC 95-15923. (Memoirs Ser.: No. 556). 144p. 1995. pap. 37.00 (*0-8218-0343-3*, MEMO/116/556) Am Math.
Pleskin, W., ed. Group Rings of Finite Groups over p-adic Integers. (Lecture Notes in Mathematics Ser.: Vol. 1026). 151p. 1983. 32.95 (*0-387-12728-3*) Spr-Verlag.
Pleskov, Yu V. & Filinovskii, V. Yu, eds. The Rotating Disc Electrode. Wroblowa, Halina S. & Conway, B. E., trs. from RUS. LC 76-22774. (Studies in Soviet Science). (Illus.). 420p. 1976. reprint ed. pap. 119.70 (*0-608-05557-3*, 2066025) Bks Demand.
Pleskov, Yurii V., jt. auth. see Myamlin, Viktor.
Pleskov, Yurri V. Solar Energy Conversion. (Illus.). x, 163p. 1989. 174.95 (*0-387-51474-0*) Spr-Verlag.
***Pleskovic, Boris, ed.** Annual Conference on Development Economics 1998. 420p. 1999. pap. 40.00 (*0-8213-4321-1*) World Bank.
Pleskovic, Boris & Stiglitz, Joseph E., eds. Annual World Bank Conference on Development Economics, 1997. 324p. 1998. pap. 40.00 (*0-8213-4115-4*, 14115) World Bank.
Pleskovic, Boris, jt. ed. see Bruno, Michael.
Plesl, Evzen, jt. auth. see Ehrich, Robert W.
Plesner, Liselotte, et al, eds. Ecto-Atpases: Recent Progress on Structure & Function. LC 97-3575. 308p. (C). 1997. text 110.00 (*0-306-45584-6*, Kluwer Plenum) Kluwer Academic.
Pless, I. A., ed. World-Wide Collaboration for Safe & Peaceful Use of Nuclear Energy: Proceedings of the International Seminar, November 1986. vii, 244p. 1986. text 135.00 (*2-88124-209-X*) Gordon & Breach.
Pless, Ivan B. The Epidemiology of Childhood Disorders. (Illus.). 552p. 1994. text 79.50 (*0-19-507516-1*) OUP.
Pless, Thomas. Let Every Heart: A Family Devotional for the Advent Season. (Illus.). 112p. 1999. 14.99 (*1-57748-573-4*) Barbour Pub.
Pless, V. S.' & Huffman, W. C., eds. Handbook of Coding Theory Pt. 1: Algebraic Coding, Vol. 1. LC 98-44056. 1212p. 1998. 201.00 (*0-444-81472-8*, North Holland) Elsevier.
Pless, Vera. Introduction to the Theory of Error-Correcting: Codes. 3rd ed. LC 97-49834. (Wiley-Interscience Series in Discrete Mathematics & Optimization). 224p. 1998. 74.95 (*0-471-19047-0*, Wiley-Liss) Wiley.
Pless, Vera, et al. Handbook of Coding Theory. LC 98-44056. 1998. 201.00 (*0-444-50087-1*); 373.50 (*0-444-50088-X*) Elsevier.
Plessas, W., jt. ed. see Mathelitsch, L.
Plessas, W., jt. ed. see Mitter, H.
Plesset, Isabel R. Noguchi & His Patrons. LC 78-66819. 320p. 1970. 38.50 (*0-8386-2347-6*) Fairleigh Dickinson.
Plessinger, James, ed. see Tharp, Robert N.
Plessis, A. G. Du, see Du Plessis, Lourens M.
Plessis, A. G. Du, see Du Plessis, L. M. & Du Plessis, A. G.
Plessis, A. G. Du, see Du Plessis, Lourens M.
Plessis, A. G. Du, see Du Plessis, Lourens M. & Du Plessis, A. G.
Plessis, A. G. Du, see Du Plessis, Lourens M.
Plessis, A. G. Du, see Du Plessis, Lourens M. & Du Plessis, A. G.
Plessis, Alain. The Rise & Fall of the Second Empire, 1852-1871. Mandelbaum, Jonathan, tr. (Cambridge History of Modern France Ser.: No. 3). (Illus.). 218p. 1988. pap. text 18.95 (*0-521-35856-6*) Cambridge U Pr.
Plessis, Contessa Villeneuve de, see Villeneuve de Plessis, Contessa.
***Plessis, F.** Fabrizio Plessi: Opus Video Sculpture. 1998. 160.00 (*3-931876-10-1*) Koelen OHG.
Plessis, F. Horatius Flaccus, Quintus, Odes, Epodes et Chant Seculaire. (GER.). lxxviii, 396p. 1966. reprint ed. write for info. (*0-318-70455-2*) G Olms Pubs.
Plessis, J. C. Du, see De Jong, M. & Du Plessis, J. C.
Plessis, J. du. Surface Segregation. (Solid State Phenomena Ser.: Vol. 11). 132p. 1990. text 92.00 (*3-908044-06-5*, Pub. by Trans T Pub) Enfield Pubs NH.
Plessis, J. Du, see Du Plessis, J.
Plessis, L. M. Du, see Du Plessis, L. M.
Plessis, Lourens Du, see Du Plessis, Lourens.
Plessis, Roger Du, see Du Plessis, Roger.
Plessis, Rosemary Du, see Du Plessis, Rosemary.
Plessis, Susan Du, see Du Plessis, Susan.
Plessix Gray, Francine Du, see Du Plessix Gray, Francine.
Plessman, C. K., jt. auth. see Lynch, R. L.
Plessmann, W., jt. auth. see Schmidt, H.
Plessner, Gerald M. The Encyclopedia of Fund Raising: A Three Volume Work on How to Organize Fund Raising Special Events, Set. (Illus.). 351p. 1980. 100.00 (*0-916555-00-3*) Fund Raisers.
— The Encyclopedia of Fund Raising: Charity Auction Management Manual. rev. ed. (Illus.). 83p. 1986. 39.00 (*0-916555-01-1*) Fund Raisers.
— The Encyclopedia of Fund Raising: Golf Tournament Management Manual. rev. ed. (Illus.). 110p. 1992. 39.00 (*0-916555-02-X*) Fund Raisers.
— The Encyclopedia of Fund Raising: Testimonial Dinner & Industry Luncheon Management Manual. (Illus.). 142p. 1980. 39.00 (*0-916555-03-8*) Fund Raisers.
Plessner, Helmuth. The Limits of Community: A Critique of Social Radicalism. Wallace, Andy, tr. from GER. 128p. 1997. 39.95 (*0-391-04071-5*) Humanities.
— The Limits of Community: A Critique of Social Radicalism. Wallace, Andrew, tr. LC 99-29377. 225p. 2000. 49.95 (*1-57392-723-6*, Humanity Bks) Prometheus Bks.
— Die Stufen des Organischen und der Mensch: Einleitung in die philosophische Anthropologie. 3rd ed. (Sammlung Goeschen Ser.: No. 2200). 373p. (C). 1975. 22.95 (*3-11-005985-1*) De Gruyter.
Plessner, Markus. Vox--Enciclopedia Cultural Tomo 2: El Hombre. (SPA.). 210p. 1977. 29.95 (*0-8288-5546-3*, S50509) Fr & Eur.
Plessner, Yakir. The Political Economy of Israel: From Ideology to Stagnation. LC 93-203. (SUNY Series in Israeli Studies). 328p. (C). 1993. text 64.50 (*0-7914-1741-7*); pap. text 21.95 (*0-7914-1742-5*) State U NY Pr.
Plessz, Nicholas G. Problems & Prospects of Economic Integration in West Africa. LC 67-29636. (Centre for Developing-Area Studies, McGill University, Keith Callard Lectures: No. 2). 102p. reprint ed. pap. 31.70 (*0-7837-1158-1*, 204168700022) Bks Demand.
Plesters, Joyce, jt. auth. see Bull, David.
Pleszczynska, Elzbieta, jt. ed. see Bromek, Tadeusz.
Pletanek, Basia, tr. see Smith, Teresa H.
Pletcher, Barbara. Readings in Business Today. (C). 1980. 12.50 (*0-256-02376-X*, Irwn McGrw-H) McGrw-H Hghr Educ.
***Pletcher, David M.** The Diplomacy of Involvement: American Economic Expansion across the Pacific, 1784-1900. 416p. 2001. 44.95 (*0-8262-1315-4*) U of Mo Pr.
Pletcher, David M. The Diplomacy of Trade & Investment: American Economic Expansion in the Hemisphere, 1865-1900. LC 97-38825. (Illus.). 440p. 1998. 44.95 (*0-8262-1127-5*) U of Mo Pr.
Pletcher, Derek. A First Course in Electrode Processes. 270p. 1991. pap. 45.00 (*0-9517307-0-3*) Electrosyn Co.
Pletcher, Jean E., et al. Memories of the Michigan City Lighthouse & Description of the United States Lighthouse Service. (Little Bit of History Ser.: Bk. 5). 24p. (Orig.). (YA). (gr. 6 up). 1991. pap. 2.00 (*0-935549-15-3*) MI City Hist.
Pletcher, Larry B. Hiking New Hampshire. (Illus.). 254p. 1996. reprint ed. pap. 14.95 (*1-56044-461-4*) Falcon Pub Inc.
— Hiking Vermont. LC 96-30389. (Illus.). 198p. (Orig.). 1996. pap. 12.95 (*1-56044-395-2*) Falcon Pub Inc.
— It Happened in Massachusetts. LC 99-25063. 1999. 9.95 (*1-56044-846-6*, Two Dot) Falcon Pub Inc.
— Roughing It Easy in New England: Outdoor Adventures Near Lodgings in CT, ME, MA, NH, RI, VT. LC 98-9395. (Illus.). 268p. 1998. pap. 15.95 (*0-89997-210-1*) Wilderness Pr.
Pletka, Radovan. Learn Czech Fast. (Intensive Cassette Ser.). 226p. 1998. spiral bd. 184.00 incl. audio (*1-58214-011-1*) Mltilngl Bks.
— Spoken Czech: Czech Fast Course. (Spoken Language Ser.). (Orig.). 1995. pap. 135.00 incl. audio (*0-87950-632-6*); pap. text 30.00 (*0-87950-630-X*) Spoken Lang Serv.
Pletnev, A., tr. see Nezlin, Mikhail V. & Snezhkin, E. N.
Plets, C., et al. Computer Tomographic Imaging & Anatomic Correlation of the Human Brain. (Series in Radiology). 1987. text 184.00 (*0-89838-811-2*) Kluwer Academic.
Pletsch, Carl. Young Nietzsche: Becoming a Genius. 261p. 1992. pap. 14.95 (*0-02-925042-0*) Free Pr.
Pletsch, Susan, jt. auth. see Palmer, Pati.
Pletsch, William. Integrated Circuits: Making the Miracle Chip. rev. ed. LC 84-90578. (Illus.). 96p. 1984. pap. text 8.00 (*0-917927-00-1*) Pletsch Assocs.
Pletscher, A. & Ladewig, D., eds. Fifty Years of LSD: Current Status & Perspectives of Hallucinogens. LC 94-8290. (Illus.). 238p. 1994. 75.00 (*1-85070-569-0*) Prthnon Pub.
Plett, Delbert F. Sarah's Prairie: A Novel. 1995. 13.99 (*1-895308-20-8*) Windflower Comns.
Plett, H. F. English Renaissance Rhetoric & Poetics: A Systematic Bibliography of Primary & Secondary Sources. (Symbola et Emblemata Ser.: No. 6). 525p. 1995. 177.00 (*90-04-10343-0*) Brill Academic Pubs.
Plett, Heinrich F., ed. Renaissance-Poetik - Renaissance Poetics. (ENG & GER.). 449p. (C). 1994. lib. bdg. 155.75 (*3-11-013964-2*) De Gruyter.
— Renaissance-Rhetorik - Renaissance Rhetoric. (ENG & GER.). ix, 391p. (C). 1993. lib. bdg. 161.55 (*3-11-013567-1*) De Gruyter.
Plett, Heinrich F., et al. Rhetorica Movet: Studies in Historical & Modern Rhetoric in Honor of Heinrich F. Plett. LC 99-29764. (Symbola et Emblemata Ser.). 1999. write for info. (*90-04-11339-8*) Brill Academic Pubs.
Plett, Heinrich F., ed. see Koll, Beate-Maria.
Plett, Henry. Wings of Hope: A Father's Story. LC 90-82600. 152p. (Orig.). 1990. pap. 8.99 (*0-8361-3527-X*) Herald Pr.
Plett, P., et al. Training for Older People: A Handbook. v, 217p. (Orig.). 1991. pap. 22.50 (*92-2-107294-0*) Intl Labour Office.
Plettenberg-Serban, Alexandra, tr. see Descouvemont, Pierre.
Plettenberg-Serban, Alexandra, tr. see Gaucher, Guy.
Plettinger, H. Anne. Table of the Sin Function & Sin Squared Function for Values from 2 Degrees to 87 Degrees. 46p. 1965. pap. 63.00 (*0-677-01100-8*) Gordon & Breach.
Pletz, John. Being Ethical. LC 97-45680. 1999. 19.50 (*1-56072-532-X*, Nova Kroshka Bks) Nova Sci Pubs.
Pletzke, Jonathan. Advanced Smalltalk. LC 96-28542. 569p. 1996. pap., pap. text 49.95 incl. cd-rom (*0-471-16350-3*) Wiley.
Pleu, Mark G., ed. Prehistoric Hunter-Gatherer Fishing Strategies. (Illus.). (Orig.). 1996. pap. 18.50 (*0-9639749-1-2*) Boise St U Dept Anthrop.
Pleune, Ruud. Strategies of Dutch Environmental Organizations: Ozone Depletion, Acidification & Climate Change. LC 98-181568. 200p. 1998. pap. 24.95 (*90-5727-016-1*, Pub. by Intl Bks) Paul & Co Pubs.
Plevan, Kenneth A. & Siroky, Miriam L. Advertising Compliance Handbook. LC 88-62454. 527p. 1988. text 10.00 (*0-318-41230-6*, G1-1008) PLI.
Plevan, Kenneth A., et al. Advertising Compliance Handbook. 2nd ed. 905p. 1991. text 140.00 (*0-87224-025-8*, G6-2007) PLI.
Plevnik, Joseph. Paul & the Parousia: An Exegetical & Theological Investigation. LC 96-10729. 352p. (C). 1997. 29.95 (*1-56563-180-3*) Hendrickson MA.
Plevyak, Thomas, jt. auth. see Aidarous, Salah.
Plevyak, Thomas, jt. ed. see Aidarous, Salah.
Plew, Mark G. An Introduction to the Archaeology of Southern Idaho. (Hemingway Western Studies). (Illus.). 51p. (Orig.). 1986. pap. 4.95 (*0-932129-03-X*) Heming W Studies.
Plew, Mark G. & Forte, Janette, eds. A Bibliography of Guyana Anthropology. 60p. 1998. pap. text 5.95 (*0-9639749-3-9*) Boise St U Dept Anthrop.
Plew, Mark G., ed. see Hurt, Wesley R.
Plew, Ronald, jt. auth. see Stephens, Ryan.
Plewa, Franklin J. & Friedlob, George T. Income Statements. LC 94-29850. 304p. 1995. pap. 19.95 (*0-471-10384-5*) Wiley.
— Income Statements. LC 94-29850. 296p. 1995. 49.95 (*0-471-10383-7*) Wiley.
Plewa, Franklin J., Jr. & Friedlob, George T. Understanding Return on Investment. LC 96-8694. (Finance Fundamentals for Nonfinancial Managers Ser.). 256p. 1996. pap. 19.95 (*0-471-10372-1*) Wiley.
Plewa, Franklin J. & Friedlob, George T., Jr. Understanding Return on Investment. LC 96-8694. (Finance Fundamentals for Nonfinancial Managers Ser.). 237p. 1996. 34.95 (*0-471-10381-0*) Wiley.
Plewa, Franklin J., jt. auth. see Friedlob, George T.
Plewe, Brandon. GIS Online: Information Retrieval Mapping & the Internet. LC 97-22624. 336p. (C). 1997. pap. 51.95 (*1-56690-137-5*) Thomson Learn.
Plewes, John. Building Birdhouses for North American Birds. (Illus.). 87p. 1990. pap. 10.95 (*0-921335-22-9*, Pub. by LVTL) Veritas Tools.
***Plewig, G., et al.** Acne & Rosacea. 3rd rev. enl. ed. 770p. 2000. (*3-540-66751-2*) Spr-Verlag.
Plewig, Gerd & Kligman, Albert M. Acne & Rosacea. 2nd rev. ed. LC 92-49778. 1992. 231.00 (*0-387-52277-8*) Spr-Verlag.
Plewig, Gerd, jt. auth. see Marks.
Plewig, Gerd, jt. ed. see Marks, R. M.
Plewis, Ian. Analysing Change: Measurement & Explanation Using Longitudinal Data. fac. ed. LC 84-22044. 194p. 1985. reprint ed. pap. 60.20 (*0-7837-8276-4*, 204905600009) Bks Demand.
— Statistics in Education. (Arnold Applications of Statistics Ser.). 180p. 1997. pap. 39.95 (*0-340-64628-4*, Pub. by E A) OUP.
Plewman, Nicholas & Dooley, Brendan. Visitors' Guide to Zambia. LC 95-164009. 200p. 1995. pap. 17.95 (*1-86812-532-7*) Menasha Ridge.
Plews, John, jt. ed. see Lorey, Christoph.
Plexus Press Staff. The Day the Music Died: A Rock'n'Roll Tribute. 160p. 1994. per. 14.95 (*0-85965-058-8*, Pub. by Plexus) Publishers Group.
***Plexus Research Inc. Staff & National Rural Electric Cooperative Association Staff.** Internet Technology for Communication among Electric Cooperatives: Project 97-07. LC 99-43284. 1999. write for info. (*0-917599-27-6*) Natl Rural.

P

***Plexus Research Staff & National Rural Electric Cooperative Staff.** Guide to Automatic Meter Reading. LC 99-32655. 1999. write for info. (0-917599-26-8) Natl Rural.

Pleydell, Sarah & Brown, Victoria. Dramatic Difference: Drama in the Preschool & Kindergarten Classroom. LC 99-25827. 1999. pap. text 22.00 (0-325-00121-9) Heinemann.

Pleyel. Six Easy Violin Duets. 1927. pap. 11.95 (0-685-69310-4, WH02927) Shawnee Pr.

***Pleyel, Ignace.** Four Viennese String Quintets. Eisen, Cliff, ed. (Recent Researches in Music of the Classic Era Ser.: Vol. RRC53). (Illus.). xiii, 181p. 1998. pap. 65.00 (0-89579-417-9) A-R Eds.

Pleyel, Ignaz. Ignaz Pleyel Nos. 1 & 14: Periodical Symphonies. Smith, Raymond R., ed. (Recent Researches in Music of the Classic Era Ser.: Vol. RRC8). (Illus.). x, 95p. 1978. pap. 35.00 (0-89579-113-7) A-R Eds.

Pleyer, Uwe, et al, eds. Immuno-Ophthalmology. 3rd ed. (Developments in Ophthalmology Ser.: Vol. 30). (Illus.). vii, 200p. 1999. 174.00 (3-8055-6863-0) S Karger.

Pleynet, Marcelin. Painting & System. Godfrey, Sima N., tr. from FRE. LC 84-209. (Illus.). 168p. (C). 1994. 17.50 (0-226-67093-7) U Ch Pr.

Pleyte, E. & Rossi, F. Paprus de Turin. 253p. reprint ed. write for info. (0-318-71390-X) G Olms Pubs.

Pleyte, Willem. Chapitres Supplementaires Du Livre Des Morts 162-174. vii, 178p. reprint ed. write for info. incl. 3.5 hd (0-318-71391-8) G Olms Pubs.

Plezia, Valerie. Polka Party Dances. (Ethnic Dance Bks.: No.280). 130p. 1982. pap. 12.00 (0-9609368-0-7) V Plezia.

Pliakas, Stephanie, ed. see Meisler, Meryl & Popper, Evelyn.

Pliakas, Stephanie, ed. see Meisser, Meryl & Popper, Evelyn.

Pliakas, Stephanie, ed. see Nayer, Judy.

Pliakas, Stephanie, ed. see Thoburn, Tina, et al.

Pliakas, Stephanie, ed. see Trumbauer, Lisa.

Plice, Steven S. Manpower & Merger: The Impact of Merger upon Personnel Policies in the Carpet & Furniture Industries. LC 76-21151. (Manpower & Human Resources Studies: No. 5). 168p. reprint ed. pap. 52.10 (0-608-14850-4, 202590900047) Bks Demand.

Plichta, Peter. God's Secret Formula. 240p. 1998. pap. 14.95 (1-86204-358-2, Pub. by Element MA) Penguin Putnam.

— God's Secret Formula: The Deciphering of the Riddle of the Universe & the Prime Number Code. LC 96-48014. 240p. 1997. pap. 27.50 (1-86204-014-1, Pub. by Element MA) Penguin Putnam.

***Plick, Grad L.** MaNejar el Comportamiento Deticil: En la Sala de Clase: Una Guia de Bolsillo Para. Weeks, Mary, tr. (Illus.). 130p. 1999. pap. write for info. (1-928633-51-X) Seacoast MS.

Plieninger, Helga, ed. see Cous, Hippocrates.

Pliester, Leon. Rubinstein Complex: Of the Nimzo Indian Defense. Berry, Jonathan, ed. (Illus.). 376p. (Orig.). 1995. pap. 24.95 (1-879479-25-7) ICE WA.

Plieth, Waldfried. Electrochemical Nanotechnology: In Situ Local Probe Techniques at Electrochemical Interfaces. Lorenz, W. J., ed. 400p. 1998. 150.00 (3-527-29520-8) Wiley.

Plievier, Theodore. Stalingrad. Winston, Richard & Winston, Clara, trs. 460p. 1984. pap. 8.95 (0-88184-108-0) Carroll & Graf.

Plikhanou, Georgi. Development of the Monist View of History. 334p. 1972. reprint ed. 25.00 (0-8464-1086-9) Beekman Pubs.

***Pilar, Barbara.** Coming Out of the Pit. 2000. pap. 8.99 (1-930027-05-2) Insght Pub.

Plimmer, Don, et al. The Environment: A Primary Teacher's Guide. (Cassell Education Ser.). (Illus.). 160p. 1996. teacher ed. 80.00 (0-304-33353-0); pap., teacher ed. 33.95 (0-304-33355-7) Continuum.

Plimmer, Frances. Rating Law & Valuation. xxix, 262p. 1998. pap. 31.00 (0-582-30250-1, 15720) Gaunt.

Plimmer, Jack R. Encyclopedia of Agrochemicals, 10 vols. write for info. (0-471-19363-1) Wiley.

Plimmer, Jack R., ed. Pesticide Chemistry in the 20th Century: A Symposium. LC 76-51748. (ACS Symposium Ser.: No. 37). (Illus.). 320p. 1977. reprint ed. pap. 99.20 (0-608-04340-0, 206512000001) Bks Demand.

— Pesticide Residues & Exposure. LC 81-20568. (ACS Symposium Ser.: No. 182). 1982. 32.95 (0-8412-0701-1) Am Chemical.

— Pesticide Residues & Exposure. LC 81-20568. (ACS Symposium Ser.: Vol. 182). 224p. 1982. reprint ed. pap. 69.50 (0-608-03107-0, 206356000007) Bks Demand.

Plimmer, John F. In the Footsteps of the Whitechapel Murders: An Examination of the Jack the Ripper Murders Using Modern Police Techniques. (Illus.). 201p. 1998. pap. 18.95 (1-85776-394-7, Pub. by Book Guild Ltd) Trans-Atl Phila.

Plimoth Plantation Staff, jt. auth. see Hornblower, Malabar.

Plimpton, jt. auth. see Marcus.

***Plimpton, Carol E. & Sweeney, Victoria J.** Physical Education for the Elementary Classroom Teacher. (Illus.). 396p. 2000. pap. write for info. (0-9671766-3-8) Huron Valley.

Plimpton, Chet. A Word in Season. 196p. (Orig.). 1993. pap. 8.95 (0-9632190-4-9) Longwood.

Plimpton, Elizebeth B., jt. auth. see Ely, Susan H.

Plimpton, George. The Best American Sportwriting 1997. 352p. 1997. pap. 13.00 (0-395-79762-4) HM.

Plimpton, George. The Best of Plimpton. LC 90-42037. 384p. 1991. pap. 12.95 (0-87113-503-5, Atlntc Mnthly) Grove-Atltic.

— The Bogey Man: A Month on the PGA Tour. 320p. 1993. pap. 15.95 (1-55821-241-8) Lyons Pr.

— Mad Ducks & Bears: Football Revisited. 256p. 1993. pap. 14.95 (1-55821-240-X) Lyons Pr.

— The Open Net: A Professional Amateur in the World of Big-Time Hockey. 288p. 1993. pap. 12.95 (1-55821-242-6) Lyons Pr.

— Out of My League. 160p. 1993. pap. 10.95 (1-55821-238-8) Lyons Pr.

— The Paris Review, 140. 1996. pap. 10.00 (0-679-77369-X) Random.

— The Paris Review, No. 13. 1995. pap. 10.00 (0-679-76053-9) Random.

— The Paris Review, No. 13. (Illus.). 304p. 1996. pap. 10.00 (0-679-76418-6) Random.

— The Paris Review, No. 142. 1997. pap. 10.00 (0-679-77846-2) Random.

— The Paris Review, Vol. 137. (Illus.). 304p. 1996. pap. 10.00 (0-679-76875-0) Random.

— Paris Review, Vol. 148. 1999. pap. 10.00 (0-375-75361-3) Random.

— Paris Review, Vol. 149. 1999. pap. 10.00 (0-375-75362-1) Random.

— Paris Review, Vol. 150. 1999. pap. 12.00 (0-375-75435-0) Random House.

— The Paris Review: Strippable, No. 134. 1995. pap. 10.00 (0-679-76299-X) Random.

— The Paris Review No. 135: Strippable. 1995. pap. 10.00 (0-679-76300-7) Random.

***Plimpton, George.** Pet Peeves: Or Whatever Happened to Doctor Rawff? LC PS3566.L5P57 2000. (Illus.). 80p. 2000. 16.95 (0-87113-820-4, Atlntc Mnthly) Grove-Atltic.

Plimpton, George. Shadow Box. 352p. 1993. pap. 14.95 (1-55821-276-0) Lyons Pr.

— Truman Capote: In Which Various Friends, Enemies, Acquaintances, & Detractors Recall His Turbulent Career. (Illus.). 544p. 1998. pap. 16.95 (0-385-49173-5) Doubleday.

— The X-Factor: A Quest for Excellence. 172p. 1996. pap. 12.00 (0-393-31468-5, Norton Paperbks) Norton.

Plimpton, George, ed. The Norton Book of Sports. 500p. 1992. 24.95 (0-393-03040-7) Norton.

— The Paris Review, 151. 304p. 1999. pap. 12.00 (0-375-75517-9) Random.

— The Paris Review, No. 138. 1996. pap. 10.00 (0-679-77143-3) Fodors Travel.

— The Paris Review, No. 139. 1996. pap. 10.00 (0-679-77144-1) Fodors Travel.

***Plimpton, George, ed.** The Paris Review, Vol. 152. 304p. 1999. pap. 12.00 (0-375-75518-7) Random.

Plimpton, George, ed. Women Writers at Work. LC 99-462452. 304p. 1998. pap. 16.95 (0-679-77129-8) Random.

— The Writer's Chapbook. LC 98-34158. (Modern Library Ser.). 400p. 1999. 18.95 (0-679-60315-8) Modern Lib NY.

***Plimpton, George & Shinder, Jason, eds.** Best American Movie Writing 1998. 240p. 1998. pap. 14.95 (0-312-18049-7) St Martin.

Plimpton, George, ed. see Stein, Jean.

Plimpton, George A. A Collector's Recollections. Plimpton, Pauline A., ed. (Illus.). 104p. (Orig.). 1993. pap. 10.00 (0-9607862-6-0) Columbia U Libs.

— Education of Chaucer. LC 74-160453. reprint ed. 32.50 (0-404-05064-6) AMS Pr.

— Education of Shakespeare. LC 76-109658. (Select Bibliographies Reprint Ser.). ix, 140p. 1977. 23.95 (0-8369-5267-7) Ayer.

Plimpton, Oakes, ed. Stories of Early Twentieth Century Life: An Oral History of Arlington, Massachusetts. LC 92-61076. 192p. 1992. per. 12.00 (0-89725-082-6, 1388, Penobscot Pr) Picton Pr.

Plimpton, Pauline A. Oakes Ames: Jottings of a Harvard Botanist. LC 79-52949. (Illus.). 401p. 1980. text 12.95 (0-674-62921-3) HUP.

Plimpton, Pauline A., ed. see Plimpton, George A.

Plimpton, Ruth. Mary Dyer: Biography of a Rebel Quaker. (Illus.). 247p. 1999. text 22.00 (0-7881-5993-3) DIANE Pub.

Plimpton, Ruth T. Mary Dyer: Biography of a Rebel Quaker. (Illus.). 300p. 1994. 21.95 (0-8283-1964-2) Branden Bks.

***Pline, James L. & Institute of Transportation Engineers Staff.** Traffic Engineering Handbook. 5th rev. ed. LC 99-41568. (Illus.). 704p. 1999. text 100.00 (0-935403-32-9) Inst Trans Eng.

Pline, Marc J. Biology 1110. 128p. (C). 1996. pap. text, spiral bd., lab manual ed. 19.95 (0-7872-1994-0) Kendall-Hunt.

Pliner, Jayne, ed. see Christie, Agatha.

Plinio, Alex J. & Scanlon, Joanne B. Resource Raising: The Role of Non-Cash Assistance in Corporate Philanthropy. 56p. 1986. pap. 10.00 (0-685-23210-7) Ind Sector.

Plinius Secundus, C. Elder Pliny's Chapters on the History of Art. 1988. reprint ed. lib. bdg. 59.00 (0-7812-0568-9) Rprt Serv.

— Epistularum Libri Duo. Cowan, James, ed. (GER.). xxxiii, 198p. 1982. reprint ed. write for info. (3-487-07229-7) G Olms Pubs.

— Konkordanz Zur Naturalis Historia des C. Plinius Elder, Set, 3 Vols. Rosumek, Peter & Najock, Dietmar, eds. 1750p. write for info. (0-318-71202-4) G Olms Pubs.

— Naturalis Historia, 6 vols. in 3. (GER.). 1784p. reprint ed. write for info. (0-318-70423-4); reprint ed. write for info. (0-318-70424-2); reprint ed. write for info. (0-318-70425-0); reprint ed. write for info. (0-318-70426-9) G Olms Pubs.

— Physica Plinii Bambergensis. Onnerfors, Alf, ed. (Bibliotheca Graeca Et Latina Ser.: Vol. II). 174p. 1975. write for info. (3-487-05873-1) G Olms Pubs.

***Plinks LLC Staff.** 50 Commemorative State Quarters Collectors Booklet. (Illus.). 2000. 14.95 (0-9701801-0-1) pLinks.

Plint & Martyr. Engine Testing & Theory. 2nd ed. LC 98-86655. 352p. 1998. 69.00 (0-7680-0314-8, R-348) Soc Auto Engineers.

Plint, M. A. & Boeswirth, L. Fluid Mechanics: A Laboratory Course. (Illus.). 186p. 1978. pap. 25.00 (0-85264-245-8) Lubrecht & Cramer.

Plint, M. A. & Martyr, Anthony. Engine Testing: Theory & Practice. 2nd ed. LC 98-33487. 352p. 1998. pap. text 74.95 (0-7506-4021-9) Buttrwrth-Heinemann.

Plint, Michael A. & Martyr, Anthony J. Engine Testing: Theory & Practice. LC 94-33331. (Illus.). 272p. 1995. pap. text 69.95 (0-7506-1668-7) Buttrwrth-Heinemann.

Plint, Thomas. Crime in England: Its Relation, Character & Extent As Developed from 1801-1848. LC 73-14175. (Perspectives in Social Inquiry Ser.). 192p. 1974. reprint ed. 13.95 (0-405-05518-8) Ayer.

Pliny. Fifty Letters of Pliny. 2nd ed. Sherwin-White, A. N., ed. 230p. 1969. pap. text 17.95 (0-19-912010-2) OUP.

— Natural History, 1. Warmington, E. H., ed. (Loeb Classical Library: No. 330, 352-353, 370-371). 372p. 1938. text 19.95 (0-674-99364-0) HUP.

— Natural History, 2. Warmington, E. H., ed. (Loeb Classical Library: No. 330, 352-353, 370-371). 674p. 1942. text 19.95 (0-674-99388-8) HUP.

— Natural History, 3. Warmington, E. H., ed. (Loeb Classical Library: No. 330, 352-353, 370-371). 626p. 1940. text 19.95 (0-674-99389-6) HUP.

— Natural History, 4. Warmington, E. H., ed. (Loeb Classical Library: No. 330, 352-353, 370-371). 564p. 1945. text 19.95 (0-674-99408-6) HUP.

— Natural History, 5. Warmington, E. H., ed. (Loeb Classical Library: No. 330, 352-353, 370-371). 562p. 1950. text 19.95 (0-674-99409-4) HUP.

— Natural History, 7. (Loeb Classical Library: No. 392-394, 418-419). 576p. 1956. text 18.95 (0-674-99432-9) HUP.

— Natural History, 8. (Loeb Classical Library: No. 392-394, 418-419). 604p. 1963. text 19.95 (0-674-99460-4) HUP.

— Natural History, 10. (Loeb Classical Library: No. 392-394, 418-419). 362p. 1962. text 19.95 (0-674-99461-2) HUP.

— Selections from Pliny's Letters. Fisher, M. B. & Griffen, M. R., eds. LC 73-80489. (Latin Texts Ser.). (Illus.). 74p. 1973. pap. text 12.95 (0-521-20298-1) Cambridge U Pr.

Plinzner, Paul. System der Reiter-Ausbildung. (Documenta Hippologica Ser.). 113p. 1997. reprint ed. 30.00 (3-487-08195-4) G Olms Pubs.

Plis, Alexander I., jt. auth. see Shikin, Eugene V.

Plischke, Elmer. Berlin: Development of Its Government & Administration. LC 70-98789. 257p. 1970. reprint ed. lib. bdg. 65.00 (0-8371-3024-7, PLB, Greenwood Pr) Greenwood.

— Contemporary U. S. Foreign Policy: Documents & Commentary. LC 90-43385. 872p. 1991. lib. bdg. 135.00 (0-313-26032-X, PEF/, Greenwood Pr) Greenwood.

— Foreign Relations: Analysis of Its Anatomy, 213. LC 88-3121. (Contributions in Political Science Ser.: No. 213). 328p. 1988. 65.00 (0-313-25245-9, PFR/, Greenwood Pr) Greenwood.

— Microstates in World Affairs: Policy Problems & Options. LC 77-1351. (AEI Studies: No. 144). 168p. reprint ed. pap. 52.10 (0-8357-4506-6, 203736300008) Bks Demand.

Plischke, Elmer, ed. U. S. Department of State: A Reference History. LC 98-53381. 800p. 1999. lib. bdg. 125.00 (0-313-29126-8) Greenwood.

Plischke, Michael, jt. auth. see Bergersen, Birger.

Plischke, Michael, jt. auth. see Bergerson, Birger.

Pliscke, Micheal & Bergersen, Birger. Equilibrium Statistical Physics: Solution Manual. 2nd ed. 112p. 1994. pap. text 21.00 (981-02-2068-5) World Scientific Pub.

Plisek, V., jt. auth. see Leskova, T.

Pliska, Stanley R. Introduction to Mathematical Finance: Discrete Time Models. LC 97-7158. (Illus.). 400p. 1997. text 55.95 (1-55786-945-6) Blackwell Pubs.

Pliska, Stanley R., jt. ed. see Dempster, M. A.

Plisken, Berniece & Sargent, Claudia K. Top Twenty-Four Spanish Word Game Hits. 1987. pap. text 18.00 (0-582-99852-2, 75277) Longman.

Pliskin. My Father. My King. 19.99 (0-89906-315-2, MYFH); pap. 16.99 (0-89906-316-0, MYFP) Mesorah Pubns.

Pliskin, Berniece & Sargent. Top Twenty-Four French Word Game Hits. 1987. pap. text 18.00 (0-582-99858-1, 75283) Longman.

Pliskin, Jacqueline J. Living, Loving, & Laughing with Pain. 272p. 1995. pap. 19.95 (0-9647480-0-2) Words & Pict.

Pliskin, Jacqueline J., ed. Through the Eyes of Women of the 20th Century. (Illus.). 378p. (Orig.). 1997. pap. 19.95 (0-9647480-1-0) Words & Pict.

Pliskin, Karen L. Silent Boundaries: Cultural Constraints on Sickness & Diagnosis of Iranians in Israel. LC 86-32492. 293p. reprint ed. pap. 90.90 (0-7837-4551-6, 208034200005) Bks Demand.

Pliskin, Zelig. N'Tzor L'Shoncha: Guard Your Tongue in Yiddish. Rosenbaum, M. G., tr. (YID.). xxxxiii, 284p. 1996. 14.00 (0-9654702-0-2) M Birnhack.

Plisnier, Andre, jt. auth. see Blaise, Denis.

Plissner. TV American Presidency. 1996. 24.95 (0-02-874033-5) Free Pr.

Plissner, Martin. The Control Room: How Television Calls the Shots in Presidential Elections. LC 98-51053. 240p. 1999. 25.00 (0-684-82731-X) Free Pr.

***Plissner, Martin.** The Control Room: How Television Calls the Shots in Presidential Elections. 256p. 2000. per. 13.00 (0-684-86772-9) S&S Trade.

Plissner, Martin, et al, eds. Campaign Seventy-Six. LC 77-78784. (Individual Publications). (Illus.). 1977. lib. bdg. 51.95 (0-405-10515-0) Ayer.

Plissner, Martin, jt. auth. see Mitofsky, Warren J.

Pliszka, Steven R., et al. ADHD with Comorbid Disorders: Clinical Assessment & Management. LC 99-29748. 325p. 1999. 38.00 (1-57230-478-2) Guilford Pubns.

Plitnik, George R., jt. auth. see Strong, William J.

***Plitt, Jane.** Martha Matilda Harper & the American Dream: How One Woman Changed the Face of American Business. LC 99-85982. (Women's Studies). (Illus.). 224p. 2000. text 26.95 (0-8156-0638-9) Syracuse U Pr.

Plivier, Theodore. The Kaiser's Coolies. Green, M., tr. from GER. 308p. 1988. reprint ed. lib. bdg. 35.00 (0-86527-378-2) Fertig.

Ploch, Beth, ed. see Junior League of Memphis Staff.

Plocharski, J. & Roth, S., eds. Electrochemistry of Conducting Polymers 88. (Materials Science Forum Ser.: Vol. 42). 260p. 1989. text 96.00 (0-87849-585-1, Pub. by Trans T Pub) Enfield Pubs NH.

Plocher, David W., jt. auth. see Kongstvedt, Peter R.

Plocher, Hermann. German Air Force Versus Russia, Nineteen Forty-One. LC 68-22547. (German Air Force in World War 2 Ser.). (Illus.). 1968. reprint ed. 23.95 (0-405-00044-8) Ayer.

— German Air Force Versus Russia, Nineteen Forty-Three. LC 68-22549. (German Air Force in World War 2 Ser.). (Illus.). 1968. reprint ed. 20.95 (0-405-00046-4) Ayer.

— German Air Force Versus Russia, Nineteen Forty-Two. LC 68-22548. (German Air Force in World War 2 Ser.). (Illus.). 1968. reprint ed. 25.95 (0-405-00045-6) Ayer.

Plochinger, B. & Prey, S. Der Wienerwald. Schnabel, W., ed. (Sammlung Geologischer Fuehrer Ser.: Band 59). (GER., Illus.). xiv, 168p. 1993. spiral bd. 30.00 (3-443-15059-4, Pub. by Gebruder Borntraeger) Balogh.

Plochinger, Benno. Salzburger Kalkalpen. (Sammlung Geologischer Fuehrer Ser.: Band 73). (GER., Illus.). x, 144p. 1983. spiral bd. 23.00 (3-443-15034-9, Pub. by Gebruder Borntraeger) Balogh.

Plochmann, George K. Richard McKeon: A Study. LC 89-28254. (Illus.). 276p. 1990. 35.95 (0-226-67109-7) U Ch Pr.

Plochmann, George K. & Robinson, Franklin E. A Friendly Companion to Plato's "Gorgias" LC 87-12884. 466p. 1987. text 51.95 (0-8093-1404-5) S Ill U Pr.

Plociennik, Eve. A Passion for Flavor: Cooking with Infused Vinegar & Oil. (Illus.). 128p. 1997. 24.95 (0-9660352-0-8) Verve Edtns.

Ploeg, Anton, jt. ed. see Levine, Hal.

Ploeg, Frederick Van der, see Van der Ploeg, Frederick, ed.

Ploeg, H. M. Van der, see Van der Ploeg, H. M.

Ploeg, J. P. Van der, see Kampman, A. A., ed.

Ploeg, J. P. Van der, see Kampman, A. A. & Van der Ploeg, J. P., eds.

Ploeg, J. P. Van der, see Kampman, A. A., ed.

Ploeg, J. P. Van der, see Kampman, A. A. & Van der Ploeg, J. P., eds.

Ploeg, Kees Van Der, see Van Der Ploeg, Kees.

Ploeg, Marcie Ver, see Bloom, Leslie B. & Ver Ploeg, Marcie.

Ploeg, Tymen J. Van der, see Van der Ploeg, Tymen J., ed.

Ploeger, Katherine. Simplified Paragraph Skills. LC 99-21759. 1999. write for info. (0-8442-0345-9) NTC Contemp Pub Co.

Ploetz, Craig T. Milo's Friends in the Dark. (Illus.). 32p. (J). (ps-4). 1992. lib. bdg. 11.95 (1-882172-00-0) Milo Prods.

— Milo's Trip to the Museum with Grandpa. (J). (ps-3). 1994. 11.95 (1-882172-01-9) Milo Prods.

Ploetz, Manfred, jt. auth. see Weeser-Krell, Lothar.

***Ploetz, R. C., ed.** Diseases of Tropical & Subtropical Fruit Crops. (CABI Publishing Ser.). (Illus.). 512p. 2001. text. write for info. (0-85199-390-7) OUP.

— Fusarium Wilt of Banana. LC 90-82570. (Illus.). 146p. (Orig.). 1990. pap. 32.00 (0-89054-112-4) Am Phytopathol Soc.

Ploetz, R. C., et al, eds. Compendium of Tropical Fruit Diseases. LC 94-70664. (Disease Compendium Ser.). (Illus.). 128p. (Orig.). 1994. pap. 42.00 (0-89054-162-0) Am Phytopathol Soc.

Plog, Barbara A., ed. Fundamentals of Industrial Hygiene. 3rd ed. LC 87-60256. (Occupational Safety & Health Ser.). (Illus.). 927p. 1988. reprint ed. pap. 200.00 (0-608-01652-7, 206320400002) Bks Demand.

Plog, Barbara A., ed. see Plogg, H.

Plog, F., ed. An Analytical Approach to Cultural Resource Management: The Little Colorado Planning Unit. (Anthropological Research Papers: No. 13). (Illus.). xiv, 293p. 1978. pap. 15.00 (0-685-19298-9) AZ Univ ARP.

Plog, Fred, jt. auth. see Bates, Daniel.

Plog, Fred, jt. auth. see Bates, Daniel G.

Plog, Fred, jt. auth. see Jolly, Clifford.

Plog, Michael & Stenzel, Norman. The Rainbow Guide to Introductory Statistics. Kirby, Belinda, ed. 150p. (Orig.). 1987. 6.95 (0-932471-05-6) Falsoft.

Plog, Stanley C. Fielding's Best & Worst: The Surprising Results of the Plog Survey. Knoles, Kathy, ed. (Illus.). 640p. 1997. pap. 19.95 (1-56952-155-7) Fielding Wrldwide.

— Leisure Travel: Making It a Growth Market... Again! 256p. 1991. 69.95 (0-471-52952-4) Wiley.

Plog, Stephen. Ancient Peoples of the American Southwest. LC 96-61017. (Ancient Peoples & Places Ser.). (Illus.). 224p. 1997. 27.50 (0-500-02116-3, Pub. by Thames Hudson) Norton.

— Ancient Peoples of the American Southwest. LC 96-61017. (Ancient Peoples & Places Ser.). (Illus.). 224p. 1998. pap. 18.95 (0-500-27939-X, Pub. by Thames Hudson) Norton.

P

An Asterisk (*) at the beginning of an entry indicates that the title is appearing for the first time.

— Stylistic Variation in Prehistoric Ceramics. (New Studies in Archaeology). (Illus.). 192p. 1980. text 59.95 (*0-521-22581-7*) Cambridge U Pr.

Plog, Stephen, ed. Spatial Organization & Exchange: Archaeological Survey on Northern Black Mesa. LC 84-23646. (Illus.). 400p. 1986. text 31.95 (*0-8093-1214-X*) S Ill U Pr.

Plog, Stephen & Powell, Shirley, eds. Papers on the Archaeology of Black Mesa, Arizona, Vol. II. LC 75-32340. (Papers in Archaeology Ser.). (Illus.). 224p. 1984. 31.95 (*0-8093-1149-6*) S Ill U Pr.

Plogg, H. Coating Thickness Measurement. (C). 1988. 150.00 (*0-85218-036-5*, Pub. by Fuel Metallurgical Jrnl) St Mut.

— Fundamentals of Industrial Hygiene. 4th rev. ed. Plog, Barbara A., ed. (Illus.). 1011p. 1995. 124.95 (*0-87912-171-8*, 15134-0000) Natl Safety Coun.

Plokhy, Serhiy, ed. see Hrushevsky, Mykhailo.

Ploman, Edward W. Space, Earth & Communication. LC 84-12969. 237p. 1984. 55.00 (*0-89930-094-4*, PSE/, Quorum Bks) Greenwood.

Ploman, Edward W., ed. International Law Governing Communications & Information: A Collection of Documents. LC 81-7036. 367p. 1982. lib. bdg. 45.00 (*0-313-23277-6*, PLC/, Greenwood Pr) Greenwood.

Ploman, Edward W., jt. ed. see Thomas, Alan M.

Plombanie, Henri De Goyon de la, see De Goyon de la Plombanie, Henri.

Plomer, Aurora. Phenomenology, Geometry & Vision: Merleau Ponty's Critique of Classical Theories of Vision. 110p. 1991. text 72.95 (*1-85628-218-X*, Pub. by Avebry) Ashgate Pub Co.

Plomer, Henry R., compiled by. Index of Wills & Administrations Now Preserved in the Probate Registry at Canterbury, 1396-1558 & 1640-1650. (British Record Society Index Library: Vol. 50). 1969. reprint ed. pap. 60.00 (*0-8115-1495-1*) Periodicals Srv.

Plomer, William. Local Colour. 14p. 1999. 85.00 (*1-893450-02-3*) Elysium Pr.

Plomer, William & Nowell-Smith, Simon. The Autobiography of William Plomer. LC 75-332046. 455 p. 1975. 7.50 (*0-224-01036-0*) Jonathan Cape.

Plomer, William C. At Home: Memoirs. LC 79-179737. (Biography Index Reprint Ser.). 1977. reprint ed. 18.95 (*0-8369-8106-5*) Ayer.

— Double Lives: An Autobiography. LC 72-179738. (Biography Index Reprint Ser.). 1977. reprint ed. 20.95 (*0-8369-8105-7*) Ayer.

Plomerova, Jaroslava & Liebermann, R. C. Geodynamics of Lithosphere & Earth's Mantle: Seismic Anisotropy As a Record of the Past & Present Dynamic Processes. LC 98-23994. (Pageoph Topical Volumes Ser.). 516p. 1998. pap. 52.00 (*3-7643-5907-2*) Spr-Verlag.

Plomerova, Jaroslava, et al. Geodynamics of Lithospere & Earth's Mantle: Seismic Anisotropy As a Record of the Past & Present Dynamic Processes. LC 98-23994. (Pageoph Topical Volumes Ser.). 1998. write for info. (*0-8176-5907-2*) Birkhauser.

Plomin. Behavioral Genetics, Vol. 1. 3rd ed. LC 96-45063. 320p. 1997. pap. text 70.95 (*0-7167-2824-9*) St Martin.

***Plomin, Robert.** Behavioral Genetics. 4th ed. LC 00-39394. 2000. pap. write for info. (*0-7167-5159-3*) W H Freeman.

Plomin, Robert. Development, Genetics, & Psychology. 384p. (C). 1986. text 79.95 (*0-89859-630-0*) L Erlbaum Assocs.

— Genetics & Experience. (Individual Differences & Development Ser.: Vol. 6). 208p. (C). 1994. pap. text 13.99 (*0-8039-5421-2*) Sage.

— Genetics & Experience: The Interplay Between Nature & Nurture. (Individual Differences & Development Ser.: Vol. 6). (C). 1994. text 48.00 (*0-8039-5420-4*) Sage.

— Nature & Nuture: An Introduction to Behavioral Genetics. LC 89-9725. 150p. (C). 1996. mass mkt. 18.00 (*0-534-10768-0*) Brooks-Cole.

Plomin, Robert & Dunn, Judy, eds. The Study of Temperament: Changes, Continuities & Challenges. 192p. 1986. text 39.95 (*0-89859-670-X*) L Erlbaum Assocs.

Plomin, Robert & McClearn, Gerald E., eds. Nature, Nurture & Psychology. 498p. 1993. pap. 19.95 (*1-55798-396-8*) Am Psychol.

Plomin, Robert, et al. Nature & Nurture During Infancy & Early Childhood. 368p. 1988. text 69.95 (*0-521-34370-4*) Cambridge U Pr.

Plomin, Robert, jt. auth. see Buss, Arnold H.

Plomin, Robert, jt. ed. see Wachs, Theodore D.

Plommer, William H. Vitruvius & Later Roman Building Manuals. LC 72-90487. (Cambridge Classical Studies). 125p. reprint ed. pap. 35.70 (*0-608-13044-3*, 2024512) Bks Demand.

Plommer, William H., ed. see Cook, John M.

Plommet, M., jt. ed. see Verger, J. M.

Plomp, T. & Ely, eds. International Encyclopedia of Educational Technology. 2nd ed. 700p. 1996. 219.75 (*0-08-042307-8*, Pergamon Pr) Elsevier.

Plomp, T., jt. ed. see Moonen, J.

Plomp, Tjeerd, jt. auth. see Ely, Donald P.

Plomp, Tjeerd, ed. see Anderson, Ronald E., et al.

Plomp, Tjeerd, jt. ed. see Pelgrum, Willem J.

Plon, jt. auth. see Mame.

Plona, Christopher. The European Bond Basis: An In-Depth Analysis for Hedgers, Speculators, & Arbitrageurs. 480p. 1996. 70.00 (*0-7863-0852-4*, Irwn Prfssnl) McGraw-Hill Prof.

Plongeon, Alice D. Le, see Le Plongeon, Alice D.

Plongeon, Augustus Le, see Le Plongeon, Augustus.

Plonien, Michael J. & Black, Stephanie J. Establishing Remote Computer Communication. 1997. ring bd. 59.00 (*0-7646-0116-4*, QRCP97) Prctnrs Pub Co.

— Mastering Computer Communication. 1997. ring bd. 59.00 (*0-7646-0098-2*, QCCP97) Prctnrs Pub Co.

— Securing Online Communication. LC 97-196227. 1997. ring bd. 59.00 (*0-7646-0117-2*, QSCP97) Prctnrs Pub Co.

Plonien, Michael J., et al. Guide to Technology Solutions, 2 vols. Incl. Vol. 1. 1996. ring bd. Not sold separately (*1-56433-921-1*); Vol. 2. 1996. ring bd. Not sold separately (*1-56433-922-X*); 140.00 (*1-56433-920-3*) Prctnrs Pub Co.

— Using Online Services & the Internet. LC 97-196210. 1997. ring bd. 59.00 (*0-7646-0118-0*, QOSP97) Prctnrs Pub Co.

Plonsey, R. & Barr, R. C. Bioelectricity: A Quantitative Approach. LC 88-22418. (Illus.). 326p. (C). 1988. text 114.00 (*0-306-42894-6*, Kluwer Plenum) Kluwer Academic.

Plonsey, Robert, jt. auth. see Malmivuo, Jaakko.

Plonsky, Kathryn A. Balancing Law & Parenthood: Part-Time Careers in the Law. (Illus.). 150p. 1999. pap. 30.00 (*0-938609-35-1*) Graduate Group.

Plonus, Martin. Applied Electromagnetics. (Illus.). 704p. (C). 1978. 101.56 (*0-07-050345-1*) McGraw.

Ploof, Ron. The Edison Effect: Success Strategies for the Information Age. (Illus.). 262p. 1995. pap. 17.95 (*0-89447-338-7*) Cypress.

Ploof, Willis H., jt. auth. see Woods, Sandra K.

Ploog, K. H. & Tapfer, L., eds. Physics & Technology of Semiconductor Quantum Devices: Proceedings of the International School Held in Mesagne, Brindisi, Italy, 21-26 September 1992. (Lecture Notes in Physics Ser.: Vol. 419). (Illus.). viii, 212p. 1993. 73.95 (*0-387-56989-8*) Spr-Verlag.

Ploog, Klaus, ed. III-V Quantum System Research. (Materials & Devices Ser.: No. 11). 357p. 1995. boxed set 125.00 (*0-85296-824-8*, ED011) INSPEC Inc.

Ploog, Klaus, jt. ed. see Chang, Leroy L.

Ploog, Randy. Benjamin West Drawings from the Historical Society of Pennsylvania, (Exhibition Catalogue) 1987th ed. (Illus.). 66p. (Orig.). 1987. pap. 7.50 (*0-911209-36-0*) Palmer Mus Art.

— Florence Putterman: A Twenty Year Survey, 1970-1990. (Illus.). 40p. 1990. pap. 7.00 (*0-911209-43-3*) Palmer Mus Art.

Plooij, Daniel. Pilgrim Fathers from a Dutch Point of View. LC 71-100509. reprint ed. 20.00 (*0-404-05065-4*) AMS Pr.

— Pilgrim Fathers from a Dutch Point of View. LC 79-131801. 1970. reprint ed. 7.00 (*0-403-00688-0*) Scholarly.

Plooij, Frans X. Behavioral Development of Free-Living Chimpanzee Babies & Infants. Lipsitt, Lewis P., ed. LC 83-25804. (Monographs on Infancy: Vol. 4). (Illus.). 224p. (Orig.). 1984. text 73.25 (*0-89391-115-1*) Ablx Pub.

Ploos van Amstel, M. J., jt. auth. see Farmer, David.

Plopper, Bruce L. Mass Communication Law in Arkansas. 105p. 1997. pap. 12.95 (*0-913507-83-0*) New Forums.

— The Problem-Solving Handbook for High School Journalism Advisers. 1992. 8.50 (*0-317-04966-6*) Quill & Scroll.

Ploquin, Genevieve. Painting on Stones. (Illus.). 48p. 1998. pap. text 11.95 (*0-85532-864-9*, Pub. by Srch Pr) A Schwartz & Co.

Ploquin, Max. Dictionnaire de l'Enfantement. (FRE.). 264p. 1974. pap. 39.95 (*0-8288-6012-2*, M6459) Fr & Eur.

Ploscik, Vince, jt. auth. see Mason, Sophia.

Ploski, Cynthia. Conversations with My Healers: My Journey to Wellness from Breast Cancer. 288p. 1995. 18.95 (*1-57178-010-6*) Coun Oak Bks.

— Conversations with My Healers: My Journey to Wellness from Breast Cancer. 278p. 1996. pap. 18.95 (*1-57178-027-0*) Coun Oak Bks.

Ploski, Harry A., compiled by. Reference Library of Black America, 5 vols. (Illus.). 1600p. 1990. lib. bdg. 179.90 (*0-685-49222-2*) Afro Am Pr.

Ploski, Harry A. & Williams, James D., eds. The Negro Almanac: A Reference Work on the Afro-American. 4th ed. LC 86-72654. (Illus.). 1550p. 1983. text 99.95 (*0-685-17467-0*) Bellwether Pub.

Ploskonka, Catherine A., ed. see Thacker, Robert M.

Plosky, Harry A. & Williams, James D., eds. The Negro Almanac: A Reference Work on the Afro-American. 5th ed. (Illus.). 1989. text 99.95 (*0-913144-09-6*) Bellwether Pub.

Ploss, Sidney I. Conflict & Decision-Making in Soviet Russia: A Case Study of Agricultural Policy, 1953-1963. LC 65-12992. 323p. 1965. reprint ed. pap. 100.20 (*0-608-03363-4*, 206407500008) Bks Demand.

Ploss, Thomas H. The Nation Pays Again: The Demise of The Milwaukee Road, 1928-1986. 3rd ed. 214p. (C). 1991. 40.00 (*0-9613788-1-6*) T M Ploss.

Plossajcsak, M., jt. ed. see Kutschers, Michael.

Plosser, Gray G., ed. see White, Marjorie L.

Plossl, George W. Effective Corporate Strategy in Manufacturing. LC 86-90412. (Illus.). 120p. 1986. 30.00 (*0-926219-03-0*) G P Ed Serv.

— Orlicky's Material Requirements Planning. 2nd ed. LC 93-41951. 311p. 1993. 49.00 (*0-07-050459-8*) McGraw.

— Production & Inventory Control: Applications. LC 83-81732. (Illus.). 320p. 1983. 45.00 (*0-926219-04-9*) G P Ed Serv.

Plossl, George W. & Wright, Oliver W. Production & Inventory Control: Principles & Techniques. 2nd ed. (Illus.). 448p. 1985. 96.00 (*0-13-725144-0*) P-H.

Plossl, Keith R. Engineering for the Control of Manufacturing. (ENG & SPA., Illus.). 240p. 1987. text 34.95 (*0-317-56749-7*) P-H.

Plossu, Bernard. The African Desert. LC 87-5021. (Illus.). 90p. 1987. pap. 8.95 (*0-8165-0934-4*) U of Ariz Pr.

Plotch, Batia, ed. NewYorkwalks: The Ninety-Second Street Y. (Walks Ser.). (Illus.). 272p. 1995. pap. 12.95 (*0-8050-1660-0*, Owl) H Holt & Co.

Plotch, Batia & Cobe, Patricia, eds. The Kosher Gourmet: The Ninety Second Street Y Kosher Cooking School. 464p. 1994. pap. 12.50 (*0-449-90959-X*) Fawcett.

Plotch, Walter, jt. ed. see Tumin, Melvin M.

Plotinus. Are the Stars Causes? 1985. pap. 3.95 (*0-916411-93-1*) Holmes Pub.

— Complete Works of Plotinus with Concordance, 4 vols. Guthrie, K. S., ed. 1977. lib. bdg. 1000.00 (*0-8490-1659-2*) Gordon Pr.

Plotinus. Ennead III.6: On the Impassivity of the Bodiless. Fleet, Barrie, tr. & comment by.Tr. of Nines. (ENG & GRE.). 338p. 1995. text 75.00 (*0-19-814965-4*) OUP.

Plotinus. An Essay on the Beautiful, 1792. Taylor, Thomas, tr. from GRE. LC 96-34847. (Revolution & Romanticism, 1789-1834 Ser.). xx, 47 p. 1997. 48.00 (*1-85477-209-0*) Continuum.

— Liber de Pulchritudine. cxlii, 574p. 1976. reprint ed. write for info. (*3-487-06054-X*) G Olms Pubs.

Plotinus. A Neo-Platonic Discourse: Being "Against the Gnostics" by Plotinus. Dodge, Early, ed. Elster, Roy, tr. from GRE. 1997. pap. 8.95 (*1-55818-380-9*) Holmes Pub.

Plotinus. On Nature, Contemplation & the One. Taylor, Thomas, ed. & tr. by. from GRE. 1989. pap. 5.95 (*1-55818-160-1*) Holmes Pub.

— Opera Vol. I: Enneades I-III cum Vita Porphyrii. Henry, Paul & Schwyzer, H. R., eds. (Oxford Classical Texts Ser.). 410p. 1964. text 49.95 (*0-19-814561-6*) OUP.

— Opera Vol. II: Enneades IV-V. Schwyzer, H. R. & Henry, Paul, eds. (Oxford Classical Texts Ser.). 338p. 1977. text 49.95 (*0-19-814582-9*) OUP.

— Opera Vol. III: Ennead VI. Schwyzer, H. R. & Henry, Paul, eds. 402p. (C). 1983. text 55.00 (*0-19-814591-8*) OUP.

— Plotinus: Essay on the Beautiful. Taylor, Thomas, tr. 1984. pap. 8.95 (*0-916411-86-9*) Holmes Pub.

— Works, 7 vols. No. 440-445, & 468. write for info. (*0-318-53221-2*) HUP.

***Plotinus & Abhayananda.** The Origin of Western Mysticism: Selected Writings of Plotinus. LC 99-38569. 2000. write for info. (*0-914557-12-2*) Atma Bks.

Plotke, A. J. Imperial Spies Invade Russia: The British Intelligence Interventions, 1918, 131. LC 92-25731. (Contributions in Military Studies Ser.: No. 131). 304p. 1993. 62.95 (*0-313-28611-6*, PBI, Greenwood Pr) Greenwood.

Plotke, David. Building a Democratic Political Order: Reshaping American Liberalism in the 1930's & 1940's. (Illus.). 399p. (C). 1996. text 49.95 (*0-521-42059-8*) Cambridge U Pr.

Plotke, David, jt. ed. see Boggs, Carl.

***Plotkin.** Tremor the Most Common Complaints. 224p. 2000. pap. 25.00 (*0-7506-7284-6*) Buttrwrth-Heinemann.

Plotkin, Albert. The Ethics of World Religions. LC 93-35756. 192p. 1993. pap. 24.95 (*0-7734-1940-3*) E Mellen.

— Rabbi Plotkin: A Memoir. Sabine, Gordon A., ed. 160p. (Orig.). 1992. lib. bdg. write for info. (*1-879286-02-5*) AZ Bd Regents.

Plotkin, Allen, jt. auth. see Katz, Joseph.

Plotkin, B. I. Universal Algebra, Algebraic Logic, & Databases. LC 93-44246. 438p. 1994. text 272.50 (*0-7923-2665-2*) Kluwer Academic.

Plotkin, B. I., et al. Algebraic Structures in Automata & Database Theory. 296p. 1992. text 61.00 (*981-02-0936-3*) World Scientific Pub.

Plotkin, Cary H. The Tenth Muse: Victorian Philology & the Genesis of the Poetic Language of Gerard Manley Hopkins. LC 88-39600. 214p. (C). 1989. 26.95 (*0-8093-1488-6*) S Ill U Pr.

Plotkin, Dave. Using Lotus Approach 3.0 for Windows. LC 93-84121. 699p. 1994. 29.99 (*1-56529-177-8*) Que.

Plotkin, Dave & Sanna, Paul. Windows 98 Complete Reference. 800p. 1998. boxed set 50.00 (*0-7615-1533-X*) Prima Pub.

***Plotkin, David N.** How to Do Everything with FrontPage 2000. (Illus.). 2000. pap. 24.99 (*0-07-212575-6*) Osborne-McGraw.

Plotkin, David N. Selling to Humans: A New Approach to Exchange. 268p. 1995. pap. 14.00 (*0-9643549-4-2*) Influence Trning.

***Plotkin, David N.** VISIO 2000 Visual Insight. LC 99-54513. (Illus.). 1999. pap. 24.99 (*1-57610-532-6*) Coriolis Grp.

Plotkin, Diane M., jt. auth. see Ritvo, Roger A.

Plotkin, Fred. Italy for the Gourmet Traveler. (Illus.). 736p. 1996. pap. 22.00 (*0-316-71070-9*) Little.

— Opera 101: A Complete Guide to Learning & Loving Opera. LC 94-9477. 512p. (J). 1994. pap. 14.45 (*0-7868-8025-2*, Pub. by Hyperion) Time Warner.

— Recipes from Paradise: Life & Food on the Italian Riviera. LC 97-1813. (Illus.). 496p. (gr. 8). 1997. 32.50 (*0-316-71071-7*) Little.

Plotkin, Fred, jt. auth. see De' Medici Stucchi, Lorenza.

Plotkin, Frederick S., jt. auth. see Neyer, Jeanie E.

Plotkin, G., jt. ed. see Huet, Gedeon.

Plotkin, G., jt. ed. see Huet, Gerard.

Plotkin, George, ed. see Milner, Robin.

Plotkin, Gordon, jt. ed. see Dezani-Ciancaglini, Mariangiola.

Plotkin, Gordon, jt. ed. see Lassez, Jean-Louis.

Plotkin, Gregory & Plotkin, Rita. Cooking the Russian Way. (Easy Menu Ethnic Cookbooks Ser.). (Illus.). 48p. (J). (gr. 5 up). 1986. lib. bdg. 19.93 (*0-8225-0915-6*, Lerner Publctns) Lerner Pub.

Plotkin, Harris M. Building a Winning Team. 1997. pap. text 24.95 (*1-882180-82-8*) Griffin CA.

Plotkin, Henry. Evolution in Mind: An Introduction to Evolutionary Psychology. LC 97-74915. ix, 288p. 1998. 27.95 (*0-674-27120-3*) HUP.

***Plotkin, Henry.** Evolution in Mind: An Introduction to Evolutionary Psychology. 2000. pap. text 16.95 (*0-674-00195-8*) HUP.

Plotkin, Henry C. Darwin Machines & the Nature of Knowledge. 287p. (C). 1994. text 27.95 (*0-674-19280-X*) HUP.

— Darwin Machines & the Nature of Knowledge. 288p. 1997. pap. text 15.95 (*0-674-19281-8*) HUP.

— The Nature of Knowledge: Concerning Adaptations, Instinct & the Evaluation of Intelligence. LC 93-39328. 1994. write for info. (*0-674-60482-2*) HUP.

Plotkin, Henry C., ed. Learning, Development, & Culture: Essays in Evolutionary Epistemology. LC 82-1947. 505p. reprint ed. pap. 156.60 (*0-608-16346-5*, 202668300051) Bks Demand.

— The Role of Behavior in Evolution. 208p. 1988. 35.00 (*0-262-16107-9*, Bradford Bks) MIT Pr.

Plotkin, Ira L. Anarchism in Japan: A Study of the Great Treason Affair, 1910-1911. LC 90-24281. (Japanese Studies: Vol. 1). 180p. 1991. lib. bdg. 79.95 (*0-88946-729-3*) E Mellen.

Plotkin, Kathy L. The Pearson Girls: A Family Memoir of the Dakota Plains. LC 98-66956. (Illus.). 260p. 1999. pap. 16.95 (*0-911042-51-2*) NDSU Inst Reg.

Plotkin, Mark J. Medicine Quest: In Search of Nature's Healing Secrets. LC 99-42822. 214p. 2000. 22.95 (*0-670-86937-6*) Viking Penguin.

— The Shaman's Apprentice. LC 97-5978. (Illus.). 40p. (YA). 1998. 16.00 (*0-15-201281-8*) Harcourt.

***Plotkin, Mark J.** Tales of a Shaman's Apprentice: An Ethnobotanist Searches for New Medicines in the Amazon Rain Forest. 2000. 25.50 (*0-8446-7132-0*) Peter Smith.

Plotkin, Mark J. Tales of a Shaman's Apprentice: An Ethnobotanist Searches for New Medicines in the Amazonian Rain Forest. (Illus.). 352p. 1994. pap. 13.95 (*0-14-012991-X*, Penguin Bks) Viking Penguin.

Plotkin, Mark J. & Famolare, Lisa, eds. Sustainable Harvest & Marketing of Rain Forest Products. LC 91-43278. 325p. 1992. text 45.00 (*1-55963-169-4*) Island Pr.

Plotkin, Martha R. A Time for Dignity: Police (Response to) & Domestic Abuse of the Elderly. LC 88-62067. 112p. (Orig.). (C). 1988. pap. 9.00 (*1-878734-05-9*) Police Exec Res.

Plotkin, Martha R. & Narr, Tony. The Police Response to the Homeless: A Status Report. LC 93-86619. 312p. (Orig.). 1993. pap. 26.00 (*1-878734-31-8*) Police Exec Res.

Plotkin, Norman C. & Novick, Amy R., contrib. by. Western Region Directory of INS Offices. 180p. 1995. 35.00 (*1-878677-92-6*, PT602) Amer Immi Law Assn.

Plotkin, R. The Intervention Handbook. 64p. pap. 8.95 (*0-318-41637-9*) Am Bartenders.

Plotkin, Rita, jt. auth. see Plotkin, Gregory.

Plotkin, Robert. The Bartender's Companion: A Complete Drink Recipe Guide. 3rd ed. 1997. spiral bd. 17.95 (*0-945562-23-3*) PSD Pub.

— The Bartender's Companion: A Complete Drink Recipe Guide. 3rd rev. ed. LC 97-165413. (Illus.). 169p. 1997. pap. 14.95 (*0-945562-22-5*) PSD Pub.

— 501 Questions Every Bartender Should Know How to Answer: A Unique Look at the Bar Business. LC 93-92667. 72p. 1993. pap. 11.95 (*0-945562-12-8*) PSD Pub.

— Increasing Bar Sales: Creative Twists to Bigger Profits. 206p. 1997. pap. 17.95 (*0-945562-15-2*) PSD Pub.

— Preventing Internal Theft: A Bar Owner's Guide. 2nd ed. 1998. pap. 19.95 (*0-945562-24-1*) PSD Pub.

***Plotkin, Robert & Flores, Raymond J.** Toma! Margaritas! The Original Guide to Margaritas & Tequila. LC 99-457869. (Illus.). 107p. 1999. 15.95 (*0-945562-26-8*, BarMedia) PSD Pub.

Plotkin, Robert A. The Commercial Bartender's Training Manual. 2nd ed. 1994. pap. 11.95 (*0-945562-14-4*) PSD Pub.

— Professional Guide to Bartending: An Encyclopedia of American Mixology. 2nd ed. LC 91-60296. (Illus.). 183p. (C). 1991. pap. 29.95 (*0-945562-10-1*) PSD Pub.

— Reducing Bar Costs: A Survival Plan for the '90s. LC 93-93670. 101p. 1993. pap. 20.00 (*0-945562-13-6*) PSD Pub.

Plotkin, S. A. & Fantini, B., eds. Vaccinia, Vaccination, Vaccinology: Jenner, Pasteur & Their Successors. 380p. 1996. pap. text 110.00 (*2-906077-83-6*) Elsevier.

Plotkin, S. A., jt. ed. see Majer, M.

Plotkin, Sidney & Scheuerman, William E. Private Interest, Public Spending: Balanced-Budget Conservatism & the Fiscal Crisis. 280p. write for info. (*1-895431-99-9*); pap. 19.99 (*1-895431-98-0*, Pub. by Black Rose) Consort Bk Sales.

Plotkin, Sidney, jt. auth. see Scheuerman, William E.

Plotkin, Stanley A., et al, eds. Preclinical & Clinical Development of New Vaccines: Symposium, Institut Pasteur, Paris, May, 1997, Vol.95. (Developments in Biological Standardization Ser.: Vol. 95). (Illus.). xii, 284p. 1998. pap. 235.00 (*3-8055-6734-0*) S Karger.

Plotkin, Stanley A. & Mortimer, Edward A., Jr. Vaccines. 2nd ed. LC 93-10761. (Illus.). 1024p. 1994. reprint ed. text 185.00 (*0-7216-6584-5*, W B Saunders Co) Harcrt Hlth Sci Grp.

Plotkin, Stanley A. & Orenstein, Walter A. Vaccines. 3rd ed. Zorab, Richard, ed. LC 98-31650. 1055p. (C). 1999. text. write for info. (*0-7216-7443-7*, W B Saunders Co) Harcrt Hlth Sci Grp.

Plotkin, V. Y. The Dynamics of the English Phonological Systems. (Janua Linguarum, Ser. Practica: No. 155). 98p. 1972. pap. text 60.75 (*90-279-2324-8*) Mouton.

Plotkin, Zalman. Even in America. (Illus.). 115p. 1998. pap. 10.00 (*0-8059-4299-8*) Dorrance.
***Plotnick.** Introduction to Psychology. 6th ed. 2001. pap. 53.25 (*0-534-57996-5*); pap. 42.00 (*0-534-57997-3*) Thomson Learn.
— The Survival Guide. 476p. (Orig.). 1999. pap. 29.99 (*0-07-212051-7*) McGraw.
Plotnick, Amy, ed. 1999/2000 Public Human Services Directory. 600p. 1999. pap. 90.00i (*0-910106-30-4*) Am Human Servs.
Plotnick, Amy J., ed. Public Welfare Directory Vol. 58: A Resource Guide to the Human Services. LC 41-4981. xx, 568p. (Orig.). 1997. pap. 80.00 (*0-910106-27-4*) Am Human Servs.
Plotnick, Charles & Leimberg, Stephan R. How to Settle an Estate: A Manual for Executors & Trustees. LC 97-32603. 352p. 1998. pap. 14.95 (*0-452-27934-8*, Plume) Dutton Plume.
Plotnick, Harvey M. Notes of a Refugee: Poems. LC 92-14940. 64p. 1992. pap. 14.95 (*0-7734-0002-8*, Mellen Poetry Pr) E Mellen.
Plotnick, Leslie & Henderson, Randi. Clinical Management of the Child & Teenager with Diabetes. LC 98-16878. (Series in Ambulatory Pediatric Medicine). 1998. 55.00 (*0-8018-5908-5*); pap. 24.95 (*0-8018-5909-3*) Johns Hopkins.
Plotnick, Robert D. The Twentieth Century Record of Inequality & Poverty in the United States. (Illus.). 67p. (C). 1999. pap. text 20.00 (*0-7881-7829-6*) DIANE Pub.
Plotnick, Robert D., jt. auth. see Waller, Maureen R.
Plotnicov, Leonard. Strangers to the City: Urban Man in Jos, Nigeria. LC 67-13928. (Illus.). 333p. (C). 1967. pap. 14.95 (*0-8229-5135-5*) U of Pittsburgh Pr.
Plotnicov, Leonard & Tuden, Arthur, eds. Essays in Comparative Social Stratification. LC 79-81666. 357p. reprint ed. pap. 110.70 (*0-608-13764-2*, 202062000018) Bks Demand.
Plotnicov, Leonard, jt. ed. see Coy, Michael W., Jr.
Plotnik. Intro to Psychology. 5th ed. (Psychology Ser.). 1998. pap. 29.95 (*0-534-36535-3*) Brooks-Cole.
— Introduction to Psychology. 3rd ed. (Psychology Ser.). Date not set. lab manual ed. 63.75 (*0-534-30798-1*) Brooks-Cole.
— Introduction to Psychology. 5th ed. LC 98-37913. (Psychology Ser.). 724p. 1998. pap. 74.95 (*0-534-35611-7*); pap., teacher ed. 47.75 (*0-534-36415-2*); mass mkt. 39.00 (*0-534-36319-9*) Brooks-Cole.
— Introduction to Psychology. 5th ed. (Psychology Ser.). 1998. pap., student ed. 16.75 (*0-534-36145-5*) Brooks-Cole.
Plotnik, et al. Psychology Lab Manual. (Adaptable Courseware Ser.). 1996. lab manual ed. 14.00 (*0-534-49746-2*) Brooks-Cole.
Plotnik, Arthur. Elements of Editing: A Modern Guide For Editors & Journalists. 176p. 1986. pap. 9.95 (*0-02-047430-X*) Macmillan Gen Ref.
— The Elements of Editing: A Modern Guide for Editors & Journalists. 32nd ed. 156p. 1996. pap. 9.95 (*0-02-861451-8*) Macmillan Gen Ref.
***Plotnik, Arthur.** The Urban Tree Book: An Uncommon Field Guide of City & Town. LC 99-42452. (Illus.). 304p. 2000. pap. 18.95 (*0-8129-3103-3*, Times Bks) Crown Pub Group.
Plotnik, Arthur, et al. The CLAST Review Book. 445p. (C). 1992. pap. text 35.00 (*0-15-500041-1*, Pub. by Harcourt Coll Pubs) Harcourt.
Plotnik, Rod. Introduction to Psychology. 3rd ed. 770p. (C). 1992. mass mkt. 49.75 (*0-534-16446-3*) Brooks-Cole.
— Introduction to Psychology. 3rd ed. 770p. (C). 1993. mass mkt., student ed. 17.00 (*0-534-16448-X*) Brooks-Cole.
— Introduction to Psychology. 3rd expanded ed. (Psychology Ser.). 1993. student ed. 14.30 (*0-534-16451-X*) Brooks-Cole.
— Introduction to Psychology. 3rd expanded ed. (Psychology Ser.). 1993. student ed. 14.30 (*0-534-16453-6*) Brooks-Cole.
— Introduction to Psychology. 4th ed. (Psychology Ser.). 760p. 1995. pap. 52.50 (*0-534-26142-6*); pap. 44.25 (*0-534-34244-2*); mass mkt. 17.00 (*0-534-33846-1*) Brooks-Cole.
— Introduction to Psychology. 4th ed. 1996. pap., teacher ed. write for info. (*0-534-33843-7*) Brooks-Cole.
— Introduction to Psychology: Test Items. 4th ed. 1995. mass mkt. write for info. (*0-534-33844-5*) Brooks-Cole.
Plotnikoff, Joyce & Woolfson, Richard. Prosecuting Child Abuse: An Evaluation of the Government's Speedy Progress Policy. LC 96-189240. 109p. 1995. pap. 33.00 (*1-85431-404-1*, Pub. by Blackstone Pr) Gaunt.
Plotnikoff, N. P., et al. Enkephalins & Endorphins: Stress & the Immune System. LC 85-23234. (Illus.). 458p. (C). 1986. text 120.00 (*0-306-42226-3*, Kluwer Plenum) Kluwer Academic.
Plotnikoff, Nicholas P. & Faith, Robert E. Cytokines Stress & Immunity. LC 98-34473. 384p. 1998. boxed set 104.95 (*0-8493-3150-1*) CRC Pr.
Plotnikoff, Nicholas P., et al. Stress & Immunity. (Illus.). 528p. 1991. lib. bdg. 129.00 (*0-8493-8845-7*, QP82) CRC Pr.
Plotnikov, A. F., ed. Electron Processes in MIS-Structure Memories. Makinen, Paul, tr. from RUS. (Proceedings of the Lebedev Physics Institute Ser.: Vol. 184). 227p. (C). 1989. text 175.00 (*0-941743-53-5*) Nova Sci Pubs.
Plotnikov, L. M. Shear Structures in Layered Geological Bodies. Sychanthavong, S. P., ed. (Russian Translation Ser.: No. 104). (Illus.). 171p. (C). 1994. text 71.00 (*90-5410-220-9*, Pub. by A A Balkema) Ashgate Pub Co.
Plotnikov, N. I. & Roginets, I. I. Hydrogeology of Ore Deposits. Viswanathan, S., tr. from RUS. (Russian Translation Ser.: No. 72). (Illus.). 298p. (C). 1990. text 123.00 (*90-6191-900-2*, Pub. by A A Balkema) Ashgate Pub Co.
Plotnitsky, Arkady. Complementarity: Anti-Epistemology after Bohr & Derrida. LC 93-29583. 328p. 1994. text 54.95 (*0-8223-1433-9*); pap. text 18.95 (*0-8223-1437-1*) Duke.
— In the Shadow of Hegel: Complementarity, History, & the Unconscious. LC 92-42561. 544p. 1993. 49.95 (*0-8130-1202-3*); pap. 29.95 (*0-8130-1203-1*) U Press Fla.
— Reconfigurations: Critical Theory & General Economy. LC 92-22271. 440p. 1993. 49.95 (*0-8130-1172-8*); pap. 29.95 (*0-8130-1173-6*) U Press Fla.
Plotnitsky, Arkady & Smith, Barbara H., eds. Mathematics, Science, & Postclassical Theory. (Special Issue of SAQ Ser.: Vol. 94, No. 2). 230p. 1995. pap. 10.00 (*0-8223-6426-3*) Duke.
Plotnitsky, Arkady, jt. ed. see Smith, Barbara H.
Plotsky, Charlotte W. About Creative Time Spaces: An International Sourcebook. 9th ed. Orig. Title: Havens for Creatives. 128p. 1996. pap. text 19.95 (*1-886527-01-6*) ACTS By C P.
— As Charlotte Tells the Story: Family Chronicles. 100p. (Orig.). 1996. pap. text 19.95 (*1-886527-02-4*) ACTS By C P.
— Impact: Belgian Jewry During WWII. 205p. 1999. pap. text 19.95 (*1-886527-03-2*) ACTS By C P.
Plott, C. & Smith, V. L. Handbook of Results in Experimental Economics, 1. (Handbooks in Economics Ser.: Vol. I). 1999. write for info. (*0-444-82642-4*) Elsevier.
Plott, John C. Global History of Philosophy, Vol. V. (C). 1989. 35.00 (*81-208-0552-6*, Pub. by Motilal Bnarsidass) S Asia.
***Plott, Michele & Umanski, Lauri, eds.** Making Sense of Women's Lives: An Introduction to Women's Studies. 2000. pap. text 38.75 (*0-939693-53-4*) Collegiate Pr.
Plott, Monte. Flashes of Fire: An American Anthology. 80p. (Orig.). 1985. pap. 10.00 (*0-932662-51-X*) St Andrews NC.
Plottel, Jeanine F., jt. ed. see Stanton, Domna C.
Plottner, Sean. UFO Files: Out of This World . . . But True? LC 97-65681. (Disney Adventures Ser.). 112p. (J). (gr. 2-5). 1997. pap. 3.95 (*0-7868-4146-X*, Pub. by Disney Pr) Time Warner.
Plotts, J. N., ed. Poetical Tributes to the Memory of Abraham Lincoln. 1972. reprint ed. lib. bdg. 20.00 (*0-8422-8105-3*) Irvington.
Plotz, Helen, ed. see Dickinson, Emily.
***Plotz, John M.** The Crowd: British Literature & Public Politics. LC 99-51794. 332p. 2000. pap. 18.95 (*0-520-21917-1*, Pub. by U CA Pr) Cal Prin Full Svc.
***Plotz, John Milton Gabriel.** The Crowd: British Literature & Public Politics. LC 99-51794. 332p. 2000. 48.00 (*0-520-21916-3*, Pub. by U CA Pr) Cal Prin Full Svc.
Plotz, Judith A. Romanticism & the Vocation of Childhood. text. write for info. (*0-312-22735-3*) St Martin.
Plotz, Rob. Dingaling. 1983. pap. 1.75 (*0-912963-01-8*) Eldridge Pub.
Plotzner, Rolf. The Integrative Use of Qualitative & Quantitative Knowledge in Physics Problem Solving. LC 94-38700. (European University Studies, Series VI, Psychology: Vol. 483). (Illus.). 265p. 1994. 47.00 (*3-631-47640-X*) P Lang Pubng.
Plouffe, Bruce. Post-War Novella in German-Language Literature: An Analysis. (Studies in German Literature & Culture: Vol. 5). 1996. write for info. (*0-404-64055-9*) AMS Pr.
Plouffe, Paul B., jt. auth. see Hatton, John.
Plouffe, Simon, jt. ed. see Sloane, Neil J.
Ploug, Niels & Kvist, Jon. Social Security in Europe: Development or Dismantlement? LC 95-45764. (Kluwer SOVAC Series on Social Security: No. 3). 100p. 1996. pap. 42.00 (*90-411-0160-8*) Kluwer Law Intl.
Plough, Alonzo, jt. auth. see Krimsky, Sheldon.
Plough, Harold H. Sea Squirts of the Atlantic Continental Shelf from Maine to Texas. LC 76-47388. (Illus.). 128p. reprint ed. pap. 39.70 (*0-608-14701-X*, 202585100046) Bks Demand.
Plough Publishing House Staff, ed. see Arnold, Emmy.
Plough Publishing House Staff, ed. see Romero, Oscar.
Plough Publishing House Staff, ed. & tr. see Baum, Markus.
Plough Publishing House Staff, ed. & tr. see Zuendel, Friedrich.
Plough Publishing House Staff, tr. see Arnold, Eberhard, ed.
Plough Publishing House Staff, tr. see Blumhardt, Christoph F.
***Plougin, Vladimir.** Russian Intelligence Services Vol. I: The Early Days. 384p. 2000. pap. 21.95 (*1-892941-52-X*, Pub. by Algora Pubng) Midpt Trade.
Plourde-Barker, Michele. Chicopee. LC 98-86557. (Images of America Ser.). (Illus.). 128p. 1998. pap. 16.99 (*0-7524-0503-9*) Arcadia Publng.
Plourde, Elizabeth L. & Plourde, M. T. The Ultimate Rape: What Every Woman Should Know about Hysterectomies & Ovarian Removal. LC 97-92836. (Informed Health Care Ser.: No. 1). 288p. 1998. 19.95 (*0-9661735-0-3*) New Voice.
Plourde, Harvey S. The Compleat Taildragger Pilot. (Illus.). 263p. (Orig.). 1991. pap. 24.95 (*0-9639137-0-0*) H S Plourde.
Plourde, Lynn. CLAS by Themes. (Illus.). 213p. 1990. pap. text 39.00 (*0-7616-7673-2*) Commun Skill.
— CLAS Preschool. (Illus.). 364p. 1989. pap. text 69.50 (*0-7616-7570-1*) Commun Skill.
— CLAS 3-4. 2nd rev. ed. (Illus.). 248p. 1997. pap. 65.00 (*0-7616-3210-7*) Commun Skill.
— Moose, of Course! LC 99-27492. (Illus.). 24p. (J). (ps-1). 1999. 14.95 (*0-89272-454-4*); pap. 9.95 (*0-89272-473-0*) Down East.
— Pigs in the Mud in the Middle of the Rud. LC 96-23098. (Illus.). 32p. (YA). (ps-2). 1997. 15.95 (*0-590-56863-9*) Scholastic Inc.
— Thank You & Good-Bye. LC 98-33763. (Illus.). (J). 2001. per. 16.00 (*0-689-81853-X*) S&S Childrens.
— Wild Child. LC 98-15476. (Illus.). 32p. (J). (gr. k-3). 1999. 17.00 (*0-689-81552-2*) S&S Bks Yung.
Plourde, Lynn & Knowles, Paul. Celebration of Maine Children's Books. (Illus.). 336p. (J). 1998. pap. 18.95 (*0-89101-093-9*) U Maine Pr.
Plourde, M. T., jt. auth. see Plourde, Elizabeth L.
Plourde, Marc, ed. & tr. see Langevin, Gilbert.
Plourde, Marc, tr. see Miron, Gaston.
Plous, Frederick K., Jr., tr. see Levine, Norman D., ed.
Plous, Frederick K., Jr., tr. see Naumov, N. P.
Plous, Phyllis. Bart Wasserman: North Wall Curving South. (Illus.). 24p. 1985. 10.00 (*0-942006-09-7*) U of CA Art.
— Carroll Dunham: Paintings & Drawings. (Illus.). 52p. 1997. pap. 19.95 (*1-880658-12-7*) San Barb CAF.
— Collaborations in Monotype II No. II: Garner Tullis Workshop. (Illus.). 48p. 1989. pap. 18.00 (*0-942006-32-1*) U of CA Art.
— Contemporary Tableaux - Constructions. (Illus.). 40p. 1977. pap. 5.00 (*0-942006-38-0*) U of CA Art.
— Dark - Light: Extensions of Photography. (Illus.). 40p. 1980. pap. 6.00 (*0-942006-39-9*) U of CA Art.
— 5 American Painters: Recent Work. (Illus.). 38p. 1973. pap. 5.00 (*0-942006-42-9*) U of CA Art.
— Guy Williams: The Paper Works. (Illus.). 47p. 1977. pap. 5.00 (*0-942006-60-7*) U of CA Art.
— Howard Fenton: Recent Paintings. (Illus.). 20p. (Orig.). 1990. pap. 7.00 (*0-942006-19-4*) U of CA Art.
— Jack Tworkov: Recent Paintings & Drawings. (Illus.). 32p. 1977. pap. 3.00 (*0-942006-58-5*) U of CA Art.
— Richard Allen Morris: Recent Work. (Illus.). 8p. 1978. pap. 2.00 (*0-942006-50-X*) U of CA Art.
— Scapes. (Illus.). 59p. 1985. 15.00 (*0-942006-10-0*) U of CA Art.
Plous, Phyllis & Baker, Kenneth. Collaborations in Monotype I No. 1: Garner Tullis Workshop. (Illus.). 68p. 1988. pap. 18.00 (*0-942006-15-1*) U of CA Art.
Plous, Phyllis & Colpitt, Frances. Abstract Options. (Illus.). 68p. 1989. pap. 14.95 (*0-295-96874-5*) U of Wash Pr.
Plous, Phyllis & Cortright, Steven. Invented Images. (Illus.). 76p. 1980. pap. 5.00 (*0-942006-47-X*) U of CA Art.
Plous, Phyllis & Gebhard, David. Paul Tuttle Design & the 80s. (Illus.). 24p. 1987. pap. 7.00 (*0-942006-13-5*) U of CA Art.
Plous, Phyllis & Guggenheim, Eileen. A Heritage Renewed: Representational Drawing Today. (Illus.). 87p. (Orig.). 1983. 15.00 (*0-942006-03-8*) U of CA Art.
Plous, Phyllis & Klein, Michael R. Figuration. (Illus.). 56p. 1982. 9.00 (*0-942006-00-3*) U of CA Art.
Plous, Phyllis & Thomas, Robert. Sculpture - 20s & 30s. (Illus.). 12p. 1971. pap. 3.00 (*0-942006-56-9*) U of CA Art.
Plous, Phyllis, et al. Contemporary Drawings: In Search of an Image. (Illus.). 58p. 1981. pap. 9.00 (*0-942006-37-2*) U of CA Art.
— Neo York: Report on a Phenomenon. (Illus.). 72p. (Orig.). 1984. 15.00 (*0-942006-08-9*) U of CA Art.
— PULSE Two: A Report on a Phenomenon. (Illus.). 160p. (Orig.). 1990. pap. 20.00 (*0-295-97036-7*) U of Wash Pr.
— Pulse 2: Report on a Phenomenon. (Illus.). 72p. 1990. pap. 20.00 (*0-942006-20-8*) U of CA Art.
Plous, Phyllis, jt. auth. see Colpitt, Frances.
Plous, Scott. The Psychology of Judgement & Decision Making. LC 92-38542. 352p. (C). 1993. pap. 29.69 (*0-07-050477-6*) McGraw.
Plouwden, D. & Worthington, C. Techniques for Evaluation of Marginal Field Development. 1989. 125.00 (*90-6314-532-2*, Pub. by Lorne & MacLean Marine) St Mut.
Plovnick, Julie, tr. see Lamblin, Bianca.
Plowden. The Machine Age, Vol. 1. 1995. text 60.00 (*0-8050-2902-8*) St Martin.
Plowden, Alison. Danger to Elizabeth: The Catholics under Elizabeth I. 1999. pap. text 15.95 (*0-7509-2196-X*) Sutton Pub Ltd.
***Plowden, Alison.** Elizabeth Regina. 224p. 2000. pap. 15.95 (*0-7509-2198-6*) Sutton Publng.
Plowden, Alison. The House of Tudor. LC 99-188171. (Illus.). 288p. 1999. 35.00 (*0-7509-1890-X*, Pub. by Sutton Pub Ltd) Intl Pubs Mktg.
Plowden, Alison. The House of Tudor. LC 76-377371. 224p. 1976. write for info. (*0-297-77147-7*, Pub. by Weidenfeld & Nicolson) Trafalgar.
Plowden, Alison. Marriage with My Kingdom: The Courtships of Elizabeth I. 2000. pap. 15.95 (*0-7509-2197-8*, Pub. by Sutton Pub Ltd) Intl Pubs Mktg.
— The Stuart Princesses. (Illus.). 240p. 1997. pap. 17.95 (*0-7509-1611-7*, Pub. by Sutton Pub Ltd) Intl Pubs Mktg.
— Tudor Women. LC 99-206190. 192p. 1998. pap. 23.95 (*0-7509-2005-X*, Pub. by Sutton Pub Ltd) Intl Pubs Mktg.
— Two Queens in One Isle: The Deadly Relationship of Elizabeth I & Mary Queen of Scots. 1999. pap. 19.95 (*0-7509-2168-4*, Pub. by Sutton Pub Ltd) Intl Pubs Mktg.
— Women All on Fire: The Women of the English Civil War. (Illus.). 218p. 1998. 36.95 (*0-7509-1221-9*, Pub. by Sutton Pub Ltd) Intl Pubs Mktg.
— Young Elizabeth The First Twenty-Five Years of Elizabeth I. LC 99-494998. 1999. pap. text 15.95 (*0-7509-2192-7*) A Sutton.
***Plowden, Alison.** Young Victoria. 2000. reprint ed. pap. 15.95 (*0-7509-2574-4*, Pub. by Sutton Publng) Intl Pubs Mktg.
Plowden, Celeste. Carousel Animals Cut & Use Stencils: 44 Full-Size Stencils Printed on Durable Stencil Paper. 81st ed. (Illus.). 64p. (Orig.). 1991. pap. 5.95 (*0-486-26889-6*) Dover.
— Carousel Animals Iron-on Transfer Patterns. 81st ed. (Transfer Patterns Ser.). (Illus.). 48p. (Orig.). 1991. pap. text 3.95 (*0-486-26653-2*) Dover.
— Favorite Birds Charted Designs. LC 94-20405. (Illus.). 48p. 1994. pap. 3.50 (*0-486-28220-1*) Dover.
— Horses Charted Designs. LC 93-18960. (Needlework Ser.). 48p. 1993. pap. 3.50 (*0-486-27578-7*) Dover.
— Wild Animals Charted Designs. (Illus.). 48p. 1989. pap. 3.95 (*0-486-25991-9*) Dover.
Plowden, D. & Worthington, C., eds. Techniques for Evaluation of Marginal Field Development. (C). 1989. 125.00 (*0-89771-742-2*, Pub. by Lorne & MacLean Marine) St Mut.
Plowden, David. The End of an Era: The Last of the Great Lakes Steamboats. (Illus.). 160p. 1992. 50.00 (*0-393-03348-1*) Norton.
— The Hand of Man on America. LC 74-127823. (Illus.). 136p. 1973. reprint ed. pap. 14.95 (*0-85699-077-9*) Chatham Pr.
— Imprints: The Photographs of David Plowden. LC 96-48891. (Illus.). 204p. (gr. 8). 1997. 60.00 (*0-8212-2323-2*) Little.
Plowden, Edwin Noel. An Industrialist in the Treasury: The Post-War Years. LC 89-185596. xix, 220 p. 1989. write for info. (*0-233-98364-3*) Andre Deutsch.
Plowden, Martha W. Olympic Black Women. LC 95-32067. (Illus.). 160p. (J). (gr. 4-7). 1995. pap. 16.95 (*1-56554-080-8*) Pelican.
Plowden, Martha Ward. Famous Firsts of Black Women. LC 93-13837. (Illus.). 160p. (J). (gr. 4-7). 1993. 18.95 (*0-88289-973-2*) Pelican.
Plowden, Philip, jt. auth. see Brayne, Hugh.
Plowden, William, jt. auth. see Blackstone, Tessa.
Plowert, Jacques. Petit Glossaire pour Servir l'Intelligence des Auteurs. McGuinness, Patrick, ed. (Exeter French Texts Ser.). (FRE.). 150p. 1998. pap. text 23.95 (*0-85989-594-7*) Univ Exeter Pr.
Plowhead, Ruth G. Lucretia Ann on the Oregon Trail. 8th ed. LC 31-25267. (Illus.). 250p. (J). (gr. 4-8). 1997. reprint ed. pap. 10.95 (*0-87004-360-9*, 036090) Caxton.
Plowman. Haematology & Immunology. 1987. pap. text 61.00 (*0-471-91449-5*) Wiley.
— Neurology & Psychiatry. 1987. pap. text 76.00 (*0-471-91450-9*) Wiley.
Plowman, Andrew. The Radical Subject: Social Change & the Self in Recent German Autobiography. LC 98-217944. (British & Irish Studies in German Language & Literature: Vol. 13). 168p. (C). 1998. pap. text 27.95 (*0-8204-3449-3*) P Lang Pubng.
Plowman, B. H. Plowman: A Register of Plowmans in America & Extr. from English & American Records. 90p. 1991. reprint ed. pap. 17.50 (*0-8328-1828-3*) Higginson Bk Co.
Plowman, Edward. A Book about Billy. 1999. text. write for info. (*0-670-81372-9*) Viking Penguin.
Plowman, Gillian. Cecily. 1992. pap. 3.50 (*0-87129-132-0*, C83) Dramatic Pub.
— Me & My Friend. 1990. pap. 5.95 (*0-87129-140-1*, M78) Dramatic Pub.
— The Wooden Pear. 1992. pap. 3.50 (*0-87129-131-2*, W71) Dramatic Pub.
Plowman, Gillian, et al. The Verity Bargate Award Plays, 1988. Keeffe, Barrie, ed. (Methuen New Theatrescripts Ser.). 110p. (Orig.). (C). 1989. pap. write for info. (*0-413-62240-1*, A0408, Methuen Drama) Methn.
Plowman, John. The Craft of Handmade Paper: A Practical Guide to Papermaking Techniques. 1997. 24.95 (*1-57715-018-X*) Knckerbocker.
— Plasterworks. (Illus.). 128p. 1996. 18.99 (*0-89134-707-0*, North Lght Bks) F & W Pubns Inc.
***Plowman, John.** Plasterworks: A Beginner's Guide to Molding & Decorating Plaster Projects from Stars & Cherubs to Shells & Sunflowers. (Illus.). 128p. 2000. reprint ed. text 19.00 (*0-7881-9276-0*) DIANE Pub.
Plowman, John. Start Sculpting. 144p. 1995. 17.98 (*0-7858-0354-8*) Bk Sales Inc.
Plowman, Kathryn J. Doctor's Letters: Interludes of War: 1944-45. 1983. pap. 8.50 (*0-9613217-0-9*) Augusta Pubs.
Plowman, Mary S. This Time. Goodfellow, Pamela R., ed. LC 93-80292. 384p. 1994. pap. 7.99 (*0-9639882-1-2*) Goodfellow Pr.
— White Powder. Goodfellow, Pamela R., ed. LC 95-75136. 1996. pap. 9.99 (*0-9639882-6-3*) Goodfellow Pr.
Plowman, Max. Subaltern on the Somme. (Great War Ser.: No. 51). 256p. 1996. reprint ed. 34.95 (*0-89839-248-9*) Battery Pr.
Plowman, P. N. Respiratory Medicine. LC 87-31999. (Illustrated Lecture Ser.). 236p. reprint ed. pap. 73.20 (*0-7837-4772-1*, 204452700003) Bks Demand.
Plowman, P. N. & Pinkerton, C. R., eds. Paediatric Oncology: Clinical Practice & Controversies. (Illus.). 672p. 1992. 132.95 (*0-442-31595-3*) Chapman & Hall.
Plowman, P. N., jt. auth. see Pinkerton, C. R.
Plowman, Paul D. Teaching the Gifted & Talented in the Social Studies Classroom. 56p. 1980. pap. 6.95 (*0-8106-0737-9*) NEA.
Plowman, Peter. Emigrant Ships to Luxury Liners: Passenger Ships to Australia & New Zealand 1945-90. (Illus.). 300p. 1993. 47.95 (*0-86840-379-2*, Pub. by New South Wales Univ Pr) Intl Spec Bk.
— The Wheels Still Turn: A History of Australian Paddleboats. (Illus.). 160p. 1993. 32.50 (*0-86417-428-4*, Pub. by Kangaroo Pr) Seven Hills Bk.
Plowman, Roscoe E. Twice Out of Sight. 122p. (Orig.). 1982. pap. 5.00 (*0-935680-11-X*) Kentucke Imprints.

An Asterisk (*) at the beginning of an entry indicates that the title is appearing for the first time.

P

— Veterinary Drug Handbook: Pocket Edition. 3rd ed. LC 98-53001. 864p. 1999. pap. text 49.95 (*0-8138-2353-6*) Iowa St U Pr.
— Veterinary Drug Handbook: Pocket Edition & CD-ROM. 3rd rev. ed. 1999. pap. 89.95 incl. cd-rom (*0-8138-1588-6*) Iowa St U Pr.
— Veterinary Drug Handbook: Pocket Edition & Companion. 3rd rev. ed. 1999. pap. 69.95 (*0-8138-0235-0*) Iowa St U Pr.
— Veterinary Drug Handbook: Pocket Edition, CD-ROM & Companion. 3rd rev. abr. ed. 1999. pap. 109.95 incl. cd-rom (*0-8138-1968-7*) Iowa St U Pr.
Plumb, G. R., ed. Nuclear Waste Reprocessing. (Illus.). 72p. 1984. pap. 44.00 (*0-08-031509-7*, Pergamon Pr) Elsevier.
Plumb, Gregory. Waterfall Lover's Guide to the Pacific Northwest: Where to Find Hundreds of Spectacular Waterfalls. 3rd ed. LC 98-36763. 288p. 1998. pap. 14.95 (*0-89886-593-X*) Mountaineers.
— Waterfalls of Tennessee: A Guide to over 200 Falls in the Volunteer State. (Illus.). 256p. (Orig.). 1996. pap. 17.95 (*1-57072-057-6*) Overmountain Pr.
Plumb, H. B. History of Hanover Township, PA, Including Sugar Notch, Ashley & Nanticoke Boroughs, & Also a History of Wyoming Valley in Luzerne Co., PA. 498p. 1990. reprint ed. lib. bdg. 51.00 (*0-8328-1633-7*) Higginson Bk Co.
Plumb, John A. Health Maintenance & Microbial Diseases of Culture Fish. 272p. 1994. lib. bdg. 99.95 (*0-8493-4614-2*) CRC Pr.
— Health Maintenance & Principal Microbial Diseases of Cultured Fishes. LC 98-38489. (Illus.). 344p. (C). 1999. text 74.95 (*0-8138-2298-X*) Iowa St U Pr.
Plumb, John H. Italian Renaissance. (American Heritage Library). 320p. 1986. pap. 15.00 (*0-8281-0485-9*) HM.
— Men & Centuries. LC 78-26300. 294p. 1979. reprint ed. lib. bdg. 52.50 (*0-313-20868-9*, PLMC, Greenwood Pr) Greenwood.
Plumb, John H., ed. Studies in Social History. LC 71-80395. (Essay Index Reprint Ser.). 1977. 24.95 (*0-8369-1063-X*) Ayer.
Plumb, Joseph C. The Last Domino? A POW Looks Ahead. 96p. 1973. text 7.95 (*1-881886-03-4*) J C Plumb.
Plumb, Lawrence. A Critique of the Human Potential Movement. LC 92-40360. (Cults & Nonconventional Religious Groups Ser.). 272p. 1993. text 40.00 (*0-8153-0777-2*) Garland.
Plumb, Pam, jt. auth. see Kelsey, Dee.
***Plumb, Ralph G.** A History of Manitowoc County Wisconsin. (Illus.). 386p. 1999. reprint ed. pap. 26.00 (*0-7884-1248-5*, P485) Heritage Bk.
Plumb, Ron, jt. auth. see LaJoie, Jim.
Plumb, Sally. A Pika's Tail: A Children's Story about Mountain Wildlife. Milligan, Sharlene, ed. (Illus.). 40p. (J). (gr. k-5). 1994. 14.95 (*0-931895-26-X*); pap. 9.95 (*0-931895-25-1*) Grand Teton NHA.
Plumb, Steve. Monzano Trails: A Hiker's Guide to Appreciate the Nature of the Sandia-Monzano Mountains. Wilde, David, ed. (Sun Also Sets Ser.). (Illus.). 50p. (Orig.). 1992. pap. 13.95 (*0-9625472-7-1*) Wilde Pub.
Plumb, Sylvia L., ed. Long Trail Guide. 24th ed. (Illus.). 238p. 1997. reprint ed. pap. 14.95 (*1-888021-01-2*) Green Mtn Club.
Plumb, Vivienne. The Wife Who Spoke Japanese in Her Sleep. 113p. 1993. pap. 24.95 (*0-908569-74-2*, Pub. by Univ Otago Pr) Intl Spec Bk.
Plumb, Wendy, jt. auth. see Gallup, George H.
Plumbe, Wilfred J. Tropical Librarianship. LC 87-19984. 334p. 1987. 45.00 (*0-8108-2057-9*) Scarecrow.
Plumber, Betty J. Tasty Blends. (Illus.). viii, 104p. 1998. pap. 15.47 (*0-9666589-0-6*, 25264) Plumbers Entrprs.
Plumbley, Philip, ed. Recruitment & Selection. 176p. (C). 1985. 90.00 (*0-85292-342-2*, Pub. by IPM Hse) St Mut.
— Recruitment & Selection. 176p. (C). 1991. pap. text 59.00 (*0-85292-459-3*, Pub. by IPM Hse) St Mut.
Plume, Alice, tr. from RUS. Salt: A Russian Folktale. LC 91-74007. (Illus.). 40p. (J). (gr. k-3). 1992. 14.95 (*1-56282-178-4*, Pub. by Hyprn Child) Little.
Plume, Ilse. The Shoemaker & the Elves. LC 88-26792. (Illus.). 32p. (J). (ps-3). 1991. 14.95 (*0-15-274050-3*, Harcourt Child Bks) Harcourt.
Plume, Ilse. The Bremen-Town Musicians. 32p. (J). (ps-3). 1998. reprint ed. pap. 6.99 (*0-440-41456-3*, Yearling) BDD Bks Young Read.
Plumer, Ada L. & Cosentino. Plumer's Principles & Practice of Intravenous Therapy. 4th ed. (Illus.). 567p. (C). 1987. text 31.50 (*0-673-39403-4*) Lppncott W & W.
Plumer, Erwin H. When You Place a Child . . . (Illus.). 258p. 1992. pap. 34.95 (*0-398-06326-5*) C C Thomas.
— When You Place a Child . . . (Illus.). 258p. (C). 1992. text 50.95 (*0-398-05770-2*) C C Thomas.
Plumer, James M., ed. see Warner, Langdon.
Plumer, Lutz. Termination Proofs for Logic Programs. Siekmann, Joerg H., ed. (Lecture Notes in Artificial Intelligence Ser.: Vol. 446). viii, 142p. 1990. 25.00 (*0-387-52837-7*) Spr-Verlag.
Plumer, Lutz, jt. auth. see Forstner, W.
Plumer, Lutz, jt. ed. see Beierle, Christoph.
***Plumer, Richard P.** Town of Suwanee, Georgia, Early History, Vol. 1. (Illus.). 2000. 20.00 (*0-914923-18-8*) Gwinnett Hist.
Plumer, W. S. Psalms. (Geneva Commentaries Ser.). 1978. 59.99 (*0-85151-209-7*) Banner of Truth.
Plumer, William, Jr. Life of William Plumer. LC 77-87384. (American History, Politics & Law Ser.). 1969. reprint ed. lib. bdg. 69.50 (*0-306-71608-9*) Da Capo.
Plumer, William S. Commentary on Romans. LC 73-155251. (Kregel Reprint Library). 648p. 1993. 25.99 (*0-8254-3501-3*, Kregel Class); pap. 26.99 (*0-8254-3543-9*, Kregel Class) Kregel.
— The Grace of Christ. 1995. 29.99 (*0-87377-185-0*) GAM Pubns.
— Jehovah-Jireh: A Treatise on Providence. 1995. 19.99 (*0-87377-186-9*) GAM Pubns.
— The Law of God. 1995. 34.99 (*0-87377-187-7*) GAM Pubns.
— The Rock of Our Salvation. 1995. 27.99 (*0-87377-188-5*) GAM Pubns.
— Vital Godliness: A Treatise on Experimental & Practical Piety. 1995. 29.99 (*0-87377-189-3*) GAM Pubns.
Plumlee, Harry J. Shadow of the Wolf: An Apache Tale. LC 96-34556. 216p. 1997. 21.95 (*0-8061-2905-0*) U of Okla Pr.
Plumlee-Schindler, Becky. Recreating Recipes: Nutritious & Delicious II. (Illus.). (Orig.). 1993. pap. 14.95 (*0-9637340-9-1*) Beckys Body.
Plumlee, Travis. Family Foundations. 128p. (Orig.). 1995. pap. 7.99 (*0-89114-225-8*) Baptist Pub Hse.
Plumley, Lisa. Lawman. 1999. mass mkt. 4.99 (*0-8217-6386-5*, Zebra Kensgtn) Kensgtn Pub Corp.
— Outlaw. 320p. 1999. mass mkt. 4.99 (*0-8217-6120-X*) Kensgtn Pub Corp.
Plumley, Rhey, jt. auth. see Hickoff, Steve.
Plumley, Sue. Documented NT Server: A Start to Finish Network Installation Plan. LC 97-20682. 496p. 1997. pap. 29.99 (*0-471-19224-4*) Wiley.
— Easy Windows 95. 265p. 1995. 19.99 (*1-56529-989-2*) Que.
Plumley, Sue. Easy Windows 95. 2nd ed. LC 97-65007. 240p. 1997. pap. 19.99 (*0-7897-1159-1*) Que.
— Home Networking Bible. 720p. 1999. pap. 34.99 (*0-7645-3399-1*) IDG Bks.
Plumley, Sue. Lotus Smartstart Essentials. 1995. teacher ed. 39.99 (*0-7897-0446-3*) Que.
***Plumley, Sue.** Microsoft Publisher 2000 Bible. LC 99-30304. (Bible Ser.). (Illus.). 877p. 1999. pap. 34.99 (*0-7645-3343-6*) IDG Bks.
Plumley, Sue. Migrating from Novell NetWare to Windows NT Server 4.0. LC 96-44767. 401p. 1997. pap. 29.95 (*0-471-17563-3*) Wiley.
***Plumley, Sue.** Network Administration Survival Guide. LC 98-30225. 864p. 1998. pap. 49.99 (*0-471-29621-X*) Wiley.
— Networking Bible. 2000. pap. 39.99 (*0-7645-3499-8*) IDG Bks.
Plumley, Sue. Office Max - MS Office Quick Reference. 1994. 14.99 (*0-7897-0699-7*) Que.
— 1-2-3 for Windows 95 Essentials. Date not set. pap. text 22.99 (*1-57576-004-5*) Que Educ & Trng.
— Sams Teach Yourself Windows 2000 Professional in 10 Minutes. 2000th ed. 210p. 2000. pap. 12.99 (*0-672-31702-8*) Macmillan.
***Plumley, Sue.** Setting up a Windows 98 Home Network. (Cliffs Notes Ser.). 128p. 1999. pap. text 8.99 (*0-7645-8541-X*) IDG Bks.
— Teach Yourself Windows NT Workstation 4 in 10 Minutes. LC 98-89463. (Teach Yourself Ser.). (Illus.). 208p. 1999. pap. 12.99 (*0-672-31580-7*) Sams.
Plumley, Sue. Teach Yourself Windows 95 in 10 Minutes. LC 98-84478. (Teach Yourself Ser.). 208p. 1998. pap. 12.99 (*0-672-31316-2*) Sams.
— 10 Minute Guide to Lotus Notes 4.5. 3rd ed. LC 96-70615. 224p. 1997. 14.99 (*0-7897-0945-7*) Que.
— 10 Minute Guide to Outlook 97. LC 96-70774. 182p. 1996. 14.99 (*0-7897-1018-8*) Que.
— 10 Minute Guide to pcANYWHERE 32. LC 97-179487. 193p. 1997. 14.99 (*0-7897-1269-5*) Que.
— 10 Minute Guide to Windows NT Workstation 4.0. LC 96-220203. 224p. 1996. 14.99 (*0-7897-0870-1*) Que.
— 10 Minute Guide to Windows 95. 2nd ed. LC 97-65011. 224p. 1997. 14.99 (*0-7897-1160-5*) Que.
— Transition to Windows 95 for 3.X Users, IM. 1996. teacher ed., ring bd. 49.99 (*1-57576-252-8*) Que Educ & Trng.
***Plumley, Sue.** Windows 2000 Administration for Dummies Quick Reference. (For Dummies). (Illus.). 224p. 2000. spiral bd. 14.99 (*0-7645-0694-3*) IDG Bks.
— Windows 2000 Server for Dummies: Quick Reference. LC 99-66512. (For Dummies Ser.). (Illus.). 224p. 2000. spiral bd. 12.99 (*0-7645-0662-5*) IDG Bks.
Plumley, Sue, jt. auth. see Thomas, Stephen A.
Plumley, Yolanda. The Grammar of 14th Century Melody: Tonal Organization & Compositional Process in the Chansons of Guillaume de Machaut & the Ars Subtilior. LC 95-49733. (Outstanding Dissertations in Music from British Universities Ser.). 335p. 1996. text 94.00 (*0-8153-2065-5*) Garland.
***Plumly, Stanley.** Boy on the Step. 2000. 17.95 (*0-88001-228-5*) HarpC.
Plumly, Stanley. Boy On The Step. 1991. pap. 9.95 (*0-88001-229-3*) HarpC.
— The Marriage In The Trees. LC 96-18589. 96p. 1997. 22.00 (*0-88001-487-3*) HarpC.
***Plumly, Stanley.** The Marriage In The Trees. LC 96-18589. 96p. 1998. pap. 14.00 (*0-88001-546-2*) HarpC.
— Now That My Father Lies Down Beside Me: New & Selected Poems, 1970-2000. LC 99-57297. 176p. 2000. 23.00 (*0-06-019659-9*, Ecco Press) HarperTrade.
Plumly, Stanley. Out-of-the-Body Travel. LC 76-46174. (American Poetry Ser.: No. 10). 1977. pap. 4.95 (*0-912946-36-9*, Ecco Press) HarperTrade.
Plumly, Stanley, jt. ed. see Collier, Michael.
Plummer. Out of the Depths or Triumph of Cross: African-American Women Writers, 1910-1940 by Plummer. LC 97-16844. 1997. 30.00 (*0-7838-1425-9*, Hall Reference) Macmillan.
Plummer. Physical Geology. 7th ed. 1995. 58.00 (*0-697-32865-1*, WCB McGr Hill) McGrw-H Hghr Educ.
Plummer. Ssg Physical Geology. 8th ed. 208p. 1998. spiral bd. 24.69 (*0-697-37407-6*) McGraw.
Plummer & McGeary. Physical Geology: Test Index File. 7th ed. 1995. teacher ed. 18.75 (*0-697-26677-X*, WCB McGr Hill) McGrw-H Hghr Educ.
Plummer, Aileen. Japan: The Silent Superpower? 1985. pap. 45.00 (*0-904404-50-1*, Pub. by P Norbury Pubns Ltd) St Mut.
Plummer, Albert. Civil War Infantry, the 48th Regiment, M. V. M., During the Civil War. (Illus.). 133p. 1995. reprint ed. lib. bdg. 29.50 (*0-8328-4636-8*) Higginson Bk Co.
Plummer, Alfred. A Commentary on St. Paul's Epistle to the Philippians. 139p. 1997. pap. 15.00 (*1-57910-058-9*) Wipf & Stock.
— Corinthians II: Critical & Exegetical Commentary. Driver, Samuel R. & Briggs, Charles A., eds. (International Critical Commentary Ser.). 462p. 1915. 39.95 (*0-567-05028-9*, Pub. by T & T Clark) Bks Intl VA.
— English Church History: From the Death of Archbishop Parker to the Death of King Charles I. 1977. lib. bdg. 59.95 (*0-8490-1772-6*) Gordon Pr.
— International Combines in Modern Industry. 2nd ed. LC 74-157354. (Select Bibliographies Reprint Ser.). 1977. reprint ed. 21.95 (*0-8369-5815-2*) Ayer.
— St. Luke: Critical & Exegetical Commentary. Driver, Samuel R. et al, eds. (International Critical Commentary Ser.). 688p. 1982. 39.95 (*0-567-05023-8*, Pub. by T & T Clark) Bks Intl VA.
Plummer, Alfred & Early, Richard E. The Blanket Makers, Sixteen Sixty-Nine to Nineteen Sixty-Nine: A History of Charles Early & Marriott Whitney Ltd. LC 69-17112. (Illus.). 205p. 1969. 24.95 (*0-678-06508-X*) Kelley.
Plummer, Alfred & Robertson, Archibald T. Corinthians One: Critical & Exegetical Commentary. Driver, Samuel R. & Briggs, Charles A., eds. (International Critical Commentary Ser.). 496p. 1914. 39.95 (*0-567-05027-0*, Pub. by T & T Clark) Bks Intl VA.
Plummer, Alfred, ed. see Driver, Samuel R.
Plummer, Alfred D., ed. see Charles, R. H.
Plummer, Brenda G. Haiti & the Great Powers, 1902-1915. LC 87-33873. (Illus.). 280p. 1988. text 40.00 (*0-8071-1409-X*) La State U Pr.
— Rising Wind: Black Americans & U. S. Foreign Affairs, 1935-1960. LC 95-36068. (Illus.). 442p. (C). 1997. pap. text 19.95 (*0-8078-4575-2*); lib. bdg. 55.00 (*0-8078-2272-8*) U of NC Pr.
Plummer, Brian & Shewan, Don, eds. City Gardens: A Survey of Open Spaces in the City of London. (Illus.). 256p. 1992. text 65.00 (*1-85293-219-8*) St Martin.
Plummer, C. Life & Times of Alfred the Great. LC 68-25261. (English Biography Ser.: No. 31). 1969. reprint ed. lib. bdg. 75.00 (*0-8383-0230-0*) M S G Haskell Hse.
Plummer, C., ed. Vitae Sanctorum Hiberniae, 2 vols. 930p. 1997. boxed set 130.00 (*1-85182-325-5*, Pub. by Four Cts Pr) Intl Spec Bk.
Plummer, Cameron M., ed. see Walter, Eugene.
Plummer, Carlyle J. Ship Handling in Narrow Channels. 3rd enl. ed. LC 78-15384. 165p. reprint ed. pap. 51.20 (*0-608-15288-9*, 202922800059) Bks Demand.
Plummer, Carol A. Preventing Sexual Abuse: Curriculum Guides for K-6, 7-12, & Special Populations. 2nd ed. LC 83-82306. (Illus.). 192p. 1997. pap. text 23.95 (*1-55691-114-9*, 149) Learning Pubns.
Plummer, Charles. Life & Times of Alfred the Great. LC 72-131802. 1970. reprint ed. 49.00 (*0-403-00689-9*) Scholarly.
Plummer, Charles, ed. Irish Litanies. (Henry Bradshaw Society Ser.: Vol. LXII). 176p. (C). 1992. 60.00 (*1-870252-02-0*, Henry Bradshaw Soc) Boydell & Brewer.
— Lives of Irish Saints, 2 vols. 1969. 49.50 (*0-19-821389-1*) OUP.
— Lives of the Saints, Vol. I. (Celtic Studies). 390p. 1997. 65.00 (*1-85182-223-2*, Pub. by Four Cts Pr); 65.00 (*1-85182-224-0*, Pub. by Four Cts Pr) Intl Spec Bk.
— Vitae Sanctorum Hiberniae, Vol. I. (Celtic Studies). 463p. 1997. 65.00 (*1-85182-225-9*, Pub. by Four Cts Pr) Intl Spec Bk.
— Vitae Sanctorum Hiberniae, Vol. II. (Celtic Studies). 463p. 1997. 65.00 (*1-85182-226-7*, Pub. by Four Cts Pr) Intl Spec Bk.
***Plummer, Charles, et al.** Ready Notes for Physical Geology. 8th ed. (C). 1998. 9.69 (*0-07-234020-7*) McGrw-H Hghr Educ.
Plummer, Charles C. & McGeary, David. Physical Geology. 6th ed. 560p. (C). 1993. text 56.55 (*0-697-13806-2*, WCB McGr Hill); text. write for info. (*0-697-13807-0*, WCB McGr Hill) McGrw-H Hghr Educ.
— Physical Geology. 6th ed. 560p. (C). 1994. text, student ed. 21.87 (*0-697-13811-9*, WCB McGr Hill) McGrw-H Hghr Educ.
Plummer, Charles C., jt. auth. see McGeary, David.
Plummer, Charles C., jt. auth. see Rutford, Robert H.
Plummer, Christopher. Stratford. LC 98-173721. (Illus.). 120p. 1998. 29.95 (*1-55046-274-1*, Pub. by Boston Mills) Genl Dist Srvs.
***Plummer, Clare.** An Island for Doctor Phillipa. large type ed. 336p. 2000. pap. 20.99 (*1-85389-996-8*, Dales) Ulverscroft.
Plummer, D. Brian. The Complete Jack Russell Terrier. (Illus.). 158p. 1980. 22.95 (*0-85115-121-3*) Howell Bks.
— Tales of a Rat-Hunting Man. LC 97-5252. (Illus.). 160p. 1997. pap. 12.95 (*1-55821-595-6*) Lyons Pr.
Plummer, David. Counting Kittens. 1997. 19.95 (*0-382-39663-4*) Silver.
***Plummer, David.** One of the Boys: Masculinity, Homophobia & Modern Manhood. LC 99-34431. 364p. (C). 1999. 49.95 (*1-56023-973-5*, Harrington Park); pap. text 24.95 (*1-56023-974-3*, Harrington Park) Haworth Pr.
***Plummer, David & Archambault, John.** ABC Chicka Boom with Me. Cernek, Kim, ed. (Happy Song Sing-Alongs Ser.: Vol. 2355). (Illus.). 64p. (J). (ps-6). 1999. pap. 12.98 incl. cd-rom (*1-57471-636-0*) Creat Teach Pr.
Plummer, David & Archambault, John. Counting Kittens. (Illus.). (J). (ps-3). 1997. 13.95 (*0-382-39650-2*); 13.95 (*0-614-29051-1*, Silver Pr NJ); 19.95 incl. audio (*0-614-29052-X*, Silver Pr NJ) Silver Burdett Pr.
Plummer, David, jt. auth. see Archambault, John.
***Plummer, David E. & Crumpton, Nancy.** Only Closers Make Big Money. 160p. 1999. pap. 14.95 (*1-881825-24-8*) Hist Pubns TX.
Plummer, Don. Colonial Wrought Iron: The Sorber Collection. LC 99-70856. (Illus.). 256p. 1999. text 44.00 (*1-879535-16-5*) Skipjack Pr.
Plummer, Elena, ed. see Zokala, Marina, et al.
Plummer, Elizabeth. A Kitty Named Wummpus. (Illus.). 12p. (J). 1997. pap. write for info. (*1-57579-089-0*) Pine Hill Pr.
Plummer, Ellen A. In Focus: Guercino's Esther. (Illus.). 16p. 1993. 6.00 (*0-912303-47-6*) Michigan Mus.
Plummer, F. B. & Sargent, E. C. Underground Waters & Subsurface Temperatures of the Woodbine Sand in Northeast Texas. (Bulletin Ser.: BULL 3138). (Illus.). 178p. 1931. pap. 1.00 (*0-686-29351-7*) Bur Econ Geology.
Plummer, George F. History of the Town of Wentworth, New Hampshire. (Illus.). 401p. 1994. reprint ed. lib. bdg. 45.00 (*0-8328-3635-4*) Higginson Bk Co.
Plummer, George W. A Masonic Compendium to the Sacred Books & Early Literature of the East (1918) 67p. 1996. reprint ed. pap. 12.00 (*1-56459-556-0*) Kessinger Pub.
— Master's Word: A Short Treatise on the Word, the Light & the Self (1913) 120p. 1998. reprint ed. pap. 14.95 (*0-7661-0505-9*) Kessinger Pub.
Plummer, George W., ed. Mercury: An Official Organ of the Societas Rosicruciana in America (1916-1921) 282p. 1998. reprint ed. pap. 24.95 (*0-7661-0707-8*) Kessinger Pub.
***Plummer, Gillian.** Failing Working Class Girls. 180p. 2000. pap. 25.00 (*1-85856-173-6*, Trentham Bks) Stylus Pub VA.
***Plummer, James D., et al.** Silicon VLSI Technology: Fundamentals, Practice, & Modeling. LC 99-42745. 700p. 2000. pap. 92.00 (*0-13-085037-3*) P-H.
Plummer, James L. QED Report on Venture Capital Financial Analysis. 217p. 1987. 295.00 (*0-9620093-0-X*) QED Research.
Plummer, Jeanne G., ed. see Kirkwood, Tim.
Plummer, John, jt. auth. see Cockerell, Sydney C.
Plummer, John F., ed. Vox Feminae: Studies in Medieval Woman's Songs. (Studies in Medieval Culture: No. 25). (Orig.). 1989. pap. 10.95 (*0-918729-12-2*) Medieval Inst.
Plummer, John F., 3rd, ed. see Chaucer, Geoffrey.
Plummer, Katherine. A Japanese Glimpse at the Outside World, 1839-1843: The Travels of Jirokichi in Hawaii, Siberia & Alaska. (Alaska History Ser.: No. 36). 1991. 28.00 (*0-919642-34-9*) Limestone Pr.
— Shogun's Reluctant Ambassadors: Japanese Sea Drifters in the North Pacific. (Illus.). 320p. 1991. pap. 19.95 (*0-87595-235-6*) Oregon Hist.
Plummer, Ken. Telling Sexual Stories: Power, Change, & Social Worlds. LC 94-1215. 288p. (C). (gr. 13). 1994. pap. 22.99 (*0-415-10296-0*, B4405) Routledge.
Plummer, Ken, ed. Chicago School, 4 vols. (Critical Assessments Ser.). 1024p. (C). 1997. 700.00 (*0-415-11639-2*) Routledge.
— Chicago School. (Critical Assessments Ser.: Vol. 3). 280p. (C). 1997. write for info. (*0-415-11642-2*) Routledge.
— Chicago School. (Critical Assessments Ser.: Vol. 4). 224p. (C). 1997. write for info. (*0-415-11643-0*) Routledge.
— Chicago School, Vol. 1. (Critical Assessments Ser.). 256p. (C). 1997. text. write for info. (*0-415-11640-6*) Routledge.
— Chicago School, Vol. 2. (Critical Assessments Ser.). 264p. (C). 1997. text. write for info. (*0-415-11641-4*) Routledge.
— Modern Homosexualities: Fragments of Lesbian & Gay Experience. LC 92-6434. 272p. (C). 1992. pap. 24.99 (*0-415-06421-X*, A7752) Routledge.
Plummer, Kenneth. Sociology. 6th ed. LC 97-47074. 1997. pap. write for info. (*0-13-664533-X*) P-H.
Plummer, Kenneth, ed. The Making of the Modern Homosexual. 280p. 1981. 56.00 (*0-389-20159-6*, N6929) B&N Imports.
Plummer, Kristin. Receiving a Prophet. 108p. (Orig.). 1997. pap. 9.99 (*1-889389-04-8*) End-Time Wave.
— Spiritual Geography. LC 98-91336. 130p. 1998. pap. 5.00 (*0-9645112-1-5*) K Plummer.
— Where the Spirit Is Lord. 89p. (Orig.). 1995. pap. 8.99 (*0-9645112-0-7*) K Plummer.
Plummer, L. Gordon. By the Holy Tetraktys: Symbol & Reality in Man & Universe. (Study Ser.: No. 9). (Illus.). 96p. (Orig.). (C). 1982. pap. 9.95 (*0-913004-44-8*) Point Loma Pub.
— From Atom to Kosmos: Journey Without End. 2nd rev. ed. (Illus.). 136p. 1987. reprint ed. 8.95 (*0-913004-49-9*) Point Loma Pub.
— From Atom to Kosmos: Journey without End. 3rd ed. LC 88-40491. 142p. 1989. reprint ed. pap. 6.95 (*0-8356-0308-3*, Quest) Theos Pub Hse.
— Mathematics of the Cosmic Mind. (Illus.). 240p. 1982. 24.95 (*0-913004-84-7*) Point Loma Pub.
— Three Steps to Infinity. 1994. pap. 10.00 (*0-913004-81-2*) Point Loma Pub.
— The Way to the Mysteries. 126p. 1992. pap. 10.00 (*0-913004-73-1*) Point Loma Pub.
Plummer, Louise. A Dance for Three. LC 99-30877. 230p. (YA). (gr. 8-12). 2000. 15.95 (*0-385-32511-8*) BDD Bks Young Read.

P

An Asterisk (*) at the beginning of an entry indicates that the title is appearing for the first time.

— Unlikely Romance. (J). 1995. 21.95 (*0-385-31002-1*) BDD Bks Young Read.
— The Unlikely Romance of Kate Bjorkman. 192p. (YA). (gr. 7 up). 1997. mass mkt. 4.50 (*0-440-22704-6*) BDD Bks Young Read.
— The Unlikely Romance of Kate Bjorkman. (J). 1997. 9.60 (*0-606-12838-7*, Pub. by Turtleback) Demco.

Plummer, M. D., jt. auth. see Lovasz, Laszlo.

Plummer, Marguerite R., jt. auth. see Joiner, Gary D.

Plummer, Mary A. Foods & Nutrition: Syllabus. 1976. pap. text 7.95 (*0-89420-001-1*, 167070); audio 58.10 (*0-89420-147-6*, 167040) Natl Book.

Plummer, Mary B. From the Pen. 1997. pap. 56.95 (*1-57553-676-5*) Watermrk Pr.

Plummer-Mcgeary. Physical Geology. 7th ed. 1995. 318.75 (*0-697-26679-6*, WCB McGr Hill) McGrw-H Hghr Educ.
— Physical Geology. 7th ed. 1996. lab manual ed. 8.75 (*0-697-31280-1*, WCB McGr Hill) McGrw-H Hghr Educ.
— Physical Geology Northridge Ea. 6th ed. 1994. 50.00 (*0-697-25607-3*, WCB McGr Hill) McGrw-H Hghr Educ.

Plummer, Michael V. & Shirer, Hampton W. Movement Patterns in a River Population of the Softshell Turtle, Trionyx Muticus. (Occasional Papers: No. 43). 26p. 1975. pap. 1.00 (*0-686-80377-9*) U KS Nat Hist Mus.

***Plummer, Norman H.** Beacons of Hooper Strait. LC 00-30331. 2000. write for info. (*0-922249-08-3*) Ches Bay Mus.

Plummer, Norman H. Lambert Wickes: Pirate or Patriot? (Illus.). 1991. pap. 6.00 (*0-922249-03-2*) Ches Bay Mus.
— Maryland's Oyster Navy: The First Fifty Years. LC 93-26694. 1993. 19.95 (*0-922249-05-9*) Ches Bay Mus.

Plummer, Ralph W., et al. Minimizing Employee Exposure to Toxic Chemical Releases. LC 87-12213. (Pollution Technology Review Ser.: No. 145). (Illus.). 257p. 1988. 44.00 (*0-8155-1131-0*) Noyes.

Plummer, Ray L. Beginner's Guide to Repairing Lionel Trains. LC 97-225324. 80p. (Orig.). 1997. pap. 14.95 (*0-89778-438-3*, 10-8095, Kalmbach Books) Kalmbach.

***Plummer, Ray L.** Toy Train Repair Made Easy: 21 Lionel Postwar Projects. (Illus.). 2000. pap. 16.95 (*0-89778-508-8*) Kalmbach.

***Plummer, Robert H.** Age 60 to 120 - Live It up in the New Millenium. LC 99-75132. 2000. 11.95 (*1-882792-88-2*) Proctor Pubns.

Plummer, Sherry K., jt. auth. see Hull, Larry A.

Plummer, Stephen E., jt. ed. see Danson, F. Mark.

Plummer, Susan E., jt. ed. see Lodoiska, Emmanuel R.

Plummer, Thomas G. Making Money in the Fitness Business: If I Knew the Fitness Business Was This Hard, I'd Have Gotten a "Real Job"! (Illus.). 352p. (Orig.). 1998. pap. 59.00 (*0-9652432-1-4*, Fitness Mgmt Bks) Fitness Mgmt.

Plummer, Thomas G., et al, eds. Film & Politics in the Weimar Republic. (Germany in the Twenties Ser.). (Illus.). 98p. 1984. pap. text 19.50 (*0-8419-7503-5*) Holmes & Meier.

Plummer, Tom. Don't Bite Me, I'm Santa Claus. LC 99-35285. 160p. 1999. 16.95 (*1-57345-538-5*, Shadow Mount) Deseret Bk.
— Eating Chocolates & Dancing in the Kitchen: Sketches of Marriage & Family. LC 97-32821. 1998. 16.95 (*1-57345-305-6*, Shadow Mount) Deseret Bk.

***Plummer, Tom.** Second Wind: Variations on a Theme of Growing Older. LC 00-38748. 2000. pap. 16.95 (*1-57345-780-9*, Shadow Mount) Deseret Bk.

Plummer, Tony. Forcasting Financial Markets: The Psychology of Successful Investing. 3rd rev. ed. 320p. 1998. pap. 55.00 (*0-7494-2585-7*) Kogan Page Ltd.
— Forecasting Financial Markets: Technical Analysis of the Dynamics of Price. LC 90-24550. (Finance Editions Ser.). 259p. 1991. 55.00 (*0-471-53408-0*) Wiley.
— Psychology of Technical Analysis: Profiting from Crowd Behavior & the Dynamics of Price. 2nd rev. ed. 275p. 1993. text 50.00 (*1-55738-543-2*, Irwn Prfssnl) McGraw-Hill Prof.

Plummer, Wilbur C. & Young, Ralph A. Sales Finance Companies & Their Credit Practices. (Financial Research Program II: Studies in Consumer Installment Financing: No. 2). 324p. 1940. reprint ed. 84.30 (*0-87014-461-8*) Natl Bur Econ Res.

Plummer, William. The Holy Goof: A Biography of Neal Cassady. (Illus.). 162p. 1994. pap. 9.95 (*1-56924-925-3*) Marlowe & Co.

***Plummer, William.** Wishing My Father Well: A Memoir of Fathers, Sons & Fly-Fishing. LC 00-25298. 160p. 2000. 23.95 (*1-58567-031-6*, Pub. by Overlook Pr) Penguin Putnam.

Plummeridge, Charles. Music Education in Theory & Practice. (Falmer Press Library on Aesthetic Education). 184p. 1991. 65.00 (*1-85000-765-9*, Falmer Pr) Taylor & Francis.

Plump, Wendy, jt. auth. see Gallup, George H., Jr.

Plumpe, J. & Quasten, J. The Epistles of St. Clement of Rome & St. Ignatius of Antioch. (Ancient Christian Writers Ser.: No. 1). 1946. 19.95 (*0-8091-0038-X*) Paulist Pr.

Plumpe, J., ed. see Augustine, Saint.

Plumpe, J., jt. ed. see Kuasten, J.

Plumpp, Sterling. Black Rituals. LC 72-80785. (Orig.). 1972. pap. 8.95 (*0-88378-024-0*) Third World.
— Ornate with Smoke. LC 97-22954. 1997. write for info. (*0-88378-193-X*); pap. 12.95 (*0-88378-198-0*) Third World.

Plumpp, Sterling D. Blues Narratives. 72p. 1999. pap. 10.95 (*1-882688-20-1*, Pub. by Tia Chucha Pr) SPD-Small Pr Dist.

Plumptie, E. H., tr. see Sophocles.

Plumpton, A. J. International Symposium on the Production & Processing of Fine Particles: Proceedings of the Metallurgical Society of the Canadian Institute of Mining & Metallurgy, Vol. 7. 930p. 1988. 96.00 (*0-08-036449-7*, Pergamon Pr) Elsevier.

Plumpton, C. A. & Macilwaine, P. S. New Tertiary Mathematics. 1250p. 1981. text 590.00 (*0-08-021646-3*) Franklin.

Plumpton, C. A., jt. auth. see Chirgwin, B. H.

Plumpton, Edward. Plumpton Correspondence. Stapleton, Thomas, ed. (Camden Society, London. Publications, First Ser.: No. 4). reprint ed. 95.00 (*0-404-50104-4*) AMS Pr.

Plumptre. Classic Plant Combinations. 1998. 35.00 (*0-7063-7722-2*, Pub. by WrLock) Sterling.

Plumptre, E. H., ed. Sophocles: Tragedies & Fragments. 30.00 (*0-8196-2891-3*) Biblo.

***Plumptre, George.** Classic Planting. (Illus.). 2000. pap. 21.95 (*1-84188-042-6*) Seven Dials.

Plumptre, George. Edward VII. (Illus.). 288p. 1997. pap. 24.95 (*1-85793-846-1*, Pub. by Pavilion Bks Ltd) Trafalgar.
— The Garden Makers: The Great Tradition of Garden Design from 1600 to the Present Day. (Illus.). 240p. 1997. pap. 24.95 (*1-85793-282-X*, Pub. by Pavilion Bks Ltd) Trafalgar.
— Garden Ornament: Five Hundred Years of History & Practice. LC 98-60310. (Illus.). 256p. 1998. pap. 29.95 (*0-500-28079-7*, Pub. by Thames Hudson) Norton.

***Plumptre, George.** Great Gardens, Great Designers. (Illus.). 2000. pap. 21.95 (*1-84188-021-3*) Seven Dials.

Plumptre, George. Great Gardens, Great Designers. (Illus.). 168p. 1997. pap. 19.95 (*0-7063-7453-3*) Ward Lock Ltd UK.
— Sotheby's the Country House Guide. (Illus.). 288p. 1996. pap. 19.95 (*0-7063-7519-X*, Pub. by WrLock) Sterling.

Plumptre, George & Moore, Derry. Royal Gardens. LC 81-175394. 224 p. 1981. write for info. (*0-00-211871-8*) Collins SF.

Plumptre, James. The Lakers. LC 90-40598. 88p. 1990. reprint ed. 40.00 (*1-85477-052-7*) Continuum.
— Observations on "Hamlet" LC 71-144672. reprint ed. 20.00 (*0-404-05066-2*) AMS Pr.

Plumptre, R. A. Some Wood Properties of Pinus Patula from Uganda & Techniques Developed. 1978. 80.00 (*0-85074-032-0*) St Mut.

Plumptree, Timothy W. Beyond the Bottom Line: Management in Government. 466p. 1988. 23.95 (*0-88645-069-1*, Pub. by Inst Res Pub) Ashgate Pub Co.

Plumridge, Diane M., et al. The Student with a Genetic Disorder: Educational Implications for Special Education Teachers & for Physical Therapists, Occupational Therapists, & Speech Pathologists. LC 92-39088. (Illus.). 382p. 1993. pap. 47.95 (*0-398-06327-3*); text 79.95 (*0-398-05839-3*) C C Thomas.

Plumsock Mesoamerican Studies Staff, ed. see Hannstein, Walter B.

Plumstead, A. W., ed. The Wall & the Garden: Selected Massachusetts Election Sermons, 1670-1775. LC 68-19742. 398p. reprint ed. pap. 123.40 (*0-608-15976-X*, 203328400084) Bks Demand.

Plumstead, J. E., jt. contrib. by see McNiven, J. D.

Plumstead, Michael. A Passion to Lead! How to Develop Your Natural Leadership Ability. Scanlon, Kelly, ed. LC 96-69147. (Self-Study Sourcebook Ser.). (Illus.). 152p. 1997. pap. 15.95 (*1-57294-051-4*, 13-0027) SkillPath Pubns.

Plumtree, Alexandra. Child Care Law: Scotland: A Summary. 80p. 1997. pap. 30.00 (*1-873868-49-9*, Pub. by BAAF) St Mut.

Plumtree, Simon, ed. see Thomas & Weedon.

Plumwood, Val. Feminism & the Mastery of Nature. LC 93-15995. (Opening Out Ser.). 1993. pap. write for info. (*0-415-50610-7*) Routledge.
— Feminism & the Mastery of Nature. 256p. (C). 1994. pap. 22.99 (*0-415-06810-X*) Routledge.

***Plunk, Roger.** Wandering Peacemaker. 2000. pap. 13.95 (*1-57174-179-8*) N D Walsch.

***Plunka, Gene A.** Jean-Claude Van Itallie & the Off-Broadway Theater. LC 98-30066. 332 p. 1999. write for info. (*0-87413-664-4*) U Delaware Pr.

Plunka, Gene A. Peter Shaffer: Roles, Rites, & Rituals in the Theater. LC 87-46010. 256p. 1988. 37.50 (*0-8386-3329-3*) Fairleigh Dickinson.
— The Rites of Passage of Jean Genet: The Art & Aesthetics of Risk Taking. LC 91-55363. 360p. 1992. 45.00 (*0-8386-3461-3*) Fairleigh Dickinson.

Plunka, Gene A., ed. Antonin Artaud & the Modern Theater. LC 93-40087. 1994. 42.50 (*0-8386-3550-4*) Fairleigh Dickinson.

Plunket, Emmeline. Calendars & Constellations of the Ancient World. (Illus.). 272p. 1998. reprint ed. pap. text 15.00 (*0-7881-5396-X*) DIANE Pub.

Plunket, Ierne A. Isabel of Castille. LC 73-14464. (Illus.). reprint ed. 45.00 (*0-404-58282-6*) AMS Pr.

Plunket, Robert, jt. auth. see Evans, Walker.

Plunkett. Accounting Information. Date not set. pap. text, teacher ed. write for info. (*0-314-02501-4*) West Pub.
— Introduction to Management. (SWC-Management Ser.). 1983. teacher ed. write for info. (*0-534-01288-4*) Sth-Wstrn College.
— Introduction to Management: Study Guide. 3rd ed. (SWC-Management Ser.). 1989. pap., student ed. 19.50 (*0-534-91757-7*) Thomson Learn.
— Management: Meeting & Exceeding Customer Expectations. 6th ed. (GC - Principles of Management Ser.). 1997. mass mkt., student ed. 21.95 (*0-538-85659-9*); mass mkt., suppl. ed. 21.95 (*0-538-86311-0*) S-W Pub.
— Management: Meeting & Exceeding Customer Expectations. 6th ed. LC 96-37322. (GC - Principles of Management Ser.). (C). 1997. mass mkt. 94.95 (*0-538-84496-5*) S-W Pub.

***Plunkett.** Supervision: Diversity & Teams in Workplace. 9th ed. LC 99-24424. (Illus.). 608p. 1999. 79.00 (*0-13-096006-3*) P-H.

Plunkett. Telecourse Guide Business of Management. 2nd ed. (SWC-Management Ser.). 1986. pap. 20.00 (*0-534-05773-X*) Thomson Learn.
— Telecourse Guide Introduction to Management. 3rd ed. (SWC-Management Ser.). 1988. pap. 20.75 (*0-534-91758-5*) Thomson Learn.

Plunkett & Attner. Introduction to Management: Student Review. (SWC-Management Ser.). 1983. pap., student ed. 13.25 (*0-534-01360-0*) Thomson Learn.
— Telecourse Guide Business of Management. (SWC-Management Ser.). 1983. pap. 13.25 (*0-534-01359-7*) Thomson Learn.

Plunkett, et al. Student Review - Intro To Management. 5th ed. (SWC-Management). 1994. mass mkt., student ed. 23.95 (*0-534-93385-8*) S-W Pub.

Plunkett, Brian, ed. see CCH Tax Law Editors.

Plunkett, Drew, et al. Four Studies on Charles Rennie Mackintosh. LC 96-71717. (Illus.). 60p. (Orig.). 1996. pap. 7.95 (*1-890053-00-7*) NY Schl Interior Des.

Plunkett, E. R., ed. Handbook of Industrial Toxicology. 1987. 100.00 (*0-8206-0321-X*) Chem Pub.

Plunkett, George A. Disappearing Norwich. 1994. pap. 40.00 (*0-86138-057-6*, Pub. by T Dalton) St Mut.

Plunkett, George A., ed. Rambles in Old Norwich. 136p. 1990. pap. 30.00 (*0-86138-078-9*) St Mut.

Plunkett, Hazel. Nicaragua in Focus: A Guide to the People, Politics & Culture. LC 99-19668. 1999. pap. 12.95 (*1-56656-286-4*) Interlink Pub.

Plunkett, J. J., jt. auth. see Dale, B. G.

Plunkett, Jack W. The Almanac of American Employers, 1998-99: The Complete Guide to America's Largest, Most Successful Employers. 4th rev. ed. 695p. 1998. pap. 149.99 incl. disk (*0-9638268-9-1*) Plunkett Res.

***Plunkett, Jack W.** The Almanac of American Employers, 2000-01: The Only Complete Guide to America's Largest, Most Successful Employers. 704p. 2000. pap. 179.99 incl. cd-rom (*1-891775-12-X*) Plunkett Res.
— Plunkett's Biotech & Genetics Industry Almanac: The Only Complete Reference to the Biotech Business. 650p. 2001. pap. 199.99 incl. cd-rom (*1-891775-18-9*) Plunkett Res.

Plunkett, Jack W. Plunkett's Companion to the Almanac of American Employers: Mid-Size Firms. LC 98-212699. 640p. 1999. pap. 149.99 incl. disk (*1-891775-02-2*) Plunkett Res.

***Plunkett, Jack W.** Plunkett's Companion to the Almanac of American Employers, 2000-2001: Mid Size Firms. 693p. 2000. pap. 149.99 incl. cd-rom (*1-891775-13-8*) Plunkett Res.

Plunkett, Jack W. Plunkett's E-Commerce & Internet Business Almanac: The Only Complete Guide to the Business Side of the Internet. 500p. 2000. pap. 199.99 incl. cd-rom (*1-891775-11-1*) Plunkett Res.
— Plunkett's Employers' Internet Sites with Careers Information: The Only Complete Guide to Careers Websites Operated by Major Employers. 701p. 1999. pap. 149.99 incl. disk (*1-891775-01-4*) Plunkett Res.
— Plunkett's Energy Industry Almanac: The Only Complete Guide to the Energy & Utilities Industry. 610p. 1999. pap. 149.99 incl. disk (*0-9638268-8-3*) Plunkett Res.
— Plunkett's Engineering & Research Industry Almanac: The Only Complete Guide to the Hottest Research & Engineering Firms. 680p. 2000. pap. 179.99 incl. cd-rom (*1-891775-10-3*) Plunkett Res.
— Plunkett's Entertainment & Media Industry Almanac: The Complete Guide to America's Publishing, Broadcasting & Entertainment Business. 626p. 1998. pap. 149.99 incl. disk (*0-9638268-6-7*) Plunkett Res.

***Plunkett, Jack W.** Plunkett's Entertainment & Media Industry Almanac, 2000-2001: The Complete Guide to America's Publishing, Broadcasting & Entertainment Business. 642p. 2000. pap. 179.99 incl. cd-rom (*1-891775-14-6*) Plunkett Res.

Plunkett, Jack W. Plunkett's Financial Services Industry Almanac, 2000-2001. 754p. 1999. pap. 179.99 incl. cd-rom (*1-891775-03-0*) Plunkett Res.
— Plunkett's Health Care Industry Almanac, 1999-2000: The Only Complete Guide to America's Health Care Industry. 740p. 1999. pap. 179.99 incl. cd-rom (*1-891775-04-9*) Plunkett Res.
— Plunkett's InfoTech Industry Almanac, 1999-2000: The Only Complete Guide to the Technologies & Companies Changing the Way the World Thinks, Works, & Shares Information. 2nd rev. ed. 695p. 1998. pap. 149.99 incl. disk (*1-891775-00-6*) Plunkett Res.
— Plunkett's On-Line Trading, Finance & Investment Web Sites Almanac: The Only Complete Guide to Investment, Finance, Accounting, Economics, Banking & Financial Services Web Sites. 547p. 2000. pap. 149.99 incl. disk (*1-891775-08-1*) Plunkett Res.
— Plunkett's Retail Industry Almanac, 1999-2000: The Only Complete Guide to the Hottest Retail Companies & Hottest Retail Trends. 648p. 1999. pap. 179.99 incl. cd-rom (*1-891775-05-7*) Plunkett Res.
— Plunkett's Telecommunications Industry Almanac: The Only Complete Guide to the Firms Changing the Way the World Communicates Via Wired & Wireless Systems. 680p. 2000. pap. 179.99 incl. cd-rom (*1-891775-06-5*) Plunkett Res.

Plunkett, James. The Boy on the Back Wall. 208p. 1987. pap. 8.95 (*0-905169-60-3*, Pub. by Poolbeg Pr) Dufour.
— The Trusting & the Maimed. 12.50 (*0-8159-6909-0*) Devin.

Plunkett, James J., jt. auth. see Dale, B. G.

Plunkett, James R. Understanding Bar Codes. 1993. pap. 22.95 (*1-882419-46-4*) News Four-Hund.

Plunkett, John & Rossetto, Louis, eds. Mind Grenades: Manifestos from the Future. LC 96-207698. (Illus.). 160p. (Orig.). 1996. pap. 32.95 (*1-888869-00-3*) Wired Bks.

Plunkett, John, jt. ed. see Wieners, Brad.

Plunkett, Joseph M. The Poems of Joseph Mary Plunkett. LC 75-28839. reprint ed. 29.50 (*0-404-13828-4*) AMS Pr.

Plunkett, Kim. Language Acquisition & Connectionism. 427p. 1998. 54.95 (*0-86377-984-0*) Taylor & Francis.
— Preliminary Approaches to Language Development. (Illus.). 154p. (C). 1985. pap. 15.95 (*87-7288-001-5*, Pub. by Aarhus Univ Pr) David Brown.

Plunkett, Kim & Elman, Jeffrey L. Exercises in Rethinking Innateness: A Handbook for Connectionist Simulations. LC 97-155473. (Neural Network Modeling & Connectionism Ser.). (Illus.). 329p. 1997. pap. text 40.00 (*0-262-66105-5*, Bradford Bks) MIT Pr.

Plunkett, Michael. Afro-American Sources in Virginia: A Guide to Manuscripts. LC 89-16616. (Carter G. Woodson Institute Series in Black Studies). 323p. 1990. text 40.00 (*0-8139-1251-2*) U Pr of Va.

Plunkett, Myles, jt. auth. see Boland, Gerry.

***Plunkett, Nancy.** Lhasa Apsos. (New Owner's Guide to Ser.). 1999. 12.95 (*0-7938-2797-3*) TFH Pubns.

Plunkett, Oliver. Letters of St. Oliver Plunkett. Hanly, John, ed. 624p. 1979. 85.00 (*0-85105-344-0*, Pub. by Smyth) Dufour.

Plunkett, P., jt. auth. see Dale, D.

Plunkett, Paul M. Shackspere of Stratford: A Monumental Design. 1995. 13.95 (*0-533-11068-8*) Vantage.

Plunkett-Powell, Karen. Remembering Woolworths. LC 99-15916. 224p. 1999. text 27.95 (*0-312-20670-4*) St Martin.

***Plunkett, Richard & Finlay, Hugh.** Delhi. 2nd ed. (Illus.). 224p. 1999. pap. 14.95 (*0-86442-675-5*) Lonely Planet.

Plunkett, Richard J. & Gordon, John E. Epidemiology & Mental Illness. Grob, Gerald N., ed. LC 78-22581. (Historical Issues in Mental Health Ser.). 1980. reprint ed. lib. bdg. 17.95 (*0-405-11933-X*) Ayer.

Plunkett, Robert L. A California Dreamer in King Henry's Court. 213p. 1989. lib. bdg. 16.95 (*0-9623139-4-7*) Silver Dawn.

Plunkett, Signe J. Standard Emergency Procedures for the Small Animal Veterinarian. LC 92-39992. 1993. pap. text 33.00 (*0-7216-6781-3*, W B Saunders Co) Harcrt Hlth Sci Grp.

***Plunkett, Susan.** Heaven's Time. 1998. mass mkt. 5.99 (*0-515-12287-4*, Jove) Berkley Pub.

Plunkett, Susan. Remember Love. (Time Passages Ser.). 368p. 1996. mass mkt. 5.99 (*0-515-11980-6*, Jove) Berkley Pub.
— Silver Tomorrows. 352p. 1997. mass mkt. 5.99 (*0-515-12047-2*, Jove) Berkley Pub.

***Plunkett, Susan.** Soul Survivor. 1999. mass mkt. 5.99 (*0-515-12684-5*, Jove) Berkley Pub.

Plunkett, Susan. Timepool. (Time Passages Romance Ser.). 314p. 1999. mass mkt. 5.99 (*0-515-12553-9*, Jove) Berkley Pub.

***Plunkett, Susan.** Untamed Time, 1 vol. 1999. mass mkt. 5.99 (*0-515-12447-8*, Jove) Berkley Pub.

Plunkett, T. J., jt. auth. see Brownstone, Meyer.

***Plunkett, W. Howard.** F-105 Thunderchiefs: A 29-Year Illustrated Operational History, with Individual Accounts of the 103 Surviving Fighter Bombers. (Illus.). 224p. 2000. 55.00 (*0-7864-0880-4*) McFarland & Co.

Plunkett, Warren R. Supervision: The Direction of People at Work. 5th ed. 416p. 1989. teacher ed. write for info. (*0-318-64394-4*, H17320) P-H.

Plunkett, Warren R. & Attner, Raymond F. Introduction To Management. LC 82-18698. (SWC-Management). 544p. 1983. pap. 33.50 (*0-534-01298-1*) PWS Pubs.
— Introduction to Management. 2nd ed. (SWC-Management). 590p. (YA). (gr. 11-12). 1986. pap. 33.00 (*0-534-05772-1*) PWS Pubs.
— Introduction To Management. 3rd ed. (SWC-Management). 640p. (C). 1988. pap. 38.00 (*0-534-91756-9*) PWS Pubs.
— Introduction to Management. 5th ed. 838p. 1993. pap. 59.00 (*0-534-93321-1*) S-W Pub.

***Plunz, Richard.** New Urbanisms: Mostar, Bosnia & Herzegovina LC 98-73349. (MSAUD New Urbanisms Ser.). 83p. 1998. write for info. (*1-883584-13-2*) CUGSA.
— Two Adirondack Hamlets in History: Keene & Keene Valley. LC 99-89183. 2000. pap. write for info. (*1-930098-04-9*) Purple Mnt Pr.

Plunz, Richard A. A History of Housing in New York City. (History of Urban Life Ser.). (Illus.). 480p. 1992. pap. 25.50 (*0-231-06297-4*) Col U Pr.

Plunz, Richard A., ed. Housing Form & Public Policy in the United States. LC 77-22686. 248p. 1980. 59.95 (*0-275-90537-3*, C0537, Praeger Pubs) Greenwood.

Plura, M., jt. auth. see Albrecht, R.

Plus, Raoul. How to Pray Well. 144p. 1996. reprint ed. text 15.95 (*0-912141-30-1*) Roman Cath Bks.
— Winning Souls for Christ: How You Can Become an Effective Apostle. LC 99-13334. Orig. Title: Rayonner le Christ. 144p. 1999. pap. 12.95 (*0-918477-94-8*) Sophia Inst Pr.

***Plusch, Jackie.** ZAP Your Junk Mail: The Quick Solution to Your Junk Mail Problems & Unwanted Telephone Calls. (Illus.). 16p. 1999. pap. 16.95 (*0-9673136-0-0*) Clutter Cut.

Pluskat, Thomas J. Real Estate to a Better Future & Financial Independence. LC 86-83019. 275p. (Orig.). (C). 1986. pap. 35.00 (*0-9618963-1-0*) Innovat Dynamics.

P

Plusquellec, Herve, et al. Modern Water Control in Irrigation: Concepts, Issues, & Applications. LC 94-3821. (World Bank Technical Papers: No. 246). 116p. 1994. pap. 22.00 (0-8213-2819-0, 12819) World Bank.

Plut-Pregelj, Leopoldina & Rogel, Carole. Historical Dictionary of Slovenia. LC 95-26566. (European Historical Dictionaries Ser.: No. 13). 450p. 1996. 67.00 (0-8108-3113-9) Scarecrow.

Pluta, Joseph. The Art of Making Choices. 402p. 1998. pap. text 45.95 (1-56226-414-1) CAT Pub.

Pluta, M. Advanced Light Microscopy Vol. 3: Measuring Techniques. 718p. 1993. 289.00 (0-444-98819-X, North Holland) Elsevier.

Pluta, Maksymilian, ed. Gradient-Index Optics in Science & Engineering. 226p. 1996. 59.00 (0-8194-2345-9) SPIE.

Pluta, Maksymilian & Wolinski, Tomasz R., eds. Polarimetry & Ellipsometry, Vol. 3094. LC 97-200960. 392p. 1997. 80.00 (0-8194-2509-5) SPIE.

***Pluta, Maksymilian, et al.** Ophthalmic Measurements & Optometry: 12-16 May 1997, Kazmierz Dolny, Poland LC 99-192200. (Proceedings Ser.). xvi, 202 p. 1998. write for info. (0-8194-3046-3) SPIE.

Pluta, Olaf. Kritker der Unsterblichkeitsdoktrin in Mittelalter und Renaissance. (Bochumer Studien zur Philosophie Ser.: Vol. 7). xii, 138p. 1986. 35.00 (90-6032-276-2, Pub. by B R Gruner) Humanities.

— Die Philosophische Psychologie des Peter von Ailly. (Beitrag zur Geschichte der Philosophie des Spaten Mittelalters Bochumer Studien zur Philosophie: Vol. 6). 366p. (C). 1987. 56.00 (90-6032-275-4, Pub. by B R Gruner) Humanities.

Pluta, Olaf, ed. Die Philosophie im 14. und 15. Jahrhundert: In Memoriam Konstanty Michalski (1879-1947) (Bochumer Studien zur Philosophie Ser.: Vol. 10). (GER.). lx, 640p. (C). 1988. 80.00 (90-6032-297-5, Pub. by B R Gruner) Humanities.

Pluta, Olaf, jt. ed. see Mojsisch, Burkhard.

Pluta, Terry, jt. auth. see Ahbe, Dottie.

Plutarch. The Age of Alexander. Scott-Kilvert, Ian, tr. & anno. by. (Classics Ser.). 448p. 1973. pap. 13.95 (0-14-044286-3, Penguin Classics) Viking Penguin.

— A Commentary on Plutarch's Life of Agesilaos: Response to Sources in the Presentation of Character. Shipley, D. R., ed. 528p. (C). 1998. text 125.00 (0-19-815073-3) OUP.

— The Education or Bringinge up of Children. Eliot, T., tr. LC 72-224. (English Experience Ser.: No. 184). 48p. 1969. reprint ed. 30.00 (90-221-0184-3) Walter J Johnson.

— Essays. Kidd, Ian, ed. Waterfield, Robin A., tr. 448p. 1993. pap. 13.95 (0-14-044564-1, Penguin Classics) Viking Penguin.

— The Fall of the Roman Republic. Warner, Rex, tr. (Classics Ser.). 368p. 1954. pap. 13.95 (0-14-044084-4, Penguin Classics) Viking Penguin.

— The Governaunce of Good Helthe, Erasmus Beynge Interpretoure. LC 68-54657. (English Experience Ser.: No. 16). 32p. 1968. reprint ed. 20.00 (90-221-0016-2) Walter J Johnson.

— Greek Lives. Stadter, Philip A., ed. Waterfield, Robin, tr. LC 98-17490. (Oxford World's Classics Ser.). (Illus.). 522p. 1999. pap. 13.95 (0-19-282501-1) OUP.

— The Greek Question of Plutarch. Halliday, W. R., tr. & comment by. LC 75-10646. (Ancient Religion & Mythology Ser.). 1978. reprint ed. 25.95 (0-405-07270-8) Ayer.

— How to Profit by Your Enemies. Draghici, Simona, ed. LC 98-14383. 112p. 1998. pap. text 5.95 (0-943045-14-2) Plutarch Pr OR.

— Life of Antony. Pelling, Christopher B. R., ed. (Illus.). 352p. 1988. text 65.00 (0-521-24066-2); pap. text 24.95 (0-521-28418-X) Cambridge U Pr.

— Life of Aratus. Connor, W. R., ed. LC 78-18593. (Greek Texts & Commentaries Ser.). (Illus.). 1979. reprint ed. lib. bdg. 19.95 (0-405-11434-6) Ayer.

— Life of Dion. Connor, W. R., ed. LC 78-18594. (Greek Texts & Commentaries Ser.). (Illus.). 1979. reprint ed. lib. bdg. 21.95 (0-405-11435-4) Ayer.

— Makers of Rome: Nine Lives by Plutarch. Scott-Kilvert, Ian, tr. & intro. by. (Classics Ser.). 368p. 1965. pap. 12.95 (0-14-044158-1, Penguin Classics) Viking Penguin.

— Moralia. Incl. Vol. 1. 19.95 (0-674-99217-2); Vol. 2. 19.95 (0-674-99245-8); Vol. 3. 19.95 (0-674-99270-9); Vol. 4. 19.95 (0-674-99336-5); Vol. 5. 19.95 (0-674-99337-3); Vol. 6. 19.95 (0-674-99371-3); Vol. 7. 19.95 (0-674-99446-9); Vol. 8. 19.95 (0-674-99466-3); Vol. 9. 19.95 (0-674-99467-1); Vol. 10. 19.95 (0-674-99354-3); Vol. 11. 19.95 (0-674-99469-8); Vol. 12. 19.95 (0-674-99447-7); Vol. 14. 19.95 (0-674-99472-8); Vol. 15. 19.95 (0-674-99473-6); write for info. (0-318-53118-6) HUP.

— Plutarch: Life of Cicero. Moles, J. L., ed. (Classical Texts Ser.). 1989. 59.99 (0-85668-360-4, Pub. by Aris & Phillips); pap. 28.00 (0-85668-361-2, Pub. by Aris & Phillips) David Brown.

Plutarch. Plutarch: Lives of Aristedes & Cato. Sansone, David, ed. (Classical Texts Ser.). 1989. 59.99 (0-85668-421-X, Pub. by Aris & Phillips) David Brown.

— Plutarch: Lives of Aristedes & Catro. Sansone, David, ed. (Classical Texts Ser.). 1989. pap. 28.00 (0-85668-422-8, Pub. by Aris & Phillips) David Brown.

Plutarch. Plutarch: The Malice of Herodotus. 1992. 59.99 (0-85668-568-2, Pub. by Aris & Phillips); pap. 22.00 (0-85668-569-0, Pub. by Aris & Phillips) David Brown.

Plutarch. Plutarch, the Parallel Lives: Agesilaus & Pompey, Pelopidas & Marcellus. 19.95 (0-674-99097-8) HUP.

Plutarch. Plutarch's Advice to the Bride & Groom & A Consolation to His Wife: English Translations, Commentary, Interpretive Essays & Bibliography. LC 98-27968. (Illus.). 240p. 1999. text 55.00 (0-19-512023-X) OUP.

— Plutarch's Lives. White, John S., ed. LC 66-28487. (Illus.). 468p. (YA). (gr. 7 up). 1995. 25.00 (0-8196-0174-8) Biblo.

— Plutarch's Lives of the Noble Grecians & Romans, 6 vols. North, Thomas, ed. LC 70-158307. (Tudor Translations, First Ser.: Nos. 7-12). reprint ed. 345.00 (0-404-51870-2) AMS Pr.

— Plutarch's Rules of Health. (Longevity Ser.). 1991. lib. bdg. 75.00 (0-8490-4183-X) Gordon Pr.

— The Rise & Fall of Athens: Nine Greek Lives. Kilvert, Ian S., tr. (Classics Ser.). 320p. 1960. pap. 12.95 (0-14-044102-6, Penguin Classics) Viking Penguin.

— Roman Lives: A Selection of Eight Lives. Stadter, Philip A., ed. Waterfield, Robin, tr. (Oxford World's Classics Ser.). (Illus.). 608p. 2000. pap. 13.95 (0-19-282502-X) OUP.

— The Roman Questions of Plutarch. Rose, Herbert J., ed. LC 75-14267. (Ancient Religion & Mythology Ser.). 1976. reprint ed. 19.95 (0-405-07272-4) Ayer.

— Selected Lives from the Lives of the Noble Grecians & Romans, 1. Turner, Paul, ed. LC DE0007.P7T8. 370p. 1963. reprint ed. pap. 114.70 (0-608-08372-0, 205132000003) Bks Demand.

— Selected Lives from the Lives of the Noble Grecians & Romans, 2. Turner, Paul, ed. LC DE0007.P7T81. 281p. 1963. reprint ed. pap. 87.20 (0-608-08373-9, 205132000002) Bks Demand.

— Les Vies des Hommes Illustres, Vol. 1. (FRE.). 1937. lib. bdg. 95.00 (0-8288-3525-X, F19161) Fr & Eur.

— Les Vies des Hommes Illustres, Vol. 2. (FRE.). 1937. lib. bdg. 95.00 (0-8288-3526-8, F19162) Fr & Eur.

— Virgil. Rose, H. J., tr. 1924. 30.00 (0-8196-0284-1) Biblo.

Plutarch, ed. see Skeat, Walter W.

Plutarco. Sobre el Amor. Guzman Guerra, Antonio, ed. & tr. by. (Nueva Austral Ser.: Vol. 127). (SPA.). 1991. pap. text 24.95 (84-239-1927-7) Elliots Bks.

— Vida de Alejandro. (Fondo 2000 Ser.). (SPA.). pap. 2.99 (968-16-5055-7, Pub. by Fondo) Continental Bk.

Plutarque. Les Vies des Homme Illustres, 2 vols., Ea. D'Amyot, tr. 37.50 (0-318-52319-1) Fr & Eur.

Plutchak, Mary. Circled in Red. 65p. 1995. pap. 8.00 (0-9630322-1-6) Carrousel Pr.

— So Small a Pocket. 68p. 1991. pap. 10.95 (0-9630322-0-8) Carrousel Pr.

Plutchik, Robert. The Emotions. rev. ed. 228p. (C). 1991. reprint ed. pap. text 19.50 (0-8191-8286-9) U Pr of Amer.

***Plutchik, Robert.** Emotions in the Practice of Psychotherapy: Clinical Implications of Affect Theories. LC 00-41612. 2000. write for info. (1-55798-694-0) Am Psychol.

Plutchik, Robert & Conte, Hope R., eds. Circumplex Models of Personality & Emotions. (Illus.). 484p. 1996. text 29.95 (1-55798-380-1) Am Psychol.

Plutchik, Robert, jt. ed. see Conte, Hope R.

Plute, M. Tool Management in Manufacturing. (Manufacturing Engineering & Materials Processing Ser.). Date not set. write for info. (0-8247-9971-2) Dekker.

Plute, Martin. Tool Management Strategies. LC 98-27327. 1998. 49.95 (1-56990-247-X) Hanser-Gardner.

Plute, Patricia J. Money Management for Women with No Money. LC 95-71267. 196p. 1995. pap. 12.95 (0-9647957-0-1) Running Coyote Pr.

Pluth, Martin, ed. Wayne Evans on AS/400 Security. LC 98-112130. (Illus.). 300p. 1997. pap. text 89.00 (1-883884-36-5, 571) Midrange Comput.

Pluth, Tamara, ed. see Rivera, John & Walker, Carol A.

Pluto. Revisions. 1997. pap. 11.95 (0-7453-0814-7, Pub. by Pluto GBR) Stylus Pub VA.

Pluto Project Staff & Semkiw, Walter. Astrology for Regular People. (For Regular People Ser.). (Illus.). xi, 198p. 1998. pap. 24.95 (0-9662982-7-6, Pub. by Pluto Proj) Partners Pubs Grp.

Pluto, Terry. Burying the Curse: How the Indians Became the Best Team in Baseball. Mezger, Ann S., ed. (Illus.). 208p. 1995. pap. 12.95 (0-9649902-3-7) Beacon Jrnl.

— The Curse of Rocky Colavito: A Loving Look at a Thirty-Year Slump. 304p. 1995. per. 12.00 (0-684-80415-8, Fireside) S&S Trade Pap.

***Pluto, Terry.** Falling from Grace: Can Pro Basketball Be Saved? 319p. 1999. reprint ed. text 23.00 (0-7881-6626-3) DIANE Pub.

Pluto, Terry. Our Tribe: A Baseball Memoir. LC 99-22125. (Illus.). 272p. 1999. 24.50 (0-684-84505-9) S&S Trade.

***Pluto, Terry.** Tall Tales: The Glory Years of the NBA. (Illus.). 413p. 2000. pap. 17.95 (0-8032-8766-6, Bison Books) U of Nebr Pr.

Pluto, Terry. Tall Tales: The Glory Years of the NBA, in the Words of the Men Who Played, Coached, & Built Pro Basketball. (Illus.). 384p. 1992. 23.00 (0-671-74279-5) S&S Trade.

— Tall Tales: The Glory Years of the NBA, in the Words of the Men Who Played, Coached, & Built Pro Basketball. 400p. 1994. pap. 12.00 (0-671-89937-6, Fireside) S&S Trade Pap.

— When All the World Was Browns Town. LC 97-14358. (Illus.). 320p. 1997. 24.50 (0-684-82246-6) S&S Trade.

Pluto, Terry, jt. auth. see Glass, Bill.

Pluto, Terry, jt. auth. see Kerr, Johnny.

***Plutschow, Herbert.** The Tea Master: A Biography of Soshitsu Sen XV. (Illus.). 2000. 35.00 (0-8348-0429-8) Weatherhill.

Plutschow, Herbert E. Chaos & Cosmos: Ritual in Early & Medieval Japanese Literature. LC 89-9761. (Japanese Studies Library: Vol. 1). xii, 284p. 1990. 94.50 (90-04-08628-5) Brill Academic Pubs.

— Introducing Kyoto. LC 79-51164. (Illus.). 72p. 1979. 28.00 (0-87011-384-4) Kodansha.

— Introducing Kyoto. LC 79-51164. (Illus.). 72p. 1989. 18.00 (0-87011-904-4) Kodansha.

— Japan's Name Culture: The Significance of Names in a Religious, Political & Social Context. (Japan Library). 256p. (C). 1995. text 55.00 (1-873410-42-5, Pub. by Curzon Pr Ltd) UH Pr.

— Matsuri: The Festivals of Japan: With a Selection from P. G. O'Neill's Photographic Archive of Matsuri. (Japan Library). 320p. (C). 1996. text 52.00 (1-873410-63-8, Pub. by Curzon Pr Ltd) UH Pr.

Plutzik, Hyam. Hyam Plutzik: The Collected Poems. (American Poets Continuum Ser.: No. 13). 313p. 1987. 30.00 (0-918526-54-X) BOA Edns.

— Hyam Plutzik: The Collected Poems. 313p. 1987. pap. 15.00 (0-918526-55-8) BOA Edns.

Pluvier, Jan M. Historical Atlas of South-East Asia. (Handbuch der Orientalistik. 3. Abteilung. Indonesien, Malaysia und die Philippinen: Band 8). (Illus.). 84 + 64p. 1995. 167.00 (90-04-10238-8) Brill Academic Pubs.

Pluvinel, Antoine De, see De Pluvinel, Antoine.

Pluymen, Bert. The Thinking Person's Guide to Sobriety. 248p. (Orig.). 1996. pap. 14.95 (1-880092-40-9) Bright Bks TX.

— The Thinking Person's Guide to Sobriety. LC 98-43649. (Orig.). 1999. text 23.95 (0-312-20034-X) St Martin.

***Pluymen, Bert.** The Thinking Person's Guide to Sobriety. (Orig.). 2000. pap., student ed. 13.95 (0-312-25428-8) St Martin.

Pluyter-Wenting, Elly S., ed. see International Conference on Nursing Use of Compute.

Pluzhnikova, G., jt. auth. see Kalashnikova, N.

Plvan. Language & Power. 2000. pap. 36.56 (0-07-235048-2) McGraw.

Plvar, William H. & Bruss, Robert J. California Real Estate Law. 3rd ed. LC 96-44158. 528p. 1997. 39.95 (0-7931-2495-6, 1523-023A) Dearborn Res.

Ply, Mary S. & Winchell, Donna H. Writer Audience Subject. (C). 1997. text 30.00 (0-673-18325-4) Addson-Wesley Educ.

Plyatskii, V. M. Extrusion Casting. LC 65-29302. (Illus.). 316p. 1965. 39.50 (0-911184-06-6) Primary.

Plykkanen. Search for Meaning: The Spirit in Science & Philosophy. 1988. pap. text 15.95 (1-85274-061-2, Pub. by Crucible Pr) Cavendish Bks.

Plymale, Sallie H. Teacher's Manual for West Virginia: Our State 2000 C. E. Rowley, James W., ed. (Illus.). 1997. pap., teacher ed. 25.00 (0-914498-15-0) WV Hist Ed Found.

Plymale, Steven F. The Prayer-Texts of Luke Acts. LC 91-18623. (American University Studies: Theology & Religion: Ser. VII, Vol. 118). 134p. (C). 1992. text 35.95 (0-8204-1658-4) P Lang Pubng.

Plymat, William, Jr. Victorian Architecture of Iowa. 2nd ed. (Illus.). 144p. 1997. 45.00 (0-9661440-1-5); pap. 25.00 (0-9661440-0-7) Palladian Pub.

***Plymell, Charles.** Hand on the Doorknob: A Charles Plymell Reader. Breithaupt, David, ed. LC 98-54825. 250p. 2000. pap. 15.95 (0-934953-59-7) Water Row Pr.

— Hand on the Doorknob: A Charles Plymell Reader. Breithaupt, David, ed. LC 98-54825. (Illus.). 250p. 2000. 27.00 (0-934953-63-5) Water Row Pr.

Plymell, Charles. The Last of the Moccasins. 1995. 20.00 (0-9636829-8-9); pap. 12.00 (0-9636829-7-0) Mother Road.

Plymen, Roger & Robinson, Paul. Spinors in Hilbert Space. (Tracts in Mathematics Ser.: No. 114). 179p. (C). 1995. text 49.95 (0-521-45022-5) Cambridge U Pr.

Plymen, Roger J., jt. ed. see Baker, Andrew J.

Plymouth County Heritage Book Committee. Plymouth County Heritage. LC 97-76566. 216 p. 1998. write for info. (1-890105-03-1) Taylor Publishing.

Plymouth Historical Society Staff. Plymouth. LC 98-86584. (Images of America Ser.). 1997. pap. 16.99 (0-7524-0518-7) Arcadia Publng.

Plymouth Press Staff. Vintage Airliners. 1998. 9.95 (1-882663-19-5) Plymouth VT.

***Plympton, Bill.** Mutant Aliens. (Illus.). 192p. 2000. pap. 10.95 (1-56163-236-8) NBM.

Plympton, Bill. The Sleazy Cartoons of Bill Plympton. (Illus.). 80p. 1996. pap. 15.00 (0-9652075-0-1) B Plympton.

— Tube Strips. 1976. pap. 100.00 (0-918266-04-1) Smyrna.

— Tube Strips. LC NC1429.P59. (Illus.). 35p. 1976. reprint ed. pap. 30.00 (0-7837-9092-9, 204984200003) Bks Demand.

— We Eat Tonight! The Bizarre Cartoons of Bill Plympton. (Illus.). 128p. 1998. pap. 5.95 (0-9652075-1-X) B Plympton.

Plympton, Tia. Homeless Youth Creating Their Own "Street Family" rev. ed. LC 96-46671. (Children of Poverty Ser.). 110p. 1997. text 34.00 (0-8153-2616-5) Garland.

PMA, Ltd. Staff. Contracts & Agreements. 156p. 1991. pap. text 80.00 (0-8403-6728-7) Kendall-Hunt.

Pma, Ltd. Staff. Executive Management Salary Survey, 1991. 208p. 1991. pap. text 225.00 (0-8403-7052-0) Kendall-Hunt.

PMA, Ltd. Staff. Human Resources Survey: Exclusively for Design Firms. 96p. 1991. pap. text 160.00 (0-8403-6812-7) Kendall-Hunt.

P'Malley, Sarah A., jt. auth. see Eimer, Robert D.

PMI Standards Committee. A Guide to the Project Management Body of Knowledge. 176p. 1996. 44.95 (1-880410-13-3); pap. 32.95 (1-880410-12-5) Proj Mgmt Inst.

Pneuma. Husband 101: Everything Your Wife Wished You Already Knew. 1997. pap. 6.99 (1-56229-116-5) Pneuma Life Pub.

— Wife 101: Everything Your Husband Wished You Already Knew. 1997. pap. 6.99 (1-56229-117-3) Pneuma Life Pub.

Pneuma Life Publishing Staff. Gods Practical Instruction Mny; 1997. pap. text 5.99 (1-56229-109-2) Pneuma Life Pub.

— Gods Practical Instruction Mrg; 1997. pap. text 5.99 (1-56229-108-4) Pneuma Life Pub.

Pnevmatikos, S. N., et al. Singular Behavior & Non-Linear Dynamics, 2 vols., I. 742p. (C). 1989. text 143.00 (9971-5-0895-8) World Scientific Pub.

— Singular Behavior & Non-Linear Dynamics, 2 vols., Set. 742p. 1989. text 113.00 (9971-5-0896-6) World Scientific Pub.

Pnevmatikos, S. N., ed. see Abdullaev, Fatkhulla K., et al.

Png, Ivan. Managerial Economics. LC 97-12043. 700p. 1997. 78.95 (1-55786-927-8) Blackwell Pubs.

Pnueli, A., jt. auth. see Manna, Zohar.

Pnueli, Amir, jt. auth. see Manna, Zohar.

Pnueli, David & Gutfinger, Chaim. Fluid Mechanics. (Illus.). 496p. (C). 1992. text 69.95 (0-521-41704-X) Cambridge U Pr.

— Fluid Mechanics. (Illus.). 496p. 1997. pap. text 37.95 (0-521-58797-2) Cambridge U Pr.

Po, Alain L. Dictionary of Evidence-Based Medicine. LC 99-170133. 163p. 1998. pap. 29.93 (1-85775-305-4, Radcliffe Med Pr) Scovill Paterson.

Po-Chia Hsia, R. & Lehmann, Hartmut, eds. In & Out of the Ghetto: Jewish-Gentile Relations in Late Medieval & Early Modern Germany. (Publications of the German Historical Insitute, Washington, D.C.). (Illus.). 352p. (C). 1995. text 80.00 (0-521-47064-1) Cambridge U Pr.

Po-Fei, Huang P., jt. auth. see Stimson, Hugh M.

Po-jen, Sung. Guide to Capturing a Plum Blossom. Pine, Red, tr. from CHI. (Illus.). 224p. (Orig.). 1995. pap. 14.95 (1-56279-077-3) Mercury Hse Inc.

Po-Yee, Iris W., jt. ed. see Sinclair, Kevin.

Poag, C. Wylie. Chesapeake Invader: Discovering America's Giant Meteorite Crater. LC 99-24115. (Illus.). 162p. 1999. 24.95 (0-691-00919-8, Pub. by Princeton U Pr) Cal Prin Full Svc.

Poag, James F. Wolfram von Eschenbach. LC 73-187627. (Twayne's World Authors Ser.). 136p. (C). 1972. lib. bdg. 17.95 (0-8290-1750-X) Irvington.

Poage, Bettyjane. The Guide to Psychic Awareness. 163p. (Orig.). 1989. pap. 12.50 (0-9625501-0-8) Parapsychology Pr.

Poage, Godfrey. In Garments All Red. 45p. 1996. 2.25 (0-911988-17-3, 42173) AMI Pr.

— St. Maria Goretti: In Garments All Red. LC 97-62521. (Illus.). xxvi, 86p. 1998. pap. 6.00 (0-89555-615-4, 1540) TAN Bks Pubs.

Poage, Greg A., jt. auth. see Moffat, Donald W.

Poage, James & Landis, Carolyn P. Contracting for Computing: A Checklist of Terms & Clauses for Use in Contracting with Vendors for Software Packages & Custom Software, Vol. II. 148p. 1975. 16.00 (0-318-14014-4); 9.00 (0-318-14015-2) EDUCOM.

Poage, M. Latam Liitellghi (Letter Recognition) rev. ed. (ESK., Illus.). 59p. (J). 1983. pap., wbk. ed. 4.50 (0-933769-89-X) Alaska Native.

Poage, Melvin L., et al. Critical Thinking Approach to Beginning Algebra. (Review Sequence in Mathematics of MTE Ser.). (Illus.). x, 298p. 1989. text 28.00 (1-888679-02-6, 5300) MTE.

— Critical Thinking Approach to Beginning Algebra. 2nd rev. ed. (Review Sequence in Mathematics of MTE Ser.). (Illus.). xii, 314p. 1994. text 30.00 (1-888679-03-4, 6300) MTE.

— Critical Thinking Approach to Competency Arithmetic. 2nd rev. ed. (Review Sequence in Mathematics of MTE Ser.). (Illus.). x, 195p. 1996. pap. text 16.00 (1-888679-00-X, 6100) MTE.

— Critical Thinking Approach to Geometric & Measurement Topics. (Review Sequence in Mathematics of MTE Ser.). (Illus.). viii, 254p. (Orig.). 1988. pap. text 16.00 (1-888679-01-8, 5200) MTE.

— Critical Thinking Approach to Pre-Calculus. (Review Sequence in Mathematics of MTE Ser.). (Illus.). xii, 405p. 1990. text 35.00 (1-888679-06-9, 5500) MTE.

Poage, Michael. The Gospel of Mary: Poems. Low, Denise, ed. 85p. 1997. pap. 7.00 (0-939391-23-6) B Woodley Pr.

Poage, Waller S. The Building Professional's Guide to Contract Documents. 375p. 1991. 64.95 (0-87629-210-4, 67261) R S Means.

Poague, Leland. Another Frank Capra. (Cambridge Studies in Film). (Illus.). 304p. (C). 1995. text 64.95 (0-521-38066-9) Cambridge U Pr.

Poague, Leland & Parsons, Kathy A. Susan Sontag. LC 99-33532. (Bibliographies of Modern Critics & Critical Schools Ser.). 2000. text 29.00 (0-8240-5731-7) Garland.

Poague, Leland, jt. auth. see Cadbury, William.

Poague, Leland, jt. ed. see Deutelbaum, Marshall.

Poague, Leland, ed. see Sontag, Susan.

Poague, William T. Gunner with Stonewall: Reminiscences of W. T. Poague. Cockrell, Monroe F., ed. (Illus.). 181p. 1989. reprint ed. 30.00 (0-916107-26-4) Broadfoot.

— Gunner with Stonewall: Reminiscences of William Thomas Poague. Cockrell, Monroe F., ed. LC 98-8000. (Illus.). 240p. 1998. pap. 12.00 (0-8032-8753-4, POAGUX) U of Nebr Pr.

***Poane, Robert.** Troubleshooting Back Pain: A Manual & Self-Help Guide for Care of the Spine. (Illus.). 150p. 1999. 14.95 (0-9671841-0-X) Gentle Pr MD.

Poarch, Candice. The Essence of Love. 1998. 4.99 (0-7860-0567-X) Kensgtn Pub Corp.

— Intimate Secrets. 1999. mass mkt. 4.99 (1-58314-033-6) BET Bks.

***Poarch, Candice.** Tender Escape. (Arabesque Ser.). 256p. 2000. mass mkt. 5.99 (1-58314-082-4, Arabesq) BET Bks.

An Asterisk (*) at the beginning of an entry indicates that the title is appearing for the first time.

Poarch, Candice. White Lightning. 288p. 1997. mass mkt. 4.99 (*0-7860-0365-0*, Pinncle Kensgtn) Kensgtn Pub Corp.
— With This Kiss. (Arabesque Ser.). 320p. 1998. mass mkt. 4.99 (*0-7860-0474-6*, Pinncle Kensgtn) Kensgtn Pub Corp.
Poarch, Candice & Sims, Janice. Love Letters. 288p. 1997. mass mkt. 4.99 (*0-7860-0366-9*, Pinncle Kensgtn) Kensgtn Pub Corp.
Poate, C. D. & Daplyn, P. F. Data for Agrarian Development. LC 92-22831. (Wye Studies in Agricultural & Rural Development). (Illus.). 397p. (C). 1993. text 95.00 (*0-521-36566-X*) Cambridge U Pr.
— Data for Agrarian Development. LC 92-22831. (Wye Studies in Agricultural & Rural Development). (Illus.). 397p. (C). 1993. pap. text 34.95 (*0-521-36758-1*) Cambridge U Pr.
Poate, John M., et al, eds. Laser-Solid Interactions & Laser Processing, 1978: Materials Research Society, Boston. LC 79-51564. (AIP Conference Proceedings Ser.: No. 50). (Illus.). 1979. lib. bdg. 26.00 (*0-88318-149-5*) Am Inst Physics.
Poate, John M. & Fan, J. C., eds. Heteroepitaxy on Silicon. (MRS Symposium Proceedings Ser.: Vol. 67). 1986. text 17.50 (*0-931837-33-2*) Materials Res.
Poate, John M., ed. see Electrochemical Society, Thin Film Phenomena-Inter.
Poate, John M., ed. see Symposium on Thin Film Interfaces & Interactions.
Poatgieter, A. Hermina, tr. see Lewis, Henry.
Poats, Susan V., jt. ed. see Feldstein, Hilary S.
Pobee, John S. Who Are the Poor? The Beatitudes As a Call to Community. (Risk Bks.: No. 32). 74p. (Orig.). 1987. pap. 5.50 (*2-8254-0884-0*) Wrld Coun Churches.
Pobee, John S. & Von Wartenberg-Potter, Barbel, eds. New Eyes for Reading: Biblical & Theological Reflections by Women from the Third World. LC 86-211225. 116p. (Orig.). reprint ed. pap. 36.00 (*0-7837-6000-0*, 204581000008) Bks Demand.
Pobee, John S., jt. ed. see Amirtham, Samuel.
Pobell, F. Matter & Methods at Low Temperatures. 319p. 1992. 79.00 (*0-387-53751-1*) Spr-Verlag.
Poberezny, Paul H., ed. Flying & Glider Manual, 1931. (Flying & Gliding Ser.). (Illus.). 80p. reprint ed. pap. 6.95 (*0-940000-84-9*, 21-14169) EAA Aviation.
— Flying Manual, 1932. LC 21-14170. (Flying & Gliding Ser.). (Illus.). 75p. reprint ed. pap. 5.95 (*0-940000-85-7*) EAA Aviation.
— Flying Manual, 1933. LC 21-14171. (Flying & Gliding Ser.). (Illus.). 75p. reprint ed. pap. 5.95 (*0-940000-86-5*) EAA Aviation.
Poberezny, Paul H., intro. Flying & Glider Manual, 1930. (Flying & Gliding Ser.). (Illus.). 80p. reprint ed. pap. 6.95 (*0-940000-83-0*, 21-14168) EAA Aviation.
Poberezny, Paul H. & Schmid, S. H., eds. Aircraft Welding Manual. rev. ed. (How to Aircraft Building Ser.). (Illus.). 94p. 1991. pap. 16.95 (*0-940000-49-0*) EAA Aviation.
— Custom Built Sport Aircraft Handbook: A Guide to Construction Standards for the Amateur Aircraft Builder. rev. ed. (Illus.). 132p. 1991. pap. 21.95 (*0-940000-43-1*) EAA Aviation.
— Wood: Aircraft Building Techniques. rev. ed. (EAA How to Ser.). (Illus.). 140p. 1991. pap. 11.95 (*0-940000-44-X*) EAA Aviation.
Poberezny, Paul H., et al. Poberezny: The Story Begins . . . LC 96-92890. (Illus.). 350p. 1997. 24.95 (*0-9655654-0-8*) Red One Pub.
— Poberezny: The Story Begins . . . limited ed. LC 96-92890. (Illus.). 350p. 1997. lthr. 46.95 (*0-9655654-1-6*) Red One Pub.
Pobil, Angel P. & Serna, Miguel A., eds. Spatial Representation & Motion Planning. LC 95-46103. (Lecture Notes in Computer Science Ser.: Vol. 1014). 242p. 1995. 49.00 (*3-540-60620-3*) Spr-Verlag.
Pobil, Angel P. Del, see Del Pobil, Angel P.
Poblador, Niceto S. The Economics of the Firm: Managerial Applications. 560p. 1997. pap. text 40.00 (*971-542-088-5*, Pub. by U of Philippines Pr) UH Pr.
Poblome, J., jt. auth. see Waelkens, M.
Poblome, J., jt. ed. see Waelkens, M.
Pobo, Ken. Yes, Irises. 32p. 1992. pap. 4.00 (*1-880286-08-4*) Singular Speech Pr.
Pobst, Dick. Trout Stream Insects: An Orvis Streamside Guide. 96p. 1991. pap. 16.95 (*1-55821-067-9*) Lyons Pr.
Pobst, Dick & Richards, Carl. The Caddisfly Handbook: An Orvis Guide. LC 98-8201. (Illus.). 128p. 1999. pap. 16.95 (*1-55821-542-5*) Lyons Pr.
Pobst, Phyllis E., ed. The Register of William Bateman, Bishop of Norwich, 1344-1355, Vol. I. (Canterbury & York Society Ser.: Vol. 84). 168p. 1996. 55.00 (*0-907239-54-4*) Boydell & Brewer.
***Pobst, Phyllis E., ed.** The Register of William Bateman, Bishop of Norwich, 1344-55 Vol. II: Norwich. (Canterbury & York Society Ser.: No. 90). 256p. 2000. 45.00 (*0-907239-60-9*, Canterbury & York Soc) Boydell & Brewer.
Pobst, Richard. Fish the Impossible Places. (Illus.). 1974. 9.95 (*0-88395-025-1*) Freshet Pr.
Poccia, Dominic. Molecular Aspects of Spermatogenesis. 155p. 1994. 94.00 (*1-57059-204-7*, LN9204) CRC Pr.
Poceski, A. Mixed Finite Element Method. (Lecture Notes in Engineering Ser.: Vol. 72). (Illus.). 352p. 1992. 100.95 (*0-387-54916-1*) Spr-Verlag.
Poceta, J. Steven & Mitler, Merrill M. Sleep Disorders: Diagnosis & Treatment. LC 98-16257. (Current Clinical Practice Ser.). (Illus.). 250p. 1998. 79.50 (*0-89603-527-1*) Humana.
Poch. Simulation: Principles & Methods. 2nd ed. 1992. write for info. (*0-318-69402-6*, CRC Reprint) Franklin.
Poch, Gerald. Combined Effects of Drugs & Toxic Agents: Modern Evaluation in Theorie & Practice. LC 92-43470. 1993. 57.95 (*0-387-82434-0*); write for info. (*3-211-82434-0*) Spr-Verlag.
Poch, M. Clementine. Always & Forever: The Life & Times of Mother Franciska Lechner. 224p. (Orig.). 1994. pap. text 12.95 (*1-883520-04-5*) Jeremiah Pr.
Poch, Pompeu F. Dictionary of the Catalan Language: Diccionari Manual de la Llengua Catalana. 9th ed. (CAT & ENG.). 1360p. 1991. 49.95 (*0-7859-4960-7*) Fr & Eur.
— General Dictionary of the Catalan Language: Diccionari General de la Llengua Catalana. 26th ed. (CAT.). 1826p. 1991. write for info. (*0-7859-4959-3*) Fr & Eur.
Poch, Robert K. Academic Freedom in American Higher Education: Rights, Responsibilities & Limitations. Fife, Jonathan D., ed. & frwd. by. (ASHE-ERIC Higher Education Reports: No. 94-4). 85p. (Orig.). 1994. pap. 24.00 (*1-878380-25-7*) GWU Grad Schl E&HD.
Pocha, J. J. An Introduction to Mission Design for Geostationary Satellites. (C). 1987. text 120.50 (*90-277-2479-2*) Kluwer Academic.
Pochat, Goetz. Figur und Landschaft. Historische Interpretation der Landschaftsmalerei von der Antike bis zur Renaissance. LC 72-87564. (Illus.). 560p. (C). 1973. 296.15 (*3-11-004104-9*) De Gruyter.
Poche, David J., jt. auth. see Fichter, Lynn.
Poche, Henry Z. Medical Biology of Yohimbine & Its Easy Use in Male Sex Erectile Dysfunction: Index of New Information with Authors, Subjects, Research Categories & References. 167p. 1997. 47.50 (*0-7883-1590-0*); pap. 44.50 (*0-7883-1591-9*) ABBE Pubs Assn.
Poche, Michelle, jt. auth. see Hilburn, Mari.
Pochedly, Carl, ed. Acute Childhood Leukemia. (Modern Problems in Pediatrics Ser.: Vol. 16). (Illus.). viii, 214p. 1975. 81.75 (*3-8055-2065-4*) S Karger.
— Childhood Lymphoblastic Leukemia. LC 85-9331. 237p. 1985. 62.95 (*0-275-90048-7*, C0048, Praeger Pubs) Greenwood.
— Neuroblastoma: Tumor Biology & Therapy. 432p. 1990. lib. bdg. 159.00 (*0-8493-0157-2*, RC280) CRC Pr.
— Non-Lymphoid Leukemias in Children. 256p. 1985. 45.00 (*0-275-90009-6*, C0009, Praeger Pubs) Greenwood.
— Reviews in Pediatric Hem-Oncology VI. LC 85-9547. 218p. 1985. 57.95 (*0-275-91306-6*, C1306, Praeger Pubs) Greenwood.
Pochedly, Carl, et al, eds. Neoplastic Diseases in Childhood, 2 vol., Set. LC 93-12664. 1600p. 1995. text 473.00 (*3-7186-5340-0*) Gordon & Breach.
Pochedly, Carl, jt. ed. see Stockman, James A., 3rd.
Pochedly, Carl, jt. ed. see Zeltzer, Paul M.
Pocher, Don & Pocher, Pat. Cape May in Vintage Postcards. (Images of America Ser.). (Illus.). 128p. 1998. pap. 16.99 (*0-7524-0856-9*) Arcadia Publng.
Pocher, Pat, jt. auth. see Pocher, Don.
Pochet, Michel. Sex Redeemed. 64p. 1991. pap. 6.95 (*0-904287-31-9*) New City.
***Pochet, Philippe, ed.** Monetary Union & Collective Bargaining in Europe. (Work & Society Ser.: Vol. 22). 288p. 2000. pap. 27.95 (*0-8204-4653-X*) P Lang Pubng.
***Pochet, Philippe & Vanhercke, Bart, eds.** Les Enjeux Sociaux de L'union Economique et Monetaire: Actes du Colloque Organise par L'observatoire Social Europeen, avec le Soutien du Ministere Belge des Affaires Sociales, de la Sante Publique et de L'environnement, en Collaboration avec le Ministere Finlandais des Affaires Sociales et de la Sante. 2nd ed. (Travail & Societe Ser.). (Illus.). 185p. 1999. 24.95 (*90-5201-904-5*, Pub. by College of Europe) P Lang Pubng.
Pochet, R., et al, eds. Calcium Binding Proteins in Normal & Transformed Cells. LC 90-6704. (Advances in Experimental Medicine & Biology Ser.: Vol. 269). (Illus.). 224p. (C). 1990. text 102.00 (*0-306-43491-1*, Kluwer Plenum) Kluwer Academic.
***Pochet, Roland.** Calcium: The Molecular Basis of Calcium Action in Biology & Medicine. LC 00-42406. (Illus.). 2000. write for info. (*0-7923-6421-X*) Kluwer Academic.
Pochi Yeh. Photorefractive Nonlinear Optics. 400p. 1995. text 86.00 (*981-02-1443-X*) World Scientific Pub.
Pochiluk, William. Autofacts 1997 Yearbook. Benko, Chris, ed. 1997. text 595.00 (*1-887363-02-5*) AUTOFACTS Intl.
— Autofacts Yearbook, 1991, Vol. 1. Nash, David, ed. 625p. 1991. text 495.00 (*1-879800-00-4*) Autofacts.
— Autofacts Yearbook, 1993, 2 vols., Set. 1993. text 595.00 (*0-9637549-0-4*) AUTOFACTS Intl.
— Autofacts Yearbook, 1993, 2 vols., Vols. 1-2. 1993. text 595.00 (*0-9637549-1-2*); text 595.00 (*0-9637549-2-0*) AUTOFACTS Intl.
— Autofacts Yearbook, 1994, Set. Benko, Christopher, ed. 1125p. 1994. text 595.00 (*0-9637549-5-5*) AUTOFACTS Intl.
— Autofacts Yearbook, 1994, Vol. 1. Benko, Christopher, ed. 525p. 1994. text 595.00 (*0-9637549-3-9*) AUTOFACTS Intl.
— Autofacts Yearbook, 1994, Vol. 2. Benko, Christopher, ed. 600p. 1994. text 595.00 (*0-9637549-4-7*) AUTOFACTS Intl.
— Autofacts Yearbook, 1996. Benko, Christopher, ed. 1115p. 1996. text 595.00 (*1-887363-01-7*) AUTOFACTS Intl.
— Autofacts Yearbook, 1996, Vol. 1. Benko, Christopher, ed. 525p. 1996. text 595.00 (*0-9637549-9-8*) AUTOFACTS Intl.
— Autofacts Yearbook, 1996, Vol. 2. Benko, Christopher, ed. 490p. 1996. text 595.00 (*1-887363-00-9*) AUTOFACTS Intl.
— Autofacts, 1995: Yearbook, Vol. 1. Ruhl, Mary, ed. 525p. 1995. text 595.00 (*0-9637549-7-1*) AUTOFACTS Intl.
— Autofacts, 1995: Yearbook, Vol. 2. Ruhl, Mary, ed. 490p. 1995. text 595.00 (*0-9637549-8-X*) AUTOFACTS Intl.
— Autofacts, 1995: Yearbook, 2 vols., Vols. 1-2. Ruhl, Mary, ed. 1115p. 1995. text 595.00 (*0-9637549-6-3*) AUTOFACTS Intl.
Pochiluk, William & Nash, David. Autofacts Yearbook, 1992. 1000p. 1992. text 495.00 (*1-879800-01-2*) Autofacts.
— Autofacts Yearbook, 1992, Vol. 1. 480p. 1992. text 495.00 (*1-879800-02-0*) Autofacts.
Pochin, Edward E. Nuclear Radiation: Risks & Benefits. (Monographs on Science, Technology & Society). (Illus.). 204p. 1985. pap. text 18.95 (*0-19-858337-0*) OUP.
— Why Be Quantitative about Radiation Risk Estimates? LC 78-61402. (Taylor Lectures: No. 2). 1978. 20.00 (*0-913392-42-1*) NCRP Pubns.
Pochin-Mould, Daphne P. Irish Pilgrimage. 1957. 12.95 (*0-8159-5816-1*) Devin.
Pochmann, Gunter. Controlling - Information im Derivativbereich: Dargestellt am Beispiel von Zinsbezogenen Optionen. (GER., Illus.). XLVIII, 333p. 1996. 64.95 (*3-631-30107-3*) P Lang Pubng.
Pochmann, Henry A. German Culture in America: Philosophical & Literary Influences 1600-1900. LC 78-5337. 865p. 1978. reprint ed. lib. bdg. 93.50 (*0-313-20378-4*, POGC, Greenwood Pr) Greenwood.
— New England Transcendentalism & St. Louis Hegelianism. LC 68-55163. (Studies in Comparative Literature: No. 35). 1969. reprint ed. lib. bdg. 75.00 (*0-8383-0610-1*) M S G Haskell Hse.
— Washington Irving. 1988. reprint ed. lib. bdg. 75.00 (*0-7812-0193-4*) Rprt Serv.
Pochmann, Henry A., ed. see Irving, Washington.
Pochmuller, W., jt. auth. see Glesner, Manfred.
Pochna, Marie-France. Christian Dior: The Man Who Made the World Look New. Savill, Joanna, tr. from FRE. LC 96-13219. 320p. 1996. 25.45 (*1-55970-340-7*, Pub. by Arcade Pub Inc) Time Warner.
— Christian Dior: The Man Who Made the World Look New. Savill, Joanna, tr. from FRE. LC 96-13219. (Illus.). 336p. 1997. pap. 15.45 (*1-55970-397-0*, Pub. by Arcade Pub Inc) Time Warner.
— Dior. (Illus.). 80p. 1996. text 18.95 (*0-7893-0065-6*) St Martin.
Pochna, N. F. Dior. (Fashion Memoir Ser.). (Illus.). 1996. 24.00 (*0-500-01721-2*) Thames Hudson.
Pochocki, Ethel. The Adventures of Pilaf, Almondine, & Tetrazzini. (Illus.). 48p. (Orig.). (J). (gr. 3-6). 1994. pap. 9.95 (*1-880812-09-6*) S Ink WA.
— More Once upon a Time Saints. LC 97-77144. (Golden Key Bks.). (Illus.). 96p. (J). (ps up). 1998. pap. 9.95 (*1-883937-34-5*, 34-5) Bethlehem ND.
— Once upon a Time Saints. rev. ed. LC 96-83473. (Golden Key Bks.). (Illus.). 96p. (J). (gr. 1 up). 1996. pap. 9.95 (*1-883937-15-9*, 15-9) Bethlehem ND.
— A Penny for a Hundred. LC 96-30287. (Illus.). 32p. (J). (gr. 3-6). 1996. 14.95 (*0-89272-392-0*) Down East.
***Pochocki, Ethel.** Rosebud & Red Flannel. LC 99-35563. (Illus.). 32p. (YA). 1999. 14.95 (*0-89272-474-9*) Down East.
Pochocki, Ethel. Saints & Heroes for Kids. (Illus.). 223p. (J). 1994. pap. 10.95 (*0-86716-194-9*) St Anthony Mess Pr.
— Saints of the Seasons for Children. (Illus.). 280p. (J). (gr. k-6). 1997. pap. 15.95 (*0-86716-319-4*, B3194) St Anthony Mess Pr.
— Soup Pot: Stories for All Seasons for Children of All Ages. (Illus.). 112p. (Orig.). 1996. pap. 8.95 (*1-878718-33-9*, Resurrection Pr) Catholic Bk Pub.
— The Wind Harp & Other Angel Tales. LC 95-199933. (Illus.). 136p. 1995. pap. 7.95 (*0-86716-255-4*) St Anthony Mess Pr.
***Pochocki, Ethel & LaGue, Peter.** The Mistletoe Girl & Other Christmas Stories. LC 99-48856. (Illus.). 64p. 1999. 15.95 (*0-939516-47-0*) Forest Peace.
Pochop, L. O., jt. auth. see Burman, R. D.
Pochta, Kiiu. M., jt. auth. see Kirabaev, N. S.
Pocius, Alphonsus V. Adhesion & Adhesive Technology: An Introduction. LC 96-31003. 1996. 89.00 (*1-56990-212-7*) Hanser-Gardner.
Pocius, Gerald L. A Place to Belong: Community Order & Everyday Space in Calvert, Newfoundland. 384p. 1991. text 29.95 (*0-7735-0805-8*) McG-Queens Univ Pr.
Pock, Max A. Consolidating Police Functions in Metropolitan Areas. LC 62-64274. (Michigan Legal Publications). v, 51p. 1985. reprint ed. lib. bdg. 35.00 (*0-89941-384-6*, 303540) W S Hein.
— Independent Special Districts: A Solution to the Metropolitan Area Problems. LC 62-63903. (Michigan Legal Publications). vii, 193p. 1985. reprint ed. lib. bdg. 36.00 (*0-89941-385-4*, 303550) W S Hein.
Pockell, ed. see Kodansha International Staff.
Pockell, ed. see Lifton, Betty J.
***Pocket Books Staff.** Are You Afraid of the Dark: Movie Novelization. (J). 1999. pap. 3.99 (*0-671-00904-4*, Pocket Books) PB.
— Full House Stephanie Boxed Set: Getting Even with the Flamingos; the Dude of My Dreams; Back to School; Picture Me Famous, 4 vols. (Full House Stephanie Ser.). (Illus.). (J). (gr. 4-6). 1996. pap., boxed set 15.96 (*0-671-85161-6*, Minstrel Bks) PB.
— Great Pet Project/Super Duper Sleepover Party/My Two Best Friends/Lucky, Lucky Day, 4 bks. (Illus.). (J). (gr. 8-12). 1996. boxed set 14.00 (*0-671-85162-4*) PB.
— Millennium Madness: Super Edition. (Sabrina, the Teenage Witch Ser.: Vol. 29). 368p. (J). (gr. 7-12). 2000. per. 4.99 (*0-671-02820-0*, Archway) PB.
— Official Postcard Book. (Illus.). 1998. pap. 8.00 (*0-671-02672-0*) PB.
— Operation Stormbird: Into the Neutral Zone. (Star Trek: The Next Generation Ser.). 2000. per. 16.00 (*0-671-03502-9*) PB.
Pocket Books Staff. Secret World of Alex Mack: Alex, You're Growing!/Are You Afraid of the Dark?... (Nick in a Box Ser.). 1996. pap. text 11.97 (*0-671-85165-9*) PB.
— Space Cases 2. (J). 1997. mass mkt. 3.99 (*0-671-00809-9*) PB.
Pocket Books Staff, ed. America's Favorite National Parks. 1988. 5.95 (*0-671-84591-8*) PB.
— Are You Afraid of the Dark. (Nickelodeon Ser.: No. 11). (J). (ps-1). 1996. pap. 3.99 (*0-671-00082-9*, Minstrel Bks) PB.
— Camp Colorado. (Camp U. S. A. Ser.). (Illus.). 80p. (Orig.). 1988. pap. 3.95 (*0-528-88275-9*) S&S Trade.
— Camp Fishmen West. 1988. mass mkt. 5.95 (*0-671-84721-X*) PB.
— Camp U. S. A. California. 1988. mass mkt. 3.95 (*0-671-88240-6*) PB.
— Camp U. S. A. Colorado. 1988. 3.95 (*0-671-88275-9*) PB.
— Camp U. S. A. Florida. 1988. 3.95 (*0-671-88241-4*) PB.
— Camp U. S. A. Texas. 1988. 3.95 (*0-671-88242-2*) PB.
— Camp U. S. A. Wisconsin. 1988. 3.95 (*0-671-88269-4*) PB.
— Camp Wisconsin. (Camp U. S. A. Ser.). (Illus.). 80p. (Orig.). 1988. pap. 3.95 (*0-528-88269-4*) S&S Trade.
— Devil's Advocate. 1993. mass mkt. 5.50 (*0-671-86986-8*) PB.
— Fishing Hotspots in Wisconsin. 1988. mass mkt. 2.95 (*0-671-88272-4*) PB.
— Greece. 1988. 5.95 (*0-671-84841-0*) PB.
— Ireland. 1988. pap. 5.95 (*0-671-84840-2*) PB.
— The Kneaded Loaf. 1995. per. 8.00 (*0-671-56845-0*) PB.
— Light Years. 1988. per. 4.50 (*0-671-65875-1*) PB.
— National Park Guide. 1988. 12.95 (*0-671-88260-0*) PB.
— Paris. 1988. pap. 5.95 (*0-671-88279-1*) PB.
— Pocket Austria & Switzerland. 1988. mass mkt. 5.95 (*0-671-88280-5*) PB.
— Pocket California Goldenwest. 1988. mass mkt. 5.95 (*0-671-84894-1*) PB.
— Pocket Holland, Belguim, Luxembourg. 1988. mass mkt. 5.95 (*0-671-84842-9*) PB.
— Portugal. 1988. 5.95 (*0-671-84890-9*) PB.
— Pot of Gold. 1994. mass mkt. 6.50 (*0-671-88600-2*) PB.
— South American Handbook. 1988. pap. 28.95 (*0-671-88271-6*) PB.
— Spain. 1988. 5.95 (*0-671-84878-X*) PB.
— Spanish Synonyms & Antonyms. 1995. 25.00 (*0-671-84868-2*) PB.
***Pocket Books Staff, ed.** Star Trek Sketchbook: The Original Series. (Illus.). 1998. per. 30.00 (*0-671-71759-6*, Pocket Books) PB.
Pocket Books Staff, ed. Star Trek Voyage 1999. 1998. mass mkt. 12.00 (*0-671-01455-2*) PB.
— Venice. 1988. 5.95 (*0-671-84407-5*) PB.
Pocket Books Staff, jt. auth. see Holland, Steve.
Pocket Books Staff, ed. see Cornwell, Patricia.
Pocket Pointers, Inc. Staff. Pocket Pointers: A Quick Reminder on Any Shot. Golf Magazine Editors, ed. 1988. pap. 3.00 (*1-878728-18-0*) Golf Gifts.
Pockets Learning Staff. Birthday Cake. (Illus.). (J). (ps-1). 1998. 30.00 (*1-888074-93-0*) Pckts Lrning.
— Bunny House. (Illus.). (ps up). 1998. 35.00 (*1-888074-94-9*) Pckts Lrning.
— Christian Celebrations Book. (Illus.). 8p. (ps up). 1998. 35.00 (*1-888074-96-5*) Pckts Lrning.
— Fire Station. (Illus.). (YA). (ps-1). 1998. 35.00 (*1-888074-95-7*) Pckts Lrning.
— Lord Is My Shepherd Book. (Illus.). 8p. (ps up). 1998. 35.00 (*1-888074-99-X*) Pckts Lrning.
— Samantha's Alaska Adventure. (Illus.). 2p. (J). (ps-1). 1998. 15.00 (*1-888074-90-6*) Pckts Lrning.
— Samantha's California Adventure. (Illus.). 2p. (ps-1). 1998. 15.00 (*1-888074-91-4*) Pckts Lrning.
— Samantha's Louisiana Adventure. (Illus.). 2p. (YA). (ps-1). 1998. 15.00 (*1-888074-92-2*) Pckts Lrning.
— Victorian Advent. (Illus.). (J). 1998. 45.00 (*1-888074-68-X*) Pckts Lrning.
— Victorian Stocking. (Illus.). (J). 1998. 20.00 (*1-888074-21-3*) Pckts Lrning.
Pockets of Learning Staff. Good Samaritan Book. (Illus.). 8p. (ps up). 1998. 35.00 (*1-888074-97-3*) Pckts Lrning.
— I Can Do It Myself Book. (Illus.). 8p. (ps up). 1998. 35.00 (*1-888074-98-1*) Pckts Lrning.
Pocklington, John. Sunday No Sabbath: A Sermon. LC 74-28881. (English Experience Ser.: No. 759). 1975. reprint ed. 20.00 (*90-221-0759-0*) Walter J Johnson.
Pocknell, ed. see Kodansha International Staff.
***Pockocki, Ethel, et al.** Animus No. 2: Return. Farnsworth, Annie, ed. (Illus.). 41p. 1999. pap. 6.00 (*0-9672567-1-2*) Sheltering Pines.
Pockrand, I. Surface Enhanced Raman Vibrational Studies at Solid-Gas Interfaces. (Tracts in Modern Physics Ser.: Vol. 104). (Illus.). 160p. 1984. 56.00 (*0-387-13416-6*) Spr-Verlag.
Pocock, Arthur. Arabs & Me: My Life with Allah's Rogues (Lovable & Otherwise) LC 96-71029. (Illus.). 272p. 1998. pap. 14.50 (*0-88739-109-5*) Creat Arts Bk.
Pocock, Barbara. Demanding Skill: Women & Technology. 1989. pap. text 18.95 (*0-04-332137-2*, Pub. by Allen & Unwin Pty) Paul & Co Pubs.
Pocock, Barbara, ed. Strife: Sex & Politics in Labour Unions. LC 97-197609. 264p. 1998. pap. 29.95 (*1-86448-312-1*, Pub. by Allen & Unwin Pty) Paul & Co Pubs.
***Pocock, Chris.** The U-2 Spyplane. (Illus.). 288p. 2000. 29.95 (*0-7643-1113-1*) Schiffer.
Pocock, D. F., tr. see Durkheim, Emile.
Pocock, David F. & MacClancy, Jeremy. Understanding Social Anthropology. rev. ed. LC 98-20721. 4p. 1998. pap. 27.95 (*0-485-12140-9*, Pub. by Athlone Pr) Transaction Pubs.

P

Pocock, Gillian. Human Physiology: The Basis of Medicine. LC 98-44801. (Illus.). 646p. 1999. text (0-19-262539-X) OUP.

Pocock, Gillian & Richardson, Christopher D. Human Physiology: The Basis of Medicine. LC 98-44801. (Oxford Core Texts Ser.). (Illus.). 648p. 1999. pap. text 49.95 (0-19-262538-1) OUP.

Pocock, Guy N. Little Room. LC 68-55854. (Essay Index Reprint Ser.). 1977. 20.95 (0-8369-0794-9) Ayer.

Pocock, J. A., et al. The Varieties of British Political Thought, 1500-1800. 384p. 1996. pap. text 24.95 (0-521-57498-6) Cambridge U Pr.

***Pocock, J. G.** Barbarism & Religion, 2 vols. 824p. 2000. 90.00 (0-521-77921-9) Cambridge U Pr.

Pocock, J. G. Barbarism & Religion Vol. 1: The Enlightenments of Edward Gibbon, 1737-1764. LC 98-41114. 384p. 2000. 49.95 (0-521-63345-1) Cambridge U Pr.

— Barbarism & Religion Vol. 2: Narratives of Civil Government. 440p. 2000. 49.95 (0-521-64002-4) Cambridge U Pr.

— The Machiavellian Moment: Florentine Political Thought & the Atlantic Republican Tradition. LC 73-2490. 576p. 1975. pap. text 29.95 (0-691-10029-2, Pub. by Princeton U Pr) Cal Prin Full Svc.

— Politics, Language & Time: Essays on Political Thought & History. viii, 304p. 1989. pap. text 16.95 (0-226-67139-9) U Ch Pr.

— Virtue, Commerce & History: Essays on Political Thought & History, Chiefly in the Eighteenth Century. (Ideas in Context Ser.). 336p. 1985. text 85.00 (0-521-25701-8); pap. text 24.95 (0-521-27660-8) Cambridge U Pr.

Pocock, J. G., jt. ed. see Ball, Terence.

Pocock, J. G., ed. see Farrington, James.

Pocock, J. G., ed. & intro. see Burke, Edmund.

Pocock, J. G. A., ed. see Burke, Edmund.

Pocock, John W. Fund-Raising Leadership: A Guide for College & University Boards. (Illus.). (Orig.). 1989. 27.95 (0-318-41355-1) Assn Gov Bds.

Pocock, L. G. Sicilian Origin of the Odyssey. Scammacca, Nina & Scammacca, Nat, trs. 206p. 1986. 36.00 (0-89304-593-4); pap. 15.00 (0-89304-568-3) Cross-Cultrl NY.

Pocock, Leslie W. Comfort Ye My People. 128p. 1986. 30.00 (0-7223-2048-5, Pub. by A H S Ltd) St Mut.

Pocock, M. A., jt. auth. see Taylor, A. H.

Pocock, Marge, jt. ed. see Mower, Mavis.

Pocock, Michael, ed. see RCC Pilotage Foundation Staff.

Pocock, Nick. Did W. D. Custead Fly First? The Story of W. D. Custead of Elm Mott - Waco, Texas - Airship Builder Before the Wrights Flew. LC 74-83996. (Illus.). 1974. pap. 25.00 (0-915376-00-8); mic. film 30.00 (0-915376-01-6) Spec Aviation.

— Grumman-Schweizer AG-CAT. LC 94-69850. (Illus.). 48p. 1994. pap. 18.95 (0-915376-02-4) Spec Aviation.

Pocock, R. F. Nuclear Power, Its History. 280p. 1984. 60.00 (0-905418-15-8, Pub. by Gresham Bks) St Mut.

Pocock, R. I. Mammalia: Primates Carnivora Families Felidae & Viveridae, Vol. 1. (Fauna of British India Ser.). xxxiv, 464p. 1985. reprint ed. 50.00 (1-55528-038-2, Pub. by Today Tomorrow) Scholarly Pubns.

Pocock, Rita. Annabelle & the Big Slide. 28p. (J). (ps). 1989. 10.95 (0-15-200407-6, Gulliver Bks) Harcourt.

Pocock, Stuart J., ed. Clinical Trials: A Practical Approach. LC 83-1316. 278p. 1984. 170.00 (0-471-90155-5, Wiley-Liss) Wiley.

***Pocock, Tom.** Battle for Empire: The Very First World War 1756-63. (Illus.). 272p. 1999. pap. 14.95 (1-85479-390-X, Pub. by M OMara) Trafalgar.

Pocock, Tom. Horatio Nelson. (Pimlico Ser.). (Illus.). 364p. 1995. 16.95 (0-7126-6123-9, Pub. by Pimlico) Trafalgar.

— Norfolk. (Pimlico County History Guides Ser.). (Illus.). 192p. 1997. pap. 19.95 (0-7126-5154-3, Pub. by Pimlico) Trafalgar.

Pocs. Human Sexuality. 19th ed. 1994. 12.74 (1-56134-279-3) McGraw.

— Marriage & Family. 1994. 12.74 (1-56134-283-1) McGraw.

Pocs, Eva, et al. Between the Living & the Dead: A Perspective on Witches & Seers in the Early Modern Age. LC 98-43986. (Illus.). 250p. (C). 1998. 39.95 (963-9116-18-1); pap. 21.95 (963-9116-19-X) Ctrl Europ Univ.

Pocs, Ollie. Our Intimate Relationships: Marriage & the Family. 2nd ed. (Illus.). 577p. (C). 1994. pap. text 28.95 (0-87563-465-6) Stipes.

Pocsik, G., jt. auth. see Csikor, F.

Pocsik, G., jt. ed. see Csikor, F.

Podach, E. The Madness of Nietzsche. 1973. 250.00 (0-87968-179-9) Gordon Pr.

Podack, Eckhard R. Cytolytic Lymphocytes & Complement: Effectors of the Immune System, Vol. I. 280p. 1988. 154.00 (0-8493-6968-1, QR185, CRC Reprint) Franklin.

— Cytolytic Lymphocytes & Complement: Effectors of the Immune System, Vol. II. 256p. 1988. 141.00 (0-8493-6969-X, 6969, CRC Reprint) Franklin.

Podall, H. E., jt. ed. see Lonsdale, H. K.

Podani, J. Multivariate Analysis in Ecology & Systematics. (Ecological Computations Ser.: Vol. 6). (Illus.). 316p. 1994. 68.00 (90-5103-094-0, Pub. by SPB Acad Pub) Balogh.

Podani, J., et al, eds. Proceedings of the IAB Conference of Bryoecology, Budapest-Vacratot, Hungary, 5-10 August 1985: Budapest-Vacratot, Hungary 5-10 August, 1985. (Symposia Biologica Hungarica Ser.: No. 35). 901p. (C). 1987. 270.00 (963-05-4633-7, Pub. by Akade Kiado) St Mut.

Podanoffsky, Michael. Dissecting DOS: A Code-Level Look at the DOS Operating System. LC 93-42508. 496p. 1994. pap. 39.95 incl. disk (0-201-62687-X) Addison-Wesley.

Podany, Jerry, jt. ed. see True, Marion.

Podaras, C., tr. see Birolini, A.

Podbrey, Pauline. White Girl in Search of the Party. (Illus.). 216p. 1993. 23.00 (0-86980-904-0, Pub. by Univ Natal Pr) Intl Spec Bk.

Podczeck, Fridrun. Particle-Particle Adhesion in Pharmaceutical Powder Handling. 260p. 1998. 48.00 (1-86094-112-5, Pub. by Imperial College) World Scientific Pub.

Podd. Get Software Out on Time. (C). 2001. pap. text 39.00 (0-13-572074-5) P-H.

Podd, Marvin H. & Seelig, Donald P. Building a Neuropsychology Practice: A Guide to Respecialization. LC 97-34797. 192p. 1998. 50.00 (0-7657-0146-4) Aronson.

***Poddar, Prem, ed.** Translating Nations. (Dolphin Ser.: Vol. 30). 269p. (C). 2000. pap. 19.95 (87-7288-381-2, Pub. by Aarhus Univ Pr) David Brown.

Podder, V. Technology in Paper Industry. 586p. 1990. 200.00 (81-209-0004-9, Pub. by Pitambar Pub) St Mut.

Podeh, Elie. The Decline of Arab Unity: The Rise & Fall of the United Arab Republic. LC 99-20797. 252p. 1999. 75.00 (1-902210-20-4, Pub. by Sussex Acad Pr) Intl Spec Bk.

— The Quest for Hegemony in the Arab World: The Struggle over the Baghdad Pact. LC 95-884. (Social, Economic & Political Studies of the Middle East: Vol. 52). xii, 281p. 1995. 99.00 (90-04-10214-0) Brill Academic Pubs.

Podell. Exceptional Learners. (C). 1998. pap. text 16.36 (0-395-90258-4) HM.

Podell, Albert, jt. auth. see Stephens, Harold.

Podell, Diane K. Thematic Atlases for Public, Academic, & High School Libraries. LC 94-4326. 208p. 1994. 29.00 (0-8108-2866-9) Scarecrow.

Podell, H., et al. UNIX Security - Course Notes. (Illus.). 416p. (Orig.). (C). 1995. pap. 45.76 (0-942891-63-5) Comp Educ.

Podell, Janet, ed. Abortion. (Reference Shelf Ser.: Vol. 62, No. 4). 231p. 1990. pap. 25.00 (0-8242-0793-9) Wilson.

— Annual Obituary, 1981. 81st ed. 1982. 100.00 (0-912289-51-1) St James Pr.

— Annual Obituary, 1982. 1983. 85.00 (0-912289-01-5) St James Pr.

Podell, Janet & Anzovin, Steven, eds. Speeches of the American Presidents. 820p. 1988. 65.00 (0-8242-0761-0) Wilson.

Podell, Janet, jt. auth. see Anzovin, Steven.

Podell, Larry & Kaye, David. Audiotex Directory & Buyer's Guide. 1989. 40.00 (0-317-93152-0) ADBG Pub.

Podell, Richard N. & Proctor, William. The G-Index Diet: The Missing Link That Makes Permanent Weight Loss Possible. 336p. 1994. mass mkt. 6.50 (0-446-36576-9, Pub. by Warner Bks) Little.

Podell, Ronald M. Contagious Emotions: Staying Well When Your Loved One is Depressed. Zion, Claire, ed. 1993. reprint ed. pap. 10.00 (0-671-70240-8) PB.

Podell, Susan K. Checklist for Your First Baby. LC 96-11909. 240p. 1997. pap. 6.99 (0-385-47797-X, Main St Bks) Doubleday.

— A Guide to Eating Right During Pregnancy. LC 92-42111. 48p. 1993. pap. 2.99 (0-385-46775-3) Doubleday.

— The Pocket Guide to Vitamins. LC 93-2344. 56p. 1994. pap. 2.99 (0-385-46823-7) Doubleday.

— Vest Pocket Cholesterol Counter. 48p. 1990. pap. 2.99 (0-385-41329-7) Doubleday.

— Vest Pocket Fat Counter. 56p. 1992. pap. 2.99 (0-385-42294-6) Doubleday.

Podelski, Andreas, ed. Constraint Programming: Basics & Trends: 1994 Chatillon Spring School, Chantillon-sur-Seine, France, May 16-20, 1994: Selected Papers. LC 95-10074. (Lecture Notes in Computer Science Ser.: No. 910). 1995. write for info. (0-387-59155-9) Spr-Verlag.

Podelski, Andreas, jt. ed. see Nivat, Maurice.

Podemski, Richard S., et al. Comprehensive Administration of Special Education. LC 94-11499. 416p. (C). 1994. 62.20 (0-02-395961-4, Macmillan Coll) P-H.

Podendorf, Illa. Animals of Sea & Shore. LC 81-38453. (New True Books Ser.). (Illus.). 48p. (J). (gr. k-4). 1982. lib. bdg. 21.00 (0-516-01615-6) Childrens.

— Animals of Sea & Shore. LC 81-38453. (New True Books Ser.). (Illus.). 48p. (J). (ps-3). 1982. pap. 5.50 (0-516-41615-4) Childrens.

— Baby Animals. LC 81-9938. (New True Books Ser.). (Illus.). 48p. (J). (ps-3). 1981. lib. bdg. 21.00 (0-516-01605-9) Childrens.

— Insects. LC 81-7689. (New True Books Ser.). (Illus.). 48p. (J). (ps-3). 1981. lib. bdg. 20.00 (0-516-01627-X) Childrens.

— Jungles. LC 82-4454. (New True Books Ser.). (J). (gr. k-4). 1982. lib. bdg. 21.00 (0-516-01631-8) Childrens.

— Spiders. LC 81-38444. (New True Books Ser.). (Illus.). 48p. (J). (gr. 3-5). 1982. pap. 5.50 (0-516-41653-7); lib. bdg. 21.00 (0-516-01653-9) Childrens.

Poder, Thomas C. Basic Concepts in Physiology: A Student's Survival Guide. (Basic Concepts Ser.). (Illus.). 320p. 1998. pap. text 25.95 (0-07-050344-3) McGraw-Hill HPD.

Poderegin, Mike B. The Dawning. 365p. (C). 1990. 49.00 (0-907855-05-9, Pub. by Honeyglen Pub Ltd); pap. 39.00 (0-907855-06-7, Pub. by Honeyglen Pub Ltd) St Mut.

Poderegin, Nadja, tr. see Bajic-Poderegin, Milka.

Poderis, Tony. It's a Great Day to Fund-Raise! A Veteran Campaigner Reveals the Development Tips & Techniques That Will Work for You. LC 96-84730. 115p. 1996. 35.00 (0-9652066-0-2); pap. 22.95 (0-9652066-1-0) FundAmerica.

***Poderscek, Anthony L., et al, eds.** Companion Animals & Us: Exploring the Relationships Between People & Pets. (Illus.). 350p. 2000. 80.00 (0-521-63113-0) Cambridge U Pr.

Podeschi, John B. Books on the Horse & Horsemanship, Riding, Hunting, Breeding, & Racing, 1400-1941. (Illus.). 427p. 1981. 50.00 (0-905005-53-8) Yale Ctr Brit Art.

— Dickens & Dickensiana: A Catalogue of the Richard Gimbel Collection in the Yale University... LC 79-66938. 1980. 70.00 (0-8457-3120-3) Yale U Lib.

Podesta, Connie. How to be the Person Successful Companies Fight to Keep: The Insider's Guide to Being #1 in the Workplace. 208p. 1998. per. 11.00 (0-684-84008-1, Fireside) S&S Trade Pap.

— Self-Esteem & the Six-Second Secret. 96p. 1992. pap. 16.95 (0-8039-6037-9) Corwin Pr.

Podesta, Connie & Gatz, Jean. How to be the Person Successful Companies Fight to Keep: The Insider's Guide to Being #1 in the Workplace. LC 96-52718. 1997. 20.50 (0-684-83032-9) S&S Trade.

Podesta, Connie & Sanderson, Vicki. Life Would Be Easy If It Weren't for Other People. LC 99-6030. (One-Off Ser.). (Illus.). 200p. 1999. 55.95 (0-8039-6864-7); pap. 24.95 (0-8039-6865-5) Corwin Pr.

Podesta, Guido A. Desde Lutecia: Anacronismo y modernidad en los escritos teatrales de Cesar Vallejo. (SPA.). 341p. 1995. pap. 18.00 (0-9640795-0-X) Latinoam Edit.

Podesta, Michael & Krody, Barron. Joy. 96p. (Orig.). 1995. pap. 4.95 (0-88028-165-0, 1343) Forward Movement.

Podesta, Patti, intro. Resolution: A Critique of Video Art. (Illus.). 131p. (Orig.). (C). 1986. pap. 10.00 (0-937335-01-0) LA Contemp Exhib.

Podesta, Robert. Robert Podesta's One Million Dollar No Joke Italian's Success System. 10.00 (0-686-23143-0) Wave Spray.

Podesta, Ronald B., et al, eds. Membrane Physiology of Invertebrates. LC 81-17534. (Illus.). 678p. reprint ed. pap. 200.00 (0-7837-0914-5, 204121900019) Bks Demand.

Podesta, Sandra & Paxton, Andrea. 201 Killer Cover Letters. LC 95-37325. 288p. 1996. pap. 16.95 (0-07-050456-3) McGraw.

Podet, Allen H. The Success & Failure of the Anglo-American Committee of Inquiry, 1945-1946: Last Chance in Palestine. LC 87-1635. (Jewish Studies: Vol. 3). 384p. 1987. lib. bdg. 99.95 (0-88946-255-0) E Mellen.

Podet, Allen Howard, jt. auth. see Modena, Leone.

Podgaetsky, V. V., jt. auth. see Pokhodnaya, I. K.

Podger, Christopher J., jt. auth. see Ioannides, Alexander C.

Podgor, Ellen S. White Collar Crime in a Nutshell. (Nutshell Ser.). 303p. 1993. pap. text 16.00 (0-314-02349-6) West Pub.

Podgor, Ellen S. & Israel, Jerold H. White Collar Crime in a Nutshell. 2nd ed. LC 97-37005. (Paralegal). 425p. (C). 1997. pap. text 19.95 (0-314-21163-2) West Pub.

Podgorecki, Adam. Higher Faculties: A Cross-National Study of University Culture. LC 96-26876. 208p. 1997. 57.95 (0-275-95616-4, Praeger Pubs) Greenwood.

— Polish Society. LC 93-25056. 208p. 1993. 62.95 (0-275-94728-9, C4728, Praeger Pubs) Greenwood.

— Social Oppression, 106. LC 93-7712. (Contributions in Sociology Ser.: No. 106). 152p. 1993. 52.95 (0-313-29024-5, GM9024, Greenwood Pr) Greenwood.

Podgorecki, Adam & Olgiati, Vittorio. Totalitarian & Post-Totalitarian Law: A Sociolegal Analysis. LC 95-46957. (Onati Series in Law & Society). (Illus.). 384p. 1996. 87.95 (1-85521-779-1, Pub. by Dartmth Pub); pap. 34.95 (1-85521-783-X, Pub. by Dartmth Pub) Ashgate Pub Co.

Podgornyi, I. M. Topics in Plasma Diagnostics. LC 72-137010. (Illus.). 228p. 1971. reprint ed. pap. 70.70 (0-608-05754-1, 205971800007) Bks Demand.

Podgurski, Mary J. Games Educators Play: Interactive Game & Role Plays. 95p. 1996. pap. write for info. (1-891032-00-3) Acad Adolescent.

Podgursky, Michael. Job Displacement & the Rural Worker. 20p. 1989. 10.00 (0-944826-14-8) Economic Policy Inst.

Podgursky, Michael, jt. auth. see Ballou, Dale.

Podgursky, Michael J., jt. auth. see Ballou, Dale.

Podhaizer, Mary E. Painless Spelling. LC 98-18313. (Illus.). 224p. 1998. pap. 8.95 (0-7641-0567-1) Barron.

— Redwall: A Teaching Guide. (Discovering Literature Ser.). (Illus.). 95p. 1998. pap. text, teacher ed. 7.95 (0-931993-91-1, GP-091) Garlic Pr OR.

***Podhaizer, Mary E.** A Teaching Guide to "The Giver" (Discovering Literature Ser.). (Illus.). 91p. 1999. pap., teacher ed. 7.95 (0-931993-97-0, GP-097) Garlic Pr OR.

Podhaizer, Mary E. A Teaching Guide to "The Hobbit" (Discovering Literature Ser.). (Illus.). 75p. (YA). (gr. 9 up). 1998. pap., wbk. ed. 7.95 (0-931993-90-3, GP-090) Garlic Pr OR.

— A Teaching Guide to "The Odyssey" (Discovering Literature Series). (Illus.). 112p. 1999. pap. text, teacher ed. 7.95 (0-931993-92-X, GP-092) Garlic Pr OR.

Podhaizer, Mary E., ed. A Guide to Independent Schools in Vermont for Families, Educators, & Policy Makers. xv, 124p. 1998. pap. 12.00 (0-9666927-0-5) Res Vermont Ed.

Podhajski, Blanche, jt. auth. see Lenchner, Orna.

Podhajsky, Alois. Complete Training of Horse & Rider. 1982. pap. 15.00 (0-87980-235-9) Wilshire.

— My Horses, My Teachers. 1997. pap. 75.00 (0-85131-692-1) Trafalgar.

— My Horses, My Teachers. Podhajsky, Eva, tr. LC 96-50410. (Illus.). 202p. 1997. pap. 17.95 (1-57076-091-8, Trafalgar Sq Pub) Trafalgar.

— The Riding Teacher: A Basic Guide to Correct Methods of Classical Instruction. (Illus.). 204p. 1993. 22.95 (0-943955-84-X, Trafalgar Sq Pub) Trafalgar.

Podhajsky, Eva, tr. see Podhajsky, Alois.

***Podhoretz, Norman.** Ex-Friends: Falling Out with Allen Ginsberg, Lionel & Diana Trilling, Lillian Hellman, Hannah Arendt & Norman Mailer. LC 98-26687. 240p. 2000. 16.95 (1-893554-17-1) Encounter Bks.

Podhoretz, Norman. Ex-Friends: Falling Out with Allen Ginsberg, Lionel & Diana Trilling, Lillian Hellman, Hannah Arendt & Norman Mailer. LC 98-26687. 256p. 1999. 24.50 (0-684-85594-1) Free Pr.

***Podhoretz, Norman.** My Love Affair with America: The Cautionary Tale of a Cheerful Conservative. LC 99-462225. 256p. 2000. 25.00 (0-7432-0051-9) Free Pr.

Podhoretz, Norman. The Present Danger. 1980. pap. 3.95 (0-671-41328-7, Touchstone) S&S Trade Pap.

Podhorsky, M. & Krips, H. Heat Exchangers: A Practical Approach to Mechanical Construction, Design & Calculations. LC 98-18447. 217p. 1998. write for info. (1-56700-117-3) Begell Hse.

***Podila, Gopi K. & Douds, David D., eds.** Current Advances in Mycorrhizae Research. 214p. 1999. 42.00 (0-89054-245-7) Am Phytopathol Soc.

Podis, Joanne M. & Podis, Leonard A. Rethinking Writing. LC 95-23479. 500p. 1995. pap. text 42.00 (0-205-14805-0) Allyn.

Podis, JoAnne M., jt. auth. see Podis, Leonard A.

Podis, JoAnne M., jt. ed. see Podis, Leonard A.

Podis, Leonard A. & Podis, JoAnne M. Rethinking Writing. (C). 1995. pap. text, teacher ed. write for info. (0-205-18703-X, H8703-4) Allyn.

Podis, Leonard A. & Podis, JoAnne M., eds. Working with Student Writers: Essays on Tutoring & Teaching. LC 98-36828. XII, 352p. 1999. pap. text 29.95 (0-8204-4032-9) P Lang Pubng.

Podis, Leonard A., jt. auth. see Podis, Joanne M.

Podis, Leonard A., jt. ed. see Saaka, Yakubu.

Podjarny, A. D., et al, eds. Crystallographic Computing 5: From Chemistry to Biology. (IUCr Crystallographic Symposia Ser.: No. 5). (Illus.). 494p. 1992. text 85.00 (0-19-855384-6) OUP.

Podjasek, Jill H. & Carney, Jennifer. Ten Habits of Naturally Slim People. (Illus.). 288p. 1998. pap. 12.95 (0-8092-2953-6, 295360, Contemporary Bks) NTC Contemp Pub Co.

***Podjen, India J.** Repercussion. Mauiner, Dan, ed. (Illus.). v, 245p. 1999. pap. 14.95 (0-9672557-0-8) Mindscape Pubng.

Podlech, D., jt. auth. see Lippert, W.

Podlecki, A. J., ed. see Holladay, A. J.

Podlecki, Anthony J. The Life of Themistocles: A Critical Survey of the Literary & Archaeological Evidence. LC 73-93001. 272p. reprint ed. pap. 84.40 (0-7837-1027-5, 204133800020) Bks Demand.

— Pericles & His Circle. LC 97-19131. 264p. (C). 1998. 65.00 (0-415-06794-4) Routledge.

Podlecki, Anthony J., ed. Aeschylus: The eumenides. (Classical Texts Ser.). 1989. pap. 28.00 (0-85668-382-5, Pub. by Aris & Phillips) David Brown.

— Aeschylus: The Eumenides. (Classical Texts Ser.). 1989. 59.99 (0-85668-381-7, Pub. by Aris & Phillips) David Brown.

Podlecki, Anthony J., tr. Euripides' Medea. (Classical Library). 92p. 1991. pap. text 6.95 (0-941051-10-2) Focus Pub-R Pullins.

Podlecki, Anthony J. & Gregory, T. E., eds. Panathenaia: Studies in Athenian Life & Thought in the Classical Age. 1979. 10.00 (0-87291-126-8) Coronado Pr.

Podles, Leon J. The Church Impotent: The Feminization of Christianity. LC 98-19150. 306p. 1999. 27.95 (1-890626-07-4) Spence Pub.

***Podles, Leon J.** The Church Impotent: The Feminization of Christianity. LC 98-19150. xviii, 290p. 1999. pap. 14.00 (1-890626-19-8) Spence Pub.

Podleski, Greta, jt. auth. see Podleski, Janet.

***Podleski, Janet.** Looneyspoons: Low-Fat Food Made Fun. (Illus.). 2000. pap. 19.95 (0-399-52563-7, Perigee Bks) Berkley Pub.

***Podleski, Janet & Podleski, Greta.** Crazy Plates: Low-Fat Food So Good, You'll Swear It's Bad for You! LC 99-40792. 192p. 2000. pap. text 19.95 (0-399-52584-X, Perigee Bks) Berkley Pub.

Podleski, Janet & Podleski, Greta. Looneyspoons: Low-Fat Food Made Fun! LC 97-13876. (Illus.). 192p. 1997. per. 19.95 (0-9680631-1-X) Granet Pub.

Podlewski, Regina. Rhetorik Als Pragmatisches System. (Philosophische Texte und Studien: Vol. 3). (GER.). xiv, 271p. 1982. write for info. (3-487-06658-0) G Olms Pubs.

Podley, Andrea & Bang, Derrick. Peanuts Collectibles Identification & Values Guide: I. 304p. 1999. pap. 24.95 (1-57432-147-1) Collector Bks.

Podlin, Sharon. Hands on Access '97. LC 97-76503. 500p. 1998. per. 40.00 (0-7615-1339-6) Prima Pub.

— Hands on Visual Basic 6. 1998. pap. 40.00 (0-7615-1635-2) Prima Pub.

— Hands on Visual InterDev 6. LC 98-66443. (Illus.). 450p. 1998. per. 40.00 (0-7615-1678-6) Prima Pub.

— SmartSuite 97 Visual Learning Guide: Visual Learning Guide. LC 97-67392. 352p. 1997. per. 16.99 (0-7615-1192-X) Prima Pub.

— Teach Yourself Excel 2000 Programming in 24 Hours. 2000th ed. LC 99-60558. (Teach Yourself ... in 24 Hours Ser.). (Illus.). 345p. 1999. pap. 19.99 (0-672-31650-1) Sams.

P

An Asterisk (*) at the beginning of an entry indicates that the title is appearing for the first time.

Podlin, Sharon, jt. auth. see Palmer, Pam.

Podlinsky, Michael, jt. auth. see Podolinsky, Michael A.

Podlubny. Fractional Differential Equations. 336p. (C). 1998. text 69.95 (*0-12-558840-2*) Acad Pr.

Podmore, Colin. The Moravian Church in England, 1728-1760. (Oxford Historical Monographs). (Illus.). 352p. 1998. text 85.00 (*0-19-820725-5*) OUP.

Podmore, Frank. The Newer Spiritualism. LC 75-7392. (Perspectives in Psychical Research Ser.). 1975. reprint ed. 26.95 (*0-405-07041-1*) Ayer.

— Robert Owen, 2 vols. LC 78-156295. (World History Ser.: No. 48). 1971. lib. bdg. 150.00 (*0-8383-1265-9*) M S G Haskell Hse.

— Robert Owen: A Biography, 2 vols. LC 68-9762. 1968. reprint ed. 65.00 (*0-678-00417-X*) Kelley.

— Studies in Psychical Research. LC 75-7393. (Perspectives in Psychical Research Ser.). 1975. reprint ed. 39.95 (*0-405-07042-X*) Ayer.

Podmore, Harry J. Trenton: Old & New. (Illus.). 166p. 1997. reprint ed. pap. 21.00 (*0-8328-6883-3*); reprint ed. lib. bdg. 29.00 (*0-8328-6882-5*) Higginson Bk Co.

Podmore, J. The Role of Fats in Human Nutrition. LC 85-5491. 210p. 1985. text 65.00 (*3-527-26219-9*, Wiley-VCH) Wiley.

Podmore, P. C. The Slide Rule for Sea & Air Navigation. (C). 1987. 40.00 (*0-85174-213-0*) St Mut.

Podmore, Ron. Signs in Success: Profiles of Deaf Americans. (Illus.). 48p. (Orig.). (J). 1995. pap. text 7.95 (*1-884362-02-8*) Butte Pubns.

Podmore, Will. Britain, Italy, Germany & the Spanish Civil War. LC 98-5719. 172p. 1998. text 79.95 (*0-7734-8491-4*) E Mellen.

Podmoshensky, Herman, jt. ed. see Rose, Seraphim.

Podnieks, Andrew. Blue & White Book: The Most Complete Toronto Maple Leafs Fact Book Ever Printed. 2nd ed. (Illus.). 550p. 1996. pap. text 18.95 (*1-55022-285-6*, Pub. by ECW) LPC InBook.

— Canada's Olympic Hockey. 1997. 26.95 (*0-385-25691-4*) Doubleday.

— The Great One: The Life & Times of Wayne Gretzky. 160p. 1999. 24.95 (*1-57243-352-3*) Triumph Bks.

***Podnieks, Andrew.** The Great One: The Life & Times of "99" (Illus.). 1999. 25.00 (*0-385-25926-3*) Doubleday.

Podnieks, Andrew. Patrick Roy. (Hockey Heroes Ser.). 1998. pap. text 6.95 (*1-55054-641-4*, Pub. by DGL) Sterling.

— Portraits of The Game: Classic Photographs from The Turofsky Collection at The Hockey Hall of Fame. LC 98-127393. (Illus.). 176p. 1997. 50.00 (*0-385-25644-2*) Doubleday.

***Podnieks, Andrew.** Portraits of the Game: Classic Photographs from the Turofsky Collection at the Hockey Hall of Fame. (Illus.). 176p. 1999. pap. 17.95 (*0-385-25801-1*) Doubleday.

Podnieks, Andrew. Return to Glory: The Leafs from Imlach to Fletcher. LC 95-230484. (Illus.). 300p. 1997. pap. 19.95 (*1-55022-242-2*, Pub. by ECW) Genl Dist Srvs.

— Shooting Stars: The Lewis Portnoy Collection at the Hockey Hall of Fame. (Illus.). 160p. 1999. 40.00 (*1-55209-314-X*) Firefly Bks Ltd.

Podnieks, Andrew, jt. auth. see Davis, Jefferson.

Podnieks, Andrews. Red Wings Book. LC 97-118585. (Illus.). 500p. 1996. pap. text 18.95 (*1-55022-283-X*, Pub. by ECW) LPC InBook.

***Podnieks, Elizabeth.** Daily Modernism: The Literary Diaries of Virginia Woolf, Antonia White, Elizabeth Smart & Anahis Nin. 424p. 2000. 65.00 (*0-7735-2021-X*, Pub. by McG-Queens Univ Pr) CUP Services.

Podobed, Vladimir V. Fundamental Astrometry: Determination of Stellar Coordinates. Vyssotsky, A. N., ed. LC 64-15810. 248p. reprint ed. pap. 76.90 (*0-608-30842-0*, 202014500016) Bks Demand.

Podolak, Cecelia. Easy Guide to Sewing Jackets. LC 95-18165. (Sewing Companion Library). (Illus.). 112p. 1995. pap. 17.95 (*1-56158-087-2*, 070215) Taunton.

***Podolefsky, Aaron & Brown, Peter J.** Applying Anthropology: An Introductory Reader. LC 00-32429. 2001. write for info. (*0-7674-1841-7*) Mayfield Pub.

Podolefsky, Aaron & Brown, Peter J. Applying Anthropology: An Introductory Reader. 5th ed. LC 98-20616. 400p. 1998. pap. text 25.95 (*0-7674-0465-3*, 0465-3) Mayfield Pub.

— Applying Anthropology Instructor's Manual: An Introductory Reader. 5th rev. ed. 44p. 1998. pap. text, teacher ed. write for info. (*0-7674-0828-4*, 0828-4) Mayfield Pub.

— Applying Cultural Anthropology: An Introductory Reader. 4th ed. LC 98-20617. 338p. 1998. pap. text 25.95 (*0-7674-0466-1*, 0466-1) Mayfield Pub.

***Podolefsky, Aaron & Brown, Peter J.** Applying Cultural Anthropology: An Introductory Reader. 5th ed. LC 00-32458. 2001. write for info. (*0-7674-1837-9*) Mayfield Pub.

Podolinsky, Michael, jt. auth. see Podolinsky, Michael A.

Podolinsky, Michael A. & Podlinsky, Michael. Smart Leadership. (Smart Tapes Ser.). 28p. 1996. pap. 19.95 incl. audio (*1-55678-063-X*, 3275) Learn Inc.

Podolinsky, Michael A. & Podolinsky, Michael. From Stress to Success. unabridged ed. (Smart Tapes Ser.). (C). 1995. pap. 19.95 incl. audio (*1-55678-055-9*, 3265) Learn Inc.

— Go for Your Goals. unabridged ed. (Smart Tape Ser.). (C). 1995. pap. 19.95 incl. audio (*1-55678-056-7*, 3255) Learn Inc.

— Winning at Work. unabridged ed. (Smart Tapes Ser.). (C). 1995. pap. 19.95 incl. audio (*1-55678-057-5*, 3255) Learn Inc.

Podoll, Brian A. Bound by Blood & Name: A History & Genealogies of the Podoll Families in Prussia & America. (Illus.). 600p. 1989. 40.00 (*0-9621809-0-4*) B A Podoll.

Podoll, David. Small Scale Turkey Growing for the Beginner. (Shorey Lost Arts Ser.). 26p. 1975. reprint ed. pap. 10.00 (*0-8466-6044-X*, U44) Shoreys Bkstore.

***Podolske, Ann.** Managing Customer Service 2000 Yearbook. annuals (Illus.). 2000p. 2000. pap. 199.00 (*1-58673-024-X*) IOMA.

— The 2000 Pay for Performance Report Yearbook. (Illus.). 200p. 1999. pap. 199.00 (*1-58673-002-9*) IOMA.

Podolski, Alfred L., ed. Massachusetts Family Law Journal. 1628p. 1985. 125.00 (*0-88063-029-9*, 81489-10, MICHIE) LEXIS Pub.

Podolski, Alfred L., et al. Massachusetts Family Law Journal. 140.00 (*0-327-12441-5*) LEXIS Pub.

Podolsky, Baruch. A Greek-Tatar-English Dictionary. (ENG, GRE & TAR.). 51p. 1986. 49.95 (*0-8288-1648-4*, M 421) Fr & Eur.

Podolsky, Boris & Kunz, Kaiser S. Fundamentals of Electrodynamics. LC 78-78828. (Illus.). 508p. reprint ed. pap. 157.50 (*0-7837-0731-2*, 204105500019) Bks Demand.

Podolsky, Edward. Red Miracle. LC 70-167402. (Essay Index Reprint Ser.). 1977. 24.95 (*0-8369-2818-0*) Ayer.

Podolsky, Joseph L. Computers & the Fortune One Thousand: Guidelines for Using PCs in the Corporate Environment. (Illus.). 304p. 1987. 19.95 (*0-13-162983-2*) P-H.

Podolsky, Kathleen M. World Point - World Line. LC 82-15164. (Illus.). 72p. (Orig.). 1982. pap. 14.95 (*0-942714-00-8*) LIM Press CA.

Podolsky, Leo, ed. Guild Repertoire: Elementary A & B. 48p. (gr. 3-12). 1960. pap. text 7.95 (*0-87487-639-7*) Summy-Birchard.

— Guild Repertoire: Elementary C & D. 48p. (gr. 3-12). 1961. pap. text 7.95 (*0-87487-640-0*) Summy-Birchard.

— Guild Repertoire: Intermediate A. 32p. (gr. 3-12). 1959. pap. text 5.95 (*0-87487-641-9*) Summy-Birchard.

— Guild Repertoire: Intermediate B. 32p. (gr. 3-12). 1959. pap. text 5.95 (*0-87487-642-7*) Summy-Birchard.

— Guild Repertoire: Intermediate C & D. 64p. (gr. 3-12). 1959. pap. text 9.95 (*0-87487-643-5*) Summy-Birchard.

— Guild Repertoire: Prepatory A. (Guild Repertoire Ser.). 48p. (Orig.). 1960. pap. text 7.95 (*0-87487-645-1*) Summy-Birchard.

Podolsky, Leo, ed. see Davison, June & Schaub, Ardella.

Podolsky, M. Lawrence. Cures out of Chaos: How Unexpected Discoveries Led to Breakthroughs in Medicine & Health. 446p. 1998. text 65.00 (*90-5702-555-8*, Harwood Acad Pubs); pap. text 32.95 (*90-5702-556-6*, Harwood Acad Pubs) Gordon & Breach.

Podolsky, M. Lawrence & Lukas, Victor. The Care & Feeding of an Iacuc: How to Organize & Manage an Institutional Animal Care & Use Committee. LC 98-51623. 216p. 1999. boxed set 59.95 (*0-8493-2580-3*) CRC Pr.

Podolsky, Nancy. Bargello Hearts. Roubal, Diane & Doheny, Marilyn, eds. (Illus.). 96p. 1996. reprint ed. pap. 22.95 (*0-945169-17-5*) Doheny Pubns.

Podolsky, Scott H. & Tauber, Alfred I. The Generation of Diversity: Clonal Selection Theory & the Rise of Molecular Immunology. LC 97-22942. (Illus.). 512p. 1998. 75.00 (*0-674-77181-8*) HUP.

Podolsky, Stephen & Viswanathan, M., eds. Secondary Diabetes: The Spectrum of the Diabetic Syndromes. fac. ed. LC 79-62976. (Illus.). 624p. pap. 193.50 (*0-7837-7267-X*, 204703800005) Bks Demand.

Podos, Arlene, jt. auth. see Cascio, Danis.

Podos, Batya. Ariadne. LC 80-70233. 52p. (Orig.). 1980. pap. 3.00 (*0-9603628-2-7*) Frog in Well.

Podoshen, Lois. The Artist. (Books for Young Learners). (Illus.). 12p. (J). (gr. k-2). 1999. pap. text 5.00 (*1-57274-137-6*) R Owen Pubs.

— The Birthday Bird. (Books for Young Learners). (Illus.). 8p. (J). (gr. k-2). 1998. pap. text 5.00 (*1-57274-154-6*, A2430) R Owen Pubs.

— La Dulceria de Abuelo. Romo, Alberto, tr. (Books for Young Learners).Tr. of Grandpa's Candy Store. (SPA., Illus.). 12p. (J). (gr. k-2). 1998. pap. text 5.00 (*1-57274-200-3*, A2850) R Owen Pubs.

— Grandpa's Candy Store. (Books for Young Learners). (Illus.). 12p. (J). (gr. k-2). 1997. pap. text 5.00 (*1-57274-113-9*, A2160) R Owen Pubs.

***Podoshen, Lois.** El Huerto de Paco. Romo, Alberto, tr. (Books for Young Learners).Tr. of Paco's Garden. (SPA., Illus.). 12p. (J). (gr. k-2). 1999. pap. text 5.00 (*1-57274-337-9*, A2869) R Owen Pubs.

Podoshen, Lois. Paco's Garden. (Books for Young Learners). (Illus.). 12p. (J). (gr. k-2). 1999. pap. text 5.00 (*1-57274-235-6*) R Owen Pubs.

— El Regalo de Cumpleanos. Romo, Alberto, tr. (Books for Young Learners).Tr. of Birthday Bird. (SPA., Illus.). 8p. (J). (gr. k-2). 1998. pap. text 5.00 (*1-57274-207-0*, A2895) R Owen Pubs.

Podovinikoff, Elaine. A Fight to the Finish. LC 97-90556. 1998. 13.95 (*0-533-12424-7*) Vantage.

Podraza, Eugene. The Memoirs of Ludwik Zychlinski: Reminiscences of the American Civil War, Siberia & Poland. LC 93-73796. 111p. 1994. 20.00 (*0-88033-289-1*, 392, Pub. by East Eur Monographs) Col U Pr.

Podrazik, Walter J., jt. auth. see Castleman, Harry.

Podrebarac, Charles. Night of the Living Bar-B-Q. Morrissey, Jake, ed. (Illus.). 160p. 1997. pap. 9.95 (*0-9604884-3-X*) Kansas Cty Star.

Podrebarac, Francis, jt. auth. see Martinez, Martin.

Podrecca, Boris, jt. auth. see Zschokke, Walter.

Podreka, Tomislav. Serendipitea: A Guide to the Varities, Origins, & Rituals of Tea. LC 98-6816. (Illus.). 208p. 1998. 16.00 (*0-688-15808-0*, Wm Morrow) Morrow Avon.

Podrid, Philip J. & Kowey, Peter R. Cardiac Arrhythmia. 2nd ed. 800p. text 129.00 (*0-7817-2486-4*) Lppncott W & W.

Podrid, Philip J. & Kowey, Peter R., eds. Cardiac Arrhythmia: Mechanisms, Diagnosis, & Management. (Illus.). 1472p. 1994. 159.00 (*0-683-06905-5*) Lppncott W & W.

— Handbook of Cardiac Arrhythmia. (Illus.). 512p. 1996. pap. 39.00 (*0-683-06909-8*) Lppncott W & W.

Podro, Michael. The Critical Historians of Art. LC 82-4934. (Illus.). 260p. 1984. reprint ed. pap. 16.00 (*0-300-03240-4*, Y-499) Yale U Pr.

— Depiction. LC 98-15247. (Illus.). 208p. 1998. 30.00 (*0-300-06914-6*) Yale U Pr.

Podrug, Junius. Frost of Heaven. LC 98-18904. 2000. 23.95 (*0-312-86683-6*, Pub. by Forge NYC) St Martin.

***Podrug, Junius.** Frost of Heaven. LC 98-18904. 425p. 2000. mass mkt. 6.99 (*0-8125-5505-8*, Pub. by Tor Bks) St Martin.

Podrug, Junius. Presumed Guilty. LC 97-16925. 384p. 1997. text 24.95 (*0-312-86242-3*) St Martin.

— Presumed Guilty. 1998. mass mkt. 6.99 (*0-8125-5507-4*, Pub. by Tor Bks) St Martin.

— Stop Being a Victim. LC 98-26464. 320p. 1998. 23.95 (*0-312-86845-6*, Pub. by Forge NYC) St Martin.

***Podrug, Junius.** Stop Being a Victim: A Survival Kit for the New Millennium. 320p. 2000. pap. text 14.95 (*0-312-86844-8*, Pub. by Forge NYC) St Martin.

***Podsen, India & Denmark, Vicki M.** Coaching & Mentoring First-Year & Student Teachers. LC 99-33809. 2000. 29.95 (*1-883001-80-3*) Eye On Educ.

Podsen, India, et al. Written Expression: The Principal's Survival Guide. LC 96-40532. (School Leadership Library Ser.). 160p. 1997. 29.95 (*1-883001-34-X*) Eye On Educ.

Podsen, India J. Disk with Workbook to Accompany Written Expression: The Principal's Survival Guide. (Illus.). 200p. 1997. pap., wbk. ed. 39.95 incl. disk (*1-883001-42-0*) Eye On Educ.

***Podskoch, Martin.** Fire Towers of the Catskills: Their History & Lore. LC 00-40246. (Illus.). 128p. 2000. pap. write for info. (*1-930098-10-3*) Purple Mnt Pr.

Podulka, Fran. Essentials: Messages in the Blood. Spelius, Carol, ed. (Illus.). 62p. (Orig.). 1989. pap. 7.95 (*0-941363-04-X*) Lake Shore Pub.

Poduska, Bernard E. For Love & Money: A Guide to Finances & Relationships. 320p. (C). 1992. mass mkt. 8.75 (*0-534-18852-4*) Brooks-Cole.

— For Love & Money: A Guide to Finances & Relationships for Latter-Day Saints. LC 95-21449. 352p. (Orig.). 1995. pap. 14.95 (*0-87579-969-8*) Deseret Bk.

***Poduska, Bernard E.** Till Debt Do Us Part: Finances, Feelings & Family Relationships. LC 00-22314. 224p. 2000. pap. 15.95 (*1-57345-587-3*, Shadow Mount) Deseret Bk.

Poduska, Paul, et al. Linux Pro - Installation & More: Why Linux? Fall in Love Again. Bolzern, Mark, ed. (Illus.). 40p. (Orig.). 1997. pap. 19.95 incl. cd-rom (*1-888894-39-3*) WrkGrp Solns.

Poduska, Paul R. Linux Pro Sampler, 5 CD-Roms. (Illus.). 134p. 1998. pap. 49.00 incl. cd-rom (*1-888894-42-3*) IPG Chicago.

Podvesko, M. L. English-Ukrainian Dictionary. 2nd ed. (ENG & UKR.). 42.50 (*0-87557-089-5*) Saphrograph.

Podvesko, M. L., ed. Ukrainian-English Dictionary. 2nd ed. (ENG & UKR.). 42.50 (*0-87557-088-7*) Saphrograph.

Podvesko, M. L. & Balla, M. I. English-Ukrainian Dictionary. LC 88-91407. (UKR & ENG.). 664p. Date not set. 34.95 (*0-920862-62-4*) Ukrainian Acad.

Podvesko, M. L. & Balla, M. J. English-Ukrainian Dictionary. (ENG & UKR.). 664p. 1980. 40.00 (*0-569-08127-0*) St Mut.

Podwal, Mark. A Book of Hebrew Letters. LC 92-20241. 64p. 1992. 25.00 (*0-87668-317-0*) Aronson.

— The Book of Tens. LC 93-43871. (Illus.). 24p. (J). 1994. 16.00 (*0-688-12994-3*, Grenwillow Bks) HarpC Child Bks.

— Golem: A Giant Made of Mud. LC 94-7865. (Illus.). 24p. (J). (gr. k up). 1995. 15.00 (*0-688-13811-X*, Grenwillow Bks) HarpC Child Bks.

— The Menorah Story. LC 97-36300. (Illus.). 24p. (YA). (gr. k-3). 1998. 15.00 (*0-688-15758-0*, Grenwillow Bks) HarpC Child Bks.

***Podwal, Mark.** The Menorah Story. LC 97-36300. (Illus.). 24p. (YA). (gr. k-3). 1998. 14.93 (*0-688-15759-9*, Grenwillow Bks) HarpC Child Bks.

Podzemny, Darrel. Every Good & Perfect Gift: An Exciting New Christian Motivational Book. 140p. (Orig.). 1996. pap. 7.50 (*1-57502-178-1*, PO802) Morris Pubng.

Podziba, Susan L., jt. auth. see Susskind, Lawrence E.

Podzorski, A. C. An Illustrated & Annotated Check-list of Diatoms from the Black River Waterways, St. Elizabeth, Jamaica. (Bibliotheca Diatomologica Ser.: No. 7). (Illus.). 178p. 1985. lib. bdg. 39.00 (*3-7682-1422-2*) Lubrecht & Cramer.

Podzorski, A. C. & Hakansson, H. Freshwater & Marine Diatoms from Palawan, a Philippine Island. (Bibliotheca Diatomologica Ser.: Vol. 13). (Illus.). 245p. 1987. pap. text 71.00 (*3-443-57004-6*, Pub. by Gebruder Borntraeger) Balogh.

Podzunas, Albert E., jt. auth. see Srikanth, Mokshagundam L.

Poe, Ann. The McGraw-Hill Handbook of More Business Letters. LC 98-24855. 416p. 1998. pap. 19.95 (*0-07-050517-9*) McGraw.

— Quilting School. LC 93-43792. (Learn-As-You-Go Guides Ser.). (Illus.). 176p. 1993. 21.00 (*0-89577-471-2*, Pub. by RD Assn) Penguin Putnam.

Poe, Ann & Schneider, Kandy. Getting Ready for Baby. LC 97-51234. (Illus.). 144p. 1999. pap. 19.95 (*0-8092-2904-8*, 290480, Contemporary Bks) NTC Contemp Pub Co.

Poe, Ann & Schneider, Kandy. The Playtime Boutique: 50 Fast, Fun & Easy-to-Make Projects. LC 99-23628. 128p. Date not set. pap. 19.95 (*0-8442-0092-1*, 00921, Contemporary Bks) NTC Contemp Pub Co.

Poe, Arthur C., jt. auth. see Lipschutz, Seymour.

Poe, Charles A., jt. auth. see Poe, Clarence.

Poe, Clarence. South at War 1861-1865 True Tales of How Families Lived & How Soldiers. 236p. Date not set. 21.95 (*0-8488-2659-0*) Amereon Ltd.

Poe, Clarence & Poe, Charles A. Poe-Pourri: A North Carolina Cavalcade. LC 87-90549. (Illus.). 157p. 1987. 11.95 (*0-9618716-0-1*) Charles Poe.

Poe, Clarence & Seymour, Betsy, eds. True Tales of the South at War: How Soldiers Fought & Families Lived, 1861-1865. LC 94-34997. (Illus.). 224p. 1995. pap. text 6.95 (*0-486-28451-4*) Dover.

Poe, Edgar Allan. Al Aaraaf, Tamerlane & Minor Poems. (Notable American Authors Ser.). 1999. reprint ed. lib. bdg. 125.00 (*0-7812-8751-0*) Rprt Serv.

— Annabel Lee. (Illus.). 24p. 1987. 19.95 (*0-88776-200-X*); pap. 5.95 (*0-88776-230-1*) Tundra Bks.

— Les Aventures d'Arthur Gordon Pym. (FRE.). 1996. pap. 5.95 (*2-87714-318-X*, Pub. by Bookking Intl) Distribks Inc.

— Les Aventures d'Arthur Gordon Pym. (FRE.). 1975. pap. 11.95 (*0-7859-4040-5*) Fr & Eur.

— The Best of Poe. (Illustrated Classics Collection 3). 64p. 1994. pap. 4.95 (*0-7854-0726-X*, 40465) Am Guidance.

— The Best of Poe. abr. ed. Farr, Naunerle C., ed. (Now Age Illustrated III Ser.). (Illus.). (J). (gr. 4-12). 1977. pap. text 2.95 (*0-88301-269-3*) Pendulum Pr.

— The Best of Poe Readalong. (Illustrated Classics Collection 3). 64p. 1994. pap. 14.95 incl. audio (*0-7854-0742-1*, 40467) Am Guidance.

— The Black Cat: Penguin Readers Level 3. (Penguin Readers : Level 3). 144p. 1999. pap. text 7.00 (*0-582-40168-2*) Longman.

— The Black Cat & Other Stories. (Cloth Bound Pocket Ser.). 240p. 1998. 7.95 (*3-89508-091-8*) Konemann.

— The Brevities: Pinakidia, Marginalia, Fifty Suggestions & Other Works, Vol. 2. Pollin, Burton R., ed. & intro. by. 640p. 1985. 100.00 (*0-87752-229-4*) Gordian.

***Poe, Edgar Allan.** The Cask of Amontillado. rev. ed. Kisner, Don, ed. 44p. (YA). (gr. 7 up). 1998. ring bd. 38.00 incl. audio (*1-878298-15-1*) Balance Pub.

Poe, Edgar Allan. A Chapter on Autobiography. (Studies in Poe: No. 23). 1974. lib. bdg. 75.00 (*0-8383-2067-8*) M S G Haskell Hse.

— Classic Poe. unabridged ed. 1994. lib. bdg. 18.95 incl. audio (*1-883049-45-8*) Sound Room.

— Classic Poe, Set. unabridged ed. (Poe Ser.). 1994. 16.95 incl. audio (*1-883049-39-3*, 390525, Pub. by Sound Room) Lndmrk Audiobks.

— Collected Stories of Edgar Allan Poe, Vol. I. (Classics Illustrated Study Guides Ser.). (Illus.). (Orig.). 1997. mass mkt. 4.99 (*1-57840-028-7*, Pub. by Acclaim Bks) Penguin Putnam.

— Collected Stories of Edgar Allan Poe, Vol. II. (Classics Illustrated Study Guides Ser.). (Illus.). (Orig.). 1997. mass mkt. 4.99 (*1-57840-036-8*, Pub. by Acclaim Bks) Penguin Putnam.

— The Collected Tales & Poems of Edgar Allan Poe. LC 92-50231. 1040p. 1992. 20.00 (*0-679-60007-8*) Modern Lib NY.

***Poe, Edgar Allan.** The Collected Tales Of Edgar Allan Poe. large type ed. 256p. 2000. pap. 22.00 (*0-06-019722-6*, HarpCollins) HarpTrade.

Poe, Edgar Allan. Collected Works of Edgar Allan Poe Vol. I: Poems. Mabbott, Thomas O., ed. LC 68-17627. (Illus.). 657p. 1969. 50.00 (*0-674-13935-6*) Belknap Pr.

— Complete Poems. LC 92-10200. 128p. 1992. 7.99 (*0-517-08245-4*) Random Hse Value.

— Complete Poems. 1992. reprint ed. lib. bdg. 13.95 (*0-89968-292-8*, Lghtyr Pr) Buccaneer Bks.

***Poe, Edgar Allan.** Complete Poems. Mabbott, Thomas Ollive, ed. 2000. reprint ed. pap. 25.00 (*0-252-06921-8*) U of Ill Pr.

Poe, Edgar Allan. The Complete Poetry of Edgar Allan Poe. LC 96-17044. 1996. mass mkt. 4.95 (*0-451-52640-6*, Sig Classics) NAL.

— The Complete Stories. LC 92-52933. 944p. 1992. 23.00 (*0-679-41740-0*) Everymns Lib.

— Complete Stories & Poems of Edgar Allan Poe. LC 66-24310. 832p. 1984. 21.95 (*0-385-07407-7*) Doubleday.

— Complete Tales & Poems of Edgar Allan Poe. 1975. 20.10 (*0-606-02981-8*, Pub. by Turtleback) Demco.

— The Complete Tales & Poems of Edgar Allan Poe. LC 75-9506. 1975. pap. 16.00 (*0-394-71678-7*) Vin Bks.

— The Complete Works of Edgar Allan Poe, 17 vols., Set. Harrison, James A., ed. LC 79-15593. reprint ed. 695.00 (*0-404-09400-7*) AMS Pr.

— The Conchologist's First Book. (Notable American Authors Ser.). 1999. reprint ed. lib. bdg. 125.00 (*0-7812-8753-7*) Rprt Serv.

— Cuentos. 1998. pap. 9.95 (*84-320-6969-8*) Planeta.

***Poe, Edgar Allan.** Dead Brides: Vampire Tales. 1999. pap. text 12.95 (*1-84068-011-3*) Creation Books.

Poe, Edgar Allan. Edgar Allan Poe. Bagert, Brod, ed. LC 94-30774. (Poetry for Young People Ser.). (Illus.). 48p. (J). 1995. 14.95 (*0-8069-0820-3*) Sterling.

— Edgar Allan Poe. (BCL1-PS American Literature Ser.). 664p. 1993. reprint ed. lib. bdg. 109.00 (*0-7812-6999-7*) Rprt Serv.

— Edgar Allan Poe: A Collection of Stories. 352p. 1994. pap. 2.50 (*0-8125-0455-0*, Pub. by Tor Bks) St Martin.

Poe, Edgar Allan. Edgar Allan Poe: Sixty-Seven Tales. 768p. 1993. 12.99 (*0-517-09290-5*) Random Hse Value.

P

An Asterisk (*) at the beginning of an entry indicates that the title is appearing for the first time.

Poe, Edgar Allan. Edgar Allan Poe Letters until Now Unpublished. Stanard, Mary N., ed. & intro. by. LC 72-11698. (Studies in Poe: No. 23). 1973. reprint ed. lib. bdg. 75.00 (*0-8383-1692-1*) M S G Haskell Hse.

***Poe, Edgar Allan.** Edgar Allan Poe Stories: Rathbone,&Basil, Set. abr. ed. 1998. audio 18.00 (*1-55994-091-3*, CPN 2104) HarperAudio.

— Edgar Allen Poe Reader. (Literary Classics Ser.). 320p. 1999. 5.98 (*0-7624-0544-9*) Running Pr.

Poe, Edgar Allan. Eight Tales of Terror. 208p. (J). (gr. 7-9). 1961. pap. 3.99 (*0-590-41136-5*) Scholastic Inc.

Poe, Edgar Allan. 18 Best Stories. 1965. 11.09 (*0-606-00600-1*, Pub. by Turtleback) Demco.

Poe, Edgar Allan. 18 Best Stories by Edgar Allan Poe. Price, Vincent & Brossard, Chandler, eds. 288p. (Orig.). (YA). (gr. 7 up). 1965. mass mkt. 6.50 (*0-440-32227-8*, LE) Dell.

— Essays & Reviews. Thompson, G. R., ed. LC 83-19923. 1544p. 1984. 40.00 (*0-940450-19-4*, Pub. by Library of America) Penguin Putnam.

— The Essential Poe. 1993. 6.98 (*0-88365-834-8*) Galahad Bks.

— The Essential Poe. 2nd ed. Smith, Dave, ed. LC 90-43745. (Essential Poets Ser.: No. 14). 104p. 1991. reprint ed. pap. 10.00 (*0-88001-478-4*) HarpC.

Poe, Edgar Allan. Essential Poe, Vol. 14. (Essential Poets Ser.: Vol. 14). 128p. (C). 1991. pap. 8.00 (*0-88001-273-0*) HarpC.

Poe, Edgar Allan. Eureka. limited ed. (Illus.). 120p. 1991. 450.00 (*0-910457-23-9*) Arion Pr.

— Eureka, Vol. 5. (Green Integer Ser.: No. 5). 210p. 1997. pap. 10.95 (*1-55713-329-8*) Green Integer.

— Eureka: A Prose Poem. LC 96-50022. (Literary Classics). 146p. 1997. pap. 7.95 (*1-57392-134-3*) Prometheus Bks.

— Eureka: A Prose Poem. (Notable American Authors Ser.). 1999. reprint ed. lib. bdg. 125.00 (*0-7812-8758-8*) Rprt Serv.

— The Fall of the House of Usher. 1995. pap. 3.50 (*0-87129-583-0*, F56) Dramatic Pub.

— The Fall of the House of Usher. (Classic Frights Ser.). 1997. 11.05 (*0-606-13375-5*, Pub. by Turtleback) Demco.

— The Fall of the House of Usher. (Classic Frights Ser.). (Illus.). 64p. (J). (gr. 4 up). 1997. reprint ed. pap. 5.95 (*0-929605-66-7*) Books of Wonder.

— The Fall of the House of Usher: In 2 Acts. Kelly, Tim, ed. 60p. 1979. pap. 4.00 (*0-88680-049-8*) I E Clark.

— The Fall of the House of Usher & Other Tales. (Signet Classics Ser.). 384p. 1998. mass mkt. 5.95 (*0-451-52675-9*, Sig Classics) NAL.

— The Fall of the House of Usher & Other Tales. (Signet Classics: No. 29). 1960. 11.05 (*0-606-00633-8*, Pub. by Turtleback) Demco.

— The Fall of the House of Usher & Other Tales, Vol. 1. large type ed. LC 97-30818. 240p. 1997. text 22.95 (*1-56000-536-X*) Transaction Pubs.

— The Fall of the House of Usher & Other Writings. Galloway, David, ed. 544p. 1986. pap. 9.95 (*0-14-043291-4*) Viking Penguin.

— Ghostly Tales & Eerie Poems of Edgar Allan Poe. LC 92-30884. (Illustrated Junior Library). (Illus.). 256p. (J). 1993. 14.95 (*0-448-40533-4*, G & D) Peng Put Young Read.

— The Gold Bug. Harris, Raymond, ed. (Classics Ser.). (Illus.). 48p. (YA). (gr. 6-12). 1982. teacher ed. 7.32 (*0-89061-269-2*, 481, Jamestwn Pub); pap. text 5.99 (*0-89061-268-4*, 479, Jamestwn Pub); audio 17.96 (*0-89061-270-6*, 480, Jamestwn Pub) NTC Contemp Pub Co.

— The Gold Bug & Other Stories: The Black Cat, The Pit & the Pendulum. (Illus.). 1962. pap. 5.95 (*0-8283-1437-3*, 22) Branden Bks.

— The Gold Bug & Other Tales. (Thrift Editions Ser.). 128p. (Orig.). 1993. pap. 1.00 (*0-486-26875-6*) Dover.

— Great Short Works of Edgar Allan Poe. (Perennial Classic Ser.). 1970. 12.60 (*0-606-02062-4*, Pub. by Turtleback) Demco.

— Great Short Works Poe. 576p. 1970. pap. 7.50 (*0-06-083093-X*) HarperTrade.

— Great Tales & Poems of Edgar Allan Poe. 432p. 1990. per. 5.99 (*0-671-72770-2*, WSP) PB.

— Great Tales & Poems of Edgar Allan Poe. 1951. 11.09 (*0-606-03490-0*, Pub. by Turtleback) Demco.

— Histoires Extraordinaires. (FRE.). 1996. pap. 7.95 (*2-87714-329-5*, Pub. by Bookking Intl) Distribks Inc.

***Poe, Edgar Allan.** Hop Frog. rev. ed. Kisner, Don, ed. (Read-Along Radio Dramas Ser.). 45p. (YA). (gr. 7 up). 1998. ring bd. 38.00 incl. audio (*1-878298-13-5*) Balance Pub.

Poe, Edgar Allan. The Imaginary Voyages: The Narrative of Arthur Gordon Pym, The Unparalleled Adventure of One Hans Pfaall, The Journal of Julius Rodman, Vol. 1. rev. ed. Pollin, Burton R., ed. LC 81-2915. 667p. 1992. 100.00 (*0-87752-238-3*) Gordian.

Poe, Edgar Allan. Imp of the Perverse. abr. ed. LC 72-750995. 1975. audio 14.00 (*0-694-50265-0*, SWC 1450, Caedmon) HarperAudio.

Poe, Edgar Allan. Letters of Edgar Allan Poe, 2 vols., Set. Ostrom, John, ed. LC 66-20025. 731p. 1966. reprint ed. 150.00 (*0-87752-085-2*) Gordian.

— Listen & Read Edgar Allan Poe's The Raven & Other Poems. 1998. pap. 6.95 incl. audio (*0-486-40130-8*) Dover.

— Listen & Read Edgar Allan Poe's The Tell-Tale Heart & Other Stories. (Illus.). 128p. (Orig.). 1996. pap. text 5.95 incl. audio (*0-486-29123-5*) Dover.

— Literary Theory & Criticism. Cassuto, Leonard, ed. LC 99-36639. 256p. 1998. pap. 11.95 (*0-486-40155-3*) Dover.

— The Man of the Crowd. unabridged ed. 1994. lib. bdg. 18.95 incl. audio (*1-883049-44-X*) Sound Room.

— The Man of the Crowd, Set. unabridged ed. (Poe Ser.). 1994. 16.95 incl. audio (*1-883049-38-5*, 391134, Pub. by Sound Room) Lndmrk Audiobks.

— Marginalia. LC 80-22585. (Illus.). 255p. reprint ed. pap. 79.10 (*0-8357-3133-2*, 203939600012) Bks Demand.

— The Masque of the Red Death. (Short Story Library). (Illus.). 32p. (YA). (gr. 4 up). 1991. lib. bdg. 18.60 (*0-88682-477-X*, Creat Educ) Creative Co.

— The Masque of the Red Death. Harris, Raymond, ed. (Classics Ser.). (Illus.). 48p. (YA). (gr. 6-12). 1982. teacher ed. 7.32 (*0-89061-272-2*, 477, Jamestwn Pub); pap. text 5.99 (*0-89061-271-4*, 475, Jamestwn Pub); audio 17.96 (*0-89061-273-0*, 476, Jamestwn Pub) NTC Contemp Pub Co.

— Maxon's Poe: Seven Short Stories & Poems. limited ed. LC 98-105667. (Cottage Classics Ser.). (Illus.). 88p. 1997. 40.00 (*0-9642922-5-4*); pap. 17.95 (*0-9642922-4-6*) Word Play Calif.

— Murders in the Rue Morgue. 240p. 1998. 7.95 (*3-89508-090-X*) Konemann.

— Murders in the Rue Morgue & Other Stories. 1998. pap. text 7.95 (*1-902058-02-X*, Pub. by Pulp Fictions) Seven Hills Bk.

— The Murders in the Rue Morgue & Other Tales, Vol. 2. large type ed. LC 97-30821. Vol. 2. 240p. 1997. text 22.95 (*1-56000-535-1*) Transaction Pubs.

— The Narrative of Arthur Gordon Pym. (Notable American Authors Ser.). 1999. reprint ed. lib. bdg. 125.00 (*0-7812-8752-9*) Rprt Serv.

— The Narrative of Arthur Gordon Pym of Nantucket. Kopley, Richard, ed. & intro. by. LC 98-50102. 320p. 1999. pap. 8.95 (*0-14-043748-7*) Viking Penguin.

— The Narrative of Arthur Gordon Pym of Nantucket & Related Tales. Kennedy, J. Gerald, ed. & intro. by. (Oxford World's Classics Ser.). 328p. 1998. pap. 8.95 (*0-19-283771-0*) OUP.

***Poe, Edgar Allan.** Nouvelles Histoires Extraordinaires. 1999. pap. 9.95 (*2-266-08285-X*) Midwest European Pubns.

Poe, Edgar Allan. Oeuvres en Prose. (FRE.). 1932. lib. bdg. 89.95 (*0-8288-3527-6*, M5172) Fr & Eur.

— Oeuvres en Prose: Histoires Extraordinaires, Adventures d'Arthur Gordon Pym, Eureka, etc. Baudelaire, Charles, tr. 1184p. 41.50 (*0-686-56551-7*) Fr & Eur.

— The Pit & the Pendulum. (Classic Short Stories on Tape Ser.). (YA). (gr. 8-12). 1993. ring bd. 38.00 (*1-878298-11-9*) Balance Pub.

— The Pit & the Pendulum. Jamestown Publishers Staff, ed. 1982. pap. 7.80 (*0-8092-0047-3*, Jamestwn Pub) NTC Contemp Pub Co.

— The Pit & the Pendulum. Harris, Raymond, ed. (Classics Ser.). (Illus.). 48p. (YA). (gr. 6-12). 1982. teacher ed. 7.32 (*0-89061-266-8*, 473, Jamestwn Pub); pap. text 5.99 (*0-89061-265-X*, 471, Jamestwn Pub); audio 17.96 (*0-89061-267-6*, 472, Jamestwn Pub) NTC Contemp Pub Co.

***Poe, Edgar Allan.** The Pit & the Pendulum. (Short Stories Ser.). 22p. 2000. pap. 3.95 (*1-86092-019-5*, Pub. by Travelman Pub) IPG Chicago.

Poe, Edgar Allan. Poe: Selected Stories & Poems. (Airmont Classics Ser.). (J). (gr. 9 up). 1962. mass mkt. 3.95 (*0-8049-0008-6*, CL-8) Airmont.

— Les Poemes d'Edgar Allan Poe. Mallarme, Stephane, tr. LC 77-11473. (FRE., Illus.). reprint ed. 57.50 (*0-404-16335-1*) AMS Pr.

— Poems. (BCL1-PS American Literature Ser.). 332p. 1992. reprint ed. lib. bdg. 89.00 (*0-7812-6831-1*) Rprt Serv.

— Poems & Essays on Poetry. Sisson, C. H., ed. & intro. by. xvi, 150p. 1995. pap. 17.95 (*1-85754-120-0*, Pub. by Carcanet Pr) Paul & Co Pubs.

— Poems & Prose. LC 95-15329. (Everyman's Library of Pocket Poets). 256p. 1995. 12.50 (*0-679-44505-6*) Knopf.

— Poems & Tales of Edgar Allan Poe at Fordham. 2nd ed. Beirne, Elizabeth, ed. (Illus.). 42p. 1999. pap. 15.00 (*0-941980-06-5*) Bronx County.

— The Poems of Edgar Allan Poe. Stovall, Floyd, ed. LC 65-23455. 400p. reprint ed. pap. 124.00 (*0-7837-1246-4*, 204138300020) Bks Demand.

— The Poems of Edgar Allan Poe. Mabbott, Thomas O., ed. LC 79-28853. 511p. reprint ed. pap. 158.50 (*0-7837-4168-5*, 205901700012) Bks Demand.

— The Poems of Edgar Allan Poe: Illustrated & Decorated by W. Heath Robinson. LC 71-536276. xxi, 225 p. 1970. write for info. (*0-7135-1603-8*) CE10.

— Poetry & Tales. Quinn, Patrick F., ed. 1408p. 1984. 37.50 (*0-940450-18-6*, Pub. by Library of America) Penguin Putnam.

— Poetry, Tales & Selected Essays. LC 96-8922. (Library of America College Editions). 1506p. (C). 1996. pap. text 16.95 (*1-883011-38-8*, Pub. by Library of America) Penguin Putnam.

— Politian: An Unfinished Tragedy. (BCL1-PS American Literature Ser.). 89p. 1992. reprint ed. lib. bdg. 59.00 (*0-7812-6832-X*) Rprt Serv.

— The Portable Edgar Allan Poe. Stern, Phillip V., ed. & selected by. LC 76-54888. (Portable Library: No. 12). 704p. 1977. pap. 15.95 (*0-14-015012-9*, Penguin Bks) Viking Penguin.

— The Prose Romances of Edgar Allan Poe. (Notable American Authors Ser.). 1999. reprint ed. lib. bdg. 125.00 (*0-7812-8755-3*) Rprt Serv.

— The Raven. LC 95-45989. (Illus.). 64p. 1996. reprint ed. pap. 6.95 (*0-486-29072-7*) Dover.

— The Raven. 4th ed. (Illus.). 48p. 1996. reprint ed. pap. 7.95 (*0-9631135-3-4*) MCE Publ Co.

— The Raven: Poem. Mallarme, Stephane, tr. from FRE. (Illustrated Book Reprints Ser.: Raven Bks.). (Illus.). 14p. 1978. reprint ed. boxed set 75.00 (*0-932256-00-7*) Pilgrim Pr Corp NY.

— The Raven & Other Favorite Poems. 64p. 1991. pap. 1.00 (*0-486-26685-0*) Dover.

— The Raven & Other Poems. 80p. (YA). (gr. 7-9). 1992. pap. 2.95 (*0-590-45260-6*, Apple Classics) Scholastic Inc.

Poe, Edgar Allan. The Raven & Other Poems. (Apple Classics Ser.). (J). 1992. 9.09 (*0-606-01929-4*, Pub. by Turtleback) Demco.

Poe, Edgar Allan. The Raven & Other Poems. 1998. lib. bdg. 13.95 (*1-56723-085-7*) Yestermorrow.

— The Raven & Other Poems. (Notable American Authors Ser.). 1999. reprint ed. lib. bdg. 125.00 (*0-7812-8757-X*) Rprt Serv.

— The Raven & The Pit & the Pendulum. Modern Library Staff, ed. LC 98-18665. 1998. pap. 12.00 (*0-375-75216-1*) Modern Lib NY.

— The Science Fiction of Edgar Allan Poe. Beaver, Harold, ed. & compiled by by. (English Library). 430p. 1976. pap. 11.95 (*0-14-043106-3*, Penguin Classics) Viking Penguin.

— The Selected Poetry & Prose. Mabbott, Thomas O., ed. (Modern Library College Editions). 427p. (C). 1951. pap. 8.44 (*0-07-553641-2*) McGraw.

— Selected Stories & Poems. Gray, Richard, ed. 320p. 1993. pap. 6.95 (*0-460-87261-3*, Everyman's Classic Lib) Tuttle Pubng.

— Selected Stories of Poe. large type ed. (Large Print Ser.). 600p. 1993. reprint ed. lib. bdg. 24.00 (*0-939495-47-3*) North Bks.

— Selected Tales. LC 90-50620. 436p. 1991. pap. 14.00 (*0-679-72524-5*) Vin Bks.

— Selected Tales. 2nd ed. Van Leer, David, ed. & intro. by. (Oxford World's Classics Ser.). 366p. 1998. pap. 7.95 (*0-19-283224-7*) OUP.

Poe, Edgar Allan. Selected Writings, 001. Davidson, E. H., ed. LC 56-13895. (Orig.). (C). 1956. pap. 13.96 (*0-395-05110-X*) HM.

— Selected Writings of Edgar Allan Poe. Thompson, G. R., ed. 1999. pap. text 16.00 (*0-393-97285-2*) Norton.

Poe, Edgar Allan. Selections from the Critical Writings of Edgar Allan Poe. Prescott, F. C., ed. & intro. by. Carlson, Eric W., intro. 425p. (C). 1981. reprint ed. 50.00 (*0-87752-182-4*) Gordian.

— The Short Fiction of Edgar Allan Poe: An Annotated Edition. annot. ed. Levine, Stuart & Levine, Susan, eds. 672p. 1990. pap. 21.95 (*0-252-06125-X*) U of Ill Pr.

— Tales. (Notable American Authors Ser.). 1999. reprint ed. lib. bdg. 125.00 (*0-7812-8756-1*) Rprt Serv.

***Poe, Edgar Allan.** Tales & Sketches Vol. 1: 1831-1842. Mabbott, Thomas Ollive et al, eds. 752p. 2000. reprint ed. pap. 25.00 (*0-252-06922-6*) U of Ill Pr.

— Tales & Sketches Vol. 2: 1843-1849. Mabbott, Thomas Ollive et al, eds. 760p. 2000. reprint ed. pap. 25.00 (*0-252-06923-4*) U of Ill Pr.

Poe, Edgar Allan. Tales & The Raven & Other Poems. LC 69-13800. 1975. pap. 4.00 (*0-675-09530-1*, Merrill Coll) P-H.

Poe, Edgar Allan. Tales of Edgar Allan Poe. pap. write for info. (*0-688-16674-1*, Wm Morrow) Morrow Avon.

Poe, Edgar Allan. Tales of Edgar Allan Poe. LC 91-3277. (Books of Wonder). (Illus.). 312p. (J). 1991. 22.00 (*0-688-07509-6*, Wm Morrow) Morrow Avon.

— Tales of Mystery & Imagination. 360p. Date not set. 22.95 (*0-8488-2555-1*) Amereon Ltd.

— Tales of Mystery & Imagination. LC 95-39315. (Illus.). (J). 1995. 22.00 (*0-15-200959-0*) Harcourt.

— Tales of Mystery & Imagination. (Fiction Ser.). (YA). 1993. pap. text 6.50 (*0-582-08483-0*, 79831) Longman.

— Tales of Mystery & Imagination. LC 88-40069. 304p. 1988. 25.00 (*0-89296-350-6*) Mysterious Pr.

— Tales of Mystery & Imagination. Hedge, Tricia, ed. (Illus.). 64p. 1994. pap. text 5.95 (*0-19-422689-1*) OUP.

— Tales of Mystery & Imagination. Clarke, Graham, ed. 576p. 1993. pap. 6.95 (*0-460-87342-3*, Everyman's Classic Lib) Tuttle Pubng.

— Tales of Mystery & Imagination. 280p. 1997. pap. 3.95 (*1-85326-013-4*, 0134WW, Pub. by Wrdsworth Edits) NTC Contemp Pub Co.

— Tales of Mystery & Imagination. 1981. reprint ed. lib. bdg. 27.95 (*0-89966-434-2*) Buccaneer Bks.

— Tales of Mystery & Terror. 20.95 (*0-8488-1127-5*) Amereon Ltd.

— Tales of Mystery & Terror. Vogel, Malvina, ed. (Great Illustrated Classics Ser.: Vol. 33). (Illus.). 240p. (J). (gr. 3-6). 1994. 9.95 (*0-86611-984-1*) Playmore Inc.

— Tales of Mystery & Terror. (Illus.). (gr. 1-4). 1995. pap. 4.99 (*0-14-036720-9*) Viking Penguin.

— Tales of Terror & Detection. unabridged ed. (Thrift Editions Ser.). 96p. 1998. reprint ed. pap. 1.00 (*0-486-28744-0*) Dover.

— Tales of the Grotesque & Arabesque. (Notable American Authors Ser.). 1999. reprint ed. lib. bdg. 125.00 (*0-7812-8754-5*) Rprt Serv.

— Tamerlane & Other Poems. (Notable American Authors Ser.). 1999. reprint ed. lib. bdg. 125.00 (*0-7812-8750-2*) Rprt Serv.

— The Tell-Tale Heart. (Classic Frights Ser.). (Illus.). 64p. (YA). (gr. 5 up). 1998. pap. 5.95 (*0-929605-86-1*, Classic Frights) Books of Wonder.

— The Tell-Tale Heart. Harris, Raymond, ed. (Classics Ser.). (Illus.). 48p. (YA). (gr. 6-12). 1982. teacher ed. 7.32 (*0-89061-263-3*, 469, Jamestwn Pub); pap. text 5.99 (*0-89061-262-5*, 467, Jamestwn Pub); audio 16.67 (*0-89061-264-1*, 468, Jamestwn Pub) NTC Contemp Pub Co.

— The Tell-Tale Heart. rev. ed. (Read-Along Radio Dramas Ser.). (YA). (gr. 6-12). 1993. reprint ed. ring bd. 38.00 (*1-878298-04-6*) Balance Pub.

— The Tell-Tale Heart & Other Writings. 432p. (gr. 7-12). 1983. mass mkt. 5.95 (*0-553-21228-1*, Bantam Classics) Bantam.

Poe, Edgar Allan. The Tell-Tale Heart & Other Writings. (Bantam Classics Ser.). 1982. 11.05 (*0-606-01761-5*, Pub. by Turtleback) Demco.

— Thirty-Two Stories. Levine, Stuart & Levine, Susan, eds. LC 99-48766. 390p. (C). 2000. pap. 12.95 (*0-87220-498-7*); lib. bdg. 37.95 (*0-87220-499-5*) Hackett Pub.

Poe, Edgar Allan. The Unabridged Edgar Allan Poe. LC 83-16023. (Illus.). 1184p. (Orig.). 1983. pap. 17.95 (*0-89471-233-0*) Running Pr.

— The Unabridged Edgar Allan Poe. unabridged ed. (Unabridged Classics Ser.). 1184p. (Orig.). 1997. 18.98 (*0-7624-0178-8*, Courage) Running Pr.

— The Unknown Poe: An Anthology of Fugitive Writings. Foye, Raymond, ed. LC 80-2431. 1980. pap. 8.95 (*0-87286-110-4*) City Lights.

— Works of Edgar Allan Poe. deluxe ed. 768p. 1990. 19.99 (*0-517-05358-6*) Random Hse Value.

— Works of Edgar Allan Poe, 10 vols, Set. Stedman, Edmund C. & Woodberry, George E., eds. LC 71-169773. (Select Bibliographies Reprint Ser.). reprint ed. 250.00 (*0-8369-5993-0*) Ayer.

— The Works of Edgar Allan Poe: With a Study of His Life & Writings by Charles Baudelaire. Curwen, H., tr. LC 77-11472. reprint ed. 42.50 (*0-404-16334-3*) AMS Pr.

— The Works of Edgar Allen Poe. (Poetry Library). 180p. 1998. pap. 7.95 (*1-85326-432-6*, 4326WW, Pub. by Wrdsworth Edits) NTC Contemp Pub Co.

Poe, Edgar Allan & Carlson, Eric W. The Fall of the House of Usher. LC 73-166123. (Merrill Literary Casebook Ser.). v, 138p. (J). 1971. write for info. (*0-675-09641-3*, Merrill Pub Co) Macmillan.

Poe, Edgar Allan & McMahon, Luella E. The Tell-Tale Heart. 26p. (YA). (gr. 10 up). 1967. pap. 3.50 (*0-87129-819-8*, T16) Dramatic Pub.

***Poe, Edgar Allan & Prunier, James.** The Pit & the Pendulum & Other Stories. (Illus.). 153p. (YA). (gr. 8 up). 1999. 25.99 (*0-670-88706-4*, Viking Child); pap. 17.99 (*0-670-88725-0*, Viking Child) Peng Put Young Read.

***Poe, Edgar Allan & Whitman, Sarah Helen.** Last Flowers: The Romance Poems of Edgar Allan Poe & Sarah Helen Whitman. 2nd rev. ed. Rutherford, Brett, ed. (Illus.). 120p. 2000. pap. 12.95 (*0-922558-08-6*) Poets Pr.

Poe, Edgar Allan & Wilmer, Lambert A. Letters & Documents in the Enoch Pratt Free Library. LC 41-10640. 192p. 1978. 50.00 (*0-8201-1199-6*) Schol Facsimiles.

Poe, Edgar Allan & Wilson, Gahan. The Raven & Other Poems. (Classics Illustrated Ser.). (Illus.). 52p. (YA). pap. 4.95 (*1-57209-000-6*) Classics Int Ent.

Poe, Edgar Allan, et al. The Fall of the House of Usher. (Classics Illustrated Ser.). (Illus.). 52p. (YA). pap. 4.95 (*1-57209-014-6*) Classics Int Ent.

Poe, Edgar Allan, jt. auth. see Hurley, Mike.

Poe, Edgar Allan, jt. auth. see Wiles, Julian.

Poe, Elizabeth A. Focus on Relationships. LC 93-21030. (Teenage Perspectives Ser.). 257p. 1993. lib. bdg. 39.50 (*0-87436-672-0*) ABC-CLIO.

— Focus on Sexuality. LC 90-43661. (Teenage Perspectives Ser.). 225p. (J). 1990. lib. bdg. 39.50 (*0-87436-116-8*) ABC-CLIO.

— Presenting Barbara Wersba. LC 97-44279. 180p. (YA). (gr. 10 up). 1998. 24.95 Mac Lib Ref.

***Poe, Elizabeth W.** Compilatio: Lyric Texts & Prose Commentaries in Troubadour Manuscript H (Vat. Lat. 3207) LC 00-130184. (Edward C. Armstrong Monographs on Medieval Literature: Vol. 11). 308p. 2000. pap. 34.50 (*0-917058-93-3*) French Forum.

Poe, Elizabeth W. From Poetry to Prose in Old Provencal. LC 83-50518. (ENG & PRO.). 133p. 1984. 16.95 (*0-917786-33-5*) Summa Pubns.

Poe, Elmer, ed. Study Guide for the CET Test-Computer Option. 4th ed. 31p. 1993. pap. 10.00 (*0-318-17467-7*) Intl Soc Cert Elect.

Poe, Francis R. Teaching & Performing Renaissance Choral Music: A Guide for Conductors & Performers. LC 93-23597. 227p. 1994. 39.50 (*0-8108-2778-6*); pap. 26.50 (*0-8108-2886-3*) Scarecrow.

***Poe, Harry L. & Davis, Jimmy H.** Science & Faith: An Evangelical Dialogue. 288p. 2000. pap. text 19.99 (*0-8054-2142-4*) Broadman.

Poe, Jerry B. An Introduction to the American Business Enterprise. 7th ed. (C). 1989. student ed. 18.50 (*0-256-07366-X*, Irwn McGrw-H) McGrw-H Hghr Educ.

Poe, John Robert. Festival Favorites. 16p. (J). 1996. pap. 3.95 (*0-87718-050-4*, 12017) Willis Music Co.

Poe, Lenora M. Black Grandparents As Parents. (Orig.). 1992. pap. text 13.95 (*0-9633992-0-9*) L M Poe.

Poe, Lori M. Beyond Miracles. LC 91-92914. 260p. 1996. pap. 23.95 (*0-9624804-4-4*) Place Light.

— Dynamic Keys to Self-Healing. LC 91-92914. 244p. 1992. pap. 23.95 (*0-9624804-5-2*) Place Light.

— Journeys to Worlds Beyond. rev. ed. LC 91-92915. 152p. 1992. pap. 23.95 (*0-9624804-3-6*) Place Light.

— Milestones to God: Healing Mind & Emotions. LC 89-92799. 260p. (Orig.). 1990. pap. 23.95 (*0-9624804-0-1*) Place Light.

— My Name Is Ana. LC 91-91466. (Illus.). 208p. 1992. pap. 23.95 (*0-9624804-9-5*) Place Light.

— Teach Me the Way. LC 91-92913. 153p. 1992. pap. 23.95 (*0-9624804-7-9*) Place Light.

Poe, Margie. The No-Cooking Cookbook for Kids. (Illus.). (J). (gr. k-6). 1985. pap. 4.95 (*0-936985-75-5*, 1096A) Kidsmart.

Poe, Marshall. Foreign Descriptions of Muscovy: An Analytic Bibliography of Primary & Secondary Sources. 233p. 1995. 27.95 (*0-89357-262-4*) Slavica.

P

Poe, Maurice & Schmidt, Barbara. Word-Wise Sourcebook: Laugh-Aloud Rhymes for Learning Language Skills: Grade Level 1-2, Level 1. (Illus.). 1997. teacher ed., spiral bd. 42.50 (*1-886050-13-9*) Egger Pub Inc.

Poe, Maurice, jt. auth. see Schmidt, Barbara.

Poe, Randy. Music Publishing: A Songwriter's Guide. rev. ed. LC 97-25566. (Illus.). 144p. 1997. pap. 18.99 (*0-89879-754-3*, Wrtrs Digest Bks) F & W Pubns Inc.

Poe, Ray W. The McGraw-Hill Handbook of Business Letters. 3rd ed. 400p. 1993. 59.50 (*0-07-911700-7*) McGraw.

Poe, Richard. Black Spark, White Fire: Did African Explorers Civilize Ancient Europe? LC 97-27713. (Illus.). 576p. 1997. 37.95 (*0-7615-0758-2*) Prima Pub.

— Einstein Factor: New Method for Increasing Intelligence. 352p. 1995. pap. 15.95 (*0-7615-0186-X*) Prima Pub.

***Poe, Richard.** Wave 4: Network Marketing in the 21st Century. LC 99-37125. 1999. pap. 15.00 (*0-7615-1752-9*) Prima Pub.

— Wave 4 Way. pap. 15.00 (*0-7615-2213-1*) Prima Pub.

Poe, Richard. Wave Three: The New Era in Network Marketing. LC 94-9089. 288p. 1994. pap. 14.95 (*1-55958-501-3*) Prima Pub.

— Wave Three: The New Era in Network Marketing. 1997. 18.95 incl. audio (*0-7615-0673-X*, 634227) Prima Pub.

— The Wave Three to Building Your Downline: Your Guide to Building a Successful Network Marketing Empire. 256p. 1996. pap. 14.95 (*0-7615-0439-7*) Prima Pub.

— The Wave Three Way to Building Your Downline: Your Guide to Building a Successful Network Marketing Empire. LC 96-32432. 1997. 18.95 incl. audio (*0-7615-0757-4*, 634202) Prima Pub.

Poe, Robert. The Black Cat. 1998. mass mkt. 6.99 (*0-8125-4932-5*, Pub. by Tor Bks) St Martin.

— Return to the House of Usher. LC 96-18270. 288p. 1996. 22.95 (*0-312-86012-9*) Forge NYC.

— Return to the House of Usher. 1997. mass mkt. 6.99 (*0-8125-4931-7*, Pub. by Tor Bks) St Martin.

Poe, Robert H. & Israel, Robert H., eds. Problems in Pulmonary Medicine for the Primary Physician. LC 82-8972. (Illus.). 426p. reprint ed. pap. 132.10 (*0-7837-1494-7*, 205719000023) Bks Demand.

Poe, Roy W. The McGraw-Hill Handbook of Business Letters. 3rd ed. LC 93-24986. 384p. 1992. 59.50 (*0-07-050425-3*) McGraw.

— The McGraw-Hill Handbook of Business Letters. 3rd ed. LC 93-24986. 363p. 1994. pap. 19.95 (*0-07-050451-2*) McGraw.

Poe, Roy W. & Fruehling, Rosemary T. Business Communication: A Case Method Approach. LC 94-21339. 1995. text, teacher ed. 15.00 (*1-56118-338-5*) Paradigm MN.

— Business Communication: A Case Method Approach. 5th ed. LC 94-21339. 425p. 1994. text 31.95 (*1-56118-337-7*) Paradigm MN.

— Business Communication: A Problem-Solving Approach. 4th ed. 406p. 1989. pap. text 28.95 (*1-56118-317-2*) Paradigm MN.

— Business Communication: A Problem-Solving Approach. 4th ed. 406p. 1989. teacher ed. 14.00 (*1-56118-318-0*); student ed. 10.00 (*1-56118-313-X*) Paradigm MN.

Poe, Roy W., et al. Getting Invloved with Business. (Illus.). 576p. (gr. 9-10). 1981. text 22.60 (*0-07-050335-4*) McGraw.

Poe, Sidney. The Gospel According to Mark: A Commentary. LC 94-15350. 400p. (Orig.). 1994. pap. 10.99 (*1-56722-024-X*) Word Aflame.

Poe, Stephen E. A Vision of the Future. (Star Trek). 1998. per. 18.00 (*0-671-53481-5*) PB.

Poe, Vidette. Building A Data Warehouse for Decision Support. 2nd ed. LC 98-104050. 340p. (C). 1997. 49.99 (*0-13-769639-6*) P-H.

Poe, Vidette & Reeves, Laura L. Building a Data Warehouse for Decision Support. LC 97-29161. (Illus.). 1997. write for info. (*0-13-590662-8*) P-H.

Poe, W. Old Person in Your Home. 1986. pap. 2.45 (*0-684-71871-5*, Scribners Ref) Mac Lib Ref.

Poe, William A. Green W. Hartsfield, A Biography: 1883-1986. LC 84-61196. (Illus.). 228p. 1984. 22.50 (*0-917898-12-5*) NSU Pr LA.

Poe-Yamagata, Eileen & Butts, Jeffrey A. Female Offenders in the Juvenile Justice System: Statistics Summary. (Illus.). 25p. (Orig.). (C). 1996. pap. text 15.00 (*0-7881-3724-7*) DIANE Pub.

Poebel, Arno. Babylonian Legal & Business Documents: From the Time of the First Dynasty of Babylon; Chiefly from Nippur. LC PJ3711.P4. (University of Pennsylvania, Babylonian Expedition, Series A: Cuneiform Texts: Vol. 6, Pt. 2). 251p. reprint ed. pap. 77.90 (*0-8357-5940-7*, 205201400027) Bks Demand.

— Grammatical Texts. LC 15-2790. (University of Pennsylvania, the University Museum, Publications of the Babylonian Section: Vol. 6, No. 1). 122p. reprint ed. pap. 37.90 (*0-608-13651-4*, 205202500026) Bks Demand.

— Historical & Grammatical Texts. LC 15-2790. (University of Pennsylvania, the University Museum, Publications of the Babylonian Section: Vol. 5). 136p. reprint ed. pap. 42.20 (*0-608-13650-6*, 205202400026) Bks Demand.

— Historical Texts. LC 15-2790. (University of Pennsylvania, the University Museum, Publications of the Babylonian Section: Vol. 4, No. 1). 242p. reprint ed. pap. 75.10 (*0-608-13649-2*, 205202300026) Bks Demand.

Poeck, Klaus. Diagnostic Decisions in Neurology. LC 85-18801. 145p. 1985. 39.00 (*0-387-15779-4*) Spr-Verlag.

Poeck, Klaus, et al, eds. New Trends in Diagnosis & Management of Stroke. (Illus.). 169p. 1988. pap. 33.10 (*0-387-18369-8*) Spr-Verlag.

Poedjosoedarmo, Soepomo, jt. auth. see Wolff, John U.

Poehlein, Gary W., jt. ed. see Tess, Roy W.

Poehling, Gary G., et al, eds. Arthroscopy of the Wrist & Elbow. LC 93-42821. 200p. 1994. text 98.00 (*0-7817-0194-5*) Lppncott W & W.

Poehlman, Elizabeth S. Darrington: Mining Town/Timber Town. (Illus.). 176p. 1995. pap. 10.95 (*0-9648572-0-0*) Gold Hill Pr.

Poehlman, John M. Breeding Field Crops. LC 93-44366. (Illus.). 740p. 1994. reprint ed. pap. 200.00 (*0-608-00033-7*, 206079900006) Bks Demand.

— Mungbean. (C). 1991. text 27.50 (*81-204-0590-0*, Pub. by Oxford IBH) S Asia.

Poehlman, John M. & Sleper, David A. Breeding Field Crops. 4th ed. LC 94-36673. (Illus.). 510p. 1995. text 66.95 (*0-8138-2427-3*) Iowa St U Pr.

Poehlman, William R., tr. see Lohse, Edward.

Poehlmann, JoAnna. Love Letters. LC 95-33393. (Post Impressions Ser.). (Illus.). 72p. 1996. bds. 5.95 (*0-7892-0091-0*) Abbeville Pr.

— Post Impressions: Cancelling Out. (Illus.). 148p. 1991. 4.98 (*1-55859-233-4*) Abbeville Pr.

— Post Impressions: Food for Thought. (Illus.). 148p. 1991. 4.98 (*1-55859-232-6*) Abbeville Pr.

— Post Impressions: Love Letters. (Illus.). 74p. 1991. 10.95 (*1-55859-231-8*) Abbeville Pr.

Poehlmann, William R., tr. see Lohfink, Gerhard.

***Poehls, D. J. & Smith, Gregory J.** Encyclopedic Dictionary of Hydrogeology. 1999. 79.95 (*0-12-558690-6*) Acad Pr.

***Poehner, Donna, ed.** Photographer's Market: 2,000 Places to Sell Your Photographs. 640p. 2000. pap. 24.99 (*0-89879-978-3*) F & W Pubns Inc.

***Poekel, Charles.** West Essex/North Caldwell. (Images of America Ser.). 128p. 1999. pap. 18.99 (*0-7385-0141-7*) Arcadia Publng.

Poekel, Wilhelm. Philologisches Schriftsteller Lexikon. 2nd ed. 1974. 95.00 (*0-7859-0844-7*, M-7582) Fr & Eur.

Poel, Cornelius Van der, see Van der Poel, Cornelius.

Poel, M. G. Van Der, see Van Der Poel, M. G.

Poel, Marc G. Van der, see Van der Poel, Marc G.

Poel, William. Shakespeare in the Theatre. LC 70-143343. reprint ed. 31.50 (*0-404-05067-0*) AMS Pr.

— Shakespeare in the Theatre. LC 67-31456. 1972. reprint ed. 19.95 (*0-405-08859-0*) Ayer.

Poeldinger, W., ed. Somatisierte Angst und Depressivitaet. (Illus.). vi, 136p. 1984. 35.00 (*3-8055-3844-8*) S Karger.

Poeldinger, W. & Taeuber, K., eds. Nomifensine-Clinical & Experimental Investigation. (Journal: International Pharmacopsychiatry: Vol. 17, Suppl. 1, 1982). iv, 148p. 1982. pap. 41.75 (*3-8055-3585-6*) S Karger.

Poeldinger, W., jt. ed. see Kielholz, P.

Poelker, Greg, ed. see Buse, John J.

Poelker, Kathy. Amazing Musical Moments. (Illus.). 48p. 1985. teacher ed. 7.95 (*0-945405-06-5*) LAM Co.

— At the Firehouse. Judge, Matt, ed. (Rhythms to Reading Ser.). (Illus.). 8p. (Orig.). (J). (ps-3). 1988. pap. text 15.00 (*0-929842-00-6*) Hawthorne Pubs.

— Look at Me. (Illus.). 64p. 1987. teacher ed. 7.95 (*0-945405-00-6*) LAM Co.

— Look at My World. (Illus.). 48p. 1983. teacher ed. 7.95 (*0-945405-04-9*) LAM Co.

— Look at the Holidays. (Illus.). 64p. (J). (ps-4). 1988. reprint ed. teacher ed. 7.95 (*0-317-91200-3*) LAM Co.

— One Little Drop of Sunshine. Judge, Matt, ed. (Rhythms to Reading Ser.). (Illus.). 8p. (Orig.). (J). (ps-3). 1988. pap. text 15.00 (*0-929842-01-4*) Hawthorne Pubs.

Poellner, Peter. Nietzsche & Metaphysics. (Oxford Philosophical Monographs). 332p. 1995. text 60.00 (*0-19-823517-8*) OUP.

***Poellner, Peter.** Nietzsche & Metaphysics. 336p. 2000. pap. 24.95 (*0-19-825063-0*) OUP.

Poellot, Luther, tr. see Chemitz, Martin.

Poelman, Anne O. The Amulek Alternative. LC 97-28687. x, 132p. 1997. 15.95 (*1-57345-322-6*) Deseret Bk.

— The Simeon Solution: One Woman's Spiritual Odyssey. LC 94-46883. vii, 151p. 1995. 14.95 (*0-87579-967-1*) Deseret Bk.

***Poelman, Anne Osborn.** Secret Santa. 2000. 15.95 (*1-57345-792-2*, Shadow Mount) Deseret Bk.

***Poelman, Catherine E.** The Soul of Adoption. LC 00-24520. 2000. pap. write for info. (*1-57345-655-1*) Deseret Bk.

Poelsema, B. & Comsa, G. Scattering of Thermal Energy Atoms from Disordered Surfaces. (Tracts in Modern Physics Ser.: Vol. 115). (Illus.). 170p. 1989. 80.95 (*0-387-50358-7*) Spr-Verlag.

Poelstra, Francine. Pull the Cord: Discover Who You Really Are. 3 Simple Steps. Mitchell, Nancy, ed. LC 98-96420. (Illus.). 144p. 1998. 9.95 (*0-9666228-0-4*) Dynamic Poss.

Poelstra, Sharon R., ed. Lifetime Memories, 1995-96: Summer Missions Handbook. rev. ed. 1995. pap. text 5.00 (*0-9621469-3-5*) Biola Student Missionary.

Poelt, J. Bestimmungsschluessel Europaeischer Flechten. (Illus.). 1969. pap. 56.00 (*3-7682-0159-7*) Lubrecht & Cramer.

Poelt, J. & Vezda, A. Bestimmungsschluessel Europaeischer Flechten. (Bibliotheca Lichenologica Ser.: No. 9, suppl. I). 1977. lib. bdg. 32.50 (*3-7682-1162-2*) Lubrecht & Cramer.

— Bestimmungsschluessel Europaeischer Flechten, Suppl. II. (Bibliotheca Lichenologica Ser.: No. 16). (GER.). 390p. 1981. text 52.00 (*3-7682-1312-9*) Lubrecht & Cramer.

Poelt, J., jt. auth. see Mayrhofer, H.

Poelt, Josef & Hinteregger, Erika. Beitrage Zur Kenntnis der Flechtenflora des Himalaya Vol. VII: Die Gattungen Caloplaca, Fulgensia und Ioplaca (Mit Englischem Bestimmungsschlussel) Wirth, Volkmar et al, eds. (Bibliotheca Lichenologica: Vol. 50). (GER., Illus.). 256p. 1993. 71.00 (*3-443-58029-7*, Pub. by Gebruder Borntraeger) Balogh.

Poelt, Josef, ed. see Kapitel, V. & Engler, Adolf.

Poem & the World Editorial Committee, ed. The Poem & the World: An International Anthology of Poetry, Bk. IV. (Orig.). 1996. pap. 10.00 (*0-9636124-4-1*) Poem & The Wrld.

Poem & the World Editorial Committee, jt. auth. see International Poets Staff.

Poem & the World Editorial Committee, ed. see International Poets Staff.

Poen, Monte M. Harry S. Truman vs. the Medical Lobby: The Genesis of Medicare. LC 96-20042. 272p. (C). 1996. pap. 16.95 (*0-8262-1086-4*) U of Mo Pr.

Poen, Monte M., ed. Strictly Personal & Confidential: The Letters Harry Truman Never Mailed. LC 99-15517. (Give 'Em Hell Harry Ser.). 224p. 1999. pap. 19.95 (*0-8262-1258-1*) U of Mo Pr.

Poenar, Daniel P. Thin Film Colour Sensors. (Illus.). 236p. (Orig.). 1996. pap. 57.50 (*90-407-1343-X*, Pub. by Delft U Pr) Coronet Bks.

Poenaru, D. N. & Greiner, W., eds. Experimental Techniques in Nuclear Physics. 690p. (C). 1997. lib. bdg. 315.55 (*3-11-014467-0*) De Gruyter.

Poenaru, Dorin N. Nuclear Decay Modes. LC 95-45782. (Fundamental & Applied Nuclear Physics Ser.). 577p. 1996. 353.00 (*0-7503-0338-7*) IOP Pub.

Poenaru, Dorin N. & Ivascu, Marin S., eds. Particle Emission from Nuclei, 3 vols., Vol. I: Nuclear Deformation Energy. 256p. 1988. 152.00 (*0-8493-4634-7*, QC793, CRC Reprint) Franklin.

— Particle Emission from Nuclei, 3 vols., Vol. II: Alpha, Proton, & Heavy Ion Radioactives. 272p. 1988. 155.00 (*0-8493-4635-5*, QC793, CRC Reprint) Franklin.

— Particle Emission from Nuclei, 3 vols., Vol. III: Fission & Beta-Delayed Decay Modes. 224p. 1988. 147.00 (*0-8493-4636-3*, QC793, CRC Reprint) Franklin.

***Poenaru, Dorin N. & Stoica, Sabin, eds.** Advances in Nuclear Physics. 400p. 2000. 86.00 (*981-02-4276-X*) World Scientific Pub.

Poenaru, Dorin N., jt. auth. see Greiner, W.

Poepoe, Karen, jt. auth. see Kahalewai, Marilyn.

Poeppig, E. & Endlicher, S. Nova Genera Ac Species Plantarum Quas in Regno Chilensi, Peruviano & in Terra Amazonica Annis 1827-32: 1835-45. 1968. 450.00 (*3-7682-0549-5*) Lubrecht & Cramer.

Poerksen, Uwe. Plastic Words: The Tyranny of a Modular Language. Mason, Jutta & Cayley, David, trs. LC 94-44589. (Illus.). 134p. 1995. 24.50 (*0-271-01476-8*) Pa St U Pr.

Poersch, Eric, ed. see Mahlo, Edwin K.

Poerschke, R., jt. ed. see Madelung, Otfried.

Poertner, Dale F., ed. see Schmidt, Stan.

Poertner, John, jt. auth. see Rapp, Charles A.

Poertner, John, ed. see Friesen, Barbara J.

Poertner, Shirley & Miller, Karen M. The Art of Giving & Receiving Feedback. LC 96-84566. (How-to Book Ser.). 101p. (Orig.). 1996. pap. 12.95 (*1-884926-53-3*, FBACK) Amer Media.

Poerwowidagdo, Judo, et al, eds. Pastoral Theology from a Global Perspective: A Case Method Approach. LC 96-24882. 224p. (Orig.). 1996. pap. 17.00 (*1-57075-079-3*) Orbis Bks.

Poesch, Jesse, jt. auth. see Cuthbert, John A.

Poesch, Jesse, jt. auth. see Green, Nancy E.

Poesch, Jessie & Bacot, Barbara S., eds. Louisiana Buildings, 1720-1940: The Historic American Buildings Survey. LC 96-16959. (Illus.). 472p. (C). 1996. 59.95 (*0-8071-2054-5*) La State U Pr.

Poesch, Jessie, et al. Newcomb Pottery: An Enterprise for Southern Women, 1895-1904. LC 83-51776. (Illus.). 208p. 1984. pap. 24.95 (*0-916838-99-4*) Schiffer.

Poesch, Jessie, jt. auth. see Green, Nancy E.

Poeschel, H. African Impressions: Wildlife in African National Parks - the View of a Scientific Illustrator. 2nd ed. (ENG & GER., Illus.). 165p. 1989. 59.00 (*3-8236-1192-5*, Pub. by Backhuys Pubs) Balogh.

Poeschke, Joachim. Michelangelo & His World: Sculpture of the Italian Renaissance. Stockman, Russell, tr. from GER. LC 95-34373. (Illus.). 272p. 1996. 125.00 (*0-8109-4276-3*) Abrams.

— Die Sieneser Domkanzel des Nicola Pisano. LC 72-81565. (Beitraege zur Kunstgeschichte Ser.: Vol. 9). (C). 1973. 62.35 (*3-11-003961-3*) De Gruyter.

Poeschl, Viktor. Die Dichtkunst Virgils. 3rd rev. ed. (GER.). (C). 1977. 46.15 (*3-11-006885-0*) De Gruyter.

Poesnecker, G. E. Chronic Fatigue Unmasked 2000. rev. ed. (Illus.). 366p. 1999. pap. 15.00 (*0-916285-61-8*) Humanitarian.

— The Circle of Lives. (Illus.). 207p. 1988. 16.95 (*0-932785-68-9*); pap. 10.95 (*0-932785-69-7*) Philos Pub.

— A Guide for the New Renaissance. (Illus.). 181p. 1986. 16.95 (*0-932785-78-6*); pap. 10.95 (*0-932785-77-8*) Philos Pub.

— In Search of Health & Happiness. 296p. 1998. 17.95 (*1-891485-16-4*); pap. 11.95 (*1-891485-15-6*) Philos Pub.

— In Search of Health & Happiness. deluxe ed. 296p. 1998. 20.00 (*1-891485-17-2*) Philos Pub.

— In Search of Love & Wisdom. 212p. 1988. 17.95 (*0-932785-84-0*); pap. 11.95 (*0-932785-83-2*) Philos Pub.

— In Search of Love & Wisdom. deluxe ed. 212p. 1988. 20.00 (*0-932785-85-9*) Philos Pub.

— It's Only Natural. 442p. 1996. pap. 15.00 (*0-916285-40-5*) Humanitarian.

Poesnecker, G. E., ed. see Lindlahr, Henry.

Poesnecker, Gerald E. Creative Sex. 62p. (Orig.). 1972. pap. 2.00 (*0-916285-26-X*) Humanitarian.

— A Guide for the New Renaissance. LC 86-63004. 184p. 1986. 16.95 (*0-318-23247-2*); pap. 10.95 (*0-318-23248-0*) Randolph Pr.

— One Flesh: Body, Mind, Spirit. (Illus.). 284p. 1996. pap. 12.00 (*0-916285-41-3*) Humanitarian.

Poesse, Walter. Internal-Line-Structure of Thirty Autograph Plays of Lope De Vega. LC 72-6787. (Studies in Drama: No. 39). (C). 1972. reprint ed. lib. bdg. 49.00 (*0-8383-1655-7*) M S G Haskell Hse.

Poessehl, G. L. South Asian Archeaology Studies. 276p. (C). 1993. text 49.00 (*1-881570-17-7*) Science Pubs.

Poest, Gordon. Raising Reindeer for Pleasure & Profit. LC 98-93377. 100p. 1998. pap. 15.00 (*1-57502-893-X*, PO2455) Morris Pubng.

Poesy, SherryLynn. Book of Lives: Poetry by SherryLynn Poesy. LC 93-14296. 48p. 1993. pap. text 15.00 (*0-934172-26-9*) WIM Pubns.

Poet of Pearl. Cleaness: An Alliterative Tripartite Poem on the Deluge, the Destruction of Sodom, & the Death of Belshazzar, 2 vols., Set. (BCL1-PR English Literature Ser.). 1992. reprint ed. lib. bdg. 150.00 (*0-7812-7181-9*) Rprt Serv.

— Patience, An Alliterative Version of Jonah. (BCL1-PR English Literature Ser.). 77p. 1992. reprint ed. lib. bdg. 59.00 (*0-7812-7190-8*) Rprt Serv.

Poet Project Staff. A Poem for You. 48p. 1998. pap. 6.00 (*0-9655816-8-3*) Wings of Dawn.

Poethig, Eunice B., jt. auth. see Palm, James E.

Poetker-Thiessen, Audrey. Standing All Night Through. 1997. pap. 7.95 (*0-88801-169-5*, Pub. by Turnstone Pr) Genl Dist Srvs.

Poeton, E., ed. see Bonham, Thomas.

Poetry Society of America, et al. Poetry in Motion: Postcard Book. 1996. pap. 7.95 (*1-56924-805-2*) Marlowe & Co.

Poetry Society of Michigan. Golden Song. LC 84-82139. 160p. 1985. write for info. (*0-8187-0056-4*) Harlo Press.

Poetry Society of Texas Staff, ed. see Anthology of Winning Poets Staff.

Poets & Patrons Club Members Staff. A Taste of Poetry . . . Chicago Style: An Anthology by Poets & Patrons Club of Chicago. LC 97-100836. 140p. 1996. pap. 9.95 (*1-887312-03-X*) P Gangas.

Poets & Writers Editors, ed. A Directory of American Poets & Fiction Writers, 1999-2000. 450p. 1999. pap. 29.95 (*0-913734-61-6*, Pub. by Poets & Writers) SPD-Small Pr Dist.

Poets & Writers, Inc. Staff. A Community of Words: A Directory of Literary Readings & Workshops in California. LC 99-13448. 245p. 1999. pap. 12.00 (*1-890771-20-1*, Pub. by Heyday Bks) SPD-Small Pr Dist.

— Into Print: Guides to the Writing Life. 212p. 1997. pap. 12.95 (*0-913734-48-9*) Poets & Writers.

Poets & Writers, Inc. Staff, compiled by. A Directory of American Poets & Fiction Writers: 1997-1998 Edition. 300p. 1997. pap. 27.95 (*0-913734-58-6*) Poets & Writers.

Poets & Writers, Inc. Staff, et al. A Writer's Guide to Copyright. 2nd ed. (Illus.). 64p. (Orig.). 1990. pap. 6.95 (*0-913734-21-7*) Poets & Writers.

Poets Club of Chicago Members. Going 60 in Chicago: 60 Years of Poetry from the Poets Club of Chicago. LC 98-173486. 140p. 1998. pap. 10.95 (*1-887312-04-8*) P Gangas.

Poets House Staff, ed. Directory of American Poetry Books, Vol. II. 3rd ed. 1997. pap. 24.95 (*1-890695-01-7*) Poets Hse.

— Directory of American Poetry Books, Vol. 3. 3rd ed. 397p. 1999. pap. 24.95 (*1-890695-02-5*, Pub. by Poets Hse) SPD-Small Pr Dist.

Poets of Little Sister Publications Staff. Songs of Sacramento. Takseena, Ana, ed. (Illus.). 43p. (Orig.). 1987. pap. text 4.00 (*0-944667-01-5*) Little Sister Pubns.

Poet's Press & Stone Ridge (NY) Poetry Society Sta. As If the World Had Not Known Sorrow. Powell, Shirley, ed. 48p. 1985. write for info. (*0-318-64096-1*) Poets Pr.

Poet's Press-Gyro Publications Staff & Murphy, Stanley. Short Poems for a Long Journey. 1972. write for info. (*0-318-64140-2*) Poets Pr.

Poet's Workshop Staff. Be Somebody Be Yourself Poetry, Bk. 1. rev. ed. 11p. (YA). (gr. 7-12). 1994. pap. 7.00 (*0-913597-98-8*) Prosperity & Profits.

— Black American History: Rap & Rhyme. 8p. (YA). (gr. 6-12). 1989. pap. text 6.00 (*0-913597-53-8*) Prosperity & Profits.

Poett, A. Dibblee. Rancho San Julian: The Story of a California Ranch & Its People. 2nd ed. (Illus.). 240p. 1993. reprint ed. pap. 14.95 (*1-56474-080-3*) Fithian Pr.

Poetter, Herausgegeben Von Jochen, see Von Jochen Poetter, Herausgegeben.

Poetter, Thomas S. Voices of Inquiry in Teacher Education. LC 96-54813. 1997. 45.00 (*0-8058-2689-0*) L Erlbaum Assocs.

Poewe, Karla, ed. Charismatic Christianity As a Global Culture. LC 94-6874. 290p. 1994. text 34.95 (*0-87249-996-0*) U of SC Pr.

Poewe, Karla, jt. auth. see Hexham, Irving.

Poewe, Karla O. Childhoood in Germany During World War II: The Story of a Little Girl. LC 88-8956. (Studies in German Thought & History: Vol. 4). 230p. 1989. lib. bdg. 89.95 (*0-88946-354-9*) E Mellen.

— The Namibian Herero: A History of Their Psychosocial Disintegration & Survival. LC 85-2991. (African Studies: Vol. 1). (Illus.). 364p. 1985. lib. bdg. 99.95 (*0-88946-176-7*) E Mellen.

— Religion, Kinship & Economy in Luapula, Zambia. LC 88-26643. (African Studies: Vol. 9). 253p. 1989. lib. bdg. 89.95 (*0-88946-190-2*) E Mellen.

Poewe, Karla O., jt. auth. see Hexham, Irving.

P

Poewe, W. & Ransmayr, G., eds. Advances in Research on Neurodegeneration: Special Edition of Journal of Neural Transmission. (Journal of Neural Transmission Ser.: Vol. 6). 150p. 1999. 109.00 (*3-211-83262-9*) Spr-Verlag.

Poey, Delia & Suarez, Virgil, eds. Iguana Dreams: New Latino Fiction. LC 92-52628. 400p. 1992. pap. 17.00 (*0-06-096917-2*, Perennial) HarperTrade.

Poey, Delia, jt. ed. see Suarez, Virgil.

Poeze, Harry A., compiled by. Politiek-Politionelle Overzichten van Nederlandsch-Indie, Deel IV, 1935-41. (Illus.). 583p. (Orig.). 1995. pap. 44.00 (*90-6718-051-3*, Pub. by KITLV Pr) Cellar.

Poff, Donna L. The Mask. 368p. 1998. mass mkt. 4.99 (*0-8439-4416-1*, Leisure Bks) Dorchester Pub Co.

Poff, Ima, ed. see White, Carter.

Poff, Jan-Michael, ed. Addresses & Public Papers of James Grubbs Martin, Governor of North Carolina, 1985-1989 Vol. 1, 1985-1989, Vol. 1. (Illus.). xlii, 1089p. 1992. 4.00 (*0-86526-250-0*) NC Archives.

— Addresses & Public Papers of James Grubbs Martin, Governor of North Carolina, 1989-1993, Vol. II. (Illus.). xxxii, 763p. 1998. 4.00 (*0-86526-265-9*) NC Archives.

Poff, Sherry. My Heavenly Bank Account. (Orig.). 1995. pap. 5.99 (*1-883602-07-6*) Atlantic Digital.

Poffenbarger, jt. auth. see McCurnin, Dennis M.

Poffenbarger, Amy & Poffenbarger, Mark. Mountain Bike America: Washington: An Atlas of Washington's Greatest Off-Road Bicycle Rides. Croxton, Ryan, ed. (Illus.). 224p. 2000. pap. 15.95 (*1-882997-09-3*, Pub. by Beachway Pr) Globe Pequot.

Poffenbarger, Mark, jt. auth. see Poffenbarger, Amy.

Poffenberger, A. T., ed. James McKeen Cattell: Man of Science. LC 73-2984. (Classics in Psychology Ser.). 1976. reprint ed. 40.95 (*0-405-05155-7*) Ayer.

Poffenberger, Dan, et al. Working Together: Leading a Task-Oriented Small Group. (People Together Ser.). (Illus.). 68p. 1998. pap. text, wbk. ed. 12.95 (*1-890676-13-6*) Beavers Pond.

Poffenberger, Donald L., jt. auth. see Campagna, Daniel S.

Poffenberger, John D. How to Coach Winning Soccer: For the Mom or Dad Who Is Suddenly Coach. Poffenberger, Nancy, ed. 24p. (Orig.). 1987. pap. 5.95 (*0-938293-50-8*) Fun Pub OH.

Poffenberger, Mark, ed. Keepers of the Forest: Land Management Alternatives in Southeast Asia. fac. ed. LC 89-38879. (Kumarian Press Library of Management for Development). (Illus.). 319p. 1994. pap. 98.90 (*0-7837-7577-6*, 204733000007) Bks Demand.

Poffenberger, Mark & McGean, Betsy, eds. Village Voices, Forest Choices: Joint Forest Management in India. LC 96-900517. (Illus.). 392p. (C). 1996. 24.95 (*0-19-563683-X*) OUP.

— Village Voices, Forest Choices: Joint Forest Management in India. (Oxford India Paperbacks Ser.). (Illus.). 376p. 1998. reprint ed. pap. text 7.95 (*0-19-564458-1*) OUP.

Poffenberger, Nancy. Instant Fun with Bells & Xylophones. 32p. 1986. pap. 3.95 (*0-938293-00-1*) Fun Pub OH.

— Instant Fun With Sacred Songs. 24p. (J). (gr. k up). 1977. reprint ed. pap. 5.95 (*0-938293-27-3*) Fun Pub OH.

— Instant Organ Fun for Christmas. 24p. 1976. pap. 5.95 (*0-938293-29-X*) Fun Pub OH.

— Instant Piano Fun, Bk. 1. 34p. (J). (gr. 4). 1985. reprint ed. pap. 10.95 (*0-938293-25-7*) Fun Pub OH.

— Instant Piano Fun, Bk. 2. 62p. 1975. pap. 12.95 (*0-938293-26-5*) Fun Pub OH.

— Instant Piano Fun for Christmas. 24p. 1986. reprint ed. pap. text 10.95 (*0-938293-28-1*) Fun Pub OH.

— Instant Piano Fun with Nursery Rhymes. (Illus.). 40p. (Orig.). (J). (ps up). 1997. pap. 12.95 (*0-938293-30-3*) Fun Pub OH.

— Instant Recorder Fun, Bk. 1. 32p. (Orig.). (J). (gr. 4). 1986. reprint ed. pap. 4.95 (*0-938293-14-1*) Fun Pub OH.

— Instant Recorder Fun Package 1. 32p. (J). (ps-3). 1986. reprint ed. 14.95 (*0-938293-15-X*) Fun Pub OH.

— Now! Instant Keyboard Fun I. 32p. (J). (gr. 4 up). 1985. reprint ed. pap. 4.95 (*0-938293-39-7*) Fun Pub OH.

— Xylo-Fun I, Vol. 1. 24p. 1995. pap. 6.95 (*0-938293-13-3*) Fun Pub OH.

Poffenberger, Nancy & Bane, Rosemary C. Instant Recorder Fun, Bk. 2. 32p. (Orig.). 1988. pap. 5.95 (*0-938293-16-8*) Fun Pub OH.

Poffenberger, Nancy, ed. see Poffenberger, John D.

Poffenberger, Thomas. Fertility & Family Life in an Indian Village. LC 75-9025. (Michigan Papers on South & Southeast Asia: No. 10). (Illus.). xii, 114p. (Orig.). 1975. pap. 3.00 (*0-89148-010-2*) Ctr S&SE Asian.

Poffenberger, Thomas & Sebaly, Kim. The Socialization of Family Size Values: Youth & Family Planning in an Indian Village. LC 76-53996. (Michigan Papers on South & Southeast Asia: No. 12). (Illus.). xiv, 159p. (Orig.). 1976. pap. 3.00 (*0-89148-012-9*) Ctr S&SE Asian.

Poffley, Frewin. Greek Island Hopping 1998. 3rd ed. (Illus.). 656p. 1998. pap. 17.95 (*0-8442-4655-7*, Passprt Bks) NTC Contemp Pub Co.

***Poffley, Frewin.** Greek Island Hopping 2000. 2nd ed. LC 99-89671. (Thomas Cook Independent Traveler's Guides Ser.). (Illus.). 544p. 2000. pap. 19.95 (*0-7627-0729-1*) Globe Pequot.

Poffley, Frewin. Greek Island Hopping 1999. 1999. pap. 18.95 (*0-8442-0634-2*) NTC Contemp Pub Co.

Poffley, Richard F. Greek Island Hopping. 544p. 1996. pap. 17.95 (*0-8442-4697-2*, Passprt Bks) NTC Contemp Pub Co.

Poffo, Lanny. Leaping Lanny! Wrestling with Rhyme. LC 87-51044. (Illus.). 144p. 6.95 (*0-318-23404-1*) Leilo Pub.

Poffo, Larry. Leaping Lanny! Wrestling with Ryme. 1988. pap. 6.95 (*0-9619169-0-7*) Leilo Pub.

Pogacar, Timothy, jt. auth. see Martin-Reynolds, Joanne.

Pogacnik, Marko. Christ Power & the Earth Goddess: A Fifth Gospel. 300p. (Orig.). 1999. pap. text 15.95 (*1-899171-92-4*) Findhorn Pr.

— Healing the Heart of Mother Earth: Restoring the Subtle Levels of Life. Spesstoesser, Carola, tr. (Illus.). 280p. 1998. pap. 14.95 (*1-899171-57-6*, Pub. by Findhorn Pr) Words Distrib.

— Nature Spirits & Elemental Beings: Working with the Intelligence in Nature. (Illus.). 256p. (Orig.). 1997. pap. 13.95 (*1-899171-66-5*, Pub. by Findhorn Pr) Words Distrib.

Pogal, Patricia. Light Imagery in the "Romancero" 160p. Date not set. 59.50 (*0-614-10347-9*) Scripta.

— Light Imagery in the Spanish Ballad. LC 98-150775. 164p. 1997. pap. 49.95 (*1-57309-233-9*) Intl Scholars.

Pogany-Balas, E. The Influence of Rome's Antique Monumental Sculptures on... 1980. pap. 105.00 (*963-05-1682-9*, Pub. by Akade Kiado) St Mut.

Pogany, Istvan, ed. Human Rights in Eastern Europe. LC 95-19496. (Law in Its Social Setting Ser.). 272p. 1995. 90.00 (*1-85898-333-9*) E Elgar.

Pogany, Istvan S. Nuclear Weapons & International Law. LC 86-31342. 226p. 1987. text 39.95 (*0-312-57986-1*) St Martin.

— Righting Wrongs in East Europe. LC 97-20341. 256p. 1998. text 79.95 (*0-7190-3042-0*) St Martin.

Pogany, Istvan S., jt. auth. see Perrott, David L.

Pogany, Susan Browning. Sex Smart: A Sexuality Resource for Teenagers. LC 98-19179. 224p. (YA). (gr. 6-12). 1998. pap. 14.95 (*1-57749-043-6*, Pub. by Fairview Press) Natl Bk Netwk.

Pogany, Willy. The Art of Drawing. (Illus.). 128p. 1996. pap. 14.95 (*1-56833-059-6*) Madison Bks UPA.

***Pogany, Willy.** Mother Goose. (Books of Wonder Ser.). (Illus.). (J). 2000. 19.95 (*1-58717-026-4*) SeaStar.

Pogarell, Reiner. Minority Languages in Europe - Past & Present: A Classified Bibliography. viii, 208p. 1983. 72.35 (*3-11-009783-4*) Mouton.

Pogash, Carol. As Real As It Gets: The Life of a Hospital at the Center of the AIDS Epidemic. 272p. 1992. 18.95 (*1-55972-127-8*, Birch Ln Pr) Carol Pub Group.

Pogel, Nancy. Woody Allen. (Twayne's Filmmakers Ser.). 240p. 1987. 23.95 (*0-8057-9297-X*) Macmillan.

Pogell, B. M., jt. ed. see McGilvery, R. W.

Poger, Sidney, jt. auth. see Magistrale, Tony.

Pogge, H. Bernhard, ed. Electronic Materials Chemistry: An Introduction to Device Processes & Material Systems. LC 95-40327. (Illus.). 640p. 1995. text 225.00 (*0-8247-9632-2*, TK7871) Dekker.

Pogge, Paul. Im Reiche des Muata Jamwo: Tagebuch Meiner im Auftrag der Deutschen Gesellschaft zur Erforschung Aequatorial-Afrikas in die Lunda- Staaten Unternommenen Reise. (B. E. Ser.: No. 159). (GER.). 1880. 35.00 (*0-8115-3075-2*) Periodicals Srv.

Pogge, Thomas W. Realizing Rawls. LC 89-42879. (Illus.). 320p. 1989. text 45.00 (*0-8014-2124-1*); pap. text 16.95 (*0-8014-9675-3*) Cornell U Pr.

Pogge von Strandmann, Hartmut, jt. ed. see Evans, Robert.

Poggeler, Franz, ed. National Identity & Adult Education: Challenge & Risk. LC 95-22939. (Illus.). 305p. 1995. 57.95 (*3-631-48353-8*) P Lang Pubng.

Poggeler, Franz, jt. ed. see Jarvis, Peter.

Poggeler, Franz, ed. see Van Gent, Bastiaan.

Poggeler, Otto. The Paths of Heidegger's Life & Thought. Bailiff, John, tr. (Contemporary Studies in Philosophy & the Human Sciences Ser.). 376p. (C). 1996. text 70.00 (*0-391-03964-4*) Humanities.

Poggemann, Martin. Schuld und Strafe In der Jungeren Entwicklung des Preubischen Steuerstrafrechts. 210p. 1997. 44.95 (*3-631-32377-8*) P Lang Pubng.

Poggendorf, J. C. Biographisch-Literarisches Handworterbuch zur Geschichte der Exacten Wissenschaften, 2 vols. (GER.). 1526p. 1996. reprint ed. 150.00 (*1-888262-85-0*) Martino Pubng.

Poggendorff, J. C. Biographisch Literarisches Handworter Buch: Zur Geschichte der Exacien Wissenschaften, 4 vols. (GER.). 3214p. 1997. reprint ed. 295.00 (*1-57898-043-7*) Martino Pubng.

Poggendorff, J. C. Concise Biographic-Literary Dictionary of the Exact Sciences: 1st Installment. 80p. 1995. pap. 32.00 (*3-05-501575-4*, Pub. by Akademie Verlag) Wiley.

— Concise Biographic-Literary Dictionary of the Exact Sciences: 2nd Installment. 80p. 1995. pap. 32.00 (*3-05-501574-6*, Pub. by Akademie Verlag) Wiley.

— Concise Biographic-Literary Dictionary of the Exact Sciences: 3rd Installment. 80p. 1996. pap. 32.00 (*3-05-501722-6*, Pub. by Akademie Verlag) Wiley.

Poggenpohl, Sharon H., ed. Graphic Design: A Career Guide & Educational Directory. (Illus.). 160p. (Orig.). 1993. pap. 25.00 (*1-884081-00-2*) Am Inst Graphic Arts.

***Poggetto, Newton D.** Sonoma: The Night of the Assassin. 295p. 1999. pap. 15.00 (*0-9672773-0-2*) Niche Pubg.

Poggi, Antonio, jt. auth. see Fabbrizzi, Luigi.

Poggi, Antonio, jt. ed. see Fabbrizzi, Luigi.

Poggi, Christine. In Defiance of Painting: Cubism, Futurism, & the Invention of Collage. LC 91-37317. (Publications in the History of Art). (Illus.). 320p. (C). 1993. 60.00 (*0-300-05109-3*) Yale U Pr.

Poggi, Gianfranco. The Development of the Modern State: A Sociological Introduction. LC 77-76148. xii, 175p. 1978. 29.50 (*0-8047-0959-9*); pap. 10.95 (*0-8047-1042-2*) Stanford U Pr.

***Poggi, Gianfranco.** Durkheim. (Founders of Modern Political & Social Thought Ser.). 250p. 2000. pap. 19.95 (*0-19-878087-7*) OUP.

Poggi, Gianfranco. Images of Society: Essays on the Sociological Theories of Tocqueville, Marx, & Durkheim. LC 79-183892. xvi, 268p. 1972. 42.50 (*0-8047-0811-8*) Stanford U Pr.

— Money & the Modern Mind: George Simmel's Philosophy of Money. LC 92-32231. 1993. 35.00 (*0-520-07571-4*, Pub. by U CA Pr) Cal Prin Full Svc.

— The State: Its Nature, Development & Prospects. LC 90-70700. 222p. 1991. 35.00 (*0-8047-1849-0*) Stanford U Pr.

Poggi, Gianfranco, ed. see Luhmann, Niklas.

Poggi, Isotta, jt. auth. see Melton, J. Gordon.

Poggi, Jack. The Monologue Workshop: From Search to Discovery in Audition & Performance. (Acting Ser.). 272p. 1990. pap. 12.95 (*1-55783-031-2*) Applause Theatre Bk Pubs.

Poggi, Jim, ed. see Ohsawa, George.

Poggi, Stefano, et al, eds. Romanticism in Science: Science in Europe, 1790-1840. LC 93-1728. (Boston Studies in the Philosophy of Science). 264p. 1994. lib. bdg. 148.50 (*0-7923-2336-X*, Pub. by Kluwer Academic) Kluwer Academic.

Poggie, John J., Jr., et al, eds. Anthropological Research: Process & Application. LC 91-16528. (SUNY Series in Advances in Applied Anthropology). (Illus.). 334p. (C). 1992. text 21.50 (*0-7914-1001-3*) State U NY Pr.

Poggie, John J., Jr. & Lynch, Robert N., eds. Rethinking Modernization. LC 72-826. 405p. 1974. 79.50 (*0-8371-6394-3*, POM/, Greenwood Pr) Greenwood.

Poggie, John J., jt. ed. see Pollnac, Richard B.

Poggio, T. A. & Glaser, D. A. Exploring Brain Functions: Models in Neuroscience. LC 00-92. (Life Sciences Research Reports: No. 52). 358p. 1993. 305.00 (*0-471-93602-2*) Wiley.

Poggio, Tomaso, jt. auth. see Vaina, Lucia M.

Poggio, Tomaso, jt. ed. see Nayar, Shree K.

Poggioli, Renato. The Spirit of the Letter: Essays in European Literature. LC 65-22064. 385p. 1965. reprint ed. pap. 119.40 (*0-7837-4179-0*, 205902800012) Bks Demand.

— The Theory of the Avant-Garde. (Belknap Ser.). 256p. 1981. pap. 18.00 (*0-674-88216-4*) HUP.

Poggiolini, Duilio, ed. Technical Guidelines for Pharmaceuticals in the European Economic Community. LC 83-9580. 73p. 1983. reprint ed. pap. 30.00 (*0-608-00650-5*, 206123800007) Bks Demand.

Poggius the Papist. Hus the Heretic. LC 97-65112. (Illus.). 78p. 1997. 9.95 (*0-9643914-3-0*) Shiloh Med.

Poglany-Balas, Edit. The Influence of Rome's Antique Monumental Sculptures on the Great Masters of the Renaissance. 116p. 1980. 135.00 (*0-569-08643-4*) St Mut.

Poglazov, B. F. Morphogenesis of T-Even Bacteriophages. (Monographs in Developmental Biology: Vol. 7). 1973. 47.00 (*3-8055-1645-2*) S Karger.

Poglia, Eho, et al, eds. Pluralite Culturelle et Education en Suisse: Etre Migrant II. 472p. 1995. 47.95 (*3-906753-56-5*, Pub. by P Lang) P Lang Pubng.

Pogliani, Giuliano, jt. ed. see Vannini, Vanio.

Pogo, Beatriz G., jt. auth. see Dales, S.

Pogodzinski, J. M., ed. Readings in Public Policy. LC 94-26134. (Illus.). 350p. (C). 1995. pap. text 35.95 (*1-55786-521-3*) Blackwell Pubs.

Pogonowski, Iwo. Jews in Poland: A Documentary History. (Illus.). 402p. 1997. pap. 19.95 (*0-7818-0604-6*) Hippocrene Bks.

***Pogonowski, Iwo C.** Poland: An Illustrated History. (Illustrated History Ser.). (Illus.). 150p. 2000. 14.95 (*0-7818-0757-3*) Hippocrene Bks.

Pogonowski, Iwo C. Polish-English - English-Polish Concise Dictionary: With Complete Phonetics. 4th rev. ed. 408p. 1993. pap. 9.95 (*0-7818-0133-8*) Hippocrene Bks.

— Polish-English - English-Polish Practical Dictionary. 15th ed. (Practical Language Dictionaries Ser.). 703p. 1993. pap. 11.95 (*0-7818-0085-4*) Hippocrene Bks.

— Polish-English - English-Polish Standard Dictionary: With Business Terms. rev. ed. (Standard Dictionaries Ser.). 780p. 1994. pap. 19.95 (*0-7818-0282-2*) Hippocrene Bks.

— Polish-English Unabridged Dictionary, 3 vols., Set. LC 97-14300. (ENG & POL.). 3800p. 1997. 200.00 (*0-7818-0441-8*) Hippocrene Bks.

— Polish Phrase Book & Dictionary. 2nd rev. ed. 252p. 1993. pap. 11.95 (*0-7818-0134-6*) Hippocrene Bks.

Pogony, G. E. Wing Beat: A Collection of Eagle Woodcuts. Graham, Douglas J., tr. from HUN. LC 76-22176. (Illus.). 120p. 1976. 20.00 (*0-933652-10-0*) Domjan Studio.

Pogorel, Gerard, ed. Global Telecommunications Strategies & Technological Changes. LC 93-44144. 376p. 1994. 99.00 (*0-444-89960-X*, North Holland) Elsevier.

Pogorel, Gerard, jt. auth. see Noam, Eli M.

Pogorel, Gerard, jt. ed. see Allouche, Jose.

Pogorelov, A. V. Bendings of Surfaces & Stability of Shells. LC 88-23511. (MMONO Ser.: No. 72). 77p. 1988. text 47.00 (*0-8218-4525-X*, MMONO/72) Am Math.

— Extrinsic Geometry of Convex Surfaces. LC 72-11851. (Translations of Mathematical Monographs: Vol. 35). 669p. 1973. text 109.00 (*0-8218-1585-7*, MMONO/35) Am Math.

— Geometry. 312p. (C). 1987. 100.00 (*0-7855-4994-3*, Pub. by Collets) St Mut.

***Pogorelov, Vladlen.** Decadent. LC 99-69793. (Illus.). 64p. 2000. pap. 14.95 (*1-892494-04-3*) Repossessed Head.

Pogorelov, Vladlen. Derelict. (Illus.). 40p. 1997. 5.00 (*1-892494-01-9*) Repossessed Head.

— The Dirty Whore. (Lost City: Poetic Broadside Ser.: Vol. 1). (Illus.). 2p. 1998. pap. 2.00 (*1-892494-07-8*) Repossessed Head.

Pogorzala, jt. auth. see Stanfield, Christine.

Pogorzelski, H. Transtheoretic Foundations of Mathematics: Goldbach Conjecture, 3 vols. LC 97-179587. (Natural Numbers Ser.: Vol. IC). 301p. 1997. pap. 29.99 (*0-9643023-5-7*) RIM.

Pogorzelski, H. & Ryan, W. Transtheoretic Foundations of Mathematics: Arithmetics, 3 vols. LC 97-179587. (Natural Numbers Ser.: Vol. IB). 217p. 1997. pap. 29.99 (*0-9643023-4-9*) RIM.

— Transtheoretic Foundations of Mathematics: Foundations. LC 97-179587. (Natural Numbers Ser.: Vol. IA). 175p. 1997. pap. 29.99 (*0-9643023-3-0*) RIM.

Pogorzelski, H. & Snyder, W., trs. from GER. What Are Numbers & What Should They Be? rev. ed. (Rim Monographs in Mathematics).Tr. of Was Sind und Was Sollen die Zahlen. (Illus.). 91p. 1995. 29.99 (*0-9643023-1-4*) RIM.

Pogorzelski, Henry A. & Ryan, William J. Foundations of Semiological Theory of Numbers, Vol. 1. LC 89-155354. 590p. (Orig.). 1982. pap. 31.50 (*0-89101-053-X*) U Maine Pr.

— Foundations of Semiological Theory of Numbers, Vol. 2. LC 89-155354. 746p. (Orig.). 1985. pap. 36.50 (*0-89101-064-5*) U Maine Pr.

— Foundations of Semiological Theory of Numbers Vol. 3: Foundations of Computability. LC 89-155354. 530p. (Orig.). 1988. pap. 41.50 (*0-89101-065-3*) U Maine Pr.

Pogorzelski, W. & Sneddon, Ian N. Integral Equations & Their Applications. LC 64-18247. (International Series of Monographs on Pure & Applied Mathematics: Vol. 1, Pts. 1-3). 1966. 314.00 (*0-08-010662-5*, Pub. by Pergamon Repr) Franklin.

Pogosian, Barbara. Experimental Exercises in General Microbiology. 2nd ed. Ardinger, Barbara, ed. (Illus.). 334p. (C). 1992. pap. text, lab manual ed. 15.50 (*0-938841-02-5*) Biocomm.

Pogosian, Barbara, jt. auth. see Bergquist, Lois M.

Pogosov, V. S. & Antoniv, V. F. Malignant Tumors of the Ear, Nose, & Throat. (Illus.). 600p. 1984. 70.00 (*0-8236-3082-X*) Intl Univs Pr.

— Microscopy & Microsurgery of Larynx & the Laryngopharynx. 1987. 37.50 (*0-8236-3363-2*, BN#03363) Intl Univs Pr.

Pogossky, A. L., tr. see Ouspensky, P. D.

Pogreba, B. A. Protecting Yourself from Crime: What to Do If Attacked! (Illus.). 16p. (Orig.). 1997. pap. 3.95 (*1-891065-01-7*) Pogreba Pub.

Pogreba, Beverly A. Chart Your Health: A 60-Day Journal. (Illus.). 1997. spiral bd. 6.95 (*1-891065-00-9*) Pogreba Pub.

Pogrebin, Bertrand B., jt. auth. see Getman, Julius G.

Pogrebin, Letty C. Deborah, Golda & Me: Being Female & Jewish in America. 416p. 1992. pap. 15.95 (*0-385-42512-0*, Anchor NY) Doubleday.

— Getting over Getting Older: An Intimate Journey. 1997. pap. 13.00 (*0-614-27342-0*) Berkley Pub.

— Getting over Getting Older: An Intimate Journey. 336p. 1997. reprint ed. pap. 13.00 (*0-425-15793-8*) Berkley Pub.

Pogrow, Stanley. Education in the Computer Age: Issues of Policy, Practice, & Reform. LC 83-11213. (Managing Information Ser.: No. 6). (Illus.). 231p. reprint ed. pap. 71.70 (*0-8357-4869-3*, 203780100009) Bks Demand.

Pogrund. Making Your Mark Health in Service Jobs. 128p. 1996. pap. 11.93 (*0-8092-0915-2*) NTC Contemp Pub Co.

— Making Your Mark in Retail Jobs. 128p. 1996. pap. 11.93 (*0-8092-0910-1*) NTC Contemp Pub Co.

Pogrund, Benjamin. Sobukwe & Apartheid. 416p. (C). 1991. pap. 16.95 (*0-8135-1693-5*); text 45.00 (*0-8135-1692-7*) Rutgers U Pr.

***Pogrund, Benjamin.** War of Words: Memoirs of a South African Journalist. LC 97-50423. (Illus.). 400p. 2000. 26.95 (*1-888363-71-1*, Pub. by Seven Stories) Publishers Group.

Pogrund, Phyllis & Grebel, Rosemary. Contemporary's Make Your Mark in Food Service. LC 96-38698. 128p. 1996. pap. 11.93 (*0-8092-0907-1*) NTC Contemp Pub Co.

— Contemporary's Make Your Mark in the Hotel Industry. LC 96-45972. 128p. 1996. pap. 11.93 (*0-8092-0913-6*) NTC Contemp Pub Co.

Pogrund, Rona L., et al, eds. Early Focus: Working with Young Blind & Visually Impaired Children & Their Families. LC 92-17874. 160p. 1992. pap. 32.95 (*0-89128-215-7*) Am Foun Blind.

Pogrund, Rona L., et al. Teaching Age-Appropriate Purposeful Skills: An Orientation & Mobility Curriculum for Students with Visual Impairments. 2nd ed. 1995. pap. 45.00 (*1-880366-18-5*) TSBVI.

Pogson, Beryl. In the East My Pleasure Lies. LC 73-20439. (Studies in Shakespeare: No. 24). 1974. lib. bdg. 75.00 (*0-8383-1760-X*) M S G Haskell Hse.

— The Work Life: Based on the Teachings of G. I. Gurdjieff, P. D. Ouspensky & Maurice Nicoll. LC 93-45899. (Illus.). 304p. (Orig.). 1994. pap. 12.95 (*0-87728-809-7*) Weiser.

Pogson, Patricia. Before the Roadshow. (C). 1988. 25.00 (*0-904524-47-7*, Pub. by Rivelin Grapheme Pr) St Mut.

Pogson, Philip, jt. auth. see Tennant, Mark.

Pogue. American Constitutional Law, Custom Pub. (C). 1993. pap. text 49.50 (*0-07-050464-4*) McGraw.

***Pogue.** How Do You Go to Bathroom in Reverse. 1999. mass mkt. write for info. (*0-8125-7632-2*) Tor Bks.

— The Ibook for Dummies. (For Dummies Ser.). 408p. 1999. pap. 19.99 (*0-7645-0647-1*) IDG Bks.

Pogue & Christoff. Understanding New York State Law, Custom Pub. (C). 1993. pap. text 36.74 (*0-07-050458-X*) McGraw.

Pogue, Bill, jt. auth. see Bova, Ben.

Pogue, Carolyn. The Language of the Heart: Rituals, Stories, & Information about Death. 160p. 1998. pap. 14.95 (*1-896836-17-8*) NStone Publ.

— Part-Time Parent: Learning to Live Without Full-Time Kids. 160p. 1998. pap. 14.95 (*1-896836-23-2*) NStone Publ.

P

Pogue, Charles E. Dragonheart. 272p. 1996. mass mkt. 5.99 (*1-57297-130-4*) Blvd Books.

***Pogue, David.** FileMaker Pro. (Missing Manuals Ser.). 2000. pap. 19.95 (*1-56592-866-0*) OReilly & Assocs.

Pogue, David. Great Macintosh Easter Egg Hunt. LC 98-168804. 160p. 1998. pap. text 9.95 (*0-425-16006-8*) Berkley Pub.

— Hard Drive. 304p. 1995. mass mkt. 5.50 (*0-441-00255-2*) Ace Bks.

***Pogue, David.** The iMac for Dummies. 2nd ed. (For Dummies Ser.). 432p. 1999. pap. 19.99 (*0-7645-0648-X*) IDG Bks.

— iMovie: The Missing Manual. 400p. 2000. pap. 19.95 (*1-56592-859-8*) OReilly & Assocs.

— Mac OS 9: The Missing Manual. (Illus.). 460p. 2000. pap. 19.95 (*1-56592-857-1*) OReilly & Assocs.

— Mac OS X. (Missing Manuals Ser.). 2000. pap. 19.95 (*1-56592-867-9*) OReilly & Assocs.

Pogue, David. MAC pour les Nuls. (FRE.). 338p. 1995. 49.95 (*0-7859-9852-7*) Fr & Eur.

Pogue, David. Macs for Dummies. (Illus.). 336p. 1993. pap. 16.95 (*1-878058-53-3*) IDG Bks.

Pogue, David. Macs for Dummies. 2nd ed. 350p. 1993. pap. 19.95 (*1-56884-051-9*) IDG Bks.

— Macs for Dummies. 3rd ed. 432p. 1995. pap. 19.99 (*1-56884-239-2*) IDG Bks.

— Macs for Dummies. 6th ed. LC QA76.8.M3P617 1998. (For Dummies Ser.). 432p. 1998. pap. 19.99 (*0-7645-0398-7*) IDG Bks.

***Pogue, David.** Macs for Dummies. 7th ed. (For Dummies Ser.). (Illus.). 432p. 2000. pap. 19.99 (*0-7645-0703-6*) IDG Bks.

Pogue, David. MacWorld Mac & Power Mac Secrets. 2nd ed. LC 94-77529. 1020p. 1994. pap. 39.95 (*1-56884-175-2*) IDG Bks.

— MacWorld Mac & Power Mac Secrets. 3rd ed. LC 95-81815. 1088p. 1996. pap. 39.99 incl. disk (*1-56884-791-2*) IDG Bks.

— MacWorld Mac Faqs. 456p. 1995. pap. 19.99 (*1-56884-480-8*) IDG Bks.

— Magic for Dummies. LC GV1547.P73 1998. (For Dummies Ser.). (Illus.). 408p. 1998. pap. 19.99 (*0-7645-5101-9*) IDG Bks.

— The Microsloth Joke Book. LC 98-183280. 128p. 1997. pap. 9.95 (*0-425-16054-8*) Berkley Pub.

— More Macs for Dummies. LC 94-75910. 432p. 1994. pap. 19.95 (*1-56884-087-X*) IDG Bks.

Pogue, David. Opera for Dummies: Pouge,&David, Set. abr. ed. 1997. audio 18.00 (*0-694-51909-X*, CPN2727) HarperAudio.

Pogue, David. PalmPilot: The Ultimate Guide. (Illus.). 489p. 1998. pap. 29.95 incl. cd-rom (*1-56592-420-7*) OReilly & Assocs.

***Pogue, David.** PalmPilot: The Ultimate Guide. 2nd ed. O'Reilly, Tim, ed. (Illus.). 520p. 1999. pap. 29.95 incl. cd-rom (*1-56592-600-5*) OReilly & Assocs.

Pogue, David. Tales from the Tech Line: Hilarious Strange-but-True Stories from the Computer Industry's Technical Support Hotlines. LC 99-163541. 112p. 1998. pap. 10.00 (*0-425-16363-6*) Berkley Pub.

Pogue, David & Peck, M. Scott. Classical Music for Dummies: Pouge,&David, Set. abr. ed. 1997. audio 18.00 (*0-694-51908-1*, 395525, Pub. by HarperAudio) Lndmrk Audiobks.

Pogue, David & Schorr, Joseph. Mac World Mac & Power Mac Secrets. 2nd ed. (Illus.). 1072p. 1998. pap. 30.00 incl. disk (*0-7881-5663-2*) DIANE Pub.

— Macworld Mac Secrets. 5th ed. LC QA76.8.M3P619 1999. (Secrets Ser.). 1344p. 1998. pap. 49.99 incl. cd-rom (*0-7645-4040-8*) IDG Bks.

— Macworld Macintosh Secrets. (Illus.). 1000p. 1993. pap. 39.95 incl. disk (*1-56884-025-X*) IDG Bks.

***Pogue, David & Seiter, Charles.** The Imac Internet Kit for Dummies. (For Dummies Ser.). 768p. 1999. pap. 29.99 (*0-7645-0573-4*) IDG Bks.

Pogue, David & Speck, Scott. Classical Music for Dummies. LC 97-80115. (For Dummies Ser.). (Illus.). 384p. 1997. pap. 24.99 incl. audio compact disk, 3.5 hd (*0-7645-5009-8*) IDG Bks.

— Opera for Dummies. LC 97-80116. (For Dummies Ser.). (Illus.). 384p. 1997. pap. 24.99 incl. audio compact disk, 3.5 hd (*0-7645-5010-1*) IDG Bks.

Pogue, David, jt. auth. see Engst, Adam.

Pogue, David, ed. see Elferdink, Jim & Reynolds, David.

Pogue, Dennis J. King's Reach & 17th Century Plantation Life. (Occasional Papers: No. 1). (Illus.). 33p. 1990. pap. 5.95 (*1-878399-05-5*) Div Hist Cult Progs.

Pogue, Dennis J. & Smolek, Michael A. An Archaeological Resource Management Plan for the Southern Maryland Region. (Manuscript Ser.). 165p. 1985. reprint ed. spiral bd. 15.00 (*1-878399-07-1*, NO. 30) Div Hist Cult Progs.

Pogue, Dennis J., jt. ed. see Reinhart, Theodore R.

Pogue, Donna, jt. auth. see Pogue, Erika.

Pogue, Erika & Pogue, Donna. Erika's Angels: The Secrets of the Locket. Winters, Kas, ed. & illus. by. 37p. (J). (gr. 3-6). 1997. pap. 5.95 (*1-892225-09-3*, ERIKA-1) Winmark Comm.

Pogue, Forrest C., ed. Access to Government Documents: Papers Presented to a Session of the American Historical Association, December, 1972. 53p. 1974. pap. text 23.00 (*0-89126-008-0*) MA-AH Pub.

Pogue, Gregory. Employee Assistance Programs on Liberal Arts Campuses. LC 97-41781. 80p. (C). 1997. 21.50 (*0-7618-0966-X*) U Pr of Amer.

Pogue, John M., ed. see Pogue, Lloyd W.

Pogue, Joseph E., jt. auth. see Gilbert, Chester G.

Pogue, Julia A. & Jones, Eileen M. A Traveler's Journey Through Time & Space. 130p. (Orig.). 1989. pap. write for info. (*0-9622814-1-7*) Anonymous & Assocs.

Pogue, Julia R. & Jones, Eileen M. Commentaries by the Inner Christ Circle. 176p. (Orig.). 1989. pap. 7.95 (*0-9622814-0-9*) Anonymous & Assocs.

Pogue, Lloyd W. Pogue-Pollock-Polk Genealogy As Mirrored in History: From Scotland to Northern Ireland-Ulster, Ohio & Westward. Pogue, John M., ed. LC 84-73111. (Illus.). 720p. 1990. 35.00 (*0-9622395-0-X*) Gateway Balto.

***Pogue, Pamela & Lee, Virginia.** Effectiveness of State Coastal Management Programs in Providing Public Access to the Shore: A National Overview. (Coastal Management Report Ser.: Vol. 2210). (Illus.). 1999. pap. write for info. (*1-885454-10-4*) Coastal Res.

***Pogue, Pamela & Lewis, Noelle.** Coastal Hazards Mitigation: An Overview of the Policies, Programs & Activities in the Coastal Northeast. (Coastal Management Report Ser.: Vol. 2216). (Illus.). 99p. 1999. pap. write for info. (*1-885454-14-7*) Coastal Res.

Pogue, Stephanie E., intro. Sources: Multicultural Influences on Contemporary African American Sculptors. LC 93-73887. 20p. (Orig.). (C). 1994. pap. 4.00 (*0-937123-30-7*) Art Gal U MD.

Pogue, Steven L. The First Year of Your Christian Life. LC 88-30066. 128p. (Orig.). Date not set. pap. 7.99 (*0-89840-195-X*) Integrtd Res.

Pogue, Thomas F., ed. State Taxation of Business: Issues & Policy Options. LC 92-15767. 360p. 1992. 65.00 (*0-275-94125-6*, C4125, Praeger Pubs) Greenwood.

Pogue, William R. Astronaut Primer. (Illus.). (Orig.). 1986. pap. 5.50 (*0-935291-00-8*) Nat Space Soc.

Pogue, William R. How Do You Go to the Bathroom in Space? LC 85-226024. 156 p. 1985. write for info. (*0-8125-4910-4*) Orb NYC.

Pogue, William R. How Do You Go to the Bathroom in Space? 160p. 1991. mass mkt. 9.99 (*0-8125-1728-8*, Pub. by Tor Bks) St Martin.

***Pogue, William R.** How Do You Go to the Bathroom in Space? 2nd ed. LC 99-36192. 192p. 1999. pap. text 11.95 (*0-312-87295-X*, Pub. by Tor Bks) St Martin.

Pogun, Sakire. Neurotransmitter Release & Uptake. LC 97-4076. (NATO ASI Series, Series H, Cell Biology). 1997. 157.00 (*3-540-62479-1*) Spr-Verlag.

Poguntke, Thomas. Alternative Politics: The German Green Party. (Environment, Politics, & Society Ser.). 288p. 1994. text 76.50 (*0-7486-0393-X*, Pub. by Edinburgh U Pr) Col U Pr.

Poguntke, Thomas, jt. ed. see Muller-Rommel, Ferdinand.

Pogzeba, Wolfgang & Overbeck, Joy. Ranchos de Taos: San Francisco de Asis Church. LC 81-82257. (Illus.). 68p. (Orig.). 1981. pap. 7.95 (*0-913504-66-1*) Lowell Pr.

Poh Choo Chua, Margaret, jt. auth. see Chua, Soon-Leng.

Poh-Kam, Wong, jt. ed. see Minden, Karen.

Poh, Lai Y., et al. Small Businesses in Singapore: Case Studies in Entrepreneurship & Strategic Management. 288p. 1992. pap. 17.50 (*981-210-009-1*, Pub. by Times Academic) Intl Spec Bk.

***Pohanish, Dick.** Machinery's Handbook Pocket Reference. 1999. text 19.95 (*0-8311-3089-X*) Indus Pr.

***Pohanish, Richard.** McGraw-Hill's Chemical Safety Guide for the Plastics Industry. (Illus.). 1000p. 2000. 125.00 (*0-07-135607-X*) McGraw-Hill Prof.

Pohanish, Richard & Greene, Stanley. Hazardous Chemicals Safety Guide: For the Machining & Metalworking Industries. LC 99-174972. (Illus.). 800p. 1998. 79.95 (*0-07-050499-7*) McGraw-Hill Prof.

Pohanish, Richard P. Hazardous Materials Handbook. (Industrial Health & Safety Ser.). 1997. 300.00 (*0-442-02220-4*, VNR) Wiley.

Pohanish, Richard P. Rapid Guide to Hazardous Chemicals in the Environment. 519p. 1997. 43.95 (*0-471-28830-6*, VNR) Wiley.

Pohanish, Richard P. Rapid Guide to Hazardous Chemicals in the Environment. LC 97-14013. 544p. 1997. pap. 29.95 (*0-442-02527-0*, VNR) Wiley.

— Rapid Guide to Trade Names & Synonyms. LC 97-44409. (References Ser.). 304p. (C). 1997. pap. 39.95 (*0-442-02594-7*, VNR) Wiley.

***Pohanish, Richard P.** Rapid Guide to Trade Names & Synonyms of Environmentally Regulated Chemicals. 850p. 1998. pap. 43.95 (*0-471-29269-9*) Wiley.

Pohanish, Richard P. & Greene, Stanley A. Electronic & Computer Industry Guide to Chemical Safety & Enviromental Compliance. LC 98-33479. 672p. 1998. pap. 84.95 (*0-471-29285-0*) Wiley.

Pohanish, Richard P. & Greene, Stanley A. Hazardous Materials Handbook: For Handling Shipping, Storage & First Response. (Industrial Health & Safety Ser.). 1840p. 1996. 175.00 (*0-471-28748-2*, VNR) Wiley.

Pohanish, Richard P. & Greene, Stanley A. Hazardous Materials Handbook: Print Version. (Industrial Health & Safety Ser.). 1620p. 1996. text 156.95 (*0-442-02212-3*, VNR) Wiley.

— Hazardous Substances Resource Guide. 2nd ed. 800p. 1996. 205.00 (*0-8103-9062-0*) Gale.

Pohanish, Richard P. & Greene, Stanley A. Rapid Guide to Chemical Incompatibilities. 866p. 1997. 43.95 (*0-471-28802-0*, VNR) Wiley.

Pohanish, Richard P. & Greene, Stanley A. Rapid Guide to Chemical Incompatibility. LC 96-37063. (Miscellaneous/Catalogs Ser.). 878p. 1997. pap. 39.95 (*0-442-02394-4*, VNR) Wiley.

Pohanka, Brian C., ed. A Summer on the Plains, Eighteen Seventy: From the Diary of Annie Gibson Roberts. (Illus.). 29.50 (*0-8488-0003-6*, J M C & Co); pap. 21.95 (*0-8488-0028-1*, J M C & Co) Amereon Ltd.

Pohanka, Brian C. & Worthington, Glenn H. Fighting for Time: The Battle of Monocacy. LC 88-20742. (Civil War Classics Ser.). 327p. 1994. reprint ed. pap. 16.95 (*0-942597-71-0*, Burd St Pr) White Mane Pub.

Pohanka, Brian C., jt. auth. see Kristofferson, L.

Pohanka, Brian C., jt. auth. see McPherson, James M.

Pohanka, Brian C., ed. see Davis, William.

Pohier, Jacques & Mieth, Dietmar, eds. One Faith, One Church, Man, Many Moralities, Vol. 150. (Concilium Ser.). 128p. 1981. 6.95 (*0-8164-2350-4*) Harper SF.

Pohill, John B. Paul & His Letters. LC 99-26826. 1999. 29.99 (*0-8054-1097-X*) Broadman.

Pohjola, Erkki & Tuomisto, Matti. Tapiola Sound. 204p. 1993. pap. text 24.95 (*1-884598-00-5*) Walton Music.

Pohl, Alice N. Committees & Boards: How to Be an Effective Participant. (Illus.). 96p. 1991. pap. 10.95 (*0-8442-5635-8*, NTC Business Bks) NTC Contemp Pub Co.

— Formal Meeting: How to Prepare & Participate. (Illus.). 224p. 1992. pap. 10.95 (*0-8442-5633-1*, NTC Business Bks) NTC Contemp Pub Co.

Pohl, Amelia E. The Florida Will. 120p. (Orig.). 2000. pap. 39.95 incl. disk (*1-892407-03-5*) Eagle Pub FL.

— Simplified Divorce: Florida. unabridged ed. (Legal Kits Ser.). (Illus.). 80p. 2000. pap. write for info. (*1-892407-00-0*) Eagle Pub FL.

— When Someone Dies in Florida: All the Legal & Practical Things You Need to Do. LC 98-68439. 200p. 1999. 24.95 (*1-892407-01-9*); pap. 16.95 (*1-892407-02-7*) Eagle Pub FL.

***Pohl, Amelia E.** When Someone Dies In Michigan: All the legal & Practical Things You Need To Do. 2000. pap. 19.95 (*1-892407-26-4*) Eagle Pub FL.

— When Someone dies In New Jersey: All the Legal & Practical Things You Need to Do. 288p. 2000. 26.95 (*1-892407-22-1*); per. 19.95 (*1-892407-23-X*) Eagle Pub FL.

— When Someone Dies in North Carolina: All the Legal & Practical Things You Need to Do. 288p. 2000. 26.95 (*1-892407-20-5*); per. 19.95 (*1-892407-21-3*) Eagle Pub FL.

— When Someone Dies In Ohio: All the Legal & Practical Things You Need to Do. LC 00-190218. (YA). (gr. 8-12). 2000. 26.95 (*1-892407-18-3*) Eagle Pub FL.

— When Someone Dies in Ohio: All the Legal & Practical Things You Need to Do. LC 00-190218. (gr. 8-12). 2000. per. 19.95 (*1-892407-19-1*) Eagle Pub FL.

— When Someone Dies in Pennsylvania: All the Legal & Practical Things You Need to Do. 288p. 2000. 26.95 (*1-892407-14-0*); per. 19.95 (*1-892407-15-9*) Eagle Pub FL.

— When Someone Dies in Texas: All the Legal & Practical Things You Need to Do. LC 00-100116. 288p. 2000. per. 19.95 (*1-892407-17-5*) Eagle Pub FL.

— When Someone Dies in Texas: All the Legal & Practical Things You Need to Do. LC 00-100116. 288p. (YA). (gr. 8-12). 2000. 26.95 (*1-892407-16-7*) Eagle Pub FL.

***Pohl, Amelia E. & Bartlet, Paul B.** When Someone Dies in Arizona: All the Legal & Practical Things You Need to Do. 270p. 2000. 25.95 (*1-892407-04-3*) Eagle Pub FL.

— When Someone Dies in Arizona: All the Practical & Legal Things You Need to Do. 270p. 2000. per. 17.95 (*1-892407-05-1*) Eagle Pub FL.

***Pohl, Amelia E. & Feder, Bruce A.** When Someone Dies in California: All the Legal & Practical Things You Need to Do. 288p. 2000. 29.95 (*1-892407-06-X*); per. 19.95 (*1-892407-07-8*) Eagle Pub FL.

***Pohl, Amelia E. & Przybylo, Chester M.** When Someone Dies in Illinois: All the Legal & Practical things You Need to Do. 288p. 2000. 26.95 (*1-892407-11-6*) Eagle Pub FL.

— When Someone Dies in Illinois: All the Legal & Practical Things You Need to Do. 2000. per. 19.95 (*1-892407-12-4*) Eagle Pub FL.

***Pohl, Amelia E. & Russo, Vincent J.** When Someone Dies in New York: All the Legal & Practical Things You Need to Do. 288p. 2000. 26.95 (*1-892407-09-4*); per. 19.95 (*1-892407-10-8*) Eagle Pub FL.

Pohl, C. F. Mozart & Haydn in London, 2 vols. in 1. LC 70-125059. (Music Ser.). 1970. reprint ed. lib. bdg. 55.00 (*0-306-70024-7*) Da Capo.

Pohl, Chris, jt. auth. see Guyomard, Irene.

***Pohl, Christian.** Methodik Und Realisation Von Systemen Zur Effizienten Wissensvermittlung Durch Hypermedia. (Illus.). 272p. 1999. 48.95 (*3-631-33919-4*) P Lang Pubng.

Pohl, Christine D. Making Room: Recovering Hospitality As a Christian Tradition. LC 99-31765. 214p. 1999. pap. 15.00 (*0-8028-4431-6*) Eerdmans.

Pohl, Christine D., jt. auth. see Hershberger, Michele.

Pohl, Dieter W. & Courjon, Daniel, eds. Near Field Optics: Proceedings of the NATO Advanced Research Workshop at Arc-et-Senans, Oct. 26-28, 1992. LC 93-25336. (NATO Advanced Study Institutes Series E, Applied Sciences: No. 242). 1993. text 264.50 (*0-7923-2394-7*) Kluwer Academic.

Pohl, Eliane, ed. & illus. see Jackson, Matthew.

Pohl, Frances K. Ben Shahn: New Deal Artist in a Cold War Climate, 1947-1954. LC 88-39304. (American Studies). (Illus.). 250p. 1989. 24.95 (*0-292-75537-6*) U of Tex Pr.

Pohl, Frederick J. The New Columbus. (Illus.). 262p. 1986. 16.00 (*0-9611422-4-3*) Security Dupont.

— Prince Henry Sinclair. LC E109. (Illus.). 232p. 1998. pap. text 14.95 (*1-55109-122-4*) Nimbus Publ.

— William Shakespeare: A Biography. Butterfield, Stephen & Burton, Bruce A., eds. 256p. 1983. 16.75 (*0-9611422-1-9*) Security Dupont.

***Pohl, Frederik.** Chasing Science. 256p. 2000. text 23.95 (*0-312-86711-5*) St Martin.

— The Far Shore of Time. 352p. 2000. mass mkt. 6.99 (*0-8125-7783-3*, Pub. by Tor Bks) St Martin.

Pohl, Frederik. The Far Shore of Time: A Tom Doherty Associates Book. LC 99-22203. 320p. 1999. 23.95 (*0-312-86618-6*, Pub. by Tor Bks) St Martin.

— Gateway. 320p. 1987. mass mkt. 5.99 (*0-345-34690-4*, Del Rey) Ballantine Pub Grp.

— Jem. 352p. 1994. per. 4.99 (*0-671-87625-2*) Baen Bks.

— Land's End. 1989. mass mkt. 4.95 (*0-8125-0024-5*, Pub. by Tor Bks) St Martin.

— Midas World. 320p. 1984. pap. 2.95 (*0-8125-4925-2*, Pub. by Tor Bks) St Martin.

— O Pioneer! 1999. mass mkt. 6.99 (*0-8125-4544-3*, Pub. by Tor Bks) St Martin.

— O Pioneer! large type ed. LC 98-42375. 1998. 23.95 (*0-7838-0397-4*, G K Hall & Co) Mac Lib Ref.

— O Pioneer! A Tom Doherty Associates Book. LC 98-9726. 256p. 1998. text 21.95 (*0-312-86164-8*) St Martin.

— The Other End of Time. 1997. mass mkt. 6.99 (*0-614-27805-8*); mass mkt. 6.99 (*0-8125-3519-7*, Pub. by Tor Bks) St Martin.

— The Siege of Eternity. 1998. mass mkt. 6.99 (*0-8125-7766-3*, Pub. by Tor Bks) St Martin.

— The Voices of Heaven. 352p. 1995. 5.99 (*0-8125-3518-9*, Pub. by Tor Bks) St Martin.

Pohl, Frederik, ed. The SFWA Grand Masters. LC 99-21933. (Science Fiction Writers Association Ser.: Vol. 1). 384p. 1999. text 24.95 (*0-312-86881-2*, Pub. by Tor Bks) St Martin.

***Pohl, Frederik, ed.** The SFWA Grand Masters, Vol. 1. Vol. 1. 384p. 2000. pap. 15.95 (*0-312-86880-4*, Pub. by Tor Bks) St Martin.

— The SFWA Grand Masters, Vol. 2. LC 99-21933. Vol. 2. 384p. 2000. 25.95 (*0-312-86879-0*, Pub. by Tor Bks) St Martin.

Pohl, Frederik & Asimov, Isaac. Our Angry Earth. 448p. 1993. mass mkt. 5.99 (*0-8125-2096-3*, Pub. by Tor Bks) St Martin.

Pohl, Frederik & Kornbluth, Cyril. The Space Merchants. 1993. reprint ed. lib. bdg. 18.95 (*0-89968-359-2*, Lghtyr Pr) Buccaneer Bks.

Pohl, Frederik & Thomas, Thomas T. Mars Plus. 352p. 1994. 20.00 (*0-671-87605-8*) Baen Bks.

— Mars Plus. 352p. 1995. mass mkt. 5.99 (*0-671-87665-1*) Baen Bks.

Pohl, Frederik & Williamson, Jack. The Starchild Trilogy. 448p. 1986. reprint ed. per. 4.99 (*0-671-65558-2*) Baen Bks.

Pohl, Gayle. Public Relations: Communication. 176p. (C). 1995. pap. text, per. 24.95 (*0-7872-0432-3*) Kendall-Hunt.

Pohl, Gerhard & Sorsa, Piritta. European Integration & Trade with the Developing World. LC 92-28788. (Policy & Research Ser.: Vol. 21). 102p. 1992. pap. 22.00 (*0-8213-2204-4*, 12204) World Bank.

Pohl, Gerhard, et al. Creating Capital Markets in Central & Eastern Europe. LC 95-32644. 44p. 1995. pap. 22.00 (*0-8213-3370-4*) World Bank.

— Creating Capital Markets in Central & Eastern Europe. (World Bank Technical Papers: No. 295). (RUS.). 56p. 1995. pap. 22.00 (*0-8213-3468-9*, 13468) World Bank.

— Privatization & Restructuring in Central & Eastern Europe: Evidence & Policy Options. LC 97-13342. (Technical Paper Ser.: No. 368). 48p. 1997. pap. 22.00 (*0-8213-3975-3*, 13975) World Bank.

Pohl, Gherhard, et al. Restructuring Large Industrial Firms in Central & Eastern Europe: An Empirical Analysis. LC 96-26383. (World Bank Technical Papers: No. 332). 48p. 1996. pap. 22.00 (*0-8213-3712-2*, 13712) World Bank.

Pohl, Gladys L. The Key to the Universe. 64p. (Orig.). 1984. pap. 5.95 (*0-939332-10-8*) J Pohl Assocs.

Pohl, H. Taschen Lexikon Sicherheit der Informationstechnik. (ENG & GER.). 184p. 1989. pap. 95.00 (*0-8288-3883-6*, F120960) Fr & Eur.

Pohl, H., ed. Hydrogen & Other Alternate Sources of Energy for Air & Ground Transportation. LC 95-17785. 224p. 1996. 130.00 (*0-471-95336-9*) Wiley.

Pohl, H., et al, eds. German Yearbook on Business History 1981. (Illus.). 127p. 1982. 36.00 (*0-387-11230-8*) Spr-Verlag.

Pohl, H. & Rudolph, B., eds. German Yearbook on Business History 1987. 160p. 1989. 46.00 (*0-387-50074-X*) Spr-Verlag.

Pohl, H., jt. ed. see Engels, W.

Pohl, Hans, jt. ed. see Bosbach, Franz.

Pohl, Hartel. Roemische Politik & Piraterie im Oestlichen Mittelmeer: Vom 3. Bis 1, Jh. v. Chr. (Untersuchungen zur Antiken Literatur und Geschichte Ser.: Band 42). (GER.). x, 310p. (C). 1993. lib. bdg. 114.70 (*3-11-013890-5*) De Gruyter.

Pohl, Heinz. Kitab Al-Mirat: Das Buch der Erbschaft des Samritaners Ibraham Abv Ishag: Kritische Edition mit Uebersetzung und Kommentar. LC 74-80633. (Studia Samaritana: Band 2). (GER.). 328p. (C). 1974. 119.25 (*3-11-002495-0*) De Gruyter.

***Pohl, Inge.** Interdisziplinaritat und Methodenpluralismus in der Semantikforschung: Beitrage der Konferenz; Interdisziplinaritat und Methodenpluralismus in der Semantikforschung/An der Universitat Koblenz-Landau/Abteilung Landau, 1998. (GER., Illus.). 393p. 1999. 57.00 (*3-631-34895-9*) P Lang Pubng.

Pohl, Inge. Methodologische Aspekte der Semantikforschung: Beitrage der Konferenz Methodologische Aspekte der Semantikforschung an der Universitat Koblenz - Landau/Abteilung Landau (1996) (GER., Illus.). 440p. 1997. 63.95 (*3-631-31326-8*) P Lang Pubng.

Pohl, Inge & Pohl, Jurgen, eds. Texte Uber Texte: Interdisziplinaere Zugaenge. (Sprache - System und Tatigkeit Ser.: Band 24). (GER., Illus.). 628p. 1998. pap. 85.95 (*3-631-31831-6*) P Lang Pubng.

Pohl, Ingrid. San Giovenale: The Iron Age Habitations in Area E. (Acta Instituti Romani Regni Sueciae, Series in 4 Degrees: Vol. XXVI:III,3). (Illus.). 124p. 1977. pap. 48.50 (*91-7042-063-7*, Pub. by P Astroms) Coronet Bks.

Pohl, Ingrid, jt. auth. see Olinder, Bjorn.

Pohl, Ira. C++ for C Programmers. 2nd ed. LC 93-30685. 384p. (C). 1993. pap. 43.95 (*0-8053-3159-X*) Benjamin-Cummings.

P

— C++ for C Programmers. 3rd ed. LC 98-37980. 512p. (C). 1998. pap. 39.95 (0-201-39519-3) Addison-Wesley.
— C++ Distilled: A Concise Ansi/ISO Reference & Style Guide. LC 96-29545. 224p. (Orig.). (C). 1996. pap. 22.95 (0-201-69587-1) Addison-Wesley.
— C++ for Fortran Programmers. LC 97-13771. 560p. (C). 1997. pap. 39.95 (0-201-92483-8) Addison-Wesley.
— C++ for Pascal Programmers. 2nd ed. 496p. (C). 1995. pap. 43.95 (0-8053-3158-1) Benjamin-Cummings.
— Easy Reference Guide to C Plus Plus. 430p. (C). 1997. pap. text. write for info. (0-8053-3164-6) Benjamin-Cummings.
— Object-Oriented Programming Using C++ (Object-Oriented Software Engineering Ser.). 512p. (C). 1993. pap. 42.95 (0-8053-5382-8) Benjamin-Cummings.
— Object Oriented Programming Using C++ 2nd ed. LC 96-48514. 576p. (C). 1996. pap. 41.95 (0-201-89550-1) Addison-Wesley.

Pohl, Ira & McDowell, Charlie. Java by Dissection. LC 99-33159. 509p. (C). 1999. pap. 68.00 (0-201-61248-8) Addison-Wesley.

Pohl, Ira, jt. auth. see Kelley, Al.

***Pohl, J. Otto.** Ethnic Cleansing in the U. S. S. R., 1937-1949, Vol. 65. LC 98-46822. (Contributions to the Study of World History Ser.: Vol. 65). 200p. 1999. 59.95 (0-313-30921-3) Greenwood.

Pohl, J. Otto. The Stalinist Penal System: A Statistical History of Soviet Repression & Terror, 1930-1953. LC 97-26939. 175p. 1997. lib. bdg. 35.00 (0-7864-0336-5) McFarland & Co.

Pohl, James W. Battle of San Jacinto. 49p. 1989. pap. 7.95 (0-87611-084-7) Tex St Hist Assn.

Pohl, John M. The Politics of Symbolism in the Mixtec Codices. Spores, Ronald M., ed. (Vanderbilt University Publications in Anthropology: No. 46). (Illus.). 157p. (Orig.). 1994. pap. 14.00 (0-935462-37-6) VUPA.

Pohl, John M. D. Exploring Mesoamerica. LC 99-56046. (Places in Time Ser.). (Illus.). 240p. 2000. 39.95 (0-19-510887-6) OUP.

Pohl, Jurgen, jt. ed. see Pohl, Inge.

***Pohl, Karl-Heinz.** Chinese Thought in a Global Context: A Dialogue Between Chinese & Western Philosophical Approaches LC 99-27727. (Sinica Leidensia Ser.). 1999. write for info. (90-04-11426-2) Brill Academic Pubs.

Pohl, Karl O. A New Monetary Order for Europe. LC HG0930.5.P6. (Per Jacobsson Lecture Ser.: Vol. 1992). 32p. reprint ed. pap. 30.00 (0-608-08739-4, 206937800004) Bks Demand.
— Un Nouvel Ordre Monetaire pour L'Europe. LC HG0930.5.P64. (Conference Per Jacobsson Ser.: Vol. 1992). (FRE.). 34p. reprint ed. pap. 30.00 (0-608-08740-8, 206937900004) Bks Demand.
— Un Nuevo Order Monetario para Europa. LC HG0930.5.P64. (Conferencia Per Jacobsson de 1992 Ser.). (SPA.). 34p. reprint ed. pap. 30.00 (0-608-08741-6, 206938000004) Bks Demand.

Pohl, Kathy, ed. Country Woman Christmas 1997. LC 96-67482. 112p. 1997. 17.95 (0-89821-211-1, 24494) Reiman Pubns.

***Pohl, Kathy, ed.** Down the Aisle Country-Style. LC 99-76346. (Illus.). 116p. 2000. 15.99 (0-89821-283-9) Reiman Pubns.

Pohl, Kathy & Thibodeau, Karen, eds. Country Woman Christmas, Vol. 1. LC 96-67482. 116p. 1996. 17.95 (0-89821-171-9, 20406) Reiman Pubns.

Pohl, Kathy, ed. see Woman Country.

Pohl, Klaus. Process-Centered Requirements Engineering. LC 96-3339. (Advanced Software Development Ser.). 342p. 1996. 84.95 (0-86380-193-5) Wiley.
— Waiting Room Germany. 80p. (Orig.). 1996. pap. 13.95 (1-85459-274-2, Pub. by N Hern Bks) Theatre Comm.

Pohl, L., et al. Liquid Crystals. (Topics in Physical Chemistry Ser.: Vol. 3). 1994. 51.95 (0-387-91421-8) Spr-Verlag.

Pohl, Linda P. The Ah-Chooo Book. (Illus.). 20p. (J). (ps-2). 1990. 3.95 (0-9625453-0-9) L P Pohl.
— The Boo Boo Book. (Illus.). 12p. (Orig.). (J). (ps-1). 1995. pap. 3.95 (0-9625453-2-5) L P Pohl.
— The Grumpy Queen. (Illus.). 16p. (J). (ps-1). 1998. pap. text 4.95 (0-9625453-3-3) L P Pohl.
— The Wiggly Tooth Book. (Illus.). 16p. (J). (ps-2). 1991. 3.95 (0-9625453-1-7) L P Pohl.

Pohl, M. D. Aztec, Mixtex, & Zapotec Armies. (Men-at-Arms Ser.: No. 239). (Illus.). 48p. pap. 12.95 (1-85532-159-9, 9197, Pub. by Ospry) Stackpole.

Pohl, Manfred, ed. Handbook on the History of European Banks. LC 93-24564. 1328p. 1994. 390.00 (1-85278-919-0) E Elgar.

***Pohl, Manfred, et al.** A Century of Banking Consolidation in Europe: The History & Archives of Mergers & Acquisitions. LC 00-44198. 2000. write for info. (0-7546-0263-X, Pub. by Ashgate Pub) Ashgate Pub Co.

Pohl, Margaret L. Teaching Function Nursing Practition. 4th ed. 176p. (C). 1981. text. write for info. (0-697-05546-9, WCB McGr Hill) McGrw-H Hghr Educ.

Pohl, Mary D., ed. Prehistoric Lowland Maya Environment & Subsistence Economy. LC 84-62626. (Peabody Museum Papers: Vol. 77). (Illus.). 209p. 1985. reprint ed. pap. 25.00 (0-87365-203-7) Peabody Harvard.

Pohl, Nicole, jt. auth. see D'Monte, Rebecca.

Pohl, Nina, ed. see Caroselli, Marlene.

Pohl, Peter & Gieth, Kinna. I Miss You, I Miss You! Greenwald, Roger, tr. from ENG. LC 97-25424. 256p. (YA). (gr. 7-12). 1998. 17.00 (91-29-63935-2, Pub. by R & S Bks) FS&G.

Pohl, R. German-English - English-German Dictionary of Hydrolic Engineering. (ENG & GER.). 1990. 38.00 (0-7859-8961-7) Fr & Eur.

Pohl, R., jt. ed. see Gershon, Samuel.

Pohl, R. O., jt. ed. see Meissner, M.

Pohl, Reinhard. Wasserbau: Englisch - Deutsch Deutsch - Englisch. 1991. 49.95 (0-685-40786-1) Fr & Eur.
— Wasserbau: Englisch-Deutsch-Englisch. (DUT & ENG.). 49.95 (0-8288-7936-2, F58909) Fr & Eur.

Pohl, Richard W., et al. Grasses. 3rd ed. (Pictured Key Nature Ser.). 208p. (C). 1978. text. write for info. (0-697-04876-4, WCB McGr Hill) McGrw-H Hghr Educ.

Pohl, Richard W., jt. auth. see Clark, Lynn G.

Pohl, Susan, ed. see Coffman, Charlotte W.

Pohl, Susan E., ed. see O'Neill, Charles R., Jr.

Pohl, Udiger, jt. auth. see Gabrisch, Hubert.

Pohl, Victoria. How to Enrich Geometry Using String Designs. LC 86-5189. (Illus.). 68p. 1986. pap. 14.95 (0-87353-227-9) NCTM.

Pohl, Walter. W. & W. E. Petrascheck's Lagerstaettenlehre: Eine Einfuehrung in die Wissenschaft von den Mineralischen Bodenschaetzen. viii, 504p. 1992. 58.00 (3-510-65150-2, Pub. by E Schweizerbartsche) Balogh.

Pohl, Walter, ed. Kingdoms of the Empire: The Integration of Barbarians in Late Antiquity. LC 97-8209. (Transformation of the Roman World Ser.: No. 1). (ENG & FRE.). 220p. 1997. 89.00 (90-04-10845-9) Brill Academic Pubs.
— Strategies of Distinction: The Construction of Ethnic Communities, 300-800. LC 97-40123. (Transformation of the Roman World Ser.: No. 2). (ENG & FRE., Illus.). 1997. 97.00 (90-04-10846-7) Brill Academic Pubs.

***Pohl, Walter, et al, eds.** Transformation of Frontiers: From Late Antiquity to the Carolingians. (Illus.). 280p. 2000. 96.00 (90-04-11115-8) Brill Academic Pubs.

Pohl, William, tr. see Husserl, Edmund.

Pohland, A. E., et al, eds. Microbial Toxins in Foods & Feeds: Cellular & Molecular Modes of Action. LC 90-14343. (Illus.). 634p. (C). 1990. text 198.00 (0-306-43716-3, Kluwer Plenum) Kluwer Academic.

Pohland, Albert E., jt. ed. see Trucksess, Mary W.

Pohland, F. G., jt. auth. see Tedder, D. W.

Pohland, Frederick G. & Britz. Anaerobic Digest VII. (Water Science & Technology Ser.: No. 30-12). 444p. 1995. pap. write for info. (0-08-042641-7, Pergamon Pr) Elsevier.

Pohland, Frederick G., jt. auth. see Tedder, D. W.

Pohland, Frederick G., jt. ed. see Malina, Joseph F., Jr.

Pohland, Frederick G., jt. ed. see Tedder, D. William.

Pohland, Frederick G., jt. ed. see Tedder, D. W.

Pohland, Frederick G., jt. ed. see Vidic, Radisav D.

Pohlandt, K. Materials Testing for the Metal Forming Industry. (Illus.). 240p. 1989. 94.95 (0-387-50651-9) Spr-Verlag.

Pohle, Joseph. Eschatology. LC 72-109823. 164p. 1971. reprint ed. lib. bdg. 55.00 (0-8371-4314-4, POES, Greenwood Pr) Greenwood.

***Pohle, Nancy C. & Selover, Ellen L.** Awakening the Real You: Awareness Through Dreams & Intuition. LC 98-43103. (Illus.). 161p. 1999. pap. 12.95 (0-87604-419-4, 488) ARE Pr.

Pohlen, Annelie, jt. auth. see Fonce, Jan.

***Pohlen, Jerome.** Oddball Illinois: A Guide to Some Really Strange Places. 2000. pap. 12.95 (1-55652-371-8, Pub. by Chicago Review) IPG Chicago.

Pohlenz, ed. Ciceronis, M. Tulli Fascicule 44: Tusculanae Disputationes. (LAT.). 1995. reprint ed. pap. 29.95 (3-519-01220-0, T1220, Pub. by B G Teubner) U of Mich Pr.

Pohlenz & Ziegler, eds. Plutarchi Vol. VI, Fascicule 3: De Musica. (GRE.). 1966. 19.95 (3-322-00248-9, T1688, Pub. by B G Teubner) U of Mich Pr.

Pohlenz, M. Freedom in Greek Life & Thought: The History of an Ideal. Lofmark, C., tr. from GER. 202p. 1966. lib. bdg. 71.50 (90-277-0009-5) Kluwer Academic.

Pohlenz, Max. Kleine Schriften, 2 vols., Set. xxxi, 1192p. 1965. write for info. (0-318-70819-1) G Olms Pubs.

Pohler, J. G. Foreign Participation in U. S. Academic Science & Engineering. (Illus.). 127p. (Orig.). (C). 1993. pap. text 40.00 (1-56806-420-9) DIANE Pub.

Pohler, Rolf J. Continuity & Change in Christian Doctrine: A Study of the Problem of Doctrinal Development. LC 98-43686. (Friedensauer Schriftenreihe. Reihe A: Theologie: No. 2). 156p. 1998. pap. text 31.95 (0-8204-3579-1) P Lang Pubng.

Pohler, Ulrike. Anwaltsgesellschaften in den U. S. A. und in Deutschland. (Europaische Hochschulschriften Reibe: No. 2, Band 2373). 327p. 1998. pap. 56.95 (3-631-33168-1) P Lang Pubng.

Pohlers, W. Proof Theory. (Lecture Notes in Mathematics Ser.: Vol. 1407). vi, 213p. 1996. pap. 39.95 (0-387-51842-8) Spr-Verlag.

***Pohlig, James N.** An Exegetical Summary of Malachi. LC 98-61751. 207 p. 1998. pap. 18.40 (1-55671-079-8) S I L Intl.

Pohlman, H. L. Justice Oliver Wendell Holmes: Free Speech & the Living Constitution. 312p. (C). 1993. pap. text 18.50 (0-8147-6622-6) NYU Pr.
— The Whole Truth? A Case of Murder on the Appalachian Trail. LC 98-28300. (Illus.). 264p. 1999. 45.00 (1-55849-165-1); pap. 16.95 (1-55849-166-X) U of Mass Pr.

Pohlman, H. L., ed. Political Thought & the American Judiciary. LC 92-30025. 344p. (C). 1993. pap. 19.95 (0-87023-830-2); lib. bdg. 45.00 (0-87023-829-9) U of Mass Pr.

Pohlman, Karl-Friedrich. Ezechielstudien: Zur Redaktionsgeschichte des Buches und zur Frage nach den Altesten Texten. (Beiheft zur Zeitschrift fuer die Alttestamentliche Wissenschaft Ser.: Bd. 202). ix, 262p. (C). 1992. lib. bdg. 106.15 (3-11-012976-0, 247-91) De Gruyter.

Pohlman, Lisa H. Factory Recipes Make Lasting Memories. 360p. 1996. pap. 13.00 (0-9653030-0-4, R2-202395) L H Pohlman.

Pohlman, Marcus D. & Kirby, Michael P. Racial Politics at the Crossroads: Memphis Elects Dr. W. W. Herenton. LC 95-32505. (Illus.). 288p. (C). 1996. pap. text 17.00 (0-87049-927-0); lib. bdg. 34.00 (0-87049-926-2) U of Tenn Pr.

***Pohlman, Randolph A., et al.** Value Driven Management: How to Create & Maximize Value over Time for Organizational Success. LC 00-21498. 240p. 2000. 24.95 (0-8144-0485-5) AMACOM.

Pohlman, Richard W., jt. auth. see Morgan, Fred.

Pohlman, Roberta, jt. auth. see Isaacs, Larry D.

Pohlman, Steven L., ed. see Electrochemical Society Staff.

Pohlmann, Horst Georg. Encounters with Hinduism. 1996. pap. 18.00 (0-334-02628-8) S C M Pr Ltd.

Pohlmann, K. Principles of Digital Audio. 3rd ed. LC 95-17259. (Illus.). 640p. 1995. pap. 44.95 (0-07-050469-5) McGraw.

Pohlmann, Ken C., jt. auth. see Bonime, Andrew.

Pohlmann, Kenneth C. The Compact Disc Handbook. 2nd ed. LC 92-13287. (Computer Music & Digital Audio Ser.: Vol. 5). (Illus.). 349p. (C). 1992. pap. 34.95 (0-89579-300-8) A-R Eds.

Pohlmann, Marcus D. Black Politics in Conservative America. 2nd ed. LC 98-17996. 272p. (C). 1998. pap. text 52.00 (0-8013-1732-0) Addison-Wesley.

Pohlmann, S., jt. auth. see Weichselberger, K.

Pohlmann, Ulrich, jt. auth. see Von Amelunxen, Hubertus.

Pohlsander, Hans A. Constantine. LC 96-10186. (Lancaster Pamphlets Ser.). (Illus.). 128p. (C). 1996. pap. 12.99 (0-415-13178-2) Routledge.
— Helena: Empress & Saint. LC 96-173814. (Illus.). 500p. 60.00 (0-89005-562-9) Ares.

Pohlsander, Hans A., ed. Greek Texts from the Fourth to the Thirteenth Centuries. (Sources for the History of Cyprus Ser.: Vol. VII). 195p. 1999. pap. 50.00 (0-9651704-7-0) Greece & Cyprus Res.

Pohly, Linda. The Barbra Streisand Companion: A Guide to Her Vocal Style & Repertoire. LC 99-31631. 304p. 2000. lib. bdg. 49.95 (0-313-30414-9) Greenwood.

Pohn, Alison, jt. auth. see Weinberger, Norman.

Pohorecky, Larissa A., et al, eds. Alcohol & Aggression: Proceedings of the Symposium on Alcohol & Aggression Held at the Center of Alcohol Studies, Rutgers University, October 1992. (Journal of Studies on Alcohol: Suppl. No. 11). 200p. 1993. pap. 26.95 (0-911290-52-4, AJS-106) Rutgers Ctr Alcohol.

Pohoryles, Ronald, et al, eds. European Transformations: Five Decisive Years at the Turn of the Century: An Innovative Reader 1988-1992. (Contemporary Trends in European Social Sciences Ser.). 432p. 1994. 77.95 (1-85628-656-8, Pub. by Avebry) Ashgate Pub Co.

Pohost, Gerald M. Principles & Practice of Cardiovascular Imaging. 1990. 135.00 (0-316-71247-7, Little Brwn Med Div) Lppncott W & W.

Pohost, Gerald M., ed. Cardiovascular Applications of Magnetic Resonance. LC 92-48279. (American Heart Association Monograph Ser.). (Illus.). 480p. 1993. 86.00 (0-87993-548-0) Futura Pub.

Pohost, Gerald M., et al. Imaging in Cardiovascular Disease. 1,120p. text 149.00 (0-397-51591-X) Lppncott W & W.

Pohozaev, S. I., jt. auth. see Kuzin, I.

Pohren, D. E. Adventures in Taste: The Wines & Folk Food of Spain. (Illus.). 302p. 1972. 19.95 (0-933224-13-3, I001, Pub. by Soc Sp Studies) Bold Strummer Ltd.
— Art of Flamenco. 1985. lib. bdg. 250.00 (0-8490-3248-2) Gordon Pr.
— Lives & Legends of Flamenco: A Biographical History. rev. ed. (Society of Spanish Studies). (Illus.). 329p. 1988. reprint ed. 29.95 (0-933224-12-5, I026, Pub. by Soc Sp Studies) Bold Strummer Ltd.
— Paco de Lucia & Family: The Master Plan. 1995. pap. 11.95 (0-933224-62-1, I140) Bold Strummer Ltd.
— A Way of Life. (Illus.). 194p. 1988. reprint ed. 24.95 (0-933224-02-8, I049, Pub. by Soc Sp Studies); reprint ed. pap. 19.95 (0-933224-03-6, I050, Pub. by Soc Sp Studies) Bold Strummer Ltd.

Pohren, D. E. & George, David. The Art of Flamenco: Society of Spanish Studies. rev. ed. (Illus.). 212p. 1996. pap. 24.95 (0-933224-38-9, I007, Pub. by Soc Sp Studies) Bold Strummer Ltd.

Pohribny, Arsen, jt. auth. see Elliott, David.

Pohrt, Richard, Jr. & Penney, David W. Bags of Friendship: Bandolier Bags of the Great Lakes Indians. (Illus.). 32p. (Orig.). 1996. pap. 20.00 (0-9617085-2-2) Morning Star Gal.

Pohrt, Tom. Coyote Goes Walking. 32p. (J). (gr. k-3). 1997. pap. text 5.95 (0-374-41380-0) FS&G.
— Coyote Goes Walking. 1997. 11.15 (0-606-12664-3, Pub. by Turtleback) Demco.
— Having a Wonderful Time. LC 98-13093. (Illus.). 32p. (YA). (ps up). 1999. pap. text 16.00 (0-374-32898-6) FS&G.

Pohrt, Tom. Coyote Goes Walking. LC 94-24096. 32p. (J). (ps-3). 1995. 16.00 (0-374-31628-7) FS&G.

Pohrt, Tom, jt. illus. see Frank, John.

Pohs, Henry A. Metric Conversion Symbols: Pohs Shop. (Illus.). 24p. 1994. pap. 7.50 (0-9641165-1-0) Flame Pubng.
— The Miner's Flame Light Book. LC 92-97415. (Illus.). 833p. 1995. 89.50 (0-9641165-0-2) Flame Pubng.

Pohst, M. & Zassenhaus, H. Algorithmic Algebraic Number Theory. (Encyclopedia of Mathematics & Its Applications Ser.: Vol. 30). (Illus.). 480p. 1997. pap. text 42.95 (0-521-59669-6) Cambridge U Pr.

Pohst, Michael E. Computational Algebraic Number Theory. LC 93-26028. (DMV Seminar Ser.: Bd. 21). 88p. 1993. 31.50 (0-8176-2913-0, Pub. by Birkhauser) Princeton Arch.

Pohst, Michael E., ed. Algorithmic Methods in Algebra & Number Theory. 135p. 1988. pap. text 44.00 (0-12-559190-X) Acad Pr.

Pohst, Michael E. & Zassenhaus, Hans. Algorithmic Algebraic Number Theory. (Encyclopedia of Mathematics & Its Applications Ser.: No. 30). (Illus.). 480p. 1989. text 120.00 (0-521-33060-2) Cambridge U Pr.

Poi, Caroline Van de, see Van de Poi, Caroline.

Poidevin, Raymond, jt. auth. see Spierenburg, Dirk.

Poidras, Henri. Critical & Documentary Dictionary of Violin Makers - Old & Modern, 2 vols., Set. 1988. reprint ed. lib. bdg. 129.00 (0-7812-0779-7) Rprt Serv.
— Critical & Documentary Dictionary of Violin Makers Old & Modern, 2 vols. in 1. LC 70-166252. 1930. reprint ed. 59.00 (0-403-01381-X) Scholarly.

***Poier Bernhard, Astrid.** Romain Gary im Spiegel der Literaturkritik. 1999. 48.95 (3-631-35273-5) P Lang Pubng.

***Poiger, Uta G.** Jazz, Rock, & Rebels: Cold War Politics & American Culture in a Divided Germany LC 99-34558. (Studies on the History of Society & Culture: Vol. 35). (Illus.). 346p. 2000. 19.95 (0-520-21139-1) U CA Pr.

Poiger, Uta G. Transactions, Transgressions, Transformations: American Culture in Western Europe & Japan. Fehrenbach, Heide, ed. LC 98-47360. (Illus.). 304p. 1999. pap. 24.00 (1-57181-108-7) Berghahn Bks.

Poiger, Uta G., jt. ed. see Fehrenbach, Heide.

Poignant, Raymond. Education & Development in Western Europe, the United States, & the U. S. S. R. A Comparative Study. LC 72-77012. (Comparative Education Studies). 361p. reprint ed. pap. 112.00 (0-608-14835-0, 202605700048) Bks Demand.

Poignard, Renee. Waxing Made Easy: A Step-By-Step Guide. LC 93-25343. (SKIN). 108p. 1993. pap. 13.95 (1-56253-171-9) Thomson Learn.

Poikolainen, Kari. Alcohol Poisoning Mortality in Four Nordic Countries. (Finnish Foundation for Alcohol Studies: Vol. 28). 1977. 8.00 (951-9191-47-X) Rutgers Ctr Alcohol.

Poiky, Patrick D. How to Beat the New & Used Boat Salesman. 102p. (Orig.). 1994. pap. 12.95 (0-9640800-0-1) Peoples Interest.

Poiletman, Robert. How to Teach Your Child the Three R's: One Parent's Method. 153p. (Orig.). 1986. pap. text 4.95 (0-937519-00-6) Poiletman Pub.

Poilin, Aodan Mac, see Mac Poilin, Aodan.

***Poillon, Christopher.** Getting Started in Emerging Markets. (Getting Started In Ser.). 2000. pap. 19.95 (0-471-39545-5) Wiley.

Poillon, Florence, ed. Dioxin Treatment Technologies. (Illus.). 80p. (Orig.). (C). 1994. pap. text 25.00 (0-7881-0576-0) DIANE Pub.

Poinar, G. O., Jr. & Thomas, G. M. Laboratory Guide to Insect Pathogens & Parasites. LC 84-9875. (Illus.). 408p. (C). 1984. text 110.00 (0-306-41680-8, Kluwer Plenum) Kluwer Academic.

Poinar, George O., Jr. Life in Amber. LC 91-5045. (Illus.). 374p. (C). 1992. 59.50 (0-8047-2001-0) Stanford U Pr.

Poinar, George O., Jr. & Jansson, Hans-Borje, eds. Diseases of Nematodes. 160p. 1988. 95.00 (0-8493-4317-8, SF997, CRC Reprint); 176.00 (0-8493-4318-6, SF997, CRC Reprint) Franklin.

Poinar, George O., Jr. & Poinar, Roberta. The Amber Forest: A Reconstruction of a Vanished World. LC 98-35388. 1999. 29.95 (0-691-02888-5, Pub. by Princeton U Pr) Cal Prin Full Svc.

Poinar, George O. & Poinar, Roberta. The Quest for Life in Amber. 240p. (C). 1995. pap. 15.00 (0-201-48928-7) Addison-Wesley.

Poinar, Roberta, jt. auth. see Poinar, George O.

Poinar, Roberta, jt. auth. see Poinar, George O., Jr.

Poincare, Henri. New Methods of Celestial Mechanics, 3 vols., Set. (History of Modern Physics & Astronomy Ser.: Vol. 13). 1600p. 1990. 199.95 (1-56396-117-2) Spr-Verlag.
— Science & Hypothesis. 271p. 1952. pap. 7.95 (0-486-60221-4) Dover.
— Science & Method. (Key Texts Ser.). 288p. 1996. pap. 24.95 (1-85506-431-6) Bks Intl VA.

***Poincare, Henri.** Science & Method. (Key Texts Ser.). 288p. 2000. reprint ed. pap. text 24.00 (1-890318-82-5, Pub. by St Augustines Pr) U Ch Pr.

Poincare, Jules Henri. Papers on Fuchsian Functions. Stillwell, John C., tr. from FRE. (Illus.). iv, 483p. 1985. 79.95 (0-387-96215-8) Spr-Verlag.

Poincare, Raymond. The Memoirs of Raymond Poincare, 4 vols., Set. Arthur, George, tr. LC 70-160452. reprint ed. 140.00 (0-404-09090-7) AMS Pr.

Poincelot, Raymond P. & Olson, Richard K., eds. Integrating Sustainable Agriculture, Ecology & Environment Policy. LC 92-13752. (Journal of Sustainable Agriculture: Vol. 2, No. 3). (Illus.). 196p. 1992. 54.95 (1-56022-023-6); pap. 24.95 (1-56022-024-4) Haworth Jrnl Co-Edits.

Poincenot, Lissa, ed. see Short, Jack.

Poindexter. E-course Netscape Communicator. (C). 1997. pap. text 16.00 (0-7600-7227-2) Thomson Learn.

Poindexter. Making Research Relevant. 1999. pap. text 53.95 (0-312-19162-6) St Martin.

Poindexter. NP Internet Using NTSCP Communicator Software. (C). 1997. pap. 18.95 (0-7600-5501-7) Course Tech.

***Poindexter, Floyd.** Bait Man Down the Road: Tales of a Tennessee Bait Dealer about Friends, Places. (Illus.). 192p. 1999. write for info. (0-9677681-0-1) Stroud Graphics.

***Poindexter, George, ed.** Homeless Veterans: VA Expands Partnerships, but Homeless Program Effectiveness Is Unclear. (Illus.). 50p. (C). 1999. pap. text 20.00 (0-7881-8425-3) DIANE Pub.

P

An Asterisk (*) at the beginning of an entry indicates that the title is appearing for the first time.

Poindexter, Hildrus A. My World of Reality. LC 72-85752. (Illus.). 349p. 1973. 9.95 (*0-913642-03-7*) Balamp Pub.

Poindexter, J. S., jt. auth. see Leadbetter, E. R.

Poindexter, Joseph. To the Summit: 50 Mountains That Lure, Inspire & Challenge. (Illus.). 336p. 1999. 39.98 (*1-57912-041-5*) Blck Dog & Leventhal.

Poindexter, Katherine. A Day with the Pet Doctor. (Look-Look Bks.). (Illus.). 24p. (J). (ps-3). 1998. pap. 3.29 (*0-307-13182-3*, 13182, Goldn Books) Gldn Bks Pub Co.

***Poindexter, Lawrence.** Comparative Analysis of the Perception of an Exemplary Middle School. 1999. pap. 9.95 (*1-56167-537-7*) Am Literary Pr.

Poindexter, Lawrence. A Comparative Analysis of the Perception of an Exemplary Middle School as Held by Administrators & Classroom Teachers. (Illus.). 80p. 1999. pap. 9.95 (*0-8059-4660-8*) Dorrance.

***Poindexter, Sandra.** New Perspectives on Internet. 1998. pap. 14.00 (*0-7600-5784-2*) Course Tech.

Poindexter, Sandra, jt. auth. see Carey, Joan.

Poindexter, Sandra E., jt. auth. see Carey, Joan.

Poindexter, Sidney. Cobrina & Mongoose-Ra. (Illus.). 40p. (J). (gr. 3-6). 1998. pap. 9.00 (*0-8059-4391-9*) Dorrance.

Poiner, Gretchen. The Good Old Rule: Gender & Other Power Relationships in a Rural Community. (Sydney University Press Publication). 216p. 1991. pap. 32.00 (*0-424-00160-8*) OUP.

Poingee, Hans A. Theraplay Als Therapeutischer Ansatz Fur die Schulische Arbeit Mit Verhaltensgestorten. (Illus.). X, 236p. 1997. 44.95 (*3-631-31417-5*) P Lang Pubng.

Poinsatte, Charles. Fort Wayne During the Canal Era, 1828-1855. 284p. 1993. pap. 13.50 (*1-885323-23-9*) IN Hist Bureau.

Poinsatte, Charles, jt. auth. see Norling, Bernard.

Poinsett, Alex. Black Power Gary Style: The Making of Mayor Richard Gordon Hatcher. LC 72-128545. 200p. 1970. 6.95 (*0-87485-042-8*) Johnson Chicago.

Poinsett, Alex. Walking with Presidents: Louis Martin & the Rise of Black Political Power. LC 97-1997. 288p. 1997. 21.95 (*1-56833-093-6*) Madison Bks UPA.

***Poinsett, Alex.** Walking with Presidents: Louis Martin & the Rise of Black Political Power. 251p. 2000. pap. 14.95 (*0-8476-9741-X*) Rowman.

Poinsett, Alex, ed. Role of Sports in Youth Development. (Illus.). 157p. (Orig.). (C). 1997. pap. text 35.00 (*0-7881-4518-5*) DIANE Pub.

Poinsett, B. OT Survey Study Guide. 1994. pap., student ed. 12.99 (*0-8054-1086-4*, 4210-86) Broadman.

***Poinsett, Brenda.** What Will I Do with the Rest of My Life? 2000. pap. 10.00 (*1-57683-151-5*) NavPress.

Poinsett, Brenda. Why Do I Feel This Way? What Every Woman Needs to Know about Depression. 180p. (Orig.). 1996. pap. 12.00 (*0-89109-924-7*, 99247) NavPress.

***Poinsett, Brenda.** Why Do I Feel This Way: What Every Woman Needs to Know about Depression. 1999. mass mkt. write for info. (*1-57683-209-0*) NavPress.

Poinsett, Doris J. John/Jean Poinset of Burlington, New Jersey & Pierre Poinset L'Aine of Charlestown, South Carolina, before 1700, & Some of Their Descendants. LC 98-213906. (Illus.). 144p. 1998. 23.00 (*0-7884-0986-7*, P535) Heritage Bk.

Poinsett, Norma & Burns, Vivian. Rainbow Children: A Racial Justice & Diversity Program for Ages 5-8. 1995. pap. 25.00 (*1-55896-292-1*) Unitarian Univ.

Poinso, Yves. Diccionario Practico de Psicopatologia. (SPA.). 324p. 1976. 29.95 (*0-8288-5618-4*, S50194); pap. 29.95 (*0-8288-5619-2*, S50186) Fr & Eur.

Poinsot, Edmond-Antoinne, see D'Heylli, Georges, pseud.

Poinsot, John. Poinsot: Tractatus de Signis (Macintosh) Deely, John, ed. & tr. by. (Past Masters Ser.). (C). write for info. (*1-57085-032-1*) Intelex.

— Poinsot: Tractatus de Signis (Windows) Deely, John, ed. (Past Masters Ser.). (C). write for info. (*1-57085-120-4*) Intelex.

Poinsotte, J. P. Dictionary of Medical Siglas: Dictionnaire des Sigles Medicaux. (ENG & FRE.). 146p. 1982. pap. text 24.95 (*0-8288-4420-8*, M9772) Fr & Eur.

Poinssot, Bernard. The Stinson Beach Salt Marsh: The Form of Its Growth. LC 77-70990. (Illus.). 1977. pap. 12.00 (*0-918540-01-1*) Stinson Beach.

Point Communications Staff. New Riders Official Internet Yellow Pages, 1996. rev. ed. 700p. 1996. pap. text 29.99 (*1-56205-623-9*) New Riders Pub.

Point Foundation Staff. Helping Nature Heal: A Whole Earth Catalog. Nilsen, Richard, ed. (Illus.). 176p. 1991. pap. 14.95 (*0-89815-425-1*) Ten Speed Pr.

***Point of Grace.** Circle of Friends: A Treasure of Inspirational Thoughts for Your Cirlce of Friends. LC 99-22751. (Illus.). 64p. 1999. 12.99 (*1-58229-057-1*) Howard Pub LA.

Point of Grace Staff & Seay, David. Life, Love & Other Mysteries: Advice & Inspiration from America's #1 Christian Pop Group. (Illus.). 240p. 1996. 23.00 (*0-671-56251-7*) PB.

Point of Grace Staff, et al. Steady On: Secured by Love. LC 98-35570. (Artists Devotional Ser.). 256p. 1998. 14.99 (*1-878990-93-4*) Howard Pub LA.

Point-of-Purchase Advertising Inst. Staff, ed. Point of Purchase Design Annual: The 40th Merchandising Awards. (Illus.). 176p. 1998. text 59.95 (*0-934590-74-5*) Visual Refer.

— Point-of-Purchase Design Annual No. 6: The 41st Annual Merchandising Awards. (Illus.). 176p. 1999. 59.95 (*0-934590-63-X*) Visual Refer.

Point of Purchase Advertising Institute Staff. Point of Purchase Design Annual, No. 5. (Illus.). 176p. 1997. 59.95 (*0-934590-96-6*) Visual Refer.

— Point of Purchase Design Annual No. 2: The 36th Merchandising Awards. 2nd ed. (Illus.). 240p. 1994. 49.95 (*0-934590-64-8*) Visual Refer.

***Point of Purchase Advertising Institute Staff, ed.** Point of Purchase Design Annual, No. 7. 176p. 2000. 59.95 (*1-58471-010-1*) Visual Refer.

Point of Purchase Advertising Institute Staff, ed. Point of Purchase Design Annual No. 4: The 38th Merchandising Awards. annuals (Illus.). 208p. 1996. 59.95 (*0-934590-88-5*) Visual Refer.

Point of Purchase Institute Staff. Point of Purchase: Design Annual, Bk. 7. 4th ed. 1998. 49.95 (*0-934590-40-0*) Watsn-Guptill.

Point Reyes Community Cookbook Committee Staff. Home on the Range: Favorite Recipes from the Point Reyes Community. (Illus.). 128p. (Orig.). 1988. pap. 12.00 (*0-9620222-2-5*) Chardon Pr.

Point Reyes National Seashore Association Staff & California Native Plant Society, Marin Chapter Sta. Wildflowers of Point Reyes National Seashore. Holbrook, Katherine H. & Ptak, Elisabeth, eds. 24p. (Orig.). 1996. pap. 5.00 (*0-911235-06-X*) Pt Reyes Natl.

Point to Point Communications Staff, ed. see Kenyon, Flip & Kenyon, Heather.

Pointe de l'Eglise Genealogical & Historical Socie. Cemetery Listings of Acadia Parish, Louisiana Vol. I: Tombstone Inscriptions from Church Point, La. & the Surrounding Area. Gremillion, Irma H., ed. 210p. 1991. pap. 15.00 (*0-926764-90-X*) LAcadie Pubng.

— Cemetery Listings of Acadia Parish, Louisiana Vol. II: Tombstone Inscriptions from Rayne, La. & the Surrounding Area. Gremillion, Irma H., ed. 260p. 1994. pap. 18.00 (*0-926764-91-8*) LAcadie Pubng.

— Cemetery Listings of Acadia Parish, Louisiana Vol. III: Tombstone Inscriptions from Cemeteries in Crowley, Louisiana. Gremillion, Irma H., ed. 238p. 1995. pap. 18.00 (*0-926764-93-4*) LAcadie Pubng.

Pointe de l'Eglise Genealogical & Historical Society Staff. Cemetery Listings of Acadia Parish, Louisiana Vol. IV: Tombstone Inscriptions from Cemeteries in Iowa, La. & the Surrounding Area. Gremillion, Irma H., ed. 174p. 1998. pap. 18.00 (*0-926764-94-2*) LAcadie Pubng.

Pointe, P. R. La, see Barton, C. C. & La Pointe, P. R.

Pointe, P. R. La, see La Pointe, P. R.

Pointer, et al. Advanced Accounting: Fall 1997 Edition (Student Solutions Manual) 1997. pap., student ed. 27.95 (*0-87393-465-2*) Dame Pubns.

Pointer, Bren. Movement Activities for Children with Learning Difficulties. 140p. 1993. pap. 24.95 (*1-85302-167-9*) Taylor & Francis.

Pointer, Dennis D. & Ewell, Charles M. Really Governing: How Health System & Hospital Boards Can Make More of a Difference. LC 94-25555. 240p. 1994. mass mkt. 42.50 (*0-8273-5577-7*) Delmar.

Pointer, Dennis D. & Orlikoff, James E. Board Work: Transforming the Governance of Health Services Organizations. LC 99-19930. (Health Ser.). 320p. 1999. text 39.95 (*0-7879-4299-5*) Jossey-Bass.

***Pointer, Fritz.** A Passion to Liberate: La Guma's South Africa-Images of District Six. LC 99-59481. 2000. pap. write for info. (*0-86543-818-8*) Africa World.

Pointer, James. Corporate Travel Management. 2nd rev. ed. Scott, Sharon, ed. LC 99-462538. 1998. spiral bd. 35.00 (*1-879982-72-2*) Educ Systs.

Pointer, Larry. In Search of Butch Cassidy. LC 77-14066. (Illus.). 312p. 1988. pap. 15.95 (*0-8061-2143-2*) U of Okla Pr.

Pointer, Lyle. Better Than Imagined: For Those Who Wonder about God. LC 99-17502. 36p. 1999. pap. 0.99 (*0-8341-1817-3*) Beacon Hill.

— Now That You're Saved. (Christian Living Ser.). 40p. (Orig.). 1987. pap. 3.50 (*0-8341-1157-8*) Beacon Hill.

Pointer, Lyle & Dorsey, Jimmy. Evangelism in Everyday Life: Sharing & Shaping Your Faith. LC 98-30194. 1998. 9.99 (*0-8341-1718-5*) Nazarene.

Pointer, Michael. Charles Dickens on the Screen: The Film, Television, & Video Adaptations. Slide, Anthony, ed. LC 94-49372. 207p. 1996. 42.50 (*0-8108-2960-6*) Scarecrow.

Pointer, Nancy, ed. see Herrmann, et al.

Pointer, Richard W. Protestant Pluralism & the New York Experience: A Study of Eighteenth-Century Religious Diversity. LC 87-45371. (Illus.). 224p. 1988. 11.95 (*0-253-34643-6*) Ind U Pr.

Pointer, Steven R. Joseph Cook, Boston Lecturer & Evangelical Apologist: A Bridge Between Popular Culture & Academia in Late Nineteenth-Century America. LC 91-26362. (Studies in American Religion: Vol. 57). 268p. 1991. lib. bdg. 89.95 (*0-7734-9702-1*) E Mellen.

Pointing, John, jt. ed. see Maguire, Mike.

Pointing, Keith, jt. auth. see Sutton, Robert.

Pointon, A. J. & Howarth, H. M. AC & DC Network Theory. 176p. 1991. pap. 30.95 (*0-442-31376-4*) Chapman & Hall.

Pointon, Anne & Davies, Chris, eds. Framed: Interrogating Disability in the Media. (Illus.). 245p. 1998. pap. 24.00 (*0-85170-600-2*, Pub. by British Film Inst); spiral bd. 24.00 (*0-85170-599-5*, Pub. by British Film Inst) Ind U Pr.

Pointon, John. Issues in Business Taxation. 239p. 1994. 78.95 (*1-85628-419-0*, Pub. by Avebry) Ashgate Pub Co.

Pointon, L. D. Revenue Law in Singapore & Malaysia: Cases & Commentary. 2nd ed. 424p. 1993. pap. write for info. (*0-409-99631-9*, MICHIE) LEXIS Pub.

Pointon, Marcia. Cartoon, Caricature, Animation. 1995. pap. 24.95 (*0-631-19487-8*) Blackwell Pubs.

— Hanging the Head: Portraiture & Social Formation in Eighteenth-Century England. LC 92-15841. (Illus.). 288p. (C). 1993. 80.00 (*0-300-05738-5*) Yale U Pr.

— Hanging the Head: Portraiture & Social Formation in Eighteenth-Century England. (Paul Mellon Centre for Studies in British Art). (Illus.). 288p. 1998. pap. 35.00 (*0-300-07368-2*) Yale U Pr.

— History of Art: A Student's Handbook. 2nd ed. (Illus.). 96p. (C). 1986. pap. text 12.95 (*0-04-701016-9*) Routledge.

— History of Art: Student's Handbook. 4th ed. (Illus.). 144p. (C). 1997. pap. 14.99 (*0-415-15181-3*) Routledge.

— Image: Music: Text. 1996. pap. text 22.95 (*0-631-20074-6*) Blackwell Pubs.

— Strategies for Showing: Women, Possession, & Representation in English Visual Culture 1665-1800. LC 97-163592. (Illus.). 452p. 1997. text 85.00 (*0-19-817411-X*) OUP.

Pointon, Marcia, ed. Pre-Raphaelites Re-Viewed. (Cultural Politics Ser.). 192p. 1989. text 29.95 (*0-7190-2821-3*, Pub. by Manchester Univ Pr) St Martin.

Pointon, Marcia & Binski, Paul. The Image in the Ancient & Early Christian Worlds. 160p. pap. text 24.95 (*0-631-19474-6*) Blackwell Pubs.

Pointon, R. C., ed. The Radiotherapy of Malignant Disease: Founded by Easson. 2nd ed. (Illus.). 496p. 1991. 198.00 (*0-387-19622-6*) Spr-Verlag.

Pointon, R. C., jt. ed. see Easson, E. C.

Points, ed. see Cota-Robles, Patricia D.

Points, Larry & Jauck, Andrea. Assateague: Island of the Wild Ponies. Nicholas, Jeff, ed. (Illus.). 32p. 1997. pap. 7.95 (*0-939365-59-6*) Panorama Intl.

— Ribbons of Sand: Exploring Atlantic Beaches. (Illus.). 32p. (Orig.). (J). 1997. pap. 7.95 (*0-939365-57-X*) Panorama Intl.

Points, Maureen. The Adventures of Pepe the Poodle & Other Stories. (Illus.). (J). 1978. pap. 3.50 (*0-9601594-1-X*) Maureen Points.

Poire, Alejandro, jt. ed. see Dominguez, Jorge I.

Poirell, Dominique, jt. auth. see Connell, Stanley W.

Poirer, R., et al. Handbook of Gaussian Basis Sets: A Compendium for Ab-Initio Molecular Orbital Calculations. (Physical Sciences Data Ser.: No. 24). 674p. 1985. 379.25 (*0-444-42493-8*) Elsevier.

Poirer, Richard. Poetry & Pragmatism. 240p. 1992. pap. 16.00 (*0-674-67991-1*) HUP.

Poiret, Pierre. Oeuvres Diverses No. 3: Petri Poireti Cogitationum Rationalium De Deo Anima et Malo. 1990. reprint ed. write for info. (*3-487-09383-9*) G Olms Pubs.

Poiriel, Doninique, jt. auth. see Connell, Stanley W.

Poirier & McKee. Understanding Human Evolution. 4th ed. 386p. 1998. pap. text 48.00 (*0-13-096152-3*) P-H.

Poirier, A. & Zaccour, G., eds. Maritime & Pipeline Transportation of Oil & Gas: Problems & Outlook - Proceedings of the Conference HEC-Montreal, April 23 & 24, 1990. 2nd ed. (Illus.). 320p. (C). 1991. pap. 95.00 (*2-7108-0606-1*, 9ET10) Gulf Pub.

— Maritime & Pipeline Transportation of Oil & Gas, Problems & Outlook: Proceedings of the Conference HEC-Montreal, April 23 & 24, 1990. 320p. 1991. 505.00 (*0-7855-2697-8*, Pub. by Edits Technip) Enfield Pubs NH.

Poirier-Bures, Simone. Candyman. LC 95-157586. 158p. 1994. 25.95 (*0-88750-977-0*, Pub. by Oberon Pr); pap. 13.95 (*0-88750-978-9*, Pub. by Oberon Pr) Pocahontas Pr.

— That Shining Place. 96p. 1995. 23.95 (*0-7780-1017-1*, Pub. by Oberon Pr); pap. 11.95 (*0-7780-1019-8*, Pub. by Oberon Pr) Pocahontas Pr.

Poirier, Charles C. Advanced Supply Chain Mangement: How to Build a Sustained Competitive Advantage. LC 98-48344. 300p. 1999. 39.95 (*1-57675-052-3*) Berrett-Koehler.

Poirier, Charles C. & Houser, William F. Business Partnering for Continuous Improvement: How to Forge Enduring Alliances among Employees, Suppliers & Customers. LC 92-23473. (Illus.). 256p. 1994. pap. 19.95 (*1-881052-39-7*) Berrett-Koehler.

Poirier, Charles C. & Reiter, Stephen E. Supply Chain Optimization: Building the Strongest Total Business Network. LC 96-7814. 312p. 1996. 34.95 (*1-881052-93-1*) Berrett-Koehler.

Poirier, Charles C. & Tokarz, Steven J. Avoiding the Pitfalls of Total Quality. LC 95-46946. (Illus.). 244p. 1996. 29.00 (*0-87389-355-7*, H0914) ASQ Qual Pr.

Poirier, Claude. Dictionary of Quebecois French: Dictionnaire du Francais Quebecois. (ENG & FRE.). 167p. 1985. pap. 29.95 (*0-8288-1093-1*, F780) Fr & Eur.

Poirier, Coburn, et al. Women & Diabetes. LC 97-3159. (Illus.). 224p. 1998. mass mkt. 6.99 (*0-553-57946-0*) Bantam.

Poirier, D. R. & Geiger, G. H. Transport Phenomena in Materials Processing. LC 94-76335. (Illus.). 645p. 1994. text 72.00 (*0-87339-272-8*, 2728) Minerals Metals.

— Transport Phenomena in Materials Processing - Solutions Manual. 25.00 (*0-87339-275-2*, 2752) Minerals Metals.

Poirier, D. R. & Poirier, E. J., eds. Heat Transfer Fundamentals for Metal Casting: With SI Units. 2nd ed. LC 94-75872. (Illus.). 82p. 1994. text 44.00 (*0-87339-274-4*, 2744) Minerals Metals.

Poirier, D. R., jt. auth. see Geiger, G. H.

Poirier, Dale J. Intermediate Statistics & Econometrics: A Comparative Approach. LC 94-28184. 1995. 77.00 (*0-262-16149-4*); pap. text 38.50 (*0-262-66094-6*) MIT Pr.

Poirier, Dale J., ed. The Methodology of Econometrics, 2 vols., Set. (International Library of Critical Writings in Economics: Vol. 6). 1008p. 1994. 375.00 (*1-85278-844-5*) E Elgar.

Poirier, David A. & Bellantoni, Nicholas F. In Remembrance: Archaeology & Death. LC 96-19555. 264p. 1997. 65.00 (*0-89789-419-7*, Bergin & Garvey) Greenwood.

***Poirier, David A. & Feder, Kenneth L., eds.** Dangerous Places: Health, Safety & Archaeology. LC 00-23726. 256p. 2000. 65.00 (*0-89789-632-7*, H632, Bergin & Garvey) Greenwood.

Poirier, E. J., jt. ed. see Poirier, D. R.

Poirier, Etienne, Jr. Three Days in July. 360p. Date not set. mass mkt. 4.99 (*1-55197-271-9*) Picasso Publ.

Poirier, Frank E., jt. auth. see Wu, Xinzhi.

Poirier, G. & Moreau, P., eds. ADP - Ribosylation Reactions. (Illus.). 410p. 1992. 128.00 (*0-387-97822-4*) Spr-Verlag.

Poirier, Gayle, jt. auth. see Bolner, Myrtle.

Poirier, J., ed. see Kirkwood, John G.

Poirier, Jacques, et al. Manual of Basic Neuropathology. 3rd ed. 292p. 1990. pap. text 40.00 (*0-7216-3464-8*, W B Saunders Co) Harcrt Hlth Sci Grp.

Poirier, Jacques R. The Giraffe Has a Long Neck: French Resistance During WW II. Brownjohn, John, tr. from FRE. (Illus.). 192p. 1995. pap. 21.95 (*0-85052-461-X*, Pub. by Leo Cooper) Trans-Atl Phila.

Poirier, Jean. Ethnologie Generale. (Methodique Ser.). (FRE.). 1932p. 1968. 95.00 (*0-7859-5538-0*) Fr & Eur.

— Ethnologie Regionale: Afrique, Oceanie, Vol. 1. 1632p. 1972. lib. bdg. 140.00 (*0-7859-3925-3*) Fr & Eur.

— Histoire des Moeurs: Themes et Systemes Culturels, Vol. 3. (FRE.). 1991. lib. bdg. 190.00 (*0-7859-3893-1*) Fr & Eur.

— Histoire des Moeurs, Vol. 1: Coordonnees de l'Homme et la Culture Materielle. (FRE.). 1989. lib. bdg. 190.00 (*0-7859-3864-8*) Fr & Eur.

— Histoire des Moeurs, Vol. 2: Modes et Modeles. (FRE.). 1991. lib. bdg. 190.00 (*0-7859-3892-3*) Fr & Eur.

— Una Historia de la Etnologia. (SPA.). pap. 6.99 (*968-16-2526-9*, Pub. by Fondo) Continental Bk.

Poirier, Jean, jt. auth. see Dorion, Henri.

***Poirier, Jean-Paul.** Introduction to the Physics of the Earth's Interior. 2nd ed. LC 99-30070. (Illus.). 272p. (C). 2000. 80.00 (*0-521-66313-X*); pap. 34.95 (*0-521-66392-X*) Cambridge U Pr.

Poirier, Jean-Paul & Nicolas, Adolphe. Crystalline Plasticity & Solid State Flow in Metamorphic Rocks. LC 75-15981. (Selected Topics in Geological Sciences Ser.). (Illus.). 490p. reprint ed. pap. 151.90 (*0-608-17611-7*, 203046100069) Bks Demand.

Poirier, Jean-Pierre. Lavoisier: Chemist, Biologist, Economist. Balinski, Rebecca, tr. LC 96-35738. (Chemical Sciences in Society Ser.). (Illus.). 544p. 1996. text 49.95 (*0-8122-3365-4*) U of Pa Pr.

— Lavoisier: Chemist, Biologist, Economist. rev. ed. Gillispie, Charles C., tr. from FRE. (Illus.). 544p. 1998. pap. 19.95 (*0-8122-1649-0*) U of Pa Pr.

Poirier, Judes. Apoptosis Techniques & Protocols. LC 97-13163. (Neuromethods Ser.: Vol. 29). (Illus.). 304p. 1997. 89.50 (*0-89603-451-8*) Humana.

Poirier, Jules R. The Life & Adventures of Monica Monarch. LC 97-73933. (Illus.). 32p. (J). 1998. boxed set 11.95 (*0-89051-189-6*) Master Bks.

***Poirier, Laurinda & Coburn, Katharine M.** Women & Diabetes. 2nd ed. LC 00-38104. 240p. 2000. pap. 14.95 (*1-58040-058-2*, 00582Q, Pub. by Am Diabetes) NTC Contemp Pub Co.

Poirier, Laurinda M. & Coburn, Katharine M. Women & Diabetes. LC 97-3159. (Illus.). 240p. 1997. pap. 14.95 (*0-945448-77-5*, 00775Q, Pub. by Am Diabetes) NTC Contemp Pub Co.

Poirier, Lionel A., et al, eds. Essential Nutrients in Carcinogenesis. LC 86-25356. (Advances in Experimental Medicine & Biology Ser.: Vol. 206). 572p. 1986. 125.00 (*0-306-42471-1*, Plenum Trade) Perseus Pubng.

***Poirier, Mark Jude.** Goats: A Novel. 240p. 2001. 22.00 (*0-7868-6680-2*, Pub. by Talk Miramax Bks) Time Warner.

Poirier, Mark Jude. Naked Pueblo: Stories. LC 99-25267. 224p. 1999. 21.00 (*0-609-60447-3*, Crown) Crown.

***Poirier, Mark Jude.** Naked Pueblo: Stories. 208p. 2001. pap. 12.95 (*0-7868-8593-9*, Pub. by Talk Miramax Bks) Time Warner.

Poirier, Miriam C. & Beland, F. A., eds. Carcinogenesis & Adducts in Animals & Humans. (Progress in Experimental Tumor Research Ser.: Vol. 31). (Illus.). viii, 116p. 1987. 103.50 (*3-8055-4457-X*) S Karger.

Poirier, Richard. The Performing Self: Compositions & Decompositions in the Languages of Contemporary Life. LC 91-37410. 224p. (Orig.). (C). 1992. reprint ed. text 40.00 (*0-8135-1794-X*); reprint ed. pap. text 16.00 (*0-8135-1795-8*) Rutgers U Pr.

— Poetry & Pragmatism. 208p. (C). 1992. 30.00 (*0-674-67990-3*) HUP.

— Robert Frost: The Work of Knowing. LC 89-60362. 384p. 1990. 47.50 (*0-8047-1741-9*); pap. 15.95 (*0-8047-1742-7*) Stanford U Pr.

***Poirier, Richard.** Trying It Out in America: Literary & Other Performances. LC 99-22467. 320p. 1999. 25.00 (*0-374-27941-1*) FS&G.

Poirier, Richard. A World Elsewhere: The Place of Style in American Literature. LC 85-40376. 272p. 1985. reprint ed. pap. 14.95 (*0-299-09934-2*) U of Wis Pr.

Poirier, Richard, ed. Raritan Reading. LC 89-36068. 400p. (Orig.). (C). 1990. pap. 17.00 (*0-8135-1505-X*); text 45.00 (*0-8135-1504-1*) Rutgers U Pr.

Poirier, Richard, ed. see Frost, Robert.

Poirier, Robert G. By the Blood of Our Alumni: Norwich University Citizen Soldiers in the Army of the Potomac. (Illus.). 366p. 1999. 29.95 (*1-882810-21-X*) Savas Pub.

Poirier, Suzanne. Chicago's War on Syphilis, 1937-40: The Times, the Trib & the Clap Doctor. LC 94-19357. 296p. 1995. text 42.50 (*0-252-02147-9*) U of Ill Pr.

Poirier, Suzanne, jt. auth. see Murphy, Timothy F.

Poirier, Suzanne, jt. ed. see Murphy, Timothy F.

Poirier, Thelma. Grasslands. (Illus.). 96p. 1990. pap. 7.95 (*1-55050-006-6*, Pub. by Coteau) Genl Dist Srvs.

Poirier, Thelma. Rock Creek. (Illus.). 164p. 1998. pap. text 12.95 (*1-55050-123-2*, Pub. by Coteau) Genl Dist Srvs.

P

An Asterisk (*) at the beginning of an entry indicates that the title is appearing for the first time.

Poirier, Thelma, ed. Cowgirls: 100 Years of Writing the Range. LC 97-910532. 295p. 1997. 14.95 (*1-55105-117-6*) Lone Pine.

Poirier, Thelma, ed. Cowgirls: 100 Years of Writing the Range. (Roundup Books). 295p. 1998. pap. 14.95 (*0-88995-168-3*, Pub. by Red Deer) Genl Dist Srvs.

Poirion, Daniel. Contexts: Style & Values in Medieval Art & Literature. Regalado, Nancy F., ed. LC PQ0153.C64. (Illus.). 290p. 1991. reprint ed. pap. 89.90 (*0-608-07855-7*, 205403800011) Bks Demand.

Poirot-Delpech, Bertrand. L' Ete '36. (FRE.). 1986. pap. 11.95 (*0-7859-4239-4*) Fr & Eur.

— Le Grand Dadais. (FRE.). 1974. pap. 8.95 (*0-7859-4032-4*) Fr & Eur.

— Les Grands de Ce Monde. (FRE.). 1984. pap. 11.95 (*0-7859-4211-4*) Fr & Eur.

Poirot, Luis. Pablo Neruda. 1990. pap. 25.00 (*0-393-30643-7*) Norton.

Poirot, Paul L., compiled by. The Farm Problem. (Freeman Library Ser.). 134p. 1986. pap. 9.95 (*0-910614-72-5*) Foun Econ Ed.

Poirot, Paul L., ed. see Read, Leonard E.

Poirrier. Writing-to-Learn. LC 96-39400. 1996. write for info. (*0-88737-723-8*) Natl League Nurse.

Poirrier & Oberleitner. Clinical Pathways in Nursing: A Guide to Managing Care from Hospital to Home. 304p. 1998. 34.95 (*0-87434-930-3*) Springhouse Corp.

Poirteir, Cathal. The Great Irish Famine. LC 98-125346. 283p. 1997. pap. 18.95 (*0-8023-1316-7*) Dufour.

— 1,500 Ceist Agam Ort t. (IRI & GAE.). 144p. 1997. pap. 9.95 (*1-85635-142-4*, Pub. by Mercier Pr) Irish Amer Bk.

Poirteir, Cathal, ed. Famine Echoes. 256p. (Orig.). 1995. pap. 18.00 (*0-7171-2314-6*, Pub. by Gill & MacMill) Irish Bks Media.

— The Great Irish Rebellion of 1798: Thomas Davis Lectures. 224p. 1998. pap. 13.95 (*1-85635-226-9*, Pub. by Mercier Pr) Irish Amer Bk.

Pois, Robert. The Great War. 368p. (C). 1995. pap. text, per. 36.95 (*0-7872-1705-0*) Kendall-Hunt.

Pois, Robert A. Friedrich Meinecke & German Politics in the Twentieth Century. LC 70-157818. 174p. reprint ed. pap. 54.00 (*0-608-18276-1*, 203151000075) Bks Demand.

***Poissant, Philip & Sinclair, Dede.** The Complete Fort Kit. (Illus.). 56p. (YA). (ps up). 1998. pap. 19.95 (*1-894042-24-7*) Somerville Hse.

— Construct-a-Kit Fort & Playhouse: With Paper Linx. (Illus.). 56p. (J). (ps up). 1998. pap. 19.95 (*1-895897-17-3*) Somerville Hse.

— Make-Your-Own Fort & Playhouse: With Paper Linx. (Illus.). 56p. (J). 1998. pap. 29.95 (*1-895897-15-7*) Somerville Hse.

Poisson, Bette J. Life's Reflections: Dreams & Memories. 64p. (Orig.). 1992. pap. 9.95 (*1-879260-03-4*) Evanston Pub.

— Thoughts: Etcetera...Etcetera. (Illus.). 96p. (Orig.). 1994. pap. 12.95 (*1-879260-21-2*) Evanston Pub.

Poisson, Camille L. Theater & the Adolescent Actor: Building a Successful School Program. LC 93-36406. (Illus.). x, 228p. (C). 1994. lib. bdg. 29.50 (*0-208-02380-1*, Archon Bks) Shoe String.

Poisson, Gretchen V., jt. auth. see Poisson, Leandre.

Poisson, Jean-Marc, tr. see Bertrand, Yves.

Poisson, Leandre & Poisson, Gretchen V. Solar Gardening: Growing Vegetables Year-Round the American Intensive Way. (Illus.). 288p. 1994. pap. 24.95 (*0-930031-69-5*) Chelsea Green Pub.

Poisson, Michel. Paris: An Illustrated Guide with Over 850 Drawings & Neighborhood Maps. Goodman, John, tr. from FRE. LC 98-42780. (Illus.). 464p. 1999. 39.95 (*0-8109-4355-7*, Pub. by Abrams) Time Warner.

***Poisson, Michel.** Paris: Buildings & Monuments : An Illustrated Guide with Over 850 Drawings & Neighborhood Maps. LC 98-42780. 144p. 2000. pap. 24.95 (*0-8109-2915-5*, Pub. by Abrams) Time Warner.

Poisson, Raymond. La Hollande Malade. Navailles, Louisette, ed. (Exeter French Texts Ser.: No. 93). (FRE.). 70p. 1995. pap. text 19.95 (*0-85989-465-7*, Pub. by Univ Exeter Pr) Northwestern U Pr.

Poisson, S. & DeGangi, G. Emotional & Sensory Processing Problems: Assessment & Treatment Approaches for Young Children & Their Families. 139p. 1991. pap. text 20.00 (*1-880341-00-X*) R S Lourie Ctr.

Poissonet, P., ed. Vegetation Dynamics in Grasslands, Heathlands & Mediterranean Ligneous Formations. 1982. text 278.00 (*90-6193-636-5*) Kluwer Academic.

Poissons, Helen F. The Old Light Cord. (Illus.). 68p. (Orig.). 1991. pap. text 9.00 (*0-9621498-7-X*, Robin Hood) R Hood Little.

Poister, J. P. The New American Bartender's Guide. 3rd ed. LC 99-212754. 640p. 1999. mass mkt. 6.99 (*0-451-19782-8*, Sig) NAL.

Poitevin, jt. auth. see Sarembaud.

Poitevin, Guy & Rairkar, Hema. Stonemill & Bhakti: From the Devotion of Peasant Women to the Philosophy of Swamis. LC 96-902185. (C). 1996. 68.00 (*81-246-0059-7*, Pub. by DK Pubs Ind) S Asia.

Poitier, Joseph Le, see Verdier, Jean-Louis & Le Poitier, Joseph, eds.

***Poitier, Sidney.** The Measure of a Man: A Spiritual Autobiography. LC 99-88322. (Illus.). 272p. 2000. 26.00 (*0-06-251607-8*, Pub. by Harper SF) HarpC.

— The Measure of a Man: A Spiritual Autobiography. large type ed. 352p. 2000. 26.00 (*0-06-019717-X*) HarpC.

Poitier, Sidney. This Life. 416p. 1981. mass mkt. 2.95 (*0-345-29407-6*) Ballantine Pub Grp.

***Poitier, Sidney.** Walking on the Edge. LC 99-88322. 2000. pap. 16.00 (*0-06-251608-6*) HarpC.

Poitras, Adrian J. & Hodges, Ray L. Computer Technology Trends: Analysis & Forecasts. 63p. 1996. pap. 95.00 (*1-884154-06-9*) Tech Futures.

Poitras, Genell, tr. see Chong-hui, Choe.

Poitras, Gilles. The Anime Companion: What's Japanese in Japanese Animation? LC 98-44487. (Illus.). 163p. 2000. pap. 16.95 (*1-880656-32-9*, Pub. by Stone Bridge Pr) SPD-Small Pr Dist.

***Poitras, Gilles.** Anime Essentials: Everything a Fan Needs to Know. (Illus.). 144p. 2000. pap. 14.95 (*1-880656-53-1*) Stone Bridge Pr.

Poitras Tucker, Bonnie, jt. auth. see Colker, Ruth.

Poix, Carol De, see De Poix, Carol.

***Poizat, Bruno.** Course in Model Theory: An Introduction in Contemporary Mathematical Logic. Klein, M., tr. from LAT. LC 99-53572. 450p. 2000. 59.95 (*0-387-98655-3*) Spr-Verlag.

Poizat, Michel. The Angel's Cry: Beyond the Pleasure Principle in Opera. Denner, Arthur, tr. LC 91-55532. 240p. 1992. text 25.00 (*0-8014-2388-0*) Cornell U Pr.

Poizner, Howard, et al. What the Hands Reveal about the Brain. (Studies in the Biology of Language & Cognition). 256p. 1990. reprint ed. pap. text 17.50 (*0-262-66066-0*) MIT Pr.

Pojar, Jim. Plants of Coastal British Columbia Including Washington, Oregon & Alaska. (Illus.). 528p. 1994. pap. 19.95 (*1-55105-042-0*) Lone Pine.

Pojar, Jim & MacKinnon, Andy. Plants of the Pacific Northwest Coast: Washington, Oregon, British Columbia, & Alaska. (Illus.). 528p. 1994. pap. 19.95 (*1-55105-040-4*) Lone Pine.

Pojeta, John, Jr. & Pope, J. K., eds. Bulletins in American Paleontology: Studies in Paleontology & Stratigraphy, Vol. 67. (Illus.). 456p. 1975. 25.00 (*0-87710-296-1*) Paleo Res.

***Pojman.** Ethics: Discovering Right & Wrong. 4th ed. (Philosophy Ser.). 2001. 26.50 (*0-534-56138-1*) Wadsworth Pub.

Pojman. Philosophy: The Pursuit of Wisdom. 3rd ed. (Philosophy Ser.). 2000. pap. 27.50 (*0-534-55818-6*) Wadsworth Pub.

***Pojman.** Philosophy: The Question for Truth. 5th ed. (Philosophy Ser.). 2002. 43.75 (*0-534-52105-3*) Wadsworth Pub.

Pojman. The Theory of Knowledge. 3rd ed. (Philosophy Ser.). 2002. pap. 47.25 (*0-534-55822-4*) Wadsworth Pub.

Pojman, John A., jt. auth. see Epstein, Irving R.

Pojman, Louis. Environmental Ethics. 2nd ed. LC 97-43410. (Philosophy Ser.). (C). 1997. 55.95 (*0-534-54469-X*) Wadsworth Pub.

— Kierkegaard's Philosophy of Religion. LC 98-33351. 256p. 1999. 74.95 (*1-57309-342-4*) Intl Scholars.

Pojman, Louis, jt. auth. see Reiman, Jeffrey.

Pojman, Louis P. The Abortion Controversy. (Philosophy Ser.). (C). 1994. pap. 28.25 (*0-534-54260-3*) Wadsworth Pub.

Pojman, Louis P. Classics of Philosophy, 2 vols., Set. 1997. pap. 39.95 (*0-19-512606-8*) OUP.

Pojman, Louis P. Environmental Ethics. (Philosophy Ser.). (C). 1994. pap. 35.25 (*0-534-54259-X*) Wadsworth Pub.

— Environmental Ethics: Readings in Theory & Application. 3rd ed. (Philosophy Ser.). 551p. 2000. 55.95 (*0-534-54371-5*) Wadsworth Pub.

— Ethical Theory: Classical & Contemporary Readings. 2nd ed. LC 94-22111. 727p. 1994. mass mkt. 44.50 (*0-534-21636-6*) Wadsworth Pub.

— Ethical Theory: Classical & Contemporary Readings. 3rd ed. LC 97-34248. (Philosophy Ser.). (C). 1997. pap. 69.95 (*0-534-52961-5*) Wadsworth Pub.

— Ethical Theory: Classical & Contemporary Readings. 4th ed. (Philosophy Ser.). 2001. 44.50 (*0-534-57033-X*) Wadsworth Pub.

— Ethics: Discovering Right & Wrong. 210p. (C). 1989. mass mkt. 19.95 (*0-534-12378-3*) Wadsworth Pub.

— Ethics: Discovering Right & Wrong. 2nd ed. LC 94-5781. 283p. 1994. 23.50 (*0-534-17832-4*) Wadsworth Pub.

— Ethics: Discovering Right & Wrong. 3rd ed. LC 98-23849. (Philosophy Ser.). 1998. pap. 36.95 (*0-534-55181-5*) Wadsworth Pub.

— Global Environmental Ethics. LC 98-53448. xiv,393p. 1999. pap. text 30.95 (*1-55934-991-3*) Mayfield Pub.

— Introduction to Philosophy. 1994. mass mkt., suppl. ed. 12.95 (*0-534-31712-X*) Wadsworth Pub.

— Introduction to Philosophy: Classical & Contemporary Readings. 2nd ed. LC 99-28148. (Philosophy). 1999. mass mkt. 56.95 (*0-534-50985-1*) Wadsworth Pub.

— Life & Death. (Philosophy Ser.). (C). 1992. 21.50 (*0-534-54257-3*) Wadsworth Pub.

— Life & Death: A Reader. (Philosophy Ser.). (C). 1992. 33.00 (*0-534-54258-1*) Wadsworth Pub.

— Life & Death: A Reader in Moral Problems. 2nd ed. LC 98-55383. (Philosophy Ser.). 1999. mass mkt. 51.95 (*0-534-50825-1*) Wadsworth Pub.

— Life & Death: Grappling with the Moral Dilemmas of Our Time. 2nd ed. LC 99-10720. (Philosophy). 190p. 1999. mass mkt. 32.95 (*0-534-50824-3*) Wadsworth Pub.

— Philosophical Traditions: A Text with Readings. LC 97-15855. (Philosophy Ser.). 465p. (C). 1997. 62.95 (*0-534-26286-4*) Wadsworth Pub.

— Philosophical Traditions: A Text with Readings. 2nd ed. (Philosophy Ser.). Date not set. 38.50 (*0-534-57042-9*) Wadsworth Pub.

— Philosophy: The Pursuit of Wisdom. 395p. 1993. mass mkt. 31.95 (*0-534-17982-7*) Wadsworth Pub.

— Philosophy: The Pursuit of Wisdom. 2nd ed. LC 97-15857. (Philosophy Ser.). (C). 1997. pap. 43.95 (*0-534-52668-3*) Wadsworth Pub.

— Philosophy: The Quest for Truth. 3rd ed. LC 94-44144. 600p. (C). 1995. pap. 40.50 (*0-534-25452-7*) Wadsworth Pub.

— Philosophy: The Quest for Truth. 4th ed. LC 98-34494. (Philosophy Ser.). 1998. 60.95 (*0-534-55187-4*) Wadsworth Pub.

— Philosophy of Religion: An Anthology. 2nd ed. 578p. (C). 1993. mass mkt. 44.25 (*0-534-20532-1*) Wadsworth Pub.

— Philosophy of Religion: An Anthology. 3rd ed. LC 97-18435. (Philosophy Ser.). (C). 1997. 69.95 (*0-534-52956-9*) Wadsworth Pub.

— Philosophy of Religion: An Anthology. 4th ed. (Philosophy Ser.). Date not set. 44.25 (*0-534-54364-2*) Wadsworth Pub.

— Religious Belief & the Will. (Problems of Philosophy Series: Their Past & Present). 256p. (C). 1986. text 44.00 (*0-7102-0399-3*, Routledge Thoemms) Routledge.

— The Theory of Knowledge: Classical & Contemporary Readings. 556p. (C). 1992. pap. 42.00 (*0-534-17826-X*) Wadsworth Pub.

— Theory of Knowledge: Classical & Contemporary Readings. 2nd ed. LC 98-17857. 1998. pap. 66.95 (*0-534-54130-5*) Wadsworth Pub.

— What Can We Know? An Introduction to the Theory of Knowledge. LC 94-30155. 340p. 1994. 23.50 (*0-534-24834-9*) Wadsworth Pub.

— What Can We Know: An Intro To The Theory Of Knowledge. 2nd ed. (Philosophy). 2000. 22.50 (*0-534-52417-6*) Wadsworth Pub.

Pojman, Louis P., ed. Classics of Philosophy. LC 97-11433. 1280p. (C). 1997. pap. 36.00 (*0-19-510931-7*) OUP.

— Classics of Philosophy: Ancient & Medieval, Vol. 1. LC 97-1134. 478p. (C). 1997. pap. 26.95 (*0-19-511645-3*) OUP.

— Classics of Philosophy: Modern & Contemporary, Vol. II. LC 97-1134. 816p. (C). 1997. pap. 29.95 (*0-19-511646-1*) OUP.

— Ethical Theory: Classical & Contemporary Readings. 665p. (C). 1988. pap. 43.95 (*0-534-09360-4*) Wadsworth Pub.

— Introduction to Philosophy: Classical & Contemporary Readings. 644p. (C). 1990. 43.00 (*0-534-14370-9*) Wadsworth Pub.

— The Moral Life: An Introduction Reader in Ethics & Literature. LC 98-46486. 960p. (C). 1999. pap. text 38.00 (*0-19-512844-3*) OUP.

— Moral Philosophy: A Reader. 2nd rev. ed. LC 98-7956. 320p. (C). 1998. pap. 16.95 (*0-87220-408-1*); lib. bdg. 34.95 (*0-87220-409-X*) Hackett Pub.

— Philosophy: The Quest for Truth. 477p. (C). 1989. pap. write for info. (*0-534-10176-3*) Wadsworth Pub.

— Philosophy: The Quest for Truth. 2nd ed. 531p. (C). 1991. pap. 33.75 (*0-534-16530-3*) Wadsworth Pub.

— Philosophy of Religion: An Anthology. 537p. (C). 1986. mass mkt. 42.95 (*0-534-06672-0*) Wadsworth Pub.

Pojman, Louis P. & Beckwith, Francis J. The Abortion Controversy: 25 Years after Roe vs. Wade, a Reader. 2nd ed. LC 98-10664. (C). 1998. pap. 50.95 (*0-534-55764-3*) Wadsworth Pub.

Pojman, Louis P. & McLeod, Owen, eds. What Do We Deserve? A Reader on Justice & Desert. LC 97-46362. 336p. (C). 1998. text 47.00 (*0-19-512217-8*); pap. text 28.95 (*0-19-512218-6*) OUP.

Pojman, Louis P. & Westmoreland, Robert, eds. Equality: Selected Readings. (Illus.). 336p. (C). 1996. pap. text 24.95 (*0-19-510250-9*) OUP.

Pok, Attila, ed. A Selected Bibliography of Modern Historiography, 24. LC 91-46699. (Bibliographies & Indexes in World History Ser.: No. 24). 304p. 1992. lib. bdg. 65.00 (*0-313-27231-X*, PBM, Greenwood Pr) Greenwood.

Pok, Attila, jt. ed. see Glatz, Ferenc.

Pok, S., jt. auth. see Ranki, Gyorgy.

Pokarna, K. L. Social Beliefs, Cultural Practices in Health & Disease. (C). 1994. 28.00 (*81-7033-254-0*, Pub. by Rawat Pubns) S Asia.

***Pokeberry, P. J.** The Huckenpuck Papers: The Tales of a Family's Secret & a Young Girl's Search for Self-Esteem. (Illus.). 88p. 2001. pap. write for info. (*0-943962-03-X*) Viewpoint Pr.

Pokeberry, P. J. The Secret of Hilhouse: An Adult Book for Teens. LC 93-60940. (Illus.). 96p. (Orig.). (J). (gr. 4 up). 1993. pap. 8.95 (*0-943962-02-1*) Viewpoint Pr.

***Pokemon Movie Animation Team Staff.** Art of Pokemon: Mewto Strikes Back! (Illus.). 64p. 1999. pap. 8.95 (*1-56931-427-6*) Viz Commns Inc.

***Pokempner, Mar.** Down at Theresa's Chicago Blues: The Pictures of Marc PoKempner. (Illus.). 100p. 2000. 49.95 (*3-7913-2300-8*, Pub. by Prestel) te Neues.

Poker, D. B., et al, eds. Ion-Solid Interactions for Materials Modification & Processing: Materials Research Society Symposium Proceedings, Vol. 396. 897p. 1996. 65.00 (*1-55899-299-5*) Materials Res.

Poker, D. B. & Ortiz, C., eds. Optical Materials - Processing & Science Vol. 152: Materials Research Society Symposium Proceedings. 298p. 1989. text 17.50 (*1-55899-025-9*) Materials Res.

Pokharel, B. Land Revenue Administration in Nepal. (C). 1991. text 75.00 (*0-7855-0147-9*, Pub. by Ratna Pustak Bhandar) St Mut.

Pokhlebkin, William. History of Vodka. 222p. (C). (gr. 13). 1992. 30.00 (*0-86091-359-7*, Pub. by Verso) Norton.

Pokhodnaya, I. K. & Podgaetsky, V. V. Welding & Surfacing Reviews: Metallurgy of Welding & Welding Materials, Vol. 1, No. 2. Paton, B. E., ed. (Soviet Technology Reviews Ser.: Vol. 1, Pt. 2). iv, 62p. 1989. pap. text 69.00 (*3-7186-4947-0*) Gordon & Breach.

Pokhodnaya, I. K., et al. Metallurgy of Arc Welding: Arc Processes & Electrode Melting. 250p. 1992. boxed set 100.00 (*1-871313-01-5*, Pub. by CISP) Balogh.

Pokhodnya, I. K. Welding with Flux-Cored Wire, Vol. 4, Issue 4. 73p. 1997. pap. text 43.00 (*3-7186-5833-X*, Harwood Acad Pubs) Gordon & Breach.

***Pokhodnya, I. K. & Paton, E. O., eds.** Advanced Materials for the 21st Century, Vol. 1. 480p. 1998. 124.00 (*1-898326-61-4*, Pub. by CISP) Balogh.

Pokhotelov, O. A., jt. auth. see Guglielmi, A. V.

Pokhotelov, Oleg, tr. see Vanshtein, S. I., et al.

Pokhozhaev, S. I., jt. auth. see Kuzin, I.

Pokhrel, Durga & Willett, Anthony. Shadow over Shangri-La: A Woman's Quest for Freedom. (Illus.). 365p. 1996. 24.95 (*1-57488-061-6*) Brasseys.

Pokierser, Herbert & Lechner, G., eds. European Scientific User Conference Somatom Plus. LC 94-3446. 1994. 115.00 (*0-387-58198-7*) Spr-Verlag.

Pokinski, Deborah F. The Development of the American Modern Style. LC 84-2565. (Studies in the Fine Arts - Architecture: No. 8). (Illus.). 165p. reprint ed. pap. 51.20 (*0-8357-1567-1*, 207057000001) Bks Demand.

***Pokki, Timo.** America's Preacher & His Message: Billy Graham's View of Conversion & Sanctification. LC 99-32718. 368p. 1999. 54.00 (*0-7618-1464-7*) U Pr of Amer.

Poklasny, Lori A., ed. Freedom of the Soul. LC 97-67072. (Illus.). 177p. (Orig.). 1997. pap. 39.95 (*0-9656699-1-2*) Delta Pubns NJ.

Poklis, Alphonse. Methods of Urine Drug Testing. (Methods in Analytical Toxicology Ser.). Date not set. boxed set 50.00 (*0-8493-7882-6*) CRC Pr.

Pokluda, William J. Understanding Managed Health Care: A Guide for Seniors. LC 96-35275. (Patient Information Ser.). 63p. 1997. 6.50 (*1-57626-021-6*) Quality Med Pub.

Pokoly, Judit, tr. see Galantai, Jozsef.

Pokoly, Judit, tr. see Lendvai, Erno.

Pokorney, B. & Slaughter, P. Journey Through the Baha'i World. (Illus.). 190p. 1999. pap. 26.95 (*1-85168-050-0*) Onewrld Pubns.

— Journey Through the Baha'i World. (Mystical Classics of the World Ser.). (Illus.). 190p. 1999. reprint ed. pap. 19.95 (*1-85168-055-1*) Onewrld Pubns.

***Pokorney, Nancy.** Happy Am I. 1999. pap. write for info. (*1-58235-104-X*) Watermrk Pr.

Pokornik, Brigitte, jt. auth. see Blume, Karin.

Pokorny, Dusan. Efficiency & Justice in the Industrial World Vol. 1: The Failure of the Soviet Experiment, Vol. I. LC 92-41002. 310p. (C). (gr. 13). 1993. text 100.95 (*1-56324-139-0*) M E Sharpe.

— Efficiency & Justice in the Industrial World Vol. 2: The Uneasy Success of Postwar Europe, Vol. 2. 350p. (C). 1996. text 87.95 (*1-56324-772-0*) M E Sharpe.

Pokorny, J. & Wu, T. M. Biophysical Aspects of Coherence & Biological Order. (Illus.). 240p. 1998. 109.00 (*3-540-64651-5*) Spr-Verlag.

Pokorny, Jan, et al, eds. Waterplants & Wetland Processes: Proceedings of the 2nd Intecol Wetland Conference, Trebon, CSSR, June 13-23, 1984. (Advances in Limnology Ser.: Vol. 27). (GER., Illus.). viii, 265p. 1987. pap. 65.00 (*3-510-47025-7*, Pub. by E Schweizerbartsche) Balogh.

Pokorny, Jaromir. Trees: Leaves, Bark & Fruit: A Magna Field Guide. Kuthanova, Olga, tr. (Illus.). 188p. 1999. reprint ed. text 25.00 (*0-7881-6098-2*) DIANE Pub.

Pokorny, Julius. A Concise Old Irish Grammar & Reader, 2 vols., Set. LC 78-72643. (Celtic Language & Literature Ser.: Goidelic & Brythonic). 240p. reprint ed. 57.50 (*0-404-17576-7*) AMS Pr.

— Indogermanisches Etymologisches Woerterbuch, 2 vols., Set. (GER.). 1648p. 1969. 395.00 (*0-8288-6602-3*, M-7478) Fr & Eur.

Pokorny, Julius, ed. see Walde, Alois.

Pokorny, Michael, jt. ed. see Clarkson, Petruska.

Pokorny, Petr. Colossians: A Commentary. Schatzmann, Siegfried S., tr. from GER. LC 91-2971. 272p. 1991. 19.95 (*0-943575-38-9*) Hendrickson MA.

— The Genesis of Christology: Foundations for a Theology of the New Testament. 282p. pap. 29.95 (*0-567-29144-8*, Pub. by T & T Clark) Bks Intl VA.

— Jesus in the Eyes of His Followers: Newly Discovered Manuscripts & Old Christian Confessions, Vol. 4. LC 98-25310. (Dead Sea Scrolls & Christian Origins Library). x, 100 p. 1998. pap. 8.95 (*0-941037-65-7*, BIBAL Press) D & F Scott.

Pokorny, Susan. Pediatric & Adolescent Gynecology. (Current Topics in Obstetrics & Gynecology Ser.). (Illus.). 250p. 1995. text 80.95 (*0-412-99471-2*, Pub. by E A) OUP.

Pokorny, Sydney, jt. auth. see Tracey, Liz.

Pokorny, V. Grundzuege der Zoologischen Mikropalaeontologie: Aus Dem Tschechischen Uebersetzte und Neu Bearbeitete Auflace, 2 vols. (GER., Illus.). 1038p. 1975. reprint ed. 117.30 (*3-87429-087-5*, 001359, Pub. by Koeltz Sci Bks) Lubrecht & Cramer.

Pokorski, Doug. Death Rehearsal. LC 95-60159. 160p. 1995. pap. 12.95 (*0-87243-215-7*) Templegate.

***Pokorski, Stefan.** Gauge Field Theories. 2nd ed. (Cambridge Monographs on Mathematical Physics). (Illus.). 420p. (C). 2000. 120.00 (*0-521-47245-8*); pap. 54.95 (*0-521-47816-2*) Cambridge U Pr.

Pokotilov, Dmitri & Loewenthal, Rudolf. History of the Eastern Mongols During the Ming Dynasty from 1368 to 1631. LC 75-32335. (Studies in Chinese History & Civilization). 148p. 1976. reprint ed. lib. bdg. 62.50 (*0-313-26956-4*, U6956) Greenwood.

***Pokrant, Bob.** Bangladesh. 2000. lib. bdg. 69.00 (*1-85109-116-5*) ABC-CLIO.

Pokrant, Marvin. Desert Storm at Sea: What the Navy Really Did, 175. LC 98-48908. (Contributions in Military Studies Ser.). 352p. 1999. 59.95 (*0-313-31024-6*) Greenwood.

Pokrant, Marvin, ed. Desert Shield at Sea: What the Navy Really Did, 174. LC 98-48907. (Contributions in Military Studies Ser.: Vol. 174). 296p. 1999. 59.95 (*0-313-31023-8*) Greenwood.

An Asterisk (*) at the beginning of an entry indicates that the title is appearing for the first time.

Pokras, Judith. Contexts in the College Curriculum. (Miscellaneous/Catalogs Ser.). 1997. pap. 24.00 (*0-8384-7262-1*) Heinle & Heinle.
— Contexts in the College Curriculum: A Reading Skills Text to Build Your Information Base. LC 95-12562. 1995. 28.50 (*0-534-24211-1*) Wadsworth Pub.
***Pokras, Robert.** Ambulatory & Inpatient Procedures in the United States, 1994. 117p. 1998. per. 11.00 (*0-16-061480-5*) USGPO.
Pokras, Robert, et al. Ambulatory & Inpatient Procedures in the United States, 1994. (Illus.). 116p. (C). 1998. pap. text 30.00 (*0-7881-7424-X*) DIANE Pub.
— Ambulatory & Inpatient Procedures in the United States, 1994. LC 97-42743. (Vital & Health Statistics Ser.: Series 13, No. 132). 1998. write for info. (*0-8406-0535-8*) Natl Ctr Health Stats.
Pokras, Sandy. Building High Performance Teams. (Better Management Skills Ser.). 1996. pap. 12.95 (*0-7494-1906-7*) Kogan Page Ltd.
— Rapid Team Deployment. Keppler, Kay, ed. LC 95-67039. (Fifty-Minute Ser.). (Illus.). 128p. (Orig.). 1995. pap. 10.95 (*1-56052-321-2*) Crisp Pubns.
— Team Problem Solving. rev. ed. Crisp, Michael & Ruvolo, Francine L., eds. LC 94-72611. (Fifty-Minute Ser.). (Illus.). 132p. 1994. pap. 10.95 (*1-56052-314-X*) Crisp Pubns.
— Working in Teams: A Fifty Minute Book. LC 96-86712. 1997. pap. text 10.95 (*1-56052-412-X*) Crisp Pubns.
Pokrass, David, jt. auth. see Bray, Gary.
Pokriots, Will, jt. auth. see Cortright, Sandy.
***Pokrovski, Vladimir N.** Physical Principles in the Theory of Economic Growth. 176p. 1999. text 61.95 (*0-7546-1118-3*, Pub. by Ashgate Pub) Ashgate Pub Co.
Pokrovskii, A. V., jt. auth. see Krasnosel'Skii, M. A.
Pokrovskii, L. N., jt. auth. see Ivovich, V. A.
Pokrovsky, Nikita E. Ralph Waldo Emerson: An Intellectual Portrait. 320p. 1994. write for info. (*0-9642968-0-2*); pap. text. write for info. (*0-9642968-1-0*) Ctr Am Studies Concord.
Pokrovsky, V. L. & Talapov, A. L. Theory of Incommensurate Crystals. (Soviet Scientific Reviews, Section A, Physics Reviews Supplement Ser.: Vol. 1). xii, 164p. 1984. text 340.00 (*3-7186-0134-6*) Gordon & Breach.
Pokrovsky, Valery, et al. Modulated Structures. (Modern Condensed Matter Physics Ser.: Vol. 3). 200p. (C). 1997. text 51.00 (*981-02-0747-6*); pap. text 28.00 (*981-02-0748-4*) World Scientific Pub.
Pokshishevsky, V. Geography of the Soviet Union: Economy, Geography, Population & Production Complexes. (Illus.). 280p. 1975. 22.95 (*0-8464-0448-6*) Beekman Pubs.
Pokshishevsky, V. V., ed. Evaluation of the Soviet Population Census, 1970. 100p. (C). 1975. pap. 23.00 (*0-08-019672-1*, Pergamon Pr) Elsevier.
Poku, Nana, jt. auth. see Graham, David T.
***Poku, Nana T.** Regionalization & Security in Southern Africa. LC 00-40461. (International Political Economy Ser.). 2000. write for info. (*0-333-74844-1*) St Martin.
Poku, Nana T. & Graham, David, eds. Redefining Security: Population Movements & National Security. LC 98-6857. 264p. 1998. 59.95 (*0-275-96097-8*, Praeger Pubs) Greenwood.
Pol. Environmental Psychology in Europe. 1993. 79.95 (*1-85628-528-6*) Ashgate Pub Co.
Pol, Balth Van Der, see Van Der Pol, Balth.
Pol, Louis G. Business Demography: A Guide & Reference for Business Planners & Marketers. LC 87-2494. 305p. 1987. 69.50 (*0-89930-218-1*, PDY/, Quorum Bks) Greenwood.
Pol, Louis G. & Thomas, Richard K. Demography for Business Decision Making. LC 96-46087. 288p. 1997. 55.00 (*1-56720-014-1*, Quorum Bks) Greenwood.
Pol, Louis G., jt. auth. see Berkowitz, Eric.
Pol, Louis G., jt. auth. see Guy, Rebecca F.
Pol, Louis G., jt. auth. see Thomas, R. K.
Pol, Louis G., jt. auth. see Thomas, Richard K.
Pol, Peter, jt. auth. see Van den Berg, Leo.
Pol, Richard A. Van Den, see Spiegle, Jan & Van Den Pol, Richard A., eds.
Pol, Richard Van den, see Neilsen, Shelley.
Pol, Rick Van Den, see Paulson, Lucy H. & Van Den Pol, Rick.
Pola, Giancarlo, et al, eds. Developments in Local Government Finance: Theory & Policy. LC 95-42286. 380p. 1996. 95.00 (*1-85898-377-0*) E Elgar.
Polacco, Patricia. Appelemando's Dreams. LC 90-19716. (Illus.). 32p. (J). (ps-3). 1991. 15.95 (*0-399-21800-9*, Philomel) Peng Put Young Read.
Polacco, Patricia. Appelemando's Dreams. 1997. 11.15 (*0-606-07203-9*, Pub. by Turtleback) Demco.
Polacco, Patricia. Aunt Chip & the Great Triple Creek Dam Affair. LC 95-10112. (Illus.). 32p. (J). (ps-3). 1996. 15.95 (*0-399-22943-4*, Philomel) Peng Put Young Read.
— Aunt Chip & the Great Triple Creek Dam Affair. (J). (gr. k-3). 1997. 27.95 incl. audio (*0-8045-6836-7*, 6836) Spoken Arts.
— Babushka Baba Yaga. LC 92-30361. (Illus.). 32p. (J). (ps-3). 1993. 15.95 (*0-399-22531-5*, Philomel) Peng Put Young Read.
— Babushka's Doll. LC 89-6122. (Illus.). 40p. (J). (ps-3). 1995. mass mkt. 6.95 (*0-689-80255-2*) Aladdin.
— Babushka's Doll. LC 89-6122. (Illus.). 40p. (J). (ps-3). 1990. 16.00 (*0-671-68343-8*) S&S Bks Yung.
— Babushka's Doll. 1995. 12.15 (*0-606-07219-5*, Pub. by Turtleback) Demco.
— Babushka's Mother Goose. LC 94-32332. (Illus.). 64p. (J). (ps-2). 1995. 17.95 (*0-399-22747-4*, Philomel) Peng Put Young Read.
***Polacco, Patricia.** Babushka's Mother Goose. (Illus.). 64p. (J). (ps-3). 2000. pap. text 6.99 (*0-698-11860-X*) Putnam Pub Group.
— Babushka's Mother Goose. (Illus.). (J). 2000. 12.34 (*0-606-18389-2*) Turtleback.
Polacco, Patricia. The Bee Tree. LC 92-8660. (Illus.). 32p. (J). (ps up). 1993. 15.95 (*0-399-21965-X*, Philomel) Peng Put Young Read.
— The Bee Tree. (Illus.). 32p. (J). (ps-3). 1998. pap. 6.99 (*0-698-11696-8*, PapStar) Peng Put Young Read.
— The Bee Tree. (J). 1998. 11.19 (*0-606-13187-6*, Pub. by Turtleback) Demco.
— Boatride with Lillian Two-Blossom. LC 87-2507. (Illus.). 32p. (J). (ps-3). 1989. 15.95 (*0-399-21470-4*, Philomel) Peng Put Young Read.
***Polacco, Patricia.** The Butterfly. LC 99-30038. (Illus.). 48p. (J). (ps-3). 2000. 16.99 (*0-399-23170-6*, Philomel) Peng Put Young Read.
Polacco, Patricia. Chicken Sunday. LC 91-16030. (Illus.). 32p. (J). (ps-3). 1992. 15.95 (*0-399-22133-6*, Philomel) Peng Put Young Read.
***Polacco, Patricia.** Chicken Sunday. (J). 1998. 11.19 (*0-606-12906-5*, Pub. by Turtleback) Demco.
— La Colcha de los Recuerdos. 10th anniversary ed. LC 99-34169. (SPA., Illus.). (gr. 3-7). 1999. 16.95 (*1-880507-54-4*) Lectorum Pubns.
Polacco, Patricia. Firetalking. LC 93-48162. (Meet the Author Ser.). (Illus.). 32p. (J). (gr. 2-5). 1994. 14.95 (*1-878450-55-7*, 709) R Owen Pubs.
— The Forever Quilt. 1988. 12.95 (*0-13-749789-X*) S&S Trade.
— I Can Hear the Sun. 40p. 1999. pap. 5.99 (*0-698-11857-X*, PuffinBks) Peng Put Young Read.
— I Can Hear the Sun: A Modern Myth. LC 95-32091. (Illus.). 32p. (J). (ps-3). 1996. 15.95 (*0-399-22520-X*, Philomel) Peng Put Young Read.
— In Enzo's Splendid Gardens. LC 96-12360. (Illus.). 32p. (J). (ps-3). 1997. 15.95 (*0-399-23107-2*, Philomel) Peng Put Young Read.
— Just Plain Fancy. (Illus.). 32p. (J). (ps-3). 1994. pap. 6.99 (*0-440-40937-3*) Dell.
— Just Plain Fancy. (Dell Picture Yearling Ser.). (Illus.). (J). 1990. 11.19 (*0-606-05898-2*, Pub. by Turtleback) Demco.
— The Keeping Quilt: 10th Anniversary Edition. LC 88-4507. (Illus.). 32p. (J). (ps-3). 1988. 16.00 (*0-671-64963-9*) S&S Bks Yung.
— The Keeping Quilt Tenth Anniversary Edition. 10th anniversary ed. LC 97-47690. (Illus.). 48p. (J). (ps-3). 1998. 16.00 (*0-689-82090-9*) S&S Childrens.
— Luba & the Wren. LC 98-16353. 32p. (J). (ps-3). 1999. 16.99 (*0-399-23168-4*, Philomel) Peng Put Young Read.
— Meteor! (Illus.). 32p. (J). (ps-3). 1996. pap. 6.99 (*0-698-11410-8*, PapStar) Peng Put Young Read.
— Meteor! (ps-3). 1999. 16.99 (*0-399-23384-9*) Putnam Pub Group.
— Meteor! (J). 1996. 11.15 (*0-606-05465-0*, Pub. by Turtleback) Demco.
— Mrs. Katz & Tush. (Illus.). (J). 1992. 15.00 (*0-553-08122-5*, Litl Rooster) BDD Bks Young Read.
— Mrs. Katz & Tush. (Illus.). 32p. (J). (ps-3). 1994. pap. 6.99 (*0-440-40936-5*) Dell.
— Mrs. Katz & Tush. 1994. 11.19 (*0-606-05930-X*, Pub. by Turtleback) Demco.
— Mrs. Mack. LC 97-52946. (Illus.). 40p. (J). (ps-3). 1998. 16.99 (*0-399-23167-6*, Philomel) Peng Put Young Read.
— My Ol' Man. LC 94-15395. (Illus.). 40p. (J). (gr. k-3). 1995. 15.95 (*0-399-22822-5*, Philomel) Peng Put Young Read.
— My Ol' Man. (Illus.). 40p. (YA). (gr. k-3). 1999. pap. 6.99 (*0-698-11770-0*, PapStar) Peng Put Young Read.
— My Rotten, Redheaded Older Brother. (Illus.). 40p. (J). (ps-2). 1994. 16.00 (*0-671-72751-6*) S&S Bks Yung.
— My Rotten, Redheaded Older Brother. LC 93-13980. (Illus.). 32p. (J). (ps-3). 1998. per. 5.99 (*0-689-82036-4*) S&S Childrens.
— Picnic at Mudsock Meadow. LC 91-7374. (Illus.). 32p. (J). (ps-3). 1992. 15.95 (*0-399-21811-4*, Philomel) Peng Put Young Read.
Polacco, Patricia. Picnic at Mudsock Meadow. LC 91-7374. (J). 1997. 11.15 (*0-606-11747-4*, Pub. by Turtleback) Demco.
Polacco, Patricia. Pink & Say. LC 93-36340. (Illus.). 48p. (J). (gr. 4 up). 1994. 15.95 (*0-399-22671-0*, Philomel) Peng Put Young Read.
— Pink y Say (Pink & Say) 1997. 15.95 (*1-880507-30-7*) Lectorum Pubns.
Polacco, Patricia. Rechenka's Eggs. LC 87-16588. (Illus.). 32p. (J). (ps-3). 1988. 15.95 (*0-399-21501-8*, Philomel) Peng Put Young Read.
Polacco, Patricia. Rechenka's Eggs. 1996. 11.15 (*0-606-09782-1*, Pub. by Turtleback) Demco.
— Some Birthday! LC 90-10381. (Illus.). 40p. (J). (ps-3). 1991. pap. 15.00 (*0-671-72750-8*) S&S Bks Yung.
— Some Birthday! LC 90-10381. 40p. (J). (ps-3). 1993. pap. 6.99 (*0-671-87170-6*) S&S Bks Yung.
— Some Birthday! 1991. 12.19 (*0-606-06012-X*, Pub. by Turtleback) Demco.
— Thank You, Mr. Falker. LC 97-18685. (Illus.). 40p. (J). (gr. k-4). 1998. 16.99 (*0-399-23166-8*, Philomel) Peng Put Young Read.
— Thunder Cake. 1997. 11.15 (*0-606-12541-8*, Pub. by Turtleback) Demco.
— Thundercake. LC 89-33405. (Illus.). 32p. (J). (ps-3). 1990. 15.95 (*0-399-22231-6*, Philomel) Peng Put Young Read.
— Tikvah Means Hope. LC 93-32311. 1996. 11.19 (*0-606-09971-9*, Pub. by Turtleback) Demco.
— The Trees of the Dancing Goats. LC 95-26670. (Illus.). 32p. (J). (gr. 4-7). 1996. 16.00 (*0-689-80862-3*) S&S Childrens.
— The Trees of the Dancing Goats. LC 55-26670. 32p. (J). (gr. 2-5). 1997. pap. 22.00 incl. audio compact disk (*0-689-81193-4*) S&S Childrens.
— Uncle Vova's Tree. LC 88-25522. (Illus.). 32p. (J). (ps-3). 1989. 15.95 (*0-399-21617-0*, Philomel) Peng Put Young Read.
— Uncle Vova's Tree. (Illus.). 32p. (J). (gr. k-3). 1995. pap. 5.95 (*0-399-22838-1*, Sandcastle Bks) Putnam Pub Group.
— Welcome Comfort. LC 98-29558. 40p. (J). (ps-3). 1999. 16.99 (*0-399-23169-2*, Philomel) Peng Put Young Read.
Polacco, Patricia. El Pollo de los Domingos (Chicken Sunday) LC 97-2237. (SPA.). (gr. 2-4). 1997. 15.95 (*1-880507-31-5*) Lectorum Pubns.
Polacco, Patricia. Appelemando's Dreams. 32p. (J). (ps-3). 1997. pap. 6.99 (*0-698-11590-2*, PapStar) Peng Put Young Read.
Polacek, Karel. What Ownership's All About. Kussi, Peter, tr. from CZE. & intro. by. LC 92-33558. 238p. 1993. 21.95 (*0-945774-19-2*, PG5038.P64D813) Catbird Pr.
Polach, Dilette, ed. Radiocarbon Dating Literature: The First 21 Years, 1947-1968 - An Annotated Bibliography. 370p. 1988. text 94.95 (*0-12-559290-6*) Acad Pr.
Polacheck, Hilda S. I Came a Stranger: The Story of a Hull-House Girl. Epstein, Dena J., ed. (Women in American History Ser.). (Illus.). 288p. 1991. pap. text 15.95 (*0-252-06218-3*) U of Ill Pr.
Polacheck, William. How to Live Forever. (Illus.). 64p. 1998. pap. 18.00 (*0-8059-4468-0*) Dorrance.
Polachek, James M. The Inner Opium War. (East Asian Monographs: No. 151). 400p. (C). 1992. 30.00 (*0-674-45446-4*) HUP.
***Polachek, Mary.** A Gift. 1999. pap. write for info. (*1-58235-015-9*) Watermrk Pr.
Polachek, Solomon, et al. Research in Labor Economics, Vol. 17. 1999. 78.50 (*0-7623-0570-3*) Jai Pr.
Polachek, Solomon W., ed. Research in Labor Economics, Vol. 16. 1997. 78.50 (*0-7623-0312-3*) Jai Pr.
— Research in Labor Economics: An Economic Analysis with Applications, No. 15. 392p. 1996. 78.50 (*0-7623-0111-2*) Jai Pr.
Polachek, Solomon W., et al, eds. Research in Labor Economics, Vol. 1. 376p. 1977. 78.50 (*0-89232-017-6*) Jai Pr.
— Research in Labor Economics, Vol. 2. 381p. 1979. 78.50 (*0-89232-097-4*) Jai Pr.
— Research in Labor Economics, Vol. 3. 389p. 1980. 78.50 (*0-89232-157-1*) Jai Pr.
— Research in Labor Economics, Vol. 4. 488p. 1982. 78.50 (*0-89232-220-9*) Jai Pr.
— Research in Labor Economics, Vol. 5. 368p. 1983. 78.50 (*0-89232-312-4*) Jai Pr.
— Research in Labor Economics, Vol. 6. 400p. 1984. 78.50 (*0-89232-418-X*) Jai Pr.
— Research in Labor Economics, Vol. 7. 376p. 1985. 78.50 (*0-89232-589-5*) Jai Pr.
— Research in Labor Economics, 2 vols., Vol. 8. 1986. 157.00 (*0-89232-653-0*) Jai Pr.
— Research in Labor Economics, Vol. 9. 1987. 78.50 (*0-89232-746-4*) Jai Pr.
— Research in Labor Economics, Vol. 10. 336p. 1989. 78.50 (*1-55938-025-X*) Jai Pr.
— Research in Labor Economics, Vol. 11: Labor Economics & Public Policy. 320p. 1991. 78.50 (*1-55938-080-2*) Jai Pr.
— Research in Labor Economics, Vol. 12. 310p. 1992. 78.50 (*1-55938-381-X*) Jai Pr.
— Research in Labor Economics, Vol. 13. 338p. 1993. 78.50 (*1-55938-473-5*) Jai Pr.
— Research in Labor Economics, Vol. 14. 1995. 78.50 (*1-55938-610-X*) Jai Pr.
— Research in Labor Economics No. 1: Evaluating Manpower Training Programs. 375p. 1982. suppl. ed. 78.50 (*0-89232-046-X*) Jai Pr.
— Research in Labor Economics No. 2: New Approaches to Labor Unions: Proceedings. 353p. 1983. suppl. ed. 78.50 (*0-89232-265-9*) Jai Pr.
Polachek, Solomon W. & Siebert, W. Stanley. The Economics of Earnings. (Illus.). 383p. (C). 1993. pap. text 24.95 (*0-521-36728-X*) Cambridge U Pr.
Polack, Frank M. Scanning Electron Microscopy: Atlas of Corneal Pathology. (Illus.). 168p. (gr. 13). 1983. 74.50 (*0-89352-203-1*) Mosby Inc.
Polack, Joel S. Manners & Customs of the New Zealanders, 2 vols. LC 75-35263. reprint ed. 64.50 (*0-404-14435-7*) AMS Pr.
Polack, Lisa, jt. auth. see Bruner, Michael.
Polack, Michael, jt. auth. see McBurnie, Grant.
Polack, Philip, ed. see Jessurun, Reheul.
Polack, Philip, ed. & tr. see De Gongora, Luis.
Polackova-Kenley, Kaca, tr. see Vaculik, Ludvik.
Polaco, Oscar J. & Guzman, Ana F. Arqueoictiofauna Mexicana. (SPA., Illus.). 100p. 1997. pap. 15.00 (*970-18-0008-7*, IN99, Pub. by Dir Gen Pubicaiones) UPLAAP.
Poladian, Vartapet T., tr. see Gulleserian, Papken.
Poladitmontri, Panurat & Lew, Judy. Thailand: The Beautiful Cookbook. (Beautiful Cookbook Ser.). (Illus.). 256p. 1992. 55.00 (*0-00-255029-6*) Collins SF.
Polaino. La Diabetes. 1997. pap. text 19.95 (*84-270-1422-8*) Planeta.
Polak, A. Laurence. Legal Fictions: A Series of Cases from the Classics. (Illus.). 127p. 1995. reprint ed. 40.00 (*1-56169-105-4*) Gaunt.
Polak, A. M. Major Timber Trees of Guyana: A Field Guide. (Tropenbos Technical Ser.: No. 2). (Illus.). 272p. 1992. pap. 65.00 (*90-5113-013-9*, Pub. by Backhuys Pubs) Balogh.
Polak, Ada, ed. see Charleston, Robert J., et al.
Polak, Alfred L. More Legal Fictions: A Series of Cases from Shakespeare. LC 73-153344. reprint ed. 27.50 (*0-404-05068-9*) AMS Pr.
Polak, Craig A., ed. see Hale, Judith A.
Polak, E. Computational Methods in Optimization. (Mathematics in Science & Engineering Ser.: Vol. 77). 1971. text 142.00 (*0-12-559350-3*) Acad Pr.
— Optimization Theory & Algorithms, Vol. 124. LC 97-2158. (Applied Mathematical Sciences Ser.). 784p. 1997. 69.95 (*0-387-94971-2*) Spr-Verlag.
Polak, Emil J. Medieval & Renaissance Letter Treatises & Form Letters: A Census of Manuscripts Found in Eastern Europe & the Former U. S. S. R. LC 92-36557. (Davis Medieval Texts & Studies: Vol. 8). xxii, 324p. 1992. 126.50 (*90-04-09667-1*) Brill Academic Pubs.
Polak, H. S., et al. Mahatma Gandhi: The Father of Modern India. 1986. 49.95 (*0-318-36651-7*) Asia Bk Corp.
Polak, J. Cyclic Plasticity & Low Cycle Fatigue Life of Metals. (Materials Science Monographs: No. 63). 316p. 1991. 168.75 (*0-444-98839-4*) Elsevier.
***Polak, J. B. & Heertje, Arnold.** Analytical Transport Economics: An International Perspective. LC 00-33171. 2001. write for info. (*1-85898-786-5*) E Elgar.
***Polak, J. J.** Streamlining the Financial Structure of the International Monetary Fund. LC 99-51504. (Essays in International Finance Ser.: No. 216). 1999. 10.00 (*0-88165-123-0*) Princeton U Int Finan Econ.
Polak, J. M., ed. Modern Visualisation of the Endothelium. (Endothelial Cell Research Ser.: Vol. 4). (Illus.). 252p. 1998. text 85.00 (*90-5702-294-X*, ECU95, Harwood Acad Pubs) Gordon & Breach.
Polak, J. M., jt. ed. see Jankowski, J. A.
Polak, Jacob B. & Van Der Kamp, Jan B., eds. Changes in the Field of Transport Studies. (Developments in Transportation Studies: No. 1). 1979. lib. bdg. 145.50 (*90-247-2147-4*) Kluwer Academic.
Polak, Jacques. Coordination of National Economic Policies. (Occasional Paper Ser.: No. 7). 21p. 1981. pap. 7.00 (*1-56708-006-5*) Grp of Thirty.
Polak, Jacques J. The Changing Nature of IMF Conditionality. LC 91-34812. (Essays in International Finance Ser.: No. 184). 76p. 1991. pap. text 10.00 (*0-88165-091-9*) Princeton U Int Finan Econ.
— Economic Theory & Financial Policy: The Selected Essays of Jacques J. Polak, 2 vols., Set. LC 94-6263. (Economists of the Twentieth Century Ser.). 876p. 1994. 195.00 (*1-85278-936-0*) E Elgar.
— Financial Policies & Development. LC 89-77720. 41p. 1990. pap. 9.95 (*1-55815-100-1*) ICS Pr.
— The World Bank & the IMF. 59p. (C). 1994. pap. 9.95 (*0-8157-7149-5*) Brookings.
Polak, Joseph F. Peripheral Vascular Sonography: A Practical Guide. (Illus.). 384p. 1992. 82.00 (*0-683-06914-4*) Lppncott W & W.
Polak, Julia & McGee, James, eds. In Situ Hybridization: Principles & Practice. 2nd ed. LC 98-39953. (Modern Methods in Pathology). (Illus.). 224p. 1999. text 59.95 (*0-19-854880-X*) OUP.
Polak, Julia & Van Noorden, Susan. Introduction to Immunocytochemistry: Current Techniques & Problems. 2nd ed. LC 97-13062. (Microscopy Handbooks Ser.). (Illus.). 144p. 1997. pap. 29.95 (*0-387-91513-3*) Spr-Verlag.
Polak, Julia M. Regulatory Peptides. (BioSeries-EXS: No. 56). 400p. 1989. 193.00 (*0-8176-1976-3*) Birkhauser.
Polak, Julia M. & Priestley, John V., eds. Electron Microscopic Immunocytochemistry. (Modern Methods in Pathology Ser.). (Illus.). 288p. 1992. spiral bd. 64.50 (*0-19-963248-0*) OUP.
Polak, Julia M., jt. ed. see Roberts, Gareth W.
Polak, Julia M., jt. ed. see Stoward, Peter J.
Polak, Julia M., jt. ed. see Wharton, John.
Polak, L. S. Immunological Aspects of Contact Sensitivity. (Monographs in Allergy: Vol. 15). (Illus.). 1979. pap. 84.50 (*3-8055-3050-1*) S Karger.
Polak, L. S. & Lebedev, Yu A., eds. Plasma Chemistry. 320p. 1995. boxed set 120.00 (*1-898326-22-3*, Pub. by CISP) Balogh.
Polak, M. V., jt. auth. see Van Rooy, R.
Polak, Michael. Bottles: Identification & Price Guide. viii, 400p. 1994. pap. 15.00 (*0-380-77218-3*, Avon Bks) Morrow Avon.
***Polak, Michael.** Bottles: Identification & Price Guide. 3rd ed. LC 00-38276. (Illus.). 512p. 2000. pap. 16.00 (*0-380-72815-X*, HarpRes) HarpInfo.
— Cc Bottles Ipg. 2nd ed. LC 96-95440. (Illus.). viii, 512p. 1997. pap. 16.00 (*0-380-72814-1*, Avon Bks) Morrow Avon.
Polak, Peter. Designing for Strength. (Illus.). 315p. (C). 1983. 55.00 (*0-333-32674-1*, Pub. by Macmillan Ed) Scholium Intl.
Polak, R., jt. ed. see Zahradnik, R.
***Polak, T. A. & Pande, C. S.** Engineering Measurements: Methods & Intrinsic Errors. 190p. 1999. 74.00 (*1-86058-236-2*) Prof Eng Pubng.
Polak, Tomas & Shores, Christopher. Stalin's Falcons. (Illus.). 384p. 1999. 59.95 (*1-902304-01-2*, Pub. by Grub St) Seven Hills Bk.
Polak, W. Compiler Specification & Verification. (Lecture Notes in Computer Science Ser.: Vol. 124). 269p. 1981. pap. 24.00 (*0-387-10886-6*) Spr-Verlag.
Polakiewicz, David M. & Mellen, Stephanie. The Teeny Tiny Voice. (Illus.). 52p. (Orig.). (J). 1992. pap. 8.95 (*1-878040-08-1*) Meltec.
Polakiewicz, Leonard A. Supplemental Materials for First Year Polish. (POL., Illus.). lxii, 212p. (Orig.). (C). 1991. pap. text 16.95 (*0-89357-215-2*) Slavica.
Polakoff, Keith I. The Politics of Inertia: The Election of 1876 & the End of Reconstruction. LC 72-96400. 357p. reprint ed. pap. 110.70 (*0-7837-8693-X*, 204943900011) Bks Demand.

P

An Asterisk (*) at the beginning of an entry indicates that the title is appearing for the first time.

Polakoff, Phillip L. Work & Health: Its Your Life, an Action Guide to Job Hazards. LC 84-61087. (Orig.). 1984. pap. 7.95 (*0-918763-00-2*) Pr Assocs.

Polakoff, Phillip L. & O'Rourke, Paul F. Healthy Worker - Healthy Workplace: The Productivity Connection. (Illus.). 65p. (Orig.). (C). 1994. pap. text 25.00 (*0-7881-0348-2*) DIANE Pub.

Polakov, Lester. We Live to Paint Again. 216p. 1993. pap. 25.00 (*0-9639720-0-6*) Logbooks Pr.

Polakova, Jolana. The Possibilities of Transcendence: Human Destructiveness & the Universality of Constructive Relations. Valeska, Jan, tr. LC 95-8655. (Problems in Contemporary Philosophy Ser.: Vol. 34). 104p. 1996. 59.95 (*0-7734-8896-0*) E Mellen.

***Polakova, Jolana.** Searching for the Divine in Contemporary Philosophy: Tensions Between the Immanent & the Transcendent. LC 99-41514. (Problems in Contemporary Philosophy Ser.: Vol. 42). 124p. 1999. text 59.95 (*0-7734-7925-2*) E Mellen.

Polakow, Valerie. Lives on the Edge: Single Mothers & Their Children in the Other America. LC 92-21977. (Illus.). 232p. (C). 1993. 22.50 (*0-226-67183-6*) U Ch Pr.

— Lives on the Edge: Single Mothers & Their Children in the Other America. x, 232p. (C). 1994. pap. 10.95 (*0-226-67184-4*) U Ch Pr.

Polakowski, N. H. & Ripling, E. Strength & Structure of Engineering Materials. 1965. text 54.00 (*0-13-851790-8*) P-H.

Polaksi, Arlene L. Fundamentals for Nursing Assistants. 944p. 1994. pap. write for info. (*0-7216-6237-4*, W B Saunders Co) Harcrt Hlth Sci Grp.

***Polan, Barbara.** Worcester: From Packahoag Hill to the Present. LC 99-51314. (History Ser.). (Illus.). 144p. 1999. 35.00 (*1-58192-005-9*) Community Comm.

***Polan, Dana.** Pulp Fiction. 2000. pap. 12.95 (*0-85170-808-0*, Pub. by British Film Inst) Ind U Pr.

Polan, Dana B. In a Lonely Place. (Illus.). 72p. 1994. pap. 10.95 (*0-85170-360-7*, Pub. by British Film Inst) Ind U Pr.

— The Political Language of Film & the Avant-Garde. Kirkpatrick, Diane, ed. LC 84-24062. (Studies in Cinema: No. 30). 151p. reprint ed. pap. 46.90 (*0-8357-1604-X*, 207075100004) Bks Demand.

Polan, Dana B., tr. see De Duve, Thierry.

Polan, Dana B., tr. see Deleuze, Gilles & Guattari, Felix.

Polan, Elaine & Taylor, Daphne. Journey Across the Life Span: Human Development & Health Promotion. LC 97-39790. (Illus.). 287p. (C). 1997. pap. text 21.95 (*0-8036-0196-4*) Davis Co.

Polan, Elaine & Taylor, Daphne C. Journey Across the Lifespan: Human Development & Health Promotion. 287p. 1998. teacher ed. 19.95 (*0-8036-0212-X*) Davis Co.

***Polan, Gregory J.** Isaiah 56-66. (Berit Olam (The Everlasting Covenant) Ser.). 2000. 0.00 (*0-8146-5068-6*) Liturgical Pr.

Polanco, Bermudez Y., tr. see Judge, William Q.

Polanco, Hector Diaz, see Diaz Polanco, Hector.

Polanco, Rafael. El Misterioso Origen Del Cristianismo: Ensayo en Religion Comparativa. (SPA., Illus.). 423p. (Orig.). 1989. pap. write for info. (*0-318-65960-3*) R Polanco.

Polanco, Vincente. Valores de Puerto Rico: Spanish Text. LC 74-14242. (Puerto Rican Experience Ser.). 178p. 1975. reprint ed. 17.95 (*0-405-06229-X*) Ayer.

Polancy, Toni. Pets in Paradise: Keeping Your Dog & Cat Healthy & Happy in Hawaii. (Illus.). 96p. 1999. pap. 12.95 (*0-9666253-1-5*, Pub. by Barefoot Pub) Booklines Hawaii.

— So You Want to Live in Hawaii: A Guide to Settling & Succeeding in the Islands. LC 98-73548. (Illus.). 304p. 1999. pap. 19.95 (*0-9666253-0-7*) Barefoot Pub.

Polancy, Toni & Lang, Holly. Love, Hawaii-Style: Stories, Spells & Fables from the World's Most Romantic Island. (Illus.). (Orig.). 1999. pap. 19.95 (*0-9666253-2-3*, Pub. by Barefoot Pub) Booklines Hawaii.

Poland & Major, eds. French Psychoanalytic Voices. (Psychoanalytic Inquiry Ser.: Vol. 4, No. 2). 1995. 20.00 (*0-88163-978-8*) Analytic Pr.

Poland, Alan & Kimbrough, Renate D., eds. Biological Mechanisms of Dioxin Action. LC 84-22955. (Banbury Report Ser.). (Illus.). 514p. Date not set. reprint ed. pap. 159.40 (*0-608-20714-4*, 207181200002) Bks Demand.

Poland, Andy. College: Everything I Wish I Knew Before My First Class. (Illus.). 48p. (YA). (gr. 11-12). 1998. pap. 8.00 (*0-8059-4194-0*) Dorrance.

***Poland, Blake D., et al.** Settings for Health Promotion: Linking Theory & Practice. LC 99-50471. 2000. write for info. (*0-8039-7419-1*) Sage.

Poland, Fiona, et al. Women & Senior Management: A Research Study of Career Barriers & Progression in the Library & Information Sector. LC 96-212793. (Illus.). 103p. reprint ed. pap. 32.00 (*0-608-20963-5*, 207183500002) Bks Demand.

***Poland, Gregory A., et al.** Immunizing Health Care Workers: A Practical Approach. (Illus.). 544p. 2000. 109.00 (*1-55642-450-7*) SLACK Inc.

Poland, James M. Understanding Terrorism: Groups, Strategies, & Responses. (Illus.). 288p. (C). 1988. pap. text 32.20 (*0-13-936113-8*) P-H.

***Poland, James M. & McCrystle, Michael J.** Practical, Tactical & Legal Perspectives of Terrorism & Hostage-Taking. LC 99-52435. (Criminology Studies: Vol. 9). 248p. 2000. 89.95 (*0-7734-7877-9*) E Mellen.

Poland, Janet. Getting to Know Your One-Year-Old. 1995. mass mkt. 4.99 (*0-312-95418-2*) St Martin.

— Making Friends with Your Three-Year Old, Vol. 1. (Magical Years Ser.: No. 3). 1995. mass mkt. 4.99 (*0-312-95627-4*) St Martin.

— Surviving Your Two-Year-Old. 1995. pap. 59.88 (*0-312-95654-1*); mass mkt. 4.99 (*0-312-95582-0*, Pub. by Tor Bks) St Martin.

Poland, Janet, jt. auth. see Malmstrom, Patricia M.

Poland, Jean A. & Johnson, Godlind. Selective Guide to Literature on Applied Optics. LC 98-168810. (Engineering Literature Guides Ser.). 20 p. ;p. 1997. write for info. (*0-87823-160-9*) Am Soc Eng Ed.

Poland, Jeffrey. Physicalism: The Philosophical Foundations. 392p. 1994. text 65.00 (*0-19-824980-2*) OUP.

Poland, Larry W. The Last Temptation of Hollywood. Holmes, Robert M., Jr., ed. 208p. (Orig.). 1988. pap. 6.95 (*0-9621692-0-X*) Mastermed Intl.

— Master Key: A Growth Experience for Christian Media Professionals. (Illus.). 160p. 1997. pap., wbk. ed. 19.95 (*0-9621692-1-8*) Mastermed Intl.

Poland, Lynn M. Literary Criticism & Biblical Hermeneutics. (American Academy of Religion Academy Ser.: No. 48). 220p. (C). 1985. pap. 15.95 (*0-89130-836-9*, 01-01-48) OUP.

Poland, Robert P. Processing Medical Documents. 2nd ed. LC 98-49590. 256p. 1998. 38.95 (*0-02-804745-1*) Glencoe.

— Processing Medical Documents Using WordPerfect. LC 94-12977. 1995. write for info. (*0-02-802536-9*) Glencoe.

Poland, Scott. Suicide Intervention in the Schools. LC 88-36988. (School Practitioner Ser.). 214p. 1989. pap. text 24.00 (*0-89862-232-8*); lib. bdg. 49.95 (*0-89862-353-7*) Guilford Pubns.

***Poland, Scott & McCormick, Jami S.** Coping with Crisis: Lessons Learned. (Illus.). 456p. 1999. pap. 35.00 (*1-57035-218-6*, 108COPE) Sopris.

Poland, Scott, jt. auth. see Pitcher, Gayle D.

Poland, Warren S. Melting the Darkness: The Dyad & Principles of Clinical Practice. 1996. 45.00 (*1-56821-816-8*) Aronson.

***Polando, Johnny.** Wings Over Istanbul: The Life & Flights of a Pioneer Aviator. LC 00-24619. (Illus.). 144p. 2000. pap. write for info. (*0-914339-84-2*, Pub. by P E Randall Pub) U Pr of New Eng.

Polangin, Richard F. & Feigenbaum, Ernest. Florida Health Care Reference, 1994-95. Nelson-Morrill, Creston, ed. LC 95-122389. 320p. 1994. pap. 12.95 (*1-879919-88-5*) HealthTrac.

Polanski, Roman. Roman by Polanski. 448p. 1985. mass mkt. 4.95 (*0-345-30512-4*) Ballantine Pub Grp.

Polansky, Bohdan S. Ukrainian Churches in New York, Vol. 1. (Illus.). 120p. 1999. 60.00 (*0-9635415-3-6*) B S P Pub.

— Ukrainian Churches in New York, Vol. 2. (Illus.). 120p. 1999. 60.00 (*0-9635415-4-4*) B S P Pub.

— Ukrainian Churches in New York, Vol. 3. (Illus.). 140p. 1999. 65.00 (*0-9635415-5-2*) B S P Pub.

Polansky, Joseph. Your Personal Horoscope for 1999: Month-by-Month Forecast for Every Sign. (Illus.). 416p. 1998. pap. 13.00 (*0-7225-3570-8*) Thorsons PA.

— Your Personal Horoscope, 1994: Month-by-Month Forecast for Every Sign. 1993. pap. 9.00 (*1-85538-281-4*, Pub. by Aqrn Pr) Harper SF.

***Polansky, Joseph.** Your Personal Horoscope 2001: The Only Horoscope Book You Need. 2000. pap. 14.00 (*0-7225-3968-1*) Thorsons.

— Your Personal Horoscope 2000: Month-by-Month Forecast for Every Sign. (Illus.). 416p. 1999. pap. 13.00 (*0-7225-3789-1*) Thorsons PA.

Polansky, Joseph, jt. auth. see Nielsen, Greg.

Polansky, Leslie, jt. auth. see Torrence, Susan.

Polansky, Norman A. Integrated Ego Psychology. 2nd ed. (Modern Applications of Social Work Ser.). 387p. 1991. lib. bdg. 58.95 (*0-202-26099-2*) Aldine de Gruyter.

Polansky, Norman A., ed. Social Work Research: Methods for the Helping Professions. rev. ed. LC 74-26798. (Illus.). 352p. 1975. lib. bdg. 21.00 (*0-226-67219-0*) U Ch Pr.

Polansky, Norman A., et al. Roots of Futility. LC 72-5894. (Jossey-Bass Behavioral Science Ser.). 286p. reprint ed. pap. 88.70 (*0-608-16919-6*, 202776600056) Bks Demand.

Polansky, O. E., jt. auth. see Gutman, I.

Polansky, Paul J., ed. see Dvorak, Otakar.

Polansky, Ronald M. Philosophy & Knowledge: A Commentary on Plato's Theaetetus. LC 90-56167. 264p. 1992. 38.50 (*0-8387-5215-2*) Bucknell U Pr.

Polansky, Ronald M., jt. ed. see Kuczewski, Mark G.

Polansky, Steven. Dating Miss Universe. LC 98-47410. 195p. 1999. pap. 16.00 (*0-8142-5019-X*); text 35.00 (*0-8142-0818-5*) Ohio St U Pr.

Polansky, Susan. Puntos de Vista en la Lectura. (Bridging the Gap Ser.). (C). 1993. mass mkt., student ed. 24.95 (*0-8384-4665-5*) Heinle & Heinle.

Polanskyi, Bohdan S. Ukrainian Churches in New England. (Illus.). 152p. 1999. 95.00 (*0-9635415-2-8*) B S P Pub.

— Ukrainian Churches in New Jersey. (Illus.). 107p. 1993. 85.00 (*0-9635415-0-1*) B S P Pub.

— Ukrainian Churches in New Jersey. deluxe ed. (Illus.). 107p. 1993. 125.00 (*0-9635415-1-X*) B S P Pub.

Polanuer, Jorge. Saxophone Styles: Book & CD Package. (Illus.). 40p. 1999. pap. 17.95 (*1-57424-069-2*) Centerstream Pub.

Polanyi. Science, Faith & Society. 1964. pap. text 7.95 (*0-226-67298-0*) U Ch Pr.

Polanyi, John C., jt. ed. see Griffiths, Franklyn.

Polanyi, Karl. The Great Transformation: The Political & Economic Origins of Our Time. 1957. pap. 18.00 (*0-8070-5679-0*) Beacon Pr.

***Polanyi, Karl.** The Great Transformation: The Political & Economic Origins of Our Time. 2001. pap. 17.00 (*0-8070-5643-X*) Beacon Pr.

Polanyi, Karl. Uncollected Works of Karl Polanyi. 1999. text. write for info. (*0-312-04803-3*) St Martin.

Polanyi-Levitt, Kari, ed. The Life & Work of Karl Polanyi, Vol. 1. LC 90-83624. (Illus.). 265p. (Orig.). (C). 1990. 48.99 (*0-921689-81-0*, Pub. by Black Rose); pap. 19.99 (*0-921689-80-2*, Pub. by Black Rose) Consort Bk Sales.

Polanyi-Levitt, Kari, jt. ed. see McRobbie, Kenneth.

Polanyi, Livia. Telling the American Story: A Structural & Cultural Analysis of Conversational Storytelling. LC 84-24196. (Language & Being Ser.). 160p. 1985. text 73.25 (*0-89391-041-4*) Ablx Pub.

Polanyi, Michael. Atomic Reactions. 1980. lib. bdg. 49.95 (*0-8490-3138-9*) Gordon Pr.

— The Contempt of Freedom: The Russian Experiment & After. LC 74-29384. (History, Philosophy & Sociology of Science Ser.). 1979. reprint ed. 18.95 (*0-405-06643-0*) Ayer.

— Knowing & Being. Grene, Marjorie, ed. LC 76-77151. 1993. pap. text 10.95 (*0-226-67285-9*) U Ch Pr.

— Knowing & Being: Essays. Grene, Marjorie, ed. LC 76-77151. 264p. reprint ed. pap. 81.90 (*0-608-16408-9*, 202721400054) Bks Demand.

— The Logic of Liberty: Reflections & Rejoinders. LC 98-5301. 1998. 16.00 (*0-86597-182-X*); pap. 9.00 (*0-86597-183-8*) Liberty Fund.

— The Logic of Liberty: Reflections & Rejoinders. LC 51-8809. (Midway Reprint Ser.). 1980. pap. text 12.95 (*0-226-67296-4*) U Ch Pr.

— Personal Knowledge: Towards a Post-Critical Philosophy. LC 58-5162. xiv, 442p. 1974. reprint ed. pap. text 17.00 (*0-226-67288-3*, P583) U Ch Pr.

— Science, Faith & Society. 96p. 1964. pap. text 8.95 (*0-226-67290-5*, P155) U Ch Pr.

— Scientific Thought & Social Reality: Essays by Michael Polanyi. Schwartz, Fred, ed. LC 74-5420. (Psychological Issues Monographs: No. 32, Vol. 8, No. 4). 168p. (C). 1974. 27.50 (*0-8236-6005-2*) Intl Univs Pr.

— Society, Economics, & Philosophy: Selected Papers. LC 96-42469. 335p. 1996. text 44.95 (*1-56000-278-6*) Transaction Pubs.

— Study of Man. LC 59-4021. 1963. pap. 9.00 (*0-226-67292-1*, P128) U Ch Pr.

— The Tacit Dimension. 1983. 25.75 (*0-8446-5999-1*) Peter Smith.

Polanyi, Michael & Prosch, Harry. Meaning. LC 75-5067. 260p. 1977. reprint ed. pap. text 15.95 (*0-226-67295-6*, P740) U Ch Pr.

Polaris Associates Staff. The Power of Values. 76p. 1996. per. 50.00 (*0-7872-2898-2*, 41289801) Kendall-Hunt.

Polaschek, Martin L., jt. auth. see Mueck, Thomas A.

Polasek, Agnes, jt. auth. see Foster, Agnes M.

Polasek, M., tr. & intro. see Schulz, Karl.

Polasek, Wolfgang, jt. ed. see Bock, Hans-Hermann.

Polaski. Luckmann's Core Princ Prac. 1996. 275.00 (*0-7216-5998-5*) Harcourt.

— Saunders Fundamental Nursing Assistance. 1994. 345.00 (*0-7216-4309-4*) Harcourt.

Polaski, Arlene L. Luckmann Core Private Practice. LC 97-115800. 1996. pap. text, student ed. 17.95 (*0-7216-6771-6*, W B Saunders Co) Harcrt Hlth Sci Grp.

Polaski, Arlene L. & Tatro, Suzanne E. Luckmann's Core Principles & Practice of Medical-Surgical Nursing. 1996. teacher ed. write for info. (*0-7216-5995-0*, W B Saunders Co) Harcrt Hlth Sci Grp.

— Luckmann's Core Principles & Practice of Medical-Surgical Nursing. Eoyang, Thomas, ed. (Illus.). 1840p. 1996. text 68.00 (*0-7216-5994-2*, W B Saunders Co) Harcrt Hlth Sci Grp.

— Luckmann's Core Principles & Practice of Medical-Surgical Nursing. LC 96-166595. 1996. pap. text 19.95 (*0-7216-6817-8*, W B Saunders Co) Harcrt Hlth Sci Grp.

— Luckmann's Core Principles & Practice of Medical-Surgical Nursing, Test Manual. 1996. write for info. (*0-7216-5996-9*, W B Saunders Co) Harcrt Hlth Sci Grp.

Polaski, Arlene L. & Warner, Judith P. Saunders Fundamentals for Nursing Assistants. (Illus.). 1994. pap., teacher ed. write for info. (*0-7216-3612-8*, W B Saunders Co) Harcrt Hlth Sci Grp.

— Saunders Fundamentals for Nursing Assistants. (Illus.). 944p. 1994. pap. text 29.95 (*0-7216-3608-X*, W B Saunders Co); pap. text, student ed. 14.95 (*0-7216-3613-6*, W B Saunders Co) Harcrt Hlth Sci Grp.

— Saunders Fundamentals for Nursing Assistants, Set. (Illus.). 944p. 1994. pap., student ed. 38.95 (*0-7216-4516-X*, W B Saunders Co) Harcrt Hlth Sci Grp.

***Polaski, Donald C.** Authorizing an End: The Isaiah Apocalypse & Intertextuality. LC 00-31151. (Biblical Interpretation Ser.). 2000. write for info. (*90-04-11607-9*) Brill Academic Pubs.

***Polaski, Sandra Hack.** Paul & the Discourse of Power. (Biblical Seminar Ser.: No. 62). 151p. 1999. pap. 19.95 (*1-85075-934-0*, Pub. by Sheffield Acad) CUP Services.

Polasky, Janet. The Democratic Socialism of Emile Vandervelde: Between Reform & Revolution. LC 94-46196. (Illus.). 288p. 1995. pap. 19.50 (*1-85973-033-7*, Pub. by Berg Pubs) NYU Pr.

Polasky, Janet L. The Democratic Socialism of Emile Vandervelde: Between Reform & Revolution. LC 94-46196. (Illus.). 288p. 1995. 55.00 (*0-85496-394-4*, Pub. by Berg Pubs) NYU Pr.

Polaso. Real Analysis: Solutions Manual. 1991. lib. bdg. write for info. (*0-8493-7870-2*) CRC Pr.

Polaszek, Andrew. African Cereal Stem Borers: Economic Importance, Taxonomy, Natural Enemies & Control. LC 97-46738. (A CAB International Publication). (Illus.). 556p. 1998. 175.00 (*0-85199-175-0*) OUP.

***Polat, Mizrap.** Der Umwandlungsproze & Beta; Vom Kalifat Zur Dynastie: Regierungspolitik und Religion Beim Ersten Umayyadenherrscher Mucawiya Ibn Abi Sufyan. (Europaische Hochschulschriften Geschichte und Ihre Hilfswissenschaften Ser.). X, 211p. 1999. 35.95 (*3-631-34968-8*) P Lang Pubng.

Polatin, Paul F. Modeling & Inversion of the Radar Response of Vegetation Canopies. LC QC0973.. (University of Michigan Reports: No. RL899). 240p. reprint ed. pap. 74.40 (*0-7837-6781-1*, 204661100003) Bks Demand.

Polatoglu, Hakan, jt. auth. see Sahin, Izzet.

Polatov, Abdummonob, ed. see Afkhami, Mahnaz & Vaziri, Haleh.

Polatschek, P. L. Twelve Etudes for Clarinet. 24p. 1984. pap. 4.95 (*0-7935-5271-0*, 00008300) H Leonard.

Polavarapu, P. L. Vibrational Spectra: Principles, Applications & Molecular Structure. LC 98-38886. (Studies in Physical & Theoretical Chemistry). 412p. 1998. text. write for info. (*0-444-89599-X*) Elsevier.

Polavarapu, Prasad L., ed. Principles & Applications of Polarization Division Interferometry. LC 97-17447. 214p. 1997. 135.00 (*0-471-97420-X*) Wiley.

Polay, E. Iniuria Types in Roman Law. 226p. (C). 1986. 75.00 (*963-05-4459-8*, Pub. by Akade Kiado) St Mut.

Polcari, Stephen. Abstract Expressionism & the Modern Experience. (Illus.). 432p. (C). 1993. pap. text 30.95 (*0-521-44826-3*) Cambridge U Pr.

Polchinski, Joseph. String Theory Vol. 1: An Introduction to the Bosonic String. LC 98-4545. (Monographs on Mathematical Physics). (Illus.). 400p. (C). 1998. 49.95 (*0-521-63303-6*) Cambridge U Pr.

— String Theory Vol. 2: Superstring Theory & Beyond. LC 98-4545. (Monographs on Mathematical Physics). (Illus.). 500p. (C). 1998. 49.95 (*0-521-63304-4*) Cambridge U Pr.

Polchinski, Joseph, ed. see Harvey, Jeffrey.

***Polcz, Alaine.** A Wartime Memoir Hungary, 1944-1945. 136p. 1999. pap. 23.00 (*963-13-4556-4*, Pub. by Corvina Bks) St Mut.

Polczinski, Len C. Ginseng Culture in Marathon County, Wisconsin: Historical Growth, Distribution & Soils Inventory. (Illus.). 143p. (Orig.). 1982. pap. text 27.95 (*1-881417-03-4*) D F Curran Prods.

Poldauf, Ivan. Czech-English, English-Czech Standard Dictionary. (CZE & ENG.). 1200p. 1998. reprint ed. 39.50 (*0-7818-0653-4*) Hippocrene Bks.

— English-Czech-English Dictionary. (CZE & ENG.). 1223p. 1991. 69.95 (*0-8288-0536-9*, M14850) Fr & Eur.

Poldauf, Ivan, ed. Czech-English Comprehensive Dictionary. rev. ed. (CZE & ENG.). 1400p. 1997. 55.00 (*0-7818-0509-0*) Hippocrene Bks.

Poldauf, Ivan, jt. auth. see Osicka, V.

Polden, Margaret, jt. auth. see Mantle, Jill.

***Polden, Patrick.** A History of the County Court, 1846-1971. LC 98-43621. (Cambridge Studies in English Legal History). 389p. (C). 1999. 85.00 (*0-521-62232-8*) Cambridge U Pr.

Polden, Richard. Endeavor: A Photographic Journey. LC 98-208240. (Illus.). 136p. 1998. 29.95 (*1-86368-227-9*, Pub. by Fremantle Arts) Intl Spec Bk.

Polder, Jacqueline A., jt. auth. see Hale, Cynthia M.

Polder, Jerome. The Comprehensive Guide to United States Air Force Pocket-Shoulder Insignia Mottos. LC 85-60227. 258p. 1985. pap. 28.95 (*0-9615456-3-1*) Aeroemblem Pubns.

— The Comprehensive Illustrated Guide to United States Air Force Insignia of the Persian Gulf. (Illustrated Guide Series to Air Force Pocket-Shoulder Insignia). (Illus.). 68p. 1994. pap. 15.00 (*0-9615456-8-2*) Aeroemblem Pubns.

— The Comprehensive Illustrated Guide to United States Air Force Pocket-Shoulder Insignia, Vol. 1. LC 85-72269. (Illus.). 235p. 1985. pap. 28.95 (*0-9615456-0-7*) Aeroemblem Pubns.

— The Comprehensive Illustrated Guide to United States Air Force Pocket-Shoulder Insignia, Vol. 2. LC 85-72269. (Illus.). 235p. 1986. pap. 28.95 (*0-9615456-1-5*) Aeroemblem Pubns.

— The Comprehensive Illustrated Guide to United States Air Force Pocket-Shoulder Insignia, Vol. 3. LC 85-72269. (Illus.). 235p. 1986. pap. 28.95 (*0-9615456-2-3*) Aeroemblem Pubns.

— The Comprehensive Illustrated Guide to United States Air Force Pocket-Shoulder Insignia, Vol. 4. LC 85-72269. (Illus.). 235p. 1987. pap. 28.95 (*0-9615456-4-X*) Aeroemblem Pubns.

— The Comprehensive Illustrated Guide to United States Air Force Pocket-Shoulder Insignia, Vol. 5. LC 85-72269. (Illus.). 238p. 1988. pap. 28.95 (*0-9615456-5-8*) Aeroemblem Pubns.

— The Comprehensive Illustrated Guide to United States Air Force Pocket-Shoulder Insignia, Vol. 6. LC 85-72269. (Illus.). 169p. 1989. pap. 28.95 (*0-9615456-6-6*) Aeroemblem Pubns.

— The Comprehensive Illustrated Guide to USAF Pocket - Shoulder Insignia Supplement 1. LC 85-872269. (Illus.). 230p. 1996. pap. 28.95 (*0-9615456-7-4*) Aeroemblem Pubns.

Polderman, J. W. & Willems, J. C. Introduction to Mathematical Systems Theory: A Behavioral Approach. Marsden, J. E. et al, eds. LC 97-20710. (Texts in Applied Mathematics Ser.: No. 26). (Illus.). 428p. 1997. 49.95 (*0-387-98266-3*) Spr-Verlag.

Polderman, Jan W., jt. auth. see Mareels, I.

Polderman, Jan W., jt. auth. see Mareels, Iven.

Poldervaart, Arie W. Black-Robed Justice. Cortes, Carlos E., ed. LC 76-1472. (Chicano Heritage Ser.). 1977. reprint ed. lib. bdg. 18.95 (*0-405-09519-8*) Ayer.

— Black-Robed Justice. LC 99-61458. (Historical Society of New Mexico Publications in History: Vol. XIII). xi, 222p. 1999. reprint ed. 75.00 (*1-56169-498-3*) Gaunt.

P

An Asterisk (*) at the beginning of an entry indicates that the title is appearing for the first time.

Poldinger, Walter & Wider, Francois. Index Psychopharmacorum. 7th expanded rev. ed. 334p. 1991. text 37.00 (*0-88937-072-9*) Hogrefe & Huber Pubs.
Pole. The Silent Road. 157p. 1960. pap. 11.95 (*0-85435-443-3*, Pub. by C W Daniel) Natl Bk Netwk.
Pole, Andy. Applied Bayesian Forecasting & Time Series Analysis. 416p. 1994. boxed set 73.95 (*0-412-04401-3*, Chap & Hall CRC) CRC Pr.
Pole, Christopher J. Implementing Records of Achievement. LC 92-18995. 176p. 1993. 123.00 (*0-335-09961-0*); pap. 34.95 (*0-335-09960-2*) OpUniv Pr.
Pole, Christopher J. & Chawla-Duggan, Rita, eds. Reshaping Education in the 1990s: Perspectives on Secondary Schooling. LC 96-221781. 208p. 1996. 79.95 (*0-7507-0528-0*, Falmer Pr); pap. 29.95 (*0-7507-0529-9*, Falmer Pr) Taylor & Francis.
Pole, Christopher J., jt. auth. see Chawla-Duggan, Rita.
Pole, J. R. Equality, Status, & Power in Thomas Jefferson's Virginia. (Foundations of America Ser.). (Illus.). 40p. (Orig.). 1986. pap. 9.95 (*0-87935-114-4*) Colonial Williamsburg.
— The Pursuit of Equality in American History. 2nd enl. rev. ed. LC 92-12928. 1993. 40.00 (*0-520-07987-6*, Pub. by U CA Pr) Cal Prin Full Svc.
Pole, J. R., jt. ed. see Greene, Jack P.
Pole, Timothy. Be Yourself: The No-Nonsense Guide to Living Effectively. LC 97-7504. 128p. 1997. pap. 9.95 (*1-86204-019-2*, Pub. by Element MA) Penguin Putnam.
Pole, Wellesley. A Man Seen Afar. 186p. 1983. pap. 7.95 (*0-85435-085-3*, Pub. by C W Daniel) Natl Bk Netwk.
Pole, Wellesley T. The Silent Road. 240p. (Orig.). pap. 17.95 (*0-8464-4290-6*) Beekman Pubs.
Pole, Wellesley T. & Lehmann, Rosamond. A Man Seen Afar. 128p. (Orig.). pap. 11.95 (*0-8464-4248-5*) Beekman Pubs.
***Polecritti, Cynthia.** Preaching Peace in Renaissance Italy: Bernardino of Siena & His Audience. LC 99-36513. 2000. 61.95 (*0-8132-0960-9*) Cath U Pr.
Poledna, Stefan. Fault-Tolerant Real-Time Systems: The Problem of Replica Determinism. (International Series in Engineering & Computer Science, Natural Language Processing & Machine Translation). 168p. (C). 1995. text 100.00 (*0-7923-9657-X*) Kluwer Academic.
Polednak, Anthony P. Racial & Ethnic Differences in Disease. (Illus.). 376p. 1989. text 59.95 (*0-19-505970-0*) OUP.
— Segregation, Poverty, & Morality in Urban African Americans. LC 96-27947. (Illus.). 192p. (C). 1997. text 39.95 (*0-19-511165-6*) OUP.
Polek, David & Anderhub, Rita. Advent Begins at Home: Family Prayers & Activities. 1979. pap. 3.95 (*0-89243-111-3*) Liguori Pubns.
Polelle, Mark. Raising Cartographic Consciousness: The Social & Foreign Policy Vision of Geopolitics in the Twentieth Century. LC 99-21214. 192p. 1999. 55.00 (*0-7391-0011-4*) Lxngtn Bks.
Polelle, Michael J. & Ottley, Bruce L. Illinois Tort Law, Issue 7. 2nd ed. 500p. 1999. ring bd. write for info. (*0-327-01084-3*, 8115914) LEXIS Pub.
Polelle, Michael J., jt. auth. see Ottley, Bruce L.
Poleman, Charlotte, jt. auth. see Peckenpaugh, Nancy J.
Poleman, Charlotte M., jt. auth. see Peckenpaugh, Nancy J.
Poleman, Horace I. Census of Indic Manuscripts in the United States & Canada. (American Oriental Ser.: Vol. 12). 1938. 45.00 (*0-527-02686-7*) Periodicals Srv.
Poleman, John. All the Famous Battles That Have Been Fought in Our Age. LC 68-54658. (English Experience Ser.: No. 64). 337p. 1968. reprint ed. 55.00 (*90-221-0064-2*) Walter J Johnson.
Poleman, Thomas T., jt. auth. see Ewell, Peter T.
Poleman, Thomas T., jt. auth. see Sharma, Rita.
Polemis, Aphrodite. From a Traditional Greek Kitchen: Vegetarian Cuisine. LC 92-18500. 192p. 1992. pap. 12.95 (*0-913990-93-0*) Book Pub Co.
Polemon, John. The Second Part of the Booke of Battailes, Fought in Our Age. LC 78-38219. (English Experience Ser.: No. 483). 196p. 1972. reprint ed. 20.00 (*90-221-0483-4*) Walter J Johnson.
Polen, Dallas A., Jr. Choice Guide: A Workbook for Arrangements at the Time of a Death. 145p. (Orig.). 1992. pap. 9.95 (*0-9634285-0-0*) Alljoy Res.
— Funeral Arrangement Choice Guide: A Workbook for Arrangements at the Time of a Death. 144p. 1994. pap., student ed. 11.95 (*0-9634285-1-9*) Alljoy Res.
Polen, Lynn. Cubs Brain Twisters. (Illus.). 160p. 1990. pap. 12.00 (*1-879216-00-0*) Stny Brook Prods.
Polen, Nehemia. The Holy Fire: The Teachings of Rabbi Kalonymus Kalman Shapira, the Rebbe of the Warsaw Ghetto. 232p. 1998. pap. 25.00 (*0-7657-6026-6*) Aronson.
***Polenberg, Richard.** The Era of Franklin D. Roosevelt, 1933-1945: A Brief History With Documents (The Bedford Series in History & Culture) 2000. text 35.00 (*0-312-22764-7*) St Martin.
— Era of Franklin Delano Roosevelt: 1932-1945. 2000. pap. text 11.95 (*0-312-13310-3*) St Martin.
— Fighting Faiths: The Abrams Case, the Supreme Court & Free Speech. LC 87-40042. 431p. 1999. pap. 18.95 (*0-8014-8618-1*) Cornell U Pr.
Polenberg, Richard. One Nation Divisible: Class, Race & Ethnicity in the United States since 1938. 1993. 25.25 (*0-8446-6676-9*) Peter Smith.
— War & Society: The United States, 1941-1945. LC 80-10734. (Critical Periods of History Ser.). 298p. 1980. reprint ed. lib. bdg. 69.50 (*0-313-22348-3*, POWS, Greenwood Pr) Greenwood.
— The World of Benjamin Cardozo: Personal Values & the Judicial Process. LC 97-2053. (Illus.). 320p. 1997. 29.95 (*0-674-96051-3*) HUP.
— The World of Benjamin Cardozo: Personal Values & the Judicial Process. 320p. 1999. pap. 19.95 (*0-674-96052-1*) HUP.
Polenske, Karen R. & Xikang, Chen. Chinese Economic Planning & Input-Output Analysis. (Illus.). 368p. 1992. text 80.00 (*0-19-585249-4*) OUP.
Polenton, Sicco. Sicconis Polentoni Scriptorum Illustrium Latinaelinguae Libri XVIII. Ullman, Berthold L., ed. LC 29-7429. (American Academy in Rome. Papers & Monographs: Vol. 6). 597p. reprint ed. pap. 185.10 (*0-608-16463-1*, 202672100051) Bks Demand.
Polentz, Lloyd M. & Hamelink, Jerry L. EIT Mechanical Review: For the Discipline Specific F.E. Exam in Mechanical Engineering. 2nd ed. (Illus.). 192p. 1999. pap. 29.95 (*1-57645-039-2*, 392) Engineering.
***Polenz, Peter Von.** Deutsche Sprachgeschichte Vom Spatmittelalter Bis Zur Gegenwart. 768p. 1999. 58.00 (*3-11-016426-4*); 40.00 (*3-11-014344-5*) De Gruyter.
Polenz, Peter Von. Geschichte der Deutschen Sprache. 9th ed. (Sammlung Goeschen Ser.: Vol. 2206). (C). 1984. 19.10 (*3-11-007998-4*) De Gruyter.
Polenz, Peter Von, see Von Polenz, Peter.
Poleo, Patty W. De, see Ferrer, Jami & De Poleo, Patty W.
Poleondakis, Regina. Before I Wake. LC 96-90065. (Orig.). 1996. pap. 14.95 (*0-533-11875-1*) Vantage.
Polese, Carolyn. Promise Not to Tell. LC 84-19767. (Illus.). 66p. (J). (gr. 3 up). 1985. 16.95 (*0-89885-239-0*, Kluwer Acad Hman Sci) Kluwer Academic.
Polese, James. Tales from the Iron Triangle: Boyhood Days in the San Francisco Bay Area of the 1920's. Polese, Richard L., ed. (Illus.). 96p. (YA). (gr. 6-12). 1995. pap. 9.95 (*0-943734-12-6*) Ocean Tree Bks.
Polese, Jean-Mari, jt. auth. see Lamaison, Jean-Louis.
Polese, Richard L. Discovering Dixie: The Best of the Deep South "Along the Magnolia Trail" LC 91-15728. (Adventure Roads Travel Ser.: Vol. 2). (Illus.). 208p. 2000. pap. 14.95 (*0-943734-31-2*) Ocean Tree Bks.
Polese, Richard L., compiled by. Prayers of the World. 96p. 2000. pap. 8.00 (*0-943734-00-2*) Ocean Tree Bks.
Polese, Richard L., ed. New Mexico's Book World: A Resource Guide. 2nd ed. 210p. 1999. pap. text 10.00 (*0-943734-37-1*) Ocean Tree Bks.
Polese, Richard L., ed. see Coates, Ruth A.
Polese, Richard L., ed. see Pinkerton, Elaine.
Polese, Richard L., ed. see Polese, James.
Polesetsky, Matthew, jt. ed. see Wekesser, Carol.
Polette, Doug, jt. auth. see Landers, Jack M.
***Polette, Keith.** Look Out! Letters Alive. (Illus.). 48p. 1999. pap. 8.95 (*1-880505-44-4*, CLC0228) Pieces of Lrning.
Polette, Keith, jt. auth. see Mallett, Jerry J.
Polette, Keith, jt. auth. see Polette, Nancy.
Polette, Nancy. The ABCs of Books & Thinking Skills: A Literature - Based thinking Skills Program. (Illus.). 144p. 1987. pap. 14.95 (*0-913839-61-2*, BL168) Pieces of Lrning.
— Activities for Any Novel. (Illus.). 112p. 1999. pap. 13.95 (*1-880505-39-8*, CLC0223) Pieces of Lrning.
— The Amelia Bedelia Thinking Book. 2nd expanded ed. (Illus.). 48p. 1984. pap. 7.95 (*1-879287-10-2*, BL020) Pieces of Lrning.
— Apple Trees to Zinnias: Research Reporting Patterns. (Illus.). 48p. 1992. pap. 7.95 (*1-879287-14-5*, BL024) Pieces of Lrning.
— Books to Begin On. (Illus.). 48p. 1994. pap. 7.95 (*1-879287-28-5*, BL038) Pieces of Lrning.
***Polette, Nancy.** Celebrating the Coretta Scott King Awards: 101 Activities & Programs. (Illus.). 100p. (J). (gr. 1-6). 2000. 16.95 (*1-57950-055-2*, Alleyside) Highsmith Pr.
— Concert Reading. 1988. pap. 7.95 (*1-880505-75-4*) Pieces of Lrning.
Polette, Nancy. Earthwatch: Booktalks & Activities. (Illus.). 48p. 1993. pap. 7.95 (*1-879287-26-9*, BL036) Pieces of Lrning.
— Eight Cinderellas. (Illus.). 48p. 1994. reprint ed. pap. 8.95 (*1-880505-57-6*, CLC0207) Pieces of Lrning.
— Enjoying Fairy Tales. (Illus.). 48p. 1991. pap. 7.95 (*0-913839-94-9*, BL004) Pieces of Lrning.
— Enjoying Tall Tales. (Illus.). 48p. 1991. pap. 7.95 (*1-880505-43-6*, BL199) Pieces of Lrning.
— Expanded First Research Projects. 2nd ed. (Illus.). 48p. 1991. pap. 7.95 (*0-913839-92-2*, BL002) Pieces of Lrning.
— Exploring Themes in Aesop's Fables & Picture Books. (Illus.). 48p. 1992. pap. 7.95 (*1-879287-12-9*, BL022) Pieces of Lrning.
Polette, Nancy. The Frog & Toad Thinking Book. 1982. pap. 7.95 (*1-880505-35-5*) Pieces of Lrning.
— Literature Based Spelling. 1993. pap. 7.95 (*1-880505-74-6*) Pieces of Lrning.
Polette, Nancy. Middle Ages: Learning Through Literature. (Illus.). 48p. 1994. pap. 7.95 (*1-879287-27-7*, BL037) Pieces of Lrning.
— Mother Goose's Animals. (Illus.). 128p. 1992. pap. 12.95 (*1-879287-13-7*, BL023) Pieces of Lrning.
— Multi-Cultural Literature: Books & Activities. (Illus.). 48p. (Orig.). 1993. pap. 7.95 (*1-879287-22-6*, BL032) Pieces of Lrning.
— Multicultural Readers Theatre Booktalks. 128p. 1994. pap. 12.95 (*1-879287-31-5*, BL041) Pieces of Lrning.
— Perfect Patterns for Reporting Fact & Fiction. (Illus.). 48p. 1998. pap. 8.95 (*1-880505-25-8*, CLC0213) Pieces of Lrning.
— Picture Books Strategies for a Balanced Reading Program K-3. (Illus.). 112p. 1998. pap. 13.95 (*1-880505-40-1*, CLC0224) Pieces of Lrning.
— Predicting the Future with the Wonderful Wizard of Oz. (Illus.). 48p. 1998. pap. 7.95 (*1-880505-27-4*, GGA2005) Pieces of Lrning.
— Readers Theater Booktalks: Novel Booktalks to Read & to Perform. 128p. 1992. pap. 12.95 (*1-879287-18-8*, BL028) Pieces of Lrning.
Polette, Nancy. Reading the World with Folktales. (Orig.). 1993. pap. 12.95 (*1-880505-60-6*) Pieces of Lrning.
Polette, Nancy. The Research Book of the Fifty States. expanded ed. (Illus.). 48p. 1991. pap. 7.95 (*1-880505-36-3*, BL013) Pieces of Lrning.
Polette, Nancy. The Research Project Book. 1992. pap. 12.95 (*1-880505-34-7*) Pieces of Lrning.
Polette, Nancy. Research Reports to Knock Your Teacher's Socks Off! (Illus.). 48p. (Orig.). 1997. pap. 8.95 (*1-880505-56-8*, CLC0206) Pieces of Lrning.
Polette, Nancy. Research Without Copying. 1991. pap. 8.95 (*1-880505-32-0*) Pieces of Lrning.
Polette, Nancy. U. S. Historical Fiction. (Illus.). 48p. 1990. pap. 7.95 (*0-913839-85-X*, BL194) Pieces of Lrning.
— U. S. History Readers Theatre. 48p. 1994. pap. 7.95 (*1-879287-30-7*, BL040) Pieces of Lrning.
— Ultimate Book Report Book: Book Reports that Teach Literature Skills. 2nd expanded ed. (Illus.). 48p. 1991. pap. 7.95 (*0-913839-95-7*, BL005) Pieces of Lrning.
— Walk in Their Shoes: Character Education for the Classroom. (Illus.). 96p. 1999. pap. 12.95 (*1-880505-47-9*, CLC0231) Pieces of Lrning.
Polette, Nancy, ed. Reading with Music. 2nd ed. (Illus.). 48p. 1992. pap. 7.95 (*1-879287-04-8*, BL014) Pieces of Lrning.
Polette, Nancy & Hamlin, Marjorie. Celebrating with Books. LC 77-3862. (Illus.). 184p. 1977. 25.00 (*0-8108-1032-8*) Scarecrow.
Polette, Nancy & Polette, Keith. Readers Theatre: From Fairy Tales, Fantasy & Myth. (Illus.). 48p. 1986. pap. 7.95 (*0-913839-56-6*, BL164) Pieces of Lrning.
Polette, Nancy J. Brain Power Through Picture Books: Help Children Develop with Books That Stimulate Specific Parts of Their Minds. LC 91-50976. (Illus.). 144p. 1992. pap. text 25.00 (*0-89950-708-5*) McFarland & Co.
***Polette, Nancy J.** Gifted Books, Gifted Readers: Literature Activities to Excite Young Minds. 310p. 2000. pap. 32.50 (*1-56308-822-3*) Libs Unl.
Poletti, Jacques, tr. see des Sagettes, Christiane.
Poletto, Cecilia. The Higher Functional Field: Evidence from Northern Italian Dialects. LC 99-20704. (Oxford Studies in Comparative Syntax). 240p. 2000. pap. 35.00 (*0-19-513357-9*); text 65.00 (*0-19-513356-0*) OUP.
Poletto, Vittoria Offredi, tr. see Maraini, Dacia.
Polevoi, Boris N. Story about a Real Man. LC 79-98870. 558p. 1970. reprint ed. lib. bdg. 75.00 (*0-8371-3993-7*, PORM, Greenwood Pr) Greenwood.
Polevoi, Rob. 3D Studio Max R3 in Depth. LC 99-44601. 1999. pap. text 49.99 (*1-57610-432-X*) Coriolis Grp.
Polevoi, V. Popular Encyclopaedia of Art, Vol. 1. (RUS.). 447p. (C). 1986. 160.00 (*0-7855-6472-1*, Pub. by Collets) St Mut.
— Popular Encyclopaedia of Art, Vol. 2. (RUS.). 432p. (C). 1986. 160.00 (*0-7855-6471-3*, Pub. by Collets) St Mut.
Polevoy, Savely. Geothermal Energy in the U. S. S. R. A Survey of Resources, Methodology, Geology & Use. Jones, Steven, ed. 144p. (Orig.). 1985. pap. text 75.00 (*1-55831-034-7*) Delphic Associates.
Polevoy, Savely & Waltz, James P. Concise Water Science & Engineering. LC 94-48014. (Illus.). 1995. pap. 24.95 (*0-412-05361-6*) Chapman & Hall.
— Concise Water Science & Engineering. LC 94-48014. (Illus.). (gr. 13). 1995. 49.95 (*0-412-05351-9*) Chapman & Hall.
Polewczak, J., jt. ed. see Greenberg, W.
Poley, Franklin W. Contact Conditioning. (Illus.). 256p. 1991. text 39.95 (*0-89876-182-4*) Gardner Pr.
Poley, Irvin C. & Poley, Ruth V. Quaker Anecdotes. (C). 1983. pap. 4.00 (*0-87574-033-2*) Pendle Hill.
***Poley, J. Ph.** Erohica: The Quest for Oil in Indonesia (1850-1898) LC 00-24141. 2000. write for info. (*0-7923-6222-5*) Kluwer Academic.
Poley, Michelle F. Mastering the Art of Communication: Your Keys to Developing a More Effective Personal Style. Scanlon, Kelly, ed. 132p. (Orig.). 1995. pap. 15.95 (*1-878542-34-6*, 13-0005) SkillPath Pubns.
— A Winning Attitude: How to Develop Your Most Important Asset! (Illus.). x, 80p. 1992. pap. 12.95 (*1-878542-28-1*, 12-0009) SkillPath Pubns.
Poley, Ruth V., jt. auth. see Poley, Irvin C.
Poley, Sue, ed. see Bonne, Dick.
Poley, Wayne, et al. Alcoholism: A Treatment Manual. LC 78-13455. 1979. text 25.00 (*0-89876-063-1*) Gardner Pr.
Poleyn, Richard, ed. see Haines, Leland M.
Polezhaev, L. V. Loss & Restoration of Regenerative Capacity in Tissues & Organs of Animals. Carlson, Bruce M., tr. LC 71-160029. 395p. 1972. 34.00 (*0-674-53920-6*) HUP.
Polfack, Robert L., et al. The Pain-Free Tryptophan Diet. 256p. 1987. 16.45 (*0-446-51317-2*); mass mkt. 3.95 (*0-446-34359-5*, Pub. by Warner Bks) Little.
Polfen, M. N. A Practical Guide to European Travel. 200p. 1981. pap. 7.95 (*0-934036-07-1*) PMF Research.
— A Practical Guide to Grand Opera. 200p. (Orig.). 1981. pap. 7.95 (*0-934036-08-X*) PMF Research.
Polgar, Agnes & Koczoh, Geza. Hungarian. LC 97-47533. (TravelWise Language Learning Ser.). (ENG & HUN., Illus.). 280p. 1998. pap. 8.95 (*0-7641-0382-2*); pap. 16.95 incl. audio (*0-7641-7107-0*) Barron.
Polgar, Antoine, ed. see Reed, Dolores M.
Polgar, L., et al, eds. Behaviour & Impact of Aphidophaga. (Illus.). 350p. 1991. 112.50 (*90-5103-064-9*, Pub. by SPB Acad Pub) Balogh.
Polgar, Laszlo. Chess: 5,334 Problems, Combinations & Games. (Illus.). 1104p. 1995. 29.98 (*1-884822-31-2*) Blck Dog & Leventhal.
— Mechanisms of Protease Action. 288p. 1989. lib. bdg. 225.00 (*0-8493-6901-0*, QP609) CRC Pr.
Polgar, Stephen & Thomas, Shane A. Introduction to Research in the Health Sciences. 2nd ed. (Illus.). 357p. 1991. pap. text 39.00 (*0-443-04363-9*) Church.
— Introduction to Research in the Health Sciences. 3rd ed. 1995. pap. text 36.95 (*0-443-05039-2*) Church.
Polgar, Steven, ed. Population, Ecology, & Social Evolution. (World Anthropology Ser.). (Illus.). x, 354p. 1975. 35.40 (*0-685-18668-7*) Mouton.
Polgar, Zsuzsa & Shutzman, Jacob. Queen of the Kings Game. LC 97-91528. (Illus.). 384p. (Orig.). 1997. pap. 24.95 (*0-9657059-7-8*) Compchess Consult.
Polge, Coral & Hunter, Kay. The Living Image. 192p. 1984. 40.00 (*0-7212-0634-4*, Pub. by Regency Pr GBR) St Mut.
Polhamus, Jean B. & Funai, M. Dinosaur Funny Bones. (J). 1980. 4.95 (*0-13-214536-7*) P-H.
Polhamus, Kristeen. Preparing Perfect Pianists. (Illus.). 75p. 1996. text 9.99 (*0-9659959-2-5*) K Polhamus.
Polheim, Karl. Die Lateinische Reiimprosa. (GER.). xxxiii, 31p. 1992. write for info. (*3-296-15010-2*, Pub. by Weidmann) Lubrecht & Cramer.
Polhemus, Allen V. Mohegan Indian Maps of Montville, Connecticut. (Illus.). 84p. 1993. 42.95 (*1-883009-00-6*) Nutmeg Pubs.
Polhemus, D. A. Systematics of the Genus Rhagovelia Mayr (Heteroptera: Veliidae) in the Western Hemisphere (Exclusive of the Angustipes Complex) (Thomas Say Publications in Entomology). (Illus.). 410p. 1997. pap. 35.00 (*0-938522-59-0*, ESATSP10) Entomol Soc.
Polhemus, Dan & Asquith, Adam. Hawaiian Damselflies: A Field Identification Guide. 122p. 1996. pap. 19.95 (*0-930897-91-9*) Bishop Mus.
Polhemus, Richard R., jt. auth. see Moore, Clarence Bloomfield.
Polhemus, Robert M. Comic Faith: The Great Tradition from Austen to Joyce. LC 79-24856. x, 408p. (C). 1982. pap. text 12.95 (*0-226-67321-9*) U Ch Pr.
— Comic Faith: The Great Tradition from Austen to Joyce. LC 79-24856. x, 408p. (C). 1996. lib. bdg. 36.00 (*0-226-67320-0*) U Ch Pr.
— Erotic Faith: Being in Love from Jane Austen to D. H. Lawrence. LC 89-20438. (Illus.). 376p. 1990. 35.95 (*0-226-67322-7*) U Ch Pr.
— Erotic Faith: Being in Love from Jane Austen to D. H. Lawrence. (Illus.). xii, 376p. 1994. pap. text 17.95 (*0-226-67323-5*) U Ch Pr.
Polhemus, Robert M. & Henkle, Roger B., eds. Critical Reconstructions: The Relationship of Fiction & Life. 370p. (C). 1994. 45.00 (*0-8047-2243-9*) Stanford U Pr.
Polhemus, Ted. Body Art, 1. 96p. (YA). 1999. pap. text 9.95 (*1-901881-24-5*, Pub. by Element MA) Penguin Putnam.
— The Customized Body. LC 96-67907. (Illus.). 120p. (Orig.). 1997. pap. 24.99 (*1-85242-522-9*) Serpents Tail.
***Polhemus, Ted.** Customized Body. (Illus.). 120p. 2000. pap. 25.00 (*1-85242-677-2*) Serpents Tail.
Polhemus, Ted. Streetstyle. LC 94-60281. (Illus.). 144p. 1994. pap. 19.95 (*0-500-27794-X*, Pub. by Thames Hudson) Norton.
— Style Surfing: What to Wear in the Third Millenium. LC 96-60190. (Illus.). 144p. (Orig.). 1996. pap. 22.50 (*0-500-27895-4*, Pub. by Thames Hudson) Norton.
Polhill. Flora of Tropical East Africa Aloaceae. 60p. 1994. pap. 28.00 (*90-6191-364-0*) Ashgate Pub Co.
Polhill, Dennis. Are Coloradans Fit to Make Their Own Laws? A Common Sense Primer on the Initiative Process. (Issue Paper #8-96 Ser.). 34p. 1996. pap. text 8.00 (*1-57655-152-0*) Independ Inst.
— Unfair Government Competition Against Small Business. (Issue Papers: No. 12-93). 24p. 1993. pap. text 8.00 (*1-57655-073-7*) Independ Inst.
— Utilities: Market Competition Is Coming. (Issue Paper #4-95 Ser.). 2p. 1995. pap. text 8.00 (*1-57655-142-3*) Independ Inst.
Polhill, Dennis, jt. auth. see Mueller, Stephen.
Polhill, Dennis, jt. auth. see Mueller, Stephen R.
Polhill, Diana. Flora of Tropical East Africa: Index to Collecting Localities. (Illus.). 398p. 1988. pap. 30.00 (*0-947643-09-5*, Pub. by Royal Botnic Grdns) Balogh.
Polhill, Edward. The Works of Edward Polhill. 360p. 1998. reprint ed. 29.95 (*1-57358-056-2*) Soli Deo Gloria.
Polhill, John B. Acts. (New American Commentary Ser.: Vol. 26). 576p. 1992. 27.99 (*0-8054-0126-1*) Broadman.
Polhill, R. M. Crotalaria in Africa & Madagascar. (Illus.). vii, 389p. (C). 1982. text 132.00 (*90-6191-090-0*, Pub. by Ashgate Pub Co) Balogh.
Polhill, R. M., ed. Flora of Tropical East Africa: Ebenaceae. 52p. 1996. pap. 16.65 (*90-6191-371-3*, Pub. by A A Balkema) Ashgate Pub Co.
— Flora of Tropical East Africa: Iridaceae. 92p. 1996. pap. 24.00 (*90-6191-372-1*, Pub. by A A Balkema) Ashgate Pub Co.
Polhill, R. M. & Raven, P. H., eds. Advances in Legume Systematics, 2 Pts., Pts. 1 & 2. (Illus.). 1050p. 1981. boxed set 60.00 (*0-85521-224-1*, Pub. by Royal Botnic Grdns) Balogh.
***Polhill, R. M. & Wiens, D.** Flora of Tropical East Africa: Loranthaceae. 128p. 1999. pap. 22.00 (*90-6191-383-7*, Pub. by A A Balkema) Ashgate Pub Co.
— Flora of Tropical East Africa: Viscaceae. 24p. 1999. pap. 10.00 (*90-6191-384-5*, Pub. by A A Balkema) Ashgate Pub Co.
Polhill, R. M., ed. see Nordal, I., et al.
Polhill, R. M., ed. see Phillips, S.
Polhill, R. M., ed. see Verdcourt, B.
Polhill, R. M., jt. ed. see Verscourt, B.
Poli, ed. Longman Political Pamphleteer. 48p. (C). 1997. pap. text 7.86 (*0-673-98329-3*) Addison-Wesley.
Poli, A. Applied Algebra, Algorithmics & Error-Correcting Codes. (Lecture Notes in Computer Science Ser.: Vol. 228). (Illus.). vi, 265p. 1986. 36.00 (*0-387-16767-6*) Spr-Verlag.
Poli, A., jt. auth. see Boothroyd, Geoffrey.

P

Poli, Bernard J. Ford Madox Ford & the "Transatlantic Review" LC 67-15880. 1967. 39.95 (*0-8156-2105-1*) Syracuse U Pr.

***Poli, Corrado.** Design for Manufacturing. (Illus.). 448p. 2001. 59.96 (*0-7506-7341-9*) Buttrwrth-Heinemann.

Poli, Corrado, jt. auth. see Dixon, John.

Poli, Costanza. Tuscany. (Places & History Ser.). (Illus.). 136p. 1997. 24.95 (*1-55670-533-6*) Stewart Tabori & Chang.

Poli, Doretta D. Beachwear & Bathing-Costume. (Twentieth Century-Histories of Fashion Ser.). (Illus.). 135p. 1996. 29.95 (*0-89676-200-9*, Costume & Fashion Pr) QSMG Ltd.

— Maternity Fashion. (Twentieth Century-Histories of Fashion Ser.). (Illus.). 119p. 1996. 29.95 (*0-89676-208-4*, Costume & Fashion Pr) QSMG Ltd.

Poli, Gianangelo, jt. auth. see Segatore, Luigi.

Poli, Giovanni De, see De Poli, Giovanni, ed.

***Poli, Giuseppe, ed.** Free Radicals in Brain Pathophysiology. (Oxidative Stress & Disease Ser.: Vol. 5). 555p. 2000. 195.00 (*0-8247-0317-0*) Dekker.

Poli, Guiseppe, et al, eds. Free Radicals: From Basic Science to Medicine. LC 93-16440. (Molecular & Cell Biology Updates Ser.). x, 528p. 1993. 138.50 (*0-8176-2763-4*) Birkhauser.

***Poli, Luigi De.** La Structure Memonique de la Divine Comedie: L'Ars Memorativa et le Nombre Cinq dans la Composition du Poeme de Dante. (Illus.). xii, 255 p. 1999. 40.95 (*3-906759-99-7*, Pub. by P Lang) P Lang Pubng.

Poli, P. A., et al, eds. Free Radicals in the Pathogenesis of Liver Injury: Proceedings of the Second Congress on Free Radicals in Liver Injury, Turin, Italy, 9-11 June 1988. (Advances in the Biosciences Ser.: No. 76). (Illus.). 330p. 1989. 120.00 (*0-08-037382-8*, Pergamon Pr) Elsevier.

Poli, R., et al, eds. Evolutionary Image Analysis, Signal Processing & Telecommunications: First European Workshop, EvolASP '99 & EuroEctTel '99 Goteborg, Sweden, May 28-29, 1999, Proceedings. LC 99-28996. (Lecture Notes in Computer Science Ser.: Vol. 1596). x, 225p. 1999. pap. 45.00 (*3-540-65837-8*) Spr-Verlag.

***Poli, R., et al, eds.** Genetic Programming: Proceedings of the 2nd European Workshop, EuroGP'99, Goteborg, Sweden, May 26-27, 1999. LC 99-28995. (Lecture Notes in Computer Science Ser.: Vol. 1598). x, 283p. 1999. pap. 52.00 (*3-540-65899-8*) Spr-Verlag.

***Poli, R., et al.** Genetic Programming: Proceedings of the Third European Conference, EuroGP 2000, Edingburgh, Scotland, UK, April 15-16, 2000. (Lecture Notes in Computer Science Ser.: Vol. 1802). x, 361p. 2000. pap. 62.00 (*3-540-67339-3*) Spr-Verlag.

Poli, Roberto, ed. The Brentano Puzzle. LC 98-71407. (Western Philosophy Ser.). 238p. 1998. text 63.95 (*1-84014-371-1*, Pub. by Ashgate Pub) Ashgate Pub Co.

— Consciousness, Knowledge, & Truth: Essays Presented to Jan Srzednicki for His 70th Birthday. LC 93-31426. 208p. (C). 1993. lib. bdg. 164.50 (*0-7923-2497-8*, Pub. by Kluwer Academic) Kluwer Academic.

Poliafico, Frank J. Emergency First Aid Care. 1996. pap., student ed. 32.60 (*0-89303-183-6*) P-H.

— Emergency First Care. 160p. 1995. pap. text 21.40 (*0-89303-181-X*) P-H.

Poliak, Gregory, ed. Vprok (To Profit From) 2nd ed. (RUS., Illus.). 100p. (Orig.). pap. 8.00 (*0-686-88508-2*) Silver Age Pub.

Poliak, Gregory, ed. see Aksyonov, Vassily.

Poliak, Gregory, ed. see Chayanov, A.

Poliak, Gregory, ed. see Khodasevich, Vladislav F.

Poliak, Gregory, ed. see Oleynikol, Nikolai.

Poliak, Gregory, ed. see Venedict, Erofeev.

Poliak, Gregory, ed. see Yanovsky, Vasily.

Poliakin, Raymond I. What You Didn't Think to Ask Your Obstetrician: Revised & Expanded. rev. expanded ed. 320p. 1994. pap. 14.95 (*0-8092-3658-3*, 365830, Contemporary Bks) NTC Contemp Pub Co.

Poliakoff, Gary A. The Law of Condominium Operations, 2 vols. LC 88-8150. (Real Property - Zoning Ser.). 1988. ring bd. 250.00 (*0-685-28164-7*) West Group.

Poliakoff, I. N., tr. see Fridman, A. M. & Polyachenko, V. I.

Poliakoff, I. N., tr. see Fridman, A. M. & Polyachenko, V. L.

Poliakoff, Michael B. Combat Sports in the Ancient World: Competition, Violence & Culture. 1995. pap. 17.00 (*0-300-06312-1*) Yale U Pr.

Poliakoff, Stephen. Close My Eyes. 102p. (Orig.). (C). 1991. pap. write for info. (*0-413-64920-2*, AO581, Methuen Drama) Methn.

— Coming in to Land. 103p. (C). 1988. pap. write for info. (*0-413-15430-0*, A0059, Methuen Drama) Methn.

— Favourite Nights & Caught on a Train. 96p. (C). 1988. pap. 8.55 (*0-413-50100-0*, A0088, Methuen Drama) Methn.

— Hitting Town & City Sugar. 134p. (C). 1988. pap. write for info. (*0-413-38880-8*, A0126, Methuen Drama) Methn.

— Playing with Trains. (Methuen Modern Plays Ser.). 106p. (Orig.). (C). 1989. pap. 9.95 (*0-413-62510-9*, A0433, Methuen Drama) Methn.

— Poliakoff: Plays One. (Methuen World Dramatists Ser.). 461p. (Orig.). (C). 1989. pap. 13.95 (*0-413-62460-9*, A0414, Methuen Drama) Methn.

— Polioakoff Plays 2, No. 2. 1995. pap. 15.95 (*0-413-68660-4*, Methuen Drama) Methn.

— Runners & Soft Targets. 112p. (C). 1988. pap. write for info. (*0-413-54150-9*, A0251, Methuen Drama) Methn.

— She's Been Away & Hidden City. (Methuen Screenplay Ser.). (Illus.). 189p. (Orig.). (C). 1989. pap. 13.95 (*0-413-52210-X*, A0399, Methuen Drama) Methn.

***Poliakoff, Stephen.** Shooting the Past: Three Television Films & Two Shorts. (Illus.). 149p. 2000. pap. 10.95 (*0-413-73140-5*, Methuen Drama) Methn.

Poliakoff, Stephen. Sienna Red. (Methuen Modern Plays Ser.). 106p. (C). 1992. pap. 10.95 (*0-413-66430-9*, A0633, Methuen Drama) Methn.

— The Summer Party. (Methuen New Theatrescripts Ser.). 59p. (C). 1988. pap. write for info. (*0-413-47600-6*, A0279, Methuen Drama) Methn.

— Sweet Panic/Blinded by the Sun. 1996. pap. 15.95 (*0-413-70700-8*, Methuen Drama) Methn.

***Poliakoff, Stephen.** The Talk of the City. LC 99-494742. 1998. pap. 10.95 (*0-413-72870-6*) Methn.

Poliakov, Leon. Harvest of Hate: The Nazi Program for the Destruction of the Jews in Europe. LC 74-110836. 338p. 1971. reprint ed. lib. bdg. 35.00 (*0-8371-2635-5*, POHH, Greenwood Pr) Greenwood.

— Harvest of Hate: The Nazi Program for the Destruction of the Jews in Europe. rev. ed. LC 78-71294. 1987. reprint ed. pap. 12.95 (*0-8052-5006-9*) Schocken.

— Harvest of Hate: The Nazi Program for the Destruction of the Jews of Europe. LC 78-71294. 350p. 1979. pap. 12.95 (*0-89604-006-2*, Holocaust Library) US Holocaust.

Poliakov, Leon & Sabille, Jacques. Jews under the Italian Occupation. LC 81-22202. 208p. (C). 1983. reprint ed. 35.00 (*0-86527-344-8*) Fertig.

Poliakov, Sergei P. Everyday Islam: Religion & Tradition in Rural Central Asia. Olcott, Martha B., ed. & intro. by. LC 91-20989. 170p. (C). (gr. 13). 1993. text 62.95 (*0-87332-673-3*) M E Sharpe.

Poliakov, Sergie P. Everyday Islam: Religion & Tradition in Rural Central Asia. Olcott, Martha B., ed. & intro. by. LC 91-20989. 170p. (C). (gr. 13). 1993. pap. text 34.95 (*0-87332-674-1*) M E Sharpe.

Poliakova, M. Poziadavky Na Prijimacie Skusky Pre Osemrocne Gymnazia - Slovensky Jazyk a Literatura (The Requirements for Admittance Examinations for 8-Year-Gymnasiums) (SLO.). 96p. 1996. pap. write for info. (*80-08-02476-3*, Pub. by Slov Pegagog Naklad) IBD Ltd.

Polian, A., et al, eds. Simple Molecular Systems at Very High Density. (NATO ASI Series B, Physics: Vol. 186). (Illus.). 449p. 1988. 135.00 (*0-306-43028-2*, Plenum Trade) Perseus Pubng.

Policastre, Patrick. Everybody's Got a Shoebox. pap. write for info. (*1-882204-48-4*) Wilde Pub.

***Policastro, Michael A.** Understanding How to Build Guitar Chords & Arpeggios. 224p. 1999. pap. 22.95 (*0-7866-4443-5*, 98287) Mel Bay.

Policastro, Michael A. Understanding How to Build Guitar Chords & Arpeggios. LC 93-85006. (C). 1993. pap. text 29.95 (*0-9637292-0-9*) Silvanus Pub.

Police Conditions of Service Committee. Minutes of Evidence of the Committee Appointed to Consider & Report Whether Any & What Changes Should Be Made in the Method of Recruiting for, the Conditions of Service of, & the Rates of Pay, Pensions, & Allowances of the Police Forces of England, Wales & Scotland. LC 70-156282. (Police in Great Britain Ser.). 1971. reprint ed. 72.95 (*0-405-03393-1*) Ayer.

— Report of the Committee on Police Conditions of Service. LC 76-156281. (Police in Great Britain Ser.). 1971. reprint ed. 21.95 (*0-405-03392-3*) Ayer.

Police Executive Research Forum Staff. Abortion Conflict & Violence: A Public Safety Perspective: A Symposium for Law Enforcement. (Illus.). 60p. 1999. pap. write for info. (*1-878734-64-4*) Police Exec Res.

Police Executive Research Forum Staff, jt. auth. see International City/County Management Association Staff.

Polich, J. Michael, et al. Training Readiness in the Army Reserve Components. LC 94-32569. 1994. pap. 15.00 (*0-8330-1586-9*, MR-474-A) Rand Corp.

Polich, Judith Bluestone. Return of the Children of Light: Inca & Maya Prophecies for a New World. 176p. 1999. pap. write for info. (*0-9671775-1-0*, Pub. by Linkage Pubns) Blessingway Bks.

***Polich, Judith Bluestone.** Return of The Children of Light: Incan & Mayan Prophecies for A New World, 1. 1999. pap. text 16.95 (*0-9671775-0-2*) Linkage Pubns.

***Polich, Laurie.** Creative Bible Lessons from the Old Testament: 12 Character Studies on Surprisingly Modern Men & Women. LC 97-32390. 128p. 1998. pap. 12.99 (*0-310-22441-1*) Zondervan.

Polich, Laurie. Facing Your Future. 64p. 1994. pap., teacher ed. 11.99 (*0-310-49171-1*) Zondervan.

— Help! I'm a Small-Group Leader! 50 Ways to Lead Teenagers into Animated & Purposeful Discussion. LC 98-22388. 96p. 1998. pap. 7.99 (*0-310-22463-2*) Zondervan.

Policoff, Stephen P. The Dreamer's Companion: A Beginner's Guide to Understanding Dreams & Using Them Creatively. LC 97-10256. (Illus.). 264p. (Orig.). (gr. 10 up). 1997. pap. 12.95 (*1-55652-280-0*) Chicago Review.

Policoff, Stephen P. & Catrow, David. Cesar's Amazing Journey. LC 99-19241. 32p. (J). (ps-3). 1999. 15.99 (*0-670-88753-6*) Viking Penguin.

Policy Coordination Study Group Staff. International Macroeconomic Policy Coordination. (Report Ser.). 46p. 1988. pap. 10.00 (*1-56708-071-5*) Grp of Thirty.

Policy Development & Review Department Staff. Private Market Financing for Developing Countries. LC 92-38191. (World Economic & Financial Surveys Ser.). vii, 80p. 1992. pap. 20.00 (*1-55775-318-0*) Intl Monetary.

Policy Research Project on Health Policy Issues in. Children's Health Care Policy Issues in Texas: Options for Financing Coverage. (Working Paper Ser.: Vol. 84). 54p. 1995. pap. 7.50 (*0-89940-562-2*) LBJ Sch Pub Aff.

— Children's Health Care Policy Issues in Texas Pt. 1: Options for Financing Coverage. (Working Paper: No. 84). 54p. 1995. pap. 7.50 (*0-614-10568-4*) LBJ Sch Pub Aff.

***Policy Research Project Staff.** Medicare Benefits for Recipients Living in Mexico: Proceedings of a Conference. (U. S. - Mexican Occasional Papers: Vol. 8). 166p. 1999. pap. 20.00 (*0-89940-580-0*) LBJ Sch Pub Aff.

— Three Technical Papers on a Research & Demonstration Waiver for Medicare Coverage in Mexico. (U. S. - Mexican Occasional Papers: Vol. 7). 79p. 1999. pap. 15.00 (*0-89940-579-7*) LBJ Sch Pub Aff.

Policy Studies Associates Staff. Issues in Establishing Skill Standards in 8 States. 20p. 1995. pap. write for info. (*1-884037-17-8*) Coun Chief St Schl Offs.

Policy Studies Associates Staff, ed. Introduction to Statistics (PS-26) rev. ed. (Illus.). 57p. (Orig.). (C). 1987. pap. text 9.50 (*0-936826-24-X*) PS Assocs Croton.

Policy Studies in Education Staff, jt. auth. see College Board Staff.

Policy Studies Organization Staff. Federal Lands Policy, 162. Foss, Philip O., ed. LC 86-14983. (Contributions in Political Science Ser.: No. 162). 228p. 1987. 57.95 (*0-313-25612-8*, FFB/, Greenwood Pr) Greenwood.

Polidori & Khalailii. English Phrasal Verbs in Japanese. 1991. pap. text. write for info. (*0-17-556098-6*) Addison-Wesley.

Polidori, John W. The Vampyre. LC 90-40020. 92p. 1990. reprint ed. 40.00 (*1-85477-053-5*) Continuum.

— The Vampyre & Ernestus Berchtold, or the Modern Oedipus. Macdonald, D. L. & Scherf, Kathleen, eds. (Illus.). 240p. 1993. text 45.00 (*0-8020-0506-3*); pap. text 17.95 (*0-8020-7465-0*) U of Toronto Pr.

— The Vampyre & Other Tales of the Macabre. Morrison, Robert & Baldick, Chris, eds. LC 97-915. (Oxford World's Classics Ser.). 312p. 1997. pap. 9.95 (*0-19-283291-3*) OUP.

— The Vampyre & Other Tales of the Macabre. Morrison, Robert & Baldick, Chris, eds. LC 97-915. (Oxford World's Classics Ser.). 312p. 2001. pap. 9.95 (*0-19-283894-6*) OUP.

— The Vampyre by Dr. Polidori. Adams, Donald K., ed. 1968. 12.50 (*0-910330-14-X*) Grant Dahlstrom.

Polidori, L. Cartographie Radar. 304p. 1997. pap. text 40.00 (*90-5699-051-9*) Gordon & Breach.

Polidori, Laurent. Cartographie Radar. (Universe de la Teledetection Ser.). 304p. 1997. text 80.00 (*90-5699-050-0*) Gordon & Breach.

Polidoro. Sports & a Physically Active Modern World. LC 99-38056. 218p. 1999. pap. text 39.00 (*0-205-27158-8*) Allyn.

Polier, Justine W. Everyone's Children, Nobody's Child: A Judge Looks at Underprivileged Children in the United States. LC 74-1698. (Children & Youth Ser.). 370p. 1974. reprint ed. 31.95 (*0-405-05975-2*) Ayer.

— Juvenile Justice in Double Jeopardy: The Distanced Community & Vengeful Retribution. 224p. 1989. 32.50 (*0-8058-0462-5*) L Erlbaum Assocs.

— The Rule of Law & the Role of Psychiatry. LC 68-12900. (Isaac Ray Award Lectures: No. 1966). 192p. reprint ed. pap. 59.60 (*0-8357-8312-X*, 203412400088) Bks Demand.

Polifka, Janine E., jt. auth. see Friedman, J. M.

Polifka, Janine E., jt. auth. see Friedman, Jan M.

Polifroni, E. Carol & Welch, Marylouise. Historical & Contemporary Perspectives on Philosophy of Science in Nursing: An Anthology. LC 98-15842. 352p. 1998. pap. text 44.95 (*0-7817-1201-7*) Lppncott W & W.

Polignac, Francois de, see De Polignac, Francois.

Poligrafa, Ediciones. Rufino Tamayo: 15 Etchings/Aguafuertes, 1979. (ENG & SPA., Illus.). 12p. 1979. pap. 15.00 (*0-8150-0010-3*) Wittenborn Art.

Polikanov, Sergei. Nuclear Physics in the Soviet Union: Current Status & Future Prospects. Jones, Steven, ed. 120p. (Orig.). 1984. pap. text 75.00 (*1-55831-035-5*) Delphic Associates.

Polikoff, Barbara G. Herbert C. Hoover: Thirty-First President of the United States. Young, Richard G., ed. LC 89-39946. (Presidents of the United States Ser.). (Illus.). 128p. (J). (gr. 5-9). 1990. lib. bdg. 21.27 (*0-944483-58-5*) Garrett Ed Corp.

— James Madison: Fourth President of the United States. Young, Richard G., ed. LC 88-24537. (Presidents of the United States Ser.). (Illus.). (J). (gr. 5-9). 1989. lib. bdg. 21.27 (*0-944483-22-4*) Garrett Ed Corp.

— Life's a Funny Proposition, Horatio. LC 91-28010. 112p. (J). (gr. 4-7). 1995. 13.95 (*0-8050-1972-3*, Bks Young Read) H Holt & Co.

— Life's a Funny Proposition, Horatio. (Illus.). 112p. (J). (gr. 3-7). 1994. pap. 4.99 (*0-14-036644-X*, PuffinBks) Peng Put Young Read.

— Life's a Funny Proposition, Horatio. (J). 1994. 10.09 (*0-606-05906-7*, Pub. by Turtleback) Demco.

— Riding the Wind. 89p. (J). (gr. 4-7). 1995. 14.95 (*0-8050-3492-7*) H Holt & Co.

— Riding the Wind. (J). (gr. 3-7). 1997. pap. 3.99 (*0-614-28896-7*, PuffinBks) Peng Put Young Read.

Polikoff, Barbara Garland. With One Bold Act: The Story of Jane Addams. LC 99-94785. (Illus.). ix, 250p. 1999. pap. 15.95 (*0-9670658-0-1*) Boswell Bks.

Polikoff, Joan, et al. Troika Vol. VI: Swimming Toward Birth; Across Roses; Death in Another Country. LC 95-62152. 96p. 1996. pap. 5.95 (*0-939395-21-5*) Thorntree Pr.

Polikov, Sheila, ed. see National Council of Jewish Women, Omaha Section St.

Polimeni. Cost Accounting. 3rd ed. 1991. student ed. 42.81 (*0-07-010555-3*) McGraw.

— Cost Accounting. 3rd ed. 1991. 57.81 (*0-07-010556-1*) McGraw.

Polimeni, Albert D. & Straight, H. Joseph. Foundations of Discrete Math. LC 84-23309. (Math). 400p. (C). 1985. mass mkt. 41.75 (*0-534-03612-0*) Brooks-Cole.

Polimeni, Carlos. Bukowski for Beginners. (Illus.). 192p. 1999. pap. 11.95 (*0-86316-285-1*) Writers & Readers.

***Polimeni, Ralph S.** Product Costing: Concepts & Applications. 3rd ed. (C). 1999. pap. 66.56 (*0-07-239084-0*) McGrw-H Hghr Educ.

Polimeni, Ralph S., et al. Cost Accounting: Concepts & Applications for Managerial Decision Making. 3rd ed. 1991. text. write for info. (*0-07-010553-7*) McGraw.

— Cost Accounting: Concepts & Applications for Managerial Decision Making. 3rd ed. (C). 1991. text 22.00 (*0-07-010559-6*) McGraw.

— Cost Accounting: Concepts & Applications for Managerial Decision Making. 3rd ed. (C). 1991. pap. text, student ed. 25.00 (*0-07-010554-5*) McGraw.

— Cost Accounting: Concepts & Applications for Managerial Decision Making. 3rd ed. (C). 1991. pap. text 42.81 (*0-07-836431-0*) McGraw.

— Schaum's Outline of Theory & Problems of Cost Accounting. 3rd ed. LC 93-23908. (Schaum's Outline Ser.). 340p. (C). 1994. pap. 14.95 (*0-07-011026-3*) McGraw.

Polin, Bonnie S. & Giedt, Frances T. The Joslin Diabetes Gourmet Cookbook: Heart-Healthy, Everyday Recipes for Family & Friends. LC 93-25887. (Illus.). 544p. 1993. 29.95 (*0-553-08760-6*) Bantam.

Polin, Bonnie S., jt. auth. see Giedt, Frances T.

Polin, Claire C. The Ap Huw Manuscript. (Wissenschaftliche Abhandlungen-Musicological Studies: Vol. 34). 1982. lib. bdg. 80.00 (*0-931902-13-4*) Inst Mediaeval Mus.

— Music of the Ancient Near East. LC 73-20879. (Illus.). 138p. 1974. reprint ed. lib. bdg. 49.50 (*0-8371-5796-X*, PONE, Greenwood Pr) Greenwood.

Polin, Daniel. Galapagos Galore. (ENG & SPA., Illus.). 100p. 1999. pap. write for info. (*0-9645795-2-9*) Light Words & Music.

— Let There Be Light, Words & Music. LC 95-94209. (Illus.). 153p. (Orig.). 1995. pap. 29.95 (*0-9645795-0-2*) Light Words & Music.

Polin, Gail K., ed. see American Institute of Certified Public Accountants.

Polin, Raymond. Plato & Aristotle on Constitutionalism: An Exposition & Reference Source. LC 98-71971. (Avebury Series in Philosophy). 346p. 1998. text 72.95 (*1-84014-301-0*, Pub. by Ashgate Pub) Ashgate Pub Co.

Polin, Richard A., et al, eds. Workbook in Practical Neonatology. 2nd ed. (Illus.). 496p. 1993. pap. text, wbk. ed. 55.00 (*0-7216-4292-6*, W B Saunders Co) Harcrt Hlth Sci Grp.

Polin, Richard A. & Ditmar, Mark F., eds. Pediatric Secrets: Questions You Will Be Asked on Rounds, in the Clinic, on Oral Exams. 2nd rev. ed. LC 96-29336. (Secrets Ser.). (Illus.). 550p. 1997. pap. text 39.00 (*1-56053-171-1*) Hanley & Belfus.

Polin, Richard A. & Fox, William W. Fetal & Neonatal Physiology. 2nd ed. LC 96-31628. 1997. write for info. (*0-7216-6017-7*, W B Saunders Co); write for info. (*0-7216-6018-5*, W B Saunders Co) Harcrt Hlth Sci Grp.

— Fetal & Neonatal Physiology, 2 vols., Set. 2nd ed. Fletcher, Judy, ed. LC 96-31628. (Illus.). 2496p. 1997. text 415.00 (*0-7216-6016-9*, W B Saunders Co) Harcrt Hlth Sci Grp.

Polin, Richard A., et al. Workbook in Practical Neonatology. 3rd ed. 475p. Date not set. pap. text, wbk. ed. write for info. (*0-7216-7986-2*, W B Saunders Co) Harcrt Hlth Sci Grp.

Polin, Zena L. & Gatward, Stephen G. The Pub, Club & Grub Guide to Washington, D. C. 3rd rev. ed. LC 95-69592. (Illus.). 173p. 1997. pap. 9.95 (*0-9647062-2-9*) Patmos Pr DC.

Polinard, J. L., et al. Electoral Structure & Urban Policy: The Impact on Mexican American Communities. LC 94-17978. (Bureaucracies, Public Administration, & Public Policy Ser.). (Illus.). 216p. (gr. 13). 1994. text 75.95 (*1-56324-348-2*) M E Sharpe.

Polinard, J. L., et al. Electoral Structure & Urban Policy: The Impact on Mexican American Communities. LC 94-17978. (Bureaucracies, Public Administration, & Public Policy Ser.). (Illus.). 216p. (gr. 13). 1994. pap. text 35.95 (*1-56324-349-0*) M E Sharpe.

Poliner, Rachel A. & Benson, Jeffrey. Dialogue: Turning Controversy into Community. 142p. 1997. pap. 16.00 (*0-942349-12-1*) Eductrs Soc Respons.

Poling, jt. auth. see Ortberg.

Poling, A. & Fuqua, R. W. Research Methods in Applied Behavior Analysis: Issues & Advances. (Applied Clinical Psychology Ser.). (Illus.). 352p. (C). 1986. 65.00 (*0-306-42127-5*, Plenum Trade) Perseus Pubng.

Poling, A., et al. Psychology: A Behavioral Overview. (Applied Clinical Psychology Ser.). (Illus.). 412p. (C). 1989. 45.00 (*0-306-43432-6*, Plenum Trade) Perseus Pubng.

Poling, Alan D. A Primer of Human Behavioral Pharmacology. (Applied Clinical Psychology Ser.). (Illus.). 262p. (C). 1986. 65.00 (*0-306-42186-0*, Plenum Trade) Perseus Pubng.

***Poling, Alan D. & Byrne, Thomas.** Introduction to Behavioral Pharmacology. LC 00-25399. 2000. write for info. (*1-878978-36-5*) Context Pr.

Poling, Alan D., et al. Fundamentals of Behavior Analytic Research. (Applied Clinical Psychology Ser.). (Illus.). 236p. (C). 1995. 51.00 (*0-306-45056-9*, Plenum Trade) Perseus Pubng.

Poling, Alan D., jt. auth. see Schlinger, Henry D., Jr.

***Poling, Bruce E.** Properties of Gases & Liquids. 5th ed. (Illus.). 2000. 115.00 (*0-07-011682-2*) McGraw.

Poling, Clark V. Kandinsky: Russian & Bauhaus Years, 1915-1933. LC 83-50760. (Illus.). 360p. 1983. 19.50 (*0-89207-044-7*) S R Guggenheim.

An Asterisk (*) at the beginning of an entry indicates that the title is appearing for the first time.

— Kandinsky - Unterricht Am Bauhaus: Farbenseminar und Analytisches Zeichnen, Dargestellt Am Beispiel Des Bauhaus-Archivs Berlin. Rump, Gerhard et al, trs. (ENG & GER., Illus.). 160p. (C). 1982. 109.00 (*3-921617-67-7*, Pub. by Knstvrlag Weingrtn) Intl Bk Import.

— Surrealist Vision & Technique: Drawings & Collages from the Pompidou Center & the Picasso Museum, Paris. (EMILOP Ser.: Vol. 8). (Illus.). 115p. (Orig.). 1996. pap. 29.95 (*0-9638169-7-7*) M C Carlos Mus.

***Poling, David & Wales, Ken.** Sea of Glory. 2001. 21.99 (*0-8054-5000-9*) Broadman.

Poling, David, jt. auth. see Marshall, George.

Poling, David, jt. auth. see Marshall, George N.

Poling, Debra & Sherbondy, Sharon. Super Sketches for Youth Ministry: Thirty Creative Topical Dramas from Willow Creek Community Church. 192p. (YA). 1991. pap. 12.99 (*0-310-53411-9*) Zondervan.

Poling, Doug, jt. auth. see Borders, Deryl.

Poling, E. Barclay, jt. ed. see Gough, Robert E.

Poling, Evangeline K. Welcome Home to Deering, New Hampshire. LC 78-808. (Illus.). 1978. 12.00 (*0-914016-48-2*) Phoenix Pub.

Poling, James N. Abuse of Power: Theological Problem. 1991. pap. 16.95 (*0-687-00684-8*) Abingdon.

— Deliver Us from Evil: Resisting Racial & Gender Oppression. LC 95-45088. 208p. 1996. pap. 19.00 (*0-8006-2904-3*, 1-2904, Fortress Pr) Augsburg Fortress.

Poling, James N., jt. auth. see Fortune, Marie M.

Poling, James N., jt. ed. see Neuger, Christie C.

Poling, Jerry. Downfield: Untold Stories of the Green Bay Packers. LC 96-29365. (Illus.). 276p. (Orig.). (YA). (gr. 9-12). 1996. pap. 14.95 (*1-879483-33-5*) Prairie Oak Pr.

Poling, Jim. Bringing up Baby. LC 97-158686. 100p. 1997. pap. 10.00 (*1-57566-147-0*, Knsington) Kensgtn Pub Corp.

— Kiss & Tell: The Movie Lover's Quotable Guide to Love & Marriage. 96p. 1997. pap. 10.00 (*1-57566-124-1*, Knsington) Kensgtn Pub Corp.

Poling, John. Painting with O'Keeffe. LC 99-10127. (Illus.). 184p. 1999. 24.95 (*0-89672-381-X*) Tex Tech Univ Pr.

***Poling, Judson.** Cover to Cover: Getting the Bible's Big Picture. (Bible 101 Ser.). 64p. 2000. pap. 4.99 (*0-8308-2063-9*) InterVarsity.

— Interpretation: Discovering the Bible for Yourself. (Bible 101 Ser.). 64p. 2000. pap. 4.99 (*0-8308-2065-5*) InterVarsity.

Poling, Judson, jt. auth. see Cousins, Don.

Poling, Judson, jt. auth. see Poole, Garry.

Poling-Kempes, Lesley. The Canyon of Remembering. 320p. 1996. 24.95 (*0-89672-363-1*) Tex Tech Univ Pr.

***Poling-Kempes, Lesley.** Canyon of Remembering. 320p. 2000. pap. write for info. (*0-89672-435-2*) Tex Tech Univ Pr.

Poling-Kempes, Lesley. Far from Home: West by Rail with the Harvey Girls. (Illus.). 32p. (Orig.). 1994. pap. 7.95 (*0-89672-330-5*) Tex Tech Univ Pr.

— The Golden Era: West by Rail with the Harvey Girls. LC 97-171307. (Illus.). 32p. (Orig.). 1997. pap. 8.95 (*0-89672-376-3*) Tex Tech Univ Pr.

— Harvey Girls: Women Who Opened the West. 252p. 1994. pap. 14.95 (*1-56924-926-1*) Marlowe & Co.

— Valley of Shining Stone: The Story of Abiquiu. LC 97-4621. 336p. 1997. 50.00 (*0-8165-1421-6*) U of Ariz Pr.

— Valley of Shining Stone: The Story of Abiquiu. LC 97-4621. (Illus.). 336p. 1997. pap. 24.95 (*0-8165-1446-1*) U of Ariz Pr.

Poling, Nancy W., ed. Victim to Survivor: Women Recovering from Clergy Sexual Abuse. LC 98-45514. 144p. 1999. pap. 15.95 (*0-8298-1323-3*) Pilgrim OH.

Poling, Sheila R., jt. auth. see Wheeler, Donald J.

Poling, Tommy H., jt. auth. see Kenny, J. Frank.

Polinger, V. Z., jt. auth. see Bersuker, Isaac B.

Polinskaya, Irene, jt. ed. see Arkhipov, Andrey.

Polinski, Roth. Psychology & A.I.D.S. Index of Modern Information. LC 88-47613. 150p. 1990. 47.50 (*1-55914-232-4*); pap. 44.50 (*1-55914-233-2*) ABBE Pubs Assn.

— Psychology of Perceptions: Index of Modern Information. rev. ed. LC 88-47983. 150p. 1991. 47.50 (*1-55914-486-6*); pap. 44.50 (*1-55914-487-4*) ABBE Pubs Assn.

Polinsky. An Introduction to Law & Economics. 144p. 1983. pap. 8.95 (*0-316-71277-9*, Aspen Law & Bus) Aspen Pub.

— Law & Economics. 2nd ed. 176p. 1989. pap. text 24.95 (*0-316-71278-7*, Aspen Law & Bus) Aspen Pub.

***Polio, Marco.** The Hole. LC 00-131486. 250p. 2000. 22.00 (*0-9700702-5-X*) Sugar Loaf.

Polioukhin, V. & Shevchuk, V. N. English Russian Military Dictionary, 2 vols., Set. 3rd ed. (ENG & RUS.). 1987. 195.00 (*0-8288-3968-9*, F39650) Fr & Eur.

Polioukhin, V., jt. ed. see Shevchuk, V. N.

Poliquin, Bud. Purely Poliquin: A Collection of 100 Writings. LC 94-21816. 1994. write for info. (*0-9629159-8-X*) Pine Tree NY.

Poliquin, Charles. The Poliquin Principles: Successful Methods for Strength & Mass Development. (Illus.). 160p. 1997. pap. 39.95 (*0-9662752-0-9*) Dayton Pubns.

***Poliquin, Charles.** Winning the Arms Race. Beldecos, Nick, ed. (Illus.). 90p. 2000. pap. 24.95 (*0-9701979-0-X*) CharlesPoliquin.

Poliquin, Charles, et al. Manly Weight Loss: For Men Who Hate Aerobics & Carrot-Stick Diets. (Illus.). 80p. 1998. pap. 19.95 (*0-9662752-1-7*) Dayton Pubns.

Polirer, Debra. Dark Voyage. 1998. pap. write for info. (*1-57553-936-5*) Watermrk Pr.

— Fields of Night. 1997. pap. 56.95 (*1-57553-585-8*) Watermrk Pr.

— The Invisible Woman. 1998. pap. write for info. (*1-57553-766-4*) Watermrk Pr.

— Secret Journey. (Orig.). 1997. pap. write for info. (*1-57553-463-0*) Watermrk Pr.

***Polirer, Debra.** Tales from the Tower. 1999. pap. write for info. (*1-58235-227-5*) Watermrk Pr.

Polis, Gary A., ed. The Biology of Scorpions. LC 84-40330. (Illus.). 614p. 1990. 95.00 (*0-8047-1249-2*) Stanford U Pr.

Polis, Gary A., jt. auth. see Brownell, Philip.

Polis, John. He Cutteth Out Rivers: Preparing for the Flow of God's Power in Your Life. 112p. 1996. pap. 7.99 (*1-884369-50-2*, EBED Pubns) McDougal Pubng.

— Take My Yoke upon You: Fulfilling Your 3 Dimensional Destiny in Christ. Nigh, Kepler, ed. LC 98-151356. 98p. 1997. pap. 7.99 (*1-884369-53-7*, EBED Pubns) McDougal Pubng.

Polis, M., ed. see Joint Automatic Control Conference Staff.

Polis, Michael, jt. auth. see Miller, Kirk.

***Polis, Michael P.** Systems Modelling & Optimization: Proceedings of the 18th Ifip Tc7 Conference. LC 98-52859. (Pitman Research Notes in Mathematics Ser.). 513p. (Orig.). 1999. pap. text 94.95 (*0-8493-0607-8*) CRC Pr.

Polisar, Barry Louis. Captured Live & in the Act. 1978. pap. 9.95 incl. audio (*0-9615696-9-7*) Rainbow Morn.

Polisar, Barry Louis. Dinosaurs I Have Known. (Illus.). 44p. (J). (ps-5). 1988. 9.95 (*0-938663-00-3*); pap. 4.95 (*0-938663-05-4*) Rainbow Morn.

— Don't Do That! A Child's Guide to Bad Manners, Ridiculous Rules & Inadequate Etiquette. (Illus.). 32p. (J). (gr. 2-6). 1995. reprint ed. 14.95 (*0-938663-20-8*) Rainbow Morn.

— Family Concert. 1990. 9.95 incl. audio (*0-938663-12-7*, 5161) Rainbow Morn.

— Haunted House Party. LC 96-103506. (Illus.). 32p. (J). (gr. 1-6). 1995. 14.95 (*0-938663-21-6*) Rainbow Morn.

— Noises from under the Rug: The Barry Louis Polisar Songbook. (Illus.). 208p. (J). (gr. k-6). 1985. 18.95 (*0-9615696-0-3*) Rainbow Morn.

— Peculiar Zoo. (Illus.). 32p. (J). (gr. k-5). 1993. 14.95 (*0-938663-14-3*) Rainbow Morn.

— The Snake Who Was Afraid of People. (Illus.). 32p. (J). (ps-2). 1993. reprint ed. 14.95 (*0-938663-16-X*) Rainbow Morn.

— Snakes! & the Boy Who Was Afraid of Them. (Illus.). 32p. (J). (ps-3). 1993. reprint ed. 14.95 (*0-938663-15-1*) Rainbow Morn.

— The Trouble with Ben. (Illus.). 32p. (J). (gr. k-5). 1992. 14.95 (*0-938663-13-5*) Rainbow Morn.

Polisar, Donna, et al. Where Do We Come From? What Are We? Where Are We Going? An Annotated Bibliography of Aging & the Humanities. LC 88-24578. (C). 1988. pap. 15.00 (*0-929596-01-3*) Gerontological Soc.

Polischuk, Darrin. Mountain Biking British Columbia: The Trail Guide & Inspirational Resource Book. 1996. pap. 24.95 (*0-9680342-1-7*) Okanagan Mtn.

***Polischuk, Pablo.** Poniendo los Puntos Sobre Lasies: Consideraciones Acerca del Liderazgo de Grupos. (SPA.). 1998. pap. 13.99 (*0-8297-0353-5*) Vida Pubs.

Polisensky, Josef V. Aristocrats & the Crowd in the Revolutionary Year 1848: A Contribution to the History of Revolution & Counter-Revolution. Snider, Frederick, tr. LC 79-14765. 245p. (C). 1980. text 21.50 (*0-87395-398-3*) State U NY Pr.

Polisevski, Dan, jt. auth. see Ene, Horia I.

Polish Academy of Science Staff. Poetic Potentials in Information of Astronomy. 1976. pap. 1.95 (*0-934982-05-8*) Primary Pr.

Polish Book Fair, HTP Staff, ed. see Kaluza, Jan.

Polish Book Fair, Inc. Staff, ed. see Choznacka, Dagmara.

Polish Book Fair, Inc. Staff, ed. see Kaluza, Jan.

Polish Book Fair, Inc. Staff, ed. see Kaluza, Jan & Kruppik, Blazej.

***Polish, Daniel F.** Bringing the Psalms to Life: How to Understand & Use the Book of Psalms. LC 00-8137. 208p. 2000. 21.95 (*1-58023-077-6*) Jewish Lights.

Polish, Daniel F., et al. Drugs, Sex & Integrity: What Does Judaism Say? LC 90-28763. (Illus.). (YA). (gr. 7-9). 1991. pap. 10.00 (*0-8074-0459-4*, 168505) UAHC.

Polish, David. Give Us a King: Legal-Religious Sources of Jewish Sovereignty. 1989. 20.00 (*0-88125-309-X*) Ktav.

Polish, David, ed. Maaglei Zedek: Rabbi's Manual. 263p. 1988. 12.50 (*0-88123-004-9*) Central Conf.

***Polish Institute of Arts & Sciences in America Sta.** Grafika Polska: Estampes Polonaises (Polish Prints, 1918-1939) (POL & ENG., Illus.). 250p. 2000. 49.95 (*0-7717-0552-2*, Pub. by McG-Queens Univ Pr) CUP Services.

Polish Institute of Arts & Sciences in America Sta. Studies in Polish Civilization: Selected Papers of the Polish Institute of Arts & Sciences in America, N. Y., 1966. Wandycz, Damian, ed. 1971. 9.00 (*0-940962-43-8*) Polish Inst Art & Sci.

Polishchuk, Alexandre Y. & Zaikov, Gennadi E. Multicomponent Transport in Polymer Systems for Controlled Release. (Polymer Science & Engineering Monographs). 1996. text 85.00 (*2-88449-160-0*); pap. text 44.00 (*2-88449-236-4*) Gordon & Breach.

Polishchuk, Alexandreya & Zaikov, Gennadi E. Multicomponent Transport in Polymer Systems for Controlled Release. (Polymer Science & Engineering Monograp Ser.). 240p. 1997. text 51.00 (*90-5699-593-6*); pap. text 27.00 (*90-5699-594-4*) Gordon & Breach.

Polishchuk, E. M. Continual Means & Boundary Value Problems in Function Spaces. (Operator Theory Ser.: No. 31). 180p. 1989. 76.00 (*0-8176-2217-9*) Birkhauser.

Polishook, Irwin H. Rhode Island & the Union, 1774-1795. LC 69-18021. (Studies in History Ser.: No. 5). 280p. reprint ed. pap. 86.80 (*0-8357-9469-5*, 201368100087) Bks Demand.

Polishook, Irwin H., jt. ed. see Judd, Jacob.

Polishuk, Peter. Life Is Good - Except for This Cancer. unabridged ed. Abramowitz, Adam, ed. (Illus.). 80p. 1996. pap. 9.95 (*1-56851-107-8*) Info Gatekeepers.

Polisky, Mildred K. Essentials of Math with Business Applications: Solving Problems on the Electronic Calculator. annot. ed. 1995. teacher ed. 48.65 (*0-02-805387-7*) Glencoe.

Polisky, Mildred K. Keeping Personal Financial Records. (General Business & Business Education Ser.). 1997. pap. 19.50 (*0-8273-6613-2*) Delmar.

— Solving Business Problems on the Electronic Calculator. 3rd ed. 256p. 1988. pap. text 13.48 (*0-07-041283-9*) McGraw.

— Solving Business Problems on the Electronic Calculator. 4th ed. LC 92-31248. 1993. 16.95 (*0-02-800417-5*) Glencoe.

— Using a Calculator: Solving Business Problems. 5th ed. LC 97-35068. 237p. 1998. pap. text 23.50 (*0-02-802559-8*) Glencoe.

Polisky, Mildred K. & Meehan, James R. Solving Business Problems on the Electronic Calculator. 2nd ed. 256p. 1983. text 16.56 (*0-07-041281-2*) McGraw.

Polit, Denise. Application Manual to Accompany Data Analysis & Statistics for Nursing Research. (C). 1996. pap. text 21.95 (*0-8385-6334-1*, A6334-5) Appleton & Lange.

Polit, Denise F. Data Analysis & Statistics for Nursing Research. LC 95-83509. 506p. 1996. pap. text 42.95 (*0-8385-6329-5*, A6329-5) Appleton & Lange.

— Essentials of Nursing Research: Methods, Appraisal & Utilization. 4th ed. LC 96-28545. 496p. 1996. pap. text 34.95 (*0-397-55368-4*); pap. text, student ed. 17.95 (*0-397-55369-2*) Lppncott W & W.

— Nursing Research. 5th ed. 304p. 1994. pap. text, student ed. 18.95 (*0-397-55139-8*) Lppncott W & W.

Polit, Denise F. & Berman, Judith. Just the Right Size: A Guide to Family Size Planning. LC 83-24534. 229p. 1984. 55.00 (*0-275-91744-4*, C1744, Praeger Pubs) Greenwood.

Polit, Denise F. & Hungler, Bernadette P. Accompany Nursing Research: Principles & Methods. 6th ed. 1998. pap. text, student ed. 17.95 (*0-7817-1563-6*) Lppncott W & W.

Polit, Denise F. & Hungler, Bernadette P. Essentials of Nursing Research: Methods, Appraisal, & Utilization. 5th ed. 544p. text 36.95 (*0-7817-2557-7*) Lppncott W & W.

Polit, Denise F. & Hungler, Bernadette P. Nursing Research: Principles & Methods. 5th ed. LC 94-30403. 720p. 1994. text 45.95 (*0-397-55138-X*) Lppncott W & W.

— Nursing Research: Principles & Methods. 6th ed. LC 98-39678. 768p. 1998. text 42.95 (*0-7817-1562-8*) Lppncott W & W.

Polit, Denise F. & Hungler, Bernadette P. Study Guide to Accompany Essentials of Nursing Research: Methods, Appraisal, & Utilization. 5th ed. pap. text. write for info. (*0-7817-2558-5*) Lppncott W & W.

Polit Status ECC Staff. Hale'Ta: I Manfayi Who's Who in Chamorro History. (Hale'-Ta Ser.). 250p. (J). (gr. 6-7). pap. text 30.00 (*1-883488-04-4*) Polit Status ECC.

Politakis, George. Modern Aspects of the Laws of Naval Warfare & Maritime Neutrality. LC 97-50129. (Illus.). xvi, 678 p. 1997. 161.50 (*0-7103-0589-3*, Pub. by Kegan Paul Intl) Col U Pr.

***Politano, et al.** Lifetime Physical Fitness. 2nd ed. 200p. (C). 2000. spiral bd. 29.95 (*0-7872-7303-1*) Kendall-Hunt.

Politano, Al. Complete Book of Chords, Scales & Arpeggios. (Illus.). 88p. 1989. pap. 8.95 (*1-57424-076-5*) Centerstream Pub.

— Graded Position Studies for Guitar. (Illus.). 51p. 1983. pap. 7.95 (*0-89898-218-9*) Centerstream Pub.

Politano, Colleen. Lost in the Woods: Child Survival for Parents & Teachers. LC 93-25700. (Illus.). 64p. 1993. reprint ed. pap. 6.99 (*0-934802-83-1*) Globe Pequot.

Politano, Colleen & Davies, Anne. Multi-Age & More. (Building Connections Ser.). 168p. 1994. pap., teacher ed. 19.00 (*1-895411-65-3*) Peguis Pubs Ltd.

Politano, Frank L., jt. auth. see Epstein, Michael A.

Politano, Frank L., jt. ed. see Epstein, Michael A.

***Polite, Frank.** Hyde. 124p. 1999. pap. 11.95 (*0-9626406-3-8*) Pangborn Bks.

Polite, Vernon & Davis, James, eds. African American Males in School & Society: Practices & Policies for Effective Education. LC 99-32817. 256p. 1999. text 54.00 (*0-8077-3871-9*); pap. text 23.95 (*0-8077-3870-0*) Tchrs Coll.

Politella, Sue, ed. see Ball, Patricia A.

Politella, Sue, ed. see Vivo, Pat.

Polites, George W. Precalculus Mathematics: A Study of Functions. (Illus.). 511p. (C). 1991. reprint ed. 83.00 (*1-878907-32-8*) TechBooks.

Politi, A., jt. ed. see Livi, Roberto.

Politi, Antonio, jt. auth. see Badii, Remo.

Politi, Giancarlo. Art Diary International 1995. 500p. 1995. pap. 25.00 (*88-7816-058-X*) Dist Art Pubs.

— Dictionary of Contemporary Artists 1995-1996. 400p. 1995. pap. 29.95 (*88-7816-067-9*) Dist Art Pubs.

***Politi Giancarlo Politi Editore Staff.** Art Diary International, 1999-2000, 1. 1999. pap. 30.00 (*88-7816-111-X*) Politi.

Politi, Leo. Song of the Swallows. (SPA., Illus.). 1996. pap. 4.99 (*0-689-80880-1*) S&S Childrens.

— Song of the Swallows. LC 49-8215. (Illus.). 32p. (J). (gr. 1-4). 1987. lib. bdg. 15.00 (*0-684-18831-7*) Scribner.

Politi, Leo. Song of the Swallows. 2nd ed. 1987. 10.15 (*0-606-02268-6*, Pub. by Turtleback) Demco.

Politi, Leo. Song of the Swallows. 2nd ed. (Illus.). 32p. (J). (gr. k-3). 1987. reprint ed. mass mkt. 4.95 (*0-689-71140-9*) Aladdin.

Politi, Marco, jt. auth. see Bernstein, Carl.

Politi, Michal, jt. auth. see Harel, David.

Politi, Stephen M., ed. Massachusetts Appellate Tax Board Reporter. 85.00 (*0-327-12433-4*) LEXIS Pub.

Political Behavior Program, Survey Research Center. American National Election Study, 1962. LC 76-5755. 1976. write for info. (*0-89138-000-0*) ICPSR.

— American National Election Study, 1966. 1977. write for info. (*0-89138-050-7*) ICPSR.

— American National Election Study, 1968. 1977. write for info. (*0-89138-061-2*) ICPSR.

Political Status Educ. Coordinating Comm. I Manfayi: Who's Who in Chamorro History, Vol. II. 250p. (J). (gr. 6-7). Date not set. pap. text 25.00 (*1-883488-06-0*) Polit Status ECC.

Political Status Education Coordinating Commission. Chamorro Tradition Values & Culture. LC 95-74981. (Hale'-Ta Ser.). 250p. pap. text. write for info. (*1-883488-05-2*) Polit Status ECC.

Politis. The Paramedic Review Manual. 3rd ed. 1992. pap. text 26.00 (*0-7216-5041-4*, W B Saunders Co) Harcrt Hlth Sci Grp.

***Politis, D. N., et al.** Subsampling. Bickel, P. et al, eds. LC 99-15017. (Series in Statistics). 376p. 1999. 79.95 (*0-387-98854-8*) Spr-Verlag.

Politis, Gustavo & Alberti, Benjamin. Archaeology in Latin America. LC 99-15661. 416p. 1999. pap. 39.99 (*0-415-22158-7*) Routledge.

***Politis, Gustavo & Alberti, Benjamin, eds.** Archaeology in Latin America. LC 99-15661. 304p. (C). 2000. text 125.00 (*0-415-13308-4*) Routledge.

***Politis, N.** The New Aspects of Interntional Law: A Series of Lectures Delivered at Columbia University in July 1926. LC 99-46126. 2000. write for info. (*1-57588-587-5*) W S Hein.

***Politis, Nicolas.** Neutrality & Peace. LC 99-45068. 1999. write for info. (*1-57588-579-4*) W S Hein.

Politis, Vasilis, ed. see Kant, Immanuel.

Polito, Jim. Life, Health & the Pursuit of Happiness. LC 97-30122. 1998. pap. 16.95 (*1-56072-466-8*, Nova Kroshka Bks) Nova Sci Pubs.

Polito, Robert. Detours. 1999. pap. write for info. (*0-679-77654-0*) Knopf.

— Doubles. LC 95-2818. (Phoenix Poets Ser.). 64p. 1995. pap. 8.95 (*0-226-67338-3*); lib. bdg. 20.00 (*0-226-67337-5*) U Ch Pr.

— A Reader's Guide to James Merrill's the Changing Light at Sandover. 280p. 1994. pap. text 17.95 (*0-472-06524-6*, 06524) U of Mich Pr.

— Savage Art: A Biography of Jim Thompson. LC 94-48455. 528p. 1995. 30.00 (*0-394-58407-4*) Knopf.

— Savage Art: A Biography of Jim Thompson. 543p. 1996. pap. 16.00 (*0-679-73352-3*) Vin Bks.

Polito, Robert, ed. see McCoy, Horace, et al.

Polito, Robert, ed. see Thompson, Jim, et al.

Polito, Ronald, ed. A Directory of Massachusetts Photographers 1839-1900. LC 92-62230. (Illus.). 605p. 1993. 89.50 (*0-929539-76-1*, 1176) Picton Pr.

Polito, Serafin. Gdzie Jest Moj Dom Rodzinny? (POL.). 70p. (Orig.). 1987. pap. text 6.00 (*0-930401-11-5*) Artex Pub.

Politoske, Daniel T. Music. 4th ed. (Illus.). 576p. (C). 1988. audio. write for info. (*0-318-62496-6*) P-H.

Politoske, Daniel T., ed. see Hoyoul, Balduin.

Politycki, Matthias. Umwertung aller Werte? Deutsche Literatur im Urteil Nietzsches. (Monographien und Texte zur Nietzscge-Forschung Ser.: Vol. 21). x, 447p. (C). 1989. lib. bdg. 161.55 (*3-11-011709-6*) De Gruyter.

Politz, Karl H. Die Verfassungen des Teutschen Staatenbundes Seit Dem Jahre 1789 Bis Auf die Neueste Zeit. (GER.). xxxiv, 1659p. 1998. reprint ed. write for info. (*3-487-10653-1*) G Olms Pubs.

Politzer, Adam. History of Otology. limited ed. Milstein, Stanley et al, trs. from GER. (Illus.). 324p. 1981. 115.00 (*0-9605972-0-4*) Columella Pr.

Politzer, Georges. Critique of the Foundations of Psychology: The Psychology of Psychoanalysis. Apprey, Maurice, tr. from FRE. LC 94-4139. 215p. (C). 1994. pap. text 22.50 (*0-8207-0257-9*) Duquesne.

— Critique of the Foundations of Psychology: The Psychology of Psychoanalysis. Apprey, Maurice, tr. from FRE. LC 94-4139. 215p. (C). 1994. text 54.00 (*0-8207-0256-0*) Duquesne.

Politzer, M. Mon Premier Dictionnaire l'Attrape-Mots-Hachette. (FRE.). 237p. 1980. 29.95 (*0-8288-1513-5*, M10420) Fr & Eur.

Politzer, P. & Murray, J. S., eds. Quantitative Treatments of Solute Solvent Interactions. LC 94-31159. (Theoretical & Computational Chemistry Ser.: 1). 380p. 1994. 261.75 (*0-444-82054-X*) Elsevier.

Politzer, P., jt. ed. see Seminario, J. M.

Politzer, R. L. & Urrutibeheity, H. N. Peldanos. LC 72-75117. 382p. (C). 1972. reprint ed. text 118.50 (*0-8357-9949-2*, 201362900086) Bks Demand.

— Peldanos: Workbook. LC 72-75117. 191p. (C). reprint ed. pap., student ed. 59.30 (*0-608-08295-3*, 201647600004) Bks Demand.

Politzer, Robert, et al. La France: Une Tapisserie. 2nd ed. (Illus.). 496p. (C). 1973. text 40.04 (*0-07-050384-2*) McGraw.

Politzer, Robert L. & Hagiwara, Michie P. Active Review of French: Selected Patterns, Vocabulary, & Pronunciation Problems for Speakers of English. LC 63-15633. 264p. reprint ed. pap. 81.90 (*0-8357-5088-4*, 205597800042) Bks Demand.

P

An Asterisk (*) at the beginning of an entry indicates that the title is appearing for the first time.

Polivanov, E. D. Selected Works: Articles on General Linguistics. Armstrong, Daniel, tr. from RUS. LC 73-83930. (Janua Linguarum, Ser. Major: No. 72). (Illus.). 386p. 1974. text 109.25 (*90-279-2693-X*) Mouton.

Polivanov, Konstantin, ed. Anna Akhmatova & Her Circle. Beriozkina, Patricia, tr. from RUS. LC 93-34633.Tr. of Anna Akhmatova i e e Okruzhenie. 286p. 1994. pap. 22.00 (*1-55728-309-5*); text 34.00 (*1-55728-308-7*) U of Ark Pr.

Polivanov, Konstantin, ed. see Ivanov, V. V., et al.

Polivanov, N. Dictionary Building Construction, German to Russian. 2nd ed. (GER & RUS.). 612p. 1996. 125.00 (*0-320-00506-2*) Fr & Eur.

Polivka, Georg, jt. auth. see Bolte, Johannes.

Poliziano, Angelo. Angeli Politiani Opera, 3 vols. in 2. xviii, 1406p. reprint ed. write for info. (*0-318-71606-2*) G Olms Pubs.

— Concordanza Delle 'Stanze' Di Poliziano. Rossi, Diego, ed. (Alpha-Omega, Series F, Italienische Autoren). xvi, 406p. 1983. write for info. incl. 3.5 hd (*3-487-06997-0*) G Olms Pubs.

— Prose Volgari Inedite e Poesi Latine e Greche Edite e Inedite. (Illus.). xxxv, 568p. 1976. reprint ed. write for info. (*3-487-06101-5*) G Olms Pubs.

— A Translation of the Orpheus of Angelo Politian & the Aminta of Torquato Tasso. LC 86-3172. 182p. 1986. reprint ed. lib. bdg. 55.00 (*0-313-25211-4*, LOTR, Greenwood Pr) Greenwood.

Polizoides, G. Short Stories for Young & Old. (GRE.). 1977. pap. text 3.00 (*0-685-81640-0*) Divry.

Polizzatti, Mark, tr. & intro. see Roche, Maurice.

Polizzi, Bernadette C. WCCN Wireless Handbook: RF Systems Integrators & Selected Software. 2nd ed. 208p. 1997. write for info. (*0-9638649-4-7*) WCCN Pubng.

Polizzi, Rick. Classic Plastic Model Kits: Identification & Value Guide. LC 96-200747. (Illus.). 352p. 1996. pap. 24.95 (*0-89145-701-1*, 4649) Collector Bks.

Polizzi, Tom. Event-Time Data Processing IDP: WCCN Wireless Handbook. (Illus.). 100p. 1994. pap. 39.95 (*0-945592-18-3*) Telecom Pubng.

— RF Terminals & LANS: WCCN Wireless Handbook. 2nd ed. (Illus.). 192p. 1995. pap. 39.95 (*0-945592-17-5*) Telecom Pubng.

Polizzi, Tom. WCCN Wireless Handbook: RF Terminals & LANs. 3rd ed. 182p. 1997. write for info. (*0-9638649-5-5*) WCCN Pubng.

Polizzoti, Mark. Revolution of the Mind: The Life of Andre Breton. LC 94-20166. (Illus.). 754p. 1995. 35.00 (*0-374-24982-2*) FS&G.

Polizzotti. Rimbaud: The Poet as Myth. Date not set. 37.50 (*0-8050-5746-3*) H Holt & Co.

Polizzotti, Mark, jt. auth. see Modiano, Patrick.

Polizzotti, Mark, tr. see Breton, Andre.

Polizzotti, Mark, tr. see Breton, Andre, ed.

Polizzotti, Mark, tr. see Chamoiseau, Patrick.

Polizzotti, Mark, tr. see Daumal, Rene.

Polizzotti, Mark, tr. see Dumas, Ann & Tinterow, Gary.

Polizzotti, Mark, tr. see Dumas, Ann, et al.

Polizzotti, Mark, tr. see Duras, Marguerite.

Polizzotti, Mark, tr. see Echenoz, Jean.

Polizzotti, Mark, tr. see Echnoz, Jean.

Polizzotti, Mark, tr. see Hoestlandt, Jo.

Polizzotti, Mark, tr. & intro. see Breton, Andre.

Polizzotto, Carolyn. Chrysalis. LC 99-165269. 1998. pap. 19.95 (*1-86368-226-0*, Pub. by Fremantle Arts) Intl Spec Bk.

Polizzotto, Lorenzo. The Elect Nation: The Savonarolan Movement in Florence, 1494-1545. LC 93-31942. (Oxford-Warburg Studies). 502p. 1995. text 90.00 (*0-19-920600-7*, Clarendon Pr) OUP.

Poljakoff-Mayber, A., jt. auth. see Mayer, A. M.

***Poljakov, Romualda.** Mit Aufrichtiger Feder Meist Gegenwartig Aufgezeichnet: RU & Beta; Landberichte Deutscher Reisender Vom 16, Bis Zum 19, Jahrhundert. (Deutsch-Russische Literaturbeziehungen - Forschungen und Materialien Ser.). 218p. 1999. 37.95 (*3-631-34921-1*) P Lang Pubng.

Poljanec, Miroslav. The Zagreb, Croatia Solists, 1954-1984. 104p. 1985. 10.00 (*0-918660-87-4*) Ragusan Pr.

Polk, ed. see Faulkner, William.

Polk, Barbara, ed. see Douglass, Janet.

Polk, Benjamin. Building for South Asia: An Architectural Autobiography. (C). 1993. 49.00 (*81-7017-300-0*, Pub. by Abhinav) S Asia.

Polk, Benjamin & Polk, Emily. India Notebook: Two Americans in the South Asia of Nehru's Time. LC 86-7229. (Illus.). 182p. 1987. reprint ed. 12.95 (*0-931228-13-1*) Arts & Arch.

Polk, Benjamin, jt. auth. see Seneviratna, Anuradha.

Polk, Betty J., jt. auth. see Abbott, Marti.

Polk, Charles & Postow, Elliot. Handbook of Biological Effects of Electromagnetic Fields. 512p. 1986. 295.00 (*0-8493-3265-6*, QP82) CRC Pr.

Polk, Charles & Postow, Elliot, eds. Handbook of Biological Effects of Electromagnetic Fields. 2nd ed. 640p. 1995. boxed set 159.95 (*0-8493-0641-8*, 641C2W) CRC Pr.

Polk County Historical Society Staff. Polk County. LC 98-85880. (Images of America Ser.). (Illus.). 128p. 1998. pap. 16.99 (*0-7524-0882-8*) Arcadia Publng.

Polk, David P. If Only I Had Known: Dramatic Monologues for Advent & Lent. 96p. (Orig.). 1994. pap. 9.99 (*0-8272-1611-4*) Chalice Pr.

— On the Way to God: An Exploration into the Theology of Wolfhart Pannenberg. LC 88-27871. 350p. (C). 1989. lib. bdg. 46.00 (*0-8191-7229-4*) U Pr of Amer.

Polk, David P., ed. Now What's a Christian to Do? 160p. (Orig.). 1993. pap. 10.99 (*0-8272-2510-5*) Chalice Pr.

— You Might Be a Disciple If . . . LC 97-17866. 56p. (Orig.). 1997. pap. 5.00 (*0-8272-4406-1*) Chalice Pr.

Polk, David P., jt. ed. see Bishop, Marsha B.

Polk, David P., jt. ed. see Campbell, Joan.

Polk, David P., jt. ed. see Merrick, Daniel B.

Polk, Dean L. Guide de Preparation a l'Examen Pour Fondements du Service a la Clientele: ACS 100. Basarich, Joel V. & Duisit, Vivian, eds. (Associate, Customer Service Program Ser.). (FRE.). 104p. (C). 1994. pap. text 22.00 (*0-939921-54-5*, Pub. by Life Office) PBD Inc.

***Polk, Dean L., et al.** Guia de Preparacion: Principios del Seguro de Vida, Salud y Rentas Vitalicias. Vallenilla, Ines, ed. (PFSL Insurance Education Program Ser.). (SPA.). 259p. (C). 1998. pap. write for info. (*1-57974-017-0*, Pub. by Life Office) PBD Inc.

Polk, Debbie, ed. see Clabough, Jean.

Polk, Dora B. The Island of California: A History of the Myth. LC 95-603. (Illus.). 399p. 1995. pap. 15.00 (*0-8032-8741-0*, Bison Books) U of Nebr Pr.

Polk, Emily, jt. auth. see Polk, Benjamin.

Polk, Hiram C., Jr., et al. Basic Surgery. 5th ed. (Illus.). 1021p. 1995. pap. 48.00 (*0-942219-74-0*) Quality Med Pub.

Polk, Irwin J. All about Asthma: Stop Suffering & Start Living. LC 96-49124. (Illus.). 252p. (C). 1997. 27.95 (*0-306-45569-2*, Plen Insight); pap. 17.95 (*0-306-45570-6*, Plen Insight) Perseus Pubng.

Polk, Jacqueline K., jt. auth. see Pasch, Brian.

Polk, James K. Polk: The Diary of a Presidency, 1845-1849, Covering the Mexican War, the Acquisition of Oregon, & the Conquest of California & the Southwest. (American Biography Ser.). 412p. 1991. reprint ed. lib. bdg. 89.00 (*0-7812-8318-3*) Rprt Serv.

Polk, Judd. Sterling: Its Meaning in World Finance. Wilkins, Mira, ed. LC 78-3945. (International Finance Ser.). (Illus.). 1979. reprint ed. lib. bdg. 29.95 (*0-405-11245-9*) Ayer.

Polk, Kenneth. When Men Kill: Scenarios of Masculine Violence. LC 94-8969. (Illus.). 230p. (C). 1994. text 59.95 (*0-521-46267-3*) Cambridge U Pr.

Polk, Kenneth, jt. auth. see Eaton, Joseph W.

Polk, Lee T. ERISA Practice & Litigation. 1993. 210.00 (*0-318-72272-0*) West Group.

Polk, N., ed. see Faulkner, William.

Polk, Noel. Children of the Dark House. 2nd ed. (Illus.). 288p. 1998. reprint ed. pap. 18.00 (*1-57806-103-2*) U Pr of Miss.

— Children of the Dark House: Text & Context in Faulkner. 2nd ed. LC 95-39505. 288p. 1998. reprint ed. 37.50 (*0-87805-867-2*) U Pr of Miss.

— Eudora Welty: A Bibliography of Her Work. (Illus.), 450p. 1993. text 65.00 (*0-87805-566-5*) U Pr of Miss.

— Faulkner's Requiem for a Nun: A Critical Study. LC 80-8099. 286p. reprint ed. pap. 88.70 (*0-7837-1759-8*, 205729500024) Bks Demand.

— Outside the Southern Myth. LC 96-50045. 1997. 45.00 (*0-87805-979-2*); pap. 17.00 (*0-87805-980-6*) U Pr of Miss.

Polk, Noel, ed. New Essays on "The Sound & the Fury" LC 93-568. (American Novel Ser.). 192p. (C). 1993. text 34.95 (*0-521-45114-0*); pap. text 15.95 (*0-521-45734-3*) Cambridge U Pr.

Polk, Noel, jt. auth. see Ross, Stephen.

Polk, Noel, jt. auth. see Ross, Stephen M.

Polk, Noel, ed. see Faulkner, William.

Polk, Patrick A. Haitian Vodou Flags. LC 97-14002. (Folk Art & Artists Ser.). (Illus.). 72p. 1998. 22.50 (*1-57806-024-9*) U Pr of Miss.

Polk, Patrick A., jt. auth. see Correll, Timothy C.

Polk, Patrick Arthur, jt. auth. see Correll, Timothy Corrigan.

Polk, Ralph Weiss. Practice of Printing, 1971. 1986. 19.96 (*0-02-665410-5*) Macmillan.

Polk, Stella G. For All Those Pupils Whose Lives Touched Mine. LC 88-29359. (Wardlaw Book Ser.). 104p. 1989. 16.95 (*0-89096-405-X*) Tex A&M Univ Pr.

Polk, Tim, ed. see Hathaway, Patti.

Polk, Timothy. The Biblical Kierkegaard: Reading by the Rule of Faith. LC 97-25261. 224p. (Orig.). 1997. pap. text 21.95 (*0-86554-539-1*, MUP/P157) Mercer Univ Pr.

Polk, Timothy. The Prophetic Persona: Jeremiah & the Language of the Self. (JSOT Supplement Ser.: No. 32). 1984. 70.00 (*0-905774-70-1*, Pub. by Sheffield Acad); pap. 23.75 (*0-905774-71-X*, Pub. by Sheffield Acad) CUP Services.

Polk, Timothy W. How to Outlive Your Lifetime! Preserving a Place in Your Family's Hearts & History. LC 94-8759. 133p. 1994. 10.95 (*0-9640587-0-7*) Fam Life Intl.

Polk, Vanessa W. Mender of My Broken Wings: An Allergy of Thanksgiving & Appreciation. (Illus.). 65p. 1997. per. 3.00 (*0-9661134-0-3*) Creat Pub.

Polk, W. Harrison. Polk Family & Kinsmen. (Illus.). 742p. 1994. reprint ed. pap. 105.00 (*0-8328-4280-X*); reprint ed. lib. bdg. 115.00 (*0-8328-4279-6*) Higginson Bk Co.

Polk, W. Timothy. Automated Tools for Testing Computer System Vulnerability. 35p. (Orig.). (C). 1993. pap. text 40.00 (*0-7881-0043-2*) DIANE Pub.

Polk, W. Timothy & Bassham, Lawrence E., III. A Guide to the Selection of Anti-Virus Tools & Techniques. 43p. (Orig.). (C). 1993. pap. text 30.00 (*0-7881-0384-9*) DIANE Pub.

Polk, W. Timothy, et al. Anti-Virus Tools & Techniques for Computer Systems. LC 94-31166. (Advanced Computing & Telecommunications Ser.). (Illus.). 79p. 1995. 24.00 (*0-8155-1364-X*) Noyes.

Polk, William H., et al. Polk Family & Kinsmen. 279p. 1993. 34.95 (*1-56869-036-3*); pap. 23.95 (*1-56869-037-1*) Oldbuck Pr.

Polk, William R. The Arab World Today. (Illus.). 480p. 1991. pap. text 15.95 (*0-674-04320-0*, POLARY) HUP.

— Arab World Today. (Illus.). 480p. 1991. 52.95 (*0-674-04319-7*) HUP.

— Neighbors & Strangers: The Fundamentals of Foreign Affairs. LC 97-2353. 366p. 1997. 24.95 (*0-226-67329-4*) U Ch Pr.

— The Opening of South Lebanon, 1788-1840: A Study of the Impact of the West on the Middle East. LC 63-13815. (Harvard Middle Eastern Studies: No. 8). 319p. reprint ed. pap. 98.90 (*0-608-30368-2*, 200601900054) Bks Demand.

***Polk, William R.** Polk's Folly: An American Family History. LC 99-24552. (Illus.). 544p. 2000. 29.95 (*0-385-49150-6*) Doubleday.

Polk, William R., ed. see Baer, Gabriel.

Polk, William R., ed. see Conference on the Beginnings of Modernization in t.

Polk, William R., ed. see Coulson, Noel J.

Polk, William R., ed. see Issawi1, Charles P.

Polk, William R., ed. see Stetkevych, Jaroslav.

Polke, M., ed. see Epple, V. & Helm, M.

Polke, Sigmar. Vanishing Picture. 220p. 1996. 85.00 (*1-881616-65-7*, Pub. by Scalo Pubs) Dist Art Pubs.

Polkey, C. E., jt. ed. see Schurr, Peter H.

Polkey, Donnell. Representing Lives C. LC 99-55929. 1999. text 65.00 (*0-312-22667-5*) St Martin.

***Polkey, Pauline.** Women's Lives into Print: The Theory, Practice & Writing of Feminist Auto/biography. LC 99-18158. 1999. text 59.95 (*0-312-22352-8*) St Martin.

Polking. Differential Equations. 2001. 20.00 (*0-13-598137-9*) P-H.

Polking, Kirk. Oceanographers & Explorers of the Sea. LC 98-36135. (Collective Biographies Ser.). 128p. (YA). (gr. 6 up). 1999. lib. bdg. 20.95 (*0-7660-1113-5*) Enslow Pubs.

— Writing Family Histories & Memoirs. 272p. 1995. pap. 14.99 (*1-55870-394-2*, Betrwy Bks) F & W Pubns Inc.

Polking, Kirk, jt. ed. see Writer's Digest Magazine Editors.

***Polkinghome, John & Welker, Michael, eds.** The End of the World & the Ends of God: Science & Theology on Eschatology. LC 99-58543. 2000. pap. 27.00 (*1-56338-312-8*) TPI PA.

Polkinghorn, Bette & Thomson, Dorothy L. Adam Smith's Daughters: Eight Prominent Women Economists from the Eighteenth Century to the Present. LC 98-22239. 144p. 1999. 60.00 (*1-85898-084-4*) E Elgar.

Polkinghorn, Donald E. Methodology for the Human Sciences: Systems of Inquiry. LC 82-5895. (SUNY Series in Transpersonal & Humanistic Psychology). 349p. (C). 1984. text 49.50 (*0-87395-663-X*) State U NY Pr.

Polkinghorn, Philip K., jt. auth. see Tullis, Mark A.

Polkinghorne, Donald E. Methodology for the Human Sciences: Systems of Inquiry. LC 82-5895. (SUNY Series in Transpersonal & Humanistic Psychology). 349p. (C). 1984. pap. text 16.95 (*0-87395-664-8*) State U NY Pr.

— Narrative Knowing & the Human Sciences. LC 87-17992. (SUNY Series in the Philosophy of the Social Sciences). 232p. (C). 1988. pap. text 19.95 (*0-88706-623-2*) State U NY Pr.

***Polkinghorne, J. C.** Faith, Science & Understanding. LC 00-26934. 224p. 2000. 19.95 (*0-300-08372-6*) Yale U Pr.

Polkinghorne, J. C. Polkinghor Quantum World. LC 83-9411. (Illus.). 112p. 1984. text 14.95 (*0-582-44682-1*) Longman.

— The Quantum World. LC 84-42953. 112p. 1985. pap. 10.95 (*0-691-02388-3*, Pub. by Princeton U Pr) Cal Prin Full Svc.

Polkinghorne, John. Beyond Science: The Wider Human Context. (Canto Book Ser.). 143p. (C). 1998. pap. 11.95 (*0-521-62508-4*) Cambridge U Pr.

— The Faith of a Physicist: Reflections of a Bottom-Up Thinker. (Theology & the Sciences Ser.). 208p. 1996. pap. 18.00 (*0-8006-2970-1*, 1-2970, Fortress Pr) Augsburg Fortress.

— The Faith of a Physicist: Reflections of a Bottom-Up Thinker - The Gifford Lectures for 1993-4. LC 93-41071. 224p. 1994. text 29.95 (*0-691-03620-9*, Pub. by Princeton U Pr) Cal Prin Full Svc.

— One World: The Interaction of Science & Theology. 128p. 1987. pap. text 13.95 (*0-691-02407-3*, Pub. by Princeton U Pr) Cal Prin Full Svc.

— Quarks, Chaos, & Christianity: Questions to Science & Religion. LC 95-30120. 120p. 1995. pap. 12.95 (*0-8245-1521-8*) Crossroad NY.

— Reason & Reality: The Relationship Between Science & Theology. LC 91-23518. 128p. (C). 1991. pap. 14.00 (*1-56338-019-6*) TPI PA.

— Science & Theology: An Introduction. LC 98-229115. 176p. 1999. pap. text 19.00 (*0-8006-3153-6*, 1-3153, Fortress Pr) Augsburg Fortress.

— Searching for Truth: Lenten Meditations on Science & Faith. LC 96-45191. 160p. 1996. pap. 12.95 (*0-8245-1655-9*) Crossroad NY.

— Serious Talk: Science & Religion in Dialogue. LC 95-6976. 128p. 1995. pap. 14.00 (*1-56338-109-5*) TPI PA.

***Polkinghorne, John C.** Belief in God in an Age of Science. LC 97-30508. (The Terry Lectures). 160p. 1998. 22.00 (*0-300-07294-5*) Yale U Pr.

— Belief in God in an Age of Science. LC 97-30508. 160p. 1999. pap. text 9.95 (*0-300-08003-4*) Yale U Pr.

Polkinghorne, John C. The Way the World Is. LC 84-1527. 140p. reprint ed. 43.40 (*0-608-16754-1*, 202754900055) Bks Demand.

Polkinghorne, John C. & Arnold, David. Ordinary Differential Equations Using Matlab. 2nd ed. LC 99-462614. (C). 1999. pap. text 15.00 (*0-13-011381-6*) P-H.

***Polkinhorn, Harry.** Blue Shift. 132p. 1999. pap. 10.00 (*0-9663224-5-2*, Pub. by Ex Hihilo) SPD-Small Pr Dist.

Polkinhorn, Harry. Mount Soledad. (Illus.). 112p. (Orig.). 1996. pap. 9.00 (*1-880516-19-5*) Left Hand Bks.

— Summary Dissolution. (Illus.). 58p. (Orig.). 1988. pap. 3.00 (*0-926935-06-2*) Runaway Spoon.

— Teraphim. 60p. (Orig.). 1995. pap. 7.00 (*0-926935-98-4*) Runaway Spoon.

— Travelling with Women. 56p. 1983. pap. 5.00 (*0-317-63763-0*) Atticus Pr.

Polkinhorn, Harry, et al, eds. The Flight of the Eagle: Poetry on the U. S. - Mexico Border. (Binational Press Ser.: No. 5). (ENG & SPA.). 270p. 1993. pap. 17.50 (*1-879691-21-3*) SDSU Press.

— The Line: Essays on Mexican - American Border Literature. (Binational Press Ser.: No. 1). (ENG & SPA.). 192p. 1988. pap. 10.00 (*0-916304-92-2*) SDSU Press.

— Open Signs: Language & Society on the U. S. - Mexico Border. (Binational Press Ser.: No. 4). (ENG & SPA.). 310p. 1993. pap. 17.50 (*1-879691-20-5*) SDSU Press.

— Visual Arts on the U. S. - Mexico Border. (Binational Press Ser.: No. 3). (ENG & SPA.). 96p. 1991. pap. 12.50 (*0-916304-93-0*) SDSU Press.

Polkinhorn, Harry & Di-Bella, Jose M., eds. Encuentro Internacional de Literatura de la Frontera, Borderlands Literature, Towards an Integrated Perspective. 338p. 1990. text 10.00 (*0-925613-04-5*) SDSU Inst Reg Studies.

Polkinhorn, Harry, et al. El Libro de Calo. rev. ed. LC 86-4693. 95p. 1987. 19.95 (*0-915745-10-0*) Floricanto Pr.

— El Libro de Calo: The Dictionary of Chicano Slang. 2nd rev. ed. 100p. 1988. pap. 19.95 (*0-685-45617-X*) Floricanto Pr.

Polkinhorn, Harry, ed. see Starr, Raymond.

Polkinhorn, Harry, tr. see Espinosa, Cesar, ed.

Polkinhorn, Harry, tr. see Gomez-Montero, Sergio.

Polkinhorn, Harry, tr. see Manuel Di Bella, Jose.

Polko, Elise. Reminiscences of Felix Mendelssohn-Bartholdy. LC 87-81563. 222p. 1987. reprint ed. 24.95 (*0-944435-01-7*) Glenbridge Pub.

***Polkosnik, Greg.** Cosmically Chic: Discovering Your Fashion Style Through Astrology. (Illus.). 240p. 2000. pap. 9.95 (*0-7407-1017-6*) Andrews & McMeel.

Polkowski, L., et al, eds. Rough Sets in Knowledge Discovery 1: Methodology & Applications. (Studies in Fuzziness & Soft Computing: Vol. 18). (Illus.). x, 576p. 1998. 121.00 (*3-7908-1119-X*) Spr-Verlag.

— Rough Sets in Knowledge Discovery 2: Applications, Case Studies & Software Systems. LC 98-33605. (Studies in Fuzziness & Soft Computing: Vol. 19). (Illus.). x, 610p. 1998. 159.00 (*3-7908-1120-3*) Spr-Verlag.

Polkowski, Lech, et al, eds. Rough Sets & Current Trends in Computing: First International Conference, RSCTC '98, Warsaw, Poland, June 22-26, 1998. Proceedings, Vol. 142. LC 98-26186. (Lecture Notes in Computer Science Ser.: Vol. 1424). xiii, 624p. 1998. pap. 89.00 (*3-540-64655-8*) Spr-Verlag.

Poll, Edward. Business of Business: Your Practical Guide to Success. 1999. pap. text 33.95 (*0-8281-1313-0*) Forb Custom Pub.

— The Professional's Business Handbook: A Guide to Successful Planning. Johnson, Harald, ed. & des. by. 74p. 1997. pap. 29.95 (*0-9654948-2-9*) E Poll & Assocs.

— Secrets of the Business of Law: Successful Practices for Increasing Your Profits! Johnson, Harald, ed. LC 98-96301. x, 168 p. 1998. pap. 49.95 (*0-9654948-3-7*) E Poll & Assocs.

— The Tool Kit for Buying or Selling a Law Practice. 38p. 1996. pap., wbk. ed. 249.00 incl. audio (*0-9654948-0-2*) E Poll & Assocs.

Poll, Edward, et al. Saugerties. (Images of America Ser.). 1999. pap. 16.99 (*0-7524-0853-4*) Arcadia Publng.

Poll, Eve D. Breaking Through the Pale: A Collection of Short Stories. 42p. (Orig.). 1995. pap. 7.00 (*1-887560-45-9*) M Poll Pub.

***Poll, Julie.** Another World 35th Anniversary: The 35th Anniversary Celebration. LC 99-14440. (Illus.). 304p. 1999. 30.00 (*0-06-019304-2*) HarpC.

Poll, Kurt. Zur Geologie des Rhenoherzynikums II. (Geotektonische Forschungen Ser.: Vol. 37). (GER.). ii, 131p. 1970. 40.00 (*3-510-50003-2*, Pub. by E Schweizerbartsche) Balogh.

Poll, Morris. Roy Rogers King Cowboys LTD. 75.00 (*0-685-69283-3*) HarperTrade.

Poll, Richard D. Working the Divine Miracle: The Life of Apostle Henry D. Moyle. Larson, Stan, ed. LC 98-43911. (Illus.). 260p. 1999. 29.95 (*1-56085-129-5*) Signature Bks.

Poll, Richard D., et al, eds. Utah's History. rev. ed. (Illus.). 757p. (C). 1989. pap. text 29.95 (*0-87421-142-5*) Utah St U Pr.

Poll, Roswitha. Literatur Zu Umweltschutz und Umweltforschung. 3rd enl. rev. ed. (GER.). x, 380p. 1984. 31.00 (*3-510-65119-7*, Pub. by E Schweizerbartsche) Balogh.

Poll, Roswitha & Boekhorst, Peter te. Measuring Quality: International Guidelines for Performance Measurement in Academic Libraries. (IFLA Publications: Vol. 76). 171p. 1996. 55.00 (*3-598-21800-1*) K G Saur Verlag.

Poll-Van de Lisdonk, M. Van, see Van Poll-Van de Lisdonk, M.

Poll, Willem Van De, see Van De Poll, Willem.

Pollack. Clinical Urography: An Atlas & Textbook of Urological Imaging, 3 vols., 1. 3168p. 1989. text 198.00 (*0-7216-1556-2*, W B Saunders Co) Harcrt Hlth Sci Grp.

— Clinical Urography: An Atlas & Textbook of Urological Imaging, 3 vols., 2. 3168p. 1989. text 198.00 (*0-7216-1557-0*, W B Saunders Co) Harcrt Hlth Sci Grp.

An Asterisk (*) at the beginning of an entry indicates that the title is appearing for the first time.

— Clinical Urography: An Atlas & Textbook of Urological Imaging, 3 vols., 3. 3168p. 1989. text 198.00 (*0-7216-1558-9*, W B Saunders Co) Harcrt Hlth Sci Grp.
— Clinical Urography: An Atlas & Textbook of Urological Imaging, 3 vols., Set. 3168p. 1989. 525.00 (*0-7216-1555-4*, W B Saunders Co) Harcrt Hlth Sci Grp.
— Introduction to Machine Design. (Mechanical Technology Ser.). 1994. pap., teacher ed. 12.00 (*0-8273-5485-1*) Delmar.
***Pollack.** New Right in Chile 1973-1997. LC 99-21776. 214p. 1999. text 65.00 (*0-312-22278-5*) St Martin.
— Newsmakers 99. 1999. 135.00 (*0-7876-2108-0*) Gale.
Pollack. Part Buy-Sell. LC 95-78497. 1995. 125.00 (*0-316-71298-1*) Little.
Pollack, Pam, jt. ed. see Ryan, Kevin.
Pollack, Pam, ed. see Sathre, Vivian.
Pollack, Aharon. Al Hasetumot Bamizmor: Commentary on the Book of Psalms. Nizri, Osnath, ed. (HEB.). 556p. 1991. text 65.00 (*965-222-230-5*, Pub. by Nezer Pubng) China Bks.
Pollack, Alan, jt. auth. see Guillemin, Victor W.
***Pollack, Albert J.** Options for Remote Monitoring & Control of Small Drinking Water Facilities. LC 99-14431. 1999. pap. 57.50 (*1-57477-072-1*) Battelle.
Pollack, Ann Lemons, see Pollack, Joe & Lemons Pollack, Ann.
Pollack, Barbara, ed. see Humphrey, Doris.
Pollack, Barry. Popular Guitar Music. 256p. 1985. 16.95 (*0-13-685629-2*) P-H.
Pollack, Betsy, jt. auth. see Stern, Matthew H.
Pollack-Brichto, Mira. The God Around Us: A Child's Garden of Prayer. rev. ed. LC 99-17465. (Illus.). 32p. (J). (ps). 1999. 12.95 (*0-8074-0701-1*, 101072) UAHC.
Pollack, Cecelia. Hip Reader Pack. rev. ed. 1978. pap. text 44.95 (*0-87594-190-7*) Book-Lab.
— Hip Reader Teacher's Manual. rev. ed. 1978. pap. text 7.45 (*0-87594-193-1*) Book-Lab.
— How Hip Are You?, Bk. 2. (Hip Reader Program Ser.). (Illus.). (J). (gr. 5-12). 1978. pap. text, student ed. 6.95 (*0-87594-162-1*) Book-Lab.
— How Hip Are You?, Bk 3. (Hip Reader Program Ser.). (Illus.). (J). (gr. 5-12). 1978. pap. text, student ed. 7.45 (*0-87594-161-3*) Book-Lab.
— How Hip Are You, Bk. 4. (Hip Reader Program Ser.). (Illus.). (J). (gr. 5-12). 1978. pap. text, student ed. 7.45 (*0-87594-163-X*) Book-Lab.
Pollack, Cecelia & Lane, Patrick R. Hip Reader, 1. Ruchlis, Hy, ed. (Hip Reader Program Ser.). (Illus.). (Orig.). (gr. 5-12). 1970. pap. text 7.45 (*0-87594-011-0*) Book-Lab.
— Hip Reader, 2. Ruchlis, Hy, ed. (Hip Reader Program Ser.). (Illus.). (Orig.). (gr. 5-12). 1970. pap. text 7.45 (*0-87594-045-5*) Book-Lab.
Pollack, D. J. The Austin Affair. 276p. 1994. 19.95 (*1-55793-041-4*) Guild Bindery Pr.
Pollack, D. S. The Algebra of Econometrics. LC 78-27237. (Wiley Series in Probability & Mathematical Statistics). 375p. reprint ed. pap. 116.30 (*0-8357-6709-4*, 203534000095) Bks Demand.
Pollack, Daniel. Social Work & the Courts: A Casebook. LC 96-44894. (Illus.). 296p. 1997. text 54.00 (*0-8153-2069-8*, SS1046); pap. text 19.95 (*0-8153-2070-1*, SS1046) Garland.
Pollack, David. The Fracture of Meaning: Japan's Synthesis of China from the Eighth Through the Eighteenth Centuries. LC 85-43305. 267p. reprint ed. pap. 82.80 (*0-8357-3424-2*, 203968200013) Bks Demand.
— Reading against Culture: Ideology & Narrative in the Japanese Novel. LC 92-52769. 272p. 1992. text 45.00 (*0-8014-2752-5*); pap. text 16.95 (*0-8014-8035-3*) Cornell U Pr.
Pollack, David, jt. ed. see Minkoff, Kenneth.
Pollack, Dennis R., jt. auth. see Kosmoski, Georgia J.
Pollack, Detlef, ed. Die Legitimitat der Freiheit: Zur Rolle der Politisch Alternativen Gruppen in der DDR. (Forschungen zur Praktischen Theologie Ser.: Bd. 8). (GER.). 245p. 1990. 53.80 (*3-631-42989-4*) P Lang Pubng.
Pollack, Doreen, et al. Educational Audiology for the Limited-Hearing Infant & Preschooler: An Auditory-Verbal Program. 3rd ed. LC 96-49202. (Illus.). 410p. 1997. pap. text 66.95 (*0-398-06751-1*) C C Thomas.
Pollack, Dorothy B. A Medley of Myths. (Illus.). 149p. (YA). (gr. 7-12). spiral bd. 4.75 (*0-939507-46-3*, B206) Amer Classical.
Pollack, Eileen. Paradise, New York: A Novel. LC 98-33591. 288p. 2000. 49.50 (*1-56639-656-5*) Temple U Pr.
***Pollack, Eileen.** Paradise, New York: A Novel. 288p. 2000. pap. 17.95 (*1-56639-789-8*) Temple U Pr.
Pollack, Eileen. The Rabbi in the Attic. 239p. 1991. 20.00 (*1-883285-08-9*) Delphinium.
Pollack, Eileen & Templeman, Kristine H. Whisper Whisper Jesse, Whisper Whisper Josh: A Story about AIDS. LC 92-72471. (Illus.). 32p. (J). (ps up). 1992. pap. 5.95 (*0-9624828-3-8*); lib. bdg. 16.95 (*0-9624828-4-6*) Advantage-Aurora.
Pollack, Elisabeth. Gathering. LC 96-70110. 212p. 1997. pap. text 19.95 (*0-945980-63-9*) Nrth Country Pr.
— The Rowantree Crop. LC 89-39542. 280p. 1989. 16.95 (*0-945980-18-3*) Nrth Country Pr.
— The Rowantree Crop. LC 89-39542. (Illus.). 280p. 1989. pap. 9.95 (*0-945980-16-7*) Nrth Country Pr.
Pollack, Ervin H. Legal Research & Materials: Ohio Edition. LC 85-60265. (Legal Bibliographic & Research Reprint Ser.: Vol. 8). vii, 216p. 1985. reprint ed. lib. bdg. 42.00 (*0-89941-401-X*, 303680) W S Hein.
Pollack, Evelyn M. Allerlei Liste fur Lehrer: A German Teachers Book of Lists. (GER.). v, 102p. (Orig.). 1996. pap. 24.95 (*0-9655052-0-0*, TL64) Applause Lrn Res.
***Pollack, Evelyn Marx.** Web Works-French: Using the Internet to Learn French. 95p. 2000. pap. text 24.95 (*0-9655052-2-7*, TL92, Target Language) Applause Lrn Res.
— Web Works-Spanish: Using the Internet to Learn Spanish. 93p. 1999. pap. text 24.95 (*0-9655052-1-9*, TL86, Target Language) Applause Lrn Res.
Pollack, Flora G. An Annotated Compilation of Cercospora Names. (Mycologia Memoir Ser.: No. 12). (Illus.). viii, 212p. 1987. 48.00 (*3-443-76002-3*, Pub. by Gebruder Borntraeger) Balogh.
Pollack, Frederick. The Adventure. (Poetry Ser.). 182p. (Orig.). 1986. 15.00 (*0-934257-05-1*); pap. 8.00 (*0-934257-04-3*) Story Line.
— Essays in the Law. LC 94-75659. xii,304p. 1994. reprint ed. 80.00 (*1-56169-088-0*) Gaunt.
— Happiness: A Novel in Verse. LC 98-7890. 160p. 1998. pap. 12.95 (*1-885266-58-8*) Story Line.
Pollack, G. H. & Sugi, Haruo, eds. Molecular Mechanism of Muscle Contraction. LC 88-4182. (Advances in Experimental Medicine & Biology Ser.: Vol. 226). (Illus.). 756p. 1988. 145.00 (*0-306-42833-4*, Plenum Trade) Perseus Pubng.
Pollack, G. H., jt. auth. see Sugi, H.
Pollack, G. H., jt. ed. see Sugi, H.
Pollack, Gerald H. Muscles & Molecules: Uncovering the Principles of Biological Motion. 300p. (C). 1990. 55.00 (*0-9626895-0-5*) Ebner & Sons.
Pollack, Gerald H., jt. auth. see Granzier, Henk.
Pollack, Gloria. The Jewish Festivals in Ancient, Medieval & Modern Sources. LC 97-33202. 168p. 1997. pap. 17.50 (*0-87203-149-7*) Hermon.
Pollack, Griselda, jt. ed. see Parker, Rozsika.
Pollack, H. From Microbes to Microwaves: Autobiography of a Medical Man. (Illus.). 1992. 20.00 (*0-685-66038-9*) San Francisco Pr.
Pollack, H., tr. see Honerkamp, Josef & Romer, Hartmann.
Pollack, H. N. & Murthy, V. Rama, eds. Structure & Evolution of the Continental Lithosphere. (Illus.). 210p. 1984. 83.00 (*0-08-030023-5*, Pergamon Pr) Elsevier.
Pollack, Harriet. Having Our Way: Women Rewriting Tradition in Twentieth-Century America. (Review Ser.: Vol. 39, No. 1). 208p. 1995. 22.00 (*0-8387-5318-3*) Bucknell U Pr.
***Pollack, Harriet & Marrs, Suzanne, eds.** Eudora Welty & Politics: Did the Writer Crusade? (Southern Literary Studies). (Illus.). 208p. 2000. 39.95 (*0-8071-2618-7*) La State U Pr.
Pollack, Harriet, jt. auth. see Smith, Alexander B.
Pollack, Herman W. Materials Science & Metallurgy. 4th ed. (Illus.). 560p. 1988. text 24.00 (*0-13-560814-7*) P-H.
Pollack, Howard. Aaron Copland: The Life & Work of an Uncommon Man. LC 98-29179. 679p. 1999. 37.50 (*0-8050-4909-6*) H Holt & Co.
— Harvard Composers: Walter Piston & His Students, from Elliott Carter to Frederic Rzewski. LC 91-46438. (Illus.). 508p. 1992. 60.00 (*0-8108-2493-0*) Scarecrow.
— Skyscraper Lullaby: The Life & Music of John Alden Carpenter. LC 93-46447. (Studies of American Musicians). (Illus.). 544p. 1994. text 65.00 (*1-56098-400-7*) Smithsonian.
Pollack, Howard M., et al. Clinical Urology. 2nd ed. LC 99-15252. 3195p. 2000. text. write for info. (*0-7216-6935-2*, W B Saunders Co) Harcrt Hlth Sci Grp.
Pollack, Irv & Howland, George, Jr. Two Left Brains: Public Radio Commentaries from KCMU-Seattle, Washington. 40p. (Orig.). 1993. 6.00 (*0-940880-44-X*, Littlebook) Open Hand.
Pollack, Jane. Decorating Eggs. (Illus.). 128p. 1998. 16.95 (*0-8069-9413-4*) Sterling.
Pollack, Jill. Kupczynski. 1997. 49.95 (*1-886388-00-8*) Flower Valley Pr.
Pollack, Jill S. Lesbian & Gay Families: Redefining Parenting in America. (Changing Family Ser.). 128p. (YA). (gr. 9-12). 1995. lib. bdg. 24.00 (*0-531-11207-1*) Watts.
— Lesbian & Gay Families: Redefining Parenting in America. (Changing Family Ser.). (Illus.). 144p. (YA). (gr. 9 up). 1995. pap. 9.00 (*0-531-15749-0*) Watts.
— Shirley Chisholm. LC 93-31175. (First Bks.). (Illus.). 64p. (J). (gr. 5-8). 1994. lib. bdg. 22.00 (*0-531-20168-6*) Watts.
— Women on the Hill: A History of Women in Congress. LC 96-33831. (Women Then - Women Now Ser.). 128p. (YA). (gr. 9-12). 1996. lib. bdg. 24.00 (*0-531-11306-X*) Watts.
Pollack, Joe. Joe Pollack's Guide to St. Louis Restaurants. 2nd ed. LC 92-3382. 304p. 1992. pap. 9.95 (*1-55652-144-8*) Chicago Review.
Pollack, Joe & Lemons Pollack, Ann. Beyond Toasted Ravioli: A Tour of St. Louis Restaurants. LC 98-60429. 1999. pap. 14.95 (*1-891442-06-6*) VA Pub Corp.
Pollack, John, jt. ed. see Cummins, Robert.
Pollack, John D. World on a String. LC 96-46478. 1995. pap. 12.95 (*0-8050-4842-1*) H Holt & Co.
Pollack-Johnson, Bruce & Borchardt, Audrey F. Mathematical Connections: A Modeling Approach to Business Calculus, Vol. 1. LC 97-34502. Vol. 1. 553p. (C). 1998. pap. text 38.33 (*0-13-576398-3*) P-H.
Pollack-Johnson, Bruce & Borchardt, Audrey F. Mathematical Connections Vol. 2: A Modeling Approach to Finite Mathematics, Vol. 2. 850p. (C). 1997. pap. text 38.33 (*0-13-576687-7*) P-H.
Pollack, Jonathan & Cha, Y. K. A New Alliance for the Next Century: The Future of U. S.-Korean Security Cooperation. 100p. 1995. pap. text 15.00 (*0-8330-2350-0*, MR-594-OSD) Rand Corp.
Pollack, Jonathan D. & Lee, Chung Min. Preparing for Korean Unifications: Scenarios & Implications. LC 99-13282. 1999. pap. 15.00 (*0-8330-2721-2*) Rand Corp.
Pollack, Jonathan D. & Thomson, James A. East Asia's Potential for Instability & Crisis: Implications for the United States & Korea. 271p. 1995. pap. text 9.00 (*0-8330-2298-9*, CF-119-CAPP) Rand Corp.
Pollack, Jonathan D. & Yang, Richard H. In China's Shadow: Regional Perspectives on Chinese Foreign Policy & Military Development. LC 98-144959. (Conference Proceedings Ser.). ix, 184 p. 1998. 15.00 (*0-8330-2591-0*) Rand Corp.
Pollack, Jonathan D., jt. auth. see Goldman, Charles A.
Pollack, Jonathan D., jt. ed. see Marwah, Onkar.
Pollack, Kenan & Heighberger, Eric. The Real Life Investing Guide: How to Buy Whatever You Want, Save for Retirement, & Take the Vacation of Your Dreams--While You're Still Young. LC 97-30507. (Illus.). 168p. 1997. pap. 12.95 (*0-07-050319-2*) McGraw.
Pollack, Kenneth & Gergen, Michael J. Energy Storage: Four Major Alternatives: Heat Storage, Cool Storage, Compressed Air Energy Storage, & Underground Pumped Hydro Storage. LC 83-80664. 277p. reprint ed. pap. 85.90 (*0-7837-0329-5*, 204064800017) Bks Demand.
Pollack, Louis. Fingerprints on the Universe: Searching for Belief & Meaning in Today's Turbulent World. 20.99 (*0-89906-613-5*, FINH); pap. 16.99 (*0-89906-614-3*, FINP) Mesorah Pubns.
Pollack, M. Noncrystalline Semiconductors, Vol. 1. LC 86-31045. 280p. 1987. reprint ed. 157.00 (*0-8493-5998-8*, CRC Reprint) Franklin.
— Noncrystalline Semiconductors, Vol. 2. LC 86-31045. 176p. 1987. reprint ed. 104.00 (*0-8493-5999-6*, CRC Reprint) Franklin.
— Noncrystalline Semiconductors, Vol. 3. LC 86-31045. 184p. 1987. reprint ed. 109.00 (*0-8493-6000-5*, CRC Reprint) Franklin.
Pollack, Mark. Sports Leagues & Teams: An Encyclopedia, 1871-1996. LC 96-50084. 716p. 1997. lib. bdg. 82.00 (*0-7864-0252-0*) McFarland & Co.
Pollack, Mark H., et al, eds. Challenges in Clinical Practice: Pharmalogic & Psychosocial Strategies. LC 96-7348. 504p. 1996. lib. bdg. 60.00 (*1-57230-067-1*, 0067) Guilford Pubns.
Pollack, Mark H., jt. auth. see Rosenbaum, J. F.
Pollack, Michael, ed. see Schuon, Frithjof.
Pollack, Nathan. Leave Dreams Be. 55p. 1988. pap. 7.00 (*0-912549-13-0*) Bread & Butter.
Pollack, Norman. The Humane Economy: Populism, Capitalism, & Democracy. LC 90-31078. 224p. (C). 1990. text 45.00 (*0-8135-1599-8*) Rutgers U Pr.
— The Just Polity: Populism, Law, & Human Welfare. LC 86-11433. 392p. 1987. text 34.95 (*0-252-01348-4*) U of Ill Pr.
— The Just Polity: Populism, Law, & Human Welfare. LC 86-11433. 388p. 1987. reprint ed. pap. 120.30 (*0-7837-8084-2*, 204783700008) Bks Demand.
— The Populist Response to Industrial America. 176p. 1976. pap. 12.50 (*0-674-69051-6*) HUP.
Pollack, Norman, ed. Populist Mind. (Orig.). (C). 1967. pap. 8.50 (*0-672-60076-5*, AHS50, Bobbs) Macmillan.
Pollack, Oliver B. Empires in Collision: Anglo-Burmese Relations in the Mid-Nineteenth Century, 1. LC 78-75239. (Contributions in Comparative Colonial Studies: No. 1). (Illus.). 214p. 1980. 65.00 (*0-313-20824-7*, PEC/, Greenwood Pr) Greenwood.
***Pollack, Pamela.** The Curse of Beetenkaumun. (Funnie Mysteries Ser.: No. 4). (Illus.). 80p. (J). (gr. 2-7). 2000. pap. 4.99 (*0-7868-4410-8*, Pub. by Disney Pr) Time Warner.
Pollack, Pamela D. Hello, Mr. Circles: An Original Imagiix Kids Book. large type ed. Larrick, Jon P., ed. LC 96-75139. (Say Hello to the Wonderful World of Shapes Ser.). (Illus.). 14p. (J). (ps). 1996. bds. write for info. (*1-888802-00-6*) Imagiix.
— Hello, Mr. Squares: An Original Imagiix Kids Book. large type ed. Larrick, Jon P., ed. LC 96-75140. (Say Hello to the Wonderful World of Shapes Ser.). (Illus.). 14p. (J). (ps). 1996. bds. write for info. (*1-888802-01-4*) Imagiix.
— Hello, Mr. Triangles: An Original Imagiix Kids Book. large type unabridged ed. Larrick, Jon P., ed. LC 96-75141. (Say Hello to the Wonderful World of Shapes Ser.). (Illus.). 14p. (J). (ps). 1996. bds. write for info. (*1-888802-02-2*) Imagiix.
Pollack, R. L., jt. auth. see Morse, D. R.
Pollack, R. S. Tumor Surgery of the Head & Neck. (Illus.). x, 206p. 1975. 63.50 (*3-8055-2092-1*) S Karger.
Pollack, Rachel. The Body of the Goddess: Sacred Wisdom in Myth, Landscape & Culture. LC 96-53329. 288p. 1997. pap. 16.95 (*1-85230-871-0*, Pub. by Element MA) Penguin Putnam.
— The Complete Illustrated Guide to Tarot: How to Unlock the Secrets of the Tarot. LC 99-14078. (Illus.). 192p. 1999. pap. 19.95 (*1-86204-212-8*, Pub. by Element MA) Penguin Putnam.
— Golden Vanity. LC 96-199929. (Science Fiction Ser.). 227 P. ;p. 1980. 1.95 (*0-425-04483-1*) Berkley Pub.
— Haindl Tarot. 1990. pap. 16.00 (*0-88079-465-8*, HD78) US Games Syst.
***Pollack, Rachel.** The Haindl Tarot: A Reader's Handbook. LC 99-36062. 1999. 12.00 (*1-57281-220-6*) US Games Syst.
Pollack, Rachel. Haindl Tarot Vol. 1: The Major Arcana. 239p. 1990. pap. 9.95 (*0-87877-155-7*) Newcastle Pub.
— Haindl Tarot Vol. 2: The Minor Arcana. 1990. pap. 9.95 (*0-87877-156-5*) Newcastle Pub.
— The New Tarot. (Illus.). 176p. 1990. 22.50 (*0-87951-395-0*, Pub. by Overlook Pr) Penguin Putnam.
— The New Tarot: Modern Variations of Ancient Images. (Illus.). 176p. 1992. pap. 14.95 (*0-87951-475-2*, Pub. by Overlook Pr) Penguin Putnam.
— The Power of Ritual. LC 99-38831. (Omega Institute Mind, Body & Spirit Bks.). 224p. 2000. pap. 12.95 (*0-440-50872-X*, Dell Trade Pbks) Dell.
— Seventy-Eight Degrees of Wisdom. rev. ed. 1998. pap. 21.00 (*0-7225-3572-4*) Thorsons PA.
— Tarot: The Open Labyrinth. 1989. pap. 8.95 (*0-85030-465-2*, Pub. by Aqrn Pr) Harper SF.
— Tarot Readings & Meditations. (Illus.). 160p. 1991. pap. 11.95 (*1-85538-049-8*, Pub. by Aqrn Pr) Harper SF.
— Temporary Agency. 202p. 1995. pap. 10.95 (*0-87951-602-X*, Pub. by Overlook Pr) Penguin Putnam.
— Unquenchable Fire. LC 91-37756. 390p. 1992. 23.95 (*0-87951-447-7*, Pub. by Overlook Pr) Penguin Putnam.
— Unquenchable Fire. LC 91-37756. 390p. 1994. pap. 13.95 (*0-87951-530-9*, Pub. by Overlook Pr) Penguin Putnam.
Pollack, Rachel, jt. auth. see Gamper, Gisela.
Pollack, Rachel, jt. auth. see Livernois, Jay.
Pollack, Rachel, jt. auth. see Mathews, Caitlin.
Pollack, Ralph P. Casino Chips & Tokens of the Dutch Caribbean: Aruba Bonaire Curacao St. Maarten. (Illus.). 60p. 1998. pap. 34.95 (*0-9666542-0-X*) R Pollack.
Pollack, Rhoda G. George S. Kaufman. (United States Authors Ser.: No. 525). 160p. 1988. 21.95 (*0-8057-7508-0*) Macmillan.
Pollack, Rhoda-Gale. A Sampler of Plays by Women. LC 89-13033. (American University Studies: English Language & Literature: Ser. IV, Vol. 52). 410p. (C). 1990. text 64.50 (*0-8204-1172-8*) P Lang Pubng.
Pollack, Rhoda-Gale, ed. see Lokvam, Marian, et al.
***Pollack, Robert.** The Faith of Biology & the Biology of Faith. 2000. 19.95 (*0-231-11506-7*) Col U Pr.
Pollack, Robert. The Missing Moment: How the Unconscious Shapes Modern Science. LC 99-26241. 240p. 1999. 25.00 (*0-395-70985-7*) HM.
— Signs of Life: The Language & Meanings of DNA. 224p. 1995. pap. 10.95 (*0-395-73530-0*) HM.
***Pollack, Robert.** Soccer for Juniors: A Guide for Players, Parents & Coaches. rev. ed. LC 99-462558. (Illus.). 180p. 1999. pap. 12.95 (*0-02-862777-6*, Pub. by Macmillan) S&S Trade.
Pollack, Robert L. & Kravitz, Edward. Nutrition in Oral Health & Disease. LC 84-27804. 499p. reprint ed. pap. 154.70 (*0-7837-2739-9*, 204311900006) Bks Demand.
Pollack, Robert L., jt. auth. see Morse, Donald R.
Pollack, Rosemary. White Hibiscus. large type ed. (Linford Romance Library). 295p. 1984. pap. 16.99 (*0-7089-6020-0*) Ulverscroft.
Pollack, S. R., jt. ed. see Brighton, C. T.
Pollack, Sandra & Knight, Denise D., eds. Contemporary Lesbian Writers of the United States: A Bio-Bibliographical Critical Sourcebook. LC 92-39468. 688p. 1993. text 115.00 (*0-313-28215-3*, PCL/) Greenwood.
Pollack, Sandra & Vaughn, Jeanne, eds. Politics of the Heart: A Lesbian Parenting Anthology. LC 87-27250. 360p. (Orig.). 1987. pap. 12.95 (*0-932379-35-4*); lib. bdg. 26.95 (*0-932379-36-2*) Firebrand Bks.
Pollack, Sara A., jt. auth. see Gruenewald, Lee.
Pollack, Sean, ed. Statistical Forecasts of the United States. 2nd ed. 813p. 1995. 99.00 (*0-8103-8935-5*, 101635) Gale.
Pollack, Shane. Baseball's Big "Starr" (Illus.). 91p. (Orig.). (YA). (gr. 7-11). 1997. pap. 4.95 (*1-889534-08-0*) Jay St Pubs.
Pollack, Sheldon D. The Failure of U. S. Tax Policy: Revenue & Politics. LC 95-26110. 1996. 29.95 (*0-271-01582-9*) Pa St U Pr.
— The Failure of U. S. Tax Policy: Revenue & Politics. 320p. 1998. pap. 18.95 (*0-271-01838-0*) Pa St U Pr.
Pollack, Sheldon V. Electrosurgery of the Skin. (Practical Manuals in Dermatologic Surgery Ser.). (Illus.). 93p. 1990. pap. text 37.95 (*0-443-08683-4*) Church.
Pollack, Steve. Ecology. LC 93-10064. (Eyewitness Books). (Illus.). 64p. (J). (gr. 4-7). 1993. 15.95 (*1-56458-326-0*) DK Pub Inc.
Pollack, Suzanne. Improving Environmental Performance. LC 94-43141. (Self-Development for Managers Ser.). 104p. (C). 1995. pap. 14.99 (*0-415-10237-5*) Thomson Learn.
Pollack, William. Real Boys: Rescuing Our Sons from the Myths of Boyhood. LC 99-10388. 447p. 1999. pap. 13.95 (*0-8050-6183-5*, Pub. by H Holt & Co) VHPS.
***Pollack, William.** Real Boys Workbook. (YA). 2001. pap. 15.95 (*0-375-75526-8*) Random Bks Yng Read.
Pollack, William, jt. ed. see Levant, Ronald.
Pollack, William, ed. see Radice, Ronald A.
***Pollack, William S. & Levant, Ronald F.** New Psychotherapy for Men. LC 98-5652. 318p. 1998. 64.50 (*0-471-17772-5*) Wiley.
***Pollack, William S. & Shuster, Todd.** Real Boys' Voices. 224p. 2000. 25.95 (*0-679-46299-6*) Random.
Pollack, William S., jt. auth. see Betcher, R. William.
Pollak. Turin, 1564-1680. 1999. pap. text 14.95 (*0-226-67344-8*) U Ch Pr.
Pollak, David E., jt. auth. see Batory, Dana M.
Pollak, Abigail, tr. see Todorov, Tzvetan.
Pollak, Andy, jt. auth. see Moloney, Ed.
***Pollak, Daniel.** Have the U. S. Supreme Court's 5th Amendment Takings Decisions Changed Land Use Planning in California? 137p. 2000. pap. write for info. (*1-58703-122-1*, CRB-00-004) CA St Libry.
Pollak, Ellen. The Poetics of Sexual Myth: Gender & Ideology in the Verse of Swift & Pope. LC 84-28125. (Women in Culture & Society Ser.). 1994. 18.95 (*0-226-67345-6*) U Ch Pr.
Pollak, Emil S., compiled by. The Stanley Catalog Collection, 1855-1898, Vol. I. (Illus.). 400p. 1989. reprint ed. pap. 22.50 (*1-879335-74-3*) Astragal Pr.
Pollak, Emil S. & Pollak, Martyl. A Guide to the Makers of American Wooden Planes. 3rd ed. (Illus.). 462p. 1994. pap. 35.00 (*1-879335-51-4*) Astragal Pr.

P

An Asterisk (*) at the beginning of an entry indicates that the title is appearing for the first time.

— Prices Realized on Rare Imprinted American Wooden Planes. (Illus.). 152p. 1993. pap. 16.95 (*1-879335-36-0*) Astragal Pr.

Pollak, Emil S. & Pollak, Martyl, eds. The Fascinating World of Early Tools & Trades: Selections from the Chronicle. (Illus.). 407p. 1991. 24.95 (*1-879335-00-X*) Astragal Pr.

Pollak, Emil S., jt. auth. see Kean, Herbert.

Pollak, Erich W. Thoracic Outlet Syndrome: Diagnosis & Treatment. (Illus.). 248p. 1986. 39.50 (*0-87993-246-5*) Fairleigh Dickinson.

Pollak, Felix. Benefits of Doubt. 200p. 1988. 15.95 (*0-944024-04-1*) Spoon Riv Poetry.

Pollak, Felix, jt. auth. see Nin, Anais.

Pollak, Gustav. International Minds & the Search for the Restful. LC 73-107734. (Essay Index Reprint Ser.). 1977. 19.95 (*0-8369-1532-1*) Ayer.

***Pollak, Heinz.** Wovon Lebt der Mensch? Uber Welterkenntnis und Selbsterkenntnis - Gedanken Eines Freimaurers. 238p. 1999. 40.95 (*3-631-34554-2*) P Lang Pubng.

Pollak, J. K. & Lee, J. W., eds. The Biochemistry of Gene Expression in Higher Organisms: Proceedings. LC 72-97960. 656p. 1973. text 283.50 (*90-277-0289-6*) Kluwer Academic.

Pollak, Karen, jt. auth. see Pollak, Oliver.

Pollak, Kay. No Chance Encounter. Gaut, Britt & Gaut, Philip, trs. from SWE. (Guidebooks for Growth Together). (Illus.). 112p. (Orig.). 1996. pap. 10.95 (*1-899171-46-0*, Pub. by Findhorn Pr) Words Distrib.

Pollak, Kurt. Knaurs Lexikon der Modernen Medizin: Knaurs Modern Lexicon of Medicine. (GER.). 1972. 19.95 (*0-8288-6404-7*, M-7519) Fr & Eur.

Pollak, Linda, jt. auth. see Berrizbeitia, Anita.

Pollak, M. & Fry, J. Commonsense Paediatrics. 1986. text 144.00 (*0-85200-945-3*) Kluwer Academic.

Pollak, M. & Shklovskii, B., eds. Hopping Transport in Solids. (Modern Problems in Condensed Matter Sciences Ser.: Vol. 28). xiv, 454p. 1991. 262.50 (*0-444-88037-2*, North Holland) Elsevier.

Pollak, M., jt. ed. see Efros, A. L.

Pollak, M., jt. ed. see Fritzsche, H.

Pollak, Martha, ed. The Education of the Architect: Historiography, Urbanism, & the Growth of Architectural Knowledge. LC 96-22057. (Illus.). 494p. 1997. 47.50 (*0-262-16164-8*) MIT Pr.

***Pollak, Martha D.** Italian & Spanish Books, Vol. 4. (Mark J. Millard Architecture Collection). (SPA, ITA & ENG.). 2000. 90.00 (*0-8076-1478-5*) Braziller.

Pollak, Martha D. Turin, 1564-1680: Urban Design, Military Culture, & the Creation of the Absolutist Capital. LC 90-44409. (Illus.). 414p. 1991. 55.00 (*0-226-67342-1*) U Ch Pr.

Pollak, Martyl, jt. auth. see Pollak, Emil S.

Pollak, Martyl, jt. ed. see Pollak, Emil S.

***Pollak, Mary Jo.** Summer Burns. 192p. 2000. pap. write for info. (*1-895837-49-9*) Insomniac.

Pollak, Michael. The Jews of Dynastic China: A Critical Bibliography. (Bibliographica Judaica Ser.: No. 13). 225p. 1993. 24.95 (*0-87820-911-5*) Hebrew Union Coll Pr.

— Mandarins, Jews & Missionaries: The Jewish Experience in the Chinese Empire. LC 98-171038. 436p. 1998. reprint ed. pap. text 22.50 (*0-8348-0419-0*) Weatherhill.

— The Second Plague of Europe: AIDS Prevention & Sexual Transmission among Men in Western Europe. LC 92-18354. 1994. pap. 9.95 (*1-56023-020-7*, Harrington Park) Haworth Pr.

— The Second Plague of Europe: AIDS Prevention & Sexual Transmission among Men in Western Europe. LC 92-18354. (Illus.). 104p. 1994. 39.95 (*1-56024-306-6*) Haworth Pr.

Pollak, Michael, ed. Noncrystalline Semiconductors, 3 vols., Set. 1987. 369.00 (*0-8493-5994-5*, QC611, CRC Reprint) Franklin.

— Noncrystalline Semiconductors, 3 vols., Vol. I. 304p. 1987. write for info. (*0-318-62343-9*, CRC Reprint) Franklin.

— Noncrystalline Semiconductors, 3 vols., Vol. II. 192p. 1987. write for info. (*0-318-62344-7*, CRC Reprint) Franklin.

— Noncrystalline Semiconductors, 3 vols., Vol. III. 192p. 1987. write for info. (*0-318-62345-5*, CRC Reprint) Franklin.

Pollak, Michael, et al, eds. AIDS: A Problem for Sociological Research. (Special Issue of Current Sociology Ser.). (Illus.). 144p. (C). 1993. text 69.95 (*0-8039-8841-9*); pap. text 22.95 (*0-8039-8840-0*) Sage.

Pollak, Michael, jt. auth. see Nelkin, Dorothy.

Pollak, Michael, ed. see Loewenthal, Rudolf.

Pollak, Nancy. Mandelstam the Reader. (Parallax). 240p. 1995. text 42.00 (*0-8018-5006-1*) Johns Hopkins.

Pollak, O. J., jt. auth. see Kritchevsky, David.

Pollak, Oliver & Pollak, Karen. Rhodesia-Zimbabwe. (World Bibliographical Ser.: No. 4). 195p. 1979. lib. bdg. 25.25 (*0-903450-14-3*) ABC-CLIO.

Pollak, Otto. The Criminality of Women. LC 77-13959. 180p. 1978. reprint ed. lib. bdg. 65.00 (*0-8371-9869-0*, POCW, Greenwood Pr) Greenwood.

— Positive Experiences in Retirement. (C). 1957. 6.50 (*0-256-00674-1*, Irwn McGrw-H) McGrw-H Hghr Educ.

— Social Aspects of Retirement. (C). 1956. 5.50 (*0-256-00675-X*, Irwn McGrw-H) McGrw-H Hghr Educ.

Pollak, P. S. Halel Vzimrah: Commentary in Hebrew on the Passover Haggadah. (ENG & YID.). 12.50 (*0-87559-100-0*); pap. 9.50 (*0-87559-099-3*) Shalom.

— Hermesh Bakomo: Commentary & Interpretation on Tractate Avoth. (ENG & HEB.). 9.50 (*0-87559-092-6*) Shalom.

— Marbin Besimho. 15.00 (*0-87559-083-7*); pap. 10.00 (*0-87559-084-5*) Shalom.

— Minhas Marheshes: Commentary on Genesis. (ENG & HEB.). 12.00 (*0-87559-101-9*) Shalom.

— Nefesh Hayah: Commentary & Interpretation on the Passover Haggadah with the Haggadah Text. (ENG & HEB.). 9.50 (*0-87559-091-8*) Shalom.

— Shaare Rahmin: Sermon Material for the High Holidays in Hebrew. (ENG & HEB.). 10.50 (*0-87559-104-3*) Shalom.

— Tal Hermon: Sermon Material for Yom Kippur & Eulogy in Hebrew. (ENG & HEB.). 12.00 (*0-87559-086-1*); pap. 7.50 (*0-87559-085-3*) Shalom.

Pollak, R., et al, eds. Electronic Packaging Materials Science VII Vol. 323: Materials Research Society Symposium Proceedings. 449p. 1994. text 71.00 (*1-55899-222-7*) Materials Res.

Pollak, Richard. Creation of Dr. B: A Biography of Bruno Bettelheim. 480p. 1998. per. 15.00 (*0-684-84640-3*, Touchstone) S&S Trade Pap.

— Up Against Apartheid: The Role & the Plight of the Press in South Africa. LC 80-22363. (Science & International Affairs Ser.). 167p. 1981. 21.95 (*0-8093-1013-9*) S Ill U Pr.

Pollak, Richard A., ed. Explore Antarctica!, Incl. laserdisc, software & tchr's. guide. (Illus.). 58p. (J). (gr. 5-9). 1991. ring bd. 99.95 (*0-922649-14-6*) ETC MN.

— Explore Antarctica! Barcode Guide. 188p. (J). (gr. 5-9). 1992. spiral bd. 69.95 (*0-922649-15-4*) ETC MN.

— Interactive Multimedia Training: Introduction to CD-ROMs: A Series of Training Workshops for Educators. (Illus.). 92p. 1994. ring bd. 299.00 incl. cd-rom (*0-922649-22-7*) ETC MN.

***Pollak, Richard A., ed.** Multimedia Compendium for Education & Training Vol. 12: 2000 Edition. rev. ed. 184p. 2000. 69.95 (*0-922649-32-4*) ETC MN.

Pollak, Robert A. & Wales, Terence J. Demand System Specification & Estimation. (Illus.). 232p. 1992. text 75.00 (*0-19-506941-2*) OUP.

— Demand System Specification & Estimation. (Illus.). 232p. 1995. reprint ed. pap. 29.95 (*0-19-510121-9*) OUP.

Pollak, Susan, jt. ed. see White, Merry I.

Pollak, Vivian R. Dickinson: The Anxiety of Gender. LC 83-45941. 260p. 1986. pap. text 16.95 (*0-8014-9370-6*) Cornell U Pr.

***Pollak, Vivian R.** The Erotic Whitman. LC 00-22229. (Illus.). 290p. 2000. 50.00 (*0-520-22189-3*, Pub. by U CA Pr); pap. 18.95 (*0-520-22190-7*, Pub. by U CA Pr) Cal Prin Full Svc.

Pollak, Vivian R., ed. New Essays on "Daisy Miller" & "The Turn of the Screw" LC 92-47280. (American Novel Ser.). 165p. 1993. text 32.95 (*0-521-41673-6*) Cambridge U Pr.

Pollak, Vivian R., ed. see Dickinson, Emily N.

***Pollalis, Spiro N.** What Is a Bridge? The Making of Calatrava's Bridge in Seville. LC 98-53516. (Illus.). 163p. 1998. 35.00 (*0-262-16174-5*) MIT Pr.

Pollan, Michael. A Place of My Own: The Education of an Amateur Builder. 336p. 1998. pap. 13.95 (*0-385-31990-8*) Delacorte.

— Second Nature: A Gardener's Education. 320p. 1992. pap. 13.95 (*0-385-31266-0*, Delta Trade) Dell.

Pollan, Stephen. Money. 2000. 30.00 (*0-06-661993-9*); 18.00 (*0-06-661994-7*) HarpC.

— Trust Me. 2000. 14.00 (*0-06-661991-2*) HarpC.

***Pollan, Stephen.** Turning No Into Yes: Six Steps to Solving Your Financial Problems (So You Can Stop Worrying) LC 99-48468. 272p. 2000. 26.00 (*0-06-661992-0*) HarpC.

Pollan, Stephen & Levine, Mark. Lifescripts: What to Say to Get What You Want in 101 of Life's Toughest Situations. 1996. pap. 19.95 (*0-614-12587-1*) Macmillan.

Pollan, Stephen, ed. see Powers, Michael D.

Pollan, Stephen M. The Field Guide to Starting a Business. 292p. 1990. pap. 11.00 (*0-671-67505-2*, Fireside) S&S Trade Pap.

— Lifescripts: What to Say to Get What You Want in 101 of Life's Toughest Situations. LC 96-17332. 464p. 1996. per. 21.95 (*0-02-036048-7*, Pub. by Macmillan) S&S Trade.

***Pollan, Stephen M.** Live Rich, Vol. 1. 2000. pap. 14.00 (*0-88730-934-8*, HarpBusn) HarpInfo.

— Live Rich: Everything You Need to Know to Be Your Own Boss, Whoever You Work For, Set. 1998. audio 18.00 (*0-694-52052-7*) HarperAudio.

Pollan, Stephen M. Surviving the Squeeze. 320p. 1994. pap. 10.00 (*0-02-081168-3*) Macmillan.

Pollan, Stephen M. & Levine, Mark. Die Broke: A Radical Four-Part Financial Plan. 1998. pap. 14.00 (*0-88730-942-9*, HarpBusn) HarpInfo.

***Pollan, Stephen M. & Levine, Mark.** Die Broke: A Radical, 4-Part Financial Plan for When the Conventional Wisdom No Longer Works. LC 97-38118. 1998. 25.00 (*0-88730-867-8*, HarpBusn) HarpInfo.

Pollan, Stephen M. & Levine, Mark. Live Rich: Everything You Need to Know to Be Your Own Boss, Whoever You Work For. LC 98-39060. 320p. 1998. 25.00 (*0-88730-935-6*, HarpBusn) HarpInfo.

Pollan, Stephen M. & Levine, Mark. Starting Over: How to Change Careers or Start Your Own Business. LC 96-21475. 256p. (Orig.). 1997. mass mkt. 10.99 (*0-446-67166-5*, Pub. by Warner Bks) Little.

Pollan, Stephen M. & Levine, Mark. The Total Negotiator. 272p. 1994. pap. 10.00 (*0-380-77019-9*, Avon Bks) Morrow Avon.

***Pollan, Stephen M. & Tower, Roni Beth.** Lifescripts for Employees. Levine, Mark, ed. LC 98-55974. (Lifescripts Ser.). (Illus.). 172p. 1999. pap. 14.95 (*0-02-862623-0*, Pub. by Macmillan) S&S Trade.

***Pollan, Steven.** Die Broke: Pollan,&Stephen M. abr. ed. 1998. audio 18.00 (*0-694-51926-X*) HarperAudio.

Pollard, Alfred W., et al, eds. A Short-Title Catalogue of Books Printed in England, Scotland, & Ireland, & of English Books Printed Abroad, 1475-1640: Vol. III: Addenda, Corrigenda, & Indexes. 2nd ed. (Illus.). 424p. 1991. text 350.00 (*0-19-721791-5*) OUP.

***Polland, Barbara K.** Every Parent's Question & Answer Handbook: A Practical Guide for Parents with Children from Birth to Age 12. 232p. 2000. pap. 12.95 (*0-89087-976-1*) Celestial Arts.

Polland, Barbara K. Feelings: Inside You & Outloud Too. (Illus.). 64p. (J). (ps-3). 1997. pap. 7.95 (*1-883672-67-8*) Tricycle Pr.

— Feelings Inside You & Outloud Too. LC 74-25835. (Illus.). 64p. (J). (ps-3). 1995. pap. 6.95 (*0-89087-006-3*) Celestial Arts.

— The Parenting Challenge: Practical Answers to Childrearing Questions. rev. ed. LC 93-48937. 232p. (J). (ps-12). 1993. reprint ed. pap. 9.95 (*1-883672-08-2*) Tricycle Pr.

— The Sensible Book: A Celebration of Your Five Senses. rev. ed. (Illus.). 64p. (J). (ps-3). 1995. pap. 7.95 (*0-89087-707-6*) Celestial Arts.

***Polland, Barbara Kay.** We Can Work It Out: Conflict Resolution for Children. LC 00-23852. (Illus.). 64p. (J). (ps-5). 2000. 13.95 (*1-58246-031-0*) Tricycle Pr.

***Polland, Barbara Kay & DeRoy, Craig.** We Can Work It Out: Conflict Resolution for Children. LC 00-23852. (Illus.). 64p. (J). (ps-5). 2000. pap. write for info. (*1-58246-029-9*) Tricycle Pr.

Polland, Leon D., jt. auth. see Chapelle, Howard I.

***Polland, Madeleine A.** Beorn the Proud. LC 98-73485. (Illus.). 208p. (YA). (gr. 5 up). 1999. pap. 12.95 (*1-883937-08-6*, 08-6) Bethlehem ND.

Polland, Madeleine A. The Pomegranate House. large type ed. (Charnwood Large Print Ser.). 1994. 27.99 (*0-7089-8794-X*) Ulverscroft.

— Rich Man's Flowers. large type ed. 576p. 1993. 27.99 (*0-7089-8697-8*) Ulverscroft.

Pollanen, Michael S. Forensic Diatomology & Drowning. LC 98-142915. 159p. 1998. 149.00 (*0-444-82844-3*) Elsevier.

Pollar, Odette. Organizing Your Workspace: A Guide to Personal Productivity. Crisp, Michael G., ed. LC 91-76238. (Fifty-Minute Ser.). 92p. 1992. pap. 10.95 (*1-56052-125-2*) Crisp Pubns.

— Organizing Your Workspace: A Guide to Personal Productivity. Woodbury, Debbie, ed. LC 98-74378. (Crisp 50-Minute Bks.). 120p. 1998. pap. 10.95 (*1-56052-522-3*) Crisp Pubns.

— Take Back Your Life: Smart Ways to Simplify Daily Living. LC 99-12640. 176p. 1999. pap. 12.95 (*1-57324-132-6*) Conari Press.

— 365 Ways to Simplify Your Work Life. LC 96-22812. 224p. 1996. pap. 8.95 (*0-7931-2281-3*, 56144801) Dearborn.

Pollar, Odette & Gonzalez, Rafael. Dynamics of Diversity: Strategic Programs for Your Organization. Keppler, Kay, ed. LC 93-73147. (Fifty-Minute Ser.). (Illus.). 80p. (Orig.). 1994. pap. 10.95 (*1-56052-247-X*) Crisp Pubns.

Pollard. Cell Biology. 1900. pap. text. write for info. (*0-7216-3997-6*, W B Saunders Co) Harcrt Hlth Sci Grp.

— Developments in Management Thought. 1986. 16.50 (*0-8448-0069-4*, Crane Russak) Taylor & Francis.

Pollard. Essays on the Industrial Revolution in Britain. 94.95 (*0-86078-794-X*) Ashgate Pub Co.

— Genesis of Modern Management. 336p. 1993. 61.95 (*0-7512-0187-1*) Ashgate Pub Co.

Pollard. Reign of Virtue. LC 98-13332. 304p. 1998. pap. text 20.00 (*0-226-67350-2*); lib. bdg. 45.00 (*0-226-67349-9*) U Ch Pr.

Pollard & Quartermaine, L., eds. Italy Today: Patterns of Life & Politics. 2nd ed. 128p. 1987. pap. text 15.00 (*0-85989-304-9*, Pub. by Univ Exeter Pr) Northwestern U Pr.

Pollard, jt. auth. see Carter, John.

***Pollard, Matt.** Bravo! A Thumb Cinema Flip Book. deluxe ed. (Illus.). 60p. 1999. pap. 3.95 (*1-893859-11-8*) Thumb Cinema.

Pollard, Matt. A Day at the Lake. (Illus.). 61p. 1999. pap. 3.95 (*1-893859-07-X*) Thumb Cinema.

— Dead Astaire. (Illus.). 56p. 1997. pap. write for info. (*1-893859-00-2*) Thumb Cinema.

— Happy Birthday. (Illus.). 40p. 1999. pap. 3.95 (*1-893859-05-3*) Thumb Cinema.

— Howdy from Iowa! (Illus.). 82p. 1999. pap. 4.95 (*1-893859-03-7*) Thumb Cinema.

— Moon over Mitosis: E=Tc Squared. (Illus.). 80p. 1999. 4.95 (*1-893859-08-8*) Thumb Cinema.

— Seasons Greetings. (Illus.). 62p. 1999. pap. 3.95 (*1-893859-04-5*) Thumb Cinema.

Pollard, Matt, ed. see Sharpnack, Joe.

Pollard, A. H., et al. Demographic Techniques. 2nd ed. (Illus.). 192p. 1981. pap. text 25.00 (*0-08-024817-9*, Pergamon Pr) Elsevier.

— Demographic Techniques. 3rd ed. (Illus.). 185p. 1990. pap. text 27.00 (*0-08-040065-5*) Elsevier.

Pollard, A. J. Middlesbrough: The Growth of a Community. LC 97-131020. 1998. 33.95 (*0-7509-1270-7*, Pub. by Sutton Pub Ltd) Intl Pubs Mktg.

Pollard, A. J. North-Eastern England During the Wars of the Roses: Lay Society, War, & Politics, 1450-1500. (Illus.). 464p. 1991. text 125.00 (*0-19-820087-0*) OUP.

Pollard, A. J. The North of England in the Reign of Richard III. LC 95-17777. 1996. text 59.95 (*0-312-12592-5*) St Martin.

— Richard III & the Princess in the Tower. 1991. text 39.95 (*0-312-06715-1*) St Martin.

Pollard, A. J., ed. The Wars of the Roses. LC 95-9735. 1995. pap. 21.95 (*0-312-12699-9*); text 55.00 (*0-312-12697-2*) St Martin.

Pollard, A. J., jt. auth. see Britnell, R. H.

Pollard, A. J., jt. ed. see Britnell, R. H.

***Pollard, A. M., ed.** Geoarchaeology. (Special Publication Ser.: No. 165). 184p. 2000. 108.00 (*1-86239-053-3*, Pub. by Geol Soc Pub Hse) AAPG.

Pollard, A. M., ed. Proceedings of the British Academy: New Developments in Archaeological Science a Joint Symposium of the Royal Society & the British Academy, February, 1991. (British Academy Ser.: Vol. 77). (Illus.). 260p. 1992. 49.95 (*0-19-726118-3*) OUP.

Pollard, A. Mark & Heron, Carl. Archaeological Chemistry. 375p. 1996. 39.00 (*0-85404-523-6*) CRC Pr.

Pollard, A. W., et al, eds. A Short-Title Catalogue of Books Printed in England, Scotland, & Ireland & of English Books Printed Abroad, 3 vols., Set. 2nd rev. ed. 1992. text 795.00 (*0-19-721797-4*) OUP.

Pollard, Alan P., ed. U. S. S. R. Facts & Figures Annual, Vol. 12-14: 1988-1990, Vol. 12-14. 1988. 97.00 (*0-87569-103-X*); 97.00 (*0-685-44198-9*) Academic Intl.

Pollard, Albert F. The History of England from the Accession of Edward Sixth to the Death of Elizabeth 1 (1547-1603) LC 75-5633. (Political History of England Ser.: No. 6). reprint ed. 45.00 (*0-404-50776-X*) AMS Pr.

— Thomas Cranmer & the English Reformation, 1849-1556. LC 83-45587. reprint ed. 42.50 (*0-404-19905-4*) AMS Pr.

Pollard, Albert F., ed. Reign of Henry VII from Contemporary Sources, 3 vols. LC 73-181970. reprint ed. 145.00 (*0-404-05140-5*) AMS Pr.

Pollard, Alfred, jt. auth. see Bartlett, Henrietta.

Pollard, Alfred F. Jesuits in Poland. LC 76-116799. (Studies in Philosophy: No. 40). 1970. reprint ed. lib. bdg. 75.00 (*0-8383-1041-9*) M S G Haskell Hse.

Pollard, Alfred M. Banking Law in the United States. LC 92-20020. 1994. 60.00 (*0-250-40753-1*, MICHIE) LEXIS Pub.

Pollard, Alfred M., et al. Banking Law in the United States, 2 vols. 2nd ed. LC 92-20020. 1993. suppl. ed. 50.00 (*0-685-74451-5*, MICHIE) LEXIS Pub.

— Banking Law in the United States, Issue 7. 1200p. 1999. ring bd. write for info. (*0-327-01307-9*, 8017714) LEXIS Pub.

— Banking Laws of the United States, Issue 6. 1998. ring bd. 185.00 (*0-327-00142-9*, 80177-13) LEXIS Pub.

Pollard, Alfred W. Catalogue of Books Mostly from the Presses of the First Printers Showing the Progress of Printing with Movable Metal Types Through the 2nd Half of the 15th Century. 358p. 1999. reprint ed. 75.00 (*1-57898-129-8*) Martino Pubng.

— Chaucer. LC 73-114911. (Select Bibliographies Reprint Ser.). 1977. 19.95 (*0-8369-5316-9*) Ayer.

— Chaucer. LC 76-174278. reprint ed. 21.50 (*0-404-05069-7*) AMS Pr.

— Chaucer. LC 69-14038. 136p. 1969. reprint ed. lib. bdg. 49.50 (*0-8371-1856-5*, POCH, Greenwood Pr) Greenwood.

— Early Illustrated Books. LC 68-26366. (Bibliophile Ser.: No. 83). 1969. reprint ed. lib. bdg. 75.00 (*0-8383-0278-5*) M S G Haskell Hse.

— Italian Book Illustrations & Early Printing. (Illus.). 263p. 1994. 185.00 (*0-614-10102-6*) Oak Knoll.

— List of Catalogues of English Book Sales, 1676-1900: Now in the British Museum. 539p. 1995. reprint ed. 90.00 (*1-888262-59-1*) Martino Pubng.

— Shakespeare's Fight with the Pirates & the Problems of the Transmission of His Text. (BCL1-PR English Literature Ser.). 110p. 1992. reprint ed. lib. bdg. 69.00 (*0-7812-7310-2*) Rprt Serv.

— Shakespeare's Fight with the Pirates & the Problems of the Transmission of the Text. LC 73-20426. (Studies in Shakespeare: No. 24). xxviii, 110p. 1974. lib. bdg. 75.00 (*0-8383-1754-5*) M S G Haskell Hse.

— Shakespeare's Hand in the Play of Sir Thomas More: Papers. (BCL1-PR English Literature Ser.). 229p. 1992. reprint ed. lib. bdg. 79.00 (*0-7812-7277-7*) Rprt Serv.

Pollard, Alfred W. & Redgrave, G. R., eds. A Short-Title Catalogue of Books Printed in England, Scotland, & Ireland & of English Books Printed Abroad, 1475-1640, 2 vols., Vol. 1. 2nd ed. (Bibliographical Society Ser.). 612p. 1987. text 350.00 (*0-19-721789-3*) OUP.

— A Short-Title Catalogue of Books Printed in England, Scotland, & Ireland & of English Books Printed Abroad, 1475-1640, 2 vols., Vol. 2. 2nd ed. (Bibliographical Society Ser.). 506p. 1976. text 250.00 (*0-19-721790-7*) OUP.

Pollard, Alfred W., ed. see Chaucer, Geoffrey.

Pollard, Alton B., III. Mysticism & Social Change: The Social Witness of Howard Thurman. (Martin Luther King, Jr., Memorial Studies in Religion, Culture, & Social Development: Vol. 2). 219p. (Orig.). (C). 1992. text 39.95 (*0-8204-1612-6*) P Lang Pubng.

— Mysticism & Social Change: The Social Witness of Howard Thurman. 2nd ed. (Martin Luther King, Jr., Memorial Studies in Religion, Culture, & Social Development: Vol. 2). 219p. (Orig.). (C). 1992. pap. text 29.95 (*0-8204-1981-8*) P Lang Pubng.

***Pollard, Andrew.** Competitor Intelligence: Strategy, Tools & Techniques for Competitive Advantage. (Illus.). 238p. 1999. pap. 49.50 (*0-273-63709-6*, Pub. by Pitman Pbg) Trans-Atl Phila.

Pollard, Andrew. An Introduction to Primary Education: For Parents, Governors, & Student Teachers. (Illus.). 176p. 1996. 70.00 (*0-304-32710-7*); pap. 33.95 (*0-304-32708-5*) Continuum.

— Reflective Teaching in Secondary Education. 1997. 90.00 (*0-304-33535-5*) Continuum.

— Reflective Teaching in the Primary School: A Handbook for the Classroom 3rd ed. LC 97-188999. (Cassell Education Ser.). x, 422 p. 1997. 29.95 (*0-304-33870-2*) Continuum.

P

An Asterisk (*) at the beginning of an entry indicates that the title is appearing for the first time.

***Pollard, Andrew.** Social World of Pupil Assessment: Strategic Biographies Through Primary School. 2000. 74.95 (0-8264-4799-6); pap. 35.95 (0-8264-4790-2) Continuum.

Pollard, Andrew, ed. Children & Their Primary Schools: A New Perspective. 265p. 1987. 69.95 (1-85000-320-3, Falmer Pr); pap. 34.95 (1-85000-321-1, Falmer Pr) Taylor & Francis.

— Readings for Reflective Teaching in the Primary School. (Education Ser.). (Illus.). 256p. 1996. pap. 37.95 (0-304-33799-4); text 95.00 (0-304-33798-6) Continuum.

Pollard, Andrew, et al, eds. Children & Their Curriculum: The Perspectives of Primary & Elementary School Children. LC 97-111405. 208p. 1996. pap. 27.95 (0-7507-0594-9, Falmer Pr) Taylor & Francis.

— Education, Training & the New Vocationalism: Experience & Policy. 192p. 1988. 113.00 (0-335-15845-5); pap. 35.95 (0-335-15844-7) OpUniv Pr.

Pollard, Andrew & Filer, Ann. The Social World of Children's Learning: Case Studies of Pupils from Four to Seven. (Cassell Education Ser.). (Illus.). 352p. 1996. pap. 37.95 (0-304-32641-0) Continuum.

Pollard, Andrew & Tann, Sarah. Reflective Teaching in the Primary School. 2nd ed. (Education Ser.). (Illus.). 224p. 1993. pap. text 35.90 (0-304-32620-8) Continuum.

Pollard, Andrew, et al. Changing English Primary Schools: The Impact of the Education Reform Act at Key Stage One. LC 93-40675. (Cassell Education Ser.). (Illus.). 224p. 1994. 100.00 (0-304-32921-5); pap. 32.50 (0-304-32923-1) Continuum.

***Pollard, Andrew, et al.** High Performance Computing Systems & Applications. 624p. 2000. 140.00 (0-7923-7774-5) Kluwer Academic.

Pollard, Andrew, jt. ed. see Woods, Peter.

Pollard, Andrew J. & Murdoch, David R. The High Altitude Medicine Handbook. LC 96-36428. 1996. write for info. (1-85775-158-2, Radcliffe Med Pr) Scovill Paterson.

— The High Altitude Medicine Handbook. LC 97-179735. (Illus.). xvi, 146p. 1997. write for info. (1-85775-174-4, Radcliffe Med Pr) Scovill Paterson.

Pollard, Andrew J. & Murdoch, David R. High Altitude Medicine Handbook. 1997. reprint ed. pap. 17.00 (81-7303-129-0, Pub. by Book Faith) S Asia.

Pollard, Andrew J. & Murdoch, David R. The High Altitude Medicine Handbook. 2nd ed. LC 98-27326. 1998. write for info. (1-85775-214-7, Radcliffe Med Pr) Scovill Paterson.

Pollard, Arthur. Crabbe: The Critical Heritage. (Critical Heritage Ser.). 510p. 1975. 69.50 (0-7100-7258-9, Routledge Thoemms) Routledge.

Pollard, Arthur, ed. Richard Hooker (1553/4-1600) Ecclesiastical Polity Selections. pap. write for info. (0-85635-860-6, Pub. by Carcanet Pr) Paul & Co Pubs.

***Pollard, Arthur, ed.** The Sermons. 140p. 2000. pap. 14.95 (1-85754-458-7, Pub. by Carcanet Pr) Paul & Co Pubs.

Pollard, Arthur, ed. The Victorians, Vol. 6. 592p. 1994. pap. 15.95 (0-14-017756-6, Penguin Bks) Viking Penguin.

Pollard, Arthur, jt. auth. see Chapple, J. A.

Pollard, Arthur, ed. see Crabbe, George.

Pollard, Arthur, ed. see Gaskell, Elizabeth.

Pollard, Asuman C. & Pollard, David. Teach Yourself Turkish Complete: A Complete Course for Beginners. 2nd ed. (ENG & TUR.). 320p. 1998. pap. 21.95 incl. audio (0-8442-3642-X, Teach Yrslf) NTC Contemp Pub Co.

— Teach Yourself Turkish Complete Course. 2nd rev. ed. (TUR., Illus.). 320p. 1997. pap. 14.95 (0-8442-3715-9) NTC Contemp Pub Co.

Pollard, B. J., ed. Applied Neuromuscular Pharmacology. (Illus.). 450p. 1994. text 135.00 (0-19-262148-3) OUP.

Pollard, Carl & Sag, Ivan A. Information-Based Syntax & Semantics. LC 87-71618. (Center for the Study of Language & Information-Lecture Notes Ser.: No. 13). 252p. 1987. 64.95 (0-937073-23-7); pap. 17.95 (0-937073-24-5) CSLI.

Pollard, Carl J. & Sag, Ivan A. Head-Driven Phrase Structure Grammar. LC 93-17533. (Studies in Contemporary Linguistics). (Illus.). 454p. 1994. pap. text 34.95 (0-226-67447-9); lib. bdg. 80.00 (0-226-67446-0) U Ch Pr.

***Pollard, clare.** The Heavy-Petting Zoo. 62p. 1999. pap. (1-85224-481-X, Pub. by Bloodaxe Bks) Dufour.

Pollard, Clarice F. Laugh, Cry & Remember: The Journal of a GI Lady! Westheimer, Mary, ed. LC 91-90262. (Illus.). 224p. (Orig.). 1992. pap. 17.95 (0-9629334-0-6) Tex Tech Univ Pr.

Pollard, D. E. Law & Policy of Producers' Associations. (C). 1984. 59.00 (0-19-825480-6) OUP.

Pollard, D. E., jt. auth. see T'ung, P. C.

Pollard, D. E., jt. auth. see Tung, P. C.

Pollard, D. E., jt. auth. see T'ung, P. C.

Pollard, Dave. The Audi Quattro Book. LC 97-77759. (Illus.). 176p. 1997. 39.95 (1-85960-403-X, Pub. by J H Haynes & Co) Motorbooks Intl.

— Classic Car Electrical Systems Repair Manual. (Illus.). 192p. 1999. 35.95 (1-85960-433-1) Haynes Manuals.

Pollard, Dave. Jaguar XJ6 Purchase & Restoration Guide. LC 97-72305. (Illus.). 192p. 1997. 34.95 (0-85429-973-4, Pub. by GT Foulis) Haynes Manuals.

Pollard, Dave. Jaguar XJ6 Restoration. (Jaguar Enthusiasts Guide Ser.). (Illus.). 124p. 1995. pap. 24.95 (1-873098-31-6, Pub. by Kelsey Pub Ltd) Motorbooks Intl.

— The Jaguar XK Engine. LC 98-70518. 1998. 36.95 (1-85960-007-7, Pub. by J H Haynes & Co) Motorbooks Intl.

— Range Rover: Purchase & Restoration Guide. LC 96-75827. (Illus.). 192p. 1996. 34.95 (0-85429-968-8, Pub. by GT Foulis) Haynes Manuals.

Pollard, Dave, jt. auth. see Porter, Lindsay.

***Pollard, David.** The Chinese Essay [ku Chin San Wen Ying I Chi]. LC 99-89425. (ENG & CHI.). 2000. pap. 49.50 (0-231-12118-0) Col U Pr.

Pollard, David. Classic Motorcycle Electrical Systems Repair Manual. (Illus.). 176p. 1999. 35.95 (1-85960-626-1, 129131AE, Pub. by Haynes Manuals) Motorbooks Intl.

— Empirical Processes: Theory & Applications. (NSF-CBMS Regional Conference Series in Probability & Statistics: Vol. 2). (Illus.). 86p. (C). 1990. pap. 20.00 (0-940600-16-1) Inst Math.

— Sourcebook on French Law. (Sourcebook Ser.). 340p. 1996. pap. 44.00 (1-85941-183-5, Pub. by Cavendish Pubng) Gaunt.

— Sourcebook on French Law. 2nd ed. LC 99-160647. (Cavendish Publishing Sourcebook Ser.). 379p. 1998. pap. 49.00 (1-85941-187-8) Gaunt.

— Tolley's Employment & Pension Rights in Corporate Insolvency. 364p. 1994. 300.00 (0-85459-737-9, Pub. by Tolley Pubng) St Mut.

Pollard, David & Hughes, David J. Constitutional & Administrative Law - Text & Materials. 450p. 1990. pap. 44.00 (0-406-50600-0, UK, MICHIE) LEXIS Pub.

Pollard, David, et al. Pollard, Parpworth & Hughes: Constitutional & Administrative Law - Cases & Materials. 2nd ed. 1997. pap. write for info. (0-406-04591-7, PHCA2, MICHIE) LEXIS Pub.

Pollard, David, jt. auth. see Pollard, Asuman C.

Pollard, David, jt. auth. see Porter, Lindsay.

Pollard, David, jt. auth. see Sollis, Bill.

Pollard, David, ed. see Le Cam, Lucien M.

Pollard, David E. A Chinese Look at Literature: The Literary Values of Chou Tso-Jen in Relation to the Tradition. LC 72-97732. 195p. reprint ed. pap. 60.50 (0-608-18502-7, 203150900075) Bks Demand.

***Pollard, David E., ed.** The Chinese Essay. 384p. 1999. 150.00 (962-7255-21-1, Pub. by Chinese Univ of Hong Kong) St Mut.

Pollard, David E., ed. Translation & Creation: Readings of Western Literature in Early Modern China, 1840-1918. LC 97-50605. (Benjamins Translation Library: Vol. 25). vi, 336p. 1998. 85.00 (1-55619-709-8) J Benjamins Pubng Co.

***Pollard, Debbie.** Penelope Penguin's Pancake Party. LC 00-131650. 32p. (J). (ps-k). 2000. write for info. (1-57197-226-9, Pub. by Pentland Pr) Assoc Pubs Grp.

Pollard, Derek. Kheperu: Poems from Tristan Tzara's Hat. unabridged ed. Henderson, Derek, ed. 8p. 1997. mass mkt. 1.00 (0-9665407-3-5) Bl Nght Pr.

— Time Bomb: Selected Writing of Thaddeus Alan. 34p. 1998. pap. 5.00 (0-9665407-0-0) Bl Nght Pr.

Pollard, Derek, et al. Prechelonian: A Literary & Fine Art Magazine. unabridged ed. 30p. 1999. mass mkt. 5.00 (0-9665407-4-3) Bl Nght Pr.

Pollard, Derek, ed. see Henderson, Derek.

***Pollard, Diane & Ajirotutu, Cheryl.** African-centered Schooling in Theory & Practice. LC 99-55888. 240p. 2000. write for info. (0-89789-728-5, Bergin & Garvey) Greenwood.

Pollard, Diane S., jt. ed. see Biklen, Sari K.

Pollard, Douglas F. Peetz: The Reel for All Time. 1997. pap. 11.95 (1-895811-48-1) Heritage Hse.

Pollard, E. & Yates, T. J. Monitoring Butterflies for Ecology & Conservation: The British Butterfly Monitoring Scheme. LC 93-12557. 288p. (gr. 13). 1993. text 88.95 (0-412-40220-3) Chapman & Hall.

Pollard, Edward A. Life of Jefferson Davis, with a Secret History of the Southern Confederacy, Gathered Behind the Scenes in Richmond. LC 75-95074. (Select Bibliographies Reprint Ser.). 1977. 36.95 (0-8369-5074-7) Ayer.

— Lost Cause. LC 74-117888. (Select Bibliographies Reprint Ser.). 1977. 60.95 (0-8369-5341-X) Ayer.

— Lost Cause Regained. LC 78-117889. (Select Bibliographies Reprint Ser.). 1977. 20.95 (0-8369-5342-8) Ayer.

— Lost Cause Regained. LC 70-174279. reprint ed. 27.50 (0-404-00097-5) AMS Pr.

— Southern History of the War, 2 vols. LC 79-95075. (Select Bibliographies Reprint Ser.). 1977. reprint ed. 72.95 (0-8369-5075-5) Ayer.

Pollard, Edward B. & Stevens, Daniel G. Luther Rice - Pioneer in Missions & Education. (Ministry Helps Ser.). 125p. 1995. pap. 5.00 (1-883265-07-X) Richbarry Pr.

Pollard, Elaine. The Oxford Paperback Dictionary. 4th rev. ed. Liebeck, Helen, ed. LC 93-43215. 960p. (C). 1994. pap. 4.99 (0-19-280012-4) OUP.

Pollard, Elaine & Liebeck, Helen, eds. The Oxford Large Print Dictionary. 2nd ed. 952p. 1996. 39.95 (0-19-861322-9) OUP.

Pollard, Elizabeth B. Visual Arts Research: A Handbook. LC 86-375. 180p. 1986. lib. bdg. 55.00 (0-313-24186-4, PVA/, Greenwood Pr) Greenwood.

Pollard, Ernest C. The Cataclysm: Just the Facts. LC 88-63019. 264p. (Orig.). 1989. text 26.00 (0-9612798-2-6) Woodburn Pr.

— Radiation: Cells & People. (Illus.). 133p. (Orig.). (C). 1991. pap. 12.00 (0-9612798-3-4) Woodburn Pr.

— Radiation: One Story of the M. I. T. Radiation Laboratory. (Illus.). 197p. (Orig.). 1982. pap. 12.95 (0-9612798-1-8) Woodburn Pr.

— Sermons in Stones: Science & People. LC 92-91167. (Illus.). 218p. 1993. pap. 10.00 (0-9612798-6-9) Woodburn Pr.

Pollard, Frank. Respuestas Divinas a Inquietudes Humanas. (Estudios Biblicos Basicos Ser.).Tr. of Timely Answers to Key Questions. (SPA.). 144p. 1997. pap. 5.95 (0-311-04369-0) Casa Bautista.

Pollard, Garland. Pamunkey Indians of Virginia. (Bureau of American Ethnology Bulletins Ser.). 99p. 1995. lib. bdg. 89.00 (0-7812-4017-4) Rprt Serv.

— The Pamunkey Indians of Virginia. 1988. reprint ed. lib. bdg. 49.00 (0-7812-0056-3) Rprt Serv.

Pollard, Gordon. Bottles & Business in Plattsburgh, New York: 100 Years of Embossed Bottles As Historical Artifacts. (Illus.). 370p. 1993. pap. 18.00 (1-890402-20-6) Clinton Cnty Hist.

Pollard-Gott, Lucy. Fictional 100: A Ranking of the Most Influential Characters in World Literature & Legend. LC 97-25476. (Illus.). 400p. 1997. 27.50 (0-8065-1905-3, Citadel Pr) Carol Pub Group.

Pollard, Graham, jt. auth. see Carter, John.

***Pollard, H. B. C. & Barclay-Smith, Phyllis.** British & American Game Birds. (Illus.). 108p. 1999. pap. 19.95 (1-56833-138-X, Pub. by Derrydale Pr) Natl Bk Netwk.

Pollard, H. L., jt. ed. see Miller, P. R.

Pollard, Harry & Diamond, Harold G. The Theory of Algebraic Numbers. 3rd unabridged ed. LC 98-28912. 176p. 1999. pap. 7.95 (0-486-40454-4) Dover.

Pollard, Harry, jt. auth. see Tenenbaum, Morris.

Pollard, Harry, tr. see Bochner, Salomon.

Pollard, Hawk, jt. ed. see Cole, John.

Pollard, Helen P. Tariacuri's Legacy: The Prehispanic Tarascan State. LC 92-37080. (Civilization of the American Indian Ser.: Vol. 209). 1993. 39.95 (0-8061-2497-0) U of Okla Pr.

Pollard, Hugh M. Pioneers of Popular Education, 1760-1850. LC 73-20922. 297p. 1975. reprint ed. lib. bdg. 35.00 (0-8371-5871-0, POPP, Greenwood Pr) Greenwood.

Pollard, I. Financial Engineering. 1988. 68.00 (0-409-49464-X, MICHIE) LEXIS Pub.

Pollard, Irina. A Guide to Reproduction: Social Issues & Human Concerns. (Illus.). 426p. (C). 1994. text 80.00 (0-521-41862-3) Cambridge U Pr.

Pollard, J. H., jt. auth. see Benjamin, B.

Pollard, J. H., jt. auth. see Benjamin, Bernard.

Pollard, Jean A. The New Maine Cooking: The Healthful New Country Cuisine. (Illus.). 288p. 1996. reprint ed. pap. 15.95 (0-89272-388-2) Down East.

Pollard, Jeanne. Building Toothpick Bridges. 1985. pap. text 9.95 (0-86651-266-7) Seymour Pubns.

Pollard, Jeffrey W. & Walker, John M., eds. Animal Cell Culture. LC 84-15696. (Methods in Molecular Biology Ser.: Vol. 5). (Illus.). 727p. 1990. 69.50 (0-89603-150-0) Humana.

— Basic Cell Culture Protocols. 2nd ed. LC 97-201830. (Methods in Molecular Biology Ser.: Vol. 75). 504p. 1997. 99.50 (0-89603-441-0) Humana.

— Basic Cell Culture Protocols. 2nd ed. (Methods in Molecular Biology Ser.: Vol. 75). (Illus.). 504p. 1997. 79.50 (0-89603-384-8) Humana.

Pollard, Jeffrey W., jt. ed. see Walker, John M.

Pollard, Jeffrey W., jt. ed. see Whitaker, Leighton C.

***Pollard, Jim.** Caring for Someone with Arthritis. 128p. 1999. pap. 30.00 (0-86242-266-3, Pub. by Age Concern Eng) St Mut.

Pollard, John. The Unknown Pope: Benedict XV (1912-1922) & the Pursuit of Peace. (Illus.). 256p. 1999. 29.95 (0-225-66844-0) Continuum.

Pollard, John F. The Fascist Experience in Italy. LC 97-31359. (Routledge Sources in History Ser.). 168p. (C). 1998. 65.00 (0-415-11631-7); pap. 20.99 (0-415-11632-5) Routledge.

***Pollard, John F.** Unknown Pope: Benedict XV (1912-1922) & the Pursuit of Peace. (Illus.). 256p. 2000. pap. 22.95 (0-225-66891-2) G Chapman.

Pollard, John F., jt. auth. see Kent, Peter C.

Pollard, John W. The Physician Manager in Group Practice. 142p. 1994. pap. 36.00 (1-56829-005-5, 3931) Med Group Mgmt.

Pollard, Joseph P. Mr. Justice Cardozo: A Liberal Mind in Action. LC 95-80916. viii, 327p. 1995. reprint ed. 75.00 (0-89941-999-2, 309020) W S Hein.

— Mister Justice Cardozo: A Liberal Mind in Action. LC 75-98790. 327p. 1970. reprint ed. lib. bdg. 65.00 (0-8371-2815-3, POJD, Greenwood Pr) Greenwood.

Pollard, Josephine. Battles of America, Vol. 2. (Illus.). 256p. (J). 1998. reprint ed. 15.00 (1-889128-43-0) Mantle Ministries.

***Pollard, Josephine.** A Child's History of the Life of Christopher Columbus, No. 6. unabridged ed. (Illus.). 240p. (YA). 2000. reprint ed. write for info. (1-889128-66-X) Mantle Ministries.

Pollard, Josephine. A Child's History of the Life of Lincoln. (Child's American History Ser.). (Illus.). 152p. (J). 1999. reprint ed. 15.00 (1-889128-59-7) Mantle Ministries.

— The History of the United States. unabridged ed. (Illus.). 176p. 1998. reprint ed. 15.00 (1-889128-42-2) Mantle Ministries.

— Life of Washington, Vol. 3. (Illus.). 136p. (J). 1998. 15.00 (1-889128-44-9) Mantle Ministries.

— Our Naval Heroes: Told in One Syllable Words, Vol. 4. (Illus.). 256p. (J). 1998. reprint ed. 15.00 (1-889128-45-7) Mantle Ministries.

Pollard, Joshua. Neolithic Britain. LC 98-150957. (Archaeology Ser.: No. 75). (Illus.). 64p. 1997. pap. 10.50 (0-7478-0353-6, Pub. by Shire Pubns) Parkwest Pubns.

Pollard, Judy & Lund, Tricia. Classic Quilts with Precise Foundation Piecing. Schneider, Sally, ed. LC 96-21436. (Illus.). 80p. (Orig.). 1996. pap. 22.95 (1-56477-161-X, B272) Martingale & Co.

Pollard, June, et al. Early Childhood Care & Education: Global Connections. Beauchamp, Edward R., ed. (Reference Books in International Education). 400p. Date not set. text 60.00 (0-8153-1557-0) Garland.

Pollard, Kathi. I Climbed a Mountain: A Mother's Diary of Tragedy, Grief & Triumph. 84p. (Orig.). 1997. pap. 7.50 (1-57502-409-8, PO1271) Morris Pubng.

***Pollard, Kathi.** I Climbed a Mountain A Mother's Diary of Tragedy, Grief & Triumph. 1999. pap. 7.95 (0-9666819-2-4) Winners Success Netwrk.

Pollard, Kathi, ed. see Jacobson, Arni.

Pollard, L. Computer & Design Architecture. (C). 1989. text 65.20 (0-13-167255-X) P-H.

Pollard, Laurel & Hess, Natalie. Zero Prep: Ready-to-Go Activities for the Language Classroom. (Illus.). xvii, 128p. 1997. pap. text 19.95 (1-882483-64-2) Alta Bk Ctr.

Pollard, Leslie J. Complaint to the Lord: Historical Perspectives on the African American Elderly. LC 95-38952. 288p. 1996. 43.50 (0-945636-80-6) Susquehanna U Pr.

Pollard, Lucille A. Women on College & University Faculties: A Historical Survey & a Study of Their Present Academic Status. Metzger, Walter P., ed. LC 76-55186. (Academic Profession Ser.). (Illus.). 1980. reprint ed. lib. bdg. 33.95 (0-405-10019-1) Ayer.

Pollard, M. Dublin's Trade in Books, Fifteen Fifty to Eighteen Hundred: Lyell Lectures, 1986-7. (Lyell Lectures in Bibliography, 1986-87). (Illus.). 296p. 1990. text 85.00 (0-19-818409-3) OUP.

Pollard, M. J., jt. ed. see Harper, Nigel J. N.

Pollard, Marcia J. & Wigal, Grace J. Hospital Staff Privileges: What Every Health Care Practitioner & Lawyer Needs to Know. LC 95-40425. 210p. 1995. pap. 19.50 (1-56793-037-9, 0972) Health Admin Pr.

***Pollard, Mark.** It's Prayer Time: Prayer & Spiritual Warfare from the African-American Perspective. 2000. pap. 12.99 (0-8307-2532-6, Gospel Light) Gospel Lght.

Pollard, Mark, jt. auth. see Glimcher, Arnold.

Pollard, Mary Nash. Pardon Gentles All. LC 96-94138. 200p. (Orig.). 1996. pap. 7.95 (0-9652662-0-6) Littlefish Ltd.

Pollard, Michael. Absolute Rulers. Stefoff, Rebecca, ed. LC 91-33297. (Pioneers in History Ser.). (Illus.). 48p. (J). (gr. 5-8). 1992. lib. bdg. 19.93 (1-56074-034-5) Garrett Ed Corp.

***Pollard, Michael.** Alexander Graham Bell. LC 00-8818. (Giants of Science Ser.). (Illus.). 64p. (gr. 4-7). 2000. write for info. (1-56711-334-6) Blackbirch.

Pollard, Michael. Beliefs & Believers. Stefoff, Rebecca, ed. LC 91-36503. (Pioneers in History Ser.). (Illus.). 48p. (J). (gr. 5-9). 1992. lib. bdg. 19.93 (1-56074-037-X) Garrett Ed Corp.

— The Clock & How It Changed the World. LC 94-15225. (History & Invention Ser.). (Illus.). 48p. (J). (gr. 4-9). 1995. 16.95 (0-8160-3142-8) Facts on File.

— Discovering English Folksong. 1982. 4.50 (0-913714-65-8, Pub. by Shire Pubns) Parkwest Pubns.

— Discovering English Folksong. 1989. pap. 25.00 (0-85263-609-1, Pub. by Shire Pubns) St Mut.

— Empire Builders. Stefoff, Rebecca, ed. LC 91-36501. (Pioneers in History Ser.). (Illus.). 48p. (J). (gr. 5-8). 1992. lib. bdg. 19.93 (1-56074-038-8) Garrett Ed Corp.

— The Lightbulb & How It Changed the World. LC 94-15226. (Illus.). 48p. 1995. 16.95 (0-8160-3145-2) Facts on File.

***Pollard, Michael.** Margaret Mead: Bringing World Cultures Together. LC 98-47864. (Giants of Science Ser.). (Illus.). 64p. (J). (gr. 5-8). 1999. lib. bdg. 18.95 (1-56711-327-3) Blackbirch.

Pollard, Michael. North Sea Surge: The Story of the East Coast Floods of 1953. 136p. (C). 1988. 65.00 (0-86138-021-5, Pub. by T Dalton) St Mut.

— People Who Care. Stefoff, Rebecca, ed. LC 91-36502. (Pioneers in History Ser.). (Illus.). 48p. (J). (gr. 5-8). 1992. lib. bdg. 19.93 (1-56074-035-3) Garrett Ed Corp.

— The Red Cross & the Red Crescent. LC 93-26383. (Organizations That Help the World Ser.). 64p. (J). 1994. pap. 7.95 (0-382-24738-8, New Dscvry Bks); lib. bdg. 13.95 (0-02-774720-4, New Dscvry Bks) Silver Burdett Pr.

— Revolutionary Power. Stefoff, Rebecca, ed. LC 91-36504. (Pioneers in History Ser.). (Illus.). 48p. (J). (gr. 5-8). 1992. lib. bdg. 19.93 (1-56074-039-6) Garrett Ed Corp.

— Roads & Tunnels. LC 96-6958. (Superstructures Ser.). (Illus.). 48p. (J). (gr. 4-8). 1996. lib. bdg. 24.26 (0-8172-4332-1) Raintree Steck-V.

— Thinkers. Stefoff, Rebecca, ed. LC 91-33296. (Pioneers in History Ser.). (Illus.). 48p. (J). (gr. 5-8). 1992. lib. bdg. 19.93 (1-56074-036-1) Garrett Ed Corp.

— United Nations: Organizations That Help the World. (YA). 1995. pap. 7.95 (0-382-24764-7, New Dscvry Bks) Silver Burdett Pr.

Pollard, Michael, jt. auth. see Wilkinson, Philip.

Pollard, Miriam. The Other Face of Love: Dialogues with the Prison Experience of Albert Speer. 180p. 1996. 17.95 (0-8245-1562-5) Crossroad NY.

Pollard, Morris, ed. Perspectives in Virology Vol. 10: The Gustav Stern Symposium. fac. ed. LC 59-8415. (Illus.). 276p. pap. 85.60 (0-7837-7155-X, 204714200010) Bks Demand.

Pollard, Nan. Friends Together. (Real Mother Goose Library). (Illus.). 32p. (J). (ps-3). 1990. 4.95 (1-56288-048-9) Checkerboard.

— Life of Christ. 1998. pap. text 1.49 (0-7847-0756-1) Standard Pub.

— Old Testament. 1998. pap. text 1.49 (0-7847-0755-3) Standard Pub.

Pollard, Nancy M. What's Love Got to Do with It? 180p. (Orig.). 1993. pap. 12.95 (0-9637705-1-9) Benchmark UT.

Pollard, Neil & McDonald, Mary. How Do You Measure Up? LC 93-20060. (Illus.). (J). 1994. pap. write for info. (0-383-03697-6) SRA McGraw.

P

Pollard, Nick. Evangelism Made Slightly Less Difficult: How to Interest People Who Aren't Interested. LC 97-45682. 192p. 1998. pap. 10.99 (*0-8308-1908-8*, 1908) InterVarsity.

— Why Do They Do That? Practical Advice to Parents on How to Tackle Teen Behavioe. LC 99-31535. 1999. pap. text 10.99 (*0-7459-4087-0*) Lion USA.

Pollard, Nigel. Soldiers, Cities & Civilians in Roman Syria. (Illus.). 338p. (C). text 49.50 (*0-472-11155-8*, 11155) U of Mich Pr.

Pollard, Patricia, jt. auth. see John, Andrew.

Pollard, Patrick. Andre Gide: The Homosexual Moralist. LC 90-27047. (Illus.). 448p. (C). 1992. 50.00 (*0-300-04998-6*) Yale U Pr.

Pollard-Patrick, Michele. Children's Special Teas: A Child's Introduction to Tea. (Illus.). 49p. (J). (gr. 2-4). 1998. 12.00 (*0-8059-4479-6*) Dorrance.

Pollard, Peter. Colombia Handbook. (Footprint Handbooks Ser.). (Illus.). 336p. 1998. 21.95 (*0-8442-4949-1*, 49491, Natl Textbk Co) NTC Contemp Pub Co.

Pollard, Richard, jt. auth. see Chan, Lois M.

Pollard, Rita, jt. auth. see Daniels, Lolee.

Pollard, Robert C., jt. auth. see Harper, William L.

Pollard, Robert D. Nazi Weapons & Munitions Code. LC 83-6169. 56p. (Orig.). 1983. pap. text 10.00 (*0-86663-986-1*) Ide Hse.

Pollard, Robert T. China's Foreign Relations, Nineteen Seventeen to Nineteen Thirty-One. LC 70-111745. (American Imperialism: Viewpoints of United States Foreign Policy, 1898-1941 Ser.). 1970. reprint ed. 23.95 (*0-405-02046-5*) Ayer.

Pollard, S. Typology of Industrialization Processes in the Nineteenth Century, Vol. 39. Lesourne, Jacques & Sonnenschein, Hugo, eds. (Fundamentals of Pure & Applied Economics Ser.: 39). viii, 106p. 1990. pap. text 59.00 (*3-7186-5007-X*) Gordon & Breach.

Pollard, Sidney. Britain's Prime & Britain's Decline: The British Economy, 1870-1914. 384p. 1989. 69.50 (*0-7131-6591-X*, Pub. by E A) Routldge.

— Democracy & Empire. 4th ed. 480p. pap. text. write for info. (*0-340-56185-8*, Pub. by E A) Routldge.

— Development of the British Economy, 1914-1967. 2nd rev. ed. LC 77-408269. ix, 518 p. 1969. write for info. (*0-7131-5450-0*) St Martin.

— A History of Labour in Sheffield. (Modern Revivals in Economic & Social History Ser.). 392p. 1993. 72.95 (*0-7512-0215-0*, Pub. by Gregg Revivals) Ashgate Pub Co.

— Integration of the European Economy since 1815. (Studies on Contemporary Europe: No. 4). 96p. (C). 1981. text 24.95 (*0-04-336069-6*); pap. text 8.95 (*0-04-336070-X*) Routledge.

— International Economy since 1945. LC 97-204887. (Making of the Contemporary World Ser.). (Illus.). 136p. (C). 1997. pap. 14.99 (*0-415-14067-6*) Routledge.

— Labour History & the Labour Movement in Britian. LC 98-54452. (Variorum Collected Studies Ser.). (Illus.). 6p. 1999. text 101.95 (*0-86078-793-1*) Ashgate Pub Co.

— Marginal Europe: The Contribution of Marginal Lands Since the Middle Ages. LC 97-1021. 334p. 1997. text 75.00 (*0-19-820638-0*) OUP.

— Peaceful Conquest: The Industrialization of Europe, 1760-1970. (Illus.). 464p. 1981. pap. text 24.95 (*0-19-877095-2*) OUP.

Pollard, Sidney & Robertson, Paul. British Shipbuilding Industry Eighteen Seventy to Nineteen Fourteen. LC 78-12500. (Studies in Business History: No. 30). (Illus.). 336p. 1979. 37.50 (*0-674-08287-7*) HUP.

Pollard, Sidney & Salt, John, eds. Robert Owen: Prophet of the Poor. LC 70-156269. 318p. 1975. 40.00 (*0-8387-7952-2*) Bucknell U Pr.

Pollard, Sidney, jt. ed. see Feinstein, Charles H.

Pollard, Sidney, jt. ed. see Mathias, P.

Pollard, Stephen. Philosophical Introduction to Set Theory. LC 89-40391. (C). 1990. text 34.50 (*0-268-01584-8*); pap. text 18.50 (*0-268-01585-6*) U of Notre Dame Pr.

Pollard, Stephen, jt. auth. see Martin, Norman M.

Pollard, Stephen F. Boatbuilding with Aluminium. 280p. 1993. 29.95 (*0-07-050426-1*) McGraw.

— Boatbuilding with Aluminum. 1993. 29.95 (*0-87742-377-6*) Intl Marine.

Pollard, Stewart M. Tied to Masonic Apron Strings. Cook, Lewis C., ed. vi, 121p. 1991. pap. 6.00 (*0-88053-059-6*, M-322) Macoy Pub.

Pollard, T. E. Fullness of Humanity: Christ's Humanness & Ours. (Almond Press Individual Titles Ser.). 126p. 1982. 46.50 (*0-907459-10-2*, Pub. by Sheffield Acad); pap. 11.50 (*0-907459-11-0*, Pub. by Sheffield Acad) CUP Services.

Pollard, Ted. King of the Road: The Beginner's Guide to RV Travel. (Illus.). 221p. (Orig.). 1995. pap. 12.95 (*0-9637125-0-0*) Remington PA.

***Pollard, Tessa & Hyatt, Susan B., eds.** Sex, Gender & Health. LC 98-32165. (Biosocial Society Symposium Ser.: Vol. 11). (Illus.). 192p. (C). 1999. 54.95 (*0-521-59282-8*); pap. 19.95 (*0-521-59707-2*) Cambridge U Pr.

Pollard, Tony & Morrison, Alex, eds. The Early Prehistory of Scotland. LC 96-164996. (Illus.). 360p. 1996. 60.00 (*0-7486-0677-7*, Pub. by Edinburgh U Pr) Col U Pr.

***Pollard, Velma.** Dread Talk: The Language of Rastafari. rev. ed. 96p. 1999. pap. 14.95 (*0-7735-2030-9*) McG-Queens Univ Pr.

— Karl & Other Stories. LC 93-24169. (Caribbean Writers Ser.). 137p. (C). 1995. pap. 16.80 (*0-582-22726-7*) Longman.

Pollard, Verlma. From Jamaican Creole to Standard English. 69p. (Orig.). 1993. pap. text 15.00 (*1-878433-14-8*) Caribbean Diaspora Pr.

Pollard, William C., Jr. Dark Friday: The Story of Quantrill's Lawrence Raid. (Illus.). 144p. 1990. 16.95 (*0-941974-13-8*) Baranski Pub Co.

Pollard, William E. Bayesian Statistics for Evaluation Research: An Introduction. LC 85-14194. (Contemporary Evaluation Research Ser.: No. 8). (Illus.). 256p. 1986. reprint ed. pap. 79.40 (*0-608-01092-8*, 205940100001) Bks Demand.

Pollard, William F., jt. ed. see Boenig, Robert.

Pollarine, Barbara. Great & Capital Changes: An Account of the Valley Forge Encampment. (Illus.). 64p. (C). 1993. pap. text 7.95 (*0-939631-54-7*) Thomas Publications.

Pollastro, R. M., jt. ed. see Guven, N.

Pollatschek. Progmg Discret Sim. 1995. pap. text 40.00 (*0-13-234584-6*) P-H.

Pollatschek, Henriette & Polt, Renata. A Thousand Kisses: A Grandmother's Holocaust Letters. LC 98-9066. (Judaic Studies). 216p. 1998. 29.95 (*0-8173-0930-6*) U of Ala Pr.

Pollatschek, Moshe A. Programming Discrete Solutions. 350p. 1996. 39.95 incl. disk (*0-87930-449-9*) C M P Books.

Pollatsek, Alexander, jt. auth. see Rayner, Keith.

Pollatsek, H., jt. ed. see O'Shea, D. B.

Pollatsek, Harriet S. & O'Shea, Donal. Laboratories in Mathematical Experimentation: A Bridge Course to Higher Mathematics. LC 96-37621. (TIMS - Texts in Mathematical Science Ser.). (Illus.). 300p. 1997. pap. 34.95 (*0-387-94922-4*) Spr-Verlag.

Pollay, Richard W., ed. Information Sources in Advertising History. LC 78-75259. 330p. 1979. lib. bdg. 65.00 (*0-313-21422-0*, PIA/, Greenwood Pr) Greenwood.

***Pollay, Vanessa.** Genealogical Periodical Annual Index, 1993 Vol. 32: Key to the Genealogical Literature. 320p. 2000. 28.00 (*0-7884-1508-5*) Heritage Bk.

Polle, Torsten, et al. Fundamentals of Information Systems. LC 99-11565. (International Series In Engineering & Computer Science). 1999. write for info. (*0-7923-8450-4*) Kluwer Academic.

Pollefeyt, Didier, ed. Jews & Christians: Rivals or Partners for the Kingdom of God? In Search of an Alternative for the Theology of Substitution. (Louvain Theological & Pastoral Monographs). 196p. 1998. pap. 25.00 (*0-8028-4487-1*) Eerdmans.

Pollen, Daniel A. Hannah's Heirs: The Quest for the Genetic Origins of Alzheimer's Disease. LC 93-66. (Illus.). 320p. (C). 1993. 30.00 (*0-19-506809-2*) OUP.

— Hannah's Heirs: The Quest for the Genetic Origins of Alzheimer's Disease. LC 97-164671. (Illus.). 336p. (C). 1996. pap. 14.95 (*0-19-510652-0*) OUP.

Pollen, Michael R. Through the Eye of the Glacier. pap. 14.95 (*1-888125-58-6*) Publ Consult.

Pollen, Pandora. Moonstruck Mongrel. 1997. 16.95 (*0-7188-2788-0*, Lutterworth-Parkwest) Parkwest Pubns.

Pollentier, Nicole. Smolt. (Poesia Tejana Ser.: Vol. 1). viii, 44p. 1999. pap. 12.00 (*0-930324-43-9*) Wings Pr.

Poller. Recent Advances in Blood Coagulants. 7th ed. 1996. text 68.00 (*0-443-05316-2*, W B Saunders Co) Harcrt Hlth Sci Grp.

Poller, H. Leonard, jt. ed. see Jaffe, Hirshel.

***Poller, Jake.** Reach. 1999. pap. 16.95 (*0-224-05296-9*, Pub. by Random) Trafalgar.

Poller, L., ed. Recent Advances in Blood Coagulation, No. 5. 5th ed. (Illus.). 312p. 1991. text 77.00 (*0-443-04343-4*) Church.

Poller, Leon & Hirsch, Jack, eds. Oral Anticoagulants: Chemical & Biological Properties & Clinical Applications. (Arnold Publication). 356p. (C). 1996. text 125.00 (*0-340-55266-2*) OUP.

Poller, Leon & Thomson, Jean M., eds. Thrombosis & Its Management. (Illus.). 272p. (Orig.). 1993. pap. text. write for info. (*0-443-04797-9*) Church.

Poller, Nidra, tr. see Kourouma, Ahmadou.

Poller, Walter. Medical Block Buchenwald. 1987. pap. 7.95 (*0-8184-0448-5*) Carol Pub Group.

Pollera, Alberto. The Native Peoples of Eritrea. Lappin, Linda, tr. from ITA. LC 99-15794. 384p. 1998. 79.95 (*1-56902-094-9*) Red Sea Pr.

— The Native Peoples of Eritrea. Lappin, Linda, tr. from ITA. LC 99-15794. 1998. pap. 24.95 (*1-56902-095-7*) Red Sea Pr.

Pollery, J. B. A Soldier's Letters to Charming Nellie. 21.95 (*0-8488-1128-3*) Amereon Ltd.

Pollet, Alison. The Guy I Left Behind. (Love Stories Ser.). 192p. (YA). (gr. 7-12). 1997. mass mkt. 3.99 (*0-553-57076-5*) Bantam.

***Pollet, Alison.** MTV's Real World: New Orleans. 160p. 2000. 16.00 (*0-7434-1127-7*) PB.

Pollet, Alison. MTV's Road Rules: Journals. LC 99-199268. 160p. 1998. pap. 18.00 (*0-671-02595-3*) PB.

***Pollet, Alison.** MTV's the Real World: True Confessions. 160p. 1999. per. 16.00 (*0-671-03701-3*) PB.

Pollet, Elizabeth, ed. & intro. see Schwartz, Delmore.

Pollet, Gilbert, jt. auth. see International Reameayarna Conference Staff.

Pollet, J. V. Julius Pflug (1499-1564) et la Crise Religieuse Dans l'Allemagne Du XVIe Siecle. (Studies in Medieval & Reformation Thought: No. 45). (FRE.). 446p. 1990. 154.00 (*90-04-09241-2*) Brill Academic Pubs.

Pollet, Lloyd E., ed. see Patterson, Vanessa L.

Pollet, Maurice. John Skelton: Poet of Tudor England. LC 73-124443. 302p. 1975. 38.50 (*0-8387-7737-6*) Bucknell U Pr.

Pollet, R. J. English-French Lexicon of Technical Terms: Lexique des Termes Techniques Anglais-Francais. (ENG & FRE.). 233p. 1981. pap. 24.95 (*0-8288-0618-7*, M6460) Fr & Eur.

— Lexicon of Amateur Photography: Lexique de la Photagraphie d'Amateur: Appareils et Accessoires. (FRE.). 127p. 1981. pap. 19.95 (*0-8288-2089-9*, M14196) Fr & Eur.

Pollett, Libby, jt. auth. see Head, Debby.

Polley. Understanding the Building Regulations. (Illus.). 208p. (Orig.). (C). 1995. pap. 25.99 (*0-419-19950-0*, E & FN Spon) Routledge.

Polley, George. Fernandez' Tale & Other Stories: Short Fiction. 172p. 1999. pap. 20.00 (*1-893901-02-5*) T & H Pubns.

— Living & Working in the 21st Century: Exciting Concepts for Making It in the Marketplace of the 21st Century. 96p. 1998. pap. 10.95 (*1-893901-01-7*) T & H Pubns.

— My Story. 27p. 1999. pap. 3.00 (*1-893901-03-3*) T & H Pubns.

***Polley, George.** Seeing: Collected Poems, 1973-1999. 44p. 2000. pap. 4.00 (*1-893901-04-1*) T & H Pubns.

Polley, George. Things I've Learned from the 'Old' Life Vignettes. 93p. 1998. pap. 10.95 (*1-893901-00-9*) T & H Pubns.

Polley, J. B. Hood's Texas Brigade. (Illus.). 357p. 1995. reprint ed. 30.00 (*0-89029-037-7*) Morningside Bkshop.

— Hood's Texas Brigade. 1993. reprint ed. lib. bdg. 75.00 (*0-7812-5893-6*) Rprt Serv.

— A Soldier's Letters to Charming Nellie. 350p. 1984. reprint ed. 32.50 (*0-942211-91-X*) Olde Soldier Bks.

Polley, L. & Pottinger, D. E., eds. Variational Calculations in Quantum Field Theory. 316p. (C). 1988. pap. 51.00 (*9971-5-0501-0*); text 100.00 (*9971-5-0500-2*) World Scientific Pub.

Polley, Louis E. The History of the Mohawk Valley & Early Lumbering. Bailey, Sue, ed. LC 84-60964. (Illus.). 144p. (Orig.). 1984. pap. 19.50 (*0-916930-09-2*) Polley Pubs.

Polley, Marian L., jt. auth. see Gelb, Joyce.

***Polley, Martin.** A to Z of Modern Europe, 1789-1999. LC 00-27724. (Illus.). 240p. 2000. 60.00 (*0-415-18597-1*); pap. 17.99 (*0-415-18598-X*) Routledge.

Polley, Martin. Sport & Society: A Contemporary History. LC 97-24974. 248p. (C). 1998. 65.00 (*0-415-14216-4*); pap. 20.99 (*0-415-14217-2*) Routledge.

Polley, Maxine. Dance Aerobics. LC 80-23906. (Illus.). 160p. (Orig.). 1980. pap. 5.95 (*0-89037-186-5*) Anderson World.

— Dance Aerobics, Vol. 2. 160p. (Orig.). 1983. pap. 6.95 (*0-89037-256-X*) Anderson World.

Polley, Michael. A Biography of George F. Kennan: The Education of a Realist. LC 89-27727. (Studies in Twentieth Century American History: Vol. 4). 256p. 1990. lib. bdg. 89.95 (*0-88946-693-9*) E Mellen.

Polley, Richard B., et al, eds. The Symlog Practitioner: Applications of Small Group Research. LC 87-37684. (Illus.). 427p. 1988. 75.00 (*0-275-92364-9*, C2364, Praeger Pubs) Greenwood.

***Polley, Rodger.** Uintah Railway Pictorial: Mack to Atchee. Collman, Russ, ed. (Illus.). 320p. 1999. 52.00 (*0-913582-68-9*) Sundance.

Polli, E. E., ed. Haematopoietic Growth Factors: Biology & Clinical Use - Journal: Acta Haematologica, Vol. 86, No. 3, 1991. (Illus.). 52p. 1992. pap. 57.50 (*3-8055-5557-1*) S Karger.

— Neurochemistry of Hepatic Coma. (Experimental Biology & Medicine Ser.: Vol. 4). 1971. 30.50 (*3-8055-1187-6*) S Karger.

Polliack, Aaron. A Handbook of Essential Drugs & Regimens in Hematological Oncology. xii, 165p. 1991. text 96.00 (*3-7186-5096-7*, Harwood Acad Pubs); pap. text 43.00 (*3-7186-5097-5*, Harwood Acad Pubs) Gordon & Breach.

— Human Leukemias. (Developments in Oncology Ser.). 1984. lib. bdg. 115.00 (*90-247-2338-8*) Kluwer Academic.

Polliack, Aaron, contrib. by. Leukemia & Lymphoma Reviews, Vol. 6. (Leukemia & Lymphoma Reviews Ser.). 408p. 1997. text 84.00 (*90-5702-198-6*, Harwood Acad Pubs) Gordon & Breach.

— Leukemia & Lymphoma Reviews, Vol. 7. (Leukemia & Lymphoma Reviews Ser.). 358p. 1997. text 75.00 (*90-5702-199-4*, Harwood Acad Pubs) Gordon & Breach.

Polliack, Aaron, ed. Advances in Chronic Lymphocytic Leukemia. 150p. 1992. text 114.00 (*3-7186-5213-7*, Harwood Acad Pubs) Gordon & Breach.

— Leukemia & Lymphoma Reviews, No. 1. 372p. 1992. text 176.00 (*3-7186-5251-X*, Harwood Acad Pubs) Gordon & Breach.

— Leukemia & Lymphoma Reviews, No. 2. 294p. 1993. 78.00 (*3-7186-5374-5*) Kluwer Academic.

— Leukemia & Lymphoma Reviews, No. 3. (Leukemia & Lymphoma Reviews Ser.). 296p. 1994. text 116.00 (*3-7186-5490-3*, Harwood Acad Pubs) Gordon & Breach.

— Leukemia & Lymphoma Reviews, No. 4. (Leukemia & Lymphoma Reviews Ser). 304p. 1995. text 105.00 (*3-7186-5760-0*, Harwood Acad Pubs) Gordon & Breach.

— Leukemia & Lymphoma Reviews, Vol. 5. (Leukemia & Lymphoma Reviews Ser.). 360p. 1997. text 72.00 (*90-5702-197-8*, Harwood Acad Pubs) Gordon & Breach.

Polliack, Aaron & Catovsky, D. Chronic Lymphocytic Leukemia, 4 vols. xii, 390p. 1988. text 240.00 (*3-7186-4802-4*) Gordon & Breach.

Polliack, Aaron, et al. A Scanning Electron Microscopy Atlas of Normal & Malignant Leukocytes. LC 92-49075. 95p. 1993. text 107.00 (*3-7186-5362-1*) Gordon & Breach.

Polliack, Aaron, jt. auth. see Dion.

Polliack, Aaron, jt. ed. see Pangalis, Gerassimos A.

Polliack, Aaron, jt. ed. see Tallman, Martin S.

Polliack, Meira. The Karaite Tradition of Arabic Bible Translation: A Linguistic & Exegetical Study of Karaite Translations of the Pentateuch from the Tenth & Eleventh Centuries C. E. LC 96-50175. 1997. 134.00 (*90-04-10267-1*) Brill Academic Pubs.

Pollice, L., ed. Hepatocellular Proliferative Process. (Journal: Applied Pathology: Vol. 6, No. 2, 1988). (Illus.). 88p. 1988. pap. 50.50 (*3-8055-4788-9*) S Karger.

Pollicini, A. A., ed. Using Toolpack Software Tools. (C). 1988. text 195.50 (*0-7923-0033-5*) Kluwer Academic.

Pollick, Steve. Starwalking with Sarah: And Other Essays. LC 94-90106. (Illus.). 144p. (Orig.). 1994. pap. 7.95 (*0-9614554-1-1*) Toledo Blade.

Pollicott, Mark. Lectures on Ergodic Theory & Pesin Theory on Compact Manifolds. (London Mathematical Society Lecture Note Ser.: No. 180). (Illus.). 170p. (C). 1993. pap. text 44.95 (*0-521-43593-5*) Cambridge U Pr.

Pollicott, Mark & Schmidt, Klaus, eds. Ergodic Theory & Zd Actions. (London Mathematical Society Lecture Note Ser.: No. 228). (Illus.). 492p. (C). 1996. pap. text 49.95 (*0-521-57688-1*) Cambridge U Pr.

Pollicott, Mark & Yuri, Michiko. Dynamical Systems & Ergodic Theory. LC 97-8812. (London Mathematical Society Student Texts Ser.: No. 40). (Illus.). 193p. (C). 1998. text 64.95 (*0-521-57294-0*); pap. text 23.95 (*0-521-57599-0*) Cambridge U Pr.

Pollin, Alice M., ed. see Garcia Lorca, Federico.

Pollin, Burton R. Dictionary of Names & Titles in Poe's Collected Works. LC 68-28982. (Paperback Ser.). 1968. pap. 32.50 (*0-306-71154-0*) Da Capo.

— Insights & Outlooks: Essays of Great Writers. LC 86-22955. 239p. 1986. 17.50 (*0-87752-237-5*) Gordian.

— Music for Shelley's Poetry. LC 74-4446. (Music Reprint Ser.). 174p. 1974. lib. bdg. 29.50 (*0-306-70640-7*) Da Capo.

Pollin, Burton R., compiled by. Images of Poe's Works: An Analysis & Descriptive Catalogue, 9. LC 89-17182. (Bibliographies & Indexes in American Literature Ser.: No. 9). 442p. 1989. lib. bdg. 85.00 (*0-313-26582-8*, PPW/, Greenwood Pr) Greenwood.

Pollin, Burton R., ed. Collected Writings of Edgar Allan Poe: Poe's Nonfiction in the Broadway Journal, Set, Vols. 3 & 4. 760p. 1986. 150.00 (*0-87752-232-4*) Gordian.

— Word Index to Poe's Fiction. 512p. (C). 1982. 50.00 (*0-87752-225-1*) Gordian.

Pollin, Burton R. & Ridgely, Joseph V., eds. The Collected Writings of Edgar Allan Poe Vol. 5: Writings in "The Southern Literary Messenger" LC 86-18426. (Illus.). 406p. 1997. 75.00 (*0-87752-242-1*) Gordian.

Pollin, Burton R. & Wilkes, John W., intros. Political Justice: A Poem in a Letter to the Right Hon. the Lord. LC 92-24282. (Augustan Reprints Ser.: No. 111). 1965. reprint ed. 14.50 (*0-404-70111-6*) AMS Pr.

Pollin, Burton R., ed. see Hansen, Thomas S.

Pollin, Burton R., ed. see Poe, Edgar Allan.

Pollin, Burton R., ed. & intro. see Poe, Edgar Allan.

Pollin, Robert. Deeper in Debt: The Changing Financial Conditions of U. S. Households. LC 90-84862. (Illus.). 82p. (Orig.). 1990. pap. 12.00 (*0-944826-37-7*) Economic Policy Inst.

Pollin, Robert, ed. The Macroeconomics of Saving, Finance, & Investment. LC 97-4499. 416p. (C). 1997. text 75.00 (*0-472-10787-9*, 10787) U of Mich Pr.

Pollin, Robert & Luce, Stephanie. The Living Wage: Building a Fair Economy. LC 98-11110. 288p. 1998. 22.50 (*1-56584-409-2*, Pub. by New Press NY) Norton.

***Pollin, Robert & Luce, Stephanie.** The Living Wage: Building a Fair Economy. 272p. 2000. pap. 15.95 (*1-56584-588-9*, Pub. by New Press NY) Norton.

Pollin, Robert, jt. auth. see Sherman, Howard J.

Pollin, Robert, jt. ed. see Dymski, Gary.

***Pollin, Shane.** Law Quickly & Easily on the Internet. (Surf Less Find More! Ser.). 34p. 1999. 9.95 (*1-893957-00-4*) SurfLess.

Pollinger, Andrew, tr. see Hoss, Rudolph.

Pollinger, Eileen. Erica. (Springsong Ser.). 192p. (YA). 1996. mass mkt. 4.99 (*1-55661-899-9*) Bethany Hse.

Pollinger, Gerald, jt. auth. see Green, William.

***Pollinger, Gina.** Treasury of Shakespeare's Verse. LC 99-88382. 96p. (J). 2000. pap. 11.95 (*0-7534-5292-8*, Kingfisher) LKC.

Pollinger, Lesley. Writing for Children & Getting Published. (Teach Yourself Ser.). 192p. (J). 1996. pap., student ed. 10.95 (*0-8442-3104-5*, Teach Yrslf) NTC Contemp Pub Co.

Pollington, Andrew & Moran, William, eds. Number Theory with an Emphasis on the Markoff Spectrum. LC 93-18075. (Lecture Notes in Pure & Applied Mathematics Ser.: Vol. 147). (Illus.). 352p. 1993. pap. text 150.00 (*0-8247-8902-4*) Dekker.

Pollington, Stephen. The English Warrior: From Earliest Times to 1066. (Illus.). 272p. 1997. pap. 27.95 (*1-898281-10-6*, Pub. by Anglo-Saxon Bks) Paul & Co Pubs.

— First Steps in Old English: An Easy to Follow Language Course for the Beginner. LC 98-114676. 224p. 1997. pap. 39.95 (*1-898281-19-X*, Pub. by Anglo-Saxon Bks) Paul & Co Pubs.

— Rudiments of Runelore. 96p. 1995. pap. 12.95 (*1-898281-16-5*) Paul & Co Pubs.

Pollingue, Alice B., jt. auth. see Shelton, Carla F.

Pollingue, Mary N., jt. auth. see Nichols, David.

Pollini, John, intro. Roman Portraiture: Images of Character & Virtue in the Late Republic & Early Principate. (Illus.). 44p. (Orig.). (C). 1990. pap. 15.00 (*0-945192-04-5*) USC Fisher Gallery.

Pollins, Donald. Church Sale. (Illus.). 50p. 1989. pap. 5.00 (*0-923621-00-8*) Infinity MD.

Pollins, Harold, jt. auth. see Glass, Ruth.

P

Pollock, Gordon D. In Search of Security: The Mormons & the Kingdom of God on Earth, 1830-1844. (Nineteenth Century American Political & Social History Ser.). 392p. 1989. reprint ed. 25.00 (*0-8240-4071-6*) Garland.

Pollock, Griselda. Differencing the Canon: Feminism & the Writing of Art's Histories. LC 98-28921. (Illus.). 345p. 1999. pap. 22.99 (*0-415-06700-6*) Routledge.

— Differencing the Canon: Feminist Desire & the Writing of Art's Histories. LC 98-28921. 1999. 75.00 (*0-415-06699-9*) Routledge.

— Mary Cassatt: Painter of Modern Women. LC 98-60039. (World of Art Ser.). (Illus.). 224p. 1998. pap. 14.95 (*0-500-20317-2*, Pub. by Thames Hudson) Norton.

Pollock, Griselda. Vision & Difference: Femininity, Feminism & the Histories of Art. (Illus.). 272p. 1988. pap. text 14.95 (*0-317-67353-X*) Routledge.

Pollock, Griselda. Vision & Difference: Femininity, Feminism & the Histories of Art. 256p. (C). 1988. pap. 21.99 (*0-415-00722-4*) Routledge.

Pollock, Griselda, ed. Generations & Geographies in the Visual Arts: Feminist Readings. LC 95-25914. (Illus.). 320p. (C). 1996. 75.00 (*0-415-14127-3*); pap. 23.99 (*0-415-14128-1*) Routledge.

Pollock, Griselda, pref. Lictenberg Ettinger, Bracha. Matrix-Borderlines. 1993. pap. 28.00 (*0-905836-80-4*, Pub. by Museum Modern Art) St Mut.

Pollock, Griselda, jt. auth. see Mainz, Valerie.

Pollock, Griselda, jt. auth. see Orton, Fred.

Pollock, Griselda, jt. auth. see Parker, Rozsika.

Pollock, Griselda, jt. ed. see Kendall, Richard.

Pollock, H. M., jt. ed. see Singer, I. L.

Pollock, Harry. Max. LC 98-101057. 1997. 12.95 (*0-88962-636-7*) Mosaic.

Pollock, Harry E. Round Structures of Aboriginal Middle America. LC 77-11514. (Carnegie Institution of Washington. Publications: No. 471). reprint ed. 37.50 (*0-404-16274-6*) AMS Pr.

Pollock, Horatio M. Family Care of Mental Patients: A Review of Systems of Family Care in America & Europe. LC 75-17236. (Social Problems & Social Policy Ser.). (Illus.). 1976. reprint ed. 21.95 (*0-405-07505-7*) Ayer.

— Mental Disease & Social Welfare. LC 75-17237. (Social Problems & Social Policy Ser.). (Illus.). 1976. reprint ed. 20.95 (*0-405-07506-5*) Ayer.

Pollock, Howard W. Rules of Order & Procedure Parliamentary Law. Garstang, Richard, ed. 63p. (Orig.). 1996. pap. 9.00 (*0-9653617-0-5*) H W Pollock.

***Pollock, J.** Kitchener - The Road to Omdurman. 1999. 40.00 (*0-09-479140-6*, Pub. by Constable & Co) Trafalgar.

Pollock, J. B. Fringing & Fossil Reefs of Oahu. (BMB Ser.: No. 55). 1969. reprint ed. 25.00 (*0-527-02161-X*) Periodicals Srv.

Pollock, J. C. Goering's List. 432p. 1995. mass mkt. 6.50 (*0-440-20519-0*) Dell.

Pollock, James K. The Hitler Decrees. 1994. reprint ed. pap. 12.50 (*1-884739-03-2*) Wahr.

— Making Michigan's Constitution. 1963. pap. 12.50 (*0-911586-25-3*) Wahr.

— Money & Politics Abroad. LC 77-37909. (Select Bibliographies Reprint Ser.). 1977. reprint ed. 24.95 (*0-8369-6747-X*) Ayer.

— Source Materials on the Government & Politics of Germany. 1964. pap. 15.00 (*0-911586-26-1*) Wahr.

Pollock, James K., et al. British Election Studies, 1950. 1951. pap. 10.00 (*0-911586-27-X*) Wahr.

Pollock, Jane, jt. auth. see Arthur, Heidi.

Pollock, Jean, jt. auth. see Pollock, Robert.

Pollock, Jean M. Side by Side: Twelve Multicultural Puppet Plays. LC 97-20542. (School Library Media). 143p. 1998. pap. 29.50 (*0-8108-3362-X*) Scarecrow.

Pollock, Jocelyn M. Ethics in Crime & Justice: Dilemmas & Decisions. 3rd ed. LC 97-22962. (C). 1997. 35.95 (*0-534-50793-X*) Wadsworth Pub.

— Sex & Supervision: Guarding Male & Female Inmates, 12. LC 86-9987. (Contributions in Criminology & Penology Ser.: No. 12). 175p. 1986. 52.95 (*0-313-25410-9*, PSS/, Greenwood Pr) Greenwood.

Pollock, John. Apostle. 1987. 12.95 (*0-89693-368-7*, Victor Bks) Chariot Victor.

— The Apostle. (American Family Portrait Ser.). 312p. (Orig.). 1994. pap. 6.50 (*1-56476-242-4*, 6-3242, Victor Bks) Chariot Victor.

— Cognitive Carpentry: A Blueprint for How to Build a Person. 391p. 1995. 45.00 (*0-262-16152-4*, Bradford Bks) MIT Pr.

— Contemporary Theories of Knowledge. LC 86-20221. (Texts in Philosophy Ser.). 224p. 1986. 60.50 (*0-8476-7452-5*); pap. 23.95 (*0-8476-7453-3*) Rowman.

— How to Build a Person: A Prolegomenon. 205p. 1989. 30.00 (*0-262-16113-3*) MIT Pr.

— Hudson & Maria. (History Makers Ser.). 208p. 1996. reprint ed. pap. 10.99 (*1-85792-223-9*, Pub. by Christian Focus) Spring Arbor Dist.

— John Wesley. 260p. 1995. pap. 10.99 (*0-87788-424-2*, H Shaw Pubs) Waterbrook Pr.

— The Master: A Life of Jesus. 240p. 1994. pap. 6.50 (*1-56476-241-6*, 6-3241, Victor Bks) Chariot Victor.

— The Master: A Life of Jesus. large type ed. (Large Print Inspirational Ser.). 1988. pap. 16.95 (*0-8027-2603-8*) Walker & Co.

— Moody: A Biography. 2nd anniversary ed. 320p. 1997. pap. 12.99 (*0-8010-5786-8*) Baker Bks.

— Moody: Special Anniversary Edition. LC 97-202436. 1997. pap. 11.99 (*1-85792-270-0*, Pub. by Christian Focus) Spring Arbor Dist.

— Moody Without Sankey. 1995. 11.99 (*1-85792-167-4*, Pub. by Christian Focus) Spring Arbor Dist.

— O Apostolo.Tr. of Apostle. (POR.). 304p. 1990. pap. 11.95 (*0-8297-1621-1*) Vida Pubs.

— On Fire for God: Great Missionary Pioneers. 173p. (Orig.). 1995. reprint ed. mass mkt. 5.99 (*1-884543-01-4*) O M Lit.

— Way to Glory: Major General Sir Henry Havelock - the Christian Soldier. (History Makers Ser.). 304p. 1996. reprint ed. pap. 11.99 (*1-85792-245-X*, Pub. by Christian Focus) Spring Arbor Dist.

Pollock, John, jt. ed. see Cummins, Robert.

Pollock, John C. The Politics of Crisis Reporting: Learning to Be a Foreign Correspondent. LC 81-15350. (Praeger Special Studies). 240p. 1981. 55.00 (*0-275-90703-1*, C0703, Praeger Pubs) Greenwood.

Pollock, John C. & Finn, Peter, eds. The Connecticut Mutual Life Report on American Values in the '80s: The Impact of Belief. (Illus.). 346p. 1984. reprint ed. pap. text 36.00 (*0-8191-4020-1*) U Pr of Amer.

Pollock, John L. The Foundations of Philosophical Semantics. LC 83-43088. 252p. 1984. reprint ed. pap. 78.20 (*0-7837-9422-3*, 206016300004) Bks Demand.

— Language & Thought. LC 82-414. 312p. 1982. reprint ed. pap. 96.80 (*0-7837-9423-1*, 206016400004) Bks Demand.

— Nomic Probability & the Foundations of Induction. 368p. 1990. text 75.00 (*0-19-506013-X*) OUP.

— Subjective Reasoning. (Philosophical Studies in Philosophy: No. 8). 266p. 1976. text 126.50 (*90-277-0701-4*, D Reidel) Kluwer Academic.

Pollock, John L. & Cruz, Joseph. Contemporary Theories of Knowledge. 2nd ed. LC 99-12525. (Studies in Epistemology & Cognitive Theory: Vol. 35). 262p. 1999. 57.50 (*0-8476-8936-0*); pap. 19.95 (*0-8476-8937-9*) Rowman.

Pollock, Joy & Waller, Elisabeth. Day-to-Day Dyslexia in the Classroom. LC 93-46700. 200p. (C). 1994. pap. 18.99 (*0-415-11132-3*, B3927) Routledge.

Pollock, Joycelyn M. Counseling Women in Prison. LC 97-33903. (Women's Mental Health & Development Ser.). 1998. 28.00 (*0-8039-7330-6*) Sage.

— Counseling Women in Prison. LC 97-33903. (Women's Mental Health & Development Ser.: vol. 3). 224p. 1998. pap. 12.99 (*0-8039-7331-4*) Sage.

— Criminal Women. LC 98-36919. 299p. (C). 1998. pap. 31.95 (*0-87084-715-5*) Anderson Pub Co.

— Ethics in Crime & Justice: Dilemmas & Decisions. 2nd ed. 236p. 1993. mass mkt. 20.95 (*0-534-21456-8*) Wadsworth Pub.

Pollock, Joycelyn M., ed. Prisons: Today & Tomorrow. LC 96-77254. 505p. 1997. 59.00 (*0-8342-0950-0*, 09500) Aspen Pub.

Pollock, Judith, jt. auth. see Vierra, Andrea.

Pollock, K. H., et al. Angler Survey Methods & Their Applications in Fisheries Management. LC 94-70490. (Special Publication Ser.: No. 25). 371p. 1994. text 101.00 (*0-913235-88-1*, 510.24C) Am Fisheries Soc.

Pollock, Kenna, jt. auth. see Brooks, Courtaney.

Pollock, Kenneth E. Two Men under a Tree: And Other Stories on the Philosophies of Life. (Illus.). 200p. 1998. pap. 12.95 (*0-9662281-0-3*) Isis Pub Hse.

Pollock, Leland W. A Practical Guide to the Marine Animals of Northeastern North America. LC 96-39284. (Illus.). 272p. 1997. text 70.00 (*0-8135-2398-2*); pap. text 29.00 (*0-8135-2399-0*) Rutgers U Pr.

Pollock, Linda. With Faith & Physics: The Life of a Tudor Gentlewoman, Lady Grace Mildmay, 1552-1620. LC 94-24503. 179p. 1995. text 45.00 (*0-312-12519-4*) St Martin.

Pollock, Linda, ed. see Mildmay, Grace.

Pollock, Linda A. Forgotten Children: Parent-Child Relations from 1500 to 1900. LC 83-5315. (Illus.). 352p. 1984. pap. text 28.95 (*0-521-27133-9*) Cambridge U Pr.

Pollock, Malcolm. Abracadabra Flute: Way to Learn. 64p. (J). (gr. k-5). 1998. pap. 6.95 (*0-7136-5685-9*, Pub. by A & C Blk) Midpt Trade.

Pollock, Marion. School Health Instruction Lessons. 3rd ed. 184p. (C). 1994. text 22.50 (*0-8151-6683-4*, WCB McGr Hill) McGrw-H Hghr Educ.

Pollock, Mark. Communication Process in a Mass-Mediated Age. 238p. (C). 1997. per. 45.95 (*0-7872-4509-7*, 41450901) Kendall-Hunt.

Pollock, Marvin E. Resale of Restricted Securities under SEC Rules 144 & 144A. 2nd ed. (Corporate Practice Ser.: Portfolio No. 46). 1990. ring bd. 92.00 (*1-55871-193-7*) BNA.

Pollock, Mary & Roth, Marcia, eds. The Educated Palate: Tasteful Recipes from A-Z. 240p. (Orig.). 1988. pap. 15.00 (*0-317-90973-8*) Calhoun Schl Parents Assn.

Pollock, Michael. Hostage to Fortune: Atlantic City & Casino Gambling. Sinding, Richard V., ed. 208p. (Orig.). 1987. 11.95 (*0-943136-01-6*) Ctr Analysis Public Issues.

Pollock, Michael & Griffiths, Mark. The Royal Horticultural Society Shorter Dictionary of Gardening: A Comprehensive & Essential Reference. (Illus.). 838p. 1999. 65.00 (*0-333-65440-4*, Pub. by Macmillan) Trafalgar.

Pollock, Michael L. & Schmidt, Donald H., eds. Heart Disease & Rehabilitation. 3rd ed. LC 94-12879. 488p. 1994. text 62.00 (*0-87322-588-0*, BPOL0588) Human Kinetics.

Pollock, Norman C., jt. auth. see Lemon, Anthony.

***Pollock, Patricia Grames.** Staying Power. 2000. pap. 9.95 (*1-55279-027-4*) Picasso Publ.

Pollock, Penny. A Christmas Journey. (J). 2000. write for info. (*0-316-71356-2*) Little.

— The Turkey Girl: A Zuni Cinderella Story. LC 93-28947. (Illus.). 32p. (J). (gr. k-3). 1996. 16.95 (*0-316-71314-7*) Little.

Pollock, Penny & Barlow, Gillian. Enchanted Horse. 1993. 14.95 (*0-399-21971-4*) Putnam Pub Group.

Pollock, Philip H., III, jt. auth. see Eismeier, Theodore J.

Pollock, Polly. Basketmaking: Get Started in a New Craft with Easy-to-Follow Projects for Beginners. (Illus.). 47p. 1999. text 25.00 (*0-7881-6040-0*) DIANE Pub.

— Start a Craft: Basket Making. 1994. 7.98 (*0-7858-0060-3*) Bk Sales Inc.

Pollock, Ralph S., ed. Renewing the Dream: National Archives Bicentennial '87 Lectures on Contemporary Constitutional Issues. LC 86-19103. (Illus.). 194p. (Orig.). (C). 1987. 42.00 (*0-8191-5664-7*); pap. text 21.00 (*0-8191-5665-5*) U Pr of Amer.

***Pollock, Raphael E.** Soft Tissue Sarcomas. (ACS Atlas of Clinical Oncology Ser.). 400p. 2000. boxed set 119.00 incl. cd-rom (*1-55009-128-X*) DEKR.

Pollock, Raphael E. Surgical Oncology. LC 97-5016. (Cancer Treatment & Research Ser.). 1997. text 384.00 (*0-7923-9900-5*) Kluwer Academic.

Pollock, Raphael E., et al, eds. Manual of Clinical Oncology. 7th ed. (UICC - International Union Against Cancer Ser.). 840p. 1999. pap. 69.95 (*0-471-23828-7*, Wiley-Liss) Wiley.

Pollock, Raphael E., ed. see Curley, Steven A.

Pollock, Rebecca. My Life As a Battered Woman. Mitchell, Steven, ed. 96p. 1998. pap. 9.00 (*0-9664975-0-3*) Cocozza Pub.

Pollock, Richard A., ed. see MacLeod, Dan & Saunders, H. Duane.

Pollock, Richard A., ed. see Macleod, Dan, et al.

Pollock, Robert. Soccer for Juniors: A Guide for Players, Parents, & Coaches. (Illus.). 208p. 1985. pap. 9.95 (*0-684-18369-2*) S&S Trade.

Pollock, Robert & Pollock, Jean. Common Campground Critters of the West: A Children's Guide. 24p. (J). (gr. 1-6). 1987. reprint ed. pap. 5.95 (*0-911797-77-7*) Roberts Rinehart.

Pollock, Ross, jt. auth. see David, Paul T.

Pollock, S. M., et al, eds. Operations Research & the Public Sector. LC 94-14930. (Handbooks in Operations Research & Management Science: Vol. 6). 740p. 1994. 165.00 (*0-444-89204-4*, North Holland) Elsevier.

Pollock, Sharon. Doc. LC 87-101427. 126p. 1986. pap. text 10.95 (*0-88754-448-7*) Playwrights.

— Walsh. rev. ed. LC 83-91363. 136p. 1983. pap. 12.95 (*0-88922-215-0*, Pub. by Talonbks) Genl Dist Srvs.

Pollock, Sheldon. Aspects of Versification in Sanskrit Lyric Poetry. (American Oriental Ser.: Vol. 61). x, 335p. 1977. 15.00 (*0-940490-61-7*) Am Orient Soc.

Pollock, Steve. Animals. (Finding Out About Ser.). (Illus.). 24p. (J). 1996. 9.95 (*0-563-37333-4*, Pub. by BBC) Parkwest Pubns.

— The Atlas of Endangered Animals. LC 92-20387. (Environmental Atlas Ser.). (Illus.). 64p. (J). (gr. 6-9). 1993. 16.95 (*0-8160-2856-7*) Facts on File.

— The Atlas of Endangered Peoples. LC 94-35296. (Illus.). 64p. 1995. lib. bdg. 16.95 (*0-8160-3283-1*) Facts on File.

— The Atlas of Endangered Places. LC 92-20388. (Environmental Atlas Ser.). (Illus.). 64p. (YA). 1993. 16.95 (*0-8160-2857-5*) Facts on File.

— The Atlas of Endangered Resources. LC 94-32549. (Illus.). 64p. (YA). (gr. 5 up). 1995. lib. bdg. 16.95 (*0-8160-3284-X*) Facts on File.

— Canon EOS Elan/EOS 100. (Magic Lantern Guides Ser.). (Illus.). 176p. (Orig.). (C). 1998. pap. 19.95 (*1-883403-21-9*, H 109, Silver Pixel Pr) Saunders Photo.

***Pollock, Steve.** Deadly Creatures. (Illus.). 24p. (gr. 5-9). 1999. reprint ed. text 14.00 (*0-7881-6479-1*) DIANE Pub.

Pollock, Steve. Dinosaurs. (Illus.). 48p. (J). (gr. 7-9). 1992. 14.95 (*0-563-34753-8*, Pub. by BBC) Parkwest Pubns.

— Dinosaurs: A Fact Finder Book. (Illus.). 48p. (J). (gr. 7-9). 1992. pap. 7.50 (*0-563-34607-8*, BBC-Parkwest) Parkwest Pubns.

***Pollock, Steve.** Ecology. (Eyewitness Books). 64p. (J). (gr. 4-7). 2000. pap. text 15.95 (*0-7894-5581-1*, D K Ink) DK Pub Inc.

Pollock, Steve. Factfinders: Human Body. (Fact Finders Ser.). (J). pap. 8.95 (*0-563-37504-3*, BBC-Parkwest) Parkwest Pubns.

— Plants. (Find Out about Ser.). (Illus.). 24p. (J). 1996. 9.95 (*0-563-37335-0*, Pub. by BBC) Parkwest Pubns.

Pollock, Steve & Richter, Gunter. Canon EOS Elan II/IIE. Ohlig, Hayley, tr. from GER. (Magic Lantern Guides Ser.). (Illus.). 176p. (C). 1998. pap. 19.95 (*1-883403-35-9*, H 113, Silver Pixel Pr) Saunders Photo.

Pollock, Sudie. Will the Dollars Stretch? Teen Parents Living on Their Own: Virtual Reality Through Stories & Check-Writing Practice. Lindsay, Jeanne W., ed. (Illus.). 96p. (Orig.). (YA). (gr. 7-12). 1996. pap. text 6.95 (*1-885356-12-9*, 56129) Morning Glory.

Pollock, Sue, jt. auth. see Farmer, Elaine.

Pollock, Susan. Ancient Mesopotamia. (Case Studies in Early Societies). (Illus.). 220p. (C). 1999. text 49.95 (*0-521-57334-3*); pap. text 17.95 (*0-521-57568-0*) Cambridge U Pr.

Pollock, T. & Mulla, B. Indian Contract & Specific Relief Act. (C). 1986. 200.00 (*0-685-25707-X*) St Mut.

Pollock, T. C. & Spaulding, J. G. General Semantics Monograph III: A Theory of Meaning Analyzed. 64p. 1942. pap. 6.95 (*0-910780-03-X*) Inst Gen Seman.

Pollock, T. M. Trials of Prophylactic Agents for the Control of Communicable Diseases: A Guide to Their Organization & Evaluation. (Monographs: No. 52). (ENG, FRE, RUS & SPA.). 92p. 1966. pap. text 7.00 (*92-4-140052-8*, 1140052) World Health.

Pollock, Thomas C. Nature of Literature: Its Relation to Science, Language & Human Experiences. LC 65-25135. 218p. 1965. reprint ed. 50.00 (*0-87752-086-0*) Gordian.

— Properties of Matter, Custom Pub. 5th ed. (Texas A&M Core Engineering Ser.). 472p. (C). 1995. pap. 41.56 (*0-07-050439-3*) McGraw.

Pollock, Thomas W. Meat & Health: Index of Modern Information with Bibliography. LC 88-47788. 150p. (Orig.). 1988. 47.50 (*0-88164-900-7*); pap. 44.50 (*0-88164-901-5*) ABBE Pubs Assn.

Pollock, Vivienne, jt. auth. see Hill, Myrtle.

Pollock, W. H. William Butler Yeats. LC 75-22355. (W. B. Yeats Ser.: No. 72). 1975. lib. bdg. 59.00 (*0-8383-2104-6*) M S G Haskell Hse.

Pollock, Walter. Jane Austen. LC 73-130248. (Studies in Fiction: No. 34). 1970. reprint ed. lib. bdg. 75.00 (*0-8383-1138-5*) M S G Haskell Hse.

Pollock, Walter I. & Steely, Carroll N., eds. Corrosion under Wet Thermal Insulation. LC 90-62320. (Illus.). 104p. 1990. pap. 43.00 (*1-877914-14-2*) NACE Intl.

Pollock, Walter I., jt. ed. see Moniz, B. J.

Pollock, Warren I., ed. see American Society for Testing & Materials Staff.

Pollock, Warren I., ed. see Dillon, C. P.

Pollock, Yevonne. The Old Man's Mitten. LC 94-30195. (Illus.). 24p. (Orig.). (J). (ps-3). 1994. pap. 4.95 (*1-879531-60-7*) Mondo Pubng.

Pollock, Zailig. A. M. Klein: The Story of the Poet. 324p. 1994. text 60.00 (*0-8020-0446-6*); pap. text 25.95 (*0-8020-7234-8*) U of Toronto Pr.

Pollock, Zailig, et al. A. M. Klein: An Annotated Bibliography. 390p. (C). 1993. text 65.00 (*1-55022-095-0*, Pub. by ECW) Genl Dist Srvs.

Pollock, Zailig, ed. see Klein, A. M.

Polloczek, Dieter. Literature & Legal Discourse: Equity & Ethics from Sterne to Conrad. LC 98-48324. 287p. (C). 1999. 59.95 (*0-521-65251-0*) Cambridge U Pr.

Pollok, Linda. Twinkles: The Story of a Christmas Star. large type ed. 18p. (Orig.). (J). (gr. k-3). 1995. pap., per. 9.95 (*0-943487-47-1*) Sevgo Pr.

Pollon, Earl K. & Matheson, Shirley S. This Was Our Valley. (Illus.). 403p. 1989. 26.95 (*0-920490-92-1*); pap. 17.95 (*0-920490-91-3*) Temeron Bks.

Pollon, Zelie, tr. see Dalai Lama XIV.

Pollot, Mark. Grand Theft & Petit Larceny: Property Rights in America. LC 91-12545. 250p. (Orig.). 1992. pap. 21.95 (*0-936488-44-1*) PRIPP.

Pollotta, Nick. American Knights. (Endless Quest Ser.). 192p. (Orig.). (J). (gr. 7-8). 1995. pap. 3.95 (*1-56076-899-1*, Pub. by TSR Inc) Random.

***Pollotta, Nick.** Doomsday Exam. (Bureau 13 Ser.: Vol. 2). 288p. 2000. pap. 12.95 (*1-930318-02-2*) Delphia Bks.

— Full Moonsters. (Bureau 13 Ser.: Vol. 3). 300p. 2000. pap. write for info. (*1-930318-03-0*) Delphia Bks.

— Judgement Night. (Bureau 13 Ser.: Vol. 1). 288p. 1999. pap. 12.95 (*1-930318-01-4*) Delphia Bks.

***Pollotta, Nick & Foglio, Phil.** Illegal Aliens. rev. ed. (Illus.). 450p. 2000. pap. 12.95 (*1-930318-04-9*) Delphia Bks.

Polloway, Edward A. & Patton, James R. Strategies for Teaching Learners with Special Needs. 6th ed. LC 96-23937. 628p. (C). 1996. pap. text 63.00 (*0-13-466666-6*) P-H.

Polloway, Edward A. & Smith, Tom E. Language Instruction for Students with Disabilities. 2nd ed. 1992. teacher ed. 49.95 (*0-89108-221-2*, 9202) Love Pub Co.

Polloway, Edward A. & Smith, Tom E. C. Language Instruction for Students with Disabilities. 2nd ed. 496p. (C). 1999. pap. text 49.95 (*0-89108-269-7*) Love Pub Co.

***Polloway, Edward A., et al.** Strategies for Teaching Learners with Special Needs. 7th ed. LC 00-28365. 624p. 2000. pap. 64.00 (*0-13-027430-5*, Merrill Coll) P-H.

Polloway, Edward A., jt. auth. see Smith, Tom E.

Polloway, Edward A., jt. ed. see Patton, James R.

Polls, A., jt. ed. see Guardiola, R.

Pollsar, Barry L. Insect Soup: Bug Poems. (Illus.). 32p. (J). 1999. 14.95 (*0-938663-22-4*, Pub. by Rainbow Morn) IPG Chicago.

Pollock, Paul Jackson. Art Mini-Pollock. (Illus.). 96p. 2000. pap. text 4.95 (*3-8290-2932-2*) Konemann.

Pollution Engineering Staff. Answering NIMBY. 240p. 1994. 34.95 (*0-934165-44-0*, 65449) Gulf Pub.

— Bioremediation Desk Manual for the Environmental Professional Bioremediation. 97p. 1990. pap. 24.95 (*0-934165-33-5*, 65339) Gulf Pub.

— Clean Air Regulation the Clean Air Act. 136p. 1994. 24.95 (*0-934165-49-1*, 65499) Gulf Pub.

— Dangerous Chemical Reactions. 324p. 1993. 34.95 (*0-934165-46-7*, 65469) Gulf Pub.

— Effective Environmental, Product Stewardship & Safety Management Practices. 84p. 1989. 24.95 (*0-934165-27-0*, 65279) Gulf Pub.

— Emerging On-Site & In Situ Hazardous Waste Treatment Technologies. 260p. 1994. 34.95 (*0-934165-32-7*, 65329) Gulf Pub.

— Environmental Acronyms & Glossary. 152p. 1993. 24.95 (*0-934165-42-4*, 65429) Gulf Pub.

— Environmental Assessments & Real Estate Transactions. 324p. 1994. 44.95 (*0-934165-50-5*, 65509) Gulf Pub.

— Environmental Law Outline. 148p. 1993. 29.95 (*0-934165-41-6*, 65419) Gulf Pub.

— Environmental Rules of Thumb. 192p. 1991. 34.95 (*0-934165-35-1*, 65359) Gulf Pub.

— EPA's Handbook: Responding to Sinking Hazardous Substances. 312p. 1988. 34.95 (*0-934165-19-X*, 65199) Gulf Pub.

— The ESE National Precipitation Databook. 888p. 1992. 89.95 (*0-934165-37-8*, 65379) Gulf Pub.

— Hazardous Waste & Toxic Substances Laws & Regulations. 308p. 1994. 49.95 (*0-934165-52-1*, 65529) Gulf Pub.

— How to Review a Part B Permit. 160p. 1990. 24.95 (*0-934165-07-6*, 65079) Gulf Pub.

P

An Asterisk (*) at the beginning of an entry indicates that the title is appearing for the first time.

— Municipal Environmental Accident & Emergency Response Planning. 164p. 1994. 29.95 (*0-934165-47-5*, 65479) Gulf Pub.

— Pollution Control Engineer's Handbook. 205p. 1988. 34.95 (*0-934165-02-5*, 65029) Gulf Pub.

— Pollution Engineering Flow Sheets: Hazardous Waste Treatment & Unit Operations. 225p. 1988. 34.95 (*0-934165-23-8*, 65239) Gulf Pub.

— Preacquisition Assessment of Commercial & Industrial Property. 96p. 1994. 24.95 (*0-934165-30-0*, 65309) Gulf Pub.

— Release Prevention Control & Counter. 66p. 1992. 24.95 (*0-934165-17-3*, 65179) Gulf Pub.

— Simplified Hazardous Materials Chemistry. 239p. 1994. 39.95 (*0-934165-39-4*, 65399) Gulf Pub.

— Underground Storage Tanks Management. 136p. 1993. 29.95 (*0-934165-43-2*, 65439) Gulf Pub.

Pollution Prevention Committee Staff, contrib. by. Controlling Vehicle Service Facility Discharges in Wastewater: How to Develop & Administer a Source Control Program. LC 95-33268. 1995. pap. 30.00 (*1-57278-016-9*) Water Environ.

Polly, Jean Armour. The Internet Kids & Family Golden Directory. 2nd ed. 608p. 1997. 28.95 (*0-07-882354-4*) Osborne-McGraw.

— The Internet Kids & Family Golden Directory. 3rd ed. pap. write for info. (*0-07-211894-6*) Osborne-McGraw.

— Internet Kids & Family Yellow Pages. 3rd ed. LC 99-193750. 742p. 1999. pap. 24.99 incl. cd-rom (*0-07-211849-0*) Osborne-McGraw.

***Polly, Jean Armour.** Internet Kids & Family Yellow Pages. 4th ed. 2000. pap. 34.99 (*0-07-212662-0*) Osborne-McGraw.

— Internet Kids & Family Yellow Pages, Millennium Ed. 1999. pap. text 34.99 (*0-07-212185-8*) Osborne.

Polly, Jean Armour. The Internet Kids Yellow Pages, Special Edition. (Illus.). 400p. (YA). (gr. 5 up). 1996. pap. text 19.95 (*0-07-882197-5*) McGraw.

Polman, A., et al, eds. Film Synthesis & Growth Using Energetic Beams. (Symposium Proceedings Ser.: Vol. 388). 446p. 1995. text 83.00 (*1-55899-291-X*) Materials Res.

Polman, Bert. Comfort Now My People: The Advent Message from Isaiah. (Scripture Alive Ser.). 1998. pap. 14.95 (*1-56212-369-6*, 2280-0080) CRC Pubns.

— The Fiery Prophet: The Story of Elijah. (Scripture Alive Ser.). 29p. 1998. pap. text 14.95 (*1-56212-331-9*, 2280-0040) CRC Pubns.

— God with Us: The Christmas Message from the Gospels. (Scripture Alive Ser.). 30p. 1998. pap. 14.95 (*1-56212-363-7*, 2280-0090) CRC Pubns.

— It Is Finished: The Passion of Christ According to John. (Scripture Alive Ser.). 22p. 1998. pap. 14.95 (*1-56212-338-6*, 2280-0020) CRC Pubns.

— Mother in Israel: The Story of Deborah. (Scripture Alive Ser.). 25p. 1998. pap. text 14.95 (*1-56212-329-7*, 2280-0050) CRC Pubns.

— My Lord & My God: Thomas Meets the Risen Christ. (Scripture Alive Ser.). 17p. 1998. pap. text 14.95 (*1-56212-336-X*, 2280-0030) CRC Pubns.

***Polman, Bert.** Scripture Alive: Esther, Savior of Her People. 32p. 2000. pap. 14.95 (*1-56212-430-7*, 415110) CRC Pubns.

— Scripture Alive: God Speaks, Creation Listens! The Story of Beginnings. 32p. 2000. pap. 14.95 (*1-56212-364-5*, 415112) CRC Pubns.

— Scriptures Alive: Heal Us Today & Stories of Jesus the Healer. 24p. 2000. pap. 14.95 (*1-56212-431-5*, 415111) CRC Pubns.

Polman, Bert. This Is My Beloved Son: The Baptism of Jesus. (Scripture Alive Ser.). 20p. 1998. pap. 14.95 (*1-56212-362-9*, 2280-0100) CRC Pubns.

— Upon This Rock: The Story of Peter. (Scripture Alive Ser.). 22p. 1998. pap. 14.95 (*1-56212-327-0*, 2280-0060) CRC Pubns.

— Were Not Our Hearts Burning: The Emmaus Story. (Scripture Alive Ser.). 16p. 1998. pap. 14.95 (*1-56212-337-8*, 2280-0010) CRC Pubns.

— Why Have You Forsaken Me? The Passion of Our Lord According to Matthew. (Scripture Alive Ser.). 24p. 1999. pap. 14.95 (*1-56212-384-X*, 2280-0070) CRC Pubns.

Polman, Bert, et al, eds. Amazing Grace: Hymn Texts for Devotional Use. 256p. (Orig.). 1994. pap. 18.95 (*0-664-25510-8*) Westminster John Knox.

Polman, Bertus F., jt. auth. see Brink, Emily R.

***Polman, Joseph L.** Designing Project-Based Science: Connecting Learners Through Guided Inquiry LC 99-36981. (Ways of Knowing in Science Ser.). 240p. 2000. pap. text 23.95 (*0-8077-3912-X*) Tchrs Coll.

— Designing Project-Based Science: Connecting Learners Through Guided Inquiry. LC 99-36981. (Ways of Knowing in Science Ser.). 240p. 2000. write for info. (*0-8077-3913-8*) Tchrs Coll.

Polmar, Norman. The Naval Institute Guide to the Ships & Aircraft of the U. S. Fleet. 16th rev. ed. (Illus.). 592p. 1996. 79.95 (*1-55750-686-8*) Naval Inst Pr.

— Spy Book. 656p. 1998. pap. 18.00 (*0-375-70249-0*) Random Ref & Info.

***Polmar, Norman.** Spyplane. (Illus.). 2000. 21.95 (*0-7603-0957-4*) Trans-Atl Phila.

***Polmar, Norman & Allen, Thomas B.** The Encyclopedia of Espionage. (Illus.). 633p. 2000. reprint ed. 30.00 (*0-7881-9329-5*) DIANE Pub.

Polmar, Norman & Allen, Thomas B. Random House Encyclopedia of World War II. 960p. 1996. pap. 22.00 (*0-679-77039-9*) Random.

— Spy Book. 1996. 30.00 (*0-614-96930-1*) Random Ref & Info.

Polmar, Norman & Bohn, John T. Strategic Air Command: People, Aircraft & Missiles. 1980. 22.95 (*0-405-13275-1*) Ayer.

Polmar, Norman & Morison, Samuel L. PT Boats at War: World War II to Vietnam. LC 99-13550. (Illus.). 160p. 1999. pap. 19.95 (*0-7603-0499-8*) MBI Pubg.

Polmar, Norman & Noot, Jurrien. Submarines of the Russian & Soviet Navies, 1718-1990. LC 90-6687. (Illus.). 400p. 1991. 67.50 (*0-87021-570-1*) Naval Inst Pr.

Polmar, Norman, et al. Chronology of the Cold War at Sea, 1945-1991. LC 97-35957. 464p. 1997. 39.95 (*1-55750-685-X*) Naval Inst Pr.

— Dictionary of Military Abbreviations. LC 93-34566. 307p. 1994. text 26.95 (*1-55750-680-9*) Naval Inst Pr.

Polmar, Norman, jt. auth. see Allen, Thomas B.

Polmar, Norman, jt. auth. see United States Navy, Office of Information Staff.

Polmar, Norman, tr. see Spassky, I. D., et al, eds.

Polmar, Stephen H. New Directions in the Clinical Use of Intravenous Immunoglobulin, Vol. IV. (Illus.). 60p. 1990. write for info. (*0-318-65782-1*) Health Dimensions.

Polmear, I. J. Light Alloys Metallurgy of the Light Metals. 224p. 1981. 110.00 (*0-685-05555-8*, Pub. by E A) Routldge.

Polmear, Ian J. Light Alloys: Metallurgy of the Light Metals. 3rd ed. LC 95-31388. 362p. 1995. pap. 99.00 (*0-470-23565-9*) Wiley.

Polmer, N. & Allen, T. The Encyclopedia of Espionage. LC 97-48494. 656p. 1998. 12.99 (*0-517-20269-7*) Random Hse Value.

Polnac, et al. The Common Sense Handbook. LC 98-33272. 447p. (C). 1999. pap. text 21.33 (*0-13-082178-0*) P-H.

Polnac, Lennis R. Purpose, Pattern & Process. 4th ed. LC 97-220153. 334p. (C). 1997. per. 33.95 (*0-7872-3799-X*) Kendall-Hunt.

Polnaszek, Frank, jt. auth. see Lautier, Jack.

Polnauer, Josef, ed. see Webern, Anton.

Polnay. Manual on Community Pediatrics. 2nd ed. 1996. pap. text 24.95 (*0-443-05352-9*, W B Saunders Co) Harcrt Hlth Sci Grp.

Polnay, L. & Hull, D., eds. Community Paediatrics. 2nd ed. (Illus.). 479p. 1993. pap. write for info. (*0-443-04250-0*) Church.

Polnay, Peter De, see De Polnay, Peter.

Polner, Murray & O'Grady, Jim. Disarmed & Dangerous: The Radical Life & Times of Daniel & Philip Berrigan, Brothers in Religious Faith & Civil Disobedience. 464p. (C). 1998. pap. 21.00 (*0-8133-3449-7*, Pub. by Westview) HarpC.

Polner, Tikhon J., et al. Russian Local Government During the War & the Union of Zemstvos. (Economic & Social History of the World War Ser.). 1930. 100.00 (*0-317-27559-3*) Elliots Bks.

***Polo, J.** Post Test Analysis of P5 Experiment in Panda Facility With TRAC-BF1 Code. 20p. 2000. pap. 2.50 (*0-16-059176-7*) USGPO.

Polo, Marco. The Book of Marco Polo, 2 vols. 1980. lib. bdg. 600.00 (*0-87968-332-5*) Krishna Pr.

— The Book of Sir Marco Polo, the Venetian, Concerning the Kingdoms & Marvels of the East, 3 vols., Set. 3rd ed. Yule, Henry, ed. & tr. LC 74-5240. reprint ed. 285.00 (*0-404-11540-3*) AMS Pr.

— The Description of the World, 2 vols., Set. LC 74-5372. reprint ed. 225.00 (*0-404-11525-X*) AMS Pr.

— Travels. 26.95 (*0-8488-0187-3*) Amereon Ltd.

— Travels. 240p. 1998. 7.95 (*3-89508-453-0*) Konemann.

— The Travels. Latham, Ronald, tr. & intro. by. (Classics Ser.). 384p. (C). 2000. pap. 13.95 (*0-14-044057-7*) Viking Penguin.

— Travels. Wright, T., ed. Marsden, tr. LC 68-57871. (Bohn's Antiquarian Library). reprint ed. 57.00 (*0-404-50023-4*) AMS Pr.

— The Travels of Marco Polo. Latham, Ronald, tr. from FRE. 318p. 1982. lib. bdg. 35.00 (*0-89835-058-1*) Abaris Bks.

— The Travels of Marco Polo. (Classics of World Literature Ser.). 1997. pap. 5.95 (*1-85326-473-3*, 4733WW, Pub. by Wrdsworth Edits) NTC Contemp Pub Co.

— The Travels of Marco Polo. 1982. reprint ed. lib. bdg. 18.95 (*0-89967-045-8*, Harmony Rain) Buccaneer Bks.

Polo, Marco, et al. The Travels of Marco Polo: The Complete Yule-Cordier Edition, 2 vols., 1. 3rd rev. ed. (Illus.). 1680p. 1993. reprint ed. pap. 17.95 (*0-486-27586-8*) Dover.

— The Travels of Marco Polo: The Complete Yule-Cordier Edition, 2 vols., 2. rev. ed. (Illus.). 1680p. 1993. reprint ed. pap. 19.95 (*0-486-27587-6*) Dover.

Poloczi-Horvath, Andras. Pechenegs, Cumans & Iasians: Steppe Peoples in Medieval Hungary. (Hereditas Ser.). (Illus.). 160p. 1999. pap. 21.00 (*963-13-2740-X*, Pub. by Corvina Bks) St Mut.

Polokhalo, Volodymyr. The Political Analysis of Postcommunism: Understanding Postcommunist Ukraine. LC 97-41505. (Eastern European Studies: No. 6). 368p. 1997. pap. 21.95 (*0-89096-783-0*) Tex A&M Univ Pr.

Poloma, Margaret M. The Assemblies of God at the Crossroads: Charisma & Institutional Dilemmas. LC 88-13761. 332p. 1989. pap. 18.95 (*0-87049-607-7*) U of Tenn Pr.

Poloma, Margaret M. & Gallup, George H., Jr. Varieties of Prayer: A Survey Report. LC 90-28578. 160p. (C). 1991. pap. 15.00 (*1-56338-007-2*) TPI PA.

Poloma, Margaret M. & Pendleton, Brian F. Exploring Neglected Dimensions of Religion in Quality of Life Research. LC 91-27334. (Studies in the Psychology of Religion: Vol. 7). 236p. 1991. lib. bdg. 89.95 (*0-7734-9672-6*) E Mellen.

Polome, Edgar C. Essays on Germanic Religion. (Journal of Indo-European Studies: No. 6). (Illus.). (Orig.). (C). 1989. pap. text 30.00 (*0-941694-34-8*) Inst Study Man.

— Research Guide on Language. (Trends in Linguistics, Studies & Monographs: No. 48). xii, 564p. (C). 1990. lib. bdg. 190.80 (*3-11-012046-1*) Mouton.

Polome, Edgar C., ed. Essays in Honor of Karl Kerenyi. (Journal of Indo-European Studies: No. 4). (Illus.). 144p. 1984. pap. 30.00 (*0-941694-20-8*) Inst Study Man.

— Homage to Georges Dumezil. (Journal of Indo-European Studies: No. 3). 172p. (Orig.). 1983. pap. 30.00 (*0-941694-28-3*) Inst Study Man.

Polome, Edgar C. & Hill, C. P., eds. Language in Tanzania. (Survey of Language Use & Language Teaching in Eastern Africa Ser.). 1981. 39.00 (*0-19-724205-7*) OUP.

— Language in Tanzania. LC 81-147648. (Ford Foundation Language Surveys Ser.). 442p. reprint ed. pap. 137.10 (*0-8357-6964-X*, 203902400009) Bks Demand.

Polome, Edgar C. & Winter, Werner, eds. Reconstructing Languages & Cultures. LC 91-45260. (Trends in Linguistics, Studies & Monographs: No. 58). ix, 550p. 1992. lib. bdg. 190.80 (*3-11-012671-0*) Mouton.

***Polome, Edgar C., et al.** Language Change & Typological Variation: Language Change & Phonology. LC 99-216999. (Journal of Indo-European Studies Monographs: Vol. 30). 319p. (C). 1999. pap. text 48.00 (*0-941694-68-2*) Inst Study Man.

Polome, Edgar C., ed. see Bader, F., et al.

Polome, Edgar C., ed. see Barber, E. J., et al.

Polome, Edgar C., jt. ed. see Skomal, Susan S.

***Polomski, Bob.** Month by Month Gardening in the Carolinas. (Illus.). 320p. 2000. pap. 18.95 (*1-888608-23-4*) Cool Springs Pr.

Polomski, Lothar, jt. compiled by see Mackenzie, Harry.

Polon, Linda. Magic Story Starters: Grade 1 to 3. (Illus.). 44p. (Orig.). 1986. pap. 6.95 (*0-673-18561-3*, GoodYrBooks) Addson-Wesley Educ.

— Paragraph Production. (Study Skills Ser.). (Illus.). 48p. (J). (gr. 4-6). 1981. pap. 6.95 (*0-88160-039-3*, LW 224) Learning Wks.

— Writing Whirlwind: Grades 2-4. (Illus.). 44p. (Orig.). 1986. pap. 6.95 (*0-673-18310-6*, GoodYrBooks) Addson-Wesley Educ.

Polon, Linda & Cantwell, Aileen. The Whole Earth Holiday Book: Grades 4-6. (Illus.). 218p. (Orig.). 1983. pap. 13.95 (*0-673-16585-X*, GoodYrBooks) Addson-Wesley Educ.

Polon, Linda B. Write a Story. (Illus.). 96p. 1997. 9.95 (*0-673-36355-4*, GoodYrBooks) Addson-Wesley Educ.

***Polon, Linda Beth.** Storywriting. (Illus.). (J). (gr. 1-3). 1999. pap. 9.95 (*0-673-57580-2*, GoodYrBooks) Addson-Wesley Educ.

— Storywriting. (Illus.). (J). (gr. 4-6). 1999. pap. 9.95 (*0-673-57726-0*, GoodYrBooks) Addson-Wesley Educ.

Polon, Linda Beth. Write a Story: Open-Ended Writing Activities for Children. (Illus.). 96p. (J). (gr. 4-6). 1997. pap. 9.95 (*0-673-36356-2*, GoodYrBooks) Addson-Wesley Educ.

Polonoff, David. Down the Yup Staircase: Decline & Fall of the Republican Empire. LC 92-91211. (Illus.). 184p. (Orig.). 1993. pap. text. write for info. (*0-9635664-4-X*) Pantagruel.

Polonski, T., jt. ed. see Shintani, H.

Polonsky, Abraham. Force of Evil: The Critical Edition. Schultheiss, John & Schaubert, Mark, eds. LC 95-83222. (Film As Literature Ser.). 208p. 1996. 30.00 (*0-9635823-1-3*) Sadanlaur Pubns.

— Odds Against Tomorrow: The Critical Edition. Schultheiss, John, ed. LC 98-74816. (Film As Literature Ser.). (Illus.). 328p. 1999. 30.00 (*0-9635823-4-8*, Pub. by Sadanlaur Pubns) SCB Distributors.

— To Illuminate Our Time: The Blacklisted Teleplays of Abraham Polonsky. Schaubert, Mark, ed. LC 92-84081. 352p. (Orig.). 1993. pap. text 20.00 (*0-9635823-0-5*) Sadanlaur Pubns.

— World Above. LC 98-45490. (Radical Novel Reconsidered Ser.). 1999. pap. text 18.95 (*0-252-06806-8*) U of Ill Pr.

— You Are There Teleplays: The Critical Edition. rev. ed. Schaubert, Mark & Schultheiss, John, eds. LC 97-67547. (Film As Literature Ser.). (Illus.). 328p. (C). 1997. text 30.00 (*0-9635823-2-1*) Sadanlaur Pubns.

Polonsky, Antony. Jews in Independent Poland, 1918-1939 Polin, Vol. 8. 1994. 59.95 (*1-874774-12-9*, Pub. by Littman Lib) Intl Spec Bk.

Polonsky, Antony, ed. From Shtetl to Socialism: Studies from Polin. LC 93-29009. (Littman Library of Jewish Civilization). (Illus.). 616p. (Orig.). 1993. pap. 29.50 (*1-874774-14-5*) Intl Spec Bk.

— Polin, Vol. 3. (Illus.). 458p. 1989. 55.00 (*0-631-16694-7*) Intl Spec Bk.

— Polin, Vol. 4. (Illus.). 502p. 1990. 55.00 (*0-631-17303-X*) Intl Spec Bk.

— Polin, Vol. 5. (Illus.). 512p. 1991. 55.00 (*0-631-17886-4*) Intl Spec Bk.

— Polin, Vol. 6. 512p. 1991. 55.00 (*0-631-18167-9*) Intl Spec Bk.

— Polin: Focusing on Religion: Aspects & Experiences. (Polin: Vol. 11). (Illus.). 480p. 1998. text 55.00 (*1-874774-05-6*, Pub. by Littman Lib); pap. text 29.50 (*1-874774-34-X*, Pub. by Littman Lib) Intl Spec Bk.

— Polin: Studies in Polish Jewry, Vol. 2. 496p. 1987. 55.00 (*1-874774-24-2*) Intl Spec Bk.

— Polin: Studies in Polish Jewry, Vol. 7. 350p. 1987. 55.00 (*0-631-18932-7*) Intl Spec Bk.

Polonsky, Antony, et al, eds. Jews, Poles, Socialists Vol. 9: The Failure of an Ideal. (Polin: Studies in Polish Jewry: Vol. 9). 368p. 1996. text 55.00 (*1-874774-21-8*, Pub. by Littman Lib) Intl Spec Bk.

***Polonsky, Antony & Adamczyk-Garbowska, Monika, eds.** Contemporary Jewish Writing in Poland: An Anthology. (Jewish Writing in the Contemporary World Ser.). 2000. text 60.00 (*0-8032-3721-9*); pap. text 35.00 (*0-8032-8767-4*) U of Nebr Pr.

Polonsky, Antony, jt. ed. see Bartal, Israel.

Polonsky, Daniel L. The Letter Bandits. (Illus.). 72p. (J). (gr. 3 up). 1991. 14.95 (*0-931474-41-8*) TBW Bks.

Polonsky, Derek C. Talking about Sex. 192p. 1995. 22.95 (*0-88048-719-4*, 8719) Am Psychiatric.

Polonsky, Derek C., jt. ed. see Nadelson, Carol C.

Polonsky, Gill. Chagall. LC 98-231814. (Colour Library). (Illus.). 128p. 1998. pap. 14.95 (*0-7148-3403-3*) Phaidon Pr.

Polonsky, Lydia, et al. Math for the Very Young: A Handbook of Activities for Parents & Children. LC 94-20861. 210p. 1995. 29.95 (*0-471-01671-3*); pap. 14.95 (*0-471-01647-0*) Wiley.

Polonsky, Marc. The Poetry Appreciation Toolkit: A Guide to Reading & Understanding Poetry. LC 97-347. 1997. write for info. (*0-8442-5989-6*) NTC Contemp Pub Co.

Polonsky, Marc. The Poetry Reader's Toolkit: A Guide to Reading & Understanding Poetry. LC 97-347. (Illus.). 176p. 1997. pap. 22.45 (*0-8442-5988-8*, 59888) NTC Contemp Pub Co.

Polonsky, Michael J. & Lozada, Hector R., eds. Environmental Issues in the Curricula of International Business: The Green Imperative. LC 93-39142. (Journal of Teaching in International Business: Vol. 5, Nos. 1-2). (Illus.). 186p. 1994. lib. bdg. 39.95 (*1-56024-467-4*) Haworth Pr.

Polonsky, Michael J. & Mintu-Wimsatt, Alma T., eds. Environmental Marketing: Strategies, Practice, Theory, & Research. LC 94-28993. (Illus.). 415p. 1995. 79.95 (*1-56024-927-7*) Haworth Pr.

— Environmental Marketing: Strategies, Practice, Theory, & Research. LC 94-28993. 415p. 1997. pap. 29.95 (*1-56024-928-5*) Haworth Pr.

Polonsky, Rachel. English Literature & the Russian Aesthetic Renaissance. LC 97-47556. (Studies in Russian Literature). (Illus.). 220p. (C). 1998. 59.95 (*0-521-62179-8*) Cambridge U Pr.

Polonsky, W. Brett. Official Microsoft FrontPage 2000 Book. LC 98-52137. 1999. pap. text 24.99 (*1-57231-992-5*) Microsoft Pr.

Polonsky, W. Brett, jt. auth. see Lehto, Kerry A.

***Polonsky, William H. & Peterson, Amy.** Diabetes Burnout: Preventing It, Surviving It, Finding Inner Peace. LC 99-44735. 256p. 1999. pap. 18.95 (*1-58040-033-7*, 00337Q, Pub. by Am Diabetes) NTC Contemp Pub Co.

Polopolus, Leo C., jt. ed. see Lopez, Rigoberto A.

Polos, Laszlo & Masuch, Michael, eds. Applied Logic: How, What & Why: Logical Approaches to Natural Language. LC 95-11570. (Synthese Library: Vol. 247). 400p. (C). 1995. lib. bdg. 129.00 (*0-7923-3432-9*, Pub. by Kluwer Academic) Kluwer Academic.

Polos, Laszlo, jt. ed. see Masuch, Michael.

Poloskei, Ference. Hungary after Two Revolutions. 148p. (C). 1980. 38.00 (*963-05-2481-3*, Pub. by Akade Kiado) St Mut.

***Poloski, J. P.** Reliability Study: Auxiliary/Emergency Feedwater System, 1987-1995. 332p. 1998. per. 26.00 (*0-16-062943-8*) USGPO.

Polotan, Kerima. Author's Choice: Selected Writings of Kerima Polotan. LC 98-947693. (Likhaan / Sentro Ng Malikhaing Pagsulat Ser.). 289 p. 1998. write for info. (*971-542-205-5*) UH Pr.

— Stories. LC 98-947597. (Philippine Writers Ser.). ix, 154 p. 1998. write for info. (*971-542-192-X*) U of Philippines Pr.

Polotsky, J. H. Collected Papers. xi, 724p. 1971. text 35.00 (*965-223-581-4*, Pub. by Magnes Pr) Eisenbrauns.

Polovets, Alexander. Beglyi Rachikhin (Figitibe Rachikhin) LC 87-82248. (RUS.). 208p. 1987. 15.50 (*0-911971-25-4*) Effect Pub.

Polovin, R. V. & Demutskii, V. P. Fundamentals of Magnetohydrodynamics. (Illus.). 352p. (C). 1990. text 120.00 (*0-306-11027-X*, Kluwer Plenum) Kluwer Academic.

Polovitz, Mike. Mayor's Alley. Zygarlicke, Eileen, ed. LC 97-222674. 160p. 1997. pap. 14.95 (*1-890939-00-5*) Century Creations.

Polowetzky, Michael. A Bond Never Broken: The Relations Between Napoleon & the Authors of France. LC 92-58944. (Illus.). 192p. 1993. 32.50 (*0-8386-3482-6*) Fairleigh Dickinson.

— Jerusalem Recovered: Victorian Intellectuals & the Birth of Modern Zionism. LC 95-3355. 167p. 1995. 55.00 (*0-275-95213-4*, Praeger Pubs) Greenwood.

— Prominent Sisters: Mary Lamb, Dorothy Wordsworth & Sarah Disraeli. LC 96-21316. 176p. 1996. 55.00 (*0-275-95716-0*, Praeger Pubs) Greenwood.

Polowniak, William. On Creating a Community: A Guide for Organizations, Personal Productivity & International Peace. 296p. 1994. 23.95 (*0-9639142-1-9*) Quantum Publications CA.

— On Creating a Community: A Guide for Organizations, Personal Productivity & International Peace. LC 93-87084. 296p. (C). 1994. pap. 14.95 (*0-9639142-0-0*) Quantum Publications CA.

Polowy, Teresa. The Novellas of Valentin Rasputin: Genre, Language & Style. (Middlebury Studies in Russian Language & Literature: Vol. 1). X, 262p. (C). 1989. text 42.50 (*0-8204-0643-0*) P Lang Pubng.

Polozhii, G. & Tee, G. Method of Summary Representation for Numerical Solution of Problems of Mathematical Physics. LC 65-13073. (International Series of Monographs in Pure & Applied Mathematics: Vol. 79). 1965. 134.00 (*0-08-011017-7*, Pub. by Pergamon Repr) Franklin.

Polprasert, Chongrak. Organic Waste Recycling. LC 88-20722. (Illus.). 371p. 1989. reprint ed. pap. 115.10 (*0-608-04000-2*, 206473700011) Bks Demand.

— Organic Waste Recycling: Technology & Management. 2nd ed. 426p. 1996. pap. 75.00 (*0-471-96482-4*) Wiley.

Pols, Cynthia M., jt. auth. see Cooper, Ronald S.

P

Pols, Edward. The Acts of Our Being: A Reflection on Agency & Responsibility. LC 81-16319. 248p. 1982. lib. bdg. 32.50 (0-87023-354-8) U of Mass Pr.
— Mind Regained: How Mind Functions As a Real Cause in the Material World. LC 98-9482. 176p. 1998. 29.95 (0-8014-3531-5) Cornell U Pr.
— Radical Realism: Direct Knowing in Science & Philosophy. LC 91-55531. 240p. 1992. text 37.50 (0-8014-2710-X) Cornell U Pr.
Pols, Louis C., jt. ed. see Van Heuven, Vincent J.
Pols, Werner. Studien Zur Bismarckzeit. (GER.). 242p. 1986. write for info. (3-487-07726-4) G Olms Pubs.
Polsby, Daniel D. Firearms & Crime. 38p. 1997. pap. 5.95 (0-945999-59-3) Independent Inst.
***Polsby, Nelson, ed.** Annual Review of Political Science, Vol. 2. 600p. 1999. 60.00 (0-8243-3302-0) Annual Reviews.
Polsby, Nelson, jt. auth. see Price, Hugh.
Polsby, Nelson W. Political Innovation in America: The Politics of Policy Initation. LC 83-14749. 200p. 1984. 37.50 (0-300-03089-4) Yale U Pr.
— The Renegotiation of the Social Contract. 1976. 1.00 (1-55614-106-8) U of SD Gov Res Bur.
Polsby, Nelson W., ed. Annual Review of Political Science, Vol. 1. 1998. text 60.00 (0-8243-3301-2) Annual Reviews.
— The Modern Presidency. LC 81-40776. 250p. 1981. reprint ed. pap. text 24.00 (0-8191-1822-2) U Pr of Amer.
Polsby, Nelson W. & Wildavsky, Aaron. Presidential Elections: Strategies & Structures in American Politics. 9th ed. LC 95-32493. (Illus.). 368p. (C). 1996. pap. text 29.95 (1-56643-029-1, Chatham House Pub) Seven Bridges.
— Presidential Elections: Strategies & Structures of American Politics. 10th ed. (Illus.). 416p. 1999. pap. text 29.95 (1-889119-26-1, Chatham House Pub) Seven Bridges.
Polsby, Nelson W. & Wildavsky, Aaron B. Presidential Elections. 6th ed. 400p. (C). 1984. pap. 57.00 (0-02-396260-7, Pub. by P-H) S&S Trade.
— Presidential Elections: Contemporary Strategies of American Electoral Politics. 7th ed. 350p. 1988. pap. 14.95 (0-02-925262-8) Free Pr.
Polsby, Nelson W. & Wolfinger, Raymond E. On Parties: Essays Honoring Austin Ranney. LC 99-22656. 13p. 1999. 21.95 (0-87772-388-5) UCB IGS.
Polsby, Nelson W., jt. ed. see Peabody, Robert L.
Polselli, Joseph. Drums of a Different War. LC 83-6443. 261p. 1984. 22.95 (0-87949-241-4) Ashley Bks.
Polsgrove, Lewis. Managing Challenging Behaviors. (C). 1999. pap. text. write for info. (0-321-03771-5) Addison-Wesley.
— Managing Challenging Behaviors. (C). 2000. pap. text. write for info. (0-321-03772-3) Addison-Wesley Educ.
Polshkov, Mikhail K., ed. Exploration Geophysics, Vol. 49. LC TN0269.P75. 174p. reprint ed. pap. 54.00 (0-608-16664-2, 205611200050) Bks Demand.
— Exploration Geophysics, Vol. 51. Keller, George V., tr. LC 68-18539. 159p. 1969. reprint ed. pap. 49.30 (0-608-05394-5, 205611200051) Bks Demand.
Polsinelli, M., et al, eds. Nitrogen Fixation. (Developments in Plant & Soil Sciences Ser.). 704p. (C). 1991. text 364.50 (0-7923-1410-7) Kluwer Academic.
Polsky, Abe. Devour the Snow. 1979. pap. 5.25 (0-8222-0304-9) Dramatists Play.
Polsky, Andrew J. The Rise of the Therapeutic State. 296p. 1991. text 47.50 (0-691-07878-5, Pub. by Princeton U Pr); pap. text 18.95 (0-691-00084-0, Pub. by Princeton U Pr) Cal Prin Full Svc.
Polsky, Howard W. Cottage Six: Social System of Delinquent Boys in Residential Treatment. LC 76-50144. (Illus.). 192p. 1977. reprint ed. pap. text 11.50 (0-88275-475-0) Krieger.
Polsky, Jeffrey D., jt. auth. see McClain, Maureen E.
Polsky, Marion. First Latin, Bk. 2. 1987. pap. text, student ed. 5.85 (0-582-99853-0, 75278) Longman.
— First Latin, Set, Vols. I & II. 1990. 22.60 (0-8013-0570-5, 78477) Longman.
— First Latin, Vol. I. 1987. pap. text, teacher ed. 31.96 (0-582-90716-0, 75230); pap. text, student ed. 5.85 (0-582-90715-2, 75229) Longman.
— First Latin, Vol. II. 1987. pap. text, teacher ed. 31.96 (0-582-99854-9, 75279) Longman.
Polsky, Michael. V Zashchitu Pravoslavnoj Vjeri Ot Sektantov.Tr. of In Defence of Orthodoxy Against Sectarians. 1950. pap. 1.00 (0-317-30261-2) Holy Trinity.
Polsky, Michael A. What Good Is Religion to Me? 1993. pap. 0.50 (0-89981-140-X) Eastern Orthodox.
Polsky, Milton. Act of Will. 20p. (Orig.). 1996. pap. 6.00 (0-88734-527-1) Players Pr.
— Celebrate Your School Namesake. LC 97-62361. 275p. 1998. 39.95 (1-56676-558-7) Scarecrow.
— SATisfaction. LC 96-30988. 55p. (Orig.). 1996. pap. 6.00 (0-88734-426-7) Players Pr.
Polsky, Milton, et al. The King of Escapes: Playscript. (Orig.). (J). (gr. 3-12). 1985. pap. 6.00 (0-88734-510-7) Players Pr.
Polsky, Milton E. Let's Improvise: Becoming Creative, Expressive & Spontaneous Through Drama. LC 97-28482. (Illus.). 315p. 1998. pap. 18.95 (1-55783-307-9) Applause Theatre Bk Pubs.
Polsky, Ned. Hustlers, Beats, & Others. 220p. 1985. reprint ed. pap. text 9.00 (0-226-67473-8) U Ch Pr.
— Hustlers, Beats, & Others. rev. ed. LC 97-43059. 1998. pap. 16.95 (1-55821-404-6) Lyons Pr.
Polsky, Richard. Art Market Guide 1997: Contemporary American Art. 160p. 1996. pap. 19.95 (1-881616-77-0, 620591) Dist Art Pubs.
Polsky, Richard H. User's Guide to the Scientific & Clinical Literature on Dog & Cat Behavior. 2nd ed. 97p. (C). 1995. pap. text, student ed. 69.95 (0-614-04772-2) Animal Behav.
— User's Guide to the Scientific & Clinical Literature on Dog & Cat Behavior. 2nd ed. 92p. 1995. write for info. (0-614-13694-6) Animal Behav.
Polsky, Walter P., ed. see Foxman, Loretta D.
Polsky, Yury. Soviet Research Institutes & the Formulation of Foreign Policy: The Institute of World Economy & International Relations (IMEMO) Michta, Andrew A. & Zimmerman, William, eds. 120p. (Orig.). 1987. pap. text 75.00 (1-55831-036-3) Delphic Associates.
Polson, Alan, ed. Periodontal Regeneration: Current Status & Directions. (Illus.). 224p. 1994. text 72.00 (0-86715-175-7) Quint Pub Co.
Polson, Alfred, ed. Virus Separation & Purification Methods. LC 93-22933. (Illus.). 312p. 1993. text 125.00 (0-8247-9149-5) Dekker.
Polson, Archer. Law & Lawyers: or Sketches & Illustrations of Legal History & Biography, 2 vols. (Illus.). 1982. reprint ed. 85.00 (0-8377-1013-8, Rothman) W S Hein.
Polson, Beth & Newton, Miller. Not My Kid: A Parent's Guide to Kids & Drugs. 224p. 1985. mass mkt. 4.50 (0-380-69997-4, Avon Bks) Morrow Avon.
***Polson, Eric & Mazurik, Martin.** ASP Fundamentals Training Course. (VP Expert Ser.). (Illus.). 138p. 1999. student ed. 139.95 incl. cd-rom (0-9673353-0-2) NW Train Syst.
Polson, Martha C., et al, eds. Foundations of Intelligent Tutoring Systems. 296p. 1989. pap. text 29.95 (0-8058-0054-9) L Erlbaum Assocs.
Polson, Nicholas G. & Tiao, George C., eds. Bayesian Inference, 2 vols., Set, Vol. 7. (International Library of Critical Writings in Econometrics: Vol. 7). 800p. 1995. 310.00 (1-85278-668-X) E Elgar.
Polsov, V. M., tr. see Gindikin, Simon G. & Volevich, L. R.
Polster, Bernd. Design Directory: Scandinavia. LC 99-22957. (Illus.). 84p. 1999. pap. 24.95 (0-7893-0336-1, Pub. by Universe) St Martin.
***Polster, Bernd.** Design Directory U. S. A. (Illus.). 2000. pap. 29.95 (0-7893-0498-8) Universe.
Polster, Bernd, jt. auth. see Patton, Phil.
Polster, Bernd, ed. see Pixis, Christian.
Polster, Burkard. A Geometrical Picturebook. LC 97-48854. (Universitext Ser.). (Illus.). 296p. (C). 1998. 39.95 (0-387-98437-2) Spr-Verlag.
Polster, Erving. A Population of Selves: A Therapeutic Exploration of Personal Diversity. LC 94-42595. (Social & Behavioral Sciences Ser.). 271p. 1995. 30.95 (0-7879-0076-1) Jossey-Bass.
Polster, Gary E. Inside Looking Out: The Cleveland Jewish Orphan Asylum, 1868-1924. LC 89-24414. 254p. 1990. 32.00 (0-87338-406-7) Kent St U Pr.
Polster, Ian. Exercises for Developing Competency in Basic Music Skills. 4th ed. 106p. (C). 1995. teacher ed. 50.00 (1-887964-01-0); pap. text 25.00 (1-887964-00-2) Prescript Music.
— Selected Exercises for Developing Competency in Basic Music Skills. 4th ed. 43p. (C). 1994. pap. text 25.00 (1-887964-02-9) Prescript Music.
Polster, Irving & Polster, Miriam. Gestalt Therapy Integrated: Contours of Theory & Practice. LC 74-3424. 1982. pap. 11.00 (0-394-71006-1, V-6) Vin Bks.
Polster, James. Brown: A Novel. 288p. 1995. 16.95 (1-56352-195-4) Longstreet.
Polster, Miriam, jt. auth. see Polster, Irving.
Polston, Betty & Golant, Susan K. Loving Midlife Marriage. LC 99-17025. 272p. (C). 1999. pap. 14.95 (0-471-31453-6) Wiley.
Polt, John D. The Individualist Papers. LC 97-90674. 62p. 1998. pap. 8.95 (0-533-12455-7) Vantage.
Polt, John H. Batilo: Estudios Sobre la Evolucion Estilistica de Melendez Valdes. LC 87-7056. (University of California Publications in Entomology: No. 119). (SPA.). 335p. 1987. pap. 103.90 (0-7837-8421-X, 204922300010) Bks Demand.
— Gaspar Melchor de Jovellanos. LC 78-147263. (Twayne's World Authors Ser.). 163p. (C). 1971. lib. bdg. 20.95 (0-8290-1740-2) Irvington.
— Los Gramaticos; Historia Chinesca: Edicion Critica. LC 76-626070. (U. C. Publ. in Modern Philology Ser.: Vol. 95). 254p. reprint ed. 78.80 (0-8357-9631-0, 201376700089) Bks Demand.
Polt, John H., jt. ed. see Herr, Richard.
Polt, John H., tr. see Casey, Calvert.
Polt, John H., tr. see Casey, Calvert & Stavans, Ilan.
Polt, John H., tr. see Cela, Camilo Jose.
Polt, John R., tr. see De Turner, Clorinda M.
***Polt, Renata, ed.** A Thousand Kisses: A Grandmother's Holocaust Letters. 216p. 1999. pap. 19.95 (0-8173-1017-7) U of Ala Pr.
Polt, Renata, jt. auth. see Pollatschek, Henriette.
Polt, Richard. Heidegger. LC 98-30460. 256p. 1998. pap. 18.95 (0-8014-8564-9) Cornell U Pr.
— Heidegger: An Introduction. LC 98-30460. 256p. 1998. 39.95 (0-8014-3584-6) Cornell U Pr.
Polt, Richard, tr. see Heidegger, Martin.
Polt, Richard, tr. see Nietzsche, Friedrich Wilhelm.
***Polt, Roger.** Crackers for Your Soup! LC 99-91059. 220p. 1999. pap. 9.95 (0-9674547-0-0) Person Person.
Poltarnees, Welleran. Amy & Nathaniel. (J). 1991. pap. 13.00 (0-671-75269-3, Green Tiger S&S) S&S Childrens.
— An Anniversary Blessing. (Illus.). 48p. 1999. 18.95 (1-883211-18-2) Laughing Elephant.
— Baby Blessing. 48p. 1995. 18.95 (1-883211-06-9) Laughing Elephant.
— Birthday Blessing. (Illus.). 48p. 1998. 18.95 (1-883211-03-4) Laughing Elephant.
— A Bridal Blessing. LC 98-233867. (Illus.). 48p. 1997. 18.95 (1-883211-11-5) Laughing Elephant.
— A Christmas Blessing. (Illus.). 48p. 1996. 18.95 (1-883211-08-5) Laughing Elephant.
— Friendly Book. (Illus.). 32p. 1995. 8.95 (1-883211-05-0) Laughing Elephant.
***Poltarnees, Welleran.** A Garden Blessing. (Illus.). 48p. 2000. 18.95 (1-883211-25-5) Laughing Elephant.
Poltarnees, Welleran. A House Blessing. LC 95-236698. (Illus.). 48p. 1994. 18.95 (1-883211-04-2) Laughing Elephant.
— Most Memorable Birthday. (J). 1993. 15.00 (0-671-77862-5, Green Tiger S&S) S&S Childrens.
— Sharing the Pleasures of Reading. (Illus.). 48p. 1999. 18.00 (1-883211-24-7, Darling & Comp) Laughing Elephant.
***Poltarnees, Welleran.** A Travel Blessing. (Illus.). 56p. 2000. 18.95 (1-883211-32-8) Laughing Elephant.
Poltarnees, Welleran, et al, eds. A. B. C. of Fashionable Animals. (Illus.). 64p. (J). 1991. 12.95 (0-88138-122-5, Green Tiger S&S) S&S Childrens.
Poltarness, Welleran. Kindness Book. LC 96-131430. (Illus.). 32p. 1995. 8.95 (1-883211-02-6) Laughing Elephant.
Polte, W. & Hein, James R. Clocks & Watches from the Landrock Collection. (Illus.). 295p. (C). 1988. 350.00 (0-569-21424-6) St Mut.
Polten, Eric P. Critique of the Psycho-Physical Identity Theory: A Refutation of Scientific Materialism & an Establishment of Mind-Matter Dualism by Means of Philosophy & Scientific Method. LC 72-94504. (Studies in the Social Sciences: No. 14). 290p. 1973. text 44.65 (90-279-7224-9) Mouton.
Polter, Dovid S. Listening to Life's Messages: Adapted from the Works of the Lubavitcher Rebbe Rabbi Menachem M. Schneerson. 80p. 1997. pap. 8.00 (1-881400-25-5) S I E.
Poltera, Orlando. Le Langage de Simonide: Etude sur la Tradition Poetique et Son Renouvellement. (Sapheneia Ser.: Bd. 1). (FRE.). 686p. 1997. 70.95 (3-906757-32-3, Pub. by P Lang) P Lang Pubng.
Polthier, K., jt. ed. see Hege, H. C.
Polti, Georges. The Thirty-Six Dramatic Situations. LC 77-8343. 1988. pap. 8.95 (0-87116-109-5) Writer.
Poltimore, Mark, jt. auth. see Hook, Philip.
***Poltl, Rene.** Die Lehre Vom Indizienbeweis im 19, Jahrhundert. (Europaische Hochschulschriften Rechtswissenschaft Ser.). XXV, 547p. 1999. 79.95 (3-631-35361-8) P Lang Pubng.
Poltner, Gunther & Vetter, Helmuth. Nietzsche Und die Musik. 140p. 1997. 32.95 (3-631-49940-X) P Lang Pubng.
Polto, Pearl B. In America Is Bad Credit a Prison Term? LC 87-83736. 65p. (Orig.). 1988. pap. 4.95 (0-916391-01-9) Free & Easy Pubns.
— Pearl Polto's Easy Guide to Good Credit. 128p. 1996. mass mkt. 5.50 (0-425-15297-9) Berkley Pub.
Polto, Pearl B. & Bell, Rick. We the People Have Credit Rights Too. 110p. (Orig.). 1993. pap. 5.95 (0-9636397-0-6) P B Polto.
Polto, Pearl B. & Oskam, B. Pearl Polto's Easy Guide to Good Credit. 1990. pap. 7.95 (0-425-12059-7) Berkley Pub.
Poltorak, Joe. Fashions in the Groove, 1960s. LC 98-85073. (Illus.). 160p. 1998. pap. 29.95 (0-7643-0620-0) Schiffer.
Poltoratsky, Nikolai P. Ivan Aleksandrovich Il'in: Zhizn', Trudy, Mirovozzrenie. LC 89-7528. (RUS.). 320p. (Orig.). 1989. pap. 17.00 (1-55779-016-7) Hermitage Pubs.
Poltorzycki, Stephen. Creating Environmental Business Value: Achieving Two Shades of Green. Christopher, Bill, ed. LC 98-73104. (Management Library: Vol. 17). 128p. 1998. pap. 12.95 (1-56052-489-8) Crisp Pubns.
Polubarinova-Kochina, P. Y. Theory of Ground Water Movement. LC 62-12616. 635p. 1962. reprint ed. pap. 196.90 (0-7837-9328-6, 206006900004) Bks Demand.
Poluchina, V., tr. see Chayanov, A.
Polugaevsky, Lev, et al. Sicilian Love: The Book of the Sicilian Defence Theme Tournament, Buenos Aires 1994. 256p. 1996. 35.00 (0-917237-13-7) Chess Combi.
Polugayevsky, Lyev. The Art of Defence in Chess: Defence & Counterattack Techniques in Chess. (Russian Chess Ser.). (Illus.). 268p. 1988. pap. 19.90 (0-08-032058-9, Pergamon Pr) Elsevier.
— Grandmaster Performance. Neat, Kenneth P., tr. (Russian Chess Ser.). (Illus.). 220p. 1984. pap. 19.90 (0-08-029749-8, Pergamon Pr) Elsevier.
— Grandmaster Preparation. Neat, Kenneth P., tr. (Russian Chess Ser.). (Illus.). 240p. 1981. 29.95 (0-08-024099-2, Pergamon Pr); pap. 19.90 (0-08-024098-4, Pergamon Pr) Elsevier.
Polugayevsky, Lyev & Damsky, I. The Art of Defence in Chess: Defence & Counterattack Techniques in Chess. (Russian Chess Ser.). (Illus.). 270p. 1988. 29.95 (0-08-032059-7, Pergamon Pr) Elsevier.
Poluhowich, John J. Argonaut: The Submarine Legacy of Simon Lake. LC 99-14779. 1999. 24.95 (0-89096-894-2) Tex A&M Univ Pr.
Polukhanov, Pavel M. The Early Slavs: Eastern Europe from the Initial Settlement to the Kievan Rus. LC 95-45474. (Illus.). 256p. (C). 1996. pap. text 23.44 (0-582-23618-5, Pub. by Addison-Wesley) Longman.
Polukhanov, Pavel M., et al. The Early Slavs: Eastern Europe from the Initial Settlement to the Kievan Rus. LC 95-45474. (Illus.). 237p. (C). 1996. 76.00 (0-582-23627-4) Longman.
Polumbaum, Nyna B., jt. auth. see Polumbaum, Ted.
Polumbaum, Ted & Polumbaum, Nyna B. Today Is Not Like Yesterday: A Chilean Journey. (Illus.). 132p. (Orig.). 1992. pap. 12.95 (0-9633526-0-1) Light & Shadow.
Polunin, Miriam. Healing Foods. LC 96-30980. (Eyewitness Garden Handbks.). 160p. 1997. 24.95 (0-7894-1456-2) DK Pub Inc.
— Healing Foods. LC 96-30980. (DK Living Ser.). (Illus.). 160p. 1999. pap. 13.95 (0-7894-4247-7) DK Pub Inc.
Polunin, Miriam & Robbins, Christopher. The Natural Pharmacy: An Illustrated Guide to Natural Medicine. (Illus.). 144p. 1992. pap. 18.95 (0-02-036041-X) Macmillan.
Polunin, N. V. C. & Robertson, C. M. Reef Fisheries. (Illus.). 496p. 1996. write for info. (0-412-60110-9) Kluwer Academic.
Polunin, Nicholas, ed. Population & Global Security. 2nd ed. (Illus.). 328p. (C). 1998. text 74.95 (0-521-56372-0); pap. text 29.95 (0-521-63539-X) Cambridge U Pr.
Polunin, Nicholas & Burnett, John H., eds. Surviving with the Biosphere: Proceedings of the Fourth International Conference on Environmental Future. (Illus.). 561p. 1994. 145.00 (0-7486-0314-X, Pub. by Edinburgh U Pr) Col U Pr.
Polunin, Nicholas & Curme, Lynn M. World Who Is Who & Does What in Environment & Conservation. LC 97-1651. 608p. 1997. text 75.00 (0-312-17448-9) St Martin.
Polunin, Oleg. The Flowers of Europe: A Field Guide. (Illus.). 832p. 1969. 65.00 (0-19-217621-8) OUP.
— Flowers of Greece & the Balkans: A Field Guide. (Illus.). 688p. 1987. pap. 28.00 (0-19-281998-4) OUP.
Polunin, Oleg & Huxley, Anthony. Flowers of the Mediterranean. 3rd ed. (Illus.). 260p. 1990. pap. 29.95 (0-7011-3695-2) Trafalgar.
Polunin, Oleg & Smythies, B. E. Flowers of South-west Europe: A Field Guide. (Illus.). 544p. 1988. pap. 28.00 (0-19-288178-7) OUP.
Polunin, Oleg & Stainton, Adam. The Concise Flowers of the Himalaya. (Illus.). 426p. 1987. 45.00 (0-19-561832-7) OUP.
— Concise Flowers of the Himalaya. LC QK379.5.H55P65 1997. (Oxford India Paperbacks Ser.). (Illus.). 424p. 1998. pap. 19.95 (0-19-564414-X) OUP.
— Flowers of the Himalaya. (Illus.). 610p. 1997. reprint ed. pap. 35.00 (0-19-564187-6) OUP.
Polunin, Oleg & Walters, Martin. A Guide to the Vegetation of Britain & Europe. (Illus.). 296p. 1985. 39.95 (0-19-217713-3) OUP.
Polunin, Vladimir. The Continental Method of Scene Painting. Beaumont, Cyril W., ed. LC 77-19083. (Series in Dance). (Illus.). 1979. reprint ed. lib. bdg. 29.50 (0-306-77578-6) Da Capo.
Polushkin, Maria. Biscotti & Other Low Fat Cookies. LC 97-20229. (Illus.). 160p. 1997. pap. 12.95 (0-312-16782-2) St Martin.
— The Dumpling Cookbook, No. 119. LC 76-25437. (Illus.). 200p. 1976. pap. 8.95 (0-911104-85-2, 119) Workman Pub.
Poluyan, Igor, tr. see Kosals, L.
Poluyanov, L. V., et al. Group Properties of the Acoustic Differential Equation: Separation of Variables, Exact Solution. 180p. 1995. 85.00 (0-7484-0280-2, Pub. by Tay Francis Ltd) Taylor & Francis.
Polvay. Slim & Healthy Italian Cooking. 1990. pap. 11.95 (0-942084-33-0) SeaSide Pub.
***Polvay, Marina.** All along the Danube. 2nd rev. exp. ed. (Illus.). 360p. 2000. pap. 14.95 (0-7818-0806-5) Hippocrene Bks.
— Dracula Cookbook. LC 00-26048. (Illus.). 272p. 2000. 8.99 (0-517-20784-2) Random Hse Value.
Polvay, Marina & LaFray, Joyce. Famous Florida! Seminole Indian Recipes. 29p. 1996. 5.95 (0-942084-35-7) SeaSide Pub.
Polver, David. GURPS Mecha: Mighty Battlesuits & Anime Fighting Machines. Punch, Sean, ed. (GURPS Ser.). (Illus.). 128p. 1997. pap. 19.95 (1-55634-239-X, 6021, Pub. by S Jackson Games) BookWorld.
Polverel, A. Parler de la Lozere. (FRE.). 83p. 1994. 34.95 (0-320-00915-7) Fr & Eur.
Polvinen, Elaine & State University College of New York--Buffalo Staf, eds. Computer Applications to Textiles & Apparel. (ITAA Monograph Ser.: Vol. 8). 1996. 35.00 (1-885715-04-8) Intl Textile.
Polvinen, Tuomo. Imperial Borderland: Bobrikov & the Attempted Russification of Finland, 1898-1904. Huxley, Steven, tr. LC 94-38507. (Illus.). 272p. 1995. text 32.95 (0-8223-1563-7) Duke.
Polwhele, Richard. The English Orator: A Didactic Poem. (Anglistica & Americana Ser.: No. 16). 201p. 1968. reprint ed. 44.20 (0-685-66504-6, 05102037) G Olms Pubs.
Polworth, Barbara. Get to Know Your Calculator. 132p. (J). (gr. k-3). pap. 15.95 (1-871098-03-3, Pub. by Claire Pubns) Parkwest Pubns.
Poly, Jean-Pierre & Bournazel, Eric. The Feudal Transformation, 900-1200. LC 90-42094. (Europe Past & Present Ser.). x, 424p. 1991. 45.00 (0-8419-1167-3) Holmes & Meier.
Polya, George. George Polya - Collected Papers, 2 vols., Vol. 1: Singularities of Analytic Functions. Boas, Ralph P., ed. 1974. 75.00 (0-262-02104-8) MIT Pr.
— George Polya - Collected Papers: Analysis, Vol. III. Rota, Gian-Carlo et al, eds. (Mathematicians of Our Time Ser.: No. 22). 548p. 1984. 65.00 (0-262-16096-X) MIT Pr.
— Mathematical Discovery Combined Volume. 464p. (C). 1981. pap. 92.95 (0-471-08975-3) Wiley.
— Mathematical Methods in Science. Bowden, Leon, ed. LC 76-25863. (New Mathematical Library: No. 26). 234p. 1977. pap. text 6.00 (0-88385-626-3, NML-26) Math Assn.
— Mathematics & Plausible Reasoning, 1. (Illus.). 296p. 1954. pap. text 19.95 (0-691-02509-6, Pub. by Princeton U Pr) Cal Prin Full Svc.

— Mathematics & Plausible Reasoning, 2. (Illus.). 200p. 1954. pap. text 19.95 (*0-691-02510-X*, Pub. by Princeton U Pr) Cal Prin Full Svc.

— Mathematik und Plausibles Schliessen, 2 vols. Incl. Vol. 2. Typen und Strukturen Plausibler Folgerung. 326p. 1980. 97.00 (*0-8176-0715-3*); (Science & Civilization Ser.: Nos. 14 & 15). write for info. (*0-318-51087-1*) Birkhauser.

— Vom Losen Mathematischer Aufgaben-Einsicht und Entdeckung, Lernen und Lehren, Vol. II. (Science & Civilization Ser.: No. 21). (Illus.). 286p. 1980. 76.00 (*0-8176-0298-4*) Birkhauser.

Polya, George & Szego, G. C. Isoperimetric Inequalities in Mathematical Physics. (Annals of Mathematics Studies). 1951. 26.00 (*0-527-02743-X*) Periodicals Srv.

Polya, George & Szego, Gabor. Problems & Theorems in Analysis. Aeppli, Dorothee, tr. from GER. LC 97-47108. (Classics in Mathematics Ser.). 1997. pap. 39.95 (*3-540-63686-2*) Spr-Verlag.

— Problems & Theorems in Analysis. Aeppli, Dorothee, tr. LC 97-47108. (Classics in Mathematics Ser.: Vol. I). 400p. 1997. pap. 39.95 (*3-540-63640-4*) Spr-Verlag.

— Problems & Theorems in Analysis I: Series, Integral Calculus, Theory of Functions. (Illus.). 1989. reprint ed. pap. 39.00 (*0-387-90224-4*) Spr-Verlag.

— Problems & Theorems in Analysis II: Theory of Functions, Zeros, Polynomials, Determinants, Number Theory, Geometry. Billigheimer, C. E., tr. (Illus.). 1990. 47.95 (*0-387-90291-0*) Spr-Verlag.

Polya, George & Szegoe, G. Problems & Theorems in Analysis I: Series, Integral Calculus, Theory of Functions. (Grundlehren der Mathematischen Wissenschaften Ser.: Vol. 193). 1978. 98.00 (*0-387-05672-6*) Spr-Verlag.

Polya, George, et al. Notes on Introductory Combinatorics. (Progress in Computer Science Ser.: Vol. 4). 1990. 21.95 (*3-7643-3123-2*); 36.50 (*0-8176-3170-4*) Birkhauser.

Polya, Geroge & Latta, Gordon. Complex Variables. LC 73-14882. 343p. reprint ed. pap. 106.40 (*0-608-30016-0*, 205526600011) Bks Demand.

Polya, Gyorgy. How to Solve It. 2nd ed. 224p. 1945. pap. text 12.95 (*0-691-02356-5*, Pub. by Princeton U Pr) Cal Prin Full Svc.

Polyachenko, V. L., jt. auth. see Fridman, A. M.

Polyachenko, V. L., jt. auth. see Fridman, A. M.

Polyaenus. Polyaenus: Strategems of War, 2 vols., Vol. I. rev. ed. Krentz, Peter & Wheeler, Everett L., eds. & trs. by. from GEC. (GRE.). xxxil, 549p. (Orig.). (C). 1994. pap. text 22.50 (*0-89005-503-3*) Ares.

Polyak, B. T. Introduction to Optimization. Balakrishnan, A. V., ed. LC 87-11290. (Translations Series in Mathematics & Engineering).Tr. of Vvedenie v optimizatsiyu. 464p. 1987. text 95.00 (*0-911575-14-6*) Optimization Soft.

Polyak, Ilya. Computatinal Statistics in Climatology. (Illus.). 376p. (C). 1996. text 75.00 (*0-19-509999-0*) OUP.

***Polyak, Ilya.** I Am Your Prisoner for Life (A Jew in the DPR) 2000. 13.95 (*0-533-13538-9*) Vantage.

Polyak, Stephen. Vertebrate Visual System. Kluver, Heinrich, ed. LC 55-5153. (Illus.). 1957. lib. bdg. 100.00 (*0-226-67494-0*) U Ch Pr.

Polyakov, A. F., ed. Thermo & Laser Anemometry. 186p. 1988. 68.95 (*0-89116-607-6*) Hemisp Pub.

Polyakov, A. M. Gauge Fields & Strings. (Contemporary Concepts in Physics Ser.: Vol. 3). x, 302p. 1987. text 83.00 (*3-7186-0393-4*); pap. text 31.00 (*3-7186-0392-6*) Gordon & Breach.

Polyakov, Evgeny G., jt. auth. see Kerridge, David H.

Polyakov, I. Y., jt. auth. see Gromov, I. M.

Polyakov, V. A., jt. auth. see Ferronsky, V. I.

Polyani, Karl & Rotsfein, Abraham. Dahomey & the Slave Trade: An Analysis of an Archaic Economy. LC 84-45535. (American Ethnological Society Monographs: No. 42). 1988. reprint ed. 39.50 (*0-404-62940-7*) AMS Pr.

Polyanin, A. D. & Dilman, Victor V. Methods of Modeling Equations & Analogies in Chemical Engineering. 310p. 1991. 125.00 (*0-89116-769-2*) Begell Hse.

Polyanin, Andrei D. & Dilman, Victor V. Methods of Modeling Equations & Analogies in Chemical Engineering. Piterman, Mark A., tr. from RUS. LC 93-2356. 368p. 1994. 212.00 (*0-8493-9914-9*) CRC Pr.

Polyanin, Andrei D. & Zaitsev, Valentin F. Handbook of Exact Solutions for Ordinary Differential Equations. LC 95-1021. 720p. 1995. boxed set 134.95 (*0-8493-9438-4*, 9438) CRC Pr.

Polybe. Histoire. 1672p. 42.95 (*0-686-56553-3*) Fr & Eur.

Polybius. Histoire. (FRE.). 1989. lib. bdg. 105.00 (*0-8288-3528-4*, F22081) Fr & Eur.

— The Histories. Badian, E., ed. Chambers, Mortimer, tr. 340p. 1986. reprint ed. 29.50 (*0-8290-2014-4*) Irvington.

— Histories, 6 vols., 1. (Loeb Classical Library: No. 128, 137-138, 159-161). 442p. 1922. 19.95 (*0-674-99142-7*) HUP.

— Histories, 6 vols., 2. (Loeb Classical Library: No. 128, 137-138, 159-161). 528p. 1922. 19.95 (*0-674-99152-4*) HUP.

— Histories, 6 vols., 3. (Loeb Classical Library: No. 128, 137-138, 159-161). 560p. 1923. 19.95 (*0-674-99153-2*) HUP.

— Histories, 6 vols., 4. (Loeb Classical Library: No. 128, 137-138, 159-161). 570p. 1925. 19.95 (*0-674-99175-3*) HUP.

— Histories, 6 vols., 5. (Loeb Classical Library: No. 128, 137-138, 159-161). 542p. 1926. 19.95 (*0-674-99176-1*) HUP.

— Histories, 6 vols., 6. (Loeb Classical Library: No. 128, 137-138, 159-161). 574p. 1927. 19.95 (*0-674-99178-8*) HUP.

— The Histories of Polybius, Discoursing of the Warres Betwixt the Romanes & Carthaginenses. Watson, Christopher, tr. LC 75-25683. (English Experience Ser.: No. 132). 1969. reprint ed. 55.00 (*90-221-0132-0*) Walter J Johnson.

— Polybius on Roman Imperialism. Bernstein, Alvin H., ed. Shuckburgh, E. S., tr. LC 79-66479. 540p. (Orig.). 1980. pap. text 10.95 (*0-89526-902-3*) Regnery Pub.

— The Rise of the Roman Empire. Scott-Kilvert, Ian, tr. 576p. 1980. pap. 14.95 (*0-14-044362-2*, Penguin Classics) Viking Penguin.

Polycarpou, Susan, jt. auth. see Shoemaker, Connie.

Polychroniou, Chronis. Marxist Perspectives on Imperialism: A Theoretical Analysis. LC 90-45483. 200p. 1991. 49.95 (*0-275-93720-8*, C3720, Praeger Pubs) Greenwood.

Polychroniou, Chronis, ed. Perspectives & Issues in International Political Economy. LC 92-7496. 288p. 1992. 65.00 (*0-275-94016-0*, C4016, Praeger Pubs) Greenwood.

— Socialism: Crisis & Renewal. LC 92-36546. 272p. 1993. 62.95 (*0-275-94089-6*, C4089, Praeger Pubs) Greenwood.

Polychroniou, Chronis & Targ, Harry R., eds. Marxism Today: Essays on Capitalism, Socialism, & Strategies for Social Change. LC 95-14301. 232p. 1996. 62.95 (*0-275-94604-5*, Praeger Pubs) Greenwood.

Polychronopoulos, C., et al, eds. High Performance Computing: Second International Symposium, ISHPC'99, Kyoto, Japan, May 26-28, 1999, Proceedings. LC 99-15828. (Lecture Notes in Computer Science Ser.: Vol. 1615). xiv, 410p. 1999. pap. 69.00 (*3-540-65969-2*) Spr-Verlag.

Polychronopoulos, C. D., et al, eds. High Performance Computing: Proceedings, International Symposium, ISHPC'97, Fukuoka, Japan, November 4-6, 1997, Vol. 133. LC 97-39204. (Lecture Notes in Computer Science Ser.: Vol. 1336). xii, 416p. 1997. pap. 67.00 (*3-540-63766-4*) Spr-Verlag.

Polydorides, Nicos. The Concept of Centrality in Urban Form & Structure. (European University Studies: Ser. 37, Vol. 2). 195p. 1983. 27.00 (*3-261-03270-7*) P Lang Pubng.

Polydoris, Nicholas, jt. auth. see Green, Orville C., III.

Polykrates, Gottfried. Beitrage zur Religionsfrage der Yanonami-Indianer. 35p. 1974. 8.95 (*87-480-0050-7*, Pub. by Aarhus Univ Pr) David Brown.

Polyme. Journal of Polymer Science. 1971. 12.00 (*0-471-99954-7*); 9.00 (*0-471-99955-5*) Wiley.

Polymetric Materials Division Staff. Particle Size Distribution: Assessment & Characterization: Symposium of the 190th Meeting, Chicago, IL, September 8-13, 1985. Provder, Theodore J., ed. LC 86-32185. (ACS Symposium Ser.: No. 332). (Illus.). x, 308p. 1987. 59.95 (*0-8412-1016-0*) Am Chemical.

Polytechnic Institute of New York Staff. Stress Relaxation in Copper-Base Alloys. 188p. 1974. 28.20 (*0-317-34549-4*, 207) Intl Copper.

Polywka, John & Gabrel, Stanley. Programming of Computer Numerical Controlled Machines. (Illus.). 288p. 1992. 36.95 (*0-8311-3035-0*) Indus Pr.

Polyzoides, G. Ancient Greek History. (GRE., Illus.). (J). (gr. 4-6). 4.00 (*0-686-79636-5*) Divry.

— History & Teachings of the Eastern Greek Orthodox Church. (Illus.). 96p. 6.00 (*0-686-83964-1*) Divry.

— History of Byzantine & Modern Greece. (GRE., Illus.). (J). (gr. 4-6). 4.00 (*0-686-79635-7*) Divry.

— Stories from the New Testament. (GRE., Illus.). 112p. vinyl bd. 4.00 (*0-686-83966-8*) Divry.

— Stories from the Old Testament. (GRE., Illus.). 71p. (J). (gr. 5 up). vinyl bd. 4.00 (*0-686-80434-1*) Divry.

— What We See & Hear in a Greek Eastern Orthodox Church. 92p. 6.00 (*0-686-83965-X*) Divry.

Polyzoides, M. Catechism of Eastern Greek Orthodox Church. 96p. 6.00 (*0-686-79625-X*) Divry.

Polyzoides, Stefanos, et al. Courtyard Housing in Los Angeles. LC 92-1072. (Illus.). 232p. 1992. reprint ed. pap. 24.95 (*0-910413-53-3*) Princeton Arch.

Polzer, Charles W. Kino: A Legacy: His Life, His Works, His Missions, His Monuments. (Illus.). 210p. 1998. pap. 18.00 (*0-9661562-0-X*) Jesuit SAZ.

— Kino: His Missions, His Monuments. (Illus.). 80p. 1998. pap. 9.00 (*0-9661562-1-8*) Jesuit SAZ.

— Kino Guide II. LC 82-50218. (Illus.). 76p. 1982. pap. 7.00 (*0-915076-07-1*) SW Mission.

Polzer, Charles W., et al, eds. The Jesuit Missions of Northern Mexico. LC 91-25507. (Spanish Borderlands Sourcebooks Ser.: Vol. 19). 592p. 1991. text 45.00 (*0-8240-2096-0*) Garland.

Polzer, Charles W. & Sheridan, Thomas E., eds. The Presidio & Militia on the Northern Frontier of New Spain Vol. II, Pt. I: A Documentary History: The Californias & Sinaloa-Sonora, 1700-1765. (Illus.). 470p. 1997. 65.00 (*0-8165-1692-8*) U of Ariz Pr.

Polzer, Charles W., et al. Tucson: A Short History. LC 85-63503. (Illus.). 160p. (Orig.). 1986. pap. 8.95 (*0-915076-11-X*) SW Mission.

Polzer, Charles W., jt. auth. see Cabat, Erni.

Polzer, Charles W., ed. see Cabat, Erni.

Polzer, Charles W., jt. ed. see Naylor, Thomas H.

Polzer-Hoditz, Ludwig C. Memories of Rudolf Steiner. 1987. pap. 9.95 (*0-916786-93-5*, Saint George Pubns) R Steiner Col.

Polzin, Paul E., et al. Some Economic Impacts of the 1988 Fires in the Yellowstone Area. (Illus.). 16p. 1997. reprint ed. 10.00 (*0-89904-610-X*, Bear Meadows Resrch Grp); reprint ed. pap. 3.00 (*0-89904-611-8*, Bear Meadows Resrch Grp) Crumb Elbow Pub.

Polzin, Richard. Worthy Is the Child. (Illus.). 132p. (J). (gr. k-6). 1995. 19.95 (*0-9645911-0-3*) Nite Lite Stories.

Polzin, Robert M. Biblical Structuralism: Method & Subjectivity in the Study of Ancient Texts. LC 76-15895. (Semeia Supplements Ser.). (Illus.). 224p. reprint ed. pap. 69.50 (*0-7837-5413-2*, 204517700005) Bks Demand.

— David & the Deuteronomist: A Literary Study of the Deuteronomic History, Pt. 3: 2 Samuel. LC 93-22056. (Literary Study of the Deuteronomic History Ser.: Pt. 3). 268p. 1993. 39.95 (*0-253-34553-7*) Ind U Pr.

— Moses & the Deuteronomist: A Literary Study of the Deuteronomic History. 224p. 1984. 17.95 (*0-8164-2456-9*); 8.95 (*0-8164-2284-2*) Harper SF.

— Samuel & the Deuteronomist: A Literary Study of the Deuteronomic History, Pt. 2: 1 Samuel. LC 92-43856. (Indiana Studies in Biblical Literature: Pt. 2). 312p. (C). 1993. 35.00 (*0-253-34552-9*); pap. 15.95 (*0-253-20849-1*) Ind U Pr.

Polzyn, Richard, ed. see Hershberger, Ervin N.

Poma, Andrea. The Critical Philosophy of Hermann Cohen. Denton, John, tr. LC 96-30131. (SUNY Series in Jewish Philosophy). 320p. (C). 1997. text 65.50 (*0-7914-3185-1*); pap. text 21.95 (*0-7914-3186-X*) State U NY Pr.

Pomada, Elizabeth. Fun Places to Go with Children in Northern California. 8th ed. LC 96-50133. 208p. 1997. pap. 10.95 (*0-8118-1514-5*) Chronicle Bks.

Pomada, Elizabeth & Larsen, Michael. The Painted Ladies Revisited: San Francisco's Resplendent Victorians Inside & Out. (Illus.). 144p. 1989. pap. 24.95 (*0-525-48508-2*, Dutt) Dutton Plume.

Pomada, Elizabeth L. Daughters/Paint Lady. 1987. pap. 23.95 (*0-525-48577-5*) NAL.

Pomaine, De. French Cooking in Ten Minutes. Hyman, Mary, tr. 146p. 1994. pap. 10.00 (*0-86547-480-X*) N Point Pr.

Pomann, Howard, jt. auth. see Foley, Barbara.

Pomar, Felipe Cossio del, see Cossio del Pomar, Felipe.

Pomaranc, Joan C., ed. see Paine McBrien, Judith.

Pomare, Maui, et al. Legends of the Maori, 2 vols., Set. LC 75-35265. (Illus.). 1976. reprint ed. 125.00 (*0-404-14350-4*) AMS Pr.

Pomarède, Vincent. Delacroix: The Late Work. LC 98-60336. (Illus.). 408p. 1998. 65.00 (*0-500-09275-3*, Pub. by Thames Hudson) Norton.

Pomarede, Vincent, jt. auth. see Wallens, Gerard de.

Pomares, Henry. George Duncan Wickham. (Illus.). 70p. 1994. 15.00 (*0-9641486-0-9*) Goshen Chamber.

Pomares, Jose M. & Thoele, Sue P. Ser Tu Misma: Meditaciones Para la Capacitacion y la Paz Mental. 2nd ed. (SPA.). 200p. 1995. pap. 10.95 (*0-943233-96-8*) Conari Press.

Pomarnatsii, A. V., jt. auth. see Glinka, V. M.

Pomarska, Krystyna, jt. auth. see Jakobson, Roman.

Pomasaka, Anna. Dinosaurs. (Illus.). 32p. (J). pap. text 1.00 (*0-486-40162-6*) Dover.

Pomaska, Anna. Invisible Cars & Trucks Magic. (Illus.). (J). (ps-3). 1998. text 1.00 (*0-486-40236-3*, 881924Q) Dover.

— Invisible Numbers Magic Picture Book. 1998. pap. 1.00 (*0-486-28421-2*) Dover.

Pomaska, A. Fun with Crossword Puzzles. (J). 1989. pap. 2.50 (*0-486-24978-6*) Dover.

— Little Halloween Activity Book. (Little Activity Bks.). (J). 1993. pap. 1.00 (*0-486-27601-5*) Dover.

Pomaska, Anna. ABC. 32p. (J). (gr. 4-8). 1997. pap. 1.00 (*0-486-29534-6*) Dover.

Pomaska, Anna. ABC Sticker Book. (Illus.). (J). 1991. pap. 1.00 (*0-486-25908-0*) Dover.

Pomaska, Anna. Alphabet Hidden Picture Coloring Book. (Illus.). (J). (gr. k-3). 1992. pap. 2.50 (*0-486-27261-3*) Dover.

***Pomaska, Anna.** Birds. (Illus.). (J). 1998. pap. 1.00 (*0-486-40080-8*) Dover.

— Birds. (Illus.). (J). 2000. pap. 1.00 (*0-486-41027-7*) Dover.

Pomaska, Anna. Create Your Own Pictures Coloring Book. (Illus.). (J). 1984. pap. 2.50 (*0-486-24614-0*) Dover.

— Cut & Assemble a Peter Rabbit. (J). 1984. pap. 6.95 (*0-486-24713-9*) Dover.

— Cut & Assemble Fairy Tale Toy Theater. 1984. text 6.95 (*0-486-24654-X*) Dover.

***Pomaska, Anna.** Decorative Sun, Moon & Stars. (Illus.). 2000. pap. 4.95 (*0-486-41070-6*) Dover.

Pomaska, Anna. Dinosaur Sticker Book, Vol. 80. (Illus.). (J). (gr. k-3). 1989. pap. 1.00 (*0-486-25907-2*) Dover.

— Dot-to-Dot. (Illus.). 32p. (J). (ps-1). pap. text 1.00 (*0-486-29535-4*) Dover.

— Easy Animal Mazes. (Illus.). (J). (gr. k-3). 1990. pap. 1.00 (*0-486-26282-0*) Dover.

— Easy Mazes Activity Book. (Activity Bk.). (Illus.). (J). (ps up). 1989. pap. 1.00 (*0-486-25531-X*) Dover.

— Easy Search-a-Word Puzzles. 1991. pap. 1.00 (*0-486-26672-9*) Dover.

— Fairy Tale Hidden Coloring Book. 80th ed. (Illus.). (J). (gr. k-3). 1982. pap. 2.50 (*0-486-24284-6*) Dover.

— Follow-the-Dots Coloring Book. (Illus.). (J). 1983. pap. 2.50 (*0-486-24543-8*) Dover.

— Fun with Letters Coloring Book. (Illus.). (J). (gr. k-3). 1986. pap. 2.50 (*0-486-25104-7*) Dover.

— Fun with Opposites Coloring Book. (Illus.). (J). (gr. 4-7). 1989. pap. 2.50 (*0-486-25983-8*) Dover.

Pomaska, Anna. Get Well-Postcard Book. (Illus.). 1991. pap. 1.00 (*0-486-26599-4*) Dover.

Pomaska, Anna. Hidden Picture Puzzle Coloring Book. (Illus.). (J). (gr. k-3). 1976. pap. 2.50 (*0-486-23909-8*) Dover.

— Hidden Pictures. (Illus.). 32p. (J). 1998. pap. 1.00 (*0-486-40353-X*) Dover.

— Invisible ABC Magic Picture Book. (Invisible Magic Picture Books). (J). (ps). 1994. pap. text 1.00 (*0-486-28393-3*) Dover.

— Invisible Animals Magic Picture Book. (Illus.). 32p. (J). 1995. pap. 1.00 (*0-486-28716-5*) Dover.

— Invisible Birds Magic Picture Book. 1996. pap. 1.00 (*0-486-29269-X*) Dover.

— Invisible Christmas Magic Picture Book. pap. 1.00 (*0-486-29138-3*) Dover.

— Invisible Circus Magic Picture Book. (Invisible Magic Picture Bks). (J). (ps). 1994. pap. text 1.00 (*0-486-28394-1*) Dover.

— Invisible Dinosaurs Magic Picture Book. 1996. pap. 1.00 (*0-486-29270-3*) Dover.

— Invisible Easter Magic Picture Book. 32p. (J). 1999. pap. 1.00 (*0-486-40331-9*) Dover.

— Invisible Fairies & Elves Magic Picture Book. (Illus.). (J). (ps-3). pap. 1.00 (*0-486-29649-0*) Dover.

— Invisible Flowers Magic Picture Book. (Illus.). (J). (ps-3). pap. 1.00 (*0-486-29650-4*) Dover.

— Invisible Mother Goose Magic Picture Book. (Illus.). 32p. (J). 1995. pap. 1.00 (*0-486-28420-4*) Dover.

— Invisible Scary Creatures Magic Picture Book. (Illus.). 32p. (J). 1995. pap. 1.00 (*0-486-28715-7*) Dover.

— Invisible Sea Life Magic Picture Book. (Illus.). 32p. (J). 1996. pap. 1.00 (*0-486-29137-5*) Dover.

— Invisible Valentines Magic Picture Book. (J). pap. 1.00 (*0-486-29945-7*) Dover.

— Let's Go. (Illus.). 32p. (J). pap. 1.00 (*0-486-40163-4*) Dover.

— Little ABC Coloring Book. (Illus.). (J). (gr. k-3). 1998. pap. 1.00 (*0-486-25156-X*) Dover.

— The Little Alphabet Follow-the-Dots Book. 70th ed. (Activity Bk.). (J). (ps up). 1988. pap. 1.00 (*0-486-25623-5*) Dover.

— The Little Christmas Activity Book, Vol. 200. (Activity Bk.). (J). (ps up). 1988. pap. 1.00 (*0-486-25679-0*) Dover.

Pomaska, Anna. Little Christmas Sticker Book. (Little Activity Bks.). (Illus.). (J). 1989. pap. 1.00 (*0-486-26069-0*) Dover.

Pomaska, Anna. The Little Dinosaur Activity Book. 80th ed. (J). (ps up). 1987. pap. 1.00 (*0-486-25344-9*) Dover.

— The Little Follow the Dots Book. 80th ed. (J). 1986. pap. 1.00 (*0-486-25157-8*) Dover.

— The Little French ABC Coloring Book. (FRE., Illus.). (J). 1991. pap. 1.00 (*0-486-26812-8*) Dover.

— Little Jemima Puddle Duck Stickers. (Illus.). (J). (gr. k-3). 1993. pap. 1.00 (*0-486-27637-6*) Dover.

— Little Mother Goose Coloring Book. 81st ed. (Illus.). (J). (gr. k-3). 1986. pap. 1.00 (*0-486-25158-6*) Dover.

— Little Numbers Coloring Book. (Illus.). (J). (gr. k-3). 1989. pap. 1.00 (*0-486-25345-7*) Dover.

— Little Old MacDonald's Farm Coloring Book, Vol. 180. (Illus.). (J). (gr. k-3). 1986. pap. 1.00 (*0-486-25159-4*) Dover.

— The Little Seashore Activity Book, Vol. 181. (Activity Bk.). (Illus.). (J). (ps up). 1988. pap. 1.00 (*0-486-25608-1*) Dover.

— The Little Spanish ABC Coloring Book. 81st ed. (SPA., Illus.). (J). 1988. pap. 1.00 (*0-486-25614-6*) Dover.

Pomaska, Anna. Little Thanksgiving Sticker Book. (Little Activity Bks.). (Illus.). (J). 1989. pap. 1.00 (*0-486-26070-4*) Dover.

Pomaska, Anna. Little Tom Kitten Stickers. (Illus.). (J). (gr. k-3). 1993. pap. 1.00 (*0-486-27640-6*) Dover.

— My Camp Book Diary. (J). (gr. k-3). 1991. pap. 1.00 (*0-486-26641-9*) Dover.

— My First Crossword Puzzle Book. (J). pap. 1.00 (*0-486-26299-5*) Dover.

— Numbers. (Illus.). 32p. (J). (ps-1). pap. 1.00 (*0-486-29545-1*) Dover.

— Opposites. (Illus.). 32p. (J). 1998. pap. 1.00 (*0-486-40354-8*) Dover.

— Peter Rabbit Bookmarks. (J). (ps up). 1989. pap. 3.95 (*0-486-25444-5*) Dover.

— Rainbow Sticker Book. (Illus.). (J). (gr. k-3). 1989. pap. 1.00 (*0-486-25910-2*) Dover.

***Pomaska, Anna.** Rhyming Words. (Illus.). (J). 1999. pap. 1.00 (*0-486-40796-9*) Dover.

Pomaska, Anna. Same & Different. (Illus.). 32p. (J). pap. 1.00 (*0-486-29546-X*) Dover.

— Sealife ABC Stickers. 1999. pap. text 1.00 (*0-486-40503-6*) Dover.

— Six Hidden Picture Postcards. (Illus.). (J). (gr. k-3). 1994. pap. 1.00 (*0-486-27926-X*) Dover.

Pomaska, Anna. Six Valentine Cards. (Little Activity Bks.). (Illus.). (J). 1989. pap. 1.00 (*0-486-26238-3*) Dover.

Pomaska, Anna. Stickers - Create Your Own Easter. (Illus.). (J). (ps-3). 1998. pap. 1.00 (*0-486-29399-8*, 256939Q) Dover.

— Stickers - Make Your Own Puss in Boots. (Illus.). (J). (ps-3). 1996. pap. 1.00 (*0-486-29391-2*, 256615Q) Dover.

Pomaska, Anna. Summer Camp-Postcard Book. (Illus.). 1991. pap. 1.00 (*0-486-26600-1*) Dover.

— Sun, Moon & Stars Sticker Book. (Little Activity Bks.). (Illus.). (J). 1999. pap. text 1.00 (*0-486-40504-4*) Dover.

— Thank You: Postcard Book. (Illus.). 1990. pap. 1.00 (*0-486-26237-5*) Dover.

Pomaska, Anna. What's Wrong. (Illus.). 32p. (J). pap. 1.00 (*0-486-29563-X*) Dover.

— What's Wrong with This Picture? Coloring Book. 81st ed. (Illus.). (J). (gr. k-3). 1983. pap. 2.50 (*0-486-24485-7*) Dover.

Pomaska, Anna, ed. Favorite Beatrix Potter Character Prints: A Portfolio of Six Self-Matted Full-Color Prints. (Illus.). (J). (gr. k-3). 1993. pap. 3.95 (*0-486-26993-0*) Dover.

Pomaska, Anna, jt. auth. see Moore, Clement Clarke.

Pomaska, Anna, jt. auth. see Potter, Beatrix.

Pomata, Gianna. Contracting a Cure: Patients & Healers in Early Modern Bologna. LC 98-5982. 280p. 1998. 42.50 (*0-8018-5858-5*) Johns Hopkins.

P

An Asterisk (*) at the beginning of an entry indicates that the title is appearing for the first time.

Pomazansky, Michael. The Old Testament in the New Testament Church. 40p. (Orig.). 1994. pap. 2.00 (*0-317-30281-7*) Holy Trinity.

— Orthodox Dogmatic Theology: A Concise Exposition. 2nd ed. Rose, Hieromonk S., tr. from RUS. LC 84-51294. (Orthodox Theological Texts Ser.). 426p. (Orig.). (C). 1997. reprint ed. pap. 19.95 (*0-938635-69-7*) St Herman Pr.

***Pomazansky, Michel.** Theologie Dogmatique Orthodoxe - Expose Concis (Orthodox Dogmatic Theology - A Concise Exposition) Vronsky, Valentine, tr. from RUS. LC 97-78199. Orig. Title: Pravoslavnoe Dogmaticheskoe Bogoslovie. (FRE.). viii, 475p. 1999. pap. 40.00 (*0-9663938-0-5*) Cornerstone Edtns.

Pombeiro, A. J. & McCleverty, J. A., eds. Molecular Electrochemistry of Inorganic, Bioinorganic & Organometallic Compounds: Proceedings of the NATO Advanced Research Workshop, Sintra, Portugal, March 25-29, 1992. LC 92-40897. (NATO Advanced Science Institutes Series C: Mathematical & Physical Sciences: Series C, Vol. 385). 692p. (C). 1992. text 355.00 (*0-7923-2077-8*) Kluwer Academic.

Pomberger, Gustav. Software Engineering Tools for Professional Workstations: The Lilith Project. 1991. boxed set 48.00 (*0-13-823485-X*) P-H.

Pomberger, Gustav & Bischofberger, W. Protyping-Oriented Software Development: Concepts & Tools. Gries, David, ed. LC 92-18009. (Texts & Monographs in Computer Science). (Illus.). xi, 215p. 1992. 61.95 (*0-387-55448-3*) Spr-Verlag.

Pomberger, Gustav & Blaschek, Gunther. Object Orientation & Prototyping in Software Engineering. 350p. 1996. pap. 60.00 (*0-13-192626-8*, Prentice Hall) P-H.

Pombo, Fernando. Doing Business in Spain. 1987. 230.00 (*0-8205-1107-2*) Bender.

Pombo, Fernando, jt. ed. see Campbell, Dennis.

***Pombo, Richard W., ed.** Country-of-Origin Labeling: Congressional Hearing. 124p. (C). 2000. pap. text 30.00 (*0-7567-0026-4*) DIANE Pub.

— Strategies & Increased Competitiveness in the American Dairy Industry: Congressional Hearing. 94p. 2000. reprint ed. pap. text 20.00 (*0-7567-0117-1*) DIANE Pub.

Pomeau, Rene, jt. auth. see Beaumarchais, Pierre De.

Pomeau, Rene, ed. see Rousseau, Jean-Jacques.

Pomeau, Rene, ed. see Voltaire.

Pomedli, Michael. Ethnophilosophical & Ethnolinguistic Perspectives on the Huron Indian Soul. LC 91-28521. 196p. 1991. lib. bdg. 79.95 (*0-7734-9618-1*) E Mellen.

— William Kurelek's Huronia Mission Paintings. LC 91-20048. (Canadian Studies: Vol. 14). (Illus.). 196p. 1991. lib. bdg. 79.95 (*0-7734-9731-5*) E Mellen.

Pomegranate. The Teacher: Eleven Aspects of the Guru Rinpoche. (Salamander Ser.: No. 1). (Illus.). 23p. 1993. reprint ed. pap. 3.95 (*1-56640-591-2*) Pomegranate Calif.

Pomegranate Publishing Staff. Georgia O'Keefe Address Book. 1996. 19.95 (*0-87654-502-9*) Pomegranate Calif.

Pomer, Marshall I. Intergenerational Occupational Mobility in the United States: A Segmentation Perspective. LC 80-20626. (University of Florida Monographs: Social Sciences: No. 66). 112p. (Orig.). reprint ed. pap. 34.80 (*0-7837-5099-4*, 204479800004) Bks Demand.

Pomer, Marshall I., jt. auth. see Klein, Lawrence R.

Pomer, S. & Hull, W. E., eds. Magnetic Resonance in Nephrourology: Clinical & Experimental Applications. LC 93-9946. 1993. 132.00 (*0-387-56450-0*) Spr-Verlag.

Pomer, S., jt. ed. see Staehler, G.

Pomeranc, Marion H. The American Wei. (Illus.). 32p. (J). (gr. k-5). 1998. lib. bdg. 15.95 (*0-8075-0312-6*) A Whitman.

— The Hand-Me-down Horse. (Illus.). 32p. (J). (gr. 2-5). 1996. lib. bdg. 15.95 (*0-8075-3141-3*) A Whitman.

Pomerance & Sakeris. Bang Bang Shoot Shoot: Essays on Guns & Pop Cults. LC 99-173221. 256p. 1998. pap. text 20.00 (*0-536-01857-X*) Pearson Custom.

Pomerance, Alan. Repeal of the Blues: How Black Entertainers Influenced Civil Rights. (Illus.). 288p. 1988. 17.95 (*0-8065-1105-2*, Citadel Pr) Carol Pub Group.

— Repeal of the Blues: How Black Entertainers Influenced Civil Rights. (Illus.). 1991. pap. 10.95 (*0-8065-1244-X*, Citadel Pr) Carol Pub Group.

Pomerance, Bernard. The Elephant Man. LC 79-7792. 96p. 1987. pap. 10.00 (*0-8021-3041-0*, Grove) Grove-Atltic.

Pomerance, C. Cryptology & Computational Number Theory. LC 90-1248. (PSAPM Ser.: Vol. 42). 171p. 1991. text 44.00 (*0-8218-0155-4*, PSAPM/42) Am Math.

Pomerance, H. H. & Bercu, Barry B., eds. Topics in Pediatrics: A Festschrift for Lewis A. Barness. xxvi, 307p. 1990. 169.00 (*0-387-96964-0*) Spr-Verlag.

Pomerance, Leon. The Phaistos Disc: An Interpretation of Astronomical Symbols. (Studies in Mediterranean Archaeology: No. 6). (Illus.). 76p. (Orig.). 1976. pap. 22.50 (*91-85058-67-X*, Pub. by P Astroms) Coronet Bks.

Pomerance, Michla. The United States & the World Court As a 'Supreme Court of the Nations' Dreams, Illusions & Disillusion: Dreams, Illusions, & Disillusion. LC 96-4896. (Legal Aspects of International Organization Ser.: No. 26). 524p. 1996. 207.00 (*90-411-0204-3*) Kluwer Law Intl.

Pomerance, Michla. Law of Self-Determination in Law & Practice. 1982. lib. bdg. 90.00 (*90-247-2594-1*) Kluwer Academic.

Pomerance, Murray. Magia d'Amore. (Classics Ser.: No. 139). 136p. (Orig.). 1998. pap. 12.95 (*1-55713-308-5*, Pub. by Sun & Moon CA) Consort Bk Sales.

***Pomerance, Murray, ed.** Ladies & Gentlemen, Boys & Girls: Gender in Film at the End of the Twentieth Century. (C). 2001. pap. text 18.95 (*0-7914-4886-X*) State U NY Pr.

— Ladies & Gentlemen, Boys & Girls: Gender in Film at the End of the Twentieth Century. (C). 2001. text 57.50 (*0-7914-4885-1*) State U NY Pr.

Pomerance, Murray, ed. Ludwig Bemelmans: A Comprehensive Bibliography. (Illus.). 416p. 1995. 75.00 (*0-87008-140-3*) JAS Heineman.

Pomerance, Susan. For Women: Monologues They Haven't Heard. 64p. 1985. pap. 8.95 (*0-9611792-6-0*, D-3) Dramaline Pubns.

— For Women: More Monologues They Haven't Heard. LC 95-25807. 1995. pap. 9.95 (*0-940669-33-1*, D-39) Dramaline Pubns.

— Modern Scenes for Women. 50p. (Orig.). 1989. pap. 8.95 (*0-940669-10-2*, D-5) Dramaline Pubns.

— Monologues for Teenage Girls. LC 98-21314. 64p. 1998. pap. 9.95 (*0-940669-39-0*, D-45) Dramaline Pubns.

— Pocket Monologues for Women. LC 97-24251. 96p. 1997. pap. 9.95 (*0-940669-36-6*, D-42) Dramaline Pubns.

— Woman: One Act Monologues for Women. 64p. 1988. pap. 8.95 (*0-940669-07-2*, D-4) Dramaline Pubns.

Pomerand, Kay K. Come for Everything but Cholent. LC 95-24943. (Illus.). 200p. (Orig.). 1995. pap. 10.95 (*0-8197-0615-9*) Bloch.

Pomeraning, Denise O. Operation Melody. LC 94-72210. (Illus.). 64p. (J). (gr. 4-7). 1994. pap. 4.99 (*0-8066-2718-2*, 9-2718, Augsburg) Augsburg Fortress.

Pomerans, Arnold, tr. see Quinodoz, Danielle.

Pomerans, Arnold J., tr. see Boehlich, Walter, ed.

Pomerans, Arnold J., tr. see Boer, Pim D.

Pomerans, Arnold J., tr. see Frank, Anne.

Pomerans, Arnold J., tr. see Friedman, Carl.

Pomerans, Arnold J., tr. see Grunberg, Arnon.

Pomerans, Arnold J., tr. see Heisenberg, Werner.

Pomerans, Arnold J., tr. see Hillesum, Etty.

Pomerans, Arnold J., tr. see Kiepenheuer, Karl O.

Pomerans, Arnold J., tr. see Molnar, Miklos.

Pomerans, Arnold J., tr. see Presser, Jacob.

Pomerans, Arnold J., tr. see Selvini, Matteo, ed.

Pomerans, Arnold J., tr. see Van Oostrom, Frits P.

Pomerans, Arnold J., tr. see Von Koenigswald, G. H.

Pomerans, Arnold J., tr. see Wesseling, H. L.

Pomerans, Erica, tr. see Friedman, Carl.

Pomerans, Erica, tr. see Grunberg, Arnon.

Pomerantz, Barbara. Who Will Lead Kiddush? (Illus.). 32p. (Orig.). (J). (gr. 1-3). 1985. pap. 6.00 (*0-8074-0306-7*, 102000) UAHC.

Pomerantz, Charlotte. The Birthday Letters. LC 99-50914. (Illus.). 32p. (J). (gr. k-3). 2000. 15.95 (*0-688-16335-1*, Grenwillow Bks); 15.89 (*0-688-16336-X*, Grenwillow Bks) HarpC Child Bks.

— The Chalk Doll. LC 88-872. (Illus.). 32p. (J). (gr. k-3). 1989. 15.00 (*0-397-32318-2*) HarpC Child Bks.

— The Chalk Doll. LC 88-872. (Illus.). 32p. (J). (ps-3). 1993. pap. 6.95 (*0-06-443333-1*, HarpTrophy) HarpC Child Bks.

Pomerantz, Charlotte. The Chalk Doll. (J). 1993. 11.15 (*0-606-05196-1*, Pub. by Turtleback) Demco.

Pomerantz, Charlotte. Halfway to Your House. LC 92-30083. (Illus.). 32p. (J). (ps up). 1993. lib. bdg. 13.93 (*0-688-11805-4*, Grenwillow Bks) HarpC Child Bks.

— Here Comes Henny. LC 93-5480. (Illus.). 24p. (J). 1994. 14.00 (*0-688-12355-4*, Grenwillow Bks); lib. bdg. 13.93 (*0-688-12356-2*, Grenwillow Bks) HarpC Child Bks.

— Here Comes Henny. (Illus.). 24p. (J). (ps-3). 1999. mass mkt. 4.95 (*0-688-16703-9*, Wm Morrow) Morrow Avon.

— How Many Trucks Can a Tow Truck Tow ? LC 96-43693. (Pictureback Ser.). (Illus.). (J). 1997. pap. 3.25 (*0-679-87810-6*, Pub. by Random Bks Yng Read) Random.

— If I Had a Paka: Poems in Eleven Languages. LC 92-33088. (Illus.). 32p. (J). (ps up). 1993. pap. 4.95 (*0-688-12510-7*, Wm Morrow) Morrow Avon.

— If I Had a Paka: Poems in Eleven Languages. (J). 1993. 10.15 (*0-606-05883-4*, Pub. by Turtleback) Demco.

— Mangaboom. LC 96-10416. (Illus.). 40p. (J). (gr. k up). 1997. 16.00 (*0-688-12956-0*, Grenwillow Bks) HarpC Child Bks.

***Pomerantz, Charlotte.** The Mousery. LC 99-6116. (Illus.). 40p. (J). (ps-3). 2000. 16.00 (*0-15-202304-6*, Harcourt Child Bks) Harcourt.

— One Duck, Another Duck. LC 83-20767. (Illus.). 24p. (J). (ps-3). 1984. 15.93 (*0-688-03745-3*, Grenwillow Bks) HarpC Child Bks.

— One Duck, Another Duck. 2000. pap. write for info. (*0-688-17719-0*, Wm Morrow) Morrow Avon.

— The Outside Dog. (I Can Read Bks.). (Illus.). 64p. (J). (gr. k-3). 1996. pap. 8.95 incl. audio (*0-694-70050-9*) HarpC.

Pomerantz, Charlotte. The Outside Dog. (I Can Read Bks.). (Illus.). 64p. (J). (gr. 2-4). 1993. lib. bdg. 15.89 (*0-06-024783-5*) HarpC Child Bks.

— The Outside Dog. (I Can Read Bks.). (Illus.). 64p. (J). (gr. 2-4). 1995. pap. 3.95 (*0-06-444187-3*, HarpTrophy) HarpC Child Bks.

— The Outside Dog. (I Can Read Bks.). (J). (gr. 2-4). 1995. 9.40 (*0-606-07983-1*) Turtleback.

— The Piggy in the Puddle. LC 73-6047. (Illus.). 32p. (J). (ps-1). 1974. lib. bdg. 15.00 (*0-02-774900-2*, Mac Bks Young Read) S&S Childrens.

Pomerantz, Charlotte. Piggy in the Puddle. (J). 1989. 10.15 (*0-606-04298-9*, Pub. by Turtleback) Demco.

Pomerantz, Charlotte. The Piggy in the Puddle. LC 88-8368. (Illus.). 32p. (J). (ps-1). 1989. reprint ed. mass mkt. 5.99 (*0-689-71293-6*) Aladdin.

— The Princess & the Admiral. LC 91-32614. (Illus.). 48p. (YA). (gr. 3 up). 1992. pap. 8.95 (*1-55861-061-8*) Feminist Pr.

— The Princess & the Admiral. LC 91-32614. (Illus.). 48p. (gr. 4-7). 1992. 17.95 (*1-55861-060-X*) Feminist Pr.

— Serena Katz. LC 90-48672. (Illus.). 32p. (J). (gr. k-3). 1992. lib. bdg. 13.95 (*0-02-774901-0*, Mac Bks Young Read) S&S Childrens.

— Where's the Bear? LC 83-1697. (Illus.). 32p. (J). (ps-1). 1984. 16.00 (*0-688-01752-5*, Grenwillow Bks) HarpC Child Bks.

Pomerantz, Charlotte. Where's the Bear. LC 83-1697. (Illus.). 32p. (J). (ps-1). 1984. 15.93 (*0-688-01753-3*, Grenwillow Bks) HarpC Child Bks.

Pomerantz, Charlotte. Where's the Bear? LC 83-1697. (Illus.). 32p. (J). (ps up). 1991. reprint ed. pap. 3.95 (*0-688-10999-3*, Wm Morrow) Morrow Avon.

— You're Not My Best Friend Anymore. LC 93-42595. (Illus.). 32p. (J). (ps-4). 1998. 15.99 (*0-8037-1559-5*, Dial Yng Read) Peng Put Young Read.

Pomerantz, Edward. Brisburial: A Feast. 1981. 14.95 (*0-913660-13-2*) Magic Cir Pr CT.

— Brisburial: A Feast. 1981. pap. 7.95 (*0-913660-14-0*) Magic Cir Pr CT.

Pomerantz, Gary M. Where Peachtree Meets Sweet Auburn: A Lisa Drew Book. (Illus.). 656p. 1996. 27.00 (*0-684-80717-3*) S&S Trade.

— Where Peachtree Meets Sweet Auburn: A Saga of Race & Family. 1997. pap. 14.95 (*0-614-27379-X*) Penguin Putnam.

— Where Peachtree Meets Sweet Auburn: A Saga of Race & Family. LC 96-10399. 656p. 1997. pap. 14.95 (*0-14-026509-0*) Viking Penguin.

— Where Peachtree Meets Sweet Auburn: The Saga of Two Families & the Making of Atlanta. LC 96-10399. 1996. write for info. (*0-02-597985-X*, Schirmer Books) Mac Lib Ref.

***Pomerantz, Gary M.** Where Peachtree Meets Sweet Auburn: The Saga of Two Families & the Making of Atlanta. (Illus.). 656p. 1999. reprint ed. text 27.00 (*0-7881-6708-1*) DIANE Pub.

Pomerantz, Jack & Winik, Lyric W. Run East: Flight from the Holocaust. LC 96-51240. 240p. 1997. 26.95 (*0-252-02325-0*) U of Ill Pr.

***Pomerantz, James.** The Flathead Saloon & Cathouse. 284p. 2000. pap. 16.95 (*1-893162-13-3*) Erica Hse.

Pomerantz, James R., jt. ed. see Lockhead, Gregory R.

Pomerantz, Kay. Come for Cholent. LC 91-35294. 90p. 1992. pap. 8.95 (*0-8197-0598-5*) Bloch.

Pomerantz, Kay K. Come for Cholent Again: Cholent Stories & More Recipes. LC 93-30062. 125p. 1993. pap. 10.95 (*0-8197-0602-7*) Bloch.

Pomerantz, Lawrence S. Allowance for Funds Used During Construction: Theory & Application. LC 75-620097. (MSU Public Utilities Studies: Vol. 1975). reprint ed. pap. 63.60 (*0-608-20510-9*, 2071762) Bks Demand.

***Pomerantz, Rachel.** As Mountains Around Jerusalem. 1999. 21.95 (*1-58330-351-0*) Feldheim.

Pomerantz, Rachel. Cactus Blossoms. 366p. 1997. pap. 16.95 (*1-56871-125-5*, Pub. by Targum Pr) Feldheim.

— A Time to Rend, A Time to Sew. 1995. 23.95 (*0-87306-743-6*); pap. 19.95 (*0-87306-744-4*) Feldheim.

— Wildflower. (Illus.). 442p. (C). 1989. 24.95 (*1-56062-020-X*, Bristol Rhein) CIS Comm.

— Wings above the Flames. 400p. (C). 1991. 22.95 (*1-56062-066-8*) CIS Comm.

Pomerantz, Roger J., jt. ed. see Laughlin, Mark A.

Pomerantz, Susan, jt. auth. see Muench, Teri.

Pomerantz, Yitzchack. Itzik, Be Strong. LC 93-72594. 300p. 1993. 24.95 (*1-56062-225-3*) CIS Comm.

Pomerantz-Zhang, Linda. Wu Tingfang (1842-1922) Reform & Modernization in Modern Chinese History. 320p. (Orig.). 1992. pap. 67.50 (*962-209-287-X*, Pub. by HK Univ Pr) Coronet Bks.

Pomerantzev, B. I. Arachnida Ixodid Ticks (Ixodae) Elbl, A. & Anastos, G., trs. 1959. 30.00 (*0-934454-08-6*) Lubrecht & Cramer.

Pomeranz. Pediatric Decision Making. (C). 2000. pap. text. write for info. (*0-7216-8246-4*, W B Saunders Co) Harcrt Hlth Sci Grp.

Pomeranz, Bruce & Stux, Gabriel. Basics of Acupuncture. (Illus.). xi, 272p. 1988. pap. 19.50 (*0-387-19336-7*) Spr-Verlag.

Pomeranz, Bruce, jt. auth. see Stux, Gabriel.

***Pomeranz, Kenneth.** The Great Divergence: China, Europe & the Making of the Modern World Economy. 371p. 2000. 39.95 (*0-691-00543-5*, Pub. by Princeton U Pr) Cal Prin Full Svc.

Pomeranz, Kenneth. The Making of a Hinterland: State, Society, & Economy in Inland North China, 1853-1937. LC 92-17008. 1993. 48.00 (*0-520-08051-3*, Pub. by U CA Pr) Cal Prin Full Svc.

Pomeranz, Kenneth & Topik, Steven. The World That Trade Created: Society, Culture & the World Economy, 1400 to the Present. LC 98-50665. 280p. (gr. 13). 1999. text 34.95 (*0-7656-0249-0*) M E Sharpe.

Pomeranz, Stephen J. Orthopaedic MRI: A Teaching File. (Illus.). 416p. 1991. text 106.00 (*0-397-51105-1*) Lppncott W & W.

Pomeranz, Virginia E. First Five Years. 1987. pap. 3.95 (*0-317-65471-3*) St Martin.

Pomeranz, Y. Functional Properties of Food Components. 2nd ed. (Food Science & Technology Ser.). (Illus.). 569p. (C). 1991. text 136.00 (*0-12-561281-8*) Acad Pr.

— Modern Cereal Science & Technology. LC 87-13364. 468p. 1987. 130.00 (*0-89573-326-9*, Wiley-VCH) Wiley.

Pomeranz, Y., ed. Advances in Cereal Science & Technology, Vol. III. LC 76-645872. 348p. 1980. pap. text 89.00 (*0-913250-16-3*) Am Assn Cereal Chem.

— Advances in Cereal Science & Technology, Vol. IV. LC 76-645872. 342p. 1981. pap. text 89.00 (*0-913250-21-X*) Am Assn Cereal Chem.

— Advances in Cereal Science & Technology, Vol. V. LC 76-645872. 294p. 1982. pap. text 89.00 (*0-913250-28-7*) Am Assn Cereal Chem.

— Advances in Cereal Science & Technology, Vol. VI. LC 76-645872. 403p. 1984. pap. text 89.00 (*0-913250-33-3*) Am Assn Cereal Chem.

— Advances in Cereal Science & Technology, Vol. VII. LC 76-645872. 362p. 1985. pap. text 89.00 (*0-913250-39-2*) Am Assn Cereal Chem.

— Advances in Cereal Science & Technology, Vol. VIII. LC 76-645872. 364p. 1986. 89.00 (*0-913250-45-7*) Am Assn Cereal Chem.

— Advances in Cereal Science & Technology, Vol. IX. LC 76-645872. (Illus.). 345p. 1988. 89.00 (*0-913250-51-1*) Am Assn Cereal Chem.

— Advances in Cereal Science & Technology, Vol. X. LC 76-645872. (Illus.). 557p. 1990. 89.00 (*0-913250-66-X*) Am Assn Cereal Chem.

— Wheat: Chemistry & Technology, Vol. I. 3rd ed. LC 88-71636. (Monograph Ser.). 514p. 1988. 79.50 (*0-913250-65-1*) Am Assn Cereal Chem.

— Wheat: Chemistry & Technology, Vol. II. 3rd ed. LC 88-71636. (Monograph Ser.). 562p. 1988. 79.50 (*0-913250-73-2*) Am Assn Cereal Chem.

— Wheat Is Unique: Structure, Composition, Processing, End-Use Properties, & Products. LC 89-84430. (Illus.). 715p. 1989. 99.00 (*0-913250-68-6*) Am Assn Cereal Chem.

Pomeranz, Y. & Meloan, Clifton E. Food Analysis: Theory & Practice. 3rd ed. LC 94-12419. 778p. 1994. pap. 73.00 (*0-412-06591-6*) Chapman & Hall.

Pomeranz, Y. & Munck, Lars, eds. Cereals: A Renewable Resource, Theory & Practice. LC 81-71369. 728p. 1981. 76.00 (*0-913250-22-8*) Am Assn Cereal Chem.

Pomeray, J. K. Ireland: Major World Nations. (Major World Nations Ser.). (Illus.). 144p. (YA). (gr. 5 up). 1999. lib. bdg. 19.95 (*0-7910-4741-5*) Chelsea Hse.

— Rwanda: Major World Nations. LC 99-35494. (Major World Nations Ser.). (Illus.). 144p. (YA). (gr. 5 up). 1998. 19.95 (*0-7910-4765-2*) Chelsea Hse.

Pomeray, Sarah G., jt. auth. see Carr, John F.

Pomerening, Klaus, jt. auth. see Mohr, Peter.

Pomerenke, jt. auth. see Varner.

Pomerinke, June. The Young Years. LC 85-90524. (Illus.). 300p. (Orig.). 1986. pap. 8.50 (*0-9616273-0-1*) Young Pr Idaho.

Pomerinke, June L. Return to Whiskey Creek. LC 94-93851. (Illus.). 200p. (Orig.). 1994. pap. 5.50 (*0-318-72778-1*) Young Pr Idaho.

Pomerleau, Cynthia S., jt. ed. see Pomerleau, Ovide F.

Pomerleau, Dean A. Neural Network Perception for Mobile Robot Guidance. LC 93-24616. (International Engineering & Computer Science Ser.: SECS 239). 1993. lib. bdg. 99.00 (*0-7923-9373-2*) Kluwer Academic.

***Pomerleau, Joel.** Plages du Maine. LC 97-940019. (Travel Guide (French Guides) Ser.). (FRE.). 1998. pap. text 13.95 (*2-89464-110-9*) Ulysses Travel.

Pomerleau, Ovide F. & Pomerleau, Cynthia S., eds. Nicotine Replacement: A Critical Evaluation. 325p. 1992. pap. 29.95 (*1-56024-250-7*) Haworth Pr.

Pomerleau, Wayne P. Philosophical Perspectives on God & Religion: Descartes, Lock, Leibniz & Hume, Vol. 1. LC 92-19362. 325p. (C). 1995. text 37.50 (*0-89341-706-8*) Hollowbrook.

— Philosophical Perspectives on God & Religion: Kant, Hegel, Kierkegaard & James, Vol. 2. LC 92-19362. 325p. (C). 1995. text 37.50 (*0-89341-713-0*) Hollowbrook.

— Twelve Great Philosophers: A Historical Introduction to Human Nature. LC 97-178999. (Illus.). 473p. (C). 1997. text 51.95 (*1-880157-54-3*) Ardsley.

— Twelve Great Philosophers Instructor's Manual: A Historical Introduction to Human Nature. 89p. (C). 1997. pap. text, teacher ed. 47.95 (*1-880157-57-8*) Ardsley.

— Western Philosophies of Religion: Great Religious & Epistomologies from Augustine to Hick. 564p. (C). 1998. text 38.95 (*1-880157-62-4*) Ardsley.

Pomerol, Charles, ed. Wines & Winelands of France: Geological Journeys. (Illus.). 370p. 1990. text 45.00 (*1-85365-108-7*, Pub. by McCarta) Seven Hills Bk.

Pomeroy, A., & Co. Staff, contrib. by. Atlas of Centre County, Pennsylvania. (Illus.). 200p. 1999. reprint ed. 45.00 (*1-887315-01-2*) Centre Cty Hist Soc.

Pomeroy, Albert A. Pomeroy, Pt. 3. (Illus.). 342p. 1994. reprint ed. lib. bdg. 63.00 (*0-8328-4372-5*) Higginson Bk Co.

— Pomeroy: Romance & History of Eltweed Pomeroy's Ancestors in Normandy & England. (Illus.). 81p. 1992. reprint ed. pap. 16.00 (*0-8328-6573-7*); reprint ed. lib. bdg. 26.00 (*0-8328-2612-X*) Higginson Bk Co.

— Pomeroy Pt. 3, Pt. 3. (Illus.). 342p. 1994. reprint ed. pap. 53.00 (*0-8328-4373-3*) Higginson Bk Co.

— Pomeroy, History & Genealogy of the Pomeroy Family: Collateral Lines in Family Groups, Nrmandy, Great Britain & America, Comprising the Ancestors & Descendants of Eltweed Pomeroy, from Beaminster, Co. Dorset, England, 1630. (Illus.). 962p. 1994. reprint ed. pap. 149.00 (*0-8328-4272-9*); reprint ed. lib. bdg. 159.50 (*0-8328-4271-0*) Higginson Bk Co.

Pomeroy, Arthur J., ed. see Didymus, Arius.

***Pomeroy, Ashley.** Little Book of Living on the Edge. (Pocket Oracle Ser.). (Illus.). 124p. 2000. mass mkt. 4.99 (*1-903222-16-8*, Pub. by Wimbledon Publishing Co) Anthem.

Pomeroy, Cheri. Tales of the Oreon Woods, Vol. I. (Illus.). 36p. (J). (gr. 2 up). 1997. pap. 5.95 (*0-9660580-0-3*) Oreon.

Pomeroy, Claire, jt. ed. see Mainous, Arch G., III.

Pomeroy, D. E. & Service. Tropical Ecology. 1987. pap. text. write for info. (*0-582-64353-8*, Pub. by Addison-Wesley) Longman.

Pomeroy, Dana R., jt. auth. see Clausen, Barry.

An Asterisk (*) at the beginning of an entry indicates that the title is appearing for the first time.

Pomeroy, Danarae. When Someone You Love Has Cancer. 176p. (Orig.). 1996. mass mkt. 5.99 (*0-425-15129-8*) Berkley Pub.

Pomeroy, Dave. The Mything Link: A Study Guide on Gospel, Culture & Media. 1990. pap. 5.95 (*0-377-00208-9*) Friendship Pr.

— Video Violence & Values: A Guide to the Use of Video. 1990. pap. 2.00 (*0-377-00213-5*) Friendship Pr.

Pomeroy, Derek, jt. auth. see Lewis, Adrian.

Pomeroy, Diana. One Potato. 28p. (J). 2000. pap. 6.00 (*0-15-202330-5*) Harcourt.

— One Potato: A Counting Book of Potato Prints. LC 95-10986. (Illus.). 32p. (J). (ps-3). 1996. 16.00 (*0-15-200300-2*) Harcourt.

— Wildflower ABC. LC 96-19748. (Illus.). 40p. (J). 1997. 16.00 (*0-15-201041-6*) Harcourt.

Pomeroy, Earl. The Far West in the Twentieth Century. 1999. 28.00 (*0-06-016786-6*) HarperTrade.

Pomeroy, Elizabeth. The Huntington. (Illus.). 144p. 1997. 25.00 (*0-85667-211-4*) Scala Books.

— The Huntington, San Marino. LC 83-50338. (Illus.). 144p. 1984. 25.00 (*0-935748-56-3*) Scala Books.

Pomeroy, Elizabeth W. Reading the Portraits of Elizabeth I. LC 88-34623. (Illus.). 98p. (C). 1989. lib. bdg. 27.50 (*0-208-02189-2*, Archon Bks) Shoe String.

Pomeroy, James, ed. see Zerler, Kathryn S.

Pomeroy, James L. Advanced Photography. LC 89-92366. (Illus.). 140p. 1991. pap. text 30.00 (*0-9625017-2-7*) Palms & Rhodes Pub.

— Basic Photography: Student Handbook. LC 89-92365. (Illus.). 144p. 1991. teacher ed. 50.00 (*0-9625017-1-9*); pap. text 30.00 (*0-9625017-0-0*) Palms & Rhodes Pub.

— Computer Graphics Fundamentals. (Illus.). 158p. 1993. pap. text 30.00 (*0-9625017-7-8*) Palms & Rhodes Pub.

— Photographic Imaging with Photoshop. (Illus.). 220p. 1997. pap. text 30.00 (*0-9625017-8-6*) Palms & Rhodes Pub.

Pomeroy, Jane R. Alexander Anderson's Life & Engravings with a Checklist of Publications Drawn from His Diary. (Illus.). 75p. 1990. pap. 8.00 (*0-944026-25-7*) Am Antiquarian.

Pomeroy, Janet. Among the Roses. 100p. 1993. pap. write for info. (*0-9636130-0-6*) Rec Ctr Handicapped.

Pomeroy, Johanna P. Content Area Reading Skills Electricity & Magnetism. (Illus.). (J). (gr. 4). 1987. pap. text 3.25 (*0-89525-859-5*) Ed Activities.

— Content Area Reading Skills Geology: Detecting Sequence. (Illus.). (J). (gr. 4). 1987. pap. text 3.25 (*1-55737-085-0*) Ed Activities.

— Content Area Reading Skills Light: Main Idea. (Illus.). (J). (gr. 3). 1989. pap. text 3.25 (*1-55737-687-5*) Ed Activities.

— Content Area Reading Skills Machines: Detecting Sequence. (Illus.). (J). (gr. 3). 1989. pap. text 3.25 (*1-55737-690-5*) Ed Activities.

— Content Area Reading Skills Matter: Locating Details. (Illus.). (J). (gr. 4). 1988. pap. text 3.25 (*1-55737-086-9*) Ed Activities.

— Content Area Reading Skills Mechanics: Cause & Effect. (Illus.). (J). (gr. 4). 1988. pap. text 3.25 (*1-55737-088-5*) Ed Activities.

— Content Area Reading Skills Oceans: Main Idea. (Illus.). (J). (gr. 4). 1987. pap. text 3.25 (*0-89525-857-9*) Ed Activities.

— Content Area Reading Skills Our Earth: Locating Details. (Illus.). (J). (gr. 3). 1989. pap. text 3.25 (*1-55737-688-3*) Ed Activities.

— Content Area Reading Skills Reproduction & Heredity: Main Idea. (Illus.). (J). (gr. 4). 1988. pap. text 3.25 (*1-55737-087-7*) Ed Activities.

— Content Area Reading Skills Solar System: Locating Details. (Illus.). (J). (gr. 4). 1987. pap. text 3.25 (*0-89525-858-7*) Ed Activities.

— Content Area Reading Skills Sound & Hearing: Detecting Sequence. (Illus.). 1987. pap. text 3.25 (*0-89525-860-9*) Ed Activities.

— Content Area Reading Skills Weather: Cause & Effect. (Illus.). (J). (gr. 3). 1989. pap. text 3.25 (*1-55737-689-1*) Ed Activities.

Pomeroy, John, jt. auth. see Carr, Harold.

Pomeroy, John N. Introduction to Municipal Law: Designed for General Readers, & for Students in Colleges & Higher Schools. 2nd enl. ed. LC 97-4208. xlvi, 570p. 1997. reprint ed. 75.00 (*0-8377-2561-5*, Rothman) W S Hein.

— An Introduction to the Constitutional Law of the United States, 3 vols., Set. 1980. lib. bdg. 250.00 (*0-8490-3169-9*) Gordon Pr.

— Introduction to the Constitutional Law of the United States: Especially Designed for Students, General & Professional. 4th enl. rev. ed. LC 97-1954. xxv, 580p. 1997. reprint ed. 67.50 (*0-8377-2560-7*, Rothman) W S Hein.

— Pomeroy's Equity Jurisprudence, 5 vols., Set. 5th ed. 1994. reprint ed. 450.00 (*0-88636-305-5*, 308730) W S Hein.

— A Treatise on Equity Jurisprudence: As Administered in the United States of America. Adapted for All the States, 1941, 5 vols., Set. 5th ed. Symons, Spencer W., ed. 4756p. 1994. reprint ed. 450.00 (*1-886363-05-6*) Lawbk Exchange.

Pomeroy, John N. & Mann, John C. Treatise on the Specific Performance of Contracts. 3rd ed. Hemholz, R. H. & Reams, Bernard D., Jr., eds. LC 86-62940. (Historical Writings in Law & Jurisprudence Ser.: No. 8). xl, 1045p. 1986. reprint ed. lib. bdg. 68.00 (*0-89941-523-7*, 304590) W S Hein.

Pomeroy, John N., jt. ed. see Pomeroy, William M.

Pomeroy, Karen, jt. auth. see Heller, Steven.

Pomeroy, L. R. & Alberts, J. J., eds. Concepts of Ecosystem Ecology. (Ecological Studies: Vol. 67). (Illus.). 345p. 1990. 117.95 (*0-387-96686-2*) Spr-Verlag.

Pomeroy, L. R. & Wiegert, R. G., eds. The Ecology of a Salt Marsh. (Ecological Studies: Vol. 38). (Illus.). 288p. 1981. 117.00 (*0-387-90555-3*) Spr-Verlag.

Pomeroy, M. J., jt. ed. see Hampshire, S.

Pomeroy, Marcus M. Nonsense: or Hits & Criticisms on the Follies of the Day. LC 70-91091. (American Humorists Ser.). reprint ed. lib. bdg. 25.50 (*0-8398-1572-7*) Irvington.

Pomeroy, Marnie. Calendar for Dinah: Foundation Edition. 1966. 6.00 (*0-912156-03-1*); 20.00 (*0-912156-04-X*) Masterwork Pr.

Pomeroy, Olive G., ed. see Pomeroy, Richard M.

Pomeroy, R. S., ed. Community Management & Common Property of Coastal Fisheries in Asia & the Pacific: Concepts, Methods & Experiences. (ICLARM Conference Proceedings Ser.: No. 45). 196p. 1994. per. write for info. (*971-8709-56-8*, Pub. by ICLARM) Intl Spec Bk.

Pomeroy, Richard M. In Search of Meaning. McCoy, Charles S. & Pomeroy, Olive G., eds. 100p. 1991. pap. 12.95 (*0-9628719-0-7*) Glen-Berkeley.

Pomeroy, Robert W. Introducing Electronic Reports. (Connecting Scholarship Ser.). (Illus.). 65p. (Orig.). (YA). (gr. 11 up). 1995. pap. text 8.00 (*0-9648943-0-0*) Serenus Pr.

— Inventory America, Jr. (Illus.). 18p. (Orig.). 1996. pap. text, teacher ed. 4.00 (*0-9648943-2-7*) Serenus Pr.

— Inventory America, Jr. (Illus.). 52p. (Orig.). (J). (gr. 6-10). 1996. pap. text, student ed. 8.00 (*0-9648943-1-9*) Serenus Pr.

Pomeroy, Robert W., III, jt. ed. see Trask, David F.

Pomeroy, Ruth F. Redbook's Guide to Buying Your First Home. 1980. pap. 4.95 (*0-686-60934-4*, 24716, Fireside) S&S Trade Pap.

Pomeroy, Sally & Tanner, Mary A. Art Center of Corpus Christi Cookbook. 102p. (Orig.). 1991. spiral bd. 9.00 (*0-9629702-0-4*) Art Ctr Corpus Christi.

Pomeroy, Sarah B. Families in Classical & Hellenistic Greece: Representation & Realities. (Illus.). 272p. 1999. reprint ed. pap. text 24.95 (*0-19-815260-4*) OUP.

— Goddesses, Whores, Wives & Slaves: Women in Classical Antiquity. 1995. pap. 16.00 (*0-8052-1030-X*) Schocken.

— Women in Hellenistic Egypt: From Alexander to Cleopatra. LC 89-24894. (Illus.). 270p. (C). 1990. reprint ed. pap. text 19.95 (*0-8143-2230-1*) Wayne St U Pr.

Pomeroy, Sarah B., ed. Women's History & Ancient History. LC 90-24488. (Illus.). xviii, 318p. (C). 1991. 59.95 (*0-8078-1949-2*); pap. 19.95 (*0-8078-4310-5*) U of NC Pr.

Pomeroy, Sarah B., et al. Ancient Greece: A Political, Social & Cultural History. (Illus.). 544p. 1998. 35.00 (*0-19-509742-4*) OUP.

— Ancient Greece: A Political, Social & Cultural History. LC 98-14544. (Illus.). 544p. (C). 1999. pap. text 29.95 (*0-19-509743-2*) OUP.

— Women in the Classical World: Image & Text. (Illus.). 448p. (C). 1995. pap. 29.95 (*0-19-509862-5*) OUP.

Pomeroy, Sarah B., ed. & tr. see Xenophon.

Pomeroy, Shirley, et al. The Gateway District. (Images of America Ser.). 1997. pap. 16.99 (*0-7524-0905-0*) Arcadia Publng.

Pomeroy, Toni L., jt. ed. see Lauriat, Peter M.

Pomeroy, Virginia A. & Pruski, Gina M. Wisconsin Juvenile Law Handbook. LC 96-34341. 660p. 1996. ring bd. 115.00 incl. disk (*0-945574-88-6*) State Bar WI.

***Pomeroy, Wambach.** The Clinical Assessment. (Social Work Ser.). 2001. wbk. ed. 31.00 (*0-534-57843-8*) Wadsworth Pub.

Pomeroy, Wardell B. Dr. Kinsey & the Institute for Sex Research. LC 82-4924. 496p. 1982. 18.00 (*0-300-02916-0*) Yale U Pr.

Pomeroy, Wardell B., jt. auth. see Steward, Samuel M.

Pomeroy, William J. American Neo-Colonialism: Its Emergence in the Philippines & Asia. LC 71-108385. 255p. reprint ed. pap. 79.10 (*0-8357-5383-2*, 202063600018) Bks Demand.

— Apartheid Axis: The United States & South Africa. LC 79-150661. 96p. reprint ed. pap. 30.00 (*0-8357-5652-1*, 202286800030) Bks Demand.

— Apartheid, Imperialism & African Freedom. Smith, Betty, ed. LC 86-10488. 276p. (C). 1986. 14.00 (*0-7178-0640-5*); pap. 6.95 (*0-7178-0632-4*) Intl Pubs Co.

— The Philippines: Colonialism, Collaboration, & Resistance. Smith, Betty, ed. LC 92-35454. vi, 352p. (Orig.). 1993. pap. 9.95 (*0-7178-0692-8*) Intl Pubs Co.

Pomeroy, William M. & Pomeroy, John N., eds. Pomeroy: History & Genealogy of the Pomeroy Family & Collateral Lines, England - Ireland - America, Comprising the Ancestors & Descendants of George Pomeroy of Pennsylvania. (Illus.). 1454p. 1995. reprint ed. pap. 175.00 (*0-8328-4822-0*); reprint ed. lib. bdg. 185.00 (*0-8328-4821-2*) Higginson Bk Co.

Pometta, D., jt. ed. see James, R. W.

Pomfret, Richard. The Economics of Regional Trading Arrangements. LC 97-26763. (Illus.). 456p. 1998. text 90.00 (*0-19-823335-3*) OUP.

— Is China a "Large Country"? China's Influence on World Markets. LC 97-224780. 68p. 1997. pap. 12.00 (*92-64-15609-7*, 41-97-12-1, Pub. by Org for Econ) OECD.

Pomfret, Richard W. Asian Economies in Transition: Reforming Centrally Planned Economies. LC 95-19492. (Illus.). 176p. 1996. 70.00 (*1-85898-291-X*) E Elgar.

— The Economies of Central Asia. LC 95-6829. 200p. 1995. text 42.50 (*0-691-04375-2*, Pub. by Princeton U Pr) Cal Prin Full Svc.

— International Trade Policy with Imperfect Competition. LC 92-30715. (Special Papers in International Economics: No. 17). 68p. 1992. pap. 13.50 (*0-88165-306-3*) Princeton U Int Finan Econ.

Pomfret, Richard W., ed. Australia's Trade Policies. (Illus.). 248p. 1995. pap. 45.00 (*0-19-553536-7*) OUP.

Pomian, Krzystof. Collectors & Curiosities: Paris & Venice, 1500-1800. 348p. 1991. 58.95 (*0-7456-0680-6*) Blackwell Pubs.

Pomiane, Edouard De, see De Pomiane, Edouard.

Pomichalek, Milan, tr. see Goetz-Stankiewicz, Marketa, ed.

Pomidor, Bill. Anatomy of a Murder. 1996. mass mkt. 5.50 (*0-451-19417-3*, Sig) NAL.

— Mind over Murder. (Cal & Plato Marley Mystery Ser.). 1998. mass mkt. 5.99 (*0-451-19216-8*, Sig) NAL.

Pomier, Natalie, ed. French Correspondence. 168p. 1997. pap. 8.95 (*0-19-860010-0*) OUP.

Pommaret, Francoise. Bhutan: The Himalayan Kingdom. 2nd ed. (Illus.). 277p. 1995. pap. 19.95 (*0-8442-9966-9*, 99669) NTC Contemp Pub Co.

Pommaret, Francoise, jt. ed. see Shicklgruber, Christian.

Pommaret, J. F. Differential Galois Theory. LC 81-6298. (Mathematics & Its Applications Ser.: Vol. 15). viii, 760p. 1983. text 697.00 (*0-677-05670-2*) Gordon & Breach.

— Lie Pseudogroups & Mechanics. (Mathematics & Its Applications Ser.: Vol. 16). x, 592p. 1988. text 480.00 (*2-88124-213-8*) Gordon & Breach.

— Partial Differential Equations & Group Theory: New Perspectives for Applications. LC 94-19352. (Mathematics & Its Applications Ser.: Vol. 293). 484p. (C). 1994. text 289.00 (*0-7923-2966-X*) Kluwer Academic.

— Systems of Partial Differential Equations & Lie Pseudogroups, Vol. 14. (Mathematics & Its Applications Ser.). xiv, 412p. 1978. text 332.00 (*0-677-00270-X*) Gordon & Breach.

Pommer, Richard. Eighteenth Century Architecture in Piedmont: The Open Structures of Juvarra, Alfieri & Vittone. LC 67-10331. 399p. reprint ed. pap. 123.70 (*0-608-11461-8*, 205032000061) Bks Demand.

Pommer, Richard & Otto, Christian F. Weissenhof, 1927 & the Modern Movement in Architecture. LC 90-33628. (Illus.). 432p. 1991. 78.00 (*0-226-67515-7*) U Ch Pr.

Pommer, Stephen D. The Green Car. LC 98-90586. 1999. pap. 7.95 (*0-533-12852-8*) Vantage.

Pommerencke, Peter, jt. auth. see Flemming, Monika.

Pommerenke, C. Boundary Behaviour of Conformal Maps. Berger, M. et al, eds. LC 92-10365. (Grundlehren der Mathematischen Wissenschaften Ser.: Vol. 299). (Illus.). 312p. 1992. 86.95 (*0-387-54751-7*) Spr-Verlag.

Pommeret, Francoise. Bhutan. LC 90-63329. (India Guides Ser.). (Illus.). 277p. 1993. reprint ed. pap. 14.95 (*0-8442-9924-3*, Passprt Bks) NTC Contemp Pub Co.

Pommerin, Reiner, ed. The American Impact on Postwar Germany. LC 94-27019. 208p. (C). 1995. 42.00 (*1-57181-004-8*) Berghahn Bks.

— The American Impact on Postwar Germany. 208p. (C). 1996. pap. 16.50 (*1-57181-095-1*) Berghahn Bks.

Pommerin, Reiner, et al, eds. Culture in the Federal Republic of Germany, 1945-1995. (German Historical Perspectives Ser.). 151p. 1996. 45.00 (*1-85973-100-7*, Pub. by Berg Pubs) NYU Pr.

— Culture in the Federal Republic of Germany, 1945-1995. (German Historical Perspectives Ser.: No. 11). 151p. 1996. pap. 16.50 (*1-85973-105-8*, Pub. by Berg Pubs) NYU Pr.

Pommernecke, Peter, jt. auth. see Flemming, Monika.

Pommersheim, Frank. Braid of Feathers: American Indian Law & Contemporary Tribal Life. LC 94-4846. 1997. pap. 16.95 (*0-520-20894-3*, Pub. by U CA Pr) Cal Prin Full Svc.

— Snaps: Poetry & Prose from a Family Album. LC 94-66152. 125p. 1994. pap. 7.95 (*0-9636224-1-2*) Rose Hill Bks.

Pommerville. The Microbiology Companion: An Illustrated Guide. (C). 2001. pap. 21.33 (*0-13-944463-7*) P-H.

Pommery, Jean. How Human the Animals. LC 78-24613. 224p. (C). 1981. pap. 6.95 (*0-8128-6086-1*, Scrbrough Hse) Madison Bks UPA.

Pommier, Jean. La Jeunesse Clericale d'Ernest Reman - Saint Sulpice. (Fac. Let. Strasbourg Ser.). 13.95 (*0-685-34961-6*) Fr & Eur.

Pommier, Jean, jt. auth. see Balzac, Honore de.

Pommier, Jean, ed. see Gautier, Theophile.

Pommier, Louis. Dictionary of Emergency Homeopathy: Dictionnaire Homeopathique d'Urgentce. 13th ed. (ENG & FRE.). 765p. 1985. 75.00 (*0-7859-4836-8*, M6461) Fr & Eur.

— Dictionnaire Homeopathique. (FRE.). 1986. 19.95 (*0-7859-7851-8*, 2-253-03815-6) Fr & Eur.

Pommois, Lise M. & Veterans Memorial Foundation, Rainbow Division Sta. Winter Storm: War in Northern Alsace, November 1944-March 1945. LC 91-66593. (Illus.). 416p. 1991. 34.95 (*1-56311-056-3*) Turner Pub KY.

Pommy-Vega, Janine. The Easter Island Bulletins of William Mulloy. LC 92-56590. (Easter Island Ser.). (Illus.). 170p. (Orig.). 1997. pap. 25.00 (*1-880636-04-2*) Easter Isl Fnd.

Pomogailo, A. D. Catalysis by Polymer-Immobilized Metal Complexes. (Illus.). 424p. 1998. text 86.00 (*90-5699-130-2*, ECU113) Gordon & Breach.

Pomogailo, Anatoly D. & Savostyanov, Vladimir S. Synthesis & Polymerization of Metal-Containing Monomers. LC 93-49461. 192p. 1994. lib. bdg. 99.50 (*0-8493-2458-2*, 2863) CRC Pr.

Pomorska, K. Themes & Variations in Pasternak's Poetics. 92p. 1975. pap. 21.00 (*0-685-53318-2*) J Benjamins Pubng Co.

Pomorska, Krystyna. Jakobsonian Poetics & Slavic Narrative: From Pushkin to Solzhenitsyn. Baran, Henryk, ed. LC 91-39157. (Sound & Meaning: The Roman Jakobson Series in Linguistics & Poetics). 352p. 1992. text 49.95 (*0-8223-1233-6*) Duke.

— Russian Formalist Theory & Its Poetic Ambience. 1968. text 55.40 (*3-10-800116-7*) Mouton.

Pomorska, Krystyna, et al. Language, Poetry & Poetics: The Generation of the 1890's: Jakobson, Trubetzkoy, Majakovskj - Proceeding of the First Roman Jakobson Colloquim. (Illus.). 364p. 1987. lib. bdg. 119.25 (*0-89925-098-X*) Mouton.

Pomorska, Krystyna, ed. see Jakobson, Roman.

Pomorski, Stanislaw. American Common Law & the Principle Nullum Crimen Sine Lege. 2nd rev. ed. Chodakowska, Elizbieta, tr. from POL. x, 219p. 1975. pap. 10.00 (*0-8377-1051-0*, Rothman) W S Hein.

Pomp, A. The Boundary-Domain Integral Method for Elliptic Systems with Application to Shells, Vol. 168. LC 98-14460. (Lecture Notes in Mathematics: Vol. 1683). (Illus.). xvi, 163p. 1998. pap. 33.00 (*3-540-64163-7*) Spr-Verlag.

Pomp, Richard D. Connecticut Tax Handbook, 1998. rev. ed. 194p. 1997. pap. text 45.00 (*0-7811-0179-4*) Res Inst Am.

— Connecticut Tax Handbook, 1999. rev. ed. Jenis, Richard E., ed. 220p. 1998. pap. text 35.75 (*0-7811-0191-3*) Res Inst Am.

Pomp, Richard D., ed. see Oldman, Oliver S.

Pompa, Delia & Reilly, Michael. Looking for America: Seven Schools Experimenting with Intergroup Relations, Vol. 2. (Illus.). 116p. (Orig.). 1995. pap. 16.95 (*1-880002-11-6*) Natl Coal Advocates.

Pompa, Delia, ed. see Gill, Lucia, et al.

Pompa, Leon. Vico's Theory of the Causes of Historical Change. 23p. 1971. pap. 6.00 (*0-9500029-2-5*, Pub. by Octagon Pr) ISHK.

Pompa, Yvette. Friends Forever: Storybook & Keychain Craft Kit. (Barbie Mini-Craft Kits Ser.). (Illus.). 16p. (J). (gr. k-3). 1999. pap. 6.99 (*1-57584-333-1*, Pub. by Rdrs Digest) Random.

***Pompa, Yvette.** Magic Moments. (Barbie Mini Craft Ser.). (Illus.). 16p. (J). (gr. k-3). 2000. 6.99 (*1-57584-412-5*, Pub. by Rdrs Digest) S&S Trade.

— The Perfect Gift. (Barbie Mini Craft Ser.). (Illus.). 16p. (J). (gr. k-3). 2000. pap. 6.99 (*1-57584-413-3*, Pub. by Rdrs Digest) S&S Trade.

Pompe, S., ed. Indonesian Law, 1949-1989: A Bibliography of Foreign-Language Materials with Brief Commentaries on the Law. LC 92-15181. 468p. (C). 1992. lib. bdg. 167.50 (*0-7923-1744-0*) Kluwer Academic.

Pompe, Wolfgang, jt. ed. see Kreher, Wolfgang.

Pompea, Stephen. Current Perspectives in Astronomy & Physics: Selected Readings. LC 95-169567. 306p. 1995. 19.95 (*0-314-05887-7*) West Pub.

Pompei, Jessica, et al, eds. ECHO 681, Vol. 1. (Publications: Vol. 21, No. 4). 147p. 1998. pap. 7.95 (*1-892184-04-4*) Beyond Baroque.

Pompeiano, O., jt. ed. see Barnes, C. D.

Pompeii, Maria T., tr. see De Jesus D'Elbee, Jean.

Pompella, Giuseppe. Menander - Lexicon Menandreum. x, 289p. 1996. write for info. (*3-487-10255-2*) G Olms Pubs.

Pompella, Guiseppe, ed. Argonautica - Index in Orphei Argonautica. (Alpha-Omega, Reihe A Ser.: Bd. XXXIX). (GER.). x, 156p. 1979. write for info. (*3-487-06949-0*) G Olms Pubs.

— Quintus Smyrnaeus - Index in Quintum Smyraneum. (Alpha-Omega, Reihe A Ser.: Bd. XLIX). v, 441p. 1982. write for info. (*3-487-07134-7*) G Olms Pubs.

Pompelli, Jean. Dress for Independence Vol. 1: How to Make & Adapt Clothing for People with a Disability. Lestina, Peggy & Baker, Dorothy, eds. (Dress for Independence: Vol. 1). (Illus.). 160p. (Orig.). 1997. per., otabind 14.95 (*0-9657197-7-4*, Disability Pubns) Wings Way Pr.

Pomper, Gerald M. The Election of 1980: Reports & Interpretations. Pomper, Marlene M., ed. LC 81-598. 208p. reprint ed. pap. 64.50 (*0-8357-4822-7*, 203775900009) Bks Demand.

— The Election of 1984: Reports & Interpretations. Pomper, Marlene M., ed. LC 85-4223. 208p. reprint ed. pap. 64.50 (*0-8357-4823-5*, 203776000009) Bks Demand.

— Passions & Interests: Political Party Concepts of American Democracy. LC 92-12328. (American Political Thought Ser.). xii, 180p. 1992. 27.50 (*0-7006-0551-7*); pap. 12.95 (*0-7006-0552-5*) U Pr of KS.

— Voters' Choice: Varieties of American Electoral Behavior. (Illus.). 276p. (C). 1983. reprint ed. pap. text 22.00 (*0-8191-3188-1*) U Pr of Amer.

— Voters, Elections, & Parties: The Practice of Democratic Theory. 320p. 1988. 44.95 (*0-88738-160-X*) Transaction Pubs.

— Voters, Elections, & Parties: The Practice of Democratic Theory. 424p. (C). 1992. pap. text 24.95 (*1-56000-561-0*) Transaction Pubs.

***Pomper, Gerald M., ed.** The Election of 2000: Reports & Interpretations. (Illus.). 350p. (C). 2001. pap. text. write for info. (*1-889119-46-6*, Chatham House Pub) Seven Bridges.

Pomper, Gerald M., ed. Party Renewal in America: Theory & Practice. LC 79-25184. 204p. 1980. 36.95 (*0-275-90539-X*, C0539, Praeger Pubs) Greenwood.

— The Political State of New Jersey. 240p. (C). 1986. text 40.00 (*0-8135-1150-X*); pap. text 16.00 (*0-8135-1151-8*) Rutgers U Pr.

Pomper, Gerald M., et al, eds. The Political Life of the American States: American Political Parties & Elections. LC 83-17756. 344p. 1984. pap. 14.95 (*0-275-91630-8*, B1630, Praeger Pubs) Greenwood.

P

Pomper, Gerald M., et al. The Election of 1996: Reports & Interpretations. LC 97-4618. (Illus.). 304p. (C). 1997. 25.00 (1-56643-056-9, Chatham House Pub); pap. text 19.95 (1-56643-055-0, Chatham House Pub) Seven Bridges.

Pomper, Gerald M., ed. see Kleppner, Paul.

Pomper, Gerald M., ed. see Smith, Paul A.

Pomper, Marlene M., ed. see Pomper, Gerald M.

Pomper, Philip. Lenin, Trotsky, & Stalin: The Intelligentsia & Power. 456p. 1990. text 61.50 (0-231-06906-5) Col U Pr.

— Lenin Trotsky Stalin. 1991. pap. 17.50 (0-685-62548-6) Col U Pr.

— The Russian Revolutionary Intelligentsia. 2nd ed. Eubank, Keith, ed. LC 92-5628. (European History Ser.). 256p. (C). 1993. pap. text 12.95 (0-88295-895-X) Harlan Davidson.

— The Structure of Mind in History: Five Major Figures in Psychohistory. LC 84-22988. 192p. 1985. text 40.50 (0-231-06064-5) Col U Pr.

Pomper, Philip, et al. World History: Ideologies, Structures & Identities. LC 97-45817. 288p. 1998. 62.95 (0-631-20898-4); pap. 31.95 (0-631-20899-2) Blackwell Pubs.

Pomper, Philip, ed. see Fay, Brian.

Pomphrey, Isabel G. My Litter Box Was Dirty . . .So I Left You a Present in Your Shoe! Behavior Modification from a Cat's Point of View. Pomphrey, Patrick J., Jr., ed. (Illus.). 114p. 1997. pap. 16.98 (0-9661487-0-3) Tunabreath.

Pomphrey, Patrick J., Jr., ed. see Pomphrey, Isabel G.

Pompian, Susan. Tokyo for Free. LC 97-37512. 1998. pap. text 19.95 (4-7700-2053-8, Pub. by Kodansha Intl) Kodansha.

Pompidou. Anthologie de la Poesie Francaise. (FRE.). (C). pap. 13.95 (0-8442-1801-4, VF1801-4) NTC Contemp Pub Co.

Pompino-Marschall, Bernd. Einfuehrung in die Phoenetik. xiv, 310p. (C). 1995. pap. text 36.95 (3-11-014763-7); lib. bdg. 90.75 (3-11-013686-4) De Gruyter.

Pompl, W. & Lavery, P., eds. Tourism in Europe: Structures & Developments. (Illus.). 384p. (Orig.). 1993. pap. text 50.00 (0-85198-852-0) OUP.

Pomponatius, Petrus, pseud. De Naturalium Effectuum Causis Sive De Incantationibus. 328p. 1970. reprint ed. write for info. (0-318-71607-0) G Olms Pubs.

Pomponazzi, Pietro, see Pomponatius, Petrus, pseud.

Pomponio, Ali, et al, eds. Children of Kilibob: Creation, Cosmos, & Culture in Northeast New Guinea. (Pacific Studies: Vol. 17, No. 4). (Illus.). 224p. (C). 1994. pap. text 15.00 (0-939154-61-7) Inst Polynesian.

Pomponio, F. & Xella, P. Les Dieux d'Ebla. (FRE.). 1998. text 69.50 (3-927120-46-4) Ugarit-Verlag.

Pomraning, Dorothy E., jt. auth. see Clark, Virginia L.

Pomraning, G. C. Linear Kinetic Theory & Particle Transport in Stochastic Mixtures. (Series on Advances in Mathematics for Applied Sciences: Vol. 7). 250p. 1991. text 61.00 (981-02-0844-8) World Scientific Pub.

Pomraning, G. C., et al. Theoretical & Computational Radiation Hydrodynamics Vol. 1: Radiation-Hydrodynamics Theoretical Considerations. LC 70-135085. 228p. 1969. 20.00 (0-403-04529-0) Scholarly.

Pomrenke, G. S., et al, eds. Rare-Earth Doped Semiconductors. (Symposium Proceedings Ser.: Vol. 301). 417p. 1993. text 30.00 (1-55899-197-2) Materials Res.

Poms, Lillian, jt. auth. see Dale, Paulette.

Pomykalski, Wanda E. The Horror Trains: A Polish Woman Veteran's Memoir of World War II. LC 99-7007. (Illus.). 350p. 1999. 50.00 (0-9634895-4-2) Minerva Ctr.

Pon, C. L., jt. ed. see Gualerzi, C. O.

Pon, Donald. Experiments for Chemistry, Vol. 30A. 90p. (C). 1999. per. 20.95 (0-7872-5710-9, 41571001) Kendall-Hunt.

— Experiments for Introductory Chemistry. 74p. (C). 1998. per. 16.95 (0-7872-5446-0, 41544601) Kendall-Hunt.

Ponasse, Daniel. Mathematical Logic. LC 72-136738. (Notes on Mathematics & Its Applications Ser.). Orig. Title: Logique Mathematique. x, 126p. (C). 1973. text 160.00 (0-677-30390-4) Gordon & Breach.

***Poncar, Jaroslav.** Tibet. (Illus.). 160p. 2000. 100.00 (3-8238-5482-8) te Neues.

Poncavage, Joanna. The Italian Kitchen Garden. LC 97-15697. (Illus.). 96p. 1997. pap. write for info. (0-8362-3258-5) Andrews & McMeel.

— Totally Sunflowers. (Totally Flowers Ser.). (Illus.). 96p. 1996. pap. 5.95 (0-89087-783-1) Celestial Arts.

Ponce, jt. ed. see Larson.

Ponce, Blanca N. De, see De Ponce, Blanca N.

Ponce, Carlos. Platicas de Mi Barrio. (SPA.). 120p. 1998. pap. 11.00 (0-927534-82-7) Biling Rev-Pr.

Ponce, Carlos Salas, see Salas Ponce, Carlos.

Ponce, Charles. The Archetype of the Unconscious & the Transfiguration of Therapy: Reflections On Jungian Psychology. 120p. (Orig.). 1990. pap. 9.95 (1-55643-070-1) North Atlantic.

— Kabbalah: An Introduction & Illumination for the World Today. LC 78-7385. (Illus.). 300p. 1978. reprint ed. pap. 14.00 (0-8356-0510-8, Quest) Theos Pub Hse.

— Papers Toward Radical Metaphysics: Alchemy. 160p. (Orig.). 1984. pap. 8.95 (0-938190-02-4) North Atlantic.

— Working the Soul: Reflections on Jungian Psychology. (Illus.). 189p. 1987. pap. 12.95 (1-55643-033-7) North Atlantic.

***Ponce De Leon.** El Arte De la Conversacion: Text with Atajo. 6th ed. (SPA.). (C). 2000. pap. 50.95 (0-8384-0823-0) Heinle & Heinle.

Ponce de Leon, Carolina & Andreus, Alejanoro. Carmen Herrera: The Black & White Paintings, 1951-1989. Chasin, Noah, ed. Marin, Clara & Zatz, Asa, trs. (SPA., Illus.). 32p. 1998. pap. 12.50 (1-882454-07-3) El Museo Barrio.

Ponce de Leon, Carolina & Torruella Leval, Susana. Beatriz Gonzalez: ". . . At This Historical Moment" Works, 1965-1997. Chasin, Noah, ed. Graham, James, tr. (SPA., Illus.). 88p. 1998. pap. write for info. (1-882454-06-5) El Museo Barrio.

Ponce de Leon, Carolina, jt. auth. see Cullen, Deborah.

Ponce de Leon, Juana, ed. see Marcos, Subcomandante Insurgente.

Ponce, F. A., et al, eds. Gallium Nitride & Related Materials. (MRS Symposium Proceedings Ser.: Vol. 395). 970p. 1996. 65.00 (1-55899-298-7, 395) Materials Res.

— Nitride Semiconductors Vol. 482: Materials Research Society Symposium Proceedings. LC 98-9636. 1224p. 1998. text 76.00 (1-55899-387-8) Materials Res.

Ponce, F. A. & Cardona, M., eds. Surface Science: Lectures on Basic Concepts & Applications - Proceedings of the Sixth Latin American Symposium on Surface Physics (SLAFS-6), Cusco, Peru, September 3-7, 1990. (Proceedings in Physics Ser.: Vol. 62). (Illus.). xiii, 525p. 1992. 144.95 (0-387-53604-3) Spr-Verlag.

Ponce, J., et al, eds. Object Representation in Computer Vision: ECCV '96 International Workshop, Cambridge, U. K., April 13-15, 1996 - Proceedings. (Lecture Notes in Computer Science Ser.: Vol. 1144). viii, 403p. 1996. pap. 68.00 (3-540-61750-7) Spr-Verlag.

Ponce, Juan G. La Cabana. (SPA.). 182p. 1982. pap. 8.00 (84-85859-38-3, 2006) Ediciones Norte.

— El Gato y Otros Cuentos. (SPA.). pap. 8.99 (968-16-4882-X, Pub. by Fondo) Continental Bk.

— Inmaculada O los Placeres de la Inocencia (Immaculate or the Pleasures of Innocence) (SPA.). 336p. 1989. 16.99 (968-16-3075-0, Pub. by Fondo) Continental Bk.

— Pasaso Presente (Past Present) (SPA.). 352p. 1993. 16.99 (968-16-4175-2, Pub. by Fondo) Continental Bk.

Ponce, Juan Garcia, see Garcia Ponce, Juan.

Ponce, Manuel. Manuel Ponce: Some of My Poems. Miller, Yvette E., ed. Rodriguez-Lee, Maria-L., tr. from SPA. & intro. by. LC 87-3407. (Discoveries Ser.). (ENG & SPA.). 126p. (C). 1987. pap. 11.50 (0-935480-28-5) Lat Am Lit Rev Pr.

Ponce, Mario. Waiting on America: A Food Server's Guide to Greater Income. Modesto, Robert, ed. (Illus.). 144p. (Orig.). (C). 1989. pap. 7.95 (0-685-27820-4) Amer Serv Pubns.

Ponce, Mary Helen. Hoyt Street: An Autobiography. LC 93-1346. 338p. 1993. 14.95 (0-8263-1446-5) U of NM Pr.

Ponce, Omar. Educate para una Mejor Condicion Fisica: Guia Basica para el Desarrollo de un Programa de Eficiencia Fisica. (SPA., Illus.). 75p. (Orig.). (YA). 1986. write for info. (0-318-64880-6) B Ponce.

Ponce, Victor Miguel. Engineering Hydrology. 1997. pap. text 31.60 (0-13-315466-1) P-H.

Ponce, Wallace Y. Our Beginnings: The History of the Epworth United Methodist Church. (Orig.). 1988. 10.00 (0-9620308-3-X); pap. 10.00 (0-9620308-8-0); text 10.00 (0-9620308-2-1); lib. bdg. 10.00 (0-9620308-9-9) Epworth United Methodist Church.

Poncein, J. P. On Playing Oboe Recorder & Flageolet. LC 91-33938. (Publications of the Early Music Institute). 128p. 1992. pap. text 15.95 (0-253-28881-9) Ind U Pr.

Poncela, Enrique J. Eloisa Esta Debajo de Almendro. (SPA.). 244p. 1974. 10.50 (0-8288-7042-X) Fr & Eur.

— Noche de Primavera sin Sueno: Comedia Humoristica en Tres Actos. Lacosta, Francisco C., ed. LC 67-25113. (SPA.). (YA). (gr. 9 up). 1967. pap. text 6.95 (0-89197-320-6) Irvington.

Poncelet, G., et al, eds. Preparation of Catalysts No. 5: Scientific Basis for the Preparation of Heterogeneous Catalysts: Proceedings of the 5th International Symposium, Louvain-la-Neuve, Sept. 3-6, 1990. (Studies in Surface Science & Catalysis: No. 63). 748p. 1991. 305.00 (0-444-88616-8) Elsevier.

Poncet, Sally. Anarctic Encounter: Destination South Georgia. LC 94-13376. (Illus.). 48p. (J). (gr. 2-5). 1995. mass mkt. 17.00 (0-02-774905-3) S&S Bks Yung.

Ponchillia, Paul E. & Panchillia, Susan V. Foundations of Rehabilitation Teaching: With Persons Who Are Blind or Visually Impaired. LC 94-32260. (Illus.). 432p. 1996. text 59.95 (0-89128-939-9) Am Foun Blind.

Ponchillia, Paul E. & Ponchillia, Susan V. Foundations of Rehabilitative Teaching: With Persons Who Are Blind or Visually Impaired. unabridged ed. 1996. digital audio 59.95 (0-89128-291-2) Am Foun Blind.

Ponchillia, Susan V., jt. auth. see Ponchillia, Paul E.

Ponciano, Roberto. Canto Indispensable (Poesias) LC 87-81864. (Coleccion Espejo de Paciencia). (SPA.). 112p. (Orig.). 1987. pap. 9.00 (0-89729-446-7) Ediciones.

Poncins. From a Chinese City: In the Heart of Peacetime Vietnam. (Illus.). 262p. 1996. reprint ed. 19.95 (1-879434-01-6); reprint ed. pap. 11.95 (1-879434-00-8) Trackless Sands Pr.

Poncins, Leon De, see De Poncins, Leon.

Poncio, J. Steve, et al, eds. Concrete: Surface Preparation, Coating & Lining, & Inspection. (Illus.). 124p. 1991. ring bd. 56.00 (1-877914-22-3) NACE Intl.

Poncy, Mark P. Manopause: Boomer Hits the Big Fifty. LC 97-90295. x, 64p. (Orig.). 1997. pap. 9.95 (0-533-12345-3) Vantage.

Poncy, O., jt. auth. see Feuillet, C.

Pond. Introduction to Engineering Technology. 4th ed. LC 98-15343. 1998. pap. text 50.00 (0-13-854812-9) S&S Trade.

Pond, William G. & Pond, Kevin R. Introduction to Animal Science. LC 99-29011. 722p. 2000. text 108.95 (0-471-17094-1) Wiley.

Pond, Barbara. A Sampler of Wayside Herbs: Rediscovering Old Uses for Familiar Wild Plants. LC 73-89773. (Illus.). 1974. 24.95 (0-85699-096-5) Chatham Pr.

Pond, Becki, jt. auth. see Jackman, Staci.

Pond, Caroline M. The Fats of Life. LC 97-46515. (Illus.). 300p. (C). 1998. text 54.95 (0-521-58321-7); pap. text 19.95 (0-521-63577-2) Cambridge U Pr.

Pond, Cliffor. For Starters. 1997. pap., student ed. 9.99 (0-946462-44-5, Pub. by Evangelical Pr) P & R Pubng.

— Our Father. 1997. pap. 7.99 (0-946462-43-7, Pub. by Evangelical Pr) P & R Pubng.

Pond, Clifford. The Beauty of Jesus. 1994. pap. text 8.99 (0-946462-33-X, Pub. by Evangelical Pr) P & R Pubng.

— Only Servants. 1991. pap. 8.99 (0-946462-24-0, Pub. by Evangelical Pr) P & R Pubng.

Pond, Cornelia J. Recollections of a Southern Daughter: A Memoir by Cornelia Jones Pond of Liberty County. unabridged ed. MacKethan, Lucinda H., ed. LC 98-22321. 160p. 1999. 24.95 (0-8203-2044-7) U of Ga Pr.

***Pond, D. J.** Evaluation of Human Factors Research for Ultrasonic Inservice Inspection. 40p. 1998. pap. 3.75 (0-16-062906-3) USGPO.

Pond, Dale & Baumgartner, Walter. Nikola Tesla's Earthquake Machine: With Tesla's Original Patents Plus New Blueprints to Build Your Own Working Model. LC 95-76243. (Illus.). 176p. (Orig.). 1995. pap. 16.95 (1-57282-008-X, D2008X) Message NM.

Pond, Dale, et al. History of the American Constitutional or Common Law: With Commentary Concerning Equity & Merchant Law. LC 94-72953. (Illus.). 144p. 1995. pap. 11.95 (1-57282-010-1) Message NM.

— The Physics of Love: The Ultimate Universal Laws. LC 95-81524. (Illus.). 152p. (Orig.). 1996. pap. 15.95 (1-57282-002-0, D20020) Message NM.

— Universal Laws Never Before Revealed: Keely's Secrets: Understanding & Using the Science of Sympathetic Vibration. rev. ed. LC 94-77879. (Illus.). 288p. 1995. pap. 19.95 (1-57282-003-9) Message NM.

***Pond, David.** Chakras for Beginners: A Guide to Balancing Your Chakra Energies. LC 99-41210. 216p. 1999. pap. text 9.95 (1-56718-537-1) Llewellyn Pubns.

Pond, David & Pond, Lucy. The Metaphysical Handbook. LC 83-91290. (Illus.). 200p. 1984. pap. 12.95 (0-915395-18-5) Reflecting Pond.

Pond, David, et al. Crystals Stones & Chakras. 1988. 15.95 (0-915395-28-2); pap. text 3.95 (0-915395-31-2) Reflecting Pond.

Pond, Doreen & McDonald, Art. The Cheyenne Journey: Morning Star Our Guiding Light. LC 96-36980. 160p. 1997. 29.95 (0-929765-50-8) Seven Locks Pr.

Pond, E. Leroy. Junius Smith: Biography of the Father of the Atlantic Liner. LC 75-179535. (Select Bibliographies Reprint Ser.). 1977. reprint ed. 23.95 (0-8369-6664-3) Ayer.

Pond, Elizabeth. After the Wall: American Policy Toward Germany - A Twentieth Century Fund Paper. 111p. (Orig.). (C). 1990. pap. 9.95 (0-87078-323-8) Century Foundation.

— Beyond the Wall: Germany's Road to Unification. 367p. (C). 1993. 42.95 (0-8157-7154-1); pap. 18.95 (0-8157-7155-X) Brookings.

— From the Yaroslavsky Station: Russia Perceived. 3rd ed. 304p. 1988. pap. 12.95 (0-87663-536-2, Pub. by Universe) St Martin.

— The Rebirth of Europe. 1999. write for info. (0-8157-7157-6) Brookings.

Pond, Elizabeth. The Rebirth of Europe. 1999. 26.95 (0-8157-7158-4) Brookings.

Pond, Elizabeth, jt. auth. see Schoenbaum, David.

Pond, Elsie. Odyssey of the Heart. LC 96-70113. (Illus.). 116p. 1997. 9.95 (0-9654936-2-8) Redwood Retreat Pr.

Pond, Jane B., jt. ed. see Schaefer, Karen M.

Pond, Jesse E., Jr. The Square Peg: A Tight Fit in a Tin Can. Powell, Lilja B., ed. LC 92-85443. 208p. (Orig.). 1992. pap. 19.95 (0-9634347-0-5) Pearl Harbor Hist.

Pond, Jonathan. New Century Family Money Book. 96p. 1995. pap. 1.11 (0-440-51333-2) Dell.

Pond, Jonathan D. The ABCs of Managing Your Money. 250p. 1993. 26.95 (1-884383-00-9) Natl Endowment.

***Pond, Jonathan D.** 4 Easy Step to Successfu. 240p. 1998. pap. 12.00 (0-380-79181-1, Avon Bks) Morrow Avon.

Pond, Jonathan D. 4 Easy Steps to Successful Investing. LC 96-46377. 240p. 1997. mass mkt. 20.00 (0-380-97472-X, Avon Bks) Morrow Avon.

— One Thousand & One Ways to Cut Your Expenses. 304p. 1992. pap. 10.95 (0-440-50495-3) Dell.

— Personal Financial Planning: With Forms & Checklists. 352p. 1987. 156.50 (0-88712-914-5) Warren Gorham & Lamont.

— Personal Financial Planning: With Forms & Checklists. 352p. 1992. suppl. ed. 165.00 (0-7913-2700-0, PFF) Warren Gorham & Lamont.

Pond, Jonathan D., ed. Professional Financial Planner's Diary & Guide: 1998 Edition. Date not set. 40.95 (1-57987-015-5) Faulkner & Gray.

Pond, Jonathon. Your Money Matters: 21 Tips for Achieving Financial Security in the 21st Century. LC 99-39267. 208p. 1999. 21.95 (0-399-14569-9, G P Putnam) Peng Put Young Read.

Pond, Joyce. Lost in the Corn. (Illus.). 31p. (Orig.). (J). (gr. 6). 1992. pap. 6.95 (0-9635877-0-6) JBP Press.

Pond, Kathleen, tr. see Auclair, Marcelle.

Pond, Kathleen L. The Professional Guide. (Illus.). 250p. 1993. text 46.95 (0-442-00148-7, VNR) Wiley.

Pond, Kathleen L. The Professional Guide: Dynamics of Tour Guiding. 288p. 1992. 59.95 (0-471-28386-X, VNR) Wiley.

***Pond, Keith & Lipscombe, Geoff.** The Business of Banking: An Introduction to the Modern Financial Services Industry. 268p. 1999. pap. 48.00 (0-85297-533-3, Pub. by Chartered Bank) St Mut.

Pond, Kevin R., jt. auth. see Pond, William G.

Pond, Lily. Pillow: Exploring the Heart of Eros. LC 98-11915. 112p. 1998. pap. 9.95 (0-89087-858-7) Celestial Arts.

— Seven Hundred Kisses: A Yellow Silk Book of Erotic Writing. LC 96-38100. 1997. pap. 14.00 (0-06-251484-9, Pub. by Harper SF) HarpC.

***Pond, Lily, ed.** Yellow Silk II: International Erotic Stories & Poems. LC 99-89343. 2000. pap. 13.95 (0-446-67531-8) Warner Bks.

Pond, Lucy, jt. auth. see Pond, David.

Pond, Marion. Shades of Yesteryear. LC 82-71114. (Illus.). 48p. (Orig.). 1982. pap. 7.50 (0-941284-13-1) J Shaw Studio.

Pond, Mike. How to Become a Credit Card Merchant Immediately Without Having to Apply at a Bank. 2nd ed. LC 94-212456. (Illus.). 96p. 1993. pap. write for info. (1-880199-49-1) Mindbuilders.

— How to Get, Keep & Use VISA, MasterCard & American Express Credit Card Merchant Status to Earn Millions: Even If You Work at Home, Operate a Mail Order Business or Just Starting a New Company. 295p. (Orig.). 1992. 69.95 (1-880199-99-8); pap. 49.95 (1-880199-95-5) Mindbuilders.

Pond, Mimi. Splitting Hairs: The Bald Truth about Bad Hair Days. (Illus.). 176p. 1998. pap. 9.95 (0-684-82643-7, Fireside) S&S Trade Pap.

Pond, Oscar L. Municipal Control of Public Utilities: A Study of the Attitudes of Our Courts Toward an Increase of the Sphere of Municipal Activity. LC 79-76676. (Columbia University. Studies in the Social Sciences: No. 65). reprint ed. 27.50 (0-404-51065-5) AMS Pr.

Pond, R. C., et al, eds. Boundaries & Interfaces in Materials: The David A. Smith Symposium, Proceedings, Indianapolis, IN, 1997. LC 97-75971. (Illus.). 348p. 1998. 116.00 (0-87339-404-6, TA401) Minerals Metals.

Pond, Roger. It's Hard to Look Cool When Your Car's Full of Sheep: Tales from the Back Forty. LC 88-92371. (Illus.). 176p. (Orig.). 1989. pap. 11.95 (0-9617766-1-7) Pine Forest Pub.

— Livestock Showman's Handbook: A Guide for Raising Animals for Junior Livestock Shows. 2nd ed. LC 96-70178. (Illus.). 214p. (J). (gr. 4-12). 1997. pap. 17.95 (0-9617766-3-3) Pine Forest Pub.

— My Dog Was a Redneck, but We Got Him Fixed. LC 96-72170. (Illus.). 176p. (Orig.). 1997. pap. 11.95 (0-9617766-4-1) Pine Forest Pub.

— Things That Go "Baa!" in the Night: Tales from a Country Kid. (Illus.). 176p. (Orig.). 1992. pap. 11.95 (0-9617766-2-5) Pine Forest Pub.

Pond, Roy. Mummy's Revenge. 160p. (J). (gr. 4-6). 1994. pap. 3.50 (0-590-48374-9) Scholastic Inc.

— Mummy's Tomb. (J). 1996. pap. 3.50 (0-590-60370-1) Scholastic Inc.

— Mummy's Tomb. (J). 1996. 8.60 (0-606-09645-0, Pub. by Turtleback) Demco.

***Pond, Russell.** Introduction to Criminology. 158p. 1999. pap. 30.00 (1-872870-42-2, Pub. by Waterside Pr) Gaunt.

Pond, S. & Pickard, George L. Introductory Dynamical Oceanography. 2nd ed. 349p. 2000. pap. text 37.95 (0-7506-2496-5, Prgamon Press) Buttrwrth-Heinemann.

Pond, Samuel W. The Dakota or Sioux in Minnesota As They Were in 1834. LC 85-31039. xxi, 192p. 1986. reprint ed. pap. 9.95 (0-87351-193-X, Borealis Book) Minn Hist.

Pond, Sarah A. Bartholomew. Collection of Family Records from Bartholomew, Botsford & Winston Lines of Genealogy. (Illus.). 60p. 1997. reprint ed. pap. 12.00 (0-8328-7393-4); reprint ed. lib. bdg. 22.00 (0-8328-7392-6) Higginson Bk Co.

Pond, Seymour G. History & Romance of Exploration, Told with Pictures. LC 65-17180. (Illus.). 126p. (Orig.). 1966. pap. 11.00 (0-8154-0182-5) Cooper Sq.

Pond, Wallace K., et al. The Lights Are on, Is Anybody Home? Education in America. (Illus.). 270p. 1998. pap. text 19.95 (1-57981-016-0) Cummngs & Hath.

Pondant, Elaine, jt. auth. see Harris, Patricia.

Ponder. Genetics of Malignant Disease. 1995. text 105.00 (0-443-05153-4, W B Saunders Co) Harcrt Hlth Sci Grp.

Ponder, B. A., et al, eds. Genetics & Cancer: A Second Look. LC 96-185636. (Cancer Surveys Ser.: Vol. 25). (Illus.). 425p. (C). 1995. 75.00 (0-87969-469-6) Cold Spring Harbor.

Ponder, B. A., jt. auth. see Waring, Michael J.

Ponder, B. A., jt. ed. see Waring, Michael J.

Ponder, Catherine. Dare to Prosper! LC 82-74520. 80p. 1983. pap. 6.95 (0-87516-511-7) DeVorss.

— Dynamic Laws of Healing. 238p. 1972. pap. 14.95 (0-87516-156-1) DeVorss.

— The Dynamic Laws of Prayer. rev. ed. LC 86-72267. 353p. 1987. reprint ed. pap. 16.95 (0-87516-583-4) DeVorss.

— The Dynamic Laws of Prosperity. 253p. 1993. reprint ed. lib. bdg. 21.95 (0-89968-318-5, Lghtyr Pr) Buccaneer Bks.

— The Dynamic Laws of Prosperity. rev. ed. LC 62-18836. 448p. 1985. reprint ed. pap. 16.95 (0-87516-551-6) DeVorss.

— The Healing Secrets of the Ages. rev. ed. LC 67-26503. 278p. 1985. reprint ed. pap. 14.95 (0-87516-550-8) DeVorss.

— The Millionaire from Nazareth. (Millionaires of the Bible Ser.). 1979. pap. 11.95 (0-87516-370-X) DeVorss.

— The Millionaire Joshua. LC 77-86719. (Millionaires of the Bible Ser.). 1978. pap. 11.95 (0-87516-253-3) DeVorss.

An Asterisk (*) at the beginning of an entry indicates that the title is appearing for the first time.

— The Millionaire Moses. LC 77-71459. (Millionaires of the Bible Ser.). 1977. pap. 11.95 (*0-87516-232-0*) DeVorss.

— The Millionaires of Genesis. (Millionaires of the Bible Ser.). 224p. 1976. pap. 11.95 (*0-87516-215-0*) DeVorss.

— Open Your Mind to Prosperity. rev. ed. LC 70-155720. 184p. 1984. reprint ed. pap. 10.95 (*0-87516-531-1*) DeVorss.

— Open Your Mind to Receive. LC 82-74283. 128p. 1983. pap. 10.95 (*0-87516-507-9*) DeVorss.

— The Prospering Power of Love. rev. ed. LC 66-25849. 126p. 1984. reprint ed. pap. 6.95 (*0-87516-525-7*) DeVorss.

— The Prospering Power of Prayer. 80p. 1983. pap. 6.95 (*0-87516-516-8*) DeVorss.

— The Prosperity Secrets of the Ages. rev. ed. LC 64-16436. 344p. 1986. reprint ed. pap. 14.95 (*0-87516-567-2*) DeVorss.

— The Secret of Unlimited Prosperity. 60p. 1981. pap. 6.95 (*0-87516-419-6*) DeVorss.

***Ponder, Daniel E.** Good Advice: Information & Policy Making in the White House. LC 99-47705. 288p. 2000. 39.95 (*0-89096-913-2*) Tex A&M Univ Pr.

Ponder, Daphne, tr. see Cormier, Michel & Michaud, Achille.

Ponder, Dorothy. The Civil War in Ripley County, Missouri. Prospect News Staff, ed. LC 92-82882. (Illus.). 102p. (Orig.). (C). 1992. pap. 5.00 (*0-9623922-1-9*) Ponder Bks.

Ponder, Jacqueline G. The Weekend Cowgirl by the Accidental Writer. pap. 11.95 (*0-9679459-5-X*) CRC Pubns.

Ponder, Jerry. The Battle of Chalk Bluff: An Account of General John S. Marmaduke's Second Missouri Raid. (Illus.). 202p. (C). 1995. pap. 13.95 (*0-9623922-3-5*) Ponder Bks.

— General Sterling Price's 1864 Invasion of Missouri. Webb, Lois G., ed. LC 99-70228. (Illus.). 216p. (YA). (gr. 7 up). 1999. pap. 17.75 (*0-9623922-9-4*) Ponder Bks.

— A History of the 15th Missouri Cavalry Regiment, C. S. A. (Illus.). 203p. (J). (ps-12). 1994. pap. 13.95 (*0-9623922-2-7*) Ponder Bks.

***Ponder, Jerry.** Major General John S. Marmaduke, C. S. A. Webb, Lois G., ed. LC 99-70227. (Illus.). 259p. (gr. 7 up). 1999. pap. 17.95 (*0-9623922-8-6*) Ponder Bks.

Ponder, Jerry & Vandiver, Eldon D. The Family of Abner Ponder. LC 89-62317. 400p. (J). (ps-12). 1989. 27.50 (*0-9623922-0-0*) Ponder Bks.

Ponder, Jim, et al. Multiplication Country. unabridged ed. (Rock 'N Learn Ser.). (Illus.). 22p. (YA). (gr. 3 up). 1993. pap. 12.99 incl. audio (*1-878489-25-9*, RL925) Rock N Learn.

Ponder, Lynn, ed. see Teykl, Terry.

Ponder, Melinda M. Hawthorne's Early Narrative Art. LC 89-13804. (Studies in American Literature: Vol. 9). 260p. 1990. lib. bdg. 89.95 (*0-88946-117-1*) E Mellen.

Ponder, Melinda M., jt. ed. see Idol, John L., Jr.

Ponder, Melvin. The Need to Be Versus Hell for Eternity. (Illus.). 141p. 1997. pap. 12.00 (*0-9660742-0-3*) Obedient Faith.

Ponder, Pearlie. Links to Ancestral Ties: George Primm, Sr., Family. 208p. 1995. text 17.00 (*0-9644034-0-4*) P Ponder.

— The Lord, Through Poetry. 208p. 1999. pap. write for info. (*0-9644034-1-2*) P Ponder.

Ponder, Purvis, jt. auth. see Hill, Everett W.

Ponder, Randall D. The Leader's Guide: 15 Essential Skills. LC 98-18539. (Illus.). 221p. 1998. pap. 19.95 (*1-55571-434-X*, LG15P) PSI Resch.

Ponder, Rhinold L. & Tuck, Michele L. The Wisdom of the Word: Faith - Great African-American Sermons. 1996. 17.00 (*0-614-19798-8*) Crown Pub Group.

***Ponder, Stephen.** Managing the Press: Origins of the Media Presidency, 1897-1933. LC 98-33865. 288p. 1999. text 45.00 (*0-312-21384-0*) St Martin.

Ponder, Suzanne. Guide to St. Louis Interior Design Professionals. (Design Registry Ser.: Vol. 1). (Illus.). 120p. 1989. 14.95 (*0-9622567-3-0*); pap. 7.95 (*0-9622567-4-9*) Design Registry.

— St. Louis Interior Design Resources. (Design Registry Ser.: Vol. 2). (Illus.). 200p. 1990. 17.95 (*0-9622567-6-5*); pap. 8.95 (*0-9622567-7-3*) Design Registry.

Ponder, William S. Educational Apartheid in a Pluralistic Society. 88p. 1995. pap. 10.00 (*1-57087-093-4*) Prof Pr NC.

Ponder, Winifred. Clara Butt: Her Life Story. LC 77-16530. (Music Reprint Ser.: 1978). (Illus.). 1978. reprint ed. lib. bdg. 35.00 (*0-306-77529-8*) Da Capo.

Ponder, Winston F., jt. auth. see Hershler, Robert.

Pondicherry. People of India, Vol. XXXVI. Singh, K. S., ed. (C). 1994. 36.00 (*81-85938-25-3*, Pub. by Manohar) S Asia.

***Pondiscio, Robert.** The Future: An Owner's Manual: What the World Will Look Like in the 21st Century & Beyond. LC 99-96354. 256p. (J). (gr. 3-7). 2000. mass mkt. 5.95 (*0-380-80335-6*, Avon Bks) Morrow Avon.

Pondiscio, Robert. Get on the Net: Everything You Need to Know about the Internet, Including Hundreds of Fun & Useful Sites. LC 98-93056. 240p. (J). (gr. 5-9). 1999. mass mkt. 5.99 (*0-380-80334-8*, Avon Bks) Morrow Avon.

***Pondiscio, Robert.** Get on the Net: Everything You Need to Know about the Internet, Including the World Wide Web & Addresses for Hours of Fun & Ease. (Illus.). (J). 1999. 14.30 (*0-606-17972-0*) Turtleback.

Pondiscio, Robert, jt. auth. see Salzman, Marian.

Pondoey, Gravrill S. Notes of a Soviet Doctor. 2nd ed. Haigh, Basil, tr. LC 59-9232. 248p. reprint ed. pap. 76.90 (*0-608-30200-7*, 202065200018) Bks Demand.

Pondrom, Cyrena N., jt. ed. see Dembo, L. S.

Pondrom, Lee G., jt. ed. see Durand, Loyal.

Pondsmith, Michael. Castle Falkenstein. (Illus.). 224p. (Orig.). 1994. 32.00 (*0-937279-51-X*, CF6002); pap. 27.00 (*0-937279-43-9*, CF6001) Talsorian.

— Chromebook 2. (Cyberpunk Ser.). (Illus.). 112p. (Orig.). 1992. pap. 12.00 (*0-614-02725-X*, CP3181) Talsorian.

Pondsmith, Michael & Winn, Ross. Listen up, You Primitive Screwheads!!! (Cyberpunk Ser.). (Illus.). 112p. (Orig.). 1994. pap. 10.00 (*0-937279-45-5*, CP3291) Talsorian.

Pondsmith, Michael, et al. Cyberpunk 2020. 2nd ed. Quintanar, Derek, ed. (Cyberpunk Ser.). (Illus.). 260p. (C). 1990. pap. 20.00 (*0-937279-13-7*, CP3002) Talsorian.

***Pondsmith, Mike.** DragonBall Z: The Anime Adventure Game. (J). 1999. pap. text 20.00 (*1-891933-00-0*) Talsorian.

Ponduck, Rona. 1 2 3 4 5. limited ed. (Illus.). 44p. 1998. pap. 25.00 (*1-892367-00-9*) H Yezerski.

Pondy, Louis R., et al, eds. Organizational Symbolism. LC 83-13542. (Monographs in Organizational Behavior & Industrial Relations: Vol. 1). 307p. 1983. 78.50 (*0-89232-366-3*) Jai Pr.

Pone, Daniel A., jt. auth. see House, Susan T.

Ponec, R. Overlap Determinant Method in the Theory of Pericyclic Reactions. (Lecture Notes in Chemistry Ser.: Vol. 65). (Illus.). 126p. 1995. 41.95 (*3-540-59189-3*) Spr-Verlag.

— Overlap Determinant Method in the Theory of Pericyclic Reactivity. LC 95-12985. (Lecture Notes in Chemistry Ser.: Vol. 65). 1995. write for info. (*0-387-59189-3*) Spr-Verlag.

Ponec, Vladimir & Bond, Geoffrey C. Catalysis by Metals & Alloys. LC 95-35574. (Studies in Surface Science & Catalysis: Vol. 95). 744p. 1995. 311.25 (*0-444-89796-8*) Elsevier.

Ponech, Trevor. What Is Non-Fiction Cinema? On the Very Idea of Motion Picture Communication. LC 98-55484. (Thinking Through Cinema Ser.). 312p. 1999. text 68.00 (*0-8133-6703-4*) Westview.

Ponemon, Lawrence. Research on Accounting Ethics, Vol. 2. 1997. 78.50 (*0-7623-0167-8*) Jai Pr.

— Research on Accounting Ethics, Vol. 4. 1998. 78.50 (*0-7623-0339-5*) Jai Pr.

Ponemon, Lawrence A., et al, eds. Research on Accounting Ethics, Vol. 1. 1995. 78.50 (*1-55938-753-X*) Jai Pr.

— Research on Accounting Ethics, Vol. 2. 1996. 78.50 (*1-55938-997-4*) Jai Pr.

Ponemon, Lawrence A. & Gadhart, D. R., eds. Auditing: Advances in Behavioral Research. (Recent Research in Psychology Ser.). (Illus.). x, 166p. 1991. 72.95 (*0-387-97619-1*) Spr-Verlag.

Ponente, Nello. Raphael. (Qui Etait Ser.). (FRE., Illus.). 150p. 1990. 65.00 (*0-7859-5024-9*) Fr & Eur.

Pong, David. A Critical Guide to the Kwangtung Provincial Archives Deposited at the Public Record Office, London. (East Asian Monographs: No. 63). 400p. 1975. pap. 20.00 (*0-674-17722-3*) HUP.

— Shen Pao-chen & China's Modernization in the Nineteenth Century. (Studies in Chinese History, Literature & Institutions). (Illus.). 415p. (C). 1994. text 59.95 (*0-521-44163-3*) Cambridge U Pr.

Pong, David & Fung, Edmund S., eds. Ideal & Reality: Social & Political Change in Modern China 1860-1949. (Illus.). 400p. 1986. pap. text 31.00 (*0-8191-4919-5*) U Pr of Amer.

***Pong, Suang-Jing.** Konjunktion Und Konjunktionale Funktion. (Europaische Hochschulschriften Ser.). 294p. 2000. 45.95 (*3-631-35824-5*) P Lang Pubng.

Pong, Ted. Quilt. LC 81-90056. (Illus.). 87p. (Orig.). 1981. pap. 1.95 (*0-939966-00-X*) Pong.

Pong, Ting-Chuen, jt. auth. see Chin, Roland T.

Pong, W. Y., et al. Wood Density-Moisture Profiles in Old-Growth Douglas-Fir & Western Hemlock. (Illus.). 36p. 1997. reprint ed. pap. 5.00 (*0-89904-697-5*, Ecosytems Resrch) Crumb Elbow Pub.

Ponge, Francis. L' Atelier Contemporain. (FRE.). 361p. 1977. pap. 59.95 (*0-7859-1595-8*, 207029630X) Fr & Eur.

— Comment une Figue de Paroles et Pourquoi. (FRE.). 213p. 1977. pap. 24.95 (*0-7859-1440-4*, 2082120023) Fr & Eur.

— La Fabrique du Pre. (FRE.). 272p. 1990. pap. 89.95 (*0-7859-1606-7*, 260500158X) Fr & Eur.

— Le Grand Recueil: Lyres, Vol. 1. (FRE.). 192p. 1987. pap. 18.95 (*0-7859-1299-1*, 2070251632) Fr & Eur.

— Lyres. (FRE.). 1980. pap. 11.95 (*0-7859-2781-6*) Fr & Eur.

— Lyres. (Poesie Ser.). (FRE.). 176p. 1980. pap. 9.95 (*2-07-032188-6*) Schoenhof.

— Methodes. (FRE.). 248p. 1988. pap. 16.95 (*0-7859-1357-2*, 2070324923) Fr & Eur.

Ponge, Francis. Methodes. (Folio Essais Ser.: No. 107). (FRE.). 1988. pap. 14.95 (*2-07-032492-3*) Schoenhof.

Ponge, Francis. The Nature of Things. Fahnestock, Lee, tr. from FRE. (French Ser.).Tr. of Parti Pris des Choses. 49p. 1995. 6.95 (*0-87376-080-8*) Red Dust.

— Nouveau Recueil. (FRE.). 240p. 1992. pap. 24.95 (*0-7859-1386-6*, 2070722880) Fr & Eur.

— Le Parti Pris des Choses. (Poesie Ser.). (FRE.). 224p. 1966. pap. 9.95 (*2-07-030223-7*) Schoenhof.

Ponge, Francis. Le Parti Pris des Choses: Douze Petits Ecrits. (FRE.). 1966. pap. 11.95 (*0-7859-2764-6*) Fr & Eur.

Ponge, Francis. Pieces. (FRE.). 1971. pap. 11.95 (*0-7859-2770-0*) Fr & Eur.

— Pieces. (Poesie Ser.). 194p. 1971. 11.95 (*2-07-031873-7*) Schoenhof.

— La Rage de l'Expression. (FRE.). 1976. pap. 14.95 (*0-7859-2780-8*) Fr & Eur.

— La Rage de l'Expression. (Poesie Ser.). (FRE.). 214p. 1976. pap. 11.95 (*2-07-032167-3*) Schoenhof.

— Le Savon. (FRE.). 140p. 1992. pap. 10.95 (*0-7859-1390-4*, 2070725537) Fr & Eur.

— Selected Poems. Williams, C. K. et al, trs. LC 93-61394. (French Poetry in Translation Ser.). 232p. 1994. 18.95 (*0-916390-59-4*); pap. 12.95 (*0-916390-58-6*) Wake Forest.

— Soap. Dunlop, Lane, tr. from FRE. LC 98-13779. (Meridian Ser.). 100p. 1998. pap. text 14.95 (*0-8047-2955-7*) Stanford U Pr.

— Tome Premier. 620p. 1965. pap. 45.00 (*0-7859-1300-9*, 2070251675) Fr & Eur.

— Vegetation. Fahnestock, Lee, tr. (French Ser.). 48p. 1987. pap. 4.00 (*0-87376-058-1*) Red Dust.

Ponge, Francis & Dunlop, Lane. Soap. LC 98-13779. (Meridian Ser.). 100p. 1998. 29.50 (*0-8047-2954-9*) Stanford U Pr.

Ponge, Francis, jt. auth. see Bly, Robert.

Ponghis, G., jt. auth. see Okun, Daniel A.

Pongo, Kodzp T. Expectation As Fulfillment: A Study in Paul Tillich's Theory of Justice. 166p. (C). 1996. lib. bdg. 36.50 (*0-7618-0227-4*) U Pr of Amer.

Pongor, Sandor, jt. ed. see Bradbury, E. Morton.

Pongratz, Gregor. Anton Weberns Variationen Fur Klavier Opus 27. (Studien und Materialien Zur Musikwissenschaft Ser.: Bd. 12). (GER.). 238p. 1997. 50.00 (*3-487-10324-9*) G Olms Pubs.

***Pongratz-Leisten, Beate.** Herrschaftswissen in Mesopotamien: Formen der Kommunikation Zwischen Gott und Konig im 2. und 1. Jahrtausend v. Chr. (State Archives of Assyria Studies: Vol. X). (GER.). xvi, 392p. 1999. pap. text 59.50 (*951-45-9041-4*, Pub. by Neo-Assyrian Text) Eisenbrauns.

***Pongraz, Christian & Perbellini, Maria Rita.** Natural Born Caadesigners: Young American Architects. (IT Revolution in Architecture Ser.). (Illus.). 96p. 2000. pap. write for info. (*3-7643-6246-4*) Birkhauser.

Pongsapich, Amara. Defining the Nonprofit Sector: Thailand. Salamon, Lester M. & Anheier, Helmut K., eds. (Working Papers of the Johns Hopkins Comparative Nonprofit Sector Project: No. 11). (Illus.). 19p. 1993. pap. text 6.00 (*1-886333-13-0*) JH Univ Inst Pol Studies.

Poniachek, Harvey A. Cases in International Finance. (Series in Finance). 656p. 1993. pap. 56.95 (*0-471-53678-4*) Wiley.

Poniachek, Harvey A., ed. International Corporate Finance. LC 88-36651. 400p. (C). (gr. 13). 1989. text 125.00 (*0-04-445394-9*) Routledge.

Poniachik, Jaime. Como Jugar y Divertirse con Su Inteligencia. LC 98-205711. (SPA., Illus.). 96p. 1998. 6.95 (*0-8069-6153-8*) Sterling.

Poniastowska, Elena. De Noche Vienes. (SPA.). pap. 14.25 (*968-411-136-3*, Pub. by Edicnes Era) Continental Bk.

— Hasta No Verte Jesus Mio. (SPA.). pap. 19.95 (*968-411-207-6*, Pub. by Edicnes Era) Continental Bk.

— Querido Diego, Te Abraza Quiela. (SPA.). pap. 12.95 (*968-411-109-6*, Pub. by Edicnes Era) Continental Bk.

— Querido Diego Te Abraza Quiela, 1. 1997. pap. text 15.29 (*968-411-214-9*) Edicnes Cast.

— Tlatelolco. (SPA.). pap. 21.95 (*968-411-220-3*, Pub. by Edicnes Era) Continental Bk.

Poniatowska, Elena. Guerrero Viejo. LC 96-79636. (ENG & SPA., Illus.). 100p. (C). 1997. 55.00 (*0-9655268-0-1*) Anchorage Pr.

***Poniatowska, Elena.** Here's to You, Jesusa! Heikkinen, Deanna, tr. from SPA.Tr. of Hasta No Verte Jesus Mio. 320p. 2001. 24.00 (*0-374-16819-9*) FS&G.

Poniatowska, Elena. Massacre in Mexico. Lane, Helen R., tr. (Illus.). 352p. (C). 1991. pap. 18.95 (*0-8262-0817-7*) U of Mo Pr.

— Mexican Color. LC 98-17169. 160p. 1998. 35.00 (*1-55670-835-1*) Stewart Tabori & Chang.

— Mexican Color. (SPA., Illus.). 160p. 1998. 35.00 (*1-55670-856-4*) Stewart Tabori & Chang.

— El Nino: Children of the Streets, Mexico City. LC 98-51520. (Illus.). 168p. 1999. 45.00 (*0-8156-0592-7*) Syracuse U Pr.

— Nothing, Nobody: The Voices of the Mexico City Earthquake. de Camacho Schimidt, Aurora & Schimidt, Arthur, trs. (Voices of Latin America Life Ser.). (Illus.). (Orig.). (C). 1995. pap. 22.95 (*1-56639-345-0*); lib. bdg. 69.95 (*1-56639-344-2*) Temple U Pr.

— Tinisima. Silver, Katherine, tr. LC 96-33810. 256p. 1996. 25.00 (*0-374-27785-0*) FS&G.

— Tinisima. Silver, Katherine, tr. from SPA. LC 96-33810. (Illus.). 353p. 1998. pap. 12.95 (*0-14-026876-6*) Viking Penguin.

Poniatowska, Elena & Stellweg, Carla. Frida Kahlo: The Camera Seduced. (Illus.). 128p. 1992. 29.95 (*0-8118-0238-8*); pap. 19.95 (*0-8118-0215-9*) Chronicle Bks.

Poniatowska, Elena, jt. auth. see Conger, Amy.

Poniatowski, Martin. HP NETServer Guide for Windows NT. LC 98-20380. (Hewlett-Packard Professional Bks.). 400p. (C). 1998. pap. text 44.99 (*0-13-989682-1*) P-H.

***Poniatowski, Martin.** Hp-ux 11.x System Administration Handbook & Toolkit. 2nd ed. LC 99-24948. 1100p. 1999. pap. text 54.00 incl. audio compact disk (*0-13-012514-8*, Prentice Hall) P-H.

Poniatowski, Martin. The HP-UX Systems Administrator's "How to" Book. LC 93-2011. (Hewlett Packard Professional Bks.). 320p. (C). 1993. pap. text 45.00 (*0-13-099821-4*) P-H.

***Poniatowski, Marty.** HP-UX 11.X System Administration "How-To" Book. 2nd ed. LC 99-461717. 848p. 1998. pap. text 49.00 (*0-13-012515-6*) P-H.

Poniatowski, Marty. HP-UX System Administration Handbook & Toolkit. LC 97-36113. 736p. (C). 1997. pap. text 49.99 incl. cd-rom (*0-13-905571-1*) P-H.

Poniatowski, Marty. HP-UX 10.X System Administration. LC 95-35659. (Hewlett-Packard Bks.). 432p. 1995. pap. 45.00 (*0-13-125873-7*) P-H.

Poniatowski, Marty. Learning the HP-UX Operating System. LC 96-18464. 336p. 1996. pap. text 34.99 (*0-13-258534-0*) P-H.

***Poniatowski, Marty.** UNIX User's Handbook. LC 00-26325. 1402p. 2000. 59.99 incl. cd-rom (*0-13-027019-9*) P-H.

Poniatowski, Marty. Windows NT & HP-UX System Administrator's "How to" Book. 1997. pap. 33.00 (*0-614-28520-8*) P-H.

— Windows NT & HP-UX System Administrator's "How to" Book. LC 97-9550. 576p. (C). 1997. pap. 52.00 (*0-13-861709-0*) P-H.

Ponichtera, Brenda J. Quick & Healthy Vol. II: More Help for People Who Say They Don't Have Time to Cook Healthy Meals. 2. LC 91-90207. (Illus.). 262p. (Orig.). 1995. pap. 16.95 (*0-9629160-1-3*) ScaleDown.

— Quick & Healthy Recipes & Ideas: For People Who Say They Don't Have Time to Cook Healthy Meals. LC 91-90207. (Illus.). 262p. (Orig.). 1991. pap. 16.95 (*0-9629160-0-5*) ScaleDown.

Ponick, Wes, jt. auth. see Pugh, Frank.

Poniewaz, Jeff. Dolphin Leaping in the Milky Way. (Illus.). 148p. 1986. reprint ed. pap. 12.95 (*0-685-44851-7*) Inland Ocean Bks.

Ponikvar, A. L., jt. ed. see Carr, D. S.

Ponit of Grace Staff, et al. Life, Love & Other Mysteries. 240p. 1997. per. 14.00 (*0-671-56249-5*) PB.

Ponjoan, Jose A. Mi Pecado Fue Quererte. LC 88-81863. (Coleccion Caniqui). (SPA.). 280p. (Orig.). 1989. pap. 15.00 (*0-89729-499-8*) Ediciones.

Ponka, P., jt. auth. see Neuwirt, J.

Ponka, Prem & Schulman. Iron Transport & Storage. LC 96-4150. (Illus.). 352p. 1990. lib. bdg. 249.00 (*0-8493-6677-1*, QP535) CRC Pr.

Ponko, Vincent, Jr. Britain in the Middle East, Nineteen Twenty-One to Nineteen Fifty-Six: An Annotated Bibliography. LC 89-2325. (Themes in European Expansion Ser.: Vol. 9). 568p. 1990. text 25.00 (*0-8240-8551-5*, 357) Garland.

Ponlisse, Nanda. The Use of Compensatory Strategies by Dutch Learners of English. (Studies on Language Acquisition). 1990. pap. 53.85 (*3-11-013110-2*) Mouton.

Ponnampalam, P. S. Another Dawn. (C). 1997. write for info. (*81-207-1503-9*); text. write for info. (*81-207-1502-0*) Sterling Pubs.

Ponnamperuma, Cyril, ed. Comets & the Origin of Life. 292p. 1981. text 121.50 (*90-277-1318-9*) Kluwer Academic.

— Cosmochemistry & the Origin of Life. 1983. text 206.50 (*90-277-1544-0*) Kluwer Academic.

Ponnamperuma, Cyril & Chela-Flores, Julian, eds. Chemical Evolution: Origin of Life. LC 93-34768. (Illus.). 336p. 1993. 50.00 (*0-937194-31-X*) A Deepak Pub.

— Chemical Evolution - the Structure & Model of the First Cell: Proceedings of the Third Trieste Conference on Chemical Evolution, the Alexander Ivanovich Oparin 100th Anniversary Conference, 29 August-September 1994. LC 95-11083. 392p. (C). 1995. lib. bdg. 230.00 (*0-7923-3562-7*) Kluwer Academic.

Ponnamperuma, Cyril & Eirich, Frederick, eds. Prebiological Self Organization of Matter: The Eighth College Park Colloquium on Chemical Evolution. LC 90-3640. (Illus.). 305p. 1990. 50.00 (*0-937194-18-2*) A Deepak Pub.

Ponnamperuma, Cyril & Gehrke, Charles W., eds. A Lunar-Based Chemical Analysis Laboratory: Proceedings of the Ninth College Colloquium on Chemical Evolution. LC 91-40702. (Illus.). 281p. 1992. 50.00 (*0-937194-25-5*) A Deepak Pub.

Ponnamperuma, Cyril & Margulis, Lynn, eds. Limits of Life. 200p. 1980. lib. bdg. 75.00 (*90-277-1155-0*) Kluwer Academic.

Ponnamperuma, Cyril N., et al. Chemical Evolution - Physics of the Origin & Evolution of Life: Proceedings of the Fourth Trieste Conference on Chemical Evolution, Trieste, Italy 4-8 September 1995. Chela-Flores, Julian, ed. LC 96-17890. 428p. (C). 1996. text 217.50 (*0-7923-4111-2*) Kluwer Academic.

Ponnusamy, S. & Victor, D. Johnson. Transportation Tunnels. (Illus.). 182p. (C). 1996. text 70.00 (*90-5410-296-9*, Pub. by A A Balkema) Ashgate Pub Co.

Ponomarenko, S. V., tr. see Samchuk, A. I. & Pilipenko, A. T.

Ponomarev, A., jt. auth. see Olshevky, V.

Ponomarev, Boris N. Communism in a Changing World. LC 82-25622. 266p. 1983. 24.95 (*0-943071-01-1*) Sphinx Pr.

— Winning for Peace: The Great Victory--Its World Impact. 136p. 1985. 40.00 (*0-7855-0966-6*) St Mut.

Ponomarev, L. I., ed. The Quantum Dice. (Illus.). 256p. 1993. 137.00 (*0-7503-0251-8*); pap. 40.00 (*0-7503-0241-0*) IOP Pub.

Ponomarev, V. I., jt. auth. see Arkangeliskii, A. V.

Ponomarev, Valerii N., jt. ed. see Ragsdale, Hugh.

***Ponomarov, Alexander.** Desperate Escape. 1999. pap. 10.99 (*0-8280-1428-0*) Review & Herald.

Ponomarov, Sergius, tr. see Chekhov, Anton.

Ponomarov, Sergius, tr. see Landes, William-Alan, ed.

Ponoroff, Lawrence, jt. auth. see Snyder, Stephen E.

Pons. Pons Fachwoerterbuch Marketing. (ENG & GER.). 1991. 75.00 (*0-8288-7269-4*, 3125179807) Fr & Eur.

— Pons Fachwoeterbuch Umwelt. (ENG & GER.). 1991. 75.00 (*0-8288-7268-6*, 3125179408) Fr & Eur.

Pons, Andrew. The Labour Relations Handbook. 272p. 1998. ring bd. 86.50 (*0-7021-2301-3*, Pub. by Juta & Co) Gaunt.

Pons, Bruno. Architecture & Panelling: The James A. de Rothschild Collection at Waddesdon Manor. (Illus.). 680p. 1996. 290.00 (*0-85667-437-0*) Sothebys Pubns.

Pons, Cathy, jt. auth. see Valdman, Albert.

P

An Asterisk (*) at the beginning of an entry indicates that the title is appearing for the first time.

Pons, Francois R. De, see De Pons, Francois R.

Pons, Frank M. The Dominican Republic: A National History. 520p. 1994. 32.00 (1-885509-00-6); pap. 22.00 (1-885509-01-4) Hispaniola Bks.

— The Dominican Republic: A National History. LC 98-19818. 544p. (C). 1998. reprint ed. text 44.95 (1-55876-191-8); reprint ed. pap. text 22.95 (1-55876-192-6) Wiener Pubs Inc.

Pons, J. M., jt. auth. see Santelli, M.

Pons, Josh. Country Life Diary: Three Years in the Life of a Horse Farm, Revised Ed. 1999. pap. text 15.95 (1-58150-019-X, Pub. by Blood-Horse) IPG Chicago.

***Pons, M.** NMR in Supramolecular Chemistry. LC 99-12333. (NATO ASI Ser.). 1999. write for info. (0-7923-5621-7) Kluwer Academic.

Pons, Marie-Noelle A., ed. Bioprocess Monitoring & Control. 365p. 1993. 120.00 (0-471-03714-1) Wiley.

Pons, Matthew A. Thru the Eyes of a Cat. (Illus.). 26p. (gr. k-3). 1999. pap. 5.95 (0-9671807-0-8) NEW START CT.

Pons, N. & Sutton, B. C. Mycological Papers No. 160: Cercospora & Similar Fungi on Yams - Dioscorea Species. (Mycological Paper Ser.: No. 160). 78p. 1989. pap. 36.00 (0-85198-622-6) C A B Intl.

***Pons, Olga, et al, eds.** Knowledge Management in Fuzzy Databases. LC 99-50039. (Studies in Fuzziness & Soft Computing). (Illus.). xiv, 384p. 2000. 90.00 (3-7908-1255-2) Spr-Verlag.

Pons, Pat & Goode, Elizabeth. Word of Mouth: Triangle Restaurant & Market Guide for 1990. (Illus.). (Orig.). 1989. pap. 8.95 (0-685-29455-2) Word Mouth NC.

Pons, Peter T. & Markovchick, V. Prehospital Emergency Care Secrets: Questions You Will Be Asked--At the Scene, in the ER, on Oral Exams. LC 97-51462. (Secrets Ser.). 1998. 34.00 (1-56053-250-5) Hanley & Belfus.

Pons, Peter T., jt. auth. see Markovchick, Vincent J.

Pons, Peter T., ed. see American College of Emergency Physicians Staff.

Pons, Stanley & Rolison, Debra R. Ultramicroelectrodes. 363p. 1987. 75.00 (0-614-04931-8) Electrosyn Co.

Pons, Valdo. Stanleyville: An African Urban Community under Belgian Administration. LC 70-396468. 384p. reprint ed. pap. 119.10 (0-8357-3222-3, 205711600010) Bks Demand.

Pons, Xavier. A Sheltered Land. 368p. 1995. pap. 29.95 (1-86373-639-5, Pub. by Allen & Unwin Pty) Paul & Co Pubs.

Ponse, Alban, et al, eds. Modal Logic & Process Algebra. (CSLI Lecture Notes Ser.). 352p. 1995. 64.95 (1-881526-95-X) CSLI.

— Modal Logic & Process Algebra: A Bisimulation Perspective. (CSLI Lecture Notes Ser.). 352p. 1995. pap. 23.95 (1-881526-96-8) CSLI.

Ponse, Alban, ed. see British Computer Society Staff.

Ponse, Alban, ed. see First Workshop on the Algebra of Communicating Pro.

Ponse, Barbara. Identities in the Lesbian World: The Social Construction of Self, 28. LC 77-84763. (Contributions in Sociology Ser.: No. 28). 228p. 1978. 38.50 (0-8371-9889-5, PLW/, Greenwood Pr) Greenwood.

Ponsen, M. B. A Histological Description of the Alimentary Tract & Related Organs of Phylloxeridae (Homoptera, Aphidoidea) LC 97-196497. (Wageningen Agricultural University Papers: No. 97.1). (Illus.). 76p. 1997. pap. 23.00 (90-73348-64-1, Pub. by Backhuys Pubs) Balogh.

Ponseti, Helena Percas De, see Percas de Ponseti, Helena.

Ponseti, Ignacio. Congenital Clubfoot: Fundamentals for Treatment. (Illus.). 150p. (C). 1996. text 125.00 (0-19-262765-1) OUP.

Ponsetto, Daniel. Walking Together: Outreach & Evangelization for Youth. Stamschror, Robert P., ed. (Illus.). 72p. 1995. pap. 14.95 (0-88489-293-X) St Marys.

Ponsky, Jeffrey L., ed. Complications of Endoscopic & Laparoscopic Surgery: Prevention & Management. LC 97-10755. 352p. 1997. text 125.00 (0-316-98927-4) Lppncott W & W.

Ponsky, Jeffrey L., jt. ed. see Greene, Frederick L.

Ponsky, Jeffrey L., jt. ed. see MacFadyen, Bruce V., Jr.

Ponsonby, Arthur. English Diaries. LC 77-175708. (Select Bibliographies Reprint Ser.). 1977. reprint ed. 26.95 (0-8369-6623-6) Ayer.

— Falsehood in Wartime: Propaganda Lies of the First World War. 2nd ed. 192p. (C). 1991. reprint ed. pap. text 6.95 (0-939484-39-0, 0339, Inst Hist Rev) Legion Survival.

— Samuel Pepys. LC 71-160987. (Select Bibliographies Reprint Ser.). 1977. reprint ed. 24.95 (0-8369-5855-1) Ayer.

Ponsonby-Fane, Richard A. Fortunes of the Emperors: Studies in Revolution, Exile, Abdication, Usurpation, & Deposition in Ancient Japan. LC 79-52920. (Studies in Japanese History & Civilization). 321p. 1979. lib. bdg. 65.00 (0-313-27025-2, U7025) Greenwood.

— Imperial Cities: The Capitals of Japan from the Oldest Times Until 1229. LC 79-52921. (Studies in Japanese History & Civilization). 239p. 1979. lib. bdg. 62.50 (0-313-27032-5, U7032, Greenwood Pr) Greenwood.

***Ponsonby, Spud Talbot.** Small Steps with Heavy Hooves. large type unabridged ed. 239p. 1999. 25.95 (0-7531-5207-X, 15207X, Pub. by ISIS Lrg Prnt) ISIS Pub.

Ponsot, Marie. The Bird Catcher. LC 97-50402. 91p. 1998. 22.00 (0-375-40135-0) Knopf.

— The Bird Catcher: Poems. 104p. 1999. pap. 15.00 (0-375-70132-X) Knopf.

Ponsot, Marie & Deen, Rosemary. Beat Not the Poor Desk: Writing: What to Teach, How to Teach It & Why. LC 81-15519. 212p. (Orig.). (C). 1981. pap. text 22.00 (0-86709-009-X, 0009, Pub. by Boynton Cook Pubs) Heinemann.

— The Common Sense: What to Write, How to Write It & Why. LC 85-4126. 166p. (Orig.). (C). 1985. pap. text 19.00 (0-86709-079-0, 0079, Pub. by Boynton Cook Pubs) Heinemann.

Ponstein, Jacob. Approaches to the Theory of Optimization. LC 79-41419. (Cambridge Tracts in Mathematics Ser.: No. 77). 217p. reprint ed. pap. 61.90 (0-8357-5697-1, 2031711) Bks Demand.

— Convexity & Duality in Optimization. (Lecture Notes in Economics & Mathematical Systems Ser.: Vol. 256). v, 142p. 1985. 39.50 (0-387-15986-X) Spr-Verlag.

Pont, Adrian C. The Type-Material of Diptera (Insecta) Described by G. H. Verrall & J. E. Collin. (Illus.). 232p. 1995. text 200.00 (0-19-854919-9) OUP.

Pont, Diana C. Du, see Du Pont, Diana C.

Pont, Gillian, jt. auth. see Pont, Tony.

Pont, Gino D. Lawyers' Professional Responsibility in Australia & New Zealand. LC 97-179426. 524p. 1996. pap. 85.00 (0-455-21441-7, Pub. by LawBk Co) Gaunt.

Pont, Gino D. & Chalmers, Don. Equity & Trusts in Australia & New Zealand with Flowchart Booklet. 880p. 1995. pap. 96.00 (0-455-21346-1, Pub. by LawBk Co) Gaunt.

Pont, Gino D., et al. Equity & Trusts: Commentary & Materials. 1064p. 1997. pap. 110.00 (0-455-21455-7, 14603, Pub. by LawBk Co) Gaunt.

Pont, Henry F. Du, see Sweeney, John A. & Du Pont, Henry F.

Pont, J. J. De, see De Pont, J. J., ed.

Pont, M. Kay du, see Du Pont, M. Kay.

Pont, Michael. Integrated Software for Engineering. (C). 1999. pap. text. write for info. (0-201-33138-1) Addison-Wesley.

— Software Engineering with C++ & Case Tools. 1996. pap. 42.19 incl. disk (0-201-87718-X) Addison-Wesley.

Pont Quer, Pio. Diccionario de Botanica. (SPA.). 1244p. 1977. 59.95 (0-8288-5313-4, S50066) Fr & Eur.

— Diccionario de Botanica: Dictionary of Botany.Tr. of Dictionary of Botany. (SPA.). 256p. 1973. 29.95 (0-7859-0888-9, S-50258) Fr & Eur.

***Pont, Sally.** Finding Their Stride: A Team of Young Runners & Their Season of Triumph. (Illus.). 240p. 2000. pap. text 13.00 (0-15-601182-4) Harcourt.

— Finding Their Stride: A Team of Young Runners Races to the Finish. LC 98-50205. 240p. 1999. 23.00 (0-15-100347-5, Harvest Bks) Harcourt.

Pont, Timothy. Topographical Account of the District of Cunningham, Ayrshire. LC 74-174280. (Maitland Club, Glasgow. Publications: No. 74). reprint ed. 37.50 (0-404-53112-1) AMS Pr.

***Pont, Tony.** Developing Effective Training Skills: A Practical Guide to Designing & Delivering Group Training. 2nd ed. Bennett, Roger, ed. (Illus.). 157p. 1999. reprint ed. pap. text 25.00 (0-7881-6311-6) DIANE Pub.

— Investing in Training & Development. 256p. 1995. text 59.95 (0-7494-1524-X, Kogan Pg Educ) Stylus Pub VA.

Pont, Tony & Pont, Gillian. Interviewing Skills for Managers. 1999. pap. 14.95 (0-7499-1882-9, Pub. by Piatkus Bks) London Brdge.

Pontac. Bump in the Night. 1995. 8.98 (1-57042-225-7) Warner Bks.

Pontalis, Jean-Baptiste. Vocabulaire de la Psychanalyse. 5th ed. Laplanche, Jean, ed. (FRE.). 1976. 85.00 (0-8288-5759-8, M6558) Fr & Eur.

Pontalis, Jean-Baptiste & Laplanche, Jean. Vocabulary of Psychoanalysis (Vocabulaire de la Psychanalyse) 10th ed. (FRE.). 544p. 1990. 105.00 (0-7859-4741-8, M14530) Fr & Eur.

Pontalis, Jean-Baptiste, jt. auth. see Laplanche, Jean.

Pontalis, Jean-Bertrand, jt. auth. see Laplanche, Jean.

***Pontbon, Marcel O. & Leon-Carribon, Jose.** Neuropsychology & the Hispanic Patient: A Clinical Handbook. LC 00-42221. 2000. write for info. (0-8058-2615-7) L Erlbaum Assocs.

Ponte. Handbook of Anesthetics & Perioper. (Illus.). 412p. 1994. pap. text 30.50 (0-7020-1689-6, W B Saunders Co) Harcrt Hlth Sci Grp.

Ponte, Alfred M. Realistic Duck Carving: A Step-by-Step Illustrated Manual. 2nd ed. (Illus.). 54p. 1997. pap. 9.95 (1-56523-086-8) Fox Chapel Pub.

***Ponte, Antonio Jose.** In the Cold of the Malecon: And Other Stories. Fravizen, Cola & Cluster, Dick, trs. 136p. 2000. pap. 10.95 (0-87286-374-3, Pub. by City Lights) Subterranean Co.

Ponte, Carol A. Free Form Chip Carving: 35 New Designs. (Illus.). 39p. 1996. pap. 7.95 (1-56523-080-9) Fox Chapel Pub.

Ponte, J. P., et al, eds. Mathematical Problem Solving & New Information Technologies: Research in Contexts of Practice. (NATO ASI Series F: Computer & Systems Science: Vol. 89). xv, 346p. 1992. 98.95 (0-387-55735-0) Spr-Verlag.

Ponte, Lucille M. & Cavenagh, Thomas D. Alternative Dispute Resolution in Business. LC 98-20396. 1998. pap. 75.95 (0-324-00071-5) Thomson Learn.

Pontecorvo. Discourse. (CI Ser.: Vol. 11, Nos. 3-4). 1994. 40.00 (0-8058-9973-1) L Erlbaum Assocs.

Pontecorvo, Clotilde, ed. Writing Development: An Interdisciplinary View. LC 97-40728. (Studies in Written Language & Literacy: Vol. 6). xxxii, 338p. 1997. lib. bdg. 69.00 (1-55619-324-6) J Benjamins Pubng Co.

Pontecorvo, Clotilde, et al, eds. Children's Early Text Construction. 384p. 1996. text 79.95 (0-8058-1504-X) L Erlbaum Assocs.

Pontecorvo, G., tr. see Balashov, V.

Pontecorvo, G. B., tr. see Ignatovich, V. K.

Pontecorvo, Giulio, ed. The Management of Food Policy. LC 75-33468. (Individual Publications). (Illus.). 1980. lib. bdg. 17.95 (0-405-06680-5) Ayer.

— The New Order of the Oceans: The Advent of a Managed Environment. LC 86-6804. 240p. 1986. text 61.50 (0-231-05870-5) Col U Pr.

Pontécorvo, Giulio, jt. auth. see Crutchfield, James A.

Ponteilhet, Hubert. Les Paves du Diable. (FRE.). 1972. pap. 8.95 (0-7859-3991-1) Fr & Eur.

Pontell, Henry N. Social Deviance: Readings in Theory & Research. 3rd ed. LC 98-10671. 447p. 1998. pap. text 35.40 (0-13-674714-0) P-H.

Pontell, Henry N., jt. auth. see Rosoff, Stephen M.

Pontelli, John P. & Reed, Ronald, eds. Children, Philosophy, & Democracy. 262p. (Orig.). 1995. pap. text. write for info. (1-55059-115-0) Detselig Ents.

Ponten, J., ed. Precancer: Biology, Importance & Possible Prevention. (Cancer Surveys Ser.: No. 32). (Illus.). 238p. (C). 1998. text 93.00 (0-87969-540-4) Cold Spring Harbor.

Ponter, Anthony & Ponter, Laura. Spirits in Stone: The New Face of African Art. rev. ed. (Illus.). 216p. 1997. reprint ed. 39.95 (1-881407-50-0) Ukama Pr.

Ponter, Laura, jt. auth. see Ponter, Anthony.

Pontercorvo, G., tr. see Klimontovich, Yu. L.

Ponterotto, Joseph G., et al, eds. Affirmative Action on Campus. LC 85-644751. (New Directions for Student Services Ser.: No. SS 52). 1991. pap. 22.00 (1-55542-816-9) Jossey-Bass.

Ponterotto, Joseph G. & Casas, J. Manuel. Handbook of Racial-Ethnic Minority Counseling Research. 208p. 1991. pap. 29.95 (0-398-06329-X) C C Thomas.

— Handbook of Racial-Ethnic Minority Counseling Research. 208p. (C). 1991. text 41.95 (0-398-05716-8) C C Thomas.

Ponterotto, Joseph G. & Pedersen, Paul B. Preventing Prejudice: A Guide for Counselors & Educators. (Multicultural Aspects of Counseling Ser.: Vol. 2). (Illus.). 238p. 1993. 42.00 (0-8039-5284-8); pap. 18.95 (0-8039-5285-6) Sage.

Ponterotto, Joseph G., et al. Handbook of Multicultural Counseling. LC 95-12874. (Illus.). 679p. 1995. 89.95 (0-8039-5506-5); pap. 38.00 (0-8039-5507-3) Sage.

Ponterotto, Joseph G., jt. auth. see Kulp, Karel.

Pontes, Edison J. Surgery of Genitourinary Pelvic Tumors: An Anatomic Atlas. 136p. 1993. 175.00 (0-471-58831-8) Wiley.

Pontes, M. De, see De Pontes, M.

Ponteva, E., jt. auth. see Pesonen, Niilo.

Pontfarcy, Y. De, see Picard, J. M. & De Pontfarcy, Y.

Pontfarcy, Y. De, see Picard, Jean-Michel & De Pontfarcy, Y.

Pontgibaud, Chevalier De, see De Pontgibaud, Chevalier.

Ponthier, Gayle. Love, Passion & Tears. 1159p. write for info. (0-9658038-0-5) G Ponthier.

— Love, Passion & Tears. Mars, Geneva et al, eds. LC 98-88599. (Illus.). 352p. 1999. pap. 14.95 (1-888224-04-5) Prestige LA.

Ponti. WNBA: Stars of Women's Basketball. (YA). 1999. mass mkt. 4.99 (0-671-03275-5) PB.

***Ponti, James.** Election Connection. (Journey of Allen Strange Ser.: No. 7). (J). (gr. 3-6). 1999. pap. 3.99 (0-671-02514-7) PB.

Ponti, James. Friends in Need. (Mystery Files of Shelby Woo Ser.: No. 14). 144p. (J). (gr. 4-7). 1999. pap. 3.99 (0-671-03465-0, Pocket Books) PB.

— Green Monster. (Mystery Files of Shelby Woo Ser.: No. 12). (J). (gr. 4-6). 1999. pap. 3.99 (0-671-02696-8) PB.

— History Mystery. (Mystery Files of Shelby Woo Ser.: No. 9). 144p. (J). (gr. 4-7). 1998. pap. 3.99 (0-671-02009-9) PB.

Ponti, Marco. Transport Networks, Vol. II-11. (Single Market Review Ser.). 1998. 80.00 (0-7494-2323-4) Kogan Page Ltd.

Ponticelli, C., et al, eds. Antiglobulins, Cryoglobulins & Glomerulonephritis. (Development in Nephrology Ser.). 1986. lib. bdg. 188.00 (0-89838-810-4) Kluwer Academic.

Ponticelli, C. & De Vecchi, A., eds. Ciclosporin in Renal Transplantation. (Contributions to Nephrology Ser.: Vol. 51). (Illus.). viii, 168p. 1987. 29.75 (3-8055-4357-3) S Karger.

Ponticelli, Christy M., ed. Gateways to Improving Lesbian Health & Health Care: Opening Doors. LC 97-30299. 114p. 1997. pap. 14.95 (1-56023-103-3, Harrington Park) Haworth Pr.

Ponticelli, Christy M., ed. Gateways to Improving Lesbian Health & Health Care: Opening Doors. LC 97-30299. 114p. 1997. 29.95 (0-7890-0350-3, Harrington Park) Haworth Pr.

Ponticelli, Claudion & Glassock, Richard J. Treatment of Primary Glomerulonephritis. (Oxford Clinical Nephrology Ser.). (Illus.). 270p. 1997. text 115.00 (0-19-262666-3) OUP.

Ponticelli, Rick, jt. auth. see Slater, Jeffrey.

Pontiero, G. An Anthology of Brazilian Modernist Poetry. 1969. 119.00 (0-08-013327-4, Pub. by Pergamon Repr) Franklin.

Pontiero, Giovanni. Florencio Sanchez: La Gringa & Barranca Abajo. LC 72-6355. 150p. 1973. 28.50 (0-8386-1264-4) Fairleigh Dickinson.

— The Translator's Dialogue: Giovanni Pontiero. Orero, Pilar & Sager, Juan C., eds. LC 97-35014. (Benjamins Translation Library: Vol. 24). xiv, 252p. 1997. lib. bdg. 67.00 (1-55619-708-X) J Benjamins Pubng Co.

Pontiero, Giovanni, ed. Duse on Tour: Guido Noccioli's Diaries, 1906-1907. LC 82-4751. (Illus.). 192p. 1982. lib. bdg. 32.00 (0-87023-369-6) U of Mass Pr.

Pontiero, Giovanni, ed. see Garcia Marquez, Gabriel.

Pontiero, Giovanni, tr. see Lispector, Clarice.

Pontiero, Giovanni, tr. see Luft, Lya.

Pontiero, Giovanni, tr. see Nunes, Lygia B.

Pontiero, Giovanni, tr. see Saramago, Jose.

Pontiero, Giovanni, tr. & afterword by see Lispector, Clarice.

Pontiero, Giovanni, tr. & afterword by see Saramago, Jose.

Pontifcal Council for Pastoral Assistance to Health. Charter for Health Care Workers. 142p. pap. 3.95 (0-8198-1538-1) Pauline Bks.

Pontifex, Zsu Z. Hungarian: A Complete Course for Beginners. (Teach Yourself Ser.). (HUN., Illus.). 320p. 1994. pap. 16.95 (0-8442-3796-5, Teach Yrslf) NTC Contemp Pub Co.

— Teach Yourrself Hungarian Complete Course. (Teach Yourself Ser.). (HUN.). 320p. 1994. pap. 27.95 incl. audio (0-8442-3864-3, Teach Yrslf) NTC Contemp Pub Co.

— Teach Yourself Hungarian. (ENG & HUN.). 1993. pap. 18.95 (0-7859-1056-5, 0-340-562862); pap. 29.95 incl. audio (0-7859-1057-3, 0-340-562889) Fr & Eur.

Pontifical Biblical Commission. The Interpretation of the Bible in the Church. 135p. pap. 4.95 (0-8198-3670-2) Pauline Bks.

Pontifical Commission for Justice & Peace. The Church & Racism. 52p. pap. 1.75 (0-8198-1490-3) Pauline Bks.

Pontifical Council for Interreligious Dialogue Sta & Bormans, Maurice. Guidelines for Dialogue Between Christians & Muslims. (Interreligious Documents Ser.: Vol. I). 1990. pap. 12.95 (0-8091-3181-1) Paulist Pr.

Pontifical Council for Promoting Christian Unity S. Directory for the Application of the Principles & Norms of Ecumenism. 125p. pap. 3.25 (0-8198-1868-2) Pauline Bks.

Pontifical Council for Social Communications Staff. New Era. 48p. 1992. pap. 4.95 (1-55586-504-6) US Catholic.

— Pastoral Instruction on the Means of Social Communication: Communio et Progressio. 77p. pap. 0.50 (0-8198-4749-6) Pauline Bks.

Pontifical Council for the Family Staff. The Truth & Meaning of Human Sexuality: Guidelines for Education Within the Family. 96p. 1996. pap. 3.50 (0-8198-7390-X) Pauline Bks.

— The Truth & Meaning of Human Sexuality: Guidelines for Education Within the Family. 60p. (C). 1996. pap. 4.95 (1-57455-090-X) US Catholic.

Pontifical Council for the Family Staff, ed. Marriage & Family: Experiencing the Church's Teaching in Married Life. LC 88-81273. 175p. (Orig.). 1989. pap. 9.95 (0-89870-218-6) Ignatius Pr.

Pontifical Institute of Medieval Studies, Toronto. Dictionary Catalog of the Pontifical Institute of Medieval Studies. 1980. 635.00 (0-8161-1257-6, G K Hall & Co) Mac Lib Ref.

— Dictionary Catalogue of the Library of the Pontifical Institute of Medieval Studies, Supplement 1. 1979. suppl. ed. 175.00 (0-8161-1528-1, G K Hall & Co) Mac Lib Ref.

Pontifical Justice & Peace Commission Staff. What Have You Done to Your Homeless Brother? The Church & the Housing Problem. 30p. (Orig.). 1987. pap. 1.95 (1-55586-203-9) US Catholic.

***Pontiggia, Elena.** Shafik. 2000. pap. 15.00 (88-8158-243-0) Charta.

Pontiggia, Giuseppe. The Invisible Player. Cancogni, Annapaola, tr. from ITA. LC 88-80809. 224p. 1989. pap. 14.00 (0-941419-15-0, Eridanos Library) Marsilio Pubs.

Pontikis, Vassilis, jt. ed. see Meyer, Madeleine.

Pontin, Jolyon, jt. auth. see East, Roger.

Pontin, R. M., jt. ed. see Ejsmont-Karabin, J.

Pontin, Rosalind M. A Key to the Freshwater Planktonic & Semi-Planktonic Rotifera of the British Isles. 1978. 60.00 (0-900386-33-9) St Mut.

Ponting, Clive. A Green History of the World: The Environment & the Collapse of Great Civilizations. 448p. 1993. pap. 14.95 (0-14-017660-8, Penguin Bks) Viking Penguin.

— 1940: Myth & Reality. 272p. 1991. text 24.95 (0-929587-68-5) I R Dee.

— 1940: Myth & Reality. LC 93-11244. 276p. 1993. reprint ed. pap. 14.95 (1-56663-036-3, Elephant Paperbacks) I R Dee.

— The Right to Know: The Inside Story of the Belgrano Affair. 1985. 25.00 (0-7855-1467-8, Pub. by NCCL) St Mut.

— The Twentieth Century: A World History. LC 98-37613. 592p. 1999. 35.00 (0-8050-6088-X) H Holt & Co.

Ponting, K.M. Computational Models of Speech Pattern Processing. LC 98-55123. (NATO ASI Ser.). xxix, 446p. 1999. 129.00 (3-540-65478-X) Spr-Verlag.

Pontious, Alfred E. Feed My Sheep. 26p. pap. text 1.95 (0-940227-01-0) Liberation FL.

Pontis, Paul R. The Real Christmas Story. LC 93-74121. 1994. pap. 7.95 (1-55673-857-9, Fairway Pr) CSS OH.

Pontius, Frederick W. SDWA Advisor: Regulatory Update Service. annuals LC 94-220153. (Illus.). ring bd. 225.00 (0-89867-736-X, 74000) Am Water Wks Assn.

— SDWA Advisor: Regulatory Update Service. annuals (Illus.). 1997. cd-rom 595.00 (0-614-10248-0, SDWACD) Am Water Wks Assn.

Pontius, John. Following the Light of Christ into His Presence. 19.95 (1-55517-358-6) CFI Dist.

— Spirit of Fire - Millennial Quest. 17.95 (1-55517-385-3) CFI Dist.

Pontius, John & Yakub, Yahya. Field Training Through Case Studies. (Technical Notes Ser.: No. 16). 21p. (Orig.). 1981. pap. 2.00 (0-932288-61-8) Ctr Intl Ed U of MA.

Pontius, John M. Following the Light of Christ Into His Presence. 3rd ed. 1998. 19.95 (1-55517-359-4) CFI Dist.

Ponton, Connie, ed. Alaska Fish & Game Laws & Regulations Annotated: 1998-99 Edition. annot. ed. 960p. 1998. write for info. (0-327-06109-X, 20345-11) LEXIS Pub.

P

An Asterisk (*) at the beginning of an entry indicates that the title is appearing for the first time.

— Virginia Corporation Law: 1998 Cumulative Supplement. 76p. 1998. suppl. ed. write for info. (*0-327-06148-0*, 35490-13) LEXIS Pub.

— Virginia Freedom of Information Act, Virginia Conflict of Interest Acts; Virginia Public Procurement Act: 1998 Edition. 163p. 1998. write for info. (*0-327-06108-1*, 34437-12) LEXIS Pub.

Ponton, Consuelo G., ed. Virginia Election Laws: 1998 Edition. 263p. 1998. write for info. (*0-327-06102-2*, 34405-15); pap. write for info. (*0-327-06101-4*, 34402-15) LEXIS Pub.

Ponton, Geoffrey. The Soviet Era: From Lenin to Yeltsin. LC 93-14804. 320p. 1994. 65.95 (*0-631-18775-8*); pap. 32.95 (*0-631-18776-6*) Blackwell Pubs.

Ponton, Geoffrey, et al. Introduction to Politics. 3rd ed. LC 92-39485. 1993. pap. 32.95 (*0-631-18784-7*) Blackwell Pubs.

Ponton, Lynn E. Romance of Risk: Why Teenagers Do the Things They Do. 320p. 1998. pap. 14.00 (*0-465-07076-0*, Pub. by Basic) HarpC.

***Ponton, Lynn E.** The Sex Lives of Teenagers: Revealing the Secret World of Adolescent Boys & Girls. 352p. 2000. 24.95 (*0-525-94561-X*) NAL.

Pontonne, S., ed. Gun Control Issues. 237p. (C). 1996. lib. bdg. 95.00 (*1-56072-406-4*) Nova Sci Pubs.

***Pontow, Regina.** Proven Resumes: Strategies That Increase Your Salary & Change Your Life! LC 99-30493. 320p. 1999. 19.95 (*1-58008-080-4*) Ten Speed Pr.

Pontow, Regina. Proven Resumes & Confidence Builders. LC 93-74727. (Orig.). 1994. pap. 19.95 (*1-884668-00-3*) Abrams & Smith.

— Proven Resumes & Confidence Builders: A Complete Job Search Program. LC 96-168729. 300p. 1994. pap. 19.95 (*1-884668-05-4*) Abrams & Smith.

Pontrkilagin, L. S. Foundations of Combinatorial Topology. LC 98-43890. 1999. pap. text 6.95 (*0-486-40685-7*) Dover.

Pontryagin, Lev S. Learning Higher Mathematics. (Soviet Mathematics Ser.). (Illus.). 320p. 1984. 82.95 (*0-387-12351-2*) Spr-Verlag.

Pontryagin, Lev S., ed. Optimal Control & Differential Games. LC 90-42913. (Proceedings of the Steklov Institute of Mathematics Ser.: Vol. 185). 278p. 1990. pap. 138.00 (*0-8218-3134-8*, STEKLO/185) Am Math.

— Theory of Functions & Its Applications. LC 77-10017. (Proceedings of the Steklov Institute of Mathematics Ser.: No. 134). 458p. 1977. pap. 112.00 (*0-8218-3034-1*, STEKLO/134) Am Math.

Pontryagin, Lev S. & Boltyanskii, V. Mathematical Theory of Optimal Processes. LC 63-15354. 1964. 154.00 (*0-08-010176-3*, Pub. by Pergamon Repr) Franklin.

Pontryagin, Lev S. & Kacinskas, L. Ordinary Differential Equations. LC 62-17075. 1962. 142.00 (*0-08-009699-9*, Pub. by Pergamon Repr) Franklin.

Pontryagin, Lev S. & O'Shea, Donal. General Topology Vol. 1: Basic Concepts & Constructions, Dimension Theory. (Encyclopedia of Mathematical Sciences Ser.: Vol. 17). (Illus.). 232p. 1990. 118.95 (*0-387-18178-4*) Spr-Verlag.

Pontryagin, Lev S. & Ostianu, N. M., eds. Geometry I: Basic Ideas & Concepts of Differential Geometry. (Encyclopedia of Mathematical Sciences Ser.: Vol. 28). (Illus.). viii, 256p. 1991. 103.95 (*0-387-51999-8*) Spr-Verlag.

***Pontti, John & Luostari, Kenneth.** Midwest Skiing: A Glance Back. (Images of America Ser.). (Illus.). 128p. 2000. pap. 18.99 (*0-7385-0124-7*) Arcadia Publng.

Ponturo, Don, jt. auth. see Nichols, David.

Pontus. Life of St. Cyprian. 1987. pap. 2.50 (*0-89981-046-2*) Eastern Orthodox.

Pontus, Hulten. The Monotypes of Sam Francis. (Illus.). 350p. 1994. 500.00 (*3-87135-013-3*, Pub. by Daco-Verlag) U of Wash Pr.

Pontuso, James F. Solzhenitsyn's Political Thought. LC 90-34241. 284p. 1990. reprint ed. pap. 88.10 (*0-608-04239-0*, 206499500012) Bks Demand.

Pontusson, Jonas. The Limits of Social Democracy: Investment Politics in Sweden. LC 92-2694. (Cornell Studies in Political Economy). (Illus.). 272p. 1992. text 39.95 (*0-8014-2652-9*) Cornell U Pr.

— The Limits of Social Democracy: Investment Politics in Sweden. LC 92-2694. (Studies in Political Economy). (Illus.). 272p. 1994. pap. text 17.95 (*0-8014-8235-6*) Cornell U Pr.

Pontusson, Jonas, jt. ed. see Golden, Miriam.

Ponwall, David. Nijinsky - Death of a Faun. (Oberon Bks.). 72p. 1997. pap. 12.95 (*1-84002-000-8*) Theatre Comm.

Ponxin, jt. auth. see Jongrong, Wu.

Pony Boy, GaWaNi. Horse, Follow Closely. LC 97-38660. (Illus.). 144p. 1998. 39.95 (*1-889540-22-6*) Bowtie Press.

— Out of the Saddle: Native American Horsemanship. LC 98-36080. (Illus.). 96p. (J). (gr. 3-6). 1998. 17.95 (*1-889540-37-4*) Bowtie Press.

— Time Well Spent: A Journal. (Illus.). 208p. 1999. 19.95 (*1-889540-42-0*) Bowtie Press.

Pony Club Staff. Correct Dress for Riding. (C). 1990. pap. 30.00 (*0-900226-30-7*, Pub. by J A Allen) St Mut.

— The Foot & Showing. 71p. (C). 1990. 35.00 (*0-900226-31-5*, Pub. by J A Allen) St Mut.

— The Instructor's Handbook. 140p. (C). 1990. 40.00 (*0-900226-40-4*, Pub. by J A Allen) St Mut.

— Keeping a Pony at Grass. 96p. (C). 1990. 30.00 (*0-900226-71-4*, Pub. by J A Allen) St Mut.

— The Pony Club Quiz Book. 112p. (C). 1990. pap. 21.00 (*0-900226-29-3*, Pub. by J A Allen) St Mut.

***Ponych, M.** Lawrence & Holloman. LC 99-174858. 128p. 1999. pap. 11.95 (*0-88922-392-0*) Talonbks.

Ponza, Michael & Pfleiderer, Joanne. Elderly Nutrition Program Evaluation Vol. I: Draft Final Report: Evalution Finding. (Illus.). 466p. 1996. reprint ed. pap. text 45.00 (*0-7881-3352-7*) DIANE Pub.

Ponzek, Debra & Schwartz, Joan. French Food, American Accent: Debra Ponzek's Spirited Cuisine. 1996. 30.00 (*0-614-95785-0*) Crown Bks Yng Read.

***Ponzek, Debra & Schwarz, Joan.** French Food - American Accent: Debra Ponzek's Spirited Cuisine. 271p. 1999. reprint ed. text 27.00 (*0-7881-6566-6*) DIANE Pub.

Ponzer, Mildred, jt. auth. see Frank, Catherine M.

***Ponzer, Mildred S. & Frank, Catherine M.** Manufacturing Job Shops. (Industry-at-a-Glance Ser.). 90p. 1999. pap. write for info. (*0-9679123-0-X*) Univ of MO-Rolla.

Ponzetti, James J., Jr., jt. auth. see Levinson, David.

Ponzetto, Pietro, jt. auth. see Bellin, Robert.

Ponzio, Augusto. Man As Sign: Essays on the Philosophy of Language. (Approaches to Semiotics Ser.: No. 89). xii, 412p. (C). 1990. lib. bdg. 129.25 (*3-11-012167-0*) Mouton.

— Signs, Dialogue & Ideology: Interdisciplinary Approaches to Language, Discourse & Ideology. Petrilli, Susan, ed. & tr. by. LC 93-33214. (Critical Theory Ser.: No. 11). xvii, 185p. 1993. 65.00 (*1-55619-179-0*) J Benjamins Pubng Co.

Ponzio, Richard & Fisher, Charles. The Joy of Sciencing: A Hands-On Approach to Developing Science Literacy & Teen Leadership Through Cross-Age Teaching & Community Action. 112p. 1998. pap. 19.95 (*1-880192-24-1*) Caddo Gap Pr.

Ponzo, Peter J. Whither Willow. 205p. mass mkt. 4.99 (*1-896329-94-2*) Picasso Publ.

***Ponzol, Dan.** Lionel: A Century of Classic Toy Trains. (Illus.). 160p. 2000. 35.00 (*1-56799-966-2*, Friedman-Fairfax) M Friedman Pub Grp Inc.

Poo, Gee S., ed. Towards Network Globalization. 500p. (C). 1991. text 118.00 (*981-02-0796-4*) World Scientific Pub.

Poo, Gee S., jt. auth. see Beauchamp, Kenneth G.

Poo, Mu-Chou. In Search of Personal Welfare: A View of Ancient Chinese Religion. LC 97-19197. (Series in Chinese Philosophy & Culture). (Illus.). 288p. (C). 1998. text 65.50 (*0-7914-3629-2*); pap. text 21.95 (*0-7914-3630-6*) State U NY Pr.

Poo, Mu-chou. Wine & Wine Offering in the Religion of Ancient Egypt. LC 95-6571. (Studies in Egyptology). 1995. write for info. (*0-7103-0501-X*) Routledge.

Pooch, Heinz. Fachwoerterbuch des Nachrichtenwesens: Technical Dictionary of Communications. 2nd ed. (ENG & GER.). 377p. 1980. 75.00 (*0-8288-0183-5*, M7390) Fr & Eur.

Pooch, Udo W. & Marti, Willis F. Modern Networking Handbook. 2001. 89.95 (*0-8493-2591-9*) CRC Pr.

Pooch, Udo W. & Wall, James A. Discrete Event Simulation: A Practical Approach. 432p. 1992. boxed set 99.95 (*0-8493-7174-0*, QA) CRC Pr.

Pooch, Udo W., et al. Telecommunications & Networking. (Illus.). 400p. 1991. lib. bdg. 79.95 (*0-8493-7172-4*, T) CRC Pr.

Pood & Jagota, S. P. Maritime Boundary. 1985. lib. bdg. 153.00 (*90-247-3133-X*, Pub. by M Nijhoff) Kluwer Academic.

***Pook, L. P.** Linear Elastic Fracture Mechanics for Engineers: Theory & Applications. 176p. (C). 2000. text 95.00 (*1-85312-703-5*, 7035) Computational Mech MA.

Pook, P. L. The Role of Crack Growth in Metal Fatigue. 157p. (Orig.). 1983. pap. text 31.50 (*0-904357-63-5*, Pub. by Inst Materials) Ashgate Pub Co.

Pook, R., tr. see Hantelmann, F.

***Pookrum, Jewel.** Vitamins & Minerals from A to Z. 3rd rev. ed. (Ethno-Conscious Ser.). 160p. 1999. pap. 10.95 (*1-886433-10-0*) A&B Bks.

***Pool, Anna, et al.** Coaching Effectiveness Survey - User's Guide. (Illus.). 15p. 1999. pap. write for info. (*1-57740-042-9*, ILW329) Intl LrningWrk.

Pool, Anna, et al. Dimensions of Coaching: Facilitator Guide. (Illus.). 53p. 1998. spiral bd. write for info. (*1-57740-069-0*, ILW176) Intl LrningWrk.

— Dimensions of Coaching: Training Package. (Illus.). 1998. spiral bd. 645.00 (*1-57740-038-0*, ILW175) Intl LrningWrk.

— Effective Coaching. (Illus.). 71p. 1998. pap. 14.95 (*1-57740-070-4*, ILW121) Intl LrningWrk.

Pool, Charles L. Vander, see Vander Pool, Charles L.

Pool, Clifford W. The California Homeowner's Guidebook: How to Deal with Home Alteration Contractors. F'Mayer, Keith I., ed. 106p. (Orig.). 1992. pap. 19.95 (*0-9635362-1-4*, TX3 401 617) Courier Pub.

Pool, Daniel. Christmas in New York. LC 97-24779. (Illus.). 160p. 1997. 17.95 (*1-888363-55-X*) Seven Stories.

— Dickens' Fur Coat & Charlotte's Unanswered Letters: The Rows & Romances of England's Great Victorian Couple. LC 96-32521. (Illus.). 304p. 1998. pap. 14.00 (*0-06-098435-X*, Perennial) HarperTrade.

***Pool, Daniel.** Dickens' Fur Coat & Charlotte's Unanswered Letters: The Rows & Romances of England's Great Victorian Novelists. (Illus.). 282p. 2000. reprint ed. pap. 20.00 (*0-7881-9314-7*) DIANE Pub.

Pool, Daniel. What Jane Austen Ate & Charles Dickens Knew: From Fox Hunting to Whits-The Facts of Daily Life in Nineteenth-Century England. 416p. 1994. per. 14.00 (*0-671-88236-8*) S&S Trade Pap.

Pool, David. Hobbyist Guide to Successful Koi Keeping. (Aquarium Digest International - Collector's Edition Ser.). (Illus.). 1992. 12.95 (*3-89356-134-X*, 16583) Tetra Pr.

— Hobbyist Guide to Successful Pond Keeping. (Illus.). 144p. 1994. 12.95 (*3-89356-135-8*, 16584) Tetra Pr.

Pool, David, jt. auth. see Loiselle, Paul V.

Pool, Elizabeth. The Unicorn Was There. LC 81-4747. (Illus.). 64p. 1981. reprint ed. pap. 8.95 (*0-87233-061-3*) Bauhan.

Pool, Gail, ed. Other People's Mail: An Anthology of Letter Stories. LC 99-49609. 286p. 2000. pap. 16.95 (*0-8262-1246-8*) U of Mo Pr.

Pool, Gary. The Bread of Wickedness. LC 95-83658. 198p. 1996. pap. 12.95 (*1-885487-20-7*) Brownell & Carroll.

Pool, Gary, ed. see Murray, Rhea.

Pool, Harbison & Page, Jane A., eds. Beyond Tracking. 293p. 1995. 35.00 (*0-87367-470-7*) Phi Delta Kappa.

Pool, Ithiel de Sola. Technologies of Freedom. 312p. 1984. pap. 17.50 (*0-674-87233-9*) Belknap Pr.

Pool, Ithiel De Sola, see De Sola Pool, Ithiel.

Pool, Ithiel De Sola, see Schramm, Wilbur L. & De Sola Pool, Ithiel.

Pool, Ithiel De Sola, see De Sola Pool, Ithiel.

Pool, J. C., ed. Mathematical Aspects of Statistical Mechanics: Proceedings of the SIAM-AMS Symposia, New York, April, 1971. LC 72-321. (SIAM-AMS Proceedings Ser.: Vol. 5). 89p. 1972. text 33.00 (*0-8218-1324-2*, SIAMS/5) Am Math.

***Pool, Jackie.** Positive Approach to Occupation with People with Dementia. LC 99-42840. (Bradford Dementia Group Good Practice Guide Ser.). 1999. pap. 22.95 (*1-85302-772-3*) Jessica Kingsley.

Pool, James. Hitler & His Secret Partners: Contributions Loot & Reward 1933. LC 97-15506. 1997. 24.00 (*0-671-75081-5*, PB Hardcover) PB.

— Hitler & His Secret Partners: Contributions, Loot & Rewards, 1933-1945. (Illus.). 432p. 1999. pap. 14.00 (*0-671-75082-3*, PB Trade Paper) PB.

— Who Financed Hitler? LC 97-15509. 1997. per. 14.00 (*0-671-75083-1*, PB Trade Paper) PB.

Pool, James M. Among These Hills: A Child's History of Harrison County. (Illus.). 240p. (J). 1985. 12.95 (*0-9615566-0-9*) Clarksburg-Harrison Bicent.

Pool, Jeff B. Against Returning to Egypt: Exposing & Resisting Credalism among Baptists. LC 97-27099. (Orig.). (C). 1997. pap. text 21.95 (*0-86554-553-7*, MUP/P152) Mercer Univ Pr.

— Sacred Mandates of Conscience: Interpretations of the Baptist Faith & Message. LC 97-11346. 192p. 1997. pap. 15.00 (*1-57312-165-7*) Smyth & Helwys.

Pool, Jo L. A Good Man is Hard to Find. 1995. pap. text 9.99 (*0-7852-8166-5*) Nelson.

Pool, John C. The ABCs of Money & Banking. (Illus.). 71p. (Orig.). (YA). (gr. 9-12). 1992. pap. text, teacher ed. 9.95 (*1-882505-01-8*) Durell Inst MSASU.

Pool, John C., et al. The ABCs of International Finance. 2nd ed. 217p. 1991. pap. 20.95 (*0-669-24522-4*) Lxngtn Bks.

Pool, John Charles & LaRoe, Ross M. The Instant Economist. 120p. 1986. pap. 12.00 (*0-201-16883-9*) Addison-Wesley.

Pool, Joyce O., photos by. More Cooking Secrets of the CIA: The Companion Book to the Public Television Series. LC 97-33978. (Illus.). 1998. pap. text 14.95 (*0-8118-1863-2*) Chronicle Bks.

Pool, Joyce Oudkerk, jt. auth. see Grunes, Barbara.

Pool, K. J. A History of Amateur Archaeology in the St. Louis Area. (Missouri Archaeologist Ser.: Vol. 50 (1989)). 1992. pap. 7.50 (*0-943414-73-3*, 115000) MO Arch Soc.

Pool, Maria L. Widower & Some Spinsters: Short Stories. LC 78-101288. (Short Story Index Reprint Ser.). 1977. 21.95 (*0-8369-3225-0*) Ayer.

Pool, Mary J., jt. auth. see Howard, Linn.

Pool, Peter E., ed. see Nevada Museum of Art Staff.

Pool, Phoebe. Impressionism. LC 84-51308. (World of Art Ser.). (Illus.). 288p. 1985. pap. 16.95 (*0-500-20056-4*, Pub. by Thames Hudson) Norton.

Pool, Robert. Beyond Engineering: How Society Shapes Technology. LC 96-34364. (Sloan Technology Ser.). 368p. 1997. 30.00 (*0-19-510772-1*) OUP.

— Beyond Engineering: How Society Shapes Technology. 368p. 1999. pap. 16.95 (*0-19-512911-3*) OUP.

— Dialogue & the Interpretation of Illness: Conversations in a Cameroon Village. LC 93-4290. (Explorations in Anthropology Ser.). 296p. 1994. 46.00 (*0-85496-873-3*, Pub. by Berg Pubs); pap. 19.50 (*1-85973-016-7*, Pub. by Berg Pubs) NYU Pr.

***Pool, Robert.** Fat: Fighting the Obesity Epidemic. (Illus.). 288p. 2001. 27.50 (*0-19-511853-7*) OUP.

— Negotiating a Good Death: Euthanasia in the Netherlands Foreign Language. LC 00-38286. (Illus.). 262p. 2000. pap. 24.95 (*0-7890-1081-X*) Haworth Pr.

— Negotiating a Good Death: Euthanasia in the Netherlands Foreign Language. LC 00-38286. (Illus.). 262p. 2000. lib. bdg. 59.95 (*0-7890-1080-1*) Haworth Pr.

Pool, Robert. Yang-Mills Fields & Extension Theory. LC 86-28809. (Memoirs of the American Mathematical Society Ser.: No. 358). 63p. 1987. pap. 15.00 (*0-8218-2422-8*, MEMO/65/358C) Am Math.

Pool, Ruth, jt. auth. see Wilson, Earl.

Pool, Sam L. Orations of Mohammad. 1994. pap. 3.50 (*1-56744-175-0*) Kazi Pubns.

Pool, Sam L., jt. auth. see Nicogossian, Arnauld E.

Pool, Thomas E. John Wesley the Soul Winner. pap. 9.99 (*0-88019-074-4*) Schmul Pub Co.

***Pool, Trey.** The Earth Grew Fangs. (Illus.). 24p. 1999. pap. 3.95 (*1-930935-06-4*, Pick Pocket Pr) Phony Lid Pubns.

Pool, William C. Eugene C. Barker: Historian. LC 76-627820. (Illus.). 228p. 1971. 13.95 (*0-87611-025-1*) Tex St Hist Assn.

— The Historical Atlas of Texas. (Illus.). 216p. 1974. 29.95 (*0-88426-033-X*) Encino Pr.

Poole. Community Practice: Theory & Action. (Social Work Ser.). 2000. mass mkt. 32.95 (*0-534-34682-0*) Brooks-Cole.

— Frommer's Budget Travel Guide Ireland on $45 a Day 96-97. 1996. per. 16.95 (*0-671-51938-7*) S&S Trade.

— Frommer's Guide New Orleans. 1993. pap. 13.00 (*0-671-84888-7*) S&S Trade.

Poole. Guide to Science & Belief. 1997. pap. 14.95 (*0-7459-3941-4*, Pub. by Lion Pubng) Trafalgar.

Poole. An Introduction to Linguistics. LC 98-47245. 224p. 1999. pap. 19.95 (*0-312-22116-9*); text 59.95 (*0-312-22115-0*) St Martin.

— Linear Algebra: A Modern Approach. (Mathematics Ser.). 2001. mass mkt. 47.00 (*0-534-34174-8*) Brooks-Cole.

— Petrography of Concrete. (C). 1996. text. write for info. (*0-582-03784-0*, Pub. by Addison-Wesley) Longman.

Poole, A. B., jt. auth. see St. John, D. A.

Poole, A. L. Southern Beeches. 1987. 27.50 (*0-477-02510-2*, Pub. by Manaaki Whenua) Balogh.

Poole, A. L. & Adams, N. M. Trees & Shrubs of New Zealand. rev. ed. 1990. 34.95 (*0-477-02603-6*, Pub. by Manaaki Whenua) Balogh.

Poole, Adrian. Coriolanus. LC 88-18051. 192p. 1988. 22.95 (*0-8057-8709-7*, Twyne); pap. 13.95 (*0-8057-8713-5*, Twyne) Mac Lib Ref.

***Poole, Adrian & Maule, Jeremy, eds.** The Oxford Book of Classical Verse. (Oxford Books of Verse). 656p. 2000. pap. 18.95 (*0-19-282528-3*) OUP.

Poole, Adrian, ed. & intro. see Dickens, Charles.

Poole, Adrian, ed. & intro. see James, Henry.

Poole, Adrian, ed. & intro. see Stevenson, Robert Louis.

Poole, Amy Lowry. How the Rooster Got His Crown: A Chinese Folktale. LC 98-12311. (Illus.). (J). (ps-3). 1999. 15.95 (*0-8234-1389-6*) Holiday.

Poole, Austin L. Domesday Book to Magna Carta, 1087-1216. 2nd ed. LC 92-32686. (Illus.). 560p. (C). 1993. pap. 22.00 (*0-19-285287-6*) OUP.

— From Domesday Book to Magna Carta, 1087-1216. 2nd ed. (Oxford History of England Ser.). 558p. 1956. text 75.00 (*0-19-821707-2*) OUP.

Poole, Austin L. Henry the Lion: The Lothian Historical Essay for 1912. LC 80-2008. reprint ed. 37.50 (*0-404-18586-X*) AMS Pr.

— Obligations of Society in the Twelfth & Thirteenth Centuries: The Ford Lectures Delivered in the University of Oxford in Michaelmas Term. LC 80-2007. reprint ed. 37.50 (*0-404-18587-8*) AMS Pr.

Poole, Barbara A. Basic Mathematics, 2nd Print. 640p. 1994. pap. text 78.00 (*0-13-342569-X*) P-H.

Poole, Barbara A. Intermediate Algebra. 2nd ed. LC 94-2931. 828p. 1994. pap. text 83.00 (*0-13-075326-2*) P-H.

Poole, Barbara A. Introductory Algebra. 2nd ed. LC 93-41608. 710p. 1993. pap. text 83.00 (*0-13-503723-9*) P-H.

Poole, Barbara C. Psychology & Medicine of Appetite Disorders: Research Subject Analysis with Reference Bibliography. rev. ed. LC 85-48101. 149p. 1994. 47.50 (*0-7883-0652-9*); pap. 44.50 (*0-7883-0653-7*) ABBE Pubs Assn.

Poole, Bernard J. Education for an Information Age. 2nd ed. LC 97-12936. 480p. (C). 1997. text. write for info. (*0-697-29887-6*, WCB McGr Hill) McGrw-H Hghr Educ.

— Education for An Information Age: Teaching in the Computerized Classroom. 480p. (C). 1994. text. write for info. (*0-697-15403-3*) Brown & Benchmark.

— Essential Microsoft Works: Tutorial for Teachers. 272p. (C). 1993. text. write for info. (*0-697-21813-9*) Brown & Benchmark.

Poole, Bernard J., jt. auth. see Sharp, Vicki.

Poole, Bernice A. The Listening Sky. 224p. 1996. mass mkt. 5.99 (*0-87067-864-7*) Holloway.

— Mary McLeod Bethune: Educator. (Black American Ser.). (Illus.). 208p. (Orig.). (YA). 1994. mass mkt. 3.95 (*0-87067-783-7*, Melrose Sq) Holloway.

Poole, Bernice Anderson. Haunted Woods. (J). 1995. pap. 3.50 (*0-590-47229-1*) Scholastic Inc.

— Haunted Woods. 1995. 8.60 (*0-606-09395-8*, Pub. by Turtleback) Demco.

Poole, Betty S., ed. see Hickson Nelson, Bobbe.

Poole, Bill, ed. see Dugopolski, Mark.

Poole, Bill, ed. see Gordon Staff.

Poole, C. F. & Poole, S. K. Chromatography Today. 1026p. 1991. 228.50 (*0-444-88492-0*); pap. 75.00 (*0-444-89161-7*) Elsevier.

Poole, C. P., Jr & Farach, H. A., eds. Handbook of Electron Spin Resonance, Vol. 2. (Illus.). 400p. 1999. 150.00 (*0-387-98660-X*) Spr-Verlag.

Poole, C. P. & Farach, Horacio A. Handbook of Electron Spin Resonance. LC 93-33834. (Illus.). 500p. 1994. text 129.95 (*1-56396-044-3*) Spr-Verlag.

Poole, C. P., Jr., jt. auth. see Owens, F. J.

Poole-Carter, Rosemary. Mossy Cape: 3 Act Drama. (Illus.). 27p. 1994. pap. 4.00 (*0-88680-396-9*) I E Clark.

Poole, Cary F. CF7 Locomotives: From Cleburne to Everywhere. (Illus.). 112p. 1997. pap. 24.99 (*0-9657709-0-7*) Railroad Pr.

— A History of Railroading in Western North Carolina. (Illus.). 200p. 1995. 49.95 (*0-932807-87-9*) Overmountain Pr.

Poole, Catherine & Parr, Elizabeth. Choosing a Nurse-Midwife: Your Guide to Safe, Sensitive Care During Pregnancy & the Birth of Your Child. 200p. 1994. pap. 12.95 (*0-471-58452-5*) Wiley.

Poole, Catherine M. & Guerry, Dupont. Melanoma: Prevention, Detection & Treatment. LC 97-39658. (Illus.). 176p. 1998. 27.50 (*0-300-07361-5*); pap. 14.00 (*0-300-07362-3*) Yale U Pr.

Poole, Cecil A. Cares That Infest. AMORC Staff, ed. LC 77-91873. 120p. 1978. 15.95 (*0-912057-28-9*, 501730) GLELJ AMORC.

— The Eternal Fruits of Knowledge. LC 76-352583. 162p. 1975. pap. 9.95 (*0-912057-27-0*, 501710) GLELJ AMORC.

— In Search of Reality. LC 80-51705. 94p. 1980. pap. 9.95 (*0-912057-31-9*, 501880) GLELJ AMORC.

P

— Mysticism - The Ultimate Experience. LC 81-86628. 166p. 1982. 16.95 (0-912057-33-5, 501900) GLELJ AMORC.

Poole, Charle P., et al. Copper Oxide Superconductors. LC 88-18569. 289p. 1988. 124.95 (0-471-62342-3) Wiley.

Poole, Charles, ed. see Hemingway, Ernest.

***Poole, Charles E.** Beyond the Broken Lights: Simple Words at Sacred Edges. LC 99-38655. 128p. 2000. pap. 13.00 (1-57312-270-X) Smyth & Helwys.

Poole, Charles E. Don't Cry Past Tuesday: Hopeful Words for Difficult Days. 1993. pap. text 9.95 (0-687-82200-9) Abingdon.

***Poole, Charles E.** Don't Cry Past Tuesday: Hopeful Words for Difficult Days. 2nd ed. LC 00-41022. 2000. write for info. (1-57312-319-6) Smyth & Helwys.

Poole, Charles E. Is Life Fair? Good Words for Hard Times. LC 99-14799. 1999. reprint ed. pap. 12.00 (1-57312-272-6) Smyth & Helwys.

— The Tug of Home: Restful Words for Weary Families. LC 97-6828. 128p. 1997. 17.00 (1-57312-150-9) Smyth & Helwys.

Poole, Charles P., Jr. Electron Spin Resonance: A Comprehensive Treatise on Experimental Techniques. 2nd unabridged ed. LC 96-35377. (Illus.). 832p. 1997. reprint ed. pap. text 22.95 (0-486-69444-5) Dover.

***Poole, Charles P.** Handbook of Superconductivity. LC 98-53079. 693p. (C). 1999. 120.00 (0-12-561460-8) Acad Pr.

— The Physics Handbook: Fundamentals & Key Equations. 493p. 1999. pap. 64.95 (0-471-31460-9) Wiley.

Poole, Charles P. & Farach, Horacio A. Theory of Magnetic Resonance. 2nd ed. LC 86-11013. 384p. 1987. 190.00 (0-471-81530-6) Wiley.

Poole, Charles P., Jr., et al. Superconductivity. (Illus.). 620p. 1996. pap. text 65.00 (0-12-561456-X) Acad Pr.

Poole, Claire, jt. auth. see Harithas, James.

Poole College Staff, et al. Pathways into Caring. 240p. 1999. pap. 32.50 (0-7487-1569-X, Pub. by S Thornes Pubs) Trans-Atl Phila.

Poole, Curtis, jt. auth. see Feldman, Ellen.

***Poole, D. C. & Kiong, D. B.** Object-Oriented Programming & Java. LC 98-18558. 250p. 1998. pap. 24.95 (981-3083-96-4, Pub. by Spr-Verlag) Spr-Verlag.

***Poole, Daaimah S.** Yo Yo Love. Armstrong, Jenice S., ed. 240p. 2000. pap. 12.95 (0-9676028-1-5) Oshun Pubg Co.

Poole, Dave, ed. see Magon, Ricardo F.

Poole, David I., et al. Computational Intelligence: A Logical Approach. LC 97-9075. (Illus.). 576p. (C). 1998. text 72.00 (0-19-510270-3) OUP.

Poole, David N. The History of the Covenant Concept from the Bible to Johannes Cloppenburg: De Foedere Dei. LC 92-11672. (Illus.). 316p. 1992. lib. bdg. 99.95 (0-7734-9814-1) E Mellen.

— Stages of Religious Faith in the Classical Reformation Tradition: The Covenant Approach to the Ordo Salutis. LC 95-7267. (Illus.). 336p. 1995. text 99.95 (0-7734-8890-1) E Mellen.

Poole, Debbie & Thrust, Emily. Interactions II: A Multi-Skills Activities Manual, Vol. 5. 3rd ed. 120p. 1998. pap. 18.13 (0-07-050453-9) McGraw.

Poole, Deborah. Vision, Race & Modernity: A Visual Economy of the Andean Image World. LC 96-45561. (Princeton Studies in Culture, Power & Modernity). 272p. 1997. text 69.50 (0-691-00646-6, Pub. by Princeton U Pr); pap. text 19.95 (0-691-00645-8, Pub. by Princeton U Pr) Cal Prin Full Svc.

Poole, Deborah & Renique, Gerardo. Peru: Time of Fear. (Latin America Bureau Ser.). 200p. (Orig.). (C). 1992. pap. 19.00 (0-85345-869-3, Pub. by Lat Am Bur) Monthly Rev.

Poole, Debra A. & Lamb, Michael E. Investigative Interviews of Children: A Guide for Helping Professionals. LC 98-16385. 295p. 1998. 39.95 (1-55798-500-6, 431-710A) Am Psychol.

Poole, Denise, ed. see Mahi.

Poole, Dennis. Electrical Distribution in Buildings. 2nd rev. ed. LC 93-24612. 1993. 59.95 (0-632-03256-1) Blackwell Sci.

Poole, Dennis L. Rural Social Welfare: An Annotated Bibliography for Educators & Practitioners. LC 80-28691. 317p. 1981. 55.00 (0-275-90704-X, C0704, Praeger Pubs) Greenwood.

Poole, Ed & Poole, Susan. Collecting Movie Posters: An Illustrated Reference Guide to Movie Art-Posters, Press Kits & Lobby Cards. LC 96-48836. (Illus.). 197p. 1997. pap. 30.00 (0-7864-0169-9) McFarland & Co.

Poole, Ernest. The Harbor. 1976. lib. bdg. 17.25 (0-89968-099-2, Lghtyr Pr) Buccaneer Bks.

— His Family. 1976. 38.95 (0-89968-100-X, Lghtyr Pr) Buccaneer Bks.

— His Second Wife. 1976. lib. bdg. 14.25 (0-89968-101-8, Lghtyr Pr) Buccaneer Bks.

Poole, Fay S. Through the Years. 1998. pap. write for info. (1-57553-881-4) Watermrk Pr.

Poole, Francis, jt. ed. see Lacey, R. Kevin.

Poole, Garry & Poling, Judson. Do Science & the Bible Conflict? (Tough Questions Ser.). 64p. 1998. pap. 5.99 (0-310-22232-X) Zondervan.

— Don't All Religions Lead to God? (Tough Questions Ser.). 64p. 1998. pap. 5.99 (0-310-22229-X) Zondervan.

— How Could God Allow Suffering & Evil? (Tough Questions Ser.). 64p. 1998. pap. 5.99 (0-310-22227-3) Zondervan.

— How Does Anyone Know God Exists? (Tough Questions Ser.). 64p. 1998. pap. 5.99 (0-310-22225-7) Zondervan.

— How Reliable Is the Bible? (Tough Questions Ser.). 64p. 1998. pap. 5.99 (0-310-22226-5) Zondervan.

— Is Jesus the Only Way? (Tough Questions Ser.). 64p. 1998. pap. 5.99 (0-310-22231-1) Zondervan.

— Tough Questions Leader's Guide. (Tough Questions Ser.). 64p. 1998. pap., teacher ed. 5.99 (0-310-22224-9) Zondervan.

— Why Become a Christian? (Tough Questions Ser.). 64p. 1998. pap. 5.99 (0-310-22228-1) Zondervan.

Poole, Gary, jt. auth. see Donato, Vince.

Poole, Gary A., ed. High-Technology Editorial Stylebook. 64p. 1989. pap. 13.95 (0-685-30787-5) Renais CA.

Poole, George W. What's the Color of Your Underwear? 100p. 1995. pap. 29.95 (0-9648565-0-6) Career Res.

Poole-Gilson, Eva, et al. Thread Winding in the Loom of Eternity: California Poets in the Schools Statewide Anthology, 1987. LC 86-71766. 91p. 1987. pap. 6.95 (0-939927-03-9) Calif Poets Schls.

Poole, Gordon, tr. see Trione, Aldo.

Poole, Gray, jt. auth. see Poole, Lynn.

Poole, Gregory G. Robertson County, Tennessee: Obituaries & Death Records, 1802-1930. 226p. 1999. pap. 30.00 (0-9650513-2-3) Land Yacht Pr.

Poole, Gregory G., ed. see Lloyd, James T.

Poole, H. J. The Last Hundred Yards: The NCO's Contribution to Warfare. LC 94-67181. (Illus.). 399p. (Orig.). 1997. pap. 19.95 (0-9638695-2-3) Posterity Pr.

Poole, Harry A. The Buoy. 344p. 1995. 25.00 (1-887189-02-5); pap. text 17.95 (1-887189-03-3) Symi Pub.

— Letters from Tarsus, 2 vols., Set. 1995. 85.00 (1-887189-09-2); pap. text 55.00 (1-887189-10-6) Symi Pub.

— Letters from Tarsus: From Pythagoras to Paul, Vol. I. 324p. 1995. 45.00 (1-887189-11-4); pap. text 29.50 (1-887189-12-2) Symi Pub.

— Letters from Tarsus: From Pythagoras to Paul, Vol. II. 296p. 1995. 45.00 (1-887189-13-0); pap. text 29.50 (1-887189-14-9) Symi Pub.

— Poetic Flights: Poems on Assorted Subjects. 70p. 1995. 15.00 (1-887189-06-8); pap. 7.50 (1-887189-15-7) Symi Pub.

— The Pollenation Wand. 77p. (J). (gr. 6-7). 1995. 15.00 (1-887189-04-1); pap. 7.95 (1-887189-05-X) Symi Pub.

— The Puritan, 2 vols. 1185p. 1995. 45.00 (1-887189-00-9); pap. text 30.00 (1-887189-01-7) Symi Pub.

Poole, Helen L. Ohio. (Whitewater Dynasty Ser.). (Orig.). 1981. mass mkt. 2.75 (0-89083-733-3, Zebra Kensgtn) Kensgtn Pub Corp.

Poole, Herbert. Theories of the Middle Range. LC 84-28402. (Libraries & Information Science). 176p. 1985. text 73.25 (0-89391-257-3) Ablx Pub.

Poole, Hilary, ed. see Hanson, Carol R., et al.

Poole, J. Hero. mass mkt. 7.95 (0-340-68320-1, Pub. by Hodder & Stought Ltd) Trafalgar.

Poole, J. B., ed. see Guthrie, R.

Poole, James. Abraham. 16p. (Orig.). 1994. pap. 2.00 (1-880573-16-4) Bible Search Pubns.

— Isaac. 16p. (Orig.). 1996. pap. 2.00 (1-880573-27-X) Bible Search Pubns.

— Jacob. 16p. (Orig.). 1994. pap. text 2.50 (1-880573-09-1) Bible Search Pubns.

Poole, James R. & Poole, Jon R. Badminton. 4th rev. ed. (Illus.). 175p. 1996. pap. text 11.50 (0-88133-892-3) Waveland Pr.

Poole, Jill. Casebook on Contract. 3rd expanded ed. 633p. 1997. pap. 42.00 (1-85431-644-3, Pub. by Blackstone Pr) Gaunt.

***Poole, Jill.** Casebook on Contract. 4th ed. 697p. 1999. pap. 36.00 (1-85431-877-2, 18418, Pub. by Blackstone Pr) Gaunt.

Poole, Jill, jt. auth. see Furmston, Michael.

Poole, John J. One More Bridge to Cross: Lowering the Cost of War. (Illus.). 123p. 1999. pap. 9.40 (0-9638695-3-1) Posterity Pr.

***Poole, John R.** Cracker Cavaliers: A Regimental History of the Second Georgia Cavalry with Forrest & Wheeler. 2000. 34.95 (0-86554-697-5, H516) Mercer Univ Pr.

Poole, Jon R., jt. auth. see Poole, James R.

Poole, Josephine. Joan of Arc. LC 97-46667. 1998. lib. bdg. 19.99 (0-679-99041-0) Knopf.

— Joan of Arc. LC 97-46667. 32p. (J). (gr. 2-5). 1998. 18.00 (0-679-89041-6) Knopf.

***Poole, Josephine.** Joan of Arc. (Illus.). 40p. (J). (gr. 3-8). 2000. pap. 6.99 (0-375-80355-6, Pub. by Knopf Bks Yng Read) Random.

Poole, Joyce. Coming of Age with Elephants: A Memoir. (Illus.). 320p. (J). 1996. 24.45 (0-7868-6095-2, Pub. by Hyperion) Time Warner.

Poole, Joyce. Coming of Age with Elephants: A Memoir. (Illus.). 336p. (J). 1997. pap. 12.45 (0-7868-8191-7, Pub. by Hyperion) Time Warner.

— Elephants. LC 97-15272. (WorldLife Library). (Illus.). 80p. (Orig.). (YA). 1997. pap. 14.95 (0-89658-357-0) Voyageur Pr.

— The Harm We Do: A Catholic Doctor Confronts Church, Moral, & Medical Teaching. LC 92-82673. 168p. (Orig.). 1993. pap. 12.95 (0-89622-543-7) Twenty-Third.

Poole, Judith. The Little Grounding Book. (Illus.). 40p. 1993. spiral bd. 9.95 (0-9674257-0-0) Pooled Res.

— More Than Meets the Eye: Energy. (Illus.). 153p. 1999. spiral bd. 17.95 (0-9674257-1-9) Pooled Res.

Poole, Judith H., et al. Hypertensive Disorders of Pregnancy. LC 97-20040. 1997. write for info. (0-86525-077-4) March of Dimes.

Poole, Judith H., jt. auth. see Wjite, Denise.

Poole, Judy. Crisis Obstetrics: Emergency & Complicated Deliveries, Part 1. 64p. (C). (gr. 13). 1994. pap. text 16.95 (0-8151-6827-6, 25470) Mosby Inc.

— Crisis Obstetrics: Hemorrhage, Part 2. 48p. (C). (gr. 13). 1994. pap. text 16.95 (0-8151-6829-2, 25472) Mosby Inc.

— Crisis Obstetrics: Hypertension in Pregnancy, Part 3. 40p. (C). (gr. 13). 1994. pap. text 16.95 (0-8151-6832-2, 25474) Mosby Inc.

Poole, Judy, et al. Crisis OB. 1994. text 99.00 (0-8151-6835-7) Mosby Inc.

Poole, Julia E. English Pottery. (Fitzwilliam Museum Publications). (Illus.). 151p. (C). 1995. text 54.95 (0-521-47521-X); pap. text 17.95 (0-521-47520-1) Cambridge U Pr.

— Italian Maiolica. (Fitzwilliam Museum Handbooks Ser.). (Illus.). 153p. (C). 1997. text 59.95 (0-521-56316-X); pap. text 19.95 (0-521-56531-6) Cambridge U Pr.

— Italian Maiolica & Incised Slipware in the Fitzwilliam Museum, Cambridge. (Fitzwilliam Museum Publications). (Illus.). 617p. (C). 1996. text 195.00 (0-521-48275-5) Cambridge U Pr.

Poole, Karuna. Getting to Joy: A Western Householder's Spiritual Journey with Mata Amritanandamayi. (Illus.). 216p. (Orig.). 1997. pap. 11.95 (0-9643629-2-9) K Poole.

— Letting Go of Suffering. (Orig.). 1994. pap. 12.95 (0-9643629-0-2) K Poole.

Poole, Kathryn, ed. see Speckman, Dolores.

***Poole, Kathy & Speckman, Dolores.** Dining Secrets of Indiana. 3rd rev. ed. 64p. 2000. pap. 7.95 (0-9657499-1-6) Poole Pub.

Poole, Keith T. & Rosenthal, Howard. Congress: A Political-Economic History of Roll Call Voting. (Illus.). 320p. 1997. text 85.00 (0-19-505577-2) OUP.

***Poole, Keith T. & Rosenthal, Howard.** Congress: A Political-Economic History of Roll Call Voting. (Illus.). 320p. 2000. pap. 18.95 (0-19-514242-X) OUP.

Poole, Kenneth. Entrepreneurial Development: Formalizing the Process. Murphy, Jenny, ed. 40p. (Orig.). 1987. pap. 17.00 (0-317-04847-3) Natl Coun Econ Dev.

— Financing Tools & Techniques: A Guide to Planning for Business Development. Murphy, Jenny, ed. 32p. (Orig.). 1987. pap. 17.00 (0-317-04819-8) Natl Coun Econ Dev.

— Marketing Strategies for Local Economic Development: From Design to Implementation. Murphy, Jenny & Kailo, Andrea, eds. 44p. (Orig.). 1986. pap. 17.50 (0-317-04902-X) Natl Coun Econ Dev.

— Non-Traditional Job Creation & Entrepreneurship. Murphy, Jenny, ed. 28p. (Orig.). 1988. pap. 18.00 (0-317-04855-4) Natl Coun Econ Dev.

— Self Emloyment Initiatives: How to Promote & Finance Micro-Enterprises. Murphy, Jenny, ed. 64p. (Orig.). 1988. pap. 20.00 (0-317-04901-1) Natl Coun Econ Dev.

— Telecommunications & Rural Economic Development. Murphy, Jenny, ed. 60p. (Orig.). 1991. pap. 22.50 (0-317-04801-5) Natl Coun Econ Dev.

— Trends in Economic Development Organizations: A Survey of Selected Metropolitan Areas. Murphy, Jenny, ed. 580p. (Orig.). 1991. pap. 225.00 (0-317-04832-5) Natl Coun Econ Dev.

— Working Capital for Small Business: Addressing the Need. Murphy, Jenny, ed. 32p. (Orig.). 1987. pap. 17.00 (0-317-04818-X) Natl Coun Econ Dev.

Poole, Kenneth, et al. Evaluating Business Development Incentives. 141p. 1999. pap. write for info. (1-889493-02-3) Nat Assn St Dev.

Poole, Kenneth, ed. see Murphy, Jenny & Welch, Wayne.

Poole, Kenyon E. German Financial Policies, Nineteen Thirty-Two to Nineteen Thirty-Nine. 1977. lib. bdg. 59.95 (0-8490-1884-6) Gordon Pr.

***Poole, Kristen.** Radical Religion from Shakespeare to Milton: Figures of Nonconformity in Early Modern England. LC 99-37800. 1999. write for info. (0-05-216404-7) Cambridge U Pr.

— Radical Religion from Shakespeare to Milton: Figures of Nonconformity in Early Modern England. (Illus.). 312p. 2000. text 59.95 (0-521-64104-7) Cambridge U Pr.

Poole, Laura, ed. see Lester, Margot C.

Poole, Laura, ed. see Rold, Cynthia L.

Poole, Lisa I. & Robinson, Dianne P. Torpedo Town, U. S. A. A History of the Naval Undersea Warfare Engineering Station, 1914-1989. LC 88-51503. (Illus.). 120p. (Orig.). 1989. pap. 8.00 (0-9621829-0-7) Diamond Anniversary.

Poole, Lois E. Ring Around the Moon: A Celebration of Life's Simple Pleasures. LC 96-70132. xii, 148p. (Orig.). 1996. pap. 12.95 (0-9653507-0-3, P-1124-1) HE Pincushion Pr.

***Poole, Lon.** Mac World OS 9 Bible. LC 99-58029. 936p. 2000. pap. 39.99 (0-7645-3414-9) IDG Bks.

— Macworld Guide to System 7.0. LC 91-72754. 356p. 1991. pap. 24.95 (1-878058-16-9) IDG Bks.

— Macworld Guide to System 7.1. 2nd ed. (Illus.). 432p. 1992. pap. 24.95 (1-878058-65-7) IDG Bks.

Poole, Lon. Macworld Mac OS 8.5 Bible. LC QA76.76.O63P6585. (Bible Ser.). (Illus.). 1008p. 1998. pap. 39.99 (0-7645-4042-4) IDG Bks.

— MacWorld System 7.5 Bible. 3rd ed. LC 94-77526. 560p. 1994. pap. 29.95 (1-56884-098-5) IDG Bks.

Poole, Lon & Rizzo, John. The Little Network Book for Windows & Macintosh. (Illus.). 280p. (C). 1999. pap. text 19.99 (0-201-35378-4) Peachpit Pr.

Poole, Lynn & Poole, Gray. History of the Ancient Olympic Games. (Illus.). 1963. 11.95 (0-8392-1049-3) Astor-Honor.

— Weird & Wonderful Ants. (Illus.). (J). (gr. 5 up). 1961. 8.95 (0-8392-3041-9) Astor-Honor.

Poole, Marie, ed. & tr. see De Paul, Vincent.

Poole, Marie J., ed. see De Paul, Vincent.

Poole, Marie J., ed. & tr. see De Paul, Vincent.

Poole, Marie J., tr. see De Paul, Vincent.

Poole, Marilee, ed. see Tharp, Grover J.

***Poole, Marilyn & Feldman, Susan, eds.** A Certain Age: Women Grower Older. 224p. 2000. pap. 24.95 (1-86448-996-0, Pub. by Allen & Unwin Pty) Paul & Co Pubs.

***Poole, Marshal Scott, et al.** Organizational Change Processes: Theory & Methods for Research. (Illus.). 768p. 2001. text 45.00 (0-19-513500-8) OUP.

Poole, Marshall S., jt. ed. see Hirokawa, Randy Y.

Poole, Marshall S., jt. ed. see Van de Ven, Andrew H.

***Poole, Marshall Scott, et al.** Organizational Change Processes: Theory & Methods for Research. (Illus.). 400p. 2000. text 45.00 (0-19-513198-3) OUP.

Poole, Mathew R., jt. auth. see Lenkert, Erika.

Poole, Matthew. A Commentary on the Holy Bible, 3 vols., Set. 1979. 159.99 (0-85151-211-9) Banner of Truth.

— A Commentary on the Holy Bible, Vol. 1. 1979. 59.99 (0-85151-054-X) Banner of Truth.

— A Commentary on the Holy Bible, Vol. 2. 1979. 59.99 (0-85151-134-1) Banner of Truth.

— A Commentary on the Holy Bible, Vol. 3. 1979. 59.99 (0-85151-135-X) Banner of Truth.

— Matthew Poole's Commentary on the Holy Bible, 3 vols. 3104p. 1985. 19.95 (0-917006-28-3) Hendrickson MA.

Poole, Matthew R. Northern California Coast Best Places. 2nd ed. (Illus.). 208p. 1999. pap. 12.95 (1-57061-173-4) Sasquatch Bks.

Poole, Matthew R., ed. Northern California Coast Best Places: A Destination Guide. 224p. (Orig.). 1996. pap. 11.95 (1-57061-051-7) Sasquatch Bks.

Poole, Matthew R., jt. auth. see Foree, Rebecca P.

Poole, Matthew R., jt. ed. see Foree, Rebecca P.

Poole, Michael. Beliefs & Values in Science Education. LC 94-41387. (Developing Science & Technology Education Ser.). 152p. 1995. pap. 29.95 (0-335-15645-2) OpUniv Pr.

— Human Resource Management: Critical Perspectives on Business & Management. LC 98-49956. 1999. text. write for info. (0-415-19336-2) Routledge.

— Industrial Relations: The Origins & Patterns of National Diversity. (Illus.). 224p. 1986. text 45.00 (0-7100-9796-4, Routledge Thoemms) Routledge.

Poole, Michael & Warner, Malcolm. IEBM Handbook of Human Resource Management. LC 99-215930. (Bus Press-New). 864p. 1998. pap. 139.95 (1-86152-166-9) Thomson Learn.

Poole, Millicent E. Education & Work. (C). 1992. pap. 35.00 (0-86431-096-X, Pub. by Aust Council Educ Res) Stylus Pub VA.

Poole, Millicent E. & Langan-Fox, Janice. Australian Women & Careers: Psychological & Contextual Influences over the Life Course. (Illus.). 312p. (C). 1997. text 69.95 (0-521-56145-0) Cambridge U Pr.

Poole, Millicent E., jt. auth. see Evans, Glen.

Poole, Monica. The Wood Engravings of John Farleigh. (Illus.). 128p. 1985. 125.00 (0-946095-09-4, Pub. by Gresham Bks); 500.00 (0-946095-15-9, Pub. by Gresham Bks) St Mut.

***Poole, Nancy W.** Christopher the Christmas Tree. (Illus.). 28p. (J). (ps-6). 1999. pap. 14.95 (0-9673359-0-6, 07) Grass Lake Pubg.

Poole, Nicola, jt. auth. see Poole, P. C.

***Poole, Owen.** Network Security. 208p. 2001. pap. 47.95 (0-7506-5033-8) Buttrwrth-Heinemann.

Poole, P. C. & Poole, Nicola. Using UNIX by Example. 416p. (C). 1986. pap. text 26.66 (0-201-18535-0) Addison-Wesley.

Poole, Patricia P. Hospital Infections - Prevention & Control: Index of New Information with References. rev. ed. 169p. 1997. 47.50 (0-7883-1552-8); pap. 44.50 (0-7883-1553-6) ABBE Pubs Assn.

— Hospital Infections & Patient Complications: Index of New Information with References. rev. ed. 167p. 1997. 47.50 (0-7883-1550-1); pap. 44.50 (0-7883-1551-X) ABBE Pubs Assn.

Poole, Peter A. The Expansion of the Vietnam War into Cambodia: Action & Response by the Governments of North Vietnam, South Vietnam, Cambodia, & the United States. LC 76-633329. (Papers in International Studies : No. 17). 137p. reprint ed. pap. 42.50 (0-608-30107-8, 200511900049) Bks Demand.

Poole, Peter A., ed. Indochina: Perspectives for Reconciliation. LC 75-620006. (Papers in International Studies: No. 36). 100p. reprint ed. pap. 31.00 (0-608-30677-0, 200745400062) Bks Demand.

Poole, Phebe-Jane. Diversity: A Business Advantage. 214p. 1997. 39.95 (0-9681416-0-9, Pub. by PlePublg Co) Soc Human Resc Mgmt.

Poole, R. K. & Gadd, Geoffrey M., eds. Metal-Microbe Interactions. (Society for General Microbiology Special Publications: Vol. 26). 146p. 1989. pap. 55.00 (0-19-963025-9) OUP.

Poole, R. W. Hunting: An Introductory Handbook. (Illus.). 192p. 1993. pap. 29.95 (0-948253-67-3, Pub. by Sportmans Pr) Trafalgar.

Poole, R. W. F. A Backwoodsman's Year. large type ed. 256p. 1991. 21.95 (1-85089-885-5, Pub. by ISIS Lrg Prnt) Transaction Pubs.

Poole, Reginald L. Exchequer in the Twelfth Century. 196p. 1973. reprint ed. 32.50 (0-7146-1510-2, Pub. by F Cass Pubs) Intl Spec Bk.

— Lectures on Art. LC 77-39677. (Essay Index Reprint Ser.). 1977. reprint ed. 16.95 (0-8369-2781-8) Ayer.

— Medieval Reckonings of Time. 1977. lib. bdg. 59.95 (0-8490-2220-7) Gordon Pr.

— Wycliffe & Movements for Reform. LC 77-84729. reprint ed. 39.50 (0-404-16129-4) AMS Pr.

Poole, Reginald L. & Davis, Henry W. Essays in History Presented to Reginald Lane Poole. LC 67-30186. (Essay Index Reprint Ser.). 1977. 30.95 (0-8369-0424-9) Ayer.

Poole, Reginald L., ed. see Bale, John.

Poole, Reginald L., jt. ed. see Hunt, William.

Poole, Richard. Inca Smiled: The Growing Pains of an Aid Worker in Ecuador. 1995. pap. 15.95 (1-85168-078-0, Pub. by Onewrld Pubns) Penguin Putnam.

— Words Before Midnight. 60p. 1981. pap. 10.95 (0-907476-03-1) Dufour.

Poole, Richard L., jt. auth. see Glenn, George D.

P

An Asterisk (*) at the beginning of an entry indicates that the title is appearing for the first time.

Poole, Robert, Jr. Diaries of Samuel Bamford. 320p. 2000. text 55.00 (0-312-21598-3) St Martin.
*Poole, Robert K. Advances in Microbial Physiology. (Advances in Microbial Physiology Ser.: Vol. 42). 288p. 2000. 129.95 (0-12-027742-5) Acad Pr.
Poole, Robert K. Advances in Microbial Physiology, Vol. 41. 356p. 1999. 99.95 (0-12-027741-7) Acad Pr.
*Poole, Robert K., ed. Advances in Microbial Physiology. (Advances in Microbial Physiology Ser.: Vol. 43). 232p. 2000. 129.95 (0-12-027743-3) Acad Pr.
Poole, Robert K., ed. Advances in Microbial Physiology, Vol. 37. (Illus.). 368p. 1995. text 104.00 (0-12-027737-9) Acad Pr.
— Advances in Microbial Physiology, Vol. 38. (Illus.). 280p. 1996. text 85.00 (0-12-027738-7) Morgan Kaufmann.
— Advances in Microbial Physiology, Vol. 39. (Illus.). 392p. 1997. text 99.95 (0-12-027739-5) Morgan Kaufmann.
— Advances in Microbial Physiology, Vol. 40. (Illus.). 384p. (C). 1998. boxed set 99.95 (0-12-027740-9) Acad Pr.
Poole, Robert K., et al, eds. Microbial Growth Dynamics. (Society for General Microbiology Special Publications: Vol. 28). (Illus.). 184p. 1990. 85.00 (0-19-963118-2) OUP.
Poole, Robert K. & Dow, Crawford S., eds. Microbial Gas Metabolism. (Society for General Microbiology Special Publications: Vol. 14). 1985. text 157.00 (0-12-561480-2) Acad Pr.
Poole, Robert M., ed. Nature's Wonderlands: National Parks of the World. 304p. 1989. 29.95 (0-87044-766-1); 39.95 (0-87044-767-X) Natl Geog.
Poole, Robert W. Lepidopterorum Catalogus, Fascicle 118, Noctuidae, 3 vols., Set. (New Ser.). xii, 500p. 1988. 195.00 (0-916846-45-8) Sandhill Crane.
— Lepidopterorum Catalogus, Fascicle 118, Noctuidae, Vol. 2. (New Ser.). 1988. write for info. (0-916846-46-6) Sandhill Crane.
— Lepidopterorum Catalogus, Fascicle 118, Noctuidae, Vol. 3. (New Ser.). 1988. write for info. (0-916846-47-4) Sandhill Crane.
— The Moths of America North of Mexico: Noctuoidea, Noctuidae (Part), Cucullii. Hodges, Ronald W., ed. LC 94-61667. (Illus.). 249p. (Orig.). 1995. pap. text 70.00 (0-933003-07-2) Wedge Entomological.
Poole, Robert W., Jr. & Postrel, Virginia I., eds. Free Minds & Free Markets: Twenty-Five Years of Reason. LC 93-20435. (Illus.). 300p. (Orig.). 1993. pap. 24.95 (0-936488-72-7) PRIPP.
Poole, Robert W., jt. auth. see Lafontaine, J. Donald.
Poole, Roger. Kierkegaard: The Indirect Communication. LC 93-18805. 304p. (C). 1993. text 39.50 (0-8139-1460-4) U Pr of Va.
Poole, Rose M. Siren Sparks. 203p. 1984. 7.95 (0-89697-173-2) Intl Univ Pr.
Poole, Ross. Morality & Modernity. 224p. (C). 1991. pap. 20.99 (0-415-03601-1, A5263) Routledge.
— Nation & Identity LC 99-23022. 208p. 1999. pap. 24.99 (0-415-12623-1) Routledge.
*Poole, Ross. Nation & Identity. LC 99-23022. (Ideas Ser.). 208p. (C). 1999. text. write for info. (0-415-12622-3) Routledge.
Poole, Russell. Old English Wisdom Poetry, Vol. 5. LC 98-27022. (Annotated Bibliographies of Old & Middle English Ser.). 432p. 1998. 99.00 (0-85991-530-1) Boydell & Brewer.
Poole, Russell G. Viking Poems on War & Peace: A Study in Skaldic Narrative. (Medieval Texts & Translations Ser.: No. 8). 224p. 1991. text 45.00 (0-8020-5867-1); pap. text 14.95 (0-8020-6789-1) U of Toronto Pr.
Poole, S. K., jt. auth. see Poole, C. F.
Poole, Scott. The Cheap Seats: Poems LC 98-53878. 80p. Date not set. pap. 12.95 (0-9668612-0-5) Lost Horse.
— New Finnish Architecture. LC 91-12431. (Illus.). 224p. 1992. pap. 35.00 (0-8478-1317-7, Pub. by Rizzoli Intl) St Martin.
*Poole, Shelia. He Redeemed My Time. 94p. 1999. pap. 8.00 (0-7392-0395-9, PO3621) Morris Pubng.
Poole, Stacey, ed. see Hanson, Frances E.
Poole, Stafford. Our Lady of Guadalupe: The Origins & Sources of a Mexican National Symbol, 1531-1797. 325p. 1996. pap. 19.95 (0-8165-1623-5) U of Ariz Pr.
Poole, Stafford & Slawson, Douglas J. Church & Slave in Perry County, Missouri, 1818-1865. LC 86-16374. (Studies in American Religion: Vol. 22). (Illus.). 252p. 1988. lib. bdg. 89.95 (0-88946-666-1) E Mellen.
Poole, Stafford, tr. see De Las Casas, Bartolome.
Poole, Stafford, tr. see Sousa, Lisa, et al, eds.
Poole, Stanley L. Aurangzib & the Decay of the Mughal Empire. 1990. reprint ed. 9.50 (81-85418-10-1, Pub. by Low Price) S Asia.
— The Moors in Spain. (African Heritage Classical Research Studies). 290p. reprint ed. 16.00 (0-938818-65-1) ECA Assoc.
Poole, Stephen. The Complete Pyrography. LC 96-147422. (Illus.). 160p. 1996. pap. 21.95 (0-946819-76-9, Pub. by Guild Master) Sterling.
— The Condemned: Inside Moves. 1997. pap. text 16.99 (1-57231-361-7) Microsoft.
— Halifax: A Color Guidebook. (Illus.). 96p. 1995. pap. 14.95 (0-88780-320-2, Pub. by Formac Publ Co) Seven Hills Bk.
— Nova Scotia. 2nd ed. (Illus.). 200p. 1998. pap. 16.95 (0-88780-436-5, Pub. by J Lorimer) Formac Dist Ltd.
— Nova Scotia: A Color Guidebook. (Illus.). 192p. 1995. pap. 19.95 (0-88780-268-0) Formac Dist Ltd.
— Pyrography Handbook. LC 98-145970. (Illus.). 136p. 1998. 14.95 (1-86108-061-1, Pub. by Guild Master) Sterling.
— Riot: Inside Moves. (gr. 8). 1998. pap. 16.99 (1-57231-837-6) Little.
Poole, Stephen J. General Eukjaryotic Genetics: Biology 130B Supplementary Material. 48p. (C). 1995. spiral bd. 7.95 (0-8403-9254-0) Kendall-Hunt.
Poole, Steve, jt. auth. see Gravelle, Karen.
*Poole, Steven R. Trigger Happy: Videogames & the Future of Entertainment. (Illus.). 2000. 25.95 (1-55970-539-6, Pub. by Arcade Pub Inc) Time Warner.
Poole, Steven R., et al. Bibliographies of Behavioral Science Literature. 55p. 1983. 5.00 (0-942295-01-3, A) Soc Tchrs Fam Med.
Poole, Susan. Frommer's Dollarwise Guide to the Southeast & New Orleans. rev. ed. (Frommer's Dollarwise Guides Ser.). (Illus.). 1987. pap. 13.95 (0-685-18518-4) P-H.
*Poole, Susan. One Sad Ungathered Rose: Schizophrenia - A Mother's Story. LC 99-222079. (Illus.). 182p. 2000. pap. 15.95 (1-898256-62-4, Pub. by Collins Press) Irish Bks Media.
Poole, Susan & Gallagher, Lyn. Frommer's Ireland's Best-Loved Driving Tours. 3rd ed. 168p. 1997. 15.95 (0-02-862238-3) Macmillan.
Poole, Susan, jt. auth. see Poole, Ed.
*Poole, Susan F., ed. Lost Legacy: Inspiring Women of Nineteenth-Century America. LC 99-35264. (Illus.). 160p. (Orig.). 1999. pap. 14.95 (0-87785-386-X, Pub. by Swedenborg) Words Distrib.
Poole, T. B., ed. see Universities Federation for Animal Welfare Staff.
*Poole, Thomas R. Out of My Mind: Musings of a Maineiac. 96p. 1999. pap. 5.95 (0-7392-0353-3, PO3538) Morris Pubng.
*Poole, Trevor. UFAW Handbook on the Care & Management of Lab Animals Vols. 1 & 2: Terrestrial Vertebrates; Amphibious & Aquatic Vertebrates & Advance Invertebrates, 2 vols., Set. 7th ed. (Illus.). 1184p. 1999. text 269.95 (0-632-05133-7, Pub. by Blckwell Science) Iowa St U Pr.
Poole, Trevor & Law, Graham. Inexpensive Ways of Improving Zoo Enclosures for Mammals. (Illus.). 1999. pap. 22.00 (0-900767-89-8, Pub. by Univs Fed Animal Welfare) St Mut.
Poole, Trevor B., et al. The UFAW Handbook on the Care & Management of Laboratory Animals. 7th ed. LC 98-51409. 1999. write for info. (0-632-05132-9) Blackwell Sci.
Poole, Valerie. Obadiah Coffee & the Music Contest. LC 89-49548. (Illus.). 32p. (J). (ps-3). 1991. 14.95 (0-06-021619-0); lib. bdg. 14.89 (0-06-021620-4) HarpC Child Bks.
*Poole, W. H. Ripe Grapes: The Fruit of the Spirit. 104p. 1999. pap. 5.99 (0-88019-395-6) Schmul Pub Co.
*Poole, Wakefield. Dirty Poole: The Autobiography of a Gay Porn Pioneer. 2000. pap. 13.95 (1-55583-561-9, Pub. by Alyson Pubns) Consort Bk Sales.
Poole, William. Money Economy. LC 78-52499. (Perspectives on Economics Ser.). (Illus.). 1978. pap. text 6.95 (0-201-08364-7) Addison-Wesley.
Poole, William, jt. auth. see Henderson, J. Vernon.
Poole, William E. House Beautiful: The Designs of William E. Poole: 70 Romantic House Plans in the Classic Tradition. LC 97-73706. (Illus.). 176p. 1997. pap. 17.95 (1-881955-40-0) Home Planners.
Poole, William F. Anti-Slavery Opinions Before the Year 1800. LC 79-110001. reprint ed. 22.50 (0-8371-4144-3, POO&) Greenwood.
— The Tyler Davidson Fountain Given by Mr. Henry Probasco to the City of Cincinnati. deluxe ed. (Illus.). 117p. 1988. reprint ed. boxed set 39.95 (0-911497-06-4) Cin Mus Ctr.
— The Tyler Davidson Fountain Given by Mr. Henry Probasco to the City of Cincinnati. (Illus.). 117p. 1988. reprint ed. pap. 19.95 (0-911497-07-2) Cin Mus Ctr.
Poole-Wilson, Philip A. Heart Failure: Scientific Principles & Clinical Practice. LC 96-46029. 1996. text 140.00 (0-443-07501-8) Church.
Pooler & Cerrato. Delmar's Administrative Medical Assisting. 416p. 1997. text, wbk. ed. 18.95 (0-8273-8526-9) Delmar.
Pooler, Marilyn S., jt. auth. see Lindh, Wilburta Q.
Pooler, Victor H. Global Purchasing: Reaching for the World. (Materials Management & Logistics Ser.). (Illus.). 288p. 1992. text 49.95 (0-442-00711-6) Chapman & Hall.
*Poolet, Michelle. Database Management Systems for Starters. (Data Systems Publications). (Illus.). 415p. (C). 1999. pap. 35.00 (0-9668835-5-1) Mt Vernon Data.
— SQL Server 2000 Design & TSQL Programming. (Database Professional's Library). 2000. pap. 44.99 (0-07-212375-3) Osborne-McGraw.
Poolet, Michelle & Reilly, Michael. Acumen Series: Access 2.0 for Windows. (C). 1999. mass mkt., teacher ed. 18.50 (0-87709-984-7) Course Tech.
*Poolet, Michelle A. Advanced Database Design & Internals. 1999. pap. write for info. (0-9668835-2-7) Mt Vernon Data.
— Introduction to Database Systems & Oracle SQLPlus Programming. (Illus.). 235p. 1999. pap. 17.00 (0-9668835-1-9) Mt Vernon Data.
Pooley, A. M., ed. see Hayashi, Tadasu.
Pooley, Beverly J. Planning & Zoning in the United States. LC 61-63301. (Michigan Legal Publications). 123p. 1982. reprint ed. lib. bdg. 37.50 (0-89941-243-2, 302330) W S Hein.
Pooley, Carol A., jt. auth. see Girman, Andrea.
*Pooley, Colin G. Migration & Mobility in Britain Since the Eighteenth Century 419p. 1998. 85.00 (1-85728-867-X) Taylor & Francis.
Pooley, Colin G., ed. Housing Strategies in Europe, 1880-1930. LC 92-9976. 1992. 69.00 (0-7185-1415-7); pap. write for info. (0-7185-1430-0) St Martin.
Pooley, Colin G. & Turnbull, Jean. Migration & Mobility in Britain Since the Eighteenth Century LC 98-186667. xix, 419 p. 1998. write for info. (1-85728-868-8) UCL Pr Ltd.
Pooley, Colin G., jt. auth. see Lawton, Richard.
Pooley, D., jt. auth. see Hughes, A. E.
Pooley, Elsa. Southern African Green Guide: Flowers, Grasses, Ferns & Fungi. LC 99-175328. (Illus.). 64p. 1999. pap. 17.95 (1-86812-748-6) Menasha Ridge.
— Southern African Green Guide: Trees. LC 99-175337. (Illus.). 64p. (Orig.). 1999. pap. 17.95 (1-86812-747-8) Menasha Ridge.
Pooley, Fred, jt. auth. see Pooley, Lorraine.
Pooley, Gale L. Environmentalism & the Gospel. 160p. (C). 1995. pap. text 9.95 (0-9646651-0-7) Analytica.
Pooley, Lorraine & Pooley, Fred. The Cobbler's Guest. 15p. 1975. 4.99 (0-8341-9147-4, MC-246) Lillenas.
Pooley, Lynn E., et al. Learning to Be Partners: An Introductory Training Program for Family Support Staff. LC 97-37872. 1997. write for info. (1-885429-16-9) Family Resource.
Pooley, Michael & Lomax, John. Real Cidermaking on a Small Scale. (Illus.). 148p. (Orig.). 1999. pap. 17.95 (1-85486-195-6, Pub. by Nexus Special Interests) Trans-Atl Phila.
Pooley, Nicola. Shiatsu: A Step-by-Step Guide. LC 98-16109. (In a Nutshell Ser.). 1998. 7.95 (1-86204-197-0, Pub. by Element MA) Penguin Putnam.
Pooley, Roger. English Prose of 17th Century. LC 92-8343. (Literature in English Ser.). (C). 1992. text 72.95 (0-582-01658-4) Longman.
Pooley, Sarah. It's Raining, It's Pouring: A Book for Rainy Days. LC 92-16859. 80p. (J). (ps up). 1993. 18.00 (0-688-11803-8, Grenwillow Bks) HarpC Child Bks.
Pooley, Timothy. Chtimi: The Urban Vernaculars of Northern France. (Applications in French Linguistics Ser.: Vol. 2). 340p. 1996. 99.00 (1-85359-345-1, Pub. by Multilingual Matters) Taylor & Francis.
Poolman, J. T., et al, eds. Gonococci & Meningococci. (C). 1988. text 542.00 (90-247-3607-2) Kluwer Academic.
Poolman, Kenneth. The Speedwell Voyage. LC 98-42419. 1999. 26.95 (1-55750-693-0) Naval Inst Pr.
*Poolman, Kenneth. Speedwell Voyage: A Tale of Piracy & Mutiny in the Eighteenth Century. (Illus.). 180p. 2000. pap. 12.00 (0-425-17438-7) Berkley Pub.
Poolman, Kenneth. The Winning Edge: Naval Technology in Action, 1939-1945. LC 96-43294. (Illus.). 256p. 1997. 32.95 (1-55750-687-6) Naval Inst Pr.
*Poolos, Nicholas P. Handbook of Neurologic Differential Diagnosis. 180p. 2000. pap. text 30.00 (0-7506-7002-9) Buttrwrth-Heinemann.
Poolugayevsky, Lyev & Damsky, Iakov. Art of Defence in Chess. 1997. pap. 24.95 (1-85744-154-0, Pub. by Cadgn Bks) Macmillan.
Poom, Rilva, tr. see Manner, Eeva L.
Poom, Ritva, jt. auth. see Pentikainen, Juha.
Poom, Ritva, jt. auth. see Pentikhainen, Juha.
Poom, Ritva, jt. ed. see Barkan, Stanley H.
Poom, Ritva, ed. & tr. see Pentikainen, Juha Y.
Poom, Ritva, tr. see Reddaway, Darlene & Pruul, Kajar, eds.
Poom, Ritva, tr. see Rummo, Paul-Eerik.
Poon, Alan. Living in America. 114p. 1996. pap. text 6.00 (1-888065-08-7) New Wrld Poetry.
Poon, Auliana. Tourism, Technology & Competitive Strategies. (Illus.). 384p. 1993. pap. text 50.00 (0-85198-950-0) OUP.
Poon, Chi-Sang. Principles of Biological Systems & Neural Network Analysis. (C). 1995. text. write for info. (0-201-57890-5) Addison-Wesley.
Poon, Jessie P. H., jt. auth. see Andersson, David E.
Poon, Leonard W. New Directions in Memory & Aging: Proceedings of the George A. Talland Memorial Conference. Fozard, James L. et al, eds. LC 79-27548. (Illus.). 572p. 1980. text 115.00 (0-89859-035-3) L Erlbaum Assocs.
Poon, Leonard W., et al, eds. Aging in the 1980s: Psychological Issues. LC 80-18515. 656p. reprint ed. pap. 200.00 (0-7837-0482-8, 204080600018) Bks Demand.
— Everyday Cognition in Adulthood & Late Life. (Illus.). 720p. (C). 1992. pap. text 32.95 (0-521-42860-2) Cambridge U Pr.
Poon, Paul W. & Brugge, John F., eds. Central Auditory Processing & Neural Modeling: Proceedings of an International Workshop Held in Kaohsiung, Taiwan, January 26-29, 1997. LC 98-4100. (Illus.). 292p. 1998. 95.00 (0-306-45836-5, Kluwer Plenum) Kluwer Academic.
Poon, Ron K. Computer Circuits Electrical Design. LC 94-34252. 408p. (C). 1995. text 57.00 (0-13-213471-3) P-H.
Poonai, Premsukh. Origin of Civilization & Language. LC 94-65864. (Illus.). 247p. (C). 1994. 29.00 (1-883122-03-1) Pearce Pub.
Poonawala, Ismail K., ed. The History of al-Tabari Vol. 9: The Last Years of the Prophet: The Formation of the State, A.D. 630-632-A.H. 8-11. LC 87-7129. (SUNY Series in Near Eastern Studies). 250p. (C). 1990. text 59.50 (0-88706-691-7); pap. text 22.95 (0-88706-692-5) State U NY Pr.
Poonawala, Ismail K., tr. see Al-Tabari.
Poonen, Ephraim, ed. see Spetsieris, Archimandrite Joachim.
Poonen, Ephraim, ed. & tr. see Joseph, Elder.
Poonja, H. W. Wake up & Roar: Satsang with H. W. L. Poonja, Vol. 1. Jaxon-Bear, Eli, ed. LC 92-80404. 171p. 1992. pap. 12.00 (0-9632194-1-3) The Gangaji Fnd.
— Wake up & Roar: Satsang with H. W. L. Poonja, Vol. 2. LC 92-80404. 175p. 1993. pap. 12.00 (0-9632194-2-1) The Gangaji Fnd.
*Poonja, H. W. L. This: Prose & Poetry of Dancing Emptiness. LC 99-54795. 136p. 2000. pap. 14.95 (1-57863-176-9) Weiser.
— The Truth Is. LC 99-54796. (Illus.). 560p. 2000. pap. 24.95 (1-57863-175-0) Weiser.
Poor, jt. auth. see Wornell.
Poor, Agnes B., ed. Pan American Poems: An Anthology. 1977. lib. bdg. 59.95 (0-8490-2400-5) Gordon Pr.
Poor, Alfred. Bailey. Genealogy of the Descendants of Richard Bailey. (Illus.). 91p. 1995. reprint ed. pap. 18.00 (0-8328-4740-2); reprint ed. lib. bdg. 28.00 (0-8328-4739-9) Higginson Bk Co.
— Cross Country: 30 VFR Flights for Microsoft Flight Simulator 5.1 & FSWin95. LC 97-113816. (Illus.). 236p. (Orig.). 1996. pap. 19.95 (0-9651975-0-6) Desktop Wings.
— The Underground Guide to PC Hardware. 356p. (C). 1996. pap. text 19.95 (0-201-48997-X) Addison-Wesley.
Poor, Alfred, jt. auth. see Stone, M. David.
Poor Clare Nuns Staff, ed. see Joy, Janet L.
Poor Clares of New Orleans Staff. The New Orleans Monastery Cookbook: Recipes from St. Clare's Kitchen. Sister Olivia Wassmer, ed. 184p. 1992. 10.95 (0-9634521-0-X) St Clares Monastery.
Poor Clares of Poligny Staff & Elizabeth. Saint Colette: In the Footsteps of Saint Francis & St. Clare. Morson, Caroline, tr. from FRE. (Alongs the Paths of the Gospel Ser.). (Illus.). 72p. (gr. 2-6). 1998. teacher ed. 9.95 (0-8198-6999-6) Pauline Bks.
Poor Clares of Rockford, ed. see Duboin, Alain-Marie.
*Poor, David M. & Mussey, Mary O. My Dear Miss: The Civil War Letters of David M. Poor & Mary O. Mussey. Travers, Douglas N. & Travers, Mary I., eds. (Illus.). 609p. 1999. 85.00 (1-929013-02-7) Oakhill Pubg.
Poor, Edith. Executive Writer: A Guide to Managing Words, Ideas, & People. LC 91-18075. 160p. 1992. pap. 12.00 (0-8021-3290-1, Grove) Grove-Atltic.
Poor, Florence. One Hundred Flowers. (Illus.). 115p. 1997. pap. 12.00 (0-9658710-0-2) F Poor.
Poor, Gene W. The Illusion of Life: Lifelike Robotics. (Illus.). 96p. (Orig.). 1991. pap. 24.95 (0-88157-000-1) Creat Learn.
Poor, H. Vincent. An Introduction to Signal Detection & Estimation. (Illus.). x, 549p. 1988. 65.00 (0-387-96667-6) Spr-Verlag.
— An Introduction to Signal Detection & Estimation. 2nd ed. LC 93-21312. (Texts in Electrical Engineering Ser.). (Illus.). 398p. 1994. 64.95 (0-387-94173-8) Spr-Verlag.
Poor, H. Vincent, jt. ed. see Blake, Ian F.
Poor, Henry V. Money & Its Laws. LC 69-19678. 623p. 1969. reprint ed. lib. bdg. 125.00 (0-8371-0618-4, POML, Greenwood Pr) Greenwood.
Poor, Janet M. & Brewster, Nancy P., eds. Plants That Merit Attention Vol. 2: Shrubs. LC 94-7957. (Illus.). 364p. 1996. 59.95 (0-88192-347-8) Timber.
Poor, Janet M., ed. see Garden Club of America, Horticultural Committee St.
Poor, Janos, jt. ed. see Gero, Andras.
Poor, Maggie. Maggie Poor. 24p. 1999. pap. 12.00 (0-933519-38-9) D W Bell Gallery.
Poorbaugh, Angela. God First! Eyerly, Carey, ed. 82p. (Orig.). 1994. pap. write for info. (1-885001-03-7) Via Press.
*Poore K. W. Associates Staff. Home Maintenance: A Guide for Home Maintenance & Repair. 2nd large type rev. ed. (Illus.). 40p. 1999. pap. write for info. (0-9673225-0-2) K Poore & Assocs.
— Housekeeping: A Guide for General Housekeeping of Your Home. 3rd rev. large type ed. (Illus.). 1999. pap. write for info. (0-9673225-1-0) K Poore & Assocs.
Poore, Alfred. A Memoir & Genealogy of John Poore: Ten Generations, 1615-1880. 333p. 1989. reprint ed. pap. 50.00 (0-8328-0975-6); reprint ed. lib. bdg. 58.00 (0-8328-0974-8) Higginson Bk Co.
Poore, Benjamin P. The Early Life & First Campaigns of Napoleon Bonaparte. (Notable American Authors Ser.). 1999. reprint ed. lib. bdg. 125.00 (0-7812-8761-8) Rprt Serv.
— The Life & Public Services of Ambrose E. Burnside: Soldier - Citizen - Statesman. (Notable American Authors Ser.). 1999. reprint ed. lib. bdg. 125.00 (0-7812-8763-4) Rprt Serv.
— The Life & Public Services of John Sherman. (Notable American Authors Ser.). 1999. reprint ed. lib. bdg. 125.00 (0-7812-8762-6) Rprt Serv.
— Life of General Zachary Taylor. (Notable American Authors Ser.). 1999. reprint ed. lib. bdg. 125.00 (0-7812-8760-X) Rprt Serv.
— Life of Ulysses S. Grant. (Notable American Authors Ser.). 1999. reprint ed. lib. bdg. 125.00 (0-7812-8764-2) Rprt Serv.
— Perley's Reminiscences of Sixty Years in the National Metropolis, 2 vols. LC 74-158970. reprint ed. 74.50 (0-404-05076-X) AMS Pr.
— Perley's Reminiscences of Sixty Years in the National Metropolis. (Notable American Authors Ser.). 1999. reprint ed. lib. bdg. 125.00 (0-7812-8766-9) Rprt Serv.
— The Rise & Fall of Louis Phillippe. (Notable American Authors Ser.). 1999. reprint ed. lib. bdg. 125.00 (0-7812-8759-6) Rprt Serv.
— Sketches of the Life & Public Services of Frederick Smyth of New Hampshire. (Notable American Authors Ser.). 1999. reprint ed. lib. bdg. 125.00 (0-7812-8765-0) Rprt Serv.
Poore, Billy. Rockabilly: A Forty-Year Journey. 304p. 1998. per. 19.95 (0-7935-9142-2) H Leonard.
— Rockabilly: A 40-Year Journey. (Illus.). 200p. (Orig.). 1995. pap. 19.95 (0-7935-3706-1, HL00330020) H Leonard.

P

***Poore, Carol.** The Bonds of Labor: German Journeys to the Working World, 1890-1990. (Kritik). (Illus.). 352p. 2001. 39.95 (0-8143-2897-0) Wayne St U Pr.

Poore, Carol, ed. see Schluter, Hermann.

Poore, Carol, ed. see Spies, August.

Poore, Charles M. Death at Briar Ridge. LC 98-97006. 192p. 1999. lib. bdg. 18.95 (0-8034-9349-5, Avalon Bks) Bouregy.

Poore, Clara. Weaving with Wheat: A Manual for Beginning Wheat Weavers, No. I. (Illus.). 16p. (YA). (gr. 3 up). 1982. pap. 5.00 (0-9613993-1-7) Wheat N Flower.

Poore, David. Zippo: The Great American Lighter. LC 96-51118. (Illus.). 196p. 1997. 39.95 (0-7643-0203-5) Schiffer.

Poore, Dawn A. The Brighton Burglar. 256p. 1993. mass mkt. 3.99 (0-8217-4104-7, Zebra Kensgtn) Kensgtn Pub Corp.

— The Cairo Cats. 256p. 1994. mass mkt. 3.99 (0-8217-4571-9, Zebra Kensgtn) Kensgtn Pub Corp.

— Miss Fortune's Folly. 256p. 1992. mass mkt. 3.50 (0-8217-3913-1, Zebra Kensgtn) Kensgtn Pub Corp.

— The Mummy's Mirror. 256p. 1995. mass mkt. 3.99 (0-8217-5050-X, Zebra Kensgtn) Kensgtn Pub Corp.

— Perilous Attraction. 1996. mass mkt. 4.50 (0-8217-5339-8, Zebra Kensgtn) Kensgtn Pub Corp.

— Saints' Haven. 256p. 1997. mass mkt. 4.99 (0-8217-5710-5, Zebra Kensgtn) Kensgtn Pub Corp.

Poore, Duncan, ed. Guidelines for Mountain Protected Areas. 56p. 1992. pap. 16.00 (2-8317-0111-2, Pub. by IUCN) Island Pr.

Poore, Duncan & Sayer, Jeffrey A. The Management of Tropical Moist Forest Lands: Ecological Guidelines. 2nd ed. (Illus.). 69p. 1991. pap. 17.00 (2-8317-0071-X, Pub. by IUCN) Island Pr.

Poore, Henry R. Composition in Art. (Illus.). 104p. 1976. reprint ed. pap. 8.95 (0-486-23358-8) Dover.

— Pictorial Compositions & the Critical Judgment of Pictures. Sobieszek, Robert A. & Bunnell, Peter C., eds. LC 76-24676. (Sources of Modern Photography Ser.). (Illus.). 1979. reprint ed. lib. bdg. 20.95 (0-405-09652-6) Ayer.

Poore, Jesse H. & Trammell, Carmen J., eds. Cleanroom Software Engineering. (Illus.). 288p. (Orig.). 1996. pap. 82.95 (1-85554-654-X) Blackwell Pubs.

Poore, Jesse H., jt. auth. see Linger, Richard C.

Poore, Jesse H., jt. ed. see Kirkland, J. R.

Poore, Jonathan. Interior Color by Design: A Design Tool for Architects, Interior Designers, & Homeowners. LC 95-198081. (Illus.). 160p. 1994. 29.99 (1-56496-037-4) Rockport Pubs.

Poore, Linda. Earth's Resources: Hands on Elementary School Science. 50p. 1994. teacher ed. 35.00 (1-883410-08-8) L Poore.

— Kindergarten Physical Science: Hands on Elementary School Science. 80p. 1994. teacher ed. 100.00 (1-883410-31-2) L Poore.

— Oceans: Hands on Elementary School Science. 57p. 1994. teacher ed. 35.00 (1-883410-10-X) L Poore.

— Spanish Worksheets: Hands on Elementary School Science. 94p. 1994. teacher ed. 75.00 (1-883410-27-4) L Poore.

— Spanish Worksheets - Earth Science: Hands on Elementary School Science. 38p. 1994. teacher ed. 25.00 (1-883410-30-4) L Poore.

— Spanish Worksheets - Life Science: Hands on Elementary School Science. 38p. 1994. teacher ed. 25.00 (1-883410-29-0) L Poore.

— Spanish Worksheets - Physical Science: Hands on Elementary School Science. 30p. 1993. teacher ed. 25.00 (1-883410-28-2) L Poore.

Poore, Luz, ed. see Thomas, Mary A.

Poore, Marge. The Complete Chicken Breast Cookbook: Easy & Delicious Everyday Recipes for the Whole Family. LC 95-1605. 224p. 1995. pap. 14.95 (0-7615-0005-7) Prima Pub.

Poore, Marjorie. The Best Grill Pan Cookbook Ever. 224p. 1999. 16.95 (0-06-018798-0) HarpC.

Poore, Marjorie Productions Staff & Newens, Jennifer, eds. Home Cooking With Amy Coleman, , Vol. 3. 144p. 1999. pap. 14.95 (0-9651095-3-4) M Poore Prods.

Poore, Patricia. The Old-House Journal. 1999. pap. 19.95 (0-452-26850-8, Plume) Dutton Plume.

Poorman, Berta & Poorman, Sonja. Spread a Little Christmas Cheer. 1982. pap. 4.95 (0-686-38388-5) Eldridge Pub.

Poorman, Karen M., jt. auth. see Poorman, Ronald J.

Poorman, Mark L. Interactional Morality: A Foundation for Moral Discernment in Catholic Pastoral Ministry. 196p. (Orig.). 1993. pap. 22.95 (0-87840-536-4) Georgetown U Pr.

Poorman, Mark L., ed. Labors from the Heart: Mission & Ministry in a Catholic University. LC 96-31823. 1997. text 25.00 (0-268-01424-8); pap. text 15.00 (0-268-01425-6) U of Notre Dame Pr.

Poorman, Ronald J. & Poorman, Karen M. Everyone's Guide to Instrumental Music Lessons: For Less Than the Cost of One Private Lesson. (Illus.). 136p. (Orig.). 1990. pap. text 7.50 (0-9625874-0-0) Univ Pub NJ.

Poorman, Sonja, jt. auth. see Poorman, Berta.

Poorman, Susan. Neal-Schuman Index to Performing & Creative Artists in Collective Biographies. 155p. 1991. pap. text 27.50 (1-55570-056-X) Neal-Schuman.

Poort, Jon M. & Carlson, Roseann J. Historical Geology: Interpretations & Applications. 5th ed. 252p. (C). 1997. pap. text 47.00 (0-13-860966-7, Pub. by P-H) S&S Trade.

Poorten, Alf J. Van De, see Van De Poorten, Alf J.

***Poorthuis, Marcel & Schwartz, Joshua.** Purity & Holiness LC 99-34025. (Jewish & Christian Perspectives Ser.). 1999. write for info. (90-04-11418-1) Brill Academic Pubs.

Poortinga, Ype H., jt. ed. see Reyes Lagunes, I.

Poortman, E. L., ed. see Nicolaus of Damascus.

Poortmans, J., et al, eds. Human Muscular Function During Dynamic Exercise. (Medicine & Sport Science Ser.: Vol. 41, 1996). (Illus.). viii, 152p. 1996. pap. 159.25 (3-8055-6274-8) S Karger.

Poortmans, J. R., ed. Principles of Exercise Biochemistry. (Medicine & Sport Science Ser.: Vol. 27). (Illus.). viii, 260p. 1988. 195.00 (3-8055-4790-0) S Karger.

— Principles of Exercise Biochemistry. 2nd rev. ed. (Medicine & Sport Science Ser.: Vol. 38). (Illus.). viii, 304p. 1993. 135.75 (3-8055-5778-7) S Karger.

Poortmans, J. R. & Marconnet, P., eds. Physiological Chemistry of Training & Detraining. (Medicine & Sport Science Ser.: Vol. 17). (Illus.). xii, 264p. 1984. 172.25 (3-8055-3764-6) S Karger.

Poortmans, J. R., jt. ed. see Di Prampero, P. E.

Poortvliet, H. M. C. Valerius Flaccus: Argonautica Book II. 357p. (Orig.). 1992. pap. text 49.50 (90-5383-022-7, Pub. by VU Univ Pr) Paul & Co Pubs.

Poortvliet, Rien. The Book of the Sandman: And the Alphabet of Sleep. (Illus.). 122p. 1989. 17.95 (0-685-27156-0) Abrams.

— Daily Life in Holland in the Year 1566: And the Story of My Ancestor's Treasure Chest. (Illus.). 208p. 1992. 39.95 (0-8109-3309-8, Pub. by Abrams) Time Warner.

— Dogs. (Illus.). 220p. 1996. reprint ed. pap. 19.98 (0-8109-8140-8, Pub. by Abrams) Time Warner.

— Dutch Treat, the Artist Life. 21.95 (0-8488-1450-9) Amereon Ltd.

— The Farm Book. (Illus.). 216p. 1994. 29.95 (0-8109-0817-4, Pub. by Abrams) Time Warner.

— Gnome Clock Book. (Illus.). 24p. (J). 1998. 8.95 (1-57909-019-2) Kabouter Prods.

— Gnome Friends: Gnomes Are Friends with All Animals. (Illus.). 10p. (J). 1997. 4.95 (1-57909-021-4) Kabouter Prods.

— Gnome Music. (Illus.). 10p. (J). 1997. 4.95 (1-57909-023-0) Kabouter Prods.

— Gnome Playtime. (Illus.). 10p. (J). 1997. 4.95 (1-57909-022-2) Kabouter Prods.

— Gnome Rhymes. (Illus.). 24p. 1998. 7.95 (1-57909-044-3) Kabouter Prods.

— Gnome Songs. (Illus.). 24p. 1998. 7.95 (1-57909-043-5) Kabouter Prods.

— A Gnome's Day: A Day in a Gnome Family. (Illus.). 10p. (J). 1997. 4.95 (1-57909-020-6) Kabouter Prods.

— Noah's Ark. (Illus.). 240p. 1992. 49.50 (0-8109-1371-2, Pub. by Abrams) Time Warner.

— Sandman. (Illus.). 40p. 1996. 13.95 (1-56937-130-X) Kabouter Prods.

Poorvliet, Rien. Bedtime Alphabet Stories. (Illus.). 40p. 1996. 13.95 (1-56937-129-6) Kabouter Prods.

Poorvu, William J. Real Estate: Case Study Approach. 464p. (C). 1992. pap. text 36.80 (0-13-763483-8) P-H.

— The Real Estate Challenge: Capitalizing on Change. LC 95-26522. 470p. 1995. pap. text 55.00 (0-13-452137-4, Pub. by P-H) S&S Trade.

Poorvu, William J. & Cruikshank, Jeffrey L. The Real Estate Game: The Intelligent Guide to Successful Investing & Decision-Making. LC 99-32272. (Illus.). 322p. 1999. 24.50 (0-684-85550-X) Free Pr.

***Poos, Thomas G.** Fonthill - The Home of Henry Chapman Mercer: An American Architectural Treasure. 2nd rev. expanded ed. LC 99-76288. (Illus.). 100p. 2000. 24.95 (0-9645844-3-3); pap. 12.95 (0-9645844-2-5) Manor Hse.

Pooser, Claire, jt. auth. see Giles, Lisa.

Pooser, Claire P. & Hibbs, Nancy L. Heart Choice Recipes from Charleston's Great Chef. (Illus.). 152p. 1992. spiral bd. 12.95 (0-9674027-1-9) MUSC Creative.

Pooser, Doris. Always in Style. rev. ed. Avedon, Phyllis, ed. LC 90-55625. (Fifty-Minute Ser.). (Illus.). 214p. 1996. pap. 16.95 (1-56052-413-8) Crisp Pubns.

— Always in Style. rev. ed. 1996. pap. text 16.95 (1-56052-398-0) Crisp Pubns.

***Pooser, Doris.** Essential Guide to Hair, Makeup & Skin Care. (Illus.). 120p. 2000. pap. 24.95 (1-56052-579-7) Crisp Pubns.

Pooser, Doris. Secrets of Style. Crisp, Michael G., ed. LC 92-10401. (Illus.). 107p. (Orig.). 1994. pap. 12.95 (1-56052-152-X) Crisp Pubns.

— Successful Style: A Man's Guide to a Complete Professional Image. Michael, Angie & Trupp, Phil, eds. LC 91-18338. (Illus.). 200p. 1990. reprint ed. 16.95 (0-931961-92-0) Crisp Pubns.

Poot, Jurrie, jt. auth. see Sandee, Bernhard.

Pootler & Pillion. Take a Ride. LC 93-86728. (Illus.). 32p. (J). (ps-1). 1994. pap. 8.95 (0-9638479-3-7) Magnolia MA.

Poovey, Mary. A History of the Modern Fact: Problems of Knowledge in the Science of Wealth & Society. LC 98-5155. (Illus.). 434p. 1998. pap. text 17.00 (0-226-67526-2) U Ch Pr.

— A History of the Modern Fact: Problems of Knowledge in the Science of Wealth & Society. LC 98-5155. 1998. lib. bdg. 49.00 (0-226-67525-4) U Ch Pr.

— Making a Social Body: British Cultural Formation, 1830-1864. LC 95-4153. 266p. 1995. pap. text 12.95 (0-226-67524-6); lib. bdg. 34.00 (0-226-67523-8) U Ch Pr.

— The Proper Lady & the Woman Writer: Ideology As Style in the Writings of Mary Wollstonecraft, Mary Shelley, & Jane Austen. LC 83-3664. 287p. (C). 1985. pap. text 10.95 (0-226-67528-9) U Ch Pr.

— The Proper Lady & the Woman Writer: Ideology As Style in the Writings of Mary Wollstonecraft, Mary Shelley, & Jane Austen. LC 83-3664. 287p. (C). 1992. lib. bdg. 20.00 (0-226-67527-0) U Ch Pr.

— Uneven Developments: The Ideological Work of Gender in Mid-Victorian England. (Women in Culture & Society Ser.). 296p. 1988. pap. text 16.00 (0-226-67530-0) U Ch Pr.

— Uneven Developments: The Ideological Work of Gender in Mid-Victorian England. (Women in Culture & Society Ser.). 224p. 1995. lib. bdg. 48.00 (0-226-67529-7) U Ch Pr.

Poovey, Mary, ed. see Nightingale, Florence.

Pooya, Ayatulla Mirza Mahdi. Essence of the Holy Qur'an. 1990. 30.00 (0-944880-02-9) Tahrike Tarsile Quran.

Pop, Calin. The Symbolic Message of Illness. Charles, Rodney & Hubert, Isabelle, eds. LC 96-69529. (Illus.). 230p. 1998. 21.95 (1-887472-16-9) Sunstar Pubng.

Pop, Iggy. I Need More. LC 97-209013. (Illus.). 152p. 1996. pap. 12.95 (1-880985-43-8) Two Thirteen Sixty-one.

***Pop, Ioan I.** Romanians & Romania: A Brief History. LC 99-73807. 2000. 27.50 (0-88033-440-1, 542, Pub. by East Eur Monographs) Col U Pr.

Pop, Snap C. & Rank, Kid. Even Mo'Yo'Mama. LC 97-192515. 112p. 1997. pap. 8.00 (1-57566-201-9, Knsington) Kensgtn Pub Corp.

— Mo' Yo' Mama! LC 96-166677. 128p. (Orig.). 1996. pap. 8.00 (0-425-15214-6) Berkley Pub.

— Yo' Mama. LC 95-157653. 128p. (Orig.). 1995. pap. 8.00 (0-425-14861-0) Berkley Pub.

— Yo'Mama: Uncensored, 100p. 1999. pap. 8.00 (1-57566-451-8) Kensgtn Pub Corp.

Pop-Up Press Staff. Elvis: A Three-Dimensional Celebration. LC 97-224603. (Illus.). 1997. 29.95 (1-888443-45-6, Pop-Up Pr) Intervisual Bks.

Popa, Constantin M. The Paradoxist Literary Movement. Muiler, R. & Xiquan Publishing House Staff, eds. (RUM.). 60p. (Orig.). (C). 1992. pap. text 6.99 (1-879585-29-4) Erhus Univ Pr.

Popa, Constantin M., ed. see Smarandache, Florentin.

Popa, Marcel, jt. auth. see Treptow, Kurt W.

Popa, Opritsa D., ed. Ceausecu's Romania: An Annotated Bibliography, 36. LC 94-13055. (Bibliographies & Indexes in World History Ser.: Vol. 36). 168p. 1994. lib. bdg. 65.00 (0-313-28939-5, Greenwood Pr) Greenwood.

Popa, Radu D., jt. ed. see Rehberg, Jeanne.

Popa, Sorin. Classification of Subfactors & Their Endomorphisms: Regional Conference Series in Mathematics; No. 86. LC 95-17877. (CBMS Regional Conference Series in Mathematics: No. 86). 110p. 1995. pap. 19.00 (0-8218-0321-2, CBMS/86) Am Math.

Popa, Vasco. Midnight Sun. Barkan, Stanley H., ed: Mikasinovich, Branko, tr. (Review Chapbook Ser.: No. 28). (ENG & SER.). 48p. 1992. 15.00 (0-89304-963-8); pap. 5.00 (0-89304-964-6) Cross-Cultrl NY.

— Midnight Sun: Mini Book. Barkan, Stanley H., ed. Mikasinovich, Branko, tr. (Review Chapbook Ser.: No. 28). (ENG & SER.). 48p. 1992. 15.00 (0-89304-965-4); pap. 5.00 (0-89304-966-2) Cross-Cultrl NY.

Popa, Vasko. Collected Poems, 1. 464p. 1999. pap. text 29.95 (0-85646-268-3) Anvil Press.

— Give Me Back My Rags. Simic, Charles, tr. from SER. (Poetry Ser.). (Illus.). (Orig.). 1985. ring bd. 9.95 (0-317-39882-2) Seluzicki Fine Bks.

— Homage to the Lame Wolf: Selected Poems. 2nd ed. Simic, Charles, tr. from SER. LC 87-60028. (Field Translation Ser.: No. 12). 163p. 1987. pap. 9.00 (0-932440-22-3) Oberlin Coll Pr.

— The Little Box. Simic, Charles, tr. LC 78-134539. 1973. 7.50 (0-910350-09-4) Charioteer.

Popa, Vasko, et al. Collected Poems. Pennington, Anne & Jones, Francis R., trs. LC 97-205615. 430p. 1997. 39.95 (0-85646-237-3, Pub. by Anvil Press) Dufour.

Popadiuk, Roman. American Ukrainian Nuclear Relations. 91p. 1997. per. 5.00 (0-16-061193-8) USGPO.

Popat. Practical Fibreoptic Endoscopy & Inhibation. 226p. pap. text 63.00 (0-7506-4496-6) Buttrwrth-Heinemann.

Popay, Jennie, et al. Men, Masculinities & Gender in Welfare. LC 97-23326. (Illus.). 368p. (C). 1998. 85.00 (0-415-11970-7); pap. 25.99 (0-415-11971-5) Routledge.

Popay, Jennie, jt. ed. see Davey, Basiro.

Popcak, Gregory K. For Better... Forever! A Catholic Guide to Lifelong Marriage. LC 98-67325. 256p. 1999. pap. 12.95 (0-87973-688-7) Our Sunday Visitor.

Popcak, Gregory K., et al. Parenting with Grace Catholic Parent Guide to Raising Almost Perfect Kids. LC 99-75099. 240p. 1999. pap. 12.95 (0-87973-730-1) Our Sunday Visitor.

Popchock, Barry, ed. Soldier Boy: The Civil War Letters of Charles O. Musser, 29th Iowa. LC 95-17660. (Illus.). 272p. 1995. 24.95 (0-87745-523-6) U of Iowa Pr.

Popcorn, Faith. EVEolution: The Eight Truths of Marketing to Women. LC 00-20983. 368p. 2000. 24.95 (0-7868-6523-7, Pub. by Hyperion) Time Warner.

***Popcorn, Faith.** EVEolution: The Eight Truths of Marketing to Women. Set. abr. ed. 2000. audio 18.00 (1-55935-339-2) Soundelux.

Popcorn, Faith. Faith Popcorn. 368p. 2000. pap. 15.95 (0-7868-8441-X, Pub. by Hyprn Ppbks) Little.

— The Popcorn Report: Faith Popcorn on the Future of Your Company, Your World, Your Life. LC 92-52682. 256p. 1992. pap. 14.00 (0-88730-594-6, HarpBusn) HarpInfo.

Popcorn, Faith & Marigold, Lys. Clicking: Sixteen Trends to Future Fit Your Life, Your Work, & Your Business. abr. ed. 1996. audio 12.00 (0-694-51533-7, CPN 10051) HarperAudio.

Popcorn, Faith & Marigold, Lys. Clicking: The Authors of the Popcorn Report Show How to Position Yourself for the Way Things Will Be. LC 96-379. 1996. write for info. (0-614-95876-8) HarpC.

— Clicking: 17 Trends That Drive America. LC 97-40278. 512p. 1998. pap. 14.00 (0-88730-857-0, HarpBusn) HarpInfo.

Pope. The Biological Bases of Human Behavior. LC 99-35084. 331p. (C). 1999. pap. text 37.00 (0-205-27993-7, Macmillan Coll) P-H.

— Federal Taxation 1998, Individual. 1997. pap. text, student ed. 21.00 (0-13-659368-2) P-H.

— The Nuclear Power Industry in America. 1999. 22.95 (0-8057-4629-3, Twyne); per. 14.95 (0-8057-4630-7, Twyne) Mac Lib Ref.

— The Turks. Date not set. pap. write for info. (0-8050-6026-X) H Holt & Co.

Pope & Lovell. Research Methods Reader. LC 99-55628. (Criminal Justice Ser.). 2000. pap. 34.95 (0-534-56376-7) Wadsworth Pub.

Pope & McGraw. Anatomy & Physiology. 212p. (C). 1995. pap. text, lab manual ed. 24.00 (0-536-58764-7) Pearson Custom.

Pope, et al. Illinois Real Estate Forms, No. 7. 250p. 1998. ring bd. write for info. (0-327-00325-1, 81131-15) LEXIS Pub.

Pope, jt. auth. see Kramer.

Pope, ed. see Post, et al.

Pope, Sarah, ed. see Zheutlin, Peter & Butler, Lee.

Pope, A. W. Self-Esteem Enhancement. (C). 1988. pap. text 54.95 (0-205-14456-X, H4456) Allyn.

Pope, Alan. The CORBA Reference Guide: Understanding the Common Object Request Broker Architecture. LC 97-38067. 432p. (C). 1997. pap. 39.95 (0-201-63386-8) Addison-Wesley.

Pope, Alan & Goin, Kenneth L. High-Speed Wind Tunnel Testing. LC 78-15823. 486p. 1978. reprint ed. lib. bdg. 52.50 (0-88275-727-X) Krieger.

Pope, Alan, Jr., jt. auth. see Rae, William H.

Pope, Albert. Ladders. LC 95-1240. (Architecture at Rice Ser.: Vol. 34). (Illus.). 208p. (Orig.). 1997. pap. 17.95 (1-885232-01-2) Princeton Arch.

***Pope, Alexander.** Alexander Pope: Selected Letters. Erskine-Hill, Howard, ed. LC 99-89798. (Illus.). 400p. 2000. text 87.00 (0-19-818565-0) OUP.

Pope, Alexander. Alexander Pope: Selected Poetry. Rogers, Pat, ed. LC 96-20897. (World's Classics Ser.). 252p. pap. write for info. (0-19-283276-X) OUP.

— Alexander Pope: Selected Poetry. Rogers, Pat, ed. LC 98-230887. (Oxford World's Classics Ser.). 252p. 1998. pap. 9.95 (0-19-283494-0) OUP.

— The Best of Pope. (BCL1-PR English Literature Ser.). 467p. 1992. reprint ed. lib. bdg. 99.00 (0-7812-7393-5) Rprt Serv.

***Pope, Alexander.** The Dunciad: In Four Books. annot. ed. Rumbold, Valerie, ed. LC 98-46876. (Longman Annotated Texts Ser.). 456p. (C). 1999. 79.95 (0-582-08924-7) Addison-Wesley.

Pope, Alexander. An Essay on Man. Brady, Frank, ed. 1965. pap. write for info. (0-672-61159-7, LLA103) Macmillan.

— Essay on Man & Other Poems. LC 93-42205. (Thrift Editions Ser.). 128p. (Orig.). 1994. pap. 1.50 (0-486-28053-5) Dover.

— Minor Poems. Ault, Norman, ed. (Twickenham Ser.). 514p. 1964. 97.50 (0-416-47750-X) Elliots Bks.

— Poems of Alexander Pope: A 1 Volume Edition of the Twickenham Text with Selected Annatations. Butt, John, ed. (Illus.). 1966. pap. 19.00 (0-300-00030-8, Y163) Yale U Pr.

— Poetical Works. Davis, Herbert, ed. (Oxford Paperbacks Ser.). (Illus.). 776p. 1978. pap. text 19.95 (0-19-281246-7) OUP.

Pope, Alexander. Poetry & Prose of Alexander Pope, 001. Williams, Aubrey, ed. LC 76-4880. (C). 1969. pap. 13.96 (0-395-05156-8, RivEd) HM.

— Poetry of Alex Pope. abr. ed. LC 66-1794. 1970. audio 14.00 (0-694-50127-1, SWC 1171, Caedmon) HarperAudio.

Pope, Alexander. Pope: Poems & Prose. (Poetry Library). 224p. 1985. pap. 11.95 (0-14-058508-7, Penguin Bks) Viking Penguin.

Pope, Alexander. The Rape of the Lock. Wall, Cynthia, ed. LC 97-74968. 400p. 1997. pap. text 17.95 (0-312-11569-5) St Martin.

Pope, Alexander. The Rape of the Lock. 3rd ed. Tillotson, G., ed. 128p. (C). 1971. pap. 12.99 (0-415-03999-1, NO. 2389) Routledge.

— Selected Poetry & Prose. 2nd ed. 514p. (C). 1972. pap. text 32.50 (0-03-083262-4, Pub. by Harcourt Coll Pubs) Harcourt.

Pope, Alexander. Selections, 1993: Alexander Pope. Rogers, Pat, ed. LC 92-23197. (Oxford Authors Ser.). (Illus.). 768p. 1993. pap. text 24.00 (0-19-281346-3) OUP.

Pope, Alexander. Works: New Edition, 10 vols., Set. (BCL1-PR English Literature Ser.). 1992. reprint ed. lib. bdg. 900.00 (0-7812-7392-7) Rprt Serv.

***Pope, Alexander.** Works of Alexander Pope. (Poetry Library). 400p. 1998. pap. 7.95 (1-85326-431-8, 4318WW, Pub. by Wrdsworth Edits) NTC Contemp Pub Co.

Pope, Alexander. The Works of Alexander Pope, 10 Vols, Set. Croker, John W. et al, eds. LC 66-29708. 5462p. 1967. reprint ed. 750.00 (0-87752-087-9) Gordian.

Pope, Alexander, jt. auth. see Beardsley, Aubrey.

Pope, Alexander, ed. see Shakespeare, William.

Pope, Alexander, tr. see Homer.

***Pope, Alice, ed.** 2000 Children's Writer's & Illustrator's Market: 800+ Editors & Art Directors Who Buy Your Writing & Illustrations. 400p. 2000. pap. 21.99 (0-89879-935-X, 10626, Wrtrs Digest Bks) F & W Pubns Inc.

***Pope, Alice W., ed.** Children's Writer's & Illustrator's Market. 400p. 2001. pap. 21.99 (1-58297-010-6) F & W Pubns Inc.

P

An Asterisk (*) at the beginning of an entry indicates that the title is appearing for the first time.

Pope, Andrew M., et al, eds. Indoor Allergens: Assessing & Controlling Adverse Health Effects. LC 93-744. (Illus.). 320p. reprint ed. pap. 99.20 (0-608-06198-0, 206653000008) Bks Demand.

Pope, Andrew M., ed. see Institute of Medicine Staff.

Pope, Anne. Hear: Solutions, Skills & Sources. 1997. 22.95 (0-614-27863-5) DK Pub Inc.

Pope, Arthur U. Masterpieces of Persian Art. LC 76-97351. (Illus.). 204p. 1970. reprint ed. lib. bdg. 41.50 (0-8371-3013-1, POPA, Greenwood Pr) Greenwood.

— A Survey of Persian Art Vol. XV: Pre-Islamic Bibliography. Ackerman, Phyllis, ed. 1980. lib. bdg. 85.00 (4-89360-020-6, Pub. by Personally Oriented) Mazda Pubs.

— A Survey of Persian Art Vol. XVI: Islamic Bibliography. Ackerman, Phyllis, ed. 1980. lib. bdg. 85.00 (4-89360-021-4, Pub. by Personally Oriented) Mazda Pubs.

— A Survey of Persian Art Vols. I-XVI: From Prehistoric Times to the Present, Set. Ackerman, Phyllis, ed. (Illus.). 3816p. 1980. lib. bdg. 1495.00 (4-89360-011-7, Pub. by Personally Oriented) Mazda Pubs.

— A Survey of Persian Art Vols. IV & IX: Potery & Faience, Set. Ackerman, Phyllis, ed. 353p. 1980. lib. bdg. 145.00 (4-89360-014-1, Pub. by Personally Oriented) Mazda Pubs.

— A Survey of Persian Art Vols. V-a & X: Art of the Book, Set. Ackerman, Phyllis, ed. (Illus.). 186p. 1980. lib. bdg. 145.00 (4-89360-015-X, Pub. by Personally Oriented) Mazda Pubs.

— A Survey of Persian Art Vols. V-b & XI: Textiles, Set. Ackerman, Phyllis, ed. (Illus.). 262p. 1980. lib. bdg. 145.00 (4-89360-016-8, Pub. by Personally Oriented) Mazda Pubs.

— A Survey of Persian Art Vols. VI-a & XII: Carpets, Set. Ackerman, Phyllis, ed. (Illus.). 209p. 1980. lib. bdg. 170.00 (4-89360-017-6, Pub. by Personally Oriented) Mazda Pubs.

Pope, B. C., ed. see Bierce, Ambrose.

Pope, Barbara M., jt. ed. see Waggoner, Ellen A.

Pope, Carla B. & Whitver, Kathryn S. It All Ads Up: An Introduction to Basic Business Math. Miller, Karen M., ed. LC 98-70742. (How-To Book Ser.). 96p. 1998. pap. 12.95 (1-884926-81-9, BMATH) Amer Media.

***Pope, Carole.** Anti-Diva. 2000. write for info. (0-679-31048-7) Random.

Pope, Charles H. Cheney Genealogy: Descendants of Wm. of Roxbury & John of Newbury. (Illus.). 582p. 1995. reprint ed. pap. 75.00 (0-8328-4756-9); reprint ed. lib. bdg. 85.00 (0-8328-4755-0) Higginson Bk Co.

— A History of the Dorchester Pope Family, 1634-1888: With Sketches of Other Popes in England & America. (Illus.). 340p. 1989. reprint ed. pap. 51.00 (0-8328-0977-2); reprint ed. lib. bdg. 59.00 (0-8328-0976-4) Higginson Bk Co.

— Merriam Genealogy in England & America. (Illus.). 515p. 1989. reprint ed. pap. 69.50 (0-8328-6570-2); reprint ed. lib. bdg. 85.00 (0-8328-0866-0) Higginson Bk Co.

— Merriam Genealogy in England & America. rev. ed. LC 86-18882. (Illus.). xxxvi, 522p. 1986. pap. 40.00 (0-9612610-1-3) Bullbrier Pr.

— The Pioneers of Maine & New Hampshire. 252p. 1985. reprint ed. pap. text 5.50 (0-935207-19-8) Danbury Hse Bks.

— The Pioneers of Maine & New Hampshire, 1623-1660. 263p. 1997. reprint ed. 26.50 (0-8063-0278-X, 4655) Clearfield Co.

— Pioneers of Massachusetts. 551p. 1985. reprint ed. pap. 15.00 (0-935207-36-8) Danbury Hse Bks.

— Pioneers of Massachusetts. 550p. 1991. reprint ed. pap. 27.50 (1-55613-398-7) Heritage Bk.

— The Pioneers of Massachusetts, 1620-1650: A Descriptive List, Drawn from Records of the Colonies, Towns & Churches. 550p. 1998. reprint ed. 35.00 (0-8063-0774-9) Genealog Pub.

Pope, Charles H. & Hooper, T. Hooper Genealogy. (Illus.). 321p. reprint ed. pap. 48.00 (0-8328-0680-3); reprint ed. lib. bdg. 56.00 (0-8328-0679-X) Higginson Bk Co.

Pope, Charles H. & Pettengell, J. M. The Pettingell Genealogy. (Illus.). 596p. 1989. reprint ed. pap. 89.00 (0-8328-0961-6); reprint ed. lib. bdg. 97.00 (0-8328-0960-8) Higginson Bk Co.

Pope, Charles H. & Tobey, R. Tobey (Tobie, Toby) Genealogy: Thomas of Sandwich & James of Kittery & Their Descendants. (Illus.). 350p. 1989. reprint ed. pap. 52.50 (0-8328-1171-8); reprint ed. lib. bdg. 60.50 (0-8328-1170-X) Higginson Bk Co.

Pope, Charles H., jt. auth. see Farlow, Charles F.

Pope, Charles H., ed. see Paine, S. C.

Pope, Chris, jt. auth. see Palmer, Richard.

Pope, Clayne L. The Impact of the Ante-Bellum Tariff on Income Distribution. LC 75-2591. (Dissertations in American Economic History Ser.). (Illus.). 1975. 21.95 (0-405-07213-9) Ayer.

Pope, Clifford H., jt. auth. see Zimmermann, Arnold A.

Pope, Clive M. A-Z of Staffordshire Dogs: A Potted History. LC 97-145308. (Illus.). 168p. 1996. 49.50 (1-85149-258-5) Antique Collect.

Pope, Clyde R., jt. auth. see Freeborn, Donald K.

Pope, Colin. Working with the Unions. 216p. 1993. 75.00 (0-85292-529-8, Pub. by IPM Hse) St Mut.

Pope, Colin & Ellis, Peter. Working with the Unions. 216p. 1995. pap. 90.00 (0-85292-608-1, Pub. by IPM Hse) St Mut.

***Pope, Constance.** Journey to the Still Point: A Twelve-Year Spiritual Odyssey Through Inner Space. 190p. 1999. pap. 12.00 (0-9670026-1-3) Sila Bks.

Pope-Cordle, Jamie & Katahn, Martin. The Low-Fat Fast Food Guide. 64p. 1993. pap. 3.99 (0-393-31007-8) Norton.

Pope-Cordle, Jamie & Katahn, Martin, eds. The T-Factor Fat Gram Counter. 1989. pap. 3.99 (0-393-30655-0) Norton.

Pope-Cordle, Jane. The Low Fat Supermarket Shopping Guide. 1993. pap. 69.80 (0-393-30982-7) Norton.

Pope County Historical Society Staff. History of Pope County, Illinois. LC 86-50883. 416p. 1986. 89.50 (0-938021-03-6) Turner Pub KY.

Pope County Historical Society Staff, jt. auth. see Turner Publishing Company Staff.

***Pope, D.** Flag 4: The Battle of Coastal Forces in the Mediterranean, 1939-1945. 1999. pap. text 21.95 (1-86176-067-1) G Duckworth.

Pope, D. H., ed. Development of Methods to Detect Sulfate-Reducing Bacteria Pub. No. 37: Agents of Microbiologically Influenced Corrosion. (Illus.). 64p. 1990. 10.00 (1-877914-19-3) NACE Intl.

Pope, Daniel. Microbiologically Influenced Corrosion in Pipelines. 240p. 55.00 (0-88415-473-4, 5473) Gulf Pub.

***Pope, Daniel, ed.** American Radicalism. 2001. 64.95 (0-631-21898-X); pap. 27.95 (0-631-21899-8) Blackwell Pubs.

Pope, Daniel & Asselin, John T. Trial Handbook for Connecticut Lawyers. 2nd ed. LC 98-88480. 700p. 1998. 130.00 (0-327-00623-4, 6870011) LEXIS Pub.

Pope, Daniel C. & Murphy, Walter L. New Hampshire Civil Jury Instructions, Issue 5. LC 92-8094. 50p. 1998. ring bd. write for info. (0-327-00510-6, 8202715) LEXIS Pub.

Pope, Daniel C. & Resmini, Ronald J. Rhode Island Actions & Remedies: Tort Law, 2 vols., Set. 1180p. 1992. ring bd. 145.00 (1-56257-270-9, MICHIE) LEXIS Pub.

Pope, Daniel C., jt. auth. see Asselin, John T.

Pope, Daniel C., jt. auth. see Murphy, Walter L.

Pope, Daniel H. Microbiologically Influenced Corrosion: A State-of-the-Art Review. LC 85-115610. (MTI Publication: No. 13). 88p. reprint ed. pap. 30.00 (0-7837-0120-9, 204039700016) Bks Demand.

Pope, Daniel H., et al. Microbiologically Influenced Corrosion: A State-of-the-Art Review. 2nd ed. LC 90-60532. (MTI Publication Ser.: No. 13). 64p. 1989. reprint ed. pap. 30.00 (0-608-06736-9, 206693300009) Bks Demand.

Pope, Daniel J. & Dombroff, Mark. Trial Objections. 2nd ed. 1995. 99.00 (1-58012-018-0) James Pub Santa Ana.

Pope, David & Alston, Lee. Australia's Greatest Asset. 336p. 1989. pap. 33.00 (1-86287-013-6, Pub. by Federation Pr) Gaunt.

Pope-Davis, Don & Coleman, Hardin L., eds. Multicultural Counseling Competence: Assessment, Education & Training, & Supervision. LC 96-25239. (Multicultural Aspects Of Counseling Ser.: Vol. 7). 416p. 1996. 55.00 (0-8039-7221-0); pap. 25.95 (0-8039-7222-9) Sage.

Pope, Deborah. Falling Out of the Sky. LC 98-51115. 64p. 1999. 19.95 (0-8071-2359-5); pap. 11.95 (0-8071-2360-9) La State U Pr.

— Fanatic Heart. Poems. LC 91-48332. 64p. 1992. pap. 8.95 (0-8071-1748-X); text 15.95 (0-8071-1747-1) La State U Pr.

— Mortal World: Poems. LC 95-10354. (C). 1995. pap. 9.95 (0-8071-1984-9); text 17.95 (0-8071-1983-0) La State U Pr.

Pope, Dudley. The Battle of the River Plate. 296p. 1990. mass mkt. 4.95 (0-380-71045-5, Avon Bks) Morrow Avon.

— The Black Ship. LC 97-41890. (Heart of Oak Sea Classics Ser.). 376p. 1998. pap. 15.00 (0-8050-5566-5) H Holt & Co.

— Black Ship. (Heart of Oak Sea Classics Ser.). 412p. 1998. 30.00 (0-8050-5832-X) H Holt & Co.

— Decision at Trafalgar: The Story of the Greatest British Naval Battle of the Age of Nelson. LC 98-54896. 384p. 1999. 30.00 (0-8050-6137-1, Pub. by H Holt & Co); pap. 15.00 (0-8050-6136-3, Pub. by H Holt & Co) VHPS.

— Decoy. large type ed. (Adventure Suspense Ser.). 560p. 1985. 27.99 (0-7089-1271-0) Ulverscroft.

***Pope, Dudley.** Governor Ramage RN. (Lord Ramage Novels Ser.: Vol. 4). 368p. 2000. pap. 15.95 (0-935526-79-X) McBooks Pr.

Pope, Dudley. Life in Nelson's Navy. (Bluejacket Bks.). (Illus.). 296p. 1996. pap. 16.95 (1-55750-516-0) Naval Inst Pr.

— Ramage. 350p. 1991. reprint ed. lib. bdg. 26.95 (0-89966-840-2) Buccaneer Bks.

***Pope, Dudley.** Ramage. LC 00-22861. (Lord Ramage Novels Ser.: No. 1). 320p. 2000. reprint ed. pap. 14.95 (0-935526-76-5) McBooks Pr.

— Ramage & the Drumbeat. (Lord Ramage Novels Ser.: No. 2). 320p. 2000. reprint ed. pap. 14.95 (0-935526-77-3) McBooks Pr.

— Ramage & the Freebooters. LC 74-414913. 384p. (YA). 1969. write for info. (0-297-17710-9, Pub. by Weidenfeld & Nicolson) Trafalgar.

— Ramage & the Freebooters. LC 00-25901. (Lord Ramage Novels Ser.: No. 3). 384p. 2000. reprint ed. pap. 15.95 (0-935526-78-1) McBooks Pr.

— Ramage & the Guillotine. (Lord Ramage Novels Ser.: Vol. 6). 320p. 2000. pap. 14.95 (0-935526-81-1) McBooks Pr.

— Ramage's Prize. (Lord Ramage Novels Ser.: Vol. 5). 352p. 2000. pap. 15.95 (0-935526-80-3) McBooks Pr.

— Ramage's Prize. LC 74-6542. 344p. (J). 1975. 8.95 (0-671-21860-3) S&S Childrens.

Pope, E., et al. Rules of Thumb for Mechanical Engineers. 400p. 1996. 79.00 (0-88415-790-3, 5790) Gulf Pub.

Pope, Eddie M., jt. auth. see Wrobel, Leo A.

Pope, Edward J., et al, eds. Sol-Gel Science & Technology: Proceedings, International Symposium on Sol-Gel Science & Technology (1st: 1994: Los Angeles, CA) LC 95-24464. (Ceramic Transactions Ser.: No. 55). 402p. 1995. 88.00 (0-944904-97-1, CT055) Am Ceramic.

Pope, Edward J., jt. ed. see Lee, Burtrand I.

Pope, Elizabeth C. Opinions IV: Philatelic Expertizing. (Opinions Ser.). (Illus.). 250p. 1987. 21.00 (0-911989-18-8) Philatelic Found.

Pope, Elizabeth C., et al. Opinions-Philatelic Expertizing: An Inside View. LC 83-60036. (Illus.). 141p. 1983. 12.00 (0-911989-00-5) Philatelic Found.

Pope, Elizabeth M. The Sherwood Ring. (J). (gr. 6 up). 1990. 27.75 (0-8446-6416-2) Peter Smith.

Pope, Ethel M. India in Portuguese Literature. 1989. reprint ed. 32.00 (81-206-0496-2, Pub. by Asian Educ Servs) S Asia.

Pope, G. U. A Compendious English Tamil Dictionary: A Handbook of the Tamil Language. LC 99-932377. (TAM & ENG.). 108p. 1998. write for info. (81-206-0314-1, Pub. by Asian Educ Servs) S Asia.

— A Compendious English Tamil Dictionary. 100p. 1986. reprint ed. 12.50 (0-8364-1680-5, Pub. by Manohar) S Asia.

— A Compendious Tamil-English Dictionary: A Handbook of the Tamil Language. 7th ed. (ENG & TAM.). 98p. 1992. 25.00 (0-8288-1724-3, M 14118) Fr & Eur.

— A Handbook of the Tamil Language. 208p. 1985. 24.00 (0-8364-1678-3, Pub. by Usha) S Asia.

— Nealartiyear The Naladiyar, or, Four Hundred Quatrains in Tamil : With Introduction, Translation & Notes Critical, Philological & Explanatory to Which Is Added a Concordance & Lexicon LC 98-904958. 440 p. 1997. write for info. (81-206-0023-1) Asian Educ Servs.

— The Sacred Kurral of Tiruvalluva Nayanar. 448p. 1986. reprint ed. 22.00 (0-8364-1681-3, Pub. by Abhinav) S Asia.

— A Tamil Prose Reader. 132p. 1986. reprint ed. 12.50 (0-8364-1679-1, Pub. by Abhinav) S Asia.

Pope, G. V. Flora Zambesiaca Vol. 12, Pt. 4: Iridaceae. (Illus.). 106p. 1993. pap. 30.00 (0-947643-57-5, Pub. by Royal Botnic Grdns) Balogh.

— Handbook of the Tamil Language. 7th ed. (ENG & TAM.). 208p. 1904. 18.95 (0-7859-9812-8) Fr & Eur.

Pope, G. V., ed. Flora Zambesiaca: Pteridophyta. (Illus.). 254p. 1970. pap. 25.00 (0-565-00950-8, Pub. by Royal Botnic Grdns) Balogh.

— Flora Zambesiaca Vol. 1, Pt. 1: Introduction, Cycadaceae, Podocarpaceae, Cupressaceae. Ranunculaceae - Polygonaceae. (Illus.). 336p. 1960. pap. 30.00 (0-565-00945-1, Pub. by Royal Botnic Grdns) Balogh.

— Flora Zambesiaca Vol. 1, Pt. 2: Caryophyllaceae - Sterculiaceae. 245p. 1961. pap. 20.00 (0-565-00946-X, Pub. by Royal Botnic Grdns) Balogh.

— Flora Zambesiaca Vol. 2, Pt. 1: Tiliaceae - Icacinaceae. (Illus.). 351p. 1963. pap. 30.00 (0-565-00947-8, Pub. by Royal Botnic Grdns) Balogh.

— Flora Zambesiaca Vol. 2, Pt. 2: Aquifoliaceae - Connaraceae. (Illus.). 300p. 1966. pap. 24.00 (0-565-00948-6, Pub. by Royal Botnic Grdns) Balogh.

— Flora Zambesiaca Vol. 3, Pt. 1: Leguminosae, Subfamily Mimosoideae. (Illus.). 153p. 1970. pap. 20.00 (0-565-00949-4, Pub. by Royal Botnic Grdns) Balogh.

— Flora Zambesiaca Vol. 4: Rosaceae - Cornaceae (Excluding Escalloniaceae & Crassulaceae) (Illus.). 658p. 1978. pap. 80.00 (0-85592-044-0, Pub. by Royal Botnic Grdns) Balogh.

— Flora Zambesiaca Vol. 5, Pt. 1: Rubiaceae, Subfamily Rubiodeae. (Illus.). 250p. 1988. pap. 50.00 (0-9507682-4-3, Pub. by Royal Botnic Grdns) Balogh.

— Flora Zambesiaca Vol. 5, Pt. 2: Rubiaceae (Tribe Vanguerieaea) (Illus.). 211p. 1998. pap. 18.00 (1-900347-41-5, Pub. by Royal Botnic Grdns) Balogh.

— Flora Zambesiaca Vol. 6, Pt. 1: Compositae, Tribes Mutisieae, Cardueae, Vernonieae, Lactuceae, Arctotideae. (Illus.). 264p. 1992. pap. 48.00 (0-947643-49-4, Pub. by Royal Botnic Grdns) Balogh.

— Flora Zambesiaca Vol. 7, Pt. 1: Escalloniaceae, Crassulaceae, Valerianaceae, Dipsacaceae & Goodeniaceae - Salvadoraceae. (Illus.). 394p. 1983. pap. 60.00 (0-9507682-0-0, Pub. by Royal Botnic Grdns) Balogh.

— Flora Zambesiaca Vol. 7, Pt. 2: Apocynaceae. (Illus.). 108p. 1985. pap. 30.00 (0-565-00952-4, Pub. by Royal Botnic Grdns) Balogh.

— Flora Zambesiaca Vol. 7, Pt. 4: Canellaceae - Boraginaceae. (Illus.). 114p. 1990. pap. 40.00 (0-9507682-7-8, Pub. by Royal Botnic Grdns) Balogh.

— Flora Zambesiaca Vol. 8, Pt. 1: Convolvulaceae - Cuscutaceae. (Illus.). 142p. 1987. pap. 46.00 (0-9507682-2-7, Pub. by Royal Botnic Grdns) Balogh.

— Flora Zambesiaca Vol. 8, Pt. 2: Scrophulariaceae. (Illus.). 179p. 1990. pap. 56.00 (0-9507682-8-6, Pub. by Royal Botnic Grdns) Balogh.

— Flora Zambesiaca Vol. 8, Pt. 3: Lentibulariaceae - Pedaliaceae. (Illus.). 118p. 1988. pap. 37.00 (0-9507682-5-1, Pub. by Royal Botnic Grdns) Balogh.

— Flora Zambesiaca Vol. 9, Pt. 1: Plantaginaceae - Phytolaccaceae. (Illus.). 179p. 1988. pap. 53.00 (0-9507682-3-5, Pub. by Royal Botnic Grdns) Balogh.

— Flora Zambesiaca Vol. 9, Pt. 4: Mozambique, Malawi, Zimbabwe, Botswana. (Illus.). 337p. 1996. pap. text 50.00 (1-900347-04-0, Pub. by Royal Botnic Grdns) Balogh.

— Flora Zambesiaca Vol. 9, Pt. 6: Ulmaceae - Ceratophyllaceae (Excluding Myricaceae) (Illus.). 135p. 1991. pap. 40.00 (0-565-01145-6, Pub. by Royal Botnic Grdns) Balogh.

— Flora Zambesiaca Vol. 10, Pt. 1: Gramineae (Bambuseae - Pappophoreae) (Illus.). 152p. 1971. pap. 20.00 (0-85592-014-9, Pub. by Royal Botnic Grdns) Balogh.

— Flora Zambesiaca Vol. 10, Pt. 3: Gramineae (Paniceae, Isachneae & Arundinelleae) (Illus.). 231p. 1989. pap. 56.00 (0-9507682-6-X, Pub. by Royal Botnic Grdns) Balogh.

— Flora Zambesiaca Vol. 11, Pt. 1: Orchidaceae. (Illus.). 328p. 1993. pap. 60.00 (0-947643-89-3, Pub. by Royal Botnic Grdns) Balogh.

Pope, G. V. & Brummitt, R. K. A Bibliography for Flora Zambesiaca. 26p. 1991. pap. 10.00 (0-947643-32-X, Pub. by Royal Botnic Grdns) Balogh.

Pope, Gail & Hammond, Keith. Fast Food Toys. 2nd rev. ed. 160p. 1998. pap. 19.95 (0-7643-0321-X) Schiffer.

— Fast Food Toys. 3rd rev. ed. LC 99-17188. (Illus.). 160p. 1999. pap. 19.95 (0-7643-0712-6) Schiffer.

Pope, Geraldine. The Empty Creel. (Illus.). 56p. (J). (ps-3). 1995. 17.95 (1-56792-044-6) Godine.

Pope, Gisele & Kern, Carla. Tailfeathers, Vol. 2. (Illus.). 84p. (J). 1999. pap. 10.50 (1-56770-451-4) S Scheewe Pubns.

Pope, Gisele, jt. auth. see Kern, Carla.

***Pope, Harrison G., Jr., et al.** The Adonis Complex: The Secret Crisis of Male Body Obsession. 288p. 2000. text 24.50 (0-684-86910-1) Free Pr.

Pope, Harrison G., Jr., jt. ed. see Hudson, James I.

Pope-Hennessey, John. Fra Angelico. (Library of Great Masters). (Illus.). 80p. 1989. reprint ed. pap. 12.99 (1-878351-01-X) Riverside NY.

Pope-Hennessy, John. Fra Angelico. (Grandes Maestros del Arte Ser.). (SPA., Illus.). 80p. 1992. pap. 12.99 (1-878351-26-5) Riverside NY.

Pope-Hennessy, John W. Cellini. LC 85-6111. (Illus.). 320p. 1985. 125.00 (0-89659-453-X) Abbeville Pr.

— Cellini. deluxe ed. LC 85-6111. (Illus.). 320p. 1985. lthr. 250.00 (0-89659-593-5) Abbeville Pr.

— Donatello Sculptor. (Illus.). 368p. 1993. 125.00 (1-55859-645-3) Abbeville Pr.

— Italian Gothic Sculpture, Vol. 1. 4th ed. (Introduction to Italian Sculpture Ser.). (Illus.). 288p. 1996. 100.00 (0-7148-3014-3, Pub. by Phaidon Press) Phaidon Pr.

— Italian High Renaissance & Baroque Sculpture, Vol. 3. 4th ed. (Introduction to Italian Sculpture Ser.). (Illus.). 560p. 1996. 150.00 (0-7148-3016-X, Pub. by Phaidon Press) Phaidon Pr.

— Italian Paintings. (Robert Lehman Collection: Vol. 1). (Illus.). 352p. 1987. 95.00 (0-691-04045-1) Metro Mus Art.

— Italian Renaissance Sculpture, Vol. 2. 4th ed. (Introduction to Italian Sculpture Ser.). (Illus.). 440p. 1996. 125.00 (0-7148-3015-1, Pub. by Phaidon Press) Phaidon Pr.

— Paradiso: The Illuminations to Dante's Divine Comedy by Giovanni di Paolo. LC 93-16598. (Illus.). 1993. 75.00 (0-679-42739-2) Random.

— The Portrait in the Renaissance: The A. W. Mellon Lectures in the Fine Arts, 1963. (Bollingen Ser.: Vol. XXXV, No. 12). (Illus.). 380p. (C). 1989. pap. text 35.00 (0-691-01825-1, Pub. by Princeton U Pr) Cal Prin Full Svc.

— The Study & Criticism of Italian Sculpture. LC 80-20651. (Illus.). 271p. 1981. 45.00 (0-87099-239-2) Metro Mus Art.

Pope-Hennessy, John Wyndham. Italian Gothic Sculpture. 288p. 1999. pap. 29.95 (0-7148-3881-0) Phaidon Pr.

— Italian High Renaissance & Baroque Sculpture. (Introduction to Italian Sculpture Ser.). 560p. 1999. pap. 49.95 (0-7148-3883-7) Phaidon Pr.

— Italian Renaissance Sculpture. (Introduction to Italian Sculpture Ser.). 444p. 1999. pap. 39.95 (0-7148-3882-9) Phaidon Pr.

Pope-Hennessy, Una B. Durham Company. LC 70-36167. (Essay Index Reprint Ser.). 1977. reprint ed. 21.95 (0-8369-2714-1) Ayer.

— Edgar Allan Poe. LC 77-92977. (Studies in Poe: No. 23). 1969. reprint ed. lib. bdg. 75.00 (0-8383-0998-4) M S G Haskell Hse.

Pope, Hugh & Pope, Nicole. Turkey Unveiled: A History of Modern Turkey. LC 98-16616. (Illus.). 373p. 1998. 29.95 (0-87951-898-7, Pub. by Overlook Pr) Penguin Putnam.

***Pope, Hugh & Pope, Nicole.** Turkey Unveiled: A History of Modern Turkey. 2000. pap. 16.95 (1-58567-096-0, Pub. by Overlook Pr) Penguin Putnam.

Pope, Ingrid B. Hosanna, Help Please: On the Loss of a Loved One. LC 98-8425. 68p. 1998. pap. 14.95 (0-7734-2841-0) E Mellen.

Pope, Isabel & Kanazawa, Masakata, eds. The Musical Manuscript Montecassino 871: A Neapolitan Repertory of Sacred & Secular Music. (Illus.). 1979. 95.00 (0-19-816132-8) OUP.

Pope, Isabel, tr. see Salazar, Adolfo.

Pope, J., ed. see Frick.

Pope, J. C., ed. Homilies of Aelfric, A Supplementary Collection, Vol. I. (EETS Original Ser.: Vol. 259). 1967. 50.00 (0-19-722261-7, Pub. by EETS) Boydell & Brewer.

— Homilies of Aelfric, A Supplementary Collection, Vol. II. (EETS Original Ser.: Vol. 259). 1968. 50.00 (0-19-722262-5, Pub. by EETS) Boydell & Brewer.

***Pope, J. Gregory.** The Gift of a Lifetime: Planned Giving in Congregational Life. LC 99-45169. 128p. 2000. pap. 14.99 (0-8054-1848-2) Broadman.

Pope, J. K., jt. ed. see Pojeta, John, Jr.

Pope, Jack, et al. John Berry & His Children. 903p. 1988. text 35.00 (0-9621053-0-9) Jack Pope.

Pope, Jacqueline. Biting the Hand That Feeds Them: Organizing Women on Welfare at the Grass Roots Level. LC 88-27505. (Illus.). 170p. 1989. 52.95 (0-275-92922-1, C2922, Praeger Pubs) Greenwood.

— Bounty Hunters, Marshals & Sheriffs: Forward to the Past. LC 98-14929. 168p. 1998. 55.00 (0-275-94629-0, Praeger Pubs) Greenwood.

P

Pope, Jaime & Katahn, Martin. The Low-Fat Supermarket Shopper's Guide: Making Healthy Choices from Thousands of Brand-Name Items. 88p. 1996. pap. 5.95 (*0-393-31488-X*, Norton Paperbks) Norton.

Pope, James E., jt. auth. see McCombs, Barbara L.

Pope, Jamie. The Last Five Pounds: How to Lose Them & Leave Them Forever. Rubenstein, Julie, ed. 384p. 1995. 23.00 (*0-671-88453-0*) PB.

— The Last Five Pounds: Liberating Guide to Living Thin. 480p. 1996. per. 6.99 (*0-671-88454-9*, PB Trade Paper) PB.

— The Low-Fat Supermarket Shopper's Guide: Making Healthy Choices from Thousands of Brand-Name Items. 72p. 1993. pap. 3.99 (*0-393-30923-1*) Norton.

Pope, Jamie & Katahn, Martin. The T-Factor Fat Gram Counter. exp. rev. ed. 80p. 1995. pap. 5.95 (*0-393-31331-X*, Norton Paperbks) Norton.

Pope, Jamie, jt. auth. see Katahn, Martin.

***Pope, Jeffery Lynn & Kondratiuk, Leonia E., eds.** Armor - Calvary Regiments: Army National Guard Lineage. (Illus.). 70p. (C). 1999. reprint ed. pap. text 20.00 (*0-7881-8206-4*) DIANE Pub.

Pope, Jeffrey L. Practical Marketing Research. 2nd rev. ed. 314p. 1993. 32.95 (*0-8144-5086-5*) AMACOM.

***Pope, Jennifer Jane.** Chain Reaction. 252p. 2000. pap. 9.95 (*1-901388-58-1*, Pub. by Chimera Pubns) Firebird Dist.

— Vesta - Painworld. 256p. 1999. pap. 9.95 (*1-901388-44-1*, Pub. by Chimera Pubns) Firebird Dist.

Pope, John. A Tour Through the Southern & Western Territories of the United States. LC 70-146411. (First American Frontier Ser.). 1971. reprint ed. 13.95 (*0-405-02875-X*) Ayer.

— A Tour Through the Southern & Western Territories of the United States of North-America: The Spanish Dominions on the River Mississippi, & the Floridas; the Countries of the Creek Nations; & Many Uninhabited Parts. Starr, J. Barton, ed. LC 78-26408. (Floridiana Facsimile & Reprint Ser.). 105p. 1979. reprint ed. 19.95 (*0-8130-0418-7*) U Press Fla.

Pope, John A. Fourteenth-Century Blue-&-White, a Group of Chinese Porcelains in Topkapu Sarayi Muzesi, Istanbul. rev. ed. (Occasional Papers: Vol. 2, No. 1). 1970. pap. 3.50 (*0-934686-03-3*) Freer.

Pope, John A., et al. The Freer Chinese Bronzes, Vol. 1. (Oriental Studies: No. 7). (Illus.). 1967. 50.00 (*0-934686-10-6*) Freer.

Pope, John C., ed. Seven Old English Poems. (Orig.). 1966. pap. 5.55 (*0-672-60976-2*, LL8, Bobbs) Macmillan.

— Seven Old English Poems. 2nd ed. 240p. (Orig.). (C). 1981. reprint ed. pap. text 14.75 (*0-393-95174-X*) Norton.

Pope, Joseph. Memoirs of the Right Honorable Sir John Alexander Macdonald, 2 vols. LC 76-137271. reprint ed. 115.00 (*0-404-05085-9*) AMS Pr.

— Memoirs of the Right Honourable Sir John Alexander Macdonald, 2 vols., Set. (BCL1 - History - Canada Ser.). 1991. reprint ed. lib. bdg. 150.00 (*0-7812-6364-6*) Rprt Serv.

Pope, Joya. Upcoming Changes: Prophecy & Pragmatism for the Late Nineties. expanded rev. ed. (Michael Book Ser.). 272p. 1995. pap. 13.95 (*0-942531-38-8*) Emerald Wave.

— The World According to Michael: An Old Soul's Guide to the Universe. rev. ed. (Michael Book Ser.). 160p. (Orig.). (C). 1987. pap. 10.95 (*0-942531-39-6*) Emerald Wave.

— World According to Michael, Further Adventures: Intriguing Secrets of Your Soul. Orig. Title: World According to Michael. 200p. 2000. pap. 14.95 (*0-942531-21-3*, Pub. by Emerald Wave) Bookpeople.

Pope, Joyce. Animal Babies. LC 91-45381. (Nature Club Ser.). (Illus.). 32p. (J). (gr. 3-6). 1993. lib. bdg. 12.95 (*0-8167-2773-2*) Troll Communs.

— Animal Homes. LC 91-45380. (Nature Club Ser.). (Illus.). 32p. (J). (gr. 3-6). 1993. lib. bdg. 17.25 (*0-8167-2775-9*) Troll Communs.

— Animal Homes. LC 91-45380. (Nature Club Ser.). (Illus.). 32p. (J). (gr. 3-6). 1997. pap. 4.95 (*0-8167-2776-7*) Troll Communs.

— Animal Journeys. LC 91-45379. (Nature Club Ser.). (Illus.). 32p. (J). (gr. 3-6). 1993. lib. bdg. 17.25 (*0-8167-2777-5*) Troll Communs.

— Animal Journeys. LC 91-45379. (Nature Club Ser.). (Illus.). 32p. (J). (gr. 3-6). 1997. pap. 4.95 (*0-8167-2778-3*) Troll Communs.

— The Children's Atlas of Natural Wonders. (Children's Atlases Ser.). (Illus.). 96p. (J). (gr. 3-6). 1995. pap. 14.95 (*1-56294-886-5*); lib. bdg. 27.40 (*1-56294-564-5*) Millbrook Pr.

***Pope, Joyce.** Crocodile. (Natural World Ser.). (Illus.). (J). 2000. 9.95 (*0-7398-3127-5*); 27.12 (*0-7398-2764-2*) Raintree Steck-V.

Pope, Joyce. Earthquakes. LC 97-31924. (Closer Look at Ser.). (Illus.). 32p. (J). (gr. 4-6). 1998. 19.90 (*0-7613-0806-7*, Copper Beech Bks) Millbrook Pr.

— Fossil Detective. LC 91-45170. (Nature Club Ser.). (Illus.). 32p. (J). (gr. 3-6). 1993. pap. 4.95 (*0-8167-2782-1*); lib. bdg. 17.25 (*0-8167-2781-3*) Troll Communs.

— Life in the Dark. LC 91-18646. (Curious Creatures Ser.). (Illus.). 48p. (J). 1992. lib. bdg. 5.00 (*0-8114-3150-9*) Raintree Steck-V.

— Living Fossils. LC 91-13998. (Curious Creatures Ser.). (Illus.). 48p. (J). 1992. lib. bdg. 5.00 (*0-8114-3151-7*) Raintree Steck-V.

— Making Contact. (Curious Creatures Ser.). (Illus.). 48p. (J). 1992. lib. bdg. 5.00 (*0-8114-3155-X*) Raintree Steck-V.

— Mistaken Identity. LC 91-17136. (Curious Creatures Ser.). (Illus.). 48p. (J). 1992. lib. bdg. 5.00 (*0-8114-3152-5*) Raintree Steck-V.

— Night Creatures. LC 91-45171. (Nature Club Ser.). (Illus.). 32p. (J). (gr. 3-6). 1997. pap. 4.95 (*0-8167-2784-8*) Troll Communs.

— On the Move. (Curious Creatures Ser.). (Illus.). 48p. (J). 1992. lib. bdg. 5.00 (*0-8114-3156-8*) Raintree Steck-V.

— Plants & Flowers. LC 91-45378. (Nature Club Ser.). (Illus.). 32p. (J). (gr. 3-6). 1993. lib. bdg. 17.25 (*0-8167-2779-1*) Troll Communs.

— Plants & Flowers. LC 91-45378. (Nature Club Ser.). (Illus.). 32p. (J). (gr. 3-6). 1996. pap. 4.95 (*0-8167-2780-5*) Troll Communs.

— Plants of the Tropics. (Plant Life Ser.). 64p. (YA). 1990. 15.95 (*0-8160-2423-5*) Facts on File.

— Practical Plants. (Plant Life Ser.). 64p. (YA). 1990. 15.95 (*0-8160-2424-3*) Facts on File.

— Seashores. LC 89-20318. (Nature Club Ser.). (Illus.). 32p. (J). (gr. 3-6). 1997. lib. bdg. 17.25 (*0-8167-1965-9*) Troll Communs.

— Sharks. LC 97-16490. (DK Pockets Ser.). 128p. (J). (gr. 3 up). 1997. pap. 6.95 (*0-7894-2045-7*) DK Pub Inc.

— Strange Nature. (Curious Creatures Ser.). (Illus.). 48p. (J). 1992. lib. bdg. 5.00 (*0-8114-3157-6*) Raintree Steck-V.

— Two Lives. LC 91-17460. (Curious Creatures Ser.). (Illus.). 48p. (J). 1992. lib. bdg. 5.00 (*0-8114-3153-3*) Raintree Steck-V.

Pope, Joyce & Lilly, Kenneth. Kenneth Lilly's Animals: Wildlife Around the World. LC 94-5309. (J). (gr. 1-5). 1995. pap. 12.99 (*1-56402-513-6*) Candlewick Pr.

Pope, Judi, ed. El Ultimo Vals de los Tiranos Vol. 1: La Profecia. Castro, Juan M., tr. (SPA.). x, 139p. (Orig.). 1993. pap. 12.00 (*0-9632573-1-0*) Sin Limites.

Pope, K. S., jt. auth. see Singer, J. L.

Pope, Keats. Imaging of Musculoskeletal Stress Injury. 2nd ed. (Illus.). 352p. (C). 1999. text 95.00 (*0-8151-3665-X*, 31335) Mosby Inc.

Pope, Kenneth S. Sexual Involvement with Therapists: Patient Assessment, Subsequent Therapy, Forensics. LC 94-11534. 249p. 1994. pap. 24.95 (*1-55798-248-1*) Am Psychol.

Pope, Kenneth S. & Brown, Laura S. Recovered Memories of Abuse: Assessment, Therapy, Forensics. LC 96-33009. (Psychotherapy Practitioner Resource Ser.). 315p. 1996. pap. 24.95 (*1-55798-395-X*) Am Psychol.

Pope, Kenneth S. & Singer, Jerome L., eds. The Stream of Consciousness: Scientific Investigations into the Flow of Human Experience. LC 78-2003. (Emotions, Personality, & Psychotherapy Ser.). 390p. 1978. reprint ed. pap. 120.90 (*0-608-08386-0*, 201780200008) Bks Demand.

Pope, Kenneth S. & Vasquez, Melba J. Ethics in Psychotherapy & Counseling: A Practical Guide for Psychologists. 2nd rev. ed. LC 98-11798. (Health & Psychology Ser.). 320p. 1998. pap. 34.95 (*0-7879-4306-1*) Jossey-Bass.

Pope, Kenneth S., et al. The MMPI, MMPI-2 & MMPI-A in Court: A Practical Guide for Expert Witnesses & Attorneys. LC 92-35352. 400p. 1993. 59.95 (*1-55798-182-5*) Am Psychol.

— The MMPI, MMPI-2, & MMPI-A in Court: A Practical Guide for Expert Witnesses & Attorneys. 2nd rev. ed. LC 99-29100. 473p. 2000. 69.95 (*1-55798-590-1*, 431-729A) Am Psychol.

— On Love & Loving: Psychological Perspectives on the Nature & Experience of Romantic Love. LC 80-8012. (Jossey-Bass Social & Behavioral Science Ser.). 397p. reprint ed. pap. 123.10 (*0-7837-2548-5*, 204270700006) Bks Demand.

— Sexual Feelings in Psychotherapy: Explorations for Therapists & Therapists-in-Training. LC 93-7139. 304p. 1993. pap. text 24.95 (*1-55798-201-5*) Am Psychol.

— Sexual Intimacy Between Therapists & Patients. LC 86-15165. (Sexual Medicine Ser.: No. 5). 196p. 1988. pap. 18.95 (*0-275-92953-1*, Praeger Pubs) Greenwood.

— Sexual Intimacy Between Therapists & Patients, 5. LC 86-15165. (Sexual Medicine Ser.: No. 5). 197p. 1986. 49.95 (*0-275-92253-7*, B2953, Praeger Pubs) Greenwood.

Pope, Kenneth S., jt. auth. see Caudill, O. Brandt, Jr.

Pope, Kenneth S., jt. auth. see Caudill, O. Brant.

***Pope, Kristian & Whebbe, Ray, Jr.** Professional Wrestling Collectibles. LC 99-68109. (Illus.). 160p. 2000. pap. 21.95 (*0-87341-878-6*, PWRES) Krause Pubns.

Pope, L. E., et al, eds. New Materials Approaches to Tribology - Theory & Applications Vol. 140: Materials Research Society Symposium Proceedings. (Symposium Proceedings Ser.). 522p. 1989. text 17.50 (*1-55899-013-5*) Materials Res.

Pope, Lawrence C., ed. Manual on Test Sieving Methods: Guidelines for Establishing Sieve Analysis Procedures. 4th ed. LC 98-22472. (Manual Ser.: Vol. 32). (Illus.). 50p. 1998. pap. 26.00 (*0-8031-2495-3*, MNL32) ASTM.

Pope, Leona. Calendars of the Indians North of Mexico. fac. ed. (University of California Publications in American Archaeology & Ethnology: Vol. 16: 4). 60p. (C). 1919. reprint ed. pap. text 7.19 (*1-55567-224-8*) Coyote Press.

Pope-Levenson, Priscilla, jt. ed. see Levenson, John R.

Pope-Levinson, Priscilla. Evangelization from a Liberation Perspective. LC 90-40762. (American University Studies: Theology & Religion: Ser. VII, Vol. 69). XII, 201p. (C). 1991. text 36.00 (*0-8204-1169-8*) P Lang Pubng.

Pope, Lillie. Guidelines for Teaching Children with Learning Problems. 333p. 1996. pap. 15.95 (*0-87594-201-6*) Book-Lab.

— Guidelines to Teaching Remedial Reading. 4th rev. ed. (Illus.). 224p. 1996. pap. 14.95 (*0-87594-357-8*) Book-Lab.

— Word Play: Dictionary of Idioms. (Illus.). 148p. (YA). (gr. 4 up). 1998. pap. 15.95 (*0-87594-375-6*) Book-Lab.

Pope, Lillie, et al. Special Needs: Special Answers. (Illus.). (J). (gr. k-6). 1979. pap. 19.95 (*0-87594-181-8*) Book-Lab.

Pope, Liston, Jr. Floriane: Stages of Love. LC 97-92679. 310p. 1998. 24.95 (*0-9638900-3-4*) Mantis Press.

— Living Like the Saints: A Novel of Nicaragua. LC 95-80678. (Works Ser.: II). 300p. 1997. 24.95 (*0-9638900-1-8*) N A Gilbert.

Pope, Liston. Millhands & Preachers: A Study of Gastonia. (Studies in Religious Education: No. 15). (Illus.). (J). 1965. reprint ed. pap. 22.50 (*0-300-00182-7*) Yale U Pr.

Pope, Liston, Jr. Redemption: A Novel of War in Lebanon. LC 93-91788. (Works Ser.: I). 294p. 1994. 24.95 (*0-9638900-0-X*) N A Gilbert.

— Redemption: A Novel of War in Lebanon. 2nd ed. 294p. 1997. reprint ed. pap. 24.95 (*0-9638900-2-6*) Mantis Press.

Pope, Liston. Religion & Class Structure. (Reprint Series in Social Sciences). (C). 1993. reprint ed. pap. text 5.00 (*0-8290-3821-3*, S-225) Irvington.

Pope, Liston, Jr., ed. The Anthology of Socialist Poetry: From Heine to Neruda. (Classics in Literary Translation Ser.: Vol. 2). 1998. pap. 15.00 (*0-9638900-4-2*) Mantis Press.

— Classic Madness: Works by Nerval, Gogol, Buechner, Pirandello, Lu Hsun. (Classics in Literary Translation Ser.: Vol. 1). (CHI, FRE, GER, ITA & RUS.). 1998. pap. 15.00 (*0-9638900-5-0*) Mantis Press.

Pope, Liston, ed. see Institute for Religious & Social Studies Staff.

Pope, Loren. Colleges That Change Lives: 40 Schools You Should Know About Even if You're Not a Straight A Student. LC 95-41331. 224p. 1996. pap. 12.95 (*0-14-023951-0*, Penguin Bks) Viking Penguin.

***Pope, Loren.** Colleges That Change Lives: 40 Schools You Should Know about Even If You're Not a Straight-A Student. rev. ed. LC 00-27877. 304p. 2000. 14.00 (*0-14-029616-6*, Penguin Bks) Viking Penguin.

Pope, Loren. Looking Beyond the Ivy League: Finding the College That's Right for You. LC 95-12252. 1995. pap. 12.95 (*0-14-023952-9*, Penguin Bks) Viking Penguin.

Pope, M. H., jt. ed. see Krag, M. H.

Pope, M. T. Heteropoly & Isopoly Oxometalates. (Inorganic Chemistry Concepts Ser.: Vol. 8). (Illus.). 190p. 1983. 119.95 (*0-387-11889-6*) Spr-Verlag.

Pope, Malcolm H., et al. Occupational Low Back Pain: Assessment, Treatment & Prevention. 2nd ed. 395p. (C). (gr. 13). 2000. text 79.95 (*0-8151-4349-4*, 30028) Mosby Inc.

Pope, Malcom H., et al. Occupational Low Back Pain: Assessment, Treatment & Prevention. (Illus.). 348p. (C). (gr. 13). 1990. text 94.00 (*0-8016-6252-4*, 06252) Mosby Inc.

Pope, Margaret M. This Chosen Generation: Armed with the Gifts of God. 160p. 1994. 12.98 (*0-88290-483-3*, 1968) Horizon Utah.

Pope, Markus W. Programming Internet Controls. LC 96-70103. 480p. 1996. per. 45.00 (*0-7615-0773-6*) Prima Pub.

Pope, Martin & Swenberg, Charles E. Electronic Processes of Organic Crystals & Polymers. 2nd ed. LC 98-34710. (Monographs on the Physics & Chemistry of Materials). (Illus.). 1360p. 1999. text 250.00 (*0-19-512963-6*) OUP.

Pope, Marvin H., ed. Job. rev. ed. (Anchor Bible Ser.: Vol. 15). 504p. 1965. 39.95 (*0-385-00894-5*, Anchor NY) Doubleday.

Pope, Marvin H., intro. Song of Songs. LC 72-79417. (Anchor Bible Ser.: Vol. 7C). (Illus.). 768p. 1977. 44.95 (*0-385-00569-5*, Anchor NY) Doubleday.

Pope, Maurice. The Story of Decipherment: From Egyptian Hieroglyphs to Maya Script. rev. ed. LC 98-61441. (Illus.). 224p. 1999. pap. 19.95 (*0-500-28105-X*, Pub. by Thames Hudson) Norton.

Pope, Michael T. & Muller, Achim, eds. Polyoxometalates: From Platonic Solids to Anti-Retroviral Activity. LC 93-27849. (Topics in Molecular Organization & Engineering Ser.). 411p. (C). 1994. text 251.00 (*0-7923-2421-8*) Kluwer Academic.

Pope, Nancy P. National History in the Heroic Poem: A Comparison of the Aeneid & the Fairie Queen. LC 90-42002. (Studies in Comparative Literature). 208p. 1990. reprint ed. 15.00 (*0-8240-5472-5*) Garland.

***Pope, Nathan R.** How to Interpret the Bible: Bible Study. 1999. 37.99 (*0-8100-0875-0*) Northwest Pub.

Pope, Nathan R. Motivation for Ministry. 1993. pap. 10.99 (*0-8100-0417-8*, 15N0546) Northwest Pub.

Pope, Nick. Open Skies, Closed Minds. LC 98-48795. (Illus.). 270p. 1999. text 23.95 (*0-87951-916-9*, Pub. by Overlook Pr) Penguin Putnam.

***Pope, Nick.** Opens Skies, Closed Minds: For the First Time a Goverment UFO Expert Speaks Out. 320p. 2000. mass mkt. 5.99 (*0-440-23489-1*) Dell.

Pope, Nick. The Uninvited: An Expose of the Alien Abduction Phenomenon. 400p. 1999. mass mkt. 5.99 (*0-440-23487-5*) Dell.

— The Uninvited: An Expose of the Alien Abduction Phenomenon. LC 98-10931. 316p. 1998. 22.95 (*0-87951-878-2*, Pub. by Overlook Pr) Penguin Putnam.

Pope, Nicole, jt. auth. see Pope, Hugh.

***Pope, Nike.** Operation Thunder Child. 320p. 2000. per. 12.00 (*0-684-82442-6*) S&S Trade.

Pope, Nolan F., jt. auth. see Woods, Lawrence A.

Pope, Nori, et al. Color by Design: Planting the Contemporary Garden. LC 98-3891. (Illus.). 160p. 1998. 30.00 (*1-57959-016-0*, SOMA) BB&T Inc.

Pope, P., jt. ed. see Loxton, R.

***Pope, Pamela.** A Collar of Jewels. 512p. 2000. 31.99 (*0-7505-1449-3*) Ulverscroft.

— The Rich Pass By. large type ed. 528p. 2000. 31.99 (*0-7505-1450-7*, Pub. by Mgna Lrg Print) Ulverscroft.

Pope, Patricia. Seashore & Wading Birds of Florida. rev. ed. (Illus.). 44p. 1975. pap. 4.95 (*0-8200-0903-2*) Great Outdoors.

— Shellcraft Animals. LC 75-15906. (Short-Time Projects for Beginners Ser.). (Illus.). 32p. (Orig.). 1975. pap. 1.00 (*0-8200-0507-X*) Great Outdoors.

***Pope, Paul.** Escapo. 1999. 19.95 (*1-882402-16-2*) NBM.

— Escapo: A Life Affirming Romance Set in a Fin-de-Siecle Circus. (Illus.). 112p. (YA). 1999. pap. text 9.95 (*1-882402-14-6*) NBM.

Pope, Paul. The One-Trick Rip-Off. 120p. 1997. 12.95 (*1-56971-244-1*) Dark Horse Comics.

Pope, Peter E. The Many Landfalls of John Cabot. LC 98-112689. (Illus.). 208p. 1997. pap. 17.95 (*0-8020-7150-3*); text 50.00 (*0-8020-0786-4*) U of Toronto Pr.

Pope, Randolph D. Understanding Juan Goytisolo. Hardin, James, ed. LC 95-11606. (Understanding Modern European & Latin American Literature Ser.). 190p. 1995. text 29.95 (*1-57003-069-3*) U of SC Pr.

Pope, Randolph D., ed. The Analysis of Literary Texts: Current Trends in Methodology (Third & Fourth York College Colloquia) LC 79-54144. (Studies in Literary Analysis). 330p. 1980. pap. text 20.00 (*0-916950-13-1*); lib. bdg. 30.00 (*0-916950-14-X*) Biling Rev-Pr.

Pope, Randolph D., tr. see Wolff, Geoffrey.

Pope, Raymond P. Seventy Two Hours in Hell. 176p. (Orig.). 1989. pap. 10.00 (*0-944765-01-7*) Agape Bks.

Pope, Rebbecca A., jt. auth. see Leonardi, Susan J.

Pope, Rex. The British Economy since 1914: A Study in Decline? LC 98-18329. (Seminar Studies in History). 128p. (C). (gr. 5). 1998. pap. 15.93 (*0-582-30194-7*) Longman.

Pope, Rex, et al, eds. Social Welfare in Britain, Eighteen Eighty-Five to Nineteen Eighty-Five. 192p. (Orig.). (C). 1986. 37.50 (*0-7099-4001-7*, Pub. by C Helm) Routldge.

Pope, Rob. The English Studies Handbook. LC 97-16912. 440p. (C). 1998. 85.00 (*0-415-12866-8*); pap. 24.99 (*0-415-12867-6*) Routledge.

***Pope, Rob.** How to Study Chaucer. LC 00-42054. (Study Guides Ser.). (C). 2000. pap. write for info. (*0-312-23806-1*) St Martin.

Pope, Rob. Textual Intervention: Critical & Creative Strategies for Literary Studies. LC 94-4022. (Interface Ser.). (Illus.). 350p. (C). (gr. 13). 1994. pap. 24.99 (*0-415-05437-0*) Routledge.

***Pope, Robert.** Seeking God's Kingdom: The Nonconformist Social Gospel in Wales, 1906-1939. 224p. 2000. 50.00 (*0-7083-1568-2*, Pub. by U Wales Pr) Paul & Co Pubs.

Pope, Robert G. Half-Way Covenant: Church Membership in Puritan New England. LC 69-18067. 333p. reprint ed. 103.30 (*0-8357-9500-4*, 201147300078) Bks Demand.

Pope, Robert G., ed. The Notebook of the Reverend John Fiske, 1644 to 1675. LC 74-81447. 256p. 1974. 17.50 (*0-88389-052-6*, PEMP185, Essx Institute) Peabody Essex Mus.

Pope, Robert H. Incidental Grace. 176p. 1985. pap. 6.95 (*0-310-34651-7*, 12743P) Zondervan.

Pope, Robert W. My Patients with Tales: The Experiences of a Wisconsin Veterinarian. (Illus.). 120p. 1999. pap. 11.25 (*0-9669829-0-8*, 0101) Pause Pub Co.

Pope, Rodney J. Andrews Field: First United States World War Two Airbase in Europe, with a Brief History of Great Saling. (Illus.). 80p. (Orig.). 1991. pap. 15.00 (*0-86025-428-3*, Pub. by I Henry Pubns) Empire Pub Srvs.

Pope, Rowena M. The Hungry Years: The Story of One Family's Struggle for Survival During the Great Depression. LC 82-71137. (Illus.). 176p. (Orig.). (gr. 11-12). 1982. pap. 8.95 (*0-9608182-0-0*) Bold Blue Jay Pubns.

— Speak the Truth in Love. 71p. (Orig.). 1988. pap. 4.00 (*0-9608182-2-7*) Bold Blue Jay Pubns.

***Pope, S. & Rinehart, Robert E.** Encyclopedia of Extreme Sports. 2001. lib. bdg. 75.00 (*1-57607-228-2*) ABC-CLIO.

Pope, Sara. Manager's Pocket Guide to Team Sponsorship. 1997. pap. text 7.95 (*0-87425-421-3*) HRD Press.

Pope, Saxton. Hunting with the Bow & Arrow. 1991. 36.00 (*1-879356-05-8*) Wolfe Pub Co.

— A Study of Bows & Arrows. fac. ed. (University of California Publications in American Archaeology & Ethnology: Vol. 13: 9). 85p. (C). 1923. reprint ed. pap. text 9.69 (*1-55567-216-7*) Coyote Press.

Pope, Saxton T. The Medical History of Ishi. fac. ed. (University of California Publications in American Archaeology & Ethnology: Vol. 13: 5). (Illus.). 38p. (C). 1920. reprint ed. pap. text 4.38 (*1-55567-214-0*) Coyote Press.

Pope-Selman, Linda, ed. see Ingold, Gerard.

Pope St. Gregory the Great. The Life of St. Benedict (480-547) 71p. 1995. pap. 2.00 (*0-89555-512-3*) TAN Bks Pubs.

Pope Staff. New Antoinette Pope School Cookbook. 1980. 22.95 (*0-02-598060-2*) Macmillan.

***Pope, Stephen.** Dictionary of the Napoleonic Wars. LC 99-48829. (Illus.). 600p. 1999. 65.00 (*0-8160-4243-8*) Facts on File.

Pope, Stephen. The Evolution of Altruism & the Ordering of Love. LC 93-37489. 176p. (C). 1994. 40.00 (*0-87840-550-X*) Georgetown U Pr.

Pope, Stephen. The Evolution of Altruism & the Ordering of Love. (Moral Traditions & Moral Arguments Ser.). 176p. (C). 1995. pap. 19.95 (*0-87840-597-6*) Georgetown U Pr.

Pope, Stephen. Hornblower's Navy: Life at Sea in the Age of Nelson. (Illus.). 111p. 1998. pap. text 22.95 (*1-56649-030-8*) Welcome Rain.

Pope, Stephen & Wheal, Elizabeth-Anne. Dictionary of the First World War. Robbins, Keith, ed. (Illus.). 561p. 1995. text 40.00 (*0-312-12931-9*) St Martin.

Pope, Stephen, jt. auth. see Wheal, Elizabeth-Anne.

P

***Pope, Stephen Bailey.** Turbulent Flows. LC QA913.P64 2000. (Illus.). 800p. (C). 2000. write for info. (*0-521-59125-2*); pap. write for info. (*0-521-59886-9*) Cambridge U Pr.

Pope, Stephen J., jt. auth. see Himes, Michael J.

Pope, Stephen T., ed. The Well-Tempered Object: Musical Applications of Object Oriented Software Technology. (Illus.). 204p. 1991. 33.50 (*0-262-16126-5*) MIT Pr.

Pope, Steven W. Patriotic Games: Sporting Traditions in the American Imagination, 1876-1926. (Sports History & Society). (Illus.). 240p. 1997. text 39.95 (*0-19-509133-7*) OUP.

Pope, Steven W., ed. The New American Sport History: Recent Approaches & Perspectives. LC 96-6137. (Sport & Society Ser.). (Illus.). 440p. 1996. pap. text 19.95 (*0-252-06567-0*) U of Ill Pr.

Pope, Susan. Damaris Tale. 1999. pap. 17.95 (*0-670-83106-9*) Viking Penguin.

Pope, Terri A. Look What I Made! Easy Holiday Crafts for Young Children. Weaver-Spencer, Jennifer, ed. (Illus.). 96p. (J). (ps-1). 1998. pap. text 10.95 (*0-88724-470-X*, CD-0060) Carson-Dellos.

Pope, Thomas, et al. Attracting Birds to Southern Gardens. LC 93-7572. 176p. 1995. 24.95 (*0-87833-830-6*, OATTRA) Claitors.

Pope, Thomas H. The History of Newberry County, South Carolina, 1860-1990, Vol. 2. LC 72-13449. (Illus.). 406p. 1992. 39.95 (*0-87249-777-1*) U of SC Pr.

Pope, Thomas L., et al. Atlas of Musculoskeletal Imaging. LC 98-27858. (Illus.). 552p. 1999. 89.00 (*0-86577-695-4*) Thieme Med Pubs.

Pope, Thomas L., Jr., jt. auth. see Ford, Kenneth L., III.

Pope, Thomas Lee, jt. auth. see Spouge, Alison R.

Pope, Thomas R. Prentice Hall's 97 Individual Federal Tax Guide. 1104p. 1996. 72.00 (*0-13-239484-7*) P-H.

***Pope, Thomas R., et al.** Prentice Hall's Federal Taxation 2001: Comprehensive. 1664p. 2000. 92.00 (*0-13-026019-3*, Prentice Hall) P-H.

Pope, Thomas R., jt. auth. see Kramer, John L.

Pope, Tom. Good Scripts, Bad Scripts: Learning the Craft of Screenwriting. LC 97-45528. 256p. 1998. pap. 14.00 (*0-609-80119-8*, Crown) Crown Pub Group.

Pope, Trey. Barbecue on My Mind. 70p. 1991. pap. 6.95 (*0-9632057-0-6*) Three Pubns.

— Barbecue on My Mind: The Thirty Best Barbecue Restaurants in Georgia. LC 92-15431. 80p. (Orig.). 1992. pap. 7.95 (*0-87797-240-0*) Cherokee.

Pope, Virginia, tr. see Papini, Giovanni.

Pope, W. C. Pope's Puns & Other Air Force Cartoons. (Illus.). 96p. 1998. pap. 8.95 (*0-9671229-0-2*) Paradox Prods NY.

***Pope, Whitney.** The Search for Freedom. LC 99-30461. 224p. 1999. text 40.00 (*0-8142-0831-2*); pap. text 17.00 (*0-8142-5033-5*) Ohio St U Pr.

Pope, Willard B., ed. see Barrett, Elizabeth B. & Haydon, Benjamin R.

Pope, Willard B., ed. see Haydon, Benjamin R.

Pope, William C. Managing for Performance Perfection: The Changing Emphasis, Vol. 1. (Illus.). 344p. (Orig.). (C). 1990. pap. text 39.95 (*0-944453-00-7*) B Brae.

Pope, William L. Israel As a Nation. Hogg, Gayle, ed. 184p. 1983. pap. text 11.50 (*0-311-72225-3*) Casa Bautista.

Popeil, Russell. RPG Error Handling Technique: Bulletproofing Your Applications. (Illus.). 164p. 1995. pap. 39.00 incl. disk (*1-882419-38-3*) News Four-Hund.

Popejoy, Lori L., jt. auth. see Rantz, Marilyn J.

Popek, Gerald J. The Locus Distributed System Architecture. (MIT Press Series in Computer Systems). (Illus.). 176p. 1986. 30.00 (*0-262-16102-8*) MIT Pr.

Popel, A. S. & Johnson, P. C., eds. Microvascular Networks: Experimental & Theoretical Studies. (Illus.). x, 226p. 1986. 172.25 (*3-8055-4323-9*) S Karger.

Popel, Aleksander, ed. see Symposium on Mathematics of Microcirculation Pheno.

***Popel, S. I.** Surface Phenomena in Melts. 400p. 1999. 160.00 (*1-898326-69-X*, Pub. by CISP) Balogh.

***Popel, S. I., et al.** Atomic Ordering in Molten & Amorphous Metals. 350p. 1999. boxed set 150.00 (*1-898326-68-1*, Pub. by CISP) Balogh.

Popelar, Carl H., jt. auth. see Kanninen, Melvin F.

Popelier, P. L. A., jt. auth. see Gillespie, R. J.

Popelka, Jan, jt. auth. see Lineman, Rose.

Popelka, Susan. Super Science with Simple Stuff! Activities for the Intermediate Grades. 256p. 1997. pap. text 21.95 (*0-201-49612-7*) Addison-Wesley.

***Popely, Rick & Riggs, L. Spencer.** Indianapolis 500 Chronicle LC 99-178274. 416p. 1998. write for info. (*0-7853-2798-3*) Pubns Intl Ltd.

***Popenhagen, Ludvika.** Nekrosius & Lithuanian Theatre. LC 98-13038. (Artists & Issues in the Theatre Ser.: Vol. 8). 200p. 1999. 43.95 (*0-8204-4062-0*) P Lang Pubng.

Popenoe. Sociology. 11th ed. LC 99-40919. 588p. 1999. pap. 48.00 (*0-13-095745-3*) P-H.

Popenoe, Cris. Japan for Westerners. (Bookshop Guides Ser.). (Illus.). 88p. (Orig.). 1986. pap. 5.95 (*0-936119-00-4*) Yes Inc.

Popenoe, David. Disturbing the Nest: Family Change & Decline in Modern Societies. (Social Institutions & Social Change Ser.). 407p. 1988. pap. text 32.95 (*0-202-30351-9*); lib. bdg. 59.95 (*0-202-30350-0*) Aldine de Gruyter.

— Life Without Father. 288p. 1996. 24.50 (*0-684-82297-0*, M Kessler Bks) Free Pr.

— Life Without Father: Compelling New Evidence That Fatherhood & Marriage Are Indispensable for the Good of Children & Society. 288p. 1999. 15.95 (*0-674-53260-0*) HUP.

— Private Pleasure, Public Plight: American Metropolitan Community Life in Comparative Perspective. LC 84-16411. 192p. 1988. pap. 24.95 (*0-88738-766-7*) Transaction Pubs.

***Popenoe, David.** Private Pleasure, Public Plight: American Metropolitan Community Life in Comparative Perspective. 2000. pap. 24.95 (*0-7658-0708-4*) Transaction Pubs.

Popenoe, David. The Suburban Environment: Sweden & the United States. LC 76-8091. (Studies of Urban Society). 288p. 1998. lib. bdg. 29.00 (*0-226-67542-4*) U Ch Pr.

Popenoe, David, ed. The Urban-Industrial Frontier: Essays on Social Trends & Institutional Goals in Modern Communities. LC 73-75680. 191p. reprint ed. pap. 59.30 (*0-7837-5636-4*, 205063100087) Bks Demand.

Popenoe, David, et al, eds. Promises to Keep: Decline & Renewal of Marriage in America. LC 96-7003. 340p. 1996. 62.50 (*0-8476-8230-7*); pap. 23.95 (*0-8476-8231-5*) Rowman.

Popenoe, Paul, jt. auth. see Gosney, E. S.

Poper, Roy. Roy Poper's Guide to the Brasswind Methods of James Stamp. 32p. (C). 1995. pap. 9.80 (*0-9630856-4-6*) Balquhidder.

Popescu, Adela. Between Us - Time. (Illus.). (Orig.). 1993. pap. 25.00 (*0-9619930-6-5*) Moonfall Pr VA.

Popescu, Bogdan M., ed. Hydrocarbon Exploration History in Eastern Central Europe. LC 93-26022. 1995. 172.95 (*0-387-55014-3*) Spr-Verlag.

Popescu, Calin M. & Charoenngam, Chotchai. Project Planning, Scheduling & Control in Construction: An Encyclopedia of Terms & Applications. LC 94-35464. 573p. 1995. 110.00 (*0-471-02858-4*) Wiley.

Popescu, Calin M. & Hamiani, Abdelwahab. Directory of Microcomputer Software for Cost Engineering. LC 85-12847. 199p. reprint ed. pap. 61.70 (*0-7837-3365-8*, 204332300008) Bks Demand.

Popescu, D., jt. ed. see Badescu, L.

Popescu, Dumitru R. The Royal Hunt. Cottrell, J. E. & Bogdan, M., trs. LC 85-4985. 188p. reprint ed. pap. 58.30 (*0-608-09865-5*, 206983000006) Bks Demand.

Popescu-Judetz, Eugenia, tr. see Neamtu, Cella.

Popescu, Julian. Bulgaria: Major World Nations. LC 99-19239. (Illus.). 144p. 1999. 19.95 (*0-7910-5380-6*) Chelsea Hse.

— Hungary: Major World Nations. LC 99-19153. (Illus.). 144p. 1999. 19.95 (*0-7910-5386-5*) Chelsea Hse.

— Italian for Commerce. 2nd ed. LC 87-10275. (Illus.). 200p. 1987. 85.00 (*0-08-033956-5*, Pub. by Pergamon Repr) Franklin.

— Poland: Major World Nations. LC 99-13405. (Major World Nations Ser.). (Illus.). 144p. 1999. 19.95 (*0-7910-5394-6*) Chelsea Hse.

— Romania: Major World Nations. LC 99-13406. (Major World Nations Ser.). (Illus.). 144p. (J). 1999. 19.95 (*0-7910-5396-2*) Chelsea Hse.

— Russia: Major World Nations. LC 97-18041. (Major World Nations Ser.). (Illus.). 144p. (YA). (gr. 5 up). 1999. lib. bdg. 19.95 (*0-7910-4750-4*) Chelsea Hse.

Popescu, Ludmila. Select Scientific Developments in Romania: The Physical Chemistry of Molten Salts: A Case Study. Dawson, Melissa, ed. (Illus.). 109p. (Orig.). 1989. pap. text 75.00 (*1-55831-097-5*) Delphic Associates.

Popescu, Marcela, jt. auth. see Dumitrescu, Constantin.

Popescu, Marcela, ed. see Ashbacher, Charles.

Popescu, Oreste. Studies in the History of Latin American Economic Thought. LC 96-33540. 336p. (C). 1997. 85.00 (*0-415-14901-0*) Routledge.

***Popescu, Paul, et al, eds.** Techniques in Animal Cytogenetics. Popescu, R., tr. from FRE. LC 00-25600. (Principles & Practice Ser.). (Illus.). xiv, 246p. 2000. 74.00 (*3-540-66737-7*) Spr-Verlag.

Popescu, Petru. Almost Adam. 1997. mass mkt. 6.99 (*0-380-72824-9*, Avon Bks) Morrow Avon.

Popescu, R., tr. see Popescu, Paul, et al, eds.

Popescu-Zeletin, R., jt. auth. see Rothermel, Kurt.

Popescu-Zeletin, Radu, jt. auth. see Magendanz, Thomas.

Popesko, Peter. Colour Atlas of Anatomy of Small Laboratory Animals, 1. (Illus.). 1992. text 165.00 (*0-7234-1822-5*) CRC Pr.

— Colour Atlas of Anatomy of Small Laboratory Animals, 2. (Illus.). 1992. text 165.00 (*0-7234-1823-3*) CRC Pr.

***Popham.** Modern Educational Measurement: Practical Guidelines for Educational Leaders. 3rd ed. LC 99-22345. 466p. (C). 1999. 64.00 (*0-205-28770-0*, Macmillan Coll) P-H.

Popham, A. E. The Drawings of Leonardo Da Vinci. (Pimlico Ser.). (Illus.). 528p. 1994. pap. 22.95 (*0-7126-6100-X*, Pub. by Pimlico) Trafalgar.

— Old Master Drawings at Holkham Hall. Lloyd, Christopher, ed. (Illus.). 152p. 1987. lib. bdg. 150.00 incl. fiche (*0-226-69273-6*) U Ch Pr.

Popham, Clarence & Williams, Lorna. Early Days in the Sagebrush Country. LC 98-65208. vi, 130 p. 1997. 15.95 (*1-57510-039-8*) Pictorial Hist.

Popham, Elizabeth A., ed. see Klein, A. M.

Popham, Estelle L., jt. auth. see Ettinger, Blanche.

Popham, James W. Classroom Assessment: What Teachers Need to Know. 2nd ed. LC 98-3070. 324p. 1998. pap. text 47.33 (*0-205-27692-X*) Allyn.

Popham, Mervyn R. & Gill, Margaret. The Latest Sealings from the Palace & Houses at Knossos. (BSA Studies: Vol. 1). (Illus.). 123p. (Orig.). 1995. pap. 38.00 (*0-904887-24-3*) Brit Sch Athens.

Popham, Mervyn R., et al. Lefkandi III: The Toumba Cemetery : The Excavations of 1981, 1984, 1986 & 1992-4. LC 97-189550. 1996. write for info. (*0-904887-27-8*) Brit Sch Athens.

Popham, Peter. Traveler's Companion: Japan. (Traveler's Companion Ser.). (Illus.). 272p. 1998. pap. 22.95 (*0-7627-0253-2*) Globe Pequot.

— Wooden Temples of Japan. (Travel to Landmarks Ser.). 1992. 24.95 (*1-85043-175-2*, Pub. by I B T) St Martin.

Popham, Richard A. A Key to the Genera of the Compositales of Northeastern North America. (Bulletin Ser.: No. 38). 1941. pap. text 2.00 (*0-86727-037-3*) Ohio Bio Survey.

Popham, W. James. Criterion-Referenced Measurement. (Illus.). 1978. pap. 19.95 (*0-685-03817-3*) P-H.

— Educational Evaluation. 3rd rev. ed. LC 92-13806. (Illus.). 372p. 1992. 83.00 (*0-205-14217-6*) Allyn.

— Modern Educational Measurement: A Practitioner's Perspective. 2nd rev. ed. (Illus.). 464p. (C). 1989. pap. text 72.00 (*0-13-593898-8*) IOX Amnt Assocs.

— Tests That Help Teaching. 43p. (Orig.). 1995. pap. 29.00 (*0-614-14879-0*) IOX Amnt Assocs.

Popic, Relja. English-Serbocroat Dictionary of Science & Technology. 1096p. (C). 1987. 300.00 (*0-7855-6456-X*, Pub. by Collets) St Mut.

— Russian-Serbocroatian Scientific-Technical Dictionary: Naucno - Tehnicki Recnik Rusko-Srpskohrvatski. (RUS & SER.). 812p. 1986. 75.00 (*0-8288-2129-1*, F28341) Fr & Eur.

Popic, Relja, et al. English-Serbocroatian Scientific & Technical Dictionary. (ENG & SER.). 1140p. 1988. 195.00 (*0-8288-0658-6*, M 9688) Fr & Eur.

Popiel, Paul A. Financial Systems in Sub-Saharan Africa: A Comparative Study. (FRE.). 106p. 1995. pap. 22.00 (*0-8213-3305-4*, 13305) World Bank.

Popielawski, J., ed. The Dynamics of Systems with Chemical Reaction. 448p. 1989. text 89.00 (*9971-5-0676-9*) World Scientific Pub.

Popielawski, J. & Gorecki, J., eds. Far from Equilibrium Dynamics of Chemical Systems. 440p. (C). 1991. text 118.00 (*981-02-0528-7*) World Scientific Pub.

Popik, Barry A., jt. auth. see Cohen, Gerald Leonard.

Popik, David S. Winning Blackjack Without Counting Cards. 216p. 1992. pap. 7.95 (*0-8216-2519-5*, Carol Paperbacks) Carol Pub Group.

Popineau, Yves, jt. ed. see Gueguen, J.

Popio, Kathryn. Heart's Rest. 1992. pap. 7.95 (*1-55673-457-3*, 7912) CSS OH.

Popivanov, Petar R., jt. auth. see Gramchev, Todor V.

Popivanov, Peter R. & Palagachev, Dian K. The Degenerate Oblique Derivative Problem for Elliptic & Parabolic Equations. LC 97-151018. 153p. 1997. 64.95 (*3-05-501757-9*, Pub. by Akademie Verlag) Wiley.

Popivanov, Peter R. & Palagachev, Dian K. The Degenerate Oblique Derivative Problem for Elliptic & Parabolic Equations. 156p. 1997. pap. 89.95 (*3-527-40112-1*) Wiley.

Popken & Hagood. Generations America. 120p. (C). 1998. pap. text 36.40 (*0-201-45656-7*) Addison-Wesley.

Popken, Penny, ed. see Steiner, Erica, et al.

Popken, Randall. Departures: Reader for Developing Writers. 3rd ed. 182p. (C). 1994. text 32.00 (*0-536-58596-2*) Pearson Custom.

Popken, Randall, et al. Departures: A Reader for Developing Writers. LC 94-29358. 350p. 1994. pap. text 30.00 (*0-205-16249-5*) Allyn.

Popken, Randall L., et al. Departures: A Reader for Developing Writers: Examination Copy. 384p. (C). 1994. pap. text. write for info. (*0-205-16902-3*, H6902-4) Allyn.

Popkes, Steve, jt. auth. see Anderson, Poul.

Popkewitz, Thomas S. Change & Stability in Schooling. 112p. (C). 1983. 45.00 (*0-7300-0002-8*, Pub. by Deakin Univ) St Mut.

— A Political Sociology of Educational Reform: Power - Knowledge in Teaching, Teacher Education, & Research. 304p. (C). 1991. text 49.00 (*0-8077-3091-2*); pap. text 22.95 (*0-8077-3090-4*) Tchrs Coll.

— Struggling for the Soul: The Politics of Schooling & the Construction of the Teacher. LC 97-52181. 1998. 48.00 (*0-8077-3729-1*); pap. 22.95 (*0-8077-3728-3*) Tchrs Coll.

Popkewitz, Thomas S., ed. Changing Patterns of Power: Social Regulation & Teacher Education Reform. LC 92-15861. (SUNY Series, Teacher Preparation & Development). 382p. (C). 1993. text 64.50 (*0-7914-1447-7*); pap. text 21.95 (*0-7914-1448-5*) State U NY Pr.

— Educational Knowledge. LC 99-20650. (Suny Ser.). 448p. (C). 2000. pap. text 23.95 (*0-7914-4404-X*) State U NY Pr.

— Educational Knowledge: Changing Relationships Between the State, Civil Society & the Educational Community. LC 99-20650. (Suny Ser.). 448p. (C). 2000. text 71.50 (*0-7914-4403-1*) State U NY Pr.

Popkewitz, Thomas S. & Brennan, Marie. Foucault's Challenge: Discourse, Knowledge, & Power in Education. LC 97-34270. 1997. 58.00 (*0-8077-3677-5*) Tchrs Coll.

Popkewitz, Thomas S. & Brennan, Marie, eds. Foucault's Challenge: Discourse, Knowledge & Power in Education. LC 97-34270. 400p. 1997. pap. 27.95 (*0-8077-3676-7*) Tchrs Coll.

Popkewitz, Thomas S. & Fendler, Lynn. Critical Theories in Education: Changing Terrains of Knowledge & Politics. LC 98-34518. (Education, Social Theory, & Cultural Change Ser.). 1999. 80.00 (*0-415-92239-9*); pap. 22.99 (*0-415-92240-2*) Routledge.

Popkewitz, Thomas S. & Tabachnick, B. Robert. The Study of Schooling: Field-Based Methodologies in Educational Research & Evaluation. LC 81-1416. 301p. 1981. 59.95 (*0-275-90705-8*, C0705, Praeger Pubs) Greenwood.

***Popkewitz, Thomas S., et al.** Cultural History & Critical Studies of Education: Dissenting Essays. LC 00-42500. 2000. write for info. (*0-415-92806-0*) Routledge.

Popkin. Comprehensive Structural COBOL. 4th ed. (Computer Science Ser.). 1993. pap., suppl. ed. 81.95 (*0-534-93580-X*) PWS Pubs.

— Introduction to Federal Income Taxation. 1987. teacher ed. write for info. (*0-8205-0292-8*) Bender.

— Introduction to Federal Income Taxation. 1990. suppl. ed. write for info. (*0-8205-0293-6*) Bender.

— Women's Health Today: Perspectives on Current Research & Clinical Practice. LC 94-22810. (Illus.). 418p. (C). 1994. text 75.00 (*1-85070-568-2*) Prthnon Pub.

***Popkin, ed.** Columbia History of Western Philosophy. 2000. 14.98 (*1-56731-347-7*, MJF Bks) Fine Comms.

Popkin, Arlene. My April Fool Book. (Illus.). (J). (ps-1). 1974. lib. bdg. 11.86 (*0-914844-04-0*) J Alden.

Popkin, Barney P., jt. ed. see Charbeneau, Randall J.

Popkin, Barry M., et al. The Infant-Feeding Triad: Infant, Mother, & Household. (Food & Nutrition in History & Anthropology Ser.: Vol. 5). xvi, 248p. 1986. text 181.00 (*2-88124-142-5*) Gordon & Breach.

Popkin, Barry M., jt. auth. see McGuire, Judith S.

Popkin, Cathy. The Pragmatics of Insignificance: Chekhov, Zoshchenko, Gogol. LC 93-7021. (Illus.). 304p. (C). 1993. 42.50 (*0-8047-2209-9*) Stanford U Pr.

Popkin, David. Vocabulary Energizers: Stories of Word Origins. 143p. (Orig.). (C). 1988. pap. text 9.95 (*0-929166-01-9*) Hada Pubns.

— Vocabulary Energizers II: Stories of Word Origins. 149p. (Orig.). (C). 1990. pap. text 9.95 (*0-929166-02-7*) Hada Pubns.

Popkin, Gary S. Comprehensive Structured COBOL. LC 83-25596. 560p. 1984. mass mkt. 29.50 (*0-534-03112-9*) PWS Pubs.

— Comprehensive Structured COBOL. 2nd ed. 708p. (YA). (gr. 11-12). 1986. mass mkt. 41.75 (*0-534-06216-4*) PWS Pubs.

— Comprehensive Structured COBOL. 4th ed. LC 92-32568. 784p. (C). 1993. mass mkt. 64.95 (*0-534-93270-3*) PWS Pubs.

Popkin, James M., jt. auth. see Scales, John K.

Popkin, Jeremy D. News & Politics in the Age of Revolution: Jean Luzac's "Gazette de Leyde" LC 89-31379. (Illus.). 304p. 1989. text 45.00 (*0-8014-2301-5*) Cornell U Pr.

— Revolutionary News: The Press in France, 1789-1799. Baker, Keith M. & Kaplan, Steven L., eds. LC 89-28511. (Bicentennial Reflections on the French Revolution Ser.). 239p. (C). 1990. text 49.95 (*0-8223-0984-X*); pap. text 15.95 (*0-8223-0997-1*) Duke.

— The Right-Wing Press in France, 1792-1800. LC 79-14067. 254p. reprint ed. pap. 78.80 (*0-7837-0310-4*, 204063200018) Bks Demand.

— A Short History of the French Revolution. 2nd ed. LC 97-11955. 166p. (C). 1997. pap. text 27.20 (*0-13-647421-7*) P-H.

Popkin, Jeremy D., ed. Media & Revolution. LC 94-31808. (Illus.). 256p. 1995. text 32.50 (*0-8131-1899-9*) U Pr of Ky.

***Popkin, Jeremy D. & Popkin, Richard H.** The Abbe Gregoire & His World. LC 00-28220. 2000. write for info. (*0-7923-6247-0*) Kluwer Academic.

Popkin, Jeremy D., jt. auth. see Mercier, Louis-Sebastien.

Popkin, Jeremy D., ed. see Mercier, Louis-Sebastien.

Popkin, Louise B., jt. ed. see Sosnowski, Saul.

Popkin, Margaret L. Civil Patrols & Their Legacy: Overcoming Militarization & Polarization in the Guatemalan Countryside. Silk, James J., ed. & intro. by. 80p. 1996. pap. text. write for info. (*1-881055-06-X*) RFK Mem Ctr HR.

— Las Patrullas Civiles y Su Legado: Superar la Militarizacion y Polarizacion del Campo Guatemalteco. Silk, James J., ed. Siebentritt, Gretta T., tr. 80p. 1996. pap. text. write for info. (*1-881055-07-8*) RFK Mem Ctr HR.

***Popkin, Margaret L.** Peace Without Justice: Obstacles to Building the Rule of Law in El Salvador. 2000. 45.00 (*0-271-01997-2*); pap. 18.95 (*0-271-01998-0*) Pa St U Pr.

Popkin, Mark & Glickman, Loren. Bassoon Reed Making. 1994. 20.00 (*0-318-37569-9*) Instrumental.

Popkin, Michael H. Active Parenting of Teens: Leader's Guide. rev. ed. Cox, Michele L., ed. (Illus.). 168p. 1998. ring bd. 25.95 (*1-880283-18-2*) Active Parenting.

— Active Parenting of Teens: Parent's Guide. rev. ed. Cox, Michele L., ed. (Illus.). 255p. (Orig.). 1998. pap. text 13.95 (*1-880283-19-0*) Active Parenting.

— Active Parenting of Teens: The Basics, Parent's Guide. (Illus.). 144p. (Orig.). 1994. pap. text 13.95 (*1-880283-10-7*) Active Parenting.

— Active Parenting Today: For Parents of 2 to 12 year Olds: Short Course Leader's Guide. (Illus.). 160p. 1995. spiral bd. 13.95 (*1-880283-12-3*) Active Parenting.

— Active Parenting Today: The Basics: A Guide for Parents of 2 to 12 Year Olds. (Illus.). 112p. (Orig.). 1993. pap. 13.95 (*1-880283-06-9*) Active Parenting.

— Active Parenting Today Leader's Guide: For Parents of 2-12 Year Olds. 168p. 1993. spiral bd. 24.95 (*1-880283-04-2*) Active Parenting.

— Active Parenting Today Parent's Guide: For Parents of 2-12 Year Olds. 168p. 1993. pap. 13.95 (*1-880283-03-4*) Active Parenting.

— Active Teaching Leader's Guide: Enhancing Discipline, Self-Esteem & Student Performance. (Illus.). 176p. 1994. spiral bd. 39.95 (*1-880283-07-7*) Active Parenting.

— Active Teaching Teacher's Handbook: Enhancing Discipline, Self-Esteem & Student Performance. (Illus.). 191p. (Orig.). 1994. pap. 14.95 (*1-880283-08-5*) Active Parenting.

— Free the Horses: Storybook & Songbook. Greathead, Susan D. & Sardinas-Wyssling, Karen, eds. (Illus.). 80p. (J). (gr. 1-3). 1991. pap. 6.95 (*0-9618020-7-3*) Active Parenting.

Popkin, Michael H. & Greathead, Susan D. Free the Horses: A Self-Esteem Adventure. (Illus.). 234p. (J). (gr. 1-4). 1991. teacher ed. 29.95 (*0-9618020-6-5*) Active Parenting.

P

Popkin, Michael H. & Hannaford, Mary J. Windows: Healing & Helping Through Loss. (Illus.). 144p. 1992. pap. text 11.95 (*0-9618020-9-X*) Active Parenting.
— Windows: Healing & Helping Through Loss: When You Have Lost. (Illus.). 16p. (Orig.). 1992. pap. text 1.50 (*1-880283-01-8*) Active Parenting.
— Windows: Healing & Helping Through Loss: When You Want to Help. (Illus.). 16p. (Orig.). 1992. pap. text 1.50 (*1-880283-02-6*) Active Parenting.
— Windows Leader's Guide: Healing & Helping Through Loss. (Illus.). 96p. 1992. spiral bd. 18.95 (*1-880283-00-X*) Active Parenting.
Popkin, Michael H., et al. Helping Your Child Succeed in School: A Guide for Parents of 4 to 14 Year Olds. (Illus.). 215p. (Orig.). 1995. pap. text 13.95 (*1-880283-15-8*) Active Parenting.
— 1, 2, 3, 4 Padres! Guia para el Lider: Techicas Efectivas para los Padres de Ninos de la 4 Anos Deedad. (SPA., Illus.). 107p. 1998. 24.95 (*1-880283-21-2*) Active Parenting.
— 1, 2, 3, 4 Parents! Leader's Guide: Parenting Children Ages 1-to-4 Leader's Guide. (Illus.). 112p. 1996. 24.95 (*1-880283-16-6*) Active Parenting.
— Parenting Your 1- to 4-Year-Old: Parent's Workbook. (Illus.). 96p. (Orig.). 1996. pap., wbk. ed. 12.95 (*1-880283-17-4*) Active Parenting.
— Parents on Board: Leader's Guide: Building Academic Success Through Parent Involvement for Parents of 4 to 14 Year Olds. 111p. 1995. spiral bd. 24.95 (*1-880283-14-X*) Active Parenting.
— Technicas Efectivas para los Padres de Ninos de la 4 Anos de Edad: Cunderno de Ejercicios para los Padres. (SPA., Illus.). 89p. 1998. pap. 12.95 (*1-880283-22-0*) Active Parenting.
Popkin, Michael K., jt. ed. see Jaranson, James M.
Popkin, P. R., jt. auth. see Hill, Leslie A.
Popkin, Richard, intro. Bayle's Dictionary: Historical & Critical, 5 vols. (Early Sources in Reference Ser.). 2100p. (C). 1997. 1070.00 (*0-415-15387-5*) Routledge.
Popkin, Richard H. The High Road to Pyrrhonism. Watson, Richard A. & Force, James E., eds. LC 93-38549. 399p. 1989. pap. text 19.95 (*0-87220-251-8*); lib. bdg. 42.95 (*0-87220-252-6*) Hackett Pub.
— The History of Scepticism from Erasmus to Spinoza. LC 78-65469. 1979. pap. 17.95 (*0-520-03876-2*, Pub. by U CA Pr) Cal Prin Full Svc.
— Philosophy of the Sixteenth & Seventeenth Centuries. LC 66-10365. (Orig.). 1966. pap. 16.95 (*0-02-925490-6*) Free Pr.
— The Second Oswald. 17.95 (*0-8488-0888-6*) Amereon Ltd.
— The Second Oswald. 19.95 (*1-56723-086-5*) Yestermorrow.
— The Third Force in Seventeenth-Century Thought. LC 91-10145. (Studies in Intellectual History: Vol. 22). vi, 380p. 1991. 121.00 (*90-04-09324-9*) Brill Academic Pubs.
Popkin, Richard H., ed. The Columbia History of Western Philosophy. LC 98-15219. 846p. 1999. 59.95 (*0-231-10128-7*) Col U Pr.
— Jewish Christians & Christian Jews: From the Renaissance to the Enlightenment. LC 93-28326. (Archives Internationales d'Histoire des Idees (International Archives of the History of Ideas) Ser.). 220p. (C). 1993. lib. bdg. 155.50 (*0-7923-2452-8*, Pub. by Kluwer Academic) Kluwer Academic.
— Scepticism in the History of Philosophy: A Pan-American Dialogue. (Archives Internationales D'Histoire des Idees Ser.: Vol. 145). 296p. (C). 1996. text 166.00 (*0-7923-3769-7*) Kluwer Academic.
Popkin, Richard H., et al, eds. Scepticism in the Enlightenment. LC 97-21896. (International Archives of the History of Ideas Ser.). 208p. 1997. text 120.50 (*0-7923-4643-2*) Kluwer Academic.
Popkin, Richard H. & Stroll, Avrum. Philosophy Made Simple. 2nd rev. ed. LC 92-34537. 336p. 1993. pap. 12.95 (*0-385-42533-3*) Doubleday.
Popkin, Richard H. & Vanderjagt, Arjo, eds. Scepticism & Irreligion in the 17th & 18th Centuries. LC 92-44598. (Brill's Studies in Intellectual History: Vol. 37). x, 374p. 1993. 125.50 (*90-04-09596-9*) Brill Academic Pubs.
Popkin, Richard H., et al. Everything Connects: In Conference with Richard H. Popkin LC 98-52412. (Studies in Intellectual History). lxxvi, 380p. 1998. 128.00 (*90-04-11098-4*) Brill Academic Pubs.
Popkin, Richard H., jt. auth. see Force, James E.
Popkin, Richard H., jt. auth. see Katz, David S.
Popkin, Richard H., jt. auth. see Popkin, Jeremy D.
Popkin, Richard H., jt. auth. see Stroll, Avrum.
Popkin, Richard H., jt. ed. see Force, James E.
Popkin, Richard H., jt. ed. see Kelley, Ronald R.
Popkin, Richard H., jt. ed. see Van der Zande, Johan.
Popkin, Richard H., ed. & intro. see Hume, David.
Popkin, Richard H., tr. see Bayle, Pierre.
Popkin, Richard H., tr. & intro. see Bayle, Pierre.
Popkin, Samuel L. The Rational Peasant: The Political Economy of Rural Society in Vietnam. LC 77-83105. 1979. pap. 17.95 (*0-520-03954-8*, Pub. by U CA Pr) Cal Prin Full Svc.
— Reasoning Voter. 332p. (C). 1994. pap. text 13.95 (*0-226-67545-9*) U Ch Pr.
— The Reasoning Voter: Communication & Persuasion in Presidential Campaigns. LC 91-7610. (Illus.). 302p. 1991. 19.95 (*0-226-67544-0*) U Ch Pr.
Popkin, Samuel L., jt. ed. see Kernell, Samuel.
Popkin Software Staff. Fundamentals of System Architect. 192p. (C). 1996. text 76.85 (*0-256-19682-6*, Irwn McGrw-H) McGrw-H Hghr Educ.
Popkin, Susan A. & Allen, Roger B. Gone Fishing! A History of Fishing in River, Bay & Sea. (Illus.). 73p. 1987. pap. 12.00 (*0-913346-14-4*) Indep Seaport.
***Popkin, Susan J., et al.** The Hidden War: Crime & the Tragedy of Public Housing in Chicago. LC 99-56789. (Illus.). 256p. 2000. text 52.00 (*0-8135-2832-1*) Rutgers U Pr.
— The Hidden War: Crime & the Tragedy of Public Housing in Chicago. LC 99-56789. (Illus.). 256p. (C). 2000. pap. 22.00 (*0-8135-2833-X*) Rutgers U Pr.
Popkin, William D. Fundamentals of Federal Income Tax Law. 3rd ed. LC 98-10822. (Cases & Materials Ser.). 1998. 56.00 (*0-8205-3185-5*) Bender.
— Materials on Legislation: Political Language & the Political Process. (University Casebook Ser.). 718p. (C). 1993. text 40.50 (*1-56662-051-1*) Foundation Pr.
— Materials on Legislation: Political Language & the Political Process. 2nd ed. LC 97-1097. (University Casebook Ser.). 940p. 1997. text 48.50 (*1-56662-519-X*) Foundation Pr.
— Materials on Legislation: Political Language & the Political Process, Teacher's Manual For. 2nd ed. (University Casebook Ser.). 237p. 1997. pap. text. write for info. (*1-56662-540-8*) Foundation Pr.
— Materials on Legislation: Political Language & the Political Process, 1994 Supplement. (University Casebook Ser.). 129p. 1994. 8.50 (*1-56662-210-7*) Foundation Pr.
***Popkin, William D.** Statutes in Court: The History & Theory of Statutory Interpretation. LC 98-43552. (Illus.). 352p. 1999. 54.95 (*0-8223-2328-1*) Duke.
Popkin, William D. Teachers Manual for Materials on Legislation: Political Language & the Political Process. (University Casebook Ser.). 179p. 1993. pap. text. write for info. (*1-56662-070-8*) Foundation Pr.
Popkin, William D., jt. auth. see Oldman, Oliver S.
Popkins, Jeremy D. A History of Modern France. LC 93-19241. 368p. (C). 1993. pap. text 26.00 (*0-13-389693-5*) P-H.
Popko, Brian, ed. Mouse Models in the Study of Genetic Neurological Disorders. LC 98-55684. (Advances in Neurochemistry Ser.: Vol. 9). (Illus.). 366p. (C). 1999. text 149.00 (*0-306-45965-5*, Kluwer Plenum) Kluwer Academic.
Popkorn, Sally. First Steps in Modal Logic. (Illus.). 328p. (C). 1995. text 47.95 (*0-521-46482-X*) Cambridge U Pr.
Popkov, Yury S. Macrosystems Theory & Its Applications: Equilibrium Models. Thoma, M., ed. LC 95-15124. (Lecture Notes in Control & Information Sciences: Vol. 203). 323p. 1995. 69.00 (*3-540-19955-1*) Spr-Verlag.
Popl, Milan, et al. Chromatographic Analysis of Alkaloids. (Chromatographic Science Ser.: Vol. 53). (Illus.). 664p. 1990. text 225.00 (*0-8247-8140-6*) Dekker.
Poplack, David G., jt. auth. see Pizzo, Philip A.
Poplack, Shana, ed. The English History of African American English. LC 99-34522. (Language & Society Ser.: Vol. 28). (Illus.). 272p. (C). 1999. text 62.95 (*0-631-21261-2*); pap. text 29.95 (*0-631-21262-0*) Blackwell Pubs.
Poplack, Shana & Pousada, Alicia. A Comparative Study of Gender Assignment to Borrowed Nouns. (Illus.). 43p. 1981. lib. bdg. 3.00 (*1-878483-15-3*) Hunter Coll CEP.
Poplar, Michael G. & Toman, James A. Fumble: The Browns, Modell & the Move. LC 97-69596. (Illus.). 300p. 1997. 24.00 (*0-936760-11-7*) Cleveland Landmarks.
Poplasen, Ilija. The Analysis of the Present. (Illus.). 348p. 1987. 20.00 (*0-935352-21-X*) MIR PA.
— The Analysis of the Present. rev. ed. (Illus.). 370p. 1989. reprint ed. 20.00 (*0-935352-23-6*) MIR PA.
***Poplasen, Ilija.** Anthem of the Final Victory. (Illus.). 380p. (YA). 2000. 20.00 MIR PA.
Poplasen, Ilija. The Authentic Existence. (Illus.). 454p. 1994. 20.00 (*0-935352-26-0*) MIR PA.
— Coming & Time. 220p. 1982. 20.00 (*0-935352-07-4*) MIR PA.
— Coming & Time. 3rd ed. (Illus.). 200p. 1978. reprint ed. 20.00 (*0-935352-00-7*) MIR PA.
— Computerized Two & Three Dimensional Finite Existents Analysis. 64p. 1982. 20.00 (*0-935352-09-0*) MIR PA.
— Computerized Two & Three Dimensional Finite Existents Analysis. 2nd ed. (Illus.). 1979. reprint ed. 20.00 (*0-935352-01-5*) MIR PA.
— The Final Battle for World Domination. (Illus.). 384p. 1985. 20.00 (*0-935352-16-3*) MIR PA.
— The Great Day of Judgment. (Illus.). 455p. 1989. 20.00 (*0-935352-22-8*) MIR PA.
— In Search for the Meaning of Existence in Cinematography. 34p. 1981. 20.00 (*0-935352-06-6*) MIR PA.
— The Medjugorje Apocalypse. (Illus.). 430p. 1991. 20.00 (*0-935352-27-9*) MIR PA.
— The Medjugorje Apocalypse. 2nd ed. (Illus.). 430p. 1992. reprint ed. 20.00 (*0-935352-34-1*) MIR PA.
— The New World Order. 301p. 1983. 20.00 (*0-935352-12-0*) MIR PA.
— The New World Order. (Illus.). 301p. 1984. 20.00 (*0-935352-17-1*) MIR PA.
— The Power & the Glory. (Illus.). 408p. 1990. 20.00 (*0-935352-24-4*) MIR PA.
— The Realism of the Coming. (Illus.). 540p. 1993. 20.00 (*0-935352-25-2*) MIR PA.
— Reference to the Present. 241p. 1982. 20.00 (*0-935352-11-2*) MIR PA.
— The Restoration of the State of Good in the World. (Illus.). 200p. (Orig.). 1980. 20.00 (*0-935352-02-3*) MIR PA.
— The Restoration of the State of Good in the World. 210p. (Orig.). 1982. 20.00 (*0-935352-08-2*) MIR PA.
— The Struggle for the Good, 2 pts., Pt. I. (Illus.). 61p. 1981. reprint ed. 20.00 (*0-935352-03-1*) MIR PA.
— The Struggle for the Good, 2 pts., Pt. II. (Illus.). 128p. 1981. reprint ed. 25.00 (*0-935352-04-X*) MIR PA.
— The Struggle for the Victory of Good, Pt. I. (Illus.). 61p. 1984. 20.00 (*0-935352-18-X*) MIR PA.
— The Struggle for the Victory of Good, Pt. II. (Illus.). 128p. 1984. 20.00 (*0-935352-19-8*) MIR PA.
— The Transfer of Power. (Illus.). 401p. 1984. 20.00 (*0-935352-15-5*) MIR PA.
— The Transition Time. (Illus.). 392p. 1984. 20.00 (*0-935352-14-7*) MIR PA.
— The Victorious Present. (Illus.). 372p. 1983. 20.00 (*0-935352-13-9*) MIR PA.
— The World Government. (Illus.). 375p. 1999. 20.00 (*0-935352-35-X*) MIR PA.
— The World History Made in the Present. (Illus.). 350p. 1986. 20.00 (*0-935352-20-1*) MIR PA.
— The World History Made in the Present. (Illus.). 403p. 1991. 20.00 (*0-935352-32-5*) MIR PA.
Poplaski, Pete, ed. R. Crumb Coffee Table Art Book. (Illus.). 256p. 1997. 40.00 (*0-87816-614-9*) Kitchen Sink.
— R. Crumb Coffee Table Art Book. deluxe ed. (Illus.). 250p. 1997. 300.00 (*0-87816-615-7*) Kitchen Sink.
Poplaski, Peter, ed. see Kane, Bob.
Poplaski, Peter, ed. see Raymond, Alex.
Poplavskii, Boris I. V Venke Iz Voska; Dirizhabl' Neizvestnogo Napravleniia. 2nd ed. Karlinsky, Simon, ed. (Modern Russian Literature & Culture Studies & Texts: Vol. 9). (RUS., Illus.). 123p. 1981. pap. 7.50 (*0-933884-19-2*) Berkeley Slavic.
Poplawski, Paul. D. H. Lawrence: A Reference Companion. LC 95-38654. 744p. 1996. lib. bdg. 105.00 (*0-313-28637-X*, Greenwood Pr) Greenwood.
— A Jane Austen Encyclopedia. LC 97-44880. (Illus.). 440p. (YA). (gr. 9 up). 1998. lib. bdg. 75.00 (*0-313-30017-8*, Greenwood Pr) Greenwood.
— Language, Art & Reality in D. H. Lawrence's St. Mawr: A Stylistic Study. LC 96-14248. 284p. 1996. text 89.95 (*0-7734-8823-5*) E Mellen.
— Promptings of Desire: Creativity & the Religious Impulse in the Works of D. H. Lawrence, 49. LC 92-42429. (Contributions to the Study of World Literature Ser.: No. 49). 224p. 1993. 52.95 (*0-313-28789-9*, GM8789, Greenwood Pr) Greenwood.
Poplawski, Thomas. Eurythmy: Rhythm, Dance & Soul. (Rudolf Steiner's Ideas in Practice Ser.). 112p. 1998. pap. 9.95 (*0-88010-459-7*, 3018) Anthroposophic.
Poplawski, Wojciech A., intro. Hydraulics in Civil Engineering, International Conference, 1994: Hydraulics Working with the Environment. (National Conference Publication Ser.: No. 94-1). (Illus.). 362p. (Orig.). 1994. pap. 72.00 (*0-85825-597-9*, Pub. by Inst Engrs Aust-EA Bks) Accents Pubns.
Pople, Anthony. Berg: "Violin Concerto" (Cambridge Music Handbooks Ser.). (Illus.). 130p. (C). 1991. pap. text 12.95 (*0-521-39976-9*) Cambridge U Pr.
— Messiaen: Quatuor pour la Fin du Temps. LC 98-23937. (Cambridge Music Handbks.). (Illus.). 128p. (C). 1998. 39.95 (*0-521-58497-3*); pap. 12.95 (*0-521-58538-4*) Cambridge U Pr.
Pople, Anthony, ed. The Cambridge Companion to Berg. LC 96-39727. (Cambridge Companions to Music Ser.). (Illus.). 319p. (C). 1997. text 64.95 (*0-521-56374-7*); pap. text 19.95 (*0-521-56489-1*) Cambridge U Pr.
— Theory, Analysis & Meaning in Music. (Illus.). 240p. (C). 1994. text 59.95 (*0-521-45236-8*) Cambridge U Pr.
Pople, Anthony, jt. ed. see Marsden, Alan.
Pople, Ian. An Introduction to Text & Discourse Analysis. (Illus.). 112p. 1998. pap. 42.50 (*0-7487-3357-4*, Pub. by S Thornes Pubs) Trans-Atl Phila.
Pople, John A., et al. Ab Initio Molecular Orbital Theory. LC 84-19524. 576p. 1986. 175.00 (*0-471-81241-2*) Wiley.
***Pople, Nicolas.** Experimental Houses. (Illus.). 240p. 2000. pap. 55.00 (*0-8230-1649-8*) Watsn-Guptill.
Pople, Stephen, jt. auth. see Taylor, Charles.
Popley, H. A. The Music of India. 1990. reprint ed. 8.00 (*81-85418-06-3*, Pub. by Low Price) S Asia.
Poplin, Cecil M. Discovery of Intracranial Ossicles in a Carboniferous North American Paleoniscid: Pisces: Actinopterygii. (Occasional Papers: No. 99). 17p. 1982. 1.00 (*0-317-04811-2*) U KS Nat Hist Mus.
Poplin, Dick. A Yard of Poplin. (Illus.). 96p. (Orig.). 1991. pap. 9.95 (*0-9624100-3-9*) Bell Buckle.
Poplin, Mary S. & Cousin, Patricia T., eds. Alternative Views of Learning Disabilities: Issues for the 21st Century. LC 96-5374. 1996. pap. text 38.00 (*0-89079-697-1*, 7819) PRO-ED.
Poplin, Robert L. & Ritchie, Thomas E. 96 Ways You Can Save Taxes in '96: Oklahoma Edition. Magee, William N., ed. 128p. (Orig.). Date not set. pap. 90.95 (*0-9644913-7-0*) Loopholes Pr.
Poploff, Michelle. Bat Bones & Spider Stew. LC 97-47763. 48p. (J). 1998. pap. 4.50 (*0-440-41440-7*) BDD Bks Young Read.
— Busy O'Brien & the Caterpillar Punch Bunch. (Illus.). 119p. (J). (gr. 2-5). 1992. 13.95 (*0-8027-8151-9*) Walker & Co.
— Busy O'Brien & the Great Bubble Gum Blowout. (Illus.). 96p. (J). (gr. 2-5). 1990. lib. bdg. 13.85 (*0-8027-6984-5*) Walker & Co.
— Busy O'Brien & the Great Bubble Gum Blowout. MacDonald, Patricia, ed. (Illus.). 96p. (J). (gr. 2-5). 1990. 12.95 (*0-8027-6983-7*) Walker & Co.
— Busy O'Brien & the Great Bubble Gum Blowout. (Illus.). 96p. (J). (gr. 2-5). 1992. reprint ed. pap. 2.99 (*0-671-74082-2*, Minstrel Bks) PB.
— Splash-a-Roo & Snowflakes. LC 95-21362. (Illus.). (J). (gr. k-3). 1996. pap. 3.99 (*0-440-41119-X*, Yearling) BDD Bks Young Read.
— Tea Party for Two. LC 96-8329. (Illus.). 48p. (J). (gr. 2-3). 1997. pap. 3.99 (*0-440-41334-6*) Delacorte.
— Tea Party for Two. 1997. 9.19 (*0-606-13839-0*, Pub. by Turtleback) Demco.
Poploff, Michelle & Mitchell, Judith A. Busy O'Brien & the Caterpillar Punch Bunch. (Illus.). (J). (gr. 2-6). 1995. reprint ed. pap. 3.50 (*0-671-79407-8*, Minstrel Bks) PB.
Poplstein, Maureen. Bringing Out the Best in Yourself & Others. Williams, Sally, ed. (Illus.). 184p. (Orig.). pap. 29.95 (*0-931571-11-1*) RP Pubng.
***Popma, Jeffrey J. & Prpic, Ross, eds.** Cardiology Board Certification Review Guide-Interventional Cardiology. LC 99-64879. (Illus.). 350p. 1999. ring bd. 195.00 (*1-58397-005-3*, CBCRG) Am Coll Cardiology.
Popma, Jeffrey J., et al. Atlas of Interventional Cardiology. LC 94-1694. (Illus.). 368p. 1994. text 110.00 (*0-7216-3569-5*, W B Saunders Co) Harcrt Hlth Sci Grp.
Popoff, B. Accounting Essentials: An Introduction for Non-Accounting Majors. 161p. 1991. pap. 36.00 (*0-409-30484-0*, Austral, MICHIE); pap. 36.00 (*0-614-05474-5*, Austral, MICHIE) LEXIS Pub.
Popoff, B. & Cowan, T. Analysis & Interpretation of Financial Statements. 3rd ed. 464p. 1989. pap. 51.00 (*0-614-05475-3*, Austral, MICHIE) LEXIS Pub.
Popoff, B. & Cowan, T. K. Analysis & Interpretation of Financial Statements. 3rd ed. 451p. 1989. pap. 54.00 (*0-409-49588-3*, Austral, MICHIE) LEXIS Pub.
Popoff, Georgia A. Coaxing Nectar from Longing. LC 97-73647. 90p. 1997. pap., per. 12.00 (*0-9643477-3-3*) Hale Mary Pr.
Popoff, Leo, jt. auth. see Prosor, Larry.
Popoff, Martin. Collector's Guide to Heavy Metal: Riff Kills Man Again. 1997. pap. 19.95 (*1-896522-32-7*) CN06.
— Goldmine Heavy Metal Record Price Guide. LC 99-67515. (Illus.). 368p. 2000. pap. 23.95 (*0-87341-811-5*, HVM1) Krause Pubns.
Popoff, Peter. America's Family Crisis. Tanner, Don, ed. LC 82-82843. 80p. 1982. pap. 2.00 (*0-938544-15-2*) Faith Messenger.
— Calamities, Catastrophies, & Chaos. Tanner, Don, ed. LC 80-69974. (Illus.). 108p. 1980. pap. 2.50 (*0-938544-01-2*) Faith Messenger.
— Demons At Your Doorstep. Tanner, Don, ed. LC 82-82842. (Illus.). 56p. 1982. pap. 1.50 (*0-938544-13-6*) Faith Messenger.
— A New Fire Is Blazing. Tanner, Don, ed. LC 80-67993. (Illus.). 194p. (Orig.). 1980. pap. 4.95 (*0-938544-02-0*) Faith Messenger.
— Set Free from Satan's Slavery. Tanner, Don, ed. LC 82-83455. 64p. 1982. pap. 2.00 (*0-938544-17-9*) Faith Messenger.
— Seven Delivery Systems for God's Healing Power. Tanner, Don, ed. LC 81-69730. (Illus.). 70p. 1981. pap. 1.50 (*0-938544-07-1*) Faith Messenger.
— Six Things Satan Uses to Rob You of God's Abundant Blessings. Tanner, Don, ed. LC 81-86521. (Illus.). 96p. 1982. pap. 2.00 (*0-938544-11-X*) Faith Messenger.
— Three Steps to Answered Prayer. Tanner, Don, ed. LC 81-70342. 92p. 1981. pap. 2.00 (*0-938544-10-1*) Faith Messenger.
— Twenty-Seven Things the Church Must Go Through Before the Great Tribulation. Tanner, Don, ed. LC 81-68675. (Illus.). 50p. 1981. pap. 1.00 (*0-938544-08-X*) Faith Messenger.
— Ye Shall Receive Power: The Amazing Miracle of Holy Spirit Baptism. Tanner, Don, ed. LC 82-71629. (Illus.). 96p. 1982. pap. 2.00 (*0-938544-14-4*) Faith Messenger.
Popoli, Richard, jt. auth. see Blackman, Samuel S.
Popoola, S. Solagbade. Practical Ifa Divination Vol. 3: Ifa Reference Manual for the Beginner & Professional. large type unabridged ed. (ENG & YOR., Illus.). 594p. 1997. pap. 49.95 (*1-890157-02-3*, Pub. by Athelia-Henrietta) BookWorld.
Popousek, Dusan. Vibrational-Rotational Spectroscopy & Molecular Dynamics. LC 97-26051. (Advanced Series in Physical Chemistry). 500p. 1997. text 95.00 (*981-02-1635-1*) World Scientific Pub.
Popov, A. A. Nganasan: The Material Culture of the Tavgi Samoyeds. Ristenen, Elaine K., tr. LC 66-63668. (Uralic & Altaic Ser.: Vol. 56). (Orig.). 1966. pap. text. write for info. (*0-87750-020-7*) Curzon Pr Ltd.
Popov, A. A., et al. Oxidation of Stressed Polymers. xiii, 335p. 1991. text 427.00 (*2-88124-735-0*) Gordon & Breach.
Popov, A. I. & Hallenga, K. Modern NMR Techniques & Their Application in Chemistry. (Practical Spectroscopy Ser.: Vol. 11). (Illus.). 680p. 1990. text 225.00 (*0-8247-8332-8*) Dekker.
Popov, Alex, tr. see Rudd, Connie.
Popov, Alexander, jt. auth. see Mamantov, Gleb.
Popov, E. P. Engineering Mechanics of Solids. 2nd ed. LC 98-15677. 864p. 1998. 101.33 (*0-13-726159-4*) P-H.
Popov, Egor P. & Medwadowski, Stefan J., eds. Concrete Shell Buckling. LC 80-69968. (SP-67 Ser.). 240p. (Orig.). 1981. pap. 38.50 (*0-686-95244-8*) ACI.
— Concrete Shell Buckling. LC 80-69968. (American Concrete Institute Publication: No. SP-67). 240p. (Orig.). 1981. reprint ed. pap. 74.40 (*0-608-01431-1*, 206219300002) Bks Demand.
Popov, Evgeni I. Merry-Making in Old Russia & Other Stories. Porter, Robert, tr. from RUS. LC 97-12449. (Writings from an Unbound Europe Ser.). 1997. 49.95 (*0-8101-1326-0*) Northwestern U Pr.
Popov, Evgeny. Merry-Making in Old Russia & Other Stories. Porter, Robert, tr. from RUS. LC 97-12449. 1997. pap. text 17.95 (*0-8101-1327-9*) Northwestern U Pr.
— The Soul of a Patriot: or Various Epistles to Ferfichkin. Porter, Robert, tr. from RUS. LC 94-18887. (Writings from an Unbound Europe). 194p. 1994. reprint ed. 49.95 (*0-8101-1203-5*); reprint ed. pap. 14.95 (*0-8101-1193-4*) Northwestern U Pr.
Popov, Evgeny, jt. auth. see Loewen, E. G.

P

An Asterisk (*) at the beginning of an entry indicates that the title is appearing for the first time.

Popov, G. A. Principles of Health Planning in the U. S. S. R. (Public Health Papers: No. 43). 1971. pap. text 9.00 (*92-4-130043-4*, 1110043) World Health.

Popov, G. B. & Fishpool, L. D. A Revision of the Grasshopper Genus Orthochtha & Allies: Orthoptera, Acrididae, Acridinae. 154p. 1992. pap. 60.00 (*0-85954-305-6*, Pub. by Nat Res Inst) St Mut.

Popov, Genrikh P., et al. Ten Plus Ten: Contemporary Soviet & American Painters. LC 89-80354. (ENG & RUS., Illus.). 176p. (Orig.). 1989. pap. write for info. (*0-929865-03-0*) Mod Art Mus Ft Worth.

Popov, Haralan. Tortured for His Faith. 1970. pap. 4.95 (*0-310-31262-0*, 18070P) Zondervan.

Popov, Linda K. Sacred Moments: Daily Meditations on the Virtues. LC 97-17813. (Orig.). 1997. pap. 12.95 (*0-452-27811-2*, Plume) Dutton Plume.

— Sacred Moments: Daily Meditations on the Virtues. 480p. (Orig.). 1996. pap. 14.95 (*0-9646633-0-9*) Virtues Comm.

Popov, Linda K., et al. The Family Virtues Guide: Simple Ways to Bring Out the Best in Our Children & Ourselves. LC 96-53423. (Illus.). 319p. 1997. pap. 14.95 (*0-452-27810-4*, Plume) Dutton Plume.

— The Virtues Guide: A Family Handbook. rev. ed. LC 96-22925. (Illus.). 280p. 1993. pap. 24.95 (*0-9697634-0-9*) Virtues Comm.

***Popov, Linda Kavelin.** The Virtues Project Educator's Guide. (Illus.). 208p. 2000. pap. text 24.95 (*1-880396-84-X*) Jalmar Pr.

***Popov, Nebojsa.** Road to War in Serbia: Trauma & Catharsis. LC 99-88378. 2000. pap. 28.95 (*963-9116-56-4*) Ctrl Europ Univ.

***Popov, Nebojsa, ed.** The Road to War in Serbia: Trauma & Catharsis. LC 99-88378. 718p. (C). 2000. 59.95 (*963-9116-55-6*) Ctrl Europ Univ.

Popov, Nikolai. Por Que? LC 98-7153. (SPA., Illus.). 48p. (J). (gr. k-3). 1998. 15.95 (*1-55858-942-2*, Pub. by North-South Bks NYC); pap. 6.95 (*1-55858-683-0*, Pub. by North-South Bks NYC) Chronicle Bks.

— The Russian People Speak: Democracy at the Crossroads. 144p. (C). 1994. 37.95 (*0-8156-0300-2*) Syracuse U Pr.

— Why? LC 95-45957. (Illus.). 48p. (J). (gr. k-3). 1998. pap. 6.95 (*1-55858-996-1*, Pub. by North-South Bks NYC) Chronicle Bks.

Popov, Oleg A., ed. High Density Plasma Sources: Design, Physics, & Performance. LC 95-4918. 430p. 1996. 125.00 (*0-8155-1377-1*) Noyes.

Popov, S. V., et al. Susceptibility Tensors for Nonlinear Optics. LC 95-12396. (Optics & Optoelectronics Ser.). (Illus.). 194p. 1995. disk 500.00 (*0-7503-0344-1*) IOP Pub.

— Susceptibility Tensors for Nonlinear Optics. LC 95-12396. (Optics & Optoelectronics Ser.). (Illus.). 194p. 1995. 210.00 (*0-7503-0253-4*) IOP Pub.

Popov, V. A., jt. auth. see Petrushev, P. P.

Popov, V. L. Gruppy, Obrazuiushchie, Sizigii i Orbity v Teorii Invariantov: English Groups, Generators, Syzygies & Orbits in Invariant Theory. LC 92-10604. (Translations of Mathematical Monographs: Vol. 100). 245p. 1992. pap. 49.00 (*0-8218-4557-8*, MMONO/100) Am Math.

Popov, V. M. Hyperstability of Control Systems. Georgescu, R., tr. from RUM. LC 73-83000. (Grundlehren der Mathematischen Wissenschaften Ser.: Vol. 204). 400p. 1973. 86.95 (*0-387-06373-0*) Spr-Verlag.

Popov, V. N. Functional Integrals & Collective Excitations. (Monographs on Mathematical Physics). 224p. 1988. text 95.00 (*0-521-30777-5*) Cambridge U Pr.

— Functional Integrals in Quantum Field Theory & Statistical Physics. 1983. text 211.50 (*90-277-1471-1*) Kluwer Academic.

Popov, V. N., ed. Operator Theory with a Random Potential, & Some Questions of Statistical Physics. LC 91-24484. (Proceedings of the Steklov Institute of Mathematics Ser.: Vol. 184). 259p. 1990. reprint ed. pap. 159.00 (*0-8218-3139-9*, STEKLO/184C) Am Math.

Popov, V. N. & Yarunin, V. S. Collective Effects in Quantum Statistics of Radiation & Matter. (C). 1988. text 153.00 (*90-277-2735-X*) Kluwer Academic.

Popov, V. N., jt. auth. see Konopleva, N. P.

Popov, Vesselin, jt. auth. see Marushiakova, Elena.

Popov, Victor & Power, Henry, eds. Landfill Emission of Gases into the Atmosphere. LC 98-84460. (Advances in Air Pollution Ser.: Vol. 4). (Illus.). 200p. 1999. 120.00 (*1-85312-616-0*, 6160, Pub. by WIT Pr) Computational Mech MA.

Popov, Yu A. & Sidorenko, S. N. Theory of Interaction of Metals & Alloys with a Corrosive Environment. 380p. 1997. boxed set 113.00 (*1-898326-47-9*, Pub. by CISP) Balogh.

Popov, Yu M., ed. Injection Lasers in Optical Communication & Information Processing Systems. Stewart, S., tr. from RUS. (Proceedings of the Lebedev Physics Institute Ser.: Vol. 185). (Illus.). 326p. (C). 1989. text 175.00 (*0-941743-58-6*) Nova Sci Pubs.

— Laser Cathode-Ray Tubes: Proceedings of the Lebedev Physics Institute, Vol. 221. LC 94-48607. 315p. (C). 1994. lib. bdg. 165.00 (*1-56072-216-9*) Nova Sci Pubs.

— Stoichiometry in Crystal Compounds & Its Influence on Their Physical Properties. (Proceedings of the Lebedev Physics Institute Ser.: Vol. 177). 303p. 1988. text 165.00 (*0-941743-21-7*) Nova Sci Pubs.

Popova, L. P. Russian & English Dictionary. (Super-Mini Ser.). (RUS & ENG., Illus.). 448p. 1995. pap. 6.95 (*0-8442-4288-8*, 42888, Natl Textbk Co) NTC Contemp Pub Co.

Popova, L. P., ed. Popular English - Russian & Russian - English Dictionary. (ENG & RUS.). 432p. 1995. 12.95 (*0-8285-5206-1*) Firebird NY.

Popova, L. P., jt. auth. see National Textbook Company Staff.

Popova, Valeriya, ed. see Silver, Raissa.

Popovic, Branko D. & Kolundzija, B. M. Analysis of Metallic Antennas & Scatterers. (Electromagnetic Waves Ser.: 38). 208p. 1994. 82.00 (*0-85296-807-8*) INSPEC Inc.

Popovic, Branko D., et al. Analysis & Synthesis of Wire-Antennas. LC 82-11078. (Electronic & Electrical Engineering Research Ser.: No. 2). (Illus.). 320p. reprint ed. pap. 99.20 (*0-8357-6011-1*, 203423300089) Bks Demand.

Popovic, D., jt. auth. see Lin, V. A.

***Popovic, Dejan B. & Sinkjr, Thomas.** Restoring Movement: Control for Rehabilitation Technology. LC 99-462017. 2000. write for info. (*1-85233-279-4*) Spr-Verlag.

Popovic, Dobrivoje & Bhatkar, Vijay P. Methods & Tools for Applied Artificial Intelligence. LC 94-1715. (Computer Aided Engineering Ser.: Vol. 5). (Illus.). 544p. 1994. text 185.00 (*0-8247-9195-9*) Dekker.

Popovic, Dobrivoje, jt. auth. see Bhatkar, Vijay P.

Popovic, Dobrivojie & Vlacic, Ljubo, eds. Mechatronics in Engineering Design & Product Development. LC 98-38127. (Illus.). 632p. 1998. text 195.00 (*0-8247-0226-3*) Dekker.

Popovic, M. M., et al, eds. Physics of Ionized Gases: Proceeding of the XII International Symposium on the Physics of Ionized Gases (SPIG) 84 Yugoslavia, Sept. 1984. 1060p. 1985. 143.00 (*9971-5-0001-9*) World Scientific Pub.

Popovic, Nenad D. Yugoslavia: The New Class in Crisis. LC 68-26995. 256p. reprint ed. pap. 79.40 (*0-608-15222-6*, 202741600055) Bks Demand.

Popovic, R. S. Hall Effect Devices: Magnetic Sensors & Characterization of Semiconductors. (Sensors Ser.). (Illus.). 320p. 1991. 158.00 (*0-7503-0096-5*) IOP Pub.

Popovic, Tatyana. Prince Marko: The Hero of South Slavic Epics. (Illus.). 280p. 1988. 45.00 (*0-8156-2444-1*) Syracuse U Pr.

Popovic, Zoya B. Modern Introductory Electromagnetics. (C). 1999. pap. text, wbk. ed. 21.33 (*0-201-32680-9*) Addison-Wesley.

***Popovic, Zoya B.** Modern Introductory Electromagnetics. LC 99-42828. 556p. (C). 1999. 100.00 (*0-201-32678-7*, Prentice Hall) P-H.

Popovic, Zoya B., jt. ed. see York, Robert A.

Popovich, Charles J. & Costello, M. Rita. Directory of Business & Financial Information Services. 9th ed. 471p. 1994. 80.00 (*0-87111-420-8*) SLA.

Popovich, Christine. How to Play with Your Dog! For Children Ages 2-5 Years. (Illus.). 24p. (Orig.). (J). (ps). 1989. pap. 5.95 (*1-886056-03-X*) Super Puppy Pr.

Popovich, Igor S. The Little Book of Awkward Questions. 160p. 1995. pap. 5.95 (*0-86417-670-8*, Pub. by Kangaroo Pr) Seven Hills Bk.

Popovich, Justin, et al. Orthodox Faith & Life in Christ: Translation, Preface, & Introduction by Asterios Gerostergios, et Al. LC 94-79270. (Illus.). 248p. 1994. pap. 17.50 (*1-884729-02-9*) Inst Byzantine.

***Popovich, Marguerite.** Daydreams. 1999. pap. write for info. (*1-58235-406-5*) Watermrk Pr.

Popovich, Mark. New Businesses, Entrepreneurship, & Rural Development: Building a State Strategy. (New Alliances for Rural America Ser.). (Orig.). 1988. pap. text 6.00 (*1-55877-016-X*) Natl Governor.

Popovich, Mark G. & Brizius, Jack A. Creating High-Performance Government Organizations: A Practical Guide for Public Managers. LC 97-52364. (Nonprofit & Public Management Ser.). xxii, 191p. 1998. 25.95 (*0-7879-4102-6*) Jossey-Bass.

***Popovich, Mary K.** 526 Marriages of Milwaukee's St. Stanislaus Parish, 1900-1909. 50p. 1999. pap. 10.00 (*0-9677819-0-6*) Archangl Pubng AZ.

Popovich, Nancy, ed. see Frischer, Carol S.

Popovich, Richard E. The Measurement of Thought: A Heuristic Approach to This Development. 2nd ed. LC 81-90419. 180p. (C). 1982. 19.95 (*0-9604876-0-3*) REP Pubs.

Popovici, C., tr. see Klein, Melanie.

***Popovici, Mattei.** Garden Seats. (Illus.). 96p. 2000. 25.00 (*2-909838-43-9*, Pub. by A Gourcuff) Antique Collect.

Popovici, Neculai N., jt. ed. see Hodge, Charles A.

Popoviciu, L., ed. see European Congress on Sleep Research Staff.

Popovics, Bob, jt. auth. see Jaworowski, Ed.

Popovics, Sandor. Concrete Materials: Properties, Specifications & Testing. 2nd ed. LC 92-8953. (Illus.). 661p. 1992. 145.00 (*0-8155-1308-9*) Noyes.

— Properties Concrete w/3.5 disk. LC 97-31766. 535p. 1998. 120.00 incl. disk (*0-471-14903-9*) Wiley.

***Popovitch, Robert L., et al.** How to Do Asset Allocation. 1999. pap. 99.00 (*0-7646-0731-6*) Prctnrs Pub Co.

— How to Monitor & Report Investment Performance, Vol. 1. 1999. 99.00 (*0-7646-0778-2*) Prctnrs Pub Co.

— How to Use Investment Strategies, Vol. 1. 1999. 99.00 (*0-7646-0749-9*) Prctnrs Pub Co.

Popoviv, Alexandre. The Revolt of African Slaves in Iraq in the III/IX Century: The Revolt of the Zanj. King, Leon, tr. from FRE. LC 98-35899.Tr. of Revolt du Esclaves en Iraq au III/IX Eme Siecle. (Illus.). 180p. (C). 1999. text 44.95 (*1-55876-162-4*); pap. text 18.95 (*1-55876-163-2*) Wiener Pubs Inc.

***Popovski, Vesna.** National Minorities & Citizenship Rights in Lithuania, 1988-1993. LC 00-33297. (Studies in Russia & East Europe). (Illus.). 2000. write for info. (*0-312-23697-2*) St Martin.

Popovsky, J., et al. Suesswasserflora von Mitteleuropa Band 6: Dinophyceae (Dinoflagellida) (Illus.). 272p. 1990. lib. bdg. 100.00 (*3-437-30405-4*) Balogh.

— Sueswasserflora von Mitteleuropa Vol. 6: Dinophyceae (Dinoflagellida) (GER., Illus.). 272p. 1990. lib. bdg. 75.00 (*3-334-00247-0*, Pub. by Gustav Fischer) Balogh.

Popovsky, Mark. The Vavilov Affair. LC 84-9342. viii, 216p. (C). 1984. lib. bdg. 29.50 (*0-208-02035-7*, Archon Bks) Shoe String.

Popovsky, Mark A. Delo Akademika Vavilova. LC 83-16435. (RUS., Illus.). 280p. (Orig.). 1983. pap. 10.00 (*0-938920-33-2*) Hermitage Pubs.

— Zhizn" I Zhitie Voino-Iasenetskogo - The Life & Religious Journey of Voino-Iasenetsky. rev. ed. (RUS., Illus.). 542p. 1996. pap. 25.00 (*1-55779-086-8*) Hermitage Pubs.

Popovsky, Mark A., ed. Transfusion Reactions. (Illus.). 404p. 1996. 99.00 (*1-56395-055-3*, PC97-PR9602) Am Assn Blood.

Popovych. Tetraphenylborates. (Solubility Data Ser.). 1981. 130.00 (*0-08-023965-X*, Pergamon Pr) Elsevier.

Popovych, Erika. New Independent States & the Baltic Republics: A Directory of Institutions in Armenia, Azerbaijan, Belarus, Estonia, Georgia, Kazakhstan, Kyrgyzstan, Latvia, Lithuania, Moldova, Russian Federation, Tajikistan, Turkmenistan, Ukraine, Uzbekistan. (Special Reports). 458p. 1995. 50.00 (*0-929851-70-6*, 5345) Am Assn Coll Registrars.

Popovych, Erika & Levin-Stankevich, Brian. The Soviet System of Education. 123p. (C). 1992. pap. text 40.00 (*0-910054-97-5*) Am Assn Coll Registrars.

Popowicz, Z., jt. ed. see Garbaczewski, P.

***Popox, Lubomir.** Facility Programming as Sociospatial Planning. Cohen, Uriel, ed. (Publications in Architecture & Urban Planning Ser.: Vol. R99-3). (Illus.). 190p. 1999. pap. 22.00 (*0-938744-99-2*) U of Wis Ctr Arch-Urban.

Popp, A. John. Neural Trauma. LC 78-24627. (Seminars in Neurological Surgery Ser.). 395p. 1979. reprint ed. pap. 125.60 (*0-608-00314-X*, 206103100007) Bks Demand.

Popp, A. John, ed. The Primary Care of Neurological Disorders. 468p. 75.00 (*1-879284-57-X*) Am Assn Neuro.

Popp, Carol, jt. auth. see Wolfe, Gerald L.

Popp, Dennis J. Night Fighter's Handbook. (Illus.). 72p. 1986. pap. 18.00 (*0-87364-361-5*) Paladin Pr.

Popp, Dolores L. The Confident Traveler: A Complete Travel Guide for the Business Woman. LC 88-60723. 128p. (Orig.). 1988. pap. 12.95 (*0-945565-00-3*) Shiro Pubs.

Popp, Edward E. The Great Cookie Jar: Taking the Mysteries Out of the Money System. LC 78-62961. 1978. pap. 2.00 (*0-9600358-2-6*) CPA Bk Pub.

— Money, Bona Fide or Non-Bona Fide. 1970. pap. 1.50 (*0-9600358-1-8*) CPA Bk Pub.

Popp, Fritz-Albert, ed. Recent Advances in Biophoton Research & Its Applications. 300p. 1992. text 98.00 (*981-02-0855-3*) World Scientific Pub.

Popp, Gwelda, ed. see Bay Village Women's Club Foundation Staff.

Popp, Helen M., jt. auth. see Chall, Jeanne S.

***Popp, Jerome A.** Cognitive Science & Philosophy of Education: Toward a Unified Theory of Learning & Teaching. LC 99-37460. 256p. 1999. pap. 24.95 (*1-880192-31-4*) Caddo Gap Pr.

Popp, Jerome A. Naturalizing Philosophy of Education: John Dewey in the Postanalytic Period. LC 97-38677. 1998. 34.95 (*0-8093-2171-8*) S Ill U Pr.

***Popp, Joseph L.** Popular Evolution: Life-Lessons from Anthropology. LC 00-105072. (Illus.). xviii, 300p. 2000. 39.95 (*0-9701255-7-7*) Man & Nature.

Popp, Marcia. Learning Journals in the K-8 Classroom: Exploring Ideas & Information in the Content Areas. LC 97-9830. 248p. 1997. pap. 23.50 (*0-8058-2430-8*) L Erlbaum Assocs.

— Teaching Language & Literature in Elementary Classrooms: A Resource Book for Professional Development. LC 95-49925. 512p. 1996. pap. 37.50 (*0-8058-2253-4*) L Erlbaum Assocs.

— Teaching Language & Literature in Elementary Classrooms: A Resource Book for Professional Development. 432p. 1996. pap. 45.00 (*0-8058-8021-6*) L Erlbaum Assocs.

Popp, Nathaniel. Holy Icons: A Study on the Meaning, Style, Painting & Use of Icons. 2nd ed. (Orthodox Christian Library: No. 21). (Illus.). 36p. 1989. reprint ed. pap. 4.95 (*1-929200-00-5*) Roman Ortho Episco.

Popp, Regine, tr. see Frich, Elisabeth.

Popp, Richard L. The Presidents of the University of Chicago: A Centennial View. LC 92-28533. (Illus.). 57p. (C). 1992. pap. 7.00 (*0-943056-18-7*) Univ Chi Lib.

Popp, Terry, jt. ed. see Dragon, Judy.

Popp, W., ed. see Soussmann, H.

Popp, Walter. History of Mathematics. 160p. 1978. pap. 21.00 (*0-685-42572-X*) OpUniv Pr.

Poppa, Terrence E. Drug Lord: The Life & Death of a Mexican Kingpin. 2nd rev. ed. LC 98-72519. (Illus.). 384p. 1998. pap. 14.95 (*0-9664430-0-4*) Demand Pubns.

— El Zar de la Droga: La Vida y la Muerte de Un Narcotraficante Mexicano. 2nd rev. ed. LC 98-72520. (SPA., Illus.). 416p. 1998. pap. 14.95 (*0-9664430-1-2*) Demand Pubns.

Poppe, Carol A. & Van Matre, Nancy A. K-3 Science Activities Kit. 280p. (J). (gr. k-3). 1988. pap. text 24.95 (*0-87628-477-2*) Ctr Appl Res.

— Language Arts Learning Centers for the Primary Grades. 266p. (C). 1991. pap. text 27.95 (*0-87628-505-1*) P-H.

— Science Learning Centers for the Primary Grades. LC 85-13284. 240p. 1985. pap. text 27.95 (*0-87628-749-6*) Ctr Appl Res.

Poppe, Erich & Ross, Bianca, eds. The Legend of Mary the Egyptian: In Medieval Insular Hagiography. LC 96-156997. 220p. 1996. boxed set 55.00 (*1-85182-187-2*, Pub. by Four Cts Pr) Intl Spec Bk.

Poppe, Erich, jt. ed. see Fife, James.

Poppe, Fred C. Fifty Rules to Keep a Client Happy. LC 87-45139. 112p. 1987. 8.95i (*0-685-18544-3*, PL 00-60-915218) HarperTrade.

Poppe, Johann H. Geschichte Aller Erfindungen und Entdekkungen Im Bereiche der Gewerbe, Kunste und Wissenschaften Von der Fruhesten Zeit Bis Auf Unsere Tage. (GER.). 1997. reprint ed. 198.00 (*3-487-04368-8*) G Olms Pubs.

Poppe, Julie, jt. auth. see Hough, Melissa.

Poppe, Laszlo & Novak, Lajos. Selective Biocatalysis: A Synthetic Approach. LC 92-9284. 320p. 1992. 175.00 (*3-527-28372-2*, Wiley-VCH) Wiley.

Poppe, Nicholas N. Heroic Epic of the Khalkha Mongols. 2nd rev. ed. (Mongolia Society Occasional Papers: No. 11). 1979. pap. 12.00 (*0-910980-51-9*) Mongolia.

— Reminiscences. Schwarz, Henry G., ed. LC 82-4544. (Studies on East Asia: Vol. 16). (Illus.). vii, 330p. 1983. 25.00 (*0-914584-16-2*) WWUCEAS.

— Tatar Manual. 2nd ed. LC 63-63142. (Uralic & Altaic Ser.: Vol. 25). 271p. 1968. write for info. (*0-87750-054-1*) Curzon Pr Ltd.

Poppe, Thomas, jt. auth. see Paungger, Johanna.

Poppe, Trygve T., jt. ed. see Bruno, David W.

Poppel, Birger, jt. ed. see Petersen, Hanne.

Poppel, Ernst. Mindworks: Time & Conscious Experience. 200p. 1988. 17.95 (*0-15-152190-5*) Harcourt.

Poppel, Karl G. Das Bild des Menschen in der Wissenschaft. (Hildesheimer Beitrage Zu Den Erziehungs und Sozial Wissenschaften Ser.: Bd. 7). (GER.). iv, 197p. 1978. 20.00 (*3-487-06552-5*) G Olms Pubs.

— Unterrichten - Grundzuge und Gestaltungsformen Des Lehrens und Lernens. (Hildesheimer Beitrage Ser.: Bd. 27). (GER.). 192p. 1992. write for info. (*3-487-09033-3*) G Olms Pubs.

Poppel, Karl G., ed. Freie Schule Als Beitrag zur Schulreform. (Hildesheimer Beitrage Zu Den Erziehungs und Sozial Wissenschaften Ser.: Bd. 3). (GER.). 169p. 1977. 20.00 (*3-487-06351-4*) G Olms Pubs.

Poppel, Martin. Heaven & Hell: The War Diary of a German Paratrooper. 256p. (C). 1991. 90.00 (*0-946771-27-8*, Pub. by Spellmnt Pubs) St Mut.

— Heaven & Hell: The War Diary of a German Paratrooper. (Illus.). 256p. 1996. 34.95 (*1-873376-64-2*, Pub. by Spellmnt Pubs) Howell Pr VA.

***Poppel, Martin.** Heaven & Hell: The War Diary of a German Paratrooper. 256p. 2000. pap. 60.00 (*1-86227-102-X*, Pub. by Spellmnt Pubs) St Mut.

Poppeliers, John C., et al. What Style Is It? A Guide to American Architecture. LC 83-19278. (Building Watchers Ser.). (Illus.). 112p. (C). 1995. pap. 14.95 (*0-471-14434-7*) Wiley.

Poppelreuter, W. Disturbances of Lower & Higher Visual Capacities Caused by Occipital Damage: With Special Reference to the Psychopathological, Pedagogical, Industrial, & Social Implications. Zihl, J., tr. (History of Neuroscience Ser.: No. 2).Tr. of Die/Psychischen Schadigungen Durch Kopfschuss in Kriege, 1914-16. (Illus.). 392p. 1991. 47.50 (*0-19-852190-1*) OUP.

Poppema, Sibrand, jt. ed. see Solez, Kim.

Poppema, Suzanne T. & Henderson, Mike. Why I Am an Abortion Doctor. LC 96-2445. 266p. 1996. 26.95 (*1-57392-045-2*) Prometheus Bks.

Poppen, Jerry D. Action Packet on Jumping Rope: Individual Rope Skills. LC 82-72160. 62p. (Orig.). 1989. pap. text 8.50 (*0-9608868-3-4*) Action Prods.

— The BEST of Games That Come Alive! (Illus.). 235p. (Orig.). (C). 1990. pap. text 18.00 (*0-9608868-4-2*) Action Prods.

— Dances That Come Alive! (Illus.). 213p. (Orig.). (C). 1993. pap. 21.50 (*0-9608868-5-0*) Action Prods.

— Fitness Zone Ahead. (Illus.). 231p. 1995. pap. text 29.50 (*0-9608868-6-9*) Action Prods.

Poppen, Nikki, jt. auth. see Paterno, Jim.

Poppen, Roger. Behavioral Relaxation Training & Assessment. 2nd ed. LC 97-45278. 206p. 1998. 28.00 (*0-7619-1200-2*); pap. 12.99 (*0-7619-1201-0*) Sage.

— Joseph Wolpe. LC 95-71355. (Key Figures in Counselling & Psychotherapy Ser.). 224p. 1995. 44.00 (*0-8039-8666-1*); pap. 18.95 (*0-8039-8667-X*) Sage.

Poppendieck, Hans-Helmut. Cochlospermaceae. LC 81-9456. (Flora Neotropica Monographs: No. 27). (Illus.). 34p. 1981. pap. 6.50 (*0-89327-231-0*) NY Botanical.

Poppendieck, Janet. Sweet Charity. 256p. 1999. pap. 13.95 (*0-14-024556-1*) Viking Penguin.

Poppenhouse, Jerry, photos by. Taste of the Territory: The Flair & Flavor of Oklahoma! (Illus.). 270p. 1996. spiral bd. 18.95 (*0-9648976-0-1*) Serv Leag Bartlesville.

Popper, A. N., jt. ed. see Fay, Richard R.

***Popper, Adrienne.** Parents Book for the Toddler Years. LC 86-90928. 1999. mass mkt. 5.98 (*0-345-43639-3*) Ballantine Pub Grp.

Popper, Arthur N., et al, eds. The Evolutionary Biology of Hearing. (Illus.). xlii, 859p. 1991. 164.95 (*0-387-97588-8*) Spr-Verlag.

— The Mammalian Auditory Pathway: Neuroanatomy. (Handbook of Auditory Research Ser.: Vol. 1). (Illus.). 448p. 1992. 89.95 (*0-387-97678-7*) Spr-Verlag.

— The Mammalian Auditory Pathway: Neuroanatomy. (Handbook of Auditory Research Ser.: Vol. 1). (Illus.). 448p. 1995. 49.95 (*0-387-97800-3*) Spr-Verlag.

— Sensory Biology of Aquatic Animals. (Proceedings in Life Sciences Ser.). (Illus.). 830p. 1987. 350.00 (*0-387-96373-1*) Spr-Verlag.

Popper, Arthur N. & Eaton, R. C., eds. Mauthner Cells & Their Auditory Interactions: Proceedings of a Symposium Entitled "Interactions Between the Auditory & Mauthner Cell Systems", Vol. 46. (Journal Ser.: Vol. 46, No. 3, 1995). (Illus.). 60p. 1995. pap. 68.00 (*3-8055-6227-6*) S Karger.

P

An Asterisk (*) at the beginning of an entry indicates that the title is appearing for the first time.

Popper, Arthur N. & Fay, Richard R., eds. Comparative Hearing: Mammals. LC 93-43309. (Handbook of Auditory Research Ser.: Vol. 4). (Illus.). 280p. 1994. 89.95 (*0-387-97841-0*) Spr-Verlag.

— Comparative Studies of Hearing in Invertebrates. (Proceedings in Life Sciences Ser.). (Illus.). 512p. 1980. 175.00 (*0-387-90460-3*) Spr-Verlag.

— Hearing by Bats. LC 94-41860. (Handbook of Auditory Research: Vol. 5). (Illus.). 544p. 1995. 89.95 (*0-387-97844-5*) Spr-Verlag.

— The Mammalian Auditory Pathway: Neurophysiology. (Handbook of Auditory Research Ser.: Vol. 2). (Illus.). 368p. 1992. 89.95 (*0-387-97690-6*) Spr-Verlag.

— The Mammalian Auditory Pathway: Neurophysiology. (Handbook of Auditory Research Ser.: Vol. 2). (Illus.). 368p. 1995. 49.95 (*0-387-97801-1*) Spr-Verlag.

Popper, Arthur N., jt. auth. see Schaffner, Fenton.

Popper, Arthur N., ed. see Fay, Jan, et al.

Popper, Arthur N., jt. ed. see Fay, Richard R.

Popper, Charles. Psychiatric Pharmacosciences of Children & Adolescents. LC 86-28826. (Progress in Psychiatry Ser.). (Illus.). 179p. 1987. reprint ed. pap. 55.50 (*0-608-06668-0*, 206686500009) Bks Demand.

Popper, Eva B. My Love, My Care, My Spouse: A Chronicle of Parkinson's Disease. LC 88-90551. 75p. (Orig.). 1988. pap. text 6.95 (*0-945520-09-3*) PSGA.

Popper, Evelyn, jt. auth. see Meisler, Meryl.

Popper, Evelyn, jt. auth. see Meisser, Meryl.

Popper, Frank. Art of the Electronic Age. LC 96-61158. (Illus.). 192p. 1997. pap. 29.95 (*0-500-27918-7*, Pub. by Thames Hudson) Norton.

Popper, Frank, et al. The Politics of Land-Use Reform. LC 80-23255. 333p. reprint ed. pap. 103.30 (*0-608-09921-X*, 206925900003) Bks Demand.

Popper, Frank J., jt. ed. see Geisler, Charles C.

Popper, Helen A. Issues in International Capital Mobility. LC 97-495. (Financial Sector of the American Economy Ser.). (Illus.). 112p. 1997. text 43.00 (*0-8153-2817-6*) Garland.

Popper, Hermine I., ed. see Stanislavski, Constantin.

Popper, Karl R. All Life Is Problem Solving. LC 98-46132. 1999. 50.00 (*0-415-17486-4*) Routledge.

— Conjectures & Refutations: The Growth of Scientific Knowledge. 5th ed. 439p. (C). 1992. pap. 28.99 (*0-415-04318-2*) Routledge.

— Knowledge & the Body-Mind Problem. 168p. (C). 1996. pap. 19.99 (*0-415-13556-7*) Routledge.

— The Lesson of This Century: With Two Talks on Freedom & the Democratic State. Camiller, Patrick, tr. LC 96-5656. 112p. (C). 1996. 30.00 (*0-415-12958-3*) Routledge.

***Popper, Karl R.** Lesson of This Century: With Two Talks on Freedom & the Democratic State. 176p. 2000. pap. 16.95 (*0-415-12959-1*) Routledge.

Popper, Karl R. The Logic of Scientific Discovery. 14th ed. 480p. (C). 1992. pap. 34.99 (*0-415-07892-X*) Routledge.

— Objective Knowledge: An Evolutionary Approach. (Illus.). 390p. (C). 1972. pap. text 26.95 (*0-19-875024-2*) OUP.

— The Open Society & Its Enemies, 2 vols. 5th rev. ed. Incl. Vol. 1. Spell of Plato. 368p. 1966. pap. text 19.95 (*0-691-01968-1*, Pub. by Princeton U Pr); 1966. write for info. (*0-318-55362-7*) Princeton U Pr.

— The Open Society & Its Enemies: The High Tide of Prophecy, Vol. II. 432p. 1966. pap. text 19.95 (*0-691-01972-X*, Pub. by Princeton U Pr) Cal Prin Full Svc.

— The Open Universe: An Argument for Indeterminism. 208p. (C). 1992. pap. 27.99 (*0-415-07865-2*) Routledge.

— Popper Selections. Miller, David, ed. LC 83-43084. 480p. 1985. pap. text 18.95 (*0-691-02031-0*, Pub. by Princeton U Pr) Cal Prin Full Svc.

— The Poverty of Historicism. 176p. (C). 1988. pap. 18.99 (*0-415-06569-0*) Routledge.

— Quantum Theory & the Schism in Physics. LC 92-23685. (Postscript to the Logic of Scientific Discovery Ser.). 256p. (C). 1992. pap. 27.99 (*0-415-09112-8*) Routledge.

— Quantum Theory & the Schism in Physics. Bartley, W. W., III, ed. LC 81-8706. (Postscript to the Logic of Scientific Discovery Ser.). 250p. 1984. pap. 23.00 (*0-8476-7389-8*) Rowman.

— Realism & the Aim of Science: From the Postscript to the Logic of Scientific Discovery. Bartley, W. W., III, ed. LC 91-45665. 463p. (C). 1992. pap. 32.99 (*0-415-08400-8*) Routledge.

— The Self & Its Brain. 400p. (C). 1984. pap. 32.99 (*0-415-05898-8*) Routledge.

— Unended Quest: An Intellectual Autobiography. rev. ed. LC 76-2155. 258p. 1982. 32.95 (*0-87548-366-6*) Open Court.

— A World of Propensities. 60p. 1990. pap. 9.95 (*1-85506-000-0*) Bks Intl VA.

Popper, Karl R. & Eccles, John C. The Self & Its Brain. rev. ed. (Illus.). 597p. 1985. 86.95 (*0-387-08307-3*) Spr-Verlag.

— The Self & Its Brain: An Argument for Interactionism. 616p. 1984. reprint ed. pap. 16.95 (*0-7100-9584-8*, Routledge Thoemms) Routledge.

Popper, Karl R., et al. The World of Parmenides: Essays on the Presocratic Enlightenment. LC 97-17466. 352p. (C). 1998. 50.00 (*0-415-17301-9*) Routledge.

Popper, Karl R., jt. auth. see Marcuse, Herbert.

Popper, Karl Raimund. In Search of a Better World. 256p. (C). 1995. pap. 24.99 (*0-415-13548-6*) Routledge.

— The Myth of the Framework. 248p. (C). 1996. pap. 24.99 (*0-415-13555-9*) Routledge.

Popper-Lynkeus, Josef. The Individual & the Value of Human Life. Haber, Joram G. & Kelley, Andrew, trs. LC 95-13950. (Studies in Social & Political Philosophy).Tr. of Individuum und die Bewertung Menschlicher Existenzen. 180p. (C). 1995. text 52.00 (*0-8476-8035-5*); pap. text 21.95 (*0-8476-8036-3*) Rowman.

Popper, Samuel H. Pathways to the Humanities in Educational Administration. LC 97-103686. 231p. (C). 1990. reprint ed. pap. text 22.95 (*0-922971-00-5*, NT3) Univ Council Educ Admin.

Popper, Steven W., et al. New Forces at Work: Industry Views Critical Technologies. LC 98-37588. 180p. 2000. pap. 15.00 (*0-8330-2651-8*, MR-1008-OSTP, Pub. by Rand Corp) Natl Bk Netwk.

Popper, Virginia S., jt. ed. see Hastorf, Christine A.

Popper, William. The Cairo Nilometer: Studies in Ibn Iaghri Birdi's Chronicles of Egypt. LC 51-9495. (University of California Publications in Social Welfare: Vol. 12). 282p. reprint ed. pap. 87.50 (*0-8357-7962-9*, 202149100021) Bks Demand.

— Egypt & Syria under the Circassian Cultans, 1382-1468 A.D. Pt. II: Systematic Notes to Ibn Taghri Birdi's Chronicles of Egypt. LC 77-4958. (Publications in Semitic Philology). reprint ed. 37.50 (*0-404-58816-6*) AMS Pr.

— Egypt & Syria under the Circassian Sultans, 1382-1468 A. D. Systematic Notes to Ibn Taghri Birdi's Chronicles of Egypt, Pt. 1. LC DT0096.. (University of California Publications in Social Welfare: Vol. 15). 136p. reprint ed. pap. 42.20 (*0-608-14178-X*, 202149300021) Bks Demand.

— Egypt & Syria under the Circassian Sultans, 1382-1468 A. D. Systematic Notes to Ibn Taghri Birdi's Chronicles of Egypt, Pt. 2. (University of California Publications in Social Welfare: Vol. 16). 134p. reprint ed. pap. 38.20 (*0-608-14177-1*, 2021494) Bks Demand.

— History of Egypt, 1382-1469 A. D. Translated from the Arabic Annals of Abu L-Mahasin Ibn Taghri Birdi. LC 54-4885. (University of California Publications in Social Welfare: Vol. 24). 116p. 1963. reprint ed. pap. 36.00 (*0-608-08280-5*, 202150000021) Bks Demand.

— History of Egypt, 1382-1469 A. D. Translated from the Arabic Annals of Abu L-Mahasin Ibn Taghri Birdi, Pt. 1. LC 54-4885. (University of California Publications in Social Welfare: Vol. 13). 230p. 1954. reprint ed. pap. 71.30 (*0-608-08285-6*, 202149200021) Bks Demand.

— History of Egypt, 1382-1469 A. D. Translated from the Arabic Annals of Abu L-Mahasin Ibn Taghri Birdi, Pt. 3. LC 54-4885. (University of California Publications in Social Welfare: Vol. 17). 188p. reprint ed. pap. 53.60 (*0-608-14176-3*, 2021495) Bks Demand.

— History of Egypt, 1382-1469 A. D. Translated from the Arabic Annals of Abu L-Mahasin Ibn Taghri Birdi, Pt. 4. LC 54-4885. (University of California Publications in Social Welfare: Vol. 18). 232p. 1958. reprint ed. pap. 72.00 (*0-608-08284-8*, 202149600021) Bks Demand.

— History of Egypt, 1382-1469 A. D. Translated from the Arabic Annals of Abu L-Mahasin Ibn Taghri Birdi, Pt. 5. LC 54-4885. (University of California Publications in Social Welfare: Vol. 19). 270p. 1960. reprint ed. pap. 83.70 (*0-608-08283-X*, 202149700021) Bks Demand.

— History of Egypt, 1382-1469 A. D. Translated from the Arabic Annals of Abu L-Mahasin Ibn Taghri Birdi, Pt. 6. LC 54-4885. (University of California Publications in Social Welfare: Vol. 22). 184p. 1960. reprint ed. pap. 57.10 (*0-608-08282-1*, 202149800021) Bks Demand.

— History of Egypt, 1382-1469 A. D. Translated from the Arabic Annals of Abu L-Mahasin Ibn Taghri Birdi, Pt. 7. LC 54-4885. (University of California Publications in Social Welfare: Vol. 23). 187p. 1960. reprint ed. pap. 58.00 (*0-608-08281-3*, 202149900021) Bks Demand.

Popper, William, tr. History of Egypt, an Extract from Abu l-Mahasin Ibn Taghri Birdi's Chronicle, Entitled Hawadith ad-Duhur fi Mada l'Ayyam wash-Shuhur (845-843 A.H.) (American Oriental Society Essays Ser.: 5). 1963. pap. 3.00 (*0-940490-95-1*) Am Orient Soc.

Poppiti, James A. Practical Techniques for Laboratory Analysis. 208p. 1994. lib. bdg. 75.00 (*0-87371-361-3*, L361) Lewis Pubs.

Popple, James. A Pragmatic Legal Expert System. (Applied Legal Philosophy Ser.). (Illus.). 416p. 1996. text 91.95 (*1-85521-739-2*, Pub. by Dartmth Pub) Ashgate Pub Co.

Popple, Keith. Analysing Community Work: Its Theory & Practice. LC 95-6959. 144p. 1995. pap. 31.95 (*0-335-19408-7*) OpUniv Pr.

Popple, L. Advanced Ropeworking. (C). 1987. 60.00 (*0-85174-137-1*) St Mut.

— Marline Spike Seamanship: The Art of Handling, Splicing & Knotting Wire. (C). 1987. 50.00 (*0-85174-138-X*) St Mut.

Popple, Philip R. Child Welfare. (C). 1999. pap. text 53.33 (*0-205-27490-0*, Macmillan Coll) P-H.

Popple, Philip R. & Leighninger, Leslie. The Policy Based Profession: An Introduction to Social Welfare Policy for Social Workers. LC 97-2260. 368p. 1997. 61.00 (*0-205-18606-8*) P-H.

***Popple, Philip R. & Leighninger, Leslie.** The Policy-Based Profession: An Introduction to Social Welfare Policy for Social Workers. 2nd ed. LC 00-41630. 2001. boxed set. write for info. (*0-205-31739-1*) Allyn.

Popple, Philip R. & Leighninger, Leslie. Social Work, Social Welfare & American Society. 4th ed. LC 98-23953. 624p. 1998. 64.00 (*0-205-27858-2*) Allyn.

Popple, Simon, jt. auth. see Harding, Colin.

Popple, William, jt. auth. see Hill, Aaron.

Popplestone, John & McPherson, Marion W. An Illustrated History of American Psychology. 2nd ed. (Illus.). 222p. 1999. pap. 29.95 (*1-884836-39-9*) U Akron Pr.

Popplestone, John A. & McPherson, Marion W. Dictionary of Concepts in General Psychology. 7. LC 88-3120. (Reference Sources for the Social Sciences & Humanities Ser.: No. 7). 391p. 1988. lib. bdg. 85.00 (*0-313-23190-7*, PGP/, Greenwood Pr) Greenwood.

Poppleton, Gary, jt. auth. see Johnson, Steve.

Poppleton, Pam, jt. auth. see Menlo, Allen.

Popplewell, Jack. Breakfast in Bed. 1963. pap. 5.25 (*0-8222-0146-1*) Dramatists Play.

— Dear Delinquent. 1958. pap. 5.25 (*0-8222-0286-7*) Dramatists Play.

— Hocus Pocus. 1963. pap. 5.25 (*0-8222-0522-X*) Dramatists Play.

***Popplewell, Keith.** Financial Planning & Divorce. 280p. 1999. pap. 60.00 (*0-85297-546-5*, Pub. by Chartered Bank) St Mut.

— Investment Portfolio Planning. 266p. 1999. pap. 60.00 (*0-85297-550-3*, Pub. by Chartered Bank) St Mut.

— Mortgages & Investment Planning. 260p. 1999. pap. 60.00 (*0-85297-548-1*, Pub. by Chartered Bank) St Mut.

— Retirement Income Planning. 240p. 1999. pap. 60.00 (*0-85297-547-3*, Pub. by Chartered Bank) St Mut.

Popplewell, L. Railways, Canals & Mines of Looe & Liskeard. 72p. (C). 1985. 75.00 (*0-85361-212-9*) St Mut.

Popplewell, Richard, jt. auth. see Childs, David.

Popplewell, Richard J. Intelligence & Imperial Defense: British Intelligence & the Defense of the Indian Empire, 1904-1924. 360p. 1995. pap. 29.50 (*0-7146-4227-4*, Pub. by F Cass Pubs) Intl Spec Bk.

— Intelligence & Imperial Defense: British Intelligence & the Defense of the Indian Empire, 1904-1924. LC 95-16884. (Studies in Intelligence). 354p. 1995. 54.50 (*0-7146-4580-X*, Pub. by F Cass Pubs) Intl Spec Bk.

***Popplewell, Sean.** Exploring Museums: Ireland. (Illus.). 85p. 2000. reprint ed. pap. 15.00 (*0-7881-9240-X*) DIANE Pub.

Poppy. The Black Crystal. (Clipper Fiction Ser.). 1993. pap. text. write for info. (*0-582-91188-5*, Pub. by Addison-Wesley) Longman.

Pops, Horace, ed. Nonferrous Wire Handbook: Principles & Practice, Vol. 3. (Illus.). 678p. (C). 1995. text 125.00 (*1-877836-20-6*) Wire Assn Intl.

Pops, Martin. Home Remedies. LC 84-2647. (Illus.). 160p. 1984. pap. 15.95 (*0-87023-449-8*); lib. bdg. 22.50 (*0-87023-448-X*) U of Mass Pr.

— Vermeer: Consciousness & the Chamber of Being. Kuspit, Donald, ed. LC 84-2564. (Studies in the Fine Arts: Criticism: No. 16). 132p. reprint ed. 41.00 (*0-8357-1525-6*, 207046000093) Bks Demand.

Popson, Nancy. Building Civil Society in Post-Communist Hungary: The Case of Autonomia Alpitvany. (Pew Case Studies in International Affairs). 50p. (C). 1997. pap. text 3.50 (*1-56927-220-4*) Geo U Inst Dplmcy.

Popst, Hans, jt. auth. see Haller, Klaus.

***Popular Hot Rodding Magazine Editors.** Small-Block Chevy Performance Trends. LC 99-59764. (Illus.). 2000. pap. 17.95 (*1-55788-334-3*, HP Books) Berkley Pub.

Popular Mechanics Co. Staff. How to Make Mission Style Lamps & Shades in Metal & Glass. rev. ed. (Illus.). 128p. 1982. reprint ed. pap. 5.95 (*0-486-24244-7*) Dover.

— Mission Furniture: How to Make It. (Illus.). vii, 342p. 1980. pap. 8.95 (*0-486-23966-7*) Dover.

Popular Mechanics Editors. How to Make Amazing Toy & Game Gadgets. pap. write for info. (*0-688-17726-3*) Morrow Avon.

— How to Make Amazing Toy & Game Gadgets. 64p. 2000. 16.95 (*0-688-17797-2*, Wm Morrow) Morrow Avon.

— How to Make Cool Gadgets for Your Room. pap. write for info. (*0-688-17727-1*) Morrow Avon.

— Popular Mechanics 1998. (Illus.). 160p. 1998. 24.95 (*0-688-16137-5*, Hearst) Hearst Commns.

Popular Mechanics Editors. Popular Mechanics Saturday Mechanic. LC 90-25333. 1994. 22.00 (*0-688-12963-3*, Hearst) Hearst Commns.

Popular Mechanics Editors, ed. Popular Mechanics Housewares. 1924. write for info. (*0-688-16399-8*, Hearst) Hearst Commns.

***Popular Mechanics Staff.** The Home How-to Sourcebook. (Illus.). 512p. 2000. 30.00 (*0-688-17707-7*, Hearst) Hearst Commns.

— Popular Mechanics Kid's. 2nd ed. 2000. pap. Morrow Avon.

— Popular Mechanics Kids. 2nd ed. 64p. 2000. 16.95 (*0-688-17798-0*, Wm Morrow) Morrow Avon.

— Saturday Mechanic. 2000. pap. write for info. (*0-688-17808-1*, Hearst) Hearst Commns.

Popular Version Staff. Spanish - Version Popular. 1991. pap. text. write for info. (*0-00-152435-6*) Collins SF.

***Popular Woodworking Books Staff.** The Insider's Guide to Buying Tools. LC 00-36306. (Illus.). 128p. 2000. pap. 22.99 (*1-55870-542-2*, Popular Woodwking Bks) F & W Pubns Inc.

Popular Woodworking Books Staff, ed. The Best of Wood Boxes. LC 97-36422. (Illus.). 128p. 1998. pap. 24.99 (*1-55870-476-0*, Popular Woodwking Bks) F & W Pubns Inc.

***Popular Woodworking Books Staff, ed.** 25 Essential Projects for Your Workshop. LC 99-462302. (Illus.). 128p. 2000. 22.99 (*1-55870-541-4*, Popular Woodwking Bks) F & W Pubns Inc.

Population Council Library Staff. Catalogue of the Population Council Library. 1979. 375.00 (*0-8161-1496-X*, G K Hall & Co) Mac Lib Ref.

Population Council Staff, jt. auth. see Miller, Robert.

Population Division of the United Nations Secretariat Staff. World Population Monitoring, 1996: Selected Aspects of Reproductive Rights & Reproductive Health. 282p. 1998. pap. 45.00 (*92-1-151319-7*) UN.

Popushoi, I. S., ed. Biological & Chemical Methods of Plant Protection. Kothekar, V. S., tr. from RUS. (Illus.). 64p. 1987. text 71.00 (*90-6191-492-2*, Pub. by A A Balkema) Ashgate Pub Co.

Popv, Yuri. Essays in Political Economy Imperialism & Developing Countries. 294p. 1984. 40.00 (*0-317-53752-0*, Pub. by Collets) St Mut.

***Popyk, Bob.** Here's My Card: Networking, from Your First Introduction to Closing the Deal. (Illus.). 208p. 2000. pap. text 10.95 (*1-58063-113-4*) Renaissance.

Popyk, Bob. It's up to You! Knowing What to Do Is One Thing...Wanting to Do It Is Another. Simpson, Kristen, ed. (Illus.). x, 159p. 1997. pap. 24.95 (*1-890614-00-9*) Bentley-Hall.

Popyk, Marilyn K. Up & Running: Microcomputer Applications. LC 86-26620. (C). 1987. pap. text 35.50 (*0-201-06274-7*) Addison-Wesley.

Popyk, Marilyn K., jt. auth. see Boyce, B. L.

Por, F. D. The Legacy of Tethys. (Monographiae Biologicae). (C). 1989. text 160.00 (*0-7923-0189-7*) Kluwer Academic.

— Sooretama: The Atlantic Forest of Brazil. (Illus.). x, 130p. 1992. pap. 35.00 (*90-5103-077-0*, Pub. by SPB Acad Pub) Balogh.

Por, F. D. & Dor, I., eds. Hydrobiology of the Mangal. (Developments in Hydrobiology Ser.). 1984. text 232.00 (*90-6193-771-X*) Kluwer Academic.

Porac & Ventresca. The Social Construction of Markets & Industries. (Tourism Social Science Ser.). 352p. 1999. text 63.00 (*0-08-042587-9*, Pergamon Pr) Elsevier.

Porac, C. & Coren, S. Lateral Preferences & Human Behavior. (Illus.). 288p. 1981. 96.95 (*0-387-90596-0*) Spr-Verlag.

Porac, Joseph F., et al, eds. Advances in Managerial Cognition & Organizational Information Processing, Vol. 5. 337p. 1994. 73.25 (*1-55938-447-6*) Jai Pr.

Porad, Francine. After Autumn Rain: Haiku, Senryu, Sketches. (Illus.). 28p. (Orig.). (C). 1987. pap. text 5.00 (*0-9618009-2-5*) Vandina Pr.

— All Eyes. (Illus.). 20p. (Orig.). 1994. pap. 6.75 (*1-887381-00-7*) Vandina Pr.

— All the Games: Haiku, Tanka, Art. (Illus.). 22p. (C). 1997. pap. 9.25 (*1-887381-10-4*) Vandina Pr.

— Blues on the Run: Haiku, Senryu, Sketches. (Illus.). 28p. (Orig.). (C). 1988. pap. text 5.00 (*0-9618009-3-3*) Vandina Pr.

— Connections: Haiku, Senryu & Sketches. (Illus.). 32p. (Orig.). (C). 1986. pap. text 5.00 (*0-9618009-0-9*) Vandina Pr.

— Extended Wings: Haiku & Tanka. 26p. (Orig.). 1996. 4.75 (*1-887381-02-3*) Vandina Pr.

— Fog Lifting: Haiku & Tanka. 32p. (C). 1997. pap. 5.75 (*1-887381-05-8*) Vandina Pr.

— Free of Clouds: Haiku, Senryu, Sketches. (Illus.). 28p. (Orig.). (C). 1989. pap. text 5.00 (*0-9618009-5-X*) Vandina Pr.

— Hundreds of Wishes: Haiku, Senryu, Sketches. (Illus.). 24p. (Orig.). (C). 1991. pap. text 5.00 (*0-9618009-6-8*) Vandina Pr.

— Joy Is My Middle Name: Haiku, Senryu, Tanka. (Illus.). 40p. (Orig.). (C). 1993. pap. text 5.00 (*0-9618009-8-4*) Vandina Pr.

— Ladles & Jellyspoons: Presentations Haiku, Senryu, Tanka. (Illus.). 48p. (Orig.). 1995. pap. 12.20 (*1-887381-01-5*) Vandina Pr.

— Pen & Inklings: Haiku, Senryu & Sketches. (Illus.). 28p. (Orig.). (C). 1986. pap. text 5.00 (*0-9618009-1-7*) Vandina Pr.

— Without Haste. (Amelia Chapbooks Ser.). 16p. (Orig.). 1990. pap. 4.50 (*0-936545-16-X*) Amelia.

Porad, Francine, et al. The Patchwork Quilt: Haiku, Senryu, Tanka, Renku, Artwork. (Illus.). 40p. (Orig.). (C). 1993. pap. text 6.75 (*0-9618009-9-2*) Vandina Pr.

Porad, Francine, jt. auth. see Major, Robert.

Porada, Edith. Ancient Art in Seals: Essays in Pierre Amiet, Nimet Ozguc, & John Boardman. LC 79-19462. (Franklin Jasper Walls Lectures). (Illus.). 153p. reprint ed. pap. 47.50 (*0-8357-4035-8*, 203672700005) Bks Demand.

Poralla, P. Prosopographia Lacaedaemoniorum. 1985. reprint ed. pap. 15.00 (*0-89005-521-1*) Ares.

Porat, Boaz. A Course in Digital Signal Processing. LC 96-38470. 632p. 1996. text 109.95 (*0-471-14961-6*) Wiley.

Porat, Dan I., jt. auth. see Barna, Arpad.

Porat, Dina. The Blue & the Yellow Stars of David: The Zionist Leadership in Palestine & the Holocaust, 1939-1945. (Illus.). 334p. 1990. 41.50 (*0-674-07708-3*) HUP.

Porat, Elisha. Messiah of la Guardia. Sacks, Alan, tr. from HEB. 180p. (Orig.). 1996. pap. 14.95 (*0-88962-614-6*) Mosaic.

Porat, Freida & Will, Mimi. The Dynamic Secretary: A Practical Guide to Achieving Success as an Executive Assistant. (Illus.). 196p. 1983. pap. 7.95 (*0-685-06199-X*) P-H.

Porat, Frieda. Creative Life Management: Stress Reduction for an Enhanced Quality of Life. LC 94-69746. 185p. (Orig.). 1994. pap. 9.95 (*0-9643745-1-X*) NewLife CA.

— Creative Retirement: Shifting Gears from a Life of Work to a World of Options. LC 94-69745. 198p. (Orig.). 1994. pap. 9.95 (*0-9643745-0-1*) NewLife CA.

Porath, Ellen. Steel & Stone. (DragonLance Meetings Sextet: Vol. 5). 320p. (Orig.). 1992. pap. 5.99 (*1-56076-339-6*, Pub. by TSR Inc) Random.

Porath, Jonathan D. Jews in Russia: The Last Four Centuries. 1973. pap. 3.75 (*0-8381-0220-4*) USCJE.

Porath, Renatus. Die Sozialkritik Im Jesajabuch: Redaktionsgeschichtliche Analyse. (Europaische Hochschulschriften Ser.: Reihe 23, Bd. 503). (GER.). 214p. 1994. 37.95 (*3-631-47039-8*) P Lang Pubng.

An Asterisk (*) at the beginning of an entry indicates that the title is appearing for the first time.

Porath, Sharon. Dead File. 352p. 1995. mass mkt. 4.99 (*0-8217-4973-0*, Pinncle Kensgtn) Kensgtn Pub Corp.
— Secret Friend. 320p. 1992. mass mkt. 4.50 (*0-8217-3906-9*, Zebra Kensgtn) Kensgtn Pub Corp.

Porath, Yehoshua. The Emergence of the Palestinian Arab National Movement, 1918-1929. 406p. 1974. pap. 27.50 (*0-7146-4181-2*, Pub. by F Cass Pubs) Intl Spec Bk.
— In Search of Arab Unity, 1930-1945. 384p. 1986. 52.50 (*0-7146-3264-3*, Pub. by F Cass Pubs); pap. 27.50 (*0-7146-4051-4*, Pub. by F Cass Pubs) Intl Spec Bk.
— The Palestinian Arab National Movement, 1929-1939 Vol. 2: From Riots to Rebellion. 414p. 1977. pap. 27.50 (*0-7146-4197-9*, Pub. by F Cass Pubs) Intl Spec Bk.

Porazinska, Janina. The Enchanted Book: A Tale from Krakow. Smith, Bozena, tr. LC 86-22918. (Illus.). 32p. (J). (gr. k-4). 1987. 13.95 (*0-15-225950-3*) Harcourt.

Porcano, Thomas. Advances in Taxation, Vol. 10. 1998. 78.50 (*0-7623-0336-0*) Jai Pr.

Porcano, Thomas M. Advances in Taxation: In Preparation, Summer 1997, Vol. 9. 1997. 78.50 (*0-7623-0166-X*) Jai Pr.

***Porcano, Thomas M., ed.** Advances in Taxation, Vol. II. 1999. 78.50 (*0-7623-0519-3*) Jai Pr.

Porcano, Thomas M., et al, eds. Advances in Taxation, Vol. 1. 210p. 1988. 78.50 (*0-89232-782-0*) Jai Pr.
— Advances in Taxation, Vol. 2. 264p. 1989. 78.50 (*0-89232-783-9*) Jai Pr.
— Advances in Taxation, Vol. 3. 259p. 1990. 78.50 (*1-55938-120-5*) Jai Pr.
— Advances in Taxation, Vol. 4. 291p. 1992. 78.50 (*1-55938-376-3*) Jai Pr.
— Advances in Taxation, Vol. 5. 272p. 1994. 78.50 (*1-55938-750-5*) Jai Pr.
— Advances in Taxation, Vol. 6. 251p. 1994. 78.50 (*1-55938-777-7*) Jai Pr.
— Advances in Taxation, Vol. 7. 194p. 1995. 78.50 (*1-55938-910-9*) Jai Pr.
— Advances in Taxation, Vol. 8. 1996. 78.50 (*1-55938-994-X*) Jai Pr.

Porcaro, Susan T. Creepy, Crawly Critters, Bugs & Bees Funbook. (J). 1997. pap. text 1.50 (*1-890570-01-X*) Huckleberry CT.
— A Dog Named Zog Funbook. (J). 1997. pap. text 1.50 (*1-890570-03-6*) Huckleberry CT.
— Excuse Me... I Think I Need Some Color! (J). 1997. pap. text 1.25 (*1-890570-02-8*) Huckleberry CT.
— Muffin Huff 'n Puff Funbook. 1997. pap. text 1.50 (*1-890570-04-4*) Huckleberry CT.

Porcasi, Judith, et al. Papers on California Prehistory 5. Breschini & Haverrat, eds. (Archives of California Prehistory Ser.: No. 45). (Illus.). 106p. (Orig.). (C). 1997. pap. text 11.88 (*1-55567-626-X*) Coyote Press.

Porceddu, E. & Jenkins, G., eds. Seed Regeneration in Cross-Pollinated Species: Proceedings of the C. E. C. - Eucarpia Seminar, Nyborg, Denmark, 15-17 July 1981. 302p. (C). 1982. text 110.00 (*90-6191-244-X*, Pub. by A A Balkema) Ashgate Pub Co.

Porcel. Risas, Aplausos y Lagrimas (Laughs, Applauses & Tears) (SPA.). 1997. 9.99 (*0-88113-134-2*, B117-1342) Caribe Betania.

Porcel, Baltasar. Horses into the Night. Getman, John L., tr. LC 94-41275. 1995. pap. 20.00 (*1-55728-333-8*) U of Ark Pr.
— Horses into the Night. Getman, John L., tr. LC 94-41275. 240p. 1995. text 30.00 (*1-55728-332-X*) U of Ark Pr.

***Porcel, Baltasar.** Springs & Autumns. Getman, John L., tr. LC 00-28627. 256p. 2000. pap. 22.00 (*1-55728-609-4*) U of Ark Pr.

Porcella, Donald R., ed. Mercury As a Global Pollutant: Proceedings of the Third International Conference Held in Whistler, British Columbia, July 10-14, 1994. 1312p. (C). 1995. text 364.50 (*0-7923-3544-9*) Kluwer Academic.

Porcella, Ronald L. Strong Motion Program Report, January-December 1983. (Illus.). 70p. 1998. reprint ed. 14.00 (*0-89904-542-1*, Cascade Geog Soc); reprint ed. pap. 8.00 (*0-89904-543-X*, Cascade Geog Soc) Crumb Elbow Pub.

Porcella, Ronald L., jt. auth. see Switzer, Josephine C.

Porcella, Stephen F. & Burns, Cameron M. California's Fourteeners: A Hiking & Climbing Guide. LC 97-147732. (Illus.). 96p. (Orig.). 1995. pap. 12.95 (*1-57540-006-5*) Falcon Pub Inc.

Porcella, Steven F. & Burns, Cameron M. Climbing California's Fourteeners: 183 Routes to the Fifteen Highest Peaks. LC 97-46406. (Illus.). 272p. 1998. pap. 19.95 (*0-89886-555-7*) Mountaineers.

Porcella, Yvonne. Colors Changing Hue. Lytle, Joyce E. & Nadel, Harold, eds. LC 94-13305. (Illus.). 96p. 1995. pap. 21.95 (*0-914881-86-8*, 10103) C & T Pub.
— Pieced Clothing. rev. ed. LC 86-90565. (Illus.). 60p. 1987. pap. 11.95 (*0-936589-01-9*) Porcella Studios.
— Six Color World: Color, Cloth, Quilts & Wearables. Jonsson, Lee, ed. LC 97-3062. (Illus.). 144p. (Orig.). 1997. pap. 26.95 (*1-57120-035-5*, 10159) C & T Pub.
— Yvonne Porcella: A Colorful Book. LC 85-90510. (Illus.). 120p. (Orig.). 1986. pap. 22.00 (*0-936589-00-0*) Porcella Studios.

Porcelli, Joe. The Lampmaking Handbook. (Illus.). 1991. 24.95 (*0-9629053-6-4*) Glass Pr.
— The Photograph. Wyrick, Charles L., Jr., ed. 346p. 1995. 22.95 (*0-941711-30-7*) Wyrick & Co.

***Porcelli, Joe.** Stained Glass: Jewels of Light. LC 00-22711. (Illus.). 2000. write for info. (*1-58663-014-8*) M Friedman Pub Grp Inc.

Porcelli, Joe. Stained Glass - Jewels of Light. LC 97-17032. (Illus.). 144p. 1998. 30.00 (*1-56799-550-0*, Friedman-Fairfax) M Friedman Pub Grp Inc.

Porcelli, Joe, ed. see Radeschi, Loretta.

Porcelli, V. Lorenzo. International Lighting Design. ID Magazine Staff, ed. (Illus.). 256p. 1991. 59.95 (*0-935603-49-2*, 30253) Rockport Pubs.

Porcellino, John. Perfect Example. 1999. pap. text 9.95 (*0-9665363-5-5*) Highwater Bks.

Porcellino, Michael R. Through the Telescope: A Guide for the Amateur Astronomer. 352p. 1989. pap. 24.95 (*0-07-156226-5*) McGraw.
— Through the Telescope: A Guide for the Amateur Astronomer. (Discovering Earth Science Ser.). (Illus.). 272p. 1989. 22.95 (*0-8306-1459-1*) McGraw-Hill Prof.
— Through the Telescope: A Guide for the Amateur Astronomer. (Discovering Earth Science Ser.). (Illus.). 272p. (YA). (gr. 9-12). 1989. pap. 19.95 (*0-8306-3159-3*) McGraw-Hill Prof.

Porch, Adelle. Your First Ferret. (Illus.). 32p. (Orig.). 1991. pap. 2.29 (*0-86622-115-8*, YF-105) TFH Pubns.

Porch, Dorris D. & Easley, Rebecca. Murder in Memphis: The True Story of a Family's Quest for Justice. LC 97-66562. 320p. 1997. 24.95 (*0-88282-157-1*) New Horizon NJ.

Porch, Douglas. The Conquest of the Sahara. LC 86-12092. 332p. 1986. reprint ed. pap. 11.95 (*0-88064-061-8*) Fromm Intl Pub.
— The French Foreign Legion: A Complete History of the Legendary Fighting Force. LC 90-55834. (Illus.). 784p. 1992. reprint ed. pap. 20.00 (*0-06-092308-3*, Perennial) HarperTrade.
— The French Secret Service: From the Dreyfus Affair to the Gulf War. LC 94-46833. 623p. 1995. text 32.50 (*0-374-15853-3*) FS&G.

***Porch, Douglas.** History of Warfare: Wars of Empire. 2000. 29.95 (*0-304-35271-3*, Pub. by Cassell) Sterling.

Porch, Ludlow. You're Sittin' on Boomey! The Best of Ludlow Porch. LC 97-71929. 176p. 1997. 18.95 (*1-56352-436-8*) Longstreet.

Porchat, J. Jacques. Three Months under the Snow: The Journal of a Young Inhabitant of the Jura. LC 98-50397. 1999. write for info. (*0-9669189-0-8*); write for info. (*0-9669189-1-6*) Prism Prods.

***Porcher, E. A. & Smith, Dwight La Vern.** A Tour of Duty in the Pacific Northwest: E. A. Porcher & H. M. S. Sparrowhawk, 1865-1868. LC 00-37709. 2000. write for info. (*1-889963-06-2*) U of Alaska Pr.

Porcher, Francis P. Resources of the Southern Fields & Forests. LC 74-125758. (American Environmental Studies). 1974. reprint ed. 46.95 (*0-405-02684-6*) Ayer.
— Resources of the Southern Fields & Forests, Medical, Economical & Agricultural. (American Civil War Medical Ser.: No. 4). 601p. 1991. reprint ed. 75.00 (*0-930405-33-1*) Norman SF.

Porcher, Philip G., Jr. What You Can Expect from an Interim Pastor & an Interim Consultant. pap. 6.75 (*1-56699-101-3*, OD71) Alban Inst.

Porchet, M., jt. ed. see Hoffmann, J.

***Porchlight Entertainment Staff, ed.** Friends Forever. (Jay Jay the Jet Plane Board Bks.: Vol. 4). (Illus.). 12p. (J). (ps). 2000. 5.99 (*0-8499-7553-0*) Tommy Nelson.
— Love Each Other. (Jay Jay the Jet Plane Board Bks.: Vol. 3). (Illus.). 12p. (J). (ps). 2000. 5.99 (*0-8499-7552-2*) Tommy Nelson.
— Share Together. (Jay Jay the Jet Plane Board Bks.: Vol. 2). (Illus.). 12p. (J). (ps). 2000. 5.99 (*0-8499-7551-4*) Tommy Nelson.
— You Are Special. (Jay Jay the Jet Plane Board Bks.: Vol. 1). (Illus.). 12p. (J). (ps). 2000. 5.99 (*0-8499-7550-6*) Tommy Nelson.

Porcino, Jane. Growing Older, Getting Better: A Handbook for Women in the Second Half of Life. LC 82-24438. (Illus.). 366p. 1983. pap. 12.95 (*0-201-05592-9*) Addison-Wesley.

Porcioles, Lluis B. Diccionari Alemany-Catala. 2nd ed. (CAT & GER.). 716p. 1990. 41.95 (*0-7859-6336-7*, 8485194187) Fr & Eur.

Porck, Henk. Mass Deacidification: An Update on Possibilities & Limitations. LC 96-231763. 54p. (Orig.). 1996. pap. 15.00 (*1-887334-52-1*) Coun Lib & Info.

Pordage, S., tr. see Willis, Thomas.

***Pordes, Laurence.** Book. (Eyewitness Books). (Illus.). (J). (gr. 4-7). 2000. 19.99 (*0-7894-6597-3*) DK Pub Inc.

Pordominsky, Zusel, tr. see Gomez-Zimmerman, Mario.

Pore, Renate. A Conflict of Interest: Women in German Social Democracy, 1919 to 1933, 26. LC 80-27183. (Contributions in Women's Studies: No. 26). (Illus.). 129p. 1981. 49.95 (*0-313-22856-6*, PCW/, Greenwood Pr) Greenwood.

Pore, Renate, jt. ed. see Justice, Betty.

Pore, Sally G. & Reed, Kathlyn L. Quick Reference to Speech-Language Pathology. LC 98-54628. 288p. 1999. pap. 41.00 (*0-8342-1278-1*) Aspen Pub.

Poree, Guy. Moeurs et Coutumes des Khmers. LC 77-87069. (Illus.). reprint ed. 42.50 (*0-404-16850-7*) AMS Pr.

Poree-Maspero, Eveline. Etude Sur les Rites Agraires De Cambodgins, 3 tomes. Incl. Tome I. 1962. pap. 22.40 (*90-279-6210-3*); (Monde d'Outre Mer Passe & Present, Etudes Ser.: No. 14). Set pap. 34.00 (*0-685-03432-1*) Mouton.

Porell, Frank W. Models of Intra-Urban Relocation. (Studies in Applied Regional Science). 1982. lib. bdg. 115.50 (*0-89838-089-8*) Kluwer Academic.

***Poremba, David.** Detroit, 1930-1969. (Images of America Ser.). 128p. 1999. pap. 18.99 (*0-7385-0150-6*) Arcadia Publng.

Poremba, David Lee. Baseball in Detroit. (Images of America Ser.). 1998. 18.99 (*0-7524-1357-0*) Arcadia Publng.

***Poremba, David Lee.** Detroit: City of Champions. (Images of America Ser.). 1999. pap. 18.99 (*0-7524-1368-6*) Arcadia Publng.

Poremba, David Lee. Detroit, 1860-1899. LC 98-85884. (Images of America Ser.). 1998. 16.99 (*0-7524-1385-6*) Arcadia Publng.

***Poresky, Louise A.** Another Way of Seeing: What "A Course in Miracles" Is All About. 2000. pap. 18.95 (*0-89334-329-3*, Humanics Pub) Humanics Ltd.

Poresky, Louise A. The Elusive Self: Psyche & Spirit in Virginia Woolf's Novels. LC 79-64503. 288p. 1981. 38.50 (*0-87413-170-7*, 170) U Delaware Pr.

Porete, Marguerite. Marguerite Porete: The Mirror of Simple Souls. LC 93-14479. (Classics of Western Spirituality Ser.).Tr. of Miroir des Simples Ames. 288p. 1993. 24.95 (*0-8091-0464-4*); pap. 17.95 (*0-8091-3427-6*) Paulist Pr.

Porete, Marguerite, et al. The Mirror of Simple Souls. LC 98-54869. (Texts in Medieval Culture Ser.). 1999. pap. text 24.00 (*0-268-01435-3*) U of Notre Dame Pr.

***Porett, Jane.** When I Was Little Like You. 1999. pap. 6.95 (*0-87868-794-7*, CWLA Pr) Child Welfare.

Poretta, Vicki. Mom's Guide to Sports. LC 97-73184. 182p. 1997. 14.95 (*0-02-861966-8*) Macmillan.

Poretta, Vicki & Borden, Marian E. Mom's Guide to Raising a Good Student. LC 97-73173. (Illus.). 183p. 1997. 14.95 (*0-02-861942-0*) IDG Bks.

Poretta, Vicki & Kogan, Marcela. Mom's Guide to Nutrition. LC 97-73176. 179p. 1997. 14.95 (*0-02-861968-4*) Macmillan.

Poretta, Vicki & Lutz, Ericka. Mom's Guide to Disciplining Your Child. LC 97-73175. 216p. 1997. 14.95 (*0-02-861950-1*) IDG Bks.

Porette, Margaret. The Mirror of Simple Souls. LC 98-54869. (Texts in Medieval Culture Ser.: Vol. 6). (C). 1999. pap. 24.00 (*0-268-01431-0*) U of Notre Dame Pr.

Poretz, Doraine. Arrival. 1994. pap. 10.00 (*0-941017-37-0*) Bombshelter Pr.
— Scattered Light. 32p. (Orig.). 1987. pap. 5.95 (*0-941017-09-5*) Bombshelter Pr.

***Porfiri, Lynne & Resnick, Robert.** Law & Mental Health Professionals: Virginia. LC 99-39617. 344p. 1999. 59.95 (*1-55798-615-0*) Am Psychol.

***Porfiriev, Boris.** Disaster Policy & Emergency Management in Russia: Theory & Practice. 257p. 1998. text 70.00 (*1-56072-421-8*) Nova Sci Pubs.

Porfiriev, Boris, jt. auth. see Voskressenski, Alexei.

Porfyrio, Pomponius. Commentum in Horatium Flaccum. x, 599p. 1967. reprint ed. write for info. incl. 3.5 hd (*0-318-71203-2*) G Olms Pubs.

Porges, Cher, jt. auth. see Lindenberger, Jan.

Porges, F. Design of Electrical Services in Buildings. 3rd ed. 350p. 1989. 69.50 (*0-419-14580-X*, E & FN Spon) Routledge.
— HVAC Engineer's Handbook. 10th ed. LC 95-24199. (Illus.). 272p. 2000. text 100.00 (*0-7506-2594-5*) Buttrwrth-Heinemann.

Porges, G. Applied Acoustics. LC 87-61230. 180p. 1987. reprint ed. 32.95 (*0-932146-18-X*) Peninsula CA.

Porges, L. Bibliographie Des Regions Du Senegal. 1977. 159.25 (*90-279-7544-2*) Mouton.

Porges, Maria. Forms of Address. (Illus.). 32p. (Orig.). 1994. pap. write for info. (*0-930495-24-1*) San Fran Art Inst.

Porile, Norbert T. Modern University Chemistry, Custom Pub. 2nd ed. (C). 1993. text 48.50 (*0-07-050639-6*) McGraw.

Poris, Ruth F. Advanced Beadwork. (Illus.). 152p. (Orig.). 1990. per. 14.99 (*0-9616422-0-3*) Golden Hands Pr.
— Step-by-Step Bead Stringing: A Complete Illustrated Professional Approach. (Illus.). 45p. 1985. pap. 7.99 (*0-9616422-1-1*) Golden Hands Pr.

Porish, Peggy. Too Many Rabbits. (J). 1976. pap. 1.50 (*0-590-10157-9*) Scholastic Inc.

Poriss, Gerry H. & Poriss, Ralph G. While My Country Is in Danger: The Life & Letters of Lieutenant Colonel Richard S. Thompson, 12th NJ Volunteers. LC 94-11305. (Illus.). 229p. 1994. 22.95 (*0-9622393-6-4*) Edmonston Publ.

***Poriss, Martin P.** Real Estate Bargains! Homes You Can Afford, but May Not Want. 2nd rev. ed. (Illus.). 96p. 1999. pap. 19.95 (*0-9668110-0-3*) Best Gift Pr.

Poriss, Ralph G., jt. auth. see Poriss, Gerry H.

Poritsky, Bertrand. Minnesota Evidence Trialbook, 1987-1990. 210p. 1994. spiral bd. 65.00 (*0-86678-279-6*, MICHIE); ring bd., suppl. ed. 39.00 (*0-86678-004-1*, MICHIE) LEXIS Pub.

Poritsky, H., jt. auth. see Dudley, Darle W.

Poritsky, Ray. Anatomy to Color & Study. (Illus.). 544p. (Orig.). 1989. student ed. 26.95 (*0-932883-18-4*) Hanley & Belfus.
— Cross Sectional Anatomy to Color & Study. LC 96-2015. (Illus.). 1996. pap. 28.00 (*1-56053-169-X*) Hanley & Belfus.

***Poritsky, Ray.** Hand & Upper Extremity to Color & Study. LC 99-. (Illus.). 150p. 2000. pap. text 19.95 (*1-56053-372-2*, Pub. by Hanley & Belfus) Mosby Inc.

Poritsky, Ray. Neuroanatomy: A Functional Atlas of Parts & Pathways. (Illus.). 300p. 1992. pap. text, student ed. 34.00 (*1-56053-008-1*) Hanley & Belfus.

Poritzky-Lauvand, Rhona, tr. see Thuries, Yves.

Porjtillo, Mariano N. Turbas Republicanas, 1900-1904. LC 90-81370. 218p. 1990. pap. 9.50 (*0-929157-07-9*) Ediciones Huracan.

Porkert, Manfred. The Essentials of Chinese Diagnostics. (Illus.). 292p. 1983. reprint ed. pap. 16.00 (*0-912379-00-6*) Ctr Traditional Acupuncture.

Porkert, Manfred & Ullmann, Christiane. Chinese Medicine. 320p. 1995. pap. 12.95 (*0-8050-1277-X*, Owl) H Holt & Co.

Porkess, Roger. The HarperCollins Dictionary of Statistics. LC 90-56000. (Illus.). 288p. 1991. pap. 16.00 (*0-06-461020-9*, Harper Ref) HarpC.

Porket, J. L. Unemployment in Capitalist, Communist, & Post-Communist Economies. LC 94-34872. 1995. text 79.95 (*0-312-12484-8*) St Martin.

Porkolab, Miklos, ed. Radio Frequency Power in Plasmas. (AIP Conference Proceedings Ser.: No. 289). (Illus.). 464p. 1993. text 135.00 (*1-56396-264-0*, AIP Pr) Spr-Verlag.

Porlier, Linda K., jt. auth. see Porlier, Terry.

Porlier, Terry & Porlier, Linda K. Living over the Limit: A Credit Card Survival Kit. 140p. 1989. student ed. write for info. (*0-9623584-1-X*); pap. text 29.95 (*0-9623584-0-1*) Emerald West.
— Living over the Limit: How to Get Out & Stay Out of the Credit Trap - the Credit Card Survival Kit. 130p. (Orig.). 1989. 49.95 incl. audio (*0-9623584-2-8*) Emerald West.

Porlier, Victor W. Y2K: An Action Plan to Protect Yourself, Your Family, Your Assets & Your Community on January 1, 2000. LC 98-45864. 192p. 1999. pap. 11.95 (*0-06-273675-2*) HarpC.

Porn, Igmar. Action Theory & Social Science. (Synthese Library: No. 120). 139p. 1977. text 85.50 (*90-277-0846-0*, D Reidel) Kluwer Academic.

Pornbacher, Ulrike, compiled by. Migration & Intercultural Education in Europe. 180p. 1990. 49.00 (*1-85359-112-2*, Pub. by Multilingual Matters) Taylor & Francis.

Pornbacher, Ulrike, et al. Migration of Intercultural Education in Europe. 1990. 49.00 (*1-85359-094-0*, Pub. by Multilingual Matters) Taylor & Francis.

Pornschlegel, H., ed. Research & Development in Work & Technology. (Illus.). xiv, 413p. 1992. pap. 89.00 (*0-387-91427-7*) Spr-Verlag.

***Poro, Susanne.** Beziehungsrelevanz in der Beruflichen Kommunikation. (Arbeiten Zu Diskurs und Stil Ser.). 206p. 1999. 35.95 (*3-631-35341-3*) P Lang Pubng.

Porosky, Peter. Beginning the Novel. LC 94-8397. 128p. (Orig.). 1994. pap. 19.50 (*0-8191-9502-2*); lib. bdg. 42.50 (*0-8191-9501-4*) U Pr of Amer.
— How to Fix Fiction: Techniques of a Professional Writing Consultant. 330p. (Orig.). (C). 1995. pap. text 23.50 (*0-7618-0056-5*); lib. bdg. 48.50 (*0-7618-0055-7*) U Pr of Amer.

Porot, Antoine. Diccionario de Psiquiatria, Vol. 1. 3rd ed. (SPA.). 650p. 1977. 59.95 (*0-7859-5924-6*, 8433566695) Fr & Eur.
— Diccionario de Psiquiatria, Vol. 2. 3rd ed. (SPA.). 650p. 1977. 59.95 (*0-7859-5925-4*, 8433566709) Fr & Eur.
— Diccionario de Psiquiatria: Dictionary of Psychiatry, 2 vols., Set. 3rd ed. (SPA.). 650p. 1977. 125.00 (*0-8288-5320-7*, S50071) Fr & Eur.

Porot, Antoine, ed. Manuel Alphabetique de Psychiatrie Clinique et Therapeutique. 6th ed. (FRE.). 768p. 1984. 135.00 (*0-7859-4832-5*, M6391) Fr & Eur.

Porot, Daniel. The Pie Method for Career Success: A New Job Search Strategy. (Illus.). 218p. (Orig.). 1995. pap. 14.95 (*1-56370-182-0*, J1820) JIST Works.

***Porot, Daniel & Haynes, Frances.** 101 Ways to Improve Your Salary. 240p. 2001. pap. 12.95 (*1-58008-230-0*) Ten Speed Pr.

Porot, Daniel & Haynes, Frances Bolles. 101 Tough Interview Questions: . . . And Answers that Win the Job! LC 99-186720. (Illus.). 206p. 1999. pap. 12.95 (*1-58008-068-5*) Ten Speed Pr.

Porot, Marie, et al. S. F. B. J. - Captivating Character Children. (Illus.). 238p. 1986. 25.00 (*0-87588-279-X*, 3302) Hobby Hse.

Porowski, James P., jt. auth. see Carlisle, Paul B.

***Porozynski, Martin.** Up-Front Sleeper: The Federal Witness "Protection" Programs: A "Letter" to Janet Reno Corrupt Jurisprudence Unchecked. 3rd rev. ed. 198p. 2000. spiral bd. 14.95 (*0-9644416-2-4*) Doublenight Pr.

Porozynski, Martin. Up-Front Sleeper the Federal Witness "Protection" Program: True Involvement with Rapico Picnocrap: A Letter to Janet Reno. 2nd rev. ed. (Corruption & Capitalism - A Disastrous Experience with Jurisprudence Unchecked Ser.: Vol. 2). (Illus.). 212p. 1999. pap. 14.95 (*0-9644416-4-0*) Doublenight Pr.

Porozynski, Martin J. Up-Front Sleeper: The Federal Witness "Protection" Program: True Involvement with Rapico Picnocrap - A "Letter" to Janet Reno. LC 94-74031. 200p. (Orig.). 1995. pap. 14.95 (*0-9644416-3-2*) Doublenight Pr.

***Porphyrios, Demetri.** Classical Architecture. LC 99-234297. (Illus.). 156p. 1998. pap. 35.00 (*1-901092-06-2*, Pub. by Andreas Papadakis) Antique Collect.

Porphyrios, Demetri. Demetri Porphyrios Selected Buildings & Writings. (Architectural Monographs: No. 25). (Illus.). 144p. 1993. pap. 38.00 (*1-85490-175-3*) Academy Ed UK.
— Sources of Modern Eclecticism. (Academy Architecture Ser.). (Illus.). 128p. 1982. 19.95 (*0-312-74673-3*) St Martin.
— Sources of Modern Eclecticism. (Academy Architecture Ser.). (Illus.). 128p. 1982. pap. 19.95 (*0-312-74674-1*) St Martin.

Porphyrios, Demetri, ed. Classicism Is Not a Style: An Architectural Design Profile. (Academy Architecture Ser.). (Illus.). 128p. 1982. pap. 19.95 (*0-312-14266-8*) St Martin.
— Leon Krier: Houses, Palaces, Cities: An Architectural Design Profile. (Illus.). 128p. 1985. pap. 21.95 (*0-312-47990-5*) St Martin.

Porphyrios, Demetri, jt. ed. see Balslev, Lisbet B.

Porphyrius. De Philosophia Ex Oraculis Haurienda Librorum Reliquiae. Wolff, Gustav, ed. vi, 253p. 1984. reprint ed. write for info. (*3-487-00202-7*) G Olms Pubs.
— Opuscula Selecta. xxiii, 320p. 1977. reprint ed. write for info. (*3-487-00421-6*) G Olms Pubs.

***Porphyrius Philosophus.** Fragmenta. Smith, Andrew & Wasserstein, David, eds. (Illus.). (C). 1998. text 165.00 (*3-8154-1721-X*) B G Teubner.

P

Porphyry. On Abstinence from Animal Food. 250p. 1989. pap. 25.00 (*0-87556-238-8*) Saifer.
— On Aristotle's Categories. Strange, Steven K., tr. LC 92-14908. (Ancient Commentators on Aristotle Ser.). 1992. text 49.95 (*0-8014-2816-5*) Cornell U Pr.
***Porphyry & Clark, Gillian.** On Abstinence from Killing Animals. LC 00-22675. (Ancient Commentators on Aristotle Ser.). 2000. write for info. (*0-8014-3692-3*) Cornell U Pr.
Porphyry the Neo-Platonist. Neo-Platonic Letter to Marcella. Zimmern, Alice, tr. from GRE. 1993. reprint ed. pap. 6.95 (*1-55818-202-0*) Holmes Pub.
Porphyry the Phoenician. Isagoge. Warren, Edward W., tr. from LAT. 65p. pap. 6.29 (*0-88844-265-3*) Brill Academic Pubs.
Porpora, Douglas V. The Concept of Social Structure, 68. LC 87-12037. (Contributions in Sociology Ser.: No. 68). 159p. 1987. 55.00 (*0-313-25646-2*, PCS/, Greenwood Pr) Greenwood.
— How Holocausts Happen: The United States in Central America. 232p. 1990. 29.95 (*0-87722-750-0*) Temple U Pr.
— How Holocausts Happen: The United States in Central America. 1992. pap. 22.95 (*0-87722-923-6*) Temple U Pr.
Porporino, Frank, jt. auth. see Zamble, E.
Porqueras-Mayo, Albert, et al. The New Catalan Short Story: An Anthology. LC 82-21927. 278p. (Orig.). 1983. pap. text 25.00 (*0-8191-2900-3*) U Pr of Amer.
Porr, Susan M., et al. A Pediatric Therapy: A Systems Approach. 5th ed. Lane, Shelly J., ed. LC 98-55693. (Pediatric Occupational Therapy Ser.). (Illus.). 624p. (C). 1999. pap. text 38.95 (*0-8036-0259-6*) Davis Co.
Porras, Agustin. Desarrollo Agrario y Cambio Demografico en Tres Regiones de Mexico: (Agricultural Development & Demographic Change in Three Regions of Mexico) (Research Reports: No. 18). (SPA.). 43p. (Orig.). (C). 1981. ring bd. 5.00 (*0-935391-17-7*, RR-18) UCSD Ctr US-Mex.
Porras Cruz, Jorge L. Estudios y Articulos. (UPREX, Estudios Literarios Ser.: No. 25). 274p. (C). 1974. pap. 1.50 (*0-8477-0025-9*) U of PR Pr.
Porras-Cruz, Jorge L. Vida y Obra De Luis G. Inclan. LC 76-1829. (Coleccion Mente y Palabra). (SPA.). 230p. (Orig.). 1976. 5.00 (*0-8477-0536-6*); pap. 4.00 (*0-8477-0537-4*) U of PR Pr.
Porras, J. I. Analisis Estructural. (SPA.). (C). 1988. pap. text 7.33 (*0-201-64416-9*) Addison-Wesley.
Porras, Jerry, jt. auth. see Collins, James C.
Porras, Jerry I. Stream Analysis: Diagnosis & Planning for Managing Organization Development. LC 86-22183. (Organization Development Ser.). (Illus.). 163p. (C). 1987. pap. text 40.00 (*0-201-05693-3*) Addison-Wesley.
Porras, Jerry I. & Kass, R. Stream Analysis. 2nd ed. (Organization Development Ser.). (Illus.). 163p. (C). 1995. pap. text. write for info. (*0-201-53971-3*) Addison-Wesley.
Porras, Jerry I., jt. auth. see Collins, James C.
Porras, Louis, jt. auth. see Wilson, Larry D.
Porrata, Carmen T. & Vargas, Maria M. Biologia Experimental. (Illus.). 245p. (C). 1996. pap. text 34.95 (*1-881375-20-X*) Libreria Univ.
Porrata, Samuel, ed. see McKay, Todd.
Porrazzo, Ed & Odell, Karen. The Parents' Guide to Personal Computers. (Illus.). 1985. 19.95 (*0-13-649963-5*) P-H.
Porrazzo, Kimberly A. The Nanny Kit: Everything You Need to Hire the Right Nanny. LC 98-30841. 96p. 1999. pap. 12.95 (*0-14-027723-4*) Viking Penguin.
Porreca, Frank, jt. ed. see Raffa, Robert B.
Porreco, Richard P., ed. Contemporary Obstetrics for Medical Students. (Illus.). 340p. 1991. pap. 22.50 (*0-916859-51-7*) Perinatology.
Porreco, Rocco, ed. The Georgetown Symposium on Ethics: Essays in Honor of Henry Babcock Veatch. 316p. (Orig.). 1984. pap. text 29.00 (*0-8191-3777-4*) U Pr of Amer.
Porrello, Rick. The Rise & Fall of the Cleveland Mafia: Corn Sugar & Blood. LC 95-707. 240p. 1995. 22.00 (*1-56980-058-8*) Barricade Bks.
— To Kill the Irishman: The War That Crippled the Mafia. LC 98-65005. (Illus.). 256p. 1998. 22.95 (*0-9662508-7-7*, 9807) Next Hat Pr.
***Porrett, Theresa & Daniel, Norma.** Essential Coloproctology for Nurses. LC 99-494978. 438p. 1999. 54.95 (*1-86156-085-0*) Whurr Pub.
Porrini, M., jt. ed. see Walter, P. J.
Porritt. Interaction Strategies. 2nd ed. 1990. pap. text 21.00 (*0-443-04214-4*, W B Saunders Co) Harcrt Hlth Sci Grp.
Porritt, Arthur, ed. Causes of War: Economic, Industrial, Racial, Religious, Scientific & Political. LC 70-99719. (Essay Index Reprint Ser.). 1977. 21.95 (*0-8369-1372-8*) Ayer.
Porritt, Edward. Evolution of the Dominion of Canada: Its Government & Its Politics. LC 72-33. (Select Bibliographies Reprint Ser.). 1977. reprint ed. 26.95 (*0-8369-9970-3*) Ayer.
***Porritt, Jonathon.** Playing Safe: Science & the Environment. LC 99-66984. (Prospects for Tomorrow Ser.). 112p. 2000. pap. 12.95 (*0-500-28073-8*, Pub. by Thames Hudson) Norton.
Porritt, Vernon L. British Colonial Rule in Sarawak, 1946-1963. LC 96-32333. (South-East Asian Historical Monographs). (Illus.). 450p. 1997. text 62.00 (*983-56-0009-0*) OUP.
Porro, Barbara. Talk It Out: Conflict Resolution in the Elementary Classroom. LC 96-5639. (Illus.). 148p. (Orig.). 1996. pap. 22.95 (*0-87120-262-X*, 196018) ASCD.
Porro, G. Bianchi, jt. ed. see Scarpignato, C.
***Porro, Gabrielle B., et al, eds.** Gastroenterology & Hepatology. (Clinical Medicine Ser.). (Illus.). 768p. 1999. pap. text 67.50 (*0-07-709519-7*) McGraw-Hill HPD.
Porrua Staff. Diccionario Castellano Ilustrado. (SPA., Illus.). pap. 17.95 (*0-7859-0429-8*, S31405) Fr & Eur.
— Diccionario de Sinonimos Espanoles. (SPA.). 9.95 (*0-7859-0422-0*, S12253) Fr & Eur.
— Diccionario Enciclopedico: Gran Omeba, 12 vols., Set. (SPA.). 450.00 (*0-7859-0430-1*, S33046) Fr & Eur.
— Diccionario Enciclopedico Ilustrado, 3 vols., Set. (SPA., Illus.). 125.00 (*0-7859-0431-X*, S33077) Fr & Eur.
— Diccionario Oriente, 4 vols., Set. (SPA.). 350.00 (*0-7859-0432-8*, S33078) Fr & Eur.
Porsche, Audrey, ed. Yuto'keca: Transitions - The Burdick Collection. (Illus.). 79p. 1987. pap. 23.95 (*1-891419-15-3*) State Hist ND.
Porsdam, Helle. Legally: Contemporary American Culture & the Law. LC 98-54186. 288p. 1999. pap. 16.95 (*1-55849-208-9*) U of Mass Pr.
— Legally Speaking: Contemporary American Culture & the Law. LC 98-54186. 288p. 1999. 50.00 (*1-55849-207-0*) U of Mass Pr.
Porshnev, B. F. Muscovy & Sweden in the Thirty Years' War, 1630-1655. Dukes, Paul, ed. Pearce, Brian, tr. 278p. (C). 1996. text 64.95 (*0-521-45139-6*) Cambridge U Pr.
Porsild, A. E. Rocky Mountain Wild Flowers. (Illus.). 454p. 1979. pap. text 11.95 (*0-660-00073-3*) U Ch Pr.
— Rocky Mountain Wildflowers. 454p. 1979. pap. 9.95 (*0-226-56495-9*) U Ch Pr.
***Porsild, Charlene.** Gamblers & Dreamers: Women, Men & Community in the Klondike. LC 98-171217. (Illus.). 264p. 1998. 75.00 (*0-7748-0650-8*); pap. text 19.95 (*0-7748-0651-6*) UBC Pr.
Porson, Richard. Adversaria, Notae et Emendationes in Poetas Graecos. xviii, 354p. 1982. reprint ed. write for info. (*3-487-07198-3*) G Olms Pubs.
Porstendorfer, Gottfried. Principles of Magneto-Telluric Prospecting. Kunetz, G. & Parasnis, D. S., eds. (Geoexploration Monographs: No. 5). (Illus.). viii, 118p. 1975. 38.00 (*3-443-13007-0*, Pub. by Gebruder Borntraeger) Balogh.
Port. Japanese Trademark Jurisprudence. LC 98-157550. 1997. 88.00 (*90-411-0701-0*) Kluwer Law Intl.
Port & Harbour Research Institute Staff. Handbook on Liquefaction Remediation of Reclaimed Land. (Illus.). 310p. (C). 1997. text 97.00 (*90-5410-653-0*, Pub. by A A Balkema) Ashgate Pub Co.
Port Adelaide Centre Joint Committee Staff, jt. auth. see Vines, Elizabeth.
Port Authority of New York & New Jersey Staff, et al. The Arts As Industry: Their Economic Importance to the New York-New Jersey Metropolitan Region. (Illus.). 136p. (Orig.). 1983. pap. text 12.00 (*0-912443-00-6*) Alliance Arts.
Port, Beverly. Antique Teddy Bear Postcards, Vol. II. Vol. II. (Illus.). 12p. 1987. pap. text 4.95 (*0-87588-315-X*) Hobby Hse.
Port, C. Dictionnaire Historique, Geographique et Biographique de Maine et Loire, 3 vols., Set. (FRE.). 896p. 1978. 595.00 (*0-8288-5197-2*, M6463) Fr & Eur.
Port, Dan. SIM-Systems Integration Methodology with Java Examples. 1998. 54.95 (*0-387-98359-7*) Spr-Verlag.
Port, Kenneth L. Comparative Law: Law & the Legal Process in Japan. LC 95-68701. (Illus.). 848p. 1996. boxed set 75.00 (*0-89089-860-X*) Carolina Acad Pr.
Port, Kenneth L., et al. Licensing Intellectual Property in the Digital Age. LC 99-22415. 604p. 1999. boxed set 80.00 (*0-89089-891-X*) Carolina Acad Pr.
Port, M. H. Imperial London: Civil Government Building in London 1850-1915. LC 94-10254. (Illus.). 288p. 1995. 75.00 (*0-300-05977-9*) Yale U Pr.
Port, Robert F. & Gelder, Timothy Van, eds. Mind as Motion: Explorations in the Dynamics of Cognition. LC 94-23127. 602p. 1995. 65.00 (*0-262-16150-8*, Bradford Bks) MIT Pr.
Port, Robert F. & Van Gelder, Timothy, eds. Mind As Motion: Explorations in the Dynamics of Cognition. (Illus.). 602p. 1998. reprint ed. pap. text 32.50 (*0-262-66110-1*, Bradford Bks) MIT Pr.
Port, Sidney, jt. ed. see Ney, Peter.
Port, Sidney C. Theoretical Probability for Applications. LC 93-114725. (Hilbert Space Methods in Reliability & Statistical Inference). 894p. 1993. 144.95 (*0-471-63216-3*) Wiley.
Port Sines Investigating Panel Staff. Failure of the Breakwater at Port Sines, Portugal. LC 82-70493. 290p. 1982. pap. 5.00 (*0-87262-298-3*) Am Soc Civil Eng.
Port, Stanley. The Management of CAD for Construction. (Illus.). 240p. (gr. 13). 1989. mass mkt. 58.95 (*0-442-23698-0*) Chapman & Hall.
***Port, Stanley & MacKrell, John.** PDM Business Appraisal Guide: Business Justification of Product Data Management Systems for Industrial Organizations. 3rd rev. ed. (Illus.). 1999. ring bd. (*1-889760-11-0*) CIMdata Inc.
Port, Stanley & MacKrell, John. PDM Case Studies: User Experiences with PDM Systems. (Illus.). 150p. 1996. ring bd. 295.00 (*1-889760-04-8*) CIMdata Inc.
Porta, Antonio. As If It Were a Rhythm. Vangelisti, Paul, tr. from ITA. 1978. 2.50 (*0-88031-051-0*) Invisible-Red Hill.
— Dreams & Other Infidelities. Molino, Anthony, tr. LC 98-39745. 100p. 1998. pap. 13.00 (*1-879378-37-X*) Xenos Riverside.
— Invasions & Other Poems. Vangelisti, Paul, ed. & tr. by. 1986. 10.00 (*0-88031-065-0*) Invisible-Red Hill.
— Kisses from Another Dream. Molino, Anthony, tr. from ITA. (Pocket Poets Ser.: No. 44). 128p. (Orig.). 1987. pap. 5.95 (*0-87286-206-2*) City Lights.
— Melusine: A Ballad & a Diary, Vol. 1. Molino, Anthony, tr. from ITA. (Essential Poets Ser.: No. 49). 88p. 1993. pap. 10.00 (*0-920717-58-6*) Guernica Editions.
— Metropolis, Vol. 184. (Sun & Moon Classics Ser.: Vol. 154). 1999. 10.95 (*1-55713-326-3*) Sun & Moon CA.
— Metropolis: A Bilingual. Verdicchio, Pasquale, tr. (Green Integer Bks.: No. 25). 102p. 1999. pap. text 10.95 (*1-892295-12-1*, Pub. by Green Integer) Consort Bk Sales.
— Passenger, Vol. 1. 80p. pap. 8.00 (*0-919349-73-0*) Guernica Editions.
***Porta, Antonio.** Passenger: Selected Poems, 1958-1979. rev. ed. Verdicchio, Pasquale, tr. (Picas Ser.: Vol. 13). 84p. 1999. pap. 8.00 (*0-920717-64-0*) Guernica Editions.
Porta, Carol B., jt. auth. see Griggs, James K.
Porta, Donatella Della, see Della Porta, Donatella.
Porta, Ernesto, ed. Lipofuscin & Ceroid Pigments. (Advances in Experimental Medicine & Biology Ser.: Vol. 266). (Illus.). 393p. 1989. 110.00 (*0-306-43519-5*, Plenum Trade) Perseus Pubng.
Porta, Giovanni. Giovanni Porta: Selected Sacred Music from the Ospedale Della Pieta. Tiedge, Faun T., ed. (Recent Researches in Music of the Baroque Era Ser.: Vol. RRB74). (Illus.). xxv, 70p. 1995. pap. 35.00 (*0-89579-318-0*) A-R Eds.
Porta, Pier L., ed. see Ricardo, David.
***Porta, Pier Luigi, et al.** Knowledge, Social Institutions & the Division of Labour. LC 00-34763. 2001. write for info. (*1-84064-335-8*) E Elgar.
Portais, Jean-Charles, jt. auth. see Barbotin, Jean-Noel.
Portal, Christopher, ed. The History Curriculum for Teachers. LC 86-29305. 175p. 1987. 60.00 (*1-85000-165-0*, Falmer Pr); pap. 34.95 (*1-85000-166-9*, Falmer Pr) Taylor & Francis.
***Portal, Jane.** Korea: Art & Archaeology. LC 99-66554. (Illus.). 240p. 2000. pap. 27.50 (*0-500-28202-1*, Pub. by Thames Hudson) Norton.
Portalatin, Aida C. Yania Tierra. Fenwick, M. J., tr. from SPA. & intro. by. LC 94-79182. 196p. 1995. pap. 12.95 (*0-9632363-9-3*) Azul Edits.
***Portale, Alfred & Friedman, Andrew.** The Twelve Seasons of Cooking. LC 99-87943. (Illus.). 448p. 2000. 45.00 (*0-7679-0606-3*) Broadway BDD.
Portale, Alfred & Gotham Bar & Grill Staff. Alfred Portale's Gotham Bar & Grill Cookbook. LC 97-6611. (Illus.). 368p. 1997. 45.00 (*0-385-48210-8*) Doubleday.
Portales, Marco. Crowding Out Latinos: Mexican Americans in the Public Consciousness. LC 99-23808. (Illus.). 240p. 2000. 59.50 (*1-56639-742-1*); pap. 19.95 (*1-56639-743-X*) Temple U Pr.
— Youth & Age in American Literature: The Rhetoric of Old Men in the Mathers, Franklin, Adams, Cooper, Hawthorne, Melville, & James. (American University Studies: American Literature: Ser. XXIV, Vol. 20). XVIII, 169p. (C). 1989. text 35.00 (*0-8204-1181-7*) P Lang Pubng.
Portalie, Eugene. A Guide to the Thought of Saint Augustine. Bastian, Ralph J., tr. from FRE. LC 75-1182. 428p. 1975. reprint ed. lib. bdg. 52.50 (*0-8371-7992-0*, POGS, Greenwood Pr) Greenwood.
Portalupi, JoAnn, jt. auth. see Fletcher, Ralph J.
Portaluppi, Francesco & Smolensky, Michael H., eds. Time-Dependent Structure & Control of Arterial Blood Pressure. LC 96-7856. (Annals of the New York Academy of Sciences Ser.: Vol. 783). 1996. pap. 100.00 (*1-57331-009-3*) NY Acad Sci.
Portaluppi, Francesco, jt. auth. see Luisada, Aldo A.
Portaro, Ron, ed. & reader see Linoner, Richard.
Portaro, Sam. Conflict & a Christian Life. LC 95-49873. 128p. (Orig.). 1996. pap. 9.95 (*0-8192-1653-4*) Morehouse Pub.
Portaro, Sam & Peluso, Gary. Inquiring & Discerning Hearts: Vocation & Ministry with Young Adults on Campus. LC 93-5720. 308p. 1993. 44.95 (*1-55540-892-3*, 000307); pap. 29.95 (*1-55540-893-1*) Duke.
Portaro, Sam A. Brightest & Best: A Companion to the Lesser Feasts & Fasts. LC 97-32498. 220p. 1998. pap. 14.95 (*1-56101-148-7*) Cowley Pubns.
***Portaro, Sam A.** Crossing the Jordan: Meditations on Vocation. LC 99-40384. xiii, 105p. 1999. pap. 8.95 (*1-56101-170-3*) Cowley Pubns.
Portas, Mary. Windows: The Art of Retail Display. LC 99-70946. (Illus.). 192p. 1999. 49.95 (*0-500-01944-4*, Pub. by Thames Hudson) Norton.
***Portavoz Editorial Staff.** Libro de Caligrafia. (Sabio & Prudente Ser.). 64p. 1999. pap. 4.99 (*0-8254-0996-9*, Edit Portavoz) Kregel.
— Manual de Exploracion. (Sabio & Prudente Ser.: Vol. 4). 96p. 1999. pap. 3.75 (*0-8254-0939-X*, Edit Portavoz) Kregel.
— Manual de Exporacion. (Sabio & Prudente Ser.: Vol. 4). 96p. 1999. pap., teacher ed. 4.99 (*0-8254-0938-1*, Edit Portavoz) Kregel.
— Mas Que Vencedores. (Sabio & Prudente Ser.: Vol. 2). 96p. 1999. pap. 4.99 (*0-8254-0945-4*, Edit Portavoz) Kregel.
— Numeros, Conceptos y Figuras Geometricas. 64p. 1999. pap. 4.99 (*0-8254-0997-7*, Edit Portavoz) Kregel.
Portch, Elizabeth, tr. see Jansson, Tove.
Portcullis Press Ltd. Staff. Securitech. 300p. 1989. 400.00 (*0-7855-1282-9*) St Mut.
Portcullis Press Ltd. Staff, ed. Glass Making Today. 1985. 220.00 (*0-7855-5988-4*, Pub. by Portcullis Pr Ltd) St Mut.
Porte. Basic Math Skill Destrez. 196p. (C). 1994. pap. text 16.80 (*0-536-58599-7*) Pearson Custom.
Porte, Barbara. Harry in Trouble. (J). 1990. pap. 4.99 (*0-440-80210-5*) Dell.
Porte, Barbara A. A Black Elephant with a Brown Ear (in Alabama) (Illus.). 48p. (J). (gr. k up). 1996. 16.00 (*0-688-14374-1*, Grenwillow Bks) HarpC Child Bks.
— Chickens! Chickens! LC 94-19552. (Illus.). 32p. (J). (ps-2). 1995. 14.95 (*0-531-06877-3*) Orchard Bks Watts.
— Chickens! Chickens! LC 94-19552. (Illus.). 32p. (J). (ps-3). 1995. lib. bdg. 15.99 (*0-531-08727-1*) Orchard Bks Watts.
— Fat Fanny, Beanpole Bertha & the Boys. LC 90-7686. (Illus.). 112p. (J). (gr. 3-5). 1991. lib. bdg. 16.99 (*0-531-08528-7*) Orchard Bks Watts.
Porte, Barbara A. Harry's Pony. LC 96-43675. (Illus.). 56p. (J). (gr. k-3). 1997. 14.93 (*0-688-14826-3*, Grenwillow Bks) HarpC Child Bks.
Porte, Barbara A. Harry's Pony. LC 96-43675. (Illus.). 56p. (J). (gr. k up). 1997. 15.00 (*0-688-14825-5*, Grenwillow Bks) HarpC Child Bks.
— Hearsay: Tales from the Middle Kingdom. LC 97-6642. (Illus.). 136p. (YA). (gr. 5-9). 1998. 15.00 (*0-688-15381-X*, Grenwillow Bks) HarpC Child Bks.
— He's Sorry, She's Sorry, They're Sorry Too. LC 97-42681. 152p. 1998. 21.00 (*1-882413-47-4*); pap. 13.00 (*1-882413-46-6*) Hanging Loose.
— Leave That Cricket Be, Alan Lee. LC 92-29401. (Illus.). 32p. (J). (gr. k up). 1993. 14.00 (*0-688-11793-7*, Grenwillow Bks) HarpC Child Bks.
***Porte, Barbara A.** Ma Jiang & the Orange Ants. LC 99-30234. (Illus.). 32p. (J). (gr. k-4). 2000. lib. bdg. 17.99 (*0-531-33241-1*) Orchard Bks Watts.
Porte, Barbara A. Something Terrible Happened. LC 94-6923. 224p. (J). (gr. 6-9). 1994. 16.95 (*0-531-06869-2*); lib. bdg. 17.99 (*0-531-08719-0*) Orchard Bks Watts.
— Something Terrible Happened. 224p. (YA). (gr. 5 up). 1996. pap. 4.50 (*0-8167-3868-8*, Troll Medallion) Troll Communs.
— Something Terrible Happened. (J). 1994. 9.60 (*0-606-08877-6*, Pub. by Turtleback) Demco.
— Surprise! Surprise! It's Grandfather's Birthday! LC 96-6342. (Illus.). 32p. (J). (gr. k up). 1997. 15.00 (*0-688-14157-9*, Grenwillow Bks); lib. bdg. 14.93 (*0-688-14158-7*, Grenwillow Bks) HarpC Child Bks.
— Tale of a Tadpole. LC 96-53890. (Illus.). 32p. (J). (ps-2). 1997. 15.95 (*0-531-30049-8*); lib. bdg. 16.99 (*0-531-33049-4*) Orchard Bks Watts.
Porte, Barbara Ann. If You Ever Get Lost: The Adventures of Julia & Evan. LC 98-32133. (Illus.). 80p. (J). (gr. 2-5). 2000. 15.95 (*0-688-16947-3*, Grenwillow Bks) HarpC Child Bks.
***Porte, Barbara Ann.** Ma Jiang & the Orange Ants. LC 99-30234. 32p. (J). (gr. k-4). 2000. 16.95 (*0-531-30241-5*) Orchard Bks Watts.
Porte, Daniel & Sherwin, Robert S. Ellenberg & Rifkin's Diabetes Mellitus: Theory & Practice. 5th ed. LC 96-17517. 1423p. (C). 1998. 225.00 (*0-8385-2041-3*, Apple Lange Med) McGraw.
Porte, G. & Lagaly, G. Trends in Colloid & Interface Science IX. (Progress in Colloid & Polymer Science Ser.: Vol. 98). 311p. 1995. 155.95 (*3-7985-1031-8*) Spr-Verlag.
Porte, J. F. Sir Charles V. Stanford. LC 76-12570. (Music Reprint Ser.). 1976. reprint ed. lib. bdg. 25.00 (*0-306-70790-X*) Da Capo.
Porte, Jacques. Encyclopedie des Musiques Sacrees: Encyclopedia of Sacred Music, 3 vols., Set. (FRE.). 1978. 295.00 (*0-8288-5233-2*, M6202) Fr & Eur.
Porte, Joel. Emerson: Prospect & Retrospect. (English Studies: No. 10). 208p. 1982. 18.50 (*0-674-24915-1*); pap. 7.95 (*0-674-24917-8*) HUP.
— Emerson & Thoreau: Transcendentalists in Conflict. LC 80-2512. (Thoreau Ser.). 240p. reprint ed. 45.00 (*0-404-19060-X*) AMS Pr.
— In Respect to Egotism: Studies in American Romantic Writing. (Cambridge Studies in American Literature & Culture: No. 53). 322p. (C). 1991. text 54.95 (*0-521-36273-3*) Cambridge U Pr.
— New Essays on "The Portrait of a Lady" (American Novel Ser.). 176p. (C). 1990. text 32.95 (*0-521-34508-1*); pap. text 14.95 (*0-521-34753-X*) Cambridge U Pr.
— Representative Man: Ralph Waldo Emerson in His Time. (Illus.). 361p. 1988. text 78.50 (*0-231-06740-2*) Col U Pr.
— The Romance in America: Studies in Cooper, Poe, Hawthorne, Melville, & James. LC 69-17795. 247p. reprint ed. pap. 76.60 (*0-608-17824-1*, 203249200079) Bks Demand.
Porte, Joel, et al, eds. Emerson's Poetry & Prose. (Critical Editions Ser.). (C). 2000. pap. 22.25 (*0-393-96792-1*, Norton Paperbks) Norton.
Porte, Joel & Morris, Saundra, eds. The Cambridge Companion to Ralph Waldo Emerson. LC 98-36892. (Cambridge Companions to Literature Ser.). 288p. (C). 1999. text 59.95 (*0-521-49611-X*); pap. text 17.95 (*0-521-49946-1*) Cambridge U Pr.
Porte, Joel, ed. see Emerson, Ralph Waldo.
Porte, John F. Chopin: The Composer & His Music. 1988. reprint ed. lib. bdg. 59.00 (*0-7812-0780-0*) Rprt Serv.
— Chopin the Composer & His Music. 1976. lib. bdg. 25.00 (*0-403-03791-3*) Scholarly.
— Sir Edward Elgar. LC 75-107827. (Select Bibliographies Reprint Ser.). (Illus.). 1977. reprint ed. 21.95 (*0-8369-5194-8*) Ayer.
— Sir Edward Elgar. 214p. 1990. reprint ed. lib. bdg. 69.00 (*0-7812-9061-9*) Rprt Serv.
Porte, Michelle, jt. auth. see Duras, Marguerite.
Portefaix, Lilian. Sisters Rejoice: Paul's Letter to the Philippians & Luke-Acts as Received by First Century Philippian Women. (Coniectanea Biblica. New Testament Ser.: No. 20). (Illus.). 260p. (Orig.). 1988. pap. 48.50 (*91-22-01201-X*) Coronet Bks.

P

An Asterisk (*) at the beginning of an entry indicates that the title is appearing for the first time.

Portela, A. Dual Boundary Element Analysis of Crack Growth. 192p. 1993. 110.00 (*1-85312-187-8*) Computational Mech MA.

Portela, A. Dual Boundary Element Analysis of Crack Growth. LC 92-75028. (Topics in Engineering Ser.: Vol. 14). 192p. 1993. 110.00 (*1-56252-116-0*, 1878) Computational Mech MA.

Portela, A. & Aliabadi, M. H. Crack Growth Analysis Using Boundary Elements. 50p. 1992. ring bd. 1036.00 incl. disk (*1-85312-186-X*) Computational Mech MA.

Portela, Jose I. Don't Lose Your Unemployment Benefits! A Handbook for Workers & the Unemployed. LC 95-2020. 176p. (Orig.). 1995. pap. 12.95 (*0-945257-66-X*) Apex Pr.

Portelance, Colette. Authentic Communication: In Praise of Intimate Relationships. LC 96-749. 200p. (Orig.). 1995. pap. 12.95 (*2-9801489-5-4*, Pub. by Cram Pubs) Seven Hills Bk.

— Helping Relationships Through Self-Love: A Creative Nondirective Approach to Psychotherapy & Education. LC 96-748. (FRE & ENG.). 420p. (Orig.). 1995. pap. 14.95 (*2-9801489-4-6*, Pub. by Cram Pubs) Seven Hills Bk.

Portell-Vila, Herminio. Los Otros Extranjeros En la Revolucion Norteamericana. LC 77-88537. (Coleccion de Estudios Hispanicos - Hispanic Studies Collection). 1978. pap. 8.00 (*0-89729-173-5*) Ediciones.

***Portella, David.** Short Order Adobe GoLive 4.0. (Illus.). 300p. 2000. pap. 19.99 (*0-7897-2171-6*) Que.

Portella, P. D., jt. auth. see Rie, K. T.

Portelli, Alessandra. Text & the Voice: Writing, Speaking, & Democracy in American Literature. 1994. 34.50 (*0-231-08498-6*) Col U Pr.

Portelli, Alessandro. The Battle of Valle Giulia: Oral History & the Art of Dialogue. LC 96-36474. 368p. 1997. 49.95 (*0-299-15370-3*); pap. 21.95 (*0-299-15374-6*) U of Wis Pr.

— The Death of Luigi Trastulli & Other Stories: Form & Meaning in Oral History. LC 89-26260. (SUNY Series in Oral & Public History). 341p. (C). 1991. pap. text 24.95 (*0-7914-0430-7*) State U NY Pr.

Portelli, John P. & Bailin, Sharon, eds. Reason & Values: New Essays in Philosophy of Education. 228p. (Orig.). (C). 1993. pap. text 20.95 (*1-55059-066-9*) Temeron Bks.

Portelli, John P., jt. ed. see Hare, William.

Porten, B., jt. auth. see Muraoka, T.

***Porten, Bezalel & Yardeni, Ada, eds.** Aramaic Documents from Ancient Egypt: Ostraca & Assorted Inscriptions. lxxiv, 304p. 1999. pap. text 80.00 (*965-350-089-9*, Pub. by Friends Archeol Inst) Eisenbrauns.

Porten, Bezalel & Yardeni, Ada, eds. Textbook of Aramaic Documents from Ancient Egypt Vol. 1: Letters, Vol. 1: Letters. (ENG & HEB.). ix, 143p. 1986. pap. text 49.00 (*965-222-075-2*) Eisenbrauns.

— Textbook of Aramaic Documents from Ancient Egypt Vol. 2: Contracts, Vol. 2: Contracts, incl. 37 plates. (ENG & HEB.). liv, 191p. 1989. pap. text 78.00 (*965-350-003-1*, Pub. by Friends Archeol Inst) Eisenbrauns.

— Textbook of Aramaic Documents from Ancient Egypt Vol. 3: Literature, Accounts, Lists, Vol. 3: Literature, Accounts, Lists, incl. 36 plt. (ENG & HEB.). ixvi, 295p. 1993. pap. text 84.00 (*965-350-014-7*, Pub. by Friends Archeol Inst) Eisenbrauns.

Porten, Bezalel, et al. The Elephantine Papyri in English, with Commentary: Three Millennia of Cross-Cultural Continuity & Change. LC 96-1797. (Documenta et Monumenta Orientis Antiqui Ser.). xviii, 621p. 1996. 254.00 (*90-04-10197-7*) Brill Academic Pubs.

Porten, Jeff. The Twentysomething Guide to Creative Self-Employment: Making Money While Keeping Your Freedom. (Illus.). 288p. 1996. per. 14.95 (*0-7615-0445-1*) Prima Pub.

Portenier, C., jt. auth. see Anger, B.

Portenier, Lillian G. Pupils of Low Mentality in High School. LC 76-177158. (Columbia University. Teachers College. Contributions to Education Ser.: No. 568). reprint ed. 37.50 (*0-404-55568-3*) AMS Pr.

Portenko, L. A. Birds of the Chukchi Peninsula & Wrangel Island, Vol. 2. 1989. 39.50 (*81-205-0088-1*, Pub. by Oxford IBH) S Asia.

Portenko, N. Generalized Diffusion Processes. LC 90-21198. (Translations of Mathematical Monographs: Vol. 83). 180p. 1990. text 84.00 (*0-8218-4538-1*, MMONO/83) Am Math.

***Portenoy, Russell & Bruera, Eduardo, eds.** Topics In Pallative Care, Vol. 5. (Illus.). 350p. 2000. text 49.95 (*0-19-513220-3*) OUP.

Portenoy, Russell K. Contemporary Diagnosis & Management of Pain in Oncological & AIDS Patients. 2nd ed. (Illus.). 206p. (Orig.). (C). 1998. pap. 28.95 (*1-884065-40-6*) Assocs in Med.

Portenoy, Russell K. & Bruera, Eduardo, eds. Topics in Pallative Care, Vol. 3. (Illus.). 328p. 1998. text 55.00 (*0-19-510246-0*) OUP.

***Portenoy, Russell K. & Bruera, Eduardo, eds.** Topics in Pallative Care Vol. 4. (Illus.). 304p. 2000. text 59.50 (*0-19-513219-X*) OUP.

Portenoy, Russell K. & Bruera, Eduardo, eds. Topics in Palliative Care, Vol. 1. LC 96-22250. (Illus.). 328p. 1997. text 55.00 (*0-19-510244-4*) OUP.

Portenoy, Russell K. & Kanner, Ronald M., eds. Pain Management: Theory & Practice. LC 95-52200. (Contemporary Neurology Ser.: No. 48). (Illus.). 384p. 1996. text 99.00 (*0-8036-0171-9*) OUP.

Portenoy, Russell K., jt. ed. see Bruera, Eduardo.

Porteous, A. Forest Folklore, Mythology & Romance. 1977. lib. bdg. 59.95 (*0-8490-1858-7*) Gordon Pr.

Porteous, Andrew. Dict of Environmental Science. 2nd ed. 652p. 1996. pap. 44.95 (*0-471-96075-6*) Wiley.

***Porteous, Andrew.** Dictionary of Environmental Science & Technology. 3rd ed. LC 00-31039. 2000. write for info. (*0-471-63470-0*) Wiley.

Porteous, Andrew, ed. Desalination Technology: Developments & Practice. (Illus.). 271p. 1983. 74.00 (*0-85334-175-3*, I-453-82) Elsevier.

Porteous, Brenda. Fun Dough: Over 100 Salt Dough Projects for All the Family. (Illus.). 76p. 1996. 18.95 (*1-870586-01-8*, D Porteous-Parkwest) Parkwest Pubns.

Porteous, David J. The Geography of Finance: Spatial Dimensions of Intermediary Behaviour. 240p. 1995. 79.95 (*1-85972-046-3*, Pub. by Avebry) Ashgate Pub Co.

Porteous, Ian. Clifford Algebras. (Studies in Advanced Mathematics: No. 50). 305p. 1995. text 57.95 (*0-521-55177-3*) Cambridge U Pr.

— Geometric Differentiation: For the Intelligence of Curves & Surfaces. (Illus.). 315p. (C). 1994. text 59.95 (*0-521-39063-X*) Cambridge U Pr.

Porteous, J. Douglas. Environment & Behavior: Planning & Everyday Urban Life. LC 76-1752. (C). 1977. text. write for info. (*0-201-05867-7*) Addison-Wesley.

— Environmental Aesthetics: Ideas, Politics & Planning. LC 95-47890. 312p. (C). 1996. pap. 22.95 (*0-415-13770-5*) Routledge.

— Landscapes of the Mind: Worlds of Sense & Metaphor. 228p. 1990. text 40.00 (*0-8020-5857-4*) U of Toronto Pr.

— Planned to Death: The Annihilation of a Place Called Howdendyke. 254p. 1989. text 47.50 (*0-8020-2661-3*) U of Toronto Pr.

Porteous, Katrina. The Lost Music. LC 97-120487. 64p. 1997. pap. 15.95 (*1-85224-380-5*, Pub. by Bloodaxe Bks) Dufour.

Porteous, Murray. Occupational Psychology. LC 96-53841. 1997. 27.57 (*0-13-227810-3*) P-H.

Porteous, R. S. Cattleman. large type ed. 368p. 1982. 27.99 (*0-7089-8070-8*, Charnwood) Ulverscroft.

Porteous, Skipp. Jesus Doesn't Live Here Anymore: From Fundamentalist to Freedom Writer. LC 91-23783. 313p. 1991. 27.95 (*0-87975-689-6*) Prometheus Bks.

Porter. At Foot of Rainbow. 22.95 (*0-685-71942-1*) Amereon Ltd.

— Baker's Biographical Dictionary of Jazz. 1200p. 1999. 95.00 (*0-02-864738-6*) Mac Lib Ref.

— Ben & Jerry's 1994 Update. (C). 1996. pap. text, student ed. 4.00 (*0-03-019109-2*) Harcourt.

— Checklist of Key Figures: Financial. (C). 1995. pap. text 1.25 (*0-15-503203-8*, Pub. by Harcourt Coll Pubs) Harcourt.

— Competition in Global Industries. 582p. 1986. 39.95 (*0-07-103262-2*) McGraw.

— Competitive Strategy. LC 98-9580. 432p. 1998. 37.50 (*0-684-84148-7*) S&S Trade.

***Porter.** Diamond Sutra. 2000. 22.00 (*1-58243-059-4*, Pub. by Counterpt DC) HarpC.

Porter. Encyclopedia of American Economic History, Vol. 2. 1980. 120.00 (*0-684-16511-2*) Mac Lib Ref.

— Encyclopedia of American Economic History, Vol. 3. 1980. 120.00 (*0-684-16512-0*) Mac Lib Ref.

— English Connections. 1994. pap. 145.00 incl. audio (*0-8092-3533-1*) NTC Contemp Pub Co.

— English Connections, Bk. 3. 1994. pap. 42.33 incl. audio (*0-8092-3537-4*) NTC Contemp Pub Co.

— The Enlightenment. 1996. text 11.95 (*0-333-45414-6*, Pub. by Macmillan) St Martin.

— Financial Accounting. 2nd ed. LC 97-65089. (C). 1997. text 93.00 (*0-03-020483-6*) Harcourt Coll Pubs.

— Financial Accounting. 2nd ed. 1998. 31.00 (*0-03-020487-9*); teacher ed. 232.00 (*0-03-020547-6*, Pub. by Harcourt Coll Pubs) Harcourt.

— Financial Accounting. 2nd ed. 1998. teacher ed. 232.00 (*0-03-020544-1*, Pub. by Harcourt Coll Pubs) Harcourt.

— Financial Accounting. 2nd ed. (C). 1998. pap. text 44.50 (*0-03-021348-7*); pap. text, student ed. 29.50 (*0-03-021338-X*) Harcourt Coll Pubs.

— Financial Accounting: The Impact on Decision Makers. 2nd ed. (C). 1998. text, student ed. 32.00 (*0-03-020519-0*) Harcourt Coll Pubs.

— Financial Accounting Kit. (C). 1996. pap. 76.25 (*0-15-504000-6*, Pub. by Harcourt Coll Pubs) Harcourt.

— The Health Care Teambook. LC 99-181996. 1998. pap. text 29.95 (*1-55664-504-X*) Mosby Inc.

— The Jazz Reader. 1997. 27.00 (*0-02-864668-1*) Mac Lib Ref.

— Late Pleistocene of U. S. Date not set. pap. text. write for info. (*0-582-30123-8*, Pub. by Addison-Wesley) Longman.

— Learning to Dance. 208p. (J). (gr. 3-7). 15.95 (*0-06-028182-0*) HarpC.

— Memphis Vol. 3, Pt. 1: Abu Rawash to Abusir. 2nd ed. (Topographical Bibliography of Ancient Egyptian Hieroglyphic Texts Ser.: Reliefs & Paintings, Vol. 3, Pt. 1). 1974. 99.00 (*0-900416-19-X*, Pub. by Aris & Phillips) David Brown.

— Memphis Vol. 3, Pt. 2, Fasc. 1: Saqqara to Dahshur. (Topographical Bibliography of Ancient Egyptian Hieroglyphic Texts Ser.: Reliefs & Paintings, Vol. 3, Pt. 2). 1978. 65.00 (*0-900416-13-0*, Pub. by Aris & Phillips) David Brown.

— Memphis Vol. 3, Pt. 2, Fasc. 2: Saqqara to Dahshur. (Topographical Bibliography of Ancient Egyptian Hieroglyphic Texts Ser.: Reliefs & Paintings, Vol. 3, Pt. 2). 1979. 75.00 (*0-900416-14-9*, Pub. by Aris & Phillips) David Brown.

***Porter.** Mg Midget, Austin Healey & Sprite Restoration Manual. (Illus.). 296p. 2000. 36.95 (*1-85960-614-8*, Pub. by Haynes Manuals) Motorbooks Intl.

Porter. Microstudy (3.5)-Fianc Acct. (C). 1995. 276.50 incl. 3.5 ld (*0-15-501671-7*) Harcourt Coll Pubs.

— The Milk Cartel in Ohio. (Case; Hb - Economics Ser.). 1997. mass mkt. 3.75 (*0-538-85806-0*) S-W Pub.

***Porter.** Mini Restoration Manual. (Illus.). 304p. 2000. 36.95 (*1-85960-440-4*, Pub. by Haynes Manuals) Motorbooks Intl.

Porter. 1998 Year Book of Vascular Surgery. (Illus.). 544p. (C). (gr. 13). 1998. text 86.00 (*0-8151-9800-0*, 25037) Mosby Inc.

— Nubia Deserts & Outside Egypt. (Topographical Bibliography of Ancient Egyptian Hieroglyphic Texts Ser.: Reliefs & Paintings, Vol. 7). 1983. 91.50 (*0-900416-04-1*, Pub. by Aris & Phillips) David Brown.

— Oht T/a Financial Accounting,alt.ed. (C). 1996. pap. text 246.00 (*0-03-019689-2*) Harcourt Coll Pubs.

— Oht T/a Financial Acctng Alt Ed, 2e. 2nd ed. (C). 1998. pap. text 221.00 (*0-03-021354-1*) Harcourt Coll Pubs.

— One Hundred Maxims in Neurology: Behavioral Neurology. 384p. (gr. 13). 1993. 43.95 (*0-340-57720-7*) Mosby Inc.

— 100 Maxims in Neurology: Parkinson Disease. 169p. 1992. 42.95 (*0-340-58947-7*) Mosby Inc.

— Paramedical Emergency Care. 3rd ed. LC 97-106333. 1996. pap., wbk. ed. 29.67 (*0-8359-5055-7*) P-H.

— Parkinson's Disease. LC 92-49799. (One Hundred Maxims in Neurology Ser.). 169p. 1992. 35.95 (*0-8016-7279-1*) Mosby Inc.

— Philosophy: Literary & Conceptual. 3rd ed. (C). 1995. pap. text 41.50 (*0-15-501862-0*, Pub. by Harcourt Coll Pubs) Harcourt.

Porter. Polyanna. (Classics Library). pap. 3.95 (*1-85326-145-9*, 1459WW, Pub. by Wrdsworth Edits) NTC Contemp Pub Co.

Porter. Procedural Review: Financial. (C). 1995. pap. text 28.50 (*0-15-502836-7*) Harcourt Coll Pubs.

— Progress in Reaction Kinetics, Vol. 5. 1970. 140.00 (*0-08-013035-6*, Pergamon Pr) Elsevier.

— Pwrpt Stud Notes T/a Fin Acctg. 2nd ed. (C). 1998. pap. text 9.00 (*0-03-021339-8*) Harcourt Coll Pubs.

— Upper Egypt Chief Temples. (Topographical Bibliography of Ancient Egyptian Hieroglyphic Texts Ser.: Reliefs & Paintings, Vol. 6). 1970. 75.00 (*0-900416-30-0*, Pub. by Aris & Phillips) David Brown.

— Victor Hugo. LC 98-55426. 12p. 1999. 48.00 (*0-8057-1652-1*, Twyne) Mac Lib Ref.

***Porter.** VW Beetle & Transporter Restoration Manual. (Illus.). 327p. 2000. 36.95 (*1-85960-615-6*, Pub. by Haynes Manuals) Motorbooks Intl.

Porter. Workbook on Intermediate Emergencies. 2nd ed. 1998. pap. text 28.20 (*0-8359-5263-0*) P-H.

Porter & Bledsoe. Patient: Paramed Eme Care. 4th ed. 288p. 1999. 46.60 (*0-13-021597-X*) S&S Trade.

***Porter & Morgan.** Porsche 911 Restoration Manual. (Illus.). 256p. 2000. pap. 32.95 (*1-85960-612-1*, Pub. by Haynes Manuals) Motorbooks Intl.

***Porter & Wesley.** Canadian Book of Lilacs. 180p. 2000. 35.00 (*1-55041-396-1*) Fitzhenry & W Ltd.

Porter, jt. auth. see Angel.

Porter, jt. auth. see Danielson, Dorothy.

Porter, jt. auth. see Delorenzo.

Porter, jt. auth. see Martin, Mick.

Porter, jt. auth. see Minicz.

Porter, jt. auth. see Samovar.

Porter, jt. auth. see Wortabet, John.

Porter, ed. see Minicz.

Porter & Associates Staff. Porter's pocket Guide to Emergency & Critical Care. 6th ed. 127p. 1999. spiral bd. 16.95 (*1-882740-07-6*) Porter & Assocs.

Porter, A. & Holland, R., eds. Theory & Practice in the History of European Expansion Overseas: Essays in Honour of R. E. Robinson. (Illus.). 214p. 1988. text 35.00 (*0-7146-3346-1*, Pub. by F Cass Pubs) Intl Spec Bk.

Porter, A. D., tr. see Borchert, Wolfgang.

Porter, A. Kingsley. Medieval Architecture, 2 vols. LC 67-4391. (Illus.). 1969. 150.00 (*0-87817-019-7*) Hacker.

Porter, A. N. & Holland, R. F., eds. Money, Finance & Empire, 1790-1960. 192p. 1985. 34.00 (*0-7146-3273-2*, Pub. by F Cass Pubs) Intl Spec Bk.

Porter, A. P. Greg LeMond: Premier Cyclist. (Sports Achievers Ser.). (Illus.). 56p. (J). (gr. 4-9). 1990. lib. bdg. 18.60 (*0-8225-0476-6*, Lerner Publctns) Lerner Pub.

— Jump at de Sun: The Story of Zora Neale Hurston. (Trailblazers Ser.). 88p. (J). (gr. 4-7). 1992. lib. bdg. 22.60 (*0-87614-667-1*, Carolrhoda) Lerner Pub.

— Jump at de Sun: The Story of Zora Neale Hurston. (Illus.). 88p. (J). (gr. 4-7). 1992. pap. 6.95 (*0-87614-546-2*, Carolrhoda) Lerner Pub.

— Jump at de Sun: The Story of Zora Neale Hurston. 1992. 12.15 (*0-606-12370-9*, Pub. by Turtleback) Demco.

— Kwanzaa. (Holiday on My Own Ser.). (Illus.). 56p. (J). (gr. k-3). 1991. pap. 5.95 (*0-87614-545-4*, Carolrhoda); lib. bdg. 18.60 (*0-87614-668-X*, Carolrhoda) Lerner Pub.

— Kwanzaa. unabridged ed. (Illus.). (J). (gr. 2-4). 1993. pap. 15.95 incl. audio (*0-87499-249-4*) Live Oak Media.

— Kwanzaa, Set. unabridged ed. (Illus.). (J). (gr. 2-4). 1993. 24.95 incl. audio (*0-87499-250-8*); pap., teacher ed. 33.95 incl. audio (*0-87499-251-6*) Live Oak Media.

— Minnesota. Lerner Geography Department Staff, ed. (Hello U. S. A. Ser.). (Illus.). 72p. (J). (gr. 3-6). 1992. lib. bdg. 19.93 (*0-8225-2718-9*, Lerner Publctns) Lerner Pub.

— Minnesota: Hello U. S. A. (Illus.). 72p. (J). 1996. pap. text 5.95 (*0-8225-9735-7*) Lerner Pub.

— Nebraska. (Hello U. S. A. Ser.). (Illus.). 72p. (J). (gr. 3-6). 1991. lib. bdg. 19.93 (*0-8225-2708-1*, Lerner Publctns) Lerner Pub.

— Nebraska: Hello U. S. A. (Hello U. S. A. Ser.). (Illus.). 72p. (J). (gr. 3-6). pap. 5.95 (*0-8225-9719-5*, First Ave Edns) Lerner Pub.

— Zina Garrison. (Sports Achievers Ser.). 56p. (J). (gr. 4-9). 1991. lib. bdg. 19.95 (*0-8225-0499-5*, Lerner Publctns) Lerner Pub.

— Zina Garrison: Ace. (Illus.). 64p. (J). (gr. 4-9). 1992. pap. 4.95 (*0-8225-9596-6*, Lerner Publctns) Lerner Pub.

Porter, A. S. Lithographic Presswork. LC Z 0252.. 316p. reprint ed. pap. 98.00 (*0-7837-0363-5*, 204068500018) Bks Demand.

Porter, A. Toomer. Led On! Step by Step: Scenes from Clerical, Military, Educational & Plantation Life in the South. LC 75-89383. (Black Heritage Library Collection). 1977. 21.95 (*0-8369-8643-1*) Ayer.

Porter, Alan C. Cordoba's Treasure. large type ed. (Linford Western Library). 240p. 1996. pap. 16.99 (*0-7089-7951-3*, Linford) Ulverscroft.

***Porter, Alan C.** Riverboat. large type ed. 256p. 1999. pap. 18.99 (*0-7089-5475-8*, Linford) Ulverscroft.

Porter, Alan G. & Rezmer, Martin G. BASIC Business Subroutines for the Apple II & Apple IIe. 160p. 1983. pap. write for info. (*0-201-05663-1*) Addison-Wesley.

Porter, Alan J. Batman: The Unauthorized Collector's Guide. LC 98-86549. (Illus.). 160p. (Orig.). 1999. pap. 29.95 (*0-7643-0683-9*) Schiffer.

Porter, Alan L., et al. Forecasting & Management of Technology. LC 90-45269. (Series in Engineering & Technology Management). 464p. 1991. 140.00 (*0-471-51223-0*) Wiley.

Porter, Alan L., jt. auth. see Becker, Henk A.

Porter, Albert O. County Government in Virginia: A Legislative History, 1607-1904. (Columbia University. Studies in the Social Sciences: No. 526). reprint ed. 37.50 (*0-404-51526-6*) AMS Pr.

Porter, Allison I. Porter's Guide to Congressional Roll Call Votes, 6 vols. Incl. Senate, 1985 (Serial & Annual) 1985. 80.00 (*0-916481-26-3*); Vol. 1. House, 1983 (Annual) 1984. 80.00 (*0-916481-07-7*); Vol. 2. Senate, 1983 (Annual) 1984. 80.00 (*0-916481-08-5*); Vol. 3. House, 1984 (Serial & Annual) 1984. 80.00 (*0-916481-09-3*); Vol. 4. Senate, 1984 (Serial & Annual) 1984. 80.00 (*0-916481-10-7*); Vol. 5. House, 1985 (Serial & Annual) 1985. 80.00 (*0-916481-25-5*); 435.00 (*0-916481-06-9*) Legis Info Pr.

Porter, Alyene. Papa Was a Preacher. 76p. 1954. pap. 5.50 (*0-87129-681-0*, P14) Dramatic Pub.

Porter, Andrew. Musical Events. 1990. 16.95 (*0-671-69656-4*) S&S Trade.

— The Oxford History of the British Empire: The Nineteenth Century, Vol. III. (Oxford History of the British Empire Ser.). (Illus.). 796p. 1999. 45.00 (*0-19-820565-1*) OUP.

— Pharmaceutical Equities: Evaluation & Trading. (International Equities Ser.). 208p. 1993. 180.00 (*1-85573-090-1*, Pub. by Woodhead Pubng) Am Educ Systs.

— Resourcing Start-Up & Companies. 192p. Date not set. write for info. (*1-85573-371-4*, Pub. by Woodhead Pubng) Am Educ Systs.

Porter, Andrew & Von Rhein, John, eds. Bravi: Lyric Opera of Chicago. LC 94-6516. (Illus.). 152p. 1994. 19.98 (*1-55859-771-9*) Abbeville Pr.

Porter, Andrew, et al. Science Companion. 144p. (J). (gr. 3-5). 1998. pap. 24.00 (*0-7487-3003-6*) St Mut.

— Science Companion. 189p. (J). (gr. 3-7). 1998. pap. 29.00 (*0-7487-3002-8*) St Mut.

— Science Homework & Classroom Assignments. 368p. 1998. pap. 150.00 (*0-7487-1997-0*) St Mut.

Porter, Andrew, jt. auth. see Beynon, Karen.

Porter, Andrew, tr. see Verdi, Giuseppe.

Porter, Andrew, tr. see Wagner, Richard.

Porter, Andrew J. R., jt. ed. see Cunningham, Charles.

Porter, Ann, jt. auth. see Johnson, Sandy.

Porter, Anna H., ed. Memories of Revolution: Russian Women Remember. LC 92-46113. (Illus.). 152p. (C). 1993. pap. 22.99 (*0-415-08807-0*, B2432) Routledge.

Porter, Anne. An Altogether Different Language: Poems 1934-1994. LC 94-14561. (Illus.). 128p. 1994. pap. 10.95 (*0-944072-45-3*) Zoland Bks.

Porter, Anne Hughes, et al. The History of First Baptist Church, Kosciusko, Mississippi, 1848-1998. LC 98-85693. (Illus.). 700p. 1998. 20.00 (*0-9665596-0-6*) FBC.

Porter, Arthur K. The Crosses & Culture of Ireland. LC 68-56480. (Illus.). 165p. 1979. reprint ed. 36.95 (*0-405-08860-4*, Pub. by Blom Pubns) Ayer.

Porter, B. Memphis Vol. 3, Pt. 2, Fasc. 3: Saqqara to Dahshur. (Topographical Bibliography of Ancient Egyptian Hieroglyphic Texts Ser.: Reliefs & Paintings, Vol. 3, Pt. 2). 1981. 85.00 (*0-900416-24-6*, Pub. by Aris & Phillips) David Brown.

Porter, B. E. & Robinson, M. B. Protected Persons & Their Property in New South Wales. xvi, 176p. 1987. pap. 41.50 (*0-455-20719-4*, Pub. by LawBk Co) Gaunt.

Porter, Barbara J. Some Answers Are Loud, Some Answers Are Soft. LC 99-28393. 32p. 1999. 12.95 (*1-57345-557-1*, Shadow Mount) Deseret Bk.

Porter, Barbara N. Images, Power, & Politics: Figurative Aspects of Esarhaddon's Babylonian Policy (681-669 B.C.) LC 92-85335. (Memoirs Ser.: Vol. 208). (Illus.). 420p. 1993. 30.00 (*0-87169-208-2*, M208-POB) Am Philos.

***Porter, Barbara Nevling, et al.** One God or Many? Concepts of Divinity in the Ancient World. (Transactions of the Casco Bay Assyriological Institute Ser.). 320p. 2000. pap. 25.00 (*0-9674250-0-X*, Pub. by Casco Bay) Univ Pr MD.

Porter, Basil & Seidelman, William E. The Politics of Reform in Medical Education & Health Services: The Negev Project, No. 14. LC 91-4826. (Medical Education Ser.). 144p. (C). 1991. text 29.95 (*0-8261-7730-1*) Springer Pub.

Porter, Bern. Eighty-Nine Offenses. 1974. pap. 0.50 (*0-911856-11-0*) Abyss.

— Found Poems. (Illus.). 1972. 50.00 (*0-87110-079-7*); pap. 20.00 (*0-87110-080-0*) Ultramarine Pub.

P

An Asterisk (*) at the beginning of an entry indicates that the title is appearing for the first time.

— I've Left. 1971. 15.00 (*0-87110-076-2*); pap. 6.00 (*0-87110-077-0*) Ultramarine Pub.
— Less Than Overweight. 500p. 1993. 30.00 (*0-9638236-0-4*) Plaster Cramp.
— Neverends. (Illus.). 50p. (Orig.). 1988. pap. 3.00 (*0-926935-03-8*) Runaway Spoon.
— Numbers. (Illus.). 52p. (Orig.). 1989. pap. 3.00 (*0-926935-20-8*) Runaway Spoon.
— Signs. 44p. 1996. pap. 3.00 (*1-57141-025-2*) Runaway Spoon.
— Symbols. 52p. 1995. pap. 3.00 (*1-57141-015-5*) Runaway Spoon.
Porter, Bern & Malok. Vocrescends. 32p. (Orig.). 1991. pap. 3.00 (*0-926935-42-9*) Runaway Spoon.
Porter, Bern, jt. ed. see Leite, George.
Porter, Bernard. Britain, Europe & the World, 1850-1986: Illusions of Grandeur. 2nd ed. 184p. 1987. pap. text 17.95 (*0-04-909040-2*) Routledge.
— Lions Share. 3rd ed. LC 95-50463. 464p. (C). 1996. pap. text 23.44 (*0-582-08943-3*, Pub. by Addison-Wesley) Longman.
— The Lions Share: A Short History of British Imperialism, 1850-1995. 3rd ed. 464p. (C). 1996. text 59.06 (*0-582-29294-8*) Addison-Wesley.
— The Origins of the Vigilant State: The London Metropolitan Police Special Branch Before the First World War. 272p. 1991. reprint ed. 60.00 (*0-85115-283-X*) Boydell & Brewer.
— Plots & Paranoia: A History of Political Espionage in Britain, 1790-1988. 304p. 1989. 34.95 (*0-04-445258-6*) Routledge.
— The Refugee Question in Mid-Victorian Politics. LC 78-73947. 254p. reprint ed. pap. 72.40 (*0-608-15274-9*, 2029224) Bks Demand.
Porter, Bill & Pine, Red, trs. from CHI. The Zen Works of Stonehouse: Poems & Talks of a Fourteenth - Century Chinese Hermit. LC 97-25577. (Illus.). 192p. (Orig.). 1998. pap. 14.95 (*1-56279-101-X*, Pub. by Mercury Hse Inc) Consort Bk Sales.
Porter, Bonita. Meriah of Sorrows. LC 94-93949. 188p. (Orig.). 1995. pap. 12.95 (*1-55673-974-5*, Fairway Pr) CSS OH.
Porter, Brenda. Principles of External Auditing. LC 96-23713. 396p. 1997. pap. 75.00 (*0-471-96212-0*) Wiley.
Porter, Brian. Mighty. 645p. (C). 1991. text 34.95 (*1-881814-99-8*); pap. text 24.95 (*0-685-62417-X*) Pace Pr MA.
— When Nationalism Began to Hate: Imagining Modern Politics in Nineteenth-Century Poland. LC 99-20039. 320p. 2000. text 45.00 (*0-19-513146-0*) OUP.
Porter, Brian, ed. see Wight, Martin.
Porter, Bruce. Bill & the Burning Bush. (Illus.). 40p. (Orig.). (J). (gr. 1 up). 1987. pap. 3.95 (*0-939925-12-5*) R C Law & Co.
***Porter, Bruce.** Blow. (Illus.). 384p. 2000. pap. 14.95 (*0-312-26712-6*, St Martin Griffin) St Martin.
Porter, Bruce. Blow: How a Small Town Boy Made 100 Million Dollars with the Medellin Cartel & Lost it All. 1993. 20.00 (*0-06-179300-0*) HarperTrade.
— Butch & the Bad Baloney. (Illus.). 40p. (Orig.). (J). (gr. 1 up). 1987. pap. 3.95 (*0-939925-15-X*) R C Law & Co.
— Jonah Gets the Jitters. (Illus.). 40p. (Orig.). (J). (gr. 3 up). 1987. pap. 3.95 (*0-939925-14-1*) R C Law & Co.
***Porter, Bruce.** Martyrs' Torch. 2000. pap. 12.99 (*0-7684-2046-6*) Destiny Image.
Porter, Bruce. The Parable of Pa Diggle's Son. (Illus.). 40p. (Orig.). (J). (gr. 3 up). 1987. pap. 3.95 (*0-939925-11-7*) R C Law & Co.
— Samuel & the Strange Sound. (Illus.). 40p. (Orig.). (J). (gr. 3 up). 1987. pap. 3.95 (*0-939925-13-3*) R C Law & Co.
— Squirt & the Super Soldier. (Illus.). 40p. (Orig.). (J). (gr. 3 up). 1987. pap. 3.95 (*0-939925-16-8*) R C Law & Co.
— War & the Rise of the State: The Military Foundations of Modern Politics. 350p. 1994. 27.95 (*0-02-925095-1*) Free Pr.
Porter, Bruce & Mooney, Raymond, eds. Machine Learning, 1990: Proceedings of the Seventh International Conference. 404p. (C). 1998. pap. text 39.95 (*1-55860-141-4*) Morgan Kaufmann.
Porter, Bruce, et al. Art in California. (Illus.). 670p. (C). 1988. reprint ed. 39.00 (*0-9610520-2-3*) Westphal Pub.
Porter, Bruce, jt. auth. see Curvin, Robert.
Porter, Bruce D. The U. S. S. R. in Third World Conflicts: Soviet Arms & Diplomacy in Local Wars, 1945-1980. LC 83-26265. (Illus.). 238p. 1986. pap. text 18.95 (*0-521-31064-4*) Cambridge U Pr.
Porter, Burton F. The Good Life: Alternatives in Ethics. 2nd ed. 301p. (C). 1995. text 39.95 (*1-880157-15-2*) Ardsley.
— Philosophy: A Literary & Conceptual Approach. 2nd ed. 496p. (C). 1980. pap. text 41.50 (*0-15-570553-9*, Pub. by Harcourt Coll Pubs) Harcourt.
— Reasons for Living: A Basic Ethics. 747p. (C). 1988. pap. text 41.00 (*0-02-396050-7*, Macmillan Coll) P-H.
Porter, C. Cole Porter Classics. 48p. 1997. pap. 12.95 incl. audio compact disk (*0-7935-7529-X*); pap. 12.95 (*0-7935-7530-3*); pap. 12.95 (*0-7935-7531-1*); pap. 12.95 (*0-7935-7532-X*) H Leonard.
Porter, C. R. Klondike Paradise: Culture in the Wilderness. LC 98-161953. (Illus.). 192p. 1997. pap. 14.95 (*0-88839-402-0*) Hancock House.
Porter, Carlos W., ed. Made in Russia: The Holocaust. 415p. 1988. pap. 7.50 (*0-939484-30-7*, 0695, Inst Hist Rev) Legion Survival.
Porter Carlyle, Linda. Beautiful Bones & Butterflies Vol. 6: A Book about Conversion. Sox, Aileen, ed. (Child's Steps to Jesus Ser.). (Illus.). 24p. (J). 1993. 7.99 (*0-8163-1123-4*) Pacific Pr Pub Assn.
— Happy Birthday Tomorrow to Me! Vol. 8: A Book about Joy in Jesus. Sox, Aileen, ed. (Child's Steps to Jesus Ser.). (Illus.). 24p. (J). 1993. 7.99 (*0-8163-1125-0*) Pacific Pr Pub Assn.
— My Very Best Friend Vol. 12: A Book about Jesus. Justinen, Kim & Sox, Aileen, eds. (Child's Steps to Jesus Ser.). (Illus.). 24p. (J). (ps-2). 1994. 7.99 (*0-8163-1184-6*) Pacific Pr Pub Assn.
— No Olives Tonight! Vol. 7: A Book about Helping Others. Sox, Aileen A., ed. (Child's Steps to Jesus Ser.). (Illus.). 24p. (J). 1993. 7.99 (*0-8163-1124-2*) Pacific Pr Pub Assn.
— No Puppy Food in the Garden Vol. 9: A Book about Trust. Sox, Aileen, ed. (Child's Steps to Jesus Ser.). (Illus.). 24p. (J). 1994. 7.99 (*0-8163-1181-1*) Pacific Pr Pub Assn.
— Red & Purple on My Feet Vol. 10: A Book about Choices. Sox, Aileen, ed. (Child's Steps to Jesus Ser.). (Illus.). 24p. (J). 1994. 7.99 (*0-8163-1182-X*) Pacific Pr Pub Assn.
— Teddy's Terrible Tangle Vol. 11: A Book about Prayer. Sox, Aileen, ed. (Child's Steps to Jesus Ser.). (Illus.). 24p. (J). 1994. 7.99 (*0-8163-1183-8*) Pacific Pr Pub Assn.
Porter, Carol & Cleland, Janell. The Portfolio As a Learning Strategy. LC 94-3522. 164p. 1994. pap. text 19.00 (*0-86709-348-X*, 0348, Pub. by Boynton Cook Pubs) Heinemann.
Porter, Carol & Hamel, Mike. Women's Ministry Handbook. 272p. 1992. 18.99 (*0-89693-885-9*, 6-1885, Victor Bks) Chariot Victor.
Porter, Carol C., jt. auth. see Halferty, Suzette.
Porter, Caroline. As Life Gets Funnier. (Illus.). 48p. (Orig.). 1995. pap. 9.00 (*0-9649750-0-9*) CPI Pubng.
Porter, Carolyn, ed. see Anderson, Camille J. & Price, Don L.
Porter, Carolyn, ed. see Reid, T. J.
Porter, Catherine. Miller's Collecting Books. (Illus.). 192p. text 35.00 (*1-85732-543-5*, Pub. by Millers Pubns) Antique Collect.
Porter, Catherine. Miller's Collecting Books. LC 96-141828. (Illus.). 192p. 1996. 30.00 (*1-85732-766-7*, Pub. by Reed Illust Books) Antique Collect.
Porter, Catherine & Minich, Elizabeth. English Connections: Grammar for Education, Bk. 3. LC 94-20479. 182p. 1994. pap. 11.93 (*0-8092-4207-9*) NTC Contemp Pub Co.
Porter, Catherine, tr. see Borch-Jacobsen, Mikkel.
Porter, Catherine, tr. see David-Menard, Monique.
Porter, Catherine, tr. see Ducrot, Oswald & Todorov, Tzvetan.
Porter, Catherine, tr. see Felman, Shoshana.
Porter, Catherine, tr. see Gauchet, Marcel & Swain, Gladys.
Porter, Catherine, tr. see Genette, Gerard.
Porter, Catherine, tr. see Goux, Jean-Joseph.
Porter, Catherine, tr. see Hollier, Denis.
Porter, Catherine, tr. see Irigaray, Luce.
Porter, Catherine, tr. see Kofman, Sarah.
Porter, Catherine, tr. see Latour, Bruno.
Porter, Catherine, tr. see Lipovetsky, Gilles.
Porter, Catherine, tr. see Marin, Louis.
Porter, Catherine, tr. see Robin, Regine.
Porter, Catherine, tr. see Todorov, Tzvetan.
Porter, Cathy. Women in Revolutionary Russia. (Women in History Ser.). (Illus.). 45p. (YA). (gr. 7-12). 1987. pap. 13.95 (*0-521-31969-2*) Cambridge U Pr.
Porter, Cathy, ed. The Writer's Drawing Book: The Russians. (Illus.). 176p. (Orig.). 1995. pap., spiral bd. 16.00 (*1-57062-193-4*, Pub. by Shambhala Pubns) Random.
Porter, Cathy, tr. see Grekova, I.
Porter, Cathy, tr. see Kollontai, Alexandra M.
Porter, Cathy, tr. see Vasilieva, Larissa.
Porter, Cathy A. & Christianson, Elin B. Special Libraries: A Guide for Management. 4th ed. LC 97-8193. 1997. 42.00 (*0-87111-466-6*) SLA.
Porter, Cecelia H. The Rhine As Musical Metaphor: Cultural Identity in German Romantic Music. LC 96-14967. (Illus.). 320p. 1996. text 55.00 (*1-55553-284-5*) NE U Pr.
Porter, Cedric W., Jr., et al. Oral Contraceptives: A Guide for Programs & Clinics. 4th ed. (ENG, POR & SPA.). 56p. 1982. 3.50 (*0-933853-12-2*) Pathfinder Fund.
Porter, Charles. Bibliology: Doctrine of the Holy Scriptures. (TEE Ser.). 138p. 1976. 5.95 (*1-879892-19-7*) Editorial Bautista.
— Doctrina de Dios. (TEE Ser.). (SPA.). 199p. 1989. 6.95 (*1-879892-13-8*) Editorial Bautista.
— Doctrina de las Sagradas Escrituras. (TEE Ser.). (SPA.). 143p. 1976. 5.95 (*1-879892-00-6*) Editorial Bautista.
— The Doctrine of God. (TEE Ser.). 211p. 1976. 6.95 (*1-879892-14-6*) Editorial Bautista.
— New Testament Survey, Pt. 2. (TEE Ser.). 216p. 1981. 6.95 (*1-879892-17-0*) Editorial Bautista.
— New Testament Survey, Vol. 1. (TEE Ser.). 223p. 1981. 6.95 (*1-879892-15-4*) Editorial Bautista.
— A Revision of the South American Species of Trachysphyrus -(Hymenoptera, Ichneumonidae) (Memoir Ser.: No. 10). (Illus.). 387p. 1967. 45.00 (*1-56665-008-9*) Assoc Pubs FL.
— Sintesis Del Antiguo Testamento, Vol. I. Meyer, Richard, ed. (SPA., Illus.). 169p. 1996. pap. text, teacher ed. 6.95 (*1-879892-67-7*, TE-180) Editorial Bautista.
— Sintesis Del Neuvo Testamento, Tomo I. (TEE Ser.). (SPA.). 221p. 1991. 6.95 (*1-879892-01-4*) Editorial Bautista.
— Sintesis Del Nuevo Testamento, Tomo II. (TEE Ser.). (SPA.). 222p. 1978. 6.95 (*1-879892-16-2*) Editorial Bautista.
Porter, Charles A. After the Age of Suspicion: The French Novel Today. (Yale French Studies). 1989. pap. 18.00 (*0-300-04386-4*) Yale U Pr.
— Chateaubriand: Composition, Imagination & Poetry. (Stanford French & Italian Studies: No. 9). vi, 146p. 1978. pap. 56.50 (*0-915838-37-0*) Anma Libri.
***Porter, Charles A.** French Studies 96: Commemorative Anthology, Fifty Years of French Studies, 1948-1998. 2000. 18.00 (*0-300-08139-1*) Yale U Pr.
Porter, Charles O., jt. auth. see Blaustein, Albert P.
Porter, Charlie. Ash. 1998. pap. text 16.95 (*0-7535-0120-1*, Pub. by Virgin Bks) London Brdge.
Porter, Charlotte, ed. see Browning, Elizabeth Barrett.
Porter, Charlotte, tr. see D'Annunzio, Gabriele.
Porter, Charlotte M. The Eagle's Nest: Natural History & American Ideas, 1812-1842. LC 85-16465. (History of American Science & Technology Ser.). (Illus.). 268p. 1986. pap. 83.10 (*0-608-05149-7*, 206571000005) Bks Demand.
Porter-Chase, Mary. The Return of Sinta Claus: A Family Winter Solstice Tale. (Illus.). (Orig.). (J). (gr. 3-12). 1991. pap. 6.00 (*0-9630798-0-8*) Samary Pr.
Porter, Cheryl. Gross Grub: Retch-ed Recipes That Taste Heavenly but Look Like Heck. LC 94-3455. (Kidbacks Ser.). (Illus.). (J). 1995. pap. 5.99 (*0-679-86693-0*) Random.
Porter, Cheryl A. Captive Angel. 320p. 1999. mass mkt. 5.99 (*0-312-96906-6*) St Martin.
— From Here to Maternity (Right Stork, Wrong Address) (Love & Laughter Ser.: No. 63). 1999. per. 3.50 (*0-373-44063-4*, 1-44063-5) Harlequin Bks.
— The Great Escape. (Love & Laughter Ser.). 1998. per. 3.50 (*0-373-44044-8*, 1-44044-5) Harlequin Bks.
— Hannah's Promise. 1997. mass mkt. 5.99 (*0-312-96170-7*) St Martin.
— Jacey's Reckless Heart, No. 2. (Lawless Women Ser.). 1997. mass mkt. 5.99 (*0-312-96332-7*) St Martin.
— A Man in Demand. (Love & Laughter Ser.: No. 21). 1997. per. 3.50 (*0-373-44021-9*, 1-44021-3) Harlequin Bks.
— Seasons of Glory. 1998. mass mkt. 5.99 (*0-312-96625-3*) St Martin.
Porter, Cheryl A., jt. auth. see Paul, Sandra.
***Porter, Cheryl Anne.** Prairie Song. 352p. 2000. mass mkt. 5.99 (*0-312-97291-1*) St Martin.
***Porter, Cheryl Anne & Knoll, Patricia.** Duets 2-in-1: Drive-By Daddy; Calamity Jo. (Duets Ser.: No. 21). 2000. per. 5.99 (*0-373-44087-1*, 1-44087-4) Harlequin Bks.
Porter, Cheryl Anne, jt. auth. see Ireland, Liz.
Porter, Claude L. Cuckoo over Vienna. 3rd ed. LC 89-92105. (Illus.). 266p. 1988. reprint ed. 21.95 (*0-9624007-0-X*) C L Porter.
Porter, Clyde. Top Golf: Peak Performance Through Brain - Body Integration. (Illus.). 150p. (Orig.). 1993. pap. 14.95 (*0-9637669-4-5*) Life Enhance.
Porter, Cole. The Complete Lyrics of Cole Porter. Kimball, Robert, ed. (Illus.). 535p. 1992. reprint ed. pap. 25.00 (*0-306-80483-2*) Da Capo.
— Lee Evans Arranges Cole Porter. 48p. 1985. pap. 7.95 (*0-7935-0932-7*, 00240176) H Leonard.
Porter, Cole. Porter Cole Easy Piano Solos. (Easy Piano Ser.). 144p. 1992. per. 20.95 (*0-7935-1516-5*, 00311576) H Leonard.
Porter, Connie Rose. Addy Boxed Set: Meet Addy; Addy Learns a Lesson; Addy's Surprise; Happy Birthday, Addy!; Addy Saves the Day; Changes for Addy. (American Girls Collection : Bks. 1-6). (Illus.). 460p. (YA). (gr. 2 up). 1994. pap., boxed set 34.95 (*1-56247-087-6*); text, boxed set 74.95 (*1-56247-088-4*) Pleasant Co.
— Addy Learns a Lesson: A School Story. LC 98-16820. (American Girls Collection : Bk. 2). (Illus.). 70p. (J). (gr. 2 up). 1993. 12.95 (*1-56247-078-7*) Pleasant Co.
— Addy Learns a Lesson: A School Story. LC 98-16820. (American Girls Collection : Bk. 2). (Illus.). 70p. (YA). (gr. 2 up). 1993. pap. 5.95 (*1-56247-077-9*) Pleasant Co.
— Addy Learns a Lesson: A School Story. (American Girls Collection: Bk. 2). (Illus.). (YA). (gr. 2 up). 1993. 11.15 (*0-606-05103-1*, Pub. by Turtleback) Demco.
— Addy Saves the Day: A Summer Story. LC 98-6718. (American Girls Collection : Bk. 5). (Illus.). 72p. (YA). (gr. 2-7). 1994. 12.95 (*1-56247-084-1*) Pleasant Co.
— Addy Saves the Day: A Summer Story. LC 98-6718. (American Girls Collection : Bk. 5). (Illus.). 72p. (YA). (gr. 2 up). 1994. pap. 5.95 (*1-56247-083-3*) Pleasant Co.
Porter, Connie Rose. Addy Saves the Day: A Summer Story. (American Girls Collection: Bk. 5). (Illus.). (YA). (gr. 2 up). 1993. 11.15 (*0-606-06160-6*, Pub. by Turtleback) Demco.
— Addy's Little Brother. LC 99-38622. (American Girls Collection). (Illus.). 56p. (YA). (gr. 2 up). 2000. 3.95 (*1-58485-033-7*) Pleasant Co.
Porter, Connie Rose. Addy's Surprise: A Christmas Story. (American Girls Collection: Bk. 3). (Illus.). (YA). (gr. 2 up). 1993. 11.15 (*0-606-05104-X*, Pub. by Turtleback) Demco.
— Addy's Surprise: A Christmas Story. rev. ed. LC 98-16821. (American Girls Collection : Bk. 3). (Illus.). (YA). (gr. 2 up). 1998. text 12.95 (*1-56247-080-9*); pap. text 5.95 (*1-56247-079-5*) Pleasant Co.
***Porter, Connie Rose.** All-Bright Court. (Illus.). 224p. (J). 2000. pap. 12.00 (*0-618-05679-3*) HM.
Porter, Connie Rose. Changes for Addy: A Winter Story. LC 98-16817. (American Girls Collection : Bk. 6). (Illus.). 80p. (YA). (gr. 2 up). 1994. text 12.95 (*1-56247-086-8*); pap. text 5.95 (*1-56247-085-X*) Pleasant Co.
Porter, Connie Rose. Changes for Addy: A Winter Story. LC 94-29298. (American Girls Collection: Bk. 6). (Illus.). (YA). (gr. 2 up). 1994. 11.15 (*0-606-06272-6*, Pub. by Turtleback) Demco.
— Happy Birthday, Addy! A Springtime Story. (American Girls Collection: Bk. 4). (Illus.). (YA). (gr. 2 up). 1994. 11.15 (*0-606-06439-7*, Pub. by Turtleback) Demco.
Porter, Connie Rose. Happy Birthday, Addy! A Springtime Story. rev. ed. LC 98-6719. (American Girls Collection : Bk. 4). (Illus.). (YA). (gr. 2 up). 1998. 12.95 (*1-56247-082-5*); pap. 5.95 (*1-56247-081-7*) Pleasant Co.
— Imani All Mine. LC 98-37722. 212p. (YA). 1999. 23.00 (*0-395-83808-8*) HM.
***Porter, Connie Rose.** Imani All Mine. LC 98-37722. (Illus.). 208p. (J). 2000. pap. 12.00 (*0-618-05678-5*) HM.
Porter, Connie Rose. Meet Addy: An American Girl. LC 98-6724. (American Girls Collection : Bk. 1). (Illus.). 69p. (YA). (gr. 2 up). 1993. pap. 5.95 (*1-56247-075-2*); lib. bdg. 12.95 (*1-56247-076-0*) Pleasant Co.
— Meet Addy: An American Girl. (American Girls Collection: Bk. 1). (Illus.). (YA). (gr. 2 up). 1993. 11.15 (*0-606-05459-6*, Pub. by Turtleback) Demco.
Porter, Cynthia J., jt. auth. see Porter, Patrick K.
Porter, Cynthia J., ed. see De Shazo, Jerry.
Porter, D. Go, Deliver! 9.99 (*1-85792-000-7*, Pub. by Christian Focus) Spring Arbor Dist.
— He Changed Them. 8.50 (*1-85792-038-4*, Pub. by Christian Focus) Spring Arbor Dist.
— Political History of Public Health. LC 98-21836. (Wellcome Institute Series in the History of Medicine). 256p. (C). 1999. 85.00 (*0-415-12244-9*) Routledge.
Porter, D. A. Phase Transformations in Metal. 2nd ed. 1992. pap. 44.95 (*0-412-45030-5*, Chap & Hall NY) Chapman & Hall.
Porter, D. A. & Easterling, K. E. Phase Transformations in Metals & Alloys. LC 92-13376. 1992. write for info. (*0-442-31638-0*) Chapman & Hall.
Porter, Dablia. The Computer Blank Book. 144p. Date not set. pap. 5.95 (*1-55850-829-5*) Adams Media.
— 365 Reflections on Daughters. LC 97-27066. 400p. 1997. pap. 6.95 (*1-55850-812-0*) Adams Media.
Porter, Dablia & Cervantes, Gabriel. 365 Reflections on Sisters. LC 97-28114. 400p. 1997. pap. 6.95 (*1-55850-810-4*) Adams Media.
— 365 Reflections on Grandmothers. LC 97-28115. 400p. 1997. pap. 7.95 (*1-55850-811-2*) Adams Media.
Porter, Dahlia. 365 Reflections on Being Single: A Woman's Guide to Living Alone & Loving It!, 1. LC 98-48178. 1999. pap. 6.95 (*1-58062-126-0*) Adams Media.
Porter, Dahlia, ed. 365 Reflections on Sex. LC 98-27566. 400p. 1998. pap. text 6.95 (*1-58062-058-2*) Adams Media.
— 365 Reflections on Dating. LC 98-27565. 400p. 1998. pap. text 6.95 (*1-58062-059-0*) Adams Media.
Porter, Dahlia & Cervantes, Gabriel. 365 Reflections on Fathers. LC 97-47046. 400p. 1998. 7.95 (*1-58062-009-4*) Adams Media.
— 365 Reflections on Mothers. LC 97-47045. 400p. 1998. pap. 7.95 (*1-58062-008-6*) Adams Media.
Porter, Dale H. The Emergence of the Past: A Theory of Historical Explanation. LC 80-27165. (Chicago Original Paperback Ser.). 288p. 1992. pap. text 19.00 (*0-226-67550-5*) U Ch Pr.
— The Emergence of the Past: A Theory of Historical Explanation. LC 80-27165. 215p. reprint ed. pap. 66.70 (*0-608-09501-X*, 205430200005) Bks Demand.
— The Life & Times of Sir Goldsworthy Gurney: Gentleman Scientist & Inventor 1793-1875. LC 97-31833. (Illus.). 288p. 1998. 43.50 (*0-934223-50-5*) Lehigh Univ Pr.
— The Thames Embankment: Environment, Technology, & Society in Victorian London. LC 97-34773. (Technology & the Environment Ser.). 1998. 49.95 (*1-884836-28-3*) U Akron Pr.
— The Thames Embankment: Environment, Technology, & Society in Victorian London. LC 97-34773. (Technology & the Environment Ser.). (Illus.). 318p. 1998. pap. 24.95 (*1-884836-29-1*) U Akron Pr.
Porter, Dan & Allan, Caroline, eds. Reform, Resiliency, & Renewal: Kids in Action. 106p. 1998. pap. 19.95 (*0-939561-28-X*) Univ South ME.
Porter, Dan, jt. auth. see Coleman, Loren.
Porter, Dan, jt. ed. see Coleman, Loren.
Porter, Daniel. Cat Got Your Tongue? The Real Meaning Behind Everyday Sayings. LC 99-202165. (Illus.). 96p. (J). (gr. 3-7). 1998. pap. 3.50 (*0-8167-4918-3*) Troll Communs.
— Taming Monster Moments: Tips for Turning on Soul Lights to Help Children Handle Fear & Danger. LC 98-30150. 32p. (J). (ps-5). 1999. pap. 5.95 (*0-8091-6655-0*) Paulist Pr.
Porter, Daniel J. The Dot Com Kids: Search for the Missing Keys. Porter, Kevin & Gordon, Kevin, eds. 100p. (J). (gr. 4-6). 1996. 12.95 (*1-889693-00-6*) Tapp Creative.
— Shalinar's Song. LC 95-46808. (Illus.). 32p. (J). (gr. 2-5). 1996. pap. 6.95 (*0-8091-6631-3*, 6631-3) Paulist Pr.
Porter, Darwin. Blood Moon. (Orig.). 1998. pap. 12.95 (*0-9668030-0-0*) Georgia Literary.
— Butterflies in Heat. LC 97-65249. 1997. reprint ed. pap. 12.95 (*1-877978-95-7*, FLF Pr) FL Lit Foundation.
— Frommer's Austria, 1995-1996. 1995. pap. 18.00 (*0-671-88476-X*) S&S Trade.
***Porter, Darwin.** Frommer's Bahamas 99. 1999th ed. 352p. 1998. 15.95 (*0-02-862270-7*) Macmillan.
— Frommer's Bahamas 2001. (Illus.). 368p. 2000. pap. 15.99 (*0-7645-6089-1*) IDG Bks.
Porter, Darwin. Frommer's Bahamas '97. 352p. 1996. 16.95 (*0-02-860919-0*) Macmillan.
***Porter, Darwin.** Frommer's Bermuda 2001. (Illus.). 240p. 2000. pap. 15.99 (*0-7645-6114-6*) IDG Bks.
Porter, Darwin. Frommer's Bermuda '97. 240p. 1996. 14.95 (*0-02-860924-7*) Macmillan.

P

An Asterisk (*) at the beginning of an entry indicates that the title is appearing for the first time.

*Porter, Darwin.** Frommer's Bermuda 99. 1999th ed. 240p. 1998. 15.95 (*0-02-862266-9*, Pub. by Macmillan) S&S Trade.

Porter, Darwin. Frommer's Budget Travel Guide England on $60 a Day, 1996. 1995. pap. 18.00 (*0-671-51875-5*) S&S Trade.

— Frommer's Caribbean Cruises Ports of Call 99. 560p. 1998. 19.95 (*0-02-862264-2*, Pub. by Macmillan) S&S Trade.

— Frommer's Caribbean from $4 a Day. 2nd ed. 656p. 1997. 18.95 (*0-02-861668-5*) Macmillan.

— Frommer's Caribbean Ports of Call. 2nd ed. 336p. 1998. 14.95 (*0-02-862269-3*) Macmillan.

***Porter, Darwin.** Frommer's Caribbean 2001. (Illus.). 800p. 2000. pap. 19.99 (*0-7645-6094-8*) IDG Bks.

Porter, Darwin. Frommer's Caribbean '97. 752p. 1996. 19.95 (*0-02-860915-8*) Macmillan.

— Frommer's Carolinas & Georgia. 3rd ed. 1996. 16.95 (*0-02-860909-3*) Macmillan.

— Frommer's Comprehensive Travel Guide Bahamas, 1996-1997. 1995. pap. 17.00 (*0-671-51767-8*) S&S Trade.

— Frommer's Comprehensive Travel Guide Bermuda, 1996-1997. 1995. pap. 15.00 (*0-671-51766-X*) S&S Trade.

— Frommer's Comprehensive Travel Guide Caribbean, 1996. 1995. pap. 18.00 (*0-671-51874-7*) S&S Trade.

— Frommer's Comprehensive Travel Guide England, 1996. 1996. pap. 18.00 (*0-671-51876-3*) S&S Trade.

— Frommer's Comprehensive Travel Guide France, 1996-1997. 1995. pap. 20.00 (*0-671-51879-8*) S&S Trade.

— Frommer's Comprehensive Travel Guide Germany, 1996. 1995. pap. 19.00 (*0-671-51880-1*) S&S Trade.

— Frommer's Comprehensive Travel Guide Italy, 1996. 1995. pap. 19.00 (*0-671-51883-6*) S&S Trade.

— Frommer's Comprehensive Travel Guide London, 1996. 1995. pap. 13.00 (*0-671-51884-4*) S&S Trade.

— Frommer's Comprehensive Travel Guide Portugal, 1996-1997. 1996. per. 16.95 (*0-671-51935-2*) S&S Trade.

— Frommer's Comprehensive Travel Guide Scotland, 1996-1997. 1996. per. 16.95 (*0-671-51949-2*) S&S Trade.

— Frommer's Comprehensive Travel Guide Switzerland & Liechtenstein, 1996-1997. 1996. pap. 18.95 (*0-671-51931-X*) S&S Trade.

— Frommer's Comprehensive Travel Guide Virgin Islands, 1996-1997. 1995. pap. 13.00 (*0-671-51768-6*) S&S Trade.

***Porter, Darwin.** Frommer's England 2001. (Illus.). 768p. 2000. pap. 20.99 (*0-7645-6138-3*) IDG Bks.

Porter, Darwin. Frommer's Europe 99. 99th ed. 1024p. 1998. 21.95 (*0-02-862254-5*, Pub. by Macmillan) S&S Trade.

***Porter, Darwin.** Frommer's France 2001. (Illus.). 2000. pap. 20.99 (*0-7645-6137-5*) IDG Bks.

— Frommer's Germany 2001. (Illus.). 2000. pap. 20.99 (*0-7645-6139-1*) IDG Bks.

Porter, Darwin. Frommer's Germany '97. 1996. 19.95 (*0-02-861104-7*) Macmillan.

***Porter, Darwin.** Frommer's Italy 2001. (Illus.). 800p. 2000. pap. 20.99 (*0-7645-6136-7*) IDG Bks.

Porter, Darwin. Frommer's Italy '97. 1996. 19.95 (*0-02-861133-0*) Macmillan.

***Porter, Darwin.** Frommer's Jamaica. (Illus.). 272p. 2000. pap. 14.99 (*0-7645-6126-X*) IDG Bks.

Porter, Darwin. Frommer's Jamaica & Barbados. 4th ed. 272p. 1998. 14.95 (*0-02-862265-0*, Pub. by Macmillan) S&S Trade.

***Porter, Darwin.** Frommer's London 2001. (Illus.). 384p. 2000. pap. 14.99 (*0-7645-6134-0*) IDG Bks.

Porter, Darwin. Frommer's London '97. 1996. 13.95 (*0-02-861146-2*) Macmillan.

— Frommer's Madrid & the Costa Del Sol, 1995-1996. 1995. pap. 13.00 (*0-671-88492-1*) S&S Trade.

— Frommer's Munich & the Bavarian Alps. 1996. 13.95 (*0-02-861147-0*) Macmillan.

***Porter, Darwin.** Frommer's Paris 2001. (Illus.). 368p. 2000. pap. 14.99 (*0-7645-6133-2*) IDG Bks.

Porter, Darwin. Frommer's Portable Bahamas. 1997. 9.95 (*0-02-862267-7*) Macmillan.

— Frommer's Portable London. 1997. 9.95 (*0-02-862268-5*) Macmillan.

— Frommer's Puerto Rico. 4th ed. 256p. 1998. 14.95 (*0-02-862271-5*, Pub. by Macmillan) S&S Trade.

— Frommer's Rome. 11th ed. 1996. 14.95 (*0-02-861208-6*, P-H Travel) Prntice Hall Bks.

— Frommer's Rome, 1995-1996. 1995. pap. 13.00 (*0-671-88497-2*) S&S Trade.

— Frommer's Scandinavia. 17th ed. 1997. 19.95 (*0-02-861223-X*, P-H Travel) Prntice Hall Bks.

— Frommer's Scandinavia, 1995-1996. 1995. pap. 20.00 (*0-671-88817-X*) S&S Trade.

— Frommer's Scotland. 4th ed. LC 99-223186. 496p. 1998. 18.95 (*0-02-861669-3*) Macmillan.

***Porter, Darwin.** Frommer's Scotland 2001. (Illus.). 2000. pap. 19.99 (*0-7645-6168-5*) IDG Bks.

Porter, Darwin. Frommer's Spain. 17th ed. 1996. 19.95 (*0-02-861202-7*, P-H Travel) Prntice Hall Bks.

***Porter, Darwin.** Frommer's Spain 2001. 2000. pap. 20.99 (*0-7645-6170-7*) IDG Bks.

Porter, Darwin. Frommer's Spain, 1995-1996. 1995. pap. 18.00 (*0-671-88499-9*) S&S Trade.

— Frommer's Vienna. 1997. 14.95 (*0-02-861222-1*, P-H Travel) Prntice Hall Bks.

***Porter, Darwin.** Midnight in Savannah. 500p. 2000. pap. 14.95 (*0-9668030-1-9*, Pub. by Georgia Literary) Bookazine Co Inc.

Porter, Darwin. Razzle-Dazzle. LC 97-62287. 480p. 1998. pap. 12.95 (*1-877978-96-5*) FL Lit Foundation.

— Scotland & Wales on $25 a Day. 300p. 1986. pap. 10.95 (*0-685-11259-4*) S&S Trade.

***Porter, Darwin & Prince, Danforth.** Frommer's Austria. 8th ed. (Frommer's Austria Ser.). (Illus.). 500p. 1999. pap. 19.95 (*0-02-862718-0*, Pub. by Macmillan) S&S Trade.

Porter, Darwin & Prince, Danforth. Frommer's Comprehensive Travel Guide Caribbean, 1995. (Illus.). 720p. 1994. pap. 18.00 (*0-671-88480-8*) P-H.

— Frommer's Denmark. 388p. 1999. pap. 17.95 (*0-02-862721-0*, Pub. by Macmillan) S&S Trade.

— Frommer's England 99. 1999th ed. (Frommer's England Ser.). 721p. 1998. pap. 19.95 (*0-02-862307-X*, Pub. by Macmillan) S&S Trade.

— Frommer's Germany 98. 656p. 1997. 19.95 (*0-02-861660-X*) Macmillan.

— Frommer's Portable Bahamas. 208p. 1997. 9.95 (*0-02-862233-2*) Macmillan.

— Frommer's Portable Charleston & Savannah. 2nd ed. (Frommer's Portable Guides Ser.). 192p. 1998. pap. 9.95 (*0-02-862445-9*, Frommer) Macmillan Gen Ref.

***Porter, Darwin & Prince, Danforth.** Frommer's Scandinavia. 18th ed. (Illus.). 610p. 1999. pap. 19.95 (*0-02-862719-9*, Pub. by Macmillan) S&S Trade.

Porter, Darwin & Prince, Danforth. Frommer's Sweden. 372p. 1999. pap. 17.95 (*0-02-862720-2*, Pub. by Macmillan) S&S Trade.

— Frommer's Switzerland. 8th ed. 496p. 1998. 19.95 (*0-02-862083-6*) Macmillan.

— Frommer's the Carolinas & Georgia. 4th ed. (Frommer's Carolinas & Georgia Ser.). 499p. 1999. pap. 16.95 (*0-02-862370-3*, Frommer) Macmillan Gen Ref.

***Porter, Darwin & Prince, Danforth.** Frommer's Vienna & the Danube Valley. 2nd ed. (Frommer's Vienna & the Danube Valley Ser.). 230p. 1999. 14.95 (*0-02-862717-2*, Pub. by Macmillan) S&S Trade.

Porter, Darwin, et al. Frommer's Austria. 7th ed. LC 91-656137. 512p. 1997. 18.95 (*0-02-861211-6*, P-H Travel) Prntice Hall Bks.

Porter, Darwin, jt. auth. see Frommer's Staff.

Porter, David. The Big Steal: The Screenplay. 1991. pap. 12.95 (*0-7022-2372-7*, Pub. by Univ Queensland Pr) Intl Spec Bk.

— Dickinson: The Modern Idiom. LC 80-24322. 325p. 1981. 43.50 (*0-674-20444-1*) HUP.

***Porter, David.** Fixed: How Goodfellas Bought Boston College Basketball. 2001. 24.95 (*0-87833-192-1*) Taylor Pub.

Porter, David. Group Interaction Modelling of Polymer Properties. LC 94-43930. (Illus.). 512p. 1995. text 195.00 (*0-8247-9599-7*) Dekker.

***Porter, David.** Over the Bent World: Poems & Images from Gerard Manley Hopkins. 175p. 1999. reprint ed. text 30.00 (*1-900507-77-3*, Pub. by Solway) OM Literature.

Porter, David. Phases of the Moon: Flowers from the Garden of Hel. (Illus.). 64p. (Orig.). 1997. pap. 5.95 (*0-9641606-9-2*) Easy Break.

— U. S. Economic Foreign Aid: A Case Study of the U. S. Agency for International Development. LC 90-3612. (Foreign Economic Policy of the United States Ser.). 292p. 1990. reprint ed. text 10.00 (*0-8240-7466-1*) Garland.

— The Vienna Passage. LC 95-16346. 288p. 1995. pap. 10.99 (*0-89107-824-X*) Crossway Bks.

Porter, David, ed. Between Men & Feminism. LC 92-10405. 208p. (C). (gr. 13). 1992. text 59.95 (*0-415-06987-4*, A9844) Routledge.

— Internet Culture. LC 96-36557. 288p. (C). 1997. 70.00 (*0-415-91683-6*); pap. 19.99 (*0-415-91684-4*) Routledge.

— Vision on Fire: Emma Goldman on the Spanish Revolution. LC 82-74015. (Illus.). 383p. (Orig.). 1983. pap. 7.50 (*0-9610348-2-3*) Commonground Pr.

— The Word on the Box. 109p. 1997. pap. text 16.99 (*0-85364-794-1*) Paternoster Pub.

***Porter, David & Garcia, Yolanda P.** Remember Who You Are Vol. 2: Re-Emergence of a Queen. Sumstine, Pat, ed. LC 99-93274. (Illus.). 273p. 1999. pap. text 14.95 (*0-9660386-1-4*) New Life AZ.

Porter, David & Stirling, David S. Integral Equations: A Practical Treatment, from Spectral Theory to Applications. (Texts in Applied Mathematics Ser.: No. 5). (Illus.). 383p. (C). 1990. pap. text 31.95 (*0-521-33742-9*) Cambridge U Pr.

Porter, David B. Remember Who You Are: The Awakening. Akca, Nancy & Sumstine, Pat, eds. LC 97-92832. Vol. 1. (Illus.). 300p. 1998. pap. 14.95 (*0-9660386-0-6*) New Life AZ.

Porter, David D. Naval History of the Civil War. LC 98-13377. 864p. 1998. pap. 34.95 (*0-486-40176-6*) Dover.

Porter, David H. Horace's Poetic Journey: A Reading of Odes 1-3. LC 86-43136. 296p. 1987. reprint ed. pap. 91.80 (*0-7837-9424-X*, 206016500004) Bks Demand.

— Only Connect: Three Studies in Greek Tragedy. LC 86-28918. 128p. (Orig.). 1987. pap. text 16.00 (*0-8191-5951-4*); lib. bdg. 39.00 (*0-8191-5950-6*) U Pr of Amer.

Porter, David L. Biographical Dictionary of American Sports: Baseball, Vol. 1. rev. expanded ed. LC 99-14840. 568p. 2000. lib. bdg. 295.00 (*0-313-31174-9*, GR1174, Greenwood Pr) Greenwood.

— Biographical Dictionary of American Sports: Baseball , Vol. 2. LC 99-14840. 760p. 2000. lib. bdg. 295.00 (*0-313-31175-7*, Greenwood Pr) Greenwood.

— Biographical Dictionary of American Sports: Baseball, Vol. 3. LC 99-14840. 672p. 2000. lib. bdg. 295.00 (*0-313-31176-5*, Greenwood Pr) Greenwood.

— Love Bitter & Sweet. LC 97-17489. (Illus.). 96p. 1997. pap. 10.00 (*0-7867-0470-5*) Carroll & Graf.

Porter, David L., compiled by. A Cumulative Index to the Biographical Dictionary of American Sports. LC 93-18030. 352p. 1993. lib. bdg. 47.95 (*0-313-28435-0*, PBN/, Greenwood Pr) Greenwood.

Porter, David L., ed. African-American Sports Greats: A Biographical Dictionary. LC 95-7189. 480p. 1995. 59.95 (*0-313-28987-5*, Greenwood Pr) Greenwood.

— Biographical Dictionary of American Sports: Baseball. LC 86-12091. 730p. 1987. lib. bdg. 75.00 (*0-313-23771-9*, PDS/, Greenwood Pr) Greenwood.

— Biographical Dictionary of American Sports: Baseball. rev. expanded ed. LC 99-14840. 2064p. 2000. lib. bdg. 295.00 (*0-313-29884-X*) Greenwood.

— Biographical Dictionary of American Sports: Basketball & Other Indoor Sports. LC 88-17776. 826p. 1989. lib. bdg. 75.00 (*0-313-26261-6*, PID/, Greenwood Pr) Greenwood.

— Biographical Dictionary of American Sports: Football. LC 86-29386. 780p. 1987. lib. bdg. 75.00 (*0-313-25771-X*, PFL/, Greenwood Pr) Greenwood.

— Biographical Dictionary of American Sports: Outdoor Sports. LC 87-31780. 748p. 1988. lib. bdg. 75.00 (*0-313-26260-8*, PRO/, Greenwood Pr) Greenwood.

— Biographical Dictionary of American Sports: 1989-1992 Supplement for Baseball, Football, Basketball & Other Sports. LC 91-28742. 784p. 1992. lib. bdg. 79.95 (*0-313-26706-5*, PAS/, Greenwood Pr) Greenwood.

— Biographical Dictionary of American Sports: 1992-1994 Supplement for Baseball, Football, Basketball, & Other Sports. LC 94-27941. 848p. 1995. lib. bdg., suppl. ed. 89.50 (*0-313-28431-8*, Greenwood Pr) Greenwood.

Porter, David T. The Art of Emily Dickinson's Early Poetry. LC 66-13182. 222p. reprint ed. pap. 68.90 (*0-7837-4125-1*, 205794800011) Bks Demand.

— Emerson & Literary Change. LC 78-6669. 248p. 1978. reprint ed. pap. 76.90 (*0-7837-2314-8*, 205740200004) Bks Demand.

Porter, David W., jt. auth. see Cummings, Val R.

Porter, David W., jt. ed. see Grotans, Anna A.

Porter, David W., tr. see Gwara, Scott, ed.

Porter, Deborah L. From Deluge to Discourse: Myth, History, & the Generation of Chinese Fiction. LC 95-41456. (SUNY Series in Chinese Philosophy & Culture). 284p. (C). 1996. text 74.50 (*0-7914-3033-2*); pap. text 24.95 (*0-7914-3034-0*) State U NY Pr.

Porter, Debra, jt. ed. see Sullivan, Steven E.

Porter, Deirdre J. G., ed. see Alexander, Jason.

Porter, Dennis. Haunted Journeys: Desire & Transgression in European Travel Writing. LC 90-37224. 353p. reprint ed. pap. 109.50 (*0-608-09577-X*, 205437900006) Bks Demand.

— The Pursuit of Crime: Art & Ideology in Detective Fiction. LC 81-3399. 277p. reprint ed. pap. 85.90 (*0-8357-3756-X*, 203648200003) Bks Demand.

— Rousseau's Legacy: Emergence & Eclipse of the Writer in France. (Illus.). 320p. 1995. text 65.00 (*0-19-509107-8*) OUP.

Porter, Diana, jt. auth. see Lee, Karen.

Porter, Diane, jt. auth. see Lee, Karen.

Porter, Diane, jt. auth. see Sarlin, Janeen A.

Porter, Dilwyn, jt. auth. see Newton, Scott.

Porter, Don, jt. ed. see Hughes, Arthur.

Porter, Donald. As If a Footnote to the Final Glory. 64p. 1974. pap. 2.00 (*0-915066-09-2*) Assembling Pr.

Porter, Donald C. Ambush. large type ed. LC 93-26719. (White Indian Ser.: Bk. VIII). 368p. 1993. lib. bdg. 22.95 (*0-8161-5846-0*, G K Hall Lrg Type) Mac Lib Ref.

— Seneca. large type ed. LC 93-27951. (White Indian Ser.). 382p. 1994. lib. bdg. 22.95 (*0-8161-5847-9*, G K Hall Lrg Type) Mac Lib Ref.

Porter, Donald J. The Cessna Citations. LC 93-18321. (Illus.). 160p. 1993. pap. 14.60 (*0-8306-4147-5*) McGraw-Hill Prof.

Porter, Donna Hechler. Metes & Bounds Vol. II: David Crews, Ancestors & Descendants. (Illus.). x, 269p. 1997. 45.00 (*0-944619-54-1*) Gregath Pub Co.

Porter, Donna V., ed. see Institute of Medicine Staff.

Porter, Dorothy. Akhenaten. 176p. 1999. pap. 13.99 (*1-85242-619-5*, Pub. by Serpents Tail) Consort Bk Sales.

— Akhenaten. 2nd ed. LC 98-212748. xiv, 160 p. 1998. write for info. (*1-86447-027-5*) HM.

— Driving Too Fast. 1989. pap. 12.95 (*0-7022-2222-4*, Pub. by Univ Queensland Pr) Intl Spec Bk.

— Health, Civilization & the State: A History of Public Health from Ancient to Modern Times. LC 98-21836. 1999. pap. 25.99 (*0-415-20036-9*) Routledge.

— The Monkey's Mask. (Mask Noir Title Ser.). 256p. 1997. pap. text 14.99 (*1-85242-549-0*) Serpents Tail.

— The Monkey's Mask: An Erotic Murder Mystery by Dorothy Porter. LC 95-17755. 272p. 1995. 19.45 (*1-55970-304-0*, Pub. by Arcade Pub Inc) Time Warner.

— The Witch Number. (YA). 1993. pap. 11.95 (*0-7022-2460-X*, Pub. by Univ Queensland Pr) Intl Spec Bk.

Porter, Dorothy, et al, eds. Negro Protest Pamphlets: A Compendium. LC 79-75853. (American Negro: His History & Literature. Series 2). 1969. reprint ed. 11.95 (*0-405-01888-6*) Ayer.

Porter, Dorothy, selected by. Early Negro Writing 1760-1837. 660p. 1995. reprint ed. 49.00 (*0-933121-60-1*) Black Classic.

— Early Negro Writing 1760-1837. (Illus.). 660p. 1995. reprint ed. pap. 24.95 (*0-933121-59-8*) Black Classic.

Porter, Dorothy & Porter, Roy. Patient's Progress: Doctors & Doctoring in 18th-Century England. LC 89-60692. (Illus.). 313p. 1989. 42.50 (*0-8047-1744-3*) Stanford U Pr.

— Patient's Progress: Sickness, Health & Medical Care in England, 1650-1850. (Medicine & Society Ser.: Vol. 4). 25.00 (*0-520-06661-8*) U CA Pr.

Porter, Dorothy B. A Working Bibliography on the Negro in the United States. LC 68-55572. 202 p. 1969. write for info. (*0-8357-0002-X*) Univ Microfilms.

***Porter, Dorothy Burnett.** The Negro in the United States. LC 99-15293. 313p. 1999. 38.00 (*0-7808-0312-4*) Omnigraphics Inc.

Porter, Doug & Linge, Godfrey J. No Place for Borders: The HIV AIDS Epidemic & Development in Asia & the Pacific. LC 96-52306. 224p. 1997. text 49.95 (*0-312-17354-7*) St Martin.

Porter, Douglas. How to Develop & Use the Gift of Evangelism: A Practical Guide for the Layperson. LC 92-225299. 1992. pap. text 7.95 (*0-941005-52-6*) Chrch Grwth VA.

Porter, Douglas, jt. auth. see Towns, Elmer.

Porter, Douglas J. Investing in the Harvest: Preparing for a Spiritual Harvest in Your Church & Community. Spear, Cindy G., ed. 56p. (Orig.). (C). 1991. pap. 2.19 (*0-941005-38-0*) Chrch Grwth VA.

Porter, Douglas R. Housing for Seniors: Developing Successful Projects. LC 95-78640. 109p. 1995. pap. text 44.95 (*0-87420-771-1*, H04) Urban Land.

Porter, Douglas R. Managing Growth in America's Communities. LC 97-14941. (Illus.). 319p. 1997. pap. text 29.95 (*1-55963-442-1*, Shearwater Bks) Island Pr.

— Special Districts: A Useful Technique for Financing Infrastructure. 2nd ed. LC 92-85303. 90p. 1992. pap. text 37.95 (*0-87420-736-3*, S38) Urban Land.

Porter, Douglas R., ed. Growth Management: Keeping on Target. LC 86-50332. (Monograph: No. 86-1). 218p. 1986. pap. 42.95 (*0-87420-655-3*, G06) Urban Land.

— State & Regional Initiatives for Managing Development: Policy Issues & Practical Concerns. LC 92-606688. 259p. 1992. pap. text 45.95 (*0-87420-727-4*, S28) Urban Land.

Porter, Douglas R., et al, eds. Mitigation Banking: Theory & Practice. 225p. (Orig.). (C). 1996. pap. text 55.00 (*1-55963-371-9*) Island Pr.

Porter, Douglas R. & Cole, Susan. Affordable Housing: Twenty Examples from the Private Sector. LC 82-83409. (Illus.). 112p. reprint ed. pap. 34.80 (*0-8357-3185-5*, 203945500012) Bks Demand.

Porter, Douglas R. & Marsh, Lindell L., eds. Development Agreements: Practice, Policy & Prospects. LC 89-51661. 160p. (Orig.). 1989. pap. text 39.95 (*0-87420-694-4*, D59) Urban Land.

Porter, Douglas R. & Peiser, Richard B. Financing Infrastructure to Promote Community Growth. LC 83-51849. 1984. 13.95 (*0-87420-626-X*, D28) Urban Land.

Porter, Douglas R. & Salveson, David A., eds. Collaborative Planning for Wetlands & Wildlife: Issues & Examples. LC 94-30143. 352p. (C). 1995. pap. text 35.00 (*1-55963-287-9*) Island Pr.

Porter, Douglas R., et al. Flexible Zoning: How It Works. LC 88-51229. 200p. (Orig.). 1988. pap. text 45.95 (*0-87420-686-3*, F14) Urban Land.

— Profiles in Growth Management. LC 96-61397. 230p. 1996. pap. text 49.95 (*0-87420-795-9*, P02) Urban Land.

Porter, Duncan M., jt. auth. see Wiggins, Ira L.

Porter, Duncan M., ed. see Darwin, Charles.

Porter, E. R. Life Enhancement One: Tips from Time Travelers from the Crysanthemum Kids. 172p. 1999. pap. 12.00 (*0-9666004-0-1*) EPC Publ.

Porter, Ebenezer, et al. Letters on the Religious Revivals Which Prevailed about the Beginning of the Present Century: With Supplementary Material Compiled by Kurt R. Linde. xx, 316p. 1992. reprint ed. pap. 6.95 (*0-9631745-0-9*) Linde Pubns.

Porter, Edgar A. Foreign Teachers in China: Old Problems for a New Generation, 1979-1989, 39. LC 89-78405. (Contributions to the Study of Education Ser.: No. 39). 216p. 1990. 55.00 (*0-313-27386-3*, PFT/, Greenwood Pr) Greenwood.

— The People's Doctor: George Hatem & China's Revolution. LC 96-3401. 1997. text 60.00 (*0-8248-1840-7*); pap. text 29.95 (*0-8248-1905-5*) UH Pr.

Porter, Edward. Are We Running Out of Oil? (Illus.). 56p. (C). 1997. reprint ed. pap. text 30.00 (*0-7881-3775-1*) DIANE Pub.

Porter, Edward A., jt. auth. see Fitch, Richard D.

Porter, Edward D. International Upstream Activity by U. S. Firms: Trends, Prospects & Policy Issues. (Illus.). 55p. (C). 1999. pap. text 20.00 (*0-7881-7813-X*) DIANE Pub.

Porter, Edwin H. The Fall River Tragedy: A History of the Borden Murders. LC 85-70910. (Illus.). 312p. 1985. reprint ed. 30.00 (*0-9614811-0-2*) King Philip Pub.

Porter, Eleanor. Just David. Clarkson, Clay, ed. (Illus.). 220p. (YA). (gr. 5-10). 1998. pap. 12.95 (*1-888692-04-9*) Whole Heart.

— Pollyanna. abr. ed. Marshall, Michael J., ed. (Core Classics Ser.: Vol. 4). (Illus.). 160p. (J). (gr. 4-6). 1997. pap. 5.95 (*1-890517-06-2*); lib. bdg. 10.95 (*1-890517-07-0*) Core Knowledge.

Porter, Eleanor H. Dawn. 25.95 (*0-8488-0309-4*) Amereon Ltd.

— Hustler Joe, & Other Stories. LC 78-128750. (Short Story Index Reprint Ser.). 1977. 19.95 (*0-8369-3641-8*) Ayer.

— Just David. 334p. Date not set. 25.95 (*0-8488-2532-2*) Amereon Ltd.

— Just David. 1976. lib. bdg. 35.95 (*0-89968-107-7*, Lghtyr Pr) Buccaneer Bks.

— Just David. Clarkson, Clay, ed. (Illus.). 240p. (J). (gr. 3-8). 1999. 15.95 (*1-888692-05-7*) Whole Heart.

— Just David. 1999. lib. bdg. 26.95 (*1-56723-151-9*) Yestermorrow.

P

— Little Pardner, & Other Stories. LC 70-142273. (Short Story Index Reprint Ser.). 1977. 20.95 (0-8369-3757-0) Ayer.
— Mary-Marie. 1976. lib. bdg. 14.25 (0-89968-102-6, Lghtyr Pr) Buccaneer Bks.
— Miss Billy. 1976. lib. bdg. 16.25 (0-89968-103-4, Lghtyr Pr) Buccaneer Bks.
— Miss Billy-Married. 1976. lib. bdg. 16.75 (0-89968-104-2, Lghtyr Pr) Buccaneer Bks.
— Miss Billy's Decision. 1976. lib. bdg. 16.25 (0-89968-105-0, Lghtyr Pr) Buccaneer Bks.
— Oh Money! Money! 23.95 (0-8488-0305-1) Amereon Ltd.
— Pollyanna. (J). 21.95 (0-8488-1445-2) Amereon Ltd.
— Pollyanna. (Andre Deutsch Classics). 224p. (J). (gr. 5-8). 1996. 9.95 (0-233-99094-1, Pub. by Andre Deutsch) Trafalgar.
— Pollyanna. (Young Reader's Christian Library). (Illus.). 224p. (J). (gr. 3-7). 1994. pap. text 1.39 (1-55748-660-3) Barbour Pub.
— Pollyanna. (Illus.). 256p. (YA). (gr. 5 up). 1996. pap. 4.99 (0-14-036682-2, PuffinBks) Peng Put Young Read.
— Pollyanna. Hanft, Joshua, ed. (Great Illustrated Classics Ser.: Vol. 43). (Illus.). 240p. (J). (gr. 3-6). 1995. 9.95 (0-86611-994-9) Playmore Inc.
— Pollyanna. (J). 1997. pap. 2.95 (0-8167-1468-1) Troll Communs.
***Porter, Eleanor H.** Pollyanna. large type ed. (Large Print Heritage Ser.). 305p. (YA). (gr. 7-12). 2000. lib. bdg. 29.95 (1-58118-069-1, 23663) LRS.
Porter, Eleanor H. Pollyanna Grows Up. (J). 21.95 (0-8488-1447-9) Amereon Ltd.
— Pollyanna Grows Up. (Illus.). (YA). (gr. 5 up). 1996. pap. 4.99 (0-14-036758-6) Viking Penguin.
— Pollyanna 'n Hollywood. (J). 17.95 (0-8488-1448-7) Amereon Ltd.
— Pollyanna's Debt of Honor. (J). 15.95 (0-8488-1446-0) Amereon Ltd.
— Pollyanna's Debt of Honor. 1980. lib. bdg. 16.95 (0-89968-253-7, Lghtyr Pr) Buccaneer Bks.
— Road to Understanding. 23.95 (0-8488-0306-X) Amereon Ltd.
— Road to Understanding. 1976. lib. bdg. 16.75 (0-89968-108-5, Lghtyr Pr) Buccaneer Bks.
Porter, Elias H. & Collins, Michael L. Relationship Awareness Theory: Manual of Administration & Interpretation. 9th ed. LC 96-69654. xviii, 145 p. 1996. write for info. (0-9628732-1-7) Prsnl Strengths.
Porter, Eliot. Down the Colorado. 1994. 19.99 (0-88486-011-6) Arrowood Pr.
— Eliot Porter. (Illus.). 280p. 1987. 15.00 (0-8212-1675-9) Amon Carter.
— Eliot Porter: Birds of North America. 1992. 19.98 (0-88486-070-1) Arrowood Pr.
— Eliot Porter's Southwest. (Illus.). 128p. 1995. pap. 29.95 (0-8050-1863-8, Owl) H Holt & Co.
***Porter, Eliot.** The Place No One Knew: Glen Canyon on the Colorado. Brower, David, ed. LC 99-88752. (Illus.). 192p. 2000. reprint ed. pap. 29.95 (0-87905-971-0) Gibbs Smith Pub.
Porter, Eliot, photos by. The West. (Illus.). 132p. 1996. reprint ed. 19.98 (1-56731-147-4, MJF Bks) Fine Comms.
Porter, Eliot & Abbey, Edward. Appalachian Wilderness: The Great Smoky Mountains. 128p. 1988. 19.98 (0-88486-012-4) Arrowood Pr.
Porter, Eliot & Auerbach, Ellen. Mexican Churches. (Illus.). 120p. 1999. pap. 18.95 (0-8118-2359-8) Chronicle Bks.
Porter, Elisabeth. Women & Moral Identity. 224p. pap. 22.95 (0-04-442332-2, Pub. by Allen & Unwin Pty) Paul & Co Pubs.
Porter, Elisabeth J. Building Good Families in a Changing World. 224p. 1995. pap. 24.95 (0-522-84648-3, Pub. by Melbourne Univ Pr) Paul & Co Pubs.
***Porter, Elisabeth J.** Feminist Perspectives on Ethics. LC 99-12366. 232p. 1999. pap. text 26.25 (0-582-35635-0) Addison-Wesley.
Porter, Elizabeth. Classic Basket Quilts. 1991. pap. 16.95 (0-89145-973-1, 2208, Am Quilters Soc) Collector Bks.
Porter, Elizabeth. Social Environment: Anthology. 752p. (C). 1995. text 53.00 (0-536-58951-8) Pearson Custom.
Porter, Enid. Victorian Cambridge: Josiah Chater's Dieries, 1844-1883. (C). 1975. 40.00 (0-85033-213-3) St Mut.
Porter, Eric, jt. ed. see Schilling, Kyle E.
Porter, Erika R. All Visitors Welcome: Accessibility in State Park Interpretive Programs & Facilities. 2nd rev. ed. Helmich, Mary A. & Pozzi, Donna C., eds. LC 94-69721. (Illus.). 260p. (Orig.). 1998. reprint ed. pap. 20.00 (0-941925-20-X) Cal Parks Rec.
Porter, Ethel. One-Sided Love Affair. 66p. 1999. pap. 6.00 (0-8059-4505-9) Dorrance.
Porter, Evan. Affirmation: A Syncreny Instruction Guide. LC 87-50822. 42p. 1987. pap. 11.95 (0-940683-01-6) Sync Society Pubng.
— Communing: A Syncreny Instruction Guide. LC 87-50821. 26p. 1987. pap. 11.95 (0-940683-02-4) Sync Society Pubng.
— Contemplation: A Syncreny Instruction Guide. LC 87-50819. 54p. 1987. pap. 11.95 (0-940683-04-0) Sync Society Pubng.
— Contemplation: The Way to Control Your Mind & Control Your Life. LC 95-92747. 240p. 1996. pap. 18.95 (0-940683-32-6) Sync Society Pubng.
***Porter, Evan.** Eyes on the Soul: Near-Death Experiences Teach Forgiveness. LC 94-68767. 217p. 1999. reprint ed. pap. 14.95 (0-940683-45-8) Sync Society Pubng.
Porter, Evan. Forgiveness: A Syncreny Instruction Guide. LC 87-50820. 49p. 1987. pap. 11.95 (0-940683-03-2) Sync Society Pubng.
— Heal Your Mind, Heal Your Body: A Practical Guide to Wellness of Body, Mind & Spirit. LC 94-65441. 290p. 1994. reprint ed. pap. 14.95 (0-940683-21-0) Sync Society Pubng.
— Positive Selfishness: Your Positive Motivations Are the Natural & Health Way to Persue a Life of Happiness & Success. LC 95-92746. 252p. 1999. pap. 18.95 (0-940683-51-2) Sync Society Pubng.
— Spiritual Self-Healing: A Syncreny Instruction Guide. LC 87-50818. 56p. 1987. pap. 11.95 (0-940683-05-9) Sync Society Pubng.
— Syncreny: An Introduction. LC 86-62684. 220p. 1987. reprint ed. pap. 19.95 (0-940683-00-8) Sync Society Pubng.
Porter, Evan, jt. auth. see Hedberg, Betsy.
Porter, F., jt. ed. see Lake, E.
Porter, Fairfield. Art in Its Own Terms: Selected Criticism, 1935-1975. LC 92-38058. 288p. 1993. pap. 10.95 (0-944072-31-3) Zoland Bks.
Porter, Fenella & Smyth, Ines. Gender Training for Policy Implementers. (Working Papers). 50p. 1998. pap. 18.95 (0-85598-398-1, Pub. by Oxfam Pub) Stylus Pub VA.
***Porter, Fenella, et al.** Gender Works. 250p. 1999. 45.00 (0-85598-414-7, Pub. by Oxfam Pub); pap. 18.50 (0-85598-407-4, Pub. by Oxfam Pub) Stylus Pub VA.
Porter, Florence C. & Gries, Clara W. Collins. Our Folks & Your Folks: A Volume of Family History & Biographical Sketches, Including the Collins, Hardison, Merrill, Teague & Oak Families, & Extending over a Period of Two Centuries. (Illus.). 246p. 1997. reprint ed. pap. 38.00 (0-8328-8018-3); reprint ed. lib. bdg. 48.00 (0-8328-8017-5) Higginson Bk Co.
Porter, Frances & Macdonald, Charlotte, eds. My Hand Will Write What My Heart Dictates: The Unsettled Lives of Women in New Zealand 1820-1915 As Revealed in Letters to Sisters, Family & Friends. 480p. 1996. pap. 34.95 (1-86940-129-8) Paul & Co Pubs.
Porter, Francis. Born to New Zealand: A Biography of Jane Maria Atkinson. 416p. 1996. pap. 24.95 (0-908912-85-4) Paul & Co Pubs.
Porter, Francis K. From Belfast to Peking, 1866-1869: A Young Irishman in China. McCracken, L. J., ed. & intro. by. LC 97-127973. 160p. 1996. 39.50 (0-7165-2599-2, Pub. by Irish Acad Pr) Intl Spec Bk.
Porter, Frank. Corrosion Resistance of Zinc & Zinc Alloys. (Corrosion Technology Ser.: Vol. 6). (Illus.). 536p. 1994. text 210.00 (0-8247-9213-0) Dekker.
— Zinc Handbook: Properties, Processing & Use in Design. (Mechanical Engineering Ser.: Vol. 73). (Illus.). 648p. 1991. text 225.00 (0-8247-8340-9) Dekker.
Porter, Frank W., III, compiled by. Native American Basketry: An Annotated Bibliography, 10. LC 87-37570. (Art Reference Collection Ser.: No. 10). 249p. 1988. lib. bdg. 55.00 (0-313-25363-3, PBY/, Greenwood Pr) Greenwood.
Porter, Frank W., III, ed. The Art of Native American Basketry: A Living Legacy, 5. LC 89-26008. (Contributions to the Study of Anthropology Ser.: No. 5). 368p. 1990. 75.00 (0-313-26716-2, PAH/, Greenwood Pr) Greenwood.
— Strategies for Survival: American Indians in the Eastern United States, 15. LC 85-30189. (Contributions in Ethnic Studies: No. 15). 248p. 1986. 55.00 (0-313-25253-X, PST/, Greenwood Pr) Greenwood.
Porter, Frank W., 3rd, ed. see DeAngelis, Therese.
Porter, Frank W., 3rd, ed. see Dramer, Kim.
Porter, Gail, ed. Guide to NIST (National Institute of Standards & Technology) 116p. (Orig.). (C). 1994. pap. text 40.00 (0-7881-0746-1) DIANE Pub.
Porter, Gail & Layman, Sue. A Perfect Rose. Scoggan, Nita, ed. LC 86-61447. 100p. (Orig.). 1986. pap. 3.95 (0-910487-09-X) Royalty Pub.
Porter, Gareth. A Peace Denied: The United States, Vietnam, & the Paris Agreement. LC 75-3890. (Illus.). 381p. reprint ed. pap. 118.20 (0-608-17410-6, 205643400067) Bks Demand.
— Vietnam: The Politics of Bureaucratic Socialism. LC 92-54976. (Politics & International Relations of Southeast Asia Ser.). (Illus.). 256p. 1993. text 32.50 (0-8014-2168-3) Cornell U Pr.
Porter, Gareth & Brown, Janet W. Global Environmental Politics. 2nd ed. LC 95-19877. (Dilemmas in World Politics Ser.). (Illus.). 256p. (C). 1995. pap. 25.00 (0-8133-2182-4, Pub. by Westview) HarpC.
Porter, Gareth, et al. Global Environmental Politics. 3rd ed. (Dilemmas in World Politics Ser.). 300p. 1999. pap. 24.00 (0-8133-6845-6) Westview.
Porter, Gareth, jt. auth. see Hildebrand, George C.
***Porter, Gary.** Go Naked 2. 80p. 1999. 14.95 (0-86719-255-0) Last Gasp.
Porter, Gary. Intro to Business Pamphlet: Fin. (C). 1995. pap. text 4.00 (0-15-502837-5) Harcourt Coll Pubs.
— Introduction to Accounting. (C). 2001. text 101.50 (0-03-024318-1) Harcourt Coll Pubs.
Porter, Gary & Norton, Curtis. Financial Accounting. 624p. (C). 1995. teacher ed. write for info. (0-15-501676-8) Harcourt Coll Pubs.
— Financial Accounting. 526p. (C). 1995. pap. text, teacher ed. 35.00 (0-15-501675-X) Harcourt Coll Pubs.
Porter, Gary, et al. Financial Accounting. 400p. 1995. pap. text. write for info. (0-614-18305-7) Harcourt Coll Pubs.
— PR Set 1 Financial Accounting. 64p. (C). 1995. student ed. 28.50 (0-15-501680-6) Dryden Pr.
Porter, Gary A. Financial Accounting. alternate ed. LC 95-71950. (Dryden Series in Accounting). 1997. 95.50 (0-03-018204-2) Harcourt Coll Pubs.
— Financial Accounting: The Impact on Decision Makers. 2nd ed. 1997. 97.50 (0-03-027099-5) Harcourt Coll Pubs.
— Financial Accounting: The Impact on Decision Makers. 2nd ed. 1998. 95.50 (0-03-022053-X) Holt R&W.
Porter, Gary A., ed. Accounting Guide for Common Interest Realty Associations: An Analysis of the AICPA Guidelines. (C). 1991. pap. 12.95 (0-941301-18-4) CAI.
Porter, Gary A., et al. PPC's Homeowners' Association Tax Library. 1997. ring bd. 125.00 (0-7646-0210-1) Prctnrs Pub Co.
***Porter, Gary A., et al.** PPC's Homeowners' Association Tax Library. 1999. ring bd. 138.00 (0-7646-0817-7) Prctnrs Pub Co.
Porter-Gaylord, Laurel. I Love My Daddy Because... LC 90-2865. (Illus.). 20p. (J). (ps-3). 1991. 7.99 (0-525-44624-9, Dutton Child) Peng Put Young Read.
— I Love My Mommy Because. . . LC 90-2792. (Illus.). 24p. (J). (ps). 1991. 7.99 (0-525-44625-7, Dutton Child) Peng Put Young Read.
Porter, Gene S. At the Foot of the Rainbow. 1990. reprint ed. lib. bdg. 27.95 (0-89968-543-9) Buccaneer Bks.
— Bird Woman. 29.95 (0-8488-1527-0) Amereon Ltd.
— Birds of the Bible. 52.95 (0-8488-0884-3) Amereon Ltd.
— Birds of the Bible. 1986. reprint ed. lib. bdg. 35.95 (0-89966-529-2) Buccaneer Bks.
— Birds of the Limberlost. 35.95 (0-8488-1526-2) Amereon Ltd.
— Birds of the Limberlost. 1998. lib. bdg. 37.95 (1-56723-127-6) Yestermorrow.
— Firebird. 60.00 (0-8488-1528-9) Amereon Ltd.
— Friends in Feathers. 1998. lib. bdg. 70.95 (1-56723-125-X) Yestermorrow.
— Homing with the Birds. 32.95 (0-8488-1449-5) Amereon Ltd.
— Homing with the Birds. 1986. reprint ed. lib. bdg. 35.95 (0-89966-530-6) Buccaneer Bks.
— Jesus of the Emeralds. 80.00 (0-8488-1525-4) Amereon Ltd.
— Jesus of the Emeralds. 1994. 80.00 (1-56723-128-4) Yestermorrow.
— Let Us Highly Resolve. 39.50 (0-8488-1529-7) Amereon Ltd.
— The Magic Garden. 1990. reprint ed. lib. bdg. 27.95 (0-89968-544-7) Buccaneer Bks.
— Morning Face. 20.95 (0-8488-0872-X) Amereon Ltd.
— Moths of the Limberlost. 42.95 (0-8488-0699-9) Amereon Ltd.
— Music of Wild, Pt. 1. 19.95 (0-8488-0611-5) Amereon Ltd.
— Music of Wild, Pt. 2. 17.95 (0-8488-0612-3) Amereon Ltd.
— Music of Wild, Pt. 3. 17.95 (0-8488-0613-1) Amereon Ltd.
— The Song of the Cardinal. 1990. reprint ed. lib. bdg. 21.95 (0-89968-545-5) Buccaneer Bks.
— Tales You Won't Believe. 25.95 (0-8488-0871-1) Amereon Ltd.
— White Flag. 30.95 (0-89190-943-5) Amereon Ltd.
— Wings. 39.95 (0-8488-0883-5) Amereon Ltd.
— Wings. 1986. reprint ed. lib. bdg. 16.95 (0-89966-531-4) Buccaneer Bks.
***Porter, Gene Stratton.** Freckles. (Great Stories Ser.). 2000. pap. 9.99 (1-56179-796-0) Focus Family.
Porter, Gene Stratton. Moths of the Limberlost. 1986. reprint ed. lib. bdg. 25.95 (0-89966-512-8) Buccaneer Bks.
Porter, George, ed. Chemistry in Microtime - Selected Writings on Flash Photolysis, Free Radicals & the Excited State. LC 97-171848. 600p. 1997. 87.00 (1-86094-015-3); 49.00 (1-86094-021-8) World Scientific Pub.
***Porter, George A.** Pet ER: Memoirs of an Animal Doctor. LC 99-61912. 248p. 1999. 24.95 (1-57736-149-0, Hillsboro Pr) Providence Hse.
Porter, George R. The Progress of the Nation: In Its Various Social & Economic Relations from the Beginning of the 19th Century. LC 77-85189. (Reprints of Economic Classics Ser.). xvi, 735p. 1970. reprint ed. 65.00 (0-678-00538-9) Kelley.
Porter, George S. Inscriptions from Gravestones in the Old Burying Ground, Norwich Town, Connecticut. (Illus.). 177p. 1996. pap. 18.00 (0-7884-0479-2, P567) Heritage Bk.
— Inscriptions from Gravestones, Norwich Town, Conn. Orig. Title: Founders of Norwich. (Illus.). 171p. 1997. reprint ed. pap. 21.00 (0-8328-5457-3) Higginson Bk Co.
— Inscriptions from Gravestones, Norwich Town, Conn., 4 vols., Vols. I-IV. Frost, Josephine C., ed. Orig. Title: Founders of Norwich. (Illus.). 171p. 1997. reprint ed. lib. bdg. 31.00 (0-8328-5456-5) Higginson Bk Co.
Porter, Georgeanne B. Germany, Federal Republic Of. LC 86-14110. (World Education Ser.). (Illus.). 192p. (Orig.). (C). 1986. pap. text 20.00 (0-910054-84-3) Am Assn Coll Registrars.
Porter, Gerald. The English Occupational Song. (Umea Studies in the Humanities: No. 105). 184p. (Orig.). 1992. pap. 55.00 (91-7174-649-8) Coronet Bks.
Porter, Gerald J. & Hill, David R. Interactive Linear Algebra in MathCAD. (Textbooks in Mathematical Sciences Ser.). 516p. 1996. pap. 42.95 (0-387-94608-X) Spr-Verlag.
Porter, Gillian, jt. ed. see Handoussa, Heba.
Porter, Ginny, jt. auth. see Holleman, Jack.
Porter, Glenn. Encyclopedia of American Economic History, 3 vols., Set. LC 79-4946. 1232p. 1980. 350.00 (0-684-16271-7, Scribners Ref) Mac Lib Ref.
— Regional Economic History: The Mid-Alantic Area since 1700. 92p. 1976. pap. write for info. (0-914650-13-0) Hagley Museum.
— The Rise of Big Business, 1865-1920. 2nd ed. Eisenstadt, A. S. & Franklin, John H., eds. (American History Ser.). (Illus.). 120p. 1992. pap. text 11.95 (0-88295-882-8) Harlan Davidson.
— The Workers' World at Hagley. rev. ed. Hinsley, Jacqueline & Kaufmann, Joy, eds. LC 92-53198. 64p. 1992. reprint ed. pap. text 9.95 (0-914650-30-0) Hagley Museum.
— The Workers' World at Hagley. rev. ed. (Illus.). 64p. 1982. pap. 9.95 (0-914650-21-1) Hagley Museum.
Porter, Glenn & Livesay, Harold C. Merchants & Manufacturers: Studies in the Changing Structure of Nineteenth-Century Marketing. LC 72-156071. 269p. reprint ed. pap. 83.40 (0-8357-6706-X, 203526800094) Bks Demand.
— Merchants & Manufacturers: Studies in the Changing Structure of 19th-Century Marketing. 276p. 1989. reprint ed. pap. text 8.95 (0-929587-10-3, Elephant Paperbacks) I R Dee.
Porter, Glenn, ed. see Blackford, Mansel G.
Porter, Glenn, ed. see Freyer, Tony A.
Porter, Glenn, ed. see Giebelhaus, August W.
Porter, Glenn, ed. see Pratt, Joseph A.
Porter, Glenn, ed. see Tedlow, Richard S.
Porter, Glenn, ed. see Yeager, Mary.
Porter, Greg. Black Death: The Bubonic Plague Board Game. 8p. 1993. pap. text 9.95 (0-943891-25-6, 6001) Blacksburg Tactical.
— Complete Omniversal Role-Playing System (CORPS) 2nd ed. (Illus.). 144p. 1995. pap. text 19.95 (0-943891-28-0, 7101) Blacksburg Tactical.
***Porter, Greg.** Corps down 'n Flames: It's the End of the World... (Illus.). 72p. 1999. pap. text 12.00 (0-943891-37-X, BTRC 7105, Pub. by Blacksburg Tactical) Alliance Bk Co.
Porter, Greg. CORPS Dreamtime: Worldbook for CORPS. (Illus.). 48p. 1995. pap. text 9.95 (0-943891-30-2, 7102) Blacksburg Tactical.
— CORPS Vehicle Design System: Any Vehicle, Any Game. (Illus.). 160p. 1998. pap. text 20.00 (0-943891-35-3) Blacksburg Tactical.
— Epiphany: The Legends of Hyperborea. (Illus.). 48p. 1996. pap. 9.95 (0-943891-33-7) Blacksburg Tactical.
— Guns! Guns! Guns! Weapon Design for Any RPG. 3rd ed. (Illus.). 136p. 1991. pap. text 16.00 (0-943891-19-1, 4001) Blacksburg Tactical.
— Macho Women with Guns. 3rd ed. (Illus.). 72p. 1994. pap. text 9.95 (0-943891-27-2, 3005) Blacksburg Tactical.
— More Guns! Weapon Compendium for Any Role-Playing Game. (Illus.). 232p. 1993. pap. text 19.95 (0-943891-26-4, 4002) Blacksburg Tactical.
— Slag! Combat on the High Frontier. 2nd ed. (Illus.). 28p. 1996. pap. text 7.95 (0-943891-32-9) Blacksburg Tactical.
— Time Capsules 2: Adventures for TimeLords. (Illus.). 60p. 1993. pap. text 8.95 (0-943891-22-1, 0004) Blacksburg Tactical.
Porter, Greg & Van Sciver. Power Quality Solutions: Case Studies for Troubleshooters. 283p. (C). 1998. 79.00 (0-13-020730-6) P-H.
Porter, Greg & VanSciver, Andy. Power Quality Solutions: 25 Case Studies for Troubleshooters. LC 98-8456. (Illus.). 277p. 1998. 79.00 (0-88173-279-6, 0420) Fairmont Pr.
Porter, Greg, et al. More Excuses to Kill Things: Adventures for Macho Women with Guns. (Illus.). 48p. 1995. pap. text 9.95 (0-943891-31-0) Blacksburg Tactical.
Porter, Greg, ed. see Rice, Ed.
Porter, H., jt. auth. see Wortabet, John.
Porter, H. Boone. The Day of Light: The Biblical & Liturgical Meaning of Sunday. 104p. 1988. pap. 7.95 (0-912405-40-6, Pastoral Press) OR Catholic.
Porter, Hal. The Extra. 250p. (Orig.). 1987. pap. text 14.95 (0-7022-2052-3, Pub. by Univ Queensland Pr) Intl Spec Bk.
— Hal Porter. Lord, Mary, ed. (Illus.). 408p. 1989. pap. 14.95 (0-7022-1466-3, Pub. by Univ Queensland Pr) Intl Spec Bk.
— The Tilted Cross. 266p. 1989. reprint ed. pap. 14.95 (0-7022-2183-X, Pub. by Univ Queensland Pr) Intl Spec Bk.
— The Watcher on the Cast-Iron Balcony. (Orig.). 1993. pap. 16.95 (0-7022-2558-4, Pub. by Univ Queensland Pr) Intl Spec Bk.
Porter, Harvey, jt. auth. see Wortabet, John.
Porter, Hayden S. Essentials of Lotus 1-2-3 for Macintosh. (Illus.). 368p. (C). 1992. disk 49.95 (1-56527-008-8); disk 24.95 (1-56527-009-6) Course Tech.
***Porter, Henry.** Remembrance Day: A Novel. LC 99-87808. 368p. 2000. pap. 25.00 (0-684-86549-1) S&S Trade.
Porter, Henry. The Two Angry Women of Abingdon. LC 70-133722. (Tudor Facsimile Texts. Old English Plays Ser.: No. 87). reprint ed. 49.50 (0-404-53387-6) AMS Pr.
Porter, Horace. Campaigning with Grant. (Illus.). 608p. 2000. pap. 19.95 (0-8032-8763-1) U of Nebr Pr.
Porter, Horace A. Stealing the Fire: The Art & Protest of James Baldwin. LC 88-27806. 240p. Date not set. reprint ed. pap. 74.40 (0-608-20690-3, 207179800002) Bks Demand.
Porter, Hugh J. & Houser, Lynn. Seashells of North Carolina. Norris, Jeannie, ed. Orig. Title: Sea Shells Common to North Carolina. (Illus.). 133p. 1998. spiral bd. 12.00 (0-9663187-0-6, Pub. by NC Sea Grant) Blair.
Porter, Ian H. Imperial Germany. (C). 1995. pap. text 15.00 (0-582-03496-5) Addison-Wesley.
Porter, J., ed. Highway Research: Sharing the Benefits. 456p. 1991. text 126.00 (0-7277-1635-2, Pub. by T Telford) RCH.
Porter, J. & McAdam, K. Tuberculosis: Back to the Future. 1993. pap. text 100.00 (0-471-94346-0) Wiley.

P

An Asterisk (*) at the beginning of an entry indicates that the title is appearing for the first time.

Porter, J. C. & Jezova, D., eds. Circulating Regulatory Factors & Neuroendocrine Function. LC 90-7365. (AEMB Candidate Ser.). (Illus.). 520p. (C). 1990. text 174.00 (*0-306-43609-4*, Kluwer Plenum) Kluwer Academic.

Porter, J. L., ed. Giant Cities of Bashan & Syria's Holy Places. 371p. (C). 1991. 125.00 (*1-85077-198-7*, Pub. by Darf Pubs Ltd) St Mut.

Porter, J. M., ed. Sophia & Praxis: The Boundaries of Politics. LC 84-12154. 160p. (Orig.). reprint ed. pap. 49.60 (*0-7837-2599-X*, 204276300006) Bks Demand.

Porter, J. R. The Illustrated Guide to the Bible. (Illus.). 288p. 1998. reprint ed. pap. 22.50 (*0-19-521462-5*) OUP.

***Porter, J. R.** The Jesus of History, the Christ of Faith. Bentley, Peter, ed. LC 98-37404. (Illus.). 240p. 1999. 35.00 (*0-19-521429-3*) OUP.

Porter, J. R., ed. The Illustrated Guide to the Bible. (Illus.). 288p. (J). 1995. ring bd. 45.00 (*0-19-521159-6*) OUP.

Porter, J. R. & Woods, R. G. Extensions & Absolutes of Hausdorff Spaces. (Illus.). 860p. 1987. 146.95 (*0-387-96212-3*) Spr-Verlag.

Porter, J. R., jt. ed. see Armstrong, J. T.

Porter, J. R., jt. ed. see Janis, A. I.

Porter, J. R., tr. see Westermann, Claus.

Porter, J. W. A Genealogy of the Descendants of Richard Porter, Who Settled at Weymouth, Mass., 1635, & Allied Families: Also Some Account of the Descendants of John Porter, Who Settled at Hingham, Mass., 1635, & Salem (Danvers) Mass., 1644. 344p. 1989. reprint ed. pap. 51.50 (*0-8328-0979-9*); reprint ed. lib. bdg. 59.50 (*0-8328-0978-0*) Higginson Bk Co.

Porter, Jack N. Confronting History & Holocaust: Collected Essays 1972-1982. (Illus.). 161p. 1997. reprint ed. pap. 10.00 (*0-932270-08-5*) Spencer Pr.

— Handbook of Cults, Sects & Self-Realization Groups. 95p. 1998. reprint ed. pap. 7.00 (*0-932270-03-4*) Spencer Pr.

— The Jew As Outsider: Historical & Contemporary Perspectives, Collected Essays. LC 80-6247. 235p. 1997. reprint ed. pap. 10.00 (*0-932270-09-3*) Spencer Pr.

— Jews & the Cults: Bibliography & Resource Guide. LC 81-67448. 55p. (YA). 1997. reprint ed. pap. 7.00 (*0-932270-20-4*) Spencer Pr.

— A Life of Mitzvah: Rabbi Joseph Mayer Jacobson: Boston's Premier Orthodox Jewish Leader. (Illus.). 125p. 1997. pap. 10.00 (*0-932270-15-8*) Spencer Pr.

— Notes of a Happy Sociologist. 30p. (Orig.). 1980. pap. 5.00 (*0-932270-04-2*) Spencer Pr.

— Student Protest & the Technocratic Society: The Case of ROTC. (Illus.). 146p. 1997. reprint ed. pap. 10.00 (*0-614-29568-8*) Spencer Pr.

Porter, Jack N., ed. Genocide & Human Rights: A Global Anthology. (Holocaust Studies). (Illus.). 362p. 1997. reprint ed. pap. 12.00 (*0-932270-07-7*) Spencer Pr.

— Jewish Partisan Poems & Stories from WWII. Ritchie, Esther, tr. (POL & YID.). 94p. 1998. pap. 10.00 (*0-932270-23-9*) Spencer Pr.

— Jewish Partisans: A Documentary of Jewish Resistance in the Soviet Union During World War II. Magal Institute Staff, tr. from HEB. LC 81-40258. Orig. Title: They Were Many. (Illus.). 311p. 1997. reprint ed. pap. 14.95 (*0-932270-10-7*) Spencer Pr.

— The Sociology of American Jews: A Critical Anthology. 2nd ed. 334p. 1997. reprint ed. pap. 10.00 (*0-932270-22-0*) Spencer Pr.

— Women in Chains: A Sourcebook on the Agunah. LC 95-9843. 288p. 1996. pap. 40.00 (*1-56821-440-5*) Aronson.

Porter, Jack N. & Doress, Irvin. Kids in Cults: Why They Join, Why They Stay, Why They Leave. 5th rev. ed. (Illus.). 22p. (Orig.). 1985. reprint ed. pap. 7.00 (*0-932270-02-6*) Spencer Pr.

Porter, Jack N. & Dreier, Peter. Jewish Radicalism: A Selected Anthology. 444p. 1997. reprint ed. pap. 20.00 (*0-932270-14-X*) Spencer Pr.

Porter, Jack N. & Glazer, Gerald S. Foreclosed Real Estate: Your Profit Opportunity. 2nd ed. (Illus.). 84p. 1995. reprint ed. pap. 24.95 (*0-932270-06-9*) Spencer Pr.

Porter, Jack N. & Merin, Yehuda, eds. Jewish Partisans Vol. 2: A Documentary of Jewish Resistance in the Soviet Union During World War II. Ritchie, Esther & Abrams, Ann, trs. from HEB. (Illus.). 314p. 1997. reprint ed. pap. 14.95 (*0-932270-11-5*) Spencer Pr.

Porter, Jack N. & Taplin, Ruth. Conflict & Conflict Resolution: A Sociological Introduction. (Illus.). 113p. 1997. 20.00 (*0-932270-18-2*); pap. 10.00 (*0-932270-19-0*) Spencer Pr.

— Conflict & Conflict Resolution: A Sociological Introduction with Updated Bibliography & Theory Section. LC 87-8215. 114p. (Orig.). (C). 1987. lib. bdg. 42.00 (*0-8191-6368-6*) U Pr of Amer.

Porter, Jack W. & Henrysson, Harald. A Jussi Bjoerling Discography. LC 82-81146. 192p. (Orig.). 1982. pap. 19.95 (*0-9608546-0-6*) J Bjoerling.

Porter, Jack W. & Stineman, William F. The Catholic Church in Greencastle, Putnam County, Indiana, 1848-1978. LC 78-65724. (Illus.). 1979. 14.95 (*0-9602352-0-5*) St Paul the Apostle.

Porter, Jack W., jt. auth. see Stineman, William F.

Porter, James, ed. Rhetorical Ethics & Internetworked Writing. LC 97-43391. 1998. pap. 24.95 (*1-56750-323-3*); text 73.25 (*1-56750-322-5*) Ablx Pub.

— Selected Reports in Ethnomusicology Vol. 3, No. 1: The Traditional Music of Europeans in America. LC 76-640181. (Illus.). vii, 260p. 1978. pap. text 11.95 (*0-88287-011-4*) UCLA Dept Ethnom.

Porter, James & Gower, Herschel. Jeannie Robertson: Emergent Singer, Transformative Voice. (Publications of the American Folklore Society). 408p. (C). 1995. text 48.00 (*0-87049-904-1*) U of Tenn Pr.

Porter, James & Racz, Attila J., eds. Issues in the Conceptualization of Music. LC 76-640181. (Selected Reports in Ethnomusicology: Vol. 7). (Illus.). xi, 176p. (Orig.). 1988. audio 22.95 (*0-318-36431-X*) UCLA Dept Ethnom.

Porter, James & Sullivan, Patricia, eds. Opening Spaces: Writing Technologies & Critical Research Practices. LC 97-22413. 1997. pap. 24.95 (*1-56750-308-X*) Ablx Pub.

Porter, James, et al. The World's Music: General Perspectives & Reference Tools. (Encyclopedia of World Music Ser.: Vol. 10). (Illus.). 800p. 1998. 150.00 (*0-8153-1084-6*) Garland.

Porter, James, ed. see Bohlman, Philip V.

Porter, James, ed. see Rahkonen, Carl.

Porter, James, ed. see Schuursma, Ann.

Porter, James, jt. ed. see Sullivan, Patricia.

Porter, James A. Modern Negro Art. LC 92-37421. (Moorland-Spingarn Ser.). (C). 1992. 24.95 (*0-88258-163-5*) Howard U Pr.

— Modern Negro Art. LC 69-18593. (American Negro: His History & Literature. Series 2). 1979. reprint ed. 15.95 (*0-405-01889-4*) Ayer.

Porter, James E. Audience & Rhetoric: An Archaeological Composition of the Discourse Community. 204p. (C). 1991. pap. text 21.00 (*0-13-050675-3*, 640601) P-H.

***Porter, James I.** Invention of Dionysus. 2000. pap. text 16.95 (*0-8047-3700-2*) Stanford U Pr.

— Nietzsche & The Philosophy of The Future. 1999. pap. text 19.95 (*0-8047-3698-7*) Stanford U Pr.

Porter, James I., ed. Constructions of the Classical Body. LC 98-48617. (Body, in Theory Ser.). (Illus.). 408p. 1999. text 54.50 (*0-472-10908-1*, 10908) U of Mich Pr.

***Porter, James W. & Porter, Karen G.** Linkages Between Ecosystems in the South Florida Hydroscape. 600p. 1999. 89.95 (*0-8493-2026-7*) CRC Pr.

Porter, James W., jt. ed. see Bareis, Charles J.

Porter, Jane. Pastor's Fire-Side, 2 vols. LC 75-162887. (Bentley's Standard Novels Ser.: Nos. 18 & 19). reprint ed. 25.00 (*0-404-54560-2*); reprint ed. write for info. (*0-318-50685-8*) AMS Pr.

— The Scottish Chiefs. LC 91-8521. (Scribners Illustrated Classics Ser.). (Illus.). 520p. (YA). 1991. 28.00 (*0-684-19340-X*) Scribner.

— The Scottish Chiefs. (Illus.). 1994. reprint ed. lib. bdg. 49.95 (*1-56849-533-1*) Buccaneer Bks.

— Thaddeus of Warsaw. rev. ed. LC 70-162883. (Bentley's Standard Novels Ser.: No. 4). (Illus.). reprint ed. 37.50 (*0-404-54404-5*) AMS Pr.

Porter, Jane, ed. see Seaward, Edward.

Porter, Janice. Could I Have Your Recipe? (Illus.). 115p. (Orig.). 1981. pap. 5.95 (*0-9607670-0-2*) J Porter Bks.

Porter, Janice L. Count Your Way Through Greece. (Illus.). 24p. (J). (gr. 1-4). 1996. pap. text 5.95 (*0-87614-973-5*) Lerner Pub.

Porter, Jean. Moral Action & Christian Ethics. (New Studies in Christian Ethics: No. 5). 252p. (C). 1999. pap. text 19.95 (*0-521-65710-5*) Cambridge U Pr.

— Natural & Divine Law: Reclaiming the Tradition for Christian Ethics. 320p. 1999. pap. 28.00 (*0-8028-4697-1*) Eerdmans.

— The Recovery of Virtue: The Relevance of Aquinas for Christian Ethics. 300p. 1990. text 28.95 (*0-664-21924-1*) Westminster John Knox.

Porter, Jeane. Key West: Conch Smiles. LC 98-25156. (Illus.). 344p. 1998. pap. 20.00 (*0-931541-64-6*) Mancorp Pub.

***Porter, Jeanne.** Leading Ladies: New Images for Leadership from Biblical & Contemporary Women. 224p. 2000. pap. 14.95 (*1-880913-45-3*, Pub. by Innisfree Pr) Consort Bk Sales.

Porter, Jeanne C. Selected Works from the Collection of Samuel Gallu: Exhibition Catalogue. (Illus.). 68p. 1981. pap. 5.00 (*0-911209-21-2*) Palmer Mus Art.

Porter, Jeanne C. & Musto, Ronald G., eds. Baroque Naples: A Documentary History: c.1600-1800. LC 99-88391. (Documentary History of Naples Ser.: Vol. 4). (Illus.). 300p. 2000. pap. 25.00 (*0-934977-52-6*) Italica Pr.

Porter, Jene. Political Philosophy: The Search for Humanity & Order. LC 98-122422. 514p. 1997. pap. text 55.00 (*0-13-063991-5*) P-H.

Porter, Jennie H. Johnson. Hannah Johnson & Olly Palmer, with Some of Their Kinsfolk. 83p. 1997. reprint ed. pap. 16.00 (*0-8328-9347-1*); reprint ed. lib. bdg. 26.00 (*0-8328-9346-3*) Higginson Bk Co.

Porter, Jennifer E. & McLaren, Darcee L., eds. Star Trek & Sacred Ground: Explorations of Star Trek, Religion & American Culture. LC 98-52147. 320p. (C). 1999. text 62.50 (*0-7914-4333-7*) State U NY Pr.

— Star Trek & Sacred Ground: Explorations of Star Trek, Religion & American Culture. LC 98-52147. 320p. (C). 1999. pap. text 20.95 (*0-7914-4334-5*) State U NY Pr.

***Porter, Jenny Lind, tr. from FRO.** Helinand of Froidmont: Verses on Death. LC 99-221487. (Cistercian Fathers Ser.: Vol. CF61). 151p. 1999. 34.95 (*0-87907-461-2*) Cistercian Pubns.

— Helinand of Froidmont: Verses on Death. (Cistercian Fathers Ser.: Vol. CF61). 151p. 1999. pap. 15.95 (*0-87907-661-5*) Cistercian Pubns.

Porter, Jessica. Unbridled Love. large type ed. (Linford Romance Library). 288p. 1992. pap. 16.99 (*0-7089-7289-6*) Ulverscroft.

Porter, Joe. Simple Changes: The Boomer's Guide to a Healthier, Happier Life. LC 98-33950. 130p. 1998. pap. 9.95 (*1-886039-35-6*) Addicus Bks.

Porter, Joe A. Eelgrass. LC 77-4996. 1977. pap. 4.95 (*0-8112-0655-6*, NDP438, Pub. by New Directions) Norton.

— The Kentucky Stories. LC 82-49067. 144p. 1983. 17.95 (*0-8018-3008-7*) Johns Hopkins.

***Porter, Joe Ashby.** Resident Aliens. 160p. 2000. 19.95 (*1-56663-332-X*, Pub. by I R Dee) Natl Bk Netwk.

Porter, John. AS/400 Information Engineering. (IBM Ser.). 352p. 1993. 45.00 (*0-07-050623-X*) McGraw.

— Creating Powerful Promotions with Non-Foods in Supermarkets. 128p. 1992. spiral bd. 19.95 (*0-9631297-5-9*) Agate MN.

— The Vertical Mosaic: An Analysis of Social Class & Power in Canada. LC 65-3947. 1965. pap. text 21.95 (*0-8020-6055-2*) U of Toronto Pr.

Porter, John, tr. Anglo-Saxon Riddles. 112p. 1995. pap. 8.95 (*1-898281-13-0*) Paul & Co Pubs.

— Beowulf: Text & Translation. 192p. (Orig.). 1992. pap. text 16.95 (*0-9516209-2-4*, Pub. by Anglo-Saxon Bks) Paul & Co Pubs.

Porter, John, et al. Lawyers in God's World: The Love Command as Modern Law. (Jubilee Ser.: No. 2). 24p. (C). pap. text 1.00 (*0-685-50070-5*) Shiloh Pubns.

Porter, John, ed. see Coffman, Taylor.

Porter, John, jt. ed. see Phillips, Marcia.

Porter, John A. The Vertical Mosaic: An Analysis of Social Class & Power in Canada. LC 78-418980. (Studies in the Structure of Power: Decision-Making in Canada: No. 2). (Illus.). 646p. reprint ed. pap. 200.00 (*0-8357-6365-X*, 203571900096) Bks Demand.

Porter, John D. & Grange, John M., eds. Tuberculosis: An International Perspective. LC 98-43593. 509p. 1999. 42.00 (*1-86094-143-5*, Pub. by Imperial College) World Scientific Pub.

Porter, John D., Jr., jt. auth. see Veazey, Steve.

Porter, John M. Vascular Surgery, 2000. 2000. 86.00 (*0-8151-2736-7*, 31319) Mosby Inc.

— Vascular Surgery, 2001. 2001. 86.00 (*0-8151-2737-5*, 31320) Mosby Inc.

— Vascular Surgery, 2002. 2002. 86.00 (*0-8151-2738-3*, 31321) Mosby Inc.

Porter, John M., ed. 1997 Book of Vascular Surgery. (Illus.). 560p. (C). (gr. 13). 1997. text 86.00 (*0-8151-6800-4*, 22715) Mosby Inc.

Porter, John M. & Taylor, Lloyd M., Jr., eds. Basic Data Underlying Clinical Decision-Making in Vascular Surgery. 198p. 1994. 75.00 (*0-942219-71-6*) Quality Med Pub.

Porter, John R. Studies in Euripides' Orestes. LC 94-16657. (Mnemosyne, Bibliotheca Classica Batava. Supplementum). 1994. 120.00 (*90-04-09662-0*) Brill Academic Pubs.

Porter, John T. New Disaster Relief Handbook. Lionheart, John H., ed. (Illus.). 91p. 1997. pap. 24.95 (*0-9666685-0-2*) Biggs Pub.

Porter, John W. Biosynthesis of Isoprenoid Compounds, Vol. 1. Spurgeon, Sandra L., ed. LC 80-28511. 574p. reprint ed. pap. 178.00 (*0-8357-7256-X*, 205630200056) Bks Demand.

— Record of Events in Norfolk County, from April 19th, 1861, to May 10th, 1862, with a History of the Soldiers & Sailors of Norfolk Co., Norfolk City & Portsmouth Who Served in the Confederate Army or Navy. (Illus.). 366p. 1997. reprint ed. lib. bdg. 42.00 (*0-8328-6516-8*) Higginson Bk Co.

***Porter, Jonathan.** Macau: The Imaginary City. LC 99-47016. 256p. 2000. pap. 16.00 (*0-8133-3749-6*, Pub. by Westview) HarpC.

Porter, Jonathan. Tseng Kuo-Fan's Private Bureaucracy. LC 72-619560. (China Research Monographs: No. 9). 148p. 1972. pap. 5.00 (*0-912966-10-6*) IEAS.

Porter, Joseph A., ed. Critical Essays on Shakespeare's Romeo & Juliet. LC 96-53884. 1997. 49.00 (*0-7838-0016-9*, G K Hall & Co) Mac Lib Ref.

Porter, Joseph A., ed. see Southeastern Renaissance Conference Staff.

Porter, Joseph C. Paper Medicine Man: John Gregory Bourke & His American West. LC 85-40943. (Illus.). 352p. 1989. pap. 17.95 (*0-8061-2218-8*) U of Okla Pr.

Porter, Joseph C., jt. auth. see Goetzmann, William H.

Porter, Joyce. Dead Easy for Dover. (Inspector Dover of Scotland Yard Ser.). 176p. 1991. reprint ed. pap. 6.50 (*0-88150-212-X*, Foul Play) Norton.

— Dover: The Collected Short Stories. LC 95-30642. (Inspector Dover of Scotland Yard Ser.). 304p. 1995. 20.00 (*0-88150-342-8*, Foul Play) Norton.

— Dover & the Claret Tappers. (Inspector Dover of Scotland Yard Ser.). 208p. 1989. pap. 6.00 (*0-88150-245-6*, Foul Play) Norton.

— Dover & the Unkindest Cut of All. (Inspector Dover of Scotland Yard Ser.). 188p. 1990. reprint ed. pap. 5.95 (*0-88150-174-3*, Foul Play) Norton.

— Dover Beats the Band. (Inspector Dover of Scotland Yard Ser.). 170p. 1993. pap. 6.00 (*0-88150-268-5*, Foul Play) Norton.

— Dover Goes to Pott. (Inspector Dover of Scotland Yard Ser.). 192p. 1990. reprint ed. pap. 5.95 (*0-88150-173-5*, Foul Play) Norton.

— Dover One. (Inspector Dover of Scotland Yard Ser.). 176p. 1989. reprint ed. pap. 6.95 (*0-88150-134-4*, Foul Play) Norton.

— Dover Strikes Again. (Inspector Dover of Scotland Yard Ser.). 202p. 1991. reprint ed. pap. 5.95 (*0-88150-211-1*, Foul Play) Norton.

— Dover Three. (Inspector Dover of Scotland Yard Ser.). 188p. 1989. reprint ed. pap. 6.50 (*0-88150-147-6*, Foul Play) Norton.

— Dover Two. (Inspector Dover of Scotland Yard Ser.). 192p. 1989. reprint ed. pap. 7.95 (*0-88150-135-2*, Foul Play) Norton.

— Humanities on the Go! 80p. (C). 1992. pap. text 13.95 (*0-8403-7848-3*) Kendall-Hunt.

— It's Murder with Dover. (Inspector Dover of Scotland Yard Ser.). 192p. 1992. pap. 6.00 (*0-88150-233-2*, Foul Play) Norton.

— A Meddler & Her Murder. 176p. 1992. pap. 5.95 (*0-89733-322-5*) Academy Chi Pubs.

Porter, Judith D. Black Child, White Child: The Development of Racial Attitudes. (Illus.). 278p. 1971. pap. 15.00 (*0-674-07611-7*) HUP.

Porter, Judy K. Cycle of Seasons: Spiral of Life. 68p. 1993. pap. write for info. (*0-9636230-0-1*) Transport Pub.

Porter, K., jt. auth. see Ellinwood, Leonard.

Porter, K. M., jt. auth. see Greaves, I.

Porter, Karen G., jt. auth. see Porter, James W.

Porter, Katherine. Katherine Porter: Paintings - Drawings. LC 91-70220. (Orig.). 1991. pap. 15.00 (*0-916606-21-X*) Bowdoin Coll.

Porter, Katherine Anne. The Collected Stories of Katherine Anne Porter. LC 79-10398. 504p. (C). 1979. pap. 16.00 (*0-15-618876-7*, Harvest Bks) Harcourt.

— The Days Before. LC 77-117827. (Essay Index Reprint Ser.). 1977. 21.95 (*0-8369-2066-X*) Ayer.

— Flowering Judas. Carr, Virginia S., ed. LC 92-35362. (Woman Writers: Text & Contexts Ser.). 216p. (C). 1993. text 32.00 (*0-8135-1978-0*); pap. text 14.00 (*0-8135-1979-9*) Rutgers U Pr.

— Flowering Judas & Other Stories. 1990. 15.95 (*0-15-131811-5*) Harcourt.

— Katherine Anne Porter's Poetry. Unrue, Darlene H., ed. & intro. by. LC 95-32494. (Illus.). 224p. 1996. 24.95 (*1-57003-084-7*) U of SC Pr.

— Letters of Katherine Anne Porter. LC 89-31240. (Illus.). 642p. 1981. pap. 16.95 (*0-87113-453-5*, Atlntc Mnthly) Grove-Atltic.

— Mae Franking's My Chinese Marriage: An Annotated Edition. Franking, Holly, ed. LC 91-12698. (Illus.). 159p. 1991. 16.95 (*0-292-75132-X*) U of Tex Pr.

— The Old Order: Stories of the South from Flowering Judas, Pale Horse, Pale Rider & The Leaning Tower. LC 66-380. 180p. (Orig.). 1955. pap. 9.00 (*0-15-668519-1*, Harvest Bks) Harcourt.

— Pale Horse, Pale Rider: Three Short Novels. 1990. 17.00 (*0-15-170755-3*) Harcourt.

— Ship of Fools. 31.95 (*0-8488-1129-1*) Amereon Ltd.

— Ship of Fools. 497p. 1984. reprint ed. pap. 13.95 (*0-316-71390-2*, Back Bay) Little.

— Uncollected Early Prose of Katherine Anne Porter. Alvarez, Ruth M. & Walsh, Thomas F., eds. LC 93-3361. (Illus.). 288p. 1994. 35.00 (*0-292-76544-4*) U of Tex Pr.

Porter, Kay, jt. auth. see Foster, Judy.

Porter, Kay M. & Foster, Judy L. Visual Athletics: Visualizations for Peak Sports Performance. 224p. 1990. pap. write for info. (*0-697-10987-9*) Brown & Benchmark.

Porter, Keith R., jt. ed. see Brinkley, B. R.

Porter, Kenneth W. The Black Seminoles: History of a Freedom-Seeking People. rev. ed. Amos, Alcione M. & Senter, Thomas P., eds. (Illus.). 352p. 1996. 29.95 (*0-8130-1451-4*) U Press Fla.

— The Negro on the American Frontier. LC 77-135872. 1973. reprint ed. 18.95 (*0-405-01983-1*) Ayer.

Porter, Kenneth W., jt. auth. see Clark, Malcolm, Jr.

Porter, Kenneth W., jt. auth. see Larson, Henrietta M.

Porter, Kent. Stretch Quick Pascal. 1990. pap. 24.95 (*0-13-851890-4*) P-H.

Porter, Kevin, ed. see Porter, Daniel J.

Porter, Keyes, ed. see Historical Records Survey Staff.

Porter, Kimberly K. Legacy in the Sand: United States Army Armament, Munitions & Chemical Command in Operations Desert Shield & Desert Storm. 240p. 1993. per. 23.00 (*0-16-061106-7*) USGPO.

Porter, Kingsley A. Construction of Lombard & Gothic Vaults. limited ed. 1911. 100.00 (*0-685-69851-3*) Elliots Bks.

Porter, Kirk H. History of Suffrage in the United States. LC 70-137272. reprint ed. 42.50 (*0-404-00207-2*) AMS Pr.

— History of Suffrage in the United States. LC 69-14039. 260p. 1969. reprint ed. lib. bdg. 38.50 (*0-8371-0620-6*, POHS, Greenwood Pr) Greenwood.

Porter, L., et al. The Law & the Treatment of Drug & Alcohol-Dependent Persons: A Comparative Study of Existing Legislation. 216p. 1986. pap. text 34.00 (*92-4-156093-2*, 1150243) World Health.

Porter-Ladousse, Gillian. Role Play. (Illus.). 192p. 1987. pap. text 13.95 (*0-19-437095-X*) OUP.

Porter-Lane, Esther. St. George & the Dragon. (J). (gr. 4 up). 1985. pap. 6.00 (*0-87602-249-2*) Anchorage.

Porter, Larry C. A Study of the Origins of the Church of Jesus Christ of Latter-Day Saints in the States of New York & Pennsylvania. (Dissertations in Latter-Day Saint History Ser.). (Illus.). 93p. Date not set. pap. 17.95 (*0-8425-2468-1*, BYU Studies) Brigham.

Porter, Larry C. & Black, Susan E., eds. The Prophet Joseph: Essays on the Life & Mission of Joseph Smith. LC 88-22638. viii, 359p. 1988. 17.95 (*0-87579-177-8*) Deseret Bk.

Porter, Larry C., jt. ed. see Black, Susan E.

***Porter, Laurence M.** Approaches to Teaching Baudelaire's Flowers of Evil. LC 99-52504. (Currents in Comparative Romance Languages & Literatures Ser.). 1999. pap. 18.00 (*0-87352-752-6*) Modern Lang.

Porter, Laurence M. The Crisis of French Symbolism. LC 89-45976. 288p. 1990. text 42.50 (*0-8014-2418-6*) Cornell U Pr.

***Porter, Laurence M., ed.** Approaches to Teaching Baudelaire's Flowers of Evil. LC 99-52504. 208p. 2000. 37.50 (*0-87352-751-8*) Modern Lang.

— A Gustave Flaubert Encyclopedia. 2001. lib. bdg. write for info. (*0-313-30744-X*) Greenwood.

Porter, Laurence M. & Gray, Eugene F., eds. Approaches to Teaching Flaubert's Madame Bovary. LC 95-13050. (Approaches to Teaching World Literature Ser.: No. 53). xv, 167p. 1995. pap. 18.00 (*0-87352-730-5*, AP53P); lib. bdg. 37.50 (*0-87352-729-1*, AP53C) Modern Lang.

P

Porter, Laurin. The Banished Prince: Time, Memory, & Ritual in the Late Plays of Eugene O'Neill. LC 88-20820. (Theater & Dramatic Studies: No. 54). 142p. reprint ed. pap. 44.10 (*0-8357-1934-0*, 2070660000l5) Bks Demand.

Porter, Lawrence M. The Interpretation of Dreams: Freud's Theories Revisited. LC 87-11940. (Masterwork Studies: No. 9). 152p. 1987. 25.95 (*0-8057-7971-X*) Macmillan.

Porter, Lee. Faculty Perceptions of Continuing Education at Syracuse University. 1970. 2.25 (*0-87060-013-3*, OCP 20) Syracuse U Cont Ed.

Porter, Les. Assessing Business Excellence. 288p. 1998. pap. text 39.95 (*0-7506-3985-7*) Buttrwrth-Heinemann.

Porter, Les, jt. auth. see Oakland, John S.

Porter, Les, jt. auth. see Tanner, Steve.

Porter, Lewis. The Jazz Reader. LC 97-25600. 1997. 29.00 (*0-02-864713-0*) Mac Lib Ref.

— John Coltrane: His Life & Music. LC 97-41995. (Michigan American Music Ser.). (Illus.). 448p. (C). 1998. 32.50 (*0-472-10161-7*, 10161) U of Mich Pr.

— John Coltrane: His Life & Music. (Michigan American Music Ser.). (Illus.). 448p. 2000. pap. 17.95 (*0-472-08643-X*, 08643) U of Mich Pr.

Porter, Lewis, ed. A Lester Young Reader. LC 90-24922. (Smithsonian Readers in American Music Ser.). (Illus.). 344p. 1991. pap. 19.95 (*1-56098-065-6*) Smithsonian.

Porter, Lewis, et al. Jazz: From Its Origins to the Present. LC 92-37368. 512p. (C). 1992. pap. text 61.00 (*0-13-512195-7*) P-H.

Porter, Lezlie. Nevada Education: Laying the Groundwork. unabridged ed. Sexton, Elizabeth, ed. 29p. 1997. 10.00 (*1-886306-14-1*) Nevada Policy.

Porter, Lindsay. The Car Bodywork Repair Manual. LC 85-61092. (Motoring Bks.). 292p. 1985. pap. write for info. (*0-85429-486-4*) GT Foulis.

— The Car Bodywork Repair Manual rev. ed. LC 91-71116. 293p. 1991. write for info. (*0-85429-919-X*) GT Foulis.

***Porter, Lindsay.** The Car Bodywork Repair Manual. 3rd rev. ed. (Illus.). 310p. 2000. 32.95 (*1-85960-657-1*, 130025AE, Pub. by Haynes Manuals) Motorbooks Intl.

Porter, Lindsay. Chevrolet Corvette: Purchase & Restoration Guide LC 95-79126. 224 p. 1996. write for info. (*0-85429-787-1*) GT Foulis.

— Chevrolet Corvette: Restoration Guide. (Illus.). 224p. 1996. pap. 21.95 (*0-7603-0325-8*) MBI Pubg.

— Classic Car Restoration Guide: The Complete Illustrated Step-By-Step Manual. (Illus.). 254p. 1994. 34.95 (*1-85010-890-0*, Pub. by J H Haynes & Co) Motorbooks Intl.

— Improve & Modify MGB. LC 88-80840. 240p. 1988. write for info. (*0-85429-749-9*) GT Foulis.

— Land Rover Defender Restoration Manual. LC 98-74169. (Illus.). 192p. 1999. 34.95 (*1-85960-600-8*, Pub. by J H Haynes & Co) Motorbooks Intl.

***Porter, Lindsay.** Land Rover Series I, II & III Restoration Manual. (Illus.). 287p. 2000. 34.95 (*1-85960-622-9*, 129320AE, Pub. by Haynes Manuals) Motorbooks Intl.

Porter, Lindsay. MG Midget & Austin-Healey Sprite: Guide to Purchase & DIY Restoration. 2nd ed. (Illus.). 288p. 1995. 29.95 (*0-85429-969-6*, Pub. by J H Haynes & Co) Motorbooks Intl.

***Porter, Lindsay.** MGB Restoration Manual. 2nd ed. (Illus.). 352p. 2000. 36.95 (*1-85960-607-5*, 128581AE, Pub. by Haynes Manuals) Motorbooks Intl.

Porter, Lindsay. Mini: Guide to Purchase & DIY Restoration. 2nd ed. LC 96-75169. (Illus.). 304p. 1996. 36.95 (*0-85429-971-8*, Pub. by J H Haynes & Co) Motorbooks Intl.

— Mini Guide to Purchase & DIY Restoration. 2nd ed. 1996. 36.95 (*0-524-29971-4*) Am Theol Lib.

— Porsche 911: Guide to Purchase & DIY Restoration. (Illus.). 256p. 1988. pap. 32.95 (*0-85429-475-9*, Pub. by GT Foulis) Haynes Manuals.

— Triumph Spitfire Guide to Purchase & DIY Restoration. (Illus.). 29.95 (*0-85429-728-6*, F728, Pub. by GT Foulis) Haynes Manuals.

— VW Beetle & Transporter: Guide to Purchase & DIY Restoration. (Illus.). 270p. 1994. 34.95 (*0-85429-474-0*, Pub. by J H Haynes & Co) Motorbooks Intl.

***Porter, Lindsay.** VW Golf & Jetta Restoration Manual. (Illus.). 192p. 2000. 34.95 (*1-85960-448-X*, 130024AE, Pub. by J H Haynes & Co) Motorbooks Intl.

Porter, Lindsay & Pollard, Dave. Ford Fiesta: Improve & Modify. (Illus.). 240p. 1990. pap. 29.95 (*0-85429-785-5*, Pub. by GT Foulis) Haynes Manuals.

— Improve & Modify Escort & Orion. (Improve & Modify Ser.). (Illus.). 240p. 1990. pap. 29.95 (*0-85429-784-7*, Pub. by GT Foulis) Haynes Manuals.

Porter, Lindsay & Pollard, David. Improve & Modify Golf/Jetta: Marks I & II, Including GTI. LC 88-80841. (Motoring Bks.). 240 p. 1988. write for info. (*0-85429-669-7*) GT Foulis.

Porter, Lindsay & Williams, Peter. Triumph Spitfire, GT6, Vitesse & Herald: Guide to Purchase & D. I. Y. Restoration. LC 88-81067. (Motoring Bks.). 307p. 1988. pap. write for info. (*0-85429-583-6*) GT Foulis.

Porter, Linn B. A Black Adonis. LC 72-2028. (Black Heritage Library Collection). 1977. reprint ed. 30.95 (*0-8369-9060-9*) Ayer.

Porter, Liz & Fons, Marianne. Quick Quilts from the Heart. 176p. 1995. pap. 19.95 (*0-8487-1442-3*) Oxmoor Hse.

***Porter, Liz & Fons, Marianne.** Quilting with Fons & Porter. (Illus.). 2000. pap. 24.95 (*0-9676310-1-7*) Fons & Porter.

— Savannah Medallion Quilt. (Illus.). 8p. 1999. pap. 9.95 (*0-9676310-0-9*) Fons & Porter.

Porter, Liz, jt. auth. see Fons, Marianne.

Porter, Lori & Cantrell, Lisa. NAGNA's CNA Code of Ethics & Federal Regulation Handbook. 31p. 1996. wbk. ed. 4.99 (*0-9662101-1-5*) NAGNA.

Porter, Lorle. Discovering Ohio's Hill Country. 2nd rev. ed. (Illus.). 276p. 1996. pap. 20.00 (*0-9643184-0-7*) Locust Grove.

— The Immigrant Cocoon Slavic Migration into the Cambridge, Ohio, Coalfield. LC 95-171441. (Illus.). 350p. 1994. 25.00 (*0-9643184-4-X*) Locust Grove.

— A People Set Apart: Scotch-Irish in Eastern Ohio. Leland, Toni M., ed. LC 98-67105. (Illus.). 986p. 1999. 59.95 (*1-887932-75-5*, New Concord Pr) Equine Graph Pubng.

— Roscoe: Generations - Regeneration. (Illus.). 442p. 1991. 18.95 (*1-880443-05-8*) Roscoe Village.

Porter, Louise. Student Behaviour: Theory & Practice for Teachers. 352p. 1996. pap. 34.95 (*1-86373-956-4*, Pub. by Allen & Unwin Pty) Paul & Co Pubs.

Porter, Louise M. & Smith, Charles B. Territorial Giants: Florida's Founding Fathers. 136p. 1990. 12.00 (*0-9636228-1-1*) St Joseph Hist.

Porter, Luree G., ed. see Gregerson, Gary L.

Porter, Lyman W. Human Relations. LC 94-42389. (History of Management Thought Ser.). (Illus.). 400p. 1995. text 163.95 (*1-85521-435-0*, Pub. by Dartmth Pub) Ashgate Pub Co.

Porter, Lyman W., ed. Annual Review of Psychology, Vol. 44. LC 50-13143. (Illus.). 1993. text 43.00 (*0-8243-0244-3*) Annual Reviews.

Porter, Lyman W., et al, eds. Annual Review of Psychology, Vol. 45. LC 50-13143. (Illus.). 1994. text 46.00 (*0-8243-0245-1*) Annual Reviews.

Porter, Lyman W., jt. auth. see Riggio, Ronald E.

Porter, Lynn, et al. Environmental Science & Technology. LC 95-77144. 720p. 1997. text 74.95 (*0-8134-3060-7*); text 19.95 (*0-8134-3062-3*); text, teacher ed. 12.95 (*0-8134-3061-5*); text, teacher ed. 15.95 (*0-8134-3063-1*) Interstate.

Porter, Lynnette R. Creating the Virtual Classroom: Distance Learning with the Internet. LC 96-38065. 288p. 1997. pap. 39.99 (*0-471-17830-6*) Wiley.

Porter, Lynnette R., jt. auth. see Coggin, William.

Porter, M. Psychology & Sociology Applied to Medicine. LC 98-44803. (Illustrated Colour Text Ser.). 1998. write for info. (*0-443-04971-8*) Church.

Porter, M., jt. auth. see Langfeldt, T.

Porter, M. E. The Competitive Advantage. 557p. (C). 1986. 275.00 (*0-7855-6523-X*, Pub. by Inst Pur & Supply) St Mut.

— Mrs. Porter's New Southern Cookery Book, & Companion for Frugal & Economical Housekeepers. LC 72-9802. (Cookery Americana Ser.). 1973. reprint ed. 17.95 (*0-405-05053-4*) Ayer.

Porter, M. Erin, jt. auth. see Gabbard-Alley, Anne.

Porter, M. Gilbert. One Flew over the Cuckoo's Nest. (Twayne's Masterwork Studies: No. 22). 136p. 1988. 29.00 (*0-8057-7988-4*, Twyne) Mac Lib Ref.

Porter, Malcolm, contrib. by. The Dillon Press Children's Atlas. LC 93-15593. (Illus.). 96p. (YA). (gr. 5 up). 1993. lib. bdg. 16.95 (*0-87518-606-8*, Dillon Silver Burdett) Silver Burdett Pr.

***Porter, Margaret E.** Improper Advances. 384p. 2000. mass mkt. 5.99 (*0-380-80773-4*, Avon Bks) Morrow Avon.

— Irish Autumn. 216p. 1990. 19.95 (*0-8027-1115-4*) Walker & Co.

Porter, Margaret E. Irish Autumn. large type ed. LC 90-21574. 335p. 1991. reprint ed. lib. bdg. 18.95 (*1-56054-086-9*) Thorndike Pr.

— Jubilee Year. large type ed. LC 96-52692. (Candlelight Romance Ser.). 274p. 1997. 18.95 (*0-7862-1016-8*) Thorndike Pr.

— Kissing a Stranger. LC 98-93177. 384p. 1998. mass mkt. 5.99 (*0-380-79559-0*, Avon Bks) Morrow Avon.

— The Proposal. 384p. 1998. mass mkt. 5.99 (*0-380-79557-4*, Avon Bks) Morrow Avon.

Porter, Margaret E. Road to Ruin. 224p. 1991. 18.95 (*0-8027-1129-4*) Walker & Co.

Porter, Margit Esser. Hope Is Contagious: The Breast Cancer Treatment Survival Handbook. LC 97-23751. 192p. 1997. pap. 11.00 (*0-684-84218-1*, Fireside) S&S Trade Pap.

***Porter, Margit Esser.** Hope Lives! The After Breast Cancer Treatment Survival Handbook. LC 00-104204. (Illus.). 192p. 2000. pap. 12.00 (*0-9700443-0-5*) hic pubng.

Porter, Marianna. The Earth Game: Discovering the Cycle Inside Your Life & the Personal Adventure of Change. LC 96-131039. 224p. (Orig.). 1996. pap. 17.95 (*0-9643464-2-7*) Clary Pr.

Porter, Marilyn. Place & Persistence in the Lives of Newfoundland Women. LC 95-23148. (Illus.). 203p. 1993. 66.95 (*1-85628-444-1*, Pub. by Avebry) Ashgate Pub Co.

***Porter, Marilyn & Judd, Ellen R.** Feminists Doing Development: A Practical Critique. LC 99-41268. 2000. pap. 25.00 (*1-85649-694-5*) Zed Books.

***Porter, Marilyn & Judd, Ellen R., contrib. by.** Feminists Doing Development: A Practical Critique. LC 99-41268. 2000. 65.00 (*1-85649-693-7*) Zed Books.

Porter, Mark. Time of Your Life. 1988. pap. 7.00 (*0-937396-71-0*) Walterick Pubs.

— Wow, What a Week! Big Book. (Wonders! Ser.). (Illus.). 24p. (Orig.). (J). (gr. 1-3). 1991. pap. text 29.95 (*1-56334-051-8*) Hampton-Brown.

— Wow, What a Week! Small Book. (Wonders! Ser.). (Illus.). 24p. (Orig.). (J). (gr. 1-3). 1991. pap. text 6.00 (*1-56334-057-7*) Hampton-Brown.

Porter, Mark C., ed. Handbook of Industrial Membrane Technology. LC 88-17876. (Illus.). 604p. 1990. 145.00 (*0-8155-1205-8*) Noyes.

Porter, Mark M. To Live, to Teach, to Learn, to Love. LC 91-90404. 113p. 1991. pap. 12.95 (*0-9629790-0-7*) Kenmark Ent.

***Porter, Marsha.** Video Movie Guide 2000. 1999. mass mkt. 7.99 (*0-345-42098-5*) Ballantine Pub Grp.

Porter, Mary, jt. auth. see Katsigris, Costas.

Porter, Mary C., jt. auth. see Tarr, G. Alan.

Porter, Mary J. Sangre de Cristo Wilderness: A Territory of the Heart. (Illus.). 48p. (Orig.). 1997. pap. 15.95 (*0-9656126-6-X*, MMP-6) Music Mtn Pr.

Porter, Mary J., ed. see Quillen, Ed.

Porter, Maya, jt. ed. see Harman, Willis.

Porter, Melinda C. Art of Love: Love Poems & Paintings. 96p. 1993. pap. 14.00 (*0-86316-167-7*) Writers & Readers.

— The Art of Love: Love Poems & Paintings. 96p. 1997. 28.00 (*0-86316-168-5*) Writers & Readers.

— Badlands. LC 96-4019. 256p. 1996. 22.00 (*0-86316-149-9*) Writers & Readers.

— Boat Child: A Comedy. LC 93-79300. 75p. 1994. pap. 9.95 (*0-937552-0-X*) Blake Pr.

— Through Parisian Eyes: Reflections on Contemporary French Arts & Culture. (Illus.). 256p. 1993. reprint ed. pap. 13.95 (*0-306-80540-5*) Da Capo.

Porter, Melvin F. Linebacker: Overview of the First 120 Days. 79p. 1993. reprint ed. pap. 12.50 (*0-923135-68-5*) Dalley Bk Service.

***Porter, Michael.** Global Competitiveness Report 2000. 2000. pap. 69.95 (*0-07-135872-2*) McGraw.

Porter, Michael. Kill Them Before They Grow: The Misdiagnosis of African American Boys in America's Classrooms. LC 99-195313. 100p. 1998. pap. 10.95 (*0-913543-54-3*) African Am Imag.

***Porter, Michael, et al.** Can Japan Compete? 2000. 27.50 (*0-465-05989-9*) Basic.

Porter, Michael A. FEA Step by Step with Algor. (Illus.). 407p. (Orig.). 1993. pap. text 99.50 (*0-9639253-0-X*) Dynamic An.

— FEA Step by Step with Algor. (Illus.). 305p. (Orig.). 1994. pap. text, student ed. 60.00 (*0-9639253-1-8*) Dynamic An.

Porter, Michael E. Cases in Competitive Strategy. (Illus.). 400p. 1983. 35.00 (*0-02-925410-8*) Free Pr.

— The Competitive Advantage of Nations. LC 98-9584. 896p. 1998. 40.00 (*0-684-84147-9*) Free Pr.

— Competitive Strategy: Techniques for Analyzing Industries & Competitors. LC 80-65200. (Illus.). 398p. 1980. 37.50 (*0-02-925360-8*) Free Pr.

— Interbrand Choice Strategy, & Bilateral Market Power. (Economic Studies: No. 146). 253p. 1976. 16.50 (*0-674-45820-6*) HUP.

— Michael Porter's Landmark Trilogy: Competitive Strategy/Competitive Advantage/Competitive Advant. 1998. 115.00 (*0-684-00577-8*) Free Pr.

— On Competition. LC 98-7643. 485p. 1998. 35.95 (*0-87584-795-1*) Harvard Busn.

Porter, Michael E., ed. Capital Choices: Changing the Way America Invests in Industry. 1994. 49.95 (*0-07-103427-7*) McGraw.

Porter, Michael E., jt. ed. see Montgomery, Cynthia A.

Porter, Michael P. Hawaii Corporation Law & Practice. (National Corporation Law Ser.). 1992. ring bd. 126.00 (*0-13-072456-4*) Aspen Law.

Porter, Micheal. Competitive Advantage. LC 98-9581. 592p. 1998. 37.50 (*0-684-84146-0*) S&S Trade.

Porter, Milly H., ed. see Dorrance, Tom.

Porter, Mimi. New Equine Sports Therapy. 1999. 29.95 (*1-58150-015-7*) Blood-Horse.

Porter, Monica. The Paper Bridge: A Return to Budapest. 256p. 1982. 17.95 (*0-7043-2296-X*, Pub. by Quartet) Charles River Bks.

Porter, N. A. Physicists in Conflict. LC 98-8669. (Illus.). 367p. 1998. 39.50 (*0-7503-0509-6*) IOP Pub.

Porter, N. E., ed. Cenus of India, 1931, Bengal & Sikkim. 1987. reprint ed. 160.00 (*0-8364-2071-3*, Pub. by Usha) S Asia.

Porter, Natalie, jt. ed. see Lerman, Hannah.

Porter, Nicole. Rescuing Treasures of Golden Hearts. (Illus.). 48p. 1999. pap. 8.00 (*0-8059-4596-2*) Dorrance.

Porter, Nina. Lady Farrington's Folly. 224p. 1993. mass mkt. 3.99 (*0-8217-4202-7*, Zebra Kensgtn) Kensgtn Pub Corp.

— A Matchmaker's Match. 1992. mass mkt. 3.50 (*0-8217-3783-X*, Zebra Kensgtn) Kensgtn Pub Corp.

Porter, Noah. American Colleges & the American Public. LC 78-89219. (American Education: Its Men, Institutions, & Ideas. Series 1). 1978. reprint ed. 17.95 (*0-405-01458-9*) Ayer.

— Books & Reading: Or What Books Shall I Read & How Shall I Read Them? 432p. 1977. 24.95 (*0-8369-2968-3*) Ayer.

— Elements of Intellectual Science (1884) 590p. 1998. reprint ed. pap. 35.00 (*0-7661-0495-8*) Kessinger Pub.

— The Human Intellect. 4th ed. LC 75-3319. reprint ed. 48.00 (*0-404-59299-6*) AMS Pr.

Porter, Norman. Rethinking Unionism: An Alternative Vision for Northern Ireland. 252p. 1997. pap. 21.95 (*0-85640-585-X*, Pub. by Blackstaff Pr) Dufour.

Porter, Norman, ed. The Republican Ideal: Current Perspectives. 208p. 1998. pap. 25.95 (*0-85640-627-9*) Blackstaff Pr.

Porter-O'Grady, Tim. Implementing Shared Governance: Creating a Professional Organization. (Illus.). 320p. (C). (gr. 13). 1992. text 43.95 (*0-8016-6318-0*, 06318) Mosby Inc.

— The Nurse Manager's Problem Solver. (Illus.). 322p. (C). (gr. 13). 1994. pap. text 33.95 (*0-8016-7945-1*, 07945) Mosby Inc.

— Reorganization of Nursing Practice: Creating the Corporate Venture. 258p. (C). 1989. 62.00 (*0-8342-0123-2*, 20123) Aspen Pub.

— Shared Governance Implementation Manual. (Illus.). 208p. (C). (gr. 13). 1992. pap. text 36.95 (*0-8016-6317-2*, 06317) Mosby Inc.

Porter-O'Grady, Tim & Finnigan, Sharon. Shared Governance for Nursing: A Creative Approach to Professional Accountability. LC 84-16814. 256p. (C). 1984. text 69.00 (*0-89443-874-3*, 43874) Aspen Pub.

Porter-O'Grady, Tim, jt. auth. see Krueger Wilson, Cathleen.

Porter-O'Grady, Timothy, et al. Implementing Whole-Systems Shared Governance: Architecture for Integration. LC 97-10153. 323p. 1997. 49.00 (*0-8342-0951-9*, 20951) Aspen Pub.

Porter, Ona L. & Rand, Miriam. From Here to There! The Workbook for Families on the Move. 114p. (Orig.). 1992. pap. 15.00 (*0-9625747-5-9*) Niche OR.

Porter, Paige. Gender & Education. 144p. (C). 1986. 57.00 (*0-7300-0400-7*, Pub. by Deakin Univ) St Mut.

— Gender & Education Policy: A Call for New Directions. 158p. (C). 1995. pap. 38.00 (*0-7300-0771-5*, ESA842, Pub. by Deakin Univ) St Mut.

Porter, Pamela, jt. auth. see Harris, Linda G.

***Porter, Pamela Boyer & Flemming, Ann Carter.** Research in Missouri. LC 99-44211. (Special Publications). 1999. pap. write for info. (*0-915156-65-2*) Natl Genealogical.

Porter, Pat & Sharp, Allen W. Active English: Understand, Practice, Communicate, Bk. 1. 224p. 1977. pap. text 13.75 (*0-13-003400-2*) P-H.

— Active English: Understand, Practice, Communicate, Bk. 2. (Illus.). 272p. 1977. pap. text 13.75 (*0-13-003418-5*) P-H.

Porter, Patricia A., et al. Communicating Effectively in English: Oral Communication for Non-Native Speakers. 2nd ed. 251p. (C). 1992. text 26.95 (*0-534-17268-7*); mass mkt., teacher ed. 7.75 (*0-534-17269-5*) Heinle & Heinle.

Porter, Patrick K. Awaken the Genius: Mind Technology for the 21st Century. De Shazo, Jerry, ed. (Illus.). 200p. (Orig.). 1994. pap. 14.98 (*0-9637611-8-8*) Positive Chngs Hypnosis.

— Awaken the Genius: Mind Technology for the 21st Century. Massengill, Paul K., ed. LC 93-86044. 200p. (Orig.). reprint ed. pap. 12.95 (*1-887630-03-1*) Renaissnce Pub.

— The Power of Your Voice: Patterns of Psycho-Linguistics. De Shazo, Jerry, ed. 180p. (Orig.). 1993. pap. 19.98 (*0-9637611-5-3*) Positive Chngs Hypnosis.

— The Power of Your Voice: Patterns of Psycho-Linguistics. Massengill, Paul K., ed. LC 93-86046. 180p. (Orig.). (C). reprint ed. pap. 19.98 (*1-887630-01-5*) Renaissnce Pub.

— Psycho-Linguistics: THe Language of the Mind. De Shazo, Jerry, ed. 240p. (Orig.). (C). 1993. pap. 19.98 (*0-9637611-7-X*) Positive Chngs Hypnosis.

— Psycho-Linguistics: The Language of the Mind. Massengill, Paul K., ed. LC 93-86045. 240p. (C). reprint ed. pap. 19.98 (*1-887630-02-3*) Renaissnce Pub.

Porter, Patrick K. & Porter, Cynthia J. Six Secrets of G. E. N. I. U. S. 72p. 1997. pap. 9.95 (*1-888316-00-4*) Positive Chngs Hypnosis.

***Porter, Penny.** Heartstrings & Tailtuggers. (Illus.). 350p. 1999. 21.95 (*1-893660-10-9*, 991101-P1) Ravenhawk.

Porter, Penny. The Keymaker: Born to Steal. LC 94-14806. (Illus.). 160p. (Orig.). (YA). (gr. 7-12). 1994. pap. 9.95 (*0-943173-99-X*) Roberts Rinehart.

— Love on the Wild Side. (Illus.). 234p. 1997. pap. 12.95 (*0-9656923-1-0*) Singing Valley.

— A Squirrel from the Moon & Other Stories . . . Wild but True. (Illus.). 140p. Date not set. pap. 10.95 (*0-9656923-0-2*) Singing Valley.

Porter, Peter. The Animal Programme. Date not set. pap. 7.95 (*0-85646-108-3*, Pub. by Anvil Press) Dufour.

— Collected Poems. 352p. 1984. pap. 7.95 (*0-19-211965-6*) OUP.

***Porter, Peter.** Collected Poems 1: 1961-1999, 2 vols. LC 98-27018. 800p. 1999. pap. 45.00 (*0-19-288099-3*) OUP.

Porter, Peter. Dragons in Their Pleasant Palaces. LC 96-44450. 64p. 1997. pap. 11.95 (*0-19-288028-4*) OUP.

— George Herbert: (T. S. Eliot) 1990. 22.50 (*0-7463-0741-1*, Pub. by Northcote House) Trans-Atl Phila.

Porter, Peter, ed. The Oxford Book of Modern Australian Verse. 310p. 1999. pap. 29.95 (*0-19-550706-1*) OUP.

Porter, Peter, jt. auth. see Boyd, Arthur.

Porter, Peter, jt. auth. see Eliot, T. S.

Porter, Peter, ed. see Moore, Geoffrey, et al.

***Porter, Phil.** Above Mackinac. (Above Ser.). (Illus.). 96p. 2000. 24.50 (*0-918684-57-9*) Cameron & Co.

Porter, Phil. Eagle at Mackinac: The Establishment of the United States Military & Civil Authority on Mackinac Island, 1796-1802. (Reports in Mackinac History & Archaeology: No. 11). (Illus.). 56p. (Orig.). 1991. pap. 9.95 (*0-911872-59-0*) Mackinac St Hist Pks.

***Porter, Phil.** Eat or Be Eaten: Jungle Warfare for the Master Corporate Politician. (Illus.). 256p. 2000. 22.00 (*0-7352-0143-9*) PH Pr.

Porter, Phil. Having It All: Body, Mind, Heart & Spirit Together Again at Last. LC 97-90211. (Illus.). 128p. (Orig.). 1997. pap. 11.95 (*0-9636755-1-6*) Wing It Pr.

— Mackinac: An Island Famous in These Regions. (Illus.). 96p. 1998. 16.95 (*0-911872-69-8*); pap. 9.95 (*0-911872-68-X*) Mackinac St Hist Pks.

— View from the Veranda: The History & Architecture of the Summer Cottages on Mackinac Island. Armour, David A., ed. LC 83-198939. (Reports in Mackinac History & Archaeology: No. 8). (Illus.). 76p. (Orig.). 1981. pap. 8.50 (*0-911872-41-8*) Mackinac St Hist Pks.

— Wonder of Mackinac: A Guide to the Natural History of MacKinte Island. (Illus.). 52p. 1984. pap. 7.00 (*0-911872-49-3*) Mackinac St Hist Pks.

Porter, Phil & Winton-Henry, Cynthia. Body & Soul: Excursions in the Realm of Physicality & Spirituality. 87p. 1993. pap. 12.95 (*0-9636755-0-8*) Wing It Pr.

— Tales of a Suburban Mystic. abr. ed. 125p. 1995. pap. 9.95 incl. audio (*0-9636755-4-0*) Wing It Pr.

P

An Asterisk (*) at the beginning of an entry indicates that the title is appearing for the first time.

Porter, Phil, jt. auth. see Cameron, Robert.

Porter, Phil, ed. see Boynton, James.

Porter, Phil, ed. see Corbusier, Harold Dunbar.

Porter, Philip. Ferrari Testarossa. (Autofolio Ser.). (Illus.). 72p. 1991. 9.95 (*0-85429-734-0*, Pub. by GT Foulis) Haynes Manuals.

— Jaguar: The Complete Illustrated History. 3rd ed. (Illus.). 216p. 1995. 39.95 (*0-85429-962-9*, Pub. by J H Haynes & Co) Motorbooks Intl.

— Jaguar E-Type: The Definitive History. (Illus.). 712p. 1997. 120.00 (*0-85429-580-1*, Pub. by GT Foulis) Haynes Manuals.

— Jaguar Sports Racing Cars: C-Type, D-Type, SKSS, & Lightweight E-Type. (Illus.). 17p. 1998. 39.95 (*1-901432-21-1*, Bay View Bks) MBI Pubg.

— Jaguar XK8: New Edition the Authorized Biography. (Illus.). 136p. 1998. 31.95 (*1-901432-19-X*, Bay View Bks) MBI Pubg.

— Original Jaguar E Type. (Original Jaguar Ser.). (Illus.). 9128p. 1990. text 34.95 (*1-870979-12-5*, Bay View Bks) MBI Pubg.

— Original Jaguar XK: The Restorers Guide to XK120, XK140 & XK150 Roadster, Drophead Coupe & Fixed-Head Coupe. (Illus.). 144p. 1998. 36.95 (*1-901432-02-5*, Bay View Bks) MBI Pubg.

Porter, Philip W. Cleveland: Confused City on a Seesaw. LC 76-21700. (Illus.). 330p. reprint ed. pap. 102.30 (*0-608-09866-3*, 206983100006) Bks Demand.

— Food & Development in the Semi-Arid Zone of East Africa. LC 79-20312. (Foreign & Comparative Studies Program, African Ser.: No. 32). (Illus.). 114p. 1979. reprint ed. pap. text 7.50 (*0-915984-54-7*) Syracuse U Foreign Comp.

Porter, Philip W. & Sheppard, Eric S. A World of Difference: Society, Nature, Development. LC 97-50336. 602p. 1998. pap. text 37.95 (*1-57230-324-7*, C0324); lib. bdg. 55.00 (*1-57230-071-X*) Guilford Pubns.

Porter, Phillip H. Let the Walls Fall Down. LC 95-83906. 180p. (Orig.). 1996. pap. 11.99 (*0-88419-424-8*) Creation House.

Porter, Phoebe A., tr. & intro. see Matute, Ana M.

***Porter, Price.** Port Calamity. 272p. 2000. 18.99 (*0-7089-5711-0*) Ulverscroft.

***Porter Publishing Editors, ed.** Complete Camping Manual. (Illus.). (C). 1999. pap. 34.95 (*1-899238-32-8*) Thomson Learn.

— Fiat Punto, 1994-1999: Repair Manual, Service Guide & Owner's Manual. (Illus.). (C). 1999. pap. 34.95 (*1-899238-27-1*) Thomson Learn.

Porter, R., ed. Voinovich: By Means of Mutual Correspondence (Putem Vzaimnoi Perepiski) (Russian Texts Ser.). (RUS.). 104p. 1996. pap. 18.95 (*1-85399-474-X*, Pub. by Brist Class Pr) Focus Pub-R Pullins.

Porter, R., ed. see CIBA Foundation Staff.

Porter, R. Bruce & Hammel, Eric. ACE! A Marine Night-Fighter Pilot in World War II. LC 85-151862. (Illus.). 278p. 1998. reprint ed. pap. 19.95 (*0-935553-31-2*) Pacifica Military.

Porter, R. C., ed. Seven Soviet Poets. 104p. (C). 1988. pap. 15.95 (*0-631-15567-8*) Blackwell Pubs.

Porter, R. F., et al. Field Guide to Birds of the Middle East. (Poyser Bird Bks.). (Illus.). 480p. 1996. text 50.00 (*0-85661-076-3*) Morgan Kaufmann.

— Flight Identification of European Raptors. 3rd ed. (Illus.). 288p. 1990. text (*0-85661-027-5*) Poyser.

Porter, R. N., jt. auth. see Karplus, M.

Porter, R. S., jt. auth. see Bynum, William F.

Porter, R. S., jt. auth. see Griffin, A. C.

Porter, R. W. Back Injury & Litigation. 140p. 1995. pap. 47.50 (*1-85996-110-X*, Pub. by Bios Sci) Coronet Bks.

Porter, R. W., jt. ed. see Aspden, R. M.

***Porter, Randy.** The Best in Tent Camping Virginia: A Guide for Campers Who Hate RV's, Concrete Slabs & Loud Portable Stereos. (Illus.). 2000. pap. 14.95 (*0-89732-316-5*, Pub. by Menasha Ridge) Globe Pequot.

Porter, Randy. Mountain Bike! Virginia. LC 97-49133. (Mountain Bike! Ser.). 352p. 1997. pap. 14.95 (*0-89732-248-7*) Menasha Ridge.

Porter, Randy & Sorrells, Nancy. A Cyclist's Guide to the Shenandoah Valley: Exploring the Past & Present on Rural Routes. LC 95-203841. 250p. 1993. pap. 14.95 (*0-9637819-0-1*) Shenand Odys.

***Porter, Ray C.** Chronology of World History, 4 vols. LC 99-19300. 3109p. (YA). 1999. lib. bdg. 375.00 (*1-57607-155-3*) ABC-CLIO.

Porter, Richard. The Economics of Water & Waste: A Case Study of Jakarta, Indonesia. LC 96-84388. 144p. 1996. 61.95 (*1-85972-350-0*, Pub. by Avebry) Ashgate Pub Co.

Porter, Richard, et al. Henry Varnum Poor, Nineteen Eighty-Seven to Nineteen Seventy: A Retrospective Exhibition: Exhibition Catalogue. (Illus.). 168p. 1983. pap. 14.50 (*0-911209-29-8*) Palmer Mus Art.

Porter, Richard, jt. auth. see Cozzens, Margaret.

Porter, Richard, jt. auth. see Cozzens, Margaret B.

Porter, Richard C. Economics at the Wheel: The Costs of Cars & Drivers. LC 98-88417. (Illus.). 266p. 1999. 59.95 (*0-12-562360-7*) Acad Pr.

— Economics at the Wheel: The Costs of Cars & Drivers. LC 98-88417. 266p. 1999. pap. 39.95 (*0-12-562361-5*) Acad Pr.

— Economics of Water & Waste in Three African Capitals. 160p. 1997. 59.95 (*1-85972-602-X*, Pub. by Ashgate Pub) Ashgate Pub Co.

Porter, Richard D. Introduction to Fibre Bundles. LC 71-8325. (Lecture Notes in Pure & Applied Mathematics Ser.: Vol. 31). (Illus.). 182p. reprint ed. pap. 56.50 (*0-608-08976-1*, 206961100005) Bks Demand.

Porter, Richard D., jt. auth. see Cozzens, Margaret B.

Porter, Richard E., jt. auth. see Samovar, Larry A.

Porter, Richard E., jt. ed. see Samovar, Larry A.

Porter, Richard N., tr. see Cizevskij, Dmitry.

Porter, Richard N., tr. see Tschizewskij, Dmitrij.

Porter, Richard W. Management of Back Pain. 2nd ed. (Illus.). 368p. 1993. text 115.00 (*0-443-04630-1*) Church.

— The Versatile Satellite. (Illus.). 1977. text 16.95 (*0-19-885104-9*) OUP.

Porter, Richard W., jt. auth. see Hughes, Sean P.

Porter, Rick, jt. auth. see Gaslin, Glenn.

Porter, Robert. Paul Hasluck: A Political Biography. 1993. 39.95 (*1-875560-20-3*, Pub. by Univ of West Aust Pr) Intl Spec Bk.

— Russia's Alternative Prose. 288p. 1994. 46.00 (*0-85496-935-7*) Berg Pubs.

Porter, Robert, ed. Studies in Neurophysiology: Presented to A. K. McIntyre. LC 78-1695. (Illus.). 470p. reprint ed. pap. 134.00 (*0-608-17523-4*, 2030614) Bks Demand.

Porter, Robert & Bledsoe, Bryan. Basic Emergency Care. (C). 2001. pap. 41.33 (*0-89303-066-X*) Appleton & Lange.

Porter, Robert & Lemon, Roger. Corticospinal Function & Voluntary Movement. (Monographs of the Physiological Society: Vol. 45). (Illus.). 446p. (C). 1995. pap. text 62.50 (*0-19-852375-0*) OUP.

Porter, Robert, jt. auth. see Bledsoe, Bryan.

Porter, Robert, jt. auth. see Crouch, Martin.

Porter, Robert, tr. see Popov, Evgeni I.

Porter, Robert, tr. see Popov, Evgeny.

Porter, Robert A., ed. Guide to Corporate Giving in the Arts 4. 4th ed. LC 87-18738. 481p. (Orig.). 1987. 25.00 (*0-915400-56-1*, ACA Bks) Am for the Arts.

***Porter, Robert C.** Clean Coal Technology: Technologies for the Combined Control of Sulfur Dioxide & Nitrogen Oxides Emissions from Coal-Fired Boilers. (Illus.). 51p. (C). 2000. pap. text 25.00 (*0-7881-8654-X*) DIANE Pub.

Porter, Robert C. Four Contemporary Russian Writers. LC 88-14816. 191p. 1989. 19.50 (*0-85496-246-8*) Berg Pubs.

Porter, Robert P. Industrial Cuba: Being a Study of Present Commercial & Industrial Conditions. Bruchey, Stuart & Bruchey, Eleanor, eds. LC 76-5029. (American Business Abroad Ser.). (Illus.). 1976. reprint ed. 51.95 (*0-405-09296-2*) Ayer.

Porter, Robert S., jt. auth. see Bledsoe, Bryan E.

Porter, Robert W. & Swatton, Richard. Intermediate Bulk Containers. 55p. (C). 1979. 100.00 (*0-906297-03-6*, Pub. by ICHCA) St Mut.

Porter, Robin. Child Labour in Hong Kong LC 76-366676. (Spokesman Pamphlet Ser.: Vol.50). 27 p. 1975. 0.35 (*0-85124-119-0*) Dufour.

Porter, Robin. Industrial Reformers in Republican China. LC 94-16058. (Studies on Modern China Ser.). 294p. (gr. 13). 1994. text 81.95 (*1-56324-393-8*, East Gate Bk) M E Sharpe.

Porter, Robin, jt. ed. see Brown, David H.

Porter, Roger, jt. ed. see Johnson, Julian F.

Porter, Roger J. & Chadwick, David W. The Epilepsies 2. LC 96-50470. (Blue Books of Practical Neurology: Vol. 18). 384p. 1997. text 85.00 (*0-7506-9824-1*) Buttrwrth-Heinemann.

Porter, Roger J. & Malone, Thomas E., eds. Biomedical Research: Collaboration & Conflict of Interest. 232p. 1992. text 45.00 (*0-8018-4400-2*) Johns Hopkins.

Porter, Roger J. & Schoenberg, Bruce S., eds. Controlled Clinical Trials in Neurological Disease. 464p. 1990. text 234.00 (*0-7923-0613-9*) Kluwer Academic.

Porter, Roger J., jt. auth. see Hall, Lisa S.

Porter, Roger J., jt. auth. see Meldrum, Brian S.

Porter, Roger J., ed. see Epilepsy International Symposium Staff.

Porter, Roger S., ed. see Zachariades, Anagnostis E.

Porter, Roger S., jt. ed. see Zachariades, Anagnostis E.

Porter, Rosalie P. Forked Tongue: The Politics of Bilingual Education. 376p. 1996. pap. text 24.95 (*1-56000-881-4*) Transaction Pubs.

***Porter, Rosalie Pedalino, ed.** Educating Language Minority Children. (Read Perspectives Ser.: Vol. 6). 142p. 2000. pap. 34.95 (*0-7658-0669-X*) Transaction Pubs.

Porter-Roth, Bud. Proposal Development: How to Respond & Win the Bid. 3rd rev. ed. LC 98-21244. (Illus.). 264p. 1998. pap. 21.95 (*1-55571-431-5*, PROPP) PSI Resch.

***Porter, Roy.** Creation of the Modern World: The Untold Story of the British Enlightenment. 608p. 2000. 35.00 (*0-393-04872-1*) Norton.

Porter, Roy. Disease, Medicine & Society in England, 1550-1860. 2nd ed. (New Studies in Economic & Social History: Vol. 3). 84p. (C). 1995. text 34.95 (*0-521-55262-1*); pap. text 10.95 (*0-521-55791-7*) Cambridge U Pr.

— English Society in the Eighteenth Century. rev. ed. 416p. 1990. pap. 14.95 (*0-14-013819-6*, Penguin Bks) Viking Penguin.

***Porter, Roy.** The Enlightenment. LC 00-41507. (Studies in European History). 2000. write for info. (*0-333-94505-0*) St Martin.

Porter, Roy. The Greatest Benefit to Mankind: A Medical History of Humanity. LC 98-10219. (Illus.). 872p. 1999. pap. 17.95 (*0-393-31980-6*, Norton Paperbks) Norton.

— The Greatest Benefit to Mankind: A Medical History of Humanity from Antiquity to the Present. LC 98-10219. (Illus.). 831p. 1998. 35.00 (*0-393-04634-6*) Norton.

Porter, Roy. London. write for info. (*0-393-03762-2*) Norton.

Porter, Roy. London: A Social History. Date not set. 29.95 (*0-614-32353-3*) HUP.

— London: A Social History. LC 94-33025. (Illus.). 448p. 1995. 33.00 (*0-674-53838-2*, PORLON) HUP.

— London: A Social History. 448p. 1999. pap. 19.95 (*0-674-53839-0*) HUP.

— The Making of Geology: Earth Science in Britain, 1660-1815. LC 76-56220. 300p. reprint ed. pap. 85.50 (*0-608-13048-6*, 2024515) Bks Demand.

— Medicine: A History of Healing: Ancient Traditions to Modern Practices. (Illus.). 224p. 1998. pap. text 24.95 (*1-56924-708-0*) Marlowe & Co.

— Mind-Forg'd Manacles: A History of Madness from the Restoration to the Regency. LC 87-8703. 424p. 1988. 49.50 (*0-674-57617-9*) HUP.

— Model Buildings Masterclass. (Illus.). 128p. 1997. 29.95 (*1-85915-063-2*, Pub. by W & G) Motorbooks Intl.

***Porter, Roy.** Quacks: Fakers & Charlatans in English Medicine. (Illus.). 224p. 2000. 39.99 (*0-7524-1776-2*, Pub. by Tempus Pubng) Arcadia Publng.

Porter, Roy, ed. The Biographical Dictionary of Scientists. 2nd ed. (Illus.). 960p. 1994. text 95.00 (*0-19-521083-2*) OUP.

— The Cambridge Illustrated History of Medicine. (Illustrated Histories Ser.). (Illus.). 400p. (C). 1996. 39.95 (*0-521-44211-7*) Cambridge U Pr.

— The Faber Book of Madness. 480p. 1993. pap. 16.95 (*0-571-14388-1*) Faber & Faber.

— Myths of the English. LC 92-28892. 272p. 1993. pap. 31.95 (*0-7456-1306-3*) Blackwell Pubs.

— Rewriting the Self: Histories from the Middle Ages to the Present. LC 96-15698. (Illus.). 296p. (C). 1996. 80.00 (*0-415-14279-2*) Routledge.

— Rewriting the Self: Histories from the Renaissance to the Present. LC 96-15698. (Illus.). 296p. (C). 1996. pap. 24.99 (*0-415-14280-6*) Routledge.

Porter, Roy, et al, eds. The Anatomy of Madness, 3 vols. 352p. 1988. text 137.50 (*0-318-35451-9*); text 65.00 (*0-415-00859-X*) Routledge.

— The Anatomy of Madness, 2 vols. 528p. 1985. 87.50 (*0-422-60350-3*, 9688, Pub. by Tavistock) Routldge.

— The Anatomy of Madness Vol. 2: Institutions & Society. 264p. 1985. 47.50 (*0-422-79440-6*, 9618, Pub. by Tavistock) Routldge.

Porter, Roy & Keller, David. There & Back: The Roy Porter Story. LC 91-18913. (Illus.). 216p. 1991. 24.95 (*0-8071-1689-0*) La State U Pr.

***Porter, Roy & Ogilvie, Marilyn B., eds.** The Biographical Dictionary of Scientists, 2 vols., Set. 3rd ed. (Illus.). 1216p. 2000. text 125.00 (*0-19-521663-6*) OUP.

Porter, Roy & Roberts, Marie M., eds. Pleasure in the Eighteenth Century. LC 96-12952. 273p. (C). 1996. text 37.50 (*0-8147-6644-7*) NYU Pr.

Porter, Roy & Rousseau, G. S. Gout: The Patrician Malady. LC 98-16881. (Illus.). 352p. 1998. pap. 16.95 (*0-300-07386-0*) Yale U Pr.

***Porter, Roy & Rousseau, G. S.** Gout: The Patrician Malady. (Illus.). 408p. 2000. pap. 16.95 (*0-300-08274-6*) Yale U Pr.

Porter, Roy & Teich, Mikulas, eds. Drugs & Narcotics in History. (Illus.). 240p. 1997. pap. text 19.95 (*0-521-58597-X*) Cambridge U Pr.

— The Scientific Revolution in National Context. 317p. (C). 1992. text 69.95 (*0-521-39510-0*); pap. text 24.95 (*0-521-39699-9*) Cambridge U Pr.

Porter, Roy & Wear, Andrew. Problems & Methods in the History of Medicine. (Welcome Institute Series in the History of Medicine). 256p. 1987. 67.50 (*0-7099-3687-7*, Pub. by C Helm) Routldge.

Porter, Roy, jt. auth. see Berrios, German E.

Porter, Roy, jt. auth. see Hall, Lesley.

Porter, Roy, jt. auth. see Hinnells, John R.

Porter, Roy, jt. auth. see Porter, Dorothy.

Porter, Roy, jt. ed. see Berrios, German E.

Porter, Roy, ed. see Bowler, Peter J.

Porter, Roy, jt. ed. see Brewer, John.

Porter, Roy, ed. see Brock, William H.

Porter, Roy, jt. ed. see Burke, Peter.

Porter, Roy, jt. ed. see Bynum, W. F.

Porter, Roy, jt. ed. see Bynum, William F.

Porter, Roy, jt. ed. see Granshaw, Lindsay.

Porter, Roy, jt. ed. see Grell, Ole Peter.

Porter, Roy, ed. see Haslam, John.

Porter, Roy, jt. ed. see Jones, Colin.

Porter, Roy, jt. ed. see Micale, Mark S.

Porter, Roy, ed. see Rousseau, George S.

Porter, Roy, ed. see Service, Robert W.

Porter, Roy, jt. ed. see Teich, Mikulas.

Porter, Roy, ed. see Trotter, Thomas.

Porter, Roy E., & Assocs. Staff. Writer's Manual. LC 75-43588. 1979. 27.95 (*0-88280-063-9*) ETC Pubns.

Porter, Rufus. Yankee Inventor's Flying Ship. Gilman, Rhoda R., ed. LC 75-95571. (Illus.). vi, 51p. 1969. 7.25 (*0-87351-052-6*) Minn Hist.

Porter, Russ. America's Rail Pictorial. LC 97-72338. (Illus.). 152p. 1997. write for info. (*0-911581-42-1*) Heimburger Hse Pub.

— Chicago & Northwestern Milwaukee Road Pictorial. LC 94-75627. (Illus.). 76p. 1996. 29.95 (*0-911581-30-8*) Heimburger Hse Pub.

— North Shore/South Shore. LC 98-75537. (Illus.). 140p. 2000. 41.95 (*0-911581-49-9*, 130235AE, Pub. by Heimburger Hse Pub) Motorbooks Intl.

Porter, Russell W. The Arctic Diary of Russell Williams Porter. Friis, Herman, ed. LC 75-45375. 184p. reprint ed. pap. 57.10 (*0-8357-5726-9*, 202027100016) Bks Demand.

Porter, Ruth B. The Story of Somerset. rev. ed. 70p. 1972. pap. 3.00 (*0-685-29128-6*) Niagara Cnty Hist Soc.

Porter, Ruth S. A Dialect Study in Dartmouth, Massachusetts. (Publications of American Dialect Society: No. 43). 60p. 1967. pap. text 6.00 (*0-8173-0643-9*) U of Ala Pr.

Porter, Sarah. Massage: For Health, Relaxation & Vitality. 1998. pap. 12.95 (*1-85967-855-6*, Lorenz Bks) Anness Pub.

Porter, Sarah H. The Life & Times of Anne Royall. LC 72-2619. (American Women Ser.: Images & Realities). 302p. 1974. reprint ed. 23.95 (*0-405-04472-0*) Ayer.

***Porter Sargent Staff.** Directory for Exceptional Children. 14th ed. 1400p. 2001. 75.00 (*0-87558-141-2*) Porter Sargent.

— Handbook of Private Schools. 80th ed. (Illus.). 1336p. 1999. 93.00 (*0-87558-140-4*) Porter Sargent.

— Handbook of Private Schools. 81st ed. 1400p. 2000. 95.00 (*0-87558-142-0*) Porter Sargent.

Porter Sargent Staff, ed. Directory for Exceptional Children. 13th ed. LC 54-4975. (Special Education Ser.). (Illus.). 1312p. 1994. 60.00 (*0-87558-131-5*) Porter Sargent.

— Guide to Summer Camps & Summer Schools. 27th ed. LC 37-4715. (Handbook Ser.). (Illus.). 560p. 1995. 35.00 (*0-87558-133-1*); pap. 25.00 (*0-87558-134-X*) Porter Sargent.

— Schools Abroad of Interest to Americans. 9th ed. LC 67-18844. (Handbook Ser.). (Illus.). 544p. 1999. 45.00 (*0-87558-138-2*) Porter Sargent.

Porter, Shirley. Me, Myself, & I, Inc. 10 Steps to Career Independence. LC 98-9771. 1998. pap. text 17.95 (*1-57023-093-5*) Impact VA.

***Porter, Shirley.** Watercolor Basics: Drawing & Painting Birds. LC 99-39811. (Watercolor Basics Ser.). (Illus.). 128p. 2000. pap. 18.99 (*0-89134-919-7*, North Lght Bks) F & W Pubns Inc.

Porter, Shirley A. But You Can't Leave Shirley. LC 92-64097. 176p. (Orig.). 1992. pap. 9.95 (*0-936029-28-5*) Western Bk Journ.

Porter, Spencer K. Remembering Galileo. LC 95-10747. 216p. (C). 1995. pap. text 29.00 (*0-8191-9963-X*); lib. bdg. 48.50 (*0-8191-9962-1*) U Pr of Amer.

Porter, Stanley, jt. ed. see McDonald, Lee Martin.

***Porter, Stanley E.** The Criteria for Authenticity in Historical-Jesus Research: Previous Discussion & New Proposals. (Journal for the Study of the New Testament, Supplement Ser.: No. 191). 320p. 2000. 85.00 (*1-84127-089-X*, Pub. by Sheffield Acad) CUP Services.

Porter, Stanley E. Handbook of Classical Rhetoric in the Hellenistic Period (330 B.C.-A.D. 400) LC 96-47335. 600p. 1997. 253.00 (*90-04-09965-4*) Brill Academic Pubs.

— Idioms of the Greek New Testament, 2. 2nd ed. (Biblical Languages (Greek) Ser.: Vol. 2). 339p. (C). 1992. pap. 29.95 (*1-85075-379-2*, Pub. by Sheffield Acad) CUP Services.

— Idioms of the Greek New Testament, 2. 2nd ed. (Biblical Languages (Greek) Ser.). 339p. (C). 1996. 95.00 (*1-85075-357-1*, Pub. by Sheffield Acad) CUP Services.

— Katallasso in Ancient Greek Literature, with Reference to the Pauline Writings. (Distributed Books in Biblical Studies). 189p. 1994. pap. text 23.75 (*84-8005-011-X*, Pub. by Sheffield Acad) CUP Services.

— Romans. (Readings Ser.). 220p. 1998. 57.50 (*1-85075-966-9*, Pub. by Sheffield Acad); pap. 19.50 (*1-85075-971-5*, Pub. by Sheffield Acad) CUP Services.

— Studies in the Greek New Testament: Theory & Practice, Vol. 6. (Studies in Biblical Greek). VI, 290p. (C). 1996. pap. 32.95 (*0-8204-2858-2*) P Lang Pubng.

— Verbal Aspect in the Greek of the New Testament, with Reference to Tense & Mood. 2nd ed. Carson, D. A., ed. (Studies in Biblical Greek: Vol. 1). XII, 582p. 1993. 49.95 (*0-8204-2423-4*) P Lang Pubng.

Porter, Stanley E., ed. A Handbook to the Exegesis of the New Testament. (New Testament Tools & Studies: Vol. 25). xi, 638p. 1997. 174.50 (*90-04-09921-2*) Brill Academic Pubs.

— The Language of the Greek New Testament: Classic Essays. (Journal for the Study of the New Testament, Supplement Ser.: No. 60). 238p. (C). 1991. 70.00 (*1-85075-325-3*, Pub. by Sheffield Acad) CUP Services.

Porter, Stanley E., ed. The Nature of Religious Language: A Colloquium. (Roehampton Institute London Papers: No. 1). 250p. 1996. pap. 24.50 (*1-85075-783-6*, Pub. by Sheffield Acad) CUP Services.

Porter, Stanley E., ed. The Nature of Religious Language: A Colloquium. LC 96-183330. (Roehampton Institute London Papers: No. 1). 250p. 1996. 70.00 (*1-85075-580-9*, Pub. by Sheffield Acad) CUP Services.

Porter, Stanley E., et al, eds. Crossing the Boundaries: Essays in Biblical Interpretation in Honor of Michael D. Goulder. LC 94-26021. (Biblical Interpretation Ser.: 8). xviii, 381p. 1994. 110.50 (*90-04-10131-4*) Brill Academic Pubs.

— Images of Christ: Ancient & Modern. (Roehampton Institute London Papers: Vol. 2). 406p. 1997. 95.00 (*1-85075-658-9*, Pub. by Sheffield Acad); pap. 28.00 (*1-85075-812-3*, Pub. by Sheffield Acad) CUP Services.

***Porter, Stanley E., et al, eds.** Resurrection. (Journal for the Study of the New Testament, Supplement Ser.: No. 186). 376p. 1999. 85.00 (*1-84127-015-6*, Pub. by Sheffield Acad); pap. 29.95 (*1-84127-016-4*, Pub. by Sheffield Acad) CUP Services.

Porter, Stanley E., et al, eds. Translating the Bible: Problems & Prospects. (JSNTS Ser.: Vol. 173). 336p. 1999. 85.00 (*1-85075-918-9*, Pub. by Sheffield Acad) CUP Services.

Porter, Stanley E. & Carson, D. A., eds. Biblical Greek Language & Linguistics: Open Questions in Current Research. (Journal for the Study of the New Testament, Supplement Ser.: No. 80). 217p. 1993. 60.00 (*1-85075-390-3*, Pub. by Sheffield Acad) CUP Services.

— Discourse Analysis & Other Topics in Biblical Greek. (Journal for the Study of the New Testament, Supplement Ser.: No. 113). 227p. 1995. 65.00 (*1-85075-545-0*, Pub. by Sheffield Acad) CUP Services.

***Porter, Stanley E. & Carson, D. A., eds.** Linguistics & the New Testament: Critical Junctures. LC 99-460563. (Journal for the Study of the New Testament, Supplement Ser.: No. 168). 304p. 1999. 75.00 (*1-85075-991-X*, Pub. by Sheffield Acad) CUP Services.

***Porter, Stanley E. & Cross, Anthony R., eds.** Baptism, the New Testament & the Church: Historical & Contemporary Studies in Honour of R. E. O. White.

P

(Journal for the Study of the New Testament, Supplement Ser.: No. 171). 497p. 1999. 85.00 (*1-85075-937-5*, Pub. by Sheffield Acad) CUP Services.

Porter, Stanley E. & Evans, Craig A., eds. The Johannine Writings: A Sheffield Reader. (Biblical Seminar Ser.: No. 32). 267p. 1995. pap. 19.95 (*1-85075-729-1*, Pub. by Sheffield Acad) CUP Services.

Porter, Stanley E. & Evans, Craig A., eds. The Pauline Writings: A Sheffield Reader. (Biblical Seminar Ser.: Vol. 34). 300p. 1995. pap. 19.95 (*1-85075-730-5*, Pub. by Sheffield Acad) CUP Services.

— The Scrolls & the Scriptures: Qumran Fifty Years After. (JSP Supplement Ser.: Vol. 26). 414p. 1997. 85.00 (*1-85075-844-1*, Pub. by Sheffield Acad); pap. 35.00 (*1-85075-845-X*, Pub. by Sheffield Acad) CUP Services.

Porter, Stanley E. & McDonald, Lee M. New Testament Introduction. LC 95-25608. (IBR Bibliographies Ser.: Vol. 12). 240p. 1996. pap. 14.99 (*0-8010-2060-3*) Baker Bks.

Porter, Stanley E. & Olbricht, Thomas H., eds. Rhetoric & the New Testament: Essays from the 1992 Heidelberg Conference. (Journal for the Study of the New Testament, Supplement Ser.: No. 90). 538p. 1993. 95.00 (*1-85075-449-7*, Pub. by Sheffield Acad) CUP Services.

— Rhetoric, Scripture & Theology: Essays from the 1994 Pretoria Conference. (JSNTS Ser.: No. 131). 438p. 1996. 85.00 (*1-85075-607-4*, Pub. by Sheffield Acad) CUP Services.

— The Rhetorical Analysis of Scripture: Essays from the 1995 London Conference. LC 98-101988. (JSNT Supplement Ser.: Vol. 146). 504p. 1997. 95.00 (*1-85075-671-6*, Pub. by Sheffield Acad) CUP Services.

Porter, Stanley E. & Reed, Jeffery T., eds. Discourse Analysis & the New Testament: Approaches & Results. (JSNTS Ser.: Vol. 170). 408p. 1999. 85.00 (*1-85075-996-0*, Pub. by Sheffield Acad) CUP Services.

Porter, Stanley E. & Stamps, Dennis L., eds. The Rhetorical Interpretation of Scripture: Essays from the 1996 Malibu Conference. (JSNTS Ser.: Vol. 180). 365p. 1999. 95.00 (*1-85075-959-6*, Pub. by Sheffield Acad) CUP Services.

Porter, Stanley E. & Tombs, David, eds. Approaches to New Testament Study. LC 96-107633. (JSNT Supplement Ser.: Vol. 120). 392p. 1995. 85.00 (*1-85075-567-1*, Pub. by Sheffield Acad) CUP Services.

Porter, Stanley E., jt. auth. see Weima, Jeffrey A.

Porter, Stanley E., jt. ed. see Evans, Craig A.

Porter, Stanley E., jt. ed. see Evans, Craig.

Porter, Stanley E., ed. see Zuntz, Gunther.

Porter, Stephanie, et al, eds. Children & Youth Assisted by Medical Technology in Educational Settings: Guidelines for Care. 2nd ed. LC 96-46463. 464p. (Orig.). 1996. spiral bd. 52.00 (*1-55766-236-3*) P H Brookes.

Porter, Stephen. Destruction in the English Civil Wars. 192p. 1994. 31.95 (*0-7509-0516-6*, Pub. by Sutton Pub Ltd) Intl Pubs Mktg.

— Destruction in the English Civil Wars. (History Paperback Ser.). (Illus.). 192p. 1997. pap. 19.95 (*0-7509-1585-4*, Pub. by Sutton Pub Ltd) Intl Pubs Mktg.

— Don Juan. 1973. pap. 5.25 (*0-8222-0323-5*) Dramatists Play.

***Porter, Stephen.** The Essential List of Films for Study. unabridged ed. Landes, William-Alan, ed. LC 99-29930. 96p. 1999. pap. write for info. (*0-88734-930-7*, Pub. by Phantom Pub) Empire Pub Srvs.

Porter, Stephen. The Great Fire of London. LC 97-158874. (History Paperbacks Ser.). (Illus.). 224p. 1998. 33.95 (*0-7509-0778-9*, Pub. by Sutton Pub Ltd); pap. 21.95 (*0-7509-1813-6*, Pub. by Sutton Pub Ltd) Intl Pubs Mktg.

***Porter, Stephen.** The Great Plague. (Illus.). 224p. 2000. 34.95 (*0-7509-1615-X*, Pub. by Sutton Publng) Intl Pubs Mktg.

— The Great Plague. 2000. reprint ed. pap. 21.95 (*0-7509-2571-X*, Pub. by Sutton Publng) Intl Pubs Mktg.

Porter, Stephen, ed. London & the Civil War. 240p. 1996. text 65.00 (*0-312-15844-0*) St Martin.

Porter, Stephen, jt. auth. see Pepper, Corey.

Porter, Stephen C. & Skinner, Brian J. Physical Geology. LC 86-32533. 750p. 1987. text 93.95 (*0-471-05668-5*) Wiley.

— Physical Geology, Study Guide. 236p. 1987. pap., student ed. 43.95 (*0-471-62946-4*) Wiley.

Porter, Stephen C., jt. auth. see Skinner, Brian J.

Porter, Stephen L. & Fife, Bruce. Get Rich with Y2K: How to Cash in on the Financial Crisis in the Year 2000. unabridged ed. LC 98-54141. 154p. 1999. pap. 24.00 (*0-941599-48-5*, Pub. by Piccadilly Bks) Empire Pub Srvs.

Porter, Stephen R. Medicine & Surgery for Dentistry. 2nd ed. LC 99-10540. (Colour Guide Ser.). 1999. write for info. (*0-443-06169-6*) Harcrt Hlth Sci Grp.

Porter, Steven. The American Musical Theatre: A Complete Musical Theatre Course. LC 87-14495. 138p. 1987. pap. 14.00 (*0-935016-97-X*, Barclay House) Zinn Pub Grp.

— The American Musical Theatre: A Complete Musical Theatre Course. 2nd ed. LC 97-39626. 1997. pap. 25.00 (*0-88734-686-3*) Players Pr.

— The Ethics of a Democracy. LC 91-62678. 144p. (C). 1994. pap. write for info. (*0-9625372-2-5*, Pub. by Phantom Pubns) Empire Pub Srvs.

— The Harmonization of the Chorale. 147p. 1995. pap. 18.00 (*0-935016-80-5*, Pub. by Zinn Pub Grp) Empire Pub Srvs.

— Music: A Comprehensive Introduction. LC 85-16847. 336p. 1986. pap. 18.00 (*0-935016-81-3*, Pub. by Zinn Pub Grp) Empire Pub Srvs.

— Music: A Comprehensive Introduction, Workbook Number 1: Music Theory, Vol. 2. 45p. 1986. pap., wbk. ed. 7.00 (*0-935016-84-8*) Zinn Pub Grp.

— New Monologues for Reader's Theater. LC 94-46526. 74p. 1995. pap. 10.00 (*0-88734-651-0*) Players Pr.

— The Prairie Man. LC 89-92532. 62p. (YA). 1990. pap. text 6.00 (*0-9625372-0-9*) Phantom Pubns.

— The Prairie Man. 2nd rev. ed. LC 92-80226. (Illus.). 70p. 1992. pap. 9.95 (*0-9625372-3-3*, Pub. by Phantom Pubns) Empire Pub Srvs.

— The Senator's Son & Other Stories. LC 90-61762. 154p. 1994. pap. 10.00 (*0-9625372-1-7*, Pub. by Phantom Pubns) Empire Pub Srvs.

— Wisdom's Passing. xii, 304p. 1989. pap. 18.00 (*0-935016-71-6*, Barclay House) Zinn Pub Grp.

Porter, Steven, compiled by. New Works for Readers' Theatre. LC 93-47112. 112p. 1994. pap. 10.00 (*0-88734-644-8*) Players Pr.

— Voices from Russia & America. LC 93-83376. (Illus.). 340p. 1994. pap. write for info. (*0-9625372-4-1*, Pub. by Phantom Pubns) Empire Pub Srvs.

Porter, Steven, ed. New Works for Readers' Theatre. 112p. 1994. pap. 10.00 (*81-87848-91-X*) Phantom Pubns.

Porter, Steven, jt. auth. see Pepper, Corey.

Porter, Steven L. Save Your Home: How to Protect Your Home & Property from Foreclosure. 2nd ed. LC 90-30371. (Illus.). 160p. 1990. pap. 16.00 (*0-941599-14-0*) Piccadilly Bks.

Porter, Stuart R. Basic Technical Mathematics with Calculus. Ernst, John F., ed. LC 84-9168. 1985. text 35.16 (*0-201-05589-9*); student ed. 13.56 (*0-201-05590-2*) Addison-Wesley.

Porter, Stuart R. & Ernst, John F. Basic Technical Mathematics. LC 84-8369. 1985. teacher ed. write for info. (*0-201-05598-8*); text. write for info. (*0-201-05586-4*); student ed. write for info. (*0-201-05587-2*) Addison-Wesley.

— Basic Technical Mathematics. 2nd ed. LC 94-12265. 1024p. (C). 1997. 98.00 (*0-673-46177-7*) Addson-Wesley Educ.

— Basic Technical Mathematics with Calculus. 2nd ed. LC 94-13873. 1344p. (C). 1997. 110.00 (*0-673-46176-9*) Addson-Wesley Educ.

Porter, Stuart R., jt. auth. see Angel, Allen.

Porter, Stuart R., jt. auth. see Angel, Allen R.

Porter, Sue. In Bed Before Dark. LC 97-19127. (J). (ps). 1997. 14.95 (*0-7894-2217-4*) DK Pub Inc.

— Little Wolf & the Giant. (J). (ps-1). 1990. pap. 13.95 (*0-671-70363-3*) S&S Bks Yung.

— One Potatoe. 32p. 1989. 12.95 (*0-385-25214-5*) Doubleday.

— Parsnip. LC 98-100920. (Illus.). 24p. (J). (ps-k). 1998. 11.95 (*0-7894-2470-3*) DK Pub Inc.

— Parsnip & the Runaway Tractor. LC 98-13778. 20p. (J). 1999. 11.95 (*0-7894-2494-0*) DK Pub Inc.

— Play It Again: Suggestions for Drama. 64p. (C). 1990. pap. 8.50 (*0-7131-0698-0*, 00641) Heinemann.

Porter, Susan E., et al. Tribal Rhythms - Creating the Village: A Curriculum Guide for Building Community with Children. 98p. 1995. pap., teacher ed. 18.95 (*0-9649688-0-0*) Cprtive Artists.

Porter, Susan L. With an Air Debonair: Musical Theatre in America, 1785-1815. LC 90-24921. (Illus.). 648p. (C). 1991. text 59.95 (*1-56098-063-X*) Smithsonian.

Porter, Susan L., ed. British Opera in America: Children in the Wood, 1795 & Blue Beard, 1811. LC 91-49049. (Nineteenth-Century American Musical Theater Ser.). (Illus.). 314p. 1994. text 84.00 (*0-8153-1368-3*) Garland.

— Women of the Commonwealth: Work, Family, & Social Change in Nineteenth-Century Massachusetts. LC 95-21715. (Illus.). 248p. (C). 1996. 45.00 (*1-55849-004-3*); pap. 16.95 (*1-55849-005-1*) U of Mass Pr.

Porter, Suzanne, jt. auth. see Hansen, Julie V.

Porter, Sylvia. Sylvia Porter's 442 Tax Saving Tips, 1989. 256p. (Orig.). 1988. mass mkt. 6.95 (*0-380-89996-5*, Avon Bks) Morrow Avon.

— Sylvia Porter's a Home of Your Own. 176p. 1989. pap. 7.95 (*0-380-89755-5*, Avon Bks) Morrow Avon.

— Sylvia Porter's 495 Tax Saving Tips: 1990 Edition. 288p. (Orig.). 1989. pap. 7.95 (*0-380-89997-3*, Avon Bks) Morrow Avon.

— Sylvia Porter's Guide to Your Health Care: How You Can Have the Best Health Care for Less. 304p. 1990. pap. 9.95 (*0-380-89758-X*, Avon Bks) Morrow Avon.

— Sylvia Porter's Love & Money. 256p. 1986. mass mkt. 3.95 (*0-380-89753-9*, Avon Bks) Morrow Avon.

— Sylvia Porter's New Money Book for the 80's. 1328p. 1980. pap. 10.95 (*0-380-51060-X*, Avon Bks) Morrow Avon.

— Sylvia Porter's Your Financial Security: Making Your Money Work at Every Stage of Your Life. 240p. 1989. reprint ed. pap. 8.95 (*0-380-89754-7*, Avon Bks) Morrow Avon.

Porter, T. Learning to Dance. 208p. (J). (gr. 3-7). Date not set. mass mkt. 5.95 (*0-06-440751-9*) HarpC.

Porter, T., jt. auth. see Cordier, J. M.

Porter, T., jt. auth. see Gilbert, N. D.

Porter, T., jt. auth. see Kamps, Klaus H.

Porter, T. E. King's Day. LC 75-20728. (Haystack Bks.). (Illus.). 64p. 1975. 6.00 (*0-913142-14-X*); pap. 3.50 (*0-913142-13-1*) Mulch Pr.

Porter, Tenah. Crafts. Nabby Crafts & Her Family. 47p. 1997. reprint ed. pap. 9.00 (*0-8328-8116-3*); reprint ed. lib. bdg. 19.00 (*0-8328-8115-5*) Higginson Bk Co.

Porter, Theodore M. The Rise of Statistical Thinking, 1820-1900. 352p. 1986. reprint ed. pap. text 19.95 (*0-691-02409-X*, Pub. by Princeton U Pr) Cal Prin Full Svc.

— Trust in Numbers: The Pursuit of Objectivity in Science & Public Life. LC 94-21440. 312p. 1995. text 37.50 (*0-691-03776-0*, Pub. by Princeton U Pr); pap. text 16.95 (*0-691-02908-3*, Pub. by Princeton U Pr) Cal Prin Full Svc.

Porter, Thomas E. Myth & Modern American Drama. LC 68-21543. (Waynebook Ser.: No. 36). 286p. reprint ed. pap. 88.70 (*0-608-10601-1*, 207122200009) Bks Demand.

— The Zemstvo & the Emergence of Civil Society in Late Imperial Russia 1864-1917. LC 91-3067. (Distinguished Dissertations Ser.: Vol. 18). 324p. 1991. lib. bdg. 99.95 (*0-7734-9972-5*) E Mellen.

Porter, Tom. The Architect's Eye. LC 97-66254. (Illus.). 168p. 1997. pap. 37.99 (*0-419-21230-2*, E & FN Spon) Routledge.

Porter, Tom. Architectural Supermodels: Physical Design Simulation. (Illus.). 192p. Date not set. 57.95 (*0-7506-4928-3*, Architectural Pr) Buttrwrth-Heinemann.

— Ayn Rand's Theory of Knowledge: A Commentary. LC 99-93040. xii, 376p. 1999. pap. 23.95 (*0-9670411-0-4*) T Porter.

— Jesse & the Baby. (Illus.). 12p. (J). (ps-3). 2000. pap. 3.00 (*0-9650312-2-5*) Cosmo Starr.

Porter, Tom. Selling Architectural Ideas LC 99-29074. 1999. pap. 40.00 (*0-419-23260-5*) Routledge.

Porter, Tom & Goodman, Sue. Design Drawing Techniques: For Architects, Graphic Designers & Artists. (Illus.). 144p. 1992. pap. 49.95 (*0-7506-0812-9*, Butterwrth Archit) Buttrwrth-Heinemann.

— Manual of Graphic Techniques, Vol. 2. (Illus.). 128p. 1982. pap. write for info. (*0-408-50007-7*, VNR) Wiley.

— Manual of Graphic Techniques, Vol. 3. (Illus.). 128p. 1983. pap. write for info. (*0-408-50008-5*, VNR) Wiley.

— Manual of Graphic Techniques, Vol. 4. (Illus.). 128p. 1985. pap. write for info. (*0-7506-1627-X*, VNR) Wiley.

— Manual of Graphic Techniques Vol. 3: For Architects, Graphic Designers & Artists, Vol. 3. (Illus.). 128p. 1983. pap. 12.95 (*0-684-18018-9*, Scribners Ref) Mac Lib Ref.

Porter, Tom & Greenstreet, Bob. Manual of Graphic Techniques, Vol. 1. (Illus.). 128p. 1980. pap. write for info. (*0-408-50012-3*, VNR) Wiley.

Porter, Tom & Greenstreet, Robert. Manual of Graphic Techniques, Vol. 1. (Illus.). 112p. 1980. pap. 15.95 (*0-684-16504-X*, Scribners Ref) Mac Lib Ref.

***Porter, Tracey.** Learning to Dance. (J). 2001. lib. bdg. 15.89 (*0-06-029239-3*) HarpC Child Bks.

Porter, Tracey. Treasures in the Dust. LC 96-54860. (Joanna Cotler Bks.). (Illus.). 160p. (J). (gr. 3-7). 1997. 15.95 (*0-06-027563-4*) HarpC Child Bks.

— Treasures in the Dust. LC 96-54860. (Joanna Cotler Bks.). (Illus.). 128p. (J). (gr. 4-8). 1997. lib. bdg. 14.89 (*0-06-027564-2*) HarpC Child Bks.

— Treasures in the Dust. LC 96-54860. 160p. (J). (gr. 3-7). 1999. pap. 4.95 (*0-06-440770-5*) HarpC Child Bks.

***Porter, Tracy.** Dream. 1999. 10.95 (*0-7407-0161-4*) Andrews & McMeel.

Porter, Tracy. Garden Spiral Journal. 1999. 14.95 (*0-8362-5380-9*) Andrews & McMeel.

— Gentle Influences: The Spirited Ties of Sisters. LC 98-182137. (Little Bks.). (Illus.). 80p. (J). 1997. 4.95 (*0-8362-3736-6*) Andrews & McMeel.

— Home Spiral Journal. 1999. 10.95 (*0-8362-5381-7*) Andrews & McMeel.

— Journey Within: A Book of Hope & Renewal. LC 98-182125. (Little Bks.). (Illus.). 80p. 1997. 4.95 (*0-8362-3737-4*) Andrews & McMeel.

— Mother's Journal. 1999. 10.95 (*0-8362-7830-5*) Andrews & McMeel.

***Porter, Tracy.** The Tarot Companion: An Essential Reference. 2000. pap. 12.95 (*1-56718-574-6*) Llewellyn Pubns.

— Tracy Porter's Inspired Gatherings. LC 99-22162. 152p. 1999. 29.95 (*0-7407-0046-4*) Andrews & McMeel.

— True Love: Mini Edition. 2000. 4.95 (*0-7407-0659-4*) Andrews & McMeel.

— Wedding Journal. (Illus.). 2000. 10.95 (*0-7407-0595-4*) Andrews & McMeel.

Porter, Tracy. Returning Home: The Poetics of Whim & Fancy. LC 98-100916. 48p. 1997. 6.95 (*0-8362-3178-3*) Andrews & McMeel.

— Woven in Sunlight: A Garden Companion. LC 98-100318. 48p. 1997. 6.95 (*0-8362-3179-1*) Andrews & McMeel.

Porter, Tracy, et al. Tracy Porter's Dreams from Home: These Are My Thoughts, This Is My Language. LC 98-6436. (Illus.). 136p. 1998. 27.95 (*0-8362-6773-7*) Andrews & McMeel.

***Porter, V. I.** Pretest Analyses of the Steel Containment Vessel Model. 158p. 1999. per. 14.00 (*0-16-062990-X*) USGPO.

***Porter, Val.** British Pigs. (Album Ser.: Vol. 340). (Illus.). 340p. 1999. pap. 25.00 (*0-7478-0413-3*, Pub. by Shire Pubns) Parkwest Pubns.

Porter, Valerie. Caring for Cows. (Illus.). 144p. text 24.95 (*0-905483-93-6*); pap. text 16.95 (*0-905483-94-4*, Pub. by Whittet Bks) Diamond Farm Bk.

— Goat Breeds of the World. (Illus.). 372p. 1996. 49.95 (*0-85236-347-8*) Diamond Farm Bk.

— Life Behind the Cottage Door. (Illus.). 128p. text 34.95 (*1-873580-01-0*, Pub. by Whittet Bks) Diamond Farm Bk.

— Pigs: A Handbook to the Breeds of the World. (Comstock Bk.). (Illus.). 272p. 1993. text 39.95 (*0-8014-2920-X*) Cornell U Pr.

Porter, Venetia. Islamic Tiles. LC 95-2034. (Illus.). 128p. (Orig.). 1995. pap. 16.95 (*1-56656-191-4*) Interlink Pub.

***Porter, Vic.** Borrowed Offenses: Satan's Number One Weapon. 148p. 1999. pap. write for info. (*0-7392-0273-1*, PO3358) Morris Pubng.

Porter, Vicki & Thornes, Robin. A Guide to the Description of Architectural Drawings. LC 94-7769. 352p. 1994. 45.00 (*0-8161-0623-1*, G K Hall & Co) Mac Lib Ref.

Porter, Vondra C. Rednecks & Niggers. 64p. 1999. reprint ed. pap. 10.00 (*1-56167-150-9*) Am Literary Pr.

Porter, W. A., et al, eds. Advances in Computing & Control. (Illus.). 374p. 1989. 70.95 (*0-387-51425-2*, 3309) Spr-Verlag.

Porter, W. A. & Kak, S. C., eds. Advances in Communications & Signal Processing. (Illus.). 384p. 1989. 70.95 (*0-387-51424-4*, 3308) Spr-Verlag.

Porter, W. A., jt. ed. see Bedrosian, S. D.

Porter, W. Arthur. The Knowledge Seekers: Creating Centers for the Performing Sciences. 63p. 1998. pap. 4.95 (*1-887406-08-5*) ICTwo Inst.

Porter, W. Thomas. Bank of America Guide to Financial Solutions. 2nd rev. ed. (Illus.). vi, 286p. 1998. pap. 15.00 (*0-9670882-0-8*) Lifesport Inc.

Porter, Wes. The Garden Book & the Greenhouse. (Illus.). 64p. (Orig.). (J). (gr. k-5). 1998. pap. 11.95 (*0-921051-21-2*) Somerville Hse.

— The Garden Book & the Greenhouse. LC 89-40372. (Illus.). 64p. (Orig.). (J). (gr. k-5). 1992. pap. 10.95 (*0-89480-346-8*, 1346) Workman Pub.

***Porter, Wesley R.** Green Side Up: Growing a Perfect Lawn in Canada. rev. ed. 1999. pap. 10.95 (*1-55041-382-1*) Fitzhenry & W Ltd.

Porter, Will. Annals of Polk County, Iowa. (Illus.). 1064p. 1993. lib. bdg. 105.00 (*0-8328-3531-5*) Higginson Bk Co.

Porter, William. Porter's EMS Protocols. 164p. 1997. ring bd. 595.00 (*1-882740-08-4*) Porter & Assocs.

— Porter's Pocket Guide to Nursing. (Illus.). 1999. pap. 18.95 (*1-882740-21-1*) Porter & Assocs.

— Porter's Pocket Guide to Pediatrics. 3rd ed. 1999. pap. 16.95 (*1-882740-20-3*) Porter & Assocs.

— Reading the Classics & Paradise Lost. LC 92-24241. xx, 222p. 1993. text 45.00 (*0-8032-3706-5*) U of Nebr Pr.

Porter, William E. Assault on the Media: The Nixon Years. LC 75-14898. 330p. reprint ed. pap. 102.30 (*0-7837-4720-9*, 205907200003) Bks Demand.

— Virginia State Government: Fun, Frustrating, & Frightening. LC 92-44977. 1993. 37.50 (*0-8191-9031-4*); pap. 18.50 (*0-8191-9032-2*) U Pr of Amer.

Porter, William F., et al. Wildlife Policies in the U. S. National Parks. LC 94-47917. 300p. (C). 1995. text 55.00 (*1-55963-404-9*); pap. text 30.00 (*1-55963-405-7*) Island Pr.

Porter, William N. A Hundred Verses from Old Japan: Being a Translation of the "Hyaku-Nin-Isshu" LC 77-83039. (Illus.). 224p. 1979. pap. 12.95 (*0-8048-1256-X*) Tuttle Pubng.

Porter, William T., ed. Big Bear of Arkansas, & Other Sketches. LC 75-144673. reprint ed. 29.50 (*0-404-05079-4*) AMS Pr.

— Quarter Race in Kentucky & Other Sketches Illustrative of Scenes, Characters & Incidents Throughout the Universal Yankee Nation. LC 78-174281. reprint ed. 32.50 (*0-404-05088-3*) AMS Pr.

Porter, Wright, Morris & Arthur Staff. Ohio Environmental Law Handbook. 4th ed. LC 99-162550. 376p. 1997. pap. text 95.00 (*0-86587-605-3*, 605) Gov Insts.

— Wetlands & Real Estate Development Handbook. 2nd ed. 218p. 1991. pap. text 79.00 (*0-86587-269-4*) Gov Insts.

Porter, Y. Professional Writing Online. (C). 2000. 40.00 (*0-205-27918-X*, Macmillan Coll) P-H.

Porter, Yves. Painters, Paintings & Books: An Essay on Indo-Persian Technical Literature 12-19th Centuries. (C). 1994. text 28.00 (*81-85425-95-7*, Pub. by Manohar) S Asia.

Porterfield. Dining by Rail. LC 98-3353. 400p. 1998. pap. 17.95 (*0-312-18711-4*) St Martin.

— Inorganic Chemistry: A Unified Approach, International Edition. 2nd ed. 1999. write for info. (*0-12-562981-8*) Acad Pr.

Porterfield, Amanda. Mary Lyon & the Mount Holyoke Missionaries. LC 96-45425. (Religion in America Ser.). (Illus.). 192p. (C). 1997. text 39.95 (*0-19-511301-2*) OUP.

— The Power of Religion: A Comparative Introduction. (Illus.). 240p. (C). 1997. pap. text 21.95 (*0-19-509329-1*) OUP.

Porterfield, Billy. Diddy Waw Diddy: The Passage of an American Son. LC 95-8910. (Southwest Life & Letters Ser.). (Illus.). 448p. 1995. pap. 12.95 (*0-87074-382-1*) SMU Press.

— A Loose Herd of Texans. LC 77-99277. 212p. 1978. 18.95 (*0-89096-044-5*) Tex A&M Univ Pr.

Porterfield, Frank B. Porterfield: The Porterfields. 345p. 1993. reprint ed. pap. 54.00 (*0-8328-3387-8*); reprint ed. lib. bdg. 64.00 (*0-8328-3386-X*) Higginson Bk Co.

Porterfield, James A. & DeRosa, Carl. Mechanical Low Back Pain: Perspectives in Functional Anatomy. 2nd ed. Biblis, Margaret, ed. LC 97-14398. (Illus.). 304p. 1998. text 45.00 (*0-7216-6837-2*, W B Saunders Co) Harcrt Hlth Sci Grp.

— Mechanical Neck Pain: Perspectives in Functional Anatomy. (Illus.). 272p. 1994. text. write for info. (*0-7216-6640-X*, W B Saunders Co) Harcrt Hlth Sci Grp.

Porterfield, Karen, jt. auth. see Fries, Bruce.

Porterfield, Karen, ed. see Fries, Bruce, et al.

Porterfield, Kay M. Coping with Codependency. (Coping Skills Library). 160p. (gr. 7-12). 1997. pap. 6.95 (*1-56838-185-9*, 1157 A) Hazelden.

— Coping with Codependency. rev. ed. (Coping Ser.). (YA). (gr. 7-12). 1994. lib. bdg. 17.95 (*0-8239-1813-0*, D1813-0) Rosen Group.

— Focus on Addictions: A Reference Handbook. LC 92-26623. (Teenage Perspectives Ser.). 1992. lib. bdg. 39.50 (*0-87436-674-7*) ABC-CLIO.

— Straight Talk about Cults. LC 94-37296. (Straight Talk Ser.). 160p. (YA). (gr. 6-12). 1995. 19.95 (*0-8160-3115-0*) Facts on File.

— Straight Talk about Cults. (Straight Talk Ser.). 160p. (YA). (gr. 6-12). 1997. reprint ed. pap. text 9.95 (*0-8160-3750-7*) Facts on File.
— Straight Talk about Divorce. LC 98-45473. (Straight Talk Ser.). 160p. (YA). (gr. 6 up). 1999. 19.95 (*0-8160-3725-6*) Facts on File.
— Straight Talk about Post-Traumatic Stress Disorder: Coping with the Aftermath of Trauma. (Straight Talk Ser.). 144p. (YA). 1996. pap. 9.95 (*0-8160-3552-0*) Facts on File.
Porterfield, Kay Marie. Straight Talk About Learning Disabilities. LC 98-55947. 160p. (YA). (gr. 6-12). 1999. 19.95 (*0-8160-3865-1*) Facts on File.
Porterfield, Marie K. Straight Talk about Post Traumatic Stress Disorder: Coping with the Aftermath of Trauma. (Straight Talk Ser.). 144p. (YA). (gr. 6-12). 1996. 16.95 (*0-8160-3258-0*) Facts on File.
Porterfield, Nolan. Jimmie Rodgers: The Life & Times of America's Blue Yodeler. rev. ed. (Music in American Life Ser.). (Illus.). 512p. (C). 1992. 16.95 (*0-252-06268-X*) U of Ill Pr.
— Last Cavalier: The Life & Times of John A. Lomax, 1867-1948. LC 95-50212. (Folklore & Society Ser.). (Illus.). 656p. 1996. 34.95 (*0-252-02216-5*) U of Ill Pr.
Porterfield, Sally F. Jung's Advice to the Players: A Jungian Reading of Shakespeare's Problem Plays, 57. LC 94-5150. (Contributions in Drama & Theatre Studies: No. 57). 136p. 1994. 45.00 (*0-313-29305-8*, Greenwood Pr) Greenwood.
Porterfield, Susan, ed. Zen, Poetry, the Art of Lucien Stryk. 360p. (C). 1993. text 45.00 (*0-8040-0975-9*) Swallow.
Porterfield, Susan P. Endocrine Physiology. (Illus.). 272p. (C). (gr. 13). 1996. pap. text 31.00 (*0-8151-8492-1*, 28438) Mosby Inc.
Porterfield, Todd B. The Allure of Empire: Art in the Service of French Imperialism, 1798-1836. LC 98-23442. 232 pages 7 1/2p. 1998. text 39.50 (*0-691-05959-4*, Pub. by Princeton U Pr) Cal Prin Full Svc.
Porterfield, William W. Inorganic Chemistry. LC 82-18485. (Illus.). 650p. 1984. text. write for info. (*0-201-05660-7*); teacher ed. write for info. (*0-201-05661-5*) Addison-Wesley.
— Inorganic Chemistry: A Unified Approach. 2nd ed. (Illus.). 921p. 1993. text 41.00 (*0-12-562980-X*) Acad Pr.
Portero, Pilar. Tu Boda. 1999. pap. text 9.95 (*84-08-02247-4*) Planeta.
Portes, Alejandro. By-Passing & Trespassing: Explorations in Boundaries & Change. (Urban Studies: No. 12). 57p. (Orig.). 1995. pap. 12.00 (*0-913749-22-2*) U MD Urban Stud.
— City on the Edge: The Transformation of Miami. 1994. pap. 17.95 (*0-520-08932-4*, Pub. by U CA Pr) Cal Prin Full Svc.
Portes, Alejandro, ed. The Economic Sociology of Immigration: Essays on Networks, Ethnicity, & Entrepreneurship. LC 94-20933. 328p. 1998. 29.95 (*0-87154-682-5*) Russell Sage.
— The Economic Sociology of Immigration: Essays on Networks, Ethnicity, & Entrepreneurship. (Illus.). 328p. (C). 1998. reprint ed. pap. 19.95 (*0-87154-681-7*) Russell Sage.
— The New Second Generation. 316p. (C). 1996. text 45.00 (*0-87154-683-3*); pap. text 19.95 (*0-87154-684-1*) Russell Sage.
Portes, Alejandro, et al, eds. The Informal Economy: Studies in Advanced & Less Developed Countries. LC 88-23004. 360p. 1989. pap. text 17.95 (*0-8018-3736-7*) Johns Hopkins.
— The Urban Caribbean: Transition to the New Global Economy. LC 96-35184. 296p. 1997. text 48.50 (*0-8018-5517-9*); pap. text 17.95 (*0-8018-5519-5*) Johns Hopkins.
Portes, Alejandro & Bach, Robert L. Latin Journey: Cuban & Mexican Immigrants in the United States. LC 83-9292. 432p. 1985. pap. 16.95 (*0-520-05004-5*, Pub. by U CA Pr) Cal Prin Full Svc.
Portes, Alejandro & Rumbaut, Ruben G. Immigrant America: A Portrait. 2nd ed. LC 96-16209. (Illus.). 421p. (C). 1996. pap. 15.95 (*0-520-20765-3*, Pub. by U CA Pr) Cal Prin Full Svc.
Portes, Alejandro, jt. ed. see Kincaid, A. Douglas.
Portes Gil, Emilio. The Conflict Between the Civil Power & the Clergy: Historical & Legal Essay. 1976. lib. bdg. 59.95 (*0-87968-928-5*) Gordon Pr.
***Portes, Jacques.** Fascination & Misgivings: The United States in French Opinion, 1870-1914. 440p. (C). 2000. text Price not set. (*0-521-65323-1*) Cambridge U Pr.
Portes, Pedro R. Making Kids Smarter: A Guide For Developing & Teaching Children Successfully. 192p. (Orig.). 1998. pap. text 19.89 (*1-884532-28-4*) Butler Bks.
Portes, Richard. Deficits & Detente: Report of an International Conference on the Balance of Trade in the Comecon Countries. 92p. (Orig.). (C). 1983. pap. text 6.00 (*0-87078-150-2*) Century Foundation.
Portes, Richard, ed. Economic Transformation in Central & Eastern Europe: A Progress Report. 312p. (C). 1994. pap. 37.50 (*1-898128-00-6*) Brookings.
Portes, Richard & Vines, David. Coping with International Capital Flows, No. 30. 64p. 1997. pap. 11.95 (*0-85092-502-9*, Pub. by Comm Sec) Stylus Pub VA.
Portes, Richard, jt. ed. see Bofinger, Peter.
Portes, Richard, jt. ed. see Faini, Riccardo.
Portes, Richard, jt. ed. see Kaser, Michael C.
Porteus, Elizabeth D. Life of Stanley D. Porteus. 10.95 (*0-914916-86-6*) Ku Paa.
Porteus, Elizabeth D., jt. auth. see Dole, Richard.
Porteus, Mark. The Gdansk Poetical Kit. 1982. 20.00 (*0-933466-03-X*); pap. 10.95 (*0-933466-02-1*) Bellevue Pr.
Porteus, Richard. The Cat Owner's Shape up Manual: Learn Aerobics from Your Cat. Carle, Cliff, ed. 96p. 1993. pap. 4.95 (*0-918259-51-7*) CCC Pubns.
— Imagination Works! 48p. 1999. pap. 8.95 (*0-590-64378-9*) Scholastic Inc.
— Last Words, Last Laughs. Vervaecke, Laura, ed. LC 97-70329. 192p. (Orig.). 1997. pap. 5.99 (*0-914839-38-1*) Gollehon Pr.
— Mega-Fun Math Skill Builders. 48p. (J). (gr. 2-3). 1999. pap. 7.95 (*0-439-04493-6*) Scholastic Inc.
— Mega Fun-Math Skill Builders. 48p. (J). (gr. 5-6). 1999. pap. 7.95 (*0-439-04494-4*) Scholastic Inc.
***Porteus, Richard.** Mega Fun Math Skill Builders. (Illus.). 48p. 1999. pap. 7.95 (*0-439-04495-2*) Scholastic Inc.
Porteus, Richard. Smart Comebacks to Stupid Questions. Carle, Cliff, ed. (Illus.). 64p. 1997. pap. 5.95 (*1-57644-040-0*) CCC Pubns.
Porteus, Stanley D. Century of Social Thinking in Hawaii. LC 62-21039. xiv, 376p. 1962. 27.95 (*0-87015-113-4*) Pacific Bks.
— Porteus Maze Test: Fifty Years' Application. LC 65-18125. (Illus.). viii, 320p. 1965. 27.95 (*0-87015-139-8*) Pacific Bks.
— A Psychologist of Sorts: The Autobiography & Publications of the Inventor of the Porteus Maze Tests. LC 68-31287. (Illus.). x, 325p. 1969. 27.95 (*0-87015-174-6*) Pacific Bks.
— The Psychology of a Primitive People: Study of the Australian Aborigine. LC 71-37910. (Select Bibliographies Reprint Ser.). 1977. reprint ed. 41.95 (*0-8369-6748-8*) Ayer.
— Streamlined Elementary Education. LC 64-23745. (Illus.). 32p. (Orig.). 1964. pap. text 3.95 (*0-87015-125-8*) Pacific Bks.
Portfleet, Dianne R. Walter Wangerin, Jr. - Shaping Our Lives with Words of Power, Vol. 1. LC 96-94304. 192p. (Orig.). (C). 1996. pap. 12.00 (*0-9652129-0-4*) Greenleaf-Witcop.
Portfolio Press Staff. Gardens of England & Wales: 1998 Edition. 1998. pap. text 8.95 (*0-900558-30-X*, Pub. by Natl Gardens) Seven Hills Bk.
Portfolio Press Staff, ed. see Miller, Barbara.
Portfolio Staff. The Peopling of America: A Timeline of Events That Helped Shape Our Nation. 4th rev. ed. Kullen, Allan S., ed. LC 91-91027. 416p. 1996. 17.95 (*1-56192-096-7*) Portfolio DC.
Porth & Saltis. Management Consulting: Theory & Tools for Small Business Interventions. LC 97-77457. 1998. pap. 32.95 (*0-87393-737-6*) Dame Pubns.
Porth, Carol M. Pathophysiology: Concepts of Altered Health States. 5th ed. LC 97-49116. 1,328p. 1998. text 64.95 (*0-397-55413-3*) Lppncott W & W.
Porth, Jacquelyn S., ed. Defense & Foreign Affairs Handbook, 1983. 5th ed. (Illus.). 1982. 117.00 (*0-9605932-1-7*) Intl Strtgc Stds Assn.
Porth, Richard H., jt. auth. see Maurer, John H.
Porti, Joan. Torsion de Reidemeister pour les Varietes Hyperboliques. LC 97-12295. (Memoirs of the American Mathematical Society Ser.: Vol. 128, No. 612). (FRE.). 139p. 1997. pap. 41.00 (*0-8218-0631-9*) Am Math.
Portice, Jack, jt. auth. see Bass, Gene.
Portier, Christopher J., jt. ed. see Wolfe, Mary S.
Portier, R. J., jt. auth. see Vernick, A. S.
***Portier-Theisz, Judith K.** Le Premier Autoportrait de Rembrandt 1628: Etude sur la Formation de Jeune Rembrandt. xii, 165p. (C). 1999. pap. text 29.95 (*3-906763-42-0*) P Lang Pubng.
Portier, William L. Isaac Hecker & the First Vatican Council, Including Hecker's Notes in Italy, 1869-1870. LC 85-3034. (Studies in American Religion: Vol. 15). 360p. 1985. lib. bdg. 99.95 (*0-88946-653-X*) E Mellen.
— Tradition & Incarnation: Foundations of Christian Theology. LC 93-42702. 1994. pap. 18.95 (*0-8091-3467-5*) Paulist Pr.
Portier, William L., jt. ed. see Mize, Sandra Y.
Portilla, Lorraine. He Brought Me out of a Horrible Pit. DeLellis, Leatrice, ed. & intro. by. (Illus.). (Orig.). pap. 5.00 (*0-9616892-0-X*) Your New Beginning.
Portilla, Miguel L. El Destino de la Palabra (Destiny of the Word) 2nd ed. (SPA.). 406p. 1997. 17.99 (*968-16-4870-6*, Pub. by Fondo) Continental Bk.
— Toltecayotl. (SPA.). 19.99 (*968-16-0532-2*, Pub. by Fondo) Continental Bk.
Portilla, Nicolas De La, see De La Portilla, Nicolas.
Portillo, Carlos E. Eternal Security Is Conditional. LC 85-52117. 150p. (Orig.). 1987. pap. write for info. (*0-937365-03-3*) WCP Pubns.
— Evil Side of Good. LC 85-52117. 200p. (Orig.). pap. write for info. (*0-937365-04-1*) WCP Pubns.
— His Revelation from Apocalypses. LC 85-52117. 150p. (Orig.). 1987. pap. write for info. (*0-937365-02-5*) WCP Pubns.
— That Unknown Day. LC 85-52117. (Illus.). 400p. (Orig.). 1986. 14.95 (*0-937365-00-9*); pap. 9.95 (*0-937365-01-7*) WCP Pubns.
Portillo, Carmen F., ed. see American Academy of Nursing Staff.
Portillo-Garcia, Rafael. Diccionario Ingles-Espanol, Espanol-Ingles de Terminoligia Teatral. (SPA.). 232p. 1986. pap. 29.95 (*0-7859-5773-1*) Fr & Eur.
Portillo, J. Diaz, see Diaz Portillo, J.
Portillo, Jo. A Step by Step Approach to Strategic Personal Planning. 75p. (YA). 1998. pap. 19.95 (*1-893167-00-3*) Terrace Trail Pr.
Portillo, Jose L., jt. auth. see Krashen, Stephen D.
Portillo, Michael. Democratic Values & the Currency. (Occasional Papers: No. 103). 31p. 1998. pap. 11.95 (*0-255-36412-1*, Pub. by Inst Economic Affairs) Coronet Bks.
Portillo, Peggy. Juguemos con Musica.Tr. of Musical Trivia. (SPA., Illus.). 24p. (J). 1994. pap. 4.99 (*0-311-32438-X*) Casa Bautista.
Portillo, Rafael. English-Spanish, Spanish-English Dictionary of Theater Terms. (ENG & SPA.). 238p. 1986. 75.00 (*0-7859-9795-4*) Fr & Eur.
Portillo y Pacheco, Jose L. They Are Coming: The Conquest of Mexico. Berler, Beatrice, tr. from SPA. LC 92-3142. (Illus.). 375p. 1992. 34.50 (*0-929398-35-1*) UNTX Pr.
Portinaro, Pierluigi. The Cartography of North America, 1500-1800. 1999. 29.99 (*0-7858-1055-2*) Bk Sales Inc.
Portinaro, Pierluigi & Knirsch, Franco. The Cartography of North America, 1500-1800. LC 87-20028. (Illus.). 320p. 1987. reprint ed. pap. 99.20 (*0-7837-9922-5*, 206064900006) Bks Demand.
Portinsky, Bertrand. Minnesota Evidence Trialbook, Vol. 9. 90p. 1997. ring bd. 79.00 (*0-86678-278-8*, 81755-19, MICHIE) LEXIS Pub.
Portis, A. M. Electrodynamics of High Temperature Superconductors. (Lecture Notes in Physics Ser.). 256p. 1993. text 86.00 (*981-02-1215-1*); pap. text 36.00 (*981-02-1248-8*) World Scientific Pub.
Portis, Charles. The Dog of the South. LC 98-47727. 246p. 1999. pap. 14.95 (*0-87951-931-2*, Pub. by Overlook Pr) Penguin Putnam.
***Portis, Charles.** Gringos. 2000. pap. 14.95 (*1-58567-093-6*, Pub. by Overlook Pr) Penguin Putnam.
— Masters of Atlantis. LC 99-86846. 272p. 2000. pap. 14.95 (*1-58567-021-9*, Pub. by Overlook Pr) Penguin Putnam.
Portis, Charles. Norwood. 1994. 24.95 (*1-56849-403-3*) Buccaneer Bks.
— Norwood. LC 99-10234. 272p. 1999. pap. 13.95 (*0-87951-703-4*, Pub. by Overlook Pr) Penguin Putnam.
— True Grit. large type ed. LC 97-32573. (Perennial Ser.). 243 p. 1998. 24.95 (*0-7838-8366-8*, G K Hall & Co) Mac Lib Ref.
Portis, Clay, jt. illus. see Johnson, Hannibal B.
Portis, Edward B. Reconstructing the Classics: Political Theory from Plato to Marx. 2nd ed. LC 97-33772. (Studies in Political Thinking). (Illus.). 224p. (C). 1997. pap. text 22.95 (*1-56643-049-6*, Chatham House Pub) Seven Bridges.
***Portis, Edward B., et al, eds.** Political Theory & Partisan Politics. LC 99-44721. (C). 2000. text 59.50 (*0-7914-4591-7*) State U NY Pr.
Portis, Edward B. & Levy, Michael B., eds. Handbook of Political Theory & Policy Science. LC 88-3119. 301p. 1988. lib. bdg. 75.00 (*0-313-25598-9*, PHP/, Greenwood Pr) Greenwood.
***Portis, Edward Bryan, et al, eds.** Political Theory & Partisan Politics. LC 99-44721. (C). 2000. pap. text 19.95 (*0-7914-4592-5*) State U NY Pr.
Portis, Hattie, ed. see Abdulai, David.
Portis, Jonathan, jt. auth. see Allen, Charles F.
Portisch, Lajos & Sarkozy, Balazs. Six Hundred Endings. Eszenyi, Sandor et al, trs. (Chess Ser.). (Illus.). 198p. 1981. 21.90 (*0-08-024137-9*, Pergamon Pr) Elsevier.
Portland Cement Association. Experiences In Biology 101 3. 3rd ed. 1995. text 16.00 (*0-07-050513-6*) McGraw.
Portland Cement Association Staff. Alternative Uses of Cement Kiln Dust. 20p. 1995. 15.00 (*0-89312-133-9*, RP327T) Portland Cement.
— Cement & Concrete Reference Guide for Editors. 120p. 1997. pap. 20.00 (*0-89312-177-0*, MS124G) Portland Cement.
— Cementitious Grouts & Grouting. (Illus.). 64p. (Orig.). (C). 1990. pap. text 23.00 (*0-89312-088-X*, EB111.01T) Portland Cement.
— Circular Concrete Tanks Without Prestressing. rev. ed. (Illus.). 52p. (C). 1993. 20.00 (*0-89312-125-8*, IS072D) Portland Cement.
— Concrete Construction & Estimating. Avery, Craig, ed. LC 80-12349. (Illus.). 576p. 1980. reprint ed. pap. 25.00 (*0-910460-75-2*) Craftsman.
— Connections for Tilt-Up Wall Construction. 43p. (Orig.). (C). 1987. pap. text 12.00 (*0-89312-086-3*, EB110D) Portland Cement.
— Design & Control of Concrete Mixtures. 13th rev. ed. 212p. (Orig.). (C). 1994. pap. 35.00 (*0-89312-087-1*, EB001T) Portland Cement.
— Detailed Illustration of Contingent Management Practices for Cement Kiln Dust. (Illus.). 52p. 1993. 28.00 (*0-89312-126-6*, SP115T) Portland Cement.
— Effects of Substances on Concrete & Guide to Protective Treatments. rev. ed. 36p. 1997. pap. 15.00 (*0-89312-193-2*, IS001.09T) Portland Cement.
— Effects on Cement of High Efficiency Separators. LC 97-153902. 30p. 1995. 30.00 (*0-89312-132-0*, RD110T) Portland Cement.
— High Strength Concrete. rev. ed. (Illus.). 60p. (C). 1994. 15.00 (*0-89312-127-4*, EB114T) Portland Cement.
— Notes on ACI 318-95 Building Code Requirements for Structural Concrete with Design Applications. 5th rev. ed. Ghosh, S. K. & Rabbat, Basile G., eds. (Illus.). 920p. 1996. pap. 30.00 (*0-89312-144-4*, EB070D) Portland Cement.
— Optimizing Surface Texture of Concrete Pavement. 112p. 1995. 40.00 (*0-89312-134-7*, RD111T) Portland Cement.
— Role of Minor Elements in Cement Manufacturing & Use. (Illus.). 44p. 1995. 30.00 (*0-89312-131-2*, RD109T) Portland Cement.
— Simplified Design: Reinforced Concrete Buildings of Moderate Size & Height. 2nd ed. (Illus.). 256p. (C). 1993. 30.00 (*0-89312-129-0*, EB104) Portland Cement.
Portland, Charles. Computer Guide: Personal Computer Reference & Training. Bray, Aree, ed. LC 97-91563. (Illus.). 240p. (Orig.). 1997. pap. 12.95 (*0-9655924-0-5*) Portland NY.
***Portland Habilitation Center Staff.** Custodial Supervision of Adults with Special Needs. 298p. 1999. pap. 46.00 (*0-944352-25-1*) Cleaning Cons.
Portland Museum of Art Staff. The Maine Collection. LC 92-85255. 254p. 1993. 12.95 (*0-9635386-0-8*) Portland Mus.
— Masterpieces of Painting. (Illus.). 1992. pap. 3.95 (*0-486-27139-0*) Dover.
Portland Press Staff. Installations 1964-1992. 1992. 20.00 (*1-57684-011-5*) Portland Pr.
Portlock, Carol S. Clinical Problems in Oncology. 1986. 10.95 (*0-316-71427-5*, Little Brwn Med Div) Lppncott W & W.
— Manual Oncology, No. 2. 1986. 15.95 (*0-316-71426-7*, Little Brwn Med Div) Lppncott W & W.
Portlock, Carol S. & Goffinet, Donald R. Manual of Clinical Problems in Oncology. 2nd ed. 1986. 27.00 (*0-316-71425-9*, Little Brwn Med Div) Lppncott W & W.
Portlock, Melinda J. Cooperative Education Student Journal. 98p. (C). 1996. pap. text 20.95 (*0-7872-2899-0*) Kendall-Hunt.
Portlock, Rob. Climbing the Church Walls. LC 91-17872. (Illus.). 104p. (Orig.). 1991. pap. 6.99 (*0-8308-1830-8*, 1830) InterVarsity.
— Families off the Wall. LC 94-18628. (Illus.). 104p. (Orig.). 1994. pap. 6.99 (*0-8308-1823-5*, 1823) InterVarsity.
— Off the Church Wall. LC 87-2774. (Illus.). 108p. (Orig.). 1987. pap. 6.99 (*0-87784-753-3*, 753) InterVarsity.
— Way off the Church Wall. LC 89-11230. (Illus.). 108p. (Orig.). 1989. pap. 6.99 (*0-8308-1281-4*, 1281) InterVarsity.
***Portman, Janet.** Renters' Rights. 2nd ed. (Quick & Legal Ser.). 2000. pap. 24.95 (*0-87337-596-3*) Nolo com.
***Portman, Janet & Stewart, Marcia.** Every Tenant's Legal Guide. 2nd ed. LC 98-25916. 448p. 1999. pap. 26.95 (*0-87337-492-4*) Nolo com.
Portman, Janet & Stewart, Marcia. Renter's Rights. LC 98-19438. (Quick & Legal Ser.). (Illus.). 220p. (Orig.). 1998. pap. 15.95 (*0-87337-411-8*) Nolo com.
Portman, Janet, jt. auth. see Steingold, Fred.
Portman, M. V. A History of Our Relations with the Andamanese, Set. (C). 1995. 94.00 (*81-206-0608-6*, Pub. by Asian Educ Servs) S Asia.
— Manual of the Andamanese Languages. 1987. 19.95 (*0-7859-9826-8*) Fr & Eur.
Portman, Rob, jt. auth. see Kerrey, Bob.
Portman, Robert M., et al. Ophthalmic Regulatory Manual. 4th rev. ed. Orig. Title: Ophthalmic Reimbursement Manual. (Illus.). 252p. 1987. ring bd. write for info. (*1-929196-00-8*) Am Opthlmc Admin.
Portman, Sally. The Smiling Country. (Illus.). 1993. pap. 12.95 (*0-9636921-0-0*) Pack & Paddle.
Portman, V. T., jt. ed. see Reshetov, D. N.
Portmann, Adolf. Essays in Philosophical Zoology: The Living Form & the Seeing Eye. Carter, Richard B., tr. from GER. LC 90-5672. (Problems in Contemporary Philosophy Ser.: Vol. 20). 296p. 1991. lib. bdg. 89.95 (*0-88946-323-9*) E Mellen.
Portmann, Didier, jt. auth. see Portmann, Michel.
***Portmann, John.** When Bad Things Happen to Other People. LC 99-26106. 256p. 1999. 26.95 (*0-415-92334-4*) Routledge.
Portmann, John. When Bad Things Happen to Other People. LC 99-26106. 2000. pap. 17.95 (*0-415-92335-2*) Routledge.
Portmann, M., et al, eds. Transplants & Implants in Otology III: Proceedings of the Third International Symposium on Transplants & Implants in Otology, Bordeaux, France, June 10-14, 1995. LC 96-4640. 1996. 146.00 (*90-6299-142-4*) Kugler Pubns.
Portmann, Michael, et al. Rhino-Otological Microsurgery of the Skull Base. LC 93-33094. (Practice of Surgery Ser.). (Illus.). 320p. 1995. text 195.00 (*0-443-04539-9*) Church.
Portmann, Michel & Portmann, Didier. Otologic Surgery: Manual of Oto-Surgical Techniques. LC 97-45064. (Illus.). 298p. 1998. pap. 185.95 (*1-56593-939-5*, 1860) Thomson Learn.
Portmess, Lisa, jt. ed. see Walters, Kerry S.
Portnay, Linda. Wishing for the Worst. 40p. 1993. pap. 10.00 (*0-942292-12-X*) Warthog Pr.
Portner, H. O. & Playle, Richard C., eds. Cold Ocean Physiology. LC 97-22063. (Society for Experimental Biology Seminar Ser.: No. 66). (Illus.). 516p. (C). 1998. text 125.00 (*0-521-58078-1*) Cambridge U Pr.
Portner, Hal. Mentoring New Teachers. LC 98-19774. (Illus.). 112p. 1998. 45.95 (*0-8039-6714-4*, 82473); pap. 19.95 (*0-8039-6715-2*, 82474) Corwin Pr.
Portner, Hal & Pauker, Robert. How to Study Less & Accomplish More: Time Management for Students. (Illus.). 44p. (Orig.). (YA). (gr. 11 up). 1983. pap. 6.95 (*0-913149-00-4*) Portner.
Portner, Hans O., et al, eds. Physiology of Cephalopod Mollusc: Lifestyle & Performance Adaptations. 214p. 1995. text 104.00 (*2-88449-027-2*) Gordon & Breach.
Portney. Foundations of Clinical Research: Applications to Practice. 2nd ed. LC 99-55198. 736p. (C). 1999. 52.00 (*0-8385-2695-0*) Appleton & Lange.
Portney, Kent E. Controversial Issues in Environmental Policy. (Controversial Issues In Public Policy Ser.: Vol. 1). (Illus.). 192p. (C). 1992. 42.00 (*0-8039-4221-4*); pap. 18.95 (*0-8039-4222-2*) Sage.
— Siting Hazardous Waste Treatment Facilities: The Nimby Syndrome. LC 90-1217. 200p. 1991. 49.95 (*0-86569-016-2*, T016, Auburn Hse) Greenwood.
Portney, Kent E., jt. auth. see Danziger, Sheldon.
Portney, Leslie G. & Watkins, Mary P. Foundations of Clinical Research: Applications to Practice. (Illus.). 560p. (C). 1993. pap. text 49.95 (*0-8385-1065-5*, A1065-0) Appleton & Lange.

P

Portney, Paul R., ed. Economic Issues in Metropolitan Growth. LC 76-15906. (Resources for the Future Ser.). 160p. 1977. 15.00 (0-8018-1885-0) Johns Hopkins.
— Economic Issues in Metropolitan Growth: Papers Presented at a Forum Conducted by Resources for the Future, May 28-29, 1975 in Washington D. C. LC 76-15906. (Illus.). 157p. reprint ed. pap. 48.70 (0-608-18095-5, 203216100078) Bks Demand.
— Public Policies for Environmental Protection. LC 89-24363. 308p. 1990. pap. 12.95 (0-915707-53-5) Resources Future.
***Portney, Paul R., ed.** Public Policies for Environmental Protection. 2nd ed. (Illus.). 308p. (C). 2000. write for info. (1-891853-03-1, Pub. by Resources Future) Johns Hopkins.
Portney, Paul R., et al, eds. Current Issues in U. S. Environmental Policy. LC 78-4328. 207p. 1978. pap. 9.95 (0-8018-2119-3) Resources Future.
Portney, Paul R. & Haas, Ruth B., eds. Current Issues in Natural Resource Policy. LC 87-47982. 300p. 1982. pap. 14.95 (0-8018-2917-8) Resources Future.
Portney, Paul R., jt. auth. see Probst, Katherine N.
Portnoff, Marc A., et al. Measurement & Analysis of Vapor Sensors Used at Underground Storage Tank Sites. (Illus.). 50p. (C). 1998. reprint ed. pap. text 20.00 (0-7881-4892-3) DIANE Pub.
Portnoi, L. M. & Dibirov, M. P. Radiodiagnosis of Endophytic Gastric Cancer. LC 95-12084.Tr. of Luchevaia Diagnostika Endofitnogo Raka Zheludka. 1995. write for info. (1-56700-028-2) Begell Hse.
Portnol, Paul, ed. Airport & Handling Agents, 98/99: Europe. (Airport & Handling Agents 98-99 Ser.). 1998. 395.00 (0-7106-1782-8) Janes Info Group.
Portnov, jt. auth. see Callner.
Portnov, Anna. Awakening: Articles & Stories about Jews & Yeshua (Jesus) (RUS.). 104p. 1991. pap. 6.99 (1-880226-01-4) M J Pubs.
— Awakening: Articles & Stories about Jews & Yeshua (Jesus) 104p. 1992. pap. 6.99 (1-880226-09-X) M J Pubs.
***Portnov, B. A. & Hare, A. P., eds.** Desert Regions: Population, Migration & Environment. LC 99-30636. (Illus.). xvi, 332p. 1999. 95.00 (3-540-65780-0) Spr-Verlag.
Portnov, Mikhall, jt. auth. see Sedov, Alexander.
Portnoy. Leadership. LC 98-27295. 220p. (C). 1998. pap. text 38.40 (0-13-921495-X) P-H.
Portnoy, jt. auth. see Callner.
Portnoy, Elliot I. The Peoples Guide to Government, the Legislative Branch. LC 98-178664. 67 p. 1991. 15.75 (1-56256-011-5) Peoples Pub Grp.
Portnoy, Dennis. Overextended & Undernourished: A Self-Care Handbook for People in Helping Roles. LC 95-53695. 60p. (Orig.). 1996. pap. 7.00 (1-56246-115-X, 3279, HazeldenJohnson Inst) Hazelden.
Portnoy, Dina. Women: The Recruiter's Last Resort. 40p. 1974. pap. 3.00 (0-916894-04-5) Recon Pubns.
Portnoy, Dorothy K. Purple Irises: A Woman in Transition Discovers Passion & Unforseen Encounters. 336p. 1998. pap. 15.95 (1-58151-000-4) BookPartners.
***Portnoy, Enid J.** Make Their Days: Activities for Residents in Long-Term Care. LC 99-11374. 112p. 1999. pap. text 18.95 (0-398-06943-3) C C Thomas.
Portnoy, Francie. One Wonderful You. LC 97-202671. (Illus.). 48p. (J). (ps-5). 1997. pap. 9.95 (0-9643051-1-9) Chldrns Home Soc.
Portnoy, Jeffrey S. Mass Communication Law in Hawaii. 122p. (C). 1994. pap. 14.95 (0-913507-56-3) New Forums.
Portnoy, Joan, jt. auth. see Portnoy, Sanford.
Portnoy, Julius. Music in the Life of Man. LC 73-9265. (Illus.). 300p. 1973. reprint ed. lib. bdg. 35.00 (0-8371-7000-1, POMU, Greenwood Pr) Greenwood.
Portnoy, Kathy L., jt. auth. see Callner, Bruce W.
Portnoy, Kenneth. Screen Adaptation: A Scriptwriting Handbook. 176p. 1991. pap. 29.95 (0-240-80095-8, Focal) Buttrwrth-Heinemann.
— Screen Adaptation: A Scriptwriting Handbook. 2nd ed. LC 98-18039. 172p. 1998. pap. 24.95 (0-240-80349-3, Focal) Buttrwrth-Heinemann.
Portnoy, Linda & Farley, Eileen. Washington Criminal Practice in Courts of Limited Jurisdiction. 2nd rev. ed. LC 98-67068. 1998. ring bd. 185.00 (0-327-00200-X, 82746-20) LEXIS Pub.
Portnoy, Linda S. & Farley, Eileen P. Washington Criminal Practice in Courts of Limited Jurisdiction, 2 vols., Set. LC 92-42802. 1150p. 1994. spiral bd. 175.00 (1-56257-834-0, 82742-10, MICHIE) LEXIS Pub.
***Portnoy, Lynn.** Going Like Lynn - New York Vol. 2: A Series of Liberating Travel Primers for Women. LC 94-12045. 112p. 2000. pap. 13.95 (0-9670099-1-X) Diam Pubs.
— Going Like Lynn-Paris Vol. I: A Series of Liberating Travel Primers for Women. Bobrow, Judy, ed. (Going Like Lynn-Paris Ser.). (Illus.). 92p. 1999. pap. 12.95 (0-9670099-0-1) Diam Pubs.
Portnoy, Marshall, jt. auth. see Wolff, Josee.
Portnoy, Mindy A. Matzah Ball. LC 93-39402. (Illus.). (J). (gr. 1-5). 1994. pap. 6.95 (0-929371-69-0) Kar-Ben.
Portnoy, Samuel A., tr. from YID. Henryk Erlich & Victor Alter: Two Heroes & Martyrs for Jewish Socialism. rev. ed. 39.50 (0-88125-357-X) Ktav.
Portnoy, Sanford & Portnoy, Joan. How to Take Great Trips with Your Kids. rev. ed. Ziedrich, Linda, ed. LC 95-7411. 176p. 1995. 16.95 (1-55832-073-3); pap. 9.95 (1-55832-074-1) Harvard Common Pr.
***Portnoy, Sanford M.** Divorce Client Relationship Training. LC 00-30614. 2000. pap. write for info. (1-57073-797-5) Amer Bar Assn.
***Portny, Stanley.** Project Management for Dummies. 384p. 2000. pap. 19.99 (0-7645-5283-X) IDG Bks.
Porto. The Craft of Legal Reasoning. LC 97-61103. (C). 1997. pap. text 24.00 (0-15-503696-3, Pub. by Harcourt Coll Pubs) Harcourt.
***Porto, Brian L.** May it Please the Court: Judicial Processes & Politics in America. LC 00-35482. 2000. pap. write for info. (0-321-03683-2) Longman.
Porto Editorial Staff. Dicionario Alamao - Portugues - German - Portuguese Dictionary. (POR.). 1991. 75.00 (0-8288-8543-5) Fr & Eur.
— Dicionario da Lingua Portuguesa. (POR.). 591p. 1992. 29.95 (0-8288-8529-X) Fr & Eur.
— Dicionario Espanhol - Portugues, Portugues - Espanhol - Portuguese - Spanish, Span ish - Portuguese Dictionary. (POR & SPA.). 1195p. 1990. 49.95 (0-8288-8533-8) Fr & Eur.
— Dicionario Frances - Portugues. (FRE & POR.). 543p. 1992. 29.95 (0-8288-8534-6) Fr & Eur.
— Dicionario Frances - Portugues, Portugues - Frances. (FRE & POR.). 1195p. 1992. 49.95 (0-8288-8532-X) Fr & Eur.
— Dicionario Italiano - Portugues - Italian - Portuguese Dictionary. (ITA & POR.). 1991. 75.00 (0-8288-8547-8) Fr & Eur.
— Dicionario Latim - Portugues - Latin - Portuguese Dictionary. (LAT.). 1991. 75.00 (0-8288-8545-1) Fr & Eur.
— Dicionario Portugues - Alemao - Portuguese - German Dictionary. (GER & POR.). 1991. 75.00 (0-8288-8544-3) Fr & Eur.
— Dicionario Portugues - Espanhol - Portuguese - Spanish Dictionary. (POR & SPA.). 594p. 1989. 29.95 (0-8288-8531-1) Fr & Eur.
— Dicionario Portugues - Frances - Portuguese French Dictionary. (FRE & POR.). 652p. 1991. 29.95 (0-8288-8530-3) Fr & Eur.
— Dicionario Portugues - Italiano - Portuguese - Italian Dictionary. (ITA & POR.). 1991. 75.00 (0-8288-8548-6) Fr & Eur.
— Dicionario Portugues - Latim - Portuguese - Latin Dictionary. (LAT & POR.). 1991. 75.00 (0-8288-8546-X) Fr & Eur.
— Dicionario Romeno - Portugues - Romanian - Portuguese Dictionary. (POR & RUM.). 1991. 75.00 (0-8288-8549-4) Fr & Eur.
Porto, Grena G., ed. The Physician's Risk Management Desk Reference. xi, 176p. 1997. pap. 15.00 (0-9629192-0-9) V H A.
Porto, Manuel, jt. auth. see McGahan, John P.
Porto Staff, ed. Diccionario de Lingua Portuguesa. 1996. audio compact disk 150.00 (0-7859-9542-0) Fr & Eur.
— Dictionary. (ENG & POR.). 1991. 75.00 (0-8288-8542-7) Fr & Eur.
— Dictionary. 1996. 125.00 incl. audio compact disk (0-7859-9540-4) Fr & Eur.
Porto, V. W., et al, eds. Evolutionary Programming VII: 7th International Conference, EP '98, San Diego, California, U. S. A., March 25-27, 1998, Proceedings. (Lecture Notes in Computer Science Ser.: Vol. 1447). (Illus.). xvi, 840p. 1998. pap. 92.00 (3-540-64891-7) Spr-Verlag.
Portocarero, Lucienne. Social Mobility in Industrial Societies: Women in France & Sweden. (Swedish Institute for Social Research Ser.: No. 3). 118p. (Orig.). 1987. pap. text 36.00 (91-7604-025-9) Coronet Bks.
Portocarrero, Ria, ed. see Gilsdorf, Mary J.
***Portoghesi, Paolo, intro.** Aldo Rossi: The Sketchbooks, 1990-97. LC 00-101551. (Illus.). 192p. 2000. 27.50 (0-500-51020-2, Pub. by Thames Hudson) Norton.
Portoghesi, Paulo. Bruno Minardi. 128p. 1997. pap. 49.95 (0-471-97854-X) Wiley.
Portoghesi, Paulo & Frampton, Kenneth, eds. Bruno Minardi. (Architectural Monographs: Vol. 49). (Illus.). 128p. 1997. pap. 38.00 (1-85490-457-4) Academy Ed UK.
***Portolano, Charles.** Inspired by Their Spirits: A Collection of Poems. 78p. 1999. pap. text 12.00 (1-55605-292-8) Wyndham Hall.
Porton, Gary G. The Stranger Within Your Gates: Converts & Conversion in Rabbinic Literature. 424p. 1994. 29.95 (0-226-67586-6) U Ch Pr.
Porton, Harriet, jt. auth. see Helmut-Muuss, Rolf E.
Porton, Richard. Film & the Anarchist Imagination. LC 99-20668. 320p. 1999. pap. text 22.00 (1-85984-261-5, Pub. by Verso) Norton.
***Porton, Richard.** Film & the Anarchist Imagination. LC 99-20668. 320p. 1999. 65.00 (1-85984-702-1, Pub. by Verso) Norton.
Portoraro, Arthur. Logic with Symlog. LC 93-14976. 512p. (C). 1993. 79.00 (0-13-327628-7) P-H.
***Ports, George.** Jazz Guitar Christmas. (Illus.). 1998. pap. 9.95 (1-57424-063-3) Centerstream Pub.
Ports, George & Sibley, Frank. Jazz Guitar Solos. (Illus.). 112p. (Orig.). (C). 1997. pap. 19.95 incl. audio compact disk (1-57424-024-2) Centerstream Pub.
Ports, Michael A., ed. Hydraulic Engineering. 1200p. 1989. pap. text 117.00 (0-87262-719-5, 719) Am Soc Civil Eng.
Portsmouth Polytechnic Staff. Immobilization of Copper by Marine Fouling Micro-Organisms. 67p. 1984. write for info. (0-318-60403-5) Intl Copper.
Portugais, Jean. Didactique des Mathermatiques et Formation des Enseignants. xxi, 312p. 1995. 51.95 (3-906753-67-0, Pub. by P Lang) P Lang Pubng.
Portugal, Ana M., ed. Mujeres e Iglesia: Sexualidad y Aborto en America Latina. (SPA., Illus.). 146p. (Orig.). 1989. pap. 10.00 (0-915365-15-4) Cath Free Choice.
Portugal, Armando S., photos by. Luis Barragan: The Architecture of Light, Color, & Form. LC 92-15545. (Illus.). 168p. 1992. 50.00 (0-8478-1482-3, Pub. by Rizzoli Intl) St Martin.
Portugal, Buddy, jt. auth. see Mark, Robert.
Portugal, Jan. ABC Sillies. LC 83-10291. (Living on This Planet Ser.). (Illus.). 56p. (Orig.). (J). (ps-1). 1983. pap. 3.00 (0-937148-13-X) Wild Horses.
***Portugal, Jean.** We Were There - The Navy, the Army & the RCAF: A Record for Canada, 7 vols. LC 99-458589. 1998. 240.00 (1-55246-054-1) Battered Silicon.
Portugal, Nancy & Main, Jody S. Potted Plant Organic Care. 3rd ed. LC 79-22173. (Living on This Planet Ser.). (Illus.). 80p. 1978. pap. 4.50 (0-9601088-7-4) Wild Horses.
Portugal, Pam Rainbear. A Place for Human Beings. 2nd ed. (Living on This Planet Ser.). (Illus.). 160p. 1978. pap. 6.95 (0-9601088-5-8) Wild Horses.
Portugali. Distribution, Allocation, Social Structure & Spatial Form: Elements of Planning Theory. (Progress in Planning Ser.: Vol. 14, Part 3). (Illus.). 83p. 1980. pap. 16.25 (0-08-026808-0, Pergamon Pr) Elsevier.
Portugali, Juval. Implicate Relations: Society & Space in the Israeli-Palestinian Conflict. 224p. 1993. lib. bdg. 109.50 (0-7923-1886-2, Pub. by Kluwer Academic) Kluwer Academic.
***Portugali, Juval.** Self-Organization & the City. Haken, H., ed. LC 99-38893. (Series in Synergetics). (Illus.). xii, 319p. 1999. 99.00 (3-540-65483-6) Spr-Verlag.
Portugali, Juval, ed. The Construction of Cognitive Maps. LC 96-1812. (GeoJournal Library: Vol. 32). 376p. (C). 1996. text 191.50 (0-7923-3949-5) Kluwer Academic.
Portuges, Catherine. Screen Memories: The Hungarian Cinema of Marta Meszaros. LC 92-2359. (International Women Filmmakers Ser.). 208p. 1993. 35.00 (0-253-34558-8); pap. 15.95 (0-253-20782-7) Ind U Pr.
Portugese, Jacqueline. Fertility Policy in Israel: The Politics of Religion, Gender & Nation. LC 97-49490. 232p. 1998. 59.95 (0-275-96098-6, Praeger Pubs) Greenwood.
Portune, Robert. Changing Adolescent Attitudes Toward Police. LC 77-358331. (Criminal Justice Ser.: Vol. 4). 285p. reprint ed. pap. 88.40 (0-8357-9036-3, 201522700094) Bks Demand.
Portuondo, Aleyda T. Vigencia Politica & Literaria de Martin Morua Delgado. (Coleccion Cuba y sus Jueces). 1978. pap. 2.00 (0-89729-205-7) Ediciones.
Portvliet, Rien. Rien Poortvliet's Horses. LC 95-69818. (Illus.). 248p. 1995. 60.00 (1-55670-430-5) Stewart Tabori & Chang.
Portway, Patrick & Lane, Carla. Guide to Teleconferencing & Distance Learning. 2nd ed. 420p. (C). 1997. pap. text 50.00 (0-9643270-1-5) Applied Busn.
Portwood, Madeleine. Developmental Dyspraxia-Identification & Intervention: A Manual for Parents & Professionals. 1998. pap. 24.95 (1-85346-573-9) Taylor & Francis.
— Understanding Developmmental Dyspraxia: A Textbook for Students & Professionals. 1999. pap. 27.95 (1-85346-574-7) David Fulton.
***Portwood, Shirley Motley.** Tell Us a Story: An African American Family in the Heartland. 2000. 49.95 (0-8093-2313-3) S Ill U Pr.
— Tell Us a Story: An African American Family in the Heartland. LC 99-40182. (Illus.). 288p. 2000. pap. 16.95 (0-8093-2314-1) S Ill U Pr.
Portwood, Timothy. Competition Law & the Environment. (Environmental Law Ser.). 250p. 1994. 135.00 (1-874698-35-X, Pub. by Federation Pr) Gaunt.
— Joint Ventures under EEC Competition Law. (European Community Law Ser.). 192p. (C). 1996. text 90.00 (0-485-70012-3, Pub. by Athlone Pr) Humanities.
— Mergers under EEC Competition Law. (European Community Law Ser.). 240p. (C). 1994. text 90.00 (0-485-70009-3, Pub. by Athlone Pr) Humanities.
Portwood, Timothy, ed. Commercial Law, Vol. 2: International Trade. 252p. (C). 1991. 72.00 (1-85352-383-6, Pub. by HLT Pubns) St Mut.
— International Trade. 260p. (C). 1991. 120.00 (1-85352-904-4, Pub. by HLT Pubns) St Mut.
Portz, John. The Politics of Plant Closings. LC 90-32817. (Studies in Government & Public Policy). x, 214p. 1990. 29.95 (0-7006-0472-3); pap. 12.95 (0-7006-0473-1) U Pr of KS.
***Portz, John, et al.** City Schools & City Politics: Institutions & Leadership in Pittsburgh, Boston, & St. Louis. LC 99-31311. (Studies in Government & Public Policy). 216p. 1999. 35.00 (0-7006-0979-2); pap. 16.95 (0-7006-0980-6) U Pr of KS.
Portz, M. Susan. The Wedding Resource Directory: An Annual Directory of Wedding Services in the Denver-Boulder Area. 3rd ed. (Illus.). 110p. 1989. pap. 8.95 (0-9617718-2-8) Bascom Pr.
— The Wedding Resource Directory: An Annual Directory of Wedding Services in the Denver-Boulder Area. 4th ed. (Illus.). 104p. 1990. write for info. (0-318-66813-0); pap. 8.95 (0-9617718-3-6) Bascom Pr.
Poruchikov, V. B. Methods of the Classical Theory of Elastodynamics. Khokhryakov, V. A., tr. from RUS. (Illus.). 336p. 1993. 104.95 (0-387-54817-3) Spr-Verlag.
Porus, A. Phonics. 1995. 6.95 (1-55708-453-X, MCC896) McDonald Pub Co.
Porus, Marcus & Porus, Shirley. Who Is Gribich? LC 95-92141. (Gribich & Friends Ser.). (Illus.). 32p. (J). (ps). 1995. 14.95 (0-9646125-0-X) Doog Pub Grp.
Porus, Marcus, et al. Poof Wolf's New House. LC 95-92693. (Gribich & Friends Ser.). (Illus.). 32p. (J). (ps). 1996. 14.95 (0-9646125-2-6) Doog Pub Grp.
— Trip to Planet Doog. LC 95-92692. (Gribich & Friends Ser.). (Illus.). 32p. (J). (ps). 1996. 14.95 (0-9646125-1-8) Doog Pub Grp.
Porus, Shirley, jt. auth. see Porus, Marcus.
Porush, jt. auth. see Faubert.
Porush, David. Rope Dances. LC 78-68135. 127p. 1979. 15.95 (0-914590-50-2); pap. 6.95 (0-914590-51-0) Fiction Coll.
— A Short Guide to Writing about Science. LC 94-3119. (Short Guide Ser.). 275p. (C). 1997. pap. text 18.75 (0-06-500754-9) Addson-Wesley Educ.
Porush, Saubert. Renal Disease in the Aged. 1991. 82.95 (0-316-71401-1, Little Brwn Med Div) Lppncott W & W.
Porwal, M. C. Remote Sensing Analysis of Environmental Resources for Planning & Development. LC 97-900701. (Illus.). xii, 302p. 1997. 42.00 (81-7024-808-6, Pub. by APH Pubng) Nataraj Bks.
Pory, John, et al. Three Visitors to Early Plymouth. LC 97-72967. 96p. 1997. reprint ed. pap. 9.95 (1-55709-463-2) Applewood.
Pory, John, tr. see Africanus, John L.
Pory, John, tr. see Leo, Johannes.
Porzak, Brian. The One. (Illus.). 395p. (Orig.). 1987. pap. 12.95 (0-937983-00-4) Copy Concepts.
***Porzecanski, Teresa, et al.** Sun Inventions & Perfumes of Carthage: Two Novellas. LC 99-50994. (Jewish Latin America Ser.). 2000. pap. write for info. (0-8263-2181-X) U of NM Pr.
Porzner, Konrad, et al, eds. Vierzig Jahre Deutscher Bundestag. (GER.). 309p. 1991. pap. 45.00 (3-7890-1962-3, Pub. by Nomos Verlags) Intl Bk Import.
Posa, Francesco, ed. SAR Image Analysis, Modeling & Techniques. (Europto Ser.: Vol. 3497). 1998. 69.00 (0-8194-2956-2) SPIE.
***Posa, Francesco, ed.** SAR Image Analysis, Modeling & Techniques II. 1999. pap. text 50.00 (0-8194-3464-7) SPIE.
Posada-Carbo, Eduardo. The Colombian Caribbean: A Regional History 1870-1950. LC 95-49561. (Oxford Historical Monographs). (Illus.). 314p. (C). 1996. text 72.00 (0-19-820628-3) OUP.
Posada, E. & Violini, Galileo, eds. Search of Gravitational Waves: Proceedings of the Workshop Held in Bogota, Columbia, March 30-April 7, 1982. (CIF Ser.: Vol. 2). 244p. 1983. 47.00 (9971-950-78-2) World Scientific Pub.
Posada, Jorge. The English-Only Restaurant, Vol. 2000. 53p. (Orig.). 1990. pap. 7.00 (0-9627499-0-7) Ediciones Pirata.
Posada, Jose G. Posada's Popular Mexican Prints. Berdecio, Robert & Appelbaum, Stanley, eds. LC 77-178994. (Illus.). 156p. (Orig.). 1972. pap. 11.95 (0-486-22854-1) Dover.
Posada, Mia. Dandelions: Stars in the Grass. LC 98-53000. (Picture Bks.). (Illus.). 32p. (J). (ps-3). 2000. 15.95 (1-57505-383-7, Carolrhoda) Lerner Pub.
Posadas, Barbara M. The Filipino Americans. LC 99-10140. (New Americans Ser.). 208p. 1999. 39.95 (0-313-29742-8) Greenwood.
Posadas, Carmen. Liliana, Bruja Urbana (Liliana, Urban Witch) (SPA., Illus.). 48p. (J). (gr. 2). 1995. pap. 5.99 (968-16-4680-0, Pub. by Fondo) Continental Bk.
— Maria Celeste. (SPA., Illus.). 44p. (J). (gr. 3-4). 1993. pap. 5.99 (968-16-4039-X, Pub. by Fondo) Continental Bk.
— Pequenas Infamias. LC 99-164545. (Autores Espanoles E Iberoamericanos Ser.). 1999. 24.95 (84-08-02847-2) Planeta Edit.
Posadskaia-Vanderbeck, Anastasia. A Revolution of Their Own: Voices of Women in Soviet History. Engel, Barbara A., ed. Hoisington, Sona, tr. LC 97-26662. 1997. pap. 75.00 (0-8133-3365-2, Pub. by Westview) HarpC.
Posadskaia-Vanderbeck, Anastasia, jt. ed. see Engel, Barbara Alpern.
Posadskaya, Anastasia, ed. Women in Russia: A New Era in Russian Feminism. Clarke, Kate, tr. from RUS. LC 94-17273. 203p. (C). 1994. pap. 20.00 (0-86091-657-X, B3661, Pub. by Verso) Norton.
Posamentier, Alfred. Challenging Problems in Geometry. 1997. text 12.95 (0-86651-428-7) Seymour Pubns.
Posamentier, Alfred S. Excursions in Advanced Euclidean Geometry. 1984. text 11.95 (0-201-20359-6) Addison-Wesley.
— Math Motivators! Investigations in Geometry. 1982. text 12.95 (0-201-05583-X) Addison-Wesley.
— Math Motivators! Investigations in Pre-Algebra. 1982. text 12.95 (0-201-05581-3) Addison-Wesley.
— Math Motivators! Investigations in Pre-Algebra & Geometry. 1983. text 15.95 (0-201-05582-1) Addison-Wesley.
— Students! Get Ready for the Mathematics SAT I: Problem-Solving Strategies & Practice Tests. 216p. 1996. wbk. ed. 49.95 (0-8039-6444-7) Corwin Pr.
— Students! Get Ready for the Mathematics SAT I: Problem-Solving Strategies & Practice Tests. LC 95-49784. (Illus.). 216p. 1996. pap. 18.95 (0-8039-6415-3) Corwin Pr.
***Posamentier, Alfred S. & Hauptman, Herbert A.** 101 Great Ideas for Secondary School Mathematics. LC 00-34558. 2000. write for info. (0-7619-7513-6) Corwin Pr.
Posamentier, Alfred S. & Krulik, Stephen. Problem-Solving Strategies for Efficient & Elegant Solutions: A Resource for the Mathematics Teacher. LC 98-19702. 264p. 1998. 69.96 (0-8039-6697-0) Corwin Pr.
— Problem-Solving Strategies for Efficient & Elegant Solutions: A Resource for the Mathematics Teacher. LC 98-19702. (1-Off Ser.). (Illus.). 264p. 1998. pap. 32.95 (0-8039-6698-9) Corwin Pr.
— Teachers! Prepare Your Students for the Mathematics SAT I: Methods & Problem-Solving Strategies. LC 96-5312. 128p. 1996. teacher ed. 61.95 (0-8039-6481-1); pap., teacher ed. 27.95 (0-8039-6416-1) Corwin Pr.
Posamentier, Alfred S. & Salkind, Charles T. Challenging Problems in Algebra. 2nd unabridged ed. (Illus.). 272p. 1996. reprint ed. pap. text 8.95 (0-486-69148-9) Dover.

P

An Asterisk (*) at the beginning of an entry indicates that the title is appearing for the first time.

— Challenging Problems in Geometry. 2nd unabridged ed. 256p. 1996. reprint ed. pap. text 7.95 (*0-486-69154-3*) Dover.

Posamentier, Alfred S. & Shulz, Wolfgang. The Art of Problem Solving: A Resource for the Mathematics Teacher. LC 95-32522. (Illus.). 480p. 1995. 74.95 (*0-8039-6361-0*); pap. 34.95 (*0-8039-6362-9*) Corwin Pr.

Posamentier, Alfred S. & Stepelman, Jay. Teaching Secondary School Mathematics: Techniques & Enrichment Units. 5th ed. LC 98-7558. 492p. 1998. pap. text 73.00 (*0-13-674805-8*, Merrill Coll) P-H.

Posamentier, Alfred S., et al. Tips for the Mathematics Teacher: Research-Based Strategies to Help Students Learn. LC 97-45401. (1-Off Ser.). 224p. 1998. 65.95 (*0-8039-6589-3*); pap. 29.95 (*0-8039-6590-7*) Corwin Pr.

Posamentier, Henry W., et al, eds. Sequence Stratigraphy & Facies Associations. LC 92-34625. (International Association of Sedimentologists Special Publication Ser.: No. 18). 1993. 110.00 (*0-632-03548-X*) Blackwell Sci.

***Posamentier, Henry W. & Allen, George P.** Siliciclastic Sequence Stratigraphy: Concepts & Applications. (Concepts in Sedimentology & Paleontology Ser.: Vol. 7). (Illus.). 216p. 1999. 67.00 (*1-56576-070-0*) SEPM.

Posamentier, Henry W., jt. ed. see Weimer, Paul.

Posavac, jt. auth. see Zechmeister.

Posavac, Emil & Carey, Raymond G. Program Evaluation: Methods & Case Studies. 5th ed. LC 96-3291. 305p. (C). 1996. 56.00 (*0-13-255332-5*) P-H.

***Poscente, Vince.** Invinceable Principles. Phelps, Janice, ed. (Invinceability Ser.). (Illus.). 224p. 1999. 25.00 (*1-893430-00-6*); pap. 18.50 (*1-893430-07-3*) V Poscente.

Posch, Robert J., Jr. The Complete Guide to Marketing & the Law, 1990 Cumulative Supplement. 240p. 1990. pap. 40.00 (*0-685-38167-6*) P-H.

Poschel, Jurgen & Trubowitz, Eugene. Inverse Spectral Theory. (Pure & Applied Mathematics Ser.). 200p. 1987. text 62.00 (*0-12-563040-9*) Acad Pr.

Poschl, Viktor. The Art of Vergil: Image & Symbol in the "Aeneid" Seligson, Gerda, tr. from GER. LC 85-27077. 216p. 1986. reprint ed. lib. bdg. 45.50 (*0-313-25053-7*, POAV, Greenwood Pr) Greenwood.

Poschlod, Peter. Vegetationsentwicklung in Abgetorften Hochmooren Des Bayerischen Alpenvorlandes Unter Besonderer Beruecksichtigung Standortskundlicher und Populationsbiologischer Faktoren. (Dissertationes Botanicae Ser.: Band 152). (Illus.). xx, 331p. 1990. pap. 100.00 (*3-443-64064-8*, Pub. by Gebruder Borntraeger) Balogh.

Poschman, William. Oral Interpretation Literature. 200p. (C). 1995. 46.95 (*0-7872-1118-4*) Kendall-Hunt.

***Poscoiu, Costel.** Classical Repertoire for Clarinet, Vol. 2. 128p. 1999. 12.95 (*0-7866-2656-9*, 96512) Mel Bay.

Poscovsky, Aaron D. Football Cards Reference Guide. Orig. Title: Football Card Checklist. (Illus.). 200p. 1982. reprint ed. pap. 8.95 (*0-943110-50-5*) Vantage Printing.

Pose, Frederick & Michello, Dennis. The Appraisal & Insurance of Fine Art & Antiques. LC 97-67947. xii, 352p. 1998. write for info. (*0-88000-150-X*) Quarterman.

Pose, K. S., jt. auth. see Smith, M. D.

Pose, K. S., jt. auth. see Smith, Malcom D.

Pose, R., ed. Computer Architecture '96: Proceedings of the 1st Australasian Conference. 250p. 1997. pap. 59.95 (*981-3083-10-7*) Spr-Verlag.

Posel, Deborah. The Making of Apartheid, 1948-1961: Conflict & Compromise. (Illus.). 310p. 1997. pap. text 32.00 (*0-19-571515-2*) OUP.

Posel, K. Quantitative Methods for Tax Planning & Decision Making. 265p. 1991. pap. 74.00 (*0-409-10962-2*, SA, MICHIE) LEXIS Pub.

Poseljanin, E. Russkije Podvizhniki Blagotchestija 19-20 Vekev.Tr. of Russian Strugglers of Piety in the 19 & 20 Centuries. 908p. reprint ed. 35.00 (*0-317-29250-1*) Holy Trinity.

Posell, Elsa. Homecoming. LC 87-7615. 224p. (YA). (gr. 7 up). 1987. 14.95 (*0-15-235160-4*, Harcourt Child Bks) Harcourt.

— Horses. LC 81-7741. (New True Books Ser.). (Illus.). 48p. (J). (gr. 3-5). 1981. pap. 5.50 (*0-516-41623-5*); lib. bdg. 21.00 (*0-516-01623-7*) Childrens.

— Whales & Other Sea Mammals. LC 82-4451. (New True Books Ser.). (J). (gr. 2-4). 1982. pap. 5.50 (*0-516-41663-4*) Childrens.

Posen, Adam S. Dollarization, Currency Blocs & U. S. Policy. 150p. 2000. pap. 16.95 (*0-88132-285-7*) Inst Intl Eco.

Several countries in Latin America are considering adopting on the dollar as their official currency. In Eastern Europe, candidate countries for membership in the European Uniion are similarly considering the euro. This study analyzes the potential effects of dollarization/euroization on the economies of the adopting countries, on ongoing economic relations between richer & poorer countries (especially the United States & Latin America, the European Union & Eastern Europe) & on the possible development of regional currency block. It offers suggestions for US responses to & management of, a process driven by the apparently growing interest of emerging markets around the world in ceding their monetary sovereignty for the sake of stability. *Publisher Paid Annotation.*

–Germany in the World Economy after the EMU. 2000. pap. 20.00 (*0-88132-279-2*) Inst Intl Eco.

German economic success in the postwar period had been the basis of claims for a viable European alternative model to those of Japan & the U.S., one combing export success with high wages, relationship banking & a generous welfare state. More recently, Germany had played a leadership role in European integration, especially since the creation of the European Monetary System (EMS). But now, just as the European Union is adopting the euro & a unified monetary policy, the German public & its political & business leadership are doubting the capacity of Germany to remain generous to Europe & its own citizens. These doubts are leading many Germans & other Europeans to question whether Germany should continue to follow the German economic model, which is perceived to be breaking down. In this study - the latest in the IIE series on individual nations ",..in the World Economy - Adam Posen assesses the actual extent of this breakdown in the German model & its likely impact on German & European economic prospects & policies. Like its Institute predecessors on China, Japan, Korea & the U.S., the book also gives an analytical overview of the institutions & performance of the German economy. German economic prospects will have direct repercussions for the future of European integration, as well as implications for broader debates over the relative importance of demand management versus structural policies & over the ability of the "third way" to differ from pure free market outcomes. *Publisher Paid Annotation.*

–Restoring Japan's Economic Growth. LC 98-29813. 1998. pap. 18.95 (*0-88132-262-8*) Inst Intl Eco.

Will the Japanese government take the decisive but manageable policy actions needed to bring about economic recovery? Despite claims to the contrary, macroeconomic expansion has yet to be seriously tried in Japan. Only one-third of the announced stimulus packages of 1992-97 were actually undertaken. In addition, monetary expansion has been insufficient to prevent deflation. Actual stimulus packages in the form of permanent tax cuts should be 4 percent of GDP before the end of calendar year 1998 & the price level must be stabilized. Criticism of current Japanese macroeconomic & financial policies is so widespread that the reasons for it are assumed to be self-evident. In this volume, Adam Posen explains in depth why a shift in Japanese fiscal & monetary policies, as well as financial reform, would be in Japan's own self-interest. He demonstrates that Japanese economic stagnation in the 1990s is the result of mistaken policies of fiscal austerity & financial laissez-faire rather than any supposed structural failures of the "Japan Model." The author outlines a program for putting the country back on the path to solid economic growth - primarily through permanent tax cuts & monetary stabilization - & draws broader lessons to be learned from recent Japanese policy actions that led to country's continuing stagnation. Dr. Posen's objective analysis & comparative examples of policies from across the OECD are enhanced by the report's timeliness. His book should be required reading for Japan's business & academic communities, US foreign policy & financial players & central bank & treasury officials. As a deep analysis of a critical episode in economic policymaking, the book will be useful supplementary text for both under- & post-graduate level courses in macroeconomics, comparative political economy, Japan or East Asia studies, public finance & international relations. *Publisher Paid Annotation.*

***Posen, Adam S. & Mikitani, Ryoichi, eds.** Japan's Financial Crisis & Its Parallels to U. S. Experience. (Special Report Ser.). 230p. 2000. pap. 20.00 (*0-88132-289-X*) Inst Intl Eco.

Posen, Adam S. & Potok, Chaim. The Chosen. Date not set. pap. 5.95 (*0-8222-1740-6*) Dramatists Play.

Posen, Adam S., jt. auth. see Laubach, Thomas.

Posen, Barry R. Inadvertent Escalation: Conventional War & Nuclear Risks. LC 91-55055. (Cornell Studies in Security Affairs). 304p. 1992. text 47.50 (*0-8014-2563-8*) Cornell U Pr.

— The Sources of Military Doctrine: France, Britain & Germany Between the World Wars. LC 84-7610. (Cornell Studies in Security Affairs). 288p. 1984. text 42.50 (*0-8014-1633-7*); pap. text 16.95 (*0-8014-9427-3*) Cornell U Pr.

Posen, David B. Always Change a Losing Game: Playing at Life to Be the Best You Can Be. 272p. 1997. pap. 14.95 (*1-55209-110-4*) Firefly Bks Ltd.

— Staying Afloat When the Water Gets Rough: How to Live in a Rapidly Changing World. 228p. 1999. pap. 16.95 (*1-55263-012-9*, Pub. by Key Porter) Firefly Bks Ltd.

Posen, I. Sheldon. You Hear the Ice Talking. (Illus.). 64p. 1986. pap. 10.00 (*1-890402-11-7*) Clinton Cnty Hist.

— You Hear the Ice Talking: The Ways of People & Ice on Lake Champlain. LC 86-29914. (Illus.). 70p. (Orig.). 1986. pap. 11.00 (*0-9617701-1-2*) C E F Lib Syst.

Posener, G. Dictionnaire de la Civilisation Egyptienne. (FRE.). 1998. 95.00 (*0-320-00298-5*) Fr & Eur.

Posener, Georges. Dictionnaire de la Civilisation Egytienne.Tr. of Dictionary of the Egyptian Civilization. (FRE.). 326p. 1988. 79.95 (*0-8288-6512-4*, M-6462) Fr & Eur.

Posener, J. France. Your Baby. 112p. 1999. spiral bd. 17.95 (*1-58238-045-7*, Whitman Coin) St Martin.

Posener, Jill, ed. see Bright, Susie.

Posener, Julius. Hans Poelzig: Reflections on His Life & Work. Teireiss, Kristin, ed. (Illus.). 301p. 1992. 55.00 (*0-262-16127-3*) MIT Pr.

Poser. Broker - Dealer. LC 95-76100. 1995. 145.00 (*0-316-71415-1*, Aspen Law & Bus) Aspen Pub.

Poser, Charles M. An Atlas of Multiple Sclerosis. LC 98-17559. (Encyclopedia of Visual Medicine Ser.). (Illus.). 134p. 1998. 85.00 (*1-85070-946-7*) Prthnon Pub.

Poser, Charles M. & Bruyn, G. W. An Illustrated History of Malaria. LC 98-50048. (Illus.). 200p. 1999. 75.00 (*1-85070-068-0*) Prthnon Pub.

Poser, Gunter, jt. auth. see Oppenlander, Karl H.

Poser, Gunter, jt. ed. see Oppenlander, Karl H.

Poser, Hans. Philosophie und Mythos. (C). 1979. text 93.10 (*3-11-007601-2*) De Gruyter.

Poser, Hans, ed. see Wright, Georg H.

Poser, N. International Securities Regulations. 1990. 175.00 (*0-316-71441-0*, Aspen Law & Bus) Aspen Pub.

Poser, Norman S. Broker-Dealer Law & Regulation. 2nd ed. LC 97-29455. 1997. write for info. (*1-56706-599-6*) Aspen Law.

***Poser, Norman S.** Broker-Dealer Law & Regulation. 3rd ed. LC 99-51529. 1999. ring bd. 70.00 (*0-7355-0129-7*) Panel Pubs.

Poser, Norman S. Broker-Dealer Law & Regulation: Private Rights of Action. 523p. ring bd. 160.00 (*0-316-71516-6*, 14151) Aspen Law.

Poser, William J., ed. Papers from the Second International Workshop on Japanese Syntax. LC 88-18763. 243p. 1989. 59.95 (*0-937073-39-3*); pap. 18.95 (*0-937073-38-5*) CSLI.

Poser, Yvonne, jt. auth. see Pfister, Guenter G.

Posern, Thomas. Strukturelle Gewalt Als Paradigma Sozialethisch-Theologischer Theoriebildung. (Europaische Hochschulschriften Ser.: Reihe 23, Bd. 465). (GER., Illus.). 445p. 1992. 66.80 (*3-631-44721-3*) P Lang Pubng.

Poses, Steven, et al. The Frog: Commissary Cookbook. LC 84-7089. (Illus.). 288p. 1985. pap. 17.95 (*0-385-18457-3*) Doubleday.

Posewitz, Jim. Beyond Fair Chase: The Ethic & Tradition of Hunting. LC 94-10052. (Illus.). 118p. 1994. 17.95 (*1-56044-302-2*) Falcon Pub Inc.

— Beyond Fair Chase: The Ethic & Tradition of the Hunt. LC 94-10052. (Illus.). 118p. (Orig.). 1994. pap. 5.95 (*1-56044-283-2*) Falcon Pub Inc.

Posey. Readers Choice. 2000. pap. text. write for info. (*0-312-16693-1*) St Martin.

Posey, Alexander. The Fus Fixico Letters. Littlefield, Daniel F., Jr. & Petty Hunter, Carol A., eds. LC 92-46061. xviii, 330p. 1993. text 55.00 (*0-8032-3704-9*) U of Nebr Pr.

Posey, Carl A. The XVIII Olympiad Tokyo, 1964 & Grenoble, 1968. LC 96-3336. (Olympic Century Ser.: Vol. 16). (Illus.). 184p. 1996. 21.95 (*1-888383-16-X*, Wrld Spt) Wld Sport Resch.

— Kiev Footprint. 256p. 1987. mass mkt. 3.95 (*0-373-62103-5*) Harlequin Bks.

— Prospero Drill. 288p. 1988. per. 3.95 (*0-373-97052-8*) Harlequin Bks.

— Red Danube. 352p. 1988. reprint ed. pap. 3.95 (*0-373-97082-X*) Harlequin Bks.

Posey, Clayton E. & Steen, Harold K. Plantation Forestry in the Amazon: The Jari Experience. LC 97-36526. 1997. pap. 12.95 (*0-89030-054-2*) Forest Hist Soc.

Posey County, Indiana Historical Society Staff. Posey County, Indiana 175th Anniversary, 1814-1989. LC 89-51786. 192p. 1989. 52.50 (*0-938021-72-9*) Turner Pub KY.

***Posey, Darrell A.** Cultural & Spiritual Values of Biodiversity. 750p. 2000. 100.00 (*1-85339-397-5*, Pub. by Intermed Tech); pap. 55.00 (*1-85339-394-0*, Pub. by Intermed Tech) Stylus Pub VA.

Posey, Darrell A. & Balee, William, eds. Resource Management in Amazonia. LC 89-9392. (Advances in Economic Botany Ser.: Vol. 7). (Illus.). 304p. 1989. pap. text 59.00 (*0-89327-340-6*) NY Botanical.

Posey, Darrell A. & Dutfield, Graham. Beyond Intellectual Property: Toward Traditional Resource Rights for Indigenous Peoples & Local Communities. 250p. 1996. pap. 20.00 (*0-88936-799-X*, Pub. by IDRC Bks) Stylus Pub VA.

— Le Marche Mondial de la Propriete Intellectuelle: Droits Traditionnels et Indigenes. LC 97-900048.Tr. of Beyond Intellectual Property. (ENG & FRE.). 1997. pap. 24.00 (*0-88936-823-6*, Pub. by IDRC Bks) Stylus Pub VA.

Posey, Edgar A. Ultimate Deception. LC 97-169105. 252p. 1997. pap. 10.99 (*1-56043-279-9*, Treasure Hse) Destiny Image.

Posey, Ellis. The Funny Side of Texas. LC 93-49648. (Illus.). 120p. 1994. pap. 7.95 (*1-55622-323-4*, Rep of TX Pr) Wordware Pub.

Posey, Ernest. Hormone Pirates of Xenobia & Dream Studs of Kama Loka. 256p. (Orig.). 1996. pap. 11.95 (*1-55583-385-3*) Alyson Pubns.

Posey, Harry H., et al, eds. Proceedings: Summitville Forum, '95. (Special Publications: No. 38). (Illus.). 375p. 1995. text 95.00 (*1-884216-51-X*) Colo Geol Survey.

Posey, John T. General Thomas Posey: Son of the American Revolution. LC 92-50243. (C). 1993. 31.95 (*0-87013-316-0*) Mich St U Pr.

Posey, Josephine M. Against Great Odds: The History of Alcorn State University. LC 93-38375. (Illus.). 224p. 1994. text 27.50 (*0-87805-681-5*) U Pr of Miss.

***Posey, Josephine McCann.** Alcorn State University: And the National Alumni Association. (College History Ser.). (Illus.). 128p. 2000. pap. 19.99 (*0-7385-0591-9*) Arcadia Publng.

***Posey, L. Michael.** APHA's Complete Review for the Pharmacy Technician. 200p. 2000. pap. 30.00 (*1-58212-009-9*) Am Pharm Assn.

Posey, Lee. Night Rabbits. LC 98-34021. (Illus.). 32p. (J). (ps-3). 1999. 15.95 (*1-56145-164-9*, 51649) Peachtree Pubs.

***Posey, Ralph E., Jr.** Legends of the Wolf Creek Basin. 222p. 1999. pap. 12.95 (*0-9700565-0-8*) Ponto Hist Soc.

Posey, Rollin B. American Government. 11th ed. LC 82-24896. (Quality Paperback Ser.). (Illus.). 394p. (Orig.). 1983. pap. 17.95 (*0-8226-0372-1*) Littlefield.

Posey, Sandra M. Rubber Soul: Rubber Stamps & Correspondence Art. LC 96-19083. (Illus.). 72p. 1996. 32.50 (*0-87805-902-4*); pap. 16.95 (*0-87805-903-2*) U Pr of Miss.

***Posey, Sandra Mizumoto.** Cafe Nation: Coffee Folklore, Magick & Divination. LC 99-59929. (Illus.). 224p. 2000. pap. 9.95 (*1-891661-11-6*, Pub. by Snta Monica) IPG Chicago.

Posey, Walter B. The Development of Methodism in the Old Southwest: 1783-1824. LC 73-18408. (Perspectives in American History Ser.: No. 19). (Illus.). 151p. 1974. reprint ed. lib. bdg. 35.00 (*0-87991-339-8*) Porcupine Pr.

Posey, Walter B., ed. Alabama in the 1830's. (Illus.). 5.95 (*0-317-68073-0*) Southern U Pr.

Posey, William J. The Hanson Connection: The Book They Don't Want You to Read. 140p. (YA). 1997. pap. 9.95 (*0-9661554-0-8*) Posey & Co.

Posey, William J., jt. auth. see Householder, Catherine L.

Posgay, Mike, jt. auth. see Warner, Ian.

***Poshardt, Ulf.** DJ Culture. 2000. pap. 20.00 (*0-7043-8098-6*, Pub. by Quartet) Interlink Pub.

Poshek, Lucy. Bed & Breakfast Guide - Southwest: Arizona, New Mexico, Texas. LC 92-24998. (Frommer's Travel Guides Ser.). 128p. 1993. per. 16.00 (*0-671-84952-2*, P-H Travel) Prntice Hall Bks.

— California Trivia. LC 98-39434. 192p. 1998. pap. text 6.95 (*1-55853-679-5*) Rutledge Hill Pr.

— Frommer's Bed & Breakfasts in Hawaii. (Frommer's Travel Guide Ser.). 128p. 1995. pap. 16.00 (*0-02-860064-9*) Macmillan.

— Offbeat Overnights: A Guide to the Most Unusual Places to Stay in California. LC 95-51139. 232p. 1996. pap. text 9.95 (*1-55853-390-7*) Rutledge Hill Pr.

Poshek, Lucy, compiled by. Inn Side Views: A Collection of Inn-Sights by B&B Guests. LC 87-91317. (Illus.). 81p. 1987. pap. 4.95 (*0-9619275-0-X*) Poshek Prodns.

Posher, Roland, tr. see Lewis, David K.

Poshka, Mary & Leone, Paul. Around Chautauqua Lake: Fifty Years of Photographs, 1875-1925. LC 98-128772. (Illus.). 112p. 1997. pap. 15.95 (*0-9658955-0-5*) Chautauqua Reg.

Poshyananda, Apinan. Modern Art in Thailand in the Nineteenth & Twentieth Centuries. (Illus.). 284p. (C). 1992. text 125.00 (*0-19-588562-7*) OUP.

Poshyananda, Apinan, contrib. by. Contemporary Art in Asia: Traditions-Tensions. LC 96-85888. (Illus.). 240p. 1997. 49.50 (*0-8109-6331-0*, Pub. by Abrams) Time Warner.

Posidonius. The Fragments, Vol. 1. 2nd ed. Edelstein, L. & Kidd, I. G., eds. (Cambridge Classical Texts & Commentaries Ser.: No. 13). 400p. (C). 1989. text 105.00 (*0-521-36298-9*) Cambridge U Pr.

— The Translation of the Fragments Vol. 3. Kidd, I. G., ed. (Classical Texts & Commentaries Ser.: Vol. 3, No. 36). (Illus.). 430p. (C). 1999. text 74.95 (*0-521-62258-1*) Cambridge U Pr.

Posin, Daniel Q. Corporate Tax Planning: Takeovers, Leveraged Buyouts, & Restructurings. 900p. 1989. 155.00 (*0-316-71403-8*, Aspen Law & Bus) Aspen Pub.

— Corporation Tax Set. 1990. 155.00 (*0-316-71405-4*, Aspen Law & Bus) Aspen Pub.

Posin, Daniel Q., Jr. Federal Income Taxation of Individuals: With Diagrams for Easy Understanding of the Leading Cases & Concepts. 2nd ed. (Hornbook Ser.). 606p. (C). 1993. text 29.00 (*0-314-01832-8*) West Pub.

Posin, Daniel Q. Federal Income Taxation of Individuals: With Diagrams for Easy Understanding of the Leading Cases & Concepts. 4th ed. LC 98-3557. (Hornbook Ser.). 650p. 1998. pap. 35.00 (*0-314-23139-0*) West Pub.

— Federal Income Taxation of Individuals with Diagrams for Easy Understanding of the Leading Cases & Comments. 3rd ed. LC 97-22405. (Hornbook Ser.). 567p. (C). 1997. pap. text, student ed. write for info. (*0-314-06667-5*) West Pub.

Positano, Rock G. Disorders of the Heel, Rearfoot & Ankle. Strauss, Marc, ed. LC 98-54193. (Illus.). 555p. (C). 1999. text 79.95 (*0-443-07838-6*) Church.

P

Poska, Allyson M. Regulating the People: The Catholic Reformation in Seventeenth-Century Spain. LC 98-6541. (Cultures, Beliefs, & Traditions Ser.). x, 178p. 1998. 82.50 (*90-04-11036-4*) Brill Academic Pubs.

Poska, Valentine J. Toy Theaters. deluxe ed. (Illus.). 48p. 1994. lthr. 45.00 (*0-88014-057-7*) Mosaic Pr OH.

***Poskanzer, Alisa.** Ethiopian Exodus. LC 99-33597. 2000. 18.95 (*965-229-217-6*) Gefen Pub Hse.

Poskanzer, Susan C. Riddles about Hanukkah. Brook, Bonnie, ed. (What Can It Be? Ser.). (Illus.). 32p. (J). (ps-3). 1990. lib. bdg. 6.95 (*0-671-70553-9*) Silver Burdett Pr.

— Riddles about Hanukkah. Brook, Bonnie, ed. (Holiday Riddle Collection). (Illus.). 32p. (J). (ps-3). 1999. pap. 8.00 (*0-382-24384-6*) Silver Burdett Pr.

— Riddles about Passover. (What Can It Be? Ser.). (Illus.). 32p. (J). (ps-3). 1950. pap. 8.00 (*0-382-24381-1*) Silver Burdett Pr.

— Riddles about Passover. (What Can It Be? Ser.). (Illus.). 32p. (J). (ps-3). 1991. lib. bdg. 6.95 (*0-671-72724-9*) Silver Burdett Pr.

Poskar, Leon. Object-Oriented C++ Primer. (Illus.). 764p. (Orig.). (C). 1997. pap. text 25.95 (*1-890005-00-2*) MBSL Commun Co.

Poskitt, Kjartan. The Rumpelstiltskin Racket: A Musical Play LC 97-171598. 85 p. 1996. write for info. (*0-573-08103-4*) French.

Poskitt, R., jt. auth. see Oxley, R.

Poslusney, Venard. Prayer, Aspiration & Contemplation. 212p. 1994. pap. 6.50 (*1-890137-27-8*) One Hund-One Fnd.

— Union with the Lord in Prayer. 26p. 1994. pap. 3.50 (*1-890137-31-6*) One Hund-One Fnd.

Posluszny, Patricia. Thomas Nashe's Summer's Last Will & Testament: A Critical Modern-Spelling Edition. LC 89-34168. (American University Studies: English Language & Literature: Ser. IV, Vol. 108). 214p. 1989. text 36.95 (*0-8204-1110-8*) P Lang Pubng.

Posman, Ellen, ed. see Lamrimpa, Gen.

Posnak, Paul. Thomas "Fats" Waller: The Great Solos, 1929-1941. 120p. 1998. otabind 16.95 (*0-7935-7279-7*) H Leonard.

Posnansky, Merrick, jt. ed. see Ehret, Christopher.

Posner. Antitrust Law. 3rd ed. (American Casebook Ser.). Date not set. text. write for info. (*0-314-06598-9*) West Pub.

Posner, Alan R. State Government Export Promotion: An Exporter's Guide. LC 84-1999. 192p. 1984. 52.95 (*0-89930-042-1*, PGE/, Quorum Bks) Greenwood.

Posner, Alice. Women in Engineering. 1995. 13.95 (*0-8442-6396-6*, VGM Career) NTC Contemp Pub Co.

***Posner, Andrea.** Baby on Board. (Shaped Little Nugget Bks.). (Illus.). 18p. (J). (ps). 1999. bds. 3.99 (*0-307-14528-X*, 14528, Goldn Books) Gldn Bks Pub Co.

Posner, Andrea. Enter the World of Sea Creatures. (Panorama Book & Sticker Sets Ser.). (Illus.). 24p. (J). (gr. 4-6). 1995. 9.95 (*0-89577-787-8*, RDYF) Rdrs Digest.

***Posner, Andrea.** Frosty Day. (Little Golden Storybooks Ser.). (Illus.). (J). 2000. 3.99 (*0-307-16608-2*); pap. 2.29 (*0-307-99509-7*, Goldn Books) Gldn Bks Pub Co.

Posner, Andrea. Fun on the Go. 48p. 1999. 4.99 (*0-307-25200-0*) Gldn Bks Pub Co.

***Posner, Andrea.** Let's Eat! (Illus.). (J). 2000. 3.99 (*0-307-14530-1*) Gldn Bks Pub Co.

Posner, Andrea. More Fun on the Go. 48p. 1999. 4.99 (*0-307-25201-9*) Gldn Bks Pub Co.

***Posner, Andrea.** Peter Cottontail Is on His Way. 20p. 2000. 3.99 (*0-307-16056-4*) Gldn Bks Pub Co.

Posner, Arlene & De Keijzer, Arne J. China: A Resource & Curriculum Guide. 2nd ed. LC 75-9061. xvi, 318p. 1993. pap. text 5.00 (*0-226-67560-2*) U Ch Pr.

— China: A Resource & Curriculum Guide. 2nd ed. LC 75-9061. xvi, 318p. 1994. lib. bdg. 22.00 (*0-226-67559-9*) U Ch Pr.

Posner, Barry I. Polypeptide Hormone Receptors. LC 84-28677. (Receptors & Ligands in Intercellular Communication Ser.: No. 4). 621p. 1985. reprint ed. pap. 192.60 (*0-608-01328-5*, 206207100001) Bks Demand.

Posner, Barry I., jt. auth. see Srivastava, Ashok K.

Posner, Barry Z. & Randolph, Alan. Effective Project Planning & Management: Getting the Job Done. LC 87-11399. (Illus.). 128p. 1987. 22.50 (*0-13-244815-7*) P-H.

Posner, Barry Z., jt. auth. see Kouzes, James M.

Posner, Barry Z., jt. auth. see Kouzes, James S.

Posner, Barry Z., jt. auth. see Randolph, Alan.

Posner, Ben. Water Island Study: Summary Report & Fiscal Analysis. 64p. 1980. 10.00 (*0-318-14621-5*) Isl Resources.

Posner, David. Geographies. 1979. 20.00 (*0-933466-01-3*); pap. 12.95 (*0-933466-00-5*) Bellevue Pr.

***Posner, David M.** The Performance of Nobility in Early Modern European Literature. LC 98-53637. (Cambridge Studies in Renaissance Literature & Culture: No. 33). 284p. (C). 1999. 59.95 (*0-521-66181-1*) Cambridge U Pr.

Posner, Donald. Watteau. LC 83-45154. (Illus.). 288p. 1983. text 100.00 (*0-8014-1571-3*) Cornell U Pr.

Posner, Donald, jt. auth. see Held, Julius.

Posner, E. C., jt. auth. see Pierce, J. R.

Posner, E. S. & Hibbs, A. N. Wheat Flour Milling. LC 96-79927. (Illus.). 341p. 1997. text 149.00 (*0-913250-93-7*) Am Assn Cereal Chem.

Posner, Edward C., jt. auth. see Pierce, John R.

Posner, Eileen. Mother of the Groom, Vol. 1. 256p. 1996. pap. 12.95 (*0-9654749-0-9*) P M G Publns.

Posner, Eileen, ed. Mother of the Groom: A Collection of Women's Voices. LC 95-11281. 256p. 1995. pap. 12.95 (*0-942963-64-4*) Distinctive Pub.

***Posner, Eric A.** Law & Social Norms. LC 99-88226. 320p. 2000. 39.95 (*0-674-00156-7*) Belknap Pr.

Posner, Ernst. American State Archives. LC 64-23425. 414p. reprint ed. pap. 128.40 (*0-8357-5401-4*, 202578800046) Bks Demand.

Posner, Gabrielle J. The Teenager's Guide to the Law. 384p. 1995. pap. 18.00 (*1-874241-00-7*, Pub. by Cavendish Pubng) Gaunt.

Posner, Gary H. An Introduction to Synthesis Using Organocopper Reagents. LC 85-4744. 160p. (C). 1988. reprint ed. lib. bdg. 24.50 (*0-89874-853-4*) Krieger.

Posner, George J. Analyzing the Curriculum. 2nd ed. LC 94-33750. 320p. (C). 1994. pap. 44.06 (*0-07-050705-8*) McGraw.

— Course Design. 5th ed. LC 96-20101. 320p. (C). 1996. pap. text 47.00 (*0-8013-1780-0*) Addison-Wesley.

— Field Experience: A Guide to Reflective Teaching. 4th ed. 168p. (C). 1996. pap. text 32.81 (*0-8013-1645-6*) Longman.

— Field Experience: A Guide to Reflective Teaching. 5th ed. LC 99-33086. 160p. (C). 1999. pap. 43.00 (*0-8013-3079-3*) Longman.

Posner, George J. & Rudnitsky, Alan N. Course Design. 3rd ed. (Illus.). 210p. (C). 1989. pap. text 23.95 (*0-582-28666-2*, 71682) Addison-Wesley.

***Posner, George J. & Rudnitsky, Alan N.** Course Design. 6th ed. 320p. 2000. pap. 33.33 (*0-8013-3250-8*) Longman.

***Posner, Gerald & Ware, John.** Mengele: The Complete Story. (Illus.). 400p. 1999. reprint ed. pap. 18.95 (*0-8154-1006-9*) Cooper Sq.

Posner, Gerald L. Case Closed: Lee Harvey Oswald & the Assassination of JFK. 624p. 1994. pap. 17.95 (*0-385-47446-6*, Anchor NY) Doubleday.

— Killing the Dream: James Earl Ray & the Assassination of Martin Luther King, Jr. LC 98-52845. 464p. 1999. pap. 15.00 (*0-15-600651-0*, Harvest Bks) Harcourt.

***Posner, Gerald L.** Killing the Dream: James Earl Ray & the Assassination of Martin Luther King, Jr. large type ed. 1998. 20.00 (*0-7838-8340-4*, G K Hall & Co) Mac Lib Ref.

Posner, Gerald L. Ross Perot & Third-Party Politics. 1996. 25.00 (*0-614-95759-1*) Random.

Posner, Helaine. Angela Grauerholz: Recent Photographs. LC 93-79813. (Illus.). 32p. (Orig.). 1993. pap. 8.00 (*0-938437-45-3*) MIT List Visual Arts.

— Kiki Smith. LC 97-78283. (Illus.). 200p. 1998. 60.00 (*0-8212-2479-4*, Pub. by Bulfinch Pr) Little.

— Per Kirkeby: Paintings & Drawings, 1982-1989. LC 91-50794. (Illus.). 48p. (Orig.). 1991. pap. 15.00 (*0-938437-39-9*) MIT List Visual Arts.

***Posner, Helaine & Gelernter, David.** Selfportrait Map: LoCurto/Outcault. (Illus.). 64p. 2000. pap. 19.95 (*0-295-97934-8*) U of Wash Pr.

Posner, Helaine, jt. auth. see Kline, Katy.

Posner, Helaine, ed. see Perchuk, Andrew, et al.

Posner, Holly & Jason, Katherine. Explorations in American Culture: Readings for Critical Thinking, Writing, & Discussion. LC 94-40613. 265p. (J). 1995. mass mkt. 33.95 (*0-8384-4069-X*) Heinle & Heinle.

Posner, Jackie. El Autobus Magico Muestra Y Cuenta: Un Libro Sobre Arqueologia. 1997. 8.19 (*0-606-10796-7*, Pub. by Turtleback) Demco.

***Posner, Jackie.** The Magic School Bus Out of This World: A Book about Space Rocks. (Magic School Bus Ser.). (Illus.). (J). (ps-3). 1999. pap. 10.55 (*0-613-00275-X*) Econo-Clad Bks.

Posner, Jackie. The Magic School Bus Out of This World: A Book about Space Rocks. LC 49-243560. (Magic School Bus Ser.). (Illus.). 32p. (J). (gr. k-2). 1996. pap. text 2.99 (*0-590-92156-8*) Scholastic Inc.

— The Magic School Bus Out of This World: A Book about Space Rocks. (Magic School Bus Ser.). (Illus.). (J). (gr. k-2). 1996. 8.19 (*0-606-10865-3*, Pub. by Turtleback) Demco.

— The Magic School Bus Shows & Tells: A Book about Archaeology. LC 49-243570. (Magic School Bus Ser.). (J). (gr. k-2). 1997. pap. text 2.99 (*0-590-92242-4*) Scholastic Inc.

— The Magic School Bus Shows & Tells: A Book about Archaeology. (Magic School Bus Ser.). (J). (gr. k-2). 1997. pap. 2.99 (*0-614-29013-9*) Scholastic Inc.

— The Magic School Bus Shows & Tells: A Book about Archaeology. (Magic School Bus Ser.). (J). (gr. k-2). 1997. 8.19 (*0-606-10866-1*, Pub. by Turtleback) Demco.

Posner, Jerome B. Neurologic Complications of Cancer. (Contemporary Neurology Ser.: No. 45). (Illus.). 496p. (C). 1995. text 99.00 (*0-8036-0006-2*) OUP.

Posner, Jerome B., jt. ed. see Reis, Donald J.

Posner, John, jt. ed. see Cohen, Adam.

Posner, John, ed. see Lewis, Kevin.

Posner, John, ed. see Niemeyer, Patrick & Knudsen, Jonathan.

Posner, John, ed. see Ray, Eric & Maden, Chris.

Posner, Judith. The Feminine Mistake: Women, Work & Identity. 256p. (Orig.). 1992. mass mkt. 4.99 (*0-446-36298-0*, Pub. by Warner Bks) Little.

Posner, Julie. Louisiana Festival & Events Guide. (Illus.). 225p. (Orig.). 1997. pap. write for info. (*0-9654906-2-9*) Huli Pub.

— 1998 Calendar of Louisiana Festivals & Events. (Illus.). 28p. (Orig.). 1997. pap. 11.95 (*0-9654906-4-5*) Huli Pub.

Posner, Julie, jt. auth. see Fry, Macon.

***Posner, Keith & Applegarth, Mike.** The Empowerment Pocketbook. 112p. 1999. pap. 8.95 (*1-870471-51-2*, Pub. by Mngmnt Pocketbks) Stylus Pub VA.

— The Project Management Pocketbook. 112p. 2000. pap. 8.95 (*1-57922-004-5*) Stylus Pub VA.

***Posner, Lauri.** The Lion & the Mouse. (Between the Lions Ser.). (Illus.). (J). 2000. pap. 3.99 (*0-307-25214-0*, Goldn Books) Gldn Bks Pub Co.

Posner, Louis. Through a Boy's Eyes: The Turbulent Years, 1926-1945. 304p. Date not set. pap. 18.95 (*0-929765-74-5*) Seven Locks Pr.

Posner, M. V. & Woolf, Stuart J. Italian Public Enterprises. LC 67-4204. 171p. 1967. 20.00 (*0-674-46951-8*) HUP.

Posner, Marc. Preventing School Injuries: A Comprehensive Guide for School Administrators, Teachers & Staff. LC 99-15070. 2000. write for info. (*0-8135-2749-X*); text 34.00 (*0-8135-2748-1*) Rutgers U Pr.

— Working Together for Youth: A Guide to Collaboration Between Law Enforcement Agencies & Programs That Serve Runaway & Homeless Youth. 122p. 1994. pap. 13.95 (*1-878848-37-2*, 166) Natl Res Ctr.

Posner, Martin. Successful Credit Control. LC 97-45614. 266p. 1998. pap. 91.50 (*0-471-97526-5*) Wiley.

Posner-Mayer, Joanne. Swiss Ball Applications for Orthopedic & Sports Medicine: A Guide for Home Exercise Programs Utilizing the Swiss Ball. Hyer, Jauna et al, eds. (Illus.). 250p. (C). 1995. pap. text 29.95 (*0-9645341-4-2*) Ball Dynam.

Posner, Michael, ed. Problems of International Money, 1972-85. ix, 191p. 1986. pap. 8.50 (*0-939934-58-2*) Intl Monetary.

— Problems of International Money, 1972-85: Papers Presented at a Seminar Organized by the IMF & the Overseas Development Institute in London in March 1985. LC 86-10480. (Illus.). 202p. reprint ed. pap. 62.70 (*0-608-18035-1*, 202908800058) Bks Demand.

— Public Expenditure: Allocation Between Competing Ends. LC 76-53522. 278p. reprint ed. pap. 79.30 (*0-608-15766-X*, 2031712) Bks Demand.

Posner, Michael, ed. see Doggett, Martha.

Posner, Michael I. Chronometric Exploration of Mind. (Illus.). 286p. 1986. reprint ed. pap. text 24.95 (*0-19-503999-8*) OUP.

Posner, Michael I., ed. The Foundations of Cognitive Science. 896p. 1989. 90.00 (*0-262-16112-5*) MIT Pr.

— The Foundations of Cognitive Science. (Illus.). 904p. 1993. pap. text 45.00 (*0-262-66086-5*, Bradford Bks) MIT Pr.

Posner, Michael I. & Raichle, Marcus E. Images of Mind. (Illus.). 256p. 1997. pap. 19.95 (*0-7167-6019-3*) W H Freeman.

Posner, Michael I., jt. auth. see Fitts, Paul M.

Posner, Michael J., ed. see Ross, James D.

Posner, Mitchell. Investing in the Emerging Markets & Stocks. (C). 1997. 16.95 (*0-13-849407-X*, Macmillan Coll) P-H.

— Profiting from Emerging Market Stocks. 352p. 1998. text 30.00 (*0-7352-0023-8*) PH Pr.

***Posner, Mitchell C., et al.** Upper Gastrointestinal Cancer: Esophagus & Stomach. (ACS Atlas of Clinical Oncology Ser.). 350p. 2000. boxed set 89.95 incl. cd-rom (*1-55009-101-8*) DEKR.

Posner, Mitchell J. Executive Essentials: The Complete Sourcebook for Success. 204p. 1987. pap. 12.95 (*0-380-75376-6*, Avon Bks) Morrow Avon.

Posner, Nathan. Call It Immortality. LC 94-94163. 260p. (Orig.). 1994. pap. 14.95 (*1-883335-12-4*) Botany Bay Pr.

Posner, Neil, ed. see Delson, Donn & Hurst, Walter E.

Posner, Neil, ed. see Delson, Donn & Michalove, Ed.

***Posner, Paul L.** Budget Function Classifications: Origins, Trends, & Implications for Current Uses. (Illus.). 52p. (C). 1999. pap. text 20.00 (*0-7881-8351-6*) DIANE Pub.

Posner, Paul L. Budget Issues: Fiscal Year 1996 Agency Spedning by Budget Function. (Illus.). 64p. 1997. pap. text 20.00 (*0-7881-4753-6*) DIANE Pub.

***Posner, Paul L.** Budgeting for Emergencies: State Practices & Federal Implications. (Illus.). 59p. (C). 2000. pap. text 20.00 (*0-7881-8987-5*) DIANE Pub.

— Compendium pf Budget Accounts: Fiscal Year 2000. 128p. (C). 2000. pap. text 25.00 (*0-7881-8516-0*) DIANE Pub.

Posner, Paul L. The Politics of Unfunded Mandates: Whither Federalism? Rabe, Barry & Tierney, John, eds. LC 98-16020. (American Governance & Public Policy Ser.). 320p. 1998. 55.00 (*0-87840-708-1*) Georgetown U Pr.

— The Politics of Unfunded Mandates: Whither Federalism? Rabe, Barry & Tierney, John, eds. LC 98-16020. (American Governance & Public Policy Ser.). (Illus.). 320p. 1998. pap. 24.95 (*0-87840-709-X*) Georgetown U Pr.

Posner, Paul L., ed. Deferred Maintenance Reporting: Challenges to Implementation. (Illus.). 69p. (C). 1998. pap. text 20.00 (*0-7881-7492-4*) DIANE Pub.

***Posner, Paul L. & Irving, Susan J., eds.** Federal Debt: Answers to Frequently Asked Questions-An Update. (Illus.). 55p. (C). 2000. pap. text 20.00 (*0-7881-8892-5*) DIANE Pub.

Posner, Paul L., jt. ed. see Stevens, L. Nye.

Posner, Raphael. Junior Judaica: Encyclopedia Judaica for Youth, 6 vols. rev. ed. 1994. 135.00 (*0-8246-0366-4*) Jonathan David.

Posner, Rebecca. Linguistic Change in French. LC 97-2027. (Illus.). 530p. (C). 1997. text 125.00 (*0-19-824036-8*) OUP.

— The Romance Languages. (Cambridge Language Surveys Ser.). 393p. (C). 1996. text 69.95 (*0-521-23654-1*); pap. text 25.95 (*0-521-28139-3*) Cambridge U Pr.

— The Romance Languages: A Linguistic Introduction. 1990. 24.75 (*0-8446-0853-X*) Peter Smith.

Posner, Rebecca & Green, John, eds. Trends in Romance Linguistics & Philology, Vol. 2. (Synchronic Romance Linguistics Ser.). 422p. 1981. 123.10 (*90-279-7896-4*) Mouton.

— Trends in Romance Linguistics & Philology Vol. 5: Bilingualism & Linguistic Conflict in Romance. (Trends in Linguistics, Studies & Monographs: No. 71). x, 630p. (C). 1993. lib. bdg. 221.55 (*3-11-011724-X*) Mouton.

Posner, Rebecca, ed. see Green, John N.

Posner, Richard. Can You Hear Me Scream? MacDonald, Pat, ed. 224p. (Orig.). (YA). (gr. 7 up). 1994. mass mkt. 3.50 (*0-671-88744-0*, Archway) PB.

— Terror Runs Deep. MacDonald, Patricia, ed. 224p. (Orig.). (YA). (gr. 7 up). 1995. mass mkt. 3.50 (*0-671-88745-9*, Archway) PB.

***Posner, Richard A.** An Affair of State: The Investigation, Impeachment & Trial of President Clinton. 288p. 2000. pap. 16.95 (*0-674-00391-8*) HUP.

Posner, Richard A. An Affair of the State: The Investigation, Impeachment & Trial of President Clinton. LC 99-24307. 276p. 1999. 24.95 (*0-674-00080-3*) HUP.

— Aging & Old Age. (Illus.). 384p. 1995. 29.95 (*0-226-67566-1*) U Ch Pr.

— Aging & Old Age. (Illus.). 384p. 1997. pap. 16.95 (*0-226-67568-8*) U Ch Pr.

— Anti-Trust Laws: An Economic Perspective. LC 76-598. 272p. 1978. pap. text 20.00 (*0-226-67558-0*, P760) U Ch Pr.

— Cardozo: A Study in Reputation. (Illus.). xii, 168p. 1993. pap. text 15.00 (*0-226-67556-4*) U Ch Pr.

— Cardozo: A Study in Reputation. LC 90-35479. 168p. 1998. 22.95 (*0-226-67555-6*) U Ch Pr.

— Economic Analysis of Law. 4th ed. 1992. 49.00 (*0-316-71444-5*, Aspen Law & Bus) Aspen Pub.

— Economic Analysis of Law. 5th ed. 744p. 1997. teacher ed. write for info. (*1-56706-560-0*, 65600) Panel Pubs.

— Economic Analysis of Law. 5th ed. LC 98-107107. 744p. 1997. boxed set 58.00 (*1-56706-562-7*, 65627) Panel Pubs.

— The Economics of Justice. (Illus.). 428p. 1981. pap. 21.50 (*0-674-23526-6*) HUP.

— The Federal Courts: Challenge & Reform. LC 96-19516. (Illus.). 432p. 1996. 40.50 (*0-674-29626-5*) HUP.

— The Federal Courts: Challenge & Reform. (Illus.). 413p. 1999. pap. 18.95 (*0-674-29627-3*) HUP.

— The Federal Courts: Crisis & Reform. LC 84-19126. 382p. 1985. pap. 118.50 (*0-7837-2315-6*, 205740300004) Bks Demand.

— Law & Legal Theory in England & America. (Claredon Law Lectures). (Illus.). 146p. 1997. text 24.95 (*0-19-826471-2*) OUP.

— Law & Literature. LC 97-28244. 416p. 1999. text 45.00 (*0-674-51470-X*) HUP.

— Law & Literature. LC 97-28244. 416p. 1999. pap. 18.95 (*0-674-51471-8*) HUP.

— Law & Literature: A Misunderstood Relation. LC 88-11210. 384p. 1988. 39.50 (*0-674-51468-8*) HUP.

— Natural Monopoly & Its Regulation. LC 99-22490. 115p. 1999. 8.95 (*1-882577-81-7*) Cato Inst.

— Overcoming Law. LC 94-12753. 608p. 1995. text 42.50 (*0-674-64925-7*, POSOVE) HUP.

— Overcoming Law. 608p. 1996. pap. 17.95 (*0-674-64926-5*) HUP.

***Posner, Richard A.** The Problematics of Moral & Legal Theory. LC 98-29596. 1999. 31.00 (*0-674-70771-0*) Belknap Pr.

Posner, Richard A. The Problems of Jurisprudence. 504p. 1990. 38.00 (*0-674-70875-X*) HUP.

— The Problems of Jurisprudence. 504p. (C). 1993. pap. 20.50 (*0-674-70876-8*) HUP.

— The Robinson-Patman Act: Federal Regulation of Price Differences. LC 76-383361. (AEI Studies: No. 131). 63p. reprint ed. pap. 30.00 (*0-8357-4528-7*, 203740500008) Bks Demand.

— Sex & Reason. 480p. (C). 1992. text 29.95 (*0-674-80279-9*) HUP.

— Sex & Reason. 472p. (C). 1994. pap. text 18.95 (*0-674-80280-2*) HUP.

— Tort Law: Cases & Economic Analysis. LC 81-82981. 792p. 1982. 40.00 (*0-316-71436-4*, Aspen Law & Bus) Aspen Pub.

Posner, Richard A. & Easterbrook, Frank H. Antitrust-Cases, Economic Notes, & Other Materials. LC 80-25590. (American Casebook Ser.). 168p. (C). 1984. pap., suppl. ed. 14.50 (*0-314-85073-2*) West Pub.

— Antitrust-Cases, Economic Notes, & Other Materials. 2nd ed. LC 80-25590. (American Casebook Ser.). 1077p. (C). 1980. reprint ed. 60.00 (*0-8299-2115-X*) West Pub.

Posner, Richard A. & Parisi, Francesco, eds. Law & Economics, 3 vols., set. LC 97-13442. (International Library of Critical Writings in Economics Ser.: No. 81). 2056p. 1997. 645.00 (*1-85278-972-7*) E Elgar.

Posner, Richard A. & Scott, Kenneth E. Economics of Corporation Law & Securities Regulation. 400p. 1981. pap. 20.95 (*0-316-71435-6*, Aspen Law & Bus) Aspen Pub.

Posner, Richard A. & Silbaugh, Katharine B. A Guide To America's Sex Laws. LC 96-3306. 256p. 1996. 26.95 (*0-226-67564-5*) U Ch Pr.

— A Guide to America's Sex Laws. 244p. 1998. pap. 14.00 (*0-226-67565-3*) U Ch Pr.

Posner, Richard A., jt. auth. see Casper, Gerhard.

Posner, Richard A., jt. auth. see Kronman, Anthony T.

Posner, Richard A., jt. auth. see Landes, William M.

Posner, Richard A., jt. auth. see Philipson, Tomas J.

Posner, Richard A., ed. see Holmes, Oliver W.

Posner, Roland. Rational Discourse & Poetic Communication: Methods of Linguistic, Literary, & Philosophical Analysis. LC 82-3502. (Janua Linguarum, Series Major: No. 103). xvi, 258p. 1982. 60.00 (*90-279-3419-3*) Mouton.

Posner, Roland, et al, eds. Semiotik - Semiotics: Ein Handbuch Zu Den Zeichentheoretischen Grundlagen von Natur und Kultur - A Handbook on the Sign-Theoretic Foundations of Nature & Culture. LC 96-49024.

An Asterisk (*) at the beginning of an entry indicates that the title is appearing for the first time.

(Handbooks of Linguistics & Communication Science Ser.: Vol. 13.1). (ENG & GER., Illus.). xxxiv, 1198p. (C). 1996. lib. bdg. 712.85 (*3-11-009584-X*) De Gruyter.
— Semiotik/Semiotics. 1200p. 1998. text 600.00 (*3-11-015661-X*) De Gruyter.
***Posner, Sarah.** Fighting Gravity. 240p. 1998. pap. 20.00 (*1-929725-05-1*) Brownout Lab.
Posner, Steve. Israel Undercover: Secret Warfare & Hidden Diplomacy in the Middle East. LC 87-18811. (Illus.). 367p. reprint ed. pap. 113.80 (*0-8357-8188-7*, 203405600088) Bks Demand.
Posner, Susan F. & Solomon, Lewis D. Tax Planning Strategies, 2 vols. 1990. 210.00 (*0-685-34491-6*) West Group.
Posner, Susan F., jt. auth. see Soloman, Lewis D.
Posner, Susan F., jt. auth. see Solomon, Lewis D.
Posner, T. Natasha. Herpes Simplex. LC 97-17152. (Experience of Illness Ser.). (Illus.). 160p. (C). 1998. pap. 24.99 (*0-415-10744-X*) Routledge.
Posner, Theodore R. Current French Security Policy: The Gaullist Legacy, 118. LC 91-21195. (Contributions in Military Studies Ser.: No. 118). 184p. 1991. 52.95 (*0-313-27934-9*, PCK, Greenwood Pr) Greenwood.
***Posner, Trisha.** This Is Not Your Mother's Menopause: One Woman's Natural Journey Through Change. LC 99-55033. 192p. 2000. 21.00 (*0-375-50398-6*) Villard Books.
Posner, Vladimir, jt. ed. see Keyssar, Helene.
Posner, Zalman I. Think Jewish: A Contemporary View of Judaism, a Jewish View of Today's World. LC 78-71323. 1979. 8.95 (*0-9602394-0-5*); pap. 4.95 (*0-9602394-1-3*) Kesher.
Posner, Zalman I., tr. see Danzinger, Eliezer Y., ed.
Posner, Zalman I., tr. see Dov Ber Schneerson, Shalom.
Posner, Zalman I., tr. see Schneersohn, Yosef Y.
Posnick, Jeffrey C. Craniofacial & Maxillofacial Surgery in Children & Young Adults. Ross, Allan, ed. LC 98-40586. (Illus.). 1195p. (C). 1999. text 395.00 (*0-7216-7710-X*, W B Saunders Co) Harcrt Hlth Sci Grp.
Posnikoff, D.V.M, Janice, jt. auth. see Pavia, Audrey.
Posnock, Ross. Color & Culture: Black Writers & the Making of the Modern Intellectual. LC 98-11604. 368p. 1998. 35.00 (*0-674-14309-4*) HUP.
***Posnock, Ross.** Color & Culture: Black Writers & the Making of the Modern Intellectual. (Illus.). 368p. 2000. pap. 17.95 (*0-674-00379-9*) HUP.
Posnock, Ross. The Trial of Curiosity: Henry James, William James & the Challenge of Modernity. 382p. 1991. pap. text 39.95 (*0-19-507124-7*) OUP.
Pospesel, Howard. Introduction to Logic: Predicate Logic. (Illus.). 224p. 1976. pap. text 43.00 (*0-13-486225-2*) P-H.
— Introduction to Logic: Propositional Logic. 3rd ed. LC 97-33465. (C). 1997. pap. text 31.80 (*0-13-164997-3*) P-H.
***Pospesel, Howard & Lycan, William G.** Introduction to Logic: Propositional Logic. 3rd ed. LC 99-47648. 276p. 1999. 36.40 (*0-13-025849-0*) P-H.
Pospesel, Howard & Marans, David. Arguments: Deductive Logic Exercises. 2nd ed. (Illus.). 192p. 1998. pap. text 48.00 (*0-13-045880-5*) P-H.
Pospesel, Howard & Rodes, Robert E. Premises & Conclusions: Symbolic Logic for Legal Analysis. LC 96-33572. 387p. (C). 1996. 67.00 (*0-13-262635-7*) P-H.
Pospeshil, Bob. The Fires of God. 46p. 1987. pap. 2.95 (*0-88144-094-9*) Christian Pub.
Pospielovsky, Dimitry. The Orthodox Church in the History of Russia. LC 98-26971. 1998. 19.95 (*0-88141-179-5*) St Vladimirs.
Pospielovsky, Dimitry V. The Russian Church under the Soviet Regime, Set. LC 84-5336. 533p. 1984. pap. 26.95 (*0-88141-033-0*) St Vladimirs.
— The Russian Church under the Soviet Regime, Vol. I. LC 84-5336. 248p. 1984. pap. 10.95 (*0-88141-015-2*) St Vladimirs.
— The Russian Church under the Soviet Regime, Vol. II. LC 84-5336. 285p. 1984. pap. 11.95 (*0-88141-016-0*) St Vladimirs.
— Soviet Antireligious Campaigns & Persecutions: A History of Soviet Atheism in Theory & Practice, & the Believer, Vol. 2. LC 87-4826. 256p. 1988. text 39.95 (*0-312-00904-6*) St Martin.
Pospischil, Hans-Georg & Kreye, Andrian. Vivir la Muerte: Rituals of Death in Latin America. (Illus.). 148p. 1996. 39.95 (*3-905514-73-7*) Dist Art Pubs.
Pospishil, Victor J. Eastern Catholic Marriage Law According to the Code of Canons of the Eastern Churches. LC 90-64249. 536p. 1991. text 42.00 (*0-9628727-0-9*) St Maron Pubns.
Pospisil, Craig. Somewhere in Between. 1996. pap. 5.25 (*0-8222-1522-5*) Dramatists Play.
Pospisil, Jan & Klemchuk, Peter P., eds. Oxidation Inhibition in Organic Materials, Vol. I. 384p. 1989. lib. bdg. 395.00 (*0-8493-4767-X*, TP156) CRC Pr.
— Oxidation Inhibition in Organic Materials, Vol. II. 400p. 1989. lib. bdg. 395.00 (*0-8493-4768-8*, TP156) CRC Pr.
— Oxidation Inhibition in Organic Materials, Vols. I-II. 1989. 311.00 (*0-685-74180-X*) CRC Pr.
Pospisil, Leopold. Kapauku Papuan Economy. LC 78-188171. (Yale University Publications in Anthropology Reprints Ser.: No. 67). 502p. 1972. pap. 30.00 (*0-87536-526-4*) HRAFP.
— Kapauku Papuans & Their Law. LC 64-20560. (Yale University Publications in Anthropology Reprints Ser.: No. 54). 296p. 1964. pap. 20.00 (*0-87536-502-7*) HRAFP.
— Obernberg: A Quantitative Analysis of a Peasant Tirolean Economy. LC 95-69512. (Memoirs of the Connecticut Academy of Arts & Sciences Ser.: Vol. 24). (Illus.). 416p. 1995. text 60.00 (*1-878508-09-1*) CT Acad Arts & Sciences.
Pospisilova, Jane, jt. ed. see Solarova, J.
Poss, Faye S. Inferior Court Records of Jackson County, Georgia 1796-1831. 352p. (C). 1994. text 30.00 (*1-883793-03-3*) Wolfe Pubng.
— Jackson County, Georgia Will Abstracts, 1803-1888, Bks. A & B. LC 95-62108. 360p. (C). 1996. write for info. (*1-883793-17-3*) Wolfe Pubng.
Poss, Jeffery S., jt. ed. see Armstrong, Paul J.
Poss, Joe & Schlesinger, Henry R. Brooklyn Bounce. 240p. (Orig.). 1994. mass mkt. 4.99 (*0-380-77337-6*, Avon Bks) Morrow Avon.
Posse, Abel. La Pasion Segun Eva. 1994. pap. 23.95 (*950-04-1452-X*) Emece.
Posse, Otto. Die Lehre von den Privaturkunden. (GER., Illus.). viii, 242p. (C). 1974. reprint ed. 350.00 (*3-11-002301-6*) De Gruyter.
Possehl, Gregory L. Harappan Civilization. 1993. 92.00 (*0-8364-2871-4*, 8714) Science Pubs.
— Indus Age: The Beginnings. LC 97-1155. (C). (gr. 13). 1997. text 98.00 (*0-8122-3417-0*) U of Pa Pr.
Possehl, Gregory L., ed. South Asian Archaeology Studies. (C). 1992. text 45.00 (*81-204-0734-2*, Pub. by Oxford IBH) S Asia.
Possehl, Gregory L. & Tosi, Maurizio, eds. Harappan Studies, Vol. 1. (Illus.). 79p. (C). 1994. text 15.00 (*1-881570-18-5*) Science Pubs.
Possehl, Suzanne R., ed. Automation of Soviet Railroads: Selected Papers with Analysis. (Illus.). 218p. (Orig.). 1990. pap. 100.00 (*1-55831-116-5*) Delphic Associates.
Possehl, Suzanne R., ed. see Belkindas, Misha V.
Possehl, Suzanne R., ed. see Litvak, Eugene.
***Possekel, A. K.** Living with the Unexpected: Linking Disaster Recovery to Sustainable Development in Montserrat. Adams, I., tr. from GER. LC 99-16184. (Illus.). 305p. 1999. 109.00 (*3-540-65709-6*) Spr-Verlag.
Possemiers, Marc, jt. auth. see Brodie, Peter.
Posset, Franz. Luther's Catholic Christology. LC 87-63002. 267p. (Orig.). 1988. pap. 10.99 (*0-8100-0275-2*, 15N0443) Northwest Pub.
***Posset, Franz.** Pater Bernhardus: Martin Luther & Bernard of Clairvaux. (Cistercian Studies: Vol. CS168). (Illus.). 432p. 2000. write for info. (*0-87907-368-3*); pap. write for info. (*0-87907-668-2*) Cistercian Pubns.
Possevino, Antonio. The Moscovia of Antonio Possevino, S. J. Graham, Hugh F., tr. & intro. by. LC 77-12648. (UCIS Series in Russian & East European Studies: No. 1). 214p. 1977. pap. 66.40 (*0-7837-8539-9*, 204935400011) Bks Demand.
Possidente, John. Ultimate Civilization II Designer's Guide to Building Scenarios. LC 98-84117. 1998. pap. 19.95 (*1-56893-904-3*) GT Interactive Software.
Possidente, William. Machiavelli, the Prince: The Official Strategy Guide. LC 95-68589. 1995. pap. text 12.95 (*0-7615-0138-X*) Prima Pub.
Possidius. The Life of Saint Augustine. Rotelle, John E., ed. O'Connell, Matthew, tr. from LAT. LC 88-71357. (Augustinian Ser.). (Illus.). 144p. 1988. pap. 7.95 (*0-941491-19-6*) Augustinian Pr.
Possman, Peter. Sense of History. mass mkt. 4.99 (*1-896329-37-3*) Picasso Publ.
Possolo, Antonio, ed. Spatial Statistics & Imaging. LC 91-77910. (IMS Lecture Notes - Monographs: Vol. 20). vii, 426p. 1992. pap. 35.00 (*0-940600-27-7*) Inst Math.
Post. Arise Ye Starvelings. 1978. pap. text 98.50 (*90-247-2140-7*, Pub. by M Nijhoff) Kluwer Academic.
— Bioethics for Students, Vol. 1. LC 98-29518. 1998. 90.00 (*0-02-864936-2*) Mac Lib Ref.
— Bioethics for Students, Vol. 2. LC 98-29518. 1998. 90.00 (*0-02-864937-0*) Mac Lib Ref.
— Bioethics for Students, Vol. 3. LC 98-29518. 1998. 90.00 (*0-02-864938-9*) Mac Lib Ref.
— Bioethics for Students, Vol. 4. LC 98-29518. 1998. 90.00 (*0-02-864939-7*) Mac Lib Ref.
— Bioethics for Students: How Do We Know What's Right, 4 vols. LC 98-29518. 832p. 1998. 295.00 (*0-02-864940-0*) Mac Lib Ref.
— Internships: Finding, Managing & Transitioning Your Career. (Paralegal Ser.). 304p. (C). 1998. text, student ed. 24.95 (*0-7668-0394-5*) Delmar.
— Management Information Systems. 2nd ed. LC 99-16364. 2000. 66.25 (*0-07-229756-5*) McGraw.
Post. Pillarization. 1989. 82.95 (*0-566-07026-X*) Ashgate Pub Co.
Post. Radiographic Evaluation of the Spine. (gr. 13). 1980. 169.00 (*0-89352-050-0*) Mosby Inc.
Post, et al. Use of Anticonvulsants in Psychiatry: Recent Advances. Pope, ed. LC 88-60779. 192p. 1988. 22.50 (*0-945986-00-9*) Health Care NJ.
Post, jt. auth. see Djinis.
Post, jt. auth. see Miller.
Post, Alan, jt. ed. see Pacheco, Larry.
Post, Alexandra M. Deep Sea Mining & the Law of the Sea. 1983. lib. bdg. 160.50 (*90-247-3049-X*) Kluwer Academic.
Post, Alfred B. Double Jeopardies: Twin Threats to Our Freedoms. LC 88-90638. 298p. (Orig.). 1988. pap. 14.95 (*0-9620117-0-3*) Roanoke Pubs.
Post Ambassador Staff. Faribault County, Minnesota. (Illus.). 343p. 1987. 40.00 (*0-88107-099-8*) Curtis Media.
Post-Anderson. Management Information Systems: Solving Business Problems with Information Technology. 1996. text, teacher ed. write for info. (*0-256-22564-8*) McGraw.
— Management Information Systems: Solving Business Problems with information Technology. 1996. pap. text 31.50 (*0-256-22566-4*) McGraw.
***Post, Austin & LaChapelle, Edward R.** Glacier Ice. rev. ed. LC 99-39066. (Illus.). 160p. 2000. pap. 27.95 (*0-295-97910-0*) U of Wash Pr.
Post, Barton L., et al. The Law of Medical Practice in Pennsylvania & New Jersey. LC 83-83245. 1984. 115.00 (*0-318-01198-0*) West Group.
— The Law of Medical Practice in Pennsylvania & New Jersey. LC 83-83245. 1992. suppl. ed. 62.50 (*0-317-03240-2*) West Group.
Post, Beverly & Eads, Sandra. Logic, Anyone? One Hundred Sixty-Five Brain-Stretching Problems. (Makemaster Bk.). (J). (gr. 5-12). 1982. student ed. 5.99 (*0-8224-4327-9*); pap. 13.99 (*0-8224-4326-0*) Fearon Teacher Aids.
Post, Beverly, jt. auth. see Eads, Sandra.
Post, C. C. Too Many Promises. 456p. 1996. 21.95 (*0-9652168-0-2*) C C Pondbank.
Post, C. Gordon, jt. auth. see Calhoun, John.
Post, Carl J. Omaha Orange: History of EMS in America. 1992. pap. 26.25 (*0-86720-187-8*) Jones & Bartlett.
Post, Carole, jt. auth. see Basta, Lofty L.
Post, Chandler R. Mediaeval Spanish Allegory. (Harvard Studies in Comparative Literature: No. 4). xii, 351p. 1971. reprint ed. 50.70 (*3-487-04058-1*) G Olms Pubs.
— Medieval Spanish Allegory. 1977. lib. bdg. 59.95 (*0-8490-2221-5*) Gordon Pr.
— Medieval Spanish Allegory. 1984. lib. bdg. 90.00 (*0-8490-3235-0*) Gordon Pr.
Post, Charles G. The Supreme Court & Political Questions. LC 78-64164. (Johns Hopkins University. Studies in the Social Sciences. Thirtieth Ser. 1912: 4). reprint ed. 29.50 (*0-404-61274-1*) AMS Pr.
Post, Charles J. The Little War of Private Post: The Spanish-American War Seen up Close. LC 99-10211. (Illus.). xviii, 340p. 1999. pap. 15.00 (*0-8032-8757-7*) U of Nebr Pr.
***Post, Christian F., et al.** Journey on the Forbidden Path: Chronicles of a Diplomatic Mission to the Allegheny Country, March-september, 1760. LC 99-13908. (Transactions of the American Philosophical Society Ser.: Vol. 89, Pt. 2). 1999. 20.00 (*0-87169-892-7*) Am Philos.
Post, Constance J. Signs of the Times in Cotton Mather's "Paterna" A Study of Puritan Autobiography. LC 91-58798. (Studies in Religious Tradition: No. 2). 1992. 39.50 (*0-404-62532-0*) AMS Pr.
Post, D., et al. High Sensitivity Moire: Experimental Analysis for Mechanics & Materials. (Mechanical Engineering). (Illus.). 472p. 1997. pap. 49.00 (*0-387-98220-5*) Spr-Verlag.
Post, D. E. & Behrisch, R., eds. Physics of Plasma-Wall Interactions in Controlled Fusion. (NATO ASI Series B, Physics: Vol. 131). 1196p. 1986. 175.00 (*0-306-42097-X*, Plenum Trade) Perseus Pubng.
Post, D. L., jt. auth. see Widdel, H.
Post, Dan. Mills of the Forties Operator's Companion. (The/Yesteryear Series). (Illus.). 192p. 1980. 12.95 (*0-934422-28-1*, BKS-100274) Mead Pub Corp.
— Mills of the Thirties Operator's Companion. (The/Yesteryear Series). (Illus.). 192p. 1979. 12.95 (*0-934422-27-3*, BKS-100273) Mead Pub Corp.
— Watling Operator's Companion. (The/Yesteryear Series). (Illus.). 192p. 1979. 12.95 (*0-934422-29-X*, BKS-100280) Mead Pub Corp.
Post, Dan, jt. auth. see Gold, Laura M.
Post, Dan, ed. see Bach, Peter.
Post, Dan, ed. see Mills.
Post, Dan R. Cord-Without Tribute to Tradition: The Front Drive Legend. LC 72-96734. (Illus.). 219p. 1974. 26.95 (*0-911160-50-7*) Post Group.
— Volkswagen: Nine Lives Later. 2nd ed. LC 82-173212. (Illus.). 320p. 1982. pap. 19.95 (*0-911160-42-6*) Post Group.
Post, Dan R., ed. Cord Model 810 & 812 Owner's Companion. 224p. 1975. 19.95 (*0-911160-54-X*) Post Group.
— Duesenberg Model J Owners Companion. 192p. 1974. 13.95 (*0-911160-53-1*) Post Group.
— Mills of the Forties Operator's Companion. LC 79-53627. (Slot Machines of Yesteryear Ser.). (Illus.). 1980. 21.95 (*0-911160-75-2*) Post Group.
— Mills of the Thirties Operator's Companion. LC 79-53627. (Slot Machines of Yesteryear Ser.). (Illus.). 1979. 21.95 (*0-911160-73-6*) Post Group.
— Watling Operator's Companion. LC 79-53627. (Slot Machines of Yesteryear Ser.). (Illus.). 1979. 21.95 (*0-911160-74-4*) Post Group.
Post, Dan R., ed. see American Bantam Car Company Staff.
Post, Dan R., ed. see Ford Motor Company, Airplane Division Staff.
Post, Dan R., ed. see Ford Motor Company Staff.
Post, Dan R., ed. see GMC, Chevrolet Division Staff.
Post, Dan R., ed. see Mills Novelty Company Staff.
Post, Dan R., jt. ed. see U. S. War Department Staff.
Post, Dan W. Porsche Owner's Companion: A Manual of Preservation & Theft Protection. LC 80-82464. (Illus.). 192p. 1981. 16.95 (*0-911160-64-7*) Post Group.
— Profit from the IBM PC: A Non-Technical Guide to Selling User Services. LC 83-82632. (Illus.). 192p. 1984. 14.95 (*0-911160-89-2*) Post Group.
Post, Daniel, et al. High Sensitivity Moire: Experimental Analysis for Mechanics & Materials. LC 93-29790. 1993. write for info. (*3-540-94149-5*) Spr-Verlag.
— High Sensitivity Moire: Experimental Analysis for Mechanics & Materials. LC 93-29790. 1995. 79.95 (*0-387-94149-5*) Spr-Verlag.
Post, Deborah W., jt. auth. see Harmon, Louise.
***Post, Don E.** Beautifying the Ugly America. 272p. 2000. pap. 24.95 (*1-881515-26-5*, Pub. by TX Review Pr) Tex A&M Univ Pr.
Post, Donna C., jt. ed. see Aronson, Miriam K.
Post, Douglas. Belongings & Longings. LC 98-221646. 1997. pap. 5.60 (*0-87129-800-7*, B83) Dramatic Pub.
— Detective Sketches & Other Short Plays. 1997. pap. 5.60 (*0-87129-801-5*, D23) Dramatic Pub.
— Drowning Sorrows. 1998. pap. 5.25 (*0-8222-1629-9*) Dramatists Play.
— Earth & Sky. 1992. pap. 5.25 (*0-8222-0348-0*) Dramatists Play.
— Murder in Green Meadows. rev. ed. 1996. pap. 5.25 (*0-8222-1518-7*) Dramatists Play.
— Wind in the Willows. 87p. 1987. pap. 5.95 (*0-87129-172-X*, W05) Dramatic Pub.
Post, E. J. Formal Structure of Electromagnetics: General Covariance & Electromagnetics. LC 97-16159. (Illus.). 218p. 1997. pap. 8.95 (*0-486-65427-3*) Dover.
Post, Elizabeth. Emily Post's Guide to Business Etiquette: Post,&Peggy. abr. ed. 1997. audio 12.00 (*0-694-51829-8*, CPN 10118) HarperAudio.
Post, Elizabeth L. Emily Post on Entertaining. rev. ed. (Illus.). 144p. (Orig.). 1994. pap. 6.00 (*0-06-274007-5*, Harper Ref) HarpC.
— Emily Post on Etique. rev. ed. 208p. 1995. pap. 7.95 (*0-06-274011-3*, Harper Ref) HarpC.
— Emily Post on Second Weddings: Answers to All Your Questions about Getting Married Again. 176p. 1991. mass mkt. 6.50 (*0-06-274000-8*, Harper Ref) HarpC.
— Emily Post on Weddings. (Illus.). 135p. (Orig.). 1992. pap. 4.95 (*0-685-52545-7*, Harper Ref) HarpC.
— Emily Post on Weddings: Revised Edition. rev. ed. (Illus.). 176p. (Orig.). 1994. pap. 7.95 (*0-06-274008-3*, Harper Ref) HarpC.
— The Emily Post Wedding Book. 1991. 34.95 (*0-06-270005-7*) HarperTrade.
***Post, Elizabeth L.** Emily Post Wedding Package. rev. ed. 2000. 34.95 (*0-06-270226-2*) HarpC.
Post, Elizabeth L. Emily Post's Advice for Every Dining Occasion. LC 93-32393. 256p. 1994. 19.00 (*0-06-270099-5*, Harper Ref) HarpC.
— Emily Post's Complete Book of Wedding Etiquette. rev. ed. LC 90-55548. (Illus.). 256p. 1991. 25.00 (*0-06-270006-5*, Harper Ref) HarpC.
— Emily Post's Etiquette. 14th ed. LC 83-48375. (Illus.). 922p. 1984. 18.45 (*0-685-42642-4*) HarperTrade.
— Emily Post's Wedding Planner. rev. ed. 96p. 1991. pap. 9.95 (*0-06-273018-5*, Harper Ref) HarpC.
Post, Elizabeth L. & Coles, Joan M. Emily Post's Teen Etiquette. rev. ed. 192p. 1995. pap. 12.50 (*0-06-273337-0*, Harper Ref) HarpC.
Post, Elizabeth L. & Staffieri, Anthony. The Complete Book of Entertaining From the Emily Post Institute. 1982. pap. 8.50 (*0-671-45083-2*, Fireside) S&S Trade Pap.
Post, Emil L. Two-Valued Iterative Systems of Mathematical Logic. (Annals of Mathematics Studies). 1941. pap. 25.00 (*0-527-02721-9*) Periodicals Srv.
***Post, Emily.** Easy Entertaining: Emily Post's Essentials. (Emily Post's Etiquette Ser.). (Illus.). 208p. 1999. mass mkt. 6.50 (*0-06-273664-7*) HarpC.
Post, Emily & Post, Peggy. Emily Post's Etiquette: 16th Edition Indexed. 16th ed. LC 96-43427. (Emily Post's Etiquette Ser.). (Illus.). 864p. 1997. 35.00 (*0-06-270078-2*) HarpC.
Post, Evert J. Quantum Reprogramming: Ensembles & Single Systems: A Two-Tier Approach to Quantum Mechanics. LC 95-17463. (Boston Studies in the Philosophy of Science: Vol. 181). 332p. 1995. lib. bdg. 137.00 (*0-7923-3565-1*, Pub. by Kluwer Academic) Kluwer Academic.
Post, F., jt. ed. see Isaacs, Anthony D.
Post, Frederick J. Laboratory Manual for Food Microbiology & Biotechnology. 3rd rev. ed. (Illus.). 280p. (C). 1997. pap. text 32.95 (*0-89863-178-5*, 178-5) Star Pub CA.
Post, Frederick J., jt. auth. see Kelley, Susan G.
Post, G. C. Flora of Syria, Palestine & Sinai. 919p. (C). 1991. text 375.00 (*0-89771-627-2*, Pub. by Intl Bk Distr) St Mut.
— Flora of Syria, Palestine & Sinai. 919p. (C). 1980. reprint ed. 375.00 (*0-7855-3121-1*, Pub. by Intl Bk Distr) St Mut.
Post, Gaines, Jr. Dilemmas of Appeasement: British Deterrence & Defense, 1934-1937. LC 92-27606. (Cornell Studies in Security Affairs). 384p. 1993. text 52.50 (*0-8014-2748-7*) Cornell U Pr.
***Post, Gaines, Jr.** Memoirs of a Cold War Son. LC 99-57732. (Singular Lives Ser.). (Illus.). 246p. 2000. 24.95 (*0-87745-701-8*) U of Iowa Pr.
Post, Gaines, Jr., ed. German Unification: Problems & Prospects. LC 92-42236. (Keck Center for International & Strategic Studies: No. 3). viii, 160p. 1992. pap. 10.95 (*0-930607-14-7*) Keck Ctr.
Post, George. Textbook of Fish Health. (Illus.). 288p. 1987. 35.95 (*0-86622-491-2*, H-1043) TFH Pubns.
***Post, Gerald.** Database Management Systems. (C). 1998. pap., student ed. 80.00 (*0-07-232415-5*) McGrw-H Hghr Educ.
Post, Gerald V. Database Management Systems: Designing & Building Business Applications. LC 98-21687. 720p. 1998. 60.50 (*0-07-289893-3*) McGraw.
***Post, Gerald V.** Management Information Systems: Solving Business Problems with Information Technology. 2nd ed. 1999. pap., student ed. 86.25 (*0-07-238217-1*) McGraw.
Post, Gerald V. & Anderson, David. Management Information Systems. 640p. (C). 1996. text 67.95 (*0-256-17956-5*, Irwn McGrw-H) McGrw-H Hghr Educ.
Post, Harry H., ed. International Economic Law & Armed Conflict. LC 94-38233. (Nova et Vetera Iuris Gentium, Series A, Modern Law). 1994. lib. bdg. 92.00 (*0-7923-3189-3*, Pub. by M Nijhoff) Kluwer Academic.

P

Post, J. E., jt. auth. see Bish, D. L.

Post, Jaap H., jt. auth. see Terluin, Ida J.

Post, James. Research in Corporate Social Performance & Policy, Vol. 15. 1998. 78.50 (*1-55938-966-4*) Jai Pr.

Post, James E. Business & Society: Corporate Strategy, Public Policy, Ethics. 9th ed. 1999. 0.10 (*0-07-428694-3*) McGraw.

Post, James E., ed. Research in Corporate Social Performance & Policy, Suppl. 2. 388p. 1997. 78.50 (*0-7623-0289-5*) Jai Pr.

Post, James E., et al, eds. Research in Corporate Social Performance & Policy, Vol. 1. 291p. 1978. 78.50 (*0-89232-069-9*) Jai Pr.

— Research in Corporate Social Performance & Policy, Vol. 2. 353p. 1980. 78.50 (*0-89232-133-4*) Jai Pr.

— Research in Corporate Social Performance & Policy, Vol. 3. 250p. 1981. 78.50 (*0-89232-184-9*) Jai Pr.

— Research in Corporate Social Performance & Policy, Vol. 4. 261p. 1982. 78.50 (*0-89232-259-4*) Jai Pr.

— Research in Corporate Social Performance & Policy, Vol. 5. 256p. 1983. 78.50 (*0-89232-412-0*) Jai Pr.

— Research in Corporate Social Performance & Policy, Vol. 7. 293p. 1985. 78.50 (*0-89232-585-2*) Jai Pr.

— Research in Corporate Social Performance & Policy, Vol. 11. 300p. 1988. 78.50 (*1-55938-017-9*) Jai Pr.

— Research in Corporate Social Performance & Policy, Vol. 12. 401p. 1991. 78.50 (*1-55938-116-7*) Jai Pr.

— Research in Corporate Social Performance & Policy, Vol. 14. 236p. 1994. 78.50 (*1-55938-732-7*) Jai Pr.

— Research in Corporate Social Performance & Policy: Empirical Studies of Business Eth & Values, Vol. 9. 240p. 1987. 78.50 (*0-89232-742-1*) Jai Pr.

— Research in Corporate Social Performance & Policy No. 1: Sustaining the Natural Environment. 388p. 1995. suppl. ed. 78.50 (*1-55938-945-1*) Jai Pr.

— Research in Corporate Social Performance & Policy Vol. 8: Center Themes in CSR Research. 378p. 1985. 78.50 (*0-89232-679-4*) Jai Pr.

— Research in Corporate Social Performance & Policy Vol. 10: International & Comparative Studies. 303p. 1988. 78.50 (*0-89232-915-7*) Jai Pr.

— Research in Corporate Social Performance & Policy Vol. 13: Markets Politics & Social Performance. 244p. 1993. 78.50 (*1-55938-521-9*) Jai Pr.

Post, James E., et al. Business & Society: Corporate Strategy, Public Policy, Ethics. 8th ed. LC 95-9391. 672p. (C). 1995. 82.19 (*0-07-050494-6*) McGraw.

— Business & Society: Corporate Strategy, Public Policy, Ethics. 9th ed. LC 98-17649. 576p. 1998. 82.19 (*0-07-292447-0*) McGraw.

Post, James E., ed. see Lee, Preston.

Post, Jan & Lundin, Carl G. Guidelines for Integrated Coastal Zone Management. LC 96-32888. (Environmentally Sustainable Development Studies & Monographs Ser.: No. 9). 22p. 1996. pap. 22.00 (*0-8213-3735-1*, 13735) World Bank.

Post, Jeffrey E., jt. auth. see National Museum of Natural History Staff.

Post, Jerrold M. & Robins, Robert S. When Illness Strikes the Leader: The Dilemma of the Captive King. LC 92-25302. 320p. (C). 1993. 35.00 (*0-300-05683-4*) Yale U Pr.

— When Illness Strikes the Leader: The Dilemma of the Captive King. 1995. pap. 17.00 (*0-300-06314-8*) Yale U Pr.

Post, Jerrold M., jt. auth. see Robins, Robert S.

Post, John D. Food Shortage, Climatic Variability & Epidemic Disease in Preindustrial Europe: The Mortality Peak in the Early 1740s. LC 85-4684. 304p. (C). 1985. 39.95 (*0-8014-1773-2*) Cornell U Pr.

— Food Shortage, Climatic Variability & Epidemic Disease in Preindustrial Europe: The Mortality Peak in the Early 1740s. LC 85-4684. 304p. reprint ed. pap. 94.30 (*0-608-20934-1*, 207203300003) Bks Demand.

— The Last Great Subsistence Crisis in the Western World. LC 76-41239. 256p. 1977. reprint ed. pap. 79.40 (*0-608-03742-7*, 206456700009) Bks Demand.

Post, John F. The Faces of Existence: An Essay in Nonreductive Metaphysics. LC 86-19894. 392p. 1987. text 45.00 (*0-8014-1968-9*) Cornell U Pr.

— Metaphysics: A Contemporary Introduction. (Issues in Philosophy Ser.). 213p. (C). 1991. pap. text 16.95 (*1-55778-204-0*) Paragon Hse.

***Post, Jonathan F.** English Lyric Poetry: The Early Seventeenth Century. LC 98-48933. 323p. 1999. text. write for info. (*0-415-02949-X*) Routledge.

Post, Jonathan F. Henry Vaughan: The Unfolding Vision. LC 82-47609. 266p. 1982. reprint ed. pap. 82.50 (*0-7837-9425-8*, 206016600004) Bks Demand.

— Sir Thomas Browne. (English Authors Ser.: No. 448). 1987. 32.00 (*0-8057-6948-X*) Macmillan.

Post, Jonathan F., ed. see Gottlieb, Sidney.

Post, Jory. Family Relationships. (Comprehensive Health for Middle Grades Ser.). (J). (gr. 6-9). 1996. 24.00 (*1-56071-461-1*, H563) ETR Assocs.

— Violence. (Comprehensive Health for Middle Grades Ser.). (J). (gr. 6-9). 1996. 24.00 (*1-56071-472-7*, H574) ETR Assocs.

Post, Jory & McPherson, Carole. HIV & STD. (Comprehensive Health for Middle Grades Ser.). (J). (gr. 6-9). 1996. 24.00 (*1-56071-459-X*, H561) ETR Assocs.

— Into Adolescence: Learning about AIDS. Middleton, Kathleen, ed. (Contemporary Health Ser.). (Illus.). 231p. (Orig.). 1988. pap., teacher ed. 23.50 (*0-941816-62-1*) ETR Assocs.

Post, Joyce A. Gerontology & Geriatrics Libraries & Collections in the United States & Canada: A History, Description & Directory. LC 91-46862. 224p. 1992. lib. bdg. 55.00 (*0-313-28443-1*, PGG, Greenwood Pr) Greenwood.

Post, Kalmon D., et al, eds. The Pituitary Adenoma. LC 79-24811. (Illus.). 531p. 1980. reprint ed. pap. 164.70 (*0-608-05439-9*, 206590800006) Bks Demand.

Post, Kalmon D. & Goodrich, James T. Plastic Techniques in Neurosurgery. (Illus.). 168p. 1991. text 155.00 (*0-86577-352-1*) Thieme Med Pubs.

Post, Kalmon D., et al. Microsurgical Anatomy of the Skull Base & Approaches to the Cavernous Sinus. (Illus.). 450p. 1996. 189.00 incl. 5.25 hd (*0-86577-598-2*) Thieme Med Pubs.

Post, Ken. Communists & National Socialists: The Foundations of a Century, 1914-1939. LC 96-37662. 256p. 1997. text 65.00 (*0-312-17319-9*) St Martin.

— Regaining Marxism. LC 95-32641. 318p. 1996. text 69.95 (*0-312-12973-4*) St Martin.

***Post, Ken.** Revolution & The European Experience, 1789-1914. LC 99-18939. 1999. text 65.00 (*0-312-22256-4*) St Martin.

Post, Ken. Revolution, Socialism & Nationalism in Viet Nam Vol. 1: An Interrupted Revolution. 366p. 1989. 77.95 (*1-85521-037-1*, Pub. by Dartmth Pub) Ashgate Pub Co.

— Revolution, Socialism & Nationalism in Viet Nam Vol. 2: Viet Nam Divided. 1989. 77.95 (*1-85521-047-9*, Pub. by Dartmth Pub) Ashgate Pub Co.

— Revolution, Socialism & Nationalism in Viet Nam Vol. 3: Socialism in Half a Country. 397p. 1989. 77.95 (*1-85521-056-8*, Pub. by Dartmth Pub) Ashgate Pub Co.

— Revolution, Socialism & Nationalism in Viet Nam Vol. 4: The Failure of Counter-Insurgency in the South. 417p. 1989. 77.95 (*1-85521-091-6*, Pub. by Dartmth Pub) Ashgate Pub Co.

— Revolution, Socialism & Nationalism in Viet Nam Vol. 5: Winning the War & Losing the Peace, 5 vols. LC 93-21341. 416p. (C). 1994. text 77.95 (*1-85521-097-5*, Pub. by Dartmth Pub) Ashgate Pub Co.

— Revolution's Other World: Communism & the Periphery, 1917-1939. LC 97-18514. 196p. 1997. text 59.95 (*0-312-17631-7*) St Martin.

Post, Ken & Wright, Philip. Socialism & under Development. 242p. 1989. 39.95 (*0-415-01627-4*) Routledge.

Post, Kenneth H., jt. auth. see Combs, Eugene.

Post, L. E., jt. ed. see Oxender, D. L.

Post, Laura. Backstage Pass: Interviews with Women in Music. LC 97-5011. 1997. pap. 16.95 (*0-934678-84-7*) New Victoria Pubs.

Post, Lauren C. Cajun Sketches: From the Prairies of Southwest Louisiana. LC 90-31294. (Illus.). 215p. 1990. pap. 16.95 (*0-8071-1605-X*) La State U Pr.

Post, Laurens Van Der, see Van Der Post, Laurens.

Post-Lauria, Sheila. Correspondent Colorings: Melville in the Marketplace. LC 95-37247. 296p. (C). 1996. 50.00 (*1-55849-002-7*); pap. 18.95 (*1-55849-003-5*) U of Mass Pr.

Post, Libby, ed. Through the Eyes of Children: Liberty & Justice for All. (Illus.). 48p. (Orig.). (J). 1989. pap. write for info. (*0-9624123-0-9*) NY State Alliance.

Post, Louis F. Deportations Delirium of Nineteen-Twenty. LC 73-114343. (Civil Liberties in American History Ser.). 1970. reprint ed. lib. bdg. 42.50 (*0-306-71882-0*) Da Capo.

Post, Melville D. The Bradmoor Murder. 297p. 1980. reprint ed. lib. bdg. 14.25 (*0-89968-197-2*, Lghtyr Pr) Buccaneer Bks.

— Corrector of Destinies: Vol. 3 of Randolph Mason Stories. LC 72-150559. (Short Story Index Reprint Ser.). 1977. reprint ed. 20.95 (*0-8369-3856-9*) Ayer.

— The Man of Last Resort. 284p. 1980. reprint ed. lib. bdg. 14.25 (*0-89968-198-0*, Lghtyr Pr) Buccaneer Bks.

— The Mountain School Teacher. 196p. 1980. reprint ed. lib. bdg. 12.75 (*0-89968-199-9*, Lghtyr Pr) Buccaneer Bks.

— The Strange Schemes of Randolph Mason. 15.95 (*0-8488-1451-7*) Amereon Ltd.

— The Strange Schemes of Randolph Mason. LC 75-32776. (Literature of Mystery & Detection Ser.). 1976. reprint ed. 24.95 (*0-405-07895-1*) Ayer.

— The Strange Schemes of Randolph Mason. 280p. 1980. reprint ed. lib. bdg. 14.25 (*0-89968-200-6*, Lghtyr Pr) Buccaneer Bks.

— Uncle Abner & the Devil's Tools. 17.95 (*0-89190-987-7*) Amereon Ltd.

— Uncle Abner & the Doomsdorf Mystery. 17.95 (*0-89190-988-5*) Amereon Ltd.

Post, Melvin, et al. The Shoulder: Operative Technique. LC 97-42619. 270p. 1998. 99.00 (*0-683-06947-0*) Lppncott W & W.

Post, P., jt. ed. see Douw, L. M.

Post, Peggy. Emily Post Weddings. LC 98-42646. 352p. 1999. 26.00 (*0-06-270227-0*) HarpC.

***Post, Peggy.** Emily Post Weddings: Post,&Peggy. abr. ed. 1999. audio 12.00 (*0-694-52086-1*) HarperAudio.

Post, Peggy. Emily Post's Entertaining: A Classic Guide to Adding Elegance & Ease to Any Festive Occasion. LC 98-7309. (Illus.). 240p. 1998. pap. 20.00 (*0-06-273640-X*, Harper Ref) HarpC.

— Emily Post's Essentials. (Emily Post's Etiquette Ser.). (Illus.). 192p. 1999. mass mkt. 6.50 (*0-06-273663-9*) HarpC.

— Emily Post's Wedding Planner. 3rd ed. LC 98-42646. (Illus.). 272p. 1999. pap. 20.00 (*0-06-273520-9*) HarpC.

Post, Peggy & Post, Peter. The Etiquette Advantage in Business: Personal Skills for Professional Success. LC 99-34644. 592p. 1999. 35.00 (*0-06-273672-8*) HarpC.

Post, Peggy, jt. auth. see Post, Emily.

Post, Peter, jt. auth. see Post, Peggy.

Post, Richard S. & Schachtsiek, David A. Security Manager's Desk Reference. 466p. 1986. 69.95 (*0-409-90014-1*) Buttrwrth-Heinemann.

Post, Richard S., et al. Security Administration: An Introduction to the Protective Services. 4th ed. (Illus.). 256p. 1990. 39.95 (*0-409-90096-6*) Buttrwrth-Heinemann.

Post, Robert. Censorship & Silencing: Practices of Cultural Regulation. Roth, Michael, ed. LC 97-25546. (Issues & Debates Ser.). 350p. 1998. pap. 35.00 (*0-89236-484-X*, Pub. by J P Getty Trust) OUP.

Post, Robert & Rogin, Michael, eds. Race & Representation: Affirmative Action. LC 97-43038. 1998. pap. 20.00 (*0-942299-49-3*) Zone Bks.

Post, Robert & Rogin, Michael P. Race & Representation: Affirmative Action. LC 97-43038. 424p. 1998. 42.00 (*0-942299-48-5*) Zone Bks.

Post, Robert, jt. ed. see Hesse, Carla.

Post, Robert C. Constitutional Domains: Democracy, Community, Management. LC 94-29882. 475p. 1995. text 51.95 (*0-674-16545-4*, POSCON) HUP.

— High Performance: The Culture & Technology of Drag Racing, 1950-1990. (Johns Hopkins Studies in the History of Technology). 448p. 1996. reprint ed. pap. 18.95 (*0-8018-5464-4*) Johns Hopkins.

— The Tancook Whalers: Origins, Rediscovery & Revival. LC 85-63457. (Illus.). 113p. (Orig.). 1985. pap. 15.00 (*0-937410-05-5*) ME Maritime Mus.

Post, Robert C., ed. Eighteen Seventy-Six: A Centennial Exhibition. (Illus.). 223p. (Orig.). 1976. pap. 6.95 (*0-685-21907-0*) Natl Mus Am.

— Law & the Order of Culture. LC 90-50927. (Representation Bks.: No. 4). 200p. 1991. 45.00 (*0-520-07500-5*, Pub. by U CA Pr); pap. 14.95 (*0-520-07337-1*, Pub. by U CA Pr) Cal Prin Full Svc.

Post, Robert C., jt. ed. see Mayr, Otto.

Post, Roy G. & Seale, Robert L., eds. Water Production Using Nuclear Energy. LC 66-24303. (Illus.). 392p. reprint ed. pap. 121.60 (*0-608-11436-7*, 205535800017) Bks Demand.

Post, Ruth N. Virgil Williams: " He Shaped the Dawn of Western Art..." Carnahan, William E., ed. LC 97-74888. (Illus.). 144p. 1998. pap. 30.00 (*0-937088-23-4*) Illum Pr.

Post, Sandra & Dean, Loral. Sandra Post & Me: A Veteran Pro Takes a New Golfer from First Swing to Tournament. (Illus.). 204p. 1998. pap. 17.95 (*0-7710-7041-1*) McCland & Stewart.

Post, Shawn A., jt. auth. see Schumm, Jeanne Shay.

Post, Stephen G. Inquiries in Bioethics. LC 93-17564. 208p. 1993. 37.50 (*0-87840-538-0*); pap. 18.95 (*0-87840-539-9*) Georgetown U Pr.

— The Moral Challenge of Alzheimer Disease. LC 95-13505. 160p. 1995. text 29.95 (*0-8018-5174-2*) Johns Hopkins.

***Post, Stephen G.** The Moral Challenge of Alzheimer Disease: Ethical Issues from Diagnosis to Dying. 2nd ed. LC 99-50625. 192p. 2000. pap. 18.95 (*0-8018-6410-0*) Johns Hopkins.

— More Lasting Unions: Christianity, the Family & Society. LC 99-86147. (Religion, Marriage & the Family Ser.). 208p. 2000. pap. 15.00 (*0-8028-4707-2*) Eerdmans.

Post, Stephen G. Spheres of Love: Toward a New Ethics of the Family. LC 94-7166. 208p. 1994. text 12.95 (*0-87074-370-8*) SMU Press.

Post, Stephen G. & Whitehouse, Peter J. Genetic Testing for Alzheimer Disease: Ethical & Clinical Issues. LC 97-42661. (Illus.). 284p. 1998. 45.00 (*0-8018-5840-2*) Johns Hopkins.

Post, Steven. The Modern Book of Feng Shui. LC 97-44961. 256p. 1998. pap. 15.95 (*0-440-50768-5*, Dell Trade Pbks) Dell.

Post-Stroke Rehabilitation Guideline Panel Staff, et al. Post-Stroke Rehabilitation: Clinical Practice Guideline. LC 95-44619. 250p. 1996. pap. 21.00 (*0-8342-0811-3*) Aspen Pub.

Post, Susan E. Women in Modern Albania: Firsthand Accounts of Culture & Conditions from over 200 Interviews. LC 97-50579. 312p. 1998. lib. bdg. 48.50 (*0-7864-0468-X*) McFarland & Co.

Post, Susan L. Hiking Illinois. LC 96-37721. (America's Best Day Hiking Ser.). (Illus.). 224p. (Orig.). 1997. pap. 19.95 (*0-88011-568-8*, PPOS0568) Human Kinetics.

Post, Susan L., et al. Illinois Wilds. (Illus.). 156p. 1995. 34.95 (*1-886154-04-X*) U of Ill Pr.

Post, Thomas R. Teaching Elementary Mathematics: Research Based Material. 496p. (C). 1988. pap. text 45.00 (*0-205-11076-2*, H1076-2) Allyn.

Post, Thomas R., jt. auth. see Ellis, Arthur.

Post, W. Ellwood. Saints, Signs & Symbols. 2nd ed. LC 62-19257. (Illus.). 96p. (J). 1990. pap. 9.95 (*0-8192-1171-0*) Morehouse Pub.

Post, Waldron K. Harvard Stories. LC 77-90589. (Short Story Index Reprint Ser.). 1977. 20.95 (*0-8369-3072-X*) Ayer.

Postacchini, F. Lumbar Disc Herniation. LC 98-54151. (Illus.). 700p. 1998. 299.00 (*3-211-83118-5*) Spr-Verlag.

— Lumbar Spinal Stenosis. (Illus.). 230p. 1989. 120.00 (*0-387-82111-2*) Spr-Verlag.

Postal, Edward S. Price Guide & Bibliography to Children's & Illustrated Books. (Illus.). 295p. (Orig.). 1995. pap. 59.95 (*0-9644800-1-8*) M & P Pr.

Postal, Paul M. Masked Inversion in French. (Illus.). 168p. 1989. 33.00 (*0-226-67569-6*) U Ch Pr.

— Studies of Passive Clauses. LC 84-26850. (SUNY Series in Linguistics). 271p. (C). 1985. text 29.50 (*0-88706-083-8*) State U NY Pr.

— Three Investigations of Extraction. LC 98-39766. (Current Studies in Linguistics: Volume 29). (Illus.). 368p. 1998. 32.50 (*0-262-16179-6*) MIT Pr.

Postal, Paul M. & Joseph, Brian D., eds. Studies in Relational Grammar, No. 3. LC 82-6945. (Illus.). 402p. 1990. pap. text 39.00 (*0-226-67573-4*) U Ch Pr.

— Studies in Relational Grammar, No. 3. LC 82-6945. (Illus.). 402p. 1996. lib. bdg. 78.00 (*0-226-67572-6*) U Ch Pr.

Postal, Paul M., jt. auth. see Johnson, David E.

Postal, Paul M., jt. ed. see Culicover, Peter W.

Postan, Cynthia, tr. see Duby, Georges.

Postan, M. M., ed. The Cambridge Economic History of Europe Vol. 1: The Agrarian Life of the Middle Ages. (Illus.). 888p. 1966. text 175.00 (*0-521-04505-3*) Cambridge U Pr.

Postan, M. M. & Miller, E., eds. The Cambridge Economic History of Europe Vol. 2: Trade & Industry in the Middle Ages. (Illus.). 1024p. 1987. text 190.00 (*0-521-08709-0*) Cambridge U Pr.

Postan, M. M., jt. ed. see Mathias, P.

Postan, M. M., ed. see Power, Eileen.

Poste, E., tr. & anno. see Aristotle.

Poste, Edward, tr. GAII Institutionum Iuris Civilis Commentarii Quatuor: Elements of Roman Law by Gaius. 2nd enl. rev. ed. LC 93-79717. 700p. 1994. reprint ed. 165.00 (*1-56169-075-9*) Gaunt.

Poste, Edward, tr. & comment see Gaius.

Poste, Edward, tr. & notes see Aristotle.

Poste, G. & Crooke, S. T. Cellular & Molecular Aspects of Inflammation. LC 87-37400. (New Horizons in Therapeutics Ser.). (Illus.). 496p. (C). 1988. text 125.00 (*0-306-42852-0*, Kluwer Plenum) Kluwer Academic.

— New Frontiers in the Study of Gene Functions. LC 86-30313. (New Horizons in Therapeutics Ser.). (Illus.). 218p. (C). 1987. text 75.00 (*0-306-42502-5*, Kluwer Plenum) Kluwer Academic.

Poste, G., et al. New Generation Vaccines: The Role of Basic Immunology. (NATO ASI Ser.: Vol. 261). (Illus.). 232p. (C). 1994. text 85.00 (*0-306-44666-9*, Kluwer Plenum) Kluwer Academic.

Poste, G., jt. auth. see Hook, J. B.

Poste, George H., et al, eds. Targeting of Drugs with Synthetic Systems. LC 86-16891. (NATO ASI Series A, Life Sciences: Vol. 113). 308p. 1986. 75.00 (*0-306-42377-4*, Plenum Trade) Perseus Pubng.

Poste, George H. & Gregoriadis, Gregory, eds. Targeting of Drugs 1: Anatomical & Physiological Considerations. LC 88-28892. (Illus.). 230p. 1988. 79.50 (*0-306-43023-1*, Plenum Trade) Perseus Pubng.

Poste, George H. & Nicholson, G., eds. Virus Infection & the Cell Surface. (Cell Surface Reviews Ser.: Vol. 2). 342p. 1980. 239.50 (*0-7204-0598-X*) Elsevier.

Poste, George H., jt. ed. see Crooke, Stanely T.

Poste, George H., jt. ed. see Crooke, Stanley T.

Poste, George H., jt. ed. see Nicolson, Garth L.

Postek, M. T., ed. Integrated Circuit Metrology, Inspection, & Process Control VI. 1992. 20.00 (*0-8194-0828-X*, 1673) SPIE.

Postek, Michael T. Critical Issues in Scanning Electron Microscope Metrology. (Illus.). 31p. (Orig.). (C). 1994. pap. text 20.00 (*0-7881-1552-9*) DIANE Pub.

Postek, Michael T. & Friedrich, Craig R., eds. Microlithography & Metrology in Micromachining II, Vol. 2880. 306p. 1996. 66.00 (*0-8194-2278-9*) SPIE.

Postel, A. Williams. Mineral Resources of Africa. (African Handbooks Ser.: Vol. 2). (Illus.). iv, 106p. 1943. pap. 10.00 (*0-686-24091-X*) U Museum Pubns.

Postel, Edward. Sense & Nonsense Vol. 1: Uplifting Humor. large type ed. (Illus.). 304p. 1997. mass mkt. 6.95 (*0-9654967-1-6*) Post-n-Tell.

Postel, Guillaume. Le Thresor des Propheties de L'Univers: Manuscrit Publie Avec Une Introduction & des Notes par Francois Secret. (International Archives of the History of Ideas Ser.: No. 27). 276p. 1969. lib. bdg. 85.50 (*90-247-0203-8*, Pub. by M Nijhoff) Kluwer Academic.

Postel, J. Dictionnaire Psychiatrie, Psychopathologie. (FRE.). 1998. 59.95 (*0-320-00379-5*) Fr & Eur.

Postel, J., jt. auth. see Knowles, J. W.

Postel, Jacques. Larousse Dictionnaire de Psychiatrie et de Psychopathologie Clinique. (FRE.). 630p. 1993. pap. 29.95 (*0-7859-7685-X*, 2037202210) Fr & Eur.

Postel, Michel. Antiquities of Himachal. (C). 1992. 100.00 (*0-8364-2869-2*, Pub. by Franco-Indian) S Asia.

— Ear Ornaments of Ancient India. (Illus.). 323p. (C). 1991. 120.00 (*0-935681-02-7*) D J Content.

— Ear Ornaments of Ancient India. (C). 1992. 160.00 (*0-8364-2870-6*, Pub. by Franco-Indian) S Asia.

Postel, Mitchell P. San Mateo: A Centennial History. (Illus.). 312p. 1994. 29.95 (*0-942087-08-9*) Scottwall Assocs.

— The University Club of San Francisco Centennial History, 1890-1990: With an Appendix on the Clubhouse. (Illus.). 112p. 1990. 30.00 (*0-9627540-0-5*) Univ Club.

Postel, Sandra. Air Pollution, Acid Rain, & the Future of Forests. LC 84-50653. (Worldwatch Papers). 1984. pap. 5.00 (*0-916468-57-7*) Worldwatch Inst.

— Altering the Earth's Chemistry: Assessing the Risks. LC 86-61917. (Worldwatch Papers). 68p. (Orig.). 1986. pap. 5.00 (*0-916468-72-0*) Worldwatch Inst.

— Conserving Water: The Untapped Alternative. LC 85-51713. (Worldwatch Papers). 1985. pap. 5.00 (*0-916468-67-4*) Worldwatch Inst.

— Defusing the Toxics Threat: Controlling Pesticides & Industrial Waste. (Worldwatch Papers). 70p. (Orig.). 1987. pap. 5.00 (*0-916468-80-1*) Worldwatch Inst.

— The Last Oasis. 2nd ed. LC 97-202393. 1997. pap. 12.95 (*0-393-31744-7*) Norton.

— Pillar of Sand: Can the Irrigation Miracle Last? 320p. 1999. pap. 13.95 (*0-393-31937-7*) Norton.

— Water: Rethinking Management in an Age of Scarcity. LC 84-52522. (Worldwatch Papers). 1984. pap. 4.00 (*0-916468-62-3*) Worldwatch Inst.

— Water for Agriculture: Facing the Limits. (Orig.). (C). 1989. pap. 5.00 (*0-916468-94-1*) Worldwatch Inst.

An Asterisk (*) at the beginning of an entry indicates that the title is appearing for the first time.

Postel, Sandra & Heise, Hori. Reforesting the Earth. (Papers). 64p. (Orig.). (C). 1988. pap. 5.00 (*0-916468-84-4*) Worldwatch Inst.

Postel-Vinay, Nicolas & International Society of Hypertension Staff. A Century of Arterial Hypertension, 1896-1996. LC 96-8699. (Illus.). 224p. 1997. 79.95 (*0-471-96788-2*) Wiley.

Postell, Alice E. Where Did the Reindeer Come From? Alaska Experience the First Fifty Years. York, Susan P., ed. LC 90-146. (Illus.). 144p. (YA). (gr. 9 up). 1990. write for info. (*0-9626090-0-5*) Amaknak Pr.

Postell, Catherine. On Toplecote Bayou. LC 72-1518. (Black Heritage Library Collection). 1977. reprint ed. 15.95 (*0-8369-9048-X*) Ayer.

***Postelle, Yvonne.** Sonnets for Sarah's Daughters & Selected Poems. LC 98-94899. 87 p. 1999. pap. 15.95 (*0-89914-066-1*) Third Party Pub.

Postels, A. & Ruprecht, F. J. Illustrationes Algarum in Itinere Circa Orben...Collectarum. 1963. reprint ed. 160.00 (*3-7682-0158-9*) Lubrecht & Cramer.

Postema. Bentham. 144.95 (*1-84014-038-0*) Ashgate Pub Co.

Postema, Donald H. Catch Your Breath: God's Invitation to Sabbath Rest. LC 96-39925. 93p. 1997. pap. 6.45 (*1-56212-239-8*, 1360-0340) CRC Pubns.

— Space for God: Leader's Guide. 2nd ed. 44p. 1997. pap., teacher ed. 7.75 (*0-933140-47-9*, 1340-0500) CRC Pubns.

— Space for God: Study & Practice of Spirituality & Prayer. 2nd ed. LC 83-15504. (Illus.). 208p. 1997. pap. text 19.95 (*0-933140-46-0*, 1341-0300) CRC Pubns.

Postema, Gerald J., ed. Racism & the Law: The Legacy & Lessons of Plessy. LC 97-221280. 110p. 1997. text 67.00 (*0-7923-4665-3*) Kluwer Academic.

Postema, Maarten H. C-Glycoside Synthesis. 400p. 1995. boxed set 139.95 (*0-8493-9150-4*, 9150) CRC Pr.

Poster, Amy G., et al. Crosscurrents: Masterpieces of East Asian Art from New York Private Collections. (Illus.). 200p. 1999. 49.50 (*0-8109-6386-8*, Pub. by Abrams) Time Warner.

— Indian Miniature Plqs in TBM. LC 94-12261. (Illus.). 352p. pap. 45.00 (*0-87273-131-6*) Bklyn Mus.

— Japanese Paintings & Prints of the Shijo School. (Illus.). 48p. 1981. pap. 1.00 (*0-87273-085-9*) Bklyn Mus.

Poster, C. D., et al. Restructuring: The Key to Effective School Management LC 98-37419. 1999. pap. write for info. (*0-415-20218-3*) Routledge.

Poster, Carol. Surrounded by Dangerous Things. 48p. 1995. pap. 7.00 (*1-880286-17-3*) Singular Speech Pr.

Poster, Carol & Utz, Richard J., eds. Constructions of Time in the Late Middle Ages. (Disputatio Ser.: Vol. 1). 250p. 1996. 59.95 (*0-8101-1541-7*) Northwestern U Pr.

— The Late Medieval Epistle: An International Journal of the Late Middle Ages. (Disputatio Ser.). 250p. 1996. text 49.95 (*0-8101-1449-6*) Northwestern U Pr.

***Poster, Carol & Utz, Richard J., eds.** Transformation, Translation, & Transubstantiation, Vol. 3. (Medieval Studies). 250p. 1998. text 59.95 (*0-8101-1646-4*) Northwestern U Pr.

***Poster, Cyril.** Restructuring: The Key to Effective School Management. Blandford, Sonia & Welton, John, eds. LC 98-37419. 1999. 85.00 (*0-415-20217-5*) Routledge.

Poster, Cyril, jt. auth. see Day, Chris.

Poster, Cyril D. & Day, Christopher, eds. Partnership in Education Management. LC 89-113195. (Educational Management Ser.). (Illus.). 239p. reprint ed. pap. 74.10 (*0-608-20330-0*, 207158300002) Bks Demand.

Poster, Donna. The Quilter's Guide to Rotary Cutting. 2nd ed. LC 98-87369. (Illus.). 208p. 1999. per. 19.95 (*0-87341-707-0*) Krause Pubns.

— Stars Galore & Even More: Speed-Cut Quilt Designs Using Hexagons & Octagons. LC 95-7314. (Contemporary Quilting Ser.). (Illus.). 208p. 1995. pap. 22.95 (*0-8019-8615-X*) Krause Pubns.

Poster, Harry. The Illustrated Price Guide to Vintage TV's & Deco Radios. 80p. 1991. pap. 15.95 (*0-9630932-0-7*) H Poster.

Poster, Jem. The Thirties Poets. LC 92-45681. (Open Guides to Literature Ser.). 112p. 1993. 102.50 (*0-335-09664-6*); pap. 27.95 (*0-335-09663-8*) OpUniv Pr.

Poster, Jem, ed. see Crabbe, George.

Poster, Mark. Critical Theory & Poststructuralism: In Search of a Context: Including 7 charts. LC 89-7262. (Illus.). 200p. 1989. pap. text 13.95 (*0-8014-9588-1*) Cornell U Pr.

— Cultural History & Postmodernity. 208p. (C). 1997. pap. 17.50 (*0-231-10883-4*) Col U Pr.

— Cultural History & Postmodernity: Disciplinary Readings & Challenges. LC 96-48854. 1997. 50.00 (*0-231-10882-6*) Col U Pr.

— The Mode of Information: Poststructuralism & Social Context. LC 90-34770. 188p. 1990. pap. text 19.95 (*0-226-67596-3*); lib. bdg. 48.00 (*0-226-67595-5*) U Ch Pr.

— The Second Media Age. LC 95-14498. 192p. 1995. text 55.95 (*0-7456-1395-0*, Pub. by Polity Pr) Blackwell Pubs.

— The Second Media Age. LC 95-14498. 192p. 1995. pap. text 28.95 (*0-7456-1396-9*, Pub. by Polity Pr) Blackwell Pubs.

Poster, Mark, ed. Politics, Theory, & Contemporary Culture. LC 92-23573. 336p. (C). 1993. pap. 20.00 (*0-231-08057-3*); text 69.00 (*0-231-08056-5*) Col U Pr.

***Poster, Mark & Aronowitz, Stanley.** The Information Subject. (Critical Voices in Art, Theory & Culture Ser.). 180p. 2000. pap. 26.00 (*90-5701-242-1*, G & B Arts); text 48.00 (*90-5701-232-4*, G & B Arts) Gordon & Breach.

Poster, Mark, ed. see Baudrillard, Jean.

Poster, Mark, tr. see Baudrillard, Jean.

Posterski, Donald C. Reinventing Evangelism. LC 89-15363. 202p. (Orig.). 1989. pap. 10.99 (*0-8308-1269-5*, 1269) InterVarsity.

Postgate, Carolyn, et al. The Excavations at Tell Al Rimah: The Pottery. (Iraq Archaeological Reports: No. 4). (Illus.). 275p. (C). 1997. pap. 95.00 (*0-85668-700-6*, Pub. by Aris & Phillips) David Brown.

Postgate, Daniel. Captain Hog: Mission to the Stars. LC 97-7302. 32p. (J). (ps-3). 1998. 4.99 (*0-7636-0410-0*) Candlewick Pr.

Postgate, J. N. Early Mesopotamia: Society & Economy at the Dawn of History. LC 93-48475. (Illus.). 392p. (C). 1994. pap. 32.99 (*0-415-11032-7*) Routledge.

Postgate, J. N., jt. auth. see Steinkeller, Piotr.

Postgate, J. P., ed. see Tibullus, et al.

Postgate, John. Microbes & Man. 4th ed. LC 99-13564. (Illus.). 352p. (C). 2000. pap. 19.95 (*0-521-66579-5*) Cambridge U Pr.

Postgate, John R. The Outer Reaches of Life. LC 93-11579. (Illus.). 288p. (C). 1994. text 25.95 (*0-521-44010-6*) Cambridge U Pr.

— The Outer Reaches of Life. (Canto Book Ser.). (Illus.). 290p. (C). 1995. pap. 12.95 (*0-521-55873-5*) Cambridge U Pr.

Postgate, John Raymond. Nitrogen Fixation. 3rd rev. ed. LC 98-15362. (Illus.). 100p. (C). 1998. 54.95 (*0-521-64047-4*); pap. 17.95 (*0-521-64853-X*) Cambridge U Pr.

Postgate, Nicholas, ed. see Roaf, Michael.

Postgate, Raymond. Verdict of Twelve. 208p. 1986. reprint ed. pap. 5.95 (*0-89733-198-2*) Academy Chi Pubs.

Postgate, Raymond, jt. auth. see Cole, G. D.

Posthofen, Renate S. Barbara Frischmuth in Contemporary Context. LC 98-29033. (Studies in Austrian Literature, Culture, & Thought). 1999. 32.50 (*1-57241-054-X*) Ariadne CA.

Posthofen, Renate S., jt. ed. see Lorenz, Dagmar C.

Posthuma, Barbara W. Small Groups in Counseling & Therapy: Process & Leadership. 3rd ed. LC 98-8516. 285p. (C). 1998. pap. text 68.00 (*0-205-29126-0*) Allyn.

Posthumus, Meyjes & Guillaume, H. M. Hugo Grotius Meletius Sive de Lis Qua Inter Christianos Conveniunt Epistola. (Studies in the History of Christian Thought: Vol. XL). (Illus.). 1987. 64.00 (*90-04-08356-1*) Brill Academic Pubs.

Postian, Charles W., jt. auth. see Pratt, Timothy.

Postic, Lionel J. Wrongful Termination: A State by State Survey. LC 94-25990. 1994. 125.00 (*0-87179-843-3*) BNA Books.

***Postiglione, Gennaro.** 1930s Scandinavia, 78. 1999. pap. text 35.00 (*88-85322-41-7*) Birkhauser.

Postiglione, Gennaro. Sverre Fehn: Works & Projects, 1949-1996. LC 97-30322. (Illus.). 320p. 1997. 75.00 (*1-885254-64-4*, Pub. by Monacelli Pr) Penguin Putnam.

Postiglione, Gerard A., ed. Education & Society in Hong Kong: Toward One Country & Two Systems. LC 90-24658. (Hong Kong Becoming China: the Transition to 1997 Ser.). 328p. (C). (gr. 13). 1992. text 68.95 (*0-87332-743-8*, East Gate Bk) M E Sharpe.

Postiglione, Gerard A. & Mak, Grace C. Asian Higher Education: An International Handbook & Reference Guide. LC 96-33072. 432p. 1997. lib. bdg. 99.50 (*0-313-28901-8*, Greenwood Pr) Greenwood.

Postiglione, Gerard A. & Ming, Julian L., eds. Education & Society in Hong Kong: Toward One Country & Two Systems. 328p. (C). 1992. pap. text 42.50 (*962-209-300-0*, Pub. by HK Univ Pr) Coronet Bks.

Postiglione, Gerard A. & Stites, Regie. China's National Minority Education: Culture, State, Schooling, & Development. Beauchamp, Edward R., ed. LC 99-29155. (Reference Books in International Education: No. 42). 275p. 1998. text 65.00 (*0-8153-2223-2*) Garland.

Postiglione, Gerard A. & Tang, James T., eds. Hong Kong's Reunion with China: The Global Dimensions. LC 97-9978. (Hong Kong Becoming China Ser.). 320p. (C). (gr. 13). 1997. pap. text 30.95 (*0-7656-0156-7*, East Gate Bk) M E Sharpe.

Postiglione, Gerard A. & Tang, James T. H., eds. Hong Kong's Reunion with China: The Global Dimensions. LC 97-9978. (Hong Kong Becoming China Ser.). 320p. (C). (gr. 13). 1997. text 72.95 (*0-7656-0155-9*, East Gate Bk) M E Sharpe.

Postiglione, Gerard A. & Wing On Lee, eds. Schooling in Hong Kong: Organization, Teaching & Social Context. LC 98-170597. 240p. 1997. pap. 36.50 (*962-209-439-2*, Pub. by HK Univ Pr) Coronet Bks.

Postiglione, Gerard A., jt. ed. see Chan, Ming K.

Postiglione, Marianne, ed. The External Environment. (Illus.). 250p. (Orig.). 1991. pap. 15.95 (*0-9625431-3-6*) ITEST Faith.

— The Human Genome Project. (Illus.). iv, 286p. (Orig.). 1993. pap. 15.95 (*0-9625431-6-0*) ITEST Faith.

— Some Christian & Jewish Perspectives on the Creation. 260p. (Orig.). 1991. pap. 15.95 (*0-9625431-4-4*) ITEST Faith.

— Transfiguration: Elements of Science & Christian Faith. (Illus.). iii, 294p. (Orig.). 1993. pap. 15.95 (*0-9625431-7-9*) ITEST Faith.

Postiglione, Marianne & Brungs, Robert A., eds. Secularism versus Biblical Secularity. 272p. (Orig.). (C). 1994. pap. 15.95 (*1-885583-00-1*) ITEST Faith.

Postiglione, Marianne, jt. ed. see Brungs, Robert A.

Postiglione, Marianne, jt. ed. see Brungs, Robert.

Postin, David. The Blacksmith & the Farmer: Rural Manufacturing in Sub-Saharan Africa. 160p. 1994. pap. 30.00 (*1-85339-127-1*, Pub. by Intermed Tech) Stylus Pub VA.

Postl, Karl, see Sealsfield, Charles, pseud.

Postle, Martin. Angels & Urchins: The Fancy Picture in Eighteenth-Century Britain. 1998. pap. text 30.00 (*0-85331-717-8*, Pub. by Lund Humphries) Antique Collect.

Postle, Martin, jt. auth. see Mannings, David.

Postle, Martin J. The Artist's Model. 128p. 1999. 40.00 (*1-85894-084-2*) Merrell Holberton.

— Sir Joshua Reynolds: The Subject Pictures. LC 93-28687. (Illus.). 396p. (C). 1995. text 85.00 (*0-521-42066-0*) Cambridge U Pr.

Postle, Ron, et al. The Mechanics of Wool Structures. (Applied Science & Industrial Technology Ser.). 462p. 1988. text 94.95 (*0-470-21000-1*) P-H.

Postles, David. The Surnames of Devon. (Illus.). 332p. 1995. 34.00 (*0-904920-25-9*, Pub. by Leopards Head Pr) David Brown.

***Postles, David.** The Surnames of Leicestershire & Rutland. (English Surnames Ser.: No. 7). (Illus.). 370p. 1999. 34.00 (*0-904920-34-8*, Pub. by Leopards Head Pr) David Brown.

Postlethwa. Exploring Life. (C). Date not set. pap. text, student ed. write for info. (*0-03-022572-8*); pap. text, lab manual ed. write for info. (*0-03-022573-6*) Harcourt Coll Pubs.

— Exploring Life. (C). Date not set. pap. text. write for info. (*0-03-022558-2*) Harcourt Coll Pubs.

Postlethwait, jt. auth. see Husen.

Postlethwait, John H. & Hopson, Janet L. The Nature of Life. 2nd ed. (C). 1991. pap. text, lab manual ed. 26.25 (*0-07-050650-7*) McGraw.

— The Nature of Life. 3rd ed. LC 94-37994. (C). 1995. text 68.00 (*0-07-050750-3*) McGraw.

— The Nature of Life: Apply & Decide Case Studies. (C). 1996. pap. text 7.25 (*0-07-050762-7*) McGraw.

— The Nature of Life: Critical Thinking Workbook. 2nd ed. (C). 1995. pap. text, wbk. ed. 21.87 (*0-07-050666-3*) McGraw.

— The Nature of Life: Preparator's Guide. 2nd ed. (C). 1991. text 26.87 (*0-07-050656-6*) McGraw.

Postlethwait, John N., et al. Biology! Bringing Science to Life. (C). 1991. text 63.74 (*0-07-050631-0*) McGraw.

Postlethwait, Virgil A. The Armstrong Report, ET's & UFO's - They Need Us, We Don't Need Them, No. 1. 150p. (Orig.). 1989. pap. 7.95 (*0-925390-33-X*) Armstrong Assocs.

Postlethwaite, Alan. The Last Days of Steam on the Southern: London, Brighton & South Coast Lines & the Isle of Wight. (Illus.). 160p. 1994. 26.95 (*0-7509-0413-5*, Pub. by Sutton Pub Ltd) Intl Pubs Mktg.

— Last Days of Team on the Southern: London & South Western. (Illus.). 160p. 1996. 30.95 (*0-7509-1205-7*, Pub. by Sutton Pub Ltd) Intl Pubs Mktg.

— Odd Corners of the Southern from the Days of Steam. LC 99-494966. 1999. 36.00 (*0-7509-1939-6*) A Sutton.

Postlethwaite, Alan, ed. The Last Days of the Steam Railway. LC 98-134098. (Illus.). 144p. 1998. 44.95 (*0-7509-1504-8*, Pub. by Sutton Pub Ltd) Intl Pubs Mktg.

Postlethwaite, Diana. Making It Whole: A Victorian Circle & the Shape of Their World. LC 84-20677. 302p. reprint ed. pap. 93.70 (*0-608-09867-1*, 206983200006) Bks Demand.

Postlethwaite, Ian, jt. auth. see Skogestad, Sigurd.

Postlethwaite, Keith. Differentiated Science Teaching: Responding to Individual Differences & to Special Education Needs. LC 92-20523. 1992. pap. 31.95 (*0-335-15706-8*) OpUniv Pr.

Postlethwaite, Kenneth E. Of Goshen & Paradise: Selected Editorial Writings of Kenneth E. Postlethwaite. LC 98-74319. 359p. 1998. pap. 16.95 (*1-893046-11-7*) Vernon Cty Hist Soc.

Postlethwaite, N. & Wiley, D. The IEA Study of Science II: Science Achievement in Twenty Three Countries. LC 91-26614. (International Studies in Educational Achievement). 1992. reprint ed. 115.00 (*0-08-041035-9*, CRC Reprint) Franklin.

Postlethwaite, R. J., jt. ed. see Eminson, D. Mary.

Postlethwaite, S. R., jt. ed. see Ford, D. G.

Postlethwaite, T. Neville, ed. The Encyclopedia of Comparative Education & National Systems of Education. LC 86-9346. (Illus.). 806p. 1988. 348.00 (*0-08-030853-8*, CRC Reprint) Franklin.

— International Encyclopedia of National Systems of Education. 2nd ed. 1050p. 1995. write for info. (*0-08-042302-7*, Pergamon Pr) Elsevier.

Postlethwaite, T. Neville, jt. auth. see Husen, Torsten.

Postlethwaite, T. Neville, jt. auth. see Trijnman, Albert C.

Postlethwaite, T. Neville, ed. see Choppin, B. H.

Postlethwaite, T. Neville, jt. ed. see Choppin, B. H.

Postlethwaite, T. Neville, jt. ed. see Husen, Torsten.

Postlethwaite, T. Neville, jt. ed. see Walberg, Herbert J.

Postlethwaite, Virgil A. Citizens Alert! Alternatives for Low-Profile Survival. Clemens, Paul M., ed. (Orig.). 1981. pap. text 7.95 (*0-931892-02-3*) B Dolphin Pub.

Postlethwayt, Malachy. Britain's Commercial Interest Explained & Improved, 2 vols., Set. LC 68-22376. (Reprints of Economic Classics Ser.). 1968. reprint ed. 95.00 (*0-678-00392-0*) Kelley.

— Great Britain's True System. LC 67-18579. (Reprints of Economic Classics Ser.). 363p. 1967. reprint ed. 57.50 (*0-678-00250-9*) Kelley.

Postlewait, Ruby. History of Jersey County, Illinois - Sesquicentennial Edition. (Illus.). 769p. 1991. 60.00 (*0-88107-182-X*) Curtis Media.

Postlewait, Thomas. Prophet of the New Drama: William Archer & the Ibsen Campaign, 20. LC 85-9878. (Contributions in Drama & Theatre Studies: No. 20). (Illus.). 210p. 1986. 55.00 (*0-313-24540-1*, POW/, Greenwood Pr) Greenwood.

Postlewait, Thomas, ed. William Archer on Ibsen: The Major Essays, 1889-1919, 13. LC 84-15744. (Contributions in Drama & Theatre Studies: No. 13). (Illus.). 323p. 1984. 65.00 (*0-313-24499-5*, PWA/, Greenwood Pr) Greenwood.

Postlewait, Thomas & McConachie, Bruce A., eds. Interpreting the Theatrical Past: Essays in the Historiography of Performance. LC 88-35045. (Illus.). 339p. 1989. pap. text 16.95 (*0-87745-238-5*) U of Iowa Pr.

Postlewait, Thomas, jt. ed. see Davis, Peter A.

Postlewait, Thomas, jt. ed. see Williams, Simon.

Postlewaite, A., ed. see Palfrey, Thomas R. & Srivastava, Sanjay.

Postlewaite, Jack A. Wisconsin Corporations: Practice Systems Library Manual. LC 79-91166. ring bd. 120.00 (*0-317-00430-1*) West Group.

— Wisconsin Corporations: Practice Systems Library Manual. LC 79-91166. 1991. suppl. ed. 67.50 (*0-317-03171-6*) West Group.

Postlewaite, Pat. Bury Me with Balloons. 250p. 1991. pap. 9.95 (*0-938577-06-9*) St Johns Pub.

Postlewaite, Philip F. International Taxation: Cases, Materials, & Problems. 349p. (C). 1999. 45.95 (*0-87084-363-X*) Anderson Pub Co.

— International Taxation: Corporate & Individual, 5 vols. 3rd ed. LC 98-84002. 4512p. 1998. ring bd. 350.00 (*0-89089-889-8*) Carolina Acad Pr.

— Taxation of Small Business Enterprise: Individual Partnership & Corporation. (American Casebook Ser.). 150p. 1996. pap. text, teacher ed. write for info. (*0-314-21812-2*) West Pub.

Postlewaite, Philip F. & Birkeland, John H. Problems & Materials on the Taxation of Small Business Enterprise: Individual, Partnership & Corporation. LC 96-36923. (American Casebook Ser.). 592p. (C). 1996. 57.50 (*0-314-06603-9*) West Pub.

Postlewaite, Philip F., et al. Taxation of Intangible Assets. LC 96-61984. 1997. write for info. (*0-7913-2960-7*) Warren Gorham & Lamont.

Postlewaite, Philip F., jt. auth. see Guerin, Sanford M.

Postlewaith, jt. auth. see Husen.

Postley, John E. Soul Medicine: Medical Challenges on Life's Uncertain Journey. 288p. (Orig.). 1995. pap. 14.95 (*0-944634-33-8*, Love & Logic Pr) Cline-Fay Inst.

Postma, D., jt. auth. see Appelo, C. A. J.

Postma, G. & Oti, M. N. Geology of Deltas. (Illus.). 340p. (C). 1995. text 149.00 (*90-5410-614-X*, Pub. by A A Balkema) Ashgate Pub Co.

Postma, H., ed. Hydrography of the Wadden Sea: Movements & Properties of Water & Particulate Matter: Final Report on Hydrography of the Wadden Sea Working Group (Report 2) 76p. (C). 1982. text 55.00 (*90-6191-052-8*, Pub. by A A Balkema) Ashgate Pub Co.

Postma, H. & Zijlstra, J. J., eds. Continental Shelves. (Ecosystems of the World Ser.: No. 27). 406p. 1988. 314.25 (*0-444-42609-4*) Elsevier.

Postma, J. Tennyson As Seen by His Parodists. LC 68-748. (Studies in Tennyson: No. 27). 1969. reprint ed. lib. bdg. 75.00 (*0-8383-0674-8*) M S G Haskell Hse.

***Postma, James M., et al.** Atmospheric Chemistry of Nitric Oxide. 5th ed. 2000. pap. text, lab manual ed. 1.95 (*0-7167-9455-1*) W H Freeman.

— Chemistry of Natural Waters. 5th ed. 2000. pap. text, lab manual ed. 1.95 (*0-7167-9440-3*) W H Freeman.

— Chemistry of Oxygen:basic & Acidic Oxides. 5th ed. 2000. pap. text, lab manual ed. 1.95 (*0-7167-9416-0*) W H Freeman.

— Chemistry of Some Nonmetals. 5th ed. 2000. pap. text 1.95 (*0-7167-9452-7*) W H Freeman.

— Chemistry of Vitamin C. 5th ed. 2000. pap. text, lab manual ed. 1.95 (*0-7167-9454-3*) W H Freeman.

— Colligative Properties/the Molar Mass. 5th ed. 2000. pap. text, lab manual ed. 1.95 (*0-7167-9433-0*) W H Freeman.

— A Cycle of Copper Reactions. 5th ed. 2000. pap. text, lab manual ed. 1.95 (*0-7167-9414-4*) W H Freeman.

— Detemination of a Chemical Formula by Titration. 5th ed. 2000. pap. text, lab manual ed. 1.95 (*0-7167-9418-7*) W H Freeman.

— Determination of a Chemical Formula: The Reaction. 5th ed. 2000. pap. text, lab manual ed. 1.95 (*0-7167-9417-9*) W H Freeman.

— Determination of an Equilibrium Constant. 5th ed. 2000. pap. text, lab manual ed. 1.95 (*0-7167-9435-7*) W H Freeman.

— Determination of Molar Mass & Ionization. 5th ed. 2000. pap. text, lab manual ed. 1.95 (*0-7167-9439-X*) W H Freeman.

— Electrochemical Cells. 5th ed. 2000. pap. text, lab manual ed. 1.95 (*0-7167-9450-0*) W H Freeman.

— Electrochemical Puzzles. 5th ed. 2000. pap. text, lab manual ed. 1.95 (*0-7167-9451-9*) W H Freeman.

— Emission Spectra & the Electronic Structure. 5th ed. 2000. pap. text, lab manual ed. 1.95 (*0-7167-9428-4*) W H Freeman.

— Enthalpy Changes in Chemical Reactions. 5th ed. 2000. pap. text, lab manual ed. 1.95 (*0-7167-9426-8*) W H Freeman.

— Enthalpy Combustion of Vegetable Oil. 5th ed. 2000. pap. text, lab manual ed. 1.95 (*0-7167-9427-6*) W H Freeman.

— Equilibria of Coordination Compounds. 5th ed. 2000. pap. text, lab manual ed. 1.95 (*0-7167-9453-5*) W H Freeman.

— Estimation Avogrados Number. 5th ed. 2000. pap. text, lab manual ed. 1.95 (*0-7167-9419-5*) W H Freeman.

— Examples of Chemical Equilibria/le Chatelier. 5th ed. 2000. pap. text, lab manual ed. 1.95 (*0-7167-9434-9*) W H Freeman.

P

An Asterisk (*) at the beginning of an entry indicates that the title is appearing for the first time.

— Factors Affecting The Rates of Chemical Ions. 5th ed. 2000. pap. text, lab manual ed. 1.95 (*0-7167-9436-5*) W H Freeman.

— Heat Capacity of Metals. 5th ed. 2000. pap. text, lab manual ed. 1.95 (*0-7167-9425-X*) W H Freeman.

— Identification of Alkaline Earth & Alkali Metal Ions. 5th ed. 2000. pap. text, lab manual ed. 1.95 (*0-7167-9444-6*) W H Freeman.

— Identification Of Ferric, Aluminum & Zinc Ions. 5th ed. 2000. pap. text, lab manual ed. 1.95 (*0-7167-9443-8*) W H Freeman.

— Identification of Silver, Lead, & Mercury. 5th ed. 2000. pap. text, lab manual ed. 1.95 (*0-7167-9442-X*) W H Freeman.

— Intermol Forces: Making & Killing Slime. 5th ed. 2000. pap. text, lab manual ed. 1.95 (*0-7167-9431-4*) W H Freeman.

— Introduction & Appendix. 5th ed. 2000. pap. text, lab manual ed. 1.95 (*0-7167-9409-8*) W H Freeman.

— Ionic & Covalent Bonding. 5th ed. 2000. pap. text, lab manual ed. 1.95 (*0-7167-9429-2*) W H Freeman.

— Liquids & Solids. 5th ed. 2000. pap. text, lab manual ed. 1.95 (*0-7167-9432-2*) W H Freeman.

— Mass & Volume Relationships. 5th ed. 2000. pap. text, lab manual ed. 1.95 (*0-7167-9411-X*) W H Freeman.

— Models of Molecular Shapes. 5th ed. 2000. pap. text, lab manual ed. 1.95 (*0-7167-9430-6*) W H Freeman.

— Molar Mass of a Gas. 5th ed. 2000. pap. text, lab manual ed. 1.95 (*0-7167-9421-7*) W H Freeman.

— Molar Volume of Dioxygen & Other Gases. 5th ed. 2000. pap. text, lab manual ed. 1.95 (*0-7167-9420-9*) W H Freeman.

— Observing The Reactionso of Household Chemicals. 5th ed. 2000. pap. text, lab manual ed. 1.95 (*0-7167-9413-6*) W H Freeman.

— Oxidation-Reduction Reactions. 5th ed. 2000. pap. text, lab manual ed. 1.95 (*0-7167-9448-9*) W H Freeman.

— Paper Chromotography. 5th ed. 2000. pap. text, lab manual ed. 1.95 (*0-7167-9447-0*) W H Freeman.

— Qualitative Analysis of Some Common Anions. 5th ed. 2000. pap. text, lab manual ed. 1.95 (*0-7167-9445-4*) W H Freeman.

— Qualitative Analysis of Unlabeled Solutions. 5th ed. 2000. pap. text, lab manual ed. 1.95 (*0-7167-9446-2*) W H Freeman.

— Rate of Chemical Reaction. 5th ed. 2000. pap. text, lab manual ed. 1.95 (*0-7167-9437-3*) W H Freeman.

— Reactivity of Metals with Hydrochloric Acid. 5th ed. 2000. pap. text, lab manual ed. 1.95 (*0-7167-9422-5*) W H Freeman.

— Redox Titration/the Oxidizing Capacity. 5th ed. 2000. pap. text, lab manual ed. 1.95 (*0-7167-9449-7*) W H Freeman.

— Scientific Measurements. 5th ed. 2000. pap. text, lab manual ed. 1.95 (*0-7167-9410-1*) W H Freeman.

— Separations of Food Dyes by Paper Chromatography. 5th ed. 2000. pap. text, lab manual ed. 1.95 (*0-7167-9412-8*) W H Freeman.

— Solubility Product Constant Calcium Iodate. 5th ed. 2000. pap. text, lab manual ed. 1.95 (*0-7167-9441-1*) W H Freeman.

— Synthesis of a Chemical Compound: Making Aluminum. 5th ed. 2000. pap. text, lab manual ed. 1.95 (*0-7167-9415-2*) W H Freeman.

Postma, Patricia D. & Prescott, Susannah S., eds. Tennessee Statistical Abstract, 1980. (Illus.). 720p. (C). 1980. pap. text 18.00 (*0-940191-04-0*) Univ TN Ctr Bus Econ.

Postma, Paul. A New Marketing Era: Marketing to the Imagination in a Technology-Driven World. LC 98-34857. 176p. 1998. 19.95 (*0-07-052675-3*) McGraw.

***Postman, Andy.** What's in an Age: Who Did What When, From Age 1 To 100. LC 99-19714. (Illus.). 208p. 1999. pap. 10.00 (*0-688-16911-2*, Wm Morrow) Morrow Avon.

Postman, Frederica. The Yiddish Alphabet Book. (Illus.). 1988. 19.50 (*1-55774-029-1*) Shalom.

Postman, Leo J. & Rau, Lucy. Retention as a Funciton of the Method of Measurement. LC 57-9951. (California University Publications in Psychology: Vol. 8, No. 3). 56p. reprint ed. pap. 30.00 (*0-608-30752-1*, 202141700021) Bks Demand.

Postman, Neil. Amusing Ourselves to Death: Public Discourse in the Age of Show Business. 184p. (C). 1986. pap. 12.95 (*0-14-009438-5*) Viking Penguin.

***Postman, Neil.** Building a Bridge to 18th Century. 2000. pap. 13.00 (*0-375-70127-3*) Knopf.

Postman, Neil. Building a Bridge to the Eighteenth Century: Ideas from the Past That Can Improve Our Future. LC 99-18923. 213p. 1999. 24.00 (*0-375-40129-6*) Knopf.

— Conscientious Objection. 1992. pap. 12.00 (*0-679-73421-X*) McKay.

— The Disappearance of Childhood. LC 94-16385. 192p. 1994. pap. 11.00 (*0-679-75166-1*) Vin Bks.

— The End of Education: Redefining the Value of Schools. 1996. pap. 12.00 (*0-679-75031-2*) Knopf.

— Technopoly: The Surrender of Culture to Technology. LC 92-50584. 1993. pap. 12.00 (*0-679-74540-8*) Vin Bks.

Postman, Neil, et al, eds. Language in America: A Report on Our Deteriorating Semantic Environment. LC 73-77137. 1969. text 29.50 (*0-672-53552-1*) Irvington.

Postman, Neil & Powers, Steve. How to Watch TV News. 160p. 1992. pap. 11.95 (*0-14-013231-7*, Penguin Bks) Viking Penguin.

Postman, Richard A. Anvils in America. unabridged ed. LC 98-91240. (Illus.). xiv, 544p. 1998. 60.00 (*0-9663256-0-5*) Postma Publ.

Postman, Robert. How to Prepare for the CLAST. LC 95-31893. 1996. pap. text 12.95 (*0-8120-9434-4*) Barron.

Postman, Robert D. How to Prepare for Praxis: Praxis Ii, NTE Core Battery, Subject Assessment, Specialty Area Tests: MSAT, Praxis I, PPST, CBT. LC 94-35579. viii, 648 p. 1995. write for info. (*0-8120-1976-8*) BARRONS WA.

Postman, Robert D. How to Prepare for the LAST/ATS-W. LC 98-38301. 320p. 1998. pap. 14.95 (*0-7641-0446-2*) Barron.

— How to Prepare for the MSAT: Multiple Subjects Assessment for Teachers. LC 97-30119. 400p. 1998. pap. 16.95 (*0-7641-0268-0*) Barron.

***Postman, Robert D.** How to Prepare for the PRAXIS. 2nd rev. ed. LC 98-29108. 700p. 1999. pap. 21.95 incl. audio compact disk (*0-7641-7140-2*) Barron.

— How to Prepare for the Praxis I PPST/CBT. 416p. 2000. pap. 13.95 (*0-7641-1443-3*) Barron.

Postman, Sheryl Lynn. Bulletproof Heart. (Intrigue Ser.). 1996. per. 3.75 (*0-373-22385-4*, 1-22385-8) Harlequin Bks.

— The Case of the Bad Luck Fiance. (Intrigue Ser.: No. 425). 1997. per. 3.75 (*0-373-22425-7*, 1-22425-2) Harlequin Bks.

— The Case of the Vanished Groom. (Intrigue Ser.: No. 424). 1997. per. 3.75 (*0-373-22424-9*, 1-22424-5) Harlequin Bks.

— Dangereuse Est la Nuit. (Rouge Passion Ser.: No. 486). (FRE.). 1998. mass mkt. 3.50 (*0-373-37486-0*, 1-37486-7) Harlequin Bks.

— Dark Knight. LC 96-447. (Intrigue Ser.). 251p. 1995. per. 3.50 (*0-373-22331-5*, 1-22331-2) Harlequin Bks.

— Dark Star. LC 96-449. (Intrigue Ser.). 248p. 1995. per. 3.50 (*0-373-22336-6*, 1-22336-1) Harlequin Bks.

— Deadly Devotion. (Intrigue Ser.). 1993. pap. 2.89 (*0-373-22223-8*, 1-22223-1) Harlequin Bks.

— Easy Loving. (Harlequin Intrigue Ser.). 249p. 1998. per. 3.99 (*0-373-22467-2*, 0-22467-5) Harlequin Bks.

— Ladykiller. (Intrigue Ser.). 1995. per. 2.99 (*0-373-22306-4*, 1-22306-4) Harlequin Bks.

— The Other Laura. (Intrigue Ser.). 1996. per. 3.75 (*0-373-22367-6*, 1-22367-6) Harlequin Bks.

— Simon Says. (Intrigue Ser.). 1994. per. 2.99 (*0-373-22258-0*, 1-22258-7) Harlequin Bks.

— Undercover Fiance: Elk River, Colorado. (Intrigue Ser.: No. 518). 1999. per. 3.99 (*0-373-22518-0*, 1-22518-4, Harlequin) Harlequin Bks.

Postman, Sheryl Lynn & Blake, Jennifer. Honeymoon Suite. 1995. mass mkt. 4.99 (*0-312-95480-8*) St Martin.

Postman, Sheryl Lynn, jt. auth. see Rimanelli, Marco.

Postman, Stevee. The Cosmic Tribe Tarot. LC 98-21449. (Illus.). 208p. 1998. pap., boxed set 32.00 (*0-89281-700-3*) Inner Tradit.

Postmus, Bouwe. George Gissing's Memorandom Book: A Novelist's Notebook (1895-1902) 1997. pap. 19.95 (*3-7052-0087-9*, Pub. by Poetry Salzburg) Intl Spec Bk.

Postmus, Bouwe, ed. George Gissing's American Notebook: Notes - G.R.G. - 1877. LC 92-45565. (Illus.). 108p. 1993. text 59.95 (*0-7734-9227-5*) E Mellen.

— The Poetry of George Gissing. LC 94-5679. 204p. 1994. 69.95 (*0-7734-9148-1*) E Mellen.

Postmus, Bouwe, ed. see Gissing, George R.

Postmus, Simon, ed. Nutrition Bibliography of Indonesia. LC 55-10494. 146p. reprint ed. pap. 45.30 (*0-608-11249-6*, 200135700076) Bks Demand.

Postnikov, A. G. Ergodic Problems in the Theory of Congruences & of Diophantine Approximations. LC 66-26640. (Proceedings of the Steklov Institute of Mathematics Ser.: Vol. 82). 128p. 1967. pap. 45.00 (*0-8218-1882-1*, STEKLO/82) Am Math.

— Introduction to Analytic Number Theory. LC 87-33428. (Translations of Mathematical Monographs: No. 68). 320p. 1988. text 138.00 (*0-8218-4521-7*, MMONO/68) Am Math.

Postnikov, A. G., ed. Tauberian Theory & Its Applications. LC 80-23821. (Proceedings of the Steklov Institute of Mathematics Ser.: No. 144). 138p. 1980. pap. 47.00 (*0-8218-3048-1*, STEKLO/144) Am Math.

Postnikov, M. M. & Swinfen, A. Foundations of Galois Theory. (International Series of Monographs on Pure & Applied Mathematics: Vol. 29). 1962. 57.00 (*0-08-009686-7*, Pub. by Pergamon Repr) Franklin.

Postnikov, M. M., jt. auth. see Boltyanskii, V. G.

Postnikov, Sergei P. Politika, Ideologiia, Byt I Uchenye Trudy Russkoi Emigratsii, 1918-1945 Bibliografiia Iz Kataloga Biblioteki R.Z.I. Arkhiva, GG, Set. Blinov, Sergei, ed. xix, 256p. 1993. lib. bdg. 135.00 (*0-88354-355-9*) N Ross.

Postol, Lawrence. Legal Guide for Handling Toxic Substances in the Workplace, No. A79. 600p. 1990. ring bd. 125.00 (*0-929576-54-3*) Busn Laws Inc.

Postolica, Vasile, jt. auth. see Isac, George.

Poston. Principles Operative Surgery. 2nd ed. 1996. pap. text 24.95 (*0-443-05019-8*, W B Saunders Co) Harcrt Hlth Sci Grp.

Poston, Carol. Tender Is the Night Notes. (Cliffs Notes Ser.). 80p. (Orig.). 1974. pap. 4.95 (*0-8220-1241-3*, Cliff) IDG Bks.

Poston, Carol & Lison, Karen C. Reclaiming Our Lives: Adult Survivors of Incest. 1989. 17.95 (*0-316-71472-0*) Little.

Poston, Carol H., ed. see Shelley, Mary Wollstonecraft.

Poston, D. L., Jr. & Yaukey, D. The Population of Modern China. LC 92-15525. (Demographic Methods & Population Analysis Ser.). (Illus.). 770p. (C). 1992. pap. 54.50 (*0-306-44138-1*, Plenum Trade) Perseus Pubng.

Poston, D. L., jt. auth. see Micklin, M.

Poston, Dudley L., Jr. & Yaukey, David, eds. The Population of Modern China. LC 92-15525. (Demographic Methods & Population Analysis Ser.). (Illus.). 770p. (C). 1992. 90.00 (*0-306-44235-3*, Plenum Trade) Perseus Pubng.

Poston, Dudley L., jt. auth. see Bouvier, Leon F.

Poston, Graeme J. Aids to Operative Surgery. LC 86-8320. (Illus.). 224p. (Orig.). (C). 1987. pap. 28.00 (*0-443-03566-0*) Church.

Poston, J. W., jt. auth. see Eichholz, Geoffrey G.

Poston, Jeffrey A. A Man Called Trouble. 192p. 1991. mass mkt. 3.50 (*0-87067-369-6*) Holloway.

— The Peacekeeper. LC 97-7300. 192p. 1997. 20.95 (*0-8027-4160-6*) Walker & Co.

Poston, John P. Land Between the Rivers. (Illus.). 323p. 1999. pap. 12.99 (*1-889893-30-7*) Emerald House Group Inc.

Poston, Jonathan. The Buildings of Charleston: A Guide to the City's Architecture. LC 96-37990. 1997. 39.95 (*1-57003-202-5*) U of SC Pr.

Poston, Kay M., jt. ed. see Epstein, Marc J.

Poston, Larry. Islamic Da'wah in the West: Muslim Missionary Activity & the Dynamics of Conversion to Islam. 210p. 1996. 29.95 (*0-614-21466-1*, 621) Kazi Pubns.

— Islamic Da'wah in the West: Muslim Missionary Activity & the Dynamics of Conversion to Islam. (Illus.). 240p. 1992. text 55.00 (*0-19-507227-8*) OUP.

***Poston, Larry & Ellis, Carl.** The Changing Face of Islam in America: Understanding & Reaching Your Muslim Neighbor. LC 99-80157. 250p. 1999. pap. 12.99 (*0-88965-168-X*, Pub. by Horizon Books) Chr Pubns.

Poston, Richard W. Small Town Renaissance: A Story of the Montana Study. LC 76-109300. 231p. 1971. reprint ed. lib. bdg. 55.00 (*0-8371-3843-4*, POST, Greenwood Pr) Greenwood.

Poston, Robert M. Automating Specification-Based Software Testing. LC 96-178. 272p. 1996. pap. 40.00 (*0-8186-7531-4*) IEEE Comp Soc.

Poston, Susan L. Nonformal Education in Latin America: An Annotated Bibliography. LC 75-620142. (Reference Ser.: Vol. 8). 268p. 1976. 16.95 (*0-87903-108-5*) UCLA Lat Am Ctr.

Poston, T., jt. auth. see Dodson, C. T.

Poston, Ted. The Dark Side of Hopkinsville: Stories by Ted Poston. Hauke, Kathleen A., ed. LC 90-11251. 144p. 1991. pap. 14.95 (*0-8203-1303-3*) U of Ga Pr.

***Poston, Ted.** A First Draft of History. Hauke, Kathleen A., ed. LC 00-36421. (Illus.). 2000. 29.95 (*0-8203-2239-3*) U of Ga Pr.

Poston, Ted M. & Purdy, Rick, eds. Aquatic Toxicology & Environmental Fate, Vol. 9. LC 86-14648. (Special Technical Publication Ser.: No. 921). (Illus.). x, 535p. 1986. text 64.00 (*0-8031-0489-8*, STP921) ASTM.

Poston, Tim & Stewart, Ian. Catastrophe Theory & Its Applications. unabridged ed. LC 96-21795. (Illus.). 510p. 1996. reprint ed. pap. text 18.95 (*0-486-69271-X*) Dover.

***Poston, Walker S. Carlos, II & Haddock, C. Keith, eds.** Food as a Drug. LC 99-88150. 172p. 2000. 49.95 (*0-7890-0959-5*); pap. text 24.95 (*0-7890-0977-3*) Haworth Pr.

Poston, William K., Jr. Making Governance Work: TQE for School Boards. LC 93-47928. (Total Quality Education Ser.: Vol. 8). 144p. 1994. pap. 18.95 (*0-8039-6144-8*) Corwin Pr.

Poston, William K., Jr., et al. Making Schools Work: Practical Management of Support Operations. LC 92-3073. 208p. 1992. pap. 21.95 (*0-8039-6016-6*) Corwin Pr.

Postone, Moishe. Time, Labor & Social Domination: A Reinterpretation of Marx's Critical Theory. 438p. (C). 1993. text 64.95 (*0-521-39157-1*) Cambridge U Pr.

— Time, Labor & Social Domination: A Reinterpretation of Marx's Critical Theory. 438p. 1996. pap. text 20.95 (*0-521-56540-5*) Cambridge U Pr.

Postow, B. C. Reasons for Action: Toward a Normative Theory & Meta-Level Criteria. LC 99-20496. (Library of Ethics & Applied Philosophy Ser.). 1999. write for info. (*0-7923-5700-0*) Kluwer Academic.

Postow, Elliot, jt. auth. see Polk, Charles.

Postow, Elliot, jt. ed. see Polk, Charles.

Postrel, Virginia. The Future & Its Enemies: The Growing Conflict over Creativity, Enterprise & Progress. 288p. 1999. per. 13.00 (*0-684-86269-7*) S&S Trade Pap.

Postrel, Virginia I. The Future & Its Enemies. 1998. 24.50 (*0-02-874108-0*) Free Pr.

— The Future & Its Enemies: The Growing Conflict Over Creativity, Enterprise, & Progress. LC 98-34090. 272p. 1998. 25.00 (*0-684-82760-3*) Free Pr.

Postrel, Virginia I., jt. ed. see Poole, Robert W., Jr.

Posudievsky, Leonid. Yulkina Skazka - Yuly's Tale. (RUS., Illus.). 50p. (Orig.). 1995. 7.95 (*1-885563-03-5*) VIA Press MD.

Posudin, Yuri I. Lasers in Agriculture. 188p. 1998. 57.50 (*1-57808-016-9*) Science Pubs.

Posusney, Marsha P. Labor & the State in Egypt, 1952-1994: Workers, Unions, & Economic Restructuring. LC 97-3929. 384p. 1997. lib. bdg. 52.00 (*0-231-10692-0*) Col U Pr.

Posusta, Steven. Don't Panic: The Procrastinator's Guide to Writing an Effective Term Paper. LC 96-84169. 64p. (Orig.). (C). 1996. pap. 9.95 (*0-942208-42-0*) Bandanna Bks.

Poswillo, David E. & Alberman, Eva, eds. Effects of Smoking on the Fetus, Neonate & Child. LC 92-13005. (Illus.). 248p. (C). 1992. 89.50 (*0-19-262260-9*) OUP.

Posy, Carl J., ed. Kant's Philosophy of Mathematics: Modern Essays. (Synthese Library). 384p. (C). 1992. lib. bdg. 185.00 (*0-7923-1495-6*, Pub. by Kluwer Academic) Kluwer Academic.

Posypaiko, V. I. & Alekseeva, E. A. Phase Equilibria in Binary Halides. LC 87-29267. (Illus.). 496p. (C). 1988. text 145.00 (*0-306-65211-0*, Kluwer Plenum) Kluwer Academic.

Posz, Joseph D. Military Heroes of New Mexico Military Institute. LC 94-65906. (Illus.). 108p. 1994. 21.67 (*0-9641019-0-4*) N Mex Military.

***Pot, Ferrie.** Employment Relations & National Culture: Continuity & Change in the Age of Globalization. LC 99-87376. (New Horizons in Institutional & Evolutionary Economics Ser.). 256p. 2000. 90.00 (*1-84064-229-7*) E Elgar.

Pot, Johan Hendril Jacob van der, see van der Pot, Johan Hendrik Jacob.

Potaman, V. N., jt. auth. see Soyfer, V. N.

Potaman, Vladimir N., jt. auth. see Soyfer, Valery N.

Potamaniou, Anna. Hope: A Shield in the Economy of Borderline States. 128p. (C). 1997. 80.00 (*0-415-12176-0*); pap. 27.99 (*0-415-12177-9*) Routledge.

Potamkin, Harry A. The Compound Cinema: The Film Writings of Harry Alan Potamkin. Jacobs, Lewis, ed. LC 76-55401. (Studies in Culture & Communication). 703p. reprint ed. pap. 200.00 (*0-608-14890-3*, 202602600048) Bks Demand.

Potamkin, Lexie B. What Is Spirit? Messages from the Heart. LC 99-23614. (Illus.). 1999. text 14.95 (*1-56170-675-2*, L458) Hay House.

Potapchouck, V. S., tr. see Akulin, V. M. & Karlov, N. V.

Potapenko, J. Selected Writings of J. Potapenko, 3 vols., Set. 1976. lib. bdg. 350.00 (*0-8490-2589-3*) Gordon Pr.

Potapov, V., jt. auth. see Kovalishina, I.

Potapov, Vadim D. Stability of Stochastic Elastic & Viscoelastic Systems. LC 99-18791. 288p. 1999. 135.00 (*0-471-98793-X*) Wiley.

Potapova, Nina F. Learn Russian, 2 vols., Set. 55.00 (*0-87557-137-9*) Saphrograph.

— Learning Russian, 4 vols. Incl. Vol. 1. (ENG & RUS.). 1985. pap. 20.95 (*0-87557-127-1*); Vol. 2. (ENG & RUS.). 1985. pap. 20.95 (*0-87557-128-X*); Vol. 3. (ENG & RUS.). 1985. pap. 20.95 (*0-87557-129-8*); Vol. 4. (ENG & RUS.). 1985. pap. 20.95 (*0-87557-130-1*); 69.50 (*0-87557-073-9*) Saphrograph.

— Russian Elementary, Vol. I. (ENG & RUS.). 27.50 (*0-87557-070-4*) Saphrograph.

— Russian Elementary, Vol. II. (ENG & RUS.). 27.50 (*0-87557-136-0*) Saphrograph.

— Russian Elementary Course, 2 vols., Vol. 1. 3rd ed. xiv, 352p. (C). 1969. text 172.00 (*0-677-20890-1*) Gordon & Breach.

Potaracke, Rochelle. Nanny's Special Gift. LC 93-26093. (Illus.). 32p. (Orig.). (J). (gr. 1-4). 1994. pap. 4.95 (*0-8091-6615-1*) Paulist Pr.

Potas, I. Sentencing Robbers in New South Wales: Principles, Policy & Practice. 201p. 1990. pap. 20.00 (*0-642-14487-7*, Pub. by Aust Inst Criminology) Advent Bks Div.

Potash, Betty, ed. Widows in African Societies: Choices & Constraints. 336p. 1986. 42.50 (*0-8047-1299-9*) Stanford U Pr.

Potash, Dorothy. El Cuento de Ned y Su Nariz. (SPA., Illus.). 24p. (J). (ps-4). 1993. lib. bdg. 13.95 (*1-879567-24-5*, Valeria Bks) Wonder Well.

— The Tale of Ned & His Nose. (Illus.). 24p. (J). (gr. k-4). 1993. lib. bdg. 13.95 (*1-879567-23-7*, Valeria Bks) Wonder Well.

Potash, Herbert M. Inside Clinical Psychology: A Handbook for Graduate Students & Interns. LC 81-82640. 135p. 1981. text 19.95 (*0-940524-00-7*); pap. text 9.95 (*0-940524-01-5*) G Handwerk.

— Pragmatic-Existential Psychotherapy with Personality Disorders. 300p. (C). 1993. text 35.00 (*0-940524-05-8*) G Handwerk.

Potash, P. Jeffrey. Vermont's Burned-Over District: Patterns of Community Development & Religious Activity, 1761-1850. LC 91-28028. (Chicago Studies in the History of American Religion Ser.: Vol. 16). 330p. 1991. 60.00 (*0-926019-52-X*) Carlson Pub.

Potash, P. Jeffrey & Hand, Samuel B. Litigious Vermonters: Court Records to 1825. (Occasional Papers: No. 2). (Illus.). 30p. (Orig.). 1979. pap. text 5.00 (*0-944277-03-9*, P67) U VT Ctr Rsch VT.

Potash, Robert A. The Army & Politics in Argentina, 1962-1973 Vol. 3: From Frondizi's Fall to the Peronist Restoration. LC 69-13182. (Illus.). 592p. 1996. 57.50 (*0-8047-2414-8*) Stanford U Pr.

Potash, Robert A. The Army & Politics in Argentina, 1928-1945: Yrigoyen to Peron. LC 69-13182. (Illus.). xiv, 314p. 1969. 45.00 (*0-8047-0683-2*) Stanford U Pr.

— The Army & Politics in Argentina, 1945-1962: Peron to Frondizi. LC 79-64220. (Illus.). xiv, 418p. 1980. 52.50 (*0-8047-1056-2*) Stanford U Pr.

— Mexican Government & Industrial Development in the Early Republic: The Banco de Avio. rev. ed. LC 82-15969.Tr. of El/Banco de Avio de Mexico: El Fomento de la Industria 1821-1846. 264p. 1983. lib. bdg. 32.50 (*0-87023-382-3*) U of Mass Pr.

Potay, Michel. The Revelation of Ares. (ENG & FRE.). 1974. 49.95 (*0-614-14575-9*, Pub. by ADIRA) BookLink Distributors.

— The Revelation of Ares. Maison de la Revelation Staff, ed. 777p. 1996. 49.50 (*2-901821-07-3*, Pub. by Herveys Bklink) Herveys Bklink.

Potchen, James, et al, eds. Pulmonary Radiology: By Members of the Fleischner Society. LC 93-3835. 600p. 1993. text 91.00 (*0-7216-4821-5*, W B Saunders Co) Harcrt Hlth Sci Grp.

Potchka, Robin, jt. auth. see Roth, Phyllis.

***Poteat, A.** Aquatic Therapy: An Evidence-Based Manual. (Illus.). 1998. pap. write for info. (*0-443-07618-9*) Church.

Poteat, Hubert M. Practical Hymnology. LC 72-1693. reprint ed. 29.50 (*0-404-09912-2*) AMS Pr.

Poteat, William H. A Philosophical Daybook: Post-Critical Investigations. LC 90-34577. 144p. 1990. text 25.00 (*0-8262-0748-0*) U of Mo Pr.

— The Primacy of Persons & the Language of Culture: Essays. Stines, James W., ed. LC 93-14356. 360p. 1993. text 49.95 (*0-8262-0919-X*) U of Mo Pr.

An Asterisk (*) at the beginning of an entry indicates that the title is appearing for the first time.

— Recovering the Ground: Critical Exercises in Recollection. LC 93-45489. 235p. (C). 1994. pap. text 16.95 (*0-7914-2132-5*) State U NY Pr.
— Recovering the Ground: Critical Exercises in Recollection. LC 93-45489. 235p. (C). 1994. text 49.50 (*0-7914-2131-7*) State U NY Pr.

Poteat, William H., jt. ed. see Langford, Thomas A.

Poteau. College Outline: Advanced Accounting. (C). 1995. pap. text 14.50 (*0-15-601510-2*) Harcourt Coll Pubs.

Poteau-Tralie, Mary L. Voices of Authority: The Criminal Obsession in Guy de Maupassant's Short Works. LC 94-902. (Currents in Comparative Romance Languages & Literatures Ser.: Vol. 30). VI, 146p. (C). 1995. text 44.95 (*0-8204-2479-X*) P Lang Pubng.

Poteet, G. Howard. Film Criticism in Popular American Periodicals, 1933-1967. (Cinema Ser.). 1976. lib. bdg. 250.00 (*0-87700-240-1*) Revisionist Pr.
— Starting up Your Own Small Business: Expert Advice from the Small Business Administration. 264p. 1990. pap. 19.95 (*0-8306-3548-3*, 3548) McGraw-Hill Prof.

Poteet, G. Howard & Petti, Michael A. Exploring Careers As a Chiropractor. rev. ed. (Careers in Depth Ser.). (YA). (gr. 7-12). 1984. lib. bdg. 7.97 (*0-8239-0383-4*) Rosen Group.

Poteet, G. Howard & Santora, Joseph C. Death & Dying: A Bibliography 1950-1974: Supplement, Vol. I: Suicide. LC 76-24093. xxii, 166p. 1978. 29.00 (*0-87875-108-4*) Whitston Pub.

Poteet, G. Howard, jt. auth. see Santora, Joseph C.

***Poteet, Michael.** The Hobbit: Study Guide. (YA). 2000. pap. 14.99 (*1-58609-173-5*) Progeny Pr WI.

Potega, Patrick H. Basics of R-C Scale. 80p. pap. 11.95 (*0-942794-00-1*) Model Agency.

Potegal, Michael & Knutson, John. The Dynamics of Aggression: Biological & Social Processes in Dyads & Groups. 352p. 1994. text 75.00 (*0-8058-0729-2*) L Erlbaum Assocs.

Potempa, John, jt. auth. see Clampitt, William H.

Potempa, Sharon. In a Heart Beat. Strand, Laurel, ed. 100p. 1998. pap. 14.95 (*0-944958-40-0*) Elfin Cove Pr.

Potemra, T. A., ed. Magnetospheric Currents. (Geophysical Monograph Ser.: Vol. 28). (Illus.). 357p. 1983. 33.00 (*0-87590-055-0*) Am Geophysical.
— Magnetospheric Substorms. (Geophysical Monograph Ser.: Vol. 64). 488p. 1991. 70.00 (*0-87590-030-5*, GM0640305) Am Geophysical.

Poterba, James & National Resesrch Council Staff, eds. Borderline Case: International Tax Policy, Corporate Research & Development, & Investment. LC 97-45343. 168p. 1998. 39.95 (*0-309-06368-X*) Natl Acad Pr.

***Poterba, James M.** Fiscal Institutions & Fiscal Performance. LC 98-31598. 1999. 53.00 (*0-226-67623-4*) U Ch Pr.

Poterba, James M., ed. International Comparisons of Household Saving. (Illus.). 286p. 1994. 42.50 (*0-226-67621-8*) U Ch Pr.
— Public Policies & Household Saving. LC 93-42088. (National Bureau of Economic Research Project Report Ser.). 212p. 1994. 36.00 (*0-226-67618-8*) U Ch Pr.
— Tax Policy & the Economy. (Tax Policy & the Economy Ser.: Vol. 7). (Illus.). 190p. 1993. 30.00 (*0-262-16135-4*); pap. text 15.00 (*0-262-66081-4*) MIT Pr.
— Tax Policy & the Economy. (Tax Policy & the Economy Ser.: Vol. 8). (Illus.). 200p. 1994. 30.00 (*0-262-16143-5*); pap. text 15.00 (*0-262-66091-1*) MIT Pr.
— Tax Policy & the Economy. (Tax Policy & the Economy Ser.: Vol. 9). 350p. 1995. 30.00 (*0-262-16153-2*); pap. text 15.00 (*0-262-66095-4*) MIT Pr.
— Tax Policy & the Economy. (Tax Policy & the Economy Ser.: Vol. 10). 163p. 1996. 30.00 (*0-262-16161-3*) MIT Pr.
— Tax Policy & the Economy. (Tax Policy & the Economy Ser.: Vol. 10). (Illus.). 163p. (C). 1996. pap. text 15.00 (*0-262-66098-9*) MIT Pr.
— Tax Policy & the Economy, No. 11. (Tax Policy & the Economy Ser.). (Illus.). 223p. 1997. 30.00 (*0-262-16167-2*) MIT Pr.
— Tax Policy & the Economy, No. 11. (Tax Policy & the Economy Ser.: Vol. 11). (Illus.). 223p. 1997. pap. text 15.00 (*0-262-66104-7*) MIT Pr.
— Tax Policy & the Economy, Vol. 6. (Illus.). 200p. 1992. 30.00 (*0-262-16130-3*); pap. text 15.00 (*0-262-66077-6*) MIT Pr.
— Tax Policy & the Economy, Vol. 12. (Illus.). 267p. 1998. 30.00 (*0-262-16176-1*) MIT Pr.
— Tax Policy & the Economy, Vol. 12. Vol. 12. (Illus.). 267p. 1998. pap. text 15.00 (*0-262-66109-8*) MIT Pr.
— Tax Policy & the Economy, Vol. 13. (Illus.). 224p. 1999. 30.00 (*0-262-16185-0*) MIT Pr.

***Poterba, James M., ed.** Tax Policy & the Economy, Vol. 14. (Illus.). 224p. 2000. 40.00 (*0-262-16191-5*); pap. 20.00 (*0-262-66164-0*) MIT Pr.

***Poterba, James M. & Rueben, Kim S.** Fiscal Rules & State Borrowing Costs: Evidence from California & Other States. LC 99-51905. (Illus.). xvii, 55p. 1999. pap. 10.00 (*1-58213-019-1*) Pub Policy Inst.

Poterba, James M., jt. auth. see Dornbusch, Rudiger.

Poterba, James M., jt. ed. see Feldstein, Martin.

Poterba, James M., jt. ed. see Noguchi, Yukio.

Poterba, James M., ed. see Powell, Richard & Reynolds, Jock.

Poterfield, James D. Teleselling: A Self-Teaching Guide. 2nd rev. ed. LC 95-38849. Orig. Title: Selling on the Phone. 240p. 1996. pap. 19.95 (*0-471-11567-3*) Wiley.

Potgieter, J. M., jt. auth. see Visser, J.

Potgieter, J. M., jt. auth. see Visser, P. J.

Potgieter, M. S., ed. see Invited, Rapporteur, & Highlight Papers Staff.

Potgieter, Pieter. Victory: The Work of the Spirit. 42p. 1984. pap. 1.45 (*0-85151-430-8*) Banner of Truth.

Poth, Dee. The Goddess Speaks: Myths & Meditations. (Illus.). 112p. 1994. pap. 29.95 (*0-9638327-2-7*) Sibyl Pubns.
— The Goddess Speaks: Myths, Meditations, Symbols & Sacred Sites (Incl. Set of Cards) 2nd rev. ed. Columbus, Marge, ed. Orig. Title: The Goddess Speaks: Myths & Meditations. (Illus.). 190p. 1998. pap., boxed set 29.95 (*1-889531-00-6*) Sibyl Pubns.

Poth, Susanne. Tea Tree Oil for Health & Well-Being. LC 99-14532. 1999. pap. 10.95 (*0-8069-4848-5*) Sterling.

***Poth, Susanne & Sauer, Gina.** The Spice Lilies: Eastern Secrets to Healing with Ginger, Turmeric, Cardamom, & Galangale. 128p. 2000. pap. 9.95 (*0-89281-890-5*, Heal Arts VT) Inner Tradit.

Pothcary, Nick. Feedforward Linear Power Amplifiers. LC 99-26568. 1999. 85.00 (*1-58053-022-2*) Artech Hse.

Pothen, K. P., jt. auth. see Singh, S. D.

Pothen, S. Divorce: Its Causes & Consequences in Hindu Society. 1996. reprint ed. pap. 12.00 (*0-7069-9341-1*, Pub. by Vikas) S Asia.

Pothering, jt. auth. see Naps.

Pothering, George J. & Naps, Thomas L. Introduction to Data Structures & Algorithm Analysis with C++ LC 94-44364. 672p. (C). 1995. mass mkt. 75.95 (*0-314-04574-0*) West Pub.

Pothering, George J., jt. auth. see Naps, Thomas L.

Pothier, Dom J. Les Melodies Gregoriennes d'Apres la Tradition. vii, 306p. 1982. reprint ed. write for info. (*3-487-07199-1*) G Olms Pubs.

Pothier, Pat. Float Tube Magic: A Fly Fishing Escape. (Illus.). 48p. 1995. pap. 15.95 (*1-878175-91-2*) F Amato Pubns.

Pothier, Robert J. Treatise on Obligations, Considered in a Moral & Legal View, 1802. Martin, Francois-Xavier, tr. from FRE. LC 98-38360. 1999. reprint ed. 75.00 (*1-886363-62-5*) Lawbk Exchange.
— A Treatise on the Law of Obligations or Contracts, 1806. LC 99-26397. 2000. write for info. (*1-886363-98-6*) Lawbk Exchange.

Pothier, Robert Joseph. Treatise on the Contract of Sale, 1839. fac. ed. Cushing, L. S., tr. from FRE. LC 99-10260. 2000. 70.00 (*1-886363-82-X*) Lawbk Exchange.

Potholm, Christian. An Insider's Guide to Maine Politics. LC 97-51622. 240p. 1998. 40.00 (*1-56833-105-3*) Madison Bks UPA.

Potholm, Christian P., et al. Just Do It: Political Participation in the 1990s. 176p. (Orig.). (C). 1993. pap. text 21.50 (*0-8191-9097-7*); lib. bdg. 49.50 (*0-8191-9096-9*) U Pr of Amer.

***Pothou, Maria Lampadaridou.** A Woman in Lemnos: Plays & Poetry. (Picas Ser.: No. 14). 200p. 2000. pap. 13.00 (*1-55071-120-2*, Pub. by Guernica Editions) Paul & Co Pubs.

Pothoven, K. Solutions Manual for College Algebra. 1988. pap. text 18.50 (*0-931541-09-3*) Mancorp Pub.
— Solutions Manual for Precalculus Algebra & Trigonometry. 1988. pap. text 18.50 (*0-931541-08-5*) Mancorp Pub.

Pothoven, K., jt. auth. see Mukherjea, A.

***Poths, Elke.** Mother Earth & Her Relations. 2000. write for info. (*1-58235-527-4*) Watermrk Pr.

Potichnvj, Peter J. Soviet Agricultural Trade Unions, 1917-70. LC 70-163810. 288p. reprint ed. pap. 89.30 (*0-608-10719-0*, 201434400090) Bks Demand.

Potichnyj, Peter J. Ukraine in the Seventies. 360p. 1985. pap. 9.95 (*0-88962-000-8*) Mosaic.

Potichnyj, Peter J., ed. Poland & Ukraine: Past & Present. LC 80-91019. xiv, 365p. pap. 9.95 (*0-920862-07-1*) Ukrainian Acad.
— Soviet Union: Party & Society. (Illus.). 272p. 1988. text 59.95 (*0-521-34460-3*) Cambridge U Pr.

Potichnyj, Peter J., et al, eds. Current Soviet Leaders. 106p. 1989. 50.00 (*0-614-08506-3*) Mosaic.
— Politics & Participation under Communist Rule. LC 82-15082. 282p. 1983. 59.95 (*0-275-91060-1*, C1060, Praeger Pubs) Greenwood.
— Soviet & Eastern European Studies: A Guide to Western Institutions. 90p. 1994. pap. 12.95 (*0-88962-260-4*) Mosaic.

Potichnyj, Peter J. & Aster, Howard, eds. Ukrainian-Jewish Relations in Historical Perspective. 2nd ed. LC 87-91424. xii, 531p. 1988. 34.95 (*0-920862-53-5*) Ukrainian Acad.

Potichnyj, Peter J., jt. auth. see Aster, Howard.

Potichnyj, Peter J., ed. see Mazlakh, Serhifi & Shakhrai, Vasyl.

Potier, D., jt. ed. see Puigjaner, R.

***Potier De Courcy, Pol, et al.** Genocide in Cambodia. LC 99-55971. (Studies in Human Rights Ser.). 2000. 79.95 (*0-8122-3539-8*) U of Pa Pr.

Potier, Kenneth R. Cedar Bay: The Alternative. 1986. 23.00 (*0-7223-2047-7*, Pub. by A H S Ltd) St Mut.

Potier, Pierre, jt. ed. see Scott, A. Ian.

Potila, Joe. The Yellow Snow Meltdown. (Illus.). iv, 100p. 1997. mass mkt. 12.95 (*0-9661724-0-X*) Shields Publng.

Potin, Armand S. La, see La Potin, Armand S., ed.

Potin, Jacques. Jesus in His Homeland. Dees, Colette J., tr. from FRE. LC 97-2647. (Illus.). 128p. 1997. 35.00 (*1-57075-143-9*) Orbis Bks.

Potin, V. M. Sylloge of Coins of the British Isles: The Hermitage Museum, St Petersburg. Part I: Anglo-saxon Coins to 1016. Vol. 50. (Illus.). 192p. 1999. text 115.00 (*0-19-726187-6*) OUP.

Potish, Roger A., jt. auth. see Khan, Faiz M.

Potkay, Adam. The Fate of Eloquence in the Age of Hume. (Rhetoric & Society Ser.). 272p. 1994. text 42.50 (*0-8014-3014-3*) Cornell U Pr.
— Minding the Body: Women & Literature in the Middle Ages, 800-1500. LC 96-36468. 1997. 33.00 (*0-8057-8981-2*, Twyne) Mac Lib Ref.

***Potkay, Adam.** Passion for Happiness: Samuel Johnson & David Hume. 2000. 42.50 (*0-8014-3727-X*) Cornell U Pr.

Potkay, Adam & Burr, Sandra, eds. Black Atlantic Writers of the Eighteenth Century: Living the New Exodus in England & the Americas. 288p. 1995. pap. 18.95 (*0-312-12518-6*); text 45.00 (*0-312-12133-4*) St Martin.

Potkay, Charles R., jt. auth. see Allen, Bem P.

Potkonjak, V., jt. auth. see Vukobratovic, M.

Potmesil, Ina & Guillot, Katherine. Czech-Out Cajun Cooking. 2nd ed. (CZE., Illus.). 1991. pap. text 15.95 (*0-9627496-0-5*) Czech Out Cajun.

Potmesil, Milan & Pinedo, Herbert M. Camptothecins: New Anti-Cancer Agents. 160p. 1994. lib. bdg. 149.00 (*0-8493-4764-5*, 4764) CRC Pr.

Potocki, Comte J. Fragments Historiques et Geographiques sur la Scythie, la Sarmatie et les Slaves, 4 vols. 1497p. reprint ed. write for info. (*0-318-71392-6*) G Olms Pubs.

***Potocki, Hallie.** What Do Men Want? 2000. pap. 8.95 (*1-57071-591-2*, Casablanca) Sourcebks.

Potocki, J., tr. see Heller, Michael.

Potocki, Jan. The Manuscript Found in Saragossa. lib. bdg. 35.95 (*0-8488-2012-6*) Amereon Ltd.
— The Manuscript Found in Saragossa. 656p. 1996. pap. 14.95 (*0-14-044580-3*, Viking) Viking Penguin.
— Tales from the Sara Gossa Manuscript: Ten Days in the Life of Alphonse Van Worden. Stableford, Brian, ed. Donougher, Christine, tr. from FRE. (European Classics). 159p. 1997. reprint ed. pap. 8.95 (*0-946626-67-7*, Pub. by Dedalus) Subterranean Co.

Potocki, Jean. La Duchessa d'Avila (Manuscrit Trouve a Saragosse) (FRE.). 320p. 1972. pap. 10.95 (*0-7859-3992-X*, 2070362159) Fr & Eur.

Potocki, John. The Colt Model 1905 Automatic Pistol: With Supplemental Coverage of the Colt M1907 Automatic Pistol & a Complete Facsimile of the Thompson-LaGarde Report. LC 97-69856. (Illus.). 200p. 1998. 28.00 (*0-917218-76-0*) A Mowbray.

Potocky, Miriam & Rodgers-Farmer, Antoinette Y., eds. Social Work Research with Minority & Oppressed Populations: Methodological Issues & Innovations. LC 97-51813. (Journal of Social Service Research Monograph Ser.: Vol. 23, Nos. 3-4). 129p. 1998. 24.95 (*0-7890-0396-1*) Haworth Pr.

Potocky-Tripodi, Miriam & Tripodi, Tony, eds. New Directions for Social Work Practice Research. LC 99-12763. 139p. 1999. 41.95 (*0-87101-305-3*) Natl Assn Soc Wkrs.

Potok, Adam. Horoskopity.Tr. of Horoscope & You. (POL.). 56p. (Orig.). 1988. pap. 6.00 (*0-930401-20-4*) Artex Pub.

Potok, Chaim. The Book of Lights. 400p. 1982. mass mkt. 6.99 (*0-449-24569-1*, Crest) Fawcett.
— The Book of Lights. 1997. pap. 12.00 (*0-449-00114-8*) Fawcett.
— The Chosen. 272p. 1987. mass mkt. 6.99 (*0-449-21344-7*) Fawcett.
— The Chosen. LC 96-96725. 1996. pap. 11.00 (*0-449-91154-3*) Fawcett.
— The Chosen. 1976. 12.09 (*0-606-00469-6*, Pub. by Turtleback) Demco.
— The Chosen. large type ed. LC 98-10150. 404p. 1998. 25.95 (*0-7838-8450-8*, G K Hall & Co) Mac Lib Ref.
— The Chosen. 1994. reprint ed. lib. bdg. 35.95 (*1-56849-319-3*) Buccaneer Bks.
— Davita's Harp. LC 85-17672. 448p. 1986. mass mkt. 6.99 (*0-449-20775-7*, Crest) Fawcett.
— Davita's Harp. 1996. pap. 11.00 (*0-449-91183-7*) Fawcett.
— The Gates of November. 272p. 1997. pap. 12.95 (*0-449-91240-X*) Fawcett.
— The Gates of November: Chronicles of the Slepak Family. LC 96-4148. 249p. 1996. 25.00 (*0-394-58867-3*) Knopf.
— The Gift of Asher Lev. 368p. 1991. mass mkt. 6.99 (*0-449-21978-X*, Crest) Fawcett.
— The Gift of Asher Lev. 1997. pap. 12.00 (*0-449-00115-6*) Fawcett.
— I Am the Clay. Date not set. mass mkt. 5.99 (*0-449-22288-8*) Fawcett.
— I Am the Clay. 256p. 1994. mass mkt. 5.99 (*0-449-22138-5*, Crest) Fawcett.
— I Am the Clay. 1997. pap. 11.00 (*0-449-00112-1*) Fawcett.
— In the Beginning. 432p. 1986. mass mkt. 6.99 (*0-449-20911-3*, Crest) Fawcett.
— My Name Is Asher Lev. 352p. 1984. mass mkt. 6.99 (*0-449-20714-5*, Crest) Fawcett.
— My Name Is Asher Lev. 369p. 1996. pap. 11.00 (*0-449-91168-3*) Fawcett.
— The Promise. 384p. 1985. mass mkt. 6.99 (*0-449-20910-5*, Crest) Fawcett.
— The Promise. 1997. pap. 12.00 (*0-449-00116-4*) Fawcett.
— The Promise. large type ed. LC 98-23278. 515p. 1998. 25.95 (*0-7838-0256-0*, G K Hall & Co) Mac Lib Ref.
— Wanderings: Chaim Potok's History of the Jews. 576p. 1987. mass mkt. 6.99 (*0-449-21582-2*) Fawcett.
— Zebra & Other Stories. (Illus.). 160p. (J). (gr. 8-12). 2000. pap. 4.99 (*0-375-80686-5*) Knopf.

Potok, Chaim. Zebra & Other Stories. LC 98-4769. (Illus.). 146p. 1998. lib. bdg. 19.99 (*0-679-95440-6*) Random.
— Zebra & Other Stories. LC 98-4769. (Illus.). 146p. (J). (gr. 6-11). 1998. 18.00 (*0-679-85440-1*) Random.

Potok, Chaim, jt. auth. see Center for Learning Network Staff.

Potok, Chaim, jt. auth. see Posen, Adam S.

Potok, Chaim, jt. auth. see Stern, Isaac W.

Potok, Chaim, jt. ed. see Sarna, Nahum M.

Potokar, Jure. Endurance. Biggins, Michael, tr. 16p. 1992. pap. text 4.00 (*1-881489-06-X*) Poetry Miscellany.

Potokar, Stanley. Peregrine: Daring, Exciting, Canoeing Adventures. 128p. 1991. pap. 7.50 (*0-9630056-0-X*) Potokar Pub.

Potomac Corral of the Westerners Staff. Great Western Indian Fights. Allred, B. W. et al, eds. LC 60-15191. (Illus.). 352p. 1966. pap. 12.95 (*0-8032-5186-6*, Bison Books) U of Nebr Pr.

Potomac Corral of The Westerners Staff. Great Western Indian Fights. (Illus.). 336p. 1997. 7.98 (*1-56731-171-7*, MJF Bks) Fine Comms.

***Potomac Institute for Policy Studies Staff.** Countering Biological Terrorism in the United States: An Understanding of Issues & Status. LC 99-10409. (Terrorism : Vol. 4). 426p. 1999. text 95.00 (*0-379-21395-8*, 7147015) Oceana.

Potonniee, Georges. The History of the Discovery of Photography. LC 72-9222. (Literature of Photography Ser.). 1978. reprint ed. 21.95 (*0-405-04929-3*) Ayer.

Potonnier, B., jt. auth. see Potonnier, Georges.

Potonnier, Georges. Woerterbuch fuer Wirtschaft: Recht und Handel, Vol. 2. 2nd rev. ed. (FRE & GER.). 1678p. 1990. 350.00 (*0-7859-4850-3*) Fr & Eur.

Potonnier, Georges & Potonnier, B. Commercial, Legal & Business Dictionary: Woerterbuch Fuer Wirtschaft, Recht und Handel, Vol. 1: Deutsch-Franzoesisch. 2nd ed. (FRE & GER.). 1595p. 1982. 175.00 (*0-8288-0812-0*, M6919) Fr & Eur.

Potparic, O., jt. auth. see Gibson, John.

Potparic, Olivera & Gibson, J. A Dictionary of Clinical Tests. (Illus.). 262p. 1993. 48.00 (*1-85070-416-3*) Prthnon Pub.
— A Dictionary of Human Oncology: A Concise Guide to Tumors. LC 93-35740. 173p. 1994. 55.00 (*1-85070-472-4*) Prthnon Pub.
— A Dictionary of Infections & Infectious Diseases. 156p. (C). 1995. 35.00 (*1-85070-607-7*) Prthnon Pub.
— A Dictionary of Sports Injuries & Disorders. 156p. 1996. 35.00 (*1-85070-686-7*) Prthnon Pub.

Potparic, Olivera & Gibson, John. A Dictionary of Congenital Malformations & Disorders. (Illus.). 192p. (C). 1995. text 55.00 (*1-85070-577-1*) Prthnon Pub.

Potparic, Olivera, jt. auth. see Gibson, J.

***Potpourri Publications Co. Staff, ed.** Show & Tell: A Celebration of Art, an Expression of Word. (Illus.). 200p. 2000. pap. 14.95 (*1-884754-30-9*) Potpourri Pubns.

Potra, F. A., tr. see Deuflhard, Peter & Hohmann, Andreas.

Potratz, Wolfgang, jt. ed. see Widmaier, Brigitta.

Potrebenko, Helen. A Flight of Average Persons: Stories & Other Writings. 228p. 1979. pap. 9.95 (*0-919888-95-X*, Pub. by New Star Bks) Genl Dist Srvs.

Potrebenko, Helen. No Streets of Gold: A Social History of Ukrainians in Alberta. 312p. 1977. pap. 9.95 (*0-919888-69-0*, Pub. by New Star Bks) Genl Dist Srvs.

Potrebenko, Helen. Riding Home. LC 96-106073. 128p. 1995. pap. 11.95 (*0-88922-356-4*, Pub. by Talonbks) Genl Dist Srvs.
— Sometimes They Sang. 104p. 1986. pap. 6.95 (*0-88974-007-0*, Pub. by Press Gang Pubs) LPC InBook.

Potrebenko, Helen. Taxi! 2nd rev. ed. 162p. 1989. pap. 9.95 (*0-919573-89-4*, Pub. by New Star Bks) Genl Dist Srvs.

Potrykus, I. & Spangenberg, G., eds. Gene Transfer to Plants: Springer Lab Manual. LC 95-7854. (Lab Manuals Ser.). (Illus.). 361p. 1995. 86.95 (*3-540-58406-4*) Spr-Verlag.

Potsch, Gerd & Michaeli, Walter. Injection Molding: An Introduction. LC 95-30571. 176p. (C). 1995. 59.95 (*1-56990-193-7*) Hanser-Gardner.

Potscher, Walter. Aspekte und Probleme der Minoischen Religion. (Religionswissenschaftliche Texte und Studien: Bd. 4). viii, 288p. 1990. write for info. (*3-487-09359-6*) G Olms Pubs.
— Hellas und Rom. (Collectanea Ser.: Bd. XXI). (GER.). xiv, 670p. 1988. write for info. (*3-487-07998-4*) G Olms Pubs.
— Vergil und die Gottlichen Machte. (Spudasmata Ser.: Bd. XXXV). (GER.). vi, 184p. 1977. write for info. (*3-487-06410-3*) G Olms Pubs.

Potschka, Martin & Dubin, Paul L., eds. Strategies in Size Exclusion Chromatography. LC 96-13254. (ACS Symposium Ser.: No. 635). (Illus.). 432p. 1996. text 115.00 (*0-8412-3414-0*, Pub. by Am Chemical) OUP.

Potsdam, Eric. Syntactic Issues in the English Imperative. LC 98-4330. (Outstanding Dissertations in Linguistics Ser.). 428p. 1998. 97.00 (*0-8153-3129-0*) Garland.

***Pott, Alexander.** Difference Sets, Sequences & Their Correlation Properties. LC 99-43423. (NATO ASI Ser.). 1999. write for info. (*0-7923-5958-5*) Kluwer Academic.

Pott, Alexander. Finite Geometry & Character Theory. LC 95-4084. (Lecture Notes in Mathematics Ser.: Vol. 1601). 1995. write for info. (*0-387-59065-X*) Spr-Verlag.
— Finite Geometry & Character Theory. LC 95-4084. (Lecture Notes in Mathematics Ser.: Vol. 1601). 188p. 1995. 33.00 (*3-540-59065-X*) Spr-Verlag.

Pott-Buter, Hettie A. Facts & Fairy Tales about Female Labour, Family & Fertility: A Seven-Country Comparison, 1850-1990. 370p. (C). 1993. pap. 39.50 (*90-5356-044-0*, Pub. by Amsterdam U Pr); text 59.50 (*90-5356-045-9*, Pub. by Amsterdam U Pr) U of Mich Pr.

Pott, Constance M. Francis Bacon & His Secret Society. LC 71-174282. reprint ed. 52.50 (*0-404-05096-4*) AMS Pr.

Pott, Henry. Francis Bacon & His Secret Society. 421p. 1992. reprint ed. pap. 29.95 (*1-56459-111-5*) Kessinger Pub.
— The Promus of Formularies & Elegancies Illustrated & Elucidated by Passages from Shakespeare. 648p. 1997. reprint ed. pap. 45.00 (*0-7661-0084-7*) Kessinger Pub.

Pott, John, tr. see Hebly, J. A.

P

An Asterisk (*) at the beginning of an entry indicates that the title is appearing for the first time.

Pott, Norm. Called Out With: Stories of Presbyterian Supporters of Gays & Lesbians. LC 97-12817. 1997. 18.95 (*0-664-25719-4*) Westminster John Knox.

Pott, Patricia G. Hair Stories. LC 98-142003. (Illus.). 144p. 1997. 39.95 (*3-908162-78-5*) Dist Art Pubs.

Pott, R. Die Pflanzengesellschaften Deutschland (The Plant Associations of Germany) 2nd rev. ed. (GER., Illus.). 622p. 1995. 52.00 (*3-8001-2693-1*, Pub. by Eugen Ulmer) Balogh.

— Farbtlas Nordseekueste und Nordseeinseln (Color Atlas of the North Sea Coast & Islands) (GER., Illus.). 288p. 1995. 26.00 (*3-8001-3350-4*, Pub. by Eugen Ulmer) Balogh.

Pottage, Dave & Evans, Mike. Workbased Stress: Prescription Is Not the Cure. 1992. pap. 30.00 (*0-902789-79-1*, Pub. by Natl Inst Soc Work) St Mut.

— Workbased Stress: Prescription Is Not the Cure. (C). 1992. 50.00 (*0-7855-0070-7*, Pub. by Natl Inst Soc Work) St Mut.

Pottage, Dave, jt. auth. see Evans, Mike.

Pottage, J. Geometrical Investigations: Illustrating the Art of Discovery in the Mathematical Field. 480p. 1983. text 55.95 (*0-201-05733-6*) Addison-Wesley.

— Mathematics Education: A Wider Perspective. 197p. 1995. pap. 66.00 (*0-7300-1585-8*, Pub. by Deakin Univ) St Mut.

Pottage, Julian, jt. auth. see Reese, Terence.

Pottasch, Stuart R. Planetary Nebulae. 1983. text 162.50 (*90-277-1672-2*) Kluwer Academic.

Pottasch, Stuart R., jt. ed. see Kwok, S.

Pottash, A. L., jt. ed. see Gold, Mark S.

Pottebaum, Gerard A. The Rites of People: Exploring the Ritual Character of Human Experience. rev. ed. (Orig.). 1992. pap. text 7.95 (*0-912405-94-5*, Pastoral Press) OR Catholic.

Potteiger, Matthew & Purinton, Jamie. Landscape Narratives: Design Practices for Telling Stories. LC 97-40015. 352p. 1998. pap. 49.95 (*0-471-12486-9*) Wiley.

Pottek, Mark, jt. auth. see Dahms, Hans-Uwe.

Potten, C. S., ed. Stem Cells. (Illus.). 496p. 1996. text 99.95 (*0-12-563455-2*) Acad Pr.

Potten, C. S. & Hendry, J. H., eds. Radiation & Gut. LC 96-105368. 328p. 1995. 288.50 (*0-444-89053-X*) Elsevier.

Pottengen, Mark, ed. Astrological Research Methods: An ISAR Anthology, Vol. 1. (Illus.). 428p. (C). 1995. pap. text. write for info. (*0-9646366-0-3*) ISAR MI.

Pottenger, Dennis, jt. auth. see Wiegand, Steve.

Pottenger, Doris. UFO's, Aliens or Demons? Smith, Don, ed. (Illus.). 128p. (Orig.). 1990. pap. 5.50 (*0-927022-02-8*) CHJ Pub.

Pottenger, Francis M., Jr. Pottengers' Cats: A Study in Nutrition. LC 83-80360. (Illus.). 126p. 1983. 5.95 (*0-916764-06-0*) Price-Pottenger.

Pottenger, John R. The Political Theory of Liberation Theology: Toward a Reconvergence of Social Values & Social Sciences. LC 88-34838. 264p. (C). 1989. pap. text 21.95 (*0-7914-0119-7*) State U NY Pr.

Pottenger, Maritha. The Art of Chart Comparison. 35p. 1986. pap. 4.95 (*0-917086-72-4*) ACS Pubns.

— Astrology, the Next Step: Complete Horoscope Interpretation. 568p. 1998. pap. 25.95 (*0-935127-63-1*) ACS Pubns.

— Chiron in Houses, Signs & Aspects. 34p. 1996. pap. 4.95 (*0-935127-24-0*) ACS Pubns.

— The East Point & the Antivertex. 35p. 1985. pap. 4.95 (*0-917086-70-8*) ACS Pubns.

— Easy Astrology Guide: How to Read Your Horoscope. 352p. (Orig.). 1996. pap. 14.95 (*0-935127-49-6*) ACS Pubns.

— Healing with the Horoscope: A Guide to Counseling. 256p. (Orig.). 1984. pap. 14.95 (*0-917086-45-7*) ACS Pubns.

— Past Lives, Future Choices: The Astrology of Reincarnation. 320p. (Orig.). 1997. pap. 16.95 (*0-935127-54-2*) ACS Pubns.

— What Are Astrolocality Maps? 31p. 1984. pap. 4.95 (*0-917086-67-8*) ACS Pubns.

— What Astrology Can Do for You. 31p. 1996. pap. 4.95 (*0-935127-37-2*) ACS Pubns.

— Wit & Wisdom: Mercury in Your Chart. 44p. (Orig.). 1997. pap. 4.95 (*0-935127-57-7*) ACS Pubns.

— Your Love Life, Venus in Your Chart. 36p. 1996. pap. 4.95 (*0-935127-40-2*) ACS Pubns.

— Your Starway to Love: Better Romance with Astrology. 2nd rev. ed. (Illus.). 352p. 1994. pap. 14.95 (*0-935127-44-5*) ACS Pubns.

Pottenger, Maritha & Dobyns, Zipporah. Planets on the Move: The Astrology of Relocation. 320p. (Orig.). 1995. pap. 15.95 (*0-935127-23-2*) ACS Pubns.

— Unveiling Your Future: Progressions Made Easy. 320p. 1998. pap. 16.95 (*0-935127-65-8*) ACS Pubns.

Pottenger, Maritha, et al. Millenium Fears, Fantasies & Facts: Astrologers Look Toward 2000. 157p. 1998. pap. 12.95 (*0-935127-62-3*) ACS Pubns.

Pottenger, Mark & Vail, Scott G. Tables for Aspect Research. 128p. 1986. pap. 9.95 (*0-917086-90-2*) ACS Pubns.

Pottenger, Milton A. Symbolism. LC 94-78131. (Astro-Cards Reprints Ser.). (Illus.). 312p. 1996. reprint ed. pap. text 30.00 (*1-885500-15-7*, AR1) Astro-Cards.

— Symbolism: A Treatise on the Soul of Things; How the Natural World Is but a Symbol of the Real World; the Modern Church, with Its Spire & Cross, & the Bible Account of Noah's Ark Symbols of the Phallic Religion. (Illus.). 312p. 1996. reprint ed. pap. 24.95 (*1-56459-464-5*) Kessinger Pub.

— Three Master Masons. 402p. 1998. reprint ed. pap. 25.00 (*0-7873-0672-X*) Hlth Research.

— Three Master Masons: A Scientific & Philosophical Explanation of the Emblems of Masonry Proving It to Be the Great Constructive Principle of the World (1916) 410p. 1996. reprint ed. pap. 23.95 (*1-56459-792-X*) Kessinger Pub.

***Potter.** The Art of Measurement: Metrology in Fundamental & Applied Physics. 192p. 1999. 45.00 (*0-13-026174-2*) P-H.

Potter. Comp Package for Fundamentals of Nursing. 3rd ed. 1993. write for info. (*0-8016-7299-6*) Mosby Inc.

— Fundamentals of Nursing, No. 3. 1992. write for info. (*0-8016-6958-8*) Mosby Inc.

***Potter.** Geographies of Development. 288p. (C). 1999. pap. 42.00 (*0-582-29825-3*) P-H.

— The Narnia Atlas. 124p. (J). (gr. 3 up). 2000. pap. 18.95 (*0-06-443485-0*) HarpC Child Bks.

Potter. Pikes Peak. 1998. 76.00 (*0-323-00685-X*) Mosby Inc.

— Pocket Guide to Health Assessment. 4th ed. LC 97-47169. (Illus.). 416p. (C). (gr. 13). 1998. text 22.95 (*0-8151-8396-8*, 31696) Mosby Inc.

Potter. Urban Caribbean in an Era of Global Change. 69.95 (*0-7546-1139-6*) Ashgate Pub Co.

Potter, et al. The City in the Developing World. 264p. (C). 1998. pap. 32.47 (*0-582-35741-1*) Longman.

Potter, jt. auth. see Lyman.

Potter, jt. ed. see Bryan.

Potter, Stephen. The Complete Upmanship: Including Gamesmanship, Lifemanship, One-Upmanship, Supermanship. LC 72-551255. 349 p. 1970. write for info. (*0-246-64000-6*) Grfton HrprCllns.

Potter, A. E. & Wilson, T. L., eds. Physics & Astrophysics from a Lunar Base. LC 90-55073. (AIP Conference Proceedings Ser.: No. 202). (Illus.). 344p. 1990. 70.00 (*0-88318-646-2*) Am Inst Physics.

Potter, Agnes H., ed. see Adamson, Bruce Campbell.

Potter, Alice. I Can Do That! LC 97-204063. 272p. 1997. mass mkt. 5.99 (*0-425-15771-7*) Berkley Pub.

— Lincoln County, Colorado War Book. (Illus.). 115p. 1993. 35.00 (*0-88107-230-3*) Curtis Media.

— The Positive Thinker: Self-Motivating Strategies for Personal Success. 240p. (Orig.). 1994. mass mkt. 5.99 (*0-425-14257-4*) Berkley Pub.

— Putting the Positive Thinker to Work. 1998. mass mkt. 5.99 (*0-425-16376-8*) Berkley Pub.

Potter, Alice H. How to Be a Lesbian with Class. LC 87-11343. (Illus.). 1989. pap. 8.95 (*0-87949-276-7*) Ashley Bks.

Potter, Ambrose G. A Bibliography of the "Rubaiyat" of Omar Khayyam. xvi, 314p. reprint ed. write for info. (*0-318-71553-8*) G Olms Pubs.

Potter, Areon. From Darkness to Light: Demonic Oppression & the Christian. LC 93-73290. 368p. (Orig.). 1994. pap. 14.95 (*0-9638782-1-2*) Adonai Res.

Potter, B. G., Jr. & Bruce, A. J., eds. Synthesis & Application of Lanthanide-Doped Materials. (Ceramic Transactions Ser.: No. 67). (Illus.). 150p. 1996. 95.00 (*1-57498-012-2*, CT067) Am Ceramic.

Potter, Barry. Macintosh OLE 2.0 Developer's Reference: Programmer's Reference. LC 94-233825. 871p. 1994. pap. 44.95 incl. cd-rom (*1-55851-420-1*, M&T Bks) IDG Bks.

Potter, Beatrix. The Adventures of Peter Rabbit. (Illus.). 24p. (J). (ps-2). 1997. reprint ed. pap. 2.49 (*1-57102-108-6*, Ideals Child) Hambleton-Hill.

— The Adventures of Peter Rabbit (& His Friends) 1994. pap. 5.50 (*0-87129-356-0*, A53) Dramatic Pub.

— Beatrix Potter Audio Gift Pack: Magic of Beatrix Potter, Vol. 1. (Audio Gift Pack Ser.). (Illus.). 96p. (J). (ps-2). 1991. 19.98 incl. audio (*1-55886-063-0*, AGP 4-202) Smarty Pants.

— Beatrix Potter Audio Gift Pack: More Tales from Beatrix Potter, Vol. 2. (Audio Gift Pack Ser.). (Illus.). 96p. (J). (ps-2). 1992. 19.98 incl. audio (*1-55886-067-3*, AGP 4-203) Smarty Pants.

— Beatrix Potter Collection, 3 vols. LC 90-112240. (Frederick Warne Picture Bks.). (J). (ps-3). 1987. pap. 28.00 (*0-7232-5163-0*, F Warne) Peng Put Young Read.

— Beatrix Potter Collection, 3 vols., Set. (Frederick Warne Picture Bks.). (J). (ps-3). 1987. write for info. (*0-317-52263-9*, F Warne) Peng Put Young Read.

***Potter, Beatrix.** Beatrix Potter Decoupage. 48p. (J). 1999. pap. 16.00 (*0-7232-4445-6*) Peng Put Young Read.

— Beatrix Potter Miniature Nursery Library. 144p. (J). 1998. 10.99 (*0-7232-4389-1*, F Warne) Peng Put Young Read.

Potter, Beatrix. Beatrix Potter Tale of Baby Da. (J). (gr. k up). 1979. 17.00 (*0-8378-8011-4*) Gibson.

***Potter, Beatrix.** Beatrix Potter Treasury-Benjamin Bunny. (World of Beatrix Potter Ser.). 8p. (J). 1999. pap. write for info. (*0-7232-4528-2*, Pub. by F Warne Pubs) Penguin Books.

Potter, Beatrix. Beatrix Potter's Classic Tales, 12 vols., Set. (Classic Tales Ser.). (Illus.). 288p. (J). (gr. 2-4). 1998. lib. bdg. 11.95 (*1-56674-923-9*) Forest Hse.

***Potter, Beatrix.** Beatrix Potter's Nursery Rhyme Book. (Illus.). 64p. (J). (ps). 2000. 12.99 (*0-7232-4650-5*) F Warne Pubs.

— Beatrix Potter's Nursery Rhyme Book. (J). 1999. bds. 10.99 (*0-7232-4686-6*, F Warne) Peng Put Young Read.

Potter, Beatrix. Beatrix Potter's Peter Rabbit: A Lift-the-Flap Rebus Book. (J). (ps-3). 1991. 12.99 (*0-7232-3798-0*, F Warne) Peng Put Young Read.

— Benjamin Bunny. (Illus.). 10p. (J). (ps). 1994. pap. 3.99 (*0-7232-0018-1*, F Warne) Peng Put Young Read.

***Potter, Beatrix.** Benjamin Bunny: Beatrix Potter Pop-up Treasury. 1999. pap. write for info. (*0-7232-4527-4*) Peng Put Young Read.

Potter, Beatrix. Benjamin Bunny's Colors Mini Board Book. (Illus.). 24p. (J). (ps). 1994. pap. 3.50 (*0-7232-4118-X*, F Warne) Peng Put Young Read.

— Bunnies Peek Through: Peter Rabbit Peek-Through Board Book. (Peter Rabbit Peek-Through Board Bks.). (Illus.). (J). 1996. bds. 4.99 (*0-614-15582-7*, F Warne) Peng Put Young Read.

— Bunnies Peek Through: Peter Rabbit Peek-Through Board Book. (Illus.). 12p. (J). (ps). 1996. pap. 4.99 (*0-7232-4308-5*, F Warne) Peng Put Young Read.

***Potter, Beatrix.** Classic Nursery Songs. LC 98-234922. (J). 1998. write for info. (*0-7853-2682-0*) Pubns Intl Ltd.

Potter, Beatrix. The Complete Adventures of Peter Rabbit. (Picture Puffin Ser.). 80p. (J). (ps-3). 1984. pap. 7.99 (*0-14-050444-3*, PuffinBks) Peng Put Young Read.

— The Complete Adventures of Peter Rabbit. (Illus.). 96p. (J). (ps-3). 1987. 13.00 (*0-7232-2951-1*, F Warne) Peng Put Young Read.

— The Complete Tales of Beatrix Potter. rev. ed. (Illus.). 400p. 1997. 35.00 (*0-7232-4404-9*, F Warne) Peng Put Young Read.

Potter, Beatrix. The Complete Tales of Peter Rabbit: And Other Favorite Stories. LC 86-10116. (Children's Illustrated Classics Ser.). (Illus.). 56p. (J). (gr. k up). 1986. 9.98 (*0-89471-460-0*, Courage) Running Pr.

Potter, Beatrix. Create Your Own Peter Rabbit Nursery. (Peter Rabbit Bks.). (Illus.). 32p. 1999. 11.99 (*0-7232-4487-1*, F Warne) Peng Put Young Read.

— El Cuento de Pedrito Conejo. Marcuse, Aida R., tr. from ENG. (SPA., Illus.). 32p. (J). (ps-3). 1993. pap. 2.95 (*0-590-46475-2*) Scholastic Inc.

Potter, Beatrix. El Cuento de Pedrito Conejo. (Mariposa Scholastica en Espanol Ser.). (SPA.). (J). 1993. 8.19 (*0-606-02622-3*, Pub. by Turtleback) Demco.

Potter, Beatrix. El Cuento de Pedro, el Conejo - The Tales of Peter Rabbit. (J). (ps-3). 1998. pap. 2.95 (*0-486-27995-2*) Dover.

— El Cuento De Pedro, El Conejo, y Otros Once Cuentos De Beatrix Potter: 11 Stories. DeZardain, Paul F. & Saludes, Esperanza G., trs. (SPA., Illus.). 96p. (J). 1995. pap. text 1.00 (*0-486-28566-9*) Dover.

— Deux Vilaines Souris. (FRE.). 59p. (J). 1990. 9.95 (*0-7859-3625-4*, 2070560708) Fr & Eur.

— Deux Vilaines Souris. (Gallimard Ser.). (FRE.). 59p. (J). 1990. 10.95 (*2-07-056070-8*) Schoenhof.

— Die Geschichte von Peterchen Hase: Ein Buntes Marchenbuch.Tr. of Peter Rabbit. (GER., Illus.). 32p. (J). 1995. pap. text 1.00 (*0-486-28557-X*) Dover.

— Giant Treasury of Peter Rabbit. (Illus.). 96p. (J). (gr. k-6). 1989. 5.99 (*0-517-31687-0*) Random Hse Value.

— The Great Big Treasury of Beatrix Potter. LC 92-12165. (Illus.). 256p. (J). 1992. 12.99 (*0-517-07246-7*) Random Hse Value.

— Jeannot Lapin. (FRE., Illus.). 58p. (J). 1990. 9.95 (*0-7859-3631-9*, 2070560945) Fr & Eur.

— Jeannot Lapin. (Gallimard Ser.). (FRE.). 58p. (J). 1990. 10.95 (*2-07-056094-5*) Schoenhof.

— Jemima Puddle-Duck. (Illus.). 10p. (J). 1988. 2.99 (*0-517-65275-7*) Random Hse Value.

— Jemima Puddle-Duck Bath Book. (Illus.). 8p. (J). (ps). 1988. pap. 3.99 (*0-7232-3512-0*, F Warne) Peng Put Young Read.

***Potter, Beatrix.** Jemima Puddle-Duck's Farmyard Friends. (Illus.). (J). 2000. pap. 4.99 (*0-7232-4593-2*, F Warne) Peng Put Young Read.

Potter, Beatrix. Jemima Puddle-Duck's Numbers. (Illus.). 24p. (J). (ps). 1994. pap. 2.99 (*0-7232-4091-4*, F Warne) Peng Put Young Read.

— Jeremie Peche-a-la-Ligne. (FRE., Illus.). 58p. (J). 1990. 9.95 (*0-7859-3628-9*, 2070560740) Fr & Eur.

— Jeremie Peche-a-la-Ligne. (Gallimard Ser.). (FRE.). 58p. (J). 1990. 10.95 (*2-07-056074-0*) Schoenhof.

— Jeremy Fisher Bath Book. (Illus.). 8p. (J). (ps). 1989. pap. 3.50 (*0-7232-3513-9*, F Warne) Peng Put Young Read.

— Letters to Children. (Illus.). 48p. (J). (gr. 2 up). 1986. pap. 5.95 (*0-8027-7293-5*) Walker & Co.

— Listen & Read the Tale of Peter Rabbit & Other Favorite Stories. (Illus.). 96p. (Orig.). (J). 1996. pap. text 5.95 incl. audio (*0-486-29299-1*) Dover.

— Little Tale of Mr. Jeremy Fisher Coloring Book. (Illus.). (J). (gr. k-3). 1992. pap. 1.00 (*0-486-27291-5*) Dover.

— Little Tale of Two Bad Mice Coloring Book. (Illus.). (J). (gr. k-3). 1994. pap. 1.00 (*0-486-27868-9*) Dover.

— Madame Piquedru. (FRE., Illus.). 58p. (J). 1990. 9.95 (*0-7859-3623-8*, 2070560686) Fr & Eur.

— Madame Piquedru. (Gallimard Ser.). (FRE.). 58p. (J). 1990. 10.95 (*2-07-056068-6*) Schoenhof.

— Madame Trotte-Menu. (FRE., Illus.). 58p. (J). 1990. 9.95 (*0-7859-3634-3*, 2070561054) Fr & Eur.

— Madame Trotte-Menu. (Gallimard Ser.). (FRE.). 59p. (J). 1990. 10.95 (*2-07-056105-4*) Schoenhof.

— Mademoiselle Mitoufle. (FRE., Illus.). 58p. (J). 1990. 9.95 (*0-7859-3633-5*, 2070561046) Fr & Eur.

— Mademoiselle Mitoufle. (Gallimard Ser.). (FRE.). 37p. (J). 1990. 10.95 (*2-07-056104-6*) Schoenhof.

— Mechant Petit Lapin. (FRE., Illus.). 58p. (J). 1990. 9.95 (*0-7859-3627-0*, 2070560732) Fr & Eur.

— Mechant Petit Lapin. (Gallimard Ser.). (FRE.). (J). (gr. 5-10). 1990. 10.95 (*2-07-056073-2*) Schoenhof.

— Mice. (Peter Rabbit Peek-Through Board Bks.). (Illus.). (J). 1996. bds. 4.99 (*0-614-15583-5*, F Warne) Peng Put Young Read.

***Potter, Beatrix.** Mrs. Tiggy-Winkle's Colorful Day. (Illus.). (J). 2000. pap. 3.99 (*0-7232-4595-9*, F Warne) Peng Put Young Read.

Potter, Beatrix. My First Year: A Beatrix Potter Baby Book. 48p. 1998. 10.00 (*0-7232-4380-8*, F Warne) Peng Put Young Read.

— My Peter Rabbit Cloth Book. (Illus.). 10p. (J). (ps). 1994. pap. 4.99 (*0-7232-0020-3*, F Warne) Peng Put Young Read.

— My Tom Kitten. (J). 1994. pap. 4.99 (*0-7232-4159-7*, F Warne) Peng Put Young Read.

— My Tom Kitten Cloth Book. (Illus.). 10p. (J). (ps). 1999. 4.99 (*0-7232-0021-1*, F Warne) Peng Put Young Read.

— Noisette l'Ecureuil. (FRE., Illus.). 58p. (J). 1990. 9.95 (*0-7859-3629-7*, 2070560759) Fr & Eur.

— Noisette l'Ecureuil. (Gallimard Ser.). (FRE.). 58p. (J). 1990. 10.95 (*2-07-056075-9*) Schoenhof.

— The One Hundredth Anniversary 1-23 Presentation Box: The World of Beatrix Potter, 23 bks., Set. (Illus.). (J). 1993. text 160.00 (*0-7232-4112-0*, F Warne) Peng Put Young Read.

— The Original Peter Rabbit Books: 13-23 Presentation Box. (J). 1990. text 65.00 (*0-7232-5178-9*, F Warne) Peng Put Young Read.

— The Original Peter Rabbit Miniature Collection, No. I. (Picture Bks.: Vol. I). (Illus.). (J). (ps-3). 1991. pap. 5.95 (*0-7232-3982-7*, F Warne) Peng Put Young Read.

— The Original Peter Rabbit Miniature Collection, No. III. (Illus.). (J). (ps-3). 1989. pap. 5.95 (*0-7232-3984-3*, F Warne) Peng Put Young Read.

— The Original Peter Rabbit Miniature Collection, Vol. II. Vol. II. (J). (ps-3). 1988. pap. 5.95 (*0-7232-3983-5*, F Warne) Peng Put Young Read.

***Potter, Beatrix.** The Original Peter Rabbit Storybook Playset. (J). 1999. pap. 18.99 (*0-7232-4557-6*) Peng Put Young Read.

Potter, Beatrix. Panache Petitgris. (FRE., Illus.). 60p. (J). 1990. 9.95 (*0-7859-3713-7*) Fr & Eur.

— Panache Petitgris. (Gallimard Ser.). (FRE.). 59p. (J). 1990. 10.95 (*2-07-056102-X*) Schoenhof.

— Peter Rabbit: Story Pak. (Graphic Learning Literature Program Series: Folk Tales). (ENG & SPA., Illus.). (J). 1992. 45.00 (*0-87746-231-3*) Graphic Learning.

— The Peter Rabbit & Benjamin Bunny Coloring Book. (Illus.). (J). (gr. 1 up). 1987. pap. 1.49 (*0-671-62987-5*) Litle Simon.

— Peter Rabbit & Friends: A Stand-Up Story Book. (Illus.). 12p. (J). 1998. 14.99 (*0-7232-4343-3*, F Warne) Peng Put Young Read.

***Potter, Beatrix.** Peter Rabbit & Friends Sticker Activity Book. (Illus.). (J). 2000. pap. 7.99 (*0-7232-4681-5*) F Warne Pubs.

Potter, Beatrix. The Peter Rabbit & Friends Treasury. (J). (ps-3). 1997. 14.99 (*0-614-29146-1*, F Warne) Peng Put Young Read.

— The Peter Rabbit & Friends Treasury, Vol. 1. (Illus.). (ps-3). 1999. 19.99 (*0-7232-4576-2*, F Warne) Peng Put Young Read.

— Peter Rabbit & His Friends. (Chubby Board Bks.). (Illus.). 16p. (YA). (ps up). 1985. bds. 3.95 (*0-671-52698-7*) Litle Simon.

— Peter Rabbit & His Friends. (Illus.). 24p. (J). (ps). 1994. pap. 2.99 (*0-7232-4093-0*, F Warne) Peng Put Young Read.

Potter, Beatrix. Peter Rabbit & Other Stories. (J). 1993. 4.98 (*0-89009-187-0*) Bk Sales Inc.

Potter, Beatrix. Peter Rabbit Bath Book: Bath Book. (Illus.). 8p. (J). (ps-k). 1989. pap. 3.99 (*0-7232-3584-8*, F Warne) Peng Put Young Read.

***Potter, Beatrix.** Peter Rabbit Giant Shaped Board Book. 2001. bds. 7.99 (*0-7232-4682-3*, F Warne) Peng Put Young Read.

— Peter Rabbit Lift the Flap. (Illus.). (J). 2000. 9.99 (*0-7232-4639-4*) F Warne Pubs.

Potter, Beatrix. The Peter Rabbit Nursery Book & Toy. (Illus.). 48p. (J). (ps-k). 1997. 21.99 (*0-7232-4413-8*, F Warne) Peng Put Young Read.

— The Peter Rabbit Nursery Book & Toy Set. (Illus.). (J). 1997. write for info. (*0-614-29325-1*, F Warne) Peng Put Young Read.

***Potter, Beatrix.** Peter Rabbit Puzzle & Board Book. 2000. bds. 10.99 (*0-7232-4580-0*, F Warne) Peng Put Young Read.

— Peter Rabbit Treasury. (J). 1997. pap. 14.98 (*0-7232-4284-4*, F Warne) Peng Put Young Read.

Potter, Beatrix. Peter Rabbit's ABC. (Peter Rabbit Bks.). (Illus.). 48p. (J). (ps-1). 1987. 4.99 (*0-7232-3423-X*, F Warne) Peng Put Young Read.

— Peter Rabbit's ABC 123. (Illus.). 48p. (J). (ps-3). 1995. 10.99 (*0-7232-4188-0*, F Warne) Peng Put Young Read.

***Potter, Beatrix.** Peter Rabbit's Board Book & Toy. abr. ed. (Illus.). (ps-k). 1999. 17.99 (*0-7232-8346-X*, F Warne) Peng Put Young Read.

Potter, Beatrix. Peter Rabbit's Christmas Activity Book. 24p. (J). 1999. pap. 4.99 (*0-7232-4547-9*, F Warne) Peng Put Young Read.

***Potter, Beatrix.** Peter Rabbit's Counting Fun. (Illus.). (J). 2000. 3.99 (*0-7232-4594-0*, F Warne) Peng Put Young Read.

— Peter Rabbit's Finger Puppet Book. 2000. bds. 10.99 (*0-7232-4605-X*, F Warne) Peng Put Young Read.

— Peter Rabbit's Garden Adventure. (Illus.). (J). 2000. pap. 4.99 (*0-7232-4592-4*, F Warne) Peng Put Young Read.

Potter, Beatrix. Peter Rabbit's One Two Three. (Peter Rabbit Bks.). (J). (ps-1). 1988. 4.99 (*0-7232-3424-8*, F Warne) Peng Put Young Read.

***Potter, Beatrix.** Peter Rabbit's Puzzle Story. (Illus.). 6p. (J). (ps-k). 2000. 4.99 (*0-7232-4577-0*, F Warne) Peng Put Young Read.

— Peter Rabbit's Touch & Feel Book. (Illus.). (ps-3). 1999. 9.99 (*0-7232-4518-5*, F Warne) Peng Put Young Read.

Potter, Beatrix. Petit-Jean des Villes.Tr. of Tale of Johnny Town-Mouse. (FRE., Illus.). 58p. (J). 1990. 9.95 (*0-7859-3632-7*, 2070560953) Fr & Eur.

— The Pie & the Patty-Pan. (Illus.). 46p. (J). 1976. reprint ed. pap. 1.95 (*0-486-23383-9*) Dover.

— Pierre Lapin: Peter Rabbit. (FRE., Illus.). 62p. (J). 1980. 9.95 (*0-7859-3624-6*, 2070560694) Fr & Eur.

— Pierre Lapin: Peter Rabbit. (Gallimard Ser.). (FRE.). 62p. (J). 1980. 10.95 (*2-07-056069-4*) Schoenhof.

— Potter Story Collection 1. (J). 1999. 6.95 (*0-453-00947-6*, NAL Bks) NAL.

P

An Asterisk (*) at the beginning of an entry indicates that the title is appearing for the first time.

— Potter Story Collection 2. (J). 1999. 6.95 (*0-453-00948-4*, NAL Bks) NAL.
— Potter Story Collection 3. (J). 1999. 6.95 (*0-453-00949-2*, NAL Bks) NAL.
— Potter Story Collection 4. (J). 1999. 6.95 (*0-453-00950-6*, NAL Bks) NAL.
— Rabbit Read Play. (Illus.). 28p. (J). 1999. pap. 4.99 (*0-7232-4373-5*, F Warne) Peng Put Young Read.
— Read & Play with Peter Rabbit. (Illus.). (J). 1997. 4.99 (*0-614-29326-X*, F Warne) Peng Put Young Read.
— Read & Play with Tom Kitten. (Illus.). (J). 1997. write for info. (*0-614-29327-8*, F Warne) Peng Put Young Read.
— Scenes from Tom Kitten. (Little Carousels Ser.). (J). 1996. 4.99 (*0-614-15581-9*, F Warne) Peng Put Young Read.
— Schaum's Outline Thermodynamics for Engineers. 1995. pap. text 38.95 (*0-07-842717-7*) McGraw.

***Potter, Beatrix.** Sly Old Cat: The Facsimile Edition. (J). 1999. write for info. (*0-7232-3661-5*) Peng Put Young Read.

Potter, Beatrix. Sophie Canetang: The Tale Jemima Puddle-Duck: French Edition. (FRE.). 58p. (J). 1990. 9.95 (*0-7859-3622-X*, 2070569678) Fr & Eur.
— The Story of a Fierce Bad Rabbit. LC 88-162517. (Original Peter Rabbit Bks.: No. 20). (Illus.). 37p. (J). (ps-3). 1987. 6.99 (*0-7232-3479-5*, F Warne) Peng Put Young Read.
— The Story of Miss Moppet. LC 88-162626. (Original Peter Rabbit Bks.: No. 21). 37p. (J). (ps-3). 1987. 6.99 (*0-7232-3480-9*, F Warne) Peng Put Young Read.
— Tailleur de Gloucester. (FRE., Illus.). 58p. (J). 1991. 9.95 (*0-7859-3630-0*, 2070560767) Fr & Eur.
— Tailleur de Gloucester. (Gallimard Ser.). (FRE.). 58p. (J). 1991. 10.95 (*2-07-056076-7*) Schoenhof.
— The Tailor of Gloucester. LC 88-11510. (Illus.). 44p. (J). (ps-3). 1991. 14.95 (*0-88708-080-4*, Rabbit Ears) Litle Simon.
— The Tailor of Gloucester. LC 88-11510. (Illus.). 40p. (J). (ps-3). 1995. pap. 10.95 incl. audio (*0-689-80362-1*, Rabbit Ears) Litle Simon.
— The Tailor of Gloucester. LC 88-162501. (Original Peter Rabbit Bks.: No. 3). 58p. (J). (ps-3). 1987. 6.99 (*0-7232-3462-0*, F Warne) Peng Put Young Read.
— The Tale of Benjamin Bunny. LC 88-162474. (Original Peter Rabbit Bks.: No.4). (Illus.). 58p. (J). (ps-3). 1987. 6.99 (*0-7232-3463-9*, F Warne) Peng Put Young Read.
— The Tale of Benjamin Bunny. LC 80-27468. (Illus.). 32p. (J). (gr. k-3). 1981. pap. 3.95 (*0-89375-485-4*); lib. bdg. 15.85 (*0-89375-484-6*) Troll Communs.
— Tale of Benjamin Bunny. (Illus.). 10p. (J). 1988. 2.99 (*0-517-65277-3*) Random Hse Value.
— Tale of Benjamin Bunny: A Tiny Tale of Benjamin Bunny. (Chubby Board Bk.). (Illus.). 8p. (J). (ps). 1999. bds. 2.99 (*0-689-82238-3*) S&S Childrens.
— Tale of Benjamin Bunny Coloring Book. (Illus.). (J). (gr. k-3). 1981. pap. 2.95 (*0-486-24114-9*) Dover.
— Tale of Benjamin Bunny-Sticker. LC 92-243434. 24p. (J). (ps-3). 1990. per. 2.95 (*0-671-69254-2*) Litle Simon.
— The Tale of Ginger & Pickles. LC 88-136658. (Original Peter Rabbit Bks.: No. 18). 59p. (J). (ps-3). 1987. 6.99 (*0-7232-3477-9*, F Warne) Peng Put Young Read.
— The Tale of Jemima Puddle-Duck. LC 88-162489. (Original Peter Rabbit Bks.: No. 9). (Illus.). 58p. (J). (ps-3). 1987. 6.99 (*0-7232-3468-X*, F Warne) Peng Put Young Read.
— The Tale of Jemima Puddle Duck. (Golden Deluxe Book & Cassette Ser.). (Illus.). 24p. (J). (ps-2). 1990. 7.98 incl. audio (*1-55886-057-6*, GDB 8003) Smarty Pants.

***Potter, Beatrix.** Tale of Jemima Puddle-Duck. LC 99-52822. (Reading Railroad Bks.). 32p. (J). 2000. pap. 3.49 (*0-448-42090-2*, G & D) Peng Put Young Read.

Potter, Beatrix. The Tale of Jemima Puddle-Duck: Full-Color Storybook. LC 95-4653. (Illus.). 32p. (J). 1996. reprint ed. pap. text 1.00 (*0-486-28821-8*) Dover.
— The Tale of Jeremy Fisher. (J). pap. 5.95 incl. audio (*0-89845-502-2*, TBC5022, Caedmon) HarperAudio.
— The Tale of Johnny Town-Mouse. LC 88-150995. (Original Peter Rabbit Bks.: No. 13). 58p. (J). (ps-3). 1987. 6.99 (*0-7232-3472-8*, F Warne) Peng Put Young Read.
— The Tale of Mr. Jeremy Fisher. LC 88-34668. (Rabbit Ears Storybook Classics Ser.). (Illus.). 32p. (J). (ps-3). 1991. 14.95 (*0-88708-094-4*, Rabbit Ears) Litle Simon.
— The Tale of Mr. Jeremy Fisher. LC 88-151029. (Original Peter Rabbit Bks.: No. 7). 58p. (J). (ps-3). 1987. 6.99 (*0-7232-3466-3*, F Warne) Peng Put Young Read.
— The Tale of Mr. Jeremy Fisher. LC 92-22584. (Illus.). 64p. (J). 1992. reprint ed. 5.95 (*0-88708-253-X*, Rabbit Ears) Litle Simon.
— The Tale of Mr. Jeremy Fisher. LC 92-22584. (Illus.). 40p. (J). (ps-3). 1992. reprint ed. 9.95 incl. audio (*0-88708-252-1*, Rabbit Ears) Litle Simon.
— Tale of Mr. Jeremy Fisher-Coloring Book. (J). 1985. pap. 2.50 (*0-486-24964-6*) Dover.
— The Tale of Mr. Toad. (Illus.). (J). (ps-3). 1996. pap. 4.99 (*0-614-15584-3*, F Warne) Peng Put Young Read.
— The Tale of Mrs. Tiggy-Winkle. (Original Peter Rabbit Bks.: No. 6). (J). 1987. 5.95 (*0-7232-3465-5*, F Warne) Peng Put Young Read.
— The Tale of Mrs. Tiggy-Winkle. (Golden Deluxe Book & Cassette Ser.). (Illus.). 24p. (J). (ps-2). 1990. 7.98 incl. audio (*1-55886-058-4*, GDB 8004) Smarty Pants.
— The Tale of Mrs. Tittlemouse. LC 88-150868. (Original Peter Rabbit Bks.: No. 11). 58p. (J). (ps-3). 1987. 6.99 (*0-7232-3470-1*, F Warne) Peng Put Young Read.
— The Tale of Mrs. Tittlemouse. (Illus.). 64p. 1986. reprint ed. pap. 1.75 (*0-486-25230-2*) Dover.
— The Tale of Peter Rabbit. (Children's Classics Ser.). (Illus.). 32p. (J). 1991. 6.95 (*0-8362-4908-9*) Andrews & McMeel.

***Potter, Beatrix.** The Tale of Peter Rabbit. (J). 1999. 7.99 incl. audio (*0-7232-4355-7*, Pub. by F Warne Pubs) Penguin Books.

Potter, Beatrix. The Tale of Peter Rabbit. (Little Golden Storybks.). (Illus.). (J). 1998. 3.99 (*0-307-16192-7*, 16192, Goldn Books) Gldn Bks Pub Co.
— The Tale of Peter Rabbit. (Talking Bookworm Ser.). (J). pap. 5.95 incl. audio (*0-89845-500-6*, TBC5006, Caedmon) HarperAudio.
— The Tale of Peter Rabbit. LC 78-18071. (Illus.). 34p. (J). (ps-3). 1991. 14.95 (*0-88708-079-0*, Rabbit Ears) Litle Simon.
— The Tale of Peter Rabbit. LC 88-11509. (Illus.). 36p. (J). (ps up). 1991. 14.95 (*0-317-89758-6*, Rabbit Ears) Litle Simon.
— The Tale of Peter Rabbit. (Illus.). 24p. (J). (gr. k-3). pap. 6.95 (*0-316-71492-5*) Little.
— The Tale of Peter Rabbit. 1992. pap. 3.99 (*0-14-054295-7*) NAL.
— The Tale of Peter Rabbit. LC 85-70809. (Pudgy Pal Board Bks.). (Illus.). 16p. (J). (ps). 1986. bds. 3.99 (*0-448-10224-2*, G & D) Peng Put Young Read.
— The Tale of Peter Rabbit. LC 88-151812. (Original Peter Rabbit Miniature Collection Ser.). (Illus.). 59p. (J). (ps-3). 1987. 6.99 (*0-7232-3460-4*, F Warne) Peng Put Young Read.
— The Tale of Peter Rabbit. (All Aboard Bks.). (Illus.). 32p. (J). (ps-3). 1991. pap. 2.99 (*0-448-40061-8*, G & D) Peng Put Young Read.

***Potter, Beatrix.** The Tale of Peter Rabbit. (Rebus Sticker Storybook Ser.). (Illus.). 16p. (J). (ps-3). 1999. pap. 3.99 (*0-7232-4521-5*, F Warne) Peng Put Young Read.
— The Tale of Peter Rabbit. LC 99-52820. (Reading Railroad Bks.). (Illus.). 32p. (J). (ps-3). 2000. 3.49 (*0-448-42089-9*, G & D) Peng Put Young Read.
— The Tale of Peter Rabbit. (Play - a - Sound Ser.). (Illus.). 24p. (J). 1993. 12.98 (*0-7853-0074-0*) Pubns Intl Ltd.

Potter, Beatrix. The Tale of Peter Rabbit. LC 78-18071. (Illus.). 10p. (J). (ps). 1988. 2.99 (*0-517-65276-5*) Random Hse Value.
— The Tale of Peter Rabbit. (Easy-to-Read Folktales Ser.). (Illus.). 32p. (J). (ps-2). 1986. pap. 2.50 (*0-590-41101-2*) Scholastic Inc.
— The Tale of Peter Rabbit. LC 78-18071. (David McPhail's Favorite Tales Ser.). (Illus.). 32p. (J). (ps-k). 1995. bds. 4.95 (*0-590-20547-1*, Cartwheel) Scholastic Inc.

Potter, Beatrix. The Tale of Peter Rabbit. (Golden Deluxe Book & Cassette Ser.). (Illus.). 24p. (J). (ps-2). 1990. 7.98 incl. audio (*1-55886-055-X*, GDB-8001) Smarty Pants.

Potter, Beatrix. The Tale of Peter Rabbit. LC 78-18071. (Illus.). 32p. (J). (gr. k-3). 1979. lib. bdg. 15.85 (*0-89375-124-3*) Troll Communs.
— The Tale of Peter Rabbit. LC 78-18071. (Illus.). 32p. (J). (ps-3). 1979. pap. 3.95 (*0-89375-102-2*) Troll Communs.
— The Tale of Peter Rabbit. LC 95-82094. (Wee Books for Wee Folks). (Illus.). 64p. (J). (ps-2). 1996. reprint ed. 6.95 (*1-55709-412-8*) Applewood.
— The Tale of Peter Rabbit. LC 92-36655. (Illus.). 40p. (J). (ps-3). 1993. reprint ed. 9.95 incl. audio (*0-88708-297-1*, Rabbit Ears) Litle Simon.
— The Tale of Peter Rabbit. LC 92-36655. (Illus.). 64p. (J). 1993. reprint ed. 4.95 (*0-88708-296-3*, Rabbit Ears) Litle Simon.
— The Tale of Peter Rabbit: A Portfolio of Art Prints. limited ed. (Illus.). 52p. 1995. boxed set 950.00 (*0-9627110-5-5*) Battledore Ltd.

***Potter, Beatrix.** The Tale of Peter Rabbit: Millennium Edition. (Illus.). 59p. (J). (ps-3). 1999. 6.99 (*0-7232-4609-2*) Peng Put Young Read.

Potter, Beatrix. The Tale of Peter Rabbit & 4 Other Full-Color Storybooks, 5 vols., Set. (Illus.). (J). 1993. pap. 8.75 (*0-486-27659-7*) Dover.
— The Tale of Peter Rabbit Coloring Book. (Illus.). (J). (gr. k-3). 1976. pap. 2.95 (*0-486-21711-6*) Dover.
— The Tale of Peter Rabbit Coloring Book. (Illus.). (J). (gr. k-3). 1986. pap. 1.00 (*0-486-25160-8*) Dover.
— The Tale of Peter Rabbit Coloring Book. (SPA., Illus.). (J). 1991. pap. 1.00 (*0-486-26794-6*); pap. 1.00 (*0-486-26793-8*) Dover.
— The Tale of Peter Rabbit Sticker Book. LC 92-243454. (Illus.). 24p. (J). (ps-3). 1990. per. 3.99 (*0-671-69255-0*) Litle Simon.
— The Tale of Pigling Bland. (Original Peter Rabbit Bks.: No. 15). (J). 1987. 6.99 (*0-7232-3474-4*, F Warne) Peng Put Young Read.
— The Tale of Samuel Whiskers. LC 88-162534. (Original Peter Rabbit Bks.: No. 16). 81p. (J). (ps-3). 1987. 6.99 (*0-7232-3475-2*, F Warne) Peng Put Young Read.
— The Tale of the Flopsy Bunnies. (Original Peter Rabbit Bks.: No. 10). (Illus.). (J). (ps-3). 1987. 5.95 (*0-7232-3469-8*, F Warne) Peng Put Young Read.
— The Tale of the Pie & the Patty-Pan. (Original Peter Rabbit Bks.: No. 17). (J). 1987. pap. 2.25 (*0-7232-3501-5*, F Warne) Peng Put Young Read.
— The Tale of Timmy Tiptoes. LC 88-136677. (Original Peter Rabbit Bks.: No. 12). 58p. (J). (ps-3). 1987. 6.99 (*0-7232-3471-X*, F Warne) Peng Put Young Read.
— Tale of Tom Kitten. (Illus.). 10p. (J). 1988. 2.99 (*0-517-65278-1*) Random Hse Value.
— The Tale of Tom Kitten. LC 87-40285. (Illus.). 24p. (J). (ps up). 1990. 6.95 incl. audio (*1-55782-018-X*) Little.
— The Tale of Tom Kitten. LC 88-136666. (Original Peter Rabbit Bks.: No. 8). (Illus.). 58p. (J). (ps-3). 1987. 6.99 (*0-7232-3467-1*, F Warne) Peng Put Young Read.

Potter, Beatrix. The Tale of Two Bad Mice. LC 88-150984. (Original Peter Rabbit Bks.: No. 5). (Illus.). 58p. (J). (ps-3). 1987. 6.99 (*0-7232-3464-7*, F Warne) Peng Put Young Read.

Potter, Beatrix. The Tale of Two Bad Mice. (Rebus Sticker Storybook Ser.). (Illus.). 16p. (J). (ps-3). 1999. pap. 3.99 (*0-7232-4520-7*, F Warne) Peng Put Young Read.
— A Tale of Two Bad Mice. LC 96-31231. (Illus.). 40p. (J). (ps-3). 1999. pap. 10.95 incl. audio (*0-689-82534-X*, Rabbit Ears) Litle Simon.
— The Tale of Two Bad Mice. deluxe ed. (J). 1997. 16.00 (*0-614-29145-3*, F Warne) Peng Put Young Read.
— Tales from Beatrix Potter. LC 86-40037. (Picture Bks.). (Illus.). 228p. (J). (ps-3). 1986. 9.99 (*0-7232-3971-1*, F Warne) Peng Put Young Read.
— The Tales of Peter Rabbit & Benjamin Bunny. (We Both Read Ser.). (Illus.). 48p. (J). (gr. k-2). 1998. 7.99 (*1-891327-01-1*) Treas Bay Inc.
— Tales of Peter Rabbit & His Friends, 2 vols. in 1. LC 84-11427. (Illus.). 160p. (J). (ps-3). 1988. 7.99 (*0-517-44901-3*) Random Hse Value.
— A Tiny Tale of Peter Rabbit. (J). 1985. pap. 3.95 (*0-671-52695-2*) Litle Simon.

***Potter, Beatrix.** A Tiny Tale of Peter Rabbit. (Chubby Board Bks.). (Illus.). 8p. (J). (ps). 1999. bds. 2.99 (*0-689-82239-1*) S&S Childrens.

Potter, Beatrix. Tom Chaton. (FRE., Illus.). 58p. (J). 1980. 9.95 (*0-7859-3626-2*, 2070560715) Fr & Eur.
— Tom Chaton. (Gallimard Ser.). (FRE.). 58p. (J). 1980. 10.95 (*2-07-056071-6*) Schoenhof.
— Tom Kitten: Bath Book. 299p. (J). 1989. pap. 3.50 (*0-7232-3585-6*, F Warne) Peng Put Young Read.

***Potter, Beatrix.** Tom Kitten's Puzzle Story. (Illus.). (J). 2000. 4.99 (*0-7232-4578-9*, F Warne) Peng Put Young Read.

Potter, Beatrix. The World of Peter Rabbit & Friends: Bedtime Stories. (Illus.). 128p. (J). (ps-3). 1995. 12.99 (*0-7232-4182-1*, F Warne) Peng Put Young Read.
— The World of Peter Rabbit & Friends: Bedtime Stories, 2. (Illus.). 128p. (ps-3). 1997. pap. 12.99 (*0-7232-4381-6*) Warner Pr.
— The World of Peter Rabbit Sticker Book. (Illus.). 32p. (J). (ps-3). 1990. pap. 6.99 (*0-7232-3645-3*, F Warne) Peng Put Young Read.

Potter, Beatrix. Les Champignons: Beatrix Potter. (FRE.). 128p. 1996. pap. 24.95 (*2-909808-21-1*, Pub. by Art Bks Intl) Partners Pubs Grp.
— Meet Jemima Puddle Duck. (Board Bks. Ser.). 12p. 1996. bds. 3.50 (*0-7232-4324-7*) Warner Juvenile Bks.
— Meet Peter Rabbit. 12p. (J). (ps-k). 1996. pap. 3.99 (*0-7232-4322-0*, F Warne) Peng Put Young Read.
— Peter Rabbit's Counting Book. 20p. (YA). (ps-3). 1999. 9.99 (*0-7232-4485-5*, F Warne) Peng Put Young Read.
— Read & Play with Tom Kitten. 7p. (J). 1999. pap. 4.99 (*0-7232-4374-3*, F Warne) Peng Put Young Read.
— The Tale of Peter Rabbit: A Story Board Book. 12p. (J). (ps-k). 1999. pap. 6.99 (*0-7232-4432-4*, F Warne) Peng Put Young Read.

Potter, Beatrix & Haster. Little Tale of Benjamin Bunny. 1990. pap. text 1.00 (*0-486-26239-1*) Dover.

Potter, Beatrix & Pomaska, Anna. El Cuento de Jemima Pata-de-Charco-The Tale of Jemima Puddle-Duck. Saludes, Esperanza G., tr. (SPA., Illus.). 32p. (J). 1995. reprint ed. pap. text 1.00 (*0-486-28695-9*) Dover.
— El Cuento de la Ardilla Nuececita. (SPA.). 32p. 1996. 1.00 (*0-486-29034-4*) Dover.
— El Cuento De Pedro, El Conejo: Libro De Cuentos En Colores - Por Beatrix Potter, Ilustrato Por Anna Pomaska. LC 94-44061. (Little Activity Bks.).Tr. of Tale of Peter Rabbit. (SPA., Illus.). 32p. (J). 1995. pap. text 1.50 (*0-486-28539-1*) Dover.
— El Cuento Del Conejito Benjamin: Libro De Cuentos En Colores - Por Beatrix Potter, Ilustrado Por Anna Pomaska. DeZardain, Paul F., tr. LC 94-43851. (Little Activity Bks.).Tr. of Tale of Benjamin Bunny. (SPA., Illus.). 32p. (J). 1995. pap. text 1.00 (*0-486-28536-7*) Dover.
— El Cuento del Gatito Tomasin-The Tale of Tom Kitten. De Zardain, Paul F., tr. (SPA., Illus.). 32p. (J). 1995. reprint ed. pap. text 1.00 (*0-486-28703-3*) Dover.
— El Cuento del Senor Jeremias Pescador. (Illus.). 32p. (J). 1997. pap. 1.00 (*0-486-29344-0*) Dover.
— L' Histoire de Jemima Cane-de-Flaque-The Tale of Jemima Puddle-Duck. Dana, Catherine, tr. (FRE., Illus.). 32p. (J). 1995. reprint ed. pap. text 1.00 (*0-486-28694-0*) Dover.
— L' Histoire de Pierre Lapin: Livre d'Histoires en Couleurs.Tr. of Peter Rabbit. (FRE., Illus.). 32p. (J). 1995. pap. text 1.00 (*0-486-28540-5*) Dover.
— L' Histoire de Tom Chaton-The Tale of Tom Kitten. Brodkey, Florence A., tr. (FRE., Illus.). 32p. (J). 1995. reprint ed. pap. text 1.00 (*0-486-28702-5*) Dover.
— L' Histoire Du Lapereau Benjamin: Livre D'Histoires En Couleurs - Par Beatrix Potter, Illustre Par Anna Pomaska. Brodkey, Florence A., tr.Tr. of Benjamin Bunny. (FRE., Illus.). 32p. (J). 1995. pap. text 1.00 (*0-486-28537-5*) Dover.
— Peter Rabbit & Friends, 10 bks., Set, incl. stickers. (Illus.). (J). 1999. pap., boxed set 10.00 (*0-486-29463-3*) Dover.
— Skazka O Zaichonke Pete - The Tale of Peter Rabbit. Maler, Elvira, tr. (RUS., Illus.). 32p. (J). 1996. reprint ed. pap. text 1.00 (*0-486-28717-3*) Dover.
— The Tale of Benjamin Bunny: Full-Color Storybook. LC 94-24672. (Little Activity Bks.). (Illus.). 32p. (Orig.). (J). 1995. pap. text 1.00 (*0-486-28538-3*) Dover.
— The Tale of Mr. Jeremy Fisher. (Illus.). 32p. (J). 1996. pap. 1.00 (*0-486-29345-9*) Dover.
— The Tale of Peter Rabbit: Full-Color Storybook. LC 94-24671. (Little Activity Bks.). (Illus.). 32p. (Orig.). (J). 1995. pap. text 1.00 (*0-486-28541-3*) Dover.
— The Tale of Peter Rabbit Sticker Storybook. (Illus.). 16p. (Orig.). (J). 1996. pap. text 1.00 (*0-486-29087-5*) Dover.
— The Tale of Squirrel Nutkin. (Illus.). 32p. (J). 1996. pap. 1.00 (*0-486-29033-6*) Dover.
— The Tale of Tom Kitten: Full-Color Storybook. LC 95-4651. (Illus.). 32p. (J). 1996. reprint ed. pap. text 1.00 (*0-486-28853-6*) Dover.

***Potter, Beatrix & Publications International, Ltd. Editorial Staff.** The Tale of Peter Rabbit & Benjamin Bunny: From the Original & Authorized Stories. LC 99-179586. (Illus.). (J). 1998. write for info. (*0-7853-2689-8*) Pubns Intl Ltd.

Potter, Beatrix & Wynne, Patricia. The Tale of Jemima Puddle-Duck in Spanish Coloring Book. (Little Activity Bks.). (J). 1994. pap. 1.00 (*0-486-27914-6*) Dover.
— The Tales of Jemima Puddle-Duck in French Coloring Book. (Little Activity Bks.). (J). 1994. 1.00 (*0-486-27913-8*) Dover.

Potter, Beatrix, jt. auth. see Frederick, Warne.

Potter, Beatrix, jt. auth. see Stewart, Pat Ronson.

Potter, Ben, et al. Introduction to Formal Specification & Z. 300p. 1991. pap. 39.00 (*0-13-478561-4*) P-H.

Potter, Ben, et al. Introduction to Fromal Specification & Z. 2nd ed. LC 96-15929. 304p. 1996. pap. 43.00 (*0-13-242207-7*) P-H.

***Potter, Benjamin.** Just a Simple Carpenter: The Story of Joseph. unabridged ed. LC 99-97617. x, 81p. 2000. pap. 10.00 (*0-9677668-0-X*) Loom & Wheel Pub.

Potter, Benjamin. Something Special at Leonards Inn: A Tale of the First Christmas. 42p. 1999. pap. 7.00 (*0-7392-0147-6*, PO3086) Morris Pubng.

Potter, Betty, ed. see Grace, Kendra.

Potter, Betty M. Chocolate Mousse & Other Fabulous Chocolate Creations. 220p. (Orig.). 1986. spiral bd. 13.95 (*0-913703-11-7*) Strawberry Pt.
— The Just for Kids Cookbook. (Illus.). 180p. (Orig.). (J). (gr. 1-6). 1985. spiral bd. 13.95 (*0-913703-06-0*) Strawberry Pt.

Potter, Beverly. Beating Job Burnout: How to Transform Work Pressure into Productivity. 2nd rev. ed. (Illus.). 302p. 1994. pap. 12.95 (*0-914171-69-0*) Ronin Pub.
— From Conflict to Cooperation: How to Mediate a Dispute. (Illus.). 192p. 1996. 14.95 (*0-914171-79-8*) Ronin Pub.
— Healing Magic of Cannabis. Joy, Dan, ed. (Illus.). 184p. 1998. pap. text 14.95 (*1-57951-001-9*) Ronin Pub.
— High Performance Goal Setting: Using Intuition to Achieve Your Goals. (Illus.). 96p. 2000. pap. 9.95 (*1-57951-012-4*, Pub. by Ronin Pub) Publishers Group.

***Potter, Beverly.** The Way of the Ronin: Riding the Waters of Change. 3rd rev. ed. (Illus.). 240p. 2000. pap. 14.95 (*1-57951-013-2*, Pub. by Ronin Pub) Publishers Group.

Potter, Beverly A. Drug Testing at Work: A Guide for Employers. 3rd rev. ed. (Illus.). 218p. (Orig.). 1999. pap. 24.95 (*1-57951-007-8*) Ronin Pub.
— Finding a Path with a Heart: How to Go from Burnout to Bliss. (Illus.). 356p. (Orig.). 1994. pap. 14.95 (*0-914171-74-7*) Ronin Pub.
— Overcoming Job Burnout: How to Renew Enthusiasm for Work. 2nd ed. (Illus.). 224p. 1998. pap. 14.95 (*1-57951-000-0*) Ronin Pub.
— Preventing Job Burnout: Transforming Work Pressures into Productivity. rev. ed. Paris, Janis, ed. LC 95-78810. (Fifty-Minute Ser.). (Illus.). 104p. (Orig.). 1995. pap. 10.95 (*1-56052-357-3*) Crisp Pubns.
— Turning Around: Keys to Motivation & Productivity. (Illus.). 292p. 1989. pap. 9.95 (*0-914171-16-X*) Ronin Pub.
— Turning Around: Keys to Motivation & Productivity. 2nd ed. (Illus.). 267p. (C). 1985. reprint ed. 19.95 (*0-914171-00-3*) Ronin Pub.
— The Way of the Ronin: Riding the Waves of Change at Work. (Illus.). 272p. 1989. reprint ed. pap. 9.95 (*0-914171-26-7*) Ronin Pub.
— The Worrywart's Companion: Twenty-One Ways to Soothe Yourself & Worry Smart. LC 97-2363. 184p. (Orig.). 1997. pap. 11.95 (*1-885171-15-3*) Wldcat Canyon.

Potter, Beverly A. & Orfali, J. Sebastian. Brain Boosters: Foods & Drugs That Make You Smarter. 257p. 1993. pap. 16.95 (*0-914171-65-8*) Ronin Pub.

Potter, Beverly A. & Orfali, Sebastian J. Fountains of Youth: How to Live Longer & Healthier. LC 96-9336. (Illus.). 320p. (Orig.). 1996. pap. 14.95 (*0-914171-76-3*) Ronin Pub.

Potter, Beverly A., et al. Pass the Test: An Employee Guide to Drug Testing. (Illus.). 180p. 1999. pap. 16.95 (*1-57951-008-6*) Ronin Pub.

Potter, Beverly A., jt. auth. see Bewicke, Dhyana.

Potter, Bill. The Mahogany Ship Relic or Legend? 130p. 1987. pap. 30.00 (*0-949759-09-0*, Pub. by Deakin Univ) St Mut.

Potter, Bill, et al. Visual Basic 4.0 Ole, Databases, & Controls SuperBible, Bk. 2. (Illus.). 1000p. 1995. pap. 44.95 (*1-57169-007-7*) Sams.

Potter, Brian. Hear We Go Kids - Another New Day. (Illus.). 24p. (J). (ps-3). 1995. 19.95 incl. audio (*0-9645529-0-6*) Hear We Go.
— Hear We Go Kids - Fun Stuff Holiday. (Illus.). 24p. (J). (ps-3). 1995. 19.95 incl. audio (*0-9645529-1-4*) Hear We Go.

Potter, Bruce, et al. Water Island Study: Economic Development Options. 170p. 1980. 20.00 (*0-318-14620-7*) Isl Resources.

Potter, C. W. History of Manchester, NH, Formerly Derryfield, in New Hampshire, Including That of Ancient Amoskeag, or the Middle Merrimack Valley. (Illus.). 764p. 1995. reprint ed. lib. bdg. 77.50 (*0-8328-4473-X*) Higginson Bk Co.
— Potter: Genealogy of the Potter Families & Their Descendants in America. (Illus.). 300p. 1990. reprint ed. pap. 47.00 (*0-8328-1521-7*); reprint ed. lib. bdg. 55.00 (*0-8328-1520-9*) Higginson Bk Co.

***Potter, Carl.** Thriving Business: A Step-by-Step Plan to Gain More Clients. 68p. 2000. pap. 12.99 (*0-9700096-0-7*) Right-Attitude.

P

Potter, Carol. Before We Were Born. LC 89-20069. 72p. 1990. pap. 9.95 (*0-914086-90-1*) Alice James Bks.

— Upside down in the Dark. (Orig.). 1995. pap. 9.95 (*1-882295-05-6*) Alice James Bks.

Potter, Caroline. Henri Dutilleux: His Life & Works. LC 96-40411. 256p. 1997. text 65.95 (*1-85928-330-6*, Pub. by Scolar Pr) Ashgate Pub Co.

Potter, Charles. This Harmonica Is for "You", No. 1. Potter, Philana, ed. LC 96-105272. (Illus.). 52p. 1995. pap. 10.17 (*0-9646765-0-8*) Charles Publns.

Potter, Charles E. Genealogies of Some Old Families of Concord, Massachusetts & Their Descendants in Part to the Present Generation. (Illus.). 143p. (Orig.). 1995. pap. text 22.50 (*0-7884-0161-0*) Heritage Bk.

Potter, Charles F. The Lost Years of Jesus Revealed. 160p. 1985. mass mkt. 5.99 (*0-449-13039-8*, GM) Fawcett.

Potter, Charles H. Perennials in the Garden for Lasting Beauty. LC 59-6124. (Illus.). 1959. 34.95 (*0-87599-094-0*) S G Phillips.

Potter, Charles L., et al. Pennsylvania Tax Handbook. 464p. 1988. 17.50 (*0-13-655994-8*) P-H.

— Pennsylvania Tax Handbook, 1985. write for info. (*0-318-58212-0*) P-H.

— Pennsylvania Tax Handbook, 1989. 430p. 1988. 18.95 (*0-13-655648-5*, Busn) P-H.

***Potter, Cheryl.** Handpaint Country: A Knitter's Journey. (Illus.). 2000. 35.00 (*1-893762-03-5*) XRX Inc.

Potter, Claire B. War on Crime: Gangsters, G-Men, & the Politics of Mass Culture. LC 97-22311. (Illus.). 272p. 1998. 50.00 (*0-8135-2486-5*); pap. 20.00 (*0-8135-2487-3*) Rutgers U Pr.

Potter, Clarkson N. Who Does What & Why in Book Publishing: Writers, Editors & Money Men. 1990. 12.95 (*1-55972-056-5*, Birch Ln Pr) Carol Pub Group.

Potter, Clifton W., Jr., ed. see Aristotle, et al.

Potter, Clive. Against the Grain: Agri-Environmental Reform in the United States & the European Union. LC 97-33664. (A CAB International Publication). 208p. (C). 1998. pap. 65.00 (*0-85199-228-5*) OUP.

Potter, Cora V. My Recitations. LC 75-39380. (Granger Index Reprint Ser.). 1977. reprint ed. 20.95 (*0-8369-6347-4*) Ayer.

***Potter, Cynthia M., ed.** Big Canyon Country Guide to Hiking in WV. deluxe ed. (Illus.). 80p. 2001. pap. 16.95 (*0-9700165-1-4*) Twin Rivers NC.

— Big Canyon Country Guide to Natural Adventures in WV. deluxe ed. (Illus.). 80p. 2001. pap. 16.95 (*0-9700165-5-7*) Twin Rivers NC.

— The Photography & Poetry of Cynlos. (Illus.). 80p. Date not set. 16.95 (*0-9700165-9-X*) Twin Rivers NC.

Potter, D., et al, eds. Industrial & Engineering Applications of Artificial Intelligence & Expert Systems. 512p. 1997. pap. text 120.00 (*90-5699-615-0*) Gordon & Breach.

Potter, D. S. & Mattingly, D. J., eds. Life, Death, & Entertainment in the Roman Empire. LC 98-40201. (Illus.). 368p. 1999. text 49.50 (*0-472-10924-3*, 10924); pap. text 18.95 (*0-472-08568-9*, 08568) U of Mich Pr.

Potter, Daniel A. Destructive Turfgrass Insects: Biology, Diagnosis, & Control. LC 97-22727. 345p. 1997. 65.00 (*1-57504-023-9*, Ann Arbor Press) Sleepng Bear.

Potter, Darwin. Frommer's England '97. 1996. 19.95 (*0-02-861132-2*) Macmillan.

— Frommer's France '97. 1996. 19.95 (*0-02-861142-X*) Macmillan.

Potter, David. A History of France, 1460-1560: The Emergence of a Nation-State. LC 94-32239. (New Studies in Medieval History). 438p. 1995. pap. 19.95 (*0-312-12480-5*); text 55.00 (*0-312-12479-1*) St Martin.

— Japan's Foreign Aid to Thailand & the Philippines. 240p. 1996. text 49.95 (*0-312-12563-1*) St Martin.

— Our Boys Have Won the Cup. 184p. 1996. pap. 59.00 (*0-85976-454-0*, Pub. by J Donald) St Mut.

— Prophets & Emperors: Human & Divine Authority from Augustus to Theodosius. LC 94-25982. (Revealing Antiquity Ser.: 7). (Illus.). 344p. 1994. text 50.95 (*0-674-71565-9*, POTPRO) HUP.

Potter, David, ed. NGOs & Environmental Policies: Asia & Africa. LC 95-26760. 352p. (Orig.). (C). 1996. pap. 22.50 (*0-7146-4215-0*, Pub. by F Cass Pubs) Intl Spec Bk.

Potter, David, et al, eds. Democratization. (Democracy Ser.). 1997. text 59.95 (*0-7456-1814-6*, Pub. by Polity Pr) Blackwell Pubs.

— Democratization. (Democracy Ser.). 1997. pap. text 31.95 (*0-7456-1815-4*, Pub. by Polity Pr) Blackwell Pubs.

Potter, David, tr. French Wars of Religion: Selected Documents. LC 97-9174. 288p. 1998. text 45.00 (*0-312-17545-0*) St Martin.

Potter, David & Thomas, Gordon L., eds. Colonial Idiom. LC 71-83669. (Landmarks in Rhetoric & Public Address Ser.). 653p. 1970. pap. 7.00 (*0-8093-9100-7*) S Ill U Pr.

Potter, David, tr. see De Ley, Gerd, ed.

Potter, David C. India's Political Administrators, 1919-1983. (Illus.). 304p. 1987. text 65.00 (*0-19-821574-6*) OUP.

— India's Political Administrators 1919-1983: From ICS to IAS. rev. ed. LC 96-220983. 320p. 1996. pap. 14.95 (*0-19-563692-9*) OUP.

Potter, David E. Computational Physics. LC 72-8613. (Wiley-Interscience Publications). 316p. reprint ed. pap. 98.00 (*0-608-12454-0*, 202520300042) Bks Demand.

Potter, David E., jt. auth. see Lamberts, David W.

Potter, David F. Maya Architecture of the Central Yucatan Peninsula, Mexico. (Publications: No. 44). (Illus.). xi, 118p. 1977. 20.00 (*0-939238-49-7*) Tulane MARI.

Potter, David M. Freedom & Its Limitations in American Life. Fehrenbacher, Don E., ed. LC 76-17786. xiv, 90p. 1976. pap. 10.95 (*0-8047-1009-0*) Stanford U Pr.

— Impending Crisis. (New American Nation Ser.). 672p. 1977. reprint ed. pap. 17.00 (*0-06-131929-5*, TB1929, Torch) HarpC.

— Lincoln & His Party in the Secession Crisis. LC 95-23562. 440p. (C). 1995. pap. 19.95 (*0-8071-2027-8*) La State U Pr.

— People of Plenty: Economic Abundance & the American Character. LC 54-12797. 229p. 1958. pap. text 11.95 (*0-226-67633-1*) U Ch Pr.

— Select Problems in Historical Interpretation, 2 vols., Set. (History - United States Ser.). 1993. reprint ed. lib. bdg. 150.00 (*0-7812-4840-X*) Rprt Serv.

— The South & the Sectional Conflict. LC 68-8941. 335p. 1968. pap. 103.90 (*0-7837-8531-3*, 204934000011) Bks Demand.

Potter, David M., ed. see De Forest, John W.

Potter, David S. Literary Texts & the Roman Historian. LC 98-8690. (Approaching the Ancient World Ser.). 265p. (C). 1999. pap. 20.99 (*0-415-08896-8*) Routledge.

— Literary Texts & the Roman Historian. LC 98-8690. (Approaching the Ancient World Ser.). (Illus.). 256p. (C). 1999. 60.00 (*0-415-08895-X*) Routledge.

Potter, Deborah. Passage Through Mourning. 29p. (Orig.). 1996. pap. 5.95 (*1-888289-24-4*) Mythspinner.

— The Wind Spinners. 31p. (Orig.). 1996. pap. 5.95 (*1-888289-18-X*) Mythspinner.

— Windfall. 31p. (Orig.). 1996. pap. 5.95 (*1-888289-15-5*) Mythspinner.

— Winds of Dawn. LC 96-94134. (Maran Chronicles Ser.: Bk. 1). 376p. (Orig.). 1996. pap. 12.95 (*1-888289-09-0*, 289090) Mythspinner.

Potter, Den E. Up Your Sales Without a Lot of Reading. xii, 110p. 1997. pap. 14.95 (*0-9657996-0-3*) D Potter.

Potter, Dennis. Karaoke & Cold Lazarus. 288p. (Orig.). 1996. pap. 16.95 (*0-571-17478-7*) Faber & Faber.

***Potter, Diane L. & Brockmeyer, Gretchen A.** Softball: Steps to Success. 2nd ed. LC 99-17942. (Illus.). 184p. 1999. pap. 15.95 (*0-87322-794-8*) Human Kinetics.

Potter, Douglas A. Design & Construction of Compilers. LC 92-288. 562p. 1992. pap. 90.00 (*0-471-55939-3*) Wiley.

Potter, Doyle. Cosmos Kids: Visit Earth Children with a Message for World Peace. large type ed. (Illus.). 60p. (J). (gr. k-6). 1984. spiral bd. 10.95 (*0-938911-15-5*) Indiv Ed - Poppy Ln.

Potter, E. B. Bull Halsey: A Biography. LC 85-15419. (Illus.). 421p. 1985. 39.95 (*0-87021-146-3*) Naval Inst Pr.

— Nimitz. LC 76-1056. (Illus.). 507p. 1976. 36.95 (*0-87021-492-6*) Naval Inst Pr.

Potter, E. B., ed. Sea Power: A Naval History. 2nd rev. ed. LC 81-81668. (Illus.). 419p. 1981. text 35.00 (*0-87021-607-4*) Naval Inst Pr.

Potter, Ed, ed. see Deavers, Ken, et al.

Potter, Edgar F. Cowboy Slang. LC 85-24930. (Illus.). 128p. (Orig.). 1986. pap. 5.95 (*0-914846-23-X*) Golden West Pub.

Potter, Edgar R. Whoa . . . Yuh Sonsabitches. (Illus.). 1977. pap. 6.95 (*0-918292-00-X*) Griggs Print.

Potter, Edith L. & Craig, John M. Pathology of the Fetus & the Infant. LC 75-16021. 711p. reprint ed. pap. 200.00 (*0-608-16240-X*, 202650500049) Bks Demand.

Potter, Edith L. & Gilbert-Barness, Enid. Potter's Atlas of Fetal & Infant Pathology. LC 98-23495. 398p. 1998. text. write for info. (*0-323-00126-2*) Mosby Inc.

Potter, Edward, et al. American Workplace Report, 1998. (Illus.). 71p. 1998. pap. 20.00 (*0-916559-24-6*, Z076) EPF.

Potter, Edward E. Quality at Risk: Are Employee Participation Programs in Jeopardy? 72p. 1991. pap. 10.00 (*0-614-06154-7*, 2034-PP-4040) EPF.

Potter, Edward E., ed. Employee Selection: Legal & Practical Alternatives to Compliance & Litigation. 2nd ed. LC 86-60481. (Monograph Ser.). 330p. 1986. pap. 19.75 (*0-916559-03-3*) EPF.

Potter, Edward E. & McGuiness, Kenneth C. Freedom of Association, the Right to Organize & Collective Bargaining: The Impact on U. S. Law & Practice of ILO Conventions No. 87 & No. 98. LC 84-80187. 118p. (Orig.). (C). 1984. pap. 15.00 (*0-916603-00-8*) Labor Pol.

Potter, Edward E. & Reesman, Ann E. The Americans with Disabilities Act: Testing & Other Employee Selection Procedures. 29p. 1990. pap. 10.00 (*0-614-06165-2*, 2023C-PP-4040) EPF.

— An Assessment of Remedies: The Impact of Compensatory & Punitive Damages on Title Vi. 110p. 1990. pap. 10.00 (*0-614-06160-1*, 2019-PP-4040) EPF.

— Compensatory & Punitive Damages under Title VII - a Foreign Perspective. 2nd ed. 11p. 1992. pap. 5.00 (*0-614-06149-0*) EPF.

— Employment Tests Are Not Medical Examinations. 17p. 1992. pap. 8.00 (*0-614-06151-2*, 2042-PP-4040) EPF.

Potter, Edward E. & Youngman, Judith A. Keeping America Competitive: Employment Policy for the Twenty-First Century. LC 94-77235. (Illus.). 434p. 1995. 27.95 (*0-944435-28-9*) Glenbridge Pub.

Potter, Edwin. Babylonian Caduceus: Or, the Magical Rod of the Mysteries; Messenger of the Gods, Fertility & Peace. Abel, R. Christopher, ed. (Orig.). 1997. pap. 5.95 (*1-55818-376-0*) Holmes Pub.

Potter-Efron, Patrica, jt. auth. see Potter-Efron, Ronald.

Potter-Efron, Patricia, jt. auth. see Potter-Efron, Ronald.

Potter-Efron, Patricia S., ed. The Treatment of Shame & Guilt in Alcoholism Counseling. LC 87-29724. (Alcoholism Treatment Quarterly Ser.: Vol. 4, No. 2). (Illus.). 218p. 1989. pap. 17.95 (*0-86656-941-3*); text 39.95 (*0-86656-718-6*) Haworth Pr.

Potter-Efron, Patricia S., jt. auth. see Potter-Efron, Ronald T.

Potter-Efron, Patricia S., jt. ed. see Potter-Efron, Ronald T.

Potter-Efron, Ron. Angry All the Time. 1996. 6.98 (*1-56731-096-6*, MJF Bks) Fine Comms.

— Angry All the Time: An Emergency Guide to Anger Control. LC 94-67046. 144p. 1994. pap. 12.95 (*1-879237-97-0*) New Harbinger.

— How to Control Your Anger (Before It Controls You) A Guide for Teens. LC 98-3184. (Illus.). 36p. (YA). (gr. 6-12). 1998. pap. 4.50 (*1-56246-179-6*, 3094, HazeldenJohnson Inst) Hazelden.

Potter-Efron, Ronald & Potter-Efron, Patrica. Letting Go of Shame: Understanding How Shame Affects Your Life. 192p. (Orig.). pap. 12.00 (*0-89486-635-4*) Hazelden.

Potter-Efron, Ronald & Potter-Efron, Patricia. Verguenza.Tr. of Letting Go of Shame. (SPA.). 192p. pap. 14.00 (*968-39-0890-X*, Pub. by Edit Patria) Hazelden.

Potter-Efron, Ronald T. Being, Belonging, Doing: Balancing Your Three Greatest Needs. LC 97-75472. 144p. 1998. pap. 10.95 (*1-57224-103-9*) New Harbinger.

— Shame, Guilt & Alcoholism: Treatment Issues in Clinical Practice. LC 88-32058. (Addiction Treatment Ser.: Vol. 2). 287p. 1988. pap. text 24.95 (*0-86656-856-5*, Harrington Park) Haworth Pr.

— Shame, Guilt & Alcoholism: Treatment Issues in Clinical Practice. LC 87-29724. (Addiction Treatment Ser.: Vol. 2). 287p. 1989. text 8.95 (*0-86656-855-7*) Haworth Pr.

— Working Anger: Preventing & Resolving Conflict on the Job. LC 98-66700. 176p. 1998. pap. 12.95 (*1-57224-119-5*) New Harbinger.

Potter-Efron, Ronald T. & Potter-Efron, Patricia S. Anger, Alcoholism & Addiction: Treating Anger in a Chemical Dependency Setting. 304p. 1992. 32.95 (*0-393-70126-3*) Norton.

— Letting Go of Anger: The Ten Most Common Anger Styles & What to Do about Them. LC 94-73923. 168p. 1995. pap. 12.95 (*1-57224-001-6*) New Harbinger.

***Potter-Efron, Ronald T. & Potter-Efron, Patricia S.** The Secret Message of Shame: Pathways to Hope & Healing. 168p. 1999. pap. 13.95 (*1-57224-170-5*) New Harbinger.

Potter-Efron, Ronald T. & Potter-Efron, Patricia S., eds. Aggression, Family Violence & Chemical Dependency. LC 89-24737. (Journal of Chemical Dependency Treatment: Vol. 3, No. 1). (Illus.). 226p. 1990. text 49.95 (*0-86656-964-2*); pap. text 17.95 (*0-86656-977-4*) Haworth Pr.

Potter, Elaine, ed. see Cyprys, Ruth A.

Potter, Eli, jt. auth. see Potter, James E.

Potter, Elisha R. Memoir Concerning the French Settlements & French Settlers in the Colony of Rhode Island. (Illus.). 138p. 1996. reprint ed. pap. 14.00 (*0-8063-0280-1*, 4690) Clearfield Co.

Potter, Elizabeth. A Hairdresser's Experience in High Life. (Schomburg Library of Nineteenth-Century Black Women Writers). (Illus.). 352p. 1991. text 42.00 (*0-19-506198-5*) OUP.

— A Hairdresser's Experience in High Life. Baxter, Annette K., ed. LC 79-8805. (Signal Lives Ser.). 1980. reprint ed. lib. bdg. 33.95 (*0-405-12851-7*) Ayer.

Potter, Elizabeth, jt. ed. see Alcoff, Linda.

Potter, Elizabeth, tr. see Cipolla, Carlo M.

Potter, Eloise F. & Funderburg, John B. Native Americans: The People & How They Lived. LC 86-61434. (Illus.). 80p. (gr. 4-12). 1986. 5.00 (*0-917134-09-5*); lib. bdg. 14.95 (*0-917134-10-9*) NC Natl Sci.

Potter, Eloise F., et al. Birds of the Carolinas. LC 79-14201. (Illus.). viii, 408p. 1986. reprint ed. pap. 18.95 (*0-8078-4155-2*) U of NC Pr.

Potter, Eloise F., jt. auth. see Taylor, Tom.

Potter, Eloise F., ed. see Ross, Steve W., et al.

Potter, Eloise F., ed. see Simpson, Marcus B., Jr.

Potter, Eugenia C., ed. NASSP Bulletin: 1990-1994 Author & Subject Index. 64p. (Orig.). (C). 1996. pap. text 7.00 (*0-88210-307-5*) Natl Assn Principals.

Potter, Eugenia C., ed. see Comras, Jay & Zerowin, Jeffrey.

Potter, Eugenia K., ed. Kentucky Women. (Illus.). 232p. 1997. 29.95 (*0-9659858-0-6*) big tree pr.

Potter, Frank & Peck, Charles. Dynamic Models in Physics: A Workbook of Computer Simulations Using Electronic Spreadsheets. Barkley, David S., ed. & illus. by. 400p. (C). 1989. pap. text 19.95 (*0-9622556-1-0*) Simonson & Co.

— Dynamic Models in Physics, Vol. I Mechanics (Templates) Microsoft Excel Templates for MacIntosh Computers. Barkley, David S., ed. (Illus.). 6p. 1990. 28.95 incl. disk (*0-9622556-5-3*) Simonson & Co.

***Potter, Frank J.** Sample Design, Sampling Weights, Imputation & Variance Estimation in the 1995 National Survey of Family Growth. 71p. 1998. pap. 6.00 (*0-16-049505-9*) USGPO.

Potter, G. Printed Bygones. 88p. 1986. pap. 25.00 (*0-7212-0742-1*, Pub. by Regency Pr GBR) St Mut.

Potter, G. A., jt. auth. see Palmer, I. C.

Potter, G. W. Analysis of Biological Molecules: An Introduction to Principles, Instrumentation & Techniques. (C). 1994. pap. text 47.95 (*0-412-49050-1*, Chap & Hall NY) Chapman & Hall.

— Lessons from a Secret War. LC 97-90286. 224p. 1997. pap. 12.95 (*0-533-12355-0*) Vantage.

Potter, Gabriel. Gauguin. 1993. 5.98 (*1-55521-825-3*) Bk Sales Inc.

— Munch. 1994. 5.98 (*0-7858-0206-1*) Bk Sales Inc.

— Picasso. 1992. 5.98 (*1-55521-764-8*) Bk Sales Inc.

***Potter, Garry.** The Bet: Truth in Science, Literature & Everyday Knowledges. LC 99-72334. (Avebury Series in Philosophy). 242p. 1999. 69.95 (*1-84014-985-X*, Pub. by Ashgate Pub) Ashgate Pub Co.

— The Philosophy of Social Science: New Perspectives LC 99-30483. 1999. write for info. (*0-582-36974-6*) Addison-Wesley.

Potter, Gary W. After the Boston Heresy Case. LC 93-79287. 229p. 1995. pap. 9.95 (*0-9620994-6-5*) Cath Treas.

— Criminal Organizations: Vice, Racketeering, & Politics in an American City. LC 94-186186. (Illus.). 213p. (C). 1993. pap. text 15.95 (*0-88133-770-6*) Waveland Pr.

Potter, Gary W. & Kappeler, Victor E. Constructing Crime: Perspectives on Making News & Social Problems. (Illus.). 357p. (C). 1998. pap. text 18.95 (*0-88133-984-9*) Waveland Pr.

Potter, Gary W., jt. auth. see Lyman, Michael D.

Potter, Gavin, jt. auth. see Czerniawska, Fiona.

Potter, Geoff. The Publisher's Guide to Binding & Finishing. (Illus.). 192p. 1991. 41.95 (*0-948905-18-2*) Chapman & Hall.

Potter, George. To the Golden Door. LC 73-3928. (Illus.). 631p. 1973. reprint ed. lib. bdg. 35.00 (*0-8371-6862-7*, POGD, Greenwood Pr) Greenwood.

Potter, George A. Dialogue on Debt: Alternative Analyses & Solutions. 160p. (Orig.). (C). 1988. pap. text 7.95 (*0-934255-06-7*) Center Concern.

Potter, Gillian, tr. see El-Gamasy, M., et al.

Potter, Giselle. Lucy's Eyes & Margaret's Dragon: The Lives of the Virgin Saints. LC 97-854. (J). (gr. 4 up). 1997. 17.95 (*0-8118-1515-3*) Chronicle Bks.

Potter, Harold. Quest of Justice. (Legal Reprint Ser.). ix, 88p. 1986. reprint ed. 25.00 (*0-421-35510-7*) W S Hein.

Potter, Harold W., Jr. & Troy, Paul E., eds. A Practical Guide to Introducing Evidence. 1998. ring bd., suppl. ed. 95.00 (*1-57589-096-8*, 98-05.55-SP) Mass CLE.

Potter, Harold W., Jr., et al. A Practical Guide to Introducing Evidence. rev. ed. LC 93-86126. 508p. 1993. ring bd. 95.00 (*0-944490-55-7*) Mass CLE.

— A Practical Guide to Introducing Evidence, 1996 Supplement. LC 93-86126. 368p. 1996. ring bd., suppl. ed. 95.00 (*1-57589-037-2*, 96-05.59-SP) Mass CLE.

***Potter, Harry.** Harry Potter Strategy Guide. (Illus.). 2000. pap. 12.95 (*0-7869-1920-5*) Wizards Coast.

Potter, Harry R., jt. ed. see Perrucci, Robert.

Potter, Henry C. The Scholar & the State: And Other Orations & Addresses. LC 72-4509. (Essay Index Reprint Ser.). 1977. reprint ed. 23.95 (*0-8369-2969-1*) Ayer.

Potter, Hugh. Pornography: Group Pressures & Individual Rights. 180p. 1996. pap. 34.00 (*1-86287-215-5*, Pub. by Federation Pr) Gaunt.

Potter, I. G., jt. ed. see Hardisty, M. W.

Potter, I. N. Carbon Dioxide Controlled Ventilation System. (C). 1994. pap. 50.00 (*0-86022-376-0*, Pub. by Build Servs Info Assn) St Mut.

— The Sick Building Syndrome. (C). 1988. pap. 60.00 (*0-86022-212-8*, Pub. by Build Servs Info Assn) St Mut.

— Ventilation Effectiveness in Mechanical Ventilation of Dwellings. (C). 1988. pap. 25.00 (*0-86022-189-X*, Pub. by Build Servs Info Assn) St Mut.

Potter, I. N., jt. auth. see Booth, W. B.

Potter, I. N., ed. see BSRIA Staff.

Potter, Israel R. The Life & Remarkable Adventures of Israel R. Potter. 1987. 15.50 (*0-8446-2752-6*) Peter Smith.

Potter, J. H. SI-Ten Asme Steam Charts, SI Metric & U. S. Customary Units. 128p. 1976. pap. text 25.00 (*0-685-62575-3*, E00090) ASME.

Potter, J. H., ed. Steam Charts: S1-10. 128p. 1976. 25.00 (*0-317-33617-7*, E00090) ASME.

Potter, J. K. Neurotica: The Darkest Art of J. K. Potter. LC 96-18136. (Illus.). 128p. 1996. pap. 27.95 (*0-87951-687-9*, Pub. by Overlook Pr) Penguin Putnam.

Potter, J. L. Associative Computing: A Programming Paradigm for Massively Parallel Computers. (Frontiers of Computer Science Ser.). (Illus.). 304p. (C). 1991. 79.50 (*0-306-43987-5*, Plenum Trade) Perseus Pubng.

Potter, J. L., ed. The Massively Parallel Processor. (Scientific Computation Ser.). (Illus.). 320p. 1985. 37.50 (*0-262-16100-1*) MIT Pr.

Potter, J. M., jt. ed. see Abelkis, P. R.

Potter, J. N. CO2 Controlled Ventilation Systems. 1994. 125.00 (*0-86033-376-0*, Pub. by Build Servs Info Assn) St Mut.

Potter, J. R., jt. auth. see Buckingham, M. J.

Potter, J. T. Secrets of Solar Biology or How to Succeed (1910) 50p. 1998. reprint ed. pap. 7.95 (*0-7661-0624-1*) Kessinger Pub.

Potter, Jack M. Thai Peasant Social Structure. 1992. lib. bdg. 22.00 (*0-226-67635-8*) U Ch Pr.

Potter, Jack M., jt. auth. see Potter, Sulamith H.

***Potter, Jacob.** Reluctant Hero. 224p. 2000. pap. 13.95 (*1-58597-013-1*) Leathers Pub.

Potter, James E. dBASE III, III Plus & IV. Garrotto, Alfred J., ed. (FasTrak Jr. Ser.). 110p. 1993. spiral bd. 18.50 (*0-9632069-4-X*) Bridge Lrn Systs.

— Jump Start Jr. MS-DOS. (Jump Start Jr. Ser.). 50p. 1996. pap. 15.95 (*1-885587-57-0*) Bridge Lrn Systs.

— Lotus 1-2-3 (for DOS) Garrotto, Alfred J., ed. (FasTrak Jr. Ser.). 52p. 1993. spiral bd. 9.00 (*0-9632069-6-6*) Bridge Lrn Systs.

***Potter, James E.** Programming 101: A Basic Introduction to Computer Programming. 140p. (C). 1999. spiral bd. 26.95 (*1-885587-66-X*) Bridge Lrn Systs.

Potter, James E. Quattro Pro. Garrotto, Alfred J., ed. (FasTrak Jr. Ser.). 21p. 1993. spiral bd. 6.00 (*0-9632069-7-4*) Bridge Lrn Systs.

***Potter, James E.** UNIX Survival Guide + 170p. 1999. spiral bd. 26.95 (*1-885587-65-1*) Bridge Lrn Systs.

Potter, James E. VM/CMS: A Survival Guide. (C). 1993. pap. text 54.95 (*0-9632069-2-3*) Bridge Lrn Systs.

***Potter, James E. & Garrotto, Alfred J.** Bridging the Internet Gap. 8th ed. 130p. 1998. 17.50 (*1-885587-62-7*) Bridge Lrn Systs.

Potter, James E. & Potter, Eli. Jump Start Jr. Power Point. (Illus.). (C). 1997. spiral bd. 16.95 (*1-885587-53-8*) Bridge Lrn Systs.

An Asterisk (*) at the beginning of an entry indicates that the title is appearing for the first time.

Potter, James E. & Potter, Jamie. Jump Start Jr. Access. (Illus.). 70p. (C). 1997. spiral bd. 16.95 (*1-885587-59-7*) Bridge Lrn Systs.

***Potter, James E. & Puschendorf, L. Robert, eds.** Spans in Time: A History of Nebraska Bridges. LC 99-93181. (Illus.). 106p. 1999. 21.95 (*0-933307-27-6*) Nebraska Hist.

Potter, James E., et al. JumpStart. 7th ed. (Illus.). 180p. (C). 1999. spiral bd. 25.95 (*1-885587-63-5*) Bridge Lrn Systs.

Potter, James L. Robert Frost Handbook. LC 79-9145. 1980. text 30.00 (*0-271-00230-1*) Pa St U Pr.

Potter, James M. Middle Paleolithic Assemblage & Settlement Variability in West-Central Jordan. (Anthropological Research Papers: No. 45). (Illus.). v, 57p. 1993. pap. 10.00 (*0-936249-08-0*) AZ Univ ARP.

Potter, Jamie & Powers, Janet. The Happy Garden. (Illus.). 52p. (Orig.). (J). (ps-4). 1985. pap. 5.95 (*0-936511-00-1*) Gopher.

Potter, Jamie, jt. auth. see Potter, James E.

Potter, Jan. Wildflowers in Candlewicking. (Illus.). 56p. 1996. pap. 14.95 (*1-86351-174-1*, Pub. by Sally Milner) Sterling.

Potter, Janet, ed. see Campbell, Carol O. & Campbell, Griffin O.

Potter, Janet, ed. see Glazov, Sheila N.

Potter, Janet, ed. see Schultz, Karen.

Potter, Janet G. Great American Railroad Stations. LC 95-51432. 270p. 1996. pap. 29.95 (*0-471-14389-8*) Wiley.

Potter, Janice. The Liberty We Seek: Loyalist Ideology in Colonial New York & Massachusetts. 256p. 1983. 41.00 (*0-674-53026-8*) HUP.

Potter, Jay H. Coyote Bait. large type ed. (Linford Western Library). 256p. 1995. pap. 16.99 (*0-7089-7770-7*, Linford) Ulverscroft.

— Murder Trail. large type ed. (Linford Western Library). 256p. 1996. pap. 16.99 (*0-7089-7882-7*, Linford) Ulverscroft.

— Sodal Valley Shoot-Out. large type ed. (Linford Western Library Ser.). 240p. 1997. pap. 16.99 (*0-7089-5151-1*) Ulverscroft.

Potter, Jean. The Flying North. (Illus.). 240p. 1977. pap. 6.95 (*0-89174-018-X*) Comstock Edns.

— Nature in a Nutshell for Kids: Over 100 Activities You Can do in Ten Minutes or Less. (Illus.). 144p. (J). (gr. 4). 1995. pap. 12.95 (*0-471-04444-X*) Wiley.

— Science in a Nutshell for Kids: Over 100 Activities You Can Do in Ten Minutes or Less. 144p. (J). 1995. pap. 12.95 (*0-471-04456-3*) Wiley.

— Science in Seconds at the Beach: Exciting Experiments You Can Do in Ten Minutes or Less. LC 97-39799. 122p. (J). 1998. pap. 12.95 (*0-471-17899-3*) Wiley.

— Science in Seconds with Toys: Over 100 Experiments You Can Do in Ten Minutes or Less. LC 97-20000. 128p. (J). (gr. 2-5). 1998. pap. 12.95 (*0-471-17900-0*) Wiley.

Potter, Jean, jt. auth. see Kohl, MaryAnn F.

Potter, Jeffrey. To a Violent Grave: An Oral Biography of Jackson Pollock. (Illus.). 1993. pap. 15.00 (*0-916366-47-2*, Pub. by Pushcart Pr) Norton.

***Potter, Jennifer.** Secret Gardens. (Illus.). 144p. 1998. 29.95 (*1-85029-962-5*, Pub. by Conran Octopus) Trafalgar.

Potter, Jeremy. The Dance of Death. LC 78-404341. 232p. 1968. write for info. (*0-09-456310-1*) Constable & Co.

— Headmaster: The Life of John Percival, Radical Autocrat. (Illus.). 320p. 1998. 40.00 (*0-09-478200-8*, Pub. by Constable & Co) Trafalgar.

Potter, Jerold. The Bible Study Organizer & Notebook. 108p. 1989. 4.97 (*1-55748-460-0*) Barbour Pub.

Potter, Jerold. Books of the Bible. (Little Library Ser.). 48p. 1994. pap. 0.99 (*1-55748-521-6*) Barbour Pub.

— How to Conquer Anger. (Little Library Ser.). 48p. 1996. pap. text 0.99 (*1-55748-888-6*) Barbour Pub.

— How to Conquer Fear. (Little Library Ser.). 48p. 1996. pap. text 0.99 (*1-55748-887-8*) Barbour Pub.

— How to Conquer Unforgiveness. (Little Library Ser.). 48p. 1996. pap. text 0.99 (*1-55748-889-4*) Barbour Pub.

— How to Conquer Worry. (Little Library Ser.). 48p. 1996. pap. text 0.99 (*1-55748-890-8*) Barbour Pub.

— My Bible Study Notebook. 108p. (YA). 1992. spiral bd. 3.97 (*1-55748-280-2*) Barbour Pub.

— My Bible Study Notebook. 1994. pap. text 2.49 (*1-55748-480-5*) Barbour Pub.

Potter, Jerold C. Books of the Bible. Bowen & Bowen Type Setters Staff, ed. 36p. (J). 1988. pap. text 1.50 (*0-925306-00-2*) WOFPPM.

Potter, Jerry. Fatal Justice: The Reinvestigation of the MacDonald Murders. LC 97-197157. 480p. 1997. pap. 14.00 (*0-393-31544-4*) Norton.

Potter, Jerry O. The Sultana Tragedy: America's Greatest Maritime Disaster. LC 91-29521. (Illus.). 312p. 1992. 24.95 (*0-88289-861-2*) Pelican.

Potter, Joan & Claytor, Constance. African-American Firsts: Famous, Little-Known & Unsung Triumphs of Blacks in America. LC 93-84716. (Illus.). 352p. (YA). 1994. pap. 14.95 (*0-9632476-1-1*) Pinto Pr.

Potter, Joan, jt. auth. see Claytor, Constance.

Potter, Joan, jt. auth. see Cross, David.

Potter, Joan, ed. see Cantin, Sadie, et al.

Potter, John. Archaeologica Graeca: Or, the Antiquities of Greece, 2 vols. LC 78-60893. (Myth & Romanticism Ser.: Vol. 19). (Illus.). 948p. 1979. text 15.00 (*0-8240-3568-2*) Garland.

— Vocal Authority: Singing Style & Ideology. LC 97-11031. (Illus.). 234p. (C). 1998. text 54.95 (*0-521-56356-9*) Cambridge U Pr.

***Potter, John, ed.** The Cambridge Companion to Singing. (Cambridge Companions to Music Ser.). (Illus.). 306p. (C). 2000. 57.95 (*0-521-62225-5*); pap. 21.95 (*0-521-62709-5*) Cambridge U Pr.

Potter, John & Warn-Varnas, Alex, eds. Ocean Variability & Acoustic Propagation: Proceedings of the Workshop Held in La Spezia, Italy, June 4-8, 1990. (C). 1991. lib. bdg. 238.00 (*0-7923-1079-9*) Kluwer Academic.

Potter, John, jt. auth. see Hooper, Alan.

Potter, John F. How to Improve Your Odds Against Cancer. 2nd rev. ed. LC 96-37089. (Illus.). 224p. (Orig.). 1998. pap. 14.95 (*0-8119-0851-8*) F Fell Pubs Inc.

***Potter, John K.** The Warehouse. LC 98-91081. 1999. pap. 12.95 (*0-533-13039-5*) Vantage.

Potter, John M. Plots Against Presidents. 2nd ed. 1969. 14.95 (*0-8392-1178-3*) Astor-Honor.

— Thirteen Desperate Days. 1964. 12.95 (*0-8392-1114-7*) Astor-Honor.

Potter, John M., ed. Fatigue in Mechanically Fastened Composite & Metallic Joints. LC 86-22288. (Special Technical Publication Ser.: No. 927). (Illus.). 288p. 1986. text 48.00 (*0-8031-0927-X*, STP927) ASTM.

Potter, John M. & Watanabe, Roy T., eds. Development of Fatigue Loading Spectra. LC 88-35065. (Special Technical Publication Ser.: No. STP 1006). (Illus.). 252p. 1989. text 54.00 (*0-8031-1185-1*, STP1006) ASTM.

Potter, John M., jt. ed. see McHenry, Harry I.

Potter, John S. Treasure Diver's Guide. (Illus.). 590p. 1988. pap. 19.95 (*0-912451-22-X*) Florida Classics.

Potter, Jon. Triple Date. 64p. 1996. pap. 5.00 (*0-87440-024-4*) Bakers Plays.

Potter, Jonathan. The Idea Man. Landes, William-Alan, ed. LC 96-38125. 55p. (Orig.). 1997. pap. 5.00 (*0-88734-370-8*) Players Pr.

— It's a Lousy Old World. unabridged ed. Landes, William-Alan, ed. LC 97-177. 11p. (Orig.). 1997. pap. 5.00 (*0-88734-372-4*) Players Pr.

— Julie. Landes, William-Alan, ed. LC 97-3603. (Orig.). 1997. pap. 5.00 (*0-88734-373-2*) Players Pr.

— Rehearsing with Rat. Landes, William-Alan, ed. LC 97-5553. 55p. 1997. pap. 5.00 (*0-88734-371-6*) Players Pr.

— Representing Reality: Discourse, Rhetoric & Social Construction. LC 96-67745. 264p. 1996. 45.00 (*0-8039-8410-3*); pap. 14.99 (*0-8039-8411-1*) Sage.

— Underwear. Landes, William-Alan, ed. LC 97-7003. 55p. (Orig.). 1997. pap. 5.00 (*0-88734-369-4*) Players Pr.

Potter, Jonathan & Wetherell, Margaret. Discourse & Social Psychology: Beyond Attitudes & Behavior. 216p. (C). 1987. text 39.95 (*0-8039-8055-8*); pap. text 14.99 (*0-8039-8056-6*) Sage.

Potter, Jonathan, jt. auth. see Edwards, Derek.

Potter, Jonathan, jt. auth. see Wetherell, Margaret.

Potter, Joy H. Five Frames for the Decameron: Communication & Social Systems in the Cornice. LC 81-47942. 241p. reprint ed. pap. 74.80 (*0-8357-3305-X*, 203952800013) Bks Demand.

***Potter, Julian & Potter, Mary.** Mary Potter: A Life of Painting. LC 98-71509. 128p. 1998. 26.95 (*1-84014-640-0*, Pub. by Ashgate Pub) Ashgate Pub Co.

Potter, K. R., ed. Gesta Stephani. 2nd ed. (Oxford Medieval Texts Ser.). (Illus.). 290p. 1976. text 62.00 (*0-19-822234-3*) OUP.

Potter, Karl H. Abhidharma Buddhism to 150 A. D. (Encyclopedia of Indian Philosophies). 1991. 0.00 (*0-691-07392-9*) Princeton U Pr.

Potter, Karl H. Encyclopaedia of Indian Philosophies, 7 vols. in 8. 1997. 2060.00 (*81-208-0307-8*, Pub. by Print Hse) St Mut.

***Potter, Karl H.** Encyclopedia of Indian Philosophies Vol. III: Buddhist Philosophy from 100 to 350 A.D. 827p. 1999. pap. 600.00 (*81-208-1553-X*, Pub. by Motilal Bnarsidass) St Mut.

Potter, Karl H. Presuppositions of India's Philosophies. (C). 1991. reprint ed. 24.00 (*81-208-0779-0*, Pub. by Motilal Bnarsidass) S Asia.

Potter, Karl H., ed. Encyclopedia of Indian Philosophies: Bibliography. 2nd rev. ed. (C). 1983. 72.00 (*0-8364-2193-0*, Pub. by Motilal Bnarsidass) S Asia.

Potter, Karl H. & Bhattacharyya, Sibajiban, eds. Encyclopedia of Indian Philosophies: Nyaya-Vaisesika from Gangesa to Raghunatha Siromani. (Indian Philosophical Analysis Ser.: Vol. VI). 633p. 1992. text 79.50 (*0-691-07384-8*, Pub. by Princeton U Pr) Cal Prin Full Svc.

***Potter, Keith.** Four Musical Minimalists: La Monte Young, Terry Riley, Steve Reich, Philip Glass. LC 99-11736. (Music in the Twentieth Century Ser.: Vol. 11). (Illus.). 275p. (C). 1999. 54.95 (*0-521-48250-X*) Cambridge U Pr.

***Potter, Keith R.** This & That: A Book of Opposites. LC 99-35297. (Doodlezoo Ser.). (Illus.). 26p. (J). (ps). 1999. bds. 6.95 (*0-8118-2179-X*) Chronicle Bks.

— Those That Float, Those That Don't. (Doodlezoo Ser.). (Illus.). (J). 1999. pap. 6.95 (*0-8118-2067-X*) Chronicle Bks.

Potter, Keith R. & Fulk, Ken. Cat Nap. LC 98-46590. (Doodlezoo Ser.). (Illus.). 48p. (J). (gr. 2-5). 1999. 12.95 (*0-8118-2069-6*) Chronicle Bks.

— Count Us In. LC 98-44737. (Doodlezoo Ser.). (Illus.). 26p. (J). 1999. 6.95 (*0-8118-2064-5*) Chronicle Bks.

— Seven Weeks on an Iceberg. LC 98-45305. (Doodlezoo Ser.). (Illus.). 48p. (J). (gr. 2-5). 1999. 12.95 (*0-8118-2068-8*) Chronicle Bks.

— Those That Float Those That Don't. LC 98-45304. (Doodlezoo Ser.). (Illus.). 26p. 1999. pap. 6.95 (*0-8118-2065-3*) Chronicle Bks.

***Potter, Keith R. & Leo, Jana.** Shake, Rattle & Roll: An Action-Packed Verb Book. LC 99-16585. (Doodlezoo Ser.). (Illus.). 26p. (J). 1999. bds. 6.95 (*0-8118-2178-1*) Chronicle Bks.

***Potter, Kenyon D.** An Educator's Guide to Finding Resources in the Public Domain. LC 99-70206. 57p. 1999. pap. 12.00 (*0-87367-815-X*) Phi Delta Kappa.

Potter, Kimberly, jt. auth. see Jacobs, James B.

Potter, L. J., ed. see Milton, John.

***Potter, Lawrence G.** The Persian Gulf in Transition. LC 97-77153. (Headline Ser.). 72p. 1998. 5.95 (*0-87124-179-X*) Foreign Policy.

Potter, Lawrence G., ed. see Sick, Gary G.

Potter, Lawrence G., jt. ed. see Sick, Gary G.

Potter, Lois. Preface Milton. 2nd ed. (Preface Bks.). 184p. (C). 1986. pap. text 30.94 (*0-582-35479-X*, 72231) Longman.

Potter, Lois, ed. Playing Robin Hood: The Legend As Performance in Five Centuries. LC 97-43695. (Illus.). 256p. 1998. 42.50 (*0-87413-663-6*) U Delaware Pr.

Potter, Lois, ed. see Shakespeare, William.

Potter, Lois, ed. see Shakespeare, William & Fletcher, John.

Potter, Lou, et al. Liberators: Fighting on Two Fronts in World War II. LC 92-18791. 1992. write for info. (*0-15-151283-3*) Harcourt.

Potter, Louis, Jr. The Art of Cello Playing. (Illus.). 236p. (Orig.). (C). 1980. pap. text 26.95 (*0-87487-071-2*) Summy-Birchard.

Potter, Louise & Cole, Jerryne. Wild Flowers: Along Mt. McKinley Park Road. LC 79-52424. (Illus.). (Orig.). 1979. pap. 5.95 (*0-9602792-0-2*) Camp Denali.

Potter, M., ed. C-Myc in B-Cell Neoplasia: 14th Workshop on Mechanics in B-Cell Neoplasia - The Workshop "Mechanisms in B-Cell Neoplasia" (Current Topics in Microbiology & Immunology Ser.: Vol. 224). (Illus.). xii, 291p. 1997. 119.00 (*3-540-62892-4*) Spr-Verlag.

Potter, M., et al, eds. Morphogenesis & Maturation of Retroviruses. (Current Topics in Microbiology & Immunology Ser.: Vol. 214). 360p. 1996. 159.00 (*3-540-60928-8*) Spr-Verlag.

Potter, M. & Melchers, F., eds. Mechanisms in B-Cell Neoplasia, 1994. (Currents Topics in Microbiology & Immunology Ser.: Vol. 194). 480p. 1994. 174.95 (*3-540-58447-1*) Spr-Verlag.

— Mechanisms in B-Cell Neoplasia, 1988. (Current Topics in Microbiology & Immunology Ser.: Vol. 141). (Illus.). 340p. 1988. 123.00 (*0-387-50212-2*) Spr-Verlag.

Potter, M. & Olsnes, S. Current Topics in Microbiology & Immunology Vol. 193: Transacting Functions of Human Retroviruses. (Illus.). 250p. 1995. 140.95 (*0-387-57901-X*) Spr-Verlag.

— Current Topics in Microbiology & Immunology Vol. 199: The Molecular Repertoire of Adenoviruses, Vol. I: Virion Structure & Infection. 336p. 1995. 145.00 (*3-540-58828-0*) Spr-Verlag.

— Current Topics in Microbiology & Immunology Vol. 199: The Molecular Repertoire of Adenoviruses, Vol. II: Molecular Biology of Virus-Cell Interacti. 320p. 1995. 141.95 (*3-540-58829-9*) Spr-Verlag.

— Current Topics in Microbiology & Immunology Vol. 199: The Molecular Repertoire of Adenoviruses, Vol. III: Biology & Pathogenesis. 350p. 1995. 152.95 (*3-540-58987-2*) Spr-Verlag.

Potter, M. & Rose, N., eds. Immunology of Silicones. 210. (Current Topics in Microbiology & Immunology Ser.: Vol. 210). 430p. 1996. 197.00 (*3-540-60272-0*) Spr-Verlag.

Potter, M., jt. ed. see Melchers, F.

Potter, M., jt. ed. see Obrams, G. I.

Potter-MacKinnon, Janice. While the Women Only Wept: Loyalist Refugee Women in Eastern Ontario. 216p. 1993. 65.00 (*0-7735-0962-3*, Pub. by McG-Queens Univ Pr) CUP Services.

— While the Women Only Wept: Loyalist Refugee Women in Eastern Ontario. 216p. 1995. pap. 22.95 (*0-7735-1317-5*, Pub. by McG-Queens Univ Pr) CUP Services.

Potter, Margaret H. Istar of Babylon: A Phantasy. Reginald, R. & Melville, Douglas, eds. LC 77-84263. (Lost Race & Adult Fantasy Ser.). 1978. reprint ed. lib. bdg. 44.95 (*0-405-11004-9*) Ayer.

Potter, Marle C., ed. GRE Time Saver: From the Professors Who Know It Best. 2nd ed. 492p. 1995. pap. 17.95 (*1-881018-09-1*) Grt Lks Pr.

Potter, Martha, et al. Exploratory Survey of the James Chase Hambleton Mound. (Illus.). 13p. 1967. pap. 1.75 (*0-318-00845-9*) Ohio Hist Soc.

Potter, Martha, jt. auth. see Baby, Raymond.

Potter, Mary. Devotion for the Dying: Mary's Call to Her Loving Children. LC 91-65351. 224p. 1994. reprint ed. pap. 9.00 (*0-89555-442-9*) TAN Bks Pubs.

Potter, Mary, jt. auth. see Potter, Julian.

Potter, Mary, ed. see Green, Robert K.

Potter, Melody M. & Milam, Erin E. Healthy Baby, Toxic World: Practical Things You Can Do to Protect Your Baby. LC 98-68754. 192p. 1999. pap. 15.95 (*1-57224-139-X*) New Harbinger.

Potter, Merle. FE/EIT Discipline Review: The Blue Book. 3rd ed. 1998. pap. text 35.95 (*1-881018-39-3*) Grt Lks Pr.

— Principles & Practice of Civil Engineering. 3rd ed. 1998. 69.95 (*1-881018-25-3*) Grt Lks Pr.

Potter, Merle, et al. Principles & Practice of Electrical Engineering: The Most Effective PE Exam Review. 500p. 1997. 69.95 (*1-881018-13-X*); teacher ed. 19.95 (*1-881018-71-7*) Grt Lks Pr.

Potter, Merle C. Engineering Thermodynamics. (C). 1995. pap. text 14.95 (*0-07-050708-2*) McGraw.

***Potter, Merle C.** Fe/EIT Discipline Review. 4th ed. 2000. pap. 29.95 (*1-881018-33-4*) Grt Lks Pr.

— Fe/EIT Quick Prep & Sample Problems with CD-ROM. 2000. pap. 29.95 incl. cd-rom (*1-881018-43-1*) Grt Lks Pr.

— Fe/EIT Review for Industrial & Chemical Engineering. 4th ed. 2000. pap. 29.95 (*1-881018-50-4*) Grt Lks Pr.

Potter, Merle C. Fundamentals of Engineering: Potter's Green Book. 9th ed. 628p. 1999. pap. 54.95 (*1-881018-19-9*) Grt Lks Pr.

***Potter, Merle C.** Fundamentals of Engineering Review. 10th ed. 2000. pap. 49.95 (*1-881018-44-X*) Grt Lks Pr.

Potter, Merle C. Mathematical Methods. 2nd ed. 1978. 69.95 (*1-881018-11-3*) Grt Lks Pr.

***Potter, Merle C.** Principles & Practice of Civil Engineering. 4th ed. 2000. 79.95 (*1-881018-47-4*) Grt Lks Pr.

Potter, Merle C. Principles & Practice of Mechanical Engineering: The Most Effective PE Exam Review. 3rd ed. 586p. 1999. 74.95 (*1-881018-42-3*) Grt Lks Pr.

— Schaum's Outline of Thermodynamics for Engineers. 1993. pap. text 13.95 (*0-07-050707-4*) McGraw.

— Solutions Manual - P&P of Mechanical Engineering: For Practice Problems in the ME/PE Review. 3rd ed. 130p. 1999. pap. 22.95 (*1-881018-35-0*) Grt Lks Pr.

***Potter, Merle C.** Solutions Manual Principles & Practice of Civil Engineering. 4th ed. 2000. pap. 19.95 (*1-881018-49-0*) Grt Lks Pr.

Potter, Merle C. & Somerton, Craig W. Engineering Thermodynamics, Set. LC 95-32826. (Schaum's Outline Ser.). 384p. (C). 1995. pap. 34.95 (*0-07-844278-8*) McGraw.

Potter, Merle C., et al. GRE Engineering Review: A Complete Review for the GRE Engineering Exam. (Illus.). 320p. 1993. 19.95 (*0-9614760-6-0*) Grt Lks Pr.

Potter, Merle C., jt. auth. see Goldberg, Jack L.

Potter, Meryl. Crazy Patchwork. (Lothian Craft Ser.). 1998. pap. text 16.95 (*0-85091-797-2*, Pub. by Lothian Pub) Seven Hills Bk.

***Potter, Michael.** Reason's Nearest Kin: Philosophies of Arithmetic from Kant to Carnap. 272p. 2000. text 45.00 (*0-19-825041-X*) OUP.

***Potter, Michael & Day, Kevin.** Lawsuits, Taxes & Asset Protection. 554p. 1999. pap. text 69.95 (*1-58275-004-1*, Pub. by Black Forest Pr) Epic Bk Promo.

Potter, Michael, jt. auth. see Azar, Henry A.

Potter, Michael C. Electronic Greyhounds: The Spruance-Class Destroyers. (Illus.). 289p. 1995. 55.00 (*1-55750-682-5*) Naval Inst Pr.

Potter, Michelle A. The Complete Saving Source Catalog: A Guide to Saving the Earth & Money. LC 96-92197. 224p. (Orig.). 1996. pap. 19.95 (*0-9652196-0-7*) Rima Wrld Pr.

Potter, Miles F. Oregon's Golden Years. LC 75-12292. 185p. 1976. pap. 14.95 (*0-87004-254-8*) Caxton.

— Oregon's Golden Years: Bonanza of the West. LC 75-12292. 194p. 1976. reprint ed. pap. 60.20 (*0-608-00727-7*, 206150200009) Bks Demand.

Potter, Murray A. Sohrab & Rustem, the Epic Theme of a Combat Between Father & Son: A Study of Its Genesis & Use in Literature & Popular Tradition. LC 75-144527. (Grimm Library: No. 14). reprint ed. 27.50 (*0-404-53557-7*) AMS Pr.

***Potter, N. I.** Air Tightness Specifications. 1998. pap. 40.00 (*0-86022-499-6*, Pub. by Build Servs Info Assn) St Mut.

Potter, N. I. & Jones, T. J. Ventilation Heat Loss in Factories & Warehouses. (C). 1992. pap. 130.00 (*0-86022-296-9*, Pub. by Build Servs Info Assn) St Mut.

Potter, Nancy. Legacies: Stories. LC 86-30851. (Illinois Short Fiction Ser.). 144p. 1987. 14.95 (*0-252-01428-6*) U of Ill Pr.

Potter, Neal & Christy, Francis T. Trends in Natural Resource Commodities: Statistics of Prices, Output, Consumption, Foreign Trade, & Employment in the United States, 1870-1957. Manning, Pauline, ed. LC 62-11711. 580p. reprint ed. pap. 179.80 (*0-608-12543-1*, 202380900034) Bks Demand.

Potter, Nelson & Timmons, Mark, eds. Morality & Universality. 348p. 1985. text 167.00 (*90-277-1909-8*, D Reidel) Kluwer Academic.

Potter, Norman N., jt. auth. see Hotchkiss, Joseph H.

Potter, Norris W. Punahou Story. LC 68-31288. (Illus.). 224p. 1969. 18.95 (*0-87015-176-2*) Pacific Bks.

Potter, O. E. & Nicklin, D. J., eds. Fluidization, No. VII. 1000p. 1992. write for info. (*0-939204-47-9*) Eng Found.

Potter, O. M. The Color of Rome, Historic, Personal & Local. 1977. lib. bdg. 59.95 (*0-8490-1645-2*) Gordon Pr.

Potter, P. E. & Pettijohn, F. J. Paleocurrents & Basin Analysis. 2nd ed. LC 76-30293. (Illus.). 1977. 138.95 (*0-387-07952-1*) Spr-Verlag.

Potter, P. E., et al. Sedimentology of Shale: Study Guide & Reference Source. (Illus.). 316p. 1984. pap. 72.00 (*0-387-90430-1*) Spr-Verlag.

Potter, Pamela M. Most German of the Arts: Musicology & Society from the Weimar Republic to the End of Hitler's Reich. LC 97-50585. 364p. 1998. 40.00 (*0-300-07228-7*) Yale U Pr.

Potter, Parker B., Jr. Public Archaeology in Annapolis: A Critical Approach to History in Maryland's "Ancient City" LC 93-20779. (Illus.). 288p. (C). 1994. pap. text 19.95 (*1-56098-410-4*) Smithsonian.

Potter, Parker B., jt. auth. see Leone, Mark P.

Potter, Pat & Wiseman, Vanessa. Improving Residential Practice: Promoting Choice in Homes for Elderly People. (C). 1989. 55.00 (*0-7855-3732-5*, Pub. by Natl Inst Soc Work); 52.00 (*0-7855-5884-5*, Pub. by Natl Inst Soc Work); 50.00 (*0-902789-55-4*, Pub. by Natl Inst Soc Work) St Mut.

Potter, Patricia. The Abduction. 1999. per. 5.99 (*0-373-83406-3*, 1-83406-8, Harlequin) Harlequin Bks.

***Potter, Patricia.** The Black Knave. 2000. mass mkt. 6.99 (*0-515-12864-3*, Jove) Berkley Pub.

Potter, Patricia. Chase the Wind: Chase the Thunder: Against the Wind, 2 vols. in 1. (By Request 2's Ser.). 2000. per. 4.99 (*0-373-21705-6*, 1-21705-8) Harlequin Bks.

P

An Asterisk (*) at the beginning of an entry indicates that the title is appearing for the first time.

— Defiant. 448p. 1995. mass mkt. 5.50 (0-553-56601-6, Fanfare) Bantam.
— Defiant. large type ed. LC 96-54646. 550p. 1997. 24.95 (0-7862-1047-8) Thorndike Pr.
— Diablo. large type ed. LC 96-43981. (Romance Ser.). 564p. 1996. lib. bdg. 24.95 (0-7862-0924-0) Thorndike Pr.
— Dragonfire. (Historical Ser.: No. 48). 1990. mass mkt. 3.25 (0-373-28648-1) Harlequin Bks.
— Fundamentals of Nursing: Critical Thinking Activities. 3rd ed. 80p. (C). (gr. 13). 1994. text, suppl. ed. 9.95 (0-8151-6403-3) Mosby Inc.
— The Heiress. 448p. 1996. mass mkt. 5.99 (0-553-57508-2, Fanfare) Bantam.
— Home for Christmas: Families Are Forever. (Intimate Moments Ser.: No. 897). 251p. 1998. per. 4.25 (0-373-07897-8, 1-07897-1) Silhouette.
— The Marshall & the Heiress. large type ed. LC 96-38771. 1997. 23.95 (0-7862-0925-9) Thorndike Pr.
— The Scotsman Wore Spurs. 448p. 1997. mass mkt. 5.99 (0-553-57506-6, Fanfare) Bantam.
— The Soldier & the Rebel: Between the Thunder; Miracle of the Heart. (By Request Ser.). 1999. per. 4.99 (0-373-83415-2, 1-83415-9, Harlequin) Harlequin Bks.
— Star Keeper. 400p. 1999. mass mkt. 5.99 (0-553-57881-2) Bantam.
— Starcatcher. 400p. 1997. mass mkt. 5.99 (0-553-57507-4) Bantam.
— Starfinder. 448p. 1998. mass mkt. 5.99 (0-553-57880-4) Bantam.
— Swamp Fire. LC 95-22357. 296p. 1995. per. 4.99 (1-55166-078-4, 1-66078-6, Mira Bks) Harlequin Bks.
— Wanted. large type ed. LC 95-5403. (Large Print Bks.). 1995. pap. 21.95 (1-56895-125-6) Wheeler Pub.

Potter, Patricia & Langan, Ruth. Ransomed Brides, 2 bks. in 1. (By Request Ser.). 1998. per. 5.99 (0-373-20150-8, 1-20150-8) Harlequin Bks.

Potter, Patricia A. Fundamentals of Nursing: Concepts, Process & Practice. 3rd ed. LC 92-49926. 1808p. (C). (gr. 13). 1992. text 31.50 (0-8016-7204-X, 07204) Mosby Inc.

Potter, Patricia A. & Perry, Anne G. Basic Nursing: A Critical Thinking Approach. 4th ed. LC 98-23777. 1998. text 57.00 (0-323-00099-1) Mosby Inc.

***Potter, Patricia A. & Perry, Anne G.** Basic Nursing: A Critical Thinking Approach. 4th ed. (Illus.). 1296p. 1998. write for info. (0-323-00499-7) Mosby Inc.
— Basic Nursing: A Critical Thinking Approach, Includes Testbank. 4th ed. (Illus.). 1296p. 1998. teacher ed. write for info. (0-323-00103-3) Mosby Inc.

Potter, Patricia A. & Perry, Anne G. Basic Nursing: Theory & Practice. 3rd ed. (Illus.). teacher ed., suppl. ed. write for info. (0-8151-6756-3) Mosby Inc.
— Clinical Nursing Skills & Techniques. 4th ed. (Illus.). 1392p. (C). (gr. 13). 1997. pap. text 52.00 (0-8151-4305-2, 29659) Mosby Inc.
— Clinical Nursing Skills & Techniques: Checklists. 4th ed. 490p. (C). (gr. 13). 1997. pap. text 14.95 (0-8151-4306-0) Mosby Inc.
— Fundamentals of Nursing: Checklists. 4th ed. 224p. (C). (gr. 13). 1996. pap. text 14.95 (0-8151-8501-4, 28445) Mosby Inc.
— Fundamentals of Nursing: Concepts, Process & Practice. 4th ed. (Illus.). student ed. write for info. (0-8151-9369-6) Mosby Inc.
— Fundamentals of Nursing: Concepts, Process & Practice. 4th ed. (Illus.). 1568p. (C). (gr. 13). 1996. text 63.00 (0-8151-6909-4, 27086) Mosby Inc.

Potter, Patricia A. & Perry, Anne G. Fundamentals of Nursing: Concepts, Process & Practice. 4th ed. (Illus.). 1568p. 1997. write for info. (0-323-00498-9); write for info. (0-8151-8502-2) Mosby Inc.

Potter, Patricia A., et al. Canadian Fundamentals of Nursing: Includes Testbank. 4th ed. 1997. teacher ed. write for info. (0-8151-2788-X) Mosby Inc.
— Fundamentals of Nursing. 4th ed. (Illus.). 400p. (C). (gr. 13). 1996. pap. text, student ed. 19.95 (0-8151-4656-6, 28985) Mosby Inc.
— Fundamentals of Nursing: A Canadian Perspective. 4th ed. LC 96-37669. (Illus.). 1568p. (C). (gr. 13). 1997. text 65.75 (0-8151-8901-X, 28983) Mosby Inc.

Potter, Patricia A., jt. auth. see Perry, Anne G.

Potter, Patrick De, see De Potter, Patrick.

Potter, Paul, ed. Hippocrates, Vol. VIII. (Loeb Classical Library: Vol. 482). (Illus.). 432p. (C). 1995. text 18.95 (0-674-99531-7) HUP.

Potter, Paul, tr. from GRE. Hippocrates, Vol. V. (Loeb Classical Library: No. 472). 349p. 1989. text 18.95 (0-674-99520-1) HUP.
— Hippocrates, Vol. VI. (Loeb Classical Library: No. 473). 377p. 1989. text 18.95 (0-674-99522-8) HUP.

Potter, Paul, jt. ed. see Wright, John P.

Potter, Philana, ed. see Potter, Charles.

Potter, Philip J. Power Plant Theory & Design. 2nd ed. LC 87-17348. 722p. 1989. reprint ed. 82.50 (0-89464-236-7) Krieger.

Potter, Phillip. Life in All Its Fullness. LC 82-5079. 183p. reprint ed. pap. 56.80 (0-608-14509-2, 202534000043) Bks Demand.

Potter, Pitman B. The Economic Contract Law of China: Legitimation & Contract Autonomy in the PRC. LC 91-36749. (Asian Law Ser.: No. 10). 246p. 1992. text 50.00 (0-295-97127-4) U of Wash Pr.

Potter, Pitman B. Foreign Business Law in China: Past Progress & Future Challenges. (Illus.). 160p. (C). 1995. text 42.50 (0-472-10637-6) U of Mich Pr.
— The Wal Wal Arbitration. LC 99-48877. (Carnegie Endowment for International Peace Monograph Ser.: Vol. 3). vii, 182p. 2000. 45.00 (1-57588-560-3, 323920) W S Hein.

Potter, Pitman B., ed. Domestic Law Reforms in Post-Mao China. LC 93-23228. (Studies on Contemporary China). 326p. (C). (gr. 13). 1994. text 85.95 (1-56324-107-2, East Gate Bk) M E Sharpe.

***Potter, Pitman B., ed.** Legislative History of the Balanced Budget Act of 1997. LC 99-48877. 2000. 4295.00 (1-57588-557-3) W S Hein.

Potter, R. The Year 2000 Problem. 1996. pap. 129.00 (1-85953-062-1, Pub. by Tech Comm) St Mut.

Potter, R. B., ed. Urbanization, Planning & Development in the Caribbean. 336p. 1989. text 120.00 (0-7201-2012-8) Continuum.

Potter, R. Charles. The "Tab-Slide-Guide" for All Major Keys of the Ten-Hole Diatonic Harmonica, No. 1. 6.95 (0-9646765-1-6) Charles Publns.
— The "Tab-Slide-Guide" for All Major Keys of the Lee Oskar Melody Maker Ten-Hole Diatonic Harmonica, No. 3. 6.95 (0-9646765-3-2) Charles Publns.
— The "Tab-Slide-Guide" for All Natural Minor Keys of the Ten-Hole Diatonic Harmonica, No. 2. 6.95 (0-9646765-2-4) Charles Publns.

Potter, R. William. Issues for the Eighties: Energy, 1981. 1981. 4.00 (0-943136-06-7) Ctr Analysis Public Issues.

Potter, Ray. 100 Best Resumes for Today's Hottest Jobs. 240p. 1998. pap. 12.95 (0-02-862187-5, Arc) IDG Bks.

Potter, Ray, jt. auth. see Reed, Jean.

Potter, Reuben. The Fall of the Alamo. Grosvenor, Charles, ed. LC 77-75152. (Illus.). 1977. reprint ed. 10.00 (0-918868-01-7) Otterden.

Potter, Rick D. Dumped! The Broken Relationship Survival Manual. (Illus.). 112p. 1983. pap. 6.95 (0-317-01200-2) Laylah Pubns.

Potter, Robert. Globe Reader's Anthology Text. (Globe Anthology Series). text. write for info. (0-8359-0065-7) Globe Fearon.

Potter, Robert, tr. see Aeschylus.

Potter, Robert, tr. see Euripides.

Potter, Robert B. St. Vincent & the Grenadines. LC 93-191849. (World Bibliographical Ser.). 242p. 1992. lib. bdg. 79.00 (1-85109-183-1) ABC-CLIO.

Potter, Robert B. & Conway, Dennis, eds. Self-Help Housing, the Poor, & the State in the Caribbean. LC 96-25220. (Illus.). 320p. 1997. 26.00 (0-87049-963-7) U of Tenn Pr.

Potter, Robert B. & Dann, Graham M. Barbados. LC 88-149402. (World Bibliographical Ser.: No. 76). 398p. 1987. lib. bdg. 70.00 (1-85109-022-3) ABC-CLIO.

Potter, Robert B. & Salau, Ademola T., eds. Cities & Developments. (Illus.). 208p. 1990. text 110.00 (0-7201-2066-7) Continuum.

Potter, Robert B. & Unwin, Tim, eds. The Geography of Urban-Rural Interaction in Developing Countries: Essays for Alan B. Mountjoy. LC 88-7632. (Illus.). 352p. reprint ed. pap. 109.20 (0-608-20373-4, 207162600002) Bks Demand.

Potter, Robert B. & Unwin, Timothy. The Geography of Urban-Rural Interaction in Developing Countries. 288p. (C). 1989. lib. bdg. 62.50 (0-415-00444-6) Routledge.

Potter, Robert E. & Logan, Linda L. A History of Teacher Education in Hawaii. xxi, 305p. (Orig.). 1995. pap. 24.95 (0-9648963-1-1) Hawaii Educ Assn.

Potter, Robert E., jt. auth. see Kamins, Robert M.

Potter, Robert G., jt. ed. see Bongaarts, John.

Potter, Robert R. Benjamin Franklin. (Pioneers in Change Ser.). (Illus.). 144p. (J). (gr. 5-9). 1992. pap. 6.95 (0-382-24178-9); lib. bdg. 13.95 (0-382-24173-8) Silver Burdett Pr.
— Buckminster Fuller. Gallin, Richard, ed. (Pioneers in Change Ser.). (Illus.). 144p. (J). (gr. 5-9). 1990. pap. 6.95 (0-382-09972-9); lib. bdg. 13.95 (0-382-09967-2) Silver Burdett Pr.
— Jefferson Davis. LC 92-16914. (American Troublemakers Ser.). (Illus.). 128p. (J). (gr. 7-10). 1992. lib. bdg. 27.11 (0-8114-2330-1) Raintree Steck-V.
— John Brown: Militant Abolitionist. LC 94-17020. (American Troublemakers Ser.). (Illus.). 128p. (J). 1994. lib. bdg. 27.11 (0-8114-2378-6) Raintree Steck-V.

Potter, Roderick. Garsh. 8p. (Orig.). 1991. pap. 2.00 (0-9627192-2-6) We Pr.

Potter, Rosanne G., ed. Literary Computing & Literary Criticism: Theoretical & Practical Essays on Theme & Rhetoric. LC 88-38159. (Illus.). 320p. (C). 1989. text 45.00 (0-8122-8156-X) U of Pa Pr.

Potter, Rosemary L. The Positive Use of Commercial Television with Children. LC 81-9646. (Analysis & Action Ser.). (Illus.). 136p. reprint ed. pap. 42.20 (0-8357-6414-1, 203577800097) Bks Demand.

***Potter, Rosemary L.** Technical Reading in the Middle School. (Fastback Ser.: No. 456). 50p. 1999. pap. 3.00 (0-87367-656-4, FB# 456) Phi Delta Kappa.

Potter, Russell A. Spectacular Vernaculars: Hip-Hop & the Politics of Postmodernism. LC 94-24990. (SUNY Series in Postmodern Culture). 197p. (C). 1995. pap. text 16.95 (0-7914-2626-2) State U NY Pr.

Potter, S. B. Fundamentals of Music. 2nd ed. (Illus.). 140p. (Orig.). 1990. pap. text 10.95 (0-910648-04-2) Gamut Music.
— A Survey of Western Music to 1750. (Illus.). 445p. (C). 1993. pap. text 17.95 (0-910648-05-0) Gamut Music.

Potter, Sally. Tango Lesson. 128p. 1997. pap. 12.95 (0-571-19166-5) Faber & Faber.

Potter Schadt, Ann, tr. see Schadt, Hermann.

***Potter, Sharyn J.** Can Efficiency & Community Service Be Symbiotic? A Longitudinal Analysis of Not-for-Profit & For-Profit Hospitals in the United States. LC 99-55076. (Health Care Policy in the United States Ser.). 2000. write for info. (0-8153-3633-0) Garland.

***Potter, Shelia & Clare, Philippa.** The Potter Guide to Higher Education: Quality of Life & Learning in U. K. Universities & Colleges. 12th ed. (Illus.). 486p. 1999. pap. 29.50 (1-870892-13-5, Pub. by Dalebank Bks) Trans-Atl Phila.

Potter, Simeon. Language in the Modern World. LC 83-8248. 205p. 1983. reprint ed. lib. bdg. 55.00 (0-313-24009-4, POLA, Greenwood Pr) Greenwood.

Potter, Simeon. Our Language. 1990. pap. 13.95 (0-14-013494-8, Pub. by Pnguin Bks Ltd) Trafalgar.

Potter, Simon M., jt. ed. see Pesaran, M. Hashem.

Potter, Stephen. D. H. Lawrence. LC 78-64051. (Des Imagistes: Literature of the Imagist Movement Ser.). 168p. reprint ed. 32.50 (0-404-17091-9) AMS Pr.
— Lifemanship. 1993. reprint ed. lib. bdg. 18.95 (1-56849-093-3) Buccaneer Bks.
— One-Upmanship. LC 96-28937. (Illus.). 177p. 1997. pap. 9.95 (1-55921-190-3) Moyer Bell.
— One-Upmanship: Being Some Account of the Activities & Teaching of the Lifemanship Correspondence College of One-Upness & Gameslifemastery LC 79-304663. 151p. 1977. write for info. (0-14-001827-1) Pnguin Bks Ltd.
— The Theory & Practice of Gamesmanship. 1993. reprint ed. lib. bdg. 18.95 (1-56849-094-1) Buccaneer Bks.
— The Theory & Practice of Gamesmanship: or The Art of Winning Games Without Actually Cheating. LC 97-35118. (Illus.). 128p. 1998. pap. 9.95 (1-55921-223-3) Moyer Bell.

Potter, Stephen, ed. see Coleridge, Sara.

Potter, Stephen R. Commoners, Tribute, & Chiefs: The Development of Algonquian Culture in the Potomac Valley. LC 92-28417. (Illus.). 288p. 1993. pap. text 14.50 (0-8139-1540-6) U Pr of Va.

Potter, Sulamith H. Family Life in a Northern Thai Village: A Study in the Structural Significance of Women. LC 76-52035. 1978. pap. 15.95 (0-520-04044-9, Pub. by U CA Pr) Cal Prin Full Svc.

Potter, Sulamith H. & Potter, Jack M. China's Peasants: The Anthropology of a Revolution. (Illus.). 358p. (C). 1990. text 64.95 (0-521-35521-4); pap. text 23.95 (0-521-35787-X) Cambridge U Pr.

Potter, Susan Harrington, ed. see Harrington, W. Frank.

Potter, T. Car Travel Games. (Travel Games Ser.). (Illus.). 32p. (J). (gr. 2 up). 1988. pap. 4.95 (0-86020-926-1) EDC.

Potter, T. Dark Waters. 1997. mass mkt. 8.95 (0-340-68754-1, Pub. by Hodder & Stought Ltd) Trafalgar.

Potter, T. Pottery. (Practical Guides Ser.). (Illus.). 48p. (J). (gr. 6-12). 1986. pap. 8.95 (0-86020-944-X) EDC.
— Pottery. (Practical Guides Ser.). (Illus.). 48p. (J). (gr. 6 up). 1999. lib. bdg. 16.95 (0-88110-319-5) EDC.

Potter, T. & Butterfield, M. Travel Games. rev. ed. (Illus.). 64p. (YA). (gr. 2-5). 2000. pap. 8.95 (0-86020-999-7, Pub. by Usbrne Pbng UK) EDC.

Potter, T., et al. Robotics. (Introductions Ser.). (Illus.). 48p. (J). (gr. 6 up). 1983. pap. 7.95 (0-7460-1466-X) EDC.
— Robotics. (Introductions Ser.). (Illus.). 48p. (J). (gr. 6 up). 1999. lib. bdg. 15.95 (0-88110-661-5) EDC.

Potter, T. W. A Faliscan Town in South Etruria (Narce) (Illus.). 331p. 1976. pap. 30.00 (0-904152-04-9, Pub. by British Schl Rome) David Brown.
— Roman Britain. 1983. pap. 9.95 (0-674-77765-4) HUP.
— Roman Britain. (Illus.). 72p. 1983. pap. 13.00 (0-674-77766-2) HUP.
— Roman Britain. LC 96-79382. (Illus.). 96p. 1997. pap. text 18.95 (0-674-77767-0) HUP.
— Roman Italy. (Exploring the Roman World Ser.: Vol. 1). 240p. 1987. pap. 22.50 (0-520-06975-7, Pub. by U CA Pr) Cal Prin Full Svc.

Potter, T. W. & Johns, Catherine. Roman Britain. LC 92-25283. (Exploring the Roman World Ser.). (C). 1993. 45.00 (0-520-08168-4, Pub. by U CA Pr) Cal Prin Full Svc.

***Potter, Ted & Yau, John.** Thomas Daniel: Into My Eyes. (Illus.). 104p. 2000. 20.00 (0-935519-22-X) Anderson Gal.

Potter, Tessa. Beowulf & the Dragon. (Myths & Legends Ser.). (Illus.). (J). 1998. (1-57572-017-5) Heinemann Lib.
— Digger: The Story of a Mole in the Fall. (Animals Through the Year Ser.). (Illus.). 32p. (J). (ps-3). 1997. pap. 5.95 (0-8172-6902-9) Raintree Steck-V.
— Digger - The Story of a Mole in the Fall. LC 96-38983. (Animals Through the Year Ser.). (Illus.). 32p. (J). (ps-3). 1997. lib. bdg. 21.40 (0-8172-4623-1) Raintree Steck-V.
— Fang - The Story of a Fox in Winter. LC 96-38990. (Animals Through the Year Ser.). (Illus.). 32p. (J). 1997. lib. bdg. 21.40 (0-8172-4622-3) Raintree Steck-V.

Potter, Tessa. Fang, the Story of a Fox in Winter. 32p. (J). (ps-3). 1997. pap. text 5.95 (0-8172-6900-2) Raintree Steck-V.

Potter, Tessa. Grayfur: The Story of a Rabbit in Summer. (Animals Through the Year Ser.). (Illus.). 32p. (J). (ps-3). 1997. pap. 5.95 (0-8172-6903-7) Raintree Steck-V.
— Grayfur - The Story of a Rabbit in Summer. LC 96-38989. (Animals Through the Year Ser.). (Illus.). 32p. (J). 1997. lib. bdg. 21.40 (0-8172-4621-5) Raintree Steck-V.
— Sam - The Story of an Otter in Spring. LC 96-35466. (Animals Through the Year Ser.). (Illus.). 32p. (J). 1997. lib. bdg. 21.40 (0-8172-4620-7) Raintree Steck-V.
— Sam - The Story of an Otter in Spring. 32p. (J). (ps-3). 1997. pap. text 5.95 (0-8172-6901-0) Raintree Steck-V.

Potter, Theodore E. The Autobiography of Theodore Edgar Potter. (Michigan Heritage Library: Vol. 1). 1978. reprint ed. 15.00 (0-915056-08-9) Hardscrabble Bks.

Potter, Thomas & Simmons, Kathleen. Composition of Petroleum Mixtures. (TPH Working Group Ser.). (Illus.). 102p. 1998. pap. 19.95 (1-884940-19-6) Amherst Sci Pubs.

Potter, Thomas A., jt. auth. see Nelson, Theron R.

Potter, Thomas F. Y2K: You Can Burn This Book! (Illus.). 224p. 1998. pap. 16.95 (0-9669889-0-6) Chef Brio.

Potter, Thomas S., et al. Voices of Inquiry in Teacher Education. LC 96-54813. 224p. 1997. pap. 24.50 (0-8058-2378-6) L Erlbaum Assocs.

Potter, Tiffany. Honest Sins: Georgian Libertinism & Plays & Novels of Henry Fielding. LC 98-90110. 1998. 55.00 (0-7735-1803-7) McG-Queens Univ Pr.

Potter, Timothy W. Towns in Late Antiquity: Iol Caesarea & Its Context. (Ian Sanders Memorial Fund, Occasional Publications: No. 2). (Illus.). 122p. 1995. pap. 22.00 (0-9521073-1-7, Pub. by Oxbow Bks) David Brown.

Potter, Tom & Parnes, Beatrice. Parenting Playfully: Dancing the Developmental Ladder, Birth to Three. (Illus.). 112p. (Orig.). 1995. pap. 12.95 (0-9646045-0-7) Parent Educ.

Potter, Tom, jt. auth. see Wurdinger, Scott.

***Potter, Tony.** Baa Baa Lamb. 1998. 7.95 (1-902553-10-1) Grimond.

Potter, Tony. Find the String Kitten. (J). (ps). 1998. 9.95 (1-902553-03-9, Pub. by Grimond) BHB Intl.
— Hide & Seek Puppy. (J). (ps). 1998. 9.95 (1-902553-02-0, Pub. by Grimond) BHB Intl.
— How Television Works: A Fact Finder Book. (Illus.). 48p. (J). (gr. 7-9). 1992. pap. 8.95 (0-563-34578-0, BBC-Parkwest) Parkwest Pubns.
— Let's Find Teddy. (J). (ps). 1998. 9.95 (1-902553-00-4, Pub. by Grimond) BHB Intl.
— Look Out Tiger. (J). (ps-3). 1998. 7.95 (1-902553-04-7) Grimond.

***Potter, Tony.** Moo Moo Cow. 1998. 7.95 (1-902553-08-X) Grimond.
— Neigh Neigh Pony. 1998. 7.95 (1-902553-11-X) Grimond.
— Oink Oink Pig. 1998. 7.95 (1-902553-09-8) Grimond.

Potter, Tony. Over Here Zebra. (J). 1998. 7.95 (1-902553-05-5) Grimond.

***Potter, Tony.** Snip Snap Crocodile. 1998. 7.95 (1-902553-06-3) Grimond.
— Watch Out Elephant. 1998. 7.95 (1-902553-07-1) Grimond.

Potter, Tony. Weather. (Fact Finders Ser.). (Illus.). 48p. (J). (gr. 7-9). Date not set. 14.95 (0-563-21428-7, BBC-Parkwest) Parkwest Pubns.
— You Need a Bath Zebra. (J). (ps). 1998. 9.95 (1-902553-01-2, Pub. by Grimond) BHB Intl.

Potter, Tony & Butterfield, Moira. Hotshots Travel Games. (Usborne Kid Kits Ser.). (Illus.). (J). (gr. 2-5). 1998. 12.95 (1-58086-143-1, Usborne) EDC.

Potter, Tony & Wright, Nicola. The Macmillan First Atlas. LC 91-31257. (Macmillan Children's Reference Ser.). (Illus.). 40p. (J). (ps-2). 1992. lib. bdg. 12.95 (0-02-774920-7, Mac Bks Young Read) S&S Childrens.

Potter, Van R. Global Bioethics: Building on the Leopold Legacy. LC 88-42901. 203p. (C). 1988. pap. 13.00 (0-87013-264-4) Mich St U Pr.

Potter, Vincent. On Understanding Understanding: A Philosophy of Knowledge. 2nd rev. ed. LC 93-7931. 179p. (C). 1993. pap. 17.00 (0-8232-1486-9) Fordham.

Potter, Vincent, ed. from LAT. John Pecham: Questions Concerning the Eternity of the World. xxi, 37p. (C). 1993. 25.00 (0-8232-1488-5) Fordham.

Potter, Vincent G. Charles S. Peirce: On Norms & Ideals. 2nd rev. ed. LC 96-53944. xxxi, 229p. 1996. reprint ed. text 30.00 (0-8232-1709-4) Fordham.
— Charles S. Peirce: On Norms & Ideals. 2nd rev. ed. LC 96-53944. Vol. 6. xxxi, 229p. 1996. reprint ed. pap. 16.00 (0-8232-1710-8) Fordham.
— Peirce's Philosophical Perspectives. Colapietro, Vincent, ed. & intro. by. (American Philosophy Ser.: No. 2). xxviii, 212p. 1996. 30.00 (0-8232-1615-2) Fordham.
— Peirce's Philosophical Perspectives. Colapietro, Vincent, ed. & intro. by. LC 96-1328. xxxiii, 212p. 1996. pap. text 16.95 (0-8232-1616-0) Fordham.

Potter, Vincent G., ed. Doctrine & Experience: Essays in American Philosophy. LC 88-82221. viii, 273p. 1988. 40.00 (0-8232-1210-6) Fordham.

Potter, Vincent G., et al. Readings in Epistemology: From Aquinas, Bacon, Galileo, Descartes, Locke, Hume, Kant. 2nd ed. Colapietro, S. J., ed. LC 92-45079. xvi, 235p. (C). 1993. 27.50 (0-8232-1493-1); pap. 15.50 (0-8232-1492-3) Fordham.

Potter, W. C., jt. ed. see Valenta, Jiri.

Potter, W. James. An Analysis of Thinking & Research about Qualitative Methods. (LEA's Communication Ser.). 400p. 1996. pap. 36.00 (0-8058-1751-4); text 79.95 (0-8058-1750-6) L Erlbaum Assocs.
— Media Literacy. LC 97-33726. 1998. 61.50 (0-7619-0925-7); lib. bdg. write for info. (0-7619-0926-5) Sage.

Potter, William C. Creating a Database on International Nuclear Commerce. (CISA Working Papers: No. 59). 27p. (Orig.). 1987. pap. 15.00 (0-86682-076-0) Ctr Intl Relations.
— A Guide to Simulating U. S.-Soviet Arms Control Negotiations. (CISA Working Papers: No. 62). 40p. (Orig.). 1988. pap. 15.00 (0-86682-079-5) Ctr Intl Relations.

Potter, William C., ed. Verification & Salt: The Challenge of Strategic Deception. LC 80-13203. (Special Studies in National Security & Defense Policy). 256p. 1980. text 52.00 (0-89158-886-8) Westview.

Potter, William C., et al. Nuclear Profiles of the Soviet Successor States. (Orig.). 1993. 9.95 (0-9633859-5-X) Ctr Nonproliferation.

Potter, William C., jt. auth. see Bertsch, Gary K.

Potter, William C., jt. ed. see Shields, John M.

An Asterisk (*) at the beginning of an entry indicates that the title is appearing for the first time.

P

Potts, T. C., tr. see Barth, E. M.

Potts, T. M. Bi-Centenary Memorial of Jeremiah Carter Who Came to the Provence of Pennsylvania in 1682, a Historic-Genealogy of His Descendents down to the Present. (Illus.). 304p. 1989. reprint ed. pap. 49.00 (*0-8328-0373-1*); reprint ed. lib. bdg. 59.00 (*0-8328-0372-3*) Higginson Bk Co.

— Potts: Historical Collection Relating to the Potts Family in Great Britain & America. (Illus.). 735p. 1990. reprint ed. pap. 104.50 (*0-8328-1523-3*); reprint ed. lib. bdg. 112.50 (*0-8328-1522-5*) Higginson Bk Co.

Potts, Timothy. Mesopotamia & the East: An Archaeological & Historical Study of Foreign Relations 3400-2000 BC. (Oxford University Committee for Archaeology Monograph Ser.: No. 37). (Illus.). 340p. 1995. 48.00 (*0-947816-37-2*, Pub. by Oxford Univ Comm Arch) David Brown.

Potts, Timothy C. Structures & Categories for the Representation of Meaning. (Illus.). 324p. (C). 1994. text 59.95 (*0-521-43481-5*) Cambridge U Pr.

***Potts, Willard.** Joyce & the Two Irelands. LC 00-25962. (Literary Modernism Ser.). (Illus.). 224p. 2001. 39.95 (*0-292-76591-6*) U of Tex Pr.

Potts, William F. McGraw-Hill Data Communications Dictionary. 268p. 1992. 34.50 (*0-07-003154-1*) McGraw.

Potty, S. N., ed. Placrosym VI. 476p. (C). 1987. 34.00 (*81-204-0239-1*, Pub. by Oxford IBH) S Asia.

Potucek, Martin. Mountain Biking Boise. LC 97-44038. (Illus.). 1998. pap. 10.95 (*1-56044-599-8*) Falcon Pub Inc.

— Mountain Biking Spokane-Coeur D'Alene. LC 99-11652. (Illus.). 120p. 1999. pap. 10.95 (*1-56044-815-6*) Falcon Pub Inc.

— Not Only the Market: The Role of the Market, Government & Civic Sector in the Development of Post-Communist Societies. LC 99-38542. 146p. 2000. 49.95 (*963-9116-52-1*); pap. 19.95 (*963-9116-51-3*) Ctrl Europ Univ.

Potuchek, Jean L. Who Supports the Family: Gender & Breadwinning in Dual-Earner Marriages. LC 96-34115. 1997. write for info. (*0-8047-2835-6*); pap. 17.95 (*0-8047-2836-4*) Stanford U Pr.

Potuto, Josephine R. Prisoner Collateral Attacks. LC 91-60701. 1991. 98.00 (*0-685-59842-X*) West Group.

Potvin, Alfred R. & Tourtellotte, Wallace W., eds. Quantitative Examination of Neurologic Functions, 2 vols., Vol. I. 272p. 1985. 147.00 (*0-8493-5926-0*, RC348, CRC Reprint) Franklin.

— Quantitative Examination of Neurologic Functions, 2 vols., Vol. II. 224p. 1985. 125.00 (*0-8493-5927-9*, CRC Reprint) Franklin.

Potvin, Charles, jt. auth. see Chretien de Troyes.

Potvin, J., ed. Computational Physics: Proceedings of the 2nd IMACS Conference. 272p. 1994. text 99.00 (*981-02-1747-1*) World Scientific Pub.

Potvin, Raymond H. & Westoff, Charles F. College Women & Fertility Values. LC 66-26589. 257p. 1967. reprint ed. pap. 79.70 (*0-7837-9478-9*, 206022000004) Bks Demand.

Poty, Bernard, jt. ed. see Roth, Etienne.

Potylitsin, A. P., jt. ed. see Pivovarov, Ju L.

Potyondy, John P., jt. ed. see Olsen, Darren S.

Potz, Richard, jt. ed. see Kuppe, Rene.

Potzl, Otto, et al. Preconscious Stimulation in Dreams, Associations & Images: Classical Studies. (Psychological Issues Monographs: No. 7, Vol. 2, No. 3). 156p. (Orig.). 1961. 27.50 (*0-8236-4260-7*) Intl Univs Pr.

Pou, P. J., et al, eds. La Edicion De Textos: Actas Del I Congreso Internacional De Hispanistas De Siglo De Oro. (Monografias A Ser.: No. CXXXIX). 256p. (C). 1990. 53.00 (*0-7293-0305-5*, Pub. by Tamesis Bks Ltd) Boydell & Brewer.

Pouba, Z. & Stemprok, M., eds. Problems of Hydrothermal Ore Deposition: The Origin, Evolution & Control of Ore-Forming Fluids. (International Association of the Genesis of Ore Deposits (IAGOD) Symposia Ser.). (Illus.). 396p. 1970. text 44.00 (*3-510-56002-7*, Pub. by E Schweizerbartsche) Balogh.

Pouch, J. J., et al, eds. Advances in High-Tc Superconductors. (Materials Science Forum Ser.: Vol.137-139). (Illus.). 802p. (C). 1993. text 266.00 (*0-87849-667-X*, Pub. by Trans T Pub) Enfield Pubs NH.

— Synthesis & Characterization of High-Temperature Superconductors. 710p. (C). 1993. text 266.00 (*0-87849-658-0*, Pub. by Trans T Pub) Enfield Pubs NH.

Pouch, J. J. & Alterovitz, S. A. Synthesis & Properties of Boron Nitride. 426p. 1990. text 175.00 (*0-87849-606-8*, Pub. by Trans T Pub) Enfield Pubs NH.

Pouch, J. J. & Alterovitz, S. A., eds. Plasma Properties, Deposition & Etching. (Materials Science Forum Ser.: Vol. 140-142). (Illus.). 749p. (C). 1993. text 266.00 (*0-87849-670-X*, Pub. by Trans T Pub) Enfield Pubs NH.

— Properties & Characterization of Amorphous Carbon Films. 714p. (C). 1990. text 213.00 (*0-87849-604-1*, Pub. by Trans T Pub) Enfield Pubs NH.

Pouchepadass, Jacques. Champaran & Gandhi: Planters, Peasants & Gandhian Politics. LC 99-939175. (French Studies on South Asian Culture & Society). 256p. 2000. text 27.95 (*0-19-564084-5*) OUP.

***Pouchepadass, Jacques.** Land, Power & Market: A Bihar District under Colonial Rule, 1890-1947. LC 99-46676. 1999. write for info. (*0-7619-9402-5*) Sage.

Poucher, J. Wilson, et al, eds. Old Gravestones of Ulster County: 22,000 Inscriptions. With Index. (Illus.). 434p. 1998. reprint ed. lib. bdg. 45.00 (*0-8328-9616-0*) Higginson Bk Co.

Poucher, W. A. The Lakeland Peaks. (Illus.). 430p. 1998. 22.95 (*0-09-477510-9*, Pub. by Constable & Co) Trafalgar.

— The Scottish Peaks N-E. (Illus.). 514p. (YA). (gr. 8). 1998. 22.95 (*0-09-475850-6*, Pub. by Constable & Co) Trafalgar.

Poucher, W. A. Welsh Peaks. 1997. text 24.95 (*0-09-475860-3*, Pub. by Constable & Co) Trafalgar.

Pouchert, Charles J. & Aldrich Chemical Company. The Aldrich Library of Ft-Ir Spectra. LC 97-73684. 1989. 495.00 (*0-941633-39-X*) Sigma-Aldrich Corp.

Pouchot, Pierre. Memoirs on the Late War in North America Between France & England. Dunnigan, Brian L., ed. Cardy, Michael, tr. from FRE. (Illus.). 568p. 1994. 24.95 (*0-941967-14-X*) Old Fort Niagara Assn.

Poudrier, Almira F., ed. see Morain, Lloyd & Morain, Mary.

Poudyal, Madhab P. Administrative Reform in Nepal. 1989. 42.50 (*81-85135-41-X*, Pub. by Natl Bk Orgn) S Asia.

— Aspects of Public Administration in Nepal. 1986. 24.00 (*0-8364-1800-X*, Pub. by Somaiya) S Asia.

Pouesi, Daniel & Igoe, Michael. The Stone Maiden & Other Samoan Fables. LC 94-72855. (Illus.). 56p. (Orig.). (YA). (gr. 6 up). 1995. pap. 10.00 (*0-9644426-0-4*) Kin Pub.

Pouessel, jt. auth. see Dumarche.

Pouget, Jean-Henri-Prosper & Prosper-Pouget, Jean-Henri. Five Hundred Fifty Authentic Rococo Designs & Motifs for Artists & Craftspeople. LC 94-25929. (Pictorial Archive Ser.). Orig. Title: Traites des Pierres Precieuses et de la Maniere de le Employer en Parure. 96p. 1994. 7.95 (*0-486-28193-0*) Dover.

Pough & Janis. Vertebrate Life. 5th ed. 767p. 1998. 86.67 (*0-13-671769-1*) P-H.

Pough, F. H. Peterson Rocks & Minerals. Vol. 19. 1998. pap. 5.95 (*0-395-93543-1*) HM.

***Pough, F. H. & Andrews, Robin M.** Herpetology. 2nd ed. 624p. 2000. pap. 81.33 (*0-13-030795-5*) P-H.

Pough, Frederick H. Peterson First Guide to Rocks & Minerals. (Peterson Field Guide Ser.). (Illus.). 128p. 1991. pap. 5.95 (*0-395-56275-9*) HM.

Pough, Harvey F. Herpetology. LC 97-19347. (Illus.). 577p. 1997. 84.00 (*0-13-850876-3*) P-H.

Pougher, Richard D. Making Wooden Dinosaurs: Plans & Instructions with Notes on Each Species. LC 97-13866. (Illus.). 224p. 1997. pap. 19.95 (*0-8117-2992-3*) Stackpole.

***Poughkeepsie Journal Staff.** The Hudson Valley: Our Heritage, Our Future. LC 00-130397. (Illus.). 402p. 2000. 60.00 (*0-9674209-0-3*) Pokeepsie Jrnl.

Pougin, Arthur. Dictionnaire Historique et Pittoresque du Theatre et des Art, 2 vols. (FRE.). 1985. 175.00 (*0-7859-7980-8*, 2-7307-0280-6) Fr & Eur.

— The Life & Music of Pierre Rode: Containing an Account of Rode, French Violinist. (Illus.). 81p. 1994. 25.00 (*0-9641631-0-1*) Lyre of Orpheus.

Pougovikin, A. P., tr. see Amusia, M. Ya & Chernysheva, L. V.

Pouh, Lieselotte. Wiener Literatur und Psychoanalyse: Felix Dormann, Jakob Julius David und Felix Salten. (GER.). 251p. 1997. 51.95 (*3-631-31445-0*) P Lang Pubng.

***Pouh, Lieselotte.** Young Vienna & Psychoanalysis: Felix Doermann, Jakob Julius David, & Felix Salten. LC 99-46198. (Austrian Culture Ser.: No. 31). 224p. 2000. text 52.95 (*0-8204-4517-7*) P Lang Pubng.

Pouillon, Jean & Maranda, Pierre, eds. Echanges & Communications, Melanges Offerts a Claude Levi-Strauss, a l'Occasion de Son 60'eme Anniversaire, 2 Vols. LC 78-91207. (Studies in General Anthropology: No. 5). 1970. 284.65 (*90-279-0540-1*) Mouton.

Pouillon, Nora. Cooking with Nora. 1996. 35.00 (*0-614-95782-6*) Park Lane Pr.

Pouillot. Telecommunications: VII-6, Liberalized Services. (Single Market Review Ser.). 1998. 70.00 (*0-7494-2318-8*) Kogan Page Ltd.

Pouissant, Alvin F. The African-American Book of Lists. LC 96-22016. 192p. 1997. pap. 12.00 (*0-399-52268-9*, Perigee Bks) Berkley Pub.

Poujol, J. Echography in Ophthalmology. (gr. 13). 1986. 34.00 (*0-89352-228-7*, MA228) Mosby Inc.

Poulain, Augustin. Revelations & Visions: Discerning the True & the Certain from the False or the Doubtful. abr. ed. Sadowski, Frank, ed. Yorke, Leonora L., tr. LC 97-207419. Orig. Title: The Graces of Interior Prayer. 152p. 1998. pap. 9.95 (*0-8189-0793-2*) Alba.

Poulain, D. A., jt. ed. see Vincent, J. D.

Poulain, Elfie. La Recherche de l'Identite Sociale dans l'Oeuvre de Siegfried Lenz: Analyse de Pragmatique Romanesque. (Contacts Ser.: Series III, Vol. 37). (FRE.). 191p. 1996. 36.95 (*3-906754-68-5*, Pub. by P Lang) P Lang Pubng.

Poulain, Michel. Charcuterie Specialties. (Illus.). 192p. 1996. 55.00 (*0-471-16063-6*) Wiley.

Poulain, R. P. The Graces of Interior Prayer, 1910. 654p. 1996. reprint ed. pap. 34.95 (*1-56459-720-2*) Kessinger Pub.

Poulain, S. J., et al. The Graces of Interior Prayer. 637p. 1996. reprint ed. 35.00 (*0-7873-0674-6*) Hlth Research.

Poulakos, John. Poulakos Class of Rhetic & Theory. LC 98-72074. 1999. pap. text 27.87 (*0-395-84995-0*) HM.

— Sophistical Rhetoric in Classical Greece. LC 94-18680. (Studies in Rhetoric-Communication). 236p. 1994. text 39.95 (*0-87249-899-9*) U of SC Pr.

Poulakos, Takis. Speaking for the Polis: Isocrates' Rhetorical Education. LC 97-4865. (Studies in Rhetoric/ Communication). 139p. 1997. 24.95 (*1-57003-177-0*) U of SC Pr.

***Poulantzas, Nicos.** State, Power, Socialism. Camiller, Patrick, tr. from GRE. (Classics Ser.). 269p. (C). 2000. pap. 20.00 (*1-85984-274-7*, Pub. by Verso) Norton.

Poulard, Johannes. Beginner's Ukrainian. (UKR.). 200p. (Orig.). 1996. pap. 11.95 (*0-7818-0443-4*) Hippocrene Bks.

Poulard, Othello W. The Expanding Role of Community-Based Organizations: Implications for Vocational Education. 13p. 1983. 2.25 (*0-318-22102-0*, OC90) Ctr Educ Trng Employ.

Poularikas, Alexander. The Handbook of Formulas & Tables for Signal Processing. LC 98-10347. (Electrical Engineering Handbook Ser.). 864p. 1998. boxed set 94.95 (*0-8493-8579-2*) CRC Pr.

***Poularikas, Alexander.** Handbook of Tables & Formulas for Signal Processing. 1999. 74.95 (*0-7803-4728-5*) Inst Electrical.

Poularikas, Alexander. The Transforms & Applications Handbook. 2nd ed. LC 99-16719. (Electrical Engineering Handbook Ser.). 1999. 125.00 (*0-8493-8595-4*) CRC Pr.

Poularikas, Alexander D., ed. The Transforms & Applications Handbook. LC 95-2513. (Electrical Engineering Handbook Ser.). 1120p. 1995. boxed set 134.95 (*0-8493-8342-0*, 8342) CRC Pr.

Poularikas, Alexander D. & Seely, Samuel. Signals & Systems. 2nd ed. LC 93-48738. 1038p. 1994. reprint ed. 120.00 (*0-89464-875-6*) Krieger.

Poulenc, Ceser. Jean Laffite Gentleman Pirate. (Illus.). 50p. (Orig.). 1987. pap. 4.95 (*0-944939-00-7*) Privateer Pr.

Poulenc, Francis. Album of Six Pieces. 1989. pap. 15.95 (*0-685-68971-9*, CH02259) Shawnee Pr.

— Dialogues of the Carmelites: Vocal Score. (ENG & FRE.). 1987. pap. 19.95 (*0-7935-5396-2*) H Leonard.

— Gloria Chorus Pt Satb/s: Solo/Orchestra. (ENG & LAT.). 1986. 8.50 (*0-7935-5504-3*, 50306950) H Leonard.

— Sonata for Recorder Quartet: For Recorder Quartet. (Contemporary Consort Ser.: No. 11). i, 40p. 1990. pap. text 12.00 (*1-56571-013-4*) PRB Prods.

Poulenez, Donovan & Rosato, Peter C. Psychologically Speaking: A Self-Assessment. 227p. 1996. pap. text 28.00 (*0-205-16364-5*, H6364-7) Allyn.

Pouler, Wilfred B. BPR Machine Trades - IG. 32p. 1995. teacher ed. 15.50 (*0-8273-6652-3*) Delmar.

— Print Reading for the Machine Trades. (Blueprint Reading & Drafting Ser.). 1984. teacher ed. 11.50 (*0-538-33351-0*); pap. 24.95 (*0-538-33350-2*) S-W Pub.

— Print Reading for the Machine Trades. 2nd ed. LC 94-25405. (Illus.). 416p. 1995. mass mkt. 43.95 (*0-8273-6651-5*) Delmar.

Poulet, Denise, jt. auth. see Carton, Fernand.

Poulet, Georges. Exploding Poetry: Baudelaire-Rimbaud. Meltzer, Francoise, tr. LC 83-18062. 160p. 1997. 20.50 (*0-226-67650-1*) U Ch Pr.

— Exploding Poetry: Baudelaire/Rimbaud. Meltzer, Francoise, tr. & intro. by. LC 83-18062. 160p. reprint ed. pap. 49.60 (*0-608-09502-8*, 205430300005) Bks Demand.

— The Metamorphoses of the Circle. Dawson, Carley & Coleman, Elliott, trs. LC 66-24406. 431p. reprint ed. pap. 133.70 (*0-608-12066-9*, 202414700035) Bks Demand.

— Proustian Space. Coleman, Elliott, tr. LC 76-47390. 120p. reprint ed. pap. 37.20 (*0-608-14759-1*, 202586400046) Bks Demand.

— Studies in Human Time. Coleman, Elliot, tr. LC 78-13572. 363p. 1979. reprint ed. lib. bdg. 69.50 (*0-8371-9348-6*, POSH, Greenwood Pr) Greenwood.

Poulet, H. & Mathieu, J. P. Spectres de Vibration et Symetrie des Cristaux. (FRE.). xiv, 438p. 1970. text 421.00 (*0-677-50180-3*) Gordon & Breach.

Poulet, N., tr. see Bogulavsky, M. M.

Poulett, G. J., jt. auth. see Scrope, George J.

Poulette, Jim. Into the Adirondacks. LC 94-45453. 1994. pap. 10.00 (*0-925168-35-1*) North Country.

Pouletti, J. Dictionnaire Pratique de Droit Medicale. (FRE.). 424p. 1982. 110.00 (*0-8288-4421-6*, M9773) Fr & Eur.

Pouliezos, A. D. & Stavrakakis, G. S. Real Time Fault Monitoring of Industrial Processes. LC 94-2137. (International Series on Microprocessor-Based & Intelligent Systems Engineering: Vol. 12). 576p. (C). 1994. text 336.00 (*0-7923-2737-3*) Kluwer Academic.

Poulik, M. D., ed. Beta Two-Microglobulin: Its Significance in Clinical Medicine. (Journal: Vox Sanguinis: Vol. 38, No. 6). (Illus.). 1980. pap. 28.75 (*3-8055-1560-X*) S Karger.

Poulin. Contemporary American Poetry, 6 vols. 6th ed. (C). 1996. pap. text 40.36 (*0-395-74532-2*) HM.

— Environmental Graphics & the 20th Century. (Design & Graphic Design Ser.). 1996. text 54.95 (*0-442-02235-2*, VNR) Wiley.

— History of Environmental Graphics. text 54.95 (*0-471-29192-7*) Wiley.

Poulin, tr. see Hebert, Anne.

Poulin, A., Jr., jt. auth. see Rilke, Rainer Maria.

Poulin, A., Jr., ed. see Logan, John.

Poulin, A., Jr., tr. see Hebert, Anne.

Poulin, A., Jr., tr. see Rilke, Rainer Maria.

Poulin, Bernard. The Complete Colored Pencil Book. (Illus.). 144p. 1992. 27.99 (*0-89134-418-7*, 30363, North Lght Bks) F & W Pubns Inc.

Poulin, Deborah W., ed. International Directory of Women's Political Leadership. 4th rev. ed. 303p. 1995. text 10.00 (*1-891464-11-6*) J M Burns Academy.

Poulin, Gil. This Quirky Unit. 12p. 1998. pap. 3.00 (*1-880743-11-6*) Dead Metaphor.

Poulin, Gilles. Longitudes et Latitudes: Des Villes, Villages et Lieux du Quebec. 117p. 1985. 14.95 (*2-920083-14-7*) Edns Roseau.

Poulin, Jacques. Mr. Blue. Fischman, Sheila, tr. from FRE. 160p. (Orig.). 1993. pap. 13.95 (*1-55065-039-4*, Pub. by Vehicule Pr) Genl Dist Srvs.

— Spring Tides. Fischman, Sheila, tr. from FRE.Tr. of Les/Grandes Marees. 166p. (Orig.). 1986. reprint ed. pap. 9.95 (*0-88784-149-X*, Pub. by Hse of Anansi Pr) Genl Dist Srvs.

Poulin, James E. Hysteria & Other Cases: A Maine Doctor Looks Back. 88p. 1993. pap. 7.95 (*0-9635457-0-1*) Mtn Greenery.

Poulin, Jeffrey S. Measuring Software Reuse: Principles, Practices & Economic Models. 224p. (C). 1996. 39.95 (*0-201-63413-9*) Addison-Wesley.

Poulin, Joseph R. Pauline in Catalepsy & Psycho Therapeutics. 78p. 1996. reprint ed. spiral bd. 10.50 (*0-7873-1263-0*) Hlth Research.

Poulin, K. C. Special Events Planning: Avoiding the Disaster. (Illus.). 44p. Date not set. spiral bd. 15.00 (*1-928987-54-0*) Intl Fdtn Protect.

Poulin, Mary. New Strategies for Innovations in Medical Information Systems. 50p. 1984. 7.50 (*0-318-19205-5*, R-61) Inst Future.

Poulin, Michel, jt. auth. see Robin, Michael.

Poulin, Pamela L., tr. see Niedt, Friederich E.

Poulin, Pamela L., tr. & comment see Bach, Johann Sebastian.

Poulin, Robert. Evolutionary Ecology of Parasites: From Individuals to Communities. 1997. pap. 44.00 (*0-412-79370-9*) Kluwer Academic.

Poulin, Robert. Evolutionary Ecology of Parasites: From Individuals to Communities. LC 97-68947. 224p. 1997. write for info. (*0-412-80560-X*) Kluwer Academic.

Poulin, Stephane. Agarren Esa Gata (Can You Catch Josephine?) (SPA., Illus.). 24p. (J). (gr. 1-4). pap. 8.95 (*980-257-116-4*, Pub. by Ediciones Ekare) Kane-Miller Bk.

— Les Amours de Ma Mere - My Mother's Loves. (FRE., Illus.). 32p. (J). 1996. pap. 6.95 (*1-55037-150-9*, Pub. by Les Editions); lib. bdg. 15.95 (*1-55037-151-7*, Pub. by Les Editions) Firefly Bks Ltd.

— As-Tu Vu Josephine? LC 86-51044. (FRE., Illus.). 24p. (J). (gr. k-4). 1988. 12.95 (*0-88776-188-7*) Tundra Bks.

— Benjamin & the Pillow Saga. (Illus.). 32p. (J). (ps-2). 1990. 14.95 (*1-55037-069-3*, Pub. by Annick); pap. 5.95 (*1-55037-068-5*, Pub. by Annick) Firefly Bks Ltd.

— Benjamin et la Saga Des Oreillers Benjamin & the Pillow Saga. (Picture Bks.). (FRE., Illus.). 32p. (J). 1996. 15.95 (*1-55037-075-8*, Pub. by Les Editions); pap. 6.95 (*1-55037-074-X*, Pub. by Les Editions) Firefly Bks Ltd.

— Can You Catch Josephine? LC 87-50374. (Illus.). 24p. (J). (gr. 1-3). 1988. pap. 6.95 (*0-88776-214-X*) Tundra Bks.

— My Mother's Loves. (Illus.). 32p. (J). (ps-3). 1990. 15.95 (*1-55037-149-5*, Pub. by Annick); pap. 5.95 (*1-55037-148-7*, Pub. by Annick) Firefly Bks Ltd.

— Peux-tu Attraper Josephine? LC 87-50375. (FRE., Illus.). 24p. (J). (gr. k-4). 1988. 12.95 (*0-88776-199-2*) Tundra Bks.

— Pourrais-Tu Arreter Josephine? LC 88-50261. (FRE., Illus.). 24p. (J). (ps-3). 1989. 12.95 (*0-88776-217-4*); pap. 6.95 (*0-88776-228-X*) Tundra Bks.

— Travels for Two: Stories & Lies from My Childhood. (Illus.). 32p. (J). (ps-2). 1991. pap. 5.95 (*1-55037-204-1*, Pub. by Annick) Firefly Bks Ltd.

— Un Voyage Pour Deux - Travels for Two. (FRE., Illus.). 32p. (J). 1996. pap. 6.95 (*1-55037-206-8*, Pub. by Les Editions); lib. bdg. 15.95 (*1-55037-207-6*, Pub. by Les Editions) Firefly Bks Ltd.

Poulin, Stephane. Could You Stop Josephine? LC 88-50260. (Josephine Ser.). 24p. (J). (ps-3). 1988. 12.95 (*0-88776-216-6*); pap. 6.95 (*0-88776-227-1*) Tundra Bks.

Poulin, Stephane, jt. auth. see Pean, Stanley.

Poulin, Thomas G., ed. Avoiding Contract Disputes. 151p. 1985. 20.00 (*0-87262-484-6*) Am Soc Civil Eng.

Pouliquen, Louis Y. Risk Analysis in Project Appraisal. LC 79-120739. (World Bank Staff Occasional Papers: No. 11). 95p. (Orig.). reprint ed. pap. 30.00 (*0-7837-0342-2*, 204066100018) Bks Demand.

— Rural Infrastructure from a World Bank Perspective: A Knowledge Management Framework. LC 98-45135. 64p. 1999. pap. 22.00 (*0-8213-4309-2*, 14309) World Bank.

***Poulisse, Nanda.** Slips of the Tongue: Speech Errors in First & Second Language Production. LC 99-42694. (Studies in Bilingualism: Vol. 20). xvi, 257p. 1999. 75.00 (*1-55619-952-X*) J Benjamins Pubng Co.

Poullada, Leila D. & Poullada, Leon B. The Kingdom of Afghanistan & the United States, 1828-1973. LC 93-73121. 280p. (C). 1995. pap. 15.95 (*0-9637515-0-6*) Dageforde Pub.

Poullada, Leon B., jt. auth. see Poullada, Leila D.

Poullaos, Chris. Making the Australian Chartered Accountant. LC 94-2646. (New Works in Accounting History). 368p. 1994. reprint ed. text 20.00 (*0-8153-1717-4*) Garland.

Poulle, Emmanuel, contrib. by. Astronomie Planetaire au Moyen Age Latin. (Collected Studies). (FRE.). 320p. 1996. text 117.95 (*0-86078-589-0*, Pub. by Variorum) Ashgate Pub Co.

Poullet, Hector. Dictionnaire Creole-Francais. (CRE & FRE.). 480p. 1991. pap. write for info. (*0-7859-0505-7*, 2868770061) Fr & Eur.

Poullet, Hector, et al. Dictionnaire Creole Francais. (FRE.). 1991. write for info. (*0-7859-8164-0*, 2-86877-006-1) Fr & Eur.

Poullet, Y. & Vandenberghe, G. P., eds. Telebanking, Teleshopping & the Law. (Computer - Law Ser.: Vol. 1). 402p. 1988. pap. 104.00 (*90-6544-349-5*) Kluwer Law Intl.

Poullet, Y., jt. ed. see Vandenberghe, G. P.

Poullier, Jean-Pierre, jt. auth. see Denison, Edward F.

Poullioun, Maria-Luisa Le, see Le Poullioun, Maria-Luisa.

Poulos. Anatomy of Criminal Justice. 1976. text 37.00 (*0-88277-364-X*) Foundation Pr.

— Biography of Homicide. 1976. pap. text 20.25 (*0-88277-421-2*) Foundation Pr.

— Dynamics of Criminal Corrections. 1976. pap. text 17.95 (*0-88277-422-0*) Foundation Pr.

Poulos, Charlotte, jt. auth. see Frank, Marjorie.

Poulos, George. A Breath of God - Portrait of a Prelate: A Biography of Archbishop Iakovos. 1984. 10.95 (*0-916586-74-X*, Pub. by Holy Cross Orthodox) BookWorld.

Poulos, George. A Breath of God - Portrait of a Prelate: A Biography of Archbishop Iakovos. 177p. 1984. pap. 10.95 (*0-916586-98-7*, Pub. by Holy Cross Orthodox) BookWorld.

— Footsteps in the Sea: A Biography of Archbishop Athenagoras Cavadas. (Illus.). 186p. 1979. pap. 9.95 (*0-916586-35-9*, Pub. by Holy Cross Orthodox) BookWorld.

— Orthodox Saints, Vol. 1. 1992. pap. 13.95 (*0-917651-64-2*, Pub. by Holy Cross Orthodox) BookWorld.

— Orthodox Saints, Vol. 2. 1992. pap. 13.95 (*0-917651-65-0*, Pub. by Holy Cross Orthodox) BookWorld.

— Orthodox Saints, Vol. 3. 1992. pap. 13.95 (*0-917651-66-9*, Pub. by Holy Cross Orthodox) BookWorld.

— Orthodox Saints, Vol. 4. 1992. pap. 13.95 (*0-917651-67-7*, Pub. by Holy Cross Orthodox) BookWorld.

— Pomfret the Golden Decade. (Illus.). xii, 320p. (Orig.). 1988. pap. 9.95 (*0-917651-50-2*) Holy Cross Orthodox.

Poulos, H. G. Marine Geotechnics. (Illus.). 448p. 1988. mass mkt. 200.50 (*0-04-620024-X*) Routledge.

Poulos, Mary, ed. see Wilde, Larry.

Poulos, Nellie. Life's Story & Healings. 160p. pap. 3.00 (*0-686-29128-X*) Faith Pub Hse.

Poulos, Norma. Landscapes, Vol. 5. 58p. 1991. pap. 9.95 (*1-57377-081-7*) Easl Pubns.

— Landscapes, Vol. 6. 62p. 1991. pap. 9.95 (*1-57377-082-5*) Easl Pubns.

— Landscapes, Vol. 7. 68p. 1992. pap. 9.95 (*1-57377-083-3*) Easl Pubns.

Poulos, Norma. Landscapes, Vol. 8. (Illus.). 68p. 1992. pap. 9.95 (*1-57377-084-1*, 019884-1150) Easl Pubns.

Poulos, Paula N. A Women's War Too: U. S. Women in the Military in World War II. (Illus.). 406p. (Orig.). 1997. pap. text 50.00 (*0-7881-4514-2*) DIANE Pub.

Poulos, Paula N., ed. A Woman's War Too: U. S. Women in the Military in World War II. LC 95-50372. 1996. 15.00 (*1-880875-09-8*, 100018) National Archives & Recs.

Poulos, Steve J., jt. ed. see Hirschfeld, Ronald C.

Pouls, Gregory & Pouls, Maile. The Supplement Shopper. LC 99-12466. (Illus.). 500p. 1999. pap. 14.95 (*1-887299-17-3*) AlternMed Bks.

Pouls, Maile, jt. auth. see Pouls, Gregory.

***Poulsen, Allan.** Freezy Breezy Fun. (Look-Look Bks.). (Illus.). (J). 2000. pap. 3.29 (*0-307-12891-1*, Goldn Books) Gldn Bks Pub Co.

Poulsen, Axel D. Plant Diversity in Forests of Western Uganda & Eastern Zaire Preliminary Results. (AAU Report Ser.: No. 36). (Illus.). 76p. 1997. pap. 13.00 (*87-87600-64-1*, Pub. by Aarhus Univ Pr) David Brown.

Poulsen, Birte, jt. ed. see Isager, Signe.

Poulsen, David. Billy & the Bearman. 192p. (YA). 1996. pap. 6.95 (*0-929141-48-2*) Napoleon Publ.

Poulsen, David A. The Hunk Machine. (Salt & Pepper Chronicles Ser.). 126p. (J). (gr. 3-7). 1997. pap. 6.95 (*1-896184-28-6*) Roussan Pubs.

— The Vampire's Visit. (Salt & Pepper Chronicles Ser.). 126p. (J). (gr. 3-7). 1996. pap. 5.95 (*1-896184-12-X*) Roussan Pubs.

Poulsen, David A., et al. The Cowboy Country Cookbook. LC 96-910774. (Roundup Books). 352p. 1998. pap. 14.95 (*0-88995-162-4*, Pub. by Red Deer) Genl Dist Srvs.

Poulsen, Ebbe & Lawesson, Jonas, eds. Dryland Degradation: Causes & Consequences. (Illus.). 136p. (C). 1991. pap. text 19.95 (*87-7288-346-4*, Pub. by Aarhus Univ Pr) David Brown.

Poulsen, Erik. Asine II Fasc. 6, Pt. 2: Results of the Excavations East of the Acropolis 1970-1974; the Photogeometric Period, the Post-Geometric Settlement Material & Tombs of the Hellenistic Period. (Acta Instituti Atheniensis Regni Sueciae Ser.: Series 4, XXIV:6:2). (Illus.). 60p. (Orig.). 1994. pap. 39.50 (*91-7916-028-X*, Pub. by P Astroms) Coronet Bks.

Poulsen, Erik B., jt. auth. see Matthews, Martin S.

Poulsen, F., jt. ed. see Lindahl, Lars-Ake.

Poulsen, Frederik. Delphi. 38.95 (*0-405-19034-4*) Ayer.

Poulsen, Gail, jt. auth. see Poulsen, Ken.

Poulsen, Hemming, jt. auth. see Dallenbach-Hellweg, G.

Poulsen, Hemming, jt. auth. see Dallenbach-Hellweg, Gisela.

Poulsen, Hemming, jt. ed. see Dallenbach-Hellweg, Gisela.

Poulsen, Henrik. Conations: On Striving, Willing & Wishing & Their Relationship with Cognition, Emotions & Motives. 160p. (C). 1991. pap. 19.95 (*87-7288-358-8*, Pub. by Aarhus Univ Pr) David Brown.

Poulsen, Ken & Poulsen, Gail. Water Workout. (Illus.). 31p. 1996. spiral bd. 20.00 (*0-9654087-0-1*) LFI Pubns.

Poulsen, O. Danish-German Correspondence Dictionary: Dansk-Tysk Ordbog for Correspondenter. (DAN & GER.). 415p. 1980. 59.95 (*0-8288-0832-5*, M1273) Fr & Eur.

Poulsen, Peter. Scandinavian Revenue Stamps: Denmark. Nelson, Paul A., ed. (Illus.). 96p. (Orig.). (C). 1989. pap. text 14.00 (*0-929850-00-9*) SPLOSC.

***Poulsen, Peter Bo, ed.** Health Technology Assessment & Diffusion of Health Technology. 303p. 1999. pap. 29.75 (*87-7838-481-8*, Pub. by Odense Universitets Forlag) Intl Spec Bk.

Poulsen, Peter D. The Ancient Truths about Marriage & Divorce: What Your Pastor, Counselor & Lawyer Won't Tell. 312p. 1998. pap. 24.95 (*0-9665898-0-7*) Consultant Spec.

Poulsen, Richard C. The Body As Text: In a Perpetual Age of Non-Reason. LC 94-22607. (Revisioning Philosophy Ser.: Vol. 18). 182p. (C). 1996. text 46.95 (*0-8204-2507-9*) P Lang Pubng.

— The Landscape of the Mind: Cultural Transformations of the American West. LC 92-2950. (American University Studies: American Literature: Ser. XXIV, Vol. 23). 136p. (C). 1992. text 33.95 (*0-8204-1375-5*) P Lang Pubng.

Poulsen, Thomas M. Nations & States: A Geographic Background to World Affairs. LC 94-13925. 480p. 1994. text 41.80 (*0-13-678913-7*) P-H.

Poulson. Economic Development. Date not set. pap. text, teacher ed. write for info. (*0-314-03365-3*) West Pub.

— Quest for the Grail: Arthurian Legend in British Art 1840-1920. LC 98-29632. (Illus.). 256p. 1999. text 79.95 (*0-7190-5379-X*) St Martin.

Poulson, Barry. Fiscal Policy & Fiscal Reform in Colorado. (Issue Paper #5-98 Ser.). 56p. 1998. pap. text 8.00 (*1-57655-167-9*) Independ Inst.

— A Quota by Any Other Name: The Cost of Affirmative Action Programs in the Construction of Denver International Airport. (Issue Paper #6-94 Ser.). 32p. 1994. pap. text 8.00 (*1-57655-134-2*) Independ Inst.

— A Quota by Any Other Name: The Cost of Affirmative Action Programs in the Construction of Denver International Airport. (Issue Papers: No. 6-94). 9p. 1994. pap. text 8.00 (*1-57655-059-1*) Independ Inst.

— Solving Colorado's Educational Finance Problems. (Issue Paper #4-98 Ser.). 17p. 1998. pap. write for info. (*1-57655-166-0*) Independ Inst.

Poulson, Barry, jt. auth. see Bickel, Vern.

Poulson, Barry M. Fiscal Policies for Economic Growth in Colorado. (Issue Papers: No. 11-86). 6p. 1986. pap. text 8.00 (*1-57655-011-7*) Independ Inst.

***Poulson, Barry W.** Back to Basics for Tax Reform in Colorado. 2000. pap. write for info. (*1-57655-177-6*) Independ Inst.

Poulson, Barry W. Colorado Tax Reform: An Economist Grades the 1987 Legislature. (Issue Papers: No. 8-87). 4p. 1987. pap. text 8.00 (*1-57655-019-2*) Independ Inst.

— Fiscal Constitution Breaking down in Colorado: Economist Sees Public Sector Failure. 8p. 1988. pap. text 8.00 (*1-57655-112-1*) Independ Inst.

— Health Vouchers Could Cure the Medicaid Crisis: Medically Indigent & State Treasury Would Both Be Healthier. (Issue Papers: No. 1-93). 10p. 1993. pap. text 8.00 (*1-57655-079-6*) Independ Inst.

— How Not to Close a Military Base: The Lowery Economic Recovery Project. (Issue Papers: No. 8-94). 11p. 1994. pap. write for info. (*1-57655-057-5*) Independ Inst.

— How Not to Close a Military Base: The Lowry Economic Recovery Project. rev. ed. (Eight-94 Ser.). 11p. 1994. pap. text 8.00 (*1-57655-136-9*) Independ Inst.

— Reforming Post Secondary Education in Colorado. (Issue Paper #9-97 Ser.). 37p. 1997. pap. text 8.00 (*1-57655-161-X*) Independ Inst.

— Reforming Post Secondary Education in Colorado. (Issue Paper #9-97 Ser.). 37p. 1998. pap. text 8.00 (*1-57655-170-9*) Independ Inst.

— Should Colorado Taxpayers Impose Tougher Spending Controls? 10p. 1988. pap. text 8.00 (*1-57655-082-6*) Independ Inst.

— Stop Looking the Books on Set-a-Sides: How Statistical Disparity Misleads & Multiple Regression Excels for Assessing Discrimination in Public Works Contracting. (Issue Papers: No. 7-93). 13p. 1993. pap. text 8.00 (*1-57655-076-1*) Independ Inst.

— Supply Side Benefits of Colorado's Flat Tax: Tinkering Could Hurt Revenues & Fairness. (Issue Papers: No. 9-91). 10p. 1991. pap. text 8.00 (*1-57655-055-9*) Independ Inst.

***Poulson, Barry W.** Surplus Expenditures in Colorado. 1999. pap. write for info. (*1-57655-185-7*) Independ Inst.

Poulson, Barry W. Value Added in Manufacturing, Mining, & Agriculture in the American Economy from 1809 to 1839. LC 75-2592. (Dissertations in American Economic History Ser.). (Illus.). 1975. 20.95 (*0-405-07214-7*) Ayer.

— What to Do with Surplus Revenue in Colorado. (Issue Paper #7-98 Ser.). 28p. 1998. pap. text 8.00 (*1-57655-171-7*) Independ Inst.

Poulson, Barry W., jt. auth. see Roche, Edward J., Jr.

Poulson, Christine. The Quest for the Grail: Arthurian Legend in British Art, 1840-1920. LC 98-29632. (Illus.). 256p. 1999. pap. 29.95 (*0-7190-5537-7*, Pub. by St Martin) St Martin.

Poulson, Christine, ed. William Morris on Art & Design. (SAP Literature Ser.). 100p. 1996. pap. 9.95 (*1-85075-611-2*, Pub. by Sheffield Acad) CUP Services.

Poulson, Clair. Samuel: Gadianton's Foe. LC 94-10385. 1994. pap. 9.95 (*1-55503-658-9*, 01111574) Covenant Comms.

— Samuel: Moroni's Young Warrior. LC 92-70859. 1993. pap. 10.95 (*1-55503-553-1*, 29004799) Covenant Comms.

— Samuel: Thunder in Paradise. LC 96-33842. 1996. pap. 10.95 (*1-55503-921-9*, 01112414) Covenant Comms.

***Poulson, Clair M.** Point of Impact. 1999. pap. 12.95 (*1-55517-403-5*) CFI Dist.

Poulson, Louise. The English Curriculum in Schools. LC 99-226229. 160p. 1998. 69.95 (*0-304-33783-8*); pap. 24.95 (*0-304-33782-X*) Continuum.

Poulson, Lynn H. Uncommon Common Sense: A Guide for Engaged & Married Couples. LC 92-46167. (Illus.). 336p. 1993. pap. 15.95 (*0-935834-98-2*) Rainbow Books.

Poulson, Thomas L. & Wells, Bethany J., eds. Cave Research Foundation Annual Report, 1979. (Illus.). 74p. (Orig.). 1981. pap. 5.00 (*0-939748-14-2*) Cave Bks MO.

Poulsson, Emilie. Finger Plays for Nursery & Kindergarten. (Illus.). 88p. (J). (ps-1). 1998. reprint ed. 15.00 (*0-89904-758-0*, Silhouette Imprints); reprint ed. spiral bd. 10.00 (*0-89904-759-9*, Silhouette Imprints) Crumb Elbow Pub.

— Finger Plays for Nursery & Kindergarten. 70th ed. LC 74-165397. (Illus.). (J). (ps). 1971. reprint ed. pap. 3.95 (*0-486-22588-7*) Dover.

Poulsson, Emilie. Lessons from the Farmyard. (Illus.). 45p. (J). (gr. k-1). 1992. pap. text 3.50 (*1-930092-25-3*, CLP29605) Christian Liberty.

Poulter, A. G., et al. Nicopolis Ad Istrum: The Finds. LC 97-47439. (Reports of the Research Committee of the Society of Antiquaries of London). (Illus.). 384p. 1999. 145.00 (*0-7185-0168-3*) Bks Intl VA.

***Poulter, Alan, et al.** The Library & Information Professional's Guide to the World Wide Web. 133p. 1999. 40.00 (*1-85604-227-8*, Pub. by Library Association) Bernan Associates.

Poulter, Allan, jt. ed. see Gyngell, Julian.

Poulter, Christine. Playing the Game. LC 90-53168. (Illus.). 150p. (Orig.). 1991. pap. 16.00 (*0-88734-611-1*) Players Pr.

Poulter, G. C. Corbould Genealogy, in England. 165p. 1994. reprint ed. pap. 25.00 (*0-8328-4144-7*); reprint ed. lib. bdg. 35.00 (*0-8328-4143-9*) Higginson Bk Co.

Poulter, J. D. Early History of Electricity Supply: The Story of the Electric Light in Victorian Leeds. Bowers, B., ed. (History of Technology Ser.: No. 5). 222p. 1986. boxed set 79.00 (*0-86341-060-X*, HT005) INSPEC Inc.

Poulter, Neil, et al, eds. Cardiovascular Disease: Risk Factors & Intervention. 1993. 99.00 (*1-870905-54-7*, Radcliffe Med Pr) Scovill Paterson.

Poulter, Nick. Growing Vines to Make Wines. (Illus.). 192p. (Orig.). 1998. pap. 18.95 (*1-85486-181-6*) Nexus Special Interests.

Poulter, Sebastian. Ethnicity, Law & Human Rights: The English Experience. 456p. 1998. text 85.00 (*0-19-825773-2*) OUP.

Poulter, Stephan, jt. auth. see Zax, Barbara.

Poulter, Virgil L. An Introduction to Old Spanish: A Guide to the Study of the History of Spanish with Selected Readings. (American University Studies: Romance Languages & Literature: Ser. II, Vol. 130). (Illus.). XIV, 190p. (C). 1990. text 41.80 (*0-8204-1170-1*) P Lang Pubng.

Poulter, Wallace. SNES Compendium. 12.99 (*1-56686-352-X*) Brady Pub.

Poultney, David. Dictionary of Western Church Music. LC 91-12325. (Illus.). 272p. 1991. 30.00 (*0-8389-0569-2*) ALA.

— Studying Music History: Learning, Reasoning & Writing about Music History & Literature. 2nd ed. LC 95-13540. 262p. (C). 1995. pap. text 52.00 (*0-13-190224-5*) P-H.

Poultney, James W., ed. see Mittenthal, Suzanne M.

***Poulton, Alan.** A Dictionary-Catalog of Modern British Composers, 82. LC 00-26439. (Music Reference Collection: Vol. 82). 2000. lib. bdg. 250.00 (*0-313-31623-6*) Greenwood.

— A Dictionary-Catalog of Modern British Composers: A-C, Vol. 1. (Music Reference Collection: Vol. 82). 608p. 2000. lib. bdg. 99.50 (*0-313-28711-2*, GR8711, Greenwood Pr) Greenwood.

— A Dictionary-Catalog of Modern British Composers: D-L, Vol. 2. (Music Reference Collection: Vol. 82). 536p. 2000. lib. bdg. 99.50 (*0-313-28712-0*, GR8712, Greenwood Pr) Greenwood.

— A Dictionary-Catalog of Modern British Composers: M-Z, Vol. 3. (Music Reference Collection: Vol. 82). 600p. 2000. lib. bdg. 99.50 (*0-313-28713-9*, GR8713, Greenwood Pr) Greenwood.

Poulton, E. C. Bias in Quantifying Judgments. 328p. 1989. 69.95 (*0-86377-105-X*) L Erlbaum Assocs.

— Fallacies in Dealing with Probabilities. LC 93-26636. (Illus.). 334p. (C). 1994. text 64.95 (*0-521-44368-7*) Cambridge U Pr.

Poulton, Gail, ed. see Pfeifer, Diane.

Poulton, Helen. Index to History of Nevada, 1881: Thompson & West. (Illus.). 1981. pap. 15.00 (*0-913814-43-1*) Nevada Pubns.

Poulton, Helen J. The Historian's Handbook: A Descriptive Guide to Reference Works. LC 71-165774. xi, 304 p. 1972. write for info. (*0-8061-0985-8*) U of Okla Pr.

Poulton, Helen J. & Howland, Marguerite S. The Historian's Handbook: A Descriptive Guide to Reference Works. LC 71-165774. 300p. 1972. pap. 19.95 (*0-8061-1009-0*) U of Okla Pr.

Poulton, Hugh. The Balkans: Minorities & States in Conflict. 2nd ed. 250p. 1993. 45.00 (*1-873194-45-5*, Pub. by Minority Rts Pubns); pap. 19.95 (*1-873194-40-4*, Pub. by Minority Rts Pubns) Paul & Co Pubs.

— The Top Hat, the Grey Wolf, & the Crescent: Turkish Nationalism & the Turkish Republic. LC 96-41941. 1997. text 40.00 (*0-8147-6648-X*) NYU Pr.

— Who Are the Macedonians? LC 94-10136. 244p. 1995. 35.00 (*0-253-34598-7*) Ind U Pr.

***Poulton, Hugh.** Who Are the Macedonians? 2nd ed. LC 99-45487. (Illus.). 274p. 2000. pap. 18.95 (*0-253-21359-2*) Ind U Pr.

Poulton, John, jt. auth. see Dally, William J.

***Poulton, Kimberly.** Hello Willow. LC 00-100669. (Illus.). 32p. (J). (ps-k). 2000. 15.95 (*0-9677929-0-8*) Moon Mt Pubng Inc.

***Poulton, M. Cody.** Spirits of Another Sort: The Plays of Izumi Kyoka. (Michigan Monograph Series in Japanese Studies: Vol. 29). 350p. 2000. 49.95 (*0-939512-01-7*, 52090, Pub. by U MI Japan) U of Mich Pr.

Poulton, M. L. Alternative Engines for Road Vehicles. LC 94-70408. 192p. 1994. 91.00 (*1-56252-224-8*, 3005) Computational Mech MA.

Poulton, M. L. Alternative Engines for Road Vehicles. 192p. 1994. 91.00 (*1-85312-300-5*, Pub. by WIT Pr) Computational Mech MA.

Poulton, M. L. Alternative Fuels for Road Vehicles. LC 94-70407. 232p. 1994. 104.00 (*1-56252-225-6*, 3013) Computational Mech MA.

Poulton, M. L. Alternative Fuels for Road Vehicles. 232p. 1994. 104.00 (*1-85312-301-3*, Pub. by WIT Pr) Computational Mech MA.

Poulton, M. L. Fuel Efficient Car Technology. LC 96-86042. 160p. 1997. 91.00 (*1-85312-447-8*, 4478, Pub. by WIT Pr) Computational Mech MA.

Poulton, Michael S., et al, eds. The Constitution of the Socialist Federal Republic of Yugoslavia. LC 76-13392. (Constitutions of the World Ser.: Vol. 1). 1976. 30.00 (*0-89304-020-7*, CCC104); pap. 15.00 (*0-89304-006-1*) Cross-Cultrl NY.

Poulton, Nick L., jt. auth. see Norris, Donald M.

Poulton, Prue, jt. auth. see Wright, David.

Poulton, Susan E., jt. auth. see Norris, Donald M.

Poulton, Terry. No Fat Chicks: How Big Business Profits by Making Women Hate Their Bodies--How to Fight Back. LC 97-19002. 256p. 1997. 21.95 (*1-55972-423-4*) Carol Pub Group.

Pouncey, Peter R. The Necessities of War: A Study of Thucydides' Pessimism. LC 80-16887. 213p. reprint ed. pap. 66.10 (*0-8357-8965-9*, 203359500086) Bks Demand.

Pouncy, Carolyn J., ed. from RUS. The Domostroi: Rules for Russian Households in the Time of Ivan the Terrible. (Illus.). 280p. 1994. text 37.50 (*0-8014-2410-0*) Cornell U Pr.

Pound. Shakespears Pound: Illuminated Cantos. 435.95 (*0-7546-0033-5*) Ashgate Pub Co.

Pound & Michaux, Henri. Signs in Action: Pound/Michaux & of Languages. Sieburth, Richard, tr. & contrib. by by. LC 87-42539. 48p. 1987. pap. 4.00 (*0-87376-057-3*) Red Dust.

Pound, Arthur. The Golden Earth: The Story of Manhattan's Landed Wealth. LC 75-1865. (Leisure Class in America Ser.). (Illus.). 1975. reprint ed. 25.95 (*0-405-06931-6*) Ayer.

— Johnson of the Mohawks. 1977. lib. bdg. 59.95 (*0-8490-2107-3*) Gordon Pr.

— Johnson of the Mohawks. 568p. 1993. reprint ed. lib. bdg. 99.00 (*0-7812-5195-8*) Rprt Serv.

— Lake Ontario. (American Lakes Ser.). lib. bdg. 26.95 (*0-8488-2013-4*) Amereon Ltd.

— Native Stock. LC 70-90674. (Essay Index Reprint Ser.). 1977. 23.95 (*0-8369-1373-6*) Ayer.

— Penns of Pennsylvania & England. 1993. reprint ed. lib. bdg. 89.00 (*0-7812-5819-7*) Rprt Serv.

Pound, Arthur & Day, Richard E. Johnson of the Mohawks. LC 75-164621. (Select Bibliographies Reprint Ser.). 1977. reprint ed. 48.95 (*0-8369-5904-3*) Ayer.

Pound, Arthur, ed. see Barron, Clarence W.

Pound, Daniel. Political Economy & Ideology in the Managerial - Technological Society. 144p. 1990. per. 31.95 (*0-8403-5697-8*) Kendall-Hunt.

Pound, Dorothy, jt. auth. see Pound, Ezra.

Pound, Ezra. ABC of Reading. LC 60-30304. 1960. pap. 10.95 (*0-8112-0151-1*, NDP89, Pub. by New Directions) Norton.

— America, Roosevelt & the Causes of the Present War. 1983. lib. bdg. 250.00 (*0-87700-462-5*) Revisionist Pr.

— Antheil & the Treatise on Harmony. (Collected Works of Ezra Pound). 150p. 1999. reprint ed. lib. bdg. 88.00 (*1-58201-808-1*) Classic Bks.

— The Cantos of Ezra Pound. LC 70-117217. 832p. 1996. pap. 22.95 (*0-8112-1326-9*, NDP824, Pub. by New Directions) Norton.

— The Cantos of Ezra Pound: No. 1-117. LC 70-117217. 1970. 42.00 (*0-8112-0350-6*, Pub. by New Directions) Norton.

— The Cantos (121-150) Andre, Michael, ed. LeWitt, Sol, tr. 120p. 69.95 (*0-934450-56-0*) Unmuzzled Ox.

— Classic Noh Theatre of Japan. LC 59-9488. Orig. Title: Noh, or Accomplishment, a Study of the Classical Stage of Japan. (C). 1959. pap. 10.95 (*0-8112-0152-X*, NDP79, Pub. by New Directions) Norton.

— The Collected Early Poems of Ezra Pound. King, Michael et al, eds. LC 76-7086. (Illus.). 352p. 1982. reprint ed. pap. 13.95 (*0-8112-0843-5*, NDP540, Pub. by New Directions) Norton.

— Confucion Analects. 136p. 1980. 30.00 (*0-7206-1850-9*, Pub. by P Owen Ltd) Dufour.

— Diptych Rome-London. LC 93-50805. (Bibelot Ser.). 64p. 1994. pap. 5.00 (*0-8112-1268-8*, NDP783, Pub. by New Directions) Norton.

— A Draft of XXX Cantos. LC 74-6379. (Studies in Pound: No. 103). 1974. lib. bdg. 75.00 (*0-8383-1997-1*) M S G Haskell Hse.

— A Draft of XXX Cantos. LC 89-13432. Vol. 690. 160p. 1990. reprint ed. pap. 10.95 (*0-8112-1128-2*, NDP690, Pub. by New Directions) Norton.

— Early Poems. unabridged ed. (Thirft Editions Ser.). 80p. 1996. reprint ed. pap. text 1.00 (*0-486-28745-9*) Dover.

Pound, Ezra. The Exile: Magazine of 1927. 127p. 1927. 25.00 (*0-87556-856-4*) Saifer.

Pound, Ezra. Exultations. (Collected Works of Ezra Pound). 51p. 1999. reprint ed. lib. bdg. 88.00 (*1-58201-809-X*) Classic Bks.

— Exultations. LC 72-10016. (Studies in Poetry: No. 38). 1973. reprint ed. lib. bdg. 75.00 (*0-8383-1683-2*) M S G Haskell Hse.

— Ezra Pound & the Visual Arts. Zinnes, Harriet, ed. LC 80-36720. 352p. 1980. 25.95 (*0-8112-0772-2*, Pub. by New Directions) Norton.

Pound, Ezra. Ezra Pound Reads: Pound,&Ezra, Set. unabridged ed. 1993. audio 19.00 (*1-55994-845-0*, DCN 2088) HarperAudio.

Pound, Ezra. Ezra Pound Translations. enl. ed. LC 78-13153. 1978. reprint ed. lib. bdg. 69.50 (*0-313-21169-8*, POTO, Greenwood Pr) Greenwood.

P

— Gaudier-Brzeska: A Memoir. LC 78-107490. 1974. pap. 9.95 (*0-8112-0527-4*, NDP372, Pub. by New Directions) Norton.

— Gold & Work. 1983. lib. bdg. 250.00 (*0-87700-461-7*) Revisionist Pr.

— Guide to Kulchur. LC 52-12142. 1968. reprint ed. pap. 13.95 (*0-8112-0156-2*, NDP257, Pub. by New Directions) Norton.

— How to Read. 1972. 200.00 (*0-87968-021-0*) Gordon Pr.

— How to Read. LC 79-169105. (American Literature Ser.: No. 49). 1971. lib. bdg. 75.00 (*0-8383-1315-9*) M S G Haskell Hse.

— Hugh Selwyn Mauberley. (Collected Works of Ezra Pound). 181p. 1999. reprint ed. lib. bdg. 88.00 (*1-58201-810-3*) Classic Bks.

— Instigations. LC 67-23261. (Essay Index Reprint Ser.). 1977. 23.95 (*0-8369-0795-7*) Ayer.

— Instigations of Ezra Pound, Together with an Essay on the Chinese Written Character by Ernest Fenollosa. (Collected Works of Ezra Pound). 388p. 1999. reprint ed. lib. bdg. 88.00 (*1-58201-811-1*) Classic Bks.

— An Introduction to the Economic Nature of the United States. 1983. lib. bdg. 250.00 (*0-87700-460-9*) Revisionist Pr.

— Letters of Ezra Pound. LC 74-11145. (Studies in Pound: No. 103). 1974. lib. bdg. 75.00 (*0-8383-1991-2*) M S G Haskell Hse.

— The Letters of Ezra Pound to Alice Corbin Henderson. Nadel, Ira B., ed. LC 93-9162. (Illus.). 296p. (C). 1993. 34.95 (*0-292-71134-4*) U of Tex Pr.

— Letters to Ibbotson. LC 78-55724. (Ezra Pound Scholarship Ser.). 145p. 1979. 15.00 (*0-915032-10-4*) Natl Poet Foun.

— Literary Essays. LC 78-13133. 464p. 1978. reprint ed. lib. bdg. 75.00 (*0-313-21167-1*, POLE, Greenwood Pr) Greenwood.

— Literary Essays. Eliot, T. S., ed. LC 54-7905. 1968. reprint ed. pap. 13.95 (*0-8112-0157-0*, NDP250, Pub. by New Directions) Norton.

— Lustra. LC 72-11762. (Studies in Poetry: No. 38). 1973. reprint ed. lib. bdg. 75.00 (*0-8383-1688-3*) M S G Haskell Hse.

— Machine Art & Other Writings. Ardizzone, Maria L., ed. & intro. by. LC 95-50858. (Illus.). 232p. 1996. pap. 16.95 (*0-8223-1765-6*); text 39.95 (*0-8223-1756-7*) Duke.

— Make It New: Essays. 1988. reprint ed. lib. bdg. 79.00 (*0-7812-0195-0*) Rprt Serv.

— Make It New: Essays. LC 71-145243. 1971. reprint ed. 59.00 (*0-403-01158-2*) Scholarly.

— Pavannes & Divagations. (Collected Works of Ezra Pound). 262p. 1999. reprint ed. lib. bdg. 88.00 (*1-58201-812-X*) Classic Bks.

— Pavannes & Divagations. LC 58-9510. 256p. 1975. reprint ed. pap. 9.95 (*0-8112-0575-4*, NDP397, Pub. by New Directions) Norton.

— Personae: The Shorter Poems of Ezra Pound. 2nd ed. LC 89-14036. 304p. 1990. reprint ed. 23.95 (*0-8112-1120-7*, Pub. by New Directions) Norton.

— Personae: The Shorter Poems of Ezra Pound. 2nd ed. LC 89-14036. 304p. 1990. reprint ed. pap. 14.95 (*0-8112-1138-X*, NDP697, Pub. by New Directions) Norton.

— Plays Modelled on the Noh (1916) Gallup, Donald C., ed. LC 87-124514. (Illus.). 38p. 1987. pap. 17.00 (*0-918160-02-2*) Friends Univ Toledo.

— Polite Essays. LC 67-22111. (Essay Index Reprint Ser.). 1977. 23.95 (*0-8369-0796-5*) Ayer.

— Pound - Joyce: Letters & Essays. LC 66-27616. (Correspondence of Ezra Pound Ser.). 1970. pap. 10.95 (*0-8112-0159-7*, NDP296, Pub. by New Directions) Norton.

— Quarterly Review of Literature: The 1940s, Special Issue, Vol. V, No. 2. 1940. pap. 10.00 (*1-888545-20-8*) Quarterly Rev.

— A Quinzaine for This Yule: Facsimile of the 1908 First Edition. 1973. 200.00 (*0-87968-087-3*) Gordon Pr.

— Selected Cantos. LC 75-11446. 1970. pap. 7.95 (*0-8112-0160-0*, NDP304, Pub. by New Directions) Norton.

— Selected Poems. LC 57-8603. 1957. pap. 8.95 (*0-8112-0162-7*, NDP66, Pub. by New Directions) Norton.

— Selected Prose, 1909-1965. Cookson, William, ed. LC 72-93978. 480p. 1975. pap. 15.95 (*0-8112-0574-6*, NDP396, Pub. by New Directions) Norton.

— Social Credit: An Impact. 1983. lib. bdg. 250.00 (*0-87700-457-9*) Revisionist Pr.

— Spirit of Romance. LC 53-5860. 1968. reprint ed. pap. 12.95 (*0-8112-0163-5*, NDP266, Pub. by New Directions) Norton.

— The Spirit of Romance. (Collected Works of Ezra Pound). 251p. 1999. reprint ed. lib. bdg. 98.00 (*1-58201-813-8*) Classic Bks.

— Translations. rev. ed. LC 53-11965. 1953. pap. 13.95 (*0-8112-0164-3*, NDP145, Pub. by New Directions) Norton.

— A Visiting Card: Ancient & Modern History of Script & Money. 1983. lib. bdg. 250.00 (*0-87700-458-7*) Revisionist Pr.

— A Walking Tour in Southern France: Ezra Pound among the Troubadours. LC 92-19890. (Illus.). 160p. 1992. 22.95 (*0-8112-1223-8*, Pub. by New Directions) Norton.

— What Is Money For? 1983. lib. bdg. 250.00 (*0-87700-459-5*) Revisionist Pr.

— What Is Money For? A Sane Man's Guide to Economics. 1982. lib. bdg. 250.00 (*0-87700-408-0*) Revisionist Pr.

— Women of Trachis. 96p. 1985. pap. 6.95 (*0-8112-0948-2*, NDP597, Pub. by New Directions) Norton.

Pound, Ezra, tr. Confucius: The Great Digest, the Unwobbling Pivot, the Analects. LC 74-87911. 1969. pap. 13.95 (*0-8112-0154-6*, NDP285, Pub. by New Directions) Norton.

— Shih-Ching: The Classic Anthology Defined by Confucius. 335p. 1976. pap. text 12.95 (*0-674-13397-8*) HUP.

Pound, Ezra & Anderson, Margaret. Pound - the Little Review: The Letters of Ezra Pound to Margaret Anderson. Scott, Thomas L. et al, eds. LC 88-3410. (Correspondence of Ezra Pound Ser.: Vol. 6). 384p. 1989. 37.50 (*0-8112-1059-6*, Pub. by New Directions) Norton.

Pound, Ezra & Ford, Ford Madox. Pound-Ford: The Story of a Literary Friendship. Seyersted, Brita L., ed. LC 82-2255. (Correspondence of Ezra Pound Ser.). 384p. (C). 1982. 22.95 (*0-8112-0833-8*, Pub. by New Directions) Norton.

Pound, Ezra & Lewis, Wyndham. Pound-Lewis: The Letters of Ezra Pound & Wyndham Lewis. Materer, Timothy, ed. LC 85-3007. (Correspondence of Ezra Pound Ser.). 384p. 1985. 37.50 (*0-8112-0932-6*, Pub. by New Directions) Norton.

Pound, Ezra & Pound, Dorothy. Ezra & Dorothy Pound: Letters in Captivity, 1945-1946. Pound, Omar & Spoo, Robert, eds. LC 97-50635. (Illus.). 448p. 1999. 35.00 (*0-19-510793-4*) OUP.

Pound, Ezra & Spann, Marcella, eds. Confucius to Cummings: An Anthology of Poetry. LC 62-17274. (C). 1964. pap. 13.95 (*0-8112-0155-4*, NDP126, Pub. by New Directions) Norton.

Pound, Ezra & Williams, William Carlos. Pound/Williams: Selected Letters of Ezra Pound & William Carlos Williams. Witemeyer, Hugh, ed. LC 95-38462. (Correspondence of Ezra Pound Ser.). 480p. 1996. 39.95 (*0-8112-1301-3*, Pub. by New Directions) Norton.

Pound, Ezra & Zukofsky, Louis. Pound - Zukofsky. LC 86-19181. (Correspondence of Ezra Pound Ser.). 384p. 1987. 38.50 (*0-8112-1013-8*, Pub. by New Directions) Norton.

Pound, Ezra, et al. Ezra Pound & Margaret Cravens: A Tragic Friendship, 1910-1912. Pound, Omar & Spoo, Robert, eds. LC 88-7156. (Illus.). 168p. 1988. text 35.95 (*0-8223-0862-2*) Duke.

— I Cease Not to Yowl: Ezra Pound's Letters to Olivia Rossetti Agresti. Tryphonopoulos, Demetres P. & Surette, Leon, eds. LC 98-8909. (Illus.). 327p. 1998. 34.95 (*0-252-02410-9*) U of Ill Pr.

Pound, Ezra, jt. auth. see Fenollosa, Ernest.

Pound, Ezra, jt. auth. see Fenollosa, Ernest F.

Pound, Ezra, tr. see Morand, Paul.

Pound, G., jt. auth. see Hirth, J.

Pound House Staff. Dylife. (C). 1985. text 25.00 (*0-906885-04-3*, Pub. by Pound Hse) St Mut.

— Frongoch Lead & Zinc Mine. (C). 1985. text 45.00 (*0-7855-6573-6*, Pub. by Pound Hse) St Mut.

— The Hereford & Gloucester Canal. 80p. (C). 1985. text 39.00 (*0-906874-05-X*, Pub. by Pound Hse) St Mut.

— The Mines of Newent & Ross. (C). 1985. text 40.00 (*0-906885-06-X*, Pub. by Pound Hse) St Mut.

— The Old Copper Mines of Snowdonia. 128p. (C). 1985. pap. text 40.00 (*0-906885-03-5*, Pub. by Pound Hse) St Mut.

— The Old Industries of Dean. (C). 1985. pap. text 45.00 (*0-7855-6572-8*, Pub. by Pound Hse) St Mut.

Pound, Jeffrey J. Ponds & Creeks: Parables of Spiritual Growth. LC 96-69311. 64p. (Orig.). 1996. pap. 8.95 (*1-57736-005-2*) Providence Hse.

Pound, Jere M. Tales from Po Biddy Road. (Illus.). 1999. pap. 14.95 (*0-9672461-9-9*) I&D Books.

Pound, John. Are Takeover Targets Undervalued? An Empirical Examination of the Financial Characteristics of Target Companies. 39p. 1986. pap. 10.00 (*0-931035-54-6*) IRRC Inc DC.

— The Long Trick of Pennywise. (C). 1990. pap. 35.00 (*0-7223-2457-X*, Pub. by A H S Ltd) St Mut.

Pound, John, ed. Immunochemical Protocols. 2nd ed. LC 97-39695. (Methods in Molecular Biology Ser.: Vol. 80). 528p. 1998. 109.50 (*0-89603-493-3*) Humana.

— Immunochemical Protocols. 2nd ed. LC 97-39695. (Methods in Molecular Biology Ser.: Vol. 80). (Illus.). 528p. 1998. spiral bd. 89.50 (*0-89603-388-0*) Humana.

Pound, John F. Military Survey of 1522 for Babergh Hundred. (Suffolk Records Society Ser.: No. XXVIII). 166p. 1986. 45.00 (*0-85115-438-7*) Boydell & Brewer.

***Pound, Linda.** Supporting Mathematical Development in the Early Years. LC 98-49817. 128p. 1998. pap. 21.95 (*0-335-19887-2*) Taylor & Francis.

Pound, Lisa. Supporting Mathematical Development in the Early Years. LC 98-49817. 128p. 1998. 75.00 (*0-335-19888-0*) Taylor & Francis.

Pound, Louise. American Ballads & Songs. (BCL1-PS American Literature Ser.). 266p. 1992. reprint ed. lib. bdg. 79.00 (*0-7812-6647-5*) Rprt Serv.

— Nebraska Folklore. LC 89-32799. x, 245p. 1989. reprint ed. pap. 11.95 (*0-8032-8724-0*, Bison Books) U of Nebr Pr.

Pound, Louise & Bradley, Francis W. The American Dialect Society - A Historical Sketch; The Press As an Ally in Collecting Folk Speech. (Publications of the American Dialect Society: No. 17). 44p. 1952. pap. 4.50 (*0-8173-0617-X*) U of Ala Pr.

Pound, Omar. Pissle & the Holy Grail. LC 86-62329. 64p. 1987. 12.95 (*0-913506-18-4*) Woolmer-Brotherson.

Pound, Omar, ed. see Pound, Ezra & Pound, Dorothy.

Pound, Omar, ed. see Pound, Ezra, et al.

***Pound, Richard W. & Osgoode Society for Canadian Legal History Staff.** Chief Justice W. R. Jackett: By the Law of the Land. 1999. pap. 39.95 (*0-7735-1898-3*) McG-Queens Univ Pr.

Pound, Ron, jt. auth. see Pritchett, Price.

Pound, Roscoe. Administrative Law: Its Growth, Procedure & Significance. x, 138p. 1981. reprint ed. 35.00 (*0-8377-1009-X*, Rothman) W S Hein.

— Contemporary Juristic Theory. viii, 83p. 1981. reprint ed. 40.00 (*0-8377-1008-1*, Rothman) W S Hein.

— Criminal Justice in America. LC 97-22744. 236p. 1997. pap. text 24.95 (*1-56000-941-1*) Transaction Pubs.

— The Future of the Common Law. 1990. 16.50 (*0-8446-1361-4*) Peter Smith.

— Interpretations of Legal History. 1990. 16.50 (*0-8446-1360-6*) Peter Smith.

— Interpretations of Legal History. LC 85-81797. (Cambridge Studies in English Legal History). 198p. 1986. reprint ed. 55.00 (*0-912004-50-9*) Gaunt.

— An Introduction to the Philosophy of Law. LC 98-9740. 315p. 1998. pap. 29.95 (*1-56000-940-3*) Transaction Pubs.

— An Introduction to the Philosophy of Law. LC 94-75666. 308p. 1994. reprint ed. 85.00 (*1-56169-090-2*) Gaunt.

— An Introduction to the Philosophy of Law. rev. ed. (Storrs Lectures). (C). 1959. pap. 15.00 (*0-300-00188-6*, Y10) Yale U Pr.

— Law & Morals. ix, 144p. 1987. reprint ed. 40.00 (*0-8377-2501-1*, Rothman) W S Hein.

— Masonic Jurisprudence. 120p. 1992. reprint ed. pap. 12.95 (*1-56459-048-8*) Kessinger Pub.

— Organization of Courts. LC 79-12700. (Judicial Administration Ser.). 322p. 1980. reprint ed. lib. bdg. 35.00 (*0-313-21998-2*, POOC, Greenwood Pr) Greenwood.

— Philosophy of Freemasonry. (Illus.). 96p. 1997. reprint ed. pap. 15.95 (*1-887560-25-4*) M Poll Pub.

— Social Control Through Law. LC 96-2793. 160p. (Orig.). 1996. pap. text 21.95 (*1-56000-916-0*) Transaction Pubs.

— Spirit of the Common Law. 224p. 1921. 20.00 (*0-8338-0227-5*) Marshall Jones.

— The Spirit of the Common Law. LC 98-24171. 250p. 1998. pap. 24.95 (*1-56000-942-X*) Transaction Pubs.

— Spirit of the Common Law. LC 95-76118. xiv, 224p. 1995. reprint ed. 45.00 (*0-89941-932-1*, 308700) W S Hein.

Pound, Roscoe, ed. National Law Library, 6 vols., Set. LC 39-8999. 1980. reprint ed. lib. bdg. 285.00 (*0-89941-262-9*, 200730) W S Hein.

Pound, Roscoe & Clements, Frederic E. The Phytogeography of Nebraska: General Survey. rev. ed. Egerton, Frank N., 3rd, ed. LC 77-74248. (History of Ecology Ser.). (Illus.). 1978. reprint ed. lib. bdg. 39.95 (*0-405-10417-0*) Ayer.

Pound, Roscoe & Harvard Law School Library Staff. The Roscoe Pound Papers. LC 89-892146. 248p. 1986. write for info. (*0-89093-814-8*) U Pubns Amer.

Pound, Roscoe & Plucknett, Theodore F., eds. Readings on the History & System of the Common Law. 3rd ed. LC 93-78456. 756p. 1993. reprint ed. 175.00 (*1-56169-043-0*) Gaunt.

Pound, Roscoe, et al. Federalism As a Democratic Process. LC 78-23818. 1980. reprint ed. 21.95 (*0-89201-031-2*) Zenger Pub.

Pound, Roscoe, ed. see Cleveland Foundation Staff.

Pound, William, jt. frwd. see Fox, Daniel M.

Pounder. Handbook of Current Diagnosis & Treatment. 1996. pap. text 28.00 (*0-443-05599-8*, W B Saunders Co) Harcrt Hlth Sci Grp.

— Recent Advances in Gastroenteritis. 10th ed. 1994. pap. text 69.95 (*0-443-05021-X*, W B Saunders Co) Harcrt Hlth Sci Grp.

Pounder & Allison. Colour Atlas of Inflammatory Bowel Disease. 1998. 75.00 (*0-7234-1888-8*) Mosby Inc.

Pounder, Diana G., ed. Restructuring Schools for Collaboration: Promises & Pitfalls. LC 97-25123. (SUNY Series, Educational Leadership). 224p. (C). 1998. pap. text 19.95 (*0-7914-3746-9*) State U NY Pr.

— Restructuring Schools for Collaboration: Promises & Pitfalls. LC 97-25123. (SUNY Series, Educational Leadership). 224p. (C). 1998. text 59.50 (*0-7914-3745-0*) State U NY Pr.

Pounder, E. Physics of Ice. LC 65-21141. 1965. 78.00 (*0-08-011148-3*, Pub. by Pergamon Repr) Franklin.

Pounder, R. E., jt. ed. see Misiewicz, J. J.

Pounder, Roy, ed. Recent Advances in Gastroenterology, Vol. 8. (Illus.). 280p. 1990. text 95.00 (*0-443-04324-8*) Church.

— Recent Advances in Gastroenterology - 9. (Illus.). 258p. 1993. text 79.95 (*0-443-04674-3*) Church.

Pounders, Donnie. Celebrity Wedding Ceremonies: Complete Ceremonies & Signed Marriage Certificates from Famous People. 192p. (Orig.). 1994. pap. 19.95 (*0-9642144-9-0*) Lucky Duck.

***Pounders, Margaret.** Laws of Love. LC 99-66955. 336p. 2000. reprint ed. pap. 12.95 (*0-87159-254-1*, 147) Unity Bks.

Pounds, Bette G., jt. ed. see Baum, Laurie A.

Pounds, Dwight R. The American Viola Society: A History & Reference. 2nd ed. 293p. 1994. write for info. (*1-886601-00-3*) Am Viola Soc.

Pounds, F. Sims. Seventy-Five Windows. LC 78-56418. 120p. 1978. 11.00 (*0-86690-143-4*, P1377-014) Am Fed Astrologers.

Pounds, Jerry, jt. auth. see Mitchell, William.

Pounds, K., jt. ed. see Beer, P.

***Pounds, Kelley.** The Awakening Fire. 2000. pap. 6.99 (*1-929613-39-3*, Echoes MI) Avid MI.

Pounds, Michael C. Race in Space: The Representation of Ethnicity in Star Trek & Star Trek, the Next Generation. LC 97-9554. 208p. 1999. text 32.50 (*0-8108-3322-0*) Scarecrow.

***Pounds, N. J.** A History of the English Parish: The Culture of Religion from Saint Augustine to Queen Victoria. LC 98-53584. (Illus.). 618p. (C). 2000. 95.00 (*0-521-63348-6*) Cambridge U Pr.

Pounds, Norman J. Church Fonts. (Album Ser.: No. 318). (Illus.). 32p. 1995. pap. 4.75 (*0-7478-0293-9*, Pub. by Shire Pubns) Parkwest Pubns.

— The Culture of the English People: Iron Age to the Industrial Revolution. (Illus.). 495p. (C). 1994. pap. text 29.95 (*0-521-46671-7*) Cambridge U Pr.

— An Economic History of Medieval Europe. 2nd ed. LC 93-27069. 544p. (C). 1995. pap. 57.00 (*0-582-21599-4*, 76669) Addison-Wesley.

— Hearth & Home: A History of Material Culture. LC 87-46367. (Illus.). 450p. 1993. pap. 18.95 (*0-253-20839-4*) Ind U Pr.

— The Medieval Castle in England & Wales: A Political & Social History. (Illus.). 375p. (C). 1991. text 80.00 (*0-521-38349-8*) Cambridge U Pr.

— The Medieval Castle in England & Wales: A Political & Social History. (Illus.). 375p. (C). 1993. pap. text 29.95 (*0-521-45828-5*) Cambridge U Pr.

Pounds, Penny, ed. Cooking for the Family: Allene & Frank Matulich. (Illus.). 70p. 1999. 19.95 (*0-9660804-4-0*) AFM LLC.

Pounds, V. H. & Rant, Lilian V. Staffordshire Bull Terriers: An Owner's Companion. (Illus.). 240p. 1995. 39.95 (*1-85223-365-6*, Pub. by Cro1wood) Trafalgar.

Pounds, Wayne. Proletarian Tales. (Illus.). 59p. (Orig.). 1987. 10.95 (*0-941720-50-0*); pap. 4.95 (*0-941720-51-9*) Slough Pr TX.

***Poundstone, Paula.** Paula Poundstone. 2001. 24.00 (*0-609-60316-7*) Crown Pub Group.

Poundstone, William. Big Secrets: The Uncensored Truth about All Sorts of Stuff You Are Never Supposed to Know. LC 85-3603. (Illus.). 256p. 1985. reprint ed. pap. 10.00 (*0-688-04830-7*, Quil) HarperTrade.

— Bigger Secrets: More Than 125 Things They Prayed You'd Never Find Out. 320p. 1989. pap. 13.00 (*0-395-53008-3*) HM.

— Biggest Secrets: More Uncensored Truth about All Sorts of Stuff You Are Never Supposed to Know. 1994. pap. 10.95 (*0-688-13792-X*, Quil) HarperTrade.

— Carl Sagan: A Life in the Cosmos, 1. LC 99-14615. (Illus.). 560p. 1999. 30.00 (*0-8050-5766-8*) H Holt & Co.

***Poundstone, William.** Carl Sagan: A Life in the Cosmos. (Illus.). 496p. 2000. pap. 16.00 (*0-8050-5767-6*, Owl) H Holt & Co.

Poundstone, William. Prisoner's Dilemma: John von Neumann, Game Theory, & the Puzzle of the Bomb. LC 92-29903. 320p. 1993. pap. 15.95 (*0-385-41580-X*, Anchor NY) Doubleday.

Pountain, Christopher J. French Grammar in Context: Analysis & Practice, a Workbook. 1999. pap. text 15.95 (*0-8442-2440-5*) NTC Contemp Pub Co.

***Pountain, Christopher J.** A History of the Spanish Language Through Texts. LC 00-38264. (SPA & ENG.). 2000. pap. write for info. (*0-415-18062-7*) Routledge.

Pountain, Christopher J. Structures & Transformations: The Romance Verb. LC 83-12287. (Illus.). 272p. 1983. 44.00 (*0-389-20436-6*, N7322) B&N Imports.

Pountain, Christopher J., jt. auth. see Batchelor, R. E.

Pountain, Christopher J., jt. auth. see De Bruyne, Jacques.

Pountain, Christopher J., jt. auth. see Ibarra, Juan K.

Pountain, Christopher J., jt. auth. see Kattan-Ibarra, Juan.

Pountain, Dick. Object-Oriented Forth. 119p. (Orig.). 1987. text 41.00 (*0-12-563570-2*) Acad Pr.

Pountney, David C., jt. auth. see Townend, M. Stewart.

Pountney, Ernie. For the Socialist Course. 80p. 1973. pap. 12.00 (*0-8464-1465-1*) Beekman Pubs.

Pountney, Rosemary. Theatre of Shadows: From All That Fall to Footfalls, Samuel Beckett's Drama 1956-1976. (Irish Literary Studies: Vol. # 28). 310p. 1988. 45.00 (*0-86140-256-1*, Pub. by Smyth) Dufour.

— Theatre of Shadows: Samuel Beckett's Drama 1956-76: From All That Fall to Footfalls with Commentaries on the Late Plays. LC 99-193977. 332p. 1999. pap. text 19.95 (*0-86140-407-6*) OUP.

Poupard, Dennis. Twentieth-Century Literary Criticism, Vol. 26. LC 76-46132. 500p. 1987. text 150.00 (*0-8103-2408-3*) Gale.

— Twentieth Century Literary Criticism, Vol. 29. 500p. 1988. text 150.00 (*0-8103-2411-3*) Gale.

Poupard, Dennis, ed. Twentieth-Century Literary Criticism, Vol. 27. LC 76-46132. 500p. 1988. text 150.00 (*0-8103-2409-1*) Gale.

— Twentieth Century Literary Criticism, Vol. 28. 500p. 1988. text 150.00 (*0-8103-2410-5*) Gale.

Poupard, Dennis & Kepos, Paula, eds. Twentieth-Century Literary Criticism, Vol. 32. 500p. 1989. text 150.00 (*0-8103-2414-8*) Gale.

Poupard, Dennis & Kronick, Jelena. Classical & Medieval Literature Criticism, Vol. 1. 500p. 1987. text 150.00 (*0-8103-2350-8*) Gale.

Poupard, Dennis, jt. ed. see Kepos, Paula.

Poupard, James, et al, eds. Antimicrobial Susceptibility Testing: Critical Issues for the 90s. (Advances in Experimental Medicine & Biology Ser.: Vol. 349). (Illus.). 200p. (C). 1994. text 75.00 (*0-306-44673-1*, Kluwer Plenum) Kluwer Academic.

Poupard, Paul. The Church & Culture: Challenge & Confrontation: Inculturation & Evangelization. Miller, John H., tr. from FRE. LC 95-150063. 160p. 1994. pap. 15.00 (*0-9626257-7-9*) CBCCU Amer.

— Dictionnaire des Religions. 2nd ed. (FRE.). 1856p. 1985. 225.00 (*0-8288-9471-X*) Fr & Eur.

— Dictionnaire des Religions, 2 vols. 3rd ed. (FRE.). 2248p. 1993. 495.00 (*0-7859-7749-X*, 2130451128) Fr & Eur.

P

An Asterisk (*) at the beginning of an entry indicates that the title is appearing for the first time.

Poupard, Paul, ed. Galileo Galilei: Toward a Resolution of 350 Years of Debate, 1633-1983. Campbell, Ian, tr. from FRE. LC 86-24125.Tr. of Galileo Galilei: 350 Ans d'histoire, 1633-1983. 208p. 1986. text 28.00 (*0-8207-0193-9*) Duquesne.

Poupart, Jean-Marie. Des Crayons Qui Trichent. (Novels in the Roman Jeunesse Ser.). (FRE.). 96p. (J). (gr. 4-7). 1993. pap. 8.95 (*2-89021-197-5*, Pub. by La Courte Ech) Firefly Bks Ltd.

— Des Photos Qui Parlent. (Novels in the Roman Jeunesse Ser.). (FRE.). 96p. (J). (gr. 4-7). 1991. pap. 8.95 (*2-89021-162-2*, Pub. by La Courte Ech) Firefly Bks Ltd.

— Des Pianos Qui S'Envolent. (Novels in the Roman Jeunesse Ser.). (FRE.). 96p. (J). (gr. 4-7). 1992. pap. 8.95 (*2-89021-173-8*, Pub. by La Courte Ech) Firefly Bks Ltd.

— Les Grandes Confidences. (Novels in the Roman Plus Ser.). (FRE.). 160p. (YA). (gr. 8 up). 1991. pap. 8.95 (*2-89021-150-9*, Pub. by La Courte Ech) Firefly Bks Ltd.

— Libre Comme l'Air. (Novels in the Roman Plus Ser.). (FRE.). 160p. (YA). (gr. 8 up). 1990. pap. 8.95 (*2-89021-135-5*, Pub. by La Courte Ech) Firefly Bks Ltd.

— Le Nombril du Monde. (Novels in the Roman Jeunesse Ser.). (FRE.). 160p. (YA). (gr. 8 up). 1990. pap. 8.95 (*2-89021-143-6*, Pub. by La Courte Ech) Firefly Bks Ltd.

Poupeney, Mollie. Daddy for Sale: Stories. (Illus.). x, 172p. 1998. pap. 12.95 (*0-9666161-0-3*, 500) Mudball.

Poupette, Jean P. Little Voodoo Kit. LC 97-12810. 1997. text 11.95 (*0-312-15415-1*) St Martin.

Poupeye, Veerle. Caribbean Art. LC 97-60254. (World of Art Ser.). (Illus.). 224p. 1998. pap. 14.95 (*0-500-20306-7*, Pub. by Thames Hudson) Norton.

Poupin, J. Faune Marine Profonde des Antilles Francaises (Deep Marine Fauna of the French West Indies) Recoltes du Navire Polka Faires en 1993 (Collected by the Ship Polka in 1993)Tr. of Deep Marine Fauna of the French West Indies Collected by the Ship Polka in 1993. (FRE.). 80p. 1994. pap. 20.00 (*2-7099-1212-0*, Pub. by LInstitut Francais) Balogh.

Poupon, R. E., jt. ed. see Reichen, J.

Pouquet, J. Earth's Science in the Age of the Satellite. LC 73-94454. Orig. Title: Les Sciences de la Terre a l'Heure des Satellites. 190p. 1974. text 106.00 (*90-277-0437-6*) Kluwer Academic.

Pour-El, Akiva, ed. Functionality & Protein Structure. LC 78-31964. (ACS Symposium Ser.: No. 92). 1979. 32.95 (*0-8412-0478-0*) Am Chemical.

— Functionality & Protein Structure. LC 78-31964. (ACS Symposium Ser.: Vol. 92). 255p. 1979. reprint ed. pap. 79.10 (*0-608-03101-1*, 206355400007) Bks Demand.

Pour-El, M. B. & Richards, J. L. Computability in Analysis & Physics. (Perspectives in Mathematical Logic Ser.). (Illus.). 220p. 1989. 126.95 (*0-387-50035-9*, 2028) Spr-Verlag.

Pour, P. M., et al, eds. Atlas of Pancreatic Exocrine Tumors: Morphology, Biology, & Diagnosis, with an International Guide for Tumor Classification. LC 94-9950. 1994. 239.00 (*0-387-70129-X*) Spr-Verlag.

Pouradier, Gerard, jt. auth. see Perucca, Fabien.

Pouratzal, Haleh & Montgomery, Roger. The Spiritual Wisdom of Hafez: Teachings of the Philosopher of Love. LC 98-17365. 240p. 1998. 22.00 (*0-89281-667-8*, Inner Trad) Inner Tradit.

Pourbaix, Marcel. Atlas of Chemical & Electrochemical Equilibria in the Presence of a Gaseous Phase. (Illus.). 160p. 1997. ring bd. 120.00 (*2-9600134-0-9*, 38215) NACE Intl.

— Lectures on Electrochemical Corrosion. 3rd expanded ed. LC 95-68977. (Illus.). 342p. (C). 1995. reprint ed. pap. text 97.00 (*1-877914-91-6*, 37555) NACE Intl.

Pourchot, Mary E. When the Land Calls: A Celebration of Country Living. LC 91-77561. (Illus.). 272p. 1992. pap. 8.95 (*0-87341-195-1*, LC01) Krause Pubns.

Pourchot, Thomas, jt. ed. see Smith, M. Cecil.

Pourciau, Pam & Townsend, Nancy G. Core Review in Emergency Nursing: A CEN Study Guide & Practice Examination. 2nd ed. 207p. (C). 1989. pap. text 19.95 (*0-9622174-4-1*) Nursing Knowledge.

Pourdeyhimi, Behnam, ed. Imaging & Image Analysis Applications for Fibers. LC 99-64221. (SPE/ PDL Ser.). 308p. 1999. 160.00 (*1-884207-81-2*) William Andrew.

Poure, Ken. God's Gusto for the Family. 176p. 1994. pap. 8.95 (*0-939497-36-0*) Promise Pub.

Pouring, A. A., ed. see Joint Applied Mechanics, Fluids Engineering & Bioe.

Pourjavady, Nasrollah, tr. see Ghazzali, Ahmad.

Pourjavady, Nosrallah. The Light of Saxina in Suhranudi's Philosophy of Illusion. 1998. pap. 4.00 (*1-883058-99-6*) Global Pubns.

***Pourmand, Rahman.** Neuromuscular Diseases: Expert Clinicians' Views. (Illus.). 520p. 2000. 95.00 (*0-7506-7019-3*) Buttrwrth-Heinemann.

— Practicing Neurology: What You Need to Know, What You Need to Do. LC 98-54985. 369p. 1999. pap. text 30.00 (*0-7506-9970-1*) Buttrwrth-Heinemann.

Pournelle, J., jt. auth. see Niven, Larry.

Pournelle, Jerry. Birth of Fire. 256p. (Orig.). 1987. per. 4.99 (*0-671-65649-X*) Baen Bks.

— Blood Feuds. (War World Ser.: No. 4). 560p. 1993. per. 5.99 (*0-671-72150-X*) Baen Bks.

— Falkenberg's Legion. 448p. (Orig.). 1990. mass mkt. 6.99 (*0-671-72018-X*) Baen Bks.

— High Justice. 288p. (Orig.). 1989. pap. 4.99 (*0-671-69877-X*) Baen Bks.

— Imperial Star: Stars at War, Vol. I. 1987. pap. 3.95 (*0-685-18046-8*) PB.

— Janissaries. 256p. 1996. mass mkt. 5.99 (*0-671-87709-7*) Baen Bks.

— King David's Spaceship. 384p. (Orig.). 1991. mass mkt. 5.99 (*0-671-72068-6*) Baen Bks.

— Prince of Mercenaries. 352p. (Orig.). 1989. mass mkt. 5.99 (*0-671-69811-7*) Baen Bks.

— Starswarm. LC 98-10260. 352p. 1998. text 23.95 (*0-312-86183-4*) St Martin.

— Starswarm. 1999. mass mkt. 5.99 (*0-8125-3893-5*, Pub. by Tor Bks) St Martin.

— That Buck Rogers Stuff. Claypool, Gavin, ed. (Illus.). 101p. 1977. 9.00 (*0-935892-01-X*) Extequer.

— Twenty-Twenty Vision. 1976. mass mkt. 0.95 (*0-380-01632-X*, Avon Bks) Morrow Avon.

Pournelle, Jerry, creator. Blood Vengeance. 1994. mass mkt. 5.99 (*0-671-72201-8*) Baen Bks.

— CoDominium: Revolt on War World. 480p. (Orig.). 1992. mass mkt. 5.99 (*0-671-72126-7*) Baen Bks.

— Invasion. (War World Ser.: Vol. IV). (Orig.). 1994. mass mkt. 5.99 (*0-671-87616-3*) Baen Bks.

Pournelle, Jerry, ed. Day of the Tyrant: There Will be War, No. 4. 352p. 1988. pap. 3.95 (*0-8125-0066-0*, Pub. by Tor Bks) St Martin.

— There Will Be War. 352p. 1990. pap. 3.95 (*0-8125-0900-5*) Tor Bks.

— There Will Be War: After Armageddon, Vol. IX. 1990. pap. 3.95 (*0-8125-4967-8*) Tor Bks.

— There Will Be War: Armageddon, Vol. VIII. 1989. pap. 3.95 (*0-8125-4965-1*) Tor Bks.

— There Will Be War: Blood & Iron, Vol. III. 384p. (Orig.). 1984. pap. 2.95 (*0-8125-4955-4*, Pub. by Tor Bks) St Martin.

— There Will Be War: Call to Battle, Vol. VII. 384p. 1988. mass mkt. 3.95 (*0-8125-4963-5*, Pub. by Tor Bks) St Martin.

— There Will Be War: Men of War, Vol. II. 320p. (Orig.). 1990. pap. write for info. (*0-8125-0902-1*, Pub. by Tor Bks) St Martin.

Pournelle, Jerry, et al, eds. The Science Fiction Yearbook. 344p. 1985. 15.95 (*0-317-27055-9*) PB.

Pournelle, Jerry & Baen, Jim. Far Frontier, Vol. VII. 1987. pap. 2.95 (*0-685-18048-4*) PB.

Pournelle, Jerry & Green, Roland. Tran. 688p. 1996. mass mkt. 6.99 (*0-671-87741-0*) Baen Bks.

Pournelle, Jerry & Sheffield, Charles. Jupiter: Higher Education. 1997. mass mkt. 5.99 (*0-614-27799-X*) Tor Bks.

Pournelle, Jerry & Stirling, S. M. The Children's Hour. 1991. per. 4.99 (*0-671-72089-9*) Baen Bks.

— Prince of Sparta. 416p. (Orig.). 1993. per. 4.99 (*0-671-72158-5*) Baen Bks.

Pournelle, Jerry, jt. auth. see Niven, Larry.

Pourrat, Henri. French Folktales. (Fairy Tale & Folklore Library). 1994. reprint ed. pap. 17.00 (*0-679-74833-4*) Pantheon.

— Le Mauvais Garcon. (FRE.). 1979. pap. 10.95 (*0-7859-4113-4*) Fr & Eur.

Pourriot, R., jt. auth. see De Smet, W. H.

Pourroy, Janine. Behind the Scenes at ER. 160p. 1995. pap. 15.00 (*0-345-40249-9*) Ballantine Pub Grp.

— The Making of Waterworld. (Illus.). 160p. (Orig.). 1995. pap. 15.00 (*1-57297-005-7*) Blvd Books.

Poursartip, Anoush & Street, Ken, eds. Proceedings of the Tenth International Conference on Composite Materials: Proceedings of the Tenth International Conference on Composite Materials, Whistler, B.C., Canada, August 14-18, 1995, 6 vols. 4906p. 1995. pap. 299.95 (*1-85573-221-1*, 732211) Technomic.

Pourtales, Guy De, see De Pourtales, Guy.

Pourtales, Guy De Comte, see De Comte Pourtales, Guy.

Pourtemour, Amir H. The Perfect Alibi: O. J. Simpson's Strategy for Murder. (Illus.). vi, 328p. (Orig.). 1996. pap. 19.95 (*0-9655126-0-6*) A H Pourtemour.

Pourzanjani, M. M. & Roberts, G. N., eds. Modeling & Control of Marine Craft: Proceedings of the International Conference, Held at Exeter, U. K., 18-20 April 1990. 432p. 1991. mass mkt. 150.95 (*1-85166-592-7*) Elsevier.

Pousada, Alicia. Puerto Rican Community Participation in East Harlem Bilingual Programs. 66p. 1987. lib. bdg. 5.00 (*1-878483-14-5*) Hunter Coll CEP.

Pousada, Alicia, jt. auth. see Poplack, Shana.

Pousada, Lidia, et al. Case Studies in Emergency Medicine for the House Officer. LC 92-48917. (Illus.). 244p. 1993. 20.00 (*0-683-06966-7*) Lppncott W & W.

— Emergency Medicine. 2nd ed. (House Officer Ser.). (Illus.). 608p. 1996. 24.95 (*0-683-06963-2*) Lppncott W & W.

***Poussaint, Alvin F. & Alexander, Amy.** Lay My Burden Down: Suicide & the Mental Health Crisis among African Americans. 2000. 25.00 (*0-8070-0960-1*) Beacon Pr.

Poussaint, Alvin F., jt. auth. see Comer, James P.

Pousse, Michel. R. K. Narayan: A Painter of Modern India, Vol. 4. (Studies of World Literature in English). XV, 211p. (C). 1995. text 49.95 (*0-8204-2768-3*) P Lang Pubng.

Pousset, Edouard. Life in Faith & Freedom: An Essay Presenting Gaston Fessard's Analysis of the Dialectic of the Spiritual Exercises of St. Ignatius. Donahue, E. L., tr. LC 79-84200. (Modern Scholarly Studies about the Jesuits, in English Translations Series II: No. 4). xxviii, 240p. 1980. 9.00 (*0-912422-41-6*); pap. 7.00 (*0-912422-39-4*) Inst Jesuit.

Poussin, Charles D., jt. auth. see Bernstein, Serge.

Poussin, Louis D. La Vallee, see La Vallee Poussin, Louis D.

Poussin, Nicolas. Drawings of Poussin. Longstreet, Stephen, ed. (Master Draughtsman Ser.). (Illus.). (Orig.). 1963. 10.95 (*0-87505-027-1*); pap. 4.95 (*0-87505-180-4*) Borden.

Pousson, Edward K. Spreading the Flame: Charismatic Churches & Missions Today. 208p. 1992. pap. 14.99 (*0-310-53331-7*) Zondervan.

Pousson, Jeanie B. Foundations & Funding Sources of Louisiana, 1994-1995: Resource Guide to Private Grants & Scholarships. 176p. (Orig.). (C). 1994. per. 53.00 (*0-9643379-0-8*) Res Review.

— Foundations of Mississippi: Resource Guide to Private Grants & Scholarships. 160p. (Orig.). (YA). 1995. per. 37.00 (*0-9643379-1-6*) Res Review.

Poussopoulos, Dimitrios I., ed. see Roussopoulos, et al.

Poustie. Hospitality & Tourism Law, Vol. 1. 1998. pap. 20.99 (*1-86152-181-2*) Thomson Learn.

Poutanban, J., jt. auth. see Nagirnev.

***Poutanen, Juri & Svensson, Roland, eds.** Gamma-Ray Bursts: The First Three Minutes. LC 99-67351. (Conference Series Proceedings: Vol. 190). 305p. 1999. text 52.00 (*1-58381-016-1*) Astron Soc Pacific.

— High Energy Processes in Accreting Black Holes, Vol. 161. (ASP Conference Series Proceedings). 449p. (C). 1999. text 52.00 (*1-886733-81-3*) Astron Soc Pacific.

Poutiatine, Olga. War & Revolution: Excerpts from the Letters & Diaries of the Countess Olga Poutiatine. Lensen, George A., ed. & tr. by. LC 74-164854. (Illus.). 111p. 1971. 12.50 (*0-910512-12-4*) Diplomatic IN.

Poutney, David, tr. see Wagner, Richard.

Poutsma, E., et al, eds. Process Innovation & Automation in Small & Medium Sized Business. 146p. (Orig.). 1987. pap. 33.50 (*90-6275-365-5*, Pub. by Delft U Pr) Coronet Bks.

Pouvillon, Emile. Bernadette. Gautier, Henri, ed. Van Dien De Coeur, Diane P., tr. from FRE. & prologue by by. LC 97-73586. (Illus.). 44p. (J). (gr. 4-12). 1998. pap. 9.95 (*1-890857-00-9*) BVD Publ.

Pouwels, P. H., et al. Cloning Vectors. 300p. 1987. pap., suppl. ed. 63.00 (*0-444-90452-2*) Elsevier.

Pouwels, Randall L., ed. see Farsy, Shaikh A.

Pouwels, Randall L., jt. ed. see Levtzion, Nehemia.

Pouyanne, Therese. Hare, Reading Level 3-4. (World Animal Library). (Illus.). 28p. (J). (gr. 2-5). 1983. 12.50 (*0-685-58818-1*) Rourke Corp.

— Hare, Reading Level 3-4. (World Animal Library). (Illus.). 28p. (J). (gr. 2-5). 1983. lib. bdg. 21.60 (*0-86592-853-3*) Rourke Enter.

— Hippo, Reading Level 3-4. (World Animal Library). (Illus.). 28p. (J). (gr. 2-5). 1983. 12.50 (*0-685-58819-X*) Rourke Corp.

— Hippo, Reading Level 3-4. (World Animal Library). (Illus.). 28p. (J). (gr. 2-5). 1983. lib. bdg. 21.27 (*0-86592-855-X*) Rourke Enter.

— Ladybug, Reading Level 3-4. (World Animal Library). (Illus.). 28p. (J). (gr. 2-5). 1983. 12.50 (*0-685-58821-1*) Rourke Corp.

— Ladybug, Reading Level 3-4. (World Animal Library). (Illus.). 28p. (J). (gr. 2-5). 1983. lib. bdg. 18.60 (*0-86592-863-0*) Rourke Enter.

Pouzar, Jay, jt. auth. see Illman, Paul E.

Povah, Nigel. Chess Training. 1995. pap. 17.95 (*1-85744-170-2*) Macmillan.

Povah, Nigel, jt. auth. see Ballantyne, Iain.

Povar, Gail J., jt. auth. see Riegelman, Richard K.

Poveda, Tony G. Rethinking White Collar Crime. LC 94-1143. (Criminology & Crime Control Policy Ser.). 184p. 1994. 59.95 (*0-275-94586-3*, Praeger Pubs) Greenwood.

Povelikhina, A., jt. auth. see Kovtun, E.

Povelikhina, A. V. & Kovtun, E. F. The Painted Signboards of Russia: Tradition & the Avant-Garde. 1990. write for info. (*0-8109-3754-9*) Abrams.

Poverman, C. E. The Black Velvet Girl. LC 76-23408. (Iowa Short Fiction Award Ser.). 272p. 1976. pap. 3.25 (*0-87745-069-2*) U of Iowa Pr.

— On the Edge. LC 96-35491. 311p. 1997. 22.95 (*0-86538-087-2*) Ontario Rev NJ.

— On the Edge. 1999. mass mkt. 6.99 (*0-312-97089-7*, St Martins Paperbacks) St Martin.

— Skin. LC 92-9249. 279p. 1992. 19.95 (*0-86538-076-7*) Ontario Rev NJ.

Poveromo, George, jt. auth. see Sosin, Mark.

Poveroy, Janine. Shooting Star: The Ewan McGregor Story. LC PN2604.M38P68 1999. 1999. mass mkt. 5.99 (*0-345-42724-6*) Ballantine Pub Grp.

Povey, Barry. Continuous Business Improvement: Profit from Quality. (Quality in Action Ser.). 1996. pap. write for info. (*0-07-709124-8*) McGraw.

Povey, Glenn & Russell, Ian. Pink Floyd. LC 99-199909. 256p. 1998. pap. 19.95 (*0-312-19175-8*) St Martin.

Povey, John F. Roy Campbell. LC 77-1358. (Twayne's World Authors Ser.). 233p. (C). 1977. lib. bdg. 17.95 (*0-8057-6277-9*) Irvington.

Povey, Malcolm J. Ultrasonic Techniques for Fluids Characterization. LC 97-9788. (Illus.). 214p. 1997. text 89.95 (*0-12-563730-6*) Morgan Kaufmann.

Povey, P., tr. see Mailer, F.

Povey, P. J. & Earl, R. A. Vintage Telephones of the World. (History of Technology Ser.: No. 9). 202p. 1988. 42.00 (*0-86341-140-1*, HT009) INSPEC Inc.

***Povh, B., et al.** Particles & Nuclei: An Introduction to the Physical Concepts. 2nd rev. enl. ed. Lavelle, M., tr. from GER. LC 99-16711. (Illus.). xviii, 376p. 1999. 36.00 (*3-540-66115-8*) Spr-Verlag.

Povh, Bogdan, et al. Particles & Nuclei: An Introduction to the Physical Concepts, Vol. IX. Lavelle, Martin, tr. from GER. (Illus.). 340p. 1995. 32.95 (*3-540-59439-6*) Spr-Verlag.

Povilus, Judith. United in His Name: Jesus in Our Midst in the Writings of Chiara Lubich. Hearne, Jerry, tr. from ITA. 160p. (Orig.). 1992. pap. 8.95 (*1-56548-003-1*) New City.

Povinec, P., ed. Rare Nuclear Processes. 350p. (C). 1992. text 98.00 (*981-02-0802-2*) World Scientific Pub.

***Povinelli, Daniel J.** Folk Physics for Apes: Chimpanzees, Tool-Use, & Causal Understanding. (Illus.). 496p. 2000. text 85.00 (*0-19-857220-4*) OUP.

Povinelli, Daniel J. & Eddy, Timothy J. What Young Chimpanzees Know about Seeing. 216p. 1996. pap. text 14.00 (*0-226-67675-7*) U Ch Pr.

Povinelli, Elizabeth A. Labor's Lot: The Power, History, & Culture of Aboriginal Action. LC 93-2511. (Illus.). 344p. 1994. lib. bdg. 64.00 (*0-226-67673-0*) U Ch Pr.

— Labors Lot: The Power, History, & Culture of Aboriginal Action. LC 93-2511. (Illus.). 344p. 1994. pap. text 19.95 (*0-226-67674-9*) U Ch Pr.

***Povlsen, Jergen, et al, eds.** Childhood & Old Age - Equals or Opposites. (Illus.). 22p. 1999. pap. 29.75 (*87-7838-490-7*, Pub. by Odense Universitets Forlag) Intl Spec Bk.

Povolayev, Valeri. Man at the Limit. (Dramatised Eyewitness Reports Ser.). 272p. 1984. 22.00 (*0-7855-1226-8*, Pub. by Collets) St Mut.

***Povolny, Joyce.** Dancing in the Wind. 1999. pap. 21.00 (*1-85072-161-0*, Pub. by W Sessions) St Mut.

Povondra, Pavel, jt. auth. see Sulcek, Zdenek.

Povsic, Frances F. Eastern Europe in Children's Literature: An Annotated Bibliography of English-Language Books, 8. LC 86-3104. (Bibliographies & Indexes in World Literature Ser.: No. 8). 226p. 1986. lib. bdg. 69.50 (*0-313-23777-8*, PVE/) Greenwood.

Povsic, Frances F., compiled by. The Soviet Union in Literature for Children & Young Adults: An Annotated Bibliography of English-Language Books, 31. LC 91-25095. (Bibliographies & Indexes in World Literature Ser.: No. 31). 320p. 1991. lib. bdg. 59.95 (*0-313-25175-4*, PSU/, Greenwood Pr) Greenwood.

Povzner, A. Y., jt. auth. see Bogaevski, V. N.

Pow, Tom. Red Letter Day. LC 96-216412. 96p. 1996. pap. 16.95 (*1-85224-368-6*, Pub. by Bloodaxe Bks) Dufour.

***Pow, Tom.** Who Is the World For? LC 99-88330. (Illus.). 32p. (YA). (ps up). 2001. 15.99 (*0-7636-1280-4*) Candlewick Pr.

Powaga, Wiesiek, ed. from POL. Dedalus Book of Polish Fantasy. (Dedalus European Fantasy Anthologies Ser.). 320p. (Orig.). 1996. pap. 18.95 (*0-7818-0292-X*) Hippocrene Bks.

— The Dedalus Book of Polish Fantasy. 2nd ed. LC 95-126522. 371p. 1999. reprint ed. pap. 14.95 (*1-873982-90-9*) Dedalus.

Powaga, Wiesiek, tr. see Smith, Teresa H.

Powanda, M. C., jt. ed. see Rainsford, K. D.

Powaski, Ronald E. The Cold War: The United States & the Soviet Union, 1917-1991. LC 96-24691. (Illus.). 368p. (C). 1997. 35.00 (*0-19-507850-0*); pap. text 21.95 (*0-19-507851-9*) OUP.

— The Entangling Alliance: The United States & European Security, 1950-1993, 42. LC 93-20830. (Contributions to the Study of World History Ser.: No. 42). 288p. 1994. 65.00 (*0-313-27275-1*, Greenwood Pr) Greenwood.

— March to Armageddon: The United States & the Nuclear Arms Race, 1939 to the Present. 318p. 1989. reprint ed. pap. 9.95 (*0-19-504411-8*) OUP.

***Powaski, Ronald E.** Return to Armageddon: The United States & the Nuclear Arms Race, 1981-1999. LC 99-19999. 304p. 2000. 30.00 (*0-19-510382-3*) OUP.

Powaski, Ronald E. Toward an Entangling Alliance: American Isolationism & Europe, 1901-1950, 22. LC 90-45604. (Contributions to the Study of World History Ser.: No. 22). 312p. 1991. 62.95 (*0-313-27274-3*, PEH, Greenwood Pr) Greenwood.

Powder & Bulk Solids Conference - Exhibition Staff. Powder & Bulk Solids Conference - Exhibition: Fifteenth Annual Proceedings of the Technical Program, June 4-7, 1990, O'Hare Exposition Center, Rosemont, IL. LC TP0156.. 676p. reprint ed. pap. 200.00 (*0-7837-2610-4*, 204277400006) Bks Demand.

— Powder & Bulk Solids Conference - Exhibition: Proceedings of the 1991 Technical Program, May 6-9, 1991, Rosemont O'Hare Exposition Center, Rosemont, IL. LC TP0156.. 584p. pap. 181.10 (*0-7837-0354-6*, 204067300018) Bks Demand.

— Powder & Bulk Solids Conference - Exhibition: Proceedings of the 1993 Technical Program, May 3- 6, 1993, Rosemont Convention Center, Rosemont, IL. LC TS0180.8.B8. (Illus.). 708p. reprint ed. pap. 200.00 (*0-7837-7033-2*, 204684800004) Bks Demand.

Powder & Bulk Solids Conference-Exhibition Staff. Powder & Bulk Solids Conference-Exhibition, 13th: Proceedings of the Technical Program, May 9-12, 1988, O'Hare Exposition Center, Rosemont, IL. LC TP0156.. 800p. reprint ed. pap. 200.00 (*0-608-18185-4*, 203291300081) Bks Demand.

Powder & Bulk Solids Handling & Processing Staff. Powder & Bulk Solids Handling & Processing: Proceedings of the Technical Program: May 12-14, 1987. LC TP0156.. (Illus.). 716p. pap. 200.00 (*0-608-17394-0*, 203023400067) Bks Demand.

— Powder & Bulk Solids Handling & Processing: Proceedings of the Technical Program, 10th, May 7-9, 1985, Rosemont, IL. LC TP0156.. 929p. reprint ed. pap. 200.00 (*0-608-12341-2*, 202519200042) Bks Demand.

Powder & Bulk Solids Handlings & Processing. Powder & Bulk Solids Handling & Processing: Proceedings of the Technical Program: 11th, O'Hare Exposition Center, Rosemont, IL, May 13-15, 1986. LC TP0156.. 786p. reprint ed. pap. 200.00 (*0-608-15442-3*, 202936700060) Bks Demand.

Powder Metallurgy Conference Staff. Powder Metallurgy Conference: Proceedings of the Twenty-Second Annual Conference Presented at the 1966 Design Engineering Conference, Chicago, Illinois, May 9-12. LC TN0695.P681. (Progress in Powder Metallurgy Ser.: No. 22). 150p. reprint ed. pap. 46.50 (*0-8357-6987-9*, 205707100009) Bks Demand.

Powder Metallurgy Equipment Association Staff. Powder Metallurgy Equipment Manual. 2nd ed. LC 76-52333. 174p. reprint ed. pap. 54.00 (*0-8357-7858-4*, 203625400002) Bks Demand.

Powder Metallurgy Technical Conference Staff. Progress in Powder Metallurgy, 1962: Proceedings of the Eighteenth Annual Powder Metallurgy Technical Conference & Magnetic Inductance Core Conference Held at the Hotel Sheraton, Philadelphia, PA, April 23-25, 1962. LC TN0695.P68. (Progress in Powder Metallurgy Ser.: Vol. 18). (Illus.). 243p. reprint ed. pap. 75.40 (*0-7837-1553-6*, 204184600018) Bks Demand.

— Progress in Powder Metallurgy, 1963: Proceedings of the Nineteenth Annual Powder Metallurgy Technical Conference Held at the Hotel Sheraton-Cadillac, Detroit, MI, April 29-May 1, 1963. LC TN0695.P68. (Progress in Powder Metallurgy Ser.: Vol. 19). (Illus.). 204p. reprint ed. pap. 63.30 (*0-7837-1554-4*, 204184700019) Bks Demand.

— Progress in Powder Metallurgy, 1964: Proceedings of the Twentieth Annual Powder Metallurgy Technical Conference Magnetic Inductance Core Conference Held at the Drake Hotel, Chicago, IL, April 27-29, 1964. LC TN0695.P68. (Progress in Powder Metallurgy Ser.: Vol. 20). (Illus.). 333p. reprint ed. pap. 103.30 (*0-7837-1555-2*, 204184800020) Bks Demand.

— Progress in Powder Metallurgy, 1969: Proceedings of the Twenty-Fifth Annual Powder Metallurgy Conference Sponsored by the Metal Powder Industries Federation & Presented at the New York Park Sheraton Hotel, May 5-7, 1969, New York, NY. (Progress in Powder Metallurgy Ser.: No. 25). 147p. reprint ed. pap. 41.90 (*0-7837-3166-3*, 2042812) Bks Demand.

Powder Metallurgy World Congress Staff. Characterization of Powder & Compacts: Preprint of a Seminar Held at the 1992 Powder Metallurgy World Congress, San Francisco, California, June 22-23, 1992. LC TN0695.P76. 212p. reprint ed. pap. 65.80 (*0-7837-6977-6*, 204678800004) Bks Demand.

— Spray Forming: Science, Technology & Applications: Preprint of a Seminar Held at the 1992 Powder Metallurgy World Congress, San Francisco, California, June 23-24, 1992. LC TN0695.P76. (Illus.). 178p. reprint ed. pap. 55.20 (*0-7837-6978-4*, 204678900004) Bks Demand.

Powderly, Terence V. Path I Trod. LC 77-181971. reprint ed. 31.50 (*0-404-05098-0*) AMS Pr.

— Thirty Years of Life & Labor, 1859-1889. rev. ed. LC 66-21692. (Reprints of Economic Classics Ser.). 372p. 1967. reprint ed. 49.50 (*0-678-00249-5*) Kelley.

Powderly, William, ed. Manual of HIV Therapeutics. LC 97-8075. (Illus.). 400p. 1997. spiral bd. 42.00 (*0-316-71510-7*) Lppncott W & W.

Powdermaker, Florence B. & Frank, Jerome D. Group Psychotherapy, Studies in Methodology of Research & Therapy. LC 72-6188. (Illus.). 615p. 1973. reprint ed. lib. bdg. 89.50 (*0-8371-6450-8*, POGP, Greenwood Pr) Greenwood.

Powdermaker, Hortense. After Freedom: A Cultural Study in the Deep South. LC 92-56923. (New Directions in Anthropological Writing Ser.). 462p. (C). 1993. reprint ed. pap. 14.95 (*0-299-13784-8*); reprint ed. lib. bdg. 25.95 (*0-299-13780-5*) U of Wis Pr.

— Hollywood: The Dream Factory; an Anthropologist Looks at the Movie-Makers. Coser, Lewis A. & Powell, Walter W., eds. LC 79-7013. (Perennial Works in Sociology). 1980. reprint ed. lib. bdg. 31.95 (*0-405-12112-1*) Ayer.

— Life in Lesu: The Study of a Melanesian Society in New Ireland. LC 76-44778. reprint ed. 40.00 (*0-404-15877-3*) AMS Pr.

— Stranger & Friend. 1967. pap. 13.95 (*0-393-00410-4*) Norton.

Powdermaker, Hortense, ed. Mass Communications Seminar: Proceedings of an Interdisciplinary Seminar Held under the Auspices of the Wenner-Gren Foundation for Anthropological Research, Inc., May 11-13, 1953. LC 65-27671. (Illus.). 157p. reprint ed. pap. 48.70 (*0-608-09185-5*, 205268900002) Bks Demand.

Powdrell, David D. Point Conception to Mexico: A Common Man Kayak Adventure. (Illus.). 110p. 1998. pap. 14.95 (*0-9663634-0-X*) Cuatro Casas.

***Powe-Allred, Alexandra.** Entering the Mother Zone. (Illus.). 256p. 2000. pap. 16.95 (*1-930546-42-4*) Wish Pub.

— Passion Rules! Inspiring Women in Business. 150p. 2000. 21.95 (*1-55571-530-3*, Pub. by PSI Resch) Midpt Trade.

Powe, B. W. A Canada of Light. enl. rev. ed. LC 97-169948. 128p. 1997. pap. (*1-895897-89-0*) Somerville Hse.

— The Solitary Outlaw. 192p. pap. 13.95 (*1-895897-79-3*) Somerville Hse.

Powe, Bruce. Outage: A Journey into Electric City. rev. ed. LC 94-42171. 1995. text 21.00 (*0-88001-418-0*) HarpC.

Powe, Gregory. Faith, Purpose & True Prosperity. Holland, David, ed. (Orig.). 1995. pap. text 5.95 (*0-9645017-0-8*) Reveal Truth.

Powe, James E. FoxPro 2.5 for Windows Developer's Library. Leventhal, Lance A., ed. LC 93-18966. (Lance A. Leventhal Microtrend Ser.). 400p. (Orig.). 1993. pap. 44.95 (*0-915391-81-3*) Slawson Comm.

Powe, Karen. Private Options for Public Schools: Ways Public Schools Are Exploring Privatization. (NSBA Best Practices Ser.). 77p. (Orig.). 1995. pap. 15.00 (*0-88364-197-6*, 04-115) Natl Sch Boards.

***Powe, Lucas A., Jr.** The Warren Court & American Politics. LC 99-47075. 600p. 2000. 35.00 (*0-674-00095-1*) HUP.

Powe, Lucas A., Jr., jt. auth. see Krattenmaker, Thomas G.

Powe, Marc B. The Emergence of the War Department Intelligence Agency, 1885-1918. 161p. 1974. pap. text 30.95 (*0-89126-013-7*) MA-AH Pub.

Powel, Harford, Jr. Walter Camp, the Father of American Football. LC 70-126246. (Select Bibliographies Reprint Ser.). (Illus.). 1977. 20.95 (*0-8369-5473-4*) Ayer.

Powel-Skoog, Betty & Kerfoot, Justine. A Life in Two Worlds. LC 96-70457. 1996. pap. 14.95 (*0-9653027-1-7*) Paper Moon Pub.

Powell. Considering Computer Contracting. 167p. 1990. pap. text 30.95 (*1-85384-022-X*) Buttrwrth-Heinemann.

— Edwardian Crisis: Britain 1901-1914. LC 96-15375. 224p. 1996. text 49.95 (*0-312-16093-3*) St Martin.

— Japan's Modern Theatre: A Century of Change & Continuity. 256p. 1999. text 55.00 (*0-312-21530-4*) St Martin.

***Powell.** Law & the Enviroment. 2nd ed. 2000. 23.75 (*0-324-02041-4*) Sth-Wstrn College.

— Law & the Enviroment. 2nd ed. 2002. pap. 46.00 (*0-324-02040-6*) Thomson Learn.

Powell. Learning & Behaviour. (Psychology Ser.). 2000. pap. 38.00 (*0-534-36585-X*) Brooks-Cole.

— Management of Pituitary Tumors. 1997. pap. text 49.00 (*0-443-06023-1*, W B Saunders Co) Harcrt Hlth Sci Grp.

— Math Competencies for Everyday Living. (MA - Academic Math Ser.). 1989. mass mkt. 22.95 (*0-538-13072-5*) S-W Pub.

— The Natural Home Physician. 164p. 1975. 11.95 (*0-85032-092-5*, Pub. by C W Daniel) Natl Bk Netwk.

— Quantitative Decision Making: Student Book. 1991. pap. text, student ed. write for info. (*0-582-06791-X*, Pub. by Addison-Wesley) Longman.

— Rethinking Management of Culturally Diversified. LC 99-86567. 336p. 2000. pap. 36.00 (*0-13-460908-5*) P-H.

— Senior Rights Movement. 1998. per. 14.95 (*0-8057-9746-7*, Twyne) Mac Lib Ref.

— Snow & Us. LC 98-11196. (Weather Ser.). (Illus.). 32p. (J). 1998. 21.30 (*1-887068-39-2*) Smart Apple.

— Thin Films, Vol. 26. LC 98-28495. (C). 1998. text. write for info. (*0-12-533026-X*) Harcourt.

— Tickets to the Devil. 5.95 (*0-910791-41-4*, 0670) Devyn Pr.

— Unreal City. Date not set. pr. 12.95 (*1-873741-04-9*, Pub. by Millvres Bks) LPC InBook.

— Wired Society. (C). 1998. pap. text 34.00 (*0-15-508353-8*, Pub. by Harcourt Coll Pubs) Harcourt.

— Wired Society. (C). 1998. pap. text, teacher ed. 26.75 (*0-15-508352-X*) Harcourt Coll Pubs.

Powell & Henderson. Contributions to West Indian Herpetology. LC 95-71882. 1996. 60.00 (*0-916984-37-0*) SSAR.

Powell & Treadgold. Sidereal Zodiac. 52p. 1979. 12.00 (*0-904693-07-4*, P2533-014) Am Fed Astrologers.

Powell & Van Dyke. Minnesota & Manitoba One Hundred Years Ago. (Historical Ser.). (Illus.). 1977. pap. 3.50 (*0-89540-056-1*, SB-056) Sun Pub.

Powell, jt. auth. see Andomus.

Powell, jt. ed. see Palmer.

***Powell, Benjamin O., Sr.** Precious Truth, Plain & Simple. 112p. 2000. 15.95 (*1-56167-586-5*) Am Literary Pr.

Powell, A. Joyce Olin, ed. see Olin, Warren G.

Powell, A. Michael. Trees & Shrubs of the Trans-Pecos & Adjacent Areas. 2nd rev. ed. LC 97-13155. (Illus.). 464p. 1998. 75.00 (*0-292-76579-7*) U of Tex Pr.

Powell, A. Michael, et al. Trees & Shrubs of the Trans-Pecos & Adjacent Areas. 2nd rev. ed. LC 97-13155. (Illus.). 464p. 1998. pap. 34.95 (*0-292-76573-8*) U of Tex Pr.

Powell, Aaron M. The National Purity Congress, Its Papers, Addresses, Portraits. LC 75-17238. (Social Problems & Social Policy Ser.). (Illus.). 1976. reprint ed. 39.95 (*0-405-07507-3*) Ayer.

Powell, Adam C., Jr. Adam on Adam: The Autobiography of Adam Clayton Powell, Jr. LC 94-20247. Orig. Title: Adam by Adam. 264p. 1994. reprint ed. pap. 12.95 (*0-8065-1538-4*, Citadel Pr) Carol Pub Group.

Powell, Adam C., Sr. Against the Tide: An Autobiography. Gaustad, Edwin S., ed. LC 79-52603. (Baptist Tradition Ser.). 1980. reprint ed. 33.95 (*0-405-12468-6*) Ayer.

— Palestine & Saints in Caesar's Household. 215p. 1998. reprint ed. pap. 35.95 (*1-58073-006-X*) BCP Bks.

— Palestine & Saints in Caesar's Household. 215p. 1998. reprint ed. pap. 35.95 (*0-933121-91-1*) Black Classic.

Powell, Addison M. Trailing & Camping in Alaska: Tales of the Valdez/Copper River Gold Rush. abr. ed. (Illus.). 1997. reprint ed. pap. 19.95 (*1-877900-06-0*) Prince W Sound.

Powell, Adriana, tr. see Decker, Ed & Hunt, Dave.

Powell, Adriana, tr. see Swindoll, Charles R.

Powell, Alan. Far Country: A Short History of the Northern Territory. 288p. 1996. pap. 24.95 (*0-522-84689-0*, Pub. by Melbourne Univ Pr) Paul & Co Pubs.

— War by Stealth: Australians & the Allied Intelligence Bureau 1942-45. LC 96-127830. 480p. 1996. 59.95 (*0-522-84691-2*, Pub. by Melbourne Univ Pr) Paul & Co Pubs.

Powell, Alan A., et al. Inside a Modern Macroeconometric Model: A Guide to the Murphy Model. (Lecture Notes in Economics & Mathematical Systems Ser.: No. 428). 1995. write for info. (*0-387-60027-2*) Spr-Verlag.

— Inside a Modern Macroeconometric Model: A Guide to the Murphy Model. 2nd ed. LC 97-26089. xviii, 455p. 1997. write for info. (*3-540-63146-1*) Spr-Verlag.

— Inside a Modern Macroeconometric Model: A Guide to the Murphy Model, Vol. XVIII. (Lecture Notes in Economics & Mathematical Systems Ser.: Vol. 428). (Illus.). 424p. 1995. 84.00 (*3-540-60027-2*) Spr-Verlag.

Powell, Alexander E. Adventures in Nepal - The Last Home of Mystery. (C). 1991. text 90.00 (*0-7855-0127-4*, Pub. by Ratna Pustak Bhandar) St Mut.

Powell, Alice & McAroy, Hazel, eds. A Taste of the Valley. (Illus.). 300p. 1988. write for info. (*0-318-64734-6*) St John Don Bosco Ch.

Powell, Allan. Maryland & the French & Indian War. 250th ed. LC 97-41130. 1998. write for info. (*0-9619995-4-3*) A R Powell.

Powell, Allan K. Utah Remembers World War II. LC 91-26877. (Illus.). 285p. reprint ed. pap. 88.40 (*0-608-20041-7*, 207131300010) Bks Demand.

Powell, Allan K., ed. Utah History Encyclopedia. LC 94-18977. (Illus.). 605p. 1994. 50.00 (*0-87480-425-6*) U of Utah Pr.

***Powell, Allen K.** A Complete Guide to Starting & Running a Co-Op Gallery. Steis, Drew, ed. (Art Calendar Guide Ser.). (Illus.). 58p. 1999. pap. 12.95 (*0-945388-24-1*) Art Calendar.

Powell, Allen K. The Next Time We Strike: Labor in Utah's Coal Fields, 1900-1933. (Illus.). 292p. 1985. pap. text 24.95 (*0-87421-161-1*) Utah St U Pr.

— The Utah Guide. 2nd ed. LC 98-28608. (Illus.). 544p. 1998. pap. 19.95 (*1-55591-413-6*) Fulcrum Pub.

Powell, Alton C. Wedgwood International Seminar: An Index to the Published Proceedings, 1956-1992. LC 94-66653. 56p. 1994. pap. text 17.00 (*0-9641682-0-0*) A C Powell.

Powell, Alton C. & Powell, Mary E. British Ceramics: A Bibliography of Works in English Through 1995. 220p. 1997. 35.00 (*0-9641682-1-9*) A C Powell.

Powell, Amanda, tr. see Arenal, Electra & Schlau, Stacey, eds.

Powell, Amanda, tr. see De la Cruz, Sor Juana Ines.

Powell, Andrew. Heirs to Tibet: Travels among the Exiles in India LC 93-231737. xii, 384p. 1992. write for info. (*0-434-59932-8*) Buttrwrth-Heinemann.

— Living Buddhism. LC 95-19685. (Illus.). 200p. 1995. pap. 27.50 (*0-520-20410-7*, Pub. by U CA Pr) Cal Prin Full Svc.

Powell, Andy. Illustrated Collector's Guide to Wishbone Ash: Includes over 100 Photos, along with Detailed... (Illus.). 1995. pap. 14.95 (*1-896522-11-4*) CN06.

Powell, Anita. Reflections of an Angel: Poetic Affirmations. 1998. pap. 10.00 (*1-57502-810-7*, PO2238) Morris Pubng.

Powell, Anna S. & Conference Board Staff. Global Quality: Competitive Successes & Challenges : A Research Report. LC 98-191562. (Conference Board Report). 32 p. 1995. write for info. (*0-8237-0572-2*) Conference Bd.

Powell, Anne. Shadows of War: British Women's Poetry of the Second World War. 1999. 45.00 (*0-7509-2257-5*) Sutton Pub Ltd.

Powell, Anne, ed. A Deep Cry: First World War Soldier - Poets Killed in France & Flanders. 496p. 1999. pap. 26.95 (*0-7509-1987-6*, Pub. by Sutton Pub Ltd) Intl Pubs Mktg.

Powell, Anne R., jt. auth. see Markova, Dawna.

Powell, Annie. Biomineralization. 1999. 98.00 (*0-85404-562-7*) Spr-Verlag.

Powell, Anthony. The Acceptance World. large type unabridged ed. (Dance to Music of Time Ser.: Vol. 3). 320p. 1998. 25.95 (*0-7531-5816-7*, 158167) ISIS Pub.

— Afternoon Men. (Classics Ser.: No. 108). 192p. 1997. pap. 10.95 (*1-55713-284-4*) Sun & Moon CA.

— At Lady Molly's. large type unabridged ed. (Dance to Music of Time Ser.: Vol. 4). 350p. 1998. 25.95 (*0-7531-5817-5*, 158175) ISIS Pub.

***Powell, Anthony.** Books Do Furnish a Room. large type unabridged ed. 284p. 1999. 25.95 (*0-7531-5823-X*, 15823X, Pub. by ISIS Lrg Prnt) ISIS Pub.

Powell, Anthony. A Buyer's Market. large type unabridged ed. (Dance to Music of Time Ser.: Vol. 2). 320p. 1998. 25.95 (*0-7531-5815-9*, 158159) ISIS Pub.

***Powell, Anthony.** Casannova's Chinese Restaurant. large type unabridged ed. 269p. 1999. 25.95 (*0-7531-5818-3*, 158183, Pub. by ISIS Lrg Prnt) ISIS Pub.

Powell, Anthony. Dance to the Music of Time. 2000. 0.00 (*0-375-40318-3*) Random.

— A Dance to the Music of Time: All Four Movements, 4 vols. Incl. Dance to Music Time First Movement. LC 94-47228. 732p. 1995. pap. 19.00 (*0-226-67714-1*); Dance to Music Time Fourth Movement. 804p. 1995. pap. 18.95 (*0-226-67718-4*); Dance to Music Time Second Movement. 724p. 1995. pap. 17.95 (*0-226-67716-8*); Dance to Music Time Third Movement. 736p. 1995. pap. 17.95 (*0-226-67717-6*); 1998. Set pap. 72.80 (*0-226-67719-2*) U Ch Pr.

— A Dance to the Music of Time: First Movement. Incl. Acceptance World. 1962. Buyer's Market. 1962. Question of Upbringing. 1962. 1962. 24.95 (*0-316-71535-2*) Little.

— A Dance to the Music of Time: Third Movement. Incl. Military Philosophers. 1971. Soldier's Art. 1971. Valley of Bones. 1971. 1971. 24.95 (*0-316-71546-8*) Little.

— Faces in My Time. LC 83-124189. viii, 230p. 1980. write for info. (*0-434-59924-7*) Buttrwrth-Heinemann.

— Hearing Secret Harmonies. 240p. 1986. mass mkt. 4.50 (*0-445-20146-0*, Pub. by Warner Bks) Little.

***Powell, Anthony.** Hearing Secret Harmonies. large type unabridged ed. 1999. 25.95 (*0-7531-5825-6*, 158256, Pub. by ISIS Lrg Prnt) ISIS Pub.

— Journals, 1990-1992. pap. 29.95 (*0-434-00423-5*, Pub. by Random) Trafalgar.

— The Kindly Ones. large type unabridged ed. (Dance to the Music of Time Ser.). 298p. 1999. 25.95 (*0-7531-5819-1*, 158191, Pub. by ISIS Lrg Prnt) ISIS Pub.

Powell, Anthony. Messengers of Day. LC 83-124205. (Keep the Ball Rolling : the Memoirs of Anthony Powell Ser.). viii, 209p. 1978. write for info. (*0-434-59923-9*) Buttrwrth-Heinemann.

***Powell, Anthony.** The Military Philosophers. large type unabridged ed. 287p. 1999. 25.95 (*0-7531-5822-1*, 158221, Pub. by ISIS Lrg Prnt) ISIS Pub.

Powell, Anthony. Miscellaneous Verdicts. 510p. 1992. 38.50 (*0-226-67710-9*) U Ch Pr.

— Oh, How the Wheel Becomes It! A Novel. LC 84-105815. 143 p. 1983. 6.95 (*0-434-59925-5*) Buttrwrth-Heinemann.

— A Question of Upbringing. large type unabridged ed. (Dance to Music of Time Ser.: Vol. 1). 261p. 1998. 25.95 (*0-7531-5813-2*, 158132) ISIS Pub.

***Powell, Anthony.** The Soldier's Art. large type unabridged ed. (Dance to the Music of Time Ser.). 253p. 1999. 25.95 (*0-7531-5821-3*, 158213, Pub. by ISIS Lrg Prnt) ISIS Pub.

— Temporary Kings. large type unabridged ed. 1999. 25.95 (*0-7531-5824-8*, 158248, Pub. by ISIS Lrg Prnt) ISIS Pub.

Powell, Anthony. Under Review: Further Writings on Writers, 1946-1990. LC 93-41020. 480p. 1994. 34.95 (*0-226-67712-5*) U Ch Pr.

***Powell, Anthony.** The Valley of Bones. large type unabridged ed. (Dance to the Music of Time Ser.). 284p. 1999. 25.95 (*0-7531-5820-5*, 158205, Pub. by ISIS Lrg Prnt) ISIS Pub.

Powell, Anthony. Venusburg. (Green Integer Bks.: No. 39). 190p. 1999. pap. text 10.95 (*1-892295-24-5*, Pub. by Green Integer) Consort Bk Sales.

— What Fools These Mortals Be: A Mediatation on Love Taken from the Works of Shakespeare. 19p. (Orig.). (YA). (gr. 6 up). 1995. pap. 3.00 (*1-57514-130-2*, 1111) Encore Perform Pub.

Powell, Anthony, jt. ed. see Good, Donnie B.

Powell, Antoinette P. The Landscape Architecture Book Catalog: A Bibliography of Holdings on the University of Kentucky Campus Through 1977. (University of Kentucky Libraries Occasional Papers: No. 3). 335p. 1982. pap. 10.00 (*0-317-27432-5*) U of KY Libs.

Powell, Anton. Ancient Greece. (Cultural Atlas for Young People Ser.). (Illus.). 96p. (YA). 1989. 19.95 (*0-8160-1972-X*) Facts on File.

— Athens & Sparta: Constructing Greek Political & Social History from 478 B.C. (Illus.). 412p. (C). 1991. pap. 27.99 (*0-415-00338-5*, A5756) Routledge.

— Londonwalks. rev. ed. 258p. 1995. pap. 12.95 (*0-8050-1300-8*, Owl) H Holt & Co.

— Roman News. LC 96-3584. 1999. pap. text 6.99 (*0-7636-0341-4*) Candlewick Pr.

— Roman Poetry & Propaganda in the Age of Augustus. (Bristol Classical Paperbacks Ser.). (Illus.). 180p. 1997. pap. text 25.95 (*1-85399-552-5*, Pub. by Brist Class Pr) Focus Pub-R Pullins.

Powell, Anton, ed. Classical Sparta: Techniques Behind Her Success. LC 88-20748. (Oklahoma Series in Classical Culture: Vol. 1). 210p. 1989. 45.00 (*0-8061-2177-7*) U of Okla Pr.

— The Greek World. LC 94-41576. (Illus.). 640p. (C). (gr. 13). 1995. 165.00 (*0-415-06031-1*, B4181) Routledge.

— Greek World. (Illus.). 640p. (C). 1997. pap. 49.99 (*0-415-17042-7*) Routledge.

Powell, Anton & Hodkinson, Stephen, eds. The Shadow of Sparta. LC 93-43480. 408p. (C). (gr. 13). 1994. 75.00 (*0-415-10413-0*) Routledge.

Powell, Anton & Steele, Philip. History News: Greek News. LC 95-48489. (Illus.). 32p. (J). 1999. pap. 6.99 (*0-7636-0340-6*) Candlewick Pr.

Powell, Anton, jt. ed. see Hodkinson, Steven.

Powell, Anton, ed. see Langley, Andrew & De Souza, Philip.

Powell, Anton, jt. ed. see Welch, Kathryn.

Powell, Ardal, ed. see Lasocki, David.

Powell, Ardal, ed. see Tromlitz, Johann G.

Powell, Ardal, ed. & tr. see Tromlitz, Johann G.

Powell, Arthur B. & Frankenstein, Marilyn, eds. Ethnomathematics: Challenging Eurocentrism in Mathematics Education. LC 96-24925. (SUNY Series, Reform in Mathematics Education). 440p. (C). 1997. text 68.50 (*0-7914-3351-X*); pap. text 24.95 (*0-7914-3352-8*) State U NY Pr.

Powell, Arthur E. The Astral Body: And Other Astral Phenomena. LC 73-4775. (Classics Ser.). 280p. 1996. reprint ed. pap. 12.00 (*0-8356-0438-1*, Quest) Theos Pub Hse.

— The Astral Body & Other Astral Phenomena (1926) 274p. 1998. reprint ed. pap. 11.00 (*0-7661-0253-X*) Kessinger Pub.

— Etheric Double: The Health Aura. LC 96-22066. (Illus.). 1969. pap. 12.00 (*0-8356-0075-0*, Quest) Theos Pub Hse.

— Mental Body. 1975. pap. 19.95 (*0-8356-5504-0*) Theos Pub Hse.

— The Solar System. 371p. 1996. reprint ed. pap. 34.50 (*0-7873-1153-7*) Hlth Research.

Powell, Arthur G. I Can Go Home Again. LC 84-6935. (Illus.). 308p. 1984. reprint ed. 18.50 (*0-87152-398-1*) Hist Chattahoochee.

— Lessons from Privilege: The American Prep School Tradition. LC 96-9157. 304p. 1996. 36.50 (*0-674-52549-3*) HUP.

— Lessons from Privilege: The American Prep School Tradition. 320p. 1998. pap. text 16.95 (*0-674-52553-1*) HUP.

— The Uncertain Profession: Harvard & the Search for Educational Authority. LC 79-26096. 361p. 1980. reprint ed. pap. 112.00 (*0-7837-4180-4*, 205902900012) Bks Demand.

***Powell, Arthur G. & Sizer, Theodore R.** A Passion for Learning. 128p. 1999. pap. 17.00 (*0-7879-5043-2*) Jossey-Bass.

Powell, Arthur J., jt. auth. see Massey, James G.

Powell, Avril A. Muslims & Missionaries in Pre-Mutiny India. (SOAS London Studies on South Asia: No. 7). 368p. (C). 1996. text 50.00 (*0-7007-0210-5*, Pub. by Curzon Pr Ltd) UH Pr.

Powell, B. B. Athenian Mythology: Erechthonius & the Three Daughters of Cecrops. (Illus.). 90p. 1976. pap. 15.00 (*0-89005-121-6*) Ares.

Powell, B. B. & Morris, I. A New Companion to Homer. LC 96-38925. (Mnemosyne, Supplements Ser.: Vol. 163). (Illus.). xviii, 755p. 1997. 250.00 (*90-04-09989-1*) Brill Academic Pubs.

Powell, Barbara. Windows into the Infinite: A Guide to the Hindu Scriptures. 488p. (Orig.). 1997. pap. 19.95 (*0-87573-072-8*) Jain Pub Co.

Powell, Barbara J. Windows into the Infinite: A Guide to the Hindu Scriptures. (Illus.). 488p. (Orig.). (C). 1996. text 30.00 (*0-87573-071-X*) Jain Pub Co.

Powell, Barry B. Classical Myth. 2nd ed. LC 96-40061. 671p. 1997. pap. text 52.00 (*0-13-716714-8*) P-H.

***Powell, Barry B.** Classical Myth. 3rd ed. LC 99-87714. 736p. 2000. pap. 44.00 (*0-13-088442-1*) P-H.

***Powell, Ben.** Skateboarding. (Extreme Sports Ser.). (Illus.). 32p. (YA). (gr. 5-9). 1999. pap. 6.95 (*0-7641-0797-6*) Barron.

Powell, Benjamin W. Man of Labrador. 234p. 1993. pap. write for info. (*1-883704-00-6*) Cleaveland.

Powell, Betty. Blessed Are the Chicken-Hearted. LC 98-50465. 224p. 1999. pap. 9.99 (*0-8254-3553-6*) Kregel.

Powell, Betty B. & Park, Jeff. I Was That Woman at the Well. (Illus.). 176p. (Orig.). 1986. pap. 5.95 (*0-939241-00-5*) Faith Print.

Powell, Beverly J. Desert Quest: The Hunt for True Gold. 192p. 1991. pap. 9.99 (*0-310-53231-0*) Zondervan.

Powell, Bill. Drawing Flowers. (How to Draw Ser.). 32p. 1997. pap. 6.95 (*1-56010-154-7*, HT255) W Foster Pub.

— Drawing Landscapes. (How to Draw Ser.). 32p. (Orig.). 1997. pap. 6.95 (*1-56010-157-1*, HT258) W Foster Pub.

— Drawing People. (How to Draw Ser.). 32p. (Orig.). 1997. pap. 6.95 (*1-56010-156-3*, HT257) W Foster Pub.

— Drawing Still Life. (How to Draw Ser.). 32p. 1997. pap. 6.95 (*1-56010-155-5*, HT256) W Foster Pub.

Powell, Bob. Scottish Agricultural Implements. (Album Ser.: No. 218). (Illus.). 32p. 1989. pap. 6.95 (*0-85263-925-2*, Pub. by Shire Pubns) Parkwest Pubns.

Powell, Bob, jt. auth. see Barnes, Ann.

Powell, Brenda J. The Metaphysical Quality of the Tragic: A Study of Sophocles, Giraudoux, & Sartre. (American University Studies: Comparative Literature: Ser. III, Vol. 27). 213p. (C). 1989. text 40.50 (*0-8204-1068-3*) P Lang Pubng.

Powell, Brian. Japan's Modern Theatre: A Century of Change & Continuity. (Japan Library). 256p. (C). 1998. text 55.00 (*1-873410-30-1*, Pub. by Curzon Pr Ltd) UH Pr.

— Kabuki in Modern Japan: Mayama Seika & His Plays. LC 89-70288. 254p. 1990. text 45.00 (*0-312-04505-0*) St Martin.

***Powell, C. A.** Study of the Eastern Tennessee Seismic Zone. 74p. 1999. pap. 7.00 (*0-16-062983-7*) USGPO.

Powell, C. E., jt. ed. see Brummitt, R. K.

Powell, C. M., jt. ed. see Veevers, J. J.

Powell, Caleb. This Seething Ocean, That Damned Eagle. LC 93-807018. 127p. (Orig.). 1993. pap. text 9.95 (*1-878815-04-0*) Reflected Images.

Powell, Carol C. A Student's Guide to the Internet. 2nd ed. LC 97-30326. 192p. (C). 1997. pap. text, student ed. 20.80 (*0-13-649112-X*) P-H.

Powell, Carol E. Along the Way: A Collection of Thoughts & Inspirational Verse. 198p. 1999. pap. 14.95 (*0-9668750-2-8*) Sycamore IN.

Powell, Carroll F., et al, eds. Vapor Deposition. LC 66-13515. (Electrochemical Society Proceedings Ser.). (Illus.). 741p. reprint ed. pap. 200.00 (*0-608-11679-3*, 205125800092) Bks Demand.

Powell, Catherine, jt. auth. see Tajima, Noriyuki.

Powell, Cecilia. Italy in the Age of Turner: The Garden of the World. LC 98-167752. (Illus.). 120p. 1998. 40.00 (*1-85894-049-4*, Pub. by Merrell Holberton) U of Wash Pr.

— Turner in the South. LC 86-26673. 216p. 1987. 50.00 (*0-300-03870-4*) Yale U Pr.

Powell, Cedric J., jt. ed. see Casper, Lawrence A.

Powell, Charles, jt. auth. see Benjamin, Charles.

Powell, Charles, jt. auth. see London, Bill.

Powell, Charles A. Choices for Employees: How to Survive As an Employee. abr. large type ed. Hope, Barbara, ed. LC 96-69986. 20p. (Orig.). 1996. pap. 5.00 (*0-9627161-2-X*) QLP CA.

— Servants of Power. LC 90-91860. 314p. 1990. 18.95 (*0-9627161-9-7*) QLP CA.

Powell, Charles C. & Lindquist, Richard K. Ball Pest & Disease Manual: Disease, Insect, & Mite Control on Flower & Foliage Crops. 2nd rev. ed. LC 96-46954. (Illus.). 448p. 1997. 64.95 (*1-883052-13-0*, B030) Ball Pub.

— El Manejo Integrado de los Insectos, Acaros, y Enfermedades en los Cultivos Ornamentales. Hoyos De Martens, Veronica, ed. LC 94-28537. (SPA., Illus.). 118p. 1994. pap. text 28.95 (*1-883052-06-8*, B022) Ball Pub.

Powell, Charles C. & Rossetti, Rosemarie. The Healthy Indoor Plant: A Guide to Successful Indoor Gardening. LC 92-90698. (Illus.). 304p. (Orig.). 1992. pap. 27.00 (*0-9631767-0-6*) Rosewell Pub.

Powell, Charles C., jt. auth. see Hodges, Larry.

***Powell, Cherith & Forde, Greg.** The Self-Hypnosis Kit. 1999. 22.95 incl. audio Courage-to-Change.

Powell, Cherith & Forde, Greg. The Self-Hypnosis Kit: Discover the Power of Hypnotherapy to Improve Your Life. (Illus.). 128p. 1996. pap. 22.95 (*0-670-86530-3*) Viking Penguin.

Powell, Chester F. Thanks for Coming By. LC 97-66268. (Illus.). 72p. (Orig.). 1997. 10.95 (*0-9632886-5-2*) Plum Lick Pub.

***Powell, Chilton L.** English Domestic Relations, 1487-1653: A Study of Matrimony & Family Life in Theory & Practice as Revealed by the Literature, Law & History of the Period. LC 00-23850. 2000. write for info. (*1-58477-096-1*) Lawbk Exchange.

Powell, Christopher. Discovering Cottage Architecture. (Handbook Ser.: No. 275). (Illus.). 104p. 1989. pap. 8.50 (*0-85263-673-3*, Pub. by Shire Pubns) Parkwest Pubns.

— Stables & Stable Blocks. (Album Ser.: No. 261). (Illus.). 32p. 1989. pap. 6.25 (*0-7478-0105-3*, Pub. by Shire Pubns) Parkwest Pubns.

Powell, Clark. Un Acompanante de Sahaj Marg - A Sahaj Marg Companion: El Sendero Natural - The Natural Path. Baez, Constanza, tr. (SPA.). 208p. 1998. pap. write for info. (*0-945242-39-5*) Shri Ram Chandra.

— A Sahaj Marg Companion: The Natural Path. 216p. 1996. 15.00 (*0-945242-31-X*) Shri Ram Chandra.

Powell, Claud, ed. see Powell, Dora.

Powell, Colin L. In His Own Words: Colin Powell. Shaw, Lisa, ed. LC 95-45856. 1995. pap. 5.99 (*0-399-52224-7*, Perigee Bks) Berkley Pub.

Powell, Colin L. & Persico, Joseph E. My American Journey: An Autobiography. 1996. mass mkt. 6.99 (*0-345-40728-8*) Ballantine Pub Grp.

— My American Journey: An Autobiography. (Illus.). 643p. 1995. 25.95 (*0-679-43296-5*) Random.

Powell, Colin L., ed. see Stilwell, Paul.

Powell, Consie. A Bold Carnivore: An Alphabet of Predators. (Illus.). 32p. (J). (ps-1). 1997. pap. 7.95 (*1-57098-143-4*) Roberts Rinehart.

— Old Dog Cora & the Christmas Tree. LC 98-53797. (Illus.). 32p. (J). (gr. 2-5). 1999. text 15.95 (*0-8075-5968-7*) A Whitman.

Powell, Conway L. & Bagaraj, D. Joseph. VA Mycorrhiza. 240p. 1984. boxed set 169.00 (*0-8493-5694-6*, QK604) CRC Pr.

Powell-Cope, Gail M., jt. auth. see Brown, Marie A.

Powell-Cotton, P. H. In Unknown Africa: A Narrative of Twenty Months Travel & Sport in Unknown Lands & among New Tribes. (B. E. Ser.: No. 163). 1904. 70.00 (*0-8115-3078-7*) Periodicals Srv.

Powell, Craig. The Ocean Remembers It Is Visible: Poems 1966-1989. (QRL Poetry Bks.: Vols. XXVIII-XXIX). 1989. 20.00 (*0-614-06430-9*) Quarterly Rev.

Powell, D. Evaluating the NHS. LC 96-39950. (State of Health Ser.). 1997. pap. 29.95 (*0-335-19530-X*) OpUniv Pr.

Powell, D., et al, eds. Delta Four: A Generic Architecture for Dependable Distributed Computing. (Research Reports ESPRIT, Project 818, 2252 Delta- 4: Vol. 1). x, 484p. 1991. 62.95 (*0-387-54985-4*) Spr-Verlag.

***Powell, D. A.** Lunch. 2000. 12.95 (*0-8195-6426-5*); pap. 12.95 (*0-8195-6427-3*) U Pr of New Eng.

Powell, D. A. Tea. LC 97-44599. (Wesleyan Poetry Ser.). 88p. 1998. 17.95 (*0-8195-6334-X*, Wesleyan Univ Pr) U Pr of New Eng.

Powell, Dale. Timothy Cratchit's Christmas Carol, 1917. LC 99-207344. 128p. 1998. pap. 15.00 (*1-893069-02-8*) DickensWrld.

Powell, Dale. Timothy Cratchit's Christmas Carol, 1917: A Sequel to the Charles Dickens Classic. write for info. (*1-893069-24-9*) DickensWrld.

***Powell, Damian X.** Sir James Whitelocke's Liber Famelicus, 1570-1632: Law & Politics in Early Stuart England. LC 99-59032. 264p. 1999. pap. text 42.95 (*0-8204-4637-8*) P Lang Pubng.

Powell, Dannye R. At Every Wedding Someone Stays Home: Poems by Dannye Romine Powell. LC 93-38795. 96p. 1994. 20.00 (*1-55728-315-X*); pap. 12.00 (*1-55728-316-8*) U of Ark Pr.

— Parting the Curtains: Interviews with Southern Writers. LC 94-24853. (Illus.). 353p. 1994. 12.95 (*0-89587-116-5*) Blair.

Powell, Darlene & Powell, Derek S. The Power of Soul: Pathways to Psychological & Spiritual Growth for African Americans. LC 97-18078. 256p. 1998. 23.00 (*0-688-15110-8*, Wm Morrow) Morrow Avon.

Powell, David. Letters from America Pt. 1: September 1860-January 1863. 135p. 1995. pap. 14.95 (*1-85756-246-1*) Paul & Co Pubs.

— Tom Paine Greatest Exile. pap. write for info. (*0-09-174193-9*) Trafalgar.

— What Can I Write About? 7000 Topics for High School Students. 111p. (YA). (gr. 7-12). 1981. 10.95 (*0-8141-5656-8*) NCTE.

— What's Left? Labour Britain & the Socialist Tradition. LC 98-193745. 352p. 1998. 39.95 (*0-7206-1041-9*, Pub. by P Owen Ltd) Dufour.

Powell, David, ed. see Clare, John.

Powell, David, tr. see Sisson, Richard, et al.

Powell, David A. George Sand. (Twayne's World Authors Ser.: No. 761). 176p. 1990. 26.95 (*0-8057-8260-5*, Twayne) Mac Lib Ref.

— George Sand Today: Proceedings of the Eighth International Georges Sand Conference - Tours, 1989. 310p. 1992. lib. bdg. 49.50 (*0-8191-8522-1*) U Pr of Amer.

Powell, David E. The Russian Health Care Crisis: History, Evaluation, & Recommendations. (Twentieth Century Fund Bk.). 120p. (C). 1997. pap. 9.95 (*0-87078-373-4*) Century Foundation.

Powell, David G., ed. Equine Infectious Diseases No. 5: Proceedings of the Fifth International Conference. LC 88-27670. 312p. 1989. text 70.00 (*0-8131-1676-7*) U Pr of Ky.

Powell, David J. Clinical Supervision: Skills for Substance Abuse Counselors. LC 79-20586. 1980. student ed. 20.95 (*0-87705-407-X*, Kluwer Acad Hman Sci); pap., student ed. 30.95 (*0-89885-442-3*, Kluwer Acad Hman Sci) Kluwer Academic.

— Clinical Supervision in Alcohol & Drug Abuse Counseling: Principles, Models, Methods, No. 1. LC 97-42941. 1998. pap. text 24.95 (*0-7879-4074-7*) Jossey-Bass.

Powell, David J., ed. Alcoholism & Sexual Dysfunction: Issues in Clinical Management. LC 89-1998. (Alcoholism Treatment Quarterly Ser.: Vol. 1, No. 3). 145p. 1984. text 49.95 (*0-86656-365-2*) Haworth Pr.

Powell, David J. & Brodsky, Archie. Clinical Supervision in Alcohol & Drug Abuse Counseling: Principles, Models, Methods. LC 93-14505. 327p. 1993. 47.95 (*0-02-925055-2*) Jossey-Bass.

Powell, David R., tr. see Freidzon, Claudio.

***Powell, David Swensen.** Bad Boys of the Book of Mormon: And What They Teach Us. LC 99-64095. (Illus.). 128p. 1999. pap. 9.95 (*1-888125-48-9*) Publ Consult.

Powell, Dawn. Angels on Toast. LC 96-23040. 273p. 1996. pap. 14.00 (*1-883642-40-X*) Steerforth Pr.

— The Bride's House. LC 98-26161. (Illus.). 187p. 1998. reprint ed. pap. 14.00 (*1-883642-78-7*) Steerforth Pr.

— Come Back to Sorrento. LC 97-29556. Orig. Title: The Tenth Moon. 185p. 1997. pap. 14.00 (*1-883642-26-4*) Steerforth Pr.

— Dance Night. LC 98-51106. 235p. 1999. pap. 14.00 (*1-883642-71-X*) Steerforth Pr.

— Dawn Powell at Her Best: Including the Novels "Dance Night" & "Turn Magic Wheel" & Selected Stories. LC 94-30416. 452p. 1994. 28.00 (*1-883642-16-7*) Steerforth Pr.

— The Diaries of Dawn Powell, 1931-1965. Page, Tim, ed. & intro. by. LC 95-40271. (Illus.). 513p. 1998. reprint ed. pap. 19.00 (*1-883642-25-6*) Steerforth Pr.

— The Diaries of Dawn Powell 1931-1965. Page, Tim, ed. & intro. by. LC 95-40271. 513p. 1995. 32.00 (*1-883642-08-6*) Steerforth Pr.

— Four Plays by Dawn Powell. Page, Tim & Sexton, Michael, eds. LC 99-43314. 453p. 1999. pap. 19.00 (*1-883642-61-2*) Steerforth Pr.

— The Golden Spur. LC 97-27438. 266p. 1997. pap. 14.00 (*1-883642-27-2*) Steerforth Pr.

— The Happy Island. LC 98-25225. 275p. 1998. reprint ed. pap. 14.00 (*1-883642-79-5*) Steerforth Pr.

— The Locusts Have No King. LC 95-46742. 286p. 1996. pap. 14.00 (*1-883642-42-6*) Steerforth Pr.

— My Home Is Far Away. LC 95-3238. 295p. 1995. pap. 14.00 (*1-883642-43-4*) Steerforth Pr.

— The Selected Letters of Dawn Powell: 1913-1965. Page, Tim, ed. & intro. by. LC 99-20423. 448p. 1999. 30.00 (*0-8050-5364-6*) H Holt & Co.

— Sunday, Monday & Always: Stories by Dawn Powell. LC 99-43312. 226p. 1999. pap. 14.00 (*1-883642-60-4*) Steerforth Pr.

— A Time to Be Born. LC 96-23039. 334p. 1996. pap. 14.00 (*1-883642-41-8*) Steerforth Pr.

— A Time to Be Born. LC 83-45842. reprint ed. 30.00 (*0-404-20206-3*, PS3531) AMS Pr.

— Turn, Magic Wheel. LC 98-51107. 230p. 1999. pap. 14.00 (*1-883642-72-8*) Steerforth Pr.

— The Wicked Pavilion. LC 96-23041. 246p. 1996. pap. 14.00 (*1-883642-39-6*) Steerforth Pr.

— The Wicked Pavilion. 1990. pap. 8.95 (*0-685-29464-1*) Vin Bks.

Powell, Debra, jt. auth. see Dolan, Bridget.

Powell, Derek S., jt. auth. see Powell, Darlene.

Powell, Dilys. Descent from Parnassus. LC 75-99720. (Essay Index Reprint Ser.). 1977. 21.95 (*0-8369-1374-4*) Ayer.

— The Dilys Powell Film Reader. Cook, Christopher, ed. (Film Reader Ser.). 486p. 1995. 39.95 (*1-55783-206-4*) Applause Theatre Bk Pubs.

— The Dilys Powell Film Reader. Cook, Christopher, ed. LC 92-12538. (The World's Classics Ser). 480p. 1993. pap. 24.95 (*0-19-283082-1*) OUP.

Powell, Don L. Literary Perspectives, Vol. 1. 2nd ed. 1000p. 1998. per. 77.95 (*0-7872-4213-6*, 41421301) Kendall-Hunt.

— Literary Perspectives, Vol. II. 448p. 1992. pap. text 49.95 (*0-8403-7871-8*) Kendall-Hunt.

Powell, Don R. Self-Care: Your Family Guide to Symptoms & How to Treat Them. (Illus.). 280p. 1996. 29.95 (*1-882606-24-8*) Peoples Med Soc.

Powell, Don R. Senior's Health at Home: Your Complete Guide to Symptoms, Solutions & Self Care. 432p. pap. 17.95 (*0-9635612-9-4*) Am Inst Prevent.

Powell, Don R. 365 Health Hints. 1999. 9.99 (*1-57866-048-3*) Galahad Bks.

— A Year of Health Hints. large type ed. 664p. 1992. lib. bdg. 13.95 (*1-56054-943-2*) Thorndike Pr.

— A Year of Health Hints: Three Hundred Sixty-Five Practical Ways to Feel Better & Live Longer. rev. ed. 374p. (C). 1997. reprint ed. 23.95 (*0-9635612-1-9*) Am Inst Prevent.

***Powell, Don R. & American Institute for Preventive Medicine Staff.** Students' Self-Care Guide. 2000. pap. 5.75 (*0-9635612-0-0*) Am Inst Prevent.

Powell, Don R., jt. auth. see American Institute for Preventive Medicine Staff.

Powell, Donald B. & Powell, Mary J. The Fightin' Texas Aggie Band. LC 93-33734. (Centennial Series of the Association of Former Students: No. 53). (Illus.). 182p. 1994. 29.95 (*0-89096-595-1*) Tex A&M Univ Pr.

— The Fightin' Texas Aggie Band. limited ed. LC 93-33734. (Centennial Series of the Association of Former Students: No. 53). (Illus.). 182p. 1994. 50.00 (*0-89096-631-1*) Tex A&M Univ Pr.

Powell, Donald M. Arizona Gathering Two, 1950-1969: An Annotated Bibliography. LC 72-82946. 214p. reprint ed. pap. 66.40 (*0-8357-4764-6*, 203769100009) Bks Demand.

Powell, Dora. Edward Elgar: Memories of a Variation. Powell, Claud, ed. (Illus.). 192p. 1994. 59.95 (*0-85967-996-9*, Pub. by Scolar Pr) Ashgate Pub Co.

Powell, Douglas & Leiss, William. Mad Cows & Mother's Milk: The Perils of Poor Risk Communication. LC 99-203404. 308p. 1997. text 65.00 (*0-7735-1618-2*, Pub. by McG-Queens Univ Pr) CUP Services.

— Mad Cows & Mother's Milk: The Perils of Poor Risk Communication. LC 99-203404. 320p. 1998. pap. 19.95 (*0-7735-1619-0*, Pub. by McG-Queens Univ Pr) CUP Services.

Powell, Douglas, jt. auth. see Shreiner, Curt.

Powell, Douglas A. Explosions & Small Geometries. Mycue, Edward, ed. (Took Modern Poetry in English Ser.: No. 15). (Illus.). 28p. (Orig.). 1991. pap. 4.00 (*1-879457-14-8*) Norton Coker Pr.

Powell, Douglas A., et al. Consequences. Mycue, Edward, ed. (Took Modern Poetry in English Ser.: No. 35). (Illus.). 32p. (Orig.). 1993. pap. 4.50 (*1-879457-37-7*) Norton Coker Pr.

Powell, Douglas H. The Nine Myths of Aging: Maximizing the Quality of Later Life, Vol. 1. LC 97-51718. 250p. 1998. pap. text 23.95 (*0-7167-3104-5*) W H Freeman.

Powell, Douglas H. & Whitla, Dean K. Profiles in Cognitive Aging. LC 94-18126. (Illus.). 256p. 1994. text 46.95 (*0-674-71331-1*, POWPRO) HUP.

Powell, Douglas R. Families & Early Childhood Programs. LC 89-61025. 141p. 1989. pap. text 6.00 (*0-935989-22-6*, NAEYC#142) Natl Assn Child Ed.

Powell, Douglas R., jt. ed. see Unger, Donald G.

Powell, E. & Taylor, D., eds. Directory of Rural Organizations. 96p. 1996. text 32.95 (*0-85236-349-4*, Pub. by Farming Pr) Diamond Farm Bk.

Powell, E. Alexander. The Last Frontier: The White Man's War for Civilization in Africa. 1976. lib. bdg. 59.95 (*0-8490-2129-4*) Gordon Pr.

— Long Roll on the Rhine: A Study of Hitler's Germany. 1976. 250.00 (*0-8490-2183-9*) Gordon Pr.

— Thunder over Europe. 1972. 250.00 (*0-8490-1213-9*) Gordon Pr.

Powell, E. Sandy. Rats. LC 93-40925. (Early Bird Nature Bks.). (Illus.). 48p. (J). (gr. 2-3). 1994. lib. bdg. 19.95 (*0-8225-3003-1*, Lerner Publctns) Lerner Pub.

Powell, Earl A., III. Thomas Cole. (Illus.). 144p. 1990. 49.50 (*0-8109-3158-3*, Pub. by Abrams) Time Warner.

Powell, Earl A., III, ed. The James A. Michener Collection, Twentieth Century American Paintings. LC 77-89177. (Illus.). 354p. 1977. pap. 12.00 (*0-935213-11-2*); text 15.00 (*0-935213-03-1*) J S Blanton Mus.

Powell, Earl A., III, et al. The Robert O. Anderson Building. LC 86-20862. (Illus.). 96p. (Orig.). 1986. pap. 14.95 (*0-87587-132-1*) LA Co Art Mus.

Powell, Earl N., ed. Designing for Product Success: Essays & Case Studies from the Triad Design Project Exhibit. (Illus.). 46p. (Orig.). 1989. pap. 20.00 (*0-9624445-0-2*) Design Mgmt Inst.

Powell, Edgar & Trevelyan, George M., eds. The Peasants' Rising & the Lollards. LC 78-63202. (Heresies of the Early Christian & Medieval Era Ser.: Second Ser.). reprint ed. 34.50 (*0-404-16238-X*) AMS Pr.

Powell, Edward. Kingship, Law & Society: Criminal Justice in the Reign of Henry V. 332p. 1990. text 85.00 (*0-19-820082-X*) OUP.

Powell, Edward A. The Army Behind the Army. LC 74-75242. (United States in World War I Ser.). (Illus.). xiii, 470p. 1974. reprint ed. lib. bdg. 55.95 (*0-89198-107-1*) Ozer.

Powell, Eileen. From Seed to Bloom: How to Grow over 500 Annuals, Perennials & Herbs. LC 94-35380. (Illus.). 320p. 1995. pap. 19.95 (*0-88266-259-7*, Garden Way Pub) Storey Bks.

Powell, Elfreda. Robert De Niro. LC 97-22648. (Superstars of Film Ser.). (Illus.). 48p. (YA). (gr. 4-7). 1999. lib. bdg. 15.95 (*0-7910-4645-1*) Chelsea Hse.

Powell, Elfreda, tr. see de Saint-Andre, Alix.

Powell, Elfreda, tr. see Lescourret, Marie-Anne.

***Powell, Elizabeth.** The Republic of Self. 64p. 2001. pap. 14.00 (*1-930974-03-5*) WMU Poetry & Prose.

Powell, Elizabeth. Sex on Your Terms: What to Say to Explain Your Limits, to Repel Sexual Pressure, to Avoid Being Falsely Accused, to Escape Disease. LC 95-23581. 350p. (C). 1995. pap. 20.00 (*0-205-17925-8*) Allyn.

Powell, Elizabeth A. Pennsylvania Butter: Tools & Processes, Vol. I. (Illus.). 27p. 1974. pap. 3.00 (*0-910302-09-X*) Bucks Co Hist.

— Pennsylvania Pottery: Tools & Processes. (Tools of the Nation Maker Ser.: Vol. II). (Illus.). 20p. 1972. pap. 3.00 (*0-910302-10-3*) Bucks Co Hist.

Powell, Ella M. Clio: A Child of Fate. LC 74-137730. (American Fiction Reprint Ser.). 1977. 16.95 (*0-8369-7029-2*) Ayer.

Powell, Ellis T. Evolution of the Money Market. 732p. 1966. reprint ed. 37.50 (*0-7146-1243-X*, Pub. by F Cass Pubs) Intl Spec Bk.

Powell, Elmer E. Spinozas Gottesbegriff. (Abhandlungen Zur Philosophie und Ihrer Geschichte Ser.: Bd. 12). (GER.). ix, 113p. 1980. reprint ed. write for info. (*3-487-06774-9*) G Olms Pubs.

Powell, Elwin H. The Design of Discord: Studies of Anomie: Suicide, Urban Society, War. 2nd ed. 288p. 1987. pap. 24.95 (*0-88738-704-7*) Transaction Pubs.

Powell, Emilie E. Gracie & the Mountain. 2nd rev. ed. (Illus.). 136p. 1996. pap. 9.95 (*1-57072-053-3*) Overmountain Pr.

Powell, Emily. Soul Flight: Poems. LC 86-62447. 72p. 1986. pap. 3.95 (*0-938875-02-7*) Pittenbruach Pr.

Powell, Ena K. Where Mountains Touch Heaven. 222p. (Orig.). 1995. pap. 14.95 (*0-88839-365-2*) Hancock House.

Powell, Enid, jt. auth. see Favro, Brian P.

P

Powell, Eric F. Building a Healthy Heart. 1961. pap. 8.95 (0-8464-0997-6) Beekman Pubs.
— A Home Course in Nutrition. 110p. pap. 7.95 (0-8464-4226-4) Beekman Pubs.
— A Home Course in Nutrition. 1978. pap. 8.95 (0-8464-1019-2) Beekman Pubs.
— Kelp, the Health Giver. 1982. pap. 2.95 (0-87904-041-6) Lust.
— The Natural Home Physician. 288p. pap. 17.95 (0-8464-4316-3) Beekman Pubs.
Powell, Esther W. Early Ohio Tax Records: Reprinted with "The Index to Early Ohio Tax Records", 2 vols. in 1. 632p. 1993. reprint ed. 40.00 (0-8063-1129-0, 4695) Genealog Pub.
Powell, Esther W., ed. Ohio Records & Pioneer Families, Vol. 12. 1971. 5.00 (0-935057-11-0) OH Genealogical.
— Ohio Records & Pioneer Families, Vol. 13. 1972. 2.50 (0-935057-12-9) OH Genealogical.
— Ohio Records & Pioneer Families, Vol. 14. 1973. 5.00 (0-935057-13-7) OH Genealogical.
— Ohio Records & Pioneer Families, Vol. 15. 1974. 5.00 (0-935057-14-5) OH Genealogical.
— Ohio Records & Pioneer Families, Vol. 16. 1975. 5.00 (0-935057-15-3) OH Genealogical.
— Ohio Records & Pioneer Families, Vol. 17. 1976. 5.00 (0-935057-16-1) OH Genealogical.
— Ohio Records & Pioneer Families, Vol. 18. 1977. 5.00 (0-935057-17-X) OH Genealogical.
— Ohio Records & Pioneer Families, Vol. 19. 1978. 5.00 (0-935057-18-8) OH Genealogical.
Powell, Evan. The Unfinished Gospel: Notes on the Quest for the Historical Jesus. 347p. (C). 1994. 23.95 (0-9639650-6-9) Symposium Bks.
Powell-Evans, Keith, jt. auth. see Gibson, William.
Powell, F. E. Windmill Construction & Generating Power. (Illus.). 93p. 1991. reprint ed. pap. 10.00 (1-877767-51-4) Univ Publng Hse.
— Windmills & Wind Motors. 1985. reprint ed. pap. 6.95 (0-917914-27-9) Lindsay Pubns.
Powell, F. G. Studies in the Lesser Mysteries (1913) 124p. 1996. reprint ed. pap. 10.95 (1-56459-787-3) Kessinger Pub.
Powell, Francis D. Theory of Coping Systems: Change in Supportive Health Organizations. 244p. 1975. boxed set 34.95 (0-87073-029-0) Transaction Pubs.
Powell, Francis D. & Wessen, Albert F. Health Care Systems in Transition: An International Perspective. LC 98-19744. 428p. 1998. write for info. (0-7619-1081-6); pap. write for info. (0-7619-1082-4) Sage.
Powell, Frank. Education of the Hearing Impaired Child. LC 84-22994. (Illus.). 200p. 1985. 34.95 (1-56593-577-2) Singular Publishing.
Powell, Frank J. & Matthews, Stanley L., eds. Thermal Insulation: Materials & Systems. LC 87-27045. (Special Technical Publication Ser.: No. 922). (Illus.). 728p. 1987. text 87.00 (0-8031-0493-6, STP922) ASTM.
Powell, Fred. Bartenders Standard Manual. 122p. 1988. 5.99 (0-517-29305-6) Random Hse Value.
Powell, Fred W. The Bureau of Mines: Its History, Activities & Organization. LC 72-3016. (Brookings Institution. Institute for Government Research. Service Monographs of the U. S. Government: No. 3). reprint ed. 39.50 (0-404-57103-4) AMS Pr.
— The Bureau of Plant Industry: Its History, Activities & Organization. LC 72-3064. (Brookings Institution. Institute for Government Research. Service Monographs of the U. S. Government: No. 47). reprint ed. 39.50 (0-404-57147-6) AMS Pr.
Powell, Fred W., ed. Hall J. Kelley on Oregon. LC 79-87635. (American Scene Ser.). (Illus.). 412p. 1972. reprint ed. lib. bdg. 49.50 (0-306-71796-4) Da Capo.
Powell, Fred W., jt. auth. see Cleveland, Frederick A.
Powell, Fred W., jt. auth. see Smith, Darrell H.
Powell, Frederick W. The Politics of Irish Social Policy, 1600-1990. LC 91-48166. 384p. 1992. lib. bdg. 99.95 (0-7734-9463-4) E Mellen.
Powell, Frona. Law & the Environment. LC 97-13286. (Miscellaneous/Catalogs Ser.). 600p. 1997. mass mkt. 76.95 (0-538-87874-6) West Pub.
Powell, G. Bingham, Jr. Contemporary Democracies: Participation, Stability & Violence. (Illus.). 294p. 1982. pap. 17.00 (0-674-16687-6) HUP.
***Powell, G. Bingham.** Elections As Instruments of Democracy: Majoritarian & Proportional Visions. LC 99-59159. (Illus.). 320p. 2000. 35.00 (0-300-08015-8); pap. 17.00 (0-300-08016-6) Yale U Pr.
Powell, G. Bingham, jt. auth. see Almond, Gabriel Abraham.
Powell, G. Bingham, Jr., jt. ed. see Almond, Gabriel Abraham.
Powell, G. E., tr. see Arnason, J. T.
Powell, G. Edward, et al, eds. AAS/AIAA Spaceflight Mechanics Meeting, Feb. 12-15, 1996, Austin, TX. LC 57-43769. (Advances in the Astronautical Sciences Ser.: Vol. 93). 1776p. 1996. 280.00 (0-87703-414-1, Am Astronaut Soc) Univelt Inc.
Powell, Gabriel. The Catholikes Supplication Unto the King's Majestie, for Toleration of Catholike Religion in England. LC 76-57406. (English Experience Ser.: No. 822). 1977. lib. bdg. 10.00 (90-221-0822-8) Walter J Johnson.
***Powell, Gareth.** Australia 2001. (Independent Traveller's Guide Ser.). (Illus.). 2000. pap. 19.95 (0-7627-0768-2) Globe Pequot.
— Independent Traveler's Guide: Australia 2000. 2000. pap. 19.95 (0-7627-0674-0) Globe Pequot.
— Signpost Guide: New Zealand. 2000. pap. 22.95 (0-7627-0677-5) Globe Pequot.
Powell, Gareth. Touring Australia: The Practical Guide to Holidays by Car, Train & Plane. (Touring... Ser.). (Illus.). 432p. 1997. pap. 18.95 (0-8442-4758-8, 47588, Passprt Bks) NTC Contemp Pub Co.
Powell, Garth, jt. auth. see Downey, R.
Powell, Gary N. Women & Men in Management. 2nd ed. (Illus.). 304p. (C). 1993. text 52.00 (0-8039-5223-6); pap. text 24.00 (0-8039-5224-4) Sage.
***Powell, Gene.** The Free Zone/Free Port Operator's Guide. 145p. 1999. pap. 14.95 (1-891929-30-5) Four Seasons.
Powell, Geoffrey. Buller: The Scapecoat?: A History of General Sir Redvers Buller, V. C. (Illus.). 256p. 1994. 34.95 (0-85052-279-X, Pub. by Leo Cooper) Trans-Atl Phila.
— The Kandyan Wars, the British Army in Ceylon. (C). 1984. reprint ed. 21.00 (0-8364-2366-6, Pub. by Navarang) S Asia.
— Men at Arnhem. 1998. 29.95 (0-85052-626-4, Pub. by Leo Cooper) Combined Pub.
— The Order of Knowledge. (Avebury Series in Philosophy). 160p. 1993. 72.95 (1-85628-555-3, Pub. by Avebury) Ashgate Pub Co.
Powell, Gerald R., et al. A Practical Guide to Texas Civil Evidence: Objections, Responses, Rules & Practice Commentary. 1995. 28.95 (1-55681-487-9) Natl Inst Trial Ad.
***Powell, Gerald R., et al.** Texas Rules of Evidence with Objections. rev. ed. (Illus.). 2000. 25.95 (1-55681-599-9) Natl Inst Trial Ad.
Powell, Gerald Reading. A Practical Guide to Texas Evidence: Objections, Responses, Rules & Practice Commentary. 2nd ed. LC 99-29254. 1999. 35.95 (1-55681-600-6) Natl Inst Trial Ad.
***Powell, Glenn.** The Agnes & Muriel's Cafe Cookbook. LC 00-105069. 144p. 2000. pap. 15.00 (1-56352-621-2) Longstreet.
Powell, Gloria J., jt. ed. see Wyatt, Gail E.
Powell, Gordon W., et al. A Fractography Atlas of Casting Alloys. LC 92-5859. (Illus.). 196p. 1992. per. 87.50 (0-935470-67-0) Battelle.
Powell, Graham. Brain & Personality. LC 79-87638. 122p. 1979. 47.95 (0-275-90408-3, C0408, Praeger Pubs) Greenwood.
Powell, Graham, jt. auth. see Lindsay, Stan.
Powell, Graham, jt. ed. see Lindsay, Stan.
Powell, Grosvenor. Language As Being in the Poetry of Yvor Winters. fac. ed. LC 79-14975. 196p. 1980. reprint ed. pap. 60.80 (0-7837-7815-5, 204757100007) Bks Demand.
Powell, H. Benjamin. Philadelphia's First Fuel Crisis: Jacob Cist & the Developing Market for Pennsylvania Anthracite. LC 77-88471. (Illus.). 1978. 30.00 (0-271-00533-5) Pa St U Pr.
Powell, H. Jefferson. The Constitution & the Attorneys General. LC 98-34688. 736p. 1998. 59.95 (0-89089-893-6) Carolina Acad Pr.
— The Moral Tradition of American Constitutionalism: A Theological Interpretation. LC 92-42290. 309p. 1993. text 42.95 (0-8223-1314-6) Duke.
Powell, H. M. Santa Fe Trail to California, 1849-1852. Watson, Douglas S., ed. LC 79-174284. (Illus.). reprint ed. lib. bdg. 125.00 (0-404-05099-9) AMS Pr.
Powell, Hickman. Ninety Times Guilty. LC 73-11909. (Metropolitan America Ser.). 356p. 1974. reprint ed. 23.95 (0-405-05411-4) Ayer.

Powell, Howard F. Index to S. T. Wiley's History of Preston County. 68p. 1971. pap. 3.00 (0-87012-100-6) McClain.

Four thousand five hundred names of people of the Preston County, West Virginia area. *Publisher Paid Annotation.*

Powell, Hugh. Fervor & Fiction: Therese von Bacheracht & Her Works. (GERM Ser.). x, 144p. (C). 1996. 55.00 (1-57113-044-6) Camden Hse.
— Historic Prints of Staten Island, N. Y., 1763-1898: A Reference Guide with Commentary. 170p. 1999. pap. 20.00 (0-9650513-3-1) Land Yacht Pr.
— Louise von Gall: Her World & Work. (GERM Ser.). x, 230p. 1993. 65.00 (1-879751-55-0) Camden Hse.
Powell, Hugh, tr. & intro. see Von Bacheracht, Therese.
Powell, I. G. F., ed. see Cicero, Marcus Tullius.
Powell, Ivor C. The Amazing Acts. LC 87-3627. (Ivor Powell Commentaries Ser.). 480p. 1987. pap. 16.99 (0-8254-3545-5) Kregel.
— Bible Cameos. LC 84-23535. 192p. 1985. reprint ed. pap. 8.99 (0-8254-3515-3) Kregel.
— Bible Mirrors: Spiritual Refections from the Word of God. LC 96-53064. 224p. 1998. pap. 9.99 (0-8254-3549-8) Kregel.
— Bible Names of Christ. LC 87-29722. 176p. 1988. pap. 9.99 (0-8254-3530-7) Kregel.
— Bible Nuggets. LC 91-24340. 192p. 1991. pap. 8.99 (0-8254-3512-9) Kregel.
— Bible Oases. 192p. 1994. pap. 8.99 (0-8254-3520-X) Kregel.
— Bible Promises. LC 93-1921. 192p. 1993. pap. 9.99 (0-8254-3542-0) Kregel.
— David: His Life & Times. LC 90-36487. 368p. 1990. pap. 14.99 (0-8254-3532-3) Kregel.
— Heaven: My Father's Country. 144p. 1995. pap. 8.99 (0-8254-3517-X, 95-028) Kregel.
— Honey from the Rock: Spiritual Refreshment from the Rock of Ages. 224p. 1996. pap. 9.99 (0-8254-3547-1) Kregel.
— John's Wonderful Gospel. LC 83-16192. (Ivor Powell Commentaries Ser.). 446p. (C). 1983. 19.99 (0-8254-3514-5) Kregel.
— Luke's Thrilling Gospel. LC 84-9637. (Ivor Powell Commentaries Ser.). 508p. 1984. lib. bdg. 19.99 (0-8254-3513-7) Kregel.
— Manna from Heaven: Spiritual Food from the Word of God. 224p. 1996. pap. 9.99 (0-8254-3546-3) Kregel.
— Mark's Superb Gospel. LC 85-25615. (Ivor Powell Commentaries Ser.). 432p. 1986. pap. 16.99 (0-8254-3510-2) Kregel.
— Matthew's Majestic Gospel. LC 86-10401. (Ivor Powell Commentaries Ser.). 526p. 1993. pap. 18.99 (0-8254-3544-7) Kregel.
— Simon Peter: Fisherman from Galilee. LC 96-30471. 224p. 1996. pap. 9.99 (0-8254-3548-X) Kregel.
— What in the World Will Happen Next? LC 85-7579. 176p. 1985. pap. 9.99 (0-8254-3524-2) Kregel.
Powell, Ivor C., tr. see Maxwell, Joseph.
Powell, J., jt. auth. see Dawber, R.
Powell, J. C. American Siberia: Or, Fourteen Years Experience in a Southern Convict Camp. LC 70-90188. (Mass Violence in America Ser.). 1969. reprint ed. 15.95 (0-405-01333-7) Ayer.
— American Siberia, or Fourteen Years' Experience in a Southern Convict Camp. LC 79-108222. (Criminology, Law Enforcement, & Social Problems Ser.: No. 105). (Illus.). 1970. reprint ed. 12.00 (0-87585-105-3) Patterson Smith.
— The American Siberia, or Fourteen Years' Experience in a Southern Convict Camp. LC 76-44514. (Floridiana Facsimile & Reprint Ser.). 1976. reprint ed. 22.95 (0-8130-0372-5) U Press Fla.
Powell, J. David, jt. auth. see Franklin, Gene F.
Powell, J. Enoch. The Evolution of the Gospel: A Commentary on the First Gospel, with Translation & Introductory Essay. LC 93-35985. 224p. 1994. 32.50 (0-300-05421-1) Yale U Pr.
— A Lexicon to Herodotus. (Olms Paperbacks Ser.: Vol. 26). x, 392p. 1977. reprint ed. pap. write for info. (3-487-01149-2); reprint ed. lib. bdg. 63.50 (3-487-00036-9) G Olms Pubs.
Powell, J. Enoch, ed. Herodotus, Bk. VIII. (GRE.). 1991. pap. 27.95 (0-86292-004-3, Pub. by Brist Class Pr) Focus Pub-R Pullins.
Powell, J. Enoch & Wood, John. Freedom & Reality. LC 79-400282. viii, 264p. 1969. write for info. (0-7134-1002-7) B T B.
— Still to Decide. LC 72-190101. vii, 246 p. 1972. write for info. (0-7134-1004-3) B T B.
Powell, J. G. An Historical Geography of Modern Australia. (Cambridge Studies in Historical Geography: No. 11). (Illus.). 420p. (C). 1991. pap. text 29.95 (0-521-40829-6) Cambridge U Pr.
Powell, J. G., ed. see Cicero, Marcus Tullius.
Powell, J. Gordon. Marriage of the Lamb. (Illus.). 296p. 1997. pap. 17.00 (0-8059-4144-4) Dorrance.
Powell, J. H. Bring Out Your Dead: The Great Plague of Yellow Fever in Philadelphia in 1793. (Studies in Health, Illness, & Caregiving). 334p. (C). 1993. reprint ed. text 35.00 (0-8122-3210-0); reprint ed. pap. text 15.95 (0-8122-1423-4) U of Pa Pr.
— Dartmoor Themes: A Walker's Guide. (Illus.). 224p. 1995. pap. 24.95 (1-85223-915-8, Pub. by Crolwood) Trafalgar.
Powell, J. L., jt. auth. see Faure, G.
Powell, J. Lewis. Executive Speaking: An Acquired Skill. 2nd ed. LC 80-395. 173p. reprint ed. pap. 53.70 (0-608-16688-X, 202679100052) Bks Demand.
Powell, J. Robin. Working Women's Guide to Managing Stress. 272p. (C). 1994. pap. text 14.95 (0-13-969213-4) P-H.
Powell, J. Robin & George-Warren, Holly. The Working Woman's Guide to Managing Stress. LC 94-11400. 1994. pap. 14.95 (0-13-969212-6) P-H.
Powell, J. T. Inflammatory & Thrombotic Problems in Vascular Surgery. Greenhalgh, R. M., ed. (Illus.). 488p. 1997. text 157.00 (0-7020-2336-1) W B Saunders.
Powell, J. U. Collectanea Alexandrina. 263p. 1981. reprint ed. 25.00 (0-89005-373-1) Ares.
Powell, J. U. & Barber, E. A., eds. New Chapters in the History of Greek Literature. 1921. 30.00 (0-8196-0286-8) Biblo.
— New Chapters in the History of Greek Literature. (Second Ser.). 1929. 30.00 (0-8196-0287-6) Biblo.
Powell, J. W. Introduction to the Study of Indian Languages with Words, Phrases & Sentences to Be Collected. 1977. lib. bdg. 69.95 (0-8490-2074-3) Gordon Pr.
Powell, J. W., jt. auth. see Boas, Franz.
Powell, Jack A. A Dying Art. (Illus.). 180p. (Orig.). 1995. pap. 10.95 (1-57532-006-1) Press-Tige Pub.
— Roadblocks to Success: A Treatise in Public Relations for Private & Public Policing. O'Donnell, Kelly, ed. (Illus.). 80p. 1998. pap. 6.99 (1-57532-196-3) Press-Tige Pub.
Powell, Jackie, jt. auth. see Lovelock, Robin.
Powell, Jacquelyn M. P. Le Bre Azza Paples: Mirrors & Windows of the World. 32p. 1998. pap. 6.99 (0-9662848-0-1) J M P Powell.
— Le' Bre' Azza Pades: Erase All Color from the Exterior. 32p. 1999. pap. write for info. (0-9662848-1-X) J M P Powell.
Powell, James. Aircraft Radio Systems. LC 92-46754. (Illus.). 255p. 1990. reprint ed. pap. text 5.95 (0-89100-356-8, JS312659) Jeppesen Sanderson.
— Derrida for Beginners. LC 98-117843. (for Beginners Ser.). (Illus.). 160p. 1997. 11.00 (0-86316-139-1) Writers & Readers.
***Powell, James.** The Triumph of Liberty: A 2000-Year History, Told Through the Lives of Freedom's Greatest Champions. 592p. 2000. 35.00 (0-684-85967-X) Free Pr.
Powell, James E. FoxPro 2 Developer's Library. Leventhal, Lance A., ed. (Lance A. Leventhal Microtrend Ser.). 400p. (Orig.). 1992. pap. 44.95 (0-915391-61-9) Slawson Comm.
— HTML Plus! (Multimedia Ser.). (Illus.). 304p. (C). 1996. 49.95 (0-534-51626-2) Wadsworth Pub.
— Mastering Lotus Approach 96 for Windows 95. 2nd ed. 816p. 1996. pap. 34.99 (0-7821-1773-2) Sybex.
— The Mule Thieves. LC 86-1622. 192p. 1986. 14.95 (0-8027-4058-8) Walker & Co.
Powell, James E., et al, eds. Nonparametric & Semiparametric Methods in Econometrics & Statistics: Proceedings of the Fifth International Symposium. (International Symposia in Economic Theory & Econometrics Ser.: No. 5). (Illus.). 507p. (C). 1991. pap. text 33.95 (0-521-42431-3) Cambridge U Pr.
Powell, James E., ed. see Barnett, William A.
Powell, James H., jt. auth. see McCright, Grady E.
Powell, James L. Extinction of Dinosaurs, Vol. 1. LC 98-13192. 250p. 1998. text 22.95 (0-7167-3117-7) St Martin.
— Pathways to Leadership: How to Achieve & Sustain Success. LC 94-43956. (Nonprofit Sector Ser.). 279p. 1995. text 28.95 (0-7879-0094-X) Jossey-Bass.
Powell, James Lawrence. Night Comes to the Cretaceous: Comets, Craters, Controversy & the Last Days of the Dinosaurs. LC 99-26503. 272p. 1999. pap. text 14.00 (0-15-600703-7, Harvest Bks) Harcourt.
Powell, James M. Albertanus of Brescia: The Pursuit of Happiness in the Early Thirteenth Century. LC 91-29777. (Middle Ages Ser.). 168p. (C). 1992. text 29.95 (0-8122-3138-4) U of Pa Pr.
— Anatomy of a Crusade, 1213-1221. LC 86-11403. (Middle Ages Ser.). (Illus.). 310p. (C). 1986. pap. text 18.95 (0-8122-1323-8) U of Pa Pr.
— Muslims under Latin Rule, 1100-1300. LC 90-34238. 229p. reprint ed. pap. 71.00 (0-608-20142-1, 207141400011) Bks Demand.
Powell, James M., ed. Innocent III: Vicar of Christ or Lord of the World? 2nd ed. LC 93-12609. 197p. (C). 1994. pap. 14.95 (0-8132-0783-5) Cath U Pr.
— The Liber Augustalis: or Constitutions of Melfi Promulgated by the Emperor Frederick the Second for the Kingdom of Sicily in 1231. LC 76-150107. 201p. reprint ed. pap. 62.40 (0-608-17477-7, 202997000067) Bks Demand.
— Medieval Studies: An Introduction. 2nd rev. ed. LC 91-31160. (Illus.). 500p. (C). 1992. text 45.00 (0-8156-2555-3); pap. text 19.95 (0-8156-2556-1) Syracuse U Pr.
Powell, James M., jt. auth. see Gervers, Michael.
Powell, James M., jt. ed. see Iggers, Georg G.
Powell, James O., ed. see Powell, Lee R.
Powell, James R., Jr. The Audiophile's Technical Guide to 78 rpm, Transcription, & Microgroove Recordings. viii, 86p. 1992. pap. 50.00 (0-9634921-2-8) Gramphne Advent.
Powell, James R., Jr. & Stehle, Randall G. Playback Equalizer Settings for 78 rpm Recordings. (Illus.). v, 89p. (Orig.). 1993. pap. 50.00 (0-9634921-3-6, 1003) Gramphne Advent.
Powell, James T. Two Hundred Thousand: A Proven Program You Can Use to Get 200,000 Miles of Reliable Transportation from Your Automobile. 200p. (Orig.). 1989. pap. 8.95 (0-911168-85-0) Prakken.
Powell, Jan, jt. auth. see Simms, Willard.
***Powell, Jane.** Bungalo Kitchens. LC 99-53493. (Illus.). 160p. 2000. 39.95 (0-87905-950-8) Gibbs Smith Pub.
Powell, Janet C., jt. auth. see Norris, Rosalie N.
Powell, Jeanne. Cadences: Poems. (Cimarron Poetry Ser.). (Illus.). 27p. (Orig.). 1996. pap. 8.00 (0-9653587-0-4) Meridien Pr.
— February Voices: First Poems. (Orig.). 1995. pap. 8.00 (0-932693-08-3) Jukebox Press.
— February Voices: First Poems. unabridged ed. (Cimarron Poetry Ser.). 24p. (Orig.). 1996. reprint ed. pap. 8.00 (0-9653587-1-2) Meridien Pr.
***Powell, Jeanne.** Tangerine Dance: Poems. unabridged ed. (Cimarton Poetry Ser.). (Illus.). 32p. 1999. mass mkt. 8.00 (1-891132-00-8) Meridien Pr.
Powell, Jeanne & Foley, Carol. Pattern Making. (Illus.). 430p. (C). 1987. pap. text 38.00 (0-13-654211-5) P-H.
Powell, Jeff, jt. auth. see Impey, Ken.
Powell, Jefferson. Languages of Power: A Source Book of Early Constitutional History. LC 90-85342. 352p. 1991. pap. 19.95 (0-89089-380-2); lib. bdg. 45.00 (0-89089-379-9) Carolina Acad Pr.
Powell, Jeffrey R. Progress & Prospects in Evolutionary Biology: The Drosophila Model. LC 96-12478. (Illus.). 576p. 1997. text 45.00 (0-19-507691-5) OUP.
Powell, Jehu Z. History of Cass County, Indiana, Set, Vols. I & II. (Illus.). 1197p. 1992. reprint ed. lib. bdg. 109.00 (0-8328-2539-5) Higginson Bk Co.
Powell, Jerry A. Biological Interrelationship of Moths & Yucca Schottii. LC 83-1308. (University of California Publications in Entomology: Vol. 100). 111p. 1984. reprint ed. pap. 34.50 (0-608-04620-5, 206530700002) Bks Demand.
Powell, Jerry A., ed. Biosystematic Studies of Conifer-Feeding Choristoneura: Lepidoptera: Tortricidae in the Western United States. LC 95-41081. (Publications in Entomology: Vol. 115). (Illus.). 284p. (C). 1995. pap. 33.00 (0-520-09796-3, Pub. by U CA Pr) Cal Prin Full Svc.
Powell, Jerry A. & Hogue, Charles L. California Insects. LC 78-62876. (California Natural History Guides Ser.: No. 44). (Illus.). 1980. pap. 17.95 (0-520-03782-0, Pub. by U CA Pr) Cal Prin Full Svc.
— California Insects. LC 78-62876. (California Natural History Guides Ser.: No. 44). (Illus.). 398p. reprint ed. pap. 123.40 (0-7837-4692-X, 204443900003) Bks Demand.
Powell, Jerry A., jt. auth. see Brown, John W.

An Asterisk (*) at the beginning of an entry indicates that the title is appearing for the first time.

Powell, Jesse J. A Study of Problem Material in High School Algebra. LC 71-177162. (Columbia University. Teachers College. Contributions to Education Ser.: No. 405). reprint ed. 37.50 (*0-404-55405-9*) AMS Pr.

***Powell, Jillian.** Adoption. LC 99-17811. (Talking about Ser.). 32p. (J). 1999. 22.83 (*0-8172-5890-6*) Raintree Steck-V.

Powell, Jillian. Ancient Art. LC 94-6079. (Arts & Artists Ser.). (Illus.). 48p. (J). (gr. 5-10). 1994. lib. bdg. 24.26 (*1-56847-216-1*) Raintree Steck-V.

***Powell, Jillian.** Animal Rights. LC 99-31569. (Talking about Ser.). 32p. (J). 1999. lib. bdg. 22.83 (*0-7398-1374-9*) Raintree Steck-V.

Powell, Jillian. Art in the Nineteenth Century: Art & Artists. LC 94-26769. (Art & Artists Ser.). (Illus.). 64p. (J). (gr. 5-10). 1994. lib. bdg. 24.26 (*1-56847-219-6*) Raintree Steck-V.

— Body Decoration. (Traditions Around the World Ser.). (Illus.). 48p. (J). (gr. 4-6). 1995. lib. bdg. 24.26 (*1-56847-276-5*) Raintree Steck-V.

— Bread. LC 96-35725. (Everyone Eats Ser.). (Illus.). 32p. (J). (gr. 2-6). 1997. lib. bdg. 22.83 (*0-8172-4763-7*) Raintree Steck-V.

— Bullying. LC 98-18226. (What Do We Think about...? Ser.). 32p. (J). 1999. lib. bdg. 22.83 (*0-8172-5535-4*) Raintree Steck-V.

***Powell, Jillian.** Disability? LC 98-35438. (Talking about Ser.). (Illus.). 32p. (gr. k-4). 1999. lib. bdg. 22.83 (*0-8172-5537-0*) Raintree Steck-V.

Powell, Jillian. Drug Trafficking. LC 96-35192. (Crimebusters Ser.). (Illus.). 32p. (J). (gr. 4-6). 1997. lib. bdg. 20.90 (*0-7613-0555-6*, Copper Beech Bks) Millbrook Pr.

— Drugs & Your Health. LC 97-19064. (Health Matters Ser.). (Illus.). 32p. (J). (gr. 1-4). 1998. lib. bdg. 22.83 (*0-8172-4928-1*) Raintree Steck-V.

— Eggs. LC 96-32830. (Everyone Eats Ser.). (Illus.). 32p. (J). (gr. 2-6). 1997. lib. bdg. 22.83 (*0-8172-4759-9*) Raintree Steck-V.

— Exercise & Your Health. LC 97-19065. (Health Matters Ser.). (Illus.). 32p. (J). (gr. 1-4). 1998. lib. bdg. 22.83 (*0-8172-4927-3*) Raintree Steck-V.

***Powell, Jillian.** Family Breakup. LC 98-35437. (Talking about Ser.). (Illus.). 32p. (J). (gr. k-4). 1999. lib. bdg. 22.83 (*0-8172-5542-7*) Raintree Steck-V.

Powell, Jillian. Fish. LC 96-32828. (Everyone Eats Ser.). (Illus.). 32p. (J). (gr. 2-6). 1997. lib. bdg. 22.83 (*0-8172-4761-0*) Raintree Steck-V.

— Food & Your Health. LC 97-3259. (Health Matters Ser.). (Illus.). 32p. (J). (gr. 1-4). 1998. lib. bdg. 22.83 (*0-8172-4925-7*) Raintree Steck-V.

— Fruit. LC 96-49675. (Everyone Eats Ser.). (Illus.). 32p. (J). (gr. 2-6). 1997. lib. bdg. 22.83 (*0-8172-4765-3*) Raintree Steck-V.

— A History of Britain Through Art. (History Through Art Ser.). (Illus.). 48p. (J). (gr. 5-6). 1996. lib. bdg. 5.00 (*1-56847-440-7*) Raintree Steck-V.

— A History of France Through Art. (History Through Art Ser.). (Illus.). 48p. (J). (gr. 5-8). 1996. lib. bdg. 5.00 (*1-56847-441-5*) Raintree Steck-V.

— Hygiene & Your Health. LC 97-3260. (Health Matters Ser.). (Illus.). 32p. (J). (gr. 1-4). 1998. 22.83 (*0-8172-4926-5*) Raintree Steck-V.

— Milk. LC 96-49126. (Everyone Eats Ser.). (Illus.). 32p. (J). (gr. 2-6). 1997. lib. bdg. 22.83 (*0-8172-4766-1*) Raintree Steck-V.

— Pasta. LC 96-32829. (Everyone Eats Ser.). (Illus.). 32p. (J). (gr. 2-6). 1997. lib. bdg. 22.83 (*0-8172-4760-2*) Raintree Steck-V.

— Potatoes. LC 96-27731. (Everyone Eats Ser.). (Illus.). 32p. (J). (gr. 2-6). 1997. lib. bdg. 22.83 (*0-8172-4762-9*) Raintree Steck-V.

— Poultry. LC 96-29686. (Everyone Eats Ser.). 32p. (J). (gr. 2-6). 1998. lib. bdg. 22.83 (*0-8172-4767-X*) Raintree Steck-V.

— Rain & Us. LC 98-11195. (Weather Ser.). (Illus.). 32p. (J). 1998. lib. bdg. 21.30 (*1-887068-38-4*) Smart Apple.

— Rice. LC 96-32831. (Everyone Eats Ser.). (Illus.). 32p. (J). (gr. 2-6). 1997. lib. bdg. 22.83 (*0-8172-4758-0*) Raintree Steck-V.

— Sun & Us. LC 98-11178. (Weather Ser.). (Illus.). 32p. (J). 1998. lib. bdg. 21.30 (*1-887068-40-6*) Smart Apple.

— The Supernatural. (Mysteries of...Ser.). (Illus.). 40p. (J). (gr. 4-6). 1996. lib. bdg. 22.90 (*0-7613-0455-X*, Copper Beech Bks) Millbrook Pr.

— The Supernatural. LC 95-40837. (Mysteries Of-- Ser.). (J). 1996. 12.15 (*0-606-09660-4*, Pub. by Turtleback) Demco.

— Terrorism. LC 96-35191. (Crimebusters Ser.). (Illus.). 32p. (J). (gr. 4-6). 1997. lib. bdg. 20.90 (*0-7613-0556-4*, Copper Beech Bks) Millbrook Pr.

— Wind & Us. (Weather Ser.). (Illus.). 32p. (YA). (gr. 3 up). 1998. lib. bdg. 21.30 (*1-887068-41-4*) Smart Apple.

Powell, Jillian, et al. Mysteries Through the Ages. LC 96-13227. (Illus.). 192p. (J). (gr. 4-6). 1996. 16.95 (*0-7613-0518-1*, Copper Beech Bks) Millbrook Pr.

Powell, Jim. Designing User Interfaces. Leventhal, Lance A., ed. LC 90-61738. (Lance A. Leventhal Data Based Advisor Ser.). 500p. (Orig.). 1990. pap. 27.95 (*0-915391-40-6*) Slawson Comm.

***Powell, Jim.** Eastern Philosophy for Beginners. (Illus.). 192p. 1999. pap. 11.95 (*0-86316-282-7*) Writers & Readers.

Powell, Jim. It Was Fever That Made the World. LC 88-20720. 86p. 1989. pap. 9.95 (*0-226-67707-9*); lib. bdg. 24.00 (*0-226-67706-0*) U Ch Pr.

— Post Modernism for Beginners. (For Beginners Ser.). (Illus.). 176p. 1998. pap. 11.00 (*0-86316-188-X*) Writers & Readers.

Powell, Jim, tr. Sappho: A Garland; the Poems & Fragments of Sappho. LC 93-73349. 65p. 1993. 15.00 (*0-374-25393-5*) FS&G.

Powell, Joanna, compiled by. Things I Should Have Said to My Father. 144p. (Orig.). 1994. pap. 10.00 (*0-380-77348-1*, Avon Bks) Morrow Avon.

Powell, Jody, jt. auth. see Payson, Parker L.

***Powell, Joey.** Cumberland County, North Carolina. (Images of America Ser.). (Illus.). 128p. 1999. pap. 18.99 (*0-7385-0270-7*) Arcadia Publng.

Powell, John. Abortion: The Silent Holocaust. LC 81-69697. 183p. (Orig.). 1981. pap. 10.95 (*0-89505-063-3*, 21056) Res Christian Liv.

— Art, Truth, & High Politics: A Bibliographic Study of the Official Lives of Queen Victoria's Ministers in Cabinet, 1843-1969. LC 96-4278. (Magill Bibliographies Ser.). 232p. 1996. 36.00 (*0-8108-3139-2*) Scarecrow.

— Challenge of Faith. 112p. 1998. pap. 10.95 (*0-88347-425-5*) T More.

— CO2 Laser Cutting. LC 92-36190. 1993. 139.95 (*0-387-19786-9*) Spr-Verlag.

— CO2 Laser Cutting 2nd ed. LC 98-20448. xviii, 248p. 1998. write for info. (*1-85233-047-3*) Spr-Verlag.

***Powell, John.** Cycling the Rhine Route: Bicycle Touring along the Historic Rhine River. (Cycling Resources Ser.). (Illus.). 288p. 2000. pap. 16.95 (*1-892495-23-6*, 236, Pub. by Van der Plas) Seven Hills Bk.

Powell, John. Fully Human, Fully Alive. (John Powell Library). (Illus.). 148p. (Orig.). 1976. reprint ed. pap. 11.95 (*0-88347-321-6*, 7321) T More.

— Happiness Is an Inside Job. (John Powell Library). (Illus.). 150p. 1989. reprint ed. pap. 11.95 (*0-88347-324-0*, 7324) T More.

— The Intermediate Technology Transfer Unit: A Handbook on Operations. 54p. 1995. pap. 12.00 (*1-85339-314-2*, Pub. by Intermed Tech) Stylus Pub VA.

— Jack London. LC 92-46766. (Arts Ser.). 112p. (YA). 1993. lib. bdg. 25.27 (*0-86625-486-2*) Rourke Pubns.

— The John Powell Library, 7 vols., Set. (Illus.). 1978. reprint ed. boxed set 79.95 (*0-88347-342-9*, 7342) Res Christian Liv.

— A Life-Giving Vision: How to Be a Christian in Today's World. LC 95-237591. (Illus.). 342p. (Orig.). 1995. pap. 17.95 (*0-88347-294-5*) Res Christian Liv.

— The Secret of Staying in Love. (Illus.). 170p. 1974. reprint ed. pap. 12.95 (*0-88347-299-6*) Res Christian Liv.

— Solving the Riddle of Self: The Search for Self-Discovery. LC 95-237671. (Illus.). 96p. (Orig.). 1995. pap. 12.95 (*0-88347-300-3*) Res Christian Liv.

***Powell, John.** A Stranger at Your Door. LC 98-50434. 136p. 1999. 10.99 (*1-56955-116-2*, Charis) Servant.

Powell, John. A Stranger at Your Door. 184p. 1996. pap. 39.95 (*0-85439-522-9*, Pub. by St Paul Pubns) St Mut.

— The Survival of the Fitter: Lives of Some African Engineers. 127p. (Orig.). 1995. pap. 18.95 (*1-85339-316-9*, Pub. by Intermed Tech) Stylus Pub VA.

— Through Seasons of the Heart. (Illus.). 384p. 1987. reprint ed. pap. 16.95 (*0-88347-343-7*, 7343) Res Christian Liv.

— Through the Eyes of Faith. (Illus.). 156p. (Orig.). 1992. reprint ed. pap. 11.95 (*0-88347-330-5*, 7330) Res Christian Liv.

— Touched by God: My Pilgrimage of Prayer. LC 97-152386. (Illus.). 96p. (Orig.). 1996. reprint ed. pap. 7.95 (*0-88347-328-3*, 7328, Pub. by T More) BookWorld.

— Unconditional Love: Love Without Limits. (Illus.). 124p. 1978. reprint ed. pap. 12.95 (*0-88347-312-7*, Pub. by T More) BookWorld.

— Why Am I Afraid to Love? Overcoming Rejection & Indifferences. (John Powell Library). (Illus.). 106p. (Orig.). 1990. reprint ed. pap. 12.95 (*0-88347-322-4*, 7322, Pub. by T More) BookWorld.

— Why Am I Afraid to Tell You Who I Am? Insights into Personal Growth. (John Powell Library Ser.). (Illus.). 153p. (Orig.). 1969. reprint ed. pap. 12.95 (*0-88347-323-2*, 7323) Res Christian Liv.

— Will the Real Me Please Stand Up? Twenty-Five Guidelines for Good Communication. 216p. 1985. pap. text 11.95 (*0-88347-316-X*) Res Christian Liv.

***Powell, John, ed.** Biographical Encyclopedia of 20th-Century World Leaders, 5 vols. LC 99-34462. 1689p. (YA). (gr. 6 up). 1999. 514.21 (*0-7614-7129-4*, Benchmark NY) Marshall Cavendish.

Powell, John, ed. Chronology of European History, 2 vols. (Illus.). 2000p. 1998. lib. bdg. 275.00 (*1-57958-052-1*) Fitzroy Dearborn.

***Powell, John, et al, eds.** Biographical Dictionary of Literary Influences: The Nineteenth Century, 1800-1914. LC 99-462057. 464p. 2000. lib. bdg. 95.00 (*0-313-30422-X*, GR0422, Greenwood Pr) Greenwood.

Powell, John, jt. auth. see Hawkins, Angus.

Powell, John, ed. see Euripides.

Powell, John, jt. ed. see Kaderjak, Peter.

Powell, John A., jt. auth. see McDonald, Laughlin.

Powell, John B. My Twenty-Five Years in China. LC 76-27721. (China in the 20th Century Ser.). 1976. reprint ed. lib. bdg. 45.00 (*0-306-70761-6*) Da Capo.

Powell, John D. Political Mobilization of the Venezuelan Peasant. LC 70-134947. (Center for International Affairs Ser.). (Illus.). 275p. 1971. 35.95 (*0-674-68626-8*) HUP.

Powell, John H. Bring Out Your Dead: The Great Plague of Yellow Fever in Philadelphia in 1793. LC 77-112567. (Rise of Urban America Ser.). (Illus.). 1976. reprint ed. 23.95 (*0-405-02471-1*) Ayer.

Powell, John J. Golden State & Its Resources. LC 78-125759. (American Environmental Studies). 1974. reprint ed. 17.95 (*0-405-02685-4*) Ayer.

***Powell, John Joseph.** An Essay on the Learning: Respecting the Creation & Execution of Powers - And Also Respecting the Nature & Effect of Leasing Powers in Which the Doctrine of the Judgment Delivered by the Court of King's Bench, in the Case of Pugh & the Duke of Leeds & the Principal Authorities for & Against It, Are Considered. 2nd ed. xiv, 582p. 1999. reprint ed. 185.00 (*1-56169-559-9*) Gaunt.

Powell, John L. & Crasemann, Bernd. Quantum Mechanics. (Illus.). 1961. write for info. (*0-201-05920-7*) Addison-Wesley.

Powell, John S. The Christian Vision: The Truth That Sets Us Free. LC 83-73231. (Illus.). 156p. 1984. pap. 10.95 (*0-89505-183-4*, 21082) Tabor Pub.

— Music & Theatre in France, 1600-1800. LC 98-7971. (Illus.). 704p. 2000. text 150.00 (*0-19-816599-4*) OUP.

Powell, John S. The Nostradamus Prophecy. LC 97-77857. 354p. 1998. 23.95 (*0-9661922-5-7*) Belladonna Pr.

***Powell, John S.** The Nostradamus Prophecy. 368p. 1999. mass mkt. 5.50 (*0-8439-4652-0*, Leisure Bks) Dorchester Pub Co.

Powell, John S., ed. see Moliere & Charpentier, Marc-Antoine.

Powell, John S., ed. & tr. see De Saint Lambert.

Powell, John S., ed. & tr. see Saint-Lambert, Michael D.

Powell, John T. Origins & Aspects of Olympism. 239p. (Orig.). (C). 1994. pap. text 17.20 (*0-87563-502-4*) Stipes.

— Track & Field Fundamentals for Teacher & Coach. 4th ed. (Illus.). 1987. spiral bd. 19.80 (*0-87563-294-7*) Stipes.

Powell, John Wesley. The Exploration of the Colorado River & Its Canyons. (Illus.). 400p. 1998. pap. 8.95 (*0-486-20094-9*) Dover.

— The Exploration of the Colorado River & Its Canyons. LC 86-16899. (Illus.). 397p. 1987. pap. 10.95 (*0-14-025569-9*) Viking Penguin.

— The Hopi Villages (the Ancient Province of Tusayan) LC 75-25049. (Wild & Woolly West Ser.). Orig. Title: Ancient Province of Tusayan. (Illus.). 48p. 1972. pap. 4.00 (*0-910584-73-7*) Filter.

— John Wesley Powell & the Anthropology of the Canyon Country. (Illus.). 30p. 1995. reprint ed. pap. 4.95 (*0-938216-26-0*) GCA.

— Learning & Change, the Problems of Evaulation in Liberal Adult Education. 1960. 2.50 (*0-87060-084-2*, PUC 12) Syracuse U Cont Ed.

— An Overland Trip to the Grand Canyon: Northern Arizona As Powell Saw It in 1870. LC 77-29657. (Wild & Woolly West Ser.: No. 28). (Illus.). 40p. 1974. pap. 4.00 (*0-910584-84-2*) Filter.

— Truth & Error: or The Science of Intellection. LC 75-3322. reprint ed. 31.50 (*0-404-59318-6*) AMS Pr.

Powell, John Wesley & Jones, William R. The Canons of the Colorado. (Illus.). 1980. reprint ed. pap. 4.95 (*0-89646-059-2*) Vistabooks.

Powell, John Wesley, et al. Campus Security & Law Enforcement. 2nd ed. LC 93-21319. 289p. 1994. 49.95 (*0-7506-9441-6*) Buttrwrth-Heinemann.

***Powell, John Wesley, et al.** Diary of John Wesley Powell: Exploring the Grand Canyon. LC 00-21572. 2000. lib. bdg. write for info. (*0-7614-1013-9*) Benchmark Bks.

***Powell, John Y.** Family-Centered Services in Residential Treatment: New Approaches for Group Care. LC 00-38856. 2000. write for info. (*0-7890-1022-4*) Haworth Pr.

Powell, Jon T. Direct Broadcast by Satellite: Issues of Regulations, Barriers to Communication. LC 85-6342. 300p. 1985. 69.50 (*0-89930-067-7*, PDP/, Quorum Bks) Greenwood.

Powell, Jon T. & Gair, Wally, eds. Public Interest & the Business of Broadcasting: The Broadcast Industry Looks at Itself. LC 88-3098. 203p. 1988. 65.00 (*0-89930-198-3*, PLI/, Quorum Bks) Greenwood.

Powell, Jonathan, ed. Cicero the Philosopher: Twelve Papers. 384p. 1999. pap. text 27.50 (*0-19-815273-6*) OUP.

Powell, Jonathan, ed. Cicero the Philosopher: Twelve Papers. 384p. 1995. text 75.00 (*0-19-814751-1*) OUP.

Powell, Jonathan, jt. auth. see Robinson, Peter J., Jr.

Powell, Jonathan, ed. see Cicero, Marcus Tullius.

Powell-Jones, Mark. Impressionism. (Color Library). (Illus.). 128p. (C). 1994. reprint ed. pap. 14.95 (*0-7148-3053-4*, Pub. by Phaidon Press) Phaidon Pr.

Powell, Joseph. Aegean Dialogs: Poetry by Joseph Powell. Bixby, Robert, ed. 31p. Date not set. 6.00 (*1-882983-41-6*) March Street Pr.

— The Art & Science of the Way of the Intercepting Fist. (Illus.). 284p. 1997. pap. text, per. 15.95 (*0-9661409-0-7*) J A P Ent.

— Counting the Change. (QRL Poetry Bks.: Vol. XXVI). 1986. 20.00 (*0-614-06417-1*) Quarterly Rev.

Powell, Joseph, Jr., jt. auth. see Hairr, John.

Powell, Joseph H. Grapes of Righteousness: Spiritual Grafting into the True Vine. LC 96-68837. 192p. 1996. pap. 10.95 (*0-914984-74-8*) Starburst.

Powell, Josh. AIDS & HIV-Related Diseases: An Educational Guide for Professionals & the Public. (Illus.). 243p. (C). 1996. 24.95 (*0-306-45085-2*, Plen Insight) Perseus Pubng.

Powell, Jouett L. Three Uses of Christian Discourse in John Henry Newman: An Example of Nonreductive Reflection on the Christian Faith. LC 75-29423. (American Academy of Religion. Dissertation Ser.: No. 10). 242p. reprint ed. pap. 75.10 (*0-7837-5487-6*, 204525200005) Bks Demand.

Powell, Judith. Fishing in the Prehistoric Aegean. (Studies in Mediterranean Archaeology & Literature: No. 137). (Illus.). 297p. (Orig.). 1996. pap. 67.50 (*91-7081-112-1*, Pub. by P Astroms) Coronet Bks.

Powell, Judith. Metodo Silva del Domino de la Mente. (SPA.). 1997. pap. 16.98 (*968-13-1902-8*, Pub. by Edit Diana) Libros Fronteras.

Powell, Judith, jt. auth. see Coates, Ken.

Powell, Judith, jt. auth. see Powell, Tag.

Powell, Judith A. Wonder, Liberty & Love: Huxley's Analogical Uses of Shakespeare. 120p. (C). 1992. text 18.95 (*0-9628916-4-9*) Vande Vere.

Powell, Judith A., ed. see Murray, Raymond L.

Powell, Judith L. Discover Your Perfect Soul Mate. rev. ed. pap. text 12.95 incl. audio (*1-56087-078-8*) Top Mtn Pub.

***Powell, Judith L. & Powell, Tag.** Silva Mind Mastery. rev. ed. Fawcett, Yvonne & Van Horn, Carol, eds. LC 91-10759. (Illus.). 254p. 2000. pap. 17.95 (*1-56087-153-9*) Top Mtn Pub.

Powell, Judith L. & Powell, Tag. Taming the Wild Pendulum: Make Decisions & Solve Problems with This Psychic Tool. Fawcett, Yvonne, ed. LC 94-11030. (Illus.). 208p. 1995. pap. 19.95 (*1-56087-057-5*) Top Mtn Pub.

Powell, Judith L. & Wattles, Wallace D. The Science of Becoming Excellent. rev. ed. LC 92-41455. 160p. 1993. pap. 8.95 (*0-914295-96-9*) Top Mtn Pub.

— The Science of Getting Rich. rev. ed. LC 92-27329. 160p. 1993. pap. 12.95 (*1-56087-017-6*) Top Mtn Pub.

— The Science of Well-Being. LC 93-17454. 160p. (Orig.). 1993. pap. 8.95 (*1-56087-059-1*) Top Mtn Pub.

Powell, Judith L., ed. see Allen, James.

Powell, Judith L., ed. see Davis, Samantha A.

Powell, Judith L., ed. see Powell, Tag.

Powell, Judith L., ed. see Powell, Tag & Mills, Carol H.

Powell, Judith L., ed. see Suggs, Jackie.

Powell, K., et al. Scale-Chord Synopticon. 634p. (Orig.). (C). 1987. pap. 29.95 (*0-926954-00-8*) Synopticon Pub.

Powell, K. A., et al. The Genus Aspergillus: From Taxonomy & Genetics to Industrial Application. (FEMS Symposium Ser.: No. 69). (Illus.). 388p. (C). 1994. text 120.00 (*0-306-44701-0*, Kluwer Plenum) Kluwer Academic.

Powell, Kara E. God Knows You're Talented (Even If You Don't!) Helping Youth Find & Use Their Spiritual Gifts & Natural Talents. 87p. 1999. 15.99 (*0-8307-2355-2*) Gospel Lght.

Powell, Kara Eckmann. The Basics of Christianity. (True Life Ser.: No. 1). 1999. pap. 14.99 (*0-8307-2407-9*, Gospel Light) Gospel Lght.

***Powell, Kara Eckmann.** Life at School, Vol. 7. (Pulse Ser.). (Illus.). 2000. pap. 14.99 (*0-8307-2508-3*) Gospel Lght.

Powell, Kara Eckmann, ed. see Pearson, Darryl.

Powell, Karen & Hardwick, Georgia. Passing the Georgia High School Social Studies Test. 2nd ed. (Illus.). 200p. (YA). (gr. 11-12). pap. text 12.00 (*0-89892-193-7*) Contemp Pub Co of Raleigh.

Powell, Karen H. How to Form a Catechumenate Team. (Font & Table Ser.). 68p. 1986. pap. 4.75 (*0-930467-53-1*, CTEAM) Liturgy Tr Pubns.

Powell, Karen H. & Sinwell, Joseph P., eds. Breaking Open the Word of God: Resources for Using the Lectionary for Catechists in the RCIA (Cycle C) 192p. (Orig.). 1988. pap. 15.95 (*0-8091-2973-6*) Paulist Pr.

Powell, Karen S. Twilight Gallery. (Illus.). 72p. (Orig.). 1996. pap. 12.95 (*0-9651406-0-1*) Silverhawke.

Powell, Katherine. Italy. (Origins Ser.). 32p. (J). 1998. lib. bdg. 20.00 (*0-531-14450-X*) Watts.

Powell, Kay, jt. ed. see Boseman, Glenn.

Powell, Kay E., ed. The Country Kitchen Stoneware Cookbook. (Illus.). 100p. (Orig.). 1983. pap. 8.00 (*0-930528-05-0*) Sassafras Pr.

Powell, Keith. Microsoft Windows 98: Quick Reference. LC 99-62269. 1999. pap. 9.99 (*0-7897-2030-2*) Que.

— Waite Group's Windows 98 How to. LC 98-86953. 1998. pap. text 39.99 (*0-672-31436-3*) Sams.

Powell, Ken. John Lyall: Urban Regeneration. 1999. pap. text 25.00 (*88-7838-051-2*) L'Arca IT.

***Powell, Kenneth.** Architecture Transformed: Converting Old Buildings to New Spaces. (Illus.). 256p. 1999. 60.00 (*0-8478-2181-1*) Rizzoli Intl.

Powell, Kenneth. Church Builders of Twentieth Century. 224p. 1997. 90.00 (*0-471-97755-1*) Wiley.

***Powell, Kenneth.** City Transformed: Urban Architecture at the Beginning of the 21st Century. (Illus.). 256p. 2000. 60.00 (*3-8238-5461-5*) te Neues.

Powell, Kenneth. Grand Central Station: New York City 1903-13 Warren & Wetmore. LC 96-154031. (Architecture in Detail Ser.). (Illus.). 60p. 1996. pap. text 29.95 (*0-7148-3346-0*, Pub. by Phaidon Press) Phaidon Pr.

— Graves Residence: Princeton 1986-93: Michael Grave. (Architecture in Detail Ser.). (Illus.). 60p. (Orig.). (C). 1995. pap. 29.95 (*0-7148-3292-8*, Pub. by Phaidon Press) Phaidon Pr.

***Powell, Kenneth.** The Jubilee Line Extension: A Celebration. 160p. 1999. 45.00 (*1-85669-184-5*, Pub. by L King Pubng) Antique Collect.

Powell, Kenneth. Lloyd's Building: London 1986, Richard Rogers Partnership. LC 95-150971. (Architecture in Detail Ser.). (Illus.). 60p. (C). 1994. pap. 29.95 (*0-7148-3006-2*, Pub. by Phaidon Press) Phaidon Pr.

— Richard Rogers. (Studio Paperback Ser.). (Illus.). 208p. 1994. pap. 29.95 (*3-7643-5582-4*, Pub. by Birkhauser) Princeton Arch.

— Richard Rogers Complete Works. (Illus.). 320p. 1999. 89.95 (*0-7148-3746-6*) Phaidon Pr.

— Structure, Space & Skin: The Work of Nicholas Grimshaw & Partners. Moore, Rowan, ed. (Illus.). 256p. 1996. pap. text 39.95 (*0-7148-3457-2*, Pub. by Phaidon Press) Phaidon Pr.

Powell, Kenneth, ed. London. (World Cities Ser.: No. 1). (Illus.). 417p. 1993. 95.00 (*1-85490-188-5*, Pub. by Wiley) Wiley.

Powell, Kenneth & Spens, Iona. Church Builders of the Twentieth Century. (Illus.). 224p. 1997. 75.00 (*1-85490-483-3*) Academy Ed UK.

Powell, Kent & Murphy, Mariam B. Utah Trivia. LC 97-2995. 192p. 1997. pap. 6.95 (*1-55853-464-4*) Rutledge Hill Pr.

Powell, Kerry. Women & Victorian Theatre. LC 97-5746. (Illus.). 216p. (C). 1998. text 52.95 (*0-521-47167-2*) Cambridge U Pr.

Powell, Kevin. In the Tradition: An Anthology of Young Black Writers. 254p. (Orig.). 1993. pap. 14.00 (*0-86316-316-5*) Writers & Readers.

— Keepin' It Real: Post-MTV Reflections on Race, Sex, & Politics. 1997. 20.00 (*0-614-20434-8*) One Wrld.

— Keepin' it Real: Post-MTV Reflections on Race, Sex & Politics. LC 97-24770. 224p. 1997. 23.00 (*0-345-40400-9*) Ballantine Pub Grp.

— Keepin it Real: Post-MTV Reflections on Race, Sex & Politics. 256p. 1998. pap. 12.95 (*0-345-42478-6*) Ballantine Pub Grp.

— Recognize. (Illus.). 128p. 1995. pap. 11.00 (*0-86316-324-6*) Writers & Readers.

***Powell, Kevin.** Step into a World: A Global Anthology of the New Black Literature. 496p. 2000. 29.95 (*0-471-38060-1*) Wiley.

Powell, Kevin, et al, eds. In the Tradition: An Anthology of Young Black Writers. 254p. (Orig.). 1993. 28.00 (*0-86316-315-7*); pap. 14.00 (*0-685-53678-5*) Writers & Readers.

***Powell, Kimberly.** Living Miracles: Stories of Hope from Parents of Premature Babies. Wilson, Kim, ed. LC 99-89725. (Illus.). 320p. 2000. text 24.95 (*0-312-24550-5*) St Martin.

Powell, Kimberly, jt. ed. see Banks, Robert.

Powell, Kirsten. Fables in Frames: La Fontaine & Visual Culture in Nineteenth-Century France. LC 95-47893. (Literature & the Visual Arts Ser.: No. 10). (Illus.). XVI, 180p. (C). 1997. text 43.95 (*0-8204-3096-X*) P Lang Pubng.

Powell, Kirsten H. & Childs, Elizabeth C. Femmes d'Esprit: Women & Satire in Daumier's Caricature. LC 89-13898. (Illus.). 156p. 1990. pap. 20.00 (*0-9625262-0-7*) Middlebury Coll Mus.

Powell, L. & Piper, D. Fundamentals of Gastroenterology. 5th ed. 1991. text 39.00 (*0-07-050617-5*) McGraw-Hill HPD.

Powell, L. C. An Introduction to Robinson Jeffers. 1992. reprint ed. lib. bdg. 75.00 (*0-7812-5075-7*) Rprt Serv.

— Manuscripts of D. H. Lawrence. 1972. 200.00 (*0-87968-020-2*) Gordon Pr.

***Powell, Lane H. & Cassidy, Dawn.** Family Life Education: An Introduction. LC 00-38687. 2000. pap. write for info. (*0-7674-0570-6*) Mayfield Pub.

Powell, Larry D. Blow the Silver Trumpets. 1991. pap. 8.50 (*1-55673-314-3*, 9135) CSS OH.

— Hunger of the Heart: Communion at the Wall. (Illus.). 112p. 1995. pap. 19.95 (*0-9641919-4-6*) Islewest Pub.

Powell, Laura J., ed. Advanced Technology Program Proposal Preparation Kit. 108p. 1999. pap. text 20.00 (*0-7881-7657-9*) DIANE Pub.

***Powell, Lawerence.** Power of the Seed. 144p. 2000. pap. 8.99 (*1-890900-32-X*) Insight Intl.

Powell, Lawrence, ed. see Olmsted, Frederick L.

Powell, Lawrence A. Senior Rights Movement. 1996. 33.00 (*0-8057-9710-6*, Twyne) Mac Lib Ref.

Powell, Lawrence C. Bookman's Progress: Selected Writings. Targ, William & Ritchie, Ward, eds. 246p. 1968. 15.00 (*0-910740-25-9*) Holmes.

— Books Are Basic: The Essential Lawrence Clark Powell. Marshall, John D., ed. LC 85-14099. 95p. 1985. 17.95 (*0-8165-0952-2*) U of Ariz Pr.

— Books in My Baggage: Adventures in Reading & Collecting. LC 73-726. 255p. 1973. reprint ed. lib. bdg. 65.00 (*0-8371-6784-1*, POBB, Greenwood Pr) Greenwood.

— Books West Southwest. 137p. 1994. pap. 12.95 (*0-614-05596-2*) Bks West SW.

— Eucalyptus Fair. 271p. 1992. 20.00 (*0-9632966-0-4*) Bks West SW.

— Eucalyptus Fair. deluxe ed. 271p. 1992. boxed set 100.00 (*0-9632966-1-2*) Bks West SW.

— Fay. 64p. 1993. 100.00 (*0-9625610-1-0*) L C Powell.

— Land of Fact. LC 92-72094. 60p. 1992. 30.00 (*0-914421-07-7*) Hist Soc So CA.

— The Little Package: Pages on Literature & Landscape from a Traveling Bookman's Life. LC 73-156705. (Essay Index Reprint Ser.). 1977. reprint ed. 20.95 (*0-8369-2422-3*) Ayer.

— Manuscripts of D. H. Lawrence. (Studies in D. H. Lawrence: No. 20). 1970. reprint ed. pap. 27.95 (*0-8383-0099-5*) M S G Haskell Hse.

— Mysterious Transformation: or When Does History Become Literature. 276p. 1993. 32.50 (*0-9632966-2-0*) Bks West SW.

— Mysterious Transformation: or When Does History Become Literature. deluxe ed. 276p. 1993. boxed set 100.00 (*0-9632966-3-9*) Bks West SW.

— A Passion for Books. LC 73-727. 249p. 1973. reprint ed. lib. bdg. 59.50 (*0-8371-6783-3*, POPB, Greenwood Pr) Greenwood.

— Robinson Jeffers: The Man & His Work. 1973. lib. bdg. 59.95 (*0-8490-0966-9*) Gordon Pr.

— Robinson Jeffers: The Man & His Work. LC 68-54176. (American Biography Ser.: No. 32). (Illus.). 1969. reprint ed. lib. bdg. 75.00 (*0-8383-0675-6*) M S G Haskell Hse.

— Southwest Classics: The Creative Literature of the Arid Lands: Essays on the Books & Their Writers. LC 82-20314. 378p. reprint ed. pap. 117.20 (*0-7837-5053-6*, 204473100004) Bks Demand.

Powell, Lawrence C., contrib. by. Next to Mother's Milk ... An Engelhard Lecture on the Book, Presented at the Library of Congress on Tuesday, April 8, 1986. LC 87-4160. 25p. 1989. reprint ed. 3.95 (*0-8444-0551-5*) Lib Congress.

Powell, Lawrence C., jt. auth. see Everson, William.

Powell, Lawrence Clark, jt. auth. see Cohen, Saul.

Powell, Lawrence N. Louisiana's Capitols: The Power & the Beauty. (Illus.). 144p. 1995. 35.00 (*0-917541-03-0*) Galerie Pr.

— New Masters: Northern Planters During the Civil War & Reconstruction. LC 98-30179. (North's Civil War Ser.: No. 9). 300p. 1999. reprint ed. 37.50 (*0-8232-1893-7*); reprint ed. pap. 17.95 (*0-8232-1894-5*) Fordham.

— Troubled Memory: Anne Levy, the Holocaust, & David Duke's Louisiana. LC 99-18568. (Illus.). 616p. 2000. 34.95 (*0-8078-2504-2*) U of NC Pr.

Powell, Lawrie W., ed. Metals & the Liver. LC 78-11947. (Liver, Normal Function & Disease Ser.: No. 1). (Illus.). 464p. reprint ed. pap. 143.90 (*0-7837-0822-X*, 204113600019) Bks Demand.

Powell, Lawrie W. & Piper, Douglas W., eds. Fundamentals of Gastroenterology. 6th ed. (Illus.). 292p. 1995. 49.00 (*0-07-470192-4*) McGraw-Hill HPD.

Powell, Lee. J. William Fulbright & America's Lost Crusade: Fulbright's Opposition to the Vietnam War. (Illus.). 264p. 1984. pap. 16.45 (*0-914546-51-1*) Rose Pub.

Powell, Lee R. J. William Fulbright & His Time. Powell, James O., ed. 650p. 1996. 29.95 (*1-55793-060-0*) Guild Bindery Pr.

Powell, Len. A Guide to the Overhead Projector. (C). 1974. pap. 50.00 (*0-85171-077-8*, Pub. by IPM Hse) St Mut.

— Lecturing to Large Groups. (C). 1979. pap. 30.00 (*0-85171-017-4*, Pub. by IPM Hse) St Mut.

Powell, Lenore S. & Courtice, Katie. Alzheimer's Disease: A Guide for Families. LC 83-3887. 288p. 1983. pap. 10.53 (*0-201-06099-X*) Addison-Wesley.

Powell, LeRoy, jt. auth. see Pfitzer, Donald W.

***Powell, Leslie.** Pocket Guide to Successful Consulting. Imeson, Harvey, ed. 50p. 2000. pap. 7.95 (*0-9625738-6-8*) Gala Pub.

***Powell, Leslie.** Food & Other Enemies: Stories of Consuming Desire. 208p. 2000. pap. 14.00 (*0-9668972-4-2*) Essex Press.

Powell, Lew. Carolina Follies: A Nose-Tweaking Look at Life in Our Two Great & Goofy States. Bledsoe, Jerry, ed. LC 90-60346. (Illus.). 96p. 1990. pap. 6.95 (*0-9624255-1-6*, Pub. by Down Home NC) Blair.

— On This Day in North Carolina. LC 95-41603. (Illus.). (Orig.). 1996. pap. 16.95 (*0-89587-139-4*) Blair.

— The Ultimate North Carolina Quiz Book. LC 99-30994. 128p. 1999. pap. 10.95 (*0-8078-4825-5*) U of NC Pr.

Powell, Lilja B., ed. see Pond, Jesse E., Jr.

Powell, Lillian L., et al. Grave Markers in Burke County, Georgia, with Thirty-nine Cemeteries in Four Adjoining Counties. 384p. 1988. reprint ed. 32.50 (*0-685-54355-2*, GA 83) Southern Hist Pr.

Powell, Linton E. A History of Spanish Piano Music. LC 79-3761. 223p. reprint ed. pap. 69.20 (*0-7837-3723-8*, 205790100009) Bks Demand.

Powell, Lucas A., Jr. The Fourth Estate & the Constitution: Freedom of the Press in America. (C). 1992. 16.95 (*0-520-08038-6*, Pub. by U CA Pr) Cal Prin Full Svc.

Powell, Lydia O. The San Antonio Missions: A Study of Their History & Development with Accompanying Activities. (Illus.). 80p. (J). (gr. 3 up). 1982. pap. 9.95 (*0-937460-06-0*) Hendrick-Long.

Powell, Lyman P. Mary Baker Eddy: A Life Size Portrait. LC 91-72519. (Twentieth-Century Biographers Ser.). (Illus.). 408p. 1992. 17.95 (*0-87510-260-3*) Writings of Mary Baker.

— Mary Baker Eddy a Life Size Portrait. 434p. 1998. reprint ed. pap. 29.95 (*0-7661-0460-5*) Kessinger Pub.

Powell, Lynn. Old & New Testaments. LC 95-16361. (Brittingham Prize in Poetry Ser.). 82p. 1995. 18.95 (*0-299-14900-5*); pap. 11.95 (*0-299-14904-8*) U of Wis Pr.

Powell, Lynn S. Resource Guide to Employee Relations for Your HVACR Contracting Business. 131p. 1996. pap. 80.00 (*1-892765-19-5*) Air Conditioning Cont.

— Resource Guide to Writing a Business Plan for Your HVAC Contracting Business. 28p. 1996. pap. 70.00 (*1-892765-18-7*) Air Conditioning Cont.

Powell, Lynn S., ed. see Healy, Tom & Briggs, Jeff.

Powell, Lynn S., ed. see Taylor, Jeffrey & Austin, Kenneth, Jr.

Powell, M. Orthopaedic Nursing in Developing Countries. (WHO Regional Publications, South-East Asia Ser.: No. 3). 147p. 1977. pap. text 16.00 (*92-9022-103-8*) World Health.

— Setting for Guitar. 8p. 1993. pap. 7.95 (*0-7935-2306-0*) H Leonard.

Powell, M. Anne. Academic Tutoring & Mentoring: A Literature Review. 67p. 1997. pap. write for info. (*1-58703-073-X*, CRB-97-011) CA St Libry.

Powell, M. Anne. Child Maltreatment & the Family: Background Briefing Report with Seminar Presentations. 94p. 1994. pap. 10.00 (*0-929722-80-9*) CA State Library Fndtn.

Powell, M. Anne. Peer Tutoring & Mentoring Services for Disadvantaged Secondary School Students, Vol. 2. 10p. 1997. pap. write for info. (*1-58703-065-9*) CA St Libry.

Powell, M. Anne, ed. Teen Pregnancy in California: Effective Prevention Strategies: Background Briefing Report with Seminar Presentations. 168p. 1994. pap. 15.00 (*0-929722-82-5*) CA State Library Fndtn.

Powell, M. Anne, et al. Welfare Reform & Family & Child Well-Being: Implications & Opportunities for Child Welfare. LC 99-159284. 86 p. 1998. write for info. (*0-929722-99-X*) CA State Library Fndtn.

Powell, M. J. Approximation Theory & Methods. (Illus.). 352p. 1981. pap. text 49.95 (*0-521-29514-9*) Cambridge U Pr.

Powell, M. J., jt. ed. see Iserles, Arieh.

Powell, Marcus. An Analysis of Policy Implementation in the Third World. LC 98-74140. 174p. (C). 1999. text 61.95 (*1-85972-702-6*) Ashgate Pub Co.

Powell, Margaret J., ed. Bible, N. T. Epistles of Paul: The Pauline Epistles Contained in Ms. (EETS, ES Ser.: No. 116). 1972. reprint ed. 55.00 (*0-527-00320-4*) Periodicals Srv.

Powell, Marianne, ed. see Sorensen, Knud.

Powell, Marie. White Wings: And Other Stories. 176p. (Orig.). 1993. pap. 9.95 (*1-56474-055-2*) Fithian Pr.

Powell, Marie B. Expressions in Poetry. (Illus.). 60p. 1990. boxed set 10.95 (*0-923568-17-4*) Wilderness Adventure Bks.

Powell, Mark. Qualify! A Guide to Successful Handling in AKC Pointing Breed Hunting Tests. LC 95-78078. (Illus.). 210p. 1995. pap. 16.95 (*0-9647671-4-7*) Attwater Pub.

Powell, Mark & Svensson, John. In-Line Skating. 2nd rev. ed. LC 97-16811. (Illus.). 208p. 1997. pap. 15.95 (*0-88011-659-5*, PPOW0659) Human Kinetics.

Powell, Mark, jt. auth. see Gaster, Jens.

Powell, Mark A. Fortress Introduction to the Gospels. LC 97-22995. 176p. 1997. pap. 16.00 (*0-8006-3075-0*, 1-3075, Fortress Pr) Augsburg Fortress.

— God with Us: A Pastoral Theology of Matthew's Gospel. LC 95-3448. 160p. 1995. pap. 16.00 (*0-8006-2881-0*, Fortress Pr) Augsburg Fortress.

— What Are They Saying about Acts? LC 91-27685. (What Are They Saying about...Ser.). 160p. 1992. pap. 8.95 (*0-8091-3279-6*) Paulist Pr.

— What Are They Saying about Luke? (What Are They Saying about...Ser.). 1989. pap. 8.95 (*0-8091-3111-0*) Paulist Pr.

— What Is Narrative Criticism? LC 90-13863. (Guides to Biblical Scholarship Ser.). 144p. (Orig.). 1991. pap. 15.00 (*0-8006-0473-3*, 1-473, Fortress Pr) Augsburg Fortress.

Powell, Mark A., compiled by. The Bible & Modern Literary Criticism: A Critical Assessment & Annotated Bibliography, 22. LC 91-38128. (Bibliographies & Indexes in Religious Studies: No. 22). 488p. 1992. lib. bdg. 79.50 (*0-313-27546-7*, PBD, Greenwood Pr) Greenwood.

***Powell, Mark A., ed.** The New Testament Today. LC 98-42329. 168p. 1999. pap. 18.00 (*0-664-25824-7*) Westminster John Knox.

Powell, Mark Allan. Jesus as a Figure in History: How Modern Historians View the Man from Galilee. LC 98-24284. 238p. 1998. pap. 22.00 (*0-664-25703-8*) Westminster John Knox.

Powell, Mark Allan & Bauer, David R., eds. Who Do You Say That I Am ? Essays on Christology. LC 99-14863. 296p. 1999. pap. 29.95 (*0-664-25752-6*) Westminster John Knox.

Powell, Mark R. Science at EPA: Information in the Regulatory Process. LC 99-20153. (Illus.). 433p. 1999. pap. 49.95 (*1-891853-00-7*) Resources Future.

Powell, Martin. A Case of Blind Fear. (Illus.). 128p. 1996. pap. 12.95 (*0-941613-93-3*, Caliber Comics) Stabur Pr.

— Scarlet in Gaslight. (Illus.). 112p. 1996. pap. 12.95 (*0-941613-92-5*, Caliber Comics) Stabur Pr.

Powell, Martin, ed. see Jones, Bruce.

Powell, Marvin. Psychology of Adolescence. 2nd ed. 678p. 1971. text 13.15 (*0-672-60782-4*, Bobbs) Macmillan.

Powell, Marvin, et al. Individual Progression. LC 74-88052. 1976. pap. 2.30 (*0-685-93230-3*, Bobbs) Macmillan.

Powell, Marvin A., ed. Labor in the Ancient Near East. (American Oriental Ser.: Vol. 68). (Illus.). xiv, 289p. (C). 1987. 32.00 (*0-940490-68-4*, #HD8656: L33) Am Orient Soc.

Powell, Marvin A., Jr. & Sack, Ronald H. Studies in Honor of Tom B. Jones. (Alter Orient und Altes Testament Ser.: Vol. 203). x, 371p. 1979. text 42.50 (*3-7887-0560-4*) NeukirchenerV.

Powell, Marvin A., ed. see Dandamaev, Muhammad A.

Powell, Mary. Orthopaedic Nursing & Rehabilitation. 9th ed. (Illus.). 640p. 1986. 53.00 (*0-443-03238-6*) Church.

— Practice Exercise Book "A" Component of Self-Tutoring Math Kit. (ENG & SPA.). 1986. pap., wbk. ed. 5.00 (*1-892302-01-2*) MATHCO Educ.

— Practice Exercise Book "B" Compcnet of Self-Tutoring Math Kit. (ENG & SPA.). 1986. pap., wbk. ed. 5.00 (*1-892302-02-0*) MATHCO Educ.

— Self-Tutoring Math Kit. (Illus.). 1986. pap. 86.00 incl. audio (*1-892302-00-4*) MATHCO Educ.

Powell, Mary, ed. Wolf Tales: Native American Children's Stories. LC 92-29690. (Illus.). 40p. (Orig.). (J). (gr. 3 up). 1993. pap. 8.95 (*0-941270-73-4*) Ancient City Pr.

Powell, Mary, jt. auth. see Chambers, Barry.

***Powell, Mary C.** Auslander: A Novel. LC 99-32491. 296p. 2000. 24.50 (*0-87565-215-8*, Pub. by Tex Christian) Tex A&M Univ Pr.

Powell, Mary C. Focus on Suzuki Piano. 76p. 1994. pap. text 12.95 (*0-87487-582-X*) Summy-Birchard.

— Queen of the Air: The Story of Katherine Stinson, 1891-1977. Petrick, Thomas W., ed. (Southwesterners Ser.). (Illus.). 121p. (YA). (gr. 4 up). 1993. pap. 9.95 (*1-880384-07-8*) Coldwater Pr.

Powell, Mary E., jt. auth. see Powell, Alton C.

Powell, Mary G. History of Old Alexandria, Virginia, from July 13, 1749 to May 24, 1861. (Illus.). 367p. 1997. reprint ed. lib. bdg. 41.00 (*0-8328-7179-6*) Higginson Bk Co.

Powell, Mary J., jt. auth. see Powell, Donald B.

Powell, Mary L. Status & Health in Prehistory: A Case Study of the Moundville Chiefdom. LC 87-23318. (Series in Archaeological Inquiry). (Illus.). 352p. (C). 1988. text 40.00 (*0-87474-756-2*) Smithsonian.

Powell, Mary L., et al, eds. What Mean These Bones? Studies in Southeastern Bioarchaeology. LC 89-20455. (Illus.). 243p. 1991. reprint ed. pap. 75.40 (*0-608-01678-0*, 206233400002) Bks Demand.

***Powell, Mary Reynolds.** A World of Hurt: Between Innocence & Arrogance in Vietnam. 190p. 2000. pap. 12.95 (*0-9665319-5-7*) Grnlf Ent.

Powell, Matthew. God Off-Broadway: The Blackfriars Theatre of New York. LC 97-29111. (Illus.). 168p. 1998. 35.00 (*0-8108-3417-0*) Scarecrow.

***Powell, Matthew.** Performing Parables: Religious Folk Tales, Legends & Fables for Readers Theatre. (Illus.). 80p. 2000. pap. 19.95 (*0-89390-502-X*) Resource Pubns.

Powell, Matthew. Solomon Islands Input-Output Table, 1987. LC 94-138181. 21 p. 1992. pap. write for info. (*0-7315-1669-9*) ANU Res Sch.

Powell, Matthew, jt. auth. see Braginski, Leon.

Powell, Meris, jt. ed. see Atkins, Dale.

Powell, Michael. Computer Contracting: How to Become a Freelance Computer Professional. 180p. 1998. pap. text 39.95 (*0-7506-3851-6*, Digital DEC) Buttrwrth-Heinemann.

***Powell, Michael.** A Life in Movies. (Illus.). 640p. 2001. pap. 25.00 (*0-571-20431-7*) Faber & Faber.

Powell, Michael. A Life in Movies: An Autobiography. 700p. 1998. 24.95 (*0-685-18173-1*) Knopf.

— Million Dollar Movie. (Illus.). 626p. 1995. 30.00 (*0-614-32303-7*) Random.

***Powell, Michael & Pressburger, Emeric.** The Red Shoes: The Classic Story. 280p. 2000. reprint ed. 18.00 (*0-7881-9370-8*) DIANE Pub.

Powell, Michael F. & Newman, Mark J., eds. Vaccine Design: The Subunit & Adjuvant Approach. LC 95-16401. (Pharmaceutical Biotechnology Ser.: Vol. 6). (Illus.). 994p. (C). 1995. text 165.00 (*0-306-44867-X*, Kluwer Plenum) Kluwer Academic.

Powell, Michael H. Compactly Covered Reflections, Extension of Uniform Dualities & Generalized Almost Periodicity. LC 52-42839. (Memoirs Ser.: No. 1/105). 235p. 1970. pap. 17.00 (*0-8218-1805-8*, MEMO/1/105) Am Math.

Powell, Michael J. From Patrician to Professional Elite: The Transformation of the New York City Bar Association. LC 88-32476. 256p. 1989. 42.50 (*0-87154-686-8*) Russell Sage.

Powell, Michelle. Decorative Stamping: On Clay & Ceramics, Fabrics & Metal, Wood & Card. 1999. pap. text 14.95 (*0-85532-877-0*) Srch Pr.

***Powell, Michelle.** Printing. LC 00-38308. (Step-by-Step Ser.). 2000. lib. bdg. write for info. (*1-57572-329-8*) Heinemann Lib.

— Printing. (Step-by-Step Children's Crafts Ser.). 32p. (J). (ps-3). 2000. pap. 8.95 (*0-85532-911-4*, Pub. by Srch Pr) Midpt Trade.

***Powell, Mike.** Information Management for Development Organizations. 160p. 1999. pap. 14.95 (*0-85598-410-4*, Pub. by Oxfam Pub) Stylus Pub VA.

Powell, Montagu. Studies in the Lesser Mysteries. 124p. 1996. reprint ed. spiral bd. 11.50 (*0-7873-0675-4*) Hlth Research.

Powell, Murella H., jt. auth. see Sullivan, Charles L.

Powell, Nancy & Mast, Jim. Bloody Sunset in St. Augustine. 251p. (Orig.). 1998. pap. 10.00 (*0-9668259-0-X*) Federal Point.

Powell, Nancy H. What to See & Do in the Lost River & South Branch Valleys. (Illus.). viii, 204p. 1997. pap. 12.95 (*0-9655938-0-0*) Lost River Educ.

Powell, Neil. At the Edge LC 77-379314. 61 p. 1977. write for info. (*0-85635-214-4*) Carcanet Pr.

— Carpenters of Light: Some Contemporary English Poets. LC 79-54320. 154p. 1980. text 38.00 (*0-06-495665-2*, N6785) B&N Imports.

— Carpenters of Light: Some Contemporary English Poets LC 80-452606. ii, 154 p. 1979. write for info. (*0-85635-305-1*) Carcanet Pr.

— The Language of Jazz. LC 98-193584. 160p. 1998. pap. 18.95 (*1-85754-164-2*, Pub. by Carcanet Pr) Paul & Co Pubs.

— Roy Fuller: Writer & Society. 320p. 1996. 45.00 (*1-85754-133-2*, Pub. by Carcanet Pr) Paul & Co Pubs.

— Selected Poems. LC 99-199530. 96p. 1998. pap. 17.95 (*1-85754-350-5*, Pub. by Carcanet Pr) Paul & Co Pubs.

— The Stones on Thorpeness Beach LC 95-149777. 71 p. 1994. write for info. (*1-85754-058-1*) Carcanet Pr.

— True Colours LC 92-145901. 102p. 1991. write for info. (*0-85635-910-6*) Carcanet Pr.

Powell, Neil, ed. Fulke Greville (1554-1628) Selected Poems. pap. write for info. (*0-85635-856-8*, Pub. by Carcanet Pr) Paul & Co Pubs.

Powell, Neil, ed. Gay Love Poetry. LC 97-29717. (Illus.). 254p. 1997. pap. 11.95 (*0-7867-0469-1*) Carroll & Graf.

Powell, Neva. The Long Crossing. LC 98-85615. (Illus.). 124p. (YA). (gr. 5-8). 1998. pap. 12.95 (*0-9661072-2-5*) Avocet Pr.

Powell, Nicholas, jt. auth. see Webster, Paul.

Powell, Norman W., jt. ed. see Krueger, Mark A.

Powell, Orrin E. Educational Returns at Varying Expenditure Levels: A Basis for Relating Expenditures to Outcomes in Education. LC 75-177163. (Columbia University. Teachers College. Contributions to Education Ser.: No. 573). reprint ed. 37.50 (*0-404-55573-X*) AMS Pr.

Powell, P. C. & Housz, A. J., eds. Engineering with Polymers. 2nd ed. 512p. (Orig.). 1998. pap. 49.95 (*0-7487-3987-4*) St Mut.

Powell, Padget. Aliens of Affection. 224p. 1999. pap. 13.00 (*0-8050-6000-6*, Owl) H Holt & Co.

An Asterisk (*) at the beginning of an entry indicates that the title is appearing for the first time.

Powell, Padgett. Aliens of Affection, Vol. 1. LC 97-10451. 221p. 1998. 22.50 (0-8050-5213-5) H Holt & Co.
— Edisto. LC 84-15871. 192p. 1995. pap. 9.95 (0-8050-1370-9, Owl) H Holt & Co.
— Edisto Revisited. LC 95-34071. 88p. 1995. 20.00 (0-8050-4237-7) H Holt & Co.
— Edisto Revisited: A Novel. 1997. pap. 12.00 (0-8050-5353-0, Owl) H Holt & Co.
***Powell, Padgett.** Mrs. Hollingsworth's Men: A Novel. 144p. 2000. 20.00 (0-618-07168-7) HM.
Powell, Padgett. Typical Stories. 192p. 1995. pap. 9.95 (0-8050-2111-6, Owl) H Holt & Co.
Powell, Pamela. The Turtle Watchers. 128p. (J). (gr. 3-7). 1994. pap. 4.99 (0-14-037077-3, PuffinBks) Peng Put Young Read.
Powell, Pamela & Murnane, Lynne C. Fire & Life Safety Educator. 2nd ed. LC 96-61966. (Illus.). 400p. 1997. pap. text 40.00 (0-87939-135-9, 35002) IFSTA.
Powell, Pamela C. Reflected Light: A Century of Photography in Chester County. (Illus.). 80p. 1988. 30.25 (0-929706-01-3); pap. 24.25 (0-929706-02-1) Chester Co Hist Soc.
Powell, Patricia. Diddle Diddle Red Hot Fiddle. (Illus.). 32p. (J). (gr. 1-8). 1990. pap. text 6.95 (0-944512-01-1) Radiant LA.
— Me Dying Trial. (Caribbean Writers Ser.). 192p. 1993. pap. 9.95 (0-435-98935-9, 98935) Heinemann.
— The Pagoda. LC 99-26980. 256p. 1999. pap. 12.00 (0-15-600829-7, Harvest Bks) Harcourt.
— The Pagoda. LC 98-14568. 256p. 1998. 23.00 (0-679-45489-6) Knopf.
— Small Gathering of Bones. (Caribbean Writers Ser.). 144p. 1994. pap. 9.95 (0-435-98936-7, 98936) Heinemann.
Powell, Patricia & Huo, Shitao. Mao's Graphic Voice: Pictorial Posters from the Cultural Revolution. LC 97-153281. (Illus.). 16p. 1996. pap. 3.00 (0-932900-41-0) Elvehjem Mus.
Powell, Patricia, ed. see Lone Dog, Louise.
Powell, Patsy K. Dulac, Dat Cajun Cat: Dulac, Dat Cajun Party Animal. LC 87-91307. (Illus.). 32p. (J). (gr. k up). 1988. pap. 6.95 (0-944512-00-3) Radiant LA.
Powell, Paul. Principles of Organometallic Chemistry. 2nd ed. (C). pap. text 58.50 (0-412-27590-2) Chapman & Hall.
Powell, Paul, et al. The Gospel of Luke: Meeting Jesus Again, Anew. (Bible Study for Texas Ser.). 144p. 2000. pap. 1.95 (0-9673424-0-6) Baptistway.
Powell, Paul W. Feet of Clay: Facing Emotions That Make Us Stumble. LC 98-30882. 1999. 12.00 (1-57312-196-7) Smyth & Helwys.
Powell, Paula & Peel, Lucy. 50's & 60's Style. (Illus.). 128p. 1996. 21.95 (1-57215-172-2) World Pubns.
Powell, Peter C. Engineering with Polymers. LC 83-7180. 1983. 69.50 (0-412-24160-9, NO. 6825) Chapman & Hall.
Powell, Peter J. Sweet Medicine: The Continuing Role of the Sacred Arrows, the Sun Dance, & the Sacred Buffalo Hat in Northern Cheyenne History, 2 vols. LC 76-88145. (Civilization of the American Indian Ser.: Vol. 100). (Illus.). 935p. 1998. 55.00 (0-8061-3028-8) U of Okla Pr.
Powell, Peter W. Confederate States of America, Markings & Postal History of Richmond, Virginia. Hartmann, Leonard H., ed. LC 87-32110. (Illus.). 188p. 1987. 50.00 (0-917528-09-3) L H Hartmann.
***Powell, Phelan.** Alicia Silverstone. (Real-Life Reader Biography Ser.). (Illus.). 32p. (J). (gr. 3-8). 2000. lib. bdg. 15.95 (1-58415-037-8) M Lane Pubs.
Powell, Phelan. Fitness Stars of Boxing. (Legends of Health & Fitness Ser.). 128p. (YA). (gr. 6-12). 2000. lib. bdg. 24.95 (1-58415-013-0) M Lane Pubs.
— Garth Brooks: Award-Winning Country Music Star. LC 99-10093. (Real-Life Reader Biography Ser.). (Illus.). 32p. (J). (gr. 4-7). 1999. lib. bdg. 15.95 (1-58415-004-1) M Lane Pubs.
— Hanson. (Galaxy of Superstars Ser.). (Illus.). 64p. (YA). (gr. 3 up). 1999. 16.95 (0-7910-5148-X) Chelsea Hse.
— Jeff Gordon. LC 99-24056. (Real-Life Reader Biography Ser.). (Illus.). 32p. (J). (gr. 3-8). 1999. lib. bdg. 15.95 (1-58415-005-X) M Lane Pubs.
— John Candy. LC 99-12312. (They Died Too Young Ser.). (Illus.). 48p. 1999. 16.95 (0-7910-5226-5) Chelsea Hse.
***Powell, Phelan.** John Jay. (Revolutionary War Leaders Ser.). 2000. 18.95 (0-7910-5979-0) Chelsea Hse.
Powell, Phelan. John LeClair. (Ice Hockey Legends Ser.). (Illus.). 64p. (YA). (gr. 3 up). 1999. lib. bdg. 16.95 (0-7910-5016-5) Chelsea Hse.
— Major Unsolved Crimes. LC 99-24140. (Crime, Justice, & Punishment Ser.). (Illus.). (YA). (gr. 8 up). 1999. lib. bdg. 19.95 (0-7910-4277-4) Chelsea Hse.
***Powell, Phelan.** Mark McGwire. (Sports Heroes Ser.). 48p. (YA). (gr. 5 up). 2000. lib. bdg. 21.26 (0-7368-0578-8, Capstone Bks) Capstone Pr.
— Nathaniel Bacon. (Colonial Leaders Ser.). (Illus.). 2000. 18.95 (0-7910-5960-X) Chelsea Hse.
— Sarah Michelle Gellar. (Real-Life Reader Biography Ser.). (Illus.). 32p. (J). (gr. 3-8). 2000. lib. bdg. 15.95 (1-58415-034-3) M Lane Pubs.
— Sir William Berkeley. (Colonial Leaders Ser.). (Illus.). 2000. pap. 8.95 (0-7910-6117-5) Chelsea Hse.
— Sir William Berkeley. (Colonial Leaders Ser.). (Illus.). (J). 2000. 18.95 (0-7910-6116-7, Chelsea Juniors) Chelsea Hse.
Powell, Phelan. Tom Cruise: Actor. LC 98-47621. (Overcoming Adversity Ser.). (Illus.). 128p. (YA). (gr. 4-7). 1999. pap. 9.95 (0-7910-4941-8) Chelsea Hse.
— Tom Cruise: Actor. (Overcoming Adversity Ser.). (Illus.). 128p. (YA). (gr. 5 up). 1999. lib. bdg. 19.95 (0-7910-4940-X) Chelsea Hse.
— Trailblazers of Physical Fitness. (Legends of Health & Fitness Ser.). (Illus.). 128p. (YA). (gr. 6-12). 2000. lib. bdg. 24.95 (1-58415-024-6) M Lane Pubs.
Powell, Phil. Microsoft Critical Depth: Inside Moves. 1997. pap. text 16.99 (1-57231-633-0) Microsoft.
Powell, Phill, et al. Microsoft Urban Assault: Inside Moves. LC 98-28533. (Inside Moves Ser.). 224p. 16.99 (1-57231-861-9) Microsoft.
Powell, Phillip W. Mexico's Miguel Caldera: The Taming of America's First Frontier, 1548-1597. LC 76-62551. 334p. reprint ed. pap. 95.20 (0-8357-8585-8, 2034956) Bks Demand.
Powell, Polly. Just Dessert. LC 94-48360. 32p. (J). (ps-3). 1996. 15.00 (0-15-200383-5) Harcourt.
Powell, R. C., ed. Selected Papers on Solid State Lasers, MS31. 1991. pap. 35.00 (0-8194-0629-5) SPIE.
— Selected Papers on Solid State Lasers, MS31/HC. 1991. 45.00 (0-8194-0628-7) SPIE.
Powell, R. E., et al, eds. San Andreas Fault System: Displacement, Palinspastic Reconstruction, & Geologic Evolution. (Memoir Ser.: No. 178). (Illus.). 1993. 57.50 (0-8137-1178-9) Geol Soc.
Powell, R. E., jt. auth. see Daugherty, J. S.
Powell, R. F. & Forrest, M. R. Noise in the Military Environment. (Land Warfare: Brassey's New Battlefield Weapons & Technology Ser.: Vol. 3). 126p. 1988. 40.00 (0-08-035830-6, Pub. by Brasseys) Brasseys.
— Noise in the Military Environment. 3rd ed. (Battlefield Weapons Systems & Technology Ser.: Vol. 3). 126p. 1988. 25.00 (0-08-035831-4, Pub. by Brasseys) Brasseys.
Powell, R. Gray. Seven Seas University (SSU) 238p. 1994. pap. text 16.00 (0-9648373-0-7) Filac Pubs.
Powell, Rachel. Powell: Family Records of the Powell & Griffiths, with Poetry of John Powell. 119p. 1994. reprint ed. pap. 19.50 (0-8328-4111-0); reprint ed. lib. bdg. 29.50 (0-8328-4110-2) Higginson Bk Co.
Powell, Ralph L. The Rise of Chinese Military Power, 1895-1912. LC 55-6247. 393p. reprint ed. pap. 121.90 (0-608-30843-9, 200027600025) Bks Demand.
Powell, Randall. Career Planning Today. 3rd ed. 528p. (C). 1994. pap. text, per. 31.95 (0-8403-8469-6, 40846901) Kendall-Hunt.
— Career Planning Today. 4th ed. 550p. 1999. per. 32.95 (0-7872-4242-X, 41424201) Kendall-Hunt.
Powell, Randy. Dean Duffy. LC 94-29037. 169p. (J). 1995. 15.00 (0-374-31754-2) FS&G.
— Dean Duffy. 176p. (gr. 7 up). 1998. pap. text 4.95 (0-374-41699-0) FS&G.
— Dean Duffy. (J). 1995. 10.05 (0-606-13323-2, Pub. by Turtleback) Demco.
— Is Kissing a Girl Who Smokes Like Licking an Ashtray? 208p. (YA). (gr. 7 up). 1994. pap. 3.95 (0-374-43627-4) FS&G.
— My Underrated Year. LC 87-46401. 184p. (YA). (gr. 7 up). 1991. pap. 4.95 (0-374-45453-1, Sunburst Bks) FS&G.
— Tribute to Another Dead Rock Star. LC 98-35522. 224p. (gr. 7-12). 1999. 17.00 (0-374-37748-0) FS&G.
— The Whistling Toilets. LC 96-10475. 256p. (YA). (gr. 7 up). 1996. 17.00 (0-374-38381-2) FS&G.
Powell, Raymond. Shakespeare The Critics Debate. LC 87-673916. vii, 167 p. 1980. student ed. write for info. (0-333-27666-3) Macmillan.
Powell, Raymond P., jt. auth. see Moorsteen, Richard H.
Powell, Rebecca L. Literacy as a Moral Imperative: Facing the Challenges of a Pluralistic Society. LC 99-15039. 168p. 1999. 55.00 (0-8476-9458-5) Rowman.
***Powell, Rebecca L.** Literacy as a Moral Imperative: Facing the Challenges of a Pluralistic Society. LC 99-15039. (Culture & Education Ser.). 168p. 1999. pap. 17.95 (0-8476-9459-3) Rowman.
Powell, Richard. Dinosaurs. (Illus.). 24p. (J). 1995. pap. 1.29 (1-884628-20-6, Flyng Frog) Allied Pub MD.
— Eye Spy a Pig! (Eye Spy Ser.). 10p. 1999. pap. 6.99 (0-8431-7530-3, Price Stern) Peng Put Young Read.
— Grandma's Cottage. (Illus.). (J). 1995. boxed set 7.99 (1-884628-01-X, Flyng Frog) Allied Pub MD.
— How to Deal with Babies. LC 91-3461. (Child's Practical Guide Ser.). (Illus.). 24p. (J). (gr. k-3). 1997. pap. 2.95 (0-8167-2421-0) Troll Communs.
— How to Deal with Friends. LC 91-15164. (Illus.). 24p. (J). (gr. k-3). 1996. pap. 2.95 (0-8167-2423-7) Troll Communs.
— How to Deal with Monsters. LC 91-14975. (Child's Practical Guide Ser.). (Illus.). 24p. (J). (gr. k-3). 1997. pap. 2.95 (0-8167-2425-3) Troll Communs.
— How to Deal with Parents. LC 91-14997. (Child's Practical Guide Ser.). (Illus.). 24p. (J). (gr. k-3). 1997. pap. 2.95 (0-8167-2419-9) Troll Communs.
— If You See a Cow. 10p. 1999. 4.99 (0-307-14611-1) Gldn Bks Pub Co.
— If You See a Mouse. 10p. 1999. 4.99 (0-307-14614-6) Gldn Bks Pub Co.
— If You See a Tiger. 10p. 1999. 4.99 (0-307-14613-8) Gldn Bks Pub Co.
— If You See a Whale. 10p. 1999. 4.99 (0-307-14612-X) Gldn Bks Pub Co.
— In the Garden. (Illus.). 20p. (J). 1994. pap. 4.99 (1-881445-28-3) Sandvik Pub.
— Let's Guess Flap Book: Baa! LC 97-100808. (Illus.). 6p. (J). 1995. 4.50 (0-689-80039-8) Litle Simon.
— Let's Guess Flap Book: Grr! LC 97-124273. (Illus.). 6p. (J). 1995. 4.50 (0-689-80040-1) Litle Simon.
— The Magistrates' Court & European Law: A Practical Guide. 220p. 1997. pap. 59.50 (1-85811-160-9, Pub. by CLT Prof) Gaunt.
— An Octopus! (Eye Spy Ser.). 10p. 1999. pap 6.99 (0-8431-7531-1, Price Stern) Peng Put Young Read.
— On the Farm. (Illus.). 20p. (J). 1994. pap. 4.99 (1-881445-27-5) Sandvik Pub.
Powell, Richard & Reynolds, Jock. Tax Policy & the Economy, Vol. 13. Poterba, James M., ed. (Illus.). 224p. 1999. pap. 15.00 (0-262-66150-0) MIT Pr.
Powell, Richard, et al. Multiracial Couples. LC 95-16778. (Understanding Families Ser.: No. 1). 305p. (C). 1995. 48.00 (0-8039-7258-X) Sage.
Powell, Richard, jt. auth. see Janda, Kenneth.
Powell, Richard, jt. auth. see Robinson, Jontyle Theresa.
Powell, Richard C. Physics of Solid-State Laser Materials. LC 97-27736. (Atomic, Molecular & Optical Physics Ser.: Vol. 1). (Illus.). 336p. 1998. 59.95 (1-56396-658-1) Spr-Verlag.
Powell, Richard C., jt. auth. see Di Bartolo, Baldassare.
Powell, Richard F. Testing Active & Passive Electronic Components. (Electrical Engineering & Electronics Ser.: Vol. 38). (Illus.). 232p. 1987. text 135.00 (0-8247-7705-0) Dekker.
Powell, Richard J. Black Art & Culture in the 20th Century. LC 96-60366. (World of Art Ser.). (Illus.). 256p. 1997. pap. 14.95 (0-500-20295-8, Pub. by Thames Hudson) Norton.
***Powell, Richard J. & Reynolds, Jock.** To Conserve a Legacy: American Art from Historically Black Colleges & Universities. LC 98-50539. (Illus.). 1999. pap. 35.00 (0-262-66151-9) MIT Pr.
Powell, Richard J., et al. Rhapsodies in Black: Art of the Harlem Renaissance. LC 97-20475. (Illus.). 183p. 1997. 60.00 (0-520-21263-0, Pub. by U CA Pr); pap. 34.95 (0-520-21268-1, Pub. by U CA Pr) Cal Prin Full Svc.
Powell, Richard R. The Law of Future Interests in California. 91p. 1980. pap. write for info. (0-318-57529-9) West Pub.
Powell, Richard R. & Rohan, Patrick J. Powell on Real Property, 17 vols. 1949. ring bd. 2235.00 (0-8205-1550-7) Bender.
Powell, Richard R., et al. Classrooms under the Influence: Addicted Families/Addicted Students. LC 95-23318. (Illus.). 168p. 1995. pap. 22.95 (0-8039-6102-2) Corwin Pr.
— Field Experience: Strategies for Exploring Diversity in Schools. LC 95-14111. 263p. 1995. pap. text 41.00 (0-02-396311-5, Macmillan Coll) P-H.
Powell, Ricky. Oh Snap Rap & Hip Hops Finest. LC 97-41181. 160p. 1998. pap. 22.95 (0-312-18149-3) St Martin.
— The Rickford Files: Classic New York Photographs. 160p. 2000. pap. 24.95 (0-312-24322-7) St Martin.
Powell, Robert. The Asian House: Contemporary Houses of Southeast Asia. 176p. 1998. 42.50 (962-593-329-8, Periplus Eds) Tuttle Pubng.
***Powell, Robert.** The Christ Mystery: Reflections on the Second Coming. (Illus.). iv, 133p. 1999. pap. 15.50 (0-945803-39-7, 00195) R Steiner Col.
Powell, Robert. Christian Hermetic Astrology: The Star of the Magi & the Life of Christ. 314p. 1998. pap. 14.95 (0-88010-461-9) Anthroposophic.
— Crisis in Consciousness: The Source of All Conflict. 200p. 1988. pap. 12.00 (0-89540-167-3, SB-167) Sun Pub.
— Depopulation Arranged, Convicted & Condemned by the Lawes of God & Man. LC 76-57407. (English Experience Ser.: No. 823). 1977. reprint ed. lib. bdg. 20.00 (90-221-0823-6) Walter J Johnson.
— Dialogues on Reality: An Exploration into the Nature of Our Ultimate Identity. LC 96-24875. 226p. (Orig.). 1996. pap. 14.00 (1-884997-16-3) Blue Dove Pr.
— Discovering the Realm Beyond Appearance: Pointers to the Inexpressible. LC 98-47968. 200p. 1999. pap. 14.00 (1-884997-17-1) Blue Dove Pr.
— The Free Mind: The Inward Path to Liberation. 185p. 1987. pap. 12.00 (0-89540-168-1, SB-168) Sun Pub.
— History of the Houses. (Illus.). 32p. (Orig.). 1996. pap. 4.95 (0-935127-56-9) ACS Pubns.
— History of the Planets. 35p. 1993. pap. 4.95 (0-935127-02-X) ACS Pubns.
***Powell, Robert.** In the Shadow of Power: States & Strategies in International Politics. LC 99-12207. (Illus.). 310p. 1999. 55.00 (0-691-00456-0, Pub. by Princeton U Pr) Cal Prin Full Svc.
— In the Shadow of Power: States & Strategies in International Politics. LC 99-12207. 310p. 1999. 19.95 (0-691-00457-9, Pub. by Princeton U Pr) Cal Prin Full Svc.
Powell, Robert. Innovative Architecture of Singapore. (Illus.). 160p. 1995. 45.00 (981-00-0683-7, Pub. by Select Bks) Weatherhill.
— Nuclear Deterrence Theory: The Search for Credibility. (Illus.). 238p. (C). 1990. text 74.95 (0-521-37527-4) Cambridge U Pr.
— Path Without Form: A Journey Into the Realm Beyond Thought. LC 98-47967. 246p. (Orig.). 1999. pap. 14.95 (1-884997-21-X) Blue Dove Pr.
— Rethinking the Skyscraper: The Complete Architecture of Ken Yeang. (Illus.). 208p. 1999. pap. 45.00 (0-8230-4553-6) Watsn-Guptill.
— The Tropical Asian House. (Illus.). 176p. 1998. 42.50 (962-593-303-4) Tuttle Pubng.
— Why Does God Allow Suffering? And Other Essays on the Spiritual Quest. LC 88-83535. 158p. reprint ed. pap. 49.00 (0-7837-5211-3, 204494200004) Bks Demand.
— The Zodiac: A Historical Survey. 31p. 1986. pap. 4.95 (0-917086-69-4) ACS Pubns.
Powell, Robert, ed. The Experience of Nothingness: Sri Nisargadatta Maharaj's Talks on Realizing the Inifinite. LC 96-24322. (Illus.). 166p. 1996. pap. 14.00 (1-884997-14-7) Blue Dove Pr.
— The Nectar of Immortality: Sri Nisargadatta Maharaj's Discourses on the Eternal. LC 95-44138. 192p. 1996. pap. 14.00 (1-884997-13-9) Blue Dove Pr.
— The Ultimate Medicine: As Prescribed by Sri Nisargadatta Maharaj. 3rd ed. LC 94-34676. 220p. (Orig.). 1995. pap. 14.00 (1-884997-09-0) Blue Dove Pr.
***Powell, Robert & Andreev, Daniel.** The Most Holy Trinosophia: The New Revelation of the Divine Feminine. 144p. 2000. pap. 16.95 (0-88010-480-5) Anthroposophic.
Powell, Robert, et al. A Key to Amphibians & Reptiles of the Continental United States & Canada. LC 98-28187. (Illus.). 150p. 1998. pap. 17.95 (0-7006-0929-6) U Pr of KS.
Powell, Robert, jt. auth. see Felder, Linda.
Powell, Robert, jt. auth. see Lake, David A.
Powell, Robert, jt. ed. see Lake, David A.
Powell, Robert A. Chronicle of the Living Christ: The Life & Ministry of Jesus Christ Foundations of Cosmic Christianity. (Illus.). 488p. 1996. pap. 25.00 (0-88010-407-4) Anthroposophic.
***Powell, Robert A.** On This Day in Kentucky. (Illus.). 96p. 1999. pap. 7.90 (0-9651406-2-8) Silverhawke.
Powell, Robert A. The Ultimate Coven. (Illus.). 224p. 1996. 19.95 (0-9651406-1-X) Silverhawke.
Powell, Robert E. Bits of Bluegrass. (Illus.). 52p. (Orig.). 1995. pap. write for info. (1-57579-007-6) Pine Hill Pr.
— The Bugle Is Silent. unabridged ed. 265p. 1998. pap. 15.95 (1-892896-16-8) Buy Books.
Powell, Robert F. Naked Strangers. LC 96-96397. (Illus.). 256p. 1996. pap. 7.95 (0-9651648-0-2) Debonair Pr.
Powell, Robert J. A Musical Gift Bk. 2: 20 Organ Preludes on Familiar Hymn Tunes. 42p. (Orig.). 1996. pap., student ed. 10.00 (1-889079-08-1) Darcey Pr.
Powell, Robert J., III, ed. see Harvey, Louis S.
Powell, Rod. Rod Powell's Flame Painting Techniques: How to Flame Hot Rods, Trucks & Motorcycles. Fetherston, David, ed. LC 96-60749. (Illus.). 128p. 1997. pap. 19.95 (0-9652005-5-8, 106) Thaxton Pr.
Powell, Roger. Equilibrium Thermodynamics in Petrology: An Introduction. 300p. (C). 1978. 60.00 (0-06-318073-1, Pub. by P Chapman) St Mut.
Powell, Roger & Hindi, K. S. Computing & Control for the Water Industry. LC 98-53238. 420p. 1998. 140.00 (0-86380-230-3) Research Studies Pr Ltd.
Powell, Roger A. The Fisher: Life History, Ecology, & Behavior. LC 81-14775. (Illus.). 235p. reprint ed. pap. 72.90 (0-8357-7667-0, 205699500097) Bks Demand.
— The Fisher: Life History, Ecology, & Behavior. 2nd ed. LC 93-3716. 256p. 1993. pap. 18.95 (0-8166-2266-3) U of Minn Pr.
Powell, Ronald R. Basic Research Methods for Librarians. 3rd ed. LC 97-28906. xii, 281 p. 1997. pap. 39.50 (1-56750-338-1); text 73.25 (1-56750-337-3) Ablx Pub.
— The Relationship of Library User Studies to Performance Measures: A Review of the Literature. (Occasional Papers: No. 181). (Orig.). 1988. pap. 2.50 (0-685-34544-0) U of Ill Grad Sch.
Powell, Ronald R., jt. auth. see Benham, Frances.
Powell, Ronald R., jt. auth. see McClure, Charles R.
Powell, Ronald R., jt. auth. see Taylor, Margaret T.
Powell, Russell H. Handbooks & Tables in Science & Technology. 3rd ed. LC 94-16149. 368p. 1994. 95.00 (0-89774-534-5) Oryx Pr.
Powell, S., jt. auth. see Land, Ailsa H.
Powell, S. R., Jr., jt. ed. see Mecholsky, J. J.
***Powell, Samuel & Carter, Lane.** Almost a Whisper: A Holistic Approach to Working with Your Horse. LC 99-34046. 1999. 24.95 (1-57779-026-X) Alpine Pubns.
Powell, Samuel & Lodahl, Michael, eds. Embodied Holiness: Toward a Corporate Theology of Spiritual Growth. LC 99-43125. 240p. 1999. pap. 19.99 (0-8308-1583-X) InterVarsity.
Powell, Sandy E. Washington. LC 92-13366. (Hello U. S. A. Ser.). (Illus.). 72p. (J). (gr. 3-6). 1993. lib. bdg. 19.95 (0-8225-2726-X, Lerner Publctns) Lerner Pub.
— Washington: Hello U. S. A. (Illus.). 72p. (J). 1996. pap. text 5.95 (0-8225-9738-1) Lerner Pub.
***Powell, Sara Davis.** Professional's Guide Block Scheduling. (Illus.). 76p. 1999. pap., teacher ed. 9.95 (1-57690-478-4, TCM 2478) Tchr Create Mat.
— Professional's Guide Standards in the Classroom. 776p. 1999. pap., teacher ed. 9.95 (1-57690-482-2, TCM 2482) Tchr Create Mat.
— Super Strategies for Succeeding on the Standardized Tests: Language Arts. 128p. 2000. pap. text 14.95 (0-439-04249-6) Scholastic Inc.
Powell, Sarah, jt. auth. see Furniss, Kim.
Powell, Scott. History of Marshall County, West Virginia. 368p. 1998. reprint ed. pap. 26.00 (0-7884-0920-4, P581) Heritage Bk.
— History of Marshall County, West Virginia. 334p. 1993. reprint ed. lib. bdg. write for info. (0-8328-2929-3) Higginson Bk Co.
Powell, Shirley. Other Rooms. 112p. 1997. pap. 19.95 (0-922558-02-7) Poets Pr.
Powell, Shirley. Rooms. 72p. 1984. write for info. (0-318-64138-0) Poets Pr.
— Rooms. 2nd enl. ed. 72p. 1986. write for info. (0-318-64139-9) Poets Pr.
Powell, Shirley, ed. Excavations on Black Mesa, 1971-1976: A Descriptive Report. LC 82-72189. (Center for Archaeological Investigations Research Paper Ser.: No. 48). xxvi, 316p. 1984. pap. 15.00 (0-88104-020-7) Center Archaeol.
— Womansong: An Anthology of Women's Poetry. 1984. write for info. (0-318-64153-4) Poets Pr.
Powell, Shirley, et al, eds. Excavation on Black Mesa, 1979: A Descriptive Report. (Center for Archaeological Investigations Research Paper Ser.: No. 18). (Illus.). xii, 516p. 1980. pap. 20.00 (0-88104-028-2) Center Archaeol.
Powell, Shirley, jt. ed. see Klesert, Anthony L.
Powell, Shirley, jt. ed. see Plog, Stephen.
Powell, Shirley, ed. see Poet's Press & Stone Ridge (NY) Poetry Society Sta.

P

An Asterisk (*) at the beginning of an entry indicates that the title is appearing for the first time.

Powell, Shirley S. Discovering the Magic of Museums: Especially Children's Museums. 32p. 1991. pap. write for info. (*0-9628995-0-X*) S Powell.

Powell, Sinclair. The Franklin Automobile Company: The History of the Innovative Firm, Its Founders, the Vehicles It Produced (1902-1934) & the People Who Built Them. LC 98-37236. 500p. 1999. 39.00 (*0-7680-0221-4*, R-208) Soc Auto Engineers.

Powell-Smith. Malaysian Standard Form of Building Contract. 171p. 1990. boxed set 60.00 (*0-409-99592-4*, MICHIE) LEXIS Pub.

Powell-Smith, V., jt. ed. see Furmston, M. P.

Powell-Smith, Vincent, ed. The Asia-Pacific Construction Law Reports, 1991. 575p. 1994. write for info. (*0-409-99705-6*, MICHIE) LEXIS Pub.

Powell-Smith, Vincent & Billington, M. J. Building Regulations. 9th ed. (Illus.). 720p. 1992. pap. 40.00 (*0-632-03378-9*) Blackwell Sci.

— Building Regulations: Explained & Illustrated. 10th ed. LC 95-3605. (Illus.). 1995. 49.95 (*0-632-03933-7*, Pub. by Blckwll Scitfc UK) Blackwell Sci.

***Powell-Smith, Vincent & Billington, M. J.** The Building Regulations: Explained & Illustrated. 11th ed. LC 99-32997. 1999. write for info. (*0-632-05069-1*) Blackwell Sci.

***Powell-Smith, Vincent & Furmston, M. P.** Powell-Smith & Furmston's Building Contract Casebook. 3rd ed. LC 99-89276. 2000. write for info. (*0-632-03991-4*) Blackwell Sci.

***Powell-Smith, Vincent, et al.** Civil Engineering Claims 3rd ed. LC 99-38807. 1999. pap. write for info. (*0-632-05197-3*) Blackwell Sci.

Powell-Smith, Vincent, et al. Construction Arbitrations: A Practical Guide. 2nd ed. LC 98-12733. 1998. pap. 85.00 (*0-632-03992-2*) Blackwell Sci.

Powell-Smith, Vincent, jt. auth. see Chappell, David.

Powell-Smith, Vincent, jt. auth. see Houghton-Brown, Jeremy.

Powell-Smith, Vincent, jt. auth. see Ivamy, E. R.

Powell, Staccato & Proctor, Dennis V. Christians under Construction: A Guide to Spiritual Growth. (Illus.). 130p. 1995. pap. 10.00 (*0-9646729-0-1*) Kairos Pr.

Powell, Stephanie. Hit Me with Music: How to Start, Manage, Record, & Perform with Your Own Rock Band. LC 95-1965. (Illus.). 144p. (YA). (gr. 7 up). 1995. lib. bdg. 22.40 (*1-56294-653-6*) Millbrook Pr.

***Powell, Stephen R.** Rushing the Growler: A History of Brewing & Drinking in Buffalo, 1795-1999. 2nd ed. (Illus.). 185p. 1999. pap. 21.95 (*0-9677119-0-8*) Apogee Prod.

***Powell, Steven M., ed.** Colorectal Cancer: Methods & Protocols. (Methods in Molecular Medicine Ser.: Vol. 50). (Illus.). 270p. 2000. 109.50 (*0-89603-767-3*) Humana.

Powell, Stuart. Returning to Study: A Guide for Professionals. LC 98-50319. 128p. 1998. pap. 23.95 (*0-335-20131-8*) OpUniv Pr.

— Returning to Study: A Guide for Professionals. LC 98-50319. 128p. 1998. 85.00 (*0-335-20132-6*) Taylor & Francis.

Powell, Stuart & Jordan, Rita, eds. Autism & Learning: A Guide to Good Practice. 144p. 1997. pap. 27.95 (*1-85346-421-X*, Pub. by David Fulton) Taylor & Francis.

Powell, Stuart, jt. auth. see Joran, Rita.

Powell, Stuart, jt. auth. see Jordan, Rita.

Powell, Sumner C. Puritan Village: The Formation of a New England Town. LC 63-8862. (Illus.). 235p. 1970. pap. 17.95 (*0-8195-6014-6*, Wesleyan Univ Pr) U Pr of New Eng.

***Powell, Susan.** New Perspectives on Middle English Texts. 256p. 2000. 75.00 (*0-85991-590-5*) Boydell & Brewer.

Powell, Susan, jt. auth. see Inserra, Rose.

Powell, Susan, jt. auth. see Pickering, O. S.

Powell, Sutter. Executive Privileges. (Orig.). 1996. mass mkt. 5.95 (*1-56333-383-X*, Badboy) Masquerade.

Powell, Suzanne. The Pueblos. LC 93-18368. (First Bks.). (Illus.). 64p. (J). (gr. 4-6). 1993. lib. bdg. 22.00 (*0-531-20068-X*) Watts.

— The Pueblos. large type ed. (First Bks.). (Illus.). 64p. (J). (gr. 5-8). 1994. pap. 6.95 (*0-531-15703-2*) Watts.

Powell, Suzanne I. The Potawatomi. LC 96-52133. (First Bk.). (Illus.). 64p. (J). (gr. 4-6). 1997. lib. bdg. 22.00 (*0-531-20268-2*) Watts.

***Powell, Suzanne K.** Advanced Case Management: Outcomes & Beyond. LC 99-40665. 416p. 1999. pap. text. write for info. (*0-7817-2234-9*) Lppncott W & W.

— Case Management: A Practical Guide to Success in Managed Care. 2nd ed. LC 99-40666. 416p. 2000. pap. text. write for info. (*0-7817-1883-X*) Lppncott W & W.

Powell, Suzanne K. Nursing Case Management: A Practical Guide to Success in Managed Care. LC 95-32575. (Illus.). 416p. 1995. pap. text 38.00 (*0-397-55234-3*) Lppncott W & W.

Powell, Suzanne K. & Ignatavicius, Donna D. CMSA Core Curriculum for Case Management. 512p. pap. text 44.95 (*0-7817-2454-6*) Lppncott W & W.

Powell, T., jt. ed. see Nobel, D.

Powell, T. G. The Celts. LC 79-63879. (Ancient Peoples & Places Ser.). (Illus.). 1983. reprint ed. pap. 16.95 (*0-500-27275-1*, Pub. by Thames Hudson) Norton.

Powell, Tag. Slash Your Mortgage in Half. Powell, Judith L. & Fawcett, Yvonne, eds. LC 91-2643. (Illus.). 96p. 1991. pap. 10.00 (*0-914295-91-8*) Top Mtn Pub.

***Powell, Tag.** Think Wealth... Put Your Money Where Your Mind Is! 160p. 2000. pap. text 12.95 (*1-56087-148-2*) Top Mtn Pub.

Powell, Tag & Mills, Carol H. ESP for Kids: How to Develop You & Your Child's Psychic Ability. Powell, Judith L. & Fawcett, Yvonne, eds. LC 92-40253. (Illus.). 194p. 1993. pap. 12.95 (*0-914295-98-5*) Top Mtn Pub.

Powell, Tag & Powell, Judith. Silva Mind Mastery for the '90s: New Spanish Edition. (Illus.). 256p. pap. 17.95 (*1-56087-027-3*) Top Mtn Pub.

Powell, Tag, jt. auth. see Allen, James.

Powell, Tag, jt. auth. see Powell, Judith L.

Powell, Talmage. Six-Gun Ladies: Tales of the Range. LC 96-2825. 1996. pap. text 9.95 (*1-57090-029-9*) Alexander Dist.

Powell, Ted V. The So-Called Mystery of the Ages: The Pre-Historic Sphinx. (Illus.). 40p. 1999. pap. 8.00 (*0-8059-4688-8*) Dorrance.

Powell, Terry. Lord, Give Me Wisdom: Practical Principles from Proverbs. LC 98-83288. 160p. 1999. pap. 9.99 (*1-57921-210-7*, Pub. by WinePress Pub) BookWorld.

— You Can Lead a Bible Discussion Group. LC 96-34702. 180p. 1996. pap. 12.99 (*0-88070-884-0*, Multnomah Bks) Multnomah Pubs.

Powell, Terry, jt. auth. see Collins, Brian.

Powell, Terry, jt. auth. see Jones, Bill.

Powell, Theodore. The School Bus Law: A Case Study in Education, Religion & Politics. LC 60-13155. 1960. 31.95 (*0-89197-392-3*); pap. text 9.95 (*0-8290-2016-0*) Irvington.

Powell, Thomas. The Attorneys Academy, or the Manner of Proceeding upon Any Suite. LC 74-80209. (English Experience Ser.: No. 684). 1974. reprint ed. 30.00 (*90-221-0684-5*) Walter J Johnson.

— Direction for Search of Records. LC 74-80208. (English Experience Ser.: No. 685). 1974. reprint ed. 20.00 (*90-221-0685-3*) Walter J Johnson.

— HTML: The Complete Reference. 2nd ed. (Illus.). 1108p. (Orig.). 1999. pap. text 39.99 (*0-07-882397-8*, Oracle Press) Osborne-McGraw.

— The Persistence of Racism in America. 344p. (Orig.). (C). 1993. pap. text 23.95 (*0-8191-8588-4*); lib. bdg. 57.50 (*0-8191-8587-6*) U Pr of Amer.

***Powell, Thomas.** Web Design: The Complete Reference. (Illus.). 756p. 2000. pap. 39.99 (*0-07-212297-8*) Osborne-McGraw.

Powell, Thomas A. Cascading Style Sheets Programmer's Reference. (Programmer's Reference Ser.). 1998. pap. text 16.99 (*0-07-882571-7*) Osborne-McGraw.

— HTML: The Complete Reference. 2nd ed. LC 99-217320. 1130p. 1999. pap. text 39.99 (*0-07-211977-2*) Osborne-McGraw.

— Web Site Engineering: Beyond Web Page Design. LC 98-156460. 288p. (C). 1998. pap. text 39.95 (*0-13-650920-7*) P-H.

Powell, Thomas A. & Whitworth, Dan. HTML Programmer's Reference. 396p. 1998. pap. text 16.99 (*0-07-882559-8*) Osborne-McGraw.

Powell, Thomas G. Mexico & the Spanish Civil War. LC 80-52280. 224p. reprint ed. pap. 69.50 (*0-608-15407-5*, 202931700060) Bks Demand.

Powell, Thomas J. Self-Help Organizations & Professional Practice. LC 86-21761. 367p. 1987. 23.95 (*0-87101-133-6*) Natl Assn Soc Wkrs.

Powell, Thomas J., ed. Understanding the Self-Help Organization: Frameworks & Findings. 345p. 1994. 55.00 (*0-8039-5487-5*); pap. 26.00 (*0-8039-5488-3*) Sage.

— Working with Self-Help. LC 89-14031. 355p. 1990. 28.95 (*0-87101-174-3*) Natl Assn Soc Wkrs.

Powell, Thomas M. Ecological Time Series. 1994. pap. 51.95 (*0-412-05201-6*, Chap & Hall NY) Chapman & Hall.

Powell, Thomas R. The Logic & Rhetoric of Constitutional Law. (Reprint Series in Social Sciences). (C). 1993. reprint ed. pap. text 5.00 (*0-8290-3097-2*, PS-230) Irvington.

— Vagaries & Varieties in Constitutional Interpretation. LC 74-181973. reprint ed. 29.50 (*0-404-05118-9*) AMS Pr.

***Powell, Timothy B.** Ruthless Democracy: A Multicultural Interpretation of the American Renaissance. LC 99-53218. 224p. 2000. 47.50 (*0-691-00729-2*, Pub. by Princeton U Pr); pap. text 15.95 (*0-691-00730-6*, Pub. by Princeton U Pr) Cal Prin Full Svc.

Powell, Timothy B., ed. Beyond the Binary: Reconstructing Cultural Identity in a Multicultural Context. LC 98-30475. 320p. (C). 1999. text 52.00 (*0-8135-2621-3*); pap. text 22.00 (*0-8135-2622-1*) Rutgers U Pr.

Powell, Timothy M. You've Gotta Hand It to God! LC 84-73557. (Radiant Life Ser.). 125p. 1985. pap. 3.95 (*0-88243-859-X*, 02-0859); pap., teacher ed. 5.50 (*0-88243-199-4*, 32-0199) Gospel Pub.

Powell, Tina. Coucou! C'est Moui le Nouveau Bebe. (FRE., Illus.). 32p. (J). (ps-2). 1997. pap. 6.95 (*0-9697079-4-0*) Genl Dist Srvs.

— Hi! I Am the New Baby. (Illus.). 32p. (J). (ps-2). 1997. pap. 6.95 (*0-9697079-3-2*) Moulin Publ.

Powell, Tony, et al, eds. The International Simulation & Gaming Yearbook Vol. 6: Simulations & Games for Emergency & Crisis Management. 288p. 1998. 65.00 (*0-7494-2610-1*, Kogan Pg Educ) Stylus Pub VA.

***Powell, Trevor J.** Stress Free Living. LC 99-54223. (Living Ser.). 144p. 2000. pap. text 13.95 (*0-7894-5119-0*, D K Ink) DK Pub Inc.

Powell, Trevor J. & Enright, Simon J. Anxiety & Stress Management. LC 89-24320. (Strategies for Mental Health Ser.). (Illus.). 208p. reprint ed. pap. 64.50 (*0-608-20374-2*, 207162700002) Bks Demand.

Powell, Victor. Improving Public Enterprise Performance: Concepts & Techniques. (Management Development Ser.: No. 22). v, 226p. (Orig.). 1991. pap. 27.00 (*92-2-105563-9*) Intl Labour Office.

Powell, Victor K. Immigration--Behaviors, Barriers, Crises, Health & Life Status: Index of New Information. 160p. 1997. 47.50 (*0-7883-1664-8*); pap. 44.50 (*0-7883-1665-6*) ABBE Pubs Assn.

Powell, Victoria A., tr. see Dandamaev, Muhammad A.

Powell, Virginia. Sugar Robin. LC 98-35733. (Illus.). (J). 1998. pap. write for info. (*1-56763-305-6*) Ozark Pub.

— Sugar Robin. LC 98-35733. (Illus.). (J). 1998. write for info. (*1-56763-304-8*) Ozark Pub.

Powell, W. H. And God Said, "Let There Be Light" 84p. (Orig.). 1994. pap. 9.95 (*0-9643370-0-2*) W H R Powell.

Powell, W. J., jt. auth. see Fynn, G. W.

Powell, W. R., ed. A History of the County of Essex, Vol. 7. (Victoria History of the Counties of England Ser.). (Illus.). 1979. 99.00 (*0-19-722720-1*) OUP.

Powell, W. R., jt. auth. see Berl, W. G.

Powell, Walter L. New London Raid. (Illus.). (C). Date not set. pap. write for info. (*1-57747-059-1*) Thomas Publications.

Powell, Walter L., intro. To Gettysburg by Train: The Gettysburg & Harrisburg Railroad Co. (Illus.). 68p. (C). 1989. pap. text 4.95 (*0-939631-17-2*) Thomas Publications.

Powell, Walter L., ed. see Hamblen, Charles P.

Powell, Walter W. Getting into Print: The Decision-Making Process in Scholarly Publishing. LC 84-23962. (Illus.). xxxii, 296p. 1985. 23.95 (*0-226-67704-4*) U Ch Pr.

Powell, Walter W. Getting into Print: The Decision-Making Process in Scholarly Publishing. LC 84-23962. (Illus.). xxxii, 292p. 1988. pap. 21.00 (*0-226-67705-2*) U Ch Pr.

Powell, Walter W. Non-Profit Sector. LC 86-15984. 464p. (C). 1989. reprint ed. pap. 30.00 (*0-300-04497-6*) Yale U Pr.

— Organizations in a World Economy. 128p. Date not set. pap. 18.95 (*0-8039-9020-0*) Pine Forge.

Powell, Walter W. & Clemens, Elisabeth S. Private Action & the Public Good. LC 97-26367. 320p. 1998. 42.00 (*0-300-06449-7*) Yale U Pr.

Powell, Walter W. & DiMaggio, Paul, eds. The New Institutionalism in Organizational Analysis. LC 91-9999. (Illus.). 486p. 1991. pap. text 27.50 (*0-226-67709-5*) U Ch Pr.

— The New Institutionalism in Organizational Analysis. LC 91-9999. (Illus.). 528p. 1993. lib. bdg. 65.00 (*0-226-67708-7*) U Ch Pr.

Powell, Walter W., ed. see Abegglen, James C.

Powell, Walter W., ed. see Aron, Raymond.

Powell, Walter W., ed. see Bernard, Luther L.

Powell, Walter W., ed. see Chapin, Francis S.

Powell, Walter W., jt. ed. see Coser, Lewis A.

Powell, Walter W., ed. see DeGre, Gerard.

Powell, Walter W., ed. see Granick, David.

Powell, Walter W., ed. see Hughes, Everett C.

Powell, Walter W., ed. see Keller, Suzanne I.

Powell, Walter W., ed. see Lazarsfeld, Paul F. & Kendall, Patricia L.

Powell, Walter W., ed. see Levy-Bruhl, Lucien.

Powell, Walter W., ed. see Pareto, Vilfredo.

Powell, Walter W., ed. see Powdermaker, Hortense.

Powell, Walter W., ed. see President's Research Committee on Social Trends.

Powell, Walter W., ed. see Rainwater, Lee, et al.

Powell, Walter W., ed. see Riesman, David & Glazer, Nathan.

Powell, Walter W., ed. see Rogoff, Natalie.

Powell, Walter W., ed. see Rosenberg, Bernard & Fliegel, Norris.

Powell, Walter W., ed. see Roth, Guenther.

Powell, Walter W., ed. see Selznick, Philip.

Powell, Walter W., ed. see Simmel, Georg.

Powell, Walter W., ed. see Sorokin, Pitirim A.

Powell, Walter W., ed. see Sumner, William G.

Powell, Walter W., ed. see Svalastoga, Kaare.

Powell, Walter W., ed. see Tiryakian, Edward A.

Powell, Walter W., ed. see United States Office of Education Staff, et al.

Powell, Walter W., ed. see Walker, Charles R. & Guest, Robert H.

Powell, Walter W., ed. see Warner, W. Lloyd & Abegglen, James C.

Powell, Walter W., ed. see Wood, Robert C.

Powell, Wanda, ed. Recipes from Hope, Arkansas: Birthplace of Bill Clinton. 178p. 1992. pap. text 12.95 (*0-9636174-0-0*) Legacy Pubs.

Powell, Warren H., jt. auth. see Fox, Robert B.

Powell, Wayne B., ed. see Tsinakis.

Powell, Weldon, jt. auth. see Wildman, John R.

Powell, Wilf, ed. Arthropod Natural Enemies in Arable Land No. III: The Individual, the Population & the Community, No. III. (ACTA Jutlandica 72.2; Natural Science Ser.: No. 11). (Illus.). 326p. 1998. pap. 27.00 (*87-7288-673-0*, Pub. by Aarhus Univ Pr) David Brown.

Powell, William. Color Mixing Recipe Cards. (Illus.). 48p. 1994. pap. 7.95 (*1-56010-382-5*, CRC1) W Foster Pub.

— How to Draw Trees. (How to Draw & Paint Ser.). (Illus.). 32p. pap. 6.95 (*1-56010-345-0*, HT 259) W Foster Pub.

Powell, William, tr. see Tarkovsky, Andrei.

Powell, William F. The Anarchist Cookbook. LC 71-127797. (Illus.). 192p. 1990. reprint ed. pap. 25.00 (*0-9623032-0-8*) Barricade Bks.

— Clouds & Skyscapes. (How to Draw & Paint Ser.). (Illus.). 32p. (Orig.). 1989. pap. 6.95 (*0-929261-48-8*, HT206) W Foster Pub.

— Color & How to Use It. (Artist's Library). (Illus.). 64p. (Orig.). 1989. pap. 7.95 (*0-929261-05-4*, AL05) W Foster Pub.

— Evaluative Criteria for a Middle School. Romano, Louis G., ed. 91p. 1988. pap. text 6.50 (*0-918449-10-3*) MI Middle Educ.

— The First Casualty. 1979. 10.00 (*0-8184-0291-1*) Carol Pub Group.

— Knife Painting. (Artist's Library). (Illus.). 64p. (Orig.). 1995. pap. 7.95 (*1-56010-126-1*, AL23) W Foster Pub.

— Oil Painting Kit. (Illus.). 32p. 1997. pap. text 19.95 (*1-56010-196-2*, K06) W Foster Pub.

— Oil Painting Materials & Their Uses. (Artist's Library). (Illus.). 64p. (Orig.). 1990. pap. 7.95 (*1-56010-056-7*, AL17) W Foster Pub.

— Perspective. (Artist's Library). (Illus.). 64p. (Orig.). 1989. pap. 7.95 (*0-929261-13-5*, AL13) W Foster Pub.

— The Record of Tung-shan. LC 86-4305. (Classics in East Asian Buddhism Ser.). 112p. 1986. pap. text 9.00 (*0-8248-1070-8*) UH Pr.

— Saudi Arabia & Its Royal Family. 384p. 1982. 14.95 (*0-8184-0326-8*) Carol Pub Group.

— Understanding Color. rev. ed. (How to Draw & Paint Ser.). (Illus.). 32p. (Orig.). 1993. pap. 6.95 (*1-56010-167-9*, HT154) W Foster Pub.

— Watercolor & Acrylic Painting Materials & Their Uses. (Artist's Library). (Illus.). 64p. (Orig.). 1990. pap. 7.95 (*1-56010-060-5*, AL18) W Foster Pub.

Powell, William F., tr. see Taylor, Richard, ed.

Powell, William J. Black Aviator: The Story of William J. Powell. LC 93-50772. (History of Aviation Ser.). (Illus.). 224p. 1994. reprint ed. pap. 17.95 (*1-56098-341-8*) Smithsonian.

Powell, William S. Annals of Progress: The Story of Lenoir County & Kinston, North Carolina. (Illus.). x, 107p. 1963. pap. 6.00 (*0-86526-124-5*) NC Archives.

— Dictionary of North Carolina Biography Vol. 6: T-Z, 6. LC 79-10106. 336p. 1996. text 60.00 (*0-8078-2225-6*) U of NC Pr.

— Higher Education in North Carolina. rev. ed. (Illus.). viii, 84p. 1970. pap. 3.00 (*0-86526-080-X*) NC Archives.

— John Pory, 1572-1636 Vol. 1, Text: The Life & Letters of a Man of Many Parts; Letters & Other Minor Writings. LC 75-45074. (Illus.). 205p. 1977. reprint ed. pap. 63.60 (*0-7837-9022-8*, 204977400001) Bks Demand.

— John Pory, 1572-1636 Vol. 2, Supplement: The Life & Letters of a Man of Many Parts; Letters & Other Minor Writings. LC 75-45074. (Illus.). 399p. 1977. reprint ed. pap. 123.70 (*0-7837-9023-6*, 204977400002) Bks Demand.

— North Carolina: A History. LC 88-40142. xvi, 232p. 1988. reprint ed. pap. 11.95 (*0-8078-4219-2*) U of NC Pr.

— The North Carolina Gazetteer. LC 68-25916. xviii, 561p. 1985. pap. 18.95 (*0-8078-1247-1*) U of NC Pr.

— North Carolina Through Four Centuries. LC 88-7691. (Illus.). xviii, 652p. (C). 1989. 37.50 (*0-8078-1846-1*); text 29.95 (*0-8078-1850-X*) U of NC Pr.

— Proprietors of Carolina. (Illus.). vi, 70p. 1968. reprint ed. pap. 4.00 (*0-86526-101-6*) NC Archives.

— The War of the Regulation & the Battle of Alamance, May 16, 1771. (Illus.). 32p. 1976. reprint ed. pap. 4.00 (*0-86526-102-4*) NC Archives.

Powell, William S., ed. Dictionary of North Carolina Biography, Vol. 2, D-G. LC 79-10106. vii, 389p. 1986. 60.00 (*0-8078-1656-6*) U of NC Pr.

— Dictionary of North Carolina Biography, Vol. 3, H-K. LC 79-10106. vii, 384p. (C). 1988. 60.00 (*0-8078-1806-2*) U of NC Pr.

— Dictionary of North Carolina Biography, Vol. 5, P-S. LC 79-10106. 530p. (C). 1994. 60.00 (*0-8078-2100-4*) U of NC Pr.

— Dictionary of North Carolina Biography Vol. 1: A-C, Vol. 1, A-C. LC 79-10106. ix, 477p. 1979. 60.00 (*0-8078-1329-X*) U of NC Pr.

— Dictionary of North Carolina Biography Vol. 4: L-O, Vol. 4, L-O. LC 79-10106. viii, 416p. (C). 1991. 60.00 (*0-8078-1918-2*) U of NC Pr.

Powell, Yolanda W., jt. auth. see Cillie, LaCheryl B.

Powellson, Jack. Holistic Economics & Social Protest. LC 83-62745. (C). 1983. pap. 4.00 (*0-87574-252-1*) Pendle Hill.

Powelson, David R. & Powelson, Melinda A. The Recycler's Manual for Business, Government, & Environmentalists. LC 92-10099. 1992. text 78.95 (*0-442-01190-3*, VNR) Wiley.

Powelson, David R. & Powelson, Melinda A. The Recycler's Manual for Business, Government, & the Environmental Community. 512p. 1992. 110.00 (*0-471-28499-8*, VNR) Wiley.

Powelson, John P. Centuries of Economic Endeavor: Parallel Paths in Japan & Europe, & their Contrast with the Third World. LC 94-17693. 496p. 1994. text 60.00 (*0-472-10547-7*, 10547) U of Mich Pr.

— Centuries of Economic Endeavor: Parallel Paths in Japan & Europe & Their Contrast with the Third World. 496p. (C). 1997. pap. text 23.95 (*0-472-08426-7*, 08426) U of Mich Pr.

— Economic Accounting. LC 70-100172. 500p. 1970. reprint ed. lib. bdg. 65.00 (*0-8371-3998-8*, POEA, Greenwood Pr) Greenwood.

Powelson, John P. The Moral Economy. (Illus.). 296p. (C). pap. text 21.95 (*0-472-08672-3*, 08672) U of Mich Pr.

Powelson, John P. The Moral Economy. LC 98-8146. 296p. 1998. text 32.50 (*0-472-10925-1*, 10925) U of Mich Pr.

— A Select Bibliography on Economic Development: With Annotations. (Special Studies in Social, Political, & Economic Development). 1979. text 51.50 (*0-89158-497-8*) Westview.

— The Story of Land: A World History of Land Tenure & Agrarian Reform. LC 87-11247. 347p. (C). 1988. text 30.00 (*0-89946-218-9*) Lincoln Inst Land.

Powelson, John P. & Stock, Richard. The Peasant Betrayed: Agriculture & Land Reform in the Third World. LC 86-21770. (Lincoln Institute of Land Policy Bk.). 322p. reprint ed. pap. 99.90 (*0-7837-5769-7*, 204543400006) Bks Demand.

— The Peasant Betrayed: Agriculture & Land Reform in the Third World. rev. ed. 400p. 1990. reprint ed. pap. 20.00 (*0-932790-74-7*) Cato Inst.

P

An Asterisk (*) at the beginning of an entry indicates that the title is appearing for the first time.

***Powelson, John P., et al.** Seeking Truth Together: Enabling the Poor & Saving the Planet in the Manner of Friends. vi, 122p. 2000. pap. 12.00 (*0-9618242-2-0*) Horizon Soc Pubns.

Powelson, Mark, jt. ed. see Borg, Marcus.

Powelson, Melinda A., jt. auth. see Powelson, David R.

Powelstock, David, tr. see Pekarkova, Iva.

Power. Estates on the Edge: The Social Consequences of Mass Housing in Northern Europe. LC 97-5324. 456p. 1997. text 69.95 (*0-312-17486-1*) St Martin.

— Health & Class: The Early Years. 224p. 1991. 97.50 (*1-56593-004-5*, 0245) Thomson Learn.

— Host of Riches. 1993. per. 2.99 (*0-373-17164-1*) Harlequin Bks.

— Native American Anthology. 1997. 15.95 (*0-8050-5092-2*) H Holt & Co.

— Questions in Irish History: Why Remeber the Boyne? 1992. pap. text. write for info. (*0-582-07320-0*, Pub. by Addison-Wesley) Longman.

Power & Sheard. Body & City. 86.95 (*1-84014-675-3*) Ashgate Pub Co.

Power, et al. Frontiers in Question: Eurasian Borderlands, 700-1700. LC 98-6882. 320p. 1999. text 59.95 (*0-312-21638-6*) St Martin.

Power, jt. auth. see Palim.

Power, Anne. Hovels to Highrise: State Housing in Europe Since 1850. LC 92-35541. (Illus.). 400p. (C). (gr. 13). 1993. 80.00 (*0-415-08935-2*, B0149) Routledge.

— Hovels to Highrise: State Housing in Europe Since 1850. LC 92-35541. 400p. 1993. pap. write for info. (*0-415-08936-0*) Routledge.

Power, Arthur. Conversations with James Joyce. Hart, Clive, ed. LC 82-1839. (Phoenix Fiction Ser.). 112p. (C). 1982. pap. 4.95 (*0-226-67720-6*) U Ch Pr.

***Power, Arthur.** Conversations with James Joyce. 128p. 2000. reprint ed. pap. 17.95 (*1-901866-41-6*, Pub. by Lilliput Pr) Irish Bks Media.

Power, Barbara. I Wish Laura's Mommy Was My Mommy. LC 79-2406. (Harper I-Like-to-Read-Bks.). (Illus.). (J). (ps-2). 1979. 11.95 (*0-397-31838-3*, Lippnctt); lib. bdg. 11.89 (*0-397-31859-6*, Lippnctt) Lppncott W & W.

***Power, Brenda & Chandler, Kelly.** Well-Chosen Words: Narrative Assessments & Report Card Comments. LC 97-45939. (Illus.). vii, 112p. 1998. pap. 12.50 (*1-57110-080-6*) Stenhse Pubs.

Power, Brenda M. Long Roads, Short Distances: Teaching Writing & Writing Teachers. LC 97-14455. 1997. pap. text 17.50 (*0-435-07240-4*) Heinemann.

— Taking Note: Improving Your Observational Notetaking. 104p. (Orig.). (C). 1996. pap. text 12.50 (*1-57110-035-0*) Stenhse Pubs.

Power, Brenda M., et al, eds. Reading Stephen King: Issues of Censorship, Student Choice, & Popular Literature. LC 97-34367. (Illus.). 247p. (YA). (gr. 8-12). 1997. pap. 19.95 (*0-8141-3905-1*) NCTE.

Power, Brenda M. & Hubbard, Ruth, eds. Literacy in Process: The Heinemann Reader. LC 90-37651. 352p. (C). 1990. pap. text 29.50 (*0-435-08532-8*, 08532); pap. text, teacher ed. 5.50 (*0-435-08533-6*, 08533) Heinemann.

Power, Brenda M. & Hubbard, Ruth S., eds. Language Development: A Reader for Teachers. LC 95-32102. 294p. (C). 1996. pap. text 34.00 (*0-13-191032-9*) P-H.

— Oops: What We Learn When Our Teaching Fails. LC 95-46907. (Illus.). 200p. (C). 1996. pap. text 17.00 (*1-57110-027-X*) Stenhse Pubs.

Power, Brenda M., jt. auth. see Hubbard, Ruth S.

Power, Christine, jt. ed. see Pigott, Rod.

Power, Clark F., et al. Lawrence Kohlberg's Approach to Moral Education. 1991. pap. text 22.50 (*0-231-05977-9*) Col U Pr.

Power, Crawford. The Encounter. LC 83-42918. 320p. 1983. 22.50 (*0-87951-199-0*, Pub. by Overlook Pr); pap. 12.95 (*0-87951-191-5*, Pub. by Overlook Pr) Penguin Putnam.

Power, D. M. Current Ornithology, Vol. 6. LC 84-640616. (Illus.). 344p. (C). 1989. 95.00 (*0-306-43056-8*, Plenum Trade) Perseus Pubng.

Power, D. M. Current Ornithology, Vol. 7. LC 84-640616. (Illus.). 402p. (C). 1990. 95.00 (*0-306-43307-9*, Plenum Trade) Perseus Pubng.

— Current Ornithology, Vol. 8. LC 84-640616. (Illus.). 350p. (C). 1990. 95.00 (*0-306-43640-X*, Plenum Trade) Perseus Pubng.

Power, D. M. Current Ornithology, Vol. 9. (Illus.). 264p. (C). 1991. 95.00 (*0-306-43990-5*, Plenum Trade) Perseus Pubng.

Power, D. M. Current Ornithology, Vol. 10. (Illus.). 398p. (C). 1992. 95.00 (*0-306-44282-5*, Plenum Trade) Perseus Pubng.

— Current Ornithology, Vol. 11. (Illus.). 306p. (C). 1993. 95.00 (*0-306-44550-6*, Plenum Trade) Perseus Pubng.

Power, Dale. Carving Miniature Carousel Animals with Dale Power. LC 97-66119. (Schiffer Book for Woodcarvers Ser.). (Illus.). 64p. 1997. pap. 14.95 (*0-7643-0312-0*) Schiffer.

— Do-It-Yourself Coffins: For Pets & People. LC 97-67262. (Illus.). 64p. 1997. pap. 14.95 (*0-7643-0337-6*) Schiffer.

— Finishes for Wood. LC 97-80051. (Schiffer Book for Woodworkers Ser.). (Illus.). 64p. 1997. pap. 14.95 (*0-7643-0338-4*) Schiffer.

— Making Wooden Boxes with Dale Power. LC 99-60109. (Illus.). 64p. 1999. pap. 14.95 (*0-7643-0848-3*) Schiffer.

— Scupting in Clay with Dale Power. LC 97-80127. 64p. 1998. pap. 14.95 (*0-7643-0113-6*) Schiffer.

Power, Dale E. Do-It-yourself Tombstones & Other Markers. LC 98-88427. (Illus.). 64p. (Orig.). 1999. pap. 14.95 (*0-7643-0745-2*) Schiffer.

Power, Dale L. Bears to Carve with Dale Power: With Dale Power. LC 94-23248. (Illus.). 64p. (Orig.). 1995. pap. 12.95 (*0-88740-719-6*) Schiffer.

— Carving Dolphins & Whales. LC 94-65851. (Illus.). 64p. (Orig.). 1994. pap. text 12.95 (*0-88740-620-3*) Schiffer.

— Carving Realistic Faces with Power. LC 93-85232. (Illus.). 64p. (Orig.). 1993. pap. 12.95 (*0-88740-486-3*) Schiffer.

Power, Dale L. & Power, Margo. Wildlife Carving with Dale Power, Vol. 1. (Illus.). 54p. (Orig.). 1940. pap. 14.95 (*1-886199-00-0*) Madison Pubng.

— Wildlife Carving with Dale Power, Vol. 2. (Illus.). 74p. (Orig.). 1994. pap. 14.95 (*1-886199-01-9*) Madison Pubng.

Power, Dale L. & Snyder, Jeffrey B. Carving the Cheetah. LC 94-66199. (Illus.). 64p. (Orig.). 1994. pap. 12.95 (*0-88740-696-3*) Schiffer.

Power, Dale L., jt. auth. see Snyder, Jeffrey B.

Power, D'Arcy. Medicine in the British Isles. LC 75-23651. (Clio Medica Ser.: No. 2). reprint ed. 32.50 (*0-404-58902-2*) AMS Pr.

— Selected Writings, 1877 to 1930. LC 78-95632. (Illus.). x, 368p. 1970. reprint ed. 45.00 (*0-678-03750-7*) Kelley.

— A Short History of Surgery. LC 75-23751. reprint ed. 32.50 (*0-404-13357-6*) AMS Pr.

Power, D'Arcy, ed. British Masters of Medicine. LC 79-99721. (Essay Index Reprint Ser.). 1977. 26.95 (*0-8369-1375-2*) Ayer.

— John Arderne: Treatises of Fistula in Ano. (EETS Original Ser.: Vol. 139). 1969. reprint ed. 30.00 (*0-19-722139-4*, Pub. by EETS) Boydell & Brewer.

— John Arderne's Treatises of Fistula in Ano, Etc. (EETS, OS Ser.: Vol. 139). 1969. reprint ed. 30.00 (*0-8115-3370-0*) Periodicals Srv.

Power, David. Gifts That Differ: Lay Ministries Established & Unestablished. 205p. 1992. pap. 12.95 (*0-8146-6043-6*, Pueblo Bks) Liturgical Pr.

Power, David & Collins, Mary, eds. The Times of Celebration. (Concilium Ser.: Vol. 142). 128p. (Orig.). 1981. 6.95 (*0-8164-2309-1*) Harper SF.

Power, David, jt. ed. see Collins, Mary.

Power, David, jt. ed. see Maldonado, Luis.

Power, David N. Culture & Theology. (Worship Ser.). 284p. (C). 1991. pap. 14.95 (*0-912405-77-5*, Pastoral Press) OR Catholic.

— The Eucharistic Mystery: Revitalizing the Tradition. 384p. 1994. reprint ed. pap. 29.95 (*0-8245-1426-2*) Crossroad NY.

— Sacrament The Language of God's Giving. LC 98-52209. 384p. 1999. 49.95 (*0-8245-1809-8*) Crossroad NY.

***Power, David N.** Sacrament: The Language of God's Giving. LC 98-52209. 1999. pap. text 24.95 (*0-8245-1798-9*) Crossroad NY.

Power, David N. The Sacrifice We Offer. 1997. 43.95 (*0-567-09445-6*, Pub. by T & T Clark) Bks Intl VA.

Power, David N., jt. ed. see Lumbala, Kabasele.

Power-deFur, Lissa A. & Orelove, Fred P. Inclusive Education: Practical Implementation of the Least Restrictive Environment. LC 96-31327. 1996. 69.00 (*0-8342-0806-7*, 08067) Aspen Pub.

Power, Dennis M., ed. Current Ornithology, Vol. 12. LC 84-640616. (Illus.). 294p. (C). 1995. 95.00 (*0-306-44978-1*, Plenum Trade) Perseus Pubng.

***Power, Derek.** Tangye: A Biography. (Illus.). 210p. 2000. 27.50 (*1-85776-478-1*, Pub. by Book Guild Ltd) Trans-Atl Phila.

Power, Dermot. A Spiritual Theology of the Priesthood: The Mystery of Christ & the Mission of the Priest. 178p. 1998. pap. text 19.95 (*0-8132-0916-1*) Cath U Pr.

Power, E. G. Modern Ireland. LC 87-3521. (Modern Times Ser.). 1988. write for info. (*0-582-22165-X*) Longman.

Power, Edward J. Educational Philosophy: A History from the Ancient World to Modern America. LC 95-24265. (Studies in the History of Education: Vol. 3). 256p. 1995. text 51.00 (*0-8153-1971-1*, SS1017) Garland.

— A Legacy of Learning: A History of Western Education. LC 90-37218. (SUNY Series, the Philosophy of Education). 400p. (C). 1991. text 64.50 (*0-7914-0610-5*); pap. text 21.95 (*0-7914-0611-3*) State U NY Pr.

— The Religion & the Public Schools in 19th Century America: Contribution of Orestes A. Brownson. LC 95-31263. 192p. (Orig.). 1996. pap. 13.95 (*0-8091-3612-0*) Paulist Pr.

Power, Effie. Bag O'Tales: A Sourcebook for Story-Tellers. LC 89-62654. 340p. 1990. reprint ed. lib. bdg. 44.00 (*1-55888-834-9*) Omnigraphics Inc.

Power, Eileen. Medieval English Nunneries. 1988. pap. 25.00 (*0-8196-0140-3*) Biblo.

— Medieval People. 1993. 24.75 (*0-8446-6685-8*) Peter Smith.

— Medieval Women. Postan, M. M., ed. (Canto Book Ser.). (Illus.). 132p. (C). 1997. pap. 10.95 (*0-521-59556-8*) Cambridge U Pr.

Power, Eileen E. The Goodman of Paris.Tr. of Le Menagier de Paris. 1977. 25.95 (*0-8369-6986-3*, 7863) Ayer.

— Medieval People. LC 91-58523. 240p. 1992. reprint ed. pap. 12.50 (*0-06-092275-3*, Perennial) HarperTrade.

— The Wool Trade in English Medieval History. LC 86-29442. 128p. 1987. reprint ed. lib. bdg. 59.50 (*0-313-25656-X*, POWT, Greenwood Pr) Greenwood.

Power, Eileen E., tr. see Boissonnade, Prosper.

***Power, Eileen Edna.** Medieval People. LC 00-29514. 2000. pap. 8.95 (*0-486-41435-3*) Dover.

Power, Eileen L. Lasher Lineage: With Supplement. 545p. 1994. reprint ed. lib. bdg. 75.00 (*1-56012-131-9*, 129) Kinship Rhinebeck.

***Power, Elizabeth.** Un Aveu Impossible. (Azur Ser.: No. 797). (FRE.). 1999. mass mkt. 3.99 (*0-373-34797-9*, 1-34797-0, Harlequin French) Harlequin Bks.

Power, Elizabeth. Cadena de Errores - Host of Riches. (Harlequin Bianca - Harlequin Presents Ser.: Vol. 361).Tr. of Host of Riches. (ENG & SPA.). 1996. per. 3.50 (*0-373-33361-7*) Harlequin Bks.

— Dulce Posesion - Sweet Possession. (SPA.). 1997. per. 3.50 (*0-373-33426-5*, 1-33426-7) Harlequin Bks.

— If Change Is All There Is, Choice Is All You've Got: A Collection of Personal Vignettes about Change & Choice. 86p. 1993. reprint ed. pap. 12.95 (*1-883307-00-7*) EPower & Assocs.

— Managing Our Selves: Building a Community of Caring. 115p. 1992. student ed. 17.95 (*1-883307-01-5*) EPower & Assocs.

— Managing Our Selves: God in Our Midst. 63p. 1993. reprint ed. student ed. 12.95 (*1-883307-02-3*) EPower & Assocs.

— Marrying the Enemy! (Presents Ser.: No. 100). 1999. mass mkt. 3.75 (*0-373-18700-9*, 1-18700-4) Harlequin Bks.

— Otages du Desir. 1998. mass mkt. 3.50 (*0-373-34718-9*, 1-34718-6) Harlequin Bks.

— Un Reve a l'Italienne. (Azur Ser.: Vol. 752). (FRE.). 1999. mass mkt. 3.50 (*0-373-34752-9*, 1-34752-5) Harlequin Bks.

— Seed of Vengeance. (Presents Ser.: No. 445). 1992. pap. 2.89 (*0-373-11445-1*, 1-11445-3) Harlequin Bks.

— Straw on the Wind. LC 96-264. 189p. 1995. per. 3.25 (*0-373-11768-X*, 1-11768-8) Harlequin Bks.

— Terms of Possession. (Presents Ser.). 1996. per. 3.50 (*0-373-11838-4*, 1-11838-9) Harlequin Bks.

— Le Vent de la Passion. (Azur Ser.). (FRE.). 1994. pap. 3.50 (*0-373-34434-1*, 1-34434-0) Harlequin Bks.

Power Engineering Society & Neural Networks Counci. 1996 International Conference on Intelligent Systems Applications to Power Systems Proceedings. Institute of Electrical & Electronics Engineers, I, ed. LC 95-81732. 500p. 1996. pap. 118.00 (*0-7803-3115-X*, 96TH8152) Inst Electrical.

Power, Eugene B. Edition of One: The Autobiography of Eugene B. Power, Founder of University Microfilms. LC 90-10808. 456p. 1990. pap. text 9.95 (*0-8357-0899-3*) UMI.

Power, F. Clark & Lapsley, Daniel K., eds. The Challenge of Pluralism: Education, Politics, & Values. LC 91-50571. (C). 1993. pap. text 19.50 (*0-268-00788-8*) U of Notre Dame Pr.

Power, F. Clark, jt. ed. see Lapsley, D. K.

***Power, Francis.** The Golden Book of Ireland. 2nd ed. (Illus.). 128p. 2000. pap. 12.95 (*0-86278-510-3*, Pub. by OBrien Pr) IPG Chicago.

Power, Garrett. Parceling Out Land in Baltimore, 1632-1796. (Illus.). 56p. (Orig.). 1993. pap. 6.00 (*0-938420-37-2*) MD Hist.

Power, Gene & Stratton, Shawn. Resistance Training for Fitness. (Illus.). 123p. 1997. pap. text 10.95 (*0-87563-754-X*) Stipes.

Power, Gordon & Parfect, Michael. Planning for Urban Quality: Urban Design in Towns & Cities. LC 96-41631. (Illus.). 264p. (C). 1997. 110.00 (*0-415-15967-9*); pap. 37.99 (*0-415-15968-7*) Routledge.

Power, Gregory. The Adventures of Huckleberry Finn Study Guide. 78p. (YA). (gr. 9-12). 1996. student ed., ring bd. 14.99 (*1-58609-165-4*) Progeny Pr WI.

— Johnny Tremain Study Guide. 66p. (YA). (gr. 6-8). 1993. student ed., ring bd. 12.99 (*1-58609-138-7*) Progeny Pr WI.

— The Red Badge of Courage. 54p. (YA). (gr. 9-12). 1994. student ed., ring bd. 14.99 (*1-58609-159-X*) Progeny Pr WI.

Power, H. Visualization & Intelligent Design in Engineering & Architecture. Connor, J. J. et al, eds. LC 92-75800. (VIDEA Ser.: Vol. 1). 672p. 1993. 295.00 (*1-56252-151-9*) Computational Mech MA.

Power, H., ed. Applications in Fluid Mechanics. (Advances in Fluid Mechanics Ser.: 4). 376p. 1995. 167.00 (*1-85312-288-2*) Computational Mech MA.

— Bio-Fluid Mechanics. LC 94-69712. (Advances in Fluid Mechanics Ser.: Vol. 3). 336p. 1995. 164.00 (*1-56252-210-8*, 2866) Computational Mech MA.

Power, H., ed. Bio-Fluid Mehcanics. 336p. 1995. 164.00 (*1-85312-286-6*) Computational Mech MA.

Power, H., et al, eds. Air Pollution VIII. (Advances in Air Pollution Ser.). 900p. 2000. 426.00 (*1-85312-822-8*, 8228, Pub. by WIT Pr) Computational Mech MA.

— Air Pollution V: Modelling, Monitoring & Management. LC 97-67018. 1056p. 1997. 395.00 (*1-85312-473-7*, 4737, Pub. by WIT Pr) Computational Mech MA.

Power, H., et al, eds. Air Pollution III, 3 vols. Incl. Air Pollution Theory & Simulation. LC 95-68890. 456p. 1995. 178.00 (*1-56252-351-1*, 4419); Air Pollution III: Air Pollution Theory & Simulation. 456p. 1995. 178.00 (*1-85312-441-9*, Pub. by WIT Pr); Vol. 2. Air Pollution Engineering & Management. LC 95-68890. 536p. 1995. 207.00 (*1-56252-352-X*, 4427); Vol. 2. Air Pollution III: Air Pollution Engineering & Management. 536p. 1995. 207.00 (*1-85312-442-7*, Pub. by WIT Pr); Vol. 3. Air Pollution III: Urban Pollution. 216p. 1995. 92.00 (*1-85312-443-5*, Pub. by WIT Pr); Vol. 3. Urban Pollution. LC 95-68890. 216p. 1995. 92.00 (*1-56252-353-8*, 4435); 1208p. 429.00 (*1-85312-311-0*, Pub. by WIT Pr) Computational Mech MA.

Power, H., et al, eds. Air Pollution III, 3 vols., Set. Incl. Air Pollution Theory & Simulation. LC 95-68890. 456p. 1995. 178.00 (*1-56252-351-1*, 4419); Air Pollution III: Air Pollution Theory & Simulation. 456p. 1995. 178.00 (*1-85312-441-9*, Pub. by WIT Pr); Vol. 2. Air Pollution Engineering & Management. LC 95-68890. 536p. 1995. 207.00 (*1-56252-352-X*, 4427); Vol. 2. Air Pollution III: Air Pollution Engineering & Management. 536p. 1995. 207.00 (*1-85312-442-7*, Pub. by WIT Pr); Vol. 3. Air Pollution III: Urban Pollution. 216p. 1995. 92.00 (*1-85312-443-5*, Pub. by WIT Pr); Vol. 3. Urban Pollution. LC 95-68890. 216p. 1995. 92.00 (*1-56252-353-8*, 4435); LC 95-68890. 1208p. 1995. 429.00 (*1-56252-235-3*, 3110) Computational Mech MA.

— Boundary Elements XVII. LC 95-68889. (BEM Ser.: Vol. 17). 696p. 1995. 288.00 (*1-56252-248-5*, 3242) Computational Mech MA.

— Simulations in Biomedicine IV. LC 97-66708. (BIOMED Ser.: Vol. 4). 392p. 1997. 199.00 (*1-85312-462-1*, 4621) Computational Mech MA.

— Urban Air Pollution. LC 94-68174. (Air Pollution Ser.: Vol. 1). 336p. 1994. text 161.00 (*1-56252-255-8*, 3315) Computational Mech MA.

Power, H., et al, eds. Urban Air Pollution, Vol. 1. (Air Pollution Ser.: Vol. 1). 336p. 1994. 161.00 (*1-85312-331-5*, Pub. by WIT Pr) Computational Mech MA.

Power, H. & Baldasano, J. M., eds. Air Pollution Emissions Inventory. LC 97-80273. (Advances in Air Pollution Ser.: Vol. 3). 256p. 1998. 117.00 (*1-85312-517-2*, 5172, Pub. by WIT Pr) Computational Mech MA.

Power, H. & Brebbia, C. A., eds. High-Performance Computing in Engineering: Applications to Partial Differential Equations. 336p. 1995. 117.00 (*1-85312-380-3*) Computational Mech MA.

— High-Performance Computing in Engineering: Introduction & Algorithms. 304p. 1995. 130.00 (*1-85312-379-X*) Computational Mech MA.

Power, H. & Casares Long, J. J., eds. Applications of High-Performance Computing in Engineering V. LC 97-67014. (Advances in High Performance Computing Ser.: Vol. 3). 352p. 1997. 159.00 (*1-85312-457-5*, 4575) Computational Mech MA.

Power, H. & Hart, R. T., eds. Computer Simulations in Biomedicine. 668p. 1995. 270.00 (*1-85312-321-8*) Computational Mech MA.

Power, H. & Hart, R. T., eds. Computer Simulations in Biomedicine. LC 95-67479. (BIOMED Ser.: Vol. 3). 668p. 1995. 270.00 (*1-56252-245-0*, 3218) Computational Mech MA.

Power, H. & Moussiopoulos, N., eds. Urban Air Pollution. LC 94-6817. (Air Pollution Ser.: Vol. 2). 272p. 1996. text 137.00 (*1-56252-296-5*, 3722) Computational Mech MA.

Power, H. & Moussiopoulos, N., eds. Urban Air Pollution, Vol. 2. (Air Pollution Ser.: Vol. 2). 272p. 1996. 137.00 (*1-85312-372-2*, Pub. by WIT Pr) Computational Mech MA.

Power, H. & Wrobel, L. C., eds. Boundary Integral Methods in Fluid Mechanics. LC 94-70411. (Computational Engineering Ser.). 344p. 1995. 118.00 (*1-56252-176-4*, 2521) Computational Mech MA.

Power, H., jt. ed. see Baldasano, J. M.

Power, H., jt. ed. see Brebbia, C. A.

Power, H., jt. ed. see Brebbia, Carlos A.

Power, H. W., jt. auth. see Litovich, E.

Power, Harry W. Foraging Behavior of Mountain Bluebirds with Emphasis on Sexual Foraging Differences. 72p. 1980. 10.00 (*0-943610-28-1*) Am Ornithologists.

Power, Helen L. Tropical Medicine in the Twentieth Century: A History of the Liverpool School of Tropical Medicine. LC 97-48878. (Illus.). 200p. 1998. 110.00 (*0-7103-0604-0*, Pub. by Kegan Paul Intl) Col U Pr.

Power, Helen W. Admissions Essay. rev. ed. LC 98-28185. 240p. 1998. pap. 12.95 (*0-8184-0600-3*, L Stuart) Carol Pub Group.

Power, Henry, et al, eds. Management of Air Pollution. (Advances in Air Pollution Ser.: Vol. 7). 300p. 2000. 145.00 (*1-85312-528-8*, 5288, Pub. by WIT Pr) Computational Mech MA.

Power, Henry, jt. ed. see Garcia-Martinez, Reinaldo.

Power, Henry, jt. ed. see Popov, Victor.

Power, Hugh. Battleship Texas. LC 92-7432. (Centennial Series of the Association of Former Students: No. 45). (Illus.). 166p. 1993. 32.95 (*0-89096-516-1*); pap. 15.95 (*0-89096-519-6*) Tex A&M Univ Pr.

— Carrier Lexington. LC 95-20213. (Centennial Series of the Association of Former Students: Vol. 61). (Illus.). 176p. 1996. pap. 14.95 (*0-89096-681-8*) Tex A&M Univ Pr.

— Carrier Lexington. LC 95-20213. (Centennial Series of the Association of Former Students: Vol. 61). (Illus.). 176p. (C). 1996. 34.95 (*0-89096-680-X*) Tex A&M Univ Pr.

Power, Ian, jt. auth. see Vickers, Michael D.

Power Instrumentation Symposium Staff. Instrumentation, Control, & Automation in the Power Industry Vol. 40, 1997: Proceedings of the Fortieth Instrumentation Symposium, 7th Annual ISA POWID-EPRI Controls & Instrumentation Conference, Presented at Hyatt Regency, Knoxville, TN, June 16-18, 1997. LC 63-25575. (Illus.). 366p. 1997. reprint ed. pap. 113.50 (*0-608-07994-4*, 20679590040) Bks Demand.

— Instrumentation, Controls, & Automation in the Power Industry: Proceedings of the 39th Power Instrumentation Symposium (6th Annual ISA POWID/EPRI Controls & Instrumentation Conference) June 1996. LC 63-25575. (Illus.). 244p. 1996. reprint ed. pap. 75.70 (*0-608-04248-X*, 206500400039) Bks Demand.

Power, J. F., jt. auth. see Prasad, Rajendra.

Power, J. Gerald & Byrd, Theresa. U. S.-Mexico Border Health: Issues for Regional & Migrant Populations. LC 98-8903. 278p. 1998. write for info. (*0-7619-0895-1*); pap. write for info. (*0-7619-0896-X*) Sage.

Power, J. M., jt. auth. see Low, N. P.

Power, J. Tracy. I Will Not Be Silent & I Will Be Heard: Martin Luther King, Jr., & the Southern Christian Leadership Conference. Brimelow, Judith M., ed. 28p. 1993. pap. 3.00 (*1-880067-16-1*) SC Dept of Arch & Hist.

— Lee's Miserables: Life in the Army of Northern Virginia from the Wilderness to Appomattox. LC 97-17724. (Civil War America Ser.). (Illus.). 488p. 1998. 34.95 (*0-8078-2392-9*) U of NC Pr.

Power, Jenny, jt. auth. see Oppenheim, Klara.

Power, Jo-Ann. Allure. 352p. 1999. per. 6.50 (*0-671-03408-1*, Sonnet Bks) PB.

P

An Asterisk (*) at the beginning of an entry indicates that the title is appearing for the first time.

— Angel of Midnight. 1995. mass mkt. 5.99 (*0-671-89705-5*) PB.

— Gifts. 1996. mass mkt. 5.99 (*0-671-52996-X*) PB.

— The Last Duchess of Wolff's Lair. 352p. 1993. mass mkt. 3.99 (*0-8217-4266-3*, Zebra Kensgtn) Kensgtn Pub Corp.

— The Mark of the Chadwicks. 288p. 1993. mass mkt. 3.99 (*0-8217-4072-5*, Zebra Kensgtn) Kensgtn Pub Corp.

— Never Again: A Darker Shade of Crimson. 306p. 1998. mass mkt. 6.50 (*0-671-00899-4*, Pocket Star Bks) PB.

— Never Before. 1998. per. 6.50 (*0-671-00898-6*) PB.

— Never Say Never. 390p. 1999. mass mkt. 6.50 (*0-671-02422-1*) S&S Trade.

— Nightingale's Song. 1997. per. 5.99 (*0-671-52997-8*, Pocket Books) PB.

— Rememberance. 400p. 1995. mass mkt. 4.99 (*0-8217-0101-0*, Zebra Kensgtn) Kensgtn Pub Corp.

— Treasures. 324p. 1996. mass mkt. 5.99 (*0-671-52995-1*, PB Trade Paper) PB.

— You & No Other. Tolley, Carolyn, ed. 352p. (Orig.). 1994. mass mkt. 5.50 (*0-671-89704-7*) PB.

Power, Jo-Ann, jt. auth. see Cummings, Barbara.

Power, John. History of Salvation. 200p. 1989. pap. 6.95 (*0-8189-0566-2*) Alba.

***Power, John.** Invincible, the Game of Shusaku. (Game Collections Ser.). 1998. pap. text 35.00 (*4-906574-01-7*) KISEIDO.

Power, John, jt. auth. see Chamberlain, Nancy.

Power, John, tr. see Oedo, Yusuke, ed.

Power, John C. History of the Early Settlers of Sangamon County, Illinois, Vol. I. (Illus.). 806p. 1998. pap. 51.50 (*0-7884-1018-0*, P582) Heritage Bk.

Power, John C. & Power, S. A. History of the Early Settlers of Sangamon County. (Illus.). 797p. 1997. reprint ed. lib. bdg. 79.50 (*0-8328-5795-5*) Higginson Bk Co.

Power, John H. Review of the Lectures of Wm. A. Smith DD, on the Philosophy & Practice of Slavery. 1977. 22.95 (*0-8369-9172-9*, 9046) Ayer.

Power, Jonathan & Holenstein, Anne-Marie. World of Hunger: A Strategy for Survival. 1977. 24.00 (*0-85117-097-8*) Transatl Arts.

Power, Joseph F. Francis de Sales: Finding God Wherever You Are. 3rd ed. 160p. (Orig.). 1993. pap. 9.95 (*1-56548-074-0*) New City.

Power, Julia. Shelley in America in the Nineteenth Century. LC 70-90370. 233p. (C). 1969. reprint ed. 50.00 (*0-87752-088-7*) Gordian.

— Shelley in America in the Nineteenth Century. LC 65-15892. (Studies in Shelley: No. 25). 1969. reprint ed. lib. bdg. 75.00 (*0-8383-0611-X*) M S G Haskell Hse.

Power, Karen E. Kajo. LC 97-90288. 123p. 1998. pap. 9.95 (*0-533-12359-3*) Vantage.

Power, Kenneth. Power Baking: A Contemporary American Baking Manual. LC 91-66742. 512p. (Orig.). 1991. pap. 149.95 (*1-880650-14-2*) YCart Pub.

Power, Kenneth, jt. auth. see Power, Lyndal.

Power, Kevin, ed. While Cuba Waits: Art from the Nineties. (ENG & SPA.). 1999. pap. text 20.00 (*1-889195-38-3*) Smart Art Pr.

Power, Kevin & Baselitz, Georg. Georg Baselitz: Hammergreen' (Illus.). 68p. 1992. 35.00 (*0-947564-39-X*, Pub. by A D'Offay Gallery) Dist Art Pubs.

Power, Kevin & Noriega, Chon. Manuel Ocampo: Heridas de la Lengua. (Illus.). 96p. 1997. pap. 30.00 (*1-889195-10-3*) Smart Art Pr.

Power, Kim. Veiled Desire: Augustine on Women. LC 96-85678. 240p. 1996. 27.50 (*0-8264-0934-2*) Continuum.

Power, Lisa. No Bath but Plenty of Bubbles: Oral History of the Gay Liberation Front 1970-73. LC 96-156570. (Lesbian & Gay Studies). 352p. 1997. 69.95 (*0-304-33195-3*); pap. 21.95 (*0-304-33205-4*) Continuum.

Power, Lyndal & Power, Kenneth. Baking Solutions: Helpful Hints for Home Baking. LC 92-64417. 320p. (Orig.). 1993. pap. 12.95 (*1-880650-12-6*) YCart Pub.

Power, M. Susan. Jacques-Maritain, (1882-1973), Christian Democrat: And the Quest for a New Commonwealth. LC 92-43733. 196p. 1993. text 79.95 (*0-7734-9219-4*) E Mellen.

— Jacques-Maritain (1882-1973) Christian Democrat & the Quest for a New Commonwealth. LC 97-38144. 196p. (C). 1997. pap. text 27.50 (*0-7618-0935-X*) U Pr of Amer.

Power, Margaret. The Egalitarians, Human & Chimpanzee: An Anthropological View of Social Organization. (Illus.). 310p. (C). 1991. text 57.95 (*0-521-40016-3*) Cambridge U Pr.

Power, Margo. Image of Conspiracy: A Mystery Adventure. LC 97-74502. 1997. pap. text 5.99 (*1-886199-02-7*) Madison Pubng.

Power, Margo, jt. auth. see Power, Dale L.

Power, Marjorie. Living with It. 60p. 1983. 5.95 (*0-931694-24-8*) Wampeter Pr.

Power, Marjory W., jt. auth. see Haviland, William A.

Power, Mark, photos by. The Shippng Forecast. (Illus.). 66p. 1996. 34.95 (*1-899823-02-6*, Pub. by Art Bks Intl) Partners Pubs Grp.

Power, Mark, jt. auth. see Veerasarn, Oi.

Power, Martin. David Sylvian: The Last Romantic. (Illus.). 208p. 1998. pap. 19.95 (*0-7119-6809-8*, OP48049) Omnibus NY.

— Manic Street Preachers: In Their Own Words. 95p. 1998. pap. text 15.95 (*0-7119-6906-X*, OP48068) Music Sales.

— Metallica Live! With Poster. rev. ed. 96p. 1998. pap. 12.95 (*0-7119-6785-7*, OP48039) Omnibus NY.

— Pearl Jam - Dark Corners: An Illustrated Biography. (Illus.). 95p. 1997. pap. 21.95 (*0-7119-6374-6*, OP47895) Omnibus NY.

Power, Mary J. In the Name of the Bee: The Significance of Emily Dickinson. LC 74-115690. (Illus.). 1970. reprint ed. 28.00 (*0-8196-0266-3*) Biblo.

— Poets at Prayer. LC 68-29239. (Essay Index Reprint Ser.). 1977. 20.95 (*0-8369-0797-3*) Ayer.

Power, Mary R. Social Awareness: Serving God in the World. (J). (ps-5). 1986. 16.25 (*1-881678-33-4*) CSEE.

Power, Michael. The Audit Society: Rituals of Verification. LC 96-50995. (Illus.). 200p. (C). 1997. text 39.95 (*0-19-828947-2*) OUP.

***Power, Michael.** The Audit Society: Rituals of Verification. LC 99-31580. 200p. 1999. pap. text 24.95 (*0-19-829603-7*) OUP.

Power, Michael. Religion in the Reich. LC 78-63706. (Studies in Fascism: Ideology & Practice). 1979. reprint ed. 41.50 (*0-404-16976-7*) AMS Pr.

Power, Michael, ed. Accounting & Science: Natural Inquiry & Commercial Reason. (Environmental Chemistry Ser.). 304p. (C). 1996. text 64.95 (*0-521-55325-3*); pap. text 21.95 (*0-521-55699-6*) Cambridge U Pr.

Power, Michael, jt. ed. see Freedman, Judith.

Power, Michael A., jt. auth. see Jacobs, George M.

Power, Michael J. & Brewin, Chris R. The Transformation of Meaning in Psychological Therapies: Integrating Theory & Practice. LC 96-48034. 1997. pap. text 38.95 (*0-471-97005-0*) Wiley.

Power, Michael J. & Champion, Lorna A., eds. Adult Psychological Problems: An Introduction. 224p. 1992. 85.00 (*0-7507-0037-8*, Falmer Pr); pap. 29.95 (*0-7507-0038-6*, Falmer Pr) Taylor & Francis.

Power, Michael J. & Dalgleish, Tim. Cognition & Emotion: From Order to Disorder. LC 97-202012. (Illus.). xii, 496p. 1997. write for info. (*0-86377-738-4*, Pub. by Psychol Pr); pap. write for info. (*0-86377-739-2*, Pub. by Psychol Pr) Taylor & Francis.

Power, Michael J., jt. auth. see Dalgleish, Tim.

Power, Mick & Brewin, Chris R. The Transformation of Meaning in the Psychological Therapies: Reconciling Theory & Practice. LC 96-48034. (Clinical Psychology Ser.). 228p. 1997. 125.00 (*0-471-95826-3*) Wiley.

Power, Mick, jt. auth. see Freeman, Christopher.

Power, P. B. A Book of Comfort. 1974. pap. 4.99 (*0-85151-203-8*) Banner of Truth.

— The I Wills of Christ. 382p. 1984. reprint ed. pap. 9.99 (*0-85151-429-4*) Banner of Truth.

— The I Wills of the Psalms. 395p. 1985. reprint ed. pap. 9.99 (*0-85151-445-6*) Banner of Truth.

Power, Patrick C. The Book of Irish Curses. 116p. 1975. pap. 5.95 (*0-87243-060-X*) Templegate.

— History of South Tipperary. 1989. 100.00 (*0-85342-885-9*) Dufour.

— Sex & Marriage in Ancient Ireland. 96p. 1997. pap. 12.95 (*0-8023-1318-3*) Dufour.

Power, Patrick C., tr. see O'Brien, Flann.

Power, Paul F., ed. The Meaning of Gandhi. LC 72-170180. 205p. reprint ed. pap. 63.60 (*0-608-18714-3*, 202703200053) Bks Demand.

Power, Paul W. A Guide to Vocational Assessment. 2nd ed. LC 90-15579. 321p. (C). 1991. pap. text 33.00 (*0-89079-426-X*, 1946) PRO-ED.

— A Guide to Vocational Assessment. 3rd ed. LC 98-19448. 1998. 33.00 (*0-89079-786-2*) PRO-ED.

Power, Paul W., et al, eds. Family Interventions Throughout Chronic Illness & Disability. (Series on Rehabilitation: No. 7). 336p. 1988. 43.95 (*0-8261-5580-4*) Springer Pub.

Power, Paul W., et al. Strengthening Aging Families: Toward Diversity in Practice & Policy. 280p. 1995. text 52.00 (*0-8039-5424-7*); pap. text 24.00 (*0-8039-5425-5*) Sage.

Power, Paul W., jt. auth. see Dell Orto, Arthur E.

Power Play Technology Staff, jt. auth. see Caruso, Raymond P.

Power Publications Staff, ed. How I Became a Nurse Entrepreneur: Tales from 50 Nurses in Business. 1998. pap. 19.95 (*1-888315-03-2*) Power NY.

Power, R. J., ed. Cooperation among Organizations: The Potential of Computer Supported Cooperative Work. (Research Reports ESPRIT, Project 688, AMICE: Vol. 1). vii, 140p. 1993. 31.95 (*0-387-56263-X*) Spr-Verlag.

Power, Ray, et al. Discover Sociology. 300p. (Orig.). (C). 1986. pap. text 26.50 (*0-273-02282-2*) Trans-Atl Phila.

***Power, Richard.** Computer Crime & the Internet Revolution. 350p. 2000. 25.00 (*0-7897-2443-X*) Que.

Power, Richard. Hungry Grass. 255p. 1988. pap. 8.95 (*1-85371-009-1*, Pub. by Poolbeg Pr) Dufour.

Power, Richard, intro. Great Song: The Life & Teachings of Joe Miller. 150p. (Orig.). 1993. pap. 16.00 (*0-9618916-8-8*) Maypop.

***Power, Richard & Scott, Donia, eds.** Using Layout for the Generation Understandings or Retrieval of Documents. 90p. 2000. spiral bd. 25.00 (*1-57735-114-2*) AAAI Pr.

Power, Richard L. Planting Corn Belt Culture: The Impress of the Upland Southerner & Yankee in the Old Northwest. LC 83-8491. (Indiana Historical Society Publications Ser.). 196p. 1983. reprint ed. lib. bdg. 55.00 (*0-313-24060-4*, POPC) Greenwood.

Power, Robert D. & Fung, Frederick Y. Workers' Compensation Handbook: A Guide to Job-Related Health Problems. LC 93-79792. (Illus.). 116p. (Orig.). 1994. pap. 10.95 (*0-929894-07-3*) K-W Pubns.

Power, Roderick P., et al. Workshops in Perception. 244p. 1981. pap. 9.95 (*0-7100-0931-3*, Routledge Thoemms) Routledge.

Power, S. A., jt. auth. see Power, John C.

Power, S. C., ed. Operators & Function Theory. 1985. text 176.50 (*90-277-2008-8*) Kluwer Academic.

Power, Sally. The Pastoral & the Academic: Conflict & Contradiction in the Curriculum. LC 97-127205. (Studies in Pastoral Care, Personal & Social Education). (Illus.). 196p. 1996. 80.00 (*0-304-33223-2*); pap. 37.95 (*0-304-33225-9*) Continuum.

***Power, Samantha & Allison, Graham T.** The Future of Human Rights. LC 00-38238. 2000. 35.00 (*0-312-23494-5*) St Martin.

Power Scheduling Staff. Power Scheduling. 96p. 1995. pap. text, per. 14.95 (*0-7872-0516-8*) Kendall-Hunt.

Power, Scott. The Historic Architecture of Pitt County, North Carolina. (Illus.). 564p. 1990. 40.00 (*0-9672394-0-0*) Pitt Cty Hist Soc.

Power, Scott. Illinois Area Retirement & Relocation Guide. large type ed. (Retirement & Relocation Guides Ser.). (Illus.). 350p. Date not set. pap. 24.95 (*1-56559-131-3*) HGI-Over Fifty.

— Let's Party! Chicago: A Quite Martini to an Outrageous Soiree. LC 96-53306. 192p. 1997. pap. 14.95 (*1-57034-073-0*) Globe Pequot.

— Musician's Little Book of Wisdom. LC 96-22582. 160p. 1996. pap. 5.95 (*1-57034-048-X*) Globe Pequot.

— Salesman's Little Book of Wisdom. LC 96-29839. (Little Books of Wisdom Ser.). 160p. (Orig.). 1997. pap. 6.95 (*1-57034-061-7*) Globe Pequot.

Power, Scott & Addison, Corran. Kayaker's Little Book of Wisdom: A Couple Hundred Suggestions, Observations, & Reminders for Kayakers to Read, Remember, & Share, Vol. 1. large type ed. LC 97-22762. 160p. 1997. pap. 6.95 (*1-57034-079-X*) Globe Pequot.

Power, Susan. The Grass Dancer. 352p. 1995. mass mkt. 6.99 (*0-425-14962-5*) Berkley Pub.

— The Grass Dancer. large type ed. LC 95-15714. 1995. 23.95 (*1-56895-215-5*) Wheeler Pub.

— The Grass Dancer. 352p. 1997. reprint ed. pap. 13.00 (*0-425-15953-1*) Berkley Pub.

— Strong Heart Society. 304p. 1998. 23.95 (*0-399-14212-6*, G P Putnam) Peng Put Young Read.

Power, T. & Whelan, K., eds. Endurance & Emergence: Catholics in Ireland in the Eighteenth Century. 216p. 1990. 39.50 (*0-7165-2420-1*, I2420, Pub. by Irish Acad Pr) Intl Spec Bk.

Power, Thomas A. Family Matters: A Layperson's Guide to Family Functioning. (Illus.). 205p. (Orig.). 1989. pap. 6.95 (*0-934080-17-8*) Elan Pub Co.

Power, Thomas C. Electronics Mathematics. LC 84-7828. 416p. (C). 1985. teacher ed. 10.00 (*0-8273-2411-1*) Delmar.

Power, Thomas G. Play & Exploration in Children & Animals. LC 99-30955. 512p. 1999. 99.95 (*0-8058-2241-0*); pap. write for info. (*0-8058-2242-9*) L Erlbaum Assocs.

Power, Thomas M. The Economic Pursuit of Quality. LC 87-12128. 224p. (C). (gr. 13). 1988. pap. text 40.95 (*0-87332-449-8*) M E Sharpe.

Power, Thomas M. The Economic Pursuit of Quality. LC 87-12128. 232p. 1988. reprint ed. pap. 72.00 (*0-7837-9987-X*, 206071400006) Bks Demand.

— Environmental Protection & Economic Well-Being: The Economic Pursuit of Quality. 2nd ed. LC 96-3646. 268p. (C). (gr. 13). 1996. pap. text 35.95 (*1-56324-735-6*) M E Sharpe.

Power, Thomas Michael. Environmental Protection & Economic Well-Being: The Economic Pursuit of Quality. 2nd ed. LC 96-3646. 268p. (YA). (gr. 12-13). 1996. text 76.95 (*1-56324-734-8*) M E Sharpe.

— Lost Landscapes & Failed Economies: The Search for a Value of Place. LC 95-32365. 316p. 1998. text 32.00 (*1-55963-368-9*) Island Pr.

— Lost Landscapes & Failed Economies: The Search for a Value of Place. 350p. 1998. pap. 17.95 (*1-55963-369-7*) Island Pr.

Power, Thomas P. Land, Politics, & Society in Eighteenth-Century Tipperary. LC 93-22481. (Illus.). 392p. (C). 1993. text 70.00 (*0-19-820316-0*, Clarendon Pr) OUP.

Power, Thomas P., jt. ed. see Nolan, William.

***Power, Timothy J.** The Political Right in Postauthoritarian Brazil: Elites, Institutions & Democratization. LC 99-56473. 2000. 55.00 (*0-271-02009-1*); pap. 19.95 (*0-271-02010-5*) Pa St U Pr.

Power, Timothy J., jt. ed. see Kingstone, Peter R.

Power, Una. The Spellbinder. large type ed. 1995. 27.99 (*0-7089-3296-7*) Ulverscroft.

Power, Valerie, jt. auth. see Garrould, Ann.

Power, Vicki. Vanity. LC 94-40133. (Very Peculiar History Ser.). (Illus.). 48p. (J). (gr. 5-8). 1995. lib. bdg. 22.00 (*0-531-14356-2*) Watts.

— Vanity. (Very Peculiar History Ser.). (Illus.). 48p. (J). (gr. 4-7). 1995. pap. 6.95 (*0-531-15273-1*) Watts.

Power, Vincent J. Competition Law in Ireland. 1995. boxed set. write for info. (*1-85475-065-8*, IE, MICHIE) LEXIS Pub.

— EC Shipping Law. (Lloyd's Shipping Law Library). 800p. 1992. 260.00 (*1-85044-312-2*) LLP.

— EC Shipping Law: First Supplement. 125p. 1994. pap. 60.00 (*1-85044-591-5*) LLP.

Power, Virginia W. Ginny's Chairs. Hartung, Nancy F., ed. LC 98-70593. (Illus.). 192p. 1998. 25.00 (*0-9644760-6-1*) Phase II Publ.

Powers. Accounting. (C). Date not set. text. write for info. (*0-395-63680-9*) HM.

***Powers.** Boundary Value Problems. 4th ed. LC 98-89676. 528p. (C). 1999. 69.95 (*0-12-563734-9*) Acad Pr.

Powers. Ecological Principles of Agriculture. LC 99-43250. (Agriculture Ser.). 433p. (C). 1999. pap. text 53.95 (*0-7668-0653-7*) Delmar.

— Financial Accounting. (C). Date not set. text. write for info. (*0-395-63681-7*) HM.

— Limit Algebras. 1993. pap. 36.54 (*0-582-08781-3*) Longman.

— Philosophy & the New Physics. 208p. (C). 1982. pap. 18.95 (*0-415-07584-X*) Routledge.

— Statistical Methods for Categorical Data Analysis. 256p. (C). 1999. 49.95 (*0-12-563736-5*) Morgan Kaufmann.

Powers, ed. The Human Form in Palaeolithic Art. 237p. 1994. pap. text 83.00 (*2-88449-025-6*) Gordon & Breach.

Powers & Dodd. Total Fitness: Exercise, Nutrition, & Wellness. 2nd ed. LC 98-50706. 382p. 1998. pap. text 36.00 (*0-205-29120-1*, Longwood Div) Allyn.

Powers, Alan. Living with Books. LC 99-11690. (Illus.). 144p. 1999. 35.00 (*1-57959-024-1*, SOMA) BB&T Inc.

Powers, Alan. Modern Block Printed Textiles. (Decorative Arts Library). (Illus.). 93p. 1997. 19.95 (*0-7445-1891-1*) Antique Collect.

Powers, Alex. Painting People in Watercolor: A Design Approach. (Illus.). 144p. 1997. pap. text 19.95 (*0-8230-3868-8*) Watsn-Guptill.

Powers, Alexis. Kiss Daddy Goodbye. Blue, Denise, ed. 175p. (Orig.). 1996. pap. 11.95 (*0-9649434-2-5*) Powers Pubng.

— Kiss My Tattoo. 123p. 1995. pap. text. write for info. (*0-9649434-0-9*) Powers Pubng.

— Kiss Your Inheritance Goodbye. 1996. pap. text. write for info. (*0-9649434-1-7*) Powers Pubng.

Powers, Alice L. Italy in Mind: An Anthology. LC 96-47864. 1997. pap. 14.00 (*0-679-77023-2*) McKay.

***Powers, Alice L.** Washington, D. C. LC 99-56182. (Travel Guides Ser.). (Illus.). 2000. 19.95 (*0-7894-5546-3*) DK Pub Inc.

***Powers, Alice Leccese.** Ireland in Mind: An Anthology. LC 99-39790. 2000. pap. 13.00 (*0-375-70344-6*) Vin Bks.

Powers, Amy R. Through Amy's Eyes. Powers, Darry E., ed. LC 98-91413. (Illus.). 164p. 1998. pap. 11.95 (*1-57579-111-0*) Pine Hill Pr.

Powers, Analine M. Silva Mind Control: An Anthropological Inquiry. LC 91-39376. (Cults & Nonconventional Religious Groups Ser.). 336p. 1992. text 25.00 (*0-8153-0770-5*) Garland.

***Powers, Ann.** Weird Like Us: My Bohemian America. 288p. 2000. 23.00 (*0-684-83808-7*) S&S Trade.

Powers, Ann, jt. ed. see McDonnell, Evelyn.

Powers, Anne. The Gallant Years. large type ed. LC 98-14586. 1998. 24.95 (*0-7862-1440-6*) Thorndike Pr.

Powers-Beck, Jeffrey. Writing the Flesh: The Herbert Family Dialogue. LC 98-25499. (Medieval & Renaissance Literary Studies). (Illus.). 300p. 1999. 54.50 (*0-8207-0293-5*) Duquesne.

***Powers, Becky C., ed.** My Roots Go Back to Loving: And Other Stories from "Year of the Family" 192p. 2000. pap. 9.95 (*0-9672134-1-X*) Canaan Home Commun.

Powers, Bernard E., Jr. Black Charlestonians: A Social History, 1822-1885. LC 94-7861. (Illus.). 384p. 1994. text 36.00 (*1-55728-364-8*) U of Ark Pr.

Powers, Bethel A. & Knapp, Thomas R. A Dictionary of Nursing Theory & Research. (Illus.). 184p. (C). 1990. text 48.00 (*0-8039-3411-4*); pap. text 22.95 (*0-8039-3412-2*) Sage.

— A Dictionary of Nursing Theory & Research. 2nd ed. 224p. 1995. text 49.95 (*0-8039-5625-8*); pap. text 22.95 (*0-8039-5626-6*) Sage.

Powers, Betty & Mall, E. Jane. Church Office Handbook for Ministers. 80p. 1983. pap. 9.00 (*0-8170-1011-4*) Judson.

***Powers, Bill.** White Knights, Dark Earls: The Rise & Fall of an Anglo-Irish Dynasty. 2000. pap. 24.95 (*1-898256-94-2*, Pub. by Collins Press) Dufour.

Powers, Bob. Instructor Excellence: Mastering the Delivery of Training. LC 91-38692. (Management Ser.). 254p. 1992. text 32.95 (*1-55542-429-5*) Jossey-Bass.

***Powers, Bob.** Make Money in MLM: Full Time, Part Time, Any Time for a Lifetime. LC 00-131114. (Illus.). 192p. 2000. pap. 15.95 (*0-9673451-0-3*) Life Long Pubg.

Powers, Bob, ed. A Family & Friend's Guide to Sexual Orientation. 256p. (C). 1996. 70.00 (*0-415-91275-X*) Routledge.

Powers, Bob & Ellis, Alan. A Manager's Guide to Sexual Orientation in the Workplace. LC 95-23654. 209p. (C). 1995. 31.99 (*0-415-91277-6*) Routledge.

Powers, Bob & Ellis, Alan, eds. A Family & Friend's Guide to Sexual Orientation. 273p. 1996. pap. 19.99 (*0-415-91276-8*) Routledge.

Powers, Bruce P. Church Administration Handbook. LC 96-26334. 1997. 19.99 (*0-8054-1061-9*, 4210-61) Broadman.

Powers, Bruce P., ed. Christian Education Handbook. enl. rev. ed. LC 80-69522. 320p. 1995. pap. 29.99 (*0-8054-1060-0*, 4210-60) Broadman.

Powers, Bruce R., jt. auth. see McLuhan, Marshall.

Powers, C. Martin. Europe: All in One Guidebook. LC 86-61916. (Illus.). 320p. pap. 11.95 (*0-933448-01-5*) Outstanding VA.

Powers, Celeste N. & Frable, William J. Fine Needle Aspiration: Biopsy of the Head & Neck. (Illus.). 155p. 1996. text 160.00 (*0-7506-9503-X*) Buttrwrth-Heinemann.

Powers, Charles. Vilfredo Pareto. Turner, Jonathan E., ed. (Matters of Social Theory Ser.: Vol. 5). (Illus.). 160p. (C). 1987. 48.00 (*0-8039-2284-1*); pap. text 19.95 (*0-8039-2285-X*) Sage.

Powers, Charles, ed. see Pareto, Vilfredo.

Powers, Charles T. In the Memory of the Forest. LC 96-36664. 384p. 1997. 22.50 (*0-684-83030-2*) S&S Trade.

— In the Memory of the Forest. 384p. 1998. pap. 12.95 (*0-14-027281-X*) Viking Penguin.

Powers, Charles W., jt. auth. see Simon, John G.

***Powers, Chase.** Bathrooms: A Professional's Illustrated Design & Remodeling Guide. LC 97-52228. (Illus.). 384p. 1998. 44.95 (*0-07-008629-X*) McGraw.

Powers, Chase. Builder's Guide to Cosmetic Remodeling. LC 96-49973. (Illus.). 352p. 1997. 44.95 (*0-07-050712-0*) McGraw.

— Kitchens: A Professional's Illustrated Design & Remodeling Guide. LC 96-46929. (Illus.). 288p. 1996. 54.95 (*0-07-050713-9*); pap. 29.95 (*0-07-050714-7*) McGraw.

***Powers, Chase.** Residential Heating. LC 98-53828. (Illus.). 450p. 1999. pap. text 39.95 (*0-07-050719-8*) McGraw-Hill Prof.

Powers, Chase M. Bathrooms: A Professional's Illustrated Design & Remodeling Guide. LC 97-52228. (Illus.). 384p. 1998. pap. 29.95 (*0-07-008628-1*) McGraw.

— Builder's Guide to Cosmetic Remodeling. LC 96-49973. (Builder's Guide Ser.). (Illus.). 324p. 1997. pap. 24.95 (*0-07-050717-1*) McGraw.

Powers, D. A. Simplified Model of Decontamination by BWR Steam Suppression Pools. 458p. 1997. per. 41.00 (*0-16-062841-5*) USGPO.

Powers, D. M. Machine Learning of Natural Language. (Illus.). x, 358p. 1989. 49.00 (*0-387-19557-2*) Spr-Verlag.

Powers, D. W., Jr., jt. auth. see Howarth, R. J.

Powers, D. W., jt. auth. see Jerald, J. P.

Powers, Daniel, jt. auth. see Lackner, Michelle Myers.

Powers, Daniel T. Jiro's Pearl. LC 95-47615. (Illus.). (J). (gr. 1-4). 1997. 15.99 (*1-56402-631-0*) Candlewick Pr.

Powers, Darry E., ed. see Powers, Amy R.

Powers, David. Right Start. 32p. (Orig.). 1976. pap. 1.50 (*0-933672-32-2*, C-1506) Star Bible.

Powers, David G. Lockheed 188 Electra. Proctor, Jon, ed. (Great Airliners Ser.: Vol. 5). (Illus.). 128p. 1999. pap. 27.95 (*1-892437-01-5*, 128565AE, Pub. by World Transport) Motorbooks Intl.

Powers, David L. Boundary Value Problems. 3rd ed. 351p. (C). 1987. text 93.00 (*0-15-505535-6*) SCP.

Powers, David R. & Powers, Mary F. Making Participatory Management Work. LC 82-49282. (Jossey-Bass Higher Education Ser.). 267p. reprint ed. pap. 82.80 (*0-8357-4916-9*, 203784600009) Bks Demand.

Powers, David S. Study in Quran & Hadith. 265p. 1996. 39.95 (*0-614-21073-9*, 1182) Kazi Pubns.

Powers, David S., tr. History of al-Tabari Vol. 24: The Empire in Transition: The Caliphates of Sulayman, Lumar, & Yazid, A. D. 715-724-A. H. 97-105. LC 88-39752. (SUNY Series in Near Eastern Studies). 218p. (C). 1989. text 57.50 (*0-7914-0072-7*); pap. text 21.95 (*0-7914-0073-5*) State U NY Pr.

Powers, David S., tr. see Al-Tabari.

Powers, Deborah D. The Court of Appeals at Austin: 1892-1992. LC 92-28116. (Illus.). 96p. 1992. 24.95 (*0-938349-92-9*) State House Pr.

Powers, Dennis M. Legal Expense Defense: How to Control Your Business' Legal Costs & Problems. Pinkham, Linda, ed. LC 95-34833. (Successful Business Library). (Illus.). 346p. (Orig.). 1998. pap. 19.95 (*1-55571-348-3*, Oasis Pr) PSI Resch.

Powers, Doris. C. P. E. Bach: A Research Guide. Marco, Guy A., ed. (Composer Resource Manuals Ser.). 300p. Date not set. text 45.00 (*0-8153-2179-1*) Garland.

Powers, Doris C. English Formal Satire: Elizabethan to Augustan. (De Proprietatibus Litterarum, Ser. Practica: No. 19). 214p. (Orig.). 1971. pap. text 33.85 (*90-279-1905-4*) Mouton.

Powers, Douglas, ed. Adoption for Troubled Children: Prevention & Repair of Adoptive Failures Through Residential Treatment. LC 83-26424. (Residential Group Care & Treatment Ser.: Vol. 2, Nos. 1-2). 201p. 1984. text 49.95 (*0-86656-245-1*) Haworth Pr.

Powers, Douglas C., et al, eds. Aging, Immunity, & Infection. LC 93-42177. 328p. 1994. 47.95 (*0-8261-8180-5*) Springer Pub.

Powers, Edna & Kriegel, Gaye. Affordable Heirlooms. LC 95-10550. (Creative Machine Arts Ser.). (Illus.). 128p. 1995. pap. 17.95 (*0-8019-8647-8*) Krause Pubns.

Powers, Edward A. In Essentials, Unity: An Ecumenical Sampler. LC 82-1446. 120p. (Orig.). 1982. reprint ed. pap. 37.20 (*0-608-00238-0*, 206074200006) Bks Demand.

— Later Life Transitions: Older Males in Rural America. 1985. lib. bdg. 145.00 (*0-89838-137-1*) Kluwer Academic.

Powers, Edwin & Witmer, Helen. Experiment in the Prevention of Delinquency: The Cambridge - Somerville Youth Study. LC 70-172573. (Criminology, Law Enforcement, & Social Problems Ser.: No. 159). 1972. reprint ed. 30.00 (*0-87585-159-2*) Patterson Smith.

Powers, Elizabeth, jt. ed. see Mandelker, Amy.

Powers, Gary D. From Gasoline to Electric: A Conversion Experience. (Illus.). 114p. 1997. pap. 12.00 (*0-9660953-0-8*) Longbarn Pr.

Powers, Gene R. Cleft Palate. LC 72-86554. (Studies in Communicative Disorders). 37p. 1973. pap. text 4.50 (*0-672-61288-7*, Bobbs) Macmillan.

— Cleft Palate. Halpern, Harvey, ed. LC 86-3062. (PRO-ED Studies in Communicative Disorders). (Illus.). 52p. 1986. pap. text 9.00 (*0-89079-094-3*, 1384) PRO-ED.

Powers, Georgia D. I Shared the Dream: The Pride Passion & Politics of the First Black Woman Senator from Kentucky. LC 94-66756. 320p. 1995. 25.95 (*0-88282-127-X*) New Horizon NJ.

Powers, Greg & Wayford, Wesley. The Internet Gold: Learn & Prosper! LC 99-90019. (Illus.). viii, 242p. 1999. pap. 19.95 (*0-9668029-0-X*) Future Today.

Powers, Harold, ed. Studies in Music History: Essays for Oliver Strunk. LC 80-14086. (Illus.). 527p. 1980. reprint ed. lib. bdg. 89.50 (*0-313-22501-X*, POSM, Greenwood Pr) Greenwood.

***Powers, Helen.** Winding Roads: A New England Notebook of Wisdom & Wit. 175p. 1999. pap. 17.50 (*0-9673783-0-3*) Ltd Edition Pr.

Powers, Helen. Winding Roads: A New England Notebook of Wisdom & Wit. LC 99-94258. 188p. 1999. pap. 17.50 (*0-7392-0164-6*) Morris Pubng.

Powers, Hiram C. The Hiram C. Powers Story: An Autobiography on Pioneer Life, Travels in the Wild West & a Legendary Feud of Western Kentucky. LC 92-37914. Date not set. write for info. (*0-941677-73-7*, Pub. by White Cliffs Media); pap. write for info. (*0-941677-72-9*, Pub. by White Cliffs Media) Words Distrib.

***Powers, Hong-Oanh & Powers, Robert F., trs. from RUS.** Hoang Hau Tuyet.Tr. of Snow Queen. (VIE., Illus.). 12p. (J). (gr. 2-4). 2000. 4.95 (*1-929482-00-0*) Rodnik.

Powers, Howley. Exercise Physiology. 4th ed. 2000. 52.25 (*0-07-235551-4*) McGraw.

Powers, Isaias. Father Ike's Stories for Children: Teaching Christian Values Through Animal Stories. LC 88-50332. (Illus.). 64p. (Orig.). (J). 1988. pap. 4.95 (*0-89622-370-1*) Twenty-Third.

— Healing Words from Jesus. LC 95-61867. 152p. (Orig.). 1996. pap. 7.95 (*0-89622-682-4*) Twenty-Third.

— Healing Words from Mary: Entering the Mysteries of the Rosary. LC 96-60655. 96p. (Orig.). 1997. pap. 7.95 (*0-89622-702-2*) Twenty-Third.

— Heart-Talks with Jesus: Guided Scripture Meditations. LC 97-61821. 144p. 1998. pap. 7.95 (*0-89622-722-7*) Twenty-Third.

— Letters from an Understanding Friend: Jesus on the Way to Jerusalem. LC 84-50409. 96p. 1985. pap. 7.95 (*0-89622-413-9*) Twenty-Third.

— Quiet Places with Jesus. LC 78-64452. 128p. (YA). (gr. 9 up). 1978. pap. 7.95 (*0-89622-086-9*) Twenty-Third.

— Women of the Gospel: Sharing God's Compassion. LC 92-81796. (Illus.). 168p. (Orig.). 1993. pap. 7.95 (*0-89622-521-6*) Twenty-Third.

Powers, Isaias & Star, Andrea. Quiet Places with Mary. LC 86-50123. 160p. (Orig.). (YA). (gr. 9 up). 1986. pap. 7.95 (*0-89622-297-7*) Twenty-Third.

***Powers, J.** Ghosts & Monsters. (Illus.). (J). 2000. pap. 3.49 (*0-525-46408-5*, Dutton Child) Peng Put Young Read.

***Powers, J., et al.** Beastly Bugs. (Illus.). 32p. (J). (gr. 4-7). 2000. pap. 3.49 (*0-525-46406-9*, Dutton Child) Peng Put Young Read.

— Fierce Predators. (Illus.). 32p. (J). (gr. 4-7). 2000. pap. 3.49 (*0-525-46407-7*, Dutton Child) Peng Put Young Read.

— Towers of Torture. (Illus.). 32p. (J). (gr. 4-7). 2000. pap. 3.49 (*0-525-46409-3*, Dutton Child) Peng Put Young Read.

***Powers, J. F.** Morte d'Urban. LC 99-45446. 336p. 2000. 12.95 (*0-940322-23-4*) NY Rev Bks.

Powers, J. F. The Old Bird, A Love Story. limited ed. (Winter Bks.: No. 4). (Illus.). 32p. 1991. pap. 65.00 (*1-879832-26-7*) MN Ctr Book Arts.

***Powers, J. F.** The Stories of J. F. Powers. LC 99-47885. 592p. 2000. 14.95 (*0-94032-22-6*) NY Rev Bks.

— Wheat That Springeth Green. LC 99-52324. 327p. 2000. pap. 12.95 (*0-940322-24-2*) NY Rev Bks.

Powers, J. H. Historical Reminiscences of Chickasaw County, Iowa. (Illus.). 332p. 1992. reprint ed. lib. bdg. 36.00 (*0-8328-2585-9*) Higginson Bk Co.

***Powers, J. M. & Stout, L. M.** Loose Screws. LC 99-90812. 1999. 25.00 (*0-7388-0538-6*); pap. 18.00 (*0-7388-0539-4*) Xlibris Corp.

Powers, J. Patrick. Construction Dewatering: New Methods & Applications. 2nd ed. LC 91-34215. (Series of Practical Construction Guides: No. 1344). 528p. 1992. 120.00 (*0-471-60185-3*) Wiley.

— Dewatering: Avoiding Its Unwanted Side Effects. (C). 1986. 115.00 (*0-7855-6709-7*, Pub. by Scientific) St Mut.

Powers, J. Patrick, ed. Dewatering - Avoiding Its Unwanted Side Effects. (C). 1987. text 65.00 (*0-7855-6902-2*, Pub. by Scientific Pubs) St Mut.

— Dewatering-Avoiding Its Unwanted Side Effects. (C). 1987. reprint ed. text 100.00 (*0-7855-3142-4*, Pub. by Scientific) St Mut.

Powers, J. Patrick, ed. see American Society of Civil Engineers Staff.

Powers, Jackson L., ed. see Patton, Pamela.

***Powers, Jacqueline K.** The 21st Century Entrepreneur: How To Start A Freelance Consulting Business. LC 99-29549. 256p. 1999. pap. 12.50 (*0-380-79712-7*, Avon Bks) Morrow Avon.

Powers, Jacqueline K., ed. see Powers, Michael D.

Powers, James. IRC & Online Chat: The Beginners Guide to Real-Time Chat on the Net. (Illus.). 256p. (Orig.). 1997. pap. 29.95 (*1-55755-333-5*, B-333) Abacus MI.

***Powers, James F.** Code of Cuenca: Municipal Law on the Twelfth-Century Castilian Frontier. LC 00-20261. 240p. 2000. 49.95 (*0-8122-3545-2*) U of Pa Pr.

Powers, James F. The Presence of Grace. LC 77-85694. (Short Story Index Reprint Ser.). 1977. 19.95 (*0-8369-3037-1*) Ayer.

Powers, James R. Rape Investigation Manual. (Illus.). 320p. 1996. pap. 50.00 (*0-87364-890-0*) Paladin Pr.

Powers, Jamilla & Gibbs, Tyson. Afro-Centric Guide to: Reflections, Affirmations, Meditations & Prayers. 130p. (Orig.). 1994. pap. 10.95 (*0-9638548-0-1*) Jamilla Powers.

Powers, Jane B. The Girl Question in Education: Vocational Training for Young Women in the Progressive Era. (Studies in Curriculum History Ser.). 224p. 1992. 59.95 (*1-85000-847-7*, Falmer Pr) Taylor & Francis.

Powers, Janet, jt. auth. see Potter, Jamie.

Powers, Jennifer, jt. ed. see Campbell, Dennis.

***Powers, Jessica, et al.** The Selected Poetry of Jessica Powers. LC 99-48356. 204p. 1999. reprint ed. pap. 11.95 (*0-935216-68-5*) ICS Pubns.

Powers, Jo-Marie. Farmers' Market Cookbook. (Illus.). 238p. 1984. pap. 12.95 (*0-7737-5005-3*) Genl Dist Srvs.

Powers, Jo-Marie, jt. auth. see Powers, Thomas F.

Powers, Joan. Tattoo You: Pisces. 1999. pap. 4.99 (*0-7214-5735-5*, Ladybrd) Penguin Putnam.

***Powers, Joan.** World Greatest Cat. (Animal Planet Ser.). (Illus.). 24p. (J). (ps-3). 2000. pap. 6.99 (*0-525-46499-9*, Dutton Child) Peng Put Young Read.

Powers, John. The Boston Handbook. (Illus.). 128p. 1999. pap. 10.95 (*1-58066-023-1*) Douglas Charles Ltd.

— Introduction to Tibetan Buddhism. 501p. 1995. text 34.95 (*1-55939-028-X*) Snow Lion Pubns.

— Introduction to Tibetan Buddhism. 504p. (C). 1995. pap. 18.95 (*1-55939-026-3*) Snow Lion Pubns.

— The Yogacara School of Buddhism: A Bibliography. LC 91-37139. (American Theological Library Association Monograph: No. 27). 267p. 1991. 34.00 (*0-8108-2502-3*) Scarecrow.

Powers, John, tr. from TIB. Wisdom of Buddha: The Samdhinirmocana Sutra. LC 94-25023. 397p. 1994. 40.00 (*0-89800-247-8*); pap. 25.00 (*0-89800-246-X*) Dharma Pub.

Powers, John, et al. The Boston Dictionary. (Illus.). 128p. (Orig.). 1996. pap. 10.95 (*0-924771-85-2*, Covered Brdge Pr) Douglas Charles Ltd.

Powers, John, jt. auth. see Fieser, James.

Powers, John, jt. ed. see Sullivan, George A.

Powers, John, tr. see Asanga & Jnanagarbha.

Powers, John A., jt. auth. see Easton, Edward J., Jr.

Powers, John D. Holy & Human: Mystics for Our Time. LC 89-50565. 140p. 1989. pap. 9.95 (*0-89622-398-1*) Twenty-Third.

— If They Could Speak: Ten Witnesses to the Passion of Jesus. Brauch, Judy, tr. LC 89-51902. (Illus.). 64p. 1990. pap. 5.95 (*0-89622-421-X*) Twenty-Third.

— Seeking Inner Peace: The Art of Facing Your Emotions. LC 87-50839. 112p. (Orig.). 1987. pap. 8.95 (*0-89622-344-2*) Twenty-Third.

Powers, John H., jt. auth. see Kluver, Randy.

Powers, John H., jt. ed. see Kluver, Randy.

Powers, John O. Prison Dreams. 200p. mass mkt. 4.99 (*1-55197-039-2*) Picasso Publ.

Powers, John P. An Introduction to Fiber Optic Systems. 1993. pap. text 26.00 (*0-256-12997-5*) McGraw.

— An Introduction to Fiber Optic Systems. LC 92-31650. (Aksen Associates Series in Electrical & Computer Engineering). 500p. (C). 1993. text 71.50 (*0-256-12996-7*, Irwn McGrw-H) McGrw-H Hghr Educ.

— An Introduction to Fiber Optic Systems. 2nd ed. 672p. (C). 1996. text 71.50 (*0-256-20414-4*, Irwn McGrw-H) McGrw-H Hghr Educ.

Powers, John R. The Last Catholic in America. 224p. 1988. mass mkt. 4.95 (*0-446-31252-5*, Pub. by Warner Bks) Little.

— The Last Catholic in America. LC 79-24431. 1981. reprint ed. lib. bdg. 18.00 (*0-8376-0439-7*) Bentley Pubs.

Powers, Jonathan. Philosophy & the New Physics. (Methuens Ideas Ser.). (Illus.). 150p. 1982. pap. 12.95 (*0-416-73480-4*, NO. 3795) Routledge.

Powers Jr., William C., jt. auth. see Fischer, David A.

***Powers, Judith.** Northern Waterway Guide 2000. (Illus.). 2000. 36.95 (*1-930188-06-4*) Intertec-Primedia.

— Waterway Guide. (Illus.). 1999. pap. 36.95 (*0-915962-97-7*) Intertec GA.

Powers, Judith, ed. Waterway Guide: Great Lakes Edition, 1994. (Illus.). 1993. pap. 33.95 (*0-915962-77-2*) Intertec GA.

— Waterway Guide: Mid-Atlantic Edition, 1997. (Illus.). 1997. pap. 33.95 (*0-915962-90-X*) Intertec IL.

— Waterway Guide: Northern Edition, 1997. (Illus.). 1997. pap. 33.95 (*0-915962-91-8*) Intertec IL.

Powers, Judy, jt. auth. see Hahn, Joan.

Powers, Katherine R. The Influence of William Godwin on the Novels of Mary Shelley. Varma, Devendra P., ed. LC 79-7469. (Gothic Studies & Dissertations). 1980. lib. bdg. 23.95 (*0-405-12657-3*) Ayer.

Powers, Kimiko, jt. auth. see Rosenblum, Robert.

Powers, Larry. Goalden Eye: The Three Step Outdoor Soccer Scoring Training Aid Journal. (Illus.). 53p. 1999. pap. 9.95 (*0-7414-0108-8*) Buy Books.

Powers, Laurie, jt. auth. see Sowers, Jo Ann.

Powers, Laurie E., et al, eds. On the Road to Autonomy: Promoting Self-Competence in Children & Youth with Disabilities. LC 96-10802. 432p. 1996. pap. text 48.00 (*1-55766-235-5*, 2355) P H Brookes.

Powers, Laurie E., jt. ed. see Singer, George H.

***Powers, Lawrence W., ed.** A River Never the Same: A History of Water in the Klamath Basin. (Illus.). 123p. 1999. 14.95 (*0-9667919-1-6*) Shaw Hist Libr.

Powers, Leigh. Sightreading on Guitar. Stang, Aaron, ed. 100p. (C). 1985. pap. text 12.95 (*0-7692-1286-7*, PMP00006) Wrner Bros.

Powers, Lorie, jt. auth. see Kirk, Lauren.

Powers, Lyall H. Faulkner's Yoknapatawpha Comedy. LC 79-23140. 295p. 1980. reprint ed. pap. 91.50 (*0-7837-5652-6*, 205907700005) Bks Demand.

— Leon Edel & Literary Art. Litz, A. Walton, ed. LC 87-19211. (Studies in Modern Literature: No. 84). (Illus.). 206p. reprint ed. pap. 63.90 (*0-8357-1839-5*, 207075300004) Bks Demand.

— The Portrait of a Lady: Maiden, Woman & Heroine. (Twayne's Masterwork Studies: No. 78). 128p. 1991. 23.95 (*0-8057-8066-1*, Twyne); pap. 18.00 (*0-8057-8550-7*, Twyne) Mac Lib Ref.

Powers, Lynn. Killer Art: Art That Has Maimed, Killed or Caused General Destruction Through the Centuries. 160p. 1999. pap. 29.95 (*1-891643-02-9*) Pontalba Pr.

Powers, Lynn & Van-Si, Laurie. Helping Children Heal from Loss: A Keepsake Book of Special Memories. 35p. (Orig.). 1994. pap. 12.95 (*0-87678-102-4*) PSU CE Pr.

***Powers, Madelon.** Face along the Bar: Lore & Order in the Workingman's Saloon, 1870-1920: Lore & Order in the Workingman's Saloon, 1870-1920. (Illus.). 332p. 1999. pap. 16.00 (*0-226-67769-9*) U Ch Pr.

Powers, Madelon. Faces Along the Bar: Lore & Order in the Workingman's Saloon, 1870-1920. LC 97-39278. (Illus.). 288p. 1998. 25.00 (*0-226-67768-0*) U Ch Pr.

Powers, Mala, ed. see Chekhov, Michael.

Powers, Marcia Grad, jt. auth. see Ellis, Albert.

***Powers, Margaret & Hendley, Joyce.** The American Diabetes Association Forbidden Foods Cookbook. 2000. 14.95 (*1-58040-005-1*) Am Diabetes.

Powers, Margaret A. Handbook of Diabetes Medical Nutrition Therapy. 2nd ed. 544p. 1996. 89.00 (*0-8342-0631-5*) Aspen Pub.

Powers, Margaret A. & Johnson, Byron P. Defensive Sites of Dinetah: Bureau of Land Management New Mexico State Office. (Cultural Resources Ser.: No. 2). (Illus.). 142p. (Orig.). 1991. reprint ed. pap. 8.00 (*1-878178-02-4*) Bureau of Land Mgmt NM.

Powers, Margaret F. Footprints: Scripture with Reflections Inspired by the Best-Loved Poem. LC 98-171908. 128p. 1998. 9.99 (*0-310-97464-X*) Zondervan.

— Footprints: The Story Behind the Poem That Inspired Millions. large type ed. LC 98-29777. 1998. pap. text 12.95 (*0-8027-2733-6*) Walker & Co.

— Footprints - RI. LC 98-154778. 112p. 1998. pap. 10.00 (*0-06-251557-8*, Pub. by Harper SF) HarpC.

— Footprints Book Of Prayers - RI. LC 98-154787. 128p. 1998. pap. 10.00 (*0-06-251558-6*, Pub. by Harper SF) HarpC.

— Footprints Daybreak. 128p. 1998. 9.99 (*0-310-97462-3*) Zondervan.

— Life's Little Inspiration, Bk. 2. 144p. 1996. pap. 8.95 (*0-00-638585-0*, Pub. by Harper SF) HarpC.

— Life's Little Inspiration Book - RI. LC 98-28710. (Footprints Bks.). 144p. 1998. pap. 9.00 (*0-06-251559-4*, Pub. by Harper SF) HarpC.

Powers Margaret Fish Staff. Footprints. 96p. 1999. 12.99 (*0-310-97502-6*) Zondervan.

Powers, Margie S., ed. Kid Smarts: The Resource Guide for Parents. 144p. 1997. pap. 5.00 (*1-891094-00-9*) Lucky Thirteen.

— Kid Smarts: The Resource Guide for Parents. 144p. 1998. pap. 5.00 (*1-891094-01-7*) Lucky Thirteen.

***Powers, Margie Spenlau, ed.** Kid Smarts: The Resource Guide for Parents. 2nd rev. ed. 144p. 1999. pap. 5.00 (*1-891094-02-5*) Lucky Thirteen.

Powers, Marian & Needles, Belverd E. General Mills, Inc. Annual Report: A Decision Case in Financial Analysis, 5 vols. 2nd ed. (C). 1995. text, teacher ed. 3.96 (*0-395-65588-9*) HM.

— Heartland Airways, Inc. Annual Report: A Financial Analysis Case, 4 vols. 4th ed. (C). 1992. text, teacher ed. 11.96 (*0-395-60615-2*) HM.

— Richland Home Centers, Inc. Annual Report: A Financial Analysis Case, 5 vols. 3rd ed. (C). 1993. text, teacher ed. 11.96 (*0-395-65551-X*) HM.

Powers, Marie. Shame: Thief of Intimacy. 1996. pap. text 4.95 (*1-56616-013-8*) Aglow Communs.

— Shame, Thief of Intimacy: Unmasking the Accuser. Anderson, Karen, ed. 200p. (Orig.). 1996. pap. 4.95 (*0-614-17634-4*, 521026) Aglow Communs.

Powers, Marie & Hansen, Jane. Fashioned for Intimacy, 10 vols., Vol. 5. (Aglow Bible Study Ser.). 115p. 1998. 6.99 (*0-8307-2321-8*) Gospel Lght.

***Powers, Marilyn & Folb, Sherry.** The Bridge: Between Two Lifetimes. 147p. 1999. pap. 16.95 (*0-9670495-0-4*) Sophia Pubns.

Powers, Marion D. The Legal Citation Directory. LC 75-25703. 302p. 1971. lib. bdg. 42.00 (*0-9600482-0-0*) Franas Pr.

Powers, Mark J. Getting Started in Commodity Futures Trading. (Illus.). 1983. pap. 12.95 (*0-914230-01-8*) Investor Pubns.

— Starting Out in Futures Trading. 5th ed. LC 93-222876. 379p. 1993. per. 24.95 (*1-55738-506-8*, Irwn Prfssnl) McGraw-Hill Prof.

Powers, Mark J. & Castelino, Mark G. Inside the Financial Futures Markets. 3rd ed. LC 91-9210. 400p. 1991. 55.00 (*0-471-53674-1*) Wiley.

Powers, Marla N. Oglala Women: Myth, Ritual, & Reality. (Women in Culture & Society Ser.). (Illus.). xvi, 272p. 1988. pap. 15.95 (*0-226-67749-4*) U Ch Pr.

Powers, Marshall K. Era Mi Mejor Amigo. Bernall, Carmen, tr. (Lucky the Cat Book Ser.). (SPA.). (YA). (gr. 8-10). 1997. 15.95 (*0-9647200-8-6*); pap. 9.95 (*0-9647200-9-4*) Gato Pr.

— The Thornton Affair. (Lucky the Cat Book Ser.). (Illus.). 35p. (J). (gr. 3-6). 1997. 12.95 (*0-9647200-4-3*); pap. 9.95 (*0-9647200-5-1*) Gato Pr.

***Powers, Martha.** Bleeding Heart. 2000. 23.00 (*0-684-86610-2*) Simon & Schuster.

— Deadly Illusion. write for info. (*1-886199-03-5*) Madison Pubng.

— Sunflower. 400p. 2000. reprint ed. per. 6.99 (*0-671-03935-0*) PB.

Powers, Martha. Sunflower: A Novel. LC 98-17853. 288p. (YA). 1998. 22.00 (*0-684-83767-6*) S&S Trade.

Powers, Martha J. Double Masquerade. large type ed. LC 90-28491. 370p. 1991. reprint ed. lib. bdg. 19.95 (*1-56054-146-6*) Thorndike Pr.

Powers, Martin J. Art & Political Expression in Early China. (Illus.). 352p. 1992. 60.00 (*0-300-04767-3*) Yale U Pr.

Powers, Mary E. Our Teacher's in a Wheelchair. Tucker, Kathleen, ed. LC 86-1623. (Albert Whitman Concept Bks.). (Illus.). 32p. (J). (ps-3). 1986. lib. bdg. 13.95 (*0-8075-6240-8*) A Whitman.

Powers, Mary F., jt. auth. see Powers, David R.

P

An Asterisk (*) at the beginning of an entry indicates that the title is appearing for the first time.

Powers, Mary G. & Macisco, John J., Jr. Los Puertorriquenos en Nueva York: Un Analisis de su Participacion Laboral y Experiencia Migratoria, 1970. vi, 201p. 1982. pap. 5.00 (*0-8477-2468-9*) U of PR Pr.

Powers, Mary G. & Macisco, John J., Jr., eds. The Immigration Experience in the United States: Policy Implications. abr. ed. LC 94-22724. 126p. 1994. 14.50 (*0-934733-84-8*) CMS.

Powers, Mary G., jt. ed. see Tomasi, Lydio F.

Powers, Mary R. A Woman's Overland Journal to California. (Illus.). 75p. 1985. reprint ed. 16.95 (*0-87770-349-3*) Ye Galleon.

Powers, Melvin. Dynamic Thinking. 1980. pap. 7.00 (*0-87980-031-3*) Wilshire.

— How to Get Rich in Mail Order. rev. ed. 1981. pap. 20.00 (*0-87980-373-8*) Wilshire.

— How to Self-Publish Your Book & Have the Fun Excitement of Being a Best-Selling Author. 1984. pap. 20.00 (*0-87980-406-8*) Wilshire.

— Making Money with Classified Ads. 1995. pap. 20.00 (*0-87980-435-1*) Wilshire.

— Practical Guide to Better Concentration. (Orig.). 1980. pap. 5.00 (*0-87980-120-4*) Wilshire.

— Practical Guide to Self-Hypnosis. (Orig.). 1960. pap. 10.00 (*0-87980-122-0*) Wilshire.

— Self-Hypnosis: Its Theory, Technique & Application. 1975. pap. 7.00 (*0-87980-138-7*) Wilshire.

Powers, Meredith A. The Heroine in Western Literature: The Archetype & Her Reemergence in Modern Prose. LC 91-52597. 240p. 1991. lib. bdg. 32.50 (*0-89950-615-1*) McFarland & Co.

Powers, Michael. How to Program a Virtual Communities. LC 97-178456. 384p. 1997. pap. text 39.99 (*1-56276-522-1*, Ziff-Davis Pr) Que.

Powers, Michael & Soares, Eric. Extreme Sea Kayaking. LC 99-10718. 128p. 1999. pap. 15.95 (*0-07-050718-X*) McGraw.

Powers, Michael D. How to Open a Franchise Business. LC 95-22645. (21st Century Entrepreneur Ser.). 288p. (Orig.). 1995. pap. 12.50 (*0-380-77912-9*, Avon Bks) Morrow Avon.

— How to Start a Mail Order Business. Pollan, Stephen, ed. LC 96-24601. (Twenty-First Century Entrepreneur Ser.). 288p. (Orig.). 1996. pap. 12.50 (*0-380-78446-7*, Avon Bks) Morrow Avon.

— How to Start a Retirement Business. Powers, Jacqueline K. & Pollan, Stephen, eds. LC 96-22183. (Twenty-First Century Entrepreneur Ser.). 288p. (Orig.). 1996. pap. 12.50 (*0-380-78447-5*, Avon Bks) Morrow Avon.

***Powers, Michael D., ed.** Children with Autism: A Parents' Guide. 2nd ed. LC 00-35165. (Illus.). 390p. 2000. pap. 17.95 (*1-890627-04-6*) Woodbine House.

Powers, Michael D., ed. see Harris, Sandra L.

***Powers, Mike.** The 21st Century Entrepreneur: How to Start a Business Website. LC 99-24021. 240p. 1999. pap. 12.50 (*0-380-79713-5*, Avon Bks) Morrow Avon.

— 21st C.i. Invest Colleg. LC 98-24671. (The 21st Century Investor Ser.). 272p. 1998. pap. 12.50 (*0-380-79064-5*, Avon Bks) Morrow Avon.

— Two for the Money: A Couples Complete Guide to Money Management. LC 99-38189. 304p. 1999. pap. 13.50 (*0-380-79065-3*, Avon Bks) Morrow Avon.

Powers, Nancy. Cooking for One Hundred. (Illus.). 256p. 1992. spiral bd. 15.95 (*0-941684-04-0*) Powers Pub. A cookbook for feeding large crowds has 357 delicious recipes, all serving 100 or more; 255 page book-art throghout: intended for camps, schools, churches, factories, similar institutions or social events: including many favorite recipes from cooks across the country. A special section with breakfast recipes: Combo binding: 3-color laminated cover. Weights, measures & equivalent charts. Since there is a constant need for a source of recipes to be served to large groups, whether adults or children this cookbook is intended to satisfy that need. Included are hundreds of interesting dishes, with recipes that range from very simple to the more complicated. In particular, the many cooks from campus & churches who contributed favorite recipes requested breakfast ideas. This volume includes a section of breakfast recipes. Cooking for 100 will reassure & inspire many cooks & will insure variety & good taste in dishes to be served to many people day after day. $15.95 each, plus $3.50 shipping & handling. Book stores receive 30 percent discount 1-4 books, 40 percent discount 5 or more books. ISBN 0-941684-04-0. Send check or Purchase Order to: POWERS PUBLISHING, 6809 Garden Oaks, Memphis, TN 38120 . (901) 756-9457, FAX (901) 753-5383.
Publisher Paid Annotation.

***Powers, Nancy R.** Grassroots Expectations of Democracy & Economy: Argentina in Comparative Perspective. (Pitt Latin American Ser). 303p. 2001. pap. 19.95 (*0-8229-5745-0*) U of Pittsburgh Pr.

Powers, Ormund. Martin Andersen: Editor, Publisher, Galley Boy. LC 96-41241. 1996. write for info. (*0-8092-3044-5*) NTC Contemp Pub Co.

***Powers, Pamela Leigh.** Chinese Power Animals: Archetypes of Transformation. LC 99-87142. (Illus.). 336p. 2000. pap. 16.95 (*1-57863-147-5*) Weiser.

Powers, Paul. Too Tough to Cry. 160p. 1998. pap. 15.00 (*0-00-638661-X*) HarpC.

Powers, Paul & Russell, Deborah. Love Your Job! Loving the Job You Have . . . Finding a Job You Love. (Illus.). 210p. (Orig.). 1993. pap. 12.95 (*1-56592-036-8*) Thomson Learn.

Powers, Paul A. They That Go down to the Sea: A Bicentennial Pictorial History of the United States Coast Guard. LC 90-61231. (Illus.). vii, 208p. 1990. 35.00 (*0-9626717-0-3*) USCG CPO Assn.

— They That Go down to the Sea: A Bicentennial Pictorial History of the United States Coast Guard. deluxe ed. LC 90-61231. (Illus.). vii, 208p. 1990. 75.00 (*0-9626717-1-1*) USCG CPO Assn.

Powers, Pauline S. & Fernandez, R. C., eds. Current Treatment of Anorexia Nervosa & Bulimia. (Biobehavioral Medicine Ser.: Vol. 4). xvi, 348p. 1984. 85.25 (*3-8055-3879-0*) S Karger.

Powers, Peggy. The Activity Gourmet. LC 91-66393. (Illus.). 135p. (Orig.). 1991. spiral bd. 15.95 (*0-910251-51-7*) Venture Pub PA.

Powers, Penny, jt. auth. see Hayes, Chuck.

Powers, Peter. Everywoman's Travel Journal. 160p. 1996. pap. 9.95 (*0-89815-802-8*) Ten Speed Pr.

— Touring California's Wine Country by Bicycle: Cycling in the Wine Growing Regions of North & Central California. 174p. 1990. pap. 10.95 (*0-944376-06-1*) Terragraphics.

— Touring New England by Bicycle: Cycling in Vermont, Maine & the Cape Islands. 174p. (Orig.). 1991. pap. 10.95 (*0-944376-08-8*) Terragraphics.

— Touring Seattle by Bicycle: Cycling in Seattle & the Lower Puget Sound Area. 174p. (Orig.). 1994. pap. 10.95 (*0-944376-02-9*) Terragraphics.

— Touring the Los Angeles Area by Bicycle: Cycling in Santa Barbara, Ventura, Los Angeles, Riverside & Orange Counties. 174p. (Orig.). 1992. pap. 12.95 (*0-944376-09-6*) Terragraphics.

— Touring the Pennsylvania Countryside by Bicycle: Cycling in Southeastern Pennsylvania & Western New Jersey. 174p. (Orig.). 1992. pap. 12.95 (*0-944376-12-6*) Terragraphics.

— Touring the San Francisco Bay Area by Bicycle: Cycling in Marin, Contra Costa, San Mateo, Alameda, Santa Clara & Santa Cruz Counties. 174p. (Orig.). 1994. pap. 11.95 (*0-944376-05-3*) Terragraphics.

— Touring the Washington D. C. Area by Bicycle: Cycling in Maryland, Virginia & D. C. 1991. pap. 12.95 (*0-944376-07-X*) Terragraphics.

Powers, Peter & Travis, Renee. Touring the Islands: Bicycling in the San Juan, Gulf, & Vancouver Islands. 174p. (Orig.). 1994. pap. 12.95 (*0-944376-01-0*) Terragraphics.

Powers, Phil. NOLS Wilderness Mountaineering. LC 93-6856. (Illus.). 256p. 1993. pap. 14.95 (*0-8117-3086-7*) Stackpole.

***Powers, Phil & National Outdoor Leadership School U. S. Staff.** Nols Wilderness Mountaineering. 2nd ed. LC 00-24094. (Illus.). 2000. pap. 14.95 (*0-8117-2861-7*) Stackpole.

Powers, Rachel, ed. see MSSD English Department Staff.

Powers, Rachell C. Kaleidoscope of Poetry. (Illus.). 36p. 1988. 10.00 (*0-9621323-0-6*) R Powers.

Powers, Remus. Kansas City BBQ Pocket Guide. 128p. (Orig.). 1992. pap. 7.95 (*0-925175-08-0*) Pig Out Pubns.

Powers, Rhea & Bantle, Gawain. Riding the Dragon: The Power of Committed Relationship. LC 94-69882. 240p. 1995. pap. 14.95 (*1-880823-09-8*) N Star Pubns.

Powers, Richard. Gain. LC 97-39647. 356p. 1998. text 25.00 (*0-374-15996-3*) FS&G.

— Gain. LC 99-18955. 368p. 1999. pap. 14.00 (*0-312-20409-4*, Picador USA) St Martin.

— Galatea 2.2: Novel, A. LC 96-2117. 336p. 1996. pap. 13.00 (*0-06-097692-6*, Perennial) HarperTrade.

— Gold Bug Variations. LC 92-52616. 640p. 1994. pap. 16.00 (*0-06-097500-8*, Perennial) HarperTrade.

— Incidental Findings. 208p. 1998. pap. 15.00 (*0-8059-4354-4*) Dorrance.

— The 1998 Crime & Disorder Act Explained. LC 99-209992. (Point of Law Ser.). 1999. 50.00 (*0-11-702685-9*, Pub. by Statnry Office) Balogh.

— Operation Wandering Soul. LC 93-49506. 352p. 1994. reprint ed. pap. 14.00 (*0-06-097611-X*, Perennial) HarperTrade.

— Pathways to Spiritual Understanding: An Exciting Introduction to the Basics of the Christian Life. 245p. 1988. pap. 16.99 (*1-56322-023-7*) Hensley Pub.

***Powers, Richard.** Plowing the Dark. LC 99-45084. 400p. 2000. 25.00 (*0-374-23461-2*) FS&G.

Powers, Richard. Prisoner's Dilemma. LC 96-54203. 352p. 1996. pap. 14.00 (*0-06-097708-6*) HarpC.

— Prisoner's Dilemma. LC 95-54203. 1996. write for info. (*0-614-95874-1*, Perennial) HarperTrade.

— Prisoner's Dilemma. LC 88-29039. 1989. write for info. (*0-07-050612-4*) McGraw.

— Quicken 98 for the Direct Investor: An Easy to Use Guide on How to Manage Your Dividend Reinvestment & Direct Stock Purchase Plans. (Illus.). 224p. 1998. pap. write for info. (*0-9666997-0-X*) Failte Pubg.

— Three Farmers on Their Way to a Dance. LC 92-52617. 352p. 1994. pap. 13.00 (*0-06-097509-1*, Perennial) HarperTrade.

***Powers, Richard B.** An Alien among Us: A Diversity Game. LC 99-39391. 41p. 1999. pap. text 19.95 (*1-877864-74-9*) Intercult Pr.

Powers, Richard G. Not Without Honor: The History of American Anti-Communism. 400p. 1996. 30.00 (*0-02-925301-2*); 29.50 (*0-684-82427-2*) Free Pr.

— Not Without Honor: The History of American Anticommunism. LC 97-80742. (Illus.). 592p. 1998. pap. 18.00 (*0-300-07470-0*) Yale U Pr.

— Secrecy & Power: The Life of J. Edgar Hoover. (Illus.). 656p. 1988. pap. 18.95 (*0-02-925061-7*) Free Pr.

Powers, Richard G. & Kato, Hidetoshi, eds. Handbook of Japanese Popular Culture. LC 87-7586. 368p. 1989. lib. bdg. 89.50 (*0-313-23922-3*, PJC/, Greenwood Pr) Greenwood.

***Powers, Robert C.** Quester. 490p. 1999. pap. 16.95 (*1-891929-41-0*) Four Seasons.

***Powers, Robert F.** English-Albanian Dictionary-Phrasebook for Aid Workers & Military Personnel. (ALB & ENG.). 2001. pap. 21.95 (*1-929482-02-7*) Rodnik.

— English-Spanish Dictionary-Phrasebook of Love. (ENG & SPA.). 640p. 2001. pap. 21.95 (*1-929482-03-5*) Rodnik.

***Powers, Robert F., ed.** International Directory of Personal Ad Columns, Introduction Services & Matrimonial Agencies: 2000. 2001. pap. 21.95 (*1-929482-04-3*) Rodnik.

Powers, Robert F., jt. auth. see Frolova, Marina.

Powers, Robert F., jt. tr. see Powers, Hong-Oanh.

Powers, Robert L. & Griffith, Jane. The Individual Psychology Client Workbook with Supplements. 45p. (Orig.). 1995. pap. text, student ed. 22.50 (*0-918287-08-1*) APA.

— Understanding Life-Style: The Psycho-Clarity Process. LC 87-13146. 336p. 1987. text 42.50 (*0-918287-02-2*); pap. text 32.50 (*0-918287-03-0*) APA.

Powers, Robert L., jt. auth. see Wedge, Thomas W.

Powers, Rodney G., jt. auth. see Sagues, Alberto A.

Powers, Roger S., et al. Protest, Power, & Change: An Encyclopedia of Nonviolent Action from ACT-UP to Women's Suffrage. LC 96-26869. (Illus.). 640p. 1997. text 95.00 (*0-8153-0913-9*, H1625) Garland.

Powers, Ron. The Beast, the Eunuch & the Glass-Eyed Child: Television in the 80's. 1990. 24.95 (*0-15-111251-7*) Harcourt.

— The Cruel Radiance: Notes of a Prosewriter in a Visual Age. LC 94-20541. 269p. 1994. 25.00 (*0-87451-690-0*) U Pr of New Eng.

— Dangerous Waters: A Biography of the Boy Who Became Mark Twain. LC 99-228994. 256p. 1999. 23.00 (*0-465-07670-X*, Pub. by Basic) HarpC.

Powers, Ron, jt. auth. see Bradley, James.

Powers, Samuel R. A Diagnostic Study of the Subject Matter of High School Chemistry. LC 79-177164. (Columbia University. Teachers College. Contributions to Education Ser.: No. 149). reprint ed. 37.50 (*0-404-55149-1*) AMS Pr.

Powers, Scott. Here's Looking at You: The Actor's Guide to Commercial Print. LC 96-32691. 1997. pap. 16.95 (*0-435-08694-4*, 08694) Heinemann.

Powers, Scott K. & Dodd, Stephen L. The Essentials of Total Fitness: Exercise, Nutrition & Wellness. LC 96-31269. 253p. 1996. pap. text 26.00 (*0-205-17902-9*) Allyn.

Powers, Scott K. & Dodd, Stephen L. The Essentials of Total Fitness: Exercise, Nutrition, & Wellness - Examination Copy. 272p. (C). 1996. pap. write for info. (*0-205-26447-6*, T6447-1) Allyn.

Powers, Scott K. & Howley, Edward T. Exercise Physiology. 2nd ed. 160p. (C). 1995. text, student ed. 18.75 (*0-697-28488-3*) Brown & Benchmark.

— Exercise Physiology. 3rd ed. LC 96-83127. 624p. (C). 1996. text. write for info. (*0-697-25798-3*); text, student ed. 19.37 (*0-697-29518-4*) Brown & Benchmark.

— Exercise Physiology: Theory. 3rd ed. 544p. (C). 1997. text. write for info. (*0-07-114805-1*) McGraw.

— Exercise Physiology: Theory & Application to Fitness & Performance. 2nd ed. 624p. (C). 1993. text 47.85 (*0-697-12657-9*) Brown & Benchmark.

Powers, Sharon B., ed. see Shelley, Percy Bysshe.

Powers, Shelley. Developing ASP Components. Petrusha, Ron, ed. (Illus.). 510p. 1999. pap. 29.95 (*1-56592-446-0*) OReilly & Assocs.

Powers, Stefanie, jt. auth. see Fenichel, Emily.

Powers, Stephen. Art of Getting Over. LC 99-20420. 176p. 1999. text 29.95 (*0-312-20630-5*) St Martin.

— Tribes of California. LC 74-7994. reprint ed. 67.50 (*0-404-11881-X*) AMS Pr.

— Tribes of California. LC 75-13150. 1977. reprint ed. pap. 18.95 (*0-520-03172-5*, Pub. by U CA Pr) Cal Prin Full Svc.

Powers, Stephen P., jt. auth. see Rothman, Stanley.

Powers, Steve. Listen to your Neighbor's Heart: A Book about the Awesome Power of Listening. LC 96-94690. 215 P. :p. 1997. write for info. (*0-9654075-0-0*) Listeners Pr OH.

Powers, Steve, jt. auth. see Postman, Neil.

Powers, Susan J. Pocket Mentor: How to Get Every Promotion You Want from Now On! 390p. 1995. 29.95 (*1-886573-02-6*); pap. 19.95 (*1-886573-01-8*) Change Pubns.

***Powers, Susan M. & Hamann, Cornelia.** The Acquisition of Scrambling & Cliticization. 516p. 2000. 214.00 (*0-7923-6249-7*) Kluwer Academic.

Powers, Susan M., jt. auth. see Krippner, Stanley.

***Powers, Thomas.** The Confirmation. LC 99-49237. 416p. 2000. 25.95 (*0-375-40020-6*) Knopf.

Powers, Thomas. Heisenberg's War: The Secret History of the German Bomb. 1999. pap. write for info. (*0-452-27135-5*, Plume) Dutton Plume.

Powers, Thomas E. Invitation to a Great Experiment: Exploring the Possibility That God Can Be Known. rev. ed. (Illus.). 352p. 1996. pap. 14.95 (*0-914896-42-3*) East Ridge Pr.

Powers, Thomas F. & Powers, Jo-Marie. Food Service Operations: Planning & Control. LC 83-10364. (Service Management Ser.). 384p. (C). 1991. reprint ed. 46.50 (*0-89464-600-1*) Krieger.

***Powers, Thomas M. & Kamolnick, Paul, eds.** From Kant to Weber: Freedom & Culture in Classical German Social Theory. LC 98-34309. (Open Forum Ser.). 31p. (C). 1999. pap. text 18.50 (*0-89464-992-2*) Krieger.

Powers, Thomas R. Integrated Circuit Hobbyist's Handbook. (Illus.). 128p. 1995. pap. 19.95 (*1-878707-12-4*) LLH Tech Pub.

— The Master Handbook of IC Circuits. pap. 18.60 (*0-8306-1370-6*) McGraw-Hill Prof.

Powers, Thomas V., jt. auth. see Stockbridge, Grant.

Powers, Tim. The Anubis Gates. 416p. 1984. mass mkt. 4.95 (*0-441-02382-7*) Ace Bks.

— The Anubis Gates. 400p. 1997. reprint ed. pap. 12.95 (*0-441-00401-6*) Ace Bks.

— The Anubis Gates. (Illus.). 396p. 1990. reprint ed. 25.00 (*0-929480-10-4*) Mark Ziesing.

Powers, Tim. Declare. Date not set. mass mkt. write for info. (*0-380-79836-0*) HarpC.

— Declare. 2000. 24.00 (*0-380-97652-8*, Wm Morrow) Morrow Avon.

Powers, Tim. The Drawing of the Dark. 1999. pap. 11.95 (*0-345-43081-6*) Ballantine Pub Grp.

— Earthquake Weather. LC 97-18592. 384p. 1997. text 24.95 (*0-312-86163-X*) St Martin.

— Earthquake Weather. 1998. mass mkt. 6.99 (*0-8125-5519-8*, Pub. by Tor Bks) St Martin.

— Expiration Date. 384p. 1995. 23.95 (*0-312-86086-2*, Pub. by Tor Bks) St Martin.

— Expiration Date. 1996. mass mkt. 6.99 (*0-8125-5517-1*, Pub. by Tor Bks) St Martin.

— Last Call. (Illus.). 576p. 1992. 150.00 (*0-927389-05-3*) Charnel Hse.

— Last Call. 544p. 1993. mass mkt. 4.99 (*0-380-71557-0*, Avon Bks) Morrow Avon.

— Last Call. LC 91-34070. 544p. 1996. pap. 13.00 (*0-380-72846-X*, Avon Bks) Morrow Avon.

— Last Call. limited ed. (Illus.). 576p. 1992. teacher ed. 650.00 (*0-927389-04-5*) Charnel Hse.

— The Stress of Her Regard. 1991. pap. 4.95 (*0-441-79097-6*) Ace Bks.

— The Stress of Her Regard. limited ed. (Illus.). 544p. 1989. 125.00 (*0-927389-01-0*); 400.00 (*0-927389-00-2*) Charnel Hse.

***Powers, Tim, frwd.** Frank Kelly Freas: As He Sees It. 2000. 29.95 (*1-85585-848-7*, Pub. by Paper Tiger) Sterling.

Powers, Tim, jt. auth. see Isaacs, Richard B.

Powers, Timothy E., jt. auth. see Fijolek, Richard M.

Powers, Tom. Great Birding in the Great Lakes: A Guide to the 50 Best Birdwatching Sites in the Great Lake States. LC 98-226821. (Illus.). 170p. 1998. pap. 17.95 (*0-9660068-0-1*) Walloon Press.

— Introduction to Management in the Hospitality Industry. 5th ed. 336p. 1995. pap., teacher ed. write for info. (*0-471-05388-0*) Wiley.

— Introduction to Management in the Hospitality Industry: Short Version. 6th ed. LC 98-30332. (Wiley Service Management Ser.). (Illus.). 656p. 1999. 64.95 (*0-471-25203-4*) Wiley.

— Introduction to Management in the Hospitality Industry 94-022961. 5th ed. LC 94-22961. (Service Management Ser.). 624p. 1995. 64.95 (*0-471-31035-2*) Wiley.

— Introduction to the Hospitality Industry. 3rd ed. 256p. 1995. pap., teacher ed. write for info. (*0-471-05692-8*) Wiley.

— Marketing Hospitality. 148p. 1990. pap., student ed., suppl. ed. 29.95 (*0-471-62298-2*) Wiley.

— Marketing Hospitality. 2nd ed. LC 96-36091. 464p. 1997. 54.95 (*0-471-12703-5*) Wiley.

— Michigan in Quotes. LC 94-207331. (Illus.). 176p. (Orig.). 1994. pap. 12.95 (*0-923756-08-6*) Friede Pubns.

— Michigan State & National Parks: A Complete Guide. 3rd rev. ed. LC 98-139754. (Illus.). 240p. (Orig.). 1997. pap. 14.95 (*0-923756-16-7*) Friede Pubns.

— Natural Michigan: A Guide to 288 Natural Attractions. expanded rev. ed. (Illus.). 260p. 1995. pap. 14.95 (*0-923756-13-2*) Friede Pubns.

Powers, Tom. Steven Spielberg: Master Storyteller. LC 96-22289. (J). 1996. lib. bdg. 23.93 (*0-8225-4929-8*) Lerner Pub.

***Powers, Tom.** Steven Spielberg: Master Storyteller. (A&E Biography Ser.). (Illus.). 128p. (YA). (gr. 4-7). 2000. pap. 7.95 (*0-8225-9694-6*, Lerner Publctns) Lerner Pub.

Powers, Tom & Barrows, Clayton W. Introduction to the Hospitality Industry. 4th ed. LC 98-30333. (Service Management Ser.). 512p. 1999. pap. 59.95 (*0-471-25244-1*) Wiley.

***Powers, Tom & Grassy, John.** Audubon Guide to the National Wildlife Refuges Northern Midwest: Northern Midwest. (Illus.). 288p. 2000. pap. 19.95 (*0-312-24315-4*) St Martin.

Powers, Treval C. John Maynard Keynes & Empirical Macroeconomics. (Illus.). 150p. (C). 1998. pap. write for info. (*0-9647121-2-1*) Benchmark CT.

— Leakage: The Bleeding of the American Economy. (Illus.). 350p. (Orig.). 1996. pap. 39.95 (*0-9647121-1-3*) Benchmark CT.

Powers, Tyrone. Eyes to My Soul: The Rise or Decline of a Black FBI Agent. LC 95-47232. ix, 487p. 1996. pap. 14.95 (*0-912469-33-1*) Majority Pr.

Powers, Vicki & Payne, Laurie, eds. Internal Communications. (Illus.). 71p. 1995. spiral bd. 195.00 (*1-928593-05-4*) Am Prodtv Qual.

Powers, Vicki, ed. see O'Dell, Carla, et al.

Powers, W. Robert. Electrical Fires in New York City, 1976. 1977. 2.50 (*0-686-22739-5*, TR 77-3) Society Fire Protect.

***Powers-Water, Alma.** Mother Seton & the Sisters of Charity. 168p. 2000. pap. 9.95 (*0-89870-766-8*, Pub. by Ignatius Pr) Midpt Trade.

An Asterisk (*) at the beginning of an entry indicates that the title is appearing for the first time.

Powers, Will & Strickland, Bob. Bowling Tough: Three Simple Methods to Improve Your Performance under Pressure. 112p. 1993. pap. text 9.95 (*0-9635919-0-8*) R H Strickland.

Powers, William. Texas Products Liability Law, Issue 3. 2nd ed. 242p. 1997. ring bd. 49.00 (*0-409-25176-3*, 83056-13, MICHIE) LEXIS Pub.

Powers, William C., Jr. Texas Products Liability Law. 380p. 1993. suppl. ed. 55.00 (*0-685-46138-6*, MICHIE) LEXIS Pub.

— Texas Products Liability Law. 2nd ed. 380p. 1994. spiral bd. 115.00 (*1-56257-955-X*, MICHIE) LEXIS Pub.

Powers, William C., jt. auth. see Fischer, David A.

Powers, William C., Jr., ed. see Fischer, David A.

Powers, William D. Uncle Isaac. LC 74-170703. (Black Heritage Library Collection). 1977. reprint ed. 22.95 (*0-8369-8893-0*) Ayer.

Powers, William F., et al, eds. AAS/AIAA Astrodynamics Conference, July 28-30, 1975, Nassau, Bahamas. LC 57-43769. (Advances in the Astronautical Sciences Ser.: Vol. 33). (Illus.). 390p. 1976. 35.00 (*0-87703-079-0*, Am Astronaut Soc) Univelt Inc.

Powers, William H. Guide to Milwaukee Taverns. rev. ed. McCaig, Barbara, ed. (Illus.). 200p. 1987. pap. 4.95 (*0-935201-24-6*) Affordable Adven.

Powers, William J. & Raichle, Marcus E., eds. Cerebrovascular Diseases: Fifteenth Research, Princeton, Conference. LC 75-25125. 396p. 1987. reprint ed. pap. 122.80 (*0-608-00399-9*, 206111300007) Bks Demand.

Powers, William K. Beyond the Vision: Essays on American Indian Culture. LC 87-40218. (Civilization of the American Indian Ser.: Vol. 184). (Illus.). 256p. 1987. 37.95 (*0-8061-2091-6*) U of Okla Pr.

— Oglala Religion. LC 76-30614. (Illus.). xxii, 237p. 1977. pap. 12.00 (*0-8032-8706-2*, Bison Books) U of Nebr Pr.

— Sacred Language: The Nature of Supernatural Discourse in Lakota. LC 86-40079. (Civilization of the American Indian Ser.: Vol. 179). (Illus.). 264p. 1992. pap. 14.95 (*0-8061-2458-X*) U of Okla Pr.

— War Dance: Plains Indian Musical Performance. LC 90-32421. (Illus.). 199p. 1993. reprint ed. pap. 12.95 (*0-8165-1365-1*) U of Ariz Pr.

— Yuwipi: Vision & Experience in Oglala Ritual. LC 81-10501. (Illus.). xiii, 113p. 1982. reprint ed. pap. 6.95 (*0-8032-8710-0*, Bison Books) U of Nebr Pr.

Powers, William T. Behavior: The Control of Perception. LC 73-75697. 309p. 1973. lib. bdg. 45.95 (*0-202-25113-6*) Aldine de Gruyter.

— Living Control Systems: Selected Papers of William T. Powers. (Illus.). 300p. (Orig.). (C). 1989. reprint ed. pap. text 19.95 (*0-9647121-3-X*) Benchmark CT.

— Living Control Systems II: Selected Papers of William T. Powers. (C). 1992. reprint ed. pap. text 19.95 (*0-9647121-4-8*) Benchmark CT.

— Making Sense of Behavior: The Meaning of Control. Forssell, Dag, ed. LC 99-216013. 186p. (C). 1998. pap. 14.95 (*0-9647121-5-6*) Benchmark CT.

— The NextPresident.com. 450p. 1999. 24.95 (*0-9672701-0-3*) Coyote Pubng.

Powers, William T., jt. ed. see Robertson, Richard J.

Powery, Emerson B., jt. ed. see Cross, Terry L.

Powhida, Elizabeth C. Anthony Mouse Goes Swimming. LC 95-77342. (Illus.). 40p. (J). (ps-5). 1995. pap. write for info. (*0-9625842-1-5*, TXU538146) Kinderhook Pubs.

Powicke, Frederick J. Cambridge Platonists. 1971. reprint ed. 45.00 (*0-8371-3999-6*, POPL) Greenwood.

— The Cambridge Platonists. (GER.). viii, 219p. 1970. reprint ed. 3.5 hd. write for info. (*0-318-70503-6*) G Olms Pubs.

— The Cambridge Platonists. (Illus.). viii, 219p. 1970. reprint ed. write for info. (*0-318-71273-3*) G Olms Pubs.

— The Cambridge Platonists: A Study. (Illus.). viii, 219p. 1970. reprint ed. 32.37 incl. 3.5 hd (*0-685-66505-4*, 05102832) G Olms Pubs.

Powicke, Frederick M. Modern Historians & the Study of History: Essays & Papers. LC 75-25496. 256p. 1976. reprint ed. lib. bdg. 35.00 (*0-8371-8428-2*, POMH, Greenwood Pr) Greenwood.

— The Thirteenth Century, 1216-1307. 2nd ed. (Illus.). 844p. 1962. text 70.00 (*0-19-821708-0*) OUP.

— Ways of Medieval Life & Thought. LC 64-13394. (Illus.). 1949. 28.00 (*0-8196-0137-3*) Biblo.

Powicke, Frederick M., ed. see Rashdall, Hastings.

Powicke, J. C. Government in the Economy. 1977. pap. text 2.40 (*0-08-018120-1*, Pergamon Pr) Elsevier.

Powicke, John Colyer, et al. Applied Economics. LC 73-157811. vi, 239 p. 1972. write for info. (*0-7131-1745-1*) St Martin.

Powicke, Maurice. The Thirteenth Century, 1216-1307. 2nd ed. (Oxford History of England Ser.: Vol. 4). (Illus.). 848p. 1991. reprint ed. pap. text 16.95 (*0-19-285249-3*) OUP.

Powicke, Maurice, ed. see Daniel, Walter.

Powis, David. The Signs of Crime: A Field of Manual for Police. LC 77-30173. (Illus.). 1978. pap. text 5.95 (*0-89444-007-1*) John Jay Pr.

Powis, David A. & Bunn, Stephen J., eds. Neurotransmitter Release & Its Modulation: Biochemical Mechanisms, Physiological Function & Clinical Relevance. (Illus.). 374p. (C). 1995. text 140.00 (*0-521-44068-8*); pap. text 59.95 (*0-521-44616-3*) Cambridge U Pr.

Powis, Garth. Metabolism & Reaction of Anti Cancer Drugs, 2 vols. 329.25 (*0-08-042355-8*, Pergamon Pr) Elsevier.

Powis, Garth, ed. Anticancer Drugs: Antmetabolite Metabolism & Natural Anticancer Agents. 524p. 1994. 197.75 (*0-08-042334-5*, Pergamon Pr) Elsevier.

— Anticancer Drugs: Reactive Metabolism & Drug Interactions. 460p. 1994. 197.75 (*0-08-042335-3*, Pergamon Pr) Elsevier.

Powis, Garth & Hackar, M., eds. The Toxicity of Anticancer Drugs: A Study in Human Toxicity. 256p. 1991. text 55.00 (*0-07-105305-0*, Pub. by PPI) McGraw.

Powis, Garth & Prough, R. A., eds. Metabolism & Action of Anti-Cancer Drugs. LC 86-23179. 336p. 1987. 138.00 (*0-85066-369-5*) Taylor & Francis.

Powis, Ivan, et al, eds. High Resolution Laser Photoionization & Photoelectron Studies. LC 95-3818. (Series in Ion Chemistry & Physics). 526p. 1995. 330.00 (*0-471-94158-1*) Wiley.

Powis, Raymond L. A Northwest Twelve-Moon Journey. (Illus.). 88p. (Orig.). 1995. pap. 19.95 (*1-888647-00-0*) Ray & Roo Enter.

Powis, Raymond L. & Powis, Wendy J. The Son of Ultrasound Physics for the Fun of It. (Illus.). 106p. 1998. pap. text 34.00 (*1-888647-03-5*) Ray & Roo Enter.

— The Son of Ultrasound Physics for the Fun of It, Animal Applications. (Illus.). 70p. (Orig.). 1996. pap. text 27.00 (*1-888647-02-7*) Ray & Roo Enter.

— A Thinker's Guide to Ultrasonic Imaging. LC 83-21704. (Illus.). 430p. 1984. 55.00 (*0-683-06961-6*) Lppncott W & W.

Powis, Raymond L. & Schwartz, Robert A. Practical Doppler Ultrasound for the Clinician. (Illus.). 208p. 1991. 60.00 (*0-683-06958-6*) Lppncott W & W.

Powis, Raymond L., ed. see Jimerfield, Steven & Schoenberg, Timothy.

Powis, Robert E. Bank Secrecy Act Compliance. 4th ed. 250p. 1993. text 90.00 (*1-55738-360-X*, Irwn Prfssnl) McGraw-Hill Prof.

— Bank Secrecy Act Compliance. 5th ed. LC 96-35874. 352p. (C). 1996. 95.00 (*1-55738-797-4*, Irwn Prfssnl) McGraw-Hill Prof.

— The Bankline Quick Reference Flipchart: Complying with the Bank Secrecy Act. 20p. (C). 1995. text 17.00 (*1-55738-798-2*, Irwn Prfssnl) McGraw-Hill Prof.

— Complying with the Bank Secrecy Act. rev. ed. 22p. 1993. text 22.00 (*1-55738-399-5*, Irwn Prfssnl) McGraw-Hill Prof.

— The Money Launderers: Lessons from the Drug Wars - How Billions of Illegal Dollars Are Washed Through Banks & Businesses. 300p. 1992. 21.95 (*1-55738-262-X*, Irwn Prfssnl) McGraw-Hill Prof.

Powis, Robert E., jt. auth. see Bai.

Powis, Stephen H. & Vaughan, Robert, eds. MHC Protocols. (Methods in Molecular Biology Ser.). 350p. 1999. 79.50 (*0-89603-548-4*) Humana.

Powis, Wendy J., jt. auth. see Powis, Raymond L.

Powitt, A. H. Hair Structure & Chemistry Simplified. (Illus.). 320p. 1977. pap. 31.95 (*0-87350-080-6*) Milady Pub.

— Lectures in Hair Structure & Chemistry for Cosmetology Teachers. (Illus.). 1991. pap. 28.95 (*0-87350-354-6*) Milady Pub.

Powlas, Joe. The Church with the Golden Roof. 1988p. 12.00 (*0-8187-0103-X*) Harlo Press.

— To Walk in Heaven. 176p. 1991. 15.00 (*0-8187-0144-7*) Harlo Press.

Powledge, Fred. Pharmacy In The Forest. LC 97-6938. 47p. (J). (gr. 5-8). 1998. 17.00 (*0-689-80863-1*) S&S Childrens.

— We Shall Overcome: Heroes of the Civil Rights Movement. LC 92-25184. (Illus.). 224p. (YA). (gr. 7 up). 1993. 17.00 (*0-684-19362-0*) Scribner.

Powledge, Tabitha M. Your Brain: How You Got It & How It Works. LC 94-14273. (Illus.). 160p. (J). (gr. 6-8). 1994. mass mkt. 14.95 (*0-684-19659-X*) S&S Trade.

Powles, Simon. Wild Energy 1998: Switch on to Wind Power. 390p. 1998. 243.00 (*1-86058-137-4*) Professional Engineering Institute.

Powles, Cyril H. Interpreting the Present Time: History, the Bible & the Church's Mission Today. 88p. 1994. 8.95 (*1-55126-094-8*) Forward Movement.

Powles, David G. Powles: The Mareva Injunction & Associated Orders. 1985. boxed set 48.00 (*0-86205-069-3*, MICHIE) LEXIS Pub.

Powles, L. D. The Land of the Pink Pearl: Recollections of Life in the Bahamas. Sealey, Neil E., ed. & intro. by. (Illus.). 192p. 1996. reprint ed. pap. 12.95 (*0-9643786-3-9*) Media Pubng.

Powles, Stephen. Herbicide Resistant Weed Management. 2000. ring bd. 99.95 (*0-8493-2219-7*) CRC Pr.

Powles, Stephen & Holtum, Joseph, eds. Herbicide Resistance in Plants: Biology & Biochemistry. 368p. 1994. lib. bdg. 99.95 (*0-87371-713-9*, L713) Lewis Pubs.

Powles, Trevor J., jt. ed. see Maslin, Anna M.

Powles, William E. Human Development & Homeostasis: The Science of Psychiatry. LC 90-15604. 600p. (C). 1992. 80.00 (*0-8236-2363-7*) Intl Univs Pr.

Powley, Edward E. Pomeroy Family - House of De La Pomerai: Annals of the Family Which Was, from the Conquest to 1548. (Illus.). 144p. 1994. 32.00 (*0-8328-9827-9*); pap. 22.00 (*0-8328-9828-7*) Higginson Bk Co.

Powley, Harrison. Il Trionfo di Dori: The 29 Madrigals of the 1592 Collection. (Renaissance Voices Ser.). 264p. 1990. pap. 25.00 (*1-888471-05-0*) Gaudia Mus & Arts.

Powley, Robyn. Border Collies: A New Owner's Guide. LC 99-199908. 1998. 12.95 (*0-7938-2803-1*) TFH Pubns.

***Powlik, James.** A Glossary of Oceanographic Terms. 2nd ed. 208p. 2000. pap. 9.95 (*0-9677304-2-2*, Raggedtooth) Raggedtooth Prod.

— Sea Change. LC 98-33242. 368p. 1999. 24.95 (*0-385-33399-4*) Delacorte.

— Sea Change. 544p. 2000. mass mkt. 6.99 (*0-440-23508-1*) Dell.

— Whistle-Stop: A Novel. 288p. 1999. pap. 9.95 (*0-9677304-0-6*) Raggedtooth Prod.

***Powlik, Roger J.** Take As Directed: Memoirs of a Life in Pharmacy. 240p. 2000. pap. 9.95 (*0-9677304-8-1*) Raggedtooth Prod.

***Powling, Chris.** Kit's Castle. (I Am Reading Ser.). (Illus.). 48p. (YA). (gr. k up). 2000. pap. 3.95 (*0-7534-5122-0*, Kingfisher) LKC.

Powling, Chris. Roald Dahl. LC 97-33403. (Tell Me About Ser.). (Illus.). 24p. (J). (gr. 2-3). 1997. 19.93 (*1-57505-274-1*, Carolrhoda) Lerner Pub.

***Powlison, David.** Pornography: Slaying the Dragon. (Resources for Changing Lives Ser.). 20p. 1999. pap. 1.75 (*0-87552-677-2*) P & R Pubng.

Powlison, David. Power Encounters: Reclaiming Spiritual Warfare. 160p. 1994. pap. 9.99 (*0-8010-7138-0*, Hour Glass) Baker Bks.

***Powlison, David.** Pre-Engagement: Five Questions to Ask Yourselves. (Resources for Changing Lives Ser.). 40p. 2000. pap. 2.25 (*0-87552-679-9*) P & R Pubng.

Powlison, Keith. Profits of the National Banks. Bruchey, Stuart, ed. LC 80-1166. (Rise of Commercial Banking Ser.). (Illus.). 1981. reprint ed. lib. bdg. 15.95 (*0-405-13676-5*) Ayer.

Powlson, David S., et al, eds. Evaluation of Soil Organic Matter Models Using Existing Long-Term Datasets: Using Existing Long-Term Datasets. LC 95-45659. (NATO ASI Ser.: Vol. 38). 429p. 1996. text 197.00 (*3-540-60602-5*) Spr-Verlag.

Powlson, David S., et al. Farming, Fertilizers & the Nitrate Problem. (Illus.). 176p. (Orig.). 1991. pap. text 35.00 (*0-85198-658-7*) OUP.

Pownall, David. Composer Plays. LC 95-129462. (Oberon Bks.). 220p. 1997. pap. 18.95 (*1-870259-41-6*) Theatre Comm.

***Pownall, David.** Pownall: Plays One. 340p. 2000. pap. 20.95 (*1-84002-076-8*) Theatre Comm.

Pownall, David. Radio Plays. (Oberon Book). 200p. 1998. pap. 18.95 (*1-84002-034-2*) Theatre Comm.

Pownall, Henry J. & Spector, Arthur A., eds. Proceedings from the Scientific Conference on Omega-3 Fatty Acids in Nutrition, Vascular Biology, & Medicine. (Illus.). 275p. write for info. (*0-614-04637-8*); pap. text. write for info. (*0-87493-007-3*) Am Heart.

Pownall, Mark. Heroin. LC 91-27815. (Illus.). 64p. (YA). (gr. 6-12). 1991. lib. bdg. 25.68 (*0-8114-3201-7*) Raintree Steck-V.

Pownall, Peter. Fisheries of Australia. (Illus.). 1978. 50.00 (*0-7855-6922-7*) St Mut.

Pownall, Thomas. The Administration of the Colonies: 1668. LC 93-36377. 470p. 1993. 75.00 (*0-8201-1487-1*) Schol Facsimiles.

— The Letter from Governor Pownall to Adam Smith: Being an Examination of Several Points of Doctrine Laid down in His Inquiry. LC 66-15563. (Reprints of Economic Classics Ser.). 48p. 1967. reprint ed. 19.50 (*0-678-00258-4*) Kelley.

— A Topographical Description of the Dominions of the United States of America. Mulkearn, Lois, ed. LC 75-22835. (America in Two Centuries Ser.). 1976. reprint ed. 23.95 (*0-405-07706-8*) Ayer.

Pownall, Tim, tr. see Caron, Jean.

Pownall, Tim, tr. see Gombert, Jean E.

Pownall, Tim, tr. see Jodelet, Denise.

Pownall, Tim, tr. see Streri, Arlette.

Powne, Michael. Ethiopian Music, an Introduction: A Survey of Ecclesiastical & Secular Ethiopian Music & Instruments. LC 80-14087. (Illus.). 160p. 1980. reprint ed. lib. bdg. 35.00 (*0-313-22161-8*, POEM, Greenwood Pr) Greenwood.

Powney, Janet & Watts, Mike. Interviewing in Educational Research. LC 87-10341. (Education Bks.). 213p. reprint ed. pap. 66.10 (*0-608-20409-9*, 207166200002) Bks Demand.

Powning, Beth. Home. 1999. pap. 17.00 (*0-375-75423-7*, Pub. by Sierra) Random.

— Seeds of Another Summer. (Illus.). 115p. 1999. text 29.95 (*0-670-86786-1*) Viking Penguin.

***Powning, Beth.** Shadow Child: An Apprenticeship in Love & Loss. 320p. 2000. 24.00 (*0-7867-0720-8*) Carroll & Graf.

Powrie, P., ed. Marie Cardinal: Les Mots pour le Dire. (FRE.). 1993. pap. 20.95 (*1-85399-336-0*, Pub. by Brist Class Pr) Focus Pub-R Pullins.

Powrie, P., jt. ed. see Atack, M.

Powrie, Phil. French Cinema in the 1980s: Nostalgia & the Crisis of Masculinity. (Illus.). 218p. 1997. pap. text 17.95 (*0-19-871119-0*) OUP.

— French Cinema in the 1980s: Nostalgia & the Crisis of Masculinity. (Illus.). 218p. (C). 1997. text 67.50 (*0-19-871118-2*) OUP.

***Powrie, Phil, ed.** French Cinema in the 1990s: Continuity & Difference. (Illus.). 304p. 2000. text 65.00 (*0-19-815958-7*); pap. text 19.95 (*0-19-815957-9*) OUP.

Powrie, Phil, tr. see Daumal, Rene.

Powrie, William. Soil Mechanics: Concepts & Applications. LC 96-70577. (Illus.). 440p. (C). (gr. 13). 1996. pap. 45.00 (*0-419-19720-6*, E & FN Spon) Routledge.

Powsner, Edward R., jt. auth. see Powsner, Rachel A.

Powsner, Rachel A. & Powsner, Edward R. Essentials of Nuclear Medicine Physics. LC 98-21578. (Illus.). 1998. pap. 42.95 (*0-632-04314-8*) Blackwell Sci.

Powszechna, Wiedza. Large French-Polish Dictionary: Grand Dictionnaire Francais-Polonais. (FRE & POL.). 2220p. 1984. 95.00 (*0-8288-0481-8*, F 53100) Fr & Eur.

Powszechna, Wiedza, et al. Wiedza Powszechna Compact Polish & English Dictionary. (Illus.). 712p. 1994. 16.95 (*0-8442-8366-5*, 83665, Natl Textbk Co) NTC Contemp Pub Co.

— Wiedza Powszechna Compact Polish & English Dictionary. LC 98-8067. (POL & ENG., Illus.). 712p. 1994. pap. 12.95 (*0-8442-8367-3*, 83673, Natl Textbk Co) NTC Contemp Pub Co.

Powter, Susan. Alto a la Enfermedad ! Coma Bien y Viva Mejor.Tr. of Stop the Insanity!. (ENG & SPA.). 336p. 1995. per. 11.00 (*0-684-81327-0*) S&S Trade Pap.

— C'mon, America, Let's Eat! (Illus.). 256p. 1996. pap. 14.00 (*0-684-81317-3*, Fireside) S&S Trade Pap.

— Daily Inspiration. 320p. 2001. per. 10.00 (*0-684-84467-2*, Fireside) S&S Trade Pap.

— Food. 1996. mass mkt. 5.99 (*0-671-56756-X*) PB.

— The Pocket Powter: Questions & Answers to Help You Change the Way You Look & Feel Forever. 224p. 1994. pap. 6.99 (*0-671-89456-0*, Fireside) S&S Trade Pap.

***Powter, Susan.** Sober . . . And Staying That Way: The Missing Link in the Cure for Alcoholism. 320p. 1999. text 23.00 (*0-7881-6398-1*) DIANE Pub.

Powter, Susan. Sober... & Staying That Way. 320p. 1999. per. 13.00 (*0-684-84797-3*) S&S Trade.

— Stop the Insanity! Grose, Bill, ed. 384p. 1995. mass mkt. 7.99 (*0-671-52292-2*) PB.

— Stop the Insanity! audio 12.00 (*0-671-88078-0*, 392922, Pub. by S&S Audio) Lndmrk Audiobks.

— Stop the Insanity! (Illus.). 320p. 1993. 22.00 (*0-671-79598-8*) S&S Trade.

— Stop the Insanity! 1996. pap. 9.95 (*0-684-82664-X*) S&S Trade.

Powton, Betty. A Penny for Them. 84p. (C). 1989. 50.00 (*0-7223-2365-4*, Pub. by A H S Ltd) St Mut.

Powys, Albert R. From the Ground Up: Collected Papers. LC 77-156706. (Essay Index Reprint Ser.). 1977. reprint ed. 12.95 (*0-8369-2292-1*) Ayer.

***Powys, David J.** Hell: A Hard Look at a Hard Question: The Fate of the Unrighteous in New Testament Thought. xxii, 478p. 1998. reprint ed. pap. 45.00 (*0-85364-831-X*, Pub. by Paternoster Pub) OM Literature.

Powys, John Cowper. Autobiography. 652p. 1994. pap. 24.95 (*0-912568-17-8*) Colgate U Pr.

— The Brazen Head. 348p. text 29.95 (*0-912568-11-9*) Colgate U Pr.

— Dostoievsky. LC 72-8975. (Studies in European Literature: No. 56). 1973. reprint ed. lib. bdg. 75.00 (*0-8383-1677-8*) M S G Haskell Hse.

— A Glastonbury Romance. 1120p. text 38.00 (*0-912568-10-0*) Colgate U Pr.

— A Glastonbury Romance. 1120p. 1996. pap. 24.95 (*0-87951-681-X*, Pub. by Overlook Pr) Penguin Putnam.

— A Glastonbury Romance. LC 87-5762. 1120p. 1987. reprint ed. 35.00 (*0-87951-282-2*, Pub. by Overlook Pr) Penguin Putnam.

— Homer & the Aether. 298p. text 27.95 (*0-912568-12-7*) Colgate U Pr.

— Letters to His Brother Llewelyn, 1902-1925, Vol. I. Elwin, Malcolm, ed. 367p. 1975. pap. text 12.95 (*0-912568-06-2*) Colgate U Pr.

— Letters to His Brother Llewelyn, 1925-1939, Vol. II. Elvin, Malcolm, ed. 284p. 1975. pap. text 12.95 (*0-912568-07-0*) Colgate U Pr.

— Maiden Castle. 496p. 1994. pap. 19.95 (*0-912568-18-6*) Colgate U Pr.

— Morwyn: Or, The Vengeance of God. Reginald, R. & Menville, Douglas A., eds. LC 75-46301. (Supernatural & Occult Fiction Ser.). 1976. reprint ed. lib. bdg. 26.95 (*0-405-08161-8*) Ayer.

— Petrushka & the Dancer: The Diaries of John Cowper Powys, 1929-1939. Krissdottir, Morine, ed. LC 95-17084. (Illus.). xxvii, 340p. 1995. text 45.00 (*0-312-12770-7*) St Martin.

— Poems: A Selection. Hopkins, Kenneth, ed. 224p. 1964. text 29.95 (*0-912568-00-3*) Colgate U Pr.

— Porius: A Romance of the Dark Ages. Albrecht, Wilbur, ed. 900p. 1994. text 48.95 (*0-912568-16-X*) Colgate U Pr.

— Rodmoor: A Romance. LC 73-77361. 1973. 33.95 (*0-912568-05-4*) Colgate U Pr.

— Visions & Revisions. 221p. text 29.95 (*0-912568-13-5*) Colgate U Pr.

— Weymouth Sands. 567p. 1999. text 35.00 (*0-87951-717-4*, Pub. by Overlook Pr) Penguin Putnam.

— Weymouth Sands. LC 99-10237. 567p. 2000. pap. 19.95 (*0-87951-706-9*, Pub. by Overlook Pr) Penguin Putnam.

— Wolf Solent. 614p. text 35.95 (*0-912568-09-7*) Colgate U Pr.

— Wolf Solent. LC 98-26452. 624p. 1998. pap. 15.00 (*0-375-70307-1*) Vin Bks.

— Wolf Solent: A Novel, 2 vols., Set. 1971. reprint ed. 79.00 (*0-403-01159-0*) Scholarly.

Powys, John Cowper & Powys, Lewellyn. Confessions of Two Brothers. LC 70-131804. 1971. reprint ed. 29.00 (*0-403-00691-0*) Scholarly.

Powys, Lewellyn, jt. auth. see Powys, John Cowper.

Powys, Littleton C. The Powys Family. LC 74-7023. (English Biography Ser.: No. 31). 1974. lib. bdg. 39.00 (*0-8383-1995-5*) M S G Haskell Hse.

Powys, Llewelyn. Baker's Dozen. LC 79-86776. (Essay Index Reprint Ser.). 1977. 19.95 (*0-8369-1153-9*) Ayer.

— Earth Memories. LC 73-90675. (Essay Index Reprint Ser.). 1977. 21.95 (*0-8369-1376-0*) Ayer.

— Earth Memories. 144p. 1983. 45.00 (*0-7855-0719-1*, Pub. by Redcliffe Pr Ltd) St Mut.

— Ebony & Ivory. 1988. 29.00 (*0-7855-0754-X*, Pub. by Redcliffe Pr Ltd) St Mut.

— Ebony & Ivory. LC 75-144168. (Short Story Index Reprint Ser.). 1977. reprint ed. 24.95 (*0-8369-3783-X*) Ayer.

— Rats in the Sacristy. LC 67-30226. (Essay Index Reprint Ser.). 1977. 19.95 (*0-8369-0798-1*) Ayer.

— Thirteen Worthies. LC 67-22112. (Essay Index Reprint Ser.). 1977. 18.95 (*0-8369-0799-X*) Ayer.

— Thirteen Worthies. 1985. 35.00 (*0-7855-0757-4*, Pub. by Redcliffe Pr Ltd) St Mut.

— The Twelve Months. 96p. (C). 1987. 50.00 (*0-948265-90-6*, Pub. by Redcliffe Pr Ltd) St Mut.

Powys, Marian. Lace & Lace Making. (Illus.). 1981. reprint ed. 50.00 (*1-55888-179-4*) Omnigraphics Inc.

P

Powys, Theodore F. Fables. 1971. reprint ed. 29.00 (0-403-01160-4) Scholarly.
— Father Adam. (C). 1990. 75.00 (0-907839-47-9, Pub. by Brynmill Pr Ltd) St Mut.
— Left Leg. LC 72-140337. (Short Story Index Reprint Ser.). 1977. 18.95 (0-8369-3729-5) Ayer.
— Mark Only. (Literature Ser.). 270p. 1972. reprint ed. 25.00 (0-403-00692-9) Scholarly.
— Mr. Tasker's Gods. LC 72-145246. 320p. 1972. reprint ed. 39.00 (0-403-01161-2) Scholarly.
— Two Thieves. LC 79-167466. (Short Story Index Reprint Ser.). 1977. reprint ed. 20.95 (0-8369-3992-1) Ayer.
— Unclay. (Literature Ser.). 328p. 1972. reprint ed. 39.00 (0-403-01162-0) Scholarly.
— White Paternoster, & Other Stories. LC 70-178455. (Short Story Index Reprint Ser.). 1977. reprint ed. 18.95 (0-8369-4056-3) Ayer.
Powzyk, Joyce A. In Search of Lemurs: My Days & Nights in a Madagascar Rain Forest. (Illus.). 48p. (J). (gr. 4-6). 1998. 17.95 (0-7922-7072-X, T07072C, Pub. by Natl Geog) S&S Trade.
Poxon, Nancy J., jt. auth. see Farrand, Scott.
Poy, Glenn, jt. auth. see Chane, Ken.
Poy-Wing, Celina. All Women's Health in the 90s Series. write for info. (0-9638783-4-4) All Womens Hlth.
— Climaxx!! Orgasmic Sex. 220p. 1995. pap. 9.95 (0-9638783-1-X) All Womens Hlth.
— Tame the Yeast Beast! Self-Help for Yeast Infections. (All Women's Health in the 90s Ser.). (Illus.). 80p. (Orig.). 1994. pap. 4.95 (0-9638783-0-1) All Womens Hlth.
***Poya, Maryam, contrib. by.** Women, Work & Islamism: Ideology & Resistance in Iran. LC 99-49833. 1999. 55.00 (1-85649-681-3) Zed Books.
***Poya, Maryann.** Women Work & Islamism: Ideology & Resistance in Iran. LC 99-49833. 208p. 1999. pap. 19.95 (1-85649-682-1) Zed Books.
Poyago-Theotoky, Joanna. Competition, Cooperation, Research & Development: The Economics of Research Joint Ventures. LC 97-11685. 1997. text 69.95 (0-312-17590-6) St Martin.
***Poyarkov, Victor, et al.** The Chornobyl Accident: A Comprehensive Risk Assessment. Vargo, George J., ed. LC 99-35803. 236p. 1999. 34.95 (1-57477-082-9) Battelle.
Poyas, Ann. Slots! LC 96-72064. 336p. (Orig.). 1997. 21.95 (0-9656167-0-3); pap. 12.95 (0-9656167-1-1) Book Creek.
Poyatos, Fernando. I Was Sick & You Visited Me: A Manual for Pastoral Care Visitation. LC 99-14352. 1998. pap. 11.95 (0-8091-3871-9) Paulist Pr.
— Paralanguage: A Linguistic & Interdisciplinary Approach to Interactive Speech & Sound. LC 92-42014. (Current Issues in Linguistic Theory Ser.: Vol. 92). xii, 478p. 1993. 125.00 (1-55619-149-9) J Benjamins Pubng Co.
Poyatos, Fernando, ed. Advances in Non-Verbal Communication: Sociocultural, Clinical, Esthetic & Literary Perspectives. LC 92-599. xxiv, 412p. 1992. 118.00 (1-55619-121-9) J Benjamins Pubng Co.
— Literary Anthropology: A New Interdisciplinary Approach to People, Signs & Literature. LC 87-21820. xxiii, 342p. (C). 1988. 97.00 (90-272-2041-7); pap. 27.95 (90-272-2059-X) J Benjamins Pubng Co.
— Nonverbal Communication in Translation: New Perspectives & Challenges in Literature, Interpretation & the Media. LC 97-1033. (Benjamins Translation Library: No. 17). xii, 361p. 1997. 94.00 (1-55619-699-7) J Benjamins Pubng Co.
Poydar, Nancy. Busy Bea. LC 93-37266. (Illus.). 32p. (J). (ps-2). 1994. pap. 14.95 (0-689-50592-2) Atheneum Yung Read.
— Cool Ali. LC 95-35213. (Illus.). 32p. (J). (ps-3). 1996. pap. 13.00 (0-689-80755-4) S&S Childrens.
Poydar, Nancy. First Day, Hooray! LC 98-19312. (Illus.). 32p. (J). (gr. k-3). 1999. 15.95 (0-8234-1437-X) Holiday.
***Poydar, Nancy.** First Day, Hooray! (Illus.). (gr. 4-7). 2000. 6.95 (0-8234-1630-5) Holiday.
— Mailbox Magic. LC 99-51776. (Illus.). 32p. (J). (ps-3). 2000. 15.95 (0-8234-1525-2) Holiday.
Poydar, Nancy. Snip, Snip . . . Snow! LC 97-9052. (Illus.). 32p. (J). (ps-3). 1997. lib. bdg. 15.95 (0-8234-1328-4) Holiday.
— Snip, Snip . . . Snow! (J). (ps-3). 1997. reprint ed. pap. text 6.95 (0-8234-1415-9) Holiday.
Poyen, Charles. Progress of Animal Magnetism. (Hypnosis & Altered States of Consciousness Ser.). 1982. reprint ed. lib. bdg. 25.00 (0-306-76163-7) Da Capo.
Poyer, David. As the Wolf Loves Winter. 352p. 1996. 23.95 (0-312-85601-6) Forge NYC.
— As the Wolf Loves Winter. 1997. mass mkt. 6.99 (0-8125-3433-6, Pub. by Forge NYC) St Martin.
— As the Wolf Loves Winter. large type ed. 1996. 24.95 (1-56895-379-8, Compass) Wheeler Pub.
— Bahamas Blue: A Tiller Galloway Thriller. 1992. mass mkt. 3.99 (0-312-92846-7) St Martin.
***Poyer, David.** China Sea. 352p. 2000. text 24.95 (0-312-20287-3) St Martin.
Poyer, David. The Circle. 1993. mass mkt. 6.99 (0-312-92964-1) St Martin.
— The Dead of Winter. 320p. 1995. 5.99 (0-8125-0787-8, Pub. by Tor Bks) St Martin.
— Down to a Sunless Sea: A Tiller Galloway Underwater Thriller. 1998. mass mkt. 5.99 (0-312-96407-2) St Martin.
— Hatteras Blue. 1992. mass mkt. 5.99 (0-312-92749-5) St Martin.
— Louisiana Blue: A Tiller Galloway Thriller, Vol. 1. 1995. mass mkt. 5.99 (0-312-95422-0) St Martin.
— The Only Thing to Fear. 480p. 1996. mass mkt. write for info. (0-614-05527-X); mass mkt. 6.99 (0-8125-4815-9, Pub. by Forge NYC) St Martin.
— The Passage. 560p. 1997. mass mkt. 6.99 (0-312-95450-6) St Martin.
— The Return of Philo T. McGiffin. LC 97-46. (Bluejacket Bks.). 288p. 1997. pap. 18.95 (1-55750-689-2) Naval Inst Pr.
***Poyer, David.** Thunder on the Mountain: A Novel of 1936. (Hemlock County Ser.). 2000. mass mkt. 6.99 (0-8125-4004-2, Pub. by Forge NYC) St Martin.
Poyer, David. Thunder on the Mountain: A Novel of 1936. LC 98-43454. 384p. 1999. 25.95 (0-312-86494-9, Pub. by Tor Bks) St Martin.
— Tomahawk. LC 97-37121. 1998. text 24.95 (0-312-17975-8) St Martin.
— Tomahawk. 480p. 1999. mass mkt. 6.99 (0-312-96561-3, St Martins Paperbacks) St Martin.
— Tomahawk. large type ed. LC 98-14024. (Americana Series). 1998. 26.95 (0-7862-1457-0) Thorndike Pr.
— Winter in the Heart. 416p. 1994. mass mkt. 5.99 (0-8125-2298-2) Tor Bks.
Poyer, Joe. The M14 Type Rifles: A Shooter's & Collector's Guide. LC 98-105024. (Illus.). 1997. pap. 14.95 (1-882391-18-7) N Cape Pubns.
— The SAFN-49. (Shooter's & Collector's Guide Ser.). (Illus.). 70p. 1998. pap. 14.95 (1-882391-22-5) N Cape Pubns.
— U. S. Winchester Trench & Riot Guns & Other U. S. Combat Shotguns. (For Collectors Only Ser.). (Illus.). 122p. (Orig.). 1992. pap. 15.95 (1-882391-02-0) N Cape Pubns.
Poyer, Joe & Riesch, Craig. The 45-70 Springfield. 3rd ed. (For Collectors Only Ser.). (Illus.). 140p. (Orig.). 1999. pap. 16.95 (1-882391-25-X) N Cape Pubns.
— The M1 Garand, 1936-1957. 2nd ed. (For Collectors Only Ser.). (Illus.). 223p. 1997. pap. 19.95 (1-882391-19-5) N Cape Pubns.
Poyer, Joe, jt. auth. see Kehaya, Steve.
Poyer, Joe, jt. auth. see Lightbody, Andy.
Poyer, Lin. The Ngatik Massacre: History & Identity on a Micronesian Atoll. LC 92-37911. (Series in Ethnographic Inquiry). (Illus.). 312p. (C). 1993. pap. text 17.95 (1-56098-262-4) Smithsonian.
***Poyer, Lin, et al.** The Typhoon of War: Micronesian Experiences of the Pacific War. LC 00-29875. 2001. write for info. (0-8248-2168-8) UH Pr.
Poyer, Lin, jt. ed. see Linnekin, Jocelyn.
Poyin, Chu. Build Your Own Network: Lan & Web Server. 200p. (Orig.). 1999. pap. text 49.95 (0-9662131-3-0) BYOS Tech.
Poynder, Michael. The Lost Magic of Christianity: Celtic Essene Connections. LC 98-105991. 180p. 1998. pap. 17.95 (1-898256-25-X) Dufour.
***Poynder, Michael.** Lost Magic of Christianity: Celtic Essene Connections. (Illus.). 192p. 2000. pap. 16.99 (0-9536631-0-8, Pub. by Green Magic) SCB Distributors.
Poynder, Michael. Price Guide to Jewellery. (Illus.). 385p. 1999. 69.50 (1-85149-309-3) Antique Collect.
— Price Guide to Jewellery, 3000 B. C.-1950 A. D. (Price Guide Ser.). (Illus.). 388p. 1980. 69.50 (0-902028-50-2) Antique Collect.
Poynder, Michael & Trevelyan, George. Pi in the Sky: A Revelation of the Ancient Celtic Wisdom Tradition. 192p. 1998. pap. 29.95 (1-898256-33-0, Pub. by Collins Press) Dufour.
Poyner, B. & Fawcett, W. H. Design for Inherent Security: Guidance for Non-Residential Buildings. 184p. 1995. 14.00 (0-7277-2040-6) Am Soc Civil Eng.
***Poyner, Barry.** Bound to Slavery. 2000. pap. 14.95 (1-56794-208-3) Star Bible.
***Poyner, David & Marshall, Ian.** The CGRP Family: CGRP, Amylin & Adrenomedullin. LC 99-34620. (Medical Intelligence Unit Ser.). 294p. 2000. 89.00 (1-57059-592-5) Landes Bioscience.
Poyner, Jack. Electroplating. (Workshop Practice Ser.: No. 11). (Illus.). 61p. (Orig.). 1987. pap. 18.50 (0-85242-862-6, Pub. by Nexus Special Interests) Trans-Atl Phila.
Poyner, Ken. Sciences, Social. 28p. 1995. pap. 5.00 (1-889806-10-2) Devils Millhopper.
Poyner, Rick. The Graphic Edge. (Illus.). 208p. 1998. pap. 39.95 (1-873968-69-8) Gingko Press.
***Poyner, Rick.** Vaughan Oliver: Visceral Pleasures. (Illus.). 224p. 2000. 49.95 (1-86154-072-8, Pub. by Booth-Clibborn) Dist Art Pubs.
Poyner, Robin. Power Concealed, Power Revealed: The Arts of Africa. Libby, Gary R. & Miller, Sandra L., eds. (Illus.). 50p. (C). 1988. pap. 5.00 (0-933053-01-0) Museum Art Sciences.
***Poyner, Thomas F.** Common Skin Diseases. LC 99-21441. (Illus.). 184p. 2000. pap. 29.95 (0-632-05134-5) Blackwell Sci.
Poynet, John, compiled by. A Shorte Treatise of Politike Power. LC 72-38220. (English Experience Ser.: No. 484). 184p. 1972. reprint ed. 35.00 (90-221-0484-2) Walter J Johnson.
Poynor, A. E. Of Moose & Men: A Skewed Look at Life in Alaska. LC 99-218014. xii, 208p. 1999. pap. 12.95 (0-9667915-0-9) O M M Bks.
Poynor, Alice. East to the Shifting Sands. (Jeff Anderson Ser.: Bk. 3). 190p. (Orig.). (J). (gr. 6-9). 1992. pap. 4.95 (981-3009-05-5) OMF Bks.
— Spice Islands Mystery. 1989. pap. 3.95 (9971-972-82-4) OMF Bks.
Poynor, Rick. Design Without Boundaries: Visual Communication in the 1990s. (Illus.). 212p. 1998. pap. 25.00 (1-86154-006-X) Gingko Press.
***Poynor, Rick.** Typography Now Two: Implosion. 2000. pap. 39.95 (1-86154-023-X) Abrams.
***Poynor, Rick & Booth-Clibborn, Edward.** Typography Now: The Nest Wave. 2000. pap. 39.95 (1-873968-42-6) Abrams.
Poynor, Robin. African Art at the Harn Museum: Spirit Eyes, Human Hands. LC 94-25648. (Illus.). 256p. 1995. 49.95 (0-8130-1325-9) U Press Fla.
Poynter. Oil Spills. (J). 1995. 14.95 (0-689-31849-9) Atheneum Yung Read.
Poynter, Dan. Book Fairs: An Exhibiting Guide for Publishers. 4th ed. LC 85-16733. (Illus.). 96p. 1986. reprint ed. pap. 7.95 (0-915516-43-8) Para Pub.
— Book Fulfillment: Order Entry, Picking, Packing & Shipping. 6th ed. (Book Publishing Consultation with Dan Poynter Ser.). (Illus.). 45p. 1999. pap. 19.95 (1-56860-037-2) Para Pub.
***Poynter, Dan.** Book Production: Composition, Layout, Editing & Design - Getting It Ready for Printing. 5th ed. (Book Publishing Consultation with Dan Poynter Ser.). 30p. 2000. 19.95 (1-56860-034-8) Para Pub.
— Book Reviews. 7th ed. (Book Publishing Consultation with Dan Poynter Ser.). 40p. 2000. student ed. 19.95 (1-56860-032-1) Para Pub.
Poynter, Dan. Brochures for Book Publishers. 5th ed. (Book Publishing Consultation with Dan Poynter Ser.). (Illus.). 25p. 1999. pap. 19.95 (1-56860-036-4) Para Pub.
— Buying Book Printing: Selecting & Working with Printers. 6th ed. (Book Publishing Consultation with Dan Poynter Ser.). (Illus.). 25p. 2000. pap., student ed. 14.95 (1-56860-055-0) Para Pub.
— Direct Mail for Book Publishers: Postal & Email. 4th ed. (Book Publishing Consultation with Dan Poynter Ser.). (Illus.). 38p. 1999. pap. 19.95 (1-56860-030-5) Para Pub.
— Expert Witness Handbook: Tips & Techniques for the Litigation Consultant. 2nd ed. (Illus.). 248p. (Orig.). 1997. 39.95 (1-56860-027-5) Para Pub.
— Exports-Foreign Rights: Selling U. S. Books Abroad. 5th ed. (Book Publishing Consultation with Dan Poynter Ser.). (Illus.). 34p. 1999. 19.95 (1-56860-035-6) Para Pub.
***Poynter, Dan.** News Releases & Book Publicity: From Pre-Publication Galleys Through a Continuing Review Program. 5th ed. (Book Publishing Consultation with Dan Poynter Ser.). (Illus.). 35p. 2000. pap. 19.95 (1-56860-054-2) Para Pub.
Poynter, Dan. The Parachute Manual Vol. 1: A Technical Treatise on Aerodynamic Decelerators. 3rd rev. ed. LC 83-13350. (Illus.). 592p. 1991. pap. 49.95 (0-915516-35-7) Para Pub.
— The Parachute Manual Vol. 2: A Technical Treatise on Aerodynamic Decelerators. 4th rev. ed. LC 91-8828. 416p. 1991. pap. 49.95 (0-915516-80-2) Para Pub.
— Parachuting I-E Course: A Program of Study to Prepare the Expert Parachutist for the USPA I/E Exam. 5th rev. ed. (Illus.). 60p. 1994. pap. 14.95 (1-56860-004-6) Para Pub.
— Parachuting Manual with Log. 9th rev. ed. (Illus.). 24p. 1999. 2.95 (1-56860-057-7, PML-8) Para Pub.
— Parachuting Manual with Log for Round Canopies. 7th rev. ed. LC 76-14106. (Illus.). 24p. 1984. pap. 1.50 (0-915516-11-X) Para Pub.
***Poynter, Dan.** Self-Publishing Manual: How to Write, Print & Sell Your Own Book. 12th ed. LC 99-57841. (Illus.). 432p. 2000. pap. 19.95 (1-56860-063-1) Para Pub.
— Successful Nonfiction: Tips & Inspiration for Getting Published. LC 99-41089. (Illus.). 144p. 1999. pap. text 14.95 (1-56860-061-5) Para Pub.
Poynter, Dan. Write & Grow Rich: Using Speech-Recognition to Dictate Your How-To Book. LC 98-29873. (Illus.). 160p. 1999. pap. 14.95 (1-56860-058-5, WGR-1) Para Pub.
***Poynter, Dan.** Writing Nonfiction: Turning Thoughts into Books. (Illus.). 160p. 2000. pap. 14.95 (1-56860-064-X) Para Pub.
Poynter, Dan & Bingham, Mindy. Is There a Book Inside You? Writing Alone or with a Collaborator. 5th rev. ed. LC 98-29872. (Illus.). 235p. 1999. pap. 14.95 (1-56860-046-1, BIY-5) Para Pub.
Poynter, Dan & Schlatter, Mark. Parachute Rigging Course: A Course of Study for the FAA Senior Rigging Certificate. 3rd rev. ed. LC 94-4950. 90p. 1994. pap. 19.95 (1-56860-005-4) Para Pub.
***Poynter, Dan & Turoff, Mike.** Parachuting: The Skydiver's Handbook. 8th ed. (Illus.). 408p. 2000. pap. text 19.95 (1-56860-062-3) Para Pub.
Poynter, Edward J. Ten Lectures on Art. 1977. 17.95 (0-8369-7325-9, 8118) Ayer.
***Poynter, Gavin.** Restructuring in the Service Industries: Management Reform & Workplace Relations in the U. K. Service Sector LC 99-37177. (Employment & Work Relations in Context Ser.). 2000. 82.95 (0-7201-2341-0) Mansell Pub.
Poynter, James. Foreign Independent Tours. (Hospitality, Travel & Tourism Ser.). viii, 299 p. 1989. 30.95 (0-8273-3120-7) Delmar.
— Foreign Independent Tours. (Hospitality, Travel & Tourism Ser.). 1989. text, teacher ed. 12.00 (0-8273-3121-5) Delmar.
— Multicultural Multinational. 176p. (C). 1995. pap. text 52.95 (0-7872-1069-2) Kendall-Hunt.
Poynter, James. Multicultural Multinational Adjustment & Readjustment. 2nd ed. 196p. (C). 1997. per. 55.95 (0-7872-4538-0) Kendall-Hunt.
— Multicultural Multinational Adjustment & Readjustment. 3rd ed. 206p. (C). 2000. per. 55.95 (0-7872-7237-X) Kendall-Hunt.
— Mysery Shopping. 2nd ed. 134p. 1998. per. 44.00 (0-7872-5540-8, 41554001) Kendall-Hunt.
Poynter, James M. Corporate Travel Management. (Illus.). 384p. 1990. text 48.80 (0-13-176140-4) P-H.
— How to Research & Write a Thesis in Hospitality & Tourism: A Step-by-Step Guide for College Students. LC 92-40805. 224p. 1993. pap. 54.95 (0-471-55240-2) Wiley.
— Travel Agency Accounting Procedures. 320p. 1991. teacher ed. 11.95 (0-8273-3390-0) Delmar.
Poynter, Margaret. Frisbee Fun. (Illus.). (J). (gr. 3-6). 1978. pap. 7.29 (0-685-00479-1, Archway) PB.
— Killer Asteroids. LC 94-49124. (Weird & Wacky Science Ser.). (Illus.). 48p. (J). (gr. 4-10). 1996. lib. bdg. 18.95 (0-89490-616-X) Enslow Pubs.
— The Leakeys: Uncovering the Origins of Humankind. LC 96-40899. (Great Minds of Science Ser.). 128p. (J). (gr. 4-10). 1997. lib. bdg. 20.95 (0-89490-788-3) Enslow Pubs.
— Marie Curie: Discoverer of Radium. LC 93-21224. (Great Minds of Science Ser.). (Illus.). 128p. (J). (gr. 4-10). 1994. lib. bdg. 20.95 (0-89490-477-9) Enslow Pubs.
— Top 10 American Women Figure Skaters. LC 97-27217. (Sports Top 10 Ser.). 48p. (YA). (gr. 4-10). 1998. lib. bdg. 18.95 (0-7660-1075-9) Enslow Pubs.
Poynter, Rhonda. Start the Car. 1998. pap. 10.00 (0-942292-15-4) Warthog Pr.
Poynter, William. The Textbook of Behavioral Managed Care: From Concept Through Management to Treatment. LC 97-33474. 153p. 1997. boxed set 37.95 (0-87630-862-0) Brunner-Mazel.
Poynter, William L. The Preferred Provider's Handbook: Building a Successful Private Therapy Practice in the Managed Care Marketplace. LC 93-38869. 184p. 1994. pap. text 23.95 (0-87630-708-X, 708X) Brunner-Mazel.
Poynting, Sarah, ed. see Montagu, Walter.
Poynton, Cate. Language & Gender: Making the Difference. 104p. (C). 1995. pap. 34.00 (0-7300-0347-7, ECS806, Pub. by Deakin Univ) St Mut.
Poynton, Cate, jt. ed. see Lee, Alison.
***Poynton, Charles A.** Digital Video & HDTV: Pixels, Pictures & Perception. (Illus.). 640p. 2000. 59.99 (0-471-38489-5) Wiley.
Poynton, Charles A. A Technical Introduction to Digital Video. LC 95-38474. 352p. 1996. 44.99 (0-471-12253-X) Wiley.
Poynton, James P. Metering Pumps: Selection & Application. LC 82-23485. (Chemical Industries Ser.: Vol. 9). (Illus.). 212p. reprint ed. pap. 65.80 (0-608-08977-X, 206961200005) Bks Demand.
Poynton, Jerome, ed. see Pratt, Mary.
Poyo, Gerald E. Tejano Origins in Eighteenth-Century San Antonio. 1995. pap. 13.95 (0-292-76566-5) U of Tex Pr.
— With All & for the Good of All: The Emergence of Popular Nationalism in the Cuban Communities of the United States, 1848-1898. LC 88-21129. (Illus.). xvii, 182p. (C). 1989. text 34.95 (0-8223-0881-9) Duke.
Poyo, Gerald E., ed. Tejano Journey, 1770-1850. (Illus.). 208p. 1996. 24.95 (0-292-76570-3) U of Tex Pr.
Poyser, Norman L. Prostaglandins in Reproduction. LC 81-181787. (Prostaglandins Research Studies Ser.: No. 2). (Illus.). 272p. reprint ed. pap. 84.40 (0-8357-8996-9, 203334800085) Bks Demand.
Poyssick. Managing Digital Workflow. (C). 2002. pap. 49.99 (0-13-010911-8) P-H.
Poyssick, Gary. Adobe Illustrator Creative Techniques. LC 94-73187. (Illus.). 320p. 1995. 35.00 (1-56830-133-2) Hayden.
— Adobe Photoshop Creative Techniques. LC 94-73186. (Illus.). 320p. 1995. 40.00 (1-56830-132-4) Hayden.
— FreeHand Production Techniques. (Illus.). 320p. (Orig.). 1995. pap. text 30.00 (1-56830-175-8) Hayden.
— PageMaker Production Techniques. (Illus.). 320p. (Orig.). 1995. pap. text 30.00 (1-56830-170-7, Alpha Ref) Macmillan Gen Ref.
— QuarkXPress Production Techniques. (Illus.). 300p. (Orig.). 1997. 35.00 (1-56830-134-0) Hayden.
Poyssick, Gary, jt. auth. see Hannaford, Steve.
Poyssick, Gary, jt. auth. see Hannaford, Steven.
***Poythress, Vern & Grudem, Wayne.** God's Word or Man's Agenda? The Gender-Neutral Bible Controversy. 320p. 2000. pap. 14.99 (0-8054-2441-5) Broadman.
***Poythress, Vern S.** The Returning King: A Guide to the Book of Revelation. 240p. 2000. pap. 14.99 (0-87552-462-1) P & R Pubng.
Poythress, Vern S. The Shadow of Christ in the Law of Moses. 435p. (C). 1995. pap. 14.99 (0-87552-375-7) P & R Pubng.
— Understanding Dispensationalists. 2nd ed. LC 93-39295. 1993. pap. 7.99 (0-87552-374-9) P & R Pubng.
Poythress, Vernon S. God-Centered Biblical Interpretation. LC 98-53148. 1999. pap. 14.99 (0-87552-376-5) P & R Pubng.
— Symphonic Theology: The Validity of Multiple Perspectives in Theology. 128p. (Orig.). 1987. pap. 9.95 (0-310-45221-X, 12358P) Zondervan.
— Understanding Dispensationalists. 144p. (Orig.). 1987. pap. 10.99 (0-310-28591-7, 13257P) Zondervan.
Poythress, Willie C. Atlanta Memories for a Lifetime. (Illus.). 30p. (Orig.). 1996. pap. text 10.95 (0-9649831-0-9) W P Atlanta.
Poza, Ernesto J. Smart Growth: Critical Choice for Business Continuity. 2nd ed. LC 97-92209. 193p. 1997. reprint ed. 28.95 (0-9645105-1-0) Ed Univ Para.
Poza, Ernesto J., et al. La Empresa Familiar por Dentro.Tr. of Inside the Family Business. (SPA., Illus.). 177p. 1998. 32.95 (0-9645105-0-2) Ed Univ Para.
Poza-Valle, Ernesto. A la Sombra del Roble: La Empresa Privada Familiar y Su Continuidad. (SPA., Illus.). 168p. 1995. 25.00 (0-9645105-9-6) Ed Univ Para.
Pozar, David M. Antenna Design Using Personal Computers. 141p. (C). 1985. pap. text. write for info. (0-89006-175-0) Artech Hse.
— Antenna Design Using Personal Computers. LC 85-47745. (Artech House Microwave Library). (Illus.). 153p. reprint ed. pap. 47.50 (0-8357-3934-1, 203666900004) Bks Demand.
***Pozar, David M.** Microwave & RF Wireless Systems. 480p. 2000. write for info. (0-471-32282-2) Wiley.

An Asterisk (*) at the beginning of an entry indicates that the title is appearing for the first time.

Pozar, David M. Microwave Engineering. 2nd ed. LC 97-20878. 736p. 1997. text 114.95 (*0-471-17096-8*) Wiley.

Pozar, David M. & Schaubert, Daniel H., eds. Microstrip Antennas: The Analysis & Design of Microstrip Antennas & Arrays. LC 95-1229. 448p. 1995. reprint ed. 89.95 (*0-7803-1078-0*, PC4325) Inst Electrical.

Pozas, Ricardo. Juan Perez Jolote. (SPA.). 1994. pap. 7.99 (*968-16-0328-1*) Fondo.

— Juan the Chamula: An Ethnological Recreation of the Life of a Mexican Indian. Kemp, Lysander, tr. (Illus.). 123p. 1962. pap. 14.95 (*0-520-01027-2*, Pub. by U CA Pr) Cal Prin Full Svc.

Pozdeeva, I. V., et al. Church Slavonic, Glagolitic & Petrine Civil Script Printed Books in the New York Public Library: A Preliminary Catalog. LC 96-40350. 1997. write for info. (*1-884445-31-4*) C Schlacks Pub.

Pozdena, Randall J. The Modern Economics of Housing: A Guide to Theory & Policy for Finance & Real Estate Professionals. LC 87-32593. 224p. 1988. 62.95 (*0-89930-231-9*, Quorum Bks) Greenwood.

Pozdeyev, A., jt. auth. see Tarnovskii, Y.

Pozdeyev, Arkady. The Hiker's Guide to Almaty. LC 98-86747. 138 p. 1998. write for info. (*0-9666926-0-8*) Real Virtuality.

Pozdof, Mary B. God's Word for Warrior: The Covenant. (Old Testament Ser.: Vol. I). 123p. 1991. teacher ed., spiral bd. 19.95 (*1-889723-08-8*) Family Harvest.

Pozdol, Mary Beth. Complete Set of 5 Books: Old Testament - New Testament. (God's Word for Warriors Ser.). 612p. 1991. teacher ed., spiral bd. 80.00 (*1-889723-13-4*) Family Harvest.

— The Covenant Vol. I: Old Testament. (God's Word for Warriors Ser.). 123p. Date not set. teacher ed., spiral bd. 19.95 (*1-889723-07-X*) Family Harvest.

— Doing the Works of Jesus. (Character Ser.: Vol. 3). Date not set. ring bd. 19.95 (*1-889723-17-7*) Family Harvest.

— Grace in the Desert Vol. II: Old Testament. (God's Word for Warriors Ser.). 133p. 1991. teacher ed., spiral bd. 19.95 (*1-889723-09-6*) Family Harvest.

— Humility Vol. I: Character Series. (God's Word for Warriors Ser.). 140p. Date not set. teacher ed., spiral bd. 19.95 (*1-889723-15-0*) Family Harvest.

— The Lamb of God Vol. I: New Testament. (God's Word for Warriors Ser.). 126p. 1991. spiral bd. 19.95 (*1-889723-11-8*) Family Harvest.

— Servants of Honor Vol. III: Old Testament. (God's Word for Warriors Ser.). 112p. 1991. teacher ed., spiral bd. 19.95 (*1-889723-10-X*) Family Harvest.

— Walking by Faith Vol. II: New Testament. (God's Word for Warriors Ser.). 118p. 1991. teacher ed., spiral bd. 19.95 (*1-889723-12-6*) Family Harvest.

— Walking in the Spirit Vol. II: Character Series. (God's Word for Warriors Ser.). 120p. Date not set. teacher ed., spiral bd. 19.95 (*1-889723-16-9*) Family Harvest.

Pozela, J. Physics of High-Speed Transistors. (Microdevices: Physics & Fabrication Technologies Ser.). (Illus.). 355p. (C). 1993. text 95.00 (*0-306-44619-7*, Kluwer Plenum) Kluwer Academic.

Pozen, Robert C. The Mutual Fund Business. LC 98-4894. 743p. 1998. 65.00 (*0-262-16177-X*); pap. text 37.50 (*0-262-66141-1*) MIT Pr.

Pozeznik, Rogen. Massage for Cyclists. LC 95-61678. 1997. pap. 14.95 (*0-941950-33-6*) Vitesse Pr.

Pozgar, George D. Case Law in Health Care Administration. 2nd ed. LC 98-44120. 228p. 1998. pap. 39.00 (*0-8342-1204-8*, 12048) Aspen Pub.

— Legal Aspects of Health Care Administration. 7th ed. teacher ed. write for info. (*0-8342-1648-5*, 16485) Aspen Pub.

— Legal Aspects of Health Care Administration. 7th ed. LC 98-39361. 600p. 1998. 50.00 (*0-8342-1197-1*, 11971) Aspen Pub.

Pozgar, George D. & Pozgar, Nina. Case Law in Health Care Administration: A Companion Guide to Legal Aspects of Health Care Administration. 6th ed. 300p. 1996. pap., suppl. ed. 38.00 (*0-8342-0742-7*) Aspen Pub.

Pozgar, George D. & Pozgar, Nina S. Legal Aspects of Health Care Administration. 6th ed. 768p. 1996. 50.00 (*0-8342-0741-9*, 20741) Aspen Pub.

Pozgar, George D., et al. Long-Term Care & the Law: A Legal Guide for Health Care Professionals. 510p. 1992. 67.00 (*0-8342-0289-1*, 20289) Aspen Pub.

Pozgar, Nina, jt. auth. see Pozgar, George D.

Pozgar, Nina S., jt. auth. see Pozgar, George D.

Pozharskaya, Militsa & Volodina, Tatiana. The Art of the Ballets Russes: The Russian Seasons in Paris, 1908-1929. (Illus.). 288p. 1991. 75.00 (*1-55859-151-6*) Abbeville Pr.

Pozharskifi, A. F., jt. auth. see Katritzky, Alan R.

Pozharskii, A. F., et al. Heterocycles in Life & Society: An Introduction to Heterocyclic Chemistry & Biochemistry & the Role of Heterocycles in Science, Technology, Medicine & Agriculture. LC 96-25878. 314p. 1997. 165.00 (*0-471-96033-0*); pap. 64.95 (*0-471-96034-9*) Wiley.

Pozin, Mikhail, compiled by. Russian-English, English-Russian Dictionary of Free Market Era Economics. LC 92-56681. 327p. 1993. lib. bdg. 45.00 (*0-89950-876-6*) McFarland & Co.

Poznanski, Andrew K. Practical Approaches to Pediatric Radiology. LC 75-16022. 478p. reprint ed. pap. 148.20 (*0-608-13468-6*, 202272800029) Bks Demand.

Poznanski, Andrew K., ed. Radiation Protection in Medicine: Proceeding of the 28th Annual Meeting. LC 92-48318. (Annual Meeting Proceedings Ser.: No. 14). 250p. (Orig.). 1993. pap. text 40.00 (*0-929600-29-0*) NCRP Pubns.

Poznanski, Kazimierz A. Stabilization & Privatization in Poland: An Economic Evaluation of the Shock Therapy Program. LC 93-885. 1993. lib. bdg. 138.50 (*0-7923-9341-4*) Kluwer Academic.

Poznanski, Kazimierz Z. Poland's Protracted Transition: Institutional Change & Economic Growth, 1971-1993. LC 97-160980. (Cambridge Russian, Soviet & Post-Soviet Studies: No. 98). 360p. (C). 1997. text 74.95 (*0-521-55396-2*); pap. text 29.95 (*0-521-55639-2*) Cambridge U Pr.

***Poznanski, Roman R.** Modeling in the Neurosciences: From Ionic Channels to Neural Networks. 555p. 1999. text 95.00 (*90-5702-284-2*, Harwood Acad Pubs) Gordon & Breach.

Poznansky, Alexander. Tchaikovsky Through Others' Eyes. Burr, Ralph C. & Bird, Robert J., trs. from RUS. LC 98-45509. (Russian Music Studies). (Illus.). 392p. 1999. text 39.95 (*0-253-33545-0*) Ind U Pr.

— Tchaikovsky's Last Days: A Documentary Study. LC 96-13332. (Illus.). 254p. 1996. text 29.95 (*0-19-816596-X*, Clarendon Pr) OUP.

Pozner, Larry S. & Dodd, Roger J. Cross-Examination: Science & Techniques. 763p. 1993. 105.00 (*1-55834-071-8*, 65985-10, MICHIE) LEXIS Pub.

— Cross-Examination: Science & Techniques, 1998 Cumulative Supplement. 57p. 1998. write for info. (*0-327-00869-5*, 6598611) LEXIS Pub.

Pozniak, A., jt. auth. see Johnson, N. I.

Pozniak, G. I. Russian-English Dictionary of Helminthology & Plant Nematology. 108p. (Orig.). (C). 1979. 125.00 (*0-89771-926-3*, Pub. by Collets) St Mut.

Pozniak, G. I., ed. Dictionary of Helminthology & Plant Nematology. (ENG & RUS.). 108p. 1979. 35.00 (*0-8288-4786-X*) Fr & Eur.

— Russian-English Dictionary of Helminthology & Plant Nematology. (ENG & RUS.). 108p. (Orig.). 1979. pap. text 39.95 (*0-85198-447-9*) OUP.

Poznyak, Alexander S. & Najim, K. Learning Automata & Stochastic Optimization, Vol. 225. LC 97-1897. (Lecture Notes in Control & Information Sciences). 1997. pap. 50.00 (*3-540-76154-3*) Spr-Verlag.

Poznyak, Alexandr S., jt. auth. see Najim, Kaddour.

Poznyak, E. G., jt. auth. see Ilyin, V. A.

Pozo, Emilio Del, see Del Pozo, Emilio, ed.

Pozo, Susan. Price Behaviour in Illegal Markets. 116p. 1996. text 58.95 (*1-85972-349-7*, Pub. by Avebry) Ashgate Pub Co.

Pozo, Susan, ed. Essays on Legal & Illegal Immigration. LC 86-24605. 128p. 1986. 19.00 (*0-88099-041-4*); pap. 9.00 (*0-88099-040-6*) W E Upjohn.

— Exploring the Underground Economy: Studies of Illegal & Unreported Activity. 170p. 1995. 34.00 (*0-88099-166-6*); pap. 15.00 (*0-88099-165-8*) W E Upjohn.

Pozo y Regueiro, Manuel, ed. Memorias del Primer Congreso del Presidio Politico Cubano. (SPA.). 1994. pap. 13.00 (*0-89729-727-X*) Ediciones.

Pozorski, Shelia & Pozorski, Thomas. Early Settlement & Subsistence in the Casma Valley, Peru. LC 87-25517. (Illus.). 160p. 1987. text 24.95 (*0-87745-183-4*) U of Iowa Pr.

Pozorski, Thomas, jt. auth. see Pozorski, Shelia.

Pozovich, Gregory J. Productive Personnel: California Employment, Training, & Management. 200p. 1994. pap. 14.95 (*0-9640592-0-7*) Pacific St Pubng.

Pozrikidis. Little Book of Streamlines. LC 98-88662. 162p. (C). 1999. text 49.95 (*0-12-563855-8*) Acad Pr.

Pozrikidis, C. Boundary Integral & Singularity Methods for Linearized Viscous Flow. (Texts in Applied Mathematics Ser.: No. 8). (Illus.). 271p. (C). 1992. text 89.95 (*0-521-40502-5*); pap. text 31.95 (*0-521-40693-5*) Cambridge U Pr.

— Introduction to Theoretical & Computational Fluid Dynamics. (Illus.). 688p. (C). 1996. text 83.00 (*0-19-509320-8*) OUP.

— Numerical Computation in Science & Engineering. LC 97-38185. (Illus.). 640p. (C). 1998. text 84.95 (*0-19-511253-9*) OUP.

Pozsgai, Frank. 54 3-D Scroll Saw Patterns. LC 96-9447. 1996. pap. 12.95 (*0-7643-0036-9*) Schiffer.

— The Scroll Saw Book. LC 95-1944. (Illus.). 64p. (Orig.). 1995. pap. 12.95 (*0-88740-774-9*) Schiffer.

— Scroll Saw Pictures. LC 95-4998. (Illus.). 64p. (Orig.). 1995. pap. 12.95 (*0-88740-775-7*) Schiffer.

Pozsonyi, G. Film Production & Cinematography, Vol. 26. 220p. 1975. 40.00 (*963-05-0592-4*, Pub. by Akade Kiado) St Mut.

Pozza, D., jt. ed. see Colpi, Giovanni M.

Pozza, Guido, et al, eds. Diet, Diabetes & Atherosclerosis. LC 84-6989. 296p. reprint ed. pap. 91.80 (*0-608-00428-6*, 206114300007) Bks Demand.

Pozzar, Geri. Geri Pozzar: Photos of My Friends. (Illus.). 64p. 1997. pap. 30.00 (*0-85449-251-8*, Pub. by Gay Mens Pr) LPC InBook.

Pozzessere. Down in New Orleans. LC 97-50359. 1998. 25.95 (*0-7862-1385-X*) Thorndike Pr.

Pozzessere, Heather G. All in the Family. (Men Made in America Ser.). 1995. per. 3.99 (*0-373-45198-9*, 1-45198-8) Harlequin Bks.

— Angel of Mercy. LC 95-22353. 250p. 1995. per. 4.99 (*1-55166-069-5*, 1-66069-5, Mira Bks) Harlequin Bks.

— An Angel's Touch. 1995. 17.95 (*0-8217-5126-3*, Knsington) Kensgtn Pub Corp.

— An Angel's Touch. 192p. 1996. mass mkt. 5.99 (*0-8217-5442-4*, Zebra Kensgtn) Kensgtn Pub Corp.

— An Angel's Touch. large type ed. LC 97-23509. 216p. 1997. 24.95 (*0-7862-1211-X*) Thorndike Pr.

— Bride of the Tiger. (Mira Bks.). 1996. mass mkt. 5.50 (*1-55166-146-2*, 0-66146-2, Mira Bks) Harlequin Bks.

— Dark Stranger. LC 96-3540. 295p. 1996. per. 4.99 (*1-55166-079-2*, 1-66079-4, Mira Bks) Harlequin Bks.

***Pozzessere, Heather G.** The Di Medici Bride. 1999. mass mkt. 5.99 (*1-55166-469-0*, Mira Bks) Harlequin Bks.

Pozzessere, Heather G. Eyes of Fire. LC 95-23315. 378p. 1995. per. 5.99 (*1-55166-089-X*, 1-66089-3, Mira Bks) Harlequin Bks.

— For All of Her Life: To Love Again. 512p. 1995. mass mkt. 5.99 (*0-8217-4950-1*, Zebra Kensgtn) Kensgtn Pub Corp.

— Forbidden Fire. (Harlequin Historical Ser.: No. 66). 1991. mass mkt. 3.95 (*0-373-28666-X*) Harlequin Bks.

— Forever My Love. 1996. per. 5.50 (*1-55166-171-3*, 1-66171-9, Mira Bks) Harlequin Bks.

— The Game of Love. 1994. per. 4.50 (*0-373-48280-9*, 5-48280-7) Silhouette.

— Hatfield & McCoy. (Intimate Moments Ser.: No. 416). 1992. per. 3.29 (*0-373-07416-6*) Silhouette.

— If Looks Could Kill. 1999. mass mkt. write for info. (*1-55166-285-X*, 0-66285-8, Mira Bks) Harlequin Bks.

— King of the Castle. 2000. mass mkt. 5.99 (*0-373-48401-1*, 1-48401-3) Harlequin Bks.

— The Last Cavalier. (Shadows Ser.: No. 1). 1993. mass mkt. 3.50 (*0-373-27001-1*) Silhouette.

— Lonesome Rider. (Historical Short Stories Ser.). 1993. per. 4.99 (*0-373-83259-1*, 1-83259-1) Silhouette.

— A Matter of Circumstance. 256p. 1994. per. 4.99 (*1-55166-005-9*, 1-66005-9, Mira Bks) Harlequin Bks.

— A Matter of Circumstance. 1994. mass mkt. 4.50 (*0-373-48281-7*, 5-48281-5) Silhouette.

— Never Sleep with Strangers. 384p. 1998. mass mkt. 5.99 (*1-55166-445-3*, Mira Bks) Harlequin Bks.

— Night Moves. 1996. per. 5.50 (*1-55166-160-8*, 1-66160-2, Mira Bks) Harlequin Bks.

— A Perilous Eden. (Mira Bks.). 1997. per. 5.50 (*1-55166-296-5*, 1-66296-4, Mira Bks) Harlequin Bks.

— Rides a Hero. (Promo Ser.). 1998. mass mkt. 5.99 (*0-373-83405-5*, 1-83405-0) Harlequin Bks.

— Slow Burn. 352p. 1994. per. 5.99 (*1-55166-000-8*, 1-66000-0, Mira Bks) Harlequin Bks.

— Snowfire. (Intimate Moments Ser.: No. 386). 1991. mass mkt. 3.25 (*0-373-07386-0*) Silhouette.

— Strangers in Paradise. 248p. 1995. per. 4.99 (*1-55166-038-5*, 1-66038-0, Mira Bks) Harlequin Bks.

— The Trouble with Andrew. (Intimate Moments Ser.). 1993. per. 3.50 (*0-373-07525-1*, 5-07525-4) Silhouette.

Pozzessere, Heather G., et al. Destined for Love, 3 bks. in 1. 1998. mass mkt. 5.99 (*0-373-20152-4*, 1-20152-4) Harlequin Bks.

Pozzessere, Heather Graham. For All of Her Life. large type ed. 1999. 27.95 (*0-7862-1900-9*) Mac Lib Ref.

***Pozzessere, Heather Graham.** Night Heat. 2001. pap. 12.95 (*1-55166-787-8*, Mira Bks) Harlequin Bks.

— Summer Fires: Dark Stranger; Rides a Hero; Apache Summer, 3 bks. 2001. mass mkt. 12.95 (*0-373-83478-0*, 1-83478-7) Harlequin Bks.

***Pozzessere, Heather Graham & Wilson, Gayle.** Home for Christmas, The Heart's Desire, 2 bks. 2000. mass mkt. 4.99 (*0-373-83455-1*, 1834555) Harlequin Bks.

Pozzessere, Heather Graham, et al. Renegades, 3 vols. LC 95-23277. 376p. 1995. per. 4.99 (*0-373-83310-5*, 1-83310-2) Harlequin Bks.

Pozzessere, Heather Graham, jt. auth. see Palmer, Diana.

Pozzetta, George E. Americanization, Social Control, & Philanthropy. LC 90-49267. (Immigration & Ethnicity Ser.: Vol. 14). 360p. 1991. reprint ed. text 66.00 (*0-8240-7414-9*) Garland.

— Emigration & Immigration: The Old World Confronts the New. LC 90-49052. (Immigration & Ethnicity Ser.: Vol. 2). 736p. 1991. reprint ed. text 105.00 (*0-8240-7402-5*) Garland.

— Folklore, Culture, & the Immigrant Mind. (Immigration & Ethnicity Ser.: Vol. 18). 376p. 1991. reprint ed. text 66.00 (*0-8240-7418-1*) Garland.

— Immigrant Institutions: The Organization of Immigrant Life. LC 90-48319. (Immigration & Ethnicity Ser.: Vol. 5). 352p. 1991. reprint ed. text 66.00 (*0-8240-7405-X*) Garland.

— Immigrant Radicals: The View from the Left. (Immigration & Ethnicity Ser.: Vol. 9). 256p. 1991. reprint ed. text 77.00 (*0-8240-7409-2*) Garland.

— Immigrants on the Land: Agriculture, Rural Life, & Small Towns. LC 90-49262. (Immigration & Ethnicity Ser.: Vol. 4). 416p. 1991. reprint ed. text 72.00 (*0-8240-7404-1*) Garland.

— Politics & the Immigrant. (Immigration & Ethnicity Ser.: Vol. 8). 480p. 1991. reprint ed. text 83.00 (*0-8240-7408-4*) Garland.

— Themes in Immigration History. LC 90-49051. (Immigration & Ethnicity Ser.: Vol. 1). 368p. 1991. reprint ed. text 66.00 (*0-8240-7401-7*) Garland.

— Unions & Immigrants: Organizations & Struggle. LC 90-49263. (Immigration & Ethnicity Ser.: Vol. 7). 368p. 1991. reprint ed. text 68.00 (*0-8240-7407-6*) Garland.

— The Work Experience: Labor, Class & Immigrant Enterprise. LC 90-48320. (Immigration & Ethnicity Ser.: Vol. 6). 528p. 1991. reprint ed. text 85.00 (*0-8240-7406-8*) Garland.

Pozzetta, George E., ed. American Immigration & Ethnicity, 20 vols. 1365.00 (*0-8240-7400-9*) Garland.

— Pane e Lavoro: The Italian American Working Class. 1978. 9.95 (*0-934675-11-2*) Am Italian.

Pozzetta, George E., jt. auth. see Mormino, Gary R.

Pozzetta, George E., jt. ed. see Colburn, David R.

Pozzetta, George E., jt. ed. see Miller, Randall M.

Pozzi, A. Application of Pade's Approximation Theory in Fluid: Advances in Mathematics for Applied Sciences Ser. 252p. 1994. text 61.00 (*981-02-1414-6*) World Scientific Pub.

Pozzi, Donna C., ed. see Porter, Erika R.

Pozzi, Dora C. & Wickersham, John M., eds. Myth & the Polis. LC 90-55716. (Myth & Poetics Ser.). 248p. 1991. text 37.50 (*0-8014-2473-9*); pap. text 14.95 (*0-8014-9734-5*) Cornell U Pr.

Pozzi, Dora C., tr. see Carlisky, Nestor J., et al.

Pozzi, Dora C., tr. see Woscoboinik, Julio.

Pozzi, Doris & Williams, Stephen. Success with Soul: New Insights to Achieving Success with Real Meaning. LC 97-60118. (Illus.). 304p. 1997. pap. 14.95 (*0-646-28692-7*) D Welles.

Pozzi, Gianni. Gram-Positive Bacteria: Vaccine Vehicles for Mucosal Immunization. Wells, Jeremy M., ed. LC 97-2675. (Biotechnology Intelligence Unit Ser.). 175p. 1997. 95.00 (*1-57059-439-2*) Landes Bioscience.

Pozzi, Gianni & Wells, Jeremy M., eds. Gram-Positive Bacteria: Vaccine Vehicles for Mucosal Immunization. LC 97-2675. (Biotechnology Intelligence Unit Ser.). (Illus.). 175p. 1997. 95.00 (*3-540-62776-6*) Spr-Verlag.

Pozzi, Gianni, et al. Chagall. LC 97-7330. (Masters of Art Ser.). (Illus.). 64p. (J). (gr. 4-7). 1997. lib. bdg. 22.50 (*0-87226-527-7*, 65277B, P Bedrick Books) NTC Contemp Pub Co.

Pozzi, Grazia Viva, jt. ed. see Ascari, Rosalia Colombo.

Pozzi, Lucio. Hender. (Illus.). 1980. 6.00 (*0-935694-01-3*) St Edns.

— Hender. deluxe ed. (Illus.). 1980. 12.00 (*0-686-34459-6*) St Edns.

Pozzo, Andrea. Perspective in Architecture. (Illus.). 224p. 1989. pap. 12.95 (*0-486-25855-6*) Dover.

— Rules & Examples of Perspective. LC 69-13450. (Illus.). 1972. reprint ed. 38.95 (*0-405-08861-2*, Pub. by Blom Pubns) Ayer.

***Pozzo, Earlene Dal & Dilts, Joann.** When It Happens to You: A Practical Guide Through Breast Cancer. LC 99-87055. (Illus.). 144p. 2000. pap. 12.95 (*0-923521-49-6*, 496, Pub. by Bull Pub) Publishers Group.

Pozzo, Laura, jt. auth. see Hillman, James.

Pozzoli, Milena E. Castles of the Loire. (Places & History Ser.). (Illus.). 136p. 1997. 24.95 (*1-55670-540-9*) Stewart Tabori & Chang.

— Paris. (Places & History Ser.). 1998. 24.95 (*1-55670-693-6*) Stewart Tabori & Chang.

PPI (Pivetta) Staff. 911: Emergency Communication Manual. 3rd ed. LC 97-212828. 512p. 1997. per. 54.50 (*0-7872-4445-7*) Kendall-Hunt.

— A Non-Technical Workbook for Public Safety. 2nd ed. 152p. 1997. spiral bd. 42.95 (*0-7872-4470-8*) Kendall-Hunt.

PPU Staff. Diccionario de Psicologia Para Educadores. (SPA.). 374p. 1989. pap. 39.95 (*0-7859-6252-2*, 8476653476) Fr & Eur.

Pq Systems, Inc. Staff. Total Quality Tools. 300p. 1995. spiral bd. 39.95 (*1-882683-01-3*) PQ Systs.

— Total Quality Tools for Education (K-12) 300p. 1995. spiral bd. 39.95 (*1-882683-02-1*) PQ Systs.

PQ Systems, Inc. Staff. Total Quality Tools for Health Care. 276p. 1997. spiral bd. 45.00 (*1-882683-04-8*) PQ Systs.

— Total Quality Transformation Improvement Tools. 338p. 1991. spiral bd. 85.00 (*1-882683-00-5*) PQ Systs.

PR Japan Staff, tr. Polynesian Cultural Center - Japanese. (JPN., Illus.). 50p. 1995. pap. write for info. (*0-9644640-1-2*) Polynesian Cult.

Pra, Roberto Dal, see Gimenez, Juan & Dal Pra, Roberto.

Pra, Vic Da, see Scott, Jay & Da Pra, Vic.

***Praag, Ganna O.** Histoire du Recit Pour la Jeunesse Au Xxe Siecle, 1929-2000. xii, 394p. 1999. 41.95 (*90-5201-905-3*, Pub. by College of Europe) P Lang Pubng.

Praag, Ganna O. Le Roman pour la Jeunesse: Approches - Definitions Techniques Narratives. 2nd rev. ed. (FRE.). 296p. 1997. 47.95 (*3-906754-13-8*, Pub. by P Lang) P Lang Pubng.

***Praag, Ganna O.** Le Roman Pour la Jeunesse: Approches--Definitions Techniques Narratives 3E Edition Revue Et Corrigee. 296p. 1999. 39.95 (*3-906763-40-4*) P Lang.

Praag, Herman M. Van, see Van Praag, Herman M., ed.

Praag, Herman M. Van, see Brown, Serena-Lynn & Van Praag, Herman M., eds.

Praag, Herman M. Van, see Van Praag, Herman M.

Praag, Herman M. Van, see Mendlewicz, Julien & Van Praag, Herman M., eds.

Praag, H.M. Van, see Mendlewicz, Julien & Van Praag, H. M., eds.

Praag, J. P. Van, see Van Praag, J. P.

Praag, Philip M. Van, see Van Praag, Philip M.

Praagh, Emmanuel Van, see Van Praagh, Emmanuel, ed.

Praamsma-Raevouri, Saskia. How I Found the Urantia Book. 364p. 1998. pap. 10.95 (*0-9666705-0-7*) Square Circles Pubg.

Praaning, Rio D. & Perry, Charles M., eds. The East-West Relations in the 1990s - Politics & Technology: Proceedings of the Third International Roundtable Conference. (C). 1988. lib. bdg. 85.00 (*90-247-3766-4*) Kluwer Academic.

Praaning, Rip, jt. ed. see Bletz, Frans.

Prabbudesai, R. K., jt. auth. see Das, D. K.

Prabhakar, Arati, ed. Delivering Results: A Progress Report from the National Institute of Standards & Technology. (Illus.). 69p. (C). 1999. reprint ed. pap. text 20.00 (*0-7881-7396-0*) DIANE Pub.

Prabhakar, Eric. Madiera at Sundown: A Raj Trilogy. (C). 1990. 23.00 (*81-7001-071-3*, Pub. by Chanakya) S Asia.

Prabhakar, Vishnu. Awara Messiah: A Biography of Sarat Chandra Chatterjee. (New World Literature Ser.). 1989. 19.50 (*81-7018-564-5*, Pub. by BR Pub) S Asia.

Prabhakara, F. S. Industrial & Commercial Power System Handbook. 592p. 1995. 69.50 (*0-07-050624-8*) McGraw.

Prabhakara, N. R. & Usha, M. N. Population Growth & Umemployment in India. 1986. 15.00 (*81-7024-041-7*, Pub. by Ashish Pub Hse) S Asia.

Prabhakaran, B. Multimedia Database Management Systems. LC 96-38503. (Kluwer International Series in Engineering & Computer Science: Multimedia Systems & Applications). 1996. text 106.50 (*0-7923-9784-3*) Kluwer Academic.

*__Prabhakaran, B. & Kavehrad, Mohsen.__ Mobile Computing Environments for Multimedia Systems LC 99-31815. 1999. write for info. (*0-7923-8549-7*) Kluwer Academic.

Prabhakaran, V. T. & Jain, J. P. Statistical Techniques for Studying Genotype Environment Interactions. (C). 1994. 24.00 (*81-7003-168-0*, Pub. by S Asia Pubs) S Asia.

Prabhanananda, Swami. First Meetings with Sri Ramakrishna. 413p. 1989. pap. 5.95 (*81-7120-484-8*, Pub. by Ramakrishna Math) Vedanta Pr.

Prabhananda, Swami. More about Ramakrishna. 276p. (Orig.). 1994. pap. 5.95 (*0-87481-242-9*, Pub. by Advaita Ashrama) Vedanta Pr.

Prabhat Rainjan Sarkar. Baba's Grace: Discourses of P. R. Sarkar. (Illus.). 197p. (Orig.). 1987. reprint ed. pap. 6.95 (*0-88476-001-4*) Ananda Marga.

— Human Society, Pt. I. 3rd rev. ed. Avadhuta, Acarya V. & Kumar, Jayanta, trs. 185p. 1989. pap. 5.95 (*0-685-33561-5*) Ananda Marga.

— Human Society, Pt. II. 3rd rev. ed. Acarya Vijayananda Avadhuta & Kumar, Jayanta, trs. from BEN. 105p. (C). 1987. pap. text 5.95 (*0-88476-015-4*) Ananda Marga.

— The Liberation of Intellect: Neo-Humanism. Avadhutika Anamda Mitra Acarya & Acarya Vijayananda Avadhuta, trs. from BEN. 102p. (Orig.). (C). 1982. pap. 4.95 (*0-88476-011-1*) Ananda Marga.

— Light Comes. 248p. (Orig.). 1989. 4.95 (*0-88476-017-0*) Ananda Marga.

— Neo-Humanism in a Nutshell, Pt. I. Avadhuta, Acarya V. & Avadhuta, Acarya M., trs. from BEN. 67p. (Orig.). (C). 1987. pap. 3.95 (*0-88476-027-8*) Ananda Marga.

— Neo-Humanism in a Nutshell, Pt. II. Acarya Mantreshwarananda Avadhuta, tr. from BEN. (Orig.). (C). 1987. pap. text 3.95 (*0-88476-028-6*) Ananda Marga.

— Problem of the Day. 64p. 1968. pap. 3.95 (*0-686-95454-8*) Ananda Marga.

— Prout in a Nutshell, Pt. 1. Acarya Vijayananda Avadhuta & Kumar, Jayanta, trs. from BEN. 62p. (Orig.). (C). 1987. pap. 3.95 (*0-88476-050-2*) Ananda Marga.

— Prout in a Nutshell, Pt. 2. Acarya Vijayananda Avadhuta & Kumar, Jayanta, trs. from BEN. 68p. (Orig.). (C). 1987. pap. text 3.95 (*0-88476-051-0*) Ananda Marga.

— Prout in a Nutshell, Pt. 3. Acarya Vijayananda Avadhuta & Kumar, Jayanta, trs. from BEN. 64p. (Orig.). (C). 1987. pap. text 3.95 (*0-88476-052-9*) Ananda Marga.

— Prout in a Nutshell, Pt. 4. 3rd ed. Acarya Vijayananda Avadhuta & Kumar, Jayanta, trs. from BEN. 53p. (Orig.). (C). 1987. pap. text 3.95 (*0-88476-053-7*) Ananda Marga.

— Prout in a Nutshell, Pt. 5. Acarya Vijayananda Avadhuta & Kumar, Jayanta, trs. from BEN. 89p. (Orig.). (C). 1987. pap. 3.95 (*0-88476-054-5*) Ananda Marga.

— Prout in a Nutshell, Pt. 6. Acarya Vijayananda Avadhuta & Kumar, Jayanta, trs. from BEN. 62p. (Orig.). (C). 1987. pap. 3.95 (*0-88476-055-3*) Ananda Marga.

— Prout in a Nutshell, Pt. 7. Acarya Vijayananda Avadhuta & Kumar, Jayanta, trs. from BEN. 67p. (Orig.). (C). 1987. pap. 3.95 (*0-88476-056-1*) Ananda Marga.

— Prout in a Nutshell, Pt. 8. Acarya Vijayananda Avadhuta & Kumar, Jayanta, trs. from BEN. 67p. (Orig.). (C). 1987. pap. 3.95 (*0-88476-057-X*) Ananda Marga.

— Prout in a Nutshell, Pt. 9. Acarya Vijayananda Avadhuta & Kumar, Jayanta, trs. from BEN. 69p. (Orig.). (C). 1987. pap. 3.95 (*0-88476-058-8*) Ananda Marga.

— Prout in a Nutshell, Pt. 10. Acarya Vijayananda Avadhuta & Kumar, Jayanta, trs. from BEN. 82p. (Orig.). (C). 1987. pap. 3.95 (*0-88476-059-6*) Ananda Marga.

— Prout in a Nutshell, Pt. 11. Acarya Vijayananda Avadhuta & Kumar, Jayanta, trs. from BEN. 62p. (Orig.). (C). 1987. pap. 3.95 (*0-88476-060-X*) Ananda Marga.

— Prout in a Nutshell, Pt. 12. Acarya Vijayananda Avadhuta & Kumar, Jayanta, trs. from BEN. 60p. (Orig.). (C). 1987. pap. 3.95 (*0-88476-061-8*) Ananda Marga.

— Prout in a Nutshell, Pt. 13. Acarya Vijayananda Avadhuta & Kumar, Jayanta, trs. from BEN. 64p. (Orig.). (C). 1988. pap. 3.95 (*0-88476-062-6*) Ananda Marga.

— Prout in a Nutshell, Pt. 14. Acarya Vijayananda Avadhuta & Kumar, Jayanta, trs. from BEN. 60p. (Orig.). (C). 1988. pap. 3.95 (*0-88476-063-4*) Ananda Marga.

— Prout in a Nutshell, Pt. 15. Acarya Vijayananda Avadhuta & Kumar, Jayanta, trs. from BEN. 64p. (Orig.). (C). 1988. pap. 3.95 (*0-88476-064-2*) Ananda Marga.

— The Thoughts of P. R. Sarkar. Avadhutika Ananda Mitra Acarya, ed. 214p. (Orig.). (C). 1981. pap. text 4.95 (*0-88476-016-2*) Ananda Marga.

— Universal Humanism: Selected Social Writings of P. R. Sarkar. Anderson, Tim & Coyle, Gary, eds. 108p. (Orig.). (C). 1983. pap. 4.95 (*0-9591792-0-8*) Proutist Universal.

— Yogic Treatments & Natural Remedies. 100p. (Orig.). 1989. text 5.95 (*0-88476-029-4*) Ananda Marga.

Prabhavananda, Swami. Eternal Companion: Brahmananda, His Life & Teachings. 3rd ed. LC 72-113256. 302p. 1960. pap. 9.95 (*0-87481-024-8*) Vedanta Pr.

*__Prabhavananda, Swami.__ Narada's Way of Divine Love: The Bhakti Sutras. 192p. 2000. pap. 9.95 (*0-87481-054-X*) Vedanta Pr.

Prabhavananda, Swami. Religion in Practice. 1960. 8.95 (*0-87481-016-7*) Vedanta Pr.

— The Sermon on the Mount According to Vedanta. LC 64-8660. 127p. 1963. 12.95 (*0-87481-002-7*) Vedanta Pr.

— The Sermon on the Mount According to Vedanta. LC 64-8660. 127p. 1991. pap. 8.95 (*0-87481-050-7*) Vedanta Pr.

— Spiritual Heritage of India. LC 63-10517. 374p. (C). 1979. reprint ed. pap. 10.95 (*0-87481-035-3*) Vedanta Pr.

— Vedic Religion & Philosophy. 4.95 (*81-7120-043-5*) Vedanta Pr.

— Yoga & Mysticism: An Introduction to Vedanta. 53p. 1984. reprint ed. pap. 4.95 (*0-87481-020-5*) Vedanta Pr.

Prabhavananda, Swami, tr. Memories of a Loving Soul. (Orig.). 1968. pap. 3.50 (*0-87481-015-9*, Pub. by Advaita Ashrama) Vedanta Pr.

Prabhavananda, Swami, et al, trs. Upanishads: Breath of the Eternal. LC 48-5935. 232p. (C). 1947. pap. 7.95 (*0-87481-040-X*) Vedanta Pr.

Prabhavananda, Swami & Isherwood, Christopher, trs. Bhagavad Gita: The Song of God. 224p. 1993. 9.95 (*0-87481-008-6*); pap. 7.95 (*0-87481-043-4*) Vedanta Pr.

— How to Know God: The Yoga Aphorisms of Patanjali. 224p. 1983. pap. 7.95 (*0-87481-041-8*) Vedanta Pr.

— How to Know God: The Yoga Aphorisms of Patanjali. 224p. 1993. 12.95 (*0-87481-010-8*) Vedanta Pr.

Prabhavananda, Swami & Manchester, Frederick, trs. The Upanishads: Breath of the Eternal. 128p. 1957. mass mkt. 5.99 (*0-451-62607-9*, MJ2298, Ment) NAL.

*__Prabhavananda, Swami, et al.__ Meditation & Its Preparation. 209p. 2000. pap. 4.95 (*81-7505-195-7*) Vedanta Pr.

Prabhavananda, Swami, tr. see Bhagavad-Gita.

Prabhavananda, Swami, tr. see Bhagavatam.

Prabhavananda, Swami, tr. see Narada.

Prabhavathi, V. Perceptions, Motivations, & Performance of Women Legislators. (C). 1991. 27.50 (*81-7054-145-X*, Pub. by Classical Pubng) S Asia.

Prabhu, Arun, jt. auth. see Padamsee, Alyque.

Prabhu, Avatar. The Revised Kama Sutra: A Novel. LC 97-61874. 480p. 1998. 22.95 (*1-887472-41-X*) Sunstar Pubng.

Prabhu, Barbara W., ed. Spotlight on New Jersey Government. 6th ed. LC 91-45493. 400p. (C). 1992. text 42.00 (*0-8135-1843-1*); pap. text 16.95 (*0-8135-1844-X*) Rutgers U Pr.

Prabhu, G. M. & Wright, Charles. Computer Architecture & Assembly Language Programming: The MC 68000. LC 95-190362. 434p. (Orig.). (C). 1994. pap. text 60.65 (*1-881991-34-2*) Scott Jones Pubng.

Prabhu, Girish V. & DelGaldo, Elisa M. Designing for Global Markets. 226p. 1999. pap. write for info. (*0-9656691-2-2*) Backhouse Pr.

***Prabhu, Gurpur M. Anita's Legacy: An Inquiry into First Cause. unabridged ed. Kumar, Prem & Gupta, Henry, eds. LC 00-190921. 300p. (YA). 2000. pap. 13.95 (0-9700645-8-6) Viresh Pubns.**

At some point in our lives, The Question of First Cause: Why is there something instead of nothing? occurs to all of us. In our quest for The Answer we are swayed into accepting opinions from specialists in the traditional camps of organized religion & organized science. Both camps, of course, have been successful in promulgating their own myths. In this visionary fiction book, Gurpur M.Prabhu puts these myths into perspective by leading us through a critical examination of world religions, philosophies & scientific methods. Profound links & parallel concepts are revealed between religious literature & cosmology. What emerges is a model of the universe, an incisive critique of the nature of science & religion, informative commentary on philosophy & history & an inspirational lesson in transcending religious boundaries instead of being dogmatic about one's own faith being superior to others. With the ever-widening breach between religion & science the goal is to unite the disciplines rather than propagate the dichotomy. The provocative, humorous & spiritually uplifting theme grips the reader from start to finish. Visit the website at www.anitaslegacy.com for pre-publication reviews, readers' comments & more information. ***Publisher Paid Annotation.***

Prabhu, Joseph, ed. The Intercultural Challenge of Raimon Panikkar. LC 96-31970. (Faith Meets Faith Ser.). 300p. (Orig.). 1996. pap. 25.00 (*1-57075-056-4*) Orbis Bks.

Prabhu, K., ed. see Osho.

Prabhu, Krishna, ed. see Osho.

Prabhu, Manjiri. Symphony of Hearts. (C). 1994. text 7.00 (*81-7167-183-7*, Pub. by Rupa) S Asia.

Prabhu, N., ed. Statistical Inference from Stochastic Processes. LC 88-31369. (Contemporary Mathematics Ser.: No. 80). 386p. 1988. pap. 44.00 (*0-8218-5087-3*, CONM/80) Am Math.

Prabhu, N. D. Excellence Through People: The Canbank Way. ix, 190p. (C). 1991. text 25.00 (*81-220-0248-X*) Advent Bks Div.

Prabhu, N. U. Foundations of Queuing Theory. LC 97-24604. (International Series in Operations Research & Management Science). 1997. lib. bdg. 99.00 (*0-7923-9962-5*) Kluwer Academic.

— Stochastic Storage Processes: Queues, Insurance Risk & Dams. (Applications of Mathematics Ser.: Vol. 15). 140p. 1980. 69.95 (*0-387-90522-7*) Spr-Verlag.

— Stochastic Storage Processes: Queues, Insurance Risk, & Data Communication. 2nd ed. Balakrishnan, A. V. et al, eds. LC 97-35361. (Applications of Mathematics Ser.: No. 15). 400p. 1997. 59.95 (*0-387-98248-5*) Spr-Verlag.

Prabhu, N. U. & Basawa, I. V., eds. Statistical Inference in Stochastic Processes. (Probability Ser.: Vol. 6). (Illus.). 288p. 1990. text 145.00 (*0-8247-8417-0*) Dekker.

Prabhu, Pandharinath. Hindu Social Organization. 400p. 1986. reprint ed. pap. 11.50 (*0-8364-1836-0*, Pub. by Popular Prakashan) S Asia.

Prabhu, R. K., ed. see Gandhi, M. K.

Prabhu, R. K., ed. see Gandhi, M. K. & Tagore, Rabindranath.

Prabhu, R. K., ed. see Gandhi, Mohandas Karamchand.

Prabhu, S. R., et al, eds. Oral Diseases in the Tropics. (Illus.). 824p. 1992. 175.00 (*0-19-262008-8*) OUP.

Prabhuddda Bharata Magazine Editors. Art, Culture & Spirituality. LC 98-908069. 360p. 1997. 15.00 (*81-7505-189-2*, Pub. by Advaita Ashrama) Vedanta Pr.

*__Prabhudesai, R. K.__ Chemical Engineering Sample Forms: For the Professional Engineer's Exam. (Illus.). 208p. 2000. pap. 29.50 (*1-57645-057-0*, 570) Engineering.

Prabhudesai, R. K., jt. auth. see Das, D. K.

Prabhudesai, R. K., jt. auth. see Das, Dilip.

Prabhudesai, Raj K., jt. auth. see Das, Dilip K.

Prabhupada, jt. auth. see Bhaktivedanta, A. C.

Prabhupada, A. C. Bhagavad-Gita As It Is. 904p. 1991. 19.95 (*0-318-37155-3*) Asia Bk Corp.

— Light of the Bhagavata. (Illus.). 147p. 1997. reprint ed. 7.95 (*91-7149-267-4*) Bhaktivedanta.

— The Quest for Enlightenment: Articles from Back to Godhead Magazine. LC 97-41422. (Illus.). 272p. 1997. 9.95 (*0-89213-292-2*) Bhaktivedanta.

Prabhupada, A. C. Bhaktivedanta. Bhagavad-Gita as It Is. deluxe ed. 1047p. 1997. 26.95 (*0-89213-285-X*) Bhaktivedanta.

*__Prabhupada, A. C. Bhaktivedanta.__ A Second Chance Set: The Story of a Near-Death Experience. 217p. 1998. pap. 7.95 (*0-89213-329-5*) Bhaktivedanta.

Prabhupada, A. C. Bhaktivedanta Swami. Beyond Birth & Death. LC 72-84844. (Illus.). 56p. 1972. pap. 2.95 (*0-912776-41-2*) Bhaktivedanta.

Prabhupada, A. C. Bhaktivedanta Swami. Bhagavad-gita As It Is. 1047p. 1989. 15.95 (*0-89213-268-X*, BGV) Bhaktivedanta.

— Bhagavad Gita as It Is. 636p. 1990. pap. 5.95 (*0-89213-134-9*, BGS) Bhaktivedanta.

— Bhagavad Gita as It Is. (Illus.). 904p. 1991. 14.95 (*0-89213-123-3*, BGH) Bhaktivedanta.

— Chant & Be Happy: The Power of Mantra Meditation. (Illus.). 118p. 1992. pap. 2.95 (*0-89213-118-7*, CBH) Bhaktivedanta.

— Civilization & Transcendence. 78p. 1991. pap. 2.95 (*0-89213-298-1*, CT) Bhaktivedanta.

— Coming Back: The Science of Reincarnation. (Contemporary Vedic Library). (Illus.). 150p. 1982. pap. 2.95 (*0-89213-114-4*, CB) Bhaktivedanta.

— Easy Journey to Other Planets. LC 70-118080. (Illus.). 85p. 1970. pap. 1.95 (*0-912776-10-2*, EJ) Bhaktivedanta.

— Elevation to Krsna Consciousness. 99p. 1997. pap. 1.95 (*0-912776-43-9*, EKC) Bhaktivedanta.

— Higher Taste: Based on Teachings of A. C. Bhaktivedanta Swami. (Contemporary Vedic Library). (Illus.). 156p. 1991. pap. 2.95 (*0-89213-128-4*, HT) Bhaktivedanta.

— The Journey of Self Discovery. (Illus.). 283p. 1990. 9.95 (*0-89213-270-1*, JSDH) Bhaktivedanta.

— Krsna Consciousness: The Topmost Yoga System. (Illus.). 112p. 1991. pap. 1.95 (*0-912776-11-0*, TY) Bhaktivedanta.

— Krsna, the Supreme Personality of Godhead, 2 vols. (Illus.). 1134p. 1997. pap. text 15.95 (*91-7149-350-6*) Bhaktivedanta.

— Nectar of Devotion: The Complete Science of Bhakti-Yoga. LC 78-118082. (Illus.). 521p. 1970. 24.95 (*0-912776-05-6*, NOD) Bhaktivedanta.

— The Nector of Instruction. (Illus.). 130p. 1990. pap. 2.95 (*0-912776-85-4*, NOI) Bhaktivedanta.

— The Path of Perfection. (Illus.). 206p. 1997. pap. 2.95 (*91-7149-171-6*, POP) Bhaktivedanta.

*__Prabhupada, A. C. Bhaktivedanta Swami.__ The Path of Yoga. 207p. (YA). 1999. pap. 7.95 (*0-89213-327-9*) Bhaktivedanta.

Prabhupada, A. C. Bhaktivedanta Swami. Perfect Questions - Perfect Answers. 108p. 1997. pap. 2.95 (*91-7149-170-8*, PQPA) Bhaktivedanta.

— Perfection of Yoga. LC 72-76302. (Illus.). 56p. 1972. pap. 2.95 (*0-912776-36-6*, POY) Bhaktivedanta.

— Raja-Vidya: The King of Knowledge. LC 72-84845. (Illus.). 133p. (YA). 1998. pap. 1.95 (*0-912776-40-4*) Bhaktivedanta.

— The Science of Self-Realization. (Illus.). 412p. 1997. pap. 4.95 (*0-89213-101-2*, SSRS) Bhaktivedanta.

— A Second Chance: The Story of a Near-Death Experience. (Illus.). 208p. 1991. 9.95 (*0-89213-271-X*, SCH) Bhaktivedanta.

— Sri Caitanya-Caritamrta: Madhya-Lila, 9 vols. (Illus.). 7300p. 1975. 350.00 (*0-912776-67-6*, CC) Bhaktivedanta.

— Sri Isopanisad. LC 93-15792. 182p. 1993. pap. 2.95 (*0-89213-280-9*, ISO) Bhaktivedanta.

— Teachings of Lord Caitanya. (Illus.). 440p. 1996. 19.95 (*0-902677-01-2*, TLC) Bhaktivedanta.

Prabhupada, A. C. Bhaktivedanta Swami, abr. Srimad Bhagavatam: Bhagavata Purana, 18 vols. (Illus.). 17900p. 1988. 400.00 (*0-89213-264-7*, SBCOMP) Bhaktivedanta.

Prabir Basu & Fraser, Scott. Circulating Fluidized Bed Boilers Design & Applications. 360p. 1991. text 89.95 (*0-7506-9226-X*) Buttrwrth-Heinemann.

*__Prabst, Hunt.__ Manual for Administration in Occupational Theraphy. 2001. pap. 44.00 (*0-7693-0096-0*) Thomson Learn.

Prach, K., et al, eds. Floodplain Ecology & Management: The Luznice River in the Trebon Biosphere Reserve, Central Europe. (Illus.). xii, 286p. 1996. 90.00 (*90-5103-128-9*, Pub. by SPB Acad Pub) Balogh.

Prachan, Babulall, jt. auth. see Addison, Donna.

Prachand, S. L. Mob Violence in India. 144p. 1979. 12.95 (*0-318-37211-8*) Asia Bk Corp.

*__Prache, Anne.__ Cathedrals of Europe. LC 00-29507. (Illus.). 290p. 2000. 90.00 (*0-8014-3781-4*) Cornell U Pr.

Prachowny, Martin F. The Goals of Macroeconomic Policy. LC 93-43158. (Illus.). 240p. (C). 1994. pap. 27.99 (*0-415-10764-4*, B3798) Routledge.

— The Goals of Macroeconomic Policy. LC 93-43158. (Illus.). 240p. (C). (gr. 13). 1994. 85.00 (*0-415-10763-6*, B3794) Routledge.

— Money in the Macroeconomy. (Illus.). 352p. 1986. pap. text 34.95 (*0-521-31594-8*) Cambridge U Pr.

— Working in the Macroeconomy: A Study of the U. S. Labor Market. LC 96-33539. (Studies in the Modern World Economy). 240p. (C). 1997. 75.00 (*0-415-14927-4*) Routledge.

*__Prachowny, Martin F. J.__ The Kennedy-Johnson Tax Cut: A Revisionist History. LC 00-37621. 240p. 2000. 80.00 (*1-84064-417-6*) E Elgar.

Pracht-Fitzell, Ilse. Blendung und Wandlung: Lessings Dramen in Psychologischer Sicht. LC 90-36425. (Enlightenment: German & Interdisciplinary Studies: Vol. 3). 361p. (C). 1993. text 59.95 (*0-8204-1374-7*) P Lang Pubng.

Pracht, Klaus & Bergmeister, Manfred. Manfred Bergmeister: Schmiedearbeiten = Smithery. LC 98-197177. (ENG & GER.). 183p. 1997. write for info. (*3-8030-5066-9*) E J Wasmuth.

*__Pracht, Louis.__ Europe in Figures. 4th ed. (Illus.). 425p. (C). 1999. reprint ed. pap. text 50.00 (*0-7881-8021-5*) DIANE Pub.

Practical Sailor Editors. Practical Boat Buying, 2 vols., Set. 4th ed. 728p. 1996. 59.95 (*1-879620-41-3*) Belvoir Pubns.

Practical Sailor Staff. Practical Boat Buying. 4th ed. 1996. pap. text 47.95 (*0-07-069869-4*) McGraw.

Practical Sailor Staff, ed. Buying & Selling, Vol. V. (Practical Sailor Library). (Illus.). 1995. pap. 14.95 (*1-879620-36-7*) Belvoir Pubns.

— Commissioning & Decommissioning, Vol. II. (Practical Sailor Library). (Illus.). 1995. pap. 14.95 (*1-879620-33-2*) Belvoir Pubns.

— Do It Yourself Improvement Projects, Vol. IV. (Practical Sailor Library). (Illus.). 1995. pap. 14.95 (*1-879620-35-9*) Belvoir Pubns.

— Maintenance & Repairs, Vol. III. (Practical Sailor Library). (Illus.). 1995. pap. 14.95 (*1-879620-34-0*) Belvoir Pubns.

— Outfitting, Vol. I. (Practical Sailor Library). (Illus.). 1995. pap. 14.95 (*1-879620-32-4*) Belvoir Pubns.

Practices National Conference of Catholic Bishops, jt. auth. see Bishops' Committee for Pastoral Research Staff.

Practices National Conference of Catholic Bishops, jt. auth. see Bishops' Committee for Pastoral Research Staff.

Practising Law Institute, jt. auth. see Cushman, Kenneth M.

Practising Law Institute, jt. auth. see Fryer, Judith D.

Practising Law Institute, jt. auth. see Gerber, David A.

Practising Law Institute, jt. auth. see Pasternack, Victor.

Practising Law Institute, jt. auth. see Rogers, William P.

Practising Law Institute, jt. auth. see Ross, Alfred J.

Practising Law Institute, jt. auth. see Shih, Bruce J.

Practising Law Institute, jt. auth. see Soderquist, Larry D.

*__Practising Law Institute Staff.__ Commercial Real Estate Financing. LC 98-162331. (Real Estate Law & Practice Course Handbook Ser.). 1998. 159.00 (*0-87224-449-0*) PLI.

Practising Law Institute Staff. Doing Deals. LC 95-125700. (Commercial Law & Practice Course Handbook Ser.). 592 p. 1995. 129.00 (*0-87224-168-8*) PLI.

— MCLE Compulsories 1994. LC 95-122392. 472 p. 1994. write for info. (*0-87224-159-9*) PLI.

— Non-Profit Organizations, 1990. (Tax Law & Estate Planning Ser.). 231p. 1990. 70.00 (*0-685-38047-5*) PLI.

— What Every Successful Lawyer Needs to Know about Accounting. LC 95-208957. (Corporate Law & Practice Course Handbook Ser.). 376 p. 1995. 129.00 (*0-87224-194-7*) PLI.

Practising Law Institute Staff, et al. The New Business of Banking. LC 97-148380. (Corporate Law & Practice Course Handbook Ser.). 832 p. 1996. 39.00 (*0-87224-297-8*) PLI.

Practising Law Institute Staff, jt. auth. see Alvarez, Guy.

Practising Law Institute Staff, jt. auth. see Barrett, William L.

Practising Law Institute Staff, jt. auth. see Bernstein, David H.

Practising Law Institute Staff, jt. auth. see Dunham, Wolcott B.

Practising Law Institute Staff, jt. auth. see Dunn, M. Douglas.

Practising Law Institute Staff, jt. auth. see Edelstein, Jeffrey S.

Practising Law Institute Staff, jt. auth. see Fellas, John.

Practising Law Institute Staff, jt. auth. see Ganz, Howard L.

Practising Law Institute Staff, jt. auth. see Geltzer, Robert L.

Practising Law Institute Staff, jt. auth. see Hammock, Edward R.

Practising Law Institute Staff, jt. auth. see Kane, Siegrun D.

Practising Law Institute Staff, jt. auth. see Kennedy, Michael J.

Practising Law Institute Staff, jt. auth. see Koeppel, Adolph.

Practising Law Institute Staff, jt. auth. see Leeds, Mathew J.

Practising Law Institute Staff, jt. auth. see Nuara, Leonard T.

P

Practising Law Institute Staff, jt. auth. see Pirkey, Louis T.

Practising Law Institute Staff, jt. auth. see Ramos, Carey R.,.

Practising Law Institute Staff, jt. auth. see Romano, Robert M.

Practising Law Institute Staff, jt. auth. see Schlesinger, Sanford J.

Practising Law Institute Staff, jt. auth. see Weinberg, Steven M.

Practitioners Publishing Co. Staff. Guide To Gaap, 1996 Edition. (SWC-Accounting). 1996. pap. 35.50 (*0-538-85829-X*) S-W Pub.

***Practitioners Publishing Co. Staff.** Performance Measurment Solutions, Vol. 1. 1999. ring bd. write for info. (*0-7646-0890-8*) Prctnrs Pub Co.

Practitioners Publishing Co. Staff. PPC Library Viewer for Windows Learning Guide, Vol. 1. 1996. write for info. (*0-7646-0076-1*) Prctnrs Pub Co.

***Practitioners Publishing Co. Staff.** The PPC Medical Focus. 1998. ring bd. write for info. (*0-7646-0476-7*, HLCN 98) Prctnrs Pub Co.

— PPC's Engagement Manager Learning Guide. 1999. ring bd. 149.00 (*0-7646-0825-8*) Prctnrs Pub Co.

— PPC's Financial Advisory Services College. 1999. ring bd. write for info. (*0-7646-0869-X*, CURP 99) Prctnrs Pub Co.

— Risk Scan Learning Guide, Vol. 1. 1998. ring bd. write for info. (*0-7646-0661-1*) Prctnrs Pub Co.

Practitioners Publishing Company Staff. PPC GuideWare for Windows. 1996. 72.00 incl. disk (*1-56433-519-4*) Prctnrs Pub Co.

— Using a Client's 1040 to Generate Tax Planning Ideas. 1996. write for info. (*0-7646-0090-7*) Prctnrs Pub Co.

Practitioners Publishing Company Staff, jt. auth. see Budak, Susan Weiss.

***Practitioners Publishing Staff.** New Issues in Audit & Accounting: PPC's Annual Audit & Accounting Update. 1999. ring bd. write for info. (*0-7646-0763-4*) Prctnrs Pub Co.

Practor, Jodie. Geography Brain Teasers. (Brain Teasers Ser.). 80p. (J). (gr. 5-8). 1998. pap. 9.95 (*1-57690-213-7*) Tchr Create Mat.

Prada & Anton. Handworterbuch German to Spanish. 11th ed. (GER & SPA.). 639p. 1996. 89.95 (*0-320-00672-7*) Fr & Eur.

Prada, Jaun Manuel De, see De Prada, Jaun Manuel.

Prada, Manuel G. Grafitos. 254p. 1.00 (*0-318-14270-8*) Hispanic Inst.

Prada, Valentin de, see De Prada, Valentin.

Prade, H., jt. auth. see Dubois, D.

Prade, Henri M., ed. see European Conference on Artificial Intelligence & European Coordinating Committee for Artificial Intelligence.

Pradeau, Alberto F. Numismatic History of Mexico. LC 77-93447. (Illus.). 1978. reprint ed. lib. bdg. 25.00 (*0-915262-20-7*) S J Durst.

Pradeau, Alberto F., tr. see Nentvig, Juan.

Pradel, J., jt. auth. see Hureau, J.

Pradel, Lucie. African Beliefs in the New World. 290p. 1998. 69.95 (*0-86543-702-5*); pap. 19.95 (*0-86543-703-3*) Africa World.

Pradell, Steven. The Alaska Family Law Handbook. 95p. 1998. pap. 9.95 (*0-9664127-0-2*) Abracadabra.

— Winning the War Against Life-Threatening Diseases. LC 94-66759. 256p. 1994. pap. 13.95 (*0-88282-125-3*) New Horizon NJ.

Prader, A., jt. ed. see Cacciari, E.

Pradera, Victor. The New State. Malley, B., tr. LC 79-180421. reprint ed. 36.00 (*0-404-56196-9*) AMS Pr.

Pradere, Alexandre. French Furniture Makers: The Art of the Ebeniste from Louis XIV to the Revolution. LC 89-60462. (Illus.). 444p. 1990. 175.00 (*0-89236-183-2*, Pub. by J P Getty Trust) OUP.

Praderie, Francoise, jt. auth. see Schatzman, Evry L.

Praderle, F. & Hudson, H. S., eds. Solar & Stellar Activity: Proceedings of Symposium 11 & of the Topical Meeting of the COSPAR Interdisciplinary Scientific Commission E (Meeting E2) of the COSPAR 26th Plenary Meeting Held in Toulouse, France, 30th Juen-11.July, 1986. (Advances in Space Research Ser.: Vol. 6). 1988. pap. 63.00 (*0-08-036643-0*, Pergamon Pr) Elsevier.

Pradervand, Pierre. Listening to Africa: Developing Africa from the Grassroots. LC 89-35347. 250p. 1989. 65.00 (*0-275-93389-X*, C3389, Praeger Pubs) Greenwood.

— Listening to Africa: Developing Africa from the Grassroots. 1990. pap. 14.95 (*0-275-93692-9*, B3692, Praeger Pubs) Greenwood.

Prades, Josep L., jt. auth. see Corbi, Josep E.

Prades, Juana de Jose, jt. auth. see Diaz, Jose Simon.

Pradham, Dhiraj K., jt. ed. see De Gyvez, Jose Pineda.

Pradham, U. C. Indian Orchids Vols. I & II: Guide to Identification & Culture, I. (C). 1988. 55.00 (*0-7855-3271-4*, Pub. by Scientific) St Mut.

— Indian Orchids Vols. I & II: Guide to Identification & Culture, II. (C). 1988. 70.00 (*0-7855-3272-2*, Pub. by Scientific) St Mut.

***Pradhan, Babu Lall.** Ratna's Nepali-English Nepali Dictionary. 1998. pap. 59.00 (*0-7855-7629-0*) St Mut.

Pradhan, Babulall. English Nepali Dictionary. 696p. (C). 1990. 55.50 (*0-89771-072-X*, Pub. by Ratna Pustak Bhandar) St Mut.

Pradhan, Bishwo. Behaviour of Nepalese Foreign Policy. 1996. pap. 104.00 (*0-7855-7365-8*, Pub. by Ratna Pustak Bhandar) St Mut.

Pradhan, Dhiraj K. Fault Tolerant Computing, Vol. I. 2nd ed. (C). 1993. boxed set 45.00 (*0-13-300963-7*) P-H.

Pradhan, G. P. India's Freedom Struggle. 1990. 22.50 (*0-86132-216-9*, Pub. by Popular Prakashan) S Asia.

Pradhan, G. P., jt. auth. see Duncan, H. C.

Pradhan, Kamal Maiya. Planning Tourism in Nepal. 1997. pap. 54.00 (*0-7855-7473-5*, Pub. by Ratna Pustak Bhandar) St Mut.

Pradhan, Krishna Bhai. A Practical Guide to the Script & Pronunciation of the Nepali Language. 53p. 1989. pap. text 5.00 (*0-9659801-2-X*) U Wisconsin-Madison.

— The Structure of Spoken Nepali. 389p. 1989. pap. text 15.00 (*0-9659801-1-1*) U Wisconsin-Madison.

Pradhan, Kumar. The Gorkha Conquests: The Process & Consequences of the Unification of Nepal, with Particular Reference to Eastern Nepal. 302p. 1991. 29.95 (*0-19-562723-7*) OUP.

Pradhan, M. M. Pancha Buddha & Dance. 1996. pap. 22.00 (*0-7855-7470-0*, Pub. by Ratna Pustak Bhandar) St Mut.

Pradhan, Mahmood, jt. auth. see Derry, Andrew.

Pradhan, Mahmood, jt. auth. see Haldane, Andrew G.

Pradhan, Menno. Sector Participation Decisions in Labor Supply Models. LC 94-41478. (LSMS Working Papers: No. 113). 44p. 1995. pap. 22.00 (*0-8213-3124-8*, 13124) World Bank.

Pradhan, Menno, jt. auth. see Prescott, Nicholas M.

Pradhan, Narindar S., jt. ed. see Chander, Jagdish.

Pradhan, Prabha, jt. auth. see Banerji, M. L.

Pradhan, Prachanda P. Local Institutions & People's Participation in Rural Public Works in Nepal. (Special Series on Rural Local Organization: No. 4). 103p. (Orig.). (C). 1980. pap. text 5.80 (*0-86731-031-6*) Cornell CIS RDC.

***Pradhan, Prasant K.** Gandhians' Rise to Power: National Movement, Power Politics & Independence, 1920-47. LC 98-908940. xx, 281p. 1998. write for info. (*81-7169-520-5*, Commonwealth) S Asia.

Pradhan, R., ed. see Metallurgical Society of AIME Staff.

Pradhan, R., ed. see Minerals, Metals & Materials Society Staff.

Pradhan, R., ed. see Symposium on High Strength Sheet Steels for the Au.

Pradhan, R. D. Debacle to Revival: Y.B. Chavan As Defense Minister, 1962-65. LC 98-915710. xii, 316p. 1999. write for info. (*81-250-1477-2*) Orient Longman Ltd.

Pradhan, Radha. Financial Management Practices in Nepal. 1994. pap. 60.00 (*0-7855-0441-9*, Pub. by Ratna Pustak Bhandar) St Mut.

Pradhan, Radhe S. Public Corporations of Nepal: A Study of Financial Ratios. 1986. 19.00 (*0-8364-1943-X*, Pub. by Natl Bk Orgn) S Asia.

Pradhan, Roger & Gupta, I., eds. Developments in the Annealing of Sheet Steels: Proceedings of an International Symposium Sponsored by the TMS Ferrous Metallurgy Committee & Held at the 1991 Fall Meeting in Cincinnati, Ohio, October 22-24. LC 92-50174. (Illus.). 556p. 1992. pap. 172.40 (*0-608-04886-0*, 206557800004) Bks Demand.

Pradhan, S. 100 Beautiful Himalayan Orchids & How to Grow Them. 1996. pap. write for info. (*0-7855-7524-3*) St Mut.

***Pradhan, S. A.** Orissan History, Culture & Archaeology: Reconstructing Indian History & Culture. LC 98-909202. xix, 477 p. 1998. write for info. (*81-246-0117-8*, Pub. by D K Printwrld) S Asia.

Pradhan, Sachin N., et al, eds. Pharmacology in Medicine: Principles & Practice. 1100p. (C). 1986. text 55.00 (*0-9617129-0-2*) SP Press Intl.

Pradhan, Sanjay. Evaluating Public Spending: A Framework for Public Expenditure Reviews. LC 96-8104. (World Bank Discussion Papers: Vol. 323). 146p. 1996. pap. 22.00 (*0-8213-3633-9*, 13633) World Bank.

Pradhan, Shubhangi S. Word-Index of Abhidharmakosa. (Bibliotheca Indo-Buddhica Ser.: No. 121). (C). 1993. text 28.00 (*81-7030-369-9*) S Asia.

Pradhan, Suresh B. International Pharmaceutical Marketing. LC 82-15022. 281p. 1983. 59.95 (*0-89930-009-X*, PPH/, Quorum Bks) Greenwood.

Pradhan, T., ed. Superstrings & Grand Unification: Proceedings of the Winter School on High Energy Physics. 148p. (C). 1989. pap. 36.00 (*9971-5-0528-2*); text 67.00 (*9971-5-0527-4*) World Scientific Pub.

Pradhan, T., jt. ed. see Khare, A.

Pradhan, U. C. & Routray. Market Centers & Rural Development: A Study in Chitwan District Nepal. 1994. pap. 80.00 (*0-7855-0460-5*, Pub. by Ratna Pustak Bhandar) St Mut.

Pradhana, Gauri. Back Home from Brothels. 1997. pap. 22.00 (*0-7855-7523-5*) St Mut.

Pradhuman, Dev. Small Cap Dynamics. 65.00 (*1-57660-029-7*, Pub. by Bloomberg NJ) Norton.

Pradier, Claire-Marie, jt. ed. see Paul, Jan.

Pradl, Gordon M. Literature for Democracy: Reading As a Social Act. LC 95-47260. 163p. (Orig.). 1996. pap. text 24.50 (*0-86709-380-3*, 0380, Pub. by Boynton Cook Pubs) Heinemann.

Pradl, Gordon M., ed. see Britton, James N.

Prado, Adelia. The Alphabet in the Park: Selected Poems. Watson, Ellen, tr. from POR. LC 89-38463. (Wesleyan Poetry in Translation Ser.). 80p. 1990. pap. 12.95 (*0-8195-1177-3*, Wesleyan Univ Pr) U Pr of New Eng.

Prado, Benjamin. Never Shake Hands with a Left-Handed Gunman. Cordero, Kristina, tr. from SPA. LC 98-31664. 176p. 1998. text 19.95 (*0-312-20084-6*) St Martin.

Prado, Bento L. De Almeida, see De Almeida Prado, Bento L.

Prado, C. G. The Last Choice: Preemptive Suicide in Advanced Age. 2nd ed. LC 98-11103. 208p. 1998. pap. 19.95 (*0-275-96150-8*, Praeger Pubs) Greenwood.

— The Last Choice: Preemptive Suicide in Advanced Age. 63. LC 98-11103. (Contributions in Philosophy Ser.: Vol. 63). 208p. 1998. 59.95 (*0-313-30584-6*, Greenwood Pr) Greenwood.

— Making Believe: Philosophical Reflections on Fiction. 25. LC 83-5693. (Contributions in Philosophy Ser.: No. 25). 169p. 1984. 52.95 (*0-313-24013-2*, PMB/, Greenwood Pr) Greenwood.

— Rethinking How We Age: A New View of the Aging Mind. 28. LC 85-9862. (Contributions in Philosophy Ser.: No. 28). 185p. 1986. 49.95 (*0-313-24785-4*, PRA/, Greenwood Pr) Greenwood.

— Starting with Foucault: An Introduction to Genealogy. 192p. (C). 1995. pap. 22.00 (*0-8133-1791-6*, Pub. by Westview) HarpC.

Prado, C. G. & Taylor, S. J. Assisted Suicide: Theory & Practice in Elective Death. LC 98-15513. 216p. 1998. 55.00 (*0-391-04086-3*); pap. 17.50 (*0-391-04087-1*) Humanities.

— Assisted Suicide: Theory & Practice in Elective Death. 216p. 1999. 49.95 (*1-57392-634-5*, Humanity Bks); pap. 18.95 (*1-57392-633-7*, Humanity Bks) Prometheus Bks.

Prado-Flores, Jose, jt. auth. see Tardif, Emiliano.

Prado, G., jt. ed. see Lahaye, Jacques.

Prado, Holly. Esperanza: Poems for Orpheus. 75p. 1998. pap. 12.00 (*0-9649240-5-6*) Cahuenga Pr.

— Specific Mysteries. 55p. 1990. pap. 8.00 (*0-9649240-1-3*) Cahuenga Pr.

Prado, J., compiled by. Fisherman's Workbook. (Illus.). 192p. 1990. pap. text 24.95 (*0-85238-163-8*) Blackwell Sci.

Prado, Jan, ed. see McGuire, J. Victor.

Prado, Jorge S. Campesinado en P. R. a Fines del Siglo XIX y Principios del XX: El Caso de Toa Alta. LC 96-84356. 112p. 1996. pap. 6.95 (*0-929157-36-2*) Ediciones Huracan.

Prado, Marcial. Advanced Spanish Grammar. 2nd ed. LC 96-18358. (Self-Teaching Guides Ser.). 336p. 1997. pap. 17.95 (*0-471-13448-1*) Wiley.

— Practical Spanish Grammar: A Self-Teaching Guide. 2nd ed. LC 96-39865. 368p. 1997. pap. 17.95 (*0-471-13446-5*) Wiley.

Prado, Marcial, ed. NTC's Dictionary of Spanish False Cognates. LC 97-49455. (ENG & SPA., Illus.). 280p. 1996. pap. 12.95 (*0-8442-7977-3*, 79773, Natl Textbk Co) NTC Contemp Pub Co.

Prado, Miguelanxo. Streak of Chalk. 88p. 1994. pap. 16.95 (*1-56163-108-6*, Comics Lit) NBM.

— Tangents. Legault, Robert, tr. from SPA. (Illus.). 48p. 1996. 16.95 (*1-56163-148-5*, Comics Lit) NBM.

Prado, Pedro. Alsino Vol. 21: Pedro Prado. Castillo-Feliu, Guillermo I., tr. LC 93-22219. (American University Studies: No. XXII). (SPA.). 191p. (C). 1995. text 39.95 (*0-8204-2148-0*) P Lang Pubng.

Prado, R. De, see De Prado, R.

Prado Velazquez, Ernesto, jt. auth. see Ocampo de Gomez, Aurora.

Pradon. Phedre et Hippolyte. Classe, ed. (Exeter French Texts Ser.: Vol. 62). (FRE.). 142p. Date not set. pap. text 19.95 (*0-85989-297-2*, Pub. by Univ Exeter Pr) Northwestern U Pr.

Prados, Edward F., ed. Neptunus Rex: Naval Stories of the Normandy Invasion, June 6, 1944: Voices of the Navy Memorial. LC 98-6151. 304p. 1998. 24.95 (*0-89141-648-X*) Presidio Pr.

Prados, John. The Blood Road: The Ho Chi Minh Trail & the Vietnam War. LC 98-9340. 432p. 1998. 35.00 (*0-471-25465-7*) Wiley.

***Prados, John.** The Blood Road: The Ho Chi Minh Trail & the Vietnam War. 448p. 2000. pap. 19.95 (*0-471-37945-X*) Wiley.

Prados, John. The Hidden History of the Vietnam War. LC 94-46662. 352p. 1995. text 27.50 (*1-56663-079-7*, Pub. by I R Dee) Natl Bk Netwk.

— The Hidden History of the Vietnam War. LC 98-9472. 352p. 1998. pap. 16.95 (*1-56663-197-1*, Elephant Paperbacks) I R Dee.

— Presidents' Secret Wars: CIA & Pentagon Covert Operations from World War II Through the Persian Gulf. rev. ed. 576p. 1996. pap. 17.95 (*1-56663-108-4*, EL134, Pub. by I R Dee) Natl Bk Netwk.

***Prados, Michael.** Brain Cancer. (ACS Atlas of Clinical Oncology Ser.). 300p. 2000. boxed set 89.95 incl. cd-rom (*1-55009-098-4*) DEKR.

Pradt, Mary A., compiled by. You Must Remember This, 1955: Milestones, Memories, Trivia & Facts, News Events, Prominent Personalities & Sports Highlights of the Year. 24p. 1995. write for info. (*0-446-51919-7*) Warner Bks.

— You Must Remember This, 1975: Milestones, Memories, Trivia & Facts, News Events, Prominent Personalities & Sports Highlights of the Year. 24p. 1995. write for info. (*0-446-51937-5*) Warner Bks.

— You Must Remember This, 1968: Milestones, Memories, Trivia & Facts, News Events, Prominent Personalities & Sports Highlights of the Year. 24p. 1995. write for info. (*0-446-51931-6*) Warner Bks.

Praechter, Karl. Kleine Schriften. (Collectanea Ser.: Vol. VII). xxiii, 474p. 1973. write for info. (*3-487-04672-5*) G Olms Pubs.

Praeger, Betzabe M. & Praeger, Frank C. Places & Occasions: Poems. LC 91-60318. 64p. (Orig.). 1991. pap. 8.00 (*0-9628816-0-0*) Keweenaw Pr.

Praeger, Cheryl E. & Soicher, Leonard H. Low Rank Representations & Graphs for Sporadic Groups. (Australian Mathematical Society Lecture Ser.: No. 8). 153p. 1997. pap. text 39.95 (*0-521-56737-8*) Cambridge U Pr.

Praeger, Cindy L. & Praeger, Michael S. Tackpot! The Step-by-Step Guide to Recovering Your Money. 287p. (Orig.). 1997. pap. text 19.95 (*0-9658482-0-5*) Infoventures.

Praeger, D. K., jt. auth. see Littlebury, F. E.

***Praeger, Dennis.** Happiness is a Serious Problem: Prager,&Dennis, Set. abr. ed. 1998. audio 18.00 (*0-694-51902-2*, CPN2708) HarperAudio.

Praeger, Frank C., jt. auth. see Praeger, Betzabe M.

Praeger, Michael S., jt. auth. see Praeger, Cindy L.

Praeger, Michele & Robbe-Grillet, Alain. Les Romans de Robert Pinget: Une Ecriture des Possibles. LC 86-80313. (French Forum Monographs: No. 65). (FRE.). 165p. 1986. pap. 12.95 (*0-917058-66-6*) French Forum.

Praeger, R. L. An Account of the Genus Sedum As Found in Cultivation. (Illus.). 1967. pap. 38.00 (*3-7682-0446-4*) Lubrecht & Cramer.

Praeger, Robert L. & Viney, Michael. The Way That I Went. LC 98-166907. 394p. 1998. pap. 19.95 (*1-898256-35-7*, Pub. by Collins Press) Dufour.

Praeger, Rosamond. The Young Stamp-Collectors. (Illus.). 56p. 1985. 15.95 (*0-9508551-1-1*, Pub. by Portmoon Pr) Asia Bk Corp.

Praeger, Sandy, frwd. Expanding Health Coverage for Children: Matching Federal Policies & State Strategies. LC 98-124749. (Illus.). 48p. 1998. pap. write for info. (*1-887748-19-9*) Milbank Memorial.

Praem, Alfred. Images of Jesus: Ten Invitations to Intimacy. 229p. 1993. pap. 9.95 (*0-86716-180-9*) St Anthony Mess Pr.

Praem, O., jt. auth. see Dorff, Francis.

Praem, O., jt. auth. see McBride, Alfred.

Praem, O., jt. auth. see Van Straaten, Werenfried.

Praetorius, Henry. An Immigrant Settler. LC 88-70298. (Illus.). 136p. 1988. pap. 7.50 (*0-8323-0460-3*) Binford Mort.

Praetorius, Hieronymms. Dedication Service for St. Gertrude's Chapel, Hamburg, 1607. Gable, Frederick K., ed. (Recent Researches in Music of the Baroque Era Ser.: Vol. RRB91). (Illus.). xli, 146p. 1998. pap. 65.00 (*0-89579-418-7*) A-R Eds.

Praetorius, Hieronymus. Hieronymus Praetorius Pt. I: Polychoral Motets for Two Choirs. Gable, Frederick K., ed. (Recent Researches in Music of the Renaissance Ser.: Vol. RRR18). (Illus.). xiv, 85p. 1974. pap. 35.00 (*0-89579-052-1*) A-R Eds.

— Hieronymus Praetorius Pt. II: Polychoral Motets for Three Choirs. Gable, Frederick K., ed. (Recent Researches in Music of the Renaissance Ser.: Vol. RRR19). (Illus.). 100p. 1974. pap. 40.00 (*0-89579-053-X*) A-R Eds.

Praetorius, Jacob, II. The Motets of Jacob Praetorius II. Gable, Frederick K., ed. (Recent Researches in Music of the Baroque Era Ser.: Vol. RRB73). (Illus.). xxiv, 102p. 1994. pap. 40.00 (*0-89579-308-3*) A-R Eds.

Praetorius, Michael. The Syntagma Musicum of Michael Praetorius Vol. 2: De Organographica. Blumenfeld, Harold, tr. LC 79-20847. (Music Reprint Ser.). (Illus.). 1980. reprint ed. 29.50 (*0-306-70563-X*) Da Capo.

— Syntagma Musicum, Tomus Secundus. Eitner, Robert, ed. (Publikation Alterer Praktischer und Theoretischer Musikwerke, XV. & XVI. Jhs. Ser.: Vol. 13). (GER., Illus.). 1966. reprint ed. lib. bdg. 75.00 (*0-8450-1713-6*) Broude.

***Praetorius, N. & Enbody, R. J.** Principles of Cognition, Language & Action - Essays on the Foundations for a Science of Psychology. 500p. 2000. pap. 55.00 (*0-7923-6231-4*) Kluwer Academic.

Praetorius, Pete & Culhane, Alys. Alaska Bicycle Touring Guide: Including Parts of the Yukon Territory & Northwest Territories. 2nd ed. (Illus.). 320p. 1992. pap. 17.50 (*0-938737-27-9*) Denali Press.

***Praetzellis, Adrian.** Death by Theory: A Tale of Mystery & Archaeological Theory. (Illus.). 160p. 2000. 59.95 (*0-7425-0358-5*); pap. 17.95 (*0-7425-0359-3*) AltaMira Pr.

Praetzellis, Mary, et al. Ceramics Marks from Old Sacramento. (Publications of the Department of Parks & Recreation: No. 22). (Illus.). 108p. (C). 1983. reprint ed. pap. text 3.15 (*1-55567-471-2*) Coyote Press.

Praff, Giora. Glimmers of Light in a Betraying Land. Schreiber, Mordecai, tr. from HEB. LC 92-82824. 122p. 1992. 18.95 (*0-88400-159-8*, Shengold Bks) Schreiber Pub.

Prag, John & Neave, Richard. Making Faces: Using Forensic & Archaeological Evidence. LC 97-18786. (Texas A&M Anthropology Ser.: No. 1). (Illus.). 256p. 1997. 39.95 (*0-89096-784-9*) Tex A&M Univ Pr.

Prag, Kay. Jerusalem. (Blue Guide Ser.). (Illus.). 1989. pap. 19.95 (*0-393-30480-9*) Norton.

Prag, Kay, ed. see Eshel, Itzak.

Pragacz, Piotr, jt. auth. see Fulton, William.

Pragai, Michael. Faith & Fulfilment. 1985. 30.00 (*0-85303-210-6*, Pub. by M Vallentine & Co) Intl Spec Bk.

Pragai, Michael J. Faith & Fulfilment. 1985. pap. 16.50 (*0-85303-211-4*, Pub. by M Vallentine & Co) Intl Spec Bk.

Prager. ERCD CCC, Vols. 1 & 2. 1997. 300.00 (*0-442-02304-9*, VNR) Wiley.

***Prager.** On Turing. 2000. pap. 8.25 (*0-534-58364-4*) Wadsworth Pub.

Prager, Annabelle. The Baseball Birthday Party. LC 93-25258. (Step into Reading Ser.: A Step 2 Book). (Illus.). 46p. (J). (ps-3). 1995. pap. 3.99 (*0-679-84171-7*, Pub. by Random Bks Yng Read) Random.

— The Baseball Birthday Party. (Step into Reading Ser.: A Step 2 Book). (J). (gr. 1-3). 1995. 9.19 (*0-606-07263-2*, Pub. by Turtleback) Demco.

— The Spooky Halloween Party. LC 88-37571. (Step into Reading Ser.: A Step 2 Book). (Illus.). 48p. (J). (ps-3). 1989. pap. 3.99 (*0-394-84961-2*, Pub. by Random Bks Yng Read) Random.

— The Spooky Halloween Party. LC 88-37571. (Step into Reading Ser.: A Step 2 Book). (Illus.). 48p. (J). (ps-3). 1989. lib. bdg. 11.99 (*0-394-94961-7*, Pub. by Random Bks Yng Read) Random.

P

An Asterisk (*) at the beginning of an entry indicates that the title is appearing for the first time.

— The Surprise Party. LC 87-20649. (Step into Reading Ser.: A Step 2 Book). (Illus.). 48p. (J). (ps-3). 1988. pap. 3.99 (*0-394-89596-7*, Pub. by Random Bks Yng Read) Random.

Prager, Annabelle. The Surprise Party. (Step into Reading Ser.: A Step 2 Book). (J). 1977. 9.19 (*0-606-03934-1*, Pub. by Turtleback) Demco.

Prager, Audrey & Gettleman, Barry. Job Creation in the Community: An Evaluation of Locally Initiated Employment Projects in Massachusetts. 186p. 1977. 34.95 (*0-89011-506-0*, EMT 114) Transaction Pubs.

Prager, Carolyn, ed. Accreditation of the Two-Year College. LC 85-644753. (New Directions for Community Colleges Ser.: No. CC 83). 110p. (Orig.). 1993. pap. 22.00 (*1-55542-718-9*) Jossey-Bass.

***Prager, Dennis.** Happiness Is a Serious Problem: A Human Nature Repair Manual. LC 97-35404. 192p. 1999. pap. 13.00 (*0-06-098735-9*, ReganBks) HarperTrade.

Prager, Dennis. Think a Second Time. 352p. 1996. pap. 14.00 (*0-06-098709-X*) HarpC.

Prager, Dennis & Telushkin, Joseph. The Nine Questions People Ask about Judaism. 224p. 1986. pap. 11.00 (*0-671-62261-7*, Touchstone) S&S Trade Pap.

— Why the Jews? The Reason for Anti-Semitism. 340p. 1985. pap. 12.00 (*0-671-55624-X*) S&S Trade.

***Prager, Ellen J.** Furious Earth: The Science & Nature of Earthquakes, Volcanoes & Tsunamis. LC 99-48386. (Illus.). 235p. 1999. 24.95 (*0-07-135161-2*) McGraw.

— Sand. LC 99-29943. (Illus.). 32p. (J). (gr. 4-6). 2000. 17.95 (*0-7922-7104-1*, Pub. by Natl Geog) S&S Trade.

***Prager, Ellen J. & Earle, Sylvia A.** The Oceans. 314p. 2000. 24.95 (*0-07-135253-8*) McGraw.

Prager, Emily. Roger Fishbite. LC 98-24408. 187p. 1999. 23.95 (*0-679-41053-8*) Random.

Prager, Herman. Global Marine Environment: Does the Water Planet Have a Future? LC 92-44141. (C). 1993. 49.00 (*0-8191-9016-0*); pap. 24.50 (*0-8191-9017-9*) U Pr of Amer.

Prager, Jan C. Environmental Containment Reference Databook, Vols. 1 & 2. 1997. 600.00 (*0-442-02436-3*, VNR) Wiley.

— Environmental Contaminant Reference Databook, 3 vols. (Environmental Engineering Ser.). 3810p. 1998. pap. 435.00 (*0-471-31459-5*, VNR) Wiley.

Prager, Jan C. Environmental Contaminant Reference Databook, Vol. 1. (Environmental Engineering Ser.). 1264p. 1995. 159.00 (*0-471-28660-5*, VNR) Wiley.

Prager, Jan C. Environmental Contaminant Reference Databook, Vol. 1. LC 94-43927. (Illus.). 1292p. 1995. text 142.95 (*0-442-01918-1*, VNR) Wiley.

— Environmental Contaminant Reference Databook, Vol. 1. 1996. write for info. (*0-442-02420-7*, VNR) Wiley.

— Environmental Contaminant Reference Databook, Vol. II. (Environmental Engineering Ser.). 1292p. 1996. text 142.95 (*0-442-01969-6*, VNR) Wiley.

— Environmental Contaminant Reference Databook, 3 vols., Vol. 3. (Environmental Engineering Ser.). 1292p. 1996. 129.95 (*0-442-01971-8*, VNR) Wiley.

Prager, Jan C. Environmental Contaminant References Databook, Vol. 2. (Environmental Engineering Ser.). 1312p. 1995. 159.00 (*0-471-28683-4*, VNR) Wiley.

Prager, Janice & LePoff, Arlene. Why Be Different? A Look into Judaism. 118p. (J). (gr. 6-8). 1986. pap. text 8.95 (*0-87441-427-X*) Behrman.

Prager, Jeffrey. Presenting the Past: Psychoanalysis & Sociology of Misremembering. LC 97-49904. 240p. 1999. text 31.00 (*0-674-56641-6*) HUP.

***Prager, Jeffrey.** Presenting the Past: Psychoanalysis & the Sociology of Misremembering. 272p. 2000. pap. 16.95 (*0-674-00419-1*) HUP.

Prager, Jeffrey, et al, eds. School Desegregation Research: New Directions in Situational Analysis. (Critical Issues in Social Justice Ser.). (Illus.). 284p. (C). 1986. 65.00 (*0-306-42151-8*, Plenum Trade) Perseus Pubng.

Prager, Jeffrey & Rustin, Michael, eds. Psychoanalytic Sociology, 2 vols., set. (Schools of Thought in Sociology Ser.: Vol. 10). (Illus.). 800p. 1993. 310.00 (*1-85278-336-2*) E Elgar.

Prager, Jonas. Intermediate Microeconomics. 608p. (C). 1992. text 68.50 (*0-256-05780-X*, Irwn McGrw-H) McGrw-H Hghr Educ.

Prager, Justin, ed. see Kline, Eric.

Prager, Karen J. The Psychology of Intimacy. LC 95-37284. (Personal Relationships Ser.). 367p. 1995. lib. bdg. 39.95 (*1-57230-006-X*, 0006) Guilford Pubns.

— The Psychology of Intimacy. LC 95-37284. (Personal Relationships Ser.). 367p. 1997. pap. text 24.00 (*1-57230-267-4*, C0267) Guilford Pubns.

***Prager, Kate, et al, eds.** Health United States 1996-97 & Injury Chart Book. (Illus.). 341p. (C). 1999. reprint ed. pap. text 45.00 (*0-7881-8248-X*) DIANE Pub.

Prager, Kate, et al. Health, United States, 1995: The Annual National Report on Health. 20th ed. (Illus.). 328p. (C). 1998. pap. text 45.00 (*0-7881-7307-3*) DIANE Pub.

Prager, Leonard. Yiddish Culture in Britain: A Guide. XIV, 776p. 1991. pap. 104.00 (*3-631-41978-3*) P Lang Pubng.

Prager, Leonard, ed. see Jewish Language Review Staff.

Prager, M., ed. Structural Integrity NDE Risk & Material Performance for Petroleum Process & Power. 373p. 1996. pap. text 120.00 (*0-7918-1783-0*, TS283) ASME Pr.

Prager, M., et al, eds. Fitness-for-Service & Decisions for Petroleum & Chemical Equipment. LC 95-77290. (Proceedings of the 1995 ASME/JSME Pressure Vessels & Piping Conference Ser.: PVP-Vol. 315). 560p. 1995. 140.00 (*0-7918-1346-0*, H00978) ASME.

Prager, Marcia. Letters of Creation. 2003. 21.00 (*0-517-70362-9*) Random Hse Value.

— The Path of Blessing: Experiencing the Energy & Abundance of the Divine. LC 98-2903. 240p. 1998. 21.00 (*0-517-70363-7*) Bell T.

***Prager, Marcia.** The Path of Blessing: Experiencing the Energy & Abundance of the Divine. 240p. 1999. reprint ed. pap. 13.00 (*0-609-80393-X*) Bell T.

Prager, Martin. Fitness for Adverse Environments in Petroleum & Power Equipment: Proceedings ASME Pressure Vessels & Piping Conference (1997, Orlando, FL) LC 97-73604. (PVP Ser.: Vol. 359). 353p. 1997. pap. 130.00 (*0-7918-1576-5*) ASME.

Prager, Martin, ed. Factors Influencing the Time-Dependent Properties of Carbon Steels for Elevated Temperature Pressure Vessels, Vol. 19. 102p. 1983. pap. text 24.00 (*0-317-02616-X*, H00265) ASME.

Prager, Martin & Tilley, Richard M., eds. Nondestructive Evalution of Utilities & Pipelines, Vol. 2947. 310p. 1996. 76.00 (*0-8194-2351-3*) SPIE.

Prager, Moshe. Rabbi Yisroel Baal Shem Tov. (HEB., Illus.). 80p. 1982. pap. 2.00 (*0-914131-51-6*, D500) Torah Umesorah.

— Rabbi Yisroel Baal Shem Tov. (Illus.). 80p. 1987. pap. 2.00 (*0-914131-50-8*, D510) Torah Umesorah.

— Sparks of Glory: Inspiring Episodes of Jewish Spiritual Resistance. (ArtScroll History Ser.). (Illus.). 208p. 1985. 17.99 (*0-89906-456-6*) Mesorah Pubns.

Prager, Susan W., jt. intro. see Carroll, William A.

Prager, W., jt. auth. see Save, M.

Prager, W., ed. see International Symposium on Stress Waves in Anelast.

Praglin, Laura, ed. Starting Your Career: The Best Resources to Help You Find the Right Job. 224p. 1998. pap. 24.95 (*1-892148-03-X*) Res Pathways.

Pragnell. Machine-God Laughs. 3.50 (*0-686-05843-7*); pap. 1.50 (*0-686-05844-5*) Fantasy Pub Co.

***Pragnell, Hubert.** Britain. 2000. 18.00 (*1-84166-002-7*, Pub. by Ellipsis) Norton.

Pragnell, Hubert. Britain: A Guide to Architectural Styles from 1066 to the Present Day. LC 96-157847. 1998. pap. 12.95 (*1-899858-04-0*) Watsn-Guptill.

Prago, Albert, jt. ed. see Bessie, Alvah C.

Pragoff, Fiona. Fiona Pragoff's Board Books: Baby Plays. (Illus.). (J). 1995. 3.95 (*0-671-89913-9*) Litle Simon.

— Fiona Pragoff's Board Books: Baby Ways. (Illus.). (J). 1995. 3.95 (*0-671-89912-0*) Litle Simon.

— It's Fun to Be One. (Illus.). 24p. (J). (ps up). 1994. mass mkt. 6.95 (*0-689-71813-6*) Aladdin.

— It's Great to Be Two. (Illus.). 24p. (J). (ps up). 1994. mass mkt. 6.95 (*0-689-71814-4*, Mac Bks Young Read) S&S Childrens.

— A Present for Alice. LC 99-202892. 20p. (J). 1999. 12.95 (*0-385-32625-4*) BDD Bks Young Read.

Prague, Cary. Access Strategies & Tactics. 1997. 39.99 (*0-7897-1253-9*) Macmillan.

Prague, Cary. Access 97 Secrets. LC 96-79764. (Secrets Ser.). 1128p. 1997. pap. 49.99 (*0-7645-3043-7*) IDG Bks.

Prague, Cary M. & Irwin, Michael R. Access 97 Bible. LC 96-78778. (Bible Ser.). 950p. 1997. pap. text 49.99 (*0-7645-3035-6*) IDG Bks.

Prague, Cary N. Access for Windows 95 Bible. 3rd ed. LC 95-80474. (Bible Ser.). 1152p. 1995. pap. 39.99 (*1-56884-493-X*) IDG Bks.

— Access 2000 Programming Weekend Crash Course. 416p. 2000. pap. 24.99 (*0-7645-4688-0*) IDG Bks.

Prague, Cary N. The dBASE IV Programming. 1991. 24.95 incl. 5.25 hd (*0-8306-6687-7*); 24.95 incl. 3.5 hd (*0-8306-6688-5*) McGraw-Hill Prof.

— The dBASE IV Programming. 2nd ed. 1990. pap. 32.95 (*0-8306-3569-6*) McGraw-Hill Prof.

Prague, Cary N. & Hammitt, James E. Advanced dBASE IV Programming. 1989. pap. 22.95 (*0-8306-9376-9*, 3076P) McGraw-Hill Prof.

— Advanced Programming with dBASE IV. 1991. 24.95 (*0-8306-6647-8*) McGraw-Hill Prof.

— The dBASE III Programming Handbook. (Illus.). 240p. 1986. pap. 16.95 (*0-8306-2676-X*, 2676P) McGraw-Hill Prof.

— dBASE IV Programming. 1989. 29.95 (*0-8306-9466-8*, 3066); pap. 26.95 (*0-8306-9366-1*, 3066P) McGraw-Hill Prof.

— The dBASE IV 1.1 Program. 2nd ed. 1991. 29.95 (*0-8306-6757-1*); 29.95 (*0-8306-8758-0*) McGraw-Hill Prof.

— Programming with dBASE II. (Illus.). 288p. (Orig.). 1984. 26.95 (*0-8306-0776-5*, 1776); pap. 16.60 (*0-8306-1776-0*, 1776P) McGraw-Hill Prof.

— Programming with dBASE III Plus. (Illus.). 384p. 1986. pap. 19.95 (*0-8306-2726-X*) McGraw-Hill Prof.

— Programming with dBASE III Plus. 1991. 24.95 (*0-8306-6632-X*) McGraw-Hill Prof.

— Programming with R: Base 5000. (Illus.). 304p. 1986. 28.95 (*0-8306-0366-2*, 2666) McGraw-Hill Prof.

Prague, Cary N. & Irwin, Michael. Microsoft Access 2000 Bible. (Bible Ser.). (Illus.). 1272p. 1999. pap. 49.99 incl. cd-rom (*0-7645-3286-3*) IDG Bks.

***Prague, Cary N. & Irwin, Michael R.** Microsoft Access 2000 Bible: Gold Edition. LC 99-38068. (Bible Ser.). 1600p. 1999. pap. 64.99 (*0-7645-3404-1*) IDG Bks.

Prague, Cary N. & Kasevich, Lawrence S. Framework Three. (Illus.). 500p. 1988. pap. 24.95 (*0-8306-9386-6*, 3086) McGraw-Hill Prof.

***Prague, Cary N., et al.** Microsoft Access 97 Bible: Gold Edition. LC 99-60125. (Bible Ser.). (Illus.). 1552p. 1999. pap. 59.99 (*0-7645-3355-X*) IDG Bks.

Prague, Cary N., et al. Programming with R: BASE for DOS. (Orig.). 1991. 24.95 (*0-8306-6676-1*); 24.95 (*0-8306-9575-3*) McGraw-Hill Prof.

Prague, Cary N., jt. auth. see Hammitt, James E.

Prague, Cary N., jt. auth. see Irwin, Michael.

Prah, Christine, jt. auth. see Johnston, Bob.

Prah, K. Beyond the Colorline: Pan-Africanist Disputations: Selected Sketches, Letters, Papers, & Reviews. LC 97-40970. 200p. 1997. pap. write for info. (*0-86543-630-4*) Africa World.

Prah, K. K. Beyond the Colorline: Pan-Africanist Disputations: Selected Sketches, Letters, Papers, & Reviews. LC 97-40970. 200p. 1997. write for info. (*0-86543-629-0*) Africa World.

Prah, Kwesi K. Capitein: A Critical Study of an 18th Century African. LC 91-78314. 175p. 1992. 29.95 (*0-86543-331-3*); pap. 8.95 (*0-86543-332-1*) Africa World.

Prah, Kwesi Kwaa, ed. Between Distinction & Extinction: Harmonisation & Standardisation of African Languages. LC 99-161142. 343p. 1999. write for info. (*1-86814-330-9*) Wtwtrsrand UPP.

Prahalad. Competitive Collaboration: Managing Strategic Alliances. 1994. 23.99 (*0-02-925411-6*) S&S Trade.

Prahalad, C. K. & Doz, Yves L. The Multinational Mission: Balancing Local Demands & Global Vision. 256p. 1987. 35.00 (*0-02-925050-1*) Free Pr.

***Prahalad, C. K., et al.** Mastering Strategy. (Illus.). 488p. 2000. pap. 34.00 (*0-273-64930-2*, Pub. by F T P-H) Trans-Atl Phila.

Prahalad, C. K., jt. auth. see Hamel, Gary.

Prahl, Earl J. & Branster, Mark. Archaeological Investigations on Mackinac Island 1983: The Watermain & Sewer Project. LC 85-622249. (Archaeological Completion Reports: No. 8). (Illus.). 125p. (Orig.). 1984. pap. 10.00 (*0-911872-50-7*) Mackinac St Hist Pks.

Prahl, Ralph & Schlegel, Jeff, eds. Market Transformation. 70p. 1996. pap. 20.00 (*0-8058-9933-2*) L Erlbaum Assocs.

Prahl, Robert J., jt. auth. see Hoopes, Doris.

Prahlad, Anand & Prahlad, S. W. African-American Proverbs in Context. LC 95-53818. 288p. (C). 1996. 45.00 (*0-87805-889-3*); pap. 20.00 (*0-87805-890-7*) U Pr of Miss.

Prahlad, S. W., jt. auth. see Prahlad, Anand.

Prain, D. Flora of Sundaribans. 370p. (C). 1979. reprint ed. 185.00 (*0-7855-3120-3*, Pub. by Intl Bk Distr) St Mut.

— Flora of Sunderbuns. 370p. (C). 1979. text 150.00 (*0-89771-629-9*, Pub. by Intl Bk Distr) St Mut.

— Some Additional Leguminosae Proceedings of the Third World Orchid Conference, London. (C). 1960. 250.00 (*0-7855-3270-6*, Pub. by Scientific) St Mut.

— The Species of Dalbergia of South-Eastern Asia: Annals of the Royal Botanic Garden, Calcutta, Vol. 10, Pt. 1. 114p. (C). 1983. 170.00 (*0-7855-3241-2*, Pub. by Scientific) St Mut.

Prain, D., ed. Index Kewensis: Supplement (from 1911 to 1915), Vol. 5. 277p. 1978. reprint ed. text 100.00 (*0-685-26520-X*) Lubrecht & Cramer.

Prain, D., jt. auth. see Royal Botanic Garden, Calcutta Staff.

Prain, E. M. Live Hands: A Key to Better Golf. LC 94-69413. (Illus.). 128p. 1994. 16.95 (*1-885198-02-7*) Sports Log Pubs.

— Live Hands: A Key to Better Golf. 1998. text 16.95 (*1-886346-50-X*) Warde Pubs.

***Prain, Gordon D. & Fujisaka, Sam.** Biological & Cultural Diversity. 192p. 1999. pap. 29.95 (*1-85339-443-2*, Pub. by Intermed Tech) Stylus Pub VA.

***Prairie Home Collection Staff, ed.** Pretty Good Joke Book. 2000. pap. 11.95 (*1-56511-368-3*, Pub. by HighBridge) Penguin Putnam.

Prairie, Michel, ed. see Barnes, Jack.

Prairie-Plains Resource Institute Staff & Whitney, William S. Microcosm of the Platte: A Guide to Bader Memorial Park Natural Area. Whitney, Jan & Twedt, Curt, eds. (Illus.). 140p. (Orig.). (YA). (gr. 10-12). 1988. pap. text 10.00 (*0-945614-00-4*) Prairie Plains Res Inst.

***Prairie View A & M University Staff, ed.** Insights of America Goverment. 424p. 1999. pap. text 50.00 (*0-536-02660-2*) P-H.

Prais, Julia R. NxLevel Small Business Guide to International Trade: Business Without Borders. (Illus.). 248p. (Orig.). 1997. pap. 35.00 (*1-890730-03-3*) NxLevel Train.

Prais, S. J. Productivity, Education & Training: Facts & Policies in International Perspective. (National Institute of Economic & Social Research Occasional Papers). 154p. 1995. pap. text 18.95 (*0-521-55667-8*) Cambridge U Pr.

Prajapati, M. K., jt. ed. see Biswas, Subhas C.

***Prajapati, Vishnu, ed.** South Asia Power & Politics. 1998. 135.00 (*81-7169-509-4*, Pub. by Commonwealth) S Asia.

Prajnakarmiti. Santideva's Bodhicharyavatara, 2 vols., Set. (C). 1990. 72.00 (*81-85179-13-1*, Pub. by Aditya Prakashan) S Asia.

Prajnananda, Swami. Christ the Savior & Christ Myth. rev. ed. 121p. 1961. 12.95 (*0-87481-652-1*, Pub. by Advaita Ashrama) Vedanta Pr.

— A History of Indian Music. 1963. pap. 8.95 (*0-87481-626-2*) Vedanta Pr.

— Music of the Nations (a Comparative Study) 223p. 1973. 12.00 (*0-614-16457-5*) Theodore Front.

Prajzner, Nancy. Natural Wonders of Massachusetts. 2nd ed. 1999. pap. 14.95 (*0-8442-4623-9*) NTC Contemp Pub Co.

— Natural Wonders of Massachusetts: A Guide to Parks, Preserves & Wild Places. LC 94-18860. (Natural Wonders Ser.). (Illus.). 130p. 1994. pap. 9.95 (*1-56626-108-2*, Cntry Rds Pr) NTC Contemp Pub Co.

***Prak, Maarten Roy.** Early Modern Capitalism: Economic & Social Change in Europe 1400-1800. LC 00-35308. 2000. write for info. (*0-415-21714-8*) Routledge.

Prakasa Rao, B. L. S. Identifiability in Stochastic Models: Characterization of Probability Distributions. (Probability & Mathematical Statistics Ser.). 253p. 1992. text 71.00 (*0-12-564015-3*) Acad Pr.

— Semimartingales & Their Statistical Inference LC 99-18142. (Statistics Ser.). 1999. write for info. (*0-8493-9672-7*) CRC Pr.

***Prakasa Rao, B. L. S.** Semimartingales & Their Statistical Inference. LC 99-18142. (Monographs on Statistics & Applied Probability). 450p. 1999. boxed set 79.95 (*1-58488-008-2*, Chap & Hall CRC) CRC Pr.

Prakash. 11th National ACCP Pulmonary Board Review. American College of Chest Physicians Staff, ed. 580p. 1996. pap. text 65.00 (*0-916609-09-X*) Am Chest Phys.

Prakash, et al. Tenth National ACCP Pulmonary Board Review Course Syllabus, 2 vols. American College of Chest Physicians Staff, ed. (Illus.). 350p. 1994. pap. text 65.00 (*0-916609-04-9*) Am Chest Phys.

Prakash, A. J. The Return Generating Models in Global Finance. LC 98-22403. (Series on International Business & Economics). 250p. 1999. 65.00 (*0-08-043058-9*, Pergamon Pr) Elsevier.

Prakash, Anand & Rao, Jagadiswari. Botanical Pesticides in Agriculture. 480p. 1996. lib. bdg. 95.00 (*0-87371-825-9*, L825) Lewis Pubs.

Prakash, Arun J., et al. Financial, Commercial, & Mortgage Mathematics & Their Applications. LC 86-30579. 255p. 1987. 59.95 (*0-275-92119-0*, C2119, Praeger Pubs) Greenwood.

***Prakash, Aseem.** Greening the Firm: The Politics of Corporate Environmentalism. (Illus.). 196p. (C). 2000. 54.95 (*0-521-66249-4*); pap. 19.95 (*0-521-66487-X*) Cambridge U Pr.

Prakash, Aseem & Hart, Jeffrey A. Globalization & Governance. LC 99-19284. 1999. text. write for info. (*0-415-21604-4*) Routledge.

Prakash, Aseem, jt. auth. see Hart, Jeffrey A.

Prakash, B. A. Kerala's Economy: Performance, Problems, Prospects. 420p. 1994. 38.95 (*0-8039-9161-4*) Sage.

Prakash, G. K. & Schleyer, Paul V., eds. Stable Carbocation Chemistry. LC 95-33695. 587p. 1996. 98.95 (*0-471-59462-8*, Wiley-Interscience) Wiley.

Prakash, Gyan. Another Reason: Science & the Imagination of Modern India. LC 99-17185. 248p. 1999. 17.95 (*0-691-00453-6*, Pub. by Princeton U Pr) Cal Prin Full Svc.

***Prakash, Gyan.** Another Reason: Science & the Imagination of Modern India. LC 99-17185. 248p. 1999. 49.50 (*0-691-00452-8*, Pub. by Princeton U Pr) Cal Prin Full Svc.

Prakash, Gyan, ed. After Colonialism: Imperial Histories & Postcolonial Displacements. LC 94-21310. 336p. 1995. pap. text 18.95 (*0-691-03742-6*, Pub. by Princeton U Pr) Cal Prin Full Svc.

— The World of the Rural Labourer in Colonial India. (Oxford in India Readings: Themes in Indian History, Oxford India Paperbacks Ser.). (Illus.). 318p. 1994. reprint ed. pap. text 10.95 (*0-19-563440-3*) OUP.

Prakash, Gyan, jt. ed. see Haynes, Douglas.

***Prakash, I. & Ghosh, P. K.** Rodents in Indian Agriculture, 2 vols. 1998. pap. 550.00 (*81-7020-111-X*, Pub. by Print Hse) St Mut.

Prakash, Ishwar. Mammals of the Thar Desert. 114p. 1995. 100.00 (*81-7233-078-2*, Pub. by Scientific Pubs) St Mut.

Prakash, Ishwar, ed. Desert Ecology. (C). 1988. text 125.00 (*0-7855-3137-8*, Pub. by Scientific) St Mut.

— Rodent Pest Management, 2 vols. 496p. 1988. 271.00 (*0-8493-6726-3*, SB994, CRC Reprint) Franklin.

Prakash, Ishwar & Ghosh, P. K. Rodents in Indian Agriculture. 1992. pap. 180.00 (*81-7233-013-8*, Pub. by Scientific Pubs) St Mut.

Prakash, Ishwar & Ghosh, P. K. Rodents in Indian Agriculture-Bibliography. Cazri, Jodhpur, ed. 707p. 1991. pap. 60.00 (*81-7233-014-6*, Pub. by Scientific Pubs) St Mut.

Prakash, Ishwar, jt. auth. see Ghosh, P. K.

Prakash, Iswar, jt. ed. see Ghosh, P. K.

Prakash, J. & Pierik, T. Plant Biotechnology: Commercial Prospects & Problems. 300p. 1993. text 79.00 (*1-881570-31-2*) Science Pubs.

Prakash, J., jt. ed. see Pierik, R. L.

Prakash, K. Authentic Folk Designs from India. LC 95-23401. (Illus.). 32p. 1995. pap. 7.95 (*0-486-28733-5*) Dover.

— Paisleys & Other Textile Designs from India. LC 93-39105. (Illus.). 160p. 1994. pap. 8.95 (*0-486-27959-6*) Dover.

— 250 Stencil Designs from India. (Design Library). (Illus.). 48p. 1996. pap. 5.95 (*0-486-29026-3*) Dover.

Prakash, Lakshmi, jt. auth. see Majeed, Muhammed.

Prakash, Madhu S. & Esteva, Gustavo. Escaping Education: Living As Learning Within Grassroots Cultures. (Counterpoints Ser.: Vol. 36). 147p. (C). 1998. pap. text 22.95 (*0-8204-3327-6*) P Lang Pubng.

Prakash, Madhu Suri, jt. auth. see Esteva, Gustavo.

Prakash, N. Mathematical Perspectives of Theoretical Physics. 300p. 1997. text 61.00 (*981-02-2160-6*) World Scientific Pub.

Prakash, Nirupama. Scheduled Castes: Socio-Economic Changes. (C). 1988. 44.00 (*81-85076-58-8*, Pub. by Chugh Pubns) S Asia.

Prakash, O. Applied Physiology in Clinical Respiratory Care. 1982. text 249.00 (*90-247-2662-X*) Kluwer Academic.

Prakash, O., ed. Critical Care of the Child. (Developments in Critical Care, Medicine, & Anesthesiology Ser.). 1984. text 129.50 (*0-89838-661-6*) Kluwer Academic.

Prakash, Om. The Dutch East India Company & the Economy of Bengal, 1630-1720. LC 84-26484. (Illus.). 304p. 1985. reprint ed. pap. 94.30 (*0-7837-9426-6*, 206016700004) Bks Demand.

P

An Asterisk (*) at the beginning of an entry indicates that the title is appearing for the first time.

— European Commercial Enterprise in Pre-Colonial India. LC 97-25536. (New Cambridge History of India Ser.: Vol. II, Pt. 5). 396p. (C). 1998. text 54.95 (*0-521-25758-1*) Cambridge U Pr.

— Precious Metals & Commerce. (Collected Studies: No. CS 443). 312p. 1994. 101.95 (*0-86078-434-7*, Pub. by Variorum) Ashgate Pub Co.

Prakash, Om, ed. European Commercial Expansion in Early Modern Asia. LC 96-3236. (Expanding World Ser.: Vol. 10). 356p. 1997. 124.95 (*0-86078-508-4*, Pub. by Variorum) Ashgate Pub Co.

Prakash, Om & Srivastava, K. C. Mango Diseases & Their Management: A World Review. 180p. 1987. 59.00 (*1-55528-101-X*, Pub. by Today Tomorrow) Scholarly Pubns.

Prakash, Om, et al. Commerce & Culture in the Bay of Bengal, 1500-1800. LC 99-932393. 416 p. 1999. write for info. (*81-7304-265-9*) S Asia.

Prakash, Omar, jt. ed. see Rahn, Herman.

Prakash, Prem. The Yoga of Spiritual Devotion: A Modern Translation of the Narada Bhakti Sutras. LC 97-49646. 160p. 1998. pap. 12.95 (*0-89281-664-3*, Inner Trad) Inner Tradit.

Prakash, Ram. Advances in Forestry Research in India, Vols. 1-8. 265p. (C). 1988. text 295.00 (*0-7855-7070-5*, Pub. by Intl Bk Distr) St Mut.

Prakash, Ram, jt. auth. see Sood, P. O. P.

Prakash, Ravi, jt. auth. see Prasad, Janardan.

Prakash, Ravi, jt. auth. see Wasan, S. K.

Prakash, Ravi, jt. ed. see Devi, Ramashwari.

Prakash, S. Dynamics of Transition Metals & Alloys. LC 98-21169. (Horizons in World Physics Ser.). 552p. 1998. 115.00 (*1-56072-574-5*) Nova Sci Pubs.

Prakash, S. S. Bonded Labour & Social Justice. 1990. 17.00 (*81-7100-197-1*, Pub. by Deep & Deep Pubns) S Asia.

— Bonded Labour & Social Justice. (C). 1990. 75.00 (*0-89771-316-8*) St Mut.

Prakash, Shamsher. Fundamentals of Soil Mechanics. (Illus.). xx, 452p. 1995. write for info. (*0-9641737-1-9*) S Prakash Fnd.

— Introduction to Prevention & Yoga. (Illus.). (Orig.). (YA). (gr. 9-12). pap. text. write for info. (*0-9641737-0-0*) S Prakash Fnd.

Prakash, Shamsher, ed. Piles under Dynamic Loads: Proceedings of Sessions Sponsored by the Geotechnical Engineering Division of the American Society of Civil Engineers in Conjunction with the ASCE National Convention, New York, New York, September 13-17, 1992. LC 92-27783. (Geotechnical Special Publications: No. 34). 164p. 1992. 28.00 (*0-87262-905-8*) Am Soc Civil Eng.

— Seismic Analysis & Design for Soil-Pile-Structure Interactions: Proceedings of a Session Sponsored by the Committee on Geotechnical Earthquake Engineering of the Geo-Institute of the American Society of Civil Engineers in Conjunction with the ASCE National Convention in Minneapolis, Minnesota, October 5-8, 1997. LC 97-28739. (Geotechnical Special Publications: No. 70). (Illus.). 144p. 1997. pap. text 20.00 (*0-7844-0287-6*, 40287-6) Am Soc Civil Eng.

Prakash, Shamsher & Pathak, K. N. Advances in Statistical Physics of Solids & Liquids. LC 90-47760. 422p. 1991. text 89.95 (*0-470-21710-3*) Halsted Pr.

Prakash, Shamsher & Sharma, Hart D. Pile Foundations in Engineering Practice. LC 89-31977. 768p. 1990. 150.00 (*0-471-61653-2*) Wiley.

Prakash, Shamsher, et al. Displacement Based Aseismic Design Charts for Rigid Walls. (Illus.). vi, 120p. (C). 1995. write for info. (*0-9641737-2-7*) S Prakash Fnd.

Prakash, Shamsher, ed. see American Society of Civil Engineers Geotechnical E.

Prakash, Shamsher, ed. see American Society of Civil Engineers Staff.

Prakash, Shri, et al, eds. India & Asean: Economic Partnership in the 1990s & Future Prospects. LC 96-904827. (Illus.). 250p. 1996. 25.00 (*81-212-0522-0*, Pub. by Gyan Publishing Hse) Nataraj Bks.

Prakash, Shyam, jt. ed. see Chopra, V. L.

Prakash, Swami S. & Vidyalankar, Pandit S. Rigveda Samhita, 10 vols. 1986. 40.00 (*0-7855-7052-7*) St Mut.

Prakash, Udaya B. Mayo Internal Medicine Board Review, 1998-1999. LC 97-34817. 1000p. 1998. pap. text 89.95 (*0-7817-1477-X*) Lppncott W & W.

Prakash, Udaya B., ed. Bronchoscopy: A Text Atlas. LC 93-7652. 560p. 1993. text 199.00 (*0-7817-0095-7*) Lppncott W & W.

— Bronchoscopy: A Text Atlas. LC 93-7652. 266p. 1994. sl. 350.00 (*0-7817-0221-6*) Lppncott W & W.

— Mayo Internal Medicine Board Review, 1996-1997. 1000p. 1996. text 89.95 (*0-9627865-2-7*) Mayo Fndtn Med Ed & Res.

— Mayo Internal Medicine Board Review, 1994-1995. 1000p. 1994. text 89.95 (*0-9627865-1-9*) Mayo Fndtn Med Ed & Res.

Prakash, Udaya B.S., jt. auth. see Mayo Clinic Department of Internal Medicine Staff.

Prakash, V. Leafy Spices. 144p. 1990. lib. bdg. 149.00 (*0-8493-6723-9*, SB351) CRC Pr.

Prakashan, V., ed. Semantic Theories & Language Teaching. (C). 1986. 17.50 (*81-7023-080-2*, Pub. by Allied Pubs) S Asia.

Prakke, Hendricus J. Drenthe in Michigan. LC 84-115348. 96p. reprint ed. pap. 30.00 (*0-608-14510-6*, 202534100043) Bks Demand.

***Prakken, Bart.** Information, Organization & Information Systems Design - An Integrated Approach to Information Problems. 240p. 2000. 99.00 (*0-7923-7784-2*) Kluwer Academic.

Prakken, Henry. Logical Tools for Modelling Legal Argument: A Study of Defeasible Reasoning in Law. LC 97-31600. (Law & Philosophy Library). 328p. 1997. lib. bdg. 147.00 (*0-7923-4776-5*) Kluwer Academic.

Prakken, Henry, ed. see Sartor, Giovanni.

Prall, Richard D. The Crabb Family, 2 vols. LC 97-65404. (Illus.). 1637p. 1997. lib. bdg. 80.00 (*0-9625633-1-5*) R D Prall.

***Prall, Robert C.** The Rights of Children in Separation & Divorce: The Essential Handbook for Parents. LC 00-27022. 61p. 2000. 15.95 (*0-933849-78-8*) Landmark Edns.

Prall, Robert L. The Master Plot of the Bible. 154p. 1997. pap. 9.95 (*0-9657835-0-2*, 001) Emmaus Bks.

Prall, Stuart E. The Bloodless Revolution: England, Sixteen Eighty-Eight. LC 79-175415. 368p. 1985. reprint ed. pap. 17.95 (*0-299-10294-7*) U of Wis Pr.

— Church & State in Tudor & Stuart England. Eubank, Keith, ed. LC 92-35135. (European History Ser.). 190p. (C). 1993. pap. text 12.95 (*0-88295-904-2*) Harlan Davidson.

— Puritan Revolution: A Documentary History. 1990. 16.50 (*0-8446-2756-9*) Peter Smith.

— The Puritan Revolution & the English Civil War. (Orig.). Date not set. pap. write for info. (*0-89464-889-6*) Krieger.

Prall, Stuart E. & Willson, David H. A History of England, Vol. I. 4th ed. (Illus.). 520p. (C). 1991. pap. text 53.00 (*0-03-033424-1*, Pub. by Harcourt Coll Pubs) Harcourt.

— A History of England, Vol. II. 4th ed. (Illus.). 416p. (C). 1991. pap. text 53.00 (*0-03-033427-6*, Pub. by Harcourt Coll Pubs) Harcourt.

Pramaggiore, Maria & Hall, Donald E., eds. RePresenting Bisexualities: Subjects & Cultures of Fluid Desire. LC 96-8977. 320p. (C). 1996. text 55.00 (*0-8147-6633-1*); pap. text 19.50 (*0-8147-6634-X*) NYU Pr.

Pramanich, S. K. Sociology of G. S. Ghurye. (C). 1995. 34.00 (*81-7033-261-3*, Pub. by Rawat Pubns) S Asia.

Pramanik, M. A. Impacts of Disasters on Environment & Development: International Cooperation. 45p. (Orig.). (C). 1993. pap. text 30.00 (*0-7881-0097-1*) DIANE Pub.

Pramanik, S. K. Fishermen Community of Coastal Villages in West Bengal. (C). 1993. 17.50 (*81-7033-186-2*, Pub. by Rawat Pubns) S Asia.

Pramas, Chris, et al. The Book of Hunts. (Illus.). 96p. 1997. pap. 14.95 (*0-9657784-0-1*) Ronin Publishing.

Pramauro, E. & Pellizzetti, E. Surfactants in Analytical Chemistry: Applications of Organized Amphiphilic Media. LC 96-226675. (Comprehensive Analytical Chemistry Ser.: Vol. 31). 540p. 1996. text 262.50 (*0-444-89033-5*) Elsevier.

Pramik-Holdaway, Mary J., ed. see Nara, Andrew R., et al.

Pramik, Janice, ed. see Matherly, Sandra & Hodges, Shannon.

Pramik, Janice, ed. see Zimmerman, David.

Pramling, Ingrid. Learning to Learn. (Recent Research in Psychology Ser.). 144p. 1989. 52.95 (*0-387-97122-X*) Spr-Verlag.

Pramoj, Khukrit. Four Reigns, 1. 663p. 1999. pap. text 16.95 (*974-7100-66-5*) U of Wash Pr.

***Pramoj, M. R. Kukrit.** Many Lives. Borthwick, Meredith, tr. 240p. 2000. pap. 14.50 (*974-7100-67-3*, Pub. by Silk Worm Bks) U of Wash Pr.

Pramokchutima, S., jt. auth. see Boonyubol, M.

Prampero, P. E. Di, see Di Prampero, P. E., ed.

Pramuk, Christopher. Surviving the Search: Sexuality, Spirituality & Love. Coffey, Kathy, ed. LC 98-159719. (Crossings). 80p. (YA). 1998. pap. 3.95 (*1-889108-26-X*) Liv Good News.

Pramuk, Christopher, et al. Confirmation: Anointed & Sealed with the Spirit: A Journal for Older Candidates, Vol. 3. (Illus.). 80p. (YA). (gr. 7-12). 1997. 5.95 (*1-889108-31-6*) Liv Good News.

Pramuk, Ken, jt. auth. see Horn, Susanna K.

Pran, Dith, jt. auth. see Hall, Kari R.

***Pran, Peter.** Peter Pran: An Architect of Poetic Movement. 144p. 1999. 45.00 (*1-901092-08-9*) Andreas Papadakis.

— Peter Pran: An Architecture of Poetic Movement. 144p. 1999. pap. 37.50 (*1-901092-07-0*) Andreas Papadakis.

Pranaitis, I. B. The Talmud Unmasked. 1979. lib. bdg. 300.00 (*0-8490-3010-2*) Gordon Pr.

Pranaitis, I. B. The Talmud Unmasked. unabridged ed. 111p. 1939. reprint ed. pap. 12.00 (*0-945001-68-1*) GSG & Assocs.

Pranavananda, Yogi. Pure Yoga: A Translation from the Sanskrit into English of the Tantric Work, the Gherandasamhita, with a Guiding Commentary. (C). 1992. text 20.00 (*81-208-0922-X*, Pub. by Motilal Bnarsidass) S Asia.

Prance, Anne E. Bark: The Formation, Characteristics, & Uses of Bark Around the World. LC 92-19569. (Illus.). 176p. 1993. 49.95 (*0-88192-262-5*) Timber.

Prance, Claude A. The Characters in the Novels of Thomas Love Peacock (1785-1866) LC 92-5982. 312p. 1992. 99.95 (*0-7734-9510-X*) E Mellen.

— Essays of a Book Collector: Reminiscences on Some Old Books & Their Authors. LC 89-12734. (Locust Hill Literary Studies: No. 3). 209p. (C). 1989. lib. bdg. 30.00 (*0-933951-30-2*) Locust Hill Pr.

Prance, G. T. Flora of Ecuador No. 80: Chrysobalanaceae. (Opera Botanica Series B). 23p. 1979. pap. 15.00 (*91-546-0267-X*, Pub. by Coun Nordic Pubs) Balogh.

— Flora of Ecuador No. 121: Dichapetalaceae. (Opera Botanica Series B). 12p. 1980. pap. 15.00 (*1-878762-58-3*, Pub. by Coun Nordic Pubs) Balogh.

Prance, Ghillean. Rainforests of the World: Water, Fire, Earth & Air. LC 97-4087. (Illus.). 304p. 1998. 45.00 (*0-609-60364-7*) Crown Pub Group.

Prance, Ghillean T. Chrysobalanaceae. LC 70-180014. (Flora Neotropica Monographs: No. 9). (Illus.). 410p. (Orig.). 1972. pap. 27.95 (*0-89327-292-2*) NY Botanical.

— Chrysobalanaceae. (Flora Neotropica Monographs: No. 9S). (Illus.). 267p. (Orig.). 1989. pap. text 50.00 (*0-89327-338-4*) NY Botanical.

— Dichapetalaceae & Rhabdodendraceae. LC 73-180015. (Flora Neotropica Monographs: No. 10-11). (Illus.). 106p. (Orig.). 1972. pap. 13.95 (*0-89327-293-0*) NY Botanical.

— Tropical Rain Forests & the World Atmosphere. 105p. 1988. pap. 125.00 (*81-7089-057-8*, Pub. by Intl Bk Distr) St Mut.

Prance, Ghillean T., ed. Biological Diversification in the Tropics: Proceedings of the Fifth International Symposium of the Association for Tropical Biology, Held at Macuto Beach, Caracas, Venezuela, February 8-13, 1979. LC 81-367. 730p. reprint ed. pap. 200.00 (*0-7837-0419-4*, 204074200018) Bks Demand.

— Reproductive Biology & Evolution of Tropical Woody Angiosperms: A Symposium from the XIVth International Botanical Congress, Berlin, 1987. LC 89-13542. (Memoirs Ser.: No. 55). (Illus.). 208p. 1990. pap. 40.50 (*0-89327-348-1*) NY Botanical.

Prance, Ghillean T. & Balick, Michael J., eds. New Directions in the Study of Plants & Peoples: Research Contributions from the Institute of Economic Botany. LC 89-13336. (Advances in Economic Botany Ser.: Vol. 8). (Illus.). 292p. 1990. pap. text 41.25 (*0-89327-347-3*) NY Botanical.

Prance, Ghillean T. & Da Silva, Marlene F. Caryocaraceae. LC 72-88119. (Flora Neotropica Monographs: No. 12). (Illus.). 75p. (Orig.). 1973. pap. 9.95 (*0-89327-294-9*) NY Botanical.

Prance, Ghillean T. & Kallunki, J. A., eds. Ethnobotany in the Neotropics. LC 84-16517. (Advances in Economic Botany Ser.: Vol. 1). (Illus.). 156p. 1984. pap. 28.00 (*0-89327-253-1*) NY Botanical.

Prance, Ghillean T. & Mori, Scott A. Lecythidaceae Pt. 1: The Actinomorphic-Flowered New World Lecythidaceae Asteranthos, Gustavia, Allantoma & Carinana. LC 79-4659. (Flora Neotropica Monographs: No. 21). (Illus.). 270p. 1979. pap. 21.00 (*0-89327-193-4*) NY Botanical.

— Lecythidaceae Pt. 2: The Zygomorphic-Flowered New World Genera (Couroupita, Corythophora, Bertholletia, Couratari, Eschweilera & Lecythis) LC 85-647083. (Flora Neotropica Monographs: No. 21). (Illus.). 384p. 1990. pap. text 51.75 (*0-89327-345-7*) NY Botanical.

Prance, Ghillean T. & Ter Welle, B. J. Phanerogams: Chrysobalanaceae Including Wood & Timber. Goerts-van-Rijn, A. R. A., ed. (Flora of the Guianas Ser.: Series A, No. 85). (Illus.). 40p. 1986. pap. 80.00 (*3-87429-266-5*, 025647, Pub. by Koeltz Sci Bks) Lubrecht & Cramer.

Prance, Ghillean T., et al. Phanerogams Fascicle 12: Lecythidaceae with Wood & Timber. Goerts-Van-Rijn, A. R., ed. (Flora of the Guianas Ser.: Series A, No. 17). (Illus.). 45p. 1992. pap. 125.80 (*1-878762-33-8*, 047883, Pub. by Koeltz Sci Bks) Lubrecht & Cramer.

Prance, Ghillean T., jt. ed. see DeWitt, Calvin B.

Prance, Ghillean T., jt. ed. see Whitmore, T. C.

Prance, Ghillean T., ed. see Yungjohann, John C.

Prandi, Julie D. Dare to Be Happy! A Study of Goethe's Ethics. LC 92-37746. 238p. 1993. lib. bdg. 44.50 (*0-8191-8991-X*) U Pr of Amer.

— Spirited Women Heroes of the Goethezeit. LC 83-48708. (American University Studies: Germanic Languages & Literature: Ser. I, Vol. 22). 151p. 1983. pap. text 15.25 (*0-8204-0033-5*) P Lang Pubng.

Prandtl, Ludwig & Tietjens, O. G. Applied Hydro- & Aeromechanics. Den Hartog, Jacob P., ed. (Illus.). 311p. 1934. pap. text 10.95 (*0-486-60375-X*) Dover.

— Fundamentals of Hydro & Aeromechanics. Rosenhead, L., tr. (Illus.). 270p. 1957. pap. text 7.95 (*0-486-60374-1*) Dover.

Prandy, Ken, ed. see Stewart, Alexander, et al.

Prane, Joseph W. Introduction to Polymers & Resins. (Illus.). 35p. 1986. pap. 30.00 (*0-934010-28-5*) Fed Soc Coat Tech.

— Sealants & Caulks. (Illus.). 28p. 1989. pap. 30.00 (*0-934010-40-4*) Fed Soc Coat Tech.

Pranevicius, L. Coating Technology: Ion Beam Deposition. 458p. 1993. text 79.00 (*0-9637993-0-4*) Satas & Assocs.

Pranevieius, Liudvikas, jt. auth. see Galdikas, Arvaidas.

Prang, Margaret. A Heart at Leisure from Itself: Caroline MacDonald of Japan. (Illus.). 384p. 1997. pap. 29.95 (*0-7748-0608-7*) U of Wash Pr.

Prange, Bette & Kelly, Maureen. Wood & Technology. LC 93-28503. (C). 1994. pap. 13.95 (*0-521-43822-5*) Cambridge U Pr.

Prange, Christine. Managing Business Networks: An Inquiry into Managerial Knowledge in the Multimedia Industry. LC 99-34927. (Illus.). XVI, 332p. 1999. pap. text 56.95 (*0-8204-3512-0*) P Lang Pubng.

Prange, Gordon W., et al. At Dawn We Slept: The Untold Story of Pearl Harbor. enl. rev. ed. LC 91-50176. (Illus.). 944p. 1991. pap. 20.95 (*0-14-015734-4*, Penguin Bks) Viking Penguin.

— December 7, 1941: The Day the Japanese Attacked Pearl Harbor. 528p. 1989. mass mkt. 14.95 (*0-446-38997-8*, Pub. by Warner Bks) Little.

— God's Samurai: Lead Pilot at Pearl Harbor. (World War II Commemorative Ser.). (Illus.). 368p. 1990. 16.95 (*0-08-037440-9*, 3773M) Brasseys.

— Miracle at Midway. (Illus.). 384p. 1983. pap. 18.95 (*0-14-006814-7*, Penguin Bks) Viking Penguin.

Prange, Janet L. & Zufelt, David L. Reading Success for Each Child Every Day. (Illus.). 184p. 1980. pap. text 14.95 (*0-89641-037-4*) American Pr.

Prange, Kathy. Muffin Mania. 1984. spiral bd. 7.95 (*0-89709-187-6*) Liberty Pub.

Prange, Marnie. Dangerous Neighborhoods. LC 93-71913. 57p. (Orig.). 1994. pap. 10.00 (*1-880834-07-3*) Cleveland St Univ Poetry Ctr.

Prange, R. E. & Girvin, S. M., eds. The Quantum Hall Effect. (Graduate Texts in Contemporary Physics Ser.). (Illus.). 440p. 1986. 32.00 (*0-387-96286-7*) Spr-Verlag.

— The Quantum Hall Effect. 2nd ed. (Graduate Texts in Contemporary Physics Ser.). (Illus.). 488p. 1989. 59.95 (*0-387-97177-7*) Spr-Verlag.

Prange, Victor H. Luke. (People's Bible Commentary Ser.). 266p. (Orig.). 1992. pap. 10.99 (*0-570-04586-X*, 12-8004) Concordia.

— Luke. LC 88-61644. (People's Bible Ser.). 266p. (Orig.). 1989. pap. 11.99 (*0-8100-0297-3*, 15N0453) Northwest Pub.

Pranger, Gary K. Philip Schaff (1819-1893) Portrait of an Immigrant Theologian. LC 96-39549. (Swiss American Historical Society Ser.: Vol. 11). 305p. (C). 1997. text 45.95 (*0-8204-2847-7*) P Lang Pubng.

Pranger, M. B. Bernard of Clairvaux & the Shape of Monastic Thought: Broken Dreams. LC 94-3716. (Studies in Intellectual History: 56). xii, 375p. 1994. 113.50 (*90-04-10055-5*) Brill Academic Pubs.

Pranger, Robert J. Action, Symbolism, & Order: The Existential Dimensions of Politics in Modern Citizenship. LC 68-20548. 235p. reprint ed. pap. 72.90 (*0-608-06264-2*, 206659300008) Bks Demand.

— American Policy for Peace in the Middle East, 1969-1971: Problems of Principle, Maneuver & Time. LC 70-188039. (Foreign Affairs Study Ser.: No. 1). 74p. reprint ed. pap. 30.00 (*0-8357-5389-1*, 201713100006) Bks Demand.

— Detente & Defense: A Reader. LC 76-44607. (Foreign Affairs Study Ser.: No. 40). 456p. reprint ed. pap. 141.40 (*0-8357-4464-7*, 203730800008) Bks Demand.

Pranger, Robert J. & Labrie, Roger P., eds. Nuclear Strategy & National Security: Points of View. LC 77-15624. (AEI Studies: No. 175). 526p. reprint ed. pap. 163.10 (*0-8357-4517-1*, 203737500008) Bks Demand.

Pranger, Robert J. & Tahtinen, Dale R. Toward a Realistic Military Assistance Program. LC 74-29150. (Foreign Affairs Study Ser.: No. 15). 56p. reprint ed. pap. 30.00 (*0-608-30776-9*, 201715100006) Bks Demand.

Pranger, Robert J., jt. ed. see Chelkowski, Peter J.

Prangishvili, D. A. Biology Reviews Vol. 10, Pt. 2: Electrogenic Reactions in Photosynthetic Reactions Centres of Purple Bacteria-Eucaryotic Features of Thermoacidophilic, Vol. 10. (Soviet Scientific Reviews Ser.: Section D). 75p. 1991. text 74.00 (*3-7186-5114-9*, Harwood Acad Pubs) Gordon & Breach.

Pranis, Eve & Cohen, Joy. GrowLab: Activities for Growing Minds. (Illus.). 307p. (Orig.). (J). (gr. k-8). 1990. pap. text 24.95 (*0-915873-32-X*) Natl Gardening Assn.

Pranis, Eve & Hendry, Joreen. Exploring Classroom Hydroponics. (Growing Ideas Ser.). (Illus.). 24p. (Orig.). 1995. pap. 7.95 (*0-915873-36-2*) Natl Gardening Assn.

— School Greenhouse Guide. (Growing Ideas Ser.). (Illus.). 24p. (Orig.). 1995. pap. 7.95 (*0-915873-37-0*) Natl Gardening Assn.

Pranis, Eve, jt. auth. see Reinhardt, Karen.

***Pranitis, I. B.** The Talmud Unmasked. Sanctuary, E. N., tr. 111p. 1998. pap. 5.00 (*0-9600358-4-2*) CPA Bk Pub.

Pranjpe, Nalina. Social Welfare in India. 1990. text 18.95 (*81-7045-051-9*, Pub. by Assoc Pub Hse) Advent Bks Div.

Pransky, George S. Divorce Is Not the Answer: A Change of Heart Will Save Your Marriage. 168p. 1991. pap. 12.95 (*0-07-156015-7*) McGraw.

— Divorce Is Not the Answer: You Can Save Your Marriage. 192p. 1990. pap. 12.95 (*0-8306-3583-1*, 3583, TAB-Human Servs Inst) TAB Bks.

Pransky, Jack. Modello: A Story of Hope for the Inner-City & Beyond. Wood, Ronni, ed. 160p. 1998. pap. 32.00 (*0-9659057-1-3*) NEHRI Pubns.

— Parenting from the Heart. Gagliardi, Martha, ed. LC 97-92271. (Illus.). 160p. (Orig.). 1997. pap. 14.00 (*0-9659057-0-5*) NEHRI Pubns.

— Prevention: The Critical Need. (Illus.). 384p. (Orig.). 1991. pap. 24.95 (*0-943741-02-5*) NEHRI Pubns.

Prante, Nancy. Speaking & Performing: Confidence - Building Activities for the Speech Arts. 96p. (J). (gr. 5-12). 1997. pap. text, teacher ed. 16.95 (*1-881641-59-7*) Pencil Point.

Prantera, Amanda. Letters to Lorenzo. 258p. 1999. 24.95 (*1-58234-018-8*) Bloomsbury Pubg.

Prantera, Cosimo & Korelitz, Burton I., eds. Crohn's Disease. (Gastroenterology Ser.: Vol. 1). (Illus.). 624p. 1996. text 125.00 (*0-8247-9410-9*) Dekker.

Prantl, Carl. Geschichte der Logik im Abendlande, 4 vols. (GER.). xl, 1864p. 1997. reprint ed. write for info. (*3-487-10513-6*) G Olms Pubs.

Pranty, Bill. A Birder's Guide to Florida. 4th rev. ed. Baicich, Paul J., ed. LC 96-83566. (ABA-Lane Birdfinding Guide Ser.). (Illus.). 400p. 1996. pap. 21.95 (*1-878788-04-3*, 175) Amer Birding Assn.

***Prantzos, Nikos.** Our Cosmic Future: Humanity's Fate in the Universe. Lyle, Stephen, tr. (Illus.). 320p. 2000. 24.95 (*0-521-77098-X*) Cambridge U Pr.

Prantzos, Nikos, et al. Primordial Nuclei & Their Galactic Evolution: Proceedings of an Issi Workshop, 6-10 May 1997, Bern, Switzerland. LC 98-23730. (Space Sciences Series of Issi). 325p. 1998. write for info. (*0-7923-5114-2*) Kluwer Academic.

Prantzos, Nikos, jt. ed. see Durouchoux, Philippe.

Pranzatelli, Michael R., jt. auth. see Tate, Elizabeth D.

Pranzo, Donard. Academic Sportfolio: Excuse Notes Are No Excuse. rev. ed. Gallup, Beth, ed. (Easy Reader Ser.). (Illus.). (J). 1985. 249.00 (*0-924086-28-9*); write for info. (*0-924086-29-7*); write for info. (*0-924086-30-0*) Acad Sportfolio.

Pranzo, Donard, ed. see Matovcik, Gerard.

P

An Asterisk (*) at the beginning of an entry indicates that the title is appearing for the first time.

Pranzo, Donard, ed. see Norberg, Jon.

Pranzo, Peter. Stress Management for Law Enforcement: Over the Edge. 200p. Date not set. pap. 24.95 (*0-87526-532-4*) Gould.

Prarie, Arleen, jt. auth. see Olenick, Rhoda.

Prartho. Everyday Miracles: An A to Z Guide to the Simple Wonders of Life. LC 98-170564. 160p. 1998. pap. 13.00 (*1-57566-260-4*, Knsington) Kensgtn Pub Corp.

Prasad. Invertebrate Zoology. 14th ed. (C). 1989. pap. 14.00 (*0-85226-929-3*) S Asia.

Prasad, jt. auth. see Sachchidananda.

Prasad, A. Zinc in Human Nutrition. LC 79-15272. 96p. 1979. 61.00 (*0-8493-0145-9*, CRC Reprint) Franklin.

Prasad, A. & Vatshapayan, A. Biological & Application of Nitrogen-Fixing Organisms: Problems & Prospects. 1994. pap. 200.00 (*0-614-11805-0*, Pub. by Scientific Pubs) St Mut.

Prasad, A. B. & Valshampayan, A., eds. Biology & Application of Nitrogen-Fixing Organisms: Problems & Prospects. 1995. pap. 120.00 (*81-7233-084-7*, Pub. by Scientific Pubs) St Mut.

Prasad, A. K., et al, eds. Contributions in Phycology: Volume in Honour of Professor T. V. Desikachary. LC 96-211738. (Nova Hedwigia, Beihefte/Supplementary Issues Ser.: Beih 112). (Illus.). xvi, 552p. 1996. pap., suppl. ed. 165.00 (*3-443-51034-5*, Pub. by Gebruder Borntraeger) Balogh.

Prasad, A. S. Biochemistry of Zinc. (Biochemistry of the Elements Ser.: Vol. 11). (Illus.). 328p. (C). 1994. text 89.50 (*0-306-44399-6*, Kluwer Plenum) Kluwer Academic.

Prasad, Ananda S. Trace Elements & Iron in Human Metabolism. LC 78-13446. (Topics in Hematology Ser.). 408p. reprint ed. pap. 126.50 (*0-608-12364-1*, 205207700033) Bks Demand.

Prasad, Anirudh. Centre & State Powers under Indian Federalism. (C). 1989. 175.00 (*0-7855-4803-3*) St Mut.

— Reservation Policy & Practice in India. (C). 1991. 67.50 (*81-7100-297-8*, Pub. by Deep & Deep Pubns) S Asia.

Prasad, Anubhuti K. Coal Industry of India. 515p. 1986. 58.50 (*81-7024-055-7*, Pub. by Ashish Pub Hse) S Asia.

Prasad, Anuradha. Entrepreneurship Development under Trysem. (C). 1988. 21.00 (*81-7022-167-6*, Pub. by Mittal Pubs Dist) S Asia.

Prasad, Ashoka J., ed. Biological Basis & Therapy of Neuroses. 208p. 1988. 119.00 (*0-8493-4899-4*, RC530, CRC Reprint) Franklin.

Prasad, B., ed. Robotics & Factories of the Future, 3 vols. 1180p. 1989. 256.95 (*0-387-51135-0*) Spr-Verlag.

— Robotics & Factories of the Future, Vol. 1. (Illus.). 468p. 1989. 120.95 (*0-387-51132-6*) Spr-Verlag.

— Robotics & Factories of the Future, Vol. 2. (Illus.). 312p. 1989. 79.95 (*0-387-51133-4*) Spr-Verlag.

— Robotics & Factories of the Future, Vol. 3. (Illus.). 400p. 1989. 107.95 (*0-387-51134-2*) Spr-Verlag.

Prasad, B., jt. ed. see Bocks, P.

Prasad, B., jt. ed. see Zaremba, M. B.

Prasad, B. K. Staining Technique in Botany. 107p. 1986. 45.00 (*81-7089-081-0*, Pub. by Intl Bk Distr) St Mut.

Prasad, B. N., ed. Role of Biotechnology in Agriculture. 252p. (C). 1992. text 65.00 (*1-881570-12-6*) Science Pubs.

Prasad, B. N., ed. see Science Publishers Inc. Staff.

Prasad, Bandreddi E., jt. ed. see Gupta, Amar.

Prasad, Bimal. Gandhi, Nehru & JP: Studies in Leadership. 1985. 25.00 (*0-8364-1366-0*, Pub. by Chanakya) S Asia.

Prasad, Bimal, ed. Regional Cooperation in South Asia. viii, 221p. 1989. text 27.95 (*0-7069-4264-7*, Pub. by Vikas) S Asia.

— A Revolutionary's Quest. 406p. 1980. 29.95 (*0-318-37198-7*) Asia Bk Corp.

Prasad, Bimal, ed. Swami Vivekananda: An Anthology. 1996. pap. 27.50 (*0-7069-9824-3*, Pub. by Vikas) S Asia.

Prasad, Bimal, ed. Swami Vivekananda: Selected Speeches & Writings. (Orig.). (C). 1994. 12.00 (*0-7069-7552-9*, Pub. by Vikas) S Asia.

Prasad, Biren. Concurrent Engineering Fundamentals: Integrated Product Development, Vol. 2. 528p. (C). 1996. 70.00 (*0-13-396946-0*) P-H.

Prasad, Biren, ed. Advances in Concurrent Engineering - CE96. LC 96-60966. 440p. 1996. pap. text 49.95 (*1-56676-485-8*) Technomic.

— Advances in Concurrent Engineering--CE 97. LC 97-61502. 560p. 1997. 110.95 (*1-56676-604-4*) Technomic.

Prasad, C. H., et al. Development of Women & Children in Rural Areas. 120p. 1996. pap. 100.00 (*81-7141-299-8*, Pub. by Print Hse) St Mut.

Prasad, C. V., jt. auth. see Khan, M. E.

Prasad, D. M. Dalit Youth: A Sociological Study. LC 97-905912. (Illus.). x, 192p. (C). 1997. 26.00 (*81-7024-898-1*, Pub. by APH Pubng) Nataraj Bks.

Prasad, D. N. Food for Peace. 172p. 1980. 9.95 (*0-210-40627-5*) Asia Bk Corp.

Prasad, Devki N. Food for Peace: U. S. Food Assistance to India. xviii, 172p. (C). 1982. pap. text 8.95 (*0-86590-011-6*) Apt Bks.

***Prasad, H. A. & Ashok, Chandra.** WTO Negotiations - Some Important Issues & Strategies for India: Selected Policy Papers. LC 99-932524. 1999. 22.00 (*81-7169-546-9*, Pub. by Commonwealth) S Asia.

Prasad, H. S. The Uttaratantra of Maitreya. (Bibliotheca Indo-Buddhica Ser.: No. 79). 436p. (C). 1991. text 30.00 (*81-7030-263-3*) S Asia.

Prasad, Hari M. The Dramatic Art of Eugene O'Neill. 113p. 1987. text 18.95 (*81-7045-003-9*, Pub. by Assoc Pub Hse) Advent Bks Div.

Prasad, Hari S., ed. Time in Indian Philosophy: A Collection of Essays. (C). 1992. 58.00 (*81-7030-267-6*) S Asia.

Prasad, Ishwari. The Life & Times of Maharaja Juddha Shumsher Jung Bahadur Rana of Nepal. viii, 358p. (C). 1996. 35.00 (*81-7024-756-X*, Pub. by Ashish Pub Hse) Nataraj Bks.

Prasad, Janardan & Prakash, Ravi. Education of Handicapped Children: Problems & Solutions. 1996. pap. 260.00 (*81-7391-153-3*, Pub. by Print Hse) St Mut.

Prasad, Joshi & Prasad, Kharbanda, eds. Supreme Court Labour Judgments, 1950-1983, 13 vols. (C). 1990. 100.00 (*0-89771-303-6*) St Mut.

Prasad, Jwala, ed. History of Indian Epistemology. 1988. 32.00 (*81-215-0072-9*, Pub. by M Manoharial) Coronet Bks.

Prasad, Jyoti N. Impact of the Foreign Corrupt Practices Act of 1977 on U. S. Export. LC 92-39946. (Foreign Economic Policy of the United States Ser.). 224p. 1993. text 10.00 (*0-8153-1107-9*) Garland.

Prasad, K. Krishna. Further Developments in Turbulence Management. LC 93-19297. (Fluid Mechanics & Its Applications Ser.: Vol. 19). 1993. text 155.50 (*0-7923-2291-6*) Kluwer Academic.

***Prasad, K. N.** Dimensions of Development: Analysis of an Underdeveloped State. LC 99-931758. 1998. write for info. (*81-7022-741-0*, Pub. by Concept) S Asia.

Prasad, K. N. India's Economic Problems: Regional Aspects. 357p. 1995. pap. 225.00 (*81-85880-74-3*, Pub. by Print Hse) St Mut.

— Poverty, Inequality & Unemployment in India: (Incorporating Their Regional - Inter-State Dimensions) 1993. 44.00 (*81-7022-459-4*, Pub. by Concept) S Asia.

Prasad, K. N., ed. Cancer & Nutrition. 360p. Date not set. 86.00 (*90-5199-377-3*) IOS Press.

— Vitamins, Nutrition & Cancer. (Illus.). xii, 320p. 1984. 172.25 (*3-8055-3846-4*) S Karger.

Prasad, K. N. & Meyskens, Frank L., eds. Modulation & Mediation of Cancer by Vitamins. (Illus.). x, 350p. 1983. 143.50 (*3-8055-3526-0*) S Karger.

***Prasad, Kamta, ed.** NGO's & Socio-Economic Development Opportunities. 2000. 38.00 (*81-7629-258-3*, Pub. by Deep & Deep Pubns) S Asia.

Prasad, Kamta & Sinha, R. K., eds. Perspectives on Economic Development & Thought. 1986. 24.00 (*0-8364-1659-7*, Pub. by Somaiya) S Asia.

Prasad, Kedar N. Handbook of Radiobiology. 304p. 1984. 173.00 (*0-8493-2938-8*, QP82, CRC Reprint) Franklin.

— Handbook of Radiobiology. 2nd ed. LC 94-30433. (Illus.). 352p. 1995. boxed set 149.95 (*0-8493-2501-3*) CRC Pr.

— Vitamins in Cancer Prevention & Treatment: A Practical Guide. rev. ed. LC 93-20960. 128p. 1993. pap. 9.95 (*0-89281-483-7*, Heal Arts VT) Inner Tradit.

Prasad, Kedar N., et al, eds. Nutrients in Cancer Prevention & Treatment. LC 95-15205. (Experimental Biology & Medicine Ser.: Vol. 27). (Illus.). 405p. 1995. 140.00 (*0-89603-318-X*) Humana.

Prasad, Kedar N. & Meyskens, Frank L., Jr., eds. Nutrients & Cancer Prevention. LC 90-4677. (Experimental Biology & Medicine Ser.: Vol. 23). (Illus.). 353p. 1990. 125.00 (*0-89603-171-3*) Humana.

Prasad, Kedar N. & Vernadakis, Antonia, eds. Mechanisms of Actions of Neurotoxic Substances. LC 79-5319. (Illus.). 235p. 1982. reprint ed. pap. 72.90 (*0-608-00589-4*, 206117600007) Bks Demand.

Prasad, Kedar N., jt. ed. see Meyskens, Frank L., Jr.

Prasad, Kharbanda, jt. ed. see Prasad, Joshi.

Prasad, Kunwar. Taxation in Ancient India. 1987. 21.00 (*0-317-89531-1*, Pub. by Mittal Pubs Dist) S Asia.

Prasad, L. & Iyengar, S. S. Wavelet Analysis with Applications to Image Processing. LC 97-11042. 304p. 1997. boxed set 74.95 (*0-8493-3169-2*) CRC Pr.

Prasad, L. C. Religion, Mortality & Politics According to Mahatma Gandhi. (C). 1991. 27.50 (*81-7054-128-X*, Pub. by Classics India Pubns) S Asia.

Prasad, Lala S. How to Live a Fruitful Hundred Years. (C). 1997. pap. 5.00 (*81-208-1406-1*, Pub. by Motilal Bnarsidass) S Asia.

Prasad, M. Madhava. Ideology of the Hindi Film: A Historical Construction. LC 98-902940. (Illus.). 268p. 1998. text 24.95 (*0-19-564218-X*) OUP.

Prasad, M. N. V. & Hagemeyer, Jurgen. Heavy Metal Stress in Plants: From Molecules to Ecosystems. LC 99-20144. 400p. 1999. 229.00 (*3-540-65469-0*) Spr-Verlag.

Prasad, M. S. Study in Law of Evidence. 292p. 1982. 45.00 (*0-7855-1350-7*) St Mut.

Prasad, Madhusudan. Contemporary Indian-English Stories: Prescribed As Non-Detailed Textbook for the Common 1st Year Degree Syllabus of A. P. Universities. 1998. pap. write for info. (*81-207-1455-5*) Sterling Pubs.

Prasad, Madhusudan, ed. Indian-English Novelists: An Anthology of Critical Essays. 240p. 1982. 24.95 (*0-940500-48-5*, Pub. by Sterling) Asia Bk Corp.

Prasad, Maheshwari. Social Aspects of Mining Towns of the Tribal Regions, Pt. I. 196p. 1986. 21.00 (*1-55528-082-X*, Pub. by Today Tomorrow) Scholarly Pubns.

— Social Aspects of Mining Towns of the Tribal Regions, Pt. II. (Illus.). 60p. 1986. 12.00 (*1-55528-083-8*, Pub. by Today Tomorrow) Scholarly Pubns.

Prasad, Marehalli G., jt. ed. see Quinlan, Daniel A.

Prasad, Mular N., ed. Plant Ecophysiology. LC 96-19477. 552p. 1996. 125.00 (*0-471-13157-1*) Wiley.

Prasad, Muni Narayana. Kena Upanisad: With the Original Text in Sanskrit & Roman Transliteration, Translation with an Extensive Commentary. (SAN.). vii, 126p. (C). 1995. pap. 7.95 (*81-246-0034-1*, Pub. by D K Printwrld) Nataraj Bks.

***Prasad, Muni Narayana.** Mundaka Upanisad: With the Original Text in Sanskrit & Roman Transliteration, Translation with an Exhaustive Commentary. LC 98-903086. vii, 142p. 1998. pap. 12.00 (*81-246-0105-4*, Pub. by D K Printwrld) Nataraj Bks.

Prasad, Muni Narayana. The Taittiriya Upanisad: With the Original Text in Sanskrit & Roman Transliteration, Translation with an Exhaustive Commentary. LC 94-902188. 211p. (C). 1994. 13.00 (*81-246-0014-7*, Pub. by D K Printwrld) Nataraj Bks.

***Prasad, Muni Narayana.** The Taittiriya Upanisad: With the Original Text in Sanskrit & Roman Transliteration, Translation with an Exhaustive Commentary. 211p. 1998. pap. 8.95 (*81-246-0023-6*, Pub. by D K Printwrld) Nataraj Bks.

Prasad, N. N. V. Thermomechanical Crack Growth Using Boundary Elements. LC 97-80287. (Topics in Engineering Ser.: Vol. 34). 216p. 1998. 115.00 (*1-85312-541-5*) Computational Mech MA.

Prasad, Nadipuram R., jt. auth. see Nguyen, Hung T.

Prasad, Nageshwar. Ideology & Organization in Indian Politics. 304p. 1980. 29.95 (*0-940500-77-9*, Pub. by Allied Pubs) Asia Bk Corp.

Prasad, Nageshwar, ed. Gandhi & the Contemporary World. 194p. 1992. 25.00 (*81-7027-187-8*, Pub. by Radiant Pubs) S Asia.

Prasad, Nandini, ed. Vision Unveiled: Women on Television. (C). 1994. 28.00 (*81-241-0243-0*, Pub. by Har-Anand Pubns) S Asia.

Prasad, Naresh, ed. Radiotherapy & Cancer Immunology. 216p. 1981. 98.95 (*0-8493-5901-5*, RC268) CRC Pr.

***Prasad, Niru.** How to Keep Your Child Safe & Healthy. (Illus.). 80p. 1998. pap. 14.95 (*0-9672833-0-2*) Think Club.

Prasad Oli, Krishna, see Oli, Krishna Prasad.

Prasad, Om P. Decay & Revival of Urban Centres in Medieval South India C.A.D. 600-1200. 1989. 14.00 (*81-7169-006-8*, Pub. by Commonwealth) S Asia.

Prasad, P. Propagation of a Curved Shock & Nonlinear Ray Theory. 1993. lib. bdg. 54.95 (*0-582-07253-0*) Longman.

Prasad, P. N. Frontiers of Polymers & Advanced Materials. (Illus.). 734p. 1994. 159.50 (*0-306-44716-9*, Kluwer Plenum) Kluwer Academic.

Prasad, P. N., et al, eds. Science & Technology of Polymers & Advanced Materials: Emerging Technologies & Business Opportunities. LC 98-21006. (Illus.). 883p. (C). 1999. text 175.00 (*0-306-45820-9*, Kluwer Plenum) Kluwer Academic.

Prasad, P. N., et al. Polymers & Other Advanced Materials: Emerging Technologies & Business Opportunities. (Illus.). 740p. (C). 1996. text 191.00 (*0-306-45210-3*, Kluwer Plenum) Kluwer Academic.

Prasad, P. S., jt. auth. see Munshi, M. Z.

Prasad, Pandit A. The Gems of Vedic Wisdom: Selected Texts from the Vedas with English Translation. LC 98-907217. 224p. 1997. pap. 100.00 (*81-7533-059-7*, Pub. by Print Hse) St Mut.

Prasad, Paras N. & Nigam, J. K., eds. Frontiers of Polymer Research. (Illus.). 638p. (C). 1992. text 186.00 (*0-306-44096-2*, Kluwer Plenum) Kluwer Academic.

Prasad, Paras N. & Ulrich, D. R., eds. Nonlinear Optical & Electroactive Polymers. 448p. 1987. 125.00 (*0-306-42768-0*, Plenum Trade) Perseus Pubng.

Prasad, Paras N. & Williams, David J. Introduction to Nonlinear Optical Effects in Molecules & Polymers. LC 90-37692. 320p. 1991. 110.00 (*0-471-51562-0*) Wiley.

Prasad, Pradhan H. Lopsided Growth: Political Economy of Indian Development. (Illus.). 136p. 1990. 14.95 (*0-19-562406-8*) OUP.

Prasad, Prem. Padmavati. (Illus.). 28p. (Orig.). (C). 1994. pap. text 5.00 (*1-878173-37-5*) Birnham Wood.

Prasad, Pushkala, et al, eds. Managing the Organizational Melting Pot: Dilemmas of Workplace Diversity. LC 96-35610. 383p. 1997. 62.00 (*0-8039-7410-8*) Sage.

Prasad, Pushpa. Sanskrit Inscriptions of Delhi Sultanate, 1191-1526. (Illus.). 292p. 1991. 32.00 (*0-19-562123-9*) OUP.

Prasad, R., ed. Candida Albicans: Cellular & Molecular Biology. (Illus.). 296p. 1991. 182.95 (*0-387-51926-2*) Spr-Verlag.

— Manual on Membrand Lipids. (Springer Lab Manuals Ser.). 224p. 1996. ring bd. 79.00 (*3-540-59448-5*) Spr-Verlag.

Prasad, R. & Ghannoum, Mahoud A., eds. Lipids of Pathogenic Fungi. LC 96-24683. 304p. 1996. boxed set 189.95 (*0-8493-4794-7*) CRC Pr.

Prasad, R., et al. Wireless Networks: Catching the Mobile Future, 4 vols., Set. LC 94-78817. (Proceedings of Two Combined Conferences Held in The Hague, The Netherlands, Sep 18-23, 1994: The Fifth Ser.). 1453p. (gr. 12). 1994. pap. 200.00 (*90-5199-193-2*) IOS Press.

Prasad, R. C. Ambedkarism. (C). 1993. text 18.50 (*81-208-1070-8*, Pub. by Motilal Bnarsidass) S Asia.

— Preface to Ambedkarism. (C). 1993. 21.00 (*81-208-1088-0*, Pub. by Motilal Bnarsidass) S Asia.

— Sraddha: The Hindu Book of the Dead. (C). 1995. pap. 8.00 (*81-208-1192-5*, Pub. by Motilal Bnarsidass) S Asia.

Prasad, R. C., ed. Maha Calisa Samgraha: An Anthology of Calisas & Aratis Forming Part of the Hindu Religious Poetry & Public Worship Text in Nagari & Roman Scripts with Hindi & English Translation. Sharma, Atma R., tr. (C). 1994. 14.00 (*81-208-1199-2*, Pub. by Motilal Bnarsidass) S Asia.

— Ramayana of Tulasidasa. Growse, F. S., tr. lx, 719p. (C). 1995. reprint ed. 28.00 (*81-208-0205-5*, Pub. by Motilal Bnarsidass) S Asia.

— Tulidasa's Shriramacharitamanasa: Compact Edition. (C). 1990. 26.00 (*81-208-0680-8*, Pub. by Motilal Bnarsidass) S Asia.

Prasad, R. C., tr. Vivaha: The Hindu Marriage Samskaras. (C). 1993. pap. 11.50 (*81-208-1132-1*, Pub. by Motilal Bnarsidass) S Asia.

Prasad, R. C., ed. see Udupa, K. N.

Prasad, R. C., ed. & tr. see Tulsidasa.

Prasad, R. N. Autonomy Movements in Mizoram. (C). 1994. text 20.00 (*0-614-04136-8*, Pub. by Vikas) S Asia.

Prasad, R. R. Development of Scheduled Caste Leather Artisans, India. (C). 1991. text 35.00 (*81-7141-141-X*) S Asia.

— Pastoral Nomadism in Arid Zones of India: Socio-Demographic & Ecological Aspects. (C). 1994. text 24.00 (*81-7141-237-8*, Pub. by Discovery Pub Hse) S Asia.

— Tribal Situation in Forest Villages: Changing Subsistence Strategies & Adaptation. (C). 1993. 27.50 (*81-7141-234-3*, Pub. by Discovery Pub Hse) S Asia.

Prasad, R. R. & Chandra, K. Suman. Bonded Labourers: A Study of Rehabilitation & Organisational Dynamics. (C). 1994. text 22.00 (*81-241-0211-2*, Pub. by Har-Anand Pubns) S Asia.

Prasad, R. R. & Jahagirdar, M. P. Social Factors in Social Forestry. (C). 1992. 21.50 (*81-85613-64-8*, Pub. by Chugh Pubns) S Asia.

Prasad, Rai G. Chronology of the North Indian Kings. 1990. 46.00 (*81-7186-003-6*, Pub. by Agam) S Asia.

Prasad, Raj. A Digest of Selected California Laws Related to Certified Personnel, 1997. 86p. 1997. per. 27.00 (*0-943397-25-1*, 115) Assn Calif Sch Admin.

— A Digest of Selected California Laws Related to Classified Personnel, Feb. 1998. rev. ed. 1998. per. 27.00 (*0-943397-41-3*) Assn Calif Sch Admin.

Prasad, Rajendra. At the Feet of Mahatma Gandhi. LC 79-156204. 1971. reprint ed. lib. bdg. 75.00 (*0-8371-6154-1*, PRMG, Greenwood Pr) Greenwood.

— Karma, Causation & Retributive Morality: Conceptual Essays in Ethics & Metaethics. 460p. 1990. reprint ed. 33.00 (*81-215-0481-3*, Pub. by M Manoharial) Coronet Bks.

— Politico-Geographical Analysis of the Arthasastra. (C). 1989. 30.00 (*81-210-0224-9*, Pub. by Inter-India Pubns) S Asia.

Prasad, Rajendra & Power, J. F. Soil Fertility Management for Sustainable Agriculture. LC 96-44795. 384p. 1997. lib. bdg. 69.95 (*1-56670-254-2*) Lewis Pubs.

Prasad, Rajendra & Utkal University Staff. Varnadharma, Nirskeama Karma & Practical Morality: A Critical Essay on Applied Ethics. LC 98-917245. (Utkal Studies in Philosophy). 291p. 1999. write for info. (*81-246-0125-9*) S Asia.

Prasad, Ram. Social Forestry in India: Experience over a Decade. LC 95-910662. 235p. 1995. pap. 79.00 (*81-7089-231-7*, Pub. by Intl Bks & Periodicals) St Mut.

Prasad, Ram C. Rajneesh: The Mystic of Feeling. 239p. 1978. 16.95 (*0-318-36385-2*) Asia Bk Corp.

— Rajneesh: The Mystic of Feeling. 2nd rev. ed. 1978. 10.95 (*0-89684-023-9*, Pub. by Motilal Bnarsidass) S Asia.

— The Upanayana: The Hindu Ceremonies of the Sacred Thread LC 97-913644. xi, 191p. 1997. write for info. (*81-208-1240-9*) Motilal Bnarsidass.

Prasad, Rama. Generation Gap. (C). 1992. 25.00 (*81-7099-351-2*, Pub. by Mittal Pubs Dist) S Asia.

— Nature's Finer Forces. 251p. 1996. reprint ed. spiral bd. 23.00 (*0-7873-1031-X*) Hlth Research.

— Nature's Finer Forces: The Science of Breath & the Philosophy of the Tattvas (1894) 261p. 1996. reprint ed. pap. 21.95 (*1-56459-803-9*) Kessinger Pub.

Prasad, Ramananda. Bhagavad-/Gita - The Song of God: With Introduction, Original Sanskrit Text & Roman Transliteration, Alucid English Rendition, Guide for the Beginners & Daily Reading, Commentaries with Verses from Other Religious Scriptures, Glossary, & Index. 1996. 14.00 (*81-208-1390-1*, Pub. by Motilal Bnarsidass) S Asia.

Prasad, Ramananda, tr. from SAN. The Bhagavad-Gita (The Song of God) 2nd rev. ed. LC 94-12045. (SAN.). 351p. 1996. text 16.95 (*0-9621099-3-2*); pap. text 13.95 (*0-614-29948-9*) Amer Gita Soc.

Prasad, Ramjee. CDMA for Wireless Personal Communications. LC 95-53774. 386p. 1996. 93.00 (*0-89006-571-3*) Artech Hse.

***Prasad, Ramjee.** Third Generation Mobile Communications Systems. LC 99-89511. 2000. 93.00 (*1-58053-082-6*) Artech Hse.

Prasad, Ramjee. Universal Wireless Personal Communications. LC 98-20073. 600p. 1998. 99.00 (*0-89006-958-1*) Artech Hse.

Prasad, Ramjee, ed. see Ojanpera, Tero.

Prasad, Ray P. Surface Mount Technology: Principles & Practice. 2nd ed. (Electrical Engineering Ser.). 1995. 69.95 (*0-442-01862-2*, VNR) Wiley.

Prasad, S. A., jt. auth. see Hussey, J.

Prasad, S. Benjamin, ed. Management in International Perspective. LC 67-10930. (Orig.). 1967. pap. text 9.95 (*0-89197-289-7*) Irvington.

Prasad, S. Benjamin, et al, eds. Advances in International Comparative Management, Vol. 1. 219p. 1982. 73.25 (*0-89232-251-9*) Jai Pr.

— Advances in International Comparative Management, Vol. 2. 267p. 1986. 73.25 (*0-89232-501-1*) Jai Pr.

— Advances in International Comparative Management, Vol. 3. 219p. 1988. 73.25 (*0-89232-770-7*) Jai Pr.

— Advances in International Comparative Management, Vol. 4. 281p. 1989. 73.25 (*0-89232-997-1*) Jai Pr.

— Advances in International Comparative Management, Vol. 5. 272p. 1990. 73.25 (*1-55938-232-5*) Jai Pr.

— Advances in International Comparative Management, Vol. 6. 250p. 1991. 73.25 (*1-55938-394-1*) Jai Pr.

— Advances in International Comparative Management, Vol. 7. 267p. 1992. 73.25 (*1-55938-518-9*) Jai Pr.

— Advances in International Comparative Management, Vol. 8. 240p. 1993. 73.25 (*1-55938-618-5*) Jai Pr.

— Advances in International Comparative Management, Vol. 9. 275p. 1994. 73.25 (*1-55938-723-8*) Jai Pr.

— Advances in International Comparative Management, Vol. 10. 252p. 1995. 73.25 (*1-55938-916-8*) Jai Pr.

P

— Advances in International Comparative Management: East European Economic Trends & East-West Trade, Suppl. 2. 152p. 1987. suppl. ed. 73.25 (*0-89232-822-3*) Jai Pr.

Prasad, S. N. Survey of Work Done in the Military History of India. 1976. 6.50 (*0-88386-939-X*) S Asia.

Prasad, Saffa A. Studies in Sinological Sex: Religion, Racism, & Nationalism. 71p. 1975. pap. text 21.95 (*0-9597151-0-X*) Transaction Pubs.

Prasad Sahu, Bhairabi, ed. Readings in Early Indian History: Land System & Rural Society in Early India. LC 97-913660. (C). 1997. text 36.00 (*81-7304-192-X*, Pub. by Manohar) S Asia.

Prasad, Saroj, jt. auth. see Chanchreek, K. L.

Prasad, Saroj, jt. ed. see Chanchreek, K. L.

Prasad, Sharad, et al, eds. Microelectronic Manufacturing Yield, Reliability & Failure Analysis IV. LC 99-194427. (Proceedings of SPIE Ser.: Vol. 3510). 248p. 1998. 69.00 (*0-8194-2969-4*) SPIE.

Prasad, Sharat, jt. auth. see Roy, Kaushik.

Prasad, Sushama S. Tribal Woman Labourers: Aspects of Economic & Physical Exploitation. 1988. 36.00 (*81-212-0193-4*, Pub. by Gian Publng Hse) S Asia.

***Prasad, Swami.** Aitareya Upanisad: With the Original Text in Sanskrit & Roman Transliteration. 2000. 9.50 (*81-246-0142-9*, Pub. by D K Printwrld) S Asia.

Prasad, Swami M. Karma & Reincarnation. LC 93-910706. (C). 1994. 7.00 (*81-246-0022-8*, Pub. by DK Pubs Ind) S Asia.

***Prasad, Swami Muni Narayana.** Katha Upanisad. LC 98-908673. 1998. pap. 12.00 (*81-246-0110-0*, Pub. by D K Printwrld) S Asia.

Prasad, V. & Arimilli, R. V., eds. Advanced Computations in Materials Processing. (HTD Ser.: Vol. 241). 92p. 1993. 35.00 (*0-7918-1154-9*, G00798) ASME.

Prasad, V. J. English Is a Foreign Language. (Language & Literature Ser.: Vol. 18). (Illus.). 1995. pap. 9.95 (*0-900891-34-3*) Oleander Pr.

Prasad, V. P., et al. Illustrated Flora of Keoladeo National Park, Bharatpur, Rajasthan: A General Guide to the Wetland Flora of the Gangetic Plains. LC 97-903280. (Illus.). 538p. (C). 1998. text 35.00 (*0-19-564227-9*) OUP.

Prasad, V. R., ed. T. S. Eliot & Eugene O'Neill: The Dream & the Nightmare. (C). 1991. 20.00 (*81-202-0313-5*, Pub. by Ajanta) S Asia.

Prasad, V. V. Five Indian Novelists: The Self, the Family & Society. 172p. 1991. text 27.50 (*81-85218-27-7*, Pub. by Prestige) Advent Bks Div.

Prasad, Vasantha. Indian Vegetarian Cooking for the American Kitchen. LC 95-21501. (Illus.). 304p. 1998. pap. 18.00 (*0-679-76438-0*) Random.

Prasad, Y. V. & Sasidhara, S., eds. Hot Working Guide: A Compendium of Processing Maps. LC 97-71612. 545p. 1997. 225.00 (*0-87170-598-2*, 6591G) ASM.

Prasada, Ajit, jt. ed. see Amristaswarupananda, Swami.

Prasada, Birendra, jt. ed. see Netravali, Arun N.

***Prasada, Rama.** Patanjali's Yoga Sutras: With the Commentary of Vyasa & the Gloss of Vachaspati Misra. 2nd ed. 2000. reprint ed. pap. 19.50 (*81-215-0964-5*, Pub. by M Manoharial) S Asia.

Prasada, Rama, tr. Patanjali's Yoga Sutras. (C). 1995. pap. 22.00 (*0-614-09975-7*, Pub. by M Manoharial) S Asia.

— Patanjali's Yoga Sutras. 2nd ed. 318p. 1981. reprint ed. 24.00 (*0-89744-220-2*, Pub. by Orient Reprint) S Asia.

— Patanjali's Yoga Sutras (The Aphorisms of Yoga, by Patanjali) With the Commentary of Vyasa & the Gloss of Vachaspati Misra. LC 73-3789. reprint ed. 29.00 (*0-404-57804-7*) AMS Pr.

Prasada, Rao D. & Salazar-Carrillo, Jorge, eds. International Comparisons of Prices, Output & Productivity. (Contributions to Economic Analysis Ser.: Vol. 231). 344p. 1996. text 98.50 (*0-444-82144-9*, North Holland) Elsevier.

Prasada, Rao D. & Selvanathan, E. Anthony. Construction of Index Numbers: A Stochastic Approach. LC 94-19429. (Illus.). 256p. 1994. text 59.50 (*0-472-10577-9*, 10577) U of Mich Pr.

Prasadd, V. N. Principles & Practices in Socialcum-Community Forestry Pub. 118p. (C). 1985. 110.00 (*81-7089-032-2*, Pub. by Intl Bk Distr) St Mut.

Prasado, Rao D., jt. ed. see Salazar-Carrillo, Jorge.

Prasanna, A. R., jt. auth. see Mukherjee, S.

Prasanna, Viktor K., jt. ed. see Hartenstein, Rainer W.

Prasansuk, Sujitra, et al, eds. Aspects of Modern Otolaryngological Practice: First Congress of the Asian Otorhinolaryngological Federation, Pattaya, 1981. (Advances in OtoRhinoLaryngology Ser.: Vol. 29). (Illus.). xii, 236p. 1983. 142.75 (*3-8055-3592-9*) S Karger.

— Otolaryngology in ASEAN Countries: 6th ASEAN Congress, Chiang, Rai, Thailand, November 1994. LC 96-44296. (Advances in OtoRhinoLaryngology Ser.: Vol. 51, 1996). (Illus.). viii, 128p. 1996. 85.25 (*3-8055-6336-1*) S Karger.

Prasas, Janardan & Kumari Kaushik, Vijay. Child Education & Social Development. 1996. pap. 275.00 (*81-7391-149-5*, Pub. by Print Hse) St Mut.

Prasas, Ram. Mahua: The Tree of the Poor. 87p. 1993. pap. 100.00 (*81-7089-168-X*, Pub. by Intl Bk Distr) St Mut.

Prashad, Baini, ed. Tabaqat-i-Akbari of Khwajah Nizamuddin Ahmad: (A History of India from the Early Musabhman Invasions to the Thirty-Eighth Year of the Reign of Akbar), 3 vols., Set. Brajendranath, tr. (C). 1992. reprint ed. 28.00 (*81-85418-90-X*, Pub. by Low Price) S Asia.

Prashad, Shashi. Multithreading Programming Techniques for C Programmers. LC 96-34490. (Illus.). 408p. 1997. pap., pap. text 49.95 incl. disk (*0-07-912250-7*) McGraw.

***Prashad, Vijay.** The Karma of Brown Folk. 248p. 2000. 24.95 (*0-8166-3438-6*) U of Minn Pr.

— Untouchable Freedom: A Social History of a Dalit Community. (Illus.). 208p. 2000. text 23.95 (*0-19-565075-1*) OUP.

Prashant Bhushan. Bofors: The Selling of a Nation. 1990. 27.50 (*81-7094-066-4*, Pub. by Vision) S Asia.

Prashant, Saroj. Drug Abuse & Society: The Indian Scenario. (Illus.). xii, 219p. 1993. 17.95 (*1-881338-34-7*) Nataraj Bks.

Prasher, Charles L. Crushing & Grinding Process Handbook. LC 85-26434. (Illus.). 483p. 1987. reprint ed. pap. 149.80 (*0-608-05304-X*, 206584200001) Bks Demand.

Prasher, Deepak. Biological Effects of Noise. (Advances in Noise Research Ser.). 1998. 82.00 (*1-86156-075-3*) Whurr Pub.

— Protection Against Noise. LC 99-169847. (Advances in Noise Research Ser.). 1998. 65.00 (*1-86156-076-1*) Whurr Pub.

***Prasher, I. B.** Fungi Flora of Chandigarth. LC 98-917872. (Illus.). 168p. 1998. pap. 120.00 (*81-7089-254-6*, Pub. by Intl Bk Distr) St Mut.

***Prasher, I. B., ed.** Fungi of Nagaland. 1998. pap. 120.00 (*0-7855-7664-9*) St Mut.

Prasher, R. G. Indian Library Literature: An Annotated Bibliography. 544p. 1971. 8.00 (*0-88065-176-8*) Scholarly Pubns.

— Managing University Libraries. (Illus.). 350p. 1991. 45.00 (*1-55528-250-4*, Pub. by Today Tomorrow) Scholarly Pubns.

Prashkov, L. Wall Painting in Bulgaria: 9th to 19th Centuries. (C). 1981. 95.00 (*0-685-34406-1*) Collets.

Prasifka, David W. Water Supply Planning. LC 93-28392. 282p. 1994. 42.50 (*0-89464-838-1*) Krieger.

Prasifka, Karol, jt. auth. see Knox, William A.

Prasil, Michal. Skoda Heavy Guns: 24cm Cannon, 38cm Howitzer, 42cm Howitzer & Others. LC 97-67429. 144p. 1997. pap. 19.95 (*0-7643-0288-4*) Schiffer.

Prask, H. J., et al. Cold Neutron Research in the U. S. Government. (Illus.). 145p. (Orig.). (C). 1993. pap. text 40.00 (*0-7881-0046-7*) DIANE Pub.

Praskash, Ravi, jt. ed. see Bhatt, B. D.

Praskiewicz, Szczepan T. Saint Raphael Kalinowski: An Introduction to His Life & Spirituality. Coonan, Thomas et al, trs. from ITA. LC 94-29713. (Illus.). 68p. 1998. pap. 8.95 (*0-935216-53-7*, RK) ICS Pubns.

Praslov, N. D., jt. auth. see Soffer, O.

***Prasolov, V. V.** Essays on Numbers & Figures. LC 99-58690. (MAWRLD Ser.: Vol. 16). 75p. 2000. 15.00 (*0-8218-1944-5*) Am Math.

Prasolov, V. V. Intuitive Topology. Sossinsky, A. B., tr. from RUS. LC 94-23133. (Mathematical World Ser.: 4). (ENG.). 93p. 1994. pap. 19.00 (*0-8218-0356-5*, MAWRLD/4) Am Math.

— Knots, Links, Braids & 3-Manifolds: An Introduction to the New Invariants in Low-Dimensional Topology. Sossinsky, A. B., tr. LC 96-22164. (Translations of Mathematical Monographs). 239p. 1996. text 99.00 (*0-8218-0588-6*) Am Math.

— Problems & Theorems in Liner Algebra. LC 94-13332. (Translations of Mathematical Monographs: Vol. 134). 225p. 1994. pap. 49.00 (*0-8218-0236-4*, MMONO/134) Am Math.

Prasolov, V. V. & Sossinsky, A. B. Knots, Links, Braids & 3-Manifolds: An Introduction to the New Invariants in Low-Dimensional Topology. LC 96-22164. (Translations of Mathematical Monographs: Vol. 154). 239p. 1996. pap. 49.00 (*0-8218-0898-2*) Am Math.

Prasolov, Viktor V. & Solovyev, Yuri. Elliptic Functions & Elliptic Integrals. LC 97-24309. (Translations of Mathematical Monographs Ser.: Vol. 170). 170p. 1997. text 79.00 (*0-8218-0587-8*) Am Math.

Prassatowics, M., jt. ed. see Jezabek, M.

Prasse, Karl G. The Tuaregs: The Blue People. (Illus.). 136p. 1995. 34.00 (*87-7289-313-3*, Pub. by Mus Tusculanum) Paul & Co Pubs.

Prasse, Keith W., jt. auth. see Duncan, J. Robert.

Prassel, Frank R. The Great American Outlaw: A Legacy of Fact & Fiction. LC 93-14675. 1993. 29.95 (*0-8061-2534-9*) U of Okla Pr.

— The Great American Outlaw: A Legacy of Fact & Fiction. LC 93-14675. (Illus.). 432p. 1996. pap. 16.95 (*0-8061-2842-9*) U of Okla Pr.

Prasser, Scott, et al, eds. Corruption & Reform: The Fitzgerald Vision. 1990. pap. 29.95 (*0-7022-2234-8*, Pub. by Univ Queensland Pr) Intl Spec Bk.

Prassides, Kosmas, ed. Mixed Valency Systems: Applications in Chemistry Physics & Biology. 464p. (C). 1991. text 234.00 (*0-7923-1381-X*) Kluwer Academic.

— Physics & Chemistry of the Fullerenes: Proceedings of the NATO Advanced Research Workshop, Aghia Pelaghia, Greece, June 7-13, 1993. (NATO Advanced Science Institutes Series C: 444). 352p. (C). 1994. text 204.50 (*0-7923-3109-5*) Kluwer Academic.

Prassidis, Stratos, jt. auth. see Hughes, Bruce.

Prassoloff, Annie, jt. auth. see Brandt, Per A.

Prast, W. & Shamoun, J. The Bird Remains: Identification System. (World Biodiversity Database Ser.). 1997. 490.00 incl. cd-rom (*3-540-14632-6*) Spr-Verlag.

Prastaro, A., ed. Geometrodynamics Proceedings 1985. 466p. 1985. 66.00 (*9971-978-63-6*) World Scientific Pub.

Prastaro, A., jt. auth. see Rassias, Themistocles M.

Prastaro, Agostino. Geometry of PDEs & Mechanics. LC 95-47858. 760p. 1996. write for info. (*981-02-2520-2*) World Scientific Pub.

***Prasthofer, Thomas & Lewis, Jeffrey.** Biochemistry for Pharmaceutical Sciences. (Illus.). 768p. 2000. Price not set. (*0-07-134151-X*) McGraw.

Prasuhn, Alan L. Fundamentals of Hydraulic Engineering. (Illus.). 528p. 1995. text 84.95 (*0-19-510732-2*) OUP.

Prat, A., ed. COMPSTAT 1996 - Proceedings in Computational Statistics. (Illus.). xii, 507p. 1996. pap. 139.50 (*3-7908-0953-5*) Spr-Verlag.

Prat, E. H. & Rassem, M., eds. Kunst und Ethos: Deutungsprobleme der Modernen Kunst. (GER., Illus.). X, 204p. 1995. 39.95 (*3-631-47190-4*) P Lang Pubng.

Prat, Georges, jt. auth. see Gardes, Francis.

Prat, Louis-Antoine, jt. auth. see Rosenberg, Pierre.

Prat, Ramon, jt. photos by see Bernado, Jordi.

Prat Turu, Clara. Diccionari Portugues-Catala, Catala-Portugues. (POR.). 512p. 1982. 31.95 (*0-7859-6216-6*, 8473061829) Fr & Eur.

Prata, Giuliana. A Systemic Harpoon into Family Games: Preventive Interventions in Therapy. LC 90-2157. 192p. 1990. text 32.95 (*0-87630-591-5*) Brunner-Mazel.

Prata, Kathleen R., et al. Symbols: Guiding Lights along the Journey of Life. LC 96-29938. (ARE Membership Ser.). (Illus.). 133p. 1998. pap. 7.95 (*0-87604-379-1*) ARE Pr.

Prata, Nicholas C. Angels in Iron. LC 97-46998. x, 305p. 1997. 29.00 (*1-889758-04-3*) Evol Pubng & Manuf.

Prata, Stephen. C++ Primer Plus with CD-ROM. LC 97-36325. 1019p. 1998. 49.99 (*1-57169-131-6*) Sams.

— Waite Group's C Primer Plus. 3rd ed. LC 98-85904. 1998. pap. 29.99 (*1-57169-161-8*) Sams.

— Waite Group's C++ Primer Plus. 3rd ed. LC 98-85890. 1998. pap. 35.00 (*1-57169-162-6*) Sams.

Prata, Stephen W. C++ Primer Plus: Teach Yourself Object-Oriented Programming. 2nd ed. 880p. 1995. 39.99 (*1-878739-74-3*) Sams.

***Pratap, Ajay.** The Hoe & the Axe: An Ethnohistory of Shifting Cultivation in Eastern India. (Studies in Social Ecology & Environmental History). (Illus.). 272p. 2000. text 26.00 (*0-19-565170-7*) OUP.

Pratap, Rita. Panorama of Jaipur Paintings. LC 95-905211. 1996. 105.00 (*81-246-0068-6*, Pub. by DK Pubs Ind) S Asia.

***Pratap, Rudra.** Getting Started with Matlab 5: A Quick Introduction for Scientists & Engineers. 2nd ed. LC 98-229068. (Illus.). 240p. (Orig.). (C). 1998. pap. text 25.00 (*0-19-512947-4*) OUP.

Pratap, Vijayendra. Beginning Yoga. (Illus.). 112p. 1997. pap. text 9.95 (*0-8048-2104-6*) Tuttle Pubng.

— A Teacher's Guide for Beginning Yoga. 2nd ed. LC 87-91956. (Illus.). 122p. 1991. pap. 9.95 (*0-944731-00-7*) Sky Fnd.

Pratap, Vijayendra, ed. from SAN. Secrets of Hatha Vidya: As Disclosed by Svatmarama in Hathapradipika. LC 96-68803. (Illus.). 160p. (Orig.). 1996. mass mkt. 9.25 (*0-944731-02-3*) Sky Fnd.

— Yoga Vision: A Selection of Yoga Sutras. LC 95-68061. (Illus.). 80p. (Orig.). 1995. mass mkt. 6.90 (*0-944731-01-5*) Sky Fnd.

Pratasik, Bennie, jt. auth. see McCormick, John.

***Pratchett.** Deaths Domain: A Discworld Map. 2000. pap. 12.95 (*0-552-14672-2*, Pub. by Transworld Publishers Ltd) Trafalgar.

— Discworld Map. 2000. pap. 10.95 (*0-552-14324-3*, Pub. by Transworld Publishers Ltd) Trafalgar.

***Pratchett, Lawrence, ed.** Renewing Local Democracy? The Modernisation Agenda in British Local Government. LC 99-40343. 152p. 2000. 49.50 (*0-7146-5046-3*, Pub. by F Cass Pubs); pap. 24.50 (*0-7146-8095-8*, Pub. by F Cass Pubs) Intl Spec Bk.

***Pratchett, Terry.** Carpe Jugulum. 400p. 2000. mass mkt. 6.99 (*0-06-102039-7*, HarpTorch) Morrow Avon.

— Carpe Jugulum: A Novel of Discworld. LC 99-29277. 296p. 1999. 24.00 (*0-06-105158-6*, HarperPrism) HarpC.

Pratchett, Terry. The Carpet People. 192p. 1992. 16.50 (*0-385-40304-6*) Doubleday.

***Pratchett, Terry.** The Color of Magic. 240p. 2000. mass mkt. 3.99 (*0-06-102071-0*, Torch) HarpC.

Pratchett, Terry. The Colour of Magic. 1990. mass mkt. 6.99 (*0-552-12475-3*) Bantam.

— The Colour of Magic. 1990. 25.00 (*0-86140-324-X*, Pub. by Smyth) Dufour.

— The Colour of Magic. large type ed. 23.95 (*1-85695-364-5*, Pub. by ISIS Lrg Prnt) Transaction Pubs.

— Diggers. 1990. 12.95 (*0-385-30343-2*) Doubleday.

— Diggers. 192p. 1990. 14.95 (*0-385-26979-X*) Doubleday.

***Pratchett, Terry.** Equal Rites. 240p. 2000. mass mkt. 3.99 (*0-06-102069-9*, Torch) HarpC.

Pratchett, Terry. Equal Rites. large type ed. 23.95 (*1-85695-387-4*, Pub. by ISIS Lrg Prnt) Transaction Pubs.

— Feet of Clay. 1997. mass mkt. 7.99 (*0-552-14237-9*) Bantam.

— Feet of Clay. 368p. 1997. mass mkt. 6.50 (*0-06-105764-9*, HarperPrism) HarpC.

***Pratchett, Terry.** The Fifth Elephant: A Novel of Discworld. LC 99-43960. 336p. 2000. 24.00 (*0-06-105157-8*, HarperPrism) HarpC.

— The First Discworld Novels. LC 99-495089. 1999. 33.95 (*0-86140-421-1*, Pub. by Smyth) Dufour.

— GURPS Dicsworld. Jackson, Steve, ed. 240p. 1998. 34.95 (*1-55634-386-8*, Pub. by S Jackson Games) BookWorld.

Pratchett, Terry. Hogfather. 1998. mass mkt. 8.99 (*0-552-14542-4*) Bantam.

— Hogfather. LC 98-17239. 304p. 1998. 24.00 (*0-06-105046-6*, HarperPrism) HarpC.

— Interesting Time. 1996. mass mkt. 6.99 (*0-552-14235-2*) Bantam.

— Interesting Times. 384p. 1998. mass mkt. 5.99 (*0-06-105690-1*, HarperPrism) HarpC.

— Interesting Times. large type ed. 23.95 (*1-85695-254-1*, Pub. by ISIS Lrg Prnt) Transaction Pubs.

— Jingo: A Novel of Discworld. LC 97-47590. 336p. (YA). 1998. 24.00 (*0-06-105047-4*) HarpC.

— Jingo: A Novel of Discworld. 448p. 1999. mass mkt. 6.50 (*0-06-105906-4*) HarpC.

— Johnny & the Bomb. 1997. mass mkt. 14.95 (*0-552-52968-0*) Bantam.

Pratchett, Terry. Johnny & the Bomb. large type ed. (Illus.). (J). 1997. pap. 16.95 (*0-7540-6000-4*, Galaxy Child Lrg Print) Chivers N Amer.

Pratchett, Terry. The Last Continent. LC 98-44160. 304p. 1999. 24.00 (*0-06-105048-2*) HarpC.

***Pratchett, Terry.** The Last Continent: A Novel of Discworld. 400p. 2000. mass mkt. 6.50 (*0-06-105907-2*, HarperPrism) HarpC.

Pratchett, Terry. The Light Fantastic. 1990. mass mkt. 6.99 (*0-552-12848-1*) Bantam.

***Pratchett, Terry.** The Light Fantastic. (Illus.). 272p. 2000. mass mkt. 3.99 (*0-06-102070-2*, Torch) HarpC.

Pratchett, Terry. The Light Fantastic. LC 86-60218. 218p. 1987. 27.95 (*0-86140-203-0*, Pub. by Smyth) Dufour.

— The Light Fantastic. large type ed. 24.95 (*1-85695-369-6*, Pub. by ISIS Lrg Prnt) Transaction Pubs.

— Lords & Ladies. 384p. 1994. mass mkt. 6.99 (*0-552-13891-6*) Bantam.

— Lords & Ladies MM. 288p. 1996. mass mkt. 6.50 (*0-06-105692-8*, HarperPrism) HarpC.

— Maskerade. 368p. 1998. mass mkt. 6.50 (*0-06-105691-X*, HarperPrism) HarpC.

— Maskerade. large type ed. (Isis Large Print Ser.). 1997. 25.95 (*0-7531-5156-1*) T T Beeler.

— Men at Arms. 1995. mass mkt. 6.99 (*0-552-14028-7*) Bantam.

***Pratchett, Terry.** Men at Arms: The Play. 2000. pap. 12.95 (*0-552-14432-0*, Pub. by Transworld Publishers Ltd) Trafalgar.

Pratchett, Terry. Men At Arms MM: Men At Arms MM. LC 99-43960. 384p. 1997. mass mkt. 6.50 (*0-06-109219-3*, HarperPrism) HarpC.

— Mort. 272p. 1989. mass mkt. 6.99 (*0-552-13106-7*) Bantam.

***Pratchett, Terry.** Mort. 2000. pap. 8.95 (*0-552-14429-0*, Pub. by Transworld Publishers Ltd) Trafalgar.

Pratchett, Terry. Only You Can Save Mankind. 176p. 1994. mass mkt. 5.99 (*0-552-13926-2*) Bantam.

— Only You Can Save Mankind. large type ed. (J). 1996. 16.95 (*0-7451-4957-X*, Galaxy Child Lrg Print) Chivers N Amer.

— Small Gods. 352p. 1994. mass mkt. 6.50 (*0-06-109217-7*, Harp PBks) HarpC.

— Soul Music. 1995. mass mkt. 6.99 (*0-552-14029-5*) Bantam.

— Soul Music. 384p. 1995. mass mkt. 6.50 (*0-06-105489-5*) HarpC.

— Soul Music. large type ed. (Isis Large Print Ser.). 1997. 26.95 (*0-7531-5157-X*) T T Beeler.

— Sourcery. 240p. 1989. mass mkt. 6.99 (*0-552-13107-5*) Bantam.

— Street of Ankh Morpork. 16p. 1994. pap. 10.95 (*0-552-14161-5*) Bantam.

— Truckers. (J). 1989. 14.95 (*0-385-26961-7*) Doubleday.

***Pratchett, Terry.** The Truth: A Novel of Discworld. LC 00-31928. 336p. 2000. 24.00 (*0-380-97895-4*) Morrow Avon.

Pratchett, Terry. Wings. 176p. 1992. mass mkt. 4.50 (*0-552-52649-5*) Bantam.

— Wings. 196p. 1991. pap. 14.95 (*0-385-40018-7*) Doubleday.

***Pratchett, Terry.** Wyrd Sisters: The Play. 2000. pap. 8.95 (*0-552-14430-4*, Pub. by Transworld Publishers Ltd) Trafalgar.

Pratchett, Terry, abr. Hogfather. 384p. 1999. mass mkt. 6.50 (*0-06-105905-6*) HarpC Child Bks.

***Pratchett, Terry & Briggs, Stephen.** A Tourist Guide to Lancre: A Discoworld Map. 32p. 2000. pap. 12.95 (*0-552-14608-0*, Pub. by Transworld Publishers Ltd) Trafalgar.

Pratchett, Terry & Gollancz. Equal Rights. 240p. 1989. mass mkt. 6.99 (*0-552-13105-9*) Bantam.

Pratchett, Terry, jt. auth. see Gaiman, Neil.

Pratchett, Terry, jt. auth. see Jordan, Robert.

Pratchett, Terry, jt. auth. see Masters, Phil.

Prate, Kit. Greenhorn Stampede. large type ed. (Linford Western Library). 352p. (Orig.). 1992. pap. 16.99 (*0-7089-7172-5*) Ulverscroft.

Pratelli, M., jt. ed. see Letta, G.

Prater, A. J. Estuary Birds of Britain & Ireland. (Illus.). 456p. 1991. text (*0-85661-029-1*, 784629) Poyser.

Prater, Andreas & Bauer, Hermann. Painting of the Baroque. (Epochs & Styles Ser.). (Illus.). 159p. 1997. pap. 14.99 (*3-8228-8253-4*) Taschen Amer.

Prater, Arnold. There Really Is a Devil! Basics for Spiritual Warfare. 202p. (Orig.). 1994. pap. 9.95 (*1-888874-00-7*) Marno Bks.

— Who Is This Ghost Called Holy? The Ministry of the Holy Spirit. Orig. Title: The Presence. 147p. 1995. write for info. (*1-888874-01-5*) Marno Bks.

Prater, Bacon & Tucker. Employee Benefits Guide, Vol. 1. 1991. 125.00 (*0-8205-1574-4*) Bender.

Prater, Bayliss & McNeal, Kathleen. Full Circle: Restoring Your Habitat to Wilderness. (Illus.). 127p. (Orig.). 1993. pap. 15.00 (*0-9635867-1-8*) Last Resort.

Prater, Burt. Family Masonic Education: Using Masonic Symbolism in Daily Life. (Illus.). 192p. (Orig.). 1993. pap., wbk. ed. 14.95 (*0-9635766-0-7*) Source.

Prater, Carol, jt. auth. see Burke, Jim.

Prater, Dennis D., et al. Evidence: The Objection Method, 1997 Edition. LC 97-70466. 1149p. 1997. text 51.00 (*1-55834-469-1*, 11360-10, MICHIE) LEXIS Pub.

Prater, Donald A. A Ringing Glass: The Life of Rainer Maria Rilke. (Illus.). 506p. 1994. reprint ed. pap. text 19.95 (*0-19-815891-2*) OUP.

— Thomas Mann: A Life. (Illus.). 572p. 1995. 39.95 (*0-19-815861-0*) OUP.

P

Prater, Gene. Snowshoeing. 4th ed. Felkley, Dave, ed. LC 97-29953. 160p. 1997. pap. text 16.95 (*0-89886-497-6*) Mountaineers.

Prater, Jeffrey. The Study of Harmony: An Historical Perspective. 384p. (C). 1991. text. write for info. (*0-697-11966-1*) Brown & Benchmark.

***Prater, John.** Again! 2000. 12.95 (*0-7641-5279-3*) Barron.

— Baby Bear Book Assortment. (Illus.). (J). 2000. 6.95 (*0-7641-7398-7*) Barron.

Prater, John. The Bear Went over the Mountain. (Baby Bear Ser.). (Illus.). 24p. (J). (ps). 1999. bds. 6.95 (*0-7641-5187-8*) Barron.

— The Gift. LC 86-43071. (Illus.). 32p. (J). (gr. 3-8). 1987. pap. 3.95 (*0-317-63653-7*, PuffinBks) Peng Put Young Read.

— The Greatest Show on Earth. LC 94-24991. (Illus.). 40p. (J). (ps-1). 1995. 14.95 (*1-56402-563-2*) Candlewick Pr.

— The Greatest Show on Earth. LC 94-24991. (Illus.). 32p. (J). (ps up). 1997. reprint ed. pap. 5.99 (*0-7636-0105-5*) Candlewick Pr.

— No! Said Joe. LC 91-71828. (J). 1996. 11.19 (*0-606-09694-9*, Pub. by Turtleback) Demco.

— No! Said Joe. (J). (ps-2). reprint ed. pap. 5.99 (*0-614-15565-7*) Candlewick Pr.

— No! Said Joe. LC 91-71828. (Illus.). 32p. (J). (ps-3). 1996. reprint ed. pap. 5.99 (*1-56402-847-X*) Candlewick Pr.

***Prater, John.** Number One, Tickle Your Tum. (Baby Bear Ser.). (Illus.). 24p. (J). 1999. bds. 6.95 (*0-7641-5185-1*) Barron.

Prater, John. Oh Where, Oh Where? (Illus.). 24p. (J). 1998. bds. 6.95 (*0-7641-5109-6*) Barron.

— On Top of the World. LC 98-16344. (J). (ps-2). 1998. 15.95 (*1-57255-649-8*) Mondo Pubng.

— Once Upon a Time. (J). 1995. 11.44 (*0-606-07969-6*) Turtleback.

— Walking Around the Garden. (Illus.). 24p. (J). 1998. bds. 6.95 (*0-7641-5111-8*) Barron.

Prater, John. Once upon a Picnic. LC 95-19912. (J). (ps-3). 1996. 14.99 (*1-56402-810-0*) Candlewick Pr.

Prater, John. Once upon a Time. LC 92-53139. 32p. (J). (ps up). 1993. 14.99 (*1-56402-177-7*) Candlewick Pr.

— Once upon a Time. LC 92-53139. (J). (ps-3). 1995. pap. 5.99 (*1-56402-456-3*) Candlewick Pr.

— Once upon a Time Big Book. LC 92-53139. 32p. (J). (ps-2). 1996. pap. 19.99 (*1-56402-806-2*) Candlewick Pr.

Prater, John, jt. auth. see McGough, Roger.

Prater, John, jt. auth. see Rogers, Paul.

Prater, Rex J. & Swift, Roger W. Manual of Voice Therapy. LC 90-50380. 288p. (C). 1984. spiral bd. 31.00 (*0-89079-279-8*, 1773) PRO-ED.

***Prater, Rex J., et al.** Manual of Voice Therapy. 2nd ed. LC 99-31323. 1999. write for info. (*0-89079-825-7*) PRO-ED.

Prater, Richard B. Bridge to Superconsciousness. LC 98-15630. (Illus.). 300p. 1999. pap. 19.95 (*0-9635766-4-X*) Source.

Prater, Robin, jt. auth. see Cook, Tony.

Prater, Ronald & Chan, Vincent S. 11th Topical Conference of Radio Frequency Power in Plasmas: Palm Springs, CA, May 17-19, 1995. (AIP Conference Proceedings Ser.: No. 355). (Illus.). 528p. 1995. 135.00 (*1-56396-536-4*) Am Inst Physics.

Prater, Tony, jt. auth. see Marchant, John.

***Prater, Vickie.** Macon, GA. (Images of America Ser.). (Illus.). 128p. 1999. pap. 18.99 (*0-7385-0200-6*) Arcadia Publng.

Prater, Yvonne. Snoqualmie Pass: From Indian Trail to Interstate. (Illus.). 167p. (Orig.). 1996. reprint ed. pap. 12.95 (*0-89886-015-6*) Mountaineers.

Prater, Yvonne & Mendenhall, Ruth D. Gorp, Glop & Glue Stew: Favorite Foods from 165 Outdoor Experts. LC 81-18836. (Illus.). 204p. (Orig.). 1981. pap. 12.95 (*0-89886-017-2*) Mountaineers.

Pratesi, R., ed. Optronic Techniques in Diagnostic & Therapeutic Medicine. (Illus.). 328p. (C). 1991. text 114.00 (*0-306-43938-7*, Kluwer Plenum) Kluwer Academic.

Prathap, G. The Finite Element Method in Structural Engineering. LC 93-30133. (Solid Mechanics & Its Applications Ser.). 424p. (C). 1993. text 219.00 (*0-7923-2492-7*) Kluwer Academic.

***Prather.** Spiritual Notes to Myself. 160p. 1998. 6.98 (*1-56731-295-0*, MJF Bks) Fine Comms.

Prather, A., jt. auth. see Prather, L.

Prather, Alfred G. & Prather, Gloria A. My First Reader & Skills Book: One Hundred Words Plus. Prather, Arden C., ed. (Illus.). 36p. (Orig.). (J). (gr. 1-3). 1988. pap. write for info. (*0-9619655-2-5*) Academic Parks Co.

Prather, Alfred G., jt. auth. see Prather, Gloria M.

Prather, Angela, ed. see Prather, Dewitt G.

Prather, Arden C., ed. see Prather, Alfred G. & Prather, Gloria A.

Prather, Arden C., ed. see Prather, Gloria M. & Prather, Alfred G.

Prather, Cathy. Life What Is It? 120p. 1998. write for info. (*0-9666959-1-7*) Cathy Prather.

— The Little Mushrooms Coloring Book, No. 50. (Illus.). 50p. (J). (ps-6). 1998. pap. 2.99 (*0-9666959-2-5*) Cathy Prather.

— Miss Louise Bos & Animal Friends. LC 98-92173. (Illus.). 136p. (J). (ps-6). 1998. text 29.95 (*0-9666959-0-9*) Cathy Prather.

Prather, Charles W. & Gundry, Lisa K. Blueprints for Innovation: How Creative Processes Can Make You & Your Organization More Competitive. (AMA Management Briefing Ser.). 1995. write for info. (*0-8144-2359-0*) AMACOM.

Prather, Charlotte. A Generous Openness: Praying the Spiritual Exercises of St. Ignatius. 112p. (Orig.). 1992. pap. 12.95 (*0-932506-85-2*) St Bedes Pubns.

Prather, Dewitt G. United States National Bank Notes & Their Seals. Prather, J. S. & Prather, Angela, eds. (Illus.). 200p. 1986. 40.00 (*0-9616836-0-0*); 60.00 (*0-317-58449-9*) D G Prather.

Prather, Eric & Prather, Joy. Color the Black Hills: A Nature Coloring & Activity Book. 32p. (J). 1998. pap. 3.95 (*0-87108-300-0*) Pruett.

Prather, Gayle, jt. auth. see Prather, Hugh.

Prather, Gloria A., jt. auth. see Prather, Alfred G.

Prather, Gloria M. & Prather, Alfred G. Especially for Special Children: The A-B-C's of Super Stars. Prather, Arden C., ed. (Illus.). 30p. (Orig.). (J). 1988. lib. bdg. write for info. (*0-9619655-3-3*) Academic Parks Co.

— The Way to Go: Academic Travel Pack. Prather, Arden C. & Smith, Ellen, eds. (Illus.). 48p. (J). (gr. k-2). 1987. student ed. write for info. (*0-9619655-0-9*) Academic Parks Co.

Prather, H. Leon, Sr. Resurgent Politics & Educational Progressivism in the New South: North Carolina, 1890-1913. LC 77-74394. (Illus.). 186p. 1979. 40.00 (*0-8386-2071-X*) Fairleigh Dickinson.

— We Have Taken a City. (Illus.). 216p. 1998. reprint ed. 24.95 (*0-9664006-0-7*) Nu-World Ent.

Prather, Hugh. Circle of a Thought. 2nd rev. ed. Helberg, Bob, ed. LC 87-73314. 80p. (YA). (gr. 9-12). 1987. reprint ed. pap. 7.95 (*0-944944-00-0*) Amethyst Aura.

***Prather, Hugh.** The Little Book of Letting Go: A Revolutionary 30 Day Program to Cleanse Your Mind, Revive Your Soul & Lift Your Spirit. 200p. 2000. pap. 14.95 (*1-57324-503-8*) Conari Press.

Prather, Hugh. Notes to Myself. 176p. 1983. mass mkt. 6.99 (*0-553-27382-5*, Bantam Classics) Bantam.

— The Quiet Answer. LC 80-2979. 176p. 1982. pap. 8.95 (*0-385-17605-8*) Doubleday.

— Spiritual Notes to Myself: Essential Wisdom for the 21st Century. LC 97-35032. (Illus.). 160p. (Orig.). 1998. pap. 18.95 (*1-57324-113-X*) Conari Press.

Prather, Hugh & Prather, Gayle. I Will Never Leave You: How Couples Can Achieve the Power of Lasting Love. 400p. 1996. pap. 12.95 (*0-553-37531-8*) Bantam.

— Spiritual Parenting. 1997. pap. 13.00 (*0-517-88831-9*) Crown Pub Group.

Prather, J. S., ed. see Prather, Dewitt G.

Prather, James E., jt. auth. see Gibson, Frank K.

Prather, Jo Beecher. Mississippi Beau. LC 93-50614. (Illus.). 32p. (J). (gr. 4-5). 1995. pap. 8.95 (*0-89015-961-0*) Sunbelt Media.

Prather, John W., Jr. Prater-Prather, Genealogy & History, 2 vols. Incl. Vol. I. Praters in Wiltshire, 1480-1670. (Illus.). 215p. 1987. 30.00 (*0-9619434-1-6*); Vol. II. Prator, Prather, Prator, Praytor, in America, 1620-1800: 1-5 Generations. LC 88-129646. 489p. 1994. 50.00 (*0-9619434-2-4*); 80.00 (*0-9619434-0-8*) J W Prather.

Prather, Joy, jt. auth. see Prather, Eric.

Prather, Judy H. Seeking Sabbath: A Planning Guide for Women's Retreats. LC 97-220762. 64p. 1997. pap. text 8.95 (*1-56309-220-4*, N974111, New Hope) Womans Mission Union.

Prather, L. & Prather, A. We Believe in Miracles. 1995. pap. 7.95 (*0-89228-002-6*) Impact Christian.

***Prather, L. Alan.** Systematics of Cobaea (Polemoniaceae) Anderson, Christiane, ed. (Systematic Botany Monographs: Vol. 57). (Illus.). 82p. 1999. pap. 11.00 (*0-912861-57-6*) Am Soc Plant.

Prather, Marilyn. Crystal-Clear Dreams. LC 98-96229. 192p. 1998. 18.95 (*0-8034-9307-X*, Avalon Bks) Bouregy.

— Ravenspire. LC 97-97217. 192p. 1998. 18.95 (*0-8034-9287-1*, Avalon Bks) Bouregy.

***Prather, Marilyn.** Sonoran Love Song. LC 99-94442. 192p. 1999. 18.95 (*0-8034-9365-7*, Avalon Bks) Bouregy.

Prather, Marla. Alexander Calder, 1898-1976. LC 97-48328. (Illus.). 376p. 1998. 65.00 (*0-300-07518-9*) Yale U Pr.

Prather, Marla, et al. Alexander Calder, 1898-1976. LC 97-48328. 1998. write for info. (*0-89468-228-8*) Natl Gallery Art.

Prather, Marla, jt. auth. see Arnason, H. Horvard.

Prather-Moses, Alice I. The International Dictionary of Women Workers in the Decorative Arts: A Historical Survey from the Distant Past to the Early Decades of the Twentieth Century. LC 81-8947. 218p. 1981. 30.00 (*0-8108-1450-1*) Scarecrow.

Prather, Patricia S. & Monday, Jane C. From Slave to Statesman: The Legacy of Joshua Houston, Servant to Sam Houston. LC 93-25464. (Illus.). 277p. 1993. 32.50 (*0-929398-47-5*) UNTX Pr.

— From Slave to Statesman: The Legacy of Joshua Houston, Servant to Sam Houston. LC 93-25464. 277p. 1995. pap. 16.95 (*0-929398-87-4*) UNTX Pr.

***Prather, Paul.** Back Porch Faith: Weekly Meditations. LC 99-15624. 224p. 1999. 16.95 (*0-7407-0047-2*) Andrews & McMeel.

Prather, Paul. Modern-Day Miracles: How Ordinary People Experience Supernatural Acts of God. 240p. 1996. 19.95 (*0-8362-2174-5*) Andrews & McMeel.

Prather, Richard S. Hot Rock Rumble & The Double Take. LC 96-119875. (Gryphon Double Novel Ser.: No. 5). 100p. 1994. per. 12.00 (*0-936071-31-1*) Gryphon Pubns.

— Shellshock. 352p. 1988. pap. 3.95 (*0-8125-0783-5*, Pub. by Tor Bks) St Martin.

Prather, Robert C., jt. auth. see Levy, Jerome S.

Prather, Ronald E. Ronald Prather: Laboratory Manual for Data Structures: To Accompany Horowitz & Sahni Fundamentals of Data Structure. 3rd ed. (Illus.). (C). 1990. 16.80 (*0-7167-8236-7*) W H Freeman.

Prather, Ronald E., jt. auth. see Demsey, David.

***Prather, Stephen E.** The New Health Partners: Renewing the Leadership of Physician Practice. LC 99-22322. 352p. 1999. 39.95 (*0-7879-4024-0*) Jossey-Bass.

Prather, Stephen E., et al. Behavioral Types & the Art of Patient Management: Improving Quality of Care with Better Understanding of Physician-Patient Relationships. Rogers, Gregg, ed. LC 95-16790. 212p. 1995. 44.95 (*1-57066-031-X*, ME018) Practice Mgmt Info.

***Prati, Alessandro & Schinasi, Garry J.** Financial Stability in European Economic & Monetary Union. LC 99-16523. (Studies in International Finance: Ser. 86). 1999. 13.50 (*0-88165-258-X*) Princeton U Int Finan Econ.

Prati, Giancarlo. Photonic Networks. LC 96-29971. 1997. 109.00 (*3-540-76143-8*) Spr-Verlag.

Pratico, Gary D. Egypt-Sinai-Negev: With Slides. Shanks, Hershel, ed. 43p. (Orig.). 1987. pap. text 119.50 (*1-880317-34-6*, 5092) Biblical Arch Soc.

— Nelson Glueck's 1938-1940 Excavations at Tell El-Kheleifeh: A Reappraisal. (Archaeological Reports: No. 3). (Illus.). 223p. 1993. reprint ed. 45.00 (*1-55540-883-4*, 85 00 03, Pub. by Am Sch Orient Res) David Brown.

Pratkanis, Anthony R. Age of Propaganda: Everyday. rev. ed. 1997. write for info. (*0-7167-3109-6*) W H Freeman.

— Age of Propaganda: Everyday Use. LC 97-8615. 1997. pap. 19.95 (*0-7167-3108-8*) W H Freeman.

Pratkanis, Anthony R., et al, eds. Attitude Structure & Function. 472p. 1989. text 89.95 (*0-89859-991-1*); pap. text 49.95 (*0-8058-0323-8*) L Erlbaum Assocs.

Pratkanis, Anthony R. & Aronson, Elliot. Age of Propaganda: The Everyday Use & Abuse of Persuasion. rev. ed. LC 97-8615. (Illus.). 352p. 1997. pap. text 24.95 (*0-7167-2862-1*) W H Freeman.

Pratkanis, Anthony R. & Aronson, Elliott. Age of Propaganda: The Everyday Use & Abuse of Persuasion. rev. ed. (Illus.). 352p. 1998. pap. 19.95 (*0-7167-2861-3*) W H Freeman.

Pratkanis, Anthony R., jt. ed. see Aronson, Elliot.

Pratl, Carol, tr. see Cayrol, Pierre.

Pratley. Electric Principles & Applicat Ions. (Electrical Engineering Ser.). 128p. 1997. pap. text 21.95 (*0-340-69275-8*, VNR) Wiley.

Pratley, Gerald. The Films of John Frankenheimer: Forty Years in Film. LC 97-50118. 300p. 1998. 55.00 (*0-934223-47-5*) Lehigh Univ Pr.

— Torn Sprockets: The Uncertain Projection of the Canadian Film. LC 83-40110. (Illus.). 336p. 1987. 65.00 (*0-87413-194-4*) U Delaware Pr.

Pratley, Jim & Robertson, Alistar, eds. Agriculture & the Environmental Imperative. (Illus.). 276p. (Orig.). pap. 49.95 (*0-643-06377-3*, Pub. by CSIRO) Accents Pubns.

Pratley, Rhiannedd. Spelling It Out. 128p. 1988. pap. 8.95 (*0-563-21437-6*, Pub. by BBC) Parkwest Pubns.

Pratney, Winkey. El Joven y Su Dios, No. 1. (Joven y Sus Inquietudes Ser.).Tr. of Handbook for Followers. 1982. 6.99 (*0-88113-163-6*) Caribe Betania.

— El Joven y Su Mundo, No. 2. (Joven y Sus Inquietudes Ser.).Tr. of Handbook for Followers. 1982. 6.99 (*0-88113-164-4*) Caribe Betania.

— El Joven y Sus Amigos, No. 3. (Joven y Sus Inquietudes Ser).Tr. of Handbook for Followers. 1982. 6.99 (*0-88113-162-8*) Caribe Betania.

— El Joven y Sus Dilemas, No. 4. (Joven y Sus Inquietudes Ser.).Tr. of Handbook for Followers. 1982. 6.99 (*0-88113-165-2*) Caribe Betania.

— Nature & Character of God. LC 88-19451. 464p. (C). 1988. pap. 15.99 (*1-55661-041-6*) Bethany Hse.

Pratney, Winkie. Dealing with Doubt: When the Light Goes Out. 192p. (Orig.). 1998. mass mkt. 5.99 (*0-8007-8650-5*, The Thomas Fact, Spire) Revell.

— Fire on the Horizon: The Shape of A Twenty-first Century Youth Awakening. LC 99-12030. 200p. 1998. pap. 10.99 (*0-8307-2426-5*, Renew) Gospel Lght.

— Guia para el Discipulado, Tomo I.Tr. of Discipleship Guide. (SPA.). 144p. (Orig.). 1988. pap. text 7.99 (*0-88113-167-9*) Caribe Betania.

— Guia para el Discipulado, Tomo II.Tr. of Discipleship Guide. (SPA.). 160p. (Orig.). 1988. pap. 7.99 (*0-88113-168-7*) Caribe Betania.

— Guia para el Discipulado, Tomo III.Tr. of Discipleship Guide. (SPA.). 128p. (Orig.). 1988. pap. 7.99 (*0-88113-169-5*) Caribe Betania.

— A Handbook for Followers of Jesus. LC 76-44385. 336p. (YA). (gr. 9-12). 1977. pap. 9.99 (*0-87123-378-9*) Bethany Hse.

— Youth Aflame. LC 82-74507. 448p. (Orig.). (YA). 1983. pap. 9.99 (*0-87123-659-1*) Bethany Hse.

Prato, jt. ed. see Gentili.

Prato, Lou. Covering the Environmental Beat: An Overview for Radio & TV Journalists. Media Institute Staff, ed. LC 91-66458. 113p. (Orig.). (C). 1991. pap. 9.95 (*0-937790-47-8*, 4390) Media Institute.

— The Penn State Football Encyclopedia: Second Edition. rev. ed. (Illus.). 750p. 2000. 39.95 (*1-58261-105-X*, Pub. by Sprts Pubng) Partners-West.

Prato, Louis. The Penn State Football Encyclopedia. (Illus.). 654p. 1998. 39.95 (*1-57167-117-X*) Sports Pub.

***Prato, Peter J. & Lynne, Rita.** Financial Freedom for Women: Exclusively for Women over $3,000,000,000 in Financial Resources. 453p. 2000. 19.95 (*0-9676695-0-2*) Stress Resource.

Prato, R. J. License Renewal Demonstration Program: NRC Observations & Lessons Learned. 24p. 1996. pap. 4.25 (*0-16-062681-1*) USGPO.

Prato, Tony. Natural Resource & Environmental Economics. LC 97-25983. (Illus.). 358p. 1997. 49.95 (*0-8138-2938-0*) Iowa St U Pr.

Pratolini, Vasco. Family Chronicle. LC 87-82245. Orig. Title: Cronaca Familiare. 136p. (Orig.). 1988. pap. 12.50 (*0-934977-07-0*) Italica Pr.

— A Tale of Poor Lovers. (Voices of Resistance Ser.). 368p. 1988. reprint ed. pap. 13.00 (*0-85345-723-9*, Pub. by Monthly Rev) NYU Pr.

Prator, Clifford H., Jr. & Robinett, Betty W. Manual Amer Engl Pronnc PB 4/E. 4th ed. LC 84-25222. 244p. (C). 1985. pap. text 20.00 (*0-03-000703-8*, Pub. by Harcourt Coll Pubs) Harcourt.

***Pratorius, Nini.** Principles of Cognition, Language & Action: Essays on the Foundations for a Science of Psychology. LC 00-27387. 2000. write for info. (*0-7923-6230-6*, Kluwer Plenum) Kluwer Academic.

Prats, A. J. The Autonomous Image: Cinematic Narration & Humanism. LC 81-50182. 192p. (C). 1981. 23.00 (*0-8131-1406-3*) U Pr of Ky.

Prats, Brian, jt. auth. see Schoen, Andrew.

Prats, Michael. Thermal Recovery. 174p. 1982. 50.00 (*0-89520-314-6*, EORMONO007) Soc Petrol Engineers.

Pratsch. Pediatric Emergencies. 2nd ed. Eichelberger, Martin, ed. LC 97-6025. 272p. 1997. pap. text 51.00 (*0-8359-5123-5*) P-H.

Pratscher, Wilhelm & Sauer, Georg, eds. Die Kirche Als Historische und Eschatologische Grobe: Festschrift Fur Kurt Niederwimmer Zum 65. Geburtstag. (GER., Illus.). 355p. 1994. 55.95 (*3-631-46067-8*) P Lang Pubng.

Pratson, Frederick. A Guide to Atlantic Canada. LC 72-93258. (Illus.). (Orig.). 1973. pap. 6.95 (*0-85699-073-6*) Chatham Pr.

Pratt. Construction Estimating IG. 56p. 1995. teacher ed. 16.95 (*0-8273-6137-8*) Delmar.

— Digital Image Processing. 3rd ed. text. write for info. (*0-471-37407-5*) Wiley.

— Financial Accounting. 4th ed. (SWC-Accounting). 1999. pap., student ed. 19.50 (*0-324-01524-0*) Thomson Learn.

— Financial Accouting in an Economic Context. 4th ed. LC 99-14477. (SWC-Accounting). 1999. pap. 96.95 (*0-324-00337-4*) Thomson Learn.

— Grammar Step-by-Step, Vol. 1. 1985. pap., teacher ed. 15.66 (*0-8442-5491-6*); pap., student ed. 18.33 (*0-8442-5490-8*) NTC Contemp Pub Co.

— Grammar Step-by-Step, Vol. 2. pap., teacher ed. 15.33 (*0-8442-5494-0*); pap., student ed. 18.33 (*0-8442-5493-2*) NTC Contemp Pub Co.

Pratt. A Guide to SQL Using Oracle. 4th ed. (C). 1997. 36.95 (*0-7600-4923-8*) Thomson Learn.

Pratt. HIV & AIDS. 4th ed. LC 95-223579. write for info. (*0-340-59233-8*, Pub. by E A) Routldge.

— HIV & AIDS: A Strategy for Nursing Care. 3rd ed. 486p. 1992. pap. 35.25 (*1-56593-544-6*, 0516) Singular Publishing.

Pratt. HIV & AIDS: A Strategy for Nursing Care. 3rd ed. 1991. 28.25 (*0-340-54841-X*) Thomson Learn.

— Legal Writing: Systematic Approach. 3rd ed. LC 99-202123. (Paralegal Ser.). (C). 1999. pap. 18.75 (*0-314-22803-9*) West Pub.

Pratt. Long-Term Care: Managing Across the Continuum. LC 98-44807. 640p. 1999. pap. 55.00 (*0-8342-1032-0*, 10320) Aspen Pub.

***Pratt.** Organic Pages: Organic Trade Association's 1999 North American Resource Directory. 272p. 1999. pap. 34.95 (*1-881427-91-9*, Pub. by OTA Press) Chelsea Green Pub.

Pratt. Transcultural Children's Literature. LC 98-27483. 402p. 1999. pap. text 38.00 (*0-13-432816-7*) P-H.

— Valuing A Business. 4th ed. 950p. 2000. 95.00 (*0-07-135615-0*) McGraw.

Pratt & Adamski. The Concepts of Database Management 3rd Ed. 3rd ed. (MIS). (C). 2000. pap. text 36.95 (*0-619-00057-0*) Course Tech.

Pratt & DePace. Anatomy. (Rypins' Intensive Reviews Ser.). 1998. pap. text 19.95 (*0-397-51552-9*) Lppncott W & W.

Pratt & Gromer. Financial Accounting Simulation Analysis. 2nd ed. 1995. 31.50 (*0-538-84107-9*) Sth-Wstrn College.

***Pratt & Hirst.** Executive Financial Accounting & Analysis. 2001. pap. 40.00 (*0-324-02246-8*) Thomson Learn.

Pratt & Kulsrud, eds. Pratt & Kulsrud Tax Series: Corporate, Partnership, Estate & Gift Taxation - 2000 Edition. 1999. 78.95 (*0-87393-858-5*); pap., student ed. 24.95 (*0-87393-859-3*) Dame Pubns.

— Pratt & Kulsrud Tax Series: Federal Taxation. 1999. 80.95 (*0-87393-850-X*); pap., student ed. 24.95 (*0-87393-851-8*) Dame Pubns.

— Pratt & Kulsrud Tax Seriesd: Individual Taxation - 2000 Edition. 1999. 77.95 (*0-87393-854-2*); pap., student ed. 23.95 (*0-87393-855-0*) Dame Pubns.

Pratt, et al. Aural Awareness. 1990. 113.00 (*0-335-09418-X*) OpUniv Pr.

— Pratt & Kulsrud Tax Series: Corporate, Partnership, Estate & Gift Taxation - 1999 Edition. 1998. 78.95 (*0-87393-755-4*) Dame Pubns.

— Pratt & Kulsrud Tax Series: Corporate, Partnership, Estate & Gift Taxation - 1999 Edition (Study Guide) 1998. pap., student ed. 24.95 (*0-87393-771-6*) Dame Pubns.

— Pratt & Kulsrud Tax Series: Federal Taxation - 1999 Edition. 1998. 80.95 (*0-87393-753-8*) Dame Pubns.

— Pratt & Kulsrud Tax Series: Federal Taxation - 1999 Edition (Study Guide) 1998. pap., student ed. 24.95 (*0-87393-772-4*) Dame Pubns.

— Pratt & Kulsrud Tax Series: Individual Taxation - 1999 Edition. 1998. 77.95 (*0-87393-754-6*) Dame Pubns.

— Pratt & Kulsrud Tax Series: Individual Taxation - 1999 Edition (Study Guide) 1998. pap., student ed. 23.95 (*0-87393-770-8*) Dame Pubns.

Pratt, A. E. Tibet Through China. (C). 1987. 28.50 (*0-8364-2348-8*, Pub. by Mittal Pubs Dist) S Asia.

Pratt, A. W. Heat Transmission in Buildings. LC 80-42021. 320p. reprint ed. pap. 99.20 (*0-608-15823-2*, 203129400074) Bks Demand.

Pratt, Alan. Pardon My Backcast. LC 96-209893. (Illus.). 80p. 1996. pap. 6.95 (*1-57188-059-3*) F Amato Pubns.

Pratt, Alan, jt. ed. see Lavalette, Michael.

Pratt, Alan R. The Dark Side: Thoughts on the Futility of Life from Ancient Greeks to the Present. LC 93-45556. 1994. 10.95 (*0-8065-1481-7*) Carol Pub Group.

P

An Asterisk (*) at the beginning of an entry indicates that the title is appearing for the first time.

Pratt, Alan R., ed. Black Humor: Critical Essays. LC 92-7387. (Studies in Humor: Vol. 2). 408p. 1992. text 72.00 (*0-8153-0619-9*, H1503) Garland.

— The Critical Response to Andy Warhol, 25. LC 96-36509. (Critical Responses in Arts & Letters Ser.: Vol. 25). 344p. 1997. lib. bdg. 69.50 (*0-313-29291-4*, Greenwood Pr) Greenwood.

Pratt, Alice D. Homesteader's Portfolio. (Northwest Reprints Ser.). 256p. 1993. reprint ed. pap. 15.95 (*0-87071-517-8*); reprint ed. text 24.95 (*0-87071-516-X*) Oreg St U Pr.

Pratt, Alice E. Use of Color in the Verse of English Romantic Poets from Langland to Keats. (English Literature Ser.: No. 33). 1970. reprint ed. pap. 39.95 (*0-8383-0061-8*) M S G Haskell Hse.

Pratt, Alma K. From No History to Total Victory. 48p. 2000. 14.95 (*1-892668-13-0*) Prospect Pr.

Pratt, Amanda & Wood, Michele J. Art Therapy in Palliative Care: The Creative Response. LC 97-51524. (Illus.). 208p. (C). 1998. 80.00 (*0-415-16156-8*) Routledge.

— Art Therapy in Palliative Care: The Creative Response. LC 97-51524. (Illus.). 208p. (C). 1998. pap. 25.99 (*0-415-16157-6*) Routledge.

Pratt, Ambrose. The Living Mummy. LC 87-60464. (Illus.). 313p. 1988. reprint ed. pap. 15.95 (*0-915431-02-5*) N American Archives.

Pratt, Andrew. Uneven Reproduction: Industry, Space & Society. (Policy, Politics, & Administration Ser.). 270p. 1994. pap. text 32.95 (*0-08-040486-3*, Prgamon Press) Buttrwrth-Heinemann.

Pratt, Andy, jt. ed. see Ball, Rick.

Pratt, Ann B. The Emlen Physick House Museum. (Cape May Ser.). (Illus.). 60p. (Orig.). 1990. pap. 6.50 (*0-925436-07-0*) Cam-Tech Pub.

Pratt, Anne, tr. see Taupin, Rene.

Pratt, Anne H. Junior Missionary Handbook. 64p. (Orig.). (J). (gr. 3-6). 1987. pap. 6.98 (*0-88290-318-7*) Horizon Utah.

Pratt, Annis. Dancing with Goddesses: Archetypes, Poetry, & Empowerment. LC 93-28442. 432p. 1994. 39.95 (*0-253-34586-3*); pap. 18.95 (*0-253-20865-3*) Ind U Pr.

Pratt, Annis, et al. Archetypal Patterns in Women's Fiction. LC 81-47167. 221p. reprint ed. pap. 68.60 (*0-8357-5719-6*, 205671600081) Bks Demand.

Pratt, Annis, jt. ed. see Dembo, L. S.

Pratt, Antoinette M. The Attitude of the Catholic Church Toward Witchcraft & the Allied Practices of Sorcery & Magic. LC 79-8116. 144p. reprint ed. 32.50 (*0-404-18429-4*) AMS Pr.

Pratt, Arden L., jt. auth. see Gillie, Angelo C.

Pratt, Arthur. How to Help & Understand the Alcoholic or Drug Addict. LC 80-82964. 127p. 1981. pap. 4.95 (*0-915216-63-9*) Marathon Intl Bk.

Pratt, Authur. Christian Revolution: Practical Answers to Welfare & Addition. LC 97-70090. 144p. 1998. pap. 9.99 (*1-56384-143-6*) Huntington Hse.

Pratt, Barbara W., jt. auth. see Lacey, Ann H.

***Pratt, Bette.** Whitewater Shining Crown. LC 99-69460. 2000. 25.00 (*0-7388-1302-8*); pap. 18.00 (*0-7388-1303-6*) Xlibris Corp.

Pratt, Bob. UFO Danger Zone: Terror & Death in Brazil. LC 96-76549. (Illus.). 349p. (Orig.). 1996. pap. 16.95 (*1-881852-14-8*) Horus Hse Pr.

Pratt, Brian & Boyden, Jo. The Field Directors Handbook: An Oxfam Guide for Development Workers. 512p. (C). 1988. pap. text 150.00 (*0-85598-073-7*, Pub. by Oxfam Pubns) St Mut.

Pratt, Brian & Loizos, Peter. Choosing Research Methods: Data Collection for Development Workers. 128p. (C). 1992. pap. 14.95 (*0-85598-177-6*, Pub. by Oxfam Pub) Stylus Pub VA.

Pratt, C. E. Police Officers Guide to Community Based Policing. (Illus.). iv, 119p. 1995. pap. text 12.95 (*0-9658709-0-1*) Police Mgmt.

Pratt, Carl R. Ecology. LC 94-10645. (Applied Science Review Ser.). (Illus.). 176p. 1994. pap. 12.95 (*0-87434-689-4*) Springhouse Corp.

***Pratt, Carlos.** Psychiatric Rehabilitation. LC 98-89453. 350p. 1999. 59.95 (*0-12-564245-8*) Acad Pr.

***Pratt, Catherine.** Resisting Fiction: The Novels of Henry Handel Richardson. 205p. 1999. pap. 29.95 (*0-7022-3053-7*, Pub. by Univ Queensland Pr) Intl Spec Bk.

Pratt, Catherine, jt. ed. see Lever, Susan.

Pratt Center Staff. Cooking in the Litchfield Hills. 224p. 1994. 15.95 (*0-9639175-0-1*) Pratt Center.

Pratt, Charles W. Fables in Two Languages & Similar Diversions: Fables en Deux Langues et Divertissements de Ce Genre. LC 94-65599. (ENG & FRE., Illus.). 48p. (Orig.). 1994. pap. 13.95 (*0-9641028-0-3*) Pomme Pr.

— In the Orchard. LC 94-67304. (Illus.). 51p. 1994. reprint ed. pap. 12.95 (*0-9641028-1-1*) Pomme Pr.

Pratt, Charles W., jt. auth. see Pratt, Joan C.

Pratt, Chris, et al, eds. Research Issues in Child Development. 208p. (C). 1986. pap. text 29.95 (*0-86861-414-9*) Routledge.

Pratt, Chris, jt. auth. see Garton, Alison E.

Pratt, Christine, jt. auth. see Johnston, Robert.

Pratt, Constance & Monafo, Janet. The Best of Pastels. (Illus.). 144p. 1996. 24.99 (*1-56496-269-5*, Quarry Bks) Rockport Pubs.

***Pratt, Constance Flavell & Monafo, Jaent, selected by.** The Best of Pastels. 2000. pap. 15.00 (*1-56496-695-X*) Rockport Pubs.

Pratt, Cranford. The Critical Phase in Tanzania, 1945-1968: Nyerere & the Emergence of a Socialist Strategy. LC 75-22979. 327p. reprint ed. pap. 93.20 (*0-608-13050-8*, 2024516) Bks Demand.

Pratt, Cranford, ed. Canadian International Development Assistance Policies: An Appraisal, second edition. 392p. 1994. 65.00 (*0-7735-1180-6*, Pub. by McG-Queens Univ Pr) CUP Services.

— Canadian International Development Assistance Policies: An Appraisal, second edition. 2nd rev. ed. 408p. 1995. pap. 22.95 (*0-7735-1409-0*, Pub. by McG-Queens Univ Pr) CUP Services.

— Internationalism under Strain: The North-South Policies of Canada, the Netherlands, Norway, & Sweden. 1989. text 37.50 (*0-8020-2695-8*) U of Toronto Pr.

— Middle Power Internationalism: The North-South Dimension. 176p. (C). 1990. pap. 60.00 (*0-7735-0725-6*, Pub. by McG-Queens Univ Pr) CUP Services.

Pratt, Cranford & Mwansasu, Bismarck U., eds. Towards Socialism in Tanzania. LC 78-10350. 1979. pap. 11.95 (*0-8020-6433-7*) U of Toronto Pr.

Pratt, Cranford, jt. ed. see Matthews, Robert O.

Pratt, Cranford, jt. ed. see Mwansasu, Bismarck U.

Pratt, D. T., jt. ed. see Smoot, L. Douglas.

Pratt, Dallas. Animal Films for Humane Education. LC 86-70683. 284p. 1986. pap. 7.95 (*0-916858-07-3*) Argus Archives.

***Pratt, Dan, ed.** The Organic Pages: Organic Trade Association's 1999 North American Resource Directory. 322p. 1999. spiral bd. (*1-881427-90-0*) OTA Press.

Pratt, Daniel D., & Associates Staff. Five Perspectives on Teaching in Adult & Higher Education. LC 96-46411. (Illus.). 304p. (C). 1997. 34.50 (*0-89464-937-X*) Krieger.

Pratt, Daniel J. Beginning Postsecondary Students Longitudinal Study Second Follow-up BPS: 90/94) Final Technical Report. 422p. 1996. pap. 26.00 (*0-16-048649-1*) USGPO.

Pratt, Darnell D., jt. auth. see Pratt, L. H.

Pratt, David. Curriculum Planning: A Handbook for Professionals. 480p. (C). 1994. text 71.00 (*0-15-501098-0*, Pub. by Harcourt Coll Pubs) Harcourt.

— Fundamentals of Construction Estimating. LC 94-21788. 448p. 1995. mass mkt. 78.95 (*0-8273-6135-1*) Delmar.

— How to Find & Measure Bias in Textbooks. LC 76-168615. 64p. 1972. pap. 24.95 (*0-87778-031-5*) Educ Tech Pubns.

Pratt, David, jt. auth. see Gork, Mardi.

Pratt, David H. Researching British Probates, 1354-1858: A Guide to the Microfilm Collection of the Family History Library, Northern England, Province of York, Vol. 1. LC 92-18338. (Illus.). 219p. 1992. 45.00 (*0-8420-2420-4*) Scholarly Res Inc.

Pratt, David H. Researching British Probates, 1354-1858 Vol. 1: A Guide to the Microfilm Collection of the Family History Library: Northern England/Province of York. 219p. 45.00 (*0-8063-4925-5*, Pub. by Clearfield Co) ACCESS Pubs Network.

Pratt, David T., jt. auth. see Heiser, William H.

Pratt, Davis. Magic Animals of Japan. LC 67-17483. (Illus.). (J). (gr. 1-4). 1967. lib. bdg. 5.88 (*0-87466-020-3*) HM.

Pratt, Debora C. Celebrating Me & My World: A Unitarian Universalist Preschool Curriculum. Hoertdoerfer, Patricia, ed. 1995. pap. 30.00 (*1-55896-328-6*) Unitarian Univ.

Pratt, Derek. Discovering London's Canals. 1989. pap. 35.00 (*0-85263-901-5*, Pub. by Shire Pubns) St Mut.

Pratt-Dewey, Beth, jt. auth. see Adler, Bill, Jr.

Pratt, Diana V. Legal Writing: A Systematic Approach. 2nd ed. LC 93-9682. (American Casebook Ser.). 426p. 1993. pap. 20.50 (*0-314-01843-3*) West Pub.

— Legal Writing: A Systematic Approach, Teacher's Manual to Accompany. 2nd ed. (American Casebook Ser.). 138p. (C). 1993. pap. text 20.00 (*0-314-02394-1*) West Pub.

Pratt, Dianne. Hey Kids! You're Cookin' Now! A Global Awareness Cooking Adventure. Eldridge, Sherri, ed. LC 98-73980. (Illus.). 159p. (J). (gr. 2-6). 1998. 19.95 (*1-886862-07-9*) Harv Hill ME.

— Let's Stir It Up! Kids' Cookbook & Earth Friendly Fun. Eldridge, Sherri, ed. (Illus.). 40p. (J). (gr. k-8). 1998. pap. 4.95 (*1-886862-29-X*, MN KIDS) Harv Hill ME.

Pratt, Douglas R. Advanced Guide to Radio Control Sport Flying. (Illus.). 128p. 1988. pap. 9.95 (*0-8306-9360-2*, 3060P) McGraw-Hill Prof.

— The Beginner's Guide to Radio Control Sport Flying. (Illus.). 144p. 1988. pap. 9.95 (*0-8306-9320-3*, 3020P) McGraw-Hill Prof.

***Pratt, Douglas R.** Doug Pratt's DVD-Video Guide. 1999. pap. 19.95 (*0-9669744-4-1*) Harbor Electronic.

Pratt, Douglas R. The Laser Video Disc Companion: A Guide to the High End Delivery System for Home Video. 2nd ed. LC 91-67114. 472p. 1992. pap. 24.95 (*0-918432-89-8*) Baseline Bks.

— 1995 Laser Video Disc Companion. Royle, Lee & Hajduk, Peter, eds. 972p. (Orig.). 1995. pap. 39.95 (*0-918432-90-1*) Baseline Bks.

***Pratt, Douglas R. & Schaeffer, John.** Solar Living Sourcebook: Complete Guide to Renewable Energy Technologies & Sustainable Living. 10th rev. ed. (Illus.). 670p. 1999. pap. 30.00 (*0-916571-03-3*, Pub. by Real Goods Pub) Chelsea Green Pub.

Pratt, Douglas R. & Schaeffer, John. Solar Living Sourcebook: The Complete Guide to Renewable Energy Technologies & Sustainable Living. (Illus.). 690p. 1996. pap. 30.00 (*0-930031-82-2*) Chelsea Green Pub.

Pratt, E. J. Pursuits Amateur & Academic: The Selected Prose of E. J. Pratt. (Collected Works of E. J. Pratt). 373p. 1995. text 50.00 (*0-8020-2907-8*) U of Toronto Pr.

Pratt, Edward E. Industrial Causes of Congestion of Population in New York City. LC 68-56682. (Columbia University. Studies in the Social Sciences: No. 109). reprint ed. 37.50 (*0-404-51109-0*) AMS Pr.

— Japan's Protoindustrial Elite The Economic Foundations of the Gono. 1999. 39.50 (*0-674-47290-X*) HUP.

Pratt, Edwin A. A History of Inland Transport & Communication in England. LC 68-58857. xii, 532p. 1970. reprint ed. 49.50 (*0-678-05560-2*) Kelley.

Pratt, Edwin J. E. J. Pratt on His Life & Poetry. Gingell, Susan, ed. LC 83-208681. (Collected Works of E. J. Pratt). 268p. reprint ed. pap. 83.10 (*0-608-16851-3*, 205612900050) Bks Demand.

Pratt, Erik K. Selling Strategic Defense: Interests, Ideologies & the Arms Race. LC 89-24351. 180p. 1990. lib. bdg. 32.00 (*1-55587-190-9*) L Rienner.

Pratt, Erma E. Waiting for God: A Journal of Missionary Work Among the Totonac Indians. LC 98-92239. 110 p. 1998. 10.00 (*0-9668303-0-X*) E Pratt.

Pratt, Fevrel, jt. auth. see Sheets, Lucille.

Pratt, Fletcher. Battles That Changed History. 348p. Date not set. 25.95 (*0-8488-2573-X*) Amereon Ltd.

***Pratt, Fletcher.** The Battles That Changed History. LC 99-54547. 2000. pap. 9.95 (*0-486-41129-X*) Dover.

Pratt, Fletcher. Secret & Urgent: The Story of Codes & Ciphers. (Cryptographic Ser.: Vol. 72). (Illus.). 284p. 1996. reprint ed. pap. 28.80 (*0-89412-261-4*, C-72) Aegean Park Pr.

— A Short History of the Civil War: Ordeal by Fire. 1998. 23.50 (*0-8446-6953-9*) Peter Smith.

— A Short History of the Civil War: Ordeal by Fire. LC 97-4264. (Illus.). 448p. 1997. reprint ed. pap. text 9.95 (*0-486-29702-0*) Dover.

Pratt, Fletcher, jt. auth. see De Camp, L. Sprague.

Pratt, Fletcher, jt. auth. see Johnson, Thomas M.

Pratt, Frances H. La Belle Zoa: or The Insurrection of Haiti. LC 72-1820. (Black Heritage Library Collection). 1977. reprint ed. 15.95 (*0-8369-9049-8*) Ayer.

Pratt, Frank G., ed. see Forselles, Charles A.

Pratt, Frank G., ed. see Pratt, Verna E.

Pratt, Frank G., ed. & photos by see Pratt, Verna E.

Pratt, Frantz, compiled by. Haiti: Guide to the Periodical Literature in English, 1800-1990, 1. LC 91-7572. (Bibliographies & Indexes in Latin American & Caribbean Studies: No. 1). 328p. 1991. lib. bdg. 65.00 (*0-313-27855-5*, PHI, Greenwood Pr) Greenwood.

Pratt, G. Vascular Surgery: Guide & Handbook. LC 75-27628. (Illus.). 416p. 1976. 32.50 (*0-87527-138-3*) Green.

Pratt, Geoff, jt. auth. see Pratt, Jean.

Pratt, George. The Dynamics of Harmony: Principles & Practice. (Illus.). 160p. 1997. pap. text 26.00 (*0-19-879020-1*) OUP.

— Enemy Ace: War Idyll. Helfer, Andrew, ed. (Illus.). 128p. 1998. mass mkt. 14.95 (*0-930289-78-1*, Pub. by Warner Bks) Little.

— Enemy Ace: War Idyll. Helfer, Andrew, ed. (Illus.). 128p. 1992. reprint ed. mass mkt. 14.99 (*0-446-39365-7*, Pub. by Warner Bks) Little.

— No Man's Land. Baisden, Greg, ed. (Illus.). 112p. 1992. pap. 14.95 (*1-879450-64-X*) Kitchen Sink.

— Process Control: A Primer for the Non-Specialist & Newcomer. 2nd rev. ed. LC 98-18882. (Illus.). 200p. 1998. pap. 35.00 (*1-55617-633-3*, RA633-3) ISA.

Pratt, George, et al. Aural Awareness: Principles & Practice. 2nd ed. LC 97-50594. (Illus.). 164p. 1998. text 65.00 (*0-19-879022-8*) OUP.

— Aural Awareness: Principles & Practice. 2nd rev. ed. LC 97-50594. (Illus.). 164p. 1998. pap. text 24.95 (*0-19-879021-X*) OUP.

Pratt, George, jt. auth. see Lansdale, Joe R.

Pratt, George C., jt. auth. see Schwartz, Martin A.

Pratt, George J., et al. A Clinical Hypnosis Primer. LC 79-92665. (C). 1984. 36.00 (*0-930626-07-9*) Psych & Consul Assocs.

— Clinical Hypnosis Primer: Updated & Expanded. enl. rev. ed. LC 88-5566. 407p. 1988. 170.00 (*0-471-61384-3*) Wiley.

Pratt, George J., jt. auth. see Lambrou, Peter T.

Pratt, Geraldine, jt. auth. see Hanson, Susan.

Pratt, Geraldine, jt. ed. see Harris, Richard.

Pratt, H. Douglas. Enjoying Birds in Hawaii. 208p. 1993. pap. 18.95 (*0-935180-00-1*) Mutual Pub HI.

— Hawaii's Beautiful Birds. LC 96-76819. (Illus.). 64p. 1996. pap. 9.95 (*1-56647-120-6*) Mutual Pub HI.

— Hawai'i's Beautiful Birds. 64p. 1998. 12.95 (*1-56647-208-3*) Mutual Pub HI.

— A Pocket Guide to Hawaii's Birds. (Illus.). 112p. 1996. pap. 8.95 (*1-56647-145-1*) Mutual Pub HI.

— Pocket Guide to Hawaii's Trees & Shrubs. (Pocket Guides Ser.). (Illus.). 136p. 1999. pap. 8.95 (*1-56647-219-9*) Mutual Pub HI.

Pratt, H. Douglas, et al. A Field Guide to the Birds of Hawaii & the Tropical Pacific. (Illus.). 640p. 1987. pap. 39.50 (*0-691-02399-9*, Pub. by Princeton U Pr) Cal Prin Full Svc.

Pratt, Harold D., et al. A Field Guide to the Birds of Hawaii & the Tropical Pacific. LC 86-4993. (Illus.). 523p. 1987. reprint ed. pap. 162.20 (*0-608-04529-2*, 206527200001) Bks Demand.

Pratt, Harvey H. Early Planters of Scituate (MA) LC 98-164522. (Illus.). 386p. 1998. pap. 30.50 (*0-7884-0885-2*, P607) Heritage Bk.

Pratt, Helen G. China & Her Unfinished Revolution. LC 75-32327. (Studies in Chinese History & Civilization). 173p. 1977. reprint ed. lib. bdg. 59.95 (*0-313-26970-X*, U6970, Greenwood Pr) Greenwood.

— The Hawaiians: An Island People. (Illus.). 214p. (YA). (gr. 6 up). 1991. reprint ed. pap. 9.95 (*0-8048-1709-X*) Tuttle Pubng.

Pratt, Henry J. Gray Agendas: Interest Groups & Public Pensions in Canada, Britain, & the United States. 256p. (C). 1993. text 49.50 (*0-472-10430-6*, 10430) U of Mich Pr.

— The Gray Lobby. LC 75-43232. 262p. 1996. reprint ed. lib. bdg. 25.50 (*0-226-67917-9*, P876) U Ch Pr.

— The Liberalization of American Protestantism: A Case Study in Complex Organizations. LC 74-38837. 304p. reprint ed. pap. 94.30 (*0-7837-3618-5*, 204348400009) Bks Demand.

Pratt-Howe, Diana, jt. auth. see Garcia, Nicholas.

Pratt, Hugo. Corto Mattese: Banana Conga. Nantier, Terry, tr. from FRE. (Corto Maltese Ser.).Tr. of Sous Le Signe du Capricorne. 96p. 1986. pap. 8.95 (*0-918348-19-6*, Comics Lit) NBM.

— Corto Mattese: Fable of Venice. Bell, Elizabeth, tr. from FRE. (Corto Maltese Ser.: No. 8). 80p. 1990. pap. 10.95 (*0-918348-96-X*, Comics Lit) NBM.

— Corto Mattese: Voodoo for the President. Nantier, Terry, tr. from FRE. (Corto Maltese Ser.).Tr. of Toujours un Peu Plus Loin. 96p. 1986. pap. 8.95 (*0-918348-25-0*, Comics Lit) NBM.

***Pratt, Hugo.** El Gaucho. Leclerc, Jacinthe, tr. from FRE. (Illus.). 148p. 1999. pap. 20.95 (*1-56163-224-4*, Comics Lit) NBM.

Pratt, Hugo, jt. auth. see Manara, Milo.

Pratt, Ian. Artificial Intelligence. (Macmillan Computer Science Ser.). (Illus.). 280p. (C). 1994. pap. text 35.00 (*0-333-59755-9*) Scholium Intl.

Pratt Institute Art Therapy Staff & Robins, Auther. Pratt Creative Arts Therapy Review, Vol. 17. (Illus.). 100p. 1997. pap. 8.00 (*0-614-31246-9*) Pratt Inst.

Pratt, J. Christmas & Easter Ideas Book. 1990. pap. 21.00 (*0-7220-7714-9*) St Mut.

Pratt, J. & Gibbons, J. D. Concepts of Nonparametric Theory. (Series in Statistics). (Illus.). 462p. 1981. 66.00 (*0-387-90582-0*) Spr-Verlag.

Pratt, J., jt. ed. see Berry, C. L.

Pratt, J. G. On the Evaluation of Verbal Material in Parapsychology. LC 70-94866. (Parapsychological Monographs: No. 10). 1969. pap. 5.00 (*0-912328-14-2*) Parapsych Foun.

Pratt, J. H. Life on the Ridge. (Illus.). 170p. 1987. pap. 9.95 (*1-55787-021-7*, NY76064, Empire State Bks) Hrt of the Lakes.

Pratt, J. N. Electrotransport in Metals & Alloys. 1973. 36.00 (*0-87849-502-9*, Pub. by Trans T Pub) Enfield Pubs NH.

Pratt, J. R., jt. ed. see Cairns, John, Jr.

Pratt, James. Database Systems. (C). 1987. mass mkt. 40.00 (*0-87835-228-7*) Course Tech.

— Principles & Practice of Veterinary Technology. LC 97-14020. (Illus.). 730p. (gr. 13). 1997. text 56.00 (*0-8151-7308-3*, 27767) Mosby Inc.

— Programming in dBase 5.O DOS. (Computer Applications Ser.). 1996. pap. 40.95 (*0-7895-0075-2*) Course Tech.

— Review Questions & Answers for Veterinary Boards: Ancillary Topics. 2nd ed. LC 97-39805. 312p. (C). (gr. 13). 1997. pap. text 36.95 (*0-8151-7468-3*, 28276) Mosby Inc.

— Review Questions & Answers for Veterinary Boards: Basic Science. 2nd ed. LC 97-37952. 264p. (C). (gr. 13). 1997. pap. text 36.95 (*0-8151-7389-X*, 28272) Mosby Inc.

— Review Questions & Answers for Veterinary Boards: Clinical Sciences. 2nd ed. LC 97-37128. 312p. (C). (gr. 13). 1997. pap. text 36.95 (*0-8151-7462-4*, 28273) Mosby Inc.

— Review Questions & Answers for Veterinary Boards: Large Animal Medicine & Surgery, No. 2. 2nd ed. LC 97-39808. 288p. (C). (gr. 13). 1997. pap. text 36.95 (*0-8151-7466-7*, 28275) Mosby Inc.

— Review Questions & Answers for Veterinary Boards: Small Animal Medicine & Surgery, No. 2. 2nd ed. LC 97-34834. 288p. (C). (gr. 13). 1997. pap. text 36.95 (*0-8151-7465-9*, 28274) Mosby Inc.

— Safeguarding Liberty: The Constitution & Citizens Militias. 1995. pap. 14.00 (*1-880692-18-X*) Legacy Comms.

— Using dBase III Plus. 324p. 1991. 15.50 (*0-685-47883-1*) Course Tech.

Pratt, James & Last. MCDMU Paradox for Windows. (C). 1994. text. write for info. (*0-318-70354-8*, BF4012) S-W Pub.

— Using Paradox for Windows. (C). 1994. text. write for info. (*0-318-70355-6*, BF3962) S-W Pub.

Pratt, James & Leidig. Microcomputer Database Management Using Access. (C). 1994. text. write for info. (*0-318-70356-4*, BF3911) S-W Pub.

Pratt, James B. Adventures in Philosophy & Religion. LC 75-3323. reprint ed. 29.50 (*0-404-59319-4*) AMS Pr.

— India & Its Faiths: A Traveler's Record (1915) 496p. 1998. reprint ed. pap. 33.00 (*0-7661-0578-4*) Kessinger Pub.

— The Pilgrimage of Buddhism & a Buddhist Pilgrimage. LC 75-3325. (Philosophy America Ser.). reprint ed. 94.50 (*0-404-59320-8*) AMS Pr.

— Pilgrimage of Buddhism & a Buddhist Pilgrimage, 2 vols. (C). 1993. reprint ed. 60.00 (*81-85326-47-9*, Pub. by Vintage) S Asia.

— The Psychology of Religious Belief. LC 75-3326. (Philosophy America Ser.). reprint ed. 54.00 (*0-404-59321-6*) AMS Pr.

— What Is Pragmatism? LC 75-3327. reprint ed. 36.00 (*0-404-59322-4*) AMS Pr.

Pratt, James Michael. The Last Valentine. 1999. mass mkt. 6.99 (*0-312-96822-1*) St Martin.

— The Last Valentine. large type ed. LC 98-10748. 1998. 24.95 (*1-57490-133-8*, Beeler LP Bks) T T Beeler.

— The Last Valentine: For Fifty Years She Waited for Him to Return Until...the Last Valentine! 268p. 1996. pap. 13.95 (*0-9651163-1-X*) Harkness Pubng.

***Pratt, James Michael.** The Lighthouse Keeper. large type ed. LC 00-39867. 2000. write for info. (*1-56895-896-X*) Wheeler Pub.

— The Lighthouse Keeper. 2001. reprint ed. pap. 6.99 (*0-312-97469-8*) St Martin.

Pratt, James N. The Tea Lover's Companion: The Ultimate Connoisseur's Guide to Buying, Brewing, & Enjoying Tea. Rosen, Diana, ed. (Illus.). 176p. 1995. 15.95 (*1-55972-323-8*, Birch Ln Pr) Carol Pub Group.

— Tea Lover's Treasury. rev. ed. (One Hundred One Productions Ser.). 240p. 1989. reprint ed. pap. 12.95 (*1-56426-565-X*) Cole Group.

Pratt, James N. Reading Tea Leaves. LC 94-31884. 1995. 12.00 (*0-517-70034-4*) C Potter.

Pratt, James W., et al, eds. Corporate, Partnership, Estate & Gift Taxation, 1992. (C). 1991. text 61.95 (*0-256-10043-8*, Irwn McGrw-H) McGrw-H Hghr Educ.

Pratt, James W. & Dalton, Thomas M. Federal Taxation, 1997. 10th ed. 240p. (C). 1996. text 21.95 (*0-256-17253-6*, Irwn McGrw-H) McGrw-H Hghr Educ.

Pratt, James W. & Kulsrud, William N. Corporate, Partnership, Estate & Gift Taxation, 1993. 1120p. 1992. text 61.95 (*0-256-10842-0*, Irwn McGrw-H) McGrw-H Hghr Educ.

— Corporate, Partnership, Estate, & Gift Taxation-1997 Edition. 10th ed. 960p. (C). 1996. text 71.25 (*0-256-16436-3*, Irwn McGrw-H) McGrw-H Hghr Educ.

— CPS - Corporate Partnership Estate & Gift Taxation 1995 Edition Chapters 13-16. 8th ed. (C). 1995. text 17.95 (*0-256-20441-1*, Irwn McGrw-H) McGrw-H Hghr Educ.

— Federal Taxation, 1997 Edition. 10th ed. 1504p. (C). 1996. text 72.50 (*0-256-16434-7*, Irwn McGrw-H) McGrw-H Hghr Educ.

— Individual Taxation 1997 Edition. 10th ed. 1168p. (C). 1996. 69.95 (*0-256-16435-5*, Irwn McGrw-H) McGrw-H Hghr Educ.

Pratt, James W., et al. Individual Taxation, 1988. 213p. (C). 1987. 13.50 (*0-256-06469-5*, Irwn McGrw-H) McGrw-H Hghr Educ.

Pratt, Jamie. Financial Accounting. LC 89-29574. 1071p. reprint ed. pap. 200.00 (*0-7837-4741-1*, 204455000004) Bks Demand.

— Financial Accounting. 2nd ed. LC 93-13807. (C). 1993. mass mkt. 79.00 (*0-538-82894-3*, AO79BA) S-W Pub.

— Financial Accounting. 2nd ed. (AB - Accounting Principles Ser.). (C). 1994. mass mkt., student ed. 18.00 (*0-538-82895-1*) S-W Pub.

— Financial Accounting. 3rd ed. LC 96-20344. (AB - Accounting Principles Ser.). 1996. mass mkt. 71.95 (*0-538-85584-3*) S-W Pub.

— Financial Accounting. 3rd ed. (AB - Accounting Principles Ser.). 1996. mass mkt., student ed. 23.95 (*0-538-85585-1*) S-W Pub.

— Financial Accounting Simulation Analysis. 2nd ed. (AB - Accounting Principles Ser.). 1995. pap. 24.95 (*0-538-84101-X*) S-W Pub.

Pratt, Jamie & Ramesh. Interactive Cases in Financial Analysis. (AM - Financial Accounting Ser.). 1999. 3.5 hd 36.95 (*0-538-85980-6*) S-W Pub.

Pratt, Jane. Beyond Beauty. LC C P Pubs. 1997. pap. 30.00 (*0-517-80148-5*) C Potter.

Pratt, Jane & Pryor, Kelli. For Real: The Uncensored Truth about America's Teenagers. 336p. (J). 1995. pap. 9.70 (*0-7868-8064-3*, Pub. by Hyperion) Time Warner.

Pratt, Jean & Pratt, Geoff. Suffolk Rambles. 64p. 1987. 50.00 (*0-905392-85-X*) St Mut.

Pratt, Jeff. The Rationality of Rural Life: Economic & Cultural Change in Tuscany, Vol. 17. (Studies in Anthropology & History). 232p. 1995. text 53.00 (*3-7186-5627-2*, Harwood Acad Pubs) Gordon & Breach.

Pratt, Jennifer L., et al, eds. Let My People Know . . . And Go. LC 96-68906. (Illus.). 85p. (Orig.). 1996. pap. 4.00 (*0-9652533-0-9*) Presby Ctr Mission.

Pratt, Jeremy M. Cessna 150: A Pilot's Guide. LC 95-16303. (Pilot's Guide Ser.). 1995. pap. 14.95 (*1-56027-213-9*, ASA-PG-C-150) ASA Inc.

— Cessna 152: A Pilot's Guide. LC 95-16302. (Pilot's Guide Ser.). 1995. pap. 14.95 (*1-56027-212-0*, ASA-PG-C-152) ASA Inc.

— Cessna 172: A Pilot's Guide. LC 95-16301. (Pilot's Guide Ser.). 1995. pap. 14.95 (*1-56027-211-2*, ASA-C-172) ASA Inc.

— PA-38 Tomahawk: A Pilot's Guide. LC 95-15209. (Pilot's Guide Ser.). 1995. pap. 14.95 (*1-56027-216-3*, ASA-PG-PA-38) ASA Inc.

— PA-28 Cherokee: A Pilot's Guide. LC 95-15210. (Pilot's Guide Ser.). 1995. pap. 14.95 (*1-56027-215-5*, ASA-PG-PA-28C) ASA Inc.

— PA-28 Warrior: A Pilot's Guide. (Pilot's Guide Ser.). 1995. pap. 14.95 (*1-56027-214-7*, ASA-PG-PA-28W) ASA Inc.

Pratt, Jerome J. The Whooping Crane: North America's Symbol of Conservation. Stevens, Susan, ed. (Illus.). 171p. 1996. pap. 12.95 (*0-9640308-3-7*) Castle R Pubng.

Pratt, Joan C. & Pratt, Charles W. Food for Thought: Essays, Recipes, Poems from Apple Annie. (Illus.). 1999. pap. write for info. (*0-9641028-3-8*) Pomme Pr.

***Pratt, Joan C. & Pratt, Charles W.** Take the Apple: Essays - Poems - Recipes from Apple Annie. (Illus.). 72p. 1999. pap. 8.00 (*0-9641028-2-X*) Pomme Pr.

Pratt, Joanne & Jacobs, Karen. Work Practice: International Perspectives. LC 97-5624. 328p. 1997. pap. text 65.00 (*0-7506-2260-1*) Buttrwrth-Heinemann.

Pratt, Joanne & West, Gil. Pressure Garments: A Manual on Their Design & Fabrication. LC 94-33550. (Illus.). 160p. 1995. pap. text 50.00 (*0-7506-2064-1*) Buttrwrth-Heinemann.

Pratt, Joanne H., et al. Environmental Encounter: Experiences in Decision-Making for the Built & the Natural Environment. (Illus.). 1979. pap. 14.95 (*0-9601902-0-1*) Reverchon Pr.

Pratt, John. Governing the Dangerous: Dangerousness, Law & Social Change. LC 98-147882. 218p. 1997. 64.00 (*1-86287-268-6*, Pub. by Federation Pr); pap. 44.00 (*1-86287-269-4*, Pub. by Federation Pr) Gaunt.

— Governing the Dangerous: Dangerousness, Law & Social Change LC 98-147882. vi, 218p. 1997. write for info. (*1-86287-267-8*) Federation Pr.

Pratt, John, et al. Introduction to Statistical Decision Theory. (Illus.). 895p. 1995. 77.00 (*0-262-16144-3*) MIT Pr.

Pratt, John C. The Laotian Fragments. (Vietnam Ser.). 240p. 1985. pap. 3.50 (*0-380-69841-2*, Avon Bks) Morrow Avon.

— The Royal Laotian Air Force, 1954-1970. 184p. 1993. reprint ed. pap. 20.00 (*0-923135-50-2*) Dalley Bk Service.

Pratt, John C., ed. Vietnam Voices: Perspectives on the War Years, 1941-1982. 696p. 1998. reprint ed. pap. 24.95 (*0-8203-1969-4*) U of Ga Pr.

Pratt, John C., ed. see Greene, Graham.

Pratt, John C., ed. see Kesey, Ken.

***Pratt, John H.** Chaucer & War. LC 99-55807. 280p. 2000. 42.50 (*0-7618-1588-0*) U Pr of Amer.

Pratt, John T. War & Politics in China. LC 78-146869. (Select Bibliographies Reprint Ser.). 1977. reprint ed. 24.95 (*0-8369-5636-2*) Ayer.

Pratt, John W. & Zeckhauser, Richard J. Principals & Agents: The Structure of Business. 250p. 1991. pap. 16.95 (*0-87584-256-9*) Harvard Busn.

Pratt, John W., ed. see Satellite Symposium on Statistical Aspects of Poll.

Pratt-Johnson, Betty. 99 Dives from the San Juan Islands to Washington to the Gulf Islands & Vancouver Island in British Columbia. 320p. 1997. pap. 28.95 (*1-895811-18-X*) Heritage Hse.

— 101 Dives from the Mainland of Washington & B. C. LC 94-910292. (Illus.). 1997. pap. 24.95 (*1-895811-20-1*) Heritage Hse.

Pratt-Johnson, Betty. Whitewater Trips & Hot Springs in the Kootenays of British Columbia: For Kayakers, Canoeists & Rafters. LC 89-85596. (Illus.). 185p. 1989. pap. 19.95 (*0-921009-18-6*, Pub. by Adventure) Heritage Hse.

— Whitewater Trips for Kayakers, Canoeists & Rafters in British Columbia: Greater Vancouver Through Whistler, Okanagan & Thompson River Regions. (Illus.). 215p. (Orig.). 1986. pap. 16.95 (*0-931397-08-1*) Adventure WA.

— Whitewater Trips for Kayakers, Canoeists & Rafters on Vancouver Island. LC 83-26190. (Illus.). 127p. (Orig.). 1984. pap. 8.95 (*0-914718-90-8*) Adventure WA.

Pratt-Johnson, John A. & Tillson, Geraldine. Management of Strabismus & Amblyopia. LC 93-28854. 1993. 57.00 (*0-86577-499-4*) Thieme Med Pubs.

Pratt, Jon, jt. ed. see Davies, Norah.

Pratt, Joseph, jt. auth. see Galambos, Louis P.

Pratt, Joseph A. The Growth of a Refining Region. Porter, Glenn, ed. LC 77-7797. (Industrial Development & the Social Fabric Ser.: Vol. 4). 313p. 1980. 73.25 (*0-89232-090-7*) Jai Pr.

Pratt, Joseph A. & Castaneda, Christopher J. Builders: Herman & George R. Brown. LC 98-29635. (Kenneth E. Montague Series in Oil & Business History: No. 10). (Illus.). 352p. 1998. 36.95 (*0-89096-840-3*) Tex A&M Univ Pr.

Pratt, Joseph A., jt. auth. see Castaneda, Christopher J.

Pratt, Joseph A., jt. auth. see Lipartito, Kenneth J.

Pratt, Joseph D. Epidemics & Disease Outbreaks: Index of New Information for Reference & Research. (Illus.). 150p. 1997. 47.50 (*0-7883-1060-7*); pap. 44.50 (*0-7883-1061-5*) ABBE Pubs Assn.

Pratt, Josiah, ed. Thought of the Evangelical Leaders: John Newton, Thomas Scott, Charles Simeon, Etc. 1978. 29.99 (*0-85151-270-4*) Banner of Truth.

Pratt, Julie, ed. On the Outside: Extraordinary People in Search of Ordinary Lives. (Illus.). 97p. 1998. pap. 6.95 (*0-9662522-0-9*) WV Dev Disabilities.

Pratt, K. J. & Bennett, S. G. Elements of Personnel Management. (Illus.). 388p. (C). (gr. 13). 1996. mass mkt. 34.95 (*0-412-38380-2*, Chap & Hall NY) Chapman & Hall.

— Elements of Personnel Management. 2nd ed. 384p. 1990. pap. 32.50 (*0-412-02721-6*, A4468, Chap & Hall NY) Chapman & Hall.

Pratt, K. J. & Stenning, R. Managing Staff Appraisal in Schools: The Training Manual. (Illus.). 160p. (Orig.). 1989. pap. 84.95 (*0-412-43710-4*, Chap & Hall NY) Chapman & Hall.

Pratt, Karen, ed. Shifts & Transpositions in Medieval Narrative: A Festschrift for Dr. Elspeth Kennedy. (Illus.). 224p. (C). 1994. 75.00 (*0-85991-421-6*, DS Brewer) Boydell & Brewer.

Pratt, Keith. Korean Painting. (Images of Asia Ser.). (Illus.). 96p. (C). 1995. text 21.00 (*0-19-585885-9*) OUP.

Pratt, Keith, ed. Korea: A Cultural & Historical Dictionary. (Durham East Asia Ser.). 240p. (C). 1998. text 49.00 (*0-7007-0464-7*, Pub. by Curzon Pr Ltd); pap. text 24.95 (*0-7007-0463-9*, Pub. by Curzon Pr Ltd) UH Pr.

Pratt, Keith, jt. auth. see Palloff, Rena M.

Pratt, Kevin & Jefferson-Brown, Michael. The Gardener's Guide to Growing Fritillaries. LC 96-39383. (Gardener's Guide Ser.). (Illus.). 160p. 1997. 29.95 (*0-88192-387-7*) Timber.

Pratt, Kristin J. Bajo las Olas. Ada, Alma F., tr.Tr. of Swim Through the Sea. (SPA., Illus.). 44p. (YA). (ps up). 1995. pap. 7.95 (*1-883220-30-0*) Dawn CA.

— A Fly in the Sky. (Illus.). 40p. (J). (ps-5). 1996. 16.95 (*1-883220-40-8*); pap. 7.95 (*1-883220-39-4*) Dawn CA.

— Un Paseo por el Bosque Lluvioso (A Walk in the Rainforest) (ENG & SPA., Illus.). 36p. (YA). (ps up). 1993. pap. 7.95 (*1-883220-02-5*) Dawn CA.

— A Swim Through the Sea. (Illus.). 40p. (YA). (ps up). 1994. 16.95 (*1-883220-03-3*); pap. 7.95 (*1-883220-04-1*) Dawn CA.

— Walk in the Rainforest. (Illus.). 32p. (J). (ps-7). 1992. 16.95 (*1-878265-99-7*); pap. 7.95 (*1-878265-53-9*) Dawn CA.

— Walk in the Rainforest. (J). 1992. 13.15 (*0-606-05685-8*, Pub. by Turtleback) Demco.

Pratt, Kristin Joy. Bajo las Olas.Tr. of Swim Through the Sea. 1995. 13.15 (*0-606-08693-5*, Pub. by Turtleback) Demco.

— Fly in the Sky. 1996. 13.15 (*0-606-09288-9*, Pub. by Turtleback) Demco.

— Un Paseo por el Bosque Lluvioso.Tr. of A Walk in the Rainforest. (SPA.). 1993. 13.15 (*0-606-06835-X*) Turtleback.

Pratt, Kristin Joy. Swim Through the Sea. 1994. 13.15 (*0-606-06793-0*, Pub. by Turtleback) Demco.

Pratt, L. H. & Pratt, Darnell D. Alice Malsenior Walker: An Annotated Bibliography. 162p. 1988. lib. bdg. 55.00 (*0-313-27705-2*, PMW/, Greenwood Pr) Greenwood.

Pratt, L. J., ed. The Physical Oceanography of Sea Straits. (C). 1990. text 299.50 (*0-7923-0905-7*) Kluwer Academic.

Pratt, Lauren, ed. see Tenney, James.

Pratt, Laurence. Saga of a Paper Mill. LC 35-4692. 77p. reprint ed. pap. 30.00 (*0-608-18660-0*, 205205000030) Bks Demand.

***Pratt, Laurence R. & Hummer, Gerhard, eds.** Simulation & Theory of Electrostatic Interactions in Solution: Computational Chemistry, Biophysics & Aqueous Solutions. (AIP Conference Proceeding Ser.: Vol. 492). (Illus.). 521p. 1999. 140.00 (*1-56396-906-8*, Pub. by Am Inst Physics) Spr-Verlag.

Pratt, Lawrence S. Homeowner or Tenant? How to Make a Wise Choice. rev. ed. (Economic Education Bulletin Ser.: No. 9). (Illus.). 75p. 1997. pap. 6.00 (*0-913610-03-8*) Am Inst Econ Res.

— How to Invest Wisely: With "Toward an Optimal Stock Selection Strategy" rev. ed. (Economic Education Bulletin Ser.: Vol. 38, No. 5). (Illus.). 139p. 1998. pap. 9.00 (*0-913610-06-2*) Am Inst Econ Res.

Pratt, Lee. Directory of Health, Education & Research Journals. LC 83-49214. 144p. 1984. 29.50 (*0-8386-3213-0*) Fairleigh Dickinson.

Pratt, Lester A. Bank Frauds: Their Detection & Prevention. 2nd ed. LC 65-21814. 282p. reprint ed. pap. 87.50 (*0-8357-5960-1*, 205517800011) Bks Demand.

Pratt, Linda W., jt. auth. see Stone, Charles P.

Pratt, Lisa M., jt. ed. see Katz, Barry J.

Pratt, Lisa M., ed. see Society of Economic Paleontologists & Mineralogist.

Pratt, Lonni C. & Homan, Daniel. Here I Am, Lord: A Prayer Journal for Teens. LC 97-69272. 176p. (YA). (gr. 9-12). 1998. pap. 9.95 (*0-87973-929-0*) Our Sunday Visitor.

***Pratt, Lonni Collins & Homan, Daniel.** In Benedict's Way: An Ancient Monk's Insights for a Balanced Life. LC 99-46790. 240p. 2000. 15.95 (*0-8294-1376-6*) Loyola Pr.

Pratt, Lonnie C., ed. The Lent Book. LC 98-50326. (ML Book Ser.). (Illus.). 176p. 1999. pap. 29.95 (*0-89390-446-5*) Resource Pubns.

Pratt, Lorien, jt. ed. see Thrun, Sebastian.

Pratt, Loring W., et al. A Century of Excellence: A 100th Anniversary History of the American Academy of Otolaryngology-Head Neck Surgery & Its Predecessor Organizations. Hill, T. Susan, ed. (Illus.). 546p. (Orig.). 1996. 50.00 (*1-56772-051-X*); pap. 40.00 (*1-56772-052-8*) AAO-HNS.

Pratt, Louis. Sing Praises to His Name. Sherer, Michael L., ed. (Orig.). 1986. pap. 7.25 (*0-89536-831-5*, 6845) CSS OH.

Pratt, Louis H., jt. ed. see Standley, Fred L.

Pratt, Louise. Lying & Poetry from Homer to Pindar: Falsehood & Deception in Archaic Poetics. LC 92-45214. (Monographs in Classical Antiquity). 270p. 1993. text 44.50 (*0-472-10417-9*, 10417) U of Mich Pr.

***Pratt, Lucy & Wooley, Lindy.** Shoes. (Fashion Accessory Ser.). (Illus.). 127p. 1999. 19.95 (*1-85177-285-5*, Pub. by V&A Ent) Antique Collect.

Pratt, Lyn. The Bullmastiff Today. 176p. 1996. 27.95 (*0-87605-064-X*) Howell Bks.

Pratt, M. J., jt. auth. see Faux, I. D.

Pratt, Malcolm, ed. Remedial Processes for Contaminated Land. 148p. 1993. pap. 30.00 (*0-85295-310-0*, 9CH88) Gulf Pub.

Pratt, Mara L. American History Stories: You Never Read in School, but Should Have. 150p. 1993. pap. text 7.95 (*0-9640546-0-4*) Randall UT.

***Pratt, Mara L.** American History Stories You Never Read in School but Should Have: The Dream. (Illus.). 158p. 2000. pap. text 8.95 (*0-9640546-1-2*) Randall UT.

Pratt, Marjorie & Meighen, Mary. Story Carnival. 10.00 (*0-614-30541-1*) NAVH.

— Story Train. 10.00 (*0-614-30543-8*) NAVH.

Pratt, Marlene, ed. see Hess, Shelley.

***Pratt, Martin & Brown, Janet Allison.** Borderlands under Stress. 480p. 2000. 159.00 (*90-411-9790-7*) Kluwer Law Intl.

Pratt, Mary. NYC A-Z, Vol. II. Poynton, Jerome, ed. LC 98-183313. (Illus.). 100p. 1998. spiral bd. 16.95 (*0-9663561-0-1*) M Pratt.

— NYC A-Z, Vol. 3. (Illus.). 140p. 1999. write for info. (*0-9663561-1-X*) M Pratt.

Pratt, Mary L. Imperial Eyes: Studies in Travel Writing & Transculturization. LC 91-21435. (Illus.). 304p. (gr. 13). 1992. pap. 24.99 (*0-415-06095-8*, A3115) Routledge.

— Toward a Speech Act Theory of Literary Discourse. LC 76-26424. 255p. reprint ed. pap. 79.10 (*0-608-18850-6*, 205673200081) Bks Demand.

Pratt, Mary L., jt. auth. see Millones, Luis.

Pratt, Mary L., jt. auth. see Traugott, Elizabeth C.

Pratt, Michael. Great Country Houses of Central Europe: Czechoslovakia, Hungary & Poland. (Illus.). 380p. 1991. 95.00 (*0-89659-942-6*) Abbeville Pr.

Pratt, Michael C. Meditations for Mother. rev. ed. Mouton, Boyce, ed. 50p. 1975. pap. 1.99 (*0-89900-651-5*) College Pr Pub.

Pratt, Michael W. & Norris, Joan E. The Social Psychology of Aging: A Cognitive Perspective. LC 94-4312. (Understanding Aging Ser.). (Illus.). 272p. 1994. pap. 27.95 (*1-55786-492-6*) Blackwell Pubs.

Pratt, Minnie B. Crime Against Nature. LC 90-2778. 128p. 1990. 18.95 (*0-932379-73-7*) Firebrand Bks.

— Rebellion: Essays 1980-1991. LC 91-35238. 248p. (Orig.). 1991. pap. 12.95 (*1-56341-006-0*); lib. bdg. 26.95 (*1-56341-007-9*) Firebrand Bks.

— S/He. LC 95-3894. 192p. 1995. pap. 11.95 (*1-56341-059-1*); lib. bdg. 24.95 (*1-56341-060-5*) Firebrand Bks.

— Walking Back up Depot Street. LC 99-6047. (Pitt Poetry Ser.). 88p. 1999. pap. 12.95 (*0-8229-5695-0*); text 25.00 (*0-8229-4096-5*) U of Pittsburgh Pr.

— We Say We Love Each Other. LC 92-24947. 112p. (Orig.). 1992. pap. 8.95 (*1-56341-023-0*); lib. bdg. 18.95 (*1-56341-024-9*) Firebrand Bks.

Pratt, Neal E. Clinical Musculoskeletal Anatomy. (Illus.). 333p. 1991. text 48.00 (*0-397-54825-7*, Lippncott) Lppncott W & W.

Pratt, Ned, jt. auth. see Shaver, Elizabeth D.

Pratt, Norma F. Morris Hillquit: A Political History of an American Jewish Socialist, 20. LC 78-55349. (Illus.). 272p. 1979. 59.95 (*0-313-20526-4*, PMH/, Greenwood Pr) Greenwood.

Pratt, Norman T. Seneca's Drama. LC 82-23791. viii, 230p. 1983. 39.95 (*0-8078-1555-1*) U of NC Pr.

Pratt, Orson. The Essential Orson Pratt. LC 89-27567. (Classics in Mormon Thought: No. 2). 440p. 1991. 22.95 (*0-941214-95-8*) Signature Bks.

— The Seer. 320p. (C). 1994. 24.95 (*0-910523-18-5*) Grandin Bk Co.

Pratt, Orson, ed. see Smith, Joseph.

Pratt, Oswald T., jt. auth. see Dikkers, Scott.

Pratt, P. Poly Experiment. LC 96-38318. 1997. 134.00 (*0-335-19564-4*) OpUniv Pr.

Pratt, P. W., ed. Medical, Surgical & Anesthetic Nursing for Veterinary Technicians. 2nd ed. LC 94-70822. 621p. 1994. 32.00 (*0-939674-49-1*) Am Vet Pubns.

Pratt, Parley P. Autobiography of Parley P. Pratt. LC 85-10264. (Illus.). 447p. 1994. pap. 14.95 (*0-87579-841-1*) Deseret Bk.

— The Essential Parley P. Pratt. LC 89-27568. (Classics in Mormon Thought Ser.: No. 1). 268p. 1990. 17.95 (*0-941214-84-2*) Signature Bks.

— Key to the Science of Theology. 200p. 1998. reprint ed. pap. 17.95 (*0-7661-0456-7*) Kessinger Pub.

Pratt, Paul W. Laboratory Procedures for Veterinary Technicians. 3rd ed. LC 96-43451. (Illus.). 672p. (C). (gr. 13). 1996. pap. text 35.00 (*0-8151-7326-1*, 27768) Mosby Inc.

***Pratt, Paul W.** Principles & Practice of Veterinary Technology. (Illus.). 1998. teacher ed. write for info. (*0-323-00051-7*) Mosby Inc.

— Review Questions & Answers for Veterinary Boards: Series. 2nd ed. 1998. write for info. (*0-323-00145-9*) Mosby Inc.

Pratt, Paula B. The End of Apartheid in South Africa. LC 94-37202. (Overview Ser.). (Illus.). (YA). (gr. 6-9). 1995. lib. bdg. 22.45 (*1-56006-170-7*) Lucent Bks.

— Ernest Hemingway. LC 98-37073. (Importance of Ser.). (Illus.). (YA). (gr. 4-12). 1998. lib. bdg. 23.70 (*1-56006-358-0*) Lucent Bks.

— Jane Goodall. (Importance of Ser.). (Illus.). (J). (gr. 4-12). 1996. lib. bdg. 22.45 (*1-56006-082-4*) Lucent Bks.

— Maps: Plotting Places on the Globe. (Encyclopedia of Discovery & Invention Ser.). (Illus.). 96p. (J). (gr. 5-9). 1995. lib. bdg. 23.70 (*1-56006-255-X*, 255X) Lucent Bks.

— Martha Graham. LC 94-10883. (Importance of...Biographies Ser.). (Illus.). 112p. (J). (gr. 5-8). 1995. lib. bdg. 22.45 (*1-56006-056-5*) Lucent Bks.

Pratt, Peter, ed. History of Japan: Compiled from the Records of the English East India Company at the Instance of the Court of Directors, 2 vols., I. LC 79-65369. (Studies in Japanese History & Civilization). 488p. 1979. reprint ed. lib. bdg. 89.50 (*0-313-26914-9*, U6914) Greenwood.

— History of Japan: Compiled from the Records of the English East India Company at the Instance of the Court of Directors, 2 vols., Vol. 2. LC 79-65369. (Studies in Japanese History & Civilization). 339p. 1979. reprint ed. lib. bdg. 72.50 (*0-313-26915-7*, U6915) Greenwood.

Pratt, Peter P. Archaeology of the Oneida Iroquois. (Occasional Publications in Northeastern Anthropology: No. 1). 1976. 5.50 (*0-686-30586-8*) Fund Anthrop.

— Archaeology of the Oneida Iroquois, Vol. 1. (Occasional Publications in Northeastern Anthropology: No. 1). (Illus.). xii, 303p. 5.50 (*0-318-22319-8*) F Pierce College.

Pratt, Phil. A Guide to SQL. (C). 1989. pap. text. write for info. (*0-318-65187-4*, BF3364) S-W Pub.

Pratt, Phil & Adamski, Joseph. Database Systems: Management & Design. 2nd ed. 848p. (C). 1991. mass mkt. 39.00 (*0-87835-579-0*) Course Tech.

Pratt, Philip. The Concepts of Database Management. LC 94-10049. (C). 1994. pap. 40.95 (*0-87709-779-8*) Course Tech.

Pratt, Philip & Timmer, Marybeth. His Grandfather's Cap. LC 94-24032. (Illus.). 80p. (Orig.). (J). (gr. 4-6). 1995. pap. 6.95 (*0-942963-62-8*) Distinctive Pub.

Pratt, Philip J. Microcomputer Database Management Using dBASE IV, Version 2.0. LC 94-1014. 1994. write for info. (*0-87709-513-2*) Course Tech.

An Asterisk (*) at the beginning of an entry indicates that the title is appearing for the first time.

— Microcomputer Database Management Using dBASE IV, Version 2.0. LC 94-1014. 539p. (C). 1994. pap. 44.95 (*0-87709-539-6*) Course Tech.

— Using dBase IV, Version 2.0. 480p. (C). 1994. pap. 24.95 (*0-87709-540-X*) Course Tech.

Pratt, Philip J. & Adamski, Joseph. Concepts of Database Management. 2nd ed. 248p. (C). 1997. 49.95 (*0-7600-4926-2*) Course Tech.

Pratt, Philip J. & Adamski, Joseph J. Database Systems Management & Design. 3rd ed. (C). 1994. mass mkt., teacher ed. 49.95 (*0-87709-116-1*) Course Tech.

Pratt, Philip J. & Last, Mary Z. Microcomputer Database Management Using Paradox for Windows. 1994. write for info. (*0-318-72549-5*) Course Tech.

Pratt, Philip J. & Leidig, Paul M. Microcomputer Database Management Using Microsoft Access, Version 2, Incl. instr. manual. (Illus.). 480p. (C). 1994. pap. 33.00 incl. 3.5 ld (*0-87709-560-4*) Course Tech.

Pratt, Pierre. Follow that Hat! (Illus.). 32p. (J). (ps-2). 1992. pap. 5.95 (*1-55037-259-9*, Pub. by Annick); lib. bdg. 16.95 (*1-55037-261-0*, Pub. by Annick) Firefly Bks Ltd.

— Hippo Beach. (Illus.). 42p. (J). (ps-2). 1997. bds. 12.95 (*1-55037-419-2*, Pub. by Annick) Firefly Bks Ltd.

— Leon sans Son Chapeau - Follow That Hat! (Picture Bks.). (FRE., Illus.). 32p. (J). (ps-2). 1992. lib. bdg. 16.95 (*1-55037-263-7*, Pub. by Annick) Firefly Bks Ltd.

— Leon sans Son Chapeau - Follow That Hat! (FRE., Illus.). 32p. (J). (ps-2). 1996. pap. 6.95 (*1-55037-262-9*, Pub. by Annick) Firefly Bks Ltd.

Pratt, Pierre, jt. auth. see Roche, Hannah.

Pratt, R. 1st & 2nd Chronicles. 1996. pap. 11.99 (*1-85792-151-8*, Pub. by Christian Focus) Spring Arbor Dist.

Pratt, R., jt. ed. see Gray, G.

***Pratt, R. W., ed.** Flight Control Systems: Practical Issues in Design & Implementation. (IEE Control Engineering Ser.: No. 57). 400p. 1999. boxed set 95.00 (*0-85296-766-7*) INSPEC Inc.

Pratt, Ray. Rhythm & Resistance: Explorations in the Political Uses of Popular Music. LC 89-16197. (Media & Society Ser.). 256p. 1990. 59.95 (*0-275-92624-9*, C2624, Praeger Pubs) Greenwood.

— Rhythm & Resistance: Political Uses of American Popular Music. LC 93-30228. 256p. 1994. pap. text 16.95 (*1-56098-351-5*) Smithsonian.

Pratt, Rebecca, ed. see Bae, Yupin, et al.

Pratt, Renate. In Good Faith: Canadian Churches Against Apartheid. LC 97-200311. (Comparative Ethics Ser.: Vol. 4). 400p. 1996. pap. 29.95 (*0-88920-280-X*) W Laurier U Pr.

Pratt, Richard. El Ingles de Los Negocios. Anton, Francisco J., tr. from FRE. (Illus.). 427p. 1984. 24.95 (*2-7005-011-X*, Pub. by Assimil) Distribks Inc.

— Ingles de Los Negocios, Incl. 3 60-min. cassettes. Anton, Francisco J., tr. from FRE. 1984. 75.00 incl. audio (*2-7005-1307-X*, Pub. by Assimil) Distribks Inc.

Pratt, Richard, jt. ed. see Smith, Zachary A.

Pratt, Richard C. & Smith, Zachary. Hawai'i Politics & Government: An American State & a Pacific Society. (Politics & Governments of the American States Ser.). 384p. 2000. pap. text 27.50 (*0-8032-8750-X*, Bison Books) U of Nebr Pr.

— Hawaii Politics & Government: An American State & a Pacific Society. LC 99-33799. (Politics & Governments of the American States Ser.). 384p. 2000. text 57.50 (*0-8032-3724-3*, Bison Books) U of Nebr Pr.

Pratt, Richard H. Battlefield & Classroom: Four Decades with the American Indian, 1867-1904. Utley, Robert Marshall, ed. LC 64-20931. (Yale Western Americana Ser.: Vol. 6). 412p. 1964. reprint ed. pap. 127.80 (*0-8357-5997-0*, 205168100001) Bks Demand.

— Battlefield & Classroom: Four Decades with the American Indian, 1867-1904. Utley, Robert Marshall, ed. LC 86-25019. 409p. 1987. reprint ed. pap. 126.80 (*0-608-00487-1*, 206130600007) Bks Demand.

***Pratt, Richard L., Jr.** Designed for Dignity: What God Has Made It Possible For You to Be. 2nd ed. 232p. 2000. pap. 10.99 (*0-87552-508-3*) P & R Pubng.

Pratt, Richard L., Jr. Every Thought Captive: A Study Manual for the Defense of Christian Truth. 1979. pap. 7.99 (*0-87552-352-8*) P & R Pubng.

— He Gave Us Stories: The Bible Student's Guide to Interpreting Old Testament Narratives. 494p. 1993. reprint ed. pap. 14.99 (*0-87552-379-X*) P & R Pubng.

***Pratt, Richard L., Jr.** 1 & 2 Corinthians. (Holman New Testament Commentary Ser.: Vol. 7). 2000. 16.99 (*0-8054-0206-3*) Broadman.

— Ora Con los Ojos Abiertos. (SPA.). 200p. pap. 10.95 (*1-55883-111-8*, 6784-1602) Libros Desafio.

Pratt, Richard L., Jr. Pray with Your Eyes Open. rev. ed. (Devotional Ser.). 224p. 1998. pap. 7.95 (*1-885216-21-1*) Evan Formosan.

— Pray with Your Eyes Open: Looking at God, Ourselves & Our Prayers. LC 87-2762. 1987. pap. 8.99 (*0-87552-378-1*) P & R Pubng.

Pratt, Richard T., et al. Thrifts Going Public. LC 83-236936. (Illus.). iv, 527p. 35.00 (*0-685-08542-2*) Harcourt.

Pratt, Robert A. The Color of Their Skin: A History of School Desegregation in Richmond, Virginia, 1954-89. (Carter G. Woodson Institute Series in Black Studies). (C). 1992. text 29.50 (*0-8139-1372-1*) U Pr of Va.

— The Color of Their Skin: Education & Race in Richmond, Virginia, 1954-89. 151p. (C). 1994. pap. text 12.50 (*0-8139-1481-7*) U Pr of Va.

Pratt, Robert J. HIV & AIDS: A Strategy for Nursing Care. 4th ed. 320p. 1995. pap. text 44.95 (*1-56593-398-2*, 0820) Singular Publishing.

Pratt, Robin. Strategic Marketing Management. 509p. 1996. pap. 120.00 (*0-85297-413-2*, Pub. by Chartered Bank) St Mut.

Pratt, Roger. The Architecture of Sir Roger Pratt. Gunther, R. T., ed. LC 72-177516. (Illus.). 324p. 1979. reprint ed. 23.95 (*0-405-08862-0*, Pub. by Blom Pubns) Ayer.

Pratt, Roger C. Unbeatable Advantages. 147p. 1998. pap. 19.95 (*0-9666815-0-9*) R Pratt.

Pratt, Rosalie, jt. auth. see Peterson, Meg.

Pratt, Rosalie, jt. ed. see Gray, Genevieve.

Pratt, Rosalie R., ed. Fourth International Symposium on Justice in Rehabilitation & Human Well-Being. (Illus.). 214p. (Orig.). 1987. pap. text 25.50 (*0-8191-5970-0*) U Pr of Amer.

— Fourth International Symposium on Justice in Rehabilitation & Human Well-Being. (Illus.). 214p. (Orig.). 1987. lib. bdg. 47.50 (*0-8191-5969-7*) U Pr of Amer.

— Music Therapy & Music Education of the Handicapped - Developments & Limitations in Practice & Research: Proceedings of the Fifth International Congress, Leeuwenhorst Congress Center, Noordwijkerhout, The Netherlands, August 23-27, 1989. LC 92-12557. 190p. 1993. 14.95 (*0-918812-73-9*) MMB Music.

Pratt, Rosalie R., pref. Music Therapy & Music in Special Education Vol. 2: The International State of the Art. (ISME Edition Ser.: No. 4). 176p. 1989. pap. 11.95 (*0-918812-62-3*, ST 191) MMB Music.

Pratt, Rosalie R. & Moog, Helmut, eds. First Research Seminar of the ISME Commission on Music Therapy & Music in Special Education. (Illus.). 172p. 1989. pap. 11.95 (*0-918812-60-7*, ST 192) MMB Music.

Pratt, S. Otis. A Perspective on Corporate America: Politics, Pitfalls & Downfalls: The Source of Human Suffering & Business Failure. Easland, Mark & Woods, Kay, eds. 166p. (Orig.). 1997. pap. 14.95 (*0-9651480-0-9*) S O Pratt Stat.

Pratt, Sally R., jt. auth. see Dressel, Paul L.

***Pratt, Sarah.** Nikolai Zabolotsky: Enigma & Cultural Paradigm. 368p. 1999. 69.95 (*0-8101-1421-6*) Northwestern U Pr.

Pratt, Sereno S. The Work of Wall Street: An Account of the Functions, Methods & History of the New York Money & Stock Markets. (Third Edition, Revised & Enlarged) LC 75-2661. (Wall Street & the Security Market Ser.). 1975. reprint ed. 41.95 (*0-405-06985-5*) Ayer.

***Pratt, Shannon P.** Business Valuation: Exam Review & Professional Reference. LC 98-26014. 336p. 1998. pap. 95.00 (*0-471-25451-7*) Wiley.

Pratt, Shannon P. Cost of Capital: Estimation & Applications. LC 97-48814. 256p. 1998. 75.00 (*0-471-19751-3*) Wiley.

***Pratt, Shannon P.** Judges & Lawyers Business Valuation Handbook. LC 00-33143. 2000. write for info. (*1-57073-829-7*) Amer Bar Assn.

— The Market Approach to Valuing Companies. 250p. 2000. 85.00 (*0-471-35928-9*) Wiley.

Pratt, Shannon P. Valuing a Property Management Company. 69p. 1988. pap. 35.00 (*0-944298-20-6*, 826) Inst Real Estate.

— Valuing Small Businesses & Professional Practices. 2nd rev. ed. LC 97-46846. 720p. 1993. text 92.50 (*1-55623-551-8*, Irwn Prfssnl) McGraw-Hill Prof.

Pratt, Shannon P., et al. Valuing a Business: The Analysis & Appraisal of Closely Held Companies. 3rd ed. 785p. 1995. text 95.00 (*1-55623-971-8*, Irwn Prfssnl) McGraw-Hill Prof.

— Valuing Small Businesses & Professional Practices. 3rd ed. LC 97-26761. (Art of M & A Ser.). 750p. 1998. 95.00 (*0-7863-1186-X*, Irwn Prfssnl) McGraw-Hill Prof.

Pratt, Sherman. Arlington County Virginia: A Modern History. LC 97-77077. ix, 513p. 1997. 24.95 (*0-9661795-0-1*, 02337106/019/57) Pratt Pursuits.

Pratt, Shirley. Don't Wait to Be Rescued: Transcending the Death Experience. LC 91-90036. 179p. (Orig.). 1991. pap. 8.50 (*0-9628951-0-5*) S Pratt.

***Pratt, Stanley E.** Pratt's Guide to Venture Capital Sources 1999. 23rd ed. 1999. 385.00 (*0-914470-97-3*) Venture Econ.

Pratt, T. K. Dictionary of Prince Edward Island English. 224p. (C). 1988. 30.00 (*0-8020-5781-0*) U of Toronto Pr.

— Dictionary of Prince Edward Island English. 224p. 1997. reprint ed. pap. 19.95 (*0-8020-7904-0*) U of Toronto Pr.

— Prince Edward Island Sayings. LC 98-209478. (Illus.). 152p. 1998. text 29.95 (*0-8020-0920-4*) U of Toronto Pr.

Pratt, Terrence W. & Zelkowitz, Marvin V. Programming Languages: Design & Implementation. 3rd ed. 654p. 1995. 74.00 (*0-13-678012-1*) P-H.

***Pratt, Terry & Zelkowitz, Marvin V.** Programming Languages: Design & Implementation. 4th ed. 660p. 2000. 74.00 (*0-13-027678-2*, Prentice Hall) P-H.

Pratt, Thedore. The Barefoot Mailman. 220p. 1993. pap. 8.95 (*0-912451-32-7*) Florida Classics.

— Big Bubble. 220p. 2000. pap. 8.95 (*0-912451-34-3*) Florida Classics.

Pratt, Theodore. The Barefoot Mailman. large type ed. 1970. 27.99 (*0-85456-010-6*) Ulverscroft.

— Flame Tree. 250p. 1994. pap. 8.95 (*0-912451-33-5*) Florida Classics.

Pratt, Thomas H. Electrostatic Ignitions of Fires & Explosions. LC 97-93919. (Illus.). 182p. 1997. text 75.00 (*0-9659092-0-4*) Burgoyne.

Pratt, Timothy. Satellite Communications: Self Study Course. (Illus.). 1989. teacher ed., student ed. 299.00 (*0-87942-459-1*, HL0410-1) Inst Electrical.

Pratt, Timothy & Postian, Charles W. Satellite Communications. 496p. 1986. text 112.95 (*0-471-87837-5*) Wiley.

Pratt, Verna E. Alaska's Wild Berries: And Berry-Like Fruit. Pratt, Frank G., ed. (Illus.). 128p. (Orig.). 1995. pap. 9.95 (*0-9623192-4-4*) Alaskakrafts Pub.

— Field Guide to Alaskan Wildflowers: Commonly Seen along Highways & Byways. Pratt, Frank G., ed. LC 89-84536. (Illus.). 144p. (Orig.). 1990. pap. 13.95 (*0-9623192-0-1*) Alaskakrafts Pub.

— Linnaea's World. Pratt, Frank G., ed. & photos by by. LC 96-83135. (Illus.). 50p. (Orig.). (J). (gr. 3-6). 1996. 19.95 (*0-9623192-6-0*); pap. 11.95 (*0-9623192-5-2*) Alaskakrafts Pub.

— Wildflowers along the Alaska Highway: From Dawson Creek, BC - to Delta Jct., AK & on to Fairbanks, AK. Pratt, Frank G., ed. LC 91-77654. (Illus.). 224p. (Orig.). 1991. pap. 19.95 (*0-9623192-1-X*) Alaskakrafts Pub.

— Wildflowers of Denali National Park. Pratt, Frank G., ed. LC 92-75672. (Illus.). 176p. (Orig.). 1993. pap. 16.95 (*0-9623192-2-8*) Alaskakrafts Pub.

***Pratt, Vernon, et al.** Environment & Philosophy. LC 99-27647. 160p. (C). 1999. pap. 20.99 (*0-415-14511-2*); text. write for info. (*0-415-14510-4*) Routledge.

Pratt, Virginia A. Coming Alive: How Mates Help Each Other Solve Problems & Find Freedom & Intimacy. LC 88-83618. 171p. (Orig.). 1989. pap. 9.50 (*0-9622749-3-3*) Green Twig Pr.

— Coming Alive: How Mates Help Each Other Solve Problems & Find Freedom & Intimacy. Best, Walter, ed. 171p. (Orig.). 1989. pap. text. write for info. (*0-9622749-0-9*) Green Twig Pr.

Pratt, W. K. Digital Image Processing. 2nd ed. 720p. 1991. 140.00 (*0-471-85766-1*) Wiley.

Pratt, W. K., jt. ed. see Arps, R. B.

***Pratt, W. T.** Approach for Estimating the Frequencies of Various Containment Failure Modes & Bypass Events. 73p. 1999. pap. 6.00 (*0-16-062988-8*) USGPO.

Pratt, Waldo S. The Music of the Pilgrims: A Description of the Psalm-Book Brought to Plymouth in Sixteen Twenty. 1980. lib. bdg. 59.00 (*0-8490-3180-X*) Gordon Pr.

— Musical Ministries in the Church. LC 74-24193. reprint ed. 36.00 (*0-404-13095-X*) AMS Pr.

— The New Encyclopedia of Music & Musicians. 969p. 1990. reprint ed. lib. bdg. 129.00 (*0-7812-9009-0*) Rprt Serv.

Pratt, Walter F. Privacy in Britain. LC 76-50289. 266p. 1979. 36.50 (*0-8387-2030-7*) Bucknell U Pr.

— The Supreme Court under Chief Justice Edward Douglass White, 1910-1921. LC 99-6156. (Chief Justiceships of the United States Supreme Court Ser.). (Illus.). 352p. 1999. 39.95 (*1-57003-309-9*) U of SC Pr.

Pratt, Wendy B., jt. auth. see Schwartz, Seymour.

Pratt, Will. A Funny Thing Happened on the Way! LC 97-109613. 1996. pap. 10.99 (*0-85412-642-2*) J Corbett.

Pratt, William. Singing the Chaos: Madness & Wisdom in Modern Poetry. 360p. (C). 1996. text 44.95 (*0-8262-1048-1*) U of Mo Pr.

Pratt, William, ed. The Fugitive Poets: Modern Southern Poetry in Perspective. rev. ed. LC 91-62453. (Southern Classics Ser.). 159p. (C). 1991. pap. 12.95 (*1-879941-00-7*) J S Sanders.

Pratt, William & Richardson, Robert, eds. Homage to Imagism. LC 91-11028. (Studies in Modern Literature: No. 20). 1992. 37.50 (*0-404-61590-2*) AMS Pr.

Pratt, William, jt. auth. see Shriver, Phillip R.

Pratt, William, ed. see Davidson, Donald.

Pratt, William, ed. see Hibbett, T. C.

Pratt, William, ed. see MacKaye, Percy & Torrence, Ridgely.

Pratt, William B. & Fekety, Robert. The Antimicrobial Drugs. LC 84-29603. (Illus.). 640p. 1986. pap. text 35.00 (*0-19-503561-5*) OUP.

Pratt, William B. & Taylor, Palmer, eds. Principles of Drug Action. 3rd ed. (Illus.). 834p. 1990. text 83.00 (*0-443-08676-1*) Church.

Pratt, William B., et al. The Anticancer Drugs. 2nd ed. (Illus.). 360p. 1994. pap. text 39.95 (*0-19-506739-8*) OUP.

— The Anticancer Drugs. 2nd ed. (Illus.). 360p. (C). 1994. text 69.95 (*0-19-506738-X*) OUP.

Pratt, William B., jt. ed. see Scholar, Eric M.

Pratt, Willis S. Lord Byron & His Circle. (Studies in Byron: No. 5). 1970. pap. 39.95 (*0-8383-0062-6*) M S G Haskell Hse.

Pratt, Willis W. Byron at Southwell. LC 72-6745. (Studies in Byron: No. 5). 1972. reprint ed. lib. bdg. 51.95 (*0-8383-1646-8*) M S G Haskell Hse.

Pratt, Yvonne K. Especially for the Single Woman. 1981. pap. 2.25 (*0-87148-295-9*) Pathway Pr.

***Pratte, Eric Lionel.** Army Men Sarge's Heroes (PSX) Prima's Official Strategy Guide. (Official Strategy Guides Ser.). (Illus.). 112p. (YA). 2000. pap. 14.99 (*0-7615-2855-5*, Prima Games) Prima Pub.

— Street Fighter EX2 Plus. LC 00-102835. (Official Strategy Guides Ser.). (Illus.). 96p. 2000. pap. 12.99 (*0-7615-2912-8*) Prima Pub.

Pratte, Francois. L' Armee Rose D'Awa. (Novels in the Premier Roman Ser.). (FRE., Illus.). 64p. (J). (gr. 2-5). 1996. pap. 7.95 (*2-89021-130-4*, Pub. by Les Editions) Firefly Bks Ltd.

— Awa Au Bout Du Monde. (Novels in the Premier Roman Ser.). (FRE., Illus.). 64p. (J). (gr. 2-5). 1996. pap. 7.95 (*2-89021-151-7*, Pub. by Les Editions) Firefly Bks Ltd.

— Awa Dans le Desert. (Novels in the Premier Roman Ser.). (FRE., Illus.). 64p. (J). (gr. 2-5). 1996. pap. 7.95 (*2-89021-111-8*, Pub. by Les Editions) Firefly Bks Ltd.

— Awa En el Desierto. (Coleccion Rosa Ser.). (SPA., Illus.). 60p. (J). (gr. 5 up). 1994. pap. 5.95 (*958-07-0066-4*) Firefly Bks Ltd.

— El Blabla de los Gemelos. (Coleccion Rosa Ser.). (SPA., Illus.). 60p. (J). (gr. 5 up). 1994. pap. 5.95 (*958-07-0068-0*) Firefly Bks Ltd.

— El Ejercito Rosado de Awa. (Coleccion Rosa Ser.). (SPA., Illus.). 60p. (J). (gr. 5 up). 1994. pap. 5.95 (*958-07-0064-8*) Firefly Bks Ltd.

— Le Secret D'Awa. (Novels in the Premier Roman Ser.). (FRE., Illus.). 64p. (J). (gr. 2-5). 1996. pap. 7.95 (*2-89021-125-8*, Pub. by Les Editions) Firefly Bks Ltd.

— El Secreto de Awa. (Coleccion Rosa Ser.). (SPA., Illus.). 60p. (J). (gr. 5 up). 1994. pap. 5.95 (*958-07-0069-9*) Firefly Bks Ltd.

Pratte, Paul A. Gods Within the Machine: A History of the American Society of Newspaper Editors, 1923-1993. LC 94-24624. 248p. 1995. 62.95 (*0-275-94976-1*, Praeger Pubs) Greenwood.

Pratte, Richard. The Civic Imperative: Examining the Need for Civic Education. (Advances in Contemporary Educational Thought Ser.). 224p. (C). 1988. text 24.00 (*0-8077-2922-1*) Tchrs Coll.

Pratten, Cliff. Overseas Investments, Capital Gains & the Balance of Payments. (Research Monographs: No. 48). 121p. (Orig.). (C). 1992. pap. 22.50 (*0-255-36303-6*, Pub. by Inst Economic Affairs) Coronet Bks.

Pratten, Clifford F. The Stock Market. LC 93-2761. (Department of Applied Economics, Occasional Papers: No. 59). (Illus.). 226p. (C). 1993. text 54.95 (*0-521-44065-3*) Cambridge U Pr.

***Pratten, John & Proctor, Nigel.** GCSE Economics. 176p. 2000. 18.95 (*1-872807-73-9*, Pub. by Tudor Business Pubg Ltd) Intl Spec Bk.

Prattis, J. Ian. Anthropology at the Edge: Essays on Culture, Symbol & Consciousness. LC 96-43225. 750p. 1996. pap. text 27.50 (*0-7618-0556-7*) U Pr of Amer.

Pratto, Felicia, jt. auth. see Sidanius, Jim.

Pratton, Norah, jt. auth. see Henifin, Karen.

Pratzel, jt. auth. see Mooney.

Pratzel, Alan D., jt. auth. see Mooney, Margaret M.

Pratzel, Alana D., jt. auth. see Mooney, Margaret M.

Pratzner, Frank C. & Russell, Jill F. The Changing Workplace: Implications of Quality of Work Life for Vocational Education. 89p. 1984. 7.25 (*0-318-22062-8*, RD249) Ctr Educ Trng Employ.

Pratzner, Frank C., jt. ed. see Lewis, Morgan V.

Prausnitz, Frederik. Score & Podium, 2 vols. Incl. A Complete Guide to Conducting. rev. ed. 544p. 2000. 49.50 (*0-8108-3420-0*); The Workbook. (Illus.). 96p. 2000. 23.50 (*0-8108-3421-9*); 96p. 1999. 65.00 (*0-8108-3425-1*) Scarecrow.

Prausnitz, John M. Molecular Thermodynamics of Fluid-Phase Equilibria. 3rd ed. LC 99-222890. 864p. 1998. 105.00 (*0-13-977745-8*) P-H.

Prauss, Gerold. Knowing & Doing: In Heidegger's Being & Time. Steiner, Gary & Turner, Jeffrey, trs. LC 97-30140. 80p. 1999. 39.95 (*1-57392-670-1*, Humanity Bks) Prometheus Bks.

— Knowing & Doing in Heidegger's Being & Time. Steiner, Gary & Turner, Jeffrey S., trs. from GER. LC 97-30140. 96p. 1998. 39.95 (*0-391-04065-0*) Humanities.

Prautzsch, Hartmut, jt. auth. see Boehm, Wolfgang.

Pravadelli, Veronica, jt. ed. see Bouchard, Norma.

Praval. Indian Army after Independence. 623p. 1987. 50.00 (*81-7062-014-7*, Pub. by Lancer India) S Asia.

Pravda & Pravdova. Francuzska Konverzacia. (SLO.). 352p. 1996. write for info. (*80-08-00777-X*, Pub. by Slov Pegagog Naklad) IBD Ltd.

— Francuzstina Pre Samoukov (Subor) (SLO.). 610p. 1996. write for info. (*80-08-00368-5*, Pub. by Slov Pegagog Naklad) IBD Ltd.

Pravda, Alex. The End of the Other Empire: Soviet Union - East European Relations in Transition. (Illus.). 256p. (C). 1992. 65.00 (*0-8039-8723-4*) Sage.

Pravda, Alex, ed. The Tauris Soviet Directory: The Elite of the U. S. S. R. Today. 700p. 1990. text 185.00 (*1-85043-090-X*) St Martin.

— Yearbook of Soviet Foreign Relations, 1991. 400p. 1991. text 110.00 (*1-85043-242-2*, Pub. by I B T) St Martin.

Pravda, Alex & Duncan, Peter J., eds. Soviet-British Relations since the 1970s. (Illus.). 275p. (C). 1990. text 69.95 (*0-521-37494-4*) Cambridge U Pr.

Pravda, Alex & Ruble, Blair A. Trade Unions in Communist States. LC 85-30717. 250p. (C). 1986. text 49.95 (*0-04-331108-3*) Routledge.

Pravda, Alex, jt. ed. see Hasegawa, Tsuyoshi.

Pravda, Jay. All the Right Answers: How to Respond When Questioned by a Lawyer. (Illus.). 30p. 1996. pap. 8.95 (*0-9663357-0-8*) Spec Pubns.

Pravda, Myra & Weiland, Jeanne. Off to Camp! LC 89-80301. (Illus.). 72p. (Orig.). (J). (gr. 2-7). 1989. pap., per. 8.95 (*0-9622328-0-7*) JSP Pub.

Pravdova, jt. auth. see Pravda.

Prave, P., et al, eds. Biotechnology Vol. 1: Fundamentals, Applications, Information: Focus 1. 436p. 1993. 152.95 (*0-471-03737-0*) Wiley.

— Biotechnology Vol. 3: Fundamentals, Applications, Information: Focus 3, Vol. 3. 516p. 1993. 152.95 (*0-471-03735-4*) Wiley.

— Fundamentals of Biotechnology. LC 87-10604. (Illus.). 792p. 1987. 265.00 (*3-527-26144-3*, Wiley-VCH) Wiley.

***Pravitera, Joseph.** Beginner's Italian. 145p. 2000. pap. 14.95 (*0-7818-0839-1*) Hippocrene Bks.

Prawat, Carolyn M. Gourd Craft: Growing, Designing, & Decorating Ornamental & Hardshell Gourds. 2nd rev. ed. (Illus.). 212p. 1989. reprint ed. write for info. (*0-9623516-0-1*) Am Gourd Soc.

Prawer, Joshua. The History of the Jews in the Latin Kingdom of Jerusalem. (Illus.). 328p. 1988. 95.00 (*0-19-822557-1*) OUP.

Prawer, Joshua, ed. The History of Jerusalem: The Early Muslim Period, 638-1099. LC 95-42754. (Illus.). 400p. (C). 1996. text 75.00 (*0-8147-6639-0*) NYU Pr.

Prawer, S. S. Breeches & Metaphysics: Thackeray's German Discourse. (Legenda Ser.: 1). 544p. (Orig.). 1998. pap. write for info. (*1-900755-03-3*, Pub. by E H R C) David Brown.

— Israel at Vanity Fair: Jews & Judaism in the Writings of

P

W. M. Thackery. LC 91-25465. (Series in Jewish Studies: Vol. 2). (Illus.). x, 442p. 1992. 170.50 (*90-04-09403-2*) Brill Academic Pubs.

Prawer, Seigbert S. Caligari's Children: The Film As Tale of Terror. (Quality Paperbacks Ser.). (Illus.). 334p. 1989. reprint ed. pap. 13.95 (*0-306-80347-X*) Da Capo.

— Heine: The Tragic Satirist: A Study of the Later Poetry, 1827-1856. LC 61-4707. 327p. reprint ed. pap. 93.20 (*0-608-13043-5*, 2024511) Bks Demand.

Prawiro, Radius. Indonesia's Struggle for Economic Development: Pragmatism in Action. (Illus.). 400p. 1999. text 45.00 (*983-56-0053-8*) OUP.

Prawitz, Dag, et al, eds. Logic, Methodology & Philosophy of Science IX: Proceedings: International Congress of Logic, Methodology, & Philosophy of Science (9th: 1991: Uppsala, Sweden) LC 94-39279. (Studies in Logic & the Foundations of Mathematics: Vol. 134). 1004p. 1995. 269.00 (*0-444-89341-5*) Elsevier.

Prawitz, Dag & Westerstahl, Dag, eds. Logic & Philosophy of Science in Uppsala: Papers from the 9th International Congress of Logic, Methodology & Philosophy of Science. LC 93-50753. (Synthese Library: Vol. 236). 620p. (C). 1994. lib. bdg. 251.00 (*0-7923-2702-0*, Pub. by Kluwer Academic) Kluwer Academic.

Prawitz, Jan, et al. A Zone Free of Weapons of Mass Destruction in the Middle East. LC 96-194507. 144p. 25.00 (*92-9045-114-9*) UN.

Prawitz, Jan, jt. ed. see Joenniemi, Pertii.

Prawn, Pete. Aerosmith: Riff by Riff. 90p. pap. 17.95 (*0-89524-921-9*, 02506320, Pub. by Cherry Lane) H Leonard.

Pray, Barbara. Grandmother Series: Path to the Spirit & Spirit Vision of a Grandmother, 2 vols., Set. 1994. pap. 21.95 (*0-922863-08-3*) Dream Wvrs Pub Co.

— Path to the Spirit. Talkington, Sandra, ed. (Grandmother Ser.). (Illus.). 77p. (Orig.). (C). 1994. pap. 12.95 (*0-922863-05-9*) Dream Wvrs Pub Co.

— Spirit Vision of a Grandmother. Talkington, Sandra, ed. (Illus.). 42p. (Orig.). (C). 1991. pap. 10.95 (*0-922863-02-4*) Dream Wvrs Pub Co.

Pray, Bobbie & Holt, Marilyn J. Kansas History: A Journal of the Central Plains, a Ten-Year Cumulative Index. LC 88-82171. 315p. 1988. pap. 15.95 (*0-87726-034-6*) Kansas St Hist.

Pray, Bobbie A. & Mann, Glennis A. Let's Go Eat: The Kansas Guide to Good Dining. LC 91-66141. 200p. (Orig.). 1991. pap. 18.00 (*0-9627361-1-2*) Turn Century Pr.

Pray, Francis C., ed. Handbook for Educational Fund Raising. LC 81-81964. (Jossey-Bass Series in Higher Education). 474p. reprint ed. pap. 147.00 (*0-8357-4917-7*, 203784700009) Bks Demand.

Pray, Isaac C. Memoirs of James Gordon Bennett & His Times. LC 73-125712. (American Journalists Ser.). 1977. reprint ed. 35.95 (*0-405-01693-X*) Ayer.

Pray, Lloyd C. & Murray, Raymond C., eds. Dolomitization & Limestone Diagenesis: A Symposium. LC 73-15328. (Society of Economic Paleontologists & Mineralogists, Special Publication Ser.: No. 13). 190p. reprint ed. pap. 58.90 (*0-608-12954-2*, 202473900038) Bks Demand.

Pray, Thomas & Strang, Daniel. Decide: A Computer-Based Decision Game. (Business Division Ser.). 120p. (C). 1981. pap., student ed. 27.50 (*0-07-554259-5*) McGraw.

Pray, W. Steven. Nonprescription Product Therapeutics. LC 98-22505. 1999. write for info. (*0-683-30126-8*) Lppncott W & W.

***Prayer Point Press Staff.** Prayer Room Intercessor's Handbook. 1999. 5.00 (*1-57892-049-3*) Prayer Pt Pr.

Prayson, Alex. An Anthology of Best Loved CAD Programs. 1999. text 21.20 (*1-56870-248-5*) RonJon Pub.

— A Love-Hate Anthology: Releasing the Bitch Within . . . (Illus.). 52p. (Orig.). 1993. pap. 10.00 (*0-9639301-0-9*) A Prayson.

***Prayson, Richard A. & Cohen, Mark L., eds.** Practical Differential Diagnosis in Surgical Neuropathology. 192p. 2000. 125.00 (*0-89603-817-3*) Humana.

Praytor, Phyllis, jt. auth. see Craig, Linda.

Praz, Mario. Conversation Pieces: A Survey of the Informal Group Portrait in Europe & America. LC 76-127380. (Illus.). 285p. 1971. 70.00 (*0-271-00132-1*) A Wofsy Fine Arts.

— The Flaming Heart. 400p. (C). 1973. reprint ed. pap. 5.50 (*0-393-00669-7*) Norton.

— Studies in Seventeenth Century Imagery, 2 vols. in 1. LC 40-3654. reprint ed. 79.00 (*0-403-07208-5*) Somerset Pub.

Prazak, Ludwig J., tr. see Huckstadt, Jurgen.

Prazak, Ludwig J., tr. see Mollmann, Gerd.

Prazan, Ceslaus. The Dukkawa of Northwest Nigeria. LC 77-365. xxvi, 210 p. 1977. write for info. (*0-391-00655-X*) Humanities.

Prazmowska, Anita J. Britain & Poland, 1939-1943: The Betrayed Ally. (Cambridge Russian, Soviet & Post-Soviet Studies: 97). 250p. (C). 1995. text 85.00 (*0-521-40309-X*); pap. text 29.95 (*0-521-48385-9*) Cambridge U Pr.

***Prazmowska, Anita J.** Eastern Europe & the Origins of the Second World War. 2000. pap. 22.95 (*0-312-23353-1*) St Martin.

— Eastern Europe & the Origins of the Second World War. 2000. text 65.00 (*0-312-23352-3*) St Martin.

Prazniak, Roxann. Dialogues Across Civilizations: Sketches in World History from the Chinese & European Experiences. (Essays in World History Ser.). (C). 1996. pap. 24.00 (*0-8133-2736-9*, Pub. by Westview) HarpC.

— Of Camel Kings & Other Things: Rural Rebels Against Modernity in Late Imperial China. LC 98-23323. (State & Society in East Asia Ser.: Vol. 113). 334p. 1999. 69.00 (*0-8476-9006-7*); pap. 24.95 (*0-8476-9007-5*) Rowman.

PRC Environmental Management, Inc. Staff. Hazardous Waste Reduction in the Metal Finishing Industry. LC 89-22922. (Pollution Technology Review Ser.: No. 176). (Illus.). 205p. 1990. 42.00 (*0-8155-1223-6*) Noyes.

PRC, Inc. Staff, ed. see Daniels, William R.

PRC Publishing, Inc. Staff, ed. see Hawkins, Jerald D.

Pre, Athena Du, see Du Pre, Athena.

Pre, Jon Du, see Du Pre, Jon.

Pre-Precalculus Grou SUNY Staff & CUNY Staff. Mathematics in Action 1. 512p. (C). 1998. pap. text 61.00 (*0-201-38317-9*) Addison-Wesley.

***Pre-Precalculus Grou SUNY Staff, et al.** Mathematics in Action 2. 504p. (C). 1998. pap. text 61.00 (*0-201-38318-7*) Addison-Wesley.

Preacher, Stephen. Anasazi Sunrise: The Mystery of Sacrifice Rock. LC 92-90872. (Illus.). 108p. (Orig.). 1992. pap. 6.95 (*1-881553-01-9*) Rugged Indiv.

Preacher's Homiletic Commentary Staff. The Preacher's Homiletic Commentary, 31. 19256p. 1990. 795.00 (*0-8010-6962-9*) Baker Bks.

Preas, Bryan & Lorenzetti, Michael, eds. Physical Design Automation of VLSI Systems. (Illus.). 510p. (C). 1988. text 59.25 (*0-8053-0142-9*) Benjamin-Cummings.

Preat, V., jt. ed. see Roberfroid, M. B.

Preator, Richard. Dyer. Descendants of John Dyer & Mary "Polly" Youngblood of Jackson Co., Tenn. 80p. 1998. pap. 16.00 (*0-8328-9651-9*); lib. bdg. 26.00 (*0-8328-9650-0*) Higginson Bk Co.

Preator, Richard E., Jr. Dyer. Descendants of James Dyer & Jane Finn of Jackson Co., Tenn. 251p. 1998. pap. 38.50 (*0-8328-9653-5*); lib. bdg. 48.50 (*0-8328-9652-7*) Higginson Bk Co.

Preaud, Maxime. Dictionnaire des Editeurs d'Estampes a Paris Sous l'Ancien Regime. (FRE.). 334p. 1987. pap. 145.00 (*0-7859-8214-0*, 2903181608) Fr & Eur.

Preaux, jt. ed. see Dick.

Preaux, Claire. L' Economie Royale des Lagides. Finley, Moses, ed. LC 79-4999. (Ancient Economic History Ser.). (FRE.). 1979. reprint ed. lib. bdg. 56.95 (*0-405-12388-4*) Ayer.

Prebal, Bernard. A Practical Guide to Molecular Cloning. 2nd ed. 811p. 1988. 385.00 (*0-471-85071-3*); pap. 215.00 (*0-471-85070-5*) Wiley.

Prebble, J. N. Mitochondria, Chloroplasts & Bacterial Membranes. LC 80-40777. (Illus.). 392p. reprint ed. pap. 121.60 (*0-8357-6216-5*, 203450600090) Bks Demand.

***Prebble, John.** Darien: The Scottish Dream of Empire. 2000. reprint ed. pap. 19.95 (*1-84158-054-6*, Pub. by Birlinn Ltd) Dufour.

Prebble, John. Dimensions in Business Finance Law. 296p. 1992. pap. 54.00 (*0-409-79011-7*, Austral, MICHIE) LEXIS Pub.

— The High Girders. large type ed. 1980. 27.99 (*0-7089-0430-0*) Ulverscroft.

— The Taxation of Companies & Corporate Investors. 64p. 1984. pap. 29.00 (*0-409-70142-4*, NZ, MICHIE) LEXIS Pub.

Prebeg, Rick A., jt. auth. see Hanna, Jack.

Prebenna, David. Macmillan Millennium Atlas of the World. LC 96-20353. (Illus.). 1996. 175.00 (*0-02-861264-7*, H M Gousha) Prntice Hall Bks.

— Planet Earth. (Macmillan World Atlas Ser.). (Illus.). 432p. 1996. 34.95 (*0-02-861266-3*, Pub. by Macmillan) S&S Trade.

Prebenna, David. Planet Earth: Macmillan World Atlas. (Illus.). 1997. 34.95 (*0-02-865339-4*) Mac Lib Ref.

Prebenna, David. Sesame Street Songbook: Sixty Favorite Songs. (Illus.). 217p. (J). (ps-3). 1992. 25.00 (*0-02-525141-4*, Mac Bks Young Read) S&S Childrens.

***Prebenna, David.** What Color Is Elmo? (Illus.). 6p. (J). 2000. 2.99 (*0-375-80236-3*, Pub. by Random Bks Yng Read) Random.

— What Does Ernie Hear? 6p. (J). 1999. 2.99 (*0-375-80238-X*) Random House.

Prebenna, David, jt. illus. see Durkee, Sarah.

Prebish, Charles S. Buddhist Monastic Discipline: Sanskrit Pratimoksa Sutras of the Mahasamghikas & Mulasarvastivadins. (C). 1996. 16.00 (*81-208-1339-1*, Pub. by Motilal Bnarsidass) S Asia.

— Historical Dictionary of Buddhism. LC 93-4247. (Historical Dictionaries of Religions, Philosophies, & Movements Ser.: No. 1). (Illus.). 425p. 1993. 50.00 (*0-8108-2698-4*) Scarecrow.

— Luminous Passage: The Practice & Study of Buddhism in America. LC 98-20767. 329p. 1999. 45.00 (*0-520-21696-2*, Pub. by U CA Pr) Cal Prin Full Svc.

***Prebish, Charles S.** Luminous Passage: The Practice & Study of Buddhism in America. LC 98-20767. 329p. 1999. pap. 18.95 (*0-520-21697-0*, Pub. by U CA Pr) Cal Prin Full Svc.

Prebish, Charles S. Religion & Sport: The Meeting of Sacred & Profane, 36. LC 92-30020. (Contributions to the Study of Popular Culture Ser.: No. 36). 264p. 1992. 55.00 (*0-313-28729-5*, GM8729, Greenwood Pr) Greenwood.

Prebish, Charles S., ed. Buddhism: A Modern Perspective. LC 74-300085. 346p. 1975. pap. 18.95 (*0-271-01195-5*) Pa St U Pr.

Prebish, Charles S. & Tanaka, Kenneth K. The Faces of Buddhism in America. LC 97-38769. (Illus.). 350p. 1998. 50.00 (*0-520-20460-3*, Pub. by U CA Pr); pap. 22.00 (*0-520-21301-7*, Pub. by U CA Pr) Cal Prin Full Svc.

Preble. Artforms: Value Edition. 5th ed. (C). 1997. pap. 56.00 (*0-321-03105-9*) Addison-Wesley Educ.

— Artforms Writing & Online Research Guide. 6th ed. 96p. (C). 1999. pap. text 10.31 (*0-321-04060-0*) Addison-Wesley Educ.

Preble, Dave, et al. Fly Fishing Offshore: Cape Cod to Cape Hatteras. (Illus.). 110p. 1998. 24.95 (*0-923155-27-9*) Fisherman Lib.

Preble, Duane, et al. Artforms. 6th ed. LC 98-3685. 530p. (C). 1998. pap. 58.00 (*0-321-00229-6*, Prentice Hall) P-H.

Preble, G. H. Genealogical Sketch of the First Three Generations in America: With an Account of Abraham Preble the Emigrant of Brig. General Jedediah Preble & His Descendants. (Illus.). 340p. 1989. reprint ed. pap. 51.00 (*0-8328-0987-X*); reprint ed. lib. bdg. 59.00 (*0-8328-0986-1*) Higginson Bk Co.

Preble, George H. Opening of Japan: A Diary of Discovery in the Far East, 1853-1856. Szczesniak, Boleslaw, ed. LC 62-16484. (Illus.). 492p. reprint ed. 152.60 (*0-8357-9737-6*, 201099800073) Bks Demand.

Preble, George H., ed. see Green, Ezra.

Preble, Jack. Land of Canaan. 114p. 1965. reprint ed. pap. 9.95 (*0-87012-012-3*) McClain.
A collection of intriguing, hilarious & sometimes tragic tales from the mountains of Tucker & Randolph counties. Fifth Printing, 1995. *Publisher Paid Annotation.*

Preble, Kevin, jt. auth. see Arnold, Mark W.

Preble, Linda M., jt. auth. see Sevarino, Ferne B.

***Precast/Prestressed Concrete Institute.** PCI Design Handbook: Precast & Prestressed Concrete. 5th ed. LC 99-233856. (Illus.). 1999. write for info. (*0-937040-60-6*) P-PCI.

***Precept Ministries International Staff.** The New Inductive Study Bible. 2240p. 2000. 42.99 (*0-7369-0016-0*); 74.99 (*0-7369-0017-9*); lthr. 89.99 (*0-7369-0018-7*) Harvest Hse.

— The New Inductive Study Bible: Indexed. 2240p. 2000. 49.99 (*0-7369-0022-5*); lthr. 81.99 (*0-7369-0023-3*); lthr. 96.99 (*0-7369-0024-1*) Harvest Hse.

Prechal, Sacha. Directives in European Community Law: A Study of Directives & Their Enforcement in National Courts. (Oxford European Community Law Library Ser.). 422p. 1995. text 85.00 (*0-19-826016-4*) OUP.

Prechal, Sacha & Burrows, Noreen. Gender Discrimination Law. 414p. 1990. text 96.95 (*1-85521-058-4*, Pub. by Dartmth Pub) Ashgate Pub Co.

Prechel, Doris. Die Gottin Ishara: Ein Beitrag zur Altorientalischen Religionsgeschichte. (Abhandlvorgen zur Literatur Alt-Syrien-Palastinas und Mesopatamieus Ser.: No. 11). 1996. text 68.00 (*3-927120-36-7*, Pub. by UGARIT) Eisenbrauns.

Prechel, H. Corporate & Class Restructuring. 2000. pap. 22.00 (*0-8133-2301-0*) HarpC.

***Prechel, Harland.** Big Business & the State: Historical Transitions & Corporate Transformation in the United States, 1880s-1990s. LC 99-54293. (C). 2000. text 75.50 (*0-7914-4593-3*) State U NY Pr.

— Big Business & the State: Historical Transitions & Corporate Transformation, 1880s-1990s. LC 99-54293. (C). 2000. pap. text 25.95 (*0-7914-4594-1*) State U NY Pr.

Precht, Dave, jt. auth. see Dalrymple, Byron.

Precht, Fred L., ed. Lutheran Worship: History & Practice. LC 93-23460. 608p. 1994. 26.00 (*0-570-04255-0*, 53-1015) Concordia.

Precht, H., et al. Temperature & Life. LC 73-13495. (Illus.). 779p. 1973. 98.00 (*0-387-06441-9*) Spr-Verlag.

Prechtel, Martin. Grandmother Sweat Bath: A Story of the Tzutujil Mana. Rodney, Janet, ed. (Illus.). 39p. (Orig.). (YA). (gr. 6 up). 1990. write for info. (*1-878460-00-5*) Weaselsleeves Pr.

— Long Life, Honey in the Heart: A Story of Initation & Eloquence from the Shores of a Mayan Lake. LC 99-27247. (Illus.). 384p. 1999. 25.95 (*0-87477-994-4*, Tarcher Putnam) Putnam Pub Group.

— Secrets of the Talking Jaguar: Memoirs from the Living Heart of a Mayan Village. LC 97-48480. (Illus.). 304p. 1998. 25.95 (*0-87477-900-6*, Tarcher Putnam) Putnam Pub Group.

— Secrets of the Talking Jaguar: Memoirs from the Living Heart of a Mayan Village. LC 97-48480. (Illus.). 304p. 1999. reprint ed. pap. 13.95 (*0-87477-970-7*, Tarcher Putnam) Putnam Pub Group.

Prechter. Elliott Wave Principle. (C). 2000. text 47.00 (*0-471-98730-1*) Wiley.

Prechter, Robert R. At the Crest of the Tidal Wave. LC 97-31513. 469p. 1997. pap. 34.95 (*0-471-97954-6*) Wiley.

Prechter, Robert R., Jr. At the Crest of the Tidal Wave: A Forecast for the Great Bear Market. LC 95-68295. (Illus.). 508p. 1995. 49.00 (*0-932750-39-7*) New Classics Lib.

— The Complete Elliott Wave Writings of A. Hamilton Bolton. (Illus.). 412p. 1994. 89.00 (*0-932750-22-2*) New Classics Lib.

— Prechter's Perspective. Kendall, Peter, ed. LC 95-72498. 267p. 1996. pap. 19.00 (*0-932750-40-0*) New Classics Lib.

— R. N. Elliott's Market Letters (1938-1946) (Illus.). 234p. 1993. 89.00 (*0-932750-20-6*) New Classics Lib.

— Utility Manual for the Precision Ratio Compass. 3rd ed. (Illus.). 70p. 1993. pap. 99.00 (*0-932750-13-3*) New Classics Lib.

***Prechter, Robert R.** The Wave Principle of Human Social Behavior & the New Science of Socionomics. LC 98-68275. (Illus.). 463p. 1999. 39.00 (*0-932750-49-4*) New Classics Lib.

Prechter, Robert R., Jr. & Frost, A. J. Elliott Wave Principle (20th Anniversary Edition) Key to Market Behavior. 9th anniversary rev. ed. LC 98-66116. (Illus.). 245p. 1998. 29.00 (*0-932750-43-5*) New Classics Lib.

Prechter, Robert R., Jr., ed. see Elliott, R. N.

Prechter, Robert R., Jr., ed. see Frost, A. J. & Russell, Richard.

Prechtl, Heinz F., ed. Continuity of Neural Functions from Prenatal to Postnatal Life. LC 65-80476. (Clinics in Developmental Medicine Ser.: No. 94). (Illus.). 255p. (C). 1991. text 59.95 (*0-521-41214-5*, Pub. by Mc Keith Pr) Cambridge U Pr.

Prechtl, Heinz F. & Beintema, David. The Neurological Examination of the Full-Term Newborn Infant. 2nd ed. (Clinics in Developmental Medicine Ser.: No. 63). (Illus.). 76p. (C). 1991. reprint ed. text 27.95 (*0-521-41199-8*, Pub. by Mc Keith Pr) Cambridge U Pr.

Preciado, Kathleen, ed. see National Gallery of Art Staff.

***Preciado Martin, Patricia.** Days of Plenty, Days of Want. LC 98-46458. 80p. 1999. pap. text 9.95 (*0-8165-1946-3*) U of Ariz Pr.

Preciado, Regina, ed. see Lickson, Charles P. & Lickson, Bryane.

Precin. The Living Skills Recovery Workbook. LC 99-225255. 224p. 1999. pap. text 35.00 (*0-7506-7118-1*) Buttrwrth-Heinemann.

Precious, B. B. The Bryant Series: My New Home. Williams, Dewilda M., ed. (Byrant Ser.). (Illus.). 16p. (J). (gr. k-2). 1995. 10.95 (*1-886493-01-4*) NBC Study Pub.

***Precious, Lisa.** Premiere Parent Los Angeles: The Survival Guide for Parents of Toddlers & Preschoolers. 2000. pap. 14.95 (*0-658-00401-8*, Natl Textbk Co) NTC Contemp Pub Co.

Precious, Lloyd, et al. Classroom TOEFL. 1993. pap., teacher ed. 14.95 (*0-8120-1517-7*); pap., teacher ed. 12.95 (*0-8120-1800-1*); audio 40.00 (*0-8120-1516-9*) Barron.

Precious, Lloyd, et al. Classroom TOEFL Teachers Kit, Set. 1993. teacher ed. 79.95 incl. audio (*0-8120-8027-0*) Barron.

***Precious Promises Staff.** Precious Promises New Testament. 1999. pap. 8.99 (*0-89957-970-1*) AMG Pubs.

— Precious Promises New Testament. 1999. pap. 1.89 (*0-89957-969-8*) AMG Pubs.

Precision Indexing Staff. Georgia Census Index, 1870, 3 vols., Set. Steuart, Bradley W., ed. 3344p. 1991. lib. bdg. 350.00 (*1-877677-11-6*) Herit Quest.

— Indianapolis (Marion County), Indiana Mortality Records, September 1872-December 1881. 651p. 1989. lib. bdg. 49.95 (*1-877677-08-6*) Herit Quest.

— Ohio Census Index, 1880, 3 vols., Set. 3252p. 1991. lib. bdg. 395.00 (*1-877677-14-0*) Herit Quest.

— The Soundex Reference Guide. Stueart, Bradley W., ed. 253p. 1990. pap. 19.96 (*1-877677-09-4*); lib. bdg. 29.95 (*1-877677-12-4*) Herit Quest.

— South Carolina Census Index, 1870, 2 vols., Set. Steuart, Bradley W., ed. 1983p. 1989. lib. bdg. 195.00 (*1-877677-10-8*) Herit Quest.

Precision Indexing Staff, jt. auth. see Steuart, Raeone Christensen.

Preconference Institute on Library Automation Staf. Library Automation: A State of the Art Review: Papers of the Preconference Institute on Library Automation, San Francisco, 1967. Salmon, Stephen R., ed. LC 73-77283. 186p. reprint ed. pap. 57.70 (*0-608-14076-7*, 202420800035) Bks Demand.

Precosky, Don. W. W. E. Ross & His Works. (Canadian Author Studies). 26p. (C). 1987. pap. text 9.95 (*0-920763-20-0*, Pub. by ECW) Genl Dist Srvs.

Precourt, K. G., jt. auth. see Sheehan, Larry.

Precupanu, T., jt. auth. see Barbu, V.

Pred, Allan. Recognizing European Modernities: A Montage of the Present. LC 94-46281. (Illus.). 304p. (C). 1995. pap. 27.99 (*0-415-12136-1*, C0003) Routledge.

Pred, Allan & Watts, Michael J. Reworking Modernity: Capitalisms & Symbolic Discontent. LC 91-42894. (Hegemony & Experience Ser.). (Illus.). 265p. (C). 1992. text 45.00 (*0-8135-1831-8*) Rutgers U Pr.

Pred, Allan R. Lost Words & Lost Worlds: Modernity & the Language of Everyday Life in Nineteenth-Century Stockholm. (Cambridge Human Geography Ser.). (Illus.). 316p. (C). 1990. text 69.95 (*0-521-37531-2*) Cambridge U Pr.

— Place, Practice & Structure: Social & Spatial Transformation in Southern Sweden, 1750-1850. LC 85-30652. 300p. 1986. 56.00 (*0-389-20615-6*, N8173) B&N Imports.

— Urban Growth & City-Systems in the United States, 1840-1860. LC 80-12098. (Studies in Urban History). (Illus.). 297p. 1980. text 43.50 (*0-674-93091-6*) HUP.

— Urban Growth & the Circulation of Information: The United States System of Cities, 1790-1840. LC 73-76384. (Studies in Urban History). 384p. (C). 1973. text 46.50 (*0-674-93090-8*) HUP.

***Pred, Allan Richard.** Even in Sweden: Racisms, Racialized Spaces & the Popular Geographical Imagination. LC 00-27181. (Illus.). 300p. 2000. pap. 18.95 (*0-520-22449-3*, Pub. by U CA Pr) Cal Prin Full Svc.

— Even in Sweden: Racisms, Racialized Spaces, & the Popular Geographical Imagination. LC 00-27181. (Illus.). 300p. 2000. 48.00 (*0-520-22332-2*) U CA Pr.

Pred, Deborah R., jt. auth. see Fiedler, Donald B.

Preda, Eugen, jt. auth. see Bogdan, Corneliu.

Predazzi, E., jt. auth. see Anselmino, Isi.

Predazzi, E., jt. ed. see Anselmino, M.

Predazzi, Enrico, jt. auth. see Leader, Elliot.

Preddy, Beth, jt. auth. see Cooney, Tim.

Preddy, Marilyn. Getting Ready for Grade 3. (Home Workbooks Ser.). (Illus.). 64p. (Orig.). (J). (gr. 3). 1996. pap., wbk. ed. 2.49 (*0-88724-363-0*, CD-6860) Carson-Dellos.

— Grade 3 Activities. (Home Workbooks Ser.). (Illus.). 64p. (Orig.). (J). (gr. 3). 1996. pap., wbk. ed. 2.49 (*0-88724-364-9*, CD-6861) Carson-Dellos.

P

An Asterisk (*) at the beginning of an entry indicates that the title is appearing for the first time.

Preddy, Shan. How to Market Design Consultancy Services: Finding, Winning & Keeping Clients. LC 96-46415. (Design Council Ser.). 200p. 1997. pap. 51.95 (*0-566-07727-2*, Pub. by Gower) Ashgate Pub Co.

Predecki, P., et al. Advances in X-Ray Analysis Vol. 38: Proceedings of the 43rd Annual Conference Held in Steamboat Springs, Colorado, August 1-5, 1994, Vol. 38. LC 58-35928. (Illus.). 814p. (C). 1995. text 159.50 (*0-306-45045-3*, Kluwer Plenum) Kluwer Academic.

Predel, B. Hg-Ho...La-Zr Subvol. G: Phase Equilibria, Crystallographic Data & Values of Thermodynamic Properties of Binary Alloys. Madelung, O., ed. (Numerical Data & Functional Relationships in Science & Technology Ser.: Vol. 5). (Illus.). xxvii, 400p. 1547.00 (*3-540-60342-5*) Spr-Verlag.

— Landolt-Bornstein Subvolume f: Ga-Gd...Hf-Zr: Phase Equilibria, Crystallographic Data & Values of Thermodynamic Properties of Binary Alloys. Madelung, Otfried, ed. (Numerical Data & Functional Relationships in Science & Technology, Group IV: Physical Chemistry Ser.: Vol. 5). (Illus.). xxvi, 408p. 1996. 1583.00 (*3-540-60344-1*) Spr-Verlag.

— Lanolt-Boernstein Numerical Data & Functional Relationships in Science & Technology: Macroscopic Properties of Matter; Phase Equilibria, Crystallographic Data, & Values of Thermodynamic Properties of Binary Alloys; Ca-Cd...Co-Zr, Group IV; Vol. 5; Subvol. C. Madelung, Otfried & Schafer, K., eds. 480p. 1993. 1441.95 (*0-387-56072-6*) Spr-Verlag.

— Numerical Data & Functional Relationships in Science & Technology. Madelung, O., ed. (Group IV Ser.: Vol. 5, Subvolume I: Ni-Np . . . Pt-Zr). xxix, 397p. 1998. 1752.00 (*3-540-61712-4*) Spr-Verlag.

***Predel, B.** Numerical Data & Functional Relationships in Science & Technology. Martienssen, W., ed. (Landolt-Bornstein Ser.: Group IV, Vol. 5, Subvol. J). (Illus.). xxxi, 365p. 1998. 1839.00 (*3-540-61742-6*) Spr-Verlag.

Predel, B. Phase Equilibria, Crystallographic & Thermodynamic Data of Binary Alloys, Vol. 5, Subvol. b: B-Ba - C-Zr. (Illus.). xxviii, 403p. 1992. 1165.00 (*0-387-55115-8*) Spr-Verlag.

Predeleanu, M. & Gilormini, P., eds. Advanced Methods in Materials Processing Defects, Vol. 45. LC 97-20157. (Studies in Applied Mechanics). 438p. 1997. 203.25 (*0-444-82670-X*, North Holland) Elsevier.

Predeleanu, M., jt. ed. see Ghosh, S. K.

Predeteanu, Constantin. The ABCs of Cosmetics. 377p. 1987. text 48.00 (*0-9619278-0-1*) Inst Predete Pub.

Predika, Bryon & Dehart, Jon, eds. Cooking with Pride. (Illus.). 104p. (Orig.). 1989. pap. text 8.25 (*0-9623939-0-8*) Act One.

Predika, Jerry. The Sausage-Making Cookbook. LC 82-19679. (Illus.). 192p. 1983. 16.95 (*0-8117-1693-7*) Stackpole.

Predko, Michael. Handbook of Microcontrollers. LC 98-16890. 859p. 1998. 79.95 (*0-07-913717-2*); pap. 54.95 (*0-07-913716-4*) McGraw.

***Predko, Michael.** PC Interfacing Pocket Reference. LC 99-35422. 592p. 1999. pap. 29.95 (*0-07-135525-1*) McGraw.

Predko, Michael. Programming & Customizing the PIC-Microcontroller. LC 97-21762. (Illus.). 352p. 1997. pap. 39.95 (*0-07-913646-X*) McGraw.

***Predko, Myke.** PC Ph.D. LC 99-35904. 960p. 1999. pap. text 59.95 incl. audio compact disk (*0-07-134186-2*) McGraw.

— Picmicro Pocket Reference. (Pocket References Ser.). (Illus.). 450p. 2000. pap. text 29.95 (*0-07-136175-8*) McGraw.

Predko, Myke. Programming & Customizing the 8051 Microcontroller. LC 98-48076. 1999. 49.95 (*0-07-134195-1*) Osborne-McGraw.

***Predko, Myke.** Programming & Customizing the 8051 Microcontroller. LC 98-48076. (Tab Electronics Technician Library Ser.). (Illus.). 541p. 1999. pap. 34.95 incl. cd-rom (*0-07-134192-7*) Osborne-McGraw.

— Programming & Customizing the Picmicro. 2nd ed. (TAB Electronics Technician Library). (Illus.). 600p. 2000. pap. text 44.95 (*0-07-136172-3*) McGraw.

Predmore, Helen, et al, eds. Cemeteries of Chester, New York. LC 77-12179. (Orange County, New York Cemeteries Ser.: No. 1). 142p. (Orig.). 1977. pap. 7.00 (*0-685-03716-9*) Orange County Genealog.

Predmore, Richard L. The World of Don Quixote. LC 67-20879. 147p. reprint ed. pap. 45.60 (*0-608-14318-9*, 201701000006) Bks Demand.

Predmore, Richard L., tr. see Machado y Ruiz, Antonio.

Predock, Antoine. Antoine Predock: Buildings & Projects, 1994-1999. LC 98-67849. (Illus.). 224p. 1999. 40.00 (*0-8478-2139-0*, Pub. by Rizzoli Intl); 60.00 (*0-8478-2138-2*, Pub. by Rizzoli Intl) St Martin.

***Predock, Antoine.** Antoine Predock Houses. (Illus.). 16p. 2000. 35.00 (*0-8478-2259-1*) Rizzoli Intl.

Predock, Antoine. Rebecca Binder: Searching for Order Within Chaos. 1999. pap. text 25.00 (*88-7838-055-5*) L'Arca IT.

— Turtle Creek Residence. LC 97-39006. 1997. pap. 19.95 (*1-885254-48-2*, Pub. by Monacelli Pr) Penguin Putnam.

Pree, Hugh De, see De Pree, Hugh.

Pree, Julia De, see De Pree, Julia.

Pree, Max De, see De Pree, Max.

Pree, Wolfgang. Design Patterns for Object-Oriented Software Development. 288p. (C). 1994. 44.95 (*0-201-42294-8*) Addison-Wesley.

— Framework Patterns. (Management Briefings Ser.). 104p. 1996. pap. 85.00 (*1-884842-54-2*, QA76) SIGS Bks & Multimedia.

Preece. Designs on the Landscape. 1991. pap. text 65.00 (*0-471-94754-7*) Wiley.

— Use of Computers in General Practice. 3rd ed. 1994. pap. text 38.00 (*0-443-04938-6*, W B Saunders Co) Harcrt Hlth Sci Grp.

Preece, et al. Cancer of the Bile Ducts & Pancreas. 320p. 1989. text 135.00 (*0-7216-2631-9*, W B Saunders Co) Harcrt Hlth Sci Grp.

Preece, Alison & Cowden, Diane. Young Writers in the Making: Sharing the Process with Parents. LC 93-24636. 144p. (YA). 1993. pap. text 19.50 (*0-435-08778-9*, 08778) Heinemann.

Preece, Alun, ed. Validation & Verification of Knowledge-Based Systems: Papers from the 1993 Workshop. (Technical Reports). (Illus.). 156p. 1994. spiral bd. 25.00 (*0-929280-65-2*) AAAI Pr.

Preece, Alun, jt. ed. see O'Leary, Daniel.

Preece, C. M., ed. see Metallurgical Society of AIME Staff.

Preece, Carolyn M., ed. see Metallurgical Society of AIME Staff.

Preece, Charles O. Edward Willis & Ellen Browning Scripps: An Unmatched Pair. LC 89-90125. (Illus.). 232p. (Orig.). 1990. text 16.95 (*0-9619349-4-8*) C O Preece.

— Teaching Without Tears: The Classroom Teachers Survival Book. rev. ed. LC 88-80829. 124p. (C). 1988. pap. 11.95 (*0-9619349-3-X*) C O Preece.

Preece, D. A., jt. ed. see Lamb, J. D.

Preece, David A. Managing the Adoption of New Technology. LC 88-18309. (Management & New Information Technology Ser.). 304p. reprint ed. pap. 94.30 (*0-608-20375-0*, 207162800002) Bks Demand.

— Organizations & Technical Change: Strategy, Objectives, & Involvement. rev. ed. LC 94-34917. (The Routledge Series in the Management of Technology). 272p. (C). 1995. pap. 80.95 (*0-415-12514-6*, B4890); pap. 18.99 (*0-415-10186-7*, C0296) Thomson Learn.

***Preece, David A.** Work, Change & Competition: Managing for Bass. LC 98-45313. 1999. text. write for info. (*0-415-18525-4*) Routledge.

Preece, David A., et al. Work, Change & Competition: Managing for Bass. LC 98-45313. (Studies in the Management of Technology & Innovation). 1999. pap. write for info. (*0-415-18526-2*) Routledge.

Preece, Debbie. From Combat Zone to Love at Home. (Illus.). 65p. 1998. pap. 12.00 (*0-9647070-0-4*) D Preece.

Preece, Gordon R. The Viability of the Vocation Tradition in Trinitarian, Credal, & Reformed Perspective: The Threefold Call. LC 98-25022. 376p. 1998. text 99.95 (*0-7734-2247-1*) E Mellen.

Preece, J. E., jt. ed. see Geneve, R. L.

Preece, Jennifer Jackson, see Jackson Preece, Jennifer.

Preece, Jenny. Guide to Usability: Human Factors in Computing. LC 93-135333. 144p. (C). 1993. pap. text 28.13 (*0-201-62768-X*) Addison-Wesley.

— Human-Computer Interaction. LC 94-16158. 760p. (C). 1994. 50.63 (*0-201-62769-8*) Addison-Wesley.

Preece, John E. & Read, Paul. The Biology of Horticulture: An Introductory Textbook. LC 92-37678. 496p. 1993. text 61.95 (*0-471-05989-7*) Wiley.

Preece, John F. The Use of Computers in General Practice. 2nd ed. (Illus.). 256p. 1989. pap. text 48.00 (*0-443-04258-6*) Church.

***Preece, Julia.** Combating Social Exclusion in University Adult Education. (Interdisciplinary Research Series in Ethnic, Gender & Class Relations). 192p. 1999. text 61.95 (*0-7546-1150-7*, Pub. by Inst Materials) Ashgate Pub Co.

— Using Foucault & Feminist Theory to Explain Why Some Adults Are Excluded from British University Continuing Education. LC 99-34497. 340p. 1999. text 99.95 (*0-7734-8001-3*) E Mellen.

***Preece, Julian.** Ghunter Grass: His Life & Work. LC 00-33353. (Illus.). 2000. write for info. (*0-312-23603-4*) St Martin.

Preece, Kathleen, ed. see Rajala, Jack.

Preece, M. A., jt. ed. see Ranke, M. B.

Preece, M. A., jt. ed. see Tanner, James M.

Preece, Paul E., et al, eds. Head & Neck Oncology for the General Surgeon. (Illus.). 1991. text 96.50 (*0-7020-1551-2*, Pub. by W B Saunders) Saunders.

Preece, R. A. Designs on the Landscape: Everyday Landscapes, Values & Practice. 283p. 1993. text 145.00 (*0-471-94752-0*) Wiley.

— An Evaluation of the General Public of Scenic Quality in the Cotswolds Area of Outstanding Natural Beauty: A Basis for Monitoring Future Change. (C). 1980. 35.00 (*0-7855-3868-2*, Pub. by Oxford Polytechnic) St Mut.

Preece, R. C., ed. Island Britain: A Quaternary Perspective. (Geological Society Special Publication Ser.: No. 96). (Illus.). 280p. 1995. 93.00 (*1-897799-40-3*, 339, Pub. by Geol Soc Pub Hse) AAPG.

Preece, R. C. & Bridgland, D. R. Late Quaternary Environmental Change in North-West Europe: Excavations at Holywell Coombe, South-East England. LC 98-70919. (ENG & FRE.). xxi, 422 p. 1998. write for info. (*0-412-83230-5*, Chap & Hall NY) Chapman & Hall.

***Preece, Rod.** Animals & Nature: Cultural Myths, Cultural Realities. 336p. 1999. 29.95 (*0-7748-0724-5*, Pub. by UBC Pr) U of Wash Pr.

Preece, Rod & Chamberlain, Lorna. Animal Welfare & Human Values. 344p. (C). 1995. pap. 19.95 (*0-88920-256-7*) W Laurier U Pr.

Preece, Rod, ed. see Nicholson, George A.

Preece, Roy. Starting Research: A New Guide to Researching & Writing Up. 264p. 1994. pap. text 17.95 (*1-85567-091-7*) Bks Intl VA.

Preece-Sandoval, Pam & Reese, Bob. Noodles. (Ten Word Book Ser.). (Illus.). (J). (gr. k-3). 1994. pap. 3.95 (*0-89868-254-1*, Read Res); lib. bdg. 9.95 (*0-89868-253-3*, Read Res) ARO Pub.

— Noodles. Schaffer-Melendez, Gloria, tr. (Un Libro de Diaz Palabras Ser.). (SPA., Illus.). (J). (gr. k-3). 1994. pap. 3.95 (*0-89868-262-2*, Read Res); lib. bdg. 9.95 (*0-89868-261-4*, Read Res) ARO Pub.

Preece-Sandoval, Pam, jt. auth. see Reese, Bob.

Preedy, M., et al. Educational Management: Strategy, Quality & Resources. LC 96-32325. (Leadership & Management in Education Ser.). 288p. 1996. 108.00 (*0-335-19798-1*); pap. 29.95 (*0-335-19797-3*) OpUniv Pr.

Preedy, Margaret, ed. Approaches to Curriculum Management. (Management in Education Ser.). 192p. 1989. 113.00 (*0-335-09249-7*) OpUniv Pr.

Preedy, Victor & Watson, Ronald, eds. Nutrition in the Infant: Practice & Procedures. (Greenwich Medical Media Ser.). (Illus.). 500p. 2000. text 195.00 (*1-900151-62-6*) OUP.

Preedy, Victor R. & Watson, Ronald R., eds. Alcohol & the Gastrointestinal Tract. 368p. 1995. boxed set 199.95 (*0-8493-2480-7*, 2480) CRC Pr.

Preeg, Ernest, jt. ed. see Roberts, Brad.

Preeg, Ernest H. The American Challenge in World Trade. LC 89-9987. (Significant Issues Ser.). 94p. (Orig.). 1989. pap. 8.95 (*0-89206-143-X*) CSIS.

— The American Challenge in World Trade: U. S. Interests in the GATT Multilateral Trading System. LC 89-9987. (Significant Issues Ser.: Vol. 11, No. 7). 116p. reprint ed. pap. 36.00 (*0-7837-6714-5*, 204634100011) Bks Demand.

— The Evolution of a Revolution: Peru & Its Relations with the United States, 1968-1980. LC 81-85655. (Committee on Changing International Realities Ser.). 76p. 1981. pap. 7.00 (*0-686-36871-1*) Natl Planning.

***Preeg, Ernest H.** Feeling Good or Doing Good with Sanctions: Unilateral Economic Sanctions & the U. S. National Interest. LC 99-21602. (Significiant Issues Ser.). 256p. (C). 1999. pap. text 21.95 (*0-89206-349-1*) CSIS.

Preeg, Ernest H. From Here to Free Trade: Essays in Post-Uruguay Round Trade Strategy. LC 97-35616. 168p. 1998. pap. text 18.00 (*0-226-67962-4*) U Ch Pr.

— From Here to Free Trade: Essays in Post-Uruguay Round Trade Strategy. LC 97-35616. (Illus.). 168p. 1998. lib. bdg. 38.00 (*0-226-67961-6*) U Ch Pr.

— Haitian Dilemma: A Case Study in Demographics, Development, & U. S. Foreign Policy. (Significant Issues Ser.). (C). 1996. pap. text 14.95 (*0-89206-277-0*) CSIS.

— Trade Policy Ahead: Three Tracks & One Question. LC 95-15804. (Significant Issues Ser.: vol. 17, no. 2). 85p. (C). 1995. pap. 7.95 (*0-89206-309-2*) CSIS.

— Traders in a Brave New World: The Uruguay Round & the Future of the International Trading System. LC 95-18585. 304p. 1995. 29.95 (*0-226-67959-4*) U Ch Pr.

Preeg, Ernest H. & Levine, Jonathan D. Cuba & the New Caribbean Economic Order. LC 93-2780. (Significant Issues Ser.: Vol. 15). 110p. (C). 1993. pap. text 8.95 (*0-89206-209-6*) CSIS.

Preeg, Ernest H., ed. see Adedeji, Adebayo, et al.

Preer, James R., et al. Integrated Science Manual. 1988. spiral bd. 16.00 (*0-88252-147-0*) Paladin Hse.

Preer, Jean L. Competence, Admissions, & Articulation: Returning to the Basics in Higher Education. Fife, Jonathan D., ed. LC 84-160913. (ASHE-ERIC Higher Education Reports: No. 83-6). 115p. (Orig.). 1983. pap. 24.00 (*0-913317-05-5*) GWU Grad Schl E&HD.

— Lawyers vs. Educators: Black Colleges & Desegregation in Public Higher Education, 61. LC 81-22567. (Contributions in American Studies: No. 61). 278p. 1982. 55.00 (*0-313-23094-3*, PLE/, Greenwood Pr) Greenwood.

Preer, Robert W. The Emergence of Technopolis: Knowledge-Intensive Technologies & Regional Development. LC 91-30616. 200p. 1992. 52.95 (*0-275-94090-X*, C4090, Praeger Pubs) Greenwood.

Preez, B. G. Du, see National Industrial Council Staff & Du Preez, B. G., eds.

Preez, Jan H. Du, see Van den Heever, Louw W. & Du Preez, Jan H.

Preez, Peter Du, see Du Preez, Peter.

Prefer, Nathan. MacArthur's New Guinea Campaign: March-August, 1944. (Illus.). 288p. 1995. 24.95 (*0-938289-51-9*, 289519) Combined Pub.

***Prefer, Nathan N.** Patton's Ghost Corps: Cracking the Siegfried Line. 288p. 2000. pap. 19.95 (*0-89141-708-7*) Presidio Pr.

— Vinegar Joe's War: The Campaigns for Burma. (Illus.). 352p. 2000. 29.95 (*0-89141-715-X*) Presidio Pr.

Preferred Health Strategies Staff. Managed Care & Contracting: A Guide for the Practicing Ophthalmologist. 3rd rev. ed. (Illus.). 1994. pap. write for info. (*1-929196-03-2*) Am Opthlmc Admin.

Preferred Hotels Worldwide Staff. Chef Prefers: Favorite Recipes by the Chef of Preferred Hotels. 1989. 19.98 (*0-8241-4010-9*) Allan Pubs.

Prefontaine, Yves. This Desert Now. Cowan, Judith, tr. from FRE. (Essential Poets Ser.: No. 52). 64p. 1994. pap. 8.00 (*0-920717-66-7*) Guernica Editions.

Pregeant, Russell. Christology Beyond Dogma: Matthew's Christ in Process Hermeneutic. LC 77-78638. (Society of Biblical Literature. Semeia Supplements Ser.: No. 7). 176p. (Orig.). reprint ed. pap. 54.60 (*0-7837-5439-6*, 204520400005) Bks Demand.

— Engaging the New Testament: An Interdisciplinary Introduction. 608p. 1997. pap. 38.00 (*0-8006-3115-3*, 1-3115) Augsburg Fortress.

Pregel, Boris, et al, eds. World Priorities. LC 75-29389. 277p. 1977. reprint ed. pap. text 21.95 (*0-87855-633-8*) Transaction Pubs.

Pregent, Richard. Charting Your Course: How to Prepare to Teach More Effectively. 1994. 21.50 (*0-912150-30-0*); pap. text 21.50 (*1-891859-06-4*) Atwood Pub LLC.

Preger, ed. Scriptores Originum Constantinopolitanarum, Fascicule 1 & 2. (GRE.). 1989. reprint ed. 43.50 (*3-322-00677-8*, T1778, Pub. by B G Teubner) U of Mich Pr.

Preger, L. Iatrogenic Diseases. LC 85-24300. 1986. 100.00 (*0-8493-5888-4*, CRC Reprint) Franklin.

Preger, Leslie. Iatrogenic Diseases, Vol. 2. LC 85-24300. 272p. 1986. 154.00 (*0-8493-5889-2*, CRC Reprint) Franklin.

Preger, Leslie, ed. Iatrogenic Diseases: Ultrasound of Iatrogenic Disease. 208p. 1986. 298.00 (*0-8493-5879-5*, RC90) CRC Pr.

Preger, T., ed. Inscriptiones Graecae Metricae: Ex Scriptoribus Praeter Anthologiam Collectae. xxvii, 215p. 1977. reprint ed. 30.00 (*0-89005-214-X*) Ares.

Preger, Theodorus, ed. Scriptores Originum Constantino-Politanarum. LC 75-7335. (Roman History Ser.). (GRE.). 1975. reprint ed. 35.95 (*0-405-07054-3*) Ayer.

***Pregi.** On Kripke. 2000. pap. 8.25 (*0-534-58366-0*) Wadsworth Pub.

Pregill, Gregory. Late Pleistocene Herpetofaunas from Puerto Rico. (Miscellaneous Publications: No. 71). 72p. 1981. 4.25 (*0-317-04884-8*) U KS Nat Hist Mus.

Pregill, Gregory, jt. ed. see Estes, Richard.

Pregill, P. Landscape in History: Europe, Vol. 1. 2nd ed. (Landscape Architecture Ser.). (C). 1998. pap. 39.95 (*0-442-02609-9*, VNR) Wiley.

Pregill, Philip & Volkman, Nancy. Landscapes in History: Design & Planning in the Western Tradition. 784p. 1992. text 72.95 (*0-442-31804-9*, VNR) Wiley.

***Pregill, Philip & Volkman, Nancy.** Landscapes in History: Designing & Planning in the Eastern & Western Traditions. 2nd ed. LC 98-25814. 864p. 1999. 89.95 (*0-471-29328-8*) Wiley.

Pregillp. Landscape in History, 2 vols., Set. 2nd ed. (Landscape Architecture Ser.). (C). 1998. pap. 79.95 (*0-442-02613-7*, VNR) Wiley.

— Landscape in History: Americas, Vol. 2. 2nd ed. (Landscape Architecture Ser.). (C). 1998. pap. 39.95 (*0-442-02612-9*, VNR) Wiley.

Pregliasco, Janice. Silent Partner. 1997. pap. text 15.95 (*0-226-67929-2*); lib. bdg. 34.95 (*0-226-67928-4*) U Ch Pr.

***Pregmon, Jeff.** Jerkwater Freight: A Collection of Poems, Essays & Short Stories. LC 99-91903. 147p. 2000. 25.00 (*0-7388-1366-4*); pap. 18.00 (*0-7388-1367-2*) Xlibris Corp.

***Pregnall, Teresa.** Special Recipes from the Charleston Cake Lady. LC 99-87686. 144p. 2000. pap. 15.00 (*0-688-17032-3*, Wm Morrow) Morrow Avon.

Pregnall, Teresa. Treasured Recipes from the Charleston Cake Lady: Fast, Fabulous, Easy-to-Make Cakes for Every Occasion. LC 95-47441. 1996. 17.00 (*0-688-13931-0*, Hearst) Hearst Commns.

Pregnancy & Infant Loss Center Staff. The Rocking Horse Is Lonely: And Other Stories of Father's Grief. Nelson, James D., ed. 28p. 1994. pap. 2.50 (*1-892254-01-8*) Preg & Infant.

Pregnoff, Michael V., et al. Michael V. Pregnoff, John E. Rinne. LC 96-3088. (Connections: the EERI Oral History Ser.). 1996. pap. 15.00 (*0-943198-53-4*) Earthquake Eng.

Pregosin, P. S. Transition Metal Nuclear Magnetic Resonance. (Studies in Inorganic Chemistry: Vol. 13). 352p. 1991. 255.00 (*0-444-88176-X*, SIC 13) Elsevier.

Preheim, Beth, ed. see Cleaver, Richard G.

***Preheim, Lois Janzem.** Roots Out of Dry Ground: First Mennonite Church -- Nampa, Idaho. LC 00-133082. (Illus.). 248p. 2000. write for info. (*1-57579-191-9*) Pine Hill Pr.

Prehistoric Society of East Anglia Staff. Report on the Excavations at Grime's Graves: Weeting, Norfolk, March - May, 1914. Clarke, W. G., ed. LC 77-86437. reprint ed. 28.00 (*0-404-16676-8*) AMS Pr.

Prehm, Herbert J. & Altman, Reuben. Improving Instruction Through Classroom Research. 1976. pap. 14.95 (*0-89108-056-2*, 7601) Love Pub Co.

Prehn, Alyene E. Prehn: Journal of a Genealogist, with Ancestral Wills, Includes Anderson, Bass, Elder, Gaddy, Griggs, Ingersoll, Kelsey, Lewis, Westall, Wright Families. (Illus.). 864p. 1994. reprint ed. pap. 115.00 (*0-8328-4099-8*); reprint ed. lib. bdg. 125.00 (*0-8328-4098-X*) Higginson Bk Co.

***Prehn, John W.** On the Edge: Striptease in a Small-Town Setting. 4th rev. ed. (Illus.). viii, 150p. 1999. pap. 25.00 (*0-9652983-1-0*) J W Prehn.

Prehn, John W. Push a Button, Pull a String. iv, 96p. (Orig.). 1996. pap. 12.00 (*0-9652983-0-2*) J W Prehn.

Prehn, Roger. Gathered & Sent: An Introduction to Worship, Leader Guide. 48p. 1999. pap. 7.99 (*0-8066-3845-1*, 3-81, Augsburg) Augsburg Fortress.

Prehn, S. & Toetenel, W. J., eds. VDM '91 Formal Software Development Methods, 4th International Symposium of VDM Europe, Noorwijkerhout, the Netherlands, October 21-25, 1991 Proceedings, Vol. 1: Conference Contributions. (Lecture Notes in Computer Science Ser.: Vol. 551). xiii, 699p. 1991. 74.95 (*0-387-54834-3*) Spr-Verlag.

— VDM '91 Formal Software Development Methods, 4th International Symposium of VDM Europe, Noorwijkerhout, the Netherlands, October 21-25, 1991 Proceedings, Vol. 2: Tutorials. (Lecture Notes in Computer Science Ser.: Vol. 552). xiv, 430p. 1991. 44.95 (*0-387-54868-8*) Spr-Verlag.

Prehofer, C. Solving Higher Order Equations: From Logic to Programming. LC 97-31142. (Progress in Theoretical Computer Science Ser.). 200p. 1997. 64.50 (*0-8176-4032-0*) Birkhauser.

Prehofer, Christian. Solving Higher-Order Equations: From Logic to Programming. LC 97-31142. (Progress in Theoretical Computer Science Ser.). 1997. write for info. (*3-7643-4032-0*) Birkhauser.

Preibel, H. G., jt. auth. see Preibel, U.

Preibel, U. & Preibel, H. G. Engels-Trompeten. Brugmansia und Datura (Angels Trumpet. Brugmansia & Datura) 2nd rev. ed. (GER., Illus.). 141p. 1997. 34.00 (*3-8001-6614-3*, Pub. by Eugen Ulmer) Balogh.

Preibisch, P. Two Studies on the Roman Pontifices. LC 75-10647. (Ancient Religion & Mythology Ser.). 1976. 23.95 (*0-405-07271-6*) Ayer.

Preibisius, jt. auth. see Eckert.

Preibisz, J. Polish Dissident Publications. LC 82-7677. 382p. 1982. 65.00 (*0-275-90878-X*, C0878, Praeger Pubs) Greenwood.

Preik, Brooks. Haunted Wilmington: And the Cape Fear Coast. LC 95-79611. (Illus.). 156p. (Orig.). 1995. pap. 9.95 (*0-9635967-3-X*) Banks Channel.

Preil, Gabriel. Sunset Possibilities & Other Poems. Friend, Robert, tr. from HEB. (Jewish Poetry Ser.). 150p. 1985. pap. 8.95 (*0-8276-0241-3*) JPS Phila.

— To Be Recorded. Barkan, Stanley H., ed. Gilson, Estelle, tr. (Review Jewish Writers Chapbook Ser.: No. 6). 48p. 1991. 15.00 (*0-89304-306-0*); pap. 5.00 (*0-89304-307-9*); audio 10.00 (*0-89304-310-9*); VHS 50.00 (*0-89304-311-7*) Cross-Cultrl NY.

— To Be Recorded: Mini Book. Barkan, Stanley H., ed. Gilson, Estelle, tr. (Review Jewish Writers Chapbook Ser.: No. 6). 48p. 1991. 15.00 (*0-89304-308-7*); pap. 5.00 (*0-89304-309-5*) Cross-Cultrl NY.

Prein, Gerald, jt. ed. see Blossfeld, Hans-Peter.

Prein, J., ed. Manual of Internal Fixation in the Cranio-Facial Skeleton: Techniques As Recommended by the AO/ASIF-Maxillofacial Group. LC 97-35559. (Illus.). 235p. 1997. 185.00 (*3-540-61810-4*) Spr-Verlag.

Prein, J., et al, eds. Atlas of Tumors of the Facial Skeleton. (Illus.). 180p. 1986. 268.00 (*0-387-16167-8*) Spr-Verlag.

Prein, J., jt. ed. see Greenberg, Alex M.

Prein, M., et al, eds. Research for the Future Development of Aquaculture in Ghana. LC 99-203311. (ICLARM Conference Proceedings Ser.: No. 42). 94p. 1995. per. write for info. (*971-8709-43-6*, Pub. by ICLARM) Intl Spec Bk.

Prein, M., et al. Assessment of Integrated Aquaculture Potential Using a Farmer-Participatory Approach: A Case Study in Ghana. (ICLARM Technical Reports). 250p. 1995. per. write for info. (*971-8709-52-5*, Pub. by ICLARM) Intl Spec Bk.

Preinreich, Gabriel A. The Nature of Dividends. Brief, Richard P., ed. LC 77-87286. (Development of Contemporary Accounting Thought Ser.). 1978. reprint ed. lib. bdg. 24.95 (*0-405-10914-8*) Ayer.

Preis, Art. Labor's Giant Step: The First Twenty Years of the CIO: 1936-55. LC 72-79771. 538p. 1972. reprint ed. pap. 26.95 (*0-87348-263-8*); reprint ed. lib. bdg. 65.00 (*0-87348-371-5*) Pathfinder NY.

Preis, Donna. Shapes. LC 97-162833. (Illus.). (J). 1997. write for info. (*0-7853-2293-0*) Pubns Intl Ltd.

Preis, Donna, jt. auth. see Siede, George.

Preis, Donna, jt. photos by see Siede, George.

Preisendorfer, R. & Sneddon, Ian N. Radiative Transfer on Discrete Spaces. LC 64-12663. (International Series of Monographs on Pure & Applied Mathematics: Vol. 74). 1965. 207.00 (*0-08-010592-0*, Pub. by Pergamon Repr) Franklin.

Preiser, Geburtstag Von Gert, see Von Gert Preiser, Geburtstag.

Preiser, Gerd. Allgemeine Krankheitsbezeichnungen im Corpus Hippocraticum: Bedeutung und Gebrauch von Nousos und Nosema. (Ars Medica, Abt. 2, Griechisch Lateinische Medizin Ser.). (C). 1976. text 101.55 (*3-11-001830-6*) De Gruyter.

Preiser, Monty. Soft Tissue Injury: 1991 Supplement. 254p. 1995. pap. text. write for info. (*0-87473-982-9*, 65916-10, MICHIE) LEXIS Pub.

Preiser, Monty L., jt. auth. see Preiser, Stanley E.

Preiser, Stanley E. & Preiser, Monty L. Handling Soft Tissue Injury Cases, 2 vols. LC 85-7567. (Kluwer Litigation Library). 1985. text 160.00 (*0-685-10618-7*, MICHIE) LEXIS Pub.

— Handling Soft Tissue Injury Cases, 2 vols., 1. 1985. text. write for info. (*0-318-59228-2*, MICHIE) LEXIS Pub.

— Handling Soft Tissue Injury Cases, 2 vols., 2. LC 85-7567. (Kluwer Litigation Library). 1985. text. write for info. (*0-930273-86-9*, MICHIE) LEXIS Pub.

— Handling Soft Tissue Injury Cases 1998 Supplement: Legal Aspects. 100p. 1998. pap. write for info. (*0-327-00890-3*, 6591612) LEXIS Pub.

Preiser, Stanley E., et al. Handling Soft Tissue Injury Cases, 2 vols. 1991. suppl. ed. 35.00 (*0-87473-634-X*, MICHIE) LEXIS Pub.

— Handling Soft Tissue Injury Cases, 2 vols. 1992. suppl. ed. 35.00 (*0-930273-52-4*, MICHIE) LEXIS Pub.

***Preiser, Stanley E., et al.** Handling Soft Tissue Injury Cases, 3 vols. 3rd ed. Incl. Vol. 1. Handling Soft Tissue Injury Cases. 3rd ed. 1999. (*0-327-10008-7*, 65911-11); Vol. 2. Handling Soft Tissue Injury Cases. 3rd ed. 1999. (*0-327-10009-5*, 65912-12); Vol. 3. Handling Soft Tissue Injury Cases. 3rd ed. 1999. (*0-327-10010-9*, 65917-12); 1500p. 1999. 195.00 (*0-327-10007-9*, 65910-11) LEXIS Pub.

Preiser, Stanley E., et al. Handling Soft Tissue Injury Cases, Cycle A. 1992. suppl. ed. write for info. (*0-614-05830-9*, MICHIE) LEXIS Pub.

— Handling Soft Tissue Injury Cases, 3 vols., Set. 1985. 240.00 (*0-930273-13-3*, 65910-10, MICHIE) LEXIS Pub.

— Preparing & Winning Medical Negligence Cases, 3 vols., Set. 2nd ed. 1989. 240.00 (*1-55834-132-3*, MICHIE) LEXIS Pub.

Preiser, Wolfgang F., ed. Building Evaluation. (Illus.). 344p. 1989. 89.50 (*0-306-43337-0*, Plenum Trade) Perseus Pubng.

Preiser, Wolfgang F. E., jt. auth. see Scheer, Brenda C.

Preisigke, Friedrich. Fachworter Des Offentlichen Verwaltungsdienstes Agyptens in Den Griechischen Papyrusurkunden der Ptolemaisch-Romischen Zeit. x, 186p. 1975. reprint ed. write for info. (*3-487-05896-0*) G Olms Pubs.

— Girowesen Im Griechischen Agypten, Enthaltend Korngiro, Geldgiro, Girobanknotariat Mit Einschlub Des Archivwesens. xvi, 575p. 1971. reprint ed. write for info. (*0-318-71002-1*) G Olms Pubs.

— Sammelbuch Griechischer Urkunden Aus Aegypten, 3 vols. 1530p. 1974. reprint ed. 500.00 (*3-11-004756-X*) De Gruyter.

Preisinger, Helmut. Strukturanalyse und Zeigerwert der Auenund Ufervegetation Im Hamburger Hafen- und Hafenrandgebiet. (Dissertationes Botanicae Ser.: Band 174). (GER., Illus.). ii, 296p. 1991. pap. 77.00 (*3-443-64086-9*, Pub. by Gebruder Borntraeger) Balogh.

Preiskel, Harold W. Overdentures Made Easy: A Guide to Implant & Root Supported Prostheses. 240p. 1996. text 98.00 (*1-85097-039-4*) Quint Pub Co.

***Preisler.** Zorro & Circle of Fire. 3rd ed. (Zorro Ser.: No. 3). 1998. mass mkt. 5.99 (*0-8125-6769-2*) Forge NYC.

Preisler, Bent. A Handbook of English Grammar on Functional Principles. 2nd rev. ed. 288p. 1997. 33.00 (*87-7288-655-2*, Pub. by Aarhus Univ Pr) David Brown.

— Linguistic Sex Roles in Conversation. (Contributions to the Sociology of Language Ser.: No. 45). (Illus.). xviii, 350p. 1986. lib. bdg. 115.40 (*0-89925-225-7*) Mouton.

Preisler, Bent, ed. see Sorensen, Knud.

Preisler, Jerome. Annihilation. (Mortal Kombat Ser.). 1997. mass mkt. 6.99 (*0-8125-3933-8*, Pub. by Tor Bks) St Martin.

— Annihilation. (Mortal Kombat Ser.). (J). 1997. mass mkt. 3.99 (*0-8125-3934-6*, Pub. by Tor Bks) St Martin.

— Homicide: Life on the Street. 1996. mass mkt. 5.99 (*1-57297-227-0*) Blvd Books.

— Homicide: White Butterflies. 1998. mass mkt. 5.99 (*0-425-16494-2*) Berkley Pub.

— Homicide No. 2: Violent Delights. 2nd ed. 1998. mass mkt. 5.99 (*1-57297-340-4*) Blvd Books.

— Last Man Standing. 1996. mass mkt. 5.99 (*1-57297-185-1*) Blvd Books.

— Zorro & the Jaguar Warriors. 224p. 1997. mass mkt. 4.99 (*0-8125-6767-6*, Pub. by Forge NYC) St Martin.

— Zorro & the Jaguar Warriors. (J). 1998. 10.09 (*0-606-13946-X*, Pub. by Turtleback) Demco.

— Zorro & the Shadow Riders. 1998. 10.09 (*0-606-13947-8*, Pub. by Turtleback) Demco.

Preisler, Jerome, jt. auth. see Alexander, David.

***Preisler, Julian H.** Jewish Genealogy Resources: Mid-Atlantic States. LC 98-74993. 127p. 1999. per. 12.00 (*1-55856-288-5*, 139) Closson Pr.

Preisler, Julian H. Pioneer American Synagogues - A State by State Guide. LC 97-211149. x, 165p. 1997. pap. 17.00 (*0-7884-0711-2*, P617) Heritage Bk.

Preisner, Olga K. Chinese Export Porcelains from the Collection of Dr. & Mrs. Harold L. Tonkin: Exhibition Catalogue. (Illus.). 48p. 1980. pap. 4.50 (*0-911209-17-4*) Palmer Mus Art.

— French Drawings from European Collections: The Former Armand Gobiet Collection. Landman, Hedy B., ed. (Illus.). 64p. 1979. pap. 5.00 (*0-911209-16-6*) Palmer Mus Art.

— Hemline, Neckline, Streamline: Women's Fashions 1890-1940 from the Collection of Beverley Birks. (Illus.). 44p. 1981. pap. 7.50 (*0-911209-23-9*) Palmer Mus Art.

— Paintings & Sculpture from Central Pennsylvania Collectors: Exhibition Catalogue. (Illus.). 80p. 1984. pap. 4.50 (*0-911209-30-1*) Palmer Mus Art.

Preisner, Olga K., ed. Bellefonte Collects: Exhibition Catalogue. (Illus.). 54p. 1989. pap. 10.00 (*0-911209-40-9*) Palmer Mus Art.

— Gods of the Greeks: Greek Coins from a Private Collection: Exhibition Catalogue. (Illus.). 24p. (Orig.). 1984. pap. 0.90 (*0-911209-31-X*) Palmer Mus Art.

— The Numismatic History of Ireland: History of Irish Coinage 1000 A. D. to the Present - Coins from a Private Collection: Exhibition Catalogue. (Illus.). 28p. 1984. pap. 2.50 (*0-911209-32-8*) Palmer Mus Art.

Preisner, Olga K. & Landman, Hedy B. The England of William Penn: 1644-1718. (Illus.). 92p. 1982. pap. 12.50 (*0-911209-26-3*) Palmer Mus Art.

Preiss. Battlestar Galactica, No. 2. 1999. mass mkt. 9.95 (*0-671-01179-0*) PB.

— Great American Baby. 1998. 19.95 (*0-671-01205-3*) S&S Trade.

— How to Raise a Drug Free Kid. 1998. mass mkt. 5.99 (*0-671-01176-6*) PB.

***Preiss, Bruno.** Data Structures & Algorithms with Object-Oriented Design Patterns in C++ LC 98-18107. 688p. 1998. text 80.95 (*0-471-24134-2*) Wiley.

Preiss, Bruno, jt. ed. see Loucks, Wayne.

Preiss, Bruno R. Data Structures & Algorithms with Object-Oriented Design Patterns in Java. LC 99-21792. 656p. 1999. text 75.95 (*0-471-34613-6*) Wiley.

***Preiss, Byron.** Isaac Asimov's Robot City, Vol. 2. 460p. 2000. reprint ed. pap. 14.00 (*0-671-03905-9*, Pub. by ibooks) S&S Trade.

Preiss, Byron. Town Mouse. (J). 1994. mass mkt. 4.99 (*0-553-54183-8*) BDD Bks Young Read.

Preiss, Byron & Huck, Kathy, eds. The Best Children's Books in the World: A Treasury of Illustrated Stories. (Illus.). 320p. (J). 1996. 29.95 (*0-8109-1246-5*, Pub. by Abrams) Time Warner.

***Preiss, Byron & Ssi.** American Heritage History of the US for Young People: Jewel Case. 1998. 6.98 (*0-671-31532-3*) S&S Trade.

Preiss, Jack. Camp William James. (Illus.). 1978. 23.00 (*0-912148-07-1*); pap. 15.95 (*0-912148-08-X*) Argo Bks.

Preiss, Jack, et al, eds. The Biochemistry of Plants, Carbohydrates Vol. 14: A Comprehensive Treatise. 529p. 1988. text 157.00 (*0-12-675414-4*) Acad Pr.

Preiss, Jack, jt. ed. see Heath, Robert L.

Preiss, Jack J. & Ehrlich, Howard J. An Examination of Role Theory: The Case of the State Police. LC 66-10874. 296p. reprint ed. pap. 91.80 (*0-8357-2943-5*, 203919900011) Bks Demand.

Preiss, Kenneth, et al. Agile Competitors & Virtual Organizations: Strategies for Enriching the Customer. (Industrial Engineering Ser.). 414p. 1994. text 34.95 (*0-442-01903-3*, VNR) Wiley.

— Cooperate to Compete: Building Agile Business Relationships. 336p. 1996. 25.95 (*0-471-28760-1*, VNR) Wiley.

— Handbook for Virtual Organization: Tools for Management of Quality Intellectual Property & Risk & Revenue Sharing. 800p. 1996. spiral bd. 245.00 (*0-9654041-0-2*); cd-rom 245.00 (*0-9654041-1-0*) Comptitve Tech.

Preiss, Linda, ed. see Baoudndi, M. Salah, et al.

Preiss, Raymond W., jt. ed. see Allen, Mike.

Preiss, Scott. Table Tennis: The Sport. 80p. (C). 1991. text. write for info. (*0-697-13635-3*) Brown & Benchmark.

Preiss, Sherry. Focus on Listening & Speaking Advanced Level. LC 97-41538. 288p. 1998. pap. text 23.10 (*0-201-57177-3*) Addison-Wesley.

Preissle, Judith, jt. auth. see LeCompte, Margaret D.

Preissle, Judith, jt. auth. see Xue Lan Rong.

Preiswerk, Matias. Educating in the Living Word: A Theoretical Framework for Christian Education. Barr, Robert R., tr. from SPA. LC 87-9221.Tr. of Educar en la Palabra la Viva: Marco Teorico para la Educacion Cristiana. 143p. reprint ed. pap. 44.40 (*0-608-20272-X*, 207153100012) Bks Demand.

Preiswerk, Roy, ed. see Kapp, K. William.

Preiswork, Roy & Perrot, Dominique. Ethnocentrism & History. LC 74-81856. 1978. 21.50 (*0-88357-071-8*); pap. 8.95 (*0-88357-072-6*) NOK Pubs.

Prejean, Andrea I., jt. auth. see Fox, Lynn H.

Prejean, Helen. Dead Man Walking: An Eyewitness Account of the Death Penalty in the United States. 276p. 1994. pap. 13.00 (*0-679-75131-9*) Vin Bks.

— Dead Man Walking: The Shooting Script. 1996. pap. text 12.00 (*0-676-51014-0*) Vin Bks.

Prejevalsky, N. Mongolia: The Tangut Country & the Solitudes of Northern Tibet. (C). 1991. reprint ed. text 74.00 (*81-206-0680-9*, Pub. by Asian Educ Servs) S Asia.

Prejovich, S, ed. Socialism: Institutional, Philosophical & Economic Issues. (C). 1987. lib. bdg. 122.00 (*90-247-3487-8*) Kluwer Academic.

Preker, Alexander S. & Feachem, Richard G. Market Mechanisms & the Health Sector in Central & Eastern Europe. (Technical Papers: Vol. 293). 64p. 1996. pap. 22.00 (*0-8213-3331-3*, 13331) World Bank.

Prekopa, A. Studies on Mathematical Programming. (Mathematical Methods of Operations Research Ser.: Vol. 1). 200p. (C). 1980. 53.00 (*963-05-1854-6*, Pub. by Akade Kiado) St Mut.

Prekopa, A., et al, eds. System Modelling & Optimization. (Lecture Notes in Control & Information Sciences: Vol. 84). (Illus.). 1060p. 1986. pap. 153.00 (*0-387-16854-0*) Spr-Verlag.

Prekopa, Andras. Stochastic Programming. LC 95-10779. (Mathematics & Its Applications Ser.). 554p. (C). 1995. lib. bdg. 289.00 (*0-7923-3482-5*) Kluwer Academic.

Prelas, Mark A., et al, eds. Wide Band Gap Electronic Materials: Proceedings of the NATO Advanced Research Workshop on "Wide Band Gap Electronic Materials-Diamond, Aluminum Nitride & Boron Nitride", Minsk, Belarus, May 4-6, 1994. LC 95-7367. (NATO Advanced Science Institutes - Partnership Sub Series 3: Vol. 1). 552p. (C). 1995. text 279.50 (*0-7923-3405-1*) Kluwer Academic.

Prelas, Mark A., et al. Handbook of Industrial Diamonds & Diamond Films. LC 97-22477. (Illus.). 1240p. 1997. text 235.00 (*0-8247-9994-1*) Dekker.

Prelasased Composites, Mark A. & Workshop on Diamond Based Composites Staff. Diamond & Related Materials Based Composites: NATO Advanced Research Workshop on Diamond Based Composites, Saint Petersburg, Russia, June 21-22, 1997. LC 97-26092. (NATO ASI Series, Partnership SubSeries 3: High Technology). 1997. text 197.50 (*0-7923-4667-X*) Kluwer Academic.

Prelec, Krsto, ed. Production & Neutralization of Negative Ions & Beams: International Symposium, Brookhaven, 1983. 3rd ed. LC 84-70379. (AIP Conference Proceedings Ser.: No. 111). 778p. 1984. lib. bdg. 53.75 (*0-88318-310-2*) Am Inst Physics.

— Production & Neutralization of Negative Ions & Beams: Seventh International Symposium/Production & Application of Light Negative Ions: Sixth European Workshop: A Joint Meeting. (AIP Conference Proceedings Ser.: No. 380). (Illus.). 624p. 1996. 155.00 (*1-56396-565-8*, AIP Pr) Spr-Verlag.

Preleit, Jim, jt. auth. see Stevens, Mark.

Preleshnik, Danielle, see Ka-Tzetnik, pseud.

Prelinger, Catherine M. Charity, Challenge, & Change: Religious Dimensions of the Mid-Nineteenth Century Women's Movement in Germany, 75. LC 86-19432. (Contributions in Women's Studies: No. 75). 225p. 1987. 59.95 (*0-313-25401-X*, PCY/) Greenwood.

Prelinger, Catherine M., ed. Episcopal Women: Gender, Spirituality, & Commitment in an American Mainline Denomination. 384p. 1996. pap. text 19.95 (*0-19-510465-X*) OUP.

***Prelinger, Elizabeth.** American Impressionism. (Treasures from the Smithsonian American Art Museum). (Illus.). 112p. 2000. 19.95 (*0-8230-0190-3*) Watsn-Guptill.

— The Gilded Age. LC 99-50977. (Treasures from the Smithsonian American Art Museum). (Illus.). 112p. 2000. pap. 19.95 (*0-8230-0192-X*) Watsn-Guptill.

Prelinger, Elizabeth. Kathe Kollwitz. (Illus.). 272p. 1994. pap. 30.00 (*0-300-06168-4*) Yale U Pr.

Prelinger, Elizabeth, et al. The Symbolist Prints of Edvard Munch: The Vivian & David Campbell Collection. LC 96-3074. (Illus.). 224p. 1996. 60.00 (*0-300-06952-9*) Yale U Pr.

Prelinger, Richard, ed. Monitor America. (Frequency Guide Ser.: No. 8). (Illus.). 608p. 1985. 14.95 (*0-939430-07-X*) Scanner Master.

Prelinger, Richard & Ries, Celeste R., eds. Footage Ninety-One: North American Film & Video Sources. LC 88-90769. 1991. pap. 115.00 (*0-927347-03-2*) Sec Line Search.

Prell, Bertrand, jt. ed. see Rodriguez, Suzanne.

Prell, Dorothy, ed. Poems from Farmers Valley: A Celebration of Rural Life. LC 99-203974. (Illus.). 256p. (Orig.). 1999. pap. 16.95 (*1-889406-00-7*) Prell Pub.

Prell, Frank. Balloon Pins, Vol. 1. LC 85-71996. (Illus.). 112p. (Orig.). 1985. per. 12.95 (*0-9615189-0-1*) Oxford Promot.

Prell, George D., ed. The Neurobiology of Histamine. (Illus.). 1999. 125.00 (*0-89603-478-X*) Humana.

Prell, Heinz-Peter & Schebben-Schmidt, Marietheres. Die Verbableitung im Fruehneuhochdeutschen. (Studia Linguistica Germanica: Vol. 41). (GER.). xxx, 424p. 1996. lib. bdg. 196.95 (*3-11-014268-6*) De Gruyter.

Prell, Jan R., jt. auth. see Orcutt, Ted L.

Prell, Riv-Ellen. Fighting to Become Americans: Jews, Gender & the Anxiety of Assimilation. LC 98-37369. 272p. 1999. 28.50 (*0-8070-3632-3*) Beacon Pr.

***Prell, Riv-Ellen.** Fighting to Become Americans: Jews, Gender & the Anxiety of Assimilation. 2000. pap. 18.00 (*0-8070-3633-1*) Beacon Pr.

Prell, Riv-Ellen. Interdisciplinary Writing Through Multidisciplinary Writing. Bridwell-Bowles, Lillian et al, eds. (Technical Reports: No. 3). 26p. (Orig.). 1993. pap. 3.00 (*1-881221-06-7*) U Minn Ctr Interdis.

— Prayer & Community: The Havurah in American Judaism. LC 88-25107. (Illus.). 336p. reprint ed. pap. 104.20 (*0-608-10599-6*, 2071220) Bks Demand.

— Prayer & Community: The Havurah Movement in American Judaism. LC 88-25107. (Illus.). 336p. 1989. pap. 21.95 (*0-8143-1935-1*) Wayne St U Pr.

Preller, James. Bugs Bunny in Space. 1996. pap. 2.95 (*0-590-98480-2*) Scholastic Inc.

— Cardinal & Sunflower. LC 97-11646. (Illus.). 32p. (J). (ps-3). 1998. 14.95 (*0-06-026222-2*) HarpC.

— The Case of Hermie the Missing Hamster. (Jigsaw Jones Ser.: No. 1). (Illus.). (J). (gr. 1-4). 1998. pap. text 3.99 (*0-590-69125-2*) Scholastic Inc.

— The Case of the Christmas Snowman. (Jigsaw Jones Ser.). (Illus.). (J). (gr. 1-4). 1998. pap. text 3.99 (*0-590-69126-0*) Scholastic Inc.

***Preller, James.** The Case of the Great Sled Race. (Jigsaw Jones Ser.: No. 8). (Illus.). 80p. (J). (gr. 1-4). 2000. pap. 4.99 (*0-439-11427-6*, Little Apple) Scholastic Inc.

— Case of the Great Sled Race. (Illus.). (J). 1999. 9.44 (*0-606-18527-5*) Turtleback.

— Case of the Mummy Mystery. (Illus.). (J). 2000. 9.44 (*0-606-18528-3*) Turtleback.

Preller, James. The Case of the Mummy Mystery, 1 vol., Vol. 6. (Jigsaw Jones Ser.: No. 6). (Illus.). 80p. (gr. 1-4). 1999. pap. text 3.99 (*0-439-08094-0*) Scholastic Inc.

— The Case of the Runaway Dog. (Jigsaw Jones Ser.: No. 7). (Illus.). (J). (gr. 1-4). 1999. mass mkt. 3.99 (*0-439-11426-8*) Scholastic Inc.

***Preller, James.** Case of the Runaway Dog. (Illus.). (J). 1999. 9.44 (*0-606-18529-1*) Turtleback.

Preller, James. The Case of the Secret Valentine. (Jigsaw Jones Ser.: No. 3). (Illus.). 80p. (gr. 1-4). 1999. pap. 3.99 (*0-590-69127-9*) Scholastic Inc.

***Preller, James.** Case of the Spooky Sleepover. (Illus.). (J). 1999. 9.44 (*0-606-16586-X*) Turtleback.

Preller, James. The Case of the Spooky Sleepover, Vol. 4. (Jigsaw Jones Ser.: No. 4). (Illus.). (J). (gr. 1-4). 1999. pap. 3.99 (*0-590-69129-5*) Scholastic Inc.

***Preller, James.** Case of the Stinky Science Project. (Illus.). (J). 2000. 9.44 (*0-606-18530-5*) Turtleback.

— The Case of the Stinky Science Project, Vol. 9. (Jigsaw Jones Ser.: No. 9). (Illus.). 144p. (J). (gr. 1-4). 2000. mass mkt. 3.99 (*0-439-11428-4*) Scholastic Inc.

Preller, James. The Case of the Stolen Baseball Card, Vol. 5. (Jigsaw Jones Ser.: No. 5). (J). (gr. 1-4). 1999. pap. text 3.99 (*0-439-08083-5*) Scholastic Inc.

***Preller, James.** Crazy for Crazy Bones, Vol. 1. (Illus.). 48p. (gr. k-3). 1999. pap. 5.99 (*0-439-14980-0*) Scholastic Inc.

Preller, James. Crazy for Crazy Bones Sticker Book, Vol. 1. (Illus.). 48p. (gr. k-3). 1999. pap. 4.99 (*0-439-15402-2*) Scholastic Inc.

— Elefante Tiene Hipo. (My First Hello Reader Ser.). (SPA.). (J). 1999. pap. 3.50 (*0-439-05112-6*) Scholastic Inc.

***Preller, James.** Godzilla Deluxe Storybook. LC 99-191021. (Godzilla Ser.). 48p. (J). (gr. 2-5). 1998. pap. text 5.98 (*0-590-57213-X*) Scholastic Inc.

— Hiccups for Elephant. (Hello Reader! Level 2 Ser.). 1994. 8.70 (*0-606-07641-7*, Pub. by Turtleback) Demco.

Preller, James. In Search of the Real Tasmanian Devil. LC 97-135100. (Kratt's Creatures Ser.). (Illus.). 32p. (J). (gr. k-3). 1996. pap. text 3.50 (*0-590-53739-3*) Scholastic Inc.

Preller, James. In Search of the Real Tasmanian Devil. (Illus.). (J). 1996. 8.95 (*0-606-18565-8*) Turtleback.

— McGwire & Sosa: A Season to Remember. (J). 1998. pap. 6.99 (*0-689-82871-3*) S&S Childrens.

Preller, James. NBA Book of Big & Little. 32p. (J). (ps-2). 1998. pap. text 4.99 (*0-590-37756-6*) Scholastic Inc.

***Preller, James.** The NBA Book of Opposites. (NBA Ser.). (Illus.). 32p. (J). (ps-2). 2000. pap. 4.50 (*0-439-14075-7*) Scholastic Inc.

Preller, James. Next Generation. 32p. (gr. 2-4). 1998. pap. text 7.99 (*0-590-37240-8*) Scholastic Inc.

— Off to Elephant School. (Kratt's Creatures Ser.). (J). (ps-3). 1996. pap. text 3.50 (*0-590-53740-7*) Scholastic Inc.

***Preller, James.** Rock Solid. (J). 2000. 4.99 (*0-439-23525-1*) Scholastic Inc.

— Smackdown! Meet the Stars of Professional Wrestling. (Illus.). (J). 2000. pap. 5.99 (*0-439-21629-X*) Scholastic Inc.

Preller, James. Sports Shots: Michael Jordan. (J). 1995. 1.49 (*0-590-62327-3*) Scholastic Inc.

***Preller, James.** Superstars; Rock Solid: The Slammin' Unauthorized Biography of the Rock. (Illus.). (gr. 4-7). 2000. pap. text 4.50 (*0-439-22221-4*) Scholastic Inc.

Preller, James. The Ultimate NBA Postcard Book. (gr. 5-7). 1997. pap. 7.99 (*0-590-13514-7*) Scholastic Inc.

— Wake Me in Spring. (Hello Reader! Ser.). (Illus.). (J). (gr. 2). 1994. pap. 2.95 (*0-590-48189-4*, Cartwheel) Scholastic Inc.

— Wake Me in the Spring. LC 93-16787. (Hello Reader! Ser.). (Illus.). 32p. (J). (ps-3). 1994. pap. 3.50 (*0-590-47500-2*, Cartwheel) Scholastic Inc.

— What's Bugging You? (Kratt's Creatures Ser.). 1997. pap. 3.50 (*0-590-53742-3*) Scholastic Inc.

Preller, James, jt. auth. see Kovacs, Deborah.

Preller, James, jt. auth. see Kovaks, Deborah.

Preller, James, jt. auth. see Layden, Joe.

Preller, Jimmy. Hiccups for Elephant. LC 94-15585. (Hello Reader! Ser.). (Illus.). 32p. (J). (ps-3). 1995. 3.50 (*0-590-48588-1*, Cartwheel) Scholastic Inc.

— Sports Shots: Deion Sanders. (J). 1995. 1.49 (*0-590-62328-1*) Scholastic Inc.

— Sports Shots: Steve Young. (J). 1995. 1.49 (*0-590-62326-5*) Scholastic Inc.

Preller, Ludwig. Griechische Mythologie Bd. I: Theogonie und Gotter. (GER.). xviii, 964p. 1964. write for info. (*3-296-15101-X*) G Olms Pubs.

— Griechische Mythologie Bd. II: Die Griechische Heldensage: Landschaftliche Sagen, Buch 1. (GER.). xii, 420p. 1966. write for info. (*3-296-15102-8*) G Olms Pubs.

— Griechische Mythologie, Buch 3 Bd. II: Die Groben Heldenepen. (GER.). write for info. (*3-296-15104-4*) G Olms Pubs.

— Griechische Mythology. Bolle, Kees W., ed. LC 77-79153. (Mythology Ser.). (GER.). 1978. lib. bdg. 68.95 (*0-405-10562-2*) Ayer.

— Griechiscshe Mythologie Bd. II, Buch 2: Die Nationalheroen. (GER.). viii, 156p. 1966. write for info. (*3-296-15103-6*) G Olms Pubs.

— Romische Mythologie, Bd. 1. xii, 455p. 1978. write for info. (*3-296-15111-7*) G Olms Pubs.

— Romische Mythologie (Roman Mythology) Bolle, Kees W., ed. LC 77-79154. (Mythology Ser.). (GER.). 1978. reprint ed. lib. bdg. 58.95 (*0-405-10563-0*) Ayer.

— Romisscshe Mythologie, Bd. 2. xi, 490p. 1978. write for info. (*3-296-15112-5*) G Olms Pubs.

Preller, Maria, ed. see Schacter, Vicki.

Preller, Victor. Divine Science & the Science of God: A Reformulation of Thomas Aquinas. LC 66-21838. 291p. reprint ed. pap. 90.30 (*0-608-30474-3*, 201054300068) Bks Demand.

Prelog, V. My 132 Semesters of Studies of Chemistry. (Profiles, Pathways & Dreams Ser.). 120p. 1991. text 36.00 (*0-8412-1772-6*) OUP.

Prelovsek, Damjan. Josef Plecnik. Crampton, Patricia, ed. Martin, Eileen, tr. LC 96-48899. (Illus.). 340p. 1997. 70.00 (*0-300-06953-7*) Yale U Pr.

Prelozni, Sue, ed. see Merrill, Russell G.

Prelusky, Burt, jt. auth. see Winnikoff, Albert.

Preluts. Polar Animals. LC 98-60344. (Animal Worlds Ser.). (Illus.). (J). (ps). 1998. 6.95 (*1-84089-009-6*, 868229) Zero to Ten.

— Rainforest Animals. LC 99-166855. (Animal Worlds Ser.). (Illus.). (J). (ps). 1998. 6.95 (*1-84089-008-8*, 868230) Zero to Ten.

— Safari Animals. LC 98-60342. (Animal Worlds Ser.). (Illus.). (J). (ps). 1998. 6.95 (*1-84089-007-X*, 868232) Zero to Ten.

Prelutsky, Jack. A. Nonny Mouse Writes Again! LC 92-5214. (Dragon Tales Ser.). (Illus.). 28p. (J). (gr. 4-7). 1996. pap. 6.99 (*0-679-88087-9*, Pub. by Random Bks Yng Read) Random.

Prelutsky, Jack. A. Nonny Mouse Writes Again!, Poems. LC 92-5214. 1996. 12.19 (*0-606-10733-9*, Pub. by Turtleback) Demco.

Prelutsky, Jack. Awful Ogre's Awful day. (J). 2001. write for info. (*0-688-07778-1*, Grenwillow Bks); lib. bdg. write for info. (*0-688-07779-X*, Grenwillow Bks) HarpC Child Bks.

— The Baby Uggs Are Hatching! LC 81-7266. (Illus.). 32p. (J). (gr. k-3). 1982. lib. bdg. 15.93 (*0-688-00923-9*, Grenwillow Bks) HarpC Child Bks.

— The Baby Uggs Are Hatching! LC 81-7266. (Illus.). 32p. (J). (ps up). 1989. mass mkt. 3.95 (*0-688-09239-X*, Wm Morrow) Morrow Avon.

— The Baby Uggs Are Hatching! (J). 1982. 9.15 (*0-606-04163-X*, Pub. by Turtleback) Demco.

— Beneath a Blue Umbrella. LC 86-19406. (Illus.). 64p. (J). (ps-3). 1990. 15.95 (*0-688-06429-9*, Grenwillow Bks) HarpC Child Bks.

— Circus. (J). 1974. 10.15 (*0-606-00579-X*, Pub. by Turtleback) Demco.

— Circus! 2nd ed. (Illus.). 32p. (J). (ps-2). 1989. reprint ed. mass mkt. 4.95 (*0-689-70806-8*) Aladdin.

— Dog Days: Rhymes Around the Year. LC 98-32373. (J). 1999. 16.00 (*0-375-80104-9*, Pub. by Random Bks Yng Read); lib. bdg. 17.99 (*0-375-90104-3*, Pub. by Random Bks Yng Read) Random.

Prelutsky, Jack. The Dragons Are Singing Tonight. LC 92-29013. (Illus.). 32p. (J). (gr. 1-4). 1993. 15.95 (*0-688-09645-X*, Grenwillow Bks); 15.89 (*0-688-12511-5*, Grenwillow Bks) HarpC Child Bks.

Prelutsky, Jack. The Dragons Are Singing Tonight. (Illus.). 40p. (J). (gr. 1-4). 1998. mass mkt. 5.95 (*0-688-16162-6*, Wm Morrow) Morrow Avon.

— The Frogs Wore Red Suspenders. (Illus.). (J). 2001. 15.95 (*0-688-16719-5*, Grenwillow Bks); lib. bdg. 15.89 (*0-688-16720-9*, Grenwillow Bks) HarpC Child Bks.

— The Gargoyle on the Roof. LC 99-10578. (Illus.). 40p. (J). (gr. 1-4). 1999. 16.00 (*0-688-09643-3*, Grenwillow Bks) HarpC Child Bks.

***Prelutsky, Jack.** The Gargoyle on the Roof. LC 99-10578. (Illus.). 40p. (J). (gr. 1-4). 1999. 15.89 (*0-688-16553-2*, Grenwillow Bks) HarpC Child Bks.

Prelutsky, Jack. The Headless Horseman Rides Tonight: More Poems to Trouble Your Sleep. ALC Staff, ed. LC 80-10372. (Illus.). 40p. (J). (gr. 1 up). 1992. mass mkt. 4.95 (*0-688-11705-8*, Wm Morrow) Morrow Avon.

— The Headless Horseman Rides Tonight: More Poems to Trouble Your Sleep. 1980. 10.15 (*0-606-01366-0*, Pub. by Turtleback) Demco.

— Headless Horseman Rides Tonight: More Poems to Trouble Your Sleep. LC 80-10372. (Illus.). 40p. (J). (gr. 1-4). 1980. 16.00 (*0-688-80273-7*, Grenwillow Bks) HarpC Child Bks.

— Imagine That! Poems of Never-Was. LC 96-45591. (Illus.). 45p. (J). (gr. k-5). 1998. 18.00 (*0-679-88206-5*, Pub. by Random Bks Yng Read); lib. bdg. 19.99 (*0-679-98206-X*, Pub. by Random Bks Yng Read) Random.

— It's Christmas. LC 81-1100. (Greenwillow Read-Alone Bks.). (Illus.). 48p. (J). (gr. 1-3). 1981. lib. bdg. 15.93 (*0-688-00440-7*, Grenwillow Bks) HarpC Child Bks.

— It's Christmas. LC 81-1100. (Greenwillow Read-Alone Bks.). (Illus.). 48p. (J). (ps-3). 1981. 16.00 (*0-688-00439-3*, Grenwillow Bks) HarpC Child Bks.

— It's Christmas. LC 81-1100. (Mulberry Read-Alone Bks.). (Illus.). 48p. (J). (ps up). 1995. mass mkt. 4.95 (*0-688-14393-8*, Wm Morrow) Morrow Avon.

— It's Christmas. 1995. 10.15 (*0-606-07720-0*, Pub. by Turtleback) Demco.

— It's Halloween. LC 77-2141. (Greenwillow Read-Alone Bks.). (Illus.). 56p. (J). (gr. 1-4). 1977. 16.00 (*0-688-80102-1*, Grenwillow Bks) HarpC Child Bks.

— It's Halloween. LC 77-2141. (Illus.). 56p. (J). (ps-3). 1996. mass mkt. 4.95 (*0-688-14733-X*, Wm Morrow) Morrow Avon.

***Prelutsky, Jack.** It's Raining Pigs & Noodles. LC 00-24707. 160p. (J). 2000. 17.95 (*0-06-029194-X*, Grenwillow Bks); lib. bdg. 17.89 (*0-06-029195-8*, Grenwillow Bks) HarpC Child Bks.

Prelutsky, Jack. It's Snowing! It's Snowing! LC 83-16583. (Illus.). 48p. (J). (gr. 1-3). 1984. 18.00 (*0-688-01512-3*, Grenwillow Bks) HarpC Child Bks.

Prelutsky, Jack. It's Snowing! It's Snowing! LC 83-16583. (Illus.). 48p. (J). (gr. 1-3). 1984. 17.93 (*0-688-01513-1*, Grenwillow Bks) HarpC Child Bks.

Prelutsky, Jack. It's Thanksgiving. LC 81-1929. (Greenwillow Read-Alone Bks.: Vol. 1). (Illus.). 48p. (J). (ps-3). 1982. 15.89 (*0-688-00442-3*, Grenwillow Bks) HarpC Child Bks.

— It's Thanksgiving. LC 81-1929. (Illus.). 48p. (J). (ps-3). 1996. mass mkt. 4.95 (*0-688-14729-1*, Wm Morrow) Morrow Avon.

— It's Thanksgiving. LC 81-1929. 1996. 10.15 (*0-606-10230-2*, Pub. by Turtleback) Demco.

— It's Valentine's Day. (Illus.). (J). 1996. mass mkt. 4.95 (*0-688-14652-X*, Wm Morrow) Morrow Avon.

— It's Valentine's Day. LC 83-1449. (Mulberry Read-Alone Ser.). 1996. 10.15 (*0-606-09483-0*, Pub. by Turtleback) Demco.

— It's Valentine's Day. (Illus.). 48p. (J). (gr. k-3). 1985. reprint ed. pap. 2.50 (*0-590-40979-4*) Scholastic Inc.

— Monday's Troll. LC 95-7085. (Illus.). 40p. (J). (gr. 1-4). 1996. 16.00 (*0-688-09644-1*, Grenwillow Bks) HarpC Child Bks.

Prelutsky, Jack. Monday's Troll. LC 95-7085. (Illus.). 40p. (J). (gr. 1-4). 1996. 15.89 (*0-688-14373-3*, Grenwillow Bks) HarpC Child Bks.

— Monday's Troll. LC 95-7085. (Illus.). 40p. (J). (ps-2). 2000. pap. 5.95 (*0-688-17529-5*, Wm Morrow) Morrow Avon.

Prelutsky, Jack. My Parents Think I'm Sleeping. LC 84-13640. (Illus.). 48p. (J). (gr. 2-4). 1985. lib. bdg. 15.93 (*0-688-04019-5*, Grenwillow Bks) HarpC Child Bks.

— My Parents Think I'm Sleeping. LC 84-13640. (Illus.). 48p. (J). (ps-3). 1985. 16.00 (*0-688-04018-7*, Grenwillow Bks) HarpC Child Bks.

— My Parents Think I'm Sleeping. LC 84-13640. (Illus.). 48p. (J). (ps-3). 1995. reprint ed. mass mkt. 4.95 (*0-688-14028-9*, Wm Morrow) Morrow Avon.

— My Parents Think I'm Sleeping Poems. (J). 1995. 10.15 (*0-606-07909-2*, Pub. by Turtleback) Demco.

— New Kid on Block. (J). (gr. 1 up). 1994. pap. 23.75 incl. cd-rom (*1-57135-072-1*) Living Bks.

— The New Kid on the Block. LC 83-20621. (Illus.). 160p. (J). (ps-3). 1984. 17.95 (*0-688-02271-5*, Grenwillow Bks) HarpC Child Bks.

Prelutsky, Jack. The New Kid on the Block. LC 83-20621. (Illus.). 160p. (J). (ps-3). 1984. 17.89 (*0-688-02272-3*, Grenwillow Bks) HarpC Child Bks.

— Nightmares Lf. LC 76-4820. (Illus.). 40p. (J). (gr. 4-7). 1976. 14.89 (*0-688-84053-1*, Grenwillow Bks) HarpC Child Bks.

Prelutsky, Jack. Pack Rats Day & Other Poems. 1974. pap. 8.50 (*0-02-775050-7*) Macmillan.

— A Pizza the Size of the Sun. LC 95-35930. (Illus.). 160p. (J). (ps-3). 1996. 18.00 (*0-688-13235-9*, Grenwillow Bks) HarpC Child Bks.

Prelutsky, Jack. A Pizza the Size of the Sun. LC 95-35930. (Illus.). 160p. (J). (ps-3). 1996. 17.93 (*0-688-13236-7*, Grenwillow Bks) HarpC Child Bks.

Prelutsky, Jack. Rainy, Rainy Saturday. LC 79-22217. (Greenwillow Read-Alone Bks.). (Illus.). 48p. (J). (gr. 1-3). 1980. lib. bdg. 15.93 (*0-688-84252-6*, Grenwillow Bks) HarpC Child Bks.

— The Random House Book of Poetry for Children. LC 81-85940. (Illus.). 248p. (J). (gr. 1-5). 1983. lib. bdg. 21.99 (*0-394-95010-0*, Pub. by Random Bks Yng Read) Random.

— The Random House Book of Poetry for Children. LC 81-85940. (Illus.). 248p. (J). (gr. 4-7). 1983. 19.00 (*0-394-85010-6*, Pub. by Random Bks Yng Read) Random.

— Ride a Purple Pelican. LC 84-6024. (Illus.). 64p. (J). (ps-3). 1986. 17.95 (*0-688-04031-4*, Grenwillow Bks) HarpC Child Bks.

— Ride a Purple Pelican. LC 84-6042. (Illus.). 64p. (J). (ps-3). 1997. mass mkt. 7.95 (*0-688-15625-8*, Wm Morrow) Morrow Avon.

— Ride a Purple Pelican. 1997. 12.15 (*0-606-11799-7*, Pub. by Turtleback) Demco.

— Rolling Harvey. LC 79-18236. (Illus.). 32p. (J). (gr. k-3). 1980. 16.00 (*0-688-80258-3*, Grenwillow Bks) HarpC Child Bks.

— Rolling Harvey Down the Hill. (J). 1993. 10.15 (*0-606-05551-1*, Pub. by Turtleback) Demco.

— Rolling Harvey Down the Hill. LC 92-24606. (Illus.). 40p. (J). (gr. 2 up). 1993. reprint ed. mass mkt. 4.95 (*0-688-12270-1*, Wm Morrow) Morrow Avon.

Prelutsky, Jack. Scranimals. 1924. write for info. (*0-688-17819-7*, Grenwillow Bks); lib. bdg. write for info. (*0-688-17820-0*, Grenwillow Bks) HarpC Child Bks.

— The Sheriff of Rottenshot. LC 81-6420. (Illus.). 32p. (J). (gr. k-3). 1982. 14.93 (*0-688-00198-X*, Grenwillow Bks) HarpC Child Bks.

Prelutsky, Jack. The Sheriff of Rottenshot. Cohn, Amy, ed. LC 81-6420. (Illus.). 48p. (J). (gr. k up). 1994. reprint ed. mass mkt. 4.95 (*0-688-13635-4*, Wm Morrow) Morrow Avon.

Prelutsky, Jack. Sheriff of Rottenshot: Poems. 1994. 10.15 (*0-606-06735-3*, Pub. by Turtleback) Demco.

Prelutsky, Jack. Snopp on the Sidewalk. LC 76-46323. (Illus.). 32p. (J). (ps-3). 1977. lib. bdg. 15.93 (*0-688-84084-1*, Grenwillow Bks) HarpC Child Bks.

— Something Big Has Been Here. LC 89-34773. (Illus.). 160p. (J). (gr. 2 up). 1990. 17.95 (*0-688-06434-5*, Grenwillow Bks) HarpC Child Bks.

— The Terrible Tiger. LC 88-7901. (Illus.). 32p. (J). (ps-2). 1989. reprint ed. pap. 3.95 (*0-689-71300-2*) Aladdin.

— The 20th Century Children's Poetry Treasury. (Illus.). 87p. (J). (gr. 1-7). 1999. 19.95 (*0-679-89314-8*) Knopf.

Prelutsky, Jack. Tyrannosaurus Was a Beast. LC 87-25131. (Illus.). 32p. (J). (ps-6). 1988. lib. bdg. 15.89 (*0-688-06443-4*, Grenwillow Bks) HarpC Child Bks.

— Tyrannosaurus Was a Beast. unabridged ed. (Follow the Reader Ser.). (J). (gr. 1-3). 1994. pap. 15.98 incl. audio (*0-8072-0302-5*, FTR 169 SP) Listening Lib.

— Tyrannosaurus Was a Beast, Set. unabridged ed. (Follow the Reader Ser.). (J). (gr. 1-3). 1999. pap. 15.98 incl. audio (*0-8072-0226-6*, EFTR169SP) Listening Lib.

Prelutsky, Jack. Tyrannosaurus Was a Beast: Dinosaur Poems. LC 87-25131. (Illus.). 32p. (J). (ps-6). 1988. 16.00 (*0-688-06442-6*, Grenwillow Bks) HarpC Child Bks.

— Tyrannosaurus Was a Beast: Dinosaur Poems. LC 87-25131. (Illus.). 32p. (J). (ps-3). 1992. mass mkt. 4.95 (*0-688-11569-1*, Wm Morrow) Morrow Avon.

— Tyrannosaurus Was a Beast: Dinosaur Poems. (J). 1992. 10.15 (*0-606-01323-7*, Pub. by Turtleback) Demco.

Prelutsky, Jack. Tyrannosaurus Was a Beast Big Book. (Illus.). 32p. (J). (ps-3). 1993. reprint ed. mass mkt. 18.95 (*0-688-12613-8*, Wm Morrow) Morrow Avon.

Prelutsky, Jack. Zoo Doings: Animal Poems. LC 82-11996. (Illus.). 80p. (J). (ps-3). 1983. lib. bdg. 14.93 (*0-688-01784-3*, Grenwillow Bks) HarpC Child Bks.

Prelutsky, Jack, ed. The 20th Century Children's Poetry Treasury. LC 99-23988. 87p. 1999. lib. bdg. 21.99 (*0-679-99314-2*) Knopf.

Prelutsky, Jack, jt. auth. see Seuss, Dr., pseud.

Prem, Anand, ed. see Osho.

Prem, Ananda, ed. see Osho.

Prem, Daulat R. Criminal Practice, Eighteen Sixty-Four to Nineteen Eighty. 7th ed. (C). 1983. 130.00 (*0-7855-4791-6*) St Mut.

Prem, Hanns J. The Ancient Americas: A Brief History & Guide to Research. Kurbjuhn, Kornelia, tr. from GER. LC 97-3127.Tr. of Geschichte Altesamerikas. (Illus.). 205p. 1997. pap. 24.95 (*0-87480-536-8*) U of Utah Pr.

Prem, Jatinder. Mastering Oracle 8. 4th ed. (Mastering Ser.). 1008p. 2000. pap. 49.99 (*0-7821-2281-7*) Sybex.

Prem, Krishna, ed. see Osho.

***Prem, Ma Ananda, ed.** Mystic Experience: Bhagwan Shree Rajneesh. Diddee, Dolly, tr. 1998. 32.00 (*81-208-1377-4*, Pub. by Motilal Bnarsidass); pap. 22.00 (*81-208-1378-2*, Pub. by Motilal Bnarsidass) S Asia.

Prem Raja Baba. The Joy Book. 156p. 1996. reprint ed. pap. 12.00 (*0-9645010-0-7*) Prem Raja Baba.

Prem, Siva. Notes Toward the Truth about the Self. 16p. 1997. pap. 2.00 (*0-938075-72-1*, Permanence Pr) Ocean View Bks.

Prem, Sri K. & Ashish, Sri Madhava. Man, the Measure of All Things: In the Stanzas of Dzyan. LC 74-87256. 1969. 16.95 (*0-8356-0006-8*, Quest) Theos Pub Hse.

Prem, T. Criminal Practice, 7 vols. (C). 1988. 1000.00 (*0-7855-3532-2*) St Mut.

Premack, David, et al, eds. Causal Cognition: A Multidisciplinary Approach. (Fyssen Foundation Symposium Ser.). (Illus.). 690p. 1996. reprint ed. pap. text 45.00 (*0-19-852402-1*) OUP.

Premare, A. Dictionary Arabic to French Maroc, 10 vols. (ARA & FRE.). 1998. 1495.00 (*0-320-00271-3*) Fr & Eur.

Premazzi, Guido & Volterra, Laura. Microphyte Toxins: A Manual for Toxin Detection, Environmental Monitoring. 338p. 1994. pap. 50.00 (*92-826-2731-4*, CL-NA-14854-ENC, Pub. by Comm Europ Commun) Bernan Associates.

Premchand. Nirmala. Rai, Alok, tr. from HIN. LC 99-933485. 230p. 1999. text 17.95 (*0-19-564580-4*) OUP.

— Widows, Wives & Other Heroines: Twelve Stories by Premchand. rev. abr. ed. Rubin, David, ed. & tr. by. from HIN. LC 98-902990. 168p. 1998. 18.95 (*0-19-564217-1*) OUP.

***Premchand, A.** Control of Public Money: The Fiscal Machinery in Developing Countries. (Illus.). 512p. 2000. text 24.95 (*0-19-565368-9*) OUP.

Premchand, A. Effective Government Accounting. LC 95-17823. 190p. 1995. pap. 21.00 (*1-55775-485-3*) Intl Monetary.

— Government Budgeting & Expenditure Controls: Theory & Practice. xii, 540p. 1983. 24.00 (*0-939934-24-8*); pap. 18.00 (*0-939934-25-6*) Intl Monetary.

— Nirmala. Rubin, David, tr. (C). 1988. 17.50 (*81-7094-030-3*, Pub. by Vision Books) Asia Bk Corp.

— Public Expenditure Management. LC 92-44308. x, 282p. 1993. pap. 20.00 (*1-55775-323-7*) Intl Monetary.

Premchand, A., ed. Government Financial Management: Issues & Country Studies. LC 90-41275. x, 374p. 1990. pap. 21.50 (*1-55775-149-8*) Intl Monetary.

Premchand, A. & Antonaya, A. L., eds. Aspectos del Presupuesto Publico. x, 285p. 1988. pap. 12.50 (*1-55775-014-9*) Intl Monetary.

Premchand, A. & Burkhead, Jesse. Comparative International Budgeting & Finance. 319p. 1984. pap. 24.95 (*0-87855-966-3*) Transaction Pubs.

Premchand, Neeta. Off the Deckle Edge: A Papermaking Journey Through India. (Illus.). 128p. 1995. 49.95 (*0-9525831-1-9*) Oak Knoll.

Premchit, Sommai, jt. auth. see Swearer, Donald K.

Premdas, Ralph R. Ethnic Conflict & Development: The Case of Fiji. (Research in Ethnic Relations Ser.). 224p. 1995. 91.95 (*1-85628-979-6*, Pub. by Avebry) Ashgate Pub Co.

— Ethnic Conflict & Development: The Case of Guyana. (Research in Ethnic Relations Ser.). 224p. 1995. 91.95 (*1-85628-995-8*, Pub. by Avebry) Ashgate Pub Co.

Premeaux, jt. auth. see Mondy.

Premerlain, William, jt. auth. see Blaha, Michael.

Premfors, R. Higher Education Organization: Conditions for Policy Implementation. 180p. (Orig.). 1984. pap. text 45.50 (*91-22-00688-5*) Coronet Bks.

Premi, Kusum K. Scheduled Castes & Scheduled Tribes in Industrial Training Institutes: A Study of Five States. 150p. 1989. 14.00 (*0-7069-4263-9*, Pub. by Vikas) S Asia.

Premier League Staff. New Testament: Classic Premier Edition. (Believer's Lifesystem Ser.). 1996. pap. 8.99 (*0-8024-2766-9*) Moody.

Preminger, Alex, et al, eds. New Princeton Encyclopedia of Poetry & Poetics. 1400p. 1996. reprint ed. 19.98 (*1-56731-152-0*, MJF Bks) Fine Comms.

Preminger, Alex & Brogan, T. V., eds. Princeton Encyclopedia of Poetry & Poetics. 3rd ed. 143p. 1993. pap. text 35.00 (*0-691-02123-6*, Pub. by Princeton U Pr) Cal Prin Full Svc.

Preminger, Alex, jt. ed. see Greenstein, Edward L.

Preminger, Glenn M., jt. ed. see Lingeman, James E.

Preminger, Victoria. Barkley Unleashed: A Pirate's Tail. (Illus.). (J). (ps-2). 1997. 14.95 incl. audio (*0-614-28717-0*, Dove Audio) NewStar Media.

Premm, Mathias. Dogmatic Theology for the Laity. 1977. pap. 20.00 (*0-89555-022-9*) TAN Bks Pubs.

Premo, Michael & Walker, Ken. Backslider: A True Story. (Illus.). 162p. (Orig.). 1995. pap. 10.00 (*1-883893-11-9*) WinePress Pub.

Premo, Steele Cassie. We Heal from Memory: Sexton Lorde Anzaldua & the Poetry of Witness. text. write for info. (*0-312-23342-6*) St Martin.

Premo, Terri L. Winter Friends: Women Growing Old in the New Republic, 1785-1835. LC 89-4980. (Women in American History Ser.). (Illus.). 216p. 1990. text 24.95 (*0-252-01656-4*) U of Ill Pr.

Premoli, Amedeo, jt. auth. see Biey, Mario.

Premoli-Droulers, Francesca. Writers' Houses. (Illus.). 200p. 1999. text 50.00 (*0-86565-964-8*) Vendome.

Premoli, Orazio M. Contemporary Church History. 1977. lib. bdg. 59.95 (*0-8490-1669-X*) Gordon Pr.

Premoli, P. Flessoni, Rime, Anagrammi: L'Italiano in Scatola di Montaggio. 1991. 85.00 (*0-8288-3920-4*, F127300) Fr & Eur.

P

An Asterisk (*) at the beginning of an entry indicates that the title is appearing for the first time.

— Italiano - Ortografia. 1991. 24.95 (*0-8288-3921-2*, F18320) Fr & Eur.

— Vocabolario Nomenclatorio. 1991. 250.00 (*0-8288-3919-0*, F83910) Fr & Eur.

Premus, Robert, jt. auth. see Liu, Lewis-Guodo.

Premuzic, Eugene T. & Woodhead, Avril D., eds. Microbial Enhancement of Oil Recovery: Recent Advances. LC 93-22897. (Developments in Petroleum Science Ser.: Vol. 39). 446p. 1993. 182.75 (*0-444-89690-2*) Elsevier.

Prend, Ashley. Transcending Loss: Understanding the Lifelong Impact of Grief & How to Make It Meaningful. LC 97-183796. 304p. 1997. pap. 12.95 (*0-425-15775-X*) Berkley Pub.

Prendergast, jt. auth. see Caws.

Prendergast, Alan. The Poison Tree: A True Story of Family Violence & Revenge. 336p. 1987. mass mkt. 4.95 (*0-380-70346-7*, Avon Bks) Morrow Avon.

***Prendergast, Alexia & O'Keefe, Sarah.** Sams Teach Yourself Regular Expressions in 24 Hours. 400p. 2000. 24.99 (*0-672-31936-5*) Sams.

Prendergast, Alice V., et al. Medical Terminology: A Text/Workbook. 4th ed. LC 96-35083. 416p. (C). 1996. pap., wbk. ed. 39.60 (*0-8053-9368-4*) Addison-Wesley.

Prendergast, Bruce T. Architecture, Nos. I & II. LC 97-78221. (MCSD Certification Ser.). 1600p. 1998. student ed. 89.99 (*0-7645-3123-9*) IDG Bks.

***Prendergast, Bruce T.** Solution Architectures MCSD. LC 99-46709. (MCSD Certification Ser.). 1120p. 1999. pap., student ed. 44.99 (*0-7645-3314-2*) IDG Bks.

Prendergast, Christine, jt. auth. see Rosenberg, Helane S.

Prendergast, Christopher. Balzac: Fiction & Melodrama. LC 78-11267. 205p. 1979. text 35.00 (*0-8419-0457-X*) Holmes & Meier.

— HarperCollins World Reader, Vol. 1. Caws, Mary Anne m, ed. 2685p. (C). 1997. pap. text 88.00 (*0-06-500750-6*) Addison-Wesley Educ.

— Napoleon & History Painting: Antoine-Jean Gros's La Bataille d'Eylau. (Illus.). 238p. 1998. reprint ed. pap. text 45.00 (*0-19-817422-5*) OUP.

— Paris & the Nineteenth Century. (Writing the City Ser.). (Illus.). 296p. 1995. pap. text 28.95 (*0-631-19694-3*) Blackwell Pubs.

***Prendergast, Christopher.** The Triangle of Representation. LC 00-22651. 2000. pap. 16.50 (*0-231-12091-5*); text 42.50 (*0-231-12090-7*) Col U Pr.

Prendergast, Christopher, ed. Cultural Materialism: On Raymond Williams. LC 94-36190. (Cultural Politics Ser.: Vol. 9). 1995. pap. 21.95 (*0-8166-2281-7*); text 49.95 (*0-8166-2280-9*) U of Minn Pr.

— Nineteenth-Century French Poetry: Introductions to Close Reading. 270p. 1990. pap. text 19.95 (*0-521-34774-2*) Cambridge U Pr.

Prendergast, Christopher, jt. auth. see Cohen, Margaret.

Prendergast, Christopher, jt. ed. see Caws, Marry Ann.

Prendergast, Curtis. Easy Gardens. Time-Life Books Editors, ed. (Encyclopedia of Gardening Ser.). (Illus.). (gr. 11). 1999. 18.95 (*0-8094-2637-4*) Time-Life.

Prendergast, Curtis, ed. Productivity: The Link to Social & Economic Progress. LC 76-19833. (Swedish-American Exchange of Views Ser.). 55p. 1976. pap. text 3.50 (*0-89361-000-3*) Work in Amer.

Prendergast, Edward J., jt. auth. see IFSTA Committee.

Prendergast, Guy L. A Complete Concordance to the Iliad of Homer. enl. rev. ed. vii, 427p. 1983. reprint ed. 128.70 incl. 3.5 hd (*3-487-04161-8*) G Olms Pubs.

Prendergast, H. D., et al, eds. Plants for Food & Medicine: Proceedings of the Joint Conference of the Society for Economic Botany & the International Society for Ethnopharmacology, London, 1-6 July 1996. (Illus.). 438p. 1998. pap. 48.00 (*1-900347-55-5*, Pub. by Royal Botnic Grdns) Balogh.

Prendergast, J. K., ed. see Sheldon, J. G. M.

Prendergast, James C. Red Flags. 1994. pap. text 59.00 (*0-7931-1203-6*, 1520-2901, Real Estate Ed) Dearborn.

Prendergast, James H., jt. auth. see Chiarito, Marian D.

Prendergast, James J., jt. auth. see Franklin, David A.

Prendergast, John. Crisis Response: Humanitarian Band-Aids in Sudan & Somalia. LC 96-34393. 176p. 1997. 49.95 (*0-7453-1156-3*, Pub. by Pluto GBR) Stylus Pub VA.

— Crisis Response: Humanitarian Band-Aids in Sudan & Somalia. 176p. 1997. pap. 18.95 (*0-7453-1155-5*, Pub. by Pluto GBR) Stylus Pub VA.

— Frontline Diplomacy: Humanitarian Aid & Conflict in Africa. LC 96-25509. 165p. (Orig.). 1996. pap. 12.95 (*1-55587-696-X*, 87696X) L Rienner.

— Jump. LC 95-12783. (First Novel Ser.). 256p. (Orig.). 1995. pap. 14.00 (*0-922811-23-7*) Mid-List.

— The Road to India: Guide to the Overland Routes to India. (Illus.). 1978. 19.50 (*0-7195-3396-1*) Transatl Arts.

Prendergast, John & Miller, Terence. A Guide for Activists: Handbook on African Hunger. 28p. (Orig.). 1993. pap. text 4.95 (*0-934255-13-X*) Center Concern.

Prendergast, John & Pauling, Sharon. Peace, Development & People of the Horn of Africa. (Hunger Policy Occasional Papers: No. 1). (Orig.). (C). 1992. pap. text 5.00 (*0-685-48887-X*) Bread for the World.

Prendergast, John, jt. auth. see Duffield, Mark.

Prendergast, John P. The Cromwellian Settlement of Ireland. LC 97-175175. 378p. 1996. 35.00 (*0-09-476620-7*, Pub. by Constable & Co) Trafalgar.

***Prendergast, John P.** The Cromwellian Settlement of Ireland (1652-1660) 3rd ed. 575p. 1999. reprint ed. pap. 45.00 (*0-8063-4701-5*, Pub. by Clearfield Co) ACCESS Pubs Network.

Prendergast, Maria T. Renaissance Fantasies: The Gendering of Aesthetics in Early Modern Fiction. LC 99-21763. 344p. 1999. text 39.00 (*0-87338-644-2*) Kent St U Pr.

Prendergast, Maurice. Beechmont. (Fine Art Jigsaw Puzzles Ser.). 1989. 9.95 (*0-934967-48-2*) Battle Rd Pr.

Prendergast, Norma, jt. ed. see Kammen, Carol.

Prendergast, Renee & Stewart, Frances, eds. Market Forces & World Development. LC 93-25823. 1994. text 85.00 (*0-312-10175-9*) St Martin.

Prendergast, Richard A. Learn PROCOMM Plus 2.0 for Windows in a Day. (Popular Applications Ser.). 144p. (Orig.). 1995. pap. 15.95 (*1-55622-443-5*) Wordware Pub.

Prendergast, Roy M. Film Music: A Neglected Art. 2nd ed. 352p. 1992. pap. 14.95 (*0-393-30874-X*) Norton.

Prendergast, Thomas A. & Kline, Barbara. Rewriting Chaucer: Culture, Authority, & the Idea of the Authentic Text, 1400-1602. LC 99-19861. (Illus.). 352p. 1999. pap. 26.00 (*0-8142-5011-4*); text 60.00 (*0-8142-0811-8*) Ohio St U Pr.

Prendergast, Thomas F. Forgotten Pioneers: Irish Leaders in Early California. LC 72-1248. (Essay Index Reprint Ser.). 1977. reprint ed. 22.95 (*0-8369-2854-7*) Ayer.

Prendergast, William E. The Merry-Go-Round of Sexual Abuse: Identifying & Treating Survivors. LC 93-17364. (Illus.). 282p. 1993. pap. 19.95 (*1-56024-388-0*); lib. bdg. 49.95 (*1-56024-387-2*) Haworth Pr.

— Sexual Abuse of Children & Adolescents: A Preventive Guide for Parents, Teachers & Counselors. LC 79-4832. 336p. 1996. 29.95 (*0-8264-0892-3*) Continuum.

— Treating Sex Offenders in Correctional Institutions & Outpatient Clinics: A Guide to Clinical Practice. 220p. 1991. 49.95 (*1-56024-206-X*); pap. 19.95 (*1-56024-207-8*) Haworth Pr.

Prendes, J. M., ed. see Menendez Pidal, Ramon.

***Prendes, Jose.** The Harbinger. LC 99-93978. 2000. pap. 11.95 (*0-533-13216-9*) Vantage.

***Prendeville, Brendan.** Realism in 20th Century Painting. LC 99-69615. (World of Art Ser.). (Illus.). 240p. 2000. pap. 14.95 (*0-500-20336-9*, Pub. by Thames Hudson) Norton.

Prendeville, Dennis E. Common Stock Price Histories: 1910-1987. 2nd ed. (Illus.). 253p. 1988. suppl. ed. 14.95 (*0-685-19812-X*); pap. 39.95 (*0-9618454-1-4*) WIT Financial Pubs.

— Common Stock Price Histories, 1910-1986. (Illus.). 208p. (Orig.). 1987. pap. 39.95 (*0-9618454-0-6*) WIT Financial Pubs.

Prendiville, W. The Clinical Management of Early Pregnancy. LC RG572.C55 1999. (Illus.). 208p. 1999. text 75.00 (*0-340-74100-7*, Pub. by E A) OUP.

Prendiville, Francis, jt. auth. see Toye, Nigel.

Prendiville, Walter, ed. Large Loop Excision of the Transformation Zone: A Practical Guide to LLETZ. LC 92-49021. 1992. write for info. (*0-442-31708-5*) Chapman & Hall.

Preneel, B., et al, eds. Business Object Design & Implementation II: OOPSLA'96, OOPSLA'97 & OOPSLA'98 Workshop Proceedings. LC 98-47151. viii, 208p. 1998. pap. 79.95 (*1-85233-108-9*) Spr-Verlag.

Preneel, Bart, ed. Fast Software Encryption: Second International Workshop, Leuven, Belgium, December 14-16, 1994: Proceedings. LC 95-45832. (Lecture Notes in Computer Science Ser.: No. 1008). 367p. 1995. 62.00 (*3-540-60590-8*) Spr-Verlag.

Preneel, Bart, et al, eds. Computer Security & Industrial Cryptography: State of the Art & Evolution: ESAT Course, Leuven, Belgium, May 21-23, 1991. LC 93-32467. (Lecture Notes in Computer Science Ser.: Vol. 741). 1993. 44.95 (*0-387-57341-0*) Spr-Verlag.

Preneel, Bart & Rijmen, Vincet, eds. State of the Art in Applied Cryptography: Course on Computer Security & Industrial Cryptography, Leuven, Belgium, June 3-6, 1997: Revised Lectures. LC 98-53824. viii, 395p. 1999. pap. 67.00 (*3-540-65474-7*) Spr-Verlag.

Preneel, Bart, jt. auth. see IFIP TC6/TC11 Joint Working Conference on Communications & Multimedia Security Staff.

Preneel, Bart, jt. ed. see Bosselaers, Antoon.

Prener, Connie, tr. see Sako, Takako.

Prengaman, R. David, ed. see Minerals, Metals & Materials Society Staff.

Prengel, Serge. Still a Dad: The Divorced Father's Journey. LC 98-96241. 224p. 1999. pap. 13.95 (*1-892482-00-2*) Mission Creat.

— Twelve Steps for the Divorced Dad. 187p. 2000. pap. 13.95 (*1-892482-02-9*, Pub. by Mission Creat) Midpt Trade.

Prenger, Suzanne, jt. auth. see Dirkx, John M.

Preniszni, Dan, ed. see American Red Cross Staff.

Prenko, Evelyn, ed. Health & Your Body. 1980. 4.95 (*1-55708-194-8*, MCR753) McDonald Pub Co.

— Sys. of the Human Body. 1979. 4.95 (*1-55708-193-X*, R751) McDonald Pub Co.

Prenn, U. L. Graham Joke Book. (Illus.). 74p. (Orig.). 1990. pap. 9.95 (*0-937041-71-8*) Systems Co.

— Introduction to Ball Lightning: Rare Events. (Illus.). 100p. (Orig.). 1992. 70.00 (*0-937041-95-5*); pap. 40.00 (*0-937041-96-3*) Systems Co.

— Introduction to Biological Radiation Effects. 2nd ed. (Illus.). 130p. 1994. 110.00 (*1-56216-205-5*); pap. 80.00 (*1-56216-206-3*) Systems Co.

— Introduction to Biological Radiation Effects: An Overview of Terrestrial & Space Radiation Effects on Humans. (Illus.). 120p. (Orig.). (C). 1992. pap. 70.00 (*1-56216-101-6*); text 100.00 (*1-56216-100-8*) Systems Co.

— Learn Successful Investment Techniques. (Illus.). 74p. (Orig.). 1990. pap. 12.00 (*0-937041-94-7*) Systems Co.

— Learn Successful Investment Techniques. 2nd ed. (Illus.). 74p. (Orig.). 1992. pap. 15.00 (*1-56216-159-8*) Systems Co.

— True Life Stories. (Illus.). 80p. (Orig.). 1991. 35.00 (*0-937041-97-1*); pap. 15.00 (*0-937041-98-X*) Systems Co.

Prenor, Connie, tr. see Yano, Shinichi.

Prenowitz, Eric, tr. see Cixous, Helene & Calle-Grubar, Mireille.

Prenowitz, Eric, tr. see Cixous, Helen & Calle-Grubar, Mireille.

Prenowitz, Eric, tr. see Derrida, Jacques.

Prenowitz, W. & Jantosciak, J. The Theory of Join Spaces: A Contemporary Approach to Convex Sets & Linear Geometry. (Undergraduate Texts in Mathematics Ser.). (Illus.). 1979. 59.95 (*0-387-90340-2*) Spr-Verlag.

Prenowitz, Walter & Jordan, Meyer. Basic Concepts of Geometry. (Illus.). 350p. 1989. pap. text 44.95 (*0-912675-48-9*) Ardsley.

Prenshaw, Peggy W., ed. Conversations with Elizabeth Spencer. LC 91-19455. (Literary Conversations Ser.). 1991. pap. 15.95 (*0-87805-528-2*); text 39.50 (*0-87805-527-4*) U Pr of Miss.

— Conversations with Eudora Welty. LC 83-21668. (Literary Conversations Ser.). 367p. 1984. pap. 17.00 (*0-87805-206-2*) U Pr of Miss.

— Eudora Welty, Thirteen Essays: Selected from Eudora Welty, Critical Essays. LC 83-6945. 272p. reprint ed. pap. 84.40 (*0-7837-1065-8*, 204158700021) Bks Demand.

— More Conversations with Eudora Welty. LC 95-25720. (Literary Conversations Ser.). 328p. 1996. 39.50 (*0-87805-864-8*); pap. 16.95 (*0-87805-865-6*) U Pr of Miss.

Prenshaw, Peggy W. & McKee, Jesse O., eds. Sense of Place, Mississippi. LC 79-26098. (Illus.). 235p. reprint ed. pap. 72.90 (*0-7837-1074-7*, 204159800021) Bks Demand.

Prensky, David, jt. auth. see Wells, William.

Prensky, Janet, jt. auth. see Martin, Arlene L.

***Prensky, Marc.** Digital Game-Based Learning. (Illus.). 2001. 29.95 (*0-07-136344-0*) McGraw.

Prenter, P. M. Splines & Variational Methods. 336p. 1989. pap. 104.95 (*0-471-50402-5*) Wiley.

Prentice. Fitness & Wellness for Life. 7th ed. 2001. 32.00 (*0-07-235333-3*) McGraw.

— Fitness for College & Life. 5th ed. 1996. (*0-8151-8863-3*) Mosby Inc.

Prentice, Alison & Theobald, Marjorie R., eds. Women Who Taught: Perspectives on the History of Women & Teaching. 304p. 1991. text 45.00 (*0-8020-2745-8*); pap. text 17.95 (*0-8020-6785-9*) U of Toronto Pr.

Prentice, Alison, jt. auth. see Houston, Susan E.

Prentice Allemano, Irene, tr. & illus. see Prentice, Sydney.

Prentice, Ann, jt. ed. see Pemberton, J. Michael.

Prentice, Ann E. Financial Planning for Libraries. LC 82-7330. 236p. 1983. 26.50 (*0-8108-1565-6*) Scarecrow.

— Financial Planning for Libraries. 2nd ed. LC 94-42908. (Library Administration: No. 12). 208p. 1996. 32.50 (*0-8108-2974-6*) Scarecrow.

Prentice, Ann E. & Shaw, Debra, eds. Public Library Networking & Interlibrary Co-Operation. (Public Library Quarterly: Vol. 2, Nos. 3-4). 113p. 1982. pap. text 24.95 (*0-86656-116-1*) Haworth Pr.

Prentice, Archibald. Historical Sketches & Personal Recollections of Manchester: Intended to Illustrate Progress of Public Opinion from 1792-1832. 3rd rev. ed. 432p. 1970. reprint ed. 35.00 (*0-7146-1353-3*, BHA-01353, Pub. by F Cass Pubs) Intl Spec Bk.

— History of the Anti-Corn Law League, 2 vols., Set. 2nd ed. 1968. reprint ed. 65.00 (*0-7146-1352-5*, Pub. by F Cass Pubs) Intl Spec Bk.

Prentice, Beatriz G. Beatriz: A Manual for Peace. LC 83-51579. (Illus.). 414p. (Orig.). 1984. pap. 9.95 (*0-915485-10-9*) World Purpose Found.

Prentice, Christine & Warrington, Lisa, eds. Playlunch: 5 Short New Zealand Plays. 112p. 1996. pap. 19.95 (*1-877133-01-9*, Pub. by Univ Otago Pr) Intl Spec Bk.

Prentice, Colin W. Monino: The Russian Air Force Museum. 1998. pap. text 29.95 (*1-85310-898-7*) Specialty Pr.

Prentice, D. D. EEC Directives on Company Law & Financial Markets. 336p. 1991. pap. 65.00 (*0-19-825259-5*) OUP.

Prentice, D. D., ed. Butterworths Company Law Cases. 1984. write for info. (*0-406-99858-2*, BCLCASET, MICHIE) LEXIS Pub.

Prentice, D. D. & Stokes, Mary, eds. Butterworths Company Law Cases, 11 vols., Set. 1988. boxed set 1500.00 (*0-406-07650-2*, UK, MICHIE) LEXIS Pub.

Prentice, D. D., jt. ed. see Micheler, Eva.

Prentice, Deborah & Miller, Dale, eds. Cultural Divides: Understanding & Overcoming Group Conflict. LC 99-19380. (Illus.). 560p. 1999. 49.95 (*0-87154-690-6*) Russell Sage.

Prentice, Diana. Public Speaking Today. 512p. 1989. 30.60 (*0-8442-5515-7*) NTC Contemp Pub Co.

Prentice, E. Parmalee & Egan, John G. Commerce Clause of the Federal Constitution. lxxv, 386p. 1981. reprint ed. 46.00 (*0-8377-2505-4*, Rothman) W S Hein.

Prentice, Geoffrey A. Electrochemical Engineering Principles. 320p. (C). 1990. text 58.60 (*0-13-249038-2*) P-H.

Prentice, George R. Poquito Amigo: A Novel. LC 97-4253. 192p. 1998. pap. 10.95 (*1-56474-221-0*) Fithian Pr.

***Prentice, Hall.** Freehand 8. 375p. 1998. pap. text 33.33 (*0-13-096171-X*) P-H.

— Labor & Employment Law Desk Book, 2000 Supplement Ed. 1999. pap. text. write for info. (*0-13-012421-4*, Prentice Hall) P-H.

— Textbook of Cosmetology. (Illus.). 1999. pap. text 15.30 (*0-13-690066-6*) P-H.

***Prentice Hall Editorial Staff.** Caples' 21 Proven Ways to Create Winning Ads. 1998. spiral bd. 9.95 (*0-13-083284-7*) P-H.

— Homemade Miracles. 1999. pap. 9.95 (*0-13-017665-6*) P-H.

Prentice-Hall Editorial Staff. 38 Proven Ways to Close the Sale. 32p. (C). 1996. pap. 11.95 (*0-13-496514-0*, Macmillan Coll) P-H.

Prentice Hall General Reference & Travel Staff, ed. Monarch Notes on Dickens' David Copperfield. (C). 3.95 (*0-671-00609-6*, Arco) Macmillan Gen Ref.

— Philosophy of Nietzsche. 1965. 4.75 (*0-671-00534-0*, Arco) Macmillan Gen Ref.

Prentice Hall International Staff, jt. auth. see Institute of Personnel Management Staff.

Prentice Hall Japan Staff, tr. see Adobe Systems Inc. Staff, et al.

Prentice Hall Japan Staff, tr. see Cohen, Luanne.

Prentice Hall Law & Business (Firm) Staff. Contemporary Corporation Forms: Text Model Forms Commentary. 2nd ed. LC 97-42932. 1998. ring bd. 495.00 (*1-56706-662-3*) Aspen Law.

Prentice-Hall Publishing Staff, jt. auth. see Roberts, Garyn G.

Prentice-Hall Staff. Advanced Mathematics. 1997. 176.75 (*0-13-715780-0*) P-H.

— Algebra 1. 1997. 108.75 (*0-13-026485-7*) P-H.

— Algebra 2 with Trigonometry. 1997. 111.50 (*0-13-026642-6*) P-H.

— All States Tax Handbook. 320p. 1987. 17.50 (*0-13-022799-4*) P-H.

— All States Tax Handbook 1989. 300p. 1988. 18.95 (*0-13-023219-X*, Busn) P-H.

— Almanac of the Federal Judiciary, 2 vols. 1994. ring bd. 295.00 (*0-13-288854-8*) Aspen Law.

— American Goverment Transparencies. 3rd ed. 1995. text. write for info. (*0-13-303983-8*) Allyn.

***Prentice-Hall Staff.** Arts Humanities Catalog '90. 1999. text. write for info. (*0-13-048125-4*, Prentice Hall) P-H.

Prentice-Hall Staff. Authors' Guidelines: A Guide to Successful Publishing. (C). 1997. pap. write for info. (*0-13-518499-1*) P-H.

***Prentice-Hall Staff.** Business Essentials. 3rd ed. (C). 2000. Price not set. (*0-13-040117-X*) P-H.

Prentice-Hall Staff. The Business of Law: A Handbook on How to Manage Law Firms. 2nd ed. 1138p. 1990. ring bd. 95.00 (*0-13-292625-3*) Aspen Law.

— California Income Tax Laws. 1100p. 1989. pap. text 41.50 (*0-13-112285-1*, Busn) P-H.

— California Tax Handbook. 1987th ed. 1986. pap. 17.00 (*0-13-112046-8*) P-H.

— Client Development Series. 1984. write for info. (*0-318-58012-8*) P-H.

— Clinical Nursing Skills. 5th ed. (C). 1999. text 26.67 (*0-8385-1075-2*, Medical Exam) Appleton & Lange.

— A Complete Guide to the Tax Reform Act of 1986. LC 87-110898. 17.50 (*0-13-160649-2*) P-H.

***Prentice-Hall Staff.** Complete Idiot's Guide to Total Nutrition. 2000. pap. 25.95 (*0-13-086722-5*, Prentice Hall) P-H.

An Asterisk (*) at the beginning of an entry indicates that the title is appearing for the first time.

Prentice-Hall Staff. Corporation, Partnership & Fiduciary Federal Income Tax Specimen Returns. 72p. 1989. pap. text 8.00 (*0-13-308651-8*, Busn) P-H.

— Corporations: Tax Choices for Business Planning-Explanation, Law & Regulations, Legislative History, Cases & Rulings, Indexes. (Illus.). ring bd. write for info. (*0-318-57847-6*) P-H.

— Cultural Diversity in Health & Illness. 5th ed. 432p. (C). 1999. pap. 36.95 (*0-8385-1536-3*, Medical Exam) Appleton & Lange.

— D. C. Federal Courts Handbook. 2nd ed. 1544p. 1993. ring bd. 116.00 (*0-13-297664-1*) Aspen Law.

— Directory of Corporate Counsel, 1994-1995, 2 vols., Set. 15th ed. 2850p. 1994. 375.00 (*0-13-165664-3*) Aspen Law.

— Directory of Environmental Attorneys, 1995. 1756p. 1994. 195.00 (*0-13-169269-0*) Aspen Law.

— Employee Benefit Plans under ERISA: Federal Regulations. 1492p. 1989. pap. text 41.50 (*0-13-275299-9*, Busn) P-H.

— Estate & Gift Taxes: Complete. 1984. write for info. (*0-318-58010-1*) P-H.

— Estate Planning, Wills, Trusts. 1964. write for info. (*0-318-58305-4*) P-H.

***Prentice-Hall Staff.** Exploring Microsoft Office Professional 2000: Proficient Certification. 825p. 1999. spiral bd. 53.33 (*0-13-085640-1*) P-H.

Prentice-Hall Staff. FDIC Enforcement Decisions, 2 vols. write for info. (*0-318-65472-5*, 115) P-H.

— Federal Income Tax Regulations. 1984. write for info. (*0-318-58009-8*) P-H.

— Federal Income Tax Regulations: 1990 Edition. 1990. pap. 52.50 (*0-13-313537-3*) P-H.

— Federal Tax Handbook. 750p. 1988. 19.50 (*0-13-313164-5*, Busn) P-H.

— Federal Tax Handbook, 1985. 1985. write for info. (*0-318-58198-1*) P-H.

— Federal Tax Handbook 1988. 750p. 1987. 19.00 (*0-13-313099-1*) P-H.

— Federal Tax Handbook 1990. 1989. pap. 21.50 (*0-13-308883-9*) P-H.

— Federal Withholding Tax Tables. 48p. 1989. pap. 8.00 (*0-13-313768-6*, Busn) P-H.

— Hammond Historical Atlas. (C). 1995. pap. text 6.40 (*0-13-228917-2*) P-H.

— Handbook on Experimental Mechanics. rev. ed. Kobayashi, Albert S., ed. & intro. by. (Illus.). 1024p. 1986. 104.00 (*0-912053-07-0*) P-H.

Prentice-Hall Staff. Heat Energy. 2nd ed. 1994. text, student ed. 13.82 (*0-13-400698-4*) P-H.

Prentice-Hall Staff. Here We Go, Level 5. 3rd ed. 112p. 1995. pap. text, student ed. 14.20 (*0-13-186073-9*) P-H.

— Here We Go, Pre-Primary. 3rd ed. 1994. pap. text, teacher ed. 28.40 (*0-13-186081-X*) P-H.

— Here We Go: Level 6. 3rd ed. (C). 1995. pap. text, student ed. 10.60 (*0-13-186966-3*) P-H.

Prentice-Hall Staff. Heredity. 2nd ed. 1994. text, student ed. 10.97 (*0-13-400490-6*) P-H.

Prentice-Hall Staff. How to get Price For Home 89. 1990. pap. text 4.95 (*0-13-396060-9*) P-H.

— How to Save Money & Retire in 89. 1990. pap. text 6.85 (*0-13-396086-2*) P-H.

— How to Save Time & Money in Filing Your 1981 Personal Tax Return: Individual Federal Income Tax Specimen Returns for Filing in 1982. LC 82-243692. (Illus.). 64p. 1982. 3.95 (*0-13-308619-4*) P-H.

— How to Save Time & Money in Filing Your 1988 Personal Tax Returns. 78p. 1988. 8.00 (*0-13-431214-7*, Busn) P-H.

***Prentice-Hall Staff.** Implementing & Supporting Microsoft Proxy Server 2.0. LC 99-38993. (MCSE Ser.). 434p. 1999. pap. text 49.99 (*0-13-011248-8*) P-H.

Prentice-Hall Staff. Information Systems, Policies & Procedures Manual 1998-1999. 1999. pap. text 39.95 (*0-13-012419-2*) P-H.

— Internal Revenue Code. 1984. write for info. (*0-318-58008-X*) P-H.

— The Lawyer's Almanac, 1995. 1300p. 1995. 116.00 (*0-13-126597-0*) Aspen Law.

— Lawyer's Desk Book: 1999 Cumulative Supplement. 10th ed. 288p. (C). 1998. pap. text 39.95 (*0-13-918350-7*) P-H.

— Legal Secretary's Desk Guide to Punctuation & Spelling. 32p. (C). 1992. 5.95 (*0-13-010786-7*, Macmillan Coll) P-H.

***Prentice-Hall Staff.** Life Management. 1999. text. write for info. (*0-13-536426-4*, Prentice Hall) P-H.

Prentice-Hall Staff. Matematicas Para Niveles Intermedios. (SPA.). 1997. 49.29 (*0-13-839689-2*); 52.63 (*0-13-839697-3*); 52.63 (*0-13-839705-8*) P-H.

Prentice-Hall Staff. Matter: Building Block. 2nd ed. 1901. text, student ed. write for info. (*0-13-402082-0*, Prentice Hall) P-H.

Prentice-Hall Staff. New Cambridge GED Program: Exercise Book for Writing Skills, Pt. 2. 1995. pap. 6.95 (*0-13-601204-3*) P-H.

— 1985 Federal Tax Course. 1984. write for info. (*0-318-58023-3*) P-H.

Prentice Hall Staff. 1997 Just-in-Time for Decision Science. (C). 1997. write for info. (*0-13-259524-9*, Macmillan Coll) P-H.

Prentice-Hall Staff. 1992 Federal Tax Course. (C). 1991. 129.00 (*0-13-310418-4*, Busn) P-H.

— Nursing Knowledge & Nursing Science. (C). 2000. text 39.95 (*0-8385-7116-6*, Medical Exam) Appleton & Lange.

— Open CPI-C Specification: Version 2. 2nd ed. LC 97-162361. 564p. (C). 1996. pap. 59.00 (*0-13-496407-1*) P-H.

— Partnership Tax Handbook. 176p. 1988. 19.50 (*0-13-697104-0*) P-H.

— Partnership Tax Handbook. 200p. 1989. 21.50 (*0-13-705873-X*, Busn) P-H.

— Personnel Management: Communications. 1984. write for info. (*0-318-58014-4*) P-H.

— Personnel Management: Compensation. 1984. write for info. (*0-318-58015-2*) P-H.

— Personnel Management: Policies & Practices. 1984. write for info. (*0-318-58013-6*) P-H.

Prentice-Hall Staff. PH Lit. Gold. 3rd ed. (Prentice-Hall Literature). 1994. text. write for info. (*0-13-722505-9*, Prentice Hall) P-H.

Prentice-Hall Staff. Prentice Hall Federal Tax Course. Rubin, Alan, ed. 1981. student ed. 21.00 (*0-685-03902-1*); pap., student ed. 7.95 (*0-685-03903-X*) P-H.

— Prentice Hall Federal Tax Treaties, 2 vols., Set. ring bd. write for info. (*0-318-57895-6*) P-H.

— Prentice Hall Inheritance Taxes. (Illus.). write for info. (*0-318-58375-5*) P-H.

— Prentice Hall Pract Problms for Individuals. 1996. pap. text 6.67 (*0-13-239401-4*) P-H.

— Prentice Hall 1040 Handbook, 1990: For Filing 1989 Individual Income Tax Returns. 1989. pap. 49.50 (*0-13-903634-2*) P-H.

— Prentice Hall's Guide to Sales & Use Taxes. 720p. 1988. 37.95 (*0-13-705881-0*, Busn) P-H.

— Prentice Hall's Social Security Deskbook, 1988. Hillman, Marvin, ed. 450p. 1988. pap. 30.00 (*0-13-703035-5*, Busn) P-H.

— Professional Corporate Guide: Organization, Administration, Termination, Employee Benefits, Forms & Laws. 1983. write for info. (*0-318-57211-7*) P-H.

— Real Estate Guide. 1966. 131.50 (*0-13-762740-8*) P-H.

— S Corporations: Tax Choices for Business Planning. 1984. write for info. (*0-318-58011-X*) P-H.

— SEC Guidelines, Rules & Regulations. 590p. 1989. pap. text 22.95 (*0-685-21947-X*, Busn) P-H.

Prentice Hall Staff. Seven Proven Strategies for Becoming a More Effective Trainee. 32p. (C). 1996. pap. 11.95 (*0-13-490582-4*, Macmillan Coll) P-H.

Prentice-Hall Staff. SPSS Base 7.0 Syntax. LC 95-72796. 1996. pap., student ed. 48.00 (*0-13-476326-2*) P-H.

— Start Your Own Catering Business. (Start Your Own Ser.). 192p. 1996. pap. text 12.95 (*0-13-603309-1*) P-H.

— Start Your Own Childcare Business. (Start Your Own Ser.). 192p. (C). 1996. pap. text 12.95 (*0-13-603325-3*) P-H.

— Start Your Own Coffee & Tea Store. (Start Your Own Ser.). 248p. (C). 1996. pap. text 12.95 (*0-13-603275-3*) P-H.

— Start Your Own Desktop Publishing Business. (Start Your Own Ser.). 192p. (C). 1996. pap. text 12.95 (*0-13-603283-4*) P-H.

— Start Your Own Gift Basket Business. (Start Your Own Ser.). 248p. (C). 1996. pap. text 12.95 (*0-13-603291-5*) P-H.

— Start Your Own Import-Export Business. (Start Your Own Ser.). 192p. (C). 1996. pap. text 13.95 (*0-13-603028-9*) P-H.

— Start Your Own Mail Order Business. (Start Your Own Ser.). 192p. (C). 1996. pap. text 12.95 (*0-13-603051-3*) P-H.

Prentice-Hall Staff. Start Your Own Money-Making Computer Business. (Start Your Own Business Ser.). 192p. (C). 1996. pap. text 12.95 (*0-13-603226-5*) P-H.

Prentice-Hall Staff. Start Your Own Newsletter Publishing Business. (Start Your Own Ser.). 192p. (C). 1996. pap. text 13.95 (*0-13-603333-4*) P-H.

— Start Your Own 101 Extra Income Ideas. (Start Your Own Ser.). 248p. (C). 1996. pap. text 12.95 (*0-13-603267-2*) P-H.

— Start Your Own Resume Writing Service. (Start Your Own Ser.). 192p. (C). 1996. pap. text 12.95 (*0-13-603234-6*) P-H.

— Start Your Own Temporary Help Agency. (Start Your Own Ser.). 248p. (C). 1996. pap. text 12.95 (*0-13-603259-1*) P-H.

— Stats. 8th ed. (C). 1999. text. write for info. (*0-13-022482-0*) P-H.

— Step-by-Step Guide to Filing 91. 1991. pap. text 7.95 (*0-13-847328-5*) P-H.

— Suzhou. 1998. pap. text 29.95 (*1-888931-15-9*) Spacemkr Pr.

— Tax-Wise Ways to Sell Your House. 30p. 1984. 2.75 (*0-685-08926-6*, 88679-6) P-H.

— Teach Top Personel Managers 1989. 1989. pap. text 6.85 (*0-13-898487-5*) P-H.

— Teen Living. 1991. 23.06 (*0-13-903964-3*) P-H.

— Ten Fast Way Turn a Corporation 87. 2nd ed. 1987. pap. text 6.85 (*0-13-903303-3*) P-H.

— 33 Model Memos for Tough Situations. (C). 1995. pap. text 5.95 (*0-13-461914-5*) P-H.

— Travel & Entertainment Deduction 88. 1987. pap. text 2.50 (*0-13-930165-8*) P-H.

— Travel & Entertainment Deduction 89. 1988. text 4.95 (*0-13-930181-X*) P-H.

— Travel & Entertainment Diary 91. 1990. pap. text 2.85 (*0-13-929373-6*) P-H.

— Twenty Tested Ways to Cash out 89. 1989. pap. text 6.85 (*0-13-935289-9*) P-H.

— Twenty Two Ways to Collection 87. 1989. pap. text 4.95 (*0-13-934894-8*) P-H.

— Twenty Two Ways to 1986 Collection. 1990. pap. text 4.95 (*0-13-935140-X*) P-H.

— Using the Graphics Calculator, Bk. 2. 2nd ed. 1997. 59.29 (*0-13-353053-1*) P-H.

— What New Tax Law Means91. 1991. pap. text 0.60 (*0-13-950866-X*) P-H.

Prentice-Hall Staff. What's Up? 1989. pap. 20.80 (*0-13-955790-3*) P-H.

— X-0pen SQL & RDA. 2nd ed. LC 97-162367. 360p. (C). 1996. pap. 54.00 (*0-13-496415-2*) P-H.

***Prentice-Hall Staff, ed.** Abnormal Psychology in a Changing World. 4th ed. LC 99-28720. 678p. (C). 1999. 85.33 (*0-13-030005-5*) P-H.

Prentice-Hall Staff, ed. Adjustment & Human Relations. (C). 2000. text. write for info. (*0-13-040050-5*) P-H.

— Adobe Illustrator 7.0: Advanced Digital Illustration. LC 98-14260. (Against the Clock Ser.). (Illus.). 384p. (C). 1998. pap. text 33.33 (*0-13-080506-8*) P-H.

— Advanced Digital Images. (Photoshop Ser.). (C). 1999. text, teacher ed. write for info. (*0-13-022084-1*) P-H.

— Algebra for College Students. (C). 2000. text. write for info. (*0-13-040176-5*) P-H.

— All You Need to Know about Individual Retirement Plans (IRAS) LC 83-177115. (Pension Planning Ser.). 1981. pap. 4.75 (*0-13-022590-8*) P-H.

***Prentice-Hall Staff, ed.** American Foreign Policy: Past, Present & Future. 4th ed. LC 99-21622. 429p. (C). 1999. pap. text 45.00 (*0-13-083579-X*) P-H.

Prentice-Hall Staff, ed. Angel. 5th ed. (Preview 2000 Ser.). (C). 2000. write for info. (*0-13-084744-5*) P-H.

— Anthology of American Literature: Colonial Through Romantic, Vol. 1. 7th ed. LC 99-34844. 2233p. (C). 1999. pap. 55.00 (*0-13-083814-4*) P-H.

— Anthropology on the Internet 1999-2000. (C). 1999. write for info. (*0-13-084766-6*) P-H.

— Applied Mathematic Business Economy Life Science &Social. 7th ed. (C). 1999. text. write for info. (*0-13-040319-9*) P-H.

***Prentice-Hall Staff, ed.** Applied Mathematics for Business & Economics, Life Sciences & Social Sciences. 7th ed. (C). 1999. text. write for info. (*0-13-040321-0*) P-H.

Prentice-Hall Staff, ed. Applied Mechanics for Engineering Technolgy. 6th ed. (C). 2000. text. write for info. (*0-13-085094-2*) P-H.

— Art on the Internet 1999-2000. (C). 1999. write for info. (*0-13-084764-X*) P-H.

— Audersirk. 2nd ed. (Preview 2000 Ser.). (C). 2000. write for info. (*0-13-013678-6*) P-H.

***Prentice-Hall Staff, ed.** Basic Criminal Procedures. LC 99-13091. 205p. (C). 1999. pap. text 52.00 (*0-13-084774-7*) P-H.

Prentice-Hall Staff, ed. Becoming an Electronic Technician: Securing Your High-Tech Future. 3rd ed. LC 99-24233. (Illus.). 304p. (C). 1999. pap. text 29.00 (*0-13-082651-0*) P-H.

— Erown Lemay. 8th ed. (Preview 2000 Ser.). (C). 2000. write for info. (*0-13-084745-3*) P-H.

***Prentice-Hall Staff, ed.** Business Communication Today. 6th ed. LC 99-20812. 741p. (C). 1999. 84.00 (*0-13-084513-2*) P-H.

— Business Essentials. 3rd ed. (C). 1999. write for info. (*0-13-022068-X*) P-H.

— Business Essentials. 3rd ed. (C). 2000. text. write for info. (*0-13-040018-1*) P-H.

— C++ Introduction to Data Structure. (C). 1999. text. write for info. (*0-13-013779-0*) P-H.

Prentice-Hall Staff, ed. Calculus & Applications. (C). 1999. text. write for info. (*0-13-040297-4*); text. write for info. (*0-13-040298-2*) P-H.

— Calculus with Analytic Geometry. 8th ed. (C). 2000. text. write for info. (*0-13-085090-X*); text. write for info. (*0-13-085102-7*) P-H.

— Calculus with Analytic Geometry. 8th ed. (C). 2000. text. write for info. (*0-13-085099-3*) P-H.

***Prentice-Hall Staff, ed.** Charles Community College Trigonometry. 58p. (C). 1998. text, suppl. ed. 3.00 (*0-13-083559-5*) P-H.

Prentice-Hall Staff, ed. Classmates. (C). 2000. 19.93 (*0-13-084798-4*) P-H.

— College Algebra Enhanced with Graph Utilities. 2nd ed. (C). 1999. text 400.00 (*0-13-040307-5*) P-H.

— College Algebra Enhanced with Graph Utilities. 2nd ed. (C). 1999. text. write for info. (*0-13-040308-3*); text. write for info. (*0-13-040313-X*) P-H.

***Prentice-Hall Staff, ed.** College Algebra Enhanced with Graph Utilities. 2nd ed. (C). 1999. text 420.00 (*0-13-040305-9*) P-H.

Prentice-Hall Staff, ed. College Algebra Enhanced with Graph Utilities. 2nd ed. (C). 1999. text. write for info. (*0-13-040311-3*); text. write for info. (*0-13-040314-8*) P-H.

— College Physics. 4th ed. 522p. (C). 1999. pap. 64.67 (*0-13-084166-8*) P-H.

— College Reading: Purpose & Strategies. (C). 1999. text. write for info. (*0-13-085097-7*) P-H.

***Prentice-Hall Staff, ed.** Color Acetates. 8th ed. (C). 1998. text. write for info. (*0-13-083758-X*) P-H.

Prentice-Hall Staff, ed. Color Tranparencies. 7th ed. (C). 2000. write for info. (*0-13-084706-2*) P-H.

***Prentice-Hall Staff, ed.** Community Policy: Classical Readings. LC 99-26033. 361p. (C). 1999. pap. text 45.00 (*0-13-080075-9*) P-H.

Prentice-Hall Staff, ed. Computer Aided Statics & Strength Materials. (C). 2000. write for info. (*0-13-084681-3*) P-H.

***Prentice-Hall Staff, ed.** Computer Web Site. (C). 1999. text. write for info. (*0-13-020998-8*) P-H.

Prentice-Hall Staff, ed. Computers. 7th ed. (Open Learning for Supervisory Management Ser.). (C). 2000. text 57.01 (*0-13-085078-0*) P-H.

***Prentice-Hall Staff, ed.** Consumer Behavior. 7th ed. LC 99-24486. 468p. (C). 1999. 94.67 (*0-13-084129-3*) P-H.

Prentice-Hall Staff, ed. Consumer Behavior. 7th ed. (C). 2000. write for info. (*0-13-084698-8*); write for info. (*0-13-084699-6*); write for info. (*0-13-084701-1*); write for info. (*0-13-084702-X*); teacher ed. write for info. (*0-13-084697-X*) P-H.

— Cost Accounting: Managerial Emphasis. 10th ed. (C). 1999. text. write for info. (*0-13-040077-7*) P-H.

— Cost Accounting: Managerial Emphasis. 10th ed. (C). 1999. text 28.00 (*0-13-040088-2*) P-H.

***Prentice-Hall Staff, ed.** Cost Accounting: Managerial Emphasis. 10th ed. (C). 1999. text 30.00 (*0-13-040099-8*) P-H.

Prentice-Hall Staff, ed. Cost Accounting: Managerial Emphasis. 10th ed. (C). 2000. text. write for info. (*0-13-040076-9*); text. write for info. (*0-13-040093-9*); text. write for info. (*0-13-040095-5*); text. write for info. (*0-13-040096-3*); text. write for info. (*0-13-040098-X*) P-H.

— Creative Impulse Introduction Arts. 5th ed. (C). 1999. text 17.33 (*0-13-040036-X*) P-H.

— Creative Impulse Introduction Arts. 5th ed. (C). 1999. cd-rom 14.67 (*0-13-040047-5*) P-H.

— Creative Impulse Introduction Arts. 5th ed. (C). 2000. text. write for info. (*0-13-040037-8*); text. write for info. (*0-13-040038-6*); text. write for info. (*0-13-040039-4*) P-H.

— Creative Impulse Introduction Arts. 5th ed. (C). 2000. text. write for info. (*0-13-040046-7*) P-H.

***Prentice-Hall Staff, ed.** Cryptography Network Security: Principal & Practice. 2nd ed. (C). 1999. text. write for info. (*0-13-013777-4*) P-H.

— Cultural Anthropology: A Global Perspective. 4th ed. LC 99-38544. 456p. (C). 1999. pap. 61.00 (*0-13-082576-X*) P-H.

Prentice-Hall Staff, ed. Data Communication Applications. (C). 1999. teacher ed. write for info. (*0-13-084754-2*) P-H.

***Prentice-Hall Staff, ed.** Data Communications: An Overview. (C). 1998. text. write for info. (*0-13-084670-8*) P-H.

Prentice-Hall Staff, ed. Digital Fundamentals. 7th ed. (C). 1999. text. write for info. (*0-13-084676-7*) P-H.

— Digital Fundamentals. 7th ed. (C). 2000. text. write for info. (*0-13-084668-6*); text. write for info. (*0-13-084669-4*); text. write for info. (*0-13-084671-6*); text. write for info. (*0-13-084673-2*); text. write for info. (*0-13-084675-9*); text. write for info. (*0-13-084667-8*) P-H.

— Digital System Integrity: More Black Magic. (C). 2000. 75.00 (*0-13-084408-X*) P-H.

— Diversity & Teams in Workplace. 9th ed. (Supervision Ser.). (C). 2000. teacher ed. write for info. (*0-13-022044-2*) P-H.

— Doing It! 52p. (Orig.). (C). 1999. pap. text 2.67 (*0-13-084108-0*) P-H.

***Prentice-Hall Staff, ed.** Effective Reading in a Changing World. 3rd ed. LC 99-41128. 656p. (C). 1999. pap. text 42.00 (*0-13-011579-7*) P-H.

Prentice-Hall Staff, ed. Electrical Circuit Analysis Using Ti85 Ti86. 88p. (C). 1999. write for info. (*0-13-084692-9*) P-H.

— Electronic Instructor's Guide. (C). 1999. text. write for info. (*0-13-020133-2*) P-H.

— Electronic Technology Journal Fall '99. (C). 2000. write for info. (*0-13-021918-5*) P-H.

***Prentice-Hall Staff, ed.** Elementary Algebra for College Students. 5th ed. (C). 1999. text 12.50 (*0-13-040292-3*); text 12.50 (*0-13-040293-1*) P-H.

Prentice-Hall Staff, ed. Elementary Algebra for College Students. 5th ed. (C). 1999. text 35.00 (*0-13-040291-5*) P-H.

— Elementary Algebra for College Students. 5th ed. (C). 2000. text. write for info. (*0-13-040216-8*); text. write for info. (*0-13-040286-9*); text 420.00 (*0-13-040287-7*); text 29.00 (*0-13-040210-9*) P-H.

***Prentice-Hall Staff, ed.** Elementary Algebra for College Students: Early Graphing. (C). 1999. text 35.00 (*0-13-040271-0*); text 12.50 (*0-13-040272-9*); text 12.50 (*0-13-040273-7*); text. write for info. (*0-13-040274-5*); text. write for info. (*0-13-040275-3*) P-H.

— Elementary Algebra for College Students: Early Graphing. (C). 1999. text 400.00 (*0-13-040260-5*) P-H.

Prentice-Hall Staff, ed. Elementary Algebra for College Students: Early Graphing. 5th ed. (C). 1999. text 400.00 (*0-13-040280-X*) P-H.

— Elementary Algebra for College Students: Early Graphing. 5th ed. (C). 2000. text. write for info. (*0-13-040177-3*); text. write for info. (*0-13-040178-1*); text. write for info. (*0-13-040179-X*); text 30.80 (*0-13-040181-1*); text. write for info. (*0-13-040219-2*); text. write for info. (*0-13-040225-7*); text 29.00 (*0-13-040226-5*); text. write for info. (*0-13-040170-6*) P-H.

— Elementary & Intermediate Algebra. (C). 1999. text. write for info. (*0-13-040278-8*); text. write for info. (*0-13-040279-6*); text. write for info. (*0-13-040281-8*); text. write for info. (*0-13-040282-6*); text 420.00 (*0-13-040276-1*) P-H.

— Energy Management. (Advanced Electronical Topics Ser.). (C). 1998. pap. text 20.00 (*0-13-910001-6*) P-H.

— Environmental Law. 3rd ed. LC 99-28184. 370p. (C). 1999. pap. text 45.00 (*0-13-014121-6*) P-H.

— Equilibrium Staged Separations. 2nd ed. (C). 2000. text. write for info. (*0-13-084780-1*) P-H.

***Prentice-Hall Staff, ed.** Essential Powerpoint 97 & Exploring the Internet. (C). 1998. pap. text 50.66 (*0-13-083428-9*) P-H.

— Essentials of Oceanography. 6th ed. (C). 1999. text. write for info. (*0-13-013872-X*) P-H.

— Essentials of Visual Basic 6.0 Programming. (C). 1999. text, teacher ed. write for info. (*0-13-022007-8*) P-H.

Prentice-Hall Staff, ed. Ethics & the Conduct of Business. 3rd ed. LC 99-24485. 417p. (C). 1999. pap. text 46.00 (*0-13-083145-X*) P-H.

***Prentice-Hall Staff, ed.** Experiencing Introductory Algebra. 448p. 1998. 27.80 (*0-13-799958-5*) P-H.

Prentice-Hall Staff, ed. The Front Matter, Dead Souls. (C). 1999. text. write for info. (*0-13-085046-2*) P-H.

P

An Asterisk (*) at the beginning of an entry indicates that the title is appearing for the first time.

— Graphic Concepts with Proengineer. 250p. (C). 2000. pap. text 21.00 (*0-13-014154-2*) P-H.
— Graphic Concepts with Solid Works. 250p. (C). 2000. pap. 20.00 (*0-13-014155-0*) P-H.
***Prentice-Hall Staff, ed.** The Guide for the Critical Reader. 60p. (C). 1998. text. write for info. (*0-13-021089-7*) P-H.
Prentice-Hall Staff, ed. History & Psychology: Main Current Psychological Thought. 5th ed. (C). 2000. text. write for info. (*0-13-040236-2*) P-H.
***Prentice-Hall Staff, ed.** Hot Topics in Introduction to Business. 2nd ed. (C). 1998. text. write for info. (*0-13-013812-6*) P-H.
Prentice-Hall Staff, ed. Industrial Electronics: Applications for Place Instrumentation & Process Control & Machines of Motor Controls. 2nd ed. LC 99-32916. (Illus.). 871p. (C). 1999. 101.00 (*0-13-012697-7*) P-H.
— Interest Groups in American National Politics: An Overview. LC 99-24488. 178p. (C). 1999. pap. text 23.20 (*0-13-914060-3*) P-H.
***Prentice-Hall Staff, ed.** Intermediate Algebra. (C). 1999. 420.00 (*0-13-014138-0*) P-H.
Prentice-Hall Staff, ed. Intermediate Algebra for College Students. (C). 1999. text. write for info. (*0-13-040246-X*) P-H.
— Intermediate Algebra for College Students. (C). 2000. text. write for info. (*0-13-040254-0*) P-H.
— Intermediate Algebra for College Students. 5th ed. (C). 1999. text. write for info. (*0-13-040248-6*) P-H.
— Intermediate Algebra for College Students. 5th ed. (C). 1999. text 30.67 (*0-13-040245-1*) P-H.
— Intermediate Algebra for College Students. 5th ed. (C). 2000. text 29.00 (*0-13-040249-4*) P-H.
— Internet Security. 300p. (C). 2000. 44.99 (*0-13-014249-2*) P-H.
***Prentice-Hall Staff, ed.** Introduction to Algebra for College Students. (C). 1999. 420.00 (*0-13-014130-5*) P-H.
Prentice-Hall Staff, ed. Introduction to Animal Science. (C). 2000. write for info. (*0-13-013701-4*); teacher ed. write for info. incl. cd-rom (*0-13-013690-5*) P-H.
— Introduction to ANSI C for Engineers & Scientists. LC 98-50974. 126p. (C). 1999. pap. text 21.33 (*0-13-011854-0*) P-H.
— Introduction to Dc Ac Circuits. (C). 1999. text. write for info. (*0-13-040232-X*) P-H.
— Introduction to Dc Ac Circuits. (C). 2000. text. write for info. (*0-13-040234-6*) P-H.
***Prentice-Hall Staff, ed.** Introduction to Digital Images. (C). 1999. text, teacher ed. write for info. (*0-13-022083-3*) P-H.
Prentice-Hall Staff, ed. Introductory Electronic Devices & Circuits. 5th ed. (C). 1999. teacher ed. write for info. (*0-13-013702-2*) P-H.
— Introductory Electronic Devices & Circuits. 5th ed. (C). 2000. write for info. (*0-13-013704-9*); write for info. (*0-13-013706-5*); lab manual ed. write for info. (*0-13-013705-7*) P-H.
— Introductory Electronic Devices & Circuits: Conventional Flow Version. 5th ed. LC 99-25419. (Illus.). 1069p. (C). 1999. text 96.00 incl. audio compact disk (*0-13-927203-8*) P-H.
— Keys to Study Skills: Opening Doors to Learning. (C). 1999. text. write for info. (*0-13-040256-7*) P-H.
***Prentice-Hall Staff, ed.** Keys to Success. (C). 1999. text. write for info. (*0-13-040257-5*) P-H.
— Keys to Success: How to Achieve Your Goal D-Cart. 2nd ed. (C). 1998. text 28.00 (*0-13-010841-3*) P-H.
— Linear Algebra for Engineers & Scientists. 420p. (C). 2000. 77.33 (*0-13-906728-0*) P-H.
Prentice-Hall Staff, ed. Listening to Music. 3rd ed. (C). 1999. text 14.00 (*0-13-040239-7*) P-H.
***Prentice-Hall Staff, ed.** Listening to Music. 3rd ed. (C). 1999. text 37.80 (*0-13-040238-9*); pap. text 40.00 (*0-13-907346-9*) P-H.
Prentice-Hall Staff, ed. Listening to Music. 3rd ed. (C). 2000. text. write for info. (*0-13-040237-0*); text. write for info. (*0-13-040241-9*); text. write for info. (*0-13-040242-7*) P-H.
***Prentice-Hall Staff, ed.** Living Religions. 4th ed. (Illus.). 485p. (C). 1999. pap. text 44.00 (*0-13-011994-6*) P-H.
Prentice-Hall Staff, ed. Management Information Systems. 6th ed. (C). 1999. text. write for info. (*0-13-040207-9*); text. write for info. (*0-13-040208-7*) P-H.
— Management Information Systems. 6th ed. (C). 1999. text. write for info. (*0-13-040202-8*) P-H.
— Management Information Systems. 6th ed. (C). 1999. text. write for info. (*0-13-040206-0*) P-H.
— Management Information Systems. 6th ed. (C). 2000. text. write for info. (*0-13-040204-4*); text. write for info. (*0-13-040201-X*); text. write for info. (*0-13-040209-5*) P-H.
— Managing World Economic Change: International Political Economy. 3rd ed. (C). 2000. text. write for info. (*0-13-040211-7*) P-H.
— Marketing for Hospitality & Tourism. 2nd ed. (C). 1999. write for info. (*0-13-013698-0*) P-H.
***Prentice-Hall Staff, ed.** Mathematical Supplement for Statistics. (C). 1999. text 21.00 (*0-13-794132-3*) P-H.
— Mathematics on the Internet, 1999. 48p. (C). 1998. text, student ed. write for info. (*0-13-083998-1*) P-H.
Prentice-Hall Staff, ed. Media & Print Resources. 8th ed. (C). 2000. text, teacher ed. write for info. (*0-13-084102-1*) P-H.
— Modeling the Enterprise: From Business Processes, to Business Oblects, to Systemarchitecture, to Code. (C). 1999. pap. text 55.00 (*0-13-013783-9*) P-H.
— Objected-Orientd Data Warehousing Design: Building Star Schema. LC 99-89100. 368p. (C). 2000. 49.00 (*0-13-085081-0*) P-H.
— Old Testament Story. 5th ed. LC 99-19378. (Illus.). 397p. (C). 1999. 57.00 (*0-13-011293-3*) P-H.
— Operations Management. 3rd ed. (C). 1999. text. write for info. (*0-13-013866-5*) P-H.
— Operations Management. 3rd ed. (C). 1999. text. write for info. (*0-13-013867-3*) P-H.
— Operations Management. 3rd ed. (C). 2000. text. write for info. (*0-13-013865-7*); text. write for info. (*0-13-013864-9*); text. write for info. (*0-13-013868-1*) P-H.
— Over the Top: A Bridge to Academic & Critical Thinking Skills. (C). 2000. pap. 28.00 (*0-13-021608-9*) S&S Trade.
***Prentice-Hall Staff, ed.** Philosophy on the Internet: 1999-2000. (C). 1998. text. write for info. (*0-13-022072-8*) P-H.
Prentice-Hall Staff, ed. Physics for Scientist & Engineers with Modern Physics. 3rd ed. 1184p. (C). 2000. 116.00 (*0-13-021517-1*) P-H.
***Prentice-Hall Staff, ed.** Physics for Scientists & Engineers, Vol. 1. 3rd ed. LC 99-40008. 576p. (C). 1999. 69.00 (*0-13-021518-X*) P-H.
Prentice-Hall Staff, ed. Physics for Scientists & Engineers, Vol. 2. 3rd ed. 468p. (C). 2000. 70.67 (*0-13-021519-8*) P-H.
— Political Ideologies: Their Origins & Impact. 7th ed. LC 99-12299. 338p. (C). 1999. pap. text 29.40 (*0-13-020888-4*) P-H.
***Prentice-Hall Staff, ed.** Political Science on the Internet: 1999-2000. (C). 1999. text. write for info. (*0-13-022075-2*) P-H.
Prentice-Hall Staff, ed. PowerPoint Electronic Transparencies. 7th ed. (C). 2000. write for info. (*0-13-084705-4*) P-H.
— Powerpoint Presentation. 9th ed. (C). 2000. write for info. (*0-13-022417-0*) P-H.
— PowerPoints. 2nd ed. (C). 1999. text. write for info. (*0-13-010289-X*) P-H.
— Precalculus Enhancd with Graphing Utilities. 2nd ed. (C). 1999. text. write for info. (*0-13-022503-7*) P-H.
— Precalculus Enhanced with Graphing Utilities. 2nd ed. (C). 1999. text. write for info. (*0-13-022504-5*); text. write for info. (*0-13-022505-3*) P-H.
— Prentice Hall Business Appointment Book 1999. (C). 1999. 29.95 (*0-13-022045-0*) P-H.
***Prentice-Hall Staff, ed.** The Prentice Hall Guide for College Writers: Brief Edition. 5th ed. LC 99-24814. 634p. (C). 1999. pap. text 42.00 (*0-13-021029-3*) P-H.
Prentice-Hall Staff, ed. Preparing for TASP. 5th ed. 40p. (C). 1998. text 6.67 (*0-13-081640-X*) P-H.
— Preparing for the CLAST. 5th ed. 48p. (C). 1999. text 6.67 (*0-13-081649-3*) P-H.
— Presentation Manager. 6th ed. (C). 1999. (*0-13-935040-3*) P-H.
***Prentice-Hall Staff, ed.** Presentation Manager. 6th ed. (C). 1999. text. write for info. (*0-13-013860-6*) P-H.
Prentice-Hall Staff, ed. Principles of Electric Circuits: Electron-Flow Version. 5th ed. LC 99-36154. 925p. (C). 1999. 96.00 incl. cd-rom (*0-13-095998-7*) P-H.
***Prentice-Hall Staff, ed.** Probation & Parole. 7th ed. LC 99-19288. (Correctional Issues Ser.). (Illus.). 504p. (C). 1999. 71.00 (*0-13-021459-0*) P-H.
Prentice-Hall Staff, ed. Probation & Parole. 7th ed. (Correctional Issues Ser.). (C). 2000. text. write for info. (*0-13-022121-X*); text. write for info. (*0-13-022122-8*) P-H.
— Production Work Flow: Concepts & Techniques. LC 99-33025. 479p. (C). 1999. pap. 61.00 (*0-13-021753-0*) P-H.
— Programmable Logic Controllers. (Advanced Electronical Topics Ser.). (C). 1998. pap. text 20.00 (*0-13-909961-1*) P-H.
— Programmable Logic Controllers. 104p. (C). 1999. text, teacher ed. write for info. (*0-13-022119-8*) P-H.
— Project Management for Its Professionals. 280p. (C). 2000. 39.99 (*0-13-021914-2*) P-H.
***Prentice-Hall Staff, ed.** Psychology on the Internet: 1999-2000. (C). 1999. text. write for info. (*0-13-022074-4*) P-H.
Prentice-Hall Staff, ed. Refrigeration & Air Conditioning. 3rd ed. 168p. (C). 1997. pap. text, lab manual ed. 17.60 (*0-13-646407-6*) P-H.
— Religion in America. 4th ed. LC 99-28719. 344p. (C). 1999. pap. text 39.80 (*0-13-020992-9*) P-H.
— Religion on the Internet 1999-2000. (C). 1999. write for info. (*0-13-022060-4*) P-H.
— Salesnet: Sales Force Automation at Picker International. 14p. (C). 1998. 4.00 (*0-13-096042-X*) P-H.
***Prentice-Hall Staff, ed.** Science on the Internet, 1999. 40p. (C). 1998. text, student ed. write for info. (*0-13-021308-X*) P-H.
Prentice-Hall Staff, ed. Social Psychology. 10th ed. LC 99-21615. 570p. (C). 1999. 74.00 (*0-13-021336-5*) P-H.
— Social Studies Content for Elementary & Middle School Teachers. (C). 2000. text. write for info. (*0-13-022480-4*) P-H.
— The Sociology of Health, Healing & Illness. 3rd ed. LC 99-26763. 403p. (C). 1999. 57.00 (*0-13-099928-8*) P-H.
— The Sociology of Health, Healing & Illness. 3rd ed. (C). 2000. text. write for info. (*0-13-021801-4*) P-H.
***Prentice-Hall Staff, ed.** Sociology on the Internet: 1999-2000. (C). 1998. text. write for info. (*0-13-022071-X*) P-H.
Prentice-Hall Staff, ed. Special Report New Minmum Wage, No. 90. 1990. pap. text 4.95 (*0-13-826223-3*) P-H.
***Prentice-Hall Staff, ed.** Spring 1999 NYT American Government: Elections '98. (C). 1999. text. write for info. (*0-13-082952-8*) P-H.
Prentice-Hall Staff, ed. Statistics. 8th ed. (C). 1999. text. write for info. (*0-13-022481-2*) P-H.
— Statistics. 8th ed. (C). 2000. text. write for info. (*0-13-022470-7*) P-H.
— Strategies for Successful Writing: A Rhetoric, Reseach Guide, Reader & Handbook D-Cart. 5th ed. (C). 1999. text 38.00 (*0-13-020662-8*) P-H.
***Prentice-Hall Staff, ed.** Structured Computer Organization. 4th ed. (C). 1999. text. write for info. (*0-13-022077-9*) P-H.
Prentice-Hall Staff, ed. Student Handbook & Solutions Manual. 6th ed. (C). 2000. pap. text 29.75 (*0-13-084436-5*) P-H.
— Supervision: Diversity & Teams in Workplace. 9th ed. (C). 2000. write for info. (*0-13-022043-4*) P-H.
— Supplements Sampler. 7th ed. (C). 2000. write for info. (*0-13-084703-8*) P-H.
— Systems Projects. 6th ed. (C). 1998. pap. text, lab manual ed. 34.00 (*0-13-010995-9*) P-H.
— Teaching Children to Read: Putting Pieces Together. 3rd ed. (C). 2000. text. write for info. (*0-13-022170-8*) P-H.
— Teaching Young Children: An Introduction. (C). 1999. write for info. (*0-13-022009-4*) P-H.
— Trigonometry Enhanced with Graphing Utilities. 2nd ed. (C). 1999. text. write for info. (*0-13-022490-1*) P-H.
— Trigonometry Enhanced with with Graphing Utilities. 2nd ed. (C). 1999. text. write for info. (*0-13-022499-5*) P-H.
***Prentice-Hall Staff, ed.** Understanding Today's Police. 2nd ed. LC 99-21212. (Illus.). 345p. (C). 1999. pap. text 50.67 (*0-13-021008-0*) P-H.
Prentice-Hall Staff, ed. Uniting the Virtual Learning Community. (C). 1999. text. write for info. (*0-13-022086-8*) P-H.
— Voices of Freedom: Souces in American History. 1987. pap. 13.27 (*0-13-943655-3*) P-H.
***Prentice-Hall Staff, ed.** Winning at Weight Loss. 32p. (C). 1998. pap. 5.95 (*0-13-021307-1*) P-H.
Prentice-Hall Staff, ed. Word by Word Basic Picture Dictionary: Teacher's Resource Book & Activity Masters. (C). 2000. 19.93 (*0-13-022164-3*) P-H.
— Word by Word Primary Picture Dictionary. (C). 1999. text 33.27 (*0-13-022160-0*) P-H.
— Word by Word Primary Picture Dictionary. (C). 2000. text 14.60 (*0-13-022166-X*) P-H.
— Word by Word Primary Picture Dictionary. (C). 2000. pap. 17.00 (*0-13-022150-3*) P-H.
— Word by Word Primary Picture Dictionary Handwriting Practice Book, Level K. (C). 2000. pap. 66.60 (*0-13-022165-1*); pap. 66.60 (*0-13-022203-8*) P-H.
— Word by Word Primary Picture Dictionary Handwriting Practice Book: Cursive. (C). 2000. pap. 13.33 (*0-13-022163-5*) P-H.
— Word by Word Primary Picture Dictionary Handwriting Practice Book: Printing. (C). 2000. pap. 47.93 (*0-13-022162-7*) P-H.
— Word by Word Primary Picture Dictionary Handwriting Practice Copymasters: D'Nealian. (C). 1999. pap. 6.00 (*0-13-022199-6*) P-H.
— Word By Word Primary Picture Dictionary Handwriting Practice Copymasters Cursive. (C). 2000. pap. 47.93 (*0-13-022201-1*) P-H.
— Word by Word Primary Picture Dictionary Handwriting Practice Copymasters Printing. (C). 2000. pap. 66.60 (*0-13-022190-2*) P-H.
— Word Indentification Strategies: Phonics from a New Perspective. 2nd ed. LC 99-20620. (Illus.). 260p. (C). 1999. pap. 26.00 (*0-13-020342-4*) P-H.
***Prentice-Hall Staff, ed.** Wordsmith: A Guide to Paragraphs & Short Essays. LC 99-13469. 495p. (C). 1999. pap. text 45.00 (*0-13-095103-X*) P-H.
Prentice-Hall Staff, ed. Writing Talk: Paragraphs & Short Essays with Readings. 2nd ed. LC 99-13318. 544p. (C). 1999. pap. 45.00 (*0-13-099697-1*) P-H.
***Prentice-Hall Staff, ed.** Your Natural Beauty Makeover. 24p. (C). 1998. text. write for info. (*0-13-021306-3*) P-H.
***Prentice-Hall Staff & Devitt, Don.** PC Netlink Server Software: Performance, Scalability & Deployment. (Official Sun Microsystems Resource Ser.). 478p. 2000. pap. text 45.00 (*0-13-026686-8*) P-H.
Prentice-Hall Staff & New York Times Staff. Debates of Our Times. 1994. pap. text 14.00 (*0-13-362773-X*) P-H.
Prentice-Hall Staff & Warach. Travel & Entertainment Diary 87. 1987. pap. text 1.55 (*0-13-930066-X*) P-H.
Prentice-Hall Staff & Wheels Series Staff. HVAC: Trainee Guide, Level 1. (Wheels of Learning Ser.). (C). 1996. student ed., ring bd. 50.00 (*0-13-266412-7*) P-H.
Prentice-Hall Staff, jt. auth. see Faber, Peter L.
Prentice-Hall Staff, jt. auth. see Wilkie, Robert C.
Prentice-Hall Staff, ed. see Virgil.
Prentice-Hall Staff, tr. see Adobe Systems Inc. Staff.
Prentice-Hall Staff, tr. see Adobe Systems Inc. Staff, et al.
Prentice, Helaine K. Through These Doors: Discovering Oakland at Preservation Park. 52p. 1996. pap. text 12.95 (*0-9650265-0-7*) Preserv Pk.
Prentice, I. C. & Van Der Maarel, Eddy, eds. Theory & Models in Vegetation Science. (Advances in Vegetation Science Ser.). (C). 1987. text 278.50 (*90-6193-646-2*) Kluwer Academic.
Prentice, J. H. Dairy Rheology: A Concise Guide. LC 92-34877. (Food Science & Technology Ser.). 165p. 1992. 95.00 (*1-56081-505-1*, Wiley-VCH) Wiley.
Prentice, J. H. Dairy Rheology: A Concise Guide. 165p. 1992. 159.00 (*0-471-18814-X*, Wiley-VCH) Wiley.
Prentice, J. H., ed. Measurements in the Rheology of Foodstuffs. (Illus.). 200p. 1984. 63.00 (*0-85334-248-2*, I-221-84) Elsevier.
Prentice, James A. Amateur Guide to Building Rockets & Motors. unabridged ed. 1999. 15.95 (*0-9672092-0-X*, 2299) United Propulsion.
Prentice, Lee, jt. auth. see Wyman, Walker D.
Prentice, Mary. Catch Them Learning: A Handbook of Classroom Strategies - Grades K-12. LC 94-78534. 107p. 1994. pap. 24.95 (*0-932935-79-6*) SkyLght.
Prentice, Mary & Yancey, Edna. The Preadolescent: A Handbook of Middle School Classroom Strategies. LC 98-150722. 92 p. 1997. write for info. (*0-8251-3267-3*) J W Walch.
Prentice, Paul. Fly-about Adventures & the Ercoupe. 129p. 17.95 (*0-614-13200-2*, 21-36072) EAA Aviation.
Prentice, Penelope. Capturing the Light: Poems. LC 96-3094. 84p. 1996. pap. 14.95 (*0-7734-2700-7*, Mellen Poetry Pr) E Mellen.
— The Pinter Ethic: The Erotic Aesthetic. LC 93-7620. (Studies in Modern Drama: Vol. 3). (Illus.). 480p. 1993. text 30.00 (*0-8153-1385-3*) Garland.
Prentice, R. L., jt. auth. see Kalbfleisch, J. D.
Prentice, Rachel, jt. auth. see Keene, Nancy.
Prentice, Richard. Change & Policy in Wales in the Era of Privatism. 305p. 1998. pap. 38.95 (*0-8464-4739-8*) Beekman Pubs.
— Change & Policy in Wales in the Era of Privatism. 305p. 1993. pap. 39.00 (*0-86383-978-9*, Pub. by Gomer Pr) St Mut.
Prentice, Robert A. Law of Business Organizations & Securities. 2nd ed. LC 93-34759. 879p. (C). 1993. 70.60 (*0-13-530189-0*) P-H.
Prentice, Robert A., jt. auth. see Allison, John R.
Prentice, Robert P. Psychology of Love According to St. Bonaventure. (Philosophy Ser.). 156p. 1957. pap. 8.00 (*1-57659-096-8*) Franciscan Inst.
Prentice, Ross L. & Thompson, Donovan J., eds. Atomic Bomb Survivor Data: Utilization & Analysis. LC 84-50378. (SIAM-SIMS Conference Ser.: No. 10). ix, 289p. 1984. pap. text 35.00 (*0-89871-194-0*) Soc Indus-Appl Math.
Prentice, Ross L., jt. ed. see Moolgavkar, Suresh H.
Prentice, Roy, ed. Teaching Art & Design: Addressing Issues & Identifying Directions. LC 97-131389. (Cassell Education Ser.). 178p. 1995. 95.00 (*0-304-33074-4*, N365, Pub. by Cassell) LPC InBook.
Prentice, Sally & Harrison, Anthony. Hospital Policy in the United Kingdom: Its Development, Its Future. LC 97-230. 229p. 1997. pap. text 22.95 (*1-56000-978-0*) Transaction Pubs.
Prentice, Sydney. Tale of the Turk: Journey of a Soul. Prentice Allemano, Irene, tr. & illus. by. LC 98-71609. 224p. 1998. 12.95 (*0-9666998-0-7*) Hermitage Pr FL.
Prentice, Tom. The Climbing Guide to Scotland. (Illus.). 205p. 1992. pap. 34.95 (*1-85223-894-1*, Pub. by Crolwood) Trafalgar.
Prentice, W. P. Police Powers Arising under the Law of Overruling Necessity. xli, 516p. 1993. reprint ed. 52.50 (*0-8377-2523-2*, Rothman) W S Hein.
Prentice, William E. Fitness & Wellness for Life. 6th ed. LC 98-3936. 1998. 30.25 (*0-07-109260-9*) McGraw.
— Healthsouth's Guide to Fitness, Training, & Injury Prevention. LC 98-41454. 1999. 5.00 (*0-07-365617-8*) McGraw.
— Quick Reference Workout Diary. 4th ed. 32p. (C). 1993. text 7.50 (*0-8151-6717-2*, WCB McGr Hill) McGrw-H Hghr Educ.
— Rehabilitation Techniques in Sports Medicine. (C). 1993. pap. text 54.95 (*0-8016-7819-6*); pap. text 54.95 (*0-8016-7820-X*) Mosby Inc.
— Rehabilitation Techniques in Sports Medicine. 3rd ed. LC 98-6338. 624p. 1998. 68.75 (*0-07-289470-9*) McGraw.
— Therapeutic Modalities in Sports Medicine. 4th ed. LC 98-10430. 416p. 1998. 67.19 (*0-07-092066-4*) McGraw.
Prentice, William E., et al. Therapeutic Modalities for Allied-Health Professionals. LC 97-48335. (Illus.). 500p. 1998. text 45.00 (*0-07-050771-6*) McGraw-Hill HPD.
Prentice, William E., jt. auth. see Arnheim, Daniel D.
Prentis, Andrew, jt. auth. see White, Kay.
Prentis, Barbara. The Bronte Sisters & George Eliot: A Unity of Difference. 208p. 1987. 57.50 (*0-389-20756-X*, N8315) B&N Imports.
Prentis, James M. Engineering Mechanics. (Oxford Engineering Science Ser.). (Illus.). 1980. pap. text 18.50 (*0-19-856206-3*) OUP.
Prentis, Joe. Dead Certain. unabridged ed. 228p. 1998. pap. 14.95 (*1-892896-08-7*) Buy Books.
Prentis, Joseph. The Garden Book & Monthly Kalendar of Joseph Prentis. Crotz, D. Keith, ed. (American Horticultural Ser.: No. 3). (Illus.). 85p. 1990. 29.95 (*0-929332-02-4*) Amer Botanist.
Prentis, Noble L. Southern Letters. 1977. text 16.95 (*0-8369-9232-6*, 9086) Ayer.
Prentis, Richard S. Passages of Retirement: Personal Histories of Struggle & Success, 23. LC 92-1131. (Contributions to the Study of Aging Ser.: No. 23). 240p. 1992. lib. bdg. 49.95 (*0-313-28493-8*, PPN/, Greenwood Pr) Greenwood.
Prentis, Steve. Biotechnology. LC 83-26571. (Illus.). 192p. 1984. 18.50 (*0-8076-1094-1*) Braziller.
Prentiss. The Embodiment of Bhakti. LC 98-45874. 288p. 2000. text 55.00 (*0-19-512813-3*) OUP.
Prentiss, Charlotte. Children of the Ice. 496p. (Orig.). 1993. mass mkt. 5.99 (*0-451-17792-4*, Onyx) NAL.
— The Ocean Tribe. 384p. 1999. mass mkt. 6.50 (*0-06-101011-1*, Harp PBks) HarpC.
Prentiss, Chris. For Once in Your Life: Be Who You Want, Have What You Want. LC 87-60641. 330p. 1987. 9.95 (*0-943015-00-6*) Power Press.
***Prentiss, Chris.** The Little Book of Secrets: 81 Secrets for Living a Happy, Prosperous & Successful Life. 163p. 2000. pap. 7.95 (*0-943015-33-2*); pap. 7.95 (*0-943015-34-0*); pap. 7.95 (*0-943015-35-9*); pap. 7.95 (*0-943015-36-7*); pap. write for info. (*0-943015-37-5*) Power Press.
***Prentiss, Elizabeth.** Aunt Jane's Hero. 1999. pap. 7.95 (*1-881545-63-6*) Angelas Bkshelf.
Prentiss, Elizabeth. Aunt Jane's Hero. deluxe ed. (Prentiss Ser.). 304p. 1999. pap. 8.95 (*1-879737-34-5*) Calvary Press.

P

An Asterisk (*) at the beginning of an entry indicates that the title is appearing for the first time.

***Prentiss, Elizabeth.** Little Susy Stories. (J). 1999. pap. 7.99 (*1-881545-70-9*) Angelas Bkshelf.

Prentiss, Elizabeth. Stepping Heavenward. 1999. pap. text 10.95 (*1-879737-29-9*) Calvary Pr.

— Stepping Heavenward. pap. 10.99 (*0-87377-078-1*) GAM Pubns.

— Stepping Heavenward. rev. ed. 288p. 1992. pap. 11.95 (*1-879737-06-X*) Calvary Press.

— Stepping Heavenward: One Woman's Journey to Godliness. rev. ed. Sanna, Ellyn, ed. LC 99-216807. 300p. 1998. reprint ed. pap. text 4.97 (*1-57748-342-1*) Barbour Pub.

***Prentiss, Elizabeth.** Urbane & His Friends. 1999. pap. 7.99 (*1-881545-68-7*) Angelas Bkshelf.

Prentiss, Elizabeth & Prentiss, George. The Little Preacher. 175p. (Orig.). 1993. pap. 8.95 (*1-879737-10-8*) Calvary Press.

Prentiss, George, jt. auth. see Prentiss, Elizabeth.

Prentiss, George L. More Love to Thee: The Life & Letters of Elizabeth Prentiss. 605p. (Orig.). 1994. pap. 18.95 (*1-879737-14-0*) Calvary Press.

Prentiss, Hervey P. Timothy Pickering As the Leader of New England Federalism, 1800-1815. LC 71-124882. (American Scene Ser.). (Illus.). 118p. 1972. reprint ed. lib. bdg. 22.50 (*0-306-71052-8*) Da Capo.

Prentiss, Lee. Explosive & Contraband Detection. Berkel, Bob, ed. (CCS SecuritySource Library: Vol. VII). (Illus.). 720p. 1995. 300.00 (*1-884674-07-0*) CCS Security.

Prentiss, Mara G. & Phillips, William D., eds. Atom Optics, Vol. 2995. LC 97-200319. 312p. 1997. 80.00 (*0-8194-2406-4*) SPIE.

Prentiss, Stan. The Complete Book of Oscilloscopes. 2nd ed. 240p. 1992. pap. 29.95 (*0-07-157781-5*) McGraw.

— The Complete Book of Oscilloscopes. 2nd ed. 320p. 1991. 26.95 (*0-8306-3909-8*); pap. 16.95 (*0-8306-3908-X*) McGraw-Hill Prof.

— Electronic Signals. (Illus.). 272p. 1991. 29.95 (*0-8306-8557-X*, 3557); pap. 19.95 (*0-8306-3557-2*) McGraw-Hill Prof.

— HDTV: High-Definition Television. 2nd ed. LC 92-43819. 1993. 29.95 (*0-8306-4296-X*); pap. 16.95 (*0-8306-4295-1*) McGraw-Hill Prof.

— Troubleshooting & Repairing TVRO Systems. (Illus.). 224p. 1988. 24.95 (*0-8306-0592-4*); pap. 16.95 (*0-8306-2992-0*) McGraw-Hill Prof.

***Prentki, Tim & Selman, Jan.** Popular Theatre in Political Culture: Britain & Canada in Focus. 224p. 2000. 35.95 (*1-84150-015-1*, Pub. by Intellect) Intl Spec Bk.

Prentki, Tim, jt. ed. see Bushrui, S. B.

***Prentky, R. A. & Burgess, Ann Wolbert.** Forensic Management of Sexual Offenders. LC 00-29631. 2000. write for info. (*0-306-46278-8*, Kluwer Plenum) Kluwer Academic.

Prentky, Robert A. Creativity & Psychopathology: A Neurocognitive Perspective. LC 80-15856. 264p. 1980. 41.95 (*0-275-90540-3*, C0540, Praeger Pubs) Greenwood.

Prentky, Robert A. & Edmunds, Stacey B., eds. Assessing Sexual Abuse: A Resource Guide for Practitioners. 148p. (Orig.). 1997. pap. 25.00 (*1-884444-41-5*) Safer Soc.

Prentout, Henri. Essai sur les Origines et la Fondation du Duche de Normandie. LC 80-2214. (FRE.). reprint ed. 42.50 (*0-404-18776-5*) AMS Pr.

— Histoire de Guillaume le Conquerant: Le Duc de Normandie, Vol. 1. LC 80-2252. reprint ed. 42.50 (*0-404-18777-3*) AMS Pr.

Prentzas, G. S. Joe Montana. LC 94-1350. (Football Legends Ser.). (Illus.). 96p. (J). (gr. 3 up). 1994. lib. bdg. 15.95 (*0-7910-2453-9*) Chelsea Hse.

— Mario Andretti. LC 95-8238. (Race Car Legends Ser.). 64p. (YA). (gr. 3 up). 1996. lib. bdg. 15.95 (*0-7910-3176-4*) Chelsea Hse.

— New Orleans. LC 98-22247. (Cities of the World Ser.). (J). 1998. 26.00 (*0-516-20788-1*) Childrens.

— New Orleans. (Cities of the World Ser.). (Illus.). 64p. (YA). (gr. 4-9). 1999. pap. text 9.95 (*0-516-26397-8*) Childrens.

— Terry Bradshaw. LC 94-5780. (Football Legends Ser.). (Illus.). 64p. (J). (gr. 3 up). 1994. lib. bdg. 15.95 (*0-7910-2451-2*) Chelsea Hse.

— Thurgood Marshall: Champion of Justice. LC 92-34222. (Junior Black Americans of Achievement Ser.). (Illus.). 76p. (J). (gr. 3-6). 1993. pap. 4.95 (*0-7910-1969-1*) Chelsea Hse.

— Thurgood Marshall: Champion of Justice. LC 92-34222. (Junior Black Americans of Achievement Ser.). (Illus.). 76p. (J). (gr. 4-7). 1993. lib. bdg. 15.95 (*0-7910-1769-9*) Chelsea Hse.

Prentzas, Scott. Tribal Law. LC 94-5531. (Native American Culture Ser.). 64p. (J). (gr. 4-8). 1994. lib. bdg. 25.27 (*0-86625-536-2*) Rourke Pubns.

***Prenz, Gina.** Loriana, Forever My Sweetheart. LC 99-62. (Illus.). 288p. 1999. pap. 12.31 (*1-55212-312-X*) Trafford Pub.

Prenzian, Sheryl. Ups & Downs. (Kid Sisters Ser.: No. 12). (Illus.). 117p. (Orig.). (J). (gr. 3-5). 1995. pap. 7.95 (*0-614-08413-X*) Targum Pr.

Prenzlau, Sheryl. Deuteronomy: Jewish Children's Bible. (Jewish Children's Bible Ser.). (Illus.). 64p. (J). (gr. 2-5). 1998. 18.95 (*0-943706-35-1*) Pitspopany.

— The Jewish Children's Bible: Exodus, Vol. 2. LC 97-200330. (Illus.). 80p. (J). (gr. 1-4). 1997. 18.95 (*0-943706-32-7*) Pitspopany.

— The Jewish Children's Bible: Genesis. LC 97-200331. (Illus.). 64p. (J). (gr. 1-4). 1996. 18.95 (*0-943706-31-9*) Pitspopany.

— Jewish Children's Bible: Numbers. (Illus.). 64p. 1998. 16.95 (*0-943706-34-3*) Pitspopany.

***Prenzlau, Sheryl.** The Jewish Children's Bible Gift Set. (Jewish Children's Bible Ser.). (Illus.). 64p. (J). (gr. 1-4). 1999. 94.95 (*0-943706-36-X*) Pitspopany.

Prenzlau, Sheryl. Leviticus: The/Jewish Children's Bible. (Jewish Children's Bible Ser.). (Illus.). 64p. (J). (gr. 2-5). 1998. 18.95 (*0-943706-33-5*) Pitspopany.

— Teacher's Pet. (B. Y. Times Kid Sisters Ser.: No. 6). (Illus.). 115p. (Orig.). (J). (gr. 4-7). Date not set. pap. 7.95 (*1-56871-025-9*) Targum Pr.

Prenzlow, Linda & Candreva, Ilene A. Faith-Building with Preschoolers. 112p. 1998. pap. 12.99 (*0-570-05328-5*) Concordia.

***Prenzlow, Linda & Candreva, Ilene Allinger.** More Faith-Building with Preschoolers: Teachers & Parents Together. 112p. 1999. pap., teacher ed. 12.99 (*0-570-05366-8*, 12-3417GJ) Concordia.

Preobrazhenskii, Evgenii A. The Decline of Capitalism. Day, Richard B., ed. & tr. by. LC 84-23592. 257p. 1985. reprint ed. pap. 79.70 (*0-7837-9954-3*, 206068100006) Bks Demand.

Preobrazhensky, B. V. Contemporary Reefs. Chakravarty, R., tr. from RUS. (Russian Translation Ser.: No. 100). (ENG., Illus.). 326p. 1993. text 142.00 (*90-6191-945-2*, Pub. by A A Balkema) Ashgate Pub Co.

***Preobrazhensky, N. G., et al.** Optogalvanic Effect in Ionized Gas. 216p. 1999. text 95.00 (*90-6994-001-9*, Lebedev Physical) Gordon & Breach.

Preparata, Franco. Introduction to Computer Engineering. 315p. (C). 1984. text 39.37 (*0-06-045271-4*) Addson-Wesley Educ.

Preparata, Franco P. Introduction to Computer Engineering. 336p. 1984. text 99.95 (*0-471-60374-0*) Wiley.

Preparata, Franco P. & Shamos, M. I. Computational Geometry: An Introduction. (Texts & Monographs in Computer Science). (Illus.). xii, 390p. 1993. 67.95 (*0-387-96131-3*) Spr-Verlag.

Preparata, Giuliano. QED Coherence in Matter. LC 95-13463. 300p. 1995. text 67.00 (*981-02-2249-1*) World Scientific Pub.

Preparticipation Physical Evaluation Task Force, jt. auth. see American Academy Of Family Physicians Staff.

Prerau, David S. & Liebowitz, Janet. Worldwide Intelligent Systems: Approaches to Telecommunications & Network Management. LC 94-77523. (Frontiers in Artificial Intelligence & Applications Ser.: Vol. 24). 279p. (YA). (gr. 12). 1994. 75.00 (*90-5199-183-5*) IOS Press.

Pres, Francois Turenne Des, see Turenne des Pres, Francois.

Pres, Terrence Des, see Des Pres, Terrence.

Pres, Terrence Des, see Gibbons, Reginald & Des Pres, Terrence, eds.

***Presa, Jose O., compiled by.** Corrupcion y Cambio. 400p. 1999. pap. 9.99 (*968-16-5879-5*) Fondo CA.

Presas, Remy A. Modern Arnis: Filipino Art of Stick Fighting. LC 83-60128. (Specialties Ser.). (Illus.). 1983. pap. 12.95 (*0-89750-089-X*, 426) Ohara Pubns.

Presas, Remy A. Modern Arnis: Philippine Style of Stick Fighting. (Illus.). 176p. 1997. reprint ed. pap. 24.95 (*0-9657796-0-2*) Modern Arnis.

— Modern Arnis: The Filipino Art of Stick Fighting. 1999. pap. text 37.95 (*1-58133-138-X*) Black Belt Mag.

Presberg, Carole, jt. auth. see Quarton, Marjorie.

***Presberg, Charles D.** Adventures in Paradox. LC 99-55297. (Studies in Romance Literatures). 2001. write for info. (*0-271-02039-3*) Pa St U Pr.

Presberg, Shirley. Death by Contract. LC 96-61732. 256p. (Orig.). 1997. pap. 12.95 (*1-888745-01-0*) Zookeeper Pubng.

Presbey, Gail M., et al, eds. The Philosophical Quest: A Cross Cultural Reader. LC 94-33149. (C). 1994. pap. text 36.25 (*0-07-062547-6*) McGraw.

***Presbey, Gail M., et al.** The Philosophical Quest: A Cross-Cultural Reader 2nd ed. LC 99-35392. 2000. write for info. (*0-07-289867-4*) McGrw-H Intl.

Presby. Using dBase IV. (C). 1989. pap. text 15.56 (*0-395-51580-7*) HM.

Presby, Herman M. Selected Papers on Silica Integrated Optical Circuits. LC 96-22981. (Milestone Ser.). 1996. 100.00 (*0-8194-2269-X*, MS125) SPIE.

***Presbyterian & Reformed Staff & Office of General Assembly Staff.** Companion to the Constitution: Policy for the Local Church. 2000. pap. 9.00 (*0-664-50146-X*) Geneva Press.

Presbyterian Church (U. S. A.), Theology & Worship & Cumberland Presbyterian Church Staff. Book of Common Worship, Pastoral Edition. deluxe ed. LC 93-4538. 368p. 1993. 26.95 (*0-664-22033-9*) Westminster John Knox.

Presbyterian Church Historical Society of Campbell. Cemeteries of the Town of Hamptonburgh, Orange County, New York. LC 80-81240. (Orange County, New York Cemeteries Ser.: No. 2). 88p. (Orig.). 1980. pap. 5.00 (*0-9604116-2-3*) Orange County Genealog.

Presbyterian Church in the United States of Americ. Records of the Presbyterian Church in the United States of America, 1706-1788. LC 75-83434. (Religion in America Ser.: Series 1). 1975. reprint ed. 33.95 (*0-405-00259-9*) Ayer.

Presbyterian Church, Theology & Worship Ministry U & Cumberland Presbyterian Church Staff. The Book of Common Worship. 1008p. 1994. text 32.95 (*0-664-21991-8*) Westminster John Knox.

Presbyterian Church, U. S. A. Office Staff & Cumberland Presbyterian Church Staff. Daily Prayer: The Worship of God. LC 87-14781. (Supplemental Liturgical Resource Ser.: Vol. 5). 434p. (Orig.). 1987. pap. 19.95 (*0-664-24089-5*) Westminster John Knox.

Presbyterian Eco-Justice Task Force Staff. Keeping & Healing the Creation. 128p. (Orig.). 1989. pap. text 3.00 (*0-317-93816-9*) PC USA ACSWP.

Presbyter's Peartree Staff, tr. see Corrales, Jose.

Presbyter's Peartree Staff, tr. see Cruz, Migdalia.

Presbyter's Peartree Staff, tr. see De-Cardenas, Raul.

Presch, William, jt. auth. see Weichert, Charles K.

Prescher, jt. auth. see Amos.

Prescher, Ray E. Plumbing & HVAC Manhour Estimates: A Guide to Competitive Bidding. LC 97-6514. (Illus.). 224p. (Orig.). 1997. pap. 28.25 (*1-57218-041-2*) Craftsman.

***Prescher, Ray E.** 2000 National Plumbing & HVAC Estimator. 8th ed. (Illus.). 384p. 1999. pap. 48.25 (*1-57218-084-6*) Craftsman.

Prescience Corp. Staff. Theorist, Student Edition. LC 93-6707. 1993. 28.95 (*0-534-20340-X*) PWS Pubs.

Prescott. Art Notebook to Accompany Microbiology. 3rd ed. 1995. student ed. 16.00 (*0-697-28328-3*, WCB McGr Hill) McGrw-H Hghr Educ.

— Basic Microorganism. 1999. text 55.00 (*0-07-235496-8*) McGraw.

***Prescott.** Early Modern Englishwoman Part 2, Vol. 5. LC 99-55937. 2000. 51.95 (*1-84014-218-9*) Ashgate Pub Co.

Prescott. Lab Research Guide - Microbiology. 2nd ed. 1992. lab manual ed. 8.50 (*0-697-14858-0*, WCB McGr Hill) McGrw-H Hghr Educ.

— Microbiology. 2nd ed. 1993. 229.06 (*0-697-09934-2*) McGraw.

— Microbiology. 3rd ed. 1996. teacher ed. 14.37 (*0-697-21864-3*, WCB McGr Hill) McGrw-H Hghr Educ.

— Microbiology. 5th ed. 2001. 74.25 (*0-07-232041-9*) McGraw.

— Microbiology & Student Study Art Notebook. 3rd ed. 1995. student ed. write for info. (*0-697-29390-4*) McGrw-H Hghr Educ.

— Microbiology V1 3E V3 2E Lab E. 3rd ed. 1995. 97.00 (*0-697-34867-9*, WCB McGr Hill) McGrw-H Hghr Educ.

Prescott & Benson. Microbiology, Vol. 1. 3rd ed. 1996. (*0-697-36542-5*, WCB McGr Hill) McGrw-H Hghr Educ.

Prescott, et al. Microbiology: Research Guide. 3rd ed. 1996. 8.25 (*0-697-21870-8*, WCB McGr Hill) McGrw-H Hghr Educ.

Prescott-Allen, Christine, et al. The First Resource: Wild Species in the North American Economy. LC 86-1657. 560p. 1986. 85.00 (*0-300-03228-5*) Yale U Pr.

***Prescott-Allen, Robert.** The Wellbeing of Nations: A Country-by-Country Index of Quality of Life & the Environment. (Illus.). 219p. 2000. 50.00 (*1-55963-830-3*, Shearwater Bks); pap. 25.00 (*1-55963-831-1*, Shearwater Bks) Island Pr.

Prescott, Andrew, jt. ed. see Hallam, Elizabeth.

Prescott, Anne L. French Poets & the English Renaissance: Studies in Fame & Transformation. LC 77-5482. 304p. reprint ed. pap. 94.30 (*0-8357-8139-9*, 203386000087) Bks Demand.

— Imagining Rabelais in Renaissance England. LC 97-31016. 264p. 1998. 32.00 (*0-300-07122-1*) Yale U Pr.

Prescott, Anne L., ed. see Spenser, Hugh.

Prescott, Anne Lake, jt. auth. see Cheney, Patrick G.

Prescott, Anne Lake, jt. auth. see Travitsky, Betty.

Prescott, Anne Lake, jt. ed. see Cheney, Patrick G.

Prescott, Arthur T., ed. Drafting the Federal Constitution: A Rearrangement of Madison's Notes, Giving Consecutive Developments of Provisions in the Constitution of the United States. LC 68-54433. (Illus.). 838p. 1969. reprint ed. lib. bdg. 105.00 (*0-8371-0196-4*, PRFC) Greenwood.

Prescott, Bryan D. Creating a World Class Organization: Ten Performance Measures of Business Success. 1998. pap. text 30.00 (*0-7494-2583-0*) Kogan Page Ltd.

Prescott, Christopher. Handbook of Ear, Nose, & Throat. (Illus.). 216p. (Orig.). 1999. pap. text 29.95 (*0-19-571585-3*) OUP.

Prescott-Clarke, Patricia, et al. Queuing for Housing: A Study of Council Housing Waiting Lists. LC 88-179541. 166p. 1988. 25.00 (*0-11-752077-2*, Pub. by Statnry Office) Bernan Associates.

Prescott-Clarke, Patricia, jt. ed. see Boreham, Richard.

Prescott, Dana. The Hydra Hypothesis: The Minefield of Allegations of Abuse, Chronic Interference, & the Needs of Children. 323p. 1997. 95.00 (*0-914339-60-5*) P E Randall Pub.

Prescott, Dana E. Maine Family Law Forms. 2nd ed. LC 98-89024. 700p. 1998. 149.00 (*0-327-00637-4*, 8164511); disk. write for info. (*0-327-00638-2*, 8164511) LEXIS Pub.

— Maine Family Law Forms: Discovery, Trial & Settlement, 2 vols., Set. LC 93-23910. 750p. 1994. spiral bd. 205.00 (*0-250-40712-4*, 81645-10, MICHIE) LEXIS Pub.

Prescott, David. Cells: Principles of Molecular Structure & Function. 640p. (C). 1988. 51.25 (*0-86720-092-8*); pap., student ed. 13.75 (*0-86720-098-7*) Jones & Bartlett.

Prescott, Edward C., jt. auth. see Parente, Stephen L.

Prescott et al. Microbiology Computerized SSG. 3rd ed. 1996. 20.00 (*0-697-21872-4*) McGraw.

Prescott, F. C., ed. & intro. see Poe, Edgar Allan.

Prescott, Frederick C. The Poetic Mind. LC 83-1547. 308p. 1983. reprint ed. lib. bdg. 69.50 (*0-313-23925-8*, PRPO, Greenwood Pr) Greenwood.

Prescott, G. W., et al. Aquatic Plants. 2nd ed. (Pictured Key Nature Ser.). 176p. (C). 1979. text. write for info. (*0-697-04775-X*, WCB McGr Hill) McGrw-H Hghr Educ.

— Freshwater Algae. 3rd ed. (Pictured Key Nature Ser.). 304p. (C). 1978. text. write for info. (*0-697-04754-7*, WCB McGr Hill) McGrw-H Hghr Educ.

Prescott, Gary R., ed. see Rowe, James G., Jr.

Prescott, George B. Bell's Electric Speaking Telephone: Its Invention, Construction, Application, Modification & History. LC 72-5069. (Technology & Society Ser.). (Illus.). 536p. 1977. reprint ed. 42.95 (*0-405-04718-5*) Ayer.

— History, Theory & Practice of the Electric Telegraph. 4th ed. (Illus.). 508p. 1972. reprint ed. 16.95 (*1-890024-00-7*, HTP) Artifax Bks.

Prescott, Gerald W., et al. A Synopsis of North American Desmids Pt. 2: Desmidiaceae: Placodermae, 5 Sections, Sect. 1. LC 70-183418. (Illus.). 285p. reprint ed. pap. 88.40 (*0-8357-3791-8*, 203652200001) Bks Demand.

— A Synopsis of North American Desmids Pt. 2: Desmidiaceae: Placodermae, 5 Sections, Sect. 2. LC 70-183418. (Illus.). 423p. reprint ed. pap. 131.20 (*0-8357-3792-6*, 203652200002) Bks Demand.

— A Synopsis of North American Desmids Pt. 2: Desmidiaceae: Placodermae, 5 Sections, Sect. 3. LC 70-183418. (Illus.). 730p. reprint ed. pap. 200.00 (*0-8357-3793-4*, 203652200003) Bks Demand.

— A Synopsis of North American Desmids Pt. 2: Desmidiaceae: Placodermae, 5 Sections, Sect. 4. LC 70-183418. (Illus.). 710p. reprint ed. pap. 200.00 (*0-8357-3794-2*, 203652200004) Bks Demand.

— A Synopsis of North American Desmids Pt. 2: Desmidiaceae: Placodermae, 5 Sections, Sect. 5. LC 70-183418. (Illus.). 127p. reprint ed. pap. 39.40 (*0-8357-3795-0*, 203652200005) Bks Demand.

Prescott, Heather M. A Doctor of Their Own: The History of Adolescent Medicine. LC 97-52222. 272p. 1998. 35.00 (*0-674-21461-7*) HUP.

Prescott, Howard. Poetry for Sailors & Sea Lovers. Knop, Judy et al, eds. LC 98-91575. 93p. 1998. pap. 9.95 (*1-892109-00-X*) Founders Hill.

— Published Works. Knop, Judy et al, eds. LC 98-88102. 1998. pap. 9.95 (*1-892109-01-8*) Founders Hill.

Prescott, Howard, et al. Seasons of Love. Knop, Judy et al, eds. LC 98-96673. 94p. 1998. pap. 9.95 (*1-892109-02-6*) Founders Hill.

Prescott, J. R. Political Frontiers & Boundaries. 320p. 1987. text 49.95 (*0-04-341030-8*) Routledge.

Prescott, J. R., jt. auth. see Davis, S. L.

Prescott, James. Le Viandier de Taillevent: Fourteenth Century Cookery. 2nd ed. LC 89-80811. (Illus.). 129p. 1989. 15.00 (*0-9623719-0-4*); pap. 8.00 (*0-9623719-1-2*) Alfarhaugr Pub Soc.

Prescott, James R., et al, eds. Urban-Regional Economics, Social Systems Accounts, & Eco-Behavioral Science. LC 94-8239. (Illus.). 1994. text 52.95 (*0-8138-2338-2*) Iowa St U Pr.

Prescott, James R. & Abu-Kishk, Bakir. Regional Economic Development in the Middle East: A Survey. (Studies in Technology & Social Change: No. 3). 61p. (Orig.). (C). 1988. pap. 6.00 (*0-945271-03-4*) ISU-CIKARD.

Prescott, Janice, jt. ed. see Dzamba, Andy.

Prescott, Janice, ed. see Schaeffer, Mary L.

Prescott, Jerry. Deadly Sweet in Ann Arbor. LC 96-70303. (Illus.). 380p. 1996. 22.50 (*1-882792-33-5*) Proctor Pubns.

***Prescott, Jerry.** Invisible Intrigue. LC 99-67092. 357p. 1999. 19.50 (*1-882792-90-4*) Proctor Pubng.

Prescott, Jerry. Mackinac Maze. LC 97-75369. (Illus.). 350p. 1997. 22.50 (*1-882792-55-6*) Proctor Pubns.

Prescott, John. In Flanders Field: The Story of John McCrae. 144p. 1998. pap. 10.95 (*0-919783-07-4*, Pub. by Boston Mills) Genl Dist Srvs.

— In Flanders Fields: The Story of John McCrae. (Illus.). 144p. (Orig.). 1919. pap. 10.95 (*0-317-05877-0*, Pub. by Boston Mills) Genl Dist Srvs.

Prescott, John E. & Gibbons, Patrick T. Global Perspectives on Competitive Intelligence. LC 93-24750. 388p. 1993. pap. 24.95 (*0-9621241-1-7*) SCIP.

***Prescott, John F., et al.** Antimicrobial Therapy in Veterinary Medicine. 3rd ed. (Illus.). 812p. 2000. text 99.95 (*0-8138-0779-4*) Iowa St U Pr.

Prescott, Joseph. Aphorisms & Other Observations. 1985. 7.95 (*0-318-18396-X*) J Prescott.

— Aphorisms & Other Observations: Second Series. 1995. 10.00 (*0-614-13046-8*) J Prescott.

Prescott, Kate, jt. auth. see Bennett, Roger.

Prescott, Kate, jt. auth. see Welford, Richard.

Prescott, Kelvyn. Annotated Summary Offences Act: (South Australia) 157p. 1992. pap. 93.00 (*0-455-21156-6*, Pub. by LawBk Co) Gaunt.

Prescott, L. F., jt. ed. see Nimmo, Walter S.

Prescott, Lansing. Microbiology. 5th ed. 2001. lab manual ed. 38.50 (*0-07-233345-6*); pap., student ed. 22.50 (*0-07-233336-7*) McGraw.

— Microbiology, Vol 1. 4th ed. 1998. pap. text 51.25 (*0-697-35440-7*) McGraw.

— Microbiology, Vol. 1. 4th ed. 512p. 1998. student ed., spiral bd. 50.31 (*0-697-35443-1*) McGraw.

— Microbiology, Vol. 1. 4th ed. 408p. 1998. spiral bd. 28.75 (*0-697-35445-8*) McGraw.

— Microbiology, Vol. 1. 5th ed. 2001. 47.00 (*0-07-233341-3*) McGraw.

Prescott, Lansing & Harley, John P. Laboratory Exercises. 3rd ed. 496p. (C). 1996. text, suppl. ed. write for info. (*0-697-21869-4*, WCB McGr Hill) McGrw-H Hghr Educ.

— Microbiology, 1. 3rd ed. 672p. (C). 1997. per. write for info. (*0-07-114628-8*, WCB McGr Hill) McGrw-H Hghr Educ.

— Mircobiology. 3rd ed. 368p. (C). 1996. text, student ed. 25.62 (*0-697-21871-6*, WCB McGr Hill) McGrw-H Hghr Educ.

Prescott, Lansing & Harley, Jonh P. Microbiology, 2. 3rd ed. 392p. (C). 1997. per. write for info. (*0-07-114629-6*, WCB McGr Hill) McGrw-H Hghr Educ.

Prescott, Lansing, et al. Microbiology. 1016p. (C). 1989. text. write for info. (*0-697-03005-9*, WCB McGr Hill) McGrw-H Hghr Educ.

— Microbiology. 2nd ed. 992p. (C). 1992. text. write for info. (*0-697-01372-3*) Brown & Benchmark.

P

— Microbiology. 2nd ed. 992p. (C). 1993. text, student ed. 28.75 (*0-697-09935-0*) Brown & Benchmark.

— Microbiology. 2nd ed. 992p. (C). 1993. text. write for info. (*0-697-16888-3*) Brown & Benchmark.

— Microbiology. 3rd ed. 1024p. (C). 1995. text. write for info. (*0-697-21863-5*, WCB McGr Hill) McGrw-H Hghr Educ.

— Microbiology, II. 2nd ed. 992p. (C). 1992. text. write for info. (*0-697-16886-7*) Brown & Benchmark.

— Microbiology, III. 2nd ed. 992p. (C). 1992. text. write for info. (*0-697-16887-5*) Brown & Benchmark.

— Microbiology, Vol. I. 3rd ed. 688p. (C). 1995. text. write for info. (*0-697-21865-1*, WCB McGr Hill) McGrw-H Hghr Educ.

— Microbiology, Vol. II. 3rd ed. 368p. (C). 1995. text. write for info. (*0-697-21866-X*, WCB McGr Hill) McGrw-H Hghr Educ.

***Prescott, Lansing, et al.** Microbiology: General Topics with Microbes in Motion II CD-ROM. 4th ed. (C). 1998. 65.63 incl. cd-rom (*0-07-232632-8*) McGrw-H Hghr Educ.

— Microbiology with Microbes in Motion II CD-ROM. 4th ed. (C). 1998. 94.06 incl. cd-rom (*0-07-232514-3*) McGrw-H Hghr Educ.

Prescott, Laurence E. Without Hatreds or Fears: Jorge Artel & the Struggle for Black Literacy Expression in Colombia. LC 99-39371. 2000. 39.95 (*0-8143-2751-6*) Wayne St U Pr.

— Without Hatreds or Fears: Jorge Artel & the Struggle for Black Literacy Expression in Colombia. LC 99-39371. (Illus.). 368p. 2000. pap. 19.95 (*0-8143-2878-4*) Wayne St U Pr.

Prescott, Laurie F. Paracetamol (Acetaminophen) A Critical Bibliographic Review. 400p. 1996. 165.00 (*0-7484-0136-9*) Taylor & Francis.

Prescott, Mary. Bull Mastiffs. (Illus.). 1997. pap. 9.95 (*0-7938-2395-1*, KW-163S) TFH Pubns.

Prescott, Michael. Comes the Dark. 400p. 1999. mass mkt. 6.99 (*0-451-19250-8*, Sig) NAL.

***Prescott, Michael.** The Shadow Hunter. 432p. 2000. mass mkt. 6.99 (*0-451-20079-9*, Sig) NAL.

— Stealing Faces. 432p. 1999. mass mkt. 6.99 (*0-451-19851-4*, Sig) NAL.

— Stealing Faces. ed. 1999. mass mkt. 6.99 (*0-451-19928-6*) Penguin Putnam.

Prescott, Michael K. & Brossman, Douglas. The Environmental Liability Handbook for Property Transfer & Financing. (Illus.). 144p. 1990. lib. bdg. 99.95 (*0-87371-360-5*, L360) Lewis Pubs.

Prescott, N. J., ed. see Welding Institute Staff.

Prescott, Nicholas, ed. Choices in Financing Health Care & Old Age Security: Proceedings of a Conference Sponsored by the Institute of Policy Studies, Singapore, & the World Bank, November 8, 1997. LC 98-197034. 111p. 1998. pap. 22.00 (*0-8213-4284-3*, 14284) World Bank.

Prescott, Nicholas M. Poverty, Social Services, & Safety Nets in Vietnam. LC 97-28972. (Discussion Paper Ser.: No. 376). 76p. 1997. pap. 22.00 (*0-8213-4024-7*, 14024) World Bank.

***Prescott, Nicholas M.** Public Expenditures & the Poor in Indonesia, Vol. 397. LC 98-53681. (World Bank Discussion Papers Ser.). 1998. write for info. (*0-8213-4315-7*) World Bank.

Prescott, Nicholas M. & Pradhan, Menno. A Poverty Profile of Cambodia. LC 97-29733. (Discussion Paper Ser.: No. 373). 94p. 1997. pap. 22.00 (*0-8213-4020-4*, 14020) World Bank.

Prescott, Orville. In My Opinion. LC 73-111857. (Essay Index Reprint Ser.). 1977. 23.95 (*0-8369-2014-7*) Ayer.

Prescott, Peter, ed. The Norton Book of American Short Stories. 1988. 29.95 (*0-393-02619-1*) Norton.

— The Norton Book of American Short Stories. (Books of...Ser.). (C). 1990. pap. text. write for info. (*0-393-96092-7*) Norton.

Prescott, Ralph P. The Simplistic Poet. Hagar, Fern, ed. LC 87-71726. (Illus.). 77p. (Orig.). 1999. reprint ed. pap. 10.80 (*0-9618378-0-2*) Parishs Poetry.

Prescott, Roger. The Second Mile. 1985. 5.25 (*0-89536-739-4*, 5823) CSS OH.

Prescott, Roger K. & Hering, Eberhard A. This Wonderful Life. 1996. pap. 7.95 (*0-7880-0681-9*) CSS OH.

Prescott, S. C. & Goldblith, S. A. Pioneers in Food Science, Vol. 1. 194p. 1993. pap. 25.00 (*0-917678-33-8*) Food & Nut Pr.

Prescott, Stephen H. Carving Blockheads: A New Simplified Approach to Carving Figures in Wood. (Illus.). 49p. (Orig.). 1996. pap. 12.95 (*1-56523-069-8*) Fox Chapel Pub.

— Cowtown Carving: Techniques & Patterns from the Texas Whittling Champion. 2nd rev. ed. (Illus.). 94p. 1994. pap. 14.95 (*1-56523-049-3*) Fox Chapel Pub.

***Prescott, Sue.** Realizing the Self Within. Strand, Laurel, ed. LC 99-72914. 200p. 2000. pap. 14.95 (*0-944958-49-4*) Elfin Cove Pr.

Prescott, Susan, jt. auth. see Muncaster, Barbara.

Prescott, Susannah S., jt. ed. see Postma, Patricia D.

Prescott, Thomas E., ed. Clinical Aphasiology, Vol. 18. 531p. (C). 1989. pap. text 49.00 (*0-89079-322-0*, 1774) PRO-ED.

— Clinical Aphasiology, Vol. 19. (Illus.). 331p. 1991. pap. text 45.00 (*0-89079-407-3*, 1587) PRO-ED.

— Clinical Aphasiology, Vol. 20. 369p. 1992. text 49.00 (*0-89079-466-9*, 1803) PRO-ED.

Prescott, W. The Prescott Memorial: A Genealogical Memoir of the Prescott Family in America. (Illus.). 667p. 1989. reprint ed. pap. 100.00 (*0-8328-0991-8*); reprint ed. lib. bdg. 108.00 (*0-8328-0990-X*) Higginson Bk Co.

Prescott, W. H. Correspondence of William Hickling Prescott, 1833-1847. Wolcott, Roger, ed. LC 76-112312. (American Public Figures Ser.). 1970. reprint ed. lib. bdg. 49.50 (*0-306-71912-6*) Da Capo.

Prescott-Walker, Robert. Collecting Lalique Glass. (Illus.). 128p. 1996. pap. 24.95 (*1-870703-46-4*, Pub. by Francis Jos Pubns) Krause Pubns.

— Wade Collectors Handbook. (Illus.). 144p. 1996. pap. 19.95 (*1-870703-61-8*, Pub. by Francis Jos Pubns) Krause Pubns.

Prescott, William H. The Art of War in Spain: The Conquest of Granada, 1481-1492. McJoynt, Albert D., ed. & intro. by. (Illus.). 288p. 1995. 40.00 (*1-85367-193-2*, Pub. by Greenhill Bks) Stackpole.

— Biographical & Critical Miscellanies. (Notable American Authors Ser.). 1999. reprint ed. lib. bdg. 125.00 (*0-7812-8770-7*) Rprt Serv.

— The Conquest of Mexico. LC 36-27495. 1979. 22.00 (*0-394-60471-7*) Modern Lib NY.

— Correspondence. (Notable American Authors Ser.). 1999. reprint ed. lib. bdg. 125.00 (*0-7812-8773-1*) Rprt Serv.

— History of Conquest of Mexico & History of the Conquest of Peru. LC 36-27495. 1288p. 1979. 15.95 (*0-685-19921-5*) Modern Lib NY.

— History of Conquest of Peru. (Notable American Authors Ser.). 1999. reprint ed. lib. bdg. 125.00 (*0-7812-8771-5*) Rprt Serv.

— History of the Conquest of Mex. LC 98-10173. 1998. 27.95 (*0-679-60299-2*) Modern Lib NY.

— History of the Conquest of Mexico. abr. ed. Gardiner, C. Harvey, ed. LC 66-20592. xxvii, 414p. 1985. reprint ed. pap. text 18.00 (*0-226-68001-0*) U Ch Pr.

— The History of the Conquest of Mexico. Gardiner, C. Harvey, ed. LC 66-20592. (Classic American Historians Ser.). 441p. reprint ed. pap. 136.80 (*0-608-09503-6*, 205430400005) Bks Demand.

— History of the Conquest of Mexico. (Notable American Authors Ser.). 1999. reprint ed. lib. bdg. 125.00 (*0-7812-8769-3*) Rprt Serv.

— History of the Conquest of Mexico & History of the Conquest of Peru. LC 99-35590. (Illus.). 1330p. 2000. reprint ed. pap. 29.95 (*0-8154-1004-2*) Cooper Sq.

— History of the Conquest of Peru. LC 98-10174. (Modern Library). 1998. 27.95 (*0-679-60304-2*) Random.

— The History of the Reign of Ferdinand & Isabella the Catholic. (Notable American Authors Ser.). 1999. reprint ed. lib. bdg. 125.00 (*0-7812-8768-5*) Rprt Serv.

— History of the Reign of Philip II. (Notable American Authors Ser.). 1999. reprint ed. lib. bdg. 125.00 (*0-7812-8772-3*) Rprt Serv.

— Life of Charles Brockden Brown. (Notable American Authors Ser.). 1999. reprint ed. lib. bdg. 125.00 (*0-7812-8767-7*) Rprt Serv.

— Works, 22 vols., Set. Munro, Wilfred H. et al, eds. LC 69-16761. reprint ed. 1250.00 (*0-404-05150-2*) AMS Pr.

Prescott, William M. History of the Conquest of Mexico & History of the Conquest of Peru. LC 36-27495. 1288p. 1989. 16.95 (*0-685-28566-9*) Random.

Prescott, William P. Business, Legal, & Tax Planning for Dental Practices. LC 94-30140. 1994. 79.95 (*0-87814-424-2*) PennWell Bks.

***Presdee, Mike.** Cultural Criminology & the Carnival of Crime. LC 00-32824. 2000. pap. write for info. (*0-415-23910-9*) Routledge.

Presedee, Mike. Cultural Criminology & the Carnival of Crime. 1999. pap. text 22.95 (*0-8153-3407-9*) Garland.

Present, David. Manual of Bone & Soft Tissue Tumors. 350p. 1996. text 79.50 (*0-397-51414-X*) Lppncott W & W.

Present, Thelma. Dear Margaret: Letters from Oak Ridge to Margaret Mead. (Illus.). 205p. 1986. 15.00 (*0-941199-07-X*) ETHS.

***Presentation Edition Publishing Company Staff.** English New Testament: Presentation Edition. 10th rev. ed. 236p. 1998. 17.99 (*0-19-101251-3*) OUP.

Presents, Elizabeth P. Elizabeth Peters Presents Malice Domestic, No. 1. Chelius, Jane, ed. 288p. 1992. mass mkt. 4.99 (*0-671-73826-7*) PB.

Preservation Alliance of Greater Philadelphia Staff, jt. auth. see Greater Philadelphia Cultural Alliance Staff.

Preservation League NYS Staff. How to Care for Religious Properties. (Illus.). 40p. 1982. pap. 2.00 (*0-942000-03-X*) Pres League NYS.

Preservation Press Staff, jt. auth. see National Park Service Staff.

Preservation Society of Asheville & Buncombe Count. Color Me Asheville. (Coloring Book for Adults & Children Ser.). (Illus.). 40p. (J). (gr. 4-8). 1987. pap. 4.00 (*0-937481-01-7*) Pres Soc Asheville.

Preservation Society of Charleston Staff. The Churches of Charleston & the Lowcountry. Jacoby, Mary M., ed. LC 93-10057. (Illus.). 136p. (C). 1994. 29.95 (*0-87249-888-3*) U of SC Pr.

Preservation Society of Newport County Staff. Newport Cooks & Collects. LC 95-72320. (Illus.). 176p. 1996. 16.95 (*0-9646888-1-6*) Preserv Soc Newport.

Presfield, Christopher. Gray Air: Poems from Prison: 1983-1999. viii, 48p. 1999. pap. 8.00 (*1-891812-15-7*, 99-015) Cedar Hill Pubns.

***Presgraves, James S.** Wythe County Chapters: A Gathering of Materials from Scarce, Rare or Out-of-Print Sources about Wythe County, Virginia. (Illus.). 367p. 2000. pap. 29.00 (*0-7884-1379-1*, 1379) Heritage Bk.

Preshaw, G. O. Banking Under Difficulties: Life on the Goldfields of Victoria, New South Wales & New Zealand, Vol. 8. LC 74-357. (Gold Ser.). 179p. 1974. reprint ed. 23.95 (*0-405-05918-3*) Ayer.

Presidencia de la Republica Staff. Dicc. Biografico del Gobierno Mexicano. (SPA.). pap. 15.99 (*968-820-466-8*, Pub. by Fondo) Continental Bk.

President of the United States, contrib. by. Economic Report of the President, 1996. 1996. per. 15.00 (*0-16-048501-0*) USGPO.

— Economic Report of the President, 1998. (Illus.). 412p. 1998. per. 20.00 (*0-16-049419-2*) USGPO.

President of the United States, Council of Economi, contrib. by. Economic Report of the President, 1997. 1997. per. 20.00 (*0-16-048928-8*) USGPO.

Presidential Commission on the Assignment of Women. Women in Combat: Report to the President. (Association of the U. S. Army Book Ser.). 413p. 1994. 38.95 (*0-02-881097-X*); pap. 20.00 (*0-02-881091-0*) Brasseys.

President's Commission. A National Agenda for the Eighties. (Illus.). 225p. 1982. pap. 5.95 (*0-13-609529-1*) P-H.

President's Commission for the Study of Ethical Pr, ed. President's Commission for the Study of Ethical Problems in Medicine & Biomedical & Behavioral Research, 16 vols. in 6 bks., Set. LC 97-80015. 1997. reprint ed. 595.00 (*1-57588-391-0*, 311430) W S Hein.

President's Commission on Campus Unrest. The Kent State Tragedy: Special Report, Including Pictures. (Mass Violence in America Ser.). (Illus.). 1989. pap. 12.95 (*0-88143-103-6*) Ayer.

President's Commission on Immigration, jt. auth. see Naturalization Staff.

President's Commission on Law Enforcement & Admini. Task Force Report: The Police. LC 73-154585. (Police in America Ser.). 1979. reprint ed. 29.95 (*0-405-03383-4*) Ayer.

President's Commission on National Goals. Goals for Americans. LC 60-53566. 1960. pap. 1.00 (*0-936904-09-7*) Am Assembly.

President's Commission on the Health Needs of the. Building America's Health: A Report, 5 vols., Set. LC 75-17239. (Social Problems & Social Policy Ser.). (Illus.). 1976. reprint ed. 134.95 (*0-405-07508-1*) Ayer.

— Building America's Health: A Report, 5 vols., Vol. 1. LC 75-17239. (Social Problems & Social Policy Ser.). (Illus.). 1976. reprint ed. 66.95 (*0-405-07509-X*) Ayer.

— Building America's Health: A Report, 5 vols., Vol. 4. LC 75-17239. (Social Problems & Social Policy Ser.). (Illus.). 1976. reprint ed. 66.95 (*0-405-07510-3*) Ayer.

President's Conference on Home Building & Home Own. Negro Housing. Gries, John M. & Ford, James, eds. LC 79-89053. 282p. 1970. reprint ed. lib. bdg. 45.00 (*0-8371-1921-9*, NEH&) Greenwood.

President's Conference on Unemployment Committee. Business Cycles & Unemployment: Proceedings. LC 75-19697. (National Bureau of Economic Research Ser.). (Illus.). 1975. reprint ed. 36.95 (*0-405-07577-4*) Ayer.

***President's Institute on the Catholic Character of Loyola Marymount University Staff & McCullough, Mary K.** The Just One Justices: The Role of Justice at the Heart of Catholic Higher Education: The 1998 President's Institute on the Catholic Character of Loyola Marymount University. LC 00-37442. 2000. pap. write for info. (*0-940866-87-0*) U Scranton Pr.

President's Research Committee on Social Trends. Recent Social Trends in the United States, 2 vols., Set. Coser, Lewis A. & Powell, Walter W., eds. LC 79-7010. (Perennial Works in Sociology). (Illus.). 1979. reprint ed. lib. bdg. 122.95 (*0-405-12107-5*) Ayer.

— Recent Social Trends in the United States, 2 vols., Vol. 1. Coser, Lewis A. & Powell, Walter W., eds. LC 79-7010. (Perennial Works in Sociology Ser.). (Illus.). 1980. reprint ed. lib. bdg. 61.95 (*0-405-12108-3*) Ayer.

— Recent Social Trends in the United States, 2 vols., Vol. 2. Coser, Lewis A. & Powell, Walter W., eds. LC 79-7010. (Perennial Works in Sociology). (Illus.). 1980. reprint ed. lib. bdg. 61.95 (*0-405-12109-1*) Ayer.

President's Scientific Research Board Staff & Steelman, John R. Science & Public Policy: A Report to the President, 5 vols. Cohen, I. Bernard, ed. LC 79-7998. (Three Centuries of Science in America Ser.). (Illus.). 1980. reprint ed. lib. bdg. 94.95 (*0-405-12586-0*) Ayer.

Presilla, Maricel E. Feliz Nochebuena, Feliz Navidad: Christmas Feasts of the Hispanic Caribbean. (J). 1995. write for info. (*0-8050-2512-X*, Bks Young Read) H Holt & Co.

— Feliz Nochebuena, Feliz Navidad: Christmas Feasts of the Hispanic Caribbean. LC 93-43009. (Illus.). 32p. (J). (gr. 4-7). 1996. pap. 6.95 (*0-8050-4905-3*, B Martin BYR) H Holt & Co.

— Feliz Nochebuena, Feliz Navidad: Christmas Feasts of the Hispanic Caribbean. LC 93-43009. 1996. 12.15 (*0-606-10183-7*, Pub. by Turtleback) Demco.

— Mola: Cuna Life, Stories, & Art. LC 95-46397. (Illus.). 32p. (YA). (gr. 7 up). 1995. 16.95 (*0-8050-3801-9*, B Martin BYR) H Holt & Co.

***Presilla, Maricel E.** The New Taste of Chocolate: A Guide to Fine Chocolate with Recipes. (Illus.). 160p. 2000. 17.95 (*1-58008-143-6*) Ten Speed Pr.

Presilla, Maricel E. & Soto, Gloria. Life Around the Lake: The Feasts of Lake Patzcuaro. LC 95-38429. (Illus.). 32p. (J). (gr. 3-6). 1995. 16.95 (*0-8050-3800-0*, Bks Young Read) H Holt & Co.

***Presing, Joseph.** Shallows & Depths. LC 98-90877. 1999. pap. 8.95 (*0-533-12961-3*) Vantage.

Presiser, Wolfgang F. E., jt. ed. see Nasar, Jack L.

Preskenis, Sheri, jt. auth. see Frank, Marjorie.

***Preskill.** Stories of Teaching. 240p. 2000. pap. 28.00 (*0-13-921248-5*) P-H.

Preskill, Hallie, jt. ed. see Larson, Colleen L.

Preskill, Hallie S. Evaluative Inquiry for Learning in Organizations. 692p. 1998. 69.95 (*0-7619-0453-0*) Sage.

Preskill, Hallie S. & Torres, Roselie T. Evaluative Inquiry for Learning in Organizations. LC 98-40122. 1998. 29.95 (*0-7619-0454-9*) Sage.

***Preskorn, Sheldon H.** Case Studies in Psychopharmacology: Drug-Drug Interactions & Clinical Outcome. 224p. 2000. pap. text 19.95 (*1-884735-48-7*) Prof Comms.

Preskorn, Sheldon H. Clinical Pharmacology of Selective Serotonin Reuptake Inhibitors. (Illus.). 255p. 1996. pap. text 19.95 (*1-884735-08-8*) Prof Comms.

— Farmacologia Clinica de los Inhibidores Selectivos de la Recaptacion de Serotonina.Tr. of Clinical Pharmacology of Selective Serotonin Reuptake Inhibitors. (SPA.). 271p. 1996. pap. text 19.95 (*1-884735-17-7*) Prof Comms.

— Klinische Pharmakologie der Selektiven Serotonin-Wiederaufnahmehemmer.Tr. of Clinical Pharmacology of Selective Serotonin Reuptake Inhibitors. (GER.). 293p. 1997. pap. text 19.95 (*1-884735-25-8*) Prof Comms.

— La Pharmacologie Clinique des Inhibiteurs Selectifs du Recaptage de la Serotonine.Tr. of Clinical Pharmacology of Selective Serotonin Reuptake Inhibitors. (FRE.). 253p. 1996. pap. text 19.95 (*1-884735-16-9*) Prof Comms.

Presland, John & Adams, Pam. Motivation Books: Same & Different, What Is It, How Many, Letters & Words, 4 bks., Set. 1995. 14.99 (*0-85953-130-9*) Childs Play.

Presler, Mel. Seven Wonders of Our Universe Vol. 1: RILUXEC. (Illus.). x, 125p. 1998. pap. 12.95 (*0-9662067-0-3*) Pres Lar Res.

Presley. Can't Help Falling in Love. 32p. 15.95 (*0-06-027796-3*) HarpC Child Bks.

Presley, Bruce. An Introduction to Desktop Publishing Using Pagemaker, Version 6.5 for Windows. LC 99-178851. 400p. 1998. text 50.60 (*1-879233-74-6*) Lawrenceville Pr.

Presley, Bruce & Brown. An Introduction to Computing Using Microsoft Works: Version 3 for Windows, 10 vols., Set. 1995. student ed. 26.65 incl. disk (*1-879233-45-2*) Lawrenceville Pr.

Presley, Bruce & Brown, Beth. A Guide to Microsoft Office Professional: Version 7 for Windows 95. LC 97-137528. 528p. 1996. text 50.60 (*1-879233-76-2*); pap. text 43.35 (*1-879233-75-4*); spiral bd. 50.60 (*1-879233-93-2*) Lawrenceville Pr.

— A Guide to Microsoft Office Professional: Version 7 for Windows 95. 500p. 1997. teacher ed., ring bd. 53.25 (*1-879233-77-0*) Lawrenceville Pr.

— A Guide to Microsoft Office Professional: Version 7 for Windows 95, 20 vols., Set. 1996. disk 40.00 (*1-879233-78-9*) Lawrenceville Pr.

— A Guide to Microsoft Office 2000 Professional. 640p. 1999. text 50.60 (*1-58003-016-5*); pap. text 43.35 (*1-58003-015-7*) Lawrenceville Pr.

— A Guide to Microsoft Office 2000 Professional. 500p. 1999. teacher ed., ring bd. 53.25 (*1-58003-017-3*) Lawrenceville Pr.

— A Guide to Programming in Microsoft Visual Basic. 512p. 1999. pap. text 51.95 (*1-879233-21-5*) Lawrenceville Pr.

— A Guide to Programming in Microsoft Visual Basic. 600p. 1999. pap. text, teacher ed. 53.25 (*1-879233-22-3*) Lawrenceville Pr.

***Presley, Bruce & Brown, Beth.** An Introduction to Computing Using Apple Works, Version 6 for Macintosh: Teacher Resource Package. 2000. teacher ed. 53.25 (*1-58003-027-0*) Lawrenceville Pr.

— An Introduction to Computing Using Apple Works, Version 6 for the Macintosh. 500p. 2000. text 48.65 (*1-58003-026-2*); pap. text 42.60 (*1-58003-025-4*) Lawrenceville Pr.

Presley, Bruce & Brown, Beth. An Introduction to Computing Using Claris Works: Version 4 for Macintosh. 528p. 1996. text 48.65 (*1-879233-82-7*); pap. text 42.60 (*1-879233-81-9*) Lawrenceville Pr.

— An Introduction to Computing Using Claris Works: Version 4 for Macintosh. 500p. 1996. teacher ed., ring bd. 53.25 (*1-879233-83-5*) Lawrenceville Pr.

— An Introduction to Computing Using Claris Works: Version 4 for Macintosh, 10 vols., Set. 1996. disk 26.65 (*1-879233-84-3*) Lawrenceville Pr.

— An Introduction to Computing Using Microsoft Works: Version 3 for Windows. 512p. 1995. text 48.65 (*1-879233-43-6*) Lawrenceville Pr.

— An Introduction to Computing Using Microsoft Works: Version 3 for Windows. 360p. 1995. teacher ed., ring bd. 53.25 (*1-879233-44-4*) Lawrenceville Pr.

— An Introduction to Computing Using Microsoft Works: Version 4 for Windows 95. 528p. 1996. text 48.65 (*1-879233-58-4*); pap. text 42.60 (*1-879233-57-6*) Lawrenceville Pr.

— An Introduction to Computing Using Microsoft Works: Version 4 for Windows 95. 500p. 1996. teacher ed., ring bd. 53.25 (*1-879233-62-2*) Lawrenceville Pr.

— An Introduction to Computing Using Microsoft Works: Version 4 for Windows 95, 10 vols., Set. 1996. disk 26.65 (*1-879233-63-0*) Lawrenceville Pr.

— An Introduction to Programming Using Microsoft Visual Basic. 512p. 1999. pap. text 44.65 (*1-879233-20-7*) Lawrenceville Pr.

Presley, Bruce & Freitas, William. An Introduction to Computing Using Microsoft Works: Version 2 for IBM & Compatibles. (Illus.). 404p. 1990. text 48.65 (*0-931717-91-4*); teacher ed., ring bd. 53.25 (*0-931717-95-7*) Lawrenceville Pr.

— Introduction to Desktop Publishing Using PageMaker: Version 5 for Macintosh. LC 94-240399. 416p. 1994. text 50.60 (*1-879233-04-5*); student ed. 26.65 incl. disk (*1-879233-37-1*) Lawrenceville Pr.

— Introduction to Desktop Publishing Using PageMaker: Version 5 for Windows. LC 94-239605. 1994. pap. text 43.35 (*1-879233-17-7*); student ed. 26.65 incl. disk (*1-879233-39-8*) Lawrenceville Pr.

— Introduction to Desktop Publishing Using PageMaker: Version 5 for Windows. 1994. teacher ed., ring bd. 53.25 (*1-879233-19-3*) Lawrenceville Pr.

Presley, Bruce, et al. A Guide to Microsoft Office Professional: For Office 97. LC 98-197716. 528p. 1997. text 50.60 (*1-879233-87-8*); pap. text 43.35 (*1-879233-85-1*) Lawrenceville Pr.

— A Guide to Microsoft Office Professional: For Office 97. 500p. 1997. teacher ed., ring bd. 53.25 (*1-879233-88-6*) Lawrenceville Pr.

— A Guide to Programming in C++ LC 98-148392. 470p. 1997. pap. text 44.65 (*1-879233-90-8*) Lawrenceville Pr.

— A Guide to Programming in C++ LC 98-148392. 470p. 1997. text 51.95 (*1-879233-91-6*) Lawrenceville Pr.

— A Guide to Programming in C++ 500p. 1997. teacher ed., ring bd. 53.25 (*1-879233-92-4*) Lawrenceville Pr.

— A Guide to Programming in Turbo Pascal Version 4.0-6.0. 2nd ed. (Illus.). 528p. 1991. pap. text 44.65 (*0-931717-72-8*) Lawrenceville Pr.

— A Guide to Programming in Turbo Pascal Version 4.0-6.0. 2nd ed. (Illus.). 410p. 1991. teacher ed., ring bd. 53.25 (*0-931717-78-7*) Lawrenceville Pr.

— An Introduction to Computing Using ClarisWorks, Version 5 for Macintosh. LC 98-203340. 528p. 1997. text 48.65 (*1-879233-97-5*); pap. text 42.60 (*1-879233-96-7*) Lawrenceville Pr.

— An Introduction to Computing Using ClarisWorks, Version 5 for Macintosh. 400p. 1997. teacher ed., ring bd. 53.25 (*1-879233-98-3*) Lawrenceville Pr.

— An Introduction to Computing Using Microsoft Works: Version 4 for Macintosh. LC 96-226023. 512p. 1996. text 48.65 (*1-879233-52-5*); teacher ed., ring bd. 53.25 (*1-879233-53-3*); student ed. 26.65 incl. disk (*1-879233-56-8*) Lawrenceville Pr.

— An Introduction to Desktop Publishing Using PageMaker, Version 6.5 for Windows. LC 99-178851. 400p. 1998. pap. text 43.35 (*1-879233-59-2*) Lawrenceville Pr.

— An Introduction to Desktop Publishing Using PageMaker, Version 6.5 for Windows. 400p. 1998. teacher ed., ring bd. 53.25 (*1-879233-60-6*) Lawrenceville Pr.

Presley, Bruce, jt. auth. see Freitas, William.

Presley, Cora A., ed. & intro. see Otieno, Wambui.

Presley, Delma E. Glass Menagerie: An American Memory. 1990. 23.95 (*0-8057-8058-0*, Twyne) Mac Lib Ref.

— Glass Menagerie: An American Memory. 1990. pap. 14.95 (*0-8057-8127-7*) Macmillan.

Presley, Delma E. & Banks, Smith C. Bulloch County. (Images of America Ser.). (Illus.). 128p. 1997. pap. 16.99 (*0-7524-0924-7*) Arcadia Publng.

Presley, Delma E., jt. auth. see Harper, Francis.

Presley, Deni. Sites & Insights: The Special Event Location & Resource Directory for Southern California. Berry, Kathryn E., ed. (Illus.). 208p. (Orig.). 1994. pap. text 24.95 (*0-9640791-0-0*) Site Network.

Presley, Elvis. Elvis: The King. (Big Note Ser.). 80p. 1996. pap. 12.95 (*0-7935-5835-2*) H Leonard.

Presley, Elvis. Elvis Presley's: The First Noel. LC 99-71518. (Illus.). 32p. 5.95 (*0-06-443615-2*) HarpC.

Presley, Elvis. Elvis Presley's The First Noel. LC 99-71518. (Illus.). 32p. (J). (ps-3). 1999. 12.95 (*0-06-028126-X*) HarpC Child Bks.

— Love Me Tender. (Illus.). 32p. (J). 15.95 (*0-06-027797-1*) HarpC.

Presley, Elvis, jt. auth. see Adler, Bill, Jr.

Presley, Frances, jt. auth. see Taylor, Marilyn.

Presley, Horton. Principles of Music & Visual Arts. LC 86-1525. (Illus.). 144p. (Orig.). 1986. pap. text 14.00 (*0-8191-5258-7*) U Pr of Amer.

— Restoring & Collecting Antique Reed Organs. 2nd ed. LC 92-15651. (Illus.). 316p. 1987. reprint ed. pap. 16.95 (*0-911572-56-2*, Vestal Pr) Madison Bks UPA.

Presley, Jennifer B., ed. Organizing Effective Institutional Research Offices. LC 85-645339. (New Directions for Institutional Research Ser.: No. IR 66). 1990. pap. 22.00 (*1-55542-829-0*) Jossey-Bass.

Presley, John & Dodd, William. Essential Reading Skills. (C). 1982. pap. text 35.00 (*0-03-058001-3*, Pub. by Harcourt Coll Pubs) Harcourt.

Presley, John R. A Directory of Islamic Banking & Financial Institutions. 384p. 1988. lib. bdg. 120.00 (*0-7099-1347-8*) Routledge.

— Robertsonian Economics: An Examination of the Work of Sir D. H. Robertson on Industry Fluctuation. LC 78-25958. 320p. 1979. 45.00 (*0-8419-0471-5*) Holmes & Meier.

Presley, John R., jt. ed. see O'Brien, D. P.

Presley, John W., compiled by. The Robert Graves Manuscripts & Letters at Southern Illinois University: An Inventory. LC 75-8383. viii, 261p. 1976. 39.00 (*0-87875-075-4*) Whitston Pub.

Presley, M. & Levin, J. R., eds. Cognitive Strategy Research: Psychological Foundations, 1. (Cognitive Development Ser.). (Illus.). 350p. 1983. 88.95 (*0-387-90818-8*) Spr-Verlag.

Presley, M. W. & McGillis, K. A. Coastal Evaporite & Tidal-Flat Sediments of the Upper Clear Fork & Glorieta Formations, Texas Panhandle. (Reports of Investigations: RI 115). (Illus.). 50p. 1982. pap. 2.00 (*0-318-03248-1*) Bur Econ Geology.

Presley, Priscilla B. Selected from Elvis & Me. abr. ed. (Writers' Voices Ser.). 64p. (Orig.). 1991. pap. text 3.95 (*0-929631-27-7*, Signal Hill) New Readers.

Presley, Priscilla B. & Jarmon, Sandra. Elvis & Me. 320p. 1997. mass mkt. 7.50 (*0-425-09103-1*) Berkley Pub.

*__Presley, Sharon.__ Think for Yourself: How to Survive in a World That Wants You to Obey & Conform. LC 99-68419. (Self-Mastery Ser.). (Illus.). 112p. 2000. pap. 12.95 (*1-57951-016-7*) Ronin Pub.

Presley, Victoria. Traded Secrets. 352p. (Orig.). 1996. mass mkt. 4.99 (*0-505-52092-3*, Love Spell) Dorchester Pub Co.

Preslo, L. M., et al. Remedial Technologies for Leaking Underground Storage Tanks. (Illus.). 728p. 1988. lib. bdg. 99.95 (*0-87371-125-4*, L125) Lewis Pubs.

Presma, Frances & Edelson, Paula. Straight Talk about Today's Families. LC 98-44901. (Straight Talk Ser.). 160p. (YA). (gr. 6 up). 1999. 19.95 (*0-8160-3905-4*) Facts on File.

Presman, E. L. & Sonon, I. N. Sequential Control with Incomplete Information. (Economic Theory, Econometrics & Mathematical Economics Ser.). 266p. 1990. text 132.00 (*0-12-564435-3*) Acad Pr.

Presnakov, Alexander. Eagle's Nest. 2000. pap. 11.99 (*1-57532-252-8*) Press-Tige Pub.

Presnall, Judith J. Animal Skeletons. (Individual Titles Ser.). (Illus.). 48p. (J). (gr. 5-7). 1995. lib. bdg. 24.00 (*0-531-11160-1*) Watts.

— Animals That Glow. LC 92-25529. (First Bks.). 64p. (J). (gr. 4-6). 1993. lib. bdg. 22.00 (*0-531-20071-X*) Watts.

— Circuses: Under the Big Top. LC 96-15142. (First Books-Performances & Entertainment). 64p. (J). 1996. lib. bdg. 22.00 (*0-531-20235-6*) Watts.

— Circuses: Under the Big Top. (First Bks.). 64p. (J). (gr. 4-6). 1997. pap. 6.95 (*0-531-15808-X*) Watts.

— The Giant Panda. LC 97-27276. (Overview Ser.). (Illus.). (YA). (gr. 4-12). 1997. lib. bdg. 22.45 (*1-56006-463-3*) Lucent Bks.

*__Presnall, Judith J.__ Life on Alcatraz. LC 00-8056. (Way People Live Ser.). 2000. write for info. (*1-56006-639-3*) Lucent Bks.

— Mount Rushmore. LC 99-31390. (Building History Ser.). (Illus.). 128p. (YA). (gr. 6-9). 2000. lib. bdg. 23.70 (*1-56006-529-X*) Lucent Bks.

Presnall, Judith J. Oprah Winfrey. LC 98-23237. (People in the News Ser.). (Illus.). 144p. (YA). (gr. 4-12). 1998. lib. bdg. 23.70 (*1-56006-360-2*) Lucent Bks.

— Rachel Carson. LC 93-49487. (Importance of... Biographies Ser.). (Illus.). 112p. (J). (gr. 5-8). 1995. lib. bdg. 22.45 (*1-56006-052-2*) Lucent Bks.

Presnell, Barbara. Unrevelings. 30p. 1999. pap. 6.00 (*0-9670994-0-4*) Longleaf Meth Coll.

Presnell, Don & McGee, Marty. A Critical History of Television's "The Twilight Zone," 1959-1964. LC 98-36576. 288p. 1998. lib. bdg. 39.95 (*0-7864-0448-5*) McFarland & Co.

Presnell, Janice K., et al. Humason's Animal Tissue Techniques. 5th ed. LC 96-26473. (Illus.). 536p. 1997. text 50.00 (*0-8018-5401-6*) Johns Hopkins.

Presnell, Lowell. Mines, Miners & Minerals of Western North Carolina's Mountain Empire. LC 98-36574. (Illus.). 272p. 1998. pap. 14.95 (*1-56664-135-7*) WorldComm.

Presnell, Mick, jt. ed. see Carter, Kathryn.

Presnell, Randy. The K Factor. 32p. 1999. 9.00 (*0-8059-4627-6*) Dorrance.

Presnell, Romaine. Taking the Trip: A Journey Through Widowhood. LC 96-22357. 1996. 4.95 (*1-56123-095-2*) Centering Corp.

Presner, Lewis A. The International Business Dictionary & Reference. LC 91-9328. 504p. 1991. 49.95 (*0-471-54594-5*) Wiley.

Presniakov, Alexander E. Emperor Nicholas the First of Russia: The Apogee of Autocracy, 1825-1855. Zacek, Judith C., tr. from RUS. LC 73-90779. (Russian Ser.: No. 23).Tr. of Apogei Samoderzhavia. (Illus.). 1974. 35.00 (*0-87569-053-X*) Academic Intl.

*__Presniakov, Alexander E.__ Lords of Death. 260p. 2000. pap. 14.95 (*1-57532-294-3*, Pub. by Press-Tige Pub) Barnes & Noble Inc.

Presniakov, Alexander E. Tsardom of Muscovy. Price, R. F., ed. & tr. by. 1978. pap. 15.00 (*0-87569-090-4*) Academic Intl.

Presno, V., jt. auth. see Fournier, Robert.

Press. Imagining Our Lives. 1993. pap. text 14.95 (*0-226-68032-0*) U Ch Pr.

— Understand Earth. 2nd ed. 1998. 59.00 (*0-7167-3305-6*) W H Freeman.

— Understanding Earth, Vol. 1. 2nd ed. 1997. 51.00 incl. audio compact disk (*0-7167-3186-X*) W H Freeman.

Press, Allan N., jt. auth. see Osterkamp, Lynn.

Press, Andrea L. Women Watching Television: Gender, Class, & Generation in the American Television Experience. LC 90-21274. 258p. (C). 1991. pap. text 17.95 (*0-8122-1286-X*) U of Pa Pr.

Press, Andrea L. & Cole, Elizabeth. Speaking of Abortion: Television & Authority in the Lives of Women. LC 98-19443. 1999. 25.00 (*0-226-68031-2*) U Ch Pr.

Press, B. Collins Wild Guide: Trees. 191p. 1996. pap. 12.95 (*0-00-220009-0*, Pub. by HarpC) Trafalgar.

Press, Barry. PC Upgrade & Repair Bible, Professional Edition. LC 97-76687. 1400p. 1998. pap. 49.99 (*0-7645-3148-4*) IDG Bks.

*__Press, Barry & Press, Marcia.__ PC Upgrade & Repair Bible 3rd ed. LC 99-38351. 1450p. 1999. 49.99 (*0-7645-3357-6*) IDG Bks.

*__Press, Bernhard.__ The Murder of the Jews in Latvia, 1941-1945. Mazzarins, Laimdota, tr. 192p. 1999. 54.95 (*0-8101-1728-2*) Northwestern U Pr.

— The Murder of the Jews in Latvia, 1941-1945. Mazzarins, Laimdota, tr. 192p. 2000. pap. 15.95 (*0-8101-1729-0*) Northwestern U Pr.

Press Boulevard Company Staff. Oxford Essential Dictionary of Foreign Terms i n English: The World's Most Trusted Dictionaries. 1999. mass mkt. 5.99 (*0-425-16995-2*) Berkley Pub.

— Oxford Essential Geographical Dictionary: The World's Most Trusted Dictionaries. 1999. mass mkt. 5.99 (*0-425-16994-4*) Berkley Pub.

— Oxford New Spanish Dictionary: The World's Most Trusted Dictionaries. 1999. mass mkt. 5.99 (*0-425-17090-X*) Berkley Pub.

Press, Charles. Primer for Board of Review Members. 4th ed. LC 87-620000. 65p. 1987. 5.00 (*0-941872-53-X*) MSU Dept Res Dev.

Press, Cody, ed. see Albin, Steven J.

Press, Daniel. Democratic Dilemmas in the Age of Ecology: Trees & Toxics in the American West. LC 94-7247. 176p. 1994. text 39.95 (*0-8223-1503-3*); pap. text 16.95 (*0-8223-1514-9*) Duke.

Press, Debbie, et al. Your Modeling Career: You Don't Have to Be a Superstar to Succeed. LC 00-24650. (Illus.). 256p. 2000. pap. 14.95 (*1-58115-045-8*) Allworth Pr.

Press, Donna, jt. photos by see Siede, George.

*__Press, Eric.__ NYT Analyzing Financial Statements: 25 Keys to Understanding the Numbers. LC 99-37749. (Illus.). 104p. 1999. pap. 12.95 (*0-86730-771-4*) Lebhar Friedman.

Press, Frank. Life in the Universe/Understanding the Earth. 1994. 37.20 (*0-7167-2616-5*) W H Freeman.

Press, Frank. Understanding Earth. 2nd ed. 1997. pap. 62.95 (*0-7167-3487-7*) W H Freeman.

Press, Frank & Siever, Raymond. Earth. 4th ed. LC 85-20581. (Illus.). 656p. (C). 1985. pap. text 65.95 (*0-7167-1743-3*) W H Freeman.

— Lecture Notes for Slides, Understanding Earth. 1994. 1.60 (*0-7167-2555-X*) W H Freeman.

— Understanding Earth. LC 93-4967. (C). 1993. pap. text. write for info. (*0-7167-2544-4*) W H Freeman.

— Understanding Earth. (C). 1993. text, teacher ed. 16.80 (*0-7167-2521-5*) W H Freeman.

Press, Gerald A. The Development of the Idea of History in Antiquity. LC 84-239837. (McGill-Queen's Studies in the History of Religion: No. 2). 191p. reprint ed. pap. 59.30 (*0-7837-1028-3*, 204133900020) Bks Demand.

Press, Gerald A., ed. Plato's Dialogues: New Studies & Interpretations. 288p. (Orig.). (C). 1993. pap. text 24.95 (*0-8476-7836-9*) Rowman.

— Who Speaks for Plato? Studies in Platonic Anonymity. LC 99-14796. 256p. 2000. 63.00 (*0-8476-9218-3*); pap. 23.95 (*0-8476-9219-1*) Rowman.

Press, H. J. Giant Book of Science Experiments. (Illus.). 384p. (J). 1996. 19.95 (*0-8069-8138-5*) Sterling.

Press, Ian & J. I. Press Staff. Ukrainian: A Comprehensive Grammar. LC 98-32358. 315p. 1999. pap. 29.99 (*0-415-15030-2*) Routledge.

Press, Ian & Pugh, Stefan. Colloquial Ukrainian. LC 93-38897. 384p. (C). (gr. 13). 1994. 39.95 incl. audio (*0-415-09204-3*) Routledge.

— Colloquial Ukrainian. LC 93-38897. (Illus.). 384p. (gr. 13). 1994. pap. 24.99 (*0-415-09202-7*) Routledge.

Press, Ian & Ramoniene, Meilute. Colloquial Lithuanian: A Complete Language Course. LC 95-39835. (Colloquials Ser.). 288p. (C). 1996. audio 27.99 (*0-415-12104-3*) Routledge.

— Colloquial Lithuanian: A Complete Language Course. LC 95-39835. (Colloquials Ser.). (Illus.). 288p. 1996. pap., boxed set 49.99 incl. audio (*0-415-12105-1*) Routledge.

— Colloquial Lithuanian: A Complete Language Course. LC 95-39835. (Colloquials Ser.). (Illus.). 400p. 1996. pap. 22.99 (*0-415-12103-5*) Routledge.

Press, Ila, ed. Texas Legal Assistant Handbook. 1995. ring bd. 89.98 (*0-938065-81-5*) James Pub Santa Ana.

Press, Irwin. Tradition & Adaptation: Life in a Modern Yucatan Maya Village. LC 75-71. (Illus.). 224p. 1975. 57.95 (*0-8371-7954-8*, PYM/, Greenwood Pr) Greenwood.

Press, J. Ian. A Grammar of Modern Breton. (Mouton Grammar Library: No. 2). (Illus.). x, 406p. 1986. lib. bdg. 89.25 (*0-89925-135-8*) Mouton.

Press, James S. Bayesian Statistics: Principles, Models & Applications. LC 88-5407. (Probability & Mathematical Statistics Ser.). 256p. 1989. 115.00 (*0-471-63729-7*) Wiley.

Press, Jenny. The Christmas Baby. 20p. (J). (ps). 1995. bds. 5.98 (*0-86112-888-5*) Brimax Bks.

Press, John, ed. The Golden Treasury of the Best Songs & Lyrical Poems in the English Language. 6th ed. (Oxford Standard Authors Ser.). 714p. 1996. pap. 15.95 (*0-19-282315-9*) OUP.

Press, John & Harvey, Charles. Art, Enterprise & Ethics: Essays on the Life & Works of William Morris. LC 96-18659. (Illus.). 350p. 1996. pap. 19.50 (*0-7146-4258-4*, Pub. by F Cass Pubs) Intl Spec Bk.

Press, John, jt. ed. see Palgrave, Francis T.

Press, Jon. The Footwear Industry in Ireland, 1922-1973. (Illus.). 224p. 1988. 39.50 (*0-7165-2439-2*, Pub. by Irish Acad Pr) Intl Spec Bk.

Press, Jon & Harvey, Charles. Art, Enterprise & Ethics: Essays on the Life & Works of William Morris. LC 96-18659. (Illus.). 245p. 1996. 45.00 (*0-7146-4712-8*, Pub. by F Cass Pubs) Intl Spec Bk.

Press, Jon, jt. auth. see Harvey, Charles.

Press, Jon, jt. ed. see Harvey, Charles.

Press, Jonathan. Professional Publishing with Ventura. (Orig.). 1989. 29.95 (*0-317-93951-3*); pap. 19.95 (*0-317-93952-1*) Jonathan Pr.

Press, Joy, jt. auth. see Reynolds, Simon.

Press, Judy. Alphabet Art: With A to Z Animal Art & Fingerplays. Williamson, Susan, ed. LC 97-13762. (Little Hands Ser.). (Illus.). 144p. (Orig.). (J). (ps-1). 1997. pap. 12.95 (*1-885593-14-7*) Williamson Pub Co.

*__Press, Judy.__ Around the World Art & Activities: Visiting the 7 Continents Through Craft Fun. (Little Hands Ser.). (Illus.). 144p. (J). (ps-2). 2000. pap. 12.95 (*1-885593-45-7*) Williamson Pub Co.

— ArtStarts for Little Hands! LC 99-89956. (Little Hands Bks.). (Illus.). 144p. (J). (ps-1). 2000. pap. 12.95 (*1-885593-37-6*) Williamson Pub Co.

Press, Judy. The Kids' Natural History Book: Making Dinos, Fossils, Mammoths & More. LC 98-30052. (Kids Can! Ser.). (Illus.). 160p. (J). (ps-5). 2000. pap. 12.95 (*1-885593-24-4*) Williamson Pub Co.

— The Little Hands Art Book: Exploring Arts & Crafts with 2-to-6 Year Olds. LC 94-13910. 1994. 18.05 (*0-606-10252-3*, Pub. by Turtleback) Demco.

— The Little Hands Art Book: Exploring Arts & Crafts with 2-to-6 Year Olds. LC 94-1391. (Little Hands Bks.: No. 1). (Illus.). 160p. (J). (ps-1). 1994. pap. 12.95 (*0-913589-86-1*) Williamson Pub Co.

— The Little Hands Big Fun Craft Book: Creative Fun for 2- to 6-Year-Olds. LC 95-17574. (Little Hands Bks.: Vol. 2). (Illus.). 144p. (J). (ps-1). 1996. pap. 12.95 (*0-913589-96-9*) Williamson Pub Co.

— Vroom! Vroom! Making 'Dozers, 'Copters, Trucks & More. Williamson, Susan, ed. LC 96-27204. (Little Hands Bks.). (Illus.). 160p. (Orig.). (J). (ps-6). 1997. pap. 12.95 (*1-885593-04-X*) Williamson Pub Co.

*__Press, Karen.__ Home. 96p. 2000. pap. 12.95 (*1-85754-478-1*, Pub. by Carcanet Pr) Paul & Co Pubs.

Press, Leonard J. Applied Concepts in Vision Therapy with Accompanying Disk. LC 96-21428. (Illus.). 416p. 1997. write for info. incl. disk (*0-8151-6729-6*, 24293) Mosby Inc.

Press, Leonard J. & Moore, Bruce D. Clinical Pediatric Optometry. (Illus.). 400p. 1992. text 79.00 (*0-7506-9080-1*) Buttrwrth-Heinemann.

Press, Leonard J., et al. Computers & Vision Therapy Programs. Corngold, Sally M., ed. (Introduction to Behavioral Optometry Ser.). (Illus.). 82p. 1992. lib. bdg. 15.00 (*0-943599-57-1*) OEPF.

*__Press, Lynne & Williams, Pamela.__ Women & Feminine Images in Giacomo Leopardi, 1798-1837: Bicentenary Essays. LC 99-41713. (Studies in Italian Literature: Vol. 7). 292p. 1999. text 89.95 (*0-7734-7929-5*) E Mellen.

Press, Marcia, jt. auth. see Press, Barry.

Press, Margaret. A Scream on the Water: A Murder in Massachusetts Bay. 1997. mass mkt. 5.99 (*0-614-27791-4*) St Martin.

Press, Margaret & Pinkham, Joan. Counterpoint: A Murder in Massachusetts Bay. Colvin, Rod, ed. (Illus.). 340p. (Orig.). 1996. pap. 16.95 (*1-886039-24-0*) Addicus Bks.

Press, Margaret L. Chemehuevi: A Grammar & Lexicon. (Publications in Linguistics: Vol. 92). 1980. pap. 25.00 (*0-520-09600-2*, Pub. by U CA Pr) Cal Prin Full Svc.

— Chemehuevi, a Grammar & Lexicon. LC 78-62874. (University of California Publications in Social Welfare: No. 92). 211p. reprint ed. pap. 65.50 (*0-608-18461-6*, 203290100081) Bks Demand.

Press, Margaret M., jt. auth. see MacKillop, Mary.

Press, Mike & Thomson, Don, eds. Solidarity for Survival: The Don Thomson Reader on Trade Union Internationalism. 161p. 1989. 49.50 (*0-85124-510-2*, Pub. by Spkesman) Coronet Bks.

Press, Mike, jt. auth. see Cooper, Rachel.

Press, Peter R., jt. auth. see Tapper, Alan.

*__Press, Petra.__ Coretta Scott King: An Unauthorized Biography. LC 99-51674. (Profile Ser.). 1999. lib. bdg. write for info. (*1-57572-496-0*) Heinemann Lib.

— Fidel Castro: An Unauthorized Biography. LC 99-51675. (Profile Ser.). 1999. lib. bdg. write for info. (*1-57572-497-9*) Heinemann Lib.

Press, Petra. The 1930's. LC 98-29895. (Cultural History of the United States Through the Decades Ser.). (Illus.). (YA). (gr. 4-12). 1998. lib. bdg. 23.70 (*1-56006-553-2*) Lucent Bks.

Press Regina. Pray the Rosary. 1993. pap. text 25.00 (*0-88271-325-6*) Regina Pr.

Press, Robert A. How to Drive into Accidents - And How Not To. LC 97-91601. (Illus.). 488p. (gr. 10-12). 1998. pap. 18.95 (*0-9655648-1-9*, PP02) Pease Pub.

*__Press, Robert M.__ The New Africa: Dispatches from a Changing Continent. LC 99-17517. (Illus.). 358p. 1999. 24.95 (*0-8130-1704-1*) U Press Fla.

Press, Skip. Awesome Almanac: California. 1994. 20.10 (*0-606-09016-9*, Pub. by Turtleback) Demco.

— Awesome Almanacs - California. (J). (gr. 4-12). 1994. pap. 14.95 (*1-880190-21-4*) B&B Pub.

— Charlie Sheen, Emilio Estevez & Martin Sheen. LC 95-11619. (Star Families Ser.). 48p. (J). (gr. 4-7). 1995. pap. 4.95 (*0-382-39180-2*, Crstwood Hse); lib. bdg. 15.95 (*0-89686-884-2*, Crstwood Hse) Silver Burdett Pr.

*__Press, Skip.__ Cliffhanger. (Take Ten Ser.). (Illus.). 47p. (YA). (gr. 4-12). 1999. pap. 3.95 (*1-58659-011-1*) Artesian.

Press, Skip. Cliffhanger. Parker, Liz, ed. (Take Ten Bks.). (Illus.). 45p. (J). (gr. 6-12). 1992. pap. text 3.95 (*1-56254-055-6*) Saddleback Pubns.

— Ken Griffey, Jr. & Ken Griffey, Sr. LC 95-11815. (Star Families Ser.). 48p. (J). (gr. 5-6). 1995. pap. 4.95 (*0-382-39189-6*, Crstwood Hse) Silver Burdett Pr.

— Ken Griffey, Jr. & Ken Griffey, Sr. deluxe ed. LC 95-11815. (Star Families Ser.). 48p. (J). (gr. 5-6). 1995. lib. bdg. 15.95 (*0-89686-881-8*, Crstwood Hse) Silver Burdett Pr.

— Knucklehead. Parker, Liz, ed. (Take Ten Bks.). (Illus.). 50p. (YA). (gr. 6-12). 1993. pap. text 3.95 (*1-56254-095-5*) Saddleback Pubns.

*__Press, Skip.__ Knucklehead. rev. ed. (Take Ten Ser.). (Illus.). 50p. (YA). (gr. 4-12). 1999. pap. 3.95 (*1-58659-033-2*) Artesian.

Press, Skip. The Kuwaiti Oil Fires. Parker, Liz, ed. (Take Ten Bks.). 46p. (YA). (gr. 6-12). 1993. pap. text 3.95 (*1-56254-097-1*) Saddleback Pubns.

— The Kuwaiti Oil Fires. (Take Ten Books Ser.). (J). 1993. 9.15 (*0-606-11542-0*, Pub. by Turtleback) Demco.

*__Press, Skip.__ The Kuwaiti Oil Fires. rev. ed. (Take Ten Ser.). (Illus.). 46p. (YA). (gr. 4-12). 1999. pap. 3.95 (*1-58659-024-3*) Artesian.

Press, Skip. Mark Twain. LC 93-1827. (Importance of Ser.). 112p. (J). (gr. 5-8). 1994. lib. bdg. 22.45 (*1-56006-043-3*) Lucent Bks.

— Melissa & Joan Rivers. LC 95-13087. (Star Families Ser.).

P

48p. (J). (gr. 5-6). 1995. pap. 4.95 (0-382-39178-0, Crstwood Hse); lib. bdg. 15.95 (0-89686-883-4, Crstwood Hse) Silver Burdett Pr.

— Michael & Kirk Douglas. LC 94-28650. (Star Families Ser.). (Illus.). (YA). (gr. 5 up). 1995. pap. 4.95 (0-382-24941-0, Crstwood Hse) Silver Burdett Pr.

— Natalie & Nat "King" Cole. LC 94-22429. (J). 1995. lib. bdg. 15.95 (0-89686-879-6, Crstwood Hse) Silver Burdett Pr.

— Natalie & Nat "King" Cole. (Star Families Ser.). (Illus.). 48p. (YA). (gr. 5 up). 1995. pap. 4.95 (0-382-24942-9, Crstwood Hse) Silver Burdett Pr.

— Tori & Aaron Spelling. LC 95-11600. (Star Families Ser.). (J). (gr. 5-6). 1995. pap. 4.95 (0-382-39179-9, Crstwood Hse); lib. bdg. 15.95 (0-89686-885-0, Crstwood Hse) Silver Burdett Pr.

— The Writer's Guide to Hollywood Producers, Directors, & Screenwriters' Agents: Who They Are! What They Want! & How to Win Them Over! LC 96-46996. 480p. 1997. per. 23.00 (0-7615-0399-4) Prima Pub.

— Writer's Guide to Hollywood Producers, Directors & Screenwriter's Agents, 1999-2000: Who They Are! What They Want! & How to Win Them Over! LC 98-42438. 432p. 1998. pap. 23.00 (0-7615-1484-8) Prima Pub.

— Wynonna & Naomi Judd. LC 94-28465. (Star Families Ser.). (Illus.). (J). (gr. 5 up). 1995. pap. 7.95 (0-382-24943-7, Crstwood Hse) Silver Burdett Pr.

Press Trust of India Staff, jt. auth. see Kumar, Arun.

Press, William H., et al. Numerical Recipes in C: The Art of Scientific Computing. 2nd ed. 1020p. (C). 1992. text 57.95 (0-521-43108-5) Cambridge U Pr.

— Numerical Recipes in C: The Art of Scientific Computing. 2nd ed. (C). 1992. disk 39.95 (0-521-43724-5) Cambridge U Pr.

— Numerical Recipes in C: The Art of Scientific Computing. 2nd ed. (C). 1993. disk 39.95 (0-521-43715-6) Cambridge U Pr.

— Numerical Recipes in FORTRAN: The Art of Scientific Computing. 2nd ed. 92p. (C). 1992. disk 39.95 (0-521-43717-2) Cambridge U Pr.

— Numerical Recipes in FORTRAN: The Art of Scientific Computing. 2nd ed. (C). 1993. disk 39.95 (0-521-43716-4) Cambridge U Pr.

— Numerical Recipes in FORTRAN 90: The Art of Parallel Scientific Computing. 2nd ed. (Fortran Numerical Recipes Ser.: Vol. 2). (Illus.). 571p. (C). 1996. text 47.95 (0-521-57439-0) Cambridge U Pr.

— Numerical Recipes in FORTRAN 77: The Art of Scientific Computing. 2nd ed. 992p. (C). 1992. text 57.95 (0-521-43064-X) Cambridge U Pr.

— Numerical Recipes in FORTRAN 77 Example Book: The Art of Scientific Computing. 2nd ed. 256p. (C). 1992. pap. text 29.95 (0-521-43721-0) Cambridge U Pr.

— Numerical Recipes in Pascal: The Art of Scientific Computing. rev. ed. (Illus.). 781p. (C). 1989. text 57.95 (0-521-37516-9) Cambridge U Pr.

— Numerical Recipes in Pascal Example Book: The Art of Scientific Computing. rev. ed. (Illus.). 231p. (C). 1989. pap. text 29.95 (0-521-37675-0) Cambridge U Pr.

— Numerical Recipes in Pascal Example Book: The Art of Scientific Computing. 2nd ed. 336p. (C). 1992. pap. text 29.95 (0-521-43720-2) Cambridge U Pr.

Pressat, Roland. Dictionnaire de Demographie. (FRE.). 304p. 1979. 75.00 (0-8288-9468-X, F70763) Fr & Eur.

Pressburger, Emeric, jt. auth. see Powell, Michael.

Pressburger, Giorgio & Pressburger, Nicola. Homage to the Eighth District: Tales from Budapest. Moore, Gerald, tr. from ITA. 200p. (Orig.). 1990. 17.95 (0-930523-75-X); pap. 9.95 (0-930523-76-8) Readers Intl.

Pressburger, Nicola, jt. auth. see Pressburger, Giorgio.

Presse Commerciale Staff. Lexique de la Geographie en Cinq Langues. (FRE.). 2248p. 1993. 75.00 (0-7859-5674-3, 7100008379) Fr & Eur.

Presse, Michele, tr. see Rodieck, Jorma.

Presseisen, Barbara Z. Critical Thinking & Thinking Skills: State-of-the-Art Definitions & Practice in Public Schools. 57p. 1986. pap. 13.95 (1-56602-011-5) Research Better.

— Learning & Thinking Styles: Classroom Interaction. 160p. 1990. pap. 15.95 (0-8106-1841-9) NEA.

— Thinking Skills: Research & Practice. (What Research Says to the Teacher Ser.). 1986. pap. 3.95 (0-8106-1073-6) NEA.

— Thinking Skills Throughout the Curriculum: A Conceptual Design. (Illus.). 109p. (Orig.). (C). 1987. pap. 8.95 (0-9618056-0-9) Pi Lambda Theta.

— Understanding Adolescence: Issues & Implications for Effective Schools. 60p. 1990. reprint ed. pap. 16.95 (1-56602-002-6) Research Better.

— The Unlearned Lessons: Current & Past Reforms for School Improvement. LC 85-29659. 258p. 1985. 65.00 (1-85000-079-4, Falmer Pr) Taylor & Francis.

***Presseisen, Barbara Z., ed.** Teaching for Intelligence I: A Collection of Articles. LC 98-61805. 406p. 1999. 30.95 (1-57517-152-X) SkyLght.

Presseisen, Barbara Z., jt. auth. see Kruse, Janice.

Presseisen, Barbara Z., ed. see Langrehr, John.

Presseisen, Ernst L. Amiens & Munich. (Comparisons in Appeasement Ser.). 1978. lib. bdg. 94.00 (90-247-2067-2) Kluwer Academic.

— Before Aggression: Europeans Prepare the Japanese Army. LC 65-20235. (Association for Asian Studies, Monographs & Papers: No. 21). 173p. reprint ed. pap. 53.70 (0-8357-7089-3, 200293200016) Bks Demand.

Pressel, Lloyd & Gardner, Robert H. Supervision for Empowered Workers: View Leadership Styles for Self-Managing Teams. 210p. 1992. 24.95 (0-9634821-0-6) Loma Linda Pub.

Pressel, Ralph, jt. auth. see Field, John.

Presser, ArLynn. Getting Out: Emily. (Loop Ser.). 1995. per. 3.50 (0-373-20207-5, 1-20207-6) Harlequin Bks.

— Love Changes Everything. (Love Stories Ser.). 176p. (Orig.). (YA). (gr. 7-12). 1995. mass mkt. 3.99 (0-553-56665-2) BDD Bks Young Read.

***Presser, Art.** The Pharmacists Smart Guide to the Top 50 Herbs. LC 99-66309. (Smart Guide Ser.). (Illus.). 128p. 2000. pap. 9.95 (1-890572-09-8, Pub. by Smart Pubns CA) Publishers Group.

Presser, Beat, photos by. Coming Attractions. (Illus.). 64p. 1984. pap. 10.95 (0-912810-42-4) Lustrum Pr.

Presser, Carole. Protection Mutual Insurance Company: The First Hundred Years. LC 87-61723. (Illus.). 72p. (Orig.). 1987. pap. write for info. (0-916371-07-7) Mobium Pr.

***Presser, Harriet B. & Sen, Gita, eds.** Women's Empowerment & Demographic Process: Moving Beyond Cairo. (International Studies in Demography). 380p. 2000. text 72.00 (0-19-829731-9) OUP.

Presser, Jacob. Ashes in the Wind: The Destruction of Dutch Jewry. Pomerans, Arnold J., tr. from DUT. LC 88-225. (Illus.). 572p. 1988. reprint ed. 49.95 (0-8143-2036-8); reprint ed. pap. 24.95 (0-8143-2037-6) Wayne St U Pr.

Presser, Stanley, jt. auth. see Converse, Jean M.

Presser, Stanley, jt. auth. see Schuman, Howard.

Presser, Stanley, jt. ed. see Singer, Eleanor.

Presser, Stephen B. The Original Misunderstanding: The English, the Americans, & the Dialectic of Federalist Jurisprudence. LC 90-85344. 284p. 1991. lib. bdg. 34.95 (0-89089-425-6) Carolina Acad Pr.

— Recapturing the Constitution. 416p. 1994. 24.95 (0-89526-492-7) Regnery Pub.

Presser, Stephen B. & Zainaldin, Jamil S. Cases & Materials on Law & Jurisprudence in American History. 3rd ed. (American Casebook Ser.). 1101p. (C). 1995. 65.00 (0-314-06359-5) West Pub.

— Law & Jurisprudence in American History, Cases & Materials: Teacher's Manual to Accompany. 3rd ed. (American Casebook Ser.). 125p. 1996. pap. text. write for info. (0-314-20346-X) West Pub.

Presser, Stephen B., jt. auth. see Kmiec, Douglas W.

Presser, William. Song for Three Viols. (Contemporary Consort Ser.: No. 20). 7p. 1992. pap. text 6.00 (1-56571-057-6, CC020) PRB Prods.

Presses de l'Universite Laval Staff. Dictionnaire Biographique du Canada, 10 vols. (FRE.). 1982. 1295.00 (0-7859-8456-9, 2-7637-6950-0) Fr & Eur.

— Dictionnaire Biographique du Canada: 1701-1740. 1969. write for info. (0-7859-8028-8, 2-7637-0007-1) Fr & Eur.

— Dictionnaire Biographique du Canada: 1741-1770. (FRE.). 1974. write for info. (0-7859-8031-8, 2-7637-6736-2) Fr & Eur.

— Dictionnaire Biographique du Canada: 1771-1800. (FRE.). 1980. 295.00 (0-7859-8033-4, 2-7637-6900-4) Fr & Eur.

— Dictionnaire Biographique du Canada: 1821-1835. (FRE.). 1987. write for info. (0-7859-8034-2, 2-7637-7099-1) Fr & Eur.

— Dictionnaire Biographique du Canada: 1861-1870, 11 vols. 1977. 2995.00 (0-7859-8032-6, 2-7637-6812-1); 2995.00 (0-7859-8592-1, 0774668113) Fr & Eur.

— Dictionnaire Biographique du Canada: 1871-1880. (FRE.). 1972. write for info. (0-7859-8029-6, 2-7637-0010-1) Fr & Eur.

Pressfield, Steven. Gates of Fire: An Epic Novel of the Battle of Thermopylae. 480p. 1999. mass mkt. 6.50 (0-553-58053-1) Bantam.

— Gates of Fire: An Epic Novel of the Battle of Thermopylae. large type ed. LC 98-56126. 636p. 1999. 28.95 (0-7838-8534-2) Thorndike Pr.

— The Legend of Bagger Vance: A Novel. LC 94-32223. 245p. 1995. 20.00 (0-688-14048-3, Wm Morrow) Morrow Avon.

***Pressfield, Steven.** The Legend of Bagger Vance: A Novel of Golf & the Game of Life. LC 94-32223. 272p. 1999. pap. 12.50 (0-380-72751-X, Avon Bks) Morrow Avon.

— The Legend of Bagger Vance: A Novel of Golf & the Game of Life. 304p. 2000. mass mkt. 6.99 (0-380-81744-6, Avon Bks) Morrow Avon.

— Tides of War: An Epic Novel of Alcibiades & the Peloponnesian War. LC 99-54829. 432p. 2000. 24.95 (0-385-49252-9) Doubleday.

Pressing, Jeff. Synthesizer Performance & Real-Time Techniques. LC 91-39700. (Computer Music & Digital Audio Ser.: Vol. 8). (Illus.). 462p. (C). 1992. 49.95 (0-89579-257-5) A-R Eds.

Pressing, Jeff, ed. Compositions for Improvisers: An Australian Perspective. 1994. pap. 34.95 (1-86324-415-8) Intl Spec Bk.

Pressl, Diana A. Beamte und Soldaten: Die Verwaltung in der 26. Dynastie in Aegypten (664-525 v. Chr.) (Europaeische Hochschulschriften Ser.: Reihe 3, Band 779). (GER., Illus.). 338p. 1998. pap. 51.95 (3-631-32586-X) P Lang Pubng.

Pressland, David. Pressland's Great Book of Tin Toys. (Illus.). 335p. 1995. 250.00 (1-872727-31-X) Pincushion Pr.

Pressler, Amy, ed. see Byers, David.

Pressler, Carolyn. The View of Women Found in the Deuteronomic Family Laws. LC 93-27800. (Beiheft zur Zeitschrift fuer die Alttestamentliche Wissenschaft Ser.: Vol. 216). ix, 127p. (C). 1993. lib. bdg. 83.10 (3-11-013743-7) De Gruyter.

Pressler, Charles A. & Dasilva, Fabio B. Sociology & Interpretation: From Weber to Habermas. LC 95-40977. 208p. (C). 1996. text 21.50 (0-7914-3043-X) State U NY Pr.

Pressler, David E. The Theory of Unity: The Final Theory. (Illus.). 162p. 1994. 39.95 (0-9638572-0-7) Primary Nuclear.

Pressler, Karen L., jt. auth. see Bunker, John Michael.

Pressler, Larry. Star Wars: The Strategic Defense Initiative Debates in Congress. LC 86-809. 193p. 1986. 57.95 (0-275-92052-6, C2052, Praeger Pubs) Greenwood.

Pressler, Larry, ed. Air Bag Safety: Hearing Before the Committee on Commerce, Science & Transportation, U. S. Senate. 84p. (C). 1998. text 20.00 (0-7881-7067-8) DIANE Pub.

***Pressler, Larry, ed.** Domestic Air Services in the Wake of Airline Deregulation: Challenges Faced by Small Carriers: Hearing Before the Committee on Commerce, Science & Transportation, U. S. Senate. 266p. (C). 2000. reprint ed. pap. text 40.00 (0-7881-7274-3) DIANE Pub.

Pressler, Larry, ed. Federal Government Use & Management of Spectrum: Hearing Before the Committee on Commerce, Science, & Transportation, U. S. Senate. 92p. (C). 1998. pap. text 20.00 (0-7881-7285-9) DIANE Pub.

— Spectrum Use & Management: Hearing Before the Committee on Commerce, Science & Transportation, U. S. Senate. 176p. (C). 1998. pap. text 30.00 (0-7881-7284-0) DIANE Pub.

Pressler, Miriam. Bitterschokolade. (Easy Reader Ser.: Level 2). (GER.). 112p. 1992. text 6.95 (3-468-96702-0) Langenscheidt.

Pressler, Miriam, ed. see Frank, Anne.

***Pressler, Mirjam.** Anne Frank: A Hidden Life. LC 99-89604. (Illus.). 192p. (J). (gr. 7-12). 2000. 15.99 (0-525-46330-5, Dutt) Dutton Plume.

— Halinka. 224p. (J). (gr. 5 up). 2000. mass mkt. 5.50 (0-440-22857-3, LLL BDD) BDD Bks Young Read.

Pressler, Mirjam. Halinka. Crawford, Elizabeth D., tr. from GER. LC 98-16088. (Illus.). 214p. (YA). (gr. 5-8). 1998. 16.95 (0-8050-5861-3) H Holt & Co.

Pressler, Mirjam, jt. auth. see Rabinovici, Schoschana.

Pressler, Mirjam, jt. ed. see Frank, Otto M.

***Pressler, Paul.** A Hill to Die On: One Southern Baptist's Journey. LC 99-19790. (Illus.). 448p. 1999. 29.99 (0-8054-1677-3) Broadman.

Pressler, Rudolf & Straub, Robin. Biedermeier Furniture. 230p. 1996. 34.95 (0-7643-0155-1) Schiffer.

***Pressley, Alison.** The Best of Times: Growing Up in Britain in the 1950s. 1999. 19.95 (1-85479-458-2, Pub. by M OMara) Trafalgar.

Pressley, Andrew & Segal, Graeme. Loop Groups. (Oxford Mathematical Monographs). (Illus.). 316p. 1988. pap. text 45.00 (0-19-853561-9) OUP.

Pressley, Andrew N., jt. auth. see Chari, Vyjayanthi.

Pressley, Leigh. City Smart: Charlotte. (City Smart Ser.). (Illus.). 240p. 1999. pap. 13.95 (1-56261-415-0, City Smart) Avalon Travel.

Pressley, M. & Brainerd, Charles J., eds. Cognitive Learning & Memory in Children. (Cognitive Development Ser.). (Illus.). 290p. 1985. 83.95 (0-387-96076-7) Spr-Verlag.

Pressley, M. & Schneider, Wolfgang. Memory Development Between 2 & 20. (Cognitive Development Ser.). (Illus.). 255p. 1988. 45.00 (0-387-96742-7) Spr-Verlag.

Pressley, M., jt. ed. see Brainerd, Charles J.

Pressley, M., jt. ed. see McDaniel, M. A.

Pressley, Michael. Reading Instruction That Works: The Case for Balanced Teaching. LC 97-44072. 300p. 1998. pap. text 26.95 (1-57230-319-0, C0319); lib. bdg. 44.95 (1-57230-308-5, C0308) Guilford Pubns.

Pressley, Michael & Afflerbach, Peter. Verbal Protocols of Reading: The Nature of Constructively Responsive Reading. 168p. 1995. pap. 17.50 (0-8058-1764-6); text 39.95 (0-8058-1537-6) L Erlbaum Assocs.

Pressley, Michael & Schneider, Wolfgang. Introduction to Memory Development During Childhood & Adolescence. LC 97-1849. 260p. 1997. write for info. (0-8058-2705-6); pap. write for info. (0-8058-2706-4) L Erlbaum Assocs.

Pressley, Michael & Woloshyn, Vera. Cognitive Strategy Instruction That Really Improves Children's Academic Performance. 2nd ed. LC 95-2310. (Cognitive Strategy Training Ser.). 266p. 1995. pap. text 27.95 (1-57129-005-2) Brookline Bks.

Pressley, Michael, et al. Promoting Academic Competence & Literacy in School. (Illus.). 506p. 1992. text 59.95 (0-12-564438-8) Acad Pr.

Pressley, Michael, jt. auth. see Schneider, Wolfgang.

Pressley, Michael, jt. ed. see Hogan, Kathleen.

Pressley, Michael, ed. see Mastropieri, Margo & Scruggs, Thomas E.

Pressley, Michael, jt. ed. see McIntyre, Ellen.

Pressley, Sara, ed. see Adams, Pamela W.

Pressley, Sara R., jt. auth. see Adams, Pamela W.

Pressley, Sara R., ed. see Adams, Pamela W.

Pressley, Thomas A. & Sabatini, Sandra, eds. The ATPases. (Journal Ser.: Vol. 22, No. 5-6). (Illus.). iv, 168p. 1996. pap. 92.25 (3-8055-6398-1) S Karger.

***Presslich, Marion.** Partitivitat und Indefinitheit: Die Entstehung und Entwicklung des indefiniten Artikels in den germanischen und romanischen Sprachen am Beispiel des Deutschen, Niederlandischen, Franzosischen und Italienischen. 2000. 47.95 (3-631-35775-3, Pub. by P Lang) P Lang Pubng.

Pressly, Thomas J., ed. The Great War at Home & Abroad: The World War I Diaries & Letters of W. Stull Holt. LC 99-188020. (Illus.). 375p. 1998. pap. 26.95 (0-89745-222-4) Sunflower U Pr.

Pressly, William L. The Formative Years at Atlanta's Westminster Schools. 212p. 1991. text. write for info. (0-9628381-0-1) McGuire Pub.

— The Life & Art of James Barry. LC 80-29665. (Paul Mellon Centre for Studies in British Art). (Illus.). 320p. 1981. 90.00 (0-300-02466-5) Yale U Pr.

Pressly, William L. & Zoffany, Johann. The French Revolution As Blasphemy: Johan Zoffany's Paintings of the Massacre at Paris, August 10, 1792. LC 98-6424. (California Studies in the History of Art). 240p. 1999. 50.00 (0-520-21196-0, Pub. by U CA Pr) Cal Prin Full Svc.

Pressman. Software Engineering. 3rd ed. 1991. text, teacher ed. 34.68 (0-07-050815-1) McGraw.

Pressman, Abraham I. Switching Power Supply Design. 2nd ed. LC 97-31668. 682p. 1997. 75.00 (0-07-052236-7) McGraw.

Pressman, Alan. Ginkgo: Nature's Brain Booster. 1999. mass mkt. 5.99 (0-380-80640-1, Avon Bks) Morrow Avon.

Pressman, Alan & Buff, Sheila. The GSH Phenomenon: Nature's Most Powerful Antioxidant & Healing Agent. 228p. 1998. text 24.00 (0-7881-5540-7) DIANE Pub.

Pressman, Alan & Goodman, Herbert D. The Physicians' Guides to Healing No. 4: Treating Gynecological Conditions. LC 97-178492. (Physicians Guides to Healing Ser.). 192p. 1997. mass mkt. 5.99 (0-425-15908-6) Berkley Pub.

Pressman, Alan, et al. The Physicians' Guides to Healing: Treating Asthma, Allergies, & Food Sensitivities. 224p. 1997. mass mkt. 5.99 (0-425-15669-9) Berkley Pub.

— The Physicians' Guides to Healing No. 3: Treating Hypertension, & Other Cardiovascular Conditions. LC 97-168749. 224p. 1997. mass mkt. 5.99 (0-425-15853-5) Berkley Pub.

— The Physicians' Guides to Healing No. 5: Treating Digestive Conditions. LC 97-225152. (The Physicians' Guide to Healing Ser.). 272p. 1997. mass mkt. 6.50 (0-425-15940-X) Berkley Pub.

— Treating Arthritis, Carpal Tunnel Syndrome, & Joint Conditions. LC 97-156061. (Physicians Guide to Healing Ser.: No. 2). 224p. 1997. mass mkt. 5.99 (0-425-15694-X) Berkley Pub.

Pressman, Alan H. Glutathione: The Ultimate Antioxidant. 1998. mass mkt. 5.99 (0-312-96432-3) St Martin.

Pressman, Alan H. & Adams, Alan H. Clinical Assessment of Nutritional Status. 2nd ed. 220p. 1990. 40.00 (0-683-06970-5) Lppncott W & W.

Pressman, Alan H. & Buff, Sheila. Complete Idiot's Guide to Vitamins & Minerals. LC 97-80861. 368p. 1997. pap. 16.95 (0-02-862116-6, Pub. by Macmillan Gen Ref) S&S Trade.

***Pressman, Alan H. & Buff, Sheila.** The Pocket Idiot's Guide to Vitamins. (Pocket Idiot's Guides Ser.). 192p. 1999. pap. 9.95 (0-02-863397-0, Pub. by Macmillan Gen Ref) S&S Trade.

Pressman, Alan H. & Burke, Nancy. St. John's Wort: The Miracle Medicine. LC 98-223315. 224p. 1998. mass mkt. 5.99 (0-440-22605-8) Dell.

***Pressman, Alan H. & Shelley, Donna.** Integrative Medicine: The Patient's Essential Guide to Conventional & Complementary Treatments for More Than 300 Common Disorders. LC 00-27966. (Illus.). 608p. 2000. 39.95 (0-312-25379-6) St Martin.

Pressman, Andy. The Fountainheadache: The Politics of Architect-Client Relations. LC 94-40081. 264p. 1995. pap. 44.95 (0-471-30992-3) Wiley.

— Professional Practice 101: A Compendium of Business & Management Strategies in Architecture. LC 96-54601. 368p. 1997. pap. 49.95 (0-471-13015-X) Wiley.

Pressman, Aron. Living Language Complete Course: Russian. (Living Language Ser.). (RUS.). 1998. 22.50 incl. audio (0-609-60268-3, 903612) Crown Pub Group.

Pressman, Barbara, et al, eds. Intervening with Assaulted Women: Current Theory, Research & Practice. 196p. (C). 1989. text 39.95 (0-8058-0456-0) L Erlbaum Assocs.

***Pressman, David.** Nolo's Patents for Beginners. LC 00-27404. (Quick & Legal Ser.). (Illus.). 200p. 2000. pap. 29.95 (0-87337-575-0) Nolo com.

Pressman, David. Patent It Yourself. 6th ed. Elias, Steve, ed. LC 97-18560. (Illus.). 480p. 1997. reprint ed. pap. 44.95 (0-87337-395-2) Nolo com.

— Patent It Yourself. 7th ed. Elias, Stephen, ed. LC 98-6526. (Illus.). 496p. 1998. pap. 46.95 (0-87337-469-X) Nolo com.

***Pressman, David.** Patent It Yourself. 8th ed. LC 99-48778. 2000. write for info. (0-87337-563-7) Nolo com.

Pressman, David, jt. auth. see EDS Staff.

Pressman, David, jt. auth. see Grissom, Fred.

Pressman, David, jt. auth. see Grissom, Fred E., Jr.

Pressman, David, jt. auth. see Lo, Jack.

Pressman, Harvey, ed. Making an Exceptional Difference: Enhancing the Impact of Microcomputer Technology on Children with Disabilities. 320p. (Orig.). 1987. pap. text 24.95 (0-930958-03-9) Excptnl Parent.

Pressman, Harvey, jt. auth. see Dublin, Peter.

Pressman, Harvey, jt. ed. see Dublin, Peter.

Pressman, Hope H. A New Resource for Welfare Reform: The Poor Themselves. LC 75-2399. 140p. reprint ed. pap. 43.40 (0-7837-2138-2, 204242400004) Bks Demand.

Pressman, Jack D. Last Resort: Psychosurgery & the Limits of Medicine. LC 97-14074. (Studies in the History of Medicine). (Illus.). 572p. (C). 1998. text 49.95 (0-521-35371-8) Cambridge U Pr.

Pressman, Jeffrey L. House vs. Senate: Conflict in the Appropriations Process. LC 66-21532. (Yale College Ser.: No. 5). 151p. reprint ed. pap. 46.90 (0-8357-8171-2, 203386100087) Bks Demand.

Pressman, Jeffrey L. & Wildavsky, Aaron B. Implementation: How Great Expectations in Washington Are Dashed in Oakland; Or, Why It's Amazing That Federal Programs Work at All, This Being a Saga of the Economic Development Administration As Told by Two Sympathetic Observers Who Seek to Build Morals on a Foundation of Ruined Hopes. 3rd ed. LC 83-17987. (Oakland Project Ser.). 304p. (C). 1984. pap. 15.95 (0-520-05331-1, Pub. by U CA Pr) Cal Prin Full Svc.

P

An Asterisk (*) at the beginning of an entry indicates that the title is appearing for the first time.

Pressman, Jeremy, jt. auth. see Kemp, Geoffrey.

Pressman, Kati. The Big Picture Book: Gift Edition, A Primer of Spiritual Qualities for Adults. 62p. 1992. pap. 5.95 (*1-881422-01-1*) Jester Pr CO.

Pressman, Mark. Handbook of Polysomnogram Interpretation. 304p. 2000. text 60.00 (*0-7506-9782-2*) Buttrwrth-Heinemann.

Pressman, Mark R. & Orr, William C., eds. Understanding Sleep: The Evaluation & Treatment of Sleep Disorders. LC 97-1393. (Application & Practice in Health Psychology Ser.: Vol. 4). 566p. 1997. 49.95 (*1-55798-419-0*, 4317870) Am Psychol.

Pressman, Maurice J., jt. auth. see Joudry, Patricia.

Pressman, Maurie. Enter The Super Mind: Discover the Power of Your Super Consciousness, 1. 1999. pap. 17.95 (*1-58501-003-0*) CeShore Pubg.

Pressman, Maurie D., jt. auth. see Joudry, Patricia.

Pressman, Michael. FORTRAN for Today & Tomorrow. 512p. (C). 1992. text 55.75 (*0-697-04483-1*, WCB McGr Hill) McGrw-H Hghr Educ.

Pressman, Norman, jt. auth. see Yuen, R. Margaret.

Pressman, Peter I., jt. auth. see Hirshaut, Yashar.

Pressman, Robert. State Law Challenges to School Discipline: An Outline of Claims & Case Summaries - Updated Edition. 3rd ed. 116p. 1995. 20.00 (*0-912585-15-3*) Ctr Law & Ed.

Pressman, Robert H., jt. auth. see Donaldson-Pressman, Stephanie.

Pressman, Robert M. & Siegler, Rodie. The Independent Practitioner: Practice Management for the Allied Health Professional. LC 82-73633. (Professional Bks.). 266p. (C). 1983. text 43.95 (*0-534-11281-1*) Brooks-Cole.

Pressman, Robert M., jt. auth. see Donaldson-Pressman, Stephanie.

Pressman, Roger S. A Manager's Guide to Software Engineering. (Illus.). 528p. 1996. pap. 34.95 (*0-07-052229-4*) McGraw.

— Software Engineering. LC 87-35396. 285p. (C). 1988. pap. 55.94 (*0-07-050790-2*) McGraw.

— Software Engineering: A Practitioner's Approach. 4th ed. LC 96-77396. (Illus.). 852p. (C). 1996. 91.88 (*0-07-052182-4*) McGraw.

***Pressman, Roger S.** Software Engineering: A Practitioner's Approach. 5th ed. LC 00-36133. (Series in Computer Science). 2001. write for info. (*0-07-365578-3*) McGraw.

Pressman, Roger S. & Herron, S. Russell. Software Shock: The Danger & the Opportunity. LC 91-20988. (Illus.). 240p. (Orig.). 1991. pap. 19.95 (*0-932633-20-X*) Dorset Hse Pub Co.

Pressman, Steven. Fifty Major Economists: A Reference Guide. LC 98-33133. 207p. 1999. pap. 20.99 (*0-415-13481-1*) Routledge.

***Pressman, Steven.** Fifty Major Economists: A Reference Guide. LC 98-33133. 1999. 60.00 (*0-415-13480-3*) Routledge.

Pressman, Steven. Poverty in America. 313p. 1994. 42.00 (*0-8108-2833-2*) Scarecrow.

— Quesnay's "Tableau Economique" A Critique & Reassessment. x, 198p. 1994. lib. bdg. 37.50 (*0-678-01471-X*) Kelley.

Pressman, Steven, ed. Interactions in Political Economy: Malvern after Ten Years. LC 95-47075. 240p. (C). 1996. 80.00 (*0-415-13393-9*) Routledge.

Pressman, Steven, jt. ed. see Holt, Richard P.

Pressman, Todd Evan. Radical Joy, 1. 304p. 1999. pap. 12.00 (*1-57566-440-2*) Kensgtn Pub Corp.

Pressment, Stanley. Choice of Business Entity Answer Book. LC 97-171681. 488p. 1997. boxed set 118.00 (*1-56706-373-X*, 6373X) Panel Pubs.

Pressnall, Debra Olson. Big Book of Music Games. 1998. pap. 19.95 (*1-56822-673-X*) Instruct Fair.

Pressnell, Jon. Fifty Years of the Morris Minor: A Celebration of a Great British Institution. (Illus.). 160p. 1998. pap. 22.95 (*0-85429-980-7*, Pub. by GT Foulis) Haynes Manuals.

***Pressnell, Jon.** Mini. (Album Ser.: No. 299). (Illus.). 32p. 1999. pap. 5.25 (*0-7478-0235-1*, Pub. by Shire Pubns) Parkwest Pubns.

Pressnell, Jon. Morris Minor: Exploring the Legend LC 98-70519. 168p. 1998. write for info. (*1-85960-429-3*) Haynes Manuals.

— Touring Caravans. (Album Ser.: No. 267). (Illus.). 32p. 1989. pap. 6.25 (*0-7478-0119-3*, Pub. by Shire Pubns) Parkwest Pubns.

Pressnell, L. S. External Economic Policy since the War Vol. 1: The Post-War Financial Settlement. xiv, 501p. 1987. 100.00 (*0-11-630186-4*, Pub. by Statnry Office) Balogh.

Presson, Dorette J., jt. auth. see Shemwell, Chris D.

Presson, Leslie. Dictionary of Homophones. LC 97-15368. 224p. 1997. pap. text 6.95 (*0-7641-0168-4*) Barron.

— What in the World Is a Homophone? (Illus.). 192p. (J). (gr. 3-7). 1996. 10.95 (*0-8120-6585-9*) Barron.

Presson, Ronald C., et al. Year 2000 Home & Business Technological Emergency Management Guide, Vol. 1. (Illus.). 60p. 1998. pap. 19.95 (*0-9665682-0-6*) EPI Inc.

— Year 2000 Home & Business Technological Emergency Management Guide, Vol. 1. 2nd rev. ed. (Illus.). 85p. 1998. per. 19.95 (*0-9665682-1-4*) EPI Inc.

Presson, Shelley. Climbing: A Woman's Guide. 176p. 2000. pap. 14.95 (*0-07-135151-5*) McGraw.

Pressouyre, G. M., ed. see International Conference on Current Solutions to H.

Pressure Vessels & Piping Conference Staff. Aspects of Fracture Mechanics in Pressure Vessels & Piping. Palusamy, S. S. & Sampath, S. G., eds. LC 82-71607. (Illus.). 329p. reprint ed. pap. 102.00 (*0-8357-6028-6*, 205681400089) Bks Demand.

— Component Support Snubbers: Design, Application, & Testing: Presented at the Pressure Vessels & Piping Conference, ASME Century 2--Emerging Technology Conferences, San Francisco, California, August 12-15, 1980. Reiff, D. D., ed. LC 80-66043. (PVP Ser.: No. 42). (Illus.). 75p. reprint ed. pap. 30.00 (*0-8357-2818-8*, 203905700010) Bks Demand.

Pressuti, Petrus. Regesta Honorii Papae III. (GER.). cxxx, 1342p. 1978. reprint ed. write for info. (*3-487-06530-4*) G Olms Pubs.

Prest, A. R. The U. K. Economy: A Manual of Applied Economics. 2nd ed. LC 77-419820. xviii 250p. 1968. write for info. (*0-297-76499-3*) Weidenfeld & Nicolson.

Prest, A. R. The U. K. Economy: A Manual of Applied Economics. 3rd ed. LC 70-862546. xx, 278 p. 1970. write for info. (*0-297-00293-7*) Weidenfeld & Nicolson.

Prest, A. R. & Coppock, D. J. The U. K. Economy: A Manual of Applied Economics. 5th ed. LC 75-302175. xviii, 292p. 1974. write for info. (*0-297-76842-5*) Weidenfeld & Nicolson.

— The U. K. Economy: A Manual of Applied Economics. 6th ed. LC 77-351999. xviii, 322p. 1976. write for info. (*0-297-77230-9*) Weidenfeld & Nicolson.

— The U. K. Economy: A Manual of Applied Economics. 7th ed. LC 79-307953. xviii, 316p. 1978. write for info. (*0-297-77533-2*) Weidenfeld & Nicolson.

— The U. K. Economy: A Manual of Applied Economics. 9th ed. LC 82-229815. xvi, 336 p. 1982. write for info. (*0-297-78181-2*) Weidenfeld & Nicolson.

Prest, A. R. & Coppock, D. J., eds. The U. K. Economy: Manual of Applied Economics. 6th ed. 1977. 24.95 (*0-8464-0942-9*) Beekman Pubs.

Prest, A. R., jt. auth. see British Association for the Advancement of Science Staff.

Prest, A. R., ed. see British Association for the Advancement of Science.

Prest, Arthur. Illustrated History of the Nigerian People. LC 73-92798. (J). (gr. 4 up). 1974. write for info. (*0-89388-138-4*) Okpaku Communications.

Prest, Colin. The Law & Practice of Interdicts. 462p. 1996. 108.00 (*0-7021-3776-6*, Pub. by Juta & Co) Gaunt.

Prest, Colin B. Interlocutory Interdicts. xxxvi, 236p. 1993. pap. 60.00 (*0-7021-3078-8*, Pub. by Juta & Co) Gaunt.

Prest, D., jt. auth. see Breckon, A.

Prest, J. M., jt. ed. see Quinn, E. V.

Prest, John. Liberty & Locality: Parliament, Permissive Legislation & Ratepayers' Democracies in the Mid-Nineteenth Century. 248p. 1990. 70.00 (*0-19-820175-3*) OUP.

Prest, M. Y. Model Theory & Modules. (London Mathematical Society Lecture Note Ser.: No. 130). 400p. 1988. pap. text 64.95 (*0-521-34833-1*) Cambridge U Pr.

Prest, M. Y., jt. auth. see Humphreys, J. F.

Prest, Thomas P. Varney, the Vampire: or The Feast of Blood, 3 vols., Set. Varma, Devendra P., ed. LC 70-120557. (Gothic Novels II Ser.). 933p. 1972. reprint ed. boxed set 64.95 (*0-405-00801-5*) Ayer.

Prest, Wilfrid. Albion Ascendant: English History, 1660-1815. LC 98-213944. (Short Oxford History of the Modern World Ser.). (Illus.). 384p. (C). 1998. text 76.00 (*0-19-820417-5*); pap. text 24.95 (*0-19-820418-3*) OUP.

Prest, Wilfrid, ed. Lawyers in Early Modern Europe & America. LC 80-22574. 224p. 1981. 39.95 (*0-8419-0679-3*) Holmes & Meier.

Prest, Wilfrid R. The Rise of the Barristers: A Social History of the English Bar, 1590-1640. (Oxford Studies in Social History). (Illus.). 458p. 1987. text 90.00 (*0-19-821764-1*) OUP.

— The Rise of the Barristers: A Social History of the English Bar, 1590-1640. (Oxford Studies in Social History). (Illus.). 458p. 1991. reprint ed. pap. text 29.95 (*0-19-820258-X*) OUP.

Prestage, Edgar. Chivalry: A Series of Studies to Illustrate Its Historical Significance & Civilizing Influence, by Members of King's College, London. LC 72-11293. (Illus.). reprint ed. 57.50 (*0-404-57491-2*) AMS Pr.

— D. Francisco Manuel De Mello. 98p. (Orig.). 1992. pap. text 10.00 (*0-87535-012-7*) Hispanic Soc.

— The Portuguese Pioneers. xiv, 352p. 1985. reprint ed. lib. bdg. 49.00 (*0-932051-44-8*) Rprt Serv.

Prestage, Edgar, ed. Chapters in Anglo-Portuguese Relations. LC 73-109826. (Illus.). 198p. 1971. reprint ed. lib. bdg. 55.00 (*0-8371-4317-9*, PRCA, Greenwood Pr) Greenwood.

Prestbo, John, jt. auth. see Sease, Douglas.

Prestbo, John, jt. auth. see Sease, Douglas R.

***Prestbo, John A., ed.** The Market's Measure: An Illustrated History of America Told Through the Dow Jones Industrial Average. (Illus.). 188p. 1999. 39.95 (*1-881944-25-5*) Dow Jones & Co.

Prestbo, John A. & Sease, Douglas R. The Wall Street Journal Book of International Investing: Everything You Need to Know about Investing in Foreign Markets. LC 96-35266. (Illus.). 288p. (J). 1997. 24.45 (*0-7868-6092-8*, Pub. by Hyperion) Time Warner.

***Prestbo, John A. & Sease, Douglas R.** The Wall Street Journal Book of International Investing: Everything You Need to Know about Investing in Foreign Markets. rev. ed. (Illus.). 384p. (J). 1998. pap. 14.45 (*0-7868-8310-3*, Pub. by Hyperion) Time Warner.

Prestbo, John A., jt. auth. see Sease, Douglas.

Prestedge, Margie, jt. auth. see Bird, Madeline.

***Prestel.** American Impressionism. 1999. 8.95 (*3-7913-2048-3*) Prestel.

— Flowers. 1999. 8.95 (*3-7913-2120-X*) Prestel.

Prestel, A. Lectures on Formally Real Fields. (Lecture Notes in Mathematics Ser.: Vol. 1093). xi, 125p. 1984. reprint ed. 29.95 (*0-387-13885-4*) Spr-Verlag.

Prestel, A. & Roquette, P. Formally P Adic Fields. (Lecture Notes in Mathematics Ser.: Vol. 1050). v, 167p. 1984. pap. 29.60 (*0-387-12890-5*) Spr-Verlag.

Prestel Art Press. Gemaldegalerie Berlin. LC 98-227928. (Illus.). 192p. 1998. pap. text 14.95 (*3-7913-1912-4*) Prestel.

***Prestel Art Press Staff, ed.** Prestel Postcard Book. (Illus.). 1999. pap. 8.95 (*3-7913-2232-X*); pap. 8.95 (*3-7913-2233-8*) Prestel Pub NY.

Prestel Staff. Fondation Beyeler. LC 98-140416. (Illus.). 352p. 1997. 65.00 (*3-7913-1814-4*, Pub. by Prestel) te Neues.

— Hamburg Kunsthalle Museum of Contemporary Art. (Prestel Museum Guides). (Illus.). 96p. 1997. pap. text 14.95 (*3-7913-1899-3*, Pub. by Prestel) te Neues.

— Icons of Art: The 20th Century. LC 98-185781. (Illus.). 216p. 1997. 29.95 (*3-7913-1862-4*, Pub. by Prestel) te Neues.

— Lovis Corinth: Postcard Book. 1997. pap. text 8.95 (*3-7913-1744-X*, Pub. by Prestel) te Neues.

Prestel Staff. Oskar Kokoschka: Postcard Book. 1997. 8.95 (*3-7913-1768-7*, Pub. by Prestel) te Neues.

Prestel Staff. Picasso, World of Children: Postcard Book. 1997. 8.95 (*3-7913-1499-8*, Pub. by Prestel) te Neues.

— The Schloss Moyland Museum: Van Der Grinten Collection. (Prestel Museum Guides). (Illus.). 192p. 1997. pap. text 14.95 (*3-7913-1877-2*, Pub. by Prestel) te Neues.

— ZKM: Center for Art & Media Karlsruhe. (Museum Guides Ser.). (Illus.). 192p. 1997. pap. text 14.95 (*3-7913-1883-7*, Pub. by Prestel) te Neues.

***Prestel-Verlag Staff, ed.** INRI 2000 Oberammergau: The Making of the Passion Play. (Illus.). 2000. 29.95 (*3-7913-2365-2*) Prestel Pub NY.

— Oberammergau: Child's Play: The Passion Play 2000. 2000. 14.95 (*3-7913-2351-2*) Prestel Pub NY.

— Oberammergau: The Passion Play 2000. 2000. 25.00 (*3-7913-2327-X*) Prestel Pub NY.

Presthus, Robert V. Elites in the Policy Process. LC 73-94135. 539p. reprint ed. pap. 153.70 (*0-608-15767-8*, 2031713) Bks Demand.

Presti, Michael, jt. auth. see Whalen, Tom.

Presti, Santo M. IRS in Action: Straight Talk from a Former Treasury Agent. (Illus.). 155p. 1983. pap. 9.95 (*0-914877-00-3*) Sherwood Comns.

Prestia, Kenneth L. Chocolates for the Pillows, Nightmares for the Guests: The Failure of the Hotel Industry to Protect the Traveling Public from Violent Crime. LC 93-5928. 1993. pap. 12.95 (*0-910155-25-9*) Bartleby Pr.

Prestia, Phyllis S. Slicing Eggplant. 32p. 1984. pap. 3.50 (*0-913719-72-2*, High Coo Pr) Brooks Books.

Prestiano, Robert. The Inland Architect: Chicago's Major Architectural Journal, 1883-1908. LC 85-1178. (Architecture & Urban Design Ser.: No. 9). (Illus.). 265p. reprint ed. pap. 82.20 (*0-8357-1680-5*, 207051800097) Bks Demand.

Prestige, George L. St. Basil the Great & Apollinaris of Laodicea. LC 82-45832. (Orhtodoxies & Heresies in the Early Church Ser.). reprint ed. 32.50 (*0-404-62399-9*) AMS Pr.

Prestine, Janice Rombold. Defiant Love. LC 99-64516. 192p. 2000. pap. 11.95 (*1-56315-219-3*, Pub. by SterlingHse) Natl Bk Netwk.

Prestine, Joan S. Family Day Care Activities A to Z. 1989. pap. 10.99 (*0-8224-3073-8*) Fearon Teacher Aids.

— Helping Children Share Their Teacher: A Practical Resource Guide for It's Hard to Share My Teacher. (Kids Have Feelings, Too Ser.). 64p. 8.99 (*0-86653-923-9*, FE0923) Fearon Teacher Aids.

— Helping Children Understand Divorce. (Kids Have Feelings, Too Ser.). 64p. (J). (ps-3). 1996. 8.99 (*0-86653-858-5*, FE3858) Fearon Teacher Aids.

— Helping Children Understand Their Feelings: A Practical Resource Guide for Sometimes I Feel Awful. (Kids Have Feelings, Too Ser.). 64p. (J). (ps-3). 8.99 (*0-86653-926-3*, FE0926) Fearon Teacher Aids.

— It's Hard to Share My Teacher. (Kids Have Feelings, Too Ser.). 32p. (J). (ps-3). 8.99 (*0-86653-924-7*, FE0924) Fearon Teacher Aids.

— It's Hard to Share My Teacher: Picture Book & Resource Guide, 2 bks., Set. (Kids Have Feelings, Too Ser.). (J). (ps-3). 16.99 (*1-56417-773-4*, FE0061) Fearon Teacher Aids.

— Mom & Dad Break Up. LC 97-104355. (Kids Have Feelings, Too Ser.). (Illus.). 32p. (J). (ps-3). 1996. 8.99 (*0-86653-857-7*, FE3857) Fearon Teacher Aids.

— Someone Special Died: Picture Book & Resource Guide, 2 bks., Set. (Kids Have Feelings, Too Ser.). (J). (ps-3). 16.99 (*1-56417-762-9*, FE0050) Fearon Teacher Aids.

— Someone Special Died, Picturebook. (J). (ps-3). 1993. pap. 8.99 (*0-86653-929-8*) Fearon Teacher Aids.

— Someone Special Died, Resource. (J). (ps-3). 1993. pap. 8.99 (*0-86653-928-X*) Fearon Teacher Aids.

— Sometimes I Feel Awful: Picture Book & Resource Guide, 2 bks., Set. (Kids Have Feelings, Too Ser.). (J). (ps-3). 15.99 (*1-56417-763-7*, FE0051) Fearon Teacher Aids.

— Sometimes I Feel Awful, Picturebook. (J). (ps-3). 1993. pap. 8.99 (*0-86653-927-1*) Fearon Teacher Aids.

***Prestinenza Puglisi, Luigi.** Hyper Architecture: Spaces in the Electronic Age. LC 99-42387. 1999. write for info. (*0-8176-6093-3*) Birkhauser.

***Presto, Fay.** Magic for Kids. LC 99-12753. 72p. 1999. pap. 10.95 (*0-7534-5210-3*) LKC.

Preston. Frommer's Comprehensive Travel Guide Delaware & Maryland. 1996. per. 14.95 (*0-671-51939-5*) S&S Trade.

— Frommer's Ireland. 1995. pap. 17.00 (*0-671-88488-3*) S&S Trade.

***Preston.** Ghosting. 2000. pap. 12.95 (*0-552-99667-X*, Pub. by Transworld Publishers Ltd) Trafalgar.

Preston. Handbook Dance Education. 1987. pap. text. write for info. (*0-582-99475-6*, Pub. by Addison-Wesley) Longman.

***Preston.** Learn Office 2000 & Cd-rom. 1999. pap. text 42.67 (*0-13-019038-1*, Prentice Hall) P-H.

— Regulation of Transport in the European Union. 61.95 (*0-7546-1034-9*) Ashgate Pub Co.

Preston. Sociology Study Guide. 2nd ed. 312p. 1999. pap. text 31.00 (*0-536-02367-0*) Pearson Custom.

Preston. Whither Transport Studies? 61.95 (*0-7546-1033-0*) Ashgate Pub Co.

Preston & Ferrett. Trainers Mnl Acc Win 95. 2nd ed. 1998. pap. text 26.00 (*1-58076-162-3*) Que Educ & Trng.

Preston, A. J. & Pagan, A. R. The Theory of Economic Policy: Statics & Dynamics. LC 81-10196. 404p. 1982. text 90.00 (*0-521-23366-6*) Cambridge U Pr.

Preston, Adrian, ed. In Relief of Gordon: Lord Wolseley's Campaign Journal of the Khartoum Relief Expedition, 1884-1885. LC 79-92562. 267p. 1975. 22.50 (*0-8386-7572-7*) Fairleigh Dickinson.

Preston, Alison. A Blue & Golden Year. 182p. 1997. pap. 14.95 (*0-88801-206-3*, Pub. by Turnstone Pr) Genl Dist Srvs.

Preston, Alistair, jt. ed. see Awerbuch, Shimon.

Preston, Anthony. Aircraft Carriers. LC 84-9669. (Modern Military Techniques Ser.). (Illus.). 48p. (J). (gr. 5 up). 1985. pap. 4.95 (*0-8225-9504-4*, Lerner Publctns) Lerner Pub.

— The Destroyers. LC 77-82132. (Illus.). 1977. 14.95 (*0-685-03827-0*) P-H.

— Warship, Vol. II. (Illus.). 287p. 1980. 41.95 (*0-87021-976-6*) Naval Inst Pr.

Preston, Anthony, ed. Warship, Vol. I. LC 78-55455. (Illus.). 256p. 1978. 41.95 (*0-87021-975-8*) Naval Inst Pr.

***Preston, Antony.** Submarine Warfare: An Illustrated History, 1 Vol. LC 99-11910. (Illus.). 1999. 17.98 (*1-57145-172-2*, Thunder Bay) Advantage Pubs.

***Preston, Antony & McLean, David, eds.** Warship, 1998-1999. (Illus.). 240p. 1998. 42.95 (*0-85177-724-4*) Naval Inst Pr.

Preston, Antony, jt. ed. see McLean, David.

Preston, Ashley L., jt. ed. see McQuillan, Alan G.

Preston, B. Bassett - Preston Ancestors: History of Ancestors in America of the Children of Edward M. & Annie Preston Bassett. 359p. 1991. reprint ed. 59.00 (*0-8328-1853-4*); reprint ed. pap. 49.00 (*0-8328-1854-2*) Higginson Bk Co.

Preston, Brenda B. Andrew Davidson Firebaugh & Susan Burgess Firebaugh: California Pioneers. LC 95-68049. (Illus.). 335p. 1995. 27.95 (*0-9645475-4-6*) Rio Del Mar Pr.

— Thomas Hildreth: Early California Cattle Baron. LC 95-73061. (Illus.). 75p. (Orig.). 1995. pap. 9.95 (*0-9645475-5-4*) Rio Del Mar Pr.

Preston, Brian J. Environmental Litigation. xxxix, 415p. 1989. 87.50 (*0-455-20898-0*, Pub. by LawBk Co) Gaunt.

Preston, C. H. Preston: Descendants of Roger Preston. (Illus.). 355p. 1991. reprint ed. pap. 56.00 (*0-8328-2081-4*); reprint ed. lib. bdg. 66.00 (*0-8328-2080-6*) Higginson Bk Co.

Preston, Caroline. Jackie by Josie. 1998. per. 11.00 (*0-684-83890-7*) S&S Trade.

— Jackie by Josie. LC 96-42177. 1997. 21.50 (*0-684-83077-9*) Scribner.

— Jackie by Josie. large type ed. LC 97-10483. (Core Ser.). 503p. 1997. lib. bdg. 26.95 (*0-7838-8200-9*, G K Hall Lrg Type) Mac Lib Ref.

***Preston, Caroline.** Lucy Crocker 2.0. LC 99-88095. 352p. 2000. 23.00 (*0-684-85449-X*) Scribner.

Preston, Cathy L. A Concordance to the Child Ballads. 1000p. 158.00 (*0-8240-8983-9*, H484) Garland.

Preston, Cathy L., ed. Folklore, Literature, & Cultural Theory. LC 95-13920. (New Perspectives in Folklore Ser.: Vol. 2). (Illus.). 280p. 1995. text 25.00 (*0-8240-7271-5*, H1395) Garland.

Preston, Cathy L. & Hardy, Thomas. A KWIC Concordance to Thomas Hardy's Tess of the D'Urbervilles. LC 89-1507. 986p. 1989. text 25.00 (*0-8240-9076-4*, 749) Garland.

Preston, Cathy L. & Preston, Michael J., eds. The Other Print Tradition: Essays on Chapbooks, Broadsides, & Related Ephemera. LC 95-23141. (New Perspectives in Folklore Ser.: Vol. 3). (Illus.). 312p. 1995. text 25.00 (*0-8153-0376-9*, H1470) Garland.

Preston, Cecilia M., ed. ASIS '98 Vol. 35: Proceedings of the 61st Annual Meeting of the American Society for Information Science: Information Access in the Global Information Economy. LC 64-8303. 604p. 1998. pap. 49.50 (*1-57387-066-8*) Info Today Inc.

***Preston, Charles.** Charles Preston's Giant Crossword Puzzle Treasury. (Illus.). 1999. pap. 9.95 (*0-399-52547-5*, Perigee Bks) Berkley Pub.

Preston, Charles. Charles Preston's Giant Crossword Puzzle Treasury, No. 14. 128p. 1997. pap. 8.95 (*0-399-52347-2*, Perigee Bks) Berkley Pub.

— Charles Preston's Giant Crossword Puzzle Treasury No. 11. 128p. (Orig.). 1994. pap. 8.95 (*0-399-52147-X*, Perigee Bks) Berkley Pub.

— Charles Preston's Giant Crossword Treasury, 13. 128p. 1996. pap. 8.95 (*0-399-52248-4*, Perigee Bks) Berkley Pub.

— Charles Preston's Giant Crossword Treasury, No. 12. 128p. 1995. pap. 8.95 (*0-399-51966-1*, Perigee Bks) Berkley Pub.

— Cross Puzzles in Large Type, 11. large type ed. (Omnibus Ser.). 1999. pap. text 10.95 (*0-399-52514-9*) Berkley Pub.

— Crossword Large Omni, No. 6. 176p. (Orig.). 1994. pap. 8.95 (*0-399-52143-7*, Perigee Bks) Berkley Pub.

— Crossword Puzzles No. 19, No. 19. large type ed. 96p. 1995. pap. 6.95 (*0-399-51912-2*, Perigee Bks) Berkley Pub.

— Crossword Puzzles No. 21. large type ed. 96p. 1997. pap. 7.95 (*0-399-52280-8*, Perigee Bks) Berkley Pub.

***Preston, Charles.** Crossword Puzzles in Large Type. Vol. 12. 176p. 2000. pap. 10.95 (*0-399-52608-0*) Berkley Pub.

P

Preston, Charles. Crossword Puzzles in Large Type, No. 10. large type ed. 1998. pap. 9.95 (*0-399-52418-5*, Perigee Bks) Berkley Pub.
— Crossword Puzzles in Large Type, No. 20. large type ed. 96p. 1996. pap. 7.95 (*0-399-51993-9*, Perigee Bks) Berkley Pub.
— Crossword Puzzles in Large Type, No. 23. 96p. 1999. pap. 7.95 (*0-399-52488-6*) Berkley Pub.
— Crossword Puzzles in Large Type Omnibus, No. 8. large type ed. 176p. 1996. pap. 9.95 (*0-399-52214-X*, Perigee Bks) Berkley Pub.
— Crossword Puzzles Omnibus No. 9. large type ed. 176p. 1997. pap. 9.95 (*0-399-52311-1*, Perigee Bks) Berkley Pub.
— Crosswords for the Connoisseur. 128p. 1998. pap. 9.95 (*0-399-52413-4*, Perigee Bks) Berkley Pub.
— Crosswords for The Connoisseur, 61. 1999. pap. text 7.95 (*0-399-52539-4*, Perigee Bks) Berkley Pub.
— Crosswords for the Connoisseur, No. 50. LC 93-30008. 80p. 1994. pap. 6.95 (*0-399-52116-X*, Perigee Bks) Berkley Pub.
— Crosswords for the Connoisseur, No. 54. 80p. 1996. pap. 7.95 (*0-399-52204-2*, Perigee Bks) Berkley Pub.
— Crosswords for the Connoisseur, No. 58. 1998. pap. 7.95 (*0-399-52408-8*, Perigee Bks) Berkley Pub.
— Crosswords for the Connoisseur, No. 59. 80p. 1998. pap. 7.95 (*0-399-52437-1*, Perigee Bks) Berkley Pub.
*__Preston, Charles.__ Crosswords for the Connoisseur, No. 62. (Illus.). 2000. pap. text 8.95 (*0-399-52587-4*, Perigee Bks) Berkley Pub.
— Crosswords for the Connoisseur, No. 63. 80p. 2000. pap. 8.95 (*0-399-52616-1*) Berkley Pub.
Preston, Charles. Crosswords for the Connoisseur No. 51. 80p. (Orig.). 1994. pap. 6.95 (*0-399-52140-2*, Perigee Bks) Berkley Pub.
— Crosswords for the Connoisseur No. 52, No. 52. 80p. (Orig.). 1995. pap. 6.95 (*0-399-51951-3*, Perigee Bks) Berkley Pub.
— Crosswords for the Connoisseur No. 56. 80p. 1997. pap. 7.95 (*0-399-52306-5*, Perigee Bks) Berkley Pub.
— Crosswords for the Connoisseur No. 57, 57. 80p. 1997. pap. 7.95 (*0-399-52340-5*, Perigee Bks) Berkley Pub.
— Crosswords for the Connoisseur Omnibus, No. 6. 128p. 1994. pap. 9.95 (*0-399-52118-6*, Perigee Bks) Berkley Pub.
— Crosswords for the Connoisseur Omnibus, No. 8. 128p. 1996. pap. 9.95 (*0-399-52209-3*, Perigee Bks) Berkley Pub.
— Crosswords for the Connoisseur Omnibus, Vol. 9. 128p. 1997. pap. 9.95 (*0-399-52302-2*, Perigee Bks) Berkley Pub.
— Crosswords for the Connoisseur Omnibus #11. 1999. pap. text 9.95 (*0-399-52509-2*, Perigee Bks) Berkley Pub.
— Crosswords for the Connoisseur, #60. 1999. pap. text 7.95 (*0-399-52504-1*) Berkley Pub.
— Crosswords for the Conoisseur No. 66, No. 55. 80p. 1996. pap. 7.95 (*0-399-52243-3*, Perigee Bks) Berkley Pub.
— Crosswords Puzzles in Large Type Omnibus 7, No. 7. large type ed. 176p. 1995. pap. 8.95 (*0-399-51964-5*, Perigee Bks) Berkley Pub.
— Giant Crossword Puzzle Treasury, No. 15. 128p. 1998. pap. 8.95 (*0-399-52452-5*, Perigee Bks) Berkley Pub.
*__Preston, Charles.__ Portfolio of Cartoons.com. (Illus.). 2000. pap. 12.00 (*1-881944-29-8*, Wall St Jrnl) Dow Jones & Co.
— Portfolio of Women in Business Cartoons. (Illus.). 2000. pap. 12.00 (*1-881944-27-1*, Wall St Jrnl) Dow Jones & Co.
— Quote Acrostic, Vol. 1. 2000. pap. 9.95 (*0-399-52633-1*, Perigee Bks) Berkley Pub.
Preston, Charles. U. S. A. Crosswords, No. 20. 80p. 1996. pap. 7.95 (*0-399-52219-0*, Perigee Bks) Berkley Pub.
— U. S. A. Crosswords, No. 21. 80p. 1997. pap. 7.95 (*0-399-52275-1*, Perigee Bks) Berkley Pub.
— U. S. A. Crosswords, No. 25. (U. S. A. Crosswords Ser.). 80p. 1999. pap. 8.95 (*0-399-52473-8*, Perigee Bks) Berkley Pub.
*__Preston, Charles.__ U. S. A. Crosswords Puzzle Book. 27th ed. 2000. pap. 8.95 (*0-399-52574-2*, Perigee Bks) Berkley Pub.
Preston, Charles. U. S. A. Today Crosswords, No. 23. 1998. pap. 7.95 (*0-399-52381-2*, Perigee Bks) Berkley Pub.
— USA Today Crosswords, No. 22. 80p. 1997. pap. 8.95 (*0-399-52315-4*, Perigee Bks) Berkley Pub.
— Wall Street Journal Book of Business Cartoons. 1999. pap. text 22.95 (*1-881944-19-0*) Dow Jones & Co.
Preston, Charles, ed. Crosswords for the Connoisseur Omnibus. (Perigree Crossword Puzzles Ser.: No. 5). 128p. 1992. pap. 8.95 (*0-399-52104-6*, Perigee Bks) Berkley Pub.
— The USA Today Crossword Puzzle Book #24, No. 24. 70p. 1998. pap. 8.95 (*0-399-52422-3*, Perigee Bks) Berkley Pub.
Preston, Charles & Kipfer, Barbara A. The U. S. A. Today Crossword Puzzle Dictionary: The Newest, Most Comprehensive & Authoritative Crossword Reference Book. 928p. (J). 1996. pap. 12.45 (*0-7868-8060-0*, Pub. by Hyperion) Time Warner.
Preston, Charles F., jt. ed. see Shoenberg, Mark B.
*__Preston, Charles R.__ Wild Bird Guides: Red-Tailed Hawk. LC 99-35582. (Wild Bird Guides Ser.). 112p. 2000. 19.95 (*0-8117-2914-1*) Stackpole.
Preston, Charles R., et al. Unbroken Spirit: The Wild Horse in the American Landscape. (Illus.). 88p. 1999. pap. 18.95 (*0-931618-62-2*) Buffalo Bill Hist Ctr.
Preston, Charlotte & Dunton, Trevor. The Little Terror: First Six Weeks. LC 99-36708. (Baby Tips Ser.: Vol. 1). (Illus.). 144p. 1999. pap. 6.95 (*1-55561-199-0*) Fisher Bks.
— The Little Terror: Good Behavior Guide. LC 99-38812. (Baby Tips Ser.: Vol. 4). (Illus.). 144p. 1999. pap. 6.95 (*1-55561-202-4*) Fisher Bks.
— The Little Terror: Good Feeding Guide. LC 99-36707. (Baby Tips Ser.: Vol. 2). (Illus.). 144p. 1999. pap. 6.95 (*1-55561-200-8*) Fisher Bks.
— The Little Terror: Good Sleeping Guide. LC 99-37067. (Baby Tips Ser.: Vol. 3). (Illus.). 144p. 1999. pap. 6.95 (*1-55561-201-6*) Fisher Bks.
Preston, Charlotte, jt. auth. see Winterowd, W. Ross.
Preston, Cheryl. Divorce Without Guilt. (Illus.). 360p. 1999. pap. 15.98 (*0-939759-01-2*, DWG-P) Ctr Dynamic Living.
Preston, Cheryl K. Believe in Yourself: Be Your Own Best Friend. 110p. 1999. per. 12.95 (*0-939759-04-7*, BIY-S) Ctr Dynamic Living.
— Finding Your Compatible Partner. 110p. 1999. spiral bd. write for info. (*0-939759-08-X*) Ctr Dynamic Living.
— How to Make Your Dream Relationship a Reality. (Illus.). 500p. 1999. ring bd. write for info. (*0-939759-07-1*) Ctr Dynamic Living.
— Your Dreams Can Come True! 150p. 1999. per. 12.95 (*0-939759-05-5*) Ctr Dynamic Living.
Preston, Chris. Enlargement & Integration in the European Union. LC 96-47506. (Illus.). 272p. (C). 1997. 85.00 (*0-415-12001-2*); pap. 25.99 (*0-415-12002-0*) Routledge.
Preston, Claire. Edith Wharton's Social Register. LC 99-16599. 2000. text 59.95 (*0-312-22557-1*) St Martin.
Preston, Claire, ed. Sir Thomas Browne: Selected Poems. 192p. 1995. pap. 18.95 (*1-85754-052-2*, Pub. by Carcanet Pr) Paul & Co Pubs.
Preston, D. Road to Culloden Moor. 1996. pap. text 22.95 (*0-09-476170-1*, Pub. by Constable & Co) Trafalgar.
Preston, Daniel, jt. ed. see Harris, C. M.
Preston, Daniel D. The Era of A. J. Tomlinson. 206p. (Orig.). 1984. pap. 6.95 (*0-934942-41-2*, 1925) White Wing Pub.
Preston, Daryl W. Experiments in Physics: A Labratory Manual for Scientists & Engineers. 312p. (C). 1985. pap. 58.95 (*0-471-80571-8*) Wiley.
Preston, David. Latin America. (C). 1996. pap. 30.53 (*0-582-30148-3*) Addison-Wesley.
Preston, David A. Latin American Development: Geographical Perspectives. 2nd ed. LC 96-153681. 313p. (C). 1996. pap. 48.00 (*0-582-23695-9*) Longman.
Preston, David A., ed. Environment, Society & Rural Change in Latin America: The Past, Present & Future in the Countryside. LC 79-41481. (Illus.). 278p. reprint ed. pap. 86.20 (*0-608-17557-9*, 203053700069) Bks Demand.
Preston, David A., jt. auth. see Odell, Peter R.
*__Preston, David E.__ Lions to Lamb. LC 99-94919. 2000. pap. 9.95 (*0-533-13222-3*) Vantage.
Preston, David G., tr. see Blocher, Henri.
Preston, David L. Exploring Sociology: A Reading & Writing Workbook. (C). 1990. pap. text 3.95 (*0-942587-03-0*) Papyrus Bks.
— Sewer People. 1999. pap. write for info. (*0-14-010611-1*, Viking); text 18.00 (*0-670-82023-7*) Viking Penguin.
— The Social Organization of Zen Practice: Constructing Transcultural Reality. (Illus.). 192p. 1988. text 69.95 (*0-521-35000-X*) Cambridge U Pr.
Preston, Dennis, jt. ed. see Long, Daniel.
Preston, Dennis R. Bituminous Coal Mining Vocabulary of the Eastern United States. (Publications of the American Dialect Society: No. 59). (Illus.). 128p. (Orig.). 1975. pap. text 12.80 (*0-8173-0659-5*) U of Ala Pr.
— Perceptual Dialectology: Nonlinguists' Views of Areal Linguistics. (Topics in Sociolinguistics Ser.: No. 7). xvi, 141p. 1989. 67.70 (*90-6765-392-6*); pap. 44.65 (*90-6765-393-4*) Mouton.
Preston, Dennis R., ed. American Dialect Research: Celebrating the 100th Anniversary of the American Dialect Society, 1888-1989. LC 93-18385. xiv, 464p. 1993. 89.00 (*1-55619-488-9*); pap. 29.95 (*1-55619-489-7*) J Benjamins Pubng Co.
*__Preston, Dennis R., ed.__ Handbook of Perceptual Dialectology, Vol. 1. LC 99-25334. xi, 413p. 1999. 145.00 (*1-55619-534-6*) J Benjamins Pubng.
Preston, Dennis R., jt. ed. see Bayley, Robert.
Preston, Dennis Richard, jt. auth. see Niedzielski, Nancy A.
*__Preston, Diana.__ The Boxer Rebellion: The Dramatic Story of China's War on Foreigners That Shook the World in the Summer of 1900. (Illus.). 432p. 2000. 27.00 (*0-8027-1361-0*) Walker & Co.
Preston, Diana. A First-Rate Tragedy: Robert Falcon Scott & the Race to the South Pole. 304p. 1998. 25.00 (*0-395-93349-8*) HM.
— A First Rate Tragedy: Robert Falcon Scott & the Race to the South Pole. (Illus.). 304p. 1999. pap. 14.00 (*0-618-00201-4*, Mariner Bks) HM.
Preston, Dickson J. Newspapers of Maryland's Eastern Shore. LC 85-40533. (Illus.). 290p. 1986. reprint ed. pap. 89.90 (*0-7837-9082-1*, 204983200003) Bks Demand.
— Talbot County: A History. Harrington, Norman, ed. LC 83-40048. (Illus.). 396p. 1983. reprint ed. pap. 122.80 (*0-7837-9091-0*, 204984100003) Bks Demand.
Preston, Dickson J. Wye Oak: The History of a Great Tree. LC 72-12911. (Illus.). 144p. 1972. reprint ed. pap. 44.70 (*0-608-02463-5*, 206310700004) Bks Demand.
Preston, Dietz. The Art of Experimental Physics. LC 90-33872. 448p. 1991. pap. 80.95 (*0-471-84748-8*) Wiley.
*__Preston, Don.__ Before They Ask: Talking about Sex from a Christian Perspective - A Guide for Parents of Children from Birth Through Age Twelve. (Orig.). 1999. pap. text 10.00 (*0-687-73855-5*) Abingdon.
Preston, Doris, jt. auth. see Lipsey, Robert E.
Preston, Doris C. Needle-Made Laces & Net Embroideries: Reticella Work, Carrickmacross Lace, Princess Lace & Other Traditional Techniques. (Illus.). 160p. 1984. reprint ed. pap. 5.95 (*0-486-24708-2*) Dover.
Preston, Douglas. Talking to the Ground: One Family's Journey on Horseback Across the Sacred Land of the Navajo. LC 95-48472. 284p. 1996. pap. 18.95 (*0-8263-1740-5*) U of NM Pr.
Preston, Douglas J. Cities of Gold: A Journey Across the American Southwest. LC 98-54583. (Illus.). 480p. 1999. pap. 15.95 (*0-8263-2086-4*) U of NM Pr.
— Cities of Gold: A Journey Across the American Southwest in Coronado's Footsteps. 480p. 1993. pap. 14.00 (*0-671-86990-6*, Touchstone) S&S Trade Pap.
— Dinosaurs in the Attic: An Excursion into the American Museum of Natural History. (Illus.). 256p. 1993. pap. 13.95 (*0-312-10456-1*) St Martin.
— Jennie. 1997. mass mkt. 6.99 (*0-8125-6533-9*, Pub. by Tor Bks) St Martin.
Preston, Douglas J. Jennie. 1997. 12.34 (*0-606-13535-9*) Turtleback.
— Relic. LC 94-44321. (J). 1996. 12.09 (*0-606-11786-5*, Pub. by Turtleback) Demco.
— Reliquary: Sequel to the Relic! 464p. 1998. mass mkt. 7.99 (*0-8125-4283-5*, Pub. by Tor Bks) St Martin.
Preston, Douglas J. Talking to the Ground: One Family's Journey on Horseback Across the Sacred Land of the Navajo. LC 94-46362. 288p. 1995. 24.00 (*0-684-80391-7*) S&S Trade.
*__Preston, Douglas J. & Child, Lincoln.__ The Ice Limit. LC 99-87229. 464p. 2000. 25.95 (*0-446-52587-1*, Pub. by Warner Bks) Little.
Preston, Douglas J. & Child, Lincoln. Mount Dragon. LC 95-41323. 349p. (J). 1996. 22.95 (*0-312-86042-0*) Forge NYC.
— Mount Dragon. LC 95-41323. (J). mass mkt. 6.99 (*0-8125-6437-5*, Pub. by Tor Bks) St Martin.
— Mount Dragon. (J). 1997. mass mkt. 6.99 (*0-614-20533-6*) Tor Bks.
— Relic. 474p. (J). 1996. mass mkt. 6.99 (*0-8125-4326-2*, Pub. by Tor Bks) St Martin.
— Relic. (J). 1996. mass mkt. 6.99 (*0-8125-6358-1*, Pub. by Tor Bks) St Martin.
— Reliquary: Sequel to the Relic! 1997. 24.95 (*0-614-27906-2*) Forge NYC.
— Reliquary: Sequel to the Relic! LC 96-53533. 384p. 1997. text 24.95 (*0-312-86095-1*) St Martin.
— Riptide. LC 97-23907. 420p. 1998. 25.00 (*0-446-52336-4*, Pub. by Warner Bks) Little.
— Riptide. 465p. 1999. mass mkt. 7.50 (*0-446-60717-7*, Pub. by Warner Bks) Little.
Preston, Douglas J. & Child, Lincoln. Thunderhead. LC 98-37557. 432p. 1999. 25.95 (*0-446-52337-2*, Pub. by Warner Bks) Little.
*__Preston, Douglas J. & Child, Lincoln.__ Thunderhead. 560p. 2000. mass mkt. 7.50 (*0-446-60837-8*) Warner Bks.
Preston, Douglas J., et al. The Royal Road: El Camino Real from Mexico City to Santa Fe. LC 97-47236. (Illus.). 179p. 1998. 55.00 (*0-8263-1935-1*); pap. 26.95 (*0-8263-1936-X*) U of NM Pr.
Preston-Dunlop, Valerie. Rudolf Laban: An Extraordinary Life. (Illus.). 360p. 39.95 (*1-85273-060-9*, Pub. by Dance Bks) Princeton Bk Co.
Preston-Dunlop, Valerie, compiled by. Dance Words. (Choreography & Dance Studies: Vol. 8). 707p. 1995. text 56.00 (*3-7186-5601-9*, ECU70, Harwood Acad Pubs); pap. text 18.00 (*3-7186-5605-1*, ECU23, Harwood Acad Pubs) Gordon & Breach.
Preston-Dunlop, Valerie, ed. Schrifttanz: German Modern Dance Writings of the 1920s & 1930s. (Illus.). 136p. 1990. pap. text 24.95 (*1-85273-016-1*, Dance Horizons) Princeton Bk Co.
Preston, E. M., jt. ed. see Lauenroth, W. K.
Preston, E. W. Life & Its Spirals: History in the Light of Theosophy. 1990. pap. 9.50 (*81-7059-137-6*, 7161, Quest) Theos Pub Hse.
Preston, Ed, jt. auth. see Kerr, Bob.
*__Preston, Edmund.__ FAA Historical Chronology: Civil Aviation & the Federal Government, 1926-1996. 375p. 1998. per. 29.00 (*0-16-062445-2*) USGPO.
Preston, Edward. How to Buy Land Cheap. 5th ed. 1998. pap. text 14.95 (*0-9666932-7-2*) Breakout Prods Inc.
Preston, Edward J. & Crawford. CAD-CAM Dictionary. (Mechanical Engineering Ser.: Vol. 43). (Illus.). 224p. 1985. text 125.00 (*0-8247-7524-4*) Dekker.
Preston, Elaine. Fishing Underground. 100p. (Orig.). 1997. pap. text 17.50 (*0-9620790-1-4*) H & H Pr.
— Look for a Field to Land: Poems. LC 94-7129. 74p. (Orig.). 1994. pap. 8.95 (*1-882593-06-5*) Bridge Wrks.
Preston, Elizabeth. Preparing your Manuscript. rev. ed. LC 93-43417. 114p. 1994. pap. 12.00 (*0-87116-172-9*) Writer.
Preston, Elizabeth, jt. auth. see Preston, Thomas.
Preston, Elizabeth, ed. see Blavatsky, Helena P.
*__Preston, Fayrene.__ The Barons of Texas: Jill. 2000. per. 3.99 (*0-373-76288-7*) Silhouette.
Preston, Fayrene. The Barons of Texas: Tess. (Desire Ser.: No. 1240). 1999. mass mkt. 3.75 (*0-373-76240-2*, 1-76240-0) Silhouette.
— In Guilty Night. 352p. 1998. mass mkt. 5.99 (*0-553-57582-1*) Bantam.
*__Preston, Fayrene.__ Suenos de Pasion. (Deseo Ser.: Vol. 225). (SPA.). 2000. mass mkt. 3.50 (*0-373-35355-3*, Harlequin) Harlequin Bks.
Preston Foster, M. Looking It Up. (J). (gr. 2-5). 1988. pap. 8.99 (*0-8224-4345-7*) Fearon Teacher Aids.
Preston-Foster, Mary. Fun With Fiction. (J). (gr. 2-5). 1988. pap. 9.99 (*0-8224-3173-4*) Fearon Teacher Aids.
*__Preston, Frank E.__ California Uninsured Motorist Practice - 12/98 Update. Waxman, Robert N., ed. LC 72-619679. 268p. 1998. ring bd. 46.00 (*0-7626-0281-3*, TO-30583) Cont Ed Bar-CA.
— California Uninsured Motorist Practice - 12/99 Update. Piatt, Norma, ed. LC 72-61979. 273p. 1999. pap. text 47.00 (*0-7626-0378-X*, TO-30584) Cont Ed Bar-CA.
Preston, Frederick. Sociology: Approaches to Issues & Everyday Applications. 222p. (C). 1997. text 39.00 (*0-536-00120-0*) Pearson Custom.
Preston, Frederick W. & Beal, John M. Basic Surgical Physiology. LC 69-13375. (Illus.). 508p. reprint ed. pap. 157.50 (*0-8357-9598-5*, 201310300085) Bks Demand.
Preston, Fredrica A. Memory Bank for Chemotherapy. 256p. 1987. spiral bd. 19.95 (*0-683-06972-1*) Jones & Bartlett.
Preston, Fredrica A. & Wilfinger, Cecila. Chemotherapy Memory Bank. 2nd ed. (Nursing-Health Science Ser.). 264p. (C). 1992. pap. text, spiral bd. 31.25 (*0-86720-629-2*) Jones & Bartlett.
Preston, Fredrica A. & Wilfinger, Cecilia. Memory Bank for Chemotherapy. 3rd ed. LC 96-21045. 1996. pap., spiral bd. 31.25 (*0-86720-740-X*) Jones & Bartlett.
Preston, G. B., jt. auth. see Clifford, A. H.
*__Preston, Gary D.__ Character Forged from Conflict. LC 99-6477. (Pastor's Soul Ser.). 176p. 1999. 16.99 (*1-55661-973-1*) Bethany Hse.
Preston, Gates & Ellis Staff. Washington Environmental Law Handbook. 3rd ed. LC 98-120549. (State Environment Law Ser.). 388p. (Orig.). 1997. pap. text 95.00 (*0-86587-556-1*) Gov Insts.
Preston, Geoffrey. Faces of the Church: Meditations on a Mystery & Its Images. LC 97-158038. 1997. pap. text 35.00 (*0-8028-4353-0*) Eerdmans.
Preston, George R., Jr. Thomas Wolfe: A Bibliography. LC 74-12760. (Illus.). 1979. reprint ed. lib. bdg. 65.00 (*0-8371-7750-2*, PRTW, Greenwood Pr) Greenwood.
Preston, Georgette. Songs of Cities. 30p. (Orig.). (C). 1992. pap. text 5.00 (*1-878173-27-8*) Birnham Wood.
Preston, Gilbert. Wilderness First Aid: When You Can't Call 911. LC 97-11567. (Illus.). 128p. 1997. pap. 6.95 (*1-56044-579-3*) Falcon Pub Inc.
Preston-Gomez, Cheryl & Reisfeld, Randi. When No Means No: A Guide to Sexual Harassment by a Woman Who Won a Million Dollar Verdict. 224p. 1992. 17.95 (*1-55972-143-X*, Birch Ln Pr) Carol Pub Group.
Preston, H. B. Mollusca Vol. 4: Freshwater Gastropoda & Pelycypoda. (Fauna of British India Ser.). xx, 246p. 1978. reprint ed. 30.00 (*0-88065-177-6*) Scholarly Pubns.
Preston, Harriet W., tr. see Sainte-Beuve, Charles-Augustin.
Preston, Harry, ed. see Teutsch, Austin.
Preston, Howard H. History of Banking in Iowa. Bruchey, Stuart, ed. LC 80-1167. (Rise of Commercial Banking Ser.). (Illus.). 1981. reprint ed. lib. bdg. 42.95 (*0-405-13677-3*) Ayer.
Preston, Howard L. Dirt Roads to Dixie: Accessibility & Modernization in the South. LC 90-37726. (Illus.). 220p. 1991. pap. 18.95 (*0-87049-677-8*); text 38.50 (*0-87049-676-X*) U of Tenn Pr.
Preston, Howard L., jt. ed. see Dunn, Joe P.
Preston, Irene F. & Seltman, Arthur J. Coinage of the Crusader States, 1098-1291. (Illus.). 1994. write for info. (*0-915018-39-X*) Attic Bks.
Preston, Ivan L. The Great American Blow-up: Puffery in Advertising & Selling. rev. ed. LC 96-8273. 252p. 1996. pap. 17.95 (*0-299-15254-5*) U of Wis Pr.
— The Tangled Web They Weave: Truth, Falsity, & Advertisers. LC 93-39166. 236p. 1996. pap. 15.95 (*0-299-14194-2*) U of Wis Pr.
Preston, Ivy. The Blue Remembered Hills. large type ed. (Linford Romance Library). 304p. 1988. pap. 10.95 (*0-7089-6594-6*, Linford) Ulverscroft.
— A Fleeting Breath. large type ed. (Romance Ser.). 1991. 27.99 (*0-7089-2556-1*) Ulverscroft.
— The House above the Bay. large type ed. (Linford Romance Library). 304p. 1996. pap. 16.99 (*0-7089-7849-5*, Linford) Ulverscroft.
— Interlude in Greece. large type ed. (Linford Romance Library). 256p. 1994. pap. 16.99 (*0-7089-7516-X*, Linford) Ulverscroft.
— Love in Las Vegas. (Rainbow Romances Ser.). 160p. 1993. 14.95 (*0-7090-4830-0*) Parkwest Pubns.
— Love in Las Vegas. large type ed. (Linford Romance Library). 1994. pap. 16.99 (*0-7089-7622-0*, Linford) Ulverscroft.
— Moonlight on the Lake. large type ed. (Linford Romance Library). 1990. pap. 16.99 (*0-7089-6886-4*, Linford) Ulverscroft.
— Mountain Magic. large type ed. (Romance Ser.). 288p. 1992. 27.99 (*0-7089-2683-5*) Ulverscroft.
— None So Blind. large type ed. (Linford Romance Library). 336p. 1989. pap. 16.99 (*0-7089-6706-X*, Linford) Ulverscroft.
— Nurse in Confusion. large type ed. (Linford Romance Library). 288p. 1996. pap. 16.99 (*0-7089-7904-1*) Ulverscroft.
— One Broken Dream. large type ed. (Dales Large Print Ser.). 257p. 1997. pap. 18.99 (*1-85389-718-3*) Ulverscroft.
— Pacific Magic. large type ed. (Romance Ser.). 320p. 1987. 27.99 (*0-7089-1690-2*) Ulverscroft.
— Petals in the Wind. large type ed. (Linford Romance Library). 320p. 1992. pap. 16.99 (*0-7089-7207-1*, Linford) Ulverscroft.
— Portrait of Pierre. large type ed. (Linford Romance Library). 320p. 1992. pap. 16.99 (*0-7089-7136-9*, Linford) Ulverscroft.
— Release the Past. large type ed. (Romance Ser.). 1989. 27.99 (*0-7089-2078-0*) Ulverscroft.

An Asterisk (*) at the beginning of an entry indicates that the title is appearing for the first time.

— Romance in Glenmore Street. large type ed. (Romance Ser.). 1991. 27.99 (*0-7089-2467-0*) Ulverscroft.

— The Secret Love of Nurse Wilson. large type ed. (Linford Romance Library). 1988. pap. 10.95 (*0-7089-6480-X*, Linford) Ulverscroft.

— Stranger from the Sea. large type ed. (Linford Romance Library). 240p. 1992. pap. 16.99 (*0-7089-7294-2*) Ulverscroft.

— Summer at Willowbank. large type ed. (Romance Ser.). 1994. pap. 16.99 (*0-7089-7611-5*, Linford) Ulverscroft.

— Sunlit Seas. large type ed. (Linford Romance Library). 304p. 1994. pap. 16.99 (*0-7089-7535-6*, Linford) Ulverscroft.

— Voyage of Destiny. large type ed. (Linford Romance Library). 1990. pap. 16.99 (*0-7089-6827-9*) Ulverscroft.

— Where Ratas Twine. large type ed. (Linford Romance Library). 336p. 1993. pap. 16.99 (*0-7089-7326-4*, Linford) Ulverscroft.

— Where Stars May Lead. large type ed. (Romance Ser.). 304p. 1995. pap. 16.99 (*0-7089-7668-9*, Linford) Ulverscroft.

Preston, Izola, jt. auth. see Morgan, Gordon D.

Preston, Izola, jt. auth. see Morgan, Marian.

Preston, J. & Ferrett, R. Access 97 Essentials: Level II. LC 97-65608. 224p. 1997. 22.99 (*1-57576-805-4*) Sams.

Preston, J., et al. Access 97 Essentials: Level III. LC 97-65614. (Illus.). 224p. 1997. 22.99 (*1-57576-804-6*) Sams.

Preston, J., jt. auth. see Lewin, M.

Preston, J., jt. ed. see Black, W. Bruce.

Preston, J. B., ed. see Battle, James.

Preston, Jack. Handbook of Fiber Science & Technology. Lewin, Menachem, ed. (International Fiber Science & Technology Ser.: Vol. 12). (Illus.). 408p. 1993. text 245.00 (*0-8247-8866-4*) Dekker.

Preston, Jack, jt. auth. see Lewin, M.

Preston, Jack, jt. ed. see Lewin, Menachem.

Preston, Jack D. Perspectives in Dental Ceramics. (Illus.). 472p. 1988. text 160.00 (*0-86715-136-6*, 1366) Quint Pub Co.

Preston, Jack D., ed. Computer in Clinical Dentistry: Proceedings of the First International Conference, Houston, Texas, September 26-29, 1991. LC 92-49188. (Illus.). 228p. 1993. pap. text 52.00 (*0-86715-229-X*) Quint Pub Co.

Preston, Jacqueline N., ed. see Bellucci, Elio C.

Preston, James. Bushfire. 1993. 18.00 (*0-86025-258-2*, Pub. by I Henry Pubns) Empire Pub Srvs.

Preston, James, jt. auth. see Alexander, Marilyn B.

Preston, James, jt. ed. see Misra, Bhabagrahi.

***Preston, James Barton.** Open Book: The Life & Times of James Barton Preston. LC 00-40016. (YA). 2000. write for info. (*0-87562-113-9*) Spec Child.

Preston, James F. Air Conditioning & Refrigeration Technician's EPA Certification Guide: Getting Certified, Understanding the Rules, & Preparation for EPA Inspections. Damp, Dennis V., ed. LC 94-71513. (Illus.). 192p. (Orig.). 1994. pap. 29.95 (*0-943641-10-1*) Bookhaven Pr.

Preston, James J. Cult of the Goddess: Social & Religious Change in a Hindu Temple. (Illus.). 109p. (C). 1985. reprint ed. pap. text 10.50 (*0-88133-135-X*) Waveland Pr.

Preston, James J., ed. Mother Worship: Theme & Variations. LC 81-3336. (Studies in Religion). (Illus.). 384p. 1982. pap. 119.10 (*0-608-05209-4*, 206574600001) Bks Demand.

***Preston, Jane.** 5 versus the Rest of the World. 96p. 1999. pap. 9.95 (*0-440-41656-6*) Dell.

Preston, Jean F. & Yeandle, Laetitia. English Handwriting, 1400-1650: An Introductory Manual. 116p. 1992. pap. 19.95 (*0-86698-086-5*, P6) Pegasus Pr.

Preston, Jeff, jt. auth. see Simon, Mary Manz.

Preston, Jill. International Business: Text & Cases. 352p. (Orig.). 1993. pap. 47.50 (*0-273-60148-2*, Pub. by Pitman Pub) Trans-Atl Phila.

Preston, John. Access for Windows 95 Essentials. LC 95-72179. 224p. 1996. pap. text 22.99 (*1-57576-263-3*) Que Educ & Trng.

— Access for Windows 95 Essentials, IM. 1995. teacher ed., ring bd. 49.99 (*1-57576-264-1*) Que Educ & Trng.

— Access for Windows 95 Essentials, Level 2. LC 95-72494. 168p. 1996. pap. text 22.99 (*1-57576-265-X*) Que Educ & Trng.

Preston, John. Access for Windows 95 Essentials, Level 2. 1996. teacher ed., ring bd. 49.99 (*1-57576-266-8*) Que Educ & Trng.

— The Arena. (Orig.). 1993. mass mkt. 4.95 (*1-56333-083-0*, Badboy) Masquerade.

Preston, John. Basic Smartstart. LC 93-86490. 233p. 1994. 25.99 (*1-56529-402-5*) Que.

Preston, John. Breastplate of Faith & Love. large type ed. 537p. 1979. reprint ed. 37.99 (*0-85151-289-5*) Banner of Truth.

***Preston, John.** Clinical Psychopharmacology Made Ridiculously Simple. 4th ed. (Illus.). 73p. 2000. pap. text 13.95 (*0-940780-44-5*) MedMaster.

Preston, John. Deadly Lies. (Mission of Alex Kane Ser.: No. 3). 1993. reprint ed. mass mkt. 4.95 (*1-56333-076-8*, Badboy) Masquerade.

— Excel for Windows Essentials. LC 94-69259. 184p. 1995. 22.99 (*0-7897-0109-X*) Macmillan USA.

— Feyerabend: Philosophy, Science & Society. LC 97-10139. 248p. 1997. 60.95 (*0-7456-1675-5*, Pub. by Polity Pr); pap. 25.95 (*0-7456-1676-3*, Pub. by Polity Pr) Blackwell Pubs.

— First Run DBase IV. 1993. 16.00 (*1-56529-419-X*) Que.

— First Run Excel for Windows. 1993. 16.00 (*1-56529-420-3*) Que.

— First Run Lotus 1-2-3 R2.X. 1993. 16.00 (*1-56529-421-1*) Que.

Preston, John. Groupwise for Windows 3.1 Essentials. 1995. pap. text 22.99 (*1-57576-271-4*) Que Educ & Trng.

Preston, John. The Heir - the King. (Orig.). 1992. mass mkt. 4.95 (*1-56333-048-2*, Badboy) Masquerade.

— Hustling: A Gentleman's Guide to the Fine Art of Homosexual Prostitution. 2nd rev. ed. (Orig.). 1997. reprint ed. mass mkt. 6.50 (*1-56333-517-4*, Badboy) Masquerade.

— I Once Had a Master: And Other Tales of Erotic Love. 121p. (Orig.). 1984. pap. 8.95 (*0-932870-51-1*) Alyson Pubns.

— In Search of a Master. 1989. pap. 7.95 (*0-8216-2005-3*, Univ Books) Carol Pub Group.

— Integrative Brief Therapy: Cognitive, Psychodynamic, Humanistic & Neurobehavioral Approaches. LC 98-7498. (Practical Therapist Ser.: Vol. 1). 272p. 1998. 27.95 (*1-886230-09-9*) Impact Pubs CA.

Preston, John. An Interactive Guide to the Internet. 240p. 1996. 75.00 (*1-57576-354-0*) Macmillan.

Preston, John. Journals of a Master: Entertainment for a Master & the Love of a Master. LC 97-11710. 311p. (Orig.). 1997. pap. 12.95 (*1-55583-401-9*) Alyson Pubns.

***Preston, John.** Learn Access, 2000. LC 98-88901. 342p. 2000. pap. text 37.33 (*1-58076-258-1*) Que Educ & Trng.

Preston, John. Lethal Silence. rev. ed. (Mission of Alex Kane Ser.). (Orig.). 1993. mass mkt. 4.95 (*1-56333-125-X*, Badboy) Masquerade.

— Lotus Smartstart Essentials. 1995. 49.99 (*0-7897-0421-8*) Que.

***Preston, John.** Mr. Benson. 2nd rev. ed. 1998. mass mkt. 6.95 (*1-56333-636-7*, Badboy) Masquerade.

Preston, John. My Life As a Pornographer & Other Indecent Acts. (Orig.). 1993. pap. 12.95 (*1-56333-135-7*, R Kasak Bks) Masquerade.

— Novell Netware Smartstart. LC 93-86488. 179p. 1994. 25.99 (*1-56529-411-4*) Que.

— Paradox 5 for Windows SmartStart. LC 94-68909. 276p. 1995. 29.99 (*0-7897-0011-5*) Que.

— Practice Using Excel 5 for Windows. LC 94-68008. 1994. wbk. ed. 27.99 (*1-56529-873-X*) Que.

Preston, John. Practice Using Windows 3.1 Wkbk. LC 93-86493. 269p. 1993. 27.99 (*1-56529-669-9*) Que.

— Practice Using Word 6 for Windows Wkbk. LC 94-68006. 343p. 1995. pap. text, wbk. ed. 27.99 (*1-56529-878-0*) Que Educ & Trng.

Preston, John. Quattro Pro 6 for Windows Essentials. LC 94-69261. 195p. 1995. 22.99 (*0-7897-0107-3*) Que.

— The Saints Daily Exercise. LC 76-57409. (English Experience Ser.: No. 824). 1977. reprint ed. lib. bdg. 60.00 (*90-221-0824-4*) Walter J Johnson.

— Secret Danger. rev. ed. (Mission of Alex Kane Ser.). (Orig.). 1993. mass mkt. 4.95 (*1-56333-111-X*, Badboy) Masquerade.

— Stolen Moments. (Mission of Alex Kane Ser.). (Orig.). 1993. reprint ed. mass mkt. 4.95 (*1-56333-098-9*, Badboy) Masquerade.

— Tales from the Dark Lord. 2nd ed. (Orig.). 1995. mass mkt. 5.95 (*1-56333-323-6*, Badboy) Masquerade.

— Tales from the Dark Lord II. (Orig.). 1994. mass mkt. 4.95 (*1-56333-176-4*, Badboy) Masquerade.

— Windows 3.1 Smartstart. 1993. teacher ed. 39.99 (*1-56529-220-0*) Que.

— Windows 3.1 First Run. 1993. 16.00 (*1-56529-425-4*) Que.

— Windows 3.1 Smartstart. 2nd ed. LC 94-68905. 255p. 1994. pap. text 29.99 (*0-7897-0010-7*) Que Educ & Trng.

— Winter's Light: Reflections of a Yankee Queer. Lowenthal, Michael, ed. & intro. by. LC 94-48734. 199p. 1995. pap. 14.95 (*0-87451-781-8*) U Pr of New Eng.

— Word for Windows 95 Essentials, IM. 1996. pap. text, teacher ed. 49.99 (*1-57576-275-7*) Que Educ & Trng.

Preston, John. Word 2.0 for Windows SmartStart. LC 93-83198. 238p. 1993. 25.99 (*1-56529-204-9*) Que.

— Works 3.0 for DOS SmartStart. LC 93-86483. 356p. 1993. 25.99 (*1-56529-396-7*) Que.

Preston, John. You Can Beat Depression: A Guide to Prevention & Recovery. 2nd rev. ed. LC 96-20175. 176p. 1996. pap. 13.95 (*1-886230-02-1*) Impact Pubs CA.

Preston, John, ed. Flesh & the Word: An Anthology of Erotic Writing. 320p. 1994. pap. 15.95 (*0-452-26775-7*, Plume) Dutton Plume.

— Friends & Lovers: Gay Men Write about the Families They Create. 1996. pap. 12.95 (*0-452-27254-8*, Plume) Dutton Plume.

— Hot Living: Erotic Stories about Safer Sex. 194p. (Orig.). 1985. pap. 8.95 (*0-932870-85-6*) Alyson Pubns.

— Personal Dispatches: Writers Confront AIDS. 208p. 1990. pap. 8.95 (*0-312-05141-7*) St Martin.

Preston, John, et al, eds. The Worst Enemy of Science? Essays in Memory of Paul Feyerabend. LC 99-13710. (Illus.). 192p. 2000. text 45.00 (*0-19-512874-5*) OUP.

Preston, John, intro. The Flesh & the Word 2. 336p. (Orig.). 1993. pap. 14.95 (*0-452-27087-1*, Plume) Dutton Plume.

***Preston, John & Ferrett, Robert.** Access for Windows 95 Essentials, Level Iii. 2nd ed. 162p. (C). 1998. pap. text 21.33 (*1-58076-156-9*) Que Educ & Trng.

Preston, John & Lowenthal, Michael, eds. Flesh & the Word No. 3: An Anthology of Gay Erotic Writing. LC 94-42651. 1995. pap. 14.95 (*0-452-27252-1*, Plume) Dutton Plume.

***Preston, John, et al.** Access 2000 Essentials Intermediate. LC 98-89902. (Illus.). 239p. 2000. pap. 18.67 (*1-58076-301-4*) Que Educ & Trng.

— Every Session Counts: Making the Most Out of Your Brief Therapy. 2nd ed. (Illus.). 140p. 2000. pap. 10.95 (*1-57224-190-X*) New Harbinger.

— Learn Excel 2000. 293p. 1999. pap. text 32.00 (*1-58076-261-1*) Que Educ & Trng.

— Learn Office 2000 with CD-ROM. 310p. (C). 1999. pap. 50.67 incl. audio compact disk (*1-58076-263-8*) Que Educ & Trng.

— Learn Word 2000. 330p. 1999. pap. text 32.00 (*1-58076-262-X*) Que Educ & Trng.

— Learn Word 97. 2nd ed. LC 98-89900. (Illus.). 240p. (C). 1999. pap. text. write for info. (*1-58076-326-X*) Que Educ & Trng.

Preston, John, et al. The Puritans on Prayer. Kistler, Don, ed. 293p. 1995. 24.95 (*1-877611-77-8*) Soli Deo Gloria.

***Preston, John, et al.** Transition from Access 3 to Access for Windows 95 Essentials. 150p. 1998. pap. text 17.33 (*1-58076-069-4*) Que Educ & Trng.

Preston, John, et al. Understanding Psychiatric Medications in the Treatment of Chemical Dependency & Dual Diagnoses. (Illus.). 134p. (C). 1995. pap. text 28.95 (*0-398-05964-0*) C C Thomas.

Preston, John, jt. auth. see Mackie, Peter.

Preston, John, ed. see Feyerabend, Paul K.

Preston, John D. Shorter Term Treatments for Borderline Personality Disorders. LC 97-66082. 184p. 1997. text 49.95 (*1-57224-092-X*) New Harbinger.

Preston, John D., et al. Consumer's Guide to Psychiatric Drugs. LC 97-75482. 272p. 1998. pap. 16.95 (*1-57224-111-X*) New Harbinger.

— Handbook of Clinical Psychopharmacology for Therapists. 2nd rev. ed. LC 97-69492. (Illus.). 264p. 1997. text 49.95 (*1-57224-094-6*) New Harbinger.

— Understanding Psychiatric Medications in the Treatment of Chemical Dependency & Dual Diagnoses. (Illus.). 134p. (C). 1995. text 39.95 (*0-398-05963-2*) C C Thomas.

Preston, John H. The Liberals. LC 74-22803. (Labor Movement in Fiction & Non-Fiction Ser.). reprint ed. 45.00 (*0-404-58460-8*) AMS Pr.

***Preston, John M.** Learn PowerPoint 2000. (Illus.). 2000. pap. text 32.00 (*1-58076-257-3*) Que Educ & Trng.

Preston, John M. & Ferret, Robert. Access for Windows 95 Smartstart. LC 95-74883. (Smartstart Ser.). (Illus.). 259p. 1997. pap. 29.99 (*1-57576-030-4*) Que Educ & Trng.

Preston, John M. & Ferrett, Robert. Word 6.0 for Windows with Style Manual References. 160p. (C). 1995. spiral bd. 21.75 (*0-697-26016-X*) Bus & Educ Tech.

— Word 6.0 For Windows with Style Manuals. 192p. (C). 1995. text 15.75 (*0-256-20437-3*, Irwn McGrw-H) McGrw-H Hghr Educ.

***Preston, John M., et al.** Access 2000 Essentials Basic. (Illus.). 238p. 2000. pap. text 18.80 (*1-58076-094-5*) Que Educ & Trng.

Preston, John M., et al. Access 97 Smartstart. LC 97-65617. 1997. 29.99 (*1-57576-818-6*) Que Educ & Trng.

Preston, Joseph H. Arundel: A History of the Town & the Castle. LC 91-51134. (Illus.). 296p. 1993. 48.50 (*0-945636-39-3*) Susquehanna.

Preston, Judy J. The Outer Banks Story. (Illus.). 117p. (Orig.). (J). (gr. 5 up). 1985. pap. 4.25 (*0-9613824-0-6*) Seabright.

***Preston, Julia.** Le Mariage Force: A Comedie-Ballet by Molier. (FRE.). 1999. pap. 24.95 (*0-85989-643-9*) Univ Exeter Pr.

Preston, K. Blake & Rossetti. LC 73-117999. (Studies in Comparative Literature: No. 35). 1970. reprint ed. lib. bdg. 75.00 (*0-8383-1054-0*) M S G Haskell Hse.

Preston, K., Jr. & Duff, M. J. Modern Cellular Automata: Theory & Applications. LC 84-11672. (Advanced Applications in Pattern Recognition Ser.). (Illus.). 368p. (C). 1984. 95.00 (*0-306-41737-5*, Plenum Trade) Perseus Pubng.

Preston, Karl. Commercialmania: The Successful TV Commercial Actor's Manual. (Illus.). 287p. 1999. pap. 24.95 (*0-9641513-6-7*) Dog Gone Bks.

— Modelmania: The Working Model's Manual. LC 98-92863. (Illus.). 232p. 1998. pap. 21.95 (*0-9641513-5-9*) Dog Gone Bks.

Preston, Karl, jt. auth. see Hullana, Lisa.

Preston, Kath. Inn of the Few: 1932-1971. 128p. 1997. pap. 52.00 (*1-873376-17-0*, Pub. by Spellmnt Pubs) St Mut.

Preston, Katharine, jt. auth. see Davis, Anita.

Preston, Katherine. Scott Joplin: Ragtime Musician. (Black American Ser.). (Illus.). 192p. (YA). (gr. 4-7). 1990. mass mkt. 3.95 (*0-87067-557-5*, Melrose Sq) Holloway.

Preston, Katherine K. Music for Hire: A Study of Professional Musicians in Washington, 1877-1900. LC 85-28399. (Sociology of Music Ser.: No. 6). (Illus.). 280p. 1992. lib. bdg. 47.00 (*0-918728-66-5*) Pendragon NY.

— Opera on the Road: Traveling Opera Troupes in the United States, 1825-60. LC 92-20644. (Music in American Life Ser.). (Illus.). 496p. (C). 1993. text 39.95 (*0-252-01974-1*) U of Ill Pr.

Preston, Katherine K., ed. Irish American Theater: The Mulligan Guard Ball (1879) & Reilly & the Four Hundred (1891), Scripts by Edward Harrigan, Music by David Braham. fac. ed. LC 94-584. (Nineteenth-Century American Musical Theater Ser.: No. 10). (Illus.). 452p. 1994. text 132.00 (*0-8153-1376-4*) Garland.

Preston, Kathleen, jt. auth. see Corbett, Kathryn L.

Preston, Ken R., jt. ed. see Rasper, Vladimir F.

Preston, Kim, jt. ed. see Sampford, Charles.

Preston, Kitty. Scott Joplin: Composer. Huggins, Nathan I., ed. (Black Americans of Achievement Ser.). (Illus.). 124p. (Orig.). (YA). (gr. 5 up). 1987. lib. bdg. 19.95 (*1-55546-598-6*) Chelsea Hse.

— Scott Joplin: Composer. Huggins, Nathan I., ed. (Black Americans of Achievement Ser.). (Illus.). 124p. (Orig.). (YA). (gr. 5 up). 1989. pap. 8.95 (*0-7910-0205-5*) Chelsea Hse.

Preston, Larry M. Freedom & the Organizational Republic. LC 92-14093. (Studies in North America: No. 6). xi, 235p. (C). 1992. lib. bdg. 113.85 (*3-11-013418-7*, 101-92) De Gruyter.

Preston, Laura G. Curtis Family: A Record of Some of the Descendants of Deodatus Curtis of Braintree, Massachusetts. 166p. 1997. reprint ed. pap. 25.00 (*0-8328-8178-3*); reprint ed. lib. bdg. 35.00 (*0-8328-8177-5*) Higginson Bk Co.

Preston, Lee E. The Rules of the Game in the Global Economy: Policy Regimes for International Business. LC 97-1578. 280p. (C). 1997. pap. text 55.00 (*0-7923-9888-2*) Kluwer Academic.

Preston, Lee E. The Rules of the Game in the Global Economy: Policy Regimes for International Business. 2nd ed. LC 97-1578. 280p. (C). 1997. lib. bdg. 125.00 (*0-7923-9887-4*) Kluwer Academic.

Preston, Lee E., ed. Business & Politics: Research Issues & Empirical Studies. LC 90-4473. (Research in Corporate Social Performance & Policy Ser.). 322p. 1990. pap. 25.75 (*1-55938-224-4*) Jai Pr.

— Corporation & Society Research: Studies in Theory & Measurement. LC 90-4604. (Research in Corporate Social Performance & Policy Ser.). 306p. 1990. pap. 25.75 (*1-55938-222-8*) Jai Pr.

— Government Regulation & Business Response: Research Issues & Empirical Studies. LC 90-4490. (Research in Corporate Social Performance & Policy Ser.). 302p. 1990. pap. 25.75 (*1-55938-226-0*) Jai Pr.

— International & Comparative Corporation & Society Research. (Research in Corporate Social Performance & Policy Ser.). 302p. 1990. pap. 25.75 (*1-55938-223-6*) Jai Pr.

Preston, Lee E., jt. ed. see Frederick, William C.

Preston, Lee H. The Rules of the Game in the Global Economy: Policy Regimes for International Business. 320p. (C). 1992. lib. bdg. 154.50 (*0-7923-9225-6*) Kluwer Academic.

Preston, Lewis T., frwd. The World Bank Policy on Disclosure of Information. LC 94-174634. 24p. 1994. pap. write for info. (*0-8213-2807-7*, 12807) World Bank.

Preston, Linda A. & Hecht, Jeffrey S. Spasticity Management: Rehabilitation Strategies. (Illus.). 1999. pap. text 20.00 (*1-56900-117-0*) Am Occup Therapy.

Preston, Lydia, jt. auth. see Alster, Tina S.

Preston, M. A. Structure of the Nucleus. (C). 1993. pap. 54.95 (*0-201-62729-9*) Addison-Wesley.

Preston-Mafham, Ken. Butterflies. (Identifying Guide Ser.). 1999. 7.99 (*0-7858-1111-7*) Bk Sales Inc.

— Frogs & Toads, Vol. 1. (Identifying Guide Ser.). 1999. 7.99 (*0-7858-1110-9*) Bk Sales Inc.

— Grasshoppers & Mantids of the World. (Illus.). 192p. 1998. pap. 17.95 (*0-7137-2381-5*, Pub. by Blandford Pr) Sterling.

— Identifying Bugs & Beetles. (Illus.). 80p. 1997. 7.98 (*0-7858-0877-9*) Bk Sales Inc.

— Madagascar: A Natural History. (Illus.). 224p. 1991. 45.00 (*0-8160-2403-0*) Facts on File.

— Spiders of the World. (Illus.). 192p. 1998. pap. 17.95 (*0-7137-2392-0*, Pub. by Blandford Pr) Sterling.

Preston-Mafham, Ken & Preston-Mafham, Rod. The Natural History of Spiders. (Illus.). 160p. 1997. 35.00 (*1-85223-966-2*, Pub. by Crolwood) Trafalgar.

Preston-Mafham, Ken, et al. Complete Identifier - Bugs, Beetles, Spiders & Snakes. (Illus.). 224p. 1999. pap. 15.95 (*1-57715-064-3*) Knckerbocker.

Preston-Mafham, Ken, jt. auth. see Preston-Mafham, Rod.

Preston-Mafham, Rod. Book of Spiders. 1998. 12.99 (*0-7858-0953-8*) Bk Sales Inc.

— Butterflies of the World. 192p. 1999. pap. text 19.95 (*0-7137-2790-X*) Blandford Pr.

— Primates of the World. 192p. 1999. pap. text 19.95 (*0-7137-2791-8*) Blandford Pr.

Preston-Mafham, Rod & Preston-Mafham, Ken. Butterflies of the World. (Of the World Ser.). (Illus.). 192p. 1988. 29.95 (*0-8160-1601-1*) Facts on File.

— Cacti: The Illustrated Dictionary. LC 96-45706. (Illus.). 224p. 1997. reprint ed. pap. 27.95 (*0-88192-400-8*) Timber.

— The Encyclopedia of Land Invertebrate Behavior. (Illus.). 320p. 1993. 50.00 (*0-262-16137-0*) MIT Pr.

— The Natural History of Insects. (Illus.). 160p. 1996. 35.00 (*1-85223-964-6*, Pub. by Crolwood) Trafalgar.

— Primates of the World. (Of the World Ser.). (Illus.). 192p. 1992. lib. bdg. 29.95 (*0-8160-2745-5*) Facts on File.

Preston-Mafham, Rod, jt. auth. see Preston-Mafham, Ken.

Preston, Margaret J. Aunt Dorothy: An Old Virginia Plantation Story. LC 72-1508. (Black Heritage Library Collection). (Illus.). 1977. reprint ed. 15.95 (*0-8369-9050-1*) Ayer.

***Preston, Margaret J.** Bible Wise Study Games & Circle of Love. 2000. pap. 10.00 (*0-8059-4940-2*) Dorrance.

Preston, Marianne K. & Morton, Jane. Fresh Herb Companion. LC 93-74031. (Traditional Country Life Recipe Ser.). (Illus.). 96p. (Orig.). 1994. pap. 9.95 (*1-883283-04-3*) Brick Tower.

Preston, Marianne K., jt. auth. see Morton, Jane W.

Preston, Marilynn. Be Well, Work Well. 100p. 1990. pap. 6.95 (*0-85013-178-2*) Dartnell Corp.

Preston, Mary. Spear - It Land. (Illus.). 177p. (Orig.). 1994. pap. 14.00 (*0-9636819-0-7*) Kairos Books.

Preston, Michael & Palley, Marian L., eds. Minorities & Policy Studies. (C). 1978. pap. 15.00 (*0-918592-29-1*) Pol Studies.

Preston, Michael B., et al, eds. Racial & Ethnic Politics in California, Vol. 2. LC 91-18676. 488p. (Orig.). (C). 1998. pap. 24.95 (*0-87772-328-1*) UCB IGS.

P

Preston, Michael D. Hypnosis: Medicine of the Mind. LC 99-182053. 232p. 1998. write for info. (0-933025-72-6) Blue Bird Pub.

Preston, Michael J., jt. ed. see Preston, Cathy L.

Preston, Monte L., jt. auth. see Preston, Ralph N.

Preston, Nathaniel S., jt. auth. see Abeles, Charles C.

Preston, Noel. Understanding Ethics. 219p. 1996. pap. 29.00 (1-86287-227-9, Pub. by Federation Pr) Gaunt.

Preston, Noel, ed. Ethics for the Public Sector: Education & Training. 277p. 1994. text 49.00 (1-86287-145-0, Pub. by Federation Pr) Gaunt.

Preston, Noel, et al, eds. Ethics & Political Practice: Perspectives on Legislative Ethics. (Studies in Public Sector Management: No. 2). 232p. (C). (gr. 13). 1998. 85.00 (0-415-19482-2, D6121) Routledge.

Preston, Noel, jt. ed. see Samford, Charles.

Preston, P. Literature in Adult Education Reflections on Practice. LC 96-175052. 1995. pap. 40.00 (1-85041-079-8, Pub. by Univ Nottingham) St Mut.

Preston, P. W. Development Theory: An Introduction. LC 95-52581. 320p. (C). 1996. 72.95 (0-631-19554-8); pap. 28.95 (0-631-19555-6) Blackwell Pubs.

— Making Sense of Development: An Introduction to Classical & Contemporary Theories of Development & Their Application to Southeast Asia. 304p. 1987. text 49.95 (0-7102-0813-8, Routledge Thoemms) Routledge.

— Theories of Development. (International Library of Sociology Ser.). 300p. 1982. 29.50 (0-7100-9055-2, Routledge Thoemms) Routledge.

Preston, Paschal, jt. ed. see Corcoran, Farrel.

Preston, Patricia T. Daytrips Ireland: 55 One Day Adventures - By Car, Rail, Bus & Walking Tours. 2nd ed. 400p. 2000. pap. 16.95 (0-8038-2003-8, Pub. by Hastings) Midpt Trade.

Preston, Paul. The Coming of the Spanish Civil War: Reform, Reaction & Revolution in the Second Republic. 1983. pap. 14.95 (0-416-35720-2, NO. 3948) Routledge.

— The Coming of the Spanish Civil War: Reform, Reaction & Revolution in the Second Republic. 2nd ed. LC 93-40967. 360p. (C). 1994. pap. 27.99 (0-415-06355-8, A7864) Routledge.

— Mother Father Deaf: Living Between Sound & Silence. LC 93-44895. 296p. (C). 1994. text 24.95 (0-674-58747-2) HUP.

— Mother Father Deaf: Living Between Sound & Silence. 288p. (C). 1995. pap. 15.95 (0-674-58748-0) HUP.

— The Politics of Revenge: Fascism & the Military in Twentieth Century Spain. 240p. (C). 1995. pap. 25.99 (0-415-12000-4, C0394) Routledge.

— Spain, EEC & NATO. 1985. pap. 10.95 (0-7100-9559-7, Routledge Thoemms) Routledge.

— The Triumph of Democracy in Spain. 263p. 1986. 35.00 (0-416-36350-4, 9880) Routledge.

— The Triumph of Democracy in Spain. 288p. 1987. pap. text 14.95 (0-416-90010-0) Routledge.

— The Triumph of Democracy in Spain. 288p. (C). 1987. pap. 25.99 (0-415-04314-X) Routledge.

Preston, Paul, ed. Revolution & War in Spain, 1931 to 1939. 320p. (Orig.). 1984. pap. 15.95 (0-416-34970-6, 9074) Routledge.

***Preston, Paul, et al.** British Documents on Foreign Affairs. LC 99-47481. 1999. write for info. (1-55655-769-8) U Pubns Amer.

— British Documents on Foreign Affairs. LC 99-55337. 1999. write for info. (1-55655-768-X) U Pubns Amer.

— British Documents on Foreign Affairs: Reports & Papers from the Foreign Office Confidential Print. LC 99-30575. 1999. write for info. (1-55655-764-7) U Pubns Amer.

— British Documents on Foreign Affairs: Reports & Papers from the Foreign Office Confidential Print. LC 00-34339. 2000. write for info. (1-55655-771-X) U Pubns Amer.

— British Documents on Foreign Affairs--Reports & Papers from the Foreign Office Confidential Print. LC 99-41498. 1999. write for info. (1-55655-770-1) U Pubns Amer.

— British Documents on Foreign Affairs--Reports & Papers from the Foreign Office Confidential Print. LC 00-26838. 2000. write for info. (1-55655-767-1) U Pubns Amer.

P

Preston, Paul, jt. auth. see Balfour, Sebastian.

Preston, Paul, jt. ed. see Lanon, Frances.

Preston, Percy. A Dictionary of Pictorial Subjects from Classical Literature: A Guide to Their Identification in Works of Art. LC 83-4470. (Illus.). 336p. 1983. 45.00 (0-684-17913-X, Scribners Ref) Mac Lib Ref.

Preston, Peter. Pacific Asia in the Global System: An Introduction. LC 97-43338. 269p. 1998. 62.95 (0-631-20237-4); pap. 29.95 (0-631-20238-2) Blackwell Pubs.

Preston, Peter, ed. Literature in the Adult Class: Tradition & Challenge. 200p. 1994. 24.95 (1-85041-072-0, Pub. by U of Nottingham) Paul & Co Pubs.

Preston, Peter & Hoare, Peter, eds. D. H. Lawrence in the Modern World. 192p. (C). 1989. text 54.95 (0-521-37169-4) Cambridge U Pr.

Preston, Peter, ed. see Bennett, Arnold.

Preston, Peter, jt. ed. see Faulkner, Peter.

Preston, Peter, jt. ed. see Morgan, W. John.

Preston, Peter W. Discourses of Development: State, Market & Polity in the Analysis of Complex Change. 256p. 1994. text 72.95 (1-85972-026-9, Pub. by Avebry) Ashgate Pub Co.

— Europe, Democracy & the Dissolution of Britain: An Essay on the Issue of Europe in U. K. Public Discourse. 232p. 1994. 72.95 (1-85521-519-5, Pub. by Dartmth Pub) Ashgate Pub Co.

— Political/Cultural Identity: Nations & Citizens in a Global Era. 208p. 1997. 69.95 (0-7619-5025-7); pap. 26.95 (0-7619-5026-5) Sage.

Preston, Philip & Kannair, Jonathan A. White Mountains-West. LC 79-66098. (Illus.). (Orig.). 1979. pap. 7.50 (0-9603106-0-6) Waumbek.

Preston, R. A., ed. Advances in Botanical Research, Vol. 13. (Serial Publication Ser.). 224p. 1987. text 104.00 (0-12-005913-4) Acad Pr.

Preston, R. C, ed. Output Measurements for Medical Ultrasound. (Illus.). xvi, 180p. 1991. 117.95 (0-387-19692-7) Spr-Verlag.

Preston, R. D., ed. Advances in Botanical Research, Vol. 6. (Serial Publication Ser.). 1979. text 174.00 (0-12-005906-1) Acad Pr.

Preston, R. D. & Woolhouse, W. H., eds. Advances in Botanical Research, Vol. 5. (Serial Publication Ser.). 1978. text 99.00 (0-12-005905-3) Acad Pr.

Preston, R. Julian. Genetic Risk Assessment: Methods & Protocols. LC 99-23532. (Methods in Molecular Biology Ser.). 1999. 79.50 (0-89603-578-6) Humana.

Preston, Ralph N. Early California Atlas: Northern Edition. 2nd ed. LC 83-72442. (Illus.). 1983. pap. 12.95 (0-8323-0313-5) Binford Mort.

— Early California Atlas: Southern Edition. 2nd ed. LC 78-57008. (Illus.). 1988. pap. 12.95 (0-8323-0314-3) Binford Mort.

Preston, Ralph N. & Preston, Monte L. Early Kansas. LC 97-91617. (Illus.). 122p. (Orig.). 1997. pap. 20.00 (0-9657558-0-0) Pioneer OR.

Preston, Raymond. Four Quartets Rehearsed. LC 74-100779. (Studies in T. S. Eliot: No. 11). 1970. reprint ed. lib. bdg. 75.00 (0-8383-0337-4, 0-8383-0337-4) M S G Haskell Hse.

Preston, Richard. Acid-Base, Fluids & Electrolytes Made Ridiculously Simple. (Illus.). 156p. (Orig.). (C). 1998. pap. text 17.95 (0-940780-31-3) MedMaster.

— The Cobra Event. 1998. mass mkt. 7.99 (0-345-40997-3) Ballantine Pub Grp.

***Preston, Richard.** An Essay in a Course of Lectures on Abstracts of Title to Facilitate the Study, & the Application of the First Principles & General Rules of the Law of Property, 3 vols. lxv,1067p. 1998. reprint ed. 385.00 (1-56169-426-6) Gaunt.

Preston, Richard. First Light: The Search fo the Edge of the Universe. 272p. 1996. 24.00 (0-679-44969-8) Random.

***Preston, Richard.** The Hot Zone. (J). 1999. 9.98 (0-671-04518-0) S&S Trade.

Preston, Richard. The Hot Zone. large type ed. LC 95-3710. (Large Print Bks.). (J). 1995. 26.95 (1-56895-205-8) Wheeler Pub.

— The Hot Zone. LC 95-5751. (Illus.). 448p. (J). 1995. reprint ed. mass mkt. 7.99 (0-385-47956-5, Anchor NY) Doubleday.

— The Hot Zone: A Terrifying True Story. 352p. (J). 1999. pap. 14.00 (0-385-49522-6) Doubleday.

Preston, Richard, ed. see Serle, Geoffrey, et al.

Preston, Richard A. Canada & Imperial Defense: A Study of the Origins of the British Commonwealth's Defense Organization, 1867-1919. LC 66-29550. (Duke University, Commonwealth-Studies Center, Publication Ser.: No. 29). 598p. 1967. reprint ed. pap. 185.40 (0-8357-7987-4, 201434500093) Bks Demand.

— Canada's RMC: A History of the Royal Military College. LC 77-413015. (Illus.). 467p. reprint ed. pap. 144.80 (0-8357-4027-7, 203671900005) Bks Demand.

— The Defence of the Undefended Border: Planning for War in North America, 1867-1939. LC 78-313309. 312p. reprint ed. pap. 96.80 (0-7837-1149-2, 204167800022) Bks Demand.

— Men in Arms. 6th ed. (C). Date not set. text. write for info. (0-15-507857-7) Harcourt Coll Pubs.

— Royal Fort Frontenac. LC 58-3089. (Champlain Society Publications, Ontario Ser.: No. 2). 547p. reprint ed. pap. 169.60 (0-7837-2050-5, 204232500004) Bks Demand.

Preston, Richard A., et al. Men in Arms: A History of Warfare & Its Interrelationships with Western Society. 5th ed. (C). 1991. pap. text 37.00 (0-03-033428-4, Pub. by Harcourt Coll Pubs) Harcourt.

Preston, Richard A., ed. see Abella, Irving M., et al.

Preston, Richard J., Jr. North American Trees: Exclusive of Mexico & Tropical Florida. 4th ed. LC 89-1944. (Illus.). 436p. (C). 1989. 49.95 (0-8138-1171-6); pap. 26.95 (0-8138-1172-4) Iowa St U Pr.

Preston, Robert, ed. see Charpentier, Marc-Antoine.

Preston, Robert, ed. see Leclair, Jean-Marie.

Preston, Robert E., ed. see Leclair, Jean-Marie.

Preston, Robert L. Building Your Fortune with Silver. 112p. 1973. pap. 1.00 (0-89036-024-3) Liahona Pub Trust.

— How to Prepare for the Coming Crash. 128p. 1971. pap. 2.95 (0-89036-025-1) Liahona Pub Trust.

Preston, Rohan. Dreams in Soy Sauce. LC 91-67066. 66p. (Orig.). 1992. pap. 6.95 (0-9624287-7-9) Tia Chucha Pr.

Preston, Rohan, jt. ed. see Wideman, Daniel J.

***Preston, Roy.** Quiz of the Century. 320p. 2000. pap. 12.95 (1-85868-858-2) Carlton Bks Ltd.

***Preston, Roy & Preston, Sue.** Pony Crosswords: 30 Fact-Filled Crosswords. 96p. (J). 2000. mass mkt. 3.99 (0-330-34107-3) Mcm Child Bks.

Preston, S. J. A Whimsical Look at Kids. (C). 1989. 35.00 (0-7223-2255-0, Pub. by A H S Ltd) St Mut.

Preston-Sabin, Jennie, jt. ed. see Hodge, Bonnie M.

Preston, Sally M., et al. PowerPoint 97 Smartstart. LC 97-65618. (Smartstart Ser.). (Illus.). 364p. 1997. 29.99 incl. disk (1-57576-820-8) Sams.

***Preston, Samuel H.** Demography: Measuring & Modeling Population Processes. 2000. pap. text 29.95 (1-55786-451-9) Blackwell Pubs.

Preston, Samuel H. Older Male Mortality & Cigarette Smoking, Vol. 6. LC 76-4875. (Population Monograph: No. 7). (Illus.). 150p. 1976. reprint ed. lib. bdg. 24.75 (0-8371-8830-X, PROM, Greenwood Pr) Greenwood.

Preston, Samuel H. & Haines, Michael R. Fatal Years: Child Mortality in Late Nineteenth-Century America. 272p. 1991. text 49.50 (0-691-04268-3, Pub. by Princeton U Pr) Cal Prin Full Svc.

***Preston, Samuel H., et al.** Demography: Measuring & Modeling Population Processes. 2000. 62.95 (1-55786-214-1) Blackwell Pubs.

Preston, Samuel H., jt. ed. see Gribble, James N.

Preston, Samuel H., jt. ed. see Martin, Linda G.

Preston, Seaton T., Jr. & Pandratz, Ronald. A Guide to the Analysis of Alcohols by Gas Chromatography. 3rd ed. 190p. 1984. pap. 35.00 (0-913106-25-9) PolyScience.

— Guide to the Analysis of Hydrocarbons by Gas Chromatography. 3rd ed. 349p. 1983. spiral bd. 45.00 (0-913106-21-6) PolyScience.

Preston, Seaton T., Jr. & Pankratz, Ronald. A Guide to Selected Liquid Phases & Absorbents Used in Gas Chromatography. 250p. 1985. spiral bd. 35.00 (0-913106-19-4) PolyScience.

— A Guide to the Analysis of Amines by Gas Chromatography. 3rd rev. ed. 176p. 1981. spiral bd. 35.00 (0-913106-20-8) PolyScience.

— A Guide to the Analysis of Thioalcohols & Thioethers: (Mercaptans & Alkyl Sulfides) by Gas Chromatography. rev. ed. 193p. 1980. spiral bd. 35.00 (0-913106-05-4) PolyScience.

Preston, Seaton T., Jr. & Pankratz, Ronald E. A Guide to the Analysis of Phenols by Gas Chromatography. 3rd rev. ed. 160p. 1985. pap. 35.00 (0-913106-26-7) PolyScience.

Preston, Shawn M. Beer Dossier. (Illus.). 96p. 1996. 29.95 (0-9647874-1-5) Mako Pubng.

— Cigar Dossier. 160p. 1995. 29.95 (0-9647874-3-1) Mako Pubng.

— Golf Dossier. (Illus.). 96p. 1996. 29.95 (0-9647874-2-3) Mako Pubng.

— Wine Dossier. (Illus.). 160p. 1995. 29.95 (0-9647874-0-7) Mako Pubng.

Preston-Shoot, Michael, jt. auth. see Braye, Suzy.

Preston-Shoot, Michael, jt. auth. see Corden, John.

***Preston-Speed Publications Staff.** By England's Aid. 2000. pap. 13.99 (1-887159-38-X) Preston-Speed.

— By Right of Conquest, Study Guide. 2000. pap. 7.99 (1-887159-46-0) Preston-Speed.

Preston Speed Publications Staff, ed. see Henty, G. A.

Preston, Stuart. Vuillard. (Masters of Art Ser.). (Illus.). 128p. 1985. 24.95 (0-8109-1706-8, Pub. by Abrams) Time Warner.

Preston, Sue, jt. auth. see Preston, Roy.

Preston, T. M., et al. Cytoskeleton & Cell Motility. (Tertiary Level Biology Ser.). (Illus.). 200p. 1990. mass mkt. 34.50 (0-412-02051-3, A3607, Chap & Hall NY) Chapman & Hall.

— Cytoskeleton & Cell Motility. (Tertiary Level Biology Ser.). (Illus.). 200p. 1990. text 69.95 (0-412-02041-6, A3603, Chap & Hall NY) Chapman & Hall.

Preston, T. W., jt. auth. see Reece, A. B. J.

Preston, Thomas. Cambises. LC 74-133723. (Tudor Facsimile Texts. Old English Plays Ser.: No. 44). reprint ed. 59.50 (0-404-53344-2) AMS Pr.

***Preston, Thomas.** The President & His Inner Circle: Leadership Style & the Advisory Process in Foreign Policy Making. 256p. 2001. text 49.50 (0-231-11620-9); pap. text 21.00 (0-231-11621-7) Col U Pr.

***Preston, Thomas & Preston, Elizabeth.** The Double Eagle Guide to Camping along the Lewis & Clark Trail Vol. 1: Search for the Northwest Passage, 1804-1805. (Double Eagle Guides Ser.). (Illus.). 206p. 2000. 21.95 (0-929760-68-9) Discovery MT.

— The Double Eagle Guide to Camping along the Lewis & Clark Trail Vol. 2: Return from the Distant Sea, 1805-1806. (Double Eagle Guides Ser.). (Illus.). 194p. 2000. 21.95 (0-929760-69-7) Discovery MT.

Preston, Thomas & Preston, Elizabeth. The Double Eagle Guide to Camping in Western Parks: Washington. large type ed. (Double Eagle Guides Ser.). (Illus.). 188p. 1995. 17.95 (0-929760-41-7) Discovery MT.

— The Double Eagle Guide to Camping in Western Parks & Forests: Arizona. large type ed. (Double Eagle Guides Ser.). (Illus.). 128p. 1995. 16.95 (0-929760-49-2) Discovery MT.

— The Double Eagle Guide to Camping in Western Parks & Forests: Arizona. 2nd large type rev. ed. (Double Eagle Guides Ser.). (Illus.). 132p. 1997. 19.95 (0-929760-79-4) Discovery MT.

— The Double Eagle Guide to Camping in Western Parks & Forests: Colorado. large type ed. (Double Eagle Guides Ser.). 190p. 1995. 17.95 (0-929760-44-1) Discovery MT.

— The Double Eagle Guide to Camping in Western Parks & Forests: Colorado. 2nd large type rev. ed. (Double Eagle Guides Ser.). (Illus.). 206p. 1997. 19.95 (0-929760-74-3) Discovery MT.

— The Double Eagle Guide to Camping in Western Parks & Forests: Idaho. large type ed. (Double Eagle Guides Ser.). (Illus.). 120p. 1995. 15.95 (0-929760-43-3) Discovery MT.

— The Double Eagle Guide to Camping in Western Parks & Forests: Idaho. 2nd large type rev. ed. (Double Eagle Guides Ser.). (Illus.). 126p. 1997. 19.95 (0-929760-73-5) Discovery MT.

— The Double Eagle Guide to Camping in Western Parks & Forests: Montana. large type ed. (Double Eagle Guides Ser.). (Illus.). 128p. 1995. 16.95 (0-929760-45-X) Discovery MT.

— The Double Eagle Guide to Camping in Western Parks & Forests: Montana. 2nd large type rev. ed. (Double Eagle Guides Ser.). (Illus.). 134p. 1997. 19.95 (0-929760-75-1) Discovery MT.

— The Double Eagle Guide to Camping in Western Parks & Forests: Nebraska & Kansas. large type ed. (Double Eagle Guides Ser.). (Illus.). 162p. 1995. 17.95 (0-929760-53-0) Discovery MT.

— The Double Eagle Guide to Camping in Western Parks & Forests: Nebraska & Kansas. 2nd large type rev. ed. (Double Eagle Guides Ser.). (Illus.). 162p. 1997. 19.95 (0-929760-83-2) Discovery MT.

— The Double Eagle Guide to Camping in Western Parks & Forests: Nevada & Utah. 2nd large type rev. ed. (Double Eagle Guides Ser.). (Illus.). 192p. 1997. 19.95 (0-929760-81-6) Discovery MT.

— The Double Eagle Guide to Camping in Western Parks & Forests: Nevada-Utah. large type ed. (Double Eagle Guides Ser.). (Illus.). 188p. 1995. 17.95 (0-929760-51-4) Discovery MT.

— The Double Eagle Guide to Camping in Western Parks & Forests: New Mexico. large type ed. (Double Eagle Guides Ser.). (Illus.). 118p. 1995. 15.95 (0-929760-50-6) Discovery MT.

— The Double Eagle Guide to Camping in Western Parks & Forests: New Mexico. 2nd large type rev. ed. (Double Eagle Guides Ser.). (Illus.). 124p. 1997. 19.95 (0-929760-80-8) Discovery MT.

— The Double Eagle Guide to Camping in Western Parks & Forests: North Dakota & South Dakota. 2nd large type rev. ed. (Double Eagle Guides Ser.). (Illus.). 146p. 1997. 19.95 (0-929760-82-4) Discovery MT.

— The Double Eagle Guide to Camping in Western Parks & Forests: North Dakota-South Dakota. large type ed. (Double Eagle Guides Ser.). (Illus.). 138p. 1995. 16.95 (0-929760-52-2) Discovery MT.

— The Double Eagle Guide to Camping in Western Parks & Forests: Northern California. large type ed. (Double Eagle Guides Ser.). (Illus.). 230p. 1995. 18.95 (0-929760-47-6) Discovery MT.

— The Double Eagle Guide to Camping in Western Parks & Forests: Northern California. 2nd large type rev. ed. (Double Eagle Guides Ser.). (Illus.). 230p. 1997. 19.95 (0-929760-77-8) Discovery MT.

— The Double Eagle Guide to Camping in Western Parks & Forests: Oklahoma. large type ed. (Double Eagle Guides Ser.). (Illus.). 150p. 1995. 16.95 (0-929760-54-9) Discovery MT.

— The Double Eagle Guide to Camping in Western Parks & Forests: Oklahoma. 2nd large type rev. ed. (Double Eagle Guides Ser.). (Illus.). 150p. 1997. 19.95 (0-929760-84-0) Discovery MT.

— The Double Eagle Guide to Camping in Western Parks & Forests: Oregon. large type ed. (Double Eagle Guides Ser.). (Illus.). 168p. 1995. 16.95 (0-929760-42-5) Discovery MT.

— The Double Eagle Guide to Camping in Western Parks & Forests: Oregon. 2nd large type rev. ed. (Double Eagle Guides Ser.). (Illus.). 188p. 1997. 19.95 (0-929760-72-7) Discovery MT.

— The Double Eagle Guide to Camping in Western Parks & Forests: Southern California. large type ed. (Double Eagle Guides Ser.). (Illus.). 220p. 1995. 18.95 (0-929760-48-4) Discovery MT.

— The Double Eagle Guide to Camping in Western Parks & Forests: Southern California. 2nd large type rev. ed. (Double Eagle Guides Ser.). (Illus.). 220p. 1997. 19.95 (0-929760-78-6) Discovery MT.

— The Double Eagle Guide to Camping in Western Parks & Forests: Texas. large type ed. (Double Eagle Guides Ser.). (Illus.). 210p. 1995. 17.95 (0-929760-55-7) Discovery MT.

— The Double Eagle Guide to Camping in Western Parks & Forests: Texas. 2nd large type rev. ed. (Double Eagle Guides Ser.). (Illus.). 210p. 1997. 19.95 (0-929760-85-9) Discovery MT.

— The Double Eagle Guide to Camping in Western Parks & Forests: Washington. 2nd large type rev. ed. (Double Eagle Guides Ser.). (Illus.). 208p. 1997. 19.95 (0-929760-71-9) Discovery MT.

— The Double Eagle Guide to Camping in Western Parks & Forests: Wyoming. large type ed. (Double Eagle Guides Ser.). (Illus.). 116p. 1995. 15.95 (0-929760-46-8) Discovery MT.

— The Double Eagle Guide to Camping in Western Parks & Forests: Wyoming. 2nd large type rev. ed. (Double Eagle Guides Ser.). (Illus.). 124p. 1997. 19.95 (0-929760-76-X) Discovery MT.

— The Double Eagle Guide to Camping in Western Parks & Forests Vol. I: Pacific Northwest. (Double Eagle Guides Ser.). (Illus.). 448p. (Orig.). 1992. pap. 12.95 (0-929760-21-2) Discovery MT.

— The Double Eagle Guide to Camping in Western Parks & Forests Vol. I: Pacific Northwest. (Double Eagle Guides Ser.). (Illus.). 238p. (Orig.). 1994. 18.95 (0-929760-27-1) Discovery MT.

— The Double Eagle Guide to Camping in Western Parks & Forests Vol. I: Pacific Northwest. 2nd rev. ed. (Double Eagle Guides Ser.). (Illus.). 264p. (Orig.). 1996. 19.95 (0-929760-61-1) Discovery MT.

— The Double Eagle Guide to Camping in Western Parks & Forests Vol. II: Rocky Mountains. (Double Eagle Guides Ser.). (Illus.). 214p. 1994. 17.95 (0-929760-22-0) Discovery MT.

— The Double Eagle Guide to Camping in Western Parks & Forests Vol. 2: Rocky Mountains. 2nd rev. ed. (Double Eagle Guides Ser.). (Illus.). 232p. 1996. 19.95 (0-929760-62-X) Discovery MT.

— The Double Eagle Guide to Camping in Western Parks & Forests Vol. 3: Far West. (Double Eagle Guides Ser.). (Illus.). 240p. 1994. 18.95 (0-929760-23-9) Discovery MT.

— The Double Eagle Guide to Camping in Western Parks & Forests Vol. 3: Far West. 2nd rev. ed. (Double Eagle Guides Ser.). (Illus.). 246p. 1996. 19.95 (0-929760-63-8) Discovery MT.

— The Double Eagle Guide to Camping in Western Parks &

An Asterisk (*) at the beginning of an entry indicates that the title is appearing for the first time.

Forests Vol. IV: Desert Southwest. (Double Eagle Guides Ser.). (Illus.). 384p. (Orig.). 1992. pap. 12.95 (*0-929760-24-7*) Discovery MT.

— The Double Eagle Guide to Camping in Western Parks & Forests Vol. IV: Desert Southwest. (Double Eagle Guides Ser.). (Illus.). 212p. (Orig.). 1994. 17.95 (*0-929760-29-8*) Discovery MT.

— The Double Eagle Guide to Camping in Western Parks & Forests Vol. 4: Desert Southwest. 2nd rev. ed. (Double Eagle Guides Ser.). (Illus.). 212p. 1996. 19.95 (*0-929760-64-6*) Discovery MT.

— The Double Eagle Guide to Camping in Western Parks & Forests Vol. 5: Northern Great Plains. 2nd rev. ed. (Double Eagle Guides Ser.). (Illus.). 182p. 1996. 19.95 (*0-929760-65-4*) Discovery MT.

— The Double Eagle Guide to Camping in Western Parks & Forests Vol. V: Northern Plains. (Double Eagle Guides Ser.). (Illus.). 170p. 1994. 16.95 (*0-929760-25-5*) Discovery MT.

— The Double Eagle Guide to Camping in Western Parks & Forests Vol. 6: Southern Great Plains. 2nd rev. ed. (Double Eagle Guides Ser.). (Illus.). 202p. 1996. 19.95 (*0-929760-66-2*) Discovery MT.

— The Double Eagle Guide to Camping in Western Parks & Forests Vol. VI: Southwest Plains. (Double Eagle Guides Ser.). (Illus.). 192p. 1994. 17.95 (*0-929760-26-3*) Discovery MT.

— The Double Eagle Guide to 1000 Great Western Recreation Destinations: Great Plains: North Dakota/South Dakota/Nebraska/Kansas/Oklahoma/Texas. (Double Eagle Guides Ser.: Vol. 4). (Illus.). 180p. 1998. 19.95 (*0-929760-20-4*) Discovery MT.

— The Double Eagle Guide to 1000 Great Western Recreation Destinations: Intermountain West: Idaho/Nevada/Utah/Arizona. (Double Eagle Guides Ser.: Vol. 2). (Illus.). 168p. 1998. 19.95 (*0-929760-18-2*) Discovery MT.

— The Double Eagle Guide to 1000 Great Western Recreation Destinations: Rocky Mountains: Montana/Wyoming/Colorado/New Mexico. (Double Eagle Guides Ser.: Vol. 3). (Illus.). 176p. 1998. 19.95 (*0-929760-60-3*) Discovery MT.

— The Double Eagle Guide to 1000 Great Western Recreation Destinations: West Coast: Washington/Oregon/California. (Double Eagle Guides Ser.: Vol. 1). (Illus.). 186p. 1998. 19.95 (*0-929760-58-1*) Discovery MT.

— The Double Eagle Guide to Western Public Campgrounds: Far West. (Double Eagle Guides Ser.: Vol. III). (Illus.). 336p. (Orig.). 1988. pap. 8.95 (*0-929760-03-4*) Discovery MT.

— The Double Eagle Guide to Western Public Campgrounds: Northern Great Plains. (Double Eagle Guides Ser.: Vol. V). (Illus.). 304p. (Orig.). 1989. pap. 8.95 (*0-929760-05-0*) Discovery MT.

— The Double Eagle Guide to Western Public Campgrounds: Pacific Northwest. (Double Eagle Guides Ser.: Vol. I). (Illus.). 336p. (Orig.). 1988. pap. 8.95 (*0-929760-01-8*) Discovery MT.

— The Double Eagle Guide to Western Public Campgrounds: Rocky Mountains. (Double Eagle Guides Ser.: Vol. II). (Illus.). 304p. (Orig.). 1988. pap. 8.95 (*0-929760-02-6*) Discovery MT.

— The Double Eagle Guide to Western Public Campgrounds: Southwest. (Double Eagle Guides Ser.: Vol. IV). (Illus.). 304p. (Orig.). 1988. pap. 8.95 (*0-929760-04-2*) Discovery MT.

— The Double Eagle Guide to Western Public Campgrounds: Southwest Plains. (Double Eagle Guides Ser.: Vol. VI). (Illus.). 336p. (Orig.). 1990. pap. 8.95 (*0-929760-06-9*) Discovery MT.

— The Double Eagle Guide to Western State Parks: Colorado/New Mexico. large type ed. (Double Eagle Guides Ser.: No. 7). (Illus.). 168p. 1998. 21.95 (*0-929760-96-4*) Discovery MT.

— The Double Eagle Guide to Western State Parks: Kansas/Oklahoma. large type ed. (Double Eagle Guides Ser.: No. 9). (Illus.). 148p. 1998. 21.95 (*0-929760-98-0*) Discovery MT.

— The Double Eagle Guide to Western State Parks: Montana/Idaho/Wyoming. large type ed. (Double Eagle Guides Ser.: No. 6). (Illus.). 176p. 1998. 21.95 (*0-929760-95-6*) Discovery MT.

— The Double Eagle Guide to Western State Parks: Nevada/Utah/Arizona. large type ed. (Double Eagle Guides Ser.: No. 5). (Illus.). 170p. 1998. 21.95 (*0-929760-94-8*) Discovery MT.

— The Double Eagle guide to Western State Parks: North Dakota/South Dakota/Nebraska. large type ed. (Double Eagle Guides Ser.: No. 8). (Illus.). 164p. 1998. 21.95 (*0-929760-97-2*) Discovery MT.

— The Double Eagle Guide to Western State Parks: Northern California. large type ed. (Double Eagle Guides Ser.: No. 3). (Illus.). 194p. 1998. 21.95 (*0-929760-92-1*) Discovery MT.

— The Double Eagle Guide to Western State Parks: Oregon. large type ed. (Double Eagle Guides Ser.: Vol. 2). (Illus.). 152p. 1998. 21.95 (*0-929760-91-3*) Discovery MT.

— The Double Eagle Guide to Western State Parks: Southern California. large type ed. (Double Eagle Guides Ser.: No. 4). (Illus.). 134p. 1998. 21.95 (*0-929760-93-X*) Discovery MT.

— The Double Eagle Guide to Western State Parks: Texas. large type ed. (Double Eagle Guides Ser.: No. 10). (Illus.). 188p. 1998. 21.95 (*0-929760-99-9*) Discovery MT.

— The Double Eagle Guide to Western State Parks: Washington. large type ed. (Double Eagle Guides Ser.: Vol. 1). (Illus.). 152p. 1998. 21.95 (*0-929760-90-5*) Discovery MT.

— The Double Eagle Guide to Western State Parks Vol. 1: Pacific Northwest. (Double Eagle Guides Ser.). (Illus.). 304p. (Orig.). 1991. pap. 11.95 (*0-929760-11-5*) Discovery MT.

— The Double Eagle Guide to Western State Parks Vol. 1: Pacific Northwest: Washington/Oregon/Idaho. 2nd rev. ed. (Double Eagle Guides Ser.). (Illus.). 194p. 1997. 19.95 (*0-929760-31-X*) Discovery MT.

— The Double Eagle Guide to Western State Parks Vol. II: Rocky Mountains. (Double Eagle Guides Ser.). (Illus.). 256p. (Orig.). 1992. pap. 10.95 (*0-929760-12-3*) Discovery MT.

— The Double Eagle Guide to Western State Parks Vol. 2: Rocky Mountains: Colorado/Montana/Wyoming. 2nd rev. ed. (Double Eagle Guides Ser.). (Illus.). 148p. 1997. 19.95 (*0-929760-32-8*) Discovery MT.

— The Double Eagle Guide to Western State Parks Vol. 3: Far West. (Double Eagle Guides Ser.). (Illus.). 320p. (Orig.). 1991. pap. 12.95 (*0-929760-13-1*) Discovery MT.

— The Double Eagle Guide to Western State Parks Vol. 3: Far West: California/Nevada. 2nd rev. ed. (Double Eagle Guides Ser.). (Illus.). 204p. 1997. 19.95 (*0-929760-33-6*) Discovery MT.

— The Double Eagle Guide to Western State Parks Vol. 4: Desert Southwest. (Double Eagle Guides Ser.). (Illus.). 224p. (Orig.). 1991. pap. 9.95 (*0-929760-14-X*) Discovery MT.

— The Double Eagle Guide to Western State Parks Vol. 4: Desert Southwest: Arizona/New Mexico/Utah. 2nd rev. ed. (Double Eagle Guides Ser.). (Illus.). 136p. 1997. 19.95 (*0-929760-34-4*) Discovery MT.

— The Double Eagle Guide to Western State Parks Vol. 5: Northern Great Plains: North Dakota/South Dakota/Nebraska/Kansas. 2nd rev. ed. (Double Eagle Guides Ser.). (Illus.). 148p. 1997. 19.95 (*0-929760-35-2*) Discovery MT.

— The Double Eagle Guide to Western State Parks Vol. 5: Northern Plains. (Double Eagle Guides Ser.). (Illus.). 150p. 1994. 16.95 (*0-929760-15-8*) Discovery MT.

— The Double Eagle Guide to Western State Parks Vol. 6: Southern Great Plains: Texas/Oklahoma. 2nd rev. ed. (Double Eagle Guides Ser.). (Illus.). 190p. 1997. 19.95 (*0-929760-36-0*) Discovery MT.

— The Double Eagle Guide to Working in Western Parks & Forests. (Double Eagle Guides Ser.). (Illus.). 224p. 1995. 19.95 (*0-929760-57-3*) Discovery MT.

— Places to Hide: Pacific Coast. (Double Eagle Guides Ser.). (Illus.). 178p. 1999. 19.95 (*0-929760-86-7*) Discovery MT.

— Places to Hide Vol. 2: Intermountain West. (Double Eagle Guides Ser.). (Illus.). 170p. 1999. 19.95 (*0-929760-87-5*) Discovery MT.

— Places to Hide Vol. 3: Rocky Mountains. (Double Eagle Guides Ser.). (Illus.). 176p. 1999. 19.95 (*0-929760-88-3*) Discovery MT.

— Places to Hide Vol. 4: Great Plains. (Double Eagle Guides Ser.). (Illus.). 174p. 1999. 19.95 (*0-929760-89-1*) Discovery MT.

Preston, Thomas A. Coronary Artery Surgery: A Critical Review. LC 76-51977. 278p. reprint ed. pap. 86.20 (*0-7837-7117-7*, 204694600004) Bks Demand.

***Preston, Thomas A.** Facing Death on Your Own Terms. 2000. 22.95 (*0-7615-2899-7*) Prima Pub.

Preston-Thomas, H., et al, eds. Basic Methods, Scales & Fixed Points, Radiation, Pt. 1. LC 62-19138. 815p. 1972. pap. 200.00 (*0-608-08465-4*, 205213300001) Bks Demand.

Preston, Thomas R., ed. see Smollett, Tobias George.

Preston, Thomas W. Historical Sketches of the Holston Valleys. (Illus.). xviii, 190p. 1997. reprint ed. pap. 20.50 (*0-7884-0721-X*, P621) Heritage Bk.

Preston, Thorgrimson, Shidler, Gates & Ellis Staff. Oregon Environmental Law Handbook. 201p. 1992. pap. text 79.00 (*0-86587-285-6*) Gov Insts.

Preston, Thorgrimson, Shidler, Gates & Ellis Staff, et al. Natural Resource Damages. 234p. 1993. pap. 79.00 (*0-86587-340-2*) Gov Insts.

Preston, Tim. The Lonely Scarecrow. LC 98-42030. (Illus.). 32p. (J). (ps-3). 1999. 14.99 (*0-525-46080-2*, Dutton Child) Peng Put Young Read.

***Preston, Tom.** The Sabre Brigade United Nations. LC 99-91793. 404p. 1999. 25.00 (*0-7388-1260-9*); pap. 18.00 (*0-7388-1261-7*) Xlibris Corp.

Preston, Tony, jt. ed. see McLean, David.

Preston, Trevor S., tr. see Klant, Johannes J.

Preston, Virginia, jt. ed. see Catterall, Peter.

Preston, W. B., jt. ed. see Wilson, L. A.

Preston, W. Curtis. UNIX Backup & Recovery. Estabrook, Gigi, ed. (Illus.). 500p. 1999. pap. 36.95 incl. cd-rom (*1-56592-642-0*) OReilly & Assocs.

Preston, Walter W. History of Harford County, from 1608 (the Year of Smith's Expedition) to the Close of the War of 1812. (Illus.). 360p. 1995. reprint ed. lib. bdg. 42.00 (*0-8328-5038-1*) Higginson Bk Co.

Preston, Ward. Storyboards: Drawing Movies. 300p. Date not set. pap. text 26.95 (*1-879505-32-0*) Silman James Pr.

— What an Art Director Does: An Introduction to Motion Picture Production Design. LC 94-30605. (Illus.). 190p. (Orig.). 1994. pap. 21.95 (*1-879505-18-5*) Silman James Pr.

Preston-Whyte, Eleanor. Speaking with Beads: Zulu Arts from Southern Africa. LC 94-60280. (Illus.). 96p. (Orig.). 1994. pap. 19.95 (*0-500-27757-5*, Pub. by Thames Hudson) Norton.

Preston-Whyte, R. A. & Tyson, P. D. The Atmosphere & Weather of Southern Africa. (Illus.). 386p. 1989. pap. 32.00 (*0-19-570496-7*) OUP.

Preston, William, Jr. Aliens & Dissenters: Federal Suppression of Radicals, 1903-1933. 2nd ed. LC 94-27501. 384p. 1995. pap. text 15.95 (*0-252-06452-6*) U of Ill Pr.

Preston, William. Preston's Masonry. 410p. 1997. reprint ed. pap. 29.95 (*0-7661-0064-2*) Kessinger Pub.

Preston, William A. Nietzsche As Anti-Socialist. 1998. 60.00 (*0-391-04076-6*) Humanities.

Preston/Speed Publications Staff, ed. see Henty, G. A.

Prestopino, Chris J. Estate Planning & Taxation, 1995. 944p. (C). 1995. per. 59.95 (*0-8403-9388-1*) Kendall-Hunt.

— Estate Planning & Taxation, 1995. abr. ed. 1048p. (C). 1994. 65.95 (*0-8403-9533-7*) Kendall-Hunt.

— Introduction to Estate Planning. 512p. 1988. text 40.00 (*1-55623-132-6*, Irwn Prfssnl) McGraw-Hill Prof.

Prestopnik, Richard J. Digital Electronics: Concepts & Applications for Digital Design. 735p. (C). 1989. text 102.00 (*0-03-026757-9*, Pub. by SCP) Harcourt.

— Digital Electronics: Concepts & Applications for Digital Design. 735p. (C). 1990. pap. text, teacher ed. 35.75 (*0-03-030867-4*); pap. text, teacher ed. 35.75 (*0-03-032017-8*); pap. text, student ed. 35.50 (*0-03-026758-7*, Pub. by SCP) Harcourt.

***Prestor, Richard.** Milwaukee. (Images of America Ser.). 128p. 1999. pap. 18.99 (*0-7385-0309-6*) Arcadia Publng.

Prestowitz, Clyde V., Jr. In Search of Survival. Date not set. pap. write for info. (*0-465-03230-3*) Basic.

Prestowitz, Clyde V. Powernomics: Economics & Strategy after the Cold War. 1991. pap. 16.95 (*0-8191-8039-4*) Madison Bks UPA.

Prestowitz, Clyde V., Jr., et al. The New North American Order: A Win-Win Strategy for U. S.-Mexico Trade. 134p. (C). 1991. pap. text 17.50 (*0-8191-8438-1*) U Pr of Amer.

Prestowitz, Clyde V., Jr., jt. ed. see Harrison, Selig S.

***Prestowitz, Michele & Streett, Lucy.** A History of Medi-Cal Physician Payment Rates. (Illus.). 24p. 2000. pap. write for info. (*1-929008-27-9*) CA HlthCare Fnd.

Prestre, Philippe Le, see Le Prestre, Philippe.

Prestressed Concrete Institute Staff. Approaches to Standardization of Architectural Precast Concrete Panels. (PCI Journal Reprints Ser.). 20p. 1985. pap. 12.00 (*0-318-19769-3*, JR200) P-PCI.

— The Baton Rouge Hilton Tower: An All Precast Prestressed Systems Building. (PCI Journal Reprints Ser.). 16p. 1976. pap. 12.00 (*0-318-19851-7*, JR185) P-PCI.

— Behavior & Design of Prestressed Concrete Beams with Large Web Openings. (PCI Journal Reprints Ser.). 32p. 1985. pap. 7.00 (*0-318-19855-X*, JR193) P-PCI.

— Considerations for the Design of Precast Concrete Bearing Wall Buildings to Withstand Abnormal Loads. (PCI Journal Reprints Ser.). 36p. 1985. pap. 14.00 (*0-318-19752-9*, JR170) P-PCI.

— Criteria for Design of Bearing Pads. 118p. 1985. ring bd. 40.00 (*0-937040-24-X*, TR-4-85) P-PCI.

— Design & Behavior of Dapped-End Beams. (PCI Journal Reprints Ser.). 18p. 1985. pap. 14.00 (*0-318-19861-4*, JR212) P-PCI.

— Design of Elastomer Bearings. (PCI Journal Reprints Ser.). 17p. 1964. pap. 12.00 (*0-318-19834-7*, JR24) P-PCI.

— Design of Partially Prestressed Flexural Members. (PCI Journal Reprints Ser.). 20p. 1977. pap. 12.00 (*0-318-19854-1*, JR189) P-PCI.

— Design Supplement to SSB-1-81. 80p. 1984. pap. 20.00 (*0-318-19822-3*, SSB-Z) P-PCI.

— Fire Resistance of Architectural Precast Concrete. 13p. 1974. pap. 12.00 (*0-318-19812-6*, JR-150) P-PCI.

— High-Range Water-Reducing Admixtures in Prestressed Concrete Operations. (PCI Journal Reprints Ser.). 18p. 1978. pap. 14.00 (*0-318-19860-6*, JR208) P-PCI.

— The Pasco-Kennewick Intercity Bridge & Geometry Control for the Intercity Bridge. (PCI Journal Reprints Ser.). 36p. 1979. pap. 8.00 (*0-318-19859-2*, JR205) P-PCI.

— Precast Trapezoidal Girders Spliced with Post-Tensioning for Highway Underpass. (PCI Journal Reprints Ser.). 4p. 1980. pap. 8.00 (*0-318-19863-0*, JR219) P-PCI.

— Recommendations for Estimating Prestress Losses. (PCI Journal Reprints Ser.). 36p. 1975. pap. 12.00 (*0-318-19842-8*, JR162) P-PCI.

— Recommended Practice for Grouting of Post-Tensioned Prestressed Concrete. (PCI Journal Reprints Ser.: No. 119). 8p. 1972. pap. 10.00 (*0-318-19838-X*, JR119) P-PCI.

— Research, Application, & Experience with Precast Prestressed Bridge Deck Panels. (PCI Journal Reprints Ser.). 24p. 1975. pap. 12.00 (*0-318-19843-6*, JR167) P-PCI.

— Stretched Out AASHO-PCI Beams Types III & IV for Longer Span Highway Bridges. (PCI Journal Reprints Ser.). 19p. 1973. pap. 12.00 (*0-318-19840-1*, JR134) P-PCI.

— A Utility's Development & Use of Prestressed Concrete Poles. (PCI Journal Reprints Ser.). 8p. 1972. pap. 10.00 (*0-318-19837-1*, JR114) P-PCI.

Prestwich, M. Documents Illustrating the Crisis of 1297-98 in England. (Camden Fourth Ser.: Vol. 24). 216p. 27.00 (*0-901050-56-3*, BAB 03307) David Brown.

Prestwich, Michael. Armies & Warfare in the Middle Ages: The/Experience of War in England. (Illus.). 352p. 1999. pap. text 18.00 (*0-300-07663-0*) Yale U Pr.

— Edward I. LC 97-60218. 640p. 1997. pap. text 20.00 (*0-300-07157-4*) Yale U Pr.

— Edward I. LC 97-60218. (Illus.). 640p. 1997. 45.00 (*0-300-07209-0*) Yale U Pr.

— English Armies in the Middle Ages. LC 95-36142. (Illus.). 352p. 1996. 50.00 (*0-300-06452-7*) Yale U Pr.

— English Politics in the Thirteenth Century. Black, Jeremy, ed. (British History in Perspective Ser.). pap. 19.95 (*0-333-41434-9*) St Martin.

— The Three Edwards: War & State in England, 1272-1377. LC 92-19386. 352p. (C). (gr. 13). 1997. pap. 21.99 (*0-415-05133-9*, A9854) Routledge.

— War, Politics & Finance under Edward I. (Modern Revivals in History Ser.). 318p. 1992. 61.95 (*0-7512-0000-X*, Pub. by Gregg Revivals) Ashgate Pub Co.

Prestwich, Michael, et al, eds. Thirteenth Century England VI: Proceedings of the Durham Conference, 1995. (Thirteenth Century England Ser.: Vol. 6). (Illus.). 203p. 1997. 75.00 (*0-85115-674-6*) Boydell & Brewer.

— 13th Century England VII: Proceedings of the Durham Conference 1997. (Thirteenth Century England Ser.). 320p. 1999. 90.00 (*0-85115-719-X*, Boydell Pr) Boydell & Brewer.

***Prestwich, P. F.** The Translation of Memories: Recollections of the Young Proust. 1999. 45.95 (*0-7206-1056-7*, Pub. by P Owen Ltd) Dufour.

Prestwich, Patricia. Drink & the Politics of Social Reform: Antialcoholism in France since 1870. LC 88-11576. 365p. 1988. 36.00 (*0-930664-08-6*) SPOSS.

Prestwood, Brian. Paradox 9 Power Programming. 701p. 1999. pap. 39.99 (*0-07-211936-5*) McGraw.

Prestwood, Edward. The Creative Writer's Phrase-Finder. LC 83-5617. 384p. 1984. 24.95 (*0-88280-104-X*) ETC Pubns.

Presutti, Michael. Quick Guide: Shelving & Storage. Bakke, Timothy O., ed. LC 97-60332. (Quick Guide Ser.). (Illus.). 80p. 1997. pap. 7.95 (*1-880029-91-X*) Creative Homeowner.

Pretat, Jane R. Coming to Age. LC 95-141052. 144p. 1995. pap. 16.00 (*0-919123-63-5*, Pub. by Inner City Bks) BookWorld.

Prete, Barbara & Strong, Gary E., eds. Literate America Emerging: Seventeen New Readers Speak Out. 128p. (Orig.). 1991. pap. 11.95 (*0-929722-45-0*) CA State Library Fndtn.

Prete, Frank. First Rays of a New Rising Sun. 302p. (Orig.). 1996. pap. 10.95 (*0-9653319-0-3*) Janvid Pubs.

Prete, Frederick R. Praying Mantids. LC 99-44360. 560p. 1999. 89.95 (*0-8018-6174-8*) Johns Hopkins.

Prete, Thomas Del, see Del Prete, Thomas.

Prete, Tony Del, see Del Prete, Tony.

Preteceille, Edmond. Jeux, Modeles et Simulations: Critique des Jeux Urbains. (Recherche Urbaine Ser.: No. 9). (FRE., Illus.). 208p. 1975. pap. text 21.55 (*90-279-7793-3*) Mouton.

Preteceille, Edmond, jt. auth. see Pickvance, C. G.

***Pretel, C.** Study of Unusual Occurrence of a Partial Core Uncovery in an SBLOCA Scenario. 36p. 2000. pap. 4.00 (*0-16-059115-5*) USGPO.

Pretenders. The Isle of View. 128p. 1996. per. 17.95 (*0-7935-6080-2*) H Leonard.

Preterm Institute Staff. Exploring Human Sexuality. 115p. 1975. pap. 13.95 (*0-87073-786-4*) Schenkman Bks Inc.

Pretes, Jeffry, ed. see Defoe, Daniel.

Preteux, Francoise, et al, eds. Mathematical Modeling & Estimation Techniques in Computer Vision, Vol. 3457. LC 99-193800. 1998. 69.00 (*0-8194-2912-0*) SPIE.

— Statistical & Stochastic Methods in Image Processing II. LC 98-122607. 264p. 1997. 59.00 (*0-8194-2589-3*) SPIE.

***Preti & Velarde.** On Fodor. 2000. pap. 8.25 (*0-534-58365-2*) Wadsworth Pub.

***Preti, et al.** Advances in Clinical Prosthodontics. (Illus.). 250p. 1999. text 156.00 (*88-299-1300-6*, Pub. by Piccin Nuova) Gordon & Breach.

Pretiz, Pablo, jt. auth. see Berg, Miguel.

Pretiz, Paul, jt. auth. see Berg, Mike.

Pretiz, Paul E., jt. auth. see Berg, Clayton L., Jr.

Pretiz, Paul E., jt. illus. see Roberts, W. Dayton.

Pretlove, John, ed. see Carey, William.

Pretlow, Theresa P., jt. ed. see Pretlow, Thomas G., II.

Pretlow, Thomas G., II & Pretlow, Theresa P., eds. Biochemical & Molecular Aspects of Selected Cancers, Vol. 2. (Illus.). 542p. 1994. text 136.00 (*0-12-564499-X*) Acad Pr.

Pretner, Janko. Russian-Slovene Dictionary: Rusko-Slovenski Slovar. (RUS & SLV.). 995p. 1986. 59.95 (*0-8288-1139-3*, F114898) Fr & Eur.

Preto, Fernando D., ed. Fluidized Bed Combustion: Proceedings; International Conference on Fluidized Bed Combustion (14th: 1997: Vancouver, Canada), 2 vols. LC 87-70969. 1314p. 1997. pap. 300.00 (*0-7918-1557-9*) ASME Pr.

Preto-Rodas, Richard A. Negritude As a Theme in the Poetry of the Portuguese-Speaking World. LC 79-107879. (University of Florida Humanities Monographs: No. 31). 98p. reprint ed. pap. 30.40 (*0-7837-5082-X*, 204478000004) Bks Demand.

Preto-Rodas, Richard A., et al, eds. Cronicas Brasileiras: Nova Fase. (Center for Latin American Studies, University of Florida). (Illus.). 352p. (C). 1994. pap. 24.95 (*0-8130-1246-5*) U Press Fla.

Preto-Rodas, Richard A. & Hower, Alfred, eds. Carlos Drummond de Andrade-Quarenta Historinhas (e Cinco Poemas) LC 84-27151. (ENG & POR.). xvi, 268p. (Orig.). (C). 1985. pap. 24.95 (*0-8130-0789-5*) U Press Fla.

Preto-Rodas, Richard A., jt. ed. see Hower, Alfred.

Pretolani, S., ed. see Fourth Workshop of the Helicobacter Pylori Study G.

Pretorius, Anika. Gifts from the Home. 96p. (C). 1989. 90.00 (*1-85368-081-8*, Pub. by New5 Holland) St Mut.

Pretorius, Diederika. Surrogate Motherhood: A Worldwide View of the Issues. (American Series in Behavioral Science & Law: No. 1085). 262p. 1994. pap. 40.95 (*0-398-06331-1*) C C Thomas.

P

Pretorius, Diederika. Surrogate Motherhood: A Worldwide View of the Issues. (American Series in Behavioral Science & Law: No. 1085). 262p. (C). 1994. text 59.95 (*0-398-05787-7*) C C Thomas.

Pretorius, F., ed. see Hall, Darrell.

Pretorius, Fransjohan. Life on Commando During the South African War, 1899-1902. 1998. pap. text 39.95 (*0-7981-3806-8*) Human & Rousseau.

— The South African War, 1899-1902. (Illus.). 96p. 1999. pap. 19.95 (*1-86872-179-5*, Pub. by Struik Pubs) BHB Intl.

Pretorius, H. L. Historiography & Historical Sources Regarding African Indigenous Churches in South Africa: Writing Indigenous Church History. LC 94-40519. (African Studies: Vol. 40). 160p. 1995. text 69.95 (*0-7734-9149-X*) E Mellen.

Pretorius, H. N. Burgerlike Prosesreg in Die Landdroshowe, Vol. 1. (AFR.). 1521p. 1986. write for info. (*0-409-02655-7*, MICHIE) LEXIS Pub.

— Burgerlike Prosesreg in Die Landdroshowe, Vol. 2. (AFR.). 1521p. 1986. write for info. (*0-409-02656-5*, MICHIE) LEXIS Pub.

Pretorius, J. R., jt. auth. see Forsyth, C. F.

Pretorius, J. T. Companies Act 61 of 1973 & Close Corporations Act 69 of 1984. 2nd ed. 634p. 1993. pap. 30.00 (*0-7021-2917-8*, Pub. by Juta & Co) Gaunt.

— Companies Act 61 of 1973 & Close Corporations Act 69 of 1984. 3rd ed. LC 97-199355. 414p. 1996. pap. 32.00 (*0-7021-3570-4*, Pub. by Juta & Co) Gaunt.

— Companies Act 61 of 1973 & Close Corporations Act 69 of 1984. 4th ed. LC 98-126557. 1998. 25.00 (*0-7021-4394-4*, Pub. by Juta & Co) Gaunt.

***Pretorius, J. T.** Companies Act 61 of 1973 & Close Corporations Act 69 of 1984. 6th ed. 1999. pap. 34.00 (*0-7021-5140-8*, Pub. by Juta & Co) Gaunt.

Pretorius, J. T. Maatskappywet 61 Van 1973 en Wet Op Beslote Korporasies 69 Van, 1984. 2nd ed. 634p. 1993. pap. write for info. (*0-7021-2918-6*, Pub. by Juta & Co) Gaunt.

***Pretorius, J. T., ed.** Companies Act 61 of 1973 & Close Corporations Act 69 of 1984: Including the Insider Trading Act 135 of 1998. 5th ed. 1999. 23.50 (*0-7021-4973-X*, Pub. by Juta & Co) Gaunt.

Pretorius, J. T., ed. Student Case Book on Business Entities. 256p. 1994. pap. 20.00 (*0-7021-3337-X*, Pub. by Juta & Co) Gaunt.

***Pretorius, J. T., et al.** Hahlo's South African Company Law Through the Cases: A Source Book: A Collection of Cases on Company Law, with Explanatory Notes & Comments. 6th ed. 629p. 1999. pap. 61.50 (*0-7021-5142-4*, 18659, Pub. by Juta & Co) Gaunt.

Pretorius, J. T., jt. auth. see Delport, H. J.

Pretorius, J. T., jt. auth. see Malan, F. R.

Pretorius, Paul. Dispute Resolutions. 1993. pap. 34.00 (*0-7021-2833-3*, Pub. by Juta & Co) Gaunt.

Pretsch, E., et al. Tables of Spectral Data for Structure Determination of Organic Compounds. 2nd ed. (Chemical Laboratory Practice Ser.). xiii, 415p. 1996. 59.95 (*0-387-51202-0*) Spr-Verlag.

Pretsch, Ern & Clerc, Jean T. Spectra Interpretation of Organic Compounds. LC 97-179448. (Spectroscopic Techniques Ser.). 190p. 1997. 128.00 incl. cd-rom (*3-527-28826-0*, QD257) Wiley.

Pretschner, D. P. Personal Computing in Nuclear Medicine. (Lecture Notes in Medical Informatics Ser.: Vol. 18). 133p. 1982. 29.95 (*0-387-11598-6*) Spr-Verlag.

Pretsell, James, intro. National Engineering Management Conference, 1991: Managing in a Changing Future. (Illus.). 202p. (Orig.). 1991. pap. 57.75 (*0-85825-541-3*, Pub. by Inst Engrs Aust-EA Bks) Accents Pubns.

Prett, David M. & Morari, Manfred. Shell Process Control Workshop. (Illus.). 392p. 1987. text 89.95 (*0-409-90136-9*) Buttrwrth-Heinemann.

Prett, David M., et al. Second Shell Process Control Workshop: Solutions to the Shell Standard Problem. 696p. 1989. text 98.95 (*0-409-90186-5*) Buttrwrth-Heinemann.

***Prettejohn, Elizabeth.** The Art of the Pre-Raphaelites. (Illus.). 304p. 2000. 49.50 (*0-691-07057-1*) Princeton U Pr.

Prettejohn, Elizabeth. Interpreting Sargent. (Illus.). 80p. 1999. pap. 16.95 (*1-55670-728-2*) Stewart Tabori & Chang.

— Rossetti & His Circle. 80p. 1997. pap. text 16.95 (*1-55670-656-1*) Stewart Tabori & Chang.

Pretti-Frontczak, Kristie, jt. ed. see Bricker, Diane B.

Pretty, Jules N. Regenerating Agriculture: Policies & Practice for Sustainability & Self-Reliance. 320p. 1995. 44.95 (*0-309-05248-3*, Joseph Henry Pr) Natl Acad Pr.

— Regenerating Agriculture: Policies & Practice for Sustainability & Self-Reliance. 320p. 1995. pap. 24.95 (*0-309-05246-7*, Joseph Henry Pr) Natl Acad Pr.

Pretty, Laurence H. Patent Law Text & Cases. (Illus.). 392p. (Orig.). 1995. pap. text 40.00 (*0-9651658-0-9*) Pasadena Legal.

— Patent Law Texts & Cases. 2nd rev. ed. 439p. 1997. pap. text 47.00 (*0-9651658-1-7*) Pasadena Legal.

Pretty, Lida. Life's Journey. 56p. 1990. 9.95 (*0-910147-90-6*) World Poetry Pr.

Pretty, Ron. The Habit of Balance. 64p. (C). 1989. 35.00 (*0-9587972-0-X*, Pub. by Five Isl Pr) St Mut.

Pretty, Ruth. Interior Design Solutions. LC 99-475009. 1999. pap. 14.95 (*0-7063-7779-6*, Pub. by WrLock) Sterling.

— The Ultimate Interior Designer. (Illus.). 256p. 1998. pap. 24.95 (*0-7063-7736-2*) Sterling.

— The Ultimate Interior Designer. LC 97-171201. (Illus.). 256p. 1997. 35.00 (*0-7063-7463-0*, Pub. by WrLock) Sterling.

Pretz, Bernhard. Dictionary of Military & Technological Abbreviations & Acronyms. 450p. 1983. 45.00 (*0-7100-9274-1*, Routledge Thoemms) Routledge.

Pretzel, Oliver. Codes & Algebraic Curves. (Oxford Lecture Series in Mathematics & Its Applications: No. 8). 208p. 1998. text 65.00 (*0-19-850039-4*) OUP.

— Error-Correcting Codes & Finite Fields. (Oxford Applied Mathematics & Computing Science Ser.). (Illus.). 412p. 1992. text 98.00 (*0-19-859678-2*) OUP.

— Error-Correcting Codes & Finite Fields. (Oxford Applied Mathematics & Computing Science Ser.). (Illus.). 356p. 1996. reprint ed. pap. text, student ed. 35.00 (*0-19-269067-1*) OUP.

Pretzer, Mary. Creative Low-Budget Publication Design. (Illus.). 144p. 1998. 29.99 (*0-89134-847-6*, North Lght Bks) F & W Pubns Inc.

Pretzer, William S., intro. Working at Inventing: Thomas Edison & the Menlo Park Experience. (Illus.). 144p. 1989. 24.95 (*0-933728-33-6*, Ford Mus); pap. 12.95 (*0-933728-34-4*, Ford Mus) Henry Ford Mus.

Pretzsch, Karl. Verzeichnis der Breslauer Universitatsschriften, 1811-1885. xv, 387p. 1975. reprint ed. write for info. (*3-487-05573-2*) G Olms Pubs.

Preu, James. The Dean & the Anarchist. LC 72-888. (Studies in Anarchy & Anarchism Ser.: No. 99). 124p. (C). 1972. reprint ed. lib. bdg. 59.00 (*0-8383-1419-8*) M S G Haskell Hse.

Preub, Olaf F. Kosten- & Deckungsbeitragsmanagement im Krankenhaus unter Besonderer Berucksichtigung von Fallpauschalen & Sonderentgelten. (GER., Illus.). XVII, 266p. 1996. 54.95 (*3-631-30735-7*) P Lang Pubng.

Preucel, Robert. Contemporary Archaeology in Theory: A Reader. Hodder, Ian, ed. LC 96-2055. (Social Archaeology Ser.). 600p. 1996. 78.95 (*0-631-19559-9*); pap. 32.95 (*0-631-19561-0*) Blackwell Pubs.

Preucel, Robert W., Jr. Seasonal Agricultural Circulation & Residential Mobility: A Prehistoric Example from the Pajarito Plateau, New Mexico. LC 90-21476. (Evolution of North American Indians Ser.). 261p. 1991. reprint ed. text 10.00 (*0-8240-2511-3*) Garland.

Preucel, Robert W., ed. Processual & Postprocessual Archaeologies: Multiple Ways of Knowing the Past. LC 90-84175. (Center for Archaeological Investigations Occasional Paper Ser.: No. 10). (Illus.). xii, 324p. (Orig.). 1991. pap. 25.00 (*0-88104-074-6*) Center Archaeol.

Preucil, Doris. Suzuki Viola School: Piano Accompaniment, Vol. 3. Suzuki, Shinichi, ed. 32p. (J). (gr. k-12). 1983. pap. text 6.95 (*0-87487-246-4*, Suzuki Method) Summy-Birchard.

— Suzuki Viola School, Viola Part, Vol. 1. Suzuki, Shinichi, ed. (Suzuki Viola School Ser.). 32p. (J). (gr. k-12). 1981. pap. text 6.95 (*0-87487-241-3*) Summy-Birchard.

— Suzuki Viola School, Viola Part, Vol. 2. Suzuki, Shinichi, ed. (Suzuki Viola School Ser.). 32p. (J). (gr. k-12). 1982. pap. text 6.95 (*0-87487-242-1*) Summy-Birchard.

Preucil, Doris & Suzuki, Shinichi, eds. Suzuki Viola School, Vol. A. (Piano Accompaniment Ser.). 64p. (J). (gr. k-12). 1982. pap. text 10.95 (*0-87487-245-6*, Suzuki Method) Summy-Birchard.

Preucil, Doris, ed. see Suzuki, Shinichi.

Preul, Reiner. Kirchentheorie: Wesen, Gestalt und Funktionen der Evangelischen Kirche. 422p. 1997. 49.00 (*3-11-015495-1*); 30.00 (*3-11-015496-X*) De Gruyter.

Preumont, Andre. Random Vibration & Spectral Analysis. (Solid Mechanics & Its Applications Ser.). 288p. (C). 1994. lib. bdg. 137.50 (*0-7923-3036-6*) Kluwer Academic.

— Vibration Control of Active Structures: An Introduction. LC 96-52589. (Solid Mechanics & Its Applications Ser.). 276p. (C). 1997. lib. bdg. 149.00 (*0-7923-4392-1*) Kluwer Academic.

Preus, Anthony. Aristotle on Africa. 29p. 1992. 3.00 (*0-9633277-8-X*, Studies Global) Global Pubns.

— Greek Philosophy: Egyptian Origins. 28p. 1992. 3.00 (*0-9633277-6-3*, Studies Global) Global Pubns.

— Notes on Greek Philosophy from Thales to Aristotle. 306p. 1996. pap. 17.00 (*1-883058-09-0*, SAG&IP) Global Pubns.

— Osiris & Appolo: Encounters Between Ancient Egypt & Greece. 1998. pap. 17.00 (*1-883058-44-9*, Intl Medieval) Global Pubns.

— Science & Philosophy in Aristotle's Biological Works. (Studien und Materialien Zur Geschichte der Philosophie Ser.: No. 1). ix, 404p. 1975. 83.20 (*3-487-05832-4*) G Olms Pubs.

***Preus, Anthony, ed.** Essays in Ancient Greek Philosophy Vol. 6: Before Plato. (C). 2001. pap. text. write for info. (*0-7914-4956-4*) State U NY Pr.

— Essays in Ancient Greek Philosophy Vol. 6: Before Plato. (C). 2001. text. write for info. (*0-7914-4955-6*) State U NY Pr.

Preus, Anthony & Anton, John P., eds. Essays in Ancient Greek Philosophy V: Aristotle's Ontology. LC 69-14648. 352p. (C). 1992. text 21.50 (*0-7914-1027-7*) State U NY Pr.

Preus, Anthony, jt. ed. see Anton, John P.

Preus, Anthony, tr. & intro. see Aristotle & Michael of Ephesus.

Preus, Daniel, jt. auth. see Preus, Robert D.

Preus, Herman A. Vivacious Daughter: Seven Lectures on the Religious Situation among Norwegians in the United States. Nichol, Todd W., ed. LC 90-212645. (Publications of the Norwegian-American Historical Association: No. 11). 246p. reprint ed. pap. 76.30 (*0-7837-0109-8*, 204038600016) Bks Demand.

Preus, J. A. The Second Martin: The Life & Theology of Martin Chemnitz. LC 94-15925. 336p. (Orig.). (C). 1994. pap. 37.00 (*0-570-04645-9*, 53-3227) Concordia.

Preus, J. A., tr. see Chemnitz, Martin.

Preus, J. A., tr. see Luther, Martin.

***Preus, J. A. O.** Just Words. 1999. pap. 12.99 (*0-570-05378-1*) Concordia.

Preus, J. Samuel. Explaining Religion: Criticism & Theory from Bodin to Freud. LC 96-46105. (American Academy of Religion Texts & Translations Ser.). 256p. 1996. reprint ed. pap. 24.95 (*0-7885-0321-9*, 01 02 16) OUP.

Preus, James S. From Shadow to Promise: Old Testament Interpretation from Augustine to the Young Luther. LC 69-12732. 313p. reprint ed. pap. 97.10 (*0-7837-2316-4*, 205740400004) Bks Demand.

Preus, Margi, jt. auth. see Lunge-Larsen, Lise.

Preus, Mary. Growing Herbs. (Cascadia Gardening Ser.). (Illus.). 104p. (Orig.). 1994. pap. 9.95 (*0-912365-98-6*) Sasquatch Bks.

***Preus, Mary.** The Northwest Herb Lover's Handbook: A Guide to Growing Herbs for Cooking, Crafts & Home Remedies. LC 99-47198. (Illus.). 224p. 2000. pap. 16.95 (*1-57061-172-6*) Sasquatch Bks.

Preus, Robert. Getting into the Theology of Concord. 1978. pap. 9.00 (*0-570-03767-0*, 12-2702) Concordia.

Preus, Robert & Rosin, W., eds. A Contemporary Look at the Formula of Concord. 320p. 1987. 19.99 (*0-570-03271-7*, 15-2716) Concordia.

Preus, Robert, ed. see Marquart, Kurt E.

Preus, Robert D. & Preus, Daniel. Justification & Rome. LC 97-47476. 1997. 14.95 (*0-570-04264-X*, 53-1024) Concordia.

Preus, Robert D., ed. see Scaer, David P.

Preusch, Deb, jt. auth. see Barry, Tom.

Preuschen, Erwin. Griechisch-Deutsches Taschenwoerterbuch zum Neuen Testament. 7th ed. (GER.). ii, 220p. (C). 1996. pap. text 22.10 (*3-11-015260-6*) De Gruyter.

Preuschoft, Holger & Chivers, David J., eds. Hands of Primates. ix, 421p. 1993. 158.95 (*0-387-82385-9*) Spr-Verlag.

Preuse, Claus J., jt. ed. see Piper, Hans M.

Preuss, Arthur, ed. see Grisar, Hartmann.

Preuss, Emil, jt. auth. see Engelmann, Wilhelm.

Preuss, Evelyn & Preuss, Gunter. Broussard's Restaurant Cookbook. LC 95-47827. (Illus.). 256p. 1996. 19.95 (*1-56554-139-1*) Pelican.

Preuss, Gehard. Theory of Topological Structures: An Approach to Categorical Topology. (C). 1987. text 174.50 (*90-277-2627-2*) Kluwer Academic.

Preuss, Gunter, jt. auth. see Preuss, Evelyn.

Preuss, Harry. Clinical Practice of Nephrology, Vol. 3. 1989. 69.00 (*0-938607-26-X*) Field & Wood Inc Medical.

— Geriatric Nephrology. 2nd ed. 1996. write for info. (*0-938607-34-0*) Field & Wood Inc Medical.

Preuss, Harry G. & Adderly, Brenda D. The Prostate Cure: The Revolutionary natural Approach to Treating Enlarged Prostates. LC 98-29437. 288p. 1998. 23.00 (*0-609-60323-X*) Crown Pub Group.

Preuss, Horst D. Old Testament Theology. Perdue, Leo G., tr. (Old Testament Library: Vol. 1). 384p. 1995. 34.00 (*0-664-21844-X*) Westminster John Knox.

Preuss, Horts D. Old Testament Theology. Purdue, Leo G., tr. from GER. (Old Testament Library: Vol. 2). 432p. 1996. 34.00 (*0-664-21843-1*) Westminster John Knox.

Preuss, Julius. Biblical & Talmudic Medicine. Rosner, Fred, ed. & tr. by. LC 93-33952. 688p. 1994. pap. 50.00 (*1-56821-134-1*) Aronson.

— Biblisch-Talmudische Medizin: Beitraege zur Geschichte der Heilkunde und der Kultur Ueberhaupt. viii, 736p. 1990. reprint ed. 174.00 (*3-8055-4976-8*) S Karger.

Preuss, Konrad T. Religion y Mitologia de los Uitotos, 2 vols. Incl. (SPA.). 232p. 1994. pap. 25.00 (*958-17-0112-5*); (SPA.). 917p. 1994. pap. 25.00 (*958-17-0113-3*); 50.00 (*958-17-0114-1*, IC004) UPLAAP.

— Visita a low Indigenas Kagaba de la Sierra Nevada de Santa Marta, 2 vols. (SPA.). 316p. 1993. pap. 16.00 (*958-612-080-5*, IC003) UPLAAP.

Preuss, Mary H. Gods of the Popol Vuh: Xmukane', K'ucumatz, Tojil & Jurakan. LC 87-81583. (Illus.). 118p. 1988. pap. 23.00 (*0-911437-25-8*) Labyrinthos.

Preuss, Mary H., ed. Beyond Indigenous Voices: LAILA/ALILA 11th International Symposium on Latin American Indian Literature (1994) LC 95-82120. (ENG & SPA., Illus.). 200p. (Orig.). (C). 1996. pap. 32.00 (*0-911437-35-5*) Labyrinthos.

— Messages & Meanings: LAILA - ALILA 12th International Symposium on Latin American Indian Literatures. LC 96-78911. (Illus.). 224p. (Orig.). (C). 1997. pap. 32.00 (*0-911437-78-9*) Labyrinthos.

— Past, Present, & Future: Selected Papers on Latin American Indian Literatures. LC 91-75066. (Illus.). 160p. (C). 1991. pap. text 32.00 (*0-911437-45-2*) Labyrinthos.

Preuss, Mary M., ed. LAIL Speaks: Selected Papers from the 7th International Symposium on Latin American Indian Literatures. LC 90-60870. (Illus.). 160p. (Orig.). (C). 1990. pap. 32.00 (*0-911437-44-4*) Labyrinthos.

Preuss, Mary M., intro. In Love & War: Hummingbird Lore & Other Selected Papers from LAILA - ALILA's 1988 Symposium. LC 89-84020. (Illus.). 120p. (Orig.). (C). 1990. pap. 25.00 (*0-911437-42-8*) Labyrinthos.

***Preuss, Paul.** Arthur C. Clarke's Venus Prime, Vol. 2. 336p. 2000. reprint ed. per. 14.00 (*0-671-03899-0*, Pub. by ibooks) S&S Trade.

Preuss, Paul. Breaking Strain. (Arthur C. Clarke's Venus Prime Ser.: Vol. 1). 272p. 1987. mass mkt. 4.99 (*0-380-75344-8*, Avon Bks) Morrow Avon.

— Broken Symmetries. LC 83-4809. 333p. 1983. 25.00 (*0-89366-151-1*) Ultramarine Pub.

— Core: A Novel. 400p. 1994. mass mkt. 5.99 (*0-380-71182-6*, Avon Bks) Morrow Avon.

— Secret Passages. 1998. mass mkt. 6.99 (*0-8125-7148-7*, Pub. by Tor Bks) St Martin.

***Preuss, Paul.** Venus Prime, Vol. 1. (J). 1999. per. 14.00 (*0-671-03888-5*) S&S Trade.

Preuss, Paul. Venus Prime: The Shining Ones, Vol. 6. 272p. (Orig.). 1991. pap. 3.95 (*0-380-75350-2*, Avon Bks) Morrow Avon.

— Venus #2: Maelstrom. (Arthur C. Clarke's Venus Prime Ser.: Vol. 2). 1988. mass mkt. 4.50 (*0-380-75345-6*, Avon Bks) Morrow Avon.

— Venus #3: Hide & Seek. (Arthur C. Clarke's Venus Prime Ser.: Vol. 3). 288p. (Orig.). 1989. pap. 3.95 (*0-380-75346-4*, Avon Bks) Morrow Avon.

— Venus #4: Medusa Encounter. (Arthur C. Clarke's Venus Prime Ser.: Vol. 4). 304p. 1990. pap. 3.95 (*0-380-75348-0*, Avon Bks) Morrow Avon.

— Venus #5: Diamond Moon. (Arthur C. Clarke's Venus Prime Ser.: Vol. 5). 1990. pap. 3.95 (*0-380-75349-9*, Avon Bks) Morrow Avon.

Preuss, Paul, jt. auth. see Clarke, Arthur C.

Preuss, Peter. Epicurean Ethics: Katastematic Hedonism. LC 93-48974. (Studies in the History of Philosophy: Vol. 35). 288p. 1994. 89.95 (*0-7734-9124-4*) E Mellen.

— Reincarnation: An Inquiry into Its Possibility & Significance. LC 88-32604. (Problems in Contemporary Philosophy Ser.: Vol. 14). 266p. 1989. lib. bdg. 89.95 (*0-88946-342-5*) E Mellen.

Preuss, Peter, tr. see Fichte, Johann G.

Preuss, Peter, tr. & intro. see Nietzsche, Friedrich Wilhelm.

Preuss, S., jt. auth. see Menge, R.

Preuss, Siegmund. Index Demosthenicus. 330p. 1975. reprint ed. write for info. (*3-487-00542-5*) G Olms Pubs.

— Index Isocrateus. 208p. 1974. reprint ed. write for info. (*3-487-04169-3*) G Olms Pubs.

— Vollstandiges Lexikon Zu den Pseudo-Casarianischen. 433p. 1964. reprint ed. write for info. (*0-318-71204-0*) G Olms Pubs.

— Vollstandiges Lexikon Zu den Pseudo-Casarianischen Schriftwerkern. 433p. 1964. reprint ed. write for info. (*0-318-72068-X*) G Olms Pubs.

Preuss, Ulrich K. Constitutional Revolution: The Link Between Constitutionalism & Progress. Schneider, Deborah L., tr. from GER. LC 94-37939.Tr. of Revolution, Fortschritt und Verfassung. 136p. (C). 1995. pap. 15.00 (*0-391-03854-0*) Humanities.

Preusser, Barbara, jt. auth. see Winningham, Maryl.

Preussische Akademie der Wissenschaften Staff, ed. see Humboldt, Wilhelm Von.

Preussische Akademie der Wissenschaften Staff, ed. see Kant, Immanuel.

Preussler, Otfried. The Satanic Mill. (J). (gr. 5-9). 1990. 26.50 (*0-8446-6196-1*) Peter Smith.

Prevallet, Elaine M. Interconnections. LC 85-61134. 32p. (Orig.). 1985. pap. 4.00 (*0-87574-261-0*) Pendle Hill.

— Reflections on Simplicity. LC 82-80439. 31p. 1982. pap. 4.00 (*0-87574-244-0*) Pendle Hill.

Prevallet, Kristin. Perturbation, My Sister: A Study of Max Ernst's "Hundred Headless Woman" 80p. (Orig.). 1997. pap. 10.00 (*1-889960-02-0*) First Intensity.

Prevas, John. Hannibal Crosses the Alps: The Enigma Re-Examinaned. (Illus.). 264p. 1998. 24.95 (*1-885119-48-8*) Sarpedon.

Prevas, John. Hannibal Crosses the Alps: The Enigma Re-examined. 264p. 1997. 80.00 (*1-873376-93-6*, Pub. by Spellmnt Pubs) St Mut.

Prevedouros, P. D., jt. auth. see Papacostas, C. S.

Prevedouros, Panos D., jt. auth. see Papacostas, C. S.

Prevel, Anne. Dictionnaire de la Cuisine de Normandie. (FRE.). 160p. 1993. 39.95 (*0-7859-8120-9*, 2862531480) Fr & Eur.

Prevelakis, Pandelis. The Cretan. Rick, Abbott & Mackridge, Peter, trs. from GRE. LC 91-62529. xvii, 480p. 1991. 35.00 (*0-932963-06-4*) Nostos Bks.

Prevendarova & Kubickova. Zaklady Rodinnej a Sexualnej Vychovy. (SLO.). 88p. 1996. write for info. (*80-08-01212-9*, Pub. by Slov Pegagog Naklad) IBD Ltd.

Prevenier, Walter, jt. auth. see Blockmans, Willem P.

Prevenslik, Frederick. The Cutty Pipe Club. large type ed. (Illus.). 32p. 1997. pap. 3.00 (*1-893151-05-0*) Weavers Old.

— I Can Still Hear the Clucking. large type ed. (Illus.). 32p. 1997. pap. 3.00 (*1-893151-07-7*) Weavers Old.

Prevention Editors, jt. auth. see Dollemore, Doug.

***Prevention Health Book Staff.** Healing Herbs: Prevention's Best. 288p. 2000. pap. 5.99 (*0-312-97584-8*, St Martins Paperbacks) St Martin.

Prevention Health Books, jt. auth. see Bauman, Alisa.

Prevention Health Books, jt. auth. see Berg, Susan G.

***Prevention Health Books Editors.** The Doctors Book of Herbal Home Remedies: Cure yourself with nature's most powerful healing agents. LC 99-50051. 608p. 2000. 29.95 (*1-57954-096-1*) Rodale Pr Inc.

— The Doctor's Book of Home Remedies for Airborne Allergies. 2000. pap. 12.95 (*1-57954-211-5*) Rodale Pr Inc.

— Doctors Book of Home Remedies for Depression: Tips to Brighten Your Mood Through Herbs, Diet & Lifestyle. 144p. 2000. pap. 12.95 (*1-57954-232-8*) Rodale Pr Inc.

Prevention Health Books Editors. The Doctor's Book of Home Remedies for Preventing Disease. LC 98-44629. 512p. 1998. 27.95 (*0-87596-415-X*) Rodale Pr Inc.

***Prevention Health Books Editors.** The Doctor's Book of Home Remedies for Sharper Memory. LC 00-36602. 2000. pap. 12.95 (*1-57954-233-6*) Rodale Pr Inc.

— Getting Thinner, Getting Younger. 2001. pap. 19.95 (*1-57954-409-6*) Rodale Pr Inc.

Prevention Health Books Editors. Healing with Motion: An All-New Approach to Health & Healing Based on Simple Mind & Body Exercises. LC 98-44631. 1999. text 29.95 (*0-87596-533-4*) Rodale Pr Inc.

— Natural Cures: More Than 1,000 Remedies from the

P

An Asterisk (*) at the beginning of an entry indicates that the title is appearing for the first time.

World of Alternative Medicine. Delgado, Abel, ed. (Spanish E. P. Ser.).Tr. of Curas Naturales. (SPA.). 1999. pap. 12.95 (*1-57954-015-5*) Rodale Pr Inc.
— Prevention's Healing with Vitamins: The Ultimate Guide to Using Nature's Powerhouse Nutrients for Preventing & Curing Disease. LC 98-19052. 593 p. 1998. 29.95 (*1-57954-064-3*) Rodale Pr Inc.
— Prevention's Healthy Heart Cookbook: Over 200 Truly Satisfying Recipes. LC 99-30421. (Illus.). 416p. 1999. text 29.95 (*0-87596-503-2*) Rodale Pr Inc.
— Your Perfect Weight: The Best Ways to Lose Weight & Stay Slim Forever. Delgado, Abel, ed. (Spanish E. P. Ser.).Tr. of Su Peso Ideal. (SPA.). 1999. pap. 12.95 (*1-57954-039-2*) Rodale Pr Inc.

***Prevention Health Books Editors, ed.** Prevention's Best. 288p. 2000. 5.99 (*0-312-97503-1*, St Martins Paperbacks) St Martin.

Prevention Health Books Editors & Yeager, Selene. Prevention's New Foods for Healing. 624p. 2000. pap. 16.95 (*1-57954-095-3*) Rodale Pr Inc.

Prevention Health Books Editors, jt. auth. see Claflin, Edward Beecher.

Prevention Health Books Editors, jt. auth. see Yeager, Selene.

Prevention Health Books Editors, jt. ed. see Delgado, Abel.

Prevention Health Books for Seniors Staff, jt. ed. see Dollemore, Doug.

***Prevention Health Books for Women Editorial Staff.** Banish Your Belly, Butt & Thighs Forever! Real Woman's Guide to Body Shaping & Weight Loss. LC 99-45686. 320p. 2000. 29.95 (*1-57954-036-8*) Rodale Pr Inc.
— Banish Your Belly, Butt & Thighs Forever! Real Woman's Guide to Body Shaping & Weight Loss. LC 99-45686. (Illus.). 320p. 2000. pap. text. write for info. (*1-57954-037-6*) Rodale Pr Inc.

***Prevention Health Books for Women Staff.** Foolproof Weight Loss: Slim-down Strategies That Work--Guaranteed. LC 00-9752. 2000. write for info. (*1-57954-279-4*) Rodale Pr Inc.

Prevention Health Books for Women Staff. Natural Remedies: Nondrug Healing Strategies That Work Best. LC 99-19847. (Women's Edge Health Enhancement Guides). 1999. write for info. (*1-57954-103-8*) Rodale Pr Inc.

Prevention Health Books for Women Staff, jt. auth. see Berg, Susan G.

***Prevention Health Books Staff.** Fat Fighters. 2001. pap. write for info. (*0-312-97706-9*, St Martins Paperbacks) St Martin.

***Prevention Health Books Staff, ed.** Prevention's Best: Vitamin Cures. 560p. 2000. mass mkt. 6.99 (*0-312-97476-0*, St Martins Paperbacks) St Martin.

Prevention Health Books Staff & Berg, Susan, eds. Natural Prescriptions for Women: What to Do - And When to Do It - To Solve More Than 100 Female Problems. LC 98-10112. (Illus.). 576p. 2000. pap. 17.95 (*0-87596-434-6*) Rodale Pr Inc.

Prevention Health Books Staff, jt. auth. see Dollemore, Doug.

Prevention Magazine Editors. Age Erasers for Women: Actions You Can Take Right Now to Look Younger & Feel Great. (Illus.). 676p. 1996. pap. 17.95 (*0-87596-406-0*) Rodale Pr Inc.
— The Complete Book of Natural & Medicinal Cures. 784p. 1996. reprint ed. mass mkt. 7.99 (*0-425-15226-X*) Berkley Pub.
— Doctor Book Home Remedy Children. 1994. mass mkt. 8.99 (*0-553-85057-1*) Bantam.
— Doctors Book, Home. 1995. mass mkt. 8.99 (*0-553-85152-7*) Bantam.
— The Doctors' Book of Home Remedies. 752p. 1991. mass mkt. 6.99 (*0-553-29156-4*) Bantam.
— Doctors' Book of Home Remedies. 1995. mass mkt. 8.99 (*0-553-85158-6*) Bantam.
— The Doctor's Book of Home Remedies for Children. 528p. 1995. mass mkt. 6.99 (*0-553-56985-6*) Bantam.
— Doctors Book of Home Remedies for Dogs & Cats: Over 1000 Solutions to Your Pet's Problems. 496p. 1997. mass mkt. 6.99 (*0-553-57781-6*) Bantam.
— The Healing Foods Cookbook. (Illus.). 552p. 1994. 17.98 (*1-56731-037-0*, MJF Bks) Fine Comms.
— Healing with Vitamins: The Most Effective Vitamin & Mineral Treatments for Everyday Health Problems & Serious Disease. Feinstein, Alice, ed. LC 97-46593. 608p. 1998. pap. 17.95 (*1-57954-018-X*) Rodale Pr Inc.
— Life-Span Plus. 422p. 1993. 8.98 (*1-56731-025-7*, MJF Bks) Fine Comms.
— Lifespan Plus: 900 Natural Techniques to Live Longer! 480p. 1996. reprint ed. mass mkt. 6.99 (*0-425-15413-0*) Berkley Pub.
— New Choices in Natural Healing for Dogs & Cats. LC 99-15692. 500p. 1999. 29.95 (*1-57954-057-0*) Rodale Pr Inc.

***Prevention Magazine Editors.** New Choices in Natural Healing for Women: Drug-Free Remedies from the World of Alternative Medicine. 592p. 1999. pap. 17.95 (*1-57954-129-1*) Rodale Pr Inc.

Prevention Magazine Editors. The Prevention "How-To Dictionary of Healing Remedies & Techniques" 1996. mass mkt. 7.99 (*0-425-15191-3*) Berkley Pub.
— The Prevention Pain-Relief System: A Total Program for Relieving Any Pain in Your Body. 752p. 1994. mass mkt. 6.99 (*0-553-56491-9*) Bantam.
— Prevention's Food & Nutrition. 1996. mass mkt. 7.99 (*0-425-15520-X*) Berkley Pub.
— Prevention's Super Foods Cookbook: Two Hundred Fifty Delicious Recipes Using Nature's Healthiest Foods. LC 92-37485. (Illus.). 320p. 1993. 24.95 (*0-87596-167-3*) St Martin.
— Sintomas, Sus Causas y Curas - Symptoms, Their Causes & Cures: How to Understand & Treat 265 Health Concerns. 1996. 29.95 (*0-87596-366-8*) Rodale Pr Inc.

***Prevention Magazine Editors, ed.** Doctors Book of Home Remedies for Managing Menopause: Over 100 Tips from Leading Experts to Reduce the Stress. 144p. 2000. pap. 12.95 (*1-57954-234-4*) Rodale Pr Inc.

Prevention Magazine Editors, ed. The Doctor's Book of Home Remedies for Women. 720p. 1998. reprint ed. mass mkt. 7.50 (*0-553-57693-3*) Bantam.

***Prevention Magazine Editors, ed.** Mas Joven que Nunca (Age Erasers for Women) Recursos Rejuvenecedores para la Mujer (Actions You Can Take) (SPA., Illus.). 656p. 2000. pap. 16.95 (*0-87596-470-2*) Rodale Pr Inc.

Prevention Magazine Editors & Bechtel, Stefan. The Practical Encyclopedia of Sex & Health: From Aphrodisiacs & Hormones to Potency, Stress, Vasectomy, & Yeast Infection. LC 92-35043. 352p. 1993. text 27.95 (*0-87596-163-0*) Rodale Pr Inc.

Prevention Magazine Editors & Bricklin, Mark. Prevention Magazine's Nutrition Advisor. 596p. 1995. reprint ed. 12.98 (*1-56731-039-7*, MJF Bks) Fine Comms.

Prevention Magazine Editors & Davis, Julie. Young Skin for Life: Your Guide to Smoother, Clearer, More Beautiful Skin--At Any Age, Vol. 1. 304p. 1995. pap. 14.95 (*0-87596-241-6*) Rodale Pr Inc.

Prevention Magazine Editors, et al. Listen to Your Body. 544p. 1994. 9.98 (*1-56731-038-9*, MJF Bks) Fine Comms.

Prevention Magazine Editors, jt. auth. see Goldberg, Philip.

Prevention Magazine Editors, ed. see Goldberg, Philip.

Prevention Magazine Editors, ed. see Turbo, Richard.

Prevention Magazine Food Editors. Fabulous No Guilt Desserts. (Illus.). 128p. 1996. 21.95 (*0-87596-328-5*) Rodale Pr Inc.

Prevention Magazine Food Editors, ed. Fabulous No Guilt Desserts: Quick & Healthy Low-Fat Cooking. (Illus.). 128p. 1996. pap. 12.95 (*0-87596-329-3*) Rodale Pr Inc.
— Healthy Hometown Favorites: America's Best-Loved Recipes from America's Community Cookbooks - Made Light by the Food Editors of Prevention Magazine. LC 95-230913. (Illus.). 308p. 1995. text 23.95 (*0-87596-251-3*) Rodale Pr Inc.

Prevention Magazine Food Editors, ed. see Rosensweig, Linda.

Prevention Magazine Health Book Editors. The Doctor's Book of Home Remedies. LC 89-38656. 688p. 1990. text 27.95 (*0-87857-873-0*, 05-627-0) Rodale Pr Inc.
— The Doctors' Book of Home Remedies: Thousands of Tips & Techniques Anyone Can Use to Heal Everyday Health Problems. 739p. 1993. text 26.95 (*0-87596-182-7*) Rodale Pr Inc.
— The Doctors' Book of Home Remedies for Children. (SPA., Illus.). 450p. 1995. text 26.95 (*0-87596-266-1*) Rodale Pr Inc.
— Prevention's Healing with Vitamins. 512p. 1996. text 27.95 (*0-87596-292-0*) Rodale Pr Inc.
— Symptoms: Their Causes & Cures. 784p. 1996. reprint ed. mass mkt. 6.99 (*0-553-56989-9*) Bantam.
— The Visual Encyclopedia of Natural Healing. (Illus.). 432p. 1996. pap. 15.95 (*0-87596-273-4*) Rodale Pr Inc.

Prevention Magazine Health Book Editors, ed. The Complete Book of Natural & Medicinal Cures: How to Choose the Most Potent Healing Agents for over 200 Conditions & Diseases. LC 94-4888. 1994. text 29.95 (*0-87596-190-8*) Rodale Pr Inc.
— Easy One-Dish Meals: Prevention Magazine's Quick & Healthy Low-Fat Cooking. 128p. 1996. pap. 12.95 (*0-87596-325-0*) Rodale Pr Inc.
— Easy One-Dish Meals: Prevention Magazine's Quick & Healthy Low-Fat Cooking. (Prevention Magazine's Quick & Healthy Low-Fat Cooking Ser.). 128p. 1998. text 21.95 (*0-87596-324-2*) Rodale Pr Inc.
— The Female Body: An Owner's Manual: a Head-to-Toe Guide to Good Health & Good Looks - at Any Age. LC 96-13237. (Illus.). 432p. 1996. pap. 19.95 (*0-87596-400-1*) Rodale Pr Inc.
— Fighting Disease: Hundreds of Strategies for Preventing, Treating, & Curing Common Illnesses & Conditions. LC 94-24202. (Family Home Remedies Collection). 136p. 1996. 6.95 (*0-87596-263-7*) Rodale Pr Inc.
— Healthy Home Cooking: Family Favorites Old & New for Today's Health-Conscious Cooks. LC 94-44421. (Prevention Magazine's Quick & Healthy Low-Fat Cooking Ser.). (Illus.). 128p. 1995. pap. 15.95 (*0-87596-244-0*) Rodale Pr Inc.
— Prevention Magazine's Quick & Healthy Low-Fat Cooking: Pastas & Sauces. 128p. 1995. pap. 15.95 (*0-87596-236-X*) Rodale Pr Inc.

Prevention Magazine Health Book Editors & Kirchheimer, Sid. The Doctors' Book of Home Remedies II: Over 1,000 New Doctor-Tested Tips & Techniques Anyone Can Use to Heal Hundreds of Everyday Health Problems. LC 93-7754. 640p. 1993. text 27.95 (*0-87596-158-4*) Rodale Pr Inc.

Prevention Magazine Health Book Editors, jt. auth. see Faelten, Sharon.

Prevention Magazine Health Book Food Editors. Healthy Italian Cooking. (Prevention Magazine's Quick & Healthy Low-Fat Cooking Ser.). 128p. 1996. 21.95 (*0-87596-326-9*) Rodale Pr Inc.

Prevention Magazine Health Book Food Editors, ed. Healthy Italian Cooking. (Prevention Magazine's Quick & Healthy Low-Fat Cooking Ser.). 128p. 1996. pap. 12.95 (*0-87596-327-7*) Rodale Pr Inc.

Prevention Magazine Health Book Staff. Age Erasers for Women: Actions You Can Take Right Now to Look Younger & Feel Great. (Illus.). 500p. 1994. text 27.95 (*0-87596-214-9*) Rodale Pr Inc.

***Prevention Magazine Health Book Staff.** The Doctors' Book of Home Remedies for Preventing Disease. 2000. mass mkt. 6.99 (*0-553-58233-X*) Bantam.

Prevention Magazine Health Books Editors. The Complete Book of Alternative Nutrition: Powerful New Ways to Use Foods As Supplements, Herbs & Special Diets to Prevent & Cure Disease. 464p. 1998. reprint ed. pap. 15.00 (*0-425-16511-6*) Berkley Pub.
— The Doctor's Book of Home Remedies for Dogs & Cats. 448p. 1998. pap. 15.95 (*1-57954-010-4*) Rodale Pr Inc.

Prevention Magazine Health Books Editors, jt. auth. see Joachim, David.

Prevention Magazine Health Books Food Editors, ed. Your Family Will Love It! Cook Book: Quick & Healthy Weekday Meals for the Hard-to-Please. (Illus.). 432p. 1997. pap. 15.95 (*0-87596-447-8*) Rodale Pr Inc.

Prevention Magazine Health Books Staff. High Speed Healing: The Fastest, Safest, & Most Effective Shortcuts to Lasting Relief. 656p. 1993. mass mkt. 6.99 (*0-553-56476-5*) Bantam.
— New Choices in Natural Healing for Women: Drug-Free Remedies from the World of Alternative Medicine. 540p. 1998. mass mkt. 6.99 (*0-553-57980-0*) Bantam.
— North Dakota Century Code. annot. ed. write for info. (*0-614-05932-1*, MICHIE) LEXIS Pub.

***Prevention Magazine Health Books Staff.** Prevention's Quick & Healthy Family Favorites Cookbook: Over 215 Delicious Recipes. LC 00-36915. (Illus.). 2000. write for info. (*1-57954-310-3*) Rodale Pr Inc.

Prevention Magazine Health Books Staff, jt. auth. see Goldberg, Philip.

Prevention Magazine Health Editors, ed. Prevention Magazine's Quick & Healthy Low-Fat Cooking: Light Ways with Poultry. (Prevention Magazine's Quick & Healthy Low-Fat Cooking Ser.). (Illus.). 127p. 1995. pap. 15.95 (*0-87596-245-9*) Rodale Pr Inc.

Prevention Magazine Staff. Healing with Vitamins. 1996. 95.85 (*0-87596-381-1*) St Martin.
— Health Hints for Women: Essential News You Can Use to Shape up, Energize & Outsmart Disease. LC 96-27693. (Illus.). 320p. 1996. pap. 12.95 (*0-87596-393-5*) Rodale Pr Inc.
— New Choices in Natural Healing. 800p. 1997. mass mkt. 6.99 (*0-553-57690-9*) Bantam.
— The Prevention How-To Dictionary of Healing Remedies & Techniques: From Acupressure & Aspirin to Yoga & Yogurt -- Over 350 Curative Options. 500p. 1994. 9.98 (*1-56731-033-8*, MJF Bks) Fine Comms.

***Prevention Magazine Staff, ed.** Doctors Book of Home Remedies for Men. 440p. 2000. mass mkt. 7.50 (*0-553-58234-8*) Bantam.

Prevention Magazine Staff, ed. The Healing Foods Cookbook: 400 Delicious Recipes with Curative Power. large type ed. (General Ser.). 855p. 1992. lib. bdg. 23.95 (*0-8161-5520-8*, G K Hall Lrg Type) Mac Lib Ref.
— The Healing Foods Cookbook in Large Print: 400 Delicious Recipes with Curative Power. large type ed. (General Ser.). 855p. 1992. 19.95 (*0-8161-5521-6*, G K Hall Lrg Type) Mac Lib Ref.

Prevention Magazine Staff, et al, eds. Symptoms: Their Causes & Cures - How to Understand & Treat 265 Health Concerns. LC 93-23014. 660p. 1994. 29.95 (*0-87596-179-7*) Rodale Pr Inc.

Prevention Magazine Staff & Mitchell, Carolyn B. Age Erasers for Women. 800p. 1997. mass mkt. 6.99 (*0-553-57687-9*) Bantam.

Prevention Magazine Staff, jt. ed. see Delgado, Abel.

Prevention Medicine Editors. The Complete Book of Natural & Medicinal Cures. 1996. pap. 7.99 (*0-425-15479-3*) Berkley Pub.
— The Prevention How-To Dictionary of Healing Remedies & Techniques. 1996. pap. 7.99 (*0-425-15475-0*) Berkley Pub.

Prevert, Jacques. Arbres. (FRE., Illus.). 69p. 1976. pap. 17.95 (*0-7859-1348-3*, 2070295222) Fr & Eur.
— Blood & Feathers: Selected Poems of Jacques Prevert. Zinnes, Harriet, tr. from FRE. (FRE.). 144p. 1993. reprint ed. pap. 11.95 (*1-55921-056-7*) Moyer Bell.
— Choses et Autres. (FRE.). 264p. 1975. pap. 10.95 (*0-7859-2355-1*, 2070366464) Fr & Eur.
— Choses et Autres. (Folio Ser.: No. 646). (FRE.). 1975. pap. 8.95 (*2-07-036646-4*) Schoenhof.
— Contes pour Enfants pas Sages. (FRE.). 89p. (J). 1977. pap. 10.95 (*0-7859-1360-2*, 2070330214) Fr & Eur.
— Contes pour Enfants pas Sages. (Folio - Cadet Bleu Ser.: No. 181). (FRE., Illus.). 88p. (J). (gr. 1-5). 1990. pap. 12.95 (*2-07-031181-3*) Schoenhof.
— Fatras & Cinquante-Sept Images Composees par l'Auteur. (Folio Ser.: No. 877). (FRE.). 285p. 1977. 8.95 (*2-07-036877-7*) Schoenhof.
— Grand Bal du Printemps & Charmes de Londres. (Folio Ser.: No. 1075). (FRE.). 168p. 1976. 6.95 (*2-07-037075-5*) Schoenhof.
— Grand Bal du Printemps suivi de Charmes de Londres. (FRE.). 154p. 1979. pap. 10.95 (*0-7859-2410-8*, 2070370755) Fr & Eur.
— Hebdromadaires. (FRE.). 192p. 1974. pap. 10.95 (*0-7859-2332-2*, 2070365220) Fr & Eur.
— Histoires. (FRE.). 256p. 1972. pap. 10.95 (*0-7859-2266-0*, 2070361195) Fr & Eur.
— Histoires. (Folio Ser.: No. 119). (FRE.). 256p. 1972. pap. 9.25 (*2-07-036119-5*) Schoenhof.
— Imaginaires. (Coll. Les Sentiers de la Creation). (FRE.). 25.00 (*0-685-37050-X*) Fr & Eur.
— Lettre des Iles Baladar. (FRE.). pap. 3.40 (*0-685-37051-8*) Fr & Eur.
— Lettre des Iles Baladar. (FRE., Illus.). 93p. 1977. pap. 10.95 (*0-7859-1361-0*, 2070330257) Fr & Eur.
— Oeuvres Completes. deluxe ed. (FRE.). 1536p. 1993. 150.00 (*0-7859-0965-6*, 2070112306) Fr & Eur.
— L' Opera de la Lune. (FRE., Illus.). 48p. 1986. pap. 10.95 (*0-7859-1381-5*, 2070391418) Fr & Eur.
— Paroles. (FRE.). 251p. 1976. pap. 10.95 (*0-7859-2400-0*, 2070367622) Fr & Eur.
— Paroles. (FRE.). (C). 1972. pap. 9.95 (*0-8442-1837-5*, VF1837-5) NTC Contemp Pub Co.
— Paroles. (Folio Ser.: No. 762). (FRE.). 1957. pap. 10.50 (*2-07-036762-2*) Schoenhof.
— Paroles: Selected Poems. rev. ed. Ferlinghetti, Lawrence, tr. from FRE. (Pocket Poets Ser.: No. 9). (FRE.). 176p. 1990. pap. 8.95 (*0-87286-249-6*) City Lights.
— La Pluie et le Beau Temps. (FRE.). 1972. pap. 10.95 (*0-7859-2264-4*, 2070360903) Fr & Eur.
— La Pluie et le Beau Temps. (Folio Ser.: No. 90). (FRE.). 256p. 1955. 8.95 (*2-07-036090-3*) Schoenhof.
— Soleil de Nuit. (FRE.). 310p. 1989. pap. 11.95 (*0-7859-2574-0*, 2070381757) Fr & Eur.
— Soleil de Nuit. (Folio Ser.). (FRE.). pap. 9.95 (*2-07-038175-7*) Schoenhof.
— Spectacle. (FRE.). 1972. pap. 11.95 (*0-7859-1628-8*, 2070361047) Fr & Eur.
— Spectacle. (Folio Ser.: No. 104). (FRE.). 1972. pap. 10.50 (*2-07-036104-7*) Schoenhof.
— Tentatives de Description d'un Diner de Tetes a Paris-France. (FRE.). 9.65 (*0-685-37053-4*) Fr & Eur.

Prevert, Jacques & Carne, Marcel. Le Jour se Leve. (FRE.). 9.95 (*0-686-54911-2*) Fr & Eur.
— Les Visiteurs du Soir. (FRE., Illus.). 256p. 1974. 25.00 (*0-686-54920-1*) Fr & Eur.

Prevert, Jacques & Guilbaud, P. Les Primitifs du XIIIe. (FRE.). 5.95 (*0-686-54917-1*) Fr & Eur.

Prevert, Jacques & Lamorisse, Albert. Bim le Petit Ane. (FRE., Illus.). 48p. 1976. pap. 10.95 (*0-7859-1445-5*, 2211040659) Fr & Eur.

Prevert, Jacques & Prevert, P. Paris la Belle. (FRE.). 5.95 (*0-686-54914-7*) Fr & Eur.

Prevert, Joseph. Fatras. (FRE.). 285p. 1977. pap. 10.95 (*0-7859-2383-7*, 2070368777) Fr & Eur.

Prevert, P., jt. auth. see Prevert, Jacques.

Prevezer, Martha, jt. ed. see Dimsdale, Nicholas.

***Previdi, Taimi.** The Best of Finnish Cooking. 242p. 2000. pap. 12.95 (*0-7818-0493-0*) Hippocrene Bks.

Preview Group, Inc. Staff. Know Your Code: A Guide to the OBBC. LC 97-162369. 329p. 1996. per. 49.50 (*0-8322-0662-8*) Banks-Baldwin.

Preview Group Staff. Know Your Code: A Guide to the OBBC. LC 98-141435. xx, 326p. 1998. write for info. (*0-8322-0681-4*) Banks-Baldwin.

Previn, Andre. Andre Previn: Impressions for Piano. 24p. 1985. pap. 6.95 (*0-7935-6148-5*) H Leonard.

***Previn, Andre.** The Andre Previn Collection. 80p. 1999. otabind 19.95 (*0-7935-9962-8*) H Leonard.

Previn, Andre. Matthew's Piano Book. 1979. pap. 9.95 (*0-685-69091-1*, HC00103) Shawnee Pr.

Previn, Dory. Midnight Baby: An Autobiography. LC 76-20544. x, 246p. 1976. write for info. (*0-02-599000-4*) Macmillan.

***Previtali, David R.** Helen's Special Picture: A Children's Story about St. Maria Faustina. (Illus.). 32p. (J). (ps-2). 2000. pap. 7.50 (*0-944203-42-6*) Marian Pr.

Previtali, David R. Raymond's 2 Crowns. (Illus.). 48p. (YA). (gr. 6-12). 1994. pap. text 3.95 (*0-9625953-3-0*) Immaculata Pr.
— Saints for Young Christians. LC 96-8390. (Illus.). 174p. (Orig.). 1996. pap. 9.95 (*0-8189-0666-9*) Alba.

Previte-Orton, Charles W. Outlines of Medieval History. 2nd ed. LC 64-25837. 1916. 30.00 (*0-8196-0147-0*) Biblo.
— Political Satire in English Poetry. 244p. (C). 1966. lib. bdg. 75.00 (*0-8383-0676-4*) M S G Haskell Hse.
— The Shorter Cambridge Medieval History: The Twelfth Century to the Renaissance, Vol. 2. LC 75-31398. 579p. reprint ed. pap. 165.10 (*0-608-15700-7*, 2031627) Bks Demand.

***Previtera, Stephen Thomas.** The Iron Time: A History of the Iron Cross. unabridged ed. (Illus.). 472p. 2000. 89.95 (*0-9673070-0-7*) Winidore Pubns.

Previts, Gary. Research in Accounting Regulation, Vol. 12. 1998. 78.50 (*0-7623-0465-0*) Jai Pr.

Previts, Gary J. A Critical Evaluation of Comparative Financial Accounting Thought in America: 1900-1920. Brief, Richard P., ed. LC 80-1517. (Dimensions of Accounting Theory & Practice Ser.). 1980. lib. bdg. 28.95 (*0-405-13496-7*) Ayer.

Previts, Gary J., ed. Research in Accounting Regulation: In Preparation, Summer 1997, Vol. 11. 1997. 78.50 (*0-7623-0168-6*) Jai Pr.

Previts, Gary J., et al, eds. Research in Accounting Regulation, Vol. 1. 235p. 1987. 78.50 (*0-89232-849-5*) Jai Pr.
— Research in Accounting Regulation, Vol. 2. 245p. 1988. 78.50 (*0-89232-941-6*) Jai Pr.
— Research in Accounting Regulation, Vol. 3. 248p. 1989. 78.50 (*0-89232-998-X*) Jai Pr.
— Research in Accounting Regulation, Vol. 4. 221p. 1990. 78.50 (*1-55938-084-5*) Jai Pr.
— Research in Accounting Regulation, Vol. 5. 211p. 1991. 78.50 (*1-55938-399-2*) Jai Pr.
— Research in Accounting Regulation, Vol. 6. 227p. 1992. 78.50 (*1-55938-417-4*) Jai Pr.
— Research in Accounting Regulation, Vol. 7. 222p. 1993. 78.50 (*1-55938-692-4*) Jai Pr.
— Research in Accounting Regulation, Vol. 8. 263p. 1994. 78.50 (*1-55938-402-6*) Jai Pr.
— Research in Accounting Regulation, Vol. 9. 252p. 1995. 78.50 (*1-55938-883-8*) Jai Pr.
— Research in Accounting Regulation, Vol. 10. 1996. 78.50 (*1-55938-996-6*) Jai Pr.

***Previts, Gary J., et al, eds.** Research in Accounting Regulation, Vol. 13. 1999. 82.50 (*0-7623-0520-7*) Jai Pr.

P

Previts, Gary J. & Taylor, Richard F. Lest We Forget . . . John Raymond Wildman, 1878-1938. (Monograph Series of the Academy of Accounting Historians: Monograph 2). 84p. 1978. pap. 5.00 (*1-879750-00-7*) Acad Acct Hist.

Previts, Gary J., jt. ed. see Brief, Richard P.

Previts, Gary J., ed. see Symposium on Financial Reporting & Standard Settin.

Previts, Gary John & Merino, Barbara Dubis. History of Accountancy in the United States: The Cultural Significance of Accounting. LC 97-24109. (Historical Perspectives on Business Enterprise Ser.). 1997. pap. text 24.95 (*0-8142-0728-6*) Ohio St U Pr.

***Previts, Gary John, et al.** Corporate Reporting of Non-Financial Performance Indicators & Operating Measures by U. S. Companies. 75p. 1999. pap. 39.75 (*1-885065-17-5*, Pub. by Finan Exec) E Elgar.

Prevo, Helen R. English That We Need. 64p. 1986. teacher ed. 1.25 (*0-88323-221-9*, 203); pap. 4.50 (*0-88323-212-X*, 109) Pendergrass Pub.

— More English That We Need. 64p. 1984. teacher ed. 1.25 (*0-88323-237-5*, 261); pap. 4.50 (*0-88323-198-0*, 155) Pendergrass Pub.

Prevorsek, Dusan C., ed. Recent Advances in Polymer Chemical Physics: Contributions of the Russian Academy of Science. 386p. 1998. text 52.00 (*90-5699-586-3*) Gordon & Breach.

Prevos, Andre J., tr. see Springer, Robert.

Prevost. Undermining of the Sandinista Revolution. 1999. pap. 22.95 (*0-312-21705-6*) St Martin.

Prevost, Abbe. Histoire du Chevalier Des Grieux et de Manon Lescaut. Deloffre & Picard, eds. (Class. Garnier Ser.). 27.95 (*0-685-34051-1*); pap. 14.95 (*0-685-34050-3*) Fr & Eur.

— Histoire du Chevalier Des Grieux et de Manon Lescaut. 1976. pap. 10.95 (*0-7859-2883-9*) Fr & Eur.

— Histoire d'un Grecque Moderne. (FRE.). 1990. pap. 16.95 (*0-7859-3000-0*) Fr & Eur.

— Manon. Waddell, Helen, tr. from FRE. LC 88-60594. 262p. 1988. reprint ed. pap. 14.95 (*0-948166-15-0*, Pub. by Soho Bk Co) Dufour.

— Manon Lescaut. (FRE.). 1976. pap. 8.95 (*0-7859-3078-7*) Fr & Eur.

— Manon Lescaut. (FRE.). (C). pap. 7.95 (*0-8442-1832-4*, VF1832-4) NTC Contemp Pub Co.

— Manon Lescaut. (Folio Ser.: No. 757). (FRE.). 249p. 1988. pap. 8.95 (*2-07-036757-6*) Schoenhof.

— Manon Lescaut. Tancock, Leonard W., tr. 192p. 1992. pap. 10.95 (*0-14-044559-5*, Penguin Classics) Viking Penguin.

— Manon Lescaut. unabridged ed. (FRE.). pap. 5.95 (*2-87714-196-9*, Pub. by Bookking Intl) Distribks Inc.

***Prevost, Abbe.** Prevost: Manon Lescaut. Byrne, Patrick, ed. (Modern Language Ser.). (FRE.). 216p. 1999. pap. text 20.95 (*1-85399-517-7*, Pub. by Brist Class Pr) Focus Pub-R Pullins.

Prevost, Abbe. The Story of a Fair Greek of Yesteryear: A Translation from the French of Antoine-Francois Prevost's "L'Histoire D'Une Grecque Moderne" Jones, James F., Jr., tr. from FRE. LC 83-51712. (Illus.). 294p. 1984. 30.00 (*0-916379-08-6*) Scripta.

Prevost, Benedict. Memoir on the Immediate Cause of Blunt or Smut of Wheat & of Several Other Diseases of Plants & on the Preventatives of Bunt. Keitt, G. W., tr. (Phytopathological Classics Ser.). 95p. 1939. 22.00 (*0-89054-007-1*) Am Phytopathol Soc.

Prevost, Bernard. God's Dream: His Plan for Us. (C). 1988. 39.00 (*0-85439-262-9*, Pub. by St Paul Pubns) St Mut.

Prevost, Dale. Update Map Co. 102p. reprint ed. spiral bd. 18.00 (*0-685-29952-X*) Update Map.

***Prevost, Dyranda & Dushkina, Natalia.** Living Places in Russia. (Illus.). 108p. 2000. pap. text 29.95 (*1-86470-087-4*, Pub. by Images) Antique Collect.

Prevost, Gary, jt. auth. see Vanden, Harry E.

Prevost, Gary, jt. ed. see Castro, Vanessa.

Prevost, Gary, jt. ed. see Chaffee, Wilbur R., Jr.

Prevost, Gary, jt. ed. see Lancaster, Thomas D.

Prevost, Jean-Pierre. How to Read the Apocalypse. (Adult Christian Formation Program Ser.). (Illus.). 160p. 1993. reprint ed. pap. 15.95 (*0-8245-1280-4*) Crossroad NY.

— How to Read the Prophets. LC 97-65490. (Illus.). 144p. 1996. pap. 19.95 (*0-8264-0943-1*) Continuum.

— A Short Dictionary of the Psalms. Misrahi, Mary M., tr. LC 96-36930. 104p. (Orig.). 1997. pap. text 9.95 (*0-8146-2370-0*, Liturg Pr Bks) Liturgical Pr.

Prevost, John F. Apple Trees. LC 96-310. 24p. (J). (ps-4). 1996. lib. bdg. 13.98 (*1-56239-614-5*) ABDO Pub Co.

— Arctic Ocean. LC 98-12071. (Oceans & Seas Ser.). (J). 2000. lib. bdg. 19.92 (*1-57765-095-6*) ABDO Pub Co.

— Atlantic Ocean. LC 98-11988. (Oceans & Seas Ser.). (J). 2002. lib. bdg. 19.92 (*1-57765-092-1*) ABDO Pub Co.

— Beluga Whales. LC 95-6374. (Illus.). 24p. (J). (ps-4). 1995. lib. bdg. 13.98 (*1-56239-477-0*) ABDO Pub Co.

— Blue Whales. LC 95-9676. (Illus.). 24p. (J). (ps-4). 1995. lib. bdg. 13.98 (*1-56239-475-4*) ABDO Pub Co.

— Bottlenose Dolphins. LC 95-3316. (Illus.). 32p. (J). (ps-4). 1995. lib. bdg. 13.98 (*1-56239-493-2*) ABDO Pub Co.

— Caribbean Sea. LC 98-12654. (Oceans & Seas Ser.). (J). 2002. lib. bdg. 19.92 (*1-57765-096-4*) ABDO Pub Co.

— Common Dolphin. LC 95-12363. (Dolphins Ser.). (Illus.). 24p. (J). (ps-4). 1995. lib. bdg. 13.98 (*1-56239-496-7*) ABDO Pub Co.

— Cottonwood Trees. LC 96-6068. (Trees Ser.). (Illus.). 24p. (J). (ps-4). 1996. lib. bdg. 13.98 (*1-56239-615-3*) ABDO Pub Co.

— Daisies. LC 96-11452. (Flowers Ser.). (Illus.). 24p. (J). (ps-4). 1996. lib. bdg. 13.98 (*1-56239-608-0*) ABDO Pub Co.

— Evergreen Trees. LC 96-6062. (Trees Ser.). (Illus.). 24p. (J). (ps-4). 1996. lib. bdg. 13.98 (*1-56239-616-1*) ABDO Pub Co.

— Freshwater Dolphins. LC 95-3315. (Dolphins Ser.). (Illus.). 24p. (J). (ps-4). 1995. lib. bdg. 13.98 (*1-56239-492-4*) ABDO Pub Co.

— Gray Whales. LC 95-9677. (Illus.). 24p. (J). (ps-4). 1995. lib. bdg. 13.98 (*1-56239-476-2*) ABDO Pub Co.

— Great White Sharks. LC 95-1511. (Sharks Ser.). (Illus.). 24p. (J). (ps-4). 1995. lib. bdg. 13.98 (*1-56239-469-X*) ABDO Pub Co.

— Hammerhead Sharks. LC 95-1171. (Illus.). 24p. (J). (ps-4). 1995. lib. bdg. 13.98 (*1-56239-471-1*) ABDO Pub Co.

— The Humpback Whale. LC 95-12367. (Whales Ser.). (Illus.). 24p. (J). (ps-4). 1995. lib. bdg. 13.98 (*1-56239-479-7*) ABDO Pub Co.

— Indian Ocean. LC 98-12653. (Oceans & Seas Ser.). (J). 1998. 14.95 (*1-57765-094-8*) ABDO Pub Co.

— Killer Whales. LC 95-2750. (Whales Ser.). (Illus.). 24p. (J). (ps-4). 1995. lib. bdg. 13.98 (*1-56239-474-6*) ABDO Pub Co.

— Lake Superior. LC 98-11983. (Lakes Ser.). (J). 2000. write for info. (*1-57765-104-9*) ABDO Pub Co.

— Mediterranean Sea. LC 98-29320. (Oceans & Seas Ser.). 2002. lib. bdg. 19.92 (*1-57765-097-2*) ABDO Pub Co.

— The Mississippi. LC 98-11984. (Rivers Ser.). (J). 2002. lib. bdg. 19.92 (*1-57765-102-2*) ABDO Pub Co.

— Orchids. LC 96-3800. (Illus.). 24p. (J). (ps-4). 1996. lib. bdg. 13.98 (*1-56239-609-9*) ABDO Pub Co.

— Pacific Ocean. LC 98-12069. (Oceans & Seas Ser.). (J). 2000. lib. bdg. 19.92 (*1-57765-093-X*) ABDO Pub Co.

— Redwood Trees. LC 96-6069. (Trees Ser.). (Illus.). 245p. (J). (ps-4). 1996. lib. bdg. 13.98 (*1-56239-617-X*) ABDO Pub Co.

— Roses. (Illus.). 24p. (J). (ps-4). 1996. lib. bdg. 13.98 (*1-56239-610-2*) ABDO Pub Co.

— Sand Sharks. LC 95-3314. (Sharks Ser.). (Illus.). 24p. (J). (ps-4). 1995. lib. bdg. 13.98 (*1-56239-470-3*) ABDO Pub Co.

— Sperm Whale. LC 95-12364. (Whales Ser.). (Illus.). 24p. (J). (ps-4). 1995. lib. bdg. 13.98 (*1-56239-478-9*) ABDO Pub Co.

— Spinner Dolphins. LC 95-12368. (Dolphins Ser.). (Illus.). 24p. (J). (ps-4). 1995. lib. bdg. 13.98 (*1-56239-497-5*) ABDO Pub Co.

— Spotted Dolphins. LC 95-12365. (Dolphins Ser.). (Illus.). 24p. (J). (ps-4). 1995. lib. bdg. 13.98 (*1-56239-495-9*) ABDO Pub Co.

— Sunflowers. LC 96-1179. (Flowers Ser.). (Illus.). 24p. (J). (ps-4). 1996. lib. bdg. 13.99 (*1-56239-611-0*) ABDO Pub Co.

— Tiger Sharks. LC 95-2749. (Sharks Ser.). (Illus.). 24p. (J). (ps-4). 1995. lib. bdg. 13.99 (*1-56239-468-1*) ABDO Pub Co.

— Tulips. (Illus.). 24p. (J). (ps-4). 1996. lib. bdg. 13.98 (*1-56239-612-9*) ABDO Pub Co.

— Violets. LC 96-10482. (Flowers Ser.). (Illus.). 24p. (J). (ps-4). 1996. lib. bdg. 13.98 (*1-56239-613-7*) ABDO Pub Co.

— Walnut Trees. LC 96-309. (Trees Ser.). 24p. (J). (ps-4). 1996. lib. bdg. 13.98 (*1-56239-618-8*) ABDO Pub Co.

— Weeping Willow Trees. LC 96-6061. (Trees Ser.). (Illus.). 24p. (J). (ps-4). 1996. lib. bdg. 13.98 (*1-56239-619-6*) ABDO Pub Co.

— Whale Sharks. LC 95-6375. (Sharks Ser.). (Illus.). 24p. (J). (ps-4). 1995. lib. bdg. 13.98 (*1-56239-473-8*) ABDO Pub Co.

— White-Sided Dolphin. LC 95-8121. (Dolphins Ser.). (Illus.). 24p. (J). (ps-4). 1995. lib. bdg. 13.98 (*1-56239-494-0*) ABDO Pub Co.

Prevost, Marie-Laure, ed. see Rolland, Romain.

Prevost, Michel & Roman-D'Amat, Jean-Claude. Dictionnaire de Biographie Francaise, 16 vols., Set.Tr. of French Biographical Dictionary. (FRE.). 8040p. 1972. 2495.00 (*0-8288-6370-9*, M-6466) Fr & Eur.

Prevost, Nancy M. Paradise in the Palouse. 35p. 1985. pap. 5.95 (*0-87770-365-5*) Ye Galleon.

Prevost, Ninon, jt. auth. see Labonte, Marie Lise.

Prevost, P. Fundamentals of Modern Agriculture. (Illus.). 236p. (C). 1997. 37.50 (*1-886106-89-4*) Science Pubs.

Prevost, P., jt. auth. see Honegger, Marc.

Prevost, Robert. Probability & Theistic Explanation. (Oxford Theological Monographs). 202p. 1990. text 75.00 (*0-19-826725-7*) OUP.

Prevost, Robert W., jt. ed. see Abraham, William J.

Prevost, Ruffin. Internet Insider. (Internet Ser.). 350p. 1995. pap. text 14.95 (*0-07-882084-7*) Osborne-McGraw.

Prevost, Ruffin & Terrell, Rob. The Mac Shareware 500: The Last Word on the Virus-Free Mac Shareware, 1994. 2nd ed. (Illus.). 458p. 1998. pap. 20.00 incl. disk (*0-7881-5767-1*) DIANE Pub.

Prevost, S. Vertex Algebras & Integral Bases for the Enveloping Algebras of Affine Lie Algebras. LC 91-44874. (Memoirs Ser.). 97p. 1977. pap. 25.00 (*0-8218-2527-5*, MEMO/96/466) Am Math.

Prevost, Toni J. Indians from New York Vol. 3: A Genealogy Reference. 241p. (Orig.). 1995. pap. 34.00 (*0-7884-0306-0*) Heritage Bk.

— Indians from New York in Wisconsin & Elsewhere: A Genealogy Reference. 228p. (Orig.). 1995. pap. text 27.00 (*0-7884-0209-9*) Heritage Bk.

Prevost, Toni Jullay. Indians from New York in Ontario & Quebec Vol. 2: A Genealogy Reference. 255p. 1995. pap. text 35.50 (*0-7884-0257-9*) Heritage Bk.

Prevot, Andre. Love, Peace & Joy: Devotion to the Sacred Heart of Jesus According to St. Gertrude. LC 84-51822. 224p. 1985. reprint ed. pap. 7.00 (*0-89555-255-8*) TAN Bks Pubs.

Prevot, Floriane. Dictionnaire de la Beaute Feminine. (FRE.). 268p. 1972. pap. 10.95 (*0-7859-1444-7*, 2203221011) Fr & Eur.

Prevot, Floriane & Roman-D'Amat, Jean-Claude. Dictionnaire de Biographie Francaise, Fasc. 1018 & 31-60. (FRE.). 230.00 (*0-685-35951-4*) Fr & Eur.

Prevots, Naima. American Pageantry: A Movement for Art & Democracy. LC 89-29255. (Theatre & Dramatic Studies: No. 61). 257p. (C). reprint ed. 79.70 (*0-8357-1991-X*, 207068200017) Bks Demand.

— Dance for Export: Cultural Diplomacy & the Cold War. LC 98-26434. (Studies in Dance History). (Illus.). 188p. 1998. 40.00 (*0-8195-6365-X*, Wesleyan Univ Pr) U Pr of New Eng.

— Dancing in the Sun: Hollywood Choreographers, 1915-1937. Brockett, Oscar G., ed. LC 87-13859. (Theater & Dramatic Studies: No. 44). (Illus.). 290p. 1987. reprint ed. pap. 89.90 (*0-8357-1825-5*, 207075400004) Bks Demand.

Prew, Sarah-Jane. Survival for Aircrew. LC 99-72608. 142p. 1999. text 61.95 (*1-84014-521-8*, Pub. by Ashgate Pub) Ashgate Pub Co.

Prewitt, Bobby W. & Butler, Kathleen A. Learning Styles & Performance Assessment: A Model Teaching Guide. 208p. (Orig.). 1993. pap. text 24.95 (*0-945852-04-5*) Learners Dimension.

***Prewitt, Charles B.** Laying the Roles to Rest. 176p. 1999. pap. 9.95 (*0-9673868-0-2*) C B Prewitt.

Prewitt, Christa, ed. Gths German Immigrant Ancestors. 248p. 15.00 (*1-57168-240-6*) Sunbelt Media.

Prewitt, Jeffrey L., ed. The Dilemma of American Political Thought. LC 95-30163. 287p. 1995. pap. text 42.00 (*0-13-371592-2*) P-H.

Prewitt, Kenneth. The Recruitment of Political Leaders: A Study of Citizen-Politicians. LC 81-6344. (Urban Government Ser.). (Illus.). 234p. 1981. reprint ed. lib. bdg. 65.00 (*0-313-22744-6*, PRRP, Greenwood Pr) Greenwood.

Prewitt, Kenneth, jt. auth. see Eulau, Heinz.

Prewitt, Roger W. & Fardo, Stephen W. Electronic Instrumentation: A Lab Text. 2nd ed. (Illus.). 220p. (C). 1983. reprint ed. pap. text 16.95 (*0-89917-387-X*) Tichenor Pub.

Prewitt, Roger W., jt. auth. see Fardo, Stephen W.

Prewitt-Salem, Cheryl. Abuse, Bruised but Not Broken. Date not set. mass mkt. 2.99 (*0-89274-587-8*, CS-587) Harrison Hse.

Prewitt, Terry J. The Elusive Covenant: A Structural-Semiotic Reading of Genesis. LC 89-46325. (Illus.). 160p. 1990. 7.95 (*0-253-34599-5*) Ind U Pr.

— The Elusive Covenant: A Structural-Semiotic Reading of Genesis. LC 89-46325. (Advances in Semiotics Ser.). (Illus.). 156p. Date not set. reprint ed. pap. 48.40 (*0-608-20566-4*, 205448000002) Bks Demand.

— German-American Settlement in an Oklahoma Town: Ecologic, Ethnic & Cultural Change. LC 89-84003. (Immigrant Communities & Ethnic Minorities in the U. S. & Canada Ser.: No. 56). 1989. 52.50 (*0-404-19466-4*) AMS Pr.

Prewitt, Terry J., et al, eds. Semiotics, 1988. LC 84-640162. (Illus.). 612p. (C). 1989. lib. bdg. 103.00 (*0-8191-7478-5*) U Pr of Amer.

Prewitt, Terry J., jt. auth. see Blanchard, Dallas A.

Prewitt, Terry J., jt. ed. see Deely, John.

Prewitt, Vana, ed. Productivity Management. (ACCRUE Ser.: Level II). 175p. 1991. ring bd. 63.00 (*1-879907-01-1*) Am Soc Hlth-Syst.

Prey, Hermann. First Night Fever. Shackelton, Andrew, tr. from GER. LC 86-6491. (Illus.). 1991. 24.95 (*0-7145-3998-8*) Riverrun NY.

Prey, Pierre D. Du, see Du Prey, Pierre D.

Prey, S., jt. auth. see Plochinger, B.

Preyde, James & Preyde, Susan. Steeple Chase: Ontario's Historic Churches. (Illus.). 72p. 1991. pap. 20.00 (*1-55046-030-7*, Pub. by Boston Mills) Genl Dist Srvs.

— Yukon Gold: High Hopes & Dashed Dreams. (Illus.). 96p. 1995. pap. 12.95 (*0-88839-362-8*) Hancock House.

Preyde, Susan, jt. auth. see Preyde, James.

Preyer, Gerhard, et al, eds. Language, Mind, & Epistemology: On Don Davidson's Philosophy. LC 94-7208. (Synthese Library). 464p. (C). 1994. lib. bdg. 204.50 (*0-7923-2811-6*, Pub. by Kluwer Academic) Kluwer Academic.

Preyer, William. Embryonic Motility & Sensitivity. (SRCD Ser.: Vol. 2, No. 6). 1937. 25.00 (*0-527-01499-0*) Periodicals Srv.

— Mental Development in the Child. Brown, H. W., tr. from GER. LC 78-72818. (Brainedness, Handedness, & Mental Abilities Ser.). reprint ed. 42.50 (*0-404-60887-6*) AMS Pr.

— The Mind of the Child, 2 vols. LC 73-2985. (Classics in Psychology Ser.). 1977. reprint ed. 47.95 (*0-405-05156-5*) Ayer.

Preyma, Nadia, et al. Management Tools. Schulz, William, ed. (Options: Guidance for Grades 1). 140p. (Orig.). (gr. 1-8). 1989. pap., teacher ed. 8.00 (*0-920541-59-3*) Peguis Pubs Ltd.

Prezbindowski, Kathleen S. A Study Guide to Accompany Anthony Textbook. 11th ed. 370p. 1983. pap. text 13.95 (*0-8016-4011-3*) Mosby Inc.

Prezbindowski, Kathleen S. & Tortora, Gerald J. Principles of Anatomy & Physiology. 8th ed. LC 95-40981. 1152p. (C). 1996. pap. text, student ed., suppl. ed. 25.31 (*0-673-99356-6*) Addson-Wesley Educ.

Prezeau, Jael, ed. see Lynde, Stan.

Prezelski, Carmen V., tr. see Cabat, Erni.

Prezelski, Carmen V., tr. see Cabat, Erni & Polzer, Charles W.

Preziosi, Donald. Architecture, Language & Meaning. (Approaches to Semiotics Ser.: No. 49). 1979. pap. text 35.00 (*90-279-7828-X*) Mouton.

— Minoan Architectural Design: Formation & Signification. LC 82-22415. (Approaches to Semiotics Ser.: No. 63). xxxi, 522p. 1983. 133.85 (*90-279-3409-6*) Mouton.

— Rethinking Art History: Meditations on a Coy Science. (Illus.). 296p. (C). 1991. reprint ed. pap. 16.00 (*0-300-04983-8*) Yale U Pr.

— The Semiotics of the Built Environment: An Introduction to Architectonic Analysis. LC 78-20404. (Advances in Semiotics Ser.). 128p. 1979. pap. 39.70 (*0-8357-3956-2*, 205705200004) Bks Demand.

Preziosi, Donald, ed. The Art of Art History: A Critical Anthology. (Oxford History of Art Ser.). (Illus.). 596p. 1998. pap. 18.95 (*0-19-284242-0*) OUP.

Preziosi, Donald & Hitchcock, Louise. Aegean Art & Architecture. (Oxford History of Art Ser.). (Illus.). 272p. 2000. pap. 17.95 (*0-19-284208-0*) OUP.

Preziosi, Giochi, tr. see Perego, Maria.

Preziosi, L., jt. auth. see Monaco, R.

Preziosi, Luigi, jt. ed. see Markov, Konstantin Z.

***Preziuso, Gennaro.** The Life of Padre Pio: Between the Altar & the Confessional. Aumann, Jordan, tr. from ITA. LC 99-40385. (Illus.). x, 241p. 2000. pap. 16.95 (*0-8189-0831-9*) Alba.

Prezwalski, Jim. The Kiss of the Whip: Explorations in SM. 256p. (Orig.). 1994. pap. 15.95 (*0-943595-51-7*) Leyland Pubns.

Prezzolini, Giuseppe. Carteggio Angelini-Prezzolini: Edizioni di Storia e Letteratura. Marchione, Margherita & Mussini, Gianni, eds. (ITA.). 330p. 1983. pap. 40.00 (*0-916322-15-7*) Am Inst Ital Stud.

— The Case of the Casa Italiana. LC 76-9908. 63p. 1976. pap. 3.00 (*0-916322-14-9*) Am Inst Ital Stud.

— Fascism. Macmillan, Kathleen, tr. LC 78-63707. (Studies in Fascism: Ideology & Practice). 1977. reprint ed. 37.50 (*0-404-16977-5*) AMS Pr.

— Giuseppe Prezzolini: Lettere a Suor Margherita, (1956-1982) Quarantotto, Claudio, ed. LC 42-49549. 378p. 1992. write for info. (*0-614-10141-7*) Am Inst Ital Stud.

— Giuseppe Prezzolini: L'Ombra di Dio. 200p. 1984. write for info. (*0-614-10139-5*) Am Inst Ital Stud.

— Incontriamo Prezzolini: Editrice La Scuola, Brescia. LC 42-49549. 210p. 1985. pap. write for info. (*0-614-10140-9*) Am Inst Ital Stud.

Prezzolini, Giuseppe, et al. Ricordi, Saggi e Testimonianze: Edizioni del Palazzo, Prato. 300p. 1983. write for info. (*0-614-10138-7*) Am Inst Ital Stud.

P.R.G. Holland Staff, jt. auth. see D. D. Prentice Staff.

Prhugl, Elisabeth. The Global Construction of Gender: Home-Based Work in the Political Economy of the 20th Century. LC 99-24851. 224p. 1999. pap. 18.50 (*0-231-11561-X*) Col U Pr.

***Prialnik, Dina.** An Introduction to the Theory of Stellar Structure & Evolution. LC 99-44948. (Illus.). 288p. (C). 2000. 64.95 (*0-521-65065-8*); pap. 24.95 (*0-521-65937-X*) Cambridge U Pr.

Priamos, James S., jt. auth. see Hughes, Joseph H., Jr.

Prianishnikoff, Boris. Novopokolentsy. (Illus.). 320p. 1986. write for info. (*0-9616413-1-2*) Multilingual.

Priban, Jiri & Young, James, eds. The Rule of Law in Central Europe: The Reconstruction of Legality, Constitutionalism & Civil Society in the Post-Communist Countries. LC 99-22607. (Socio Legal Studies). 286p. 1999. text 87.95 (*1-84014-719-9*, Pub. by Ashgate Pub) Ashgate Pub Co.

Pribaum, Karl H., ed. Brain & Values. LC 98-17067. (INNS Series of Texts, Monographs, & Proceedings). 560p. 1998. pap. 95.00 (*0-8058-3154-1*) L Erlbaum Assocs.

Pribble, Wayne I., jt. auth. see DuBois, J. Harry.

Pribchevich-Zoric, Christina, jt. auth. see Pavic, Milorad.

***Pribersky, Andreas & Unfried, Berthold.** Symbole und Rituale des Politischen: Ost-Und Westeuropa im Vergleich. (Historisch-Anthropologische Studien Ser.). (Illus.). 300p. 1999. 56.95 (*3-631-31862-6*) P Lang Pubng.

Pribersky, Andreas, jt. ed. see Plasser, Fritz.

Pribic, Rado, ed. Nobel Laureates in Literature: A Biographical Dictionary. LC 89-11803. 497p. 1990. text 25.00 (*0-8240-5741-4*, H849) Garland.

Pribic, Rado, jt. ed. see Wollenberg, Jorg.

Pribicevic-Zoric, Christina, tr. see Pavic, Milorad.

Pribicevic-Zoric, Christina, tr. see Samokovlija, Isak, et al.

Pribichevich, Stoyan. Macedonia: Its People & History. LC 82-80455. (Illus.). 304p. 1982. 32.50 (*0-271-00315-4*) Pa St U Pr.

Pribil, F. Analytical Application of EDTA & Related Compounds. 368p. (C). 1972. 172.00 (*0-08-016363-7*, Pub. by Pergamon Repr) Franklin.

Pribitkin, Edmund, 2nd, jt. auth. see Goode, Richard L.

Pribor, Hugo C., et al. Drug Monitoring & Pharmacokinetic Data. LC 79-90657. 190p. 1980. 29.50 (*0-930376-10-2*) Chem-Orbital.

Pribram, Alfred F. Austria-Hungary & Great Britain, 1908-1914. LC 70-138174. 328p. 1972. reprint ed. lib. bdg. 65.00 (*0-8371-5631-9*, PRAG, Greenwood Pr) Greenwood.

Pribram, K. H., jt. auth. see Isaacson, R. L.

Pribram, Karl H. Brain & Perception: Holonomy & Structure in Figural Processing. (John M. MacEachran Lectures Ser.). 400p. 1991. 79.95 (*0-89859-995-4*) L Erlbaum Assocs.

— Cartel Problems: An Analysis of Collective Monopolies in Europe with American Application: The Institute of Economics of the Brookings Institution, No. 69. (Business Enterprises Reprint Ser.). x, 287p. 1986. reprint ed. lib. bdg. 40.00 (*0-89941-479-6*, 304060) W S Hein.

— A History of Economic Reasoning. LC 82-13042. 832p. (C). 1983. text 75.00 (*0-8018-2291-2*) Johns Hopkins.

— Languages of the Brain: Experimental Paradoxes & Principles in Neuropsychology. 5th ed. 432p. 1982. reprint ed. text 35.00 (*0-913412-22-8*) Brandon Hse.

An Asterisk (*) at the beginning of an entry indicates that the title is appearing for the first time.

Pribram, Karl H., ed. Origins: Brain & Self Organization. (INNS Ser.). 728p. 1994. text 135.00 (*0-8058-1786-7*) L Erlbaum Assocs.

— Rethinking Neural Networks: Quantum Fields & Biological Data. 568p. 1993. pap. 125.00 (*0-8058-1466-3*) L Erlbaum Assocs.

Pribram, Karl H. & King, Joseph, eds. Learning As Self-Organization. (INNS Series of Texts, Monographs, & Proceedings). 608p. (C). 1996. pap. 125.00 (*0-8058-2586-X*) L Erlbaum Assocs.

Pribram, Karl H., jt. ed. see Isaacson, Robert L.

Pribram, Karl H., jt. ed. see King, Joseph.

Pribula. Lab Manual Experiments to General Chemistry by P. W. Atkins. (C). 1995. 4.00 (*0-7167-2042-6*) W H Freeman.

Pribus, Marilyn, ed. see Williamson, Bonnie.

Pribyl, Virginia M. Recipes for Living. (Illus.). 160p. (Orig.). 1988. pap. 9.95 (*0-9621089-0-1*) VMP Servs.

Pribytkov, Victor, ed. Soviet U. S. Relations: The Selected Speeches & Writings of Chernenko. LC 84-23789. 218p. 1984. 47.95 (*0-275-91243-4*, C1243, Praeger Pubs) Greenwood.

Pricard, B. Serbo-Croatian-English Dictionary of Maritime Terms. (CRO, ENG & SER.). 285p. 1989. 29.95 (*0-8288-7251-1*, 8603992088) Fr & Eur.

Price. Biological Evolution. LC 95-68932. (C). 1995. text 83.50 (*0-03-096843-7*, Pub. by Harcourt Coll Pubs) Harcourt.

— California Government Today. 5th ed. (C). 1995. pap. text, teacher ed. 28.00 (*0-534-25999-5*) Harcourt.

***Price.** Composition Skills Activities Workbook. 2000. pap. 5.95 (*0-13-019964-8*) P-H.

— Computing with Clarisworks V 2.0. (Computer Applications Ser.). 1994. pap. 35.95 (*0-538-63479-0*) Sth-Wstrn College.

Price. Cross-Cultural Perspectives. 2nd ed. 1995. mass mkt. 10.50 (*0-314-06946-1*) West Pub.

— Cross Cultural Perspectives. 3rd ed. LC 98-29102. (Psychology Ser.). 1998. pap. 15.95 (*0-534-35570-6*) Brooks-Cole.

— Cross-cultural Perspectives In Introductory Psychology. (Psychology). 1992. pap. text 11.00 (*0-314-01115-3*) West Pub.

— Daily Plannng: Writing Lesson & Actvty Plans for the Diversified Classroom. LC 99-173217. (Special Education Ser.). 1998. mass mkt. 30.95 (*0-534-34917-X*) Wadsworth Pub.

— Documents on the French Revolution 1848. LC 96-7530. (Illus.). 240p. 1997. text 45.00 (*0-312-16128-X*) St Martin.

***Price.** Fun with Digital Imaging: The Official Hewlett-Packard Guide. LC 99-25397. 376p. 1999. pap. 19.99 (*0-7645-3307-X*) IDG Bks.

— A Guide to Starting Psychotherapy Groups. 172p. (C). 1999. 34.95 (*0-12-564745-X*) Acad Pr.

Price. Husband Hunting Made Easy. LC 98-11545. 240p. 1998. pap. 12.95 (*0-312-18727-0*) St Martin.

— Larry's Landscape. 2nd ed. (AB - Accounting Principles Ser.). 1995. mass mkt. 21.95 (*0-538-86089-8*) S-W Pub.

— Live Long & Prosper. 210p. (C). 1998. pap. text 12.00 (*0-536-01444-2*) Pearson Custom.

— Managing Health Care Resources. LC 98-4643. (Illus.). 336p. (C). (gr. 13). 1998. pap. text 34.95 (*0-8151-2298-5*, 27516) Mosby Inc.

— Mountain Research in Europe: An Overview of MAB Research from the Pyreness to Siberia. LC 94-27565. (Man & the Biosphere Ser.: Vol. 14). 254p. 1995. 65.00 (*1-85070-570-4*) Prthnon Pub.

— Other Paths. 1999. mass mkt. 3.95 (*0-445-40276-8*, Pub. by Warner Bks) Little.

***Price.** Philosophy Through the Ages. LC 99-16079. (Philosophy Ser.). 400p. 1999. pap. text 54.95 (*0-534-56700-2*) Brooks-Cole.

Price. Pre-Algebra. 1997. 41.99 (*0-02-825031-1*) McGraw.

— Revolution of 1848. 1996. text 11.95 (*0-333-36609-3*, Pub. by Macmillan) St Martin.

— Securities Compliance Handbook: 1994 Edition. 1994. per. 60.00 (*1-55738-706-0*, Irwn Prfssnl) McGraw-Hill Prof.

— Workbook for Affective Legal Research. 5th ed. 1979. 9.95 (*0-316-71855-6*, Aspen Law & Bus) Aspen Pub.

Price & Birkin. Worldwide Resort Timesharing Industry, 1992. 56p. 1992. 20.00 (*0-614-04633-5*, 21300) ARDA.

Price & Blount. Environmental Science: Laboratory Exercises. 90p. (C). 1997. spiral bd., lab manual ed. 19.95 (*0-7872-4293-4*) Kendall-Hunt.

Price, et al. Dressing Up. 24p. (ps-3). 1999. pap. 4.99 (*0-8431-7471-4*, 190788, Price Stern) Peng Put Young Read.

***Price, et al.** Pre-Algebra. 1999. student ed. 43.99 (*0-02-833240-7*); wbk. ed. 7.47 (*0-02-825041-9*) Glencoe.

— Pre-Algebra: An Integrated Transition to Algebra & Geometry, Teacher's Wraparound Edition. 1999. teacher ed. 56.51 (*0-02-833241-5*) Glencoe.

Price, et al. Trains, Trucks, & More: A Draw With Shapes Book. 24p. (ps-3). 1999. pap. 4.99 (*0-8431-7472-2*, Price Stern) Peng Put Young Read.

Price, jt. auth. see Grossman, Michael.

Price, jt. auth. see House.

Price, jt. auth. see Mahoney.

Price, jt. auth. see Miller.

Price, jt. auth. see Morozumi, Atsuko.

Price, jt. auth. see Morozuoi.

Price, ed. see De Cervantes Saavedra, Miguel.

Price, David W. History Made, History Imagined: Contemporary Literature, Poiesis & the Past. LC 98-58031. 360p. 1999. pap. text 23.95 (*0-252-06776-2*) U of Ill Pr.

— History Made, History Imagined: Contemporary Literature,Poiesis & the Past. LC 98-58031. 360p. 1999. 49.95 (*0-252-02468-0*) U of Ill Pr.

***Price, Jennifer.** Flight Maps: Adventures with Nature in Modern America. LC 99-215197. 212p. 1999. 23.00 (*0-465-02485-8*, Pub. by Basic) HarpC.

— Flight Maps: Adventures with Nature in Modern America. (Illus.). 325p. 2000. pap. text 14.00 (*0-465-02486-6*, Pub. by Basic) HarpC.

Price, A. Late Marque Spitfire Aces, 1942-45 Vol. 5: Aircraft of the Aces. (Illus.). 96p. Date not set. pap. 17.95 (*1-85532-575-6*, Pub. by Ospry) Stackpole.

Price, A. D. Financing International Projects. LC 96-113425. (International Construction Management Ser.: Vol. 3). xv, 138p. 1995. pap. 13.50 (*92-2-108747-6*) Intl Labour Office.

— International Project Accounting. LC 95-193511. (International Construction Management Ser.: Vol. 1). xiii, 152p. 1995. pap. 13.50 (*92-2-108264-4*) Intl Labour Office.

Price, A. F. & Mou-Lam, Wong, trs. The Diamond Sutra & the Sutra of Hui-Neng. 1974. pap. 9.95 (*0-394-73019-4*, Pub. by Shambhala Pubns) Random.

— The Diamond Sutra & the Sutra of Hui Neng. LC 78-237407. 192p. 1990. reprint ed. pap. 14.00 (*0-87773-005-9*, Pub. by Shambhala Pubns) Random.

Price, A. Grenfell, ed. see Cook, James.

Price, A. Lindsay. Cranes: The Shining Marks: In Natural History & Cultural Lore. (Illus.). 200p. 1999. pap. 14.00 (*1-888809-14-0*) La Alameda Pr.

— Swans of the World: In Nature, History, Myth & Art. (Illus.). 196p. 1995. 26.95 (*0-933031-81-5*) Coun Oak Bks.

Price, A. S. Buying a Shop. 128p. (Orig.). 1990. pap. 20.95 (*0-8464-1373-6*) Beekman Pubs.

Price, A. W. Love & Friendship in Plato & Aristotle. 278p. 1990. reprint ed. pap. text 27.00 (*0-19-824899-7*) OUP.

— Mental Conflict. LC 94-3935. (Issues in Ancient Philosophy Ser.). 208p. (C). 1994. pap. 27.99 (*0-415-11557-4*, B4617) Routledge.

Price, Alan. End of the Age of Innocence. 238p. 1997. pap. 17.95 (*0-312-17677-5*) St Martin.

— The End of the Age of Innocence: Edith Wharton & the First World War. LC 95-38196. (Illus.). 238p. 1996. text 35.00 (*0-312-12938-6*) St Martin.

— Human Resource Management in a Business Context. 384p. 1997. pap. 20.99 (*1-86152-182-0*) Thomson Learn.

Price, Alan, jt. ed. see Joslin, Katherine.

Price, Alfred. Air Battle Central Europe. 208p. 1990. mass mkt. 4.95 (*0-446-36047-3*, Pub. by Warner Bks) Little.

— Battle of Britain Day: 15 September 1940. LC 99-16874. (Illus.). 192p. 1999. 34.95 (*1-85367-375-7*, Pub. by Greenhill Bks) Stackpole.

***Price, Alfred.** Battle of Britain Day: 15 September, 1940. LC 00-38074. (Illus.). (J). 2000. pap. write for info. (*1-85367-419-2*) Stackpole.

Price, Alfred. Focke Wulf FW 190 in Combat. LC 98-155028. (Aviation History Ser.). (Illus.). 192p. 1998. 32.95 (*0-7509-1634-6*, Pub. by Sutton Pub Ltd) Intl Pubs Mktg.

— The Luftwaffe Data Book. LC 97-18382. (Illus.). 240p. 1997. 34.95 (*1-85367-293-9*, Pub. by Greenhill Bks) Stackpole.

— Luftwaffe in Camera: The Years of Victory, 1939-1942. (Illus.). 192p. 1998. 35.95 (*0-7509-1635-4*, Pub. by Sutton Pub Ltd) Intl Pubs Mktg.

— The Luftwaffe in Camera, 1942-1945: The Years of Desperation. (Illus.). 192p. 1998. 39.95 (*0-7509-1636-2*, Pub. by Sutton Pub Ltd) Intl Pubs Mktg.

— Sky Battles: Dramatic Air Warfare Actions. (Cassell Military Classics Ser.). 1999. pap. text 9.95 (*0-304-35103-2*) Continuum.

***Price, Alfred.** Sky Warriors: Classic Air War Battles. (Military Classics). (Illus.). 208p. 1999. pap. 9.95 (*0-304-35130-X*, Pub. by Cassell) Sterling.

Price, Alfred. Spitfire Mark V Aces, 1941-45 - Aircraft of the Aces. (Aircraft of the Aces Ser.: No. 16). (Illus.). 96p. 1997. pap. 17.95 (*1-85532-635-3*, Pub. by Ospry) Motorbooks Intl.

— Spitfire Mark I/II Aces, 1938-41. (Aircraft of the Aces Ser.: No. 12). (Illus.). 96p. 1996. pap. 17.95 (*1-85532-627-2*, Pub. by Ospry) Motorbooks Intl.

Price, Alfred & Spick, Mike. Great Aircraft of WWII. (Illus.). 328p. 1997. 17.98 (*0-7858-0669-5*) Bk Sales Inc.

Price, Alfred, jt. auth. see Ethell, Jeffrey L.

Price, Alfred, jt. auth. see Weal, John.

Price, Alfred, ed. & intro. see Deichmann, Paul.

Price, Alice L., ed. see Baron, Enid.

Price, Alice Lindsay, ed. see Walton, John Brooks.

Price, Allison. Writing from the Source: Techniques for Re-Scripting Your Life. 1999. pap. 16.00 (*0-7225-3683-6*) Thorsons PA.

Price, Alvin H. & Parry, Jay A. Discipline: One Hundred One Alternatives to Nagging, Yelling & Spanking. (Illus.). 172p. (C). 1983. pap. 9.95 (*0-944803-68-7*) Brite Music.

Price, Alvin H., jt. auth. see Scoresby, A. Lynn.

Price, Ann M. The Western Dance Master. (Illus.). 156p. 1997. 34.95 (*1-891448-01-3*, CB003) Chivalry Bkshelf.

Price, Anne & Dana, Nancy B. The Working Woman's Guide to Breastfeeding. 146p. 1987. pap. 7.00 (*0-671-63624-3*) S&S Trade.

Price, Anne & Yaakov, Juliette, eds. Middle & Junior High School Library Catalog. 7th ed. LC 95-38272. (Standard Catalog Ser.). 1008p. 1995. 175.00 (*0-8242-0880-3*) Wilson.

Price, Anne J., jt. auth. see Morton, Herbert C.

Price, Anthony. The Alamut Ambush. large type ed. (Adventure Suspense Ser.). 406p. 1988. 27.99 (*0-7089-1854-9*) Ulverscroft.

— The Eyes of the Fleet: A Popular History of Frigates & Frigate Captains, 1793-1815. 1996. text 25.00 (*0-07-052444-0*) McGraw.

— Gunner Kelly. 192p. 1989. mass mkt. 4.95 (*0-445-40253-9*, Pub. by Warner Bks) Little.

— Gunner Kelly. large type ed. (Adventure Suspense Ser.). 416p. 1988. 27.99 (*0-7089-1918-9*) Ulverscroft.

— Here Be Monsters. 256p. 1986. 15.95 (*0-89296-154-6*, Pub. by Mysterious Pr) Little.

— The Labyrinth Makers. large type ed. 369p. 1981. 27.99 (*0-7089-0711-3*) Ulverscroft.

— A New Kind of War. LC 87-40385. 272p. 1988. 17.95 (*0-89296-281-X*, Pub. by Mysterious Pr) Little.

— The Old Vengeful. 224p. 1989. mass mkt. 4.95 (*0-445-40257-1*, Pub. by Warner Bks) Little.

Price, Anthony. Sign Crossing. 1986. 15.45 (*0-89296-114-7*, Pub. by Mysterious Pr) Little.

Price, Anthony. War Game. large type ed. (Adventure Suspense Ser.). 512p. 1988. 27.99 (*0-7089-1870-0*) Ulverscroft.

Price, Antonia. Ambergris: A Novel. 246p. 1997. 42.50 (*1-85776-296-7*, Pub. by Book Guild Ltd) Trans-Atl Phila.

Price, Archibald G. The Western Invasions of the Pacific & Its Continents: A Study of Moving Frontiers & Changing Landscapes, 1513-1958. LC 80-14037. (Illus.). 236p. 1980. reprint ed. lib. bdg. 38.50 (*0-313-22433-1*, PRWE, Greenwood Pr) Greenwood.

— White Settlers & Native Peoples: An Historical Study of Racial Contacts Between English-Speaking Whites & Aboriginal Peoples in the United States, Canada, Australia, & New Zealand. LC 71-142320. (Illus.). 232p. 1972. reprint ed. lib. bdg. 59.75 (*0-8371-5923-7*, PRWH) Greenwood.

— White Settlers in the Tropics. LC 75-41217. reprint ed. 72.50 (*0-404-14731-3*) AMS Pr.

Price, Arnold H., ed. Missionary to the Malagasy: The Madagascar Diary of the Rev. Charles T. Price, 1875-1877. (American University Studies: History: Ser. IX, Vol. 60). 273p. (C). 1989. text 48.00 (*0-8204-1083-7*) P Lang Pubng.

***Price, Arthur, et al.** Fabric Science. 7th ed. LC 98-73426. 544p. 1999. ring bd. 52.00 (*1-56367-160-3*) Fairchild.

Price, Ashland. Sweet Sorcery. 384p. 1997. mass mkt. 4.99 (*0-8217-5604-4*, Zebra Kensgtn) Kensgtn Pub Corp.

— When Last We Met. 320p. 1998. pap. 4.99 (*0-8217-5866-7*, Zebra Kensgtn) Kensgtn Pub Corp.

Price, B. B. Ancient Economic Thought. LC 96-33564. 256p. (C). 1997. 80.00 (*0-415-14930-4*) Routledge.

— Medieval Thought: An Introduction. 256p. (C). 1991. pap. text 28.95 (*0-631-17509-1*) Blackwell Pubs.

Price, B. Bryon, ed. see Gober, Jim.

Price, B. Byron. Cowboys of the American West. unabridged ed. LC 96-23380. (Illus.). 224p. 1996. 9.99 (*1-57145-032-7*, Thunder Bay) Advantage Pubs.

— Imagining the Open Range, Erwin E. Smith, Cowboy Photographer: Erwin E. Smith, Cowboy Photographer. LC 97-45729. (Illus.). 187p. 1998. 149.99 (*0-88360-090-0*) Amon Carter.

— Lougheed. (Illus.). 148p. 1991. 65.00 (*0-9620327-2-7*) Nygard Pub.

Price, Barry. The Creation Science Controversy. rev. exp. ed. LC 89-12120. 1989. write for info. (*0-85574-889-3*) E J Dwyer.

Price, Barry, jt. ed. see Boesiger, W.

Price, Ben, jt. auth. see Dooley, Kirk.

Price, Benjamin Lewis. Nursing Fathers: American Colonists' Conception of English Protestant Kingship: 1688-1776. LC 98-53034. 272p. 1999. 45.00 (*0-7391-0051-3*) Lxngtn Bks.

Price, Bertram, jt. auth. see Chatterjee, Samprit.

Price, Betsy, jt. ed. see Hamouda, Omar F.

Price, Bette. Rejecting Rejection: How to Take Control of Your Life in Uncontrolled Times. 136p. 1996. pap. text, per. 14.95 (*0-7872-2681-5*) Kendall-Hunt.

Price, Betty. Through the Fire & Through the Water: My Triumph over Cancer. LC 98-206655. 1997. 14.99 (*1-883798-20-5*) Faith One.

***Price, Betty.** Through the Fire & Through the Water: My Triumph over Cancer. 2000. pap. 7.99 (*1-883798-33-7*) Faith One.

Price, Betty G. & Caujolle, Claude. See Me Read. (Illus.). (J). (ps). 1985. pap. 19.95 (*0-9614374-0-5*) Prof Reading Serv.

***Price, Betty R.** Lifestyles of the Rich & Faithful: A Handbook for Successful Christian Living. 110p. 1999. pap. 7.99 (*1-883798-40-X*) Faith One.

Price, Beverly, jt. auth. see Kurleto, Betsey.

Price, Bill. BMC-BL Competitions Department - 25 Years in Motorsport, the Cars, the People, the Events. (Illus.). 392p. 1998. 60.95 (*1-85960-439-0*, Pub. by J H Haynes & Co) Motorbooks Intl.

— Close Calls: Two Tours with the 350th Fighter SQ, 353rd Fighter Group. Frisque, Tom, ed. (Illus.). 128p. (Orig.). 1992. pap. 17.95 (*0-9623080-3-X*) Aviation Usk.

Price, Bobby G. Visualize. 58p. (Orig.). 1986. pap. 10.00 (*0-932662-60-9*) St Andrews NC.

Price, Bren T. Basic Composition Activities Kit. LC 82-12962. 240p. 1982. pap. text 29.95 (*0-87628-169-2*) Ctr Appl Res.

Price, Brena. Giving, Christian Stewardship: Teaching Bks. (Illus.). 14p. (J). (gr. 1-8). 1971. pap. text 4.50 (*0-86508-154-9*) BCM Pubn.

— Our Bodies: Learning to Use Them to Please God. (BMC Teaching Bks.). (Illus.). 20p. (J). (gr. 1-8). 1983. pap. 4.50 (*0-86508-157-3*) BCM Pubn.

Price, Brian. Book of the Tournament. 1995. boxed set 25.00 (*1-886094-23-3*) Chicago Spectrum.

Price, Brian R. Pas D'Armes & Round Tables: Re-enacting Medieval Feats of Arms. (Illus.). 296p. 1998. 39.95 (*1-891448-02-1*, CB004) Chivalry Bkshelf.

Price, Brick & Clymer Publications Staff. Toyota: Service-Repair Handbook: Corona, Mark II, Celica, Crown, Stout & Hi-Lux, 1968-1976 4th rev. ed. LC 77-352171. 242 p. 1976. write for info. (*0-89287-118-0*) Clymer Pub.

Price, Bronte. School Industry Links. (C). 1990. 59.00 (*0-86431-100-1*, Pub. by Aust Council Educ Res) St Mut.

Price, Bruce. American Dreams. LC 83-63241. 266p. 1985. 22.00 (*0-932966-37-3*); pap. 16.00 (*0-932966-62-4*) Permanent Pr.

Price, Bruce D. 1880 Cocke County Census: Cocke County, Tennessee. 288p. 1999. pap. 26.00 (*1-56664-154-3*) WorldComm.

— 1877-1900 Cocke County Marriage Bonds. 208p. 1999. pap. 26.00 (*1-56664-153-5*) WorldComm.

— 1900-1920 Sevier County Census. 80p. 1999. pap. 26.00 (*1-56664-155-1*) WorldComm.

— Too Easy. 1994. 21.00 (*0-671-88673-8*) S&S Trade.

Price, Bruce R. Before the Pilgrims - The Virginia Cavaliers. LC 97-50511. 192p. 1998. 15.95 (*0-944957-93-5*) Rivercross Pub.

Price, Bud & Engler, John. The Grass Really Isn't Greener: A Spiritual Perspective of the Other Side of God's Fence. Geissler, Rex & Wakefield, Tad, eds. 1997. pap. 8.95 (*0-9653469-5-1*) GCI Books.

Price, C. Matthew. 1997. pap. 10.99 (*1-85792-285-9*, Pub. by Christian Focus) Spring Arbor Dist.

Price, C. E., jt. auth. see McNeil, J. A.

***Price, C. Houston.** Collector Knives. 13th ed. 2000. pap. 17.95 (*0-676-60189-8*, Pub. by Crown Pub Group) Random House.

Price, C. Houston, jt. auth. see Hughes, B. R.

Price, C. Houston, ed. see Hibben, Gil.

Price, C. J., ed. see Sheridan, Richard Brinsley.

Price, Camille C., jt. auth. see Carter, Michael W.

Price, Carl F. Yankee Township (East Hampton) (Illus.). 212p. 1998. reprint ed. lib. bdg. 32.00 (*0-8328-9738-8*) Higginson Bk Co.

Price, Catherine. Glimpses of God: Jesus Parables for Youth. 48p. 1998. pap. 8.95 (*0-687-72798-7*) Abingdon.

— The Oglala People, 1841-1879: A Political History. LC 95-23153. (Illus.). xiv, 244p. 1998. pap. text 16.00 (*0-8032-8758-5*) U of Nebr Pr.

Price, Catherine, jt. ed. see Jackson, Peter.

Price, Catherine M. Welfare Economics in Theory & Practice. LC 77-363325. 175 p. 1977. write for info. (*0-333-19122-6*) Macmillan.

***Price, Cathy Nelson.** Nurseries. LC 00-20492. (For Your Home Ser.). (Illus.). 72p. 2000. pap. 12.95 (*1-56799-919-0*, Friedman-Fairfax) M Friedman Pub Grp Inc.

***Price, Charles.** The Cock's Spur. 290p. 2000. 19.95 (*0-89587-230-7*) Blair.

Price, Charles. Lines of Thought. (Illus.). 48p. 1997. pap. 18.00 (*1-880897-17-2*) Lyme Hist.

— The Real Faith for Healing. rev. ed. Chadwick, Harold J., ed. LC 97-73698. Orig. Title: The Real Faith. 1997. pap. 9.99 (*0-88270-739-6*, Logos NJ) Bridge-Logos.

— Thomas W. Nason: New England Virtues Aged in Wood. (Illus.). 61p. (Orig.). 1993. pap. 13.95 (*1-880897-03-2*) Lyme Hist.

Price, Charles, ed. The American Golfer. rev. ed. 1988. 28.00 (*0-940889-15-3*) Classics Golf.

Price, Charles, et al. The Parker Story, Vol. 1 & 2. (Illus.). 450p. 1997. write for info. (*0-9657748-1-3*); pap. write for info. (*0-9657748-2-1*) Double Gun.

Price, Charles, jt. auth. see Mather, Eleanore P.

Price, Charles, jt. ed. see Hoeber, Thomas R.

Price, Charles A. Malta & the Maltese: A Study in Nineteenth Century Migration. LC 77-87724. reprint ed. 32.50 (*0-404-16516-8*) AMS Pr.

Price, Charles E. Danger Train. 128p. (Orig.). 1995. pap. 8.95 (*1-57072-027-4*) Overmountain Pr.

— The Day They Hung the Elephant. (Illus.). 64p. 1992. pap. 5.95 (*0-932807-75-5*) Overmountain Pr.

— Demon in the Woods: Tall Tales & True from East Tennessee. 74p. 1992. pap. 7.95 (*0-932807-82-8*) Overmountain Pr.

— Diggin' up Bones. 96p. (Orig.). 1996. pap. 12.95 (*1-57072-048-7*) Overmountain Pr.

— Haints, Witches & Boogers: Tales from Upper East Tennessee. LC 92-12664. 104p. 1992. 11.95 (*0-89587-093-2*) Blair.

— Haunted Jonesborough. 79p. 1993. pap. 7.95 (*0-932807-93-3*) Overmountain Pr.

— Haunted Tennessee. (Illus.). 144p. (Orig.). 1995. pap. 9.95 (*1-57072-037-1*) Overmountain Pr.

— I'd Rather Have a Talking Frog. 96p. 1993. pap. 7.95 (*0-932807-98-4*) Overmountain Pr.

— The Infamous Bell Witch of Tennessee. (Illus.). 142p. (Orig.). 1994. pap. 9.95 (*1-57072-008-8*) Overmountain Pr.

— The Infamous Bell Witch of Tennessee. (Illus.). 142p. (Orig.). 1994. 14.95 (*1-57072-015-0*) Overmountain Pr.

— Lullaby Aggie of Sweet Potato Cave. 80p. 1996. pap. 6.95 (*1-57072-055-X*) Overmountain Pr.

— The Mystery of Ghostly Vera & Other Haunting Tales of Southwest Virginia. 128p. 1993. 12.95 (*0-932807-88-7*) Overmountain Pr.

— Something Evil Lurks in the Woods. 126p. (Orig.). 1995. pap. 8.95 (*1-57072-039-8*) Overmountain Pr.

***Price, Charles Edwin.** More Haunted Tennessee. (Illus.). 143p. 1999. pap. 12.95 (*1-57072-089-4*) Overmountain Pr.

— Mysterious Knoxville. (Illus.). 112p. 1999. pap. 12.95 (*1-57072-103-3*, Silver Dagger) Overmountain Pr.

P

— Mystery in the Old Dark Attic. 2000. 22.50 (*1-57072-118-1*); pap. 12.50 (*1-57072-134-3*) Overmountain Pr.

Price, Charles F. Freedom's Altar. LC 98-55781. 192p. 1999. 19.95 (*0-89587-177-7*) Blair.

— Hiwassee: A Novel of the Civil War. LC 95-50688. 193p. 1996. 20.00 (*0-89733-429-9*) Academy Chi Pubs.

Price, Charles M. & Bell, Charles G. California Government Today: Politics of Reform. 5th ed. LC 95-13452. 310p. (C). 1995. pap. text 50.00 (*0-534-25998-7*) Harcourt.

Price, Charles M., jt. auth. see Hoeber, Thomas R.

Price, Charles M., jt. ed. see Hoeber, Thomas R.

Price, Charles P. The Prayer Book in the Church. 24p. (Orig.). 1997. pap. 1.95 (*0-88028-195-2*, 1452) Forward Movement.

Price, Charles P. & Weil, Louis. Liturgy for Living. (Church's Teaching Ser.: Vol. 5). 1984. 5.95 (*0-8164-0422-4*) Harper SF.

Price, Charles T., jt. ed. see Beaty, James H.

Price, Charles W. Alive in Christ: How to Find Renewed Spiritual Power. LC 94-37821. 128p. 1995. pap. 7.99 (*0-8254-3551-X*) Kregel.

— Christ for Real: How to Grow into God's Likeness. 136p. 1995. pap. 7.99 (*0-8254-3550-1*) Kregel.

Price, Charlie, photos by. Planet Colors. (Illus.). 42p. 1997. pap. 25.00 (*0-9661580-0-8*) Planet Pub Intl.

***Price, Chris.** Computer-Based Diagnostic Systems. LC 99-36325. 200p. 1999. pap. 54.95 (*3-540-76198-5*) Spr-Verlag.

Price, Chris. Landfall. 1995. pap. 15.00 (*0-614-07568-8*, Pub. by Univ Otago Pr) Intl Spec Bk.

Price, Chris, ed. Landfall 193. 184p. 1997. pap. 21.95 (*1-877133-28-0*, Pub. by Univ Otago Pr) S Asia.

Price, Chris, jt. auth. see Simpson, Peter.

Price, Christine A. Women & Retirement: The Unexplored Transition. LC 98-28461. (Studies on the Elderly in America). (Illus.). 194p. 1998. 49.00 (*0-8153-3148-7*) Garland.

Price, Christopher. Baseball by the Beach: A History of America's National Pastime on Cape Cod. (Illus.). 224p. 1998. pap. 14.96 (*0-940160-71-4*) Parnassus Imprints.

***Price, Christopher.** Internet Entrepreneurs. 256p. 2000. pap. 20.00 (*0-273-64921-3*, Pub. by F T P-H) Trans-Atl Phila.

Price, Christopher P. & Newman, David J., eds. Principles & Practice of Immunoassay. 2nd ed. 650p. 1997. 140.00 (*1-56159-175-0*) Groves Dictionaries.

Price, Christopher P. & Spencer, Kevin C., eds. Centrifugal Analysers in Clinical Chemistry. LC 80-81330. (Illus.). 520p. 1980. 125.00 (*0-275-91339-2*, C1339, Praeger Pubs) Greenwood.

Price, Christopher P., jt. ed. see Hicks, Jocelyn M.

Price, Clara I. Scribe of a Soul (1901) 202p. 1998. reprint ed. pap. 17.95 (*0-7661-0576-8*) Kessinger Pub.

Price, Clelia. Life under Lake Siskiyou: A Way of Life on a Ranch Many Years Ago. (Illus.). 40p. (J). (gr. k-4). 1997. pap. 8.95 (*0-9628801-2-4*) Coyote Pub.

Price, Clement A. Many Voices, Many Opportunities: Cultural Pluralism & American Arts Policy. LC 93-34290. (Illus.). 96p. (Orig.). 1993. pap. 10.00 (*1-879903-16-4*, ACA Bks) Am for the Arts.

Price, Clive. Glorious Awakenings: First-Hand Experiences of Revival. 1999. pap. text 10.95 (*0-281-05093-7*) Society Prom Christ Know.

Price-Cohen, Cynthia. Human Rights of Indigenous Peoples. LC 98-25991. 1998. lib. bdg. 115.00 (*0-941320-93-6*) Transnatl Pubs.

Price-Cohen, Cynthia, jt. auth. see Lawrence, Leslie.

Price, Colin, jt. auth. see Dauphinais, G. William.

Price, Colin, jt. auth. see Evans, Richard.

Price, Con. Memories of Old Montana. (American Autobiography Ser.). 154p. 1995. reprint ed. lib. bdg. 69.00 (*0-7812-8620-4*) Rprt Serv.

— Trails I Rode. (American Autobiography Ser.). 262p. 1995. reprint ed. lib. bdg. 79.00 (*0-7812-8621-2*) Rprt Serv.

Price, Courtney. Courtney Price Answers the Most Asked Questions from Entrepreneurs. LC 94-2310. 1994. 29.95 (*0-07-050830-5*) McGraw.

— The Group Practice Personnel Policies Manual. rev. ed. 785p. 1997. pap. 150.00 incl. disk (*1-56829-081-0*, 4987) Med Group Mgmt.

— Health Care Innovations & Venture Trends. 1992. pap. 41.95 (*0-8273-4964-5*) Delmar.

***Price, Courtney.** 101+ Answers to the Most Frequently Asked Questions from Entrepreneurs. LC 98-40649. 320p. 1999. pap. 16.95 (*0-471-31572-9*) Wiley.

Price, Courtney. Waltzing with a Moose: Following the Wizard's Path to Corporate Creativity. 70p. 1991. pap. 8.95 (*0-944303-08-0*) Entre Ed Fndtn.

Price, Courtney & Baker, Dianne. Creatively Designing Your Future. 124p. 1988. pap. 14.95 (*0-944303-05-6*) Entre Ed Fndtn.

***Price, Courtney & Davis, R. Mack.** Corporate Entrepreneurship: Providing Direction for Your Business. 2nd rev. ed. 340p. 1999. pap. write for info. (*0-944303-97-8*, Premier Ent) Entre Ed Fndtn.

— Corporate Entrepreneurship Planning Guide. 2nd rev. ed. 1999. ring bd. write for info. (*0-944303-96-X*, Premier Ent) Entre Ed Fndtn.

Price, Courtney & Davis, R. Mack. The Entrepreneur's Fast Trac I Handbook with Fast Trac Business Resources CD. 1998. pap. write for info. incl. cd-rom (*0-944303-32-3*) Entre Ed Fndtn.

— The Entrepreneur's Fast Trac II Handbook with Fast Trac Business Resources CD. 1998. pap. write for info. incl. cd-rom (*0-944303-33-1*) Entre Ed Fndtn.

— University Fast Trac I Instructor Manual. (Illus.). 1998. pap., teacher ed. write for info. (*0-944303-38-2*) Entre Ed Fndtn.

— University Fast Trac II Instructor Manual. (Illus.). 1998. pap., teacher ed. write for info. (*0-944303-39-0*) Entre Ed Fndtn.

Price, Courtney & Novak, Alys. Job Description Manual for Medical Practices. 612p. 1999. pap. 125.00 (*1-56829-095-0*) Med Group Mgmt.

— The Medical Practice Performance Management Manual: How to Evaluate Employees. (Employee Performance Management Ser.). 234p. (Orig.). 1993. pap. 85.00 (*1-56829-027-6*) Med Group Mgmt.

Price, Courtney, et al. The Entrepreneur's Fast Trac I Handbook. rev. ed. 293p. 1998. pap. 25.00 (*0-944303-50-1*) Entre Ed Fndtn.

— The Entrepreneurs Fast Trac II Handbook. rev. ed. 406p. 1997. pap. 30.00 (*0-944303-12-9*) Entre Ed Fndtn.

— The Entrepreneur's Resource Handbook. 178p. 1997. pap. 20.00 (*0-944303-24-2*) Entre Ed Fndtn.

— Sample Business Plan. rev. ed. 266p. 1994. pap. 20.00 (*0-944303-15-3*) Entre Ed Fndtn.

Price, Courtney H. & Allen, Kathleen. Tips & Traps for Entrepreneurs: Real-Life Ideas & Solutions for the Toughest Problems Facing Entrepreneurs. LC 97-52332. 272p. 1998. pap. 15.95 (*0-07-052676-1*, BusinessWeek Bks) McGraw.

Price, Courtney H. & Davis, R. Mack. Entrepreneur's Fast Trac 2 Handbook. (SPA.). 400p. 1998. spiral bd. write for info. (*0-944303-21-8*) Entre Ed Fndtn.

— Fast Trac I & II Administrator's Manual. 1998. ring bd. write for info. (*0-944303-29-3*) Entre Ed Fndtn.

— El Manual de Planeacion Empresarial. Orig. Title: Entrepreneur's Fast Trac Planning Handbook. (SPA.). 150p. 1998. spiral bd. write for info. (*0-944303-23-4*) Entre Ed Fndtn.

Price, Courtney M., ed. Asbestos in Buildings, Facilities & Industry: Legal, Regulatory, Insurance & Economic Strategies. 296p. 1987. pap. text 73.00 (*0-86587-727-0*) Gov Insts.

Price, Craig G. & Dennie, Ronald W. Impairment & Disability Ratings: A Guide to the Guides. 186p. 1992. write for info. (*1-882678-00-1*) Meriah-Morgan.

Price, Curtis, ed. Purcell Studies. (Illus.). 317p. (C). 1995. text 69.95 (*0-521-44174-9*) Cambridge U Pr.

Price, Curtis, et al. Italian Opera in Late Eighteenth-Century London Vol. 1: The King's Theatre, Haymarket, 1778-1791. (Illus.). 736p. 1995. text 95.00 (*0-19-816166-2*) OUP.

Price, Curtis, ed. see Purcell, Henry.

Price, D. Butterworth's Student Companions - Constitutional Law. LC 95-192620. 112p. 1995. pap. write for info. (*0-409-31035-2*, MICHIE) LEXIS Pub.

— Is Any One of You Sick. 1997. pap. 15.99 (*1-85792-242-5*, Pub. by Christian Focus) Spring Arbor Dist.

Price, D. & Todd, J. F., eds. Dynamic Mass Spectrometry, Vol. 6. LC 80-641839. 338p. reprint ed. pap. 104.80 (*0-608-16332-5*, 202667900006) Bks Demand.

Price, D., jt. auth. see Burroughs, A.

Price, D., ed. see European Symposium on the Time-of-Flight Mass Spec.

Price, D., jt. ed. see Horrocks, A. R.

Price, D., ed. see International Dynamic Mass Spectrometry Symposium.

Price, D. G., ed. Proceedings: Sixth International Congress International Association of Engineering Geology, Amsterdam, 6-10 August 1990, 6 vols., Set. (Illus.). 2530p. (C). 1990. text 899.00 (*90-6191-130-3*, Pub. by A A Balkema) Ashgate Pub Co.

Price, D. L., et al. Neurodegenerative Disorders: Mechanisms & Prospects for Therapy. (Dahlem Workshop Reports - Life Sciences). 301p. 1991. 165.00 (*0-685-70063-1*, Wiley-Liss) Wiley.

Price, D. Michael. Across the River: Walter & Oliver's Amazing Adventure. LC 97-43706. (Illus.). 48p. (J). (gr. k-4). 1998. 15.95 (*0-86713-047-4*) Greenwich Wrkshop.

Price, D. Porter. Beef Production, Science & Economics, Application & Reality. LC 81-51944. (Illus.). 358p. 1985. 32.00 (*0-9606246-0-0*); pap. text 24.95 (*0-9606246-3-5*) SWI.

— Intelligent Dieting for Weight Loss & Prevention of Disease. LC 82-61578. (Illus.). 200p. (Orig.). 1982. pap. 13.95 (*0-9606246-2-7*); lib. bdg. 17.95 (*0-9606246-1-9*) SWI.

— Real World Answers to Cattle Management Problems. (Illus.). 250p. (Orig.). 1991. pap. 37.50 (*0-685-50311-9*) SWI.

Price, D. Porter, et al. Modern Agriculture: Science, Finance, Production & Economics. (Illus.). 361p. 1989. pap., teacher ed. 27.95 (*0-9606246-7-8*); pap., student ed. 14.95 (*0-9606246-8-6*); lib. bdg. 34.50 (*0-9606246-6-X*) SWI.

***Price, Dan.** How to Write a Journal. LC 99-25687. (Illus.). 96p. 1999. pap. text 7.95 (*1-58008-093-6*) Ten Speed Pr.

— Moonlight Chronicles: A Wandering Artist's Journal. LC 99-58200. (Illus.). 160p. 2000. pap. 12.95 (*1-58008-171-1*) Ten Speed Pr.

Price, Daniel. Without a Woman to Read: Toward the Daughter in Postmodernism. LC 96-43583. (SUNY Series in Radical, Social & Political Theory). 372p. (C). 1997. text 65.50 (*0-7914-3459-1*); pap. text 21.95 (*0-7914-3460-5*) State U NY Pr.

Price, Daniel E. Islamic Political Culture, Democracy & Human Rights: A Comparative Study. LC 98-44397. 240p. 1999. 59.95 (*0-275-96187-7*, Praeger Pubs) Greenwood.

Price, Danny, tr. see French Ramblers Association Staff.

Price, Darryl, jt. auth. see Welch, Jennifer G.

Price, David. Appeals. 439p. 1982. 104.00 (*0-906840-42-2*, Pub. by Fourmat Pub) St Mut.

— Appeals Procedure. 1981. 100.00 (*0-7855-7328-3*, Pub. by Fourmat Pub) St Mut.

— Before the Bulldozer: The Nambiquara Indians & the World Bank. LC 89-6065. 212p. 1989. 18.95 (*0-932020-67-4*) Seven Locks Pr.

— Cancan! LC 98-21956. (Illus.). 272p. 1998. 48.50 (*0-8386-3820-1*) Fairleigh Dickinson.

— Janus Secundus. (Medieval & Renaissance Texts & Studies: Vol. 143). (Illus.). 128p. 1996. 22.00 (*0-86698-180-2*, MR143) MRTS.

***Price, David.** Legal & Ethical Aspects of Organ Transplantation. 350p. (C). 2000. text Price not set. (*0-521-65164-6*) Cambridge U Pr.

Price, David. The Political Dramaturgy of Nicodemus Frischlin: Essays on Humanist Drama in Germany. LC 89-16733. (Germanic Languages & Literatures Ser.: No. 111). xii, 156p. (C). 1990. 37.50 (*0-8078-8111-2*) U of NC Pr.

— The Second Civil War: Examining the Indian Demand for Ethnic Sovereignty. unabridged ed. 219p. 1998. pap. 14.95 (*0-9663728-0-8*) Second MN.

— World Fibre Supplies. 140p. 1996. pap., per. 920.00 (*1-85802-153-7*, Pub. by Pira Internatl) Bks Intl VA.

— World Tissue & Other Disposable Markets. 132p. 1996. pap. 760.00 (*1-85802-195-2*, Pub. by Pira Internatl) Bks Intl VA.

Price, David. Birds & Beasts. 80p. (J). (gr. 1-6). write for info. (*0-7136-5653-0*, Pub. by A & C Blk) Midpt Trade.

— Charles Dickens, Eighteen Hundred Twelve to Eighteen Seventy. 1970. pap. 8.00 (*0-87959-009-2*) U of Tex H Ransom Ctr.

— An Exhibition of Judaica & Hebraica. 26p. 1973. pap. 7.00 (*0-87959-034-3*) U of Tex H Ransom Ctr.

— Johannes Kepler, 1571 to 1630: An Exhibit of Books, Manuscripts, & Related Materials. LC 70-180652. 1971. pap. 10.00 (*0-87959-014-9*) U of Tex H Ransom Ctr.

— John Herschel & Victorian Science. (Orig.). 1966. pap. 8.00 (*0-87959-005-X*) U of Tex H Ransom Ctr.

— Siegfried Sassoon: A Memorial Exhibition. LC 77-628295. 1969. pap. 8.00 (*0-87959-007-6*) U of Tex H Ransom Ctr.

— The Stanley Marcus Collection of Christmas Books. (Orig.). 1968. pap. 10.00 (*0-87959-029-7*) U of Tex H Ransom Ctr.

Price, David. Katherine Mansfield: An Exhibition. LC 75-620027. 1975. pap. 10.00 (*0-87959-018-1*) U of Tex H Ransom Ctr.

***Price, David & Willshaw, David.** Mechanisms of Cortical Development. LC 99-39684. (Monographs of the Physiological Society: No. 48). (Illus.). 336p. 2000. text 59.95 (*0-19-262427-X*) OUP.

Price, David, et al. The Reformation of the Bible: The Bible of the Reformation. LC 95-38683. 197p. 1996. 50.00 (*0-300-06667-8*); pap. write for info. (*0-941881-18-0*) Yale U Pr.

Price, David, jt. auth. see Hacker, Jonathan.

***Price, David E.** Congressional Experience. 2nd ed. (Transforming American Politics Ser.). 350p. 2000. pap. 25.00 (*0-8133-6812-X*) Westview.

Price, David E. The Congressional Experience: A View from the Hill. LC 92-13949. (Transforming American Politics Ser.). 208p. (C). 1992. pap. 25.00 (*0-8133-1156-X*, Pub. by Westview) HarpC.

— Who Makes the Laws? Creativity & Power in Senate Committees. 380p. 1972. ring bd., boxed set 34.95 (*0-87073-298-6*) Transaction Pubs.

Price, David H. Atlas of World Cultures: A Geographical Guide to Ethnographic Literature. 160p. (C). 1990. text 52.00 (*0-8039-3240-5*); pap. text 22.95 (*0-8039-4075-0*) Sage.

Price, David L. Magic: A Pictoral History of Conjurers in the Theater. LC 81-68623. 544p. 1985. 60.00 (*0-8453-4738-1*, Cornwall Bks) Assoc Univ Prs.

Price, David R. & Lees-Haley, Paul R., eds. The Insurer's Handbook of Psychological Injury Claims. (Illus.). 428p. 1995. text 149.00 (*0-9634957-2-0*) Insuranceweek.

Price, David T., ed. see Apps, Michael J.

Price, David T., jt. ed. see Apps, Michael J.

Price, Deb & Murdoc, Joyce. Courting Justice: Gay & Lesbian Americans vs. the Supreme Court. 320p. Date not set. 25.00 (*0-465-01513-1*) Basic.

***Price, Deborah.** Start Investing Online Today. LC 99-56325. 270p. 2000. pap. 14.95 (*1-58062-270-4*) Adams Media.

***Price, Deborah L.** Money Therapy: Using the Eight Money Types to Create Wealth & Prosperity. 176p. 2000. 18.00 (*1-57731-157-4*, Pub. by New Wrld Lib) Publishers Group.

Price, Deirdra. Healing the Hungry Self: The Diet-Free Solution to Lifelong Weight Management. (Illus.). 232p. 1996. pap. 21.95 (*0-9655583-0-4*) Diet Free Soln.

Price, Dennis, ed. Dynamic Mass Spectrometry: Invited Papers & Specially Commissioned Reviews Embracing the Whole Field of Dynamic Mass Spectrometry, Vol. 2. LC 73-107612. 282p. reprint ed. pap. 87.50 (*0-608-11848-6*, 202254400027) Bks Demand.

Price, Diadra. The Return of the Dove: Empowerment to Ascension Is Written in Your Heart. 2nd ed. 1995. pap. 12.95 (*1-887884-00-9*) Wings of Spirit.

— The Return of the Dove: Empowerment to Ascension Is Written in Your Heart, 3 Tapes, Set. 1995. digital audio 15.95 (*1-887884-01-7*) Wings of Spirit.

Price, Diadra, jt. auth. see Price, John A.

***Price, Diana.** Shakespeare's Unorthodox Biography: New Evidence of an Authorship Problem, 94. LC 00-22333. (Contributions in Drama & Theatre Studies: Vol. 94). 352p. 2000. 42.00 (*0-313-31202-8*, GM1202, Greenwood Pr) Greenwood.

Price, Dick, intro. Young British Art: The Saatchi Decade. (Illus.). 608p. 1999. 125.00 (*0-8109-6389-2*, Pub. by Abrams) Time Warner.

Price, Dick, text. The New Neurotic Realism. (Illus.). 208p. 1999. 45.00 (*0-9527453-8-0*, Pub. by Saatchi) Dist Art Pubs.

Price, Dierdra. Healing the Hungry Self: The Diet-Free Solution to Lifelong Weight Management. LC 97-29000. 240p. 1998. pap. 14.95 (*0-452-27940-2*, Plume) Dutton Plume.

Price, Don. Secrets of Personal Marketing Power. 208p. (Orig.). 1995. pap. text 19.95 (*0-8403-9392-X*) Kendall-Hunt.

Price, Don C. Russia & the Roots of the Chinese Revolution, 1896-1911. LC 74-80443. (Harvard East Asian Ser.: No. 79). 318p. reprint ed. pap. 98.60 (*0-7837-3858-7*, 204368000010) Bks Demand.

Price, Don K. America's Unwritten Constitution: Science, Religion, & Political Responsibility. LC 83-5439. (Miller Center Series on the American Presidency). 220p. 1983. pap. 68.20 (*0-7837-8468-6*, 204927300010) Bks Demand.

— America's Unwritten Constitution: Science, Religion & Political Responsibility. 224p. 1985. pap. 15.50 (*0-674-03142-3*) HUP.

— Government & Science: Their Dynamic Relation in American Democracy. LC 81-6584. 203p. 1981. reprint ed. lib. bdg. 65.00 (*0-313-23108-7*, PRGS, Greenwood Pr) Greenwood.

— The Parliamentary & Presidential Systems. (Reprint Series in Social Sciences). (C). 1993. reprint ed. pap. text 5.00 (*0-8290-3375-0*, PS-232) Irvington.

— The Scientific Estate. LC 65-22047. 343p. 1965. 41.50 (*0-674-79485-0*) Belknap Pr.

Price, Don K., ed. Secretary of State. LC 60-53378. 1960. 3.50 (*0-317-02964-9*, 79749-C) Am Assembly.

Price, Don K. & Evans, Robert H. Political Transitions & Foreign Affairs in Britain & France: Their Relevance for the United States. Mosher, Frederick C., ed. & intro. by. (Papers on Presidential Transitions & Foreign Policy: Vol. III). 100p. (Orig.). (C). 1986. pap. text 15.00 (*0-8191-5314-1*) U Pr of Amer.

— Political Transitions & Foreign Affairs in Britain & France: Their Relevance for the United States. Mosher, Frederick C., ed. & intro. by. (Papers on Presidential Transitions & Foreign Policy: Vol. III). 100p. (Orig.). (C). 1986. lib. bdg. 34.50 (*0-8191-5313-3*, Pub. by White Miller Center) U Pr of Amer.

Price, Don L., jt. auth. see Anderson, Camille J.

***Price, Donald D.** Psychological Mechanisms of Pain & Pain Modulation. LC 99-39682. (Progress in Pain Research & Management Ser.). 248p. 1999. 69.00 (*0-931092-29-9*) Intl Assn Study Pain.

Price, Donald L. Procedure Manual for the Diagnosis of Intestinal Parasites. LC 93-7450. 288p. 1994. boxed set 78.95 (*0-8493-8654-3*, RC862) CRC Pr.

— What No One Told You about Health Care: A Look at Some Health Care Problems & Some Possible Solutions. 160p. 1997. text 55.95 (*1-85972-569-4*, Pub. by Avebry) Ashgate Pub Co.

Price, Doris K. The Bump in the Road. LC 98-42568. (Illus.). 1998. write for info. (*0-945084-73-0*) J Stuart Found.

Price, Doug, jt. auth. see Ilvento, Joseph C.

Price, E. A., jt. auth. see Godfrey, Charles.

***Price, E. Bruce.** God's Channel of Truth: Is It the Watch Tower? 96p. 1999. reprint ed. pap. 2.95 (*1-57258-163-8*) Teach Servs.

Price, E. Hoffman. Grubstake. (Orig.). 1980. mass mkt. 1.95 (*0-89083-577-2*, Zebra Kensgtn) Kensgtn Pub Corp.

Price, E. W. Acts in Prayer. LC 74-15278. 32p. 1974. pap. 0.99 (*0-8054-9209-7*, 4292-09) Broadman.

Price, Edna C. Burro Bill & Me. 2nd ed. (Illus.). 300p. (C). 1993. reprint ed. pap. 5.00 (*1-878900-28-5*) DVNH Assn.

Price, Edward A. Alricks. Jacob Alricks & His Nephew Peter Alricks. (Illus.). 60p. 1998. reprint ed. pap. 12.00 (*0-8328-9633-0*); reprint ed. lib. bdg. 22.00 (*0-8328-9632-2*) Higginson Bk Co.

Price, Edward R., ed. see Denny, Hugh W.

Price, Edward R., ed. see Georgopoulos, Chris J.

Price, Edward R., ed. see Mardiguian, Michael.

Price, Edward T. Dividing the Land: Early American Beginnings of Our Private Property Mosaic. (Geography Research Papers: Vol. 238). 432p. 1995. pap. text 26.00 (*0-226-68065-7*) U Ch Pr.

Price, Elizabeth. The Mountain Brook Jokebook. 96p. (Orig.). 1996. pap. 5.95 (*1-878561-53-7*) Seacoast AL.

Price, Elizabeth & Bolton, Mike. Thank God for Mississippi. 144p. 1997. pap. 5.95 (*1-878561-58-8*) Seacoast AL.

Price, Enoch S., tr. see Swedenborg, Emanuel.

Price, Erica J., jt. auth. see Lipow, Hershel.

Price, Esther & Lipsett, Linda O. Chocolate Covered Cherries: Esther Price's Memories. LC 91-42370. (Illus.). 112p. 1991. pap. 11.99 (*0-9629399-1-9*) Halstead Meadows.

Price, Eugenia. At Home on St. Simons. LC 81-1412. (Illus.). 96p. 1981. 16.95 (*0-931948-16-9*) Peachtree Pubs.

— Beauty from Ashes. 1996. mass mkt. 6.99 (*0-312-95917-6*) St Martin.

— Beauty from Ashes, Vol. 3. large type ed. LC 94-38912. 640p. 1995. 23.50 (*0-385-26703-7*) Doubleday.

— Before the Darkness Falls. 1990. mass mkt. 7.50 (*0-515-10538-4*, Jove) Berkley Pub.

— The Beloved Invader. 288p. 1977. mass mkt. 6.99 (*0-553-26909-7*) Bantam.

***Price, Eugenia.** The Beloved Invader. LC 00-32335. 320p. 2000. pap. 14.95 (*1-57736-204-7*) Providence Hse.

Price, Eugenia. The Beloved Invader. 1977. 12.09 (*0-606-00608-7*, Pub. by Turtleback) Demco.

— The Beloved Invader. large type ed. LC 91-15592. 456p. 1991. reprint ed. lib. bdg. 21.95 (*1-56054-182-2*) Thorndike Pr.
— Beloved World: The Story of God & People as Told from the Bible. 480p. 1991. pap. 10.00 (*0-385-41716-0*) Doubleday.
— Bright Captivity. 704p. 1992. mass mkt. 6.50 (*0-553-29523-3*) Bantam.
— Bright Captivity. 1996. mass mkt. 6.99 (*0-312-95968-0*) St Martin.
— The Burden Is Light. large type ed. (Large Print Inspirational Ser.). 1985. pap. 11.95 (*0-8027-2514-7*) Walker & Co.
— The Burden Is Light: A Spiritual Autobiography. 192p. 1991. pap. 8.00 (*0-385-41776-4*) Doubleday.
Price, Eugenia. The Burden Is Light! The Autobiography of a Transformed Pagan Who Took God at His Word. LC 73-9986. 326 p. 1973. write for info. (*0-8161-6137-2*, G K Hall & Co) Mac Lib Ref.
Price, Eugenia. Don Juan McQueen. 1997. reprint ed. lib. bdg. 39.95 (*1-56849-598-6*) Buccaneer Bks.
— Getting Through the Night: Finding Your Way after the Loss of a Loved One. large type ed. 112p. 1985. pap. 10.95 (*0-8027-2482-5*) Walker & Co.
— Getting Thru the Night. 1986. mass mkt. 5.99 (*0-345-34196-1*) Ballantine Pub Grp.
— God Speaks to Women Today. 192p. 1984. reprint ed. pap. 8.99 (*0-310-31301-5*, 10530P) Zondervan.
— Inside One Author's Heart: A Deeply Personal Sharing with My Readers. 128p. 1992. 15.00 (*0-385-42321-7*) Doubleday.
— Leave Yourself Alone. 128p. 1982. pap. 6.70 (*0-310-31431-3*, 16240P) Zondervan.
— Lighthouse. 352p. 1972. mass mkt. 6.99 (*0-553-26910-0*) Bantam.
— Lighthouse. large type ed. LC 91-30413. 546p. 1992. reprint ed. lib. bdg. 20.95 (*1-56054-185-7*) Thorndike Pr.
— Make Love Your Aim. 160p. 1989. mass mkt. 3.95 (*0-515-10039-0*, Jove) Berkley Pub.
— Margaret's Story. large type ed. LC 92-18864. 723p. 1993. 22.95 (*1-56054-468-6*) Thorndike Pr.
— Maria. 432p. 1984. mass mkt. 6.99 (*0-553-26362-5*) Bantam.
— Maria. large type ed. LC 92-20070. 701p. 1993. 22.95 (*1-56054-467-8*) Thorndike Pr.
— New Moon Rising. 320p. 1985. mass mkt. 6.99 (*0-553-26848-1*) Bantam.
***Price, Eugenia.** New Moon Rising. LC 99-57799. 352p. 2000. pap. 14.95 (*1-57736-181-4*) Providence Hse.
— New Moon Rising. pap. 12.95 (*0-8027-2607-0*) Walker & Co.
Price, Eugenia. New Moon Rising. large type ed. LC 91-18383. 483p. 1991. reprint ed. lib. bdg. 19.95 (*1-56054-184-9*) Thorndike Pr.
— No Pat Answers. 144p. 1983. reprint ed. pap. 6.95 (*0-310-31331-7*, 16244P) Zondervan.
— Share My Pleasant Stones. 1982. 7.70 (*0-310-31341-4*, 10585P) Zondervan.
— Stranger in Savannah. 1990. pap. 7.99 (*0-515-10344-6*, Jove) Berkley Pub.
— To See Your Face Again. 1997. mass mkt. 6.99 (*0-312-96233-9*) St Martin.
— To See Your Face Again. 1997. reprint ed. lib. bdg. 39.95 (*1-56849-597-8*) Buccaneer Bks.
— The Unique World of Women. large type ed. 218p. 1995. 21.95 (*0-7838-1194-2*, G K Hall Lrg Type) Mac Lib Ref.
— The Waiting Time. LC 96-8250. 384p. 1997. 23.95 (*0-385-47938-7*) Doubleday.
— The Waiting Time. large type ed. LC 97-339. 1999. 25.95 (*0-7862-1065-6*) Thorndike Pr.
— The Waiting Time, Vol. 1. 352p. 1998. pap. 6.99 (*0-312-96506-0*, Pub. by Tor Bks) St Martin.
— Where Shadows Go. 1996. mass mkt. 6.99 (*0-312-95969-9*) St Martin.
— Woman to Woman. 1996. mass mkt. 5.50 (*0-310-21514-5*) Zondervan.
— Woman to Woman. large type ed. (Large Print Inspirational Ser.). 396p. 1986. pap. 16.95 (*0-8027-2562-7*) Walker & Co.
— A Woman's Choice: Living Through Your Problems. 192p. 1983. reprint ed. pap. 6.95 (*0-310-31381-3*, 16217P) Zondervan.
***Price, Eugenia, ed.** Lighthouse: Eugenia Price Commemorative Edition. LC 99-27182. (St. Simons Trilogy Ser.: Vol. 1). 344p. 1999. pap. 14.95 (*1-57736-154-7*) Providence Hse.
— Maria: Eugenia Price Commemorative Edition. LC 99-23553. (Florida Trilogy Ser.: Vol. 1). 408p. 1999. pap. 14.95 (*1-57736-152-0*) Providence Hse.
Price, Evans D. Genetic Factors in Drug Therapy: Clinical & Molecular Pharmacogenetics. (Illus.). 681p. (C). 1994. text 190.00 (*0-521-41296-X*) Cambridge U Pr.
Price, F. Right Every Time. 182p. (C). 1990. 270.00 (*0-7855-5713-X*, Pub. by Inst Pur & Supply) St Mut.
Price, Frances. Healthy Cooking for Two or Just You: Low-Fat Recipes with Half the Fuss & Double the Taste. 1997. pap. text 15.95 (*0-87596-448-6*) Rodale Pr Inc.
Price, Francis, tr. see Ousmane, Sembene.
Price, Frank. Loving Work. 255p. 1995. 56.95 (*0-566-07634-9*, Pub. by Gower) Ashgate Pub Co.
— Right Every Time. 200p. 1993. pap. 22.95 (*0-566-07419-2*, Pub. by Gower) Ashgate Pub Co.
— Right First Time: Using Quality Control for Profit. 296p. 1984. pap. 29.95 (*0-7045-0522-3*, Pub. by Gower); text 74.95 (*0-566-02467-5*, Pub. by Gower) Ashgate Pub Co.
Price, Frank. Right Every Time: Using the Deming Approach. 216p. 1990. text 75.00 (*0-8247-8328-X*) Dekker.
Price, Frank W., tr. see Yat-sen Sun.
Price, Fred. Beware of the Lies of Satan. LC 96-204785. 1995. pap. 11.00 (*1-883798-16-7*) Faith One.
— Beware the Lies of Satan. LC 96-204785. 1995. 18.00 (*1-883798-08-6*) Faith One.
— Chastening of the Lord. LC 96-209957. 1995. pap. 4.99 (*1-883798-10-8*) Faith One.
— Identified with Christ. LC 96-199030. 1995. pap. 5.99 (*1-883798-11-6*) Faith One.
— Testing the Spirits. LC 96-209915. 1995. pap. 4.99 (*1-883798-09-4*) Faith One.
***Price, Fred T., et al, eds.** Environmental Toxicology & Risk Assessment: Recent Achievements in Environmental Fate & Transport. (STP Ser.: Vol. 1381). 282p. 2000. text 110.00 (*0-8031-2861-4*, STP1381) ASTM.
Price, Fred W. The Planet Observer's Handbook. (Illus.). 430p. (C). 1994. text 39.95 (*0-521-44257-5*) Cambridge U Pr.
— The Planet Observer's Handbook. (Illus.). 432p. (C). 1998. reprint ed. pap. 19.95 (*0-521-62708-7*) Cambridge U Pr.
***Price, Fred William.** The Planet Observer's Handbook. 2nd ed. (Illus.). 450p. 2000. pap. 24.95 (*0-521-78981-8*) Cambridge U Pr.
Price, Frederick K. The Christian Family Practical Insight for Family Living. 1996. 17.99 (*1-883798-17-5*) Faith One.
— Concerning Them Which Are Asleep. (Mini-Bks.). 32p. 1989. pap. 1.00 (*0-89274-603-3*, HH-603) Harrison Hse.
— Faith, Foolishness, or Presumption. 160p. (Orig.). 1979. pap. 7.99 (*0-89274-103-1*, HH-103) Harrison Hse.
— The Faithfulness of God. 53p. (Orig.). 1993. pap. 3.99 (*1-883798-02-7*) Faith One.
— Faith's Greatest Enemies. LC 95-176757. 80p. 1994. pap. 5.99 (*0-89274-920-2*, HH-920) Harrison Hse.
— Five Little Foxes' of Faith. 68p. 1998. pap. 5.99 (*1-883798-19-1*) Faith One.
— The Holy Spirit: The Helper We All Need. 1996. pap. 7.99 (*1-883798-18-3*) Faith One.
— The Holy Spirit: The Missing Ingredient. 29p. 1978. pap. 3.99 (*0-89274-081-7*, HH-081) Harrison Hse.
— Homosexuality: State of Birth. 56p. (Orig.). 1993. mass mkt. 2.99 (*1-883798-04-3*, FP-804) Faith One.
— How Faith Works. 300p. 1979. pap. 6.99 (*0-89274-001-9*, HH-001) Harrison Hse.
— How Faith Works. rev. ed. LC 97-152691. 304p. 1996. pap. 12.99 (*0-89274-975-X*, HH-975) Harrison Hse.
— How to Believe God for a Mate. 32p. (Orig.). 1987. pap. 1.00 (*0-89274-453-7*, HH-453) Harrison Hse.
— How to Obtain Strong Faith: Six Principles. 192p. 1977. pap. 7.99 (*0-89274-042-6*, HH-042) Harrison Hse.
— Is Healing for All? 127p. (Orig.). 1979. pap. 7.99 (*0-89274-005-1*, HH-005) Harrison Hse.
— Living in the Realm of the Spirit. 41p. (Orig.). 1995. pap. 2.99 (*1-883798-07-8*) Faith One.
— Living in the Realm of the Spirit. 50p. (Orig.). 1989. pap. 4.99 (*0-89274-569-X*) Harrison Hse.
— Name It & Claim It! 192p. 1992. pap. 8.99 (*0-89274-857-5*, HH-857) Harrison Hse.
— A New Law for a New People. 92p. (Orig.). 1993. pap. 6.99 (*1-883798-01-9*) Faith One.
— Now Faith Is. 32p. 1984. pap. 1.00 (*0-89274-302-6*, HH-302) Harrison Hse.
— Origin of Satan. 32p. 1988. pap. 1.00 (*0-89274-544-4*, HH-544) Harrison Hse.
— Practical Suggestions for Successful Ministry. 112p. (Orig.). 1991. pap. 6.99 (*0-89274-880-X*, HH880) Harrison Hse.
— The Promise Land. 27p. (Orig.). 1993. pap. 1.99 (*1-883798-03-5*) Faith One.
— Prosperity on God's Terms. 112p. (Orig.). 1990. pap. 5.99 (*0-89274-670-X*, HH670) Harrison Hse.
***Price, Frederick K.** Race, Religion & Racism. 331p. 1999. 23.95 (*1-883798-36-1*) Faith One.
Price, Frederick K. Thank God for Everything, Mini bk. 32p. 1977. pap. 1.00 (*0-89274-056-6*, HH-056) Harrison Hse.
— Three Keys to Positive Confession. 71p. (Orig.). 1994. pap. 5.99 (*1-883798-05-1*) Faith One.
***Price, Frederick K.** The Truth About... Death: Do I Have a Say in When I Die? 59p. 1999. pap. 0.99 (*1-883798-25-6*) Faith One.
— The Truth About... Fear: Assault on the Mind. 32p. 1999. pap. 0.99 (*1-883798-30-2*) Faith One.
— The Truth About... Homosexuality: Is It Natural or Not? 32p. 1999. pap. 0.99 (*1-883798-31-0*) Faith One.
— The Truth About... Race: Did God Course Black People? 51p. 1999. pap. 0.99 (*1-883798-32-9*) Faith One.
— The Truth About... The Bible: Is It True or Not? 1999. pap. 0.99 (*1-883798-38-8*) Faith One.
— The Truth About... Worry: How to Leave Your Cares Behind. 1999. pap. 0.99 (*1-883798-43-4*) Faith One.
Price, Frederick K. Victorious Overcoming Life. 159p. (Orig.). 1993. pap. 7.99 (*1-883798-00-0*) Faith One.
— The Way, the Walk, the Warfare of the Believer. 403p. (Orig.). 1994. pap. 10.99 (*1-883798-06-X*) Faith One.
Price, Frederick K. C. Building on a Firm Foundation: A Guide to Developing Your Christian Walk. LC 99-176599. 64 p. 1998. 3.99 (*1-883798-21-3*) Faith One.
— Dr. Price's Golden Nuggets: A Treasury of Wisdom for Both Ministers & Laypeople. LC 99-176604. 125 p. 1998. 5.99 (*1-883798-23-X*) Faith One.
— High Finance: God's Financial Plan: Tithes & Offerings. 1995. pap. 7.99 (*1-883798-15-9*) Faith One.
***Price, Frederick K. C.** Higher Finance: How to Live Debt-Free. 2000. pap. 10.99 (*1-883798-41-8*) Faith One.
— Integrity: Would You Sin Against God? 2000. pap. 8.99 (*1-883798-42-6*) Faith One.
Price, G. B. Multivariable Analysis. (Illus.). 995p. 1984. 79.95 (*0-387-90934-6*) Spr-Verlag.
Price, Gareth. Thermodynamics of Chemical Processes. (Oxford Chemistry Primers Ser.: No. 56). (Illus.). 90p. 1998. pap. text 12.95 (*0-19-855963-1*) OUP.
Price, Geoffrey L., jt. ed. see McKnight, Stephen A.
Price, George M. Modern Factory: Safety, Sanitation & Welfare. LC 74-89758. (American Labor, from Conspiracy to Collective Bargaining Ser., No. 1). 574p. 1975. reprint ed. 51.95 (*0-405-02144-5*) Ayer.
Price, George R. Thomas Dekker. LC 68-17241. (Twayne's English Authors Ser.). 1969. pap. text 5.95 (*0-8290-2006-3*); lib. bdg. 20.95 (*0-8057-1148-1*) Irvington.
Price, George R., ed. see Easton, Hosea.
Price, George R., ed. see Middleton, Thomas & Rowley, William D.
Price, Gillel. Sunday Times Self Help Directory. 300p. 1980. 15.95 (*0-8464-1241-1*) Beekman Pubs.
Price, Gillian. Walking in Tuscany. LC 99-39087. 304p. 2000. pap. 15.95 (*1-56656-344-5*) Interlink Pub.
Price, Gina White, jt. auth. see Chepesiuk, Ron.
Price, Glanville. Ireland & the Celtic Connection: With a Celtic Bibliography. (Princess Grace Irish Library Lecture: Vol. 4). 47p. 1987. pap. 8.95 (*0-86140-269-3*, Pub. by Smyth) Dufour.
Price, Glanville, ed. The Celtic Connection. 361p. (C). 1994. lib. bdg. 76.50 (*0-86140-248-0*, Pub. by Smyth) B&N Imports.
Price, Glanville, ed. An Encyclopedia of the Languages of Europe. LC 97-29542. (Illus.). 520p. 2000. text 110.95 (*0-631-19286-7*, Pub. by Blackwell Publishers) Blackwell Pubs.
***Price, Glanville, ed.** An Encyclopedia of the Languages of Europe. (Illus.). 520p. 2000. pap. text 32.95 (*0-631-22039-9*, Pub. by Blackwell Publishers) Blackwell Pubs.
Price, Glanville, ed. see Manoliu-Manea, Maria.
Price, Glenn W. Los Origenes de la Guerra Con Mexico (Origins of the War with Mexico) (SPA.). 290p. 1974. pap. 8.99 (*968-16-2417-3*, Pub. by Fondo) Continental Bk.
Price-Goff, Claire. The Manatee. LC 98-53230. (Overview Ser.). (Illus.). 128p. (YA). (gr. 4-12). 1999. lib. bdg. 23.70 (*1-56006-445-5*) Lucent Bks.
Price, Greer, ed. see Scott, Sandra.
Price, Gregory A. Mastering Tournament Fighting: The Art of Winning the Game of Point Tournament Fighting. LC 98-28367. (Illus.). ix, 174p. 1998. pap. 29.95 (*0-9665309-0-X*) Renshi Prince.
Price-Gresty, David. The Hymnal. (Amelia Chapbooks Ser.). 48p. (Orig.). 1989. pap. 10.95 (*0-936545-08-9*) Amelia.
Price, Griffit Baley. An Introduction to Multicomplex Spaces & Functions. (Pure & Applied Mathematics Ser.: Vol. 140). (Illus.). 424p. 1990. text 155.00 (*0-8247-8345-X*) Dekker.
Price-Groff, Claire. Extraordinary Women Journalists. (Extraordinary People Ser.). (YA). (gr. 6 up). 1998. pap. 16.95 (*0-516-26242-4*) Childrens.
***Price-Groff, Claire.** Great Conquerors. LC 99-41983. (History Makers Ser.). (Illus.). 144p. (YA). (gr. 6-9). 2000. lib. bdg. 23.70 (*1-56006-612-1*) Lucent Bks.
— Queen Elizabeth I. LC 00-9247. (Importance of Ser.). (Illus.). (J). 2001. write for info. (*1-56006-700-4*) Lucent Bks.
Price-Groff, Claire. Twentieth-Century Women Political Leaders. LC 97-32373. (Global Profiles Ser.). (Illus.). 142p. (YA). (gr. 7-10). 1998. lib. bdg. 19.95 (*0-8160-3672-1*) Facts on File.
***Price Guide Editors of Sports Collectors Digest.** Standard Catalogue of Basketball Cards 2001. 4th rev. ed. LC 97-73043. (Illus.). 368p. 2000. pap. 21.95 (*0-87341-937-5*, SCBC4) Krause Pubns.
— Standard Catalogue of Football Cards 2001. 4th rev. ed. LC 97-73033. (Illus.). 592p. 2000. pap. 22.95 (*0-87341-935-9*, SCFC4) Krause Pubns.
— 2000 Baseball Card Price Guide. 14th ed. LC 87-80033. (Illus.). 832p. 2000. pap. 16.95 (*0-87341-583-3*, BP14) Krause Pubns.
***Price Guide Editors of Sports Collectors Digest, ed.** 2000 Standard Catalog of Basketball Cards. 3rd ed. LC 97-73043. (Illus.). 352p. 1999. pap. 19.95 (*0-87341-776-3*) Krause Pubns.
— 2000 Standard Catalog of Football Cards. 3rd ed. LC 97-73033. (Illus.). 560p. 1999. pap. 21.95 (*0-87341-772-0*) Krause Pubns.
Price, H., tr. see Weil, Simone.
Price, H. H. Essays in the Philosophy of Religion: Based on the Sarum Lectures, 1971. 1972. 13.95 (*0-19-824376-6*) OUP.
— Thinking & Representation. (Studies in Philosophy: No. 40). (C). 1977. lib. bdg. 24.95 (*0-8383-0117-7*) M S G Haskell Hse.
Price, H. Marcus, III. Disputing the Dead: U. S. Law on Aboriginal Remains & Grave Goods. 152p. 1991. text 37.50 (*0-8262-0779-0*) U of Mo Pr.
Price, Harry. Fifty Years of Psychical Research: A Critical Survey. LC 75-7394. (Perspectives in Psychical Research Ser.). (Illus.). 1975. reprint ed. 34.95 (*0-405-07043-8*) Ayer.
— Short Title Catalogue of Works on Psychical Research. (Hypnosis & Altered States of Consciousness Ser.). 468p. 1982. lib. bdg. 49.50 (*0-306-76166-1*) Da Capo.
Price, Harry & Dingwall, Eric J. Revelations of a Spirit Medium. LC 75-7395. (Perspectives in Psychical Research Ser.). 1975. reprint ed. 31.95 (*0-405-07044-6*) Ayer.
Price, Harry Edward & Music Educators National Conference (U. S.) Staff. Music Education Research: An Anthology from the Journal of Research in Music Education. LC 98-211644. xviii, 840p. 1998. 40.00 (*1-56545-109-0*) MENC.
Price, Haydn & Fisher, Rod. Shoeing for Performance: In the Sound & Lame Horse. (Illus.). 144p. 1995. pap. 16.95 (*1-57076-033-0*, Trafalgar Sq Pub) Trafalgar.
Price, Helen M. Poems from the Hearth. 133p. 1992. pap. 14.95 (*0-9635029-0-5*) W Price & Assocs.
Price, Henry H. Belief: The Gifford Lectures Delivered at the University of Aberdeen in 1960. LC 76-390002. (Muirhead Library of Philosophy, The Gifford Lectures: 1960). 493p. reprint ed. pap. 152.90 (*0-8357-7120-2*, 201217100080) Bks Demand.
— Perception. LC 81-13236. 332p. 1982. reprint ed. lib. bdg. 65.00 (*0-313-23153-2*, PRPT, Greenwood Pr) Greenwood.
Price, Henry R. Hawkins County, Tennessee: A Pictorial History. LC 96-24860. 1996. write for info. (*0-89865-974-4*) Donning Co.
Price, Hickman, jt. auth. see Ford, Franklin.
Price, Hilary B. Rhymes with Orange. (Illus.). 128p. (Orig.). 1997. pap. 9.95 (*0-614-30607-8*) Andrews & McMeel.
— Rhymes with Oranges. LC 97-71634. (Illus.). 128p. 1997. pap. 9.95 (*0-8362-3655-6*) Andrews & McMeel.
Price, Hope. Angels. 240p. (Orig.). 1994. mass mkt. 5.99 (*0-380-72331-X*, Avon Bks) Morrow Avon.
Price, Houston. Collector Knives. 12th ed. 1998. pap. 17.95 (*0-676-60136-7*) Hse Collectbls.
***Price, Hugh & Polsby, Nelson.** Explorations in the Evolution of Congress. LC 98-41407. xv, 207p. 1998. 21.95 (*0-87772-384-2*) UCB IGS.
Price, Hugh B. Up Jumped the Devil. LC 97-3155. 304p. 1997. mass mkt. 22.00 (*0-380-97420-7*, Avon Bks) Morrow Avon.
***Price, Hugh B., ed.** The State of Black America: The New Millennium. 2000. 24.95 (*1-56584-649-4*, Pub. by New Press NY) Norton.
Price, Hugh B., jt. auth. see Lewis, Reginald F.
Price, Huw. Time's Arrow & Archimedes' Point: New Directions for the Physics of Time. (Illus.). 320p. 1997. reprint ed. pap. 15.95 (*0-19-511798-0*) OUP.
— Time's Arrow & Archimedes' Point: Philosophical Reflections on Time & Physics. (Illus.). 320p. 1996. 30.00 (*0-19-510095-6*) OUP.
Price, I. Marshall. Old Buckingham by the Sea on the Eastern Shore of Maryland. (Illus.). 252p. 1997. reprint ed. lib. bdg. 32.50 (*0-8328-7112-5*) Higginson Bk Co.
***Price, Ira Marc & Comac, Linda.** Coping with Macular Degeneration: A Guide for Patients & Families to Understand & Live with This Degenerative Vision Disorder. 224p. 2000. pap. 13.95 (*0-89529-996-8*, Avery) Penguin Putnam.
Price, J. A. Operation Nighthawk. 1985. pap. 3.50 (*0-8217-1696-4*) NAL.
Price, J. C. Interpretation of Thermal Infrared Data: The Heat Capacity Mapping Mission, Vol.1, Vol. 1, No. 2. (Remote Sensing Reviews Ser.: Vol. 1, Pt. 2). 198p. 1986. pap. text 195.00 (*3-7186-0289-X*) Gordon & Breach.
Price, J. G., et al. Annotated Bibliography of Mineral Deposits in Trans-Pecos Texas. (Mineral Resource Circular Ser.: MRC 73). (Illus.). 108p. 1983. pap. 5.00 (*0-318-17363-8*) Bur Econ Geology.
Price, J. H., et al, eds. The Shore Environment Vol. 2: Ecosystems. (Systematics Association Special Ser.: No. 17). 1981. text 199.00 (*0-12-564702-6*) Acad Pr.
Price, J. L. The Dutch Republic in the Seventeenth Century. LC 98-24084. (European History in Perspective Ser.). 184p. 1998. pap. 21.95 (*0-312-21733-1*); text 59.95 (*0-312-21732-3*) St Martin.
— Holland & the Dutch Republic in the Seventeenth Century: The Politics of Particularism. 320p. 1994. text 70.00 (*0-19-820383-7*) OUP.
Price, J. W. Tin & Tin-Alloy Plating. 1982. 240.00 (*0-7855-7300-3*) St Mut.
— Tinand Tin Alloy Plating. 148p. 1997. pap. 210.00 (*0-901150-12-6*) St Mut.
Price, J. W. & Smith, R. Tin. (Handbook of Analytical Chemistry Ser.: Vol. 4, Pt. 3, Section A, Y). (Illus.). 1978. 117.95 (*0-387-08234-4*) Spr-Verlag.
Price, Jack. Wild Horse Country in Wyoming. (Illus.). 188p. 1996. write for info. (*1-57579-050-5*); pap. write for info. (*1-57579-049-1*) Pine Hill Pr.
***Price, Jack.** Wild Horse Robbins. 100p. 1999. pap. write for info. (*1-57579-160-9*) Pine Hill Pr.
Price, Jacob. Overseas Trade & Traders: Essays on the Commercial, Financial & Political Challenges of British Atlantic Merchants, 1600-1775. LC 96-26142. (Collected Studies: No. CS554). 320p. 1996. 98.95 (*0-86078-591-2*, Pub. by Variorum) Ashgate Pub Co.
Price, Jacob M. The Atlantic Frontier of the Thirteen Colonies & States. (Collected Studies: CS532). 280p. 1996. text 97.95 (*0-86078-586-6*, Pub. by Variorum) Ashgate Pub Co.
— Capital & Credit in British Overseas Trade: The View from the Chesapeake 1770-1776. LC 80-13815. 233p. 1980. 36.50 (*0-674-09480-8*) HUP.
— Perry of London: A Family & a Firm on the Seaborne Frontier, 1615-1753. (Historical Studies: Vol. No. III). (Illus.). 208p. 1992. text 30.00 (*0-674-66306-3*) HUP.
— Tobacco in Atlantic Trade: The Chesapeake, London & Glasgow, 1675-1775. LC 95-30952. (Collected Studies: Vol. CS513). 336p. 1995. 98.95 (*0-86078-548-3*, Pub. by Variorum) Ashgate Pub Co.
Price, James D. Concordance of the Hebrew Accents in the Hebrew Bible Vol. 2: Concordance of the Hebrew Accents Used in the Former Prophets: Includes Joshua, Judges, 1 Samuel, 2 Samuel, 1 Kings, 2 Kings. LC 95-23903. (Mellen Biblical Press Ser.: Vol. 43). 252p. 1996. text 89.95 (*0-7734-2397-4*, Mellen Biblical Pr) E Mellen.
— Concordance of the Hebrew Accents in the Hebrew Bible Vol. 3: Concordance of the Hebrew Accents Used in the Latter Prophets: Isaiah, Jeremiah, Ezekiel, the Twelve Minor Prophets: Hosea, Joel, Amos, Obadiah, Jonah,

P

Micah, Nabum, Habakkuk, Zephaniah, Haggai, Zechariah, Malachi. LC 95-23903. (Mellen Biblical Press Ser.: Vol. 44). 328p. 1996. text 99.95 (*0-7734-2399-0*, Mellen Biblical Pr) E Mellen.

— Concordance of the Hebrew Accents in the Hebrew Bible Vol. 4: Concordance of the Hebrew Accents Used in the Writings (Kethubim) LC 95-23903. (Mellen Biblical Press Ser.: Vol. 45). 268p. 1996. text 89.95 (*0-7734-2401-6*, Mellen Biblical Pr) E Mellen.

— Concordance of the Hebrew Accents in the Hebrew Bible Vol. 5: Concordance of the Hebrew Accents Used in the Poetic Books: Includes Psalms, Job, Proverbs. LC 95-23903. (Mellen Biblical Press Ser.: Vol. 46). 204p. 1996. text 89.95 (*0-7734-2403-2*, Mellen Biblical Pr) E Mellen.

— Concordance of the Herbrew Accents in the Hebrew Bible Vol. 1: Concordance of the Hebrew Accents Used in the Pentateuch: Includes Genesis, Exodus, Leviticus, Numbers, Deuteronomy. LC 95-23903. (Studies in the Bible & Early Christianity: Vols. 34A-34E). 288p. 1996. text 89.95 (*0-7734-2395-8*, Mellen Biblical Pr) E Mellen.

— The Syntax of Masoretic Accents in the Hebrew Bible. LC 90-20265. (Studies in the Bible & Early Christianity: Vol. 27). 344p. 1990. lib. bdg. 99.95 (*0-88946-510-X*) E Mellen.

Price, James E. Analysis of a Middle Mississippian House in Butler County, Missouri. LC 70-628940. (Museum Briefs Ser.: No. 1). (Illus.). iv, 31p. 1969. pap. 1.70 (*0-913134-00-7*) Mus Anthro MO.

— Masons & Methodists in Utica, Mississippi. 167p. 1998. pap. 17.00 (*1-885480-24-5*) Pioneer Pubng.

Price, James E. & Griffin, James B. The Snodgrass Site of the Powers Phase of Southeast Missouri. (Anthropological Papers Ser.: No. 66). (Illus.). (Orig.). 1979. pap. 3.00 (*0-932206-77-8*) U Mich Mus Anthro.

Price, James E. & Krakker, James J. Dalton, Occupation of the Ozark Border. Feldman, L. H., ed. LC 75-327206. (Museum Briefs Ser.: No. 20). (Illus.). vii, 41p. 1975. pap. 3.00 (*0-913134-20-1*) Mus Anthro MO.

Price, James E., et al. Recent Investigations at Towosahgy State Historic Site & Towosahgy State Historic Site & Its Physical Environment. Wood, W. Raymond, ed. (Missouri Archaeologist Ser.: Vol. 51). (Illus.). 91p. 1993. pap. 6.50 (*0-943414-74-1*) MO Arch Soc.

Price, James F. & Schweigert, Bernard S., eds. Science of Meat & Meat Products. 3rd ed. 639p. 1987. 98.00 (*0-917678-21-4*) Food & Nut Pr.

Price, James H., jt. auth. see Steen, Edwin B.

Price, James L. Handbook of Organizational Measurement. 1986. 28.00 (*0-88730-386-2*, HarpBusn) HarpInfo.

— The Study of Turnover. LC 76-56377. (Illus.). 170p. 1977. reprint ed. pap. 52.70 (*0-608-00105-8*, 206087000006) Bks Demand.

Price, James L. & Mueller, Charles W. Absenteeism & Turnover of Hospital Employees. Bacharach, Samuel B., ed. LC 85-23779. (Monographs in Organizational Behavior & Industrial Relations: Vol. 5). 282p. 1986. 78.50 (*0-89232-441-4*) Jai Pr.

— Handbook of Organizational Measurement. LC 85-8136. 304p. 1986. text 28.00 (*0-685-10496-6*, HarpBusn) HarpInfo.

— Professional Turnover: The Case of Nurses. (Health Systems Management Ser.). 218p. (C). 1980. 25.00 (*0-88331-184-4*) R B Luce.

Price, Jammie. Navigating Differences: Friendships Between Gay & Straight Men. LC 98-28103. (Illus.). 172p. 1998. pap. 19.95 (*1-56023-952-2*); lib. bdg. 39.95 (*0-7890-0619-7*, Harrington Park) Haworth Pr.

Price, Jan. The Other Side of Death. 192p. 1996. pap. 10.00 (*0-449-90992-1*) Fawcett.

Price, Jane. Motherhood. 1989. pap. 10.95 (*0-86358-211-7*, Pub. by Pandora) Harper SF.

***Price, Janet.** Feminist Theory & the Body: A Reader. 1999. pap. 24.99 (*0-415-92566-5*) Routledge.

***Price, Janet & Shildrick, Margrit.** Feminist Theory & Body: Reader. 504p. (C). 1999. text 75.00 (*0-415-92565-7*) Routledge.

Price, Janet, jt. ed. see Shildrick, Margrit.

Price, Janet, jt. ed. see Shildrik, Margrit.

Price, Janet R., et al. The Rights of Students: Basic ACLU Guide to Racial Minority Rights. LC 87-9890. (American Civil Liberties Union Handbook Ser.). 181p. 1988. pap. 11.95 (*0-8093-1423-1*) S Ill U Pr.

Price-Janney, Rebecca. The Major League Mystery. LC 93-45633. (Heather Reed Mystery Ser.: Vol. 5). (J). 1994. 5.99 (*0-8499-3535-0*) Word Pub.

— Reins of Danger. LC 94-43616. (Heather Reed Mystery Ser.: Vol. 8). (J). 1995. pap. 5.99 (*0-8499-3632-2*) Word Pub.

Price, Jeanne & Zamkoff, Bernard. Grading Techniques for Fashion Design. 2nd ed. LC 95-60516. (Illus.). 223p. (C). 1995. 51.00 (*1-56367-046-1*) Fairchild.

Price, Jeanne, jt. auth. see Zamkoff, Bernard.

Price, Jeff, et al, eds. The Summer Atlas of North American Birds. (Illus.). 364p. 1995. text 51.00 (*0-12-564660-7*) Acad Pr.

Price, Jeffrey, et al. 1.2: New Perspectives on Central Appalachian Low-Sulfur Coal Supplies. (Illus.). 265p. (Orig.). (C). 1992. pap. 55.00 (*1-878907-63-8*) TechBooks.

Price, Jeffrey T. Language & Being in Wittgenstein's "Philosophical Investigations" 1973. pap. text 26.95 (*90-279-2443-0*) Mouton.

Price, Jeffrey W. The Songs of Vittorio Giannini on Poems by Karl Flaster. 112p. 1994. per. 16.95 (*0-8403-9398-9*) Kendall-Hunt.

***Price, Jeremy Nicholas.** Against All Odds: The Meaning of School & Relationships in the Lives of Six African American Men. LC 99-53991. (Issues in Curriculum Theory, Policy & Research Ser.). 1999. write for info. (*1-56750-497-3*) Ablx Pub.

Price, Jerome A. Power & Compassion: Working with Difficult Adolescents & Abused Parents. LC 96-29012. (Family Therapy Ser.). 196p. 1996. lib. bdg. 30.00 (*1-57230-141-4*, 0141) Guilford Pubns.

— Power & Compassion: Working with Difficult Adolescents & Abused Parents. (Family Therapy Ser.). 196p. 1999. pap. text 18.00 (*1-57230-470-7*) Guilford Pubns.

Price, Jerome B. The Antinuclear Movement. 1995. text 40.00 (*0-8161-7268-4*, G K Hall & Co) Mac Lib Ref.

— The Antinuclear Movement. rev. ed. (Social Movements Past & Present Ser.). 240p. 1989. pap. 14.95 (*0-8057-9735-1*, Twyne) Mac Lib Ref.

***Price, Joan.** The Complete Idiot's Guide to Online Medical Resources. 380p. 2000. pap. 18.95 (*0-7897-2297-6*) Que.

Price, Joan. Hawk in the Wind. 124p. (J). (gr. 3-6). 1999. pap. 9.99 (*0-88092-446-2*, 4462) Royal Fireworks.

— The Honest Truth about Losing Weight & Keeping It Off. (Illus.). (Orig.). 1991. pap. text 9.95 (*0-9627708-1-7*) NordicPress.

— Truth Is a Bright Star: A Hopi Adventure. LC 82-1345. 156p. (J). (gr. 3-7). 1995. pap. 9.95 (*0-89087-333-X*) Celestial Arts.

— Truth Is a Bright Star: A Hopi Adventure. 156p. (J). (gr. 3-7). 1997. pap. 9.95 (*1-883672-62-7*) Tricycle Pr.

Price, Joan E. Louis Comfort Tiffany: The Painting Career of a Colorist. (American University Studies, Series XX: Vol. 28). XXIV, 111p. (C). 1996. text 32.95 (*0-8204-2770-5*) P Lang Pubng.

Price, Joanne K. Applied Math for Wastewater Plant Operators. LC 90-71881. 488p. 1991. student ed. 51.95 (*0-87762-809-2*); write for info. (*0-87762-810-6*) Technomic.

— Applied Math for Water Plant Operators. LC 91-65983. 535p. 1991. 48.95 (*0-87762-874-2*); write for info. (*0-87762-875-0*) Technomic.

— Basic Math Concepts for Water & Wastewater Plant Operators. LC 90-71880. 368p. 1991. 39.95 (*0-87762-808-4*) Technomic.

Price, Jody. A Map with Utopia: Oscar Wilde's Theory for Social Transformation. LC 94-22374. (American University Studies IV: Vol. 162). 249p. (C). 1996. text 44.95 (*0-8204-2069-7*) P Lang Pubng.

Price, John. Japan Works: Power & Paradox in Postwar Industrial Relations. (IRL Press Book: No. 30). (Illus.). 328p. 1996. text 45.00 (*0-8014-3285-5*); pap. text 17.95 (*0-8014-8360-3*) Cornell U Pr.

— Pub Walks Around Portsmouth & the South Downs. (C). 1989. 39.00 (*1-85455-070-5*, Pub. by Ensign Pubns & Print) St Mut.

Price, John, jt. auth. see Rees, John.

Price, John, jt. auth. see Stevens, Anthony.

Price, John A. A Gathering of Light: Eternal Wisdom for a Time of Transformation. rev. ed. 1998. reprint ed. pap. write for info. (*1-887884-06-8*) Wings of Spirit.

— Our Boundless Self: A Call to Awake. 2000. pap. write for info. (*1-887884-07-6*) Wings of Spirit.

— Roswell Vol. 1: A Quest for the Truth. Tilley, John, ed. (Illus.). 213p. (Orig.). 1997. pap. 9.95 (*0-939040-01-8*) Truth Seeker.

— Tijuana: Urbanization in a Border Culture. LC 72-1264. (Illus.). 217p. 1973. reprint ed. pap. 67.30 (*0-608-00889-3*, 206168300010) Bks Demand.

Price, John A. & Price, Diadra. Soular Reunion: Journey to the Beloved: Remembering the Love of Self, Soulmates & Twin Souls. rev. ed. 165p. 1997. reprint ed. pap. 12.95 (*1-887884-05-X*) Wings of Spirit.

Price, John-Allen. Doomsday Ship. 1982. mass mkt. 3.25 (*0-8217-1107-5*, Zebra Kensgtn) Kensgtn Pub Corp.

— Eagle's Revenge. 432p. 1993. mass mkt. 4.50 (*0-8217-4404-6*, Zebra Kensgtn) Kensgtn Pub Corp.

— Phoenix Caged. 448p. 1993. mass mkt. 4.50 (*0-8217-4192-6*, Zebra Kensgtn) Kensgtn Pub Corp.

— Siege of Ocean Valkyrie. 1992. mass mkt. 4.50 (*0-8217-3662-0*, Zebra Kensgtn) Kensgtn Pub Corp.

Price, John E., et al. College Accounting. 7th ed. LC 93-19084. 1993. 82.84 (*0-02-801441-3*) Glencoe.

— College Accounting. 8th ed. LC 95-20805. 1995. write for info. (*0-02-804056-2*) Glencoe.

— College Accounting. 9th ed. LC 98-29086. 1998. 56.00 (*0-02-804612-9*) Glencoe.

***Price, John E., et al.** College Accounting, Chpts. 1-13. 9th ed. 1999. teacher ed. 73.86 (*0-02-804638-2*); student ed. 33.91 (*0-02-804614-5*) Glencoe.

— College Accounting, Chpts. 1-32. 9th ed. 1999. teacher ed. 73.86 (*0-02-804637-4*) Glencoe.

— College Accounting, Vol. 1-25. 9th ed. 1999. student ed. 45.68 (*0-02-804613-7*) Glencoe.

Price, John F., ed. Derivatives & Financial Mathematics. LC 97-41236. 191p. 1997. 59.00 (*1-56072-511-7*) Nova Sci Pubs.

Price, John F., jt. auth. see Kholodnyi, Valery A.

***Price, John M.** The Art of Moderation: An Alternative to Alcoholism. Jones, Sharon, ed. LC 99-71333. 128p. 1999. 14.00 (*1-56550-083-0*); pap. 10.00 (*1-56550-084-9*) Vis Bks Intl.

Price, John R. The Abundance Book. LC 96-24377. 96p. (Orig.). 1996. reprint ed. pap. 7.00 (*1-56170-347-8*, 830) Hay House.

— Angel Energy: How to Harness the Power of Angels in Your Everyday Life. LC 95-90164. 240p. 1995. pap. 12.00 (*0-449-90983-2*) Fawcett.

— The Angels Within Us. 336p. (Orig.). 1993. pap. 12.00 (*0-449-90784-8*, Columbine) Fawcett.

— Empowerment. LC 96-32493. 160p. (Orig.). 1996. reprint ed. pap. 10.95 (*1-56170-350-8*, 833) Hay House.

— Estate Planning, Set. 1360p. 1993. 145.00 (*0-316-71861-0*, Aspen Law & Bus) Aspen Pub.

— Estate Planning: 1994. 1994. suppl. ed. 75.00 (*0-316-71808-4*, Aspen Law & Bus) Aspen Pub.

— Living a Life of Joy. LC 97-21724. 256p. 1997. pap. 12.00 (*0-449-91138-1*) Fawcett.

— The Love Book. 112p. 1998. pap. 7.00 (*1-56170-503-9*, 869) Hay House.

— The Meditation Book. LC 98-3340. 112p. 1998. pap. 7.00 (*1-56170-502-0*, 866) Hay House.

— 1995 Supplement to Estate Planning. 1995. suppl. ed. 82.50 (*0-316-71864-5*, Aspen Law & Bus) Aspen Pub.

— Practical Spirituality. LC 96-38831. 160p. (Orig.). 1996. reprint ed. pap. 10.95 (*1-56170-351-6*, 834) Hay House.

— Price on Contemporary Estate Planning. 1360p. 1992. boxed set 145.00 (*0-316-71859-9*, Aspen Law & Bus) Aspen Pub.

— A Spiritual Philosophy for the New World: The 60-Day Non-Human Program to Rise above the Ego. 2nd rev. ed. LC 96-53038. 160p. 1997. pap. 10.95 (*1-56170-360-5*, 842) Hay House.

— The Success Book. LC 97-32367. 112p. 1998. pap. text 7.00 (*1-56170-474-1*) Hay House.

— The Superbeings. 160p. (Orig.). 1988. reprint ed. mass mkt. 5.99 (*0-449-21543-1*) Fawcett.

— The Superbeings: They Are with Us Now...Demonstrating What We All Can Become. 2nd rev. ed. LC 96-44149. 160p. 1997. pap. 12.00 (*1-56170-358-3*, 399) Hay House.

— The Wellness Book. LC 97-47697. 112p. 1998. pap. 7.00 (*1-56170-500-4*, 864) Hay House.

— With Wings As Eagles: Discovering the Master Teacher in the Secret School Within. 2nd rev. ed. LC 96-46850. 112p. 1996. pap. 9.95 (*1-56170-359-1*, 840) Hay House.

— The Workbook for Self-Mastery: A Course of Study on the Divine Reality. LC 97-12686. 200p. (Orig.). 1997. pap., wbk. ed. 10.95 (*1-56170-362-1*, 845) Hay House.

Price, John R., jt. auth. see Stein, Robert A.

***Price, John Randolph.** The Alchemist's Handbook. 176p. 2000. pap. 8.95 (*1-56170-747-3*, 5031) Hay House.

Price, John Randolph. The Jesus Code. LC 99-15923. 160p. 2000. pap. 11.95 (*1-56170-671-X*, 5008) Hay House.

***Price, John Randolph.** Removing the Masks That Bind Us. 176p. 2001. pap. 11.95 (*1-56170-672-8*, 5009) Hay House.

Price, John V. David Hume. (Twayne's English Authors Ser.: TEAS No. 77). 160p. 1991. text 24.95 (*0-8057-7004-6*, Twayne) Mac Lib Ref.

— The Ironic Hume: 1965 Edition. 208p. 1996. reprint ed. 48.00 (*1-85506-171-6*) Bks Intl VA.

Price, John V., intro. Aesthetics: Sources in the Eighteen Century, 8 Vol. 2822p. 1998. 795.00 (*1-85506-599-1*) Thoemmes Pr.

— Collected Works of Henry Home (Lord Kames), 13 vols. 5766p. (C). 1993. 1195.00 (*0-415-08104-1*) Routledge.

Price, John V., jt. intro. see Vesey, Godfrey.

Price, John W. Food Habits of Some Lake Erie Fishes. (Bulletin New Ser.: Vol. 2, No. 1). 1962. pap. text 3.00 (*0-86727-048-9*) Ohio Bio Survey.

Price, Jonathan. LOGO for the Apple IIc: The Magic Turtle. write for info. (*0-318-58181-7*) P-H.

— Outlining Goes Electronic. LC 98-51776. (ATTW Contemporary Studies in Technical Communications). 1999. pap. write for info. (*1-56750-379-9*) Ablx Pub.

***Price, Jonathan.** Outlining Goes Electronic. LC 98-51776. (ATTW Contemporary Studies in Technical Communications). 1999. 63.50 (*1-56750-378-0*) Ablx Pub.

Price, Jonathan, ed. Critics on Robert Lowell. LC 78-161435. (Readings in Literary Criticism Ser.: No. 17). 124p. 1972. 19.95 (*0-87024-210-5*) U of Miami Pr.

Price, Jonathan & Korman, Henry. How to Communicate Technical Information: A Handbook of Software & Hardware Documentation. 2nd ed. 448p. (C). 1993. pap. 47.95 (*0-8053-6829-9*) Benjamin-Cummings.

Price, Jonathan, jt. auth. see Coulombre, Rich.

Price, Jonathan J. Jerusalem under Siege: The Collapse of the Jewish State, 66-77 C.E. LC 91-40266. (Brill's Series in Jewish Studies: Vol. 3). 372p. 1992. 120.00 (*90-04-09471-7*) Brill Academic Pubs.

Price, Jonathan L., jt. auth. see Campanelli, Jeanne F.

Price, Joseph G., ed. The Triple Bond: Audience, Actors & Renaissance Playwrights. LC 74-15140. 256p. 1975. 40.00 (*0-271-01177-7*) Pa St U Pr.

Price, Joseph G., jt. ed. see Parfenov, Alexandr T.

***Price, Joseph L.** From Season to Season: Sports as American Religion. 2000. 29.95 (*0-86554-694-0*, H513) Mercer Univ Pr.

Price, Joseph L., ed. see Musser, Donald W.

Price, Joseph L., jt. ed. see Musser, Donald W.

Price, Joseph M., jt. ed. see Ingram, Rick E.

Price, Joseph P. Park, Recreation, Leisure Film Bibliography: Annotated & Cross Indexed Bibliography of Audiovisual Materials Relating to Parks, Recreation & Leisure. LC GV0014.6.S59. 119p. reprint ed. pap. 36.90 (*0-7837-1545-5*, 204183000024) Bks Demand.

Price, Joy. Rum-Tum-Tum: Mississippi Recipes for a Festive Southern Christmas. (Illus.). 48p. (Orig.). 1985. reprint ed. pap. 5.00 (*0-945301-01-4*) Druid Pr.

Price, Juanita B., compiled by. Child's World: Children's Books: A Bibliography of 315 Oregon Authors & 60 Illustrators of Children's Books in the 20th Century. 4th ed. 62p. (Orig.). (J). (ps-12). 1995. pap. 19.95 (*0-9621683-3-5*) Price Prodns.

Price, Judy. Tips on Godly Eating, Vol. 1. large type ed. 215p. (Orig.). 1997. pap. 7.95 (*0-9659438-0-1*) Praise Him.

Price, Julia, ed. see Mendez-Faith, Kienzle.

Price, Julia, ed. see Speroni, Charles & Golino, Carlo L.

Price, Julie, ed. see Cuvier, Remi.

Price, June. Avoiding Attendants from Hell: A Practical Guide to Finding, Hiring & Keeping Personal Care Attendants. LC 98-89122. (Illus.). 120p. 1998. pap. 16.95 (*1-888725-19-2*); spiral bd. 16.95 (*1-888725-18-4*) Sci & Human Pr.

Price, June C., jt. auth. see Koch, Etta.

Price, Justin J., jt. auth. see Flanders, Harley.

Price, K. F., jt. auth. see Niehaus, R. J.

Price, K. F., jt. ed. see Niehaus, Richard J.

Price, Karen. Scent Science. (Illus.). 32p. (J). (gr. 2). 1998. boxed set 6.95 (*1-58295-010-5*, Pub. by Pace Prods) Andrews & McMeel.

— Scrapbooking for Kids. (Illus.). 24p. (J). 1999. ring bd. 9.95 (*1-58295-013-X*, Pub. by Pace Prods) Andrews & McMeel.

Price, Kathleen M. The Lady & the Unicorn. LC 94-75989. (Illus.). 32p. 1994. 14.95 (*1-880851-16-4*) Greene Bark Pr.

Price, Kathy A. The Zen of Bowel Movements: A Spiritual Approach to Constipation. 184p. (Orig.). 1995. pap. 19.95 (*0-9642906-6-9*) Rock Rose Pubng.

***Price, Keith A.** Thirsting after God. 336p. 2000. pap. 14.99 (*0-87509-820-7*) Chr Pubns.

Price, Kenneth. The Eagle Christian. (Illus.). (Orig.). 1984. pap. 7.95 (*0-685-22528-3*) Old Faithful.

— The Eagle Christian. rev. ed. LC 88-92413. (Illus.). (Orig.). 1989. reprint ed. 8.95 (*0-9621224-0-8*); reprint ed. pap. 7.95 (*0-9621224-1-6*) Old Faithful.

Price, Kenneth M. Whitman & Tradition: The Poet in His Century. LC 89-27380. 191p. 1990. reprint ed. pap. 59.30 (*0-608-07845-X*, 205402100011) Bks Demand.

Price, Kenneth M., ed. Walt Whitman: The Contemporary Reviews. (American Critical Archives Ser.: No. 9). 380p. (C). 1996. text 105.00 (*0-521-45387-9*) Cambridge U Pr.

Price, Kenneth M. & Leitz, Robert C., III. Critical Essays on George Santayana. (Critical Essays on American Literature Ser.). 288p. 1991. 49.00 (*0-8161-7303-6*, Hall Reference) Macmillan.

Price, Kenneth M. & Oliver, Lawrence J., eds. Critical Essays on James Weldon Johnson. 1997. 47.00 (*0-7838-0041-X*) Mac Lib Ref.

Price, Kenneth M. & Smith, Susan B., eds. Periodical Literature in Nineteenth-Century America. (Illus.). 352p. (C). 1995. text 45.00 (*0-8139-1629-1*); pap. text 19.50 (*0-8139-1630-5*) U Pr of Va.

Price, Kenneth M., ed. see Whitman, Thomas J.

Price, Kent A., ed. The Dilemmas of Choice. LC 86-195396. 270p. reprint ed. pap. 83.70 (*0-7837-0116-0*, 204039300016) Bks Demand.

— Regional Conflict & National Policy. LC 82-47983. xviii, 142p. 1982. pap. 14.95 (*0-8018-2919-4*) Resources Future.

Price, Kent A., jt. ed. see Castle, Emery N.

Price, Kevin S. Leadership: An Exploration. LC 93-85063. 132p. (Orig.). (C). 1993. pap. text 9.95 (*0-9637452-0-4*) Proactive Pubs.

Price, Kingsley, ed. On Criticizing Music: Five Philosophical Perspectives. LC 81-47597. 127p. reprint ed. pap. 39.40 (*0-608-15319-2*, 202924100059) Bks Demand.

Price, L. Greer. Grand Canyon: The Story Behind the Scenery. Morales, Brigitte, tr. (GER., Illus.). 48p. 1998. pap. 8.95 (*0-88714-826-3*) KC Pubns.

— Grand Canyon: The Story Behind the Scenery. 4th rev. ed. LC 91-60043. (Illus.). 64p. 1991. pap. 7.95 (*0-88714-060-2*) KC Pubns.

***Price, L. Greer.** An Introduction to Grand Canyon Geology. Scott, Sandra, ed. LC 98-75044. (Illus.). 64p. 1999. pap. 9.95 (*0-938216-68-6*) GCA.

Price, L. Greer, ed. see Anderson, Michael F.

Price, L. Greer, ed. see Duffield, Wendell A.

Price, L. Greer, jt. ed. see Haralson, Carol.

Price, Larkin B., ed. Marcel Proust: A Critical Panorama. LC 72-83033. 302p. reprint ed. pap. 93.70 (*0-608-13934-3*, 202022600016) Bks Demand.

Price, Larry. No (World Version) 1990. pap. 7.00 (*84-87467-04-0*, Pub. by Zasterle Pr) SPD-Small Pr Dist.

Price, Laurence W. Make Landscaping Your Business. LC 97-71227. (Illus.). 136p. (Orig.). 1997. pap. 9.95 (*0-9611966-2-9*) Botany Bks.

— Starting & Operating a Landscape Maintenance Business. (Illus.). 133p. (Orig.). (C). 1989. pap. text 8.95 (*0-9611966-1-0*) Botany Bks.

Price, Laurie. Except for Memory. (Orig.). pap. 8.95 (*1-880766-06-X*) Pantograph Pr.

Price, Lawrence M. Reception of English Literature in Germany. LC 68-21223. 1972. reprint ed. 36.95 (*0-405-08863-9*) Ayer.

***Price, Leah Palmer.** The Anthology & the Rise of the Novel from Richardson to George Eliot: From Richardson to George Eliot. LC 99-59206. 238p. (C). 2000. Price not set. (*0-521-78208-2*) Cambridge U Pr.

Price, Leland. Parted on Her Wedding Morn. 1942. pap. 3.25 (*0-8222-0873-3*) Dramatists Play.

Price, Len, jt. auth. see Price, Shirley.

***Price, Leo.** The Grumpy Tree. rev. ed. LC 99-26651. Orig. Title: The Tree That Always Said No!. (Illus.). 40p. (J). (gr. k-2). 1999. pap. 6.95 (*0-8198-3097-6*) Pauline Bks.

Price, Leon C. Beyond Survival to Victory: A Practical Guide for Victorious Christian Living. 96p. 1993. pap. 6.00 (*0-9637311-0-6*) Genesis Comm Inc.

***Price, Leon Carter.** Prophesy to These Bones: These Bones Can Live! 144p. 1999. pap. 7.95 (*1-58169-038-X*, Gazelle Pr) Genesis Comm Inc.

Price, Leontyne. Aida. (Illus.). 32p. 1996. pap. 5.00 (*0-15-200987-6*, Voyager Bks) Harcourt.

— Aida. LC 89-36481. (Illus.). 32p. (J). 1997. pap. 7.00 (*0-15-201546-9*) Harcourt.

— Aida. 1997. 12.20 (*0-606-12161-7*, Pub. by Turtleback) Demco.

Price, Lesley Anne. Kids' Knits. 1984. pap. write for info. (*0-345-31500-6*) Ballantine Pub Grp.

Price, Leslie, jt. ed. see Ayton, Andrew.

Price, Lew P. Aquarian Anastasis. LC 65-9503. 1975. pap. 15.00 (*0-917578-01-5*) L Paxton Price.

P

— Astrology: The Music of Life. 1984. pap. 25.00 (*0-917578-05-8*) L Paxton Price.
— Creating & Using Grandfather's Flute. (Illus.). 52p. (Orig.). 1995. pap. 10.00 (*0-917578-11-2*) L Paxton Price.
— Creating & Using Larger Native American Flutes. (Illus.). 1998. pap. 10.00 (*0-917578-19-8*) L Paxton Price.
— Creating & Using Older Native American Flutes. (Illus.). 47p. (Orig.). 1995. pap. 10.00 (*0-917578-13-9*) L Paxton Price.
— Creating & Using Smaller Native American Flutes. (Illus.). 56p. (Orig.). 1995. pap. 10.00 (*0-917578-14-7*) L Paxton Price.
— Creating & Using the Largest Native American Flutes. (Illus.). 1998. pap. 10.00 (*0-917578-20-1*) L Paxton Price.
— Creating & Using the Native American Concert Flute. (Illus.). 54p. 1996. pap. 10.00 (*0-917578-16-3*) L Paxton Price.
— Creating & Using the Native American Love Flute. (Illus.). 1994. pap. 10.00 (*0-917578-09-0*) L Paxton Price.
— Creating & Using Very Small Native American Flutes. (Illus.). 1998. pap. 12.00 (*0-917578-22-8*) L Paxton Price.
— Dimensions in Astrology. 1986. pap. 12.00 (*0-917578-06-6*) L Paxton Price.
— More Secrets of the Flute: More of the Physics, Math, & Design of Non-Mechanical Folk Flutes. (Illus.). 66p. (C). 1997. pap. 15.00 (*0-917578-17-1*) L Paxton Price.
— Native North American Flutes. (Illus.). 1990. pap. 5.00 (*0-917578-07-4*) L Paxton Price.
— The Oldest Magic: The History & Early Influence of Music. (Illus.). 200p. 1995. pap. 26.00 (*0-917578-10-4*) L Paxton Price.
— Secrets of the Flute: The Physics, Math, & Design of Non-Mechanical Folk Flutes. (Illus.). 80p. (Orig.). (C). 1991. pap. 15.00 (*0-917578-08-2*) L Paxton Price.
***Price, Lew Paxton.** Behind Light's Illusion - Electromagnetism: The Nature of Electrons, Magnetism, & Radio. (Behind Light's Illusion Ser.: Vol. 3). (Illus.). 57p. 1999. pap. 12.00 (*0-917578-25-2*) L Paxton Price.
— Behind Light's Illusion - Light: The Nature of the Illuminating Energy of Our Universe. (Behind Light's Illusion Ser.: Vol. 4). (Illus.). 56p. 1999. pap. 12.00 (*0-917578-26-0*) L Paxton Price.
— Behind Light's Illusion - Time: The Creation & Nature of Time & Our Universe. (Behind Light's Illusion Ser.: Vol. 5). (Illus.). 60p. 2000. pap. 12.00 (*0-917578-27-9*) L Paxton Price.
Price, Linda. Dare to Dream. 416p. (Orig.). 1989. mass mkt. 4.50 (*0-380-75361-8*, Avon Bks) Morrow Avon.
Price, Lindy H. Sports & New Exercise Research: Index of Current Information. 150p. 1994. 47.50 (*0-7883-0068-7*); pap. 44.50 (*0-7883-0069-5*) ABBE Pubs Assn.
— Sports & New Exercise Research: Index of Current Information. 171p. 1997. 47.50 (*0-7883-1608-7*); pap. 44.50 (*0-7883-1609-5*) ABBE Pubs Assn.
Price, Lisa & Jonathan. The Best of Online Shopping: The Prices' Guide to Fast & Easy Shopping on the Web. LC 99-32180. 1999. pap. 16.00 (*0-345-43681-4*) Ballantine Pub Grp.
Price, Llewellyn I., jt. auth. see Romer, Alfred S.
Price, Lorna. Masterpieces from the Los Angeles County Museum of Art Collection. LC 87-36685. (Illus.). 154p. (Orig.). 1988. pap. text 9.95 (*0-87587-146-1*) LA Co Art Mus.
Price, Lorna, ed. Fourth Newport Biennial: Southern California 1993. LC 93-35628. (Illus.). 56p. (Orig.). 1993. pap. text 12.95 (*0-917493-20-6*) Orange Cnty Mus.
Price, Lorna & Sunden, Larry, eds. Ann Hogle: The Refocused Frame. (Illus.). 44p. 1998. pap. 20.00 (*0-932325-36-X*) Fresno Arts Mus.
Price, Lorna, ed. see Guenther, Bruce.
Price, Lorna, ed. see Lee, Sarah.
Price, Lorna, ed. see Stevenson, John.
Price, Louise. Creative Group Work on the Campus: A Developmental Study of Certain Aspects of Student Life. LC 76-177166. (Columbia University. Teachers College. Contributions to Education Ser.: No. 830). reprint ed. 37.50 (*0-404-55830-5*) AMS Pr.
Price, Lucien, ed. see Whitehead, Alfred North.
Price, Lucy K., jt. auth. see Salam, Debera J.
Price, Lucy M. Sydney: Sydney-Smith & Clagett-Price Genealogy, with the Lewis, Montgomery, Harrison, Hawley, Moorhead, Rixey, et al. (Illus.). 324p. 1992. reprint ed. pap. 49.50 (*0-8328-2741-X*); reprint ed. lib. bdg. 59.50 (*0-8328-2740-1*) Higginson Bk Co.
Price, Lynn F. Bless Mom in . . . Whatever She Does: Making the Most of Motherhood. 96p. 1996. pap. 9.98 (*0-88290-590-2*, 2068) Horizon Utah.
— Every Person in the Book of Mormon: A Chronological Reference & Synopsis. 1995. pap. 14.98 (*0-88290-533-3*) Horizon Utah.
— Every Person in the Doctrine & Covenants. 240p. 1997. pap. 17.98 (*0-88290-597-X*, 1076) Horizon Utah.
— Find a Silver Lining. 176p. (Orig.). 1996. pap. 13.98 (*0-88290-573-2*, 1038) Horizon Utah.
Price, Lynne. Faithful Uncertainty: Leslie D. Weatherhead's Methodology of Creative Evangelism. Hollenweger, Walter J., ed. (Studies in the Intercultural History of Christianity: Vol. 100). (GER.). 260p. 1996. pap. 51.95 (*3-631-30237-1*) P Lang Pubng.
— Faithful Uncertainty: Leslie D. Weatherhead's Methodology of Creative Evangelism. Hollenweger, Walter J., ed. LC 96-9299. (Studies in the Intercultural History of Christianity: Vol. 100). 260p. 1996. pap. 51.95 (*0-8204-3190-7*) P Lang Pubng.
— Interfaith Encounter & Dialogue: A Methodist Pilgrimage. (Studies in the Intercultural History of Christianity: Vol. 70). IX, 181p. 1991. pap. 36.80 (*3-631-43735-8*) P Lang Pubng.
Price, Lynne, et al, eds. Mission Matters. (Studies in the Intercultural History of Christianity: Vol. 103). 232p. 1997. pap. 44.95 (*3-631-31513-9*) P Lang Pubng.
— Mission Matters. (Studies in the Intercultural History of Christianity: Vol. 103). 232p. 1997. pap. 44.95 (*0-8204-3265-2*) P Lang Pubng.
***Price, M.** Coins of the Macedonians. (Illus.). 2000. pap. 15.00 (*0-915262-79-7*) S J Durst.
Price, M. F., et al, eds. Global Change in the Mountains: Proceedings of the European Conference on Environmental & Societal Change in Mountain Regions: Oxford, U. K., 18-20 December 1997. LC 98-46934. 218p. 1999. pap. 34.50 (*1-85070-062-1*) Prthnon Pub.
***Price, M. J.** The Pet Sitters Diary & the Jam Packed Information Manual. 400p. 1999. pap. 17.95 (*0-7392-0398-3*, PO3626) Morris Pubng.
Price, M. Philip. Economic Problems of Europe, Pre-War & After. (Business Enterprises Reprint Ser.). 218p. 1986. reprint ed. lib. bdg. 42.00 (*0-89941-503-2*, 304360) W S Hein.
Price, M. Philips & Rose, Tania. Dispatches from the Revolution: Russia, 1915-18. LC 96-49027. 1997. write for info. (*0-7453-1210-1*, Pub. by Pluto GBR) Stylus Pub VA.
Price, M. R. Pembroke & Tenby Railway. 112p. (C). 1985. 45.00 (*0-85361-327-3*) St Mut.
Price, M. R., jt. auth. see Rush, R. W.
Price-Machado, Donna. Skills for Success: Working & Studying in English. 216p. (C). 1998. pap. text 18.95 (*0-521-65742-3*) Cambridge U Pr.
***Price, Maggie.** Dangerous Liaisons. (Intimate Moments Ser.: Bk. 1043). 2000. mass mkt. 4.50 (*0-373-27113-1*, 1-27113-9) Silhouette.
Price, Maggie. The Man She Almost Married. (Intimate Moments Ser.: No. 838). 1998. per. 4.25 (*0-373-07838-2*, 1-07838-5) Silhouette.
— Most Wanted: Men in Blue. (Intimate Moments Ser.: Vol. 948). 1999. per. 4.25 (*0-373-07948-6*, 1-07948-2) Silhouette.
***Price, Maggie.** On Dangerous Ground. (Intimate Moments Ser.: Vol. 989). 2000. mass mkt. 4.50 (*0-373-07989-3*) Silhouette.
Price, Maggie. Prime Suspect. 1997. per. 3.99 (*0-373-07816-1*, 1-07816-1) Silhouette.
Price, Marean J. For the Things He Has Done. (Illus.). 98p. (Orig.). pap. text 9.95 (*1-883372-01-1*) Rondelle Pub.
— Lord, Why Not Me? A Mother's Story of an Autistic Child. (Illus.). 104p. (Orig.). pap. text 14.95 (*1-883372-00-3*) Rondelle Pub.
***Price, Margaret.** Classic Japanese Inns & Country Getaways. 1999. pap. 20.00 (*4-7700-1873-8*, Pub. by Kodansha Intl) Kodansha.
Price, Margaret. I Can Read at Last. Carlin, Chip, ed. 42p. 1988. 60.00 (*0-685-23147-X*) Lit Vol Am.
Price, Margaret, et al. Management Handbook for Volunteer Programs. McKallip, Jonathan & Lawson, V. K., eds. 1984. pap. text 6.50 (*0-930713-37-0*) Lit Vol Am.
Price, Margaret S. What You Need to Know about Divorce. LC 98-93823. 250p. 1998. pap. 19.95 (*0-9666394-7-2*) Fillmore Pubg.
— What You Need to Know after Divorce. 250p. 2000. pap. 19.95 (*0-9666394-3-X*) Fillmore Pubg.
Price, Marian. Reader-Response Criticism: A Test of Its Usefulness in a First-Year College Course in Writing about Literature. LC 89-2444. (American University Studies: English Language & Literature: Ser. IV, Vol. 109). XI, 161p. 1989. text 34.95 (*0-8204-1115-9*) P Lang Pubng.
Price, Marilyn, et al. Instructor's Manual-Key to Tape Program to Accompany The Machine Transcriptionist. 3rd ed. 432p. (C). 1995. pap. text, teacher ed. 47.75 (*0-03-002627-X*) Dryden Pr.
Price, Marilyn E., et al. The Machine Transcriptionist. 3rd ed. LC 94-72573. 398p. (C). 1994. pap. text 38.00 (*0-03-094917-3*) Dryden Pr.
Price, Marilyn L. Scriptural Prayers for America: Minibook. 53p. 1998. pap. 3.00 (*0-9649773-2-X*) New Jruslm.
Price, Marilyn L., ed. see Bohrer, Brian L.
***Price, Marion H., Sr.** Never Quit Praying for Your Loved Ones. 12p. 1999. pap. 1.49 (*1-56632-103-4*) Revival Lit.
Price, Marla. David Bates: Forty Paintings. Sweeney, Jane, ed. LC 88-62325. (Illus.). 100p. (Orig.). 1988. pap. 20.00 (*0-929865-00-6*) Mod Art Mus Ft Worth.
— George Segal: Still Lifes & Related Works. LC 89-64288. (Illus.). 64p. (Orig.). 1990. pap. 19.95 (*0-929865-04-9*) Mod Art Mus Ft Worth.
— Milton Avery: Works from the Nineteen Fifties. LC 90-61490. (Illus.). 48p. (Orig.). 1990. 19.95 (*0-929865-05-7*) Mod Art Mus Ft Worth.
Price, Marla, frwd. Drawing Rooms: Jonathan Borofsky, Sol Le-Witt, Richard Serra. LC 94-73343. 124p. (Orig.). 1994. pap. 29.95 (*0-929865-10-3*) Mod Art Mus Ft Worth.
— History & Memory: Paintings by Christopher Brown. (Illus.). 104p. (Orig.). pap. 25.00 (*0-929865-11-1*) Mod Art Mus Ft Worth.
— Metal & Stone: Six Young Sculptors. (Illus.). 76p. (Orig.). 1992. pap. 11.95 (*0-929865-08-1*) Mod Art Mus Ft Worth.
Price, Martin. Forms of Life: Character & Moral Imagination in the Novel. LC 82-16064. 400p. 1983. 47.50 (*0-300-02867-9*) Yale U Pr.
Price, Martin, ed. Restoration & the Eighteenth Century, Vol. 3. (Illus.). 818p. 1973. pap. text 31.95 (*0-19-501614-9*) OUP.
Price, Martin & Heywood, Ian, eds. Mountain Environments & GIS. 300p. 1994. 99.00 (*0-7484-0088-5*, Pub. by Tay Francis Ltd) Taylor & Francis.
Price, Martin, jt. ed. see Casson, Lionel.
Price, Martin, jt. ed. see Clayton, Peter.
Price, Martin, ed. see Morcom, John.
Price, Martin, ed. see Swift, Jonathan.
Price, Martin F., ed. People & Tourism in Fragile Environments. LC 96-1057. 254p. 1997. 110.00 (*0-471-96584-7*) Wiley.
Price, Martin J. & Trell, Bluma L. Coins & Their Cities: Architecture on the Ancient Coins of Greece, Rome, & Palestine. LC 78-321015. (Illus.). 300p. reprint ed. pap. 93.00 (*0-7837-3593-6*, 204345700009) Bks Demand.
Price, Martin J., jt. auth. see Carradice, Ian.
Price, Martin L., jt. auth. see Meitzner, Laura S.
Price, Mary. Photograph: A Strange, Confined Space. 1997. pap. text 14.95 (*0-8047-2964-6*) Stanford U Pr.
— The Photograph: A Strange, Confined Space. LC 93-31698. xiv, 204p. 1994. 32.50 (*0-8047-2308-7*) Stanford U Pr.
Price, Mary, jt. auth. see Price, Vincent.
Price, Mary K. & Axtmann, Margaret M., eds. Setting the Legal Information Agenda for the Year 2000: Based on a Workshop of the American Association of Law Libraries, National Legal Resources Committee, Washington, D. C., October 23-26, 1988, 3 vols. LC 91-21935. (AALL Publications Ser.: No. 42). 1992. 240.00 (*0-8377-0142-2*, Rothman) W S Hein.
Price, Mary S., ed. see Apfel, Iris B.
Price, Mary S., ed. see Reynolds, Valrae.
Price, Mathew. Don't Worry, Alfie. LC 98-66403. (Illus.). 14p. (J). (ps-k). 1999. 9.95 (*0-531-30127-3*) Orchard Bks Watts.
***Price, Mathew.** Dumbo. (Illus.). 32p. (J). (ps up). 2000. 16.99 (*0-7868-3274-6*) Disney Pr.
— Dumbo Picture Book. 32p. (J). 2001. lib. bdg. 17.49 (*0-7868-2538-3*, Pub. by Disney Pr) Time Warner.
— Little Red Car in the Snow. LC 00-29744. (Illus.). (J). 2000. 0.00 (*0-7892-0674-9*, Abbeville Kids) Abbeville Pr.
— Patch & the Rabbits. LC 99-75919. (Illus.). 12p. (J). (ps-k). 2000. 5.95 (*0-531-30265-2*) Orchard Bks Watts.
— Patch Finds a Friend. LC 99-7518. (Illus.). 12p. (J). (ps-k). 2000. 5.95 (*0-531-30264-4*) Orchard Bks Watts.
— Tell Me Another! Read Along Stories for the Very Young. LC 99-28768. (Illus.). 64p. (J). (ps-k). 2000. 16.95 (*0-375-80539-7*, Pub. by Knopf Bks Yng Read) Random.
Price, Mathew. Where's Alfie? LC 98-66402. (Illus.). 14p. (J). (ps-k). 1999. 9.95 (*0-531-30126-5*) Orchard Bks Watts.
***Price, Mathew & Augarde, Steve.** Little Red Car Has an Accident. LC 00-35523. (Illus.). 2000. write for info. (*0-7892-0673-0*) Abbeville Pr.
— Little Red Car Plays Taxi. LC 00-29997. (Illus.). (J). 2000. write for info. (*0-7892-0675-7*) Abbeville Pr.
Price, Matthew, jt. auth. see Collins, Michael.
Price, Matthew C. Justice Between Generations: The Growing Power of the Elderly in America. LC 97-19234. 184p. 1997. 57.95 (*0-275-96012-9*, Praeger Pubs) Greenwood.
Price, Max B. Comprendamos al Escolar de Hoy: Understanding Today's Children. Bedford, Nancy A., tr. from ENG. (SPA.). 160p. (Orig.). 1992. pap. 6.50 (*0-311-11902-6*) Casa Bautista.
***Price, Meghan.** Surfing Safely.Com. 2000. pap. 4.99 (*0-9683303-6-3*) TUM.
Price, Michael. The Account Book for the Borough of Swansea, Wales 1640-1660: A Study in Local Administration During the Civil War & Interregnum. LC 90-5645. (Welsh Studies: Vol. 1). (Illus.). 340p. 1990. lib. bdg. 99.95 (*0-88946-480-4*) E Mellen.
— Doombook. 68p. 1998. pap. 10.00 (*0-935724-94-X*) Figures.
— Famine in Far-Go. 1982. 5.50 (*0-394-52595-7*) Random.
— Introducing Groundwater. (Special Topics in Geology Ser.: No. 2). (Illus.). 176p. 1985. text 60.00 (*0-04-553005-X*); pap. text 19.95 (*0-04-553006-8*) Routledge.
— OS/2 Warp for the SoHo Environment: Making the Most of the Small Office Home Office PC. LC 95-41544. 1995. write for info. (*0-07-709200-7*) McGraw.
— SOHO Windows 95. LC 96-297. 1995. pap. write for info. (*0-07-709199-X*) McGraw.
Price, Michael & Turner, George E. Forgotten Horrors. (Illus.). 320p. 1999. pap. 20.00 (*1-887664-20-3*) Midnght Marquee Pr.
***Price, Michael E.** Stories with a Moral: Literature & Society in Nineteenth-Century Georgia. LC 99-25524. 392p. 1999. pap. text 45.00 (*0-8203-2132-X*) U of Ga Pr.
Price, Michael F. Power Bankers: Sales Culture Secrets of High Performance Banks. LC 91-35803. 224p. 1992. 89.95 (*0-471-55555-X*) Wiley.
Price, Michael H. & Turner, George. Southern-Fried Homicide. (Illus.). 80p. 1998. pap. 7.95 (*0-9663766-0-9*, Cremo Studios) Shel-Tone.
Price, Michael H., jt. auth. see Turner, George E.
Price, Michael R., jt. ed. see Rye, Phil D.
Price, Mike, jt. auth. see Williams, Marsha P.
Price, Milburn, jt. auth. see Furr, Gary.
Price, Milburn, jt. auth. see Music, David W.
Price, Milburn, jt. auth. see Reynolds, William J.
Price, Moe. The Reindeer Christmas. (Illus.). 32p. (J). (ps-3). 1993. 15.95 (*0-15-266199-9*, Harcourt Child Bks) Harcourt.
— The Reindeer Christmas. (Illus.). (J). 1997. reprint ed. pap. 6.00 (*0-15-201570-1*, Harcourt Child Bks) Harcourt.
Price, Molly. The Iris Book. (Illus.). 224p. 1973. reprint ed. pap. 6.95 (*0-486-21522-9*) Dover.
***Price, Monroe E.** Broadcasting Reform In India: Media Law from a Global Perspective. LC 98-909284. 396p. 1999. text 29.95 (*0-19-564564-2*) OUP.
Price, Monroe E. Shattered Mirrors: Our Search for Identity & Community in the AIDS Era. LC 89-33265. 160p. 1989. text 32.00 (*0-674-80590-9*) HUP.
— Television, the Public Sphere, & National Identity. 308p. 1996. text 65.00 (*0-19-818362-3*); pap. text 28.00 (*0-19-818338-0*) OUP.
Price, Monroe E., ed. The V-Chip Debate: Content Filtering from Television to the Internet. LC 98-26402. (LEA's Communication Ser.). 344p. 1998. write for info. (*0-8058-3061-8*); pap. 36.00 (*0-8058-3062-6*) L Erlbaum Assocs.
Price, Monroe E., jt. ed. see Noll, Roger G.
Price, Morgan P. America after Sixty Years: Diaries of Two Generations of Englishmen. LC 73-13146. (Foreign Travelers in America, 1810-1935 Ser.). (Illus.). 242p. 1974. reprint ed. 23.95 (*0-405-05470-X*) Ayer.
— Dispatches from the Revolution: Russia 1916-1918. Rose, Tania, ed. LC 97-12014. xii, 181p. 1998. pap. 16.95 (*0-8223-2073-8*) Duke.
Price, Morgan Phillips. Dispatches from the Weimar Republic: Versailles & German Fascism. Rose, Tania, ed. LC 98-52780. (Illus.). 256p. 1999. 29.95 (*0-7453-1425-2*, Pub. by Pluto GBR) Stylus Pub VA.
Price, Morgan Samuel. Oil Painting with a Basic Palette. LC 98-31052. (Illus.). 128p. 1999. 27.99 (*0-89134-882-4*, 31366, North Lght Bks) F & W Pubns Inc.
Price, Munro. Preserving the Monarchy: The Comte de Vergennes, 1774-1787. 268p. (C). 1995. text 59.95 (*0-521-46566-4*) Cambridge U Pr.
Price, N., et al, eds. The Methyl Bromide Issue. LC 95-42367. (Agrochemicals & Plant Protection Ser.: Vol. 1). 412p. 1997. 235.00 (*0-471-95521-3*) Wiley.
Price, N. C., ed. Proteins Labfax. (Labfax Ser.). (Illus.). 318p. 1996. text 70.00 (*0-12-564710-7*) Acad Pr.
Price, Nancy. Night Woman. 352p. 1993. mass mkt. 5.99 (*0-671-74994-3*, Pocket Star Bks) PB.
— Night Woman. large type ed. LC 92-33705. 550p. 1993. reprint ed. lib. bdg. 18.95 (*1-56054-583-6*) Thorndike Pr.
Price, Nancy W., jt. auth. see Van der Meulen, Jan.
Price, Nelson. Indiana Legends: Famous Hoosiers from Johnny Appleseed to David Letterman. 300p. 1997. 24.95 (*1-57860-006-5*) Guild Pr IN.
***Price, Nelson.** Indianapolis: Leading the Way. LC 00-33769. (Urban Tapestry Ser.). (Illus.). 2000. write for info. (*1-881096-82-3*) Towery Pub.
Price, Nelson L. Servants, Not Celebrities. 2nd ed. 162p. (Orig.). 1999. reprint ed. pap. 9.99 (*1-889893-26-9*) Emerald House Group Inc.
***Price, Neville J.** Major Impacts & Plate Tectonics: A Model for the Phanerzoic Evolution of the Earth's Lithosphere. LC 00-37717. (Illus.). 2000. pap. write for info. (*0-7484-0850-9*) Taylor & Francis.
Price, Nicholas & Stevens, Lewis. Fundamentals of Enzymology. LC 99-25876. (Illus.). 496p. 1999. text 110.00 (*0-19-850230-3*) OUP.
— Fundamentals of Enzymology: The Cell & Molecular Biology of Catalytic Proteins. 3rd ed. LC 99-25876. (Illus.). 496p. 2000. pap. text 50.00 (*0-19-850229-X*) OUP.
Price, Nicholas C. & Stevens, Lewis. Fundamentals of Enzymology. 2nd ed. (Illus.). 544p. (C). 1989. pap. text 44.95 (*0-19-855296-3*) OUP.
Price, Nicholas S., ed. The Conservation of the Orpheus Mosaic at Paphos, Cyprus. LC 91-19192. (Illus.). 88p. 1991. pap. 25.00 (*0-89236-188-3*, Pub. by J P Getty Trust) OUP.
Price, Nicholas S., et al, eds. Historical & Philosophical Issues in the Conservation of Cultural Heritage. LC 95-44736. (Readings in Conservation Ser.). (Illus.). 520p. 1996. 55.00 (*0-89236-250-2*, Pub. by J P Getty Trust) OUP.
— Historical & Philosophical Issues in the Conservation of Cultural Heritage. LC 95-44736. (Illus.). 520p. 1996. pap. 39.95 (*0-89236-398-3*, Pub. by J P Getty Trust) OUP.
Price, Nick. The Swing: Mastering the Principles of the Game. LC 98-50676. 1999. pap. 15.00 (*0-375-70513-9*) Knopf.
Price, Nick & Rubinstein, Lorne. The Swing: Mastering the Principles of the Game. LC 96-52267. 240p. 1997. 30.00 (*0-679-44670-2*) Knopf.
Price, Norman. Notes on Mada Phonology. LC 88-63673. (Language Data, African Ser.: No. 23). 51p. 1989. pap. text 4.15 (*0-88312-600-1*) S I L Intl.
Price, Olive. Three Golden Rivers. large type ed. LC 99-6495. 272p. (YA). (gr. 4-9). 1999. pap. 12.95 (*0-8229-5707-8*) U of Pittsburgh Pr.
Price, Oliver R. High Leverage Real Estate Investments: Inside Secrets of Using OPM. 1978. pap. 5.95 (*0-685-03912-9*, Busn) P-H.
***Price, Oliver W.** The Power of Praying Together: Forgotten Secrets of a Growing Prayer Group. LC 99-24711. 192p. 1999. pap. 10.99 (*0-8254-3552-8*) Kregel.
Price-Owen, Anne, jt. ed. see Humfrey, Belinda.
Price, P. J. Competency in English: A Life Skills Approach. 180p. (Orig.). (C). 1990. pap. 18.75 (*0-07-556988-4*) McGraw.
Price, Pamela, jt. auth. see Price, Richard.
Price, Pamela G. Kingship & Political Practice in Colonial India. (University of Cambridge Oriental Publications: No. 51). (Illus.). 241p. (C). 1996. text 54.95 (*0-521-55247-8*) Cambridge U Pr.
Price, Pamela V. Wines of the Graves. (Illus.). 388p. 1998. text 37.00 (*0-7881-5648-9*) DIANE Pub.
Price, Pat, jt. auth. see Casper, Wayne.
Price, Pat, ed. see Manuscriptors Guild Members.

P

Price, Pat L. & Ouvry, Philip. Ocean Yachtmaster: Celestial Navigation. rev. ed. (Illus.). 215p. 1996. 40.00 (*0-7136-4553-9*) Sheridan.
— Ocean Yachtmaster Exercises. (Illus.). 128p. 1997. pap. 30.00 (*0-7136-4830-9*) Sheridan.
— Yachtmaster: An Examination Handbook with Exercises. 2nd ed. (Illus.). 288p. 1993. 35.00 (*0-7136-3772-2*) Sheridan.
— Yachtmaster Exercises. 2nd ed. (Illus.). 128p. 1993. pap. 29.50 (*0-7136-3810-9*, Pub. by Adlard Coles) Sheridan.
Price, Patricia. Transformational Breathwork: The Basics of Renewal & Rebirth. 100p. (Orig.). 1989. pap. text 10.00 (*0-926625-88-8*) Trilogy Pubns.
Price, Patrick L., jt. ed. see Greenberg, Martin H.
Price, Paula A. Changing of the Guard. 35p. 1994. pap. text 5.95 (*1-886288-02-X*) Everlsting Life.
— Everlasting Life Ministries, Ministerial Training School: Instructor-Student Workbook & Training Manual-Curriculum. (C). 1986. pap. text, teacher ed., student ed. write for info. (*1-886288-33-X*) Everlsting Life.
— The Five Fold Offices of the Lord Jesus Christ. 225p. (C). 1994. pap. text 29.95 (*1-886288-13-5*) Everlsting Life.
— God's Apostle Revived. (C). 1995. pap. text 26.95 (*1-886288-32-1*) Everlsting Life.
Price, Peter W. Evolutionary Biology of Parasites. LC 79-3227. (Monographs in Population Biology: Vol. 15). 251p. 1980. reprint ed. pap. 77.90 (*0-608-02908-4*, 206397200008) Bks Demand.
— Insect Ecology. 3rd ed. LC 96-47739. 888p. 1997. 125.00 (*0-471-16184-5*) Wiley.
Price, Peter W., et al, eds. Plant-Animal Interactions: Evolutionary Ecology in Tropical & Temperate Regions. LC 90-39766. 639p. 1991. 200.00 (*0-471-50937-X*) Wiley.
Price, Peter W., jt. ed. see Cappuccino, Naomi.
Price, Philips M. & Rose, Tania. Dispatches from the Revolution: Russia, 1915-1918. LC 97-12014. 1998. lib. bdg. 49.95 (*0-8223-2059-2*) Duke.
Price, Phyllis. Holy Fire: A Personal Journey of Conversion & Renewal. LC 98-28973. 128p. 1998. pap. 8.95 (*0-8091-3819-0*) Paulist Pr.
Price, Planaria J. Competency in English: A Life Skills Approach. 208p. (Orig.). (C). 1988. pap. text. write for info. (*0-318-62869-4*) Random.
— Eureka! Discovering American English & Culture Through Proverbs, Fables, Myths, & Legends. LC 99-233636. (Illus.). 232p. 1999. pap. text 17.95 (*0-472-08547-6*, 08547) U of Mich Pr.
***Price, Planaria J.** Eureka! Discovering American English & Culture Through Proverbs, Fables, Myths, & Legends. (Illus.). 232p. (C). 1999. pap. text 42.50 (*0-472-08594-8*, 08594) U of Mich Pr.
Price, Planaria J. Open Sesame: Understanding American English & Culture Through Folktales & Stories. LC 90-60157. 248p. 1997. pap. text 16.95 (*0-472-08388-0*, 08388) U of Mich Pr.
***Price, Planaria J.** Open Sesame: Understanding American English & Culture Through Folktales & Stories. LC 96-60157. (Illus.). 248p. (C). 1998. pap. text 42.50 incl. audio (*0-472-08506-9*, 08506) U of Mich Pr.
— Realistically Speaking: A Practical Approach to the Basic Sounds & Rhythms of American English. (C). 1999. pap. 19.06 (*0-07-239102-2*) McGrw-H Hghr Educ.
Price, Polly S. Sand in Our Shoes: A Guide Book to Pharaonic Egypt. (Illus.). 307p. 1979. pap. text 8.50 (*0-9604012-0-2*) P S Price.
Price, R. En Busca de los Tesoros del Templo.Tr. of In Search of Temple Treasures. 1997. pap. 13.99 (*1-56063-971-7*, 497385) Editorial Unilit.
Price, R. El Secreto de los Rollos del Mar Muerto.Tr. of Secret of Dead Sea Scrolls. (SPA.). write for info. (*0-7899-0424-1*, 498655) Editorial Unilit.
Price, R. Wanderers. LC 99-15175. 1999. pap. 12.00 (*0-395-97774-6*) HM.
Price, R. F. Marx & Education in Late Capitalism. LC 86-3541. 318p. 1986. 53.00 (*0-389-20617-2*, N8175) B&N Imports.
Price, R. F., ed. & tr. see Presniakov, Alexander E.
Price, R. M., tr. see Cyril of Scythopolis.
Price, R. M., tr. see De Cervantes Saavedra, Miguel.
Price, R. M., tr. see Theodoret.
Price, R. N. Proud to Serve: The Saga of Wolfgang O'Neill. Lewis, Lynne E., ed. LC 94-792250. 418p. (Orig.). 1996. pap. 12.95 (*1-885487-08-8*) Brownell & Carroll.
Price, Randall. The Coming Last Days' Temple: The Latest Development in Bible Prophecy. LC 99-15415. (Answer Ser.). 350p. 1999. pap. 14.99 (*1-56507-901-9*) Harvest Hse.
— Jerusalem: The Vortext of Bible Prophecy. LC 98-4079. 350p. 1998. pap. 12.99 (*1-56507-783-0*) Harvest Hse.
***Price, Randall.** La Piedras Claman. (SPA.). 2000. mass mkt. 13.99 (*0-7899-0421-7*) Editorial Unilit.
Price, Randall. Secrets of the Dead Sea Scrolls: The Controversy & Intrigue Behind the... 350p. 1996. pap. 14.99 (*1-56507-454-8*) Harvest Hse.
— The Stones Cry Out: New Archeological Discoveries of the Bible. LC 97-16947. (Illus.). 250p. 1997. pap. 12.99 (*1-56507-640-0*) Harvest Hse.
Price, Ray, et al. List of Military & Armored Fighting Vehicle Photographs in the World War II Collection of Seized Enemy Records Group Rg-242-Gap in the National Archives. 2nd rev. ed. (World War II Monograph: Vol. 14). (Illus.). 44p. 1997. 17.95 (*1-57638-048-3*, M14H) Merriam Pr.
— List of Military & Armored Fighting Vehicle Photographs in the World War II Collection of Seized Enemy Records Group Rg-242-Gap in the National Archives: In the World War II Collection of Seized Enemy Records Group RG-242-GAP in the National Archives. 2nd rev. ed. (World War II Monograph Ser.: Vol. 14). (Illus.). 35p. 1997. pap. 7.95 (*1-57638-041-6*, M14S) Merriam Pr.
Price, Ray B. & Cox, Gale R. How to Acquire Wealth: One Man's Odyssey. LC 90-61189. 87p. (Orig.). (YA). 1990. pap. text 8.95 (*0-9626318-0-9*) Price Pub SC.
Price, Raymond A. & Douglas, R. J., eds. Variations in Tectonic Styles in Canada. LC 73-331222. (Geological Association of Canada. Special Paper: No. 11). 698p. reprint ed. pap. 200.00 (*0-608-17208-1*, 202784200056) Bks Demand.
Price, Realto E. History of Clayton County, Iowa, 2 vols., Set. (Illus.). 953p. 1992. reprint ed. lib. bdg. 94.00 (*0-8328-2552-2*) Higginson Bk Co.
Price, Realto E., ed. History of Lee County, Iowa: A History of the County, Its Citizens, Towns; A Biographical Directory of Its Citizens. (Illus.). 887p. 1992. reprint ed. lib. bdg. 87.50 (*0-8328-2586-7*) Higginson Bk Co.
Price, Reese E., jt. ed. see Gilligan, Stephen G.
Price, Reynolds. August Snow. 1991. pap. 5.25 (*0-8222-0075-9*) Dramatists Play.
— Back Before Day. LC 89-62735. 64p. 1989. 25.00 (*0-933598-16-5*) NC Wesleyan Pr.
— Better Days. 1991. pap. 5.25 (*0-8222-0111-9*) Dramatists Play.
— Blue Calhoun. 416p. 1992. 23.00 (*0-689-12146-6*) Atheneum Yung Read.
***Price, Reynolds.** Blue Calhoun. 416p. 2000. per. 13.00 (*0-684-86782-6*) S&S Trade.
Price, Reynolds. Blue Calhoun. 2nd ed. 373p. 1992. 100.00 (*0-689-12171-7*) Atheneum Yung Read.
— Clear Pictures: First Loves, First Guides. 304p. 1989. 19.95 (*0-689-12075-3*) Atheneum Yung Read.
— Clear Pictures: First Loves, First Guides. LC 98-141801. (Scribner Classics Ser.). 320p. 1998. 25.50 (*0-684-84752-3*) Scribner.
— Collected Poems. LC 96-53117. 496p. 1997. 37.50 (*0-684-83203-8*, Scribners Ref) Mac Lib Ref.
— The Collected Poems. 496p. 1999. pap. 20.00 (*0-684-86002-3*) S&S Trade.
— The Collected Stories of Reynolds Price. 672p. 1993. 25.00 (*0-689-12147-4*) Atheneum Yung Read.
***Price, Reynolds.** Feasting the Heart: Fifty-Two Commentaries for the Air. 128p. 2000. 22.00 (*0-7432-0369-0*) Scribner.
Price, Reynolds. The Foreseeable Future. 288p. 1991. 21.95 (*0-689-12110-5*, Pub. by Ctrl Bur voor Schimmel) Macmillan.
— Full Moon & Other Plays. LC 92-44383. 312p. 1993. pap. 13.95 (*1-55936-064-X*) Theatre Comm.
— Home Made. deluxe ed. LC 90-63100. (Illus.). 64p. 1990. 55.00 (*0-933598-23-8*) NC Wesleyan Pr.
— House Snake. 24p. 1986. 50.00 (*0-935716-38-6*) Lord John.
— Kate Vaiden. LC 85-48143. 352p. 1986. 17.00 (*0-689-11787-6*) Atheneum Yung Read.
— Kate Vaiden. 384p. 1987. mass mkt. 5.99 (*0-345-34358-1*) Ballantine Pub Grp.
— Kate Vaiden. 320p. 1998. per. 13.00 (*0-684-84694-2*) S&S Trade.
— Learning a Trade: A Craftsman's Notebooks, 1955-1997. LC 98-26692. (Illus.). 640p. 1998. 34.95 (*0-8223-2112-2*) Duke.
***Price, Reynolds.** Learning a Trade: A Craftsman's Notebooks, 1955-1997. 624p. 2000. reprint ed. pap. 21.95 (*0-8223-2588-8*) Duke.
Price, Reynolds. Letter to a Young Man in the Fire: Does God Exist & Does He Care? LC 98-54197. 108p. 1999. 20.00 (*0-684-85626-3*) S&S Trade.
— A Long & Happy Life. LC 61-12790. 208p. 1987. 20.00 (*0-689-11947-X*); pap. 4.95 (*0-689-10224-0*) Atheneum Yung Read.
— New Music: A Trilogy. LC 90-48090. 240p. 1990. 22.95 (*1-55936-015-1*); pap. 10.95 (*1-55936-016-X*) Theatre Comm.
— Night Dance. 1991. pap. 5.25 (*0-8222-0819-9*) Dramatists Play.
***Price, Reynolds.** A Perfect Friend. LC 99-55397. (J). (gr. 7). 2000. 16.00 (*0-689-83029-7*) Atheneum Yung Read.
Price, Reynolds. The Promise of Rest. 368p. 1996. per. 13.00 (*0-684-82510-4*) S&S Trade.
— Real Copies. LC 88-62140. (Orig.). 1988. pap. 10.00 (*0-933598-08-4*) NC Wesleyan Pr.
***Price, Reynolds.** Roxanna Slade. LC 97-39167. 301p. 1999. pap. 12.00 (*0-684-85373-6*, Scribner Pap Fic) S&S Trade Pap.
Price, Reynolds. Roxanna Slade. LC 97-39167. 301p. 1998. 25.00 (*0-684-83292-5*) Scribner.
— Roxanna Slade. large type ed. LC 98-23616. 1998. 27.95 (*0-7862-1518-6*) Thorndike Pr.
— A Singular Family: Rosacoke & Her Kin. LC 99-17175. 640p. 1999. pap. 15.00 (*0-684-85188-1*) S&S Trade.
— The Source of Light. 336p. 1995. per. 12.00 (*0-684-81338-6*) S&S Trade.
— The Surface of Earth. 512p. 1995. per. 14.00 (*0-684-81339-4*) S&S Trade.
— Three Gospels: The Good News According to Mark, The Good News According to John, An Honest Account of a Memorable Life. 288p. 1996. 22.00 (*0-684-80336-4*) S&S Trade.
— Three Gospels: The Good News According to Mark, The Good News According to John, An Honest Account of a Memorable Life. 1997. per. 12.00 (*0-684-83281-X*, Touchstone) S&S Trade Pap.
— The Tongues of Angels. 176p. 1990. 17.95 (*0-689-12093-1*) Atheneum Yung Read.
— The Tongues of Angels. 244p. 1991. mass mkt. 5.99 (*0-345-37102-X*) Ballantine Pub Grp.
***Price, Reynolds.** The Tongues of Angels: A Novel. 2000. pap. 11.00 (*0-7432-0221-X*, Scribner Pap Fic) S&S Trade Pap.
Price, Reynolds. A Whole New Life: An Illness & a Healing. 224p. 1994. 20.00 (*0-689-12197-0*, Pub. by Ctrl Bur voor Schimmel) Macmillan.
***Price, Reynolds.** A Whole New Life: An Illness & a Healing. 224p. 2000. 21.50 (*0-684-87255-2*) S&S Trade.
Price, Reynolds. A Whole New Life: An Illness & a Healing. large type ed. LC 94-48471. 1995. pap. 12.95 (*0-452-27473-7*, Plume) Dutton Plume.
Price, Richard. Alabi's World. LC 89-15488. (Illus.). 480p. 1990. pap. 22.50 (*0-8018-3956-4*) Johns Hopkins.
— Augustine. Vardy, Peter, ed. LC 96-52491. (Great Christian Thinkers Ser.). 112p. 1997. reprint ed. pap. 9.00 (*0-7648-0118-X*, Liguori Triumph) Liguori Pubns.
— Bloodbrothers. LC 99-15176. 1999. pap. 12.00 (*0-395-97773-8*) HM.
— Bloodbrothers. 288p. 1993. pap. 9.00 (*0-380-77476-3*, Avon Bks) Morrow Avon.
— British Society, 1680-1880: Dynamism, Containment & Change. LC 99-11993. 340p. 1999. 59.95 (*0-521-65172-7*) Cambridge U Pr.
— British Society, 1680-1880: Dynamism, Containment & Change. 340p. (C). 1999. pap. write for info. (*0-521-65701-6*) Cambridge U Pr.
— Clockers. 640p. 1993. mass mkt. 6.99 (*0-380-72081-7*, Avon Bks) Morrow Avon.
***Price, Richard.** Color of Money, Sea of Love, Night & the City: Three Screenplays. LC 99-51706. 384p. 2000. reprint ed. pap. 14.50 (*0-8021-3669-9*, Pub. by Grove-Atltic) Publishers Group.
Price, Richard. The Convict & the Colonel. Chasman, Deborah, ed. (Illus.). 304p. 1998. pap. 18.00 (*0-8070-4651-5*) Beacon Pr.
— Discourse on the Love of Our Country, 1789. (Revolution & Romanticism Ser.). 104p. 1992. reprint ed. 40.00 (*1-85477-108-6*) Continuum.
— Equatoria. 296p. (C). (gr. 13). 1994. pap. 24.99 (*0-415-90895-7*, Pub. by Tavistock) Routldge.
— Fabulous Matter of Fact. 1992. text 35.00 (*0-7486-0259-3*, Pub. by Edinburgh U Pr) Col U Pr.
— First-Time: The Historical Vision of an Afro-American People. LC 83-29. (Studies in Atlantic History & Culture). 224p. 1983. pap. text 15.95 (*0-8018-2985-2*) Johns Hopkins.
— Four Dissertations, 1768. 478p. 1996. reprint ed. 60.00 (*1-85506-054-X*) Bks Intl VA.
— Freedomland. LC 98-10527. 560p. 1998. 25.00 (*0-7679-0024-3*) Broadway BDD.
— Freedomland. 721p. 1999. mass mkt. 7.99 (*0-440-22644-9*, Island Bks) Dell.
— The Guiana Maroons: A Historical & Bibliographical Introduction. LC 76-8498. (Johns Hopkins Studies in Atlantic History & Culture Ser.). 196p. reprint ed. pap. 60.80 (*0-7837-2649-X*, 204300300006) Bks Demand.
— Labour in British Society: An Interpretive History. 288p. 1986. 49.95 (*0-85664-736-5*, Pub. by C Helm) Routldge.
— Ladies' Man. LC 99-15174. 1999. pap. 12.00 (*0-395-97772-X*) HM.
— Ladies' Man. 272p. 1993. pap. 9.00 (*0-380-77475-5*, Avon Bks) Morrow Avon.
— Neil M. Gunn: The Fabulous Matter of Fact. (Modern Scottish Writers Ser.). 224p. 1995. pap. 25.00 (*0-7486-0536-3*, Pub. by Edinburgh U Pr) Col U Pr.
— Observations on the Importance of the American Revolution & the Means of Making It a Benefit to the World. LC 75-31129. reprint ed. 37.50 (*0-404-13607-9*) AMS Pr.
— Political Writings. Thomas, D. O., ed. (Cambridge Texts in the History of Political Thought Ser.). 234p. (C). 1992. text 59.95 (*0-521-40162-3*); pap. text 19.95 (*0-521-40969-1*) Cambridge U Pr.
— A Review of the Principal Questions in Morals. 1986. reprint ed. pap. 27.95 (*0-935005-26-9*); reprint ed. lib. bdg. 43.95 (*0-935005-25-0*) Lincoln-Rembrandt.
— The Wanderers. 256p. 1993. pap. 9.00 (*0-380-77474-7*, Avon Bks) Morrow Avon.
Price, Richard, ed. Maroon Societies: Rebel Slave Communities in the Americas. 3rd ed. LC 96-26927. 445p. 1996. reprint ed. pap. text 16.95 (*0-8018-5496-2*) Johns Hopkins.
Price, Richard & Al Tamimi Essam. United Arab Emirates Court of Cassation Judgements. LC 98-17229. (Arab & Islamic Laws Ser.). 1998. 110.00 (*90-411-1005-4*) Kluwer Law Intl.
***Price, Richard & Price, Pamela.** Joseph Smith Fought Polygamy Vol. 1: How Men Nearest the Prophet Attached Polygamy to His Name in Order to Justify Their Own Polygamous Crimes. LC 99-41763. (Illus.). 270p. 2000. pap. 10.00 (*1-891353-05-5*) Price Pub.

–Joseph Smith Fought Polygamy Vol. 1: How Men Nearest the Prophet Attached Polygamy to His Name in Order to Justify Their Own Polygamous Crimes. LC 99-41763. 272p. 2000. pap. 8.00 (*1-891353-06-3*) Price Pub.
Joseph Smith Fought Polygamy provides definite evidence that Joseph Smith, Jr. founder of the Latter Day Saint church, was not a polygamist, but actually fought against the practice. Polygamy was adopted from the Cochranite denomination & brought into the Mormon Church by Brigham Young & others. Price Publishing Company 915 E. 23rd St., Independence, MO 64055, Phone: 816-461-5659, Fax: 816-461-5565 *Publisher Paid Annotation.*

Price, Richard & Price, Sally. Enigma Variations. LC 95-1362. (Illus.). 176p. (C). 1995. 18.95 (*0-674-25726-X*) HUP.
— Enigma Variations. (Illus.). 176p. 1997. reprint ed. 12.95 (*0-674-25728-6*) HUP.
— Maroon Arts: Cultural Vitality in the African Diaspora. LC 98-29572. (Illus.). 384p. 1999. 37.50 (*0-8070-8550-2*) Beacon Pr.
— On the Mall: Presenting Maroon Tradition-Bearers at the 1992 Festival of American Folklife. (Special Publications: No. 4). (Illus.). 123p. (C). 1995. text 25.00 (*1-879407-07-8*) IN Univ Folk Inst.
— On the Mall: Presenting Maroon Tradition-Bearers at the 1992 Festival of American Folklore. (Illus.). 122p. 1995. pap. 12.00 (*0-87940-706-9*); text 25.00 (*0-87940-707-7*) Ind U Pr.
— Two Evenings in Saramaka: Afro-American Tale-Telling in the Suriname Rain Forest. LC 90-35941. (Illus.). 432p. 1991. pap. text 23.95 (*0-226-68062-2*) U Ch Pr.
— Two Evenings in Saramaka: Afro-American Tale-Telling in the Suriname Rain Forest. LC 90-35941. (Illus.). 432p. 1991. lib. bdg. 66.00 (*0-226-68061-4*) U Ch Pr.
Price, Richard, jt. auth. see Mintz, Sidney W.
Price, Richard, jt. auth. see Paterson, Audrey.
Price, Richard, jt. auth. see Price, Sally.
Price, Richard, jt. auth. see Priestley, Joseph.
Price, Richard, jt. ed. see Belchem, John.
Price, Richard, ed. see Iversen, Eleni-Dayle.
Price, Richard, ed. see Stedman, John G.
Price, Richard, jt. ed. see Van Der Linden, Marcel.
Price, Richard H. Contemporary Secrets to Finding Love. 172p. 1994. pap. 12.95 (*1-885280-09-2*) Golf Supplies.
Price, Richard H., et al, eds. Fourteen Ounces of Prevention: A Casebook for Practitioners. LC 88-14471. 191p. 1988. pap. 29.95 (*1-55798-036-5*) Am Psychol.
— Prevention in Mental Health: Research, Policy & Practice. LC 80-14676. (Sage Annual Reviews of Community Mental Health Ser.: No. 1). 320p. reprint ed. pap. 99.20 (*0-8357-4846-4*, 203777700009) Bks Demand.
Price, Richard J., et al. Navy Laboratories: Plans for Consolidation & Progress Toward Implementation. (Illus.). 50p. (C). 1997. reprint ed. pap. text 30.00 (*0-7881-4130-9*) DIANE Pub.
Price, Richard L., jt. auth. see Murvin, Harry J.
Price, Richard M. The Chemical Weapons Taboo. LC 96-24320. 256p. 1996. text 32.50 (*0-8014-3306-1*) Cornell U Pr.
Price, Richard W. & Perry, Samuel W., III, eds. HIV, AIDS, & the Brain. LC 93-36006. (Association for Research in Nervous & Mental Disease Research Publications: Vol. 72). 352p. 1993. text 99.00 (*0-7817-0063-9*) Lppncott W & W.
Price, Richard W. & Perry, Samuel W., eds. HIV, AIDS & the Brain. LC 93-36006. (Association for Research in Nervous & Mental Disease Research Publications: Vol. 72). (Illus.). 352p. reprint ed. pap. 109.20 (*0-608-09731-4*, 206989400007) Bks Demand.
Price, Richard W. & Sidtis, John J., eds. The Cellular Basis of Central Nervous System HIV-1 Infection & the AIDS Dementia Complex. 1996. 49.95 (*1-56024-774-6*, Hawrth Medical) Haworth Pr.
Price, Richard W., jt. ed. see Martin, John H.
Price, Richard W., jt. ed. see Whitehouse, David B.
Price, Rini, ed. see Seed, Sally.
***Price, Robert.** Entrepeneurship 2000-2001. 2nd ed. (Annual Editions Ser.). 240p. (C). 2000. pap. 16.56 (*0-07-236509-9*) McGrw-H Hghr Educ.
Price, Robert. Scotland's Golf Courses: An Extraordinary Variety of Experience. (Illus.). 254p. 1989. 25.00 (*0-08-036591-4*, Pub. by Aberdeen U Pr) Macmillan.
— Tsathoggua Cycle. (Mythos Ser.). 1998. pap. text 12.95 (*1-56882-131-X*) Chaosium.
Price, Robert, ed. UFOs over Hampshire & the Low. (C). 1989. 50.00 (*1-85455-037-3*, Pub. by Ensign Pubns & Print) St Mut.
Price, Robert, jt. auth. see Finley, Eddy.
Price, Robert, ed. see Lovecraft, H. P., et al.
Price, Robert C., jt. auth. see Mead, Tray C.
Price, Robert E. Blues Blood: New & Selected Poems. LC 94-72477. 83p. (Orig.). 1994. pap. 12.00 (*0-9642183-0-5*) CAC Press.
Price, Robert F. Mixail Soloxov in Yugoslavia: Reception & Literary Impact. (East European Monographs: No. 4). 180p. 1973. text 69.00 (*0-231-03748-1*, Pub. by East Eur Monographs) Col U Pr.
Price, Robert F., jt. auth. see Sljivic-Simsic, Biljana.
Price, Robert J. Glacial & Fluvioglacial Landforms. LC GB0581.P74. (Geomorphology Texts Ser.: No. 5). 250p. reprint ed. pap. 77.50 (*0-608-13535-6*, 202253300027) Bks Demand.
— Highland Landforms. (Illus.). 110p. 1991. pap. 13.95 (*0-08-041196-7*, Pub. by Aberdeen U Pr) Macmillan.
Price, Robert M. The Apartheid State in Crisis: Political Transformation of S. Africa, 1975-1990. (Illus.). 328p. (C). 1991. pap. text 25.95 (*0-19-506750-9*) OUP.
— Deconstructing Jesus. LC 99-48140. 275p. 2000. 31.95 (*1-57392-758-9*) Prometheus Bks.
— Ithaqua Cycle. 1997. pap. text 12.95 (*1-56882-124-7*) Chaosium.
— Lin Carter: A Look Behind His Imaginary Worlds. LC 93-242547. (Starmont Studies in Literary Criticism: No. 36). vi, 172p. 1991. pap. 21.00 (*1-55742-229-X*) Millefleurs.
Price, Robert M., intro. Tales of the Lovecraft Mythos. (C). 1991. 25.00 (*1-878252-02-X*) Fedogan & Bremer.
Price, Robert M., ed. see Bloch, Robert, et al.
Price, Robert M., ed. see Lovecraft, H. P., et al.
Price, Robert M., ed. see Silverberg, Robert, et al.
Price, Robert M., ed. see Tierney, Richard L.
Price, Robert M., ed. & intro. see Ambuehl, James.

P

An Asterisk (*) at the beginning of an entry indicates that the title is appearing for the first time.

Price, Robert R., jt. auth. see Finley, Eddy.

Price, Robert S. & Magnotta, George. ABCs of Industrial Development Bonds. 5th ed. 336p. (Orig.). 30.00 (*0-685-71083-1*) Packard Pr Fin.

Price, Robert W. Entrepreneurship, 1999-2000. (Annual Ser.). (Illus.). 240p. 1998. pap. text 12.25 (*0-07-290474-7*, Dshkn McG-Hill) McGrw-H Hghr Educ.

Price, Robin. Healing Within: Medicine, Health & Wholeness. 19p. 1986. pap. 7.00 (*0-904674-11-8*, Pub. by Octagon Pr) ISHK.

Price, Robin & Shinohara, Keiji. Altar Book for Gorecki: "The Symphony of Sorrowful Songs" by Henryk Gorecki: Lyrics in Polish & English Translation. (ENG & POL.). 7p. 1996. 450.00 (*0-924433-05-1*) R Price.

Price, Robin, ed. see Romero, Pepe.

Price, Roger. A Concise History of France. (Cambridge Concise Histories Ser.). (Illus.). 396p. (C). 1993. pap. 17.95 (*0-521-36809-X*); text 54.95 (*0-521-36239-3*) Cambridge U Pr.

***Price, Roger.** Mad Libs for President. (Illus.). 48p. (J). (gr. 4-7). 2000. pap. 3.99 (*0-8431-7623-7*, Price Stern) Peng Put Young Read.

Price, Roger. Mad Libs Halloween: Night of the Living Mad Libs-Monster Mad Libs, Vol. 1. 1999. pap. 3.99 (*0-8431-7466-8*, Price Stern) Peng Put Young Read.

— Mad Libs on the Road: World's Greatest Word Game. (Mad Libs Ser.). 48p. (J). (gr. 4-7). 1999. pap. 3.99 (*0-8431-7498-6*, Price Stern) Peng Put Young Read.

— A Social History of Nineteenth-Century France. LC 87-22684. (Illus.). 370p. (C). 1988. 49.50 (*0-8419-1165-7*) Holmes & Meier.

Price, Roger & Stern, Leonard. Camp Daze Mad Libs: World's Greatest Party Game. (Mad Libs Ser.). (Illus.). 48p. (J). (gr. 2 up). 1988. pap. 3.99 (*0-8431-2239-0*, Price Stern) Peng Put Young Read.

— Christmas Fun Mad Libs. (Mad Libs Ser.). (Illus.). 48p. (Orig.). (J). (gr. 3 up). 1985. pap. 3.99 (*0-8431-1238-7*, Price Stern) Peng Put Young Read.

— Goofy Mad Libs: World's Greatest Party Game, No. 5. (Mad Libs Ser.: Vol. 5). (Illus.). 48p. (Orig.). (J). (gr. 4-7). 1993. pap. 3.99 (*0-8431-0059-1*) Peng Put Young Read.

— Kid Libs. (Mad Libs Ser.). (Illus.). 48p. (Orig.). (J). (gr. 2 up). 1990. pap. 3.99 (*0-8431-2827-5*, Price Stern) Peng Put Young Read.

***Price, Roger & Stern, Leonard.** Mad Libs. (J). 1999. pap. 10.99 (*0-8431-7464-1*, Price Stern) Peng Put Young Read.

— Mad Libs 2001 Desk Calendar. 640p. 2000. pap. 10.99 (*0-8431-7573-7*) Peng Put Young Read.

Price, Roger & Stern, Leonard. Mad Mad Mad Mad Libs: World's Greatest Word Game. (Mad Libs Ser.). 48p. (J). 1998. pap. 3.99 (*0-8431-7441-2*, Price Stern) Peng Put Young Read.

Price, Roger & Stern, Leonard. Monster Mad Libs, No. 4. (Mad Libs Ser.). (Illus.). 48p. (Orig.). (J). (gr. 4-7). 1974. pap. 3.99 (*0-8431-0058-3*, Price Stern) Peng Put Young Read.

Price, Roger & Stern, Leonard. Night of the Living Mad Libs: World's Greatest Word Game. LC 96-153860. (Mad Libs Ser.). (Illus.). 48p. (J). (gr. 3 up). 1994. pap. 3.99 (*0-8431-3735-5*, Price Stern) Peng Put Young Read.

— Slam Dunk Mad Libs. (Mad Libs Ser.). (Illus.). 48p. (Orig.). (J). (gr. 2 up). 1994. pap., bds. 3.99 (*0-8431-3722-3*, Price Stern) Peng Put Young Read.

Price, Roger & Stern, Leonard. Sooper Dooper Mad Libs, No. 3. (Mad Libs Ser.). (Illus.). 48p. (Orig.). (J). (gr. 4-7). 1974. pap. 3.99 (*0-8431-0057-5*, Price Stern) Peng Put Young Read.

Price, Roger & Stern, Leonard. Vacation Fun Mad Libs. (Mad Libs Ser.). (Illus.). 48p. (Orig.). (J). (gr. 3 up). 1987. pap. 3.99 (*0-8431-1921-7*, Price Stern) Peng Put Young Read.

Price, Roger, jt. auth. see Stern, Leonard.

Price, Roger, ed. see Inskip, John S., et al.

Price, Roger D. Napoleon III & the French Second Empire. LC 98-205522. (Lancaster Pamphlets Ser.). 96p. (C). 1997. pap. 11.99 (*0-415-15433-2*) Routledge.

Price, Rohan. The Principles of Unemployment Law. LC 97-179973. 350p. 1996. pap. 35.00 (*0-455-21433-6*, Pub. by LawBk Co) Gaunt.

Price, Ron. The Healthy Business Opportunity. 120p. 1995. pap. 5.00 (*0-9647484-1-X*) AIM Intl.

Price, Ronald J. Ask for the Order! Pugh, Mary A., ed. 138p. (Orig.). 1995. pap. 12.95 (*0-9646724-0-5*) R J Price.

Price, Ross E. Search the Scriptures, Old Testament Vol. 14: Isaiah. 1969. pap. 1.99 (*0-8341-0041-X*) Beacon Hill.

— You Can Be Sanctified Wholly. 1959. pap. 0.75 (*0-8341-0436-9*) Nazarene.

Price, Rumi K., et al, eds. Social Psychiatry Across Cultures: Studies from North America, Asia, Europe & Africa. (Topics in Social Psychiatry Ser.). (Illus.). 244p. (C). 1995. 45.00 (*0-306-44971-4*, Plenum Trade) Perseus Pubng.

Price, Russell, ed. see Machiavelli, Niccolo.

Price, Ruth. Rebel: A Biography of Agnes Smedley. 400p. 1994. text 24.95 (*0-02-925452-3*) Free Pr.

Price, S. Bone Dog. (Illus.). (J). mass mkt. 8.95 (*0-340-71031-4*, Pub. by Hodder & Stought Ltd) Trafalgar.

Price, S. Crazy Ballet Game. (Crazy Games Ser.). (Illus.). (J). (gr. 1 up). 1998. pap. 2.99 (*0-8431-7912-0*, Price Stern) Peng Put Young Read.

Price, S. Nightcomers. 1997. mass mkt. 11.95 (*0-340-65605-0*, Pub. by Hodder & Stought Ltd) Trafalgar.

— Signature Hauntings. 1995. mass mkt. 11.95 (*0-340-62655-0*, Pub. by Hodder & Stought Ltd) Trafalgar.

— Story Collector. (J). mass mkt. 8.95 (*0-340-70902-2*, Pub. by Hodder & Stought Ltd) Trafalgar.

Price, S. L. Fidel's Wicked Curve: Journeys Through the Country of Sport. LC 99-21292. 1999. write for info. (*0-88001-650-7*, Ecco Press) HarperTrade.

***Price, S. L.** Pitching Around Fidel: A Journey into the Heart of Cuban Sports. LC 00-20523. (Illus.). 288p. 2000. 24.00 (*0-06-019660-2*, Ecco Press) HarperTrade.

Price, S. R. Rituals & Power: The Roman Imperial Cult in Asia Minor. (Illus.). 320p. 1985. pap. text 27.95 (*0-521-31268-X*) Cambridge U Pr.

Price, Sabra L., jt. auth. see Hein, George E.

Price, Sally. Afro-American Arts of the Suriname Rain Forest. 240p. 1996. pap. 19.95 (*0-614-21565-X*, 16) Kazi Pubns.

— Co-Wives & Calabashes. 2nd ed. LC 92-43700. (Women & Culture Ser.). (Illus.). 264p. 1993. pap. text 16.95 (*0-472-08218-3*, 08218) U of Mich Pr.

— Primitive Art in Civilized Places. LC 89-4932. (Illus.). xii, 160p. 1991. pap. 13.95 (*0-226-68064-9*) U Ch Pr.

— Primitive Art in Civilized Places. (Illus.). 208p. 1993. 19.95 (*0-226-68063-0*) U Ch Pr.

***Price, Sally & Price, Richard.** Maroon Arts: Cultural Vitality in the African Diaspora. 2000. pap. 25.00 (*0-8070-8551-0*) Beacon Pr.

Price, Sally, jt. auth. see Price, Richard.

Price, Sally, ed. see Stedman, John G.

Price, Sandra B. California Probate Workflow Manual. 2 vols. rev. ed. Tom, Janette, ed. LC 79-53359. 136p. 1996. ring bd. 48.00 (*0-88124-965-3*, ES-31566) Cont Ed Bar-CA.

— California Probate Workflow Manual. rev. ed. Tom, Janette, ed. LC 79-53359. 286p. 1997. ring bd. 53.00 (*0-7626-0133-7*) Cont Ed Bar-CA.

Price, Sandy. Exploring the Flea Markets of France: A Companion Guide for Visitors & Collectors. LC 99-12531. 1999. pap. 14.00 (*0-609-80411-1*) Harmony Bks.

***Price, Sean.** Ancient Greece: A Complete Resource Filled with Background Information, Cross-Curricular Activities. (Illus.). 2000. pap. 12.95 (*0-439-05919-4*) Scholastic Inc.

Price, Seymour G. A Guide to Monitoring & Controlling Utility Costs. LC 73-88887. (BNA Operations Manual Ser.). 121p. reprint ed. pap. 37.60 (*0-608-12752-3*, 202433800037) Bks Demand.

Price, Sharon. My All Sufficient One. 159p. (Orig.). 1985. pap. 5.95 (*0-917595-08-4*) Kingdom Pubs.

Price, Sharon J., et al, eds. Families Across Time: A Life Course Perspective (Readings) LC 99-34263. 290p. (Orig.). (C). 2000. pap. text. write for info. (*1-891487-25-6*) Roxbury Pub Co.

Price, Sharon J. & Mckenry, Patrick C. Divorce. (Family Studies Text Ser.: Vol. 9). 160p. (C). 1988. text 42.00 (*0-8039-2356-2*); pap. text 18.95 (*0-8039-2357-0*) Sage.

Price, Sharon J. & McKenry, Patrick C. Divorce. LC 87-26959. (Family Studies Text Ser.: No. 9). 160p. 1988. reprint ed. pap. 49.60 (*0-7837-9908-X*, 206063400006) Bks Demand.

Price, Sharon J., jt. auth. see McKenry, Patrick C.

Price, Sharon J., jt. ed. see Brubaker, Timothy H.

Price, Sharon J., jt. ed. see Elliott, Barbara A.

Price, Sharon J., jt. ed. see Gelles, Richard J.

Price, Sharon M., jt. auth. see Miami Valley Career Tech Ctr Staff.

***Price, Shirley.** Aromatherapy & Your Emotions: How to Use Essential Oils to Balance Mind & Body. 2000. pap. 15.95 (*0-7225-3862-6*) Thorsons PA.

Price, Shirley. Aromatherapy for Common Ailments: A Gaia Original. (Illus.). 96p. 1991. pap. 13.95 (*0-671-73134-3*, Fireside) S&S Trade Pap.

***Price, Shirley.** Practical Aromatherapy: How to Use Essential Oils to Restore Health & Vitality. 2000. pap. 12.00 (*0-7225-3906-1*, Pub. by Thorsons PA) HarpC.

Price, Shirley. Practical Aromatherapy: How to Use Essential Oils to Restore Health & Vitality. 3rd ed. 1994. pap. 11.00 (*0-7225-2850-7*) Thorsons PA.

Price, Shirley & Price, Len. Aromatherapy for Health Professionals. LC 95-20316. 1995. pap. text 30.00 (*0-443-04975-0*) Church.

Price, Simon. Everything: A Book about Manic Street Preachers. (Illus.). 160p. 1998. pap. 24.95 (*0-7535-0139-2*, Pub. by Virgin Bks) London Brdge.

— Religions of the Ancient Greeks. LC 98-39104. (Key Themes in Ancient History Ser.). (Illus.). 218p. (C). 1999. text 59.95 (*0-521-38201-7*); pap. text 19.95 (*0-521-38867-8*) Cambridge U Pr.

Price, Simon, jt. ed. see Murray, Oswyn.

Price, Stanley E. The Antediluvian Giants & the Prophecy of Noah. 149p. (Orig.). 1992. pap. 8.50 (*1-879366-24-X*) Hearthstone OK.

— Why Me? A Comedy. LC 86-215599. ii, 76p. 1986. write for info. (*0-573-01621-6*) S French Trade.

Price, Stephen, jt. auth. see Kiess, Werner.

***Price, Stern S.** Turkey Time! (Illus.). 14p. (J). (ps-3). 2000. 4.99 (*0-8431-4396-7*, G & D) Peng Put Young Read.

Price, Stern Sloan. Mythological Monsters: Visuals & Learning Activities. 32p. (Orig.). 1999. pap. 5.99 (*0-8431-7517-6*, Price Stern) Peng Put Young Read.

***Price, Stern Sloan.** Shiny Little Engine That Could. (Illus.). 12p. (ps). 1999. pap. 3.99 (*0-8431-7523-0*, Price Stern) Peng Put Young Read.

Price, Stern, Sloan Publishing Staff. Film Review Annual 1995. 1996. 184.75 (*5-552-86811-0*, Price Stern) Peng Put Young Read.

Price, Stern, Sloan Publishing Staff, jt. auth. see Abrams, Jodell.

Price, Stern, Sloan Publishing Staff, jt. auth. see Whyte, Malcolm.

Price Stern Sloan Staff. Doodle Art Medium Tube Seascape. (J). (gr. 2 up). 1995. pap. 8.95 (*0-8431-6536-7*, Price Stern) Peng Put Young Read.

Price Stern Sloan Staff. The Egyptian Gods. (Troubador Color & Story Albums Ser.). (Illus.). 32p. (gr. 1-7). 1999. pap. 5.99 (*0-8431-7516-8*, Price Stern) Peng Put Young Read.

— Flowers. (Doodle Art Postcard Bks.). (Illus.). 48p. (gr. 4-7). 1998. pap. 4.99 (*0-8431-7824-8*, Price Stern) Peng Put Young Read.

— Tropical Fish. (Doodle Art Postcard Bks.). 48p. 1998. pap. 4.99 (*0-8431-7825-6*, Price Stern) Peng Put Young Read.

***Price, Steve.** America's 50 Best Bass Waters. LC 99-86261. (Illus.). 250p. 2000. pap. 18.95 (*1-56044-775-3*) Falcon Pub Inc.

Price, Steve. Bare. 200p. 1994. pap. 7.00 (*0-9642048-0-0*) North Mtn.

— Seasonal Guide to the Natural Year: Texas. (Seasonal Guides to the Natural Year Ser.). (Illus.). 360p. (Orig.). 1996. pap. 16.95 (*1-55591-272-9*) Fulcrum Pub.

Price, Steve, jt. auth. see Gilewicz, Alicia.

Price, Steve, jt. auth. see Hedges, Burke.

Price, Steve, ed. see Hedges, Burke.

Price, Steve, ed. see Keller, Jeff.

Price, Steve, ed. see Lever, Charles.

Price, Steve, ed. see Quain, Bill.

Price, Steven, jt. auth. see Gibson, Eva.

Price, Steven, jt. auth. see Tydeman, William.

Price, Steven C. A Long Interstate 80: Ohio. 76p. 1998. pap. 9.95 (*0-9667091-0-1*) Educ Tours.

— Pennsylvania: Along Interstate 80. 64p. 1993. pap. 6.95 (*0-9667091-1-X*) Educ Tours.

Price, Steven D. The Adult Rider. 1999. 22.00 (*0-609-60263-2*, Crown) Crown Pub Group.

— The American Quarter Horse: An Introduction to Selection, Care & Enjoyment. LC 98-19132. (Illus.). 320p. 1999. 35.00 (*1-55821-643-X*) Lyons Pr.

— The Beautiful Baby Naming Book. (Illus.). 96p. (Orig.). 1984. pap. 5.95 (*0-671-43171-4*) S&S Trade.

***Price, Steven D.** Essential Riding: A Realistic Approach to Horsemanship. (Illus.). 2000. pap. 19.95 (*1-58574-002-0*) Lyons Pr.

— Horseman's Illustrated Dictionary. 2000. 40.00 (*1-58574-146-9*) Lyons Pr.

— Kids' Book of the American Quarter Horse: Two Bits' Guide to Owning, Riding & Caring for Your Horse. LC 99-34868. 1999. pap. write for info. (*1-55821-975-7*) Lyon Press.

Price, Steven D. The Ultimate Fishing Guide: Where to Go, When to Leave, What to Take, What to Wear, What to Know, How to Find Out, & Other Indispensable Information for the Angler. LC 95-19028. (Illus.). 336p. (Orig.). 1996. pap. 22.00 (*0-06-273290-0*, Harper Ref) HarpC.

Price, Steven D., ed. The Quotable Horse Lover. LC 99-16537. (Illus.). 320p. 1999. 20.00 (*1-55821-950-1*) Lyons Pr.

— The Whole Horse Catalog. LC 98-39589. (Illus.). 320p. 1998. per. 20.00 (*0-684-83995-4*) S&S Trade.

Price, Steven D. & Spector, David A. The Whole Horse Catalogue: Revised & Updated for the 1990's. 2nd ed. (Illus.). 288p. 1993. per. 18.00 (*0-671-86681-8*, Fireside) S&S Trade Pap.

Price, Stuart. The Franchise Paradox: New Directions, Different Strategies. LC 58-9331. 640p. (Orig.). 1999. pap. 41.50 (*0-304-70468-7*) Continuum.

Price, Susan. Ghost Dance. LC 94-9841. 228p. (J). (gr. 4-7). 1995. 16.00 (*0-374-32537-5*) FS&G.

— The Ghost Drum. 176p. (J). (gr. 3 up). 1989. pap. 3.50 (*0-374-42547-7*) FS&G.

— Ghost Song. LC 92-6154. 160p. (YA). (gr. 7 up). 1992. 15.00 (*0-374-32544-8*) FS&G.

***Price, Susan.** Online Investing with Quicken 2000. (Official Guides Ser.). 448p. 2000. pap. 24.99 (*0-07-212392-3*) McGraw.

— The Sterkarm Handshake. 320p. (YA). (gr. 6). mass mkt. 5.95 (*0-06-447236-1*) HarpC.

— The Sterkarm Handshake. LC 99-54844. 428p. (YA). (gr. 4-7). 2000. lib. bdg. 17.89 (*0-06-029392-6*) HarpC Child Bks.

— The Sterkarm Handshake. LC 99-54844. 428p. (YA). (gr. 6 up). 2000. 17.95 (*0-06-028959-7*) HarpC Child Bks.

Price, Susan, ed. The C & T Index, 1987-1996: To Find Authors, Subjects & Articles in Cosmetics & Toiletries Magazine. 107p. 1997. pap. 59.00 (*0-931710-61-8*) Allured Publishing Corp.

Price, Susan, tr. from RUS. The Law of God, for Study at Home & School.Tr. of Zakon Bozhi. (Illus.). 650p. (J). (gr. 1-7). 1993. 50.00 (*0-88465-044-8*) Holy Trinity.

Price, Susan & Horse, Harry, compiled by. Horror Stories. LC 95-7088. (Story Library). (Illus.). 260p. (J). (gr. 1 up). 1995. 7.95 (*1-85697-592-4*) LKC.

Price, Susan, jt. auth. see Hartsough, Cheryl.

Price, Susan, jt. auth. see Settle, Miriam B.

Price, Susan C. & Price, Tom. The Working Parents Help Book: Practical Advice for Dealing with the Day-to-Day Challenges of Kids & Careers. LC 94-19035. 285p. 1994. pap. 12.95 (*1-56079-333-3*) Petersons.

— Working Parents Help Book: Practical Advice for Dealing with the Day-to-Day Challenges of Kids & Careers. 2nd rev. ed. 400p. 1996. pap. 16.95 (*1-56079-579-4*) Petersons.

Price, Susan C., jt. auth. see Binder, David A.

Price, Susan Davis. Minnesota Gardens: An Illustrated History. 168p. 1995. 35.00 (*1-890434-36-1*) Afton Hist Soc.

— Putting down Roots. LC 99-38320. 2000. pap. write for info. (*0-8166-3306-1*) U of Minn Pr.

Price, Susanna. Click. LC 96-37211. (J). 1998. 7.95 (*0-8069-9652-8*) Sterling.

Price, Susanna & Stephens, Tim. Click! Fun with Photography. LC 96-37211. (Illus.). 48p. (J). 1997. 14.95 (*0-8069-9541-6*) Sterling.

Price, Sylvia A. & Wilson, Lorraine M. Pathophysiology: Clinical Concepts of Disease Processes. 5th ed. (Illus.). teacher ed. write for info. (*0-8151-2543-7*) Mosby Inc.

Price, Sylvia Anderson. Pathophysiology: Clinical Concepts of Disease Processes. 5th ed. Wilson, Lorraine McCarty, ed. LC 96-15023. (Illus.). 1232p. (C). (gr. 13). 1996. text 66.00 (*0-8151-6621-4*, 24418) Mosby Inc.

Price, T. A. Sunday Sermons: Thoughts of Meditation for Ministers. LC 95-60633. 192p. (Orig.). 1995. pap. 10.00 (*0-936029-38-2*) Western Bk Journ.

Price, T. D. & Feinman, G. M. Foundations of Social Inequality. (Fundamental Issues in Archaeology Ser.). (Illus.). 308p. (C). 1995. 47.50 (*0-306-44979-X*, Kluwer Plenum) Kluwer Academic.

Price, T. D., jt. auth. see Kroll, E. M.

***Price, T. Douglas, ed.** Europe's First Farmers. LC 99-15477. (Illus.). 350p. (C). 2000. 64.95 (*0-521-66203-6*); pap. 24.95 (*0-521-66572-8*) Cambridge U Pr.

Price, T. Douglas & Feinman, Gary M. Images of the Past. 2nd rev. ed. LC 96-22728. (Illus.). 534p. (C). 1996. pap. text 45.00 (*1-55934-694-9*, 1694) Mayfield Pub.

— Images of the Past: Instructor's Manual. 2nd ed. LC 96-22728. (Orig.). 1997. pap. text, teacher ed. write for info. (*1-55934-695-7*, 1695) Mayfield Pub.

Price, T. Douglas & Gebauer, Anne B. Adventures in Fugawiland - Macintosh Version: A Computer Simulation in Archaeology. 2nd rev. ed. LC 96-273314. (Illus.). 118p. (C). 1996. pap. text 26.95 incl. disk (*1-55934-531-4*, 1531) Mayfield Pub.

— Adventures in Fugawiland - Windows Version: A Computer Simulation in Archaeology. 2nd rev. ed. LC 96-273314. (Illus.). x, 118p. (C). 1996. pap. text 26.95 (*1-55934-530-6*, 1530) Mayfield Pub.

— Adventures in Fugawiland Instructor's Manual. 2nd rev. ed. (Illus.). 23p. 1996. pap. text. write for info. (*1-55934-828-3*, 1828) Mayfield Pub.

Price, T. Douglas & Gebauer, Anne B., eds. Last Hunters - First Farmers: New Perspectives on the Prehistory Transition to Agriculture. (School of American Research - Advanced Seminar Ser.). (Illus.). 354p. 1995. 50.00 (*0-933452-90-X*); pap. 24.95 (*0-933452-91-8*) Schol Am Res.

Price, T. E. Analog Electronics with PSPICE. LC 96-29174. 700p. 1996. pap. 86.00 (*0-13-242843-1*, Prentice Hall) P-H.

Price, T. R. Listo Para Reedificar.Tr. of Ready to Rebuild. 1997. pap. text 10.99 (*1-56063-514-2*, 498445) Editorial Unilit.

Price, Taff. Fly Patterns: An International Guide. 3rd ed. (Illus.). 240p. 1997. pap. 21.95 (*0-7137-2599-0*, Pub. by Blandford Pr) Sterling.

Price, Ted. Miracle Town: Creating America's Bavarian Village in Leavenworth, Washington. LC 96-92027. (Illus.). 208p. 1997. 40.00 (*0-9651206-1-9*); pap. 24.95 (*0-9651206-0-0*) Price & Rodgers.

Price, Theron D. Revelation & Faith: Theological Reflections on the Knowing & Doing of Truth. LC 86-33224. 192p. 1987. 29.95 (*0-86554-260-0*, MUP H-221); pap. 14.95 (*0-86554-261-9*, P045) Mercer Univ Pr.

Price, Thomas. Dramatic Structure & Meaning in Theatrical Productions. LC 92-21128. 364p. 1992. pap. text 34.95 (*0-7734-9897-4*) E Mellen.

— Slavery in America. LC 71-92449. 1837. 15.00 (*0-403-00170-6*) Scholarly.

Price, Thomas, jt. auth. see Shepperson, George.

Price, Thomas, ed. see Colman, George.

Price, Thomas R. Construction & Types of Shakespeare's Verse As Seen in the Othello. LC 78-168837. (Shakespeare Society of New York. Publications: No. 8). reprint ed. 27.50 (*0-404-54208-5*) AMS Pr.

Price, Thomas R. & Nelson, Erland, eds. Cerebrovascular Diseases: Eleventh Princeton Conference. fac. ed. LC 75-25125. (Illus.). 424p. pap. 131.50 (*0-7837-7191-6*, 204710800005) Bks Demand.

***Price-Thompson, Tracy.** Black Coffee. 336p. 2000. pap. 16.95 (*0-595-09631-X*, Writers Club Pr) iUniversecom.

Price, Tim. Fun with the Piano. (Fun Bks.). 32p. 1974. pap. 4.95 (*0-87166-456-9*, 93343) Mel Bay.

***Price, Tim R.** The Serpent's Kiss: The Original Screenplay. LC 99-234843. (Illus.). 180p. 1999. pap. 19.95 (*0-7528-1303-X*, Pub. by Orion Media) Trafalgar.

Price, Todd M. Freedom from Pain. 61p. 1992. pap. 4.00 (*0-9633584-0-5*) T M Price.

— Searching for Hidden Treasure. 102p. 1998. pap. 10.00 (*0-9633584-1-3*) T M Price.

Price, Tom. Memorable Baseball Moments. (Century of Gamecocks Ser.: Vol. 3). (Illus.). 208p. pap. 5.00 (*1-887714-02-2*) Summerhse Pr.

— Memorable Basketball Moments. (Century of Gamecocks Ser.: Vol. 2). (Illus.). 208p. pap. 5.00 (*1-887714-01-4*) Summerhse Pr.

— Memorable Football Moments. (Century of Gamecocks Ser.: Vol. 1). (Illus.). 208p. pap. 5.00 (*1-887714-00-6*) Summerhse Pr.

Price, Tom, jt. auth. see Burke, David.

Price, Tom, jt. auth. see Price, Susan C.

Price, Tony, ed. see Ball, John.

Price, V., jt. auth. see Daniels, D.

Price, V. B. Chaco Trilogy: Poems. 120p. 1998. pap. 14.00 (*1-888809-10-8*) La Alameda Pr.

— City at the End of the World. LC 92-9028. (Illus.). 171p. 1992. 13.95 (*0-8263-1371-X*) U of NM Pr.

Price, V. B., jt. ed. see Morrow, Baker H.

Price, Victor. The Other Kingdom. LC 97-141035. 240p. 1996. pap. text 14.95 (*1-55821-451-8*, 14518, Pub. by Breakaway Bks) Consort Bk Sales.

P

Price, Victor, tr. & intro. see Buchner, Georg.

***Price, Victoria.** Vincent Price: A Daughter's Biography. (Illus.). 384p. 2000. pap. 17.95 (*0-312-26789-4*) St Martin.

Price, Victoria H. Christian Allusions in the Novels of Thomas Pynchon. (American University Studies: English Language & Literature: Ser. IV, Vol. 89). VIII, 264p. (C). 1989. text 37.95 (*0-8204-0859-X*) P Lang Pubng.

Price, Vincent. Drawings of Delacroix. (Master Draughtsman Ser.). (Illus.). 1966. pap. 4.95 (*0-87505-159-6*) Borden.

— I Want a Woman: Nine Poems by Vincent Price. 22p. 1993. pap. text 4.00 (*1-885902-00-X*) Printable Arts.

— Public Opinion. (Communication Concepts Ser.: Vol. 4). 112p. (C). 1992. text 28.00 (*0-8039-4022-X*); pap. text 11.95 (*0-8039-4023-8*) Sage.

Price, Vincent. Tales of Terror Audio. abr. ed. LC 75-750997. (J). 1987. audio 11.95 (*0-89845-753-X*, CPN 1497, Caedmon) HarperAudio.

Price, Vincent & Price, Mary. A Treasury of Great Recipes. (Illus.). 1995. reprint ed. lib. bdg. 75.00 (*1-56849-540-4*) Buccaneer Bks.

Price, Vincent, ed. see Poe, Edgar Allan.

Price, Vincent B. Semblances (1962-1971) Poems. 1976. pap. 4.95 (*0-913270-64-4*) Sunstone Pr.

Price, Virginia P., ed. Iron Horse in the Pinelands. expanded ed. (Illus.). 1991. pap. 9.95 (*0-939566-01-X*) Pensacola Hist.

Price, W. A., jt. ed. see Abbott, M. B.

Price, W. C., ed. see International Organization of Citrus Virologists S.

Price, W. D. Lifting the Veil of Oil Infections. (Technical Papers: Vol. P58). (Illus.). 7p. 1926. pap. text 30.00 (*1-55589-353-8*) AGMA.

Price, W. F., jt. auth. see Bamforth, P. B.

Price, W. G. & Keane, A. J., eds. Statistical Energy Analysis: An Overview, with Applications in Structural Dynamics. LC 95-49979. (Illus.). 149p. (C). 1997. text 49.95 (*0-521-55175-7*) Cambridge U Pr.

Price, W. G., jt. auth. see Bishop, R. E.

Price, W. L., jt. auth. see Davies, D. W.

Price, W. L., jt. ed. see Chaum, David.

Price, W. V., jt. auth. see Van Slyke, L. L.

Price, Walter, ed. see Carreras, Jose.

Price, Warren C. Eugene Register-Guard. LC 76-15203. (Illus.). 384p. 1977. 15.00 (*0-8323-0271-6*) Binford Mort.

— The Literature of Journalism: An Annotated Bibliography. LC 59-13522. 507p. reprint ed. pap. 157.20 (*0-608-11245-3*, 200100600053) Bks Demand.

Price Waterhouse Change Integration Team Staff. The Paradox Principles; How High Performance Companies Manage Chaos Complexity & Condradiction to Achieve Superior Results. LC 95-23346. 1995. 24.95 (*0-7863-0499-5*, Irwn Prfssnl) McGraw-Hill Prof.

Price Waterhouse Change Interg. Staff. Better Change: Best Practices for Transforming Your Organization. LC 94-10542. 208p. 1994. text 30.00 (*0-7863-0342-5*, Irwn Prfssnl) McGraw-Hill Prof.

Price Waterhouse LLP Staff. The Price Waterhouse Personal Financial Adviser. 320p. 1995. text 15.00 (*0-7863-0461-8*, Irwn Prfssnl) McGraw-Hill Prof.

— Secure Your Future: Your Personal Companion for Understanding Lifestyle & Financial Aspects of Retirement. 1996. 10.80 (*0-7863-1218-1*) McGraw.

— Secure Your Future: Your Personal Companion for Understanding Lifestyle & Financial Aspects of Retirement. 352p. 1995. pap. 16.95 (*0-7863-0526-6*, Irwn Prfssnl) McGraw-Hill Prof.

— Taxation of U. S. Corporations Doing Business Abroad: U. S. Rules & Competitiveness Issues. LC 95-83617. 101p. (Orig.). 1996. pap. 35.00 (*1-885065-06-X*, 096-05) Finan Exec.

Price Waterhouse Staff. Canada Business Corporations Act. 3rd ed. 136p. 1987. pap. 25.00 (*0-409-80656-0*, MICHIE) LEXIS Pub.

— Consumer Compliance Handbook: 1995 Edition. 3rd ed. 225p. (C). 1995. per. 65.00 (*1-55738-762-1*, Irwn Prfssnl) McGraw-Hill Prof.

— Consumer Compliance Handbook: 1996-1997 Edition. 4th ed. 256p. (C). 1996. per. 65.00 (*0-7863-0954-7*, Irwn McGrw-H) McGrw-H Hghr Educ.

— Consumer Compliance Handbook, 1994. 2nd ed. 1994. per. 60.00 (*1-55738-708-7*, Irwn Prfssnl) McGraw-Hill Prof.

— Corporate Tax Strategy, 1994-95. 128p. 1994. pap. 30.00 (*0-409-91614-5*, MICHIE) LEXIS Pub.

— A Guide to TIN Compliance: Interest, Dividend, Backup Withholding & Related IRS Reporting Issues. 6th ed. 225p. 1995. per. 75.00 (*1-55738-387-1*, Irwn Prfssnl) McGraw-Hill Prof.

— Hospital Financial Reports: A Survey. 150p. (C). 1987. per. 35.00 (*0-930228-52-9*) Hlthcare Fin Mgmt.

— Personal Tax. 280p. 1995. mass mkt. 12.95 (*0-385-25497-0*) Doubleday.

— The Price Waterhouse Guide to TIN Compliance: Interest, Divident, Backup Withholding & Related IRS Reporting Issues, 1996-1997 Edition. 7th ed. LC 96-34764. 288p. 1996. pap. 75.00 (*0-7863-1105-3*, Irwn Prfssnl) McGraw-Hill Prof.

— Price Waterhouse Investment Tax Advisor. 1990. pap. 5.50 (*0-13-717463-2*) P-H.

— The Price Waterhouse Personal Financial Adviser: Special Edition. 1996. text 25.00 (*0-7863-1141-X*, Irwn Prfssnl) McGraw-Hill Prof.

— The Price Waterhouse Personal Tax Adviser, 1994-1995. 1994. text 2.17 (*0-7863-0434-0*, Irwn Prfssnl) McGraw-Hill Prof.

— Price Waterhouse Retirement Advisor. 1990. pap. 5.50 (*0-13-717471-3*) P-H.

— Price Waterhouse Tax Strategy '97. (Illus.). 288p. 1996. mass mkt. 16.95 (*0-385-25615-9*) Doubleday.

— Real Estate Interest Reporting: A Compliance Guide to IRS Reporting Requirements. 1994. pap. text 75.00 (*1-55738-703-6*, Irwn Prfssnl) McGraw-Hill Prof.

— The Regulatory Reporting Compliance Handbook: 1995-96 Edition. 3rd ed. 124p. (C). 1995. pap. 65.00 (*1-55738-765-6*, Irwn Prfssnl) McGraw-Hill Prof.

— Regulatory Reporting Handbook: 1996-1997 Edition. 4th ed. 160p. (C). 1996. per. 65.00 (*0-7863-0955-5*, Irwn Prfssnl) McGraw-Hill Prof.

— The Regulatory Risk Management Handbook, 1996-1997. 1997. text 65.00 (*0-7863-1201-7*, Irwn McGrw-H) McGrw-H Hghr Educ.

— Safety & Soundness Compliance Handbook: 1995-96 Edition. 3rd ed. 180p. (C). 1995. pap. 65.00 (*1-55738-763-X*, Irwn Prfssnl) McGraw-Hill Prof.

— Secure Your Child's Future: Financial Strategies to Safeguard Your Child's College Education. 125p. 1996. pap. 15.95 (*0-7863-1003-0*, Irwn Prfssnl); pap. 16.00 (*0-614-12583-9*, Irwn Prfssnl) McGraw-Hill Prof.

— Secure Your Future. 1996. text 16.95 (*0-7863-1049-9*, Irwn Prfssnl) McGraw-Hill Prof.

— The Securities Compliance Handbook: 1995-96 Edition. 3rd ed. 136p. (C). 1995. per. 65.00 (*1-55738-766-4*, Irwn Prfssnl) McGraw-Hill Prof.

— The Standard Trust Income Tax Guide, 1992-1993. 230p. 1993. pap. 28.00 (*0-409-07654-6*, SA, MICHIE) LEXIS Pub.

— The Standard Trust Income Tax Guide, 1994-95. 248p. 1995. pap. write for info. (*0-409-07656-2*, MICHIE) LEXIS Pub.

— Tolley's Estate Planning, 1993-94. 450p. 1993. 90.00 (*0-85459-785-9*, Pub. by Tolley Pubng) St Mut.

— The Trust Compliance Handbook: 1995-96 Edition. 3rd ed. 158p. (C). 1995. per. 65.00 (*1-55738-764-8*, Irwn Prfssnl) McGraw-Hill Prof.

— VAT in the Single Market: The Price Waterhouse Guide Through the Maze. 128p. (C). 1993. lib. bdg. 53.00 (*1-85333-944-X*, Pub. by Graham & Trotman) Kluwer Academic.

Price Waterhouse Staff, ed. Guide to VAT in Europe. (C). 1989. lib. bdg. 64.00 (*1-85333-306-9*, Pub. by Graham & Trotman) Kluwer Academic.

— The Price Waterhouse A-Z of Vat. 160p. 1990. lib. bdg. 45.00 (*1-85333-308-5*, Pub. by Graham & Trotman) Kluwer Academic.

— VAT in the Single Market: The Price Waterhouse Guide Through the Maze. LC 93-39924. 128p. (C). 1993. lib. bdg. 61.00 (*1-85333-923-7*) G & T Inc.

Price Waterhouse Staff, et al. Accounting for Income Taxes: Analysis & Commentary. 1990. 39.50 (*0-7913-0115-X*) Warren Gorham & Lamont.

Price Waterhouse Staff, jt. auth. see Department of the Environment Staff.

Price, Wendel S., ed. see International Symposium on Artificial Insemination.

Price, Weston A. Nutrition & Physical Degeneration. 6th ed. LC 97-41920. 528p. 1997. pap. 20.95 (*0-87983-816-7*, 38167K, Keats Publng) NTC Contemp Pub Co.

— Nutrition & Physical Degeneration. 9th ed. (Illus.). 560p. 1977. 34.95 (*0-916764-00-1*) Price-Pottenger.

Price, Will. Relational Database: Using dBASE III Plus. 1988. pap. text. write for info. (*0-07-555426-7*) McGraw.

Price, William, jt. ed. see Claiborne, Jack.

Price, William A. Illinois Law Office Practice Forms, 2 vols. LC 95-78507. 1995. 160.00 (*1-55834-249-4*, 66011, MICHIE) LEXIS Pub.

— Sea-Level Fluctuation & Coastal Evolution: Based on a Symposium in Honor of William Armstrong Price. Nummedal, Dag et al, eds. LC 88-140434. (Society of Economic Paleontologists & Mineralogists Ser.: Vol. 41). (Illus.). 267p. reprint ed. pap. 82.80 (*0-608-08593-6*, 206911600002) Bks Demand.

Price, William B. Tales & Lore of the Mountaineers. 176p. 1963. reprint ed. pap. 10.00 (*0-685-53558-4*) McClain. This book tells legends of Indians, of haunted houses, stories of the early Baltimore & Ohio Railroad, tales of the old inns & taverns & of the early moonshiners who so artfully distilled their potent beverages in mountain hideouts. In addition, there are chapters on superstitions, games & recipes. Fourth Printing, 1996. *Publisher Paid Annotation.*

Price, William C. & Chissick, Seymour S., eds. The Uncertainty Principle & Foundations of Quantum Mechanics: A Fifty Year Survey. LC 76-18213. 590p. reprint ed. pap. 182.90 (*0-608-18825-5*, 203047800069) Bks Demand.

Price, William H. Civil War Handbook: A Civil War Research Associates Series. (Illus.). 72p. 1960. reprint ed. pap. 2.95 (*1-879295-00-8*) L B Prince.

— The English Patents of Monopoly. LC 75-41218. reprint ed. 37.50 (*0-404-14759-3*) AMS Pr.

Price, William J. Spectrochemical Analysis by Atomic Absorption. LC QD0096.A8P74. 404p. 1983. reprint ed. pap. 125.30 (*0-8357-7033-8*, 202668200051) Bks Demand.

Price, William L. A Manual of Photographic Manipulation Treating of the Practice of the Art & Its Various Applications to Nature. 2nd ed. LC 72-9223. (Literature of Photography Ser.). 1973. reprint ed. 24.95 (*0-405-04930-7*) Ayer.

Price, William S., Jr. Not a Conquered People: Two Carolinians View Parliamentary Taxation. (Illus.). 49p. 1975. pap. 4.00 (*0-86526-111-3*) NC Archives.

— There Ought to Be a Bill of Rights: North Carolina Enters a New Nation. (Illus.). 19p. (Orig.). (YA). (gr. 8-12). 1991. pap. 4.00 (*0-86526-254-3*) NC Archives.

Price, William S., Jr., ed. North Carolina Higher-Court Records, 1702-1708. (Colonial Records of North Carolina Ser.: Vol. 4). xxxix, 533p. 1974. 16.00 (*0-86526-025-7*) NC Archives.

Price-Williams, Douglass, jt. auth. see Johnson, Allen W.

Price-Williams, Douglass R. Explorations in Cross-Cultural Psychology. LC 74-28740. (Publications in Anthropology & Related Fields). 144p. 1975. 7.50 (*0-88316-515-5*) Chandler & Sharp.

Price, WIlliam S., Jr., ed. North Carolina Higher-Court Minutes, 1709-1723. (Colonial Records of North Carolina Ser.: Vol. 5). xliii, 631p. 1977. 21.00 (*0-86526-026-5*) NC Archives.

Price, Wilson. First Look at dBASE IV, Version 1.5-2.0 for DOS. (C). 1993. pap. text 10.74 (*0-07-051075-X*) McGraw.

Price, Wilson & Olson, Jack. Modern COBOL Programming. 480p. 1987. pap. text 32.00 (*0-317-54024-6*) Mitchell Pub.

Price, Wilson & Stamper, David A. Database Design & Management: An Applied Approach. 1990. text. write for info. (*0-07-557994-4*) McGraw.

Price, Wilson, jt. auth. see Welburn, Tyler.

Price, Wilson T. Elements of Computer Programming (FORTRAN) 2nd ed. LC 71-107432. xv, 456p. 1970. write for info. (*0-03-081476-6*) H Holt & Co.

Price, Zane H. Atom to Adam: A Model of Theistic Evolution. (Illus.). ix, 115p. (Orig.). 1966. pap. 19.95 (*0-9651258-0-7*) Probe Bks CA.

Priceman, Marjorie. Emeline at the Circus. LC 98-28873. (Illus.). 40p. (gr. k-3). 1999. lib. bdg. 16.99 (*0-679-97685-X*, Pub. by Random Bks Yng Read) Random.

— Emeline at the Circus. LC 98-28873. (Illus.). 40p. (J). (gr. k-3). 1999. pap. 15.00 (*0-679-87685-5*, Pub. by Random Bks Yng Read) Random.

***Priceman, Marjorie.** Emeline at the Circus. (J). 2000. pap. 6.99 (*0-375-80351-3*, Pub. by Random Bks Yng Read) Random.

— Froggie Went a-Courting. LC 99-25703. (Illus.). 32p. (J). (ps-3). 1999. 14.95 (*0-316-71227-2*) Little.

Priceman, Marjorie. How to Make an Apple Pie & See the World. LC 93-12341. (Dragon Tales Ser.). (Illus.). 32p. (J). (ps-3). 1996. pap. 6.99 (*0-679-88083-6*, Pub. by Random Bks Yng Read) Random.

— How to Make an Apple Pie & See the World. (J). 1996. 12.19 (*0-606-10848-3*, Pub. by Turtleback) Demco.

Priceman, Marjorie. For Laughing Out Loud: Poems to Tickle Your Funnybone. LC 90-33010. 96p. (J). (gr. 1-5). 1991. 17.00 (*0-394-82144-0*, Pub. by Knopf Bks Yng Read); lib. bdg. 15.99 (*0-394-92144-5*, Pub. by Knopf Bks Yng Read) Random.

Priceman, Marjorie & Clio. My Nine Lives by Clio. LC 97-47565. (Illus.). 48p. (J). (gr. 2-6). 1998. 16.00 (*0-689-81135-7*) S&S Childrens.

***PricewaterhouseCoopers LLP Accounting Technical Dept.** Students Manual of Accounting: The Guide to UK Accounting Law & Practice. LC 99-231312. (ITBP Textbooks Ser.). (Illus.). 1999. pap. 29.99 (*1-86152-506-0*) Thomson Learn.

PricewaterhouseCoopers Staff. The Commercial Banking Regulatory Handbook. (PricewaterhouseCoopers Regulatory Handbook Ser.). 216p. (gr. 13). 1998. pap. text 71.95 (*0-7656-0268-7*, Sharpe Prof) M E Sharpe.

— Compliance Link. (PricewaterhouseCoopers Regulatory Handbook Ser.). 52p. (gr. 13). 1998. pap. text 16.95 (*0-7656-0271-7*, Sharpe Prof) M E Sharpe.

— The Consumer Banking Regulatory Handbook. (PricewaterhouseCoopers Regulatory Handbook Ser.). 248p. (gr. 13). 1998. pap. text 71.95 (*0-7656-0267-9*, Sharpe Prof) M E Sharpe.

***PricewaterhouseCoopers Staff.** Memos to the President: Management Advice from the Nation's Top CEOs. Schiro, James J., ed. 256p. 2000. 27.95 (*0-471-39338-X*) Wiley.

PricewaterhouseCoopers Staff. PricewaterhouseCoopers Regulatory Handbook Series, Set. (PricewaterhouseCoopers Regulatory Handbook Ser.). 1213p. (gr. 13). 1998. pap. text 329.95 (*0-7656-0379-9*, Sharpe Prof) M E Sharpe.

— The Regulatory Reporting Handbook. (PricewaterhouseCoopers Regulatory Handbook Ser.). 152p. (gr. 13). 1998. pap. text 71.95 (*0-7656-0270-9*, Sharpe Prof) M E Sharpe.

— The Regulatory Risk Management Handbook. (PricewaterhouseCoopers Regulatory Handbook Ser.). 208p. (gr. 13). 1998. pap. text 71.95 (*0-7656-0266-0*, Sharpe Prof) M E Sharpe.

— The Securities Regulatory Handbook. (PricewaterhouseCoopers Regulatory Handbook Ser.). 144p. (gr. 13). 1998. pap. text 71.95 (*0-7656-0269-5*, Sharpe Prof) M E Sharpe.

— The Trust Regulatory Handbook. (PricewaterhouseCoopers Regulatory Handbook Ser.). 176p. (gr. 13). 1998. pap. text 71.95 (*0-7656-0265-2*, Sharpe Prof) M E Sharpe.

***PricewaterhouseCoopers Staff, ed.** A Guide to VAT in the EU: 1998-1999 Update. (Yearbook Guide to the VAT in the European Community Ser.: Vol. 5). 376p. 1999. pap. 75.00 (*90-411-9749-4*) Kluwer Law Intl.

PricewaterhouseCoopers Staff, jt. auth. see Stuttard, John.

Pricha, W., jt. auth. see O'Hara, J. G.

Prichard, A. M. Read: Allied Families of Read, Corbin, Luttrell, & Bywaters of Culpepper Co., Va. (Illus.). 292p. 1991. reprint ed. pap. 46.00 (*0-8328-1876-3*); reprint ed. lib. bdg. 56.00 (*0-8328-1875-5*) Higginson Bk Co.

Prichard, Arthur C. An Appalachian Legacy: Mannington Life & Spirit. 330p. 1983. 18.00 (*0-9612788-0-3*) McClain. A story of an Appalachian town - Mannington, West Virginia. This historically accurate account highlights some events & people whose lives have been involved in the town through the years. *Publisher Paid Annotation.*

Prichard, Bob, ed. see West, W. B., Jr.

Prichard, Caradog. One Moonlit Night. LC 96-139705. xv, 76 p. 1995. write for info. (*0-86241-530-6*) Canongate Books.

— One Moonlit Night. Mitchell, Philip, tr. from WEL. LC 96-51842. (New Directions Classic). 304p. 1997. pap. 12.95 (*0-8112-1342-0*, NDP835, Pub. by New Directions) Norton.

Prichard Committee for Academic Excellence Staff. The Path to a Larger Life: Creating Kentucky's Educational Future. 2nd ed. LC 89-78107. 176p. 1990. pap. text 15.00 (*0-8131-0199-9*) U Pr of Ky.

***Prichard, Craig.** Making Managers in Universities & Colleges. LC 99-41464. 2000. pap. 34.95 (*0-335-20485-6*) OpUniv Pr.

— Managing Knowledge. 2000. text 69.95 (*0-312-23363-9*) St Martin.

Prichard, Doris, jt. compiled by see Sicignano, Robert.

Prichard, E. F., Jr., ed. see Frankfurter, Felix.

Prichard, Ed. Wholesome Example. 172p. 1993. pap. 9.95 (*0-917851-71-4*) Bristol Hse.

Prichard, Elizabeth R., et al. Geriatrics & Thanatology, 1. LC 84-3286. 224p. 1984. 55.00 (*0-275-91447-X*, C1447, Praeger Pubs) Greenwood.

Prichard, F. Elizabeth. Quality in the Analytical Chemistry Laboratory: Analytical Chemistry by Open Learning. (Analytical Chemistry by Open Learning Ser.). 334p. 1995. pap. 69.95 (*0-471-95470-5*) Wiley.

Prichard, F. Elizabeth, jt. auth. see James, Arthur M.

Prichard, Guy. Constructive Dismissal. 96p. 1995. pap. 36.50 (*1-85811-035-1*, Pub. by CLT Prof) Gaunt.

— Industrial Tribunals: Procedure & Appeals. 220p. 1995. pap. 46.50 (*1-85811-062-9*, Pub. by CLT Prof) Gaunt.

— Redundancies. 140p. 1995. pap. 36.50 (*1-85811-037-8*, Pub. by CLT Prof) Gaunt.

Prichard, H. Hesketh. Sniping in France: How the British Army Won the Sniping War in the Trenches. 211p. 1993. 25.00 (*1-884849-08-3*) R&R Bks.

Prichard, H. M., et al, eds. Magmatic Processes & Plate Tectonics. (Geological Society Special Publication Classic Ser.: No. 76). (Illus.). 536p. 1997. pap. 40.00 (*1-897799-87-X*, Pub. by Geol Soc Pub Hse) AAPG.

Prichard, Hesketh. Where Black Rules White. LC 70-161272. (Black Heritage Library Collection). 1977. reprint ed. 27.95 (*0-8369-8831-0*) Ayer.

Prichard, James C. Eastern Origin of the Celtic Nations. 1977. lib. bdg. 59.95 (*0-8490-1744-0*) Gordon Pr.

— Researches into the Physical History of Man. Stocking, George W., Jr., ed. LC 75-190425. (Classics in Anthropology Ser.). 716p. 1973. lib. bdg. 30.00 (*0-226-68120-3*) U Ch Pr.

— A Treatise on Insanity & Other Disorders Affecting the Mind. LC 73-2412. (Mental Illness & Social Policy; the American Experience Ser.). 1973. reprint ed. 26.95 (*0-405-05222-7*) Ayer.

— World Civilizations Vols. 1-5: Race, Tribes & Cultures, 5 vols. 1996. 3300.00 (*81-7305-093-7*, Pub. by Print Hse) St Mut.

— World Civilizations - Races, Tribes & Culture Vol. 1: General Introduction: A Historical Survey of Characteristics, Societies, Customs, Languages, Mythologies, Traditions, Flora, Fauna etc. of Natives of the World. (Illus.). xvi, 380p. 1996. 80.00 (*81-7305-088-0*, Pub. by Aryan Bks Intl) Nataraj Bks.

— World Civilizations - Races, Tribes & Culture Vol. 2: Africa: A Historical Survey of Characteristics, Societies, Customs, Languages, Mythologies, Traditions, Flora, Fauna etc. Natives of the World. (Illus.). xiv, 373p. 1996. 80.00 (*81-7305-089-9*, Pub. by Aryan Bks Intl) Nataraj Bks.

— World Civilizations - Races, Tribes & Culture Vol. 3: Europe: A Historical Survey of Characteristics, Societies, Customs, Languages, Mythologies, Traditions, Flora, Fauna etc. of Natives of the World. (Illus.). xvi, 507p. 1996. 80.00 (*81-7305-090-2*, Pub. by Aryan Bks Intl) Nataraj Bks.

— World Civilizations - Races, Tribes & Culture Vol. 4: Asia: A Historical Survey of Characteristics, Societies, Customs, Languages, Mythologies, Traditions, Flora, Fauna etc. of Natives of the World. (Illus.). xv, 631p. 1996. 80.00 (*81-7305-091-0*, Pub. by Aryan Bks Intl) Nataraj Bks.

— World Civilizations - Races, Tribes & Culture Vol. 5: Oceanaica & America: A Historical Survey of Characteristics, Societies, Customs, Languages, Mythologies, Traditions, Flora, Fauna etc. of Natives of the World. (Illus.). xv, 570p. 1996. 80.00 (*81-7305-092-9*, Pub. by Aryan Bks Intl) Nataraj Bks.

Prichard, Janet, jt. auth. see Carrano, Frank M.

Prichard, Jo G. Making Things Grow: The Story of Mississippi Chemical Corporation. (Illus.). 260p. 1998. 40.00 (*1-57806-109-1*) U Pr of Miss.

Prichard, Jones K., jt. auth. see Adams, John.

***Prichard, Julia & Jordan, Louis.** Maximising Performance in Insurance Operations LC 99-33737. 1999. write for info. (*0-8493-0688-4*) CRC Pr.

Prichard, Julia & Jordan, Louis. Maximizing Performance in Insurance Operations. 192p. 1999. 120.00 (*1-85573-438-9*) Am Educ Systs.

P

Prichard, Katharine S. Tribute: Selected Stories of Katharine Susannah Prichard. Throssell, Ric, ed. (Orig.). 1989. pap. 16.95 (*0-7022-2166-X*, Pub. by Univ Queensland Pr) Intl Spec Bk.

Prichard, Keith W. & Sawyer, R. McLaran, eds. Handbook of College Teaching: Theory & Applications. LC 93-30982. (Educators' Reference Collection). 488p. 1994. lib. bdg. 79.50 (*0-313-28142-4*, Greenwood Pr) Greenwood.

Prichard, Lillian & Key, Alexander. Stormy, the Brave Sponge Diver. 1955. pap. 0.75 (*0-614-05558-X*) Dietz.

Prichard, Lillian & Venos, Fannie. Can the Greeks Cook. 1950. spiral bd. 8.75 (*0-87517-002-1*) Dietz.

Prichard, Mari, jt. auth. see Carpenter, Humphrey.

Prichard, Nancy. The I Hate to Train Performance Guide for Climbers. LC 96-167899. (How to Rock Climb Ser.). (Illus.). 58p. (Orig.). 1994. pap. 5.95 (*0-934641-65-X*) Falcon Pub Inc.

Prichard, Pete. Submarine Badges & Insignia of the World: An Illustrated Reference for Collectors. LC 96-72253. (Illus.). 136p. 1997. 45.00 (*0-7643-0255-8*) Schiffer.

Prichard, Peter. The Making of McPaper: The Inside Story of U. S. A. Today. 1989. mass mkt. 5.95 (*0-312-91168-8*) St Martin.

— The Making of McPaper: The Inside Story of U. S. A. Today. 1989. pap. 5.95 (*0-318-42582-3*) St Martin.

Prichard, R. E. Eyes of the Doll. 200p. 1999. pap. 15.00 (*0-8059-4530-X*) Dorrance.

Prichard, Rebecca. Yard Gal. Date not set. pap. 5.95 (*0-8222-1775-9*) Dramatists Play.

— Yard Gal. 96p. 2000. pap. 9.00 (*0-571-19591-1*) Faber & Faber.

***Prichard, Rebecca B.** Sensing the Spirit: The Holy Spirit in Feminist Perspective. LC 99-38561. 160p. 1999. 15.99 (*0-8272-3442-2*) Chalice Pr.

Prichard, Robert W. History of the Episcopal Church. rev. ed. LC 99-22978. 368p. 1999. pap. 23.95 (*0-8192-1828-6*) Morehouse Pub.

— Theological Consensus in the Episcopal Church, 1801-73. LC 96-25380. 232p. 1997. text 29.95 (*0-252-02309-9*) U of Ill Pr.

Prichard, Robert W. & Robinson, Robert E. Twenty Thousand Medical Words. 288p. (gr. 13). 1972. pap. text 11.95 (*0-07-050874-7*) Mosby Inc.

Prichard, Rosalind M. Reconstructing Education: East German Schools after Unification. LC 98-7436. (International Educational Studies: No. 2). 288p. 1998. 59.95 (*1-57181-954-1*) Berghahn Bks.

Prichard, Samuel. Masonry Dissected. 50p. 1996. reprint ed. pap. 12.95 (*1-56459-982-5*) Kessinger Pub.

Prichard, Susan P. Film Costume: An Annotated Bibliography. LC 81-5274. 577p. 1981. 52.00 (*0-8108-1437-4*) Scarecrow.

Prichett, et al. Fundamentals of Quantitative Business Methods. 2nd ed. 1999. pap. 79.06 (*0-07-236824-1*) McGraw.

Prichett, Gordon D. & Saber, John C. CPS - Mathematics with Applications In Management & Economics: Quantitative Business Tools I. 7th ed. 584p. (C). 1995. text 42.95 (*0-256-20484-5*, Irwn McGrw-H) McGrw-H Hghr Educ.

— Mathematics with Applications in Management & Economics. 7th rev. ed. LC 92-36042. 1088p. (C). 1993. text 72.75 (*0-256-09237-0*, Irwn McGrw-H) McGrw-H Hghr Educ.

Prick, L. G., jt. ed. see Voorbach, J. T.

Prickel, Donald, jt. auth. see Mitchell, Robert.

Prickett, Carol A., jt. ed. see Madsen, Clifford K.

Prickett, Glenn T., jt. ed. see Bowles, Lan A.

Prickett, Hugh T. & Duncan, Earlene, eds. Coping with the Multi-Handicapped Hearing Impaired: A Practical Approach. 90p. 1988. pap. 20.95 (*0-398-06333-8*) C C Thomas.

— Coping with the Multi-Handicapped Hearing Impaired: A Practical Approach. 90p. (C). 1988. text 30.95 (*0-398-05412-6*) C C Thomas.

Prickett, Jeanne G., et al. Hand in Hand: A Trainer's Manual. LC 95-8265. 1995. pap., teacher ed. 29.95 (*0-89128-940-2*) Am Foun Blind.

Prickett-Ramutkowski, Barbara. Administrative Procedures for Medical Assisting: A Patient-Centered Approach. LC 98-26411. (Illus.). (YA). (gr. 6-12). 1999. student ed. 29.31 (*0-02-804863-6*) Glencoe.

— Medical Assisting: A Patient-Centered Approach to Administrative & Clinical Competencies. (Illus.). (gr. 6-12). 1999. student ed., wbk. ed. 19.75 (*0-02-802429-X*) Glencoe.

Prickett, Robert. Cantrell. 304p. (Orig.). 1989. spiral bd. 3.95 (*0-373-97090-0*) Harlequin Bks.

Prickett, Stephen. Origins of Narrative: The Romantic Appropriation of the Bible. (Illus.). 304p. (C). 1996. text 64.95 (*0-521-44543-4*) Cambridge U Pr.

— The Romantics: The Context of English Literature. 270p. 1981. text 37.50 (*0-8419-0723-4*); pap. text 19.50 (*0-8419-0724-2*) Holmes & Meier.

Prickett, Stephen, jt. auth. see Jasper, David.

Prickett, William. Risk in the Afternoon: Some of the Pleasures & Perils of Foxchasing. (Illus.). 230p. 1998. 30.00 (*0-9665352-0-0*) Red Fox DE.

Pricl, Sabrina & Lapasin, Romano. Rheology of Industrial Polysaccharides: Theory & Applications. 620p. 1995. 209.00 (*0-8342-1686-8*) Aspen Pub.

Prida, Dolores. Beautiful Senoritas & Other Plays. Weiss, Judith, ed. LC 90-1239. 180p. 1991. pap. 12.95 (*1-55885-026-0*, Pub. by Arte Publico) Empire Pub Srvs.

Priddle, J., jt. auth. see Medlin, L.

Priddy, A. Paul, jt. auth. see Li, Kam W.

Priddy, B. L. Fly-Fishing the Texas Hill Country. 3rd ed. (Illus.). 128p. 2000. pap. 21.95 (*0-935072-23-3*) W T Taylor.

Priddy, Eugene. Doctrina Cristiana Basica - Basic Christian Doctrine. (SPA.). 326p. 1996. write for info. (*0-7899-0247-8*) Editorial Unilit.

— How Not to Get Burned! Bible Truth Made Clear. 3rd rev. ed. LC 98-150875. vi, 282p. 1997. pap. 10.00 (*0-9660012-0-6*, BBI Pubns) Bible Basics.

— How Not to Get Burned! Bible Truth Made Clear (KJV) 3rd rev. ed. vi, 282p. 1997. spiral bd. 10.00 (*0-9660012-2-2*, BBI Pubns) Bible Basics.

— How Not to Get Burned! Bible Truth Made Clear (NASB) 3rd rev. ed. vi, 282p. 1997. spiral bd. 10.00 (*0-9660012-1-4*, BBI Pubns) Bible Basics.

***Priddy, Kevin L., et al, eds.** Applications & Science of Computational Intelligence II. 542p. 1999. pap. text 103.00 (*0-8194-3196-6*) SPIE.

***Priddy, Laurance L.** Critical Evidence: A Courtroom Suspense Novel. 192p. 2000. 26.95 (*0-86534-306-3*) Sunstone Pr.

Priddy, Laurance L. Son of Durango: A Novel. LC 95-34873. 176p. 1996. 22.95 (*0-86534-242-3*) Sunstone Pr.

— Winning Passion: A Novel. LC 93-13982. 288p. (Orig.). 1994. pap. 14.95 (*0-86534-200-8*) Sunstone Pr.

Priddy, Neil. Men & Cancer. 1999. pap. text 11.95 (*0-85969-793-2*) S C K Pubns.

Priddy, Robert. Source of the Dream: My Way to Sathya Sai Baba. LC 97-25620. (Illus.). 312p. 1997. pap. 16.95 (*1-57863-028-2*) Weiser.

Priddy, Roger. Baby's Book of Animals. LC 92-54921. (J). (ps). 1993. 9.95 (*1-56458-278-7*) DK Pub Inc.

— Baby's Book of Nature. LC 94-40836. (Illus.). 24p. (J). (ps-3). 1995. 9.95 (*0-7894-0003-0*) DK Pub Inc.

— Baby's Book of the Body. (Baby's Bk.). (Illus.). 24p. (J). 1995. 9.95 (*0-7894-0198-3*) DK Pub Inc.

***Priddy, Roger.** Baby's Book of Trucks. LC 00-30302. (Illus.). (J). 2000. write for info. (*0-7894-6795-X*) DK Pub Inc.

Priddy, Roger, jt. illus. see Schakell, John.

Priddy, Stewart, jt. auth. see Mahowald, Mark E.

Priddy, Stewart, jt. ed. see Mahowald, Mark.

Priddy, Wayne & Summers, B. J. Value Guide to Gas Station Memorabilia. 192p. 1995. 24.95 (*0-89145-638-4*, 3977) Collector Bks.

Pride, Anne, ed. see Ippolito, Donna.

Pride, Armistead S. & Wilson, Clint C., II. A History of the Black Press. LC 97-2791. (Illus.). 344p. 1997. pap. 21.95 (*0-88258-192-9*, PRHBP) Howard U Pr.

Pride, Charley. Pride: The Charley Pride Story. 1995. pap. 10.00 (*0-688-14232-X*, Quil) HarperTrade.

Pride, Emrys. Pride in Britain's High Tech Progress. 72p. (C). 1989. 59.00 (*0-905928-47-4*, Pub. by D Brown & Sons Ltd) St Mut.

Pride, Glen L. The Kingdom of Fife: An Illustrated Architectural Guide. (Illus.). 208p. (C). 1990. pap. 40.00 (*1-85158-256-8*, Pub. by Rutland Pr) St Mut.

Pride, John. NTC's Dictionary of Common Mistakes in Spanish. (BBC Phrase Bks.). (SPA & ENG., Illus.). 256p. 1995. 14.95 (*0-8442-7255-8*, 72558, Passprt Bks) NTC Contemp Pub Co.

— NTC's Dictionary of Common Mistakes in Spanish: Common Errors of English Speakers in Spanish & How to Avoid Them. (ENG & SPA.). 256p. 1998. pap. 10.95 (*0-8442-7252-3*, 72523) NTC Contemp Pub Co.

Pride, Mary. All the Way Home: Power for Your Family to Be Its Best. LC 87-71897. 284p. 1989. pap. 13.99 (*0-89107-465-1*) Crossway Bks.

***Pride, Mary.** The Big Book of Home Learning: Each Volume Is over 500 Pages & Includes Full Contact Information for Every Product Reviewed, 3 vols., Vol. 1-3. 1999. pap. 69.00 (*0-7403-0083-0*) Alpha AZ.

— The Big Book of Home Learning: Getting Started: Introduces All Major Home School Methods & Answers Your Most Frequently Asked Questions, Vol. 1. 2000. pap. 25.00 (*0-7403-0006-7*) Alpha AZ.

— The Big Book of Home Learning: Junior High through College: Latest Information & Educational Products for Grade 7 & Up. 1999. pap. 25.00 (*0-7403-0008-3*) Alpha AZ.

— The Big Book of Home Learning: Preschool & Elementary: Reviews Hundreds of Products & Provides You with Teaching Tips for All Academic Subjects. 1999. pap. 25.00 (*0-7403-0007-5*) Alpha AZ.

Pride, Mary. Schoolproof: How to Help Your Family Beat the System & Learn to Love Learning the Easy, Natural Way. LC 87-72953. 1988. pap. 10.99 (*0-89107-480-5*) Crossway Bks.

— The Way Home: Beyond Feminism, Back to Reality. LC 84-73078. 240p. 1985. pap. 12.99 (*0-89107-345-0*) Crossway Bks.

Pride, Mary, jt. auth. see DeParrie, Paul.

Pride, N. B., jt. ed. see Calverley, P. M.

Pride, Richard A. The Confession of Dorothy Danner: Telling a Life Story. LC 95-20853. (Illus.). 288p. 1995. 24.95 (*0-8265-1270-4*) Vanderbilt U Pr.

Pride, Richard A. & Woodard, J. David. The Burden of Busing: The Politics of Desegregation in Nashville, Tennessee. LC 85-5302. (Illus.). 317p. reprint ed. pap. 98.30 (*0-7837-7081-2*, 204689300004) Bks Demand.

Pride, William M. Business, 5 vols. (C). 1995. pap., teacher ed. 11.96 (*0-395-74897-6*) HM.

— Business, 3 vols. 3rd ed. (C). 1990. pap. text, teacher ed. 3.96 (*0-395-57313-0*); pap. text, teacher ed. 3.96 (*0-395-57312-2*) HM.

— Business, 4 vols. 4th ed. (C). 1992. pap. text, student ed. 18.36 (*0-395-64015-6*) HM.

— Business, 5 vols. 5th ed. (C). 1995. text 67.56 (*0-395-76127-1*); pap. text 36.36 (*0-395-74461-X*); pap. text, student ed. 21.56 (*0-395-74895-X*) HM.

— Business Spanish, 5 vols. (C). 1992. pap. 11.96 (*0-395-64017-2*) HM.

— Marketing, 9 vols. (C). Date not set. pap., teacher ed., suppl. ed. 11.96 (*0-395-72150-4*); pap., teacher ed., suppl. ed. 11.96 (*0-395-72149-0*) HM.

— Marketing, 9 vols. (C). 1995. text 80.76 (*0-395-73890-3*) HM.

— Marketing, 9 vols. 9th ed. LC 94-76541. (C). 1994. pap. text 43.96 (*0-395-70746-3*) HM.

— Marketing, 10 vols. 10th ed. (C). 1996. pap. text 43.96 (*0-395-78574-X*) HM.

— Marketing Cases, 9 vols. 9th ed. (C). 1988. pap. text 31.96 (*0-395-49594-6*) HM.

Pride, William M. & Ferrell, O. C. Marketing: Basic Concepts & Decisions. LC 83-83389. 768p. (C). 1984. disk 45.00 (*0-395-36498-1*) HM.

— Marketing: Basic Concepts & Decisions. 6th ed. 1988. write for info. (*0-318-63331-0*); trans., VHS. write for info. (*0-318-63332-9*) HM.

— Marketing: Concepts & Strategies, 10 vols. 10th ed. (C). 1996. pap. text, student ed. 15.16 (*0-395-83689-1*) HM.

— Marketing: Concepts & Strategies, 10 vols. 10th ed. (C). 1997. pap. text, teacher ed. 11.96 (*0-395-83685-9*) HM.

***Pride, William M. & Ferrell, O. C.** Marketing, 2000 Edition. 2000. pap. 39.57 (*0-395-97483-6*) HM.

Pride, William M. & Hult, G. Tomas M., eds. AMA Marketing Educators' Proceedings, 1997 Vol. 8: Enhancing Knowledge Development in Marketing. 346p. 1997. pap. 50.00 (*0-87757-266-6*) Am Mktg.

Pride, William M., et al. Business. 6th ed. LC 98-71539. xxxi, 591p. 1999. text 33.87 (*0-395-90079-4*) HM.

— Business, 5 vols., Vol. I. 5th ed. (C). 1995. text, teacher ed. 11.96 (*0-395-74896-8*) HM.

Prideaux, Gary D. Syntax of Japanese Honorifics. (Janua Linguarum, Series Practica: No. 102). 1970. pap. text 50.00 (*90-279-0741-2*) Mouton.

Prideaux, Gary D., ed. Perspectives in Experimental Linguistics: Papers from the University of Alberta Conference on Experimental Linguistics, Edmonton, 1-14 Oct. 1978. (Current Issues in Linguistic Theory Ser.: No. 10). xi, 176p. 1979. 46.00 (*90-272-3503-1*) J Benjamins Pubng Co.

Prideaux, Gary D. & Baker, William J. Strategies & Structures: The Processing of Relative Clauses. LC 86-26863. (Current Issues in Linguistic Theory Ser.: Vol. 46). vii, 195p. 1987. 52.00 (*90-272-3540-6*) J Benjamins Pubng Co.

Prideaux, James. The Housekeeper. 1984. pap. 5.25 (*0-8222-0537-8*) Dramatists Play.

— Knowing Hepburn & Other Curious Experiences. 336p. 1998. pap. 14.95 (*0-571-19941-0*) Faber & Faber.

— The Last of Mrs. Lincoln. 1973. pap. 5.25 (*0-8222-0638-2*) Dramatists Play.

— Laughter in the Shadow of the Trees & Four Other Plays. 1996. pap. 5.25 (*0-8222-1512-8*) Dramatists Play.

— Lemonade, & the Autograph Hound: Two Short Plays. 1969. pap. 5.25 (*0-8222-0081-3*) Dramatists Play.

— Mixed Couples. 1981. pap. 5.25 (*0-8222-0766-4*) Dramatists Play.

— The Orphans: A Play in Two Acts. 1980. pap. 5.25 (*0-8222-0864-4*) Dramatists Play.

— Postcards. 1970. pap. 3.25 (*0-8222-0907-1*) Dramatists Play.

— Stuffings & an American Sunset: Two Plays. 1973. pap. 5.25 (*0-8222-0037-6*) Dramatists Play.

Prideaux, P. From Spear to Pearl-Shell-Somerset, Cape York Peninsula, 1864-1877. 206p. (C). 1990. 75.00 (*0-9589799-1-X*, Pub. by Boolarong Pubns) St Mut.

Prideaux, Sarah. An Historical Sketch of Bookbinding, Vol. 11. (History of Bookbinding & Design Ser.). 300p. 1989. text 30.00 (*0-8240-4024-4*) Garland.

Prideaux, W. F. A Bibliography of the Works of Robert Louis Stevenson. 401p. 1998. reprint ed. 65.00 (*1-57898-118-2*) Martino Pubng.

***Pridgen, Allen.** Walker Percy's Sacramental Landscapes: The Search in the Desert. LC 00-30120. (Illus.). 2001. 43.50 (*1-57591-040-3*) Susquehanna U Pr.

Pridgen, Dee. Consumer Credit & the Law. LC 90-37060. 1990. ring bd. 135.00 (*0-87632-742-0*) West Group.

— Consumer Protection & the Law. LC 86-6825. 1987. ring bd. 135.00 (*0-87632-501-0*) West Group.

Pridgen, Dee, et al. Eyewitness Identification: Legal & Practical Problems. 2nd ed. LC 81-17043. (Criminal Law Ser.). 1981. ring bd. 135.00 (*0-87632-367-0*) West Group.

***Pridgen, Jodi.** Adobe Dreams. LC 00-132927. 250p. 2001. 24.00 (*0-9701033-1-X*); pap. 12.00 (*0-9701033-0-1*) Post Pubng.

Pridgen, Wardea. It's Mine Just for the Asking: After All, My Heavenly Father Owns This World. unabridged ed. 52p. 1996. 6.00 (*1-56411-156-3*, 4BBG0157) Untd Bros & Sis.

Pridgen, William. Night of the Dragon's Blood. LC 96-78145. 192p. 1997. 17.95 (*0-9636512-6-9*) Hodge & Braddock.

Pridgeon, Alec, ed. The Illustrated Encyclopedia of Orchids. (Illus.). 304p. 1992. 39.95 (*0-88192-267-6*) Timber.

Pridgeon, Alec M. Genera Orchidacearum: Apostasioideae & Cypripedioideae. (Illus.). 214p. 1999. text 75.00 (*0-19-850513-2*) OUP.

***Pridgeon, Alec M., et al, eds.** Genera Orchidacearum Volume 2: Orchidoideae (part 1) (Illus.). 448p. 2001. text 120.00 (*0-19-850710-0*) OUP.

Pridgeon, Alec M., jt. ed. see Arditti, Joseph.

Pridham, Arthur. Notes on Romans. 461p. 1977. 15.99 (*0-8254-3519-6*, Kregel Class) Kregel.

Pridham, Brian R., ed. Oman: Economic, Social & Strategic Developments. 59.95 (*0-7099-4056-4*, Pub. by C Helm) Routldge.

***Pridham, Geoffrey.** The Dynamics of Democratization: A Comparative Approach. 288p. 2000. 90.95 (*0-8264-5038-5*) Continuum.

Pridham, Geoffrey. Political Parties & Coalitional Behavior in Italy: An Interpretive Study. 256p. 1987. lib. bdg. 57.50 (*0-415-00503-5*) Routledge.

Pridham, Geoffrey, ed. Coalitional Behaviour in Theory & Practice: An Inductive Model for Western Europe. (Illus.). 328p. 1986. text 69.95 (*0-521-30537-3*) Cambridge U Pr.

— Encouraging Democracy: The International Context of Regime Transition in Southern Europe. LC 91-15987. 240p. 1991. text 55.00 (*0-312-06708-9*) St Martin.

— Transitions to Democracy: Comparative Perspectives from Southern Europe, Latin America & Eastern Europe. LC 94-47359. (International Library of Politics & Comparative Government). 1995. 219.95 (*1-85521-424-5*, Pub. by Dartmth Pub) Ashgate Pub Co.

***Pridham, Geoffrey & Gallagher, Tom.** Experimenting with Democracy: Regime Change in Balkans. LC 99-31059. (Studies of Societies in Transition). 1999. text. write for info. (*0-415-18726-5*) Routledge.

Pridham, Geoffrey & Lewis, Paul. Stabilizing Fragile Democracies: New Party Systems in Southern & Eastern Europe. LC 95-25092. 288p. (C). 1995. pap. 27.99 (*0-415-11803-4*) Routledge.

Pridham, Geoffrey & Vanhanen, Tatu. Democratization in Eastern Europe: Domestic & International Perspectives. LC 94-7513. 272p. (C). 1994. pap. 25.99 (*0-415-11064-5*, B4713) Routledge.

Pridham, Geoffrey, et al. Building Democracy? The International Dimension of Democratisation in Eastern Europe. 2nd ed. LC 96-31335. 256p. 1997. 85.00 (*0-7185-0099-7*) Bks Intl VA.

Pridham, Geoffrey, jt. ed. see Muller-Rommel, Ferdinand.

Pridham, Geoffrey, jt. ed. see Noakes, Jeremy.

Pridmore-Brown, Philip, ed. see Cumiskey, Gregory J.

Pridmore, F. West Indies, Vol. III. 55.00 (*0-686-52275-3*) S J Durst.

Pridmore, Jay. A Century of Success: The AmerUs Life Story. (Illus.). 200p. 1996. write for info. (*0-944641-21-0*) Greenwich Pub Group.

— Chicago Botanic Garden: Portrait of a Garden. Sherman, Marilyn, ed. (Illus.). 48p. 1999. pap. write for info. (*0-939914-06-9*) Chi Horticult.

— Classic American Bicycles. LC 99-38302. (Enthusiast Color Ser.). (Illus.). 96p. 1999. pap. text 13.95 (*1-58068-001-1*, Pub. by MBI Pubg) Motorbooks Intl.

— A Garden for All Seasons. (Illus.). 136p. 1990. pap. 14.95 (*0-685-31711-0*) Chi Horticult.

— Inventive Genius: The History of the Museum of Science & Industry, Chicago. LC 96-13546. (Illus.). 1996. write for info. (*0-9638657-4-9*); pap. write for info. (*0-9638657-5-7*) Mus of Sci.

— John Gunther: Inside Journalism. LC 90-83522. (Illus.). 64p. (Orig.). 1990. pap. 5.00 (*0-943056-13-6*) Univ Chi Lib.

— Many Hearts & Many Hands: The History of Ferry Hall & Lake Forest Academy. Gendler, Anne, ed. 264p. 1994. 50.00 (*0-9643350-0-X*) Lke Forest Acad.

***Pridmore, Jay.** Northwestern University: Celebrating 150 Years. LC 00-8901. 2000. write for info. (*0-8101-1829-7*) Northwestern U Pr.

Pridmore, Jay. The Richardson Story: A Family Enterprise at 150 Years. LC 98-86844. 1998. Price not set. (*0-944641-31-8*) Greenwich Pub Group.

Pridmore, Jay & Hurd, Jim. Schwinn Bicycles: The First 100 Years. LC 96-21887. (Illus.). 192p. 1996. 29.95 (*0-7603-0127-1*) MBI Pubg.

Pridmore, Jay, jt. auth. see Hurd, James L.

Pridmore, Jay, jt. auth. see Larson, George A.

***Pridmore, Pat.** Children as Partners for Health. 2000. pap. 22.50 (*1-85649-636-8*); text 59.95 (*1-85649-635-X*) Zed Books.

Pridmore, R. D., jt. auth. see Etheridge, M. K.

Pridmore, Tony, jt. auth. see Ablameyko, Sergey V.

Prieb, Wesley, ed. Peter C. Hiebert: He Gave Them Bread. (Illus.). 149p. (Orig.). 1990. pap. 10.00 (*1-877941-02-6*) Ctr Mennonite Brethren Studies.

Prieb, Wesley J., jt. auth. see Loewen, Jacob A.

Priebe, Dabmar. Kommunikation und Massenmedien in Englischen und Amerikanischen Utopien des 20. Jahr hunderts: Interpretation Aus Systemtheoretischer Sicht. (Neue Studien zur Anglistik und Amerikanistik: Bd.72). (GER.). VIII, 243p. 1998. 45.95 (*3-631-33151-7*) P Lang Pubng.

Priebe, Duane A., tr. see Ebeling, Gerhard.

Priebe, H. J. & Skarvan, K., eds. Cardiovascular Physiology. 200p. (Orig.). (C). 1995. pap. text 53.00 (*0-7279-0781-6*, Pub. by BMJ Pub) Login Brothers Bk Co.

Priebe, Hermann, jt. ed. see Knickel, Karlheinz.

***Priebe, Mac.** The Bald Eagle: Endangered No More. LC 99-75943. (Wildlife Winners). (Illus.). 32p. (J). (gr. 2-6). 2000. 15.95 (*0-9669551-8-8*, Pub. by Mindfull Pubg) ACCESS Pubs Network.

Priebe, Mac. The Peregrine Falcon: Endangered No More. LC 98-74803. (Wildlife Winners). (Illus.). 32p. (J). (gr. 2-6). 1999. 15.95 (*0-9669551-9-6*) Mindfull Pubg.

Priebe, Paul D. Modern Commercial Sailing Ship Fundamentals. LC 85-47838. 255p. 1986. reprint ed. pap. 79.10 (*0-608-02454-6*, 206309800004) Bks Demand.

Priebe, Richard & Hale, Thomas, eds. Artist & Audience: African Literature As a Shared Experience. LC 79-89930. (Annual Selected Papers of the African Literature Association). 203p. (Orig.). 1979. pap. 14.00 (*0-89410-123-4*) Cornell AS&RC.

Priebe, Richard, jt. ed. see Hale, Thomas.

Priebe, Richard K. Myth, Realism & the African Writer. Arnold, Stephen H. & Lang, George, eds. LC 88-71174. (Comparative Studies in African-Caribbean Literature Ser.). 200p. (C). 1988. 35.00 (*0-86543-097-7*); pap. 11.95 (*0-86543-098-5*) Africa World.

P

Priebe, Richard K., ed. Ghanaian Literatures. 120. LC 88-16110. (Contributions in Afro-American & African Studies: No. 120). 320p. 1988. 65.00 (*0-313-26438-4*, PGL/, Greenwood Pr) Greenwood.

Priebe, Stefan, et al. Quality of Life & Mental Health Care. LC 99-12782. 1999. 75.00 (*1-871816-40-8*) Taylor & Francis.

Priebe, Vel. Wendy's Gift. (Kinderbook Ser.). (Illus.). 24p. (J). (ps-2). 1988. pap. 1.50 (*0-919797-67-9*) Kindred Prods.

Priebe, Waldemar, ed. Anthracycline Antibiotics: New Analogues, Methods of Delivery, & Mechanisms of Actions. LC 94-38929. (ACS Symposium Ser.: No. 574). (Illus.). 380p. 1995. text 104.95 (*0-8412-3040-4*, Pub. by Am Chemical) OUP.

Prieberg, Fred K. Trial of Strength: Wilhelm Furtwangler in the Third Reich. Dolan, Christopher, tr. 394p. 1994. text 35.00 (*1-55553-196-2*) NE U Pr.

Prieditis, Armand E. Analogica. LC 86-33749. (Research Notes in Artificial Intelligence Ser.). (Illus.). 176p. (Orig.). (C). 1988. pap. text 34.95 (*0-934613-37-0*) Morgan Kaufmann.

Priehs, T. J., ed. see Arnberger, Leslie P.

Priehs, T. J., ed. see Barey, Pat.

Priehs, T. J., ed. see Berkowitz, Alan.

Priehs, T. J., ed. see Bleser, Nicholas J.

Priehs, T. J., ed. see Bogard, Travis.

Priehs, T. J., ed. see Bowers, Janice E.

Priehs, T. J., ed. see Brown, Joseph E.

Priehs, T. J., ed. see Cunningham, Richard L.

Priehs, T. J., ed. see Dodge, Natt N.

Priehs, T. J., ed. see Dowty, Robert R.

Priehs, T. J., ed. see Evans, Doris.

Priehs, T. J., ed. see Fisher, Pierre C.

Priehs, T. J., ed. see Gardner, Mark.

Priehs, T. J., ed. see Gnesios, Gregory.

Priehs, T. J., ed. see Hansen, Wallace.

Priehs, T. J., ed. see Hodge, Carle.

Priehs, T. J., ed. see Houk, Rose.

Priehs, T. J., ed. see Jorgen, Randolph.

Priehs, T. J., ed. see Keith, Sandra L.

Priehs, T. J., ed. see Lamb, Susan.

Priehs, T. J., ed. see Lister, Robert H. & Lister, Florence C.

Priehs, T. J., ed. see Mabery, Marilyne V.

Priehs, T. J., ed. see Murphy, Daniel O.

Priehs, T. J., ed. see Nabhan, Gary P.

Priehs, T. J., ed. see Parent, Laurence E.

Priehs, T. J., ed. see Phillips, Arthur M., 3rd.

Priehs, T. J., ed. see Rubissow, Ariel.

Priehs, T. J., ed. see Sperry, T. J.

Priehs, T. J., ed. see Threlkeld, Kay.

Priehs, T. J., ed. see Thybony, Scott.

Priehs, T. J., ed. see Torres, Luis.

Priehs, T. J., ed. see Trimble, Stephen A.

Priehs, T. J., ed. see Udall, Stewart L. & Haury, Emil W.

Priehs, T. J., ed. see Utley, Robert M.

Priel, V. Multi-Coordinate Data Presentation. 1977. 35.00 (*0-8464-0657-8*) Beekman Pubs.

Priemer, R., ed. Introductory Signal Processing. (Advanced Series in Electrical & Computer Engineering: Vol. 6). 752p. (C). 1990. text 90.00 (*9971-5-0919-9*); pap. text 55.00 (*9971-5-0920-2*) World Scientific Pub.

***Priemus, H., et al, eds.** Towards Undivided Cities in Western Europe: New Challenges for Urban Policy. (Illus.). 96p. 1998. 18.95 (*90-407-1545-9*, Pub. by Delft U Pr) Coronet Bks.

Priemus, Hugo, et al. European Monetary, Economic & Political Union: Consequences for National Housing Policies. (Housing & Urban Policy Studies: Vol. 6). (Illus.). 57p. (Orig.). (C). 1993. pap. 22.50 (*90-6275-840-1*, Pub. by Delft U Pr) Coronet Bks.

Prien, Jochen. Jadgeschwader 53: A History of the "Pik As" Geschwader, Vol. 2: May 1942-1944. Johnston, David, tr. from GER. LC 96-70419. 352p. 1998. 89.95 (*0-7643-0292-2*) Schiffer.

— Jagdgeschwader 53: A History of the "Pik As" Geschwader, January 1944-May 1945. 464p. 1999. 89.95 (*0-7643-0556-5*) Schiffer.

— Jagdgeschwader 53: A History of the "Pik As" Geschwader March 1937-May 1942. Johnston, David, tr. from GER. LC 96-70419. (Illus.). 400p. 1997. 89.95 (*0-7643-0175-6*) Schiffer.

Prien, Jochen & Rodeike, Peter. Messerschmitt Bf 109 F/G/K/ Series: An Illustrated Study. LC 92-81713. (Illus.). 208p. 1992. 35.00 (*0-88740-424-3*) Schiffer.

***Prien, Margaret S.** Character Links. Cory, Beverly, ed. (Illus.). 140p. (J). (ps-3). 1999. pap. 49.95 (*0-9673095-0-6*) Paw Impressions.

Prien, Robert F. & Mavissakalian, Matig R., eds. Long-Term Treatments of Anxiety Disorders. 464p. 1996. 58.00 (*0-88048-656-2*, 8656) Am Psychiatric.

Prien, Robert F. & Robinson, Donald S., eds. Clinical Evaluation of Psychotropic Drugs: Principles & Guidelines. LC 94-12397. 752p. 1994. text 89.00 (*0-7817-0143-0*) Lppncott W & W.

Priencen, Thomas. Intermediaries in International Conflict. 279p. 1992. pap. text 18.95 (*0-691-00163-4*, Pub. by Princeton U Pr) Cal Prin Full Svc.

Prier, Raymond A. Thauma Idesthai: The Phenomenology of Sight & Appearance in Archaic Greek. 312p. 1989. 49.95 (*0-8130-0919-7*) U Press Fla.

Pries, Ludger. Wege und Visionen Von Erwerbsarbeit. (Illus.). X, 433p. 1997. 76.95 (*3-631-31415-9*) P Lang Pubng.

Pries, Ludger, ed. Migration & Transportation Social Spaces. LC 98-72623. (Research in Ethnic Relations Ser.). 226p. 1998. text 61.95 (*1-84014-580-3*, Pub. by Ashgate Pub) Ashgate Pub Co.

Pries, Susan, jt. auth. see Snyder, Eleanor.

Priesack, Tim. One World, Level 1. 1994. pap. text, teacher ed. 26.80 (*0-13-157140-0*) P-H.

— One World, Level 3. 1995. pap. text, wbk. ed. 11.00 (*0-13-188145-0*) P-H.

— One World, Level 3. 1995. pap. text, teacher ed. 26.80 (*0-13-188137-X*) P-H.

Priesack, Tim & Tomscha, Terry. One World, Bk. 3. LC 91-45157. (Cassell Secondary English Course Ser.). 1993. wbk. ed. 11.90 (*0-13-635608-7*) P-H.

— One World, Coursebook 4. LC 94-26090. (English Language Teaching Ser.). 1994. 10.50 (*0-13-635616-8*) P-H.

— One World, Level 1. LC 94-16067. 128p. 1995. pap. text, student ed. 21.20 (*0-13-157132-X*) Prentice ESL.

— One World, Level 2. 1994. pap. text, teacher ed. 26.80 (*0-13-186008-9*) P-H.

— One World, Level 4. 1995. pap. text, wbk. ed. 11.00 (*0-13-188921-4*) P-H.

— One World: American English Student Book+, Level 3. 160p. 1995. pap. text, student ed. 21.20 (*0-13-188129-9*) P-H.

— One World: American English Student Book, Level 4. 160p. 1995. pap. text, student ed. 21.20 (*0-13-188160-4*) P-H.

— One World Level 2: American English Student Book. (Illus.). 128p. 1994. pap. text 21.20 (*0-13-185992-7*) P-H.

Priescha, Tim & Tomscha, Terry. One World Level 4, Level 4. 1995. pap. text, teacher ed. 26.80 (*0-13-188236-8*) P-H.

Priesing, Dorothy, jt. auth. see Zimmerman, Marian.

Priesmeyer, H. Richard. Organization & Chaos: Defining the Methods of Nonlinear Management. LC 92-7486. 272p. 1992. 59.95 (*0-89930-630-6*, PMM, Quorum Bks) Greenwood.

— Strategy: A Business Unit Simulation. 2nd ed. (C). 1992. text. write for info. (*0-538-80776-8*, GH72B8H81) S-W Pub.

Priesmeyer, Scottie. The Cheaters: The Walter Scott Murder. LC 96-61234. (Illus.). 256p. (Orig.). 1997. pap. 10.95 (*0-9654668-3-3*) Tula Pub.

— Silent Justice. LC 97-9106. 252p. 1999. pap. 12.95 (*0-9654668-4-1*, Pub. by Tula Pub) Booksource.

Priesner, H. Die Thysanopteren Europas. 1963. reprint ed. 77.00 (*90-6123-121-3*) Lubrecht & Cramer.

Priesnitz, Wendy. Markham: Canada's Community of the Future. 1990. 34.95 (*0-89781-327-8*) Am Historical Pr.

Priessnitz, Vincent. The Cold Water Cure. 48p. 1996. reprint ed. spiral bd. 12.50 (*0-7873-0677-0*) Hlth Research.

Priest. Drugs in Conception Pregnancy. 1998. pap. 16.00 (*0-7225-3594-5*) Thorsons PA.

Priest, A. W., jt. auth. see Kriege, Theodore.

Priest, Alan. Costumes from the Forbidden City. LC 74-168427. (Metropolitan Museum of Art Publications in Reprint). (Illus.). 72p. 1974. reprint ed. 23.95 (*0-405-02265-4*) Arno Press.

Priest, Alan, jt. auth. see Metropolitan Museum of Art Staff.

Priest, Carolyn. Her Reflection of His Image. 174p. 1996. pap. 6.95 (*0-89137-465-5*) Quality Pubns.

Priest, Christine, jt. auth. see Rimm, Sylvia B.

Priest, Christopher. The Extremes. LC 99-19147. 400p. 1999. text 24.95 (*0-312-20541-4*) St Martin.

***Priest, Christopher.** The Extremes. 400p. 2000. mass mkt. 12.95 (*0-446-67645-4*) Warner Bks.

Priest, Christopher. Indoctrinaire. LC 76-123984. 1970. 25.00 (*0-06-013406-2*) Ultramarine Pub.

— Prestige. 1999. 36.00 (*0-671-71924-6*) S&S Trade.

— Prestige. LC 97-19381. 416p. 1997. pap. 14.95 (*0-312-85886-8*) St Martin.

Priest, Crystal, et al. Designing Your Dream House: Learning & Using Mathematics. (Illus.). 123p. 1998. pap. text 18.00 (*0-9663943-0-5*) Fox Run Pub.

***Priest, Deborah.** Louis Laloy (1874-1944) on Dubussy, Ravel & Stravinsky. LC 99-31934. (Illus.). 340p. 1999. text 83.95 (*1-84014-628-1*, Pub. by Ashgate Pub) Ashgate Pub Co.

Priest, E. Louise, ed. see Council for National Cooperation in Aquatics Staff.

Priest, E. R. Solar Flare Magnetohydrodynamics, Vol. 1. LC 80-67417. (Fluid Mechanics of Astrophysics & Geophysics Ser.). xii, 564p. 1981. text 500.00 (*0-677-05530-7*) Gordon & Breach.

Priest, E. R., ed. Dynamics & Structure of Quiescent Solar Prominences. (C). 1988. pap. text 85.50 (*90-277-2834-8*); lib. bdg. 130.00 (*90-277-2833-X*) Kluwer Academic.

— Solar System Magnetic Fields. 1985. lib. bdg. 109.50 (*90-277-2137-8*) Kluwer Academic.

Priest, E. R. & Baker, D. N. Reconnection in the Solar Corona & Magnetospheric Substorms. (Advances in Space Research Ser.: Vol. 19). 230p. 1997. pap. 100.50 (*0-08-043292-1*, Pergamon Pr) Elsevier.

Priest, E. R. & Krishan, V., eds. Basic Plasma Processes on the Sun. (C). 1990. pap. text 76.50 (*0-7923-0880-8*); lib. bdg. 180.50 (*0-7923-0879-4*) Kluwer Academic.

***Priest, Eric & Forbes, Terry.** Magnetic Reconnection: MHD Theory & Applications. LC 99-14939. (Illus.). 451p. (C). 2000. 85.00 (*0-521-48179-1*) Cambridge U Pr.

***Priest, Eric E.** Kick Your Habit. (Illus.). 55p. 2000. 14.95 (*0-9701995-0-3*) Taran.

Priest, Eric R. & Hood, Alan W., eds. Advances in Solar System Magnetohydrodynamics. (Illus.). 451p. (C). 1991. text 74.95 (*0-521-40325-1*) Cambridge U Pr.

Priest, F. G., et al. Bacterial Diversity & Systematics. (FEMS Symposium Ser.: 75). (Illus.). 340p. (C). 1994. text 110.00 (*0-306-44832-7*, Kluwer Plenum) Kluwer Academic.

Priest, F. G., jt. auth. see Campbell, I.

***Priest, George E.** The Great Winged Monster of the Piasa Valley: The Legend of the Piasa. (Illus.). 123p. (YA). (gr. 4-12). 1998. 17.00 (*0-9678461-0-2*); pap. 15.00 (*0-9678461-1-0*) Alton Mus Hist.

Priest, Graham. In Contradiction: A Study of the Transconsistent. 294p. 1987. lib. bdg. 176.50 (*90-247-3630-7*, Pub. by M Nijhoff) Kluwer Academic.

***Priest, Graham.** Logic. (Very Short Introductions Ser.). (Illus.). 114p. 2000. pap. 8.95 (*0-19-289320-3*) OUP.

Priest, Graham, et al, eds. Paraconsistent Logic: Essays on the Inconsistent. (Analytica Ser.). 704p. 1989. 265.00 (*3-88405-058-3*) Philosophia Pr.

Priest, Harold M. Divine Comedy II: Purgatorio Notes. (Cliffs Notes Ser.). 120p. 1964. pap. 4.95 (*0-8220-0394-5*, Cliff) IDG Bks.

— Divine Comedy III: Paradiso. (Cliffs Notes Ser.). 120p. 1972. pap. 4.95 (*0-8220-0396-1*, Cliff) IDG Bks.

— Faerie Queene Notes. (Cliffs Notes Ser.). 136p. 1968. pap. 4.95 (*0-8220-0452-6*, Cliff) IDG Bks.

— Utopia & Utopian Literature Notes. (Cliffs Notes Ser.). 64p. (Orig.). 1975. pap. text 4.95 (*0-8220-1318-5*, Cliff) IDG Bks.

Priest, James D. Kirins: The Flight of the Ain. LC 91-91110. (Kirins, A Trilogy Ser.: Bk. 2). (Illus.). 336p. (Orig.). (YA). (gr. 6-12). 1992. pap. 11.95 (*0-9626225-5-9*) Yellow Pr MN.

— Kirins: The Spell of No'an. LC 90-90174. (Illus.). 470p. (Orig.). (YA). 1990. pap. 11.95 (*0-9626225-4-0*) Yellow Pr MN.

***Priest, James E.** A Religion Library Vol. 1: God's Fullness. LC 99-90807. 2000. 24.95 (*0-533-12930-3*) Vantage.

Priest, Jean, & Associates Staff. The Effective Education Secretary. LC 88-6885. (Effective School Administration Ser.: No. 2). (Illus.). 128p. 1989. pap. 12.95 (*0-88280-093-0*) ETC Pubns.

Priest, Jean H. Medical Cytogenetics & Cell Culture. 2nd ed. LC 76-7402. 364p. reprint ed. pap. 112.90 (*0-608-15343-5*, 205221300061) Bks Demand.

Priest, Jim. Family Talk. 200p. 1998. pap. 12.95 (*1-885473-98-2*) Wood N Barnes.

Priest, Joan. Sir Harry Gibbs: Without Fear Or Favour. 207p. 1995. 43.00 (*0-646-23693-8*) Gaunt.

Priest, John. Scholars & Gentlemen. 336p. (C). 1990. 78.00 (*0-86439-013-0*, Pub. by Boolarong Pubns) St Mut.

Priest, John M. Antietam: The Soldiers Battle. LC 89-5557. (Illus.). 463p. 1989. 34.95 (*0-942597-09-5*) White Mane Pub.

— Antietam: The Soldiers' Battle. LC 92-46293. (Illus.). 424p. 1994. pap. 17.95 (*0-19-508466-7*) OUP.

— Antietam Vol. 1: The Soldiers Battlefield: A Self-Guided Mini-Tour. LC 94-10648. (Illus.). 78p. (Orig.). 1994. pap. 6.95 (*0-942597-67-2*) White Mane Pub.

— Before Antietam: The Battle for South Mountain. LC 92-18927. (Illus.). 433p. 1993. 34.95 (*0-942597-37-0*) White Mane Pub.

— Into the Fight: Picketts's Charge at Gettysburg. large type ed. LC 98-7695. 280p. 1998. 34.95 (*1-57249-138-8*) White Mane Pub.

— Nowhere to Run: The Wilderness, May 4th & 5th, 1864, Vol. I. LC 95-2000. (Illus.). 316p. 1995. 29.95 (*0-942597-74-5*) White Mane Pub.

— Stephen Elliott Welch of the Hampton Legion. LC 94-10652. (Civil War Heritage Ser.: Vol. III). (Illus.). 101p. 1994. pap. 12.00 (*0-942597-66-4*, Burd St Pr) White Mane Pub.

— Victory Without Triumph: The Wilderness, May 6th & 7th, 1864. LC 96-30236. (Illus.). 368p. 1996. 34.95 (*1-57249-009-8*) White Mane Pub.

Priest, John M., ed. John T. McMahon's Diary of the 136th New York, 1861-1864. LC 92-37207. (Illus.). 148p. 1993. 24.95 (*0-942597-46-X*) White Mane Pub.

— One Surgeon's Private War: Doctor William W. Potter of the 57th New York. LC 96-19886. (Illus.). 158p. 1996. 19.95 (*1-57249-021-7*) White Mane Pub.

Priest, John M. & Brown, Robert, eds. Captain James Wren's Civil War Diary: From New Bern to Fredericksburg. (Illus.). 181p. (Orig.). 1997. reprint ed. pap. 10.00 (*0-7881-5050-2*) DIANE Pub.

Priest, John Michael. Before Antietam: The Battle for South Mountain. (Illus.). 464p. (C). 1996. pap. 17.95 (*0-19-510712-8*) OUP.

Priest, John W. Engineering Design for Producibility & Reliability. (Quality & Reliability Ser.: Vol. 14). (Illus.). 328p. 1988. text 135.00 (*0-8247-7708-5*) Dekker.

Priest, Joseph. Energy: Principles, Problems, Alternatives. 5th ed. 530p. (C). per. write for info. (*0-7872-6737-6*) Kendall-Hunt.

Priest, Joseph. Energy: Principles Problems Alternatives. 4th ed. (Illus.). 399p. (C). 1991. 52.00 (*0-201-50356-5*) Addison-Wesley.

Priest, Josiah. Slavery As It Relates to the Negro or African Race: The Light of Circumstances History & the Holy Scriptures. Grob, Gerald N., ed. LC 76-46096. (Anti-Movements in America Ser.). (Illus.). 1977. reprint ed. lib. bdg. 29.95 (*0-405-09969-X*) Ayer.

Priest, Josiah & Brown, W. S. Bible Defence of Slavery. LC 74-92439. 1851. 95.00 (*0-403-00171-4*) Scholarly.

Priest, Josiah, jt. auth. see Brown, W. S.

Priest, Judy & Schott, Judith. Leading Antenatal Classes. (Illus.). 256p. 1991. pap. text 37.50 (*0-7506-0050-0*) Buttrwrth-Heinemann.

Priest, Keith, jt. auth. see Royal, Lyssa.

Priest, Lisa. Operating in the Dark. 2000. pap. write for info. (*0-385-25722-8*) Bantam.

***Priest, Lisa.** Operating in the Dark. 336p. 2000. pap. 13.95 (*0-385-25898-4*) Doubleday.

Priest, Louise, ed. see Council for National Cooperation in Aquatics Staff.

Priest, Lyman W. The Chitty Family: Benjamin & Sarah (Palmer) Chitty & Their Descendants. LC 96-161780. 250p. 1996. pap. 77.50 (*0-608-04800-3*, AU0048500004) Bks Demand.

— The Penick Family: Descendants of Edward Penick-Penix-Pinix of St. Peter's Parish, New Kent County, Virginia. LC 82-82022. 344p. reprint ed. pap. 106.70 (*0-8357-4711-5*, AU0040700009) Bks Demand.

Priest, Mary W. Diary of Courage: Coping with Life-Threatening Illness. 176p. (Orig.). 1990. pap. 9.95 (*0-89407-099-1*) Strawberry Hill.

Priest, Nancy, ed. see Silverstein, Stuart.

Priest, Nicholas D., ed. Metals in Bone. 1985. text 225.00 (*0-85200-909-7*) Kluwer Academic.

Priest, Nicholas D. & Van De Vyver, Frank L. Trace Metals & Fluoride in Bones & Teeth. 400p. 1990. lib. bdg. 259.00 (*0-8493-6190-7*, QP88) CRC Pr.

Priest Nikolai Deputatov. Revnitel' Blagochestija 19-Go Vjeka, Episkop Teofan Zatvornik.Tr. of A/Zealot for Piety in the 19th Century Bishop Theophan the Recluse. 71p. 1971. pap. 3.00 (*0-317-29261-7*) Holy Trinity.

Priest, Patricia J. Public Intimacies: Talk Show Participants & Tell All TV. Dervin, Brenda, ed. LC 95-3929. (Communication Series). 192p. 1995. pap. text 21.95 (*1-57273-003-X*) Hampton Pr NJ.

— Public Intimacies: Talk Show Participants & Tell All TV. Dervin, Brenda, ed. LC 95-3929. (Communication Series). 192p. (C). 1995. text 49.50 (*1-57273-002-1*) Hampton Pr NJ.

Priest, Prudence, ed. & pref. see Taylor, Joseph.

Priest, R., ed. see Annual Conference for Psychosomatic Research Staff.

***Priest, Robert.** The Old Pirate of Central Park. LC 98-11913. 32p. (J). (ps-3). 1999. 15.00 (*0-395-90505-2*) HM.

Priest, Robert. Resurrection in the Cartoon. LC 97-168800. 112p. 1997. pap. 12.00 (*1-55022-313-5*, Pub. by ECW) Genl Dist Srvs.

— The Town That Got Out of Town. LC 88-46108. (Illus.). 32p. (J). 1989. 14.95 (*0-87923-786-4*) Godine.

Priest, Simon. Preparing Effective Outdoor Pursuit Leaders (People) 122p. 1987. pap. write for info. (*0-943272-18-1*) Inst Recreation Res.

Priest, Simon & Gass, Michael A. Effective Leadership in Adventure Programming. LC 97-7791. (Illus.). 336p. 1997. text 40.00 (*0-87322-637-2*, BPRI0637) Human Kinetics.

***Priest, Simon & Rohnke, Karl.** 101 of the Best Corporate Team Building Activities We Know. 114p. 1999. per. 39.95 (*0-7872-6601-9*) Kendall-Hunt.

Priest, Simon & Welch, Jim. Creating a Stress-Free Office: A Gower Management Workbook. LC 97-48984. (Management Handbook Ser.). 120p. 1998. pap. 33.95 (*0-566-07973-9*, Pub. by Gower) Ashgate Pub Co.

Priest, Simon, jt. auth. see Miles, John C.

Priest, Simon, jt. ed. see Miles, John C.

Priest, Stephen. Merleau-Ponty. LC 97-50003. (Arguments of the Philosophers Ser.). 336p. (C). 1998. 65.00 (*0-415-06263-2*) Routledge.

Priest, Stephen. Theories of the Mind. 1991. pap. 16.95 (*0-14-013069-1*, Pub. by Pnguin Bks Ltd) Trafalgar.

Priest, Stephen, ed. Hegel's Critique of Kant. (Modern Revivals in Philosophy Ser.). 241p. 1992. 61.95 (*0-7512-0064-6*, Pub. by Gregg Revivals) Ashgate Pub Co.

Priest, Stephen D. Hemispherical Projection Methods in Rock Mechanics. (Illus.). 128p. (C). 1984. pap. text 24.95 (*0-04-622007-0*) Routledge.

Priest, Susanna H. Doing Media Research: An Introduction. LC 95-36401. 256p. 1995. 48.00 (*0-8039-7292-X*); pap. 22.95 (*0-8039-7293-8*) Sage.

Priest, William L. Swear Like a Trooper: A Dictionary of Military Terms & Phrases. LC 99-89486. (Illus.). 256p. 2000. 34.95 (*1-883522-13-7*, Rockbridge) Howell Pr VA.

***Priest, William L.** Swear Like a Trooper: A Dictionary of Military Words & Phrases. 256p. 2000. 80.00 (*1-86227-064-3*, Pub. by Spellmnt Pubs) St Mut.

Priestland, Gerald. The Unquiet Suitcase. large type ed. 224p. 1991. 19.95 (*1-85089-306-3*, Pub. by ISIS Lrg Prnt) Transaction Pubs.

Priestland, J., ed. The Buraimi Dispute, 1950-1961, 10 vols. LC 98-195909. (Illus.). 6600p. 1992. reprint ed. lib. bdg. 2495.00 (*1-85207-420-5*, Pub. by Archive Editions) N Ross.

— Records of Jordan, 1919-1965, 14 vols. 10,000p. 1996. reprint ed. lib. bdg. 3995.00 (*1-85207-645-3*, Pub. by Archive Editions) N Ross.

Priestland, R. Radcliffe on Trent, 1710-1837. (C). 1985. text 50.00 (*0-7855-3206-4*, Pub. by Univ Nottingham) St Mut.

Priestley. An Inspector Calls. 1991. pap. text. write for info. (*0-582-06012-5*, Pub. by Addison-Wesley) Longman.

Priestley, Alice. Someone Is Reading This Book. (Illus.). 32p. (J). (ps-1). 1998. 18.95 (*1-55037-448-6*, Pub. by Annick) Firefly Bks Ltd.

Priestley, Alice, jt. auth. see Gilmore, Rachna.

Priestley, Anne, selected by. Animal Poems. (Jarrold Poets Ser.). 146p. 1994. 5.95 (*0-7117-0676-X*) Seven Hills Bk.

Priestley, Brian. Mingus: A Critical Biography. LC 83-26155. (Quality Paperbacks Ser.). (Illus.). 320p. 1984. pap. 11.95 (*0-306-80217-1*) Da Capo.

Priestley, Charles H. Turbulent Transfer in the Lower Atmosphere. LC 59-10427. 138p. reprint ed. pap. 42.80 (*0-608-30841-2*, 201123400074) Bks Demand.

Priestley, David T., ed. Memory & Hope: Strands of Canadian Baptist History. viii, 211p. 1996. pap. 24.95 (*0-88920-267-2*) W Laurier U Pr.

Priestley, Eric. Abracadabra. Peditto, C. Natale, ed. LC 94-12721. (Open Mouth Poetry Ser.). 118p. (Orig.). 1994. pap. 9.95 (*1-884773-02-8*) Heat Press.

An Asterisk (*) at the beginning of an entry indicates that the title is appearing for the first time.

Priestley, Herbert I. Jose de Galvez, Visitor General of New Spain, 1765-1771. LC 78-10953. (Perspectives in Latin American History Ser.: No. 1). (Illus.). xiii, 449p. 1980. reprint ed. lib. bdg. 49.50 (*0-87991-605-2*) Porcupine Pr.
— Tristan de Luna, Conquistador of the Old South: A Study of Spanish Imperial Strategy. LC 80-21168. (Perspectives in American History Ser.: No. 49). (Illus.). 215p. 1980. reprint ed. lib. bdg. 37.50 (*0-87991-375-4*) Porcupine Pr.
Priestley, Herbert I., ed. The Luna Papers, 2 vols, Set. LC 75-165803. (Select Bibliographies Reprint Ser.). 1977. reprint ed. 49.95 (*0-8369-5959-0*) Ayer.
Priestley, Hilary A. Introduction to Complex Analysis. 2nd rev. ed. (Illus.). 228p. 1990. pap. text 35.00 (*0-19-853428-0*) OUP.
— Introduction to Integration. LC 98-113423. (Illus.). 320p. 1997. text 75.00 (*0-19-850124-2*); pap. text 35.00 (*0-19-850123-4*) OUP.
Priestley, J. B. Angel Pavement. (Phoenix Fiction Ser.). iv, 494p. 1983. pap. 8.95 (*0-226-68210-2*) U Ch Pr.
— Balconinny. LC 70-99645. (Essay Index Reprint Ser.). 1977. 23.95 (*0-8369-1426-0*) Ayer.
— Bright Day. (Phoenix Fiction Ser.). vi, 364p. 1994. pap. 7.95 (*0-226-68211-0*) U Ch Pr.
— Delight. LC 70-117828. (Essay Index Reprint Ser.). 1977. 20.95 (*0-8369-2015-5*) Ayer.
— English Journey: Jubilee Edition. LC 83-40619. (Illus.). 320p. 1997. 29.95 (*0-226-68212-9*) U Ch Pr.
— English Novel. Hawke, Edward G., ed. LC 75-158906. 1971. reprint ed. 14.00 (*0-403-01311-9*) Scholarly.
— Figures in Modern Literature. LC 70-93372. (Essay Index Reprint Ser.). 1977. 19.95 (*0-8369-1772-3*) Ayer.
— The Good Companions. 1980. lib. bdg. 21.95 (*0-89967-044-X*, Harmony Rain) Buccaneer Bks.
— The Good Companions. (Phoenix Fiction Ser.). 640p. 1992. pap. 9.95 (*0-226-68223-4*) U Ch Pr.
— I for One. LC 67-23262. (Essay Index Reprint Ser.). 1977. reprint ed. 19.95 (*0-8369-0800-7*) Ayer.
— An Inspector Calls. 1948. pap. 5.25 (*0-8222-0572-6*) Dramatists Play.
Priestley, J. B. Lost Empires. 1986. mass mkt. 4.95 (*0-394-74686-4*) Random.
Priestley, J. B. The Magicians. LC 90-43613. 160p. 1996. 17.95 (*0-913720-73-9*) Beil.
— The Other Place: And Other Stories of the Same Sort. LC 72-167467. (Short Story Index Reprint Ser.). 1977. reprint ed. 20.95 (*0-8369-3993-X*) Ayer.
— Self-Selected Essays. (Essay Index Reprint Ser.). 1977. 20.95 (*0-8369-0801-5*) Ayer.
— The Shapes of Sleep. large type ed. 266p. 1990. 19.95 (*1-85089-299-7*, Pub. by ISIS Lrg Prnt) Transaction Pubs.
— Too Many People & Other Reflections. LC 71-128289. (Essay Index Reprint Ser.). 1977. 21.95 (*0-8369-2016-3*) Ayer.
Priestley, J. B. & Brett, R. L. William Hazlitt. LC 95-218347. (Writers & Their Work Ser.). 95p. (Orig.). 1996. pap. text 15.00 (*0-7463-0745-4*, Pub. by Northcote House) U Pr of Miss.
Priestley, J. B., ed. see Moore, Thomas.
Priestley, John, ed. Essayists Past & Present. LC 67-30227. (Essay Index Reprint Ser.). 1977. 20.95 (*0-8369-0802-3*) Ayer.
Priestley, John B. The English Comic Characters. (BCL1-PR English Literature Ser.). 276p. 1992. reprint ed. lib. bdg. 79.00 (*0-7812-7126-6*) Rprt Serv.
— The English Novel. (BCL1-PR English Literature Ser.). 79p. 1992. reprint ed. lib. bdg. 59.00 (*0-7812-7115-0*) Rprt Serv.
— Figures in Modern Literature. (BCL1-PR English Literature Ser.). 215p. 1992. reprint ed. lib. bdg. 79.00 (*0-7812-7066-9*) Rprt Serv.
— George Meredith. (BCL1-PR English Literature Ser.). 204p. 1992. reprint ed. lib. bdg. 79.00 (*0-7812-7597-0*) Rprt Serv.
— George Meredith. LC 70-131807. vi, 204 p. 1970. reprint ed. 25.00 (*0-403-00694-5*) Scholarly.
— Thomas Love Peacock. (BCL1-PR English Literature Ser.). 215p. 1992. reprint ed. lib. bdg. 79.00 (*0-7812-7617-9*) Rprt Serv.
Priestley, John V., jt. ed. see Polak, Julia M.
Priestley, Joseph. Autobiography of Joseph Priestley. 1975. 25.00 (*0-8386-7831-9*) Fairleigh Dickinson.
— Disquisitions Relating Matter & Spirit, 2 vols. in 1. Wellek, Rene, ed. LC 75-11248. (British Philosophers & Theologians of the 17th & 18th Centuries Ser.: Vol. 47). 1976. reprint ed. lib. bdg. 51.00 (*0-8240-1799-4*) Garland.
— Disquisitions Relating to Matter & Spirit. LC 74-26285. (History, Philosophy & Sociology of Science Ser.). 1975. reprint ed. 29.95 (*0-405-06612-0*) Ayer.
— Historical Account of the Navigable Rivers, Canals & Railways Throughout Great Britain. (Illus.). 776p. 1967. reprint ed. 60.00 (*0-7146-1067-4*, Pub. by F Cass Pubs) Intl Spec Bk.
— History & Present State of Discoveries Relating to Vision, Light, & Colours. Cohen, I. Bernard, ed. LC 80-2142. (Development of Science Ser.). (Illus.). 1981. lib. bdg. 77.95 (*0-405-13897-0*) Ayer.
— Jesus & Socrates Compared. 64p. 1994. reprint ed. pap. 9.95 (*1-56459-454-8*) Kessinger Pub.
— Letters to Burke, 1791. LC 96-34849. (Revolution & Romanticism Ser.). 1997. 65.00 (*1-85477-215-5*) Continuum.
— Political Writings. Miller, Peter, ed. LC 92-27753. (Cambridge Texts in the History of Political Thought Ser.). 189p. (C). 1993. text 49.95 (*0-521-41540-3*); pap. text 16.95 (*0-521-42561-1*) Cambridge U Pr.
— The Theological & Miscellaneous Works, 25 vols. in 26. 1974. reprint ed. pap. 1900.00 (*0-527-72751-2*) Periodicals Srv.
Priestley, Joseph & Price, Richard. Free Discussion of the Doctrine of Materialism & Necessity: 1778 Edition. 472p. 1996. reprint ed. 75.00 (*1-85506-326-3*) Bks Intl VA.
Priestley, Lee. Journeys of Faith: The Story of Preacher & Edith Lewis. (Illus.). 212p. (Orig.). 1992. pap. 14.95 (*0-9623682-2-9*) Arroyo Pr.
— Within Sound of the Bugle. LC 95-61958. (Illus.). 74p. 1996. pap. 7.95 (*1-881325-18-0*) Yucca Tree Pr.
Priestley, Lee & Peterson, Marquita. Billy the Kid: The Good Side of a Bad Man. rev. ed. LC 93-61580. (Illus.). 72p. 1993. pap. 7.95 (*1-881325-10-5*) Yucca Tree Pr.
Priestley, M. B., ed. Spectral Analysis & Time Series, 2 vols. (Probability & Mathematical Statistics Ser.). 1983. pap. text 56.00 (*0-12-564922-3*) Acad Pr.
Priestley, M. J., et al. Seismic Design & Retrofit of Bridges. LC 95-35406. (Illus.). 704p. 1996. 130.00 (*0-471-57998-X*) Wiley.
Priestley, M. J., jt. auth. see Paulay, Tom.
Priestley, Mark. Disability Politics & Community Care. LC 99-198128. 1998. pap. 29.95 (*1-85302-652-2*) Taylor & Francis.
— Practical Object-Oriented Design. LC 96-8873. 1996. write for info. (*0-07-709176-0*) McGraw.
— Practical Object-Oriented Design. (Illus.). 350p. 1996. pap., pap. text 45.00 incl. disk (*0-07-913018-6*) McGraw.
Priestley, Mary. Essays on Analytical Music Therapy. 358p. (C). 1994. pap. text 30.00 (*0-9624080-2-6*) Barcelona Pubs.
***Priestley, Mary P. & Carpenter, Jill, eds.** The Year on Sewanee Mountain: Harry Yeatman's Nature Notes. 2000. pap. 16.95 (*0-9666674-1-7*) Ione Pr.
***Priestley, Philip.** Early Watch Case Makers of England 1631-1720. (Illus.). 104p. 2000. 20.25 (*0-9668869-1-7*) Nat Assoc of Watch.
Priestley, Philip. Jail Journeys: The English Prison Experience, 1918-1986. 256p. 1989. lib. bdg. 39.95 (*0-415-03458-2*) Routledge.
Priestley, Philip, jt. auth. see McGuire, James.
Priestley, Raymond E. Antarctic Adventure: Scott's Northern Party. LC 75-317902. x, 382p. 1974. 20.00 (*0-7710-7183-3*) McCland & Stewart.
— Antarctic Adventure: Scott's Northern Party. LC 76-363375. x, 382 p. 1974. write for info. (*0-522-84069-8*) Melbourne Univ Pr.
Priestley, Susan. South Melbourne: A History. 448p. 1995. 59.95 (*0-522-84649-1*, Pub. by Melbourne Univ Pr) Paul & Co Pubs.
Priestley, Tracey B. Juggling Jobs & Kids: A Practical Guide for Today's Families. 208p. (Orig.). 1996. pap. 14.95 (*0-923000-23-2*) Summer Run Pub.
Priestley, W. M. Calculus: An Historical Approach. (Undergraduate Texts in Mathematics Ser.). (Illus.). 1995. 49.95 (*0-387-90349-6*) Spr-Verlag.
Priestley, William M. Calculus: A Liberal Art. 2nd ed. Gehring, F. W. & Halmos, P. R., eds. LC 97-41813. (Undergraduate Texts in Mathematics Ser.). (Illus.). 400p. 1998. text 49.95 (*0-387-98379-1*) Spr-Verlag.
Priestly, A. J., jt. ed. see Kolarik, L. O.
Priestly, David A. Seed Aging: Implications for Seed Storage & Persistence in the Soil. LC 85-21334. (Comstock Bk.). (Illus.). 304p. (C). 1986. text 47.50 (*0-8014-1865-8*) Cornell U Pr.
Priestly, E. B., et al. Introduction to Liquid Crystals. LC 75-34195. 356p. 1975. 69.50 (*0-306-30858-4*, Plenum Trade) Perseus Pubng.
Priestly, H. A. & Davey, B. A. Introduction to Lattices & Order. (Illus.). 256p. (C). 1990. pap. text 26.95 (*0-521-36766-2*) Cambridge U Pr.
Priestly, H. E. English Home. 1971. 20.00 (*0-584-10076-0*) Transatl Arts.
Priestly, J. B. Tom Moore's Diary. 1988. reprint ed. lib. bdg. 75.00 (*0-7812-0039-3*) Rprt Serv.
Priestly, John B. Thomas Love Peacock. LC 74-131808. 1970. reprint ed. 49.00 (*0-403-00695-3*) Scholarly.
Priestly, Joseph. Disquisitions Relating to Matter & Spirit. 356p. 1993. reprint ed. pap. 21.00 (*1-56459-314-2*) Kessinger Pub.
— The Doctrines of Heathen Philosophy. LC 87-26848. 320p. 1987. 50.00 (*0-8201-1426-X*) Schol Facsimiles.
Priestly, M. B., ed. see Rao, T. Subba.
Priestly, Michael. Performance Assessment in Education & Training: Alternative Techniques. LC 81-19598. (Illus.). 280p. 1982. 39.95 (*0-87778-181-8*) Educ Tech Pubns.
Priestly, Michael, ed. see Stearns, Brian, et al.
Priestly, Philip. Victorian Prison Lives. (Illus.). 250p. 1985. 27.50 (*0-416-34770-3*, 9594) Routledge.
Priestman, Martin. Crime Fiction: From Poe to the Present. Armstrong, Isobel & Loughrey, Bryan, eds. LC 99-217218. (Writers & Their Work Ser.). 1997. pap. 17.00 (*0-7463-0854-X*, Pub. by Northcote House) U Pr of Miss.
***Priestman, Martin.** Romantic Atheism: Poetry & Freethought, 1780-1830. LC 99-17133. (Cambridge Studies in Romanticism: No. 37). (Illus.). 355p. (C). 1999. 59.95 (*0-521-62124-0*) Cambridge U Pr.
Priestman, T. J. Cancer Chemotherapy. 3rd ed. 225p. 1989. pap. 45.00 (*0-387-19551-3*) Spr-Verlag.
***Priests for Equality Staff.** Inclusive Hebrew Scriptures Vol. III: The Writings. 1999. pap. 24.95 (*0-9644279-5-8*) Priests for Equality.
Priests for Equality Staff. The Inclusive New Testament. 470p. (Orig.). (C). 1994. pap. 19.95 (*0-9644279-0-7*) Priests for Equality.
Priests for Equality Staff, ed. The Inclusive Psalms. 204p. (Orig.). 1997. pap. 14.95 (*0-9644279-2-3*) Priests for Equality.
Prieto. Pablo's Petunias. LC 72-190269. (Illus.). 32p. (J). (gr. 3-5). 1972. lib. bdg. 9.95 (*0-87783-058-4*) Oddo.
— Pablo's Petunias. deluxe ed. LC 72-190269. (Illus.). 32p. (J). (gr. 3-5). 1972. pap. 3.94 (*0-87783-102-5*) Oddo.
Prieto, A., et al, eds. Artificial Neural Networks: International Workshop IWANN '91 Granada, Spain, September 17-19, 1991 Proceedings. (Lecture Notes in Computer Science Ser.: Vol. 540). xiii, 476p. 1991. pap. 44.00 (*0-387-54537-9*) Spr-Verlag.
— New Trends in Neural Computation: Proceedings of the International Workshop on Artificial Neural Networks IWANN '93, Sitges, Spain, June 9 - 11, 1993. (Lecture Notes in Computer Science Ser.: Vol. 686). xvi, 746p. 1993. 108.95 (*0-387-56798-4*) Spr-Verlag.
***Prieto-Diaz, Julio & Souza-Dias, Carlos R.** Strabismus. 4th ed. LC 99-23502. 554p. 1999. text 175.00 (*0-7506-7129-7*) Buttrwrth-Heinemann.
Prieto, F. English-Spanish Dictionary of Media Terms. (ENG & SPA.). 387p. 1991. pap. 52.50 (*84-86168-62-7*) IBD Ltd.
Prieto, Florencio. Diccionario Terminologico de Medios De Communicacion: Ingles-Espanol. (SPA.). 400p. 1991. pap. 55.00 (*0-7859-6392-8*, 8486168627) Fr & Eur.
Prieto, Guillermo. Algunas Memorias de Mis Tiempos. (Fondo 2000 Ser.). (SPA.). pap. 2.99 (*968-16-5216-9*, Pub. by Fondo) Continental Bk.
Prieto, J., et al, eds. Hepatobiliary Diseases. LC 91-5205. (Illus.). xxv, 1128p. 1992. 207.00 (*0-387-54326-0*) Spr-Verlag.
Prieto, Jorge. Cosecha de Esperanzas: La Peregrinacion de un Medico Mexico-Norteamericano.Tr. of Harvest of Hope. (SPA.). 184p. (Orig.). 1997. pap. 15.00 (*0-268-00823-X*) U of Notre Dame Pr.
— Harvest of Hope: The Pilgrimage of a Mexican-American Physician. LC 89-40024. 168p. (C). 1989. text 24.50 (*0-268-01087-0*) U of Notre Dame Pr.
— Harvest of Hope: The Pilgrimage of a Mexican-American Physician. LC 89-40024. 168p. (C). 1990. pap. text 16.00 (*0-268-01092-7*) U of Notre Dame Pr.
— The Quarterback Who Almost Wasn't. LC 93-29314. 128p. 1994. pap. 9.95 (*1-55885-109-7*) Arte Publico.
***Prieto, Jose Manuel.** Nocturnal Butterflies of the Russian Empire. 2000. 24.00 (*0-8021-1665-5*, Grove) Grove-Atltic.
Prieto, Mejia. Habla el Mexicano 2nd ed. (SPA.). 1997. pap. 8.98 (*968-38-0122-6*) Panorama Edit.
Prieto, Muriel H. Vocabulary Made Easy for Spanish Speakers: Teacher's Guide. LC 76-3732. 49p. 1978. pap. text 2.50 (*0-8477-2635-5*) U of PR Pr.
Prieto, Norma I. Beautiful Flowers of the Maquiladora: Life Histories of Women Workers in Tijuana. Stone, Michael & Winkler, Gabrielle, trs. from SPA. LC 97-13339. (Illus.). 128p. 1997. 20.00 (*0-292-73868-4*) U of Tex Pr.
Prieto, Norma I. Beautiful Flowers of the Maquiladora: Life Histories of Women Workers in Tijuana. Stone, Michael & Winkler, Gabrielle, trs. from SPA. LC 97-13339. (Illus.). 128p. 1997. pap. 11.95 (*0-292-73869-2*) U of Tex Pr.
***Prieto, Pamela J. H.** Cooperative Lesson Plans for Plane Geometry. 89p. 2000. 60.00 (*0-9679595-0-0*) Huge Enter.
***Prieto, Rene.** Body of Writing: Figuring Desire in Spanish American Literature. LC 99-49778. 336p. 2000. pap. 19.95 (*0-8223-2488-1*) Duke.
Prieto, Rene. Miguel Angel Asturias's Archaeology of Return. LC 92-24500. (Studies in Latin American & Iberian Literature: Vol. 7). 319p. (C). 1993. text 64.95 (*0-521-43412-2*) Cambridge U Pr.
Prieto, Ulises. Los Mascarones De Oliva. LC 78-55925. (Coleccion Espejo de Paciencia). 1978. pap. 5.00 (*0-89729-195-6*) Ediciones.
Prietula, Michael, et al, eds. Simulating Organizations: Computational Models of Institutions & Groups. LC 97-51313. (AAAI Press Ser.). (Illus.). 270p. 1998. pap. text 45.00 (*0-262-66108-X*) MIT Pr.
Prietula, Michael J., jt. ed. see Carley, Kathleen M.
Prietula, Mike, ed. AI & Theories of Groups & Organizations - Conceptual & Empirical Research: Papers from the 1993 Workshop. (Technical Reports). (Illus.). 102p. (Orig.). 1994. spiral bd. 25.00 (*0-929280-55-5*) AAAI Pr.
Prietz, G. Huf und Klauenkunde mit Hufbeschlaglehre. (GER., Illus.). 166p. 1985. 43.50 (*3-8055-4003-5*) S Karger.
Prieur, Annick. Mema's House, Mexico City: On Transvestites, Queens & Machos. LC 97-25986. 1997. pap. 16.95 (*0-226-68257-9*); lib. bdg. 50.00 (*0-226-68256-0*) U Ch Pr.
Prieur, Benoit. Atlantic Canada. 2nd ed. Ulysses Travel Guide Staff, ed. (Travel Guide Ser.). (Illus.). 304p. 1998. pap. 17.95 (*2-89464-113-3*) Ulysses Travel.
Prieur, Benoit, et al. Montreal. 2nd rev. ed. Ulysses Travel Guide Staff, ed. (Illus.). 400p. 1996. pap. text 13.95 (*2-921444-80-1*) Ulysses Travel.
Prieur, Benoit, jt. auth. see Couture, Pascale.
Prieur, Karin, jt. auth. see Prieur, Michel.
***Prieur, Michel & Prieur, Karin.** A Type Corpus of the Syro-Phoenician Tetradrachmsand Their Fractions from 57 B. C. to A. D. 253. (Illus.). 232p. 2000. 99.00 (*0-9636738-5-8*) Classical Numismatic Grp.
Priever, Beth & Robinette, Martin. Otoacoustic Emissions: From Research to Practice. (Illus.). 75p. 1997. pap. 45.00 incl. audio (*0-910329-92-3*, 0112021) Am Speech Lang Hearing.
***Priewe, Jens.** Wine: From Grape to Glass. LC 99-41865. 256p. 1999. 35.00 (*0-7892-0608-0*) Abbeville Pr.
Priez, Marie-Aude. Bassam. (Illus.). 88p. 1999. 24.95 (*2-911589-35-1*, Pub. by Editions dIndochine) BHB Intl.
Priezzhev, Alexander V., et al, eds. Optical Diagnostics of Biological Fluids & Advanced Techniques in Analytical Cytology, Vol. 2982. LC 97-175337. 510p. 1997. 107.00 (*0-8194-2393-9*) SPIE.
— Optical Diagnostics of Biological Fluids III. LC 98-227283. (Proceedings of SPIE Ser.: Vol. 3252). 204p. 1998. 69.00 (*0-8194-2691-1*) SPIE.
***Priezzhev, Alexander V., et al, eds.** Optical Diagnostics of Biological Fluids IV. 206p. 1999. pap. text 72.00 (*0-8194-3069-2*) SPIE.
Priezzhev, V. B., jt. auth. see Shirkov, D. V.
Prifitera, Auerelio & Saklofske, Don, eds. WISC III Clinical Use & Interpretation: Scientist-Practitioner Perspectives. LC 97-80798. (Illus.). 336p. 1997. text 49.95 (*0-12-564930-4*) Morgan Kaufmann.
Prifti, Peter R. Confrontation in Kosovo: The Albanian-Serb Struggle, 1969-1998. 300p. 1999. 32.50 (*0-88033-435-5*, 537, Pub. by East Eur Monographs) Col U Pr.
Prifti, William A. Securities: Public & Private Offerings, 2 vols. LC 82-24495. (Securities Law Ser.). 1983. ring bd. 250.00 (*0-317-11924-9*) West Group.
Prifti, William M. Securities: Public & Private Offerings. write for info. (*0-318-57517-5*) West Pub.
— Securities: Public & Private Offerings. 2nd ed. LC 95-39401. 1995. write for info. (*0-87632-745-5*) West Group.
— Securities: Public & Private Offerings, 2 vols., Set. 2nd ed. (Securities Ser.). 1995. ring bd. write for info. (*0-614-06274-8*) West Group.
Prigal, Alan. Federal Tax Guidebook. 2nd ed. 1972. ring bd. 225.00 (*0-8205-1589-2*) Bender.
Prigarin, S. M., jt. auth. see Ogorodnikovv, V. A.
***Prigarina, Natalia.** Mirza Ghalib: A Creative Biography. Faruqi, M. Osama, tr. 400p. 2000. 29.95 (*0-19-577945-2*) OUP.
Prigatano, George P. Principles of Neuropsychological Rehabilitation. LC RC387.5.P754 1999. (Illus.). 374p. 1999. text 49.95 (*0-19-508143-9*) OUP.
Prigatano, George P. & Schacter, Daniel L., eds. Awareness of Deficit after Brain Injury: Clinical & Theoretical Issues. (Illus.). 290p. 1991. text 52.50 (*0-19-505941-7*) OUP.
***Prigent, Helene & Rosenberg, Pierre.** Chardin: An Intimate Art. (Discoveries Ser.). 128p. 2000. pap. 12.95 (*0-8109-2864-7*, Pub. by Abrams) Time Warner.
Prigmore, Richard D. The Joy of Living. Harricharan, John et al, eds. ix, 182p. (Orig.). 1997. pap. 12.95 (*0-9661708-0-6*) Bright Angel.
Prigoff, Arline. Economics for Social Workers: Social Outcomes of Economic Globalization with Strategies for Community Action. LC 98-39721. 300p. (C). 1999. pap. text 57.95 (*0-8304-1535-1*) Thomson Learn.
Prigoff, James, jt. auth. see Chalfant, Henry.
Prigoff, James, jt. auth. see Dunitz, Robin J.
Prigogine & Rice. Advances in Chemical Physics, Vol. 111. 650p. 2000. 175.00 (*0-471-34990-9*) Wiley.
Prigogine, I. & Rice, Stuart A. Advances in Chemical Physics, Vol. 103. 412p. 1998. 215.00 (*0-471-24752-9*, Wiley-Interscience) Wiley.
— Advances in Chemical Physics, Vol. 104. 328p. 1998. 215.00 (*0-471-29338-5*, Wiley-Interscience) Wiley.
***Prigogine, I. & Rice, Stuart A.** Advances in Chemical Physics, Vol. 110. Vol. 110. 557p. 1999. 195.00 (*0-471-33180-5*) Wiley.
— Advances in Chemical Physics, Vol. 112. 656p. 2000. text 150.00 (*0-471-38002-4*) Wiley.
— Advances in Liquid Crystals: A Special Volume of Advances in Chemical Physics. LC 99-51838. 512p. 2000. 145.00 (*0-471-18083-1*) Wiley.
Prigogine, I. & Rice, Stuart A., eds. Advances in Chemical Physics, Vol. 89. (Progress in Clinical & Biological Research Ser.: Vol. 89). 422p. 1994. 220.00 (*0-471-05157-8*) Wiley.
— Advances in Chemical Physics, Vol. 90. LC 58-9935. 398p. 1995. 215.00 (*0-471-04234-X*) Wiley.
— Advances in Chemical Physics, Vol. 91. LC 58-9935. 600p. 1995. 215.00 (*0-471-12002-2*) Wiley.
— Advances in Chemical Physics, Vol. 92. LC 58-9935. (Advances in Chemical Physics Ser.: Vol. 92). 488p. 1996. 215.00 (*0-471-14320-0*, CP10, Wiley-Interscience) Wiley.
— Advances in Chemical Physics, Vol. 96. 330p. 1996. 195.00 (*0-471-15652-3*, Wiley-Interscience) Wiley.
— Advances in Chemical Physics, Vol. 98. (Advances in Chemical Physics Ser.). 623p. 1997. 195.00 (*0-471-16285-X*) Wiley.
— Advances in Chemical Physics, Vol. 102. (Advances in Chemical Physics Ser.). 395p. 1997. 215.00 (*0-471-19144-2*) Wiley.
— Advances in Chemical Physics, Vol. 109. LC 58-9935. 592p. 1999. 215.00 (*0-471-32920-7*) Wiley.
— Advances in Chemical Physics: Chemical Reactions & Their Control on the Femtosecond Time Scale, 101. (Advances in Chemical Physics Ser.). 947p. 1997. 235.00 (*0-471-18048-3*) Wiley.
— Advances in Chemical Physics: New Methods in Computational Quantum Mechanics, Vol. 93, New Methods in Computational Quantum Mech. LC 58-9935. (Advances in Chemical Physics Ser.). (Illus.). 812p. 1997. pap. 69.95 (*0-471-19127-2*) Wiley.
— Advances in Chemical Physics: Polymeric Systems, Vol. 94. LC 58-9935. (Advances in Chemical Physics Ser.). (Illus.). 752p. 1997. pap. 69.95 (*0-471-19143-4*) Wiley.
Prigogine, I. & Rice-Stuart, A., eds. Advances in Chemical Physics: Resonances, Instability, & Irreversibility, Vol. 99. LC 58-9935. (Advances in Chemical Physics Ser.). 456p. 1996. 195.00 (*0-471-16526-3*) Wiley.
Prigogine, I. & Rice, Stuart A., eds. Advances in Chemical Physics Vol. 93: New Methods in Computational Quantum Mechanics, Vol. 93. LC 58-9935. 812p. 1996. 215.00 (*0-471-14321-9*, CP10) Wiley.
— Advances in Chemical Physics Vol. 94: Polymeric Systems, Vol. 94. LC 58-9935. 742p. 1996. 195.00 (*0-471-14324-3*, CP10) Wiley.

P

Prigogine, I. & Stuart, A. R. Surface Properties: Advances in Chemical Physics, 95. (Advances in Chemical Physics Ser.: Vol. 95). 432p. 1997. pap. 69.95 (*0-471-19956-7*) Wiley.

Prigogine, I. & Stuart, A. R., eds. Advances in Chemical Physics, Vol. 95, Surface Properties, Vol. 95, Surface Properties. LC 58-9935. (Advances in Chemical Physics Ser.: Vol. 95). 432p. 1996. 195.00 (*0-471-15430-X*, Wiley-Interscience) Wiley.

Prigogine, I., et al. Chaotic Dynamics & Transport in Fluids & Plasmas. (Research Trends in Physics Ser.). 256p. 1992. 120.00 (*0-88318-923-2*) Am Inst Physics.

Prigogine, I., jt. auth. see Defay, Raymond.

Prigogine, I., jt. auth. see Kondepudi, D. K.

Prigogine, I., ed. see Leckie, Robert.

Prigogine, Ilya. End of Certainty. LC 97-3001. 1997. 24.00 (*0-684-83705-6*) S&S Trade.

— From Being to Becoming: Time & Complexity in the Physical Sciences. (Illus.). 272p. (Orig.). 1980. pap. text 14.40 (*0-7167-1108-7*) W H Freeman.

Prigogine, Ilya, et al, eds. Modern Nonlinear Optics, Vol. 2. (Advances in Chemical Physics Ser.: Vol. 85B, Pt. 2). 835p. 1993. 249.00 (*0-471-57546-1*) Wiley.

Prigogine, Ilya & Nocolis, G. Exploring Complexity. LC 88-33555. 384p. 1989. pap. text 24.95 (*0-7167-1859-6*) W H Freeman.

Prigogine, Ilya & Rice, Stuart A., eds. Advances in Chemical Physics, Vol. 77. LC 58-9955. 645p. 1990. 299.00 (*0-471-51609-0*) Wiley.

— Advances in Chemical Physics, Vol. 78. 299p. 1990. 210.00 (*0-471-52666-5*) Wiley.

— Advances in Chemical Physics, Vol. 79. 322p. 1990. 220.00 (*0-471-52768-8*) Wiley.

— Advances in Chemical Physics, Vol. 80. 489p. 1991. 275.00 (*0-471-53281-9*) Wiley.

— Advances in Chemical Physics, Vol. 81. 832p. 1992. 325.00 (*0-471-54570-8*) Wiley.

— Advances in Chemical Physics, Vol. 83. 752p. 1992. 350.00 (*0-471-54018-8*) Wiley.

— Advances in Chemical Physics, Vol. 84. 560p. 1993. 275.00 (*0-471-58726-5*) Wiley.

— Advances in Chemical Physics, Vol. 86. 433p. 1993. 220.00 (*0-471-59845-3*) Wiley.

— Advances in Chemical Physics, Vol. 100. LC 58-9935. (Advances in Chemical Physics Ser.). 688p. 1997. 195.00 (*0-471-17458-0*) Wiley.

Prigogine, Ilya, et al. Chaos: The New Science. Holte, John, ed. LC 92-34498. (Nobel Conference Ser.). (Illus.). 144p. (Orig.). 1993. pap. 21.00 (*0-8191-8934-0*); lib. bdg. 47.50 (*0-8191-8933-2*) U Pr of Amer.

Prigogine, Ilya, jt. auth. see Nicolis, G.

Prigozy, Ruth, jt. ed. see Delamater, Jerome H.

Prigozy, Ruth, ed. see Fitzgerald, F. Scott.

***Prihar, S. S., et al.** Intensive Cropping: Efficient Use of Water, Nutrients & Tillage. LC 99-39143. 264p. 1999. 79.95 (*1-56022-881-4*, Food Products); pap. 49.95 (*1-56022-899-7*, Food Products) Haworth Pr.

Prihar, S. S., jt. auth. see Jalota, S. K.

Prihoda, Deborah. "Mommy Why Are They Holding Hands?" Tuhacek, Carla & Aiken, Steve, eds. (Illus.). (J). (gr. 3-6). 1998. pap., teacher ed. 49.95 (*0-9663380-1-4*, 222) Cutting PA.

Priiatkina, Alla F., jt. auth. see Brown, James E.

Prijatel, Patricia, jt. auth. see Johnson, Sammye.

Prijatelj, Kruno. Dalmatian Painting of the Fifteenth & Sixteenth Centuries. 125p. 1983. 30.00 (*0-918660-44-0*) Ragusan Pr.

Prijs, B. Chymia Basiliensis. (Illus.). x, 126p. 1983. 17.50 (*3-8055-3786-7*) S Karger.

Prijs, Leo. Judische Tradition in der Septuaginta: Die Grammatikalische Terminologie des Abraham Ibn Esra, 2 vols. in 1. (GER.). 329p. 1987. reprint ed. write for info. (*3-487-07918-6*) G Olms Pubs.

Prikarpatskii, A. V. & Mikitiuk, I. V. Algebraic Integrability of Nonlinear Dynamical Systems on Manifolds: Classical & Quantum Aspects. LC 98-21021. (Mathematics & Its Applications Ser.). 1998. 243.00 (*0-7923-5090-1*) Kluwer Academic.

Priklonsky, Alexander. Blessed Athanasia & the Desert Ideal. 2nd ed. St. Herman of Alaska Brotherhood Staff, ed. & tr. by. from RUS. LC 89-62427. (Modern Matericon Ser.). (Illus.). 109p. 1994. pap. 5.00 (*0-938635-40-9*) St Herman Pr.

Prikry, K., jt. auth. see Jech, Thomas J.

Prikrylova, Daniela. Mathematical Modeling of the Immune Response. 224p. 1992. boxed set 125.00 (*0-8493-6753-0*, QR186) CRC Pr.

***Prilepko, A. I., et al.** Methods for Solving Inverse Problems in Mathematical Physics. LC 99-15462. (Monographs & Textbooks in Pure & Applied Mathematics). (Illus.). 744p. 1999. text 195.00 (*0-8247-1987-5*) Dekker.

Prileszky, Csilla, jt. auth. see Erdos, Jozsef.

Prilik, Pearl Ketover. Becoming an Adult Stepchild: Adjusting to a Parent's New Marriage. 160p. 1998. 22.95 (*0-88048-870-0*, 8870) Am Psychiatric.

Prilipko, L., et al, eds. Free Radicals in the Brain: Aging, Neurological, & Mental Disorders. LC 92-49895. (Illus.). xi, 181p. 1992. 89.00 (*3-540-55619-2*) Spr-Verlag.

Prill, Clarence E. Radionics - Psionics Phenomena: The Prill Method of Monitoring. Templar, Thor, ed. 75p. (Orig.). 1996. spiral bd. 18.00 (*1-57179-047-0*) Intern Guild ASRS.

Prill, D., tr. see Ahiezer, N. I. & Krein, M. G.

Prill, David. Second Coming Attractions. LC 97-36515. 1998. text 22.95 (*0-312-18173-6*) St Martin.

— Unnatural. 1995. 21.00 (*0-312-11910-0*) St Martin.

Prill, H. J. & Stauber, M., eds. Advances in Psychosomatic Obstetrics & Gynecology, Berlin 1980: Proceedings. (Illus.). 560p. 1982. pap. 59.00 (*0-387-11710-5*) Spr-Verlag.

***Prill, Ulrich.** Wer Bist Du - Alle Mythen Zerrinnen: Benito Perez Galdos Als Mythoklast und Mythograph. (Perspectivas Hispanicas Serie: Bd. 13). 302p. 1999. 45.95 (*3-906761-85-1*, Pub. by P Lang) P Lang Pubng.

Prillaman, A. Renee, et al, eds. The Tapestry of Caring: Education as Nurturance. LC 93-46343. 224p. 1994. pap. 39.50 (*1-56750-075-7*); text 73.25 (*0-89391-971-3*) Ablx Pub.

Prillaman, Helen R. A Place Apart: A Brief History of the Early Williamson Road & North Roanoke Valley Residents & Places. 187p. 1997. reprint ed. pap. 29.95 (*0-8063-4706-6*) Clearfield Co.

— Places Near the Mountain: Botetourt & Roanoke Counties, Virginia, from the Community of Amsterdam, Virginia up the Road to Catawba, on the Waters of the Catawba & Tinker Creeks, along the Carolina Road as It Approached Big Lick & Other Areas, Primarily North Roanoke. (Illus.). 397p. 1999. reprint ed. pap. 49.95 (*0-8063-4606-X*) Clearfield Co.

***Prillaman, William C.** The Judiciary & Democratic Decay in Latin America: Declining Confidence in the Rule of Law. LC 99-4603. 208p. 2000. write for info. (*0-275-96849-9*, Praeger Pubs); pap. write for info. (*0-275-96850-2*, Praeger Pubs) Greenwood.

Prilleltensky, Isaac. The Morals & Politics of Psychology: Psychological Discourse & the Status Quo. LC 93-37494. (SUNY Series, Alternatives in Psychology). 283p. (C). 1994. pap. text 21.95 (*0-7914-2038-8*) State U NY Pr.

— The Morals & Politics of Psychology: Psychological Discourse & the Status Quo. LC 93-37494. (SUNY Series, Alternatives in Psychology). 283p. (C). 1994. text 64.50 (*0-7914-2037-X*) State U NY Pr.

Prilleltensky, Isaac, jt. ed. see Fox, Dennis.

Prilliwitz, Siegmund, jt. ed. see Joachim, Guido H.

Prillwitz, Siegmund & Vollhaber, Tomas, eds. Current Trends in European Sign Language Research. (International Studies on Sign Language & the Communication of the Deaf: Vol. 9). 406p. 1990. pap. text 39.95 (*3-927731-03-X*, Pub. by Signum-Verlag) Gallaudet Univ Pr.

— Sign Language Research & Application. (International Studies on Sign Language & the Communication of the Deaf: Vol. 13). 304p. 1990. text 39.95 (*3-927731-12-9*, Pub. by Signum-Verlag) Gallaudet Univ Pr.

Prim, Bryan & Prim, Natalie F. The Natalie Years - Sharing Some Success: Municipal Government Improvements & Experiences. 224p. (Orig.). 1996. pap. 19.95 (*0-9650826-0-1*) Martin Hse.

Prim, Natalie F., jt. auth. see Prim, Bryan.

Prima. Age of Empires. 2nd ed. 240p. 1999. pap. 19.99 (*0-7615-1906-8*, Prima Games) Prima Pub.

***Prima.** Anachronox. 2000. pap. 19.99 (*0-7615-2609-9*) Prima Pub.

— Babylon. 5th ed. 1999. pap. 19.99 (*0-7615-1980-7*) Prima Pub.

— Civilization II: Test of Time: Official Strategy Guide. 1999. pap. 19.99 (*0-7615-2408-8*) Prima Pub.

— Create Your First Web Animation. 2000. pap. 24.99 (*0-7615-2443-6*) Prima Pub.

— Darkstone: Official Strategy Guide. 240p. 1999. pap. 19.99 (*0-7615-2223-9*) Prima Pub.

— Deluxe Word 2000 for Law Firms. 2000. pap. 29.99 (*0-7615-2442-8*) Prima Pub.

— Dino Crisis: Official Strategy Guide. LC 99-633281. (Illus.). 110p. 1999. pap. 12.99 (*0-7615-2239-5*, Prima Games) Prima Pub.

— Grand Theft Auto 2: Official Strategy Guide. (Illus.). 96p. 1999. pap. 12.99 (*0-7615-2455-X*, Prima Games) Prima Pub.

— Managing with Microsoft Project. 2000. pap. 39.95 (*0-7615-1986-6*) Prima Pub.

— Natural Pharmacist: Discover Natural. 176p. 1999. pap. 9.99 (*0-7615-2462-2*, Prima Health); pap. 9.99 (*0-7615-2463-0*, Prima Health); pap. 9.99 (*0-7615-2465-7*, Prima Health); pap. 9.99 (*0-7615-2467-3*, Prima Health); pap. 9.99 (*0-7615-2469-X*, Prima Health); pap. 9.99 (*0-7615-2471-1*, Prima Health) Prima Pub.

— Natural Pharmacist: Your Complete. 1999. pap. 9.99 (*0-7615-2476-2*, Prima Health) Prima Pub.

— Pac Man World. 20th anniversary ed. LC 99-67319. (Illus.). 80p. 1999. pap. 12.99 (*0-7615-2631-5*) Prima Pub.

Prima. Pharaoh. 240p. 1999. pap. 19.99 (*0-7615-2146-1*) Prima Pub.

***Prima.** Pro Pilot 2000. 1999. pap. 19.99 (*0-7615-2612-9*, Prima Games) Prima Pub.

Prima. Rollcage: Official Stragedy Guide. 1999. pap. 5.99 (*0-7615-2155-0*) Prima Pub.

— Swat 3. 1999. pap. 19.99 (*0-7615-2147-X*) Prima Pub.

***Prima.** Urban Chaos. LC 99-67119. (Illus.). 314p. 1999. pap. 12.99 (*0-7615-2607-2*) Prima Pub.

— Virtua Fighter 3TB: Official Strategy Guide. LC 99-65503. (Illus.). 128p. 1999. pap. 12.99 (*0-7615-2431-2*) Prima Pub.

— Windows 2000 Administrator's Guide. 2000. pap. 50.99 (*0-7615-2441-X*) Prima Pub.

— WWF Attitude. pap. 12.99 (*0-7615-2361-8*) Prima Pub.

Prima Comp. U. S. A. Exclusive Staff. X-Files: Official Strategy Guide. 1998. pap. text 19.99 (*0-7615-1719-7*) Prima Pub.

Prima Creative Services Staff. Big Playstation Book: Prima's Unauthorized Game Secrets, Vol. 2. 1999. pap. 14.99 (*0-7615-1645-X*) Prima Pub.

Prima Creative Services Staff. Bomberman 64. LC 97-75602. 96p. 1997. pap. 12.99 (*0-7615-1418-X*) Prima Pub.

Prima Creative Services Staff. Mortal Kombat IV: Official Arcade Game Secrets. LC 96-72647. 96p. 1997. per. 12.99 (*0-7615-1076-1*) Prima Pub.

— San Francisco Rush: Extreme Racing: The Official Strategy Guide. LC 97-69773. (Secrets of the Game Ser.). 96p. 1997. per. 12.99 (*0-7615-1313-2*) Prima Pub.

— Tactics Ogre: The Official Strategy Guide. LC 97-69922. 96p. 1998. per. 14.99 (*0-7615-1330-2*) Prima Pub.

Prima Creative Services Staff & Hill, Simon. Secret of Evermore: Authorized Power Play Guide. LC 95-71634. 160p. 1995. pap. 12.95 (*0-7615-0394-3*) Prima Pub.

Prima Creative Services Staff & Matthews, Vince. Playstation Game Secrets Unauthorized, Vol. 6. 96p. 1998. per. 12.99 (*0-7615-1643-3*) Prima Pub.

***Prima Developers Staff.** Cool Boarders 4: Official Strategy Guide. LC 99-64222. (Illus.). 95p. 1999. pap. 12.99 (*0-7615-2317-0*) Prima Pub.

Prima Development Staff. The Big Book of Retro Games. Date not set. pap. 14.99 (*0-7615-1695-6*) Prima Pub.

— Brigandine: Prima's Official Strategy Guide. 96p. 1998. per. 12.99 (*0-7615-1874-6*) Prima Pub.

***Prima Development Staff.** Castlevania: Resurrection. (Official Strategy Guides Ser.). (Illus.). 96p. 2000. pap. 12.99 (*0-7615-2504-1*) Prima Pub.

— Crash Bandicoot 3: Warped Greatest Hits. (Prima's Official Strategy Guides). (Illus.). 112p. 2000. pap. 9.99 (*0-7615-2891-1*) Prima Pub.

— Crusader: No Regret: Unauthorized Secrets. 192p. 1996. pap., per. 19.99 (*0-7615-0925-9*) Prima Pub.

— Donkey Kong 64. 1999. pap. 14.99 (*0-7615-2279-4*) Prima Pub.

— Essential Guide to Reporting in SAP R/3. (Illus.). 500p. 1999. pap. 49.99 (*0-7615-2496-7*) Prima Pub.

Prima Development Staff. Exchange Server Administrator's Guide: Administrator's Guide. 800p. 1998. 50.00 (*0-7615-1390-6*) Prima Pub.

— Extreme Warfare: Prima's Official Strategy Guide. 244p. 1998. pap. 19.99 (*0-7615-1679-4*) Prima Pub.

***Prima Development Staff.** GameShark Pocket Power Guide. 6th ed. (Official Strategy Guides Ser.). (Illus.). 384p. (YA). 2000. pap. 9.99 (*0-7615-2783-4*) Prima Pub.

— Gameshark Pocket Power Guide: Official Strategy Guide. 5th ed. 240p. 1999. pap. 9.99 (*0-7615-2184-4*) Prima Pub.

— Gauntlet Legends: Prima's Official Strategy Guide. 1999. pap. 12.99 (*0-7615-2327-8*, Prima Games) Prima Pub.

— Gran Turismo Greatest Hits. (Official Strategy Guides Ser.). (Illus.). 128p. 2000. pap. 9.99 (*0-7615-2892-X*) Prima Pub.

Prima Development Staff. Hands On. (Illus.). 500p. 1998. pap. 40.00 (*0-7615-1415-5*) Prima Pub.

***Prima Development Staff.** Hands-On SQL Server 7 with Access. 500p. 2000. pap. 40.00 (*0-7615-1386-8*) Prima Pub.

— Hot Wheels: Official Strategy Guide. 1999. pap. 12.99 (*0-7615-2291-3*, Prima Games) Prima Pub.

— Hybrid Heaven: Official Strategy Guide. 1999. pap. 14.99 (*0-7615-2273-5*, Prima Games) Prima Pub.

— Install, Configure & Customize LinuxPPC. (Illus.). 2000. pap. 39.99 (*0-7615-2685-4*, Prima Tech) Prima Pub.

— Jet Force Gemini. 1999. pap. 12.99 (*0-7615-2276-X*) Prima Pub.

— Jet Moto 3: Official Strategy Guide. 1999. pap. 12.99 (*0-7615-2286-7*) Prima Pub.

— Knockout Kings 2000: Official Strategy Guide. LC 99-63705. (Illus.). 91p. 1999. pap. 12.99 (*0-7615-2288-3*) Prima Pub.

— Legacy of Kain: Soul Reaver (DC) LC 98-73122. (Official Strategy Guides Ser.). (Illus.). 128p. (YA). 2000. pap. 14.99 (*0-7615-2757-5*, Prima Tech) Prima Pub.

— Madden NFL 2000: Official Strategy Guide. 1999. pap. 12.99 (*0-7615-2293-X*, Prima Games) Prima Pub.

— Metal Gear Solid Greatest Hits. (Prima's Official Strategy Guides). (Illus.). 104p. 2000. pap. 9.99 (*0-7615-2889-X*) Prima Pub.

— Nascar 2000: Official Strategy Guide. 1999. pap. 12.99 (*0-7615-2290-5*) Prima Pub.

— NBA Live 2000: Official Strategy Guide. 1999. pap. 14.99 (*0-7615-2292-1*) Prima Pub.

— Need for Speed: Motor City. 1999. pap. 19.99 (*0-7615-2322-7*) Prima Pub.

— NFL Blitz 2000: Prima's Official Strategy Guide. 1999. pap. 12.99 (*0-7615-2325-1*, Prima Games) Prima Pub.

— NHL 2000: Official Strategy Guide. 1999. pap. 12.99 (*0-7615-2294-8*) Prima Pub.

Prima Development Staff. Pokemon (Blue) Official Strategy Guide. 96p. 1999. pap. 12.99 (*0-7615-2282-4*, Prima Games) Prima Pub.

***Prima Development Staff.** Pokemon Snap. 1999. pap. 12.99 (*0-7615-2275-1*) Prima Pub.

— Privateer 2: The Darkening: Origin's Strategy Guide. LC 96-70912. 288p. 1996. pap., per. 19.99 (*0-7615-0934-8*) Prima Pub.

— Quake II: Official Strategy Guide. LC 99-62819. (Illus.). 81p. 1999. pap. 12.99 (*0-7615-2200-X*) Prima Pub.

— Ready 2 Rumble: Prima's Official Strategy Guide. 1999. pap. 12.99 (*0-7615-2328-6*) Prima Pub.

— Resident Evil 2 Greatest Hits. (Prima's Official Strategy Guides). (Illus.). 160p. 2000. pap. 9.99 (*0-7615-2888-1*) Prima Pub.

— Road Rash: Official Strategy Guide. LC 99-63704. (Illus.). 127p. 1999. pap. 14.99 (*0-7615-2289-1*) Prima Pub.

— Set up Your Home Network. (In a Weekend Ser.). 400p. 2000. pap. 19.99 (*0-7615-2507-6*) Prima Pub.

— Sonic Adventure: Prima's Official Strategy Guide. 1999. pap. 12.99 (*0-7615-2337-5*, Prima Games) Prima Pub.

— Star Wars: Episode 1 Racer. (Illus.). 112p. 2000. pap. 14.99 (*0-7615-2946-2*) Prima Pub.

— Starshot: Official Strategy Guide. 1999. pap. text 12.99 (*0-7615-2295-6*) Prima Pub.

Prima Development Staff. Syndicate Wars Unauthorized Secrets. LC 96-67999. 240p. 1996. per. 19.99 (*0-7615-0089-8*) Prima Pub.

***Prima Development Staff.** Theme Park, Vol. 2. 1999. pap. text 19.99 (*0-7615-2287-5*) Prima Pub.

Prima Development Staff. Thousand Arms. 1999. pap. text 14.99 (*0-7615-2274-3*) Prima Pub.

***Prima Development Staff.** Thrill Kill: Official Strategy Guide. 96p. 1998. pap. 12.99 (*0-7615-1902-5*) Prima Pub.

Prima Development Staff. Tomorrow Never Dies 007. LC 99-61524. (Illus.). 81p. 1999. pap. 14.99 (*0-7615-2144-5*) Prima Pub.

— Tonic Trouble: Prima's Official Strategy Guide. LC 98-67880. (Prima Games Ser.). 96p. 1999. pap. 12.99 (*0-7615-1912-2*, Prima Games) Prima Pub.

***Prima Development Staff.** Twisted Metal, Vol. 4. LC 99-64218. (Illus.). 80p. 1999. pap. 12.99 (*0-7615-2318-9*) Prima Pub.

— Twisted Metal Compendium. 96p. 1999. pap. 12.99 (*0-7615-2285-9*) Prima Pub.

Prima Development Staff. Ultima 9: The Official Strategy Guide. 240p. 1998. pap., per. 19.99 (*0-7615-0040-5*) Prima Pub.

Prima Development Staff. Ultima Online: The Official Strategy Guide. LC 96-71344. 304p. 1997. pap., per. 19.99 (*0-7615-0926-7*) Prima Pub.

— Vandal Hearts II. (Official Strategy Guides Ser.). 1999. pap. 14.99 (*0-7615-2503-3*) Prima Pub.

— Xena: Warrior Princess: Prima's Official Strategy Guide. 1999. pap. 12.99 (*0-7615-2349-9*, Prima Games) Prima Pub.

— Legend of Zelda: The Ocarina of Time: Prima's Official Game Secrets. LC 97-66163. 96p. 1998. pap., per. 14.99 (*0-7615-0920-8*) Prima Pub.

***Prima Development Staff, ed.** Big Code Book. 1999. pap. 14.99 Prima Pub.

— E-Commerce Solutions with MySQL. 2000. pap. 39.99 (*0-7615-2445-2*) Prima Pub.

***Prima Development Staff & Murray, Katherine.** Learn Quickbooks 6 in a Weekend. LC 98-66465. 342p. 1998. per. 19.99 (*0-7615-1384-1*) Prima Pub.

***Prima Development Staff, et al.** Perfect Dark. LC 99-63698. (Official Strategy Guides Ser.). 174p. 2000. pap. 14.99 (*0-7615-2280-8*) Prima Pub.

— Pokemon Stadium: Prima's Official Strategy Guide. LC 99-63696. (Illus.). 111p. 2000. pap. 12.99 (*0-7615-2278-6*) Prima Pub.

— Resident Evil CODE: Veronica. LC 00-10076. (Official Strategy Guides Ser.). (Illus.). 144p. 2000. pap. 14.99 (*0-7615-2768-0*) Prima Pub.

Prima Game Secrets Staff. Crash Bandicoot 2 - Cortex Strikes Back: Prima Game Secrets. LC 97-69796. 96p. 1997. per. 12.99 (*0-7615-1319-1*) Prima Pub.

Prima, P., jt. auth. see Desikachary, T. V.

***Prima Pub Staff.** Army Men Sarge's Heroes: Official Strategy Guide. LC 99-65390. (Illus.). 111p. 1999. pap. 12.99 (*0-7615-2434-7*, Prima Games) Prima Pub.

— Battletanx II: Global Assault Official Strategy Guide. LC 99-65505. (Illus.). 117p. 1999. pap. 12.99 (*0-7615-2433-9*, Prima Games) Prima Pub.

— Big Code Book: Winter 1999 Edition. 1999. pap. 14.99 (*0-7615-2350-2*) Prima Pub.

— Flight Combat: Thunder over Europe. 2000. pap. 19.99 (*0-7615-2492-4*, Prima Games) Prima Pub.

— Flight Unlimited III Official Strategy Guide. LC 99-65713. (Illus.). 206p. 1999. pap. 19.99 (*0-7615-2494-0*) Prima Pub.

— Mortal Kombat Gold: Official Strategy Guide. LC 99-65216. (Illus.). 95p. 1999. pap. 12.99 (*0-7615-2329-4*) Prima Pub.

— Natural Pharmacist. 1999. text 491.32 (*0-7615-9016-1*) Prima Pub.

— Organize Your Business Finances with QuickBooks 99 in a Weekend. LC 98-68643. (In a Weekend Ser.). (Illus.). 342p. 1999. pap. 19.99 (*0-7615-2031-7*) Prima Pub.

— Silver. LC 99-65914. (Illus.). 206p. 1999. pap. 19.99 (*0-7615-2497-5*) Prima Pub.

— System Shock 2: Official Strategy Guide. 1999. pap. 19.99 (*0-7615-2493-2*) Prima Pub.

— WCW Mayhem. LC 99-62513. (Illus.). 77p. 1999. pap. 12.99 (*0-7615-2196-8*, Prima Games) Prima Pub.

***Prima Pub Staff, ed.** Indiana Jones & the Infernal Machine. 240p. 1999. pap. 19.99 (*0-7615-2195-X*) Prima Pub.

Prima Publication Staff. Oregon Trail II: Official Strategy Guide. 1995. pap. text 19.95 (*0-7615-0376-5*) Prima Pub.

***Prima Publishers Staff.** Turbo Tax Fast & Easy. 1999. pap. 16.99 (*0-7615-2303-0*) Prima Pub.

***Prima Publishers Staff, et al.** Centipede: Prima's Official Strategy Guide. LC 99-66897. (Illus.). 130p. (J). 1999. pap. 14.99 (*0-7615-2633-1*) Prima Pub.

Prima Publishing. Thief - The Dark Project: Prima's Official Strategy Guide. (Secrets of the Games Ser.). 244p. 1998. per. 19.99 (*0-7615-1747-2*) Prima Pub.

***Prima Publishing Staff.** Abomination: The Nemesis Project. (Illus.). 240p. 1999. pap. 19.99 (*0-7615-2606-4*) Prima Pub.

— Advanced Genealogy Techniques. 2000. pap. 32.99 (*0-7615-2449-5*) Prima Pub.

Prima Publishing Staff. Alien Resurrection: Prima's Official Strategy Guide. LC 98-65314. 96p. 2000. per. 14.99 (*0-7615-1569-0*) Prima Pub.

— Batman & Robin: Prima's Official Strategy Guide. LC 98-65940. 96p. 1998. per. 12.99 (*0-7615-1641-7*) Prima Pub.

— Battleship/Risk: Prima's Official Strategy Guide. 96p. 1998. pap. 9.99 (*0-7615-1735-9*) Prima Pub.

An Asterisk (*) at the beginning of an entry indicates that the title is appearing for the first time.

— Battlespire: Elder Scrolls Leg. 1997. pap. 19.99 (*0-7615-1416-3*) Prima Pub.

***Prima Publishing Staff.** Big Nintendo Book. (Official Strategy Guides Ser.). (Illus.). 192p. (YA). 2000. pap. 14.99 (*0-7615-2799-0*) Prima Pub.

Prima Publishing Staff. Blade Runner: The Unauthorized Strategy Guide. LC 97-69759. 168p. 1998. per. 19.99 (*0-7615-1303-5*) Prima Pub.

***Prima Publishing Staff.** Braveheart. 1999. pap. 19.99 (*0-7615-2063-5*) Prima Pub.

Prima Publishing Staff. Caesar 3: Prima's Official Strategy Guide. LC 98-65449. 244p. 1998. per. 19.99 (*0-7615-1577-1*) Prima Pub.

***Prima Publishing Staff.** Castlevania. LC 99-66236. (Illus.). 126p. 1999. pap. 12.99 (*0-7615-2500-9*) Prima Pub.

— Commandos: Beyond the Call of Duty - Prima's Official Strategy Guide. LC 99-70396. (Illus.). 159p. 1999. pap. 16.99 (*0-7615-2127-5*) Prima Pub.

Prima Publishing Staff. Custom Diablo with Moves Card. 1998. pap. write for info. (*0-7615-1619-0*) Prima Pub.

— Custom Starcraft Hint Book. 1998. pap. write for info. (*0-7615-1421-X*) Prima Pub.

— Custom Tekken 3 with Cards. Date not set. pap. write for info. (*0-7615-1621-2*) Prima Pub.

— Custom Tekken 3 with Poster. 1998. pap. write for info. (*0-7615-1638-7*) Prima Pub.

— Dark Forces, Official Strategy Guide. 1995. pap. text 19.95 (*0-7615-9993-2*) Prima Pub.

— Dark Side of the Moon: Prima's Official Strategy Guide. LC 98-66588. 244p. 1998. per. 19.99 (*0-7615-1737-5*) Prima Pub.

***Prima Publishing Staff.** Die Hard 64. (Illus.). 96p. 2000. pap. 12.99 (*0-7615-2597-1*) Prima Pub.

Prima Publishing Staff. Dig Official Strategy Guide. 1995. pap. text 19.95 (*0-7615-9996-7*) Prima Pub.

Prima Publishing Staff. Duke Nukem 3D: Unauthorized Game Secrets. LC 96-68689. 272p. 1996. pap., per. 14.99 (*0-7615-0783-3*) Prima Pub.

— Dungeon Keeper: Prima's Official Strategy Guide. 240p. 1999. pap. 19.99 (*0-7615-1805-3*) Prima Pub.

— Fighting Force 2. LC 99-67119. (Illus.). 94p. 1999. pap. 14.99 (*0-7615-2602-1*) Prima Pub.

Prima Publishing Staff. Final Fantasy: Prima's Official Strategy Guide. 1995. pap. text 14.95 (*0-7615-9992-4*) Prima Pub.

— Final Fantasy: Prima's Official Strategy Guide, 5. (Secrets of the Game Ser.). 240p. 1998. per. 19.99 (*0-7615-1698-0*) Prima Pub.

— Full Throttle Official Strategy Guide. 1996. pap. text 19.99 (*0-7615-9994-0*) Prima Pub.

— Galapagos: The Official Strategy Guide. 1997. pap. 19.99 (*0-7615-0598-9*) Prima Pub.

— Game Boy. 1998. pap. 12.99 (*0-7615-1707-3*) Prima Pub.

— Game Boy Pocket Power Guide: Unauthorized. LC 97-69762. (Secrets of the Game Ser.). 96p. 1997. per. 7.99 (*0-7615-1302-7*) Prima Pub.

***Prima Publishing Staff.** Games Troubleshooting Guide Vol. 2: More Simple Solutions to Common Problems. 160p. 1998. per. 7.99 (*0-7615-1708-1*) Prima Pub.

— German Oddworld. 1999. pap. write for info. (*3-933841-13-5*) Prima Pub.

Prima Publishing Staff. Gran Turismo: Prima Guide To. LC 98-65938. 128p. 1998. per. 14.99 (*0-7615-1655-7*) Prima Pub.

***Prima Publishing Staff.** Half-Life Opposing Forces. (Illus.). 240p. 1999. pap. 19.99 (*0-7615-2590-4*) Prima Pub.

Prima Publishing Staff. Heart of Darkness: Unauthorized Game Secrets. 1996. pap. text 19.99 (*0-7615-0548-2*) Prima Pub.

***Prima Publishing Staff.** Juggernaut. LC 99-67115. (Illus.). 73p. 1999. pap. 12.99 (*0-7615-2593-9*) Prima Pub.

Prima Publishing Staff. Kartia: Prima's Official Strategy Guide. LC 98-65922. 96p. 1998. per. 14.99 (*0-7615-1682-4*) Prima Pub.

— Legacy of Kain: Soul Reaver: Prima's Unauthorized Game Secrets. 96p. 1999. per. 12.99 (*0-7615-1796-0*, Prima Games) Prima Pub.

— Longbow No. 2: The Official Strategy Guide. LC 97-69335. 304p. 1997. per. 19.99 (*0-7615-1206-3*) Prima Pub.

— Metal Gear Solid: Prima's Unauthorized Strategy Guide. (Secrets of the Games Ser.). 144p. (gr. 7). 1998. per. 12.99 (*0-7615-1766-9*) Prima Pub.

***Prima Publishing Staff.** Mission Impossible. (Official Strategy Guides Ser.). (Illus.). 94p. (YA). 1999. pap. 12.99 (*0-7615-2758-3*) Prima Pub.

— Mortal Kombat: Mythologies: Special. 96p. 2000. pap. 14.99 (*0-7615-2326-X*) Prima Pub.

Prima Publishing Staff. Mortal Kombat IV: Official Game Secrets. LC 96-72648. (Secrets of the Game Ser.). 96p. 1998. per. 12.99 (*0-7615-1077-X*) Prima Pub.

— Mortal Kombat Mythology: Official Game Secrets. LC 97-69326. (Secrets of the Game Ser.). 96p. 1997. per. 12.99 (*0-7615-1215-2*) Prima Pub.

— Mortal Kombat 2: Custom Power Play Guide. 1995. 9.95 (*1-55958-839-X*) Prima Pub.

— Nightmare Creatures 64: Prima's Official Strategy Guide. LC 98-73121. (Secrets of the Game Ser.). 96p. 1998. per. 12.99 (*0-7615-1795-2*) Prima Pub.

— Nintendo 64 Game Secrets Unauthorized, Vol. 3. 144p. 1998. per. 12.99 (*0-7615-1464-3*) Prima Pub.

— Nintendo 64 Pocket Power Guide Vol. 2: Unauthorized. LC 96-70916. (Secrets of the Game Ser.). 96p. 1997. per. 7.99 (*0-7615-1121-0*) Prima Pub.

— Nintendo 64 Unauthorized Game Secrets, Vol. 2. 144p. 1997. per. 12.99 (*0-7615-1155-5*) Prima Pub.

— Nuclear Strike: Official Game Secrets. LC 97-69327. 112p. 1997. per. 12.99 (*0-7615-1214-4*) Prima Pub.

— Ogre Battle: Official Secrets & Solutions. LC 97-68840. 144p. 1997. per. 12.99 (*0-7615-1224-1*) Prima Pub.

***Prima Publishing Staff.** Omikron. LC 99-67120. (Illus.). 175p. 1999. pap. 19.99 (*0-7615-2605-6*) Prima Pub.

Prima Publishing Staff. Penny Racers: Prima's Official Strategy Guide. 80p. 1999. per. 12.95 (*0-7615-1894-0*, Prima Games) Prima Pub.

***Prima Publishing Staff.** Planet of the Apes. (Illus.). 96p. 2000. pap. 12.99 (*0-7615-2596-3*) Prima Pub.

Prima Publishing Staff. PlayStation Game Secrets Unauthorized, Vol. 5. 144p. 1998. per. 12.99 (*0-7615-1463-5*) Prima Pub.

— PlayStation Pocket Power Guide, Vol. 3. LC 96-70918. Vol. 3. 96p. 1998. per. 7.99 (*0-7615-1466-X*) Prima Pub.

— PlayStation Pocket Power Guide: Unauthorized. LC 96-70918. 96p. 1996. pap. 7.99 (*0-7615-0973-9*) Prima Pub.

— Playstation Pocket Power Guide Vol. 2: Unauthorized. LC 96-70918. (Secrets of the Game Ser.). 96p. 1997. per. 7.99 (*0-7615-1120-2*) Prima Pub.

— PlayStation Power Pocket Guide Vol. 4: Prima's Unauthorized Game Secrets. LC 96-70918. (Games Ser.). 96p. 1998. per. 7.99 (*0-7615-1818-5*) Prima Pub.

— Prey: Prima's Unauthorized Game Secrets. 244p. 1998. per. 19.99 (*0-7615-1417-1*) Prima Pub.

— Prima Hurt Book. 1997. pap. write for info. (*0-7615-9988-6*); pap. write for info. (*0-7615-9989-4*) Prima Pub.

— Prince of Persia 3D: Prima's Official Strategy Guide. 244p. 1998. per. 19.99 (*0-7615-1729-4*) Prima Pub.

***Prima Publishing Staff.** Programming Techniques in EMACS. 400p. 2000. pap. 39.99 (*0-7615-2446-0*) Prima Pub.

Prima Publishing Staff. Rebel Assault II: Official Strategy Guide. 1996. pap. 19.95 (*0-7615-9995-9*) Prima Pub.

***Prima Publishing Staff.** Requiem: Avenging Angel. LC 98-73113. (Illus.). 369p. 1999. pap. 19.99 (*0-7615-1793-6*) Prima Pub.

Prima Publishing Staff. Revenant: Prima's Official Strategy Guide. LC 98-66749. (Secrets of the Game Ser.). (Illus.). 244p. 1999. per. 19.99 (*0-7615-1746-4*) Prima Pub.

— Sega Saturn Pocket Power Guide Vol. 2: Unauthorized. LC 96-70917. (Secrets of the Game Ser.). 96p. 1997. per. 7.99 (*0-7615-1122-9*) Prima Pub.

— Silent Hunter Official Secrets & Solutions. 1996. pap. text 14.99 (*0-7615-0144-4*) Prima Pub.

***Prima Publishing Staff.** Sim Theme Park. LC 99-67744. 1999. pap. 14.99 (*0-7615-2599-8*) Prima Pub.

Prima Publishing Staff. South Park. 1998. pap. 12.99 (*0-7615-2071-6*, Prima Games) Prima Pub.

— StarCon: Prima's Official Strategy Guide, Vol. 4. 244p. 1998. per. 19.99 (*0-7615-1594-1*) Prima Pub.

— Suikoden 2. 96p. 1998. pap. 14.99 (*0-7615-1768-5*) Prima Pub.

— Tekken 3: Unauthorized Game Secrets. LC 97-67338. 160p. 1998. per. 12.99 (*0-7615-1185-7*) Prima Pub.

***Prima Publishing Staff.** Tomb Raider: The Last Revolution. LC 99-61524. (Illus.). 175p. 1999. pap. 14.99 (*0-7615-2604-8*) Prima Pub.

— Tribes Extreme. 1999. pap. 19.99 (*0-7615-2611-0*) Prima Pub.

Prima Publishing Staff. 20,000 Leagues: The Adventure Continues: Prima's Official Strategy Guide. 244p. 1999. pap. 19.99 (*0-7615-1738-3*) Prima Pub.

— Ultima Collection: The Offical Strategy Guide. LC 97-76270. 320p. 1998. pap. 19.99 (*0-7615-1485-6*) Prima Pub.

— Ultimate Nintendo 64 Pocket Power Guide: Prima's Official Strategy Guide. LC 98-73123. (Secrets of the Game Ser.). 96p. 1998. per. 7.99 (*0-7615-1794-4*) Prima Pub.

— Uprising 2: Prima's Official Strategy Guide. LC 98-73114. 244p. 1998. per. 19.99 (*0-7615-1792-8*) Prima Pub.

***Prima Publishing Staff.** Warzone 2100: Official Strategy Guide. (Illus.). 206p. 1999. pap. 19.99 (*0-7615-2062-7*) Random.

Prima Publishing Staff. Wing Commander - Prophecy: The Official Strategy Guide. LC 97-69345. 256p. 1997. per. 19.99 (*0-7615-1207-1*) Prima Pub.

***Prima Publishing Staff.** The X-Files. LC 99-67117. (Illus.). 80p. 1999. pap. 12.99 (*0-7615-2595-5*) Prima Pub.

Prima Publishing Staff. Zork Grand Inquisitor: Unauthorized Game Secrets. LC 97-69334. 208p. 1997. per. 16.99 (*0-7615-1230-6*) Prima Pub.

Prima Publishing Staff, contrib. by. War Gods Official Game Secrets. 96p. 1997. per. 12.99 (*0-7615-1080-X*) Prima Pub.

***Prima Publishing Staff, ed.** Army Men, Vol. 2. LC 99-70165. 1999. pap. 19.99 (*0-7615-2075-9*) Prima Pub.

— Black & White. (Official Strategy Guides Ser.). (Illus.). 240p. 2000. pap. 19.99 (*0-7615-2485-1*) Prima Pub.

— Candlemaking for Fun & Profit. (For Fun & Profit Ser.). (Illus.). 2000. pap. 19.99 (*0-7615-2040-6*) Prima Pub.

— Jewelry Making for Fun & Profit. (For Fun & Profit Ser.). (Illus.). 2000. pap. 19.99 (*0-7615-2044-9*) Prima Pub.

— Relocating to Atlanta & Surrounding Areas. (Relocating Ser.). (Illus.). 400p. 2000. pap. 16.95 (*0-7615-2564-5*) Prima Pub.

— Relocating to Houston & Surrounding Areas. (Relocating Ser.). (Illus.). 400p. 2000. pap. 16.95 (*0-7615-2565-3*) Prima Pub.

— Relocating to Los Angeles & Orange County. (Relocating Ser.). 400p. 2000. pap. 16.95 (*0-7615-2566-1*) Prima Pub.

— Relocating to Seattle & Surrounding Areas. (Relocating Ser.). 400p. 2000. pap. 16.95 (*0-7615-2568-8*) Prima Pub.

— Sports Car GT: Official Strategy Guide. LC 98-68702. (Illus.). 160p. 1999. pap. 12.99 (*0-7615-2056-2*) Prima Pub.

— Team Fortress 2. 240p. 1999. pap. 19.99 (*0-7615-2145-3*) Prima Pub.

***Prima Publishing Staff & Bell, Joe Grant.** Ground Control: Prima's Official Strategy Guide. (Illus.). 240p. 2000. pap. 19.99 (*0-7615-2591-2*) Prima Pub.

Prima Publishing Staff & Knight, Michael. Rainbow Six: Prima's Official Strategy Guide. LC 98-66589. 244p. 1998. pap. 19.99 (*0-7615-1736-7*) Prima Pub.

Prima Publishing Staff & Mathews, Vince. Quake 64: The Official Strategy Guide. LC 97-69347. 112p. 1998. per. 12.99 (*0-7615-1216-0*) Prima Pub.

Prima Publishing Staff & Wright, Esther. Why I Teach: Inspirational True Stories from Teachers Who Make a Difference. LC 99-30814. 208p. 2000. pap. 12.95 (*0-7615-1099-0*) Prima Pub.

***Prima Publishing Staff, et al.** Shadow Madness: Official Strategy Guide, 1999 Edition. (Illus.). 128p. 1999. pap. 14.99 (*0-7615-2125-9*) Prima Pub.

Prima Publishing Staff, et al. Yoshi's Story: Prima's Unauthorized Game Secrets, No. 64. 96p. 1998. pap. 12.99 (*0-7615-1177-6*) Prima Pub.

Prima Publishing Staff, jt. auth. see Walher, Mark.

Prima Publishing Staff, jt. auth. see Ward, Kip.

***Prima Staff.** Desert Fighters. 1999. pap. 19.99 (*0-7615-2613-7*, Prima Games) Prima Pub.

— Diplomacy. (Official Strategy Guides Ser.). (Illus.). 200p. 1999. pap. text 19.99 (*0-7615-2634-X*, Prima Games) Prima Pub.

— F/A-18. 1999. pap. 19.99 (*0-7615-2499-1*, Prima Games) Prima Pub.

— Hexen 64: Official Secrets & Solutions. LC 97-67540. 128p. 1997. per. 12.99 (*0-7615-1203-9*) Prima Pub.

— Nintendo 64 Game Secrets 1999. LC 99-209836. (Illus.). 144p. 1999. pap. 14.99 (*0-7615-2103-8*) Prima Pub.

— Pro Pilot 4. (Official Strategy Guides Ser.). 240p. (YA). 2000. pap. 19.95 (*0-7615-2614-5*) Prima Pub.

— Sega Dreamcast Collection. LC 99-67317. (Official Strategy Guides Ser.). (Illus.). 120p. (YA). 1999. pap. 14.99 (*0-7615-2620-X*) Prima Pub.

Prima Staff. Seven Kingdoms II: Official Strategy Guide. 1999. pap. 19.99 (*0-7615-2208-5*) Prima Pub.

***Prima Staff.** Thief Gold: Prima's Official Strategy Guide. 1999. pap. 0.00 (*0-7615-2619-6*) Prima Pub.

— Tomb Raider: The Last Revelation. 1999. pap. 12.99 (*0-7615-1375-2*, Pub. by Prima Pub) Random House.

— Tribes 2. 240p. (YA). 2000. pap. 19.99 (*0-7615-2615-3*) Prima Pub.

— Worms Armageddon. LC 99-67745. (Official Strategy Guides Ser.). (Illus.). 112p. 1999. pap. 12.99 (*0-7615-2598-X*) Prima Pub.

— WWF: Wrestlemania 2000. 1999. pap. 12.99 (*0-7615-2651-X*, Prima Games) Prima Pub.

***Prima Staff, contrib. by.** Fifa 2000. 96p. 1999. 12.99 (*0-7615-1352-3*) Prima Pub.

***Prima Staff & Cohen, Mark.** Lara Croft: The Art of Virtual Seduction. LC 00-10073. (Official Strategy Guides Ser.). (Illus.). 139p. (YA). 2000. pap. 19.99 (*0-7615-2696-X*) Prima Pub.

***Prima Staff & Dobson, Linda.** Homeschoolers' Success Stories: 15 Adults & 12 Young People Share the Impact That Homeschooling... 224p. 2000. pap. 16.95 (*0-7615-2255-7*) Prima Pub.

***Prima Temp Authors.** Arcanum. (Official Strategy Guides Ser.). (Illus.). 240p. (YA). 2000. pap. 19.99 (*0-7615-2800-8*) Prima Pub.

Prima Temp Authors. GameShark Pocket Power Guide Code Revolution. LC 98-65361. 96p. 1998. per. 7.99 (*0-7615-1550-X*) Prima Pub.

***Prima Temp Authors.** Gunship 3. (Prima's Official Strategy Guides). (Illus.). 240p. 2000. pap. 19.99 (*0-7615-2671-4*) Prima Pub.

— Homeworld Cataclysm. (Illus.). 240p. 2000. pap. 19.99 (*0-7615-2592-0*) Prima Pub.

— House of the Dead 2: Official Strategy Guide. (Illus.). (J). 1999. pap. 9.99 (*0-7615-2417-7*) Prima Pub.

— Jet Moto 2124. (Official Strategy Guides Ser.). (Illus.). 112p. (YA). 2000. pap. 12.99 (*0-7615-2794-X*) Prima Pub.

— M1 Tank Platoon 3. (Illus.). 240p. 2000. pap. 19.99 (*0-7615-2670-6*) Prima Pub.

— Ogre Battle 64. (Official Strategy Guides Ser.). (Illus.). 144p. (YA). 2000. pap. 14.99 (*0-7615-2784-2*, Prima Tech) Prima Pub.

— X-Com Alliance. (Illus.). 240p. 2000. pap. 19.99 (*0-7615-2667-6*) Prima Pub.

***Prima Temp Authors, ed.** Big PlayStation Book 2000. (Official Strategy Guides Ser.). (Illus.). 544p. (YA). 2000. pap. 15.99 (*0-7615-2782-6*) Prima Pub.

Prima Temp Authors, ed. see Neuse, Alex.

***Prima Temp Staff.** Sanity. (Official Strategy Guides Ser.). (Illus.). 2000. pap. 19.99 (*0-7615-2813-X*) Prima Pub.

— Tom Clancy's Rainbow Six Rogue Spear: Platinum Edition. (Official Strategy Guides Ser.). (Illus.). 240p. (YA). 2000. pap. text 14.99 (*0-7615-2871-7*) Prima Pub.

***Prima Temp Staff, ed.** Army Men Air Combat. (Official Strategy Guides Ser.). (Illus.). 112p. (YA). 2000. pap. text 14.99 (*0-7615-2875-X*) Prima Pub.

— Might & Magic VIII: Day of the Destroyer. LC 00-10174. (Official Strategy Guides Ser.). (Illus.). 396p. (YA). 2000. pap. 19.99 (*0-7615-2841-5*) Prima Pub.

— Simon the Sorcerer 3D. (Official Strategy Guides Ser.). (Illus.). 208p. (YA). 2000. pap. text 19.99 (*0-7615-2862-8*) Prima Pub.

— Sword of the Beserk: Gut's Rage. LC 00-101857. (Illus.). 125p. (YA). 2000. pap. 14.99 (*0-7615-2869-5*) Prima Pub.

Prima Temp Staff, ed. see Kolmos, Keith M.

Primack, Alice L. Journal Literature of the Physical Sciences: A Manual. LC 92-29762. (Illus.). 220p. 1992. 32.50 (*0-8108-2592-9*) Scarecrow.

Primack, J., jt. ed. see Bonometto, S.

Primack, Karen. Jews in Places You Never Thought Of. LC 98-12292. 1998. 23.00 (*0-88125-608-0*) Ktav.

Primack, Marshall P., jt. auth. see Henley, Arthur.

Primack, Martin, jt. auth. see Willis, James.

Primack, Martin L. Farm Formed Capital in American Agriculture, 1850-1910. Bruchey, Stuart, ed. LC 76-45108. (Nineteen Seventy-Seven Dissertations Ser.). 1977. lib. bdg. 30.95 (*0-405-09920-7*) Ayer.

Primack, Martin L. & Willis, James F. Exploration in Macroeconomics Study Guide. 4th rev. ed. 144p. (C). 1996. pap. text, student ed. 18.25 (*1-56226-333-1*) CAT Pub.

— Exploration in Microeconomics. 4th rev. ed. (C). 1996. pap. text, teacher ed. write for info. (*1-56226-340-4*); pap. text, student ed. 18.25 (*1-56226-334-X*) CAT Pub.

— Explorations in Economics: Instructor's Manual. 4th rev. ed. 196p. (C). 1996. pap. text, teacher ed. write for info. (*1-56226-341-2*) CAT Pub.

— Explorations in Economics Study Guide. 4th rev. ed. 240p. (C). 1996. pap. text 22.25 (*1-56226-335-8*) CAT Pub.

— Explorations in Economics Test Bank. 4th rev. ed. 220p. (C). 1996. pap. text. write for info. (*1-56226-338-2*) CAT Pub.

— Explorations in Macroeconomics. 4th ed. 616p. (C). 1996. pap. text 39.46 (*1-56226-330-7*) CAT Pub.

— Explorations in Macroeconomics Test Bank. 4th rev. ed. 136p. (C). 1996. pap. text. write for info. (*1-56226-336-6*) CAT Pub.

— Explorations in Microeconomics. 4th rev. ed. 590p. (C). 1996. pap. text 37.65 (*1-56226-331-5*) CAT Pub.

— Instructors Manual for Explorations in Macroeconomics. 4th rev. ed. (C). 1996. pap. text, teacher ed. write for info. (*1-56226-339-0*) CAT Pub.

Primack, Martin L., et al. Economics for Managers. 830p. (C). 1996. pap. text 52.00 (*1-56226-316-1*) CAT Pub.

— Exploration in Macroeconomics. 136p. (C). 1996. pap. text, student ed. 19.95 (*1-56226-309-9*) CAT Pub.

— Exploration in Macroeconomics Test Bank. 130p. (C). 1996. pap. text. write for info. (*1-56226-311-0*) CAT Pub.

— Exploration in Microeconomics. (C). 1996. pap. text, teacher ed. write for info. (*1-56226-314-5*); pap. text, student ed. 19.95 (*1-56226-310-2*) CAT Pub.

— Exploration in Microeconomics. (C). 1996. pap. text, teacher ed. write for info. (*1-56226-322-6*); pap. text, student ed. 14.85 (*1-56226-320-X*) CAT Pub.

— Exploration in Microeconomics Test Bank. (C). 1996. pap. text. write for info. (*1-56226-312-9*) CAT Pub.

— Explorations in Economics. 598p. (C). 1993. pap. text 50.56 (*1-56226-142-8*) CAT Pub.

— Explorations in Economics. 4th ed. 666p. (C). 1995. pap. text 42.95 (*1-56226-257-2*) CAT Pub.

— Explorations in Economics. 4th ed. 576p. (C). 1996. pap. text 46.55 (*1-56226-292-0*) CAT Pub.

— Explorations in Economics: Applications. 254p. (C). 1993. pap. text 21.35 (*1-56226-143-6*) CAT Pub.

— Explorations in Economics & Business Applications. 410p. (C). 1995. pap. text 37.50 (*1-56226-263-7*) CAT Pub.

— Explorations in Macroeconomics. 318p. (C). 1995. pap. text 37.50 (*1-56226-262-9*) CAT Pub.

— Explorations in Macroeconomics. 3rd ed. 258p. (C). 1993. pap. text 37.02 (*1-56226-153-3*) CAT Pub.

— Explorations in Macroeconomics. 4th ed. 542p. (C). 1994. pap. text 35.63 (*1-56226-167-3*) CAT Pub.

— Explorations in Macroeconomics. 4th ed. 588p. (C). 1996. pap. text 48.75 (*1-56226-290-4*) CAT Pub.

— Explorations in Macroeconomics. 4th ed. 448p. (C). 1996. pap. text 43.95 (*1-56226-299-8*) CAT Pub.

— Explorations in Microeconomics. 440p. (C). 1995. pap. text 37.50 (*1-56226-226-2*) CAT Pub.

— Explorations in Microeconomics. 616p. (C). 1996. pap. text 50.00 (*1-56226-323-4*) CAT Pub.

— Explorations in Microeconomics. rev. ed. 306p. 1997. pap. text 45.00 (*1-56226-375-7*) CAT Pub.

— Explorations in Microeconomics. 3rd ed. 348p. (C). 1993. pap. text 39.27 (*1-56226-152-5*) CAT Pub.

— Explorations in Microeconomics. 4th ed. 502p. (C). 1995. pap. text 34.95 (*1-56226-244-0*) CAT Pub.

— Explorations in Microeconomics. 4th rev. ed. 554p. (C). 1996. pap. text 42.85 (*1-56226-295-5*) CAT Pub.

— Explorations in Microeconomics, First Canadian. 654p. (C). 1991. pap. text 50.61 (*1-56226-014-6*) CAT Pub.

— Instructors Manual for Exploration in Macroeconomics & Transparencies. (C). 1996. pap. text, teacher ed. write for info. (*1-56226-313-7*) CAT Pub.

— Microeconomic Fundamentals for Managerial Economics. 574p. (C). 1994. pap. text 44.89 (*1-56226-182-7*) CAT Pub.

— Microeconomic Horizons. 452p. 1998. pap. text 48.60 (*1-56226-413-3*) CAT Pub.

— Microeconomics: A Framework of Theory, Policies & Values. 476p. (C). 1993. pap. text 40.39 (*1-56226-149-5*) CAT Pub.

— Microeconomics Principles & Applications. 6th rev. ed. 656p. (C). 1997. pap. text 45.95 (*1-56226-374-9*) CAT Pub.

— Principles of Economics. 2nd ed. 964p. (C). 1998. pap. text 56.25 (*1-56226-392-7*) CAT Pub.

— Principles of Macroeconomics. 358p. (C). 1994. pap. text 42.75 (*1-56226-175-4*) CAT Pub.

— Principles of Microeconomics. 476p. (C). 1994. pap. text 42.75 (*1-56226-174-6*) CAT Pub.

— Principles of Microeconomics. 3rd ed. 322p. (C). 1992. pap. text 39.32 (*1-56226-106-1*) CAT Pub.

Primack, Richard B. Essentials of Conservation Biology. 2nd ed. LC 98-3507. (Illus.). 660p. (C). 1998. text 57.95 (*0-87893-721-8*) Sinauer Assocs.

— A Primer of Conservation Biology. LC 95-13972. (Illus.). 246p. (C). 1995. pap. text 31.95 (*0-87893-730-7*) Sinauer Assocs.

P

***Primack, Richard B.** A Primer of Conservation Biology. 2nd ed. LC 00-29693. 2000. pap. write for info. (*0-87893-732-3*) Sinauer Assocs.

Primack, Richard B. Timber, Tourists & Temples: Conservation & Development in the Maya Forest of Belize. LC 97-34519. 420p. 1997. pap. text 35.00 (*1-55963-542-8*) Island Pr.

Primack, Richard B. & Bray, David, eds. Timber, Tourists & Temples: Conservation & Development in the Maya Forest of Belize, Guatemala & Mexico. LC 97-34519. 420p. 1997. text 55.00 (*1-55963-541-X*) Island Pr.

Primack, Richard B. & Lovejoy, Thomas E., eds. Ecology, Conservation, & Management of Southeast Asia Rainforests. LC 94-45878. 304p. 1995. 40.00 (*0-300-06234-6*) Yale U Pr.

***Primal Pictures Staff.** Interactive Foot & Ankle. 1999. 250.00 (*1-902470-10-9*) Primal Pict.

— Interactive Skeleton, Kinetic & Sports Ed. 1999. 99.00 (*1-902470-07-9*) Primal Pict.

— Interactive Skeleton Version 2. 1998. 39.95 (*1-902470-09-5*) Primal Pict.

Primary Comm. Research Centre Staff, ed. Scholary Publishers Guide: Financial & Legal Aspects. 1979. 40.00 (*0-906083-08-7*) St Mut.

Primary Production Department, Singapore Staff, ed. Regulations for Agricultural Products Derived from Biotechnology: Proceedings of the ASEAN Workshop Singapore 1-2 April 1998. 132p. 1998. pap. 36.00 (*981-02-3634-4*) World Scientific Pub.

Primary Research Group Staff. The Academic Library Budget & Expenditure Report, 1999 Edition. 146p. 1998. per. 72.00 (*1-57440-016-9*) Primary Research.

— Corporate/Government Partnerships with Higher Education in Training & Human Resource Development. 139p. 1998. per. 97.50 (*1-57440-012-6*) Primary Research.

— Enrollment Growth Data Report. 85p. 1998. per. 75.00 (*1-57440-013-4*) Primary Research.

— Marketing the College. 110p. 1998. per. 85.00 (*1-57440-015-0*) Primary Research.

— Profiles of College & University Distance Learning Programs. 100p. Date not set. 80.00 (*1-57440-009-6*) Primary Research.

— The Survey of College Marketing Programs. 240p. 1998. per. 205.00 (*1-57440-020-7*) Primary Research.

— The Survey of College Marketing Programs, Vol. III. 80p. 1998. per. 80.00 (*1-57440-019-3*) Primary Research.

— The Survey of College Marketing Programs Vol. I: Management Practices. 80p. 1998. per. 80.00 (*1-57440-017-7*) Primary Research.

— The Survey of College Marketing Programs Vol. II: Print Advertising & Marketing. 80p. 1998. per. 80.00 (*1-57440-018-5*) Primary Research.

Primary Research Staff. The Law Library Budget & Expenditure Report. 110p. 1993. ring bd. 75.00 (*0-9626749-4-X*) Primary Research.

— The Medical Library Budget & Expenditure Report. 110p. 1994. 82.50 (*0-9626749-6-6*) Primary Research.

— The Report on Corporate Library Spending. 112p. 1995. pap. 75.00 (*1-57440-000-2*) Primary Research.

— The Scientific & Technical Library Budget & Expenditure Report. 120p. 1993. ring bd. 65.00 (*0-9626749-5-8*) Primary Research.

— The Scientific & Technical Library Budget & Expenditure Report, 1995. Date not set. pap. 80.00 (*1-57440-001-0*) Primary Research.

Primary Source Medic Staff. The Eighteenth Century Guide to the Microfilm Collection, Vol. 1, Units 18-198. 1809p. 1997. lib. bdg. 400.00 (*1-57803-132-X*, Resch Pubns) Primary Srce Media.

Primas, Hans, et al. On Quanta, Mind & Matter: Hans Primas in Context. LC 99-20457. (Fundamental Theories of Physics Ser.). 1999. write for info. (*0-7923-5696-9*) Kluwer Academic.

***Prima's Temp Authors Staff.** Grandia: Unauthorized Strategy Guide. LC 99-67321. (Illus.). 150p. (J). 1999. pap. 14.99 (*0-7615-2652-8*) Prima Pub.

— Hasbro's Family Gaming Pak. (Official Strategy Guides Ser.). (Illus.). (J). 1999. pap. 24.99 (*0-7615-2636-6*) Prima Pub.

— Mircosoft Flight Simulator 2000: Unauthorized Strategy Guide. (Illus.). 300p. (J). 2000. pap. 29.99 (*0-7615-2657-9*) Prima Pub.

— Power Stone. (Official Strategy Guides Ser.). 1999. pap. 12.99 (*0-7615-2578-5*, Prima Games) Prima Pub.

— Spyro 2: Ripto's Rage. LC 99-68165. (Official Strategy Guides Ser.). (Illus.). 127p. (J). 1999. pap. 14.99 (*0-7615-2666-8*) Prima Pub.

***Prima's Temp Authors Staff, ed.** Galerians. (Official Strategy Guides Ser.). (Illus.). 112p. (YA). 2000. pap. text 14.99 (*0-7615-2880-6*) Prima Pub.

Primate of the Ecumenical Catholic Church Staff, ed. The Holy Eucharist & Other Sacramental Rites: Liturgy Book of the Ecumenical Catholic Church. 356p. (Orig.). 1993. pap. 12.50 (*1-881568-03-2*) Healing Spirit.

Primate of the Ecumenical Catholic Church Staff & Shirilau, Mark S. Canon Law of the Ecumenical Catholic Church: Together with Doctrinal & Procedural Policies. 5th rev. ed. 346p. 1996. pap. 15.00 (*1-881568-11-3*); ring bd. 20.00 (*1-881568-10-5*) Healing Spirit.

Primatesta, Paola, ed. see TSO Staff.

Primaudaye, Peter P. De La, see De La Primaudaye, Peter P.

Primavera, Dorothy E., ed. see Primavera, Robert E.

***Primavera, Elise.** Auntie Claus. LC 98-4781. (Illus.). 40p. (J). 1999. 16.00 (*0-15-201909-X*, Harvest Bks) Harcourt.

— Auntie Claus: She's Back! (J). 2001. write for info. (*0-15-202441-7*) Harcourt.

Primavera, Elise. Basil & Maggie. LC 82-48455. (Illus.). 32p. (J). (gr. 1-3). 1983. 9.82 (*0-397-32027-2*); lib. bdg. 11.89 (*0-397-32028-0*) HarpC Child Bks.

***Primavera Foundation Staff.** Tucson Cooks! (Illus.). 200p. 2000. pap. 24.95 (*0-9643613-4-5*) Fiesta Pubng.

Primavera, Louis, jt. auth. see Heaney-Hunter, Joann.

Primavera, Robert E. Vertigo Explained. 2nd rev. ed. Primavera, Dorothy E., ed. (Illus.). 56p. 1998. pap. text 5.95 (*0-9667942-0-6*, VT-001) CommData.

Primavera Systems, Inc. Staff. Expedition: Construction Contract Control Software User Guide. abr. rev. ed. (Illus.). 786p. 1992. write for info. incl. disk (*0-926282-60-3*) Primavera Syst.

Primavesi, Anne. From Apocalypse to Genesis Ecology, Feminism & Christianity. 336p. 1994. pap. 27.00 (*0-86012-174-7*, Pub. by Srch Pr) St Mut.

Primavesi, Anne & Henderson, Jennifer. Our God Has No Favourites: A Liberation Theology of the Eucharist. 112p. 1994. pap. 20.00 (*0-86012-170-4*, Pub. by Srch Pr) St Mut.

Primavesi, Oliver, jt. auth. see Martin, Alain.

Primc, M., jt. auth. see Lepowsky, James.

Prime. Introduction to Pathology for Radiographers. (Illus.). 336p. (Orig.). (C). 1987. pap. text 29.50 (*0-06-318362-5*) HarpC.

Prime, Carol, jt. ed. see Szumski, Bonnie.

Prime, D. De Nuevo en Vacaciones. (Serie Sara y Pablo - Sarah & Paul Ser.: No. 6).Tr. of Go on Vacation. (SPA.). (J). write for info. (*0-7899-0495-0*, 498900) Editorial Unilit.

— Hacen un Album de Recortes. (Serie Sara y Pablo - Sarah & Paul Ser.: No. 4).Tr. of Make a Scrapbook. (SPA.). (J). write for info. (*0-7899-0498-5*, 498898) Editorial Unilit.

— Van al Museo. (Serie Sara y Pablo - Sarah & Paul Ser.: No. 5).Tr. of Go to the Museum. (SPA.). (J). write for info. (*0-7899-0499-3*, 498899) Editorial Unilit.

Prime, Daniel N. Prime: The Autobiography of an Octogenarian, with the Genealogy of His Ancestors & Sketches of Their History. 293p. 1992. reprint ed. pap. 44.00 (*0-8328-2397-X*); reprint ed. lib. bdg. 54.00 (*0-8328-2396-1*) Higginson Bk Co.

Prime, Derek. Bible Guidelines. Date not set. pap. 8.50 (*1-871676-26-6*, Pub. by Christian Focus) Spring Arbor Dist.

— Created to Praise. Date not set. pap. 5.99 (*1-871676-66-5*, Pub. by Christian Focus) Spring Arbor Dist.

— Directions for Christian Living. 6.99 (*1-85792-111-9*, Pub. by Christian Focus) Spring Arbor Dist.

— Go Back to School. (Sarah & Paul Ser.). (J). 3.99 (*1-871676-18-5*, Pub. by Christian Focus) Spring Arbor Dist.

— Go to the Museum. (Sarah & Paul Ser.). (J). 3.99 (*1-871676-36-3*, Pub. by Christian Focus) Spring Arbor Dist.

— Go to the Seaside. (Sarah & Paul Ser.). (J). 3.99 (*1-871676-34-7*, Pub. by Christian Focus) Spring Arbor Dist.

— Have a Visitor. (Sarah & Paul Ser.). (J). 3.99 (*1-871676-19-3*, Pub. by Christian Focus) Spring Arbor Dist.

— James. (Focus on the Bible Commentary Ser.). 8.50 (*1-85792-129-1*, Pub. by Christian Focus) Spring Arbor Dist.

***Prime, Derek.** Let's Study Second Corinthians. 151p. 2000. pap. 10.99 (*0-85151-779-X*) Banner of Truth.

Prime, Derek. Make a Scrapbook. (Sarah & Paul Ser.). (J). 3.99 (*1-871676-35-5*, Pub. by Christian Focus) Spring Arbor Dist.

— On Holiday Again. (Sarah & Paul Ser.). 3.99 (*1-871676-37-1*, Pub. by Christian Focus) Spring Arbor Dist.

— Practical Prayer. Date not set. 6.99 (*1-871676-51-7*, Pub. by Christian Focus) Spring Arbor Dist.

— Questions on the Christian Faith. Date not set. 6.99 (*1-871676-82-7*, Pub. by Christian Focus) Spring Arbor Dist.

Prime, E. D. Prime: Notes - Genealogical, Biographical & Bibliographical - of the Prime Family. 118p. 1992. reprint ed. pap. 19.50 (*0-8328-2709-6*); reprint ed. lib. bdg. 29.50 (*0-8328-2708-8*) Higginson Bk Co.

Prime, H. A. Multilingual Dictionary of Automatic Control Technology. (IFAC Ser.). 342p. 1994. 96.50 (*0-08-041913-5*, Pergamon Pr) Elsevier.

Prime, H. A. & Work, Ants, eds. Multilingual Dictionary of Automatic Control Technology: English, French, German, Spanish, Italian, Japanese, Chinese & Russian. (IFAC Workshop Ser.). (CHI, ENG, FRE, GER & ITA.). 390p. 1995. 132.25 (*0-08-037192-2*, Pergamon Pr) Elsevier.

Prime, Honor. The Lamb White Days. LC 81-453444. 179p. 1980. write for info. (*0-7188-2437-7*) Lutterwrth.

***Prime, Jim & Nowlin, Bill.** Tales from the Red Sox Dugout. (Illus.). 224p. 2000. 19.95 (*1-58382-054-X*) Sports Pub.

Prime, Jim, jt. auth. see Williams, Ted.

Prime, Nathaniel S. History of Long Island from Its First Settlement by Europeans to the Year 1845. (Illus.). 420p. 1997. reprint ed. lib. bdg. 45.00 (*0-8328-6165-0*) Higginson Bk Co.

***Prime, P., et al.** Global Economics. 2nd ed. 2000. 12.00 (*1-886855-45-5*) Tavenner Pub.

Prime Partners Staff. Game Plan for College Success. (CA - Career Development Ser.). (C). 1992. 38.00 (*0-538-70973-1*) S-W Pub.

Prime, Ranchor. Ramayana. 1998. 15.95 (*1-55670-711-8*) Stewart Tabori & Chang.

***Prime, Ranchor.** Ramayana: A Journey. abr. ed. (Illus.). 160p. 1999. pap. 16.95 (*1-56649-069-3*) Welcome Rain.

Prime, Samuel. The Power of Prayer. rev. ed. 265p. 1998. pap. 12.50 (*0-85151-758-7*) Banner of Truth.

Prime, Samuel I. The Life of Samuel F. B. Morse, L. L. D: Inventor of the Electro-Magnetic Recording Telegraph. LC 74-4691. (Telecommunications Ser.). (Illus.). 816p. 1974. reprint ed. 60.95 (*0-405-06054-8*) Ayer.

Prime, Temple. Some Account of the Temple Family. (Illus.). 100p. 1990. reprint ed. pap. 18.00 (*0-8328-1541-1*); reprint ed. lib. bdg. 26.00 (*0-8328-1540-3*) Higginson Bk Co.

— Some Account of the Temple Family. 2nd ed. (Illus.). 111p. 1990. reprint ed. pap. 19.50 (*0-8328-1543-8*); reprint ed. lib. bdg. 27.50 (*0-8328-1542-X*) Higginson Bk Co.

— Some Account of the Temple Family. 3rd ed. (Illus.). 146p. 1990. reprint ed. pap. 22.00 (*0-8328-1545-4*); reprint ed. lib. bdg. 30.00 (*0-8328-1544-6*) Higginson Bk Co.

— Some Account of the Temple Family. 4th ed. (Illus.). 77p. 1990. reprint ed. pap. 16.00 (*0-8328-1547-0*); reprint ed. lib. bdg. 24.00 (*0-8328-1546-2*) Higginson Bk Co.

Prime, Terence. Commercial Law. (C). 1990. 110.00 (*1-85431-087-9*, Pub. by Blackstone Pr) St Mut.

— Contract & Tort. (Student Statutes Ser.). 192p. 1993. pap. text 20.00 (*0-406-02300-X*, UK, MICHIE) LEXIS Pub.

***Prime, Terence.** European Intellectual Property Law. LC 99-46213. (European Business Law Library). 324p. 2000. text 78.95 (*1-85521-566-7*, Pub. by Ashgate Pub) Ashgate Pub Co.

Prime, Terence. The Law of Copyright. 337p. 1992. 110.00 (*1-85190-180-9*, Pub. by Tolley Pubng) St Mut.

— Prime: International Bonds & Certificates of Deposit. 380p. 1990. boxed set 160.00 (*0-406-11460-9*, MICHIE) LEXIS Pub.

Prime, Terence & Scanlan, Gary. The Law of Private Limited Companies. 458p. 1996. write for info. (*0-406-04508-9*, MICHIE) LEXIS Pub.

Prime, William C. Tent Life in the Holy Land. Davis, Moshe, ed. LC 77-70734. (America & the Holy Land Ser.). (Illus.). 1977. reprint ed. lib. bdg. 42.95 (*0-405-10278-X*) Ayer.

Primeau, John K., jt. auth. see Sickinger, Raymond L.

***Primeau, Liz.** Grow a Butterfly Garden. (Plant-a-Page Bks.). (Illus.). 24p. (J). (gr. k-5). 2000. pap. 6.99 (*1-58184-024-1*) Somerville Hse.

— Grow a Salad. (Plant-a-Page Bks.). (Illus.). 24p. (J). (gr. k-5). 2000. pap. text 6.99 (*1-58184-023-3*) Somerville Hse.

Primeau, Ronald. Beyond Spoon River: The Legacy of Edgar Lee Masters. LC 80-25825. (Dan Danciger Publications). 231p. reprint ed. pap. 71.70 (*0-7837-5193-1*, 204492700004) Bks Demand.

— Romance of the Road: The Literature of the American Highway. LC 96-6221. 171p. 1996. 34.95 (*0-87972-697-0*); pap. 17.95 (*0-87972-698-9*) Bowling Green Univ Popular Press.

Primeaux, Joan, jt. auth. see Troy, Anne.

Primeaux, Martha, jt. auth. see Henderson, George.

Primeaux, Patrick. Richard R. Niebuhr on Christ & Religion: The Four-Stage Development of His Theology. LC 81-38369. (Toronto Studies in Theology: Vol. 4). (Illus.). xiv, 288p. 1981. lib. bdg. 89.95 (*0-88946-973-3*) E Mellen.

Primeaux, Patrick & Stieber, John A. Profit Maximization: The Ethical Mandate of Business. (Illus.). 118p. 1995. 44.95 (*1-57292-025-4*); pap. 24.95 (*1-57292-024-6*) Austin & Winfield.

Primeaux, Patrick D. Humanizing the City: Politics, Religion, the Arts in Critical Conversation. LC 96-39231. 224p. 1997. 69.95 (*1-57309-021-2*); pap. 49.95 (*1-57309-020-4*) Intl Scholars.

— The Moral Passion of Bruce Springsteen. (ISP Ser.). (Illus.). 142p. 1996. 54.95 (*1-57309-037-9*); pap. 32.95 (*1-57309-036-0*) Intl Scholars.

— Reinventing the American Dream: The Ethics of Business & the Business of Ethics. LC 97-44061. 210p. 1999. 49.95 (*1-57309-252-5*); pap. 29.95 (*1-57309-251-7*) Intl Scholars.

Primeaux, Walter J. Direct Electric Utility Competition: The Natural Monopoly Myth. LC 85-20487. 312p. 1985. 59.95 (*0-275-90032-0*, C0032, Praeger Pubs) Greenwood.

— Foundations of Business Economics: The Contributions of Joel Dean. LC 83-26094. 239p. 1984. reprint ed. pap. 74.10 (*0-608-04503-9*, 206524800001) Bks Demand.

***Primel, Louis, ed.** Aggregates: Geology - Prospection - Environment - Testing Extraction - Specifications - Processing Plants Equipment - Quality. (Illus.). 516p. (C). 2000. text 125.00 (*90-5410-795-2*, Pub. by A A Balkema) Ashgate Pub Co.

Primer. Mandeville Studies. (International Archives of the History of Ideas Ser.: No. 81). 1975. lib. bdg. 126.50 (*90-247-1686-1*) Kluwer Academic.

Primer, Ben & American Civil Liberties Union Staff. American Civil Liberties Union Archives: The Roger Baldwin Years, 1917-1950. LC 96-2220. 1996. 75.00 (*0-8420-4150-8*) Scholarly Res Inc.

Primer, Irwin, ed. Seneca Unmasqued: Aphra Behn's Translation of la Rochefoucauld's Maxims. (Studies in the Eighteenth Century: No. 29). 1995. reprint ed. write for info. (*0-404-63529-6*) AMS Pr.

Primerano, Lisa. Off the Beaten Aisle: America's Quirky Spots to Tie the Knot. LC 98-7804. (Illus.). 224p. 1998. pap. 12.95 (*0-8065-2003-5*, Citadel Pr) Carol Pub Group.

Primet, Laurette D., jt. ed. see Knight, David W.

Primi, John. Charging System Explained. LC 80-730673. 1980. student ed. 7.00 (*0-8064-0137-0*, 436) Bergwall.

— Troubleshooting with the Vat Forty. LC 80-730756. (Orig.). 1980. student ed. 5.00 (*0-8064-0147-8*, 441); audio, VHS 359.00 (*0-8064-0148-6*) Bergwall.

Primicerio, M., jt. ed. see Fasano, A. P.

Primio, Franco Di, see Christaller, Thomas.

Primm. Medical Assistant. LC 97-35234. (Careers Without College Ser.). 48p. (J). (gr. 3-4). 1998. 19.00 (*1-56065-705-7*) Capstone Pr.

Primm, Clyde, ed. The Musical! Where to Find It. 219p. 1984. pap. 24.95 (*0-918933-00-5*) Magnetic Inds.

— The Musical! Where to Find It. 371p. 1985. pap. 29.95 (*0-918933-01-3*) Magnetic Inds.

Primm, E. Russell. Emergency Medical Technician. LC 97-35231. (Careers Without College Ser.). (Illus.). 48p. (YA). (gr. 4-7). 1998. 19.00 (*1-56065-702-2*) Capstone Pr.

— Emergency Medical Technician. (Careers Without College Ser.). (Illus.). 48p. (J). (gr. 3-7). 1998. 19.00 (*0-516-21281-8*) Childrens.

— Medical Assistant. (Careers Without College Ser.). (Illus.). 48p. (J). (gr. 3-7). 1998. 19.00 (*0-516-21284-2*) Childrens.

— Surgical Technician. LC RD32.3.P75 1998. (Careers Without College Ser.). (YA). (gr. 3 up). 1998. 19.00 (*1-56065-709-X*) Capstone Pr.

— Surgical Technician. (Careers Without College Ser.). (Illus.). 48p. (J). (gr. 3-7). 1998. 19.00 (*0-516-21288-5*) Childrens.

Primm, E. Russell, jt. auth. see Clinton.

Primm, E. Russell, jt. auth. see Simon.

Primm, James N. Lion of the Valley: St. Louis, Missouri, 1764-1980. 3rd rev. ed. LC 98-20315. (Illus.). 621p. 1998. 35.95 (*1-883982-24-3*, Pub. by MO Hist Soc); pap. 27.95 (*1-883982-25-1*) MO Hist Soc.

Primm, Ronald G., jt. auth. see Lewis, John S.

***Primm, Russ, ed.** Career Exploration Through Children's Literature, Grades 6-8: Correlation to the National Career Development Guideline. LC 99-49267. 256p. 1999. pap. 34.95 (*0-89434-286-X*) Ferguson.

Primm, Russell, ed. Elementary Career Awareness Through Children's Literature: A K-2 Correlation to the National Career Development Guidelines, Vol. 1. LC 98-47741. 256p. (J). (gr. k-2). 1999. spiral bd. 34.95 (*0-89434-270-3*, 7113) Ferguson.

Primm, Russell E. Elementary Career Awareness Through Children's Literature: A 3-5 Correlation to the National Career Development Guidelines, Vol. 2. LC 98-42776. 256p. (J). (gr. 3-5). 1999. spiral bd. 34.95 (*0-89434-271-1*, F114) Ferguson.

Primmer, Brian. The Berlioz Style. LC 83-18920. (Music Reprint Ser.). 202p. 1983. reprint ed. lib. bdg. 29.50 (*0-306-76223-4*) Da Capo.

Primo, A. R. M. Modelling Sintering Processes with Boundary Elements. (Topics in Engineering Ser.). 270p. 2000. 143.00 (*1-85312-754-X*, 754X, Pub. by WIT Pr) Computational Mech MA.

Primo, Angeli. Making People Respond: Design for Marketing & Communication. LC 97-214110. (Illus.). 144p. 1997. pap. text 34.95 (*0-8230-2966-2*) Watsn-Guptill.

Primo, Pauline. Vida Saludable. (SPA Ser.). 84p. 1990. pap. 9.95 (*0-685-51944-9*) Woodland UT.

Primo, Quintin E. The Making of a Black Bishop. (Illus.). xvii, 172p. 1998. pap. 18.95 (*1-892142-02-3*, 110) Cedar Tree Bks.

Primorac, Karen & Adorni, Sergio. English Grammar for Students of Italian. 2nd ed. Morton, Jacqueline, ed. 194p. 1995. pap. 12.95 (*0-934034-20-6*) Olivia & Hill.

Primoratz, Igor. Ethics & Sex. LC 98-48882. 1999. 75.00 (*0-415-09333-3*); pap. 24.99 (*0-415-09334-1*) Routledge.

— Justifying Legal Punishment. 209p. 1999. pap. 18.95 (*1-57392-410-5*, Humanity Bks) Prometheus Bks.

— Justifying Legal Punishment. 2nd ed. LC 98-101560. 216p. (C). 1997. pap. 17.50 (*0-391-04036-7*) Humanities.

Primoratz, Igor, ed. Human Sexuality. LC 97-24589. (International Research Library of Philosophy). 544p. 1997. text 185.95 (*1-85521-870-4*, Pub. by Ashgate Pub) Ashgate Pub Co.

Primosch, Robert E., jt. auth. see Mathewson, Richard J.

Primozic, Edward, et al. Strategic Choices: Supremacy, Survival or Sayonara. 256p. 1991. 24.95 (*0-07-051036-9*) McGraw.

Primozich, Jean & Strandness, D. E. Techniques of Cerebrovascular Sonography. Date not set. text. write for info. (*0-941022-30-7*); VHS. write for info. (*0-941022-33-1*) Davies Pubng.

Primrose, Carol & Gray, Carl, eds. Arts of the Chesapeake: Directory for Arts & Crafts Events. 2nd ed. (Illus.). 256p. 1998. pap. 14.95 (*0-9656840-1-6*) Huntergreen.

Primrose, David W. Civil War "Letters to Tabitha" Civil War Letters. Lunetta, Steven, ed. (Illus.). 430p. 1996. 35.00 (*0-9651549-0-4*) Prim Pr.

Primrose, E., tr. see Burago, Yu D., et al, eds.

Primrose, E., tr. see Resehtnyak, Y. G.

***Primrose, Mary & Zinck, Marian.** Wildflowers of Nova Scotia, New Brunswick & Prince Edward Island: The Photographs of Mary Primrose. (Illus.). 112p. 1998. write for info. (*0-88780-451-9*, Pub. by Formac Publ Co) Formac Dist Ltd.

Primrose, P. Investment in Manufacturing Technology. LC 91-10103. 256p. 1990. mass mkt. 89.95 (*0-412-40920-8*, A6260) Chapman & Hall.

Primrose Path Staff & Kooler, Donna. Country-Style Painted Wood Projects. (Illus.). 128p. 1997. pap. text 14.95 (*0-8069-3151-5*, Chapelle) Sterling.

Primrose, S. B. Molecular Biotechnology. 2nd ed. (Illus.). 208p. 1991. 75.00 (*0-632-03233-2*); pap. 49.95 (*0-632-03053-4*) Blackwell Sci.

— Principles of Genome Analysis: A Guide to Mapping & Sequencing DNA from Different Organisms. LC 95-6173. 1995. pap. 32.95 (*0-86542-946-4*) Blackwell Sci.

P

An Asterisk (*) at the beginning of an entry indicates that the title is appearing for the first time.

*Primrose, S. B. Principles of Genome Analysis: A Guide to Mapping & Sequencing DNA from Different Organisms. 2nd ed. LC 97-36818. (Illus.). 1998. pap. 47.95 (0-632-04983-9) Blackwell Sci.

Primrose, S. B., jt. auth. see Dimmock, N. J.

Primus, Ginger & Westlake, Barbara. Shape It Up. 112p. (C). 1994. spiral bd. 25.95 (0-8403-9936-7) Kendall-Hunt.

Primus, John H. Holy Time: Moderate Puritanism & the Sabbath. LC 89-12471. (C). 1990. pap. 16.95 (0-86554-350-X, MUP/P80) Mercer Univ Pr.

— Richard Graham: The Portrait of an Elizabethan Pastor. LC 98-5027. 240p. 1998. text 35.00 (0-86554-578-2, H433) Mercer Univ Pr.

Primus, Rebecca & Brown, Addie. Beloved Sisters & Loving Friends: Letters from Rebecca Primus of Royal Oak, Maryland & Addie Brown of Hartford, Connecticut, 1854-1868. Griffin, Farah J., ed. LC 98-52930. (Illus.). 320p. 1999. 26.00 (0-679-45128-5) Knopf.

Primus, Richard A. The American Language of Rights. LC 98-43627. (Ideas in Context Ser.: No. 54). 280p. 1999. 54.95 (0-521-65250-2) Cambridge U Pr.

Prin, John, ed. see Miller, Dennis & Hunt, Amelia.

Prina, Stephen. Stephen Prina: Monochrome Painting. (Illus.). 42p. 1989. pap. 10.00 (0-941548-17-1) Ren Soc U Chi.

Prina, Stephen & Tillman, Lynn. Stephen Prina: "It Was the Best He Could Do at the Moment" (Illus.). 104p. (Orig.). 1992. pap. 35.00 (90-6918-094-4, Pub. by Boymans Mus) Dist Art Pubs.

Prince. Exploring Theatre. LC 96-147736. 1996. mass mkt. 34.75 (0-314-07016-8) West Pub.

— Exploring Theatre. annot. ed. LC 96-147736. Date not set. text, teacher ed. write for info. (0-314-07017-6) West Pub.

Prince, A. Fatso's Rat. (Illus.). (J). 1997. mass mkt. 7.95 (0-340-69370-3, Pub. by Hodder & Stought Ltd) Trafalgar.

— Fergus' Fabulous Ferret. (Illus.). (J). 1997. mass mkt. 7.95 (0-340-69369-X, Pub. by Hodder & Stought Ltd) Trafalgar.

Prince-A-Cuba, ed. Our Mecca Is Harlem: Clarence 13X (Allah) & the Five Percent. (Illus.). 69p. (Orig.). 1995. reprint ed. pap. 6.95 (1-56411-076-1, YBBG0081) Untd Bros & Sis.

Prince, Alan, jt. ed. see Savitsky, Evgeny M.

Prince, Alison. Hans Christian Anderson: The Fan Dancer. LC 99-232683. (J). 1999. text 36.00 (0-7490-0346-4) Allison & Busby.

***Prince, Alison.** Hans Christian Anderson: The Fan Dancer. 2000. pap. 16.95 (0-7490-0478-9, Pub. by Allison & Busby) Intl Pubs Mktg.

— The Sherwood Hero. 112p. (J). 2000. mass mkt. 4.99 (0-330-33724-6) Mcm Child Bks.

Prince, Amy D., tr. see Galeana, Benita.

Prince, Anne. Crash Course - Excel 95. LC 98-121023. (Illus.). 83p. 1997. pap. 15.00 (0-911625-96-8) M Murach & Assoc.

— VS COBOL II: A Guide for Programmers & Managers. 2nd ed. LC 89-13671. 271p. 1990. pap. 27.50 (0-911625-54-2) M Murach & Assoc.

— Work Like a Pro with Excel 5 for Windows. LC 95-19201. 247p. 1995. pap. 20.00 (0-911625-89-5) M Murach & Assoc.

— Work Like a Pro with Excel for Windows 95. LC 96-9531. (Illus.). 339p. (Orig.). 1996. pap. 25.00 (0-911625-92-5) M Murach & Assoc.

Prince, Anne & Koop, Ed. Client - Server Programming: Visual Basic 5. LC 98-13129. 457p. 1998. pap. 40.00 (1-890774-00-6) M Murach & Assoc.

Prince, Anne & Murach, Joel. Client/Server Programming: Access 97. LC 98-40934. 558p. 1998. pap. 40.00 (1-890774-01-4) M Murach & Assoc.

Prince, Anne, jt. auth. see Garvin, Curtis.

Prince, Anne, jt. auth. see McQuillen, Kevin.

Prince, Anthony, jt. auth. see Collins, Trish.

Prince, Barbara. Talking with Your Child about AIDS. LC 92-42452. (Growing Together Ser.). 1993. pap. 2.25 (0-8298-0865-5) Pilgrim OH.

Prince, Barbara Jean. Margaret, Tom, & Mary's Authentic Hungarian Cookbook. (Illus.). 56p. 1998. pap. 9.95 (0-8059-4160-6) Dorrance.

Prince, Benjamin F., ed. Standard History of Springfield & Clark County: Authentic Narrative of the Past, with Particular Attention to the Modern Era in the Commercial, Industrial, Educational, Civic & Social Development. (Illus.). 999p. 1997. reprint ed. lib. bdg. 106.00 (0-8328-6363-7) Higginson Bk Co.

***Prince, Benny D.** Why Tithing Is Not for the Church. 133p. 1999. pap. 12.95 (0-7414-0024-3) Buy Books.

Prince, Beth. Christmas Collectibles. 1993. 12.98 (1-55521-910-1) Bk Sales Inc.

***Prince, Betty.** High Performance Memories: New Architecture Drams & Srams--Evolution & Function. rev. ed. LC 99-13562. 354p. 1999. 115.00 (0-471-98610-0) Wiley.

Prince, Betty. Semiconductor Memories: A Handbook of Design Manufacturing & Application. 2nd ed. 822p. 1996. pap. 145.00 (0-471-94295-2) Wiley.

Prince, Carl E. Brooklyn's Dodgers: The Bums, the Borough & the Best of Baseball, 1947-1957. (Illus.). 224p. 1997. reprint ed. pap. 12.95 (0-19-511578-3) OUP.

— New Jersey's Jeffersonian Republicans: The Genesis of an Early Party Machine, 1789-1817. LC 67-15103. 282p. reprint ed. pap. 87.50 (0-8357-3919-8, 203665400004) Bks Demand.

— Texas, 1844-45. 1993. reprint ed. lib. bdg. 75.00 (0-7812-5962-2) Rprt Serv.

Prince, Carl E., ed. The Papers of William Livingston, Vol. III. 576p. (C). 1986. text 50.00 (0-8135-1144-5) Rutgers U Pr.

Prince, Carl E., et al, eds. The Papers of William Livingston: April 1783-1790, Vol. V. (Illus.). 683p. 1988. 75.00 (0-8135-1297-2) Rutgers U Pr.

Prince, Carl E. & Keller, Mollie. The U. S. Customs Service: A Bicentennial History. LC 89-600730. (Illus.). 320p. (C). 1989. pap. text 12.00 (0-317-93799-5) DT US Customs.

Prince, Carl E. & Lustig, Mary L., eds. The Papers of William Livingston, Vol. IV. (Illus.). 590p. 1987. text 50.00 (0-8135-1213-1) Rutgers U Pr.

Prince, Cynthia & Lawrence, Leslie. The National Education Goals Report: Building a Nation of Learners (1996) 6th ed. (Illus.). 161p. 1997. pap. text 40.00 (0-7881-3747-6) DIANE Pub.

Prince, D. S. Bendicion o Maldicion: Usted Puede Escoger.Tr. of Blessing or Curse: You Can Choose. (SPA.). 282p. 1995. 8.99 (1-56063-746-3, 550072) Editorial Unilit.

Prince, D. S. El Espiritu Santo en Usted.Tr. of Holy Spirit in You. (SPA.). 3.50 (0-7899-0118-8, 550085) Editorial Unilit.

Prince, D. S. El Frasco de la Medicina de Dios.Tr. of God's Medicine Bottle. (SPA.). 32p. 1996. 3.50 (0-7899-0241-9, 550092) Editorial Unilit.

— La Guerra Espiritual.Tr. of Spiritual Warfare. (SPA.). 110p. 1996. 3.99 (0-7899-0210-9, 550090) Editorial Unilit.

Prince, D. S. Paginas del Libro de Mi Vida.Tr. of Pages from My Life's Book. (SPA.). 3.99 (0-7899-0115-3, 550082) Editorial Unilit.

— La Paternidad.Tr. of Fatherhood. (SPA.). 3.50 (0-7899-0242-7, 550093) Editorial Unilit.

— El Plan de Dios para Su Dinero.Tr. of God's Plan for Your Money. (SPA.). 3.50 (0-7899-0114-5, 550081) Editorial Unilit.

Prince, D. S. Proposito en la Vida: Hacer la Voluntad de Dios.Tr. of Objective for Living: To Do God's Will. (SPA.). 28p. 1996. 3.50 (0-7899-0208-7, 550088) Editorial Unilit.

— El Remedio de Dios para el Rechazo.Tr. of God's Remedy for Rejection. (SPA.). 68p. 1996. 3.50 (0-7899-0209-5, 550089) Editorial Unilit.

Prince, D. S. Si Deseas lo Mejor de Parte de Dios.Tr. of If You Want God's Best. (SPA.). 3.99 (0-7899-0120-X, 550087) Editorial Unilit.

— Su Lengua Necesita Sanidad?Tr. of Does Your Tongue Need Healing?. (SPA.). 3.50 (0-7899-0117-X, 550084) Editorial Unilit.

Prince, Danforth, jt. auth. see Porter, Darwin.

Prince, David & Gage, Julia. Put Your English to Work. (Illus.). 160p. (C). 1986. pap. text 9.95 (0-13-744350-1) P-H.

Prince, David L., jt. auth. see Iacono, Domenic J.

Prince, Dawn E., ed. Libro del Trasoro. (Dialect Ser.: No. 15). xxxii, 235p. 1995. 35.00 (1-56954-040-3) Hispanic Seminary.

— Text & Concordance of the Aragonese Translation of Brunetto Latini's Li Livres dou Tresor, Garona Cathedral, MS20-2-5. (Dialect Ser.: No. 11). (SPA.). 16p. 1990. 10.00 incl. fiche (0-940639-46-7) Hispanic Seminary.

Prince, Dennis. Supporting SAP R/3. LC 98-66993. 550p. 1998. 50.00 (0-7615-1750-2) Prima Pub.

Prince, Dennis L. Online Auctions at E-bay: Bid with Confidence, Sell with Success. LC 99-70113. (Illus.). 16p. 1999. pap. 19.99 (0-7615-2070-8) Prima Pub.

***Prince, Dennis L.** Online Auctions at Ebay: Bid with Confidence, Sell with Success. 2nd ed. LC 99-65391. 495p. 1999. pap. 19.99 (0-7615-2414-2) Prima Pub.

— Treasure Hunters Guide to Online Auctions. 1999. pap. 19.99 (0-7615-2316-2) Prima Pub.

***Prince, Derek.** Atonement, Your Appointment with God. 224p. 2000. pap. 11.99 (0-8007-9277-7) Chosen Bks.

Prince, Derek. Baptism in the Holy Spirit. 80p. 1995. mass mkt. 5.99 (0-88368-377-6) Whitaker Hse.

***Prince, Derek.** Blessing or Curse: You Can Choose! 272p. 2000. pap. 10.99 (0-8007-9280-7) Revell.

Prince, Derek. Blessing or Curse: You Can Choose. LC 90-38671. 264p. (YA). (gr. 10). 1990. pap. 9.99 (0-8007-9166-5) Chosen Bks.

— Derek Prince on Experiencing God's Power. LC 98-40533. 528p. 1999. pap. 17.99 (0-88368-551-5) Whitaker Hse.

— Does Your Tongue Need Healing. 100p. 1993. mass mkt. 5.99 (0-88368-239-7) Whitaker Hse.

— Faith to Live By. LC 97-46142. 171p. 1998. pap. 6.99 (0-88368-519-1) Whitaker Hse.

— Fasting. 63p. 1993. mass mkt. 4.99 (0-88368-258-3) Whitaker Hse.

— God's Medicine Bottle. 62p. 1995. mass mkt. 4.99 (0-88368-332-6) Whitaker Hse.

— God's Plan for Your Money. 95p. 1993. mass mkt. 5.99 (0-88368-287-7) Whitaker Hse.

— God's Remedy for Rejection. 112p. 1997. mass mkt. 5.99 (0-88368-483-7) Whitaker Hse.

— Holy Spirit in You. 112p. 1993. mass mkt. 5.99 (0-88368-238-9) Whitaker Hse.

— How to Fast Successfully. 76p. 1995. mass mkt. 5.99 (0-88368-345-8) Whitaker Hse.

***Prince, Derek.** Husbands & Fathers: Rediscover the Creator's Purpose for Men. LC 99-38439. 160p. 2000. pap. 9.99 (0-8007-9274-2) Chosen Bks.

Prince, Derek. Last Word on the Middle East. 1992. pap. 5.95 (0-934920-40-0, B-34) Derek Prince.

— El Manual del Cristiano Lleno del Espiritu.Tr. of Spirit Filled Believer's Handbook. (SPA.). 500p. 1996. 14.99 (1-56063-745-5, 550071) Editorial Unilit.

— The Marriage Covenant. 121p. 1995. mass mkt. 5.99 (0-88368-333-4) Whitaker Hse.

— Objective for Living: To Do God's Will. 64p. 1996. mass mkt. 4.99 (0-88368-464-0) Whitaker Hse.

***Prince, Derek.** Receiving God's Best. Orig. Title: If You Want God's Best. 106p. 1999. mass mkt. 5.99 (0-88368-593-0) Whitaker Hse.

Prince, Derek. Self Study Bible Course Workbook. 61p. 1996. pap. 8.99 (0-88368-421-7, B-90) Whitaker Hse.

— Shaping History Through Prayer & Fasting. 219p. 1994. mass mkt. 5.99 (0-88368-339-3) Whitaker Hse.

— The Spirit-Filled Believer's Handbook Bible: Foundations for Christian Living from the. 1993. 20.99 (0-88419-329-2, B-52) Creation House.

— Spiritual Warfare. 137p. 1992. mass mkt. 5.99 (0-88368-256-7) Whitaker Hse.

— They Shall Expel Demons: What You Need to Know about Demons - Your Invisible Enemies. LC 97-43975. 256p. (Orig.). 1998. pap. 10.99 (0-8007-9260-2) Chosen Bks.

Prince, Derek & Prince, Ruth. God Is a Matchmaker. LC 85-29891. 192p. 1986. pap. 8.99 (0-8007-9058-8) Chosen Bks.

— Prayers & Proclamations. 77p. 1999. reprint ed. mass mkt. 5.99 (0-88368-226-5, B-59) Whitaker Hse.

***Prince, Don & Hoppe, Michael.** Communicating Across Cultures. 30p. 2000. pap. 6.95 (1-882197-59-3) Ctr Creat Leader.

Prince, E. Mathematical Techniques in Crystallography & Materials Science. (Illus.). 192p. 1982. 54.00 (0-387-90627-4) Spr-Verlag.

Prince, E. M., tr. see Bordewijk, Ferdinand.

Prince, Edward. Mathematical Techniques in Crystallography & Materials Science. 2nd ed. LC 94-17913. 1994. 99.95 (0-387-58115-4) Spr-Verlag.

***Prince, Eldred E. & Simpson, Robert R.** Long Green: The Rise & Fall of Tobacco in South Carolina. LC 99-43773. (Illus.). 304p. 2000. 40.00 (0-8203-2176-1) U of Ga Pr.

Prince, Eleanor F. & Collier, Gaydell M. Basic Horse Care. 336p. 1989. pap. 16.95 (0-385-26199-3) Doubleday.

— Basic Training for Horses: English & Western. 448p. 1989. pap. 21.95 (0-385-26238-8) Doubleday.

Prince, Ezra M. & Burnham, John H., eds. History of McLean County. With Biographical Sketches (Published Without Historical Encyclopedia of Illinois) (Illus.). 615p. 1997. reprint ed. lib. bdg. 65.00 (0-8328-5769-6) Higginson Bk Co.

Prince, F. T. Collected Poems, 1935-1992. LC 92-33032. 319p. (C). 1993. pap. 19.95 (1-878818-16-3, Pub. by Sheep Meadow) U Pr of New Eng.

— Later On. Date not set. pap. 14.95 (0-85646-103-2, Pub. by Anvil Press) Dufour.

— Walks in Rome. Date not set. pap. 34.00 (0-85646-196-2, Pub. by Anvil Press); pap. 14.95 (0-85646-197-0, Pub. by Anvil Press) Dufour.

Prince, F. T., ed. see Milton, John.

Prince, F. T., ed. see Shakespeare, William.

Prince, Francie & Pi, Douglas. Every Woman's Guide to Investing: 11 Steps to Financial Independence & Security. (Illus.). 240p. 1996. pap. 14.95 (0-7615-0285-8) Prima Pub.

Prince, Francine. The Diabetic Gourmet. 320p. 1994. 32.92 (0-9631701-3-9) R A Rapaport.

— Francine Prince's New Jewish Cuisine. 224p. 1992. pap. 12.00 (0-399-51755-3, Perigee Bks) Berkley Pub.

Prince, Frank A. Awakening the Imagination: A Step by Step Process for Visualization & Guided Imagery. (Illus.). 111p. 1991. pap. 12.95 (1-893013-03-0) Unleash Your Mind.

— C & His Map of the World: A Parable on Diversity. (Mr. C Parable Ser.: Vol. 3). (Illus.). 52p. 1995. pap. 12.95 (1-893013-02-2) Unleash Your Mind.

— C Gets Reorganized. (Mr. C Parable Ser.: Vol. 2). (Illus.). 70p. 1993. pap. 12.95 (1-893013-01-4) Unleash Your Mind.

***Prince, Frank A. & Morrison, David C.** The Nuts & Bolts of Facilitation: Tools for the Art of Facilitation. (Illus.). 75p. 1998. pap. 12.95 (1-893013-00-6) Unleash Your Mind.

Prince, Gail, jt. auth. see Kaplan, Basha.

***Prince George's County Historical Trust Staff, et al.** Prince George's County, Maryland. (Images of America Ser.). (Illus.). 128p. 1999. pap. 18.99 (0-7385-0265-0) Arcadia Publng.

Prince, Gerald. A Dictionary of Narratology. LC 87-4998. x, 118p. 1987. pap. text 13.95 (0-8032-8714-3, Bison Books) U of Nebr Pr.

— A Grammar of Stories: An Introduction. LC 73-85691. (De Proprietatibus Litterarum, Ser. Minor: No. 13). 106p. 1974. pap. text 20.80 (90-279-2535-6) Mouton.

— Narrative As Theme: Studies in French Fiction. LC 91-22481. x, 161p. 1992. text 40.00 (0-8032-3699-9) U of Nebr Pr.

Prince, Gerald, jt. ed. see Motte, Warren F., Jr.

Prince, Gregory A. Having Authority: The Origins & Development of Priesthood During the Ministry of Joseph Smith. LC 93-10136. (John Whitmer Historical Association Monographs). 93p. 1993. pap. text 2.00 (0-8309-0635-5) Herald Pub Hse.

— Power from on High: The Development of Mormon Priesthood. LC 95-7802. 240p. 1995. 24.95 (1-56085-071-X) Signature Bks.

Prince, Harold B., compiled by. A Presbyterian Bibliography. LC 83-10116. (American Theological Library Association Monograph: No. 8). 466p. 1983. pap. 41.50 (0-8108-1639-3) Scarecrow.

Prince, Heather B. Knowledge in the Hands. LC 94-214750. 102p. 1994. pap. 10.95 (0-86492-180-2, Pub. by Goose Ln Edits) Genl Dist Srvs.

Prince, Heather B. Where Water & Gravel Meet. 7.50 (0-920635-11-3) Genl Dist Srvs.

Prince, Hugh. Wetlands of American Midwest: An Historical Geography of Changing Attitudes. LC 97-22226. 296p. 1997. pap. text 21.00 (0-226-68283-8) U Ch Pr.

Prince, J. Dyneley. Assyrian Primer: An Inductive Method of Learning the Cuneiform Characters. LC 17-31948. (Columbia University. Contributions to Oriental History & Philology Ser.: No. 3). reprint ed. 20.00 (0-404-50533-3) AMS Pr.

Prince, J. Dyneley & Budge, E. A. Wallis. Assyrian Primer & Assyrian Texts. 104p. 1978. pap. 15.00 (0-89005-226-3) Ares.

Prince, J. Dyneley & Speck, Frank. A Vocabulary of Mohegan-Pequot. LC 99-19303. (American Language Reprints Ser.: Vol. 9). 81p. 1998. 16.00 (1-889758-02-7) Evol Pubng & Manuf.

Prince, J. Dyneley & Thomas, Gabriel. An Ancient New Jersey Indian Jargon. LC 97-46385. (American Language Reprints Ser.: No. 5). (CRP.). 58p. 1997. lib. bdg. 16.00 (0-9644234-8-0) Evol Pubng & Manuf.

***Prince, Jan.** Tahiti & French Polynesia Guide. 2nd ed. 568p. 2000. pap. 18.95 (1-892975-35-1) Open Rd Pub.

Prince, Jan & Chamberlaine, Sally. From the Inside Out: Building a Healthy Identity. (Illus.). 1992. per. 21.95 (0-9644385-0-X) Chamberlaine & Prince.

***Prince, Janet McKenzie.** Duff at First Sight: A Love Story. LC 99-95439. (Illus.). xvi, 93p. 2000. pap. 16.95 (0-9667286-1-0) Burley Creek Studio.

— Watching Heather Bloom. LC 99-95434. (Illus.). vii, 53p. 2000. pap. 7.95 (0-9667286-2-9) Burley Creek Studio.

***Prince, Jeffrey M. & Heiser, Lisa.** Essentials of Career Interest Assessment. (Essentials of Psychological Assessment Ser.). 256p. 2000. pap. 29.95 (0-471-35365-5) Wiley.

Prince, Jeffrey M., jt. auth. see Fleenor, John W.

Prince, John D. Fragments from Babel. LC 39-13100. reprint ed. 27.50 (0-404-05136-7) AMS Pr.

— Passamaquoddy Texts. LC 73-3545. (American Ethnological Society Publications: No. 10). reprint ed. 20.00 (0-404-58160-9) AMS Pr.

Prince, John L., jt. auth. see Senthinathan, Ramesh.

Prince, Judith S., jt. auth. see Miller, Theodore K.

Prince, K., tr. see Ibach, Harald & Luth, Hans.

Prince, Karen. Aimee Three Dimensional Paper Doll & Trunk. (Illus.). 32p. 1996. pap. text 5.95 (0-87588-458-X) Hobby Hse.

— Danielle Three Dimensional Paper Doll & Trunk. (Illus.). 1996. pap. text 5.95 (0-87588-459-8) Hobby Hse.

Prince, Karen D., illus. see Larson, Mary.

Prince, Katie. Boring Records: Communication, Speech, & Writing in Social Work. LC 95-41381. 250p. 1996. pap. 24.95 (1-85302-325-6, Pub. by Jessica Kingsley) Taylor & Francis.

Prince, Keith R., ed. see American Water Resources Association Staff.

Prince, Kevin C. Photoelectron Spectroscopy of Solids & Surfaces. (Synchrotron Radiation Techniques & Applications Ser.). 300p. 1997. text 55.00 (981-02-2164-9) World Scientific Pub.

Prince, L. Bradford. Spanish Mission Churches of New Mexico. LC 77-1749. (Beautiful Rio Grande Classics Ser.). (Illus.). 535p. 1977. reprint ed. lib. bdg. 50.00 (0-87380-126-1) Popular E Commerce.

Prince, Laura. Breaking the Silence. LC 96-166. (Death, Value & Meaning Ser.). 149p. 1996. text 29.95 (0-89503-137-X) Baywood Pub.

Prince, Len. About Glamour. LC 97-20758. (Illus.). 160p. 1997. 40.00 (0-684-83623-8) Simon & Schuster.

Prince, Leslie. The Farrier & His Craft. 280p. 1990. 60.00 (0-85131-353-1, Pub. by J A Allen) Trafalgar.

Prince, M. R., et al. 3D Contrast MR Angiography. LC 97-6972. 128p. 1997. pap. 39.00 (3-540-62577-1) Spr-Verlag.

Prince, Maggie. The House on Hound Hill. LC 97-42159. 256p. (YA). (gr. 5 up). 1998. 15.00 (0-395-90702-0) HM.

***Prince, Martin R. & Banerjee, Sube.** Mental Health of Older Populations. (Illus.). 224p. 2001. pap. 45.00 (0-7506-4860-0) Buttrwrth-Heinemann.

Prince, Mary, et al. Six Women's Slave Narratives, 1831-1909. (Schomburg Library of Nineteenth-Century Black Women Writers). 384p. 1988. text 38.00 (0-19-505262-5) OUP.

Prince, Mary M. Bieber's Dictionary of Legal Abbreviations. 5th rev. ed. 1993. 45.00 (1-57588-408-9, 311530) W S Hein.

— Bieber's Dictionary of Legal Abbreviations: Reference Guide for Attorneys, Legal Secretaries, Paralegals & Law Students. 4th ed. LC 93-13817. iv, 792p. 1993. 45.00 (0-89941-847-3, 307830) W S Hein.

— Bieber's Dictionary of Legal Citations: Reference Guide for Attorneys, Legal Secretaries, Paralegals & Law Students. 4th ed. LC 92-27176. vi, 372p. 1992. 29.00 (0-89941-824-4, 307710) W S Hein.

Prince, Mary M. & Bieber, Doris M. Bieber's Dictionary of Legal Citations. 5th ed. LC 97-21987. x,441,xv,368p. (C). 1997. 39.50 (1-57588-285-X, 311270) W S Hein.

Prince, Mary M. & Kavass, Igor I., eds. World Dictionary of Legal Abbreviations, 4 vols., Set. 1991. 235.00 (1-57588-383-X, 307320) W S Hein.

Prince, Matthew S. & New Life Inc. Staff. Building Your Relationship with Christ. 1988. pap. text 3.00 (0-942026-02-0) ATAP Corp.

Prince, Michael. Chasing Light. 1995. 17.95 (0-9648319-0-2) Mystic Sun Pr.

— Forgotten Monarchy of Scotland: The True Story of the Royal House of Stewart & the Hidden Lineage of the Kings & Queens of Scots. LC 98-4773. 240p. 1998. 24.95 (1-86204-234-9, Pub. by Element MA) Penguin Putnam.

— Indigo. LC 98-91331. 134 p. 1998. write for info. (0-9648319-1-0) Mystic Sun Pr.

P

— New Guide to Washington. rev. ed. (Illus.). 96p. 1998. pap. 6.50 (*1-879295-25-3*) L B Prince.
— The Pigs of Lake Hood. 64p. 1994. pap. 6.95 (*0-9642662-0-2*) Sundog Pubng.
— The Totems of Seldovia. 160p. (J). (gr. 5-6). 1994. pap. 8.95 (*0-9642662-1-0*) Sundog Pubng.
— Washington D. C. Picture Book: Nation's Capital. rev. ed. (Illus.). 32p. 1997. pap. 3.95 (*1-879295-19-9*) L B Prince.

Prince, Michael B. New Guide to Washington D. C. 8 Tours with 80 Photos - City Maps. (Illus.). 82p. 1990. pap. 5.95 (*1-879295-03-2*) L B Prince.
— Philosophical Dialogue in the British Enlightenment: Theology, Aesthetics, & the Novel. (Studies in Eighteenth-Century English Literature & Thought: No. 31). 296p. (C). 1997. text 59.95 (*0-521-55062-9*) Cambridge U Pr.

Prince, Michael B. Coloring & Activity Book of Washington. 8p. (Orig.). (J). 1996. pap. 1.95 (*1-879251-48-5*) L B Prince.

***Prince Michael of Albany.** The Forgotten Monarchy of Scotland: The True Story of the Royal House of Stewart & the Hidden Lineage of the King & Queens of Scots. (Illus.). 528p. 2000. reprint ed. pap. 19.95 (*1-86204-702-2*) Element MA.

Prince Michael of Greece. Imperial Palaces of Russia. (Illus.). 228p. 1992. 59.50 (*1-85043-566-9*, Pub. by I B T) St Martin.

Prince, Michele. Mandatory Celibacy in the Catholic Church: A Handbook for the Laity. LC 92-16145. 114p. (C). 1992. pap. 9.95 (*0-932727-60-3*, N Paradigm Bks); lib. bdg. 16.95 (*0-932727-61-1*, N Paradigm Bks) Hope Pub Hse.

Prince, Morton. Clinical & Experimental Studies in Personality. rev. ed. LC 72-100197. (Illus.). 671p. 1970. reprint ed. lib. bdg. 89.50 (*0-8371-3995-3*, PRPE, Greenwood Pr) Greenwood.

Prince, Morton. The Dissociation of a Personality. 585p. 120.00 (*1-85506-690-4*) Thoemmes Pr.

Prince, Morton. Dissociation of a Personality: A Biographical Study in Abnormal Psychology. LC 69-10148. 575p. 1969. reprint ed. lib. bdg. 35.00 (*0-8371-1988-X*, PRAP, Greenwood Pr) Greenwood.
— Psychotheraphy & Multiple Personality: Selected Essays. Hale, Nathan G., Jr., ed. LC 74-82574. 336p. 1975. 41.50 (*0-674-72225-6*) HUP.
— The Unconscious: The Fundamentals of Human Personality Normal & Abnormal. 2nd ed. LC 73-2411. (Mental Illness & Social Policy; the American Experience Ser.). 1973. reprint ed. 44.95 (*0-405-05221-9*) Ayer.

Prince, Morton, et al. Psychotherapeutics: A Symposium. LC 75-16728. (Classics in Psychiatry Ser.). 1976. reprint ed. 18.95 (*0-405-07451-4*) Ayer.

Prince, Nancy. A Black Woman's Odyssey Through Russia & Jamaica: The Narrative of Nancy Prince. LC 89-24945. (Topics in World History Ser.). (Illus.). 124p. (Orig.). (C). reprint ed. text 19.95 (*1-55876-028-8*); reprint ed. pap. text 9.95 (*1-55876-019-9*) Wiener Pubs Inc.

Prince, Pamela & Handel, Jane, eds. You're the Top: A Song by Cole Porter. LC 98-37785. (Illus.). 64p. 1999. 12.95 (*0-684-85560-7*, S&S Edns) Simon & Schuster.

Prince, Pamela, ed. see Baudelaire, Charles.

Prince, Patricia. The Contreras Clinic Laetrile Cookbook. LC 79-89609. (Illus.). 248p. 1979. pap. 12.00 (*0-8159-5221-X*) Devin.

Prince, Richard. Adult Comedy Action Drama. (Illus.). 240p. 1995. 70.00 (*1-881616-36-3*, Pub. by Scalo Pubs) Dist Art Pubs.
— Amor Extravagante.Tr. of Extravagant Love. (SPA.). 4.50 (*0-7899-0113-7*, 550080) Editorial Unilit.
— Corvette Restoration Guide, 1968-1982. LC 99-49083. (Authentic Restoration Guides Ser.). (Illus.). 256p. 1999. pap. 29.95 (*0-7603-0657-5*, 128913AP) Motorbooks Intl.
— Inside World. (Illus.). 88p. 1989. pap. 750.00 (*1-878607-09-X*) Kent Gallery.

Prince, Richard, photos by. 4 X 4. (Illus.). 120p. 1999. pap. 40.00 (*1-57687-034-0*, pwerHse Bks) pwerHse Cultrl.

Prince, Richard A. From Bondage to Freedom. LC 92-75259. (Illus.). 153p. (Orig.). (C). 1992. pap. text 7.95 (*1-879667-12-6*) Dove Pr TX.

***Prince, Richard E.** Atlantic Coast Line Railroad: Steam Locomotives, Ships & History. LC 99-41987. (Illus.). 232p. 2000. 49.95 (*0-253-33694-5*) Ind U Pr.
— Seaboard Air Line Railway: Steam Boats, Locomotives & History. LC 99-41988. (Illus.). 272p. 2000. 49.95 (*0-253-33695-3*) Ind U Pr.

Prince, Robert H. Why a Woman Should Not Be Called a Preach: Victory Collection. 4th ed. Koger, Dorothy P., ed. 20p. 1999. reprint ed. pap. 5.00 (*1-882821-02-5*) DPK Pubns.

Prince, Robert M. The Death of Psychoanalysis: Murder? Suicide? or Rumor Greatly Exaggerated. LC 97-37074. 408p. 1998. pap. 50.00 (*0-7657-0147-2*) Aronson.
— The Legacy of the Holocaust: Psychohistorical Themes in the Second Generation. LC 84-24036. (Research in Clinical Psychology Ser.: No. 12). 239p. reprint ed. pap. 74.10 (*0-8357-1627-9*, 207041100088) Bks Demand.
— The Legacy of the Holocaust: Psychohistorical Themes in the Second Generation. LC 99-25641. 223p. 1999. reprint ed. pap. 25.00 (*1-892746-26-3*, 46263) Other Pr LLC.

Prince, Russ A. & File, Karen F. The Seven Faces of Philanthropy: A New Approach to Cultivating Major Donors. LC 94-8095. (Nonprofit Sector Ser.). 247p. 1994. text 30.95 (*0-7879-0008-7*) Jossey-Bass.

Prince, Russ A. & File, Karen M. Building Your Business: Marking Your Way to a $100 Million Investment Advisory Business. LC 97-211051. 250p. 1997. pap. 40.00 (*0-9658391-0-9*) HNW Pr.
— Cultivating the Affluent Vol. 1: How to Segment & Service the High-Net-Worth Market. (Illus.). 121p. 1995. 95.00 (*0-9619446-4-1*) Institutional Investor.
— Cultivating the Affluent Vol. 2: Leveraging High-Net-Worth Client & Advisor Relationships. (Illus.). 144p. 1997. 195.00 (*0-9619446-5-X*) Institutional Investor.

Prince, Russ A., et al. The Perfect Legacy: How to Establish Your Own Private Foundation. LC 99-164255. (Illus.). 80p. 1998. pap. 19.95 (*0-9658391-1-7*) HNW Pr.
— Physician Financial Planning in a Changing Environment. 300p. (Orig.). 1996. reprint ed. pap. text 44.95 (*1-57066-104-9*, ME115) Practice Mgmt Info.

Prince, Ruth, jt. auth. see Prince, Derek.

Prince, Stephanie. The Pledge Class, Vol. 2. (Sorority Sisters Ser.: No. 2). 224p. (J). 1997. mass mkt. 4.50 (*0-06-106508-0*) HarpC Child Bks.
— Rush Week, Vol. 1. (Sorority Sisters Ser.: No. 1). 208p. (J). (gr. 7-12). 1997. mass mkt. 4.50 (*0-06-106507-2*) HarpC Child Bks.

***Prince, Stephen.** History of the American Cinema: A New Pot of Gold, Vol. 10. LC 99-38369. 450p. 1999. 85.00 (*0-684-80493-X*) Mac Lib Ref.

Prince, Stephen. Savage Cinema: Sam Peckinpah & the Rise of Ultraviolent Movies. LC 97-32696. (Illus.). 308p. 1998. 35.00 (*0-292-76581-9*); pap. 18.95 (*0-292-76582-7*) U of Tex Pr.
— Visions of Empire: Political Imagery in Contemporary American Film. LC 91-44449. (Political Communication Ser.). 232p. 1992. 57.95 (*0-275-93661-9*, C3661, Praeger Pubs); pap. 19.95 (*0-275-93662-7*, B3662, Praeger Pubs) Greenwood.
— The Warrior's Camera. LC 99-24982. 432p. 1999. pap. 19.95 (*0-691-01046-3*, Pub. by Princeton U Pr) Cal Prin Full Svc.
— The Warrior's Camera: The Cinema of Akira Kurosawa. (Illus.). 370p. 1991. pap. text 19.95 (*0-691-00859-0*, Pub. by Princeton U Pr) Cal Prin Full Svc.

Prince, Stephen, ed. Sam Peckinpah's "The Wild Bunch" LC 98-25117. (Cambridge Film Handbks.). (Illus.). 224p. (C). 1999. 49.95 (*0-521-58433-7*); pap. 14.95 (*0-521-58606-2*) Cambridge U Pr.

***Prince, Stephen, ed.** Screening Violence. LC 99-54344. (Depth of Field Ser.). (Illus.). 240p. 2000. text 50.00 (*0-8135-2817-8*); pap. text 19.00 (*0-8135-2818-6*) Rutgers U Pr.

Prince, Stephen R. Movies & Meaning: An Introduction to Film. LC 95-43380. 397p. 1996. pap. text 51.00 (*0-02-396806-0*, Macmillan Coll) P-H.

Prince, Sue A., ed. The Old Guard & the Avant-Garde: Modernism in Chicago, 1910-1940. LC 90-35236. (Illus.). 312p. 1990. 42.00 (*0-226-68284-6*) U Ch Pr.

Prince, Thane. Quick & Easy Soups. (Illus.). 1996. pap. 9.95 (*0-563-36949-3*, BBC-Parkwest) Parkwest Pubns.
— Quick Cook. (Illus.). 192p. 1992. 19.95 (*0-7011-6181-7*, Pub. by Chatto & Windus) Trafalgar.

Prince, Thomas. A Chronological History of New England in the Form of Annals. LC 75-31100. reprint ed. 49.50 (*0-404-13517-X*) AMS Pr.

Prince, Thomas & Mayberry, Edward. Bottom Line Billing & Collections for the Medical Practice. 500p. (C). Date not set. 169.00 (*1-56329-405-2*) St Anthony Pub.
— Managed Care Operational Strategies: A Medical Office Survival Guide. LC 97-204049. 500p. (C). 1997. 169.00 (*1-56329-404-4*) St Anthony Pub.

Prince, Thomas R. Strategic Management for Health Care Entities: Creative Frameworks for Financial & Operational Analysis. LC 98-9419. 543p. 1998. write for info. (*1-55648-214-0*) AHPI.

Prince, Tony, jt. tr. see Buzo, Adrian.

Prince, W. Bartlett. Pilot - Take Charge. (C). 1987. 60.00 (*0-85174-139-8*) St Mut.

Prince, Walter F. The Enchanted Boundary: Being a Survey of Negative Reactions to Claims of Psychic Phenomena, 1820-1930. LC 75-7396. (Perspectives in Psychical Research Ser.). 1975. reprint ed. 29.95 (*0-405-07045-4*) Ayer.

Prince, William S. Crusade & Pilgrimage: A Soldier's Death, a Mother's Journey, & a Grandson's Quest. (Illus.). 128p. (Orig.). 1986. pap. 14.95 (*0-87595-160-0*) Oregon Hist.

Prince, Wilson. Relational Database: Using dBASE III Plus. 2nd ed. (C). 1988. text 49.95 (*0-07-051043-1*) McGraw.

Princelle, Jean L. Authentic Guide to Russian & Soviet Cameras. (Illus.). 190p. 1996. pap. text 45.00 (*1-874031-63-0*, Pub. by Hove Foto) Watsn-Guptill.

Princen, Thomas. Beagle Channel Negotiations. (Pew Case Studies in International Affairs). 50p. (C). 1995. pap. text 3.50 (*1-56927-401-0*) Geo U Inst Dplmcy.
— Intermediaries in International Conflict. (Illus.). 264p. 1992. text 47.50 (*0-691-07897-1*, Pub. by Princeton U Pr) Cal Prin Full Svc.

Princen, Thomas, jt. auth. see Olsen, Jennifer.

Princenthal, Nancy. Mary Miss: Photo - Drawings. (Illus.). 68p. (C). 1991. pap. text 25.00 (*0-941972-12-7*) Freedman.

Princenthal, Nancy & Philbrick, Harry, texts. Landscape Reclaimed. (Illus.). 72p. 1996. pap. 19.95 (*1-888332-03-4*, 620823) Aldrich Mus.

Princenthal, Nancy, et al. Album: 30 Years at the Lower East Side Printshop, 1968-1998. Sinaiko, Eve, ed. LC 98-88087. (Illus.). 68p. 1998. pap. 10.00 (*0-9667505-0-0*) Lower East Side.

Princenthal, Nancy, jt. auth. see Lauterbach, Ann.

Princess Chichibu, et al. The Silver Drum: A Japanese Imperial Memoir. Britton, Dorothy, tr. (Illus.). 210p. 1999. 24.95 (*1-86034-004-0*, Pub. by Global Bks) Midpt Trade.

Princess Grace Irish Library Staff. Irishness in a Changing Society. LC 88-7828. 280p. 1988. lib. bdg. 53.00 (*0-389-20857-4*, N8415) B&N Imports.

***Princess Ivori.** Living in Girlfriend's House: Real Woman Survival Tips. 112p. 2000. pap. 10.95 (*0-615-11871-2*) Linden & Farmer.

Princess, Takamado Hih. Lulie: The Iceburg. (J). (gr. 3 up). 1998. 17.00 (*1-56836-272-2*) Kodansha.

Princeton Architectural Press Staff. Winka Dubbeldam, Architect. (Illus.). 60p. 1996. pap. 35.00 (*1-56898-102-3*) Princeton Arch.

Princeton Conference on Cerebrovascular Disease. Cerebrovascular Diseases. Ginsberg, Myron D. & Dietrich, W. Dalton, eds. LC 75-25125. 483p. 1989. reprint ed. pap. 149.80 (*0-608-03411-8*, 206410900008) Bks Demand.

Princeton, Douglas C. Manual of HIV - AIDS Therapy, 1997 Edition: Current Clinical Strategies. 2nd ed. 102p. 1997. pap. 12.75 (*1-881528-05-7*) Current Clin Strat.

***Princeton, Douglas C.** Manual of HIV-AIDS Therapy: 2001 Edition. rev. ed. (Current Clinical Strategies Ser.). 83p. 2000. pap. 28.95 incl. cd-rom (*1-881528-88-X*) Current Clin Strat.

Princeton, Douglas C. Manual of HIV-AIDS Therapy, 2001 Edition: Current Clinical Strategies. rev. ed. 1999. pap. 12.95 (*1-881528-87-1*) Current Clin Strat.

Princeton Institute Staff. Twenty-First Century Roberts Rules of Order. Rozakis, Laurie E. & Lichtenstein, Ellen, eds. LC 95-236066. 224p. 1995. mass mkt. 6.50 (*0-440-21722-9*) Dell.

Princeton Language Institute. 21st Century Synonym & Antonym Finder. (21st Century Reference Ser.). 1993. 11.09 (*0-606-05097-3*, Pub. by Turtleback) Demco.

Princeton Language Institute Staff. Twenty-First Century Dictionary of Quotations. LC 93-225023. 624p. 1993. mass mkt. 6.50 (*0-440-21447-5*) Dell.
— Twenty-First Century Dictionary of Slang. 352p. 1994. mass mkt. 5.99 (*0-440-21551-X*) Dell.
— Twenty-First Century Guide to Improving Your Writing. 272p. 1995. mass mkt. 5.99 (*0-440-21727-X*) Dell.
— Twenty-First Century Guide to Increasing Your Reading Speed. 240p. 1995. mass mkt. 5.99 (*0-440-21724-5*) Dell.
— Webster's 21st Century Large-Print Dictionary. large type ed. 608p. 1996. pap. 19.95 (*0-385-31643-7*, Delta Trade) Dell.

Princeton Language Institute Staff, ed. see Kipfer, Barbara A.

Princeton Language Institute Staff, ed. see Read, Elizabeth.

***Princeton Publishing Staff.** Princeton Review America's Top Internships 2001. 8th ed. 416p. 2000. pap. 21.00 (*0-375-75637-X*, Pub. by PRP NY) Random.
— Princeton Review Best Distance Learning. 2nd ed. 336p. 2000. pap. 21.00 (*0-375-75636-1*, Pub. by PRP NY) Random.
— Princeton Review Internship Bible 2001. 672p. 2000. pap. 25.00 (*0-375-75638-8*, Pub. by PRP NY) Random.

Princeton Rev Staff. Math Smart Jr. II: More Math Made Easy. LC 98-229112. (Princeton Review Ser.). (J). 1998. pap. 10.00 (*0-679-78377-6*) Random.
— Reading Smart Junior: Becoming a Star Reader. LC 98-232311. (Princeton Review Ser.). (J). 1998. pap. 10.00 (*0-679-78376-8*) Random.

***Princeton Review Publishing Staff.** African American: Student's Guide. 2000. pap. write for info. (*0-375-75632-9*) PRP NY.
— Biology. (Cracking the Golden State Ser.). (Illus.). 263p. 2000. pap. 16.00 (*0-375-75356-7*, Pub. by PRP NY) Random.

Princeton Review Publishing Staff. Biology Smart. LC 97-208383. 1996. pap. 12.00 (*0-679-76908-0*) Random.

***Princeton Review Publishing Staff.** Biology 2000-2001. 4th ed. 2000. pap. 17.00 (*0-375-75495-4*, Pub. by PRP NY) Random.
— Calculus AB & BC 2000-2001, 4th ed. 2000. pap. 18.00 (*0-375-75499-7*, Pub. by PRP NY) Random.

Princeton Review Publishing Staff. Careers in Law. Date not set. pap. write for info. (*0-679-76929-3*) Random Ref & Info.

***Princeton Review Publishing Staff.** Chemistry. (Cracking the Golden State Ser.). (Illus.). 233p. 2000. pap. 16.00 (*0-375-75357-5*, Pub. by PRP NY) Random.
— Chemistry Exam 2000, 3rd ed. (Illus.). 413p. 2000. pap. 6.95 (*0-375-75554-3*, Pub. by PRP NY) Random.
— Chemistry 2000-2001, 4th ed. 2000. pap. 17.00 (*0-375-75497-0*, Pub. by PRP NY) Random.

Princeton Review Publishing Staff. The Complete Book of Colleges. 2nd ed. (Princeton Review Ser.). 288p. 1998. pap. 21.00 (*0-375-75167-X*) Random.

***Princeton Review Publishing Staff.** Complete Book of Colleges 2000. 1632p. 1999. pap. 26.95 (*0-375-75462-8*, Pub. by PRP NY) Random.
— Complete Book of Colleges 2001. 1824p. 2000. pap. 26.95 (*0-375-76152-7*, Pub. by PRP NY) Random.

Princeton Review Publishing Staff. Cracking the Act: With Simple Tests on Cd-Rom, 1999-2000 Edition. 1999. pap. 29.95 (*0-375-75281-1*) Pantheon.

***Princeton Review Publishing Staff.** Cracking the ACT 2000-2001. 5th ed. 2000. pap. 29.95 (*0-375-75501-2*, Pub. by PRP NY) Random.
— Cracking the ACT 2000-2001. 9th ed. 2000. pap. 18.00 (*0-375-75500-4*, Pub. by PRP NY) Random.
— Cracking the AP: Economics (Macro & Micro), 2000-2001. 2000. pap. 17.00 (*0-375-75507-1*, Pub. by PRP NY) Random.
— Cracking the AP: Spanish 2000-2001. 2000. pap. 17.00 (*0-375-75481-4*, Pub. by PRP NY) Random.
— Cracking the AP Psychology 2000-2001. 336p. 2000. pap. 17.00 (*0-375-75480-6*) Random.

Princeton Review Publishing Staff. Cracking the GMAT CAT with Sample Tests on CD-ROM 2000. 1999. pap. 34.95 (*0-375-75406-7*) Random.
— Cracking the GRE Biology. 2nd ed. 1997. pap. 18.00 (*0-679-78408-X*) Random.
— Cracking the GRE CAT with Sample Tests on CD-ROM 2000. 1999. pap. 29.95 (*0-375-75408-3*) Random.
— Cracking the GRE CAT 2000. 1999. pap. 20.00 (*0-375-75407-5*) Random.

***Princeton Review Publishing Staff.** Cracking the NCLEX-RN 2000-2001. 2000. pap. 34.95 (*0-375-75543-8*, Pub. by PRP NY) Random.
— Cracking the New York State 8th Grade Math Test. 2000. pap. 16.00 (*0-375-75555-1*, Pub. by PRP NY) Random.
— Cracking the Regents Earth Science Exam 2000, 3rd ed. 2000. pap. text 6.95 (*0-375-75552-7*, Pub. by PRP NY) Random.
— Crash Course for the Act. 208p. 2000. pap. 9.95 (*0-375-75326-5*, Pub. by PRP NY) Random.
— Economics. (Cracking the Golden State Ser.). (Illus.). 272p. 2000. pap. 16.00 (*0-375-75355-9*, Pub. by PRP NY) Random.
— English Literature 2000-2001. 4th ed. 2000. pap. 17.00 (*0-375-75493-8*, Pub. by PRP NY) Random.
— European History 2000-2001, 2nd ed. 2000. pap. 17.00 (*0-375-75498-9*, Pub. by PRP NY) Random.
— First Year Algebra. (Illus.). 282p. 2000. pap. 16.00 (*0-375-75352-4*, Pub. by PRP NY) Random.
— Geometry. (Illus.). 242p. 2000. pap. 16.00 (*0-375-75353-2*, Pub. by PRP NY) Random.
— Global History Exam 2000. 3rd ed. 2000. pap. 6.95 (*0-375-75551-9*, Pub. by PRP NY) Random.

Princeton Review Publishing Staff. GRE Math, 1997. Date not set. pap. write for info. (*0-679-76923-4*) Random Ref & Info.
— Great Math Workout. (Princeton Review Ser.). 1998. pap. 16.00 (*0-679-78373-3*) Random.
— GRE/GMAT Math. Date not set. pap., wbk. ed. write for info. (*0-679-76936-6*) Random Ref & Info.
— Guide to Your Career 1999. 3rd ed. 1998. pap. 21.00 (*0-375-75156-4*) Random.
— High School Biology Review. (Princeton Review Ser.). 1998. pap. 10.95 (*0-375-75081-9*) Random.
— High School Chemistry Review. LC 98-4596. 1998. pap. 9.95 (*0-375-75082-7*) Random.
— High School Comprehensive English Review. large type ed. 1998. pap. 9.95 (*0-375-75076-2*) Random.
— High School Earth Science Review. LC 98-14847. (Princeton Review Ser.). 1998. pap. 12.95 (*0-375-75080-0*) Random.
— High School Global Studies Review. LC 98-3066. (Princeton Review Ser.). 1998. pap. 11.95 (*0-375-75079-7*) Random.
— High School Math II Review, No. 2. LC 98-2985. (Princeton Review Ser.). 1998. pap. 10.95 (*0-375-75074-6*) Random.
— High School Math III Review. 1998. pap. 9.95 (*0-375-75075-4*) Random.
— High School Spanish Review. LC 98-4592. 304p. 2000. pap. 10.95 (*0-375-75077-0*) Random.
— Illustrated Word Smart: A Visual Vocabulary Builder. 288p. 1999. pap. 12.95 (*0-375-75189-0*) Random.
— Law School Companion. (Princeton Review Ser.). 288p. 1995. pap. 15.00 (*0-679-76150-0*) Random.
— Mythology Smart Junior. LC 97-27239. 1997. pap. 10.00 (*0-679-78375-X*) Random.
— NCLEX-RN Questions & Answers: More Than 2,000 Quetions & Answers for NCLEX-RN Success. 1999. pap. 27.95 (*0-375-75291-9*) Random.
— NYCLEX, 1997. (Princeton Review Ser.). 1997. pap. 20.00 (*0-679-76915-3*) Random Ref & Info.

***Princeton Review Publishing Staff.** Physics 2000-2001. 2nd ed. 2000. pap. 19.00 (*0-375-75492-X*, Pub. by PRP NY) Random.
— PR Cracking the GED 2001. 608p. 2000. pap. 18.00 (*0-375-75619-1*, Pub. by PRP NY) Random.
— PR Cracking the GMAT- CAT 2001. 416p. 2000. pap. 18.00 (*0-375-75623-X*, Pub. by PRP NY) Random.
— PR Cracking the GMAT CAT. 432p. 2000. pap. 34.95 incl. cd-rom (*0-375-75624-8*, Pub. by PRP NY) Random.
— PR Cracking the GRE CAT 2001. 400p. 2000. pap. 20.00 (*0-375-75625-6*, Pub. by PRP NY); pap. 31.00 incl. audio compact disk (*0-375-75626-4*, Pub. by PRP NY) Random.
— PR Cracking the LSAT 2001. 400p. 2000. pap. 20.00 (*0-375-75628-0*, Pub. by PRP NY); pap. 34.95 incl. cd-rom (*0-375-75629-9*, Pub. by PRP NY) Random.
— PR Cracking the SSAT/ISEE 2001. 576p. 2000. pap. 18.00 (*0-375-75630-2*, Pub. by PRP NY) Random.
— PR Crash Course for the GMAT. 208p. 2000. pap. 9.95 (*0-375-75618-3*, Pub. by PRP NY) Random.
— PR Guide to Your Career. 4th ed. 464p. 2000. pap. 21.00 (*0-375-75620-5*, Pub. by PRP NY) Random.

Princeton Review Publishing Staff. The Princeton Review: GRE Subject, Vol. 6. Date not set. pap. write for info. (*0-679-76935-8*) McKay.
— Princeton Review: Inside the GRE. 144p. 1996. 36.95 incl. cd-rom (*1-884536-57-3*) Villard Books.
— Princeton Review: Inside the SAT. 1996. 34.95 incl. cd-rom (*1-884536-56-5*) Villard Books.
— The Princeton Review Law School Course Summary, Vol. 3. Date not set. pap. write for info. (*0-679-76918-8*) McKay.
— The Princeton Review Law School Course Summary, Vol. 4. 1998. pap. 20.00 (*0-679-76930-7*) McKay.
— The Princeton Review Law School Course Summary, Vol. 7. Date not set. pap. write for info. (*0-679-76933-1*) McKay.
— The Princeton Review Law School Course Summary No. 6, Vol. 6. Date not set. pap. write for info. (*0-679-76932-3*) McKay.

***Princeton Review Publishing Staff.** Princeton Review SAT Math Workout. 2nd ed. 256p. 2000. pap. 16.00 (*0-375-76177-2*, Pub. by PRP NY) Random.
— Princeton Review SAT Verbal Workout. 2nd ed. 240p. 2000. pap. 16.00 (*0-375-76176-4*, Pub. by PRP NY) Random.

Princeton Review Publishing Staff. The Princeton Review Science Smart, Jr. LC 97-193671. 1996. pap. 12.00 (*0-679-76906-4*) McKay.
— The Princeton Review Student Guide to Finance. Date not set. pap. write for info. (*0-679-76937-4*) McKay.
— R. N., 1997. Date not set. pap. write for info. (*0-679-76916-1*) Random Ref & Info.
— Review Smart. LC 97-51714. (Princeton Review Ser.). 1998. pap. 12.95 (*0-375-75078-9*) Random.
— Rookie's Guide to Money Management: How to Keep Score of Your Finances. LC 98-148380. 1997. pap. 12.00 (*0-679-77882-9*) Random.

***Princeton Review Publishing Staff.** Sequential Math III Exam 2000. 3rd ed. 540p. 2000. pap. 6.95 (*0-375-75547-0*, Pub. by PRP NY) Random.
— Sequential Math II Exam 2000. 3rd ed. 2000. pap. 6.95 (*0-375-75546-2*, Pub. by PRP NY) Random.

Princeton Review Publishing Staff. High School Math I Review. 1998. pap. 10.95 (*0-375-75073-8*) Random.

***Princeton Review Publishing Staff.** Spanish Exam 2000. 3rd ed. 2000. pap. 6.95 (*0-375-75549-7*, Pub. by PRP NY) Random.
— U. S. Government & Politics 1999-2000. 3rd ed. 2000. pap. 17.00 (*0-375-75496-2*, Pub. by PRP NY) Random.
— U. S. History. (Cracking the Golden State Ser.). 248p. 2000. pap. 16.00 (*0-375-75354-0*, Pub. by PRP NY) Random.
— U. S. History 2000-2001. 4th ed. 2000. pap. 17.00 (*0-375-75494-6*, Pub. by PRP NY) Random.

Princeton Review Publishing Staff. Work Smart: How to Think, Look & Act on the Job. (Princeton Review Ser.). 1998. pap. 12.00 (*0-679-78388-1*) Random.

Princeton Review Publishing Staff, ed. Best Graduate Programs: Engineering. 2nd ed. (Princeton Review Ser.). 1998. pap. 21.00 (*0-375-75205-6*) Villard Books.

***Princeton Review Publishing Staff, ed.** Best 331 Colleges 2001. (Illus.). 768p. 2000. pap. 20.00 (*0-375-75633-7*, Pub. by PRP NY) Random.
— Crackig the COOP/HSPT. (Illus.). 2000. pap. 18.00 (*0-375-76143-8*, Pub. by PRP NY) Random.
— Cracking the SAT 2001. 372p. 2000. pap. 29.95 (*0-375-75622-1*, Pub. by PRP NY) Random.
— Pocket Guide to Colleges 2001. (Illus.). 2000. pap. 9.95 (*0-375-75631-0*, Pub. by PRP NY) Random.

Princeton Review Publishing Staff, ed. Princeton Review GRE Computer Diagnostics 95: IBM Version. 1995. pap. text 15.25 incl. 3.5 hd (*1-884536-11-5*) Villard Books.

Princeton Review Publishing Staff, ed. Princeton Review Sat Version 2.0: Mac Version. 1995. 15.25 incl. disk (*1-884536-10-7*) Villard Books.

Princeton Review Publishing Staff & Lerner, Marcia. Math Smart Junior: Grade School Math Made Easy. (J). (gr. 6-8). 1995. pap. 12.00 (*0-679-75935-2*) Villard Books.

***Princeton Review Publishing Staff, et al.** Cracking the SAT 2000. 624p. 1999. pap., student ed. 18.00 (*0-375-75403-2*) Random.

Princeton Review Publishing Staff, et al. Cracking the SAT with Sample Tests on CD-ROM. 624p. 1999. pap., student ed. 29.95 incl. cd-rom (*0-375-75404-0*) Random.

Princeton Review Publishing Staff, jt. auth. see Alcamo, I. Edward.

Princeton Review Publishing Staff, jt. auth. see Goddin, Nell.

Princeton Review Publishing Staff, jt. auth. see Lerner, Marcia.

Princeton Review Publishing Staff, jt. auth. see Robinson, Adam.

Princeton Symposium on Mathematical Programming St. Proceedings of the Princeton Symposium on Mathematical Programming. Kuhn, Harold W., ed. LC 75-140280. (Illus.). 626p. 1970. reprint ed. pap. 194.10 (*0-608-06611-7*, 206680800009) Bks Demand.

Princeton Training Staff. Doing Business Internationally, Self-Paced Workbook. 1995. text 49.50 (*1-882390-00-8*, Irwn Prfssnl) McGraw-Hill Prof.

Princeton Un Staff. Physics for Scientist & Engineers: Learning Guide. 2nd ed. 1995. pap. text. write for info. (*0-13-231705-2*) Allyn.

Princeton University Art Museum Staff. Princeton Alumni Collections: Works on Paper. LC 81-80640. (Illus.). 264p. 1981. text 44.50 (*0-691-03977-1*, Pub. by Princeton U Pr) Cal Prin Full Svc.

Princeton University Conference on Discrimination. Discrimination in Labor Markets. Rees, Albert E. & Ashenfelter, Orley C., eds. LC 72-4037. 195p. 1973. reprint ed. pap. 60.50 (*0-608-02877-0*, 206394100007) Bks Demand.

Princeton University Library Staff, et al. Handlist of Arabic Manuscripts in the Princeton University Library. LC 84-42613. (Princeton Studies on the Near East). 417p. 1987. reprint ed. pap. 129.30 (*0-608-07168-4*, 206739300009) Bks Demand.

Princeton University Staff. Dictionary Catalog of the Princeton University Plasma Physics Laboratory Library. 1994. 205.00 (*0-7838-2281-2*, G K Hall & Co) Mac Lib Ref.
— Morgantina, Vol. 6. (Morgantina Studies: No. 6). 1998. 85.00 (*0-691-04017-6*, Pub. by Princeton U Pr) Cal Prin Full Svc.
— Morgantina, Vol. 7. (Morgantina Studies: No. 7). 1999. 85.00 (*0-691-04018-4*, Pub. by Princeton U Pr) Cal Prin Full Svc.
— Population Index Bibliography Cumulated 1935 to 1968 by Authors & Geographical Areas. 1971. 500.00 (*0-8161-1437-4*, G K Hall & Co) Mac Lib Ref.
— Population Index Bibliography Cumulated, 1935 to 1968 by Geographical Areas. 1971. 520.00 (*0-8161-1398-X*, G K Hall & Co) Mac Lib Ref.
— Princeton Manuscripts: A Guide to Modern Manuscripts in the Princeton University Library. (Library Reference Ser.). 2000p. 1989. 290.00 (*0-8161-0469-7*, G K Hall & Co) Mac Lib Ref.

Princeton University Staff, jt. auth. see Hourihane, Colum.

Princeton/Masters Press Staff, ed. see Gerberg, Bob.

Princeton/SSI Conference on Space Manufacturing Staff & Faughnan, Barbara. Space Manufacturing 11: The Challenge of Space, Past & Future: Proceedings of the 13th SSI/Princeton Conference on Space Manufacturing, May 8-11, 1997. LC 97-166203. xi, 381 p. 1997. write for info. (*0-9622379-1-4*) SSIP.

Princetonians Staff, et al. Princetonians Vol. 5: A Biographical Dictionary, 1791-1794. LC 81-47074. 641p. 1991. reprint ed. pap. 198.80 (*0-608-07126-9*, 206735200005) Bks Demand.

***Princewill, Mpaka.** Engineering Forecasting Mythology: Parking Demand Analysis: Newark Central Business District. LC 99-91655. 2000. 25.00 (*0-7388-1154-8*); pap. 18.00 (*0-7388-1155-6*) Xlibris Corp.

***Princeyal, Albert.** Girls of the Rue Pigalle. 192p. 1999. mass mkt. 7.95 (*1-56201-151-0*) Blue Moon Bks.

***Princing & Ewend Staff.** Saginaw County: Visions of the Valley. LC 99-47579. (American Enterprise Ser.). (Illus.). 208p. 1999. 35.00 (*1-58192-006-7*) Community Comm.

***Principato, Tom.** Open-string Guitar Chords: An Encyclopedia of Over 4,000 Unique & Practical Voicings for All Styles & Levels. 104p. 1999. otabind 9.95 (*0-634-00478-6*) H Leonard.

Principe, Angelo. The Darkest Side of the Fascist Years: The Italian-Canadian Press: 1920-1942. (Essay Ser.: Vol. 42). 200p. 1999. pap. 18.00 (*1-55071-083-4*) Guernica Editions.

Principe, Angelo A. World War II War Birds: Solid Wood Airplane Modeling. (Illus.). 200p. 1993. spiral bd. 19.95 (*0-9634736-0-3*) Hist In Wood.

***Principe, Concetta.** Interference. LC 98-75179. (Essential Poets Ser.: Vol. 91). 96p. 1999. pap. 10.00 (*1-55071-089-3*, Pub. by Guernica Editions) Paul & Co Pubs.

Principe, Concetta. Stained Glass. LC 96-78722. 96p. 1997. pap. 10.00 (*1-55071-062-1*) Guernica Editions.

Principe, David del, see Del Principe, David.

Principe, Jacob. El Otro Lado de la Biblia (The Other Side of the Bible) Lo Que la Teologia No Ha Revalado - What Theology Has Not Revealed - un Amanecev a la Realidad - a Dawn to Reality. (SPA.). 250p. (Orig.). pap. write for info. (*0-9641776-0-9*) El Otro Lado.

***Principe, Jose C., et al.** Neural & Adaptive Systems: Fundamentals Through Simulations. LC 99-27794. 658p. 1999. 80.90 incl. cd-rom (*0-471-35167-9*) Wiley.

Principe, Lawrence & Boyle, Robert. The Aspiring Adept. LC 97-41793. 381p. 1998. text 45.00 (*0-691-01678-X*, Pub. by Princeton U Pr) Cal Prin Full Svc.

***Principe, Lawrence M.** Aspiring Adept: Robert Boyle & His Alchemical Quest. 381p. 2000. pap. 19.95 (*0-691-05082-1*) Princeton U Pr.

Principe, Walter H. Faith, History & Cultures: Stability & Change in Church Teachings. LC 90-64240. (Pere Marquette Lectures). 1991. 15.00 (*0-87462-546-7*) Marquette.
— The Theology of the Hypostatic Union in the Early Thirteenth Century Vol. 4: Philip the Chancellor's Theology of the Hypostatic Union. 234p. pap. 33.14 (*0-88844-032-4*) Brill Academic Pubs.

Principe, William L., Jr., jt. auth. see Clements, James F.

Prindl, Andreas R. & Prodhan, Bimal, eds. Ethical Conflicts in Finance: The A. C. T. Guide To. 272p. 1994. 49.95 (*1-85573-256-4*, Pub. by Woodhead Pubng) Am Educ Systs.

Prindle, Anthony & Prindle, Katie. Math the Easy Way: Your Key to Learning. 3rd ed. Farley, Eugene J., ed. LC 95-20390. (Barron's Easy Way Ser.). (Illus.). 232p. 1996. pap. 11.95 (*0-8120-9139-6*) Barron.

Prindle, David F. Petroleum Politics & the Texas Railroad Commission. LC 81-7535. (Elma Dill Russell Spencer Foundation Ser.: No. 12). (Illus.). 240p. (C). 1984. pap. 10.95 (*0-292-76449-8*) U of Tex Pr.
— The Politics of Glamour: Ideology & Democracy in the Screen Actors Guild. LC 88-40194. (Illus.). 240p. (C). 1988. 27.95 (*0-299-11810-X*) U of Wis Pr.

Prindle, Dennis, jt. auth. see Kent, Conrad.

Prindle, F. C. Prindle Genealogy, Embracing the Descendants of William Pringle, the First Settler, & Also the Ancestors & Descendants of Zalmon Prindle, 1654-1906. 352p. 1989. reprint ed. pap. 52.75 (*0-8328-0995-0*); reprint ed. lib. bdg. 60.75 (*0-8328-0994-2*) Higginson Bk Co.

Prindle, Katie, jt. auth. see Prindle, Anthony.

Prindle, Katie, jt. auth. see Williams, Edward.

Prindle, Paul W. Van DerWerken - Van DerWerker Family. (Illus.). 370p. 1998. reprint ed. pap. 56.00 (*0-8328-9695-0*); reprint ed. lib. bdg. 66.00 (*0-8328-9694-2*) Higginson Bk Co.

Prindle, Peter H. Tinglatar: Socio-Economic Relationship of a Brahmin Village in Eastern Nepal. 1983. 75.00 (*0-7855-0237-8*, Pub. by Ratna Pustak Bhandar); 70.00 (*0-7855-0322-6*, Pub. by Ratna Pustak Bhandar) St Mut.

Prindle, Peter H., ed. Tinglatar: Socio-Economic Relationship of a Brahmin Village in Eastern Nepal. 157p. (C). 1989. 125.00 (*0-89771-126-2*, Pub. by Ratna Pustak Bhandar) St Mut.

Prindle, Tamae, ed. see Watanabe, Kazuo.

***Prindle, Tamae K.** Japan in the Twentieth Century. LC 99-27892. (Japan Studies). 1999. write for info. (*0-9650254-2-X*) Teikyo Loretto.

Prindle, Tamae K. Kinjo the Corporate Bouncer: And Other Stories from Japanese Business. 1992. pap. 9.95 (*0-8348-0254-6*) Weatherhill.

Prindle, Tamae K., tr. from JPN. Made in Japan & Other Japanese 'Business Novels' LC 89-4218. 200p. (C). (gr. 13). 1990. 53.95 (*0-87332-529-X*, East Gate Bk); pap. 27.50 (*0-87332-772-1*, East Gate Bk) M E Sharpe.

Prindle, Tamae K., ed. & tr. see Shimizu, Ikko.

Prindle, Wilford. I Hear You Talking Job. 100p. (Orig.). 1988. pap. 6.99 (*0-8341-1257-4*) Beacon Hill.

Prindle, William D. Bible Word Comparison: Four Traditional Bibles Compared with Twelve Contemporary Bibles. LC 98-61723. ix, 70 p. 1998. pap. 4.50 (*1-892833-01-8*) Third Mill SD.

Prine, James S. Night Flyer: Tales from the Id. 125p. (Orig.). Date not set. pap. 12.95 (*0-9653752-1-8*) J S Prine.
— The Real Police: Stories from the Crescent City. LC 96-92574. 142p. (Orig.). 1996. pap. 12.95 (*0-9653752-0-X*) J S Prine.

Prine, Mary, jt. auth. see Rosenbaum, Jean.

Prinetti, Emanuela S. Salads. Wertz, Laurie, ed. LC 92-18191. (Williams-Sonoma Kitchen Library). (Illus.). 108p. 1993. pap. write for info. (*0-7835-0238-9*) Time-Life.
— Salads. Wertz, Laurie, ed. LC 92-18191. (Williams-Sonoma Kitchen Library). (Illus.). 108p. (J). (gr. 11). 1999. 18.95 (*0-7835-0237-0*) Time-Life.

Pring, Adele. Women of the Centre. 192p. (C). 1990. 51.00 (*0-947087-23-0*, Pub. by Pascoe Pub) St Mut.

Pring, David, jt. auth. see Bradshaw, Kenneth.

Pring, George W. & Canan, Penelope. SLAPPs: Getting Sued for Speaking Out. LC 95-13610. 352p. (C). 1996. pap. text 24.95 (*1-56639-369-8*); lib. bdg. 69.95 (*1-56639-368-X*) Temple U Pr.

***Pring, J. T., ed.** The Pocket Oxford Greek Dictionary. 592p. 2000. pap. 15.95 (*0-19-860327-4*) OUP.

Pring, Julian T., ed. The Oxford Dictionary of Modern Greek. rev. ed. (GEC.). 592p. 1995. pap. 15.95 (*0-19-864197-4*) OUP.

Pring, Martin J. All-Season Investor: Successful Strategies for Every Stage in the Business Cycle. LC 91-34336. 337p. 1992. 34.95 (*0-471-54977-0*) Wiley.
— The Complete Stock Book. 1996. text 27.95 (*0-07-050934-4*) McGraw.
— Investment Psychology Explained: Classic Strategies to Beat the Markets. LC 92-15914. 288p. 1992. 27.95 (*0-471-55721-8*) Wiley.
— Investment Psychology Explained: Classic Strategies to Beat the Markets. LC 92-15914. 288p. 1995. pap. 19.95 (*0-471-13300-0*) Wiley.
— Martin Pring on Market Momentum. 335p. 1997. pap. 29.95 (*0-7863-1176-2*, Irwn Prfssnl) McGraw-Hill Prof.
— Martin Pring's Introduction to Technical Analysis: A CD-ROM Seminar & Workbook. 1997. pap. text, wbk. ed. write for info. (*0-07-913621-4*) McGraw.

***Pring, Martin J.** Martin Pring's Introduction to Technical Analysis: A CD-ROM Seminar & Workbook. LC 97-9028. (Illus.). 304p. 1998. pap. 49.95 incl. cd-rom (*0-07-032933-8*) McGraw.

Pring, Martin J. Technical Analysis Explained: The Successful Investor's Guide to Spotting Investment Trends & Turning Points. 3rd ed. LC 91-9075. (Illus.). 544p. 1991. 49.95 (*0-07-051042-3*) McGraw.

Pring-Mill, R. D. La Estructuracion del Mundo Ejemplar Vol. 175: Estudios Sobre la Prosa y el Teatro del Siglo de Oro. (Monagrafias A Ser.). 340p. 1999. 63.00 (*1-85566-059-8*, Pub. by Tamesis Bks Ltd) Boydell & Brewer.

Pring-Mill, Robert, ed. see Cardenal, Ernesto.

Pring, Richard & Walford, Geoffrey, eds. Affirming the Comprehensive Ideal. 224p. 1997. 79.95 (*0-7507-0619-8*, Falmer Pr); pap. 29.95 (*0-7507-0620-1*, Falmer Pr) Taylor & Francis.

***Pring, Roger.** WWW.Color. (Illus.). 192p. 2000. pap. 29.95 (*0-8230-5857-3*) Watsn-Guptill.
— WWW.Type: Effective Typographic Design for the World Wide Web. (Illus.). 192p. 2000. pap. write for info. (*0-8230-5860-3*) Watsn-Guptill.

Pring, S. W., tr. see Lourie, Arthur.

Pring, S. W., tr. see Sabaneev, Leonid L.

Pringeheim, Fritz. Der Kauf mit Frimdem Geld. Vlastos, Gregory, ed. (Morals & Law in Ancient Greece Ser.). (GER, GRE & LAT.). 1979. reprint ed. lib. bdg. 17.95 (*0-405-11568-7*) Ayer.

***Pringle.** Brand Spirit. LC 99-13354. 306p. (C). 1999. 32.95 (*0-471-98776-X*) Wiley.
— Hollywood: The Best 100 Novels. 59.95 (*1-85928-161-3*) Ashgate Pub Co.

Pringle. Imagine a Dragon. (J). 1995. 14.95 (*0-684-19741-3*) Atheneum Yung Read.
— Men, Masculinities & Social Welfare. LC 95-9566. 1995. 65.00 (*1-85728-401-1*, Pub. by UCL Pr Ltd); pap. write for info. (*1-85728-402-X*, Pub. by UCL Pr Ltd) Taylor & Francis.

Pringle, A., jt. auth. see Burtt, E. T.

Pringle, A. Denis & Hanna, Justice, contrib. by. The Statute Law of the Irish Free State, 1922-1928. xxiv, 101p. 1999. reprint ed. 69.00 (*1-56169-509-2*) Gaunt.

Pringle, Alexander, jt. auth. see Craddock, Sacha.

Pringle, Allan R., et al. Drugs of Abuse Digest: A Prevention Guide for the Family, School & Workplace. rev. ed. (Illus.). 112p. 1998. pap. 12.95 (*0-935847-11-1*) Inst Subs Abuse Res.

Pringle, Bruce D. Colorado Law Annotated, 2 vols., Set. 2nd ed. LC 91-75646. 1991. 248.00 (*0-317-04259-9*) West Group.

Pringle, C. R. Respiratory Syncytial Virus. (Perspectives in Medical Virology Ser.: Vol. 1). write for info. (*0-317-15191-6*) Elsevier.

Pringle, Catherine M., jt. ed. see Almeda, Frank.

Pringle, Catherine S. Across the Plains in 1844. 41p. 1995. pap. 6.95 (*0-87770-463-5*) Ye Galleon.

Pringle, Colombe, jt. auth. see Universe Publishing Incorporated Staff.

Pringle, Cyrus. Civil War Diary of Cyrus Pringle: Record of Quaker Conscience. LC 62-18328. Orig. Title: Record of a Quaker Conscience. (Orig.). 1962. pap. 4.00 (*0-87574-122-3*) Pendle Hill.

Pringle, David. Earth Is the Alien Planet: J. G. Ballard's Four-Dimensional Nightmare. LC 79-13065. (Milford Ser.: Popular Writers of Today: Vol. 26). 63p. 1979. pap. 13.00 (*0-89370-238-2*) Millefleurs.
— Imaginary People: A Who's Who of Fictional Characters from the 18th Century to the Present Day. 2nd ed. 306p. 1996. 69.95 (*1-85928-162-1*, Pub. by Scolar Pr) Ashgate Pub Co.
— Imaginary People: A Who's Who of Modern Fictional Characters. (Illus.). 528p. 1988. text 24.95 (*0-88687-364-9*) Wrld Almnc.
— Science Fiction: The 100 Best Novels. LC 97-28181. 224p. 1997. pap. 10.95 (*0-7867-0481-0*) Carroll & Graf.
— The Ultimate Encyclopedia of Science Fiction. 1996. 24.99 (*1-57215-212-5*, JG1212) World Pubns.
— The Ultimate Guide to Science Fiction: An A-Z of Science Fiction Books by Title. 2nd ed. 480p. 1995. 69.95 (*1-85928-071-4*, Pub. by Scolar Pr) Ashgate Pub Co.

Pringle, David, ed. The Ant Men of Tibet & Other Stories. 320p. 1999. text 7.95 (*1-902058-22-4*, Pub. by Pulp Fictions) Seven Hills Bk.
— St. James Guide to Fantasy Writers. (St. James Guide to Fantasy Writers Ser.). 711p. 1995. 140.00 (*1-55862-205-5*) St James Pr.
— St. James Guide to Horror, Ghost & Gothic Writers. 746p. (YA). (gr. 9 up). 1998. 140.00 (*1-55862-206-3*, 00007321) St James Pr.
— The Ultimate Encyclopedia of Fantasy. LC 99-10503. (Illus.). 256p. 1999. text 29.95 (*0-87951-937-1*, Pub. by Overlook Pr) Penguin Putnam.

Pringle, Denys. Churches of the Crusader Kingdom of Jerusalem Vol. 1: A Corpus: A-K (Excluding Acre & Jerusalem) (Illus.). 356p. (C). 1993. text 150.00 (*0-521-39036-2*) Cambridge U Pr.
— The Churches of the Crusader Kingdom of Jerusalem: A Corpus Vol. 2: L-Z (Excluding Tyre) (Illus.). 470p. (C). 1998. text 150.00 (*0-521-39037-0*) Cambridge U Pr.
— Secular Buildings in the Crusader Kingdom of Jerusalem: An Archaeological Gazetteer. LC 96-31664. (Illus.). 180p. (C). 1998. text 74.95 (*0-521-46010-7*) Cambridge U Pr.

Pringle, Denys, jt. auth. see Harper, Richard P.

Pringle, Denys, jt. auth. see Johns, C. N.

Pringle, Denys, ed. see Lawrence, T. E.

Pringle, Elizabeth A. Rab & Dab. limited ed. Blythe, Anne, ed. & intro. by. 1985. 27.50 (*0-685-13973-5*) Seajay Society.

Pringle, Heather. In Search of Ancient North America: An Archaeological Journey to Forgotten Cultures. LC 95-43781. (Illus.). 227p. 1996. 24.95 (*0-471-04237-4*) Wiley.

Pringle, Henry F. Alfred E. Smith: A Critical Study. LC 75-101271. reprint ed. 20.00 (*0-404-00627-2*) AMS Pr.
— Alfred E. Smith: A Critical Study. (History - United States Ser.). 402p. 1992. reprint ed. lib. bdg. 99.00 (*0-7812-6217-8*) Rprt Serv.
— Theodore Roosevelt: A Biography. LC 56-13739. 456p. 1956. pap. 16.00 (*0-15-688943-9*, HB15, Harvest Bks) Harcourt.
— William Howard Taft Vol. 1: The Life & Times. Speirs, Katherine E., ed. (Signature Ser.). (Illus.). 550p. 1998. reprint ed. 35.00 (*0-945707-19-3*) Amer Political.
— William Howard Taft Vol. 2: The Life & Times. Speirs, Katherine E., ed. (Signature Ser.). (Illus.). 556p. 1998. reprint ed. 35.00 (*0-945707-20-7*) Amer Political.

Pringle, J. E., jt. ed. see Eggleton, P. P.

Pringle, J. F. Lunenburgh: or The Old Eastern District: Its Settlement & Early Progressm with Personal Recollections of the Town of Cornwall from 1824. (Illus.). 423p. 1996. reprint ed. lib. bdg. 46.00 (*0-8328-5156-6*) Higginson Bk Co.

Pringle, J. M. China Struggles for Unity. 1976. lib. bdg. 59.95 (*0-8490-1609-6*) Gordon Pr.

Pringle, J. S. Flora of Ecuador Nos. 159A & 159B: Gentianaceae, Menyanthaceae. (Opera Botanica Series B). 147p. 1995. pap. 60.00 (*87-88702-80-4*, Pub. by Coun Nordic Pubs) Balogh.

***Pringle, Jack.** Colditz Last Stop. large type unabridged ed. 168p. 1999. pap. 19.95 (*0-7531-5445-5*, 154455, Pub. by ISIS Lrg Prnt) ISIS Pub.

Pringle, Jack. Colditz Last Stop: Eleven Prisons, Four Countries, Six Escapes. large type unabridged ed. 2000. 25.95 (*0-7531-5443-9*, 154439, Pub. by ISIS Lrg Prnt) ISIS Pub.

Pringle, James R. Pringle's History of Gloucester: New, Indexed Edition. 2nd ed. (Illus.). 416p. 1997. reprint ed. pap. 19.95 (*0-938459-10-4*) Ten Pound Isl Bk.

Pringle, Janice, et al. Treatment of the Pregnant Addict. 135p. 1994. pap. 49.97 (*1-884937-16-0*) Manisses Communs.

Pringle, John J. & Harris, Robert S. Essentials of Managerial Finance. 2nd ed. LC 86-31333. (Illus.). 945p. reprint ed. pap. 200.00 (*0-7837-4747-0*, 204455600004) Bks Demand.

Pringle, John K., jt. auth. see Allen, Dana G.

Pringle, Keith. Children & Social Welfare in Europe. LC 97-31569. (Illus.). 218p. 1998. 89.00 (*0-335-19702-7*); pap. 27.95 (*0-335-19701-9*) OpUniv Pr.

P

***Pringle, Keith & Harder, Margit, eds.** Through Two Pairs of Eyes: A Comparative Study of Danish Social Policy & Child Welfare. (Comparative Study & Child Welfare Ser.: Vol. 2). 177p. 1999. pap. 27.95 (*87-7307-620-1*, Pub. by Aalborg Univ) David Brown.

Pringle, Kenneth. Waters of the West. 1976. lib. bdg. 59.95 (*0-8490-2809-4*) Gordon Pr.

Pringle, Larry. Taking Care of the Earth: Kids in Action. LC 95-76352. (Illus.). 64p. (J). (gr. 2-5). 1997. pap. 7.95 (*1-56397-64-X*) Boyds Mills Pr.

Pringle, Laurence. Animal Rights Controversy. LC 89-11095. 112p. (YA). (gr. 7-12). 1989. 16.95 (*0-15-203559-1*) Harcourt.

— Animals at Play. LC 85-901. (Illus.). 70p. (J). (gr. 3-7). 1985. 17.95 (*0-15-203554-0*, Harcourt Child Bks) Harcourt.

— Antarctica. (Illus.). 64p. (J). (gr. 3-7). 1992. pap. 16.00 (*0-671-73850-X*) S&S Bks Yung.

— Bats: Strange & Wonderful! LC 95-83192. (Illus.). 32p. (J). (gr. 4-7). 2000. 15.95 (*1-56397-327-8*) Boyds Mills Pr.

— Being a Plant. LC 82-45915. (Illus.). 96p. (YA). (gr. 7 up). 1983. 12.95 (*0-690-04346-5*); lib. bdg. 12.89 (*0-690-04347-3*) HarpC Child Bks.

— Coral Reefs. LC 94-5875. (Illus.). 48p. (J). (ps-3). 1995. 16.00 (*0-689-80286-2*) S&S Bks Yung.

— Dinosaurs! Strange & Wonderful. LC 92-71273. (Illus.). 32p. (J). (ps-2). 1995. 15.95 (*1-878093-16-9*) Boyds Mills Pr.

— Dinosaurs: Strange & Wonderful. 1996. 10.19 (*0-606-11259-6*, Pub. by Turtleback) Demco.

— Dolphin Man: Exploring the World of Dolphins. (J). 1995. 15.00 (*0-684-19733-2*) Atheneum Yung Read.

— Dolphin Man: Exploring the World of Dolphins. Marshall, Marcia, ed. LC 95-5290. (Illus.). 48p. (YA). (gr. 5 up). 1995. 17.00 (*0-689-80299-4*) Atheneum Yung Read.

— The Earth Is Flat & Other Great Mistakes. (Illus.). 80p. (J). 1995. pap. 3.99 (*0-380-72319-0*, Avon Bks) Morrow Avon.

— Elephant Woman: Cynthia Moss Explores the World of Elephants. LC 96-40241. (Illus.). 48p. (J). (gr. 4-8). 1997. 16.00 (*0-689-80142-4*) Atheneum Yung Read.

— The Environmental Movement: From Its Roots to the Challenges of a New Century. LC 99-32110. (Illus.). 144p. (YA). (gr. 5-9). 2000. 16.95 (*0-688-15626-6*, Wm Morrow) Morrow Avon.

— Everybody Has a Belly Button: Your Life Before You Were Born. LC 95-83168. (Illus.). 32p. (J). (ps-3). 1997. 14.95 (*1-56397-009-0*) Boyds Mills Pr.

— Explore Your Senses Boxed Set, 5. 2000. 113.93 (*0-7614-0733-2*, Benchmark NY) Marshall Cavendish.

— An Extraordinary Life: The Story of a Monarch Butterfly. LC 96-31482. (Illus.). 64p. (J). (gr. 3-7). 1997. 18.95 (*0-531-30002-1*); lib. bdg. 19.99 (*0-531-33002-8*) Orchard Bks Watts.

***Pringle, Laurence.** An Extraordinary Life: The Story of a Monarch Butterfly. LC 96-31482. (Illus.). 64p. (J). 2000. pap. 7.95 (*0-531-07169-3*) Orchard Bks Watts.

— Extraordinary Life: The Story of a Monarch Butterfly. (Illus.). (J). 2000. 13.30 (*0-606-18330-2*) Turtleback.

Pringle, Laurence. Fire in the Forest: A Cycle of Growth & Renewal. LC 92-32257. (Illus.). 32p. (J). (gr. 3-6). 1995. per. 16.00 (*0-689-80394-X*) Atheneum Yung Read.

— Fire in the Forest: A Cycle of Growth & Renewal. LC 92-32257. (Illus.). 32p. (J). 1994. text 16.00 (*0-02-775215-1*, Mac Bks Young Read) S&S Childrens.

— Gambling. (J). 1924. write for info. (*0-688-16609-1*, Wm Morrow) Morrow Avon.

— Killer Bees. LC 90-34658. (Illus.). 64p. (J). (gr. 3 up). 1990. pap. 6.95 (*0-688-09618-2*, Wm Morrow) Morrow Avon.

— Listen to the Crows. LC 75-43535. (Illus.). 40p. (J). (gr. 3-7). 1976. lib. bdg. 12.89 (*0-690-01069-9*) HarpC Child Bks.

***Pringle, Laurence.** Naming the Cat. (Illus.). 32p. (J). (gr. k-3). 1999. reprint ed. pap. 6.95 (*0-8027-7565-9*) Walker & Co.

Pringle, Laurence. Nature! Wild & Wonderful. LC 96-53268. (Meet the Author Ser.). (Illus.). 32p. (J). (gr. 2-5). 1997. 14.95 (*1-57274-071-X*, 718) R Owen Pubs.

— Octopus Hug. LC 92-73830. (Illus.). 32p. (J). (ps-3). 1996. pap. 6.95 (*1-56397-559-9*) Boyds Mills Pr.

— Oil Spills. LC 92-30348. (Save-the-Earth Ser.). (Illus.). 64p. (J). (gr. 3 up). 1993. lib. bdg. 14.93 (*0-688-09861-4*, Wm Morrow) Morrow Avon.

— One Room School. LC 96-84154. (Illus.). 32p. (J). (gr. 1-5). 1998. 15.95 (*1-56397-583-1*) Boyds Mills Pr.

— Scorpion Man: Exploring the World of Scorpions. LC 93-34936. (Illus.). 48p. (YA). (gr. 5 up). 1994. mass mkt. 15.95 (*0-684-19560-7*) S&S Trade.

— Smoking. LC 96-5359. (Save the Earth Ser.). (Illus.). 128p. (J). (gr. 4-7). 1996. 16.00 (*0-688-13039-9*, Wm Morrow) Morrow Avon.

— Vanishing Ozone. LC 94-25928. (Save the Earth Ser.). (Illus.). 64p. (J). (gr. 3 up). 1995. lib. bdg. 15.93 (*0-688-04158-2*, Wm Morrow) Morrow Avon.

— Water Plants. LC 74-23942. (Let's-Read-&-Find-Out Science Bks.). (Illus.). 40p. (J). (gr. k-3). 1975. lib. bdg. 12.89 (*0-690-00738-8*) HarpC Child Bks.

— What Shall We Do with the Land? LC 81-43034. (Illus.). 160p. (J). (gr. 5 up). 1981. 11.95 (*0-690-04108-X*) HarpC Child Bks.

Pringle, Laurence P. Animal Monsters: The Truth about Scary Creatures. LC 96-27604. (Illus.). 64p. (J). (gr. 3-7). 1997. 15.95 (*0-7614-5003-3*) Marshall Cavendish.

***Pringle, Laurence P.** Chemical & Biological Warfare: The Cruelest Weapons. rev. ed. LC 99-40269. (Issues in Focus Ser.). 112p. (gr. 6 up). 2000. lib. bdg. 20.95 (*0-7660-1241-7*) Enslow Pubs.

Pringle, Laurence P. Hearing. LC 98-28041. (Explore Your Senses Ser.). (Illus.). 32p. (YA). (gr. 2-4). 1999. lib. bdg. 22.79 (*0-7614-0735-9*, Benchmark NY) Marshall Cavendish.

— Naming the Cat. LC 97-443. (Illus.). 32p. (J). (ps-3). 1997. lib. bdg. 16.85 (*0-8027-8622-7*) Walker & Co.

— Naming the Cat. LC 97-443. (Illus.). 32p. (J). (gr. k-3). 1999. 15.95 (*0-8027-8621-9*) Walker & Co.

— Sight. LC 98-28040. (Explore Your Senses Ser.). (J). (gr. 2-4). 1999. lib. bdg. 19.95 (*0-7614-0734-0*, Benchmark NY) Marshall Cavendish.

— Taste. LC 98-28042. (Explore Your Senses Ser.). (J). (gr. 2-4). 1999. lib. bdg. 22.79 (*0-7614-0736-7*, Benchmark NY) Marshall Cavendish.

***Pringle, Laurence P. & Marstall, Bob.** A Dragon in the Sky: The Story of a Green Darner Dragonfly. LC 00-39156. (Illus.). (J). 2001. lib. bdg. write for info. (*0-531-33315-9*) Orchard Bks Watts.

Pringle, Lawrence. Coral Reefs. LC 94-5875. (J). (gr. 3 up). 1995. write for info. (*0-671-79166-4*) S&S Bks Yung.

— Drinking: A Risky Business. LC 97-7807. (Illus.). 128p. (J). (gr. 3-7). 1997. 16.00 (*0-688-15044-6*, Wm Morrow) Morrow Avon.

Pringle, Lillie. Methodological Perception of Imagery Literature. (Orig.). 1990. pap. 12.50 (*0-913412-30-9*) Brandon Hse.

Pringle, M. & Naidoo, Sandhya. Early Child Care in Britain, Vol. 5. LC 74-80075. (International Monographs on Early Child Care). (Illus.). xii, 175p. 1975. text 104.00 (*0-677-05200-6*) Gordon & Breach.

Pringle, M. A. Journey in East Africa: Towards the Mountains of the Moon. LC 72-3957. (Black Heritage Library Collection). 1977. reprint ed. 35.95 (*0-8369-9105-2*) Ayer.

Pringle, M. K. Needs of Children. 3rd ed. 192p. (C). (gr. 13). 1989. pap. text 19.99 (*0-09-170251-8*) Elsevier Applied Sci.

Pringle, Malcolm S., et al, eds. The Mesozoic Pacific: Geology, Tectonics, & Volcanism. LC 93-33017. (Geophysical Monograph Ser.: No. 77). 435p. 1993. 54.00 (*0-87590-036-4*) Am Geophysical.

Pringle, Marian J., jt. auth. see Brock, Susan.

Pringle, Mary B. John Grisham. LC 96-35026. (Critical Companions to Popular Contemporary Writers Ser.). 160p. 1997. 29.95 (*0-313-29637-5*, Greenwood Pr) Greenwood.

Pringle, Mary L. & Ellis, Joseph. "We Don't Need Drugs to Be OK," with Gillie the Knowbot & Sis & Chris. rev. ed. (Educational Story Coloring Book Ser.). Orig. Title: Sis & Chris & the Knowbots in "We Don't Need Drugs to Be OK". (Illus.). 32p. (J). (ps-3). 1998. 1.95 (*0-935847-12-X*) Inst Subs Abuse Res.

***Pringle, Michael, et al.** A Guide to the MLA Style of Documentation, in a Nutshell. 2nd rev. ed. 30p. (C). 1998. pap. text 2.50 (*0-9674026-0-3*) Nutshell.

Pringle, Mike, et al. A Guide for New Principles. (Oxford General Practice Ser.). (Illus.). 222p. 1996. pap. text 39.50 (*0-19-262536-5*) OUP.

Pringle, Nancy G. Family Law. (C). 1996. 40.00 (*0-13-396805-7*, Macmillan Coll) P-H.

Pringle, Norman & Thompson, Paul. Social Work, Psychiatry & the Law. rev. ed. LC 98-52026. 250p. 1999. pap. 39.95 (*1-85742-416-6*) Ashgate Pub Co.

— Social Work, Psychiatry & the Law. 2nd rev. ed. LC 98-52026. 211p. 1999. text 65.95 (*1-85742-415-8*) Ashgate Pub Co.

Pringle, Patrick. Hue & Cry: The Birth of the British Police. (Criminology Ser.). 1992. lib. bdg. 300.00 (*0-8490-5300-5*) Gordon Pr.

Pringle, Peter. Cornered: Big Tobacco at the Bar of Justice. LC 97-47008. 307p. 1998. text 27.50 (*0-8050-4292-X*) St Martin.

Pringle, Peter K. & Clinton, Helen E. Radio & Television: A Selected, Annotated Bibliography; Supplement Two: 1982-1986. LC 88-23968. 249p. 1989. 32.00 (*0-8108-2158-3*) Scarecrow.

Pringle, Peter K., et al. Electronic Media Management. 3rd rev. ed. (Illus.). 448p. 1994. pap. 39.95 (*0-240-80199-7*, Focal) Buttrwrth-Heinemann.

— Electronic Media Management. 4th ed. LC 99-11797. (Illus.). 440p. 1999. pap. 44.95 (*0-240-80332-9*, Focal) Buttrwrth-Heinemann.

Pringle, Robert. Cold Front. 35p. 1998. pap. 7.95 (*0-944754-48-1*) Pudding Hse Pubns.

Pringle, Robert, jt. auth. see Deane, Marjorie.

Pringle, Rosemary. Sex & Medicine: Gender, Power & Authority in the Medical Profession. LC 97-46532. 256p. (C). 1998. text 64.95 (*0-521-57093-X*); pap. text 22.95 (*0-521-57812-4*) Cambridge U Pr.

Pringle, Rosemary, jt. auth. see Game, Ann.

Pringle, Rosemary, jt. ed. see Caine, Barbara.

Pringle, Terry. This Is the Child: A Father's Story of His Young Son's Battle with Leukemia. LC 91-52776. 208p. 1992. reprint ed. pap. 10.95 (*0-87074-332-5*); reprint ed. text 19.95 (*0-87074-335-X*) SMU Press.

Pringle, Thomas. African Poems of Thomas Pringle. Pereira, Ernest & Chapman, Michael, eds. (Killie Campbell Africana Library Publication: No. 4). 204p. 1989. pap. 20.00 (*0-86980-686-6*, Pub. by Univ Natal Pr) Intl Spec Bk.

Pringsheim, E. G. Farblose Algen. Ein Beitrag zur Evolutionsforschung. (GER., Illus.). 471p. 1963. lib. bdg. 66.00 (*3-437-30046-6*) Lubrecht & Cramer.

— Die Gattungen Chlorogonium und Hyalogonium: Volvocales. (Nova Hedwigia Ser.: No. 18). (Illus.). 38p. 1969. pap. text 20.00 (*3-7682-0662-9*) Lubrecht & Cramer.

Pringsheim, Klaus H. Neighbors Across the Pacific: The Development of Economic & Political Relations Between Canada & Japan, 90. LC 82-11713. (Contributions in Political Science Ser.: No. 90). 241p. 1983. 59.95 (*0-313-23507-4*, PRN/) Greenwood.

— Neighbours Across the Pacific: Canadian-Japanese Relations, 1870-1982. 242p. 1995. pap. 14.95 (*0-88962-216-7*) Mosaic.

Pringsheim, Klaus H. & Bosen, Victor. Man of the World: Memoirs of Europe, Asia & North America (1930s to 1980s) (Illus.). 180p. 1995. pap. 18.95 (*0-88962-584-0*) Mosaic.

Prinn, R. G. Global Atmospheric-Biospheric Chemistry. LC 94-22508. (Environmental Science Research Ser.: Vol. 48). (Illus.). 270p. (C). 1994. 89.50 (*0-306-44884-X*, Plenum Trade) Perseus Pubng.

Prinn, R. G., jt. auth. see Bras, R. L.

Prins & Statlib. The Student's Statistical Software Library. (C). 1995. pap. text 17.74 (*0-07-912913-7*) McGraw.

Prins, Adriann H. The Swahili-Speaking Peoples of Zanzibar & the East African Coast: Arabs, Shirazi & Swahili. LC 68-5550. (Ethnographic Survey of Africa: East Central Africa Ser.: Pt. 12). 157p. reprint ed. pap. 48.70 (*0-8357-6965-8*, 203902500009) Bks Demand.

Prins, Bob, ed. see Fracassi, Linda F.

Prins, Corien, jt. ed. see Meijboom, Alfred P.

Prins, Eliezer, jt. auth. see Lehmann, Marcus.

Prins, Gwyn. Threats Without Enemies: Facing Environmental Insecurity. 192p. (Orig.). 1992. 26.00 (*1-85383-157-3*, Pub. by Escan Pubns) Island Pr.

Prins, Gwyn, ed. Spring in Winter: The Nineteen Eighty-Nine Revolutions. 160p. 1991. 29.95 (*0-685-38699-6*, Pub. by Manchester Univ Pr); text 27.95 (*0-7190-3445-0*, Pub. by Manchester Univ Pr) St Martin.

***Prins, Gwyn & Tromp, Hylke.** The Future of War. LC 00-33109. (Law Specials Ser.). 2000. pap. write for info. (*90-411-1399-1*, Kluwer Law) Kluwer Academic.

***Prins, H. H. T., et al.** Conservation of Wildlife by Sustainable Use. LC 00-20449. (Conservation Biology Ser.). 2000. write for info. (*0-412-79730-5*, Kluwer Plenum) Kluwer Academic.

Prins, Harald E. Mi'kmaq: Resistance, Accommodation & Cultural Survival. (Case Studies in Cultural Anthropology). 1997. pap. 25.00 (*0-03-053427-5*) Harcourt Coll Pubs.

Prins, Herschel A. Dangerous Behaviour, the Law & Mental Disorder. 240p. (C). 1986. pap. text 18.95 (*0-422-79220-9*, 9931, Pub. by Tavistock) Routldge.

— Fire-Raising: Its Motivation & Management. LC 93-7385. 224p. (C). (gr. 13). 1993. text 49.95 (*0-415-05984-4*, B0870) Routledge.

— Offenders, Deviants or Patients? 2nd ed. LC 94-34150. (Illus.). 304p. (C). 1995. 80.00 (*0-415-10220-0*, C0116) Routledge.

Prins, Herschel A. Will They Do It Again? Risk Assessment & Management in Criminal Justice & Psychiatry. LC 99-21513. 1999. pap. write for info. (*0-415-16018-9*) Routledge.

***Prins, Herschel A.** Will They Do It Again? Risk Assessment & Management in Criminal Justice & Psychiatry. LC 99-21513. 176p. (C). 1999. text. write for info. (*0-415-16017-0*) Routledge.

Prins, J. Egbert, jt. ed. see Wunderlich, W. O.

Prins, Jack. Quality Control Chart. LC 92-37808. (Six Sigma Research Institute Ser.). 1993. 295.95 (*0-201-63403-1*) Addison-Wesley.

— Six Sigma Quality Control Charts. LC 92-37808. (Six Sigma Research Institute Ser.). (C). 1993. write for info. (*0-201-63441-4*) Addison-Wesley.

Prins, Jack & Harry, Mikel J. Six Sigma Metrics. LC 92-37809. (Six Sigma Research Institute Ser.). (C). 1993. write for info. (*0-201-63440-6*) Addison-Wesley.

— Six Sigman Metrics. LC 92-37809. (Six Sigma Research Institute Ser.). 1993. 241.95 (*0-201-63405-8*) Addison-Wesley.

Prins, Jack, et al. Basic Statistics: The Six Sigma Research Institute Series. LC 92-41299. (Six Sigma Research Institute Ser.). 1993. pap. text 19.95 (*0-201-63406-6*) Addison-Wesley.

Prins, Jez, jt. auth. see Hammond, Derek.

Prins, Johanna C., tr. see Stevens, Martin & Wright, Stephen, eds.

Prins, Johanna H., tr. see Pelgrom, Els.

Prins, Johanna W., tr. see Pelgrom, Els.

Prins, Piet. Anak, the Eskimo Boy. Kanis, Wim & Veenendaal, Alice, trs. from DUT. (Illus.). 115p. (J). 1989. pap. 6.30 (*0-921100-11-6*) Inhtce Pubns.

— Dispelling the Tyranny. Rustenberg-Bootsma, Paulina M., tr. from DUT. LC 94-38670. (Struggle for Freedom Ser.: No. 2). (Illus.). 152p. (Orig.). (J). 1994. pap. 8.90 (*0-921100-40-X*) Inhtce Pubns.

— The Partisans. Van Oosterom, James C., tr. from DUT. (Illus.). 102p. (J). 1989. pap. 7.20 (*0-921100-07-8*) Inhtce Pubns.

— Sabotage. Van Oosterom, James C., tr. from DUT. (Shadow Ser.: No. 5). (Illus.). 120p. (J). 1989. pap. 7.20 (*0-921100-08-6*) Inhtce Pubns.

— Scout: The Secret of the Swamp. LC 97-19929. (ENG & DUT.). 176p. (J). 1997. pap. 8.90 (*0-921100-50-7*) Inhtce Pubns.

— When the Morning Came. Deboer, Gertrude, tr. from DUT. LC 98-12403. (Struggle for Freedom Ser.: No. 1). (Illus.). 158p. (Orig.). (J). 1989. pap. 8.90 (*0-921100-12-4*) Inhtce Pubns.

Prins, R., jt. ed. see Koningsberger, D. C.

Prins, R., jt. ed. see Schuit, G. C.

Prins, R. A. & Stewart, C. S., eds. Micro-Organisms in Ruminant Nutrition. 249p. 1999. pap. 160.00 (*1-897676-54-9*, Pub. by Nottingham Univ Pr) St Mut.

Prins, Yopie. Victorian Sappho. LC 98-28067. 256p. 1998. pap. text 17.95 (*0-691-05919-5*, Pub. by Princeton U Pr) Cal Prin Full Svc.

— Victorian Sappho. LC 98-28067. (Illus.). 256p. 1998. text 55.00 (*0-691-05918-7*, Pub. by Princeton U Pr) Cal Prin Full Svc.

Prins, Yopie & Shreiber, Maeera, eds. Dwelling in Possibility: Women Poets & Critics on Poetry. LC 97-25507. (Reading Women Writing Ser.). (Illus.). 360p. 1997. pap. 19.95 (*0-8014-8294-1*); text 49.95 (*0-8014-3199-9*) Cornell U Pr.

Prinsen, Gerry L. Ecossais or Perfect Elect of the Lodge. 50p. 1998. reprint ed. pap. 12.95 (*0-7661-0693-4*) Kessinger Pub.

Prinsen, Gerry L., ed. The Bonseigneur Rituals a Collection of 18th Century Ecossais Rituals, Vols. 1 & 2. 234p. 1998. reprint ed. pap. 29.95 (*0-7661-0696-9*) Kessinger Pub.

— Cayers Macconiques Rituals of the Lodge of Perfection. 186p. 1998. reprint ed. pap. 24.95 (*0-7661-0695-0*) Kessinger Pub.

— Documents of Mirecourt. 130p. 1998. reprint ed. pap. 19.95 (*0-7661-0694-2*) Kessinger Pub.

— Miscellaneous Masonic Documents. 58p. 1998. reprint ed. pap. 12.95 (*0-7661-0692-6*) Kessinger Pub.

— The Story of les Elus Parfaits, the Mother-Ecossais Lodge of Bordeaux. 50p. 1998. reprint ed. pap. 12.95 (*0-7661-0687-X*) Kessinger Pub.

— The Story of the Ecossais Lodge of Toulouse. 54p. 1998. reprint ed. pap. 12.95 (*0-7661-0691-8*) Kessinger Pub.

— The Story of the Ecossais Lodges in the Isle San Domingo. 50p. 1998. reprint ed. pap. 12.95 (*0-7661-0689-6*) Kessinger Pub.

— The Story of the Ecossais of New Orleans. 64p. 1998. reprint ed. pap. 12.95 (*0-7661-0690-X*) Kessinger Pub.

— The Story of the Lodge la Parfaite Union in the Island of Martinique. 60p. 1998. reprint ed. pap. 12.95 (*0-7661-0688-8*) Kessinger Pub.

Prinsep, James. Essays on Indian Antiquities: Historic, Numismatic & Palaeographic, 2 vols. (C). 1995. reprint ed. 88.00 (*81-206-1036-9*, Pub. by Asian Educ Servs) S Asia.

Prinsley, Roslyn T., ed. The Role of Trees in Sustainable Agriculture: Review Papers Presented at the Australian Conference, Albury, Victoria, Australia, October 1991. LC 92-36592. (Forestry Sciences Ser.: Vol. 43). 192p. (C). 1992. text 119.00 (*0-7923-2030-1*) Kluwer Academic.

Prinsloo, K., jt. auth. see Lanham, L. W.

Prinsloo, Mastin & Breier, Mignonne, eds. The Social Uses of Literacy: Theory & Practice in Contemporary South Africa. LC 96-14789. (Studies in Written Language & Literacy: Vol. 4). viii, 279p. 1996. pap. 24.95 (*1-55619-321-1*); lib. bdg. 69.00 (*1-55619-320-3*) J Benjamins Pubng Co.

Prinsloo, Willem S. The Theology of the Book of Joel. (Beiheft zur Zeitschrift fuer die Alttestamentliche Wissenschaft Ser.: Vol: 163). viii, 136p. 1985. 70.00 (*3-11-010301-X*) De Gruyter.

Print India Staff. Encyclopaedia of Fishes of the World, 2 vols. 1996. pap. 179.50 (*81-86505-20-2*, Pub. by Print Hse) St Mut.

— Encyclopaedia of Scientific Development Inventions & Discoveries, 5 vols. 1996. pap. 1121.00 (*81-86505-15-6*, Pub. by Print Hse) St Mut.

— The Masterpiece Library of Buddhis, 10 vols. 1996. 3700.00 (*81-7305-106-2*, Pub. by Print Hse) St Mut.

Print India Staff & Gopal, Ram. Hindu Culture During & after Muslim Rule: Survival & Subsequent Challenges. LC 93-911131. 199p. (C). 1994. pap. 125.00 (*81-85880-26-3*, Pub. by Print Hse) St Mut.

Print, Murray. Curriculum Development & Design. 256p. 1993. pap. 29.95 (*1-86373-362-0*, Pub. by Allen & Unwin Pty) Paul & Co Pubs.

Print Project Staff. Buy Wholesale-by-Mail 1998: The Consumer's Bible to Shopping by Mail, Phone, or On-Line. 20th anniversary ed. 672p. 1997. pap. 19.00 (*0-06-273438-5*, Harper Ref) HarpC.

***Print Project Staff, ed.** Wholesale by Mail & Online 2000. 22nd ed. 688p. 1999. pap. 20.00 (*0-06-273676-0*) HarpC.

Print Staff & Rotovision Staff. European Regional Design Annual 1997. (Illus.). 144p. 1997. pap. 25.00 (*2-88046-287-8*, Rotovision) Watsn-Guptill.

Printen, Kenneth J., jt. ed. see Griffen, Ward O., Jr.

Printers, Franz, ed. see Lockridge, Elaine.

***Prints India Staff.** Encyclopaedia of Practical Management Training, 20 vols. 1998. pap. 4750.00 (*81-242-0131-5*, Pub. by Print Hse) St Mut.

Prints India Staff. Great Books on Indian Education, 18 vols., Set. (C). 1988. 995.00 (*0-7855-0041-3*, Pub. by Print Hse) St Mut.

***Prints India Staff.** Indian Art Collection, 22 vols. 1998. pap. 12500.00 (*81-7020-589-1*, Pub. by Print Hse) St Mut.

Prints India Staff. Indian Art Collection, 22 vols., Set. (C). 1988. 4000.00 (*0-7855-0049-9*, Pub. by Print Hse) St Mut.

— Indian Historical Researches, 78 vols., Set. (C). 1988. 5000.00 (*0-7855-0045-6*, Pub. by Print Hse) St Mut.

— Landmarks in Indian Anthropology, 74 vols., Set. (C). 1988. 5000.00 (*0-7855-0046-4*, Pub. by Print Hse) St Mut.

— Loudon's Encyclopaedia of Plants, 3 vols., Set. (C). 1988. 500.00 (*0-7855-0053-7*, Pub. by Print Hse) St Mut.

— Max Muller's Encyclopaedia of Languages, 2 vols., Set. (C). 1988. 395.00 (*0-7855-0060-X*, Pub. by Print Hse) St Mut.

— The New Gesham World Encyclopaedia, 12 vols., Set. (C). 1988. 1000.00 (*0-7855-0043-X*, Pub. by Print Hse) St Mut.

— Rediscovering India-Indian Philosophy Library, 71 vols. (C). 1988. 1600.00 (*0-7855-0047-2*, Pub. by Print Hse) St Mut.

— Sir Aurel Stein's Central Asia, 12 vols., Set. (C). 1988. 4000.00 (*0-7855-0048-0*, Pub. by Print Hse) St Mut.

P

An Asterisk (*) at the beginning of an entry indicates that the title is appearing for the first time.

— Story of the Civilisation, 15 vols., Set. (C). 1988. 1500.00 (*0-7855-0042-1*, Pub. by Print Hse) St Mut.
— The William Shakespeare Encyclopaedia, 8 vols. (C). 1988. 1000.00 (*0-7855-0044-8*, Pub. by Print Hse) St Mut.
Printup, A. D., II. History of New York Indians & the Printup Family. LC 83-72027. (Illus.). 89p. 1985. 66.66 (*0-685-09879-6*) DeWitt & Sheppard.
— N. Y. Indians & the Printup Family. Harder, Arvid, ed. LC 83-72027. (Illus.). 99p. 1983. 66.66 (*0-685-07429-3*); pap. 33.33 (*0-685-07430-7*) Clark Inc.
— The Scatterings (Based upon a True Story) LC 85-71343. 192p. 1986. pap. 6.95 (*0-685-10438-9*, TS-027) DeWitt & Sheppard.
Printup, A. D., II, et al. How I Lost Weight. LC 84-71480. 84p. 1985. pap. 5.25 (*0-932365-00-0*) DeWitt & Sheppard.
Printz, Charles T. The Printz-Prince Family: Into the Family. LC 94-80149. 450p. 1995. 98.00 (*0-9636320-2-7*) Nuggets Wisdom.
Printz, Neil, et al. Texas Art. LC 88-60136. 25p. 1988. pap. 5.00 (*0-939594-09-9*, Menil Collection) Menil Found.
Printz, Neil, jt. auth. see Hopps, Walter.
Printz, Stacey. The Best 50 Salad Dressings. LC 99-213385. (Best 50 Ser.). 80p. 1998. pap. 4.95 (*1-55867-211-7*) Bristol Pub Ent CA.
Printzen, Christian. Die Flechtengattung Biatora in Europa. (Bibliotheca Lichenologica Ser.: No. 60). (GER., Illus.). 275p. 1995. 70.80 (*3-443-58039-4*, Pub. by Gebruder Borntraeger) Balogh.
Prinz, Christopher. Cohabiting, Married or Single: Portraying, Analyzing, & Modeling New Living Arrangements in the Changing Societies in Europe. 224p. 1995. 72.95 (*1-85972-187-7*, Pub. by Avebry) Ashgate Pub Co.
Prinz, Friedrich B. Rapid Prototyping in Europe & Japan Vol. II: Site Reports. unabridged ed. (JTEC Panel Reports). (Illus.). 127p. (Orig.). 1996. pap. write for info. (*1-883712-43-2*) Intl Tech Res.
Prinz, G. A., jt. auth. see Hadjipanayis, G. C.
Prinz, Jessica. Art Discourse - Discourse in Art. LC 90-19388. (Illus.). 225p. (C). 1991. pap. text 16.00 (*0-8135-1734-6*) Rutgers U Pr.
Prinz, Johannes. John Wilmot, Earl of Rochester: His Life & Writings. 1988. reprint ed. lib. bdg. 59.00 (*0-7812-0228-0*) Rprt Serv.
— John Wilmot, Earl of Rochester: His Life & Writings. 1971. reprint ed. 69.00 (*0-403-01165-5*) Scholarly.
— John Wilmot, Earl of Rochester: His Life & Writings. reprint ed. 59.00 (*0-403-04129-5*) Somerset Pub.
Prinz, Karl. Epitaphios Logos: Struktur, Funktion und Bedeutung der Bestattungsreden im Athen des 5. und 4. Jahrhunderts. (Europaische Hochschulschriften Ser.: Reihe 3, Bd. 747). (GER.). 365p. 1997. 63.95 (*3-631-31808-1*) P Lang Pubng.
Prinz, Martin, et al. Simon & Schuster's Guide to Rocks & Minerals. (Illus.). 1978. pap. 15.00 (*0-671-24417-5*) S&S Trade.
Prinz, Phyllis & Saia, Stephanie. Private Moments in Public Places. LC 79-64330. (Illus.). 72p. 1979. pap. 16.00 (*0-932966-04-7*) Permanent Pr.
Prinz, Richard. Endocrine Surgery. (Vademecum Ser.). 1999. spiral bd. 45.00 (*1-57059-574-7*) Landes Bioscience.
Prinz, Ronald J., ed. Advances in the Behavioral Assessment of Children & Families, Vol. 5. 320p. 1991. 85.00 (*1-85302-069-9*) Taylor & Francis.
Prinz, Ronald J., jt. ed. see Ollendick, Thomas H.
Prinz, Tom. Dragon-Slaying for Couples. 240p. 1995. pap. 14.95 (*0-933025-44-0*) Blue Bird Pub.
— Dragon Slaying for Parents. LC 91-75194. 336p. 1992. pap. 9.95 (*0-914984-35-7*) Starburst.
Prinz, Tom & Elliott, Reed. The Lost Aspect of Love. LC 98-60060. 144p. 1998. pap. 9.99 (*1-57921-098-8*, Pub. by WinePress Pub) BookWorld.
Prinz, W. & Sanders, A. F., eds. Cognition & Motor Processes. (Illus.). 385p. 1984. 89.95 (*0-387-12855-7*) Spr-Verlag.
Prinz, Wolfgang & Bridgeman, Bruce, eds. Handbook of Perception & Action Vol. 1: Perception, Vol.1. (Illus.). 456p. 1996. text 99.95 (*0-12-516161-1*) Acad Pr.
Prinz, Wolfgang, jt. auth. see Hommel, Bernhard.
Prinzba, jt. auth. see Streith.
***Prinzenberg, Ernest D.** Ginseng: Stay Young & Vital. LC 99-39011. 96p. 1999. pap. text 11.95 (*0-8069-6571-1*) Sterling.
Prinzhorn, Hans. Artistry of the Mentally Ill: A Contribution to the Psychology & Psychopathology of Configuration. Von Brockdorff, Eric, tr. LC 95-18.Tr. of Bildnerei der Geisteskranken. (ENG & GER., Illus.). 300p. 1995. 45.00 (*3-211-82639-4*) Spr-Verlag.
Prinzhorn, M., jt. ed. see Haider, H.
Prinzing, Fred W. Handling Church Tensions Creatively. LC 86-80687. 216p. (Orig.). 1986. pap. 5.95 (*0-935797-23-8*) Harvest IL.
Prinzing, Friedrich. Epidemics Resulting from Wars. Westergaard, Harold, ed. 1977. lib. bdg. 59.95 (*0-8490-1781-5*) Gordon Pr.
Prioh, John G., jt. ed. see Clive, Williams S.
Priola, J. John, photos by. Onced Removed: Portraits by J. John Priola. (Illus.). 128p. 1998. text 65.00 (*0-9657280-3-X*, 810311) Arena Editions.
Prioli, Carmine. Hope for a Good Season: The Ca'e Bankers of Harkers Island. (Illus.). 119p. 1998. pap. 15.95 (*1-878086-65-0*, Pub. by Down Home NC) Blair.
Prioli, Carmine A., ed. see Patton, George S., Jr.
Priolo, F., et al. New Trends in Ion Beam Processing of Materials & Beam Induced Nanometric Phenomena: Proceedings of Symposium I & Symposium K of the 1996 E-MRS Spring Conference, Strasbourg, France, June 4-7, 1996. 640p. 1997. 373.00 (*0-444-20506-3*) Elsevier.
Priolo, Lou. As for Me & My House. 210p. 1977. mass mkt. 5.99 (*0-88368-245-1*) Whitaker Hse.
***Priolo, Lou.** Complete Husband. 1999. pap. text 13.95 (*1-879737-35-3*) Calvary Press.
Priolo, Lou. The Heart of Anger: Practical Help for the Prevention & Cure of Anger in Children. (Christian Counsel Ser.). Orig. Title: How to Help Angry Kids. 208p. 1997. pap. 13.95 (*1-879737-28-0*) Calvary Press.
Priolo, Pierluigi, ed. Experimental Techniques & Design in Composite Materials, No. 3. (Key Engineering Materials Ser.: Vol. 144). (Illus.). 316p. (C). 1998. text 98.00 (*0-87849-778-1*, Pub. by Trans T Pub) Enfield Pubs NH.
Prior, Allan. Script to Screen: From Z Cars to the Charmer. (Distributed for the British Film Institute Ser.). (Illus.). 256p. 1996. pap. 17.50 (*0-9527512-0-8*, Pub. by British Film Inst) Ind U Pr.
***Prior, Amy, ed.** Retro, Retro, Fictional Flashbacks. 256p. 2000. 15.00 (*1-85242-644-6*) Serpents Tail.
Prior, Arthur N. Logic & the Basis of Ethics. 124p. 1949. text 17.95 (*0-19-824157-7*) OUP.
— Objects of Thought. Geach, Peter T., ed. 1971. 49.95 (*0-19-824354-5*) OUP.
— Time & Modality. LC 78-26696. (Illus.). 148p. 1979. reprint ed. lib. bdg. 35.00 (*0-313-20911-1*, PRTI, Greenwood Pr) Greenwood.
Prior, Arthur N. & Fine, Kit. Worlds, Times & Selves. LC 76-45042. 176p. 1977. 25.00 (*0-87023-227-4*) U of Mass Pr.
Prior, B., jt. auth. see Dench, D.
Prior, C. & Lomer, C. J., eds. Biological Control of Locusts & Grasshoppers. 394p. 1992. pap. 64.50 (*0-85198-779-6*) C A B Intl.
Prior, C., jt. auth. see Keane, P. J.
Prior, Colin & Linklater, Magnus. Highland Wilderness: A Photogrpahic Essay of the Scottish Highlands. (Illus.). 256p. 1998. 50.00 (*0-09-471560-2*, Pub. by Constable & Co) Trafalgar.
Prior, David. The Message of Joel, Micah & Habakkuk. LC 98-54078. (Bible Speaks Today Ser.). (Illus.). 279p. 1999. pap. 14.99 (*0-8308-1241-5*, 1241) InterVarsity.
— Parish Renewal at the Grassroots. 1987. 14.95 (*0-310-38370-6*, 18409) Zondervan.
Prior, David B., jt. auth. see Coleman, James M.
Prior, David B., jt. ed. see Brunsden, Denys.
Prior, E., ed. Dispositions. (Scots Philosophical Monographs: No. 7). 176p. 1985. text 31.95 (*0-08-032418-5*, Pub. by Aberdeen U Pr) Macmillan.
Prior, Elizabeth Brown. Clara Barton. LC 80-607838. (Official National Park Handbook Ser.: No. 110). (Illus.). 80p. 1981. pap. 7.50 (*0-912627-07-7*) Natl Park Serv.
Prior, G. & Field, J. Pensions & Divorce. (DSS Research Report Ser.). 1996. write for info. (*0-11-762423-3*, Pub. by Statnry Office) Bernan Associates.
Prior, G., jt. auth. see Field, J.
Prior, Ian. The History of Gaelic Games. (Illus.). 80p. 1997. 14.95 (*0-86281-663-7*, Pub. by Appletree Pr) Irish Bks Media.
Prior, Jean C. Landforms of Iowa. LC 91-16136. (Bur Oak Original Ser.). (Illus.). 168p. 1991. pap. 15.95 (*0-87745-347-0*); text 34.95 (*0-87745-350-0*) U of Iowa Pr.
Prior, Jennifer. The Games of Africa. (Illus.). 48p. (J). (gr. 2 up). 1994. 17.95 (*0-694-00597-5*, HarpFestival) HarpC Child Bks.
— Technology Connections for Creepy Crawlies. (Technology Connections Ser.). 48p. (J). (gr. 3-8). 1998. pap. 7.95 (*1-57690-399-0*) Tchr Create Mat.
— Technology Connections for Native American. (Technology Connections Ser.). 48p. (J). (gr. 3-8). 1998. pap. 7.95 (*1-57690-398-2*) Tchr Create Mat.
— Technology Connections for Weather. (Technology Connections Ser.). 48p. (J). (gr. 1-3). 1997. pap. 7.95 (*1-57690-397-4*) Tchr Create Mat.
***Prior, Jennifer Overend.** Bats: Thematic Unit. Hale, Janet A., ed. (Illus.). 80p. (J). 1999. pap., teacher ed. 9.95 (*1-57690-376-1*, TCM2376) Tchr Create Mat.
— Bugs: Early Childhood Thematic Unit. (Illus.). 80p. (J). 1999. pap., teacher ed. 9.95 (*1-57690-620-5*, TCM2620) Tchr Create Mat.
— How to Make a Book Report. Buehler, Stephanie J., ed. (Illus.). 48p. (J). (gr. 1-3). 1999. pap., teacher ed. 7.95 (*1-57690-503-9*, TCM2503) Tchr Create Mat.
— How to Write a Simple Report. Guckian, Mary Ellen, ed. (Illus.). 48p. (J). (gr. 1-3). 1999. pap., teacher ed. 7.95 (*1-57690-502-0*, TCM2502) Tchr Create Mat.
— Magnets: Thematic Unit. Hale, Janet A., ed. (Illus.). 80p. (J). 1999. pap., teacher ed. 9.95 (*1-57690-377-X*, TCM2377) Tchr Create Mat.
— Thematic Unit Numbers: Early Childhood. (Illus.). 80p. 2000. pap., teacher ed. 9.95 (*1-57690-617-5*, TCM 2617) Tchr Create Mat.
— Thematic Unit Shapes: Early Childhood. (Illus.). 80p. 2000. pap., teacher ed. 9.95 (*1-57690-615-9*, TCM 2615) Tchr Create Mat.
***Prior, Jennifer Overend & Burton, Cassandra K.** 20th Century Inventions, Discoveries & Highlights. (Twentieth Century Ser.). (Illus.). 80p. (J). 1999. pap., teacher ed. 9.95 (*1-57690-352-4*, TCM2352) Tchr Create Mat.
***Prior, Jennifer Overend & Miller, Beth A.** Thematic Unit Alphabet: Early Childhood. (Illus.). 80p. 2000. pap., teacher ed. 9.95 (*1-57690-614-0*, TCM 2614) Tchr Create Mat.
Prior, John. The Gower Handbook of Training & Development. 2nd ed. 750p. 1994. 109.95 (*0-566-07446-X*, Pub. by Gower) Ashgate Pub Co.
Prior-Jonson, Elizabeth. AIDS: Myths, Facts & Ethics. 165p. 1989. pap. text 17.00 (*0-08-034434-8*, Pergamon Pr) Elsevier.
***Prior, Judith.** Aladdin's Take-Out. unabridged ed. 48p. 1999. pap. 10.00 (*0-88734-047-4*) Players Pr.
Prior, Judith. Barney's Fair. Landes, William-Alan, ed. LC 97-17296. 50p. (Orig.). 1997. pap. 10.00 (*0-88734-015-6*) Players Pr.
— Girls' Night Out. Landes, William-Alan, ed. LC 97-4491. 55p. (Orig.). 1997. pap. 6.00 (*0-88734-019-9*) Players Pr.
— Jest at the West. Landes, William-Alan, ed. LC 97-3631. 55p. (Orig.). 1997. pap. 10.00 (*0-88734-016-4*) Players Pr.
— Jest Call Me Cowboy. unabridged ed. LC 98-19494. 55p. 1998. pap. 10.00 (*0-88734-022-9*) Players Pr.
— Jungle Juice. 55p. (Orig.). 1996. pap. 10.00 (*0-88734-021-0*) Players Pr.
***Prior, Judith.** Lady Godiva. unabridged ed. Landes, William-Alan, ed. 52p. 2000. pap. 10.00 (*0-88734-046-6*) Players Pr.
Prior, Judith. Phantom of the Music Hall. 55p. 1996. pap. 10.00 (*0-88734-017-2*) Players Pr.
— Sailing South. LC 96-29689. 55p. (Orig.). 1996. pap. 10.00 (*0-88734-018-0*) Players Pr.
— Strudelfest. LC 99-10474. 1998. pap. 10.00 (*0-88734-023-7*) Players Pr.
***Prior, Judith.** Uncle Jack. unabridged ed. Landes, William-Alan, ed. LC 99-55861. 40p. 2000. pap. 10.00 (*0-88734-024-5*) Players Pr.
Prior, Judith. A Wink at the Sphinx. LC 96-51654. 55p. (Orig.). 1996. pap. 10.00 (*0-88734-020-2*) Players Pr.
Prior, Julian. Pastoral Development Planning. LC 95-204569. 160p. (C). 1994. 39.95 (*0-85598-203-9*, Pub. by Oxfam Pub); pap. 14.95 (*0-85598-204-7*, Pub. by Oxfam Pub) Stylus Pub VA.
Prior, K. Gospel in a Pagan Society. 1996. 6.99 (*1-85792-142-9*, Pub. by Christian Focus) Spring Arbor Dist.
— The Way of Holiness. 7.99 (*1-85792-109-7*, Pub. by Christian Focus) Spring Arbor Dist.
Prior, Karen Swallow, jt. auth. see Cohen, Marilyn.
Prior, Katherine. Indian Subcontinent. LC 96-2133. (Origins Ser.). (J). (gr. 5-8). 1997. lib. bdg. 19.30 (*0-531-14418-6*) Watts.
— Initiation Customs. LC 93-516. (Comparing Religions Ser.). (Illus.). 32p. (J). (gr. 4-8). 1993. lib. bdg. 22.83 (*1-56847-035-5*) Raintree Steck-V.
— Ireland. (Origins Ser.). (J). 1997. lib. bdg. 20.00 (*0-531-14415-1*) Watts.
— Pilgrimages & Journeys. LC 93-16318. (Comparing Religions Ser.). (Illus.). 32p. (J). (gr. 4-8). 1993. lib. bdg. 22.83 (*1-56847-032-0*) Raintree Steck-V.
***Prior, Katherine & Adamson, John.** Maharajas' Jewels. (Illus.). 208p. 2000. 67.50 (*0-86565-218-X*) Vendome.
***Prior, Lily.** La Cucina: A Novel of Rapture. 288p. 2000. 24.00 (*0-06-019538-X*) HarpC.
Prior, Lindsay. The Social Organization of Mental Illness. (Illus.). 240p. (C). 1993. text 69.95 (*0-8039-8499-5*) Sage.
Prior, Margot. Understanding Specific Learning Difficulties. 192p. 1996. 45.00 (*0-86377-712-0*); pap. 21.50 (*0-86377-713-9*) L Erlbaum Assocs.
Prior, Mary. Women in English Society, 1500-1800. 304p. 1985. pap. 13.95 (*0-416-35710-5*, 9177) Routledge.
Prior, Mary, jt. auth. see Robinson, Barbara.
Prior, Matthew. The Shorter Poems of Matthew Prior. 1977. 16.95 (*0-8369-7120-5*, 7954) Ayer.
Prior, Michael. The Bible & Colonialism: A Moral Critique. (Biblical Seminar Ser.: Vol. 48). 342p. 1997. pap. 24.95 (*1-85075-815-8*, Pub. by Sheffield Acad) CUP Services.
Prior, Michael. Jesus the Liberator Vol. 3: Nazareth Liberation Theology (Luke 4.16-30) (Biblical Seminar Ser.: Vol. 26). 228p. 1995. pap. 28.50 (*1-85075-524-8*, Pub. by Sheffield Acad) CUP Services.
— Paul the Letter-Writer & the Second Letter to Timothy. (JSNT Supplement Ser.: No. 23). 300p. 1989. 85.00 (*1-85075-147-1*, Pub. by Sheffield Acad) CUP Services.
***Prior, Michael.** Zionism & State of Israel: Moral Inquiry. LC 99-10921. 304p. (C). 1999. text. write for info. (*0-415-20462-3*) Routledge.
Prior, Mike & Purdy, Dave. Out of the Ghetto: A Path to Socialist Rewards. 193p. 1979. pap. 19.95 (*0-85124-260-X*, Pub. by Spkesman) Coronet Bks.
Prior, Mike, jt. auth. see Warren, Bill.
Prior, Moody E. Science & the Humanities. LC 62-13293. 136p. reprint ed. 42.20 (*0-8357-9470-9*, 201530600095) Bks Demand.
Prior, Natalie J. Bog Bodies: Mummies & Curious Corpses. 1997. pap. text 6.95 (*1-86448-243-5*, Pub. by Allen & Unwin Pty) IPG Chicago.
— Caves, Graves & Catacombs: Secrets from Beneath the Earth. (True Stories Ser.). (Illus.). 96p. (Orig.). (J). (gr. 3-7). 1997. pap. 6.95 (*1-86448-389-X*, Pub. by Allen & Unwin Pty) IPG Chicago.
— Dance Crazy: Star Turns from Ballet to Belly Dancing. (Illus.). 96p. (Orig.). (J). (gr. 3-7). 1997. pap. 6.95 (*1-86448-390-3*, Pub. by Allen & Unwin Pty) IPG Chicago.
— London Calling. LC 97-207107. 200p. (YA). 1997. pap. 12.95 (*0-7022-2948-2*, Pub. by Univ Queensland Pr) Intl Spec Bk.
— Mysterious Ruins. 1996. pap. 6.95 (*1-86448-247-8*) IPG Chicago.
— Tasha's Witch. (Storybridge Ser.). 96p. (J). (gr. 4-7). 1995. pap. 9.95 (*0-7022-2793-5*, Pub. by Univ Queensland Pr) Intl Spec Bk.
— West End Shuffle. (YA). 1996. pap. 12.95 (*0-7022-2882-6*, Pub. by Univ Queensland Pr) Intl Spec Bk.
— Yesterday's Heroes. (YA). 1995. pap. 11.95 (*0-7022-2808-7*, Pub. by Univ Queensland Pr) Intl Spec Bk.
Prior, O. H., ed. Caxton's Mirrour of the World: With All the Woodcuts. (EETS, ES Ser.: Vol. 110). 1972. reprint ed. 35.00 (*0-8115-3410-3*) Periodicals Srv.
Prior, Paul, jt. ed. see Bridwell-Bowles, Lillian.
Prior, Paul, ed. see Fang, Irving E.
Prior, Paul A. Writing/Disciplinarity: A Sociohistoric Account of Literate Activity in the Academy. LC 97-50354. (Rhetoric, Knowledge & Society Ser.). 220p. 1998. write for info. (*0-8058-2296-8*); pap. write for info. (*0-8058-2297-6*) L Erlbaum Assocs.
Prior, Pauline. Gender & Mental Health. LC 99-24151. 1999. pap. text 18.50 (*0-8147-6675-7*) NYU Pr.
— Mental Health & Politics: A History of the Mental Health Services in Northern Ireland. 208p. 1993. 66.95 (*1-85628-540-5*, Pub. by Avebry) Ashgate Pub Co.
***Prior, Pauline M.** Gender & Mental Health. LC 99-24151. 240p. 1999. text 55.00 (*0-8147-6674-9*) NYU Pr.
Prior, Philippe, et al, eds. Bacterial Wilt Disease: Molecular & Ecological Aspects. LC 97-52209. (Illus.). 490p. 1998. 129.00 (*3-540-63887-3*) Spr-Verlag.
Prior, R. W. The Great Monarch Butterfly Chase. LC 92-7423. (Illus.). 32p. (J). (ps-3). 1993. text 14.95 (*0-02-775145-7*, Bradbury S&S) S&S Childrens.
Prior, Richard B., ed. Clinical Applications of the Limulus Amoebocyte Lysate Test. 192p. 1990. lib. bdg. 129.00 (*0-8493-6209-1*, RC116) CRC Pr.
Prior, Richard B., jt. ed. see Spagna, Vincent A.
Prior, Richard E. 501 Latin Verbs. LC 94-73692. (LAT.). 1995. pap. text 13.95 (*0-8120-9050-0*) Barron.
***Prior, Robin & Wilson, Trevor.** The First World War. (Illus.). 224p. 2000. 29.95 (*0-304-35256-X*, Pub. by Cassell) Sterling.
Prior, Robin & Wilson, Trevor. Passchendaele: The Untold Story. (Illus.). 256p. 1996. 40.00 (*0-300-06692-9*) Yale U Pr.
— Passchendaele: The Untold Story. 256p. 1998. pap. 16.00 (*0-300-07227-9*) Yale U Pr.
Prior, Robin, jt. auth. see O'Connor, Joseph.
Prior, Roger, jt. auth. see Lasocki, David.
Prior, Sandra P. Fayre Formez of the Pearl Poet. LC 95-69180. 222p. 1996. 37.95 (*0-87013-460-4*) Mich St U Pr.
— The Pearl Poet Revisited. (Twayne's English Authors Ser.: No. 512). 176p. 1994. 32.00 (*0-8057-4516-5*, Twyne) Mac Lib Ref.
Prior, Stephen. Object Relations in Severe Trauma: Psychotherapy of the Sexually Abused Child. LC 95-32752. 200p. 1996. 40.00 (*1-56821-554-1*) Aronson.
Prior, Terrance M. & Siembor, Natalie J. Around Oswego. LC 96-231227. (Images of America Ser.). 1996. pap. 16.99 (*0-7524-0416-4*) Arcadia Publng.
Prior, William J., ed. Socrates: Critical Assessments, 4 vols., Set. LC 95-51962. (Critical Assessments of Leading Philosophers Ser.: .). 1208p. (C). 1996. text, boxed set 655.00 (*0-415-10968-X*) Routledge.
Prior, Yehiam, et al, eds. Methods of Laser Spectroscopy. LC 86-12304. (Fritz Haber International Symposium Ser.). 510p. 1986. 125.00 (*0-306-42285-9*, Plenum Trade) Perseus Pubng.
Priore, Anthony, jt. auth. see Sterne, Jim.
Priore, Domenic. Look! Listen! Vibrate! Smile! 5th rev. ed. (Dumb Angel Gazette Ser.: Vol. 2). (Illus.). 200p. 1995. pap. 19.95 (*0-86719-417-0*) Last Gasp.
Priore, Domenic, ed. The Dumb Angel Gazette: Potpourri, No. 3. 145p. (Orig.). 1989. pap. 6.00 (*0-9621744-1-6*) Surfin Colours.
Priore, Frank V. Getting Your Acts Together: Selling Plays to the School Market. (Illus.). 222p. (Orig.). 1997. pap. 14.95 (*0-9637498-4-6*) Toad Hall PA.
Priore, Frank W. Holiday Play, Vol. 2. 1985. pap. 4.95 (*0-687-17259-4*) Abingdon.
Prioreschi, Plinio. A History of Human Responses to Death: Mythologies, Rituals & Ethics. LC 89-38896. (Studies in Health & Human Services: Vol. 17). 504p. 1990. lib. bdg. 119.95 (*0-88946-142-2*) E Mellen.
— A History of Medicine Vol. 1: Primitive & Ancient Medicine. 2nd enl. rev. ed. LC 95-81354. 596p. 1996. 115.00 (*1-888456-01-9*) Horatius Pr.
— A History of Medicine Vol. 2: Greek Medicine. 2nd enl. rev. ed. 660p. 1996. text 135.00 (*1-888456-02-7*) Horatius Pr.
— A History of Medicine Vol. 3: Roman Medicine. LC 91-29934. (C). 1998. text 150.00 (*1-888456-03-5*) Horatius Pr.
— Masks: Six Plays. LC 98-70675. 370p. 1998. text 35.00 (*1-888456-25-6*) Horatius Pr.
— Mellen History of Medicine, 8 vols. Incl. Vol. 1. Primitive & Ancient Medicine. LC 91-29934. 672p. 1991. lib. bdg. 129.95 (*0-7734-9661-0*); write for info. (*0-7734-9715-3*) E Mellen.
Priority Associates Staff. Practical Christian Living: Teacher's Guide. 149p. Date not set. pap., teacher ed. 15.00 (*1-57902-082-8*, 5401g) Integrtd Res.
— Practical Christian Living Vol. 1: Lessons 1-9, Nos. 1-9. 106p. Date not set. 11.00 (*1-57902-080-1*) Integrtd Res.
— Practical Christian Living Vol. 2: Lessons 10-18, Nos. 10-18. 218p. Date not set. 6.00 (*1-57902-081-X*) Integrtd Res.
Priority Staff. In the National Interest: The 1990 Urban Summit: With Related Analyses Transcript, & Papers. 1991. pap. text 10.95 (*0-87078-332-7*) Century Foundation.
Priou, A., et al, eds. Advances in Complex Electromagnetic Materials: Proceedings of the NATO Advanced Research Workshop on Electromagnetics of Chiral, Bi-Isotropic & Bi-Anisotropic Media (Chiral '96), St.

Petersburg-Moscow, Russia, 23-30 July 1996. LC 97-8140. (NATO ASI Series: Partnership Sub-Series 3). 1997. text 217.50 (*0-7923-4503-7*) Kluwer Academic.

Priozzolo, F., jt. ed. see Johnston, C. W.

Pripps, Robert A. Illustrated John Deere Two-Cylinder Tractor Buyer's Guide. (MBI Illustrated Buyer's Guide Ser.). (Illus.). 160p. 1992. pap. 17.95 (*0-87938-659-2*) MBI Pubg.

Pripps, Robert A. & Morlands, Andrew. Oliver Tractors: Oliver, Hart-Parr & Cockshutt. (Tractor Color Histories Ser.). (Illus.). 128p. 1994. pap. text 21.95 (*0-87938-853-6*) MBI Pubg.

***Pripps, Robert N.** The Big Book of Caterpillar: The Complete History of Caterpillar Bulldozers & Tractors, Plus Collectibles, Sales Memorabilia & Brochures. LC 99-50035. (A Town Square Book). (Illus.). 208p. 2000. 39.95 (*0-89658-366-X*) Voyageur Pr.

Pripps, Robert N. The Field Guide to Vintage Farm Tractors. LC 98-31448. (Illus.). 160p. 1999. 19.95 (*0-89658-365-1*) Voyageur Pr.

— How to Restore Your Farm Tractor. (Illus.). 176p. 1992. pap. 21.95 (*0-87938-593-6*) MBI Pubg.

— Illustrated Ford & Fordson Tractors Buyer's Guide. (MBI Illustrated Buyer's Guide Ser.). (Illus.). 159p. 1994. pap. 17.95 (*0-87938-890-0*) MBI Pubg.

— Illustrated International Harvestor Buyers Guide. (Illustrated Tractor Buyer's Guide Ser.). (Illus.). 160p. 1995. pap. 17.95 (*0-7603-0011-9*) MBI Pubg.

— John Deere Model B Restoration Guide. LC 94-39847. (Authentic Restoration Ser.). (Illus.). 192p. 1995. pap. 19.95 (*0-87938-974-5*) MBI Pubg.

— John Deere Photographic History. (Motorbooks International Ser.). (Illus.). 240p. 1995. pap. 24.95 (*0-7603-0058-5*) MBI Pubg.

— Vintage Ford Tractor. LC 97-1858. (American Legends Ser.). (Illus.). 160p. 1997. 29.95 (*0-89658-354-6*) Voyageur Pr.

Pripps, Robert N. & Morland, Andrew. Big Green: John Deere GP Tractors. (Farm Tractor Color History Ser.). (Illus.). 128p. 1994. pap. 21.95 (*0-87938-937-0*) MBI Pubg.

Pripps, Robert N. & Morland, Andrew. Case General Purpose Tractors. LC 96-22154. (Farm Tractor Color History Ser.). (Illus.). 128p. 1996. pap. 21.95 (*0-7603-0116-6*) MBI Pubg.

Pripps, Robert N. & Morland, Andrew. Farmall Tractors. LC 93-13162. (Farm Tractor Color History Ser.). (Illus.). 128p. 1993. pap. 21.95 (*0-87938-763-7*) MBI Pubg.

— Ford Tractors: N-Series, Fordson, Ford & Ferguson 1914-1954. (Farm Tractor Color History Ser.). (Illus.). 128p. 1990. pap. 21.95 (*0-87938-471-9*) MBI Pubg.

Pripstein, Marsha P. Labor & the State in Egypt, 1952-1994: Workers, Unions, & Economic Restructuring. LC 97-3929. 384p. 1997. pap. 18.50 (*0-231-10693-9*) Col U Pr.

Pris, Claude. Une Grande Entreprise Francaise sous l'Ancien-Regime: La Manufacture Royale des Glaces des Saint-Gobain, 1665-1830, 2 vols., Set. Bruchey, Stuart, ed. LC 80-2824. (Dissertations in European Economic History Ser.: NO. 2).Tr. of A/Large French Enterprise Under the Ancient Regime: the Glassworks of Saint Gobain 1665-1830. (Illus.). 1981. lib. bdg. 72.95 (*0-405-14008-8*, 12919) Ayer.

Prisant, Carol. Antiques Roadshow Primer: The Introductory Guide to Antiques & Collectibles from the Most-Watched Show on PBS. LC 99-29960. (Illus.). 366p. 2000. 28.95 (*0-7611-1775-X*) Workman Pub.

***Prisant, Carol.** Antiques Roadshow Primer: The Introductory Guide to Antiques & Collectibles from the Most-Watched Show on PBS. LC 99-29960. (Illus.). 366p. 2000. pap. 19.95 (*0-7611-1624-9*) Workman Pub.

Priscian, jt. auth. see Simplicius.

Priscilla Publishing Co. Staff. Irish Crochet: Techniques & Projects. (Illus.). 48p. 1984. reprint ed. pap. 3.95 (*0-486-24705-8*) Dover.

Priscilla Publishing Co. Staff, ed. Traditional Hardanger Embroidery. (Illus.). 32p. 1985. reprint ed. pap. 3.50 (*0-486-24906-9*) Dover.

Prisco, G. Di, see Di Prisco, G.

***Prisco, Pete.** Mark Brunnell: Super Southpaw. (SuperStar Series: Vol. 5). 96p. (J). 1999. pap. 4.95 (*1-58261-166-1*, Pub. by Sprts Pubng) Partners-West.

Priscu, John C., ed. Ecosystem Dynamics in a Polar Desert: The McMurdo Dry Valleys, Antarctica. LC 97-46526. (Antarctic Research Ser.: Vol. 72). 1998. 70.00 (*0-87590-899-3*) Am Geophysical.

Priscu, Radu, et al. Earthquake Engineering for Large Dams. LC 84-3730. 407p. reprint ed. pap. 126.20 (*0-7837-4013-1*, 204384300011) Bks Demand.

Prishvin, Mikhail. The Lake & the Woods: or Nature's Calendar. Goodman, W. L., tr. from RUS. LC 75-27685. (Illus.). 258p. 1975. reprint ed. lib. bdg. 55.00 (*0-8371-8465-7*, PRLW, Greenwood Pr) Greenwood.

Prisk, Court, jt. ed. see Manwaring, Max G.

Prism Staff. Competing Values Self-Assessment. (Prism Ser.: Vol. 1). 1992. pap. 11.95 (*1-55542-454-6*) Jossey-Bass.

Prism Staff & Quinn, Robert E. Competing Values Associate Assessment. (Prism Ser.: Vol. 2). 1992. pap. 17.95 (*1-55542-455-4*) Jossey-Bass.

— Competing Values Developmental Tool. (Prism Ser.: Vol. 3). 39p. 1992. pap. 20.95 (*1-55542-456-2*) Jossey-Bass.

Prisma. Italian/Swedish/Italian Dictionary. (ITA & SWE.). 560p. 1997. 69.95 (*0-320-00654-9*) Fr & Eur.

— Swedish-English Dictionary. 3rd ed. LC 97-27430. (SWE.). 1997. pap. 19.95 (*0-8166-3163-8*) U of Minn Pr.

Prisma Staff. Dutch-English Dictionary (New Prisma) (DUT & ENG.). 438p. 1996. pap. 20.00 (*90-274-5148-6*) IBD Ltd.

— English-Dutch Dictionary (New Prisma) (DUT & ENG.). 496p. 1996. pap. 20.00 (*90-274-5149-4*) IBD Ltd.

— English-Swedish-English Dictionary. (ENG & SWE.). 275p. 1981. pap. 29.95 (*0-7859-0913-3*, M9449) Fr & Eur.

— Finnish-Swedish-Finnish Dictionary. (FIN & SWE.). 272p. 1981. pap. 29.95 (*0-8288-4659-6*, M9444) Fr & Eur.

— French-Swedish-French Dictionary. (FRE & SWE.). 370p. 1980. pap. 19.95 (*0-8288-4702-9*, M9445) Fr & Eur.

— Italian-Swedish-Italian Dictionary. (ITA & SWE.). 279p. 1978. pap. 19.95 (*0-8288-5248-0*, M9446) Fr & Eur.

— Prisma's Abridged English-Swedish & Swedish-English Dictionary. abr. ed. LC 94-49413. (ENG & SWE.). 480p. 1995. 26.95 (*0-8166-2734-7*) U of Minn Pr.

— Prisma's English-Swedish Dictionary. 3rd ed. LC 97-27429. (SWE.). 1997. write for info. (*0-8166-3162-X*) U of Minn Pr.

— Prisma's Lilla Modern French-Swedish, Swedish-French Dictionary: Prismas Lilla Moderna Fransk-Svensk Och Svensk-Franska Ordbok. (FRE & SWE.). 585p. 1983. 75.00 (*0-8288-1680-8*, F31845) Fr & Eur.

— Prisma's Unabridged Swedish-English & English-Swedish Dictionary. 3rd ed. LC 99-230157. (ENG & SWE.). 1997. 69.95 (*0-8166-3231-6*) U of Minn Pr.

***Prisman, Eli.** Derivative Securities with Maple V. 760p. 2000. 99.95 (*0-12-564915-0*) Morgan Kaufmann.

Prison Discipline Society Boston Staff. Reports of the Prison Discipline Society, Boston: Reports 1-29, 1826-1854 (With Intro. essay & Analytical Index Added), 6 vols. LC 71-129322. (Criminology, Law Enforcement, & Social Problems Ser.: No. 155). (Illus.). 1972. 175.00 (*0-87585-155-X*) Patterson Smith.

***Priss, Uta.** Proceedings of the Tenth Midwest Artificail Intelligense & Cognitive Science Conference. (Technical Reports). (Illus.). 115p. 1999. pap. 35.00 (*1-57735-082-0*) AAAI Pr.

Prisse, D'Avennes. Arabic Designs in Color. (Pictorial Archive Ser.). (Illus.). 46p. 1978. pap. 8.95 (*0-486-23658-7*) Dover.

Prisse d'Avennes, E. L' Atlas de l'Art Egyptien: Atlas of Egyptian Art. rev. ed. (FRE.). 405p. 1993. reprint ed. lib. bdg. 495.00 (*0-7859-3710-2*, 9775170001) Fr & Eur.

Prista, Alexander R. Essential Portuguese Grammar. 114p. (Orig.). 1966. pap. 5.95 (*0-486-21650-0*) Dover.

— Say It in Portuguese (European Usage) LC 77-73311. 1979. pap. 3.95 (*0-486-23676-5*) Dover.

Pristash, David J. Power Economics for the Next Generation. Yuschak, Catherine L., ed. (Illus.). 266p. (C). 1997. pap. 29.95 (*0-9657318-0-4*) Pub Systs.

Prisuta, Mike. Awe Inspiring, The Storied History of Spartan Hockey. 200p. 1997. 29.95 (*0-9658933-1-6*) Visions Sports.

Priszter, J., ed. see Csapody, V. & Javorka, S.

Priszter, S. Trees & Shrubs of Europe. (ENG, FRE, GER, HUN & ITA.). 300p. 1983. 95.00 (*0-8288-0070-7*, M15341) Fr & Eur.

Priszter, S. Z., ed. Dictionary of Trees & Shrubs of Europe: A Dictionary in Eight Languages. 300p. 1983. 62.00 (*963-05-2946-7*, Pub. by Akade Kiado) IBD Ltd.

Pritam, Amrita. Forty-Nine Days. 1981. 11.00 (*0-8364-0798-9*, Pub. by Chanakya) S Asia.

— The Haunted House & the Thirteenth Sun: Two Novels. 155p. 1993. text 15.95 (*0-685-66338-8*, Pub. by Vikas) S Asia.

— Life & Poetry of Sara Shagufta. LC 93-911494. (Orig.). (C). 1994. 8.50 (*81-7018-771-0*, Pub. by BR Pub) S Asia.

Pritch, jt. auth. see Morgan.

Pritchard. Indigenous Peoples United Nations, Vol. 1. 1998. text. write for info. (*1-85649-593-0*, Pub. by Zed Books); text 25.00 (*1-85649-594-9*) Zed Books.

— Lighting. 1985. pap. text. write for info. (*0-582-30529-2*, Pub. by Addison-Wesley) Longman.

— Lighting. 5th ed. (C). 1995. pap. text. write for info. (*0-582-23422-0*, Pub. by Addison-Wesley) Longman.

— Practical Geography Africa. 1984. pap. text. write for info. (*0-582-60366-8*, Pub. by Addison-Wesley) Longman.

— Reinforced Plastics Durability. 1999. ring bd. 159.95 (*0-8493-0547-0*) CRC Pr.

— Using the Magnetic Forces of Your Mind. 1957. pap. 4.95 (*0-87505-094-8*) Borden.

— Wills & Administrative Estates: 1989 Supplement. 5th ed. 1989. pap. 225.00 (*0-87215-833-0*, 66049-10, MICHIE) LEXIS Pub.

Pritchard & Trebbau. Turtles of Venezuela. LC 83-51450. 1984. write for info. (*0-916984-11-7*) SSAR.

Pritchard, jt. auth. see Harris, Charles E.

Pritchard, Stuart. A Murder in Lincoln County. LC 98-91569. 177p. 1998. write for info. (*1-892508-03-6*) Jingle Bob Pr.

Pritchard, A. J., ed. see IFAC Symposium Staff.

Pritchard, Adam C., jt. auth. see Boudreaux, Donald J.

Pritchard, Allan, ed. Vancouver Island Letters of Edmund Hope Verney, 1862-65. LC 96-187325. (Pioneers of British Columbia Ser.). (Illus.). 324p. 1996. 65.00 (*0-7748-0554-4*, FC3822); pap. 25.95 (*0-7748-0573-0*) U of Wash Pr.

Pritchard, Andrea, et al, eds. Alien Discussions: Proceedings of the Abduction Study Conference Held at M. I. T. Cambridge, MA. LC 95-69530. (Illus.). 684p. 1994. 39.95 (*0-9644917-0-2*) N Cambridge Pr.

Pritchard, Andrew. The Microscope Cabinet. (History of Microscopy Ser.). 256p. 1987. reprint ed. 62.40 (*0-940095-02-5*) Sci Heritage Ltd.

Pritchard, Annette, jt. auth. see Morgan, Nigel.

Pritchard, Annette, jt. auth. see Morgan, Nigel J.

Pritchard, Anthony. A Century of Grand Prix Motor Racing. (Illus.). 272p. 1998. 39.95 (*1-899870-38-5*) Motor Racing.

Pritchard, Arnold. Catholic Loyalism in Elizabethan England. LC 78-10208. 255p. reprint ed. pap. 79.10 (*0-7837-6851-6*, 204668000003) Bks Demand.

Pritchard, Audrey, jt. auth. see Pritchard, Raymond F.

Pritchard, B. Continuous & Integral Bridges. (Illus.). 320p. (C). 1994. 125.00 (*0-419-19030-9*, E & FN Spon) Routledge.

Pritchard, B., tr. see Ferrero, Guglielmo.

Pritchard, Brian. Bridge Design for Economy & Durability: Concepts for New, Strengthened & Replacement Bridges. (Illus.). 172p. 1992. 79.00 (*0-7277-1671-9*, Pub. by T Telford) RCH.

Pritchard, Brian, ed. Antonio Caladara: Essays on His Life & Time. 424p. 1987. 113.95 (*0-85967-720-6*, Pub. by Scolar Pr) Ashgate Pub Co.

— Bridge Modification 2: Stronger & Safer Bridges. 2nd ed. LC 97-200304. 145p. 1997. 71.00 (*0-7277-2589-0*) Am Soc Civil Eng.

Pritchard, Carl. Precedence Diagram: Successful Schedule in a Team Environment. (Project Management Nuts & Bolts Ser.: Vol. 3). 1999. pap. write for info. (*1-890367-20-6*) ESI Int.

Pritchard, Carl. How to Build a Work Breakdown Structure: The Cornerstone of Project Management. Weaver, Angela, ed. LC 99-191664. (Project Management Nuts & Bolts Ser.: Vol. 1). 70p. 1998. pap. 24.95 (*1-890367-12-5*) ESI Int.

Pritchard, Carol. Avoiding Rape on & off Campus. 2nd ed. 68p. (Orig.). 1988. pap. 8.00 (*1-877858-24-2*, AROOC2) Amer Focus Pub.

Pritchard, Clive. Sorting & Matching, Animal Lotto. 1995. pap. 12.99 (*0-85953-705-6*) Childs Play.

Pritchard, Colin. Suicide: The Ultimate Rejection; a Psycho-Social Study. LC 94-43417. 209p. 1995. pap. 31.95 (*0-335-19032-4*) OpUniv Pr.

Pritchard, Colin, jt. auth. see Taylor, Richard.

***Pritchard, D. Brine.** The Right Way to Play Chess. (Illus.). 224p. 2000. pap. 12.95 (*1-58574-046-2*) Lyons Pr.

Pritchard, D. J. & Scott, C. J., eds. Applications of Transputers Two: Proceedings of the 2nd International Conference on Applications of Transputers, Southampton, U. K. July 11-13, 1990. (Transputer & Occam Engineering Ser.). 587p. (gr. 12). 1990. pap. 110.00 (*90-5199-035-9*, Pub. by IOS Pr) IOS Press.

Pritchard, Dale J. A Philosophy: (And Fitness) 112p. (Orig.). 1997. pap., wbk. ed. 19.95 (*0-9649856-6-7*) Christina Pub.

— A Philosophy: The Workbook on Life. 1998. 19.96 (*0-9649856-1-6*) Christina Pub.

— Weird Weddings: True Stories about Nonsense in Nuptials. 109p. (Orig.). 1997. pap., wbk. ed. 19.95 (*0-9649856-9-1*) Christina Pub.

***Pritchard, David.** Popular Chess Variants: Tournament. (Chess Bks.). (Illus.). 112p. 2000. pap. text 14.95 (*0-7134-8578-7*) B T B.

Pritchard, David & Lysaght, Alan. The Beatles: An Oral History. LC 98-19090. 320p. 1998. 23.95 (*0-7868-6436-2*, Pub. by Hyperion) Time Warner.

— The Beatles: An Oral History. 352p. 1999. pap. 14.00 (*0-7868-8489-4*, Pub. by Hyperion) Time Warner.

Pritchard, David & Reeve, Jeff. Euro-Par'98 Parallel Processing: 4th International Euro-Par Conference, Southampton, UK, September 1-4, 1998, Proceedings, Vol. 147. Goos, G. et al, eds. LC 98-38786. (Lecture Notes in Computer Science Ser.: Vol. 1470). xxii, 1157p. 1998. pap. 119.00 (*3-540-64952-2*) Spr-Verlag.

Pritchard, David A., jt. auth. see Hall, Harold V.

***Pritchard, David Hemmings, ed.** Holding the Media Accountable: Citizens, Ethics & the Law. LC 99-37764. 240p. 2000. pap. 16.95 (*0-253-21357-6*); lib. bdg. 39.95 (*0-253-33662-7*) Ind U Pr.

Pritchard, David W., jt. auth. see Foy, Chester L.

Pritchard, Derek. Soldering, Brazing & Welding: A Manual of Techniques. (Illus.). 160p. 1997. 35.00 (*1-85223-991-3*, Pub. by Crolwood) Trafalgar.

Pritchard Dodge, Ellen. Communication Lab 1: A Classroom Communication Program. LC 98-223274. (Illus.). 150p. 1998. reprint ed. pap. 39.95 (*0-7693-0006-5*, 1992) Thomson Learn.

Pritchard, Donna L., jt. auth. see Colorado Assoc. of Legal Secretaries Staff.

Pritchard, Donna L., ed. see Colorado Assoc. of Legal Secretaries Staff.

Pritchard, Doris. Monmouth Court: Boston. LC 81-3589. (Illus.). 1981. 15.00 (*0-87233-064-8*) Bauhan.

Pritchard, Douglas J., ed. Instructional Course Lectures, Vol. 45. (Illus.). 550p. 1996. 120.00 (*0-89203-145-X*) Amer Acad Ortho Surg.

Pritchard, E. B., ed. Mars: Past, Present, & Future. (PAAS Ser.: Vol. 145). 324p. 1992. 69.95 (*1-56347-043-8*, V-145) AIAA.

Pritchard, Earl H. & Pritchard, Phil, eds. Journal of William Fowler Pritchard: Indiana to California, 1850, Return Via Nicaragua, 1852. LC 95-39741. 173p. 1996. 24.95 (*0-87770-569-0*); pap. 14.95 (*0-87770-570-4*) Ye Galleon.

Pritchard, Eileen R. & Scott, Paula. Literature Searching in Science, Technology & Agriculture. rev. ed. LC 95-39491. 216p. 1996. lib. bdg. 65.00 (*0-313-26212-8*, Greenwood Pr) Greenwood.

***Pritchard, Elaine & Reeves, Richard.** Quality Assurance & the Law. 224p. 2000. pap. text 54.95 (*0-7506-4176-2*, Newnes) Buttrwrth-Heinemann.

Pritchard, Ernest M. & Cary, Emily P. Duet-Two Accounts of the Pritchard-Stuart Heritage. (Illus.). 112p. 1991. pap. 9.00 (*0-614-15836-2*) McClain. Shaped by their upbringing in turn-of-the-century West Virginia, Ernest Pritchard & Adelaide Stuart became master teachers who touched the lives of grateful students for fifty years. Ernest Pritchard's reflections about growing up in a Methodist parsonage are combined with Emily Pritchard Cary's account of the Stuart family's misfortunes that reached a happy conclusion: her parent's marriage.
Publisher Paid Annotation.

Pritchard, Evan T. From the Temple Within: The Fourth Book of Light. (Illus.). 160p. (Orig.). 1993. pap. 8.95 (*0-9637990-0-2*) Resonance Comm.

— No Word for Time: The Way of the Algonquin People. LC 97-7492. 114p. (Orig.). 1997. pap. 12.95 (*1-57178-042-4*) Coun Oak Bks.

— The Secrets of Whole-Hearted Thinking: 100 Sayings, Ideas & Paradoxes That Can Make Your Life Fuller, Happier & Less Complicated. LC 93-33283. 1993. pap. 8.95 (*0-88268-160-5*) Station Hill Pr.

Pritchard, G. Anti-Corrosion Polymers: PEEK, PEKK, & Other Polyaryls. 118p. 1994. 137.00 (*1-85957-043-7*, 6038) ASM.

Pritchard, G., ed. Reinforced Plastics Durability. 350p. 1998. boxed set 170.00 (*1-85573-320-X*, Pub. by Woodhead Pubng) Am Educ Systs.

Pritchard, G. A. Willow Creek Seeker Services: Evaluating a New Way of Doing Church. LC 95-21487. 336p. 1995. pap. 16.99 (*0-8010-5274-2*) Baker Bks.

Pritchard, George. The Aggressions of the French at Tahiti & Other Islands in the Pacific. De Deckker, P. T., ed. (Illus.). 1983. 59.00 (*0-19-647994-0*) OUP.

Pritchard, Gerylin, ed. see Dunn, Edith B.

Pritchard, Gretchen W. Alleluia! Amen: The Sunday Paper's Communion Book for Children - A Guide to the Holy Eucharist, Rite II. (Illus.). 78p. (Orig.). (J). (gr. k-6). 1984. pap. 5.75 (*0-9614022-0-2*) Sunday Paper.

— Go, Tell It on the Mountain: Three Christmas Pageants for Church Schools. (Illus.). 63p. (Orig.). 1985. pap. 12.50 (*0-9614022-1-0*) Sunday Paper.

— New Life: The Sunday Paper's Baptism Book. (Illus.). 80p. (Orig.). (J). (gr. k-6). 1986. pap. 5.75 (*0-9614022-2-9*) Sunday Paper.

— Offering the Gospel to Children. LC 92-23900. 219p. 1992. pap. 13.95 (*1-56101-065-0*) Cowley Pubns.

— Risen with Christ: Celebrating the Paschal Mystery with the Parish Family. (Illus.). 118p. (Orig.). 1988. pap. 15.00 (*0-9614022-3-7*) Sunday Paper.

***Pritchard, Gretchen Wolff.** I Love Christmas. (Illus.). 76p. (J). (gr. 3-6). 1999. pap. 16.50 (*0-9614022-4-5*) Sunday Paper.

— Learning to Love. LC 99-86141. (Journeybook Ser.). 2000. pap. write for info. (*0-89869-322-5*) Church Pub Inc.

Pritchard, H. Baden. About Photography & Photographers. LC 72-9225. (Literature of Photography Ser.). 1973. reprint ed. 19.95 (*0-405-04931-5*) Ayer.

— The Photographic Studios of Europe. LC 72-9226. (Literature of Photography Ser.). 1973. reprint ed. 23.95 (*0-405-04932-3*) Ayer.

Pritchard, J. M. Africa: Geography of a Changing Continent. LC 71-145838. 248p. 1972. 39.50 (*0-8419-0071-X*, Africana) Holmes & Meier.

Pritchard, Jacki. The Abuse of Older People: A Training Manual for Detection & Prevention. 2nd rev. ed. LC 95-11795. Orig. Title: The Abuse of Elderly People. 204p. 1995. pap. 27.00 (*1-85302-305-1*, Pub. by Jessica Kingsley) Taylor & Francis.

— Good Practice in Working with Elder Abuse in Britain & Canada, Vol. 7. (Good Practice Ser.). 1998. pap. text 49.95 (*1-85302-704-9*) Taylor & Francis.

— Working with Elder Abuse: A Training Manual for Home Care, Residential & Day Care Staff. 200p. 1996. pap. 34.95 (*1-85302-418-X*, Pub. by Jessica Kingsley) Taylor & Francis.

Pritchard, Jacki, ed. Good Practice in Supervision: Statutory & Voluntary Organisations. LC 95-102904. 190p. 1994. pap. 26.00 (*1-85302-279-9*) Taylor & Francis.

Pritchard, Jacki, jt. auth. see Kemshall, Hazel.

Pritchard, Jacki, jt. ed. see Kemshall, Hazel.

Pritchard, Jacki, jt. ed. see Owen, Hilary.

Pritchard, James. Anatomy of a Naval Disaster: The 1746 French Expedition to North America. LC 96-154384. (Illus.). 344p. 1995. 49.95 (*0-7735-1325-6*, Pub. by McG-Queens Univ Pr) CUP Services.

Pritchard, James, contrib. by. Preserving Natural Conditions: Science & the Perception of Nature in Yellowstone National Park. LC 98-51144. (Illus.). 1999. text 45.00 (*0-8032-3722-7*) U of Nebr Pr.

Pritchard, James, ed. Proceedings of the 18th Symposium on Naval Hydrodynamics: (Actes du Dix-Huitieme Colloque de la Societe d'Histoire Coloniale Francaise. Montreal. Mai 1992) v, 116p. 1993. text 30.00 (*1-884679-00-5*) Fr Colonial Hist.

— Proceedings of the Nineteenth Meeting of the French Colonial Historical Society, Providence, R. I., May, 1993.Tr. of Actes du Dix-Neuvieme Colloque de la Societe D'Histoire Coloniale Francaise, Providence, R. I., Mai 1993. (ENG & FRE., Illus.). v, 228p. (C). 1994. text 30.00 (*1-884679-01-3*) Fr Colonial Hist.

Pritchard, James, jt. auth. see Pritchard, Peter.

Pritchard, James B. Archaeology & the Old Testament. LC 58-10053. 279p. reprint ed. pap. 86.50 (*0-8357-5716-1*, 201601100006) Bks Demand.

— The Bronze Age Cemetery at Gibeon. (University Museum Monographs: No. 25). (Illus.). ix, 181p. 1963. pap. 20.00 (*0-934718-17-2*) U Museum Pubns.

— The Cemetery at Tell es-Sa'idiyeh, Jordan. (University Museum Monographs: No. 41). (Illus.). xxi, 103p. (Orig.). (C). 1980. pap. 25.00 (*0-934718-32-6*) U Museum Pubns.

— Gibeon, Where the Sun Stood Still: The Discovery of the Biblical City. LC 62-11963. (Illus.). 244p. reprint ed. pap. 75.70 (*0-7837-6765-X*, 204659500003) Bks Demand.

P

An Asterisk (*) at the beginning of an entry indicates that the title is appearing for the first time.

— HarperCollins Concise Atlas of The Bible. 152p. 1997. pap. 25.00 (*0-06-251499-7*, Pub. by Harper SF) HarpC.
— Recovering Sarepta, a Phoenician City: Excavations at Sarafand, Lebanon, 1969-1974, by the University Museum of the University of Pennsylvania. LC 77-28304. (Illus.). 178p. 1978. reprint ed. pap. 55.20 (*0-608-07160-9*, 206738500009) Bks Demand.
— Tell Es-Sa'Idiyeh: Excavations on the Tell, 1964-1966. (University Museum Monographs: No. 60). (ARA & ENG., Illus.). 88p. 1985. text 60.00 (*0-934718-60-1*) U Museum Pubns.
— Winery, Defenses, & Soundings at Gibeon. (University Museum Monographs: No. 26). (Illus.). viii, 85p. 1964. pap. 15.00 (*0-934718-18-0*) U Museum Pubns.
Pritchard, James B., ed. Ancient Near East in Pictures. 2nd ed. Incl., 2 vols. 424p. 1969. text 99.50 (*0-691-03502-4*, Pub. by Princeton U Pr); An Anthology of Texts & Pictures. 320p. 1976. pap. text 18.95 (*0-691-00209-6*, Pub. by Princeton U Pr); An Anthology of Texts & Pictures. 380p. 1958. pap. text 19.95 (*0-691-00200-2*, Pub. by Princeton U Pr); Pictures. 1969. (*0-691-03610-1*); 1969. pap. write for info. (*0-318-70291-6*) Princeton U Pr.
— Ancient Near Eastern Texts: Relating to the Old Testament. 3rd ed. LC 78-76499. 734p. reprint ed. pap., suppl. ed. 200.00 (*0-8357-8801-6*, 205227600085) Bks Demand.
— Ancient Near Eastern Texts Relating to the Old Testament, Set. 3rd ed. 548p. 1969. text 100.00 (*0-691-03503-2*, Pub. by Princeton U Pr) Cal Prin Full Svc.
Pritchard, James B., et al. Sarepta: A Preliminary Report on the Iron Age. (University Museum Monographs: No. 35). (Illus.). ix, 114p. 1975. pap. 30.00 (*0-934718-24-5*) U Museum Pubns.
Pritchard, James S. Louis XV's Navy, 1748-1762: A Study of Organization & Administration. 304p. 1987. 60.00 (*0-7735-0570-9*, Pub. by McG-Queens Univ Pr) CUP Services.
Pritchard, Jane, jt. ed. see Henry, Christine.
***Pritchard, Jason.** COM & CORBA Side by Side: Architectures, Strategies, & Implementations. LC 99-23779. 464p. (C). 1999. pap. text 44.95 (*0-201-37945-7*) Addison-Wesley.
Pritchard, Jeffrey J. Low-Risk High-Performance Investing with Convertible Bonds. 256p. 1990. 39.95 (*0-88730-396-X*, HarpBusn) HarpInfo.
Pritchard, Jenette S. Anti-Depressants in America - Therapeutic Use & Effects: Index of New Information. 160p. Date not set. 47.50 (*0-7883-1884-5*); pap. 44.50 (*0-7883-1885-3*) ABBE Pubs Assn.
Pritchard, Jim. The Man with the Buzzer in His Throat. (Chapbook Ser.). (Illus.). 6p. 1995. pap. 10.00 (*0-9652505-2-0*) Synaesthesia.
— The Neighbors. (Chapbook Ser.). 8p. 1995. pap. 10.00 (*0-9652505-0-4*) Synaesthesia.
Pritchard, John. Guide to the Law. 1088p. pap. 29.95 (*0-14-051253-5*, Pub. by Pnguin Bks Ltd) Trafalgar.
Pritchard, John, ed. see Dunn, Edith B.
Pritchard, John, ed. see Nelson-Giavanni, Marcus.
Pritchard, John, ed. see Voorhees, Russell.
Pritchard, John, ed. see Walker, Jim.
Pritchard, John G. Poly(Vinyl Alcohol), Vol. 10. (Polymer Monographs). (Illus.). xii, 140p. 1970. text 190.00 (*0-677-01670-0*) Gordon & Breach.
***Pritchard, John R., Jr.** Breathing New Life into Lent Vol. 2: A Collection of Creative Worship Resources. 96p. 2000. pap. 14.00 (*0-8170-1340-7*) Judson.
Pritchard Jones, K. V., jt. auth. see Adams, John N.
Pritchard, Juanita & Stone, Karla. From the Classroom to the Workplace, Vol. I. (Illus.). 304p. 1997. pap. 34.00 (*1-884135-34-X*, M440) Mayer-Johnson.
— From the Classroom to the Workplace, Vol. II. (Illus.). 192p. 1997. pap. 29.00 (*1-884135-35-8*, M441) Mayer-Johnson.
***Pritchard, Kara.** RHCE Exam Cram. LC 99-45281. (Exam Cram Ser.). (Illus.). 380p. 1999. pap. 29.99 (*1-57610-487-7*) Coriolis Grp.
Pritchard, Kathleen W. Swiss Timepiece Makers, 1775-1975, 2 vols. LC 97-4050. 1800p. 1997. 125.00 (*0-914659-79-0*) Phoenix Pub.
Pritchard, L., jt. ed. see Lawrence, M.
Pritchard, Lawrence W., jt. auth. see Walker, Deward E., Jr.
Pritchard, Louise. Cars, Trucks & Buses: Vehicle Stickers. (Illus.). 8p. (J). 1998. pap. text 3.95 (*0-7894-3103-3*) DK Pub Inc.
— Dump Trucks, Tractors & Bulldozers: Vehicle Stickers. (Illus.). 8p. (J). 1998. pap. text 3.95 (*0-7894-3102-5*) DK Pub Inc.
— Fire Trucks & Rescue Vehicles: Vehicle Stickers. (Illus.). 8p. (J). 1998. pap. text 3.95 (*0-7894-3101-7*) DK Pub Inc.
— Race Cars, Bikes & Boats: Vehicle Stickers. (Illus.). 8p. (J). 1998. pap. text 3.95 (*0-7894-3164-5*) DK Pub Inc.
Pritchard, M., et al. Utilization of Small Pelagic Fish Species in Asia. 1996. pap. 60.00 (*0-85954-467-2*, Pub. by Nat Res Inst) St Mut.
Pritchard, M. L. Psychological Aspects of Rheumatoid Arthritis. (Recent Research in Psychology Ser.). (Illus.). xv, 208p. 1989. 59.95 (*0-387-97116-5*) Spr-Verlag.
Pritchard, Margaret B., jt. ed. see Meyers, Amy R.
Pritchard, Mark. Too Beautiful, 1. 1999. pap. text 7.95 (*1-58419-006-X*) Masq Bks.
Pritchard-Martinez, Carol, ed. see Devlin, Keith J.
Pritchard, Melissa. The Instinct for Bliss. 160p. (Orig.). 1997. reprint ed. pap. 12.95 (*0-944072-79-8*) Zoland Bks.
— Phoenix. LC 91-71514. 133p. (Orig.). (C). 1991. pap. text 8.95 (*0-943433-08-8*) Cane Hill Pr.
— Selene of the Spirits. LC 98-28729. 217p. 1998. 22.00 (*0-86538-094-5*); pap. 14.00 (*0-86538-095-3*) Ontario Rev NJ.
— Spirit Seizures. LC 87-5932. (Flannery O'Connor Award for Short Fiction Ser.). 186p. 1987. 19.95 (*0-8203-0959-1*) U of Ga Pr.
Pritchard, Michael S. On Becoming Responsible. LC 90-41613. x, 278p. 1991. 29.95 (*0-7006-0444-8*) U Pr of KS.
— Reasonable Children: Moral Education & Moral Learning. LC 96-25633. 192p. 1996. 29.95 (*0-7006-0796-X*); pap. 12.95 (*0-7006-0797-8*) U Pr of KS.
Pritchard, Michael S., jt. auth. see Jaksa, James A.
Pritchard, Michael S., jt. ed. see Robison, Wade L.
Pritchard, Paul. Deep Play: A Climber's Odyssey from Llanberis to the Big Walls. LC 98-128185. 192 p. 1997. write for info. (*1-898573-14-X*) Baton Wicks Pubns.
— Deep Play: A Climber's Odyssey from Llanberis to the Big Walls. (Illus.). 192p. 1998. 22.95 (*0-89886-565-4*) Mountaineers.
— An Introduction to Programming with Macintosh Pascal. (Illus.). 608p. (C). 1988. pap. text 33.00 (*0-201-17539-8*) Addison-Wesley.
***Pritchard, Paul.** The Totem Pole: And a Whole New Adventure. (Illus.). 216p. 2000. 22.95 (*0-89886-696-0*) Mountaineers.
Pritchard, Paul C., ed. Views of the Green: Presentations from New Directions for the Conservation of Parks; An International Working Conference. 154p. 1985. 14.95 (*0-940091-14-3*); pap. 9.95 (*0-940091-13-5*) Natl Parks & Cons.
Pritchard, Peter & Pritchard, James. Teamwork for Primary & Shared Care. 2nd ed. (Practical Guides for General Practice Ser.). (Illus.). 160p. 1994. pap. text 29.95 (*0-19-262527-6*) OUP.
Pritchard, Peter C. The Galapagos Tortoises: Nomenclatural & Survival Status. Rhodin, Anders G., ed. LC 97-101342. (Chelonian Research Monographs: No. 1). (Illus.). 85p. 1996. 29.00 (*0-9653540-0-8*); pap. 19.00 (*0-9653540-1-6*) Chelonian Res.
— Rare & Endangered Biota of Florida, Vol. 6 - 1982. LC 78-12121. (Illus.). 153p. 1982. reprint ed. pap. 47.50 (*0-608-04478-4*, 206522300006) Bks Demand.
Pritchard, Peter M. Manual of Primary Health Care: Its Nature & Organization. 2nd ed. (Illus.). (C). 1981. pap. text 18.95 (*0-19-261355-3*) OUP.
Pritchard, Phil, jt. ed. see Pritchard, Earl H.
Pritchard, Philip J. MathCAD: A Tool for Engineering Problem Solving. LC 97-47318. 336p. 1998. pap. 28.75 (*0-07-012189-3*) McGraw.
Pritchard, R. E., ed. Mary Sidney, Countess of Pembroke (1561-1621) & Sir Philip Sidney: The Sidney Psalms. pap. write for info. (*0-85635-983-1*, Pub. by Carcanet Pr) Paul & Co Pubs.
Pritchard, R. John, ed. The Tokyo Major War Crimes Trial Vol. 1: The Records of the International Military Tribunal for the Far East/with an Authoritative Commentary & Comprehensive Guide. 1998. text 99.95 (*0-7734-8295-4*) E Mellen.
— The Tokyo Major War Crimes Trial Vol. 2: The Records of the International Military Tribunal for the Far East/with an Authoritative Commentary & Comprehensive Guide. LC 98-38299. 1998. text 99.95 (*0-7734-8297-0*) E Mellen.
— The Tokyo Major War Crimes Trial Vol. 3: The Records of the International Military Tribunal for the Far East/with an Authoritative Commentary & Comprehensive Guide. 1998. text 99.95 (*0-7734-8299-7*) E Mellen.
— The Tokyo Major War Crimes Trial Vol. 4: The Records of the International Military Tribunal for the Far East/with an Authoritative Commentary & Comprehensive Guide. 1998. text 99.95 (*0-7734-8301-2*) E Mellen.
— The Tokyo Major War Crimes Trial Vol. 5: The Records of the International Military Tribunal for the Far East/with an Authoritative Commentary & Comprehensive Guide. 1998. text 99.95 (*0-7734-8303-9*) E Mellen.
— The Tokyo Major War Crimes Trial Vol. 6: The Records of the International Military Tribunal for the Far East/with an Authoritative Commentary & Comprehensive Guide. 1998. text 99.95 (*0-7734-8305-5*) E Mellen.
Pritchard, R. John, jt. auth. see International Military Tribunal for the Far East Staff.
Pritchard, Ray. The ABC's of Wisdom: Building Character with Solomon. 320p. 1997. 14.99 (*0-8024-8182-5*, 1) Moody.
***Pritchard, Ray.** An Anchor for the Soul: Help for the Present, Hope for the Future. LC 00-33869. 2000. write for info. (*0-8024-1535-0*) Moody.
Pritchard, Ray. Green Pastures, Quiet Waters. 331p. 1999. 14.99 (*0-8024-8157-4*) Moody.
— Keep Believing: God in the Midst of Our Deepest Struggles. LC 97-200116. 224p. 1997. pap. 11.99 (*0-8024-3199-2*, 194) Moody.
— Man of Honor: Living the Life of Godly Character. LC 96-10520. 1996. pap. 12.99 (*0-89107-899-1*) Crossway Bks.
— Names of the Holy Spirit. (Names of Ser.). mass mkt. 4.99 (*0-8024-6045-3*, 401) Moody.
— The Road Best Traveled: Knowing God's Will for Your Life. LC 95-15381. 224p. 1995. pap. 10.99 (*0-89107-851-7*) Crossway Bks.
— Something New under the Sun: Ancient Wisdom for Contemporary Living. 316p. 1998. 14.99 (*0-8024-8156-6*) Moody.
— What a Christian Believes: An Easy to Read Guide to Understanding. LC 98-23783. 176p. 1998. pap. 9.99 (*1-58134-016-8*) Crossway Bks.
Pritchard, Ray, jt. auth. see Briner, Bob.
Pritchard, Raymond F. & Pritchard, Audrey. Driving the Pan-American Highway to Mexico & Central America: A Complete Guidebook for Do-it-Yourself Planning, Preplanning for & Driving Through Mexico & Central America. 6th rev. ed. Howard, Chris, ed. (Illus.). 162p. (Orig.). 1997. pap. 18.95 (*1-881233-48-0*) Costa Rica Bks.
***Pritchard, Rhonda.** When Parents Part, How Kids Adapt: What Hurts, What Heals. LC 99-194278. 1998. 24.95 (*0-14-027790-0*) Penguin Books.
Pritchard, Robert, ed. Economic Development, Foreign Investment & the Law: Promoting Economic Development Through Private Sector Involvement, Foreign Investment & the Rule of Law. LC 96-6841. (International Bar Association Ser.). 272p. 1996. 102.00 (*90-411-0891-2*) Kluwer Law Intl.
Pritchard, Robert, jt. ed. see Spangenberg-Urbschat, Karen.
Pritchard, Robert D. Helping Teachers Teach Well: A New System for Measuring & Improving Teaching Effectiveness in Higher Education. LC 97-25642. 1997. 39.00 (*0-7879-3965-X*) Jossey-Bass.
— Measuring & Improving Organizational Productivity: A Practical Guide. LC 90-34680. 264p. 1990. 65.00 (*0-275-93668-6*, C3668, Praeger Pubs) Greenwood.
Pritchard, Robert D., ed. Productivity Measurement & Improvement: Organizational Case Studies. LC 94-32932. 400p. 1995. 79.50 (*0-275-93907-3*) Greenwood.
Pritchard, Robert E. & Hindelang, Thomas J. The Strategic Evaluation & Management of Capital Expenditures. LC 80-69702. 336p. reprint ed. pap. 104.20 (*0-608-12970-4*, 202392500034) Bks Demand.
Pritchard, Robert Tbobb. Sponsorship Made Simple. 1998. pap. 15.95 (*1-86351-200-4*, Pub. by Sally Milner) Sterling.
Pritchard, Roger M. Housing & the Spatial Structure of the City: Residential Mobility & the Housing Market in an English City since the Industrial Revolution. LC 75-3859. (Cambridge Geographical Studies: No. 7). 244p. reprint ed. pap. 69.60 (*0-608-17524-2*, 2030615) Bks Demand.
Pritchard, Ron. Shakespeare's England: Life in Elizabethan & Jacobean Times. 256p. 2000. 34.95 (*0-7509-2112-9*, Pub. by Sutton Publng) Intl Pubs Mktg.
Pritchard, Rosalind M. The End of Elitism? The Democratisation of the West German University System. LC 89-39611. 256p. 1991. 19.50 (*0-85496-661-7*) Berg Pubs.
Pritchard, Russ A., jt. auth. see Davis, William C.
Pritchard, Samuel. Jachin & Boaz: An Authentic Key to the Door of Freemasonry Calculated Not Only for the Instruction of Every New-Made Mason but Also for the Information of All Who Intend to Become Brethren As Practiced in 1762. 60p. 1992. reprint ed. pap. 7.00 (*1-56459-246-4*) Kessinger Pub.
— The Three Distinct Knocks: On the Door of the Most Ancient Freemasonry; Being a Universal Description of All Its Branches from Its First Rite to This Present Time. 73p. 1992. reprint ed. pap. 9.00 (*1-56459-247-2*) Kessinger Pub.
Pritchard, Sara, ed. 1995 AACE International Transactions. (Illus.). 450p. (Orig.). 1995. pap. text 19.95 (*1-885517-01-7*) AACE Intl.
— 1997 Transactions of AACE International. (Illus.). 500p. (Orig.). 1997. pap. 47.95 (*1-885517-06-8*) AACE Intl.
— 1996 AACE International Transactions. (Illus.). 500p. (Orig.). 1996. pap. text 47.95 (*1-885517-04-1*) AACE Intl.
Pritchard, Sarah M. Chinese Massage Manual: The Healing Art of Tui Na. LC 99-39009. 144p. 1999. pap. text 17.95 (*0-8069-1967-1*) Sterling.
Pritchard, Sarah M., ed. The Women's Annual, No. 4: 1983-1984. 248p. 1984. 39.95 (*0-8161-8725-8*, Hall Reference) Macmillan.
Pritchard, Sonia Z. Oil Pollution Control. 240p. 1987. 59.95 (*0-7099-2094-6*, Pub. by C Helm) Routldge.
Pritchard, Steve. Linux Administration Black Book. (Black Book Ser.). 1999. pap. text 49.99 (*1-57610-419-2*) Coriolis Grp.
Pritchard, Syd. A Golfer's Guide to Shakespeare. 114p. (C). 1988. pap. 35.00 (*0-7212-0799-5*, Pub. by Regency Pr GBR) St Mut.
Pritchard, T. & Alloway, K. Medical Neuroscience. (Integrated Medical Sciences Ser.). (C). 1998. pap. 22.95 (*1-889325-29-5*) Fence Crk Pubng.
Pritchard, Thomas J. Representative Bodies. 213p. (C). 1988. 39.00 (*0-86383-403-5*, Pub. by Gomer Pr) St Mut.
Pritchard, Tom. Madderlake's Trade Secrets: Finding & Arranging Flowers Naturally. 1994. 27.50 (*0-517-88158-6*, Crown) Crown Pub Group.
Pritchard, W. E. Tolley's Tax Planning for New Businesses. 150p. 1993. 90.00 (*0-85459-565-1*, Pub. by Tolley Pubng) St Mut.
Pritchard, W. E., et al. Papers on Merced County Prehistory. (Publications of the Department of Parks & Recreation: No. 21). (Illus.). 111p. (C). 1983. reprint ed. pap. text 3.15 (*1-55567-470-4*) Coyote Press.
Pritchard, Wendy, jt. auth. see Beckhard, Richard.
Pritchard, Wilbur L. & Sciulli, Joseph A. Communications Satellite Systems Engineering. (Illus.). 352p. (C). 1986. text 42.95 (*0-685-10916-X*) P-H.
Pritchard, Wilbur L., et al. Satellite Communication Systems Engineering. 2nd ed. LC 92-2361. 544p. (C). 1993. text 99.00 (*0-13-791468-7*) Prntice Hall Bks.
Pritchard, William E. Archeology of the Menjoulet Site, Merced County, California. (Publications of the Department of Parks & Recreation: No. 13). (Illus.). 154p. (C). 1970. reprint ed. pap. text 16.88 (*1-55567-464-X*) Coyote Press.
Pritchard, William H. English Papers: A Teaching Life. LC 95-77952. 176p. 1995. 22.95 (*1-55597-234-9*) Graywolf.
— Frost: A Literary Life Reconsidered. 2nd ed. LC 92-36872. (Illus.). 312p. (C). 1993. pap. 18.95 (*0-87023-838-8*) U of Mass Pr.
— Lives of the Modern Poets. rev. ed. LC 96-15041. 334p. 1997. reprint ed. pap. text 19.95 (*0-87451-787-7*) U Pr of New Eng.
— Playing It by Ear: Literary Essays & Reviews. LC 94-12255. 288p. (C). 1994. pap. 18.95 (*0-87023-948-1*); lib. bdg. 45.00 (*0-87023-947-3*) U of Mass Pr.
— Randall Jarrell: A Literary Life. 1990. 25.00 (*0-374-24677-7*) FS&G.
— Randall Jarrell: A Literary Life. 1992. pap. 14.95 (*0-374-52277-4*) FS&G.
— Talking Back to Emily Dickinson, & Other Essays. LC 98-10322. 304p. 1998. 29.95 (*1-55849-138-4*) U of Mass Pr.
— Under Criticism: Essays for William H. Pritchard. Sofield, David & Tucker, Herbert F., eds. LC 97-37650. 300p. 1998. text 39.95 (*0-8214-1224-8*) Ohio U Pr.
***Pritchard, William H.** Updike: America's Man of Letters. 320p. 2000. 27.00 (*1-58642-002-X*, Pub. by Steerforth Pr) Publishers Group.
Pritchard, William H., ed. see Jarrell, Randall.
Pritchet, Christopher J. The Extragalactic Distance Scale. Van Den Bergh, Sidney, ed. (ASP Conference Series Proceedings: Vol. 4). (Illus.). 397p. 1988. 34.00 (*0-937707-21-X*) Astron Soc Pacific.
Pritchett. Ghosts of Kings. 1999. 25.95 (*0-7862-1963-7*) Mac Lib Ref.
Pritchett, B. Michael. Financing Growth: A Financial History of American Life Insurance Through 1900. LC 84-62400. (S. S. Huebner Foundation Monographs: No. 13). 90p. (Orig.). 1985. pap. 17.95 (*0-918930-13-8*) Huebner Foun Insur.
Pritchett, Bradley L. Grammatical Competence & Parsing Performance. LC 91-43480. (Illus.). 208p. 1992. pap. text 21.95 (*0-226-68442-3*); lib. bdg. 60.00 (*0-226-68441-5*) U Ch Pr.
Pritchett, Bruce M. A Study of Capital Mobilization: The Life Insurance Industry of the 19th Century. Bruchey, Stuart, ed. LC 76-45109. (Nineteen Seventy-Seven Dissertations Ser.). (Illus.). 1977. lib. bdg. 41.95 (*0-405-09921-5*) Ayer.
Pritchett, Charles H., jt. auth. see Murphy, Walter F.
Pritchett, Frances W. Nets of Awareness: Urdu Poetry & Its Critics. LC 92-43826. 1994. 48.00 (*0-520-08194-3*, Pub. by U CA Pr); pap. 18.95 (*0-520-08386-5*, Pub. by U CA Pr) Cal Prin Full Svc.
— The Romance Tradition in Urdu. 1991. text 44.00 (*0-231-07164-7*) Col U Pr.
Pritchett, Frances W. & Farrukhi, Asif, trs. An Evening of Caged Beasts: Seven Post-Modernist Urdu Poets. 262p. 2000. pap. 10.95 (*0-19-579145-2*) OUP.
Pritchett, Frances W. & Farrukhi, Asif A., eds. An Evening of Caged Beasts: Seven Post-Modernist Urdu Poets. 282p. 1999. 19.95 (*0-19-579020-0*) OUP.
Pritchett, Harry H., Jr., et al. God Is a Surprise Songbook. 2nd rev. unabridged ed. (Illus.). 24p. (J). (gr. 4-12). 1975. mass mkt. 5.95 (*1-884877-13-3*, CML199218SB) Creat Mats Lib.

Pritchett, Jamie A. Lots of Love & a Spanking! A Common Sense Discipline Plan for Children from Birth to Age Twelve - That Works! LC 96-95392. 144p. (Orig.). 1997. pap. 9.95 (*0-9656087-1-9*) Little Palm.
A discipline plan for children using the old-fashioned method of spanking to teach obedience & respect. Spanking!? Yes, but spanking with a difference. NOT the screaming, red-faced, violent beating that many people imagine when they hear the word; but a "few hard whacks on the bottom given by a calm parent, followed by a loving talk explaining how much the child is loved, why he got a spanking, & how to avoid getting one in the future." Author Jamie Pritchett maintains that well behaved children are not just born that way to very lucky parents, but that parents of well behaved, polite, & cheerful children do something differently - they use a system that works! This book explains why current discipline philosophies are not producing polite, obedient & cheerful children, & that our entire country is seeing the results of those inadequate discipline methods. LOTS OF LOVE & A SPANKING! combines the "firm hand" approach of our forefathers with the self-esteem & anti-violence concerns of the 90s. A one-of-a-kind book! To order, contact Little Palm Press, P.O Box 541215, Merritt Island, FL 32954-1215. Phone (407) 453-2949, FAX: (407) 452-4880. *Publisher Paid Annotation.*

Pritchett, Jennifer. Providing Reference Service in Church & Synagogue Libraries. LC 87-15776. (Guide Ser.: No. 15). 60p. 1987. pap. 9.75 (*0-915324-26-1*) CSLA.
Pritchett, Kay, tr. see Urzagasti, Jesus.
Pritchett, Martha. Still Speaking to Your Builder. 100p. 1998. spiral bd. write for info. (*1-888701-16-1*) Jarrett Pr.
***Pritchett, Marty Y.** God's Easy--Just Do It His Way. LC 99-93696. 1999. pap. 8.95 (*0-533-13108-1*) Vantage.
***Pritchett, Matthew.** The Best of Matt 1999: Cartoons from the Daily Telegraph. 1999. pap. 11.95 (*0-7528-2706-5*, Pub. by Orion Pubng Grp) Trafalgar.

P

An Asterisk (*) at the beginning of an entry indicates that the title is appearing for the first time.

Pritchett, Michael. The Venus Tree. LC 88-21795. (John Simmons Short Fiction Award Ser.). 138p. 1988. 11.50 (*0-87745-220-2*) U of Iowa Pr.

Pritchett, Nash L. One Flower While I Live: Elvis As I Remember Him. LC 87-32391. (Illus.). 154p. 1987. pap. 10.95 (*0-942179-05-6*) Shelby Hse.

Pritchett, Norm, jt. auth. see Stiverson, Carla.

Pritchett, Norman M. & Richardson, William G. Cooks in Cadence. LC 94-74894. (Illus.). 220p. (Orig.). 1995. pap. 15.00 (*0-943335-04-3*) Marblehead Pub.

***Pritchett, Patrick.** Reside. 44p. 1999. pap. 5.00 (*1-880743-14-0*) Dead Metaphor.

Pritchett, Price. After the Merger: Managing the Shockwaves. LC 84-73046. 140p. 1985. text 45.00 (*0-87094-627-7*, Irwn Prfssnl) McGraw-Hill Prof.

— After the Merger: The Authoritative Guide for Integration Success. 2nd rev. ed. LC 97-13951. 1997. text 45.00 (*0-7863-1239-4*, Irwn Prfssnl) McGraw-Hill Prof.

— Culture Shift: The Employee Handbook for Changing Corporate Culture. 35p. (Orig.). 1993. pap. 5.95 (*0-944002-12-9*) Pritchett Assocs.

— Culture Shift: The Employee Handbook for Changing Corporate Culture. (POR.). 30p. (Orig.). 1996. pap. 5.95 (*0-944002-51-X*) Pritchett Assocs.

— Culture Shift: The Employee Handbook for Changing Corporate Culture. (SPA.). 30p. (Orig.). 1996. pap. 5.95 (*0-944002-53-6*) Pritchett Assocs.

— The Employee Handbook of New Work Habits for a Radically Changing World: Thirteen Ground Rules for Job Success in the Information Age. 42p. (Orig.). 1994. pap. 5.95 (*0-944002-15-3*) Pritchett Assocs.

— The Employee Handbook of New Work Habits for a Radically Changing World: 13 Ground Rules for Job Success in the Information Age. (GER.). 51p. 1996. pap. 5.95 (*0-944002-66-8*); pap. 5.95 (*0-944002-65-X*); pap. 5.95 (*0-944002-64-1*); pap. 5.95 (*0-944002-63-3*) Pritchett Assocs.

— The Employee Handbook of New Work Habits for a Radically Changing World: 13 Ground Rules for Job Success in the Information Age. (SPA.). 51p. 1997. pap. 5.95 (*0-944002-67-6*) Pritchett Assocs.

— The Employee Survival Guide to Mergers & Acquisitions. 22p. (Orig.). Date not set. pap. 4.95 (*0-944002-06-4*) Pritchett Assocs.

— The Employee Survival Guide to Mergers & Acquisitions. 94p. (Orig.). 1988. pap. write for info. (*0-944002-00-5*) Pritchett Assocs.

— The Employee Survival Guide to Mergers & Acquisitions. (ENG & FRE.). 22p. (Orig.). 1996. pap. 5.95 (*0-944002-23-4*) Pritchett Assocs.

— The Ethics of Excellence. 25p. (Orig.). 1991. pap. 5.95 (*0-944002-09-9*) Pritchett Assocs.

— Fast Growth: A Career Acceleration Strategy. 46p. 1997. pap. 6.95 (*0-944002-72-2*) Pritchett Assocs.

— Firing up High Commitment During Organizational Change. LC 97-170683. 42p. (Orig.). 1994. pap. 5.95 (*0-944002-14-5*) Pritchett Assocs.

Pritchett, Price. Managing the 4th Level of Change Pb. Date not set. pap. 14.00 (*0-88730-975-5*, HarpBusn) HarpInfo.

Pritchett, Price. Mindshift: The Employee Handbook for Understanding the Changing World of Work. 60p. 1996. pap. text 5.95 (*0-944002-50-1*) Pritchett Assocs.

— Outsourced: The Employee Handbook: 12 New Rules for Running Your Career in an Interconnected World. 56p. (Orig.). 1997. pap. 5.95 (*0-944002-68-4*) Pritchett Assocs.

— The Quantum Leap Strategy. 90p. (Orig.). 1991. pap. 5.95 (*0-944002-08-0*) Pritchett Assocs.

— Resistance: Moving Beyond the Barriers to Change. 34p. 1996. pap. 5.95 (*0-944002-18-8*) Pritchett Assocs.

— Service Excellence! 31p. (Orig.). 1989. pap. 5.95 (*0-944002-02-1*) Pritchett Assocs.

— The Team Member Handbook for Teamwork. 60p. (Orig.). 1992. pap. 5.95 (*0-944002-11-0*) Pritchett Assocs.

Pritchett, Price & Cover, Fred. The Human Resources Planning Guide to Mergers & Acquisitions. 126p. Date not set. wbk. ed. 89.00 (*0-944002-05-6*) Pritchett Assocs.

Pritchett, Price & Gilbreath, Robert D. Mergers: Growth in the Fast Lane. 27p. 1996. pap. 5.95 (*0-944002-17-X*) Pritchett Assocs.

— Mergers: Growth in the Fast Lane. (FRE.). 27p. 1996. pap. 5.95 (*0-944002-22-6*) Pritchett Assocs.

Pritchett, Price & Muirhead, Brian. The Mars Pathfinder Approach to "Faster-Better-Cheaper" Hand of from the NASA - JPL Pathfinder Team on How Limitations Can Guide You to Breakthroughs. LC 98-154527. (Illus.). 85p. 1998. pap. 9.95 (*0-944002-74-9*) Pritchett Assocs.

Pritchett, Price & Pound, Ron. Business As Unusual. (SPA.). 28p. Date not set. pap. 5.95 (*0-944002-59-5*); pap. 5.95 (*0-944002-60-9*); pap. 5.95 (*0-944002-61-7*); pap. 5.95 (*0-944002-62-5*) Pritchett Assocs.

— Business As Unusual: The Handbook for Managing & Supervising Organizational Change. 27p. 1988. pap. 5.95 (*0-944002-01-3*) Pritchett Assocs.

— The Employee Handbook for Organizational Change. 1990. pap. 5.95 (*0-944002-07-2*) Pritchett Assocs.

— The Employee Handbook for Organizational Change. (SPA.). 40p. 1996. pap. 5.95 (*0-944002-55-2*); pap. 5.95 (*0-944002-56-0*); pap. 5.95 (*0-944002-57-9*); pap. 5.95 (*0-944002-58-7*) Pritchett Assocs.

— High-Velocity Culture Change: A Handbook for Managers. 44p. (Orig.). 1993. pap. 5.95 (*0-944002-13-7*) Pritchett Assocs.

— High-Velocity Culture Change: A Handbook for Managers. (SPA.). 44p. (Orig.). 1996. pap. 5.95 (*0-944002-52-8*) Pritchett Assocs.

— High-Velocity Culture Change: A Handbook for Managers. (POR.). 44p. (Orig.). 1996. pap. 5.95 (*0-944002-54-4*) Pritchett Assocs.

— Smart Moves: A Crash Course on Merger Integration Management. (Orig.). 1989. pap. 5.95 (*0-944002-03-X*) Pritchett Assocs.

— A Survival Guide to the Stress of Organizational Change. 30p. (Orig.). 1995. pap. 5.95 (*0-944002-16-1*) Pritchett Assocs.

— A Survival Guide to the Stress of Organizational Change. (FRE.). 30p. (Orig.). 1996. pap. 5.95 (*0-944002-24-2*) Pritchett Assocs.

— Team ReConstruction: High Velocity Moves for Repairing Work Groups Rocked by Change. 24p. (Orig.). 1992. pap. 5.95 (*0-944002-10-2*) Pritchett Assocs.

***Pritchett, Price, et al.** The Leadership Engine: Building Leaders at Every Level. 47p. 1998. pap. 5.95 (*0-944002-25-0*) Pritchett Assocs.

Pritchett, Ron. Cougar City. large type ed. (Linford Western Library). 256p. 1992. pap. 16.99 (*0-7089-7150-4*) Ulverscroft.

***Pritchett, Ron.** Peaceful Guns. large type ed. 256p. 1999. pap. 18.99 (*0-7089-5542-8*, Linford) Ulverscroft.

Pritchett, S. Travis. Risk Management. 7th ed. Date not set. pap. text, teacher ed. write for info. (*0-314-06445-1*) West Pub.

Pritchett, S. Travis & Wilder, Ronald P. Stock Life Insurance Company Profitability & Workable Competition. LC 85-61668. (S. S. Huebner Foundation Monographs: No. 14). (Illus.). 1986. pap. 20.95 (*0-918930-14-6*) Huebner Foun Insur.

Pritchett, S. Travis, et al. Risk Management & Insurance. 7th ed. LC 95-45304. 750p. (C). 1996. mass mkt. 98.95 (*0-314-06427-3*) West Pub.

Pritchett, Sue, ed. see Harlan, Timothy S.

Pritchett, Sue, ed. see Spicer, Myrna R.

Pritchett, V. S. A Cab at the Door & Midnight Oil. 432p. 1994. 16.00 (*0-679-60103-1*) Modern Lib NY.

— Complete Collected Stories. LC 91-58068. 1992. pap. 20.00 (*0-06-797389-2*) Vin Bks.

— The Gentle Barbarian: The Life & Work of Ivan Turgenev. 243p. (C). 1986. reprint ed. pap. 9.50 (*0-88001-120-3*) HarpC.

— George Meredith & English Comedy. LC 79-512245. (Clark Lectures for 1969). 127p. 1970. write for info. (*0-7011-1565-3*) Chatto & Windus.

***Pritchett, V. S.** London Perceived. (Illus.). 2001. pap. 19.95 (*1-56792-148-5*) Godine.

Pritchett, V. S. The Pritchett Century. LC 97-15360. 800p. 1997. 23.00 (*0-679-60244-5*) Modern Lib NY.

— The Pritchett Century. LC 98-21226. 1999. pap. 14.95 (*0-375-75217-X*) Modern Lib NY.

Pritchett, V. S., ed. The Oxford Book of Short Stories. 558p. 1988. pap. 15.95 (*0-19-282113-X*) OUP.

Pritchett, V. S., selected by. The Oxford Book of Short Stories. 576p. 1981. text 35.00 (*0-19-214116-3*) OUP.

Pritchett, V. S., jt. auth. see Turgenev, Ivan Sergeevich.

Pritchett, V. S., ed. see Bronte, Emily Jane.

***Pritchett, Virginia Aten.** A Fine Thin Thread: Poems by Virginia Aten Pritchett. Kriebel, David L., ed. LC 99-62948. (Illus.). 91p. 1999. pap. 9.95 (*0-9641622-1-0*) Lite Circle.

Pritchett, W. Kendrick. Essays in Greek History. LC 95-108914. (Illus.). 340p. 1994. lib. bdg. 74.00 (*90-5063-316-1*, Pub. by Gieben) J Benjamins Pubng Co.

— Greek Archives, Cults & Topography. (Archaia Hellas Ser.: Vol. 2). (Illus.). 278p. 1996. lib. bdg. 64.00 (*90-5063-147-9*, Pub. by Gieben) J Benjamins Pubng Co.

— The Greek State at War, Vol. Pt. 1. LC 71-633960. 1974. 60.00 (*0-520-02758-2*, Pub. by U CA Pr) Cal Prin Full Svc.

— The Greek State at War, Vol. Pt. 2. LC 74-77991. 1975. 65.00 (*0-520-02565-2*, Pub. by U CA Pr) Cal Prin Full Svc.

— The Greek State at War, Vol. Pt. III. 1979. 65.00 (*0-520-03781-2*, Pub. by U CA Pr) Cal Prin Full Svc.

— The Greek State at War, Vol. Pt. IV. LC 75-312653. 1985. 65.00 (*0-520-05379-6*, Pub. by U CA Pr) Cal Prin Full Svc.

— The Greek State at War, Vol. Pt. V. LC 75-312653. 545p. 1991. 65.00 (*0-520-07374-6*, Pub. by U CA Pr) Cal Prin Full Svc.

— The Liar School of Herodotus. 350p. 1993. 74.00 (*90-5063-088-X*, Pub. by Gieben) J Benjamins Pubng Co.

***Pritchett, W. Kendrick.** Pausanias Periegetes. LC 98-195507. 1998. 55.00 (*90-5063-518-0*, Pub. by Gieben) J Benjamins Pubng Co.

— Pausanias Periegetes II. (Monographs on Ancient Greek History & Archaeology Ser.: No. 7). 363p. 1999. pap. 55.00 (*90-5063-138-X*, Pub. by Gieben) J Benjamins Pubng Co.

Pritchett, W. Kendrick. Studies in Ancient Greek Topography, Pt. VII. 238p. 1991. pap. 97.00 (*90-5063-071-5*, Pub. by Gieben) J Benjamins Pubng Co.

— Studies in Ancient Greek Topography, Pt. VIII. (Illus.). 185p. 1993. pap. 97.00 (*90-5063-087-1*, Pub. by Gieben) J Benjamins Pubng Co.

— Thucydides' Pentekontaetia & Other Essays. LC 96-107729. (Archaia Hellas Ser.: Vol. 1). 287p. 1995. lib. bdg. 60.00 (*90-5063-487-7*, Pub. by Gieben) J Benjamins Pubng Co.

Pritchett, William K. Ancient Greek Military Practices, Part 1. LC 71-633960. (University of California Publications: Vol. 7). 177p. reprint ed. pap. 54.90 (*0-8357-5465-0*, 201103700072) Bks Demand.

— Studies in Ancient Greek Topography, Vol. Pt. V. (UC Publications in Classical Studies: Vol. 31). 1986. pap. 50.00 (*0-520-09698-3*, Pub. by U CA Pr) Cal Prin Full Svc.

— Studies in Ancient Greek Topography: Battlefields, Part 2. LC 65-65210. (University of California Publications: Classical Studies: Vol. 4). 292p. reprint ed. pap. 90.60 (*0-608-14165-8*, 202126100021) Bks Demand.

— Studies in Ancient Greek Topography Pt. III: (Roads) (UC Publications in Classical Studies: Vol. 22). 436p. 1981. pap. 50.00 (*0-520-09635-5*, Pub. by U CA Pr) Cal Prin Full Svc.

— Studies in Ancient Greek Topography Pt. 4: Passes. LC 65-65210. (University of California Publications, Classical Studies: No. 28). (Illus.). 374p. reprint ed. pap. 116.00 (*0-8357-6855-4*, 203555300095) Bks Demand.

Pritchett, William L. & Fisher, Richard F. Properties & Management of Forest Soils. 2nd ed. LC 86-22421. 512p. 1987. text 109.95 (*0-471-89572-5*) Wiley.

Prithvi Ram Mudiam. India & the Middle East. 192p. 1994. text 59.50 (*1-85043-703-3*, Pub. by I B T) St Martin.

Priti, R. Operation Principles of the High Sliding Gears. (Technical Papers: Vol. P109.33). (Illus.). 7p. 1973. pap. text 30.00 (*1-55589-201-9*) AGMA.

Pritikin, Enid & Reece, Trudy. Parentcare Survival Guide: Helping Your Folks Through the Not-So-Golden Years. 256p. 1993. pap. 8.95 (*0-8120-4975-6*) Barron.

Pritikin, Ilene, jt. auth. see Pritikin, Nathan.

Pritikin, Karin. The King & I: A Little Gallery of Elvis Impersonators. (Illus.). 95p. 1998. text 10.00 (*0-7881-5387-0*) DIANE Pub.

Pritikin, Nathan. The Pritikin Promise. 1991. mass mkt. 5.99 (*0-671-73267-6*) PB.

Pritikin, Nathan & McGrady, Patrick. The Pritikin Program for Diet & Exercise. 464p. 1984. mass mkt. 6.99 (*0-553-27192-X*) Bantam.

Pritikin, Nathan & Pritikin, Ilene. The Official Pritikin Guide to Dining Out. LC 83-3853. 224p. 1984. write for info. (*0-672-52773-1*) Macmillan.

Pritikin, Renny, et al. The Hall of Fame Hall of Fame. (Illus.). 64p. (Orig.). 1996. pap. 15.00 (*1-889195-04-9*) Smart Art Pr.

***Pritikin, Robert.** The Pritikin Principle: The Calorie Density Solution. LC 99-89980. (Illus.). 224p. 2000. 24.95 (*0-7370-1616-7*) T-L Custom Pub.

Pritikin, Robert. The Pritikin Weight Loss Breakthrough: Five Easy Steps to Outsmart Your Fat Instinct. 371p. 1999. mass mkt. 6.99 (*0-451-19572-8*, Sig) NAL.

Pritikin, Robert C. Christ Was an Ad Man: How to Create the Miracle Ads. 3rd rev. ed. (Illus.). 201p. 1980. pap. 14.95 (*0-9659069-0-6*) Bay-Court Pubs.

— The New Pritikin Program. Rubenstein, Julie, ed. 464p. 1991. reprint ed. per. 6.99 (*0-671-73194-7*) PB.

Pritsak, Omeljan. On the Writing of History in Kievan Rus' 40p. 1994. write for info. (*0-9609822-9-9*) Ukrainian Studies Fund.

— The Origin of Russia, Vol. I. (Series in Ukrainian). 850p. (C). 1982. 50.00 (*0-674-64465-4*) HUP.

— The Origins of the Old Rus' Weights & Monetary Systems: Two Studies in Western Eurasian Metrology & Numismatics in the Seventh to Eleventh Centuries. LC 92-54345. (Harvard Series in Ukrainian Studies). (Illus.). 160p. (C). 1998. text 29.00 (*0-916458-48-2*) Harvard Ukrainian.

— When & Where Was Ol'ga Baptized? 24p. 1994. write for info. (*0-940465-01-9*) Ukrainian Studies Fund.

Pritsak, Omeljan, ed. Lev Krevza's Obrona iednosci cerkiewney & Zaxarija Kopystens'kyj's Palinodija. LC 87-81952. (Harvard Library of Early Ukrainian Literature: Vol. 3). (POL & UKR., Illus.). 596p. (C). 1987. text 15.00 (*0-916458-22-9*) Harvard Ukrainian.

Pritsak, Omeljan & Subtelny, Orest, intros. The Diariusz Podrozny of Pylyp Orlyk: (1727-1730) LC 88-84116. (Harvard Library of Early Ukrainian Literature: Vol. 6). xxviii, 868p. (C). 1989. text 15.00 (*0-916458-26-1*) Harvard Ukrainian.

Pritsak, Omeljan, ed. see Berindei, Mihnea & Veinstein, Gilles.

Pritsak, Omeljan, jt. intro. see Subtelny, Orest.

Pritscher, Tom. Practicing the Presence: A Course in Meditation. LC 95-90643. (Illus.). 108p. (YA). (gr. 11 up). 1999. pap. 19.95 (*0-9648165-1-2*) Thou Art.

— Practicing the Presence Bk. 1: A Course in Meditation. LC 95-90643. (Illus.). 108p. (Orig.). 1996. pap. 13.00 (*0-9648165-0-4*) Thou Art.

Pritsker, A. Alan B. Introduction to Simulation & SLAM II. 4th ed. (Illus.). 839p. 1995. 130.00 (*0-470-23457-1*) Wiley.

— Papers - Experiences - Perspectives. (QM - Quantitative Methods Ser.). (C). 1993. mass mkt. 57.00 (*0-89426-245-9*) S-W Pub.

— Papers, Experiences, Perspectives. 250p. 1990. 30.00 (*0-938974-03-3*, PR-1) Soc Computer Sim.

***Pritsker, A. Alan B.** Simulation with Visual SLAM & AweSim. 2nd ed. LC 99-24351. 890p. 1999. 115.95 (*0-471-35293-4*) Wiley.

Pritsker, A. Alan B. Slam II: Network Models for Decision Support. (QM - Quantitative Methods Ser.). (C). 1993. pap. 67.95 (*0-89426-248-3*) S-W Pub.

Pritsker, A. Alan B. & O'Reilly, Jean J. Solutions Book for Simulation with Visual SLAM & AweSim. (Illus.). 1997. pap. write for info. (*0-938974-05-X*) Systems Pub.

Pritsker, A. Alan B. & Young, Robert E. Simulation with GASP-PL-I: A PL-I Based Continuous-Discrete Simulation Language. LC 75-23182. 351p. reprint ed. pap. 108.90 (*0-608-11634-3*, 202249000027) Bks Demand.

Pritsker, A. Alan B., et al. Introduction to Simulation & SLAM II, Solutions Manual. (Illus.). 305p. 1986. 50.00 (*0-938974-01-7*) Systems Pub.

— Simulation with Visual SLAM & AweSim. (Illus.). 811p. 1997. text 94.95 (*0-470-23738-4*) Halsted Pr.

Pritt, Mark D., jt. auth. see Ghiglia, Dennis C.

Prittie, Joni. The Victorian Home. (Illus.). 76p. 1990. 11.95 (*0-937769-81-9*) Mark Inc CA.

Pritts, Kim D. Ginseng: How to Find, Grow & Use America's Forest Gold. LC 95-7210. (Illus.). 160p. 1995. pap. 16.95 (*0-8117-2477-8*) Stackpole.

— The Mystery of Sadler Marsh. LC 92-26454. (Illus.). 112p. (Orig.). (J). (gr. 3-7). 1993. pap. 5.99 (*0-8361-3618-7*) Herald Pr.

Pritts, Marvin & Handley, David, eds. Bramble Production Guide. (Illus.). 190p. 1989. ring bd. 45.00 (*0-935817-21-2*, 35) NRAES.

Pritts, Marvin & Handley, David, eds. Strawberry Production Guide: For the Northeast, Midwest, & Eastern Canada, Vol. 88. 162p. 1998. ring bd. 45.00 (*0-935817-23-9*, NRAES-88) NRAES.

Pritts, Marvin P., jt. auth. see Eames-Sheavly, Marcia.

Prittwitz, Karl L. von. Berlin 1848: Das Erinnerungswerk des Generalleutnants Karl Ludwig von Prittwitz und Andere Quellen zur Berliner Maerzrevolution und zur Geschichte Preussens um die Mitte des 19 Jahrunderts. (Veroeffentlichungen der Historischen Kommission zu Berlin, Band 67, Beitraege zu Inflation und Wiederaufbau in Deutschland und Europa 1914-1924: Vol. 60, Quellenwerke Band 7). (GER., Illus.). lxvi, 518p. 1985. 115.40 (*3-11-008326-4*) De Gruyter.

Pritz, Alan L. Pocket Guide to Meditation. LC 97-26037. (Crossing Press Pocket Ser.). (Illus.). 112p. (Orig.). 1997. pap. 6.95 (*0-89594-886-9*) Crossing Pr.

Pritz, Ray A. Nazarene Jewish Christianity: From the End of the New Testament Period until Its Disappearance in the Fourth Century. 153p. 1992. 18.00 (*965-223-798-1*, Pub. by Magnes Pr) Gefen Bks.

Pritzel, George August. Thesaurus of Botanical Literature. 576p. 1995. reprint ed. 90.00 (*1-888262-60-5*) Martino Pubng.

Pritzker, Barry. Native Americans: An Encyclopedia of History, Culture & Peoples, 2 vols., Vols. I & II. LC 98-21718. (Illus.). 868p. 1998. lib. bdg. 175.00 (*0-87436-836-7*, FN-1644) ABC-CLIO.

***Pritzker, Barry M.** Native America Today: A Guide to Community Politics & Culture. LC 99-52306. 453p. 1999. lib. bdg. 75.00 (*1-57607-077-8*) ABC-CLIO.

***Pritzker, Barry M., ed.** A Native American Encyclopedia: History, Culture, & Peoples. (Illus.). 576p. 2000. 45.00 (*0-19-513897-X*) OUP.

Pritzker, Steven, jt. ed. see Runco, Mark A.

Pritzlaff, John A., ed. International Safety Standard Guidelines for the Operation of Tourist Submersibles. 311p. 1993. 56.00 (*0-939773-14-7*, R-39); 76.00 (*0-614-06720-0*) Soc Naval Arch.

Privacy Rights Clearinghouse Staff & Givens, Beth. The Privacy Rights Handbook: How to Take Control of Your Personal Information. LC 97-16596. 336p. 1997. pap. 12.50 (*0-380-78684-2*, Avon Bks) Morrow Avon.

Prival, Jody & Stadolsky, Daniel, eds. Guide to Living in Pittsburgh: A Narrative for New Pittsburghers. 1994. pap. 7.95 (*0-9642186-8-2*) Dec Five.

Privalko, V. P. & Novikov, V. V. The Science of Heterogeneous Polymers: Structure & Thermophysical Properties. LC 94-19288. 254p. 1995. 250.00 (*0-471-94167-0*) Wiley.

Privalko, V. P., jt. ed. see Godovsky, Y. K.

Privara, I., et al, eds. Mathematical Foundations of Computer Science, 1994, 841. (Lecture Notes in Computer Science Ser.: Vol. 841). 628p. 1994. pap. text 82.00 (*0-387-58338-6*) Spr-Verlag.

— Mathematical Foundations of Computer Science, 1997: 22nd International Symposium, MFCS'97, Bratislava, Slovakia, August 25-29, 1997, Proceedings. (Lecture Notes in Computer Science Ser.: Vol. 1295). x, 519p. 1997. pap. 79.00 (*3-540-63437-1*) Spr-Verlag.

Private Fostering Special Interest Group Staff & Batty, Daphne, compiled by. Caring for Other People's Children: A Guide for Private Foster Carers. 1995. pap. 22.00 (*1-873868-23-5*, Pub. by BAAF) St Mut.

Private Philanthropy & Public Need Commission. Research Papers, 5 vols. in 6 bks. 1986. reprint ed. lib. bdg. 325.00 (*0-89941-446-X*, 303990) W S Hein.

Private Sector Conference. The Academic Health Center & Health Care Reform: Proceedings of the Duke Private Sector Conference, 1994. Snyderman, Ralph et al, eds. LC 95-7174. 128p. 1995. text 60.00 (*0-7817-0326-3*) Lppncott W & W.

Priven, Judith S. Hello! U. S. A. Everyday Living for International Residents & Visitors. (Orig.). 1996. pap. 16.95 (*0-9635633-2-7*) Hello America.

— Hello! Washington: A Handbook on Everyday Living for International Residents. 250p. 1993. pap. 16.95 (*0-9635633-0-0*) Hello America.

Priven, Judy. Easy Writer: Basics to GED. (Cambridge Writing Ser.). 160p. (C). 1991. pap. text 6.50 (*0-13-971136-8*, 640304) P-H.

Priver, David, jt. auth. see Leveen, Louis.

Privett, Dave. Rod Puppet Flower Pattern: With Moving Mouth Mechanism. (Illus.). 16p. 1997. ring bd. 13.00 (*1-58302-084-5*, PAT-06) One Way St.

Privett, Dave & Brown, Keann. Note Puppet Pattern. (Illus.). 18p. 1998. pap. 15.00 (*1-58302-052-7*) One Way St.

Privett, Dave, jt. auth. see Liebenow, Todd.

Privett, Judy & Privett, Tony. What America's Teachers Wish Parents Knew. LC 93-79657. 144p. 1993. pap. 5.95 (*1-56352-104-0*) Longstreet.

Privett, Katherine H. The Dreams of Exiles. LC 82-2886. (Kestrel Chapbks.). 24p. 1982. pap. 3.00 (*0-914974-34-3*) Holmgangers.

Privett, Tony, jt. auth. see Privett, Judy.

Privette, Eleanor T. The Living Christmas Card. 32p. 1990. pap. 4.25 (*0-687-22288-5*) Abingdon.

Privitera, Bettina, jt. auth. see Privitera, Joseph F.

Privitera, James R. Olive Leaf Extract: A New/Old Healing Bonanza for Mankind. (Orig.). 1996. pap. write for info. (*0-9655872-0-7*) J Privitera.

P

An Asterisk (*) at the beginning of an entry indicates that the title is appearing for the first time.

Privitera, James R. & Stang, Alan. Silent Clots, Life's Biggest Killers: Lockstep Medicine's Conspiracy to Suppress the Test That Should Be Done in Emergency Rooms Throughout the World. large type unabridged ed. LC 96-72237. (Illus.). 290p. (Orig.). 1997. pap. 19.95 (0-9656313-0-3) Catacombs Pr.

Privitera, Joseph. Beginner's Sicilian. (Beginner's Guides Ser.). 150p. 1998. pap. 11.95 (0-7818-0640-2) Hippocrene Bks.

— Treasury of Italian Cuisine: Recipes, Sayings & Proverbs in Italian & English. (Hippocrene Bilingual Cookbooks Ser.). (ENG & ITA., Illus.). 142p. 1999. 11.95 (0-7818-0740-9) Hippocrene Bks.

Privitera, Joseph F. Basic Sicilian: A Brief Reference Grammar. LC 98-24106. 92p. 1998. text 49.95 (0-7734-8335-7) E Mellen.

— Faustus in Love & Other Poems: In English & Other Tongues. LC 98-46264. 68p. 1999. pap. 14.95 (0-7734-3106-3, Mellen Poetry Pr) E Mellen.

***Privitera, Joseph F.** Italy: An Illustrated History. (Illus.). 150p. 2000. 14.95 (0-7818-0819-7) Hippocrene Bks.

Privitera, Joseph F. & Privitera, Bettina. Language As Historical Determinant: The Normans in Sicily (1061-1200) LC 95-77606. 136p. 1995. pap. 18.00 (1-877965-03-0, PA2001) AIBDC.

Privitera, Joseph F., tr. see Pirandello, Luigi.

***Privitera, Joseph Frederic & Alighieri, Dante.** A Reference Grammar of Medieval Italian According to Dante, with a Dual Edition of the Vita Nova. LC 00-33949. (Studies in Italian Literature: Vol.. 11). 124p. 2000. 69.95 (0-7734-7727-6) E Mellen.

Privitera, Walter. Problems of Style: Michel Foucault's Epistomology. Keller, Jean, tr. from GER. LC 94-10398. (SUNY Series in Social & Political Thought). 168p. (C). 1995. text 49.50 (0-7914-2333-6); pap. text 16.95 (0-7914-2334-4) State U NY Pr.

Privman, V. Finite Size Scaling & Numerical Simulation of Statistical Systems. 528p. (C). 1990. text 101.00 (981-02-0108-7) World Scientific Pub.

Privman, V. & Svrakie, N. M. Directed Models of Polymers, Interfaces & Clusters: Scaling & Finite-Size Properties. (Lecture Notes in Physics Ser.: Vol. 338). vi, 120p. 1989. 34.95 (0-387-51429-5, 3454) Spr-Verlag.

Privman, Vladimir, ed. Nonequilibrium Statistical Mechanics in One Dimension. LC 96-45965. (Illus.). 488p. (C). 1997. text 110.00 (0-521-55974-X) Cambridge U Pr.

Privott, Christine R., ed. Fieldwork Anthology: A Classic Research & Practice Collection. LC 98-139903. 468p. 1998. pap. text 40.00 (1-56900-092-1, 1176) Am Occup Therapy.

***Privratsky, Bruce G.** Muslim Turkistan: Razak Religion & Collective Memory. (Illus.). 336p. 2000. 85.00 (0-7007-1297-6, Pub. by Curzon Pr Ltd) Paul & Co Pubs.

***Prix, Wolf D.** Prinz Eisenbeton 2: Projects '96 To '99. (Illus.). 360p. 2000. pap. 35.00 (3-211-83323-4) Spr-Verlag.

Priya, Jacqueline V. Birth Traditions & Modern Pregnancy Care. 1992. pap. 10.95 (1-85230-321-2, Pub. by Element MA) Penguin Putnam.

Priz, Edward J. Comp Control: Secrets of Reducing Workers' Compensation Costs. Doyle, Kathleen, ed. LC 95-17314. (Successful Business Library). (Illus.). 160p. 1995. pap. 19.95 (1-55571-355-6, Oasis Pr) PSI Resch.

Prizant, Barry M., jt. auth. see Wetherby, Amy M.

Prizel, Ilya. Latin America Through Soviet Eyes: The Evolution of Soviet Perceptions During the Brezhnev Era 1964-1982. (Cambridge Russian, Soviet & Post-Soviet Studies: No. 72). 267p. (C). 1990. text 69.95 (0-521-37303-4) Cambridge U Pr.

— National Identity & Foreign Policy: Nationalism & Leadership in Poland, Russia & Ukraine. LC 97-44352. (Russian, Soviet & Post-Soviet Studies: No. 103). 460p. (C). 1998. text 54.95 (0-521-57157-X); pap. text 24.95 (0-521-57697-0) Cambridge U Pr.

Prizel, Ilya & Michta, Andrew A., eds. Polish Foreign Policy Reconsidered: Challenges of Independence. LC 94-35327. 224p. 1995. text 45.00 (0-312-12293-4) St Martin.

Prizel, Ilya, ed. see Michta, Andrew A.

Prizer, Joshua, ed. see Sakach, Deborah.

Prizio, Diana. Beyond Granola: An Evolutionary Approach to Natural Foods. 63p. (Orig.). 1990. pap. text 4.00 (0-9621498-1-0, Robin Hood) R Hood Little.

Prizzi, Elaine & Hoffman, Jeanne. Functional Reading Set, 3 bks., Set. (J). (gr. 4-6). 22.99 (1-56417-725-4, FE0001S) Fearon Teacher Aids.

— Reading Around the World. (J). (gr. 4-6). 1985. pap. 7.99 (0-8224-3182-3) Fearon Teacher Aids.

— Reading Around Town. (J). (gr. 4-6). 1985. pap. 7.99 (0-8224-3181-5) Fearon Teacher Aids.

— Reading Everyday Stuff. (J). (gr. 4-6). 1985. pap. 7.99 (0-8224-3180-7) Fearon Teacher Aids.

— Teaching off the Wall. LC 80-81836. (J). (gr. 2-5). 1981. pap. 9.99 (0-8224-6830-1) Fearon Teacher Aids.

Prizzi, Elaine & Hoffmann, Jeanne. Beginning Book Reporting. LC 83-63175. 1984. pap. 12.99 (0-8224-2175-5) Fearon Teacher Aids.

— Interactive Bulletin Boards. LC 82-63176. (J). (gr. 1-4). 1984. pap. 12.99 (0-8224-6256-7) Fearon Teacher Aids.

Prizzi, Elaine, jt. auth. see Hoffman, Jeanne.

Prlando, Louise. Multicultural Game Book: More Than 70 Traditional Games from 30 Countries. LC 94-196979. 110p. 1993. pap., teacher ed. 14.95 (0-590-49409-0) Scholastic Inc.

Pro Football Weekly Editors & Buchsbaum, Joel. Pro Football Weekly Draft Preview, 1996. (Illus.). 184p. (Orig.). 1996. pap. 18.95 (1-888924-00-4) Pro Football.

Pro Football Weekly Editors, jt. auth. see Buchsbaum, Joel.

Pro-West. Fundamentals of Case Management: Guidelines for Practicing Case Managers. LC 97-16816. (Illus.). 272p. (C). (gr. 13). 1997. pap. text 33.95 (0-8151-2498-8, 31049) Mosby Inc.

***Proag, V.** Water Resources in Small Islands. 300p. 2000. 143.00 (1-85312-797-3, Pub. by WIT Pr) Computational Mech MA.

Proakis. Digital Communications. 4th ed. 2000. 77.50 (0-07-232111-3) McGraw.

Proakis, John G. Bookware Companion: Community Systems with Matlab. LC 97-31815. (Electrical Engineering Ser.). 320p. (C). 1998. pap. 41.95 (0-534-93804-3) PWS Pubs.

— Digital Communications. 3rd ed. LC 94-41620. (Electrical & Computer Engineering Ser.). 912p. (C). 1995. 102.81 (0-07-051726-6) McGraw.

— Digital Communications. 3rd ed. (McGraw-Hill Series in Electrical & Computer Engineering). 1995. pap. text, teacher ed. write for info. (0-07-051727-4) McGraw.

Proakis, John G. & Ingle, Vinay K. Digital Signal Processing Using MATLAB: A BookWare Companion Problems Book. LC 96-178311. 416p. (C). 1996. pap., mass mkt. 42.95 incl. disk (0-534-93805-1) PWS Pubs.

Proakis, John G. & Manolakis, Dimitris G. Digital Signal Processing: Principles, Algorithms & Applications. 3rd ed. LC 95-9117. 1016p. 1995. 105.00 (0-13-373762-4) P-H.

Proakis, John G. & Salehi, Masoud. Communications Systems Engineering. LC 93-23109. 889p. (C). 1993. 105.00 (0-13-158932-6) P-H.

Proal, Jean. Farandole. deluxe limited ed. (Ediciones Especiales y de Bibliofilo Ser.). (FRE., Illus.). 1993. 7500.00 (84-343-0108-3) Elliots Bks.

Proal, Louis. Political Crime. LC 70-172565. (Criminology, Law Enforcement, & Social Problems Ser.: No. 146). 1973. reprint ed. 24.00 (0-87585-146-0) Patterson Smith.

Proano, Franklin. La Poesia Femenina Actual de Sudamerica. 59.50 (1-882528-04-2) Scripta.

Proaps, Linda. Capitol Punishment. (Illus.). 295p. 1991. 24.95 (1-879563-03-7) Lexicon CA.

Probabilistic Conference Staff. Probabilistic Methods in Differential Equations: Proceedings of the Probabilistic Conference, University of Victoria, August 1974. (Lecture Notes in Mathematics Ser.: Vol. 451). 190p. (Orig.). 1975. 23.95 (0-387-07153-9) Spr-Verlag.

Probart, M. E., et al. The Properties & Management of Vertisols. 36p. (Orig.). 1987. pap. text 45.00 (0-85198-601-3) OUP.

Probasco, Lisa, ed. see Freeman, Holly.

Probasco, Lisa, ed. see Freeman, Holly & Oliver, Jim.

Probasco, Steve. The Art of Fly Tying: An Angler's Complete Handbook & Kit. 96p. 1996. per. 25.00 (0-684-80067-5, Fireside) S&S Trade Pap.

— Big Hole River. (River Journal Ser.: Vol. 3, No. 3). (Illus.). 48p. 1995. pap. 15.95 (1-57188-006-2) F Amato Pubns.

— Fishing Washington's Endless Season: A Year 'Round Fishing Guide. LC 97-61614. (Illus.). 176p. (Orig.). 1997. pap. 19.95 (0-916473-12-0) Flying Pencil.

— Fly Fishing Desert & High Arid Lakes. (Illus.). 56p. 1995. pap. 19.95 (1-57188-026-7) F Amato Pubns.

— Hoh River, WA. (Steelhead River Journal Ser.: Vol. 3, No. 2). (Illus.). 48p. 1999. pap. 15.95 (1-57188-033-X) F Amato Pubns.

***Probasco, Steve.** Montana Blue-Ribbon Fly Fishing Guide. (Illus.). 96p. 2001. pap. 24.95 (1-57188-165-4) F Amato Pubns.

Probasco, Steve. Olympic Peninsula Rivers Guide: Floating & Fishing the Peninsula's Best Streams. LC 99-43817. 1999. pap. 15.95 (0-9639705-5-0) Ecopress.

— Yakima River, WA. (River Journal Ser.: Vol. 2, No. 2). (Illus.). 48p. 1994. pap. 14.95 (1-878175-75-0) F Amato Pubns.

Probasco, Teri. Blue Jean Gum. 35p. (J). (ps-4). pap. 5.90 (0-932970-95-8) Prinit Pr.

— Edge of the Night Sky. (Illus.). 32p. (Orig.). (J). (ps-5). 1995. pap. 10.00 (1-888305-00-2) Friends Genl Conf.

— Imprints. 177p. (J). (gr. 3-8). 1994. pap. 10.95 (0-932970-99-0) Prinit Pr.

— Simple Things. 36p. (J). (ps-6). 1994. pap. 5.90 (0-932970-98-2) Prinit Pr.

Probdorf, Henrik. Telekommunikation in Mittelosteuropa: Die Reform der Festnetzkommunikation in Polen, Tschechien & Ungarn. (GER., Illus.). XVI, 207p. 1996. 51.95 (3-631-30205-3) P Lang Pubng.

Probdorf, Siegfried & Silbermann, Bernd. Numerical Analysis for Integral & Related Operator Equations. (Mathematische Lehrbucher und Monographien: Abt. II, Band 84). 540p. 1991. text 236.25 (3-05-500696-8, Pub. by Akademie Verlag) Wiley.

***Prober, Paula & King, Kay.** Ten Tips for Women Who Want to Change the World Without Losing Their Friends, Shirts or Minds. LC 00-190031. (Illus.). 82p. 2000. per. 9.95 (0-9676842-0-X) TCC Pr.

Probert, Belinda & Wilson, Bruce W., eds. Pink Collar Blues: Work, Gender & Technology. 192p. (Orig.). 1993. pap. 19.95 (0-522-84520-7, Pub. by Melbourne Univ Pr) Paul & Co Pubs.

Probert, Christina & Lee-Potter, Charlie. Fashion in Vogue since 1910: Lingerie. LC 81-14926. (Accessories in Vogue Ser.). (Illus.). 96p. (Orig.). 1982. pap. 6.98 (0-89659-268-5) Abbeville Pr.

— Fashion in Vogue since 1910: Sportswear. LC 83-26574. (Accessories in Vogue Ser.). (Illus.). 96p. 1984. pap. 6.98 (0-89659-499-8) Abbeville Pr.

Probert, D. Cloze Clues. (Learning Works Reading Ser.). (Illus.). (J). (gr. 4-6). 1988. pap. 6.95 (0-88160-166-7, LW276) Learning Wks.

Probert, David. Developing a Make or Buy Strategy for Manufacturing Business. 132p. 1997. 55.00 (0-85296-863-9) INSPEC Inc.

Probert, Ellen, jt. auth. see Schueler, Sally H.

Probert, Henry. The Forgotten Air Force: The Royal Air Force in the War Against Japan 1941-1945. (Illus.). 350p. 1995. 44.95 (1-85753-065-9, Pub. by Brasseys) Brasseys.

Probert, Ian. Internet Spy. LC 96-173. (Classified Ser.). 96p. (YA). (gr. 5 up). 1996. pap. 5.95 (0-7534-5007-0, Kingfisher) LKC.

***Probert, Leslie D. & Harkness, Lisa L.** Emergency Food in a Nutshell. (Illus.). 170p. 1999. 16.95 (0-9676791-0-9) Purely Simple Pubng.

Probert, M. E., ed. A Search for Strategies for Sustainable Dryland Cropping in Semi-Arid Eastern Kenya. 134p. 1992. pap. 78.00 (1-86320-068-1, Pub. by ACIAR) St Mut.

Probert, Martin. Scenarios in IT Pack 2: Communicating & Handling Information. 112p. 1998. pap. 120.00 (0-7487-3968-8) St Mut.

Probert, P., jt. auth. see Cameron, S.

***Probert, Randall.** Courier de Bois. 358p. 2000. pap. 14.95 (0-9667308-2-8) Randall Entprs.

Probert, Randall. An Eloquent Caper. 1999. pap. 12.95 (0-9667308-1-X) Randall Entprs.

— A Forgotten Legacy: The Mata Gamon Region. (Illus.). 222p. 1998. pap. 19.95 (0-9667308-0-1) Randall Entprs.

— Katrina's Valley. LC 90-27842. 226p. 1991. pap. 14.95 (0-87949-350-X) Ashley Bks.

Probert, Richard E. Fishing Hot Spots (of the Upper Fraser Valley) 96p. 1992. pap. 8.95 (0-88839-307-5) Hancock House.

Probert, Robert. Archie's Way: A Memoir about Friendship & Craftsmanship. LC 98-3149. 192p. 1998. 19.95 (1-55821-704-5) Lyons Pr.

Probert, Sidney, ed. see Schueler, Sally H. & Probert, Ellen.

Probleme der Sprachwissenschaft Staff. Beitrage zur Linguistik. (Janua Linguarum, Ser. Minor: No. 118). 1971. pap. text 64.60 (90-279-1797-3) Mouton.

Probosz, Kathilyn. Alvin Ailey. (J). 1994. pap. 3.99 (0-553-85042-3) BDD Bks Young Read.

Probosz, Kathilyn S. Martha Graham. LC 94-8992. (People in Focus Ser.). (Illus.). (YA). (gr. 5 up). 1995. pap. 7.95 (0-382-24961-5, Dillon Silver Burdett) Silver Burdett Pr.

Probst. Expeditions into English 1. 160p. 1989. pap. text 26.40 (0-13-025487-8) P-H.

Probst, Brad, jt. auth. see Probst, Jeffrey.

Probst, Charles O. Bosch Fuel Injection & Engine Management Handbook. (Illus.). 224p. 29.95 (0-8376-0300-5) Bentley Pubs.

— Ford Fuel Injection & Electronic Engine Control: All Ford-Lincoln-Mercury Cars & Light Trucks, 1980 to 1987. LC 95-40935. (Illus.). 330p. 1995. 29.95 (0-8376-0302-1) Bentley Pubs.

— Ford Fuel Injection & Electronic Engine Control: How to Understand, Service & Modify, 1988-1993. LC 93-7168. (Illus.). 454p. 1993. pap. 29.95 (0-8376-0301-3) Bentley Pubs.

Probst, D. K., jt. ed. see Bochmann, G. V.

Probst, Eugen. Fischereiwirtschaft Band IV: Geschichte der Binnenfischerei, Teichwirtschaft und Kunstliche Fischzucht. (Handbuch der Binnenfischerei Mitteleuropas Ser.: Lieferung 4). (GER., Illus.). iii, 76p. 1934. 15.00 (3-510-41019-X, Pub. by E Schweizerbartsche) Balogh.

Probst, G. J., jt. ed. see Ulrich, H.

Probst, George E., intro. The Happy Republic: A Reader in Tocqueville's America. 1990. 16.50 (0-8446-1368-1) Peter Smith.

Probst, George T. & Reichmann, Eberhard. The Germans in Indianapolis, Vol. 1. (Illus.). xii, 200p. 1989. 16.00 (0-614-04948-2) MKGAC & IGHS.

Probst, Gerhard F. Erwin Piscator & the American Theatre. LC 90-28359. (American University Studies: Theatre Arts: Ser. XXVI, Vol. 6). (Illus.). XIV, 213p. (C). 1991. text 45.95 (0-8204-1591-X) P Lang Pubng.

Probst, Gerhard F. & Bodine, Jay F., eds. Perspectives on Max Frisch. LC 80-5181. 232p. 1982. 27.50 (0-8131-1438-1) U Pr of Ky.

***Probst, Gilbert.** British Roots. LC 99-37215. 368p. 1999. 45.00 (0-471-99768-4) Wiley.

Probst, Jeffrey. Backpacking Sense. (Illus.). 144p. (Orig.). 1996. pap. 7.95 (0-9655871-1-8) Outland Pub.

Probst, Jeffrey & Probst, Brad. High Uintas Backcountry. (Illus.). 303p. (Orig.). 1996. pap. 13.95 (0-9655871-2-6) Outland Pub.

***Probst, Jeffrey & Probst, Kyle.** High Uintas Fishing. (Illus.). 112p. 2000. pap. 8.95 (0-9655871-3-4) Outland Pub.

***Probst, Katherine N. & Beierle, Thomas C.** The Evolution of Hazardous Waste Programs: Lessons from Eight Countries. (Illus.). 102p. (C). 2000. pap. text 25.00 (0-7881-8405-9) DIANE Pub.

Probst, Katherine N. & Beierle, Thomas C. The Evolution of Hazardous Waste Programs: Lessons from Eight Countries. LC 99-21298. (Illus.). 102p. 1999. pap. text 12.95 (1-891853-01-5) Resources Future.

Probst, Katherine N. & McGovern, Michael H. Long-Term Stewardship & the Nuclear Weapons Complex: The Challenge Ahead. LC 98-23013. (Illus.). 67p. 1998. pap. text 9.95 (0-915707-97-7) Resources Future.

Probst, Katherine N. & Portney, Paul R. Assigning Liability for Superfund Cleanups: An Analysis of Policy Options. 62p. 1992. pap. text 15.00 (0-915707-64-0) Resources Future.

Probst, Katherine N., et al. Footing the Bill for Superfund Cleanups: Who Pays & How? LC 94-37702. (Illus.). 176p. (C). 1994. text 38.95 (0-8157-2994-4) Brookings.

— Footing the Bill for Superfund Cleanups: Who Pays & How? LC 94-37702. (Illus.). 176p. (C). 1994. pap. text 16.95 (0-8157-2995-2, Pub. by Resources Future) Johns Hopkins.

Probst, Ken, photos by. Pornegrafik. (Illus.). 96p. 1998. 50.00 (0-944092-52-7) Twin Palms Pub.

— Pornegrafik. limited ed. (Illus.). 96p. 1998. 400.00 (0-944092-53-5) Twin Palms Pub.

Probst, Kyle, jt. auth. see Probst, Jeffrey.

***Probst, Louis.** Complex Cases with LASIK: Advanced Techniques & Complication Management. LC 99-40823. (Illus.). 528p. 1999. text 175.00 (1-55642-404-3, 64043) SLACK Inc.

***Probst, Louis E.** Complex Cases with LASIK: Advanced Techniques & Complications Management. (SPA., Illus.). 528p. 2000. 175.00 (1-55642-445-0) SLACK Inc.

***Probst, Louis E. & Doane, John F.** Color Synopsis of Refractive Surgery. (Illus.). 275p. 2000. 79.00 (0-86577-914-7) Thieme Med Pubs.

***Probst, Martina.** Nu Wache UF, Sunder Trage. 186p. 1999. 37.95 (3-631-34562-3) P Lang Pubng.

Probst, Raymond R. Good Offices in the Light of Swiss International Practice & Experience. (C). 1989. lib. bdg. 94.50 (0-7923-0141-2) Kluwer Academic.

Probst, Robert E. Response & Analysis: Teaching Literature in Junior & Senior High School. LC 87-24509. 279p. (Orig.). (C). 1987. pap. text 23.00 (0-86709-203-3, 0203, Pub. by Boynton Cook Pubs) Heinemann.

Probst, S. & Flaxa, R. The Power LINUX: Linux 1.2 - LST Distribution 2.1. Dereig, A., tr. 200p. 1997. pap. text 49.95 incl. cd-rom (3-540-14556-7, AIP Pr) Spr-Verlag.

Probst, S., et al. The Power LINUX Kit. 1997. pap. 65.95 incl. audio compact disk (0-387-98263-9) Spr-Verlag.

Probst, Volker G. Arno Breker, das Bildnis des Menschen. (Illus.). 160p. (Orig.). 1981. pap. 15.00 (0-914301-26-8, Pub. by Marco) West-Art.

— Der Bildhauer Arno Breker. (Illus.). 168p. (Orig.). 1978. pap. 15.00 (0-914301-25-X, Pub. by Marco) West-Art.

— Schriften: Collected Writings of Arno Breker. (Illus.). 192p. 1983. text 20.00 (0-914301-28-4, Pub. by Marco) West-Art.

Probst, Volker G., ed. see Breker, Arno.

Probstein, Bobbie. Healing Now: A Personal Guide Through Challenging Times. (Illus.). 64p. (Orig.). 1992. pap. 9.95 (1-880823-00-4) N Star Pubns.

— Return to Center. LC 85-70723. (Illus.). 256p. (Orig.). 1985. pap. 10.95 (0-87516-554-0) DeVorss.

Probstein, Ian. Elegies: A Book of Poems. LC 94-74408. (RUS., Illus.). 80p. 1996. pap. 8.00 (1-882725-10-7) Arch-Arcada.

Probstein, Ian, ed. see Shatrov, Nikolai.

Probstein, Ian E., ed. see Murphy, Remington.

Probstein, Ian E., ed. see Ogniedou, Altan.

Probstein, Jan. Vita Nuoja: A Book of Poems Written in English & Translated from Russian by the Author. Graves, Michael, ed. 64p. (Orig.). 1993. pap. 4.00 (0-9635200-3-2) R E M Pr.

Probstein, Jan E. Requiem: A Book of Poems. (RUS., Illus.). 92p. (Orig.). 1994. pap. text 8.00 (0-911971-86-6) Effect Pub.

— Vremion Naskvozniake: A Book of Poems.Tr. of In the Draught of Time. (RUS., Illus.). 112p. (Orig.). 1993. pap. text 8.00 (0-911971-85-8) Effect Pub.

— Zhemchuzhina - A Pearl: A Book of Poems. Kazakova, Natalia, ed. LC 94-94446. (RUS.). 104p. 1994. pap. text 8.00 (1-882725-09-3) Arch-Arcada.

Probstein, Ronald F. Physicochemical Hydrodynamics. 353p. 1989. text 89.95 (0-7506-9401-7) Buttrwrth-Heinemann.

— Physiochemical Hydrodynamics. 2nd ed. 400p. 1994. 89.95 (0-471-01011-1) Wiley.

— Physiochemical Hydrodynamics: An Introduction. 2nd ed. 133p. 1995. teacher ed. write for info. (0-471-11703-X) Wiley.

Proby, Kathryn H. Audubon in Florida: With Selections from the Writings of John James Audubon. LC 72-85114. (Illus.). 384p. 1974. pap. 24.95 (0-87024-301-2) U of Miami Pr.

Probyn, Clive T. Jonathan Swift: The Contemporary Background. LC 78-12270. (Literature in Context Ser.). 219p. 1978. 17.50 (0-7190-0697-X) St Martin.

— The Sociable Humanist: Life & Work of James Harris, 1709-1740: Provincial & Metropolitan Culture in Eighteenth-Century England. (Illus.). 392p. 1991. 105.00 (0-19-818563-4) OUP.

Probyn, Clive T., ed. see Fielding, Henry & Fielding, Sarah.

***Probyn, Elspeth.** Carnal Appetite: Food Sex Identities. 2000. 75.00 (0-415-22304-0); pap. 19.99 (0-415-22305-9) Routledge.

Probyn, Elspeth. Outside Belongings. LC 95-26496. 181p. (C). 1996. 80.00 (0-415-91583-X); pap. 21.99 (0-415-91584-8) Routledge.

— Sexing the Self: Gendered Positions in Cultural Studies. LC 92-22143. 208p. (C). 1993. pap. 21.99 (0-415-07356-1, B0135) Routledge.

Probyn, Elspeth, jt. ed. see Grosz, Elizabeth.

Probyn, John W., ed. Systems of Land Tenure in Various Countries. LC 75-153000. (Select Bibliographies Reprint Ser.). 1977. reprint ed. 30.95 (0-8369-5752-0) Ayer.

Procassini, Andrew A. Competitors in Alliance: Industry Associations, Global Rivalries & Business. LC 94-39659. 360p. 1995. 65.00 (0-89930-962-3, Quorum Bks) Greenwood.

Proceedings of the Kew Chromosome Conference - Jodrell Laboratory, England. Molten Slags & Fluxes 3rd Intl Conf. 1989. 76.00 (0-901462-54-3) Institute of Management Consultants.

Proceedings of the 2nd European Conference on Adva. Euromat 91: Proc. 2nd European Conf. of Advanced Materials & Processes, 3 vols., Set. 1800p. 1991. 100.00 (0-901716-14-6, Pub. by Inst Materials) Ashgate Pub Co.

P

Proceedings of the 2nd Int'l Conference on the Beh. Advanced Machining for Quality & Productivity: Proc. 2nd Int'l Conf. on the Behaviorial Materials in Machining. 176p. 1991. 80.00 (*0-901716-24-3*, Pub. by Inst Materials) Ashgate Pub Co.

Procella, Yvonne. Yvonne Porcella: Art & Inspirations. LC 98-4700. 144p. 1998. 35.95 (*1-57120-056-8*, 10180) C & T Pub.

— Yvonne Porcella: Art & Inspirations. LC 98-4700. (Art & Inspirations Ser.). (Illus.). 144p. 1998. pap. text 29.95 (*1-57120-050-9*, 10174) C & T Pub.

Procesi, Claudio, ed. Geometry Today: Giornate Di Geometria, Roma 1984. (Progress in Mathematics Ser.: Vol. 60). 1985. 49.00 (*0-8176-3290-5*) Birkhauser.

Process Data Exchange Institute Staff. PDXI Activity Model Vol. 2: Includes Entire Activity Model. 344p. 1997. pap. 150.00 (*0-8169-0756-0*, I-2) Am Inst Chem Eng.

— PDXI Data Models, Vol. 1. 380p. 1997. pap. 300.00 (*0-8169-0755-2*, I-1) Am Inst Chem Eng.

Process Management Institute Staff & Gitlow, Howard S. Planning for Quality, Productivity & Competitive Position, ASQC Edition. 172p. 1990. text 17.47 (*1-55623-466-X*, Irwn Prfssnl) McGraw-Hill Prof.

Process Management Work Group Staff. The Road to Excellence: Becoming a Process-Based Company. 177p. 1997. 30.00 (*1-890783-01-3*) CAM-I.

Process Measurement & Control Division & New Orlea, ed. see ISA Final Control Elements Symposium Staff.

Process Technology Conference Staff. New Ironmaking & Steelmaking Processes: Proceedings of the 7th Process Technology Conference, April 17-20, 1988, Toronto, Ontario. LC 82-197229. (Illus.). 307p. reprint ed. pap. 95.20 (*0-8357-5552-5*, 203518100093) Bks Demand.

***Processional Edition Staff.** Lectionary for Sunday Mass Cycle C: Precessional Edition. 2000. 59.00 (*0-89942-072-9*) Catholic Bk Pub.

Proch, D., jt. auth. see Gower, M.

Proch, Kathleen Ohman, see Hess, Peg M. & Ohman Proch, Kathleen.

Prochaska & Norcross. Systems of Psychotherapy. 4th ed. LC 98-28468. (Counseling Ser.). 1998. pap. 76.95 (*0-534-35704-0*) Brooks-Cole.

Prochaska, Bernadette. The Myth of the Fall & Walker Percy's Last Gentleman. LC 91-42105. (American University Studies: American Literature: Ser. XXIV, Vol. 32). XI, 148p. 1993. pap. 29.95 (*0-8204-1806-4*) P Lang Pubng.

Prochaska, F. K. Philanthropy & the Hospitals of London: The King's Fund, 1897-1990. (Illus.). 320p. 1992. text 75.00 (*0-19-820266-0*) OUP.

— Women & Philanthropy in Nineteenth-Century England. (Illus.). 316p. 1980. pap. text 22.50 (*0-19-822628-4*) OUP.

Prochaska, Frank. The Rise of the Welfare Monarchy. LC 95-12271. 1996. 42.00 (*0-300-06453-5*) Yale U Pr.

Prochaska, Georg. A Dissertation on the Functions of the Nervous System. Laycock, T., tr. LC 78-72819. (Brainedness, Handedness, & Mental Abilities Ser.). reprint ed. 34.50 (*0-404-60888-4*) AMS Pr.

Prochaska, James O. Systems of Psychotherapy: A Transtheoretical Analysis. 2nd ed. 442p. (C). 1984. pap. 47.25 (*0-534-10708-7*) Brooks-Cole.

Prochaska, James O. & Norcross, John C. Systems of Psychotherapy: A Transtheoretical Analysis. 3rd ed. 1994. mass mkt., teacher ed. write for info. (*0-534-22291-9*) Brooks-Cole.

Prochaska, James O. & Norcross, John C. Systems of Psychotherapy: A Transtheoretical Analysis. 3rd ed. LC 93-41023. 540p. 1996. pap. 51.00 (*0-534-22290-0*) Brooks-Cole.

Prochaska, James O., et al. Changing for Good. 304p. 1995. reprint ed. pap. 12.50 (*0-380-72572-X*, Avon Bks) Morrow Avon.

Prochaska, Michael. Leistungsmotivation Methoden, Soziale Erwunschtheit und das Konstrukt: Ansatzpunkte Zur Entwicklung Eines Neuen Eignungsdiagnostischen Verfahrens. (Psychologie Ser.: Bd. 612). (GER., Illus.). VIII, 182p. 1998. 37.95 (*3-631-33162-2*) P Lang Pubng.

Prochazka, A., et al. Signal Analysis & Prediction. LC 98-4740. (Applied & Numerical Harmonic Analysis Ser.). 432p. 1998. text 59.95 (*0-8176-4042-8*) Birkhauser.

Prochazka, Alex. Signal Analysis & Prediction. LC 98-4740. (Applied & Numerical Harmonic Analysis Ser.). 1998. write for info. (*3-7643-4042-8*) Birkhauser.

Prochazka, Theodore, Jr. Saudi Arabian Dialects. 400p. 1987. text 82.50 (*0-7103-0204-5*) Routledge.

Prochazka, V., ed. Narodni Divadlo, Slovnik Umelcu Divadel Vlastenskeho, Stavovskeho, Prozatimniho a Narodniho. (CZE.). 624p. 1990. 70.00 (*0-317-03839-7*) Szwede Slavic.

Prochazka, Zelimir, tr. see Vecera, Miroslav.

Prochelo, Barbara B. Draw from Within: A Workbook for Self-Expression & Self-Discovery. (Illus.). 66p. (Orig.). 1990. pap. 9.95 (*0-9626838-0-9*) Sun Dance Creat.

Prochnau, William. Once upon a Distant Star: David Halberstam, Neil Sheehan, Peter Arnett--Young War Correspondents & Their Early Vietnam Battles. 576p. 1996. pap. 15.00 (*0-679-77265-0*) McKay.

— Once upon a Distant War: Young War Correspondents & the Early Vietnam Battles. 1996. pap. 15.00 (*0-614-20772-X*) Vin Bks.

Prochnicky, Jerry & Russo, Joe. Jim Morrison: My Eyes Have Seen You. LC 96-92143. (Illus.). 170p. (Orig.). 1996. pap. 20.00 (*0-9651481-9-X*) J Prochnicky.

Prochnicky, Jerry, jt. auth. see Riordan, James.

Prochnow, Dave. Experiments in CMOS Technology. (Advanced Technology Ser.). (Illus.). 304p. 1988. 24.95 (*0-8306-9262-2*, 3062); pap. 16.95 (*0-8306-9362-9*, 3062) McGraw-Hill Prof.

— Experiments with E-PROMs. 240p. 1988. pap. 22.95 (*0-07-156490-X*) McGraw.

— Experiments with EPROMs. (Advanced Technology Ser.). (Illus.). 208p. 1988. 24.95 (*0-8306-0362-X*); pap. 17.95 (*0-8306-2962-9*) McGraw-Hill Prof.

— Flight Simulator & Flight Simulator II: 82 Challenging New Adventures. 1987. 19.95 (*0-8306-0462-6*, 2862); pap. 12.95 (*0-8306-2862-2*) McGraw-Hill Prof.

— Jet: Eighty-Two Challenging New Adventures. 1987. pap. 12.95 (*0-8306-2872-X*) McGraw-Hill Prof.

— Superconductivity: Experiments in a New Technology. (Advanced Technology Ser.). (Illus.). 208p. 1988. pap. 14.95 (*0-8306-3132-1*, 3132) McGraw-Hill Prof.

— Yo-Yo Book. Date not set. write for info. (*0-8069-5725-5*) Sterling.

Prochnow, Dave & Knott. One Thousand One Things to Do with Your Amiga. 1991. 24.95 (*0-8306-6427-0*) McGraw-Hill Prof.

Prochnow, Dave & Prochnow, Kathy. How? More Experiments for the Young Scientist. (Illus.). 160p. (J). 1992. 16.95 (*0-8306-4024-X*, 4177) McGraw-Hill Prof.

— How? More Experiments for the Young Scientist. (Illus.). 160p. (J). (gr. 6-8). 1992. pap. 9.95 (*0-8306-4025-8*, 4177) McGraw-Hill Prof.

— How? More Experiments for the Young Scientist. 2nd ed. 160p. 1993. pap. 10.95 (*0-07-051052-0*) McGraw.

— Why? Experiments for the Young Scientist. (Illus.). 160p. (J). (gr. 4-7). 1992. 16.95 (*0-8306-4015-0*, 4176); pap. 9.95 (*0-8306-4023-1*, 4176) McGraw-Hill Prof.

Prochnow, Dave & Sawusch, Mark R. One Thousand One Things to Do with Your IBM PS-2. 1991. 24.95 (*0-8306-8686-X*) McGraw-Hill Prof.

Prochnow, Dave, jt. auth. see Prochnow, Kathy.

Prochnow, David W. & Prochnow, Kathy. How? LC 97-24043. (Experiments for Young Scientists Ser.). (Illus.). 152p. (YA). (gr. 5 up). 1999. lib. bdg. 22.95 (*0-7910-4846-2*) Chelsea Hse.

Prochnow, Herbert. A Funny Thing Happened on the Way to the Podium: The Speaker's Complete Guide to Great Jokes, Anecdotes & Stories. LC 98-26824. 368p. 1998. per. 15.95 (*0-7615-1452-X*) Prima Pub.

Prochnow, Herbert V. American Financial Institutions. LC 76-128290. (Essay Index Reprint Ser.). 1977. 47.95 (*0-8369-2017-1*) Ayer.

— A Funny Thing Happened on the Way to the Podium: The Speaker's Complete Guide to Great Jokes, Anecdotes & Stories. LC 99-29782. 2000. pap. text 7.99 (*0-517-20651-X*) Random Hse Value.

— Speaker's & Toastmaster's Handbook. 368p. 1992. pap. 14.95 (*1-55958-146-8*) Prima Pub.

— The Speaker's & Toastmaster's Handbook: 1,000 Quips, Stories, & Illustrations for All Occasions. LC 72-92120. (Illus.). 220p. 1973. write for info. (*0-513-01172-2*) Denison.

— The Speaker's Treasury of Stories for All Occasions. 344p. 1982. 16.95 (*0-685-05562-0*) P-H.

Prochnow, Herbert V., ed. Great Stories from Great Lives. LC 77-111858. (Essay Index Reprint Ser.). 1977. 29.95 (*0-8369-2018-X*) Ayer.

***Prochnow, Kathy & Prochnow, Dave.** The Art of Fine Furniture Building: A Guide to Designing, Constructing & Finishing High-Quality Furniture. (Illus.). 174p. 1999. reprint ed. pap. text 17.00 (*0-7881-6784-7*) DIANE Pub.

Prochnow, Kathy, jt. auth. see Prochnow, Dave.

Prochnow, Kathy, jt. auth. see Prochnow, David W.

Prochnow, Peter-Michael. Staat Im Wachstum Versucheiner Finanzwirthschaftlichen Analyse der Preussischen Haushaltsrechungen, 1871-1913, 2 vols. Bruchey, Stuart, ed. LC 80-2825. (Dissertations in European Economic History Ser.). (Illus.). 1981. lib. bdg. 35.95 (*0-405-14009-6*) Ayer.

Prochorov, A. M. Dictionary of Micro-Electronics. (DUT, ENG, FRE, GER & RUS.). 150.00 (*0-8288-9438-8*) Fr & Eur.

— Encyclopedia Dictionary of Physics. (RUS.). 928p. 1983. 85.00 (*0-8288-2240-9*, M15362) Fr & Eur.

Prochownik, Edda. Funfundsiebzig Deutsche Balladen. (GER.). 120p. 1968. 9.80 (*3-296-40200-4*, Pub. by Weidmann) Lubrecht & Cramer.

Procidano. Dimensions of Personality. (C). 1999. text 53.50 (*0-15-500127-2*, Pub. by Harcourt Coll Pubs) Harcourt.

Procidano, Mary & Fisher, Celia B. Contemporary Families: A Handbook for School Professionals. 336p. (C). 1992. text 29.00 (*0-8077-3166-8*) Tchrs Coll.

Proclus. The Elements of Theology. 2nd ed. Dodds, Eric R., tr. & comment by. (Illus.). 396p. 1992. pap. text 35.00 (*0-19-814097-5*) OUP.

— Elements of Theology, or Divine Arithmetic. Holmes, J. D., ed. Ionides, A., tr. from GRE. 1993. 45.00 (*1-55818-204-7*) Holmes Pub.

— Proclus' Commentary on Plato's "Parmenides" Morrow, Glenn R. & Dillon, John M., trs. 664p. 1987. pap. text 39.50 (*0-691-02089-2*, Pub. by Princeton U Pr) Cal Prin Full Svc.

Proclus & Felty, David. The Nature of the Universe. 2nd ed. LC 97-24982. (Lynchburg College Symposium Readings Ser.). 1997. pap. write for info. (*0-7618-0829-9*) U Pr of Amer.

Proclus & Taylor, Thomas. Fragments of the Lost Writings of Proclus. 2nd ed. Robb, R. I., ed. LC 87-51458. 128p. 1988. reprint ed. 14.00 (*0-913510-58-0*) Wizards.

Procope, J. F., ed. see Seneca, Lucius Annaeus.

Procopic, Richard, photos by. Maine: A Coastal Portrait. (Illus.). 32p. 1996. pap. 9.95 (*1-881535-20-7*) New Eng Pr VT.

Procopio, Glenn. So That's Why I Keep Doing This! 52 Devotional Stories of Encouragement & Inspiration for Youth Workers. LC 98-7636. 128p. 1998. pap. 14.99 (*0-310-22456-X*) Zondervan.

Procopio, Luanne. For the Golfer. 59p. (Orig.). 1992. pap. text 6.95 (*0-9633986-0-1*) L Prods.

Procopio, Richard, photos by. Maine Scenes & Seasons. LC 92-81160. (Illus.). 80p. (Orig.). 1992. pap. 14.95 (*0-933050-95-X*) New Eng Pr VT.

Procopiow. The Elements of Legal Prose. LC 98-48345. 196p. 1999. pap. 15.00 (*0-205-28225-3*) Allyn.

Procopiow, Norma. Robert Lowell, the Poet & His Critics. LC 84-467. (Poet & His Critics Ser.). 352p. reprint ed. pap. 109.20 (*0-608-17000-3*, 202772600056) Bks Demand.

Procopis, Peter G. & Kewley, Geoff D., eds. Current Paediatric Practice. (Illus.). 336p. 1991. pap. text 71.00 (*0-7295-0397-6*) Bailliere Tindall.

Procopius. The Secret History. Williamson, G., tr. & intro. by. (Classics Ser.). 208p. 1966. pap. 15.99 (*0-14-044182-4*, Penguin Classics) Viking Penguin.

— Secret History. Atwater, Richard, tr. 166p. 1961. pap. text 12.95 (*0-472-08728-2*, 08728, Ann Arbor Bks) U of Mich Pr.

Procter. Nurses, Computers & Information Technology. 118p. 1992. pap. 34.95 (*1-56593-019-3*, 0262) Thomson Learn.

Procter, Ben. Just One Riot: Episodes of Texas Rangers in the Twentieth Century. (Illus.). 192p. 1991. 18.95 (*0-89015-806-1*) Sunbelt Media.

— William Randolph Hearst: The Early Years, 1863-1910. (Illus.). 384p. 1998. 30.00 (*0-19-511277-6*) OUP.

Procter, Ben & McDonald, Archie P. The Texas Heritage. 3rd ed. LC 97-6788. (Illus.). 288p. (C). 1998. pap. text 18.95 (*0-88295-976-X*) Harlan Davidson.

Procter, Ben H. The Battle of the Alamo. LC 86-50749. (Illus.). 36p. 1986. pap. 7.95 (*0-87611-081-2*) Tex St Hist Assn.

Procter, Bryan W. The Life of Edmund Kean, 2 vols., 1 bk. LC 70-82840. 560p. 1972. reprint ed. 39.95 (*0-405-08864-7*, Pub. by Blom Pubns) Ayer.

Procter, David E. Enacting Political Culture: Rhetorical Transformations of Liberty Weekend 1986. LC 90-7462. (Praeger Series in Political Communication). 144p. 1990. 47.95 (*0-275-93489-6*, C3489, Praeger Pubs) Greenwood.

Procter, Evelyn S. Alfonso X of Castile, Patron of Literature & Learning. LC 80-10508. (Norman Macoll Lectures Ser.: 1949). 149p. 1980. reprint ed. lib. bdg. 35.00 (*0-313-22347-5*, PRAL, Greenwood Pr) Greenwood.

— Curia & Cortes in Leon & Castile, 1072-1295. LC 79-51750. (Cambridge Iberian & Latin American Studies). 336p. reprint ed. pap. 95.80 (*0-608-16937-4*, 2027259) Bks Demand.

Procter, Everett. Christian Controversy in Alexandria: Clement's Polemic Against the Basilideans & Valentinians. LC 93-37342. (AUS VII: Vol. 172). XI, 121p. (C). 1995. text 37.95 (*0-8204-2378-5*) P Lang Pubng.

Procter, Garry. Asymmetric Synthesis. (Illus.). 246p. 1997. pap. text 37.00 (*0-19-855725-6*) OUP.

— Asymmetric Synthesis. (Illus.). 246p. (C). 1997. text 85.00 (*0-19-855726-4*) OUP.

— Stereoselectivity in Organic Synthesis. (Oxford Chemistry Primers Ser.: No. 63). (Illus.). 96p. (C). 1998. pap. text 12.95 (*0-19-855957-7*) OUP.

Procter, George H. The Fisherman's Memorial & Record Book. (Illus.). 192p. 1989. reprint ed. lib. bdg. 39.00 (*0-8328-1397-4*) Higginson Bk Co.

Procter, Ian & Padfield, Maureen. Young Adult Women, Work & the Family: Living a Contradiction. LC 97-33501. (Employment & Work Relations in Context Ser.). 272p. 1998. 75.00 (*0-7201-2336-4*, Pub. by Mansell Pub) Cassell.

***Procter, James.** Writing Black Britain, 1948-1998: An Interdisciplinary Anthology. LC 99-49700. 2000. pap. write for info. (*0-7190-5382-X*); text. write for info. (*0-7190-5381-1*) Manchester Univ Pr.

***Procter, Jody.** Toil: Building Yourself. LC 99-58370. (Illus.). 224p. 2000. 22.95 (*1-890132-67-5*) Chelsea Green Pub.

***Procter, Margaret & Cook, Michael.** Manual of Archival Description. 3rd ed. LC 00-21004. 352p. 2000. 104.95 (*0-566-08258-6*, Pub. by Ashgate Pub) Ashgate Pub Co.

Procter, Margaret, jt. auth. see Cook, Michael.

Procter, Margaret, jt. auth. see Northey, Margot.

Procter, Maurice. The Midnight Plumber. 1996. 19.50 (*0-7451-8682-3*, Black Dagger) Chivers N Amer.

Procter, Pam, jt. auth. see Schoen, Allen M.

***Procter, Paul.** Renaissance. (Illus.). 40p. (J). (gr. 3-7). 2000. 16.95 (*0-87226-618-4*, 66184B, P Bedrick Books) NTC Contemp Pub Co.

Procter-Smith, Marjorie. In Her Own Rite: Constructing Feminist Liturgical Tradition. 160p. 1990. pap. 11.95 (*0-687-18790-7*) Abingdon.

— Shakerism & Feminism: Reflections on Women's Religion & the Early Shakers. (Illus.). 24p. 1991. pap. text 4.95 (*0-937942-16-2*) Shaker Mus.

— Women in Shaker Community & Worship: A Feminist Analysis of Religious Symbolism. LC 85-13776. (Studies in Women & Religion: Vol. 16). 253p. 1985. lib. bdg. 89.95 (*0-88946-533-9*) E Mellen.

Procter, Sue, jt. ed. see Reed, Jan.

Procter, Thomas. Of the Knowledge & Conduct of Warres. LC 79-25921. (English Experience Ser.: No. 268). 96p. 1970. reprint ed. 20.00 (*90-221-0268-8*) Walter J Johnson.

— A Profitable Worke to This Whole Kingdome Concerning the Mending of All Highways, As Also for Waters & Iron Workes. LC 77-7425. (English Experience Ser.: No. 885). 1977. reprint ed. lib. bdg. 15.00 (*90-221-0885-6*) Walter J Johnson.

Proctor. Psychology: The Adaptive Mind. 2nd ed. (Psychology Ser.). 1999. pap. 20.25 (*0-534-36774-7*) Brooks-Cole.

Proctor & Van Zandt. Human Factors in Simple & Complex Systems. 576p. 1994. pap. text, wbk. ed. 28.00 (*0-205-14005-X*) P-H.

Proctor, jt. auth. see Bruijnzeel.

Proctor, jt. auth. see Cooper, Kenneth H.

Proctor, jt. auth. see Livesey.

Proctor, jt. auth. see Walters, D. Eric.

Proctor, Alan. A Doreset Downs Walk. (C). 1988. pap. text 40.00 (*0-904110-96-6*, Pub. by Thornhill Pr) St Mut.

— A Severn to Solent Walk. (C). 1988. pap. 35.00 (*0-904110-91-5*, Pub. by Thornhill Pr) St Mut.

— The Wessex Way. (C). 1988. pap. 40.00 (*0-904110-83-4*, Pub. by Thornhill Pr) St Mut.

Proctor, Alexander P. Alexander Phimister Proctor, Sculptor in Buckskin: An Autobiography. Proctor, Hester E., ed. LC 77-108803. (Illus.). 281p. reprint ed. 87.20 (*0-8357-9716-3*, 201625100002) Bks Demand.

Proctor, Alison. Flowers for Cakes: How to Create over 40 Lifelike Sugar Flowers. 1999. pap. text 12.95 (*1-85391-432-0*) Merehurst Ltd.

Proctor, Allan. Multiple Choice Questions in Preparation for the AP United States History Examination. 3rd ed. 1996. pap. 16.95 (*1-878621-43-2*) D & S Mktg Syst.

— Teacher's Manual to Accompany Multiple Choice Questions in Preparation for the AP United States History Examination. 3rd ed. 1996. pap., teacher ed. write for info. (*1-878621-44-0*) D & S Mktg Syst.

Proctor, Anne, et al. Learning to Teach in the Primary Classroom. LC 94-25720. (Illus.). 208p. (C). 1995. pap. 20.99 (*0-415-11065-3*, B4208) Routledge.

Proctor, Arthur M. Safeguarding the School Board's Purchase of Architects' Working Drawings. LC 73-177168. (Columbia University. Teachers College. Contributions to Education Ser.: No. 474). reprint ed. 37.50 (*0-404-55474-1*) AMS Pr.

Proctor, Bruce. Chronic Progressive Deafness: Resume of World-Wide Publications 1952-1959. LC 63-19171. 758p. pap. 200.00 (*0-608-16549-2*, 202766100055) Bks Demand.

— Surgical Anatomy of the Ear & Temporal Bone. (Illus.). 240p. 1989. text 79.00 (*0-86577-295-9*) Thieme Med Pubs.

Proctor, C. R., ed. see Materials Handling Conference Staff.

***Proctor, Candice.** The Last Knight. 416p. 2000. mass mkt. 6.99 (*0-8041-1930-9*) Ivy Books.

Proctor, Candice. Night in Eden. 1997. mass mkt. 5.99 (*0-449-00125-3*, GM) Fawcett.

— Night in Eden. 1997. mass mkt. 5.99 (*0-8041-1758-6*) Ivy Books.

***Proctor, Candice.** September Moon. 1999. mass mkt. 5.99 (*0-449-00127-X*, GM) Fawcett.

Proctor, Candice E. The Bequest. 1998. mass mkt. 5.99 (*0-8041-1827-2*) Ivy Books.

— The Bequest. large type ed. LC 98-22091. (Large Print Book Ser.). 439 p. 1998. 22.92 (*1-56895-608-8*) Wheeler Pub.

***Proctor, Candice E.** September Moon. large type ed. LC 00-40420. (Large Print Book Ser.). 2000. write for info. (*1-56895-917-6*) Wheeler Pub.

Proctor, Candice E. Women, Equality & the French Revolution, 115. LC 90-2963. (Contributions in Women's Studies: No. 115). 224p. 1990. 55.00 (*0-313-27245-X*, PWE, Greenwood Pr) Greenwood.

Proctor, Charles, jt. ed. see Colliver, Douglas.

***Proctor, Chris.** Chris Proctor/Only Now. 72p. 1999. pap. 19.95 incl. audio compact disk (*0-7866-3841-9*, 96903BCD) Mel Bay.

Proctor, Claude O. NTC's Multilingual Dictionary of American Sign Language. (FRE, ENG, DUT, CHI & ARA., Illus.). 767p. 1994. 49.95 (*0-8442-0731-4*) NTC Contemp Pub Co.

— NTC's Multilingual Dictionary of American Sign Language. LC 98-16218. (Illus.). 767p. 1996. pap. 29.95 (*0-8442-0732-2*, 07322, Natl Textbk Co) NTC Contemp Pub Co.

***Proctor, Claude O.** Signing in 14 Languages: A Thirteen Language Dictionary of 2,500 American Sign Language Words. (ENG, ARA, CHI, DUT & FRE., Illus.). 767p. 2000. 17.98 (*1-57912-099-7*, 81099) Blck Dog & Leventhal.

Proctor, Custis N., jt. auth. see Dillon, Mary J.

Proctor, D. Experience of Thucydides. 1980. pap. 40.00 (*0-85668-206-3*, Pub. by Aris & Phillips) David Brown.

Proctor, D. L. Grain Storage Techniques - Evolution & Trends in Developing Countries. (Agricultural Services Bulletin Ser.: No. 109). 288p. 1994. pap. 45.00 (*92-5-103456-7*, F34567, Pub. by FAO) Bernan Associates.

Proctor, David. The Quotable Vampire. LC 97-222005. 96p. 1997. pap. 7.00 (*1-57566-218-3*, Knsington) Kensgtn Pub Corp.

Proctor, Dennis V., jt. auth. see Powell, Staccato.

Proctor, Donald F., ed. A History of Breathing Physiology. LC 95-9619. (Lung Biology in Health & Disease Ser.: Vol. 83). (Illus.). 416p. 1995. text 150.00 (*0-8247-9653-5*) Dekker.

Proctor, Dorothy & Rosen, Fred. Chameleon: The Lives of Dorothy Proctor from Street Criminal to International Special Agent. LC 94-66762. 304p. 1994. 22.95 (*0-88282-099-0*) New Horizon NJ.

Proctor, Emma J. Cherish. (Illus.). 64p. 1997. pap. 8.00 (*0-8059-4248-3*) Dorrance.

Proctor, Enola, jt. auth. see Davis, Larry.

***Proctor, Enola Knisley, et al.** Mental Health Services & Sectors of Care LC 99-17012. 1999. write for info. (*0-7890-0760-6*) Haworth Pr.

Proctor, F. J., jt. auth. see Currah, L.

Proctor, Frank. Growing Through an Effective Church School. 160p. (Orig.). 1990. pap. 9.99 (*0-8272-1235-6*) Chalice Pr.

Proctor, Frederick M., ed. Open Architecture Control Systems & Standards. Vol. 2912. LC 96-69764. 232p. 1997. 56.00 (*0-8194-2314-9*) SPIE.

An Asterisk (*) at the beginning of an entry indicates that the title is appearing for the first time.

Proctor, G. R. Flora of the Cayman Islands. (Kew Bulletin Additional Ser.: Vol. XI). xii, 834p. 1984. 70.00 (*0-11-242548-8*, Pub. by Royal Botnic Grdns) Balogh.

Proctor, George A. Canadian Music of the Twentieth Century. LC 81-143054. (Illus.). 323p. reprint ed. pap. 100.20 (*0-7837-0531-X*, 204085900019) Bks Demand.

Proctor, George R. Ferns of Puerto Rico & the Virgin Islands. LC 89-13193. (Memoirs Ser.: No. 53). (Illus.). 396p. 1989. text 39.75 (*0-89327-341-4*) NY Botanical.

Proctor, George R. & Redpath, James. Moncyclic Azepines: The Syntheses & Chemical Properties of the Monocyclic Azepines, Vol. 56, Vol. 56. LC 95-48039. 632p. 1997. 435.00 (*0-471-96372-0*) Wiley.

Proctor, Henry. Perpetual Youth: An Occult & Historical Romance. 115p. 1993. reprint ed. spiral bd. 13.00 (*0-7873-0678-9*) Hlth Research.

Proctor, Henry H. Between Black & White. LC 79-173611. (Black Heritage Library Collection). 1977. reprint ed. 20.95 (*0-8369-8903-1*) Ayer.

Proctor, Hester E., ed. see Proctor, Alexander P.

Proctor, J. The Ecology of Areas with Serpentinized Rocks: A World Review. Roberts, B. A., ed. 440p. 1992. text 341.00 (*0-7923-0922-7*) Kluwer Academic.

— Mineral Nutrients in Tropical Forests & Savannah Ecosystems. 1989. 125.00 (*0-632-02559-X*) Blackwell Sci.

***Proctor, James D.** Geography & Ethics: Journeys in Moral Terrain. LC 98-47914. 1999. pap. write for info. (*0-415-18969-1*); text. write for info. (*0-415-18968-3*) Routledge.

Proctor, Jesse H., ed. Islam & International Relations. LC 80-1914. 1981. reprint ed. 27.50 (*0-404-18969-5*) AMS Pr.

Proctor, John C. Heintz. Johannes Heintz (John Hines) & His Descendants (Emigrants from Prussia to Pennsylvania in 1751) (Illus.). 111p. 1997. reprint ed. pap. 17.50 (*0-8328-9084-7*); reprint ed. lib. bdg. 27.50 (*0-8328-9083-9*) Higginson Bk Co.

Proctor, John M. Viktor, Vodka & Raw Fish: The Last Crossing of the U. S. S. R. LC 94-60891. (Illus.). 300p. (Orig.). 1994. pap. 19.95 (*0-9639519-4-7*) Whitewing Pr.

Proctor, Jon. Convair 880 & 990, Vol. 1. (Great Airliners Ser.: No. 1). (Illus.). 128p. 1996. pap. 24.95 (*0-9626730-4-8*, 2501) World Transport.

Proctor, Jon, ed. see Archer, Robert D.

Proctor, Jon, ed. see Powers, David G.

Proctor, Joyce A. Recipes from the Flying Kitchen: On Pacific Tour in an Albatross. (Illus.). 200p. (YA). 1996. 29.95 (*0-9653893-0-8*) Albatross Trvls.

Proctor, June. We Are Eucharist. 96p. 1996. pap. 39.95 (*0-85439-521-0*, Pub. by St Paul Pubns) St Mut.

Proctor, Kate. Bittersweet Yesterdays. (Presents Ser.). 1994. per. 2.99 (*0-373-11710-8*, 1-11710-0) Harlequin Bks.

— Contract to Love. 1994. per. 2.99 (*0-373-11661-6*, 1-11661-5) Harlequin Bks.

— A Passionate Deceit. (Presents Ser.: Vol. 89). 1998. per. 3.75 (*0-373-18689-4*, 1-18689-9) Harlequin Bks.

— Prince of Darkness. LC 96-259. 186p. 1995. per. 3.25 (*0-373-11767-1*, 1-11767-0) Harlequin Bks.

Proctor, L. B. Lawyer & Client: Or, the Trials & Triumphs of the Bar; Illustrated by Scenes in the Court-Room, Etc., Etc. (Illus.). xii, 324p. 1995. reprint ed. 45.00 (*0-8377-2553-4*, Rothman) W S Hein.

Proctor, M. R., et al, eds. Solar & Planetary Dynamos. (Publications of the Newton Institute). (Illus.). 378p. (C). 1994. text 59.95 (*0-521-45470-0*) Cambridge U Pr.

Proctor, M. R. & Gilbert, A. D., eds. Lectures on Solar & Planetary Dynamos. (Publications of the Newton Institute: No. 2). (Illus.). 389p. (C). 1995. text 85.00 (*0-521-46142-1*); pap. text 31.95 (*0-521-46704-7*) Cambridge U Pr.

Proctor, M. R., jt. ed. see Fearn, D. R.

Proctor, Mara. The Beveled Rose: And Other Stories. 123p. (Orig.). 1994. pap. 8.00 (*0-9647975-0-X*) Willow Pond Pubs.

***Proctor, Maryjane, compiled by.** Family Chronicles of the Paterson Intelligencer Newspaper: Marriages & Deaths, 1825-1856. 166p. 1999. spiral bd. 15.00 (*0-9674344-4-0*) Passaic Co Hist.

Proctor, Maurine J. & Proctor, Scot F. Charting a New Millennium: The Latter-Day Saints in the Coming Century. LC 98-25988. 1998. write for info. (*1-56236-236-4*, Pub. by Aspen Bks) Origin Bk Sales.

— The Gathering: Mormom Pioneers on the Trail to Zion. LC 95-49742. 224p. 1996. 49.95 (*1-57345-087-1*) Deseret Bk.

— Light from the Dust: A Photographic Exploration into the Ancient World of the Book of Mormon. LC 93-72676. (Illus.). 208p. 1993. 39.95 (*0-87579-680-X*) Deseret Bk.

— Source of the Light: A Witness & Testimony of Jesus Christ, the Savior & Redeemer of All. LC 92-27973. (Illus.). 208p. 1992. 39.95 (*0-87579-648-6*) Deseret Bk.

Proctor, Maurine J., jt. ed. see Proctor, Scot F.

Proctor, Michael, et al. The Natural History of Pollination. LC 96-198390. (Illus.). 487p. 1996. pap. 27.95 (*0-88192-353-2*) Timber.

Proctor, Minna, tr. see Eco, Umberto & Martini, Carlo M.

Proctor, Minna, tr. see Vinci, Simona.

Proctor, Mortimer R. The English University Novel: University of California Publications, No. 15, 1977. Metzger, Walter P., ed. LC 76-55197. (Academic Profession Ser.). 1977. reprint ed. lib. bdg. 20.95 (*0-405-10030-2*) Ayer.

Proctor, Nigel, ed. The Aims of Primary Education & the National Curriculum. (Contemporary Analysis in Education Ser.). 220p. 1990. pap. 37.95 (*1-85000-560-5*) Taylor & Francis.

Proctor, Nigel, jt. auth. see Pratten, John.

Proctor, Noble. Garden Birds: How to Attract Birds to Your Garden. 160p. 1996. pap. 16.95 (*0-87596-950-X*) Rodale Pr Inc.

Proctor, Noble S. Manual of Ornithology: Avian Structure & Function. (Illus.). 352p. 1993. pap. 25.00 (*0-300-07619-3*) Yale U Pr.

— Manual of Ornithology: Avian Structure & Function. LC 92-17066. (Illus.). 352p. (C). 1993. 50.00 (*0-300-05746-6*) Yale U Pr.

Proctor, Noble S. & Lynch, Patrick J. Bird Anatomy No. 2: Avian Structure & Function. 1993. 75.00 incl. mac hd (*0-300-05403-3*) Yale U Pr.

Proctor, Pam, jt. auth. see Newburger, Amy E.

Proctor, Pam, jt. auth. see Schoen, Allen M.

Proctor, Paul, ed. The Cambridge International Dictionary of English. 1795p. 1995. pap. 30.95 (*0-521-48469-3*) Cambridge U Pr.

— The Cambridge International Dictionary of English. LC 99-11164. (Illus.). 1795p. (C). 1995. pap. text 26.95 (*0-521-48421-9*) Cambridge U Pr.

— The Cambridge International Dictionary of English. LC 99-11164. (Illus.). 1795p. (C). 1995. text 32.95 (*0-521-48236-4*) Cambridge U Pr.

— Longman Dictionary of Contemporary English. (Illus.). 1229p. (C). 1987. pap. text 25.95 (*0-582-84223-9*, 75140) Longman.

Proctor, Paul D. & Shirts, Morris A. Silver Sinners & Saints: A History of Old Silver Reef, Utah. (Illus.). 225p. (Orig.). 1991. text 19.95 (*0-9625042-1-1*); pap. text 17.95 (*0-9625042-2-X*) Paulmar.

Proctor, Paul D., et al. Mineral-Rock Handbook. LC 89-205367. (Illus.). 272p. (Orig.). 1989. lib. bdg. 14.95 (*0-9625042-0-3*) Paulmar.

Proctor, R. W. & Reeve, T. G., eds. Stimulus-Response Compatibility: An Integrated Perspective. (Advances in Psychology Ser.: No. 65). 508p. 1989. 199.00 (*0-444-88092-5*, North Holland) Elsevier.

Proctor, R. W. & Weeks, D. J. The Goal of B. F. Skinner & Behavior Analysis. (Recent Research in Psychology Ser.). (Illus.). ix, 223p. 1991. 39.95 (*0-387-97236-6*) Spr-Verlag.

Proctor, Raymond L. Hitler's Luftwaffe in the Spanish Civil War, 35. LC 83-5526. (Contributions in Military History Ser.: No. 35). (Illus.). 289p. 1983. 45.00 (*0-313-22246-0*, PCC/, Greenwood Pr) Greenwood.

Proctor, Richard, jt. auth. see Hirschman, Robert.

Proctor, Richard, jt. ed. see Pipkin, Bernard.

Proctor, Richard A. Chance & Luck. 263p. 1996. reprint ed. spiral bd. 16.50 (*0-7873-0679-7*) Hlth Research.

— Wages & Wants of Science-Workers. 270p. 1970. reprint ed. 38.00 (*0-7146-1627-3*, Pub. by F Cass Pubs) Intl Spec Bk.

Proctor, Richard M. Principles of Pattern Design. (Illus.). 144p. 1990. pap. 8.95 (*0-486-26349-5*) Dover.

Proctor, Richard M. & Lew, Jennifer F. Surface Design for Fabric. LC 81-7420. (Illus.). 192p. 1984. pap. 24.95 (*0-295-96087-6*) U of Wash Pr.

***Proctor, Rob.** The Cutting Garden: Plants for Gorgeous Bouquets All Year Round. LC 99-28990. (Taylor's Weekend Gardening Guide Ser.). 128p. 2000. pap. 14.00 (*0-395-82945-3*) HM.

Proctor, Rob. Herbs in the Garden: The Art of Intermingling. LC 97-37411. (Illus.). 160p. 1997. 29.95 (*1-883010-25-X*) Interweave.

— Naturalizing Bulbs. LC 97-1972. (Illus.). 256p. 1995. 35.00 (*0-8050-4631-3*) H Holt & Co.

— The Outdoor Potted Bulb. LC 93-6664. (Illus.). 128p. 1993. 20.00 (*0-671-87034-3*) S&S Trade.

Proctor, Rob, photos by. Colorado's Great Gardens: Plains, Mountains & Plateaus. LC 98-15965. (Illus.). 144p. 1998. 14.98 (*1-56579-284-X*) Westcliffe Pubs.

Proctor, Rob, text. Annuals & Bulbs. LC 95-13796. (Successful Organic Gardening Ser.). (Illus.). 160p. 1995. text 24.95 (*0-87596-669-1*) Rodale Pr Inc.

Proctor, Robert. An Index to the Early Printed Books in the British Museum from the Invention of Printing to the Year MDC. 1000p. 1999. reprint ed. 100.00 (*1-57898-136-0*) Martino Pubng.

***Proctor, Robert.** Nazi War on Cancer. (Illus.). 365p. 2000. pap. 16.95 (*0-691-07051-2*) Princeton U Pr.

Proctor, Robert. The Printing of Greek in the Fifteenth Century. (Monographs: No. 8). (Illus.). 222p. 1966. reprint ed. 50.70 (*0-685-66506-2*, 05101254) G Olms Pubs.

Proctor, Robert E. Defining the Humanities. 2nd ed. LC 98-18653. 264p. 1998. pap. 15.95 (*0-253-21219-7*) Ind U Pr.

— Defining the Humanities: How Rediscovering a Tradition Can Improve Our Schools: With a Curriculum for Today's Students. 2nd ed. LC 98-18653. 264p. 1998. 35.00 (*0-253-33421-7*) Ind U Pr.

— Education's Great Amnesia: Reconsidering the Humanities from Petrarch to Freud with a Curriculum for Today's Students. LC 87-46002. 252p. 1988. 32.50 (*0-253-34925-7*) Ind U Pr.

— Herbs in Pots: A Practical Guide to Container Gardening Indoors & Out. LC 99-24679. 1999. 24.95 (*1-883010-52-7*) Interweave.

Proctor, Robert J., ed. The Consumer Privacy Kit: Stop Junk Mail & Unwanted Telephone Calls. 16p. 1998. mass mkt. 3.95 (*0-9665441-0-2*, 125-110) Consumer Resource.

Proctor, Robert N. Cancer Wars: How Politics Shape What We Know & Don't Know about Cancer. (Illus.). 368p. 1996. pap. 17.50 (*0-465-00859-3*, Pub. by Basic) HarpC.

— The Nazi War on Cancer. LC 98-49405. (Illus.). 380p. 1999. 24.95 (*0-691-00196-0*, Pub. by Princeton U Pr) Cal Prin Full Svc.

— Racial Hygiene: Medicine under the Nazis. (Illus.). 496p. 1988. pap. text 18.50 (*0-674-74578-7*) HUP.

— Value-Free Science? Purity & Power in Modern Knowledge. (Illus.). 352p. (C). 1991. 46.50 (*0-674-93170-X*) HUP.

Proctor, Robert W. & Dutta, Addie. Skill Acquisition & Human Performance. (Advanced Psychology Texts Ser.: Vol. 1). 400p. 1994. 58.00 (*0-8039-5010-1*) Sage.

Proctor, Robert W., et al. Human Factors in Simple & Complex Systems. LC 93-10148. 576p. 1993. 102.00 (*0-205-13999-X*) Allyn.

Proctor, Robert W., jt. auth. see Capaldi, E. John.

Proctor, Roscoe. Black Workers & the Class Struggle. 40p. 1972. pap. 0.45 (*0-87898-078-4*) New Outlook.

Proctor, Russell F., 2nd. Communication in Film II: Teaching Communication Courses Using Feature Films. 9th ed. 80p. (C). 1997. pap. text 31.00 (*0-15-505788-X*) Harcourt Coll Pubs.

Proctor, S., jt. auth. see Reed, J.

Proctor, Samuel. Eighteenth Century Florida & Its Borderlands. LC 74-31385. (Illus.). 173p. 1975. reprint ed. pap. 53.70 (*0-8357-6731-0*, 203537300095) Bks Demand.

— Napoleon Bonaparte Broward: Florida's Fighting Democrat. 2nd ed. LC 92-39694. (Florida Sand Dollar Bk.). (Illus.). 416p. 1993. pap. 17.95 (*0-8130-1191-4*) U Press Fla.

Proctor, Samuel, ed. Eighteenth Century Florida & the Revolutionary South. LC 77-23576. (Papers of the Annual Bicentennial Symposium: No. 4). 125p. 1978. 16.95 (*0-8130-0584-1*) U Press Fla.

Proctor, Samuel, ed. see Bicentennial Symposium Staff.

Proctor, Samuel, ed. see Florida Technological University, Bicentennial Sym.

Proctor, Samuel, jt. ed. see Milanich, Jerald T.

Proctor, Samuel, jt. ed. see Milanich, Jerald.

Proctor, Samuel D. Certain Sound of the Trumpet: Crafting a Sermon of Authority. 152p. 1994. pap. 14.00 (*0-8170-1202-8*) Judson.

— How Shall They Hear? Effective Preaching for Vital Faith. 112p. 1992. pap. 12.00 (*0-8170-1172-2*) Judson.

— Samuel Proctor: My Moral Odyssey. 176p. 1989. pap. 14.00 (*0-8170-1151-X*) Judson.

— The Substance of Things Hoped For: A Memoir of African-American Faith. LC 98-54388. 288p. 1999. pap. 18.00 (*0-8170-1325-3*) Judson.

Proctor, Samuel D. & Taylor, Gardner C. We Have This Ministry: The Heart of the Pastor's Vocation. LC 96-34975. 160p. (Orig.). 1996. pap. 15.00 (*0-8170-1248-6*) Judson.

Proctor, Samuel D. & Watley, William D. Sermons from the Black Pulpit. 128p. 1984. pap. 12.00 (*0-8170-1034-3*) Judson.

Proctor, Scot F. Witness of the Light: A Photographic Journey in the Footsteps of the American Prophet, Joseph Smith. LC 91-71335. (Illus.). 208p. 1995. pap. 24.95 (*1-57345-056-1*) Deseret Bk.

Proctor, Scot F. & Proctor, Maurine J., eds. The Revised & Enhanced History of Joseph Smith by His Mother. rev. ed. LC 97-100826. 1996. 21.95 (*1-57008-267-7*) Bookcraft Inc.

Proctor, Scot F., jt. auth. see Proctor, Maurine J.

Proctor-Smith, Marjorie. Praying with Our Eyes Open: Engendering Feminist Liturgical Prayer. LC 95-38861. 256p. 1995. pap. 16.95 (*0-687-39122-9*) Abingdon.

Proctor-Smith, Marjorie & Walton, Janet R., eds. Women at Worship: Interpretations of North American Diversity. 272p. 1993. pap. 20.00 (*0-664-25253-2*) Westminster John Knox.

Proctor, Susan, jt. auth. see Hull, Jonathan.

Proctor, T. Marketing Management: Integrating Theory & Practice. (Illus.). 528p. 1995. pap. 24.99 (*0-412-62350-1*) Thomson Learn.

Proctor, T. & LaTorre, D. R. Calculator Enhancement for Differential Equations: A Manual of Applications Using the HP-48S & HP-28S Calcuators. (Clemson Calculator Enhancement Ser.). 140p. (C). 1992. pap. text 19.00 (*0-03-092730-7*) SCP.

Proctor, T. Gilmer. Differential Equations Using the HP 48 G/GX. (Illus.). 158p. (C). 1995. pap. 15.95 (*1-886801-19-3*) Thomson Learn.

Proctor, Thom, ed. Belwin Master Duets Vol. 1: Flute (Intermediate) 28p. (C). 1986. pap. text 6.95 (*0-7692-1777-X*, EL03240) Wrner Bros.

— Belwin 21st Century Band Method: B Flat Bass Clarinet. 1996. pap. text 5.95 (*1-57623-412-6*, B21105) Wrner Bros.

— Belwin 21st Century Band Method: B Flat Tenor Sax. 1996. pap. text 5.95 (*1-57623-414-2*, B21107) Wrner Bros.

— Belwin 21st Century Band Method: B Flat Trumpet. 1996. pap. text 5.95 (*1-57623-416-9*, B21109) Wrner Bros.

— Belwin 21st Century Band Method: Baritone B. C. 1996. pap. text 5.95 (*1-57623-419-3*, B21112) Wrner Bros.

— Belwin 21st Century Band Method: Baritone T. C. 1996. pap. text 5.95 (*1-57623-420-7*, B21113) Wrner Bros.

— Belwin 21st Century Band Method: Bassoon. 1996. pap. text 5.95 (*1-57623-411-8*, B21103) Wrner Bros.

— Belwin 21st Century Band Method: Clarinet. 1996. pap. text 5.95 (*1-57623-407-X*, B21104) Wrner Bros.

— Belwin 21st Century Band Method: Conductor. 1996. pap. text 49.95 (*1-57623-408-8*, B21100) Wrner Bros.

— Belwin 21st Century Band Method: E Flat Alto Sax. 1996. pap. text 5.95 (*1-57623-413-4*, B21106) Wrner Bros.

— Belwin 21st Century Band Method: E Flat Baritone Sax. 1996. pap. text 5.95 (*1-57623-415-0*) Wrner Bros.

— Belwin 21st Century Band Method: Electric Bass Guitar. 1996. pap. text 5.95 (*1-57623-440-1*, B21117) Wrner Bros.

— Belwin 21st Century Band Method: Flute. 1996. pap. text 5.95 (*1-57623-409-6*, B21101) Wrner Bros.

— Belwin 21st Century Band Method: Guitar. 1996. pap. text 5.95 (*1-57623-441-X*, B21118) Wrner Bros.

— Belwin 21st Century Band Method: Horn in F. 1996. pap. text 5.95 (*1-57623-417-7*, B21110) Wrner Bros.

— Belwin 21st Century Band Method: Keyboard Percussion. 1996. pap. text 5.95 (*1-57623-422-3*, B21115) Wrner Bros.

— Belwin 21st Century Band Method: Oboe. 1996. pap. text 5.95 (*1-57623-410-X*, B21102) Wrner Bros.

— Belwin 21st Century Band Method: Percussion. 1996. pap. text 5.95 (*1-57623-423-1*, B21116) Wrner Bros.

— Belwin 21st Century Band Method: Trombone. 1996. pap. text 5.95 (*1-57623-418-5*, B21111) Wrner Bros.

— Belwin 21st Century Band Method: Tuba. 1996. pap. text 5.95 (*1-57623-421-5*, B21114) Wrner Bros.

— Classic Festival Solos: Baritone (Piano Accompaniment) 40p. (C). 1986. pap. text 6.95 (*0-7692-1773-7*, EL03745) Wrner Bros.

— Classic Festival Solos: Bb Clarinet (Solo Book) 16p. (C). 1992. pap. text 4.95 (*0-7692-1762-1*, EL03724) Wrner Bros.

— Classic Festival Solos: Eb Alto Saxophone (Solo Book) 16p. (C). 1986. pap. text 4.95 (*0-7692-1770-2*, EL03732) Wrner Bros.

— Classic Festival Solos: Eb Baritone Saxophone (Solo Book) 16p. (C). 1986. pap. text 4.95 (*0-7692-1771-0*, EL03736) Wrner Bros.

— Classic Festival Solos: Flute (Solo Book) 16p. (C). 1986. pap. text 4.95 (*0-7692-1769-9*, EL03720) Wrner Bros.

— Classic Festival Solos: Trombone (Piano Accompaniment) 44p. (C). 1986. pap. text 6.95 (*0-7692-1772-9*, EL03743) Wrner Bros.

— Duets for Alto Saxophone Students: Level Two (Intermediate) (Student Instrumental Course Ser.). 16p. (C). 1970. pap. text 4.95 (*0-7692-1764-8*, BIC00235) Wrner Bros.

— First Division Band Method Pt. 1: Alto Clarinet. 36p. (C). 1962. pap. text 5.95 (*0-7692-1606-4*, FDL00005) Wrner Bros.

— First Division Band Method Pt. 1: Baritone B. C. 36p. (C). 1962. pap. text 5.95 (*0-7692-1613-7*, FDL00016); pap. text 5.95 (*0-7692-1612-9*, FDL00017) Wrner Bros.

— First Division Band Method Pt. 1: Baritone Saxophone. 36p. (C). 1962. pap. text 5.95 (*0-7692-1609-9*, FDL00011) Wrner Bros.

— First Division Band Method Pt. 1: Bass Clarinet. 36p. (C). 1962. pap. text 5.95 (*0-7692-1607-2*, FDL00006) Wrner Bros.

— First Division Band Method Pt. 1: Bassoon. 36p. (C). 1962. pap. text 5.95 (*0-7692-1610-2*, FDL00008) Wrner Bros.

— First Division Band Method Pt. 1: F Horn. 36p. (C). 1962. pap. text 5.95 (*0-7692-1611-0*, FDL00013) Wrner Bros.

— First Division Band Method Pt. 1: Tenor Saxophone. 36p. (C). 1962. pap. text 5.95 (*0-7692-1608-0*, FDL00010) Wrner Bros.

— First Division Band Method Pt. 2: Baritone B. C. 36p. (C). 1963. pap. text 5.95 (*0-7692-1617-X*, FDL00108) Wrner Bros.

— First Division Band Method Pt. 2: Baritone T. C. 36p. (C). 1963. pap. text 5.95 (*0-7692-1616-1*, FDL00109) Wrner Bros.

— First Division Band Method Pt. 2: Bass Clarinet. 36p. (C). 1963. pap. text 5.95 (*0-7692-1614-5*, FDL00098) Wrner Bros.

— First Division Band Method Pt. 2: Conductor's Score. 100p. (C). 1963. pap. text 19.95 (*0-7692-1618-8*, FDL00093) Wrner Bros.

— First Division Band Method Pt. 2: Tenor Saxophone. 36p. (C). 1963. pap. text 5.95 (*0-7692-1615-3*, FDL00102) Wrner Bros.

— Flute Solos: Piano Accompaniment, Level One. 40p. (C). 1984. pap. text 6.95 (*0-7692-1767-2*, EL03105) Wrner Bros.

— Solo Sounds for Flute: Piano Accompaniment (Levels 3-5) 40p. (C). 1986. pap. text 6.95 (*0-7692-1765-6*, EL03326) Wrner Bros.

— Treasury of Scales: Alto Clarinet. 12p. (C). 1952. pap. text 4.95 (*0-7692-1597-1*, EL01875) Wrner Bros.

— Treasury of Scales: Baritone B. C. 12p. (C). 1952. pap. text 4.95 (*0-7692-1603-X*, EL01894) Wrner Bros.

— Treasury of Scales: Baritone Saxophone. 12p. (C). 1952. pap. text 4.95 (*0-7692-1600-5*, EL01882) Wrner Bros.

— Treasury of Scales: Baritone T. C. 12p. (C). 1952. pap. text 4.95 (*0-7692-1602-1*, EL01893) Wrner Bros.

— Treasury of Scales: Bass Clarinet. 12p. (C). 1952. pap. text 4.95 (*0-7692-1598-X*, EL01876) Wrner Bros.

— Treasury of Scales: Bassoon. 12p. (C). 1952. pap. text 4.95 (*0-7692-1601-3*, EL01878) Wrner Bros.

— Treasury of Scales: Conductor's Score. 28p. (C). 1952. pap. text 6.95 (*0-7692-1594-7*, EL01868) Wrner Bros.

— Treasury of Scales: Flute. 12p. (C). 1952. pap. text 4.95 (*0-7692-1595-5*, EL01869) Wrner Bros.

— Treasury of Scales: Oboe. 12p. (C). 1952. pap. text 4.95 (*0-7692-1596-3*, EL01877) Wrner Bros.

— Treasury of Scales: Percussion. 12p. (C). 1952. pap. text 4.95 (*0-7692-1605-6*, EL01897) Wrner Bros.

— Treasury of Scales: Tenor Saxophone. 12p. (C). 1952. pap. text 4.95 (*0-7692-1599-8*, EL01881) Wrner Bros.

— Treasury of Scales: Tuba. 12p. (C). 1952. pap. text 4.95 (*0-7692-1604-8*, EL01895) Wrner Bros.

— Trios for Brass Vol. 1: Bass Clef Instruments. 16p. (C). 1986. pap. text 6.50 (*0-7692-1751-6*, EL03278) Wrner Bros.

— Trumpet Solos: Solos Only, Level One. 16p. (C). 1984. pap. text 4.95 (*0-7692-1766-4*, EL03114) Wrner Bros.

— Tunes for Trombone Technic: Level Three (Advanced Intermediate) (Student Instrumental Course Ser.). 32p. (C). 1971. pap. text 5.95 (*0-7692-1763-X*, BIC00358) Wrner Bros.

— 25 16th & 17th Century Dance Tunes & Airs: Bass. 16p. (C). 1959. pap. text 4.50 (*0-7692-1592-0*, EL01383) Wrner Bros.

P

An Asterisk (*) at the beginning of an entry indicates that the title is appearing for the first time.

— 25 16th & 17th Century Dance Tunes & Airs: Cello. 16p. (C). 1959. pap. text 4.50 (*0-7692-1591-2*, EL01382) Wrner Bros.
— 25 16th & 17th Century Dance Tunes & Airs: Conductor's Score. 40p. (C). 1959. pap. text 11.00 (*0-7692-1593-9*, EL01377) Wrner Bros.
— 25 16th & 17th Century Dance Tunes & Airs: Viola. 16p. (C). 1959. pap. text 4.50 (*0-7692-1590-4*, EL01381) Wrner Bros.
— 25 16th & 17th Century Dance Tunes & Airs: Violin 2. 16p. (C). 1959. pap. text 4.50 (*0-7692-1588-2*, EL01379) Wrner Bros.
— 25 16th & 17th Century Dance Tunes & Airs: Violin 3. 16p. (C). 1959. pap. text 4.50 (*0-7692-1589-0*, EL01380) Wrner Bros.
— 25 16th & 17th Century Dance Tunes & Airs: Violin 1. 16p. (C). 1959. pap. text 4.50 (*0-7692-1587-4*, EL01378) Wrner Bros.
Proctor, Thom, ed. see American School Band Directors Association Staff.
Proctor, Thom, ed. see Applebaum, Samuel.
Proctor, Thom, ed. see Bullock, Jack & Maiello, Anthony.
Proctor, Thom, ed. see Erickson, F., et al.
Proctor, Thom, ed. see Farberman, Harold.
Proctor, Thom, ed. see Harris, Brian.
Proctor, Thom, ed. see Hovey, Nilo W.
Proctor, Thom, ed. see Lombardo, Mario.
Proctor, Thom, ed. see Lowry, Robert & Ployhar, James.
Proctor, Thom, ed. see Ryden, William.
Proctor, Thom, ed. see Swearingen, Jim.
Proctor, Thom, ed. see Yaus, Grover C.
Proctor, Thom, ed. see Zepp, George.
Proctor, Thomas E. Building Trades Printreading Pt. 1: Residential Construction. 3rd ed. LC 99-175372. (Illus.). 218p. 1998. 29.96 (*0-8269-0407-6*) Am Technical.
— Building Trades Printreading Pt. 2: Residential & Light Commercial Construction. 2nd ed. LC 96-198928. (Illus.). 370p. 1999. 36.96 (*0-8269-0421-1*) Am Technical.
Proctor, Thomas E. & Gosse, Jonathan F. Printreading for Welders. 2nd ed. LC 97-19353. (Illus.). 348p. 1997. 28.96 (*0-8269-3030-1*) Am Technical.
Proctor, Thomas E. & Mazur, G. A. Troubleshooting Electric Motors. 2nd ed. (Illus.). 299p. 1997. 30.96 (*0-8269-1765-8*) Am Technical.
Proctor, Thomas E. & Mazur, Glen A. Electrical/Electronic Systems. (Illus.). 490p. 1995. text 46.96 (*0-8269-1772-0*) Am Technical.
— Troubleshooting Electrical/Electronic Systems. LC 94-10801. (Illus.). 476p. 1994. pap. text 39.96 (*0-8269-1775-5*) Am Technical.
Proctor, Thomas E. & Rockis, Gary. Residential Wiring. 2nd ed. (Illus.). 260p. 1994. 24.96 (*0-8269-1652-X*) Am Technical.
Proctor, Thomas E., et al. Machine Trades Printreading. LC 95-171166. (Illus.). 298p. 1995. 28.96 (*0-8269-1864-6*) Am Technical.
Proctor, Thomas E., jt. auth. see Mazur, Glen A.
Proctor, Thomas H. The Banker's Dream: A Fiction - an Argument for the Free Coinage of Silver. LC 74-30648. (American Farmers & the Rise of Agribusiness Ser.). 1975. reprint ed. 24.95 (*0-405-06820-4*) Ayer.
***Proctor, Tony.** Creative Problem Solving in Management. LC 98-39630. 1999. write for info. (*0-415-19678-7*); pap. write for info. (*0-415-19679-5*) Routledge.
Proctor, Tony. The Essence of Management Creativity. LC 95-12260. 192p. (C). 1995. pap. text 19.95 (*0-13-356536-X*) P-H.
Proctor, Tony. Essentials of Marketing Research. (Illus.). 360p. 1997. pap. 62.50 (*0-273-62531-4*, Pub. by Pitman Pub) Trans-Atl Phila.
— Essentials of Marketing Research. 2nd ed. LC 00-21895. (Illus.). 400p. 2000. pap. 52.50 (*0-273-64200-6*) F T P H.
— Strategic Marketing: An Introduction. LC 99-87270. 384p. 2000. write for info. (*0-415-20810-6*); pap. write for info. (*0-415-20811-4*) Routledge.
Proctor, W. L. A Genealogy of the Descendants of Robert Proctor of Concord & Chelmsford, Mass., with Notes of Some Connected Families. (Illus.). 315p. 1989. reprint ed. pap. 48.50 (*0-8328-0997-7*); reprint ed. lib. bdg. 56.50 (*0-8328-0996-9*) Higginson Bk Co.
Proctor, Wesley, tr. see Meredith, Howard L. & Milan, Virginia E.
Proctor, Wesley, tr. see Meredith, Howard L. & Sobral, Virginia M., eds.
***Proctor, William.** The Gospel According to the New York Times: How the World's Most Powerful News Organization Shapes Your Mind & Values. 304p. 2000. pap. 14.99 (*0-8054-2347-8*) Broadman.
— Introduction to Bibliographical & Textual Studies. 3rd ed. LC 99-14326. 184p. 1999. text 37.50 (*0-87352-267-2*); pap. text 18.00 (*0-87352-268-0*) Modern Lang.
— The Last Star: A Novel. 288p. 2000. pap. 14.99 (*0-7852-6810-3*) Nelson.
Proctor, William. The Resurrection Report: A Journalist Investigates the Most Debated Event in History. LC 97-33608. 300p. (Orig.). 1998. pap. 13.99 (*0-8054-6372-0*) Broadman.
— The Templeton Touch. 1983. 14.95 (*0-385-18302-X*) Templeton Fnd.
— Terrible Speller. 192p. 1995. pap. 7.95 (*0-688-14229-X*, Wm Morrow) Morrow Avon.
Proctor, William & Minear, Ralph E. Kids' Symptoms: From Birth to Teens. 352p. (Orig.). 1992. pap. 12.50 (*0-380-76228-5*, Avon Bks) Morrow Avon.
Proctor, William, jt. auth. see Benna, Theodore.
Proctor, William, jt. auth. see Benson, Herbert.
Proctor, William, jt. auth. see Boa, Kenneth.
Proctor, William, jt. auth. see Mickey, Paul A.
Proctor, William, jt. auth. see Minear, Ralph E.
Proctor, William, jt. auth. see Podell, Richard N.
Proctor, William, jt. auth. see Robertson, Arthur K.
Proctor, William, jt. auth. see Yoder, Jean.
Procyk, Anna M. Russian Nationalism & Ukraine: The Nationality Policy of the Volunteer Army During the Civil War. xvi, 202p. 1995. 39.95 (*1-895571-04-9*) Ukrainian Acad.
Procyk, Oksana, et al. Famine in the Soviet Ukraine Nineteen Thirty-Two to Nineteen Thirty-Three. (College Library). (Illus.). 116p. 1986. pap. 12.95 (*0-674-29426-2*) HUP.
Proczek, Zygmunt. The Servant of Mary Immaculate: Fr. Casimir Wyszynski. write for info. (*0-944203-27-2*) Marian Pr.
Prodano, Sylvio. Pension Funds: Investment & Performance. (C). 1987. 260.00 (*0-7855-4065-2*, Pub. by Witherby & Co) St Mut.
Prodanov, Vasil & Stoyanova, Maria, eds. Morality & Public Life in a Time of Change No. 1: Bulgarian Philosophical Studies. LC 93-11927. (Cultural Heritage & Contemporary Change Series IVA: Vol. 6). 200p. (Orig.). 1994. pap. 17.50 (*1-56518-055-0*) Coun Res Values.
— Morality & Public Life in a Time of Change No. 1: Bulgarian Philosophical Studies. LC 93-11927. (Cultural Heritage & Contemporary Change Series VI: Foundations of Moral Education,: Vol. IVA,6). 200p. (Orig.). 1994. 45.00 (*1-56518-054-2*) Coun Res Values.
Proddow, Penny & Fasel, Marion. Diamonds: A Century of Spectacular Jewels. LC 96-3548. (Illus.). 192p. 1996. 49.50 (*0-8109-3229-6*, Pub. by Abrams) Time Warner.
Proden, Robert, jt. auth. see Honek, Walter.
***Proder, Jack V.** Fossils: Index of New Information for Reference & Research. rev. ed. 153p. 1999. 47.50 (*0-7883-2146-3*); pap. 44.50 (*0-7883-2147-1*) ABBE Pubs Assn.
Prodger, Mich J. Vintage Flying Helmets: Aviation Headgear Before the Jet Age. LC 94-69862. (Illus.). 336p. 1995. 75.00 (*0-88740-776-5*) Schiffer.
Prodger, Mick J. Luftwaffe vs. RAF: Flying Equipment Of The Air War, 1939-45. LC 97-80324. 144p. 1998. 49.95 (*0-7643-0249-3*) Schiffer.
— Luftwaffe vs. RAF-Flying Clothing of the Air War, 1939-1945, Vol. I. LC 96-70829. (Illus.). 160p. 1997. 49.95 (*0-7643-0234-5*) Schiffer.
Prodger, Phillip. An Annotated Catalogue of the Illustrations of Human & Animal Expression from the Collection of Charles Darwin: An Early Case Use of Photography in Scientific Research. LC 97-53663. (Illus.). 144p. 1997. text 69.95 (*0-7734-8467-1*) E Mellen.
Prodgers, Jeanette. The Only Good Bear Is a Dead Bear. 2nd ed. 224p. 1997. pap. text 9.95 (*1-56044-552-1*) Falcon Pub Inc.
Prodgers, Jeannette, ed. see Smith, Victor G.
Prodhan, Bimal. Multinational Accounting: Segment Disclosure & Risk. (International Accounting Ser.). 320p. 1986. 55.00 (*0-7099-4010-6*, Pub. by C Helm) Routldge.
Prodhan, Bimal, jt. ed. see Prindl, Andreas R.
Prod'homme, J. G. Les Symphonies de Beethoven. 13th ed. LC 76-52485. (Music Reprint Ser.). (FRE., Illus.). 1977. reprint ed. lib. bdg. 55.00 (*0-306-70859-0*) Da Capo.
Prod'homme, J. G., ed. Ecrits de Musiciens. (Music Reprint Ser.). (FRE.). 455p. 1984. reprint ed. lib. bdg. 49.50 (*0-306-76246-3*) Da Capo.
Prod'Homme, Jacques G. Gluck. LC 76-43934. (Music & Theatre in France in the 17th & 18th Centuries Ser.). (FRE.). reprint ed. 49.50 (*0-404-60185-5*) AMS Pr.
— Nicolo Paganini. LC 74-24195. reprint ed. 29.50 (*0-404-13096-8*) AMS Pr.
Prodi, G., et al, eds. Cancer Metastasis: Biological & Biochemical Mechanisms & Clinical Aspects. (Advances in Experimental Medicine & Biology Ser.: Vol. 233). (Illus.). 504p. 1988. 125.00 (*0-306-42907-1*, Plenum Trade) Perseus Pubng.
Prodi, Giovanni, jt. auth. see Ambrosetti, Antonio.
***Prodi, Romano.** Europe as I See It. 2000. 59.95 (*0-7456-2496-0*, Pub. by Polity Pr); pap. 24.95 (*0-7456-2497-9*, Pub. by Polity Pr) Blackwell Pubs.
Prodsky, Joseph, ed. see Khodasevich, Vladislav F.
Product Communication Ltd. Staff. Hotels & Restaurants of Britain 2000: The Essential Guide for the Traveller in Britain for over 70 Years. 72nd ed. (Illus.). 320p. 2000. pap. text 18.95 (*0-7627-0503-5*) Globe Pequot.
Product Design Special Committee Staff. Preparation of Calibration Procedures: RP-3. (NCSL Recommended Practices Ser.). 1990. 15.00 (*0-614-18742-7*) Natl Conf Stds Labs.
Production Consulting & Construction Staff. Americans with Disabilities Act Compliance Evaluation Survey: A Do-It-Yourself Assessment. 237p. 1992. pap. 85.00 (*1-883337-29-1*) Ctr Energy Envir.
Production Systems Staff. Aquaponic Farming. (Illus.). 120p. 1997. text 99.95 (*1-58100-000-6*) Beckley Cardy.
***Productivity Development Staff.** Cellular Manufacturing: One-Piece Flow for Workteams. LC 98-50439. (Illus.). 96p. 1999. pap. 25.00 (*1-56327-213-X*) Productivity Inc.
***Productivity Development Team (Productivity Press) Staff.** Focused Equipment Improvement for TPM Teams: Learning Package. LC 00-20947. (Illus.). 2000. write for info. (*1-56327-230-X*) Productivity Inc.
— Oee for Operators: Overall Equipment Effectiveness. LC 99-34532. 1999. 25.00 (*1-56327-221-0*) Productivity Inc.
— One-Point Lessons: Rapid Transfer of Best Practices to the Shopfloor. LC 00-32336. 2000. write for info. (*1-56327-224-5*) Productivity Inc.
Productivity Point Internation Staff. Certified Microsoft Office User, Frontpage 97 Exam Guide. 1997. 19.99 (*0-7897-1296-2*) Que.
Productivity Point International Staff. Internet Information Server 4 & Index Server Exam Guide. 900p. 1997. 99.99 (*0-7897-1387-X*) Que.
— Microsoft Certified Professional Training Kit for Excel 7. 1100p. 1996. pap. text 99.99 incl. cd-rom (*0-7897-0761-6*) Que.
***Productivity Press Development Team Staff.** 5S for Safety Implementation Toolkit: Facilitator's Guide. LC 00-34158. 2000. write for info. (*1-56327-220-2*) Productivity Inc.
Productivity Press Development Team Staff. Just-in-Time for Operators. LC 97-52252. (Shopfloor Ser.). (Illus.). 85p. 1998. pap. 25.00 (*1-56327-133-8*) Productivity Inc.
— Just-in-Time for Operators Learning Package. (Shopfloor Ser.). (Illus.). 1998. ring bd. 295.00 (*1-56327-134-6*) Productivity Inc.
Productivity Press Staff. T.P.M. Development. 85.00 (*0-915299-46-1*) Productivity Inc.
Productivity Press Staff, jt. auth. see Shingo, Shigeo.
Products Finishing Staff. Electrocoat Conference Proceedings 1992. 246p. 1992. pap. 45.00 (*1-56990-074-4*) Hanser-Gardner.
— Electroless Nickel Conference Proceedings, 1991. 302p. 1991. pap. 45.00 (*0-685-67268-9*) Hanser-Gardner.
— Electroless Nickel Conference Proceedings, 1993. 700p. 1993. pap. 65.00 (*1-56990-075-2*) Hanser-Gardner.
— Pretreat Conference Proceedings, 1990. 347p. 1990. pap. 45.00 (*1-56990-076-0*) Hanser-Gardner.
— Pretreat Conference Proceedings, 1993. 360p. 1993. pap. 45.00 (*1-56990-077-9*) Hanser-Gardner.
— Qualifinish Conference Proceedings, 1993. 405p. 1993. pap. 45.00 (*1-56990-078-7*) Hanser-Gardner.
Proefriedt, William A. How Teachers Learn: Toward a More Liberal Teacher Education. LC 94-8960. 168p. (C). 1994. text 37.00 (*0-8077-3359-8*); pap. text 16.95 (*0-8077-3358-X*) Tchrs Coll.
Proehl, Carl W. The Fourth Marine Division in World War II. (Elite Unit Ser.). (Illus.). 238p. 1988. reprint ed. 49.95 (*0-89839-116-4*) Battery Pr.
Proehl, Geoffrey S. Coming Home Again: American Family Drama & the Figure of the Prodigal. LC 96-13831. 224p. 1997. 36.00 (*0-8386-3547-4*) Fairleigh Dickinson.
Proehl, Jean A. Adult Emergency Nursing Procedures. (Nursing-Health Science Ser.). 619p. (C). 1993. text 57.50 (*0-86720-328-5*) Jones & Bartlett.
— Emergency Nursing Procedure. 2nd ed. Wood, Terri, ed. LC 98-36264. (Illus.). 540p. 1999. text. write for info. (*0-7216-7589-1*, W B Saunders Co) Harcrt Hlth Sci Grp.
Proehl, Jean A. & Jones, Linell M. Mosby's Emergency Department Patient Teaching Guides. LC 97-15759. (Illus.). 128p. (C). (gr. 13). 1997. text 69.95 (*0-8151-3829-6*, 30305) Mosby Inc.
***Proehl, Jean A. & Jones, Linell M.** Mosby's Emergency Department Patient Teaching Guides. (Illus.). 168p. 1998. write for info. (*1-55664-564-3*) Mosby Inc.
Proehl, Karl H. & Shupe, Barbara. Long Island Gazetteer. 370p. 1984. 29.95 (*0-935912-15-0*) LDA Pubs.
Proell, Wayne. High Efficiency Internal Combustion Engines. LC 92-75671. (Illus.). 512p. 1993. text 200.00 (*0-9635505-1-9*) Cloud Hill.
— SuperCarnot Heat Engines. 439p. 1994. text 200.00 (*0-9635505-0-0*) Cloud Hill.
***Proenneke, Richard & Keith, Sam.** One Man's Wilderness: An Alaskan Odyssey. 26th ed. LC 98-27704. 223p. 1999. pap. 14.95 (*0-88240-513-6*, Alaska NW Bks) Gr Arts Ctr Pub.
Proes & Serena. Children of the Sun: The Great Aton Family. 240p. 1987. pap. 8.99 (*0-9639066-1-5*) Crystal Star.
— Eden Isles: A Journey Through Time & Space with Spirit Teachers & Guides. 130p. 1986. pap. 3.95 (*0-9639066-0-7*) Crystal Star.
Proescholdt, Kevin & Rapson, Rip. Troubled Waters: The Fight for the Boundary Waters Canoe Area. LC 95-37239. (Illus.). 333p. (Orig.). 1995. pap. 19.95 (*0-87839-100-2*) North Star.
Proescholdt, Ludwig, jt. ed. see Warnke, Karl.
Proett, Jackie & Gill, Kent. The Writing Process in Action: A Handbook for Teachers. 61p. 1986. teacher ed. 8.95 (*0-8141-5872-2*) NCTE.
Proface, Dom. College Men: Their Making & Unmaking. LC 67-26772. (Essay Index Reprint Ser.). 1977. 20.95 (*0-8369-0803-1*) Ayer.
***Proferes, Nicholas.** Film Directing Fundamentals. (Illus.). 304p. 2001. pap. 29.95 (*0-240-80422-8*, Focal) Buttrwrth-Heinemann.
Professional Books Staff. Assessing Math Problem-Solving Skills. LC 97-197742. 1997. pap. text 14.95 (*0-590-27051-6*) Scholastic Inc.
— Brain-Boosting Math Activities: More Than 50 Great Activities that Reinforce Problem-Solving. (Professional Bks.). 1997. pap. 9.95 (*0-590-06543-2*); pap. 9.95 (*0-590-06544-0*); pap. 9.95 (*0-590-06545-9*); pap. 9.95 (*0-590-06557-2*); pap. 9.95 (*0-590-06558-0*); pap. text 9.95 (*0-590-06546-7*) Scholastic Inc.
***Professional Books Staff.** Johnny Tremaine. (Illus.). 16p. 1999. pap. text 3.95 (*0-590-38930-0*) Scholastic Inc.
Professional Books Staff. Let's Write. LC 97-198078. 1997. pap. text 15.95 (*0-590-93102-4*) Scholastic Inc.
***Professional Books Staff.** Month-by-Month Poetry: September, October & November. 1999. pap. 9.95 (*0-590-37898-8*) Scholastic Inc.
— Penguins: The Hands-on Way to Build Reading Skills!, 1 vol. (Illus.). 4p. 1999. 7.95 (*0-439-04323-9*) Scholastic Inc.
Professional Books Staff. Poem a Day: More Than 200 Cross-Curricular Poems That Teach & Delight. LC 97-198073. 1997. pap. text 14.95 (*0-590-29433-4*) Scholastic Inc.
— 10 Minute Math Mind-Stretchers: Quick Problems & Activities to Help Reinforce Essential Math Skills. (J). 1997. pap. text 14.95 (*0-590-86563-3*) Scholastic Inc.
***Professional Books Staff, ed.** Havest Time: The Hands-On Way to Build Reading Skills. (Illus.). 4p. 1999. pap. 7.95 (*0-439-06157-1*) Scholastic Inc.
Professional Builder & Remodeler Magazine Staff. Custom Creations Inc. 152p. pap. 29.95 (*1-56056-004-5*) Cahners Busn Info.
Professional Communication Univ. Staff. Handbook: A Guide to Effective Spoken & Written Communication. 1993. pap. text 34.00 (*0-7021-3077-X*, Pub. by Juta & Co) Gaunt.
Professional Computer Staff. Templus Multiplan. 1985. 79.95 (*0-13-903048-4*) P-H.
— Templus Supercalculus. 1985. 79.95 (*0-13-903089-1*) P-H.
— Templus Visicalc I. 1985. 79.95 (*0-13-903105-7*) P-H.
Professional Engineer Review Course Staff. Chapman & Hall's Complete Fundamentals of Engineering Exam Review Workbook. LC 97-43131. (Professional Engineer Workbook Ser.). 1070p. 1998. 39.95 (*0-412-14961-3*) Chapman & Hall.
Professional Engineering Associates Inc. Staff, compiled by. Handbook of Underground Storage Tank Safety & Correction Technology. (Science Information Research Center Ser.). 196p. 1988. 78.95 (*0-89116-824-9*) Hemisp Pub.
Professional Ethics Committee of the FBA, contrib. by. Standards for Civility in Professional Conduct, 1998. 10p. 1998. pap. 2.00 (*1-56986-023-8*, ETH-98-10) Federal Bar.
Professional Photographers of America Staff, photos by. Kodak Gallery Award Collection Album. (Illus.). 100p. (Orig.). 1997. pap. 54.95 (*0-9658571-0-7*) Marathon NE.
Professional Picture Framers Assn. Staff. Art Print & Graphics Glossary. LC 85-155639. (Orig.). 1985. pap. 10.00 (*0-88445-017-1*) Prof Picture Frame.
Professional Practice Division Staff. Practice Standards of ASHP, 1997-1998. 424p. 1997. reprint ed. pap. text 38.00 (*1-879907-75-5*, P510) Am Soc Hlth-Syst.
— Practice Standards of ASHP, 1998-1999. rev. ed. 552p. 1998. pap. text 38.00 (*1-879907-87-9*) Am Soc Hlth-Syst.
Professional Publications Editors, ed. How to Become a Professional Engineer. 5th ed. LC 96-33320. 92p. (Orig.). 1996. pap. 19.95 (*0-912045-99-X*) Prof Pubns CA.
Professional Publications Staff. Maine Probate Forms, Issue 5. 30p. 1998. ring bd. 43.00 (*0-327-00525-4*, 8167215) LEXIS Pub.
Professional Registration Committee. Study Guide for the Professional Registration of Mining/Mineral Engineers. (Illus.). 120p. 1996. pap. 25.00 (*0-87335-145-2*, 427-4) SMM&E Inc.
Professional Report Editors & Kirk, John. Incorporating Your Business: The Complete Guide That Tells All You Should Know about Establishing & Operating a Small Corporation. LC 94-46796. 192p. 1986. reprint ed. pap. 14.95 (*0-8092-5902-8*, 59028) NTC Contemp Pub Co.
Professional Resource Group Staff. Closing & Funding Standards & Practices. (Illus.). vii, 161p. 1997. ring bd. 345.00 (*1-929246-06-4*) Schl Mortg Lend.
— Conventional Processing. (Learning System Ser.). (Illus.). xv, 495p. 1998. ring bd. 395.00 (*1-929246-03-X*) Schl Mortg Lend.
— FHA/VA Processing. (Learning System Ser.). (Illus.). xv, 520p. 1998. ring bd. 395.00 (*1-929246-04-8*) Schl Mortg Lend.
— Fundamentals of Mortgage Lending. (Learning System Ser.). (Illus.). xxiii, 679p. 1998. ring bd. 395.00 (*1-929246-01-3*) Schl Mortg Lend.
— Principles of Mortgage Origination. (Learning System Ser.). (Illus.). xviii, 399p. 1999. ring bd. 395.00 (*1-929246-02-1*) Schl Mortg Lend.
— Regulatory Study Guide: Federal Statutes & Washington State Statutes. (Learning System Ser.). (Illus.). xvii, 800p. 1998. ring bd. 395.00 (*1-929246-00-5*) Schl Mortg Lend.
— Underwriting Standards for Mortgage Lending. (Learning System Ser.). (Illus.). xxvi, 437p. 1998. ring bd. 395.00 (*1-929246-05-6*) Schl Mortg Lend.
Professional Resources, Inc. Staff. Preventing Sexual Harassment in the Workplace. 300p. 1994. ring bd. 125.00 (*0-87425-979-7*) HRD Press.
Professional Scholastic. Around-The-Year Mini-Books, 1. 160p. 1999. pap. text 14.95 (*0-590-51308-7*) Scholastic Inc.
Professional Ski Instructors of America, Inc. Staf. The American Teaching System: Snowboard Skiing. LC 92-61802. (Illus.). (Orig.). 1992. pap. 35.90 (*1-882409-01-9*) Prof Ski Instructors.
Professional Symposium on Human Services & Profess. Human Services & Social Work Responsibility: Papers. Richan, Willard C., ed. LC 72-108195. 382p. reprint ed. pap. 118.50 (*0-608-15428-8*, 202927600059) Bks Demand.
Professional Translating Services, Inc. Staff, tr. see Lipcon, Charles R.
Professional Translation Services, Inc. Staff, tr. see Vacca, Marie, ed.
***Professional Truck Driver Institute, Inc. Staff.** Straight Truck Driver: Handbook/Workbook. Klein, William C., ed. LC 97-69110. (Illus.). 500p. 1998. pap. text 35.95 (*0-89262-503-1*) Career Pub.
— Straight Truck Driver: Overhead Masters. Klein, William C., ed. 250p. 1998. teacher ed., ring bd. 139.95 (*0-89262-505-8*) Career Pub.
— Tractor-Trailer Driver: Handbook/Workbook. Martin, Marilyn M., ed. Dzur, Carlos Lopez, tr.Tr. of Camionaje Manual del Camionero de Tractor-Remolques Ubro de Ejercicios. (SPA., Illus.). 850p. 1995. spiral bd., wbk. ed. 49.95 (*0-89262-487-6*) Career Pub.

P

An Asterisk (*) at the beginning of an entry indicates that the title is appearing for the first time.

— Tractor-Trailer Driver: Instructor's Guide. Martin, Marilyn M., ed. Dzur, Carlos Lopez, tr.Tr. of Camionaje Manual del Camionelo de Tractor-Remolques Guias del Instructor. (SPA., Illus.). 850p. 1995. teacher ed., ring bd. 249.95 (*0-89262-488-4*) Career Pub.

— Tractor-Trailer Driver: Overhead Masters. Martin, Marilyn M., ed. Dzur, Carlos Lopez, tr.Tr. of Camionaje Manual del Camionero de Tractor Remolques Diaposiriuas. (SPA., Illus.). 305p. 1995. teacher ed., ring bd. 199.95 (*0-89262-489-2*) Career Pub.

Professional Truck Driving Institute, Inc. Staff. Trucking: Tractor-Trailer Driver Instructor's Guide. Martin, Marilyn M., ed. 600p. 1993. ring bd. 199.95 (*0-89262-501-5*) Career Pub.

— Trucking: Tractor-Trailer Driver Overhead Masters. Martin, Marilyn M., ed. 305p. 1993. teacher ed., ring bd. 149.95 (*0-89262-502-3*) Career Pub.

Professional Truck Driving Institute of America (P. Trucking: Tractor-Trailer Driver Handbook-Workbook. Martin, Marilyn M., ed. LC 92-74427. 600p. 1999. pap. text 39.95 (*0-89262-500-7*) Thomson Learn.

Professional Truth Driver Institute Staff. Straight Truck Driver. Klein, William C., ed. 1999. teacher ed., ring bd. 169.95 (*0-89262-504-X*) Career Pub.

Professional/Scholarly Publishing Division, Electr. Professional & Scholarly Publishing in the Digital Age. Grycz, Czeslaw J., ed. 144p. 1997. per. 25.00 (*0-933636-34-2*) AAP.

***Professor.** The Drunk Dictionary. 134p. 2000. pap. 15.00 (*0-9672965-0-1*) Siole.

Professor, Herausgegeben von, see von Professor, Herausgegeben.

Professor Hooper. Jake the Snake. large type ed. Morisie, Sandy, ed. (Professor Hooper's Library). (Illus.). 24p. (J). (ps-3). 1996. 12.00 (*1-889803-00-6*) Prof Hooper.

Professor Ima Kook. Atomic Physics: Putting Together Atoms & Nuclei. LC 98-96239. (As Dreamed by Itsy Ser.: Vol. 7). 30p. (J). (gr. k-3). 2000. 14.95 (*1-892298-09-0*) Abique.

— Big Bang Theory: The Bang That Created Our Universe. LC 98-96236. (As Dreamed by Itsy Ser.: Vol. 4). (Illus.). 30p. (J). (gr. k-3). 2000. 14.95 (*1-892298-06-6*) Abique.

— Chemical Bonding: 100 Kinds of Atoms Make Everything. LC 98-96237. (As Dreamed by Itsy Ser.: Vol. 6). (Illus.). 26p. (J). (gr. k-3). 2000. 14.95 (*1-892298-07-4*) Abique.

— Einstein's Theory of Relativity: Go Too Fast & Strange Things Happen. LC 98-96239. (As Dreamed by Itsy Ser.: Vol. 8). (Illus.). 32p. (J). (gr. k-3). 2000. 14.95 (*1-892298-10-4*) Abique.

— Kinetic Theory: Gases Are Atoms Shooting About. LC 98-96234. (As Dreamed by Itsy Ser.: Vol. 2). (Illus.). 30p. (J). (gr. k-3). 2000. 14.95 (*1-892298-04-X*) Abique.

— Physics of Liquids & Boiling: Heat Makes Molecules Shake & Liquids Boil. LC 98-96235. (As Dreamed by Itsy Ser.: Vol. 3). (Illus.). 26p. (J). (gr. k-3). 2000. 14.95 (*1-892298-05-8*) Abique.

Professor Jay. Happiness Is . . . A Time to Rhyme: Over 5,000 Lines of Rhyming Verse Bliss. deluxe ed. (Illus.). 200p. (J). (gr. 2-12). 1997. vinyl bd. 26.50 (*1-886197-21-0*) Joy Books.

Professor Solomon. Japan in a Nutshell. unabridged ed. LC 97-147912. (Illus.). 151p. (Orig.). 1997. pap. 9.95 (*0-912509-06-6*) Top Hat.

Profet, Margie. Pregnancy Sickness: Using Your Body's Natural Defenses to Protect Your Baby-to-Be. 1997. pap. 11.00 (*0-614-28115-6*) Addison-Wesley.

— Protecting Your Baby to Be. LC 97-7307. 1997. pap. 10.00 (*0-201-15492-7*) Addison-Wesley.

— Protecting Your Baby-to-Be: Preventing Birth Defects in the First Trimester. LC 95-4873. (Illus.). 168p. 1995. 20.00 (*0-201-40768-X*) Addison-Wesley.

Proffat, John. Treatise on Trial by Jury: Including Questions of Law & Fact, with an Introductory Chapter on the Origin & History of Jury Trial. viii, 608p. 1986. reprint ed. 54.00 (*0-8377-2506-2*, Rothman) W S Hein.

Proffatt, John. Curiosities & Law of Wills. LC 89-85976. xvii, 216p. 1989. reprint ed. lib. bdg. 40.00 (*0-89941-707-8*, 306060) W S Hein.

Proffer, Carl R. Widows of Russia. 1992. pap. 12.00 (*0-679-74262-X*) Vin Bks.

Proffer, Carl R., compiled by. Nineteenth-Century Russian Literature in English: A Bibliography of Criticism & Translations. (Illus.). 260p. 1990. 49.50 (*0-88233-943-5*) Ardis Pubs.

Proffer, Carl R., ed. From Karamzin to Bunin: An Anthology of Russian Short Stories. LC 79-85097. 480p. 1969. pap. 18.95 (*0-253-32506-4*) Ind U Pr.

Proffer, Carl R., et al, eds. Russian Literature of the Twenties: An Anthology. 480p. 1987. 39.50 (*0-88233-820-X*); pap. 22.95 (*0-88233-821-8*) Ardis Pubs.

Proffer, Carl R. & Proffer, Ellendea C., eds. The Barsukov Triangle, the Two-Toned Blonde & Other Stories. LC 84-387. 360p. 1984. 29.50 (*0-88233-805-6*) Ardis Pubs.

Proffer, Carl R., tr. see Bulgakov, Mikhail Afanasevich.

Proffer, Carl R., tr. see Sokolov, Sasha (Aleksandr).

Proffer, Ellendea C., ed. Marina Tsvetaeva: A Pictorial Biography. (Illus.). 1980. pap. 15.95 (*0-88233-359-3*) Ardis Pubs.

— A Pictorial Biography of M. Bulgakov - Fotobiografiia M. Bulgakova. 140p. 1984. pap. 15.00 (*0-88233-813-7*) Ardis Pubs.

Proffer, Ellendea C., ed. see Bulgakov, Mikhail Afanasevich.

Proffer, Ellendea C., jt. ed. see Proffer, Carl R.

Proffer, Ellendea C., tr. see Bulgakov, Mikhail Afanasevich.

Proffit, Brian. OS/2 Warp Survl Kit Pk, Set. 144p. 1995. 19.95 incl. disk (*0-201-40915-1*) Addison-Wesley.

Proffit, Judy. Sunshine for Life's Shadows. (Illus.). 146p. (Orig.). 1997. pap. 9.95 (*1-57090-072-8*, Mountain Chrch) Alexander Dist.

***Proffit, William R. & Fields, Henry W., Jr.** Contemporary Orthodontics. LC 99-24758. (Illus.). 710p. (C). 1999. text. write for info. (*1-55664-553-8*) Mosby Inc.

Proffit, William R., et al. Contemporary Orthodontics. 2nd ed. LC 92-22056. (Illus.). 688p. (C). (gr. 13). 1992. text 81.00 (*0-8016-6393-8*, 06393) Mosby Inc.

Proffitt, Bettina, tr. see Hutchinson, Hanna.

Proffitt, Bettina, tr. see Hutchinson, Hanna, ed.

***Proffitt, Brian.** Staroffice 5.1 Fast & Easy. 2000. pap. 16.99 (*0-7615-2447-9*) Prima Pub.

— Staroffice 5.1 for Linux. 1999. pap. 34.99 (*0-7615-2454-1*) Prima Pub.

— Sun StarOffice 5.1 for Windows. (Illus.). 500p. 2000. pap. 29.99 (*0-7615-2693-5*) Prima Pub.

Proffitt, Brian & Spilker, Kim. Teach Yourself Microsoft Outlook 97 in 24 Hours. LC 96-72165. 432p. 1997. 19.99 (*0-672-31044-9*) Sams.

Proffitt, Brian, jt. auth. see Zupan, Ann.

Proffitt, Edward. The Organized Writer: A Brief Rhetoric. LC 91-36782. 191p. (C). 1992. pap. text 28.95 (*1-55934-118-1*, 1118) Mayfield Pub.

— The Organized Writer: Instructor's Manual. (C). 1992. pap. text, teacher ed. write for info. (*1-55934-129-7*, 1129) Mayfield Pub.

— Reading & Writing about Literature: Fiction, Poetry, Drama, & the Essay. 1030p. (C). 1990. pap. text 46.50 (*0-15-575526-9*, Pub. by Harcourt Coll Pubs); pap. text 3.50 (*0-15-575527-7*) Harcourt Coll Pubs.

— Reading & Writing about Short Fiction. 605p. (C). 1988. pap. text 31.50 (*0-15-575520-X*, Pub. by Harcourt Coll Pubs) Harcourt.

Proffitt, Judith S., jt. auth. see Thompson, Charles A.

Proffitt, Margaret T., jt. auth. see Darden, Mary M.

Proffitt, Mark A. & Yang, Chen-Jui. A Story of Innovation: The Alexian Village Health Center, Milwaukee. (Illus.). xi, 75p. (C). 1995. per. 15.00 (*0-938744-86-0*, R94-5) U of Wis Ctr Arch-Urban.

Proffitt, Michael, ed. Oxford English Dictionary Additions Series, Vol. 3. 418p. (C). 1997. 55.00 (*0-19-860027-5*) OUP.

Proffitt, Nicholas. Gardens of Stone. rev. ed. 446p. 1987. mass mkt. 4.50 (*0-88184-312-1*) Carroll & Graf.

— Homestand. 1999. pap. 24.95 (*0-670-84991-X*) Viking Penguin.

Proffitt, Pamela, ed. Notable Women Scientists. LC 99-35741. 700p. (J). 1999. 85.00 (*0-7876-3900-1*, GML00299-113696, Gale Res Intl) Gale.

Proffitt, Ray, jt. ed. see Glennon, Eric.

Proffitt, T. D., III. Tijuana: The History of a Mexican Metropolis. abr. ed. LC 94-1124. 426p. (C). 1993. pap. text 29.50 (*0-916304-90-6*); lib. bdg. 66.00 (*1-879691-01-9*) SDSU Press.

Profile Corp. Staff. Buckle down! on Ohio Writing: Student Workbook. 88p. 1994. 30.00 (*0-7836-1313-X*, BD21) Buckle Down Publ.

Profile Staff. Advanced Road Transport Telematics Systems. LC 96-116027. 1995. 1960.00 (*1-85617-245-7*, Pub. by Elsvr Adv Tech) Elsevier.

PROFILE Staff. European Market for Electromagnetic Compatability. LC 95-131933. pap. 933.50 (*1-85617-236-8*) Elsevier.

— No Clean Technology: An Assessment of Market & Technological Potential. LC 96-118074. pap. 463.00 (*1-85617-237-6*) Elsevier.

Profile Staff. Profile of the International Technical Textiles Industry. 1996. 630.00 (*1-85617-194-9*, Pergamon Pr) Elsevier.

— Profile of the International Valve Industry. LC 96-115956. 1995. 776.75 (*1-85617-265-1*, Pub. by Elsvr Adv Tech) Elsevier.

Profiles Co. Staff. Buckle down! on American Citizenship: Student Text. 2nd ed. (Illus.). 73p. (YA). (gr. 7-12). 1992. pap. text 30.00 (*0-7836-1302-4*, ST BD01) Buckle Down Publ.

— Buckle down! on American Citizenship: Teacher's Guide. 2nd ed. (Illus.). 73p. 1992. 14.00 (*0-7836-1303-2*, ST BD02) Buckle Down Publ.

— Buckle down on Ohio Mathematics: Student Workbook. (Illus.). 120p. (Orig.). (YA). (gr. 7-12). 1992. 30.00 (*0-7836-1246-X*, ST BD51) Buckle Down Publ.

— Buckle down on Ohio Mathematics: Teacher's Guide. (Illus.). 120p. (Orig.). 1992. 40.00 (*0-7836-1248-6*, ST BD52) Buckle Down Publ.

Profiles Co., Staff. Buckle down! on Ohio Reading: Workbook & Diagnostic Tests. (Illus.). 168p. 1994. 35.00 (*0-7836-1316-4*, BD15) Buckle Down Publ.

Profiles Co. Staff. Inside the SAT. (Illus.). 80p. (YA). (gr. 11-12). 1992. student ed. 15.95 (*0-7836-1306-7*, 2103) Buckle Down Publ.

Profilet, Cynthia. Kamal's Quest. (Illus.). 40p. (J). (gr. 5-6). 1993. 15.95 (*0-9637735-0-X*) Sterling Pr MS.

Profillidis, Vassilios. Railway Engineering. 287p. 1995. pap. text 109.95 (*0-291-39828-6*, TF145, Pub. by Avebury Technical) Random.

Profio, A. Edward. Biomedical Engineering. LC 92-27830. 296p. 1993. 145.00 (*0-471-57768-5*) Wiley.

— Radiation Shielding & Dosimetry. LC 78-15649. (Illus.). 559p. reprint ed. pap. 173.30 (*0-608-18205-2*, 205660900078) Bks Demand.

Profit, Richard. Systemic Safety Management int he Air Traffic Services. 135p. 1998. pap. write for info. (*1-85564-470-3*) Euromoney.

Profit, Vera B. Menschlich: Gesprache Mit Karl Krolow. (Studies in Modern German Literature: Vol. 78). (GER.). 154p. (C). 1996. text 39.95 (*0-8204-2794-2*) P Lang Pubng.

— Ein Portrat Meiner Selbst: Karl Krolow's Autobiographical Poems (1945-1958) & Their French Sources. LC 90-22033. (American University Studies: Germanic Languages & Literature: Ser. I, Vol. 74). 214p. (C). 1991. text 37.95 (*0-8204-0851-4*) P Lang Pubng.

***Profit, W. R., et al.** The Enigma of the Vertical Dimension. McNamara, J. A., Jr., ed. (Craniofacial Growth Ser.: Vol. 36). (Illus.). 310p. 2000. 85.00 (*0-929921-32-1*) UM CHGD.

***Profitlich, Florian.** Berlin Images. (Illus.). 2000. 45.00 (*3-931321-57-6*) Jovis Verlags.

***Profitt, Norma Jean, ed.** Women Survivors, Psychological Trauma & the Politics of Resistance. LC 99-462147. 200p. (C). 2000. 49.95 (*0-7890-0890-4*); pap. text 24.95 (*0-7890-1113-1*) Haworth Pr.

Profor. Initiation to Building & Public Works Vocabulary: Initiation au Vocabulaire du Batiment et des Travaux Publics. (FRE.). 176p. 1979. 65.50 (*0-8288-4812-2*, M6467) Fr & Eur.

Profos, P. Dictionary - Lexicon of Industrial Measurement. (ENG, FRE & GER.). 417p. 1986. spiral bd. 95.00 (*0-8288-7941-9*) Fr & Eur.

Profos, P. & Domeisen. Lex., Dictionary Industrial Measuring Technology. 3rd ed. (GER & ENG.). 251p. 1993. 120.00 (*0-320-03038-5*) Fr & Eur.

Profozich, David M. Managing Change with Business Process Simulation. LC 97-30380. 224p. (C). 1997. 34.95 (*0-13-905837-0*) P-H.

Proft, R. J. & DeMars, Mitch, eds. United States of America's Congressional Medal of Honor Recipients & Their Official Citations. 2nd rev. ed. (Illus.). 1225p. 1999. 44.00 (*0-9644590-1-9*) Highland House.

— United States of America's Congressional Medal of Honor Recipients & Their Official Citations. 3rd rev. ed. LC 95-173588. (Illus.). 1136p. 1997. reprint ed. 44.00 (*0-9644590-0-0*) Highland House.

Profumo, Paola, jt. auth. see Gastaldo, Paola.

***Profy, Vince.** Yardley. (Images of America Ser.). 1999. pap. 18.99 (*0-7385-0072-0*) Arcadia Publng.

Proga. Basic Math. 3rd ed. (Mathematics Ser.). 1991. teacher ed. 24.25 (*0-534-92470-0*) Brooks-Cole.

Proga, Rosanne. Arithmetic & Algebra. 2nd ed. (Math). 650p. (C). 1989. mass mkt. 38.25 (*0-534-91596-5*) PWS Pubs.

— Arithmetic & Algebra. 3rd ed. (Math). 688p. 1992. mass mkt. 48.50 (*0-534-92997-4*) PWS Pubs.

— Arithmetic & Algebra. 4th ed. LC 95-20925. (Mathematics Ser.). 1995. mass mkt. 51.50 (*0-534-94758-1*) PWS Pubs.

— Basic Math. 420p. (C). 1984. mass mkt. 25.50 (*0-87150-452-9*, 3000) PWS Pubs.

Progelhof, Richard C. & Throne, James L. Polymer Engineering Principles: Properties, Processes, & Tests for Design. LC 93-34614. 720p. 1993. 159.00 (*1-56990-150-3*) Hanser-Gardner.

— Polymer Engineering Principles: Properties, Processes, & Tests for Design. LC 93-34614. 720p. (C). 1993. pap. 79.95 (*1-56990-151-1*) Hanser-Gardner.

— Polymer Engineering Principles: Properties, Processes, & Tests for Designs. LC 92-26915. 1993. write for info. (*0-19-520977-X*) OUP.

Proger, Phillip A. & Henry, Brian R. Antitrust Aspects of Mergers & Acquisitions. 2nd ed. (Corporate Practice Ser.: No. 56). 1994. 95.00 (*1-55871-307-7*) BNA.

Proger, Phillip A., et al. Health Care Networks & Managed Care: Antitrust Aspect of Integration & Exclusion. (BNA's Health Law & Business Ser.: No. 2500). 1996. 125.00 (*1-55871-331-X*) BNA.

Progoff, Ira. At a Journal Workshop: Writing to Access the Power of the Unconscious & Evoke Creative Ability. 2nd rev. ed. LC 91-36435. 422p. (Orig.). 1992. pap. 16.95 (*0-87477-638-4*, Tarcher Putnam) Putnam Pub Group.

Progoff, Ira. Life-Study: Experiencing Creative Lives by the Intensive Journal Method. LC 83-72877. 302p. (Orig.). 1983. pap. text 14.95 (*0-87941-012-4*) Dialogue Hse.

Program Committee for the Comittee for Economic De. Prescription for Progress: The Uruguay Round in the New Global Economy: Version of July 7, 1994. LC 94-34588. 1994. 10.00 (*0-87186-118-6*) Comm Econ Dev.

Program for Art on Film Staff. Art on Screen: A Directory of Films & Videos on the Visual Arts. (Illus.). 350p. (C). 1992. 75.00 (*0-8161-7294-3*, G K Hall & Co) Mac Lib Ref.

— Art on Screen: A Directory of Films & Videos on the Visual Arts. (Illus.). 350p. (C). 1992. pap. 45.00 (*0-8161-0538-3*, G K Hall & Co) Mac Lib Ref.

Program of the Lesbian & Gay Community Community S , jt. auth. see Lesbian & Gay Community Services, National Museum.

Program of the Lesbian & Gay Community Services St, jt. auth. see National Museum & Archive of Lesbian & Gay History.

***Program on Energy, the Environment, and the Economy (Aspen Institute).** Uncovering Value: Integrating Environmental & Financial Performance. LC 99-201977. 1998. write for info. (*0-89843-254-5*) The Aspen Inst.

Program Unit on Education & Community Life Ministr, contrib. by. Family Life: Christian Family in Today's World. LC 95-33740. 1995. pap. write for info. (*0-86642-055-X*) Ortho Church Am.

Programming Press Staff & Marchuk, Michael. Building Internet Applications with Visual Basic. LC 95-68633. (Illus.). 480p. (Orig.). 1995. 39.99 (*0-7897-0214-2*) Que.

Progress & Freedom Foundation. The Digital State. 107p. 1998. pap. 30.00 (*0-9659578-3-7*) Progress & Freedom.

Progress in Behavior Modification Staff. Progress in Behavior Modification, Vol. 22. Hersen, Michel et al, eds. LC 75-646720. (Illus.). 286p. reprint ed. pap. 88.70 (*0-608-09793-4*, 206996700022) Bks Demand.

— Progress in Behavior Modification, Vol. 23, 1988. Hersen, Michel et al, eds. LC 75-646720. (Illus.). 230p. reprint ed. pap. 71.30 (*0-608-09794-2*, 206996700023) Bks Demand.

— Progress in Behavior Modification, Vol. 24, 1989. Hersen, Michel et al, eds. LC 75-646720. (Illus.). 260p. reprint ed. pap. 80.60 (*0-608-09795-0*, 206996700024) Bks Demand.

— Progress in Behavior Modification, Vol. 27, 1991. Hersen, Michel et al, eds. LC 75-646720. (Illus.). 168p. reprint ed. pap. 52.10 (*0-608-09798-5*, 206996700027) Bks Demand.

Progress in Behavior Modification Staff. Progress in Behavior Modification, Vol. 25, 1990. Hersen, Michel et al, eds. LC 75-646720. (Illus.). 224p. reprint ed. pap. 69.50 (*0-608-09796-9*, 206996700025) Bks Demand.

— Progress in Behavior Modification, Vol. 26, 1990. Hersen, Michel et al, eds. LC 75-646720. (Illus.). 230p. reprint ed. pap. 71.30 (*0-608-09797-7*, 206996700026) Bks Demand.

Progress in Mathematics Staff. Progress in Mathematics, Vol. 2. Gamkrelidze, R. V., ed. LC 67-27902. (RUS.). 169p. 1968. reprint ed. pap. 52.40 (*0-608-08312-7*, 202630500002) Bks Demand.

Progress in Pesticide Biochemistry & Toxicology St. Progress in Pesticide Biochemistry & Toxicology, Vol. 2. fac. ed. LC 80-41419. (Wiley-Interscience Publications). (Illus.). 238p. pap. 73.80 (*0-7837-7379-X*, 204329500002) Bks Demand.

Progress in Powder Metallurgy Staff. Progress in Powder Metallurgy: Proceedings of the Twenty-Fourth Annual Powder Metallurgy Conference, Chicago, IL, April 22-25, 1968, Vol. 24. LC 79-18458. (Illus.). 96p. reprint ed. pap. 30.00 (*0-7837-1559-5*, 204185100024) Bks Demand.

— Progress in Powder Metallurgy, 1960: Proceedings of the 16th Annual Meeting of the Metal Powder Industries Federation. LC 79-18458. (Progress in Powder Metallurgy Ser.: Vol. 16). (Illus.). 215p. reprint ed. pap. 66.70 (*0-7837-1552-8*, 204184500016) Bks Demand.

Progress Publishers, Moscow Staff, ed. Fundamentals of Soviet Legislation of the U. S. S. R. & the Union Republics. 387p. (C). 1974. 24.95 (*0-8464-0439-7*) Beekman Pubs.

Progressive Diagnostics Staff & Young, Kasey. Wavefile Autopro Software. 465.95 (*0-7668-0773-8*, Pub. by Delmar) Thomson Learn.

Progressive Education Assn. Staff. Social Frontier, 1934 to 1943: A Journal of Educational Criticism & Reconstruction, 5 vols. LC 70-168564. 1971. reprint ed. 217.95 (*0-405-03723-6*) Ayer.

Progressive Staff. Progressive Bengali English Dictionary. 1992. reprint ed. 29.95 (*0-8288-8474-9*) Fr & Eur.

— Progressive English-Bengali Dictionary. 1992. reprint ed. 29.95 (*0-8288-8475-7*) Fr & Eur.

Progris. Go Baroque with That Jazz Feeling. 1990. 6.95 (*0-685-47128-4*, K743) Hansen Ed Mus.

— Go for Baroque with That Jazz Feeling. 1990. 6.95 (*0-685-32165-7*, K742) Hansen Ed Mus.

— The Heart of Dixieland: Tenor Saxophone. 1990. 4.95 (*0-685-32215-7*, B083) Hansen Ed Mus.

— The Heart of Jazz. 1990. 4.95 (*0-685-32173-8*, B137) Hansen Ed Mus.

— The Heart of Jazz: Alto Saxophone. 1990. 4.95 (*0-685-32209-2*, B139) Hansen Ed Mus.

— The Heart of Jazz: Tenor Saxophone. 1990. 4.95 (*0-685-32214-9*, B140) Hansen Ed Mus.

Progris, jt. auth. see Dentato.

Progris, jt. auth. see Lee.

Progris, J. Modern Method for Keyboard, a Study Vol. 1: Supplement. 136p. 1986. per. 10.95 (*0-7935-3901-3*, 50449660) H Leonard.

Progris, James. A Modern Method for Keyboard, 2. 160p. 1986. per. 14.95 (*0-634-01330-0*) H Leonard.

Prohaska, Elizabeth, jt. auth. see Kino Learning Center Staff.

Prohaska, Mark, jt. auth. see Scogin, Forrest.

Prohaska, Wolfgang. The Kunsthistorisches Museum, Vienna: The Paintings Collection. (Illus.). 128p. 1997. 35.00 (*1-85759-124-0*) Scala Books.

Prohaszka, Marianne. Reflections from the Dead: The Metal Finds from the Pantanello Necropolis at Metaponto; a Comprehensive Study of Grave Goods from the 5th to the 3rd Centuries B. C. 2nd ed. (Studies in Mediterranean Archaeology: Vol. CX). (Illus.). 297p. 1995. pap. 87.75 (*91-7081-106-7*, Pub. by P Astroms) Coronet Bks.

Prohias, Antonio. Fifth MAD Report on Spy vs. Spy. 1989. mass mkt. 3.95 (*0-446-35793-6*, Pub. by Warner Bks) Little.

— The Fourth Mad Declassified Papers on Spy vs. Spy. (Illus.). 192p. 1989. mass mkt. 3.95 (*0-446-35797-9*, Pub. by Warner Bks) Little.

— Prohias Spy. 1999. mass mkt. 2.95 (*0-446-34565-2*, Pub. by Warner Bks) Little.

— Third MAD Dossier on Spy vs. Spy. 1989. mass mkt. 3.95 (*0-446-35801-0*, Pub. by Warner Bks) Little.

Prohl, Marga. International Strategies & Techniques for Future Local Government; Practical Aspects Towards I. 1998. pap. text 22.95 (*3-89204-275-6*) Bertelsmann Stiftung.

Prohle, Wilhelm. Vergleichende Syntax der Uralaltaischen (Turanischen) Sprachen. (Bibliotheca Nostratica Ser.: Vol. 4). 229p. 1978. 66.00 (*3-447-02003-2*) Eurolingua.

Prohofsky, Earl. Statistical Mechanics & Stability of Macromolecules: Application to Bond Disruption, Base Pair Separation, Melting, & Drug Dissociation of the DNA Double Helix. (Illus.). 237p. (C). 1995. text 54.95 (*0-521-45184-1*) Cambridge U Pr.

P

Prohorov, Y. V., et al, eds. Probability Theory & Mathematical Statistics: Proceedings of the 4th Vilnius Conference, U. S. S. R., 1985, 2 Vols., Set. 1298p. 1986. lib. bdg. 255.00 (*90-6764-069-7*, Pub. by VSP) Coronet Bks.

Prohorov, Y. V. & Rozanov, J. A. Probability Theory: Basic Concepts, Limit Theorems, Random Processes. Krickeberg, K. & Urmitzer, H., trs. (Grundlehren der Mathematischen Wissenschaften Ser.: Vol. 157). (Illus.). 1969. 75.00 (*0-387-04508-2*) Spr-Verlag.

Prohorov, Y. V. & Sazonov, V. V., eds. Bernoulli Society, U. S. S. R. Proceedings of the First World Congress, 1986, 2 vols. 1690p. 1987. lib. bdg. 387.50 (*90-6764-103-0*, Pub. by VSP) Coronet Bks.

Prohorov, Y. V., ed. see Hannan, E. J., et al.

Prohovnik, I., et al, eds. Vascular Dementia: A Review of Concepts & Ideas. LC 95-45454. 362p. 1996. 234.95 (*0-471-95294-X*) Wiley.

Proietti, Gerald. Xenophon's Sparta: An Introduction. (Mnemosyne, Bibliotheca Classica Batava Ser.: Vol. 98). (Orig.). 1987. pap. 34.50 (*90-04-08338-3*) Brill Academic Pubs.

Proietti, Maria L., ed. Image, Word & Self: Proceedings of the International Symposium on Recent Receptions of Freud on Both Sides of the Atlantic. LC 96-30184. LII, 198p. (C). 1996. text 49.95 (*0-8204-1630-4*) P Lang Pubng.

Proietti, Maurizio, ed. Logic Program Synthesis & Transformation: 5th International Workshop, LOPSTR'95, Utrecht, the Netherlands, September 20-22, 1995: Proceedings. LC 96-10638. (Lecture Notes in Computer Science Ser.: Vol. 1048). x, 267p. 1996. pap. 49.00 (*3-540-60939-3*) Spr-Verlag.

Proimos, James. As a Cat Thinketh. (Illus.). 168p. (Orig.). 1994. pap. 5.95 (*1-56245-089-1*) Great Quotations.

***Proimos, James.** Joe's Wish. LC 97-40837. (Illus.). 32p. (J). (ps-7). 1998. 13.00 (*0-15-201831-X*) Harcourt.

Proimos, James. The Loudness of Sam. LC 98-29884. (Illus.). 32p. (J). (ps-3). 1999. 13.00 (*0-15-202087-X*) Harcourt.

***Proimos, James.** The Many Adventures of Johnny Mutton. LC 00-9219. (Illus.). (J). 2001. write for info. (*0-15-202413-1*) Harcourt.

Prois, Karyn S., jt. auth. see Brown, James I.

Project Adventure Inc. Staff. Adventure in the Classroom. LC 97-218430. 256p. 1996. pap. text, per. 24.00 (*0-7872-2459-6*) Kendall-Hunt.

— Bridges to Accessibility. 144p. 1996. per. 14.00 (*0-8403-7891-2*) Kendall-Hunt.

Project Adventure Inc. Staff, jt. auth. see Fortier.

Project Air Force Desert Shield Assessment Team St. Project Air Force Assessment of Operation Desert Shield: The Buildup of Combat Power. LC 94-7952. 1994. pap. text 13.00 (*0-8330-1521-4*, MR-356-AF) Rand Corp.

Project Air Force Staff, jt. auth. see Ramey, Timothy.

Project Censored Staff. The Progressive Guide to Alternative Media & Activism. LC 98-30137. (Open Media Pamphlet Ser.: No. 8). 128p. 1999. pap. 10.00 (*1-888363-84-3*) Seven Stories.

Project Censored Staff & Jensen, Carl. 20 Years of Censored News. LC 97-24373. (Illus.). 352p. 1997. pap. 16.95 (*1-888363-52-5*) Seven Stories.

Project Censored Staff, jt. auth. see Jensen, Carl.

Project Censored Staff, jt. auth. see Phillips, Peter.

Project Command Staff, jt. auth. see Phillips, Peter.

Project Group on Data Protection Staff, jt. auth. see Council of Europe Staff.

Project Gutenberg Staff. Inaugural Addresses: Presidents of the United States from George Washington to . . . 2004. LC 97-97209. (Illus.). 280p. 1998. pap. 16.95 (*1-888725-07-9*) Sci & Human Pr.

Project Impact Staff. Child Sexual Abuse: Impact & Aftershocks. Freese, Sue, ed. 272p. (Orig.). 1989. pap. 7.00 (*0-9622478-0-4*) Project Impact.

Project Inform Staff & Mitchell, Carolyn B. The HIV Drug Book. rev. ed. LC 99-180938. 704p. 1998. per. 18.00 (*0-671-01490-0*, PB Trade Paper) PB.

Project Management Institute Staff. Experience, Cooperation & the Future: The Global Status of the Project Management Profession. Pennypacker, James S., ed. LC 97-13463. (Illus.). 194p. (Orig.). 1997. pap. 39.95 (*1-880410-04-4*) Proj Mgmt Inst.

***Project Management Institute Staff.** The Fact Book. LC 99-41944. 1999. pap. write for info. (*1-880410-62-1*) Proj Mgmt Inst.

— The Future of Project Management: The First PMI Forecast & Assessment of the Future of the Project Management Profession & the Future of the Project Management Institute. LC 99-35893. 1999. pap. write for info. (*1-880410-71-0*) Proj Mgmt Inst.

Project Management Institute Staff. Project Management: The Next Century: Proceedings of the 28th Annual Project Management Institute Seminars & Symposium, Chicago, IL, September 26-October 2, 1997. LC 97-33556. 1997. pap. 169.95 (*1-880410-33-8*) Proj Mgmt Inst.

***Project Management Institute Staff.** Project Management Experience & Knowledge Self-Assessment Manual. LC 00-27972. 2000. write for info. (*1-880410-24-9*) Proj Mgmt Inst.

Project Management Institute Staff. Project Management Software Survey, 1998. LC 99-230980. 100p. 1998. pap. 249.95 (*1-880410-52-4*) Proj Mgmt Inst.

Project Management Institute Staff, ed. The PMI Book of Project Management Forms. LC 97-27953. 416p. 1997. ring bd. 49.95 (*1-880410-31-1*) Proj Mgmt Inst.

Project Management Institute Staff, jt. auth. see Webster, Francis M.

Project on Disney Staff. Inside the Mouse: Work & Play at Disney World. LC 94-40192. (Post-Contemporary Interventions Ser.). (Illus.). 264p. 1995. text 49.95 (*0-8223-1607-2*); pap. text 16.95 (*0-8223-1624-2*) Duke.

Project on Religion & Human Rights Staff. Religion & Human Rights. 144p. (Orig.). 1994. pap. 10.00 (*1-56432-141-X*) Hum Rts Watch.

Project Open Hand Staff. Comforting Foods. LC 95-11422. 320p. 1995. pap. 25.00 (*0-02-566401-8*) Macmillan.

Project Squid Workshop on Combustion Measurement i. Combustion Measurements: Modern Techniques & Instrumentation Proceedings. Goulard, Robert J., ed. LC 76-25999. 495p. reprint ed. pap. 153.50 (*0-608-10064-1*, 205532600016) Bks Demand.

Project Success Enrichment Staff. Language Arts Manual: Introductory Unit & Bibliography. 152p. 1996. pap. text, spiral bd. 50.00 (*0-7872-2643-2*, 41264301) Kendall-Hunt.

— Language Arts Manual: Literary Analysis Unit. 190p. 1996. pap. text, spiral bd. 40.00 (*0-7872-2644-0*) Kendall-Hunt.

— Language Arts Manual: Short Story Unit. 108p. 1996. pap. text, spiral bd. 40.00 (*0-7872-2645-9*) Kendall-Hunt.

— Training Manual. 116p. 1996. pap. text, spiral bd. 50.00 (*0-7872-2641-6*, 41264101) Kendall-Hunt.

— Visual Art Introductory Unit. 244p. 1996. pap. text, spiral bd. 50.00 (*0-7872-2642-4*) Kendall-Hunt.

Project, Tims. Math Trailblazers: Adventure Book Big Book. 136p. (gr. 3). 1996. student ed., spiral bd. 15.90 (*0-7872-0249-5*) Kendall-Hunt.

Project Zero, Harvard Graduate School of Education. Portfolio Practices: Assessing & Thinking Through Children's Work. 160p. (Orig.). 1997. pap. 16.95 (*0-8106-1858-3*, 1858-3) NEA.

Project 2061 (American Association for the Advancement of Science). Dialogue on Early Childhood Science, Mathematics & Technology Education. LC 99-17184. 1999. write for info. (*0-87168-629-5*) AAAS.

Prokai, L. Field Desorption Mass Spectrometry. (Practical Spectroscopy Ser.: Vol. 9). (Illus.). 304p. 1989. text 160.00 (*0-8247-8303-4*) Dekker.

Prokasy, William F., ed. Classical Conditioning. LC 65-16466. (Century Psychology Ser.). (Illus.). 1965. 32.50 (*0-89197-082-7*) Irvington.

Prokes, Jaroslav, ed. see Zhyvotko, Arkadii.

Prokes, M. Timothy. Women's Challenge: Ministry in the Flesh. 1969. pap. 4.95 (*0-87193-006-4*) Dimension Bks.

Prokes, Mary T. Toward a Theology of the Body. 208p. 1996. pap. text 21.00 (*0-8028-4339-5*) Eerdmans.

Prokes, S. M., et al, eds. Control of Semiconductor Surfaces & Interfaces. LC 97-13302. (Materials Research Society Symposium Proceedings Ser.: No. 448). 505p. 1997. text 62.00 (*1-55899-352-5*) Materials Res.

— Surface/Interface & Stress Effects in Electronic Materials Nanostructures: Materials Research Society Symposium Proceedings. (MRS Symposium Proceedings Ser.: Vol. 405). 546p. 1996. 73.00 (*1-55899-308-8*, 405) Materials Res.

Prokesch-Osten, Anton F. Denkwurdigkeiten und Erinnerungen Aus Dem Orient, 3 vols. lvi, 2080p. reprint ed. write for info. (*0-318-71554-6*) G Olms Pubs.

Prokh, L. Z. Dictionary of Winds. (RUS.). 312p. 1983. 19.95 (*0-8288-1402-3*, M15586) Fr & Eur.

Prokhorenko, V. Y. & Fortov, V. E. Thermophysical Properties & Structure of Molten Metals under Extreme Conditions, Vol. 2. (Thermal Physics Ser.: Vol. 2, Pt. 2). iv, 72p. 1989. pap. text 75.00 (*3-7186-4908-X*) Gordon & Breach.

Prokhoris, Sabine. The Witch's Kitchen: Freud, "Faust" & the Transference. Goshgarian, G. M., tr. 200p. 1995. text 39.95 (*0-8014-3043-7*); pap. text 16.95 (*0-8014-8315-8*) Cornell U Pr.

Prokhorov, A. Soviet Encyclopaedic Dictionary. (RUS.). 1600p. (C). 1981. 160.00 (*0-7855-6470-5*, Pub. by Collets) St Mut.

Prokhorov, A., et al. Coherent Radiation Generation & Particle Accelerators. (Research Trends in Physics Ser.). 528p. 1992. 99.95 (*0-88318-926-7*) Spr-Verlag.

Prokhorov, A. M. Dictionary of Microelectronics: English, Russian, German, French, Dutch. (DUT, ENG, FRE, GER & RUS.). 544p. 1991. 95.00 (*0-7859-1084-0*, 5200006376) Fr & Eur.

Prokhorov, A. M. & Kuz'minov, Yu S. Ferroelectric Crystals for Laser Radiation Control. (Optics & Optoelectronics Ser.). (Illus.). 468p. 1990. 212.00 (*0-7503-0047-7*) IOP Pub.

— Physics & Chemistry of Crystalline Lithium Niobate. (Optics & Optoelectronics Ser.). (Illus.). 392p. 1990. 208.00 (*0-85274-002-6*) IOP Pub.

Prokhorov, A. M., et al. Ferroelectric Thin-Film Waveguides in Integrated Optics & Optoelectronics. 370p. 1995. boxed set 130.00 (*1-898326-10-X*, Pub. by CISP) Balogh.

— Laser Heating of Metals. (Optics & Optoelectronics Ser.). (Illus.). 260p. 1990. 130.00 (*0-7503-0040-X*) IOP Pub.

Prokhorov, Alexander M., ed. Lasers in Synthesis, Characterization & Processing of Diamond, Vol. 3484. LC 99-192241. 250p. 1998. write for info. (*0-8194-2942-2*) SPIE.

***Prokhorov, Alexander M., et al, eds.** Novel Laser Methods in Medicine & Biology. 188p. 1999. pap. text 62.00 (*0-8194-3315-2*) SPIE.

Prokhorov, Alexander M. & Fotakis, Costas, eds. Laser Methods for Biomedical Applications Vol. 2965: ALT '96 International Symposium. 212p. 1996. 59.00 (*0-8194-2369-6*) SPIE.

Prokhorov, B. Frunze, A Guide. (Illus.). 124p. (C). 1984. 40.00 (*0-7855-5204-9*, Pub. by Collets) St Mut.

Prokhorov, Gleb. Art under Socialist Realism: Soviet Painting 1930-1950. (Illus.). 120p. 1995. text 26.00 (*976-8097-83-3*) Gordon & Breach.

Prokhorov, K. I., et al. English-Russian Dictionary of Microelectronics. 2nd rev. ed. (ENG & RUS.). 391p. (C). 1993. pap. 16.95 (*0-8285-5098-0*) Firebird NY.

Prokhorov, V. A., jt. auth. see Rusanov, Anatolii I.

Prokhorov, Y. V. & Shiryaev, A. N., eds. Probability Theory III: Stochastic Calculus. (Encyclopaedia of Mathematical Sciences Ser.: Vol. 45). 262p. 1998. 99.95 (*3-540-54687-1*) Spr-Verlag.

Prokhorov, Y. V. & Skorohod, A. V. Probability Theory IV: Markov Processes. LC 92-27610. (Encyclopedia of Mathematical Sciences Ser.: Vol. 46). 1993. write for info. (*0-387-54688-X*) Spr-Verlag.

Prokhorov, Y. V., jt. ed. see Watanabe, S.

Prokhorov, Yu V., ed. see Bentkus, V., et al.

Prokhovnik, Raia. Rational Woman: A Feminist Critique of Dualism. LC 98-47963. 1999. write for info. (*0-415-14618-6*) Routledge.

— Rhetoric & Philosophy in Hobbes's Leviathan. rev. ed. LC 91-10709. (Political Theory & Political Philosophy Ser.). 268p. 1991. 20.00 (*0-8153-0142-1*) Garland.

Prokhovnik, S. J. Light in Einstein's Universe: The Role of Energy in Cosmology & Relativity. LC 85-14183. 1985. text 138.50 (*90-277-2093-2*) Kluwer Academic.

— The Logic of Special Relativity. LC 67-13854. 142p. reprint ed. pap. 40.50 (*0-608-30418-2*, 2050785) Bks Demand.

Prokofieff, Sergei O. Case of Valentin Tomberg: Anthroposophy or Jesuitism? 1998. pap. 19.95 (*0-904693-85-6*, Pub. by Temple Lodge) Anthroposophic.

— The Cycle of the Seasons & the Seven Liberal Arts. Michell, Richard, tr. (Illus.). 48p. 1995. pap. 9.95 (*0-904693-73-2*, Pub. by Temple Lodge) Anthroposophic.

— The Cycle of the Year As a Path of Initiation: Leading to an Experience of the Christ Being an Esoteric Study of the Festivals. 2nd rev. ed. De Lange, Simon B., tr. from RUS. (Illus.). 496p. 1995. 49.95 (*0-904693-70-8*, Pub. by Temple Lodge) Anthroposophic.

— The East in the Light of the West Pt. 1: Two Eastern Streams of the Twentieth Century in the Light of Christian Esotericism: Agni Yoga. De Lange, Simon B., tr. 176p. 1993. pap. 17.95 (*0-904693-57-0*, 1757, Pub. by Temple Lodge) Anthroposophic.

***Prokofieff, Sergei O.** Encounter with Evil & Its Overcoming Through Spiritual Science. 2000. pap. 19.00 (*1-902636-10-4*) Temple Lodge.

Prokofieff, Sergei O. Eternal Individuality: Towards a Karmic Biography of Novalis. De Lange, Simon B., tr. from RUS. (Illus.). 400p. 1992. 52.50 (*0-904693-39-2*, Pub. by Temple Lodge) Anthroposophic.

— The Heavenly Sophia & the Being Anthroposophia. De Lange, Simon B., tr. from RUS. 312p. 1996. 35.00 (*0-904693-86-4*, Pub. by Temple Lodge) Anthroposophic.

— The Occult Significance of Forgiveness. 3rd ed. De Lange, Simon B., tr. from RUS. 208p. 1995. 31.95 (*0-904693-71-6*, Pub. by Temple Lodge) Anthroposophic.

— Peter & the Wolf. 1994. 22.95 incl. audio (*0-679-86156-4*) Random Hse Chldrns.

— Prophecy of the Russian Epic: How the Holy Mountains Released the Mighty Russian Heroes from Their Rocky Caves. De Lange, Simon B., tr. from RUS. 64p. 1993. pap. 10.95 (*0-904693-49-X*, Pub. by Temple Lodge) Anthroposophic.

— Rudolf Steiner & the Founding of the New Mysteries. 2nd expanded rev. ed. King, Paul & De Lange, Simon B., trs. from RUS. (Illus.). 480p. 1994. 39.95 (*0-904693-61-9*, Pub. by Temple Lodge) Anthroposophic.

— Rudolpf Stainer's Research into Karma & the Mission of the Anthroposophical Society. Michell, Richard, tr. 48p. 1995. pap. 10.95 (*0-904693-69-4*, Pub. by Temple Lodge) Anthroposophic.

— The Spiritual Origins of Eastern Europe & the Future Mysteries of the Holy Grail. De Lange, Simon B., tr. (Illus.). 560p. 1993. 49.95 (*0-904693-55-4*, Pub. by Temple Lodge) Anthroposophic.

— The Twelve Holy Nights & the Spiritual Hierarchies. 2nd ed. De Lange, Simon B., tr. from RUS. 208p. 1993. 29.95 (*0-904693-54-6*, Pub. by Temple Lodge) Anthroposophic.

Prokofiev, Oleg, ed. & tr. see Prokofiev, Sergei.

Prokofiev, S. Complete Piano Sonatas. 296p. 1985. per. 24.95 (*0-7935-2259-5*, 00123085) H Leonard.

— 4 Pieces, Opus 4. 20p. 1985. pap. 4.95 (*0-7935-4014-3*, 00123082) H Leonard.

— Sonata, Opus 94: For Flute or Violin & Piano. 64p. 1985. pap. 10.95 (*0-7935-1343-X*, 00121734) H Leonard.

Prokofiev, Sergei. Classical Symphony, Romeo & Juliet & Other Works in Original Transcriptions for Solo Piano. 224p. pap. 13.95 (*0-486-28551-0*) Dover.

— Complete Piano Sonatas. 288p. pap. 12.95 (*0-486-25689-8*) Dover.

***Prokofiev, Sergei.** Peter & the Wolf. LC 99-18979. (Illus.). 32p. (J). (gr. k-2). 1999. 15.95 (*0-7358-1188-1*, Pub. by North-South Bks NYC) Chronicle Bks.

— Peter & the Wolf. LC 99-18979. (Illus.). 32p. (J). (gr. k-3). 1999. lib. bdg. 15.88 (*0-7358-1189-X*, Pub. by North-South Bks NYC) Chronicle Bks.

Prokofiev, Sergei. Peter & the Wolf. Carlson, Maria, tr. LC 86-3217. (Picture Puffin Ser.). (Illus.). 32p. (J). (ps-3). 1986. pap. 5.99 (*0-14-050633-0*, PuffinBks) Peng Put Young Read.

— Peter & the Wolf. Johnson, Joe, tr. from FRE. (Illus.). 22p. (J). (gr. 4-8). 1998. 15.95 (*1-56163-200-7*) NBM.

— Peter & the Wolf. large type ed. (Illus.). 1993. 9.50 (*0-614-09851-3*, L-34092-00) Am Printing Hse.

— Peter & the Wolf. unabridged ed. Carlson, Maria, tr. (Illus.). (J). (gr. 1-5). 1987. pap. 15.95 incl. audio (*0-87499-073-4*) Live Oak Media.

— Peter & the Wolf, 4 bks., Set. Carlson, Maria, tr. (Illus.). (J). (gr. 1-5). 1987. pap., teacher ed. 33.95 incl. audio (*0-87499-075-0*) Live Oak Media.

Prokofiev, Sergei. Peter & the Wolf & Tubby the Tuba. unabridged ed. (J). (gr. k-5). 1988. audio 14.95 (*0-89845-816-1*, CPN 1623, Caedmon) HarperAudio.

Prokofiev, Sergei. Peter & the Wolf Pop-up-Book. (Illus.). (J). (gr. k-12). 1986. 19.99 (*0-670-80849-0*, Viking Child) Peng Put Young Read.

***Prokofiev, Sergei.** Sarcasms, Visions, Fugitives & Other Short Works for Piano. 2000. pap. 14.95 (*0-486-41091-9*) Dover.

Prokofiev, Sergei. Soviet Diary, 1927 & Other Writings. Prokofiev, Oleg, ed. & tr. by. from RUS. Palmer, Christopher, ed. 290p. 1992. text 45.00 (*1-55553-120-2*) NE U Pr.

Prokofiev, Sergey. Peter & the Wolf. (J). 1986. 10.19 (*0-606-01425-X*, Pub. by Turtleback) Demco.

Prokofiev, Sergey, jt. auth. see Vagin, Vladimir Vasil'evich.

Prokofieva, Rose, tr. see Vigdorova, F.

Prokop, Ales, et al, eds. Bioartificial Organs Vol. 831: Science Medicine, & Technology. LC 97-46923. 1997. 100.00 (*1-57331-098-0*) NY Acad Sci.

Prokop, Ales, et al. Bioartificial Organs Vol. 831: Science, Medicine, & Technology. LC Q11.N5 vol. 831RD13. (Annals of the New York Academy of Sciences Ser.). 1997. pap. 100.00 (*1-57331-099-9*) NY Acad Sci.

Prokop, Dave, ed. The Dart Book. LC 77-85322. (Illus.). 109p. 1978. pap. 4.95 (*0-89037-124-5*) Anderson World.

Prokop, David. Supplements for Athletes: Using Nutritional Supplements to Enchance Athletic Performance, 1. 1998. pap. text 7.95 (*1-58054-029-5*) Woodland UT.

Prokop, Friedrich W. The Future Economic Significance of Large Lowgrade Copper & Nickel Deposits. (Monograph Series on Mineral Deposits: No. 13). (Illus.). viii, 67p. 1975. text 27.00 (*3-443-12013-X*, Pub. by Gebruder Borntraeger) Balogh.

Prokop, Lori. Employee No More: How to Stay Home & Still Make Money. 192p. (Orig.). 1997. pap. 19.97 (*0-9651842-7-7*) Who You Are.

— How I Cured My Allergies to Cats & Dogs & You Can, Too. (Illus.). 100p. (Orig.). 1998. pap. 9.95 (*0-9651842-6-9*) Who You Are.

***Prokop, Lori.** Jesus Teenager: How to Be the Coolest Kid Around. (Illus.). (YA). 2000. pap. 9.95 (*1-929737-00-9*) Who You Are.

— The Result Is Money: The Tax People.Net Phenomenon! 256p. 2000. pap. 19.95 (*1-929737-02-5*) Who You Are.

Prokop, Lori, jt. auth. see Maloney, Dayle.

Prokop, M. S. The Divorce Group Counseling Program. 1996. wbk. ed. 209.95 incl. audio (*0-933879-42-3*) Alegra Hse Pubs.

— Kids' Confidence & Creativity Kit. 1988. 8.95 (*0-933879-33-4*) Alegra Hse Pubs.

Prokop, M. S. Prokop Divorce Adjustment Inventory: Divorce Test for Children. 1986. audio 10.40 (*0-933879-30-X*) Alegra Hse Pubs.

Prokop, Manfred. Learning Strategies for Second Language Users: An Analytical Appraisal with Case Studies. LC 88-39605. (Studies in Education: Vol. 2). 250p. 1989. lib. bdg. 89.95 (*0-88946-937-7*) E Mellen.

Prokop, Marian, ed. see Takehara, Jan C.

Prokop, Mathias, jt. auth. see Galanski, Michael.

Prokop, Michael S. Divorce Happens to the Nicest Kids: A Rational Self-Help Book for Children (3-15), Parents & Counselors. rev. ed. Peters, Robert C., ed. LC 85-72180. (Illus.). 224p. (J). (gr. k-8). 1996. pap. 14.95 (*0-933879-41-5*) Alegra Hse Pubs.

— Kids Divorce Workbook: A Self-Help Book for Kids (3-15) & Adults. Peters, Robert C., ed. LC 85-72180. (Illus.). 96p. (Orig.). (J). (ps-8). 1996. pap., wbk. ed. 6.95 (*0-933879-27-X*) Alegra Hse Pubs.

Prokop, Nora, ed. Kids Only: Snacks. (Illus.). 111p. 1997. pap. 12.99 (*1-896891-14-4*) Companys Coming.

***Prokop, Paul.** The True Story of Santa Claus. LC 00-8967. (Illus.). (J). 2000. pap. write for info. (*0-8198-7406-X*) Pauline Bks.

Prokop, Phyllis S. Two Birds Flying. Goodman, Frances B., ed. (Illus.). 1984. 12.95 (*0-89896-150-5*) Larksdale.

***Prokop, Richard.** Piano Power: A Breakthrough Approach to Improving Your Technique. unabridged ed. Newton, Jean, ed. LC 99-65769. (Illus.). 115p. 1999. pap. 34.95 (*1-929583-00-1*) Greenacres Pr.

— Piano Power Exercises: For Large Hands. unabridged ed. 74p. 1999. pap. 12.95 (*1-929583-03-6*) Greenacres Pr.

— Piano Power Exercises: For Medium Hands. unabridged ed. 74p. 1999. pap. 12.95 (*1-929583-02-8*) Greenacres Pr.

— Piano Power Exercises: For Small Hands. unabridged ed. 74p. 1999. pap. 12.95 (*1-929583-01-X*) Greenacres Pr.

Prokopchak, Mary, jt. auth. see Prokopchak, Steve.

Prokopchak, Steve. Be Angry & Sin Not: Identifying & Dealing with Anger. 48p. 1996. pap. 2.95 (*1-886973-14-8*) Dove Chr Fel.

— Recognizing Emotional Dependency: Identifying & Dealing with Emotionally Dependent Relationships. 32p. 1995. pap. 2.95 (*1-886973-12-1*) Dove Chr Fel.

***Prokopchak, Steve.** Resolving Conflicts in Marriage. 48p. 1999. pap. 2.95 (*1-886973-41-5*) Dove Chr Fel.

Prokopchak, Steve. Thinking Right in a World That Thinks Wrong: Change - How Does It Happen? 40p. 1995. pap. 2.95 (*1-886973-13-X*) Dove Chr Fel.

***Prokopchak, Steve & Prokopchak, Mary.** Called Together: A Marriage Preparation Workbook. rev. ed. 275p. 1999. pap. 12.99 (*0-88965-171-X*, Pub. by Horizon Books) Chr Pubns.

An Asterisk (*) at the beginning of an entry indicates that the title is appearing for the first time.

Prokopchak, Steve & Prokopchak, Mary. Called Together: Building a Foundation for a Christian Marriage. 160p. 1992. pap. text. write for info. (*0-9634951-0-0*) S&M Prokopchak.

Prokopczyk, Czeslaw. Truth & Reality in Marx & Hegel: A Reassessment. LC 80-7976. 144p. 1980. lib. bdg. 22.50 (*0-87023-307-6*) U of Mass Pr.

Prokopczyk, Czeslaw Z., ed. see Schultz, Bruno.

Prokopenko, J., ed. Management Development: A Guide for the Profession. 1998. pap. 40.00 (*92-2-109196-1*) Intl Labour Office.

Prokopenko, Joseph. Productivity Management: A Practical Handbook. xiv, 287p. (Orig.). 1992. pap. 36.00 (*92-2-105901-4*) Intl Labour Office.

Prokopenko, Joseph, ed. Management for Privatization: Lessons from Industry & Public Service. LC 96-145880. (Management Development Ser.: Vol. 32). xiii, 300p. 1995. pap. 33.75 (*92-2-109198-8*) Intl Labour Office.

Prokopenko, Joseph & Pavlin, Igor, eds. Entrepreneurship Development in Public Enterprises. (Management Development Ser.: No. 29). vi, 208p. 1991. pap. 24.75 (*92-2-107286-X*) Intl Labour Office.

Prokopenko, Joseph, jt. auth. see Kubr, Milan.

Prokopetz, Andrew T. Safety in the Chemistry & Biochemistry Laboratory. Picot, Andre et al, eds. Dodd, Robert H., tr. LC 94-38824. 1994. 49.95 (*1-56081-040-8*, Wiley-VCH) Wiley.

Prokopiw, Orysia, ed. see Teliha, Olena.

Prokopp, Maria. Italian Trecento Influence on Murals in East Central Europe, Particularly Hungary. 200p. (C). 1983. text 300.00 (*0-569-08765-1*, Pub. by Collets) St Mut.

Prokopy, Joshua, jt. auth. see Smith, Christian.

Prokosch, Frederic. The Asiatics: A Novel. LC 70-138620. (Illus.). 371p. 1972. reprint ed. lib. bdg. 62.50 (*0-8371-5732-3*, PRAS, Greenwood Pr) Greenwood.

— A Ballad of Love. LC 74-178787. 311p. 1972. reprint ed. lib. bdg. 38.50 (*0-8371-6287-4*, PRBL, Greenwood Pr) Greenwood.

— The Idols of the Cave. LC 78-178788. 373p. 1973. reprint ed. lib. bdg. 38.50 (*0-8371-6289-0*, PRIC, Greenwood Pr) Greenwood.

— Night of the Poor. LC 71-178789. 359p. 1972. reprint ed. lib. bdg. 52.50 (*0-8371-6288-2*, PRNP, Greenwood Pr) Greenwood.

— A Tale for Midnight. LC 76-178790. 354p. 1973. reprint ed. lib. bdg. 38.50 (*0-8371-6281-5*, PRTM, Greenwood Pr) Greenwood.

Prokosch, H. U. & Dudeck, J., eds. Hospital Information Systems: Design & Development Characteristics, Impact & Future Architecture. LC 95-20592. (Medical Artificial Intelligence Ser.: Vol. 2). 414p. 1995. 244.00 (*0-444-82129-5*, R858) Elsevier.

Prokosh, Eric. The Technology of Killing: A Military & Political History of Anti-Personnel Weapons. 256p. (C). 1995. text 59.95 (*1-85649-357-1*, Pub. by Zed Books); text 22.50 (*1-85649-358-X*, Pub. by Zed Books) St Martin.

Proksa, M. Chemia a My (Chemistry & Us) (SLO.). 200p. 1997. pap. 100.00 (*80-08-02455-0*, Pub. by Slov Pegagog Naklad) IBD Ltd.

Proksch, B., jt. auth. see Kaulbach, B.

Proksch, Reinhard, jt. ed. see Campbell, Dennis.

Prokscha, Susanne. Practical Guide to Clinical Data Management. LC 99-21232. 1999. 189.00 (*1-57491-100-7*) Interpharm.

Prokudin, A. V., jt. ed. see Petrov, V. A.

Prokup, Steve, jt. auth. see Harte, Lawrence.

Prokurat, Michael, et al. Historical Dictionary of the Orthodox Church. LC 95-37165. 528p. 1996. 89.00 (*0-8108-3081-7*) Scarecrow.

Prokurat, Michael, tr. see Leskov, Nikolai.

Prol-Ledesma, Rosa M. El Calor de la Tierra. (Ciencia Para Todos Ser.). (SPA.). pap. 6.99 (*968-16-2865-9*, Pub. by Fondo) Continental Bk.

Prolla, Joao C. & Kirsner, Joseph B. Handbook & Atlas of Gastrointestinal Exfoliative Cytology. LC 72-80621. (Illus.). 152p. (C). 1994. lib. bdg. 25.00 (*0-226-68451-2*) U Ch Pr.

Prollop, Rowlan. Using Norton Utilities: Special Edition. 1995. 29.99 incl. cd-rom (*0-7897-0686-5*) Que.

Prolman, Marilyn. The Constitution. LC 94-35657. (Cornerstones to Freedom Ser.). (Illus.). 32p. (J). (gr. 4-7). 1995. lib. bdg. 19.50 (*0-516-06692-7*) Childrens.

— The Constitution. LC 94-35657. (Cornerstones to Freedom Ser.). (Illus.). 32p. (gr. 4-7). 1995. pap. 5.95 (*0-516-46692-5*) Childrens.

Promack, Jennie. Seasons of the Moose. (Illus.). 128p. (Orig.). 1992. pap. 19.95 (*0-87905-455-7*) Gibbs Smith Pub.

Prombaum, Ephraim H., tr. from YID. The Drama of Slavuta by Saul Moiseyevich Ginsburg. 172p. (C). 1991. lib. bdg. 39.00 (*0-8191-8297-4*) U Pr of Amer.

Prometheus Research Library Staff, ed. Guidelines on the Organizational Structure of Communist Parties, on the Methods & Content of Their Work: Prometheus Research Ser., No. 1. 93p. 1993. 5.00 (*0-9633828-3-7*) Spartacist Pub.

— In Memoriam, Richard S. Fraser: An Appreciation & Selection of His Work. 2nd ed. (Prometheus Research Ser.: No. 3). (Illus.). 109p. 1994. 6.00 (*0-9633828-5-3*) Spartacist Pub.

Prometheus Research Library Staff, ed. see Norden, Jan.

***Promey, Sally M.** Painting Religion in Public: John Singer Sargent's Triumph of Religion at the Boston Public Library. LC 99-12158. (Illus.). 376p. 1999. 45.00 (*0-691-01565-1*, Pub. by Princeton U Pr) Cal Prin Full Svc.

Promey, Sally M. Spiritual Spectacles: Vision & Image in Mid-Nineteenth-Century Shakerism. LC 92-19337. (Religion in North America Ser.). 320p. (C). 1993. 37.50 (*0-253-34614-2*) Ind U Pr.

Promey, Sally M., jt. auth. see Morgan, David.

Promis, Jose. The Identity of Hispanoamerica: An Interpretation of Colonial Literature. Kelley, Alita & Kelley, Alec E., trs. from SPA. LC 91-9979. 137p. 1991. 29.95 (*0-8165-1251-5*) U of Ariz Pr.

Promis, Jose & Roman-Lagunas, Jorge, eds. La Prosa Hispanoamericana: Evolucion y Antologia. LC 88-18742. 502p. (Orig.). (C). 1988. lib. bdg. 64.00 (*0-8191-7098-4*) U Pr of Amer.

***Promise Keepers Mens Study Staff.** Biblia de Hombres: Cumplidores de Promesas. (SPA.). 2000. pap. 29.99 (*0-8297-2407-9*) Vida Pubs.

Promise Keepers Speakers Staff. A Life of Integrity: 12 Outstanding Leaders Raise the Standard for Today's Christian Men. Hendricks, Howard, ed. LC 96-40127. 160p. 1997. 14.99 (*1-57673-136-7*, Multnomah Bks) Multnomah Pubs.

Promise Keepers Staff. Biblia de Hombres: Cumplidores de Promesas. 1999. pap. 29.99 (*0-8297-1971-7*) Vida Pubs.

***Promise Keepers Staff.** Biblia de Hombres: Cumplidores de Promesas. 1999. 59.99 (*0-8297-2174-6*) Vida Pubs.

— Biblia de Hombres: Cumplidres de Promesas. 1999. 34.99 (*0-8297-2173-8*) Vida Pubs.

Promise Keepers Staff. Standing Strong: Stories of Changed Lives, 1. (Illus.). 96p. 1999. 12.99 (*0-8499-5501-7*) Word Pub.

Promise, N. T. King James Version Black: Personal Promise. 1995. pap. 2.09 (*0-529-10457-1*) World Publng.

Promislow, Sharon. Making the Brain/Body Connection: A Playful Guide to Releasing Mental, Physical & Emotional Blocks to Success. LC 97-901126. (Illus.). 1998. 15.95 (*0-9681066-2-5*) Kinetic Pub.

***Promislow, Sharon.** Making the Brain/Body Connection: A Playful Guide to Releasing Mental, Physical & Emotional Blocks to Success. 2000. pap. 15.95 (*0-9681066-3-3*) Kinetic Pub.

***Prommel, Harald H.** Two Hearts Talking. Jackson, Donna, ed. (Illus.). 64p. 2000. 14.95 (*0-9626335-9-3*, Pub. by C&G Pub CO) Quality Bks IL.

Promotional Reprint Company Staff. The World Between the Wars. 1938p. 1995. write for info. (*1-57215-090-4*) World Pubns.

***Prompt Publications Staff.** Simplified Digital Signal Processing. LC 97-69159. 127p. 1998. pap. text 29.95 (*0-7906-1136-8*) Prompt Publns.

Pron, Nick. Lethal Marriage. 1996. mass mkt. 5.99 (*0-345-39055-5*) Ballantine Pub Grp.

— Lethal Marriage: The Unspeakable Crimes of Paul Bernardo & Karla Homolka. LC 97-201464. 352p. 1995. pap. 8.99 (*0-7704-2710-3*) Bantam.

Pronay, Andreas. C Marius Victorinus: Liber de Definitionibus. 290p. 1997. 54.95 (*3-631-30757-8*) P Lang Pubng.

Pronay, Nicholas & Taylor, John. Parliamentary Texts of the Later Middle Ages. 1980. 68.00 (*0-19-822368-4*) OUP.

Prone, Terry. Just a Few Words. 182p. 1989. pap. 10.95 (*1-85371-031-8*, Pub. by Poolbeg Pr) Dufour.

— Racing The Moon. 448p. 1997. 25.00 (*1-86023-048-2*, Pub. by Martello Bks) Irish Amer Bk.

— Write & Get Paid for It. 198p. 1989. pap. 9.95 (*1-85371-030-X*, Pub. by Poolbeg Pr) Dufour.

Pronek, Neal. Land Hermit Crabs. (Illus.). 96p. 1989. 9.95 (*0-86622-967-1*, KW-098) TFH Pubns.

— Oscars. 96p. 1972. 11.95 (*0-86622-212-X*, PS-687) TFH Pubns.

— Tropical Fish. LC 98-7568. (Fish Ser.). (Illus.). 64p. (YA). (gr. 3 up). 1999. lib. bdg. 17.95 (*0-7910-5094-7*) Chelsea Hse.

— Tropical Fish. (Illus.). 64p. 1996. pap. 6.95 (*0-7938-0367-5*, RE618) TFH Pubns.

Pronger, Brian. The Arena of Masculinity: Sports, Homosexuality, & the Meaning of Sex. LC 91-29264. (Stonewall Inn Editions Ser.). (Illus.). 320p. 1992. pap. 15.95 (*0-312-06293-1*) St Martin.

— The Arena of Masculinity: Sports, Homosexuality, & the Meaning of Sex. 1992. pap. text 19.95 (*0-8020-7705-6*) U of Toronto Pr.

***Pronic, Ron, ed.** Introduction to Access 2000. (Illus.). 200p. 1999. pap. write for info. (*1-58264-077-7*) ActiveEd.

— Introduction to Outlook 2000. (Illus.). 200p. 1999. pap. 20.00 (*1-58264-079-3*) ActiveEd.

— Introduction to Power Point 2000. (Illus.). 200p. 1999. pap. write for info. (*1-58264-078-5*) ActiveEd.

— Introduction to Word 2000. (Illus.). 200p. 1999. pap. 20.00 (*1-58264-076-9*) ActiveEd.

***Pronilover, Eduard.** Chast Tretya, Pt. 3. Sergeeva, Emilia, ed. LC 99-95151. (RUS.). 104p. 1999. pap. 4.75 (*0-9667160-1-9*) Voice & Friends Pubg.

***Pronilplvcr, Eduard & Sergeeva, Emilia.** Kovcheg (The Ark) LC 98-90682. (RUS., Illus.). 208p. 1999. pap. 12.75 (*0-9667160-0-0*) Voice & Friends Pubg.

Pronin, Alex. Russian Vocabulary Builder, Seven Verbs a Day. (RUS.). 1971. 8.00 (*0-87505-314-9*) Borden.

Pronin, Barbara. Substitute Teaching: A Handbook for Hassle-Free Subbing. 6th ed. (Illus.). 241p. 1983. pap. 12.95 (*0-312-77484-2*) St Martin.

— West Covina: Fulfilling the Promise. 1989. 29.95 (*0-89781-291-3*) Am Historical Pr.

Pronin, P. I. & Obukhov, Yu N., eds. Modern Problems of Theoretical Physics. 360p. (C). 1991. text 101.00 (*981-02-0259-8*) World Scientific Pub.

Pronina, I. A. Decorative Art in the Academy of Arts. (RUS.). 312p. 1983. 60.00 (*0-7855-1584-4*) St Mut.

Pronk, C., tr. see Van Genderen, J.

Pronk, Cornelis, tr. see Bakker, Frans.

Pronk, Fredrika, tr. see Bakker, Frans.

Pronk, Nico & Gorman, Barry. Soccer Everyone. 160p. 1991. pap. text 14.95 (*0-88725-137-4*) Hunter Textbks.

***Pronk, Ron.** Access 2000 Advanced. (Illus.). 200p. 1999. pap. 20.00 (*1-58264-086-6*) ActiveEd.

— Access 2000 Intermediate. (Illus.). 200p. 1999. pap. 20.00 (*1-58264-082-3*) ActiveEd.

— Crystal Reports 7 Advanced. (Illus.). 200p. 1999. pap. 65.00 (*1-58264-084-X*) ActiveEd.

— Excel 2000 Intermediate. (Illus.). 200p. 1999. pap. 20.00 (*1-58264-083-1*) ActiveEd.

— Fundamentals of Visual Basic 6 Programming. (Illus.). 200p. 1999. pap. 95.00 (*1-58264-085-8*) ActiveEd.

— Introduction to Excel 2000. (Illus.). 200p. 1999. pap. 20.00 (*1-58264-080-7*) ActiveEd.

Pronk, Ron. Microsoft Works Version 2.0 IBM PCs & Compatibles: Increasing Your Productivity. 1993. pap. 26.33 (*0-02-800326-8*) Glencoe.

Pronk, Ron. PowerPoint 97 - What's New. 70p. 1997. 20.00 (*1-58264-029-7*) ActiveEd.

— Word 2000 Intermediate. (Illus.). 200p. 1999. pap. 20.00 (*1-58264-081-5*) ActiveEd.

Pronk, Ron, ed. Access 97 - Advanced. (Illus.). 180p. 1997. pap. 20.00 (*1-58264-007-6*, 122) ActiveEd.

— Access 97 - Intermediate. (Illus.). 180p. 1997. pap. 20.00 (*1-58264-002-5*, 116) ActiveEd.

— Access 97 - Introduction. (Illus.). 180p. 1997. pap. 20.00 (*1-58264-067-X*, 111) ActiveEd.

— Access 97 Expert Test Preparation. (Illus.). 120p. 1997. pap. 20.00 (*1-58264-026-2*, 144) ActiveEd.

— Access 97 (MOUS) - Advanced. (Illus.). 180p. 1997. pap. 20.00 (*1-58264-014-9*, 130) ActiveEd.

— Access 97 (MOUS) - Intermediate. (Illus.). 180p. 1997. pap. 20.00 (*1-58264-013-0*, 129) ActiveEd.

— Access 97 (MOUS) - Introduction. (Illus.). 180p. 1997. pap. 20.00 (*1-58264-012-2*, 128) ActiveEd.

— Access 7.0 for Windows 95 - Advanced. (Illus.). 180p. 1996. pap. 20.00 (*1-58264-059-9*, 04) ActiveEd.

— Access 7.0 for Windows 95 - Introduction. (Illus.). 180p. 1996. pap. 20.00 (*1-58264-052-1*, 87) ActiveEd.

— Access 7.0 for Windows 95 - Intermediate. (Illus.). 180p. 1996. pap. 20.00 (*1-58264-053-X*, 88) ActiveEd.

— ACT! 3.0 - Using. (Illus.). 180p. 1997. pap. 20.00 (*1-58264-003-3*, 118) ActiveEd.

— ACT! 2.0 for Windows - Introduction. (Illus.). 180p. 1996. pap. 20.00 (*1-58264-054-8*, 89) ActiveEd.

— Crystal Reports 6.0: Level 1. (Illus.). 200p. 1998. pap. 100.00 (*1-58264-072-6*, 165) ActiveEd.

— Excel 97 - Advanced. (Illus.). 180p. 1997. pap. 20.00 (*1-58264-011-4*, 127) ActiveEd.

— Excel 97 - Advanced. rev. ed. (Illus.). 180p. 1998. pap. 20.00 (*1-58264-040-8*, 159) ActiveEd.

***Pronk, Ron, ed.** Excel 97 - Advanced. rev. ed. (Illus.). 154p. 1998. pap. 20.00i (*1-58264-100-5*) ActiveEd.

Pronk, Ron, ed. Excel 97 - Intermediate. (Illus.). 180p. 1997. pap. 20.00 (*1-58264-001-7*, 117) ActiveEd.

— Excel 97 - Intermediate. rev. ed. (Illus.). 180p. 1997. pap. 20.00 (*1-58264-038-6*, 157) ActiveEd.

— Excel 97 - Introduction. (Illus.). 180p. 1997. pap. 20.00 (*1-58264-064-5*, 105) ActiveEd.

— Excel 97 - Introduction. rev. ed. (Illus.). 180p. 1997. pap. 20.00 (*1-58264-037-8*, 156) ActiveEd.

— Excel 97 - What's New. (Illus.). 180p. 1997. pap. 20.00 (*1-58264-006-8*, 121) ActiveEd.

— Excel 97 Expert Test Preparation. (Illus.). 120p. 1997. pap. 20.00 (*1-58264-023-8*, 141) ActiveEd.

— Excel 97 (MOUS) - Intermediate. (Illus.). 180p. 1997. pap. 20.00 (*1-58264-016-5*, 132) ActiveEd.

— Excel 97 (MOUS) - Introduction. (Illus.). 180p. 1997. pap. 20.00 (*1-58264-015-7*, 131) ActiveEd.

— Excel 97 Proficient Test Preparation. (Illus.). 120p. 1997. pap. 20.00 (*1-58264-022-X*, 140) ActiveEd.

— Excel 7.0 for Windows 95 - Introduction. (Illus.). 180p. 1995. pap. 20.00 (*1-58264-047-5*, 81) ActiveEd.

— Excel 7.0 for Windows 95 - Intermediate. (Illus.). 180p. 1995. pap. 20.00 (*1-58264-050-5*, 83) ActiveEd.

***Pronk, Ron, ed.** Excel 2000 Advanced. (Illus.). 221p. 1999. pap. 20.00i (*1-58264-089-0*) ActiveEd.

Pronk, Ron, ed. FrontPage 98. (Illus.). 200p. 1998. pap. 20.00 (*1-58264-041-6*, 160) ActiveEd.

— GroupWise 5 - Using. (Illus.). 180p. 1997. pap. 20.00 (*1-58264-034-3*, 152) ActiveEd.

***Pronk, Ron, ed.** GroupWise 5.5 - Using. (Illus.). 200p. 1999. pap. 20.00 (*1-58264-075-0*) ActiveEd.

— Introduction to Outlook 98. (Illus.). 190p. 1998. pap. 20.00 (*1-58264-099-8*) ActiveEd.

— Introduction to Outlook 97. (Illus.). 148p. 1997. pap. 20.00i (*1-58264-096-3*) ActiveEd.

— Introduction to Outlook 97 (MOUG Version) (Illus.). 153p. 1997. pap. 20.00i (*1-58264-097-1*) ActiveEd.

— Introduction to Photodraw 2000. (Illus.). 224p. 1999. pap. 25.00i (*1-58264-088-2*) ActiveEd.

— Introduction to Windows 98. (Illus.). 232p. 1998. pap. 20.00i (*1-58264-092-0*) ActiveEd.

Pronk, Ron, ed. Microsoft Exchange 4.0: Introduction. (Illus.). 120p. 1996. pap. 20.00 (*1-58264-010-6*, 85) ActiveEd.

— Microsoft Internet Explorer 4 - Introduction. (Illus.). 180p. 1997. pap. 20.00 (*1-58264-031-9*, 149) ActiveEd.

— Microsoft Office for Windows 95. (Illus.). 180p. 1996. pap. 20.00 (*1-58264-056-4*, 92) ActiveEd.

— Microsoft Office 97 Quick Reference. (Illus.). 130p. 1997. pap. 20.00 (*1-58264-009-2*, 126) ActiveEd.

— Microsoft Publisher 98 - Using. (Illus.). 232p. 1998. pap. 20.00 (*1-58264-071-8*, 168) ActiveEd.

— Netscape Communicator 4. (Illus.). 180p. 1997. pap. 20.00 (*1-58264-030-0*, 148) ActiveEd.

Pronk, Ron, ed. Outlook 97 - Customizing (MOUG Version) (Illus.). 134p. 1997. pap. write for info. (*1-58264-098-X*) ActiveEd.

Pronk, Ron, ed. Outlook 97 Expert Test Preparation. (Illus.). 120p. 1997. pap. 20.00 (*1-58264-028-9*, 146) ActiveEd.

***Pronk, Ron, ed.** Outlook 2000 Intermediate. (Illus.). 2000p. 1999. pap. 20.00i (*1-58264-094-7*) ActiveEd.

Pronk, Ron, ed. Personal Computers - Introduction to Using Windows 95. (Illus.). 180p. 1997. pap. 20.00 (*1-58264-065-3*, 107) ActiveEd.

— PowerPoint 97 - Intermediate. (Illus.). 180p. 1997. pap. 20.00 (*1-58264-004-1*, 119) ActiveEd.

— PowerPoint 97 - Introduction. (Illus.). 180p. 1997. pap. 20.00 (*1-58264-068-8*, 112) ActiveEd.

— PowerPoint 97 - Introduction. rev. ed. (Illus.). 180p. 1997. pap. 20.00 (*1-58264-039-4*, 158) ActiveEd.

— PowerPoint 97 Expert Test Preparation. (Illus.). 120p. 1997. pap. 20.00 (*1-58264-027-0*, 145) ActiveEd.

— PowerPoint 97 (MOUS) - Introduction. (Illus.). 180p. 1997. pap. 20.00 (*1-58264-020-3*, 136) ActiveEd.

— PowerPoint 7.0 for Windows 95 - Introduction. (Illus.). 180p. 1996. pap. 20.00 (*1-58264-049-1*, 84) ActiveEd.

— PowerPoint 7.0 for Windows 95 - Intermediate. (Illus.). 180p. 1996. pap. 20.00 (*1-58264-051-3*, 86) ActiveEd.

***Pronk, Ron, ed.** PowerPoint 2000 - Intermediate. (Illus.). 154p. 1999. pap. 20.00 (*1-58264-101-3*) ActiveEd.

— Project 98 - Intermediate. (Illus.). 220p. 1998. pap. 20.00i (*1-58264-091-2*) ActiveEd.

Pronk, Ron, ed. Project 98 - Introduction. (Illus.). 200p. 1998. pap. 20.00 (*1-58264-042-4*, 163) ActiveEd.

— QuickBooks Pro 4.0 - Introduction. (Illus.). 180p. 1996. pap. 20.00 (*1-58264-057-2*, 93) ActiveEd.

— QuickBooks Pro 5.0 - Using. (Illus.). 180p. 1997. pap. 20.00 (*1-58264-000-9*, 115) ActiveEd.

— QuickBooks 6 - Using. (Illus.). 200p. 1998. pap. 20.00 (*1-58264-074-2*, 174) ActiveEd.

— Quicken 98 - Using. (Illus.). 240p. 1998. pap. 20.00 (*1-58264-070-X*, 164) ActiveEd.

— Upgrading to Windows 95. (Illus.). 180p. 1995. pap. 20.00 (*1-58264-044-0*, 78) ActiveEd.

***Pronk, Ron, ed.** Using ACT! 4.0. (Illus.). 244p. 1998. pap. 20.00i (*1-58264-090-4*) ActiveEd.

Pronk, Ron, ed. What's New in Office 97 - Professional. (Illus.). 200p. 1997. pap. 20.00 (*1-58264-069-6*, 114) ActiveEd.

***Pronk, Ron, ed.** Windows 98 - Intermediate. (Illus.). 200p. 1998. pap. 20.00i (*1-58264-093-9*) ActiveEd.

Pronk, Ron, ed. Windows 95 - Intermediate. (Illus.). 180p. 1995. pap. 20.00 (*1-58264-045-9*, 79) ActiveEd.

— Windows 95 - Introduction. rev. ed. (Illus.). 1998. pap. 20.00 (*1-58264-043-2*, 167) ActiveEd.

— Windows NT 4.0 - Intermediate. (Illus.). 180p. 1996. pap. 20.00 (*1-58264-061-0*, 100) ActiveEd.

— Windows NT 4.0 Introduction. (Illus.). 180p. 1996. pap. 20.00 (*1-58264-060-2*, 98) ActiveEd.

— Word 97 - Advanced. (Illus.). 180p. 1997. pap. 20.00 (*1-58264-008-4*, 123) ActiveEd.

— Word 97 - Intermediate. (Illus.). 180p. 1997. pap. 20.00 (*1-58264-066-1*, 109) ActiveEd.

— Word 97 - Intermediate. rev. ed. (Illus.). 180p. 1997. pap. 20.00 (*1-58264-036-X*, 155) ActiveEd.

— Word 97 - Introduction. (Illus.). 180p. 1997. pap. 20.00 (*1-58264-063-7*, 103) ActiveEd.

— Word 97 - Introduction. rev. ed. (Illus.). 180p. 1997. pap. 20.00 (*1-58264-035-1*, 154) ActiveEd.

— Word 97 - What's New. (Illus.). 180p. 1997. pap. 20.00 (*1-58264-005-X*, 120) ActiveEd.

— Word 97 Expert Test Preparation. (Illus.). 120p. 1997. pap. 20.00 (*1-58264-025-4*, 143) ActiveEd.

— Word 97 (MOUS) - Advanced. (Illus.). 180p. 1997. pap. 20.00 (*1-58264-019-X*, 135) ActiveEd.

— Word 97 (MOUS) - Intermediate. (Illus.). 180p. 1997. pap. 20.00 (*1-58264-018-1*, 134) ActiveEd.

— Word 97 (MOUS) - Introduction. (Illus.). 180p. 1997. pap. 20.00 (*1-58264-017-3*, 133) ActiveEd.

— Word 97 Proficient Test Preparation. (Illus.). 120p. 1997. pap. 20.00 (*1-58264-024-6*, 142) ActiveEd.

— Word 7.0 for Windows 95 - Introduction. (Illus.). 180p. 1995. pap. 20.00 (*1-58264-046-7*, 80) ActiveEd.

— Word 7.0 for Windows 95 - Intermediate. (Illus.). 180p. 1995. pap. 20.00 (*1-58264-048-3*, 82) ActiveEd.

— Word 7.0 for Windows 95 - Advanced. (Illus.). 180p. 1996. pap. 20.00 (*1-58264-055-6*, 90) ActiveEd.

— WordPerfect 8.0 - Intermediate. (Illus.). 180p. 1997. pap. 20.00 (*1-58264-033-5*, 151) ActiveEd.

— WordPerfect 8.0 - Introduction. (Illus.). 180p. 1997. pap. 20.00 (*1-58264-032-7*, 150) ActiveEd.

— WordPerfect 7 for Windows 95 - Introduction. (Illus.). 180p. 1996. pap. 20.00 (*1-58264-058-0*, 97) ActiveEd.

— WordPerfect 7 for Windows 95 - Intermediate. (Illus.). 180p. 1997. pap. 20.00 (*1-58264-062-9*, 102) ActiveEd.

Pronk, Ron, ed. see Palmer, Scott.

Pronko, Evelyn C. & Switzer, Stephen E. Test Taking: Math. 1980. 4.95 (*1-55708-250-2*, R833) McDonald Pub Co.

Pronko, Leonard C. Avant Garde: The Experimental Theater in France. LC 77-26017. (Illus.). 225p. 1978. reprint ed. lib. bdg. 38.50 (*0-313-20096-3*, PRAV, Greenwood Pr) Greenwood.

Pronko, N. H. From AI to Zeitgeist: A Philosophical Guide for the Skeptical Psychologist, 11. LC 87-14921. (Contributions in Psychology Ser.: No. 11). 281p. 1988. lib. bdg. 59.95 (*0-313-25888-0*, PPT/, Greenwood Pr) Greenwood.

Pronks, Ron, ed. PowerPoint 97 (MOUS) - Intermediate. (Illus.). 180p. 1997. pap. 20.00 (*1-58264-021-1*, 137) ActiveEd.

Pronsky, Zaneta M. Food-Medication Interactions. 9th ed. Epstein, Solomon et al, eds. 310p. (C). 1995. pap. text 18.95 (*0-9606164-5-4*) FMI.

— Food-Medication Interactions. 10th rev. ed. Epstein, Solomon et al, eds. 300p. 1997. pap. text 19.95 (*0-9606164-6-2*) FMI.

P

An Asterisk (*) at the beginning of an entry indicates that the title is appearing for the first time.

Pronych, Peter M., jt. auth. see Christen, Arden G.

Pronzato, Allessandro. Meditations on the Sand. (C). 1988. 60.00 (0-85439-218-1, Pub. by St Paul Pubns) St Mut.

Pronzato, L., jt. auth. see Walter, E.

***Pronzato, Luc, et al.** Dynamical Search: Applications of Dynamical Systems in Search & Optimization. LC 99-32954. (Interdisciplinary Statistics Ser.). 240p. 1999. boxed set 69.95 (0-8493-0336-2) CRC Pr.

Pronzini, Bill. Best Western Stories of Bill Pronzini. Greenberg, Martin M., ed. LC 89-21778. (Best Western Stories Ser.). 200p. 1990. 24.95 (0-8040-0932-5) Swallow.

— Best Western Stories of Bill Pronzini. LC 89-21778. (Best Western Stories Ser.). 200p. 1991. pap. 14.95 (0-8040-0933-3) Swallow.

— Blue Lonesome. 240p. 1999. reprint ed. pap. 8.95 (0-8027-7561-6) Walker & Co.

— Boobytrap: A Nameless Detective Mystery. 256p. 1998. 23.00 (0-7867-0505-1) Carroll & Graf.

Pronzini, Bill. Boobytrap: A Nameless Detective Mystery. large type ed. LC 98-31480. Date not set. 30.00 (0-7862-1718-9) Thorndike Pr.

Pronzini, Bill. Carpenter & Quincannon, Professional Detective Services. LC 99-173187. 200p. 1998. pap. 16.00 (1-885941-25-0) Crippen & Landru.

***Pronzini, Bill.** CrazyBone. 208p. 2000. 23.00 (0-7867-0730-5, Pub. by Carroll & Graf) Publishers Group.

Pronzini, Bill. Dead Run. (Mystery Scene Bk.). 194p. 1992. pap. 3.95 (0-88184-838-7) Carroll & Graf.

— Demons. large type ed. 1994. 65.95 (0-7862-9982-7, G K Hall Lrg Type) Mac Lib Ref.

— Epitaphs. large type ed. 372p. 1993. reprint ed. lib. bdg. 19.95 (1-56054-593-3) Thorndike Pr.

— Great Tales of Horror & the Supernatural. 1988. 9.98 (0-88365-699-X) Galahad Bks.

***Pronzini, Bill.** Illusions: A 'Nameless Detective' Novel. 254p. 1999. 26.95 (0-7351-0222-8) Replica Bks.

Pronzini, Bill. Jackpot. large type ed. (General Ser.). 342p. 1991. lib. bdg. 20.95 (0-8161-5037-0, G K Hall Lrg Type) Mac Lib Ref.

— The Jade Figurine. 208p. 1991. pap. 3.95 (0-88184-773-9) Carroll & Graf.

— Masques. 272p. 1999. mass mkt. 4.99 (0-8439-4501-X) Dorchester Pub Co.

***Pronzini, Bill.** Night Freight. 368p. 2000. pap. 5.50 (0-8439-4706-3, Leisure Bks) Dorchester Pub Co.

Pronzini, Bill. Nothing but the Night. LC 98-43720. 272p. 1999. 23.95 (0-8027-3330-1) Walker & Co.

***Pronzini, Bill.** Nothing but the Night. large type ed. 2000. 24.95 (1-57490-266-0, Beeler LP Bks) T T Beeler.

— Nothing but the Night. 272p. 2000. reprint ed. pap. 8.95 (0-8027-7582-9) Walker & Co.

Pronzini, Bill. Sentinels: A "Nameless Detective" Mystery. large type ed. LC 96-29613. 1996. lib. bdg. 23.95 (1-57490-074-9, Beeler LP Bks) T T Beeler.

— Sentinels: A Nameless Detective Novel. 288p. 1996. 20.00 (0-7867-0311-3) Carroll & Graf.

— Six-Gun in Cheek: An Affectionate Guide to the "Worst" in Western Fiction. LC 99-162695. 190p. 1997. pap. 16.00 (0-9628870-2-1) Crossover Pr.

— Six-Gun in Cheek: An Affectionate Guide to the "Worst" in Western Fiction. limited ed. LC 99-162695. 190p. 1997. 50.00 (0-9628870-1-3) Crossover Pr.

***Pronzini, Bill.** Sleuths. LC 98-44598. 1999. 20.95 (0-7862-1702-2, Five Star MI) Mac Lib Ref.

Pronzini, Bill. Snowbound. 256p. 1994. mass mkt. 4.95 (0-7867-0108-0) Carroll & Graf.

— Son of Gun in Cheek. LC 87-7872. 192p. 1988. 9.95 (0-89296-952-0) Mysterious Pr.

— Spadework: A Collection of "Nameless Detective" Stories. LC 97-133603. 192p. 1996. pap. 16.00 (1-885941-07-2) Crippen & Landru.

— Spadework: A Collection of "Nameless Detective" Stories. limited ed. 192p. 1996. 30.00 (1-885941-06-4) Crippen & Landru.

— A Wasteland of Strangers. LC 96-50927. 256p. 1997. 21.95 (0-8027-3301-8) Walker & Co.

— A Wasteland of Strangers. 264p. 1999. reprint ed. pap. 8.95 (0-8027-7560-8) Walker & Co.

— With an Extreme Burning. 304p. 1994. 19.95 (0-7867-0139-0) Carroll & Graf.

— With an Extreme Burning. large type ed. LC 95-7489. 536p. 1995. lib. bdg. 22.95 (0-7862-0460-5) Thorndike Pr.

Pronzini, Bill, ed. Great Tales of Mystery & Suspense. 1994. 9.98 (0-88365-700-7) Galahad Bks.

— Great Tales of the West. 1994. 10.98 (0-88365-702-3) Galahad Bks.

— Riders in the Shadowlands: Western Stories by H. A. Derosso. large type ed. 1999. 20.00 (0-7862-0760-4) Thorndike Pr.

Pronzini, Bill, ed. Wild Westerns. 192p. 1986. 14.95 (0-8027-4066-9) Walker & Co.

Pronzini, Bill & Adrian, Jack, eds. Hardboiled: An Anthology of American Crime Stories. 544p. 1997. reprint ed. pap. 16.95 (0-19-510353-X) OUP.

Pronzini, Bill & Greenberg, Martin H., eds. The Best of the West II: More Stories That Inspired Classic Western Films. 224p. 1990. pap. 3.95 (0-317-02737-9, Sig) NAL.

— Great Modern Police Stories. 192p. 1986. pap. 11.95 (0-8027-7291-9) Walker & Co.

Pronzini, Bill & Lutz, John. The Eye. LC 83-63042. 277p. 1999. 15.45 (0-89296-075-2, Pub. by Mysterious Pr) Little.

— The Eye. 1986. mass mkt. 3.95 (0-445-40294-6, Pub. by Warner Bks) Little.

Pronzini, Bill & Wallman, Jeffrey. Day of the Moon. 192p. 1993. mass mkt. 3.95 (0-88184-976-6) Carroll & Graf.

Pronzini, Bill & Wilcox, Collin. Twospot. 272p. 1993. mass mkt. 4.95 (0-7867-0042-4) Carroll & Graf.

Pronzini, Bill, jt. auth. see Greenberg, Martin Harry.

Pronzini, Bill, jt. auth. see Loomis, Noel M.

Pronzini, Bill, jt. auth. see Muller, Marcia.

Pronzini, Bill, jt. ed. see Adrian, Jack C.

Pronzini, Bill, ed. see Bonham, Frank.

Pronzini, Bill, ed. see Cheshire, Gifford P.

Pronzini, Bill, ed. see DeRosso, H. A.

Pronzini, Bill, ed. see Gorman, Ed.

Pronzini, Bill, ed. see Greenberg, Martin H.

Pronzini, Bill, jt. ed. see Greenberg, Martin Harry.

Pronzini, Bill, jt. ed. see Greenberg, Martin H.

Pronzini, Bill, ed. see Jakes, John.

Pronzini, Bill, ed. see Johnson, Ryerson.

Pronzini, Bill, ed. see Loomis, Noel M.

Pronzini, Bill, jt. ed. see Muller, Marcia.

Pronzini, Bill, ed. see Overholser, Wayne D.

Pronzini, Bill, ed. see Patten, Lewis B.

Pronzini, Bill, ed. see Savage, Les, Jr.

Pronzinni, Bill, jt. auth. see Muller, Marcia.

Proof Theory Symposium Staff. Proof Theory Symposium Keil 1974: Proceedings. Muller, G. H. & Diller, J., eds. (Lecture Notes in Mathematics Ser.: Vol. 500). 1976. 28.95 (0-387-07533-X) Spr-Verlag.

***Proops, Ian.** Logic & Language in Wittgenstein's Tractatus. LC 00-26427. (Studies in Philosophy). 2000. pap. write for info. (0-8153-3793-0) Garland.

Proops, John L., et al. Reducing CO B2 S Emissions: A Comparative Input-Output Study for Germany & the U. K. LC 92-34932. 1993. 97.00 (0-387-55947-7) Spr-Verlag.

Proops, John L., jt. auth. see Faber, Malte.

Proops, John L. R., jt. auth. see Barry, John.

Proost, J., jt. auth. see Van De Fliert, E.

Proost, Stef & Braden, John B., eds. Climate Change, Transport & Environmental Policy: Empirical Applications in a Federal System. LC 97-29927. (New Horizons in Environmental Economics Ser.). 272p. 1998. 90.00 (1-85898-599-4) E Elgar.

Proost, Stef, jt. ed. see Braden, John B.

Proot, Kevin G. Adobe PageMaker 6 for Windows - Illustrated. (Illus.). 384p. 1997. 18.50 (0-7600-3508-3) Course Tech.

— Adobe PageMaker 6 for Macintosh - Illustrated, Incl. instr. resource kit, test mgr., Web pg. (Illustrated Ser.). (Illus.). 384p. 1996. text, mass mkt. 32.95 incl. 3.5 ld (0-7600-3765-5) Course Tech.

— Adobe PageMaker 6 for Windows 95 - Illustrated, Incl. instr. resource kit, test mgr., Web pg. (Illustrated Ser.). (Illus.). 384p. 1996. text, mass mkt. 29.95 incl. 3.5 ld (0-7600-3834-1) Course Tech.

Proot, Kevin G. Adobe Pagemaker 6.5. (Illustrated Ser.). (Illus.). (C). 1997. pap. 34.95 (0-7600-5569-6) Course Tech.

Prop, G., jt. ed. see Parnham, Michael J.

Propecy Study Staff. Marked Reference Prophecy Study Bible: New International Version. 1999. bond lthr. 59.99 (0-310-90864-7) Zondervan.

— Marked Reference Prophecy Study Bible: New International Version, Indexed. 1999. bond lthr. 69.99 (0-310-90865-5) Zondervan.

Proper, C. B. Social Elements in English Prose Fiction Between 1700 & 1832. LC 68-1013. 1970. reprint ed. lib. bdg. 75.00 (0-8383-0612-8) M S G Haskell Hse.

Proper, Datus. Pheasants of the Mind. 154p. 1994. 25.00 (1-885106-07-6) Wild Adven Pr.

— Pheasants of the Mind: A Hunter's Search for a Mythic Bird. limited ed. (Illus.). 166p. 1995. lthr. 95.00 (1-885106-08-4) Wild Adven Pr.

— What the Trout Said: About the Design of Trout Flies & Other Mysteries. rev. ed. (Illus.). 304p. 1989. reprint ed. pap. 16.95 (1-55821-187-X) Lyons Pr.

Proper, Datus C. The Last Old Place: A Search Through Portugal. LC 92-22628. 1993. 22.00 (0-671-78226-6) S&S Trade.

Proper, David R. Lucy Terry Prince: Singer of History. LC 97-65748. (Illus.). 56p. (Orig.). 1997. pap. 5.95 (1-882374-02-9) Pocumtuck Valley Mem.

Proper, Emberson E. Colonial Immigration Laws. LC 04-2636. (Columbia University. Studies in the Social Sciences: No. 31). reprint ed. 31.50 (0-404-51031-0) AMS Pr.

Proper, Ida S. Monhegan, Maine, the Cradle of New England. (Illus.). 275p. 1997. reprint ed. lib. bdg. 35.00 (0-8328-7106-0) Higginson Bk Co.

Proper, Stan. And Justice for All. 24p. (Orig.). (C). 1988. pap. 2.00 (0-9619992-1-7) Walden Sudbury.

— And Justice for All - II. rev. ed. 36p. (Orig.). (C). 1995. pap. 2.00 (0-9619992-2-5) Walden Sudbury.

— And This Is What They Said. (Illus.). 24p. (Orig.). (C). 1988. pap. 2.00 (0-9619992-0-9) Walden Sudbury.

— Dachau: Remembering Europe 1945. 32p. (C). 1995. pap. 2.00 (0-9619992-5-X) Walden Sudbury.

— Love Lyrics. 40p. 1996. pap. 2.00 (0-9619992-7-6) Walden Sudbury.

— Poetry Essays: From Context Journal. 32p. (Orig.). (C). 1995. pap. 2.00 (0-9619992-4-1) Walden Sudbury.

— Portraits: Kith, Kin & Neighbors. 40p. 1998. pap. 5.00 (0-9619992-8-4) Walden Sudbury.

— Ravensbruch Chronicles, 1940-45. (Illus.). 36p. (Orig.). (C). 1995. pap. 2.00 (0-9619992-3-3) Walden Sudbury.

— Views of Spaceship Earth. 1985. 3.00 (0-932593-02-X) Black Bear.

Properce. Elegiae. (Alpha-Omega Ser.: Reihe A, Bd. CLXXXVII). 377p. 1997. 125.00 (3-487-10323-0) G Olms Pubs.

Propert, W. A. The Russian Ballet in Western Europe, 1909-1920. LC 72-86601. (Illus.). 1972. reprint ed. 36.95 (0-405-08865-5, Pub. by Blom Pubns) Ayer.

Propertius. Carmina. xxviii, 413p. 1973. reprint ed. write for info. (3-487-04626-1) G Olms Pubs.

— Die Elegien, Bd. 1: Buch 1 & 2. Rothstein, Max, ed. vi, 500p. 1966. write for info. (3-296-15151-6) G Olms Pubs.

— Die Elegien, Bd. 2: Buch 3 & 4. Rothstein, Max, ed. 418p. 1966. write for info. (3-296-15152-4) G Olms Pubs.

— Elegies, 3 bks. Camps, W. A., ed. 112p. 1977. pap. text 19.95 (0-521-29210-7) Cambridge U Pr.

— The Poems: Translated with Explanatory Notes. Lee, Guy, tr. LC 93-42190. 230p. (C). 1994. text 55.00 (0-19-814497-0, Clarendon Pr) OUP.

— Propertius: Elegies, Bk. IV. Connor, W. R. & Camps, W. A., eds. LC 78-67126. (Latin Texts & Commentaries Ser.). (ENG & LAT.). 1979. reprint ed. lib. bdg. 20.95 (0-405-11597-0) Ayer.

Propes, Steve & Gart, Galen. Los Angeles R&B Groups & Duo's, 1945-1965. 200p. 1998. pap. write for info. (0-936433-18-3) Big Nickel.

Prophecy Study Staff. Marked Reference Prophecy Study Bible. 1999. bond lthr. 59.99 (0-310-92065-5) Zondervan.

— Marked Reference Prophecy Study Bible: Indexed. 1999. bond lthr. 69.99 (0-310-92067-1) Zondervan.

— Marked Reference Prophecy Study Bible: King James Version. 1700p. 1999. bond lthr. 59.99 (0-310-92068-X) Zondervan.

— Marked Reference Prophecy Study Bible: New International Version. 1999. bond lthr. 59.99 (0-310-90863-9) Zondervan.

— Marked Reference Prophecy Study Bible: New International Version, Indexed. 1999. bond lthr. 69.99 (0-310-90866-3) Zondervan.

— Prophecy Study Bible, Supersaver ed. 1999. 19.97 (0-7852-0736-8) Nelson.

— Prophecy Study Bible, Supersaver ed. 1999. 29.97 (0-7852-0107-6) Nelson.

— Prophecy Study Marked Reference. 1999. 69.99 (0-310-92066-3); 79.99 (0-310-92070-1) Zondervan.

Propher, John. The Councillor. (C). 1987. pap. 50.00 (0-7219-0851-9, Pub. by Scientific) St Mut.

Prophet, et al. AFIP Methodos Histotecnologicos. Heffes, Mullick, tr. Orig. Title: AFIP Laboratory Methods in Histotechnology. (SPA., Illus.). 280p. 1995. pap. text 35.00 (1-881041-21-2) Am Registry Path.

Prophet, Elizabeth C. La Ciencia de la Palabra Hablada. 262p. 1991. pap. write for info. (0-318-71307-1) Edic Gran Dir.

— La Ciencia de la Palabra Hablada. Garces, Soledad, tr. from ENG. (SPA.). 262p. 1991. pap. write for info. (1-883482-00-3) Edic Gran Dir.

— Las Ensenanzas Perdidas de Jesus, 4 vols. Garces, Soledad, tr. from ENG. (SPA.). pap. write for info. (1-883482-01-1) Edic Gran Dir.

— Las Ensenanzas Perdidas de Jesus, No. 1. (SPA.). 404p. 1990. pap. write for info. (0-318-71310-1) Edic Gran Dir.

— Las Ensenanzas Perdidas de Jesus, No. 2. 404p. 1990. pap. write for info. (0-318-71309-8) Edic Gran Dir.

— Las Ensenanzas Perdidas de Jesus, No.3. (SPA.). 446p. 1991. pap. write for info. (0-318-71308-X) Edic Gran Dir.

— Las Ensenanzas Perdidas de Jesus, Vol. I. Garces, Soledad, tr. from ENG. (SPA.). 404p. 1990. pap. write for info. (1-883482-02-X) Edic Gran Dir.

— Las Ensenanzas Perdidas de Jesus, Vol. II. Garces, Soledad, tr. from ENG. (SPA.). 404p. 1990. pap. write for info. (1-883482-03-8) Edic Gran Dir.

— Las Ensenanzas Perdidas de Jesus, Vol. III. Garces, Soledad, tr. from ENG. (SPA.). 446p. 1991. pap. write for info. (1-883482-04-6) Edic Gran Dir.

— Quietly Comes the Buddha: Awakening Your Inner Buddha-Nature. 1998. pap. text 9.95 (0-922729-40-9) Summit Univ.

***Prophet, Elizabeth Clare.** Accede al Poder de Tu Yo Superior. (SPA.). 2000. pap. 4.95 (968-19-0580-6) Aguilar.

Prophet, Elizabeth Clare. Access the Power of Your Higher Self. 1998. pap. 4.95 (0-922729-36-0) Summit Univ.

***Prophet, Elizabeth Clare.** Art of Practical Spirituality: How to Bring More Passion, Creativity & Balance into Everyday Life. (Pocket Guides to Practical Spirituality Ser.). 2000. pap. 5.95 (0-922729-55-7) Summit Univ.

— Como Trabajar Con los Angeles. (SPA.). 2000. pap. 4.95 (968-19-0516-4) Aguilar.

Prophet, Elizabeth Clare. Creative Power of Sound: Affirmations to Create, Heal & Transform. 1998. pap. 4.95 (0-922729-42-5) Summit Univ.

***Prophet, Elizabeth Clare.** Fallen Angels & Orgins of Evil. 2000. pap. text 7.99 (0-922729-43-3) Summit Univ.

Prophet, Elizabeth Clare. How to Work with Angels. 1998. pap. 4.95 (0-922729-41-7) Summit Univ.

***Prophet, Elizabeth Clare.** Llama Violeta: Para Sanar Cuerpo, Mente y Alma. (SPA.). 2000. pap. 4.95 (968-19-0565-2) Aguilar.

Prophet, Elizabeth Clare. Nurturing Your Baby's Soul: A Spiritual Guide for Expectant Parents. LC 98-60410. 1998. pap. 12.95 (0-922729-39-5) Summit Univ.

***Prophet, Elizabeth Clare.** The Path of Self-Transformation. 2000. pap. 7.99 (0-922729-54-9) Summit Univ.

— El Poder Creativo del Sonido. (SPA.). 2000. pap. 4.95 (968-19-0581-4) Aguilar.

— Profecias de Saint Germain Para el Nuevo Milenio. (SPA.). 2000. pap. 12.95 (968-19-0605-5) Aguilar.

Prophet, Elizabeth Clare. Saint Germain's Prophecy for the New Millennium: A Spiritual Approach to Self-Discovery & Soul. 1999. pap. 7.99 (0-922729-45-X) Summit Univ.

— Soul Mates & Twin Flames: The Spiritual Dimension of Love & Relationships. 1999. pap. text 5.95 (0-922729-48-4) Summit Univ.

— Violet Flame to Heal the Body, Mind & Soul. 1998. pap. 4.95 (0-922729-37-9) Summit Univ.

***Prophet, Elizabeth Clare.** Your Seven Energy Centers: A Holistic Approach to Physical, Emotional & Spiritual Vitality. (Pocket Guides to Practical Spirituality Ser.). 2000. pap. 6.95 (0-922729-56-5) Summit Univ.

Prophet, John, ed. Fair Rents. (C). 1985. pap. 100.00 (0-7219-0702-4, Pub. by Scientific) St Mut.

***Prophet, Mark L.** Foundations of The Path. 1999. 14.95 (0-922729-53-0) Summit Univ.

Prophet of Islam. Letters of the Holy Prophet. Qureshi, Ahmed, tr. 125p. (Orig.). 1985. pap. 7.50 (1-56744-323-0) Kazi Pubns.

Prophet, Sue. Health Information Management Compliance: A Model Program for Healthcare Organizations. (Illus.). 86p. 1998. pap. text 40.00 (1-58426-012-2, AB102198) Am Hlth Info.

Prophit, Penny, jt. auth. see Long, Lynette.

Prophyrius. On the Methodology of Architectural History. 1982. pap. 14.95 (0-312-53149-4) St Martin.

Propp, James, jt. ed. see Aldous, David J.

Propp, Karen. The Pregancy Project: Encounters with Reproductive Therapy. LC 99-6058. (Emerging Writers in Creative Nonfiction Ser.). 175p. 1999. 24.95 (0-8207-0302-8) Duquesne.

Propp, Vera W. When the Soldiers Were Gone. LC 97-50169. 112p. (YA). (gr. 5 up). 1999. 14.99 (0-399-23325-3) Putnam Pub Group.

Propp, Vladimir. Morphology of the Folktale. 2nd ed. Wagner, Louis A., ed. Scott, Laurence, tr. from RUS. (American Folklore Society Bibliographical & Special Ser.: No. 9). 184p. 1968. pap. 9.95 (0-292-78376-0) U of Tex Pr.

— Theory & History of Folklore. Liberman, Anatoly, ed. Martin, Ariadna Y. & Martin, Richard P., trs. LC 83-14840. (Theory & History of Literature Ser.: Vol. 5). (RUS., Illus.). 288p. 1984. pap. 19.95 (0-8166-1182-3) U of Minn Pr.

Propp, William H. Exodus 1-18: A New Translation with Introduction & Commentary. LC 97-37301. (Anchor Bible Ser.). 704p. 1999. 44.95 (0-385-14804-6) Doubleday.

Propp, William H., et al, eds. The Hebrew Bible & Its Interpreters. LC 89-23372. (Biblical & Judaic Studies from the University of California, San Diego: No. 1). vi, 225p. 1990. text 34.50 (0-931464-52-8) Eisenbrauns.

Propper, Bob. The Bear, Reading Level 3-4. (World Animal Library). (Illus.). 28p. (J). (gr. 2-5). 1983. lib. bdg. 21.27 (0-86592-865-7) Rourke Enter.

— Dolphin, Reading Level 3-4. (World Animal Library). (Illus.). 28p. (J). (gr. 2-5). 1983. 12.50 (0-685-58815-7) Rourke Corp.

— Dolphin, Reading Level 3-4. (World Animal Library). (Illus.). 28p. (J). (gr. 2-5). 1983. lib. bdg. 21.27 (0-86592-861-4) Rourke Enter.

— The Giraffe, Reading Level 3-4. (World Animal Library). (Illus.). 28p. (J). (gr. 2-5). 1983. lib. bdg. 21.27 (0-86592-860-6) Rourke Enter.

— Panda, Reading Level 3-4. (World Animal Library). (Illus.). 28p. (J). (gr. 2-5). 1983. 12.50 (0-685-58822-X) Rourke Corp.

— Turtle, Reading Level 3-4. (World Animal Library). (Illus.). 28p. (J). (gr. 2-5). 1983. lib. bdg. 12.50 (0-685-58828-9) Rourke Corp.

— Turtle, Reading Level 3-4. (World Animal Library). (Illus.). 28p. (J). (gr. 2-5). 1983. lib. bdg. 21.27 (0-86592-856-8) Rourke Enter.

Propper, Bob, et al. World Animal Library, 17 bks. (Illus.). 476p. (J). (gr. 2-5). 1983. lib. bdg. 361.53 (0-86592-850-9) Rourke Enter.

— World Animal Library, 17 bks., Reading Level 3-4. (Illus.). 476p. (J). (gr. 2-5). 1983. lib. bdg. 212.50 (0-685-58814-9) Rourke Corp.

***Propper, Eugene M.** Corporate Fraud Investigations & Compliance Programs. LC 99-55585. 2000. 110.00 (0-379-21410-5, 7195028) Oceana.

Propping, Peter, jt. ed. see Bouchard, Thomas J., Jr.

Propst, C. & Perun, Thomas. Computer-Aided Drug Design: Methods & Applications. (Illus.). 516p. 1989. text 175.00 (0-8247-8037-X) Dekker.

Propst, C. & Perun, Thomas, eds. Nucleic Acid Targeted Drug Design. LC 92-17585. (Illus.). 644p. 1992. text 225.00 (0-8247-8662-9) Dekker.

Propst, H. Dean, ed. see Winthrop, Theodore.

Propst, Milam M. A Flower Blooms on Charlotte Street. LC 98-46966. 176p. 1999. 18.95 (0-86554-626-6) Mercer Univ Pr.

Propst, Nell B. Those Strenuous Dames of the Colorado Prairie. LC 95-178591. (Illus.). 310p. 1994. reprint ed. pap. 15.95 (0-9634839-6-X) Tamarack Bks.

Propst, Rebecca L. Psychotherapy in a Religious Framework: Spirituality in the Emotional Healing Process. LC 86-27582. 209p. 1987. 38.95 (0-89885-350-8, Kluwer Acad Hman Sci) Kluwer Academic.

Propst, Robert. The Office: A Facility Based on Change. 71p. 1986. 8.50 (0-936658-01-0) H Miller Res.

Prorok, Carolyn V., et al. Asian Women & Their Work: A Geography of Gender & Development. LC 98-145518. (Pathways Ser.: Vol. 17). (Illus.). 131p. 1998. pap. text 12.95 (1-884136-12-5) NCFGE.

Prorok, Paul. In Pursuit of Giant Bass. (Illus.). 375p. (Orig.). 1992. pap. 19.95 (0-9633120-0-6) Giant Bass Pub.

Pros, Jorge S. Diccionario de Axiomas, Juicios y Reflexiones. (SPA.). 1040p. 1991. 95.00 (0-7859-5883-5, 8430206132) Fr & Eur.

— Diccionario de la Felicidad. 2nd ed. (SPA.). 1046p. 1988. pap. 75.00 (0-7859-4897-X) Fr & Eur.

P

An Asterisk (*) at the beginning of an entry indicates that the title is appearing for the first time.

— Diccionario de Maximas Pensamientos y Sentacias. 9th ed. (SPA.). 744p. 1989. write for info. (0-7859-5026-5) Fr & Eur.

— Diccionario Humoristico. 3rd ed. (SPA.). 552p. 1982. pap. 50.00 (0-7859-4898-8) Fr & Eur.

— Dictionary of Celebrated Phrases: Diccionario de Frases Celabres. 6th ed. (ENG & SPA.). 1000p. 1988. 89.95 (0-7859-5025-7) Fr & Eur.

Prosapio, Richard. Intuitive Tarot. LC 96-223834. 1997. pap. text 10.95 (0-88079-495-X, BK112) US Games Syst.

Prosch, Charles. Reminiscences of Washington Territory. enl. ed. 128p. 1969. 16.95 (0-87770-022-2) Ye Galleon.

Prosch, Gina, jt. auth. see Prosch, Richie.

Prosch, Gus J., Jr., jt. auth. see Di Fabio, Anthony.

Prosch, Harry. Michael Polanyi: A Critical Exposition. LC 85-27849. (SUNY Series in Cultural Perspectives). 354p. (C). 1986. text 64.50 (0-88706-277-6); pap. text 21.95 (0-88706-276-8) State U NY Pr.

Prosch, Harry, jt. auth. see Polanyi, Michael.

Prosch, Kevin. Kiss the Son - Come to the Light Songbook. (Illus.). 122p. 1997. spiral bd. 15.00 (0-9658465-0-4) Seventh Time.

Prosch, Richie & Prosch, Gina. The Windburnt Plains of Wonder. (Illus.). 170p. (Orig.). 1996. pap. 11.95 (1-57502-343-1, PO1137) Morris Pubng.

Proschan, Frank, jt. auth. see Barlow, Richard.

Proschan, Frank, jt. auth. see Hollander.

Proschek, L., jt. ed. see Gaetan, Jasmin.

***Prosci Research Staff.** Best Practices in Business Process Reengineering & Process Design. (Illus.). 32p. 1999. 115.00 (1-930885-06-7) Prosci Rsrch.

— Best Practices in Business Process Reengineering & Process Design with the Future Role of IT. (Illus.). 48p. 1999. 145.00 (1-930885-07-5) Prosci Rsrch.

— Best Practices in Call Center Management, Operations & Technology. (Illus.). 44p. 1999. 149.00 (1-930885-05-9) Prosci Rsrch.

— Best Practices in Managing Change Report. (Illus.). 32p. 1998. 125.00 (1-930885-04-0) Prosci Rsrch.

— Business Case Toolkit. (Illus.). 1999. 289.00 (1-930885-02-4, RTA 3) Prosci Rsrch.

— Call Center Measurement Vol. I: How to Measure & Improve Call Center Performance. (Illus.). 2000. write for info. (1-930885-08-3) Prosci Rsrch.

— Change Management Toolkit. (Illus.). 1999. 289.00 (1-930885-03-2, RTA 4) Prosci Rsrch.

— Innovative Practices in Human Resources. (Illus.). 1999. 249.00 (1-930885-09-1) Prosci Rsrch.

— Project Planning Toolkit. (Illus.). 1999. 189.00 (1-930885-00-8, RTA 1) Prosci Rsrch.

— Reengineering Design Toolkit. (Illus.). 1999. 389.00 (1-930885-01-6, RTA 2) Prosci Rsrch.

Prosdocimo de'Beldomandi. Brief Treatise on Ratios That Pertain to Music & A Little Treatise on the Method of Dividing the Monochord. Herlinger, Jan, ed. & tr. by. LC 87-10818. (Greek & Latin Music Theory Ser.). x, 182p. 1987. text 40.00 (0-8032-3677-8) U of Nebr Pr.

Prose, Francine. The Angels Mistake: Stories of Chelm. LC 96-7465. (Illus.). 24p. (J). (gr. k up). 1997. 15.00 (0-688-14905-7, Grenwillow Bks) HarpC Child Bks.

Prose, Francine. The Angel's Mistake: Stories of Chelm. LC 96-7465. (Illus.). 24p. (J). (gr. k up). 1997. 14.89 (0-688-14906-5, Grenwillow Bks) HarpC Child Bks.

Prose, Francine. Bigfoot Dreams. LC 97-31403. 288p. 1998. pap. 12.00 (0-8050-4860-X) H Holt & Co.

***Prose, Francine.** Blue Angel: A Novel. LC 99-40564. 320p. 2000. 25.00 (0-06-019541-X) HarpC.

— The Demons' Mistake: A Story from Chelm. LC 99-56245. 32p. (J). 2000. lib. bdg. 15.89 (0-688-17566-X, Grenwillow Bks) HarpC Child Bks.

— The Demons' Mistake: A Story from Chelm. LC 99-56245. 32p. (J). (gr. k up). 2000. 15.95 (0-688-17565-1, Grenwillow Bks) HarpC Child Bks.

Prose, Francine. Dybbuk: A Story Made in Heaven. LC 95-22825. (Illus.). (J). (gr. k up). 1996. 16.00 (0-688-14307-5, Grenwillow Bks) HarpC Child Bks.

— Guided Tours of Hell: Novellas. 256p. 1997. 23.00 (0-8050-4861-8) H Holt & Co.

— Guided Tours of Hell: Novellas. 224p. 1998. pap. text 12.00 (0-8050-5586-X) H Holt & Co.

— Household Saints. 208p. 1993. mass mkt. 4.99 (0-8041-1165-0) Ivy Books.

— Hunters & Gatherers. LC 95-3569. 256p. 1995. text 20.00 (0-374-17371-0) FS&G.

— Hunters & Gatherers. write for info. (0-8050-5375-1, Owl) H Holt & Co.

— Hunters & Gatherers: A Novel. LC 96-35461. 256p. 1997. pap. 13.00 (0-8050-4896-0) H Holt & Co.

— The Peaceable Kingdom. LC 93-10080. 231p. 1993. 20.00 (0-374-23042-0) FS&G.

— The Peaceable Kingdom. LC 98-21553. 240p. 1998. pap. 12.00 (0-8050-5939-3, Owl) H Holt & Co.

— Primitive People. 250p. 1992. 20.00 (0-374-23722-0) FS&G.

— You Never Know: A Legend of the Lamed-Vavniks. LC 97-24764. (Illus.). 24p. (J). (gr. k-3). 1998. 15.00 (0-688-15806-4, Grenwillow Bks) HarpC Child Bks.

***Prose, Francine.** You Never Know: A Legend of the Lamed-Vavniks. LC 97-24764. (Illus.). 24p. (J). (gr. k-3). 1998. 14.93 (0-688-15807-2, Grenwillow Bks) HarpC Child Bks.

Prose, Francine, intro. Master Breasts: Objectified, Aesthetisized, Fantasized, Eroticized, Feminized by Photography's Most Titillating Masters . . . LC 98-84498. (Illus.). 16p. 1998. 60.00 (0-89381-803-8) Aperture.

Prose, Francine, tr. see Fink, Ida.

***Proseck'y, Jir'i, ed.** Intellectual Life of the ANE: Papers Presented at the 43rd Recontre Assyriologique International Prague, July 1-5, 1996. 482p. 1999. pap. text 60.00 (80-85425-30-0) Eisenbrauns.

Prosek, James. The Complete Angler: A Connecticut Yankee Follows in the Footsteps of Walton. (Illus.). Date not set. lib. bdg. 13.00 (0-06-092931-6) HarpC.

— The Complete Angler: A Connecticut Yankee Follows in the Footsteps of Walton. LC 98-55756. (Illus.). 336p. 1999. 30.00 (0-06-019189-9) HarpC.

***Prosek, James.** Early Love & Brook Trout. (Illus.). 128p. 2000. 24.95 (1-58574-039-X) Lyons Pr.

Prosek, James. 41st Latitude. 2000. 25.00 (0-06-019379-4); pap. 13.00 (0-06-093199-X) HarpC.

— Joe & Me: An Education in Fishing & Friendship. LC 97-10039. (Illus.). 200p. 1997. 23.00 (0-688-15316-X, Wm Morrow) Morrow Avon.

— Trout: An Illustrated History. 168p. 1996. 29.95 (0-679-44453-X) Knopf.

Prosen, jt. auth. see Chan.

Prosen, Harry, jt. auth. see Sperry, Len.

Proser, Maria A., ed. & tr. see Lara, Jesus.

Proser, Maria A., tr. see De Jesus, Teresa.

Proser, Maria A., tr. see Mellibovsky, Matilde.

Proser, Matthew, tr. see Mellibovsky, Matilde.

Proser, Matthew N. The Gift of Fire: Aggression & the Plays of Christopher Marlowe. LC 94-21588. (Renaissance & Baroque Studies & Texts: Vol. 12). VII, 226p. (C). 1995. text 30.95 (0-8204-2276-2) P Lang Pubng.

— The Heroic Image in Five Shakespearian Tragedies. LC 78-17428. 259p. 1978. reprint ed. 50.00 (0-87752-200-6) Gordian.

Proshansky, Harold M., ed. Genetic Destiny: Scientific Controversy & Social Conflict, No. 11. LC 76-5964. (Studies in Modern Society: Political & Social Issues). 32.50 (0-404-10130-5) AMS Pr.

Proshchakov, Vitold. In the Friendly Family of Fraternal Peoples. 120p. 1983. 22.00 (0-7855-1223-3, Pub. by Collets) St Mut.

Prosise, Jeff. How Computer Graphics Work. LC 95-105171. (How It Works Ser.). (Illus.). 182p. (Orig.). 1994. pap. 24.95 (1-56276-242-7, Ziff-Davis Pr) Que.

— PC Magazine DOS 5 Memory Management with Utilities. (Techniques & Utilities Ser.). (Illus.). 244p. (Orig.). 1992. pap. 34.95 incl. disk (1-56276-050-5, Ziff-Davis Pr) Que.

— PC Magazine DOS 5 Techniques & Utilities. (Techniques & Utilities Ser.). (Illus.). 1012p. (Orig.). 1991. pap. 39.95 incl. disk (1-56276-007-6, Ziff-Davis Pr) Que.

— PC Magazine DOS 6 Techniques & Utilities. 1072p. 1993. pap. 39.95 incl. disk (1-56276-095-5, Ziff-Davis Pr) Que.

— PC Magzine Guide to DOS 6 Memory Management with Utilities. (Techniques & Utilities Ser.). 432p. 1993. pap. 29.95 incl. disk (1-56276-097-1, Ziff-Davis Pr) Que.

— Programming Windows 95 with MFC: Create Object-Oriented Programs Quickly with the Microsoft Foundation Class Library. 1024p. 1996. pap. 49.95 incl. cd-rom (1-55615-902-1) Microsoft.

— Programming Windows with MFC. 2nd ed. LC 99-13028. 1200p. 1998. 49.99 incl. cd-rom (1-57231-695-0) Microsoft.

— Windows Desktop Utilities. (Techniques & Utilities Ser.). 480p. 1994. pap. 34.95 incl. disk (1-56276-098-X, Ziff-Davis Pr) Que.

Prosise, Michael, jt. auth. see Ramirez, Ron.

Prosise, Roger. Beyond Rules & Consequences for Classroom Management. LC 96-67179. (Fastback Ser.: No. 401). 37p. (Orig.). 1996. pap. 3.00 (0-87367-601-7) Phi Delta Kappa.

***Prosise, Roger.** Strategic Planning for School Administrators. (Fastback Ser.: No. 457). 50p. 1999. pap. 3.00 (0-87367-657-2, FB#457) Phi Delta Kappa.

Proskauer, et al. New York Employment Discrimination Handbook. LC 92-41658. 1993. write for info. (0-8205-2788-2) Bender.

Proskauer, Heinrich O. The Rediscovery of Color. (Illus.). 180p. 1990. pap. 16.95 (0-88010-088-5, 1055) Anthroposophic.

Proske, Beatrice G. Archer Milton Huntington. (Illus.). 1965. 5.00 (0-87535-098-4) Hispanic Soc.

— Brookgreen Gardens Sculpture. rev. ed. (Illus.). 574p. (C). 1968. text 15.00 (0-9638206-0-5) Brookgreen.

— Castilian Sculpture: Gothic to Renaissance. (Illus.). 1988. reprint ed. 15.00 (0-87535-069-0) Hispanic Soc.

— Catalogue of Sculpture (13th to 15th Centuries) in the Collection. (Illus.). 360p. 1932. 10.00 (0-87535-030-5) Hispanic Soc.

— Catalogue of Sculpture (16th to 18th Centuries) in the Collection. (Illus.). 1930. 10.00 (0-87535-027-5) Hispanic Soc.

— Juan Martinez Montanes, Sevillian Sculptor. (Illus.). 199p. 1967. 35.00 (0-87535-107-7) Hispanic Soc.

— Pompeo Leoni: Work in Marble & Alabaster in Relation to Spanish Sculpture. (Illus.). 1956. 5.00 (0-87535-088-7) Hispanic Soc.

— Sculpture by Anna Hyatt Huntington. (Illus.). 24p. 1957. pap. text 0.50 (0-87535-093-3) Hispanic Soc.

Proske, Beatrice G. & Salmon, Robin R. Brookgreen Gardens Sculpture & Brookgreen Gardens Sculpture Vol. II. (Illus.). 885p. (C). 1993. text 30.00 (0-9638206-2-1) Brookgreen.

Proske, Uwe, jt. ed. see Ferrell, William R.

Proskine, Alec. Adirondack Canoe Waters: South & West Flow. 2nd rev. ed. LC 88-34398. (Canoe Guide Ser.: Vol. 2). 176p. 1998. reprint ed. pap. 12.95 (0-935272-50-X) ADK Mtn Club.

Proskouriakoff, Tatiana. An Album of Maya Architecture. LC 63-17166. 1976. reprint ed. pap. 21.95 (0-8061-1351-0) U of Okla Pr.

— Jades from the Cenote of Sacrifice, Chichen Itza, Yucatan. LC 74-77555. (Peabody Museum Memoirs Ser.: Vol. 10, No. 1). (Illus.). 218p. 1974. pap. 42.00 (0-87365-682-2) Peabody Harvard.

Proskouriakoff, Tatiana, jt. ed. see Knorozov, Yuri V.

Proskouriakoff, Tatiana A. A Study of Classic Maya Sculpture. LC 77-11515. (Carnegie Institution of Washington. Publications: No. 593). reprint ed. 62.50 (0-404-16275-4) AMS Pr.

Proskurin, Nikolai. Cubic Metaplectic Forms & Theta Functions. Dold, A. & Takens, F., eds. LC 97-45869. (Lecture Notes in Mathematics Ser.: Vol. 1677). vii, 196p. 1998. pap. 41.00 (3-540-63751-6) Spr-Verlag.

Proskurina, Vera, ed. & intro. see Gershenzon, Mikhail.

Proskurovsky, D. I., jt. auth. see Mesyats, G. A.

Proskurowski, W. The Fruits from My Garden: A Selection of Endgames. 49p. (Orig.). 1993. pap. 6.00 (0-945470-37-1) Chess Ent.

Prosky, Leon, jt. ed. see Cho, Sungsoo.

***ProsoftTraining.com Staff.** ProsoftTraining.com Technology Terms A4. 2000. pap. write for info. (1-58143-104-X) Prosoft I-net.

— ProsoftTraining.com Technology Terms. 2000. pap. write for info. (1-58143-103-1) Prosoft I-net.

Prosor, Larry & Moreno, Richard. Nevada: Desert Lows & Mountain Highs. Lippert, Laurel H., ed. (Illus.). 174p. 1994. 39.95 (1-885515-00-6) Fineline Productions.

Prosor, Larry & Popoff, Leo. Lake Tahoe: A Photo Essay of the Lake Tahoe Region. Lippert, Laurel H., ed. (Illus.). 150p. (Orig.). (C). 1992. pap. 19.95 (0-9620148-0-X) Fineline Productions.

— Lake Tahoe: A Photo Essay of the Lake Tahoe Region. 2nd ed. Lippert, Laurel H., ed. (Illus.). 135p. (Orig.). 1993. 34.95 (0-9620148-2-6) Fineline Productions.

Prosorova, L. P. & Kreizer, V. L. English-Russian Television Dictionary. (ENG & RUS.). 429p. 1960. 24.95 (0-8288-6837-9, M-9065) Fr & Eur.

Prospect News Staff, ed. see Ponder, Dorothy.

Prosper, Charles. How to Become a Balloon Artist & Make up to One Hundred Thousand Dollars a Year: An Expert's Step-by-Step Guide. LC 87-81325. (Illus.). 165p. (Orig.). 1987. pap. 35.00 (0-943845-77-7) Global Pub CA.

Prosper, Harrison B., jt. auth. see Bhat, Pushpalatha C.

Prosper, Peter A., Jr. Concentration & the Rate of Change of Wages in the United States, 1950-1962. Bruchey, Stuart, ed. LC 76-4511. (Nineteen Seventy-Seven Dissertations Ser.). (Illus.). 1977. lib. bdg. 23.95 (0-405-09922-3) Ayer.

Prosper-Pouget, Jean-Henri, jt. auth. see Pouget, Jean-Henri-Prosper.

Prosper, Saint. St. Prosper of Aquitaine, Defense of St. Augustine. Burghardt, Walter J. et al, eds. LC 78-62463. (Ancient Christian Writers Ser.: No. 32). 235p. 1963. 16.95 (0-8091-0263-3) Paulist Pr.

— St. Prosper of Aquitaine, the Call of All Nations. Burghardt, Walter J. et al, eds. (Ancient Christian Writers Ser.: No. 14). 250p. 1952. 16.95 (0-8091-0253-6) Paulist Pr.

Prospere, Peter. The Secrets of Successful Selling. LC 96-94758. 64p. (Orig.). 1996. pap. text 8.95 (0-9654374-1-8) Integrated Mktg Sys.

Prospere, Susan. Sub Rosa: Poems. 96p. 1993. pap. 8.95 (0-393-31003-5) Norton.

Prosperetti, A., jt. ed. see Arndt, R. E.

Prosperi, D., et al, eds. First International Course on Condensed Matters. 348p. (C). 1988. text 85.00 (9971-5-0743-9) World Scientific Pub.

Prosperi, G. M. & Brambilla, N. Quark Confinement & the Hadron Spectrum: Proceeding of the International Conference. 396p. 1995. text 112.00 (981-02-2085-5) World Scientific Pub.

Prosperity & Profits Unlimited Staff. Party Plan Sales: A Reference & Workbook. rev. ed. 1992. ring bd. 29.95 (0-317-04782-5) Prosperity & Profits.

***Prospero, Ann.** Almost Night: A Novel. LC 99-87713. 288p. 2000. 23.95 (0-525-94532-6, Dutt) Dutton Plume.

Prospero Press Staff. Prospero's Almanac, 1997 Vol. 1: The Theatre Lover's Guide to the World at Large. (Illus.). 96p. (Orig.). 1996. mass mkt. 7.95 (0-937657-21-2) Feedbk Theabks & Prospero.

Prosperoso, Rico. Silhouette Designs for Artists & Craftspeople. LC 94-37319. (Illus.). 48p. 1995. pap. 4.50 (0-486-28452-2) Dover.

Pross, Addy. Theoretical & Physical Principles of Organic Reactivity. LC 95-21389. 312p. 1995. 74.95 (0-471-55599-1) Wiley.

Pross, Christian. Paying for the Past: The Struggle over Reparations for Surviving Victims of the Nazi Terror. Cooper, Belinda, tr. from GER. LC 97-39245. 276p. 1998. 29.95 (0-8018-5824-0) Johns Hopkins.

Pross, Paul E. Winter Songs & Final Dreams: Memoirs of a Wayward Cherub. 120p. 1995. write for info. (0-9630307-1-X) Vertex Pr.

Pross, Paul E. & Yungclas, Jack H. The Sound of Sleigh Bells: A Christmas Story for All Seasons. 70p. 1991. 13.95 (0-9630307-0-1) Vertex Pr.

— The Sound of Sleigh Bells: A Christmas Story for All Seasons. rev. ed. 70p. 1993. 13.95 (0-9630307-2-8) Vertex Pr.

Prossdorf, S. & Silbermann, Bernd. Numerical Analysis for Integral & Related Operator Equations. (Operator Theory Ser.: Vol. 52). 560p. 1991. 234.00 (0-8176-2620-4) Birkhauser.

Prossdorf, S., jt. auth. see Michlin, S. G.

Prossdorf, S., tr. see Maz'ya, V. G. & Nikol'skij, S. M.

Prosser, Albert L. Nasson: The Seventy Years. D'Abate, Richard, ed. LC 93-25217. (Illus.). 376p. 1993. 30.00 (0-914659-63-4) Phoenix Pub.

Prosser, Alex & Meredith, Carol. The Font Directory, Version 1.0 for Windows. LC 96-35486. (Illus.). 90p. (Orig.). 1992. spiral bd. 11.95 (0-9696751-0-0, Pub. by Beaver Pnd) DIMI Pr.

Prosser, Bo & Qualls, Charles. Lessons from the Cloth: 501One-Minute Motivators for Leaders. LC 98-30883. 96p. 1999. pap. 10.00 (1-57312-252-1) Smyth & Helwys.

Prosser, C. Ladd. Comparative Animal Physiology, 2 vols., Pt. A, Set. 4th ed. LC 90-27165. 592p. 1991. 155.00 (0-471-85767-X) Wiley.

***Prosser, C. Ladd.** A History of Nerve & Muscle Physiology. (People & Ideas Ser.). (Illus.). 450p. 2000. 75.00 (0-19-511354-3) OUP.

Prosser, C. Ladd, ed. Comparative Animal Physiology, 2 vols., Set. 4th ed. 1378p. 1991. 250.00 (0-471-56093-6) Wiley.

Prosser, C. Ladd, ed. Neural & Integrative Animal Physiology: Comparative Animal Physiology, Vol. 2. 4th ed. LC 90-27164. 786p. 1991. 155.00 (0-471-56071-5) Wiley.

Prosser, D. J., jt. ed. see Hartley, A. J.

Prosser, D. J., jt. ed. see North, C. P.

Prosser, David. TEC Course - Advanced C Workshop: Algorithms & Data Structures. 1990. ring bd. write for info. (0-201-41891-6) Addison-Wesley.

Prosser, Eleanor. Hamlet & Revenge. 2nd ed. LC 71-120745. xvi, 302p. 1971. 42.50 (0-8047-0316-7); pap. 14.95 (0-8047-0317-5) Stanford U Pr.

Prosser, J. I., ed. Nitrification. (Society for General Microbiology Special Publications: Vol. 20). 228p. (C). 1987. 75.00 (1-85221-013-3); pap. text 44.00 (1-85221-001-X) OUP.

Prosser, James I., jt. auth. see Bazin, Michael J.

Prosser, James I., jt. ed. see Bazin, Michael J.

***Prosser, Jay.** Second Skins: The Body Narratives of Transsexuality. LC 97-32529. (Gender & Culture Ser.). (Illus.). 288p. 1998. pap. 17.00 (0-231-10935-0) Col U Pr.

— Second Skins: The Body Narratives of Transsexuality. LC 97-32529. (Gender & Culture Ser.). (Illus.). 288p. 1998. 50.00 (0-231-10934-2) Col U Pr.

Prosser, Jerry. Aliens: Harvest. 2nd ed. (Illus.). 136p. 1995. pap. 14.95 (1-56971-122-4) Dark Horse Comics.

— Aliens Harvest. (Aliens Ser.). (Illus.). 1997. pap. 16.95 (1-56971-198-4) Dark Horse Comics.

Prosser, Jerry, see Mayakovsky, Stanislaw, pseud.

Prosser, Jerry, ed. see Miller, Frank.

Prosser, Jerry, ed. see Miller, Frank & Darrow, Geof.

Prosser, Jerry, ed. see Verheiden, Mark, et al.

Prosser, Jon. Image-Based Research: A Sourcebook for Qualitative Researchers. 318p. 1998. 85.00 (0-7507-0706-2, Falmer Pr); pap. 29.95 (0-7507-0649-X, Falmer Pr) Taylor & Francis.

Prosser, Kevin, jt. contrib. by see Anderson, Julie.

Prosser, M. Learning & Teaching in Higher: The Experience in Higher Education. LC 98-23978. 1998. pap. 115.00 (0-335-19832-5) OpUniv Pr.

— Understanding Learning & Teaching. LC 98-23978. ix, 194p. 1998. pap. 36.95 (0-335-19831-7) OpUniv Pr.

Prosser, Michael, jt. auth. see Sitaram, K. S.

***Prosser, Michael H. & Sitaram, K. S.** Civic Discourse: Intercultural, International & Global Media. LC 98-28941. (Civic Discource for the Third Millennium Ser.). xiv, 508 p. 1999. pap. 42.50 (1-56750-417-5) Ablx Pub.

Prosser, Michael H. & Sitaram, K. S. Civic Discourse Vol. 2: Intercultural, International & Global Media. LC 98-28941. (Civic Discource for the Third Millenium Ser.: Vol. 2). 520p. 1999. 78.50 (1-56750-416-7) Ablx Pub.

Prosser, Michael H., jt. auth. see Donahue, Ray T.

Prosser, Michael H., jt. auth. see Sitaram, K. S.

Prosser, Michael H., jt. ed. see Benson, Thomas W.

Prosser, Peter E., ed. Dispensationalist Eschatology & Its Influence on American & British Religious Movements. LC 99-26121. (Texts & Studies in Religion: Vol. 82). 372p. 1999. text 99.95 (0-7734-8000-5) E Mellen.

Prosser, Reese T. A New Formulation of Particle Mechanics. LC 52-42839. (Memoirs Ser.: No. 1/61). 57p. 1980. reprint ed. pap. 17.00 (0-8218-1261-0, MEMO/1/61) Am Math.

— On the Ideal Structure of Operator Algebras. LC 52-42839. (Memoirs of the American Mathematical Society Ser.: No. 45). 28p. 1974. reprint ed. pap. 17.00 (0-8218-1245-9, MEMO/1/45C) Am Math.

Prosser, Robert. Places & Cases Teacher's Resource Pack: The World. 64p. 1998. pap. 77.50 (0-7487-3477-5, Pub. by S Thornes Pubs) Trans-Atl Phila.

— The World: Places & Cases. (Illus.). 96p. (YA). (gr. 9-11). 1998. pap. 22.50 (0-7487-2914-3, Pub. by S Thornes Pubs) Trans-Atl Phila.

Prosser, Sharon S. Spanish on the Job: Quick, Easy Word Guide. 107p. (Orig.). 1990. pap. 6.95 (0-923176-09-8) SW Pr.

***Prosser, Thomas.** Naked Hemingway. LC 99-72165. (Illus.). 218p. 1999. pap. 19.95 (0-9669614-0-4) Cappuccino Prodns.

Prosser, Tony. Law & the Regulators. LC 97-12130. 332p. (C). 1997. text 78.00 (0-19-876391-3) OUP.

Prosser, Tony, jt. auth. see Graham, Cosmo.

Prosser, Tony, jt. ed. see Moran, Michael.

Prosser, William L. Torts: Adaptable to Courses Utilizing Materials by Prosser. 3rd ed. LC 87-116625. (Legalines Ser.). 362p. 13.95 (0-685-18533-8) Harcourt.

Prosser, William L., ed. Judicial Humorist: A Collection of Judicial Opinions & Other Frivolities. xvii, 248p. 1989. reprint ed. 45.00 (0-8377-2518-6, Rothman) W S Hein.

Prosser, William L. & Keeton. Part to Torts. 5th ed. (C). 1987. 13.50 (0-314-24253-8) West Pub.

Prosser, William L. & Keeton, Page. Prosser & Keeton on Torts: Lawyers Edition. 5th ed. LC 83-19714. (Hornbook Ser.). 1456p. 1985. reprint ed. text. write for info. (*0-314-74442-8*) West Pub.

Prosser, William L., et al. Torts. 5th ed. Keeton, Page et al, eds. LC 83-19830. (Paralegal). 1286p. 1998. reprint ed. text 39.50 (*0-314-74880-6*) West Pub.

— Torts, Cases & Materials On. 8th ed. (University Casebook Ser.). 1266p. 1991. reprint ed. text 39.75 (*0-88277-641-X*) Foundation Pr.

Prost, Andre, jt. auth. see Le Bris, Pierre.

Prost, Antoine. In the Wake of War: Les Anciens Combattants & French Society. McPhail, Helen, tr. from FRE. LC 92-13236. (Legacy of the Great War Ser.).Tr. of Les/Anciens Combattants et la Societe Francaise. 160p. 1992. pap. 16.50 (*0-85496-337-5*) Berg Pubs.

Prost, Antoine & Vincent, Gerard, eds. A History of Private Life Vol. 5: Riddles of Identity in Modern Times, Vol. 2. (Illus.). 640p. 1994. pap. text 19.95 (*0-674-40004-6*, PROHIX) Belknap Pr.

Prost, Charles. Garden of Claude Monet: Mini Edition. (Illus.). 48p. 1997. 5.95 (*0-7641-5035-9*) Barron.

Prost, Gary. English-Spanish & Spanish-English Glossary of Geoscience Terms. 376p. 1997. text 62.00 (*90-5699-561-8*); pap. text 38.00 (*90-5699-562-6*) Gordon & Breach.

Prost, Gary L. Remote Sensing for Geologists: A Guide to Image Interpretation. LC 93-50702. 326p. 1994. text 140.00 (*2-88449-101-5*) Gordon & Breach.

Prost, Helen, jt. auth. see Young, Blanche.

Prost, J., jt. auth. see DeGennes, P. E.

***Prost, Raymond Joseph.** Murder Matters. LC 00-190109. 2000. 25.00 (*0-7388-1554-3*); pap. 18.00 (*0-7388-1555-1*) Xlibris Corp.

Prostano, Christina. New York for Less. (Illus.). 288p. 1997. pap. 19.95 (*0-9525437-8-8*, Pub. by Metropolis International) IPG Chicago.

— New York for Less Compact Guide: 2nd Ed. 2nd ed. 1999. pap. text 19.95 (*1-901811-31-X*) Metropolis International.

— Paris for Less: The Total Guidebook. (For Less Guidebook Ser.). (Illus.). 288p. 1998. pap. 19.95 (*1-901811-15-8*, Pub. by Metropolis International) IPG Chicago.

Prostano, Emannel T. & Prostano, Joyce S. The School Library Media Center. 5th ed. LC 98-49990. (Library & Information Science Text Ser.). 200p. 1999. 47.50 (*1-56308-461-9*); pap. 35.00 (*1-56308-564-X*) Teacher Ideas Pr.

Prostano, Joyce S., jt. auth. see Prostano, Emannel T.

Prosten, David, ed. The Union Steward's Complete Guide: A Survival Manual from the Publishers of "Steward Update" Newsletter. (Illus.). 226p. 1997. pap. 19.95 (*0-9659486-0-9*, UCS1) Union Commun.

Prosterman, Leslie. Ordinary Life, Festival Days: Aesthetics in the Midwestern County Fair. LC 93-49385. (Illus.). 352p. 1994. pap. text 24.95 (*1-56098-408-2*) Smithsonian.

Prosterman, Roy & Hanstad, Tim, eds. Legal Impediments to Effective Rural Land Relations in Eastern Europe & Central Asia: A Comparative Perspective. LC 99-28652. (Technical Paper Ser.: No. 436). 330p. 1999. pap. 30.00 (*0-8213-4501-X*, 14501) World Bank.

Prosterman, Roy L., et al, eds. Agrarian Reform & Grassroots Development: Ten Case Studies. LC 90-8493. 342p. 1990. lib. bdg. 40.00 (*1-55587-231-X*) L Rienner.

Prosterman, Roy L. & Riedinger, Jeffrey M. Land Reforms & Democratic Development. LC 87-4188. (Johns Hopkins Studies in Development). 328p. reprint ed. pap. 101.70 (*0-608-06187-5*, 206651900008) Bks Demand.

Prosyniuk, Joann R. Modern Arts Criticism, Vol. 2. 1991. 115.00 (*0-8103-7874-4*) Gale.

— Modern Arts Criticism, Vol. 3. 1992. 115.00 (*0-8103-8310-1*) Gale.

— Modern Arts Criticism, Vol. 4. 1993. 115.00 (*0-8103-8311-X*) Gale.

Prosyniuk, Joann R., ed. Modern Arts Criticism, Vol. 1. (Illus.). 575p. 1990. 115.00 (*0-8103-7689-X*) Gale.

Prot, R. Dictionnaire de la Radio, 75 Ans Radiodiffusion. (FRE.). 1998. 125.00 (*0-320-00309-4*) Fr & Eur.

Prot, Viviane A. The Story of Birth. Bogard, Vicki, tr. from FRE. LC 90-50777. (Young Discovery Library). (Illus.). 38p. (J). (gr. k-5). 1991. 5.95 (*0-944589-34-0*, 340) Young Discovery Lib.

Prota, Guiseppe. Melanins & Melanogenesis. (Illus.). 290p. 1992. text 69.00 (*0-12-565970-9*) Acad Pr.

***Protasevich, E. T.** Cold Nonequillibrium Plasma: Generation, Properties, Applications. 280p. 1999. boxed set 103.00 (*1-898326-44-4*, Pub. by CISP) Balogh.

***Protasevich, E. T. & Grigor'ev, V. P.** Application of Electromagnetic Radiation & Plasma for Solving Ecological Problems. 200p. 2000. boxed set 100.00 (*1-898326-66-5*, Pub. by CISP) Balogh.

Protasi, M., jt. ed. see Ausiello, G.

Protasio, John. To the Bottom of the Sea: True Accounts of Major Ship Disasters. 1990. 18.95 (*0-8184-0530-9*) Carol Pub Group.

***Protasoni, Sara.** City, Architecture & Municipality in Post-War Europe. (Rassegna Ser.). 1999. pap. text 35.00 (*88-85322-38-7*) Birkhauser.

Protasov, Taisa Nikolajevna, ed. see Dratva, Tomas & Buznova, Viktoria.

Proteau, L. & Elliott, D. Vision & Motor Control. (Advances in Psychology Ser.: Vol. 85). 478p. 1992. 160.50 (*0-444-88816-0*, North Holland) Elsevier.

Protected Areas Data Unit of the Conservation Moni & IUCN Commission on National Parks & Protected Area. The IUCN Directory of Afro-Tropical Protected Areas. (International Union for the Conservation of Nature & Natural Resources: A Belhaven Press Book Ser.). (Illus.). 1054p. 1986. 60.00 (*2-88032-804-7*, Pub. by IUCN) Island Pr.

Protein-Ligand Interactions Symposium Staff. Proceedings of the Protein-Ligand Interactions Symposium, University of Konstanz, Germany, Sept. 1974. Blauer, Gideon & Sund, Horst, eds. (C). 1975. 188.50 (*3-11-004881-7*) De Gruyter.

Protej, Vittoria B. Teach Yourself Italian Vocabulary. (Teach Yourself Ser.). (ENG & ITA., Illus.). 224p. 1996. pap. 9.95 (*0-8442-3987-9*, Teach Yrslf) NTC Contemp Pub Co.

Protess, D. & McCombs, M., eds. Agenda Setting: Readings on Media, Public Opinion & Policymaking. (Communication Textbook (Journalism) Ser.). 328p. (C). 1991. pap. 32.50 (*0-8058-0841-8*) L Erlbaum Assocs.

Protess, David & Warden, Robert. A Promise of Justice: The Eighteen Year Fight to Save Four Innocent Men. LC 97-36431. 288p. (J). 1998. 23.95 (*0-7868-6294-7*, Pub. by Hyperion) Time Warner.

Protess, David L., et al. The Journalism of Outrage: Investigative Reporting & Agenda Building in America. LC 91-8932. (Communication Ser.). 301p. 1991. lib. bdg. 42.00 (*0-89862-314-6*) Guilford Pubns.

— The Journalism of Outrage: Investigative Reporting & Agenda Building in America. LC 91-8932. (Communication Ser.). 301p. 1992. pap. text 23.00 (*0-89862-591-2*) Guilford Pubns.

Protestant Episcopal Church Staff. The Hymnal Nineteen Forty Companion. 741p. 1993. reprint ed. lib. bdg. 109.00 (*0-7812-9680-3*) Rprt Serv.

Proteus Group Staff. Playstation Games Secrets. (Illus.). 153p. (Orig.). 1995. 9.99 (*1-56686-408-9*) Brady Pub.

Protevi, John. Time & Exteriority: Aristotle, Heidegger, Derrida. LC 93-49860. 1994. 38.50 (*0-8387-5229-2*) Bucknell U Pr.

Proth, J. M. & Hillion, H. P. Mathematical Tools in Production Management. (Competitive Methods in Operations Research & Data Analysis Ser.). (Illus.). 400p. (C). 1990. 110.00 (*0-306-43358-3*, Plenum Trade) Perseus Pubng.

Proth, Jean-Marie & Xie, Xiaolan. Petri Nets: A Tool for Design & Management of Manufacturing Systems. LC 96-28024. 298p. 1997. 85.00 (*0-471-96770-X*) Wiley.

Prothero, Donald A. Bringing Fossils to Life: An Introduction to Paleontology. LC 97-30208. 480p. (C). 1997. pap. 58.13 (*0-07-052197-2*) McGraw.

Prothero, Donald R. The Eocene-Oligocene Transition: Paradise Lost. (Illus.). 208p. 1994. 72.00 (*0-231-08090-5*); pap. 27.00 (*0-231-08091-3*) Col U Pr.

— Interpreting the Stratigraphic Record. 409p. (C). 1989. pap. text 72.95 (*0-7167-1854-5*) W H Freeman.

— Sedimentary Geology. LC 95-50846. 575p. (C). 1996. pap. text 81.95 (*0-7167-2726-9*) W H Freeman.

Prothero, Donald R. & Berggren, William A. Eocene-Oligocene Climatic & Biotic Evolution. (Geology & Paleontology Ser.). 568p. 1992. text 125.00 (*0-691-08738-5*, Pub. by Princeton U Pr); pap. text 49.50 (*0-691-02542-8*, Pub. by Princeton U Pr) Cal Prin Full Svc.

Prothero, Donald R. & Emry, Robert J., eds. The Terrestrial Eocene-Oligocene Transition in North America. (Illus.). 704p. (C). 1996. text 100.00 (*0-521-43387-8*) Cambridge U Pr.

Prothero, Donald R. & Schoch, Robert M., eds. The Evolution of Perissodactyls. (Oxford Monographs on Geology & Geophysics: No. 15). (Illus.). 560p. 1989. text 100.00 (*0-19-506039-3*) OUP.

Prothero, Donald R., jt. auth. see Dott, Robert H., Jr.

Prothero, George. Bibliography on the Great War. (Reference Ser.: No. 8). 440p. 1995. reprint ed. 39.95 (*0-89839-230-6*) Battery Pr.

Prothero, George W., ed. Select Statutes & Other Constitutional Documents Illustrative of the Reigns of Elizabeth & James I. 4th ed. LC 83-1740. 490p. 1983. reprint ed. lib. bdg. 150.00 (*0-313-23973-8*, PRSE, Greenwood Pr) Greenwood.

Prothero, Iorwerth. Radical Artisans in England & France, 1830-1870. LC 96-45550. 440p. (C). 1997. text 74.95 (*0-521-58299-7*) Cambridge U Pr.

Prothero, Jon C. Driving & Surviving. LC 80-82627. (Illus.). 73p. (Orig.). (gr. 10-12). 1980. pap. 5.00 (*0-938026-01-1*) Instruct Res.

Prothero, Rowland E. English Farming Past & Present. LC 72-83276. 519p. 1972. reprint ed. 30.95 (*0-405-08866-3*, Pub. by Blom Pubns) Ayer.

Prothero, Rowland E., ed. see Gibbon, Edward.

***Prothero, Stephen.** Purified by Fire: A History of Cremation in America. (Illus.). 279p. 2001. 27.50 (*0-520-20816-1*) U CA Pr.

Prothero, Stephen. The White Buddhist: The Asian Odyssey of Henry Steel Olcott. LC 95-22092. (Religion in North America Ser.). 256p. 1996. 35.00 (*0-253-33014-9*) Ind U Pr.

Prothero, Stephen, jt. ed. see Tweed, Thomas A.

Prothero, Steve, jt. auth. see Regli, Phil.

***Prothero, Walter.** Complete Book of Mule Deer Hunting. (Illus.). 192p. 2000. pap. 24.95 (*1-58574-098-5*) Lyons Pr.

Prothero, Walter. The Hunting Adventures of Me & Joe. (Illus.). 220p. 1995. 22.50 (*1-57157-015-2*) Safari Pr.

***Prothero, Walter.** Safari: A Dangerous Affair. limited ed. (Illus.). 210p. 2000. 65.00 (*1-57157-093-4*) Safari Pr.

Prothero, Walter. Stalking Big Game. LC 92-754. (Illus.). 224p. 1992. 19.95 (*0-8117-0282-0*) Stackpole.

— Stalking Trophy Mule Deer. 240p. 1993. 18.98 (*0-88290-476-0*, 1240) Horizon Utah.

Protherough. Effective Teaching of English. 1989. pap. text. write for info. (*0-582-29720-6*, Pub. by Addison-Wesley) Longman.

Protherough, Robert. Students of English. 200p. 1989. 59.95 (*0-415-01637-1*) Routledge.

— Teaching Literature for Examinations. LC 86-754. (English, Language & Education Ser.). 160p. 1986. pap. 31.95 (*0-335-15076-4*) OpUniv Pr.

Protherough, Robert & Atkinson, Judith. The Making of English Teachers. (English, Language & Education Ser.). 176p. 1991. pap. 31.95 (*0-335-09374-4*) OpUniv Pr.

Protho Williams, Kimberly, jt. auth. see Lampl, Elizabeth J.

Prothro, Crystaline J. I'm a Kid but I'm Not Kiddin' I Love the Lord. Curry, Rosalynn A. & Johnson, Charmaine, eds. (Illus.). 100p. (J). (gr. 4-7). 1998. pap. 9.95 (*0-9662919-3-X*) Robot Pubg.

Prothro, Edwin T. Child Rearing in the Lebanon. LC 61-18039. (Middle Eastern Monographs: No. 8). (Illus.). 194p. 1961. pap. 4.50 (*0-674-11500-7*) HUP.

Prothro, Edwin T. & Diab, Lutfy N. Changing Family Patterns in the Arab East. 1974. 34.95 (*0-8156-6039-1*) Syracuse U Pr.

Prothro, James S. Apostles, the Missing Link of the Five-Fold Ministry. Curry, Rosalynn A. & Johnson, Charmaine, eds. (Illus.). 135p. 1998. pap. 12.95 (*0-9662919-2-1*) Robot Pubg.

— Man, God's Robot. 1998. pap. text 19.95 (*0-9662919-0-5*) Robot Pubg.

***Prothro, James S.** Man, God's Robot Workbook. Curry, Rosalynn A., ed. 51p. 1999. pap. 9.95 (*0-9662919-8-0*) Robot Pubg.

— Slices from the Loaf of Wisdom, Menu 1. Curry, Rosalynn A. & Johnson, Charmaine, eds. (Illus.). 63p. 1999. pap. 5.99 (*0-9662919-6-4*) Robot Pubg.

— Slices from the Loaf of Wisdom, Menu 2. Curry, Rosalynn A. & Johnson, Charmaine, eds. (Illus.). 63p. 1999. pap. 5.99 (*0-9662919-7-2*) Robot Pubg.

— Water for Dry Seasons: Bitterness - Blame - Bondage. Curry, Rosalynn A. & Johnson, Charmaine, eds. LC 98-68542. (Illus.). 223p. 1998. pap. 15.95 (*0-9662919-4-8*) Robot Pubg.

Prothro, James S., ed. see Hamdon, Marshall.

Prothro, James W. Dollar Decade: Business Ideas in the 1920s. LC 70-88923. 256p. 1970. reprint ed. lib. bdg. 65.00 (*0-8371-2299-6*, PRDD, Greenwood Pr) Greenwood.

Prothro, James W., jt. auth. see Matthews, Donald R.

Prothro, Lonnie, III, ed. see Crosby, D'Arcy R.

Prothrow-Stith, Deborah. Deadly Consequences. LC 90-55938. 288p. 1993. pap. 13.00 (*0-06-092402-0*, Perennial) HarperTrade.

— Violence Prevention Curriculum for Adolescents. (Illus.). 80p. (Orig.). 1987. pap. 29.95 (*0-89292-093-9*) Educ Dev Ctr.

Protic, Jelica, et al, eds. Distributed Shared Memory: Concepts & Systems. LC 97-11392. 272p. 1997. pap. 70.00 (*0-8186-7737-6*, BP07737) IEEE Comp Soc.

Proto, A. N. & Aliaga, J. L., eds. Condensed Matter Theories, Vol. 7. (Illus.). 440p. (C). 1992. text 186.00 (*0-306-44201-9*, Kluwer Plenum) Kluwer Academic.

Proto, Anthony V., et al. Chest Disease (Fourth Series) Test & Syllabus. (Professional Self-Evaluation & Continuing Education Program Ser.: Vol. 27). (Illus.). 814p. 1989. 165.00 (*1-55903-027-5*) Am Coll Radiology.

Proto, Louis. Be Your Own Best Friend: How to Achieve Greater Self-Esteem, Health, & Happiness. 176p. 1994. reprint ed. mass mkt. 5.99 (*0-425-14296-5*) Berkley Pub.

— Increase Your Energy: How to Fight Fatigue & Stress & Find a New Enthusiasm for Life. 192p. 1997. mass mkt. 5.99 (*0-425-16046-7*) Berkley Pub.

— Increase Your Energy: The Science of Smart Living. LC 92-23075. 144p. (Orig.). 1992. pap. 8.95 (*0-87728-755-4*) Weiser.

— Self Healing. 1997. mass mkt. 5.99 (*0-425-16192-7*) Berkley Pub.

Protologik Computer Systems Staff. VirtualEscapes. (Illus.). 1995. 49.95 (*1-888410-00-0*, SS4101) Elgin Intractve.

Protopappas, John J. & McNeal, Alvin R., eds. Washington on Foot: Twenty-Three Walking Tours of Washington, D. C., & Old Town Alexandria. 4th rev. ed. LC 83-12880. (Illus.). 224p. 1992. pap. 8.95 (*1-56098-176-8*) Smithsonian.

Protopopova, I., ed. see Viatiutnev, M. N. & Sosenko, E.

Protopresbyter Michael Pomazansky. Bog Nash na Njbesi i na zjemli.Tr. of Our God is in Heaven & on Earth. 140p. 1985. pap. 5.00 (*0-317-29087-8*) Holy Trinity.

— O Zhizni o Vjere o Tzerkvje, 2 vols.Tr. of On Life, Faith & the Church. 650p. 1976. pap. 23.00 (*0-317-29072-X*) Holy Trinity.

Protopsaltis, Byron, jt. ed. see Katz, Casimir.

Protsman, Erin O., ed. A Season of Celebrating Cookbook. LC 97-75240. (Illus.). 160p. 1997. 18.95 (*0-9638657-6-5*) Mus of Sci.

Protter & Protter. Calculus. 4th ed. (Illus.). (C). 1988. pap. text, student ed. 27.50 (*0-86720-110-X*) JB Pubns.

Protter, jt. auth. see Protter.

Protter, B., jt. auth. see Travin, S.

Protter, Eric. Painters on Painting. LC 97-34498. (Illus.). 312p. pap. 8.95 (*0-486-29941-4*) Dover.

Protter, M. & Weinberger, Hans F. Maximum Principles in Differential Equations. (Illus.). 1984. 60.95 (*0-387-96068-6*) Spr-Verlag.

Protter, M. H. Basic Elements of Real Analysis. LC 98-16913. (Undergraduate Texts in Mathematics Ser.). 272p. 1998. 39.95 (*0-387-98479-8*) Spr-Verlag.

Protter, Murray H. Calculus. 4th ed. 1000p. (C). 1988. text 45.00 (*0-86720-093-6*) Jones & Bartlett.

Protter, Murray H., intro. Reviews in Partial Differential Equations, 1980-1986, 5 vols. LC 88-6681. 3998p. 1988. pap. 355.00 (*0-8218-0103-1*, REVPDE/86) Am Math.

Protter, Murray H. & Morrey, Charles B., Jr. Calculus with Analytic Geometry: A First Course. 3rd ed. LC 76-12801. (Mathematics Ser.). (C). 1977. text 34.36 (*0-201-06037-X*); student ed. write for info. (*0-318-50136-8*) Addison-Wesley.

— College Calculus with Analytic Geometry. 3rd ed. LC 76-12800. (Mathematics Ser.). (C). 1977. text 40.00 (*0-201-06030-2*) Addison-Wesley.

— A First Course in Real Analysis. LC 76-43978. (Undergraduate Texts in Mathematics Ser.). 1987. 39.80 (*0-387-90215-5*) Spr-Verlag.

— A First Course in Real Analysis. 2nd ed. Ewing, J. H. et al, eds. (Undergraduate Texts in Mathematics Ser.). (Illus.). xviii, 534p. 1997. 44.95 (*0-387-97437-7*) Spr-Verlag.

— Intermediate Calculus. 2nd ed. (Undergraduate Texts in Mathematics Ser.). (Illus.). 600p. 1996. 49.95 (*0-387-96058-9*) Spr-Verlag.

— Modern Mathematical Analysis. 1964. text 68.95 (*0-201-05995-9*) Addison-Wesley.

— PSI Student Study Guide to Calculus. 3rd ed. LC 76-12800. (Mathematics Ser.). (C). 1977. student ed. 8.75 (*0-201-06036-1*) Addison-Wesley.

Protter, P. Stochastic Integration & Differential Equations. (Applications of Mathematics Ser.: Vol. 21). x, 302p. 1995. 69.00 (*0-387-50996-8*) Spr-Verlag.

Protter, P., jt. auth. see Jacod, J.

Protti, Maria E., ed. Webster vs. Reproductive Health Services: Briefs & Related Documents. LC 90-83331. 818p. 1990. lib. bdg. 195.00 incl. fiche (*0-89941-741-8*, 306660) W S Hein.

Protype Ltd. Staff, ed. see Graves, Carmen.

Protz, Roger. Classic Bottled Beers of the World. (Classic Drink Ser.). (Illus.). 192p. 1997. 16.95 (*1-85375-219-3*, Pub. by Prion) Trafalgar.

— Classic Stout & Porter. (Classic Drink Ser.). (Illus.). 192p. 1997. 16.95 (*1-85375-220-7*) Trafalgar.

— English Village Pubs. (Illus.). 160p. 1992. 27.50 (*1-55859-409-4*) Abbeville Pr.

— The European Beer Almanac. (Illus.). 168p. 1991. per. 16.99 (*0-948403-28-4*, Pub. by Camra Bks) All About Beer.

— The Great British Beer Book. (Illus.). 156p. 1987. pap. 12.99 (*0-245-54599-9*, Pub. by Camra Bks) All About Beer.

— The Real Ale Almanac. 4th ed. 320p. 1996. pap. 14.95 (*1-897784-34-1*, Pub. by N Wilson Pubng) Interlink Pub.

— The Real Ale Almanac. 5th ed. 352p. 1998. pap. 15.00 (*1-897784-67-8*, Pub. by N Wilson Pubng) Interlink Pub.

— The Real Ale Drinker's Almanac. 3rd ed. (Illus.). 320p. 1993. per. 14.99 (*1-897784-17-1*, Pub. by Camra Bks) All About Beer.

***Protz, Roger.** World Beer Guide. (Illus.). 368p. 2000. 24.95 (*1-85868-975-9*, Pub. by Carlton Bks Ltd) Natl Bk Netwk.

Protz, Roger, ed. Beer, Bed & Breakfast: The Essential Guide to Pubs with Good Value Accomodations & Excellent Food & Beer. 4th ed. (Illus.). 222p. 1991. pap. 10.95 (*0-86051-785-3*, Pub. by Robson Bks) Parkwest Pubns.

Protz, Roger & Sykes, Homer. The Village Pub. (Country Ser.). (Illus.). 160p. 1997. pap. 17.95 (*0-297-83561-0*, Pub. by Orion Pubng Grp) Trafalgar.

— The Village Pub. (Country Ser.). (Illus.). 160p. 1998. pap. 17.95 (*0-7538-0434-4*, Pub. by Orion Pubng Grp) Trafalgar.

Protz, Roger & Wheeler, Graham. Brew Your Own Real Ale at Home. (Illus.). 187p. (Orig.). 1993. pap., per. 14.99 (*1-85249-113-2*, Pub. by Camra Bks) All About Beer.

Protz, Roger, jt. auth. see Wheeler, Graham.

Protzman, John M. Confounded Interest. (Illus.). 44p. (Orig.). 1982. pap. 11.95 (*0-9608898-0-9*, 2-EJD) JMP Mfg.

Prou, Jean. Le Chant Gregorien et la Sanctification des Fideles. (FRE.). 24p. (C). 1985. pap. 5.95 (*1-55725-128-2*, 4080, Pub. by Abbey St Peter Solesmes) Paraclete MA.

Prou, Suzanne. Les Amis de Monsieur Paul Level C. text 8.95 (*0-8219-1218-6*) EMC-Paradigm.

Proud-Bailey Co. Ltd., Staff. British Post Office in the Far East. (C). 1989. 175.00 (*1-872465-09-9*, Pub. by Proud Bailey) St Mut.

Proud Bailey Co. Ltd., Staff. History of the Australian Military Postal Service 1914 - 1950. 1989. 190.00 (*1-872465-60-9*, Pub. by Proud Bailey) St Mut.

— History of the South African Postal Service. 1989. 180.00 (*1-872465-76-5*, Pub. by Proud Bailey) St Mut.

Proud-Bailey Co. Ltd., Staff. The Postal History of British Airmails. (C). 1989. 175.00 (*1-872465-72-2*, Pub. by Proud Bailey) St Mut.

Proud Bailey Co. Ltd., Staff. The Postal History of Hong Kong. 1989. 175.00 (*1-872465-07-2*, Pub. by Proud Bailey) St Mut.

— The Postal History of Kenya. 1989. 175.00 (*0-614-01353-4*, Pub. by Proud Bailey) St Mut.

Proud-Bailey Co. Ltd., Staff. The Postal History of Tanganyika. 1989. 175.00 (*1-872465-06-4*, Pub. by Proud Bailey) St Mut.

Proud Bailey Co. Ltd., Staff. The Postal History of the Naval & R. A. F. Postal Services. (C). 1989. 175.00 (*1-872465-62-5*, Pub. by Proud Bailey) St Mut.

— The Postal History of the Occupation of Malaya & British Borne. (C). 1989. 175.00 (*1-872465-73-0*, Pub. by Proud Bailey) St Mut.

Proud-Bailey Co. Ltd., Staff. The Postal History of Uganda & Zanzibar. 1989. 175.00 (*1-872465-08-0*, Pub. by Proud Bailey) St Mut.

Proud, Jean. Understanding Obstetric Ultrasound: Its Use & Interpretation. 2nd ed. LC 97-200254. 104p. 1997. pap. text 29.00 (*1-898507-60-0*, RG527) Buttrwrth-Heinemann.

Proud, John F. Master Production Scheduling: The Practical Guide for Managing World Class MPS. LC 93-60667. 400p. 1994. 150.00 (*0-939246-36-8*, TM7638) Wiley.

P

An Asterisk (*) at the beginning of an entry indicates that the title is appearing for the first time.

— Master Scheduling: A Practical Guide to Competitive Manufacturing. 560p. 1995. 60.00 (*0-471-13219-5*) Wiley.
— Master Scheduling: A Practical to Competitive Manufacturing. LC 99-13999. (Oliver Wright Manufacturing Ser.). 640p. 1999. 74.95 (*0-471-24322-1*) Wiley.
Proud, Joseph M. & Luessen, Lawrence H., eds. Radiative Processes in Discharge Plasmas. (NATO ASI Series B, Physical Sciences: Vol. 149). 600p. 1987. 135.00 (*0-306-42550-5*, Plenum Trade) Perseus Pubng.
Proud, Judith, jt. ed. see Bickerton, David.
Proud, Judith K., ed. see D'Eglantine, P. Fabre.
Proud, L. Designing with Photographs. 1998. 35.00 (*2-88046-353-X*, Rotovision) Watsn-Guptill.
Proud, Richard F. Portrait of a Legislature. 413p. 1989. 15.95 (*0-9621473-0-3*) Duorp Pr.
Proudfit, Charles L., ed. see Landor, Walter Savage.
Proudfoot, Alex J. & Hutchings, Lawrence. Teacher Beware: A Legal Primer for the Classroom Teacher. 391p. (Orig.). (C). 1988. pap. text 28.95 (*0-920490-82-4*) Temeron Bks.
Proudfoot, Alex J., jt. auth. see Giles, T. E.
Proudfoot, Amanda E. I., et al, eds. Chemokine Protocols. (Methods in Molecular Biology Ser.: Vol. 138). 332p. 2000. 99.50 (*0-89603-722-3*) Humana.
Proudfoot, Anna. Teach Yourself Italian Grammar. (Teach Yourself Ser.). 1992. 15.95 (*0-8288-8360-2*) Fr & Eur.
***Proudfoot, Anna.** Teach Yourself Italian Grammar. 2nd ed. (Teach Yourself... Grammar Ser.). 256p. 2000. pap. 11.95 (*0-8442-1333-0*, 13330, Teach Yrslf) NTC Contemp Pub Co.
Proudfoot, Anna. Teach Yourself Italian Grammar: A Modern Guide. (ENG & ITA., Illus.). 224p. 1995. pap. 9.95 (*0-8442-3803-1*, Teach Yrslf) NTC Contemp Pub Co.
Proudfoot, Anna & Cardo, Francesco. Modern Italian Grammar. LC 99-204903. 144p. (C). 1999. pap., wbk. ed. 14.99 (*0-415-12095-0*) Routledge.
— Modern Italian Grammar: A Practical Guide. LC 96-1193. (ENG & ITA.). 440p. (C). 1997. 75.00 (*0-415-09849-1*); pap. 25.99 (*0-415-09850-5*) Routledge.
Proudfoot, C. Noel, ed. Handbook of Photographic Science & Engineering, Vol. PM50. 768p. 1998. 135.00 (*0-8194-2615-6*) SPIE.
Proudfoot, Elsie B. Deep in the Heart of Them Thar Hills. Truster, Lena B., ed. (Deep in the Heart of Ser.: Vol. 2). (Illus.). 127p. (J). (ps-6). 1997. 19.95 (*0-9659329-1-5*) E B Proudfoot.
Proudfoot, Elsie R. Deep in the Heart of Potatoes. Truster, Lena B., ed. (Deep in the Heart of Ser.: Vol. 1). (Illus.). 127p. (J). (ps-6). 1995. 19.95 (*0-9659329-0-7*) E B Proudfoot.
Proudfoot, G. R., ed. Tom a Lincoln. (Malone Society Reprints Ser.: No. 153). (Illus.). 126p. 1992. text 45.00 (*0-19-729030-2*) OUP.
Proudfoot, Helen. Gardens in Bloom: Jocelyn Brown & Her Sydney Gardens of the '30s & '40s. LC 89-218554. (Illus.). 124p. 1989. write for info. (*0-86417-238-9*, Pub. by Kangaroo Pr) Intl Spec Bk.
Proudfoot, Kenneth. Children's Book of Home Rules. 100p. (Orig.). 1995. pap. 6.95 (*1-887671-00-5*); text 17.50 (*1-887671-01-3*) Shoreline Pr.
— The Dogfish Ate My Homework: And Other Flukes. (Illus.). 150p. (Orig.). 1995. pap. 9.95 (*1-887671-02-1*) Shoreline Pr.
Proudfoot, L. J., jt. ed. see Graham, B. J.
Proudfoot, Lindsay, ed. Down: History & Society. LC 97-226223. (County History & Society Ser.). (Illus.). 820p. 1997. pap. 79.95 (*0-906602-80-7*, Pub. by Geography Pubns) Irish Bks Media.
Proudfoot, Lindsay J. Urban Patronage & Social Authority: The Management of the Duke of Devonshire's Towns in Ireland, 1764-1891. LC 94-22416. 398p. 1995. 69.95 (*0-8132-0819-X*) Cath U Pr.
Proudfoot, Malcolm J. Population Movements in the Caribbean. LC 75-109359. 187p. 1970. reprint ed. lib. bdg. 35.00 (*0-8371-3634-2*, PCA&, Greenwood Pr) Greenwood.
Proudfoot, Mary M. & Perham, Margery F. Britain & the United States in the Caribbean: A Comparative Study in Methods of Development. LC 74-385. (Illus.). 434p. 1977. reprint ed. lib. bdg. 35.00 (*0-8371-7382-5*, PRBR, Greenwood Pr) Greenwood.
Proudfoot, Merrill. Diary of a Sit-in. 2nd ed. (Blacks in the New World Ser.). (Illus.). 272p. 1990. pap. text 14.95 (*0-252-06062-8*) U of Ill Pr.
Proudfoot, Peter. Seaport Sydney. (Illus.). 267p. 1995. pap. 39.95 (*0-86840-007-6*, Pub. by New South Wales Univ Pr) Intl Spec Bk.
— The Secret Plan of Canberra. 160p. 1994. 29.95 (*0-86840-030-0*, Pub. by New South Wales Univ Pr) Intl Spec Bk.
Proudfoot, Richard, et al, eds. The Arden Shakespeare Complete Works: Complete Series. 3rd ed. 1500p. 1998. 250.00 (*0-17-443615-7*, 9345) Thomson Learn.
Proudfoot, Robert. Even the Birds Don't Sound the Same Here: The Laotian Refugees Search for Heart in American Culture. (American University Studies Anthropology & Sociology: Ser. XI, Vol. 28). (Illus.). XVI, 276p. (C). 1990. text 52.95 (*0-8204-0841-7*) P Lang Pubng.
Proudfoot, Wayne. God & the Self: Three Types of Philosophy of Religion. LC 75-28983. 241p. 1976. 34.50 (*0-8387-1769-1*) Bucknell U Pr.
— Religious Experience. LC 84-23928. 1985. pap. 16.95 (*0-520-06128-4*, Pub. by U CA Pr) Cal Prin Full Svc.
Proudhon, P. J. Proudhon's Solution of the Social Problem. Cohen, Henry E., ed. (Men & Movements in the History & Philosophy of Anarchism Ser.). 1980. lib. bdg. 250.00 (*0-87700-044-1*) Revisionist Pr.
— What Is Property. 1972. 300.00 (*0-8490-1287-2*) Gordon Pr.
Proudhon, Pierre J. System of Economic Contradictions: or The Philosophy of Misery. Tucker, Benjamin R., tr. LC 75-38261. (Evolution of Capitalism Ser.). 482p. 1978. reprint ed. 30.95 (*0-405-04134-9*) Ayer.
Proudhon, Pierre-Joseph. General Idea of Revolution in the Nineteenth Century. 301p. (C). 1989. pap. text 23.00 (*0-85305-067-8*) Westview.
— General Idea of the Revolution in the Nineteenth Century. Robinson, John B., ed. (Studies in Individualist Anarchism & Mutualism). 1992. lib. bdg. 250.00 (*0-87968-009-1*) Gordon Pr.
— General Idea of the Revolution in the Nineteenth Century. LC 70-92978. (World History Ser.: No. 48). 1970. reprint ed. lib. bdg. 75.00 (*0-8383-1005-2*) M S G Haskell Hse.
— The Principle of Federation. Vernon, Richard, tr. & intro. by. LC 79-4192. 136p. reprint ed. pap. 42.20 (*0-8357-3504-4*, 203403500089) Bks Demand.
Proudhon, Pierre-Joseph, et al. What Is Property? LC 93-16214. (Cambridge Texts in the History of Political Thought Ser.). 267p. (C). 1994. text 59.95 (*0-521-40555-6*); pap. text 19.95 (*0-521-40556-4*) Cambridge U Pr.
Proudler, I. K., jt. ed. see McWhirter, J. G.
Proudlove, A., jt. auth. see Lichfield, N.
Proudman, Robert D., jt. auth. see Birchard, William, Jr.
Prough, R. A., jt. ed. see Powis, Garth.
Proulx, Ronald J., et al, eds. AAS/AIAA Spaceflight Mechanics Meeting, Feb. 13-16, 1995, Albuquerque, NM. LC 57-43769. (Advances in the Astronautical Sciences Ser.: Vol. 89). (Illus.). 1774p. 1995. 280.00 (*0-87703-401-X*, Am Astronaut Soc) Univelt Inc.
Prouix, Suzanne. Bad Blood. 1999. mass mkt. 5.99 (*0-449-00420-1*, GM) Fawcett.
***Prouix, Suzanne.** Bad Luck: A Big-City Hospital Just Received a Lethal Dose of... 320p. 2000. mass mkt. 6.50 (*0-449-00421-X*) Fawcett.
Proukakes, Charalampos & Katsaros, N. The New Role of the Academies of Sciences in the Balkan Countries. LC 97-34490. (NATO ASI Ser.). 237p. 1997. lib. bdg. 144.00 (*0-7923-4773-0*) Kluwer Academic.
Proulx, Brenda Z., ed. L. O. V. E. Works: Photojournalism by the Leave Out Violence Kids. LC 99-181481. 1999. 19.95 (*0-7737-6008-3*) Genl Dist Srvs.
Proulx, Daniel. The Kitchen Cabinetmaker's Building & Business Manual. LC 98-9883. (Illus.). 133p. 1998. pap. 19.95 (*0-941936-42-2*) Linden Pub Fresno.
Proulx, Danny. Build Your Own Kitchen Cabinets. (Illus.). 136p. 1997. pap. 22.99 (*1-55870-461-2*, Betrwy Bks) F & W Pubns Inc.
***Proulx, Danny.** Building Cabinet Doors & Drawers. LC 99-54627. (Illus.). 128p. 2000. pap. 21.95 (*0-941936-56-2*, Pub. by Linden Pub Fresno) IPG Chicago.
— Fast & Easy Techniques for Building Modern Cabinetry. LC 00-22530. (Illus.). 128p. 2000. pap. 22.99 (*1-55870-537-6*, Popular Woodwking Bks) F & W Pubns Inc.
Proulx, Danny. How to Build Classic Garden Furniture. LC 98-39468. (Illus.). 128p. 1999. pap. 24.99 (*1-55870-483-3*, Popular Woodwking Bks) F & W Pubns Inc.
— Smart Shelving & Storage Solutions. LC 99-21730. (Illus.). 144p. 1999. pap. 24.99 (*1-55870-509-0*, 70445, Popular Woodwking Bks) F & W Pubns Inc.
Proulx, E. Annie. Accordion Crimes. Date not set. 25.00 (*0-614-98011-9*, Scribners Ref) Mac Lib Ref.
— Accordion Crimes. LC 96-16299. 381p. 1996. 25.00 (*0-684-19548-8*) S&S Trade.
— Accordion Crimes. 432p. 1997. per. 13.00 (*0-684-83154-6*, Scribner Pap Fic) S&S Trade Pap.
Proulx, E. Annie. Accordion Crimes. 544p. 1996. per. 7.50 (*0-684-83282-8*) Scribner.
— Close Range: Wyoming Stories. 288p. 1999. per. 7.99 (*0-684-86726-5*, Scribners Ref) Mac Lib Ref.
— Close Range: Wyoming Stories. 288p. 2000. per. 13.00 (*0-684-85222-5*) S&S Trade.
Proulx, E. Annie. Close Range: Wyoming Stories. LC 98-56066. (Illus.). 288p. 1999. 23.50 (*0-684-85221-7*) Scribner.
— Close Range: Wyoming Stories. large type ed. LC 99-32480. (Illus.). 379p. 1999. pap. 28.95 (*0-7838-8677-2*, G K Hall Lrg Type) Mac Lib Ref.
— Heart Songs & Other Stories. LC 93-34060. 224p. 1995. per. 10.00 (*0-02-036075-4*, Pub. by Macmillan) S&S Trade.
— Postcards. 320p. 1994. per. 12.00 (*0-684-80087-X*) S&S Trade.
— Postcards. 1996. 21.50 (*0-684-83368-9*) S&S Trade.
— The Shipping News. LC 93-33221. 352p. 1994. pap. 10.00 (*0-02-036078-9*) Macmillan.
***Proulx, E. Annie.** The Shipping News. LC 99-234809. 352p. 1999. 25.00 (*0-684-85791-X*) S&S Trade.
Proulx, E. Annie. The Shipping News. LC 94-16863. 352p. 1994. per. 12.00 (*0-671-51005-3*, Scribner Pap Fic) S&S Trade Pap.
Proulx, E. Annie, ed. The Best American Short Stories 1997. 381p. 1997. pap. 13.00 (*0-395-79865-5*) HM.
Proulx, E. Annie & Nichols, Lew. Cider: Making, Using & Enjoying Sweet & Hard Cider. 2nd ed. LC 97-12169. (Illus.). iv, 219p. 1997. pap. 14.95 (*0-88266-969-9*) Storey Bks.
Proulx, Earl. Yankee Magazine's Make It Last: Over 1,000 Ingenious Ways to Extend the Life of Everything You Own. 416p. 1996. text 27.95 (*0-87596-296-3*) Rodale Pr Inc.
***Proulx, Earl.** Yankee Magazine's Make It Last: Over 1,000 Ingenious Ways to Extend the Life of Everything You Own. 1999. pap. 15.95 (*0-87596-517-2*) Rodale Pr Inc.
Proulx, Earl. Yankee's Practical Problem Solver: 1001 Ingenious Solutions to Everyday Dilemmas. LC 97-43248. 416p. 1998. 27.95 (*0-89909-375-2*) Rodale Pr Inc.
***Proulx, Earl & Gustafson, Eric.** Yankee Magazine's Vinegar, Duct Tape, Milk Jugs & More: 1,500 Ingenious Ways to Use Common Household Items to Repair, Restore, Revise, or Replace Just about Everything in Your Life. LC 99-28952. 400p. 1999. 27.95 (*0-89909-379-5*) Rodale Pr Inc.
Proulx, Earl, jt. auth. see Yankee Magazine Editors.
Proulx, Kevin E. Fear to the World: Eleven Voices in a Chorus of Horror. LC 93-242564. (Starmont Studies in Literary Criticism: No. 35). x, 243p. 1992. pap. 25.00 (*1-55742-173-0*) Millefleurs.
***Proulx, Matt.** The Photographer's Assistant Handbook. LC 99-87666. (Illus.). 176p. 2000. pap. 29.95 (*0-240-80413-9*, Focal) Buttrwrth-Heinemann.
Proulx, Paul G. Heather on the Vale: A Story about Paradise, Dreams, & the Agony of Eternal Life. LC 98-5973. 240p. 1998. pap. 14.95 (*1-880090-67-8*) Galde Pr.
Proulx, Richard. Love Is His Word. pap. write for info. (*1-58459-068-8*, 4037) Wrld Lib Pubns.
— More Sublime Chant. 1999. 15.95 (*5-550-71988-6*); pap. 10.95 (*5-550-71992-4*) Nairi.
Proulx, Richard, jt. auth. see Haugen, Marty.
Proum, Im, jt. auth. see Huffman, Franklin E.
Proum, Im, jt. ed. see Huffman, Franklin E.
Prouse, Derek, tr. see Ionesco, Eugene.
Prouse, Robert. Ticket to Hell. (Illus.). 183p. 1982. mass mkt. 4.95 (*0-88780-132-3*, Pub. by Formac Publ Co) Formac Dist Ltd.
Prousis, Theophilus C. Russian Society & the Greek Revolution. LC 94-7870. 269p. 1994. lib. bdg. 32.00 (*0-87580-193-5*) N Ill U Pr.
Proussis, Costas M., jt. ed. see Arnakis, George G.
Proust, Marcel. A la Recherche du Temps Perdu, 4 vols., Vol. 1. Tadie, Jacques, ed. 1987. lib. bdg. 145.00 (*0-7859-3879-6*) Fr & Eur.
— A la Recherche du Temps Perdu, Vol. 1. deluxe ed. (Pleiade Ser.). (FRE.). 400p. 1969. 89.95 (*2-07-011126-1*) Schoenhof.
— A la Recherche du Temps Perdu, Vol. 2. Tadie, Jean-Yves, ed. (FRE.). 1988. lib. bdg. 145.00 (*0-7859-3882-6*) Fr & Eur.
— A la Recherche du Temps Perdu, Vol. 2. deluxe ed. (Pleiade Ser.). (FRE.). 376p. 1969. 89.95 (*2-07-011136-9*) Schoenhof.
— A la Recherche du Temps Perdu, Vol. 3. Tadie, Jean-Yves, ed. (FRE.). 1988. lib. bdg. 150.00 (*0-7859-3884-2*) Fr & Eur.
— A la Recherche du Temps Perdu, Vol. 3. deluxe ed. (Pleiade Ser.). (FRE.). 488p. 1969. 89.95 (*2-07-011143-1*) Schoenhof.
— A la Recherche du Temps Perdu, Vol. 4. Tadie, Jean-Yves, ed. (FRE.). 1989. lib. bdg. 155.00 (*0-7859-3886-9*) Fr & Eur.
— A la Recherche du Temps Perdu, Vol. 4. deluxe ed. (Pleiade Ser.). (FRE.). 504p. 1989. 89.95 (*2-07-011164-4*) Schoenhof.
— A l'Ombre des Jeunes Filles en Fleurs. (FRE.). 492p. 1992. pap. 24.95 (*0-7859-1639-3*, 2070724913) Fr & Eur.
— A l'Ombre des Jeunes Filles en Fleurs. (Folio Ser.: No. 1946). (FRE.). 568p. 1988. pap. 12.95 (*2-07-038051-3*, 1428) Schoenhof.
— A l'Ombre des Jeunes Filles en Fleurs, Vol. 9. (FRE.). 1965. 12.95 (*0-685-74005-6*, F52240) Fr & Eur.
— A l'Ombre des Jeunes Filles en Fleurs: A la Recherche du Temps Perdu, Bk. 2. (FRE.). 1972. pap. 13.95 (*0-8288-3758-9*, F119540) Fr & Eur.
— Albertine Disparu La Fugitive Bk. 7: A la Recherche du Temps Perdu. (FRE.). 1990. pap. 15.95 (*0-8288-3759-7*, F119550) Fr & Eur.
— Albertine Disparue: (La Fugitive) (Folio Ser.: No. 2139). (FRE.). 374p. 1984. pap. 9.95 (*2-07-038233-8*, 2127) Schoenhof.
— Un Amour de Swann. (FRE.). 1976. pap. 10.95 (*0-8288-3760-0*, F119603) Fr & Eur.
— Un Amour de Swann. Sonnenfeld, Albert, ed. (FRE.). 278p. 1986. 3.95 (*0-88332-466-0*) Schoenhof.
— Un Amour de Swann. (Folio Ser.: No. 780). (FRE.). 254p. 1987. 8.95 (*2-07-036780-0*) Schoenhof.
— Un Amour de Swann. unabridged ed. (FRE.). pap. 6.95 (*2-87714-221-3*, Pub. by Bookking Intl) Distribks Inc.
— Autour de la Recherche: Lettres. (FRE.). 1988. pap. 24.95 (*0-7859-3311-5*, 2870272650) Fr & Eur.
— Briquebec: Prototype d' A l'Ombre des Jeunes Filles en Fleurs. Bales, Richard, ed. (FRE., Illus.). 330p. 1989. text 69.00 (*0-19-815857-2*) OUP.
— The Captive & The Fugitive, Vol. 5. (In Search of Lost Time Ser.: No. 5). 980p. 1993. 24.00 (*0-679-42477-6*) Modern Lib NY.
— Captive the Fugitive Time, Vol. III. 1982. pap. 22.00 (*0-394-71184-X*) Vin Bks.
— Combray. Bree, Germaine & Lynes, Carlos, Jr., eds. (FRE.). (Orig.). (C). 1952. pap. text 17.40 (*0-13-152439-9*) P-H.
— Combray. Hodson, L., ed. (French Texts Ser.). (FRE.). 1996. pap. 20.95 (*1-85399-456-1*, Pub. by Brist Class Pr) Focus Pub-R Pullins.
— Contre Sainte-Beuve. (FRE.). write for info. (*0-318-63466-X*) Fr & Eur.
— Contre Sainte-Beuve. (Folio Ser.: No. 68). (FRE.). pap. 11.95 (*2-07-032428-1*) Schoenhof.
— Contre Sainte-Beuve, Etc. (FRE.). 1971. lib. bdg. 99.50 (*0-8288-3529-2*, F119354) Fr & Eur.
— Contre Sainte-Beuve, Pastiches et Melanges, Essais et Articles. deluxe ed. (Pleiade Ser.). (FRE.). 1022p. 1971. 64.95 (*2-07-010651-9*) Schoenhof.
— Correspondance avec Gaston Gallimard. (Gallimard Ser.). (FRE.). pap. 49.95 (*2-07-071629-5*) Schoenhof.
— Correspondance avec Sa Mere. (FRE.). 1992. pap. 16.95 (*0-7859-3205-4*, 2264017929) Fr & Eur.
— Cote de Guermantes. (FRE.). 354p. 1988. pap. 12.95 (*0-7859-1377-7*, 2070381900) Fr & Eur.
— Le Cote de Guermantes. unabridged ed. (FRE.). pap. 8.95 (*2-87714-209-4*, Pub. by Bookking Intl) Distribks Inc.
— Cote de Guermantes, Tome 1. (Folio Ser.: No. 2005). (FRE.). pap. 11.95 (*2-07-038094-7*) Schoenhof.
— Cote de Guermantes, Tome 2. (Folio Ser.: No. 2006). (FRE.). pap. 11.95 (*2-07-038190-0*) Schoenhof.
— Cote de Guermantes: A la Recherche du Temps Perdu: Avec: Sodome et Gomorrhe, Vol. 4. (FRE.). 504p. 1992. pap. 29.95 (*0-685-74008-0*, 207072638X) Fr & Eur.
— La Cote de Guermantes Vol. 1, Bks. 3-4: A la Recherche du Temps Perdu. (FRE.). 1988. pap. 11.95 (*0-8288-3761-9*, FC1509); pap. 11.95 (*0-8288-3762-7*, FC1510) Fr & Eur.
— Du Cote de Chez Swann. (FRE.). (C). pap. 16.95 (*0-8442-1751-4*, VF1751-4) NTC Contemp Pub Co.
— Du Cote de Chez Swann. (Folio Ser.: No. 1924). (FRE.). 1965. pap. 13.75 (*2-07-037924-8*) Schoenhof.
— Du Cote de Chez Swann. unabridged ed. (FRE.). pap. 7.95 (*2-87714-136-5*, Pub. by Bookking Intl) Distribks Inc.
— Du Cote de Chez Swann: A la Recher che du Temps Perdu, Bk. 1. (FRE.). 527p. 1989. pap. 16.95 (*0-7859-4618-7*, F119560) Fr & Eur.
— La Fugitive. (FRE.). 1986. pap. 16.95 (*0-7859-3399-9*) Fr & Eur.
— The Guermantes Way. (In Search of Lost Time Ser.: Vol. 3). 1993. 18.50 (*0-685-62549-4*) Modern Lib NY.
— The Guermantes Way. rev. ed. Scott-Moncrieff, C. K. & Kilmartin, Terence, trs. 1993. write for info. (*0-318-69701-7*) Modern Lib NY.
— The Guermantes Way, Vol. 3. Scott-Moncrieff, C. K. & Kilmartin, Terence, trs. (In Search of Lost Time Ser.: No. 3). (Illus.). 770p. 1993. 21.00 (*0-679-60028-0*) Modern Lib NY.
— In Search of Lost Time, 4. 1999. pap. 13.95 (*0-375-75310-9*) Modern Lib NY.
— In Search of Lost Time, 5. 1999. pap. 14.95 (*0-375-75311-7*) Modern Lib NY.
— In Search of Lost Time, 6. 1999. pap. 13.95 (*0-375-75312-5*) Modern Lib NY.
— In Search of Lost Time, Vol. 2. 1998. pap. 13.95 (*0-375-75219-6*) Modern Lib NY.
— In Search of Lost Time Vol. III: The Guermantes Way, Vol. III. (Modern Library Ser.). 1998. pap. 14.95 (*0-375-75233-1*) Modern Lib NY.
— L' Indifferent: Nouvelle. (FRE.). 1978. pap. 10.95 (*0-7859-1351-3*, 2070297713) Fr & Eur.
— Jean Santeuil. (FRE.). 1971. lib. bdg. 89.95 (*0-8288-3530-6*, F119353) Fr & Eur.
— Jean Santeuil, les Plaisirs et las Jours. deluxe ed. (Pleiade Ser.). (FRE.). 1123p. 1987. 63.95 (*2-07-010650-0*) Schoenhof.
— Lettres a Bibesco. (FRE.). 11.95 (*0-685-37066-6*) Fr & Eur.
— Lettres a Reynaldo Hahn. (FRE.). pap. 6.50 (*0-685-37068-2*) Fr & Eur.
— Lettres Retrouvees. (FRE.). 6.95 (*0-685-37069-0*) Fr & Eur.
— Marcel Proust on Art & Literature, 1896-1919. Warner, Sylvia T., tr. LC 97-17483. 416p. 1997. pap. 13.95 (*0-7867-0454-3*) Carroll & Graf.
— L' Ombre des Jeunes Filles en Fleurs. unabridged ed. (FRE.). pap. 7.95 (*2-87714-142-X*, Pub. by Bookking Intl) Distribks Inc.
— On Reading Ruskin. Burford, William, ed. & tr. by. LC 86-22467. (Illus.). 192p. 1987. 15.00 (*0-300-03513-6*) Yale U Pr.
— Par les Yeux de Marcel Proust. Muhlstein, ed. (FRE.). 16.50 (*0-685-37070-4*) Fr & Eur.
— Les Pastiches de Proust. Milly, ed. (FRE.). 48.25 (*0-685-37071-2*) Fr & Eur.
— Pastiches et Melanges. (FRE.). 1970. pap. 8.95 (*0-7859-2836-7*) Fr & Eur.
— Les Plaisirs et les Jours. (FRE.). 1979. pap. 17.95 (*0-7859-2743-3*) Fr & Eur.
— Les Plaisirs et les Jours. (Imaginaire Ser.). (FRE.). 1924. reprint ed. pap. 13.95 (*2-07-028613-4*) Schoenhof.
— Pleasures & Days: And Other Writings. Varese, Louise et al, trs. from FRE. LC 78-2432. 1978. reprint ed. 35.00 (*0-86527-293-X*) Fertig.
— Pleasures & Regrets. 236p. 1986. reprint ed. 33.00 (*0-7206-0655-1*) Dufour.
— Pleasures & Regrets. Varese, Louise, tr. from FRE. LC 84-6120. (Neglected Books of the 20th Century Ser.). 221p. 1984. reprint ed. pap. 7.50 (*0-88001-063-0*) HarpC.
— La Prisonniere. (Folio Ser.: No. 785). (FRE.). 499p. 1987. pap. 12.95 (*2-07-038177-3*) Schoenhof.
— La Prisonniere Bk. 6: A la Recherche du Temps Perdu. (FRE.). 1989. pap. 15.95 (*0-8288-3764-3*, F119580) Fr & Eur.
— Remembrance of Things Past, Vol. 2. 1982. pap. 22.00 (*0-394-71183-1*) Vin Bks.
— Remembrance of Things Past, 3 vols., Vol. 3. Scott-Moncrieff, C. K. et al, trs. from FRE. LC 82-40052. (C). 1982. boxed set 64.00 (*0-394-71243-9*) Vin Bks.
— Marcel Proust: Selected Letters, 1880-1903. Kolb, Philip, ed. Manheim, Ralph, tr. (Illus.). xxviii, 376p. 1997. pap. text 20.50 (*0-226-68459-8*) U Ch Pr.
— Sodom & Gomorrah. Scott-Moncrieff, C. K. & Kilmartin, Terence, trs. LC 92-27272. (In Search of Lost Time Ser.: Vol. 4). 700p. 1993. 21.00 (*0-679-60029-9*) Modern Lib NY.

P

An Asterisk (*) at the beginning of an entry indicates that the title is appearing for the first time.

— Sodome et Gomorrhe. (FRE.). 1966. write for info. (0-318-63599-2, 1641) Fr & Eur.
— Sodome et Gomorrhe. (Folio Ser.: No. 2047). (FRE.). 599p. 1985. pap. 16.50 (2-07-038135-8, 1641) Schoenhof.
— Sodome et Gomorrhe Bk. 5: A la Recherche du Temps Perdu. (FRE.). 1972. pap. 18.95 (0-8288-3765-1, F119590) Fr & Eur.
— Sur Baudelaire, Flaubert et Morand. (FRE.). 1987. pap. 24.95 (0-7859-3309-3, 2870271980) Fr & Eur.
— Swann's Way. Scott-Moncrieff, C. K., tr. 551p. (C). 1964. pap. 8.44 (0-07-553647-1, T67) McGraw.
Proust, Marcel. Swann's Way. Scott-Moncrieff, C. K. & Kilmartin, Terence, trs. 1982. pap. 20.00 (0-394-71182-3) Random.
Proust, Marcel. Swann's Way. Kilmartin, Terence & Mancrief, C. K. Scott, trs. from FRE. LC 98-217411. 496p. 1998. pap. 12.95 (0-14-118058-7, Penguin Bks) Viking Penguin.
— Swann's Way. Scott-Moncrieff, C. K. & Kilmartin, Terence, trs. (International Ser.). 480p. 1989. pap. 12.00 (0-679-72009-X) Vin Bks.
— Swann's Way. 1986. reprint ed. lib. bdg. 21.95 (0-89966-581-0) Buccaneer Bks.
***Proust, Marcel.** Swann's Way, Set. unabridged ed. (Remembrance of Things Past Ser.: Pt. 1). (C). 1999. 77.95 incl. audio (1-55685-607-5) Audio Bk Con.
Proust, Marcel. Swann's Way: In Search of Lost Time, Vol. 1. Scott-Moncrieff, C. K. & Kilmartin, Terence, trs. from FRE. LC 92-25657. (In Search of Lost Time Ser.). 644p. 1992. 21.95 (0-679-60005-1) Modern Lib NY.
— Swann's Way: In Search of Lost Time, Vol. 1. 640p. 1998. pap. 12.95 (0-375-75154-8) Modern Lib NY.
***Proust, Marcel.** Swan's Way. 496p. 1999. pap. 13.95 (0-14-028326-9) Viking Penguin.
Proust, Marcel. Le Temps Retrouve. (Folio Ser.: No. 2203). (FRE.). 442p. 1987. pap. 10.95 (2-07-038293-1) Schoenhof.
— Le Temps Retrouve Bk. 8: A la Recherche du Temps Perdu. (FRE.). 1990. pap. 16.95 (0-8288-3766-X, F128080) Fr & Eur.
Proust, Marcel. Time Regained, Vol. 6. Mayor, Andreas & Kilmartin, Terence, trs. (In Search of Lost Time Ser.: No. 6). 770p. 1993. 24.00 (0-679-42476-8) Modern Lib NY.
Proust, Marcel. Within a Budding Grove. Scott-Moncrieff, C. K. & Kilmartin, Terence, trs. from FRE. LC 92-25656. (In Search of Lost Time Ser.: Vol. 2). 784p. 1992. 21.00 (0-679-60006-X) Modern Lib NY.
Proust, Marcel & Riviere, Jacques. Correspondance, 1914-1922. Kolb, Phillip, ed. (FRE.). 353p. 1976. pap. 18.95 (0-7859-1594-X, 2070292420X) Fr & Eur.
Proust, Marcel, jt. auth. see Seymour, Gabriel N.
Prout, Alan. The Body, Childhood & Society. LC 98-49901. 240p. 1999. text 59.95 (0-312-22144-4) St Martin.
Prout, Alan, et al, eds. Children, Medicines, & Culture. LC 95-17497. 420p. (C). 1997. pap. 19.95 (0-7890-0210-8, Pharmctl Prods) Haworth Pr.
Prout, Alan, jt. auth. see James, Allison.
Prout, Alan, jt. ed. see James, Allison.
Prout, Brian J. & Cooper, J. G. An Outline of Clinical Diagnosis. 2nd ed. (Illus.). 280p. 1987. pap. 18.00 (0-318-35047-5) Mosby Inc.
Prout, Brian J. & Cooper, John G. An Outline of Clinical Diagnosis. 264p. 1987. pap. text 39.00 (0-7506-2106-0) Buttrwrth-Heinemann.
Prout, Ebenezer. Applied Forms: A Sequel to Musical Form. LC 77-10853. 1971. reprint ed. 7.00 (0-403-00329-6) Scholarly.
— Applied Forms: A Sequel to "Musical Form" 307p. 1990. reprint ed. lib. bdg. 79.00 (0-7812-0784-3) Rprt Serv.
— Applied Forms: A Sequel to Musical Form. 3rd ed. LC 71-155615. reprint ed. 34.50 (0-404-05138-3) AMS Pr.
— Counterpoint: Strict & Free. LC 73-108530. 1970. 7.00 (0-403-00325-3) Scholarly.
— Counterpoint: Strict & Free. 249p. 1990. reprint ed. lib. bdg. 69.00 (0-7812-9141-0) Rprt Serv.
— Counterpoint: Strict & Free. 2nd ed. LC 70-149692. reprint ed. 45.00 (0-404-05139-1) AMS Pr.
— Double Counterpoint & Canon. LC 68-25300. (Studies in Music: No. 42). 1969. reprint ed. lib. bdg. 75.00 (0-8383-0312-9) M S G Haskell Hse.
— Fugue. LC 68-25301. (Studies in Music: No. 42). 1969. reprint ed. lib. bdg. 75.00 (0-8383-0313-7) M S G Haskell Hse.
— Fugue. 258p. 1990. reprint ed. lib. bdg. 69.00 (0-7812-9134-8) Rprt Serv.
— Fugue. LC 71-108527. 1970. reprint ed. 14.00 (0-403-00328-8) Scholarly.
— Fugue. 4th ed. LC 69-14043. 258p. 1970. reprint ed. lib. bdg. 65.00 (0-8371-1872-7, PRFU, Greenwood Pr) Greenwood.
— Harmony: Its Theory & Practice. 342p. 1990. reprint ed. lib. bdg. 79.00 (0-7812-9137-2) Rprt Serv.
— Harmony, Its Theory & Practice. rev. ed. LC 79-151598. reprint ed. 34.50 (0-404-05144-8) AMS Pr.
— Instrumentation. LC 68-25302. (Studies in Music: No. 42). (Illus.). 1969. reprint ed. lib. bdg. 75.00 (0-8383-0314-5) M S G Haskell Hse.
— Instrumentation. 144p. 1990. reprint ed. lib. bdg. 59.00 (0-7812-9150-X) Rprt Serv.
— Musical Form. 257p. 1990. reprint ed. lib. bdg. 69.00 (0-7812-9147-X) Rprt Serv.
— Musical Form. LC 78-108526. 1970. reprint ed. 6.50 (0-403-00327-X) Scholarly.
— The Orchestra. 1990. reprint ed. lib. bdg. 140.00 (0-7812-9151-8) Rprt Serv.
— The Orchestra, 2 vols. (Illus.). 577p. reprint ed. 59.00 (0-403-00322-9) Scholarly.
— The Orchestra: The Works of Ebenezer Prout, 2 vols. reprint ed. lib. bdg. 99.00 (0-7812-0781-9) Rprt Serv.

P

Prout, G. Motor Boating for Beginners. (C). 1987. 25.00 (0-85174-142-8) St Mut.
— Simple Boat Building. (C). 1987. 40.00 (0-85174-143-6) St Mut.
Prout, H. Thompson & Brown, Douglas T. Counseling & Psychotherapy with Children & Adolescents: Theory & Practice for School & Clinic Settings. 3rd ed. LC 98-16412. 456p. 1998. 65.00 (0-471-18236-2) Wiley.
Prout, H. Thompson, jt. auth. see Brown, Douglas T.
Prout, H. Thompson, jt. auth. see Knoff, Howard M.
Prout, H. Thompson, jt. auth. see Strohmer, Douglas C.
Prout, H. Thompson, jt. ed. see Strohmer, Douglas C.
Prout, Henry G. A Life of George Westinghouse. LC 72-5068. (Technology & Society Ser.). (Illus.). 406p. 1977. reprint ed. 34.95 (0-405-04719-3) Ayer.
Prout, James H. Acoustics for You. LC 88-7699. 276p. (C). 1991. reprint ed. 31.50 (0-89464-328-2) Krieger.
***Prout, Linda.** Live in the Balance: The Ground-Breaking East-West Nutrition Program. (Illus.). 304p. 2000. pap. 16.95 (1-56924-615-7) Marlowe & Co.
Prout, Quintin. Nobe's Kitchen: Poems. LC 98-23115. 64p. 1998. pap. 10.00 (0-914278-75-4) Copper Beech.
Prout, T. P. Industrial Market Research Workbook. 240p. 1973. 35.00 (0-8464-0509-1) Beekman Pubs.
Prouty, Charles T. Contention & Shakespeare's 2 Henry V. 1954. 59.50 (0-685-69852-1) Elliots Bks.
— George Gascoigne. LC 65-19620. 363p. 1972. 23.95 (0-405-08867-1, Pub. by Blom Pubns) Ayer.
— The Sources of Much Ado about Nothing. LC 76-128893. (Select Bibliographies Reprint Ser.). 1977. reprint ed. 19.95 (0-8369-5513-7) Ayer.
Prouty, Charles T., ed. Shakespeare: Of an Age & for All Time. LC 72-960. reprint ed. 27.50 (0-404-05146-4) AMS Pr.
Prouty, Charles T., ed. see Kyd, Thomas.
Prouty, Chris. Empress Taytu & Menilek II: Ethiopia, 1883-1910. 430p. 1987. 29.95 (0-932415-10-5); pap. 11.95 (0-932415-11-3) Red Sea Pr.
Prouty, Chris & Rosenfeld, Eugene. Historical Dictionary of Ethiopia & Eritrea. 2nd ed. LC 93-29501. (African Historical Dictionaries Ser.: No. 56). (Illus.). 644p. 1994. 69.50 (0-8108-2663-1) Scarecrow.
Prouty, Dick, jt. auth. see Shelton, David C.
***Prouty, Dow E.** Grandpa's Book of Rules: Rules & Guidelines for Raising Your Kids, Your Grandkids, & Maybe Your Neighbor's Kids. LC 97-75226. (Illus.). 1998. 21.95 (0-911119-82-5) Igram Pr.
Prouty, Garry. Theoretical Evolutions in Person-Centered - Experiential Therapy: Applications to Schizophrenic & Retarded Psychoses. LC 93-42143. 144p. 1994. 55.00 (0-275-94543-X, Praeger Pubs) Greenwood.
Prouty, Graciela P., tr. see Rubio, Pedro.
Prouty, Howard H. Variety Television Reviews, 1923-1990: Index. LC 89-17088. (Variety Television Reviews Ser.: Vol. 15). 450p. 1991. reprint ed. text 195.00 (0-8240-3794-4) Garland.
Prouty, Howard H., ed. Variety Television Reviews, 1951-1953. LC 89-17088. (Variety Television Reviews Ser.: Vol. 4). 528p. 1989. text 80.00 (0-8240-2590-3) Garland.
— Variety Television Reviews, 1983-1986. LC 89-17088. (Variety Television Reviews Ser.: Vol. 13). 544p. 1989. text 80.00 (0-8240-3792-8) Garland.
— Variety Television Reviews, 1987-1988. LC 89-17088. (Variety Television Reviews Ser.: Vol. 14). 328p. 1990. text 80.00 (0-8240-3793-6) Garland.
— Variety Television Reviews, 1989-1990. LC 89-17088. (Variety Television Reviews Ser.: Vol. 16). 592p. 1992. text 180.00 (0-8240-3795-2) Garland.
— Variety Television Reviews, 1957-1959. LC 89-17088. (Variety Television Reviews Ser.: Vol. 6). 536p. 1989. text 80.00 (0-8240-2592-X) Garland.
— Variety Television Reviews, 1946-56. LC 89-17088. (Variety Television Reviews Ser.: Vol. 1). 776p. 1990. text 80.00 (0-8240-2587-3) Garland.
— Variety Television Reviews, 1970-1973. LC 89-17088. (Variety Television Reviews Ser.: Vol. 10). 472p. 1989. text 80.00 (0-8240-2596-2) Garland.
— Variety Television Reviews, 1974-1977. LC 89-17088. (Variety Television Reviews Ser.: Vol. 11). 464p. 1989. text 80.00 (0-8240-2597-0) Garland.
— Variety Television Reviews, 1978-1982. LC 89-17088. (Variety Television Reviews Ser.: Vol. 12). 424p. 1989. text 80.00 (0-8240-2598-9) Garland.
— Variety Television Reviews, 1966-1969. LC 89-17088. (Variety Television Reviews Ser.: Vol. 9). 560p. 1989. text 80.00 (0-8240-2595-4) Garland.
— Variety Television Reviews, 1923-1950. LC 89-17088. (Variety Television Reviews Ser.: Vol. 3). 528p. 1989. text 80.00 (0-8240-2589-X) Garland.
— Variety Television Reviews, 1923-1990, 16 vols. 1992. 3015.00 (0-8153-0363-7) Garland.
— Variety Television Reviews, 1923-1990, 16 vols., Ea. 1992. 165.00 (0-318-69656-8) Garland.
— Variety Television Reviews, 1957-60. LC 88-17088. (Variety Television Reviews Ser.: Vol. 2). 496p. 1990. text 80.00 (0-8240-2588-1) Garland.
— Variety Television Reviews, 1960-1962. LC 89-17088. (Variety Television Reviews Ser.: Vol. 7). 496p. 1989. text 80.00 (0-8240-2593-8) Garland.
— Variety Television Reviews, 1963-1965. LC 89-17088. (Variety Television Reviews Ser.: Vol. 8). 520p. 1989. text 80.00 (0-8240-2594-6) Garland.
Prouty, John C., et al. The ACC Basketball Stat Book. 362p. 1993. pap. 11.95 (0-9640369-0-8) Willow Oak.
Prouty, L. Fletcher. JFK: The CIA, Vietnam & the Plot to Assassinate John F. Kennedy. 352p. 1992. 22.00 (1-55972-130-8, Birch Ln Pr) Carol Pub Group.
— JFK: The CIA, Vietnam & the Plot to Assassinate John F. Kennedy. (Illus.). 408p. 1996. pap. 18.95 (0-8065-1772-7, Citadel Pr) Carol Pub Group.

Prouty, L. Fletcher, jt. ed. see Ratcliffe, David T.
Prouty, Olive H. Now, Voyager. 340p. 1991. reprint ed. lib. bdg. 25.95 (0-89966-791-0) Buccaneer Bks.
Prouty, Raymond W. Helicopter Performance, Stability & Control. 746p. 1995. 98.50 (0-89464-929-9) Krieger.
— Military Helicopter Design Technology. LC 97-28755. (Illus.). 148p. (C). 1998. reprint ed. text 38.50 (1-57524-067-X) Krieger.
Prouty, Vicki L. & Fagan, Michele. Language Strategies for Children: Keys to Classroom Success. LC 97-9031. 1997. pap. 39.00 (1-888222-01-8) Thinking Pubns.
Prouty, Vicki L., jt. auth. see Fagan, Michele.
Prouty, William W. Bill Prouty's Chapel Hill. unabridged ed. (Illus.). 116p. (Orig.). 1979. pap. 5.95 (0-940715-05-8) Chapel Hill Hist.
***Prouve, Jean.** Jean Prouve. 1999. pap. text. write for info. (2-909187-04-7) Galerie Jousse-Seguin.
Prouxl, E. A. Great Grapes Grow the Best Eve. 1983. pap. 2.95 (0-88266-228-7, Storey Pub) Storey Bks.
— Make Your Own Insulated Window. 1983. pap. 2.95 (0-88266-294-5, Storey Pub) Storey Bks.
— Making the Best Apple Cider. 1983. pap. 2.95 (0-88266-222-8, Storey Pub) Storey Bks.
Provan. Digital Typography Pocket Guide. (Graphic Communications Ser.). 1997. pap. 15.95 (0-8273-7428-3) Delmar.
Provan, A. MCQ's in Medicine for MRCP, Pt. 1. 208p. 1989. pap. write for info. (0-443-04220-9) Church.
***Provan, Andrew & Gribbin, John, eds.** Molecular Haematology. LC 99-16528. (Illus.). 240p. 2000. 195.00 (0-632-05037-3) Blackwell Sci.
Provan, Drew. The Oxford Handbook of Clinical Haematology. LC 98-28128. 640p. 1998. pap. 39.95 (0-19-262903-4) OUP.
Provan, Drew & Henson, Andrew, eds. A B C of Clinical Haematology. 80p. 1997. pap. text 27.00 (0-7279-1206-2, Pub. by BMJ Pub) Login Brothers Bk Co.
Provan, Drew, et al. Clinical Haematology: A Postgraduate Exam Companion. LC 96-53901. 336p. 1997. pap. text 47.50 (0-7506-2920-7) Buttrwrth-Heinemann.
Provan, Iain. First & Second Kings. expanded rev. ed. (New International Biblical Commentary Ser.). 306p. 1995. pap. 11.95 (1-56563-053-X) Hendrickson MA.
Provan, Iain W. 1 & 2 Kings. (Old Testament Guides Ser.: Vol. 11). 125p. 1997. 12.50 (1-85075-802-6, Pub. by Sheffield Acad) CUP Services.
— Hezekiah & the Books of Kings: A Contribution to the Debate about the Composition of the Deuteronomistic History. (Beiheft zur Zeitschrift fuer die Alttestamentliche Wissenschaft Ser.: Vol. 172). 218p. (C). 1988. lib. bdg. 69.25 (3-11-011557-3) De Gruyter.
— Ideologies, Literary & Critical: Reflections on Recent Writings on the History of Israel. 36p. 1998. reprint ed. pap. 5.50 (1-57383-094-1, Regent Coll Pub) Regent College.
Provan, Iain W. Lamentations. (New Century Bible Ser.). 142p. 1991. pap. 14.95 (0-551-02323-6, Pub. by Sheffield Acad) CUP Services.
Provan, James W., ed. Probabilistic Fracture Mechanics & Reliability. 1986. text 326.50 (90-247-3334-0) Kluwer Academic.
Provan, James W., jt. ed. see Sih, G. C.
Provan, John. Berlin Airlift: The Effort & the Aircraft. Davies, R. E., ed. (Illus.). 80p. 1998. lib. bdg. 30.00 (1-888962-05-4) Paladwr Pr.
Provanzano, Steven A. Blue Collar Resumes: Job-Winning Resumes for Artisans, Beauticians, Carpenters... X-ray Technicians, Yarn Dyers, Zookeepers & Everything in Between. LC 99-22502. 224p. 1999. pap. 11.99 (1-56414-412-7) Career Pr Inc.
Provder, Theodore. Chromatography of Polymers: Hyphenated & Multidimensional Techniques. LC 99-25837. (ACS Symposium Ser.: No. 731). (Illus.). 336p. 1999. text 120.00 (0-8412-3661-5, Pub. by Am Chemical) OUP.
Provder, Theodore, ed. Chromatography of Polymers: Characterization by SEC & FFF. LC 93-186. (ACS Symposium Ser.: No. 521). (Illus.). 338p. 1993. text 105.00 (0-8412-2625-3, Pub. by Am Chemical) OUP.
— Computer Applications in Applied Polymer Science. LC 82-13735. (ACS Symposium Ser.: No. 197). 469p. 1982. lib. bdg. 54.95 (0-8412-0733-X) Am Chemical.
— Computer Applications in Applied Polymer Science. LC 82-13735. (ACS Symposium Ser.: Vol. 197). 478p. 1982. reprint ed. pap. 148.20 (0-608-03120-8, 206357300007) Bks Demand.
— Computer Applications in Applied Polymer Science No. 2: Automation, Modeling, & Simulation. LC 89-17602. (Symposium Ser.: No. 404). (Illus.). 551p. 1989. text 120.00 (0-8412-1662-2, Pub. by Am Chemical) OUP.
— Computer Applications in the Polymer Laboratory. LC 86-10831. (ACS Symposium Ser.: No. 313). (Illus.). 321p. 1986. 76.95 (0-8412-0977-4) Am Chemical.
— Computer Applications in the Polymer Laboratory. LC 86-10831. (ACS Symposium Ser.: Vol. 313). 336p. 1986. reprint ed. pap. 104.20 (0-608-03518-1, 206423700008) Bks Demand.
— Detection & Data Analysis in Size Exclusion Chromatography. LC 87-19480. (Symposium Ser.: No. 352). (Illus.). ix, 370p. 1987. 76.95 (0-8412-1429-8) Am Chemical.
— Detection & Data Analysis in Size Exclusion Chromatography. LC 87-19480. (ACS Symposium Ser.: Vol. 352). 320p. 1987. reprint ed. pap. 99.20 (0-608-03875-X, 206432200008) Bks Demand.
— Particle Size Distribution: Assessment & Characterization. LC 86-32185. (ACS Symposium Ser.: Vol. 332). 320p. 1987. reprint ed. pap. 99.20 (0-608-03544-0, 206426300008) Bks Demand.
— Particle Size Distribution III: Assessment & Characterization. LC 98-16110. (Symposium Ser.: No. 693). (Illus.). 368p. 1998. text 120.95 (0-8412-3561-9, Pub. by Am Chemical) OUP.
— Particle Size Distribution II: Assessment & Characterization. LC 91-25166. (ACS Symposium Ser.: No. 472). (Illus.). 408p. 1991. 89.95 (0-685-50550-2) Am Chemical.
Provder, Theodore, et al, eds. Chromatographic Characterization of Polymers: Hyphenated & Multidimensional Techniques. LC 95-22137. (Advances in Chemistry Ser.: No. 247). (Illus.). 314p. 1995. text 135.00 (0-8412-3132-X, Pub. by Am Chemical) OUP.
— Film Formation in Waterborne Coatings. LC 96-31614. (ACS Symposium Ser.: No. 648). (Illus.). 562p. 1996. text 145.00 (0-8412-3457-4, Pub. by Am Chemical) OUP.
Provder, Theodore & Urban, Marek W. Advances in Polymer Characterization. (ACS Symposium Ser.). 130.00 (0-8412-3621-6, Pub. by Am Chemical) OUP.
Provder, Theodore & Urban, Marek W., eds. Multidimensional Spectroscopy of Polymers: Vibrational, NMR, & Fluorescence Techniques. LC 95-17880. (ACS Symposium Ser.: No. 598). (Illus.). 586p. 1995. text 155.00 (0-8412-3262-8, Pub. by Am Chemical) OUP.
Provder, Theodore, ed. see American Chemical Society Division of Polymeric Ma, et al.
Provder, Theodore, jt. ed. see Craver, Clara D.
Provder, Theodore J., ed. Size Exclusion Chromatography: Methodology & Characterization of Polymers & Related Materials. LC 83-27515. (ACS Symposium Ser.: No. 245). 391p. 1984. lib. bdg. 72.95 (0-8412-0826-3) Am Chemical.
— Size Exclusion Chromatography: Methodology & Characterization of Polymers & Related Materials. LC 83-27515. (ACS Symposium Ser.: Vol. 245). 401p. 1984. reprint ed. pap. 124.40 (0-608-03125-9, 206357800007) Bks Demand.
— Size Exclusion Chromatography (GPC) LC 80-22015. (ACS Symposium Ser.: No. 138). 1980. 41.95 (0-8412-0586-8) Am Chemical.
— Size Exclusion Chromatography (GPC) LC 80-22015. (ACS Symposium Ser.: No. 138). (Illus.). 320p. 1980. reprint ed. pap. 99.20 (0-608-03227-1, 206374600007) Bks Demand.
Provder, Theodore J., ed. see Polymetric Materials Division Staff.
Provencal, Yvon. The Mind of Society: From a Fruitful Analogy of Minsky to a Prodigious Idea of Teilhard de Chardin. (World Futures General Evolution Studies: Vol. 12). 124p. 1998. text 29.00 (90-5700-514-X, ECU38, Harwood Acad Pubs) Gordon & Breach.
Provence, Sally. Guide for the Care of Infants in Groups. LC 67-26025. 104p. (C). 1967. pap. 12.95 (0-87868-061-6) Child Welfare.
Provence, Sally, ed. Infants & Parents: Clinical Case Reports. LC 83-18441. (Clinical Infant Reports: No. 2). xix, 306p. (C). 1983. 47.50 (0-8236-2636-9) Intl Univs Pr.
Provence, Sally & Lipton, Rose C. Infants in Institutions: A Comparison of Their Development During the First Year of Life with Family-Reared Infants. LC 62-21560. 191p. 1967. 31.50 (0-8236-2648-2) Intl Univs Pr.
Provence, Sally, et al. The Challenge of Daycare. LC 75-43331. 313p. reprint ed. pap. 97.10 (0-7837-3307-0, 205770900006) Bks Demand.
Provence, Sally, jt. ed. see Fenichel, Emily.
Provencer, Ronald, ed. Crossroads: General Issue. (Interdisciplinary Journal of Southeast Asian Studies: Vol. 1.2). 113p. 1983. pap. 12.00 (1-877979-81-3) SE Asia.
— Crossroads: General Issue. (Interdisciplinary Journal of Southeast Asian Studies: Vol. 2.1). 69p. 1984. pap. 12.00 (1-877979-83-X) SE Asia.
— Crossroads: Philippine Studies Issue. (Interdisciplinary Journal of Southeast Asian Studies: Vol. 1.1). 85p. 1983. pap. 12.00 (1-877979-80-5) SE Asia.
Provencer, Ronald, ed. Crossroads Vol. 2, No. 3: An Interdisciplinary Journal of Southeast Asian Studies. 155p. 1984. pap. 12.00 (1-877979-85-6) SE Asia.
Provencer, Ronald, ed. Southeast Asian Studies & International Business. (Crossroads Ser.: Ser. 1.3). 123p. 1983. pap. 12.00 (1-877979-82-1) SE Asia.
— Two Hundred Years of the Chakri Dynasty. (Crossroads Ser.: Ser. 2.2). 145p. 1985. pap. 12.00 (1-877979-84-8) SE Asia.
Provencher, Denis M., jt. auth. see Geno, Marie Gontier.
***Provencher, Estella.** Pro's Poetry. 1999. pap. write for info. (1-58235-197-X) Watermrk Pr.
Provencher, R. G. Arson 1976. 1976. 3.25 (0-686-17605-7, TR 76-3) Society Fire Protect.
***Provencher, Rose-Marie.** Mouse Cleaning. 2001. text 15.95 (0-8050-6240-8) St Martin.
Provensen, Alice. The Buck Stops Here: The Presidents of the United States. LC 88-35036. (Illus.). 56p. (J). (gr. 2 up). 1990. 18.00 (0-06-024786-X) HarpC Child Bks.
— The Buck Stops Here: The Presidents of the United States. rev. ed. LC 96-53997. (Illus.). 64p. (J). 1997. pap. 10.00 (0-15-201628-7, Harcourt Child Bks) Harcourt.
— The Glorious Flight: Across the Channel with Louis Bleriot, July 25, 1909. LC 86-25473. (Picture Puffin Ser.). (Illus.). (J). 1987. 11.19 (0-606-01975-8, Pub. by Turtleback) Demco.
— My Fellow Americans: A Family Album. LC 95-15527. (Illus.). 64p. (J). (gr. 4 up). 1995. 19.95 (0-15-276642-1, Harcourt Child Bks) Harcourt.
— An Owl & Three Pussycats. 1981. 8.99 (0-224-01821-3) Random.
***Provensen, Alice.** Tales from Two Fortune Cookies. LC 99-462275. (Illus.). (J). 2001. write for info. (0-689-83232-X) S&S Childrens.

Provensen, Alice & Provensen, Martin. The Glorious Flight: Across the Channel with Louis Bleriot. (Illus.). 40p. (J). (gr. 3-8). 1987. pap. 4.95 (*0-317-63651-0*, PuffinBks) Peng Put Young Read.
— The Glorious Flight: Across the Channel with Louis Bleriot. (J). (gr. 4-6). 1987. pap. 6.99 (*0-14-050729-9*, PuffinBks) Peng Put Young Read.
— Town & Country. LC 93-44749. (Illus.). 32p. (J). (ps-3). 1994. 16.95 (*0-15-200182-4*, Harcourt Child Bks) Harcourt.

Provensen, Martin, jt. auth. see Brown, Margaret Wise.

Provensen, Martin, jt. auth. see Provensen, Alice.

Provenson, Alice & Provenson, Martin. The Glorious Flight: Across the Channel with Louis Bleriot. unabridged ed. (J). (gr. 4-6). 1987. 22.95 incl. audio (*0-87499-062-9*) Live Oak Media.
— The Glorious Flight: Across the Channel with Louis Bleriot, 4 bks., Set. (J). (gr. 4-6). 1987. pap., teacher ed. 33.95 incl. audio (*0-87499-063-7*) Live Oak Media.

Provenson, Martin, jt. auth. see Provenson, Alice.

Provenza, Dominic V. Oral Histology: Inheritance & Development. 2nd ed. LC 84-20140. 497p. reprint ed. pap. 154.10 (*0-7837-2740-2*, 204312000006) Bks Demand.

Provenza, Frederick D., et al, eds. Proceedings - Symposium on Plant - Herbivore Interactions. (Illus.). 188p. 1997. reprint ed. 25.00 (*0-89904-665-7*, Bear Meadows Resrch Grp); reprint ed. pap. 20.00 (*0-89904-666-5*, Bear Meadows Resrch Grp) Crumb Elbow Pub.

Provenzale, A., jt. ed. see Castagnoli, G. Cini.

Provenzale, James. Duke Radiology Boards Review. LC 97-34795. 640p. 1997. pap. text 75.00 (*0-397-51613-4*) Lppncott W & W.

Provenzale, James M. & Taveras, Juan M. Clinical Cases in Neuroradiology. LC 93-629. (Illus.). 400p. 1993. 89.00 (*0-8121-1590-2*) Lppncott W & W.

Provenzano, Antonino. Vinissi ... I'd Love to Come ..., Vol. IV. Cipolla, Gaetano, ed. & tr. by. LC 95-41987. (Pueti D'arba Sicula - Poets of ARBA Sicula). (ITA.). 200p. 1995. pap. 16.00 (*1-881901-08-4*) LEGAS.

Provenzano, Jim. Pins: A Novel. LC 99-90529. 285p. 1999. pap. 14.95 (*0-9672382-0-X*, Pub. by Myrmidude Pr) Alamo Sq Dist.

Provenzano, Richard G. Remembering Saugus: Growing up in a Small Town. (Saugus Historical Society Booklet Ser.: Vol. 6). 1995. write for info. (*0-936363-09-6*) Saugus Hist.

Provenzano, Steven A. The Guide to Basic Cover Letter Writing. (Illus.). 96p. 1994. pap. 7.95 (*0-8442-8196-4*, 81964, VGM Career) NTC Contemp Pub Co.
— Slam Dunk Resumes. Kennedy, Sarah, ed. LC 93-45862. (Illus.). 160p. (Orig.). 1994. pap. 7.95 (*0-8442-8191-3*, 81913, VGM Career) NTC Contemp Pub Co.

***Provenzano, Steven A.** Top Secret Executive Resumes: What It Takes to Create the Perfect Resume for the Best Top-Level Jobs. LC 99-51919. 256p. 2000. pap. 14.99 (*1-56414-431-3*) Career Pr Inc.

Provenzano, Steven A. Top Secret Resumes & Cover Letters. LC 95-16477. (Illus.). 208p. (Orig.). 1995. reprint ed. pap. text 12.95 (*0-7931-1359-8*, 5614-3401) Dearborn.
— Top Secret Resumes of the '90s: Discover What Really Works, & the Secrets "Professional" Resume Writers Won't Tell You. rev. ed. Desktop Publishing Inc. Staff, ed. LC 93-70858. (Careers-Resume Writing Ser.). 214p. (Orig.). 1994. reprint ed. pap. 10.95 (*0-9633558-1-3*) DeskTop IL.

Provenzo, Asterie B. Favorite Board Games You Can Make & Play. (Illus.). 256p. 1990. pap. 7.95 (*0-486-26410-6*) Dover.

Provenzo, Asterie B., jt. auth. see Provenzo, Eugene F.

Provenzo, Asterie B., jt. auth. see Provenzo, Eugene F., Jr.

Provenzo, E. Pursuing the Past. 1984. text, teacher ed., student ed. 16.95 (*0-201-20124-0*) Addison-Wesley.

Provenzo, Eugene F. Beyond the Gutenberg Galaxy: Microcomputers & the Emergence of Post-Typographic Culture. LC 86-1938. 128p. (Orig.). reprint ed. pap. 39.70 (*0-7837-4629-6*, 204435200002) Bks Demand.
— The Educator's Brief Guide to Computers in the Schools. LC 96-5258. 250p. 1996. 29.95 (*1-883001-22-6*) Eye On Educ.
— The Educator's Brief Guide to the Internet & the World Wide Web. LC 97-25293. 200p. 1997. pap. 25.95 (*1-883001-43-9*) Eye On Educ.

Provenzo, Eugene F., Jr. The Internet & the World Wide Web for Preservice Teachers. LC 99-185352. 138p. (C). 1998. pap. text 14.00 (*0-205-28857-X*, Longwood Div) Allyn.
— Religious Fundamentalism & American Education: The Battle for the Public Schools. LC 89-4456. (SUNY Series, Frontiers in Education). 134p. (C). 1990. text 59.50 (*0-7914-0217-7*); pap. text 19.95 (*0-7914-0218-5*) State U NY Pr.
— Video Kids: Making Sense of Nintendo. (Illus.). 192p. 1991. pap. text 10.95 (*0-674-93709-0*) HUP.

Provenzo, Eugene F., Jr. & Brett, Arlene. The Complete Block Book. (Illus.). 182p. 1983. text 45.00 (*0-8156-2300-3*) Syracuse U Pr.

Provenzo, Eugene F. & Carlebach, Michael, Jr. Farm Security Administration Photographs of Florida. LC 93-2846. (Illus.). 144p. (C). 1993. 29.95 (*0-8130-1212-0*); pap. 19.95 (*0-8130-1213-9*) U Press Fla.

Provenzo, Eugene F., Jr. & Fradd, Sandra H. Hurricane Andrew, the Public Schools, & the Rebuilding of Community. LC 94-28873. (SUNY Series in Education & Culture). 177p. (C). 1995. text 44.50 (*0-7914-2481-2*); pap. text 14.95 (*0-7914-2482-0*) State U NY Pr.

Provenzo, Eugene F., Jr. & McCloskey, Gary N., eds. Schoolteachers & Schooling: Ethoses in Conflict. LC 96-22351. (Social & Policy Issues in Education Ser.). 194p. 1996. pap. 24.95 (*1-56750-248-2*); text 73.25 (*1-56750-247-4*) Ablx Pub.

Provenzo, Eugene F., Jr. & Provenzo, Asterie B. Easy-to-Make Old-Fashioned Toys. (Illus.). xvi, 272p. 1989. pap. 8.95 (*0-486-25958-7*) Dover.

Provenzo, Eugene F. & Provenzo, Asterie B. Forty-Seven Easy to Do Classic Science Experiments. (Illus.). 128p. 1990. pap. 3.95 (*0-486-25856-4*) Dover.

Provenzo, Eugene F., Jr., et al. Computers, Curriculum, & Cultural Change: An Introduction for Teachers. LC 98-23042. 312p. 1998. pap., teacher ed. 34.50 (*0-8058-2268-2*) L Erlbaum Assocs.

Provenzo, Eugene F., Jr., jt. auth. see Brett, Arlene.

Provenzo, Eugene F., Jr., ed. see Lewis, Mary H.

Provenzo, Therese M., ed. see Lewis, Mary H.

Prover, Jorja. No One Knows Their Names: Screenwriters in Hollywood. LC 94-70377. 176p. (C). 1994. 37.95 (*0-87972-657-1*); pap. 17.95 (*0-87972-658-X*) Bowling Green Univ Popular Press.

Provey, Joe. Parent's Complete Guide to Soccer. LC 99-16818. 2000. pap. 14.95 (*0-7615-1697-2*) Prima Pub.

Provey, Joe & Robinson, Kris. Better Lawns, Step-by-Step. Soderstrom, Neil, ed. LC 98-84957. (Illus.). 160p. 1999. pap. 14.95 (*1-58011-051-7*) Creative Homeowner.

Providencia, Joao Da, see Dreizler, Reiner M., ed.

Providencia, Joao Da, see Dreizler, Reiner M. & Da Providencia, Joao, eds.

Providencia, Joao Da, see Dreizler, Reiner M.

***Provident Music Publishing Staff, ed.** Celebrate Gospel 2000 Shopping Guides. 2000. pap. 0.00 (*0-7601-3528-2*) Brentwood Music.

Province, Charles M. Patton's One-Minute Messages: Tactical Leadership Skills for Business Managers. (Illus.). 104p. 1995. pap. 9.95 (*0-89141-546-7*, Pub. by Presidio Pr) Natl Bk Netwk.

Provincial Congress of Massachusetts Colony, 1775. Narrative of the Excursions & Ravages of the King's Troops under Command of General Gage. LC 67-29008. (Eyewitness Accounts of the American Revolution Ser.). 1968. reprint ed. 14.95 (*0-405-01119-9*) Ayer.

Provine, Doris M. Case Selection in the United States Supreme Court. LC 79-25967. 224p. 1980. lib. bdg. 25.50 (*0-226-68468-7*) U Ch Pr.
— Judging Credentials: Nonlawyer Judges & the Politics of Professionalism. LC 85-16516. xviii, 264p. 1986. pap. text 17.00 (*0-226-68471-7*) U Ch Pr.
— Judging Credentials: Nonlawyer Judges & the Politics of Professionalism. LC 85-16516. xviii, 248p. 1994. lib. bdg. 30.00 (*0-226-68470-9*) U Ch Pr.

Provine, Dorothy S. District of Columbia Free Negro Registers, 1821-1861, 2 vols. LC 96-216196. (Orig.). 1996. pap. 94.00 (*0-7884-0506-3*, P658) Heritage Bk.
— District of Columbia Indentures of Apprenticeship, 1801-1893. 400p. 1998. pap. 38.00 (*1-888265-28-0*) Willow Bend.
— District of Columbia Marriage Records, 1870-1877. 333p. 1997. pap. 28.00 (*1-888265-23-X*) Willow Bend.
— Index to District of Columbia Wills, 1801-1920. 218p. pap. 18.50 (*0-8063-1354-4*, 4705) Clearfield Co.
— Index to District of Columbia Wills, 1921-1950. 351p. 1996. pap. 37.50 (*1-888265-01-9*) Willow Bend.

Provine, Dorothy S., compiled by. Alexandria County, Virginia, Free Negro Registers, 1797-1861. 358p. (Orig.). 1991. pap. 35.00 (*1-55613-416-9*) Heritage Bk.

Provine, Rick, jt. auth. see Brancolini, Kristine.

Provine, Robert R. Laughter: A Scientific Investigation. 288p. 1999. 24.00 (*0-316-71102-0*) Little.

***Provine, Robert R.** Laughter: A Scientific Investigation. (Illus.). 256p. 2000. 24.95 (*0-670-89375-7*, Viking) Viking Penguin.

Provine, William B. Darwinian Revolutions. Date not set. 21.95 (*0-393-02946-8*) Norton.
— The Origins of Theoretical Population Genetics. LC 73-153711. (Chicago History of Science & Medicine Ser.). xii, 214p. 1999. pap. text 19.00 (*0-226-68466-0*) U Ch Pr.
— Sewall Wright & Evolutionary Biology. LC 85-24651. (Illus.). xvi, 560p. 1989. pap. text 23.00 (*0-226-68473-3*) U Ch Pr.
— Sewall Wright & Evolutionary Biology. LC 85-24651. (Illus.). xvi, 560p. 1997. 45.00 (*0-226-68474-1*) U Ch Pr.

Provine, William B., jt. auth. see Mayr, Ernst W.

Provine, William B., ed. see Wright, Sewall.

***Provinzano, A. M.** Green Milk: Burning Hues of Lost Edens. 250p. 2000. pap. 12.95 (*1-930185-01-4*, 102) Joan of Arc Pubng.
— The Penitents: A Story about Love, Death & Freedom. 200p. 2000. pap. 11.95 (*1-930185-02-2*, 103) Joan of Arc Pubng.
— The Race of Leaves: A Rebels' Fable. 200p. 2000. pap. 11.95 (*1-930185-03-0*, 104) Joan of Arc Pubng.

–The Secret Spring of Edith Cooley. LC 99-96367. 138p. 2000. pap. 11.95 (*1-930185-00-6*, 101) Joan of Arc Pubng.

Inspired by a true story & set in a Greenwich Village Brownstone, The Secret Spring of Edith Cooley is a multilayered novel with compelling social & psychological implications. Edith Cooley, an aging scholar, sets a stage one spring for a mysterious chain of events in which she seems to purposely involve Natalie Tanner, a shy young art student. Also pivotal are Jake Laslo, a gifted & misanthropic artist for whom Tanner feels an inexplicable responsibility & 'King', a still-handsome middle-aged jazz composer with whom Edith has a curious involvement & with whom Tanner will also become involved. Revolving around the modern blight of loneliness & disenchantment, the novel's central riddle also compels new & exhilarating views of the trials "of youth, of old age, of the dangers (or benefits) of narcissism, of the eternal quest for love, all faces of, even Platonic or imaginary..." Provinzano, who restores to 'psychological' the root 'psyche' which meant 'soul' to the ancient Greeks, has a refreshingly metaphysical approach to a seductive mosaic of ironies in all her writings. Combining timeless echos of Conrad & Dostoevsky with an analytical playfulness of a Borges or Marquez, The Secret Spring of Edith Cooley is a must for every serious reader, or modern soul in pain. To order: e-mail: wjoandarc@cs.com *Publisher Paid Annotation.*

Provis, Chris, jt. ed. see Hunt, Ian.

Provisional Government of Ireland Staff. The Irish Proclamation: Easter, 1916. McCormick, Malachi, ed. 16p. 1982. pap. text 7.00 (*0-943984-04-1*) Stone St Pr.

Provisor, Janis. Bada Shanren & Me. (Illus.). 16p. 1991. pap. 5.00 (*0-930495-11-X*) San Fran Art Inst.

Provizer, Norman W., ed. Analyzing the Third World: Essays from "Comparative Politics" 510p. 1978. pap. 24.95 (*0-87073-943-3*) Transaction Pubs.
— Analyzing the Third World: Essays from Comparative Politics. LC 77-13286. 509p. reprint ed. pap. 157.80 (*0-8357-5430-8*, 205658300077) Bks Demand.

Provo Craft (Group). Decorative Painted Wood Projects. LC 96-24640. (Illus.). 128p. 1997. 24.95 (*0-8069-8141-5*) Sterling.

Provo Craft Combination Artists Staff. Everyday Cookie Keepers & Gifts. (Illus.). 48p. 1997. 9.99 (*1-58050-017-X*, 40-6146) Provo Craft.
— Holiday Cookie Keepers & Gifts. (Illus.). 52p. 1997. 9.99 (*1-58050-018-8*, 40-6147) Provo Craft.

Provo Craft Combined Artists Staff. Fill Your Pockets. (Illus.). 56p. 1998. 9.99 (*1-58050-039-0*, 40-6162) Provo Craft.

Provo Craft Designers Staff. Carefree Collectibles. (Illus.). 1998. 6.99 (*1-58050-055-2*, HO-6179) Provo Craft.

***Provo Craft Designers Staff.** Carefree Collectibles: Christmas Edition. (Illus.). 28p. 1999. 7.99 (*1-58050-070-6*, 40-6199) Provo Craft.
— Carefree Collectibles: Christmas Edition. 2nd ed. (Illus.). 28p. 1999. 7.99 (*1-58050-071-4*, 40-6205) Provo Craft.
— Cheery Holiday Greetings. (Illus.). 16p. 1999. write for info. (*1-58050-068-4*, 40-6200) Provo Craft.
— Christmas Medley. (Illus.). 44p. 2000. write for info. (*1-58050-090-0*, 40-6219) Provo Craft.
— Frosty Friends. (Illus.). 56p. (YA). 2000. write for info. (*1-58050-094-3*, 40-6220) Provo Craft.
— Holly Days Glass Jars & Ornaments. (Illus.). 24p. 1999. write for info. (*1-58050-079-X*, 40-6198) Provo Craft.
— Nutcracker Company. (Illus.). 24p. 1998. write for info. (*1-58050-066-8*, 40-6197) Provo Craft.
— Outdoor Decor. (Illus.). 22p. 1999. write for info. (*1-58050-086-2*) Provo Craft.
— Paper Pockets & Boxes. (Illus.). 32p. 1998. 7.99 (*1-58050-061-7*, 40-6196) Provo Craft.

Provo Craft Designers Staff. Pocket Full of Posies. (Illus.). 24p. 1998. 7.99 (*1-58050-060-9*, 40-6178) Provo Craft.

***Provo Craft Designers Staff.** Rusty Simple Shapes Idea Book. (Illus.). 28p. 1999. 7.99 (*1-58050-067-6*, 40-6204) Provo Craft.
— Simply the Best Everyday. (Illus.). 40p. 2000. write for info. (*1-58050-087-0*, 40-6202) Provo Craft.
— Simply the Best for the Holidays. (Illus.). 44p. 2000. write for info. (*1-58050-088-9*, 40-6203) Provo Craft.

Provo Craft Group Staff. Decorative Painted Wood Projects. 1999. pap. text 14.95 (*0-8069-8142-3*) Sterling.

Provo, Diane & Bott, Diane. Kids Are Great . . . When You Know How They Work: An Owners Manual. 2nd ed. (Illus.). 72p. 1992. pap. 11.95 (*0-9631607-2-9*) Kid Are Great.

Provo, Joanne, jt. auth. see Herling, Richard W.

Provo, Patti. Inspiration Tarot. (Illus.). 1992. pap. 12.00 (*0-88079-524-7*, IT78) US Games Syst.

Provoost, jt. ed. see Wolff.

Provoost, Anne. My Aunt Is a Pilot Whale. Bleumer, Ria, tr. 150p. (YA). pap. 8.95 (*0-88961-202-1*, Pub. by Womens Pr) LPC InBook.

Provorse, Carl, jt. auth. see Carpenter, Allan.

Provost. Advanced Indoor Exercise. (Runner's World Ser.). 1981. pap. 16.95 (*0-02-499470-7*, Macmillan Coll) P-H.

***Provost.** Online Investor. 2000. 29.95 (*0-07-135884-6*) McGraw.

Provost Beller, Susan. Medical Practices in the Civil War. LC 92-14960. (Illus.). 96p. 1998. reprint ed. pap. 9.99 (*0-9663758-0-7*, 01) OurStory.

Provost, C. Antonio. Modern Renaissance Poetry & Philosophy. Kroll, William, ed. LC 92-96848. (Illus.). 148p. (YA). (gr. 9-12). 1992. 14.00 (*0-317-05253-5*); pap. 10.00 (*0-317-05254-3*) Provost.
— Opening of the American Mind. LC 89-64102. 1990. 15.95 (*0-87212-246-8*); pap. 9.95 (*0-87212-235-2*) Libra.
— The Reformation of Society Through Adequate Education. LC 94-69192. 159 p. 1996. 15.95 (*0-8158-0511-X*) Chris Mass.

Provost, C. Antonio & Blaney, Worth. The Senior Olympics, Preventive Medicine, & Findings Pertaining to Health & Longevity. 1981. 6.00 (*0-686-32025-5*) Provost.

Provost, David H. & Hyink, Bernard L. Politics & Government in California. 13th ed. 272p. (C). 1997. pap. 45.00 (*0-673-99304-3*) Addson-Wesley Educ.

Provost, Foster. Columbus: An Annotated Guide to the Scholarship on His Life & Writings, 1750-1988. (Illus.). 225p. 1991. lib. bdg. 54.00 (*1-55888-157-3*) Omnigraphics Inc.
— Columbus: Dream & Act. 70p. 1986. 15.00 (*0-916617-23-8*) J C Brown.
— A Columbus Dictionary. 142p. 1991. lib. bdg. 54.00 (*1-55888-158-1*) Omnigraphics Inc.

Provost, Gary. Across the Border: The True Story of the Satanic Cult Killings in Matamoros, Mexico. 256p. 1989. mass mkt. 4.50 (*0-671-69319-0*) PB.
— Baffled in Boston. 256p. (Orig.). 1996. mass mkt. 5.50 (*0-425-15183-2*) Berkley Pub.
— One Hundred Ways to Improve Your Writing. 1985. mass mkt. 5.99 (*0-451-62721-0*, Ment) NAL.
— Perfect Husband. Zion, Claire, ed. 264p. 1992. reprint ed. mass mkt. 5.50 (*0-671-72494-0*) PB.
— Story Sense. 1999. pap. 12.95 (*0-452-27395-1*, Plume) Dutton Plume.
— Without Mercy: Obsession & Murder under the Influence. Zion, Claire, ed. 328p. 1990. reprint ed. mass mkt. 5.99 (*0-671-66997-4*) PB.

Provost, Gary & Levine-Provost, Gail. David & Max. 196p. (J). (gr. 5-9). 1991. pap. 9.95 (*0-8276-0392-4*) JPS Phila.

Provost, Gary & Rubie, Peter. How to Tell a Story: The Secrets of Writing Captivating Tales. LC 98-11454. 240p. 1998. 17.99 (*0-89879-809-4*, Wrtrs Digest Bks) F & W Pubns Inc.

Provost, J. & Walf, Knut, eds. Studies in Canon Law: Presented to P. J. M. Huizing. (Annua Nuntia Lovaniensia Ser.: No. 32). 270p. (Orig.). 1991. pap. 57.50 (*90-6186-439-9*, Pub. by Leuven Univ) Coronet Bks.

Provost, J. C. Obedient to God's Word. LC 92-75258. 200p. (Orig.). 1992. pap. 7.95 (*1-879667-11-8*) Dove Pr TX.

Provost, James & Walf, Knut, eds. Catholic Identity. (Concilium Ser.). 125p. (Orig.). 1994. pap. 15.00 (*0-88344-880-7*) Orbis Bks.

Provost, James, jt. ed. see Walf, Knut.

Provost, Janine & Schmider, Francois-Xavier, eds. Sounding Solar & Stellar Interiors. (International Astronomical Union Symposia Ser.: No. 181). 468p. 1997. pap. text 83.00 (*0-7923-4839-7*) Kluwer Academic.
— Sounding Solar & Stellar Interiors: Proceedings of the 181st Symposium of the International Astronomical Union Held in Nice, France, September 30-October 3, 1996. LC 97-31928. (International Astronomical Union Symposia Ser.: No. 181). 468p. 1997. 165.00 (*0-7923-4838-9*) Kluwer Academic.

Provost, Jerry. Salvaged Memories: The Raising of the Minnehaha. LC 96-94657. (Illus.). 110p. (Orig.). 1996. pap. 10.95 (*0-9653839-0-3*) In Depth Pub.

Provost, John F. Nurse Shark. LC 95-1173. (Sharks Ser.). (Illus.). 24p. (J). (ps-4). 1995. lib. bdg. 18.60 (*1-56239-472-X*, Checkerboard Library) ABDO Pub Co.

Provost, Judith A. A Casebook: Applications of the Myers-Briggs Type Indicator in Counseling. 2nd ed. LC 93-41360. 124p. 1993. pap. 12.00 (*0-935652-17-5*) Ctr Applications Psych.
— Procrastination: Using Psychological Type Concepts to Help Students. 11p. 1988. 5.00 (*0-935652-14-0*) Ctr Applications Psych.
— Strategies for Success: Using Type to Do Better in High School & College. 13p. 1992. 4.50 (*0-935652-15-9*) Ctr Applications Psych.
— Work, Play, & Type: Achieving Balance in Your Life. 128p. 1990. pap. 11.95 (*0-89106-040-5*, 7484, Davies-Black Pub) Consulting Psychol.

Provost, Louis. Honore Daumier: A Thematic Guide to His Oeuvre. LC 89-11898. 300p. 1989. text 160.00 (*0-8240-9302-X*) Garland.

Provost, Rene, tr. see Conforti, Benedetto.

Provost, Rhoda, jt. auth. see Benyo, Rich.

Provost, Rhonda, jt. auth. see Benyo, Rich.

Provost, Richard. The Art & Technique of Performance. 62p. (Orig.). (C). 1995. pap. text 14.95 (*0-9627832-4-2*, DK 10020) Guitar Solo.
— The Art & Technique of Practice. 53p. (Orig.). (C). 1992. pap. text 14.95 (*0-9627832-0-X*) Guitar Solo.

Provost, S. B., jt. auth. see Mathai, A. M.

Provost, Sarah. Inland, Thinking of Waves. LC 90-83468. (CSU Poetry Ser.: No. XXX). 70p. (Orig.). 1991. 12.00 (*0-914946-80-3*); pap. 8.00 (*0-914946-81-1*) Cleveland St Univ Poetry Ctr.

***Provost, Thomas T., et al.** Cutaneous Medicine. 700p. 2000. boxed set 195.00 incl. cd-rom (*1-55009-100-X*) DEKR.

Provost, Thomas T., jt. ed. see Sontheimer, Richard D.

Prow, Cameron, ed. see Demarco, Ric.

Prowant, Christopher B., jt. auth. see Lung, Haha.

Prowant, Yvonne, jt. auth. see Schmidt, Wayne.

Prowe, Diethelm. Weltstadt in Krisen: Berlin, 1949-1958. (Veroeffentlichungen der Historischen Kommission zu Berlin, Band 67, Beitraege zu Inflation und Wiederaufbau in Deutschland und Europa 1914-1924: Vol. 42). x, 359p. (C). 1973. 112.35 (*3-11-003876-5*) De Gruyter.

Prowe, Gunhild. The Oxford-Duden German Minidictionary. 2nd rev. ed. Schneider, Jill, ed. 710p. 1999. vinyl bd. 6.50 (*0-19-860252-9*) OUP.

P

Prowe, Gunhild & Schneider, Jill, compiled by. The Oxford Color German Dictionary: German-English, English-German; Deutsch-Englisch, Englisch-Deutsch. rev. ed. 528p. 1998. pap. 8.95 (*0-19-860189-1*) OUP.

Prowell, George R. History of Camden County, New Jersey. (Illus.). 769p. 1992. reprint ed. lib. bdg. 77.50 (*0-8328-2442-9*) Higginson Bk Co.

— History of York County, PA, Vol. I. (Illus.). 1118p. 1993. reprint ed. lib. bdg. 109.00 (*0-8328-2861-0*) Higginson Bk Co.

— History of York County, PA, Vol. II. (Illus.). 1058p. 1993. reprint ed. lib. bdg. 99.00 (*0-8328-2862-9*) Higginson Bk Co.

— History of York County, Pa., Index Vols. I & II. (Illus.). 474p. 1994. reprint ed. lib. bdg. 47.50 (*0-8328-4431-4*) Higginson Bk Co.

Prowell, Sandra West. By Evil Means. 384p. 1995. mass mkt. 5.99 (*0-553-56966-X*) Bantam.

— By Evil Means. 216p. 1993. 19.95 (*0-8027-1248-7*) Walker & Co.

— The Killing of Monday Brown: A Phoebe Siegel Mystery. 304p. 1996. mass mkt. 5.99 (*0-553-56969-4*) Bantam.

— The Killing of Monday Brown: A Phoebe Siegel Mystery. 240p. 1994. 19.95 (*0-8027-3184-8*) Walker & Co.

— When Wallflowers Die: A Phoebe Siegel Mystery. 368p. 1997. mass mkt. 5.99 (*0-553-56970-8*, Crimeline) Bantam.

— When Wallflowers Die: A Phoebe Siegel Mystery. 336p. 1996. 22.95 (*0-8027-3254-2*) Walker & Co.

Proweller, Amira. Constructing Female Identities: Meaning Making in an Upper Middle Class Youth Culture. LC 97-35900. (SUNY Series, Power, Social Identity, & Education). 284p. (C). 1998. text 59.50 (*0-7914-3771-X*); pap. text 19.95 (*0-7914-3772-8*) State U NY Pr.

Prowense, Mary J. Pamela & the Revolution. Schatz, Molly, ed. (Illus.). 130p. (J). (gr. 7 up). 1993. 12.95 (*0-9635107-2-X*) Marc Anthony.

***Prowle, Malcolm.** A Professional Guide to Management in the Public Sector. LC 00-26417. 288p. 2000. 99.95 (*0-566-08216-0*, Pub. by Ashgate Pub) Ashgate Pub Co.

Prowler, David. A Telegram from Marcel Duchamp. LC 90-91685. (Illus.). (Orig.). 1990. pap. 15.00 (*0-9628062-1-8*) Ready Made Pr.

***Prown, Jules & Haltman, Kenneth, eds.** American Artifacts: Essays in Material Culture. 368p. 2000. pap. 32.95 (*0-87013-524-4*) Mich St U Pr.

Prown, Jules D. John Singleton Copley, 2 vols. Incl. Vol. 1. In America, 1738 to 1774. LC 66-13183. (Illus.). 1966. Vol. 2. In England, 1774 to 1815. LC 66-13183. (Illus.). 1966. LC 66-13183. (Aisla Mellon Bruce Studies in American Art). 1966. 40.00 (*0-674-48000-7*) HUP.

Prown, Jules D., et al. Discovered Lands, Invented Pasts: Transforming Visions of the American West. LC 92-53537. (Illus.). 232p. 1994. pap. 27.00 (*0-300-05731-8*) Yale U Pr.

Prown, Pete. Great Model Riffs for Guitar. 23p. (YA). pap., pap. text 17.95 incl. cd-rom (*0-89524-945-6*, 02503466, Pub. by Cherry Lane); pap., pap. text 12.95 incl. audio (*0-89524-944-8*, 02503461) Cherry Lane.

Prown, Pete & Newquist, H. P. Legends of Rock Guitar. 300p. 1996. 19.95 (*0-614-20105-5*, 00330019) H Leonard.

— Legends of Rock Guitar: The Essential Reference of Rock's Greatest Guitarists. LC 97-180000. (Illus.). 264p. (Orig.). 1997. per. 22.95 (*0-7935-4042-9*, HL00330019) H Leonard.

Prowse, Brad. Jerky Making: For the Home, Trail, & Campfire. LC 97-17016. (Illus.). 48p. (Orig.). 1997. pap. 7.95 (*0-87961-247-9*) Naturegraph.

Prowse, C., et al, eds. Hepatitis A Virus Transmission by Blood Products. (Journal: Vox Sanguinis: Vol. 67, Supplement 1, 1994). (Illus.). iv, 86p. 1994. pap. 39.25 (*3-8055-6006-0*) S Karger.

Prowse, Philip, jt. auth. see Sinclair, Barbara.

Proxmire, Bill. Your Joy Ride to Health. LC 93-93538. 318p. 1994. 24.95 (*0-9637988-2-0*) B Proxmire.

Proxmire, William. Can Small Business Survive? Bruchey, Stuart & Carosso, Vincent P., eds. LC 78-18974. (Small Business Enterprise in America Ser.). 1979. reprint ed. lib. bdg. 21.95 (*0-405-11477-X*) Ayer.

Proxmire, William, ed. see Waller, Douglas C. & Bruce, James T., III.

Proyect, Mitchell M., jt. auth. see Wall, Deborah K.

Proyen, Mark Van, see Van Proyen, Mark.

Proysen, Alf. Christmas Eve at Santa's. LC 91-42059. (Illus.). 32p. (J). (ps-1). 1992. 12.72 (*91-29-62066-X*, 734270, Pub. by R & S Bks) FS&G.

— Little Old Mrs. Pepperpot. (J). (gr. 1-4). 1960. 12.95 (*0-8392-3021-4*) Astor-Honor.

— Mrs. Pepperpot Again. (Illus.). (J). (gr. 1-4). 1961. 12.95 (*0-8392-3023-0*) Astor-Honor.

— Mrs. Pepperpot to the Rescue. (Illus.). (J). (gr. 1-4). 1988. pap. 3.50 (*0-317-69648-3*, PuffinBks) Peng Put Young Read.

Prozan, Charlotte. Construction & Reconstruction of Memory: Dilemmas of Childhood Sexual Abuse. LC 95-51701. 256p. 1997. pap. 50.00 (*1-56821-787-0*) Aronson.

— Feminist Psychoanalytic Psychotherapy. LC 91-47122. 384p. 1992. 60.00 (*0-87668-456-8*) Aronson.

— The Technique of Feminist Psychoanalytic Psychotherapy. LC 93-20278. 584p. 1993. 60.00 (*0-87668-268-9*) Aronson.

Prozendaal, P., jt. auth. see Jack, R. D.

Prozesky, Martin. A New Guide to the Debate about God. 200p. 1992. pap. write for info. (*0-86980-877-X*, Pub. by Univ Natal Pr) Intl Spec Bk.

Prozesky, Martin & De Gruchy, John, eds. Living Faiths in South Africa. LC 95-16661. 256p. 1995. text 45.00 (*0-312-12776-6*) St Martin.

Prozesky, Martin, jt. ed. see Brown, Judith M.

Prozier, Norman W., jt. ed. see Pederson, William D.

Prozorova, L. A., jt. auth. see Kotyuzhanskii, B. Y.

Prpic, George J. Croatia & the Croatians: An Annotated Bibliography. LC 80-66277. (Illus.). 315p. 1982. pap. 9.95 (*0-910164-02-9*) Assoc Bk Pubs.

— Croatian & the Croatians: An English-Language Bibliography & Resource Guide. rev. ed. Kapetanovic, Ruzica, ed. (Illus.). 450p. 1993. pap. 17.95 (*0-910164-24-X*) Assoc Bk Pubs.

Prpic, K. J & Davey, B. R., eds. The Genus Yersinia: Epidemiology, Molecular Biology & Pathogenesis. (Contributions to Microbiology & Immunology Ser.: Vol. 9). (Illus.). x, 346p. 1987. 243.50 (*3-8055-4482-0*) S Karger.

Prpic, Ross, jt. ed. see Popma, Jeffrey J.

Prsad, B. K. Tropical Techniques in Botany. 107p. 1989. pap. 125.00 (*0-614-10280-4*) St Mut.

Prssat, Roland. Diccionario de Demografia. (SPA.). 248p. 1987. 75.00 (*0-7859-5853-3*, 8428105979) Fr & Eur.

Prubhupada, A. C., tr. see Wilson, Karen.

Pruce, Earl. Synagogues, Temples & Congregations of Maryland, 1830-1990. 255p. 1993. pap. 15.00 (*1-883312-00-0*) Jewish Museum MD.

Pruch, Charles C. How to Jumpstart a Stalled Career. LC 93-3897. (Illus.). 192p. 1994. pap. 12.95 (*0-8442-4171-7*, 41717, VGM Career) NTC Contemp Pub Co.

Pruch, Margarete. Die Lacke der Westlichen Han-Zeit (206 v. - 6. n. Chr.) Bestand und Analyse. (Europaische Hochschulschriften, Reihe 28: Bd. 299). (GER., Illus.). 617p. 1997. 95.95 (*3-631-30105-7*) P Lang Pubng.

Prucha, Cristine, ed. Wisconsin Poets' Calendar, 1998. (Illus.). 163p. (Orig.). 1997. pap. 9.95 (*0-9618384-0-X*) Wisconsin Fellowship of Poets.

Prucha, David J., tr. see Paulus, Trina.

Prucha, Edward, ed. Health Reference Series Cumulative Index: A Comprehensive Index to All Volumes of the Health Reference Series, 1990-1998. LC 99-52056. (Health Reference Ser.). 900p. 1999. lib. bdg. 78.00 (*0-7808-0382-5*) Omnigraphics Inc.

— Pediatric Cancer Sourcebook: Basic Consumer Health Information. LC 99-41613. (Health Reference Ser.). (Illus.). 600p. 1999. lib. bdg. 78.00 (*0-7808-0245-4*) Omnigraphics Inc.

***Prucha, Edward J., ed.** Breast Cancer Sourcebook: Basic Consumer Information about Breast Cancer. (Health Reference Ser.). 600p. 2000. lib. bdg. 78.00 (*0-7808-0244-6*) Omnigraphics Inc.

Prucha, Edward J., ed. Cancer Sourcebook. 3rd ed. (Health Reference Ser.). (Illus.). 1100p. 1999. lib. bdg. 78.00 (*0-7808-0227-6*) Omnigraphics Inc.

Prucha, Frances P. American Indian Treaties: The History of a Political Anomaly. LC 93-36297. (Illus.). 1997. pap. 21.95 (*0-520-20895-1*, Pub. by U CA Pr) Cal Prin Full Svc.

Prucha, Francis P. Atlas of American Indian Affairs. LC 90-675000. (Illus.). x, 191p. 1990. text 60.00 (*0-8032-3689-1*) U of Nebr Pr.

— Broadax & Bayonet: The Role of the United States Army in the Development of the Northwest, 1815-1860. LC 94-44363. (Illus.). xix, 277p. 1995. pap. text 14.00 (*0-8032-5151-3*, Bison Books) U of Nebr Pr.

— The Great Father: The United States Government & the American Indians. abr. ed. LC 85-5875. (Illus.). xii, 426p. 1986. pap. text 25.00 (*0-8032-8712-7*, Bison Books) U of Nebr Pr.

— The Great Father: The United States Government & the American Indians, 2 vols., Set. unabridged ed. LC 83-16837. (Illus.). xxxii, 1355p. 1995. pap. text 60.00 (*0-8032-8734-8*, Bison Books) U of Nebr Pr.

— Handbook for Research in American History: A Guide to Bibliographies & Other Reference Works. 2nd rev. ed. LC 93-4240. xiii, 214p. (C). 1994. pap. text 14.00 (*0-8032-8731-3*, Bison Books) U of Nebr Pr.

— Indian Peace Medals in American History. LC 95-8353. 1995. pap. write for info. (*0-9630731-4-1*) Rivilo Bks.

— Indian Policy in the United States: Historical Essays. LC 81-1667. (Illus.). 282p. reprint ed. pap. 87.50 (*0-7837-1895-0*, 204209900001) Bks Demand.

— Indian-White Relations in the United States: A Bibliography of Works Published 1975-1980. LC 81-14722. viii, 179p. 1982. pap. text 12.00 (*0-8032-8705-4*, Bison Books) U of Nebr Pr.

— The Indians in American Society: From the Revolutionary War to the Present. LC 85-1023. (Quantum Bks.: No. 29). 1985. 45.00 (*0-520-05503-9*, Pub. by U CA Pr); pap. 13.95 (*0-520-06344-9*, Pub. by U CA Pr) Cal Prin Full Svc.

— U. S. Indian Policy: A Critical Bibliography. LC 77-6920. (Bibliographical Ser.). 64p. reprint ed. pap. 30.00 (*0-608-18470-5*, 205671400081) Bks Demand.

Prucha, Francis P., ed. Documents of United States Indian Policy. 2nd expanded ed. LC 89-16408. (Illus.). xiii, 338p. 1990. pap. text 20.00 (*0-8032-8726-7*, Bison Books) U of Nebr Pr.

Prucha, Francis P., ed. see Croghan, George.

***Prucha, Francis Paul, ed.** Documents of United States Indian Policy. 3rd ed. LC 99-89969. (Illus.). 352p. 2000. 50.00 (*0-8032-3728-6*); pap. 25.00 (*0-8032-8762-3*) U of Nebr Pr.

Prucha, Ingmar R., jt. auth. see Pitscher, Benedikt M.

Prucha, Isabel D. Your Library: A Friend. Duy, Hoang Chu, tr. (ENG & VIE., Illus.). 77p. (Orig.). 1986. pap. 10.95 (*0-937319-00-7*) Golden Palm Pr.

Prucha, Jan. Information Sources in Psycholinguistics: Biographical Handbook. 1972. pap. text 19.25 (*90-279-2362-0*) Mouton.

— Pragmalinguistics: East European Approaches. (Pragmatics & Beyond: An Interdisciplinary of Language Studies: Vol. IV:5). v, 103p. 1983. pap. 38.00 (*0-915027-28-3*) J Benjamins Pubng Co.

— Soviet Psycholinguistics. (Janua Linguarum, Ser. Minor: No. 143). 117p. (Orig.). 1972. pap. text 53.10 (*90-279-2317-5*) Mouton.

***Pruchnicki, Janice Ferraro.** Divine Soldier: A Biography of Samuel Wheelock Fiske. 100p. 1999. pap. 9.95 (*0-9673740-0-6*) Quickstep Pub.

Pruchnik, F. P. Organometallic Chemistry of the Transition Elements. (Modern Inorganic Chemistry Ser.). (Illus.). 774p. (C). 1990. text 165.00 (*0-306-43192-0*, Kluwer Plenum) Kluwer Academic.

Pruchno, Bill. ShapeSheet Programming for the Visio Masters. 1998. pap. text 59.95 (*1-55622-669-1*) Wordware Pub.

— Tips & Tricks of the Visio Masters. 1998. pap. text 39.95 (*1-55622-671-3*) Wordware Pub.

***Pruchno, Billy.** Learn Visio 2000 for the Masters. (Illus.). 2000. pap. text 39.95 (*1-55622-713-2*) Wordware Pub.

Prudden, Bonnie. Bonnie Prudden's after Fifty Fitness Guide. 1987. pap. 10.95 (*0-345-31807-2*, Ballantine) Ballantine Pub Grp.

— Exer-Sex. (Illus.). 1980. pap. 6.50 (*0-553-10698-8*) Bonnie Prudden.

— How to Keep Your Family Fit & Healthy. (Illus.). 1975. 10.00 (*0-88349-041-2*) Bonnie Prudden.

— Pain Erasure: The Bonnie Prudden Way. 1985. pap. 12.00 (*0-345-33102-8*) Ballantine Pub Grp.

— Teach Your Baby to Swim. LC 73-79534. (Illus.). 1978. pap. text 12.95 (*0-9602146-0-7*) Bonnie Prudden.

Prudden, Horton R. Prudden: Rev. Peter Prudden & His Descendants in America, 2 vols. 1351p. 1996. reprint ed. pap. 155.00 (*0-8328-5613-4*); reprint ed. lib. bdg. 175.00 (*0-8328-5612-6*) Higginson Bk Co.

Prudden, P. M. Further Study of Prehistoric Small House-Ruins in the San Juan Watershed. LC 18-15717. (American Anthropological Association Memoirs Ser.: No. 21). 1918. pap. 25.00 (*0-527-00520-7*) Periodicals Srv.

Prudden, Suzy. Suzy Prudden's Exercise Program for Young Children. LC 82-40506. (Illus.). 192p. 1983. pap. 6.95 (*0-89480-371-9*, 371) Workman Pub.

***Prude, George B.** No Time to Waste: On the Run to Be Ready to Meet Jesus. 85p. 1999. pap. 10.00 (*0-7392-0343-6*, PO3518) Morris Pubng.

Prude, Jonathan. The Coming of Industrial Order: Town & Factory Life in Rural Massachusetts, 1810-1860. LC 98-55713. 400p. 1999. pap. 19.95 (*1-55849-204-6*) U of Mass Pr.

Prude, Jonathan, jt. ed. see Hahn, Steven.

Pruden, Betty K. Home Free. LC 96-48124. 234p. 1997. 21.95 (*1-880664-20-8*) E M Pr.

Pruden, Caroline. Conditional Partners: Eisenhower, the United Nations, & the Search for a Permanent Peace. LC 97-43275. (Eisenhower Center Studies on War & Peace). (Illus.). 344p. 1998. text 35.00 (*0-8071-2204-1*) La State U Pr.

Pruden, Donald. Around Town Cycling. LC 75-20739. (Illus.). 112p. 1975. pap. 2.95 (*0-89037-066-4*) Anderson World.

Pruden, Durward. A Sociological Study of a Texas Lynching. (Reprint Series in Sociology). (C). 1993. reprint ed. pap. text 1.00 (*0-8290-2939-7*, S-479) Irvington.

Pruden, Leo M., tr. see De La Vallee Poussin, Louis.

Pruden, Leo M., tr. see Lamotte, Etienne.

Pruden, Leo M., tr. see Numata Center for Buddhist Translation & Research.

Pruden, Wesley. America in the Gelded Age. unabridged ed. (Best of the Washington Times Ser.). (Illus.). 70p. 1996. pap. 8.95 (*1-889984-00-0*) News Wrld Comm.

Pruden, Wesley & Linberg, Tod, eds. Shaping the Debate. unabridged ed. (Best of the Washington Times Ser.). (Illus.). 40p. 1996. pap. 5.95 (*1-889984-02-7*) News Wrld Comm.

Pruden, Wesley, ed. see Fields, Suzanne.

Prudentius. Poems, Vol. 1. Eagan, M. Clement, tr. LC 63-5499. (Fathers of the Church Ser.: Vol. 43). 280p. 1962. 31.95 (*0-8132-0043-1*) Cath U Pr.

— Poems, Vol. 2. Eagan, M. Clement, tr. LC 63-5499. (Fathers of the Church Ser.: Vol. 52). 230p. 1965. 31.95 (*0-8132-0052-0*) Cath U Pr.

— Works, 2 vols. No. 387, 398. write for info. (*0-318-53222-0*) HUP.

— Works, 2 vols., 1. (Loeb Classical Library: No. 387, 398). 19.95 (*0-674-99426-4*) HUP.

— Works, 2 vols., 2. (Loeb Classical Library: No. 387, 398). 19.95 (*0-674-99438-8*) HUP.

Prudenziati, M., ed. Thick Film Sensors. LC 94-29429. (Handbook of Sensors & Actuators Ser.: 1). 482p. 1994. 168.75 (*0-444-89723-2*) Elsevier.

Prudhoe, J., tr. see Goethe, Johann Wolfgang Von.

Prudhomme, Enola C. E. C. Prudhomme's Gun Engraving Review. (Illus.). 200p. 1995. 60.00 (*1-884849-18-0*) R&R Bks.

— Enola Prudhomme's Low-Calorie Cajun Cooking. LC 90-5244. (Illus.). 224p. 1991. pap. 19.95 (*0-688-09255-1*, Hearst) Hearst Commns.

— Enola Prudhomme's Low-Fat Favorites: Enjoy Low-Fat Versions of Your Favorite Southern Dishes. LC 94-6973. 326p. 1994. pap. 19.95 (*0-688-11894-1*, Hearst) Hearst Commns.

Prudhomme, Frances & Sternberg, Susan T. The Gift of the Greeks: Art & Civilization of Ancient Greece. 24p. (Orig.). (J). (gr. 4-7). 1982. pap. 8.95 (*0-935213-04-X*) J S Blanton Mus.

Prudhomme, Jacques. Bily Love Bites: A Cookbook for Romantic Encounters. (Illus.). 152p. 1999. pap. 12.50 (*1-58446-001-6*, Legacy OH) Temple Pubg.

— Z'Art of Gourmet Seduction: A Culinary Express of Love. xviii, 164p. 1998. 24.95 (*1-892509-57-1*) Chambers Pubg Grp.

— Z'Art of Romantic Seduction: An Expression of Love. xviii, 164p. 1998. pap. 19.95 (*1-892509-22-9*) Chambers Pubg Grp.

Prudhomme, Jeff O. God & Being: Heidegger's Relation to Theology. LC 96-26272. (Contemporary Studies in Philosophy & the Human Science Ser.). 256p. (C). 1997. 55.00 (*0-391-03965-2*) Humanities.

Prud'Homme, Paul. Chef Paul Prudhomme's Kitchen Expedition. unabridged ed. (Illus.). 1997. 15.95 (*0-9656348-0-9*) P Prudhomme Foods.

— Chef Paul Prudhomme's Louisiana Tastes: Exciting Flavors from the State That Cooks. LC 99-35611. (Illus.). 352p. 2000. 25.00 (*0-688-12224-8*, Morrow Cookbks) HarpInfo.

— Chef Prudhommes Louis Ki. LC 83-63236. (Cookbook Library). (Illus.). 344p. 1984. 25.00 (*0-688-02847-0*, Wm Morrow) Morrow Avon.

— Fiery Foods That I Love. LC 95-34370. 48p. 1995. 25.00 (*0-688-12153-5*, Wm Morrow) Morrow Avon.

— Prudhomme-Pure Magic. LC 94-46213. (Illus.). 206p. 1995. 12.95 (*0-688-14202-8*, Wm Morrow) Morrow Avon.

— Prudhomme's-Fork in T Ro. LC 93-25836. 281p. 1993. 23.00 (*0-688-12165-9*, Wm Morrow) Morrow Avon.

— Seasoned Amer Chef Paul. (Illus.). 384p. 1991. 23.00 (*0-688-05282-7*, Wm Morrow) Morrow Avon.

Prud'Homme, Paul, tr. see Walling, Regis M. & Rupp, N. Daniel, eds.

Prud'homme, Robert K., ed. Foams. (Surfactant Science Ser.: Vol. 57). (Illus.). 608p. 1995. text 225.00 (*0-8247-9395-1*) Dekker.

Prud'homme, Robert K., jt. ed. see Harland, Ronald S.

Prud'homme, Robert K., jt. ed. see Herb, Craig A.

Prud'homme van Reine, W. F. European Sphacelariaceae (Sphacelariales, Phaeophyceae) (Leiden Botanical Ser.: No. 6). (Illus.). x, 293p. 1982. pap. 31.00 (*90-04-06597-0*, Pub. by Rijksherbarium) Balogh.

Prudhommeaux, Jules. Icarie et Son Fondateur, Etienne Cabet: Contribution a l'Etude Du Socialisme Experimental. LC 72-187458. (American Utopian Adventure Ser.). xl, 688p. 1972. reprint ed. lib. bdg. 65.00 (*0-87991-005-4*) Porcupine Pr.

Prud'hon, Pierre-Paul. The Language of the Body: Drawings by Pierre-Paul Prud'hon. LC 96-10851. 224p. 1996. 75.00 (*0-8109-3585-6*, Pub. by Abrams) Time Warner.

Prudic, David E., jt. auth. see Harrill, James R.

Prudnikov, A., ed. Proceedings of the Conference Different Aspects of Differentiality. 220p. 1996. pap. text 58.00 (*90-5699-044-6*) Gordon & Breach.

Prudnikov, A., jt. auth. see Ditkin, V.

Prudnikov, A. P. Integrals & Series, 2 vols., Vol. 5. 1,214p. 1992. text 498.00 (*2-88124-836-5*) Gordon & Breach.

— Inverse Laplace Transform, Vol. 5. 595p. 1992. text 279.00 (*2-88124-838-1*) Gordon & Breach.

Prudnikov, A. P., et al. Direct Laplace Transforms, Vol. 4. (Integrals & Ser.). 618p. 1992. text 279.00 (*2-88124-837-3*) Gordon & Breach.

— Integrals & Series, 2 vols., Set. Queen, N. M., tr. from RUS. 1560p. 1986. text 382.00 (*2-88124-089-5*) Gordon & Breach.

— Integrals & Series, 2 Vols., Vol. 2. Queen, N. M., tr. from RUS. viii, 1548p. 1986. text 615.00 (*2-88124-097-6*) Gordon & Breach.

— Integrals & Series: More Special Functions, Vol. 3. Gould, G. G., tr. from RUS. ii, 800p. 1990. text 293.00 (*2-88124-682-6*) Gordon & Breach.

— Tables of Indefinite Integrals. 192p. 1989. text 110.00 (*2-88124-710-5*) Gordon & Breach.

Prudnikov, A. P., jt. auth. see Brychkov, Yu A.

Prue, Bernadette S., ed. see Prue, Bernard P.

Prue, Bernard P. Nathan Starr Arms. Prue, Bernadette S., ed. (Illus.). 214p. 1999. lib. bdg. 32.50 (*0-8328-9811-2*) Higginson Bk Co.

***Prue, Bernard P.** Nathan Starr Arms. Prue, Bernadette S., ed. (Illus.). 214p. 1999. pap. 22.50 (*0-8328-9812-0*) Higginson Bk Co.

Prue, J. E. Ionic Equilibria. 1966. 65.00 (*0-08-011344-3*, Pub. by Pergamon Repr) Franklin.

Prue, Lucinda K. Atlas of Mammographic Positioning. LC 92-49800. (Illus.). 176p. 1993. text 43.00 (*0-7216-3683-7*, W B Saunders Co) Harcrt Hlth Sci Grp.

Pruemers, Walther. Spinozas Religionsbegriff. (Abhandlungen Zur Philosophie und Ihrer Geschichte Ser.: Bd. 23). (GER.). 73p. 1980. reprint ed. write for info. (*3-487-06780-3*) G Olms Pubs.

Pruen, S. Tristram. The Arab & the African. 368p. 1986. 250.00 (*1-85077-136-7*, Pub. by Darf Pubs Ltd) St Mut.

Pruente, Christian & Flammer, Josef, eds. Das Glaukom in der Praxis: Glaucoma Meeting Basel, Maerz 1996. (GER., Illus.). x, 334p. 1997. 121.75 (*3-8055-6316-7*) S Karger.

Pruessen. Those Damn Islands: Quemoy, Matsu & Nuclear Brinkmanship, 1945-58. 1994. 22.95 (*0-02-925475-2*) S&S Trade.

Prueter, Shelley, jt. auth. see Solomon, Ed.

Pruett, Barbara J. Marty Robbins: Fast Cars & Country Music. LC 90-8709. (Illus.). 621p. 1990. 62.50 (*0-8108-2325-X*) Scarecrow.

— Popular Entertainment Research: How to Do It & How to Use It. LC 92-3800. 593p. 1992. 66.00 (*0-8108-2501-5*) Scarecrow.

***Pruett, Darrell.** The Pact at Star's Crossing. LC 00-24222. 224p. 1999. pap. 13.95 (*0-87714-503-2*) Denlingers.

Pruett, David J., jt. ed. see Gump, Barry H.

An Asterisk (*) at the beginning of an entry indicates that the title is appearing for the first time.

Pruett, Gordon, intro. Life & Exploits of S. Glenn Young: A Reprint of the 1925 Biography of S. Glenn Young, Southern Illinois' Most Infamous Law Officer. (Illus.). 253p. 1989. reprint ed. 16.95 (*0-685-28059-4*); reprint ed. pap. 12.95 (*0-685-28060-8*) Crossfire Pr.

Pruett, Gordon E. As a Father Loves His Children: The Image of the Supreme Being As Loving Father in Judaism, Christianity, & Islam. LC 94-12974. (Catholic Scholars Press Ser.). 1994. 54.95 (*1-883255-69-4*); pap. 34.95 (*1-883255-68-6*) Intl Scholars.

Pruett, Harold L. & Brown, Vivian B., eds. Crisis Intervention & Prevention. LC 85-644751. (New Directions for Student Services Ser.: No. SS 49). 1990. pap. 22.00 (*1-55542-836-3*) Jossey-Bass.

Pruett, James. Black Mist: Anguish of the Mist. (Illus.). 112p. (Orig.). 1995. pap. 12.95 (*0-941613-70-4*, Caliber Comics) Stabur Pr.

Pruett, James & Rigsby, Lee. Selective Music Bibliography from the Period, 1663-1763. (Illus.). vii, 53p. 1962. pap. 2.00 (*0-86526-109-1*) NC Archives.

Pruett, James M. Fundamentals of Programming with FORTRAN 77. LC 86-21331. (Independent Learning Module from the Instrument Society of America Ser.). (Illus.). 309p. 1987. reprint ed. pap. 95.80 (*0-7837-9048-1*, 204979900003) Bks Demand.

Pruett, James W., compiled by. Studies in Musicology: Essays in History, Style & Bibliography of Music in Memory of Glenn Haydon. LC 76-7574. (Illus.). 286p. 1976. reprint ed. lib. bdg. 65.00 (*0-8371-8883-0*, PRSM, Greenwood Pr) Greenwood.

Pruett, James W. & Slavens, Thomas P. Research Guide to Musicology. fac. ed. LC 84-24379. (Sources of Information in the Humanities Ser.: No. 4). 178p. 1985. pap. 55.20 (*0-7837-7314-5*, 204724100007) Bks Demand.

Pruett, Joe, ed. Negative Burn: Best of Year One. (Illus.). 128p. 1995. 9.95 (*0-941613-69-0*) Stabur Pr.

— Negative Burn: Best of Year Two. (Illus.). 128p. (Orig.). 1996. pap. 9.95 (*0-941613-84-4*, Caliber Comics) Stabur Pr.

Pruett, John H. The Parish Clergy under the Later Stuarts: The Leicestershire Experience. LC 78-8174. (Illus.). 213p. 1978. reprint ed. pap. 66.10 (*0-7837-8085-0*, 204783800008) Bks Demand.

Pruett, Judy, jt. auth. see Pruett, Scott.

Pruett, Kenneth M. Chemical Resistance Guide for Elastomers II: A Guide to Chemical Resistance of Rubber & Elastomeric Compounds. (Illus.). 440p. 1994. 110.00 (*1-889712-02-7*, CRGE) Compass CA.

— Chemical Resistance Guide for Metals & Alloys: A Guide to Chemical Resistance of Metals & Alloys. (Illus.). 437p. 1995. 130.00 (*1-889712-00-0*, CREM) Compass CA.

— Chemical Resistance Guide for Plastics: A Guide to Chemical Resistance of Engineering Thermoplastics, Fluoropolymers, Fibers & Thermoset Resins. Orig. Title: Compass Corrosion Guide II. 688p. 2000. 170.00 (*1-889712-03-5*, 83) Compass CA.

— Compass Corrosion Guide II: A Guide to Chemical Resistance of Metals & Engineering Plastics. 2nd rev. ed. (Illus.). 236p. 1983. 69.00 (*1-889712-01-9*, CCG2) Compass CA.

*__Pruett, Kyle D.__ Fatherneed: Why Father Care Is as Essential as Mother Care for Your Child. LC 99-50214. 256p. 2000. 24.00 (*0-684-85775-8*) Free Pr.

Pruett, Kyle D. Me, Myself & I: How Children Build Their Sense of Self 18-36 Months. LC 99-60433. (Goddard Parenting Guides Ser.). 256p. 1999. pap. 19.95 (*0-9666397-5-8*) Goddard Pr.

— Me, Myself & I: How Children Build Their Sense of Self 18-36 Months. LC 99-60433. (Goddard Parenting Guides Ser.). 216p. 1999. 24.95 (*0-9666397-4-X*) Goddard Pr.

Pruett, Mary Jane. Color the Wild Rockies! Discover the Great Outdoors. 32p. 1999. pap. text 3.95 (*0-87108-301-9*) Pruett.

Pruett, Nancy J. Scientific & Technical Libraries, Vol. 2. (Library & Information Science Ser.). 1986. text 89.95 (*0-12-566042-1*) Acad Pr.

Pruett, Nancy J., ed. see Geoscience Information Society Staff.

Pruett, R. H., ed. see Fleming, Dorothy.

Pruett, Robert H., ed. see Chewning, Alpheus J.

Pruett, Robert H., ed. see Williams, Jane S.

Pruett, Sarah C., tr. see Tarango, Yolanda, et al.

Pruett, Scott & Pruett, Judy. Twelve Little Race Cars. Eytchison, Glen, ed. LC 99-90127. (Illus.). 32p. (J). (ps-3). 1999. 12.95 (*0-9670600-0-1*) Word Weaver.

Pruett, Sven. How-to Build & Modify Ford 60 Degree V-6 Engines. LC 94-26702. (Power Pro Ser.). (Illus.). 160p. 1994. pap. 9.98 (*0-87938-914-1*) MBI Pubg.

Pruette, Lorine. G. Stanley Hall. LC 73-126247. (Select Bibliographies Reprint Ser.). 1977. 20.95 (*0-8369-5474-2*) Ayer.

— Women & Leisure: A Study of Social Waste. LC 72-2620. (American Women Ser.: Images & Realities). 230p. 1974. reprint ed. 17.95 (*0-405-04473-9*) Ayer.

Pruetz, Rick. Putting Transfer of Development Rights to Work in California. 232p. (Orig.). 1993. pap. text 25.00 (*0-923956-29-8*) Solano Pr.

— Saved by Development: Preserving Environmental Areas, Farmland & Historic Landmarks with Transfer of Development Rights. LC 97-70105. (Illus.). 436p. 1997. pap. 39.95 (*0-9658314-0-X*) Arje Pr.

Prufer, Christopher B. Der Konzentrationsprozeb Auf Dem Europaischen Entsorgungsmarkt: Chancen, Gefahren und Zukunftige Entwicklungen Fur Unternehmen. (Europaische Hochschulschriften Ser.: Reihe 5, Bd. 2132). (GER., Illus.). 101p. 1997. 29.95 (*3-631-32142-2*) P Lang Pubng.

Prufer, Kevin. Strange Wood. 64p. 1998. pap. 12.00 (*0-8071-2350-1*) La State U Pr.

*__Prufer, Kevin, ed.__ The New Young American Poets: An Anthology. LC 99-37043. 264p. 2000. pap. 16.95 (*0-8093-2309-5*) S Ill U Pr.

Prufer, Olaf H. Raven Rocks: A Specialized Late Woodland Rockshelter Occupation in Belmont County, Ohio. LC 80-28085. No. 1. 103p. reprint ed. pap. 32.00 (*0-7837-1343-6*, 204149100020) Bks Demand.

Prufer, Olaf H. & Long, Dana A. The Archaic of Northeastern Ohio. LC 86-33. (Kent State Research Papers in Archaeology: No. 6). 95p. reprint ed. pap. 30.00 (*0-7837-1344-4*, 204149200020) Bks Demand.

Prufer, Olaf H. & McKenzie, Douglas H., eds. Studies in Ohio Archaeology. rev. ed. LC 75-45380. 400p. reprint ed. pap. 124.00 (*0-608-13548-8*, 202545200044) Bks Demand.

Prufer, Olaf H. & Shane, Orrin C. Blain Village & the Fort Ancient Tradition in Ohio. LC 79-99082. (Kent Studies in Anthropology & Archaeology: No. 1). 295p. reprint ed. pap. 91.50 (*0-7837-0300-7*, 204062100018) Bks Demand.

Prufer, Olaf H., et al. Krill Cave: A Stratified Rockshelter in Summit County, Ohio. LC 88-30600. (Research Papers in Archaeology: No. 8). (Illus.). 109p. 1989. pap. 12.50 (*0-87338-379-6*) Kent St U Pr.

*__Prufer, Ralf M.__ Die Verpackungsverordnung Und Ihre Okologischen Alternativen. (Illus.). XIII, 196p. 1999. 37.95 (*3-631-34398-1*) P Lang Pubng.

Prufer, Sabine. The Individual at the Crossroads: The Works of Robert Bolt, Novelist, Dramatist, Screenwriter. (European University Studies: Vol. 349). 208p. (C). 1998. pap. text 37.95 (*0-8204-3641-0*) P Lang Pubng.

Prufer, Thomas. Recapitulations: Essays in Philosophy. LC 91-44978. (Studies in Philosophy & the History of Philosophy: Vol. 26). 112p. 1993. 34.95 (*0-8132-0764-9*) Cath U Pr.

Prufer, Thomas, jt. auth. see Fulda, Daniel.

*__Pruger, Elizabeth & Zernone, Michelle.__ Smart Start! A Preparatory Guide. (Illus.). 64p. (YA). (gr. 4). 1999. pap. 5.95 (*1-893110-06-0*) Silver Moon.

Pruger, Elizabeth, jt. auth. see La Raja, Taryn.

Pruger, Heidelinde. The Righteousness of Life Vol. 344: William Soutar: A Poet's Scottish Predilection for Philosophy. LC 98-26130. (European University Studies Anglo-Saxon Languages & Literature: No. 14). (Illus.). 210p. 1998. pap. text 37.95 (*0-8204-3601-1*) P Lang Pubng.

Pruger, Robert. Efficiency & the Social Services. (Administration in Social Work Ser.: Vol. 15, Nos. 1 & 2). (Illus.). 187p. 1991. text 49.95 (*1-56024-113-6*) Haworth Pr.

Pruger, Robert, jt. auth. see Gambrill, Eileen.

Pruger, Robert, jt. auth. see Thyer, Bruce.

Prugh, Dane G. The Psychosocial Aspects of Pediatrics. LC 81-8289. 700p. reprint ed. pap. 200.00 (*0-7837-2741-0*, 204312100006) Bks Demand.

Prugh, Dane G., jt. ed. see Stuart, Harold C.

Prugh, Jean. All My Relations - Mitakuye Oyasin: The Sioux, the Pueblo & the Spirit World. Susswein, Deborah, ed. (Illus.). 118p. (Orig.). 1996. pap. 5.95 (*1-57502-283-4*, PO986) Morris Pubng.

Prugh, Thomas. Natural Capital & Human Economics Survival. LC 95-78332. 1995. 24.95 (*1-887490-01-9*) Int Soc Ecol.

Prugh, Thomas & Costanza, Robert. Natural Capital & Human Economic Survival 2nd ed. LC 99-12121. 1999. 39.95 (*1-56670-398-0*) Lewis Pubs.

Prugh, Thomas, et al. Natural Capital & Human Economics Survival. 216p. 1995. 18.95 (*1-887490-02-7*) Int Soc Ecol.

*__Prugl, Elisabeth.__ The Global Construction of Gender: Home-Based Work in the Political Economy of the 20th Century. LC 99-24851. 224p. 1999. 49.50 (*0-231-11560-1*) Col U Pr.

Prugl, Elisabeth, jt. ed. see Boris, Eileen.

Prugl, Elisabeth, jt. ed. see Meyer, Mary K.

Prugovecki, Eduard. Principles of Quantum General Relativity. 376p. 1995. pap. 36.00 (*981-02-2138-X*) World Scientific Pub.

— Quantum Geometry: A Framework for Quantum General Relativity. (Fundamental Theories of Physics Ser.). 544p. (C). 1992. text 247.50 (*0-7923-1640-1*) Kluwer Academic.

— Stochastic Quantum Mechanics & Quantum Spacetime. 1984. text 166.50 (*90-277-1617-X*) Kluwer Academic.

Prugovecki, Edward. Principles of Quantum General Relativity. LC 94-41518. 376p. 1995. text 74.00 (*981-02-2077-4*) World Scientific Pub.

Pruijt, Hans D. Job Design & Technology; Taylorism vs. Anti-Taylorism. LC 97-3829. (Advances in Management & Business Studies). 208p. (C). 1997. 75.00 (*0-415-15869-9*) Routledge.

Pruim, R., tr. see Schoning, U.

Pruit, Virginia D., jt. ed. see Faulkner, Howard J.

Pruitt. Health Style. (C). 1994. pap. text 11.50 (*0-03-015033-7*) Harcourt Coll Pubs.

— Health Styles: Decisions for Living Well (Interactive Edition) 2nd ed. 1998. pap. 42.50 (*0-205-29996-2*) Allyn.

— Human Sexuality. (C). Date not set. pap. text, teacher ed. 15.00 (*0-03-007604-8*) Harcourt Coll Pubs.

— Human Sexuality. (C). 1999. pap. text, student ed. 19.50 (*0-03-007607-2*) Harcourt Coll Pubs.

— Surgeon General's Report on. (C). 1994. pap. text 20.50 (*0-03-010248-0*) Harcourt Coll Pubs.

Pruitt, ed. Decision Making & Nursing Management. (C). 1989. write for info. (*0-673-39855-2*) Addison-Wesley.

Pruitt, et al. Health Styles: Decisions for Living Well. 2nd ed. LC 98-14502. 600p. 1998. pap. text 62.00 (*0-205-27229-0*) Allyn.

Pruitt, A. B. Abstracts of Land Entries: Gates, Chowan, Perquimans, Pasquotank, Camden, & Currituck Cos, NC. (Illus.). 198p. (Orig.). 1992. pap. 18.75 (*0-944992-44-7*) ABP Abstracts.

— Abstracts of Lincoln Co, NC, Deeds (1786-1793) Books 3, 4, & 16. (Illus.). 159p. (Orig.). 1988. pap. 14.50 (*0-944992-12-9*) ABP Abstracts.

— Abstracts of Sales of Confiscated Land & Property in North Carolina. (Illus.). 249p. (Orig.). 1990. pap. 23.00 (*0-944992-26-9*) ABP Abstracts.

— Colonial Petitions for Land Resurveys, Land Warrants, & Caveats. 142p. 1993. pap. 14.50 (*0-944992-47-1*) ABP Abstracts.

— Glasgow Land Fraud Papers Seventeen Eighty-Three - Eighteen Hundred: North Carolina Revolutionary War Bounty Land in Tennessee. (Illus.). xxviii, 541p. (Orig.). 1988. pap. text 47.30 (*0-944992-14-5*) ABP Abstracts.

— Petitions for Land Grant Suspensions in North Carolina. (Illus.). 402p. (Orig.). 1993. pap. 39.00 (*0-944992-48-X*) ABP Abstracts.

Pruitt, A. Kelly. I Will Always Come Home, Vol. 1. (Illus.). 185p. 1997. 29.50 (*1-891029-49-5*) Henderson Pub.

Pruitt, Albert B. Spartanburg County - District, South Carolina, Deed Abstracts, Book A-T, 1785-1827. 872p. 1988. 55.00 (*0-89308-553-7*, SC 86) Southern Hist Pr.

Pruitt, Anne S., ed. In Pursuit of Equality in Higher Education. LC 86-80125. 236p. 1987. text 38.95 (*0-930390-68-7*) Gen Hall.

Pruitt, B. E. Health Styles: Decisions for Life. LC 93-86348. (C). 1993. pap. text 62.50 (*0-03-094072-9*) Harcourt Coll Pubs.

— Health Styles: Decisions for Life. (C). 1994. pap. text, teacher ed., suppl. ed. 33.75 (*0-03-044779-8*) Harcourt Coll Pubs.

— Health Styles: Decisions for Life. rev. ed. (C). Date not set. pap. text. write for info. (*0-03-005917-8*) Harcourt Coll Pubs.

Pruitt, Bernadette. The Man Next Door. LC 98-96612. 192p. 1998. 18.95 (*0-8034-9323-1*, Avalon Bks) Bouregy.

— Salt of the Earth. LC 87-83381. 71p. 1988. 12.00 (*0-934188-27-0*) Evans Pubns.

Pruitt, Bettye H. The Making of Harcourt General: A History of Growth Through Diversification, 1922-1992. LC 93-50567. 320p. 1994. 35.00 (*0-87584-509-6*) Harvard Busn.

— Timken: From Missouri to Mars - A Century of Leadership in Manufacturing. LC 98-42263. 552p. 1999. 39.95 (*0-87584-887-7*) Harvard Busn.

Pruitt, Bettye H., ed. The Massachusetts Tax Valuation List of 1771. LC 97-81345. 960p. 1998. reprint ed. 125.00 (*0-89725-318-3*, 1839) Picton Pr.

Pruitt, Burnadette. The Biggest Heart in Choctaw Hollow. LC 96-95280. 192p. 1997. 18.95 (*0-8034-9190-5*, Avalon Bks) Bouregy.

Pruitt, Buzz E. Human Sexuality. 704p. (C). 1998. text 68.00 (*0-03-007603-X*) SCP.

Pruitt, Carolyn, jt. auth. see Hazelwood, Joanna.

*__Pruitt, David.__ Your Adolescent. 400p. 2000. pap. 18.00 (*0-06-095676-3*, HarpRes) HarpInfo.

Pruitt, David. Your Child: A Parent's Guide to the Changes & Challenges of Childhood, Vol. 1. LC 98-9503. (Illus.). 496p. 1998. 27.50 (*0-06-270158-4*, Harper Ref) HarpC.

Pruitt, David, jt. auth. see American Academy of Child & Adolescence Staff.

Pruitt, David B. & American Academy of Child & Adolescent Psychiatry Staff. Your Adolescent: Emotional, Behavioral & Cognitive Development from Early Adolescence through Teen Years. LC 98-34587. 400p. 1999. 27.50 (*0-06-270182-7*) HarpC.

Pruitt, Dean G. & Carnevale, Peter J. Negotiation in Social Conflict. Manstead, Anthony S., ed. (Mapping Social Psychology Ser.). 192p. 1993. 9.00 (*0-335-09866-5*); pap. 30.95 (*0-335-09865-7*) OpUniv Pr.

Pruitt, Elisabeth A., ed. see MacLane, Mary.

Pruitt, Ethel. A Pearl of Great Price. 40p. 1998. pap. 8.00 (*0-8059-4289-0*) Dorrance.

Pruitt, Fred. The New Testament Church & Its Symbols. 131p. 3.00 (*0-686-29157-3*) Faith Pub Hse.

— Past, Present & Future of the Church. 72p. pap. 2.00 (*0-686-29133-6*) Faith Pub Hse.

Pruitt, Fred & Pruitt, Lawrence. God's Gracious Dealings. (Illus.). 496p. 8.00 (*0-686-29110-7*) Faith Pub Hse.

Pruitt, Gerald R., ed. Selected Papers on Cryogenic Optical Systems. LC 94-11392. (Milestone Ser.: Vol. MS 98). 1994. pap. 45.00 (*0-8194-1632-0*) SPIE.

— Selected Papers on Cryogenic Optical Systems. LC 94-11392. (Milestone Ser.: Vol. MS 98/HC). 1994. 55.00 (*0-8194-1633-9*) SPIE.

Pruitt, Ida. Old Madam Yin: A Memoir of Peking Life. LC 78-68782. xii, 129p. 1979. 24.50 (*0-8047-1038-4*) Stanford U Pr.

Pruitt, Ida, ed. see T'ai-t'ai, Ning L.

*__Pruitt, J. Crayton.__ A Crusade for Stroke Prevention. LC 99-6775. 168p. 1999. write for info. (*1-879852-63-2*) Univ Tampa.

*__Pruitt, James.__ Firewall. (Checkered Flag Ser.: Vol. 2). 2000. mass mkt. 5.99 (*0-515-12887-2*) Berkley Pub.

— Healed by Prayer. LC 99-94454. 192p. 1999. mass mkt. 5.99 (*0-380-79758-5*, Avon Bks) Morrow Avon.

— Southern Runnin' (Checkered Flag Ser.: Vol. 1). 208p. 2000. mass mkt. 5.99 (*0-515-12805-8*, Jove) Berkley Pub.

Pruitt, James N. Angels Beside You. 224p. (Orig.). 1994. reprint ed. mass mkt. 5.50 (*0-380-77766-5*, Avon Bks) Morrow Avon.

— The Complete Angel: Angels Through the Ages - All You Need to Know. 256p. (Orig.). 1995. reprint ed. mass mkt. 5.50 (*0-380-78045-3*, Avon Bks) Morrow Avon.

— Fire Force. 192p. (Orig.). 1992. mass mkt. 3.99 (*0-380-76617-5*, Avon Bks) Morrow Avon.

— Lobo One. 240p. (Orig.). 1992. mass mkt. 4.50 (*0-380-76616-7*, Avon Bks) Morrow Avon.

Pruitt, Jim. Coaching Beginning Basketball. (Coaching Ser.). (Illus.). 138p. 1980. 12.95 (*0-8092-7089-7*); pap. 14.95 (*0-8092-7088-9*, 70889) NTC Contemp Pub Co.

— Play Better Basketball. (Illus.). 160p. (Orig.). 1982. pap. 12.95 (*0-8092-5799-8*) NTC Contemp Pub Co.

Pruitt, John, jt. auth. see Reddy, Kumuda.

Pruitt, John E., jt. auth. see Reddy, Kumuda.

Pruitt, Jon E., jt. auth. see Reddy, Kumuda.

Pruitt, K. Wayne, jt. auth. see Lee, Jackson F., Jr.

Pruitt, Kenneth & Tenovuov. The Lactoperoxidase System: Chemistry & Biological Significance. (Immunology Ser.: Vol. 27). (Illus.). 272p. 1985. text 155.00 (*0-8247-7298-9*) Dekker.

*__Pruitt, Kristin A. & Durham, Charles.__ Living Texts: Interpreting Milton. LC 00-34442. (Illus.). 2001. 47.50 (*1-57591-042-X*) Susquehanna U Pr.

Pruitt, Kristin A., jt. ed. see Durham, Charles W.

Pruitt, Lawrence, jt. auth. see Pruitt, Fred.

Pruitt, Leonard E. Namemaker's Handbook: Creative Selections for Constant Connections. LC 98-90492. xiv, 400p. 1998. lib. bdg. 25.00 (*0-9665145-1-3*) Wordway Pubg Co.

Pruitt, Mary L. C++ for Engineers. (C). 2001. teacher ed. write for info. (*0-201-35097-1*); pap. text 31.00 (*0-201-35096-3*) Addison-Wesley.

*__Pruitt, Nancy L., et al.__ Bioinquiry Learning System 1.2: Making Connections in Biology. LC 99-38867. 576p. 1999. 88.95 incl. cd-rom (*0-471-19280-5*) Wiley.

Pruitt, Pamela, et al. Henry Box Brown; Struggle for Freedom; Wildfire. 2nd ed. McCluskey, John A., ed. (Stories from Black History Series II: Vol. 1). (Illus.). (Orig.). (J). (gr. 4-7). 1993. pap. 2.00 (*0-913678-25-2*) New Day Pr.

Pruitt, Pamela, jt. auth. see Johnston, Brenda A.

Pruitt, Patricia. Construction Work. 36p. 1991. 6.00 (*0-9630045-0-6*) Longwood MA.

— Sessions, Sections I-IV. 28p. 1998. 4.00 (*1-893032-02-7*) Jensen Daniels.

*__Pruitt, Ramona.__ Paint Shop Pro 6 Visual Insight. LC 99-49157. 1999. pap. text 29.99 (*1-57610-525-3*) Coriolis Grp.

— Photoshop X Visual Insight. (Illus.). 280p. 2000. pap. 24.99 (*1-57610-747-7*) Coriolis Grp.

Pruitt, Raymond M. Fundamentals of the Faith. 1981. 16.95 (*0-934942-21-8*) White Wing Pub.

Pruitt, Rhonda R. Flames of Fire: Biographical Accounts of Pentecost Through the Centuries. (Orig.). pap. text. write for info. (*0-318-59338-6*) Faith Print.

Pruitt, Robert G., Jr. Digest of Mining Claim Laws. 5th ed. LC 97-123758. (Illus.). 244p. (Orig.). 1996. pap. 32.00 (*0-929047-62-1*, DMC5) Rocky Mtn Mineral Law Found.

Pruitt, Robert J. And Then Shall the End Come. 1979. pap. 2.25 (*0-934942-20-X*) White Wing Pub.

— The Death of the Third Nature. 1975. pap. 2.50 (*0-934942-04-8*) White Wing Pub.

— The Kingdom of God & the Church of God. 1977. pap. 2.25 (*0-934942-09-9*) White Wing Pub.

Pruitt, Scott K., ed. see D'Amico, Thomas A.

Pruitt, Sharon. Art of the Cameroon: Selections from the Spelman College Collection of African Art. (Illus.). 40p. 1990. pap. 7.50 (*0-915977-05-2*) Georgia Museum of Art.

Pruitt, Sheryl K., jt. auth. see Dornbush, Marilyn P.

*__Pruitt, Victoria E. Murray.__ An Intimate Account: My Twenty-Five Year Battle Before & after the Diagnosis of Scleroderma & Periarthritis. LC 99-93617. 2000. pap. 8.95 (*0-533-13092-1*) Vantage.

Pruitt, Virginia D., jt. ed. see Faulkner, Howard J.

Prum, Bernard & Fort, Jean C. Stochastic Processes on a Lattice & Gibbs Measures. (Mathematical Physics Studies). (C). 1991. text 160.00 (*0-7923-1069-1*) Kluwer Academic.

Prum, Deborah M. Rats, Bulls & Flying Machines: A History of the Renaissance & Reformation. Holdren, John, ed. (Core Chronicles Ser.: Vol. 1). (Illus.). (J). (gr. 5-9). 1999. pap. 11.95 (*1-890517-18-6*) Core Knowledge.

— Rats, Bulls & Flying Machines: A History of the Renaissance & Reformation. Holdren, John, ed. (Core Chronicles Ser.: Vol. 1). (Illus.). 106p. (YA). (gr. 5-10). 1999. 21.95 (*1-890517-19-4*) Core Knowledge.

Prumm, Hans-Joachim. Film-Script - William Shakespeare: Eine Untersuchung der Film-Bearbeitungen von Shakespeares Dramen am Beispiel ausgewahlter Tragodien-Verfilmungen von 1945-1985. (Munchner Studien zur Neueren Englischen Literatur: Band 3). (GER.). 439p. 1987. 50.00 (*90-6032-287-8*, Pub. by B R Gruner) Humanities.

Prummer, Dominic M. Handbook of Moral Theology. Shelton, Gerald W., ed. 513p. 1995. reprint ed. 29.95 (*0-912141-29-8*) Roman Cath Bks.

Prunckun, Henry W., Jr. Shadow of Death: An Analytic Bibliography on Political Violence, Terrorism, & Low-Intensity Conflict. LC 93-32400. (Illus.). 432p. 1995. 81.00 (*0-8108-2773-5*) Scarecrow.

— Special Access Required: A Practitioner's Guide to Law Enforcement Intelligence Literature. LC 90-46292. (Illus.). 212p. 1990. 32.00 (*0-8108-2371-3*) Scarecrow.

Prunet, Antoine. Ferrari Legend: The Road Cars. 2nd ed. LC 87-81363. (Illus.). 446p. 1981. 45.00 (*0-393-01475-4*, F613, Pub. by GT Foulis) Haynes Manuals.

*__Prunet, Antoine.__ Pininfarina: Seventy Years. (Illus.). 308p. 2000. text 95.00 (*0-8478-2243-5*) Rizzoli Intl.

Prunet, Jean-Francois, jt. ed. see Paradis, Carole.

P

Prunetti, Luigi. Viking Explorers. LC 96-33. (Voyages of Discovery Ser.). (Illus.). 48p. (J). (gr. 4-7). 1996. 18.95 (*0-87226-486-6*, 64866B, P Bedrick Books) NTC Contemp Pub Co.

Prungel, Elizabeth & Spyer, Heather. The Top Ramen Noodle Cookbook: Over 175 Delicious, Quick, Easy & Inexpensive Recipes Using America's Favorite Noodle. LC 94-21450. 224p. 1994. pap. 10.95 (*1-55958-565-X*) Prima Pub.

Prunier, Gerard. The Rwanda Crisis: History of a Genocide. LC 95-18203. 250p. 1995. 42.00 (*0-231-10408-1*) Col U Pr.

— The Rwanda Crisis: History of a Genocide. 1997. pap. 18.00 (*0-231-10409-X*) Col U Pr.

Prunier, J. & Galeron, Henri. Dinosaure. (Gallimard - Mes Premieres Decouvertes Ser.: No. 30). (FRE.). (J). (ps-1). 1991. 17.95 (*2-07-056642-0*) Schoenhof.

Prunier, James. Livre des As et des Heros: Histoire de l'Aviation, No. 2. (Gallimard - Decouverte Cadet Ser.: No. 48). (FRE.). 77p. (J). (gr. 4-9). 1988. 13.95 (*2-07-039548-0*) Schoenhof.

— Livre des Trains. (Gallimard - Decouverte Cadet Ser.: No. 27). (FRE.). 93p. (J). (gr. 4-9). 1986. 15.95 (*2-07-039527-8*) Schoenhof.

Prunier, James, jt. auth. see Delafosse, Claude.

Prunier, James, jt. auth. see Poe, Edgar Allan.

Prunier, Michael L., jt. ed. see Scaros, Michael.

Prunieras, M., ed. Epidermal Keratinocyte Differentiation & Fibrillogenesis. (Frontiers of Matrix Biology Ser.: Vol. 9). (Illus.). viii, 192p. 1981. 104.50 (*3-8055-0893-X*) S Karger.

Prunieres, Henry. Monteverdi: His Life & Work. MacKie, Marie D., tr. LC 70-100830. (Illus.). 293p. 1973. reprint ed. lib. bdg. 55.00 (*0-8371-3996-1*, PRMO, Greenwood Pr) Greenwood.

— Monteverdi: His Life & Work. 293p. 1990. reprint ed. lib. bdg. 69.00 (*0-7812-9075-9*) Rprt Serv.

— A New History of Music: The Middle Ages to Mozart. (Music Book Index Ser.). 413p. 1992. reprint ed. lib. bdg. 99.00 (*0-7812-9465-7*) Rprt Serv.

— La Vie Illustre et Libertine de Jean-Baptiste Lully. LC 76-43934. (Music & Theatre in France in the 17th & 18th Centuries Ser.). reprint ed. 52.50 (*0-404-60186-3*) AMS Pr.

Prunieres, Henry, ed. see Lully, Jean-Baptiste.

Prunkl, Peter R. & Berry, Rebecca L. Death Week: Exploring the Dying Process. (Death Education, Aging & Health Care Ser.). 240p. 1988. 89.95 (*0-89116-784-6*); pap. 33.95 (*0-89116-112-0*) Hemisp Pub.

Prunskiene, Kazimiera & Altvater, Elmar, eds. East-West Scientific Co-Operation: Science & Technology Policy of the Baltic States & International Co-Operation. LC 97-26119. (NATO ASI Ser.). 168p. 1997. 110.50 (*0-7923-4689-0*) Kluwer Academic.

Prunskiene, Kazimiera, ed. see Altvater, Elmara & Lithuanian European Institute Staff.

Prunster, Nicole, jt. ed. see Cicioni, Mirna.

Prunty, Jacinta. Dublin Slums, 1800-1925: A Study in Urban Geography. (Illus.). 384p. 1998. 49.50 (*0-7165-2538-0*); pap. 32.50 (*0-7165-2690-5*) Irish Acad Pr.

***Prunty, Jacinta.** Maps & Map-Making in Local History. (Maynooth Research Guides for Irish Local History Ser.). 64p. 2000. pap. 14.50 (*0-7165-2727-8*, Pub. by Irish Acad Pr) Intl Spec Bk.

Prunty, Jacinta. Margaret Aylward, 1810-1889: Lady of Charity, Sister of Faith. LC 99-198046. 192p. 1999. pap. 19.95 (*1-85182-438-3*, Pub. by Four Cts Pr) Intl Spec Bk.

Prunty, John J. A Critical Reformulation of Educational Policy Analysis. 113p. (C). 1984. 65.00 (*0-7300-0113-X*, Pub. by Deakin Univ) St Mut.

Prunty, Wyatt. The Run of the House: Poems. LC 92-43034. (Poetry & Fiction Ser.). 68p. 1993. pap. 12.95 (*0-8018-4626-9*) Johns Hopkins.

— Since the Noon Mail Stopped: Poetry. LC 97-4993. (Poetry & Fiction Ser.). 88p. 1997. 16.95 (*0-8018-5646-9*) Johns Hopkins.

— Unarmed & Dangerous: New & Selected Poems. LC 99-27613. (Johns Hopkins). 192p. 1999. 24.95 (*0-8018-6290-6*) Johns Hopkins.

***Prunty, Wyatt, ed.** Sewanee Writers on Writing. (Southern Literary Studies). 168p. 2000. 42.50 (*0-8071-2631-4*); pap. 22.50 (*0-8071-2652-7*) La State U Pr.

Prupas, Marilynne, jt. auth. see Rosenfeld, Linda.

Pruppacher, Hans R. Microphysics of Clouds & Precipitation: An Introduction to Cloud Chemistry & Cloud Electricity. 2nd enl. rev. ed. 976p. (C). 1997. pap. text 99.00 (*0-7923-4409-X*); lib. bdg. 290.00 (*0-7923-4211-9*) Kluwer Academic.

Pruppacher, Hans R. & Klett, James D. Microphysics of Atmospheric Clouds & Precipitation. 1978. lib. bdg. 145.00 (*90-277-0515-1*) Kluwer Academic.

Prus, Bolesiaw. The Doll. Welsh, David et al, trs. LC 97-147052. (Central European Classics Ser.). 704p. (C). 1996. pap. 19.95 (*1-85866-065-3*, Pub. by Ctrl Europ Univ) Bks Intl VA.

— The Doll. 700p. 1993. pap. 16.95 (*0-7818-0158-3*) Hippocrene Bks.

— The Sins of Childhood & Other Stories. Johnston, Bill, tr. from POL. 250p. 1997. 42.95 (*0-8101-1274-4*); pap. 14.95 (*0-8101-1462-3*) Northwestern U Pr.

Prus, Robert. Beyond the Power Mystique: Power As Intersubjective Accomplishment. LC 98-43622. 320p. (C). 1999. text 71.50 (*0-7914-4069-9*); pap. text 23.95 (*0-7914-4070-2*) State U NY Pr.

— Subcultural Mosaics & Intersubjective Realities: An Ethnographic Research Agenda for Pragmatizing the Social Sciences. LC 96-32485. 349p. (C). 1997. text 65.50 (*0-7914-3239-4*); pap. text 21.95 (*0-7914-3240-8*) State U NY Pr.

— Symbolic Interaction & Ethnographic Research: Intersubjectivity & the Study of Human Lived Experience. LC 94-49571. 301p. (C). 1995. pap. text 21.95 (*0-7914-2702-1*) State U NY Pr.

Prusa, Thomas. International Trade Policies & Incentives. LC 90-3526. (Foreign Economic Policy of the United States Ser.). 165p. 1990. reprint ed. text 10.00 (*0-8240-7473-4*) Garland.

Prusaczyk, J. E., et al. Fire Performance Characteristics in Rooms as the Result of Increased Insulation. 1978. 4.00 (*0-686-12079-5*, TR 78-2) Society Fire Protect.

Prusaensis, Dio. Quae Exstant Omnia, Vol. I. Von Arnim, Hans F., ed. xl, 338p. 1962. write for info. (*3-296-12301-6*) G Olms Pubs.

— Quae Exstant Omnia, Vol. II. Von Arnim, Hans F., ed. xiv, 380p. 1962. write for info. (*3-296-12302-4*) G Olms Pubs.

Prusak, Bernard P., ed. Raising the Torch of Good News: Catholic Authority & Dialogue with the World. LC 87-31695. (College Theology Society Annual Publications: Vol. 32). 342p. (Orig.). (C). 1988. pap. text 27.00 (*0-8191-6700-2*); lib. bdg. 51.00 (*0-8191-6699-5*) U Pr of Amer.

Prusak, Larry & Matarazzo, Jim. Information Management & Japanese Success. 15p. 1992. 16.00 (*0-87111-383-X*) SLA.

Prusak, Laurance, jt. auth. see Davenport, Thomas H.

Prusak, Laurence, jt. auth. see Cohen, Don.

Prusak, Laurence, jt. auth. see Matarazzo, James M.

Prusak, Laurence, jt. auth. see McGee, James.

Prusak, Lawrence, jt. auth. see Davenport, Thomas H.

Prusek, Jaroslav. Chinese History & Literature: Collection of Studies. LC 77-133129. 586p. 1970. lib. bdg. 171.00 (*90-277-0175-X*) Kluwer Academic.

— Chinese Statelets & the Northern Barbarians in the Period 1400-300 B. C. LC 70-154745. 312p. 1971. lib. bdg. 121.50 (*90-277-0225-X*) Kluwer Academic.

Prushan, Victor H. No-Nonsense Marketing: 101 Practical Ways to Win & Keep Customers. LC 96-42473. 282p. 1997. pap. 19.95 (*0-471-15707-4*) Wiley.

***Prusiner, Stanley B., ed.** Prion Biology & Diseases. (Monographs). (Illus.). 710p. (C). 1999. 125.00 (*0-87969-547-1*) Cold Spring Harbor.

Prusinkiewicz, P. The Algorithmic Beauty of Plants. (Virtual Laboratory Ser.). 228p. 1996. 29.95 (*0-387-94676-4*) Spr-Verlag.

Prusinkiewicz, P. & Hanan, Joe J. Lindenmayer Systems, Fractals, & Plants. (Lecture Notes in Biomathematics Ser.: Vol. 79). viii, 120p. 1992. 43.95 (*0-387-97092-4*) Spr-Verlag.

Prusinkiewicz, P. & Lindenmayer, A. The Algorithmic Beauty of Plants. Cutter, M., ed. (Virtual Laboratory Ser.). (Illus.). xii, 228p. 1991. 49.95 (*0-387-97297-8*) Spr-Verlag.

Pruski, Gina M., jt. auth. see Pomeroy, Virginia A.

Pruski, Linda, et al. TAAS Master Science, Grade 8. LC 94-234008. (Illus.). 1994. pap. text, teacher ed. 20.95 (*0-944459-93-5*) ECS Lrn Systs.

Prusmack, Florence. Khan. 412p. 1992. pap. 4.00 (*0-9633903-0-9*) Ashby-Ferguson.

Pruss, Adrian, jt. auth. see Spencer, John.

Pruss, Jan. Evolutionary Integral Equations & Applications. LC 93-20736. (Monographs in Mathematics: Vol. 87). 366p. 1993. 149.50 (*0-8176-2876-2*) Birkhauser.

Prussack, Tracy, jt. auth. see Foster, Sandra.

Prussia Kriegministerium Staff. War in South Africa. Du Cane, Hubert, tr. LC 69-19361. 374p. 1970. reprint ed. lib. bdg. 59.75 (*0-8371-5089-2*, PRW&, Greenwood Pr) Greenwood.

Prussia Kriegsministerium Staff. Regulations for the Prussian Infantry: To Which Is Added the Prussian Tactick. LC 68-54803. 444p. 1969. reprint ed. lib. bdg. 38.50 (*0-8371-0625-7*, PRPI, Greenwood Pr) Greenwood.

Prussia, Stanley E., jt. ed. see Shewfelt, Robert L.

Prussian, Claire, jt. ed. see Frantz, Claire W.

Prussian General Staff. The Campaign of 1866 in Germany. (European War Ser.: No. 2). (Illus.). 672p. 1994. 54.95 (*0-89839-201-2*) Battery Pr.

Prussin, Labelle. African Nomadic Architecture: Space, Place, & Gender. LC 94-43109. (Illus.). 320p. 1995. text 55.00 (*1-56098-358-2*) Smithsonian.

— African Nomadic Architecture: Space, Place & Gender. (Illus.). 320p. 1997. pap. text 27.50 (*1-56098-756-1*) Smithsonian.

— Hatumere: Islamic Design in West Africa. 300p. 1996. 29.95 (*0-614-21577-3*, 377) Kazi Pubns.

Prussing, John E. & Conway, Bruce A. Orbital Mechanics. LC 92-41505. (Illus.). 208p. (C). 1993. text 52.95 (*0-19-507834-9*) OUP.

Prusski, Jeffrey. Bring Back the Deer. LC 86-33605. (Illus.). 32p. (J). (ps-3). 1988. 13.95 (*0-15-200418-1*, Gulliver Bks) Harcourt.

Prusski, Jeffrey J. Bring Back the Deer. 1988. 13.95 (*0-15-211418-1*) Harcourt.

Prust, Jim, et al. The Czech & Slovak Federal Republic: An Economy in Transition. LC 90-47707. (Occasional Papers: No. 72). vii, 70p. 1990. pap. 10.00 (*1-55775-169-2*) Intl Monetary.

Prust, Randall & Luzader, Susan. Conquering Pain. 1997. mass mkt. 5.99 (*0-425-16118-8*) Berkley Pub.

Prust, Z. A. Graphic Communications: The Printed Image. LC 98-7572. 1998. 45.28 (*1-56637-464-2*) Goodheart.

Pruter, A. T. & Alverson, Dayton L., eds. The Columbia River Estuary & Adjacent Ocean Waters: Bioenvironmental Studies. LC 79-178705. (Illus.). 882p. 1972. 40.00 (*0-295-95177-X*) U of Wash Pr.

Pruter, Bishop K. The Strange Partnership of George Alexander McGuire & Marcus Garvey. LC 86-17628. 50p. 1986. pap. 13.00 (*0-912134-08-9*) Millefleurs.

Pruter, Karl. The Catholic Priest: A Guide to Holy Orders. LC 92-45059. (St. Willibrord Studies in Philosophy & Religion: No. 2). 88p. 1993. pap. 15.00 (*0-912134-15-1*, 27181559); lib. bdg. 25.00 (*0-912134-14-3*, 27181559) Millefleurs.

— The Mystic Path. LC 96-48219. (St. Willbrords Studies in Philosophy & Religion: No. 5). 80p. 1997. 23.00 (*0-912134-32-1*); pap. 13.00 (*0-912134-33-X*) Millefleurs.

— Neo-Congregationalism. LC 85-13416. 90p. 1985. reprint ed. pap. 17.00 (*0-912134-02-X*) Millefleurs.

— The Old Catholic Church: A History & Chronology. expanded rev. ed. LC 95-3866. (Autocephalous Orthodox Churches Ser.: No. 3). (Illus.). 96p. 1996. pap. 17.00 (*0-912134-19-4*) Millefleurs.

— One Day with God: A Guide to Retreats & the Contemplative Life. rev. ed. LC 91-35733. (St. Willibrord Studies in Philosophy & Religion: No. 1). 56p. 1991. pap. 13.00 (*0-912134-11-9*); lib. bdg. 23.00 (*0-912134-10-0*) Millefleurs.

— The People of God. LC 85-13417. v, 162p. 1985. reprint ed. pap. 21.00 (*0-912134-03-8*) Millefleurs.

— The Priest's Handbook. 2nd expanded rev. ed. LC 96-25022. (St. Willibrord Studies in Philosophy & Religion: No. 4). 62p. 1996. 23.00 (*0-912134-28-3*, 35008104); pap. 13.00 (*0-912134-29-1*, 35008104) Millefleurs.

— The Teachings of the Great Mystics. LC 85-13306. 118p. 1985. reprint ed. pap. 17.00 (*0-912134-00-3*) Millefleurs.

— The Theology of Congregationalism. LC 85-12844. 100p. 1985. reprint ed. pap. 17.00 (*0-912134-09-7*) Millefleurs.

Pruter, Karl & Melton, J. Gordon. The Old Catholic Sourcebook. LC 83-47610. 254p. 1983. text 30.00 (*0-8240-9111-6*) Garland.

Pruter, Robert. Chicago Soul. (Music in American Life Ser.). (Illus.). 464p. 1992. 21.95 (*0-252-06259-0*) U of Ill Pr.

— Doowop: The Chicago Scene. LC 95-19593. (Music in American Life Ser.). 360p. 1996. 19.95 (*0-252-06506-9*) U of Ill Pr.

***Pruthi, Devi & Devi, eds.** Encyclopaedia of Status & Empowerment of Women in India, 4 vols. 1999. 185.00 (*81-7594-039-5*, Pub. by Mangal Deep) S Asia.

Pruthi, Raj & Sharma, Bela R. Aryans & Hindu Women. (C). 1995. 32.00 (*81-7488-084-4*, Pub. by Anmol) S Asia.

— Buddhism, Jainism, & Women. (C). 1995. 30.00 (*81-7488-085-2*, Pub. by Anmol) S Asia.

— Education & Modernisation of Women in India. (C). 1995. 32.00 (*81-7488-096-8*, Pub. by Anmol) S Asia.

— Islam & Women. (C). 1995. 30.00 (*81-7488-086-0*, Pub. by Anmol) S Asia.

— Sikhism & Women. (C). 1995. 32.00 (*81-7488-087-9*, Pub. by Anmol) S Asia.

— Trend in Women Studies. (C). 1995. 29.00 (*81-7488-082-8*, Pub. by Anmol) S Asia.

***Pruthi, Raj & Sharma, Bela Rani.** Encyclopaedia of Women Society & Culture, 15 vols. 1998. pap. 2750.00 (*81-7488-002-X*, Pub. by Print Hse) St Mut.

Prutkovsky, Alexander. Phosphorus Research & Production in the U. S. S. R. Michta, Andrew A., ed. 118p. (Orig.). 1987. pap. text 75.00 (*1-55831-037-1*) Delphic Associates.

Prutton, Martin. Electronic Properties of Surfaces. (Illus.). 202p. 1984. 90.00 (*0-85274-773-X*) IOP Pub.

— Introduction to Surface Physics. LC 93-31100. (Illus.). 204p. (C). 1994. pap. text 31.95 (*0-19-853476-0*, Clarendon Pr) OUP.

Prutz, Hans. Kulturgeschichte der Kreuzzuge. xxxi, 642p. 1994. reprint ed. write for info. (*3-487-00489-5*) G Olms Pubs.

Prutzman, Deborah S. A Banker's Guide to Loan Participations. 2nd ed. 77p. (C). 1994. 134.00 (*0-89982-376-9*) Am Bankers.

Prutzman, Priscilla, et al. CCRC'S Friendly Classroom & Communities for Young Children: A Manual of Conflict Resolution Activities & Resources. (Illus.). 120p. 1998. pap. write for info. (*1-891955-03-9*) Creative Resp.

Prutzman, Priscilla, jt. auth. see Johnson, Judith M.

Pruul, Kajar, jt. ed. see Reddaway, Darlene.

Pruyn, John V. Catalogue of Books Relating to the Literature of the Law. 300p. 1982. reprint ed. 38.50 (*0-8377-1015-4*, Rothman) W S Hein.

Pruyn, Marc. Discourse Wars in Gotham-West: A Latino Immigrant Urban Tale of Resistance & Agency. LC 98-229695. (Edge Ser.). 240p. 1998. text 59.00 (*0-8133-9067-2*, Pub. by Westview) HarpC.

Pruyne, Ellen, ed. An End to Debt: Operational Guidelines for Credit Projects. 111p. (Orig.). 1993. pap. 15.95 (*0-912917-44-X*) UNIFEM.

Pruyne, Gwen, jt. auth. see Hines, Edward R.

Pruys, Karl Hugo. Kohl, Genius of the Present: A Biography of Helmut Kohl. LC 96-23379. (Illus.). 416p. 1996. 26.95 (*1-883695-10-4*) Edition Q.

— Tigers Tender Touch. 18p. 1995. 21.95 (*1-883695-12-0*) Edition Q.

Pruyser, Paul W. The Minister As Diagnostician: Personal Problems in Pastoral Perspective. LC 76-8922. 144p. 1976. pap. 14.95 (*0-664-24123-9*) Westminster John Knox.

— The Psychological Examination: A Guide for Clinicians. LC 78-70234. 311p. 1979. 47.50 (*0-8236-5605-5*) Intl Univs Pr.

Pruyser, Paul W., ed. Changing Views of the Human Condition. LC 86-31067. 256p. 1987. pap. text 13.95 (*0-86554-230-9*, MUP\P032) Mercer Univ Pr.

Pruyt, Hans. Database Management with DBASE & SQL: A Practical Introduction. Lewis, Mike, tr. LC 92-38822. (DUT & ENG.). 1992. mass mkt. 46.50 (*0-412-47750-5*) Chapman & Hall.

Pruzan, Elliot R. The Concept of Justice in Marx. (American University Studies: Political Science: Ser. X, Vol. 13). XII, 238p. (C). 1988. text 37.00 (*0-8204-0665-1*) P Lang Pubng.

Pruzanski, W. & Vadas, P., eds. Novel Molecular Approaches to Anti-Inflammatory Therapy. LC 95-1382. (Agents & Actions Supplements Ser.: Vol. 46). 1995. 69.50 (*0-8176-5096-2*) Birkhauser.

Pruzhan, V. Bakst - Set & Costume Designs, Book Illustrations, Paintings & Graphic Works. (C). 1990. pap. 130.00 (*0-7855-4475-5*, Pub. by Collets) St Mut.

Pruzinsky, Thomas, jt. ed. see Cash, Thomas F.

Pruzzo, C., jt. ed. see Cabello, F. C.

Pry, Daniel J. Star Flower Essences: The Andean Orchids. Riparetti, Star & Ederer, Maria, eds. (Illus.). 139p. 1998. pap. 14.44 (*1-892457-00-8*) Laughng Star Pr.

Pry, Mark E. The Town on the Hassayampa: A History of Wickenburg, Arizona. LC 97-207665. (Illus.). 176p. 1997. pap. 12.95 (*0-9657377-0-5*) Desert Cab.

***Pry, Peter Vincent.** War Scare: Russia & America on the Nuclear Brink. LC 98-56630. 360p. 1999. 25.95 (*0-275-96643-7*, Praeger Pubs) Greenwood.

Pryakhin, Vladimir, jt. auth. see Sevstyanov, Vitali.

Prybot, Peter K. White-Tipped Orange Masts: Gloucester's Fishing Draggers a Time of Change, 1970-1972. (Illus.). 228p. 1998. pap. 24.95 (*1-892839-01-6*) Curious Traveller Pr.

Prybyla, Jan S. Issues in Socialist Economic Modernization. LC 80-18647. 121p. 1981. 49.95 (*0-275-90706-6*, C0706, Praeger Pubs) Greenwood.

— Market & Plan under Socialism: The Bird in the Cage. (Publication Ser.: No. 422). 348p. (C). 1987. text 15.98 (*0-8179-8351-1*); pap. text 7.58 (*0-8179-8352-X*) Hoover Inst Pr.

Prybyla, Jan S., ed. Comparative Economic Systems. LC 69-17707. (C). 1969. 44.50 (*0-89197-097-5*); pap. text 24.50 (*0-89197-707-4*) Irvington.

Prybylowski, Douglas. Comex ASVAB-AFCT. (Illus.). 360p. 1996. pap. text 17.95 (*1-56030-022-1*) Comex Systs.

Pryce, Huw. Native Law & the Church in Medieval Wales. LC 92-25903. (Oxford Historical Monographs). (Illus.). 306p. 1993. text 75.00 (*0-19-820362-4*, Clarendon Pr) OUP.

Pryce, Huw, et al, contrib. by. Literacy in Medieval Celtic Societies. LC 97-9721. (Studies in Medieval Literature: No. 33). (Illus.). 314p. (C). 1998. text 64.95 (*0-521-57039-5*) Cambridge U Pr.

Pryce, Huw, ed. see Maund, K. L.

Pryce, John D. Numerical Solution of Sturm-Liouville Problems. (Monographs on Numerical Analysis). (Illus.). 336p. 1994. text 59.00 (*0-19-853415-9*) OUP.

Pryce-Jones. The Strange Death of the Soviet Empire. Date not set. pap. write for info. (*0-8050-4155-9*) St Martin.

Pryce-Jones, David. The Strange Death of the Soviet Empire. 89p. 1995. 30.00 (*0-8050-4154-0*) H Holt & Co.

— You Can't Be Too Careful. LC 92-50291. (Illus.). 80p. 1992. pap. 4.95 (*1-56305-156-7*, 3156) Workman Pub.

***Pryce, Maggie.** Decoupage. (New Crafts Collections). (Illus.). 2000. 16.95 (*0-7548-0489-5*, Lorenz Bks) Anness Pub.

Pryce, Mark. Finding a Voice: Men, Women & the Community of the Church. 1997. pap. 17.00 (*0-334-02662-8*) TPI PA.

Pryce, Melinda. Loving Spirits. 208p. 1994. mass mkt. 4.50 (*0-515-11474-X*, Jove) Berkley Pub.

— Rose for Lady Edwina. 1990. mass mkt. 3.95 (*1-55817-368-4*, Pinncle Kensgtn) Kensgtn Pub Corp.

Pryce, Paula. Keeping the Lakes Way: Reburial & Re-Creation of a Moral World amoung an Invisible People. 240p. 1999. text 45.00 (*0-8020-4419-0*); pap. text 17.95 (*0-8020-8223-8*) U of Toronto Pr.

Pryce-Phillips, William. Companion to Clinical Neurology. LC 94-19605. 1009p. 1995. text 99.95 (*0-316-72041-0*, Little Brwn Med Div) Lppncott W & W.

Pryce, Roy, ed. The Dynamics of European Union. LC 87-592. 288p. 1986. 55.00 (*0-7099-4327-X*, Pub. by C Helm) Routldge.

Pryce, Roy, ed. see Duff, Andrew, et al.

Pryce, W. T., ed. From Family History to Community History. (Studying Family & Community History Ser.: No. 2). 256p. (C). 1994. text 59.95 (*0-521-46002-6*); pap. text 19.95 (*0-521-46578-8*) Cambridge U Pr.

Prychitko, David, ed. Individuals, Institutions, Interpretations: Hermeneutics Applied to Economics. LC 95-75559. 186p. 1995. 61.95 (*1-85628-968-0*, Pub. by Avebry) Ashgate Pub Co.

Prychitko, David L. Marxism & Workers' Self-Management: The Essential Tension, 123. LC 91-9152. (Contributions in Economics & Economic History Ser.: No. 123). 176p. 1991. 57.95 (*0-313-27854-7*, PPY, Greenwood Pr) Greenwood.

Prychitko, David L., ed. Why Economists Disagree: An Introduction to the Alternative Schools of Thought. LC 97-1725. (SUNY Series, Diversity in Contemporary Economics). 415p. (C). 1997. pap. text 21.95 (*0-7914-3570-9*) State U NY Pr.

— Why Economists Disagree: An Introduction to the Alternative Schools of Thought. LC 97-1725. (SUNY Series, Diversity in Contemporary Economics). 415p. (C). 1997. text 65.50 (*0-7914-3569-5*) State U NY Pr.

Prychitko, David L. & Vanek, Jaroslav, eds. Producer Cooperatives & Labor-Managed Systems, 2 vols., Set. LC 95-42011. (International Library of Critical Writings in Economics: Vol. 62). 864p. 1996. 325.00 (*1-85898-189-1*) E Elgar.

Prychitko, David L., jt. ed. see Boettke, Peter J.

Pryde, A. & Gilbert, M. T. Application of High Performance Liquid Chromatography. 1979. 35.00 (*0-412-14220-1*, NO.6229) Chapman & Hall.

Pryde, Everett H., ed. Fatty Acids. 644p. (C). 1979. 40.00 (*0-935315-04-7*) Am Oil Chemists.

P

An Asterisk (*) at the beginning of an entry indicates that the title is appearing for the first time.

Pryde, George S., ed. Treaty of Union of Scotland & England. LC 78-24202. 120p. 1979. reprint ed. lib. bdg. 45.00 (*0-313-20829-8*, SCTR, Greenwood Pr) Greenwood.

Pryde, Marion J., jt. auth. see Fleming, Beatrice J.

Pryde, Paul, jt. auth. see Green, Shelley.

Pryde, Paul, jt. auth. see Green, Shelly.

Pryde, Philip R., ed. Environmental Resources & Constraints in the Former Soviet Republics. (C). 1995. pap. 34.00 (*0-8133-2965-5*, Pub. by Westview) HarpC.

Pryde-Sunbelt, Philip R. San Diego: An Introduction to the Region. 3rd ed. (Illus.). 320p. 1992. per. 18.95 (*0-8403-7094-6*) Kendall-Hunt.

Prydz, H., ed. The Cell Biology of Triggers in Coagulation. (Journal: Haemostasis: Vol. 14, No. 5). (Illus.). 68p. 1985. pap. 48.75 (*3-8055-4046-9*) S Karger.

***Pryer, Ada & Morgan, Susan.** A Decade in Borneo. LC 00-55656. (Literature of Novel, Exploration & Empire Ser.). 2001. write for info. (*0-7185-0197-7*, Pub. by Leicester U Pr) Continuum.

Pryer, Jane & Crook, Nigel. Cities of Hunger: Urban Malnutrition in Developing Countries. (Illus.). 112p. (C). 1988. pap. 12.95 (*0-85598-155-5*, Pub. by Oxfam Pub) Stylus Pub VA.

— Cities of Hunger: Urban Malnutrition in Developing Countries. (Illus.). 120p. (C). 1990. 39.95 (*0-85598-154-7*, Pub. by Oxfam Pub) Stylus Pub VA.

Pryer, Peter. Jottings: Historical & Political. (C). 1990. text 50.00 (*0-7223-2519-3*, Pub. by A H S Ltd) St Mut.

— The New Communism. 108p. 1988. 40.00 (*0-7223-2044-2*, Pub. by A H S Ltd) St Mut.

Pryer, Richard R., tr. see Detrie, Philippe.

Prygoski, Phil. Constitutional Law. 2nd rev. ed. (Quick Review Ser.). 358p. (C). 1996. pap. text 18.95 (*0-614-30136-X*) Sum & Substance.

***Prygoski, Phil.** Constitutional Law. 5th ed. 1999. pap. 18.95 (*0-314-24290-2*) West Pub.

Pryke, E. J. Redactional Style in the Marcan Gospel: A Study of Syntax & Vocabulary as Guides to Redaction in Mark. LC 76-52184. (Society for New Testament Studies,: No. 33). 206p. reprint ed. pap. 58.80 (*0-608-15768-6*, 2031714) Bks Demand.

***Pryke, John.** Building City Scenery for Your Model Railroad. (Model Railroader Ser.). (Illus.). 2000. pap. 17.95 (*0-89024-343-3*) Kalmbach.

Pryke, Julie & Thomas, Martin. Domestic Violence & Social Work. LC 98-12738. 178p. 1998. text 59.95 (*1-85742-357-7*, HV6626.23.G7P79, Pub. by Ashgate Pub) Ashgate Pub Co.

Pryke, Kenneth G. Nova Scotia & Confederation, 1864-74. LC 79-322022. (Canadian Studies in History & Government: No. 15). 252p. reprint ed. pap. 78.20 (*0-608-15418-0*, 202934500060) Bks Demand.

— Profiles of Canada. (C). 1992. pap. text 33.95 (*0-7730-5188-0*) Addison-Wesley.

Pryke, Martin. A Quest for Perfection: The Story of the Making of the Stained-Glass Windows in the Bryn Athyn Cathedral & Glencairn. 40p. (Orig.). 1990. pap. 2.75 (*0-910557-24-1*) Acad New Church.

— You & the Opposite Sex. (Illus.). 90p. (Orig.). 1986. pap. 3.80 (*0-910557-14-4*) Acad New Church.

Pryke, Paula. Candles: Home Dcorating Workbooks with 20 Step-by-Step Projects on Fold-Out Pages. 112p. 1998. pap., wbk. ed. 19.95 (*0-8230-0552-6*) Watsn-Guptill.

— Festive Flowers. LC 97-66477. (Illus.). 168p. 1997. 37.50 (*0-8478-2039-4*, Pub. by Rizzoli Intl) St Martin.

— Flair with Flowers. LC 95-7852. Orig. Title: Flower Variations. (Illus.). 192p. 37.50 (*0-8478-1892-6*, Pub. by Rizzoli Intl) St Martin.

— Flowers, Flowers! Inspired Arrangements for All Occasions. LC 93-862. (Illus.). 192p. 1993. 39.95 (*0-8478-1679-6*, Pub. by Rizzoli Intl) St Martin.

— Simple Flowers. 1998. write for info. (*0-609-60139-3*) C Potter.

— Simple Flowers. (Illus.). 27.50 (*0-8478-2177-3*, Pub. by Rizzoli Intl) St Martin.

— Wreaths & Garlands: Home Decorating Workbook with 20 Step-by-Step Projects & Fold-Out Pages. (Illus.). 1998. pap., wbk. ed. 19.95 (*0-8230-5876-X*) Watsn-Guptill.

Pryke, Susan. Explore Muskoka. (Illus.). 176p. 1999. pap. 13.95 (*1-55046-241-5*, Pub. by Boston Mills) Genl Dist Srvs.

— Explore Muskoka Lakes. (Illus.). 144p. 1990. 24.95 (*1-55046-010-2*, Pub. by Boston Mills) Genl Dist Srvs.

— Windermere House: The Tradition Continues. (Illus.). 96p. 1999. 14.95 (*1-55046-288-1*, Pub. by Boston Mills) Genl Dist Srvs.

Pryles, Michael, ed. Dispute Resolution in Asia. LC 97-35845. 352p. 1998. 136.50 (*90-411-0484-4*) Kluwer Law Intl.

Pryles, Michael C., jt. auth. see Sykes, E. I.

Pryles, Michael C., jt. auth. see Sykes, Edward I.

Pryluck, Calvin. Sources of Meaning in Motion Pictures & Television. Lowett, Garth S., ed. LC 75-21434. (Dissertations on Film Ser.). 1976. lib. bdg. 23.95 (*0-405-07535-9*) Ayer.

Prymak, Gregory. Authority in the RLDS Theological Tradition: Two Views. Brown, Richard, ed. (Graceland-Park Press Theological Monographs). 144p. (Orig.). 1995. pap. text 10.00 (*0-8309-0698-3*) Herald Pub Hse.

Prymak, Thomas M. Mykhailo Hrushevsky: The Politics of National Culture. 432p. 1987. text 40.00 (*0-8020-5737-3*) U of Toronto Pr.

Pryme, Ian, jt. ed. see Hesketh, J. E.

Pryne, et al. The Incredible Journey: Literature Unit. (Literature Units Ser.). 48p. 1995. pap. text, wbk. ed. 7.95 (*1-55734-521-X*) Tchr Create Mat.

Pryne, Abram, jt. auth. see Brownlow, William G.

Pryne, Jane. Mrs. Frisby & the Rats of NIMH. (Literature Unit Ser.). (Illus.). 48p. 1998. pap., teacher ed. 7.95 (*1-55734-523-6*) Tchr Create Mat.

— Summer of the Swans. (Literature Units Ser.). 48p. (J). (gr. 5-8). 1997. pap. 7.95 (*1-55734-532-5*) Tchr Create Mat.

***Prynne, Edward.** Boy in Hob-Nailed Boots. large type unabridged ed. 1999. 25.95 (*0-7531-5088-3*, 150883, Pub. by ISIS Lrg Prnt) ISIS Pub.

Prynne, J. H. Poems. (Agneau 2 Paperbook Ser.: 1). 320p. 1982. pap. 18.00 (*0-907954-01-4*, Pub. by Allardyce Barnett) SPD-Small Pr Dist.

— Poems. 440p. 1998. 59.95 (*1-85224-491-7*, Pub. by Bloodaxe Bks); pap. 29.95 (*1-85224-492-5*, Pub. by Bloodaxe Bks) Dufour.

Prynne, William. Mount-Orgueil. LC 83-20361. 232p. 1984. reprint ed. 50.00 (*0-8201-1392-1*) Schol Facsimiles.

— The Unlovelinesse of Love-Lockes. LC 76-57410. (English Experience Ser.: No. 825). 1977. reprint ed. lib. bdg. 25.00 (*90-221-0825-2*) Walter J Johnson.

Pryor, et al. Strategic Quality Management: A Strategic Systems Approach to Continuous Improvement. LC 97-77450. 1998. pap. 49.95 (*0-87393-416-4*) Dame Pubns.

Pryor, jt. auth. see Phillips.

Pryor, Aaron & Terrell, Marshall. Flight of the Hawk: The Aaron Pryor Story. (Illus.). 236p. (Orig.). 1998. pap. 14.95 (*1-881542-29-7*) Book World Inc.

***Pryor, Alton.** Classic Tales in California Histroy. 193p. 1999. pap. 9.95 (*0-9660053-2-5*) Stagecoach Pub.

Pryor, Alton. Little Known Tales in California History. 2nd rev. ed. (Illus.). 200p. 1997. reprint ed. pap. 9.95 (*0-9660053-1-7*) Stagecoach Pub.

Pryor, Andrew J. Browns Ferry Nuclear Plant Fire. 1977. 4.25 (*0-686-22684-4*, TR 77-2) Society Fire Protect.

Pryor, Anthony, et al. The Compleat Alchemist. 2nd ed. (Illus.). 72p. 1993. pap. 10.95 (*1-880992-09-4*) Wizards Coast.

Pryor, Anthony, jt. auth. see Pearson, Charles S.

Pryor, Austin. Sound Mind Investing: A Step-by-Step Guide to Financial Stability & Growth. pap. 24.99 (*0-8024-7947-2*, 288) Moody.

Pryor, Betsy & Holst, Sanford. Kombucha Phenomenon: The Miracle Health Tea: How to Safely Make & Use Kombucha. 2nd rev. ed. LC 95-72008. (Illus.). 160p. 1996. pap. 11.95 (*1-887263-11-X*) Sierra Sunrise Pub.

***Pryor, Bonnie.** American Adventures: Joseph's Choice-1861. LC 00-20132. (American Adventures Ser.). (Illus.). 176p. (J). (gr. 3-7). 2000. 14.95 (*0-688-17633-X*) Morrow Avon.

— American Adventures: Joseph's Choice-1861. (American Adventures Ser.). (Illus.). 176p. (J). (gr. 3 up). 2000. 14.89 (*0-06-029226-1*) Morrow Avon.

— American Adventures: Luke on the High Seas. LC 99-46226. (American Adventures Ser.). (Illus.). 176p. (YA). (gr. 4-7). 2000. 14.95 (*0-688-17134-6*, Wm Morrow) Morrow Avon.

— American Adventures: Thomas in Danger-1779. LC 99-15286. (American Adventures Ser.). 176p. (J). 2000. mass mkt. 4.95 (*0-380-73212-2*) Morrow Avon.

— American Adventures: Thomas in Danger-1779. 2nd ed. LC 99-15286. (American Adventures Ser.). (Illus.). 160p. (J). (gr. 3-7). 1999. 15.00 (*0-688-16518-4*, Wm Morrow) Morrow Avon.

— American Adventures: Thomas: 1778--Patriots on the Run. LC 98-9199. (American Adventures Ser.). (Illus.). 160p. (J). (gr. 3-7). 2000. mass mkt. 4.50 (*0-380-73088-X*, Avon Bks) Morrow Avon.

Pryor, Bonnie. The Dream Jar. (Illus.). (J). (gr. k-3). 1996. lib. bdg. 15.93 (*0-688-13062-3*, Wm Morrow) Morrow Avon.

— Grandpa Bear's Christmas. 32p. 1999. mass mkt. 4.95 (*0-688-17066-8*, Grenwillow Bks) HarpC Child Bks.

— Greenbrook Farm. LC 89-11573. (Illus.). 40p. (J). (ps-2). 1993. pap. 4.95 (*0-671-79606-2*) S&S Bks Yung.

Pryor, Bonnie. The House on Maple Street. ALC Staff, ed. LC 86-12648. (Illus.). 32p. (J). (gr. k-3). 1992. mass mkt. 5.95 (*0-688-12031-8*, Wm Morrow) Morrow Avon.

Pryor, Bonnie. The House on Maple Street. 1992. 10.15 (*0-606-01360-1*, Pub. by Turtleback) Demco.

— Joseph: 1861 - A Rumble of War. LC 98-47497. (American Adventures Ser.). (Illus.). 176p. (YA). (gr. 3-7). 1999. 15.00 (*0-688-15671-1*, Wm Morrow) Morrow Avon.

***Pryor, Bonnie.** Joseph: 1861 - A Rumble of War. LC 98-47497. (American Adventures Ser.). (Illus.). 176p. (J). (gr. 3-7). 2000. mass mkt. 4.50 (*0-380-73103-7*, Avon Bks) Morrow Avon.

— Joseph: 1861-A Rumble of War. (Illus.). (J). 2000. 9.85 (*0-606-17975-5*) Turtleback.

— Joseph's Choice - 1861. (American Adventures Ser.). (J). Date not set. pap. write for info. (*0-380-73321-8*) Morrow Avon.

Pryor, Bonnie. Louie & Dan Are Friends. LC 96-32444. (Illus.). 32p. (J). 1997. lib. bdg. 15.93 (*0-688-08561-X*, Wm Morrow) Morrow Avon.

— Louie & Dan Are Friends. LC 96-32444. (Illus.). 32p. (J). (ps-3). 1997. 16.00 (*0-688-08560-1*, Wm Morrow) Morrow Avon.

— Luke: 1849 - On the Golden Trail. LC 98-47498. (American Adventures Ser.). (Illus.). 176p. (YA). (gr. 3-7). 1999. 15.00 (*0-688-15670-3*, Wm Morrow) Morrow Avon.

***Pryor, Bonnie.** Luke: 1849 - On the Golden Trail. LC 98-47498. (American Adventures Ser.). (Illus.). 176p. (J). (gr. 3-7). 2000. mass mkt. 4.50 (*0-380-73102-9*, Avon Bks) Morrow Avon.

— Luke: 1849-On the Golden Trail. (Illus.). (J). 2000. 9.85 (*0-606-17977-1*) Turtleback.

— Luke on the High Seas. (American Adventures Ser.). (J). Date not set. pap. 4.95 (*0-380-73286-6*, Wm Morrow) Morrow Avon.

— Marvelous Marvin & the Pioneer Ghost. LC 94-33237. (Illus.). 144p. (J). (gr. 2 up). 1995. 15.00 (*0-688-13886-1*, Wm Morrow) Morrow Avon.

Pryor, Bonnie. Marvelous Marvin & the Wolfman Mystery. LC 93-49686. (Illus.). 144p. (YA). (gr. 7 up). 1994. 15.00 (*0-688-12866-1*, Wm Morrow) Morrow Avon.

— Mr. Munday & the Space Creatures. (J). (gr. k-3). 1991. pap. 4.95 (*0-671-73620-5*) S&S Bks Yung.

— The Plum Tree War. LC 88-32426. (Illus.). 128p. (J). (gr. 4-7). 1989. 14.00 (*0-688-08142-8*, Wm Morrow) Morrow Avon.

— Poison Ivy & Eyebrow Wigs. LC 92-38881. (Illus.). 176p. (J). (gr. 3 up). 1993. 15.00 (*0-688-11200-5*, Wm Morrow) Morrow Avon.

— Poison Ivy & Eyebrow Wigs. (J). 1995. 10.30 (*0-606-08026-0*) Turtleback.

— Poison Ivy & Eyebrow Wigs. LC 92-38881. (Illus.). 176p. (J). (gr. 3 up). 1995. reprint ed. pap. 4.95 (*0-688-13562-5*, Wm Morrow) Morrow Avon.

Pryor, Bonnie. The Porcupine Mouse. LC 87-12305. (Illus.). 32p. (J). (ps-2). 1988. 15.93 (*0-688-07154-6*, Wm Morrow) Morrow Avon.

— Thomas. LC 98-9199. (Illus.). 144p. (J). (gr. 3-7). 1998. 14.95 (*0-688-15669-X*, Wm Morrow) Morrow Avon.

Pryor, Bonnie. Toenails, Tonsils And Tornadoes. (Illus.). 176p. (gr. 3-7). 1999. mass mkt. 4.95 (*0-688-16675-X*, Wm Morrow) Morrow Avon.

— Toenails, Tonsils, Tornadoes. LC 96-30637. (Illus.). 160p. (J). (gr. 3 up). 1997. 15.00 (*0-688-14885-9*, Wm Morrow) Morrow Avon.

— Vinegar Pancakes & Vanishing Cream. LC 86-31085. (Illus.). 128p. (J). (gr. 4-7). 1987. 16.00 (*0-688-06728-X*, Wm Morrow) Morrow Avon.

— Vinegar Pancakes & Vanishing Cream. LC 86-31085. (J). (gr. 4-7). 1996. mass mkt. 4.95 (*0-688-14744-5*, Wm Morrow) Morrow Avon.

— Vinegar Pancakes & Vanishing Cream. LC 86-31085. (J). 1996. 10.05 (*0-606-10016-4*, Pub. by Turtleback) Demco.

Pryor, Burt, jt. auth. see Andersen, Sue.

Pryor, Burt, jt. auth. see Anderson, Susan.

***Pryor, Caroline.** Democratic Practice: Activities for the Field Experience. 208p. (C). 1999. pap., wbk. ed. 23.43 (*0-07-232568-2*) McGrw-H Hghr Educ.

Pryor, Carolyn, jt. auth. see Carpenter, Doug.

Pryor, Cheryl. Legacy: A Story of Your Family History to Pass down from Generation to Generation & Keep the History Alive. (Illus.). 200p. (Orig.). 1995. pap. 18.00 (*1-886541-09-4*) Higher Priority.

— Write Now! A Home Study Course That Teaches the Essentials on Writing Fiction & Nonfiction. 112p. 1997. pap. 14.95 (*1-886541-02-7*, Pub. by Higher Priority) Southern Bk Service.

Pryor, Chris. Your Marketing Plan. 2nd ed. (Oregon SBDC Network Workbook Ser.). 79p. (C). 1996. wbk. ed. 20.00 (*1-878475-14-2*) Oregon Small Busn Dev Ctr.

Pryor, Deborah. The Love Talker. 1992. pap. 5.25 (*0-8222-1384-2*) Dramatists Play.

Pryor, Douglas W. Unspeakable Acts: Why Men Sexually Abuse Children. 300p. (C). 1996. text 55.00 (*0-8147-6637-4*) NYU Pr.

— Unspeakable Acts: Why Men Sexually Abuse Children. 352p. 1999. reprint ed. pap. 18.95 (*0-8147-6666-8*) NYU Pr.

***Pryor, Elizabeth Brown.** Clara Barton: Clara Barton National Historic Site, Maryland. 80p. 1998. per. 7.50 (*0-16-061689-1*) USGPO.

Pryor, Eric. Escape from the Dark Side: The Eric Pryor Story. St. Clair, A. Wendell, ed. 155p. (Orig.). 1994. pap. write for info. (*1-884920-01-2*) Jubilee Christian Ctr.

***Pryor, Esther & Kraines, Minda G.** Keep Moving! Fitness Through Aerobics & Step. 4th ed. LC 99-29763. 224p. 1999. pap. text 16.95 (*0-7674-1200-1*) Mayfield Pub.

Pryor, Esther, jt. auth. see Kraines, Minda G.

Pryor, Esther, jt. auth. see Kraines, Minda Goodman.

Pryor, Francis. A Catalogue of British & Irish Prehistoric Bronzes in the Royal Ontario Museum. (Illus.). 88p. 25.71 (*0-88854-240-2*) Brill Academic Pubs.

— Excavation at Fengate, Peterborough, England: The First Report. (Illus.). 60p. pap. 11.43 (*0-88854-035-3*) Brill Academic Pubs.

— Excavation at Fengate, Peterborough, England: The Second Report. (Illus.). 260p. pap. 28.57 (*0-88854-213-5*) Brill Academic Pubs.

***Pryor, Francis.** Farmers in Prehistoric Britain. (Illus.). 176p. 1998. 29.99 (*0-7524-1403-8*, Tempus Publng) Arcadia Publng.

— Farmers in Prehistoric Britain. (History & Archaeology Ser.). (Illus.). 176p. 1999. pap. 24.99 (*0-7524-1477-1*, Tempus Publng) Arcadia Publng.

Pryor, Frederic L. Economic Evolution & Structure: The Impact of Complexity on the U. S. Economic System. (Illus.). 415p. (C). 1995. pap. text 21.95 (*0-521-55924-3*) Cambridge U Pr.

— Economic Evolution & Structure: The Impact of Complexity on the U. S. Economic System. (Illus.). 415p. (C). 1996. text 69.95 (*0-521-55097-1*) Cambridge U Pr.

— Poverty, Equity, & Growth in Malawi & Madagscar. (World Bank Publication). (Illus.). 488p. 1991. text 39.95 (*0-19-520823-4*) OUP.

— Public Expenditures in Communist & Capitalist Nations. LC 68-14872. 550p. reprint ed. pap. 170.50 (*0-8357-8292-1*, 203386200087) Bks Demand.

— The Red & the Green: The Rise & Fall of Collectivized Agriculture in Marxist Regimes. LC 91-32459. 563p. reprint ed. pap. 174.60 (*0-608-02568-2*, 206321300004) Bks Demand.

— Revolutionary Grenada: A Study in Political Economy. LC 86-8109. 415p. 1986. 69.50 (*0-275-92155-7*, C2155, Praeger Pubs) Greenwood.

Pryor, Frederic L. & Schaffer, David L. Who's Not Working & Why: Employment, Cognitive Skills, Wages & the Changing U. S. Labor Market. LC 98-39048. (Illus.). 320p. (C). 1999. 34.95 (*0-521-65152-2*) Cambridge U Pr.

***Pryor, Frederic L. & Schaffer, David L.** Who's Not Working & Why: Employment, Cognitive Skills, Wages & the Changing U. S. Labor Market. 314p. (C). 2000. pap. write for info. (*0-521-79439-0*) Cambridge U Pr.

Pryor, Gale. Nursing Mother, Working Mother: The Essential Guide for Breastfeeding & Staying Close to Your Baby after You Return to Work. LC 96-46491. (Illus.). 208p. 1997. 19.95 (*1-55832-116-0*); pap. 10.95 (*1-55832-117-9*) Harvard Common Pr.

Pryor, George L. Neither Bond nor Free. LC 79-144674. reprint ed. 36.00 (*0-404-00208-0*) AMS Pr.

Pryor, Glyn, jt. auth. see Parker, Martyn J.

Pryor, Harold, ed. see Armstrong, Emma P.

Pryor, Hugh C. Graded Units in Student-Teaching. LC 71-177170. (Columbia University. Teachers College. Contributions to Education Ser.: No. 202). reprint ed. 37.50 (*0-404-55202-1*) AMS Pr.

***Pryor, J. A. & Webber, B. A., eds.** Physiotherapy for Respiratory & Cardiac Problems. 2nd ed. (Illus.). 556p. 1998. pap. write for info. (*0-443-05841-5*) Church.

Pryor, J. B. & Day, J. D., eds. The Development of Social Cognition. (Illus.). 268p. 1985. 86.95 (*0-387-96138-0*) Spr-Verlag.

Pryor, J. P. & Chisholm, Geoffrey D., eds. Urological Prostheses, Appliances & Catheters. (Clinical Practice in Urology Ser.). (Illus.). xii, 288p. 1992. 196.00 (*0-387-17490-7*) Spr-Verlag.

Pryor, J. P., jt. auth. see Jordan, Thomas.

Pryor, J. P., jt. ed. see Kelami, A.

Pryor, Jennifer A., ed. Respiratory Care. (International Perspectives in Physical Therapy Ser.: Vol. 7). (Illus.). 244p. 1991. pap. text 44.95 (*0-443-03611-X*) Church.

Pryor, John, ed. see Karamanoukian, Hratch L., et al.

Pryor, John B. & McKinney, Kathleen, eds. Research Advances in Sexual Harassment. 136p. 1995. pap. 20.00 (*0-8058-9935-9*) L Erlbaum Assocs.

Pryor, John B. & Reeder, Glenn, eds. The Social Psychology of HIV Infection. 376p. 1993. text 75.00 (*0-8058-0991-0*) L Erlbaum Assocs.

Pryor, John H. Commerce, Shipping & Naval Warfare in the Medieval Mediterranean. (Collected Studies: No. CS259). (Illus.). 348p. (C). 1987. reprint ed. lib. bdg. 115.95 (*0-86078-207-7*, Pub. by Variorum) Ashgate Pub Co.

Pryor, John J., jt. ed. see Gregoire, Alain.

Pryor, Judith, jt. auth. see Murin, William J.

Pryor, Karen. Dolphin Societies: Discoveries & Puzzles. (Illus.). 405p. 1998. pap. 22.00 (*0-520-21656-3*, Pub. by U CA Pr) Cal Prin Full Svc.

— Don't Shoot the Dog: The New Art of Teaching & Training. rev. ed. LC 99-14695. 224p. 1999. pap. 12.95 (*0-553-38039-7*) Bantam.

— Getting Started: Clicker Training for Dogs: Including a Dog & a Dolphin. 64p. 1999. pap. 6.95 (*1-890948-00-4*) Sunshine MA.

— Nursing Your Baby. 1991. mass mkt. 6.99 (*0-671-74548-4*) PB.

— On Behavior: Essays & Research. (Illus.). 280p. (Orig.). 1995. pap. 14.95 (*0-9624017-1-4*) Sunshine MA.

Pryor, Karen & Norris, Kenneth S., eds. Dolphin Societies: Discoveries & Puzzles. (Illus.). 405p. 1990. 45.00 (*0-520-06717-7*, Pub. by U CA Pr) Cal Prin Full Svc.

Pryor, Kelli, jt. auth. see Pratt, Jane.

Pryor, Louise, ed. Plan Execution: Problems & Issues: Papers from the Fall Symposium. (Technical Reports). (Illus.). 155p. 1996. spiral bd. 25.00 (*1-57735-015-4*) AAAI Pr.

Pryor, Mary. On Occasion: Selected Poems, 1968-92. 1992. per. 5.00 (*0-941127-12-5*) Dacotah Terr Pr.

Pryor, Mary J. Jelly Side Up! Finding Time for What's Important in Your Life. LC 97-92619. (Illus.). 110p. 1997. pap. 6.95 (*1-887587-01-2*, Old Rivers Pr) Pryor Grp.

— Start Now! Life Is Too Short. LC 95-92312. 120p. 1995. pap. 5.95 (*1-887587-00-4*) Pryor Grp.

Pryor, Neale T. You Can Trust Your Bible. 1980. 5.45 (*0-89137-524-4*); student ed. 1.65 (*0-89137-568-6*) Quality Pubns.

Pryor, R. W., et al. Disorder & Order in the Solid State: Concepts & Devices. LC 88-12574. (Institute for Amorphous Studies). (Illus.). 272p. (C). 1988. text 95.00 (*0-306-42926-8*, Kluwer Plenum) Kluwer Academic.

Pryor, Richard & Gold, Todd. Pryor Convictions: And Other Life Sentences. (Illus.). 288p. 1997. pap. 12.00 (*0-375-70048-X*) Pantheon.

Pryor, Richard "Cactus". Playback. LC 95-10561. (Illus.). 176p. 1995. 19.95 (*0-292-76567-3*) U of Tex Pr.

Pryor, Robert E., jt. auth. see Phillips, Jerry J.

Pryor, Roger A. Reminiscences of Peace & War. LC 77-126248. (Select Bibliographies Reprint Ser.). 1977. 25.95 (*0-8369-5475-0*) Ayer.

Pryor, S. N. An Economic Analysis of Silvicultural Options for Broadleaved Woodlands, Vol. I. 1982. 60.00 (*0-85074-041-X*) St Mut.

Pryor, T. M. Wealth Building Lessons of Booker T. Washington. LC 95-67017. (Illus.). 150p. 1995. 15.95 (*1-878647-21-0*) APU Pub Grp.

Pryor, Timothy R. & North, Walter, eds. Applying Automated Inspection. LC 85-61377. (Manufacturing Update Ser.). (Illus.). 287p. reprint ed. pap. 89.00 (*0-8357-6495-8*, 203586600097) Bks Demand.

Pryor, Tom. Pryor Convictions: 31 Insights into ABM. (Illus.). 52p. 1998. pap. 9.95 (*1-886933-05-7*) ICMS TX.

P

An Asterisk (*) at the beginning of an entry indicates that the title is appearing for the first time.

Pryor, Tom, et al, eds. Activity Dictionary: A Comprehensive Reference Tool for ABM & ABC. 202p. 1992. pap. 99.95 (*1-886933-01-4*) ICMS TX.

Pryor, Tom & Sahm, Julie. Using Activity Based Management for Continuous Improvement. (Illus.). 190p. 1994. pap. 29.95 (*1-886933-00-6*) ICMS TX.

Pryor, W. J. Draught Animal Power in the Asian Australasian Region. 135p. (Orig.). 1993. pap. 96.00 (*1-86320-079-7*) St Mut.

Pryor, William A., ed. Organic Free Radicals. LC 78-1672. (ACS Symposium Ser.: Vol. 69). 495p. 1978. reprint ed. pap. 153.50 (*0-608-03928-4*, 206437500009) Bks Demand.

Pryor, William A., jt. ed. see Diana, John N.

Pryputniewicz, Ryszard J., et al, eds. Laser Interferometry VIII Vol. 2861: Applications. 310p. 1996. 76.00 (*0-8194-2249-5*) SPIE.

— Laser Interferometry IX Vol. 3479: Applications. LC 98-233176. (Proceedings of SPIE Ser.: Vol. 3479). 366p. 1998. 80.00 (*0-8194-2934-1*) SPIE.

Pryputniewicz, Ryszard J., et al. Interferometry VII--Applications: 13-14 July 1995, San Diego, California. LC 95-68560. (Proceedings of the SPIE--the International Society of Optical Engineering Ser.). x, 434p. 1995. write for info. (*0-8194-1904-4*) SPIE.

Prys, Elined, jt. ed. see Kotsching, Walter M.

Prys-Jones, A. G. Collected Poems of A. G. Prys-Jones. (C). 1989. pap. 30.00 (*0-86383-419-1*, Pub. by Gomer Pr) St Mut.

— The Fountain of Life: Prose & Verse from the Bible. large type ed. 1979. 27.99 (*0-7089-0311-8*) Ulverscroft.

Prys-Roberts, C., jt. ed. see Hutton, P.

Prys-Roberts, Cedric & Brown, Burnell R., Jr., eds. International Practice of Anaesthesia, 2 vols. 6th ed. LC 97-104572. 1536p. 1996. text 265.00 (*0-7506-0240-6*) Buttrwrth-Heinemann.

Prysby, Charles & Scavo, Carmine. American Voting Behavior: In Presidential Elections 1972 to 1992. (Setups Ser.). (Orig.). (C). 1995. pap. 6.00 (*1-878147-21-8*) Am Political.

— Voting Behavior: The 1988 Election. (SETUPS Ser. - Supplementary Empirical Teaching Units in Political Science). 70p. (C). 1989. pap. text 5.25 (*0-915654-87-3*) Am Political.

— Voting Behavior: The 1992 Election. (Setups Ser.). 87p. (Orig.). (C). 1993. pap. 5.25 (*1-878147-11-0*) Am Political.

Prysby, Charles & Scavo, Carmine. Voting Behavior: The 1996 Election. (SETUPS Series - Supplementary Empirical Teaching Units in Political Science). 52p. (C). 1997. pap. 6.90 (*1-878147-28-5*) Am Political.

Prysby, Charles L., jt. auth. see Books, John W.

Pryse, tr. see Morgan, James M.

Pryse, James M. The Adorers of Dionysos. (Illus.). 166p. 1993. reprint ed. pap. 14.95 (*1-56459-413-0*) Kessinger Pub.

— The Apocalypse Unsealed. LC 76-41124. (Illus.). 222p. 1977. reprint ed. pap. 9.50 (*0-912504-02-1*) Sym & Sign.

— The Apocalypse Unsealed: Being an Esoteric Interpretation of the Initiation of Ioannes Commonly Called the Revelation of St. John. 232p. 1993. reprint ed. pap. 17.50 (*1-56459-336-3*) Kessinger Pub.

— The Magical Message According to Ioannes. 230p. 1996. reprint ed. spiral bd. 15.50 (*0-7873-0685-1*) Hlth Research.

— The Magical Message According to Ioannes St. John. 240p. 1993. reprint ed. pap. 14.95 (*1-56459-337-1*) Kessinger Pub.

— A New Presentation of the Prometheus Bound of Aischylos: Wherein is Set Forth the Hidden Meaning of the Myth (1925) 209p. 1996. reprint ed. pap. 17.95 (*1-56459-823-3*) Kessinger Pub.

— Prometheus Bound of Aischylos: A New Presentation. 207p. 1996. reprint ed. spiral bd. 18.00 (*0-7873-0681-9*) Hlth Research.

— Reincarnation in the New Testament. 92p. 1996. reprint ed. spiral bd. 10.00 (*0-7873-0682-7*) Hlth Research.

— Reincarnation in the New Testament. 92p. 1994. reprint ed. pap. 8.95 (*1-56459-451-3*) Kessinger Pub.

— The Restored New Testament, 2 vols., Set. 3rd ed. 1996. reprint ed. spiral bd. 48.50 (*0-7873-0683-5*) Hlth Research.

— The Restored New Testament: The Hellenic Fragments, Freed from the Pseudo-Jewish Interpolations, Harmonized, & Done Into English Verse & Prose (1925): With Introductory Analyses, & Commentaries, Giving an Interpretation According to Ancient Philosophy & Psychology & a New Literal Translation of the Synoptic Gospels, with Commentaries & Illustrations. (Illus.). 840p. 1994. reprint ed. pap. 45.00 (*1-56459-433-5*) Kessinger Pub.

— The Sermon on the Mount & Other Extracts from the New Testament. 80p. 1984. reprint ed. spiral bd. 13.50 (*0-7873-0684-3*) Hlth Research.

Pryse, James M., comment. The Sermon on the Mount & Other Selections from the New Testament. 1994. pap. 8.50 (*0-913004-92-8*) Point Loma Pub.

Pryse, James M., tr. Apocalypse Unsealed. 222p. 1996. reprint ed. spiral bd. 18.50 (*0-7873-0680-0*) Hlth Research.

Pryse, John M. Spiritual Light: New Scripture by Many Authors & Translations from Ancient Manuscripts, Previously Unpublished. 193p. 1994. reprint ed. pap. 15.00 (*1-56459-440-8*) Kessinger Pub.

Pryse, Marjorie. The Mark & the Knowledge: Social Stigma in Classic American Fiction. LC 78-23229. 189p. reprint ed. pap. 58.60 (*0-608-09868-X*, 206983300006) Bks Demand.

— Selected Stories of Freeman. (C). 1991. pap. text 14.75 (*0-393-30106-0*, Norton Paperbks) Norton.

Pryse, Marjorie, ed. see Austin, Mary.

Pryse, Marjorie, jt. ed. see Feterley, Judith.

Pryse, Marjorie, jt. ed. see Fetterley, Judith.

Prystowsky, Eric N. & Klein, George. Cardiac Arrhythmias: An Integrated Approach for the Clinician. (Illus.). 452p. 1994. text 67.00 (*0-07-050984-0*) McGraw-Hill HPD.

Prystowsky, Eric N., jt. auth. see Klein, George J.

Prystowsky, Eric N., jt. ed. see DiMarco, John P.

***Prytherch, Ray.** Harrod's Librarians' Glossary & Reference Book: A Directory of over 9600 Terms, Organizations, Projects & Acronyms in the Areas of Information Management, Library Science, Publishing & Archive Management. 9th ed. LC 99-73658. 806p. 1999. 166.95 (*0-566-08018-4*, Pub. by Gower) Ashgate Pub Co.

Prytherch, Raymond John. The Basics of Reader's Advisory Work. LC 87-48257. 112p. 1988. reprint ed. pap. 34.80 (*0-7837-9258-1*, 204999800004) Bks Demand.

— Gower Handbook of Library & Information Management. LC 98-7776. 432p. 1998. 131.95 (*0-566-08052-4*, Pub. by Gower) Ashgate Pub Co.

— Handbook of Library Training Practice. 400p. (Orig.). 1986. text 86.95 (*0-566-03543-X*, Pub. by Gower) Ashgate Pub Co.

— Handbook of Library Training Practice, Vol. 2. 288p. (Orig.). 1991. text 78.95 (*0-566-03633-9*, Pub. by Gower) Ashgate Pub Co.

— Harrod's Librarians' Glossary: Nine Thousand Two Hundred Terms Used in Information Management, Library Science, Publishing, the Book Trades & Archive Management. 8th ed. 1995. 99.95 (*0-566-07533-4*) Gower.

— Information Management & Library Science: A Guide to the Literature. LC 94-165859. 331p. 1994. 78.95 (*0-566-07467-2*, Pub. by Gower) Ashgate Pub Co.

— Sources of Information in Librarianship & Information Science. 2nd ed. 190p. 1987. text 57.95 (*0-566-05509-0*, Pub. by Gower) Ashgate Pub Co.

Prytherch, Raymond John, jt. auth. see Hicken, Mandy.

Prytherch, Raymond John, jt. auth. see MacDougall, Alan F.

Prywes, Ruth W. The United States Labor Force: A Descriptive Analysis. LC 99-13717. 408p. 2000. 75.00 (*1-56720-266-7*, Quorum Bks) Greenwood.

***Pryzby, Phyllis.** Wildflowers of the Berkshires: Where & When They Bloom. (Illus.). xx, 170p. 2000. pap. 18.95 (*0-9700509-1-7*) P M Pryzby.

Pryzwansky, jt. auth. see Brown.

Pryzwansky, Walter B. Professional & Ethical Issues in Psychology: Foundations of Practice. LC 99-26042. 256p. 1999. 39.00 (*0-393-70285-5*) Norton.

Pryzwansky, Walter B., jt. auth. see Brown, Duane.

Przbyla. Understanding Human Sexuality. 5th ed. 1993. student ed. 48.12 (*0-07-031725-9*) McGraw.

Przbylski, R. & McDonald, B., eds. Development of Vegetable Oils in Human Nutrition. 144p. 1995. 70.00 (*0-935315-66-7*) Am Oil Chemists.

Przebienda, Edward, ed. Cumulative Personal Author Indexes for the Monthly Catalog of U. S. Government Publications, 1941-1975, 5 vols., Set. Incl. Decennial Cumulative Personal Author Index, 1941-50. LC 04-18088. 1971. 49.50 (*0-87650-007-6*); Decennial Cumulative Personal Author Index, 1951-60. LC 04-18088. 1971. 49.50 (*0-87650-008-4*); Quinquennial Cumulative Personal Author Index, 1961-65. LC 04-18088. 1971. 49.50 (*0-87650-009-2*); Quinquennial Cumulative Personal Author Index, 1966-70. LC 04-18088. 1972. 49.50 (*0-87650-016-5*); Quinquennial Cumulative Personal Author Index, 1971-75. LC 04-18088. 1979. 49.50 (*0-87650-097-1*); LC 04-18088. (Cumulative Author Index Ser.: No. 2). 1979. 225.00 (*0-686-76934-1*) Pierian.

Przebinda, T. The Oscillator Duality Correspondence for the Pair 0(2,2), SP(2,R) LC 89-6540. (Memoirs Ser.: No. 79/403), 105p. 1989. pap. 20.00 (*0-8218-2464-3*, MEMO/79/403) Am Math.

Przedwojski, B., et al. River Training Techniques: Fundamentals, Design & Applications. LC 99-227590. (Illus.). 648p. (C). 1995. text 176.00 (*90-5410-196-2*, Pub. by A A Balkema) Ashgate Pub Co.

Przelecki, Marian, et al, eds. Formal Methods in the Methodology of Empirical Sciences. (Synthese Library: No. 103). 457p. 1977. text 176.50 (*90-277-0698-0*, D Reidel) Kluwer Academic.

Przemieniecki, J. S. Mathematical Methods in Defense Analyses. 2nd ed. LC 94-25921. (Illus.). 425p. 1994. 74.95 (*1-56347-092-6*, 92-6) AIAA.

***Przemieniecki, J. S.** Mathematical Methods in Defense Analyses. 3rd ed. LC 00-33138. 2000. write for info. (*1-56347-397-6*) AIAA.

Przemieniecki, J. S. Theory of Matrix Structural Analysis. (Illus.). 480p. 1985. reprint ed. pap. 12.95 (*0-486-64948-2*) Dover.

Przemieniecki, J. S., ed. Acquisition of Defense Systems. LC 93-27833. (Education Ser.). 358p. 1993. 61.95 (*1-56347-069-1*) AIAA.

— Critical Technologies for National Defense. (Educ Ser.). (Illus.). 318p. 1991. 46.95 (*1-56347-009-8*, 09-8) AIAA.

Przepiorka, Donna & Sollinger, Hans, eds. Recent Developments in Transplantation Medicine: New Immunosuppressive Drugs. LC 94-65128. (Illus.). 208p. 1994. 42.95 (*0-614-05152-5*) Phys Sci Pub.

Przepiorkowski, Adam, jt. ed. see Borsley, Robert.

Przetacznik, Franciszek. Protection of Officials of Foreign States According to International Law. 1983. lib. bdg. 160.50 (*90-247-2721-9*) Kluwer Academic.

Przetacznik, Frank. The Catholic Concept of Genuine & Just Peace As a Basic Collective Human Right. LC 90-44321. (Roman Catholic Studies: Vol. 2). 352p. 1990. lib. bdg. 99.95 (*0-88946-239-9*) E Mellen.

— The Philosophical & Legal Concept of War. LC 93-16073. 680p. 1994. text 129.95 (*0-7734-9256-9*) E Mellen.

Przeworska-Rolewicz, Danuta. Logarithms & Antilogarithms: An Algebraic Analysis Approach. LC 98-10806. (Mathematics & Its Applications Ser.). 348p. 1998. 159.00 (*0-7923-4974-1*) Kluwer Academic.

Przeworska-Rolewicz, Dauta. Algebraic Analysis. (C). 1988. text 346.50 (*90-277-2443-1*) Kluwer Academic.

Przeworski, Adam. Capitalism & Social Democracy. (Studies in Marxism & Social Theory). 284p. 1986. pap. text 23.95 (*0-521-33656-2*) Cambridge U Pr.

— Democracia y Mercado - Democracy & the Market: Reformas Politicas y Economicas En la Europa Del Este y America Latina - Political & Economic Reforms in Eastern Europe & Latin America. Abello, Mireia B., tr. (SPA., Illus.). 370p. (C). 1995. pap. 16.95 (*0-521-47645-3*) Cambridge U Pr.

— Democracy & the Market: Political & Economic Reforms in Eastern Europe & Latin America. (Studies in Rationality & Social Change). (Illus.). 224p. (C). 1991. pap. text 19.95 (*0-521-42335-X*) Cambridge U Pr.

— The State & the Economy under Capitalism, Vol. 31. (Fundamentals of Pure & Applied Economics Ser.). viii, 126p. 1990. pap. text 58.00 (*3-7186-5006-1*, Harwood Acad Pubs) Gordon & Breach.

— Sustainable Democracy. 155p. (C). 1995. pap. text 15.95 (*0-521-48375-1*) Cambridge U Pr.

***Przeworski, Adam, et al, eds.** Democracy, Accountability & Representation. LC 98-50663. (Studies in the Theory of Democracy). (Illus.). 344p. (C). 1999. 59.95 (*0-521-64153-5*); pap. 22.95 (*0-521-64616-2*) Cambridge U Pr.

Przeworski, Adam & Sprague, John. Paper Stones: A History of Electoral Socialism. LC 86-6984. (Illus.). vi, 230p. (C). 1986. 29.95 (*0-226-68497-0*) U Ch Pr.

— Paper Stones: A History of Electoral Socialism. LC 86-6984. (Illus.). vi, 224p. (C). 1994. pap. text 11.95 (*0-226-68498-9*) U Ch Pr.

Przeworski, Adam & Teune, Henry. Logic of Comparative Social Inquiry. LC 81-19332. 168p. 1982. reprint ed. lib. bdg. 23.50 (*0-89874-462-8*) Krieger.

***Przeworski, Adam, et al.** Democracy & Development: Political Institutions & Well-Being in the World, 1950-1990. (Cambridge Studies in the Theory of Democracy). (Illus.). 312p. (C). 2000. 19.95 (*0-521-79032-8*); pap. Price not set. (*0-521-79379-3*) Cambridge U Pr.

Przeworski, Joanne F. The Decline of the Copper Industry in Chile & the Entrance of North American Capital, 1870 to 1916. Bruchey, Stuart, ed. LC 80-609. (Multinational Corporations Ser.). 1981. lib. bdg. 36.95 (*0-405-13379-0*) Ayer.

Przewoznik, J. & Pein, Malcolm. The Blumenfeld Gambit. (PECH Pergamon Chess Ser.). 128p. 1991. pap. 14.95 (*0-08-037133-7*, 6201, Pub. by CHES) Macmillan.

— The Blumenfeld Gambit. (PECH Pergamon Chess Ser.). 128p. 1991. write for info. (*0-08-037132-9*, 6201, Pub. by CHES) Macmillan.

Przexecki, Marian & Wojcicki, Ryszard, eds. Twenty-Five Years of Logical Methodology in Poland. LC 76-7064. (Synthese Library: No. 87). 743p. 1977. text 220.00 (*90-277-0601-8*, D Reidel) Kluwer Academic.

Przirembel, Janet L. How to Conduct Supplier Surveys & Audits. LC 95-47471. (Illus.). (Orig.). 1997. pap. text 14.95 (*0-945456-24-7*) PT Pubns.

Przirembel, Janet L., ed. see PT Publications Staff.

Przuntek, H., et al, eds. Instrumental Methods & Scoring in Extrapyramidal Disorders. (Illus.). 344p. 1995. 86.95 (*0-387-57875-7*) Spr-Verlag.

Przuntek, H. & Muller, T., eds. Diagnosis & Treatment of Parkinson's Disease - State of the Art Suppl. 56: Special Edition of Journal of Neural Transmission. LC 99-19306. (Journal of Neural Transmission Ser.). (Illus.). 150p. 1999. 119.00 (*3-211-83276-9*) Spr-Verlag.

Przuntek, H., et al. Instrumental Methods & Scoring in Extrapyramidal Disorders. LC 95-40048. 1995. pap. write for info. (*3-540-57875-7*) Spr-Verlag.

Przuntek, H., jt. ed. see Riederer, P.

Przybilla, B. & Ring, Johannes, eds. New Trends in Allergy, No. III. (Illus.). 568p. 1991. 249.00 (*0-387-52993-4*) Spr-Verlag.

Przybille, Crystal. Bible Stories with Songs & Fingerplays: Stories Come Alive for Young Children. (Whole People of God Library). 64p. 1998. pap. 9.95 (*1-55145-297-9*, Pub. by Wood Lake Bks) Logos Prods.

Przyblyski, Jeannene M., jt. ed. see De la Motte, Dean.

Przybyhek, Stephanie. Around Auburn, Vol. II. (Images of America Ser.). (Illus.). 128p. 1998. pap. 16.99 (*0-7524-1200-0*) Arcadia Publng.

Przybylek, Stephanie E. Around Cayuga County. LC 96-231030. (Images of America Ser.). 128p. 1996. pap. 16.99 (*0-7524-0431-8*) Arcadia Publng.

Przybylek, Stephanie E., et al. Breaking the Silence on Film: The History of the Case Research Laboratory. (Illus.). viii, 200p. 1999. 25.00 (*0-9673366-0-0*); pap. 17.99 (*0-9673366-1-9*) Cayuga Mu.

Przybylek, Stephanie E., jt. auth. see Jones, Peter Lloyd.

Przybylo, Chester M., jt. auth. see Pohl, Amelia E.

Przybylowicz, Donna. Desire & Repression: The Dialectic of Self & Other in the Late Works of Henry James. LC 84-24068. 367p. 1986. pap. 113.80 (*0-7837-8399-X*, 205921000009) Bks Demand.

Przybylski, Roberta, jt. auth. see Filson, Yolande.

Przybylski, Roger, et al. Trends & Issues, 1997: Illinois Criminal Justice Information Authority. (Illus.). 232p. (C). 1998. pap. text 35.00 (*0-7881-4944-X*) DIANE Pub.

Przybylski, Steven A. Cache & Memory Hierarchy: A Performance Directed Approach. 223p. (C). 1990. text 53.95 (*1-55860-136-8*) Morgan Kaufmann.

Przybyszewska, Stanislawa. The Danton Case & Thermidor. 297p. 1989. pap. 15.95 (*0-8101-0806-2*) Northwestern U Pr.

Przybyszewski, Linda. The Republic According to John Marshall Harlan. LC 99-13686. (Studies in Legal History). (Illus.). 352p. 1999. pap. 19.95 (*0-8078-4789-5*); lib. bdg. 49.95 (*0-8078-2493-3*) U of NC Pr.

Przybyszewski, Stanislaw. Homo Sapiens. Seltzer, Thomas, tr. reprint ed. 49.50 (*0-404-05147-2*) AMS Pr.

Przyklenk, Karin, et al, eds. Ischemic "Preconditioning" The Concept of Endogenous Cardioprotection. LC 93-21904. (Developments in Cardiovascular Medicine Ser.). 224p. (C). 1993. text 141.50 (*0-7923-2410-2*) Kluwer Academic.

Przyklenk, Karin, jt. ed. see Kloner, Robert A.

Przyluski, Jan. Conducting Polymers: Electrochemistry. (Solid State Phenomena Ser.: Vols. 13 & 14). 394p. 1991. 191.00 (*3-908044-10-3*, Pub. by Scitec Pubns) Enfield Pubs NH.

Przyluski, Jan & Roth, S., eds. Conducting Polymers-Transport Phenomena. 280p. (C). 1993. text 100.00 (*0-87849-659-9*, Pub. by Trans T Pub) Enfield Pubs NH.

Przyluski, Jan & Roth, Siegmar, eds. Electrochemistry of Conducting Polymers. (Materials Science Forum Ser.: Vol. 21). 220p. 1987. text 100.00 (*0-87849-562-2*, Pub. by Trans T Pub) Enfield Pubs NH.

— New Materials: Conjugated Double Bond Systems. (Materials Science Forum Ser.: Vol. 191). (Illus.). 296p. (C). 1995. 100.00 (*0-87849-695-5*, Pub. by Trans T Pub) Enfield Pubs NH.

Przystup, James J., jt. ed. see Holmes, Kim R.

Przytulski, Karen R., jt. auth. see Lutz, Carroll A.

Przytycki, Jozef H. Algebraic Topology Based on Knots. (Series on Knots & Everything: Vol. 18). 300p. 1999. 46.00 (*981-02-3622-0*) World Scientific Pub.

Przytycki, Jozef H., jt. auth. see Murasugi, Kunio.

Przywara, Erich. Heart of Newman. LC 96-78014. 1997. pap. text 14.95 (*0-89870-624-6*) Ignatius Pr.

Psacharopoulos, George. Building Human Capital for Better Lives. (Directions in Development Ser.). 56p. 1995. pap. 22.00 (*0-8213-3392-5*, 13392) World Bank.

— Encyclopedia of Computer Education. (Advances in Education Ser.). 1988. 95.00 (*0-08-034252-3*, Pergamon Pr) Elsevier.

— Why Educational Policies Can Fail: An Overview of Sellected African Experiences. (Discussion Papers: No. 82). 34p. 1990. pap. 22.00 (*0-8213-1549-8*, 11549) World Bank.

Psacharopoulos, George, ed. Economics of Education: Research & Studies. 500p. 1987. 221.00 (*0-08-033379-6*, Pub. by Pergamon Repr) Franklin.

— Essays on Poverty, Equity & Growth: A Comparative Study. LC 90-26780. 416p. 1991. 191.00 (*0-08-040805-2*, Pub. by Pergamon Repr) Franklin.

Psacharopoulos, George & Nguyen, Nguyen X. The Role of Government & the Private Sector in Fighting Poverty. LC 96-46315. (Technical Paper Ser.: No. 346). 104p. 1997. pap. 22.00 (*0-8213-3817-X*, 13817) World Bank.

Psacharopoulos, George & Patrinos, Harry A., eds. Indigenous People & Poverty in Latin America: An Empirical Analysis. (World Bank Ser.). 256p. 1996. 77.95 (*1-85972-228-8*, Pub. by Avebry) Ashgate Pub Co.

— Indigenous People & Poverty in Latin America: An Empirical Analysis. LC 94-26584. 256p. 1994. pap. 22.00 (*0-8213-2958-8*, 12958) World Bank.

Psacharopoulos, George & Tzannatos, P. Zafiris, eds. Case Studies on Women's Employment & Pay in Latin America. LC 92-40880. 488p. 1993. pap. 30.00 (*0-8213-2308-3*, 12308) World Bank.

Psacharopoulos, George & Woodhall, Maureen. Education for Development: An Analysis of Investment Choices. 352p. 1986. text 29.95 (*0-19-520477-8*) OUP.

Psacharopoulos, George, et al. Poverty & Income Distribution in Latin America: The Story of the 1980s. LC 96-36910. (Technical Paper Ser.: No. 351). 328p. 1997. pap. 22.00 (*0-8213-3831-5*) World Bank.

Psaedaens, J., et al. The Structure of the Relational Database Model. (EATCS Monographs on Theoretical Computer Science: Vol. 17). (Illus.). 231p. 1989. 58.95 (*0-387-13714-9*) Spr-Verlag.

Psakhis, Lev. The Complete French. (Batsford Chess Library). 256p. 1995. pap. 22.95 (*0-8050-2641-X*, Owl) H Holt & Co.

Psaki, Regina, ed. Jean Renart: The Romance of the Rose or of Guillaume de Dole (Roman de la Rose ou de Guillaume de Dole) LC 95-509. (Library of Medieval Literature: Vol. 92A). 324p. 1995. text 66.00 (*0-8153-0400-5*) Garland.

***Psalidopoulos, M.** The Canon in the History of Economics: Critical Essays. LC 99-47824. 272p. 2000. 90.00 (*0-415-19154-8*) Routledge.

***Psalm 150, compiled by.** At the Cross: A Celebration of the Resurrection. 1999. 6.99 (*5-552-41257-5*) Diamante Music Grp.

Psaltis, Demetri, jt. ed. see Javidi, Bahram.

Psaris, Jett, jt. auth. see Lyons, Marlena.

Psarouthakis, John, jt. auth. see Hendrickson, Lorraine U.

Psarouthakis, John, jt. auth. see Tanter, Raymond.

Psathas, George. Conversation Analysis: The Study of Talk-in-Interaction. (Qualitative Research Methods Ser.: Vol. 35). 96p. 1994. 24.00 (*0-8039-5746-7*); pap. 10.50 (*0-8039-5747-5*) Sage.

— Phenomenological Sociology: Issues & Applications. LC 73-2805. 384p. reprint ed. pap. 119.10 (*0-608-14030-9*, 205551500023) Bks Demand.

Psathas, George, ed. Everyday Language. 302p. (C). 1979. text 29.50 (*0-8290-0872-1*) Irvington.

— Everyday Language. 302p. 1989. pap. text 16.95 (*0-8290-1042-4*) Irvington.

— Interaction Competence. 300p. (C). 1989. text 29.95 (*0-8290-1459-4*) Irvington.

P

An Asterisk (*) at the beginning of an entry indicates that the title is appearing for the first time.

Psathas, George, jt. ed. see Ten Have, Paul.

Psathas, Irene. Sister Irene's Culinary Journal: A Notebook Filled with Love, Faith & Recipes, Many Blessed Years of Cooking, Serving & Caring. LC 98-7651. (Illus.). 222p. 1998. pap. 19.95 (*1-55725-205-X*, 930-035, Pub. by Paraclete MA) BookWorld.

Pschorr, Elizabeth. A Privileged Marriage: The Autobiography of Elizabeth Pschorr. LC 94-15618. 368p. 1994. 24.95 (*0-915269-13-9*) Windgate Pr.

Pschyrembel, Willibald. Clinical Dictionary: Klinisches Woerterbuch. (GER.). 1876p. 1993. 95.00 (*0-8288-1839-8*, 3110126923) Fr & Eur.

— Klinisches Woerterbuch Data Disk. (GER.). 1994. write for info. (*0-614-00371-7*, 357011001X) Fr & Eur.

— Woerterbuch Radioaktivitat, Strahlenwirkung, Strahlenschutz. 2nd ed. (GER.). 108p. 1987. 39.95 (*0-7859-8270-1*, 3110113430) Fr & Eur.

Pschyrembel, Willibald & Dudenhausen, J. W. Grundriss der Perinatalmedizin. (GER., Illus.). 336p. (C). 1972. 29.25 (*3-11-003694-0*) De Gruyter.

PSECC Staff. Hale'-Ta: Governing Guam: Before & After the Wars. (Hale'-Ta Ser.). 300p. (YA). (gr. 8). 1994. 40.00 (*1-883488-02-8*) Polit Status ECC.

— Hale'-Ta: Insights: The Chamorro Identity. (Hale'-Ta Ser.). 200p. (YA). (gr. 12). 1993. 25.00 (*1-883488-01-X*) Polit Status ECC.

— Hale'-Ta: Issues in Guam's Political Development: The Chamorro Perspective. (Hale'-Ta Ser.). 100p. (YA). (gr. 9). 1994. 25.00 (*1-883488-03-6*) Polit Status ECC.

— Hale'Ta: Hestorian Taotao Tano': History of the Chamorro People. (Hale'-Ta Ser.). 100p. (J). (gr. 5). 1993. 30.00 (*1-883488-00-1*) Polit Status ECC.

Psellus, Michael. Fourteen Byzantine Rulers. Sewter, E. R., tr. 400p. 1966. pap. 13.95 (*0-14-044169-7*) Viking Penguin.

— The History (Chronographia) Sachas, Constantine, ed. x, 385p. write for info. (*0-318-71003-X*) G Olms Pubs.

— The History of Psellus. LC 76-24929. (Byzantine Texts: No. 1). reprint ed. 55.00 (*0-404-60001-8*) AMS Pr.

Psencik, I., et al. Seismic Waves in Laterally Inhomogeneous Media. LC 96-48399. (Pageoph Topical Ser.). 1996. write for info. (*0-8176-5648-0*) Birkhauser.

— Seismic Waves in Laterally Inhomogeneous Media, Pt. II. (Pageoph Topical Volumes Ser.: Vol. 148, Nos. 3 & 4, 1996). 370p. 1996. pap. 34.50 (*3-7643-5651-0*) Birkhauser.

Psenner, Roland & Gunatilaka, Amarasinha, eds. Proceedings of the 1st International Workshop on Sediment Phosphorus, March 1986. (Advances in Limnology Ser.: Vol. 30). (GER., Illus.). vii, 115p. 1988. pap. text 32.00 (*3-510-47028-1*, Pub. by E Schweizerbartsche) Balogh.

Pseudo-Athanasius. The Life & Regimen of The Blessed & Holy Teacher Syncletica. Bongie, Elizabeth B., tr. (Translation Ser.). 85p. 1996. pap. 10.00 (*0-920669-46-8*, Pub. by Peregrina Pubng) Cistercian Pubns.

Pshenichny, Boris N. The Linearization Method for Constraint Optimization. Wilson, Steven S., tr. from RUS. LC 94-1938. (Computational Mathematics Ser.: Vol. 22).Tr. of Metod Linearizatsii. viii, 147p. 1994. 103.95 (*0-387-57037-3*) Spr-Verlag.

Pshenichnyi, B. N. Necessary Conditions for an Extremum. (Pure & Applied Mathematics Ser.: Vol. 4). (Illus.). 248p. 1971. text 135.00 (*0-8247-1556-X*) Dekker.

Psi. Psi Model Curriculum for Office Careers. (Office Procedures Ser.). Date not set. 11.50 (*0-538-63279-8*) S-W Pub.

***PSI Research Editors.** SmartStart Your West Virginia Business. (Smart Start Your Business Ser.). 300p. 2000. pap. 19.95 (*1-55571-478-1*, Pub. by PSI Resch) Midpt Trade.

***PSI Research Staff.** SmartStart Your Alabama Business. LC 98-50166. (Illus.). 350p. 1999. pap. 19.95 (*1-55571-467-6*) PSI Resch.

PSI Research Staff. SmartStart Your Alaska Business. LC 99-10594. 350p. 2000. pap. 19.95 (*1-55571-477-3*, SSAKP) PSI Resch.

— SmartStart Your Colorado Business. LC 97-36436. (Illus.). 360p. (Orig.). 1997. pap. 19.95 (*1-55571-411-0*, Oasis Pr) PSI Resch.

— SmartStart Your Kansas Business. LC 99-10577. (Illus.). 340p. 1999. pap. 19.95 (*1-55571-468-4*) PSI Resch.

***PSI Research Staff.** SmartStart Your Louisiana Business. LC 98-50168. (Smartstart Ser.). (Illus.). 340p. 1999. pap. 19.95 (*1-55571-469-2*) PSI Resch.

PSI Research Staff. SmartStart Your Minnesota Business. LC 98-50169. (Illus.). 340p. 1999. pap. 19.95 (*1-55571-470-6*) PSI Resch.

— SmartStart Your Wisconsin Business. LC 98-6052. (Illus.). 340p. 1998. pap. 19.95 (*1-55571-445-5*, SSWIP) PSI Resch.

PSI Research Staff, jt. auth. see Oasis Press Editors.

PSI Research Staff, ed. see Jenkins, Michael D.

PSI Research Staff, jt. ed. see Oasis Press Editors.

Psichari, Henriette, ed. see Renan, Ernest.

Psillakis, Jorge, ed. Deep Face Lifting Techniques. (Illus.). 232p. 1994. 129.00 (*0-86577-530-3*) Thieme Med Pubs.

Psillakis, Jorge, et al. Color Atlas of Aesthetic Surgery of the Abdomen. (Illus.). 96p. 1991. text 115.00 (*0-86577-343-2*) Thieme Med Pubs.

Psillas, Benjamin S. Washington Job Source: Everything You Need to Land the Internship, Entry-Level or Middle Management Job of Your Choice. 3rd ed. 436p. 1995. pap. 15.95 (*0-9635651-2-5*) Benjamin Scott.

Psillas, Benjamin S. & McMahon, Mary. Washington Job Source. 4th ed. 480p. 1997. 16.95 (*0-9635651-7-6*) Benjamin Scott.

Psillas, Benjamin S., ed. see McMahon, Mary.

***Psillas, Thomas G.** Millionaire Bootcamp: Basic Training. 325p. 1999. pap. 24.95 (*0-9674683-0-2*) Tamion.

***Psillos, Stathis.** Scientific Realism: How Science Tracks Truth LC 99-29721. 1999. pap. 27.99 (*0-415-20819-X*) Routledge.

— Scientific Realism: How Science Tracks Truth. (Philosophical Issues in Science Ser.). 352p. (C). 1999. text 90.00 (*0-415-20818-1*) Routledge.

Psimmenos, Iordanis. Globalisation & Employee Participation. LC 97-72074. (Illus.). 240p. 1997. text 64.95 (*1-85972-454-X*, Pub. by Avebry) Ashgate Pub Co.

Psomiades, Harry J. & Scourby, Alice, eds. The Greek American Community in Transition. LC 82-81628. 290p. 1982. pap. text 11.00 (*0-918618-22-3*) Pella Pub.

Psomiades, Harry J. & Thomadakis, Stavros B., eds. Greece, the New Europe, & the Changing International Order. LC 93-84826. 440p. (Orig.). 1993. pap. text 20.00 (*0-918618-56-8*) Pella Pub.

Psomiades, Kathy A. Beauty's Body: Femininity & Representation in British Aestheticism. LC 96-27398. 1997. write for info. (*0-8047-2784-8*) Stanford U Pr.

Psomiades, Kathy A., jt. ed. see Schaffer, Talia.

Psota, Sunshine. Native American Use of Non-Quarry Obsidian in Northern Sonoma County: A Preliminary Assessment. 198p. (C). 1994. pap. text 21.25 (*1-55567-111-X*) Coyote Press.

Psotka, Joseph, et al, eds. Intelligent Tutoring Systems: Lessons Learned. 576p. 1988. text 125.00 (*0-8058-0023-9*); pap. text 65.00 (*0-8058-0192-8*) L Erlbaum Assocs.

Psotka, Joseph, jt. ed. see Farr, Marshall J.

Psrcas, Ben & Hicks, Donna C., eds. Virginia Job Source: Over 7,000 Professional Job Contacts, Web Site Addresses & Job Hotlines to Virginia's Largest Companies. (Job Source Ser.: Vol. 6). 424p. 1998. pap. 16.95 (*0-9635651-3-3*, Metcom) Benjamin Scott.

P.S.R.F. Mathijsen Staff. Guide to European Union Law, Vol. 1. 6th ed. 1994. pap. text 42.00 (*0-421-51230-X*, Pub. by Sweet & Maxwll) Gaunt.

Psuik, Karrie. Love Letters, Lust Letters. 45p. (Orig.). 1994. pap. 7.95 (*0-9645010-1-5*, Karrie Angel) Prem Raja Baba.

Psuty, N. P., jt. ed. see Kelletat, D. H.

Psuty, Norbert, et al, eds. Coastal Dunes: Form & Process. LC 90-34519. (Coastal Morphology & Research Ser.). 410p. 1991. 340.00 (*0-471-91842-3*) Wiley.

Psv, N., tr. see Tsereteli, O. D., ed.

Psv, N., tr. see Vinogradov, I. M.

Psychic Research Co. Staff. Psychic Skills: Lessons in Clairvoyance, Personal Magnetism, Auto-Suggestion, Concentration, & Mind Reading (1901) 105p. 1996. reprint ed. pap. 14.95 (*1-56459-650-8*) Kessinger Pub.

Psychology Staff, ed. see Fallowfield, Lesley & Clark, Andrew.

Psychopedis, Kosmas, jt. auth. see Bonefeld, Werner.

Psychos. The New Guide to Palmistry: The Mystery of Your Palm & How It Affects Your Life. 200p. 1995. pap. 6.95 (*0-572-01378-7*, Pub. by Foulsham UK) Assoc Pubs Grp.

Psychosomatic Medicine, Editorial Committee. Psychosomatic Classics: Selected Papers from Psychosomatic Medicine, 1939-1958. 1971. pap. 31.00 (*3-8055-1232-5*) S Karger.

***Psychoundakis, George.** Cretan Runner: His Story of the German Occupation. 320p. 1998. pap. 12.95 (*0-14-027322-0*, Pub. by Pnguin Bks Ltd) Trafalgar.

PT Publications Staff. The Glossary of Key Purchasing Terms, Acronyms, & Formulas. Przirembel, Janet L., ed. LC 95-39697. 135p. (Orig.). 1996. pap. text 14.95 (*0-945456-22-0*) PT Pubns.

P'taah, jt. auth. see King, Jani.

Ptacek, James. Battered Women in the Courtroom: The Power of Judicial Response. LC 98-48853. (Gender, Crime & Law Ser.). 1999. text 50.00 (*1-55553-391-4*) NE U Pr.

— Battered Women in the Courtroom: The Power of Judicial Responses. LC 98-48853. (Northeastern Series on Gender, Crime, & Law). 224p. 1999. pap. 20.00 (*1-55553-390-6*) NE U Pr.

Ptacek, Greg. Champion for Children's Health: A Story about Dr. S. Josephine Baker. LC 93-10482. (Illus.). (J). (gr. 3-6). 1994. lib. bdg. 19.93 (*0-87614-806-2*, Carolrhoda) Lerner Pub.

Ptacek, Greg, jt. auth. see Ullis, Karlis.

Ptacek, Greg, jt. auth. see Vare, Ethlie A.

Ptacek, Greg, jt. auth. see Woodruff, Cheryl.

Ptacek, Kathryn, ed. Women of Darkness II. 1994. pap. write for info. (*0-8125-0837-8*) Tor Bks.

Ptacnik, Donald J. The EMT Review Manual. 5th ed. 2000. pap. text. write for info. (*0-7216-5081-3*, W B Saunders Co) Harcrt Hlth Sci Grp.

— The EMT Review Manual: Self-Assessment Practice Tests for Basic Life Support Skills. 4th ed. 326p. 1993. pap. text 26.00 (*0-7216-5043-0*, W B Saunders Co) Harcrt Hlth Sci Grp.

— Review Manual for the Emt-Intermediate: Self-Assessment Practice Tests. 3rd ed. 246p. 1993. pap. 27.00 (*0-7216-5042-2*, W B Saunders Co) Harcrt Hlth Sci Grp.

Ptacnik, Donald J., jt. auth. see Childs, B. J.

Ptak, Carol A. MRP & Beyond: A Toolbox for Integrating People & Systems. LC 96-3311. 264p. 1996. text 40.00 (*0-7863-0554-1*, Irwn Prfssnl) McGraw-Hill Prof.

Ptak, Diane S. The American Loyalists: Origin & Nominal Lists. LC 95-92173. 15p. 1995. pap., suppl. ed. 17.00 (*1-886905-07-X*) D S Ptak.

— The American Loyalists: Origins & Nominal Lists. LC 95-92175. 40p. 1993. pap. 17.00 (*1-886905-05-3*) D S Ptak.

— Cast in Stone: Selected Albany, Rensselaer & Saratoga County, New York Burials. LC 90-224405. (Illus.). 168p. 1990. 35.00 (*1-56012-108-4*, 101) Kinship Rhinebeck.

— Chasing Elusive Women: A Historian's Guide. 30p. 1997. 17.00 (*1-886905-11-8*) D S Ptak.

— A Compilation of American & Canadian Passenger - Emigration Registers. LC 95-92172. 25p. 1993. pap. 17.00 (*1-886905-02-9*) D S Ptak.

— A Compilation of American & Canadian Passenger/Emigration Registers: Supplement. (Illus.). 15p. (Orig.). 1995. pap. 11.00 (*1-886905-09-6*) D S Ptak.

— Lost & Found: Albany NY Area Church & Synagogue Vital Record Compendium. 30p. 1993. pap. 17.00 (*1-886905-03-7*) D S Ptak.

— Lost & Found: Albany NY Area Church & Synagogue Vital Record Compendium, 1654-1925 - Supplement. LC 95-92177. (Illus.). 15p. (Orig.). 1995. pap. 11.00 (*1-886905-10-X*) D S Ptak.

— A Passage in Time: The Ships That Brought Our Ancestors. LC 95-92203. 30p. 1992. pap. 17.00 (*1-886905-01-0*) D S Ptak.

— Surnames: Determining Origins with Biographical & Ethnic References. LC 95-92174. 30p. 1995. pap. 17.00 (*1-886905-06-1*) D S Ptak.

— Surnames: Their Meanings & Origins. LC 95-92176. 30p. 1993. pap. 17.00 (*1-886905-04-5*) D S Ptak.

Ptak, Elisabeth, ed. see Point Reyes National Seashore Association Staff & California Native Plant Society, Marin Chapter Sta.

Ptak, Elizabeth, ed. see Romo, Terezita & Mesa-Bains, Amalia.

Ptak, Pavel & Pulmannova, Sylvia. Orthomodular Structures As Quantum Logics: Intrinsic Properties, State Space & Probabilistic Topics. (C). 1991. text 166.50 (*0-7923-1207-4*) Kluwer Academic.

Ptak, Richard, et al. Manager's Guide to Distributed Environments. LC 98-8275. 368p. 1998. 39.99 (*0-471-19712-2*) Wiley.

Ptak, Roderich. China & the Asian Seas: Trade, Travel & Visions of the Others (1400-1750) LC 98-29800. (Variorum Collected Studies: Vol. CS638). 350p. 1998. text 103.95 (*0-86078-775-3*, Pub. by Variorum) Ashgate Pub Co.

— China's Seaborne Trade with South & Southeast Asia (1200-1750) LC 98-42913. (Variorum Collected Studies Ser.). 352p. 1999. text 110.95 (*0-86078-776-1*, Pub. by Variorum) Ashgate Pub Co.

Ptak, Roger. Sky Stories: Ancient & Modern. LC 97-41659. (Illus.). 237p. 1998. pap. 45.00 (*1-56072-507-9*) Nova Sci Pubs.

Ptashne, Mark. A Genetic Switch. 2nd ed. (Illus.). 192p. (Orig.). 1992. pap. 34.95 (*0-86542-209-5*) Blackwell Sci.

PTI-AMHCA Staff. Clinical Mental Health Counselor Handbook & Study Guide. 496p. 1998. 225.00 (*0-7872-5300-6*) Kendall-Hunt.

***PTI-AMHCA Staff & AMHCA Staff.** Mental Health Counselors Clinical Practice Companion: A Continuing Education Program. 1999. pap. text 195.00 (*0-7872-6384-2*) Kendall-Hunt.

***Ptito, Maurice & AMHCA Staff.** Clinical Mental Health Counselor Crossword Puzzle. 32p. 1998. pap. text 18.00 (*0-7872-5301-4*) Kendall-Hunt.

PTM Staff. Creation or Evolution? (Illus.). 75p. (Orig.). 1995. per. 9.95 (*1-889973-00-9*) Plain Truth Minst.

***Ptok, Daniela.** Social Competence ALS Gesellschaftlicher Imperative: Eine Untersuchung Zu Grundlagen, Pragung und Bedeutung Interpersonaler Fertigkeiten in der Nordamerikanischen Kultur. 355p. 1999. 52.00 (*3-631-34821-5*) P Lang Pubng.

Ptolemy, Claudius. Geographia, 3 vols. in 1. Nobbe, C. F., ed. (GER.). xxxvi, 760p. 1990. reprint ed. write for info. (*3-487-01236-7*) G Olms Pubs.

— The Geography. Orig. Title: Geography of Claudius Ptolemy. (Illus.). 304p. 1991. reprint ed. pap. 19.95 (*0-486-26896-9*) Dover.

— Geography of Claudius Ptolemy. Stevenson, Edward L., ed. LC 70-174287. reprint ed. 245.00 (*0-404-05148-0*) AMS Pr.

— Harmonicorum Libri Tres. fac. ed. Wallis, John, ed. & tr. by. (Monuments of Music & Music Literature in Facsimile, II Ser.: Vol. 60). (Illus.). 1977. lib. bdg. 55.00 (*0-8450-2260-1*) Broude.

— Die Harmonielehre des Claudios Ptolemy. During, Ingemar, ed. cvi, 147p. 1982. reprint ed. write for info. (*3-487-07263-7*) G Olms Pubs.

— Tetrabiblos. (Loeb Classical Library: No. 435). 502p. (C). 1980. text 19.95 (*0-674-99479-5*) HUP.

— Tetrabiblos. LC 76-41123. 1974. pap. 7.50 (*0-912504-24-2*) Sym & Sign.

— Tetrabiblos, Together with the Centiloquy. Ashmand, J. M., tr. LC 76-41123. 165p. 1974. pap. 7.50 (*0-912504-31-5*) Sym & Sign.

Pu, F. C., et al, eds. Aspects of Modern Magnetism: Lecture Notes of the 8th Chinese International Summer School of Physics: Beijing, 28 August-7 September, 1995. LC 96-4813. 288p. 1996. write for info. (*981-02-2601-2*) World Scientific Pub.

Pu, Ning. Flower Terror: Suffocating Stories of China. Ferris, Richard J., Jr. & Morton, Andrew, trs. from CHI. LC 98-87238. 256p. 1998. pap. 13.95 (*0-9665421-0-X*) Hcma & Sekey.

Pu, Pearl, jt. ed. see Maher, Mary L.

Pu, S. C. & McCoy-Thompson, Steven, eds. Technology in the Pacific Century: Trade, Security & Competitiveness. (US-Asia Institute National Leadership Conference Ser.: No. 6). (Illus.). 224p. (C). 1989. pap. 35.00 (*0-9621762-0-6*) US-Asia Inst.

Pu, Songling. Strange Tales from Make-Do Studio. Mair, Denis C. & Mair, Victor H., trs. from CHI. 446p. (Orig.). 1989. pap. 12.95 (*0-8351-2256-5*) China Bks.

Pu, Yushu. The Cosmos: A Book of Poetry. (Illus.). 24p. (Orig.). 1989. pap. 2.95 (*0-9612480-0-9*) Mount Pr DE.

Pub Group Woodtones Staff. Art of Poncho. 1998. 14.95 (*1-892107-04-X*) Woodtones Publ.

— Dedicated Dads. 1998. 12.95 (*1-892107-03-1*) Woodtones Publ.

— Small Friends & Company. 1998. 12.95 (*1-892107-01-5*) Woodtones Publ.

— Spirit of Black Men. 1998. 14.95 (*1-892107-00-7*) Woodtones Publ.

Pub. Services Central Office. Britain's Legal Systems. 2nd ed. (Aspects of Britain Ser.). (Illus.). 118p. 1996. pap. 12.00 (*0-11-702026-5*, HM20265, Pub. by Statnry Office) Bernan Associates.

Pub. Services COI Staff. Local Government. LC 97-135863. (Aspects of Britain Ser.). (Illus.). 97p. 1996. pap. 12.00 (*0-11-702037-0*, HM020370, Pub. by Statnry Office) Bernan Associates.

Pubantz, Jerry, jt. auth. see Moore, John A., Jr.

Publassist Staff. Out of This Kitchen: A History of the Ethnic Groups & Their Foods in the Steel Valley. 2nd ed. (Illus.). 186p. 1998. lib. bdg. 15.00 (*0-9638745-0-0*, TX-3-619-596) Publassist.

Public Affairs Research Council of Louisiana Staff. Citizen's Guide to the 1973 Constitutional Convention. (Illus.). 58p. 1973. write for info. (*0-318-58239-2*) Pub Aff LA.

Public Agenda Foundation. America's Role in the World. 1991. 9.50 (*0-07-041728-8*) McGraw.

Public Agenda Foundation Staff. Admissions Decisions: Should Immigration Be Restricted? 52p. (C). 1994. 12.19 (*0-07-051824-6*) McGraw.

— Contested Values: Tug-of-War in the Schoolyard. (C). 1994. pap. text 9.50 (*0-07-051825-4*) McGraw.

— Criminal Violence: What Direction Now for the War on Crime? 45p. (C). 1992. 12.19 (*0-07-051081-4*) McGraw.

— The Four Trillion Dollar Debt: Tough Choices about Soaring Federal Deficits. 45p. (C). 1993. 12.19 (*0-07-051549-2*) McGraw.

— The Health Care Cost Explosion: Why It's So Serious, What Should Be Done. 45p. (C). 1993. 11.56 (*0-07-051547-6*) McGraw.

— Kids Who Commit Crimes: What Should Be Done about Juvenile Violence? 48p. (C). 1994. 12.19 (*0-07-051828-9*) McGraw.

— Pocket Pressures: Who Benefits from Economic Growth? 48p. (C). 1995. pap. 12.19 (*0-07-052213-8*) McGraw.

— The Poverty Puzzle: What Should Be Done to Help the Poor. 45p. (C). 1993. 12.19 (*0-07-051548-4*) McGraw.

— Prescription for Prosperity: Four Paths to Economic Renewal. 45p. (C). 1992. 12.19 (*0-07-051082-2*) McGraw.

— Reexamining America's Global Role. 45p. (C). 1995. pap. 12.19 (*0-07-052214-6*) McGraw.

— The Troubled American Family: Which Way Out of the Storm? 52p. (C). 1995. pap. 12.19 (*0-07-052212-X*) McGraw.

Public Agenda Staff, et al. Here to Stay: The Domestic & International Priorities of Latino Leaders. 24p. 1998. pap. 10.00 (*1-889483-54-0*) Public Agenda.

Public Archives Staff of Canada Ottawa. Catalogue of the Public Archives Library of Canada: Collection of Published Material with a Chronological List of Pamphlets. 1979. 1575.00 (*0-8161-0316-X*, G K Hall & Co) Mac Lib Ref.

Public Broadcasting Foundation of Northwest Ohio S. What's Good to Eat? The Best of Northwest Ohio. 200p. 1995. 24.95 (*0-9649111-0-8*) Public Broadcsting.

Public Citizen Environmental Working Group Staff, et al. Trading Away U. S. Food Safety. 100p. (C). 1994. pap. text 20.00 (*0-937188-54-9*) Pub Citizen.

Public Citizen Health Group Staff, et al. Worst Pills, Best Pills: A Consumer's Guide to Preventing Drug-Induced Death or Illness. 720p. 1999. per. 16.00 (*0-671-01918-X*, PB Trade Paper) PB.

Public Citizen Health Research Group Staff. Worst Pills, Best Pills News Collection March 1995 - April 1996: Recent Articles about Prescription & Over-the-Counter Drugs. Wolfe, Sidney M., ed. 94p. (Orig.). 1996. pap. 10.00 (*0-937188-09-3*) Pub Citizen.

Public Citizen Staff. A Million for Your Thoughts: The Industry-Funded Campaign Against the FDA by Conservative Think Tanks. 53p. (Orig.). 1996. pap. 20.00 (*0-937188-57-3*) Pub Citizen.

Public Citizen Staff, et al. Power for the People: A Public Interest Blueprint for Electricity Restructuring. 20p. (Orig.). 1996. pap. 20.00 (*0-937188-27-1*) Pub Citizen.

Public Citizen's Critical Mass Energy Project Staf. Renewable Source: A National Directory of Resources, Contacts, & Companies. 240p. (C). 1994. pap. text 40.00 (*0-937188-93-X*) Pub Citizen.

Public Citizen's Global Trade Watch Staff. NAFTA's Broken Promises: A Border Betrayed U. S. - Mexico Border Environment & Health Decline in NAFTA's First Two Years. (SPA., Illus.). 100p. (Orig.). 1996. pap. text 15.00 (*0-937188-03-4*) Pub Citizen.

Public Domain. Deck the Halls. 6p. (ps up). bds. 6.95 (*0-694-01561-X*) HarpC.

— Santa Claus Is Coming to Town. 6p. (ps up). bds. 6.95 (*0-694-01559-8*) HarpC.

— Take Me Out to the Ball Game. 6p. (ps up). bds. 6.95 (*0-694-01560-1*) HarpC.

— We Wish You a Merry Christmas. 6p. (ps up). bds. 6.95 (*0-694-01558-X*) HarpC.

— Yankee Doodle. 6p. (ps up). bds. 6.95 (*0-694-01557-1*) HarpC.

Public Domain Research Staff, jt. auth. see Simon, Carly.

P

An Asterisk (*) at the beginning of an entry indicates that the title is appearing for the first time.

Public Employee Retirement Administration Staff. Retirement Sample, Vol. 1. 113p. 1973. 7.00 (*0-317-34952-X*) Municipal.

Public Health & Labor Institutes Staff. Corporate Power & the American Dream: Toward an Economic Agenda for Working People. 9th rev. ed. (Illus.). 200p. 1997. wbk. ed. 14.00 (*0-945257-89-9*) Apex Pr.

Public Health Service Staff, et al. Health Characteristics of Large Metropolitan Statistical Areas: United States, 1988-1989. LC 93-7390. (Vital & Health Statistics Ser. 10: Data from the National Health Interview Survey: No. 187). 1993. write for info. (*0-8406-0479-3*) Natl Ctr Health Stats.

Public Library Assn. Job & Career Information Serv. Guide to Basic Resume Writing. LC 90-50722. (Illus.). 96p. (YA). (gr. 9 up). 1995. pap. 7.95 (*0-8442-8123-9*, 81239, VGM Career) NTC Contemp Pub Co.

Public Library Assn. Staff. The Library Connection: Essays Written in Praise of Public Libraries. LC 77-24687. 96p. reprint ed. pap. 30.00 (*0-608-17133-6*, 202735600055) Bks Demand.

Public Library of Cleveland Staff. Catalog of Folklore, Folklife & Folk Songs, 3 vols. 1994. 325.00 (*0-7838-2289-8*, G K Hall & Co) Mac Lib Ref.

Public Media Center Staff. The Impact of Homophobia & Other Social Biases on AIDS: A Special Report by Public Media Center. 40p. (Orig.). 1995. pap. text 5.00 (*0-915287-00-5*) Pub Media Ctr.

Public Policy Institute of California Staff, ed. see Neuman, Michael & Whittington, Janice.

Public Policy National University of Singapore Sta, jt. auth. see Asher, Mukul G.

***Public Record Office Staff.** Domesday: A Souvenir Guide. (Illus.). 2000. pap. 4.95 (*1-873162-85-5*) PRO Pubns.

— Getting Started in Family History. (Pocket Guides to Family History Ser.). (Illus.). 63p. 2000. 8.00 (*1-873162-87-1*, Pub. by PRO Pubns) Balogh.

— Souvenir Guide to the Public Record Office. 1999. pap. 5.95 (*1-873162-71-5*) PRO Pubns.

— Titanic: 14th-15th April 1912 The Official Story. 1999. 21.95 (*1-873162-37-5*) PRO Pubns.

— Titanic: The Official Enquiry: Court of Enquiry Report & Evidence. 1999. 120.00 (*1-873162-70-7*) PRO Pubns.

— Using Army Records. (Pocket Guides to Family History Ser.). (Illus.). 64p. 2000. 8.00 (*1-873162-91-X*, Pub. by PRO Pubns) Balogh.

— Using Birth, Marriage & Death Records. (Pocket Guides to Family History Ser.). (Illus.). 64p. 2000. 8.00 (*1-873162-88-X*, Pub. by PRO Pubns) Balogh.

— Using Census Returns. (Pocket Guides to Family History Ser.). (Illus.). 63p. 2000. 8.00 (*1-873162-89-8*, Pub. by PRO Pubns) Balogh.

— Using Wills. (Pocket Guides to Family History Ser.). (Illus.). 63p. 2000. 8.00 (*1-873162-90-1*, Pub. by PRO Pubns) Balogh.

Public Service Co. of New Mexico Staff. Cocinas de New Mexico. 79p. (Orig.). 1995. 11.95 (*0-9649026-0-5*) Pblic Serv Co NM.

Public Technology, Inc. Staff, ed. Solutions for Technology-Sharing Networks, 1986. (Annual Ser.). 436p. (Orig.). 1986. pap. 10.00 (*1-55657-001-5*) Pub Tech Inc.

— Solutions for Technology-Sharing Networks, 1987. 400p. (Orig.). 1987. pap. 10.00 (*0-317-60094-X*) Pub Tech Inc.

Public Utilities Reports, Inc. Staff. Electric Cooperatives: On the Threshold of a New Era. 232p. 1996. pap. 79.00 (*0-910325-63-4*) Public Util.

Public Utilities Reports Staff. Public Utilities Reports Fourth Series: Containing Decisions of the Regulatory Commissions & of State & Federal Courts. Vols. 1 to 74, 1974-1986. LC KF2085.A2P84. 604p. pap. 187.30 (*0-608-16093-8*, 202959800001) Bks Demand.

Public Works & Government Services Staff, jt. ed. see Canada Translation Services Staff.

Public Works & Government Servre Canada-Translation, ed. Le Guide du Redacteur. 2nd rev. ed. LC 96-980276. (FRE.). 319p. 1996. pap. 23.95 (*0-660-95300-5*, Pub. by Canadian Govt Pub) Accents Pubns.

Public Works Committee, jt. auth. see United States National Resources Committee.

***Publicacion Pastoral Rednetorista Staff.** La Confirmacion: Preguntas y Respuestas. (SPA.). 1999. pap. 2.95 (*0-7648-0438-3*, Libros Liguori) Liguori Pubns.

— Devocionario Catolico. LC 98-67858. (SPA.). 64p. 1999. pap. 1.95 (*0-7648-0399-9*, Libros Liguori) Liguori Pubns.

Publications Committee, ASJA Staff. Soil Mechanics 14th Intl, Vol. 1. LC 99-496398. 1997. 259.00 (*90-5410-892-4*) Ashgate Pub Co.

— Soil Mechanics 14th Intl, Vol. 2. LC 99-496398. 1997. 259.00 (*90-5410-893-2*) Ashgate Pub Co.

— Soil Mechanics 14th Intl, Vol. 3. LC 99-496398. 1997. 259.00 (*90-5410-894-0*) Ashgate Pub Co.

Publications Committee of the XII ICSMFE Staff, ed. Proceedings of the 12th International Conference on Soil Mechanics & Foundation Engineering, Rio de Janeiro, 13-18 August 1989, 5 vols. 2500p. (C). 1989. text 1288.00 (*90-6191-890-1*, Pub. by A A Balkema) Ashgate Pub Co.

***Publications Committee Staff.** Soil Mechanics 14th Intl, Vol. 4. LC 99-496398. 1999. 259.00 (*90-5410-895-9*) Ashgate Pub Co.

Publications Committee XIII ICSMFE Ser. Proceedings of the Thirteenth Annual International Conference on Soil Mechanics & Foundations Engineering, New Dehli, January 1994. (Illus.). 3500p. (C). 1994. text 970.00 (*90-5410-370-1*, Pub. by A A Balkema) Ashgate Pub Co.

Publications Committee XIII ICSMFE Ser. Soil Mechanics 13th Intl. 1994. 181.00 (*90-5410-375-2*) Ashgate Pub Co.

— Soil Mechanics 13th Intl, Vol. 1. 440p. 1994. 181.00 (*90-5410-371-X*) Ashgate Pub Co.

— Soil Mechanics 13th Intl, Vol. 2. 400p. 1994. 181.00 (*90-5410-372-8*) Ashgate Pub Co.

— Soil Mechanics 13th Intl, Vol. 3. 400p. 1994. 181.00 (*90-5410-373-6*) Ashgate Pub Co.

— Soil Mechanics 13th Intl, Vol. 4. 400p. 1994. 181.00 (*90-5410-374-4*) Ashgate Pub Co.

Publications Department of the American TFP Staff, ed. & tr. see Del Campo, Carlos P.

Publications International, Ltd. Editorial Staff. America's Favorite Brand Name Easy Home Cooking. LC 98-65958. 384 p. 1998. write for info. (*0-7853-2806-8*) Pubns Intl Ltd.

— America's Favorite Brand Name Light Cooking. LC 97-75575. 384 p. 1998. write for info. (*0-7853-2788-6*) Pubns Intl Ltd.

***Publications International, Ltd. Editorial Staff.** Baby Ducklings. LC 98-130383. (Wonder Window Ser.). (Illus.). 1998. write for info. (*0-7853-2685-5*) Pubns Intl Ltd.

Publications International, Ltd. Editorial Staff. Cars of the Sizzling '60s: A Decade of Great Rides & Good Vibrations LC 97-67074. 416p. 1997. write for info. (*0-7853-2435-6*) Pubns Intl Ltd.

— Chocolate Lover's Collection. LC 98-184247. 128p. 1998. write for info. (*0-7853-2766-5*) Pubns Intl Ltd.

— Christmas Cottage, 4 vols. LC 98-141204. (Illus.). (J). 1997. write for info. (*0-7853-2636-7*) Pubns Intl Ltd.

— Christmas Snowman LC 98-140513. (Wonder Window Ser.). 1997. write for info. (*0-7853-2464-X*) Pubns Intl Ltd.

***Publications International, Ltd. Editorial Staff.** Classic Animal Tales. LC 98-227497. (Illus.). 88 p. (J). 1998. write for info. (*0-7853-2699-5*) Pubns Intl Ltd.

— Classic Bedtime Stories. LC 98-227758. (Illus.). 88p. (J). 1998. write for info. (*0-7853-2700-2*) Pubns Intl Ltd.

— Classic Children's Stories. LC 98-227773. 88p. (J). 1998. write for info. (*0-7853-2701-0*) Pubns Intl Ltd.

Publications International, Ltd. Editorial Staff. Cookies. LC 98-224232. 128 p. 1998. write for info. (*0-7853-2765-7*) Pubns Intl Ltd.

— Cooking Class Chocolate Cookies & Brownies Cookbook. LC 95-198073. 94 p. 1994. write for info. (*0-7853-0667-6*) Pubns Intl Ltd.

Publications International, Ltd. Editorial Staff. Donald Duck Sound Board. pap. 7.98 (*0-7853-1128-9*) Pubns Intl Ltd.

Publications International, Ltd. Editorial Staff. Favorite Brand Name Best-Loved Chocolate Recipes. LC 96-68274. 384p. 1996. write for info. (*0-7853-1791-0*) Pubns Intl Ltd.

— Favorite Brand Name Match-A-Meal Light Recipes: Over 100,000 Meals. LC 98-224964. 95 p. 1998. write for info. (*0-7853-2748-7*) Pubns Intl Ltd.

— The First Christmas LC 98-140489. (Wonder Window Ser.). (Illus.). 1997. write for info. (*0-7853-2461-5*) Pubns Intl Ltd.

— Great American Favorite Brand Name Cookbook: Collector's Edition. LC 97-66765. 576p. 1997. 34.95 (*0-7853-2471-2*) Pubns Intl Ltd.

— Great-tasting Recipes with Spam Luncheon Meat. LC 96-227490. 94 p. 1996. write for info. (*0-7853-1402-4*) Pubns Intl Ltd.

— Kermit Sound Board Bk. 7.98 (*0-7853-1247-1*) Pubns Intl Ltd.

Publications International, Ltd. Editorial Staff. Lion King Look & Find. pap. 6.98 (*0-7853-1189-0*) Pubns Intl Ltd.

Publications International, Ltd. Editorial Staff. 101 Cookie Recipes: A Collection of Your Favorites. LC 98-66091. 192p. 1998. write for info. (*0-7853-2810-6*) Pubns Intl Ltd.

— 101 Pasta Recipes: A Collection of Your Favorites. LC 97-75998. 192p. 1998. write for info. (*0-7853-2801-7*) Pubns Intl Ltd.

— 101 Wraps & More: A Collection of your Favorites. LC 98-65616. 192 p. 1998. write for info. (*0-7853-2475-5*) Pubns Intl Ltd.

— Players of Cooperstown: Baseball's Hall of Fame. 1992. 29.95 (*1-56173-230-3*) Pubns Intl Ltd.

— Secret Santa. LC 98-140485. (Wonder Window Ser.). (J). 1997. write for info. (*0-7853-2462-3*) Pubns Intl Ltd.

— 365 Favorite Brand Name Diabetic Recipes. LC 97-75996. 336p. 1998. write for info. (*0-7853-2750-9*) Pubns Intl Ltd.

— 365 Favorite Brand Name Slow Cooker Recipes & More. LC 98-65617. (Illus.). 336 p. 1998. write for info. (*0-7853-2805-X*) Pubns Intl Ltd.

— Treasury of Baby Animal Stories. LC 98-218906. (Illus.). 384 p. (J). 1998. write for info. (*0-7853-2680-4*) Pubns Intl Ltd.

— Treasury of Country Crafts: Easy Step-by-Step Designs. LC 97-76072. 240p. 1998. 29.95 (*0-7853-2862-9*) Pubns Intl Ltd.

Publications International, Ltd. Editorial Staff, et al. Peekaboo Baby. LC 98-208306. 1998. write for info. (*0-7853-2777-0*) Pubns Intl Ltd.

— Players of Cooperstown: Baseball's Hall of Fame. (Illus.). 256p. 1992. 29.95 (*0-7853-0336-7*) Pubns Intl Ltd.

— Southwest Expressions. (Illus.). 256p. 1992. 29.95 (*1-56173-585-X*) Pubns Intl Ltd.

Publications International, Ltd. Editorial Staff, jt. auth. see Baker, Darrell.

Publications International, Ltd. Editorial Staff, jt. auth. see Burris, Priscilla.

Publications International, Ltd. Editorial Staff, jt. auth. see Johnston, Jane.

Publications International, Ltd. Editorial Staff, jt. auth. see Matieu, Kristen.

Publications International, Ltd. Editorial Staff, jt. auth. see Mitchell, Kathy.

Publications International, Ltd. Editorial Staff, jt. auth. see Potter, Beatrix.

Publications International, Ltd. Editorial Staff, jt. auth. see Thorburgh, Anne H.

Publications International, Ltd. Editorial Staff, jt. auth. see Wolf, Conor.

Publications International, Ltd. Editorial Staff, jt. illus. see Morgan-Vanroyen, Mary.

***PUBLICATIONS, LEMA.** Helicopters. 1999. 16.95 (*84-95323-16-8*) LEMA.

— Materials & Techniques. 1999. 16.95 (*84-95323-09-5*) LEMA.

***PUBLICATIONS REIMAN.** Best of Country Cookies. Schnittila, Julie, ed. LC 99-70498. (Illus.). 118p. 1999. 15.99 (*0-89821-260-X*) Reiman Pubns.

PUBLICATIONS REIMAN & Taste of Home Staff. The Best of Country Cooking: 1999 Edition. Steiner, Jean, ed. (Illus.). 186p. 1999. 24.99 (*0-89821-256-1*) Reiman Pubns.

Publicola Staff. New Vade Mecum: Or a Pocket Companion for Lawyers, Deputy Sheriffs & Constables; Suggesting Many Grievous Abuses & Alarming Evils, Which Attend the Present Mode of Administering the Laws of New Hampshire: Together with the Most Obvious Means of Redressing & Removing Them. LC 94-26147. xv, 155p. 1995. reprint ed. 42.50 (*0-8377-2551-8*, Rothman) W S Hein.

Publicover, Robert J. My Unicorn Has Gone Away. 112p. 1993. 14.00 (*0-9634759-0-8*) Powder Hse Pub.

Publishers Design Works Staff, ed. see Mitchell, Pam.

***Publishers Editorial Staff.** Callaghan's Michigan Digest, Fall 1999 Interim Supplement, 42 vols. 42p. 1999. write for info. (*0-327-01677-9*, 7654512) LEXIS Pub.

Publisher's Editorial Staff. Decisions of the U.S. Supreme Court, 35 Vols. 2000.00 (*0-327-12376-1*) LEXIS Pub.

— European Community Customs Code Annotated, 2 Vols. pap. 195.00 (*0-327-11401-0*) LEXIS Pub.

— Florida Criminal & Traffic Law Manual: 1999-2000 Edition. 19.50 (*0-327-10397-3*) LEXIS Pub.

Publisher's Editorial Staff. Instructions for Virginia & West Virginia, 4 vols. 3rd ed. Michie Company Editorial Staff, ed. 1987. 240.00 (*0-87473-287-5*, 73055-10, MICHIE) LEXIS Pub.

— Michigan Law & Practice, 31 vols. Date not set. text 1790.00 (*0-318-57515-9*, 63830, MICHIE) LEXIS Pub.

— Michigan Law & Practice, 31 vols. 1998. text 1790.00 (*0-327-00088-0*, 63830, MICHIE) LEXIS Pub.

— Minnesota Legal Forms: Minnesota Limitations Manual. 2nd ed. 352p. 1989. ring bd. 95.00 (*0-86678-835-2*, MICHIE) LEXIS Pub.

Publisher's Editorial Staff. Motor Vehicle Laws of North Carolina with Cd-rom: 1999 Edition. 1083p. pap. 34.00 (*0-327-10153-9*) LEXIS Pub.

— New Hampshire Court Rules of Evidence--Desk Copy: 1999-2000 Edition. 230p. 1999. pap. 45.00 (*0-327-10179-2*, 4566015) LEXIS Pub.

Publisher's Editorial Staff. Pennsylvania Law Encyclopedia, 57 vols. Date not set. text 2399.00 (*0-318-57516-7*, 63620-10, MICHIE) LEXIS Pub.

— Pennsylvania Law Encyclopedia, 53 vols. 1986. text 2399.00 (*0-327-00963-2*, 63620-10, MICHIE) LEXIS Pub.

Publisher's Editorial Staff, compiled by. Delaware Code Annotated, 20 Vols. 845.00 (*0-327-10880-0*) LEXIS Pub.

— Michie's Annotated Code of Maryland, 40 Vols. 725.00 (*0-327-11754-0*) LEXIS Pub.

— New York Standard Civil Practice Service Desk Book: 2000 Supplement. 2000. pap. write for info. (*0-327-10181-4*, 6891111) LEXIS Pub.

Publisher's Editorial Staff, ed. Ballentine's Law Dictionary with Pronunciations. 3rd ed. LC 68-30931. 1429p. 1969. 25.00 (*0-686-14540-2*) West Group.

— Nichols Cyclopedia of Legal Forms, 1925-1990, 31 vols. LC 73-165177. 1320.00 (*0-685-09239-9*) West Group.

Publishers Marketing Association Staff, jt. auth. see Book Industry Study Group Staff.

***Publishers of Today's Collector Staff.** Today's Hottest Collectibles. 2nd rev. ed. LC 98-84625. (Illus.). 356p. 2000. pap. 24.95 (*0-87341-907-3*, CGA02) Krause Pubns.

Publishers of Toy Shop Staff & Publishers of Warman's Today's Collector Staff, eds. Today's Hottest Collectibles. LC 98-84625. (Illus.). 400p. 1998. pap. 24.95 (*0-87341-372-5*, CGA01) Krause Pubns.

Publishers of Warman's Today's Collector Staff, jt. ed. see Publishers of Toy Shop Staff.

***Publisher's Resource Group Staff, ed.** Payroll Practice Fundamentals: 2000 Edition. 250p. 2000. 95.95 (*1-930471-06-8*, 0100) American Payroll.

Publisher's Staff & Michie Company Editorial Staff. Colorado Court Rules. 1140p. 1989. ring bd. 70.00 (*0-685-07733-0*, MICHIE) LEXIS Pub.

***Publishing Company Staff.** Discovering Careers for Your Future. LC 00-37661. 2000. pap. write for info. (*0-89434-361-0*) Ferguson.

Publishing Group Affinity. Dance. 384p. 1999. 6.95 (*1-928684-04-1*, Pub. by Affinity Pubg) BookWorld.

Publishing Group Staff, ed. see Lowry, Linda.

Publishing Images Staff. R. M. Kliment & Frances Halsband Architects. (Master Architect Ser.). 1998. 59.95 (*1-875498-88-5*) Images Aust AT.

Publishing Nelson Staff. Assorted Fall Christmas, 1. 1998. 14.99 (*0-8499-7159-4*) Focus Family.

Publishing Resources Staff, ed. see National Campaign for Freedom of Expression.

Publishing West. Hazen's Hornbook on Securities Regulation. 3rd ed. 1998. pap. 33.00 (*0-314-23431-4*) West Pub.

Publishing West Staff. Brain's Quick Review Contracts. 5th ed. (Sum & Substance Quick Review Ser.). 1998. pap. 19.95 (*1-57793-052-5*) West Pub.

— Levine's Quick Review Torts. 2nd ed. (Sum & Substance Quick Review Ser.). 1998. pap. 18.95 (*1-57793-010-X*) West Pub.

— Miller & Friedenthal's Quick Review on Civil Procedure. 3rd ed. (Sum & Substance Quick Review Ser.). 1998. pap. 19.95 (*1-57793-050-9*) West Pub.

— Prygoski's Quick Review Constitutional Law. 4th ed. (Sum & Substance Quick Review Ser.). 1998. pap. 18.95 (*1-57793-051-7*) West Pub.

Publishing Woodland Staff. Juicing. (Woodland Health Ser.). (Orig.). 1998. pap. 3.95 (*1-58054-003-1*) Woodland UT.

Publishing Zondervan Staff. Jesus: That the World May Know. (Faith Lessons Ser.). 1998. 48.99 (*0-310-67888-9*) Zondervan.

Publitec Publications Staff. Who's Who in Lebanon, 1999-2000. 496p. 1998. 169.00 (*3-598-07672-X*) K G Saur Verlag.

Publitec Publications Staff, ed. Who's Who in Lebanon, 1997-1998. 482p. 1996. 245.00 (*3-598-07647-9*) K G Saur Verlag.

Publitech Publications Staff, ed. Who's Who in the Arab World, 1999-2000. 976p. 1998. write for info. (*3-598-07671-1*) K G Saur Verlag.

Publow, Barry. Speed on Skates. LC 98-39168. (Illus.). 352p. 1998. pap. 21.95 (*0-88011-721-4*, PPUB0721) Human Kinetics.

***Pubs, Struik.** Evolution: A Novel. LC 98-220227. 188p. 1998. write for info. (*1-86872-248-1*) Struik Pubs.

Puc, Krystyna. Poland's Commitment to Its Past: A Report on 2 Study Tours. LC 85-21716. (Illus.). 48p. (Orig.). 1985. pap. 7.00 (*0-941182-16-9*) Partners Livable.

Pucacco, G., jt. auth. see Boccaletti, D.

Puccetti, A., ed. The Programming & Proof System ATES: Advanced Techniques Integration into Efficient Scientific Software. (Research Reports ESPRIT, Project 1158: Vol. 1). viii, 341p. 1991. 39.00 (*0-387-54188-8*) Spr-Verlag.

Puccetti, Patricia I., ed. see Nacelewicz, Barbara.

Pucci, Idanna. The Trials of Maria Barbella: The True Story of a Nineteenth Century Crime of Passion. Fumo, Stefania, tr. from ITA. LC 95-30008.Tr. of Il Fuoco Dell'Anima. (Illus.). 324p. 1996. 22.00 (*1-56858-061-4*) FWEW.

— The Trials of Maria Barbella: The True Story of a 19th Century Crime of Passion. Fumo, Stefania, tr. LC 96-28269.Tr. of Il Fuoco Dell'Anima. 296p. 1997. pap. 14.00 (*0-679-77604-4*) Random.

Pucci, Joseph M. The Full-Knowing Reader: Allusion & the Power of the Reader in the Western Literary Tradition. LC 97-18238. 256p. 1998. 35.00 (*0-300-07152-3*) Yale U Pr.

Pucci, Joseph M., jt. auth. see Harrington, Karl P.

Pucci, Linda, jt. auth. see Copen, Lynn M.

Pucci, Linda M. & Copen, Lynn M. Finding Your Way: What Happens When You Tell about Abuse. 61p. (J). (gr. 5-12). 1995. pap. text 8.95 (*0-9647822-0-0*) Tree of Serenity.

Pucci, Linda M., jt. auth. see Copen, Lynn M.

Pucci, Pietro. Hesiod & the Language of Poetry. LC 76-234. 160p. reprint ed. pap. 49.60 (*0-7837-1109-3*, 204163900021) Bks Demand.

— Odysseus Polutropos: Intertextual Readings in the "Odyssey" & the "Iliad" (Studies in Classical Philology). 264p. 1995. pap. text 17.95 (*0-8014-8270-4*) Cornell U Pr.

— Oedipus & the Fabrication of the Father: The Oedipus Tyrannus in Modern Criticism & Philosophy. 240p. 1992. text 38.50 (*0-8018-4340-5*) Johns Hopkins.

— The Song of the Sirens & Other Essays. LC 97-39863. 208p. (C). 1997. pap. text 21.95 (*0-8226-3059-1*); lib. bdg. 52.50 (*0-8226-3058-3*) Rowman.

— The Violence of Pity in Euripides' Medea. LC 79-52501. (Cornell Studies in Classical Philology: No. 41). (Illus.). 239p. reprint ed. pap. 74.10 (*0-608-18390-3*, 203023100067) Bks Demand.

Puccia, Charles J. & Levins, Richard. Qualitative Modeling of Complex Systems: An Introduction to Loop Analysis & Time Averaging. (Illus.). 256p. 1986. 54.00 (*0-674-74110-2*) HUP.

Pucciani, O. F. Langue & Langage. 5th ed. LC 86-29439. (FRE.). 655p. (C). 1996. pap. text 67.50 (*0-15-504317-X*) Harcourt Coll Pubs.

Pucciani, Oresta F., ed. The French Theater since Nineteen Thirty: Six Contemporary Full-Length Plays. LC PQ1223.P8. 406p. reprint ed. pap. 125.90 (*0-608-10984-3*, 205511600008) Bks Demand.

Pucciani, Oreste. Langue et Langage. 5th ed. (C). 1987. pap. text, lab manual ed. 27.75 (*0-03-004042-6*) Harcourt.

— Langue et Langage. 5th ed. (C). 1987. pap. text, teacher ed. 25.75 (*0-03-004039-6*) Harcourt Coll Pubs.

Pucciani, Oreste & Hamel, Jacqueline. Langue et Language: Le Francais par le Francais. 5th ed. 608p. (C). 1987. text 45.25 (*0-03-004037-X*) Harcourt Coll Pubs.

Pucciani, Oreste, jt. auth. see Cottino-Jones, Marga.

Pucciani, Oreste F., ed. & tr. see Racine, Jean.

Puccinelli, Patricia M. Yardsticks: Retarded Characters & Their Roles in Fiction. LC 92-43532. (AUS IV: Vol. 155). VIII, 104p. (C). 1995. text 32.95 (*0-8204-2001-8*) P Lang Pubng.

Puccini. La Fanciulla del West in Full Score. 1998. pap. 19.95 (*0-486-29712-8*) Dover.

Puccini, Dario. Una Mujer en Soledad (A Woman in Solitude) (SPA.). 238p. 1997. pap. 16.99 (*968-16-5036-0*, Pub. by Fondo) Continental Bk.

***Puccini, G.** Stephens Development. (Puccini Opus). 48p. 1998. pap. 9.95 (*0-7935-9218-6*) H Leonard.

P

An Asterisk (*) at the beginning of an entry indicates that the title is appearing for the first time.

Puccini, Giacomo. La Boheme. John, Nicholas, ed. Pinkerton, P. & Grist, W., trs. from ITA. (English National Opera Guide Series: Bilingual Libretto, Articles: No. 14). (Illus.). 128p. 1983. pap. 9.95 (*0-7145-3938-4*) Riverrun NY.
— La Boheme in Full Score. 416p. pap. 16.95 (*0-486-25477-1*) Dover.
— La Boheme Librettos. (ENG & ITA.). 80p. 1986. pap. 4.95 (*0-7935-2229-3*, 50340200) H Leonard.
— La Boheme Opera: Vocal Score. (ENG & ITA.). 300p. 1986. pap. 24.95 (*0-7935-3852-1*, 50337870) H Leonard.
— Early Puccini for Soprano: Five Arias from Le Villi & Edgar. 32p. 1992. pap. 6.95 (*0-7935-1561-0*, 00747028) H Leonard.
— Gianni Schicchi from Il Trittico: Vocal Score. (ENG & ITA.). 1986. pap. 24.95 (*0-7935-5366-0*) H Leonard.
— Letters of Giacomo Puccini. Makin, Ena, ed. LC 71-140038. reprint ed. 32.50 (*0-404-05149-9*) AMS Pr.
— Madam Butterfly. John, Nicholas, ed. Ellcin, R. H., tr. from ITA. (English National Opera Guide Series: Bilingual Libretto, Articles: No. 26). (Illus.). (Orig.). 1984. pap. 9.95 (*0-7145-4038-2*) Riverrun NY.
— Madama Butterfly: Vocal Score. (ENG & ITA.). 1986. pap. 19.95 (*0-7935-5388-1*); pap. 24.95 (*0-7935-4416-5*, 50338200) H Leonard.
— Madama Butterfly in Full Score. 496p. 1990. pap. 19.95 (*0-486-26345-2*) Dover.
— Madama Butterfly Libretto. 64p. 1986. pap. 4.95 (*0-7935-2614-0*, 50340150) H Leonard.
— Manon Lescaut in Full Score. 496p. pap. text 22.95 (*0-486-28590-1*) Dover.
— Puccini's La Boheme. (Music (General) Ser.). 96p. 1984. pap. 2.95 (*0-486-24607-8*) Dover.
— Puccini's Madama Butterfly. (Opera Libretto Ser.). 79p. (Orig.). 1983. pap. 2.95 (*0-486-24465-2*) Dover.
— La Rodine Arias: For Soprano Canzone di Doretta Ore Dolci e Divine. 16p. 1992. pap. 5.95 (*0-7935-1571-8*, 00747029) H Leonard.
— Suor Angelica: Vocal Score. (ENG & ITA.). 1986. pap. 19.95 (*0-7935-5373-3*) H Leonard.
— Tosca. John, Nicholas, ed. & tr. by. from ITA. (English National Opera Guide Series: Bilingual Libretto, Articles: No. 16). (Illus.). 128p. (Orig.). 1982. pap. 9.95 (*0-7145-3772-1*) Riverrun NY.
— Tosca: Vocal Score. (ENG & ITA.). 320p. 1986. pap. 28.95 (*0-7935-4708-3*, 50337970) H Leonard.
— Tosca in Full Score. 448p. pap. 19.95 (*0-486-26937-X*) Dover.
— Tosca Liberetto. (ENG & ITA.). 88p. 1986. pap. 4.95 (*0-7935-2607-8*, 50340040) H Leonard.
— Il Trtfico in Full Score: "Il Tabarro"/"Suor Angelica"/"Gianni Schicchi" 416p. pap. 19.95 (*0-486-29329-7*) Dover.
— Turandot. John, Nicholas, ed. (English National Opera - Royal Opera House Guide Ser.: No. 27). (Illus.). 1984. pap. 9.95 (*0-7145-4039-0*) Riverrun NY.
— Turandot: Vocal Score. (ENG & ITA.). 1987. pap. 29.95 (*0-7935-5374-1*) H Leonard.
— Turandot Libretto. (ENG & ITA.). 1987. pap. 8.95 (*0-7935-5362-8*) H Leonard.
— Turandot Libretto. 1987. pap. 6.95 (*0-7935-5363-6*) H Leonard.
Puccini, Giacomo & Foil, David. La Boheme. (Black Dog Opera Library). (Illus.). 160p. 1996. 19.98 (*1-884822-83-5*) Blck Dog & Leventhal.
***Puccini, Michael, ed.** Our Goal Is Gold: The Official 1998 U. S. A. Hockey Team Publication: The Pictorial Profile of the U. S. A. Hockey Team. (Illus.). 200p. 1999. reprint ed. text 25.00 (*0-7881-6606-9*) DIANE Pub.
***Puccio, Kristin, et al.** Adventures in Real Problem Solving: Facilitating Creatiave Problem Solving with Primary Students. 89p. 2000. pap. 19.95 (*1-882664-61-2*) Prufrock Pr.
Puccio, Kristin, jt. auth. see Keller-Mathers, Susan.
***Pucel, David J.** Beyond Vocational Education: Career Majors, Tech Prep, Schools Within Schools, Magnet Schools & Academies. LC 00-55154. 2001. write for info. (*1-930556-04-7*) Eye On Educ.
Pucel, David J. Performance-Based Instructional Design. (C). 1989. student ed. 31.50 (*0-943919-01-0*) Perf Trning Systs.
Pucel, David J. & Fruehling, Rosemary T. Working in Teams: Interaction & Communication. LC 96-32309. 184p. (C). 1997. pap. 15.95 (*1-56118-739-9*) Paradigm MN.
— Working in Teams: Interaction & Communication. 68p. (C). 1997. pap. text, teacher ed. 8.00 (*1-56118-740-2*) Paradigm MN.
Pucelik, Frank, jt. auth. see Lewis, Byron A.
Puchala, Donald J. The Ethics of Globalism, Vol. 3. LC 96-165524. (Reports & Papers). 28p. 1995. pap. text. write for info. (*1-880660-11-3*) Acad Coun UN Syst.
— Fiscal Harmonization in the European Communities. 1992. text 45.00 (*0-86187-465-X*, Pub. by P P Pubs) Cassell & Continuum.
Puchala, Donald J., ed. see Bonanate, Luigi.
Puchala, Donald J., jt. ed. see Hopkins, Raymond F.
Puchala, Donald J., ed. see Modelski, George & Thompson, William R.
Puchala, Donald J., ed. see Most, Benjamin A. & Starr, Harvey.
Puchala, Donald J., ed. see Ray, James L.
Puchalla, Debra Durocher, ed. see Fischetti, Patrick R.
Puchalski, Steve. Slimetime: A Guide to Sleazy, Mindless, Movie Entertainment. (Illus.). 200p. (Orig.). 1996. pap. 19.95 (*0-9523288-5-2*, Pub. by Headpress) AK Pr Dist.
Puchelle, E., jt. ed. see Koch, Charles.
***Pucher, Estella.** Kidnapped! "Bitte, Wo Ist Mein Sohn?" (Illus.). 168p. 2000. write for info. (*0-9638589-4-7*) Wein Pr.
Puchkov, V. P. Political Development of Bangladesh. (C). 1989. 32.00 (*81-7050-084-2*) S Asia.
Puchner, Willy. Sally & Joe: Penguins Traveling the World. (Illus.). 82p. 1999. 19.95 (*3-8290-1412-0*, 521194) Konemann.
***Puchovsky, Milosh T.** Automatic Sprinkler Systems Handbook, 1, 8. LC 99-75956. (Illus.). 1042p. 2000. 18.00 (*0-87765-443-3*, 13HB99) Natl Fire Prot.
Puchovsky, Milosh T., et al. Fire Pump Handbook. LC 97-76287. x, 486p. 1998. 81.00 (*0-87765-431-X*) Natl Fire Prot.
Puchta, H., jt. auth. see Gerngross, G.
Puchta, Herbert & Gerngross, Gunter. Pictures in Action. 160p. (C). 1992. pap. 18.75 (*0-13-675182-2*) P-H.
Pucik, Vladimir, et al, eds. Globalizing Management: Creating & Leading the Competitive Organization. LC 92-1084. 368p. 1992. 99.95 (*0-471-50821-7*) Wiley.
Pucillo, Gladys. Medical Terminology Challenge. (Medical Terminology Ser.). 1995. 79.95 (*0-8273-7430-5*, VNR) Wiley.
Pucillo, Gladys, compiled by. God, Grant Me Serenity. 1982. 6.95 (*0-8378-2030-8*) Gibson.
— A Little Book about Baby. 1981. 6.95 (*0-8378-1932-6*) Gibson.
— A Little Book of Friendship. 1981. 5.95 (*0-8378-1931-8*) Gibson.
Puck Productions Staff. Asian-American Yellow Pages. 1999. pap. 19.95 (*0-8050-5652-1*, Owl) H Holt & Co.
— Hispanic-American Yellow Pages. 1998. pap. 19.95 (*0-8050-5651-3*, Owl) H Holt & Co.
Puck, Susan T. Sacrifice at Vicksburg: Letters from the Front. LC 96-49465. 112p. 1997. 24.95 (*1-57249-047-0*) White Mane Pub.
Puck, Theodore T. The Mammalian Cell As a Microorganism: Genetic & Biochemical Studies in Vitro. LC 73-188127. 219p. (C). 1972. 28.95 (*0-8162-6980-7*); pap. text 26.95 (*0-8162-6970-X*) Holden-Day.
Puck, Theodore T., et al. Rhythmic & Synthetic Processes in Growth. Rudnick, Dorothea, ed. LC 55-10678. (Society for the Study of Development & Growth, Symposium Ser.: 15th). 233p. reprint ed. pap. 72.30 (*0-7837-0245-0*, 204055400017) Bks Demand.
Puck, Wolfgang. The Wolfgang Puck Cookbook. LC 86-10155. (Illus.). 320p. 1986. 26.95 (*0-394-53366-6*) Random.
— The Wolfgang Puck Cookbook. (Illus.). 304p. 1996. pap. 16.00 (*0-679-76125-X*) Random.
— Wolfgang Puck's Modern French Cooking for the American Kitchen: Recipes from the James Beard Award-Winning Owner of Spago. 2nd ed. 288p. 1998. pap. 18.00 (*0-395-93520-2*) HM.
***Puck, Wolfgang & Gethers, Judy.** Wolfgang Puck's Pizza, Pasta & More! LC 00-38715. (Illus.). 224p. 2000. 35.00 (*0-679-43887-4*) Random.
Puck, Wolfgang & Trillin, Calvin. Adventures in the Kitchen. Epstein, Jason, ed. (Illus.). 264p. 1991. 34.95 (*0-394-55895-2*) Random.
Puckahtikom, Chanpen, jt. auth. see Brau, Eduard H.
Pucke, Lawrence, jt. auth. see Stark, Thomas.
Pucker, Bernard H. & St. Florian, Ilaria L., eds. A Tribute to Sandra A. Wadsworth, A. I. A. (Illus.). (Orig.). 1995. pap. write for info. (*0-9635318-1-6*, Pucker Art) Pucker Gallery.
Puckering, Gary, tr. see Jorgensen, Stig.
Puckering, R. D. & Brough, S. Electronics for Electrical Installation Engineers. (Illus.). 224p. 1992. pap. 34.95 (*0-632-03266-9*) Blackwell Sci.
Puckering, R. D. & Miller, Henry Arthur. Electrical Installation Practice, Bks. 1-3. 4th ed. LC 92-39982. (Illus.). 144p. (C). 1993. pap. text 21.95 (*0-632-02542-5*) Blackwell Sci.
Puckett. Teaching Young Children. LC 98-72360. (C). 1998. pap. text 60.50 (*0-15-503216-X*) Harcourt Coll Pubs.
Puckett, Andrew. Blood-Hound. large type ed. (Dales Mystery Ser.). 317p. 1993. pap. 18.99 (*1-85389-410-9*, Dales) Ulverscroft.
— Shadows Behind a Screen. LC 99-15491. 192p. 1999. text 20.95 (*0-312-20586-4*) St Martin.
Puckett, Andrew A. Terminus. large type ed. 368p. 1992. 27.99 (*0-7089-2751-3*) Ulverscroft.
Puckett, Anita. Seldom Ask, Never Tell: Labor & Discourse in Appalachia. LC 99-40241. No. 25. (Illus.). 256p. 2000. text 65.00 (*0-19-510277-0*) OUP.
Puckett, Ann, jt. compiled by see Kelly, Elizabeth S.
Puckett, Barry & Henderson, Helene, eds. Holidays & Festivals Index. 885p. 1995. 84.00 (*0-7808-0012-5*) Omnigraphics Inc.
Puckett, Christine S. Hoots from Owl's Hollow. 1998. pap. write for info. (*0-9633116-2-X*) Starr Pub AL.
— In My Time. 36p. 1997. pap. 3.95 (*0-9633116-1-1*, 2-97) Starr Pub AL.
Puckett, Christine S. & Barnes, Joe. A Panorama of Northeast Alabama & Etowah County: Lookout Mountain Meets the Coosa. 2nd ed. (Illus.). 136p. (Orig.). (J). (gr. 4 up). 1992. reprint ed. pap. 8.95 (*0-9633116-0-3*) Starr Pub AL.
Puckett, Dale & Dibble, Peter. The Complete Rainbow Guide to OS-9. Falk, Lawrence C. & Noe, Courtney, eds. (Illus.). 420p. (Orig.). (C). 1985. pap. 19.95 (*0-932471-00-5*) Falsoft.
— The Complete Rainbow Guide to OS-9 Level II. Arnott, JoAnne, ed. (Illus.). (Orig.). 1987. pap. 19.95 (*0-932471-09-9*) Falsoft.
Puckett, David H. Reflections from a Teacher's Heart: The Affective Side of Middle Grades Education. LC 99-11947. 40 p. 1999. write for info. (*1-56090-159-4*) Natl Middle Schl.
Puckett, David H., Sr., ed. The Blue Spaders at the Battle of Ap Gu: 31 March-1 April 1967. LC 97-67562. 28p. (Orig.). 1997. pap. write for info. (*1-890093-08-4*) Cantigny Frst Div.
Puckett, David L. John Calvin's Exegesis of the Old Testament. LC 94-31595. (Columbia Series in Reformed Theology). 192p. 1995. 19.00 (*0-664-22044-4*) Westminster John Knox.
***Puckett, G. Douglas, et al.** PPC'S Guide to Roth IRAs. 1998. ring bd. 153.00 (*0-7646-0619-0*) Prctnrs Pub Co.
Puckett, Hugh W. Germany's Women Go Forward. LC 30-8154. reprint ed. 27.50 (*0-404-05173-1*) AMS Pr.
Puckett, James H., ed. see Gibbs, Michael D.
Puckett, James M. & Reese, Hayne W., eds. Mechanisms of Everyday Cognition. (West Virginia Series on Lifespan Developmental Psychology). 256p. 1993. text 59.95 (*0-8058-0976-7*) L Erlbaum Assocs.
Puckett, Jay A., jt. auth. see Barker, Richard M.
Puckett, John L. Foxfire Reconsidered: A Twenty-Year Experiment in Progressive Education. LC 88-17106. (Illus.). 376p. 1989. text 29.95 (*0-252-01574-6*) U of Ill Pr.
Puckett, John R. Five Photo-Textual Documentaries from the Great Depression. LC 84-8536. (Studies in Photography: No. 6). (Illus.). 183p. reprint ed. pap. 56.80 (*0-8357-1582-5*, 207057100001) Bks Demand.
Puckett, Katharyn E. & Laughlin, Sara, eds. Directory of Indiana Children's Authors & Illustrators. 2nd rev. ed. 48p. 1991. pap. 6.95 (*0-9624180-1-3*) Stone Hills Area Lib Servs.
Puckett, Kelley. Batman: The Collected Adventures, Vol. 2. Kahan, Bob, ed. (Illus.). 144p. 1994. mass mkt. 5.95 (*1-56389-124-7*, Pub. by DC Comics) Time Warner.
Puckett, Kelley. Batman's Dark Secret. LC 99-15262. (Hello Reader! Ser.). (Illus.). 32p. (J). (gr. 1-3). 2000. mass mkt. 3.99 (*0-439-09551-4*) Scholastic Inc.
***Puckett, Kelley.** Batman's Dark Secret. (Hello, Reader! Ser.). (Illus.). (J). 2000. 9.44 (*0-606-18517-8*) Turtleback.
Puckett, Kelly. Batman: The Collected Adventures, Vol. 1. Kahan, Bob, ed. (Illus.). 144p. (YA). 1993. mass mkt. 5.95 (*1-56389-098-4*, Pub. by DC Comics) Time Warner.
Puckett, Kent, jt. auth. see Lindrall, Ella K.
Puckett, Kent, ed. see Rorty, Richard McKay.
Puckett, Kirby. Be the Best You Can Be. (Illus.). 40p. (J). (gr. 2 up). 1994. 14.95 (*0-931674-20-4*) Waldman Hse Pr.
Puckett, Kirby & Gutielle, Andrew. Kirby Puckett's Baseball Games. LC 96-10192. (Illus.). 112p. (J). (gr. 1-4). 1996. pap. 13.95 (*0-7611-0155-1*, 10155) Workman Pub.
Puckett, Linda J. Cast a Long Shadow. 228p. 1984. 25.00 (*0-9613539-0-2*) Jay Banks.
— Cast a Long Shadow. limited ed. 228p. 1984. 125.00 (*0-614-29825-3*) Jay Banks.
Puckett, Margaret B. & Black, Janet K. Authentic Assessment of the Young Child: Celebrating Development & Learning. 2nd ed. LC 99-35056. 384p. (Orig.). (C). 1999. pap. 37.00 (*0-13-080271-9*, Macmillan Coll) P-H.
Puckett, Margaret B., jt. auth. see Black, Janet K.
Puckett, Newbell N. Folk Beliefs of the Southern Negro. LC 68-55780. (Criminology, Law Enforcement, & Social Problems Ser.: No. 22). (Illus.). 1968. reprint ed. 35.00 (*0-87585-022-7*) Patterson Smith.
Puckett, Renee, ed. see Cerny, Laurie A.
Puckett, Richard. Windows NT Automated Deployment & Customization. LC 97-76476. 1998. pap. text 35.00 (*1-57870-045-0*) Macmillan Tech.
***Puckett, Ron.** The Presidents, the First Ladies & the Other Ladies. Brooks, Pamela, ed. (Illus.). 64p. 1999. pap. 9.95 (*1-929940-00-9*) Hert Pub Kentucky.
— Yesterday in Kentucky. (Illus.). 64p. 1999. pap. 7.95 (*1-929940-01-7*) Hert Pub Kentucky.
Puckett, Ruby. Dietary Manager Training, 1998. rev. ed. Brown, Laurel, ed. (Dietary Manager Training for Pre-Certification Ser.). (Illus.). 704p. 1998. spiral bd. write for info. (*0-9652609-1-7*) U Fla Div Cont Educ.
— Safety, Security & Sanitation for Food Service Operations, 1996. Brown, Laurel, ed. (Illus.). 336p. student ed., spiral bd. write for info. (*0-9652609-2-5*) U Fla Div Cont Educ.
Puckett, Ruby P. & Danks, Sheryl. Nutrition, Diet Modifications & Meal Patterns. 356p. (C). 1996. pap. text, per. 52.95 (*0-7872-2638-6*) Kendall-Hunt.
Puckett, Ruby P. & Norton, L. Charnette. HACCP the Future Challenge: Practical Application for the Foodservices Administrator. 195p. 1998. pap. text 75.00 (*0-9644447-6-3*) Norton Grp.
Puckett, Susan. A Cook's Tour of Iowa. LC 87-35751. (Bur Oak Original Ser.). (Illus.). 310p. 1988. pap. 16.95 (*0-87745-289-X*) U of Iowa Pr.
— Dips. (Illus.). 96p. 1995. 14.95 (*1-56352-241-1*) Longstreet.
Puckett, Susan, jt. auth. see Auchmutey, Jim.
Puckle, Bertram S. Funeral Customs: Their Origin & Development. LC 89-63010. (Illus.). xiv, 399p. 1990. reprint ed. lib. bdg. 48.00 (*1-55888-750-4*) Omnigraphics Inc.
Puckler, Furst, jt. auth. see Kameke, Rochus.
Puddephatt. Puddephatt's Primers. 110p. 1976. pap. 2.95 (*0-85032-136-0*, Pub. by C W Daniel) Natl Bk Netwk.
Puddephatt, Neal, jt. auth. see Pullein-Thompson, Diana.
Puddephatt, Noel. Homeopathic Correspondence Course: Advanced Level. 92p. 1996. reprint ed. spiral bd. 14.00 (*0-7873-1076-X*) Hlth Research.
Puddester, R. P. Catalogue of British Historical Medals. 245p. 1987. 150.00 (*0-9511308-2-X*, Pub. by R C Senior) St Mut.
Puddey & Mackay. Art Works!, Bk. 2. 1991. pap. text. write for info. (*0-582-87057-7*, Pub. by Addison-Wesley) Longman.
Puddey & MacKay. Art Works! Bk. 1. 1990. pap. text. write for info. (*0-582-86862-9*, Pub. by Addison-Wesley) Longman.
***Puddington, Arch.** Broadcasting Freedom: The Cold War Triumph of Radio Free Europe & Radio Liberty. LC 99-89785. (Illus.). 288p. 2000. 27.50 (*0-8131-2158-2*) U Pr of Ky.
***Puddlepot, Bing.** Jimmy Jonny Brownie Stays up All Night. LC 99-88135. (Illus.). 32p. (J). (ps-3). 2000. 14.95 (*0-9676148-1-3*) Bing Puddle.
Pudemat, Petra. Auslandische Direktinvestitionen Im Verarbeitenden Gewerbe Portugals: Strukturwandel Im Zuge der Europaischen Integration. (GER., Illus.). 254p. 1997. 51.95 (*3-631-31299-7*) P Lang Pubng.
Puder, Arno. Mico Is Corba: A Corba 2.0 Compliant Implementation. (C). 1998. pap. text 39.95 (*3-932588-11-8*) Morgan Kaufmann.
***Puder, Arno.** MICO is CORBA: A CORBA 2.2 Compliant Implementation. 170p. 1998. pap. 39.95 incl. cd-rom (*3-932588-42-8*) Morgan Kaufmann.
***Puder, Arno & Rhomer, Kay.** MICO: An Open Source Corba Implementation. 3rd ed. LC 99-86924. (Illus.). 180p. 2000. pap. 39.95 (*1-55860-666-1*) Morgan Kaufmann.
Puderbaugh, Tom K. Change Your Life...& Do It NOW! Seven Secret Strategies to Help You Design (& Live!) the Life of Your Dreams. LC 96-84624. (Illus.). 168p. (Orig.). 1997. pap. 14.95 (*1-889132-01-2*) Develop Dynam.
— Violence in the Workplace: Managing People in the Age of Rage. LC 96-85604. (Illus.). 80p. (Orig.). 1997. pap., wbk. ed. 24.95 (*1-889132-00-4*) Develop Dynam.
Pudlak, P., jt. auth. see Hajek, P.
Pudlak, Pavel, jt. auth. see Hajek, Petr.
Pudney, Peter, jt. auth. see Howlett, Philip.
Pudney, Warwick, jt. auth. see Whitehouse, Eliane.
PUDOC Staff. Prosea, Vol. II. Westphal, E. & Jansen, P. C., eds. 324p. (C). 1991. text 650.00 (*0-89771-634-5*, Pub. by Intl Bk Distr) St Mut.
— PROSEA Vol. I: (Pulses) Van Maesen, L. J., ed. 108p. (C). 1991. text 250.00 (*0-89771-632-9*, Pub. by Intl Bk Distr) St Mut.
— PROSEA Vol. III: (Plant Resources of South-East Asia) Siemonsma, J. S. & Wolijarni-SoetJipto, N., eds. 337p. (C). 1991. text 695.00 (*0-89771-635-3*, Pub. by Intl Bk Distr) St Mut.
— Pulses by L. J. G. Van der Maesen (Prosea No. 1) 108p. 1993. pap. 125.00 (*81-7089-150-7*, Pub. by Intl Bk Distr) St Mut.
PUDOC Staff, et al. Advances in Research & Technology of Seeds, Pts. I & II. (C). 1991. text 2500.00 (*0-89771-631-0*, Pub. by Intl Bk Distr) St Mut.
PUDOC Staff, ed. see Mannetje, L. T. & Jones, R. M.
Pudovik, A. N. Chemistry of Organophosphorus Compounds. 1990. 68.00 (*0-8493-7124-4*, QD) CRC Pr.
Pudritz, Ralph E. & Fich, Michel, eds. Galactic & Extragalactic Star Formation. (C). 1988. text 321.00 (*90-277-2725-2*) Kluwer Academic.
Pudup, Mary B., et al, eds. Appalachia in the Making. LC 94-47135. 402p. 1995. pap. text 19.95 (*0-8078-4534-5*); lib. bdg. 59.95 (*0-8078-2229-9*) U of NC Pr.
Pue & Sugarman. Lawyers Culture. 70.95 (*1-84014-766-0*) Ashgate Pub Co.
***Pue, W. Wesley, ed.** Pepper in Our Eyes: The APEC Affair. (Illus.). 232p. 2000. 32.95 (*0-7748-0779-2*, Pub. by UBC Pr) U of Wash Pr.
Puebla, Manuel De La, see De La Puebla, Manuel, ed.
Puech, Alain. Use of Anchors in Offshore Petroleum Operations. (Illus.). 160p. (C). 1984. 280.00 (*2-7108-0453-0*, Pub. by Edits Technip) Enfield Pubs NH.
— The Use of Anchors in Offshore Petroleum Operations. Marshall, Nissim, tr. from FRE. LC 84-71684. (Illus.). 155p. 1984. reprint ed. pap. 48.10 (*0-608-04201-3*, 206493600011) Bks Demand.
Puech, Claude & Reischuk, Rudiger, eds. STACS, '96: 13th Annual Symposium on Theoretical Aspects of Computer Science, Grenoble, France, February 22-24, 1996: Proceedings. LC 96-6926. (Lecture Notes in Computer Science Ser.: Vol. 1046). xii, 690p. 1996. pap. 106.00 (*3-540-60922-9*) Spr-Verlag.
Puech, Claude, jt. auth. see Sillion, Francois X.
Puech, Henri-Charles. Histoire des Religions, 3 vols. (FRE.). 1520p. 1970. 125.00 (*0-7859-4552-0*) Fr & Eur.
— Histoire des Religions, 3 vols., Vols. 1 & 2. (Historique Ser.). 59.95 (*0-686-56461-8*) Fr & Eur.
— Histoires des Religions, Vol. 2. (FRE.). 1973. lib. bdg. 130.00 (*0-7859-3820-6*) Fr & Eur.
— Histoires des Religions, Vol. 3. (FRE.). 1976. lib. bdg. 135.00 (*0-7859-3826-5*) Fr & Eur.
— Le Manicheisme: Son Fondateur, Sa Doctrine (Musee Guimet. Bibliotheque de diffusion, t. 56) LC 82-45821. (Orthodoxies & Heresies in the Early Church Ser.). reprint ed. 27.50 (*0-404-62391-3*) AMS Pr.
Puech, Mile, ed. Qumran Grotte 4: Textes Hebreux (4Q521-4Q578), 25. (Discoveries in the Judaean Desert Ser.: Vol. XXV). (Illus.). 264p. 1998. text 105.00 (*0-19-826948-X*) OUP.
Puello, Andres D. Brevisima Historia de Fray Bartolome de las Casas, Obispo de Chiapas. (Cuadernos Panamericanos Ser.). 44p. 1994. spiral bd. 11.95 (*0-9631210-2-2*) DPA Intl.
— Jose Marti en el Exilio. (SPA., Illus.). 44p. 1991. 9.95 (*0-9631210-0-6*) DPA Intl.
— Public Holidays in Latin America. (International Business Reports). 45p. 1993. spiral bd. 14.95 (*0-9631210-1-4*) DPA Intl.
— Sor Juana Ines de la Cruz, Fenix de America. (Cuadernos Panamericanos: Vol. 2). 1997. spiral bd. write for info. (*0-9631210-3-0*) DPA Intl.
***Puente.** Leopard Gecko: An Owner's Guide to a Happy, Healthy Pet. (Illus.). 128p. 2000. 12.95 (*1-58245-165-6*) Howell Bks.

Puente, Antonio E., et al, eds. Teaching Psychology in America: A History. LC 92-32027. 578p. 1992. text 34.95 (1-55798-181-7); pap. text 29.95 (1-55798-183-3) Am Psychol.

Puente, Antonio E., jt. ed. see McCaffrey, Robert J.

Puente, Debbie. Deceptively Simple: A Minimun Effort Cookbook with Very Impressive Results. 60p. (Orig.). 1996. pap. 9.95 (0-9653010-0-1) Piccolo Pr CA.
— Elegantly Easy Creme Brulee & Other Custard Desserts. LC 97-46767. (Illus.). 80p. 1998. 14.95 (1-58063-008-1) Renaissance.

Puente-Duany, N. Aventuras de Amor del Doctor Fonda (la Sombra de Helena) LC 78-73151. (Coleccion Caniqui). (Illus.). 1979. pap. 5.95 (0-89729-215-4) Ediciones.

Puente, E. A. & Nemes, L., eds. Information Control Problems in Manufacturing Technology 1989: Selected Papers from the Sixth IFAC-IFORS-IMACS Symposium, Madrid, Spain, 26-29 September 1989, 2 vols., Set. LC 90-7005. (IFAC Proceedings Ser.: No. IFPS 9013). 710p. 1990. 297.00 (0-08-037023-3, Pergamon Pr) Elsevier.

Puente, Julius I. Foreign Consul: His Juridical Status in the United States. xv, 157p. 1987. reprint ed. 34.00 (0-8377-2513-5, Rothman) W S Hein.
— International Law As Applied to Foreign States: Being an Analysis of the Juidical Status of Foreign States in American Jurisprudence. xxiii, 299p. 1983. reprint ed. 46.00 (0-8377-1017-0, Rothman) W S Hein.

Puente, Ramon. Hombres de la Revolucion: Calles. (SPA.). pap. 9.99 (968-16-4379-8, Pub. by Fondo) Continental Bk.

Puente, Rene de La, see De la Puente, Rene.

***Puente, Tito, et al.** Tito Puente: Drumming with the Mambo King. (Illus.). 200p. 2000. pap. 32.95 (0-634-01956-2) H Leonard.

Puentes, Nancy O., jt. auth. see Bresenhan, Karoline P.

***Pueppke, M. D.** Fuzzy the Cat & His Adventures in St. Augustine. 48p. (J). 1999. pap. 11.00 (0-9678352-0-8) Hlth Trust.

Puerta, A., jt. ed. see Duke, D. J.

Puerta, Mauricio, jt. auth. see Chaves, Alvaro.

Puertas-Donoso, Benjamin. Across the Footsteps of Africa: The Experiences of an Ecuadorian Doctor in Malawi & Mozambique. LC 98-34380. 265p. 1998. 69.95 (0-86543-639-8) Africa World.
— Across the Footsteps of Africa: The Experiences of an Ecuadorian Doctor in Malawi & Mozambique. LC 98-34380. 1998. pap. 19.95 (0-86543-640-1) Africa World.

Puerto, Cecilia. Latin American Women Artists, Kahlo & Look Who Else: A Selective, Annotated Bibliography, 21. LC 96-7150. (Art Reference Collection Ser.). 260p. 1996. lib. bdg. 77.95 (0-313-28934-4, Greenwood Pr) Greenwood.

Puerto Rican Forum Staff. The Puerto Rican Community Development Project. LC 74-14243. (Puerto Rican Experience Ser.). (Illus.). 162p. 1975. reprint ed. 13.95 (0-405-06230-3) Ayer.

***Puerto Rico.** Puerto Rico Insurance Laws & Related Laws. LC 98-66240. 1999. write for info. (0-89246-500-X) NILS Pub.

Puerto Rico. Office of the Commissioner of Insurance. Puerto Rico Regulations: Containing Regulations, Selected Circular Letters, & Selected Rulings of the Office of the Commissioner of Insurance. LC 97-69921. (Illus.). 1997. write for info. (0-89246-484-4) NILS Pub.

Puerto Rico, Universidad. Facultad de Humanidades,, ed. Despachos de los Consules Norteamericanos en Puerto Rico: 1818-1868, Tomo I. LC 77-12721. 1395p. 1982. 25.00 (0-8477-0845-4) U of PR Pr.

Puerto Rico. Universidad. Facultad de Humanidades., ed. Problemas de la Traduccion: Problems in Translation. LC 77-12171. 187p. 1982. pap. 5.00 (0-8477-3187-1) U of PR Pr.

Puertolas, Julio R., ed. El No Importa de Espana y la Verdad en el Potro. (Textos B Ser.: No. 15). (SPA.). 205p. 1973. pap. 51.00 (0-900411-57-0, Pub. by Tamesis Bks Ltd) Boydell & Brewer.

Puertolas, Soledad. Bordeaux (Burdeos) Gonzalez-Arias, Francisca, tr. from SPA. LC 97-21478. (European Women Writers Ser.). 275p. 1998. pap. 15.00 (0-8032-8748-8); text 35.00 (0-8032-3715-4) U of Nebr Pr.

Puertorriqueno, Ateneo. Problemas de la Cultura en Puerto Rico (Foro Auspiciado por el Ateneo Puertorriqueno En 1940) LC 76-10701. (SPA.). 272p. (Orig.). 1976. 8.00 (0-8477-2430-1) U of PR Pr.

Puerzer, Richard J., ed. see Cleland, David I. & Vlasak, A. Yaroslav.

Pues, Sylvester. I've Got Style! You've Got Style! Understanding & Teaching to Learning Styles. 65p. (Orig.). (C). 1994. teacher ed. 15.00 (1-880830-49-3) AEON-Hierophant.

Pueschel, Jeanette K. & Pueschel, Siegfried M. Sindrome de Down: Problematica Biomedica. (SPA.). 352p. 1994. pap. 55.00 (84-458-0202-X, Pub. by Ediciones Cientificas) P H Brookes.

***Pueschel, R. F., et al.** Bertreibung aus Peterswald. unabridged ed. (GER.). 118p. 1999. pap. 11.75 (0-9663968-0-4) RFP.

Pueschel, Siegfried M. An Overview of Down Syndrome. rev. ed. 26p. 1986. pap. 4.00 (0-318-22870-X, 10-6) Arc of the US.
— Sindrome de Down: Hacia un Futuro Mejor Guia Para los Padres. (SPA.). 286p. 1993. pap. 25.00 (84-345-2429-5, Pub. by Ediciones Cientificas) P H Brookes.
— The Young Child with Down Syndrome. 371p. 1984. 45.95 (0-89885-120-3, Kluwer Acad Hman Sci) Kluwer Academic.

Pueschel, Siegfried M., ed. A Parent's Guide to Down Syndrome: Toward a Brighter Future. (Illus.). 336p. (C). 1990. pap. text 22.95 (1-55766-060-3, 0603) P H Brookes.

Pueschel, Siegfried M., et al, eds. Lead Poisoning in Childhood. LC 95-41441. 1996. 31.95 (1-55766-232-0) P H Brookes.

Pueschel, Siegfried M. & Sustrova, Maria. Adolescents with Down Syndrome. LC 96-52748. 1997. 35.95 (1-55766-281-9) P H Brookes.

Pueschel, Siegfried M., et al. The Special Child: A Source Book for Parents of Children with Developmental Disabilities. 2nd ed. LC 94-1018. 464p. (Orig.). 1994. pap. 29.95 (1-55766-167-7) P H Brookes.

Pueschel, Siegfried M., jt. auth. see Pueschel, Jeanette K.

Pueschel, Siegfried M., jt. ed. see Marino, Bruno.

***Pueschul, Rudolf.** Expulsion from Czechoslovakia, 1945-46. unabridged ed. 28p. 1999. pap. 5.50 (0-9663968-2-0) RFP.

Pueschul, Rudolf, ed. & intro. see Aner, Walter.

Puett, Barbara & Apfelbaum, Jim. Golf Etiquette. (Illus.). 176p. 1992. text 12.95 (0-312-07686-X) St Martin.
— A Woman's Own Golf Book: Simple Lessons for New Golfers. LC 99-32244. 1999. text 21.95 (0-312-20393-4) St Martin.

Puett, Joseph E., Jr. LifeLines: The Esoteric Work. (Illus.). 50p. (Orig.). 1997. pap., spiral bd. 12.00 (0-9656662-6-3) LifeLines Pub.

Puett, Minnie S. History of Gaston County. LC 96-29798. (Illus.). 1998. 40.00 (0-9624488-8-5) Laney-Smith.

Puette, William J. Tale of Genji: A Reader's Guide. 196p. 1993. pap. 12.95 (0-8048-1879-7) Tuttle Pubng.
— Through Jaundiced Eyes: How the Media View Organized Labor. 240p. (Orig.). 1992. text 39.95 (0-87546-184-0, ILR Press); pap. text 16.95 (0-87546-185-9, ILR Press) Cornell U Pr.

Puetz, Belinda & Shinn, Linda J. The Nurse Consultant's Handbook. LC 96-47041. 248p. 1997. 39.95 (0-8261-9520-2) Springer Pub.

Puetz, C. J., ed. Arkansas County Maps. (Illus.). 152p. (Orig.). 1987. pap. 16.85 (0-916514-07-2) Cnty Maps.
— Florida County Maps. rev. ed. (Illus.). 160p. 1995. pap. 16.85 (0-916514-08-0) Cnty Maps.
— Indiana County Maps. rev. ed. (Illus.). 128p. 1996. pap. 16.85 (0-916514-09-9) Cnty Maps.
— Kentucky County Maps. rev. ed. (Illus.). 136p. 1997. pap. 16.85 (0-916514-10-2) Cnty Maps.
— Ohio County Maps & Recreational Guide. rev. ed. (Illus.). 136p. 1996. pap. 16.85 (0-916514-12-9) Cnty Maps.
— Pennsylvania County Maps. rev. ed. (Illus.). 144p. 1995. pap. 16.85 (0-916514-13-7) Cnty Maps.
— South Carolina County Maps. rev. ed. (Illus.). 128p. 1995. pap. 16.85 (0-916514-14-5) Cnty Maps.
— Tennessee County Maps. rev. ed. (Illus.). 144p. 1999. pap. 16.85 (0-916514-15-3) Cnty Maps.
— West Virginia County Maps. rev. ed. (Illus.). 144p. (Orig.). 1995. pap. 16.85 (0-916514-16-1) Cnty Maps.

Puetz, Cy, ed. North Carolina County Maps. rev. ed. (Illus.). 156p. 1996. pap. 16.85 (0-916514-11-0) Cnty Maps.

Puetz, Detlev, jt. ed. see Von Braun, Joachim.

Puetz, Martin & Dirven, Rene, eds. The Construal of Space in Language & Thought. LC 96-3459. (Cognitive Linguistics Research Ser.: Vol. 8). xxiii, 704p. (C). 1996. lib. bdg. 155.75 (3-11-015243-6) Mouton.

Pueyo-Mena, F. J. Biblia Romanceada: MS. BNM 10.288. 470p. 1996. 40.00 (1-56954-059-4) Hispanic Seminary.

Pueyo, X., et al, eds. Rendering Techniques, '96: Proceedings of the Eurographics Workshop in Porto, Portugal, June 17-19, 1996. (Eurographics Ser.). (Illus.). ix, 294p. 1996. pap. 89.50 (3-211-82883-4) Spr-Verlag.

Pufall, Peter, jt. ed. see Beilin, Harry.

Pufall, Peter, jt. ed. see Forman, George E.

Pufendorf, Samuel. On the Duty of Man & Citizen According to Natural Law. Tully, James, ed. Silverthorne, Michael, tr. (Cambridge Texts in the History of Political Thought Ser.). 248p. (C). 1991. text 59.95 (0-521-35195-2); pap. text 19.95 (0-521-35980-5) Cambridge U Pr.
— On the Natural State of Men. Seidler, Michael, tr. LC 89-77198. (Studies in History of Philosophy: Vol. 13). (ENG & LAT.). 152p. 1990. lib. bdg. 69.95 (0-88946-299-2) E Mellen.
— The Political Writings of Samuel Pufendorf. Carr, Craig L., ed. Seidler, Michael J., tr. 304p. 1994. text 65.00 (0-19-506560-3) OUP.

Pufendorf, Samuel & Freiherr, Von. Les Devoirs De l'Homme et Du Citoyen, 2 vols in 1. (FRE.). lii, 523p. 1992. reprint ed. write for info. incl. 3.5 hd (3-487-09562-9) G Olms Pubs.

Puff, C. Flora of Southern Africa Series, Vol. 31, Pt. 1. (Illus.). 79p. 1986. 25.00 (0-621-08876-5, Pub. by Natl Botanical Inst) Balogh.

Puff, C., ed. The Genus Paederia L: A Multidisciplinary Study. (Opera Botanica Belgica Ser.: Vol. 3). (Illus.). 376p. 1991. 87.00 (90-72619-04-8, Pub. by Natl Botanic Grdn Belgium) Balogh.

Puff, Robert E. Anger Work: Stomping Your Way Down the Path of Healing. LC 98-90860. 1999. 17.95 (0-533-12956-7) Vantage.

Puffenbarger, Charles E. Dictionary of Computer Terms. 1993. pap. 9.95 (1-882912-00-4) Sunrise TN.

Puffer, Andrew, jt. ed. see Laska, Shirley.

Puffer, J. H. & Ragland, P. C., eds. Eastern North American Mesozoic Magmatism. (Special Papers: No. 268). 1992. pap. 39.00 (0-8137-2268-3) Geol Soc.

Puffer, Sheila M. Business & Management in Russia. LC 96-431. 352p. 1996. 90.00 (1-85898-361-4) E Elgar.
— Managerial Insights from Literature. 334p. (C). 1991. 37.95 (0-534-92481-6) S-W Pub.
— Managing Across Cultures: Insights from Fiction & Practice. 390p. (C). 1996. pap. text 36.95 (1-55786-673-2) Blackwell Pubs.

Puffer, Sheila M., ed. The Russian Management Revolution: Preparing Managers for the Market Economy. LC 92-9034. 320p. (gr. 13). 1992. text 93.95 (1-56324-042-4) M E Sharpe.

Puffer, Sheila M., ed. The Russian Management Revolution: Preparing Managers for the Market Economy. LC 92-9034. 320p. (gr. 13). 1992. pap. text 42.95 (1-56324-043-2) M E Sharpe.

Puffer, Sheila M., et al, eds. Managerial Cognition & Organizational Information Vol. 3: The Cross-Functional Link of Basic & Application Research. 286p. 1985. 73.25 (0-89232-689-1) Jai Pr.

***Puffer, Sheila M., et al.** The Russian Capitalist Experiment: From State-Owned Organizations to Entrepreneurships. LC 99-45193. 296p. 2000. 90.00 (1-85898-633-8) E Elgar.

Puffer, Yvonne. Family Mini-Series. 1999. pap. text 19.95 (1-891024-12-4) Dist Art Pubs.

Puffert, Douglas J. Unrecorded Media: Industry & Trade Summary. (Illus.). 22p. (Orig.). (C). 1995. pap. text 20.00 (0-7881-2102-2) DIANE Pub.

Puffett, Derrick, tr. see Nattiez, Jean-Jacques.

Puffin Books Staff. The Night the Heads Came. (Illus.). 160p. (J). 1998. pap. 4.99 (0-14-038441-3, PuffinBks) Peng Put Young Read.

Puffin Books Staff, ed. Martina Navratilova. (Women of Our Time Ser.). (J). (gr. 2-6). 1989. pap. 3.50 (0-14-033218-9, PuffinBks) Peng Put Young Read.
— Mary McLeod Bethune. (Women of Our Time Ser.). (J). (gr. 2-6). 1989. pap. 3.50 (0-14-042219-6, PuffinBks) Peng Put Young Read.

Puffin Books Staff, ed. see Costain, Meredith.

Puffr, jt. auth. see Kubanek, V.

Puffr, Rudolf & Kubanek, V. Lactam Based Polyamides, Vol. II. 368p. 1991. lib. bdg. 225.00 (0-8493-4966-4, QD383) CRC Pr.

Puga, Alvaro & Wallace, Kendall, eds. Molecular Biology in Toxicology. LC 98-17547. 582p. 1998. text 135.00 (1-56032-592-5) Hemisp Pub.

Puga, Maria L. La Ceremonia de Iniciacion (The Initiation Ceremony) (SPA.). (YA). 1994. pap. 6.99 (968-16-4066-7, Pub. by Fondo) Continental Bk.

Pugach, Marleen. On the Border of Opportunity. LC 98-22068. 256p. 1998. write for info. (0-8058-2463-4); pap. write for info. (0-8058-2464-2) L Erlbaum Assocs.

Pugach, Marleen C. & Johnson, Lawrence J. Collaborative Practitioners, Collaborative Schools. LC 94-75177. 266p. (Orig.). (C). 1994. pap. text 36.00 (0-89108-234-4) Love Pub Co.

Pugach, Marleen C. & Warger, Cynthia L., eds. Curriculum Trends, Special Education, & Reform: Refocusing the Conversation. LC 96-9469. (Special Education Ser.: Vol. 16). 288p. (C). 1996. text 46.00 (0-8077-3563-9); pap. text 22.95 (0-8077-3562-0) Tchrs Coll.

Pugachenkova, G. A. A Museum in the Open: The Architectural Treasures of Uzbekistan. 236p. 1981. 275.00 (0-569-08712-0) St Mut.

Pugachev, V. S. Lectures on Functional Analysis & Applications. LC 99-26757. 1999. pap. text 38.00 (981-02-3723-5) World Scientific Pub.

Pugeat, M., jt. auth. see Forest, M. G.

Pugel, Thomas A. & Lindert, Peter H. International Economics. 10th ed. 272p. (C). 1996. text, student ed. 23.12 (0-256-14027-8, Irwn McGrw-H) McGrw-H Hghr Educ.

Pugel, Thomas A., jt. auth. see Lindert, Peter H.

Pugh. Britain Since 1789. LC 99-18933. 1999. pap. 18.95 (0-312-22359-5) St Martin.

***Pugh.** Britain Since 1789. LC 99-18933. 264p. 1999. text 45.00 (0-312-22358-7) St Martin.
— Sheep & Goat Medicine. 2002. text. write for info. (0-7216-9052-1, W B Saunders Co) Harcrt Hlth Sci Grp.

Pugh, A., ed. Assembly Automation. (Illus.). 450p. 1988. 153.00 (0-387-19324-3) Spr-Verlag.
— Robot Sensors: Tactile & Non-Vision, Vol. 2. (International Trends in Manufacturing Technology Ser.). 350p. 1986. 118.95 (0-387-16126-0) Spr-Verlag.
— Robot Sensors: Vision, Vol. 1. (International Trends in Manufacturing Technology Ser.). 300p. 1986. 111.95 (0-387-16125-2) Spr-Verlag.
— Robotic Technology. (Control Engineering Ser.: No. 23). 168p. 1983. boxed set 79.00 (0-86341-004-9, CE 023) INSPEC Inc.

Pugh, A., jt. auth. see Wong, A. K.

Pugh, A., jt. ed. see Warwick, K.

Pugh, A. K., jt. ed. see Mayor, Barbara.

Pugh, Aelwyn & Pugh, Lesley. Music in the Early Years. LC 97-45590. (Teaching & Learning in the First Three Years of School Ser.). 224p. (C). 1998. pap. 20.99 (0-415-14181-8) Routledge.

Pugh, Alexander L., III, jt. auth. see Richardson, George P.

Pugh, Ann & Utter, Betty. Heidi: 2-Act Musical Dramatization. LC 79-53859. (Illus.). 68p. (J). (gr. k up). 1962. pap. 4.50 (0-88680-082-X) I E Clark.
— It Happened in Hamelin: Musical Dramatization of the Pied Piper Story. (Illus.). 56p. (J). (gr. k up). 1973. pap. 4.50 (0-88680-095-1) I E Clark.

Pugh, Ann B. Across-the-Curriculum Guide for Diggy Armadillo Goes to Fort Worth Stock Show & Rodeo: 140 Creative Activites. (Illus.). 60p. (Orig.). 1992. 10.00 (1-879465-01-9) Diggy & Assocs.
— Diggy Armadillo Goes to Fort Worth Stock Show & Rodeo. LC 93-73103. (Adventures of Arnie Armadillo Ser.: Bk. 1). (ENG & SPA., Illus.). 54p. (Orig.). (J). (gr. 3-6). 1993. reprint ed. 5.00 (1-879465-00-0) Diggy & Assocs.
— Westy the Hare Goes to the National Western Stock Show & Rodeo. (ENG & SPA., Illus.). (J). 1995. 5.00 (0-9643660-0-2) Diggy & Assocs.

Pugh, Ann B., et al. Diggy Armadillo Goes to Fort Worth Stock Show & Rodeo Bk. 2: Further Adventures: "Finding Rosita" LC 93-73103. (Illus.). 54p. (J). (gr. 3-6). 1993. 5.00 (1-879465-02-7) Diggy & Assocs.

Pugh, Anthony. The Birth of a la Recherche du Temps Perdu. LC 87-80816. (French Forum Monographs: No. 68). 147p. (Orig.). 1987. pap. 13.95 (0-917058-69-0) French Forum.
— Polyhedra: A Visual Approach. LC 92-227036. 15.95 (0-86651-538-0) Seymour Pubns.

Pugh, Anthony R. Balzac's Recurrring Characters. LC 72-190348. (University of Toronto Romance Ser.: No. 24). 544p. reprint ed. pap. 168.70 (0-8357-5955-5, 202934400060) Bks Demand.
— The Composition of Pascal's Apologia. (Romance Ser.: No.49). 656p. 1984. text 75.00 (0-8020-5611-3) U of Toronto Pr.

Pugh, Barbara & Spencer, Donald W. Cemetaries of Phelps County Missouri Vol. II: Arlington, Liberty, Spring Creek, West Cold Spring Townships. rev. ed. xii, 171p. 1996. pap. 40.00 (1-893474-09-7) Phelps Cnty Gene.
— Cemeteries of Phelps County Missouri Vol. II: East Cold Spring, Dawson, North Dillon, South Dillon, North Meramec, South Meramec, St. James Townships. (Illus.). xix, 204p. 1996. pap. 40.00 (1-893474-10-0) Phelps Cnty Gene.

Pugh, Barbara, et al. The Rolla Weekly Herald, 1890-1899 Obituaries & Death Notices. i, 241p. 1989. pap. 40.00 (1-893474-11-9) Phelps Cnty Gene.

Pugh, Barbara S., jt. auth. see McFarland, Twilah S.

Pugh, Burton H. A Better Way to Make Money. (Illus.). 1987. 35.00 (0-939093-09-X) Lambert Gann Pub.
— Mastering Cotton. (Illus.). 27p. (C). 1976. pap. 25.00 (0-939093-14-6) Lambert Gann Pub.
— Science & Secrets of Wheat Trading, Vol. 6. 234p. 1980. pap. text 60.00 (0-939093-10-3) Lambert Gann Pub.
— Traders Instruction Book. (Illus.). 1980. pap. 25.00 (0-939093-08-1) Lambert Gann Pub.

Pugh, Cedric. Housing & Urbanization: A Study of India. (Illus.). 298p. (C). 1990. text 32.00 (0-8039-9655-1) Sage.

Pugh, Charles. The Griot. 288p. (YA). 1993. mass mkt. 3.95 (0-87067-697-0) Holloway.
— The Hospital Plot. Young, Billie, ed. LC 78-54163. 1979. 22.95 (0-87949-116-7) Ashley Bks.

Pugh, Charles & Day, Martyn. Pollution & Personal Injury: Toxic Torts II. 297p. 1995. 84.00 (1-874698-16-3, Pub. by Cameron May) Gaunt.
— Toxic Torts. (Environmental Law Ser.). 220p. 1992. pap. 80.00 (1-874698-00-7, Pub. by Cameron May) Gaunt.

Pugh, Clifford A., ed. see American Society of Civil Engineers, Hydraulics Di.

Pugh, Corky. Family & Friends. 112p. 1994. pap. 8.95 (0-9642888-0-X) Longbeard Pub.

***Pugh, Craig.** Ganja Tales. (Illus.). 128p. 2000. pap. 20.00 (0-9701140-0-1) Pugh Pr.

Pugh, Cynthia T. Saved, Single & Sanctified. 50p. (Orig.). 1996. pap. 5.00 (1-57502-356-3, PO1159) Morris Pubng.

Pugh, D. Michael & Tarazona, Jose V. Regulation for Chemical Safety in Europe: Analysis, Comment, & Criticism. LC 98-36875. (Environment & Policy Ser.). 1998. 105.00 (0-7923-5269-6) Kluwer Academic.

Pugh, D. S., ed. Organization Theory: Selected Readings. 4th ed. 608p. 1997. reprint ed. pap. 24.95 (0-14-025024-7, Pub. by Pnguin Bks Ltd) Trafalgar.

Pugh, D. S. & Hickson, D. J. Writers on Organizations. 4th ed. 240p. (C). 1989. text 48.00 (0-8039-3507-2); pap. text 22.95 (0-8039-3508-0) Sage.

Pugh, D. S., jt. auth. see Phillips, Estelle M.

Pugh, Darrell. Looking Back . . . Moving Forward. 140p. 1988. 27.95 (0-936678-10-0); pap. 17.95 (0-685-25268-X) Am Soc Pub Admin.

Pugh, David. The Book of Baltimore Orioles Lists. 2nd rev. ed. (Illus.). 224p. (Orig.). 1999. pap. 9.95 (1-56167-523-7) Am Literary Pr.
— Dialectic of Love: Platonism in Schiller's Aesthetics. LC 98-134402. (McGill-Queen's Studies in the History of Religion Ser.). 456p. 1997. 60.00 (0-7735-1020-6, Pub. by McG-Queens Univ Pr) CUP Services.

Pugh, David, jt. auth. see Bowen-Simpkins, Peter.

Pugh, David G. Sons of Liberty: The Masculine Mind in Nineteenth Century America, 68. LC 83-10755. (Contributions in American Studies: No. 68). 186p. 1983. 45.00 (0-313-23934-7, PSL/, Greenwood Pr) Greenwood.

Pugh, David G., et al. Proposing to Win. (Illus.). 240p. 1994. write for info. (1-57740-006-2, ILW005) Intl LrningWrk.

Pugh, David V. Schiller's Early Dramas: A Critical History. (Studies in German Literature, Linguistics & Culture). 265p. 2000. 55.00 (1-57113-153-1) Camden Hse.

Pugh, Deborah & Tietjen, Jeanie. I Have Arrived Before My Words: Autobiographical Writings of Homeless Women. LC 96-43936. 224p. (Orig.). 1997. pap. 14.00 (0-9647124-2-3) C River Pr.

Pugh, Derek. The Aston Programme, 3 vols. LC 98-73547. (Classic Research in Management Ser.). 8p. 1998. 450.95 (1-84014-057-7, Pub. by Ashgate Pub) Ashgate Pub Co.
— Unveiling Creation: Eight is the Key. 1999. pap. text 18.95 (1-886656-43-6) Sunstar Pubng.

Pugh, Derek, jt. auth. see Pugh, Nirmal.

Pugh, Derek S. & Hickson, David J., eds. Great Writers on Organisations: The Omnibus Edition. 4th ed. 396p. 1993. 49.95 (1-85521-383-4, Pub. by Dartmth Pub) Ashgate Pub Co.

An Asterisk (*) at the beginning of an entry indicates that the title is appearing for the first time.

Pugh, Derek S., et al. Writers on Organizations. 5th ed. LC 96-25180. 288p. 1996. 48.00 (*0-7619-0475-1*); pap. 22.95 (*0-7619-0476-X*) Sage.

Pugh, Derek S., jt. auth. see Phillips, Estelle M.

Pugh, Dianne G. Cold Call. Issacson, Dana, ed. 288p. 1994. mass mkt. 5.50 (*0-671-77842-0*) PB.

— Fast Friends. LC 96-36271. 320p. 1997. 22.00 (*0-671-51912-3*) PB.

— Fast Friends. 1998. per. 6.50 (*0-671-51913-1*) PB.

— Fool Proof. 1999. per. 6.50 (*0-671-01425-0*, Pocket Star Bks) PB.

— Foolproof. LC 97-52306. 344p. 1998. 23.00 (*0-671-01424-2*, PB Hardcover) PB.

— Slow Squeeze: An Iris Thorne Mystery. 1995. mass mkt. 5.99 (*0-671-77844-7*) PB.

Pugh, Donna J., et al. Judicial Rulemaking: A Compendium. LC 83-73160. 307p. 1984. lib. bdg. 59.95 (*0-313-27057-0*, U7057, Greenwood Pr) Greenwood.

Pugh, Edwin W. Charles Dickens: Apostle of the People. LC 75-176497. (Studies in Dickens: No. 52). 1971. reprint ed. lib. bdg. 75.00 (*0-8383-1364-7*) M S G Haskell Hse.

— Charles Dickens: The Apostle of the People. LC 78-148287. reprint ed. 37.50 (*0-404-08894-5*) AMS Pr.

— The Charles Dickens Originals. LC 71-148288. (Illus.). reprint ed. 48.50 (*0-404-08895-3*) AMS Pr.

Pugh, Emerson W. Building IBM: Shaping an Industry & Its Technology. LC 94-21609. 432p. 1995. 35.00 (*0-262-16147-8*) MIT Pr.

— Memories That Shaped an Industry: Decisions Leading to IBM System 360. (History of Computing Ser.). (Illus.). 336p. 1984. 35.00 (*0-262-16094-3*) MIT Pr.

***Pugh, Emerson W.** Memories That Shaped an Industry: Decisions Leading to IBM System-360. (Illus.). 323p. 2000. pap. 30.00 (*0-262-66167-5*) MIT Pr.

Pugh, Emerson W., et al. IBM's 360 & Early 370 Systems. 848p. 1991. 49.50 (*0-262-16123-0*) MIT Pr.

Pugh, Eric. Pugh's Dictionary of Acronyms & Abbreviations: Abbreviations in Management, Technology, & Information Science. 5th ed. LC 86-17352. 372p. 1987. reprint ed. pap. 115.40 (*0-608-02474-0*, 206311800004) Bks Demand.

Pugh, Francis, jt. auth. see Baynes, Ken.

Pugh, Frank & Ponick, Wes. Experiments in Basic Electronics. 2nd ed. 296p. 1989. pap. text 29.19 (*0-07-050987-5*) McGraw.

Pugh, G. Allen. Industrial Experiments Without Statistical Pain. LC 94-6301. 56p. 1994. pap. 15.00 (*0-87389-278-X*, MB101) ASQ Qual Pr.

***Pugh-Gannon, Joanne.** Encyclopedia of Sewing Machine Techniques. 224p. 1999. 34.95 (*0-8069-6393-X*) Sterling.

Pugh-Gannon, Joanne. Making the Most of Your Sewing Machine & Serger Accessories. LC 98-50985. 1999. 27.95 (*0-8069-8453-8*) Sterling.

***Pugh-Gannon, Joanne.** Serger Shortcuts: Tips, Tricks & Techniques. 128p. 1999. pap. text 14.95 (*0-8069-2455-1*) Sterling.

Pugh, Geoffrey, jt. auth. see Lange, Thomas.

***Pugh, Gillian.** Unlocking the Past: The Impact of Access to Barnardo's Childcare Records. 134p. 1999. text 56.95 (*0-7546-1040-3*, Pub. by Ashgate Pub) Ashgate Pub Co.

Pugh, Gillian, ed. Contemporary Issues in the Early Years: Working Collaboratively for Children. 176p. 1992. pap. 27.00 (*1-85396-173-6*, Pub. by P Chapman) Taylor & Francis.

— Contemporary Issues in the Early Years: Working Collaboratively for Children. 2nd ed. LC 96-223371. 272p. 1996. pap. text 24.95 (*1-85396-323-2*, Pub. by P Chapman) Taylor & Francis.

Pugh, Gillian & Hollows, Anne, eds. Child Protection in Early Childhood Services. 108p. 1995. 22.50 (*1-874579-19-9*, Pub. by Natl Childrens Bur) Paul & Co Pubs.

Pugh, Gillian, et al. Confident Parents, Confident Children: Policy & Practice in Parent Education & Support. 288p. 1995. 25.50 (*1-874579-37-7*, Pub. by Natl Childrens Bur) Paul & Co Pubs.

Pugh, Gillian, jt. auth. see Abbott, Lesley.

Pugh, Harry F. German Airborne Insignia 1956-1992. LC 92-81930. (Elite Insignia Guides Ser.). (Illus.). 128p. (Orig.). 1992. pap. 16.00 (*0-9633231-0-5*) C&D Ent.

— U. S. Special Forces Shoulder & Pocket Insignia. LC 93-72379. (Elite Insignia Guides Ser.). (Illus.). 320p. (Orig.). 1993. pap. 24.00 (*0-9633231-2-1*) C&D Ent.

Pugh, Harry F. & Bragg, Robert. Portugal Elite Forces Insignia, 1951-Present. LC 95-67552. (Elite Insignia Guides Ser.). (Illus.). 140p. (Orig.). 1995. pap. 16.00 (*0-9633231-4-8*) C&D Ent.

Pugh, Harry F. & Clark, Thomas. Canadian Airborne Insignia, 1942-Present. LC 94-70190. (Elite Insignia Guides Ser.). (Illus.). 160p. (Orig.). 1994. pap. 16.00 (*0-9633231-3-X*) C&D Ent.

Pugh, Harry F. & Piotti, Vittorio. Italian Airborne Insignia, 1938-Present. LC 92-7891. (Elite Insignia Guides Ser.). (Illus.). 224p. (Orig.). 1993. pap. 20.00 (*0-9633231-1-3*) C&D Ent.

Pugh, J. T. For Preachers Only. LC 86-10976. 192p. (Orig.). 1971. pap. 7.99 (*0-912315-35-0*) Word Aflame.

— How to Receive the Holy Ghost. 63p. (Orig.). 1969. pap. 3.99 (*0-912315-45-8*) Word Aflame.

Pugh, Jeffrey C. The Anselmic Shift: Christology & Method in Karl Barth's Theology. LC 90-34802. (American University Studies: Theology & Religion: Ser. VII, Vol. 68). XIII, 179p. (C). 1990. text 42.95 (*0-8204-1121-3*) P Lang Pubng.

Pugh, Jennie L. Colors for Living: Baths. Ragan, Sandra, ed. 128p. 1995. 24.99 (*1-56496-103-6*) Rockport Pubs.

— Colors for Living: Baths. (Colors for Living Ser.). (Illus.). 128p. 1998. pap. 19.99 (*1-56496-552-X*) Rockport Pubs.

— Colors for Living: Bedrooms. Ragan, Sandra, ed. 128p. 1996. 24.99 (*1-56496-105-2*) Rockport Pubs.

— Colors for Living: Bedrooms. (Colors for Living Ser.). (Illus.). 128p. 1998. pap. 19.99 (*1-56496-550-3*) Rockport Pubs.

Pugh, June B. & Woodard-Smith, Mary A. Nurse Manager: A Practical Guide to Better Employee Relations. 2nd ed. Eoyang, Thomas, ed. (Illus.). 125p. 1996. pap. text 14.95 (*0-7216-6445-8*, W B Saunders Co) Harcrt Hlth Sci Grp.

Pugh, Kenneth. Learn C & Save Your Job: C for COBOL Programmers. 360p. 1993. pap. 29.95 (*0-89435-431-0*) Wiley.

— UNIX for the MS-DOS User. LC 93-46801. 240p. (C). 1994. pap. text 18.80 (*0-13-146077-3*) P-H.

Pugh, Kenneth, jt. auth. see Killeen, Leslie.

Pugh, Kenneth, jt. ed. see Killeen, Leslie.

Pugh, Lesley, jt. auth. see Pugh, Aelwyn.

Pugh, Lisa & Pugh, Virginia Y. Keep Your Finger on the Boat. LC 89-84931. 104p. (Orig.). 1990. pap. 8.95 (*0-942419-01-4*) Ana Pub.

Pugh, Luise R., tr. see Gruen, Anselm.

***Pugh, Lyndon.** Change Management in Information Services. 216p. 2000. 79.95 (*0-566-08253-5*, Pub. by Ashgate Pub) Ashgate Pub Co.

Pugh, Marie-Luce. Very Simple French. 1996. pap. write for info. (*1-86034-007-5*, Pub. by Global Bks) Midpt Trade.

Pugh, Martin. Lloyd George. 1989. text 46.25 (*0-582-02387-4*, Pub. by Addison-Wesley) Longman.

— Lloyd George. (Illus.). 206p. (C). 1988. pap. text 23.95 (*0-582-55268-0*, 79762) Longman.

— The Making of Modern British Politics, 1867-1939. 2nd ed. LC 92-22093. 344p. 1993. pap. 32.95 (*0-631-17928-3*) Blackwell Pubs.

***Pugh, Martin.** The March of the Women: A Revisionist Analysis of the Campaign for Women's Suffrage, 1866-1914. 320p. 2000. text 35.00 (*0-19-820775-1*) OUP.

Pugh, Martin. State & Society: A Social & Political History of Britain, 1870-1997. 416p. 1999. pap. 45.00 (*0-340-71919-2*, Pub. by E A) OUP.

— State & Society: British Political & Social History, 1870-1992. 384p. 1995. text 74.95 (*0-340-50711-X*, B2315, Pub. by E A); pap. text 19.95 (*0-340-50710-1*, B2319, Pub. by E A) OUP.

— Women & the Women's Movement in Britain. 249p. (C). 1994. 49.95 (*1-56924-855-9*) Marlowe & Co.

***Pugh, Martin.** Women & the Women's Movement in Britain, 1914-1999. LC 00-26942. 2000. write for info. (*0-312-23491-0*) St Martin.

Pugh, Martin, ed. The Blackwell Companion to Modern European History, 1871-1945. (Illus.). 416p. (Orig.). 1997. 68.95 (*0-631-19217-4*) Blackwell Pubs.

— The Blackwell Companion to Modern European History, 1871-1945. (Illus.). 416p. (Orig.). (C). 1997. pap. text 28.95 (*0-631-19218-2*) Blackwell Pubs.

Pugh, Mary A., ed. see Price, Ronald J.

Pugh, Mary J. Providing Reference Services for Archives & Manuscripts. (Archival Fundamentals Ser.). 124p. 1992. pap. 27.00 (*0-931828-82-1*) Soc Am Archivists.

Pugh, Maud. Capon Valley: Its Pioneers & Their Descendants, 1698 to 1940. (Illus.). 350p. 1995. reprint ed. pap. 28.50 (*0-8063-4551-9*, 9292) Clearfield Co.

— Capon Valley Vol. 1 & 2: Its Pioneers & Their Descendants, 1698 to 1940, 2 vols. (Illus.). 842p. 1995. reprint ed. pap. 49.50 (*0-7884-0231-5*) Heritage Bk.

Pugh, Michael. The ANZUS Crisis, Nuclear Visiting & Deterrence. (Cambridge Studies in International Relations: No. 4). (Illus.). 304p. (C). 1989. text 69.95 (*0-521-34355-0*) Cambridge U Pr.

***Pugh, Michael.** Regeneration of War-torn Societies. LC 99-54960. 288p. 2000. text 65.00 (*0-312-23113-X*) St Martin.

Pugh, Michael, ed. Maritime Security & Peacekeeping. LC 94-28597. (Illus.). 240p. 1995. text 29.95 (*0-7190-4563-0*, Pub. by Manchester Univ Pr) St Martin.

Pugh, Michael, jt. auth. see Rushbrook, Philip.

Pugh, Michael, jt. ed. see Whitman, Jim.

Pugh, Michael C., ed. European Security - Towards Two Thousand. LC 91-4025. 200p. 1992. text 29.95 (*0-7190-3576-7*, Pub. by Manchester Univ Pr) St Martin.

— The U. N., Peace, & Force. LC 97-9826. (Cass Series in Peacekeeping: No. 2). 209p. 1997. 42.50 (*0-7146-4759-4*, Pub. by F Cass Pubs); pap. 19.50 (*0-7146-4320-3*, Pub. by F Cass Pubs) Intl Spec Bk.

Pugh, Nirmal & Pugh, Derek. Unveiling Creation. LC 97-61869. (Illus.). 400p. 1998. pap. 18.95 (*1-887472-43-6*) Sunstar Pubng.

Pugh, Olin S., jt. auth. see Kreps, Clifton H.

Pugh, Pat'rick N. Calif of Fornia. LC 93-92578. 216p. 1993. pap. 9.95 (*1-883184-08-8*) PNP.

— Cuisine Is Poetry. LC 93-92597. 1995. pap. 7.95 (*1-883184-12-6*) PNP.

— Paris on the March Thru the Heartland of California at 65 MPH. (Illus.). (Orig.). pap. 7.95 (*1-883184-17-7*) PNP.

— Poet Tree Proof! 1995. 18.00 (*1-883184-15-0*); pap. 9.95 (*1-883184-11-8*) PNP.

— Recollections of Regret. (Illus.). (Orig.). pap. 7.95 (*1-883184-16-9*) PNP.

— Sword Dance of the Generalissimos. 1995. pap. 7.95 (*1-883184-14-2*) PNP.

***Pugh, Pat'rick N.** Sword Dance of the Generalissimos. LC 99-93503. 64p. 1999. pap. 7.95 (*1-883184-22-3*) PNP.

— Usherance of an Unknown Poet. LC 99-93504. 64p. 1999. pap. 7.95 (*1-883184-23-1*) PNP.

***Pugh, Peter.** Introducing Keynesian Economics. (Illus.). 176p. 2000. pap. 11.95 (*1-84046-157-8*) Totem Bks.

— The Magic of a Name: The Rolls-Royce Story (the First Forty Years) 320p. 2000. 50.00 (*1-84046-151-9*) Totem Bks.

Pugh, R. Effective Language in Health & Social Work. (Illus.). 184p. (Orig.). 1996. pap. 54.25 (*1-56593-324-9*, 0654) Singular Publishing.

***Pugh, R. B.** Sources for Colonial Studies in the Public Record Office: Public Record Office Handbook No. 3: Records of the Colonial & Dominions Office. rev. expanded ed. Thurston, Anne, ed. (British Documents on the End of Empire Series C: Vol. 2). xi, 565p. 1998. 132.00 (*0-11-440247-7*, Pub. by Statnry Office) Balogh.

Pugh, Richard C., ed. International Income Taxation Code & Regulations: Selected Sections (1997-1998 Editions) rev. ed. 1500p. (C). 1997. pap. text 65.00 (*0-8080-0186-8*) CCH INC.

— International Income Taxation Code & Regulations - Selected Sections: 1998-1999 Edition. 1568p. 1998. pap. text 44.00 (*0-8080-0262-7*) CCH INC.

Pugh, Robert J. & Bergstrom, Lennourt, eds. Surface & Colloid Chemistry in Advanced Ceramics Processing. (Surfactant Science Ser.: Vol. 51). (Illus.). 376p. 1993. text 185.00 (*0-8247-9098-7*) Dekker.

Pugh, Ronnie. Ernest Tubb: The Texas Troubadour. LC 96-7918. (Illus.). 536p. 1996. text 29.95 (*0-8223-1859-8*) Duke.

— Ernest Tubb: The Texas Troubadour. (Illus.). 512p. 1998. pap. text 16.95 (*0-8223-2190-4*) Duke.

Pugh, S. F. An Introduction to Grain Boundary Fracture in Metals. 238p. 1991. 63.00 (*0-901462-59-4*, Pub. by Inst Materials) Ashgate Pub Co.

Pugh, Sharon L., et al. Metaphorical Ways of Knowing: The Imaginative Nature of Thought & Expression. LC 96-47982. (Illus.). 222p. (Orig.). 1997. pap. 19.95 (*0-8141-3151-4*) NCTE.

Pugh, Sharon L., jt. auth. see Pace, David.

Pugh, Sheenagh. Earth Studies & Other Voyages. 42p. 1982. pap. 7.95 (*0-907476-16-3*) Dufour.

— Id's Hospit. LC 97-205613. 64p. 1997. pap. 17.95 (*1-85411-177-9*, Pub. by Seren Bks) Dufour.

— Selected Poems. 148p. 1990. pap. 15.95 (*1-85411-029-2*, Pub. by Seren Bks) Dufour.

— Sing for the Taxman. 63p. 1993. pap. 14.95 (*1-85411-085-3*, Pub. by Seren Bks) Dufour.

***Pugh, Sheenagh.** Stonelight. 64p. 1999. pap. (*1-85411-243-0*, Pub. by Seren Bks) Dufour.

Pugh, Shirley. In One Basket. (J). 1972. 6.00 (*0-87602-140-2*) Anchorage.

***Pugh, Stefan.** A Comprehensive Grammar. LC 98-32358. (Grammars Ser.). 1999. 100.00 (*0-415-15029-9*) Routledge.

Pugh, Stefan, jt. auth. see Press, Ian.

Pugh, Stefan M. Testament to Ruthenian: A Linguistic Analysis of the Smotryc'kyj Variant. (Series in Ukrainian Studies). (Illus.). 314p. 1996. text 39.95 (*0-916458-75-X*) Harvard Ukrainian.

Pugh, Stuart. Total Design: Steps along the Way. 592p. (C). 1996. 63.00 (*0-201-63485-6*) Addison-Wesley.

Pugh, Virginia Y., jt. auth. see Pugh, Lisa.

Pugh, W. C., jt. ed. see Katz, R. L.

Pugh, Wesly, jt. auth. see Rogal, Owen.

Pugh, William O. A Good Place for Relics & Other Things: An Account of the Yakima Valley Museum & Historical Association from Its Beginnings Through 1983. (Illus.). 60p. 1987. pap. 5.00 (*1-928707-05-X*) Yakima Valley Mus.

***Pugh/Hickson.** Great Writers on Organization 2nd Edition. LC 99-58935. 1999. 65.00 (*0-7546-2041-7*) Ashgate Pub Co.

Pughe, Thomas. Comic Sense: Reading Robert Couver, Stanley.Elkin, Philip Roth. LC 94-6568. (International Cooper Series in English Language & Literature). 1994. 35.00 (*0-8176-5023-7*) Birkhauser.

Pugin, A. Welby. Floriated Ornament Designed by A. Welby Pugin. (Illus.). 72p. 1996. pap. 18.95 (*0-903685-36-1*, Pub. by R Dennis) Antique Collect.

Pugin, Augustus C. Pugin's Gothic Ornament: The Classic Sourcebook of Decorative Motifs-with 100 Plates. (Pictorial Archive Ser.). (Illus.). 112p. 1987. reprint ed. pap. 8.95 (*0-486-25500-X*) Dover.

Pugliano, Carol. Easy-to-Read Folk & Fairy Tale Plays. LC 97-148453. 56p. 1997. pap. 9.95 (*0-590-93088-5*) Scholastic Inc.

***Pugliano, Carol.** Just Right Plays: 25 Emergent Reader Plays Around the Year. 64p. 1999. pap. 10.95 (*0-439-10564-1*) Scholastic Inc.

Pugliano, Carol. 25 Just-Right Plays for Emergent Readers: Reproducible, Thematic, with Cross-Curricular Extension. 1998. pap. text 9.95 (*0-590-18945-X*) Scholastic Inc.

— 25 Spanish Plays for Emergent Readers: Reproducible-thematic-with Cross-curricular Extension Act, 1 vol. (Illus.). 64p. 1999. pap. text 10.95 (*0-439-10546-3*) Scholastic Inc.

— What's That Noise?, Level 2, No. 16. (Disney's First Readers Ser.). (Illus.). (J). (gr. 1-3). 1998. pap. 2.95 (*0-7868-4229-6*, Pub. by Disney Pr) Time Warner.

Pugliatti, Paola. Shakespeare the Historian. LC 95-31651. 224p. 1996. text 49.95 (*0-312-12840-1*) St Martin.

Pugliese, Frank. Aven'u Boys. 1994. pap. 6.95 (*0-88145-114-2*) Broadway Play.

Pugliese, Gina & Weinstein, Robert A. Issues & Controversies in Prevention & Control of VRE, Vancomycin-Resistant Enterococci. LC 98-35461. 1998. pap. write for info. (*0-9659973-1-6*) ETNA Communs.

Pugliese, M. Dicionario de Expressoes Idiomaticas: Locucoes Mas Usuais da Lingua Portuguesa. (POR.). 309p. 1981. pap. 14.95 (*0-8288-1996-3*, M14432) Fr & Eur.

Pugliese, Michael A. The Ultimate Do-It-Yourself Survival Shelter Construction Manual. rev. ed. (Illus.). 126p. (Orig.). 1994. pap. 19.95 (*1-886774-02-1*) M & M Engr.

— The Ultimate Potato Bazooka: Hair Spray Powered Vegetable Gun. 36p. 1994. pap. write for info. (*1-886774-05-6*) M & M Engr.

— The Ultimate 7.62 X 39 mm SKS-AK-47-MAX 90 Muffler Pipe Silencer Plans. (Illus.). 28p. (Orig.). pap. text. write for info. (*1-886774-00-5*) M & M Engr.

— The Ultimate SKS Full Auto Plans. (Illus.). 28p. (Orig.). pap. text. write for info. (*1-886774-01-3*) M & M Engr.

Pugliese, Patt, ed. see Pugliese, Peter T.

Pugliese, Peter T. Advanced Professional Skin Care. Pugliese, Susan et al, eds. (Illus.). 428p. (C). 1991. text 119.95 (*0-9630211-0-9*) P T Pugliese.

— Devour Disease: With Shark Liver Oil. LC 99-60314. 63p. 1999. pap. text. write for info. (*1-890694-15-0*) IMPAKT Communs.

— Skin, Sex & Longevity: The Search for Happiness. Pugliese, Patt, ed. (Illus.). 200p. 1998. mass mkt. 16.95 (*0-9630211-1-7*, 070249) P T Pugliese.

Pugliese, Ricardo M. El Matrimonio Bendecido por Dios. (Serie Guia de Bolsillo - Pocket Guides Ser.).Tr. of Marriage Blessed by God. (SPA.). 1990. pap. 2.79 (*1-56063-011-6*, 498053) Editorial Unilit.

***Pugliese, Stanislao G.** Carlo Rosselli: Socialist Heretic & Antifascist Exile. LC 99-31395. 352p. 1999. 35.00 (*0-674-00053-6*) HUP.

Pugliese, Susan, ed. see Pugliese, Peter T.

***Pugliese, Tina L.** Public Relations for Pharmacists. 150p. 2000. pap. 28.00 (*1-58212-011-0*) Am Pharm Assn.

Pugliesi, Richard. Angie's Kids. LC 96-72532. 310p. (Orig.). 1996. pap. 18.95 (*0-9653899-5-2*) Digi Print.

***Puglionesi, Peter S.** Compliance Guidance & Model Risk Management Program for Water Treatment Plants. LC 99-172628. (Illus.). 1998. write for info. (*0-89867-965-6*) Am Water Wks Assn.

Puglisi-Allegra, Stefan, ed. Psychobiology of Stress: Proceedings of the NATO Advanced Research Workshop Held in Sorrento, Italy, August 28 - September 2, 1988. (C). 1990. text 195.50 (*0-7923-0682-1*) Kluwer Academic.

***Puglisi, Catherine.** Caravaggio. 2000. pap. 39.95 (*0-7148-3966-3*) Phaidon Pr.

Puglisi, Catherine. Caraviggio. LC 99-185355. (Illus.). 400p. 1998. 59.95 (*0-7148-3416-5*) Phaidon Pr.

Puglisi, Catherine, jt. auth. see Wilson-Smith, Timothy.

Puglisi, Catherine R. The Bondmate Chronicles. LC 98-87509. 325p. 1998. pap. 15.00 (*0-7388-0100-3*) Xlibris Corp.

— Dreams of Torment. LC 98-87515. 325p. 1998. 25.00 (*0-7388-0111-9*) Xlibris Corp.

— A Framework for the Design & Implementation of Competition Law & Policy. LC 98-40938. 160p. 1998. 95.00 (*0-8213-4288-6*, 14288) World Bank.

— Haze of Joran. LC 98-87508. 325p. 1998. pap. 15.00 (*0-7388-0098-8*) Xlibris Corp.

— The King That Never Was. LC 98-88287. 325p. 1998. pap. 15.00 (*0-7388-0136-4*) Xlibris Corp.

— The Marriage Plan. LC 98-88292. 325p. 1998. pap. 15.00 (*0-7388-0146-1*) Xlibris Corp.

— Y2K. LC 98-87822. 537 p. 1998. pap. 15.00 (*0-7388-0118-6*) Xlibris Corp.

Puglisi, Catherine R. & Brooker, Alan M. Bad Blood. LC 98-87513. 325p. 1998. pap. 15.00 (*0-7388-0108-9*) Xlibris Corp.

— The Battle for Barnstable. LC 98-87514. 325p. 1998. 25.00 (*0-7388-0109-7*); pap. 15.00 (*0-7388-0110-0*) Xlibris Corp.

— Dreams of Charni. LC 98-87512. 325p. 1998. 25.00 (*0-7388-0105-4*); pap. 15.00 (*0-7388-0106-2*) Xlibris Corp.

— Dreams of Torment. LC 98-87515. 325p. 1998. pap. 15.00 (*0-7388-0112-7*) Xlibris Corp.

Puglisi, Catherine R. & Casey, Betty. Arcane America. LC 98-87854. 602 p. 1998. pap. 15.00 (*0-7388-0128-3*) Xlibris Corp.

Puglisi, Catherine R. & Espinosa, Resurreccion. Waking Dream. LC 98-86295. 140p. 1998. 25.00 (*0-7388-0061-9*); pap. 18.00 (*0-7388-0062-7*) Xlibris Corp.

Puglisi, Catherine R. & Hetherington, Grant. Evolution of the Vampire. LC 98-87511. 180p. 1998. pap. 18.00 (*0-7388-0104-6*) Xlibris Corp.

Puglisi, Catherine R., et al. Francesco Albani. LC 98-40709. (Illus.). 244p. 1999. 75.00 (*0-300-06799-2*) Yale U Pr.

Puglisi, Catherine R., jt. auth. see Brooker, Alan M.

Puglisi, Catherine R., ed. see World Bank Staff.

Puglisi, James F. The Process of Admission to Ordained Ministry Vol. 2: Reformed, Anglican, Lutheran, & Wesylan Rites. Misrahi, Mary M., tr. (Reformed Anglican, Lutheran, & Wesleyan Rites Ser.). 252p. (Orig.). 1997. pap. text 39.95 (*0-8146-6129-7*, Pueblo Bks) Liturgical Pr.

— The Process of Admission to Ordained Ministry Vol. 3: A Comparative Study: The Contemporary Rites & General Conclusions. 1999. pap. 39.95 (*0-8146-6130-0*, M Glazier) Liturgical Pr.

— The Process of Admission to Ordained Ministry, a Comparative Study Vol. 1: Epistemological Principles & Roman Catholic Rites. Driscoll, Michael S. & Misrahi, Mary M., trs. (Process of Admission to Ordained Ministry Ser.). 278p. (Orig.). 1996. pap. 39.95 (*0-8146-6128-9*, M Glazier) Liturgical Pr.

***Puglisi, James F., ed.** Petrine Ministry & the Unity of the Church: Toward a Patient & Fraternal Dialogue. LC 98-33867. 211p. 1999. pap. 19.95 (*0-8146-5936-5*) Liturgical Pr.

***Puglisi, Luigi Prestinenza.** Hyper Architecture: Space in the Electronic Age. LC 99-42387. 96p. 1999. pap. 12.50 (*3-7643-6093-3*) Birkhauser.

Puglisi, M., et al, eds. New Techniques for Future Accelerators. LC 87-20248. (Ettore Majorana International Science Series, Life Sciences: Vol. 29). (Illus.). 292p. 1987. 85.00 (*0-306-42608-0*, Plenum Trade) Perseus Pubng.

— New Techniques for Future Accelerators II: RF &

Microwave Systems. (Ettore Majorana International Science Series, Life Sciences: Vol. 36). (Illus.). 322p. 1989. 95.00 (0-306-43090-8, Plenum Trade) Perseus Pubng.

Puglisi, Michael J. Puritans Beseiged: The Legacies of King Philip's War in the Massachusetts Bay Colony. 256p. (Orig.). 1991. pap. text 28.00 (0-8191-8291-5); lib. bdg. 51.50 (0-8191-8278-8) U Pr of Amer.

Puglisi, Michael J., ed. Diversity & Accomodation: Essays on the Cultural Composition of the Virginia Frontier. LC 96-35612. (Illus.). 324p. 1997. 45.00 (0-87049-969-6) U of Tenn Pr.

Puglisi, Steven E. First Lights. 64p. (Orig.). 1990. pap. 8.00 (0-937179-06-X) Blue Scarab.

***Pugmire, David.** Rediscovering Emotion. 2000. pap. 28.00 (0-7486-1126-6, Pub. by Edinburgh U Pr) Col U Pr.

Pugmire-Stoy, M. C. Spontaneous Play in Early Childhood. 128p. (C). 1991. mass mkt. 24.75 (0-8273-3660-8) Delmar.

— Spontaneous Play in Early Childhood. 128p. 1992. teacher ed. 10.50 (0-8273-3661-6) Delmar.

Pugmireoffers, Jennifer, jt. auth. see Woolley, Deborah J.

Pugnaire & Valladares, eds. Handbook of Functional Plant Ecology. LC 99-18797. (Books in Soils, Plants & the Environment Ser.). (Illus.). 920p. 1999. text 250.00 (0-8247-1950-6) Dekker.

Pugne, Melina S. The Communication Planning Process in the Philippine Commission on Population. (East-West Communication Institute Case Studies: No. 6). xii, 136p. (Orig.). 1983. pap. 5.00 (0-86638-005-1) EW Ctr HI.

Pugnetti, Gino. Mozart: Portraits of Greatness. Lawrence, Helen, tr. from ITA. (Illus.). 75p. 1989. reprint ed. 17.50 (0-918367-35-2); reprint ed. pap. 12.50 (0-918367-29-8) Elite.

Pugni, Johanna, et al. ESL: Beginner Level. 256p. Date not set. pap. 22.95 incl. audio (0-87891-083-2) Res & Educ.

Pugsley, Betty C., jt. auth. see Pugsley, Richard J.

Pugsley, Christopher, jt. auth. see Moses, John A.

Pugsley, Clement. In Sorrow's Lone Hour. (C). 1990. pap. 24.00 (0-85305-104-6, Pub. by Arthur James) St Mut.

Pugsley, John. The Twilight of the Gene: From Genesis to Genocide. 240p. 1998. pap. 19.95 (1-85756-397-2, Pub. by Janus Pubng) Paul & Co Pubs.

Pugsley, Keith. Enquiries of Local Authorities: A Practical Guide. 192p. 1991. 60.00 (1-85190-133-7) St Mut.

— Enquiries of Local Authorities: A Practical Guide. 3rd ed. 196p. (C). 1994. pap. 125.00 (0-85459-947-9, Pub. by Tolley Pubng) St Mut.

Pugsley, M. Neil, jt. auth. see Bannerman, Glenn Q.

Pugsley, Michael K., jt. ed. see Walker, Michael J.

Pugsley, Richard J. & Pugsley, Betty C. The Sound Eternal: Two Opinionated Musicians Discover the Gregorian Chant, 2 vols. Incl. Vol. I. Sound Eternal. LC 87-61191. 1987. pap. 9.95 (0-941478-50-5); LC 87-61191. 1987. Set pap. 18.95 (0-941478-92-0) Paraclete MA.

Pugsley, Steven, ed. Devon Gardens: An Historical Survey. (Illus.). 192p. 1994. 35.95 (0-7509-0055-5, Pub. by Sutton Pub Ltd) Intl Pubs Mktg.

Puhakka, Kaisa. Knowledge & Reality: A Comparative. (C). 1994. text 8.00 (81-208-1174-7, Pub. by Motilal Bnarsidass) S Asia.

Puhala, Bob. 52 Illinois Weekends. (52 Weekends Ser.). (Illus.). 180p. (Orig.). 1995. pap. 9.95 (1-56626-083-3, Cntry Rds Pr) NTC Contemp Pub Co.

***Puhala, Bob.** 52 Illinois Weekends: Great Getaways & Adventures for Every Season. 2nd ed. LC 98-34155. (Fifty-Two... Weekends Ser.). (Illus.). 256p. (Orig.). 1998. pap. 14.95 (1-56626-133-3, 61333, Cntry Rds Pr) NTC Contemp Pub Co.

Puhala, Bob. 52 Michigan Weekends. 2nd rev. ed. LC 97-2222. (52 Weekends Ser.). (Illus.). 200p. 1997. pap. 14.95 (1-56626-180-5, Cntry Rds Pr) NTC Contemp Pub Co.

— 52 Michigan Weekends. 3rd ed. LC 99-51809. (Fifty-Two... Weekends Ser.). 184p. 1999. pap. 14.95 (1-56626-147-3, 61473, Cntry Rds Pr) NTC Contemp Pub Co.

— 52 Wisconsin Weekends. LC 93-30998. (52 Weekends Ser.). (Illus.). 148p. (Orig.). 1993. pap. 9.95 (1-56626-057-4, Cntry Rds Pr) NTC Contemp Pub Co.

— 52 Wisconsin Weekends. 2nd rev. ed. LC 97-2220. (52 Weekends Ser.). (Illus.). 180p. (Orig.). 1997. pap. 14.95 (1-56626-181-3, Cntry Rds Pr) NTC Contemp Pub Co.

***Puhala, Bob.** Recommended Country Inns: The Midwest. 7th ed. (Recommended Country Inns Ser.). 356p. 1999. pap. text 16.95 (0-7627-0296-6) Globe Pequot.

— Wisconsin: Great Getaways & Adventures for Every Season. 3rd ed. LC 99-29876. (Fifty-Two... Weekends Ser.). (Illus.). 176p. (Orig.). 1993. reprint ed. pap. 14.95 (1-56626-027-2, 60272, Cntry Rds Pr) NTC Contemp Pub Co.

***Puhallo, Mike.** Meadow Muffins Vol. 1: Cowboy Rhymes & Other B. S. (Illus.). 64p. 1999. pap. 7.95 (0-88839-436-5) Hancock House.

Puhallo, Mike & Brannon, Brian. Can't Stop Rhymin' on the Range. (Illus.). 64p. 1997. pap. 7.95 (0-88839-398-9) Hancock House.

— Still Rhymin' on the Range. (Illus.). 64p. 1996. pap. 7.95 (0-88839-388-1) Hancock House.

Puhallo, Mike, et al. Rhymes on the Range. 64p. 1995. pap. 6.95 (0-88839-368-7) Hancock House.

Puhalo, Lazar. Akathist Hymn for Our Lady, Joy of Canada. 24p. Date not set. pap. 5.00 (1-879038-77-3, 9047) Synaxis Pr.

— Auke Lake Tales. (Illus.). 50p. (J). (gr. k-6). Date not set. pap. 5.50 (1-879038-86-2, 9056) Synaxis Pr.

— Baptism & Ekonomy. 28p. Date not set. pap. 3.50 (1-879038-65-X, 9035) Synaxis Pr.

— Basil the Elder. Date not set. pap. 6.00 (1-879038-87-0, 9057) Synaxis Pr.

— The Beginning & the End. 55p. Date not set. pap. 5.00 (1-879038-76-5, 9046) Synaxis Pr.

— Creation & Fall. 36p. (Orig.). 1986. pap. text 4.00 (0-913026-97-2) Synaxis Pr.

— The Creation & Fall. 54p. Date not set. pap. 5.00 (1-879038-70-6, 9040) Synaxis Pr.

— Cycle of Orthodox Divine Services. 32p. Date not set. pap. 4.00 (1-879038-67-6, 9037) Synaxis Pr.

— Evidence of Things Not Seen. 63p. Date not set. pap. 8.00 (1-879038-89-7, 9059) Synaxis Pr.

— Gender As Prophecy & Revelation. Date not set. pap. 4.00 (1-879038-96-X, 9062) Synaxis Pr.

— Guardian Angel: Contemplations. 47p. Date not set. pap. 6.00 (1-879038-50-1, 9019) Synaxis Pr.

— Ikon As Scripture. (Illus.). 54p. Date not set. pap. write for info. (1-879038-55-2, 9025) Synaxis Pr.

— Ikon Corner Prayer Book. 21p. Date not set. pap. 4.00 (1-879038-80-3, 9050) Synaxis Pr.

— Infant Baptism. 42p. Date not set. pap. 3.50 (1-879038-58-7, 9028) Synaxis Pr.

— Innokenty of Alaska. (Illus.). 86p. (Orig.). (J). (gr. 8 up). 1986. pap. 5.00 (0-913026-86-7) Synaxis Pr.

— Lives of Saints for Young People: Twelve Saints. 28p. (YA). (gr. 7-12). Date not set. pap. 4.50 (1-879038-34-X, 9002) Synaxis Pr.

— Lives of Saints for Young People: Twelve Saints, Vol. 1. 28p. (YA). (gr. 7-12). Date not set. pap. 4.50 (1-879038-33-1, 9001) Synaxis Pr.

— Lives of Saints for Young People: Twelve Saints, Vol. 3. 32p. (YA). (gr. 7-12). Date not set. pap. 4.50 (1-879038-35-8, 9003) Synaxis Pr.

— Lives of Saints for Young People: Twelve Saints, Vol. 4. 42p. (YA). (gr. 7-12). Date not set. pap. 4.50 (1-879038-36-6, 9004) Synaxis Pr.

— Lives of Saints for Young People: Twelve Saints, Vol. 5. 32p. (YA). (gr. 7-12). Date not set. pap. 4.50 (1-879038-37-4, 9005) Synaxis Pr.

— Lives of Saints for Young People: Twelve Saints, Vol. 6. 28p. (YA). (gr. 7-12). Date not set. pap. 4.50 (1-879038-38-2, 9006) Synaxis Pr.

— Lives of Saints for Young People: Twelve Saints, Vol. 7. 78p. (YA). (gr. 7-12). Date not set. pap. 6.50 (1-879038-39-0, 9007) Synaxis Pr.

— Lives of Saints for Young People: Twelve Saints, Vol. 8. 32p. (YA). (gr. 7-12). Date not set. pap. write for info. (1-879038-40-4, 9008) Synaxis Pr.

— Lives of Saints for Young People: Twelve Saints, Vol. 9. 28p. (YA). (gr. 7-12). Date not set. pap. 4.50 (1-879038-41-2, 9009) Synaxis Pr.

— Lives of Saints for Young People: Twelve Saints, Vol. 10. 28p. (YA). (gr. 7-12). Date not set. pap. write for info. (1-879038-42-0, 9010) Synaxis Pr.

— Meaning of Mysticism. 48p. Date not set. pap. write for info. (1-879038-63-3, 9033) Synaxis Pr.

— Missionary Handbook. 42p. (Orig.). Date not set. pap. 5.50 (1-879038-57-9, 9027) Synaxis Pr.

— Missionary Handbook. 49p. (Orig.). 1985. pap. text 3.00 (0-911523-00-6) Synaxis Pr.

— Most Holy Theotokos: Contemplations. 57p. Date not set. pap. 6.00 (1-879038-51-X, 9020) Synaxis Pr.

— Mystery & Meaning of Love & Marriage. 45p. Date not set. pap. 4.00 (1-879038-54-4, 9024) Synaxis Pr.

— On Angels. 32p. Date not set. pap. 3.50 (1-879038-60-9, 9030) Synaxis Pr.

— On Commemoration of the Dead. 40p. Date not set. pap. 5.00 (1-879038-95-1, 9061) Synaxis Pr.

— On Evil Spirits. 28p. Date not set. pap. 4.00 (1-879038-61-7, 9031) Synaxis Pr.

— On Fasting. 36p. Date not set. pap. 5.00 (1-879038-59-5, 9029) Synaxis Pr.

— Out-of-Body Experiences. 32p. Date not set. pap. 4.00 (1-879038-64-1, 9034) Synaxis Pr.

— Paschal Service: Hymnal. 52p. Date not set. pap. 6.00 (1-879038-78-1, 9048) Synaxis Pr.

— Sacraments or Holy Mysteries. 24p. Date not set. pap. 4.00 (1-879038-66-8, 9036) Synaxis Pr.

— Scriptural & Spiritual Meaning of Monasticism. 38p. Date not set. pap. 4.00 (1-879038-62-5, 9032) Synaxis Pr.

— Scripture & the Divine Liturgy: Scripture in the Liturgy. 60p. Date not set. pap. 5.50 (1-879038-94-3, 9060) Synaxis Pr.

— Sermons on Matthew. 67p. Date not set. pap. 5.00 (1-879038-71-4, 9041) Synaxis Pr.

— Soul, Body & Death. 94p. Date not set. pap. 8.00 (1-879038-68-4, 9038) Synaxis Pr.

— The Soul, the Body & Death. 2nd ed. 1989. pap. 8.00 (0-911523-03-0) Synaxis Pr.

— Twelve Great Feast Days. (Illus.). 45p. (J). Date not set. pap. 5.00 (1-879038-43-9, 9011) Synaxis Pr.

— Veneration of the Theotokos. 38p. Date not set. pap. 4.00 (1-879038-56-0, 9026) Synaxis Pr.

Puhalo, Lazar, ed. Paschal Service: Priest's Service Book. 55p. Date not set. pap. 6.00 (1-879038-79-X, 9049) Synaxis Pr.

Puhalo, Lazar, jt. auth. see Veniaminox, Innocent.

Puhalo, Lazar, tr. see Khrapovitsky, Antony.

Puhalo, Ron, Jr. Morning Dew: Contemplations. 48p. Date not set. pap. 5.00 (1-879038-52-8, 9021) Synaxis Pr.

***Puhani, P. A.** Evaluating Active Labour Market Policies: Empirical Evidence for Poland During Transition. LC 99-50368. (ZEW Economic Studies: Vol. 5). (Illus.). xvi, 239p. 1999. pap. 67.00 (3-7908-1234-X) Spr-Verlag.

***Puhe, J., et al.** Global Climate Change & Human Impacts on Forest Ecosystems: Postglacial Development, Present Situation & Future Trends in Central Europe. LC 00-41037. (Ecological Studies). 2000. write for info. (3-540-67127-7) Spr-Verlag.

Puhek, Ronald E. The Abyss Absolute: The Autobiography of a Suicide. 146p. 1998. pap. 10.00 (1-892590-07-7) Out Your Bk.

— A Guide to the Nature & Practice of Seminars in Integrative Studies. 145p. 1998. pap. 10.00 (1-892590-09-3) Out Your Bk.

— Killer Competitiveness. 130p. 1998. pap. 10.00 (1-892590-08-5) Out Your Bk.

— Meaning & Creativity. 118p. 1998. pap. 10.00 (1-892590-06-9) Out Your Bk.

— The Metaphysical Imperative: A Critique of the Modern Approach to Science. 2nd ed. 135p. 1998. pap. 10.00 (1-892590-03-4) Out Your Bk.

— Mind, Soul & Spirit: An Inquiry into the Spiritual Derailments of Modern Life. 148p. 1998. pap. 10.00 (1-892590-02-6) Out Your Bk.

— The Powers of Knowledge. 83p. 1998. pap. 10.00 (1-892590-04-2) Out Your Bk.

— Social Consciousness: Renewed Theory in the Social Sciences. 202p. 1998. pap. 10.00 (1-892590-00-X) Out Your Bk.

— Spiritual Meditations. 171p. 1998. pap. 10.00 (1-892590-10-7) Out Your Bk.

— Stephen of the Holy Mountain. 94p. 1998. pap. 10.00 (1-892590-01-8) Out Your Bk.

— Violence. 82p. 1998. pap. 10.00 (1-892590-05-0) Out Your Bk.

Puhk, Heino. Estonia Estonorum Eesti 1940: Ajalooline Geograafia (Historical Geography) LC 96-68141.Tr. of Estonia of the Estonians Estonia 1940 Historical Geography. (EST., Illus.). 571p. 1996. 135.00 (0-9652245-0-3) Heino Puhk.

Puhl, Albert E. Remembrances: A Russian Family Migrates from the Steppes of Russia to Colorado, the Puhl Family. (Illus.). 196p. 1998. pap. 25.00 (0-9653419-2-5) Lazuli Pr.

Puhl, Jacqueline L. & Brown, C. Harmon, eds. The Menstrual Cycle & Physical Activity: Proceedings of the Seminar Held February 24-26, 1984, at the Olympic Training Center, Colorado Springs, Colorado, under Sponsorship of the U. S. Olympic Committee Sports Medicine Council in Cooperation with Tampax Incorporated. LC 85-22427. (Illus.). 174p. reprint ed. pap. 54.00 (0-608-07036-X, 206724300009) Bks Demand.

Puhl, Jacqueline L., ed. see Women & Sports Science Conference (1985, Colorado Springs, CO) Staff.

Puhl, Klaus, ed. Meaning Scepticism. (Foundations of Communication & Cognition Ser.). ix, 258p. (C). 1991. lib. bdg. 109.25 (3-11-011833-5) De Gruyter.

Puhl, Louis J. The Spiritual Exercises of St. Ignatius: Based on Studies in the Language of the Autograph. (Request Reprint Ser.). (SPA.). 216p. 1968. pap., per. 5.95 (0-8294-0065-6, PUHL) Loyola Pr.

Puhl, Susan M., jt. ed. see Buskirk, Elsworth R.

Puhler, A., ed. see Timmis, K. N.

Puhn, Adele. The 5-Day Miracle Diet. 1997. pap. 6.00 (0-345-40909-4); mass mkt. 6.99 (0-345-41998-7) Ballantine Pub Grp.

— 5-Day Miracle Diet. 1998. mass mkt. 6.99 (0-345-91314-0) Ballantine Pub Grp.

— The 5-Day Miracle Diet: Conquer Food Cravings, Lose Weight, & Feel Better Than You Ever Have in Your Life! 1996. 22.00 (0-614-96793-7) Ballantine Pub Grp.

— Healing from the Inside Out: A Natural Health Program That Reveals the True & Surprising Source of Your Symptoms. LC 97-30085. 288p. 1998. 25.00 (0-345-41990-1) Ballantine Pub Grp.

— Healing from the Inside Out: A Natural Health Program That Reveals the Truth - And Surprising - Source of Your Symptoms. 1999. pap. 14.00 (0-345-41991-X) Ballantine Pub Grp.

Puhvel, Jaan. Comparative Mythology. LC 86-20882. (Illus.). 320p. 1989. reprint ed. pap. text 16.95 (0-8018-3938-6) Johns Hopkins.

— Hittite Etymological Dictionary Vol. 3: Words Beginning with H. (Trends in Linguistics, Documentation Ser.: No. 14). x, 462p. 1991. 168.00 (3-11-011547-6) Mouton.

— Hittite Etymological Dictionary Vol. 4: Words Beginning with K. (Trends in Linguistics Ser.: Vol. 14). x, 333p. (C). 1997. lib. bdg. 183.70 (3-11-015491-9) Mouton.

— Hittite Etymological Dictionary, Vol. 3: Words Beginning with H. (Trends in Linguistics, Documentation Ser.: No. 5). x, 462p. (C). 1991. lib. bdg. 183.10 (0-89925-431-4) Mouton.

Puhvel, Jaan, et al. Indo-European Religion after Dumezil. LC 96-183883. (Journal of Indo-European Studies: Vol. 16). (ENG & FRE.). 212p. (C). 1996. pap. text 36.00 (0-941694-51-8) Inst Study Man.

Puhvel, Madli, tr. see Tode, Emil.

Puhvel, Martin. Beowulf & Celtic Tradition. LC 80-473645. ix, 142 p. 1979. write for info. (0-88920-063-7) W Laurier U Pr.

Puhvel, Martin. The Crossroads in Folklore & Myth. (American University Studies: English Language & Literature: Ser. IV, Vol. 88). XIII, 131p. (C). 1989. text 31.75 (0-8204-0839-5) P Lang Pubng.

Pui, Ching-Hon, ed. Childhood Leukemias. LC 98-46407. (Illus.). 600p. (C). 1999. text 120.00 (0-521-58176-1) Cambridge U Pr.

Pui-Lan, Kwok. Chinese Women & Christianity, 1860-1927. (American Academy of Religion Academy Ser.). 229p. (C). 1992. 29.95 (1-55540-669-6, 010175) OUP.

Pui-Lan, Kwok. Chinese Women & Christianity, 1860-1927. (American Academy of Religion Academy Ser.). 229p. (C). 1992. pap. 19.95 (1-55540-670-X) OUP.

Pui-Lan, Kwok. Discovering the Bible in the Non-Biblical World. LC 95-10028. (Bible & Liberation Ser.). 160p. (Orig.). 1995. pap. 17.00 (0-88344-997-8) Orbis Bks.

Pui-Lan, Kwok, jt. ed. see Fiorenza, Elizabeth S.

Puia. Case-Chateau de Charmes Wines Limited. (GC - Principles of Management Ser.). (C). 1997. pap. 3.50 (0-538-88012-0) S-W Pub.

— Case-Salary Supplements. (GC - Principles of Management Ser.). (C). 1997. pap. 3.50 (0-538-88018-X) S-W Pub.

— Case-Westbrook Farm. (GC - Principles of Management Ser.). (C). 1997. pap. 3.50 (0-538-88014-7) S-W Pub.

Puig, Evelyn. Chico the Street Boy. (Illus.). 85p. (J). (gr. 4-8). 1984. 3.95 (0-901269-79-4) Grosvenor USA.

Puig, Idoya, ed. see Casas, Luis Puig.

Puig, J. J., jt. auth. see Parramon, J. M.

Puig, L. On the Local Structure of Morita & Rickard Equivalences Between Brauer Blocks. LC 99-15831. (Progress in Mathematics Ser.: Vol. 178). 268p. 1999. 98.00 (3-7643-6156-5) Birkhauser.

Puig, Manuel. El Beso de la Mujer Arana.Tr. of Kiss of the Spider Woman. (SPA.). pap. 12.95 (84-322-3026-X, Pub. by E Seix Barral) Continental Bk.

— El Beso de la Mujer Arana.Tr. of Kiss of the Spider Woman. (SPA.). 304p. 1994. pap. 12.00 (0-679-75545-4) Vin Bks.

— El Beso de la Mujer Arana. 12th ed.Tr. of Kiss of the Spider Woman. (SPA.). 287p. 1992. pap. 14.95 (0-7859-0562-6, 843223026X) Fr & Eur.

— Blood of Requited Love. Grayson, Jan L., tr. from SPA. LC 99-30998. 202p. 1999. pap. 15.95 (0-8166-3535-8, Pub. by U of Minn Pr) Chicago Distribution Ctr.

— Boquitas Pintadas. (SPA.). 240p. 1996. pap. 11.95 (0-14-025579-6, Viking) Viking Penguin.

Puig, Manuel. The Buenos Aires Affair: A Detective Novel. (SPA.). 1997. pap. 7.95 (84-322-3031-6, Pub. by E Seix Barral) Continental Bk.

Puig, Manuel. Eternal Curse on the Reader of These Pages. LC 99-31003. 240p. 1999. pap. 15.95 (0-8166-3536-6, Pub. by U of Minn Pr) Chicago Distribution Ctr.

— Heartbreak Tango: A Serial. LC 96-204566. 224p. 1996. pap. 11.95 (0-14-018997-1, Viking) Viking Penguin.

— Kiss of the Spider Woman. LC 90-50626. Orig. Title: El Beso De la Mujer Arana. 23.95 (0-8488-0614-X) Amereon Ltd.

Puig, Manuel. Kiss of the Spider Woman. Colchie, Thomas, tr. from SPA. LC 90-50626. Orig. Title: El Beso De la Mujer Arana. 288p. 1991. pap. 13.00 (0-679-72449-4) Vin Bks.

— Pubis Angelical. 2000. pap. write for info. (0-8166-3681-8) U of Minn Pr.

— Tropical Night Falling. Levine, Suzanne J., tr. 192p. 1993. pap. 8.95 (0-393-30908-8) Norton.

Puig, Manuel. Under a Mantle of Stars. rev. ed. Christ, Ronald J., tr.Tr. of Bajo un Manto de Estrellas. 64p. (Orig.). 1993. pap. 10.00 (0-930829-32-8) Lumen Inc.

Puig, Manuel, et al. Drama Contemporary: Latin America. Woodyard, G. W., ed. 224p. 1986. pap. 16.95 (1-55554-005-8) PAJ Pubns.

— Kiss of the Spider Woman & Two Other Plays. LC 94-6549. 1994. pap. 10.95 (0-393-31148-1) Norton.

Puig, Olive De, see De Puig, Olive.

Puig-Pey, J. Computer Aided Engineering Systems Handbook. (Illus.). 650p. 1987. 287.95 (0-387-17936-4) Spr-Verlag.

Puig-Pey, J. & Brebbia, Carlos A., eds. Computer Aided Engineering Systems Handbook, Vol. 2. LC 87-70842. 280p. 1987. 75.00 (0-931215-25-0) Computational Mech MA.

Puig Torne, Juan. Computers Dictionary: Diccionario de Informatica. 2nd ed. (SPA.). 208p. 1986. pap. 19.00 (0-7859-4926-7) Fr & Eur.

Puig Zaldivar, Raquel. Roberto Va de Pesco (Robert Goes Fishing) (Illus.). 32p. (J). (gr. 1-3). 1992. 12.95 (1-880507-00-5) Lectorum Pubns.

— Women Don't Need to Write. 1998. pap. 13.95 (1-55885-257-3) Arte Publico.

Puigdefabergas, C., jt. ed. see Marzo, M.

Puigdomenech, Ignasi, jt. ed. see Grenthe, Ingmarr.

Puigdomenech, Pedro, jt. ed. see Coruzzi, Gloria.

Puiggros, Adriana. Neoliberalism & Education in Latin America. LC 98-49326. 224p. 1999. text 69.00 (0-8133-2909-4, Pub. by Westview) HarpC.

— Neoliberalism & Education in Latin America. 2000. pap. 20.00 (0-8133-2910-8) Westview.

Puigjaner, R., et al, eds. Computer Performance Evaluation: 10th International Conference, Tools'98, Palma de Mallorca, Spain, September 14-18, 1998, Proceedings. Modelling Techniques & Tools. (Lecture Notes in Computer Science Ser.: Vol. 1469). xiii, 376p. 1998. pap. 59.00 (3-546-49492-X) Spr-Verlag.

— Computer Performance Evaluation: 10th International Conference, Tools'98, Palma de Mallorca, Spain, September 14-18, 1998, Proceedings. Modelling Techniques & Tools, Vol. 146. LC 98-38789. (Lecture Notes in Computer Science Ser.: Vol. 1469). xiii, 376p. 1998. pap. 59.00 (3-540-64949-2) Spr-Verlag.

Puigjaner, R. & Potier, D., eds. Modeling Techniques & Tools for Computer Performance Evaluation. (Illus.). 466p. 1989. 110.00 (0-306-43368-0, Plenum Trade) Perseus Pubng.

Puije, Patrick D. Van Der, see Van Der Puije, Patrick D.

Puije, Patrick Van der, see Elgerd, Olle I.

Puippe, Jean-Claude & Leaman, Frank. Theory & Practice of Pulse Plating. (Illus.). 250p. 1986. 57.00 (0-936569-02-6); pap. 47.00 (0-936569-01-8) Am Electro Surface.

Puisis, Michael. Clinical Practice in Correctional Medicine. LC 98-34369. (Illus.). 450p. (C). (gr. 13). 1998. text 86.00 (0-8151-2704-9, 31339) Mosby Inc.

Puiszis, Stephen. Illinois Municipal Tort Liability: 1996 Edition, 1997 Supplement. LC 96-77676. 921p. 1996. text, suppl. ed. 95.00 (1-55834-397-0, 66015-10, MICHIE) LEXIS Pub.

Puiszis, Steven M. Illinois Municipal Tort Liability. 1996. 105.00 (1-55834-386-5, 66015, MICHIE) LEXIS Pub.

An Asterisk (*) at the beginning of an entry indicates that the title is appearing for the first time.

— Illinois Municipal Tort Liability: 1998 Cumulative Supplement. 1998. 40.00 (*0-327-00134-8*, 66016-11) LEXIS Pub.

— Illinois Municipal Tort Liability, 1999 Cumulative Supplement. 335p. 1999. pap. 45.00 (*0-327-01151-3*, 6601612) LEXIS Pub.

Puite, K. J. Progress Plant Protoplasm. 1988. lib. bdg. 185.00 (*90-247-3688-9*, Pub. by M Nijhoff) Kluwer Academic.

Pujado, Lynda. Child of the Star. 25p. 1993. pap. 6.95 (*1-877871-56-7*, 2563) Ed Ministries.

— Dramatic Resources for Advent. 61p. 1995. pap. 9.95 (*1-877871-90-7*, 2582) Ed Ministries.

— Dramatic Resources for Lent. 28p. 1994. pap. 9.95 (*1-877871-62-1*, 2682) Ed Ministries.

— The Faithful Men of God: Six Monologues of Biblical Heroes. LC 97-187728. 40p. (Orig.). 1997. pap. 6.50 (*0-7880-0763-7*) CSS OH.

— The Last Covenant: An Easter Worship Service. LC 96-164471. 34p. (Orig.). 1996. pap. 4.95 (*0-7880-0226-0*) CSS OH.

— The Last Straw in Egypt: A Rhyming Play about Moses & Pharaoh. 32p. 1999. pap. 4.95 (*0-7880-1344-0*) CSS OH.

— Mary of Nazareth: A Dramatic Monologue for Lent or Easter. 20p. (Orig.). 1995. pap. 4.50 (*0-7880-0332-1*) CSS OH.

— Mothers of the Bible: A Worship Service for Mother's Day or Other Special Occasions. 52p. (Orig.). 1995. pap. 6.95 (*0-7880-0370-4*) CSS OH.

— The Trials of Christ: Readers' Theater for Easter. 16p. 1999. pap. 3.75 (*0-7880-1315-7*) CSS OH.

Pujals, E. Historia de la Literatura Inglesa. (SPA.). 830p. 1993. 150.00 (*84-249-0952-6*) Elliots Bks.

Pujals, Enrique J. La Obra Narrativa de Carlos Montenegro. LC 79-52537. (SPA., Illus.). 153p. (Orig.). 1980. pap. 9.95 (*0-89729-231-6*) Ediciones.

— Vida y Memorias de Carlos Montenegro. LC 88-80535. (SPA., Illus.). 81p. (Orig.). 1988. pap. 9.00 (*0-89729-469-6*) Ediciones.

Pujals, Josefina A. El Bosque Indomado...Donde Chilla el Obsceno Pajaro de la Noche. LC 81-69533. (SPA.). 134p. (Orig.). 1982. pap. 15.95 (*0-89729-304-5*) Ediciones.

Pujante, Angel-Luis, ed. & tr. see Shakespeare, William.

***Pujol, Carlos.** Emma's Eggs. (Illus.). (J). 1999. 12.20 (*0-606-16547-9*) Turtleback.

Pujol, Emilio. Guitar School: A Theoretical-Practical Method for the Guitar, Based on the Principles of Francisco Tarrega, Bks. 1 & 2. Ophee, Matanya, ed. Jeffery, Brian, tr. from SPA. LC 82-84565.Tr. of Escuela Razonada de la Guitarra. xxii, 192p. 1983. pap. 27.00 (*0-936186-07-0*) Edit Orphee.

— Guitar School, Bk. III: A Theoretical-Practical Method for the Guitar, Based on the Principles of Francisco Tarrega. Segal, Peter, ed. & tr. by. LC 82-64565. 144p. (Orig.). (C). 1991. pap. 18.00 (*0-936186-57-7*, RTFT-2) Edit Orphee.

Pujol, Ernesto, jt. contrib. by see Alvarez, Lupe.

Pujol, Laura, tr. see Woolf, Virginia.

Pujol, Louis. Tres Visiones Del Amor en la Obra de Jose Marti. LC 88-83427. (SPA.). 87p. 1989. pap. 9.95 (*0-89729-517-X*) Ediciones.

Pujol, Michele A. Feminism & Anti-Feminism in Early Economic Thought. 240p. 1992. text 95.00 (*1-85278-456-3*) E Elgar.

— Feminism & Anti-Feminism in Early Economic Thought. LC 91-23888. 240p. 1999. pap. 25.00 (*1-85898-884-5*) E Elgar.

Pujol, R. Microorganisms in Activated Sludge & Biofilm Processes: Proceedings fo the IAWQ 1st International Specialized Conference on Microorganisms in Activated Sludge & Biofilm Processes, Held in Paris, France, 27-28 September 1993. (Water Science & Technology Ser.). 392p. pap. 197.75 (*0-08-042538-0*, Pergamon Pr) Elsevier.

Pujolle, G., ed. High-Capacity Local & Metropolitan Area Networks: Architecture & Performance Issues. (NATO ASI Series F: Computer & Systems Sciences, Special Programme AET: Vol. 72). x, 536p. 1991. 136.95 (*0-387-53767-8*) Spr-Verlag.

***Pujolle, G., et al, eds.** Networking 2000: Broadband Communications, High Performance Networking & Performance of Communication Networks: Proceedings of the IFIP-TC6/European Union International Conference, Paris, France, May 14-19, 2000. (Lecture Notes in Computer Science Ser.: Vol. 1815). xx, 981p. 2000. pap. 129.00 (*3-540-67506-X*) Spr-Verlag.

Pujolle, G., jt. auth. see Gelenbe, E.

Pujolle, Jean. Lexique-Guide D'Acoustique Architecturale. (FRE.). 152p. 1971. 59.95 (*0-8288-6470-5*, M-6470) Fr & Eur.

Puka, Bill. Towards Moral Perfectionism. (Harvard Dissertations in Philosophy Ser.). 488p. 1990. reprint ed. text 10.00 (*0-8240-3208-X*) Garland.

Puka, Bill, ed. Caring Voices & Women's Moral Frames: Gilligan's View, Vol. 6. LC 94-462. (Moral Development: a Compendium Ser.: No. 6). (Illus.). 544p. 1994. reprint ed. text 90.00 (*0-8153-1553-8*) Garland.

— Defining Perspectives in Moral Development, Vol. 1. LC 94-462. (Moral Development: a Compendium Ser.: No. 1). (Illus.). 264p. 1994. reprint ed. text 60.00 (*0-8153-1548-1*) Garland.

— Fundamental Research in Moral Development, Vol. 2. LC 94-462. (Moral Development: a Compendium Ser.: No. 2). (Illus.). 416p. 1994. reprint ed. text 80.00 (*0-8153-1549-X*) Garland.

— The Great Justice Debate: Kohlberg Criticism, Vol. 4. LC 94-462. (Moral Development: a Compendium Ser.: No. 4). (Illus.). 352p. 1994. reprint ed. text 70.00 (*0-8153-1551-1*) Garland.

— Kohlberg's Original Study of Moral Development, Vol. 3. LC 94-462. (Moral Development: a Compendium Ser.: No. 3). 520p. 1994. reprint ed. text 90.00 (*0-8153-1550-3*) Garland.

— Moral Development: A Compendium, 7 Vols., Set. LC 94-462. 2784p. 1995. 454.00 (*0-8153-1547-3*) Garland.

— New Research in Moral Development, Vol. 5. LC 94-462. (Moral Development: a Compendium Ser.: No. 5). (Illus.). 448p. 1994. reprint ed. text 85.00 (*0-8153-1552-X*) Garland.

Puka, Bill, ed. Reaching Out: Caring Altruism, & Prosocial Behavior, Vol. 7. LC 94-462. 360p. 1994. text 70.00 (*0-8153-1554-6*) Garland.

***Pukalo, Linda A.** Thoughts from Both Sides of the Rainbow. (Illus.). 80p. 1999. pap. 14.95 (*1-880849-15-1*) Chapel Hill NC.

***Pukanszky, L.** Characters of Connected Lie Groups LC 99-29967. (Mathematical Surveys & Monographs). 1999. write for info. (*0-8218-1088-X*) Am Math.

Pukelsheim, Friedrich. Optimal Design of Experiments. LC 00-279. (Probability & Mathematical Statistics: Applied Probability & Statistics Section Ser.). 480p. 1993. 109.95 (*0-471-61971-X*) Wiley.

Pukhov, G. E., jt. ed. see Frank, P. M.

Pukite, Jan, jt. auth. see Pukite, Paul.

Pukite, John. A Field Guide to Cows: How to Identify & Appreciate America's 52 Breeds. LC 96-12469. (Illus.). 144p. 1998. pap. 11.95 (*0-14-027388-3*) Viking Penguin.

— A Field Guide to Pigs. LC 99-38988. (Illus.). 140p. 1999. pap. 9.95 (*1-56044-877-6*) Falcon Pub Inc.

— Hiking Minnesota. LC 97-41155. (Illus.). 224p. 1998. pap. 14.95 (*1-56044-565-3*) Falcon Pub Inc.

Pukite, Paul & Pukite, Jan. Modeling for Reliability Analysis: Markov Modeling for Reliability, Maintainability, Safety, & Supportability Analysis of Complex Systems. LC 97-46570. (Series on Engineering of Complex Computer Systems). 288p. 1998. pap. 89.95 (*0-7803-3482-5*) Inst Electrical.

Pukkala, Eero. Cancer Risk by Social Class & Occupation: A Survey of 109,000 Cancer Cases among Finns of Working Age. LC 95-1186. (Contributions to Epidemiology & Biostatistics Ser.: Vol. 7). (Illus.). x, 278p. 1995. 104.50 (*3-8055-6152-0*) S Karger.

Pukui, Mary K. Na Mele Welo: Songs of Our Heritage. 238p. 1995. pap. 21.95 (*0-930897-87-0*) Bishop Mus.

Pukui, Mary K. & Curtis, Caroline. Hawai'i Island Legends: Pikoi, Pele & Others. LC 96-130376. Orig. Title: Pikoi & Other Legends of the Island of Hawaii. (Illus.). 252p. (Orig.). (YA). (gr. 7-12). 1995. pap. 11.95 (*0-87336-032-X*) Kamehameha Schools.

Puku'i, Mary K. & Curtis, Caroline. Tales of the Menehune. rev. ed. LC 96-130329. (Illus.). 130p. (YA). (gr. 7-12). 1994. pap. 8.95 (*0-87336-010-9*) Kamehameha Schools.

— The Water of Kane: And Other Legends of the Hawaiian Islands. rev. ed. LC 96-130298. (Illus.). 221p. (YA). (gr. 7-12). 1994. pap. 9.95 (*0-87336-020-6*) Kamehameha Schools.

Pukui, Mary K. & Elbert, Samuel H. Hawaiian Dictionary: Hawaiian-English, English-Hawaiian. enl. rev. ed. LC 85-24583. 600p. 1986. 29.95 (*0-8248-0703-0*) UH Pr.

— New Pocket Hawaiian Dictionary. rev. ed. LC 91-25854. 272p. 1992. pap. 4.95 (*0-8248-1392-8*) UH Pr.

Pukui, Mary K. & Korn, Alfons L., trs. The Echo of Our Song: Chants & Poems of the Hawaiians. LC 72-91620. 250p. 1979. pap. 12.95 (*0-8248-0668-9*) UH Pr.

Pukui, Mary K., et al. Nana I Ke Kumu, Vol. 1. LC 72-93779. 1972. pap. 12.00 (*0-9616738-0-X*) Hui Hanai.

— Nana I Ke Kumu, Vol. 2. LC 72-93779. 1979. pap. 12.00 (*0-9616738-2-6*) Hui Hanai.

— Place Names of Hawaii. 2nd ed. LC 73-85582. 310p. 1974. pap. 10.95 (*0-8248-0524-0*) UH Pr.

— Pocket Place Names of Hawaii. LC 88-27747. (Illus.). 96p. (Orig.). 1989. pap. 3.95 (*0-8248-1187-9*) UH Pr.

Pukui, Mary K., jt. auth. see Craighill Handy, E. S.

Pukui, Mary K., jt. auth. see Elbert, Samuel H.

Pukui, Mary K., jt. auth. see Handy, E. S.

Pukui, Mary K., tr. see Kamakau, S. M.

Pukui, Mary K., tr. see Kamakau, Samuel M.

Pukui, Mary K., tr. see Li, John Papa.

Pukui, Mary Kawena. Olelo No'eau: Proverbs & Poetical Sayings, No. 71. (Special Publication Ser.). (Illus.). 368p. 1983. pap. 24.95 (*0-910240-93-0*) Bishop Mus.

Pula, Faafouina I., jt. auth. see Copp, John D.

Pula, James S. For Liberty & Justice. 288p. 1978. 20.00 (*0-942211-45-6*) Olde Soldier Bks.

***Pula, James S.** Poles in the Central & Western States, Vol. IV. 2001. 59.95 (*0-8132-0923-4*) Cath U Pr.

Pula, James S. The Polish Americans. LC 94-20514. (Twayne's Immigrant Heritage of America Ser.). 1995. 33.00 (*0-8057-8427-6*, Twyne); pap. 20.00 (*0-8057-8438-1*, Twyne) Mac Lib Ref.

Pula, James S. The Sigel Regiment: A History of the 26th Wisonsin Volunteer Infantry, 1862-1865. (Illus.). 504p. 1997. 29.95 (*1-882810-20-1*) Savas Pub.

— Thaddeus Kosciuszko: The Purest Son of Liberty. LC 98-44025. (Illus.). 350p. 1999. 29.95 (*0-7818-0576-7*) Hippocrene Bks.

Pula, James S. & Biskupski, M. B., eds. Polish Democratic Thought from the Renaissance to the Great Emigration: Essays & Documents. (East European Monographs: No. 289). 224p. 1990. 44.50 (*0-88033-186-0*) East Eur Monographs.

— Selected Essays from the Fiftieth Anniversary Congress of the Polish Institute of Arts & Sciences in America. 755p. 1994. 104.00 (*0-88033-287-5*, 390, Pub. by East Eur Monographs) Col U Pr.

Pula, James S. & Dziedzic, Eugene E. United We Stand: The Role of Polish Workers in the New York Mills Textile Strikes, 1912 & 1916. (East European Monographs: No. 286). 320p. 1990. 56.50 (*0-88033-183-6*, Pub. by East Eur Monographs) Col U Pr.

Pula, James S., ed. see Kruszka, Waclaw.

Pula, Judith J., et al. Controversy: Issues for Reading & Writing. LC 98-10093. 335p. (C). 1998. pap. text 32.20 (*0-13-598103-4*) P-H.

Pula, Robert, ed. General Semantics Bulletin: Official Annual Journal of the Institute of General Semantics. annuals 1996. 15.00 (*0-910780-00-5*) Inst Gen Seman.

***Pula, Robert P.** A General-Semantics Glossary: Pula's Guide for the Perplexed. (Illus.). 136p. 2000. pap. text 19.95 (*0-918970-49-0*) Intl Gen Semantics.

Pula, Robert P., ed. see Muller, Robert J.

Pulacio, Enrique. Panoramic Colombia. LC 98-199846. 1998. 65.00 (*958-9393-38-1*) Villegas Ed.

Pulakos, Elaine, jt. ed. see Ilgen, Daniel R.

Pulaski County Board of Commissioners. Pulaski County Illinois, 1819-1987. LC 87-71197. 408p. 1988. 55.00 (*0-938021-21-4*) Turner Pub KY.

Pulaski High School Drama Club Staff & Mueller, Tobin J. I Want to Know! A Musical Time Line about the History of Science & Invention. (Classroom Musicals Ser.). (Illus.). 55p. (J). (gr. 4-12). 1991. 14.95 (*1-56213-059-5*) Ctr Stage Prodns.

Pulaski, Jack. The St. Veronica Gig Stories. LC 86-50657. 178p. (Orig.). 1986. 15.95 (*0-939010-10-0*); pap. 8.95 (*0-939010-09-7*) Zephyr Pr.

— The St. Veronica Gig Stories. deluxe ed. LC 86-50657. 178p. (Orig.). 1986. 25.00 (*0-685-13535-7*) Zephyr Pr.

Pulaski, Mary Ann S. Step by Step Guide to Correct English. 2nd ed. 160p. 1985. per. 11.95 (*0-671-86955-8*, Arc) IDG Bks.

Pulat, B. Mustafa. Fundamentals of Industrial Ergonomics. 2nd rev. ed. LC 98-115918. (Illus.). 439p. (C). 1997. text 59.95 (*0-88133-949-0*) Waveland Pr.

Pulat, B. Mustafa & Alexander, David C., eds. Industrial Ergonomics Case Studies. 334p. 1991. pap. text 34.95 (*0-89806-099-0*, INERGO) Eng Mgmt Pr.

Pulat, P. Simin, jt. auth. see Badiru, Adedeji B.

Pulawski, Wojciech J. Revision of North American Tachysphex Wasps Including Central American & Caribbean Species: Hymenoptera: Sphecidae. LC 88-70114. (Memoirs of the California Academy of Sciences Ser.: No. 10). (Illus.). 1988. pap. 30.00 (*0-940228-16-5*) Calif Acad Sci.

— The Wasp Genus Gastrosericus Spinola, 1839: Hymenoptera: Sphecidae. LC 95-71265. (Memoirs of the California Academy of Sciences Ser.: No. 18). (Illus.). 1995. 40.00 (*0-940228-36-X*) Calif Acad Sci.

Pulawski, Wojciech J., jt. auth. see Krombein, Karl V.

Pulbrook, jt. auth. see Gould.

Pulci, Antonia. Florentine Drama for Convent & Festival: Seven Sacred Plays. Cook, James W. & Cook, Barbara C., eds. 167p. 1996. pap. text 15.00 (*0-226-68517-9*) U Ch Pr.

— Florentine Drama for Convent & Festival: Seven Sacred Plays. Cook, James W., ed. & tr. by. Cook, Barbara C., ed. LC 96-12766. 167p. 1996. lib. bdg. 33.00 (*0-226-68516-0*) U Ch Pr.

Pulci, Luigi. Morgante: The Epic Adventures of Orlando & His Giant Friend Morgante. Tusiani, Joseph, tr. LC 97-44991. (Indiana Masterpiece Editions Ser.). 975p. 1998. 49.95 (*0-253-33399-7*) Ind U Pr.

Pulcini, Theodore. Exegesis As Polemical Discourse: Ibn Hazm on Jewish & Christian Scriptures. LC 97-30055. (AAR the Religions Ser.). 220p. 1998. pap. 19.95 (*0-7885-0395-2*, 011202) OUP.

Pulcini, Theodore & Laderman, Gary. Exegesis As Polemical Discourse: Ibn Hazm on Jewish & Christian Scriptures. LC 97-30055. (AAR the Religions Ser.). 210p. 1998. 44.95 (*0-7885-0396-0*, 011202) OUP.

Pulcino, Paola & Pal, S. B. Another Look at Sobriety: Walk with Us to Freedom. (Illus.). 96p. 1999. pap. 11.95 (*0-9662542-6-0*) Etta Pub Co.

Pule, John P. Burn My Head in Heaven (Tugi e Ulu Haaku He Langi) LC 98-119271. 279p. 1998. write for info. (*0-14-027374-3*, Penguin Bks) Viking Penguin.

Pulec. Atlas of Otology. 2000. pap. 154.50 (*0-7693-0011-1*) Singular Publishing.

Puledda, Salvatore. On Being Human: Interpretations of Humanism from the Renaissance to the Present. Hurley, Andrew, tr. from SPA. LC 96-3253. (New Humanism Ser.). Orig. Title: Interpretaciones del Humanismo. 224p. (Orig.). 1997. pap. 11.95 (*1-878977-18-0*, 18-0) Latitude Pr.

— The Tokarev Report. Tooby, Paul, tr. from SPA. 140p. (Orig.). 1999. pap. 14.95 (*1-878977-17-2*) Latitude Pr.

Puleo, Alicia H. Como Leer a Julio Cortazar. 42.50 (*0-685-69533-6*) Scripta.

Puleo, Mev. The Struggle Is One: Voices & Visions of Liberation. LC 93-37873. 251p. (C). 1994. pap. text 19.95 (*0-7914-2014-0*) State U NY Pr.

Puleo, Nancy F., jt. auth. see Weber, James M.

Puleston, Dennis E. Tikal Report No. 13: The Settlement Survey of Tikal. (University Museum Monographs: No. 48). (Illus.). 136p. 1983. text 30.00 (*0-934718-47-4*) U Museum Pubns.

Puleston, William D. Influence of Sea Power in World War II. LC 71-104248. 310p. 1971. reprint ed. lib. bdg. 49.50 (*0-8371-3997-X*, PUSP, Greenwood Pr) Greenwood.

Pulfer, Laura. I Beg to Differ: Politically Incorrect, Proudly Midwestern, Potentially Funny. LC 98-26623. 216p. 1998. 24.95 (*1-882203-24-0*) Orange Frazer.

Pulfer, Laura, ed. see Hair, Deidra.

Pulford, Florence. Morning Star Quilts. (Illus.). 80p. 1989. 34.95 (*0-942786-00-9*); pap. 24.95 (*0-942786-28-9*) Eddies Q Bee.

— Morning Star Quilts: A Presentation of the Work & Lives of Northern Plains Indian Women. (Illus.). 80p. 1996. text 9.95 (*0-486-29466-8*) Dover.

Pulford, Kevin, et al. A Quantitative Approach to Software Management: The AMI PRO Handbook. Ware, A. & Harutunian, Katherine, eds. LC 95-37088. 200p. (C). 1996. pap. 44.95 (*0-201-87746-5*) Addison-Wesley.

Pulgar, M., jt. auth. see Timms, W. W.

Pulgram, Ernst. Syllable, Word, Nexus, Cursus. (Janua Linguarum, Ser.: No. 81). 1970. pap. text 40.80 (*90-279-0706-4*) Mouton.

Pulgram, Ernst, ed. Romanitas: Studies in Romance Linguistics. LC 81-50963. (Michigan Romance Studies: No. 4). (Illus.). 262p. 1984. pap. 15.00 (*0-939730-03-0*) Mich Romance.

Pulham, Grace, jt. auth. see Eder, Enelle G.

Pulham, J. R. General Relativity: Proceedings of the Forty Sixth Scottish Universities Summer School in Physics, Aberdeen, July 1995. LC 96-30968. (Scottish Universities Sunner School in Physics, NATO Advanced Study Institute Ser.: Vol. 46). 422p. 1996. 200.00 (*0-7503-0395-6*) IOP Pub.

Pulham, J. R., jt. auth. see Hall, Graham.

Puli, Ali. The Center of Nature Concentrated: Or, The Regenerated Salt of Nature. 1988. pap. 5.95 (*1-55818-110-5*) Holmes Pub.

***Puliafito, Carmen A.** Photodynamic Therapy for Macular Degeneration. 250p. (C). 2000. text 190.00 (*1-55642-490-6*) SLACK Inc.

Puliafito, Carmen A., ed. Lasers in Surgery & Medicine: Principles & Practice. LC 95-36635. 484p. 1996. 129.95 (*0-471-12070-7*, Wiley-Liss) Wiley.

Puliafito, Carmen A., et al. Optical Coherence Tomography of Ocular Diseases. LC 95-20538. (Illus.). 384p. 1995. 175.00 (*1-55642-295-4*, 62954) SLACK Inc.

Puliafito, Carmen A., jt. auth. see Reichel, Elias.

Puliafito, Carmen A., jt. auth. see Steinert, Roger F.

Pulich, Warren M. The Birds of North Central Texas. LC 87-9143. (W. L. Moody, Jr. Natural History Ser.: No. 9). (Illus.). 472p. 1988. 45.00 (*0-89096-319-3*) Tex A&M Univ Pr.

Pulickal, Joseph, jt. compiled by see Brys, Aurel.

***Pulido, Alberto L.** The Sacred World of the Penitentes. LC 00-26523. 2000. pap. write for info. (*1-56098-394-9*) Smithsonian.

Pulido, Brian. Between Heaven & Hell. (Lady Death Ser.). 1997. pap. text 12.95 (*0-9642260-3-0*) Chaos Comics.

— Odyssey. LC 98-134116. (Lady Death Ser.). 1997. pap. text 9.95 (*0-9642260-5-7*) Chaos Comics.

— Reckoning. LC 97-220105. (Lady Death Ser.). (Illus.). 1997. pap. text 12.95 (*0-9642260-8-1*) Chaos Comics.

— Revenge! LC 97-220101. (Evil Ernie Ser.). (Illus.). 1997. pap. text 12.95 (*0-9642260-4-9*) Chaos Comics.

— Theatre of Pain. (Chastity Ser.). 1997. pap. text 9.95 (*1-891243-00-4*) Chaos Comics.

— Vampires Myth. (Purgatori Ser.). (Illus.). 1997. pap. text 12.95 (*0-9642260-6-5*) Chaos Comics.

— Youth Gone Wild. LC 98-134116. (Evil Ernie Ser.). 1997. pap. text 9.95 (*0-9642260-2-2*) Chaos Comics.

***Pulido, Jose.** Requisites in Ophthalmology: Retina, Choroid & Vitreous. (Illus.). 475p. (C). 1999. text. write for info. (*0-323-00237-4*) Mosby Inc.

Pulido, Laura. Environmentalism & Economic Justice: Two Chicano Struggles in the Southwest. LC 95-32449. (Society, Environment, & Place Ser.). (Illus.). 282p. (C). 1996. 47.50 (*0-8165-1424-0*); pap. 18.95 (*0-8165-1605-7*) U of Ariz Pr.

Puligandla, R. & Rama Rao, P. Indian Philosophy: Past & Future. (C). 1982. 28.00 (*0-8364-0670-2*); text 18.50 (*0-8364-0789-X*) S Asia.

Puligandla, R. Fact & Fiction in B. F. Skinner's Science & Utopia. LC 73-21001. 114p. 1974. 10.00 (*0-87527-130-8*) Green.

Puligandla, Ramakrishma & Miller, David L., eds. Buddhism & the Emerging World Civilization: Essays in Honor of Nolan Pliny Jacobson. LC 93-3267. 256p. (C). 1995. 26.95 (*0-8093-1842-3*) S Ill U Pr.

Puligandla, Ramakrishna. Fundamentals of Indian Philosophy. xix, 362p. (C). 1997. 25.00 (*81-246-0086-4*, Pub. by D K Printwrld); pap. 14.95 (*81-246-0087-2*, Pub. by D K Printwrld) Nataraj Bks.

Puligandla, Ramakrishna. Jnana-Yoga: The Way of Knowledge, an Analytical Interpretation. xix, 140p. 1997. 13.00 (*81-246-0088-0*, Pub. by D K Printwrld) Nataraj Bks.

Pulinka, Steven M. Discover the Historic Houses of Odessa. LC 99-25545. 1999. pap. text 7.95 (*0-912724-48-X*) Winterthur.

Pulippani, U. S., ed. Biorhythms of Natal Moon: Mysteries of Pancha Pakshi. (C). 1994. 16.00 (*0-8364-2900-1*, Pub. by Ranjan Pubs) S Asia.

Pulis, Bonnie, jt. auth. see Huey, Lois.

Pulis, John W., ed. Moving On: Black Loyalists in the Afro-Atlantic World. LC 98-41807. (Crosscurrents in African American History Ser.). 222p. 1999. 49.00 (*0-8153-2748-X*, H2049) Garland.

***Pulis, John W., ed.** Religion, Diaspora & Cultural Identity: A Reader in the Anglophone Caribbean. 411p. 1999. pap. 43.00 (*90-5700-546-8*, Harwood Acad Pubs) Gordon & Breach.

— Religion, Diaspora & Cultural Identity: A Reader in the Anglophone Caribbean. 436p. 1999. text 58.00 (*90-5700-545-X*, Harwood Acad Pubs) Gordon & Breach.

Pulitzer, Copey, pseud. How to Manage Your Parents. (Illus.). 144p. (Orig.). 1992. pap. 7.95 (*0-9633496-0-0*) S C Pulitzer.

Pulitzer, Lisa. The Blue Blood Murder. Spicer, C., ed. LC 99-179447. 1999. mass mkt. 6.50 (*0-312-96833-7*) St Martin.

P

An Asterisk (*) at the beginning of an entry indicates that the title is appearing for the first time.

***Pulitzer, Lisa.** Romance Novelist Case. 2000. mass mkt. write for info. (0-312-97580-5) St Martin.

Pulitzer, Lisa B. Crime on Deadline: Police Reporters Tell Their Most Unforgettable Stories. LC 97-108391. 288p. 1996. pap. 13.00 (1-57297-175-4) Blvd Books.

Pulitzer, Ralph. New York Society on Parade. LC 75-1866. (Leisure Class in America Ser.). (Illus.). 1975. reprint ed. 15.95 (0-405-06932-4) Ayer.

Pulitzer, Roxanne. The Palm Beach Story. 288p. 1997. mass mkt. 5.99 (1-57566-167-5, Knsington) Kensgtn Pub Corp.

Pulitzer, Roxanne & Maxa, Kathleen. The Prize Pulitzer: The Scandal That Rocked Palm Beach - The Real Story. 1988. 19.95 (0-317-66206-6) Villard Books.

Pulitzer, Sidney C., see Pulitzer, Copey, pseud.

Puljiz. Social Policy in Croatia. 61.95 (1-85972-150-8) Ashgate Pub Co.

Pulker, Hans K. Coatings on Glass. (Thin Films Science & Technology Ser.: Vol. 6). 502p. 1984. 222.00 (0-444-42360-5, I-230-84) Elsevier.

— Wear & Corrosion Resistant Coatings by CVD & PVD. 1989. text 99.00 (0-470-21638-7) P-H.

***Pulker, H.K.** Coatings on Glass. 2nd rev. ed. LC 99-13856. 540p. 1999. 190.50 (0-444-50103-7) Elsevier.

***Pulker, H.K., et al, eds.** Coatings on Glass 1998. 466p. 1999. 139.50 (0-444-50247-5) Elsevier.

Pulkina, I. M. Russian: A Practical Grammar with Exercises. 582p. (C). 1997. 24.95 (0-8285-4993-1) Firebird NY.

— A Short Russian Grammar. 352p. 1984. 65.00 (0-7855-0940-2) St Mut.

— A Short Russian Reference Grammar. 2nd ed. Kuznetsov, P. S., ed. ii, 352p. 1969. text 87.00 (0-677-20820-0) Gordon & Breach.

Pulkina, I. M. & Zakhlava-Nekrasova, E., eds. Russian: A Practical Grammar with Exercises. 584p. (C). 1988. 80.00 (0-569-09174-8, Pub. by Collets) St Mut.

Pulkkinen, Helj A. Microsoft Excel 97. LC 97-41633. (Paradigm Visual Ser.). 1997. 18.68 (0-7638-0091-0) Paradigm MN.

Pulkkinen, Helja & Valtanen, E. Paradigm Visual Series: Microsoft Excel 7: Text with disk, 3.5. 128p. 14.95 incl. cd-rom (0-7638-0015-5) EMC-Paradigm.

Pulkkinen, Helja & Valtanen, Esko. Excel 7. LC 96-9746. (Paradigm Visual Ser.). 1996. write for info. (0-7638-0014-7) Paradigm MN.

Pulkkinen, Jarmo. The Threat of Logical Mathematism: A Study on the Critique of Mathematical Logic in Germany at the Turn of the 20th Century. LC 94-26760. 187p. 1994. 36.00 (3-631-47409-1) P Lang Pubng.

Pulkkinen, Tuija. The Postmodern & Political Agency. 250p. pap. 24.95 (951-39-0660-4, Pub. by SoPhi Academic) Intl Spec Bk.

Pulkrabek, Willard W. Engineering Fundamentals of the Internal Combustion Engine. LC 96-54259. 411p. (C). 1997. 105.00 (0-13-570854-0) P-H.

Pullaiah, T. Embryology of Compositae. (International Bioscience Monographs: No. 13). 192p. 1984. 19.00 (1-55528-029-3) Scholarly Pubns.

Pullaiah, T. & Chennaiah, E., eds. Flora of Andhra Pradesh, Vols. 1 & 2. 1997. pap. 520.00 (81-7233-137-1, Pub. by Scientific Pubs) St Mut.

Pullam, Hugh. Atlantic Schooners. (Illus.). 64p. 1998. pap. text 6.95 (1-55109-191-7) Nimbus Publ.

Pullan, jt. auth. see McGladrey.

Pullan, Brian. The Jews of Europe & the Inquisition of Venice, 1550-1670. 368p. 1998. pap. text 19.95 (1-86064-357-4, Pub. by I B T) St Martin.

— Poverty & Charity: Europe, Italy, Venice, 1400-1700. LC 94-5846. (Collected Studies). 1994. 106.95 (0-86078-446-0, Pub. by Variorum) Ashgate Pub Co.

Pullan, Dorothy. Corny the Pigeon Saves Christmas. (Illus.). 11p. (J). (gr. 1-4). 1997. pap. 10.00 (0-8059-3956-3) Dorrance.

Pullan, Linda M. & Patel, Jitendra, eds. Neurotherapeutics: Emerging Strategies. LC 95-381027. (Contemporary Neuroscience Ser.). (Illus.). 444p. 1995. 125.00 (0-89603-306-6) Humana.

***Pullan, Wendy & Bhadeshia, H. K. D. H., eds.** Structure: In Science & Art. LC 00-21912. (Darwin College Lectures). (Illus.). 240p. 2000. write for info. (0-521-78258-9) Cambridge U Pr.

Pullar, G. C. A Shifting Town: Glass Plate Images of Clermont & Its People. LC 86-16070. (Illus.). 232p. 1987. text 49.95 (0-7022-2012-4, Pub. by Univ Queensland Pr) Intl Spec Bk.

Pullar, Laurence, jt. auth. see Murray, John.

Pullar, Philippa, jt. auth. see Bek, Lilla.

Pullee, Caroline. 20th Century Jewellery. (Illus.). 128p. 10.99 (1-57215-249-4, JG2494) World Pubns.

Pullein-Thompson, Christine. More Horse Stories. 1999. pap. 7.95 (0-7534-5169-7, Kingfisher) LKC.

Pullein-Thompson, Diana. Classic Horse & Pony Stories: The World's Best Horse & Pony Stories in Their Real-life Setti. LC 99-26011. 96p. (J). (gr. 4-6). 1999. 16.95 (0-7894-4896-3) DK Pub Inc.

— This Pony Is Dangerous. 174p. (C). 1990. pap. 29.00 (0-85131-520-8, Pub. by J A Allen) St Mut.

***Pullein-Thompson, Diana & Puddephatt, Neal.** Classic Horse & Pony Stories. LC 99-86031. (Read & Listen Ser.). (J). 2000. pap. write for info. incl. cd-rom (0-7894-6362-8) DK Pub Inc.

Pullein-Thompson, J. Gin & Murder. large type ed. (Linford Mystery Library). 1990. pap. 16.99 (0-7089-6848-1) Ulverscroft.

— Murder Strikes Pink. large type ed. (Linford Mystery Library). 1990. pap. 16.99 (0-7089-6839-2, Linford) Ulverscroft.

— They Died in the Spring. large type ed. (Linford Mystery Library). 1990. pap. 16.99 (0-7089-6897-X) Ulverscroft.

Pullein-Thompson, Joseph. The Hidden Horse. 197p. (C). 1990. pap. 21.00 (0-85131-490-2, Pub. by J A Allen) St Mut.

Pullein-Thompson, Josephin. Star Riders. 127p. (C). 1990. pap. 21.00 (0-85131-519-4, Pub. by J A Allen) St Mut.

Pullen, jt. auth. see McGladre.

***Pullen, Bruce Reed.** Discovering Celtic Christianity: It's Roots, Relationship & Relevance. LC 98-60275. (Illus.). 168p. 1999. pap. 12.95 (0-89622-927-0) Twenty-Third.

Pullen-Burry, Bessie. Ethiopia in Exile: Jamaica Revisited. LC 76-157376. (Black Heritage Library Collection). 1977. 21.95 (0-8369-8814-0) Ayer.

Pullen-Burry, Henry B. Qabalism. 167p. 1972. reprint ed. 15.00 (0-911662-45-6) Yoga.

Pullen, Charles H. Miss Columbia's Public School. LC 70-85687. (American Fiction Reprint Ser.). 1977. 17.95 (0-8369-7016-0) Ayer.

Pullen, Gerald, jt. auth. see Grubbs, Bill.

Pullen, Helen R., jt. auth. see Baker, Georgia O.

Pullen, Ian, jt. auth. see Hume, Clephane.

Pullen, Ian, jt. auth. see Hume, Clephane A.

Pullen, Ian, jt. ed. see Emery, Alan E.

Pullen, J. A., jt. auth. see Faiola, Theodora.

Pullen, J. M. Unpublished Papers of T. R. Malthus in the Collection of Kanto Gakuen University. 164p. (C). 1998. text 57.95 (0-521-58138-9) Cambridge U Pr.

Pullen, J. Mark. Understanding Internet Protocols Through Hands-On Programming. (Illus.). 304p. 2000. pap. text 49.99 incl. cd-rom (0-471-35626-3) Wiley.

Pullen, John. The Twentieth Maine. 338p. 1980. reprint ed. pap. 17.50 (0-89029-755-X) Morningside Bkshop.

— The Twentieth Maine: A Volunteer Regiment in the Civil War. 338p. 1980. reprint ed. 35.00 (0-89029-055-5) Morningside Bkshop.

Pullen, John, ed. see Malthus, Thomas Robert.

Pullen, John J. Joshua Chamberlain: A Hero's Life & Legacy, 1. LC 99-17606. (Illus.). 256p. 1999. 22.95 (0-8117-0886-1) Stackpole.

Pullen, John J. A Shower of Stars: The Medal of Honor & the 27th Maine. LC 96-43138. 288p. 1997. 24.95 (0-8117-0075-5) Stackpole.

— A Shower of Stars: The Medal of Honor & the 27th Maine. large type ed. LC 99-41064. (American History Ser.). 1999. 26.95 (0-7838-8757-4, G K Hall & Co) Mac Lib Ref.

Pullen, John J., ed. see Judson, Amos.

***Pullen, L. Larry.** Christian Ethics & U. S. Foreign Policy. 176p. 2000. 50.00 (0-7391-0110-2) Lxngtn Bks.

Pullen, Martha. Madeira Applique by Machine: Plus Heirloom Sewing from A to Z. LC 97-65222. (Marth'a Sewing Room Ser.). (Illus.). 107p. (Orig.). 1997. text 19.95 (1-878048-12-0) M Pullen.

— Martha's Attic: Program Guide for Public T. V. Series 400. McMakin, Kathy, ed. LC 96-920960. (Illus.). 344p. 1996. text 19.95 (1-878048-06-6) M Pullen.

Pullen, Martha C. Antique Embroidery LC 98-68426. 63 p. 1998. write for info. (1-878048-18-X) M Pullen.

— Beautiful Vests & All the Rest. LC 97-76441. (Martha's Sewing Room Ser.: No. 700). (Illus.). 240p. 1997. pap. text 19.95 (1-878048-13-9) M Pullen.

— A Christmas to Remember: Martha's Sewing Room. (Illus.). 108p. 1996. pap. 12.00 (1-878048-10-4) M Pullen.

— Grandmother's Hope Chest: French Sewing by Machine. (Illus.). 400p. 1992. 39.95 (1-878048-01-5) M Pullen.

— Heirloom Doll Clothes for Gotz. LC 96-94552. (Illus.). 336p. 1996. pap. text 24.95 (1-878048-08-2) M Pullen.

— Making Memories: Martha's Sewing Room Series 600. LC 96-71614. (Illus.). 276p. (Orig.). 1997. pap. text 19.95 (1-878048-11-2) M Pullen.

— Martha's Sewing Room: Program Guide for Public T. V. Series-100. (Illus.). 274p. 1994. 19.95 (1-878048-03-1) M Pullen.

— The New Zealand Blouse. LC 99-70132. (Illus.). 72p. 1999. 19.95 (1-878048-20-1) M Pullen.

— Sewing Inspirations from Yester Year: Martha's Sewing Room Series 500. LC 96-70808. (Illus.). 218p. 1996. pap. text 19.95 (1-878048-09-0) M Pullen.

— Silk Ribbon Treasures: Smocking & Embroidery. LC 96-92281. (Illus.). 240p. (Orig.). 1996. pap. text 24.95 (1-878048-07-4) M Pullen.

— Victorian Sewing & Crafts: Program Guide for Public T. V. Series 200. McMakin, Kathy, ed. (Illus.). 360p. 1995. 19.95 (1-878048-04-X) M Pullen.

Pullen, Martha C. & Walters, Lilly. You Can Make Money from Your Hobby: Building a Business Doing What You Love. LC 98-43079. 192p. 1999. pap. 12.99 (0-8054-1657-9) Broadman.

Pullen, Martha C., et al. Heirloom Sewing for Women: French Sewing by Machine. (Illus.). 350p. 1993. 39.95 (1-878048-02-3) M Pullen.

***Pullen, Martha Campbell.** Three Best Friends Heirloom Doll Clothes. LC 98-68284. 125 p. 1998. write for info. (1-878048-16-3) M Pullen.

***Pullen, Mike & Ris, Birgit.** EU E-Commerce - Law & Policy. 152p. 2000. pap. write for info. (1-902558-37-5, Pub. by Palladian Law) Gaunt.

Pullen, Robert & Taylor, Stephen. Montserrat Caballe: Casta Diva. LC 94-36295. 1995. text 29.95 (1-55553-228-4) NE U Pr.

Pullen, Virginia A. They Chose This Valley. Mills, Charlotte, ed. LC 89-71479. (Illus.). 168p. (Orig.). 1991. pap. 8.95 (0-9625483-0-8) Dewey Pr.

Puller, Lewis B. Fortunate Son: The Autobiography of Lewis B. Puller. 464p. 1993. mass mkt. 6.99 (0-553-56076-X) Bantam.

***Puller, Lewis B., Jr.** Fortunate Son: The Autobiograpy of Lewis B. Puller, Jr. (Illus.). 400p. 2000. pap. 13.00 (0-8021-3690-7, Pub. by Grove-Altic) Publishers Group.

Puller, Malcolm. Deep Excavations: A Practical Manual. LC 96-233467. 448p. 1996. 154.00 (0-7277-1987-4) Am Soc Civil Eng.

Pullerits, Albert. Estonia: Population, Cultural & Economic Life. LC 77-87536. reprint ed. 37.50 (0-404-16604-0) AMS Pr.

Pulley. Patricia Wright. (J). 1995. lib. bdg. 13.95 (0-8050-2212-0) H Holt & Co.

Pulley, Dean. Michalopoulos. Cass, Jim, ed. & des. by. Foster, David, des. (Illus.). 128p. 1997. 60.00 (0-9659554-0-0) Cattywompus Pr.

Pulley, Dennis. Open Water Diver Study Guide. 3rd ed. 24p. 1995. pap. text 12.95 (1-880229-30-7) Concept Sys.

Pulley, Dennis, jt. auth. see Clark, Laurie K.

Pulley, James W. Rays of Light: Scripture Verses & References for. LC P02099. 130p. 1998. pap. 10.00 (1-57502-759-3) Morris Pubng.

***Pulley, Kelly R.** Noah's Ark. LC 99-178960. (Beginner's Bible Ser.). 1998. write for info. (0-7853-2676-6) Pubns Intl Ltd.

Pulley, Leland E. The Parent-Child Development Program. 400p. 1999. 34.95 (0-9611282-2-4); pap. 29.95 (0-9611282-3-2) Stewardship Enters.

***Pulley, Lloyd.** Walk in Love: Following God's Plan for Marriage. (Illus.). 68p. 1999. pap. 4.95 (0-9676414-0-3) Bridging.

Pulley, Mary L. Losing Your Job, Reclaiming Your Soul: Stories of Resilience, Renewal & Hope. LC 97-4700. 1997. 24.50 (0-7879-0937-8) Jossey-Bass.

Pulley, Mary L., jt. auth. see Horowitz, Leonard G.

Pulley, Nancy. Tremolo of Light. (Indiana Poetry Chapbook Contest Ser.: No. 2). 40p. 1992. pap. 3.95 (1-880649-28-4) Writ Ctr Pr.

Pulley, R., jt. auth. see Mantin, Peter.

Pulley, Richard, jt. auth. see Mantin, Peter.

Pulley-Sayre, April. Coral Reef. (Exploring Earth's Biomes Ser.). (J). (gr. 5-8). 1995. lib. bdg. 20.40 (0-8050-4087-0) TFC Bks NY.

Pulleyblank, Douglas. Tone Lexical Phonology. 1986. lib. bdg. 120.00 (90-277-2123-8, Pub. by Kluwer Academic) Kluwer Academic.

Pulleyblank, Douglas, jt. auth. see Archangeli, Diana B.

Pulleyblank, Edwin G. The Background of the Rebellion of An Lu-Shan. LC 82-6200. (London Oriental Ser.). (Illus.). 264p. 1982. reprint ed. lib. bdg. 55.00 (0-313-23549-X, PUBA, Greenwood Pr) Greenwood.

— Outline of Classical Chinese Grammar. LC 95-173932. 206p. 1996. pap. 36.95 (0-7748-0541-2, PL1101, Pub. by UBC Pr) U of Wash Pr.

Pulleyn, Micah & Bracken, Sarah. Kids in the Kitchen: 100 Delicious, Fun, & Healthy Recipes to Cook & Bake. LC 93-39111. (Illus.). 112p. (J). 1995. pap. 12.95 (0-8069-0446-1) Sterling.

— Kids in the Kitchen: 100 Delicious, Fun, & Healthy Recipes to Cook & Bake. LC 93-39111. (Illus.). 112p. (J). (gr. 4 up). 1994. reprint ed. 24.95 (0-8069-0447-X, Sterling-Main St) Sterling.

Pulleyn, Rob & Mautor, Claudette. Everlasting Floral Gifts. LC 89-21909. (Illus.). 144p. 1990. 27.95 (0-8069-5826-X) Sterling.

Pulleyn, Rob, et al. Everlasting Floral Gifts. LC 89-21909. (Illus.). 144p. 1991. pap. 14.95 (0-8069-5827-8) Sterling.

Pulleyn, Simon. Prayer in Greek Religion. LC 97-20423. (Oxford Classical Monographs). (Illus.). 260p. 1998. text 75.00 (0-19-815088-1) OUP.

Pulliam. Nursing Assistant. 2nd ed. 1997. pap., teacher ed. 23.20 (0-8359-5161-8); pap., wbk. ed. 13.27 (0-8359-5162-6) P-H.

Pulliam, Becca, jt. auth. see Isacoff, Stuart.

Pulliam, H. Ronald & Dunford, Christopher. Programmed to Learn: An Essay on the Evolution of Culture. LC 79-17941. (Illus.). 1980. text 41.00 (0-231-04838-6) Col U Pr.

Pulliam, Henry, ed. see Saunders, Lesley.

Pulliam, John D. & Van Patten, James J. History of Education in America. 7th ed. LC 98-6873. 320p. (C). 1998. pap. text 38.00 (0-13-849654-4, Scribners Ref) Mac Lib Ref.

Pulliam, Jolynn. The Nursing Assistant: Acute, Subacute, & Long-Term Care. 2nd ed. LC 97-12604. 336p. 1997. pap. text 30.00 (0-8359-5141-3) P-H.

Pulliam, June M., jt. auth. see Fonseca, Anthony J.

Pulliam, Linda B. A Chicken Named Ruth: A Collection of True, Amusing Tales. 174p. (Orig.). 1995. pap. 12.95 (1-886951-05-5) Ahh Cappella.

Pulliam, Lynn, jt. auth. see Gupta, Kapil.

Pulliam, Mark S., jt. auth. see Haggard, Thomas R.

Pulliam, Tom. New York Times Crossword Dictionary. 3rd ed. 656p. 1997. pap. 18.00 (0-8129-2823-7, Times Bks) Crown Pub Group.

— New York Times Puzzle Dictionary. 3rd ed. 1995. 27.50 (0-8129-2373-1) Random.

Pulliam, Tom & Grundman, Claire. NY Times Crossword Puzzle Dictionary. 3rd ed. LC 84-40108. 1457p. 1999. pap. 7.99 (0-8129-3122-X, Times Bks) Crown Pub Group.

Pulliam, Tom & Grundman, Clare. The New York Times Crossword Puzzle Dictionary. 2nd ed. 624p. 1989. pap. 15.99 (0-446-38265-5) Warner Bks.

— The New York Times Crossword Puzzle Dictionary. 3rd rev. ed. LC 95-11416. 640p. 1995. 27.50 (0-8129-2606-4, Times Bks) Crown Pub Group.

Pullias, Earl & Young, James D. A Teacher Is Many Things. LC 68-14612. 314p. reprint ed. pap. 97.40 (0-8357-6671-3, 205684900094) Bks Demand.

Pullicino, Patrick M., et al, eds. Cerebral Small Artery Disease. LC 92-48462. (Advances in Neurology Ser.: Vol. 62). 256p. 1993. text 103.00 (0-7817-0051-5) Lppncott W & W.

Pullin, Beatriz, tr. see McKee, David.

Pullin, Jorge, jt. auth. see Gambini, Rodolfo.

Pullin, R. S. & Casal, C. V., eds. Consultation on Fish Genetic Resources. 61p. 1997. pap. 32.00 (971-8709-90-8, Pub. by ICLARM) Intl Spec Bk.

Pullin, Roger S., ed. Tilapia Genetic Resources for Aquaculture. (Conference Proceedings Ser.: No. 16). 108p. 1988. pap. 7.40 (971-10-2244-3, Pub. by ICLARM) Intl Spec Bk.

Pullin, Roger S., et al, eds. Aquaculture Research & Development in Rural Africa. (ICLARM Conference Proceedings Ser.: No. 27). 52p. 1991. write for info. (0-614-23051-9, Pub. by ICLARM) Intl Spec Bk.

— Environment & Aquaculture in Developing Countries. (ICLARM Conference Proceedings Ser.: No. 31). 359p. 1995. per. 22.00 (971-8709-05-3, Pub. by ICLARM) Intl Spec Bk.

— Second International Symposium on Tilapia in Aquaculture. 1990. 58.00 (971-10-2260-5, Pub. by ICLARM); pap. text 45.00 (971-10-2258-3, Pub. by ICLARM) Intl Spec Bk.

Pullin, Roger S., jt. ed. see Acosta, B. O.

Pullin, Roger S., jt. ed. see Moriarty, D. J.

***Pulling, Alexander.** The Order of the Coif. LC 99-37829. 2000. 75.00 (1-58477-025-2) Lawbk Exchange.

Pulling, Alexander. Order of the Coif. Mersky, Roy M. & Jacobstein, J. Myron, eds. LC 75-15318. (Classics in Legal History Reprint Ser.: Vol. 28). 288p. 1975. reprint ed. lib. bdg. 45.00 (0-89941-027-8, 301220) W S Hein.

***Pulling, Anne Frances.** Northern Cambria. LC 00-104041. (Images of America Ser.). (Illus.). 128p. 2000. pap. 18.99 (0-7385-0415-7) Arcadia Publng.

— Wind & Water Mills of Long Island. (Images of America Ser.). 128p. 1999. pap. 18.99 (0-7385-0288-X) Arcadia Publng.

Pulling, Pierre. Canoeing the Indian Way: Straight Talk for Modern Paddlers from the Dean of American Canoeists. LC 88-19206. (Illus.). 128p. 1989. reprint ed. pap. 8.95 (0-8117-2241-4) Stackpole.

Pulling, Sr. Anne Francis. Around Central Islip. (Images of America Ser.). (Illus.). 128p. 1998. pap. 16.99 (0-7524-0492-X) Arcadia Publng.

— Around Cresson & the Alleghenies. LC 97-170813. (Images of America Ser.). 1997. pap. 16.99 (0-7524-0505-5) Arcadia Publng.

— Babylon by the Sea. (Images of America Ser.). (Illus.). (Orig.). 1999. pap. 18.99 (0-7385-0091-7) Arcadia Publng.

Pullinger, D. J. The SuperJournal Project. 60p. 1994. pap. 58.00 (0-7503-0102-3) IOP Pub.

Pullinger, Diana. Final Legal Fictions: A Series of Cases from Folk-Lore & Opera. 117p. 1995. reprint ed. 39.00 (1-56169-106-2) Gaunt.

— More Legal Fictions: A Series of Cases from Shakespeare. 134p. 1995. reprint ed. 42.00 (1-56169-107-0) Gaunt.

Pullinger, Jackie. Chasing the Dragon. 236p. 1980. pap. 7.99 (0-89283-151-0, Vine Bks) Servant.

***Pullinger, John, et al.** Social Focus on the Unemployed. LC 98-175903. (Illus.). 1998. write for info. (0-11-621039-7) Statnry Office.

Pullinger, Kate. Where Does Kissing End? (Masks Ser.). 132p. 1995. pap. 12.99 (1-85242-277-7) Serpents Tail.

Pullinger, Kate, jt. auth. see Campion, Jane.

Pullinger, Kate, ed. see Gellner, David N.

Pullins, ed. see Baker, David & Engel, Robert.

Pullins, ed. see Bloomfield, Derek I.

Pullins, ed. see Goodman, Arthur & Hirsch, Lewis R.

Pullins, ed. see Hirsch, Lewis R. & Goodman, Arthur.

Pullins, ed. see Lissner, David.

Pullins, ed. see Myers, Nancy.

Pullins, ed. see Piascik, Chester.

Pullins, ed. see Pinet, Paul R.

Pullins, ed. see Plascik, Chester.

Pullis, Cheryl. Principles of Speedwriting Shorthand. 1984. pap. 14.50 (0-02-679840-9) Macmillan.

— Speedwriting Regency SW PP 98503. 1984. pap. 14.50 (0-02-679430-6) Macmillan.

Pullis, Cheryl, jt. auth. see Pullis, Joe M.

Pullis, Joe. Principles of Speedwriting Shorthand, Regency Professional Edition (First Course) 1987. text 27.64 (0-02-685100-8) Glencoe.

Pullis, Joe M. Speedwriting for Notetaking & Study Skills. 1990. 27.15 (0-02-685155-5) Macmillan.

— Speedwriting Shorthand Dictation & Transcription, Regency Professional Edition (Second Course) 1985. text 40.18 (0-02-685130-X) Glencoe.

Pullis, Joe M. & Bippen, Linda. Principles of Speedwriting Shorthand: Regency Edition. (Speedwriting Shorthand Ser.). 304p. (gr. 10-12). 1984. teacher ed. write for info. (0-672-98502-0); text. write for info. (0-672-98501-2); student ed. write for info. (0-672-98503-9) Macmillan.

Pullis, Joe M. & Pullis, Cheryl. Speedwriting Shorthand Abridged Dictionary: Regency Edition. (Speedwriting Shorthand Ser.). 192p. (gr. 10-12). 1984. text. write for info. (0-672-98504-7) Macmillan.

Pullis, Joe M., et al. Speedwriting Shorthand Dictation & Transcription: Regency Edition. (Speedwriting Shorthand Ser.). 352p. (gr. 10-12). 1984. teacher ed. write for info. (0-317-00348-8); text. write for info. (0-672-98506-3) Macmillan.

Pullis, Laura T. Information Investigation: Discovering Non-Fiction Books with Children. (Illus.). 240p. (J). (gr. 3-6). 1998. pap. text 17.95 (1-55591-955-3) Fulcrum Pub.

Pullis, T. Speedwriting. 2nd ed. 1983. pap. 12.65 (0-02-679660-0) Macmillan.

***Pullman.** Count Karstein. (J). 2000. pap. 5.95 (0-440-86266-3, Pub. by Transworld Publishers Ltd) Trafalgar.

Pullman, Alberte. Nuclear Magnresonance. (The Jerusalem Symposia on Quantum Chemistry & Biochemistry Ser.). 1978. text 184.00 (90-277-0932-7) Kluwer Academic.

P

An Asterisk (*) at the beginning of an entry indicates that the title is appearing for the first time.

— Nucleic Acids Vectors. (The Jerusalem Symposia on Quantum Chemistry & Biochemistry Ser.). 1983. text 261.50 (*90-277-1655-2*) Kluwer Academic.

Pullman, Alberte, et al, eds. Modelling of Biomolecular Structures & Mechanisms: Proceedings of the Jerusalem Symposium on Quantum Chemistry & Biochemistry (27th: 1994: Jerusalem, Israel) LC 94-32858. (The Jerusalem Symposia on Quantum Chemistry & Biochemistry Ser.: Vol. 27). 479p. 1995. text 217.50 (*0-7923-3102-8*) Kluwer Academic.

— Transport Through Membranes: Carriers, Channels & Pumps. (C). 1988. text 304.50 (*90-277-2831-3*) Kluwer Academic.

Pullman, Alberte & Dordrecht, Joshua, eds. Membrane Proteins - Structures, Interactions & Models: Proceedings of the Twenty-Fifth Jerusalem Symposium on Quantum Chemistry & Biochemistry Held in Jerusalem, Israel, May 18-21, 1992. LC 92-26604. (Jerusalem Symposia on Quantum Chemistry & Biochemistry Ser.: Vol. 25). 516p. (C). 1992. text 302.00 (*0-7923-1951-6*) Kluwer Academic.

Pullman, Bernard. The Atom in the History of Human Thought. Reisinger, Axel R., tr. (Illus.). 416p. 1998. 32.50 (*0-19-511447-7*) OUP.

— Emergence of Complexity in Mathematics, Physics, Chemistry, & Biology. 494p. 1997. pap. text 39.50 (*0-691-01238-5*, Pub. by Princeton U Pr) Cal Prin Full Svc.

Pullman, Bernard, ed. Catalysis in Chemistry & Biochemistry: Theory & Experiment. (Jerusalem Symposia on Quantum Chemistry & Biochemistry Ser.: No. 12). 1979. text 141.50 (*90-277-1039-2*) Kluwer Academic.

— Intermolecular Interactions: From Diatomics to Biopolymers. LC 77-24278. (Perspectives in Quantum Chemistry & Biochemistry Ser.: Vol. 2). 457p. reprint ed. pap. 141.70 (*0-608-17581-1*, 203041900069) Bks Demand.

— Quantum Mechanics of Molecular Conformations. LC 75-43927. (Perspectives in Quantum Chemistry & Biochemistry Ser.). 422p. reprint ed. pap. 130.90 (*0-7837-0195-0*, 204049100017) Bks Demand.

— Specificity in Biological Interactions. 1984. text 270.00 (*90-277-1813-X*) Kluwer Academic.

Pullman, Bernard, et al, eds. Carcinogenesis: Fundamental Mechanisms & Environmental Effects. (Jerusalem Symposia on Quantum Chemistry & Biochemistry Ser.: No. 13). 560p. 1980. text 191.50 (*90-277-1171-2*) Kluwer Academic.

— Dynamics on Surfaces. 1984. text 232.00 (*90-277-1830-X*) Kluwer Academic.

— Interrelationship among Aging, Cancer & Differentiation. 1985. text 176.50 (*90-277-2117-3*) Kluwer Academic.

Pullman, Bernard & Goldblum, Nathan, eds. Excited States in Organic Chemistry & Biochemistry. (Jerusalem Symposia on Quantum Chemistry & Biochemistry Ser.: No. 10). 1977. text 171.00 (*90-277-0853-3*) Kluwer Academic.

Pullman, Bernard & Jortner, Joshua, eds. Molecular Basis of Specificity in Nucleic Acid-Drug Interactions. (C). 1990. text 341.00 (*0-7923-0897-2*) Kluwer Academic.

Pullman, Bernard, jt. ed. see Bergmann, Ernst.

Pullman, Bernard, jt. ed. see Daudel, Raymond.

Pullman, Bernard, ed. see International Congress of Quantum Chemistry Staff.

Pullman, Bernard, ed. see Jerusalem Symposium on Quantum Chemistry & Biochem.

Pullman, Bernard, jt. ed. see Jortner, Joshua.

Pullman, Bernard, jt. ed. see Lowdin, Per-Olov.

Pullman, Geoffrey K., jt. ed. see Derbyshire, Desmond C.

Pullman, N. J. Matrix Theory & Its Applications: Selected Topics. LC 75-40845. (Pure & Applied Mathematics Ser.: Vol. 35). 252p. reprint ed. pap. 78.20 (*0-608-16666-9*, 202781600054) Bks Demand.

Pullman, Philip. The Amber Spyglass. (His Dark Materials Trilogy: Bk. 3). 400p. (YA). 2000. 19.95 (*0-679-87926-9*, Pub. by Knopf Bks Yng Read) Random.

— The Broken Bridge. (Illus.). 224p. (YA). (gr. 7 up). 1994. pap. 4.99 (*0-679-84715-4*, Pub. by Random Bks Yng Read) Random.

Pullman, Philip. Broken Bridge. 1994. 10.09 (*0-606-06945-3*, Pub. by Turtleback) Demco.

Pullman, Philip. Clockwork or All Wound Up. LC 97-27458. (Illus.). 128p. (J). (gr. 3-7). 1998. 16.95 (*0-590-12999-6*, A A Levine) Scholastic Inc.

— Clockwork or All Wound Up. LC 97-27458. (Illus.). 112p. (J). (gr. 3-7). 1999. pap. 4.99 (*0-590-12998-8*, Pub. by Scholastic Inc) Penguin Putnam.

***Pullman, Philip.** Count Karlstein. 256p. (YA). 2000. pap. 4.99 (*0-375-80348-3*) Knopf.

Pullman, Philip. Count Karlstein. LC 97-44160. (J). 1998. lib. bdg. 18.99 (*0-679-99255-3*, Pub. by Random Bks Yng Read) Random.

— Count Karlstein. LC 97-44160. 176p. (J). (gr. 3-8). 1998. 17.00 (*0-679-89255-9*, Pub. by Random Bks Yng Read) Random.

— Detective Stories. LC 97-41367. (Story Library). (Illus.). 244p. (J). (gr. 4-9). 1998. 14.95 (*0-7534-5157-3*); pap. 7.95 (*0-7534-5146-8*, Kingfisher) LKC.

***Pullman, Philip.** The Firework-Maker's Daughter. 1999. 16.95 (*0-7540-6055-1*) Chivers N Amer.

Pullman, Philip. The Firework-Maker's Daughter. LC 98-41048. (Illus.). 97p. (J). (gr. 3-6). 1999. 15.95 (*0-590-18719-8*, Pub. by Scholastic Inc) Penguin Putnam.

— The Fireworkmaker's Daughter. LC 98-41048. (Illus.). 1999. pap. write for info. (*0-590-12943-0*, A A Levine) Scholastic Inc.

— The Golden Compass. (His Dark Materials Trilogy: Bk. 1). (YA). 1998. pap. 5.99 (*0-345-91365-5*) Ballantine Pub Grp.

— The Golden Compass. (His Dark Materials Trilogy: Bk. 1). 351p. (YA). 1999. mass mkt. 5.99 (*0-345-41335-0*, Del Rey) Ballantine Pub Grp.

***Pullman, Philip.** The Golden Compass. (His Dark Materials Trilogy: Bk. 1). (YA). 1999. mass mkt. 5.99 (*0-345-91640-9*) Ballantine Pub Grp.

Pullman, Philip. The Golden Compass. LC 95-33397. (His Dark Materials Trilogy: Bk. 1). (Illus.). 416p. (YA). (gr. 7-12). 1996. 20.00 (*0-679-87924-2*) Knopf.

— The Golden Compass. (His Dark Materials Trilogy: Bk. 1). 420p. (YA). 1998. pap. 10.00 (*0-679-89310-5*, Pub. by Random Bks Yng Read) Random.

— The Golden Compass, Vol. 1. (His Dark Materials Trilogy: Bk. 1). (YA). 1997. 11.09 (*0-606-12945-6*, Pub. by Turtleback) Demco.

— I Was a Rat. LC 99-31806. (Illus.). 192p. (J). (gr. 3-5). 2000. lib. bdg. 17.99 (*0-375-90176-0*, Pub. by Knopf Bks Yng Read) Random.

— I Was a Rat! LC 99-31806. 192p. (J). (gr. 3-5). 2000. 15.95 (*0-375-80176-6*, Pub. by Knopf Bks Yng Read) Random.

Pullman, Philip. The Ruby in the Smoke. (J). 1985. 10.09 (*0-606-04047-1*, Pub. by Turtleback) Demco.

Pullman, Philip. The Ruby in the Smoke. LC 86-20983. 240p. (YA). (gr. 7 up). 1988. reprint ed. pap. 4.99 (*0-394-89589-4*, Pub. by Knopf Bks Yng Read) Random.

Pullman, Philip. Shadow in the North. (J). 1988. 10.09 (*0-606-04320-9*, Pub. by Turtleback) Demco.

Pullman, Philip. The Subtle Knife. (His Dark Materials Trilogy: Bk. 1). (YA). 1999. mass mkt. 5.99 (*0-345-41336-9*, Del Rey) Ballantine Pub Grp.

— The Subtle Knife. (His Dark Materials Trilogy: Bk. 1). (YA). 1999. mass mkt. 5.99 (*0-345-91641-7*) Ballantine Pub Grp.

— The Subtle Knife. (His Dark Materials Trilogy: Bk. 2). 352p. (YA). (gr. 7-12). 1999. pap. 10.00 (*0-375-80211-8*) Random.

— The Subtle Knife. LC PZ7.P968Su 1997. (His Dark Materials Trilogy: Bk. 2). 352p. (YA). 1997. 20.00 (*0-679-87925-0*, Pub. by Random Bks Yng Read) Random.

***Pullman, Philip.** The Subtle Knife. (His Dark Materials Trilogy: Bk. 1). (YA). 1998. 11.09 (*0-606-13822-6*, Pub. by Turtleback) Demco.

Pullman, Philip. Tiger in the Well. 1996. 10.09 (*0-606-09969-7*, Pub. by Turtleback) Demco.

— The Tin Princess. LC 93-38305. (Illus.). 304p. (YA). (gr. 9-12). 1994. 16.00 (*0-679-84757-X*, Pub. by Knopf Bks Yng Read) Random.

Pullman, Philip. The Tin Princess. 304p. (J). (gr. 5). 1996. pap. 4.99 (*0-679-87615-4*) Random.

Pullman, Philip. The Tin Princess. 1996. 10.09 (*0-606-09979-4*, Pub. by Turtleback) Demco.

Pullman, Philip. The White Mercedes. 1997. 10.09 (*0-606-12846-8*, Pub. by Turtleback) Demco.

Pullman, Philip. The White Mercedes. 176p. (J). (gr. 7). 1997. reprint ed. pap. 4.99 (*0-679-88623-0*) Knopf.

Pullman, Phillip. White Mercedes. 1992. pap. 15.99 (*0-679-93198-8*) McKay.

***Pullman, Phyllis.** How to Solve Word Problems in Arithmetic. (How to Solve Word Problems Ser.). (Illus.). 160p. 2000. pap. 9.95 (*0-07-136271-1*) McGraw.

Pullman, Wesley E. African American Men in Crisis: Proactive Strategies for Urban Youth. rev. ed. LC 95-9660. (Children of Poverty Ser.). (Illus.). 290p. 1995. text 77.00 (*0-8153-2141-4*) Garland.

Pullmann, B., jt. ed. see Bergmann, E. D.

Pullum, G. K., jt. ed. see Derbyshire, Desmond C.

Pullum, Geoffrey K. The Great Eskimo Vocabulary Hoax: And Other Irreverent Essays on the Study of Language. LC 90-11286. 246p. 1991. pap. 17.00 (*0-226-68534-9*) U Ch Pr.

— The Great Eskimo Vocabulary Hoax: And Other Irreverent Essays on the Study of Language. LC 90-11286. 200p. 1993. lib. bdg. 42.95 (*0-226-68533-0*) U Ch Pr.

Pullum, Geoffrey K. & Ladusaw, William A. Phonetic Symbol Guide. LC 86-7036. xxx, 266p. (C). 1993. lib. bdg. 35.00 (*0-226-68531-4*) U Ch Pr.

— Phonetic Symbol Guide. LC 86-7036. xxx, 296p. (C). 1997. pap. text 13.95 (*0-226-68532-2*) U Ch Pr.

— Phonetic Symbol Guide. 2nd ed. 335p. 1996. pap. text 20.00 (*0-226-68536-5*); lib. bdg. 75.00 (*0-226-68535-7*) U Ch Pr.

Pullum, Geoffrey K., jt. auth. see Jacobson, Pauline.

Pullum, Stephen J. Foul Demons, Come Out! The Rhetoric of Twentieth-Century American Faith Healing. LC 98-47817. 200p. 1999. 55.00 (*0-275-96083-8*, Praeger Pubs) Greenwood.

Pulman. Let Us Have Music for Violin, Vol. 2. (Illus.). 80p. 1944. pap. 10.95 (*0-8258-0247-4*, 0-3207) Fischer Inc NY.

Pulman, S. G. Word Meaning & Belief. LC 83-2622. 192p. 1983. text 73.25 (*0-89391-201-8*) Ablx Pub.

Pulmannova, Sylvia, jt. auth. see Dvureicenskij, Anatolij.

Pulmannova, Sylvia, jt. auth. see Ptak, Pavel.

Pulmano, V. A. & Murti, V., eds. Impact of Computational Mechanics on Engineering Problems: Proceedings, Sydney, Australia, August 1993. (Illus.). 198p. 1993. text 78.00 (*90-5410-324-8*, Pub. by A A Balkema) Ashgate Pub Co.

Pulmonary Circulation Symposium Staff. Pulmonary Circulation: Proceedings of the Symposium, Prague, 1969. Widimsky, J. et al, eds. (Progress in Respiratory Research Ser.: Vol. 5). 1971. 125.25 (*3-8055-1152-3*) S Karger.

Pulos, Arthur J. The American Design Adventure. (Illus.). 450p. 1990. reprint ed. pap. text 30.00 (*0-262-66068-7*) MIT Pr.

***Pulp & Paper Canada Staff.** Gadget Competition Booklet 1998 (Publication sur le Concours de Gadgets 1998) (ENG & FRE.). 143p. 1998. 13.60 (*1-896742-41-6*) Pulp & Paper.

— Gadget Competition Booklet 1997 (Publicaiton sur le Concours de Gadgets 1997) (ENG & FRE.). 135p. 1997. 13.60 (*1-896742-22-X*) Pulp & Paper.

— Gadget Competition Booklet 1996 (Publicaiton sur le Concours de Gadgets 1996) (FRE & ENG.). 127p. 1996. 13.60 (*1-896742-12-2*) Pulp & Paper.

— Gadget Competition Booklet 1995 (Publication sur le Concours de Gadgets 1995) (FRE & ENG.). 91p. 1995. 13.60 (*1-895288-91-6*) Pulp & Paper.

— Gadget Competition Booklet 1994 (Publication sur le Concours de Gadgets 1994) (ENG & FRE.). 80p. 1994. 13.60 (*1-895288-71-1*) Pulp & Paper.

— Gadget Competition Booklet 1993 (Publication sur le Concours de Gadgets 1993) (FRE & ENG.). 100p. 1993. 13.60 (*1-895288-52-5*) Pulp & Paper.

— Gadget Competition Booklet 1992 (Publication sur le Concours de Gadgets 1992) (FRE & ENG.). 66p. 1992. 13.60 (*1-895288-35-5*) Pulp & Paper.

Pulp & Paper Fundamental Research Soceity Staff. Proceedings of the 11th Fundamental Research Symposium Vol. 3: The Fundamentals of Papermaking Materials. 1998. 120.00 (*1-85802-211-8*, Pub. by Pira Internatl) Bks Intl VA.

Pulp & Paper Magazine Editors. Process, Quality & Information Control in the Worldwide Pulp & Paper Industry. (Illus.). 189p. 1996. pap. 59.00 (*0-87930-400-6*, 510) Miller Freeman.

Pulp & Paper Manufacture Staff. Pulp & Paper Manufacture Vol. 1: Pulping of Wood. 2nd ed. 1969. text 97.15 (*0-07-050924-7*) Glencoe.

— Pulp & Paper Manufacture Vol. 2: Control, Secondary Fiber, Structural Board, Coating. 2nd ed. 1969. text 119.92 (*0-07-050925-5*) McGraw.

***Pulpit Bible Staff.** Santa Biblia Para Pulpito RVA.Tr. of Pulpit Bible. 2000. 39.99 (*0-311-48789-0*) Baptist Spanish.

Puls, Barbara A. Working Together for a Competitive Workforce: A Handbook for State Policy Teams. LC 95-623347. (Investing in People Ser.: Vol. 6). 42p. 1994. 15.00 (*1-55516-330-0*, 3127) Natl Conf State Legis.

Puls, Barbara A., et al. Breaking New Ground: Community-Based Development Organizations. (Capitols & Communities Ser.). 21p. 1991. pap. text 15.00 (*1-55516-804-3*, 3908) Natl Conf State Legis.

Puls, Grace, jt. auth. see Gregory, Dave.

Puls, Herta. Textiles of the Kuna Indians of Panama. (Ethnography Ser.: No. 6). (Illus.). 72p. 1989. pap. 30.00 (*0-85263-942-2*, Pub. by Shire Pubns) Parkwest Pubns.

Puls, Jane E. & Osburn, A. E., eds. Pediatrics. 2nd ed. LC 96-13501. (Oklahoma Notes Ser.). 390p. 1996. 17.95 (*0-387-94634-9*) Spr-Verlag.

Puls, Joan. Every Bush Is Burning: A Spirituality for Today. 2nd ed. LC 85-51476. 120p. 1985. reprint ed. pap. 5.95 (*0-89622-280-2*) Twenty-Third.

— Hearts Set on the Pilgrimage: The Challenge of Discipleship in the World Church. LC 89-51385. 128p. (Orig.). 1989. pap. 7.95 (*0-89622-403-1*) Twenty-Third.

— A Spirituality of Compassion. LC 87-51633. 144p. 1988. pap. 7.95 (*0-89622-352-3*) Twenty-Third.

***Puls, Richard C.** Software for the Souls of the Next Millennium: An Archetypal Paradigm for Spiritual Development. LC 99-97838. 124p. 2000. pap. write for info. (*1-930344-00-7*) Narvard Enter.

Puls, W., jt. ed. see Kuhlman, Jochen.

Pulsiano, Phillip. An Annotated Bibliography of North American Doctoral Dissertations on Old English Language & Literature. LC 87-51125. (Medieval Texts & Studies: No. 3). 332p. 1988. 48.00 (*0-937191-06-X*) Mich St U Pr.

Pulsiano, Phillip & Skaptason, Jon. Barthar Saga. LC 83-48240. (Library of Medieval Literature). 178p. 1984. text 20.00 (*0-8240-9424-7*) Garland.

Pulsiano, Phillip & Treharne, Elaine M., eds. Anglo-Saxon Manuscripts & Their Heritage. LC 97-51288. (Illus.). 304p. 1998. text 78.95 (*1-85928-158-3*, Z106.5.G72E543, Pub. by Ashgate Pub) Ashgate Pub Co.

Pulsiano, Phillip, jt. ed. see Doane, A. N.

Pulsifer, David. Records of the Colony of New Plymouth in New England: Deeds & C., 1620-1651 & Book of Indian Records for Their Lands. 280p. 1999. pap. 23.00 (*0-7884-1119-5*, P850) Heritage Bk.

— Records of the Colony of New Plymouth in New England Vol. IX: Acts of the Commissioners of the United Colonies of New England, 1643-1651. 504p. 1999. reprint ed. pap. 21.00 (*0-7884-1051-2*, P847) Heritage Bk.

— Records of the Colony of New Plymouth in New England Vol. X: Acts of the Commissioners of the United States of New England, 1653-1679. 504p. 1999. reprint ed. pap. 35.50 (*0-7884-1068-7*, P848) Heritage Bk.

— Records of the Colony of New Plymouth in New England Vol. XI: Laws 1623-1682. 288p. 1999. pap. 22.00 (*0-7884-1093-8*, P849) Heritage.

Pulsifer, David, jt. ed. see Shurtleff, Nathaniel B.

Pulsifer, Gary, ed. Paul Bowles by His Friends. (Illus.). 160p. 1992. pap. 24.00 (*0-7206-0866-X*, Pub. by P Owen Ltd) Dufour.

Pulsinelli, jt. see Miller.

Pulsinelli, jt. auth. see Miller.

Pulsinelli, jt. ed. see Miller, Roger L.

Pulsinelli, Linda. Intermediate Algebra. 3rd ed. LC 90-35859. 820p. 1990. pap. text 88.00 (*0-02-396994-6*, Macmillan Coll) P-H.

— Microview. 7th ed. (C). 1991. pap. 22.00 (*0-06-045353-2*) Addson-Wesley Educ.

Pulsinelli, Linda & Hooper, Patricia. Essential Mathematics: An Interactive Approach. 800p. (C). 1990. pap. text 48.80 (*0-02-357170-5*, Macmillan Coll) P-H.

— Introductory Algebra: An Interactive Approach. 3rd ed. 673p. (C). 1990. pap. text 88.00 (*0-02-396984-9*, Macmillan Coll) P-H.

Pulsinelli, Robert W., jt. auth. see Miller, Roger L.

Pulsinelli, William A., ed. see Research (Princeton-Williamsburg) Conference on Cerebrovascular Diseases Staff.

Pulsipher, Gerald, jt. auth. see Hanks, Kurt.

***Pulsipher, Lydia M.** World Regional Geography. 1999. pap. text, student ed., wbk. ed. 25.95 (*0-7167-3449-4*) W H Freeman.

***Pulsipher, Lydia M., et al.** World Regional Geography LC 99-28227. 1999. pap. text 70.95 (*0-7167-3092-8*) W H Freeman.

Pulst, Stefan-M., ed. Neurogenetics. LC 99-22365. (Contemporary Neurology Ser.: No. 57). (Illus.). 488p. 1999. text 110.00 (*0-19-512975-X*) OUP.

Pultar, Gonul. Technique & Tradition in Beckett's Trilogy of Novels. LC 96-6281. 194p. 1996. lib. bdg. 42.00 (*0-7618-0306-8*) U Pr of Amer.

Pultorak, Edward G. Customizing Your Resume for Teaching Positions. LC 92-34092. 52p. (Orig.). (C). 1993. pap. text 18.50 (*0-8191-8938-3*) U Pr of Amer.

***Pultz, David, ed.** A Preaching Ministry: Twenty-One Sermons Preached by Harry Emerson Fosdick. 400p. 2000. pap. 25.00 (*0-9606818-1-7*) First Presbyterian Church in City.

Pultz, Jane W., ed. see Rappolt, Miriam E.

Pultz, John. The Body & the Lens: Photography 1839 to the Present. LC 94-37844. (The Perspectives Ser.). (Illus.). 176p. 1995. 16.95 (*0-8109-2703-9*, Pub. by Abrams) Time Warner.

Pulu, Tupou. Koyukon Athabaskan Songs. (Illus.). 45p. 1978. reprint ed. pap. 7.95 (*1-878051-34-2*, CP070) Circumpolar Pr.

***Pulver, Andrew & Davies, Steven Paul.** Brat Pack: Confidential. 2000. pap. 23.95 (*0-7134-8685-6*, Pub. by B T B) Bks Intl VA.

Pulver, Carol, jt. auth. see Haigh, Rosemary.

Pulver, Dale. Linn's Introduction to the Stamps of Mexico. 112p. 1992. 30.00 (*0-940403-49-8*) Linns Stamp News.

— Linn's Introduction to the Stamps of Mexico. (Illus.). 112p. 1992. pap. 14.95 (*0-940403-48-X*) Linns Stamp News.

Pulver, David. Complete Druid's Handbook. (Advanced Dungeons & Dragons, 2nd Edition Ser.). 1994. 20.00 (*1-56076-886-X*, Pub. by TSR Inc) Random.

— GURDS Technomancer: High Magic, High Tech, High Adventure. Purch, Sean, ed. (Illus.). 128p. 1998. pap. 19.95 (*1-55634-359-0*, 6087, Pub. by S Jackson Games) BookWorld.

— GURPS Bio-Tech: The Next Step in Human Evolution. Punch, Sean, ed. (Illus.). 144p. 1998. pap. 20.95 (*1-55634-336-1*, 6524, Pub. by S Jackson Games) BookWorld.

Pulver, David. GURPS Psionics: Fantastic Powers of Mind over Matter. Steve Jackson Games Staff & McCubbin, Chris, eds. (GURPS Ser.). (Illus.). 128p. 1991. pap. 19.95 (*1-55634-196-2*, 6040, Pub. by S Jackson Games) BookWorld.

Pulver, David. Gurps Reign of Steel: The War Is Over. The Robots Won. Pinsonneault, Susan, ed. (Illus.). 128p. 1997. pap. 19.95 (*1-55634-330-2*, 6079) S Jackson Games.

— Gurps Robots: Bold Experiments, Faithful Servants, Soulless Killers. Pinsonneault, Susan, ed. (Illus.). 128p. 1997. pap. 19.95 (*1-55634-233-0*, 6511) S Jackson Games.

— GURPS Traveller: Alien Races 1: Zhodani, Vagr & Other Races of the Spinward Marches. Wiseman, Loren, ed. (Illus.). 144p. 1998. pap. 20.95 (*1-55634-361-2*, 6603, Pub. by S Jackson Games) BookWorld.

Pulver, David. GURPS Ultra-Tech: A Sourcebook of Weapons & Equipment for Future Ages. 2nd rev. ed. Punch, Sean, ed. 1996. 19.95 (*1-55634-315-9*, Pub. by S Jackson Games) BookWorld.

Pulver, David. GURPS Ultra-Tech 2: Hard-Core, Hard-Wired Hardware, 2 vols. Seabolt, Gene & Punch, Sean, eds. (Illus.). 128p. 1997. pap. 19.95 (*1-55634-337-X*, 6525, Pub. by S Jackson Games) BookWorld.

— GURPS Vehicles: From Chariots to Cybertanks...and Beyond! 2nd ed. Punch, Sean, ed. (Illus.). 208p. 1998. pap. 24.95 (*1-55634-325-6*, 6505) S Jackson Games.

Pulver, Glen. New Alliances for Community Education & Technical Assistance in Rural Areas. (New Alliances for Rural America Ser.). (Orig.). 1988. pap. text 6.00 (*1-55877-020-8*) Natl Governor.

Pulver, Jeff. The Internet Telephone Toolkit. LC 96-17987. 201p. 1996. pap. text 29.95 incl. cd-rom (*0-471-16352-X*) Wiley.

Pulver, Jeffrey. A Biographical Dictionary of Old English Music. LC 69-16666. (Music Ser.). 538p. 1973. reprint ed. lib. bdg. 59.50 (*0-306-71103-6*) Da Capo.

— A Biographical Dictionary of Old English Music. 537p. 1990. reprint ed. lib. bdg. 99.00 (*0-7812-9008-2*) Rprt Serv.

— Paganini, the Romantic Virtuoso. (Music Book Index Ser.). 328p. 1992. reprint ed. lib. bdg. 89.00 (*0-7812-9470-3*) Rprt Serv.

Pulver, Joseph S., Sr. Nightmare's Disciple. (Call of Cthulhu Fiction Ser.). 396p. 1999. pap. 14.95 (*1-56882-118-2*, Chaosium Fiction) Chaosium.

Pulver, Kathryn. Is That So? LC 96-90932. 345p. 1997. 18.95 (*0-533-12218-X*) Vantage.

Pulver, Kathryn, jt. auth. see Mouseglib, Pomfret.

P

Pulver, Kathryn. Encore, Mouseglib, Encore! LC 96-90611. 1996. 16.95 (*0-533-12106-X*) Vantage.

Pulver, Kathryn, ed. see Talbert, Debra.

***Pulver, Marco.** Tribut der Seuche Oder: Seuchenmythen Als Quelle Sozialer Kalibrierung: Eine Rekonstruktion Des Aids-Diskurses Vor Dem Hintergrund Von Studien Zur Historizitat Des Seuchendispositivs. (GER., Illus.). 868p. 1999. 97.00 (*3-631-34512-7*) P Lang Pubng.

Pulver, Mary M. Show Stopper: A Kori & Peter Brichter Mystery. 204p. 1992. 19.95 (*0-8027-3210-0*) Walker & Co.

Pulver, Robin. Axle Annie. LC 98-8696. (Illus.). (J). 1999. lib. bdg. 16.01 (*0-8037-2097-1*, Dial Yng Read) Peng Put Young Read.

— Axle Annie. Kane, Cindy, ed. LC 98-8696. (Illus.). 32p. (J). (ps-3). 1999. 15.99 (*0-8037-2096-3*, Dial Yng Read) Peng Put Young Read.

— Mrs. Toggle & the Dinosaur. (J). 1995. 9.15 (*0-606-07896-7*) Turtleback.

— Mrs. Toggle's Beautiful Blue Shoe. LC 92-40824. (Illus.). 32p. (J). (ps-2). 1994. mass mkt. 13.95 (*0-02-775456-1*, Four Winds Pr) S&S Childrens.

— Mrs. Toggle's Zipper. LC 88-37251. (Illus.). 32p. (J). (ps-2). 1990. lib. bdg. 13.95 (*0-02-775451-0*, Four Winds Pr) S&S Childrens.

— Mrs. Toggle's Zipper. (J). 1993. 10.15 (*0-606-05484-7*, Pub. by Turtleback) Demco.

— Mrs. Toggle's Zipper. LC 92-39355. (Illus.). 32p. (J). (ps-2). 1993. reprint ed. mass mkt. 4.95 (*0-689-71689-3*) Aladdin.

— Nobody's Mother Is in Second Grade. LC 91-16395. (Illus.). 32p. (J). (gr. k-3). 1992. 15.99 (*0-8037-1210-3*, Dial Yng Read) Peng Put Young Read.

— Way to Go, Alex! LC 99-10683. (Illus.). 32p. (J). (gr. 1-3). 1999. lib. bdg. 14.95 (*0-8075-1583-3*) A Whitman.

***Pulver, Robin & Alley, R. W.** Mrs. Toggle's Class Picture Day. LC 99-58609. (J). 2000. pap. write for info. (*0-590-11741-6*) Scholastic Inc.

Pulver, Robin, ed. see Dorman, Gayle.

Pulverer, Gerhard, et al, eds. Pathogenicity & Clinical Significance of Coagulase-Negative Staphylococci. (Zentralblatt fur Bakteriologie Ser.: Vol. 16). 290p. 1987. lib. bdg. 140.00 (*0-89574-242-X*, Pub. by Gustav Fischer) Balogh.

Pulvino, Charles J. Communicating with Clients: A Guide for Financial Professionals. LC 87-153498. 1987. pap. 25.00 (*0-13-153578-1*) P-H.

Pulvino, Charles J., jt. auth. see Lee, James L.

Pulvirenti, M., jt. ed. see Bellomo, Nicola.

Pulvirenti, Mario, jt. auth. see Marchioro, Carlo.

Pulvirenti, Mario, jt. ed. see Cercignani, Carlo.

Pulwarty, Roger S., jt. auth. see Diaz, Henry F.

Pulyer, Y. M. Electromagnetic Devices for Motion Control & Signal Processing. (Illus.). 472p. 1992. 89.95 (*0-387-97827-5*) Spr-Verlag.

Pulzer, Peter. German Politics, 1945-1995. (Illus.). 210p. 1996. pap. text 16.95 (*0-19-878111-3*) OUP.

— Germany, 1870-1945: Politics, State Formation & War. LC 96-43074. (Illus.). 190p. 1997. pap. text 17.95 (*0-19-878135-0*) OUP.

— Germany, 1870-1945: Politics, State Formation & War. LC 96-43074. (Illus.). 192p. (C). 1997. text 65.00 (*0-19-878134-2*) OUP.

Pulzer, Peter. The Rise of Political Anti-Semitism in Germany & Austria. rev. ed. LC 88-15062. 384p. 1988. pap. 21.50 (*0-674-77166-4*) HUP.

Pulzer, Peter, jt. auth. see Luther, Kurt R.

***Puma, Michael & Drury, Darrel.** Exploring New Directions: Title I in the Year 2000. unabridged ed. 69p. 2000. 16.00 (*0-88364-231-X*) Natl Sch Boards.

Puma, J. Extended Scale Playing for Guitar. 48p. 1993. pap. 7.95 (*0-7935-1686-2*, 00697237) H Leonard.

Puma, John La, see La Puma, John.

Puma, Richard D. De, see De Puma, Richard D., ed.

Puma, Richard D. De, see Begley, Vimala & De Puma, Richard D., eds.

Puma, Richard D. De, see De Puma, Richard D.

Pumarega. Ingles en Veinte Lecciones. (SPA.). 1997. pap. text 6.98 (*968-403-429-6*) Selector.

Pumari, Antonio N. & Rodriguez, Jose A. Co-Existence & Persistence of Strange Attractors, Vol. 165. LC 97-11974. (Lecture Notes in Mathematics Ser.). 1997. pap. write for info. (*3-540-62731-6*) Spr-Verlag.

Pumarino, Jose Maria & Reyes, Gustavo. Ahora O Nunca! (SPA., Illus.). 146p. 1997. pap. 8.98 (*968-403-997-2*) Selector.

Pume, N. D. & Magnyickij, A. V. Agricultural Dictionary in Eight Languages, 2 vols., Set. (BUL, CZE, ENG, GER & HUN.). 1720p. 1970. write for info. (*0-8288-7191-4*) Fr & Eur.

Pumfrey, Peter D. Improving Children's Reading in the Junior School: Challenges & Responses. 400p. 1991. pap. text 37.95 (*0-304-31723-3*) Continuum.

Pumfrey, Peter D. & Elliot, Colin D., eds. Children's Difficulties in Reading, Spelling & Writing: Challenges & Responses. 260p. 1990. pap. 39.95 (*1-85000-691-1*) Taylor & Francis.

Pumfrey, Peter D. & Verma, Gajendra K., eds. The Foundation Subjects & Religious Education in Primary Schools. LC 93-27228. (Cultural Diversity & the Curriculum Ser.: Vol. 3). 216p. 1993. 89.95 (*0-7507-0143-9*, Falmer Pr); pap. 29.95 (*0-7507-0144-7*, Falmer Pr) Taylor & Francis.

Pumfrey, Peter D. & Verman, Gajendra K., eds. The Foundation Subjects & Religious Education in Secondary Schools. LC 92-39723. (Cultural Diversity & the Curriculum Ser.: Vol. 1). 256p. 1993. pap. 39.95 (*0-7507-0140-4*, Falmer Pr) Taylor & Francis.

Pumfrey, Peter D., jt. auth. see Verma, Gajendra K.

Pumfrey, Peter D., jt. ed. see Owen, Pamela.

Pumfrey, Peter D., jt. ed. see Verma, Gajendra K.

Pumilio, J. M. Access to Asset Protection & Insider Secrets No. 1: Legally Safeguard Your Personal Wealth. large type ed. (Illus.). 180p. 1998. 29.95 incl. cd-rom (*0-9665330-0-3*, TMGCD51001) Tech Mktg Grp.

Pummer, K., ed. Biological Modulation of Solid Tumours by Interferons. LC 94-5664. (European School of Oncology Monographs). (Illus.). viii, 75p. 1994. 73.95 (*0-387-57764-5*) Spr-Verlag.

Pummer, Reinhard. The Samaritans. (Iconography of Religions Ser.: Vol. XXIII-5). (Illus.). xiv, 46p. 1987. pap. 54.00 (*90-04-07891-6*) Brill Academic Pubs.

***Pump, Anna, et al.** Country Weekend Entertaining: Seasonal Recipes from Loaves & Fishes & the Bridgehampton Inn. LC 98-8311. (Illus.). 384p. 1999. 30.00 (*0-385-48827-0*) Doubleday.

Pumpel-Mader, Maria, et al. Deutsche Wortbildung: Typen und Tendenzen der Gegenwartssprache. Institut fur Deutsche Sprache Staff, ed. (Sprache der Gegenwart Ser.: No. 80). (GER.). xx, 340p. (C). 1992. lib. bdg. 136.95 (*3-11-012445-9*) De Gruyter.

Pumpelly, Raphael. Census of the United States: Tenth Decennial Census, 1880: Report of the Mining Industries of the United States (Exclusive of the Precious Metals), with Special Investigations into the Iron Resources of the Republic & into the Cretaceous Coals of the Northwest, 22 vols., Vol. 15, Series 38. LC 07-18862. (Illus.). xxxviii, 1025p. 1991. reprint ed. lib. bdg. 400.00 (*0-88354-438-5*) N Ross.

Pumphrey, Caroline. Charlbury of our Childhood. 1999. pap. 21.00 (*1-85072-050-9*, Pub. by W Sessions) St Mut.

Pumphrey, Jane, jt. ed. see Ansley, Norman.

Pumphrey, Jean. Sheltered at the Edge. 56p. 1981. 30.00 (*0-941490-32-7*) Solo Pr.

Pumphrey, Linda, et al. Mountain Mist Blue Book of Quilts. (Illus.). 56p. (Orig.). 1996. pap. 8.95 (*0-9652122-0-3*) Stearns Tech.

Pumphrey, Margaret B. Stories of the Pilgrims. McHugh, Michael J., ed. (Illus.). 244p. (J). (gr. 3-5). 1991. pap. text 6.00 (*1-930092-36-9*, CLP29545) Christian Liberty.

— Stories of the Pilgrims: Answer Key. McHugh, Michael J., ed. 1991. 1.00 (*1-930092-37-7*) Christian Liberty.

Pumphrey, W. Jerome. Creepy Things are Scaring Me. (Illus.). 32p. (ps-3). 14.95 (*0-06-028962-7*) HarpC.

— Creepy Things Are Scaring Me. (Illus.): 32p. (ps-3). 14.89 (*0-06-028963-5*); 5.95 (*0-06-443680-2*) HarpC.

Pumpian-Mindlin, Eugene, ed. Psychoanalysis As Science: The Hixon Lectures on the Scientific Status of Psychoanalysis. LC 70-106692. 174p. 1970. reprint ed. lib. bdg. 59.50 (*0-8371-3365-3*, PUMP, Greenwood Pr) Greenwood.

Pumpin, Cuno. The Essence of Corporate Strategy. 160p. 1987. text 78.95 (*0-566-02565-5*, Pub. by Gower) Ashgate Pub Co.

— The Essence of Corporate Strategy. (Business Enterprise Ser.). 196p. 1989. pap. text 28.95 (*0-7045-0638-6*, Pub. by Gower) Ashgate Pub Co.

— How World Class Companies Become World Class: Studies in Corporate Dynamism. 218p. 1993. pap. 33.95 (*0-566-07478-8*, Pub. by Gower) Ashgate Pub Co.

Pumplun, D., jt. auth. see Rohrl, H.

Pumroy, Eric L. & Brockman, Paul. A Guide to Manuscript Collections of the Indiana Historical Society & Indiana State Library. LC 86-18593. xviii, 513p. 1986. 20.00 (*0-87195-006-5*) Ind Hist Soc.

Pumroy, Eric L. & Rampelmann, Katja, compiled by. Research Guide to the Turner Movement in the United States, 33. LC 96-5846. (Bibliographies & Indexes in American History Ser.: No. 33). 392p. 1996. lib. bdg. 89.50 (*0-313-29763-0*, Greenwood Pr) Greenwood.

Pumtree, Anne. Something New, 3 vols., Set. McLeod, Deborah, ed. (Broadview Literary Texts Ser.). 250p. 1996. pap. 12.95 (*1-55111-079-2*) Broadview Pr.

Pun, Gheorghe. Marcus Contectual Grammars. LC 97-34636. (Studies in Linguistic & Philosophy 7). 392p. 1997. text 140.50 (*0-7923-4783-8*) Kluwer Academic.

Pun, Pattle. Evolution: Nature & Scripture in Conflict? - Chinese Edition. (CHI.). 311p. 1999. pap. 10.00 (*1-56582-014-2*) Christ Renew Min.

Punancy, Karlene & Cosentino, Edmund. Basic Immigration: A Simple Survival Guide. 2nd large type ed. (CRP, ENG & SPA., Illus.). 330p. 1997. pap. text 12.95 (*0-9660444-0-1*) Multiculture Resrch.

Puncel, Maria. Abuelita Opalina. 15th ed. (Barco de Vapor Ser.). (SPA.). 1991. 11.05 (*0-606-05101-5*, Pub. by Turtleback) Demco.

— El Amigo Nuevo. (Illus.). 32p. (Orig.). (J). (gr. 3-5). pap. text 7.50 (*1-56492-108-5*) Laredo.

— El Premio. (Illus.). 32p. (Orig.). (J). (gr. 3-5). pap. text 7.50 (*1-56492-107-7*) Laredo.

Puncel, Maria, ed. Las Cosas de Cada Dia - Everyday Things. Aixela, Javier F., tr. (Diccionarios Visuales Altea Ser. - Visual Dictionary Ser.). (SPA., Illus.). 64p. (YA). (gr. 5-12). 1992. write for info. (*84-372-4527-3*) Santillana.

Puncel, Maria & Basquez, Juan J., eds. Cuerpo Humano - The Human Body. Secanell, Jose M., tr. (Diccionarios Visuales Altea Ser. - Visual Dictionary Ser.). (SPA., Illus.). 63p. (YA). (gr. 5-12). 1992. write for info. (*84-372-4528-1*) Santillana.

Puncel, Maria, tr. see Ahlberg, Janet & Ahlberg, Allan.

Puncel, Maria, tr. see Steig, William.

Punch. Coping with Corruption. 1993. pap. text 40.00 (*90-6544-715-6*) Kluwer Academic.

Punch, Keith F. Introduction to Social Research: Quantitative & Qualitative Approaches. LC 98-61492. 319 p. 1998. write for info. (*0-7619-5812-6*) Sage.

***Punch, Keith F.** Introduction to Social Research: Quantitative & Qualitative Approaches. 336p. 1998. pap. 25.95 (*0-7619-5813-4*) Sage.

Punch, Maurice. Dirty Business: Exploring Corporate Misconduct: Analysis & Cases. 304p. 1996. 79.95 (*0-8039-7603-8*); pap. 28.95 (*0-8039-7604-6*) Sage.

— The Politics & Ethics of Fieldwork. (Qualitative Research Methods Ser.: No. 3). 96p. 1985. text 24.00 (*0-8039-2562-X*); pap. text 10.50 (*0-8039-2517-4*) Sage.

Punch, Maurice, ed. Control in the Police Organization. (Organization Studies: No. 4). 368p. 1983. 45.00 (*0-262-16090-0*) MIT Pr.

***Punch, Sean.** Gurps GM's Screen. 1999. 10.95 (*1-55634-397-3*, Pub. by S Jackson Games) BookWorld.

Punch, Sean. GURPS Wizards. Elmy, Jack, ed. (Illus.). 128p. 1998. pap. 19.95 (*1-55634-270-5*, 6411, Pub. by S Jackson Games) BookWorld.

Punch, Sean & Seabolt, Gene, eds. GURPS Black Ops: Find the Truth--And Kill It. 128p. 1997. pap. 19.95 (*1-55634-333-7*, Pub. by S Jackson Games) BookWorld.

Punch, Sean, ed. see Barton, William A.

Punch, Sean, ed. see Blankenship, Loyd.

Punch, Sean, ed. see Carella, C. J.

Punch, Sean, ed. see Dale, Malcolm & Thomas, Klaude.

Punch, Sean, ed. see Daniels, Steve & MacLean, Jim.

Punch, Sean, ed. see Godwin, Russell, et al.

Punch, Sean, ed. see Jackson, Steve, et al.

Punch, Sean, ed. see Polver, David.

Punch, Sean, ed. see Pulver, David.

Punch, Sean, ed. see Rose, Greg.

Punch, Sean, ed. see Seabolt, Gene.

Punch, Terrence M., ed. Genealogist's Handbook for Atlantic Canada Research. 2nd ed. LC 97-26232. 150p. 1997. 15.00 (*0-88082-067-5*) New Eng Hist.

Punchard, Lorraine. Playtime Pottery & Porcelain: From Europe & Asia. LC 95-52684. (Illus.). 192p. (YA). (gr. 10-13). 1996. pap. write for info. (*0-88740-974-1*) Schiffer.

— Playtime Pottery & Porcelain: From the United Kingdom & the United States. LC 95-44164. (Illus.). 160p. (YA). (gr. 10-13). 1996. pap. 29.95 (*0-88740-958-X*) Schiffer.

Punchard, Neville & Kelly, Frank, eds. Free Radicals: A Practical Approach. (Practical Approach Ser.: Vol. 168). (Illus.). 334p. (C). 1996. text 110.00 (*0-19-963560-9*); pap. text 55.00 (*0-19-963559-5*) OUP.

Punchard, Neville A., jt. ed. see Cason, John.

Punches, Laurie C. How to Simply Cut Children's Hair. Martinez, Carla, ed. LC 89-90694. (How to Simply Ser.: Vol. 2). (Illus.). 1015p. (Orig.). 1989. pap. 7.95 (*0-929883-10-1*) Punches Prodns.

— How to Simply Cut Hair. Martinez, Carla et al, eds. LC 88-92443. (How to Simply Ser.: Vol. 1). (Illus.). 109p. (Orig.). (YA). (gr. 11 up). 1989. pap. 8.95 (*0-929883-06-3*) Punches Prodns.

— How to Simply Cut Hair Even Better: Advanced Haircutting. LC 88-92468. (How to Simply Ser.: Vol. 5). (Illus.). 129p. (Orig.). (YA). (gr. 11 up). 1989. pap. 9.95 (*0-929883-08-X*) Punches Prodns.

— How to Simply Highlight Hair. LC 88-92469. (How to Simply Ser.: Vol. 4). (Illus.). 79p. (Orig.). (YA). (gr. 11 up). 1989. pap. 6.95 (*0-929883-02-0*) Punches Prodns.

— How to Simply Perm Hair. LC 88-92467. (How to Simply Ser.: Vol. 3). (Illus.). 74p. (Orig.). (YA). (gr. 11 up). 1989. pap. 6.95 (*0-929883-04-7*) Punches Prodns.

Puncochar, Daniel E. Interpretation of Geometric Dimensioning & Tolerancing. 2nd rev. ed. (Illus.). 160p. 1997. pap. 25.95 (*0-8311-3072-5*) Indus Pr.

Pundeff, Marin V. Bulgaria: A Bibliographic Guide. LC 65-60006. (Bibliographic Guides Ser.). 1968. reprint ed. 12.95 (*0-405-00059-6*) Ayer.

— Bulgaria in American Perspective: Political & Cultural Issues. 334p. 1994. 51.50 (*0-88033-295-6*, 398, Pub. by East Eur Monographs) Col U Pr.

Punderson, James M., 4th & O'Rourke, Charles M. How to Sue Your Stockbroker Without a Lawyer. LC 98-85212. (Illus.). 274p. 1998. pap. 49.95 (*0-9663989-0-4*, ACP9801) AllCourt.

Pundik, Herbert. In Denmark It Could Not Happen. LC 98-10650. 176 p. 1998. 16.95 (*965-229-176-5*) Gefen Bks.

Pundt, Helen M. AHEA: A History of Excellence. 1980. 21.00 (*0-8461-5042-5*) AAFCS.

Pundt, Hermann G. Schinkel's Berlin: A Study in Environmental Planning. LC 75-172325. (Illus.). 283p. reprint ed. pap. 87.80 (*0-7837-4181-2*, 205903000012) Bks Demand.

Puner, Helen W. Sigmund Freud: His Life & Mind. 295p. (C). 1992. pap. 24.95 (*1-56000-611-0*) Transaction Pubs.

Puner, Linda P. Starting Out Suburban: A Frosh Year Survival Guide. LC 96-67384. 240p. (Orig.). (YA). 1996. pap. 16.95 (*0-9651403-0-X*) New Forge.

Puner, Morton, jt. ed. see Melby, Ernest O.

Pung, H. K. Networks: The Next Millennium. Ngoh, L. H. & Biswas, J., eds. 490p. 1997. text 60.00 (*981-02-3129-6*) World Scientific Pub.

Pungente, John J. & O'Malley, Martin. More Than Meets the Eye: Watching Television Watching Us. 272p. 1999. 24.95 (*0-7710-7100-0*) McCland & Stewart.

Pungetti, Gloria, jt. auth. see Makhzoumi, Jala.

***Pungier, Jean.** John Baptist de la Salle: The Message of His Catechism. Rummery, Gerard, ed. Murdoch, Oswald, tr. from FRE. LC 99-71585. (Lasallian Resources: Vol. 4).Tr. of Jean-Baptiste de la Salle: Le Message de Son Catechisme. (Illus.). xvi, 273p. 1999. pap. 20.00 (*0-944808-22-0*) Lasallian Pubns.

Pungitore, Verna L. Innovation & the Library: The Adoption of New Ideas in Public Libraries, 86. LC 95-3808. 208p. 1995. 55.00 (*0-313-28673-6*, Greenwood Pr) Greenwood.

— Public Librarianship: An Issues - Oriented Approach, 63. LC 89-2189. (Contributions in Librarianship & Information Science Ser.: No. 63). 240p. 1989. 55.00 (*0-313-26072-9*, PPB/, Greenwood Pr) Greenwood.

Pungor, E. Coulometric Analysis. 302p. 1979. 175.00 (*0-569-08551-9*, Pub. by Collets) St Mut.

Pungor, E., ed. Bioelectroanalysis No. 2: Second Symposium Held at Matrafured, Hungary 11-15 October, 1992. (Illus.). 450p. 1993. 75.00 (*963-05-6529-3*, Pub. by Akade Kiado) Intl Spec Bk.

Pungor, E. & Buzas, I. Bioelectroanalysis: 1st Symposium Held at Matrafured, Hungary on October 6-8, 1986. 433p. (C). 1987. 150.00 (*963-05-4641-8*, Pub. by Akade Kiado) St Mut.

— Coulometric Analysis: Conference Held at Matrafured, Hungary, October 17-19, 1978. 301p. (C). 1979. 100.00 (*963-05-2021-4*, Pub. by Akade Kiado) St Mut.

Pungor, Erno. Ion-Selective Electrodes. 264p. 1977. 110.00 (*0-569-08470-9*, Pub. by Collets) St Mut.

— Ion-Selective Electrodes 5: Proceedings of the Fifth Symposium Held at Matrafured, Hungary 9-13, October, 1988. 674p. (C). 1989. 150.00 (*963-05-5623-5*, Pub. by Akade Kiado) St Mut.

— Practical Guide to Instrumental Analysis. 400p. 1994. boxed set 99.95 (*0-8493-8681-0*) CRC Pr.

Pungor, Erno, et al, eds. Dynamic Characteristics of Ion-Selective Electrodes. 192p. 1988. 89.00 (*0-8493-6493-0*, QD571, CRC Reprint) Franklin.

Pungur, Joseph. Theology Interpreted: A Guide to Christian Doctrine - God, the World & Mankind, Vol. I. LC 87-8250. (Christian Doctrine of God, Revelation, Creation, Providence, Man & Sin Ser.). 246p. (Orig.). (C). 1987. pap. text 24.00 (*0-8191-6355-4*); lib. bdg. 43.50 (*0-8191-6354-6*) U Pr of Amer.

— Theology Interpreted, Vol. 2: A Guide to Christian Doctrine. 226p. (Orig.). (C). 1992. pap. text 27.50 (*0-8191-8892-1*); lib. bdg. 54.00 (*0-8191-8891-3*) U Pr of Amer.

Punia, Deep. Social Values in Folklore. (C). 1993. 19.50 (*81-7033-193-5*, Pub. by Rawat Pubns) S Asia.

Punia, R. K., jt. ed. see Sharma, M. L.

Punica, George. Messerschmitt ME 210-410 in Action. LC 95-118258. (Aircraft in Action Ser.). (Illus.). 50p. 1994. pap. 9.95 (*0-89747-320-5*) Squad Sig Pubns.

Puniello, Francoise S. & Rusak, Halina R. Abstract Expressionist Women Painters: An Annotated Bibliography: Elaine de Kooning, Helen Frankenthaler, Grace Hartigan, Lee Krasner, Joan Mitchell, Ethel Schwabacher. LC 95-21924. 372p. 1996. 55.00 (*0-8108-2998-3*) Scarecrow.

Punin, N. N., et al. The Diaries of Nikolay Punin: 1904-1953. LC 98-58095. (Harry Ransom Humanities Research Centre Imprint Ser.). (GER.). 268p. 1999. 29.95 (*0-292-76589-4*) U of Tex Pr.

Punithalingam, E. Mycological Papers No. 159: Ascochyta II. Species on Monocotyledons (excluding grasses), Cryptograms & Gymnosperms. 235p. (C). 1987. pap. text 41.50 (*0-85198-592-0*) C A B Intl.

Punja, Shobita. This is India. 1998. 39.95 (*1-85368-409-0*, Pub. by New5 Holland) Sterling.

Punjab Law Agency Staff, ed. Cases & Material on Arbitration Act, (1940-1988) 2nd ed. (C). 1989. 175.00 (*0-7855-4760-6*) St Mut.

***Punjab University Staff.** Sikh Religion & Human Civilization. Singh, Jodh, ed. LC 99-933156. xxxiv, 164 p. 1999. 15.00 (*81-7380-518-0*, Pub. by Pubn Bureau) S Asia.

Punjaba, Tomas J. Medical Aspects of Food Handling: Medical Subject Research Analysis with Bibliography. LC 84-45737. 150p. 1986. pap. 44.50 (*0-88164-253-3*) ABBE Pubs Assn.

Punjabi University Staff, jt. auth. see Singh, Navtej.

Punk Magazine Editors. Punk: The Original. LC 97-104585. (Illus.). 128p. 1996. pap. text 19.95 (*0-9647858-5-4*) Trans-High Corp.

***Punka, George.** Fiat CR32/CR42 in Action. (Aircraft in Action Ser.: Vol. 172). (Illus.). 50p. 2000. pap. 8.95 (*0-89747-411-2*) Squad Sig Pubns.

Punka, George. FW-189 in Action. (Aircraft in Action Ser.). (Illus.). 50p. 1994. pap. 9.95 (*0-89747-310-8*) Squad Sig Pubns.

— Hungarian Air Force. (Foreign Airforces Ser.). (Illus.). 64p. 1995. pap. 11.95 (*0-89747-349-3*) Squad Sig Pubns.

Punley, Randolph J., ed. see Frazier, Gregory W.

Punnett, Betty J. & Shenkar, Oded, eds. Handbook for International Management Research. LC 95-1581. 450p. 1995. pap. 47.95 (*1-55786-500-0*) Blackwell Pubs.

Punnett, Betty J., et al. Global Management. LC 94-28076. (Illus.). 600p. (C). 1994. text 66.95 (*1-55786-635-X*) Blackwell Pubs.

Punnett, Dick. Help Dress Priscilla. LC 84-23030. (Rhyme Time Library). (Illus.). 32p. (J). (ps-2). 1985. lib. bdg. 21.36 (*0-89565-217-X*) Childs World.

— Peek-a-Boo Sue. LC 84-23003. (Rhyme Time Library). (Illus.). 32p. (J). (ps-2). 1985. lib. bdg. 21.36 (*0-89565-305-2*) Childs World.

— Racing on the Rim: A History of the Annual Automobile Racing Tournaments Held on the Sands of the Ormond/Daytona Beach, Florida 1903-1910. Punnett, Yvonne, ed. LC 97-90095. (Illus.). vi, 106p. (Orig.). 1997. pap. 22.95 (*0-9657211-0-8*) Tomoka.

Punnett, Dick & Punnett, Yvonne. Thrills, Chills & Spills: A Photographic History of Early Aviation on the World's Most Bizarre Airport - The Beach at Daytona Beach, Florida - 1906-1929. LC 90-42545. (Illus.). 120p. (Orig.). 1990. pap. text 17.95 (*1-877633-09-7*) Luthers.

Punnett, Neil, jt. auth. see Webber, Peter.

Punnett, R. M. British Government & Politics. 6th ed. (Illus.). 608p. (C). 1994. text 77.95 (*1-85521-497-0*, Pub. by Dartmth Pub); pap. text 28.95 (*1-85521-508-X*, Pub. by Dartmth Pub) Ashgate Pub Co.

Punnett, Yvonne, jt. auth. see Punnett, Dick.

Punnett, Yvonne, ed. see Punnett, Dick.

Punola, John A. Fishing Catskill Trout. rev. ed. 106p. 1996. pap. 10.95 (*0-939888-19-X*) Outdoors USA.

— Fishing Delaware River. (Illus.). 108p. 1993. pap. 9.95 (*0-939888-17-3*) Outdoors USA.

P

An Asterisk (*) at the beginning of an entry indicates that the title is appearing for the first time.

— Fishing Delaware River. rev. ed. (Illus.). 108p. Date not set. pap. write for info. (*0-939888-21-1*) Outdoors USA.
— Fishing New Jersey Lakes. rev. ed. (Illus.). 128p. Date not set. pap. 9.95 (*0-939888-22-X*) Outdoors USA.
— Guide to New Jersey Lakes. (Illus.). 124p. (Orig.). 1993. pap. 9.95 (*0-939888-16-5*) Outdoors USA.
— Guide to New Jersey Saltwater Fishing. (Illus.). 120p. (Orig.). 1991. pap. 8.95 (*0-939888-13-0*) Outdoors USA.
— Guide to Pennsylvania Trout. 2nd ed. (Illus.). 104p. (Orig.). 1990. reprint ed. pap. 7.95 (*0-939888-09-2*) Outdoors USA.
— New Jersey Trout. (Illus.). 124p. (Orig.). 1994. pap. 9.95 (*0-939888-18-1*) Outdoors USA.
Punongbayan, Raymundo S., jt. ed. see Newhall, Christopher G.
Punsalan, Victoria J., jt. compiled by see Miller, A. Carolyn.
Punset, Eduardo & Sweeney, Gerry P. Information Resources & Corporate Development. 280p. 1992. 54.00 (*0-86187-720-9*, Pub. by P P Pubs) Cassell & Continuum.
Punshon, John. Alternative Christianity. LC 81-85560. (C). 1982. pap. 1.00 (*0-87574-245-9*) Pendle Hill.
Punshon, John. Encounter with Silence: Reflections from the Quaker Tradition. LC 87-181. 156p. (Orig.). 1987. pap. 10.50 (*0-913408-96-4*) Friends United.
— Letter to a Universalist. LC 89-60789. (Orig.). 1989. pap. 4.00 (*0-87574-285-8*) Pendle Hill.
Punt, Capelle. International Dictionary of Law, Commerce, & Finance: German-English-French-Spanish. (ENG, FRE & GER.). 600p. 1992. 105.00 (*0-7859-8341-4*, 3409199438) Fr & Eur.
Punt, Neal. Baker's Textual & Topical Filing System. deluxe ed. LC 60-53376. 628p. 1989. reprint ed. 54.95 (*0-945315-15-5*) Northland Bks.
— Unconditional Good News: Toward an Understanding of Biblical Universalism. LC 80-10458. 179p. reprint ed. pap. 55.50 (*0-608-14617-X*, 202322200032) Bks Demand.
— What's Good about the Good News? The Plan of Salvation in a New Light. LC 87-63576. 156p. (Orig.). 1988. pap. 8.95 (*0-945315-07-4*) Northland Bks.
Punt, W., et al, eds. The Northwest European Pollen Flora, Vol. 5. 154p. 1988. 150.00 (*0-444-87268-X*) Elsevier.
Punt, W. & Blackmore, Stephen. The Northwest European Pollen Flora, Vol. VI. 276p. 1991. 191.50 (*0-444-89164-1*) Elsevier.
Punt, W. & Clarke, G. C., eds. The Northwest European Pollen Flora, Vol. 3. 138p. 1981. 136.50 (*0-444-41996-9*) Elsevier.
— The Northwest European Pollen Flora, Vol. 7. (Illus.). 282p. 1995. 200.75 (*0-444-82392-1*) Elsevier.
Puntel, Lorenz B. Grundlagen Einer Theorie der Wahrheit. (Grundlagen der Kommunikation & Kognition (Foundations of Communication & Cognition) Ser.). (GER.). xiii, 408p. (C). 1990. lib. bdg. 152.35 (*3-11-012079-8*) De Gruyter.
Puntenney, Pamela J., ed. Global Ecosystems: Creating Options Through Anthropological Perspectives. LC 95-1455. (NAPA Bulletin Ser.: Vol. 15). 1995. write for info. (*0-913167-70-3*) Am Anthro Assn.
Punter, David. Gothic Pathologies: The Text, the Body & the Law LC 97-38767. xi, 251p. 1998. write for info. (*0-333-65802-7*) Macmillan.
Punter, David, ed. A Companion to the Gothic. LC 99-31099. (Blackwell Companions to Literature & Culture Ser.). 400p. 1999. 99.95 (*0-631-20620-5*) Blackwell Pubs.
Punter, John. Design Guidelines in American Cities: A Review of Design Policies & Guidance in Five West-Coast Cities. (Illus.). 8p. 1998. pap. 24.95 (*0-85323-893-6*, Pub. by Liverpool Univ Pr) Intl Spec Bk.
Punter, John & Carmona, Matthew. The Design Dimension of Planning: Theory, Content, & Best Practice for Design Policies. LC 97-66017. 1997. write for info. (*0-419-22410-6*) Routledge.
Puntillo, Kathleen A. Pain in the Critically Ill: Assessment & Management. 276p. 1991. text 52.00 (*0-8342-0222-0*, 20222) Aspen Pub.
***Puntillo, Timothy & Cardone, Christine.** The Birthday Book. 120p. 2000. 22.95 (*0-9700192-0-3*); 22.95 (*0-9700192-1-1*) Ink.
Puntillo, Timothy, jt. auth. see Cardone, Christine.
Punwar, Alice & Peloquin, Suzanne. Occupational Therapy: Principles & Practice. 3rd ed. 312p. pap. text 37.95 (*0-683-30453-4*) Lppncott W & W.
Punwar, Alice J. Occupational Therapy: Principles & Practice. 2nd ed. LC 92-48838. (Illus.). 304p. 1994. 35.00 (*0-683-06975-6*) Lppncott W & W.
Punzo, Fred. The Biology of Camel-Spiders (Arachnida, Solifugae) LC 98-16274. 312p. 1998. 135.00 (*0-7923-8155-6*) Kluwer Academic.
***Punzo, Fred.** Desert Arthropods: Life History Variations. LC 99-42825. (Adaptations of Desert Organisms Ser.). (Illus.). 220p. 2000. 129.00 (*3-540-66041-0*) Spr-Verlag.
Punzo, L. F., jt. ed. see Bohm, B.
Punzo, Richard. Managing Across Cultures. (Management Booklets Ser.). Date not set. write for info. (*1-882390-94-6*) Princeton Trng.
— Managing Global Projects. (Management Booklets Ser.). Date not set. write for info. (*1-882390-92-X*) Princeton Trng.
Puolanne, E., et al, eds. Pork Quality: Genetic & Metabolic Factors. (CAB International Publication). (Illus.). 336p. 1993. text 95.00 (*0-85198-836-9*) OUP.
Puoplo, Gerard. Building Network Management Tools with TCL/TK. 448p. (C). 1998. 58.00 (*0-13-080727-3*) P-H.
Puopolo, Vito. Music Fundamentals. LC 75-4316. (Illus.). 219p. (C). 1976. 19.00 (*0-02-871890-9*, Schirmer Books) Mac Lib Ref.
Puoskari, Mauri. Integral Equation Theories of Simple Classical & Bose Liquids LC 98-149240. 320 p. 1997. write for info. (*952-90-8833-7*, Pub. by Finnish State) Dist Art Pubs.
Puotinen, Arthur E. Finnish Radicals & Religion in Midwestern Mining Towns: 1865-1914. Scott, Franklyn D., ed. LC 78-15851. (Scandinavians in America Ser.). (Illus.). 1979. lib. bdg. 30.95 (*0-405-11657-8*) Ayer.
Puotinen, C. J. Encyclopedia of Natural Pet Care. LC 97-43372. 520p. 1997. pap. 19.95 (*0-87983-797-7*, 37977K, Keats Publng) NTC Contemp Pub Co.
— Herbal Teas. Herman, Phyllis, ed. (Good Health Guides Ser.). 48p. 1996. pap. 3.95 (*0-87983-707-1*, 37071K, Keats Publng) NTC Contemp Pub Co.
— Herbs for Detoxification. LC 97-4291. (Good Herb Guides Ser.). 46p. (Orig.). 1997. pap. 4.95 (*0-87983-795-0*, 37950K, Keats Publng) NTC Contemp Pub Co.
— Herbs for Improved Digestion. (Good Herb Guides Ser.). 96p. (Orig.). 1996. pap. 4.95 (*0-87983-742-X*, 3742XK, Keats Publng) NTC Contemp Pub Co.
— Herbs to Help You Breathe Freely. LC 96-24278. (Good Herb Guides Ser.). 96p. 1996. pap. 4.95 (*0-87983-741-1*, 37411K, Keats Publng) NTC Contemp Pub Co.
— Natural Remedies for Dogs & Cats. LC 99-26191. 244p. 1998. pap. 14.95 (*0-87983-827-2*, 38272K, Keats Publng) NTC Contemp Pub Co.
— Nature's Antiseptics: Tea Tree Oil & Grapefruit Seed Extract. (Good Health Guides Ser.). (Orig.). 1997. pap. 3.95 (*0-87983-714-4*, 37144K, Keats Publng) NTC Contemp Pub Co.
Puotinen, CJ. Herbs to Relieve Arthritis. LC 96-27547. (Keats Good Herb Guide Ser.). 96p. (Orig.). 1996. mass mkt. 4.95 (*0-87983-743-8*, Keats Publng) NTC Contemp Pub Co.
Pupello, Anthony J. The Sax Man's Case. (Illus.). 64p. 1998. pap. 10.00 (*0-9657818-6-0*, Pnd Frog) Red Moon Pr.
Pupello, Tony, jt. ed. see Kauan, Jim.
Pupeter, Jean A. All the Presidents' Dates: The Presidential Trivia Book Every American Household Should Have. (Illus.). 130p. 1999. pap. 12.95 (*1-892896-72-9*) Buy Books.
Pupeza, Lori K. Custom Bikes. LC 97-53097. (Ultimate Motorcycle Ser.). (J). 1999. lib. bdg. 14.95 (*1-57765-000-X*) ABDO Pub Co.
— Eco-Gardens. LC 98-29326. (Gardening Ser.). (J). 2002. lib. bdg. 19.92 (*1-57765-033-6*) ABDO Pub Co.
— Flower Gardens. LC 98-11205. (How-To Gardening for Kids Ser.). (J). 1999. 13.95 (*1-57765-031-X*) ABDO Pub Co.
— Minibikes. LC 98-10606. (Ultimate Motorcycle Ser.). (J). 1998. lib. bdg. 14.98 (*1-57765-002-6*) ABDO Pub Co.
— Patio Gardens. LC 98-11987. (How-To Gardening for Kids Ser.). (J). 2002. lib. bdg. 13.95 (*1-57765-034-4*) ABDO Pub Co.
— Scooters. LC 97-53098. (Ultimate Motorcycle Ser.). 1999. lib. bdg. 14.98 (*1-57765-001-8*) ABDO Pub Co.
— Scooters. LC 97-53098. (Ultimate Motorcycle Ser.). (J). 1999. 14.95 (*1-57765-003-4*) ABDO Pub Co.
— Sport Bikes. LC 97-53091. (Ultimate Motorcycle Ser.). (J). 1999. lib. bdg. 14.98 (*1-57765-004-2*) ABDO Pub Co.
— Street Bikes. LC 97-53096. (Ultimate Motorcycle Ser.). (J). 1999. lib. bdg. 14.98 (*1-57765-005-0*) ABDO Pub Co.
— Wildlife Gardens. LC 98-16910. (How-To Gardening for Kids Ser.). (J). 1998. 13.98 (*1-57765-032-8*) ABDO Pub Co.
Pupil, A. The Serene Life. 1981. pap. 2.00 (*0-911794-47-6*) Saraydarian Inst.
Pupils of Farr Secondary School Staff & Temperley, Alan. Tales of the North Coast: The Beautiful & Remote North Coast of Scotland from Melvich to Tongue. (Illus.). 224p. 1999. pap. 14.95 (*0-946487-18-9*, Pub. by Luath Pr Ltd) Midpt Trade.
Pupin, Michael. From Immigrant to Inventor. Cohen, I. Bernard, ed. LC 79-7983. (Three Centuries of Science in America Ser.). (Illus.). 1980. reprint ed. lib. bdg. 37.95 (*0-405-12565-8*) Ayer.
— New Reformation: From Physical to Spiritual Realities. 300p. 1998. reprint ed. pap. 19.95 (*0-7661-0414-1*) Kessinger Pub.
Puplesis, R. Nepticulidae of Eastern Europe & Asia. Western, Central & Eastern Parts. (Illus.). 552p. 1994. 140.00 (*90-73348-29-3*, Pub. by Backhuys Pubs) Balogh.
Puplick, C. Banting's Dog & Schrodinger's Cat: Animals & Experiments. 1994. pap. 35.00 (*0-646-20678-8*, Pub. by Univs Fed Animal Welfare) St Mut.
Pupo-Walker, Enrique, ed. Castaways - Alvar Nunez Cabeza de Vaca: The Narrative of Alvar Nunez Cabeza de Vaca. Lopez-Morillas, Frances M., tr. LC 92-25645. (C). 1993. pap. 15.95 (*0-520-07063-1*, Pub. by U CA Pr) Cal Prin Full Svc.
Pupo-Walker, Enrique, jt. ed. see Echevarria, Roberto G.
Pupolin, S., jt. ed. see DeNatale, F.
Pupolin, S., jt. ed. see Louise, M.
Puppe, F., ed. see German Conference on Knowledge-Based Systems.
Puppe, C. Distorted Probabilities & Choice under Risk. Beckmann, Martin J. & Krelle, W., eds. (Lecture Notes in Economics & Mathematical Systems Ser.: Vol. 363). (Illus.). viii, 100p. 1991. 28.95 (*0-387-54247-7*) Spr-Verlag.
Puppe, Frank. Systematic Introduction to Expert Systems: Knowledge Representations & Problem Solving Methods. LC 93-14650. 1993. 59.00 (*0-387-56255-9*) Spr-Verlag.
Puppe, Volker, jt. auth. see Allday, Christopher.
Puppe, Wolfgang G., ed. Conversion of Military Enterprises - A Practical Approach of Industry & Science: Proceedings of the NATO Advanced Research Workshop, St. Petersburg, Russia, November 20-23, 1995. LC 96-49529. (NATO ASI Series: Partnership Sub-Series 4). 116p. (C). 1996. lib. bdg. 92.50 (*0-7923-4342-5*) Kluwer Academic.
Puppel, Stanislaw. The Biology of Language. LC 94-49701. x, 300p. 1995. 84.00 (*1-55619-480-3*) J Benjamins Pubng Co.
Puppel, Stanislaw, jt. ed. see Fisiak, Jacek.
Puppo, P., jt. ed. see Giuliani, L.
***Pura, Murray A.** Mizzly Fitch: The Light, the Sea, the Storm. 2nd ed. 1999. reprint ed. pap. 18.95 (*1-57383-127-1*, Regent Coll Pub) Regent College.
Puranas, Bhagavatapurana. The Bhakti-Ratnavali: With the Commentary of Visnu Puri. LC 73-3794. (Sacred Books of the Hindus: No. 7 Pt.3). reprint ed. 25.00 (*0-404-57835-7*) AMS Pr.
— Brahma-Vaivarta Puranam, 2 vols., Set. LC 73-3817. reprint ed. 74.50 (*0-404-57824-1*) AMS Pr.
— The Matsya Puranam, 2 vols., Set. LC 73-3808. reprint ed. 74.50 (*0-404-57817-9*) AMS Pr.
Puranas, Brahmandapurana. The Adhyatma Ramayana. Nath, Lala B., tr. LC 73-3828. (Sacred Books of the Hindus: Extra Vol. 1). reprint ed. 25.00 (*0-404-57846-2*) AMS Pr.
***Purandare, S.** The Sena Story. LC 99-937301. 1998. pap. 125.00 (*81-7693-015-6*, Pub. by Business Pubns) St Mut.
Purani, A. B. The Life of Sri Aurobindo. 4th ed. 440p. 1987. pap. 15.00 (*81-7058-080-3*, Pub. by SAA) E-W Cultural Ctr.
Purani, A. B. Sri Aurobindo's Savitri: An Approach & a Study. 3rd ed. 397p. 1996. pap. 8.50 (*81-7058-442-6*, Pub. by SAA) E-W Cultural Ctr.
Purani, A. B., ed. Evening Talks with Sri Aurobindo. 3rd ed. 786p. 1995. 19.95 (*81-7060-093-6*, Pub. by SAA) E-W Cultural Ctr.
Purari, Peter. Tropical Environment. (Mobi Ser.). 1983. text 417.00 (*90-6193-104-5*) Kluwer Academic.
Puravs, Grace, et al, eds. Accessing English Literary Periodicals: A Guide to the Microfilm Collection with Title, Subject, Editor, & Reel Number Indexes. LC 81-16124. 1981. 30.00 (*0-8357-0231-6*) Univ Microfilms.
Puravs, Grace, ed. see University Microfilms International Staff.
***Purba, Sanjiv.** Microsoft SQL Server 7 for Client/Server Developers. LC 98-53557. 506p. 1999. pap. 39.99 (*0-471-19233-3*) Wiley.
— Data Management Handbook. 3rd ed. LC 99-49200. 1048p. 1999. boxed set 95.00 (*0-8493-9832-0*) CRC Pr.
— Designing & Developing High-Performance Databases for the Web. LC 00-44173. (Best Practices Ser.). 2000. write for info. (*0-8493-0882-8*) Auerbach.
Purba, Sanjiv. Developing Client-Server Systems Using Sybase SQL Server System 11. LC 96-13745. 544p. 1996. pap. 49.99 (*0-471-15338-9*) Wiley.
— Using SQL Windows & Centura: Techniques for Building Client/Server Solutions. LC 96-21161. 458p. 1996. pap. 44.95 incl. cd-rom (*0-471-13089-3*) Wiley.
Purba, Sanjiv, et al. How to Manage a Successful Software Project: Methodologies, Techniques, Tools. LC 95-13371. 400p. 1995. pap. 49.99 (*0-471-04401-6*) Wiley.
Purbhoo. Simply Accounting Windows. 2nd ed. (C). 1996. spiral bd. write for info. (*0-201-83918-0*) Addison-Wesley.
Purce, Jill. The Mystic Spiral: Journey of the Soul. (Art & Imagination Ser.). (Illus.). 128p. 1980. reprint ed. pap. 15.95 (*0-500-81005-2*, Pub. by Thames Hudson) Norton.
Purcel, John. Linux Complete Command Reference. LC 97-66202. 1495p. 1997. 49.99 (*0-672-31104-6*) Sams.
***Purcell.** Complete Keyboard Works I: Individual Pieces. 1999. pap. text 7.95 (*963-8303-89-1*) Kone Music.
— Complete Keyboard Works II: Suites. (Music Scores Ser.). 1999. pap. text 7.95 (*963-8303-72-7*) Kone Music.
Purcell. Heaven Sent. 1999. pap. 17.95 (*0-9666750-4-5*, Pub. by Nocturnum Pr) Consort Bk Sales.
— Inorganic Chemistry. 2nd ed. (C). 1999. text 37.50 (*0-03-058437-X*) Harcourt Coll Pubs.
Purcell, Arthur H. Life Cycle Analysis for Environmental Problem Solving. Date not set. 59.95 (*0-87371-854-2*) Lewis Pubs.
Purcell, Brendan, ed. & tr. see Voegelin, Eric.
Purcell, Brendan M. The Drama of Humanity: Towards a Philosophy of Humanity in History. LC 96-23685. (Illus.). X, 295p. 1996. pap. 57.95 (*0-8204-3188-5*) P Lang Pubng.
— The Drama of Humanity: Towards a Philosophy of Humanity in History. (Illus.). x, 295p. 1996. pap. 57.95 (*3-631-49099-2*) P Lang Pubng.
Purcell, C. M., ed. see Sillers, Molly.
Purcell, Catherine. Canadian Professional Schools Factsheets, 1996-98. rev. ed. 367p. 1996. pap. 28.00 (*1-55022-262-7*, Pub. by ECW) Genl Dist Srvs.
— Checklist of Professional Schools in Canada. 300p. (C). 1993. pap. text 28.00 (*1-55022-194-9*, Pub. by ECW) Genl Dist Srvs.
— Guide to Law Schools in Canada. 266p. (C). 1992. pap. text 14.95 (*1-55022-160-4*, Pub. by ECW) Genl Dist Srvs.
— Guide to Law Schools in Canada, 1996-1998. 3rd rev. ed. 332p. 1996. pap. 14.95 (*1-55022-294-5*, Pub. by ECW) Genl Dist Srvs.
— Guide to MBA Schools in Canada 1995-97. 3rd rev. ed. 320p. 1995. pap. 14.95 (*1-55022-261-9*, Pub. by ECW) Genl Dist Srvs.
Purcell, Charles H. Washington, Oregon & Alaska Limited Liability Company Forms & Practice Manual, 2 vols. LC 96-37712. 800p. 1997. ring bd. 239.90 (*1-57400-026-8*) Data Trace Pubng.
Purcell, Cindy. From Glass to Boat. LC 97-22706. (Changes Ser.). (gr. 2-3). 1997. lib. bdg. 24.00 (*0-516-20736-9*) Childrens.
— From Glass to Boat. LC 97-22706. (Changes Ser.). (J). (gr. 2-3). 1998. pap. text 6.95 (*0-516-20367-3*) Childrens.
Purcell, David W., jt. ed. see Cabaj, Robert P.
Purcell, Deidre. On Lough Derg. (Illus.). 122p. 1989. 39.00 (*1-85390-095-8*, Pub. by Veritas Pubns) St Mut.
Purcell, Deirdre. The Place of Stones. 448p. (Orig.). 1993. mass mkt. 5.99 (*0-451-17329-5*, Sig) NAL.
— Roses after Rain. 496p. 1996. mass mkt. 5.99 (*0-451-18630-3*, Sig) NAL.
Purcell, Dennis L. & Anderson, Jock R. Agricultural Extension & Research: Achievements & Problems in National Systems. (World Bank Operations Evaluation Study Ser.). 304p. 1997. pap. 40.00 (*0-8213-3878-1*, 13878) World Bank.
Purcell, E. M. Berkeley Physics Course: Electricity & Magnetism, Vol. 2. 2nd ed. (C). 1984. 95.31 (*0-07-004908-4*) McGraw.
Purcell, Edward, jt. rev. see Purcell, Mary.
Purcell, Edward A., Jr. Brandeis & the Progressive Constitution: Erie, the Judicial Power & the Politics of the Federal Courts in Twentieth-Century America. LC 99-31555. (Illus.). 430p. 2000. 37.50 (*0-300-07804-8*) Yale U Pr.
— The Crisis of Democratic Theory: Scientific Naturalism & the Problem of Value. LC 72-91669. 344p. 1973. reprint ed. pap. 19.00 (*0-8131-0141-7*) U Pr of Ky.
Purcell, Edward A. Litigation & Inequality: Federal Diversity Jurisdiction in Industrial America, 1870-1958. 464p. 1992. text 75.00 (*0-19-507329-0*) OUP.
Purcell, Edward L. Who Was Who in the American Revolution. LC 99-11767. 1999. 17.99 (*0-517-20378-2*) Random Hse Value.
Purcell, Edward L., jt. auth. see Burg, David F.
Purcell, Edward M. Berkeley Physics Course Vol. II: Electricity & Magnetism, Vol. 2. 2nd ed. (C). 1985. pap. text, teacher ed. 24.00 (*0-07-050960-3*) McGraw.
Purcell, Edwin J. Calculus with Analytic Geometry. 3rd ed. (Illus.). 1978. 36.95 (*0-13-112052-2*); pap. 6.95 (*0-13-112037-9*) P-H.
Purcell, Edwin J., jt. auth. see Varberg, Dale.
Purcell, Edwin J., jt. auth. see Varberg, Dale E.
Purcell, Elizabeth F., ed. The Role of the University Teaching Hospital: An International Perspective: Report of a Conference. LC 82-83988. 266p. reprint ed. pap. 82.50 (*0-608-16369-4*, 202669600051) Bks Demand.
— World Trends in Medical Education: Faculty, Students, & Curriculum. LC 79-144335. (Josiah Macy Foundation Ser.). 248p. reprint ed. 76.90 (*0-8357-9292-7*, 201569300095) Bks Demand.
Purcell, Elizabeth F., jt. ed. see Bowers, John Z.
Purcell, Elizabeth F., jt. ed. see Bradley, Stanley.
Purcell, Elizabeth F., jt. ed. see Friedman, Charles P.
Purcell, Elizabeth F., jt. ed. see Warren, Kenneth S.
Purcell, Gary R., jt. auth. see Hernon, Peter.
Purcell-Gates, Victoria. Other People's Words: The Cycle of Low Literacy. LC 94-31073. (Illus.). 256p. 1995. text 31.00 (*0-674-64497-2*, PUROTH) HUP.
— Other People's Words: The Cycle of Low Literacy. (Illus.). 256p. 1997. pap. text 18.00 (*0-674-64511-1*) HUP.
Purcell, Gervais. Japan Journal: The Private Notes of Gervais Purcell 1874-1900. limited ed. Purcell, Hugh D., ed. (Illus.). 64p. 1975. 50.00 (*0-317-06150-X*) Rare Oriental Bk Co.
Purcell, Gordon, jt. auth. see McDonald, Brian.
***Purcell, H.** Fairy Queen in Full Score. 2000. pap. 16.95 (*0-486-41190-7*) Dover.
Purcell, H. J., ed. see Society for the Environmental Therapy, Inaugural C.
Purcell, Henry. A Choice Collection of Lessons for the Harpsichord or Spinnet. fac. ed. (Monuments of Music & Music Literature in Facsimile, I Ser.: Vol. 26). (Illus.). 1978. lib. bdg. 40.00 (*0-8450-2026-9*) Broude.
— Dido & Aeneas, an Opera. Price, Curtis, ed. (Critical Scores Ser.). (C). 1986. pap. text 15.50 (*0-393-95528-1*) Norton.
— Dido & Aeneas in Full Score. 112p. pap. 8.95 (*0-486-28746-7*) Dover.
— Harpsichord Works, Bk. 1. 1987. pap. 13.95 (*0-685-69071-7*, CH55559) Shawnee Pr.
— Keyboard Works. 96p. pap. 7.95 (*0-486-26363-0*) Dover.
— Orpheus Britannicus. fac. ed. (Monuments of Music & Music Literature in Facsimile, I Ser.: Vol. 1). (Illus.). 1965. lib. bdg. 75.00 (*0-8450-2001-3*) Broude.
Purcell, Henry, et al. Late-Seventeenth-Century English Keyboard Music. Bailey, Candace et al, eds. (Recent Researches in Music of the Baroque Era Ser.: Vol. RRB81). (Illus.). xv, 104p. 1997. pap. 40.00 (*0-89579-382-2*) A-R Eds.
Purcell, Henry, jt. auth. see Playford, John.
Purcell, Hugh D., ed. see Purcell, Gervais.
***Purcell, J. O. & Purcell, Juanita.** How to Stay Sane When Life Doesn't Make Sense. 1999. pap. 6.29 (*0-87227-199-4*) Reg Baptist.
***Purcell, Jeanne H. & Renzulli, Joseph S.** Total Talent Portfolio: A Systematic Plan to Identify & Nurture Gifts & Talents. 122p. 1998. pap. 19.95 (*0-936386-72-X*) Creative Learning.
***Purcell, John.** Linux: The Complete Reference. 7th ed. (Illus.). 2000. pap. text 39.95 (*1-57176-165-9*) Walnut Creek.
— Linux: The Complete Reference Advanced. 7th ed. (Illus.). 1999. pap. text 39.95 (*1-57176-249-3*) Walnut Creek.

P

Purcell, John, ed. Linux Man: The Essential Man Pages for Linux. 1218p. 1996. 29.95 (*1-885329-07-5*, Iman) Linux Syst.

— Register of Research, 1987. 96p. (C). 1987. 60.00 (*0-85292-399-6*) St Mut.

Purcell, John & Ahlstrand, Bruce. Human Resource Management in the Multi-Divisional Company. LC 93-42896. (Illus.). 246p. 1995. pap. text 29.95 (*0-19-878020-6*) OUP.

Purcell, John F. Trade Conflicts & U. S. - Mexican Relations. (Research Reports: No. 38). 49p. (Orig.). (C). 1982. pap. 5.00 (*0-935391-37-1*, RR-38) UCSD Ctr US-Mex.

Purcell, John W. African Animals. LC 82-9541. (New True Books Ser.). (Illus.). 48p. (J). (gr. k-4). 1982. lib. bdg. 21.00 (*0-516-01665-2*) Childrens.

Purcell, Juanita. Be Patient - I'm Not Perfect Yet. (Women's Ser.). 120p. (Orig.). 1993. reprint ed. pap. 6.29 (*0-87227-178-1*, RBP5214) Reg Baptist.

— Be Still, My Child: 366 Devotional Readings from the Psalms. LC 97-195621. (RBP Women's Studies). 384p. 1997. lib. bdg. 15.99 (*0-87227-191-9*) Reg Baptist.

— How Can I Love Those Prickly People? The "One Anothers" of the Bible. (Women's Studies). 120p. (Orig.). 1995. pap. 6.29 (*0-87227-187-0*, RBP5224) Reg Baptist.

— Joyous Journeys Around the Detours: The Book of Philippians. (Women's Studies). 120p. (Orig.). 1994. pap. 6.29 (*0-87227-182-X*, RBP5219) Reg Baptist.

— Stretch My Faith, Lord. (Women's Ser.). 104p. (Orig.). 1992. reprint ed. pap. text 6.29 (*0-87227-174-9*, RBP5207) Reg Baptist.

— Trials - Don't Resent Them As Intruders. (Women's Ser.). 96p. (Orig.). 1991. reprint ed. pap. text 6.29 (*0-87227-161-7*, RBP5184) Reg Baptist.

***Purcell, Juanita.** Why Cope When You Can Conquer? Studies in Selected Psalms. 128p. 1999. pap. 6.29 (*0-87227-203-6*) Reg Baptist.

Purcell, Juanita, jt. auth. see Purcell, J. O.

Purcell, Julia A. Angioplasty: For Narrowed Heart, Kidney or Leg Arteries. LC 86-25378. (Illus.). 24p. 1999. pap. text 5.75 (*0-939838-22-2*) Pritchett & Hull.

***Purcell, Julia A.** Blood Pressure Control: A Matter of Choices. large type ed. Carpentieri, J. D., ed. (Illus.). 48p. 2000. pap. 5.95 (*0-939838-53-2*) Pritchett & Hull.

Purcell, Julia A. Cardiac Catheterization: And Other Cardiac Diagnostic Tests & Radiological Procedures. rev. ed. Hull, Nancy R., ed. LC 82-10133. (Illus.). 32p. 1995. pap. 5.95 (*0-939838-10-9*) Pritchett & Hull.

— Off the Beat: A Book about Abnormal Heart Rhythms. Hull, Nancy R., ed. LC 91-33673. (Illus.). 24p. 1996. pap. text 6.25 (*0-939838-32-X*) Pritchett & Hull.

Purcell, Julia A. & Fletcher, Barbara J. A Stronger Pump: A Guide for People with Heart Failure. rev. ed. Hull, Nancy R., ed. LC 80-10191. (Illus.). 40p. 1994. pap. text 6.50 (*0-939838-05-2*) Pritchett & Hull.

Purcell, Julia A., et al. Angina Pectoris: Learn about Coronary Heart Disease & How to Prevent It. rev. ed. LC 84-26382. (Illus.). 32p. 1994. pap. text 5.50 (*0-939838-17-6*) Pritchett & Hull.

— Despue's De Un Ataque Cardi'aco: Qu'e Sigue? Hull, Nancy R., ed. De la Vega, Olimpia, tr. LC 90-27143. (Illus.). 68p. (Orig.). 1994. pap. text 9.95 (*0-939838-30-3*) Pritchett & Hull.

— Heart Attack: Bouncing Back. LC 96-50006. (Illus.). 48p. (Orig.). 1997. pap. 5.75 (*0-939838-45-1*) Pritchett & Hull.

— Heart Attack: What's Ahead? rev. ed. Hull, Nancy R., ed. LC 80-25793. (Illus.). 64p. (Orig.). 1993. reprint ed. pap. text 9.95 (*0-939838-02-8*) Pritchett & Hull.

Purcell, Julia A., jt. auth. see Fletcher, Barbara J.

Purcell, Julia Ann. Using the ECG to Detect MI: CE Booklet. 28p. pap. text 39.95 (*0-7817-1899-6*) Lppncott W & W.

Purcell, Julie Ann. Pacemaker Primer. write for info. (*0-7817-1900-3*) Lppncott W & W.

Purcell, Katherine. Falize: A Dynasty of Jewelers. LC 99-70848. (Illus.). 320p. 1999. 85.00 (*0-500-01911-8*, Pub. by Thames Hudson) Norton.

Purcell, Keith F. & Kotz, John C. An Introduction to Inorganic Chemistry. 600p. (C). 1980. text 101.50 (*0-03-056768-8*) SCP.

Purcell, L. Edward. Immigration. LC 94-38677. (Social Issues in American History Ser.). (Illus.). 216p. 1995. 29.95 (*0-89774-873-5*) Oryx Pr.

— Who Was Who in the American Revolution. 560p. 1993. lib. bdg. 60.00 (*0-8160-2107-4*) Facts on File.

Purcell, L. Edward, ed. Suggested State Legislation, 1986, Vol. 45. 220p. (Orig.). 1986. pap. 15.00 (*0-87292-060-7*) Coun State Govts.

— The Vice Presidents: A Biographical Dictionary. LC 97-9164. (Illus.). 480p. 1997. 50.00 (*0-8160-3109-6*) Facts on File.

Purcell, L. Edward & Garraty, John A., intros. The World Almanac of the American Revolution. (Illus.). 408p. 1992. text 35.00 (*0-88687-574-9*); text 18.95 (*0-88687-665-6*) Wrld Almnc.

***Purcell, L. Edward & Purcell, Sarah J.** Encyclopedia of Battles in North America: 1517 to 1916. LC 99-38634. (Illus.). 400p. 2000. 60.00 (*0-8160-3350-1*) Facts on File.

Purcell, L. Edward, jt. ed. see Grant, H. Roger.

Purcell, Laurie. Main Progressions in Eidetic Analysis. (Orig.). 1990. pap. 11.00 (*0-913412-29-5*) Brandon Hse.

— Secondary Progressions in Eidetic Analysis. 121p. 1993. pap. 11.00 (*0-913412-69-4*) Brandon Hse.

***Purcell, Lee.** CD-R/DVD: Digital Recording to Optical Media. (Video/Audio Engineering Ser.). 500p. 2000. pap. text 49.95 (*0-07-135715-7*) McGraw-Hill Prof.

Purcell, Lee. Web Developer.com Guide to Creating Web Channels. LC 98-14351. (Web Developer.com Ser.). 736p. 1998. pap. 39.99 (*0-471-25168-2*) Wiley.

Purcell, Lee & Hemphill, Jordan. Internet Audio Sourcebook. LC 97-36220. 553p. 1997. pap., pap. text 44.99 incl. cd-rom (*0-471-19150-7*) Wiley.

Purcell, Lee, jt. auth. see Jost, Martin.

Purcell, Mary. Matt Talbot: His Life & Times. 238p. 1977. pap. 8.95 (*0-8199-0657-3*, Frncscn Herld) Franciscan Pr.

— Remembering Matt Talbot. 142p. (Orig.). 1990. pap. 11.95 (*1-85390-185-7*, Pub. by Veritas Pubns) St Mut.

— The World of Monsieur Vincent. 256p. 1989. pap. 22.00 (*1-85390-019-2*, Pub. by Veritas Pubns) St Mut.

Purcell, Mary & Purcell, Edward, revs. Pastor's Complete Book of Model Speeches. (C). 1992. text 39.95 (*0-13-653387-6*) P-H.

Purcell, Mia. The Industrial Incubator. Murphy, Jenny & Kailo, Andrea, eds. 20p. (Orig.). 1984. pap. 15.00 (*0-317-04906-2*) Natl Coun Econ Dev.

— Marketing & Managing Local Enterprise Zones. Kailo, Andrea, ed. 32p. (Orig.). 1985. pap. 16.00 (*0-317-04905-4*) Natl Coun Econ Dev.

— Revolving Loan Funds. Young, Laurie B., ed. 40p. (Orig.). 1983. pap. 13.00 (*0-317-04848-1*) Natl Coun Econ Dev.

— SBA's Section Five Hundred Three Program. Sampson, Stephanie, ed. 24p. (Orig.). 1983. pap. 11.00 (*0-317-04826-0*) Natl Coun Econ Dev.

Purcell, Michael. Mystery & Method: The Other in Rahner & Levinas. LC 98-8986. (Studies in Theology: Vol. 15). 400p. 1998. 40.00 (*0-87462-639-0*) Marquette.

Purcell, Nadine H., jt. ed. see Moore, Richard E.

Purcell, Nicholas, jt. auth. see Horden, Peregrine.

Purcell, Norah, tr. see Saint-Exupery, Antoine de.

***Purcell, Paul.** The Case File. 70p. 1999. ring bd. 49.95 (*0-942369-01-7*) InfoQuest Investigators.

Purcell, Paul E. The Complete Guide to Homemade Income. 128p. (Orig.). 1987. pap. 7.95 (*0-942369-00-9*) InfoQuest Investigators.

Purcell, Randall B., ed. The Newly Industrializing Countries in the World Economy: Challenges for U. S. Policy. LC 89-30730. 250p. 1989. lib. bdg. 37.00 (*1-55587-154-2*) L Rienner.

Purcell, Randall B. & Morrison, Elizabeth, eds. U. S. Agriculture & Third World Development: The Critical Linkage. LC 86-29860. 240p. 1987. lib. bdg. 36.50 (*1-55587-011-2*) L Rienner.

Purcell, Rebecca. Decorating ABC's. LC 97-34689. 1998. 30.00 (*0-688-14894-8*, Hearst) Hearst Commns.

Purcell, Robert Y. & Sharif, Gunseli S., eds. Handbook of Control Technologies for Hazardous Air Pollutants. (Science Information Research Center Ser.). 176p. 1988. 63.95 (*0-89116-825-7*) Hemisp Pub.

Purcell, Rosamond W. Special Cases: Natural Anomalies & Historical Monsters. LC 97-26754. 159p. 1998. 24.95 (*0-8118-1568-4*) Chronicle Bks.

Purcell, Rosamond W., photos by. Finders, Keepers: Eight Collectors. (Illus.). 128p. 1992. 50.00 (*0-393-03054-7*) Norton.

Purcell, Royal. The Concept of Being Human. 173p. (Orig.). 1985. pap. 9.95 (*0-933189-00-1*) Purcell Pub.

— Ethics, Morality, & Mores. 177p. (Orig.). 1986. pap. 9.95 (*0-933189-01-X*) Purcell Pub.

— Purcell's Thesaurus of Knowledge. (Illus.). 301p. 1993. ring bd. 19.95 (*0-933189-04-4*) Purcell Pub.

Purcell, Sally. Dark of Day. 48p. 1977. pap. 11.95 (*0-85646-029-X*, Pub. by Anvil Press) Dufour.

— Fossil Unicorn. LC 98-148373. 64p. 1998. pap. 15.95 (*0-85646-282-9*, Pub. by Anvil Press) Dufour.

— Gaspara Stampa. (C). 1990. 35.00 (*0-906887-15-1*, Pub. by Greville Pr) St Mut.

— The Holly Queen. Date not set. 14.95 (*0-900977-81-7*, Pub. by Anvil Press) Dufour.

Purcell, Sarah J., jt. auth. see Purcell, L. Edward.

Purcell, Sherri M. This Songs for You: Poetry for Ministers of Music. (Illus.). 100p. 1998. pap. 19.95 (*0-9664532-0-4*) A Valued Voice.

Purcell, Steve. The Collected Sam & Max. (Illus.). 160p. 1995. 22.50 (*1-56924-812-5*); pap. 12.95 (*1-56924-814-1*) Marlowe & Co.

— The Collected Sam & Max. limited ed. (Illus.). 160p. 1995. 50.00 (*1-56924-837-0*) Marlowe & Co.

Purcell, Stuart, ed. see Billac, Pete.

Purcell, Susan K. Cuba's Cloudy Future. 1990. 3.00 (*0-685-37920-5*) Cuban Amer Natl Fndtn.

— Is Cuba Changing? 1989. 3.00 (*0-685-47389-9*) Cuban Amer Natl Fndtn.

Purcell, Susan K., ed. Mexico - United States Relations, 34. LC 80-70867. 213p. 1981. 49.95 (*0-275-90707-4*, C0707, Praeger Pubs) Greenwood.

Purcell, Susan K. & Roett, Riordan. Brazil under Cardoso. LC 97-13956. 119p. 1997. pap. 12.95 (*1-55587-452-5*) L Rienner.

Purcell, Susan K. & Rubio, Luis, eds. Mexico under Zedillo. LC 97-32753. (Americas Society Ser.). 152p. 1998. pap. 13.50 (*1-55587-315-4*) L Rienner.

Purcell, Susan K. & Simon, Francoise, eds. Europe & Latin America in the World Economy. LC 94-14624. 218p. 1995. pap. text 5.00 (*1-55587-498-3*) L Rienner.

***Purcell, Susan Kaufman & Rothkopf, David, eds.** Cuba: The Contours of Change. (Americas Society Ser.). 160p. 2000. pap. 13.95 (*1-55587-933-0*) L Rienner.

Purcell, T. Robert. Doors to the Future: Steps to English Proficiency. rev. ed. (Illus.). 154p. (C). 1989. pap. text. write for info. (*1-878251-00-7*) English Tutors.

— Doors to the Future Vol. 2: Steps to English Proficiency. rev. ed. (Illus.). 120p. (C). 1990. text. write for info. (*0-318-65773-2*) English Tutors.

— Keys to the Future Vol. 1: Steps to English Proficiency. rev. ed. (Illus.). 140p. (C). 1990. text. write for info. (*0-318-65771-6*) English Tutors.

— Roads to the Future: Steps to English Proficiency, Vol. 3. (Illus.). 114p. (C). 1989. text. write for info. (*0-318-65772-4*) English Tutors.

Purcell, Theodore F. Blue Collar Man: Patterns of Dual Allegiance in Industry. Stein, Leon, ed. LC 77-70524. (Illus.). 1977. reprint ed. lib. bdg. 34.95 (*0-405-10192-9*) Ayer.

Purcell, Theresa. Teaching Children Dance: Becoming a Master Teacher. LC 94-2170. (Illus.). 136p. 1994. pap. text 16.00 (*0-87322-479-5*, BPUR0479) Human Kinetics.

Purcell, Theresa M. Teaching Children Dance. (Becoming a Master Teacher Ser.). 136p. 1994. pap. text 31.95 incl. VHS (*0-87322-705-0*, AMTP0308) Human Kinetics.

Purcell, Trevor W. Banana Fallout: Class, Color, & Culture among West Indians in Costa Rica. (Afro-American Culture & Society Monographs: Vol. 12). 198p. (Orig.). (C). 1993. pap. text 15.95 (*0-934934-37-1*) CAAS Pubns.

Purcell, Trip. Sunset Beach. 320p. (Orig.). 1996. pap. 12.95 (*1-884570-47-X*) Research Triangle.

Purcell, Victor W. Malaya: Communist or Free? LC 75-30076. (Institute of Pacific Relations Ser.). reprint ed. 32.50 (*0-404-59553-7*) AMS Pr.

Purcell, W. R., Jr. Understanding a Company's Finances: A Graphic Approach. (Illus.). 143p. (C). 1998. reprint ed. pap. text 10.00 (*0-7881-5184-3*) DIANE Pub.

Purcell, Wayne. Marketing Agricultural Commodities. Reynold, Ralph & Drummond, H. Evan, eds. (Farm Business Management Ser.). (Illus.). (Orig.). 1995. pap. text, student ed. 25.95 (*0-86691-219-3*, FBM14601W) Deere & Co.

— Marketing Agricultural Commodities. Reynold, Ralph & Drummond, H. Evan, eds. (Farm Business Management Ser.). (Illus.). (Orig.). (C). 1995. pap. text, teacher ed. 44.95 (*0-86691-218-5*, FBM14501T) Deere & Co.

Purcell, Wayne D. Agricultural Futures & Options: Principles & Strategies. 2nd ed. LC 98-27294. 400p. 1998. 100.00 (*0-13-779943-8*) P-H.

Purcell, William L. An Introduction to Asian Music, 1966: Asia Society Guides. 44.00 (*0-685-43152-5*, 10753) Ayer.

Purcell, William M. Ars Poetriae: Rhetorical & Grammatical Invention at the Margin of Literacy. Benson, Thomas, ed. LC 95-4401. (Studies in Rhetoric & Communication). (Illus.). 200p. 1996. text 34.95 (*1-57003-059-6*) U of SC Pr.

Purcell, William P., et al. Strategy of Drug Design: A Guide to Biological Activity. LC 72-13240. 200p. reprint ed. pap. 62.00 (*0-8357-9983-2*, 205515600008) Bks Demand.

Purch, Sean, ed. see Pulver, David.

Purchas, ed. Handbook of Filter Media. LC 97-126138. 1996. text 154.00 (*1-85617-278-3*) Elsevier.

Purchas, John. Death on the Isles of Scilly: The Grave in California Field. (C). 1989. 35.00 (*0-907566-79-0*, Pub. by Dyllansow Truran) St Mut.

Purchas, Samuel. Hakluytus Posthumus: or Purchas His Pilgrimes, 20 vols. LC 07-23966. reprint ed. 1530.00 (*0-404-05180-4*) AMS Pr.

Purchase, Edna, jt. auth. see Skinner, Joyce.

***Purchase, Eric.** Out of Nowhere: Disaster & Tourism in the White Mountains. LC 98-28897. (Illus.). xiii, 192p. 1999. write for info. (*0-8018-6013-X*) Johns Hopkins.

Purchase, Graham. Anarchism & Ecology. 216p. 1996. text 48.99 (*1-55164-027-9*, Pub. by Black Rose); pap. text 19.99 (*1-55164-026-0*, Pub. by Black Rose) Consort Bk Sales.

— My Journey with Aristotle to the Anarchist Utopia. 128p. (Orig.). 1994. pap. 7.00 (*0-9622937-6-8*) III Pub.

Purchase, Rupert, ed. The Laboratory Environment. 270p. 1994. 89.95 (*0-85186-605-0*, R6605); 89.95 (*0-85186-050-8*, R6605) CRC Pr.

Purchase, Shirley. Australian Writers' Dictionary. LC 97-158764. 1997. write for info. (*0-19-554080-8*) OUP.

Purchon, Nerys. Health & Beauty the Natural Way: Simple, Safe Recipes for All Your Health & Beauty Needs. LC 97-10920. (Illus.). 256p. 1997. 24.98 (*1-56799-529-2*, MetroBooks) M Friedman Pub Grp Inc.

Purchon, R. D. & Kerkut, G. The Biology of the Mollusca. 2nd ed. LC 76-10804. (International Series of Monographs on Pure & Applied Mathematics: No. 57). 1977. 254.00 (*0-08-021028-7*, Pub. by Pergamon Repr) Franklin.

***Purdam, Stanley H. & Mulhern, Kathleen.** Focus on John: A Study Guide for Groups & Individuals. (Focus Bible Study Ser.). 176p. 2000. pap. 11.95 (*1-889108-66-9*) Liv Good News.

Purday, Richard, ed. Document Sets for the South in U. S. History. 256p. (C). 1991. pap. text 9.56 (*0-669-27108-X*) HM Trade Div.

Purdie, ed. Hebbel: Herodes und Mariamne. (Bristol German Texts Ser.). (GER.). 206p. 1943. 16.95 (*0-631-01330-X*) Blackwell Pubs.

Purdie, Bob. Politics in the Street. 352p. 1990. pap. 19.95 (*0-85640-437-3*, Pub. by Blackstaff Pr) Dufour.

Purdie, Catherine. Wenn Ihr Nicht Werdet Wie die Kinder: The Significance of the Child in the World-View of Ilse Aichinger. (European University Studies: No. 1, Vol. 1681). 127p. 1998. pap. 28.95 (*3-631-33544-X*) P Lang Pubng.

— Wenn Ihr Nicht Werdet Wie die Kinder: The Significance of the Child in the World-View of Ilse Aichinger. LC 98-20569. (European University Studies: Series 1, Vol. 1681). 127p. (C). 1998. pap. text 28.95 (*0-8204-3606-2*) P Lang Pubng.

Purdie, Erica M., ed. Response to Love. (C). 1988. 35.00 (*0-7212-0825-8*, Pub. by Regency Pr GBR) St Mut.

Purdie, N., ed. see Brittain, H. G.

Purdie, P. W. & Noble, I. R., eds. Mountain Ecology in the Australian Region. 178p. (C). 1983. text 75.00 (*0-909436-05-3*, Pub. by Surrey Beatty & Sons) St Mut.

Purdie, Robert A., jt. auth. see La Follette, Maryly.

Purdie, Robin B. & Earnest, Sam L. Pure Practice in 12-Lead ECG's. (Illus.). 576p. 1997. pap. text 34.95 (*0-8151-4669-8*) Mosby Inc.

— Pure Practice in 12-Lead ECGS Instructor's Kit. (Illus.). 576p. (C). 1997. text, teacher ed. write for info. (*0-8151-4670-1*) Mosby Inc.

Purdie, Susan. Comedy: The Mastery of Discourse. LC 92-95214. 186p. 1993. text 45.00 (*0-8020-2980-9*); pap. text 17.95 (*0-8020-7437-5*) U of Toronto Pr.

Purdom, C. B. The God-Man: The Life, Journeys & Work of Meher Baba with an Interpretation of His Silence & Spiritual Teaching. LC 72-175960. (Illus.). 464p. 1971. 20.00 (*0-913078-03-4*) Sheriar Pr.

Purdom, Charles, jt. auth. see Schloss, Malcolm.

Purdom, Laura. New England. 2nd ed. (Traveler's Companion Ser.). (Illus.). 296p. 1999. pap. text 23.95 (*0-7627-0486-1*) Globe Pequot.

Purdom, Laura, jt. auth. see Carroll, Donald.

Purdom, Misty, ed. see Mulkern, Dawn.

Purdom, P. Walton, ed. Environmental Health. 2nd ed. LC 79-51672. 1980. text 94.00 (*0-12-567860-6*) Acad Pr.

Purdom, Paul W. & Brown, Cynthia A. The Analysis of Algorithms. (Illus.). 560p. (C). 1995. text 66.95 (*0-03-072044-3*) OUP.

Purdon, Douglas. Color Secrets for Glowing Oil Paintings. LC 98-4123. (Illus.). 128p. 1998. 27.99 (*0-89134-831-X*, North Lght Bks) F & W Pubns Inc.

***Purdon, Eric.** Black Company: The Story of Subchaser 1264. LC 00-30573. (Bluejacket Bks.). 2000. write for info. (*1-55750-658-2*) Naval Inst Pr.

Purdon, Liam O. & Vitto, Cindy L., eds. The Rusted Hauberk: Feudal Ideals of Order & Their Decline. (Illus.). 352p. (C). 1994. 49.95 (*0-8130-1281-3*); pap. 19.95 (*0-8130-1282-1*) U Press Fla.

Purdon, Nicholas. Carpet & Textiles Patterns. (Illus.). 144p. 1996. 29.95 (*1-85669-081-4*, Pub. by L King Pubng) Antique Collect.

Purdue. Second World War. LC 98-32355. 1999. pap. 19.95 (*0-312-22214-9*); text 55.00 (*0-312-22213-0*) St Martin.

***Purdue, A. W. & Golby, John.** Kings & Queens of Empire: British Monarchs 1760-2000. (Illus.). 160p. 2000. pap. 25.99 (*0-7524-1775-4*, Pub. by Tempus Pubng) Arcadia Publng.

Purdue, A. W., jt. auth. see Golby, John M.

Purdue, Basil, ed. see Mason, Ken.

Purdue, Elizabeth, jt. auth. see Purdue, Howell.

Purdue, Howell & Purdue, Elizabeth. Patrick Cleburne. 499p. 1973. reprint ed. 35.00 (*0-942211-03-0*) Olde Soldier Bks.

Purdue, James R., et al, eds. Beamers, Bobwhites, & Blue-Points: Tributes to the Career of Paul W. Parmalee. 436p. 1991. pap. 19.50 (*0-89792-134-8*) Ill St Museum.

Purdue, James R. & Styles, Bonnie W. Dynamics of Mammalian Distribution in the Holocene of Illinois. (Reports of Investigations: No. 41). 63p. (Orig.). 1986. pap. 5.00 (*0-89792-107-0*) Ill St Museum.

Purdue, Joretta, ed. see Maynard, Edwin H.

Purdue, Leo G., tr. see Preuss, Horts D.

Purdue, Matt. Adventure Guide to Nevada. (Adventure Guides Ser.). (Illus.). 300p. 1998. pap. 15.95 (*1-55650-842-5*) Hunter NJ.

Purdue, Matt, jt. auth. see Sullivan, Lynne M.

Purdue, Michael. Planning Appeals: A Critique. (Studies in Law & Politics Ser.). 72p. 1991. pap. 25.95 (*0-335-09630-1*) OpUniv Pr.

Purdue Research Foundation Staff, contrib. by. Federally Registered Pesticides. 5th ed. 1100p. 1997. pap. 96.00 (*1-889750-07-7*) Nrth Amer Compendiums.

Purdue University Staff. Guia Cientifica de Truman Para Operaciones de Control de Plagas. 4th ed. Ituarte, Ricardo & Granovsky, Ted, trs. (SPA., Illus.). 504p. 1996. 74.95 (*0-929870-37-9*) Advanstar Commns.

— Navigating a Professional Vision. 144p. (C). 1997. per. 19.95 (*0-7872-4170-9*) Kendall-Hunt.

Purdue University Staff, et al, eds. Continuity & Discontinuity of Experience in Child Care. LC 85-645444. (Advances in Applied Developmental Psychology Ser.: Vol. 2). 222p. 1987. text 73.25 (*0-89391-406-1*) Ablx Pub.

— Parent Education As Early Childhood Intervention: Emerging Directions in Theory, Research & Practice. (Advances in Applied Developmental Psychology Ser.: Vol. 3). 256p. (C). 1988. text 73.25 (*0-89391-502-5*) Ablx Pub.

Purdue University, Thermophysical Properties Resea. Thermophysical Properties of High Temperature Solid Materials, Vols. 1-6. LC 67-15295. 1294p. reprint ed. pap. 200.00 (*0-608-16095-4*, 205656500001) Bks Demand.

— Thermophysical Properties of Matter: Specific Heat - Metallic Elements & Alloys. LC 73-129616. (TPRC Data Ser.: Vol. 4). 814p. 1970. reprint ed. pap. 200.00 (*0-608-08483-2*, 205569700004) Bks Demand.

— Thermophysical Properties of Matter: Specific Heat Nonmetallic Liquids & Gases, Vol. 6. LC 73-129616. 383p. 1970. reprint ed. pap. 118.80 (*0-608-08484-0*, 205595300006) Bks Demand.

— Thermophysical Properties of Matter: The TPRC Data Series, Vol. 1: Thermal Conductivity; Metallic Elements & LC 73-129616. (TPRC Data Ser.). 1597p. 1970. reprint ed. pap. 200.00 (*0-608-08481-6*, 205577700001) Bks Demand.

— Thermophysical Properties of Matter: The TPRC Data Series, Vol. 6 Supplement: Specific Heat: Nonmetallic Liqu. LC 73-129616. (TPRC Data Ser.). 169p. 1976. reprint ed. pap. 52.40 (*0-608-08485-9*, 205577800006) Bks Demand.

— Thermophysical Properties of Matter: The TPRC Data

Series, Vol 12: Thermal Expansion: Metallic Elements & Alloys. LC 73-129616. 1443p. 1971. reprint ed. pap. 200.00 (*0-608-08491-3*, 202272600012) Bks Demand.

— Thermophysical Properties of Matter: Thermal Conductivity - Nonmetallic Liquids & Gases. LC 73-129616. (TPRC Data Ser.: Vol. 3). 707p. 1970. reprint ed. pap. 200.00 (*0-608-08482-4*, 205569600003) Bks Demand.

— Thermophysical Properties Research Literature Retrieval Guide, Bk. 1. 2nd ed. Touloukian, Y. S. et al, eds. LC 60-14226. 844p. 1967. reprint ed. pap. 200.00 (*0-608-08493-X*, 202272400001) Bks Demand.

— Thermophysical Properties Research Literature Retrieval Guide, Bk. 2. 2nd ed. Touloukian, Y. S. et al, eds. LC 60-14226. 634p. 1967. reprint ed. pap. 196.60 (*0-608-08494-8*, 202272400002) Bks Demand.

— Thermophysical Properties Research Literature Retrieval Guide, Bk. 3. 2nd ed. Touloukian, Y. S. et al, eds. LC 60-14226. 1328p. 1967. reprint ed. pap. 200.00 (*0-608-08495-6*, 202272400003) Bks Demand.

Purdue University, Thermophysical Properties Resea & Touloukian, Y. S. Thermal Diffusivity, Vol. 10. LC 73-129616. 761p. 1973. pap. 200.00 (*0-608-08489-1*, 201941200010) Bks Demand.

— Thermal Radiative Properties: Coatings, Vol. 9. LC 73-129616. 1570p. 1972. pap. 200.00 (*0-608-08488-3*, 201941200009) Bks Demand.

— Thermal Radiative Properties: Metallic Elements & Alloys, Vol. 7. LC 73-129616. 1562p. 1970. pap. 200.00 (*0-608-08486-7*, 201941200007) Bks Demand.

— Thermal Radiative Properties: Nonmetallic Solids, Vol. 8. LC 73-129616. 1890p. 1972. pap. 200.00 (*0-608-08487-5*, 201941200008) Bks Demand.

— Thermophysical Properties of Matter: Thermal Expansion-Nonmetallic Solids. LC 73-129616. (TPRC Data Ser.: Vol. 13). 1786p. 1977. reprint ed. pap. 200.00 (*0-608-08492-1*, 205569800030) Bks Demand.

— Viscosity, Vol. 11. LC 73-129616. 791p. 1975. pap. 200.00 (*0-608-08490-5*, 201941200011) Bks Demand.

Purdue Workshop on Standardization of Industrial-Computer Languages, Glossary Committee. Dictionary of Industrial Digital Computer Terminology. LC 72-81778. 96p. reprint ed. pap. 30.00 (*0-608-30906-0*, 205111700078) Bks Demand.

Purdum, Elizabeth D., jt. ed. see Fernald, Edward A.

Purdum, Elizabeth D., ed. see Winsberg, Morton D.

Purdum, Stan. Roll Around Heaven All Day: A Piecemeal Journey Across America by Bicycle. LC 97-92439. (Illus.). 306p. 1998. pap. 14.95 (*0-930921-11-9*, RAH) Comm Res OH.

Purdum, Stan, ed. see Bodo, John, et al.

Purdum, Stan, ed. see Ford, Joe T.

Purdum, Stan, ed. see Peacock, Larry J., et al.

Purdy. Emotions. (C). 1994. pap. text 38.36 (*0-395-66539-6*) HM.

— World Champions at Work. Date not set. pap. 25.00 (*0-938650-81-5*) Thinkers Pr.

Purdy & Hutchings. How Purdy Won: The Correspondence Chess Career of a World Champion. 1998. pap. 18.00 (*0-938650-80-7*) Thinkers Pr.

Purdy & Steiner. The Chess World Editors. Date not set. pap. write for info. (*0-938650-82-3*) Thinkers Pr.

Purdy, A. Jane. He Will Never Remember: Caring for the Victims of Child Abuse. Mueller, Phyllis, ed. LC 89-31362. 180p. (Orig.). 1989. pap. 13.95 (*0-932419-22-4*) Cherokee.

Purdy, A. T. Needle-Punching. 1986. 75.00 (*0-7855-7206-6*) St Mut.

Purdy, Al, ed. Sing for the Inner Ear: The Winning Poems of the 1997 Sandburg-Livesay Anthology Contest. LC 98-16064. 122p. 1998. pap. 12.00 (*1-884206-04-2*) Unfinish Monumnt.

***Purdy, Al & Beardsley, Doug, eds.** The Man Who Outlived Himself: An Appreciation of John Donne: A Dozen of His Best Poems. 109p. 2000. pap. 14.95 (*1-55017-219-0*) Harbour Pub Co.

Purdy, Al, jt. auth. see Beardsley, Doug.

Purdy, Alexander. The Reality of God: Thoughts on the Death of God Controversy. LC 67-23314. (Orig.). 1967. pap. 4.00 (*0-87574-154-1*) Pendle Hill.

Purdy, Andrew J. Master of the Courts. limited ed. LC 72-96446. (Illus.). 44p. 1973. 20.00 (*0-912292-31-8*) Smith.

Purdy, Anthony. A Certain Difficulty of Being: Essays on the Quebec Novel. 200p. (C). 1990. text 60.00 (*0-7735-0770-1*, Pub. by McG-Queens Univ Pr) CUP Services.

Purdy, Anthony, jt. auth. see Elliot, Bridget.

Purdy, Barbara A. Florida's Prehistoric Stone Technology: A Study of the Flintworking Techniques of Early Florida Stone Implement Makers. LC 80-24726. (Illus.). xvi, 165p. 1981. 35.95 (*0-8130-0697-X*) U Press Fla.

— How to Do Archaeology the Right Way. LC 95-38050. (Illus.). 216p. (C). 1996. 29.95 (*0-8130-1392-5*) U Press Fla.

— Indian Art of Ancient Florida. LC 96-7798. (Illus.). 152p. 1996. 34.95 (*0-8130-1462-X*) U Press Fla.

Purdy, Barbara A., ed. Wet Site Archaeology. (Illus.). 450p. 1990. lib. bdg. 59.95 (*0-936923-08-3*); boxed set 59.95 (*0-936923-07-5*, Q) CRC Pr.

Purdy, Bryn. A. S. Neill: Bringing Happiness to a Few Children. LC 98-120167. 1997. pap. 13.95 (*1-900219-03-4*, Pub. by Educ Heretics) Intl Spec Bk.

Purdy, C. J. S. The Search for Chess Perfection: The Life, Games, & Writings of C.J.S. Purdy. 310p. 1997. pap. 22.00 (*0-938650-78-5*) Thinkers Pr.

Purdy, Carol. Least of All. LC 86-12613. (Illus.). 32p. (J). (gr. 1-4). 1987. lib. bdg. 12.95 (*0-689-50404-7*) McElderry Bks.

Purdy, Carol. Mrs. Merriwether's Musical Cat. LC 92-43934. (J). 1997. 11.15 (*0-606-11647-8*, Pub. by Turtleback) Demco.

Purdy, Carol. Nesuya's Basket. (Council of Indian Education Ser.). (Illus.). 110p. (Orig.). (J). (gr. 3-7). 1997. pap. 8.95 (*1-57098-087-X*) Roberts Rinehart.

Purdy, D. L. & Laidler, David E., eds. Inflation & Labor Markets. (Studies in Inflation: No.2). 272p. 1993. reprint ed. text 56.95 (*0-7512-0199-5*, Pub. by Gregg Revivals) Ashgate Pub Co.

Purdy, Daniel L. The Tyranny of Elegance: Consumer Cosmopolitanism in the Era of Goethe. LC 98-13582. (Illus.). 368p. 1998. 48.00 (*0-8018-5874-7*) Johns Hopkins.

Purdy, Dave, jt. auth. see Prior, Mike.

***Purdy, Don.** Aerocrafter: Homebuilt Aircraft Sourcebook. 7th rev. ed. (Illus.). 480p. 2000. pap. 35.00 incl. audio compact disk (*0-9636409-6-8*) BAI Commun.

Purdy, Don, ed. Aerocrafter: Homebuilt Aircraft Sourcebook. 432p. 1998. pap. 28.00 (*0-9636409-4-1*) BAI Commun.

***Purdy, Don, ed.** AeroCrafter: Homebuilt Aircraft Sourcebook. 6th ed. 432p. 1999. pap. 29.00 (*0-9636409-5-X*, Pub. by BAI Commun) ACCESS Pubs Network.

Purdy, Dwight H. Biblical Echo & Allusion in the Poetry of W. B. Yeats: Poetics & the Art of God. LC 93-9005. 1994. 32.50 (*0-8387-5254-3*) Bucknell U Pr.

— Joseph Conrad's Bible. LC 83-40331. 160p. 1984. 29.95 (*0-8061-1876-8*) U of Okla Pr.

Purdy, Edward G. & Bertram, George T. Carbonate Concepts from the Maldives, Indian Ocean. (Studies in Geology: No. 34). (Illus.). 56p. (Orig.). 1993. pap. 10.00 (*0-89181-042-0*, 579) AAPG.

Purdy, Gary. Comparison of God: Jonah 4. (Inter Acta Ser.). (Illus.). 6p. (C). 1994. teacher ed., ring bd. 1.25 (*1-885702-51-5*, 741-027t, Inter Acta); student ed., ring bd. 3.25 (*1-885702-50-7*, Inter Acta) WSN Pr.

— Fear of God: Jonah 1. (Inter Acta Ser.). (Illus.). (C). 1994. teacher ed., ring bd. write for info. (*1-885702-45-0*, 741-024t, Inter Acta); student ed., ring bd. 3.25 (*1-885702-44-2*, 741-024s, Inter Acta) WSN Pr.

— New I.D. Your New Identity in Christ. (Inter Acta Ser.). (Illus.). 6p. (C). 1994. teacher ed., ring bd. 1.25 (*0-9629245-6-3*, 741-003t, Inter Acta); student ed., ring bd. 3.25 (*0-9629245-5-5*, 741-003s, Inter Acta) WSN Pr.

— Perspective of God: Jonah 3. (Inter Acta Ser.). (Illus.). 6p. (C). 1994. teacher ed., ring bd. 1.25 (*1-885702-49-3*, 741-026t, Inter Acta); student ed., ring bd. 3.25 (*1-885702-48-5*, 741-026s, Inter Acta) WSN Pr.

— Submission to God: Jonah 2. (Inter Acta Ser.). (Illus.). 6p. (C). 1994. teacher ed., ring bd. 1.25 (*1-885702-47-7*, 741-025t, Inter Acta); student ed., ring bd. 3.25 (*1-885702-46-9*, 741-025s, Inter Acta) WSN Pr.

Purdy, Gary & Swanson, Eric. The Price Is Right: Discipleship Requirements. (Inter Acta Ser.). (Illus.). 4p. (C). 1994. student ed., ring bd. 3.25 (*1-57334-000-6*, 741-050s, Inter Acta) WSN Pr.

— The Price Is Right: Discipleship Requirements. rev. ed. (Inter Acta Ser.). (Illus.). 6p. (C). 1995. teacher ed., ring bd. 1.25 (*1-57334-007-3*, 741-050t, Inter Acta) WSN Pr.

Purdy, Graeme. Trees & Shrubs. (Illus.). 128p. pap. 12.95 (*1-86447-040-2*, Pub. by Hyland Hse) Seven Hills Bk.

Purdy, J., et al. Medical Accelerator Safety Considerations: Report of AAPM Radiation Therapy Committee Task Group, No. 35. (AAPM Report Ser.: No. 56). 16p. 1996. reprint ed. write for info. (*1-888340-01-0*) AAPM.

Purdy, J. Gerry. Running Trax: Computerized Running Training Programs. LC 97-148672. 128p. (Orig.). 1996. pap., spiral bd. 17.50 (*0-911521-48-8*) Tafnews.

***Purdy, J. Gerry.** ThinkPad: A Different Shade of Blue. 1999. 25.00 (*0-672-31756-7*) Sams.

Purdy, J. M., jt. auth. see Edwards, R. G.

Purdy, James. Brooklyn Branding Parlors. limited ed. Gosciak, Josh & Kenny, Maurice, eds. LC 85-18994. (Illus.). 24p. (Orig.). (C). 1986. pap. 10.00 (*0-936556-13-7*) Contact Two.

— The Candles of Your Eyes. 160p. (Orig.). 1991. pap. 7.95 (*0-87286-256-9*) City Lights.

— Color of Darkness. LC 74-26739. 175p. 1975. reprint ed. lib. bdg. 55.00 (*0-8371-7874-6*, PUCD, Greenwood Pr) Greenwood.

— Garments the Living Wear. 160p. (Orig.). 1989. pap. 7.95 (*0-87286-239-9*) City Lights.

***Purdy, James.** Gertrude of Stony Island Avenue. 192p. 1999. pap. 13.00 (*0-688-17226-1*, Quil) HarperTrade.

Purdy, James. Gertrude of Stony Island Avenue. LC 98-10746. 144p. 1998. 19.95 (*0-688-15901-X*, Wm Morrow) Morrow Avon.

— Gertrude of Stony Island Avenue. 256p. 1996. 27.95 (*0-7206-1011-7*, Pub. by P Owen Ltd) Dufour.

— House of the Solitary Maggot. 360p. 1986. 28.00 (*0-7206-0662-4*, Pub. by P Owen Ltd) Dufour.

— In a Shallow Grave. 160p. 1988. reprint ed. pap. 8.95 (*0-87286-234-8*) City Lights.

Purdy, James. Malcolm. LC 94-28945. 196p. 1995. pap. 12.99 (*1-85242-368-4*) Serpents Tail.

Purdy, James. Malcolm. adapted ed. 1966. pap. 5.25 (*0-8222-0719-2*) Dramatists Play.

— Mourners Below. 295p. 1984. 28.00 (*0-7206-0621-7*, Pub. by P Owen Ltd) Dufour.

— Narrow Rooms. 185p. 1997. reprint ed. pap. 12.95 (*0-907040-57-8*, Pub. by Gay Mens Pr) LPC InBook.

— Out with the Stars. 192p. 1993. pap. 9.95 (*0-87286-284-4*) City Lights.

— Out with the Stars. 192p. 1993. 30.00 (*0-7206-0861-9*, Pub. by P Owen Ltd) Dufour.

Purdy, James A., ed. Advances in Radiation Oncology Physics: Dosimetry, Treatment Planning, & Brachytherapy. LC 92-81653. (American Association of Physicists in Medicine Symposium Ser.: No. 19). 1099p. 1993. 75.00 (*1-56396-054-0*, Pub. by Am Inst Physics) Med Physics Pub.

Purdy, James A., jt. ed. see Smith, Alfred R.

Purdy, Jeanne. Alix in Academe. LC 98-83078. 160p. 2000. pap. 13.95 (*0-88739-245-8*) Creat Arts Bk.

Purdy, Jeannine M. Common Law & Colonised Peoples: Studies in Trinidad & Western Australia. LC 96-41978. (Law, Social Change & Development Ser.). (Illus.). 328p. 1997. 78.95 (*1-85521-916-6*, Pub. by Dartmth Pub) Ashgate Pub Co.

***Purdy, Jedediah.** For Common Things: Irony, Trust & Commitment in America Today. LC 99-31055. 226p. 1999. 20.00 (*0-375-40708-1*) Knopf.

— For Common Things: Irony, Trust & Commitment in America Today. 256p. 2000. pap. 12.00 (*0-375-70691-7*) Vin Bks.

Purdy, Jim, jt. auth. see Roffman, Peter.

Purdy, John L. Word Ways: The Novels of D'Arcy McNickle. LC 89-27106. 167p. 1990. 30.95 (*0-8165-1157-8*) U of Ariz Pr.

Purdy, John L., ed. The Legacy of D'Arcy McNickle: Writer, Historian, Activist. LC 95-25863. (American Indian Literature & Critical Studies Ser.: Vol. 21). 288p. 1996. 29.95 (*0-8061-2806-2*) U of Okla Pr.

***Purdy, John L. & Ruppert, James.** Nothing But the Truth: An Anthology of Native American Literature. 800p. 2000. pap. 37.33 (*0-13-011642-4*) P-H.

Purdy, Laura M. In Their Best Interest? The Case Against Equal Rights for Children. LC 91-55550. 272p. 1992. pap. text 15.95 (*0-8014-9956-9*) Cornell U Pr.

— Reproducing Persons: Issues in Feminist Bioethics. 304p. 1996. text 45.00 (*0-8014-3243-X*); pap. text 17.95 (*0-8014-8322-0*) Cornell U Pr.

Purdy, Laura M., jt. ed. see Donchin, Anne.

Purdy, Laura M., jt. ed. see Holmes, Helen B.

Purdy, Linda, jt. auth. see Woodard, James.

***Purdy, Michael & Banks, David.** Health & Exclusion: Policy & Practice in Health Provision. LC 98-51639. 1999. write for info. (*0-415-18016-3*) Routledge.

Purdy, Michael & Banks, David. Health & Exclusion: Policy & Practice in Health Provision. LC 98-51639. 1999. pap. write for info. (*0-415-18017-1*) Routledge.

Purdy, Michael & Borisoff, Deborah, eds. Listening in Everyday Life: A Personal & Professional Approach. 2nd ed. LC 96-9654. 360p. 1996. pap. text 26.50 (*0-7618-0461-7*); lib. bdg. 52.00 (*0-7618-0460-9*) U Pr of Amer.

Purdy, Michael, jt. ed. see Borisoff, Deborah.

Purdy, P. F., et al. Phantoms for Performance Evaluation & Quality Assurance of CT Scanners. (AAPM Reports: No. 1). 23p. (Orig.). 1977. pap. 10.00 (*1-888340-04-5*) AAPM.

Purdy, Penny T., ed. see Purdy, Warren F.

Purdy, R. Allan, jt. auth. see Rapoport, Alan M.

Purdy, Ralph E. & Boucek, Mark Jr. Handbook of Cardiac Drugs. 2nd ed. LC 94-22278. 400p. 1994. pap. text 38.00 (*0-316-72246-4*) Lppncott W & W.

Purdy, Richard L., ed. see Hardy, Thomas.

Purdy, Rick, jt. ed. see Poston, Ted M.

Purdy, Rob R. Fugitives' Reunion: Conversations at Vanderbilt, May 3-5, 1956. LC 59-9772. (Vanderbilt Studies in the Humanities: No. 3). 226p. reprint ed. pap. 70.10 (*0-8357-3267-3*, 203948800013) Bks Demand.

Purdy, Scott. Time Management for Teachers: Essential Tips & Techniques. (Orig.). (C). 1995. pap. 10.00 (*0-9641366-3-5*) Write Time.

Purdy, Strother B. The Hole in the Fabric: Science, Contemporary Literature & Henry James. LC 76-6667. (Critical Essays in Modern Literature Ser.). 240p. reprint ed. pap. 74.40 (*0-608-20006-9*, 207128200010) Bks Demand.

Purdy, Susan. Christmas Gifts for You to Make. LC 76-10160. (Illus.). (J). (gr. 4-6). 1976. lib. bdg. 12.89 (*0-397-31695-X*) HarpC Child Bks.

— The Family Baker. LC 99-20469. 256p. 1999. 25.00 (*0-7679-0261-0*) Bantam.

***Purdy, Susan G.** The Perfect Pie: 150 All-Time Favorite Pies & Tarts. LC 99-45530. (Illus.). 384p. 2000. pap. 17.95 (*0-7679-0262-9*) Broadway BDD.

Purdy, Tim I. Eagle Lake. (Illus.). 136p. 1988. 12.95 (*0-938373-04-8*) Lahontan Images.

***Purdy, Tim I.** Fruit Growers Supply Company: A History of the Northern California Operations. deluxe ed. (Illus.). 164p. 2000. 39.95 (*0-938373-19-6*) Lahontan Images.

Purdy, Tim I. Honey Lake Justice: The Never Sweats of the 1860s. (Illus.). 104p. 1993. pap. 9.95 (*0-938373-08-0*) Lahontan Images.

— Sacred Heart Church. LC 97-191147. (Illus.). 105p. 1995. pap. 10.00 (*0-938373-16-1*) Lahontan Images.

— Sagebrush Reflections: The History of Amedee & Honey Lake. (Illus.). 66p. (Orig.). 1993. pap. 9.45 (*0-938373-11-0*) Lahontan Images.

***Purdy, Verity.** Luckiest Girl in the World. LC 98-232365. (Illus.). 192p. 1998. pap. 18.95 (*1-895811-57-0*) Heritage Hse.

Purdy, Virginia C. Portrait of a Know-Nothing Legislature: The Massachusetts General Court of 1855. (Nineteenth Century American Political & Social History Ser.). 298p. 1989. reprint ed. 20.00 (*0-8240-4073-2*) Garland.

Purdy, Virginia C. & Gruber, Robert, eds. American Women & the U. S. Armed Forces: A Guide to the Records of Military Agencies in the National Archives Relating to Women. rev. ed. LC 91-40430. (Illus.). 368p. (C). 1992. text 25.00 (*0-911333-90-8*, 100022) National Archives & Recs.

Purdy, Warren F. Profits from Successful Management or Working for Profits. Purdy, Penny T., ed. (Illus.). 353p. Date not set. 99.50 (*0-9661965-0-3*) W F Purdy.

Purdy, Warren G. The Complete Bus Planning Gde. (SWC-Management Ser.). 336p. 1997. pap. 19.95 (*1-880394-27-8*) Thomson Learn.

— The Guide to Retail Business Planning. 304p. 1997. pap. 19.95 (*1-880394-31-6*) Thomson Learn.

Purdy, William M. An Outline of the History of the Flaming Gorge Area. (Upper Colorado Ser.: No. 1). reprint ed. 20.00 (*0-404-60637-7*) AMS Pr.

Pure. Pixy Junket-Comic. (Illus.). 192p. 15.95 (*1-56931-239-7*) Viz Commns Inc.

Pure Mathematics Staff. Applications of Categorical Algebra. Heller, A., ed. LC 72-89866. (Proceedings of Symposia in Pure Mathematics Ser., Humboldt State University, Arcata, CA, July 29-August 16, 1974: Vol. 17). 231p. 1970. text 45.00 (*0-8218-1417-6*, PSPUM/17) Am Math.

Pure Mathematics Symposium Staff. Algebraic Geometry - Arcata 1974. Hartshorne, Robin, ed. LC 75-9530. (Proceedings of Symposia in Pure Mathematics Ser., Humboldt State University, Arcata, CA, July 29-August 16, 1974: Vol. 29). 642p. 1975. pap. 62.00 (*0-8218-1429-X*, PSPUM/29) Am Math.

— Algebraic Groups & Discontinuous Subgroups: Proceedings. Borel, Armand & Mostow, G. D., eds. LC 66-18581. (Proceedings of Symposia in Pure Mathematics Ser.: Vol. 9). 426p. 1966. reprint ed. pap. 49.00 (*0-8218-1409-5*, PSPUM/9) Am Math.

— Algebraic Topology, Vol. 22. Liulevicius, Arunas, ed. LC 72-167684. (Proceedings of Symposia in Pure Mathematics Ser., Humboldt State University, Arcata, CA, July 29-August 16, 1974). 294p. 1971. text 55.00 (*0-8218-1422-2*, PSPUM/22) Am Math.

— Analytic Number Theory. Diamond, H. G., ed. LC 72-10198. (Proceedings of Symposia in Pure Mathematics Ser., Humboldt State University, Arcata, CA, July 29-August 16, 1974: Vol. 24). 344p. 1973. pap. 67.00 (*0-8218-1424-9*, PSPUM/24) Am Math.

— Axiomatic Set Theory, 2 pts., Pt. 1. LC 78-125172. (Proceedings of the Symposia in Pure Mathematics Ser.: Vol. 13). 474p. 1970. pap. 52.00 (*0-8218-0245-3*, PSPUM/13.1) Am Math.

— Axiomatic Set Theory, 2 pts., Pt. 2. LC 78-125172. (Proceedings of the Symposia in Pure Mathematics Ser.: Vol. 13). 222p. 1975. text 73.00 (*0-8218-0246-1*, PSPUM/13.2) Am Math.

— Axiomatic Set Theory, 2 pts., Set. LC 78-125172. (Proceedings of the Symposia in Pure Mathematics Ser.: Vol. 13). 696p. 1970. pap. 114.00 (*0-8218-1413-3*, PSPUM/13) Am Math.

— Combinatorics. Motzkin, T. S., ed. LC 74-153879. (Proceedings of Symposia in Pure Mathematics Ser., Humboldt State University, Arcata, CA, July 29-August 16, 1974: Vol. 19). 255p. 1971. text 59.00 (*0-8218-1419-2*, PSPUM/19) Am Math.

— Differential Geometry. Allendoerfer, Carl B., ed. LC 50-1183. (Proceedings of Symposia in Pure Mathematics Ser., Humboldt State University, Arcata, CA, July 29-August 16, 1974: Vol. 3). 200p. 1961. reprint ed. pap. 36.00 (*0-8218-1403-6*, PSPUM/3) Am Math.

— Differential Geometry, 2 pts. Chern, Shiing-Shen & Osserman, Robert, eds. LC 75-6593. (Proceedings of Symposia in Pure Mathematics Ser., Humboldt State University, Arcata, CA, July 29-August 16, 1974: Vol. 27). 451p. 1975. reprint ed. pap. 66.00 (*0-8218-0247-X*, PSPUM/27.1); reprint ed. pap. 73.00 (*0-8218-0248-8*, PSPUM/27.2) Am Math.

— Differential Geometry, 2 pts., Set. Chern, Shiing-Shen & Osserman, Robert, eds. LC 75-6593. (Proceedings of Symposia in Pure Mathematics Ser., Humboldt State University, Arcata, CA, July 29-August 16, 1974: Vol. 27). 894p. 1975. reprint ed. pap. 113.00 (*0-8218-1427-3*, PSPUM/27) Am Math.

— Harmonic Analysis on Homogeneous Spaces: Proceedings. Moore, Calvin C., ed. LC 73-10456. (Proceedings of Symposia in Pure Mathematics Ser.: Vol. 26). 467p. 1974. reprint ed. pap. 58.00 (*0-8218-1426-5*, PSPUM/26) Am Math.

— Institute on Finite Groups, 1960. Hall, M., Jr., ed. LC 62-10812. (Proceedings of Symposia in Pure Mathematics Ser.: Vol. 6). 114p. 1961. reprint ed. pap. 31.00 (*0-8218-1406-0*, PSPUM/6) Am Math.

— Lattice Theory. Dilworth, R. P., ed. LC 50-1183. (Proceedings of Symposia in Pure Mathematics Ser.: Vol. 2). 208p. 1961. text 33.00 (*0-8218-1402-8*, PSPUM/2) Am Math.

— Mathematical Developments Arising from the Hilbert Problems: Proceedings, 2 pts, Set. LC 76-20437. (Proceedings of Symposia in Pure Mathematics Ser.: Vol. 28). 628p. 1976. reprint ed. pap. 34.00 (*0-8218-1428-1*, PSPUM/28) Am Math.

— Partial Differential Equations. Spencer, D. C., ed. LC 72-4071. (Proceedings of Symposia in Pure Mathematics Ser.: Vol. 23). 505p. 1973. reprint ed. pap. 61.00 (*0-8218-1423-0*, PSPUM/23) Am Math.

— Recursive Function Theory. Dekker, J., ed. LC 50-1183. (Proceedings of Symposia in Pure Mathematics Ser.: Vol. 5). 247p. 1962. reprint ed. pap. 42.00 (*0-8218-1405-2*, PSPUM/5) Am Math.

— Singular Integrals: Proceedings. Calderon, A. P., ed. LC 67-16553. (Proceedings of Symposia in Pure Mathematics Ser.: Vol. 10). 375p. 1968. reprint ed. pap. 51.00 (*0-8218-1410-9*, PSPUM/10) Am Math.

— Theory of Numbers. Whiteman, A. L., ed. LC 65-17382. (Proceedings of Symposia in Pure Mathematics Ser.: Vol. 8). 216p. 1965. reprint ed. pap. 38.00 (*0-8218-1408-7*, PSPUM/8) Am Math.

P

Pure Mind Foundation Staff. Beyond Forever: Unlocking the Door to Eternal Life. 304p. 1999. 23.95 (*0-9666854-0-7*, Pub. by Wheelbarrow Pubng) ACCESS Pubs Network.

Purefoy, George W. History of the Sandy Creek Baptist Association, from Its Organization in A. D. 1758 to 1858. Gaustad, Edwin S., ed. LC 79-52604. (Baptist Tradition Ser.). (Illus.). 1980. reprint ed. lib. bdg. 29.95 (*0-405-12469-4*) Ayer.

Puregger, Marjorie. Australian Guide to Chairing Meetings. 1998. pap. 19.95 (*0-7022-3010-3*, Pub. by Univ Queensland Pr) Intl Spec Bk.

— Mr. Chairman: A Guide to Meeting Procedure & Forms of Address. 5th ed. 1989. pap. text 16.95 (*0-7022-1769-7*, Pub. by Univ Queensland Pr) Intl Spec Bk.

Purello, Joseph T., jt. auth. see Schmid, A. Allan.

Puretz, Susan, et al. The Woman's Guide to Peak Performance. LC 97-42142. 400p. 1998. pap. 21.95 (*0-89087-841-2*) Celestial Arts.

Puretz, Susan L., jt. auth. see Haas, Adelaide.

***Purewal Jasjit, et al.** The Food of India: Authentic Recipes from the Spicy Subcontinent, 13 vols. LC 98-18182. (World Cookbks.). (Illus.). 132p. 1998. 16.95 (*962-593-391-3*, Periplus Eds) Tuttle Pubng.

Purewal, Tol S. Metered Dose Inhaler Technology. Grant, David J., ed. LC 97-41982. (Illus.). 280p. 1998. 194.00 (*1-57491-065-5*) Interpharm.

Purgathofer, W. & Schonhut, J., eds. Advances in Computer Graphics 5. (Eurographic Seminars Ser.). (Illus.). viii, 221p. 1989. 91.95 (*0-387-51420-1*, 3290) Spr-Verlag.

Purgathofer, W., jt. ed. see Hanrahan, P. M.

Purgraski, Carolyn B. Sorting Life Out. 36p. 1978. student ed. write for info. (*0-318-51257-2*); 24.00 (*0-930004-00-0*) C E M Comp.

Purgraski, Carolyn B., et al. Sorting Out Money Values & Student Packet of Ready-to-Be-Duplicated Worksheets. rev. ed. LC 59-4503. (Sorting Life Out Ser.). 292p. (C). 1981. teacher ed. 25.00 (*0-930004-02-7*); student ed. write for info. (*0-318-51258-0*) C E M Comp.

Puri. Digital Video Compression. (Electrical Engineering Ser.). 1995. 59.95 (*0-442-02039-2*, VNR) Wiley.

— Essentials of Psychiatry. 1995. pap. text 21.00 (*0-7020-1877-5*, W B Saunders Co) Harcrt Hlth Sci Grp.

— Statistics for Clinicians. 1996. pap. text 28.50 (*0-7020-1876-7*, W B Saunders Co) Harcrt Hlth Sci Grp.

— Textbook of Psychiatry. 1996. pap. text 35.00 (*0-443-04911-4*, W B Saunders Co) Harcrt Hlth Sci Grp.

Puri, Jyoti. Woman, Body, Desire in Post-Colonial India: Narratives of Gender & Sexuality. LC 99-23522. 224p. 1999. pap. 17.99 (*0-415-92128-7*) Routledge.

Puri, Asha, tr. see Sorman, Guy.

***Puri, Atul & Chen, Tsuhan, eds.** Multimedia Systems, Standards & Networks. LC 00-24108. (Signal Processing Ser.). 636p. 2000. pap. 195.00 (*0-8247-9303-X*) Dekker.

Puri, B. B. Mass Scale Housing for Hot Climate. (C). 1993. 18.00 (*81-204-0797-0*, Pub. by Oxford IBH) S Asia.

Puri, B. N. Buddhism in Central Asia. (C). 1993. 25.00 (*81-208-0366-3*, Pub. by Motilal Bnarsidass) S Asia.

— The Changing Horizon. 249p. (C). 1986. 125.00 (*81-85009-19-8*, Pub. by Print Hse) St Mut.

— The Gupta Administration. 1990. 18.50 (*81-7018-598-X*, Pub. by BR Pub) S Asia.

— India in the Time of Patanjali. 1990. 34.00 (*0-685-40066-2*, Pub. by M Manoharial) S Asia.

Puri, Balraj. Jammu & Kasmir: Triumph & Tragedy of Indian Federalisation. 280p. 1981. 33.95 (*0-940500-47-7*, Pub. by Sterling) Asia Bk Corp.

Puri, Basant & McKee, Heather. Psychiatry Vade-Mecum. (An Arnold Publication). (Illus.). 288p. 1998. pap. text 24.95 (*0-340-69171-9*, Pub. by E A) OUP.

Puri, Basant K. Statistics in Practice: An Illustrated Guide to SPSS. (Illus.). 144p. 1996. pap. text 26.50 (*0-340-66209-3*, Pub. by E A) OUP.

Puri, Basant K. & Hall, Anne D. Complete MCQs in Psychiatry: Self-Assessment for Parts 1 & 2 of the MRCpsych. 496p. 1999. pap. text 39.95 (*0-340-74035-3*, Pub. by E A) OUP.

— Revision Notes in Psychiatry. LC 97-30185. (An Arnold Publication). (Illus.). 464p. 1998. pap. text 42.95 (*0-340-66227-1*) OUP.

Puri, Basant K. & Sklar, John. Revision for MRCPsych, Pt. 1. 232p. 1990. pap. text 28.00 (*0-443-04331-0*) Church.

Puri, Basant K. & Tyrer, Peter J. Sciences Basic to Psychiatry. 2nd ed. LC 98-14946. (C). 1998. pap. text 65.00 (*0-443-05514-9*) Church.

P

Puri, C. P. & Van Look, P. F. Current Concepts in Fertility Regulation & Reproduction: Proceedings of an International Conference on Fertility Regulation, Nov. 5-8, 1992, Bombay. 1994. write for info. (*81-224-0695-5*, Pub. by Wiley Estrn) Franklin.

Puri, G. S., et al. Forest Ecology, Vol. 1. (C). 1985. 31.00 (*0-8364-2433-6*, Pub. by Oxford IBH) S Asia.

— Forest Ecology, Vol. 2. (C). 1988. 50.00 (*81-204-0364-9*, Pub. by Oxford IBH) S Asia.

Puri, Geeta. Bharatiya Jana Sangh: Organization & Ideology. 292p. 1980. 24.95 (*0-940500-26-4*) Asia Bk Corp.

***Puri, H. S.** Neem: The Divine Tree, Azadirachta Indica. 196p. 1999. text 75.00 (*90-5702-348-2*, Harwood Acad Pubs) Gordon & Breach.

Puri, Harish. Ghadar Movement: Ideology, Organisation & Strategy. 1984. 18.50 (*0-8364-1113-7*, Pub. by Nanak Dev Univ IA) S Asia.

***Puri, Harish K., et al.** Terrorism in Punjab: Understanding Grassroots Reality. LC 99-938874. (Illus.). 200p. 1999. 29.50 (*81-241-0619-3*, Pub. by Har-Anand Pubns) Nataraj Bks.

Puri, Ishwar C. Beyond Logic & Reason. Ingram, Leonard, ed. 59p. 1983. pap. 3.00 (*0-937067-00-8*) Insti Study Aware.

— Go Within. Scott, Edward D., ed. 177p. (Orig.). 1986. pap. 6.00 (*0-937067-07-5*) Insti Study Aware.

— The Healing Arts. Crothers, Marta, ed. 37p. (Orig.). 1988. pap. 3.00 (*0-937067-10-5*) Insti Study Aware.

— Human Consciousness: The Key to Higher Knowledge. Ingram, Leonard, ed. 84p. (Orig.). 1983. pap. 5.00 (*0-937067-02-4*) Insti Study Aware.

— Journey to Totality. Scott, Edward D., ed. 121p. (Orig.). 1985. pap. 6.00 (*0-937067-05-9*) Insti Study Aware.

— Know Thyself. Ingram, Leonard, ed. 66p. 1983. pap. 3.00 (*0-937067-01-6*) Insti Study Aware.

— New Age-Old Path. Scott, Edward D., ed. 54p. (Orig.). 1985. pap. 3.00 (*0-937067-04-0*) Insti Study Aware.

— On Love. Scott, Edward D., ed. 28p. (Orig.). 1984. pap. 2.00 (*0-937067-03-2*) Insti Study Aware.

— Spirituality & Total Health. Scott, Edward D., ed. 29p. (Orig.). 1986. pap. 2.00 (*0-937067-08-3*) Insti Study Aware.

Puri, Ishwar K. Environmental Implications of Combustion Processes. 336p. 1993. boxed set 136.95 (*0-8493-4423-9*) CRC Pr.

Puri, K. N. Excavations at Rairh: During Samvat Years 1995 & 1996 (1938-39 & 1939-40 A. D.) 1998. 64.00 (*81-86782-27-3*, Pub. by Publicat Schem) S Asia.

Puri, Kamal, ed. Indigenous People: In the Wake of Mabo. 262p. 1997. pap. 16.95 (*0-909991-89-8*) Bahai.

Puri, M. L., jt. ed. see Vilaplana, J. P.

Puri, Madan L., et al, eds. Mathematical Statistics & Probability Theory: Theoretical Aspects, Vol. A. (C). 1987. lib. bdg. 154.50 (*90-277-2580-2*) Kluwer Academic.

— New Perspectives in Theoretical & Applied Statistics. LC 86-22401. 544p. 1987. 298.00 (*0-471-84800-X*) Wiley.

Puri, Madan L. & Sen, Pranab K. Nonparametric Methods in Multivariate Analysis. LC 90-19772. 456p. (C). 1993. reprint ed. lib. bdg. 74.50 (*0-89464-551-X*) Krieger.

Puri, Madan L., ed. see International Symposium on Nonparametric Technique.

Puri, Mohinder, ed. see Singer, Hans W.

Puri, Narottam. Power Quiz Book of Cricket. (C). 1987. 14.00 (*81-220-0045-2*, Pub. by Konark Pubs) S Asia.

Puri, P., ed. Congenital Diaphragmatic Hernia. (Modern Problems in Pediatrics Ser.: Vol. 24). (Illus.). 164p. 1989. 104.50 (*3-8055-4807-9*) S Karger.

— Surgery & Support of the Premature Infant. (Modern Problems in Pediatrics Ser.: Vol. 23). (Illus.). x, 210p. 1985. 141.75 (*3-8055-4073-6*) S Karger.

Puri, Prem & Surana, Rajendra, eds. Neonatal Tumours. LC 96-13126. 150p. 1996. 125.00 (*3-540-19938-1*) Spr-Verlag.

Puri, Prem, jt. ed. see Hoey, Hilary M.

Puri, Prem, jt. ed. see Holschneider, Alexander M.

Puri, R., jt. ed. see Aggarwal, B. B.

Puri, Raj, jt. auth. see Aggarwal, Bharwat.

Puri, Rama. Antartica, a Natural Reserve: A Study in International Environmental Politics. LC 98-900198. (Illus.). 352p. 1997. 27.00 (*81-85952-46-9*, Pub. by Indian Inst) Nataraj Bks.

Puri, Rashmi-Sudha. Gandhi on War & Peace. LC 86-20489. 259p. 1986. 59.95 (*0-275-92303-7*, C2303, Praeger Pubs) Greenwood.

Puri, S. & Khosla, P. K. Nursery Technology for Agroforestry: Application in Arid & Semi-Arid Regions. (Winrock Ser.). 392p. (C). 1993. text 75.00 (*1-881570-11-8*) Science Pubs.

Puri, Subash C. Stepping up to ISO 14000: Integrating Environmental Quality with ISO 9000 & TQM. LC 96-13221. (Illus.). 280p. 1996. 39.00 (*1-56327-129-X*) Productivity Inc.

***Puri, Subhash C.** Retention Management: The Art of Keeping, Motivating, Challenging the Workforce. 2000. pap. text 22.00 (*0-9691919-1-X*, Capital Pubng) S-QMG.

Puri, Sunil, ed. Tree Improvement: Applied Research & Technology Transfer. 324p. 1998. 80.00 (*1-57808-027-4*) Science Pubs.

Puri, Sunita. Advent of Sikh Religion: A Socio-Political Perspective. 271p. 1993. 38.50 (*81-215-0572-0*, Pub. by M Manoharial) Coronet Bks.

Puri, Swami B. The Heart of Krishna: Vaisnava Aparadha & the Path of Spiritual Caution. 108p. 1995. 19.95 (*0-945475-06-3*, 1100C, Pub. by Mandala Pub Grp); pap. 14.95 (*0-945475-35-7*, 1100L, Pub. by Mandala Pub Grp) Words Distrib.

Puri, Vishnu. Bhakti Ratnavali: An Anthology from the Bhagavata. Bhagavatam, tr. from SAN. 256p. 1980. 5.95 (*0-87481-499-5*, Pub. by Ramakrishna Math) Vedanta Pr.

Puri, Yogesh. Party Politics in the Nehru Era: (A Study of Congress in Delhi) (C). 1993. 28.50 (*81-85135-72-X*) S Asia.

Puric, J. & Belic, D., eds. Physics of Ionized Gases: Proceedings of the XIII Symposium on Sibenik, Yugoslavia, September 1-5, 1986. 528p. 1987. text 148.00 (*9971-5-0292-5*) World Scientific Pub.

Puricelli, Luigi, jt. auth. see Cristini, Ermanno.

***Purich.** Enzymology, Vol. 73. 283p. 1999. 129.95 (*0-471-24644-1*) Wiley.

Purich. Enzymology, Vol. 74. 388p. 2000. 125.00 (*0-471-34921-6*) Wiley.

— Handbook of Biochemical Kinetics. LC 99-63958. (Illus.). 1200p. 1999. 150.00 incl. disk (*0-12-568048-1*) Acad Pr.

Purich, Daniel L. Advances in Enzymology & Related Areas of Molecular Biology: Amino Acid Metabolism, Vol. 72. (Advances in Enzymology & Related Areas of Molecular Biology Ser.). 448p. 1998. 149.95 (*0-471-24643-3*, Wiley-Interscience) Wiley.

Purich, Daniel L., et al, eds. Contemporary Enzyme Kinetics & Mechanisms. 2nd ed. LC 82-16265. (Selected Methods in Enzymology Ser.). (Illus.). 541p. 1996. pap. text 59.95 (*0-12-568052-X*) Acad Pr.

Purich, Donald. The Inuit & Their Land. 176p. 29.95 (*1-55028-383-9*, Pub. by J Lorimer); pap. 19.95 (*1-55028-382-0*, Pub. by J Lorimer) Formac Dist Ltd.

Purificacion Zabia, Maria, ed. Text & Concordance of MS1-17: Biblioteca Colombina, Tesoro de los Remedios. (Medieval Spanish Medical Texts Ser.: No. 22). (SPA.). 6p. 1987. 10.00 incl. fiche (*0-940639-20-3*) Hispanic Seminary.

— Tratado Nuevo: Alvarez Chanca, Biblioteca Nacional, Madrid, I-51. (Medieval Spanish Medical Texts Ser.: No. 19). (SPA.). 6p. 1987. 10.00 incl. fiche (*0-940639-15-7*) Hispanic Seminary.

— Tratado Util, Licenciado Fores: Biblioteca Nacional de Madrid, I-51. (Medieval Spanish Medical Texts Ser.: No. 17). (SPA.). 6p. 1987. 10.00 incl. fiche (*0-940639-13-0*) Hispanic Seminary.

Purificacion Zabia, Maria, ed. see Alvarez, Fernando.

Purificacion Zabia, Maria, ed. see De Taranto, Vasco.

Purifoy. Awake My Soul & Sing. 1994. pap. 6.95 (*1-55897-913-1*) Brentwood Music.

— Carols Communion & Candlelight. 1995. pap. 6.95 (*0-7601-0143-4*) Brentwood Music.

— Sing We Now of Christmas. 1994. pap. 6.95 (*1-55897-840-2*) Brentwood Music.

Purinton, Edward. The Philosophy of Fasting. 140p. 1984. reprint ed. pap. text 15.00 (*0-87556-382-1*) Saifer.

Purinton, Edward E. The Philosophy of Fasting. 130p. 1996. reprint ed. spiral bd. 15.00 (*0-7873-0686-X*) Hlth Research.

Purinton, Jamie, jt. auth. see Potteiger, Matthew.

Purinton, Marjean D. Romantic Ideology Unmasked: The Mentally Constructed Tyranies in Dramas of William Wordsworth, Lord Byron, Percy Shelley, & Joanna Baillie. LC 93-41730. 1994. 36.50 (*0-87413-499-4*) U Delaware Pr.

***Purinton, Mike.** Purely Fun: The Humor Book: Techniques for Adding Life to Your Years & Years to Your Life. LC 99-91527. (Illus.). 128p. 1999. 10.00 (*0-9674996-0-7*) Lakeside Pubng.

Purintun, Ann-Elizabeth, jt. ed. see Kraft, Robert A.

Puris, Martin. Comeback: How Seven Straight-Shooting CEOs Turned Around Troubled Companies. LC 98-27592. (Illus.). 240p. 1999. 23.00 (*0-8129-3127-0*, Times Bks) Crown Pub Group.

Puritt, Paul, jt. auth. see Moore, Sally F.

Puritz, Patricia & Scali, Mary Ann. Beyond the Walls: Improving Conditions of Confinement for Youth in Custody. LC 98-127266. (OJJDP Report Ser.). 1998. write for info. (*1-57073-425-9*) Amer Bar Assn.

***Puritz, Patricia & Scali, Mary Ann.** Beyond the Walls: Improving the Conditions of Confinement for Youth in Custody. 100p. 1999. pap. text 25.00 (*0-7881-7890-3*) DIANE Pub.

Purj. 199 Things to Do with a Politician. Jackson, Mike et al, eds. (Illus.). 168p. (Orig.). 1994. pap. 5.95 (*1-56245-088-3*) Great Quotations.

***Purjavady, Nasrollah, ed.** The Splendour of Iran, 3 vols. (Illus.). 1550p. 2000. 475.00 (*1-86154-011-6*, Pub. by Booth-Clibborn) Dist Art Pubs.

Purkait, Biswa R. Indian Renaissance & Education. (C). 1992. 18.00 (*0-8364-2770-X*, Pub. by Firma KLM) S Asia.

Purkart, Josef, ed. see Boncompagno da Signa.

Purkayastha, R. K., jt. ed. see Das, Gurudas.

Purkayastha, R. P. & Chandra, Aindrila. Manual of Indian Edible Mushrooms. (International Bioscience Monographs: No. 16). 267p. 1985. 37.00 (*1-55528-070-6*) Scholarly Pubns.

Purkayastha, R. P. & Chendra, Anidrila. Manual of Indian Edible Mushrooms. Jain, R. K., ed. (International Bioscience Monographs: Vol. 16). (Illus.). xvi, 267p. (C). 1985. lib. bdg. 37.00 (*1-55528-001-3*) Scholarly Pubns.

Purkayastha, R. P., jt. ed. see Daniel, M.

Purke, Terry, ed. see Andrews, Larry L.

Purkey, Becky W. & Garside, Larry J. Geologic & the Natural History Tours in the Reno Area. (Special Publications: No. 19). (Illus.). 212p. (Orig.). 1996. pap. 10.95 (*1-888035-01-3*) Nev Bureau Mines & Geol.

Purkey, Becky W., et al. Geologic Tours in the Las Vegas Area. (Special Publications: No. 16). (Illus.). 156p. (Orig.). (C). 1995. pap. 10.95 (*1-888035-00-5*) Nev Bureau Mines & Geol.

***Purkey, Mike.** Reverse the Devil's Decision. 2000. pap. 12.99 (*0-88419-699-2*) Creation House.

Purkey, Ruth A. The Haunted Carousel: One-Act Tragedy about Missing Children. (Illus.). 22p. 1982. pap. 3.25 (*0-88680-080-3*) I E Clark.

Purkey, William W. Inviting School Success: A Self-Concept Approach to Teaching & Learning. 128p. (C). 1978. pap. write for info. (*0-534-00566-7*) Wadsworth Pub.

Purkey, William W. & Novak, John M. Inviting School Success: A Self-Concept Approach to Teaching & Learning. 2nd ed. 159p. (C). 1984. mass mkt. 18.75 (*0-534-02891-8*) Wadsworth Pub.

Purkey, William W. & Schmidt, John J. Invitational Counseling: A Self-Concept Approach to Professional Practice. LC 95-8766. 215p. 1995. mass mkt. 50.95 (*0-534-33902-6*) Brooks-Cole.

— Invitational Learning for Counseling & Development. 136p. 1990. pap. 16.95 (*1-56109-002-6*) CAPS Inc.

Purkey, William W. & Stanley, Paula H. Invitational Teaching, Learning, & Living: A Guide for Teaching, Learning, & Living. (Analysis & Action Ser.). 96p. (Orig.). 1991. pap. 10.95 (*0-8106-3049-4*, 3049-4) NEA.

— The Inviting School Treasury: 1,001 Ways to Invite Student Success. LC 97-71382. 223p. 1997. reprint ed. 35.00 (*0-9626185-2-7*) Brookcliff Pubs.

Purkey, William W. & Strahan, David B. Positive Discipline: A Pocketful of Ideas. 50p. 1986. 9.00 (*1-56090-031-8*) Natl Middle Schl.

***Purkey, William Watson.** What Students Say to Themselves: Internal Dialogue & School Success. LC 99-6722. (Illus.). 120p. (C). 1999. 39.95 (*0-8039-6694-6*); pap. 16.95 (*0-8039-6695-4*) Corwin Pr.

Purkircher, G. Opera Quae Supersunt Omnia. (FRE.). 1989. pap. 120.00 (*963-05-4790-2*, Pub. by Akade Kiado) St Mut.

Purkis. Chronicle of Books. 1994. pap. text. write for info. (*0-582-12456-5*, Pub. by Addison-Wesley) Longman.

Purkis, John. Preface to Wilfred Owen. 1999. 62.95 (*0-582-27651-9*); pap. text 29.81 (*0-582-27652-7*) Addison-Wesley.

— Teach Yourself Greek Civilization. (Teach Yourself Ser.). 192p. 1999. pap. 12.95 (*0-8442-2676-9*, Teach Yrslf) NTC Contemp Pub Co.

Purkis, Jon & Bowen, James. Twenty-First Century Anarchism: Unorthodox Ideas for the New Millennium. LC 96-43321. (Global Issues Ser.). (Illus.). 224p. 1997. 75.00 (*0-304-33742-0*) Continuum.

Purkis, Jon & Bowen, James, eds. Twenty-First Century Anarchism: Unorthodox Ideas for the New Millennium. LC 96-43321. (Global Issues Ser.). (Illus.). 214p. 1997. pap. 23.95 (*0-304-33743-9*) Continuum.

Purkiser, W. T. Adventures in Truth. 1960. pap. 1.50 (*0-8341-0990-5*) Nazarene.

— Beliefs That Matter Most. 96p. 1959. pap. 7.99 (*0-8341-0310-9*) Beacon Hill.

— The Biblical Foundations, 3 Vols. (Exploring Christian Holiness Ser.: Vol. 1). 256p. 1983. 21.99 (*0-8341-0843-7*) Beacon Hill.

— Called unto Holiness, Vol. 2. 356p. 1983. 27.99 (*0-8341-0868-2*) Beacon Hill.

— Conflicting Concepts of Holiness. 96p. 1972. pap. 7.99 (*0-8341-0278-1*) Beacon Hill.

— The Gifts of the Spirit. 80p. 1975. pap. 6.99 (*0-8341-0347-8*) Beacon Hill.

— Hebrews, James, 1 & 2 Peter Vol. 11. Greathouse, William M. & Taylor, Willard H., eds. (Bible Exposition Ser.: Vol. 11). 232p. 1974. 14.99 (*0-8341-0322-2*) Beacon Hill.

— The New Testament Image of the Ministry. 148p. 1969. pap. 9.99 (*0-8341-0509-8*) Beacon Hill.

— A Primer on Prayer. (Christian Living Ser.). 48p. (Orig.). 1987. pap. 3.50 (*0-8341-1191-8*) Beacon Hill.

— Search the Scriptures, Old Testament Vol. 7: I & II Samuel. 1965. pap. 1.99 (*0-8341-0034-7*) Beacon Hill.

— Search the Scriptures, Old Testament Vol. 12: Psalms. 1969. pap. 1.99 (*0-8341-0039-8*) Beacon Hill.

— Security: The False & the Truth. 64p. 1974. pap. 5.99 (*0-8341-0048-7*) Beacon Hill.

Purkiser, W. T., ed. Exploring Our Christian Faith. 552p. 1978. 26.99 (*0-8341-0552-7*) Beacon Hill.

— Exploring the Old Testament. 472p. 1955. kivar 24.99 (*0-8341-0007-X*) Beacon Hill.

Purkiser, W. T., jt. ed. see Harper, Albert F.

Purkiss. Timelines Information. 1993. pap. text. write for info. (*0-582-22771-2*, Pub. by Addison-Wesley) Longman.

Purkiss, David, ed. & illus. see Jaffe, Merle & Cappello, Sharyn.

Purkiss, Diane. The Witch in History: Early Modern & Twentieth-Century Representations. LC 96-11316. 304p. 1996. pap. 17.95 (*0-415-08762-7*) Routledge.

— The Witch in History: Early Modern & Twentieth-Century Representations. LC 96-11316. (Illus.). 304p. (C). 1996. 90.00 (*0-415-08761-9*) Routledge.

Purkiss, Diane, ed. Renaissance Women: The Plays for Elizabeth Carry & the Poems of Aemilia Lanyer. (Women's Classics Ser.). 256p. 1995. 55.00 (*1-85196-029-5*, Pub. by Pickering & Chatto) Ashgate Pub Co.

Purkiss, Dianne, jt. ed. see Brant, Clare.

Purkitt. Annual Editions: World Politics, 97-98. 18th ed. 256p. (C). 1997. text. write for info. (*0-697-37371-1*) Brown & Benchmark.

— World Politics. 15th ed. 1994. 12.74 (*1-56134-290-4*) McGraw.

— World Politics. 17th annot. ed. 1996. teacher ed. (*0-697-31683-1*, WCB McGr Hill) McGrw-H Hghr Educ.

— World Politics, 1996-1997. annuals 17th ed. 256p. (C). 1996. text. write for info. (*0-697-31682-3*) Brown & Benchmark.

Purkitt, Helen, ed. Annual Editions: World Politics, 95-96. 16th rev. ed. (Illus.). 288p. (C). 1995. text 12.95 (*1-56134-376-5*, Dshkn McG-Hill) McGrw-H Hghr Educ.

Purkitt, Helen E. World Politics, 98-99. 19th ed. (Annual Ser.). (Illus.). 256p. 1998. pap. text 12.25 (*0-697-39190-6*, Dshkn McG-Hill) McGrw-H Hghr Educ.

Purks, James. Habitat for Humanity: Building Around the World. Kroitzsh, Gregory J., ed. (Illus.). 96p. (Orig.). 1991. pap. 18.95 (*0-9627262-3-0*) Five Corners.

Purks, Stacy, ed. see Holmes, Nicole C.

Purkus, Christina. Peta's Pence. (Livewire Ser.). (YA). (gr. 6-9). pap. 6.95 (*0-7043-4923-X*, Pub. by Womens Press) Trafalgar.

Purl, Benjamin F. Republic of Texas, Second Class Headrights: March 2, 1836-October 1, 1837. 261p. 1994. reprint ed. lib. bdg. 32.50 (*0-8328-3873-X*) Higginson Bk Co.

Purl, JoAnna. Blue Reality: From the Police Academy to Working the Streets. LC 96-25427. 212p. (Orig.). 1996. pap. 14.95 (*0-89896-325-7*) Larksdale.

Purl, Mara. Closer Than You Think: Milford-Haven, Bk. 2. LC 98-70317. 190p. (Orig.). 1998. pap. 11.95 (*0-9659480-2-1*) Haven Bks CA.

An Asterisk (*) at the beginning of an entry indicates that the title is appearing for the first time.

— What the Heart Knows: Milford-Haven, Bk. 1. x, 152p. 1997. pap. 11.95 (*0-9659480-1-3*, 62900) Haven Bks CA.

Purl, Mara & Gray, Erin. Act Right: Everything You Need to Know That They Didn't Teach You in Acting Class. LC 98-70321. 190p. 1998. pap. 19.95 (*0-9659480-0-5*) Haven Bks CA.

Purl, Sandy & Lewis, Gregg. Am I Alive? A Surviving Flight Attendant's Struggle & Inspiring Triumph over Tragedy. abr. ed. (Illus.). 200p. 1996. pap. text 15.00 (*1-883581-06-0*) Chevron Pub.

Purmort, Charles H. Purmort Genealogy, Consisting of Nineteen Generations, Nine in England, Ten in America. (Illus.). 148p. 1995. reprint ed. pap. 21.00 (*0-8328-4886-7*); reprint ed. lib. bdg. 31.00 (*0-8328-4885-9*) Higginson Bk Co.

Purna. The Truth Will Set You Free. 160p. 1993. pap. 13.95 (*1-85230-015-9*, Pub. by Element MA) Penguin Putnam.

Purna, Svami. A Practical Introduction: Yoga. LC 97-39389. 96p. 1998. pap. 14.95 (*1-86204-164-4*, Pub. by Element MA) Penguin Putnam.

Purnell. Rhyme Time Books: Humpty Dumpty. (J). 1989. 1.98 (*0-671-09369-X*) S&S Trade.

Purnell, Dick. Becoming a Friend & Lover. LC 93-35575. 276p. 1995. pap. 10.99 (*0-7852-7957-1*) Nelson.

Purnell, Geoff. The Motorcycle Restores Workshop Manual. (Illus.). 160p. 1992. 32.95 (*1-85260-393-3*) Haynes Manuals.

Purnell, Herbert C., ed. Miao & Yao Linguistic Studies: Selected Articles in Chinese. LC 73-155571. (Cornell University, Southeast Asia Program, Data Paper Ser.: No. 88). 306p. reprint ed. pap. 94.90 (*0-8357-3677-6*, 203640100003) Bks Demand.

Purnell, Herbert C., Jr., ed. see Lombard, Sylvia J.

***Purnell, Jennie.** Popular Movements & State Formation in Revolutionary Mexico: The Agraristas & Cristeros of Michoacan. 1999. write for info. (*0-8223-2282-X*) Duke.

— Popular Movements & State Formation in Revolutionary Mexico: The Agraristas & Cristeros of Michoacan. LC 98-46237. (Illus.). 288p. 1999. pap. 17.95 (*0-8223-2314-1*) Duke.

***Purnell, Karl H.** A Mountain Too Far: A Father's Search for Meaning in the Climbing Death of His Son. LC 00-132565. 304p. 2001. 24.95 (*0-88282-204-7*, Pub. by New Horizon NJ) Natl Bk Netwk.

Purnell, Kathi. Dating.Com. 160p. 1999. pap. 13.95 (*0-7414-0029-4*) Buy Books.

— Dating.Com: Diary of an Internet Romance. LC 97-93586. 160p. (Orig.). 1997. pap. 9.95 (*0-9657900-0-2*) Mastercraft Pubns.

Purnell, Larry D. Conversational Medical Spanish. 240p. (C). 1995. spiral bd. 29.34 (*0-7872-0740-3*) Kendall-Hunt.

Purnell, Larry D. & Paulanka, Betty J., eds. Transcultural Health Care: A Culturally Competent Approach. LC 97-5282. (Illus.). 511p. (C). 1997. pap. text 34.95 (*0-8036-0208-1*) Davis Co.

Purnell, Nancy. And I Love You So. (Illus.). 32p. (Orig.). 1996. pap. 20.00 (*0-9654515-0-X*) N Purnell.

***Purnell, Pamela.** Denny & the Magic Pool. 133p. (J). 1998. pap. 11.95 (*0-8464-4841-6*) Beekman Pubs.

Purnell, S. W., et al. Implementation of the Study of Teaching in the Dodds-Germany Region. LC 97-34880. xxiii, 124p. 1998. pap. text 9.00 (*0-8330-2553-8*) Rand Corp.

Purnell, Susanna, et al. A Formative Assessment of the General Electric Foundation's College Bound Program. LC 94-3462. 1994. pap. text 13.00 (*0-8330-1563-X*, MR-463-GEF) Rand Corp.

Purner, John F. The $100 Hamburger: A Guide to Pilots' Favorite Fly-In Restaurants. LC 98-16271. (Illus.). 352p. 1998. pap. 24.95 (*0-07-083714-7*) McGraw.

***Purney-Mark, Susan & Greig, Daphne.** Quilted Havens, City Houses, Country Homes. LC 99-59946. 128p. 1999. per. 22.95 (*1-57432-731-3*) Collector Bks.

Purohit, B. D. Handbook of Reservation for Scheduled Castes & Scheduled Tribes. (C). 1990. 125.00 (*0-89771-296-X*) St Mut.

Purohit, B. D. & Purohit, S. D. Handbook Reservation for Scheduled Castes & Scheduled Tribes. ii, 438 p. (C). 1990. 38.00 (*81-85287-05-8*, Pub. by Ashish Pub Hse) S Asia.

Purohit, Mahesh, et al. Fiscal Policy for the National Capital Region. 171p. 1993. text 25.00 (*0-7069-6382-2*, Pub. by Vikas) S Asia.

Purohit, R. K. Fundamentals of Fluid Mechanics. 1996. pap. 200.00 (*81-7233-144-4*, Pub. by Scientific Pubs) St Mut.

— Thermal Engineering (S. I. Unites) (C). 1992. text 145.00 (*81-7233-048-0*, Pub. by Scientific Pubs) St Mut.

Purohit, S. D., jt. auth. see Purohit, B. D.

Purohit, S. K. Ancient India Legal Philosophy: Its Relevance to Contemporary Jurisprudential Thought. (C). 1994. 27.50 (*81-7100-583-7*, Pub. by Deep & Deep Pubns) S Asia.

Purohit, S. S., ed. Hormonal Regulation of Plant Growth & Development. LC 85-11634. (Advances in Agricultural Biotechnology Ser.). 1985. text 247.50 (*90-247-3198-4*) Kluwer Academic.

— Hormonal Regulation of Plant Growth & Development, Vol. 2. (Advances in Agricultural Biotechnology Ser.). 1986. text 176.50 (*90-247-3435-5*) Kluwer Academic.

Purohit, V. B., ed. Recent Advances in Ecology & Environment. (Recent Researches in Ecology, Environment & Pollution Ser.: Vol. 1). 200p. 1988. 35.00 (*1-55528-157-5*) Scholarly Pubns.

Puroto Gyarakushi Editorial Staff, ed. see Sato, Gen T.

Purpel, David E. The Moral & Spiritual Crisis in Education: A Curriculum for Justice & Compassion in Education. LC 88-16602. (Critical Studies in Education). 192p. (Orig.). 1988. 55.00 (*0-89789-153-8*, H153, Bergin & Garvey); pap. 18.95 (*0-89789-152-X*, G152, Bergin & Garvey) Greenwood.

***Purpel, David E.** Moral Outrage in Education. LC 98-37877. (Counterpoints Ser.: Vol. 102). viii, 258p. (C). 1999. pap. text 29.95 (*0-8204-4169-4*) P Lang Pubng.

Purpel, David E. & Shapiro, Svi. Beyond Liberation & Excellence: Reconstructing the Public Discourse on Education. LC 94-39191. (Critical Studies in Education & Culture). 256p. 1995. 65.00 (*0-89789-416-2*, Bergin & Garvey); pap. 20.95 (*0-89789-417-0*) Greenwood.

Purpel, David E., jt. auth. see Giroux, Henry A.

Purpel, David E., jt. ed. see Gress, James.

Purpel, David E., jt. ed. see Shapiro, H. Svi.

Purple, Edwin R. Perilous Passage: A Narrative of the Montana Gold Rush, 1862-1863. Owens, Kenneth N., ed. LC 95-33196. (Illus.). x, 211p. 1995. 25.95 (*0-917298-35-7*); pap. 15.95 (*0-917298-37-3*) MT Hist Soc.

Purple, Samuel S. Records of the Dutch Reformed Church in New Amsterdam & New York. 1972. 50.00 (*0-8490-0936-7*) Gordon Pr.

— Records of the Reformed Dutch Church in New Amsterdam & New York. LC 98-117268. 351p. 1998. reprint ed. pap. 26.50 (*0-7884-0795-3*, P866) Heritage Bk.

***Purpura, James E. & Pinkley, Diane.** On Target 1: Intermediate. 2nd ed. LC 99-36749. 1999. 15.67 (*0-201-57978-2*) Addison-Wesley.

Purpura, Lia. The Brighter the Veil. LC 95-34708. 80p. 1996. pap. 12.95 (*0-914061-56-9*) Orchises Pr.

***Purpura, Lia.** Increase. LC 99-44066. 2000. 24.95 (*0-8203-2232-6*) U of Ga Pr.

— Stone Sky Lifting. (Journal Award Ser.). 80p. 2000. 35.00 (*0-8142-0862-2*); pap. 15.00 (*0-8142-5065-3*) Ohio St U Pr.

Purpura, Philip P. Criminal Justice. (Criminal Justice Ser.). 1996. pap., teacher ed. 12.00 (*0-8273-6349-4*) Delmar.

— Criminal Justice: An Introduction. (Illus.). 368p. 1996. pap. 36.95 (*0-7506-9630-3*) Buttrwrth-Heinemann.

— Criminal Justice: An Introduction. (Criminal Justice Ser.). 1996. text 56.21 (*0-8273-6348-6*) Delmar.

— Retail Security & Shrinkage Protection. 336p. 1993. 44.95 (*0-7506-9274-X*) Buttrwrth-Heinemann.

— Security & Loss Prevention. 3rd ed. LC 97-38810. 384p. 1998. 44.95 (*0-7506-9642-7*) Buttrwrth-Heinemann.

— The Security Handbook. 288p. (C). 1991. mass mkt. 38.50 (*0-8273-3825-2*) Delmar.

— The Security Handbook. 288p. 1991. pap., teacher ed. 11.95 (*0-8273-3826-0*) Delmar.

***Purr, Jane.** Moving House with Feng Shui: Use Effective Feng Shui Principles - Create a Feel-Good Factor Inside & Out - Harmonise Your Home. (Essentials Ser.). (Illus.). 64p. 2000. pap. 9.95 (*1-85703-569-0*, Pub. by How To Bks) Midpt Trade.

— Sell Your Home Using Feng Shui: Energise Your House - Discover What Attracts & Repels Buyers - Create a Feel-Good Factor Inside & Out. (Essentials Ser.). (Illus.). 64p. 2000. pap. 9.95 (*1-85703-570-4*, Pub. by How To Bks) Midpt Trade.

Purrington, Robert D. Physics in the Nineteenth Century. LC 96-49115. 320p. (C). 1997. text 55.00 (*0-8135-2441-5*); pap. text 22.00 (*0-8135-2442-3*) Rutgers U Pr.

Purrington, Robert D., jt. auth. see Durham, Frank.

Purrington, Sandra, et al. Music! Words! Opera!, 4 vols., Level 1. LC 90-19274. (Illus.). 264p. (J). (gr. k-2). 1990. teacher ed. 65.00 (*0-918812-65-8*, SE0694) MMB Music.

— Music! Words! Opera!, 3 vols., Set, Level 1. LC 90-19274. (Illus.). 264p. (J). (gr. k-2). 1990. student ed. 3.50 (*0-918812-67-4*, SE0695-SE0697) MMB Music.

Purroy, Carol, ed. see Rivers-Moore, Judith.

Pursak, Laurence. Knowledge in Organizations. LC 96-47427. (Resources for the Knowledge-Based Economy Ser.). 240p. 1997. pap. 21.95 (*0-7506-9718-0*) Buttrwrth-Heinemann.

Pursall, B. Mediterranean Tortoises. (Illus.). 64p. 1995. pap. 9.95 (*0-7938-0284-9*, RE135) TFH Pubns.

Pursall, K. R. Computer Risk Manager. x, 168p. 1992. 310.00 (*1-85617-172-8*, Pub. by Elsvr Adv Tech) Elsevier.

Purschel, Heiner & Bartsch, Elmar, eds. Intercultural Communication: Proceedings of the 17th Internations L. A. U. D. Symposium Duisburg, 23-27 March 1992. LC 94-26629. (Duisburg Papers on Research in Language & Culture: Bd. 20). II, 563p. 1994. 58.00 (*3-631-47614-0*) P Lang Pubng.

***Purse, Bill.** The Finale Primer: Mastering the Art of Music Notation with Finale. 2nd ed. (Illus.). 245p. 2000. pap. 24.95 (*0-87930-602-5*) Miller Freeman.

Purse, Bill. Getting Started with Finale: A Quickstart Method for the Leading Music Notation Program. 160p. 1996. pap. text 14.95 (*0-7935-6700-9*, 00330240) H Leonard.

Purse, Bill, adapted by. Bach Chorales for Guitar. 216p. 1994. spiral bd. 23.95 incl. audio (*0-7866-1189-8*, 95050P) Mel Bay.

Purse, Bill, et al, eds. Strategies for Teaching Middle-Level & High School Guitar. LC 99-178533. 92p. 1998. pap. 20.00 (*1-56545-091-4*) MENC.

Pursel, Jach, jt. auth. see Lazaris.

Pursell, Carroll. The Machine in America: A Social History of Technology. (Illus.). 256p. 1995. text 45.00 (*0-8018-4817-2*); pap. text 17.95 (*0-8018-4818-0*) Johns Hopkins.

— White Heat: People & Technology. 1994. pap. 19.95 (*0-520-08905-7*, Pub. by U CA Pr) Cal Prin Full Svc.

***Pursell, Carroll, ed.** American Technology. 2000. 64.95 (*0-631-21996-X*); pap. 29.95 (*0-631-21997-8*) Blackwell Pubs.

Pursell, Carroll W., Jr., ed. Technology in America: A History of Individuals & Ideas. 2nd ed. (Illus.). 334p. 1990. pap. text 18.50 (*0-262-66067-9*) MIT Pr.

Pursell, Cleo. Facing Death & Dying. 1982. pap. 1.95 (*0-89265-080-X*) Randall Hse.

— Triumph over Suffering. 1982. pap. 1.95 (*0-89265-079-6*) Randall Hse.

Pursell, Donald E. & Deichert, Jerome A. The Economic Impact of the University of Nebraska. 1984. write for info. (*0-318-58380-1*) Bur Busn Res U Nebr.

Pursell, Donald E., jt. auth. see Bare, Charles L.

***Pursell, Garry.** Indian Trade Policies in the 1990s. 104p. 2000. text 15.95 (*0-19-564246-5*) OUP.

Pursell, John W. Why Do They Call It Topeka? How Places Got Their Names. LC 94-17790. 224p. 1994. 9.95 (*0-8065-1588-0*, Citadel Pr) Carol Pub Group.

Pursell, Joshua R. & Miller, Richard K. The 1997 Sports Business Market Research Handbook. 260p. 1997. pap. 275.00 (*1-881503-72-0*) R K Miller Assocs.

Purser, Ann. Mixed Doubles. large type ed. LC 98-44589. 1999. 30.00 (*0-7862-1712-X*) Thorndike Pr.

— New Every Morning. large type ed. LC 97-23293. 1997. pap. 21.95 (*0-7862-1152-0*) Thorndike Pr.

— Orphan Lamb. 320p. 1997. pap. 8.95 (*0-7528-0245-3*, Pub. by Orion Pubng Grp) Trafalgar.

— Orphan Lamb. large type ed. LC 96-9843. 1996. pap. 20.95 (*0-7862-0802-3*) Thorndike Pr.

— Pastures New. large type ed. (General Ser.). 518p. 1996. pap. 20.95 (*0-7862-0666-7*) Thorndike Pr.

— Spinster of the Parish. 288p. 1996. pap. 8.95 (*0-7528-0279-8*, Pub. by Orion Pubng Grp) Trafalgar.

— Spinster of the Parish. large type ed. 445p. 1996. pap. 20.95 (*0-7862-0667-5*) Thorndike Pr.

— Thy Neighbor's Wife. large type ed. LC 97-42551. 1998. 21.95 (*0-7862-1370-1*) Thorndike Pr.

Purser, B. H., ed. see Freytet, Pierre & Plaziat, Jean-Claude.

Purser, B. H., jt. ed. see Schroeder, J. H.

Purser, Bruce, ed. see Tucker, Maurice E.

Purser, Harry & Rowley, David. Clinical Information Technology: A Practical Guide to Personal Computing for Healthcare Clinicians & Managers. 220p. 1987. 59.25 (*1-56593-580-2*, 0064) Singular Publishing.

Purser, John W. The Literary Works of Jack B. Yeats. (Princess Grace Irish Library). 220p. (C). 1990. text 75.00 (*0-389-20929-5*) B&N Imports.

Purser, Louis C., ed. see Apuleius, Lucius.

Purser, Michael. Data Communications for Programmers. 256p. (C). 1986. pap. text 15.96 (*0-201-12918-3*) Addison-Wesley.

— Introduction to Error-Correcting Codes. LC 94-32112. 133p. 1994. 67.00 (*0-89006-784-8*) Artech Hse.

Purser, Paul E., et al, eds. Manned Spacecraft: Engineering Design & Operation. LC 64-24708. (Illus.). 523p. reprint ed. pap. 162.20 (*0-608-11525-8*, 201174500079) Bks Demand.

Purser, Ronald & Cabana, Steven. The Self-Managing Organization: Transforming the Work of Teams Through Participative Design. LC 98-27061. 256p. 1998. 28.00 (*0-684-83734-X*) Free Pr.

Purser, Ronald & Montuori, Alfonso, eds. Social Creativity, Vol. 2. (Perspectives on Creativity Ser.). 368p. 1998. text 76.50 (*1-57273-130-3*) Hampton Pr NJ.

— Social Creativity, Vol. 2. (Perspectives on Creativity Ser.). 368p. 1999. pap. text 28.50 (*1-57273-131-1*) Hampton Pr NJ.

Purser, Ronald, jt. ed. see Montuori, Alfonso.

Purser, Ronald E., jt. auth. see Emery, Merrelyn.

Purser, William. My Guardian Angel: The Invisible Crewman. 2nd ed. LC 97-94118. (Illus.). vi, 178p. 1997. pap. 18.95 (*0-9659414-0-X*) Bonnie Pr.

— My Guardian Angel - The Invisible Crewman. 2nd rev. ed. Giddens, Kathy P., ed. LC 97-94118. (Illus.). 210p. 1997. pap. 12.95 (*0-9659414-2-6*) Bonnie Pr.

Pursey, H. J. Merchant Ship Construction. (Illus.). (C). 1987. 120.00 (*0-7855-6054-8*) St Mut.

— Merchant Ship Construction. 7th ed. 217p. 1983. text 48.00 (*0-85174-454-0*) Sheridan.

— Merchant Ship Stability: Metric Edition. 6th rev. ed. (Illus.). 207p. (C). 1992. text 48.00 (*0-85174-442-7*) Sheridan.

Pursglove, Glyn. A Bibliography of the Writings of Peter Russell. LC 99-211519. (Studies in English Literature). xv, 250p. 1995. write for info. (*3-7052-0729-6*, Pub. by Poetry Salzburg) Intl Spec Bk.

Pursglove, Glyn. Francis Warner & Tradition: An Introduction to the Plays. 232p. 1981. 26.00 (*0-86140-083-6*, Pub. by Smyth) Dufour.

— Francis Warner's Poetry: A Critical Assessment. 348p. 1989. 40.00 (*0-86140-271-5*, Pub. by Smyth) Dufour.

Pursglove, Glyn, jt. ed. see Gortschacher, Wolfgang.

Pursglove, M., ed. Gogol: Nevsky Prospect (Nevskii Prospekt) (Bristol Russian Texts Ser.). (RUS.). 96p. 1995. pap. 18.95 (*1-85399-348-4*, Pub. by Brist Class Pr) Focus Pub-R Pullins.

— Tolstoy: Childhood (Detstvo) (Bristol Russian Texts Ser.). (RUS.). 152p. 1993. pap. 16.95 (*1-85399-294-1*, Pub. by Brist Class Pr) Focus Pub-R Pullins.

— Tolstoy: Sebastopol in December (Sevastopol' V Dekabre Mesyatse) (Bristol Russian Texts Ser.). (RUS.). 1994. pap. 16.95 (*1-85399-353-0*, Pub. by Brist Class Pr) Focus Pub-R Pullins.

Pursglove, Michael, ed. see Tsukerman, V. A. & Azarkh, Z. A.

Pursglove, Paul D., ed. Zen in the Art of Close Encounters: Crazy Wisdom & UFO's. LC 94-80141. (Illus.). 333p. (Orig.). (C). 1995. pap. 14.50 (*0-9638691-0-8*) New Being Proj.

Pursh, Frederick. Flora Americae Septentrionalis. (Historia Naturalis Classica Ser.: 104). 1979. reprint ed. lib. bdg. 80.00 (*3-7682-1242-4*) Lubrecht & Cramer.

Pursiful, Darrell J. The Cultic Motif in the Spirituality of the Book of Hebrews. LC 93-21560. (Biblical Press Ser.: Vol. 14). 208p. 1993. text 89.95 (*0-7734-2376-1*, Mellen Biblical Pr) E Mellen.

***Pursiful, Nola.** Nola's Daily Doses: Registration Preparation. 23p. 1999. student ed., ring bd. 10.00 (*1-884048-30-7*) Natl Assn Parliamentarians.

Pursifull, Carmen, ed. & intro. see Mihalas, Dimitri.

***Pursifull, Carmen M.** Brimmed Hat with Flowers: Multi-Tasking.com. Mamaril, Marie, ed. (Illus.). 140p. 2000. pap. 22.00 (*1-881900-06-1*, Pub. by Hawk Prods) C M Pursifull.

Pursifull, Carmen M. Elsewhere in a Parallel Universe. Walker, Ruth S., ed. (Hawk Production Ser.). 124p. (Orig.). 1992. pap. 10.00 (*0-932884-99-7*) Red Herring.

— The Many Faces of Passion. LC 95-82261. (Illus.). 112p. 1996. pap. 10.00 (*1-881900-04-5*) Hawk Prods.

Pursifull, Carmen M. & Walker, Ruth S., eds. Matrix 15: Anthology of Red Herring Poets. 15th ed. 156p. 1990. pap. 7.95 (*0-932884-45-8*) Red Herring.

— Matrix 16: Anthology of Red Herring Poets. 16th ed. 72p. 1991. pap. 8.00 (*0-932884-46-6*) Red Herring.

Pursifull, Carmen M., ed. see Mihalas, Dimitri.

Pursley, Duane, jt. auth. see Deems, Eugene F., Jr.

***Pursley, Joan Muyskens & Bischoff, Karen.** The World's Most Beautiful Dolls. (Illus.). 160p. 1999. 24.95 (*0-942620-24-0*) Portfolio Pr.

Pursley, Michael B. Introduction to Digital Communications. (Electrical Engineering Ser.). (Illus.). 640p. (C). 2000. 95.00 (*0-201-18493-1*) Addison-Wesley.

Pursley, Robert D. Introduction to Criminal Justice. 6th ed. LC 93-16649. (Criminal Justice Ser.). 720p. (C). 1993. 91.00 (*0-02-396941-5*, Macmillan Coll) P-H.

Pursley, Robert D., jt. auth. see Albanese, Jay S.

Purslow, Frances A. City-Smart: Calgary. (City Smart Ser.). (Illus.). 216p. 1998. pap. 12.95 (*1-56261-322-7*, City Smart) Avalon Travel.

Purslow, Vicki T. Jazz Appreciation: A Listener's Notebook. 85p. 1999. pap. text, wbk. ed. 8.25 (*1-893438-03-1*) Lighthse Pubg.

— Music Appreciation. (Listener's Notebook Ser.). 98p. 1998. pap. text, wbk. ed. 8.25 (*1-893438-01-5*) Lighthse Pubg.

— Music Fundamentals for the Recreational Musician. 2nd rev. ed. (Illus.). 49p. 1998. pap. text 9.95 (*1-893438-00-7*) Lighthse Pubg.

— Music Word Search Puzzles. 56p. 1999. pap. 7.95 (*1-893438-02-3*) Lighthse Pubg.

***Purt-Nichols, Tanya.** The Colouring Book. (Illus.). 26p. 2000. 14.99 (*0-615-11430-X*) Purnichols.

Purtee, Les. Death Dressed in White. 310p. 1995. 21.50 (*0-9644420-0-0*) Flag Pub.

Purtell, April, et al. The A to Z Guide to Educational Field Trips. Harris, Gregg, ed. 206p. 1993. pap. text 19.95 (*1-56857-081-3*) Noble Pub Assocs.

Purtell, April, jt. auth. see Fudge, Thomas A.

Purtell, April L. The Gospel Syllabus. (Illus.). 15p. (YA). 1993. pap. 3.50 (*0-913717-71-1*, 1904) Hewitt Res Fnd.

Purtell, April L. & Dillon, Christine J. Across America Student Workbook: Second-Grade Curriculum. (Illus.). 339p. 1994. ring bd. 30.00 (*0-913717-59-2*, 2010) Hewitt Res Fnd.

Purtell, L. P., jt. ed. see Dutton, J. C.

Purtill, John, Jr., ed. see CAAS Inc. Staff.

Purtill, John S. Controllers Manual. 96th ed. 1997. pap. text 69.00 (*0-15-601854-3*) Harcourt.

Purtill, Mark, jt. auth. see Ridge, M. D.

Purtill, Richard L. Enchantment at Delphi. LC 85-30556. (YA). (gr. 7 up). 1986. 14.95 (*0-15-200447-5*, Gulliver Bks) Harcourt.

— Logical Thinking. 174p. (C). 1992. reprint ed. pap. text 19.50 (*0-8191-8493-4*) U Pr of Amer.

— Thinking about Ethics. 147p. 1976. pap. text 45.00 (*0-13-917716-7*) P-H.

— Thinking about Religion: A Philosophical Introduction to Religion. 1978. pap. text 12.95 (*0-13-917724-8*) P-H.

Purtilo, Ruth. Ethical Dimensions in the Health Professions. 3rd ed. Allen, Andrew, ed. (Illus.). 300p. (C). 1998. pap. text. write for info. (*0-7216-7799-1*, W B Saunders Co) Harcrt Hlth Sci Grp.

Purtilo, Ruth B. Ethical Dimensions in the Health Professions. 2nd ed. LC 92-49438. (Illus.). 288p. 1993. pap. text 30.00 (*0-7216-3550-4*, W B Saunders Co) Harcrt Hlth Sci Grp.

Purtilo, Ruth B & Haddad, Amy. Health Professional & Patient Interaction. 5th ed. Biblis, Margaret, ed. 416p. 1996. pap. text 30.00 (*0-7216-6048-7*, W B Saunders Co) Harcrt Hlth Sci Grp.

Purtle, Jane, et al. Spiritual Autographs: Southern Women Tell Their Stories. (Illus.). 280p. 1999. pap. 20.00 (*1-58374-003-1*) Chicago Spectrum.

Purtle, Jane H. Food from the Hills of East Texas. LC 90-84194. (Illus.). 228p. (Orig.). 1990. pap. 10.00 (*0-9627944-0-6*) FoxLair Pubns.

***Purton, Michael.** I Can Make Music. (Illus.). 40p. (J). 2000. pap. 7.95 (*0-7548-0223-X*, Lorenz Bks) Anness Pub.

Purton, Peter, et al. Butterworths Planning Law Service. 1990. ring bd. 440.00 (*0-406-34050-1*, U.K., MICHIE) LEXIS Pub.

Purton, Valerie, ed. see Dickens, Charles.

Purtscheller, F. Oetztaler und Stubaier Alpen. 2nd ed. (Sammlung Geologischer Fuehrer Ser.: Band 53). (GER., Illus.). viii, 128p. 1978. spiral bd. 18.00 (*3-443-15022-5*, Pub. by Gebruder Borntraeger) Balogh.

***Purtscher, P. T.** Structure-property Relationships in Steel Produced in Hot-strip Mills. 71p. 1999. pap. 7.00 (*0-16-058912-6*) USGPO.

Purtschert, R., ed. Advances in Vaccination Against Virus Diseases. (Monographs in Pediatrics: Vol. 11). (Illus.). 1979. pap. 27.25 (*3-8055-3046-3*) S Karger.

P

PuruShotam & Srirekam, Nirmala. Negotiating Language, Constructing Race: Disciplining Difference in Singapore. LC 97-40999. (Contributions to the Sociology of Language Ser.: No. 79). 294p. 1997. 118.65 (*3-11-015679-2*) De Gruyter.

***Purushotam, Nirmala.** Negotiating Multiculturalism: Disciplining Difference in Singapore. LC 00-25550. 2000. write for info. (*3-11-015680-6*) De Gruyter.

Purushotham, Daniel P. & Wilson, Stephanie Y. Building Pay Structures: An Approach to Establishing the Foundation for a Compensation Program. (Building Blocks Ser.: Vol. 8). (Illus.). 24p. (Orig.). 1993. pap. 24.95 (*1-57963-011-1*, A0022) Am Compensation.

Purushotham, P., jt. auth. see Moulik, T. K.

Purushothaman, Sahasranaman & Zwarico, Amy, eds. NAPAW '92: Proceedings of the First North American Process Algebra Workshop, Stony Brook, NY, 28 August 1992. LC 92-44291. 1993. 69.00 (*0-387-19822-9*) Spr-Verlag.

Purushothaman, Sangeetha. The Empowerment of Women in India: Grassroots Women's Networks & the State. LC 97-31053. 384p. 1997. 38.00 (*0-8039-9395-1*); pap. write for info. (*0-8039-9396-X*) Sage.

Purver, Jonathan M. & Taylor, Lawrence. Handling Criminal Appeals. LC 80-81271. 1980. 120.00 (*0-685-59836-5*) West Group.

Purver, Jonathan M., et al. Trial Lawyer's Book: Preparing & Winning Cases. LC 90-60301. 1990. 100.00 (*0-317-02942-8*) West Group.

— Trial Lawyer's Book: Preparing & Winning Cases. 1993. suppl. ed. 32.50 (*0-317-04629-2*) West Group.

Purves. Life. 5th ed. 1997. 46.00 (*0-7167-3354-4*) W H Freeman.

— Life. 5th ed. 1998. student ed. write for info. (*0-7167-3393-5*) W H Freeman.

PURVES. Life, Vol. 1, 3. 5th ed. 1997. 50.00 (*0-7167-3353-6*) W H Freeman.

Purves. Life, Vol. 1 & 2. 5th ed. 1997. 50.00 incl. cd-rom (*0-7167-3351-X*) W H Freeman.

— Life, Vols. 1, 2 & 3. 5th ed. 1998. student ed. 87.00 incl. cd-rom (*0-7167-3447-8*) W H Freeman.

— Life: Science of Biology. 4th ed. 2000. 58.00 (*0-7167-3020-0*); lab manual ed. 78.00 (*0-7167-3037-5*) W H Freeman.

Purves. Life: Science of Biology. 5th ed. 1997. pap. text 4.95 (*0-7167-3372-2*, Pub. by W H Freeman) VHPS.

Purves. Life: Science of Biology. 5th ed. 280p. 1997. 18.00 (*0-7167-3219-X*); teacher ed. 20.00 (*0-7167-3220-3*) Worth.

— Life: Science of Biology, 2. 4th ed. Date not set. 43.00 (*0-7167-3017-0*) W H Freeman.

— Life: Science of Biology, Vol. I. 1997. pap. text 35.95 (*0-7167-3274-2*) W H Freeman.

— Life: Science of Biology, Vol. 1. 4th ed. Date not set. 60.00 (*0-7167-3014-6*); 43.00 (*0-7167-3015-4*) W H Freeman.

— Life: Science of Biology, Vol. 1. 5th ed. 1997. pap. 40.95 (*0-7167-3326-9*) W H Freeman.

— Life: Science of Biology, Vol. 1 & 2. Date not set. 74.00 (*0-7167-3018-9*) W H Freeman.

— Life: Science of Biology, Vol. 2. 4th ed. Date not set. 58.00 (*0-7167-3021-9*) W H Freeman.

— Life: Study of Biology. 5th ed. (Illus.). 413p. 1997. pap. text, student ed. 24.95 (*0-7167-3221-1*) St Martin.

Purves, Alan C. How Porcupines Make Love. 4th ed. (C). 1998. pap. text. write for info. (*0-8013-1870-X*) Addison-Wesley.

— The IEA Study of Written Composition II. (International Studies in Educational Achievement: Vol. 6). 300p. 1992. 97.75 (*0-08-041397-8*, Pergamon Pr) Elsevier.

— The Web of Text & the Web of God: An Essay on the Third Information Transformation. LC 98-2995. 230p. 1998. lib. bdg. 36.95 (*1-57230-249-6*, C0249) Guilford Pubns.

Purves, Alan C., ed. The Idea of Difficulty in Literature. LC 90-43101. (SUNY Series, Literacy, Culture, & Learning: Theory & Practice). 182p. (C). 1991. pap. text 21.95 (*0-7914-0674-1*) State U NY Pr.

— Writing Across Languages & Cultures: Issues in Contrastive Rhetoric. LC 88-80974. (Written Communication Annual Ser.: No. 2). 309p. reprint ed. pap. 95.80 (*0-7837-6720-X*, 204634700011) Bks Demand.

Purves, Alan C., et al, eds. Encyclopedia of English Studies & Language Arts: A Project of the National Council of Teachers of English. LC 93-33627. 1995. 150.00 (*0-590-49268-3*, pe65.e47 1994) Scholastic Inc.

— Using Portfolios in the English Classroom. LC 98-104325. 288p. 1996. pap. text, teacher ed. 36.95 (*0-926842-62-5*) CG Pubs Inc.

Purves, Alan C. & Quattrin, Joseph A. Creating the Literature Portfolio: A Guide for Students. 1996. pap., teacher ed. 26.79 (*0-8442-5951-9*) NTC Contemp Pub Co.

Purves, Alan C. & Quattrini, Joseph A. Creating the Literature Portfolio: A Guide for Students. LC 96-14224. 272p. 1996. write for info. (*0-8442-5950-0*) NTC Contemp Pub Co.

Purves, Alan C., et al. Creating the Writing Portfolio. 1995. pap., teacher ed. 12.66 (*0-8442-5818-0*); pap., student ed. 22.59 (*0-8442-5817-2*) NTC Contemp Pub Co.

— How Porcupines Make Love, 2. rev. ed. 256p. (C). 1990. pap. text 23.00 (*0-8013-0382-6*, 78161) Longman.

— How Porcupines Make Love, 3. 2nd rev. ed. LC 94-6629. 215p. (C). 1995. pap. text 38.44 (*0-8013-1260-4*) Longman.

Purves, Alan C., jt. ed. see Jennings, Edward M.

Purves, Alan C., jt. ed. see Niles, Olive S.

Purves, Alan C., jt. ed. see Westbury, Ian.

***Purves, Andrew.** Encountering God: Christian Faith in the Turbulent Times. 176p. 2000. pap. 15.95 (*0-664-22242-0*) Westminster John Knox.

Purves, Andrew, jt. auth. see Achtemeier, Mark.

Purves, Andrew, jt. auth. see Achtemeier, P. Mark.

Purves, Bill. Barefoot in the Boardroom. 192p. pap. 19.95 (*1-86373-038-9*, Pub. by Allen & Unwin Pty) Paul & Co Pubs.

— Barefoot in the Boardroom: Venture & Misadventure in the People's Republic of China. 190p. (Orig.). 1992. pap. 14.95 (*1-55021-079-3*, Pub. by NC Ltd) U of Toronto Pr.

***Purves, Bill.** Living with Landmines: From International Treaty to Reality. (Illus.). 208p. 2000. pap. 19.99 (*1-55164-174-7*) Black Rose.

Purves, Bryan. The Austin Seven Source Book. (Source Book Ser.). (Illus.). 592p. 1990. 59.95 (*0-85429-557-7*, Pub. by J H Haynes & Co) Motorbooks Intl.

Purves, Dale. Body & Brain: A Trophic Theory of Neural Connections. LC 88-764. (Illus.). 272p. 1988. 52.00 (*0-674-07715-6*) HUP.

— Body & Brain: A Trophic Theory of Neural Connections. (Illus.). 272p. 1990. pap. 22.50 (*0-674-07716-4*) HUP.

Purves, Dale, et al, eds. Neuroscience. LC 96-43031. 562p. (C). 1996. text 62.95 (*0-87893-747-1*) Sinauer Assocs.

Purves, Dale & Lichtman, Jeff W. Principles of Neural Development. LC 84-10566. (Illus.). 433p. 1985. text 62.95 (*0-87893-744-7*) Sinauer Assocs.

Purves, David. A Scots Grammar: Scots Grammar & Usage. 1993. pap. 32.00 (*0-85411-068-2*, Pub. by Saltire Soc) St Mut.

***Purves, Geoffry.** Healthy Living Centers Planning & Designing for Primary Health Care. 192p. 2000. 100.00 (*0-7506-4602-0*, Architectural Pr) Buttrwrth-Heinemann.

Purves, George T. The Testimony of Justin Martyr to Early Christianity. 1977. lib. bdg. 59.95 (*0-8490-2735-7*) Gordon Pr.

Purves, Jock. Fair Sunshine. 206p. 1990. reprint ed. pap. 8.99 (*0-85151-136-8*) Banner of Truth.

— Sweet Believing: Eight Character Studies of the Scottish Covenantors. 3rd ed. 97p. (Orig.). 1998. reprint ed. pap. text 8.99 (*1-84030-044-2*) Ambassador Prodns Ltd.

— The Unlisted Legion. 1978. pap. 6.99 (*0-85151-245-3*) Banner of Truth.

Purves, John. Italian Dictionary. (Routledge Pocket Dictionaries Ser.). (ITA.). 862p. 1980. pap. 12.95 (*0-7100-0602-0*, Routledge Thoemms) Routledge.

— Italian-English - English-Italian Pocket Dictionary. (ENG & ITA.). 833p. 1980. pap. 16.95 (*0-8288-4706-1*, M9364) Fr & Eur.

Purves, L. Holy Smoke. text 35.00 (*0-340-72151-0*, Pub. by Hodder & Stought Ltd) Trafalgar.

Purves, Libby, et al. The English & Their Horses. 1989. 24.95 (*0-370-31175-2*) Random.

Purves, Lloyd. Lloyd Purves on Closing Sales. 1978. 4.95 (*0-13-539130-X*, Parker Publishing Co) P-H.

Purves, M. J. The Physiology of Cerebral Circulation. LC 70-169577. (Monographs of the Physiological Society: No. 28). 436p. reprint ed. pap. 124.30 (*0-608-15770-8*, 2031716) Bks Demand.

Purves, Pamela. Decorating Eggs: In the Style of Faberge. Dace, Rosalind, ed. (Illus.). 96p. (Orig.). (YA). 1996. reprint ed. pap. 19.95 (*0-85532-644-1*, 644-1, Pub. by Srch Pr) A Schwartz & Co.

Purves, R. D. Microelectrode Methods for Intracellular Recording & Ionophoresis. (Biological Techniques Ser.). 1981. text 79.00 (*0-12-567950-5*) Acad Pr.

Purves, William K. Life. (C). teacher ed. 16.00 (*0-7167-2705-6*) W H Freeman.

— Life. 3rd ed. (C). 1992. pap. text 20.00 (*0-7167-2329-8*) W H Freeman.

— Life. 4th ed. teacher ed. 16.80 (*0-7167-2656-4*) W H Freeman.

— Life, Vol. 1. 4th ed. Date not set. student ed. 30.00 (*0-7167-3011-1*) W H Freeman.

— Life, Vol. II. 4th ed. Date not set. student ed. 36.00 (*0-7167-3012-X*) W H Freeman.

— Life, Vol. III. Date not set. student ed. 36.00 (*0-7167-3013-8*) W H Freeman.

— Life: Science of Biology. 4th ed. (C). 1995. text 16.80 (*0-7167-2936-9*) W H Freeman.

— Life: The Science of Biology. 5th ed. 1997. pap. text 83.95 (*0-7167-3325-0*) W H Freeman.

— Life: The Science of Biology, Sampler. 4th ed. 1994. write for info. (*0-7167-2737-4*) W H Freeman.

***Purves, William K., et al.** Life: Science of Biology. 6th ed. 2000. pap. text, student ed. write for info. (*0-7167-3951-8*) W H Freeman.

Purves, William K., et al. Life: Science of Biology, Vol. 1. 5th ed. (Illus.). 1997. pap. text 35.95 (*0-7167-3275-0*) W H Freeman.

— Life: The Science of Biology. (Illus.). 1200p. (C). 1992. student ed. 40.00 (*0-7167-2279-8*); student ed. 6.40 (*0-7167-2280-1*) W H Freeman.

— Life: The Science of Biology. rev. ed. (Illus.). 1200p. (C). 1991. disk 48.00 (*0-7167-2330-1*); disk 48.00 (*0-7167-2277-1*) W H Freeman.

— Life: The Science of Biology. rev. ed. (Illus.). 360p. (C). 1992. 40.00 (*0-7167-2278-X*) W H Freeman.

— Life: The Science of Biology. 3rd rev. ed. (Illus.). 1200p. (C). 1992. text 52.00 (*0-7167-2276-3*) W H Freeman.

Purves, William K., jt. auth. see Lillard, Jeremiah V.

Purvey, P. F. Coins of England & the United Kingdom. (Illus.). 1997. lib. bdg. 24.95 (*0-900652-69-1*) S J Durst.

Purviance, Edwin. The Best of Mable. 100p. 1995. pap. text 4.00 (*0-9620694-4-2*) E & M Purviance.

Purviance, Edwin & Purviance, Mable. Preachers Do the Craziest Things! 150p. (Orig.). 1993. pap. text 3.95 (*0-9620694-3-4*) E & M Purviance.

Purviance, Mable, jt. auth. see Purviance, Edwin.

Purvin, Robert. Franchise Fraud: How to Protect Yourself Before & After You Invest. 275p. 1994. 27.95 (*0-471-59947-6*) Wiley.

***Purvin, Robert L.** Franchise Fraud: How to Protect Yourself Before & after You Invest. 304p. 1998. pap. 16.95 (*0-471-25371-5*) Wiley.

Purvins, John J., jt. auth. see Lesperance, Gary L.

Purvis. Applications of Liquid Crystal Devices. (Illus.). 288p. (C). 1997. text. write for info. (*0-412-63340-X*, Chap & Hall NY) Chapman & Hall.

— Interdependence. (C). 1992. pap. text 51.50 (*0-15-500005-5*, Pub. by Harcourt Coll Pubs) Harcourt.

— Media & Politics. (C). 1999. pap. text 34.50 (*0-15-503643-2*, Pub. by Harcourt Coll Pubs) Harcourt.

— Women's History: Britain, 1850-1945. (Women's History Ser.). 1995. write for info. (*1-85728-319-8*, Pub. by UCL Pr Ltd); pap. write for info. (*1-85728-320-1*, Pub. by UCL Pr Ltd) Taylor & Francis.

Purvis, Alston W. Dutch Graphic Design: 1918-1945. (Illus.). 228p. 1992. text 46.95 (*0-442-00444-3*, VNR) Wiley.

Purvis, Alston W. Dutch Graphic Design, 1918-1945. (Illus.). 234p. 1992. 46.95 (*0-471-28404-1*, VNR) Wiley.

Purvis, Andrea, jt. auth. see Clay, Diskin.

Purvis, C. J. The Offensive Art: The Liberation of Poetic Imagination in Augustan Satirre. 232p. (C). 1989. 100.00 (*0-907839-34-7*, Pub. by Brynmill Pr Ltd) St Mut.

Purvis, Cynthia M., ed. see Cooke, Edward S., Jr.

Purvis, Cynthia M., ed. see Museum of Fine Arts Curatorial Staff.

Purvis, Cynthia M., ed. see Stebbins, Theodore E., Jr.

Purvis, Cynthia M., ed. see Stebbins, Theodore E., Jr., et al.

Purvis, Edie A. The Gallant Gladden. (Illus.). 359p. 1997. 35.00 (*1-887301-02-X*) Palmetto Bookworks.

Purvis, Heidi, ed. see Foreman, George & Merydith, Connie.

Purvis, Hoyt. Interdependence: An Introduction to International Affairs. (C). 1992. text. write for info. (*0-318-69125-6*) Harcourt Coll Pubs.

— Media Issues & Trends: A Mass Communication Reader. 148p. (C). 1998. per. 38.95 (*0-7872-5468-1*, 41546801) Kendall-Hunt.

Purvis, Hoyt, jt. auth. see Weintraub, Sidney.

Purvis, Hoyt, jt. ed. see Kelley, Donald R.

Purvis, Hoyt H. The Presidency & the Press. (Symposia Ser.). 120p. 1976. pap. 3.00 (*0-89940-405-7*) LBJ Sch Pub Aff.

— The Press: Free & Responsible? (Symposia Ser.). 114p. 1982. pap. 6.00 (*0-89940-411-1*) LBJ Sch Pub Aff.

Purvis, Hoyt H., jt. auth. see Radin, Beryl A.

Purvis, I. Handbook of Industrial Materials. 2nd ed. 804p. 1992. 190.25 (*0-946395-83-7*, Pub. by Elsvr Adv Tech) Elsevier.

Purvis, James D. Jerusalem, the Holy City: A Bibliography. LC 87-4758. (American Theological Library Association Monograph: No. 20). 513p. 1988. 50.00 (*0-8108-1999-6*) Scarecrow.

— Jerusalem, the Holy City Vol. II: A Bibliography. (American Theological Library Association Monograph: No. 20). 545p. 1991. 57.50 (*0-8108-2506-6*) Scarecrow.

***Purvis, Jean.** The History of Medicine in Butler County. 80p. 2000. 30.00 (*0-929690-52-4*) Herit Pubs AZ.

***Purvis, June.** Women's History: Britain 1850-1945: An Introduction. LC 00-35273. (Women's & Gender History Ser.). 2000. pap. write for info. (*0-415-23889-7*) Routledge.

Purvis, June & Holton, Sandra, eds. Votes for Women. LC 99-10066. (Illus.). 288p. 1999. 66.00 (*1-85728-767-3*, Pub. by UCL Pr Ltd) Taylor & Francis.

Purvis, June, jt. auth. see Holton, Sandra Stanley.

Purvis, June, jt. ed. see Griffin, Gabriele.

Purvis, June, ed. see Jackson, Margaret.

Purvis, June, jt. ed. see Maynard, Mary.

Purvis, June, jt. ed. see Oldfield, Sybil.

Purvis, Kenneth. The Male Sexual Machine: An Owner's Manual. (Illus.). 210p. 1998. pap. text 11.00 (*0-7881-5449-4*) DIANE Pub.

Purvis, Leslie K. The P. R. E. P. Guide: To the Real Estate Licensing Exams. (Orig.). 1995. pap. text 24.95 (*0-9638207-4-5*) Purvis Real Est.

— The Prep Guide: Texas Real Estate Sales Licensing Exams. 4th ed. Purvis, Lynn, ed. (Illus.). 220p. 1999. pap. text 29.95 (*0-9638207-2-9*) Purvis Real Est.

— Real Estate: Exam PREP Guide-Texas. Purvis, Lynn, ed. (Illus.). 320p. (Orig.). 1996. pap. text 29.95 (*0-9638207-9-6*) Purvis Real Est.

— Real Estate: Exam Prep-Texas. 3rd ed. Purvis, Lynn, ed. (Illus.). 1998. pap. text 29.95 (*0-9638207-8-8*, 98EPBK) Purvis Real Est.

Purvis, Lynn, ed. see Purvis, Leslie K.

Purvis, Nancy. Let's Face It: The Ultimate Skin Care Consultation. 70p. 1998. pap. 8.95 (*0-9664402-0-X*) N Purvis.

Purvis, Peggy, jt. auth. see Leeburg, Verlene.

Purvis, Ronald L., et al. Life-Cycle Cost Analysis for Protection & Rehabilitation of Concrete Bridges Relative to Reinforcement Corrosion. 289p. (C). 1994. pap. text 25.00 (*0-309-05755-8*, SHRP-S-377) SHRP.

Purvis, Sally. The Power of the Cross: Foundations for a Christian Feminist Ethic of Community. LC 92-41372. 160p. (Orig.). 1993. pap. 6.78 (*0-687-33206-0*) Abingdon.

Purvis, Sally B. The Stained-Glass Ceiling: Churches & Their Women Pastors. 112p. (Orig.). 1995. pap. 15.95 (*0-664-25608-2*) Westminster John Knox.

Purvis, Scott C., jt. auth. see Burton, Philip W.

Purvis, T. T. Hagar, the Singing Maiden: With Other Stories & Rhymes. LC 77-174289. reprint ed. 45.00 (*0-404-00100-9*) AMS Pr.

Purvis, Thomas L. Colonial America to 1763. Balkin, Richard, ed. LC 98-29007. (Almanacs of American Life Ser.). (Illus.). 381p. 1999. lib. bdg. 75.00 (*0-8160-2527-4*) Facts on File.

— A Dictionary of American History. 512p. 1997. lib. bdg. 26.95 (*1-57718-099-2*) Blackwell Pubs.

— Proprietors, Patronage, & Paper Money: Legislative Politics in New Jersey, 1703-1776. LC 85-27895. 360p. 1986. lib. bdg. 45.00 (*0-8135-1161-5*) Rutgers U Pr.

— Revolutionary America, 1763-1800. LC 93-38382. (Almanacs of American Life Ser.). (Illus.). 400p. 1995. 75.00 (*0-8160-2528-2*) Facts on File.

***Purvis, William.** Lichens. LC 00-29146. (Illus.). 2000. pap. 14.95 (*1-56098-879-7*) Smithsonian.

***Purwin, Patricia.** Grampa's a Scientist. (Illus.). 24p. (ps-6). 1999. pap. 12.95 (*0-9673408-0-2*) Collage Storybk Pr.

Puryear, Anne. Stephen Lives! His Life, Suicide & Afterlife. (Illus.). 400p. 1993. pap. 14.95 (*0-9634964-3-3*) N Paradigm.

— Stephen Lives! My Son Stephen: His Life, Suicide & Afterlife. 1997. per. 14.00 (*0-671-53664-8*) PB.

Puryear, Douglas A. Helping People in Crisis: A Practical, Family-Oriented Approach to Effective Crisis Intervention. LC 79-88108. (Social & Behavioral Science Ser.). 237p. 1979. 35.95 (*0-87589-421-6*) Jossey-Bass.

***Puryear, Edgar F., Jr.** American Generalship - Character Is Everything: The Art of Command. LC 99-48919. 432p. 2000. 34.95 (*0-89141-658-7*) Presidio Pr.

Puryear, Edgar F., Jr. 19 Stars: A Study in Military Character & Leadership. LC 81-14365. 464p. 1997. reprint ed. pap. 17.95 (*0-89141-148-8*) Presidio Pr.

Puryear, Herbert B. The Edgar Cayce Primer. 272p. (Orig.). 1982. mass mkt. 6.99 (*0-553-25278-X*) Bantam.

— Sex & the Spiritual Path: Uniting the Spirit & the Body. 304p. 1999. pap. 6.99 (*0-312-97183-4*, St Martins Paperbacks) St Martin.

— Why Jesus Taught Reincarnation: A Better News Gospel. 262p. (Orig.). 1993. pap. 14.95 (*0-9634964-9-2*) N Paradigm.

Puryear, Jeffrey M. Thinking Politics: Intellectuals & Democracy in Chile, 1973-1988. LC 93-47402. (C). 1994. text 42.50 (*0-8018-4839-3*); pap. text 15.95 (*0-8018-4841-5*) Johns Hopkins.

Puryear, Jeffrey M. & Burnner, Jose J., eds. Education, Equity & Economic Competitiveness in the Americas, Vol. 1. LC 94-877. (INTERAMER Ser.: No. 37). 1994. write for info. (*0-8270-3314-1*) OAS.

Puryear, Kay & Brown, Tracy. Today's Wedding Austin. Crowell, Lynda, ed. 260p. 1998. pap. 21.95 (*0-938934-36-8*) LCN.

— Today's Wedding Dallas/Ft. Worth. Crowell, Lynda, ed. 260p. 1998. pap. 21.95 (*0-938934-37-6*) LCN.

— Today's Wedding Houston. 260p. (Orig.). 1998. pap. 21.95 (*0-938934-38-4*) LCN.

— Today's Wedding San Antonio. Crowell, Lynda, ed. 260p. 1998. pap. 21.95 (*0-938934-39-2*) LCN.

Puryear, Kay & Corry, Tracy. Today's Wedding - Austin. Crowell, Lynda, ed. 250p. 1995. pap. 21.95 (*0-938934-30-9*) LCN.

— Today's Wedding - San Antonio. Crowell, Lynda, ed. 260p. (Orig.). pap. 21.95 (*0-938934-34-1*) LCN.

— Today's Wedding - San Antonio. Crowell, Lynda, ed. 225p. (Orig.). 1993. pap. 18.95 (*0-938934-31-7*) LCN.

— Today's Wedding Dallas-Ft. Worth - Metroplex. Crowell, Lynda, ed. 260p. (Orig.). pap. 21.95 (*0-938934-33-3*) LCN.

— Today's Wedding Houston. Crowell, Lynda, ed. 260p. (Orig.). pap. 21.95 (*0-938934-32-5*) LCN.

Puryear, Meredith A. Healing Through Meditation & Prayer. 108p. 1997. pap. 12.95 (*0-87604-104-7*, 290) ARE Pr.

Puryear, Vernon J. France & the Levant from the Bourbon Restoration to the Peace of Kutiah. LC 42-89. (University of California Publications in Social Welfare: Vol. 27). 265p. reprint ed. pap. 82.20 (*0-608-13929-7*, 202144600021) Bks Demand.

Purzer, Angelika. Der Ansatz Einer Ganzheitsphilosophie Bei Arnold Gehlen. (Europaische Hochschulschriften Ser.: Reihe 20, Bd. 526). (GER.). 217p. 1996. 42.95 (*3-631-31152-4*) P Lang Pubng.

Purzycki, Robert H., jt. auth. see Semer-Purzycki, Jeanne.

Pusateri, Mike, jt. auth. see Napolitano, Lisa.

Puscariu, Sextil. Etudes de Linguistique Roumaine. xix, 508p. 1973. reprint ed. write for info. (*3-487-05005-6*) G Olms Pubs.

Puscas, George. Dandies, Eh? 50 Years of Sports History. 1996. pap. 9.95 (*0-937247-57-X*) Detroit Pr.

Pusch, Annekatrin. Friedrich Holderlin Als Ubersetzer Lucans. (Europaische Hochschulschriften Ser.: Reihe 1, Bd. 1578). (GER.). 229p. 1996. 44.95 (*3-631-50002-5*) P Lang Pubng.

Pusch, Hans. Working Together on Rudolf Steiner's Mystery Dramas. LC 80-67024. (Steiner's Mystery Dramas Ser.). (Illus.). 144p. (Orig.). 1980. 15.95 (*0-910142-90-4*); pap. 9.95 (*0-910142-91-2*) Anthroposophic.

Pusch, Hans, tr. see Steiner, Rudolf.

Pusch, Margaret D., ed. Multicultural Education: A Cross-Cultural Training Approach. LC 79-92379. 276p. (Orig.). 1979. pap. text 14.95 (*0-933662-06-8*) Intercult Pr.

Pusch, R. Rock Mechanics on a Geological Base. LC 95-3973. (Developments in Geotechnical Engineering Ser.: Vol. 77). 518p. 1995. 215.00 (*0-444-89613-9*) Elsevier.

— Waste Disposal in Rocks. LC 93-48194. (Developments in Geotechnical Engineering Ser.: Vol. 76). 510p. 1994. 205.00 (*0-444-89449-7*) Elsevier.

Pusch, Ruth. Waldorf Schools: Kindergarten & Early Grades, Vol. 1. pap. 13.00 (*0-929979-29-X*, 1828) Merc Pr NY.

An Asterisk (*) at the beginning of an entry indicates that the title is appearing for the first time.

— Waldorf Schools: Upper Grades & High School, Vol. 2. pap. 13.00 (*0-929979-30-3*, 1829) Merc Pr NY.
Pusch, Ruth, tr. see Steiner, Rudolf.
Pusch, Ruth, tr. & intro. see Gabert, Erich.
***Pusch, Steffi.** Exemplarisch DDR Geschichte leben: Ostberliner Dokumentarfilme 1989, 1990. 2000. 26.95 (*3-631-35398-7*) P Lang Pubng.
Puscheck, John, jt. auth. see Sinnes, A. Cort.
Puschel, Ulrich, jt. ed. see Sandig, Barbara.
Puschendorf, Bernd, jt. auth. see Mair, Johannes.
Puschendorf, L. Robert, jt. ed. see Potter, James E.
Puschett, Jules B. Disorders of Fluid & Electrolyte Balance: Diagnosis & Treatment. (Illus.). 259p. (Orig.). 1985. pap. text 36.95 (*0-443-08318-5*) Church.
Puschmann-Nalenz, Barbara. Science Fiction & Postmodern Fiction: A Genre Study. LC 91-21112. (American University Studies: General Literature: Ser. XIX, Vol. 29). 268p. (C). 1992. text 46.95 (*0-8204-1670-3*) P Lang Pubng.
Puschnigg, Michael. Asymptotic Cyclic Cohomology, Vol. XXIII. LC 96-39705. (Lecture Notes in Mathematics Ser.: Vol. 1642). 238p. 1996. pap. 52.00 (*3-540-61986-0*) Spr-Verlag.
Puscoiu, Costel. Christmas Solos for Beginning Pan Flute: Beginning-Intermediate Level. 40p. 1997. pap. 14.95 incl. audio compact disk (*0-7866-2076-5*, 95972BCD) Mel Bay.
— Classical Repertoire for Clarinet, Vol. 3. 80p. 2000. pap. 12.95 (*0-7866-2657-7*, 96513) Mel Bay.
— Classical Repertoire for Clarinet: Beginning-Intermediate Level, Vol. 1. 144p. 1998. pap. 12.95 (*0-7866-2655-0*, 96511) Mel Bay.
— Classical Repertoire for Flute, Vol. 1. 120p. 1995. pap. 12.95 (*0-7866-0367-4*, 95395) Mel Bay.
— Classical Repertoire for Flute, Vol. 2. 128p. 1995. spiral bd. 14.95 (*0-7866-0724-6*, 95599) Mel Bay.
— Classical Repertoire for Flute, Vol. 3. 110p. 1995. pap. 14.95 (*0-7866-0725-4*, 95600) Mel Bay.
— Classical Repertoire for Pan Pipes. 120p. 1995. pap. 14.95 (*0-7866-0291-0*, 95332) Mel Bay.
— Classical Repertoire for Recorder. 96p. 1995. pap. 12.95 (*0-7866-0292-9*, 95333) Mel Bay.
— Classical Repertoire for Saxophone, Vol. 2. 96p. 2000. pap. 12.95 (*0-7866-2733-6*, 96589) Mel Bay.
— Classical Repertoire for Saxophone, Vol. 3. 80p. 2000. pap. 12.95 (*0-7866-2734-4*, 96590) Mel Bay.
— Classical Repertoire for Saxophone Vol. 1: Beginning-Intermediate Level. 144p. 1998. pap. 12.95 (*0-7866-2075-7*, 95970) Mel Bay.
— Classical Repertoire for Violin, Vol. 1. 136p. 1997. pap. 12.95 (*0-7866-1626-1*, 95680) Mel Bay.
— Classical Repertoire for Violin Vol. 2: Intermediate Level. 136p. 1997. pap. 14.95 (*0-7866-2023-4*, 95968) Mel Bay.
— Classical Repertoire for Violin Vol. 3: Intermediate-Advanced Level. 96p. 1997. pap. 12.95 (*0-7866-2024-2*, 95969) Mel Bay.
— Complete Pan Flute. 208p. 1997. pap. 22.95 (*0-7866-1625-3*, 95679) Mel Bay.
— Easiest Pan Flute. 24p. 1996. pap. 14.95 incl. audio compact disk (*0-7866-1627-X*, 95681BCD) Mel Bay.
— International Carols for Alto Saxophone. 120p. 1998. pap. 19.95 incl. audio compact disk (*0-7866-3821-4*, 97528BCD) Mel Bay.
— International Carols for Flute. 120p. 1998. pap. 19.95 incl. audio compact disk (*0-7866-3822-2*, 97529BCD) Mel Bay.
— International Carols for Pan Flute: Beginning-Intermediate Level. 84p. 1996. pap. 19.95 incl. audio compact disk (*0-7866-2077-3*, 95978BCD) Mel Bay.
— International Carols for Recorder: Beginning-Intermediate Level. 88p. 1996. pap. 19.95 incl. audio compact disk (*0-7866-2078-1*, 95971BCD) Mel Bay.
— International Carols for Violin. 120p. 1998. pap. 19.95 incl. audio compact disk (*0-7866-3823-0*, 97530BCD) Mel Bay.
— Solo Pieces for the Beginning Pan Flutist. 24p. 1994. pap. 5.95 (*0-7866-0079-9*) Mel Bay.
— You Can Teach Yourself Pan Flute. 96p. 1997. pap. 9.95 (*0-7866-1628-8*, 95682) Mel Bay.
— You Can Teach Yourself Pan Flute. 97p. 1997. pap. 24.95 incl. audio compact disk (*0-7866-1631-8*, 95682CDP); pap. 18.95 incl. audio (*0-7866-1632-6*, 95682P) Mel Bay.
Pusey, Alyssa M., jt. auth. see Wright, Elena D.
***Pusey, C. D., ed.** The Treatment of Glomerulonephritis. 227p. 1999. 129.00 (*0-7923-5332-3*) Kluwer Academic.
Pusey, Charles D., ed. Immunology of Renal Disease. (Immunology & Medicine Ser.). (C). 1991. text 174.50 (*0-7923-8964-6*) Kluwer Academic.
Pusey, Charles D. & Reese, Andrew J., eds. Rapidly Progressive Glomerulonephritis. LC 97-16817. (Oxford Clinical Nephrology Ser.). (Illus.). 290p. 1998. text 129.50 (*0-19-262636-1*) OUP.
Pusey, Edward Bouverie. Daniel, the Prophet. 592p. 1987. lib. bdg. 22.99 (*0-8254-5219-8*, Kregel Class) Kregel.
Pusey, Edward Bouverie, tr. see Augustine, Saint.
Pusey, Edward E., jt. auth. see Nicoll, A.
Pusey, James R. China & Charles Darwin. (East Asian Monographs: No. 100). 556p. 1983. 30.00 (*0-674-11735-2*) HUP.
— Lu Xun & Evolution. LC 97-13018. (SUNY Series in Philosophy & Biology). 288p. (C). 1998. text 65.50 (*0-7914-3647-0*); pap. text 21.95 (*0-7914-3648-9*) State U NY Pr.
— Wu Han: Attacking the Present Through the Past. (East Asian Monographs: No. 33). 94p. 1969. pap. 20.00 (*0-674-96275-3*) HUP.
Pusey, M. Jurgen Habermas. (Key Sociologists Ser.). 160p. (C). 1988. pap. 17.99 (*0-415-10451-3*) Routledge.
Pusey, Merlo J. The Supreme Court Crisis. LC 74-171699. (FDR & the Era of the New Deal Ser.). 108p. 1972. reprint ed. lib. bdg. 19.50 (*0-306-70389-0*) Da Capo.
Pusey, Michael. Economic Rationalism in Canberra: A Nation-Building State Changes Its Mind. 318p. (C). 1992. text 74.95 (*0-521-33422-5*) Cambridge U Pr.
— Jurgen Habermas. 1987. pap. 12.95 (*0-7458-0117-X*) Routledge.
Pusey, Nathan M. American Higher Education 1945-1970: A Personal Report. 240p. 1978. 29.00 (*0-674-02425-7*) HUP.
Pusey, Pennock. Crane Hook Church, Predecessor of Old Swede's Church: Wilmington. (Illus.). 28p. 1998. reprint ed. pap. 6.00 (*0-8328-9592-X*) Higginson Bk Co.
— History of Lewes. (Illus.). 32p. 1998. reprint ed. pap. 6.50 (*0-8328-9590-3*) Higginson Bk Co.
Pusey, Walter C., III, jt. ed. see Wantland, Kenneth F.
Pusey, William A. The History & Epidemiology of Syphilis. LC 75-23753. reprint ed. 32.50 (*0-404-13359-2*) AMS Pr.
— The History of Dermatology. LC 75-23754. reprint ed. 55.00 (*0-404-13360-6*) AMS Pr.
***Push & Silcott, Mireille.** On 'E' Ecstasy. 200p. 1999. 19.95 (*0-7119-7519-1*) Omnibus NY.
***Push, Richard Crowford, ed.** International Income Taxation Code & Regulations: Selected Sections, 1999-2000 Edition. 1720p. 1999. pap. text 45.00 (*0-8080-0373-9*) CCH INC.
Pushcart Prize Editors, ed. see Henderson, Bill.
Pushcart Prize Editors, jt. ed. see Henderson, Bill.
Pushcart Prize Staff & Henderson, Bill, eds. Pushcart Prize XIX: Best of the Small Presses, 1994-95 Edition. 580p. 1995. pap. 15.00 (*0-916366-98-7*, Pub. by Pushcart Pr) Norton.
***Pushies, Fred J.** U. S. Air Force Special Ops. LC 99-52217. (Power Ser.). (Illus.). 128p. 2000. pap. 16.95 (*0-7603-0733-4*, 129829AP, Pub. by MBI Pubg) Motorbooks Intl.
Pushkar, Dolores, et al, eds. Improving Competence Across the Lifespan: Building Interventions Based on Theory & Research: Proceedings of a Conference Held in Montreal, Canada, November 15-17, 1996. LC 98-5154. (Illus.). 216p. 1998. 85.00 (*0-306-45814-4*, Kluwer Plenum) Kluwer Academic.
Pushkarev, Sergei. Rol' Pravoslavnoi Tserkvi V Istorii Rosii: The Role of the Orthodox Church in Russian History. LC 85-80831. (RUS.). 125p. 1985. 9.50 (*0-911971-13-0*) Effect Pub.
Pushkarev, V. A. Watercolours & Drawings: Akvareli i Risunki v Gosudarstvennom Russkom Muzee. (Illus.). 1982. 125.00 (*0-7855-1684-0*) St Mut.
Pushkarev, V. V., et al. Treatment of Oil-Containing Wastewater. LC 83-70667. viii, 214p. 1983. 42.50 (*0-89864-004-0*) Allerton Pr.
Pushkareva, Natalia. Women in Russian History: From the Tenth to the Twentieth Century. Levin, Eve, ed. & tr. by. LC 96-30667. (The New Russian History Ser.). (ENG & RUS.). 336p. (C). 1997. pap. text 38.95 (*1-56324-798-4*) M E Sharpe.
— Women in Russian History: From the Tenth to the Twentieth Century. Levin, Eve, ed. & tr. by. LC 96-30667. (The New Russian History Ser.). (ENG & RUS., Illus.). 336p. (C). (gr. 13). 1997. text 74.95 (*1-56324-797-6*) M E Sharpe.
Pushkarov, D. I., ed. Quasiparticle Theory of Defects in Solids. 200p. (C). 1991. text 36.00 (*981-02-0180-X*) World Scientific Pub.
Pushker, Gloria T. A Belfer Bar Mitzvah. LC 95-9209. (Illus.). 32p. (J). (gr. 4-7). 1995. 14.95 (*1-56554-095-6*) Pelican.
— Toby Belfer Never Had a Christmas Tree. LC 91-14514. (Illus.). 32p. (J). (gr. k-3). 1991. reprint ed. 14.95 (*0-88289-855-8*) Pelican.
— Toby Belfer's Seder: A Passover Story Retold. LC 93-5585. (Illus.). 32p. (J). (ps-3). 1994. 14.95 (*0-88289-987-2*) Pelican.
***Pushker, Gloria T. & Hierstein, Judy.** Toby Belfer & the High Holy Days. LC 99-89424. (J). 2000. write for info. (*1-56554-765-9*) Pelican.
Pushkin, Aleksandr. Alexander Pushkin: Complete Prose Fiction. Debreczeny, Paul, tr. from RUS. LC 81-85450. 560p. 1983. pap. 19.95 (*0-8047-1800-8*) Stanford U Pr.
— Boris Godunov. Barbour, Philip L., tr. & notes by. LC 75-31441. (Columbia Slavic Studies). 196p. 1976. reprint ed. lib. bdg. 55.00 (*0-8371-8522-X*, PUBG, Greenwood Pr) Greenwood.
— The Captain's Daughter. 248p. 1987. 40.00 (*0-7855-2316-2*) St Mut.
— The Captain's Daughter. 1957. pap. 10.00 (*0-394-70714-1*) Vin Bks.
— The Captain's Daughter & Other Stories. 24.95 (*0-89190-231-7*) Amereon Ltd.
— Collected Narrative & Lyrical Poetry. Arndt, Walter, tr. from RUS. 475p. 1984. pap. 18.95 (*0-88233-826-9*) Ardis Pubs.
— The Collected Stories. 1999. 20.00 (*0-375-40549-6*) Everymns Lib.
— Complete Prose Fiction. lib. bdg. 32.95 (*0-8488-1891-1*) Amereon Ltd.
— Eugene Onegin. Johnston, Charles, tr. (Classics Ser.). 240p. 1979. pap. 9.95 (*0-14-044394-0*) Viking Penguin.
— Eugene Onegin: A Novel in Verse. Hofstadter, Douglas R., tr. from RUS. LC 99-224060. (Illus.). 224p. 1999. 22.00 (*0-465-02093-5*, Pub. by Basic) HarpC.
***Pushkin, Aleksandr.** Eugene Onegin: A Novel in Verse. 1999. 12.50 (*0-375-40672-7*) Evlntry Pubns.
Pushkin, Aleksandr. Eugene Onegin: A Novel in Verse. Nabokov, Vladimir, tr. from RUS. LC 80-8730. (Bollingen Ser.: No. LXXII). 362p. (C). 1964. pap. text 16.95 (*0-691-01905-3*, Pub. by Princeton U Pr) Cal Prin Full Svc.
— Eugene Onegin: A Novel in Verse. unabridged ed. Deutsch, Babette, tr. from RUS. LC 98-36323. (Illus.). 192p. 1998. pap. text 8.95 (*0-486-40423-4*) Dover.
***Pushkin, Aleksandr.** Eugene Onegin a Novel in Verse. 276p. 1998. pap. 8.95 (*0-19-283899-7*) OUP.
Pushkin, Aleksandr. Evgenij Onegin: A Novel in Verse. LC 52-12257. 360p. 1953. reprint ed. pap. 111.60 (*0-7837-1684-2*, 205721400024) Bks Demand.
— Golden Cockerel. Hulick, Elizabeth C., tr. (Illus.). 1962. 10.95 (*0-8392-1039-6*) Astor-Honor.
— Mozart & Salieri: The Little Tragedies. Wood, Antony, tr. from RUS. 96p. 1982. reprint ed. 23.00 (*0-946162-02-6*, Pub. by Angel Bks) Dufour.
— Mozart & Salieri: The Little Tragedies. Wood, Antony, tr. from RUS. LC 87-13480. 96p. 1987. reprint ed. pap. 15.95 (*0-8023-1282-9*) Dufour.
— Povesti Belkina (Tales of Belkin) (Voices from Russia Ser.). (RUS.). 52p. 1996. pap. text 9.50 (*1-58085-009-X*) Interlingua VA.
— Prose. unabridged ed. (World Classic Literature Ser.). (RUS.). pap. 8.95 (*2-87714-270-1*, Pub. by Bookking Intl) Distribks Inc.
— The Prose Tales of Alexander Pushkin. Keane, T., tr. from RUS. LC 78-150484. (Short Story Index Reprint Ser.). 1977. reprint ed. 24.95 (*0-8369-3825-9*) Ayer.
— Pushkin: Eugene Onegin (Eugenii Onegin) (Bristol Russian Texts Ser.). (RUS.). 282p. (C). 1993. reprint ed. pap. 20.95 (*1-85399-396-4*, Pub. by Brist Class Pr) Focus Pub-R Pullins.
— Pushkin - Eugene Onegin. Arndt, Walter, tr. from RUS. & intro. by. 224p. 1993. reprint ed. pap. 12.95 (*0-87501-106-3*) Ardis Pubs.
— Pushkin - Eugene Onegin. unabridged ed. (World Classic Literature Ser.). (RUS.). pap. 6.95 (*2-87714-256-6*, Pub. by Bookking Intl) Distribks Inc.
— Pushkin on Literature. Wolff, Tatiana, ed. & tr. by. LC 98-16799. (Studies in Russian Literature & Theory). 592p. 1998. pap. text 24.95 (*0-8101-1615-4*) Northwestern U Pr.
— Pushkin Threefold: Narrative, Lyric, Polemic & Ribald Verse, the Originals with Linear & Metric Translations. 2nd ed. Arndt, Walter, tr. & intro. by. 455p. 1993. reprint ed. pap. 18.95 (*0-87501-107-1*) Ardis Pubs.
— The Queen of Spades & Other Stories. Edmonds, Rosemary, tr. from RUS. & intro. by. (Classics Ser.). 320p. 1978. pap. 12.95 (*0-14-044119-0*, Penguin Classics) Viking Penguin.
— The Queen of Spades & Other Stories. Keane, T., tr. from RUS. 128p. 1994. reprint ed. pap. 1.50 (*0-486-28054-3*) Dover.
— The Queen of Spades & Other Stories. 128p. 1999. reprint ed. pap. 6.95 (*1-57002-096-5*) Univ Publng Hse.
— Secret Journal, 1836-1837. 2nd ed. Armalinskii, Mikhail, tr. from RUS. & intro. by. 91p. 1991. reprint ed. pap. 10.00 (*0-916201-07-4*) M I P Co.
— Tales of Belkin. Aitken, Gillon & Budgen, David, trs. 136p. 1983. 27.00 (*0-946162-04-2*) Dufour.
— Tales of Belkin & Other Prose Writings. Wilks, Ronald, tr. from RUS. LC 98-167584. xxi,194p. 1998. pap. 10.95 (*0-14-044675-3*) Viking Penguin.
— The Tales of Ivan Belkin. 16.95 (*0-8488-0111-3*) Amereon Ltd.
— Tales of the Late Ivan Petrovich Belkin, the Queen of Spades, the Captain's Daughter, Peter the Great's Blackamoor. Kahn, Andrew, ed. Myers, Alan, tr. (Oxford World's Classics Ser.). 330p. 1999. pap. 10.95 (*0-19-283954-3*) OUP.
— Tayniye Zapiski, 1836-1837. LC 86-90457. (RUS.). 104p. 1997. reprint ed. pap. 10.00 (*0-916201-02-3*) M I P Co.
— Yevgeny Onegin. rev. ed. Briggs, A. D., ed. Elton, Oliver, tr. (Everyman Paperback Classics Ser.). 272p. (C). 1995. pap. 7.95 (*0-460-87595-7*, Everyman's Classic Lib) Tuttle Pubng.
***Pushkin, Aleksandr & Anderson, Nancy K.** The Little Tragedies. LC 99-46416. (Russian Literature & Thought Ser.). (Illus.). 160p. 2000. 13.00 (*0-300-08027-1*) Yale U Pr.
Pushkin, Aleksandr, et al. Armenia Observed. Baliozian, Ara, ed. LC 79-21946. 1979. 10.95 (*0-933706-10-3*); pap. 5.95 (*0-933706-11-1*) Ararat Pr.
— Eugene Onegin. Obolensky, George, tr. 60p. 1996. pap. 5.50 (*0-87129-602-0*, E34) Dramatic Pub.
— Liubvi Bezumnoe Tomlen'e: Rasskazy I Povesti Russkikh Pisateli XIX Veka. Efimov, Igor, ed. LC 94-47189. (Klassiki Russkoi Literatury (Russian Classics) Ser.). (RUS.). 290p. (Orig.). 1995. pap. 12.00 (*1-55779-081-7*) Hermitage Pubs.
***Pushkin, Alexander.** After Pushkin. Feinstein, Elaine, ed. & intro. by. 96p. 2000. pap. 16.95 (*1-85754-444-7*, Pub. by Carcanet Pr) Paul & Co Pubs.
Pushman, Muriel G. We All Wore Blue: The Funny, Romantic & Moving Adventures of a Young Girl in the Wartime WAAF. (Illus.). 175p. 1995. pap. 10.95 (*0-86051-940-6*, Robson-Parkwest) Parkwest Pubns.
***Pushman, Muriel Gane.** One Family's War: Where's Your Medal Mother? (Illus.). 128p. 2000. pap. 19.99 (*0-7524-2002-X*, Pub. by Tempus Pubng) Arcadia Publng.
Pushong, Carlyle A. Tarot of the Magi. 112p. 1994. pap. 10.95 (*0-87877-192-1*) Newcastle Pub.
Pushpamma, P. Choosing Sorghum as Food in the Semi-Arid Tropics: Studies in Dryland Communities. 91p. 1993. pap. write for info. (*0-88936-657-8*) IDRC Bks.
Pushpangadan, P., ed. Conservation & Economic Evaluation of Biodiversity. 2 vols. (Illus.). 690p. 1997. 110.00 (*1-57808-023-1*) Science Pubs.
Pushparajah, E., jt. ed. see Craswell, E. T.
Pusic, Eugen. Social Welfare & Social Development. LC 79-189707. (Institute of Social Studies Publications: No. 5). (Illus.). 251p. (Orig.). 1972. pap. text 19.25 (*90-279-1969-0*) Mouton.
Pusic, Milenko, jt. auth. see Vukovic, Milan.
***Pusins.** Computer Concepts Basics. (Computer Applications Ser.). 2000. student ed. 12.00 (*0-538-69502-1*) S-W Pub.
— Computer Concepts Basics. (Computer Applications Ser.). (C). 2000. text 26.50 (*0-538-69501-3*) S-W Pub.
Pusins. West's Essential Lotus 1-2-3 for Windows Release 5. LC 95-220645. 1995. mass mkt. 17.95 (*0-314-04641-0*) West Pub.
— West's Essentials of Lotus 1-2-3 for Windows R5. LC 95-212625. (DF - Computer Applications Ser.). 1995. mass mkt. 13.95 (*0-314-04632-1*) West Pub.
Pusins, Dolores. Metro Web Kit. 1998. teacher ed. 22.99 (*1-58076-005-8*) Que Educ & Trng.
Pusins, Dolores W. & Ross, Steven C. Understanding & Using Lotus 1-2-3 for Windows 5.0. 5th ed. 645p. (C). 1995. mass mkt. 36.95 (*0-314-04651-8*) West Pub.
Puska, P. & Leparski, E. Comprehensive Cardiovascular Community Control Programmes in Europe. (Euro Reports & Studies Ser.: No. 106). 91p. 1988. pap. text 6.00 (*92-890-1272-2*) World Health.
Puskar, A. High-Frequency Fatigue of Materials. 320p. 1999. 124.00 (*1-898326-58-4*, Pub. by CISP) Balogh.
Puskar, Anton. Internal Friction of Materials. 350p. 1997. boxed set 113.00 (*1-898326-50-9*, Pub. by CISP) Balogh.
Puskar, Arno, jt. auth. see Burke, John J.
Puskas, Charles B. Introduction to the New Testament. LC 89-48242. 298p. 1989. text 19.95 (*0-913573-45-0*) Hendrickson MA.
***Puskas, Charles B.** An Introduction to the New Testament. 300p. 1999. pap. 19.95 (*1-56563-484-5*) Hendrickson MA.
Puskas, Charles B., Jr. The Letters of Paul: An Introduction. (Good News Studies: Vol. 25). 232p. (Orig.). 1993. pap. 14.95 (*0-8146-5690-0*, M Glazier) Liturgical Pr.
Puskas, Ildiko. India Bibliography: Bibliotheca Orientalis Hungarica 35. (Bibliotheca Orientalis Hungarica Ser.). (ENG & HUN.). 602p. (C). 1991. 135.00 (*963-05-5591-3*, Pub. by Akade Kiado) St Mut.
Puskas, Julianna. From Hungary to the United States, 1880-1914. 3rd ed. (Studia Historica Academiae Scientiarum Hungaricae: Vol. 184). 225p. (C). 1982. 60.00 (*963-05-3020-1*, Pub. by Akade Kiado) St Mut.
Puskas, Julianna & Akademiai Kiado Staff. Overseas Migration from East-Central & Southeastern Europe, 1880-1940. (Studia Historica Academiae Scientiarum Hungaricae Ser.: No. 191). 246p. (C). 1990. 78.00 (*963-05-4992-1*, Pub. by Akade Kiado) St Mut.
***Puskbas, Genoveva, ed.** Word Order in Hungarian: The Syntax of A-Positions. LC 99-88715. (Linguistik Aktuell/Linguistics Today Ser.: No. 33). xvi, 395p. 2000. 95.00 (*1-55619-917-1*) J Benjamins Pubng Co.
Puskina, Druz'ta. Perepiska, Vospominaniia, Dnevniki, 2 vols. 642p. 1984. 75.00 (*0-7855-2931-4*) St Mut.
Pusser. Angelettes & Cosmic Sex. LC 88-81436. 120p. (Orig.). 1988. pap. 9.95 (*0-941404-86-2*) New Falcon Pubns.
Pust, Brian C., jt. auth. see Smith, Ronald.
***Pust, Joel.** Intuitions As Evidence. (Studies in Philosophy). 146p. 1999. 45.00 (*0-8153-3763-9*) Garland.
Pust, Ron, jt. auth. see Krogh, Christopher.
Pustak Bhandar, Ratna, see Bhandar, Ratna Pustak.
Pustan, Regina, tr. & intro. see Gonzalez, Luisa.
Pustav, jt. auth. see Griffin.
Pustay, John S., jt. auth. see Griffin.
Pustay, Michael W., jt. auth. see Griffin, Ricky W.
Pustejovsky, James. The Generative Lexicon. (Language, Speech & Communication Ser.). 298p. 1995. 39.50 (*0-262-16158-3*, Bradford Bks) MIT Pr.
***Pustejovsky, James.** The Generative Lexicon. (Language, Speech & Communication Ser.). (Illus.). 312p. 1998. reprint ed. pap. text 17.50 (*0-262-66140-3*, Bradford Bks) MIT Pr.
Pustejovsky, James, ed. Semantics & the Lexicon. LC 92-28758. (Studies in Linguistics & Philosophy: Vol. 49). 416p. (C). 1993. lib. bdg. 158.50 (*0-7923-1963-X*) Kluwer Academic.
Pustejovsky, James, et al, eds. Lexical Semantics & Knowledge Representation: First SIGLEX Workshop, Berkeley, CA, U. S. A., June 1991, Proceedings. LC 92-26469. (Lecture Notes in Computer Science, Lecture Notes in Artificial Intelligence Ser.: Vol. 627). xiii, 381p. 1992. 57.00 (*0-387-55801-2*) Spr-Verlag.
Pustejovsky, James & Boguraev, Branimir, eds. Lexical Semantics: The Problem of Polysemy. (Illus.). 220p. 1997. pap. text 32.00 (*0-19-823662-X*) OUP.
Pustejovsky, James, jt. ed. see Boguraev, Branimir.
Pustejovsky, James, jt. ed. see Tenny, Carol L.
Puster, Rolf W., ed. Veritas Filia Temporis? Philosophiehistorie Zwischen Wahrheit und Geschichte. (GER.). 319p. (C). 1995. lib. bdg. 133.85 (*3-11-014170-1*) De Gruyter.
***Pustogarov, V. V. & Butler, William Elliott.** Our Martens: F. F. Martens, International Lawyer & Architecht of Peace. LC 00-28721. 2000. write for info. (*1-898029-50-4*) Kluwer Academic.
Pustol, Colleen A. Bower. The Bower - Winchcomb Connection: Being a Record of the Descendants of Isaac N. Bower. (Illus.). xxviii, 294p. 1996. 55.00 (*0-944619-45-2*) Gregath Pub Co.
Pustovalova, N., jt. auth. see Kolesova, I.
Pustovoy, Vladimir I., ed. ALT '97 International Conference on Laser Surface Processing, Vol. 3404. LC 98-233182. 474p. 1998. 89.00 (*0-8194-2855-8*) SPIE.

P

An Asterisk (*) at the beginning of an entry indicates that the title is appearing for the first time.

Pustylnik, B. I., ed. Heavy Ion Physics: Scientific Report, Flerov Laboratory of Nuclear Reactions of Jinr, Dubna, Russia. (Illus.). 420p. 1993. pap. text 70.00 (0-911767-67-3) Hadronic Pr Inc.

Pustylnik, B. I., jt. ed. see Kristiak, J.

Pusty'nikov, A. M., jt. auth. see Butkovsky, A. G.

Pustz, Matthew J. Comic Book Culture: Fanboys & True Believers. LC 99-31140. (Studies in Popular Culture). (Illus.). 232p. 1999. 48.00 (1-57806-200-4) U Pr of Miss.

— Comic Book of Culture: Fanboys & True Believers. LC 99-31140. (Studies in Popular Culture). (Illus.). 232p. 1999. pap. 18.00 (1-57806-201-2) U Pr of Miss.

Pusztai, Arpad. Plant Lectins. (Chemistry & Pharmacology of Natural Products Ser.). 271p. (C). 1992. text 80.00 (0-521-32824-1) Cambridge U Pr.

Pusztai, Arpad & Bardocz, Susan, eds. Lectins: Biomedical Perspectives. 368p. 1994. 99.50 (0-7484-0177-6, Pub. by Tay Francis Ltd) Taylor & Francis.

Pusztai, Joseph, jt. auth. see Sava, Michael.

Put, Ed Van, see Van Put, Ed, ed.

Put, Eddy, jt. auth. see Harline, Craig.

Put, Marius van der, see Van Der Put, Marius.

Puta, Mircea. Hamiltonian Mechanical Systems & Geometric Quantization. LC 93-13189. (Mathematics & Its Applications Ser.: Vol. 260). 288p. (C). 1993. text 164.50 (0-7923-2306-8) Kluwer Academic.

Putanec, Valentin. French - Serbocroatian Dictionary: Francusko-Hrvatski ili Srpski Rjecnik. (FRE & SER.). 1152p. 1988. write for info. (0-8288-1047-8, F97152) Fr & Eur.

Putatunda, Susil K., jt. ed. see Strauss, Bernard M.

Puter, S. A. Looters of the Public Domain. LC 70-38833. (Illus.). 495p. 1972. reprint ed. lib. bdg. 59.50 (0-306-70449-8) Da Capo.

Puterbaugh, Donald L., jt. auth. see Fling, Paul N.

Puterbaugh, Ed & Borneman, Eric. A Practical Guide to Corals for the Reef Aquarium. 2nd rev. ed. LC 96-86765. (Illus.). 112p. 1997. 34.95 (0-945738-99-4) Crystal KY.

Puterbaugh, Geoff. Twins & Homosexuality: A Casebook. LC 90-31756. (Gay & Lesbian Studies: Vol. 2). 164p. 1990. text 15.00 (0-8240-6149-7, 627) Garland.

Puterbaugh, Parke. Southeastern Wetlands: A Guide to Selected Sites in Georgia, North Carolina, South Carolina, Tennessee, & Kentucky. Derby, Jennifer, ed. (Illus.). 208p. 1998. mass mkt. 16.95 (1-880686-00-7) Terrene Inst.

***Puterbaugh, Parke & Bisbort, Alan.** Foghorn Outdoors: California Beaches: The Only Guide to the Best Places to Swim, Play, Eat & Stay on Every Beach in the Golden State. 2nd ed. (Illus.). 640p. 1999. pap. 19.95 (1-57354-060-9, Foghorn Outdoors) Avalon Travel.

Puterbaugh, Parke & Bissort, Alan. Foghorn Outdoors: Florida Beaches: The Only Guide to the Best Places to East, Stay, Swim & Play on Every Beach in the Sunshine State. (Illus.). 650p. 1999. pap. text 19.95 (1-57354-054-4, Foghorn Outdoors) Avalon Travel.

Puterbaugh, Parke & Derby, Jennifer. Southeastern Wetlands: A Guide to Selected Sites in Georgia, North Carolina, South Carolina, Tennessee & Kentucky. LC 98-220750. 208p. 1997. 16.95 (0-9659726-0-7) Environ Protect.

Puterbaugh, Parke, jt. auth. see Bisbort, Alan.

Puterbaugh, Rex. 50 Smart Dogs: Veterinarians Share Warm Recollections. LC 98-19095. (Illus.). 192p. 1998. 16.95 (1-55972-476-5, Birch Ln Pr) Carol Pub Group.

***Puterbaugh, Rex.** 50 Smart Dogs: Veterinarians Share Warm Recollections. large type unabridged ed. 2000. 25.95 (0-7531-5482-X, 15482X, Pub. by ISIS Lrg Prnt) ISIS Pub.

Puterman, Martin L. Markov Decision Processes: Discrete Stochastic Dynamic Programming. (Series in Probability & Mathematical Statistics). 672p. 1994. 129.95 (0-471-61977-9) Wiley.

Putfarcken, Jan. Jazz Portraits. 1994. 40.00 (3-926048-40-9, Pub. by Nieswand-Verlag) Dist Art Pubs.

Puth, Robert C. American Economic History. 3rd ed. LC 92-72940. 732p. (C). 1993. text 91.00 (0-03-096905-0, Pub. by Harcourt Coll Pubs) Harcourt.

— Supreme Life: The History of a Negro Life Insurance Company. LC 75-41780. (Companies & Men: Business Enterprises in America Ser.). 1976. 27.95 (0-405-08095-6) Ayer.

Puthenkandathil, Eldho. Philos: A Designation for the Jesus-Disciple Relationship, an Exegetico-Theological Investigation of the Term in the Fourth Gospel. LC 93-3470. XXIV, 379p. 1993. 61.00 (3-631-45841-X) P Lang Pubng.

Puthenparampil, J. Philip, jt. ed. see Bickley, Verner C.

Puthenpurackal, J. Heidegger Through Authentic Totality to Total Authenticity: A Unitary Approach to His Thought in Its Two Phases. (Louvain Philosophical Studies: No. 2). 360p. (Orig.). 1987. pap. 47.50 (90-6186-203-5, Pub. by Leuven Univ) Coronet Bks.

Puthenpurakal, Joseph. Baptist Missions in Nagaland. 1984. 22.50 (0-8364-1138-2, Pub. by Mukhopadhyaya) S Asia.

Puthli, Ram S., et al, eds. Proceedings of the Second (1992) International Offshore & Polar Engineering Conference, Vol. IV. LC 91-78280. 628p. (Orig.). 1992. pap. 100.00 (1-880653-04-4) ISOPE.

— The Proceedings of the Third International Offshore & Polar Engineering Conference, 1993, 4 vols., 4. LC 92-76219. 732p. (Orig.). 1993. pap. 100.00 (1-880653-09-5) ISOPE.

Puthucheary, Mavis. The Politics of Administration: The Malaysian Experience. 1978. 32.50 (0-19-580386-8) OUP.

Puthusserypady, Sadasivan, jt. auth. see Haykin, Simon.

***Putin, Vladimir, et al.** First Person: An Astonishingly Frank Self Portrait by Russia's President Vladimir Putin. Fitzpatrick, Caterine A., tr. (Illus.). 208p. 2000. pap. 15.00 (1-58648-018-9, Pub. by PublicAffairs NY) HarpC.

Putinar, M., jt. auth. see Eschmeier, J.

Putinar, M., jt. auth. see Martin, M.

Putini, Elisabetta, jt. auth. see Petren, Birgitta.

Putinski, Nancy A. & Kocik, Michael J. A Farewell to Failure: Creating Quality in Our Schools. 200p. 1993. spiral bd. 29.95 (1-883296-00-5) Par Excell.

***Putis, Robert.** Outdogs, Undercasts, & Other Superzeroes: A Collection. 142p. 1999. pap. 15.00 (0-9669874-1-1, 002) Maple Leaf.

***Putkowski, Julian.** Shot at Dawn. 2nd rev. ed. 1998. 36.95 (0-85052-613-2, Pub. by Leo Cooper) Trans-Atl Phila.

Putland, Helen. Duck Keeping for Beginners. 56p. 1998. pap. 12.95 (0-86417-963-4, Pub. by Kangaroo Pr) Seven Hills Bk.

Putlitz, Gisbert Z. Atomic Physics Methods in Modern Research: Selection of Papers Dedicated to Gisbert zu Putlitz on the Occasion of His 65th Birthday. Jungmann, K. et al, eds. LC 97-43416. (Lecture Notes in Physics Ser.: Vol. 499). ix, 448p. 1997. 110.00 (3-540-63716-8) Spr-Verlag.

Putman. Legal Analysis & Writing for Paralegals, IML. 160p. 1997. teacher ed. 17.95 (0-314-13022-5) Delmar.

Putman, Andree, ed. The International Design Yearbook 7, Vol. 7. (International Design Yearbooks Ser.). (Illus.). 240p. 1992. 65.00 (1-55859-285-7) Abbeville Pr.

Putman, Anthony O. Marketing Your Services: A Step-by-Step Guide for Small Businesses & Professionals. 256p. 1990. 39.95 (0-471-50948-5) Wiley.

Putman, Anthony O. & Davis, Keith E., eds. Advances in Descriptive Psychology, Vol. 5. 320p. 1990. 70.00 (0-9625661-0-1) Descriptive Psych Pr.

Putman, Bluford H. & Wilford, D. Sykes, eds. The Monetary Approach to International Adjustment. rev. ed. LC 85-28314. 396p. 1986. 65.00 (0-275-92024-0, C2024, Praeger Pubs) Greenwood.

Putman, Bob, et al. Is This Missions Thing for Real? For Students Who Have Their Doubts. (Illus.). 128p. 1990. teacher ed., ring bd. 49.95 incl. VHS (0-935797-32-7) Harvest IL.

Putman, Byron W. Digital & Microprogram Electronics: Theory Application Troubleshooting. (Illus.). 416p. (C). 1986. text 52.00 (0-13-214354-2) P-H.

— RS-232 Simplified: Connecting, Interfacing & Troubleshooting Peripheral Devices. (Illus.). 264p. (C). 1986. 24.95 (0-13-783499-3) P-H.

Putman, Charles E., ed. Diagnostic Imaging of the Lung. (Lung Biology in Health & Disease Ser.: Vol. 46). (Illus.). 752p. 1990. text 275.00 (0-8247-8318-2) Dekker.

Putman, Charles E. & Ravin, Carl E. Textbook of Diagnostic Imaging, 2 vols. 2nd ed. LC 94-4061. (Illus.). 2368p. 1994. text 310.00 (0-7216-3697-7, W B Saunders Co) Harcrt Hlth Sci Grp.

Putman, Charles E., jt. auth. see Chiles, Caroline.

Putman, Daniel A. Human Excellence: Dialogues on Virtue Theory. 144p. (C). 1998. 44.00 (0-7618-1161-3); pap. 24.50 (0-7618-1162-1) U Pr of Amer.

***Putman, Eileen.** Never Kiss a Duke. 384p. 2000. mass mkt. 5.99 (0-380-80290-2) Morrow Avon.

— Never Trust a Rake. 384p. 1999. mass mkt. 5.99 (0-380-80289-9, Avon Bks) Morrow Avon.

Putman, Eileen. Reforming Harriet. 1998. mass mkt. 4.99 (0-451-19493-4) NAL.

Putman, Hilary. Philosophical Papers, Set. 1986. pap. 85.00 (0-521-31020-2) Cambridge U Pr.

— Philosophical Papers Vol. 1: Mathematics, Matter & Method. 2nd ed. (Illus.). 374p. 1979. pap. text 35.95 (0-521-29550-5) Cambridge U Pr.

— Philosophical Papers Vol. 2: Language & Reality. (Illus.). 457p. 1975. 47.50 (0-317-66588-X); pap. 18.95 (0-317-66589-8) Cambridge U Pr.

— Philosophical Papers Vol. 3: Reason, Truth & History. (Illus.). 312p. 1985. pap. text 26.95 (0-521-31394-5) Cambridge U Pr.

Putman, Marc R., jt. auth. see Engstrom, Robert E.

Putman, Perry. Guide to Owning a Gerbil. (Illus.). 64p. 1997. pap. 6.95 (0-7938-2152-5, RE-503) TFH Pubns.

Putman, Peter H. The Toastmasters International Guide to Audiovisual Presentations. 2nd rev. ed. (Illus.). 106p. 1997. pap. 9.95 (0-9658991-0-1) Toastmasters.

Putman, R. J. Community Ecology. 2nd ed. LC 93-33026. 178p. 1993. write for info. (0-412-56690-7, Chap & Hall NY) Chapman & Hall.

Putman, Rory. The Natural History of Deer. LC 88-22856. (Comstock Bk.). (Illus.). 224p. 1989. text 32.50 (0-8014-2283-3) Cornell U Pr.

Putman, Stephen H. Urban Residential Location Models. (Studies in Applied Regional Science: Vol. 13). 1979. lib. bdg. 73.50 (0-89838-011-1) Kluwer Academic.

Putnam. Bricklaying. 1995. pap. 11.50 (0-15-505548-8) Harcourt Coll Pubs.

***Putnam.** Essential Welder: Oxyacetelene Welding. (Welding Ser.). (C). 2000. pap., student ed. 15.00 (0-8273-7625-1) Delmar.

Putnam, A. A., jt. auth. see Abrishaman, M.

Putnam, A. W. History of Middle Tennessee: Or, Life & Times of General James Robertson. (Illus.). 668p. 1997. reprint ed. lib. bdg. 69.50 (0-8328-6922-8) Higginson Bk Co.

Putnam, Annie C., ed. see Wynne, Madeline Y.

Putnam, Bertha H. The Place in Legal History of Sir William Shareshull. LC 85-48163. (Cambridge Studies in English Legal History). 346p. 1986. reprint ed. 85.00 (0-912004-33-9) Gaunt.

Putnam, Bertha H., ed. Enforcement of the Statutes of Labourers During the First Decade After the Black Death, 1349-59. LC 70-127447. (Columbia University Social Science Studies: No. 85). reprint ed. 37.50 (0-404-51085-X) AMS Pr.

Putnam, Bluford H. Applying Quantitative Discipline to Asset Allocation. (Illus.). 1995. pap. 180.00 (1-85564-529-7, Pub. by Euromoney) Am Educ Systs.

Putnam, Bluford H. & Wilford, D. Sykes, eds. The Monetary Approach to International Adjustment. LC 78-19753. 299p. 1979. 36.95 (0-275-90409-1, C0409, Praeger Pubs); pap. 15.95 (0-275-91480-1, B1480, Praeger Pubs) Greenwood.

Putnam, Calvin R. Commutation Properties of Hilbert Space Operators & Related Topics. (Ergebnisse der Mathematik und Ihrer Grenzgebiete Ser.: Vol. 36). 1967. 89.95 (0-387-03778-0) Spr-Verlag.

Putnam, Carleton. Race & Reality. LC 67-19407. 192p. 1980. pap. 12.00 (0-914576-14-3) Howard Allen.

— Race & Reason. LC 61-8447. 125p. 1977. pap. 12.00 (0-914576-08-9) Howard Allen.

Putnam-Carlson. Diccionario de Arquitectura: Ingles - Espanol Construccion y Obras Publicas. (SPA.). 1991. write for info. (0-7859-3685-8, 8428315604) Fr & Eur.

Putnam, Claudia, jt. auth. see Malville, J. McKim.

Putnam, Constance E., jt. auth. see Hayward, Oliver S.

Putnam, Cora M. The Story of Houlton: With Supplement. (Illus.). 431p. 1997. reprint ed. lib. bdg. 47.00 (0-8328-5861-7) Higginson Bk Co.

***Putnam, Dave.** The Working American Bulldog. (Illus.). 189p. 1999. 49.95 (0-9672710-0-2) Bulldog Pr.

Putnam, Douglas. Controversies of the Sports World. LC 98-38217. (Contemporary Controversies Ser.). 272p. 1999. 45.00 (0-313-30558-7, Greenwood Pr) Greenwood.

Putnam Dunkle, Laura. Carving Whimsical Birds: An Artistic Approach. 44p. 1999. pap. 12.95 (1-56523-113-9) Fox Chapel Pub.

Putnam, E. History of the Putnam Family in England & America (Including "Putnam Leaflets"), 2 vols. in 1. (Illus.). 720p. 1989. reprint ed. pap. 99.00 (0-8328-0999-3); reprint ed. lib. bdg. 117.00 (0-8328-0998-5) Higginson Bk Co.

Putnam, E. C. & Putnam, J. J. Jackson: Honorable Jonathan Jackson & Hannah Tracy Jackson, Their Ancestors & Descendants. (Illus.). 70p. 1991. reprint ed. pap. 14.00 (0-8328-1749-X) Higginson Bk Co.

Putnam, Eben. Lt. Joshua Hewes, a New England Pioneer, & Some of His Descendants. (Illus.). 673p. 1989. reprint ed. pap. 101.00 (0-8328-0654-4); reprint ed. lib. bdg. 109.00 (0-8328-0653-6) Higginson Bk Co.

Putnam, Eben, ed. see Osgood, I.

Putnam, Emily J. Candaules' Wife, & Other Old Stories. LC 72-169559. (Short Story Index Reprint Ser.). 1977. reprint ed. 19.95 (0-8369-4022-9) Ayer.

— The Lady: Studies of Certain Significant Phases of Her History. LC 70-108990. 1993. pap. 1.95 (0-226-68564-0, P362) U Ch Pr.

Putnam, F. W. The Manufacture of Bone Fish Hooks in the Little Miami Valley. (Ohio History, Prehistoric Indians, Archaeology Ser.). (Illus.). 8p. (C). 1994. reprint ed. pap. 1.30 (1-56651-105-4) A W McGraw.

— The Serpent Mound of Ohio: Site Excavation & Park Construction. (Ohio History, Archaeology, Prehistoric Indians Ser.). (Illus.). 8p. (C). 1994. reprint ed. lib. bdg. 2.80 (1-56651-091-0) A W McGraw.

Putnam, F. W., et al, eds. Author & Title Index: Volumes 1-26, 1903-1929. (University of California Publication in American Archaeology & Ethnology Ser.). 18p. 1929. pap. text 2.19 (1-55567-882-3) Coyote Press.

Putnam, Frank B., jt. auth. see Cleland, Robert G.

Putnam, Frank W. Diagnosis & Treatment of Multiple Personality Disorder. LC 88-11217. (Foundations of Modern Psychiatry Ser.). 351p. 1989. lib. bdg. 42.00 (0-89862-177-1) Guilford Pubns.

— Dissociation in Children & Adolescents: A Developmental Perspective. LC 97-20444. 423p. 1997. lib. bdg. 44.00 (1-57230-219-4, 0218) Guilford Pubns.

Putnam, Frederic C. A Cumulative Index to the Grammar & Syntax of Biblical Hebrew. LC 95-33708. 338p. 1996. pap. 24.50 (1-57506-007-8); text 34.50 (1-57506-001-9) Eisenbrauns.

— Hebrew Bible Insert: A Student's Guide to the Syntax of Biblical Hebrew. 64p. (Orig.). 1997. pap. text 4.95 (1-887070-03-6) Stylus Publ.

Putnam, Frederic W. The Archaeological Reports of Frederic Ward Putnam. LC 78-178422. (Harvard University. Peabody Museum of Archaeology & Ethnology. Antiquities of the New World Ser.: No. 8). (Illus.). reprint ed. 62.50 (0-404-57308-8) AMS Pr.

— The Selected Archaeological Papers of Frederic Ward Putnam. LC 76-178419. (Harvard University. Peabody Museum of Archaeology & Ethnology. Antiquities of the New World Ser.: No. 5). (Illus.). reprint ed. 110.00 (0-404-57305-3) AMS Pr.

Putnam, Frederic W., ed. see Goddard, P. E.

Putnam, Frederic W., ed. see Goddard, Pliny E.

Putnam, Frederick, ed. Author & Title Index University of California Publications in American Archaeology & Ethnology Vols. 1-50: 1903-1964. (Contributions of the University of California Archaeological Research Facility: No. 32). 83p. (C). 1976. reprint ed. pap. text 9.38 (1-55567-594-8) Coyote Press.

Putnam, George G. Salem Vessels & Their Voyages Vol. 2: A History of the "George", "Glide", "Taria Topan" & "St. Paul" in Trade with Calcutta, East Coast of Africa, Madagascar & the Phillippine Islands. LC 30-1353. 1925. 19.95 (0-88389-106-9, PEMP196) Peabody Essex Mus.

Putnam, George H. Censorship of the Church of Rome & Its Influence upon the Production & Distribution of Literature, 2 vols. LC 67-12455. 1972. reprint ed. 60.95 (0-405-08869-8) Ayer.

— Censorship of the Church of Rome & Its Influence upon the Production & Distribution of Literature, 2 vols., Vol. 1. LC 67-12455. 1976. reprint ed. 30.95 (0-405-08870-1) Ayer.

— Censorship of the Church of Rome & Its Influence upon the Production & Distribution of Literature, 2 vols., Vol. 2. LC 67-12455. 1976. reprint ed. 30.95 (0-405-08871-X) Ayer.

— Question of Copyright: A Summary of the Copyright Laws at Present in Force in the Chief Countries of the World. xii, 412p. 1996. reprint ed. 65.00 (0-8377-2555-0, Rothman) W S Hein.

Putnam, Greta, jt. auth. see Finch, Karen.

Putnam, H. G., ed. see Olivo, C. Thomas.

Putnam, Harold. Yankee Journal. LC 98-91329. 210p. 1998. pap. 14.00 (1-57502-762-3, PO2105) Morris Pubng.

Putnam, Herbert, et al. Essays Offered to Herbert Putnam by His Colleagues & Friends on His Thirtieth Anniversary As Librarian of Congress, April 5, 1929. LC 67-23214. (Essay Index Reprint Ser.). 1977. pap. 30.95 (0-8369-0430-3) Ayer.

Putnam, Hilary. Philosophical Papers, 2 vols. Incl. Vol. 2. Mind, Language & Reality. 474p. 1979. pap. text 35.95 (0-521-29551-3); 1975. write for info. (0-318-51290-4) Cambridge U Pr.

— Philosophical Papers Vol. 3: Reason, Truth & History. LC 81-6126. 224p. 1981. pap. text 21.95 (0-521-29776-1) Cambridge U Pr.

— Philosophy of Mathematics: Selected Readings. 2nd ed. Benacerraf, Hilary, ed. LC 85-25257. 624p. 1984. pap. text 37.95 (0-521-29648-X) Cambridge U Pr.

— Pragmatism: An Open Question. 128p. 1995. pap. 20.95 (0-631-19343-X) Blackwell Pubs.

— Realism with a Human Face. 424p. (C). 1992. pap. 20.50 (0-674-74945-6) HUP.

— Renewing Philosophy. LC 92-10854. 234p. (Orig.). 1992. 34.95 (0-674-76093-X) HUP.

— Renewing Philosophy. 248p. (Orig.). (C). 1995. pap. text 16.50 (0-674-76094-8) HUP.

— Representation & Reality. (Illus.). 154p. 1991. pap. text 13.00 (0-262-66074-1) MIT Pr.

***Putnam, Hilary.** The Threefold Cord: Mind, Body & World. LC 99-38458. 256p. 2000. 27.50 (0-231-10286-0) Col U Pr.

Putnam, Hilary. Words & Life. Conant, James, ed. LC 93-39799. 544p. 1994. 55.00 (0-674-95606-0) HUP.

— Words & Life. 608p. (C). 1995. pap. text 22.50 (0-674-95607-9) HUP.

Putnam, Howard D. & Busnar, Gene. The Winds of Turbulence. 256p. 1991. 23.00 (0-88730-458-3, HarpBusn) HarpInfo.

Putnam, J. J., jt. auth. see Putnam, E. C.

Putnam, Jackson K. Modern California Politics. 4th ed. Hundley, Norris, Jr. & Schutz, John A., eds. (Golden State Ser.). (Illus.). 160p. 1990. 12.00 (0-929651-02-2) MTL.

Putnam, James. Amazing Facts about Ancient Egypt. (Illus.). 64p. (J). 1994. 10.95 (0-8109-1953-2, Pub. by Abrams) Time Warner.

— Ancient Egypt Treasure Chest: 3000 Years of Mystery to Unlock & Discover. LC 95-232155. (Treasure Chest Ser.). (Illus.). 32p. (J). (gr. 4-7). 1994. student ed. 19.95 (1-56138-462-3) Running Pr.

***Putnam, James.** Make Your Own Egyptian Pyramid. 24p. 1999. pap. 9.95 (0-688-17019-6, Wm Morrow) Morrow Avon.

***Putnam, James.** Pyramid. (Eyewitness Books). (Illus.). (J). (gr. 4-7). 2000. 19.99 (0-7894-6602-3) DK Pub Inc.

— Pyramid. (Eyewitness Books). (J). (gr. 4-7). 2000. 15.95 (0-7894-5898-5) DK Pub Inc.

Putnam, James. Pyramid. LC 94-8804. (Eyewitness Books). (Illus.). 64p. (YA). (gr. 5 up). 1994. lib. bdg. 20.99 (0-679-96170-4, Pub. by Knopf Bks Yng Read) Random.

Putnam, James J. Human Motives. LC 73-2413. (Mental Illness & Social Policy; the American Experience Ser.). 1973. reprint ed. 19.95 (0-405-05223-5) Ayer.

— James Jackson Putnam & Psychoanalysis: Letters Between Putnam & Sigmund Freud, Ernest Jones, William James, Sandor Ferenczi & Morton Prince, 1877-1917. Hale, Nathan G., Jr., ed. Heller, Judith B., tr. LC 70-150010. (Commonwealth Fund Publications). (Illus.). 400p. 1971. 37.00 (0-674-47170-9) HUP.

Putnam, Jeff. Bottoms Up. LC 92-75410. 320p. 1993. 20.00 (0-9627509-4-8) Baskerville.

— By the Wayside. LC 91-77771. 343p. 1992. 19.00 (0-9627509-5-6) Baskerville.

— Demigod. LC 93-70994. 320p. 1993. 20.00 (1-880909-09-X) Baskerville.

— Good Men. LC 92-70842. 253p. 1992. 18.00 (0-9627509-7-2) Baskerville.

— Sellout. Chase, Sam, ed. 338p. 1995. 22.00 (1-880909-35-9) Baskerville.

Putnam, Jeff, ed. see Bateman, Paul.

Putnam, Jeff, ed. see Black, Simon.

Putnam, Jeff, ed. see Eisner, William.

Putnam, Jeff, ed. see Wheelis, Allen.

Putnam, Jim. The Joshua Chronicles. 310p. (Orig.). 1995. pap. 13.95 (0-9645993-0-9) Ivy Hollow.

— Mummy. (Eyewitness Books). (Illus.). (J). (gr. 4-8). 2000. 19.99 (0-7894-6593-0) DK Pub Inc.

— Mummy. (Eyewitness Books). (J). (gr. 4-7). 2000. 15.95 (0-7894-5856-X) DK Pub Inc.

Putnam, Jim. Mummy. LC 92-1591. (Eyewitness Books). (Illus.). 64p. (J). (gr. 5 up). 1993. 19.00 (0-679-83881-3, Pub. by Knopf Bks Yng Read) Random.

P

Putnam, Joanne. Cooperative Learning in Diverse Classrooms. 217p. (C). 1996. pap. text 38.00 (*0-02-397043-X*, Macmillan Coll) P-H.

Putnam, Joanne W. Cooperative Learning & Strategies for Inclusions: Celebrating Diversity in the Classroom. 2nd ed. LC 97-45507. 1998. pap. 26.95 (*1-55766-346-7*) P H Brookes.

Putnam, Joe B., Jr., jt. auth. see Franco, Kenneth L.

Putnam, Joyce. Seven Years with the Group of Seven. (Illus.). 160p. 1991. 39.95 (*1-55082-013-3*, Pub. by Quarry Pr) LPC InBook.

Putnam, Karen & Cramer, Marianne. New York's 50 Best Places to Discover & Enjoy in Central Park. LC 99-20604. 144p. 1998. pap. 12.00 (*1-885492-64-2*) City & Co.

Putnam, Ken, jt. auth. see Wallace, Judi Lawson.

Putnam, Lawrence. Measures for Excellence: Reliable Software on Time, Within Budget. 400p. 1991. 77.00 (*0-13-567694-0*, Pub. by P-H) S&S Trade.

Putnam, Lawrence H. & Myers, Ware. Industrial Strength Software: Effective Management Using Measurement. 328p. 1997. 42.00 (*0-8186-7532-2*) IEEE Comp Soc.

Putnam, Lillian R. How to Become a Better Reading Teacher: Strategies for Assessment & Intervention. LC 94-44805. 347p. 1995. pap. text 24.00 (*0-02-397045-6*, Macmillan Coll) P-H.

— Stories to Talk About: Helping Students Make Ethical Choices. LC 95-113146. 1994. pap. 12.95 (*0-590-48922-4*) Scholastic Inc.

Putnam, Lillian R., ed. Readings on Language & Literacy: Essays in Honor of Jeanne S. Chall. LC 97-11360. (Orig.). 1997. pap. text 24.95 (*1-57129-039-7*) Brookline Bks.

Putnam, Linda L. & Roloff, Michael E. Communication & Negotiation. (Annual Reviews of Communication Research Ser.: Vol. 20). 304p. (C). 1992. text 58.00 (*0-8039-4011-4*); pap. text 26.00 (*0-8039-4012-2*) Sage.

Putnam, Lynn & Finlayson, Christine. Clackamas River Watershed Atlas. (Illus.). 1997. spiral bd. 24.00 (*0-9662473-0-2*, 1997-10251-GMS) Metro Region.

*Putnam, Mark & Chamberlain, Donald, eds. Effective Participation by the HIV/AIDS Community in HUD's Consolidated Plan. 60p. 1999. pap. write for info. (*0-9636595-6-1*) AIDS Hse WA.

*Putnam, Mark S. Ethics for a Modern Workforce: Facilitator's Guide. (Ethics for a Modern Workforce Training Curriculum Ser.). 103p. 2000. 89.00 (*0-9679729-0-6*) Character Training.

— Ethics for a Modern Workforce: Participant Workbook. (Ethics for a Modern Workforce Training Curriculum Ser.). 42p. 2000. wbk. ed. 29.00 (*0-9679729-1-4*) Character Training.

Putnam, Mary, jt. ed. see Gibson, Brad.

Putnam, Mary T. Record of an Obscure Man. LC 70-82213. (Anti-Slavery Crusade in America Ser.). 1970. reprint ed. 25.95 (*0-405-00652-7*) Ayer.

Putnam, Melanie K. & Schaefgen, Susan. Ohio Legal Research Guide. LC 96-16186. xv, 371p. 1997. 65.00 (*1-57588-087-3*, 306700) W S Hein.

*Putnam, Michael. Silent Screens: The Decline & Transformation of the American Movie Theater. LC 99-53226. (Creating the North American Landscape Ser.). (Illus.). 2000. 39.95 (*0-8018-6329-5*) Johns Hopkins.

Putnam, Michael C. Artifices of Eternity: Horace's Fourth Book of Odes. (Studies in Classical Philology - Townsend Lectures). 352p. 1996. pap. text 18.95 (*0-8014-8346-8*) Cornell U Pr.

— Essays on Latin Lyric, Elegy, & Epic. LC 81-47944. (Princeton Collected Essays Ser.). 371p. 1982. reprint ed. pap. 115.10 (*0-608-02593-3*, 206325000004) Bks Demand.

— The Poetry of the Aeneid. LC 88-47774. 256p. 1988. pap. text 14.95 (*0-8014-9518-0*) Cornell U Pr.

— Tibullus: A Commentary. (American Philological Association Ser.: Vol. 3). 222p. 1979. pap. 16.95 (*0-8061-1560-2*) U of Okla Pr.

— Virgil's Aeneid--Essays in Interpretation & Influence. LC 94-19891. 420p. 1995. pap. text 19.95 (*0-8078-4499-3*); lib. bdg. 55.00 (*0-8078-2191-8*) U of NC Pr.

— Virgil's Epic Designs: Ekphrasis in the Aeneid. LC 97-43717. 272p. (ps up). 1998. 35.00 (*0-300-07353-4*) Yale U Pr.

*Putnam, Michael C. J. Horace's Carmen Saeculare: Ritual Magic & the Poet's Art. LC 00-38154. (Illus.). 2001. write for info. (*0-300-08333-5*) Yale U Pr.

Putnam, Milt, jt. auth. see Putnam, Patti.

Putnam, Oliver. Tracts on Sundry Topics of Political Economy. LC 68-56567. (Reprints of Economic Classics Ser.). viii, 156p. 1970. reprint ed. 35.00 (*0-678-00600-8*) Kelley.

Putnam, Patti & Putnam, Milt. North America's Favorite Butterflies: A Pictorial Guide. LC 97-9334. (Illus.). 136p. 1997. pap. 9.95 (*1-57223-109-2*, 1092) Willow Creek Pr.

Putnam, Paul A., ed. Handbook of Animal Science. (Illus.). 401p. 1991. text 83.00 (*0-12-568300-6*) Acad Pr.

Putnam, Peter B. Love in the Lead: The Miracle of the Seeing Eye Dog. 2nd ed. LC 97-15322. (Illus.). 304p. 1997. reprint ed. pap. 16.95 (*0-7618-0777-2*) U Pr of Amer.

Putnam Publishing Group Staff, ed. Jill's Dream Surprise. (J). Date not set. pap. 4.95 (*0-448-40900-3*) Putnam Pub Group.

— Supergirl Popup Book. (J). Date not set. pap. 2.95 (*0-448-15300-9*) Putnam Pub Group.

— Those Playful Bunnies. (J). Date not set. pap. 4.95 (*0-448-40902-X*) Putnam Pub Group.

Putnam Publishing Staff, ed. Crazy Frog Game. (Crazy Games Ser.). (Illus.). (J). (ps up). 1989. 3.99 (*0-8431-2478-4*, Price Stern) Peng Put Young Read.

— Crazy Penguin Game. (Crazy Games Ser.). (Illus.). (J). (ps up). 1989. 3.99 (*0-8431-2479-2*, Price Stern) Peng Put Young Read.

Putnam, R. E. Spanish-English Dictionary of Architecture & Construction: With English Vocabulary. (ENG & SPA., Illus.). 535p. 1988. pap. 68.25 (*84-283-1560-4*, Pub. by Paraninfo) IBD Ltd.

Putnam, Richard, jt. auth. see Weyrick, Jeannie.

Putnam, Richelle. Fall Out. 325p. 1999. pap. 6.99 (*1-57532-141-6*) Press-Tige Pub.

Putnam, Rita J. As Your Parents Age: Your 94-Minute Guide to Information, Help, Peace of Mind, Set. 124p. (Orig.). 1994. pap. 21.95 incl. digital audio (*1-886909-03-2*) Dynam Comm.

— Our Positively Golden Years Vol. 1: Reflections on Aging. large type ed. (Illus.). 200p. (Orig.). Date not set. pap. write for info. (*1-886909-04-0*) Dynam Comm.

Putnam, Robert. Builder's Comprehensive Dictionary. 3rd ed. (Illus.). 513p. 1996. reprint ed. pap. 29.95 (*1-889892-00-9*) Builders Bk Inc.

Putnam, Robert D. The Beliefs of Politicians: Ideology, Conflict, & Democracy in Britain & Italy. LC 72-75207. (Yale Studies in Political Science: No. 24). 322p. reprint ed. pap. 99.90 (*0-8357-7121-0*, 202203200024) Bks Demand.

— Bowling Alone: The Collapse & Revival of American Community. LC 00-27278. (Illus.). 384p. 2000. 26.00 (*0-684-83283-6*) Simon & Schuster.

— Democracy & the Civic Community: Tradition & Change in an Italian Experiment. (Illus.). 288p. 1992. text 39.50 (*0-691-07889-0*, Pub. by Princeton U Pr) Cal Prin Full Svc.

— Making Democracy Work: Civic Traditions in Modern Italy. 258p. 1992. pap. text 16.95 (*0-691-03738-8*, Pub. by Princeton U Pr) Cal Prin Full Svc.

Putnam, Robert D. & Bayne, Nicholas. Hanging Together: Co-operation & Conflict in the Seven-Power Summits. 2nd ed. 304p. (C). 1988. text 45.00 (*0-8039-8101-5*); pap. text 17.95 (*0-8039-8102-3*) Sage.

— Hanging Together: Cooperation & Conflict in the Seven-Power Summits. rev. ed. LC 87-23593. 296p. 1988. pap. 18.95 (*0-674-37226-3*) HUP.

— Hanging Together: The Seven-Power Summits. (Illus.). 276p. 1985. 37.95 (*0-674-37225-5*) HUP.

Putnam, Robert D., jt. ed. see Pharr, Susan J.

Putnam, Robert E. Basic Blueprint Reading: Residential. LC 80-80673. (Illus.). 256p. reprint ed. pap. 79.40 (*0-8357-5974-1*, 201784200010) Bks Demand.

— Bricklaying Skill & Practice. 3rd ed. LC 73-84363. (Illus.). 272p. reprint ed. pap. 84.40 (*0-8357-7401-5*, 200641200059) Bks Demand.

— Modern Masonry. 395p. (C). 1988. teacher ed. write for info. (*0-15-562066-5*, MASON IM); text 53.00 (*0-15-562065-7*, MASON, Pub. by SCP) Harcourt.

Putnam, Robert E. & Burnett, John. Concrete Block Construction. 3rd ed. LC 73-75302. (Illus.). 232p. reprint ed. pap. 72.00 (*0-608-11526-6*, 201156700078) Bks Demand.

Putnam, Roger, jt. auth. see Hopkins, David.

Putnam, Roy C. In It to Win It. 1973. pap. 3.95 (*0-87508-440-0*) Chr Lit.

Putnam, Rufus, jt. auth. see Finley, Isaac J.

Putnam, Russell, jt. auth. see McKay, Ray.

Putnam, Ruth. Alsace & Lorraine from Caesar to Kaiser 58 B.C.-1871 A.D. LC 75-160988. (Select Bibliographies Reprint Ser.). 1977. reprint ed. 33.95 (*0-8369-5856-X*) Ayer.

— Charles the Bold. LC 73-14465. (Heroes of the Nations Ser.). reprint ed. 30.00 (*0-404-58283-4*) AMS Pr.

— William the Silent. LC 73-14466. (Heroes of the Nations Ser.). reprint ed. 30.00 (*0-404-58284-2*) AMS Pr.

Putnam, Ruth, tr. see Blok, Petrus J.

Putnam, Ruth A., ed. The Cambridge Companion to William James. LC 96-29099. (Cambridge Companions to Philosophy Ser.). 418p. (C). 1997. text 59.95 (*0-521-45278-3*); pap. text 20.95 (*0-521-45906-0*) Cambridge U Pr.

Putnam, S. An Empirical Model of Regional Growth. (Monographs: No. 6). 1975. 22.00 (*1-55869-037-9*) Regional Sci Res Inst.

Putnam, Sallie B. Richmond During the War: Four Years of Personal Observation. LC 96-20643. xxi, 373p. 1996. pap. 16.95 (*0-8032-8745-3*, Bison Books) U of Nebr Pr.

Putnam, Samuel. Francois Rabelais, Man of the Renaissance: A Spiritual Biography. 1977. 31.95 (*0-8369-7167-1*, 7999) Ayer.

Putnam, Samuel, tr. from FRE. Kiki's Memoirs. LC 96-27746. (Illus.). 176p. 1996. 23.00 (*0-88001-496-2*) HarpC.

Putnam, Samuel, tr. see Amado, Jorge.

Putnam, Samuel, tr. see Cunha, Euclydes Da.

Putnam, Samuel, tr. see De Cervantes Saavedra, Miguel.

Putnam, Stan P. How I Made Four Hundred Twenty-Three Thousand Dollars with a "Fool Idea" A Proven Money Building Plan of Success in Real Estate, I. (Illus.). (Orig.). (C). 1987. pap. 10.00 (*0-944047-01-7*) Res Improvement Inst.

— How I Made Four Hundred Twenty-Three Thousand Dollars with a "Fool Idea" A Proven Money Building Plan of Success in Real Estate, II. (Illus.). (Orig.). (C). 1987. pap. 10.00 (*0-944047-02-5*) Res Improvement Inst.

— How I Made Four Hundred Twenty-Three Thousand Dollars with a "Fool Idea" A Proven Money Building Plan of Success in Real Estate, Set. (Illus.). (Orig.). (C). 1987. pap. 20.00 (*0-944047-00-9*) Res Improvement Inst.

— How to Analyze Handwriting for Fun & Profit: A Manual Showing How to Analyze, Interpret & Provide Behavior Modification Through Handwriting. (Illus.). 120p. 1987. 20.00 (*0-318-22857-2*); pap. 12.00 (*0-318-22858-0*) Res Improvement Inst.

— How to Never Be Fat Again: A Proven Physical Fitness Plan for Health, Looks & Physique Using Exercise, Diet & Behavior Modification. (Illus.). 120p. 1987. 20.00 (*0-318-22859-9*); pap. 12.00 (*0-318-22860-2*) Res Improvement Inst.

— How to Test & Improve Your Sex Appeal: A Psychographological (Handwriting Analysis) Plan to Test & Improve Basic Sex Appeal. (Illus.). (Orig.). 1987. pap. text 10.00 (*0-944047-03-3*) Res Improvement Inst.

— Momento, Souvenir, Keepsake, & Collector's Kit on the Life & Music of Elvis. (Illus.). 1988. reprint ed. pap. 10.00 (*0-944047-08-4*) Res Improvement Inst.

— Money Making Secrets of the Self-Made Millionaires: A Proven Plan for Structuring & Implementing a Path Toward Riches As Has Been Done by Self-Made Millionaires. (Illus.). (Orig.). 1987. pap. 10.00 (*0-944047-04-1*) Res Improvement Inst.

— New Found Facts & Memorabilia about Elvis Presley: A Manual on the Life & Times of Elvis Presley Using Psychographology (Handwriting Analysis) with Related Memorabilia. (Illus.). 100p. 1987. 20.00 (*0-318-22861-0*); pap. 12.00 (*0-318-22862-9*) Res Improvement Inst.

Putnam, Tim, jt. auth. see Alfrey, Judith.

Putnam, Walter, III. Paul Valery Revisited. LC 94-12619. (Twayne's World Authors Ser.: No. 850). 200p. 1994. 32.00 (*0-8057-8291-5*, Twyne) Mac Lib Ref.

Putnam, Walter C., III. L' Aventure Litteraire de Joseph Conrad et d'Andre Gide. (Stanford French & Italian Studies: Vol. 67). (FRE.). 276p. 1991. pap. 56.50 (*0-915838-83-4*) Anma Libri.

Putnam, William. Legal Analysis & Writing for Paralegals. LC 97-10303. 384p. (C). 1997. mass mkt. 45.95 (*0-314-12830-1*) West Pub.

Putnam, William L. The Explorers of Mars Hill: A Centennial History of Lowell Observatory. LC 93-49057. (Illus.). 320p. 1994. 30.00 (*0-914659-69-3*) Phoenix Pub.

— The Great Glacier & Its House: The Story of the First Center of Alpinism in North America, 1885-1925. LC 80-69728. (Illus.). 224p. 1982. 28.50 (*0-930410-13-0*) Amer Alpine Club.

— Green Cognac: The Education of a Mountain Fighter. (Illus.). 256p. 1991. 24.95 (*0-930410-50-5*) Amer Alpine Club.

— Green Cognac: The Education of a Mountain Fighter. (Illus.). 242p. 1998. text 25.00 (*0-7881-5731-0*) DIANE Pub.

— John Peter Zenger & the Fundamental Freedom. LC 97-14213. 205p. 1997. lib. bdg. 30.00 (*0-7864-0370-5*) McFarland & Co.

— A Yankee Image: The Life & Times of Roger Lowell Putnam. LC 91-36425. (Illus.). 172p. 1991. 25.00 (*0-914659-55-3*) Phoenix Pub.

Putnam, William L., jt. auth. see Kauffman, Andrew J.

Putney, Albert H. United States Constitutional History & Law. 599p. 1985. reprint ed. 58.00 (*0-8377-1021-9*, Rothman) W S Hein.

*Putney, Carolyn M. Japanese Treasures: The Art of Netsuke Carving in the Toledo Museum of Art. (Illus.). 48p. 2000. pap. 11.95 (*0-935172-08-4*) Art Media Resources.

Putney, Christopher. Russian Devils & Diabolic Conditionality in Nikolai Gogol's "Evenings on a Farm Near Dikanka" LC 97-12512. (Middlebury Studies in Russian Language & Literature: Vol. 15). XIII, 250p. (C). 1999. text 51.95 (*0-8204-3770-0*, 37700) P Lang Pubng.

Putney, Erika K., jt. auth. see Kuhn, Walter N., Jr.

Putney, James W., Jr. Capacitative Calcium Entry. LC 96-52387. (Molecular Biology Intelligence Unit Ser.). 210p. 1997. 99.00 (*1-57059-431-7*) Landes Bioscience.

Putney, James W. Methods in Calcium Signaling. LC 99-43588. (Methods in Life Sciences - Signal Transduction Ser.). 400p. 1999. boxed set 129.95 (*0-8493-3386-5*) CRC Pr.

Putney, James W., Jr., ed. Inositol Phosphates & Calcium Signalling. LC 88-646597. (Advances in Second Messenger & Phosphoprotein Research Ser.: No. 26). (Illus.). 416p. 1992. reprint ed. pap. 129.00 (*0-608-05795-9*, 205976000007) Bks Demand.

Putney, James W., Jr., jt. ed. see Mitchell, Robert H.

Putney, Martha S. Black Sailors: Afro-American Merchant Seamen & Whalemen Prior to the Civil War. 103. LC 86-22822. (Contributions in Afro-American & African Studies: No. 103). (Illus.). 184p. 1987. 49.95 (*0-313-25639-X*, PBS/, Greenwood Pr) Greenwood.

— When the Nation Was in Need: Blacks in the Women's Army Corps During World War II. LC 92-24084. (Illus.). 245p. 1992. 40.00 (*0-8108-2531-7*) Scarecrow.

Putney, Mary Jo. Angel Rogue. 384p. (Orig.). 1995. pap., mass mkt. 6.99 (*0-451-40598-6*, Topaz) NAL.

— The Bargain. 384p. 1999. mass mkt. 6.99 (*0-451-19864-6*, Sig) NAL.

*Putney, Mary Jo. The Bargain. large type ed. LC 00-21928. (Basic Ser.). 2000. pap. 29.95 (*0-7862-2462-2*) Thorndike Pr.

Putney, Mary Jo. Burning Point. Date not set. write for info. (*0-449-00035-4*) Fawcett.

*Putney, Mary Jo. The Burning Point. 352p. 2000. mass mkt. 6.99 (*0-425-17428-X*) Berkley Pub.

— The China Bride. 480p. 2000. 22.95 (*0-345-43335-1*, Ballantine) Ballantine Pub Grp.

— The China Bride. large type ed. LC 00-32506. 2000. write for info. (*1-56895-916-8*) Wheeler Pub.

Putney, Mary Jo. Dancing on the Wind. 384p. (Orig.). 1994. mass mkt. 6.99 (*0-451-40486-6*, Topaz) NAL.

— Dearly Beloved. (Historical Romance Ser.). 416p. (Orig.). 1990. mass mkt. 6.99 (*0-451-40185-9*, Sig) NAL.

— The Diabolical Baron. (Regency Romance Ser.). 240p. 1987. mass mkt. 5.99 (*0-451-15042-2*, Sig) NAL.

— One Perfect Rose. LC 98-96114. 421p. 1998. mass mkt. 5.99 (*0-449-00018-4*, Crest) Fawcett.

— One Perfect Rose. large type ed. LC 97-29620. (Large Print Book Ser.). 1997. 24.95 (*1-56895-476-X*) Wheeler Pub.

— Petals in the Storm. 384p. (Orig.). 1993. mass mkt. 6.99 (*0-451-40445-9*, Topaz) NAL.

— The Rake. 384p. 1998. mass mkt. 6.99 (*0-451-40686-9*, Topaz) NAL.

*Putney, Mary Jo. The Rake. LC 98-29237. 1998. 25.95 (*1-56895-623-1*) Wheeler Pub.

Putney, Mary Jo. River of Fire. 1996. mass mkt. 6.99 (*0-451-18864-0*, Sig) NAL.

— Shattered Rainbows. 384p. 1996. mass mkt. 5.99 (*0-451-40614-1*, Topaz) NAL.

— Silk & Secrets. 400p. (Orig.). 1992. mass mkt. 6.99 (*0-451-40301-0*, Onyx) NAL.

— Silk & Shadows. 432p. 1991. mass mkt. 6.99 (*0-451-40277-4*, Onyx) NAL.

*Putney, Mary Jo. Silk & Shadows. 2000. mass mkt. 6.99 (*0-451-20206-6*, Sig) NAL.

Putney, Mary Jo. Thunder & Roses. 384p. (Orig.). 1993. mass mkt. 6.99 (*0-451-40367-3*, Topaz) NAL.

*Putney, Mary Jo. Tormenta de Pasiones. (SPA.). 496p. 2000. pap. 9.50 (*0-553-06122-4*) Bantam.

Putney, Mary Jo. Uncommon Vows. 384p. (Orig.). 1991. mass mkt. 6.99 (*0-451-40244-8*, Onyx) NAL.

— Veils of Silk. 384p. (Orig.). 1992. mass mkt. 6.99 (*0-451-40348-7*, Onyx) NAL.

— The Wild Child. LC 99-15271. 1999. 19.95 (*0-345-43315-7*) Ballantine Pub Grp.

*Putney, Mary Jo. The Wild Child. (J). 2000. mass mkt. 6.99 (*0-449-00584-4*, GM) Fawcett.

— The Wild Child. large type ed. LC 99-48205. (Large Print Book Ser.). 1999. 27.95 (*1-56895-791-2*) Wheeler Pub.

*Putney, Mary Jo, et al. Bride by Arrangement. 2000. mass mkt. 6.50 (*0-373-83437-3*, 1-83437-3) Harlequin Bks.

Putney, Mary Jo, et al. Faery Magic. 352p. 1998. mass mkt. 6.50 (*0-8217-5817-9*, Zebra Kensgtn) Kensgtn Pub Corp.

— Faery Magic. 320p. 1999. pap. 12.00 (*1-57566-379-1*) Kensgtn Pub Corp.

— Promised Brides. 1994. per. 4.99 (*0-373-83296-6*, 1-83296-3) Harlequin Bks.

Putney, Michael. The Average Student's Guide to Mastering Money in the Real World. 90p. (Orig.). (C). 1996. pap. 9.95 (*0-9650201-0-X*) Putney & Co.

Putney, Scott D. & Bolognesi, Dani P. AIDS Vaccine Research & Clinical Trials. 504p. 1990. text 150.00 (*0-8247-8221-6*) Dekker.

Putnicki, Patti. Celibacy Is Better Than Really Bad Sex: And Other Classic Rules for Single Women. LC 94-33737. (Illus.). 176p. 1994. pap. 9.95 (*0-944042-35-X*) CorkScrew Pr.

Putnik, Edwin. Art of Flute Playing. LC 75-146521. (Illus.). 96p. 1970. pap. 14.95 (*0-87487-077-1*) Summy-Birchard.

*Putnik, Edwin. El Arte de Tocar la Flauta. Gutierrez, Raul, tr. 96p. 1999. pap. text 16.95 (*0-87487-834-9*) Summy-Birchard.

Putnis, Andrew. An Introduction to Mineral Sciences. LC 92-8420. (Illus.). 479p. (C). 1992. pap. text 44.95 (*0-521-42947-1*) Cambridge U Pr.

— An Introduction to Mineral Sciences. LC 92-8420. (Illus.). 479p. (C). 1993. text 125.00 (*0-521-41922-0*) Cambridge U Pr.

*Putnoi, Johanna. Senses Wide Open: Living the Body, Mind, Spirit Connection. 240p. 2000. pap. text 14.95 (*1-56975-201-X*) Ulysses Pr.

Putnum, A. W. History of Middle Tennessee, Or, Life & Times of Gen. James Robertson. LC 73-146412. (First American Frontier Ser.). (Illus.). 1971. reprint ed. 49.95 (*0-405-02876-8*) Ayer.

Putseys, Y., jt. auth. see De Geest, W.

Putseys, Yvan, jt. auth. see Dirven, Rene.

Putt, Arlene M. General Systems Theory Applied to Nursing. 1978. 14.00 (*0-316-72300-2*, Little Brwn Med Div) Lppncott W & W.

Putt, Judy & Higgins, Karl, eds. Violence Against Women in Australia: Key Research & Data Issues. LC 98-145405. 64p. 1999. pap. 25.00 (*0-642-24031-0*, Pub. by Aust Inst Criminology) Advent Bks Div.

Puttanil, Thomas. A Comparative Study of the Theological Methodology of Irenaeus of Lyon & Sankaracharya. Burkle, Horst & Klimkeit, Hans-Joachim, eds. (Religionswissenschaft Ser.: Band 4). VI, 379p. 1990. pap. 64.00 (*3-631-41970-8*) P Lang Pubng.

*Puttaswamaiah, K. Cost-Benefit Analysis: With Reference to Environment & Ecology. 2000. 39.95 (*0-7658-0706-8*) Transaction Pubs.

Puttaswamaiah, K. Cost Benefit Analysis for Irrigation & Drought Proofing. (C). 1988. 27.50 (*81-204-0369-X*, Pub. by Oxford IBH) S Asia.

— Irrigation Projects in India: Towards a New Policy. (C). 1994. text 28.00 (*81-7387-007-1*, Pub. by Indus Pub) S Asia.

*Puttaswamaiah, K. John Hicks: His Contributions to Economic Theory & Application. 2000. pap. 29.95 (*0-7658-0703-3*) Transaction Pubs.

Putte, Katherine. Thematic Learning Centers. (Illus.). 144p. (J). 1998. pap., teacher ed. 14.95 (*1-57690-033-9*, TCM2033) Tchr Create Mat.

Putte, M. J. Van Den, see Van Den Putte, M. J.

Putte, Van De, see Van De Putte.

Putte, Vaude. More Thematic Learning Centers. 208p. (J). (gr. 5-8). 1997. pap. 15.95 (*1-57690-064-9*) Tchr Create Mat.

P

Puttenham, George. The Arte of English Poesie. LC 79-26413. (English Experience Ser.: No. 342). 258p. 1971. reprint ed. 30.00 (*90-221-0342-0*) Walter J Johnson.

— The Arte of English Poesie. Walker, Alice & Willcock, G. D., eds. 471p. reprint ed. pap. 134.30 (*0-8357-5768-4*, 2024510) Bks Demand.

Puttenham, Richard. The Arte of English Poesie: Contrived into Three Bookes: The First of Poets & Poesie, the Second of Proportion, the Third of Ornament. LC 71-85107. (Kent English Reprints, the Renaissance Ser.). 340p. reprint ed. pap. 105.40 (*0-7837-6150-3*, 204587200009) Bks Demand.

Putter, Ad. Gawain Poet Longman Lib. LC 96-11182. (Longman Medieval & Renaissance Library). 272p. (C). 1996. pap. text 24.38 (*0-582-22574-4*, Pub. by Addison-Wesley) Longman.

— An Introduction to the Gawain-Poet. LC 96-11182. 272p. (C). 1996. 66.00 (*0-582-22575-2*) Longman.

— Sir Gawain & the Green Knight & the French Arthurian Romance. 292p. 1995. text 60.00 (*0-19-818253-8*) OUP.

***Putter, Ad.** Spirit of Medieval Popular Romance: A Historical Introduction. 336p. 2000. pap. 29.95 (*0-582-29888-1*) Longman.

***Putter, Ad & Gilbert, Jane.** Spirit of Medieval Popular Romance: A Historical Introduction. 336p. 2000. 85.95 (*0-582-29880-6*) Longman.

Putter, Ann M., ed. The Memorial Rituals Book for Healing & Hope. LC 96-28349. (Death, Value & Meaning Ser.). 88p. 1997. pap. text 23.95 (*0-89503-143-4*) Baywood Pub.

Putter, C. A., jt. ed. see Keane, P. J.

Putter, Irving, tr. see De Chateaubriand, Francois-Rene.

Putter, Johann S. Versuch Einer Academischen Gelehrtengeschichte Von der Georg-Augustus-Universitat Zu Gottingen, 4 vols. reprint ed. write for info. (*0-318-71942-8*) G Olms Pubs.

Putterford, Mark. Aerosmith Live! LC 95-188010. (Illus.). 32p. (Orig.). (YA). (gr. 9 up). 1995. pap. 9.95 (*0-7119-4246-3*, OP 47707) Omnibus NY.

— Metallica: In Their Own Words. LC 95-158816. (In Their Own Words Ser.). (Illus.). 96p. pap. 15.95 (*0-7119-3866-0*, OP 47592) Omnibus NY.

— Over the Top: The True Story of Guns & Roses. (Illus.). 192p. 1997. pap. 16.95 (*0-7119-5222-1*, OP 47793) Omnibus NY.

— Phil Lynott: The Rocker. (Illus.). 288p. 1998. pap. 19.95 (*0-7119-6972-8*, OP48089) Omnibus NY.

Putterman, Allen M. Cosmetic Oculoplastic Surgery: Eyelid, Forehead, & Facial Techniques. 2nd ed. Lampert, Richard, ed. (Illus.). 400p. (C). 1998. text 145.00 (*0-7216-7076-8*, W B Saunders Co) Harcrt Hlth Sci Grp.

Putterman, Louis. Continuity & Change in China's Rural Development: Collective & Reform Eras in Perspective. (Illus.). 400p. 1993. text 75.00 (*0-19-507872-1*) OUP.

— Division of Labor & Welfare: An Introduction to Economic Systems. (Library of Political Economy). (Illus.). 264p. 1990. text 70.00 (*0-19-877299-8*) OUP.

Putterman, Louis, ed. Peasants, Collectives, & Choice: Economic Theory & Tanzania's Villages. LC 86-2915. (Contemporary Studies in Economic & Financial Analysis: Vol. 57). 389p. 1986. 78.50 (*0-89232-684-0*) Jai Pr.

Putterman, Louis & Kroszner, Randall S., eds. The Economic Nature of the Firm: A Reader. 2nd ed. (Illus.). 400p. (C). 1996. pap. text 28.95 (*0-521-55628-7*) Cambridge U Pr.

— The Economic Nature of the Firm: A Reader. 2nd ed. (Illus.). 400p. (C). 1996. text 80.00 (*0-521-47092-7*) Cambridge U Pr.

Putterman, Louis & Rueschemeyer, Dietrich, eds. State & Market in Development: Synergy or Rivalry? LC 92-17038. (Emerging Global Issues Ser.). 277p. 1992. lib. bdg. 49.95 (*1-55587-311-1*) L Rienner.

Putterman, Louis, jt. auth. see Bonin, John P.

Putterman, Louis, jt. ed. see Ben-Ner, Avner.

***Puttfarken, Thomas.** Discovery of Pictorial Composition: Theories of Visual Order in Painting, 1400-1800. LC 99-57910. (Illus.). 288p. 2000. 45.00 (*0-300-08156-1*) Yale U Pr.

Putti, Joseph. Theology as Hermeneutics: Paul Ricoeur's Theory of Text Interpretation & Method in Theology. LC 93-39087. 1995. 64.95 (*1-883255-23-6*); pap. 54.95 (*1-883255-22-8*) Intl Scholars.

Putti, Joseph M. & Ser, Toh T. Cases in Human Resource Management. 2nd ed. 344p. 1990. pap. 22.50 (*981-00-1477-5*, Pub. by Times Academic) Intl Spec Bk.

Putti, Joseph M., et al. Essentials of Management: An Asian Perspective LC 98-837349. xvi, 576p. 1998. write for info. (*0-07-115524-4*) McGraw.

Puttick & Simpson. Bibliotheca Mejicana. LC 71-168027. reprint ed. 40.00 (*0-404-02388-6*) AMS Pr.

Puttick, Elizabeth. Women in New Religions. LC 96-46619. 284p. 1997. pap. 18.95 (*0-312-17260-5*) St Martin.

Puttick, Elizabeth & Clarke, Peter B., eds. Women As Teachers & Disciples in Traditional & New Religions. LC 93-30865. (Studies in Women & Religion: Vol. 32). 152p. 1993. text 69.95 (*0-7734-9346-8*) E Mellen.

Puttick, G. & Van Esch, S. D. The Principles & Practice of Auditing. 7th ed. LC 99-215274. 1997. pap. write for info. (*0-7021-3772-3*, Pub. by Juta & Co) Intl Spec Bk.

Puttick, K. Challenging Delegated Legislation. (Waterlow Practitioner's Library). 336p. 1988. 59.00 (*0-08-033071-1*, K125, K130, Pergamon Pr) Elsevier.

Puttick, Keith. Wages & the Law. 190p. (C). 1989. pap. 75.00 (*0-7219-1110-2*, Pub. by IPM Hse) St Mut.

— Wages & the Law. (C). 1988. pap. 125.00 (*0-7855-2307-3*, Pub. by Scientific) St Mut.

***Puttick, Keith.** Welfare Benefits 1999-2000. 160p. 1999. pap. 21.50 (*1-85811-211-7*, Pub. by CLT Prof) Gaunt.

Puttick, Richard, jt. auth. see Tkach, Daniel.

Puttkammer, Ernst W. Administration of Criminal Law. LC 53-8736. 1994. lib. bdg. 21.00 (*0-226-68665-5*) U Ch Pr.

Puttnam, David. Movies & Money: Undeclared War Between Europe & America. LC 97-31244. 1998. 27.50 (*0-679-44664-8*) McKay.

Puttner, Herta & Rohrer, Eva. Tips & Tricks for Cat Owners. (Illus.). 160p. 1997. pap. 6.95 (*0-7938-0469-8*, TS-277) TFH Pubns.

— Tips & Tricks for Dog Owners. (Illus.). 160p. 1997. pap. 6.95 (*0-7938-0468-X*, TS-276) TFH Pubns.

Puttock, J. S., ed. Stably Stratified Flow & Dense Gas Dispersion. (Institute of Mathematics & Its Applications Conference Series, New Ser.: New Series 15). (Illus.). 448p. 1988. 95.00 (*0-19-853615-1*) OUP.

Putu Phalgunadi, I. Gusti. Pararaton: A Study of the Southeast Asian Chronicle. 1996. 52.00 (*81-85067-97-X*, Pub. by Sundeep Prak) S Asia.

Putuwar, Sunanda. The Buddhist Sangha: Paradigm of the Ideal Human Society. 136p. (C). 1991. pap. text 21.50 (*0-8191-7842-X*); lib. bdg. 39.00 (*0-8191-8279-6*) U Pr of Amer.

Putz-Anderson, Vern, ed. Cumulative Trauma Disorders: A Manual for Musculoskeletal Diseases of the Upper Limbs. 151p. 1988. 29.95 (*0-85066-405-5*) Taylor & Francis.

Putz, George. The Maine Coast. (Illus.). 175p. 1997. 15.98 (*0-89009-882-4*) Bk Sales Inc.

— Wood & Canvas Kayak Building. (Illus.). 144p. 1990. pap. text 17.95 (*0-87742-258-3*) Intl Marine.

— Wood & Canvas Kayak Building. (Illus.). 196p. 1990. pap. 18.95 (*0-07-155939-6*) McGraw.

Putz, George & Conkling, Philip W., eds. Island Journal: An Annual Publication of the Island Institute, Vol. II. 70p. 1985. pap. 7.95 (*0-942719-02-6*) Island Inst.

— Island Journal: An Annual Publication of the Island Institute, Vol. III. (Illus.). 72p. 1986. pap. 7.95 (*0-942719-03-4*) Island Inst.

Putz, George & Island Journal Staff, eds. Killick Stones: A Collection of Maine Island Writing, Vol. 1. (Illus.). 117p. (Orig.). 1987. pap. text 6.95 (*0-942719-05-0*) Island Inst.

Putz, Gregory B. Facilitation Skills: Helping Groups Make Decisions. LC 98-25716. (Illus.). 80p. 1998. pap. 29.95 (*0-9664456-0-0*) Deep Space Tech.

***Putz, Johanna.** In Beziehung zur Geschichte Sein: Frauen und Manner der Dritten Generation in Ihrer Auseinandersetzung Mit Dem Nationalsozialismus. (Studien Zur Bildungsreform Ser.). 164p. 1999. 28.95 (*3-631-34706-5*) P Lang Pubng.

Putz, Manfred, ed. Nietzsche in American Literature & Thought. LC 95-9731. (GERM Ser.). vi, 382p. (C). 1995. 75.00 (*1-57113-028-4*) Camden Hse.

Putz, Martin. Language Contact & Language Conflict. LC 93-46217. xvii, 256p. 1994. lib. bdg. 59.00 (*1-55619-479-X*) J Benjamins Pubng Co.

Putz, Martin, ed. Discrimination Through Language in Africa? Perspectives on the Nambian Experience. LC 95-35833. (Contributions to the Sociology of Language Ser.: No. 69). x, 338p. (C). 1995. lib. bdg. 136.95 (*3-11-014817-X*) Mouton.

— Language Choices: Conditions, Constraints & Consequences. LC 96-6512. (Impact: Studies in Language & Society: Vol. 1). xxi, 430p. 1997. lib. bdg. 127.00 (*1-55619-850-7*) J Benjamins Pubng Co.

— Thirty Years of Linguistic Evolution: Studies in Honor of Rene Dirven on the Occasion of His 60th Birthday. LC 92-22941. xl, 632p. 1992. 106.00 (*1-55619-462-5*) J Benjamins Pubng Co.

Putz, Martin, et al, eds. The Cultural Context in Foreign Language Teaching. (Duisburg Papers on Research in Language & Culture Ser.: Vol. 32). (Illus.). viii, 245p. 1997. 51.95 (*3-631-32338-7*) P Lang Pubng.

***Putz, Martin & Verspoor, Marjolijn, eds.** Explorations in Linguistic Relativity. LC 00-21132. (Current Issues in Linguistic Theory Ser.: Vol. 199). xvi, 369p. 2000. 80.00 (*1-55619-977-5*) J Benjamins Pubng Co.

Putz, R., et al, eds. Sobotta Atlas of Human Anatomy, 2 vols., Set. 12th ed. Taylor, Anna N., tr. LC 96-10269. (Illus.). 1996. write for info. (*0-683-30030-X*) Lppncott W & W.

— Sobotta Atlas of Human Anatomy, Vol. 1, Head, Neck, Upper Limbs. 12th ed. Taylor, Anna N., tr. from GER. LC 96-10269. (Illus.). 400p. 1997. write for info. (*0-683-18209-9*) Lppncott W & W.

— Sobotta Atlas of Human Anatomy, Vol. 2, Thorax, Abdomen, Pelvis, Lower Limb. 12th ed. Taylor, Anna N., tr. LC 96-10269. (Illus.). 401p. 1997. write for info. (*0-683-18210-2*) Lppncott W & W.

Putz, R. & Pabst, R., eds. Sobotta Atlas of Human Anatomy, Vol. 2. 12th ed. 820p. 170.00 (*0-683-30047-4*) Lppncott W & W.

Putz, Robyn, ed. see Maurer, Tracy M. & Woolf, Joni W.

Putzar, Edward. Japanese Literature: A Historical Outline. LC 70-189229. 278p. reprint ed. pap. 86.20 (*0-608-10796-4*, 202275400029) Bks Demand.

Putzel, James. A Captive Land: The Politics of Agrarian Reform in the Philippines. LC 92-12667. 427p. 1992. pap. 24.00 (*0-85345-842-1*, Pub. by Monthly Rev) NYU Pr.

Putzel, Max. Genius of Place: William Faulkner's Triumphant Beginnings. LC 84-10057. (Southern Literary Studies). 352p. 1985. pap. 109.20 (*0-7837-8515-1*, 204932400011) Bks Demand.

— The Man in the Mirror: William Marion Reedy & His Magazine. LC 97-46994. 376p. 1998. pap. 19.95 (*0-8262-1178-X*) U of Mo Pr.

Putzel, Steven. Reconstructing Yeats: "The Secret Rose" & "The Wind among the Reeds" LC 85-22986. 256p. 1986. 53.00 (*0-389-20600-8*, N8158) B&N Imports.

Putzell, Sara M., jt. auth. see McGuire, Peter J.

Putzer, H. Metallogenetische Provinzen in Suedamerika. xii, 316p. 1976. 68.00 (*3-510-65074-3*, Pub. by E Schweizerbartsche) Balogh.

Putzer, Hannfrit. Die Geologie Von Paraguay. (Beitraege Zur Regionalen Geologie der Erde. Ser.: Vol. 2). (Illus.). xii, 184p. 1962. 52.00 (*3-443-11002-9*, Pub. by Gebruder Borntraeger) Balogh.

Putzer, Thomas C., ed. Population & Related Organizations: International Address List. LC 93-49526. (APLIC Special Publication Ser.: No. 6). (Orig.). 1994. pap. write for info. (*0-933438-20-6*) APLIC Intl.

***Putzi, Sibylla.** Global Road Warrior: 100-Country Handbook for the International Business Traveler. 3rd ed. (Illus.). 2000. pap. 65.00 (*1-885073-86-0*) Wrld Trade Pr.

Putzki, Ellen. Literarische Spurensuche Psychischer und Physischer Konsequenzen der Sudafrikanischen Apartheidspolitik. (Europaische Hochschulschriften, Reihe 14: No. 335). 327p. 1997. 57.95 (*3-631-31302-0*) P Lang Pubng.

***Puu, T. Onu.** Attractors, Bifurcations & Chaos: Nonlinear Phenomena in Economics. xii, 507p. 2000. (*3-540-66862-4*) Spr-Verlag.

Puu, T. Onu. Nonlinear Economic Dynamics. 4th enl. rev. ed. LC 97-14351. (Illus.). x, 288p. 1997. 83.00 (*3-540-62768-5*) Spr-Verlag.

Puu, Tonu. Mathematical Location & Land Use Theory: An Introduction. LC 96-52372. (Advances in Spatial Science Ser.). (Illus.). 294p. 1997. 109.00 (*3-540-61819-8*) Spr-Verlag.

— Nonlinear Economic Dynamics. (Lecture Notes in Economics & Mathematical Systems Ser.: Vol. 336). (Illus.). viii, 119p. 1989. pap. 17.80 (*0-387-51438-4*) Spr-Verlag.

— Nonlinear Economic Dynamics. 2nd enl. rev. ed. (Illus.). x, 151p. 1991. 39.00 (*0-387-53351-6*) Spr-Verlag.

— Nonlinear Economic Dynamics. 3rd enl. rev. ed. LC 92-35868. 1993. 69.95 (*0-387-56145-5*) Spr-Verlag.

Puu, Tonu, jt. auth. see Beckmann, Martin J.

***Puuronen.** Youth in a Changing Karelia. 266p. 2000. 89.95 (*0-7546-2028-X*) Ashgate Pub Co.

Puvogel, Renate. Carl Larsson. (Illus.). 95p. 1997. pap. 9.99 (*3-8228-8572-X*) Taschen Amer.

Puxley, Frank L. In African Game Tracks: Wanderings with a Rifle Through Eastern Africa. limited ed. (Illus.). 320p. 1993. 65.00 (*1-882458-01-X*) Trophy Rm Bks.

Puxley, Lavallin. Samoyeds. deluxe ed. 80p. 1995. 20.00 (*0-614-04550-9*) Donald R Hoflin.

Puxley, Ray. Cockney Rabbit: A Dick'n'Arry of Rhyming Slang. (Illus.). 230p. 1995. pap. 10.95 (*0-86051-827-2*, Robson-Parkwest) Parkwest Pubns.

***Puxley, Ray.** Fresh Rabbit: Dick 'n' Arry of Contemporary Rhyming Slang. 134p. 1999. pap. text 9.95 (*1-86105-221-9*) Robson.

Puxon, Grattan, jt. auth. see Kenrick, Donald.

Puxty, A. G. The Social & Organizational Context of Management Accounting. (Advanced Management Accounting & Finance Ser.). (Illus.). 163p. 1993. pap. text 18.00 (*0-12-568660-9*) Acad Pr.

Puxty, A. G. & Dodds, J. C. Financial Management: Method & Meaning. (Accounting & Finance Ser.). (Illus.). 664p. (C). 1996. mass mkt. 44.95 (*0-412-40970-4*, A5655) Chapman & Hall.

Puxty, Anthony, jt. auth. see Tinker, Tony.

Puxty, John, jt. auth. see Fox, Roy A.

Puy, Candace De, see De Puy, Candace.

Puy-Costa, M. Modern Langenscheidt French-Spanish, Spanish-French Dictionary: Diccionario Moderno Langenscheidt Frances-Espanol-Frances. 11th ed. (FRE & SPA.). 512p. 1981. 19.95 (*0-8288-0740-X*, S39863) Fr & Eur.

Puy-Costa, M., ed. Dictionnaire Pratique. 2nd ed. (FRE.). 1966. write for info. (*0-7859-8602-2*, 203220620X); write for info. (*2-03-220620-X*) Fr & Eur.

Puy, David Du, see Du Puy, David.

Puy, Henry F. De, see De Puy, Henry F.

Puyear, Robert B., jt. auth. see Hansen, David A.

Puymbroeck, W. Van, see Van Puymbroeck, W., ed.

Puymbroeck, W. Van, see Withnell, S. & Van Puymbroeck, W., eds.

Puymbroeck, W. Van, see Van Puymbroeck, W.

Puyol Montero, F. Dictionary of Constitutional Rights & Procedural Guarantees Spanish. (SPA.). 459p. 1996. pap. 91.50 (*84-8151-313-X*, Pub. by Comares Edit) IBD Ltd.

Puytorac, P. De, see De Puytorac, P.

Puza, Richard & Weib, Andreas, eds. Iustitia in Caritate: Festgabe Fur Ernst Robler Zum 25Jahrigen Dienstjubilaum Als Offizial der Diozese Rottenburg-Stuttgart. (Adnotationes in ius Canonicum Ser.: Bd. 3). (GER., Illus.). 810p. 1997. 63.95 (*3-631-31004-8*) P Lang Pubng.

Puzak, P. P., jt. ed. see Holt, John M.

Puzinauskas, V. P. Properties of Asphalt Cements. 72p. 1980. 15.00 (*0-318-13396-2*, RR-80-2) Asphalt Inst.

Puzio, Henry & Johnson. Practical Heating, Ventilation, & Air Conditioning. 96p. 1995. teacher ed. 14.95 (*0-8273-5592-0*) Delmar.

Puzio, Henry & Johnson, Jim. Practical Heating, Ventilation, Air Conditioning, & Refrigeration. LC 94-30878. 1995. pap. 45.75 (*0-8273-5591-2*) Delmar.

Puzio, Michelle T., ed. A Morehead Family Day Book. (Illus.). (Orig.). 1996. pap. 6.25 (*0-9647647-1-7*) Preserv Greensboro.

Puzman, J. & Kubin, B. Public Data Networks: From Separate PDNs to the ISDN. (Illus.). x, 241p. 1991. 116.95 (*0-387-19580-7*) Spr-Verlag.

Puzo, Mario. Fools Die: A Novel. 531p. 1979. mass mkt. 7.99 (*0-451-16019-3*, Sig) NAL.

— The Fortunate Pilgrim. 304p. 1998. pap. 12.95 (*0-449-00358-2*) Fawcett.

— The Fortunate Pilgrim. LC 96-46329. 1997. 23.00 (*0-679-45778-X*) Random.

Puzo, Mario. The Fortunate Pilgrim. large type ed. LC 97-15411. (Core Ser.). 378p. 1997. lib. bdg. 26.95 (*0-7838-8237-8*, G K Hall Lrg Type) Mac Lib Ref.

Puzo, Mario. The Godfather. 444p. 1983. mass mkt. 7.99 (*0-451-16771-6*, Sig) NAL.

— The Godfather. 1969. 24.95 (*0-399-10342-2*, G P Putnam) Peng Put Young Read.

Puzo, Mario. The Godfather. Set. abr. ed. 1996. 24.95 incl. audio (*1-882071-84-0*) B&B Audio.

Puzo, Mario. The Last Don. 1997. mass mkt. 7.99 (*0-345-41221-4*) Ballantine Pub Grp.

— The Last Don. 1997. mass mkt. 7.99 (*0-345-91220-9*) Ballantine Pub Grp.

***Puzo, Mario.** Omerta: A Novel. LC 00-28082. 316p. 2000. 25.95 (*0-375-50254-8*) Random.

— Omerta: A Novel. large type ed. LC 00-21660. 512p. 2000. 25.95 (*0-375-43058-X*) Random Hse Lrg Prnt.

Puzo, Mario. Selected from The Godfather. abr. ed. (Writers' Voices Ser.). 64p. (Orig.). 1991. pap. text 3.95 (*0-929631-22-6*, Signal Hill) New Readers.

— The Sicilian. large type ed. (Charnwood Large Print Ser.). 1986. 11.50 (*0-7089-8317-0*, Charnwood) Ulverscroft.

Puzo, Michael J., jt. auth. see Muir, Douglas A.

Puzon, Bridget, ed. Women Religious & the Intellectual Life: The North American Achievement. 145p. 1995. text 64.95 (*1-883255-77-5*); pap. text 44.95 (*1-883255-76-7*) Intl Scholars.

***Puzzo, Dante A.** Apple Pie & Bourbon Whiskey. 200p. 2000. pap. 9.95 (*0-9634503-4-4*) Randatamp Pr.

— By the Dawn's Early Light. 125p. 2000. pap. 9.95 (*0-9634503-5-2*) Randatamp Pr.

— Chicago. 125p. 2000. pap. 9.95 (*0-9634503-6-0*) Randatamp Pr.

Puzzo, Dante A. Myth & the Cold War. 98p. (Orig.). 1995. pap. 12.00 (*0-9634503-2-8*) Randatamp Pr.

— The Partisans & the War in Italy. LC 92-10256. (Studies in Modern European History: Vol. 7). 101p. (C). 1993. text 38.95 (*0-8204-1951-6*) P Lang Pubng.

— Peering into the Darkness. LC 92-62457. 118p. (Orig.). 1993. pap. 12.00 (*0-9634503-0-1*) Randatamp Pr.

— Spain & the Great Powers, 1936 to 1941. LC 72-3101. (Select Bibliographies Reprint Ser.). 1980. reprint ed. 23.95 (*0-8369-6868-9*) Ayer.

***Puzzo, Dante A.** The Temptation of Adam & Other Stories. 180p. 2000. pap. 9.95 (*0-9634503-3-6*) Randatamp Pr.

PWN, Polish Scientific Publishers Staff, ed. see Szmydt, Zofia.

PWN, Polish Scientific Publishers Staff, ed. see Topolski, Jerzy.

Pwu, Jean L. East Wind, West Rain: Poems. LC 96-53096. 92p. 1997. pap. 14.95 (*0-7734-2709-0*, Mellen Poetry Pr) E Mellen.

Py, Bernard, jt. ed. see Grossen, Michele.

Pyadyshen, Boris D., ed. Russia & the World: New Views on Foreign Policy. 352p. 1991. 21.95 (*1-55972-087-5*, Birch Ln Pr) Carol Pub Group.

Pyakuryal, S., jt. auth. see Adhikari, S.

Pyarelal. Mahatma Gandhi, 10 vols., Set. Incl. Vol. I. Early Phase, 1869-1896. 875p. 1983. 40.00 (*0-934676-41-0*); Vol. II. Discovery of Satyagraha, 1896-1902. 445p. 1983. 65.00 (*0-934676-42-9*); Vol. III. Birth of Satyagraha, 1902-1906. 648p. 1983. 40.00 (*0-934676-73-9*); Vol. IX. Last Phase, 1944-7 (Part One) (Illus.). 742p. 1983. 75.00 (*0-934676-43-7*); (Illus.). 7200p. 1983. 585.00 (*0-934676-86-0*) Greenlf Bks.

Pyarelel. Gandhian Techniques in the Modern World. 70p. (Orig.). 1983. pap. 2.00 (*0-934676-45-3*) Greenlf Bks.

Pyatakhin, M. V. & Suchkov, A. F. Spatiotemporal Characteristics of Laser Emission. (Proceedings of the Lebedev Physics Institute Ser.: Vol. 199). (Illus.). 249p. (C). 1994. lib. bdg. 115.00 (*1-56072-163-4*) Nova Sci Pubs.

Pyatetskii-Shapiro, I. I. Automorphic Functions & the Geometry of Classical Domains, Vol. 8. (Mathematics & Its Applications Ser.). viii, 264p. 1969. text 274.00 (*0-677-20310-1*) Gordon & Breach.

***Pyatnitsky, Yuri I., et al, eds.** Introduction to Non-Linear Cinetics in Heterogeneous Catalysis. 2000. lib. bdg. 89.00 (*1-56072-819-1*) Nova Sci Pubs.

Pyatov, P. N. & Solodukhin, S. N. Geometry & Integrable Models. 232p. 1996. text 81.00 (*981-02-2330-7*) World Scientific Pub.

Pyatt, Buford H. Tall Green Grass: Lot's of Open Range. 226p. 1997. pap. 18.25 (*1-57502-621-X*, PO1774) Morris Pubng.

Pyatt, D. W., ed. Safety Engineering & Risk Analysis, 1998; Proceedings: ASME International Mechanical Engineering Congress & Exposition (1998: Anaheim, CA) LC 99-182513. 65p. 1998. pap. 60.00 (*0-7918-1587-0*) ASME Pr.

— Safety Engineering & Risk Analysis, 1995 Vol. 4: Safety Engineering & Risk Analysis - 1995. LC 95-81258. (1995 ASME International Mechanical Engineering Congress & Exposition Ser.: SERA-Vol. 4). 148p. 1995. 60.00 (*0-7918-1727-X*, H01009) ASME.

Pyatt, D. W., jt. ed. see Ellia, F. A.

Pyatt, F. Graham & Roe, Alan. Social Accounting for Development Planning with Special Reference to Sri Lanka. LC 76-30553. 222p. reprint ed. pap. 63.30 (*0-608-14565-3*, 2024943) Bks Demand.

Pyatt, Richard I. People's Medical Answer Book: Plain Answers to One Thousand One Hundred Common Questions from Thirty-Six Leading Specialists. 1984. 21.95 (*0-13-656596-4*); pap. 10.95 (*0-13-656588-3*) P-H.

Pyatt, Rosina. Unquestionable Lady. 1994. pap. 3.99 (*0-8217-4444-5*) NAL.

Pyatt, Sherman. Apartheid, 1979-1988: A Selective Annotated Bibliography. LC 89-7710. 190p. 1989. text 15.00 (*0-8240-7637-0*, 55587) Garland.

P

An Asterisk (*) at the beginning of an entry indicates that the title is appearing for the first time.

Pyatt, Sherman E., compiled by. Martin Luther King, Jr. An Annotated Bibliography, 12. LC 86-7593. (Bibliographies & Indexes in Afro-American & African Studies: No. 12). 166p. 1986. lib. bdg. 55.00 (*0-313-24635-1*, PML/, Greenwood Pr) Greenwood.

Pyatt, Sherman E. & Johns, Alan. A Dictionary & Catalog of Southern African American Folklife of the South. LC 97-26906. 232p. 1999. lib. bdg. 75.00 (*0-313-27999-3*, Greenwood Pr) Greenwood.

Pybrum, Steven. Money & Marriage: Making It Work Together. LC 96-83730. 1996. pap. text 17.95 (*0-9651277-2-9*) Abundance Pub.

Pybus, Beverly E., ed. The Privileging Quick Reference Guide. 130p. 1998. pap. text 97.00 (*1-57839-022-2*) Opus Communs.

Pybus, Beverly E., jt. auth. see Black, Christina W.

***Pybus, Cassandra.** The Devil & James McAuley. (Illus.). 321p. 1999. 34.95 (*0-7022-3111-8*, Pub. by Univ Queensland Pr) Intl Spec Bk.

Pybus, Cassandra. Till Apples Grow on an Orange Tree. 1998. pap. 24.95 (*0-7022-2986-5*, Pub. by Univ Queensland Pr) Intl Spec Bk.

— Till Apples Grow on an Orange Tree. 1998. pap. 18.95 (*0-7022-3036-7*, Pub. by Univ Queensland Pr) Intl Spec Bk.

Pybus, Cassandra, ed. Columbus' Blindness & Other Essays. LC 95-107359. 1994. pap. 16.95 (*0-7022-2745-5*, Pub. by Univ Queensland Pr) Intl Spec Bk.

Pybus, D. & Sell, C. The Chemistry of Fragrances. (RCS Paperbacks Ser.). 18p. 1998. 39.00 (*0-85404-528-7*) Am Chemical.

Pybus, Elizabeth. Human Goodness: Generosity & Courage. 154p. 1991. text 40.00 (*0-8020-5939-2*) U of Toronto Pr.

Pybus, Paul, see Notrik, Paul, pseud.

Pybus, Roger. Safety Management: Strategy & Practice. (Illus.). 192p. 1996. 69.95 (*0-7506-2519-8*) Buttrwrth-Heinemann.

Pybus, Victoria. Kibbutz Volunteer. 192p. 1997. pap. 15.95 (*1-85458-142-2*, Pub. by Vac Wrk Pubns) Seven Hills Bk.

— Kibbutz Volunteer. rev. ed. 192p. 2000. pap. 17.95 (*1-85458-228-3*, Pub. by Vac Wrk Pubns) Seven Hills Bk.

— Live & Work in France. 2nd ed. (Live & Work Abroad Guides Ser.). 248p. 1997. pap. 16.95 (*1-85458-111-2*, Pub. by Vac Wrk Pubns) Seven Hills Bk.

— Live & Work in France. 3rd ed. (Live & Work Abroad Guides Ser.). 288p. 1998. pap. 17.95 (*1-85458-180-5*, Pub. by Vac Wrk Pubns) Seven Hills Bk.

— Live & Work in Germany. (Live & Work Abroad Guides Ser.). 200p. (Orig.). 1997. pap. 16.95 (*1-85458-071-X*, Pub. by Vac Wrk Pubns) Seven Hills Bk.

— Live & Work in Germany. 2nd ed. (Live & Work Abroad Guides Ser.). 256p. (Orig.). 1998. pap. 17.95 (*1-85458-184-8*, Pub. by Vac Wrk Pubns) Seven Hills Bk.

— Live & Work in Italy. 2nd ed. (Live & Work Abroad Guides Ser.). 224p. (Orig.). 1998. pap. 17.95 (*1-85458-182-1*, Pub. by Vac Wrk Pubns) Seven Hills Bk.

— Live & Work in Japan. (Live & Work Ser.). 256p. 1999. pap. 19.95 (*1-85458-209-7*, Pub. by Vac Wrk Pubns) Seven Hills Bk.

***Pybus, Victoria.** Saudi & the Gulf. (Live & Work Ser.). 2000. pap. 19.95 (*1-85458-239-9*) Vac Wrk Pubns.

Pybus, Victoria. Working in Ski Resorts: Europe & North America. 304p. (Orig.). 1997. pap. 16.95 (*1-85458-109-0*, Pub. by Vac Wrk Pubns) Seven Hills Bk.

— Working in Ski Resorts: Europe & North America. 4th ed. (Illus.). 320p. (Orig.). 1997. pap. 17.95 (*1-85458-176-7*, Pub. by Vac Wrk Pubns) Seven Hills Bk.

— Working with Animals: U. K., Europe & Worldwide. 1999. pap. 19.95 (*1-85458-224-0*) Seven Hills Bk.

Pybus, Victoria & Dunne, Susan. Live & Work in Scandinavia. (Live & Work Abroad Guides Ser.). 320p. (Orig.). 1997. pap. 16.95 (*1-85458-121-X*, Pub. by Vac Wrk Pubns) Seven Hills Bk.

Pybus, Victoria & Robinson, Richard. Live & Work in Italy. (Live & Work Abroad Guides Ser.). 168p. (Orig.). 1997. pap. 15.95 (*1-85458-067-1*, Pub. by Vac Wrk Pubns) Seven Hills Bk.

Pycior, Helena M. Symbols, Impossible Numbers, & Geometric Entanglements: British Algebra Through the Commentaries on Newton's "Universal Arithmetick" LC 96-25469. (Illus.). 339p. (C). 1997. text 74.95 (*0-521-48124-4*) Cambridge U Pr.

Pycior, Helena M., et al, eds. Creative Couples in the Sciences. LC 94-41059. (Lives of Women in Science Ser.). (Illus.). 250p. (C). 1995. text 50.00 (*0-8135-2187-4*); pap. text 18.95 (*0-8135-2188-2*) Rutgers U Pr.

Pycior, Julie L. LBJ & Mexican Americans: The Paradox of Power. LC 96-48458. (Illus.). 392p. 1997. pap. 19.95 (*0-292-76578-9*) U of Tex Pr.

— LBJ & Mexican Americans: The Paradox of Power. LC 96-48458. (Illus.). 392p. 1997. 45.00 (*0-292-76577-0*) U of Tex Pr.

Pycke, Nestor, jt. ed. see Verhelst, Daniel.

Pycock, Jonathan F. Self-Assessment Color Review of Equine Reproduction & Stud Medicine. LC 97-179510. (Illus.). 208p. 1997. pap. 34.95 (*0-8138-2303-X*) Iowa St U Pr.

Pye. Respond to the AIDS Challenge. Date not set. pap. text. write for info. (*0-582-06434-1*, Pub. by Addison-Wesley) Longman.

Pye, Chris. Carving on Turning. (Illus.). 176p. 1995. pap. 14.95 (*0-946819-88-2*, Pub. by Guild Master) Sterling.

***Pye, Chris.** Elements of Woodcarving. (Illus.). 2000. pap. 17.95 (*1-86108-108-1*, Pub. by Guild Master) Sterling.

Pye, Chris. Lettercarving in Wood: A Practical Course. LC 98-110394. (Illus.). 256p. 1997. pap. text 18.95 (*1-86108-043-3*, Pub. by Guild Master) Sterling.

— Relief Craving in Wood: A Practical Introduction. LC 99-216481. 1999. pap. text 19.95 (*1-86108-096-4*) Guild Master.

— Woodcarving Tools, Materials & Equipment. (Illus.). 362p. 1995. pap. 26.95 (*0-946819-49-1*) Sterling.

Pye, David. The Nature & Aesthetics of Design. 6th ed. (Illus.). 160p. 1995. reprint ed. pap. 22.95 (*0-9643999-1-1*, 9911) Cambium Pr.

— The Nature & Art of Workmanship. rev. ed. (Illus.). 144p. 1995. reprint ed. pap. 22.95 (*0-9643999-0-3*, 9903) Cambium Pr.

Pye, David L., et al, eds. The Physics of Non-Crystalline Solids. 900p. 1992. 135.00 (*0-7484-0050-8*, Pub. by Tay Francis Ltd) Taylor & Francis.

Pye, Diana & Greenall, Simon. CAE Listening & Speaking Skills. 136p. 1997. pap. text 13.95 (*0-521-48533-9*) Cambridge U Pr.

***Pye, Donna-Marie.** America's Best Slow Cooker Recipes. (Illus.). 192p. 2000. pap. 18.95 (*0-7788-0022-9*, Pub. by R Rose Inc) Firefly Bks Ltd.

Pye, Douglas, jt. ed. see Cameron, Ian.

Pye, Ethel, ed. see Adrine-Robinson, Kenyette.

Pye, Ethel, ed. see Ceasor, Ebraska D.

Pye, Ethel, ed. see Durant, Charlotte T.

Pye, Geralyn, jt. auth. see Pettavino, Paula J.

Pye, J. & Jago, W. Effective Communication in Practice. (Illus.). 240p. 1998. pap. write for info. (*0-443-05993-4*) Church.

Pye, James. The Invisible Children: Who Are the Real Losers at School? 216p. 1989. 32.00 (*0-19-215958-5*) OUP.

Pye, K., ed. The Dynamics & Environmental Context of Aeolian Sedimentary Systems. (Geological Society Special Publications: No. 72). (Illus.). viii, 336p. (C). 1993. 97.00 (*0-903317-88-5*, 285, Pub. by Geol Soc Pub Hse) AAPG.

Pye, K. & Lancaster, Nicholas, eds. Aeiolian Sediments. LC 92-36454. (International Association of Sedimentologists Special Publication Ser.: No. 16). 167p. 1993. pap. 65.00 (*0-632-03544-7*) Blackwell Sci.

Pye, Keith & Yates, Richard, eds. British Politics: Ideas & Concepts. 304p. (C). 1990. pap. 29.00 (*0-7487-0227-X*, Pub. by S Thornes Pubs) Trans-Atl Phila.

Pye, Kenneth, ed. Sediment Transport & Depositional Processes. LC 93-17446. 330p. 1994. pap. 59.95 (*0-632-03112-3*) Blackwell Sci.

Pye, L. D., et al, eds. Borate Glasses: Structure, Properties, Applications. LC 78-9108. (Materials Science Research Ser.: Vol. 12). 648p. 1978. 135.00 (*0-306-40016-2*, Plenum Trade) Perseus Pubng.

Pye, L. D. & Joseph, I. Glass-Forming Metals Handbook. Date not set. write for info. (*0-8247-9621-7*) Dekker.

Pye, Lloyd. Everything You Know Is Wrong: Human Origins. 2nd rev. ed. (Illus.). 311p. 1998. reprint ed. pap. 20.00 (*0-9660134-3-3*) Adamu Pr.

— Everything You Know Is Wrong Bk. 1: Human Evolution. LC 97-94383. (Illus.). xii, 311p. 1997. pap. 20.00 (*0-9660134-1-7*) Adamu Pr.

Pye, Lucian W. Chinese Negotiating Style: Commercial Approaches & Cultural Principles. LC 91-32748. 136p. 1992. 55.00 (*0-89930-724-8*, PCN/, Quorum Bks) Greenwood.

— Guerrilla Communism in Malaya: Its Social & Political Meaning. LC 81-4591. 369p. 1981. reprint ed. lib. bdg. 65.00 (*0-313-23017-X*, PYGC, Greenwood Pr) Greenwood.

— The Mandarin & the Cadre: China's Political Cultures. LC 88-27727. (Michigan Monographs in Chinese Studies: No. 59). 224p. 1989. pap. text 20.00 (*0-89264-083-9*) Ctr Chinese Studies.

— The Non-Western Political Process. (Reprint Series in Social Sciences). (C). 1993. reprint ed. pap. text 5.00 (*0-8290-3099-9*, PS-351) Irvington.

— The Spirit of Chinese Politics. 2nd ed. 288p. (C). 1992. pap. text 19.50 (*0-674-83240-X*) HUP.

Pye, Lucian W., ed. Political Science & Area Studies: Rivals or Partners? LC 74-15711. 253p. reprint ed. 78.50 (*0-8357-9234-X*, 201583200097) Bks Demand.

Pye, Lucian W. & Pye, Mary W. Asian Power & Politics: The Cultural Dimensions of Authority. LC 85-2581. 432p. 1985. reprint ed. pap. 22.50 (*0-674-04979-9*) HUP.

Pye, Mary E., jt. ed. see Clark, John E.

Pye, Mary W., jt. auth. see Pye, Lucian W.

Pye, Michael. The Drowning Room: A Novel of New Amsterdam. 256p. 1997. pap. 11.95 (*0-14-014149-9*) Penguin Putnam.

— The Drowning Room: A Novel of New Amsterdam. 1997. pap. 11.95 (*0-14-014122-7*) Viking Penguin.

— The Study of Kanji. 340p. 1997. pap. 35.95 (*4-590-00714-2*, Pub. by Hokuseido Pr) Book East.

— Taking Lives. LC 98-28256. 304p. 1999. 23.00 (*0-375-40260-8*) Knopf.

***Pye, Michael.** Taking Lives. large type ed. LC 99-16584. 1999. 26.95 (*0-7862-2096-1*) Mac Lib Ref.

Pye, Patrick. The Time Gatherer: El Greco & the Sacred Theme. (Illus.). 126p. 1991. 25.00 (*1-85182-084-1*, Pub. by Four Cts Pr) Intl Spec Bk.

Pye, Richard J., jt. ed. see Champion, Robert H.

***Pye, Smith C.** Rebels & Outcasts: A Journey Through Christian India. 288p. 1998. pap. 15.95 (*0-14-024462-X*, Pub. by Pnguin Bks Ltd) Trafalgar.

Pye-Smith, Charlie. The Philippines: An Oxfam Country Profile. LC 98-131254. (Oxfam Country Profiles Ser.). (Illus.). 64p. (C). 1997. pap. 9.95 (*0-85598-367-1*, Pub. by Oxfam Pub) Stylus Pub VA.

Pye-Smith, Charlie, et al. The Wealth of Communities: Stories of Success in Local Environmental Management. LC 94-75606. (Library of Management for Development). (Illus.). x, 213p. (Orig.). 1994. pap. 18.95 (*1-56549-038-X*) Kumarian Pr.

Pyefinch, Mary. Access 2000 Client/Server Gold Book. LC 99-51342. (Illus.). 737p. 1999. pap. 49.99 (*1-57610-417-6*) Coriolis Grp.

— SQL from the Ground Up. 510p. 1999. pap. 34.99 (*0-07-211974-8*) McGraw.

Pyenson, Bruce. Managing Risk: A Leader's Guide to Creating a Successful Managed Care Provider Organization. LC 98-5830. 1998. 35.95 (*1-55648-213-2*) AHPI.

Pyenson, Bruce S., ed. Calculated Risk: A Provider's Guide to Assessing & Controlling the Financial Risk of Managed Care. 78p. 1995. pap. text 32.00 (*1-55648-131-4*, 131001) AHPI.

Pyenson, Lewis. Civilizing Mission: Exact Sciences & French Overseas Expansion, 1830-1940. LC 92-22577. (Illus.). 352p. 1993. text 49.95 (*0-8018-4421-5*) Johns Hopkins.

— Neohumanism & the Persistence of Pure Mathematics in Wilhelmian Germany. LC 82-72156. (American Philosophical Society, Memoirs Ser.: No. 150). 148p. reprint ed. pap. 45.90 (*0-7837-4333-5*, 204404400012) Bks Demand.

— Teaching & Research in the University. (Publications of the Graduate School, University of Southwestern Louisiana: Vol. 2). (Illus.). 90p. (Orig.). (C). 1996. pap. 10.00 (*1-889911-00-3*) U SW LA Grad.

— The Young Einstein: The Advent of Relativity. (Illus.). 272p. 1995. 65.00 (*0-85274-779-9*) IOP Pub.

Pyenson, Lewis, ed. Disciplines & Interdisciplinarity in the New Century. (Publications of the Graduate School, University of Southwestern Louisiana: Vol. 4). 107p. 1997. pap. 5.00 (*1-889911-02-X*) U SW LA Grad.

Pyenson, Lewis, et al, eds. Historical Studies in the Physical Sciences, Vol. 10. LC 77-75220. 344p. 1979. reprint ed. pap. 106.70 (*0-8357-8166-6*, 203414400010) Bks Demand.

Pyenson, Lewis & McCormmach, Russell K., eds. Historical Studies in the Physical Sciences, Vol. 8. LC 77-75220. 313p. 1977. reprint ed. pap. 97.10 (*0-608-03737-0*, 206456200008) Bks Demand.

— Historical Studies in the Physical Sciences, Vol. 9. LC 77-75220. 374p. 1978. reprint ed. pap. 116.00 (*0-608-04797-X*, 202632800009) Bks Demand.

Pyenson, Lewis & Sheets-Pyenson, Susan. The Norton History of Science in Society. (Illus.). 512p. 1999. pap. 17.95 (*0-393-31736-6*) Norton.

— Servants of Nature. LC 98-53198. (Illus.). 496p. 1999. 32.50 (*0-393-04614-1*) Norton.

Pyenson, Lewis, et al. Writing & the Graduate Experience. 2nd rev. ed. (Publications of the Graduate School, University of Southwestern Louisiana: Vol. 3). (Illus.). 40p. (C). 1996. pap. 5.00 (*1-889911-01-1*) U SW LA Grad.

Pyenson, Lewis, ed. see Infeld, Leopold.

Pyeritz, Reed E. Molecular Biology in Critical Medicine. 1995. pap. text 30.00 (*0-07-051102-0*) McGraw.

Pyeritz, Reed E. & Gasner, Cheryll. The Marfan Syndrome. 4th ed. (Illus.). 48p. 1994. pap. 4.00 (*0-918335-09-4*) Natl Marfan Foun.

— The Marfan Syndrome. 5th ed. (Illus.). 44p. Date not set. pap. text 5.00 (*0-918335-10-8*) Natl Marfan Foun.

Pyes, Craig. Picnics of Tuscany: Italian Country-Style Picnics to Enjoy at Home of Abroad. LC 93-34448. 64p. 1994. 14.00 (*0-671-87015-7*) S&S Trade.

Pyhrr, Stephen A., et al. Real Estate Investment: Strategy, Analysis, Decisions. 2nd ed. LC 88-27961. 992p. 1989. text 95.95 (*0-471-87953-3*) Wiley.

Pyhrr, Stuart W., et al. Heroic Armor of the Italian Renaissance: Filippo Negroli & His Contemporaries. LC 98-24942. (Illus.). 368p. 1999. 75.00 (*0-8109-6529-1*, Pub. by Abrams) Time Warner.

— Heroic Armor of the Italian Renaissance: Filippo Negroli & His Contemporaries. LC 98-24942. 1998. 65.00 (*0-87099-872-2*) Metro Mus Art.

Pykacz, J., et al, eds. Problems in Quantum Physics II: Gdansk '89. 536p. (C). 1990. text 130.00 (*981-02-0177-X*) World Scientific Pub.

Pykacz, Jaroslaw, jt. auth. see Aerts, Diederik.

Pykare, Nina. Affair of the Heart. 1980. per. 1.50 (*0-373-58005-3*) Harlequin Bks.

***Pykare, Nina.** The Haunting of Grey Cliffs. LC 99-54474. 2000. 24.95 (*0-7862-2350-2*) Thorndike Pr.

Pykare, Nina C. A Question of Trust. LC 98-96611. 192p. 1998. 18.95 (*0-8034-9322-3*, Avalon Bks) Bouregy.

***Pykare, Nina Coombs.** Death Comes for Desdemona. LC 99-31279. (Romances Ser.). 1999. 24.95 (*0-7862-2042-2*, Five Star MI) Mac Lib Ref.

Pyke, David F., jt. ed. see Johnson, M. Eric.

Pyke, Frank S. Industrial Development Through Small-Firm Cooperation Theory & Practice. vi, 69p. (Orig.). 1992. pap. 11.25 (*92-2-108256-3*) Intl Labour Office.

Pyke, Helen G. Cancer at 3 A.M. 154p. (Orig.). 1995. pap. 8.99 (*0-8280-0943-0*) Review & Herald.

— Doctor, Doctor. LC 92-37123. 1993. pap. write for info. (*0-8280-0683-0*) Review & Herald.

Pyke, Kaye & Landy, Lynne. Kay Pyke's Elegant Embroidery. (Illus.). 128p. 1993. 29.95 (*0-04-442357-8*, Pub. by Allen & Unwin Pty) IPG Chicago.

— Kaye Pyke's Elegant Embroidery. (Illus.). 128p. 1995. pap. 20.00 (*1-86373-876-2*, Pub. by Allen & Unwin Pty) IPG Chicago.

Pyke, Kaye, et al. Kaye Pyke's Classic Cushions. (Illus.). 128p. 1993. 34.95 (*1-86373-332-9*, Pub. by Allen & Unwin Pty) IPG Chicago.

— Kaye Pyke's Classic Cushions. (Illus.). 128p. 1995. pap. 20.00 (*1-86373-877-0*, Pub. by Allen & Unwin Pty) IPG Chicago.

Pyke, Steve, photos by. I Could Read the Sky. LC 98-110491. (Illus.). 176p. 1998. 24.00 (*1-86046-318-5*, Pub. by Harvill Press) FS&G.

— Philosophers. (Illus.). 168p. 1995. 50.00 (*0-9518371-8-4*) Dist Art Pubs.

— Philosophers. (Illus.). 168p. 1995. reprint ed. pap. 27.50 (*0-9518371-7-6*) Dist Art Pubs.

Pyke, Steve, jt. auth. see O'Grady, Timothy.

Pykett. "Improper" Feminine: Women's Sensation Novel & the New Woman Writing. 240p. (C). Date not set. pap. write for info. (*0-415-16262-9*) Routledge.

— Wilkie Collins. LC 97-32203. 256p. 1998. pap. 19.95 (*0-312-21270-4*); text 49.95 (*0-312-21269-0*) St Martin.

Pykett, Derek. Michael Ripper Unmasked. (Illus.). 192p. 1999. pap. 20.00 (*1-887664-27-0*) Midnght Marquee Pr.

Pykett, Lyn. Emily Bronte. 200p. (C). 1989. pap. 19.00 (*0-389-20881-7*); text 53.00 (*0-389-20880-9*) B&N Imports.

— Engendering Fictions: The English Novel in the Early Twentieth Century. (Writing in History Ser.). 224p. 1995. text 49.95 (*0-340-64577-6*, Pub. by E A) St Martin.

— Reading Fin de Siecle Fictions. (Critical Readers Ser.). 256p. (C). 1996. pap. 29.06 (*0-582-23390-9*) Longman.

— Reading Fin De Siecle Fictions. 21st ed. (Critical Readers Ser.). 256p. (C). 1996. 76.00 (*0-582-23392-5*) Addison-Wesley.

— The Sensation Novel. (Writers & Their Work Ser.). 95p. (Orig.). 1996. pap. text 15.00 (*0-7463-0725-X*, Pub. by Northcote House) U Pr of Miss.

— Sensations Novels. 1990. pap. 25.00 (*0-7463-0752-7*, Pub. by Northcote House) Trans-Atl Phila.

Pykett, Lyn, ed. see Braddon, Mary Elizabeth.

Pykh, Yuri A. & Malkina-Pykh, I. G., eds. The Method of Response Function in Ecology. (Advances in Ecological Sciences Ser.: Vol. 7). 246p. 2000. 125.00 (*1-85312-662-4*, 6624, Pub. by WIT Pr) Computational Mech MA.

Pykitt, David, jt. auth. see Barber, Chris.

Pylant. Standard Haircutting Manual. (Cosmetology Ser.). 1997. student ed. 17.95 (*1-56253-335-5*) Milady Pub.

Pylant, Della. Borrowed Joy: Victory over Tragedy. LC 90-83324. (Illus.). 144p. (Orig.). 1991. 14.95 (*0-9628285-3-X*); pap. 9.95 (*0-9628285-5-6*); write for info. (*0-9628285-1-3*); write for info. (*0-9628285-2-1*); write for info. (*0-9628285-4-8*) ABBA Pub.

Pylant, James, ed. Genealogies of Texas Families: Biographical Notes of Pioneer Settlers. LC 88-51835. (Illus.). 400p. (C). 1989. 37.50 (*0-9622746-1-5*) Datatrace Systems.

— Genealogies of Texas Families: Biographical Notes of Pioneer Settlers, Vol. 2. LC 92-81935. (Illus.). 200p. (C). 1992. text 27.50 (*0-9622746-2-3*) Datatrace Systems.

Pyle, A. M. Trouble Making Toys. LC 84-29162. 192p. 1985. 13.95 (*0-8027-5610-7*) Walker & Co.

Pyle, Andrew. Atomism & Its Critics. 756p. 1997. pap. 40.00 (*1-85506-502-9*) Thoemmes Pr.

Pyle, Andrew. Key Philosophers in Conversation: The Cogito Interviews. LC 98-40026. 1999. 65.00 (*0-415-18036-8*); pap. 20.99 (*0-415-18037-6*) Routledge.

***Pyle, Andrew.** Liberty: Contemporary Responses to John Stuart Mill. LC 99-52296. (Key Issues Ser.). 466p. 2000. pap. text 25.00 (*1-890318-43-4*) St Augustines Pr.

***Pyle, Andrew, ed.** The Dictionary of Seventeenth-Century: British Philosophers, 2 vols. 1000p. 2000. 550.00 (*1-85506-704-8*) Thoemmes Pr.

Pyle, Andrew, ed. The Origins of Modern Philosophy of Science, 1830-1914, 12 vols., Set. 2715p. (C). 1996. 1485.00 (*0-415-13267-3*) Routledge.

Pyle, Andrew, ed. Agnosticism: Contemporary Responses to Spencer & Huxley. (Key Issues Ser.). 328p. 1995. 72.00 (*1-85506-405-7*) Bks Intl VA.

— Liberty: Contemporary Responses to John Stuart Mill. LC 94-183793. (Key Issues Ser.). 466p. 1994. pap. 24.95 (*1-85506-245-3*) Bks Intl VA.

— Population: Contemporary Responses to Thomas Malthus. (Key Issues Ser.). 320p. 1994. 72.00 (*1-85506-344-1*) Bks Intl VA.

— Population: Contemporary Responses to Thomas Malthus. (Key Issues Ser.). (Illus.). 320p. 1994. pap. 24.00 (*1-85506-345-X*) Bks Intl VA.

Pyle, Andrew, ed. The Subjection of Women: Contemporary Responses to John Stuart Mill. (Key Issues Ser.). 340p. 1995. 72.00 (*1-85506-409-X*) Bks Intl VA.

Pyle, Andrew, ed. The Subjection of Women: Contemporary Responses to John Stuart Mill. (Key Issues Ser.). 340p. 1995. pap. 24.00 (*1-85506-408-1*) Bks Intl VA.

Pyle, Andrew, jt. ed. see Harris, Roy.

Pyle, Andrew, jt. ed. see Stapleton, Julia.

Pyle, Andrew, ed. & intro. see Mongiovi, Gary & Petri, Fabio.

***Pyle, Christopher H.** Extradition, Politics & Human Rights. 472p. 2001. 89.50 (*1-56639-822-3*); pap. 29.95 (*1-56639-823-1*) Temple U Pr.

Pyle, D. L., ed. Separations for Biotechnology 3: Proceedings of the International Symposium, Reading, UK, 1994. 618p. 1994. 184.00 (*0-85186-724-3*, R6724) CRC Pr.

***Pyle, David.** What Every Artist Needs to Know about Paints & Colors. LC 99-69484. (Illus.). 144p. 2000. 29.95 (*0-87341-831-X*, ARTPC) Krause Pubns.

Pyle, David J. Cutting the Costs of Crime: The Economics of Crime & Criminal Justice. (IEA Hobart Paper Ser.: No. 129). 68p. 1995. pap. 16.95 (*0-255-36373-7*, Pub. by Inst Economic Affairs) Coronet Bks.

Pyle, David J., jt. auth. see MacDonald, Ziggy.

P

Pyle, Dorian. Data Preparation for Data Mining. LC 99-17280. 540p. 1999. pap. 49.95 incl. cd-rom (*1-55860-529-0*, Pub. by Morgan Kaufmann) Harcourt.

Pyle, Douglas C. Clean, Sweet, Wind: The Watermen of the West Indies. LC 97-49256. (Illus.). 231p. 1998. 21.95 (*0-07-052679-6*) Intl Marine.

Pyle, Ernest. Home Country. 30.95 (*0-89190-771-8*) Amereon Ltd.

Pyle, Ernest W. New Techniques for Welding & Extending Sprinkler Pipes. 1976. 2.50 (*0-686-17608-1*, TR 76-2) Society Fire Protect.

Pyle, Ernie. Brave Men. 31.95 (*0-89190-770-X*) Amereon Ltd.

— Brave Men. 320p. 1983. reprint ed. lib. bdg. 26.95 (*0-89966-464-4*) Buccaneer Bks.

— Brave Men. LC 74-70. 474p. 1974. reprint ed. lib. bdg. 35.00 (*0-8371-7368-X*, PYBM, Greenwood Pr) Greenwood.

— Here Is Your War. Kohn, Richard H., ed. LC 78-22393. (American Military Experience Ser.). (Illus.). 1980. reprint ed. lib. bdg. 27.95 (*0-405-11869-4*) Ayer.

Pyle, Forest. The Ideology of Imagination: Subject & Society in the Discourse of Romanticism. LC 94-20154. xiii , 225p. 1995. 39.50 (*0-8047-1649-8*) Stanford U Pr.

— Ideology of Imagination: Subject & Society in the Discourse of Romanticism. 1997. pap. text 15.95 (*0-8047-2862-3*) Stanford U Pr.

Pyle, Gayle M. Nut Salad: Bompa & Me. Shaw, Thomas & Klemke, Anita, eds. LC 94-68040. (Illus.). 116p. (Orig.). 1994. pap. 12.95 (*0-9633371-1-4*) Carson St Pub.

Pyle, Gayle M., ed. see Shaw, Thomas E. & Klemke, Anita.

Pyle, Gerald F. The Diffusion of Influenza: Patterns & Paradigms. LC 86-1780. (Illus.). 240p. (C). 1986. 60.50 (*0-8476-7429-0*, R7429) Rowman.

— Heart Disease, Cancer, & Stroke in Chicago: A Geographical Analysis with Facilities, Plans, for 1980. LC 77-167941. (University of Chicago, Department of Geography, Research Paper Ser.: No. 134). 318p. 1971. reprint ed. pap. 98.60 (*0-608-02262-4*, 206290300004) Bks Demand.

Pyle, Gerald F., et al. The Spatial Dynamics of Crime. LC 74-80718. (University of Chicago, Department of Geography, Research Paper Ser.: No. 159). (Illus.). 234p. reprint ed. pap. 72.60 (*0-8357-3722-5*, 203644400003) Bks Demand.

Pyle, Hilary. The Different Worlds of Jack B. Yeats: His Cartoons & Illustrations. (Illus.). 344p. 1994. 49.50 (*0-7165-2521-6*, Pub. by Irish Acad Pr) Intl Spec Bk.

— Images in Yeats. (Illus.). 88p. 1990. pap. 32.95 (*0-9510228-3-0*, Pub. by Art Bks Intl) Partners Pubs Grp.

— Jack B. Yeats. (Illus.). 128p. 1997. pap. 15.95 (*1-86059-053-5*) Roberts Rinehart.

— Jack B. Yeats: A Biography. (C). 1989. lib. bdg. 52.50 (*0-389-20892-2*, N 8449) B&N Imports.

— Jack B. Yeats: His Watercolours, Drawings & Pastels. (Illus.). 224p. (C). 1993. 95.00 (*0-7165-2477-5*, Pub. by Irish Acad Pr) Intl Spec Bk.

— Jack B. Yeats: His Watercolours, Drawings & Pastels. (Illus.). 224p. 1994. pap. 29.50 (*0-7165-2606-9*, Pub. by Irish Acad Pr) Intl Spec Bk.

*__Pyle, Hilary.__ Red-Headed Rebel: Susan L. Mitchell: Poet & Mystic of the Irish Cultural Renaissance. LC 99-165672. (Illus.). 266p. 1998. pap. 24.95 (*0-9528453-7-7*, Pub. by Woodfield Pr) Irish Bks Media.

Pyle, Hilary. Yeats: Portrait of an Artistic Family. LC 97-224226. (Illus.). 304p. 1997. 60.00 (*1-85894-040-0*) Merrell Holberton.

Pyle, Hilary, ed. The Sligo-Leitrim World of Kate Cullen, 1832-1913: A 19th Century Memoir Revealed. LC 97-212381. (Illus.). 149p. 1997. pap. 19.95 (*0-9528453-2-6*, Pub. by Woodfield Pr) Irish Bks Media.

Pyle, Howard. The Adventures of Robin Hood. (Young Collector's Illustrated Classics Ser.). (Illus.). 192p. (J). (gr. 3-7). write for info. (*1-56156-454-0*) Kidsbks.

— Bearskin. LC 96-32451. (Books of Wonder Ser.). (Illus.). 48p. (J). (gr. k-3). 1997. 16.00 (*0-688-09837-1*, Wm Morrow) Morrow Avon.

Pyle, Howard. Bearskin. LC 96-32451. (Books of Wonder). (Illus.). 48p. (J). (gr. k-3). 1997. 15.93 (*0-688-09838-X*, Wm Morrow) Morrow Avon.

Pyle, Howard. Champions of the Round Table. 25.95 (*0-89190-661-4*) Amereon Ltd.

— Empty Bottles. 1975. 9.50 (*0-686-23319-0*) Rochester Folk Art.

— The Garden Behind the Moon: The Real Story of the Moon Angel. 2nd ed. (Illus.). 176p. (J). (gr. 6-8). 1988. reprint ed. pap. 10.95 (*0-930407-22-9*) Parabola Bks.

— Howard Pyle's Book of Pirates. 25.95 (*0-8488-0758-8*) Amereon Ltd.

— King Arthur. Hinkle, Don, ed. LC 87-15461. (Illus.). 48p. (J). (gr. 3-6). 1988. lib. bdg. 19.95 (*0-8167-1213-1*) Troll Communs.

— King Arthur. Hinkle, Don, ed. LC 87-15461. (Illus.). 48p. (J). (gr. 3-6). 1989. pap. 5.95 (*0-8167-1214-X*) Troll Communs.

— King Arthur & the Knights of the Round Table. Hanft, Joshua, ed. (Great Illustrated Classics Ser.: Vol. 31). (Illus.). 240p. (J). (gr. 3-6). 1993. 9.95 (*0-86611-982-5*) Playmore Inc.

— Men of Iron. (Airmont Classics Ser.). (Illus.). (J). (gr. 6 up). 1965. mass mkt. 3.95 (*0-8049-0093-0*, CL-93) Airmont.

— Men of Iron. 25.95 (*0-8488-1131-3*) Amereon Ltd.

— Men of Iron. 220p. (YA). 1993. pap. 6.49 (*0-89084-694-4*, 070466) Bob Jones Univ.

— Men of Iron. LC 89-33926. (Illustrated Classics Ser.). (Illus.). 48p. (J). (gr. 3-6). 1990. pap. 5.95 (*0-8167-1872-5*) Troll Communs.

Pyle, Howard. Men of Iron. (Illus.). (J). 1965. 9.30 (*0-606-17899-6*) Turtleback.

Pyle, Howard. The Merry Adventures of Robin Hood. (YA). 1986. mass mkt. 4.95 (*0-451-52284-2*, Sig Classics) NAL.

— The Merry Adventures of Robin Hood. (Illus.). (J). (gr. 4-8). 1990. 24.00 (*0-8446-2765-8*) Peter Smith.

— The Merry Adventures of Robin Hood. Vogel, Malvina, ed. (Great Illustrated Classics Ser.: Vol. 13). (Illus.). 240p. (J). (gr. 3-6). 1990. 9.95 (*0-86611-964-7*) Playmore Inc.

— The Merry Adventures of Robin Hood. (Illus.). 288p. (J). (gr. 6-9). 1977. 45.00 (*0-684-14838-2*) Scribner.

— The Merry Adventures of Robin Hood. Mattern, Joanne, ed. LC 92-12702. (Illustrated Classics Ser.). (Illus.). 48p. (J). (gr. 3-6). 1992. lib. bdg. 19.95 (*0-8167-2858-5*, BM210) Troll Communs.

— Merry Adventures of Robin Hood. 27.95 (*0-8488-0858-4*) Amereon Ltd.

— The Merry Adventures of Robin Hood. LC 68-55820. (Illus.). 296p. (J). (gr. 3-6). 1968. reprint ed. pap. 7.95 (*0-486-22043-5*) Dover.

Pyle, Howard. Merry Adventures of Robin Hood: Of Great Renown, in Nottinghamshire. (J). 1985. 10.05 (*0-606-01909-X*, Pub. by Turtleback) Demco.

Pyle, Howard. Otto of the Silver Hand. (Illus.). 173p. (J). (gr. 5-9). 1967. pap. 6.95 (*0-486-21784-1*) Dover.

Pyle, Howard. A Peninsular Canaan. 1996. 6.00 (*1-886706-08-5*) Hickory Hse.

Pyle, Howard. Robin Hood. abr. ed. (Illustrated Classics Ser.). (Illus.). 128p. (Orig.). (J). 1991. pap. 2.95 (*1-56156-028-6*) Kidsbks.

— Sixth Merry Adventure of Robin Hood. 1986. pap. 2.95 (*0-317-38208-X*, Sig Classics) NAL.

— The Story of King Arthur & His Knights. (Illus.). xviii, 313p. (YA). (gr. 7 up). 1996. pap. 8.95 (*0-486-21445-1*) Dover.

— The Story of King Arthur & His Knights. (Illus.). 1986. mass mkt. 5.95 (*0-451-52488-8*, Sig Classics) NAL.

— The Story of King Arthur & His Knights. (Signet Classics). (J). 1986. 10.60 (*0-606-01952-9*, Pub. by Turtleback) Demco.

— Story of King Arthur & His Knights. 25.95 (*0-89190-662-2*); lib. bdg. 25.95 (*0-8488-2107-6*) Amereon Ltd.

— Story of King Arthur & His Knights. (YA). (gr. 6-12). 1990. 23.00 (*0-8446-2766-6*) Peter Smith.

— The Story of King Arthur & His Knights. deluxe ed. (Illus.). (YA). (gr. 7 up). 1978. reprint ed. lib. bdg. 13.00 (*0-932106-01-3*, Pub. by Marathon Press) S J Durst.

— The Story of King Arthur & His Knights. LC 84-50167. (Illus.). 320p. (J). (gr. 5 up). 1984. reprint ed. 21.00 (*0-684-14814-5*) Scribner.

— The Story of Sir Lancelot & His Companions. (Illus.). 368p. 1991. pap. 9.95 (*0-486-26701-6*) Dover.

— The Story of the Champions of the Round Table. lib. bdg. 25.95 (*0-8488-2106-8*) Amereon Ltd.

— The Story of the Champions of the Round Table. (Illus.). 329p. (J). (ps-4). 1968. pap. 8.95 (*0-486-21883-X*) Dover.

— The Story of the Champions of the Round Table. LC 84-13881. (Illus.). 352p. (YA). (gr. 7 up). 1984. lib. bdg. 19.95 (*0-684-18171-1*) Scribner.

— Story of the Grail & the Passing of Arthur. 276p. Date not set. 23.95 (*0-8488-2660-4*) Amereon Ltd.

— The Story of the Grail & the Passing of Arthur. unabridged ed. LC 92-29058. (Illus.). 272p. (J). 1992. reprint ed. pap. text 8.95 (*0-486-27361-X*) Dover.

— Wonder Clock. (Illus.). (J). (gr. 5 up). 1990. 23.00 (*0-8446-2767-4*) Peter Smith.

— The Wonder Clock or, Four & Twenty Marvelous Tales, Being One for Each Hour of the Day. (Illus.). 319p. (J). (gr. 3-6). 1965. pap. 8.95 (*0-486-21446-X*) Dover.

— Young King Arthur. Date not set. 14.95 (*0-399-21723-1*) Putnam Pub Group.

Pyle, Howard, ed. The Buccaneers & Marooners of America. (Illus.). 420p. 1990. reprint ed. pap. 15.00 (*0-87380-173-3*) Popular E Commerce.

Pyle, Howard & Greene, Ellin. The Swan Maiden. LC 93-34605. (Illus.). 32p. (J). (gr. k-3). 1994. lib. bdg. 15.95 (*0-8234-1088-9*) Holiday.

Pyle, Howard & Wyeth, Nc & A/j. Wondrous & Strange: Special Edition. 1998. 14.00 (*0-8212-2570-7*, Pub. by Bulfinch Pr) Little.

Pyle, Howard, ed. see Delaware Art Museum Staff, et al.

Pyle, Hugh F. Truth about Tongues. LC 76-8730. 128p. 1976. write for info. (*0-916406-19-9*) Accent CO.

— The Truth About Tongues & the Charismatic Movement / LC 89-220422. 148p. 1989. write for info. (*0-87398-846-9*) Sword of Lord.

Pyle, Jack. Boost Your Credibility As a Leader. 24p. 1993. student ed. 7.00 (*1-882843-02-9*) Faceway Pub.

Pyle, Jack R. The Sound of Distant Thunder: An Appalachian Novel LC 98-73972. 228p. 1998. write for info. (*0-9663666-2-X*) AAcorn Bks.

Pyle, Jack R. & Reese, Taylor. Raising with the Moon: The Complete Guide to Gardening -- & Living -- by the Signs of the Moon. Jackson, Dot, ed. LC 93-70246. (Illus.). 147p. 1993. pap. 13.95 (*1-878086-18-9*, Pub. by Down Home NC) Blair.

Pyle, Jack R., jt. auth. see Reese, Taylor.

Pyle, Jean L. The State & Women in the Economy: Lessons from Sex Discrimination in the Republic of Ireland. LC 89-26160. (Series on Women & Work). 202p. (C). 1990. pap. text 21.95 (*0-7914-0380-7*) State U NY Pr.

Pyle, Jeanne. The Best in Tent Camping: Washington & Oregon. 3rd ed. 200p. 2000. pap. 13.95 (*0-89732-298-3*) Menasha Ridge.

Pyle, Jeanne L. The Best in Tent Camping, Washington & Oregon: A Guide for Campers Who Hate RVs, Concrete Slabs, & Loud Portable Radios. 2nd ed. LC 97-9556. 200p. 1996. pap. 13.95 (*0-89732-211-8*) Menasha Ridge.

Pyle, Joseph G. The Life of James J. Hill, Vol. 2. 1990. 14.50 (*0-8446-1369-X*) Peter Smith.

Pyle, Kenneth B. The Japanese Question: Power & Purpose in a New Era. 2nd ed. LC 96-18512. 200p. 1996. pap. 12.95 (*0-8447-3799-2*, AEI Pr) Am Enterprise.

— The Making of Modern Japan. 2nd ed. 240p. (C). 1995. pap. text 27.96 (*0-669-20020-4*) HM Trade Div.

— The New Generation in Meiji Japan: Problems of Cultural Identity, 1885-1895. LC 69-13183. viii, 240p. 1969. 29.50 (*0-8047-0697-2*) Stanford U Pr.

Pyle, Kenneth B., jt. ed. see Hellmann, Donald C.

Pyle, Leo, jt. ed. see Van Buren, Ariane.

Pyle, Linda M. Peaks, Palms & Picnics: Day Journeys in the Mountains & Deserts of Palm Springs. LC 99-61932. 365p. 1999. 25.00 (*0-7388-0362-6*); pap. 15.00 (*0-7388-0363-4*) Xlibris Corp.

Pyle, Michael A. Advanced Practice for the TOEFL. 2nd rev. ed. (Cliffs Test Preparation Ser.). 101p. (Orig.). (C). 1995. pap. text 24.95 incl. audio (*0-8220-2080-7*, Cliff) IDG Bks.

— Cliffs Advanced Practice for the Toefl 2nd ed. LC 95-238014. xi, 267 p. 1995. write for info. (*0-8220-2082-3*, Cliff) IDG Bks.

*__Pyle, Michael A.__ TOEFL Preparation Guide. 5th ed. (Cliffs Preparation Guides Ser.). 2000. pap. 24.99 (*0-7645-8609-2*) IDG Bks.

Pyle, Michael A. & Munoz, Mary E. TOEFL Preparation Guide with 2 Cassettes: Test of English As a Foreign Language. 5th rev. ed. (Cliffs Test Preparation Ser.). 101p. (C). 1995. pap. text 29.95 incl. audio (*0-8220-2079-3*, Cliff) IDG Bks.

*__Pyle, Paul, ed.__ I've Been Wondering... 160p. 1999. pap. write for info. (*0-9673835-0-1*) Dayton Christian.

Pyle, Paul, jt. auth. see Sligh, Mike.

Pyle, Paula A. Just Around the Corner. (Illus.). 112p. 1999. pap. 12.95 (*1-56664-151-9*) WorldComm.

Pyle, Peter. Flight-Feather Molt Patterns & Age in North American Owls. Able, Kenneth P., ed. LC 97-71955. (Monographs in Field Ornithology: Vol. 2). (Illus.). 32p. 1997. 9.95 (*1-878788-36-1*, 957) Amer Birding Assn.

Pyle, Peter, et al. Identification Guide to North American Passerines. LC 87-90700. (Illus.). 283p. (Orig.). 1987. pap. 19.50 (*0-9618940-0-8*) Slate Creek Pr.

Pyle, Ralph E. Persistence & Change in the Protestant Establishment. LC 96-10426. (Religion in the Age of Transformation Ser.). 176p. 1996. 57.95 (*0-275-95487-0*, Praeger Pubs) Greenwood.

Pyle, Ransford, jt. auth. see Hall, Daniel E.

Pyle, Ransford C. Family Law. LC 93-25985. (Paralegal Ser.). 482p. (C). 1993. mass mkt. 65.95 (*0-8273-5479-7*) Delmar.

— Family Law: Instructor's Guide. 83p. 1994. 12.75 (*0-8273-5480-0*) Delmar.

— Foundations of Law. 2nd ed. (C). 1996. text 39.95 (*0-8273-7976-5*) Delmar.

— Foundations of Law: Cases, Commentary & Ethics. 2nd ed. (Paralegal Ser.). 480p. (C). 1995. mass mkt. 74.95 (*0-8273-7194-2*) Delmar.

— Foundations of Law for Paralegals. 1992. text 42.95 (*0-8273-4572-0*) Delmar.

— Foundations of Law for Paralegals. 1992. pap., teacher ed. 12.50 (*0-8273-4573-9*) Delmar.

— Foundations of Law for Paralegals: Cases, Commentary, & Ethics. 2nd ed. (Paralegal Ser.). 32p. 1996. teacher ed. 15.00 (*0-8273-7195-0*) Delmar.

Pyle, Robert L. All That Remains: A West Virginia Archaeologists Discoveries. 2nd rev. ed. Wiley, Betty L., ed. (Illus.). 96p. 1998. pap. 19.95 (*0-9629050-0-3*) Arch Archives.

Pyle, Robert M. Handbook for Butterfly Watchers. (Illus.). 288p. 1992. pap. 14.00 (*0-395-61629-8*) HM.

— The Thunder Tree: Lessons from an Urban Wildland. LC 98-14030. 240p. 1998. pap. 14.95 (*1-55821-703-7*) Lyons Pr.

— Where Bigfoot Walks. (Illus.). 352p. 1997. pap. 13.00 (*0-395-85701-5*) HM.

Pyle, Robert M., jt. auth. see Audubon Society Staff.

Pyle, Robert M., ed. see Nabokov, Vladimir.

Pyle, Robert Michael. Chasing Monarchs: Migrating with the Butterflies of Passage. LC 99-12266. 288p. 1999. 24.00 (*0-395-82820-1*) HM.

*__Pyle, Robert Michael.__ Walking the High Ridge: Life As Field Trip. (Credo Ser.). 172p. 2000. pap. 12.00 (*1-57131-242-0*) Milkweed Ed.

— Walking the High Ridge: Life As Field Trip. deluxe ed. (Credo Ser.). 172p. 2000. 20.00 (*1-57131-243-9*) Milkweed Ed.

Pyle, Robert W., jt. auth. see Svenson, Henry K.

Pyle, S. Idell, jt. auth. see Greulich, William W.

Pyle, Sandra J. Mirth & Morality of Shakespeare's Holy Fools. LC 97-47267. (Studies in British Literature: Vol. 33). 284p. 1998. text 89.95 (*0-7734-8480-9*) E Mellen.

Pyle, Stephen J., jt. auth. see Newhof, Susan.

Pyle, Susan Newhof, see Newhof Pyle, Susan, ed.

Pyle, Theresa P. The Teacher's Dependency Load. LC 79-177172. (Columbia University. Teachers College. Contributions to Education Ser.: No. 782). reprint ed. 37.50 (*0-404-55782-1*) AMS Pr.

Pyle, Thomas H. Project Finance Training Manual. 1995. 295.00 (*1-85564-355-3*, Pub. by Euromoney) Am Educ Systs.

Pyle, Trussell, ed. see North, Max M., et al.

Pyle, Vera. Current Medical Terminology. 6th rev. ed. Pitman, Sally C., ed. LC 96-221591. 1996. pap. 37.00 (*0-934385-67-X*) Hlth Prof Inst.

Pyle, W. R., ed. Solar Hydrogen Chronicles. (Illus.). 118p. 1998. pap. 25.00 (*0-9663703-0-9*, CHRON-1) H-Ion.

Pyle, William E., jt. auth. see Larson, Kermit D.

Pyle, William T. & Seals, Mary A., eds. Experiencing Ministry Supervision. LC 94-6860. 168p. 1994. 17.99 (*0-8054-1163-1*, 4211-63) Broadman.

Pyle, William W. & Larson. Elementary Accounting No. II. 1979. pap. 12.00 (*0-256-02131-7*, Irwn McGrw-H) McGrw-H Hghr Educ.

Pyle, William W. & Zin, Michael. Initiation a la Comptabilite Financiere Administrative la Monographie. (C). 1975. 7.45 (*0-256-01766-2*, Irwn McGrw-H) McGrw-H Hghr Educ.

Pyle, William W., et al. Comptabilite Financiere Tome, Vol. 2. 528p. (C). 1988. per. 32.95 (*0-256-06629-9*, Irwn McGrw-H) McGrw-H Hghr Educ.

Pyler, Ernst J. Baking Science & Technology, 2 vols. (Illus.). 1988. 78.00 (*1-882005-02-3*); write for info. (*1-882005-00-7*); write for info. (*1-882005-01-5*) Sosland Pub.

Pyles, James C., jt. auth. see Cabin, William D.

Pyles, Marian S. Death & Dying in Children's & Young People's Literature: A Survey & Bibliography. LC 87-46386. 187p. 1988. lib. bdg. 28.50 (*0-89950-335-7*) McFarland & Co.

Pyles, Raymond A. & Shulman, Hyman L. United States Air Force Fighter Support in Operation Desert Storm. LC 95-33017. 126p. (Orig.). 1995. pap. text 13.00 (*0-8330-2291-1*, MR-468-AF) Rand Corp.

Pyles, Rebecca A., jt. auth. see Duellman, William E.

*__Pyles, Stephan.__ New Tastes from Texas. LC 99-23443. 1999. pap. 21.95 (*0-609-80497-9*) Crown Pub Group.

Pyles, Stephan. Southwestern Vegetarian. LC 99-45619. (Illus.). 240p. 2000. 30.00 (*0-609-60118-0*) C Potter.

Pyles, Stephan & Harisson, John. The New Texas Cuisine. LC 92-31496. 448p. 1993. 38.95 (*0-385-42336-5*) Doubleday.

Pyles, Stephen, jt. auth. see Miller, Mark.

Pyles, Thomas. Selected Essays on English Usage. Algeo, John, ed. LC 78-18833. 237p. 1983. reprint ed. pap. 73.50 (*0-7837-4904-X*, 204456900004) Bks Demand.

Pyles, Thomas & Algeo, John. The Origins & Development of the English Language. 3rd ed. 383p. (C). 1982. teacher ed. write for info. (*0-318-52971-8*) Harcourt Coll Pubs.

— The Origins & Development of the English Language. 4th ed. (Illus.). 425p. (C). 1992. text. write for info. (*0-318-68953-7*) Harcourt Coll Pubs.

— The Origins & Development of the English Language. 4th ed. 416p. (C). 1993. text 59.00 (*0-15-500168-X*, Pub. by Harcourt Coll Pubs) Harcourt.

Pylkkannen, P. & Havel, I., eds. Brain, Mind & Physics. LC 95-8175. (Frontiers in Artificial Intelligence & Applications Ser.: Vol. 33). 300p. (YA). (gr. 12). 1997. 110.00 (*90-5199-254-8*, 254-8) IOS Press.

Pylkko, Pauli. The Aconceptual Mind: Heideggerian Themes in Holistic Naturalism. LC 98-16141. (Advances in Consciousness Research Ser.: Vol. 11). xxvi, 297p. 1998. pap. 34.95 (*1-55619-191-X*) J Benjamins Pubng Co.

Pylyshyn, Zenon, jt. ed. see Lepore, Ernest.

Pylyshyn, Zenon W. Computation & Cognition: Toward A Foundation for Cognitive Science. 320p. (C). 1986. pap. text 17.50 (*0-262-66058-X*, Bradford Bks) MIT Pr.

— Constraining Cognitive Theories: Issues & Options. LC 96-32728. (Tutorial Monographs in Cognitive Science Ser.). 230p. 1998. pap. 39.50 (*1-56750-300-4*); text 73.25 (*1-56750-299-7*) Ablx Pub.

Pylyshyn, Zenon W., ed. Robot's Dilemma: The Frame Problem in Artificial Intelligence. LC 86-10801. (Theoretical Issues in Cognitive Science Ser.: Vol. 4). 156p. 1987. text 73.25 (*0-89391-371-5*) Ablx Pub.

Pylyshyn, Zenon W. & Demopoulos, William, eds. Meaning & Cognitive Structure: Issues in the Computational Theory of Mind. LC 86-10801. (Theoretical Issues in Cognitive Science Ser.: Vol. 3). 264p. (C). 1986. text 78.50 (*0-89391-372-3*) Ablx Pub.

Pylyshyn, Zenon W., ed. see Dennett, Daniel Clement, et al.

*__Pym, Barbara.__ Crampton Hodnet. LC 99-43636. 216p. 2000. pap. 12.95 (*1-55921-243-8*, Pub. by Moyer Bell) Publishers Group.

Pym, Barbara. Excellent Women. 1988. pap. 13.95 (*0-452-26730-7*, Plume) Dutton Plume.

*__Pym, Barbara.__ A Few Green Leaves. LC 98-37759. 250p. 1999. pap. 12.95 (*1-55921-228-4*) Moyer Bell.

Pym, Barbara. Jane & Prudence. LC 98-45061. 256p. 1999. pap. 12.95 (*1-55921-226-8*) Moyer Bell.

— Quartet in Autumn. 1992. pap. 12.95 (*0-452-26934-2*, Plume) Dutton Plume.

*__Pym, Barbara.__ Quartet in Autumn. LC 99-87259. 218p. 2000. pap. 11.95 (*1-55921-278-0*) Moyer Bell.

Pym, Barbara. Some Tame Gazelle. LC 98-28858. 252p. 1999. pap. 11.95 (*1-55921-264-0*) Moyer Bell.

— An Unsuitable Attachment. LC 98-53774. 256p. Date not set. pap. 12.95 (*1-55921-234-9*) Moyer Bell.

Pym, Dora & Silver, Nancy. Alive on Men's Lips. 150p. (C). 1982. pap. text 50.00 (*0-7855-5992-2*, Pub. by Old Vicarage) St Mut.

Pym, Francis, et al. Europe, America, & South Africa. Treverton, Gregory F., ed. 144p. (C). 1989. text 35.00 (*0-8147-8180-2*) NYU Pr.

Pym, Hilary & Wyatt, Honor. A La Pym: The Barbara Pym Cookery Book. (Illus.). 101p. 1995. 20.00 (*0-907325-61-0*, Pub. by Prospect) Food Words.

*__Pym, Jim.__ Listening to the Light: How to Bring Quaker Simplicity & Integrity into Our Lives. 192p. 2000. pap. 14.95 (*0-7126-7020-3*, Pub. by Rider) Trafalgar.

Pym, John. Film Guide. 6th ed. LC 98-130203. (Time Out Ser.). 1184p. 1998. pap. 22.95 (*0-14-026564-3*, Penguin Bks) Viking Penguin.

— Film on Four: A Survey, 1982-1991. (Illus.). 228p. (C). 1993. 42.00 (*0-85170-345-3*, Pub. by British Film Inst) Ind U Pr.

P

An Asterisk (*) at the beginning of an entry indicates that the title is appearing for the first time.

— Merchant Ivory's English Landscape: Rooms, Views, & Anglo-Saxon Attitudes. LC 94-32106. 132p. 1995. 35.00 (*0-8109-4275-5*, Pub. by Abrams) Time Warner.

— The Palm Beach Story. LC 98-215541. (Film Classics Ser.). (Illus.). 80p. 1998. pap. 10.95 (*0-85170-671-1*) Ind U Pr.

***Pym, John, ed.** Film. 8th ed. (Time Out Guide Ser.). 1248p. 1999. pap. 22.95 (*0-14-028365-X*) Viking Penguin.

Pyman, Avril. A History of Russian Symbolism. LC 93-30418. 499p. (C). 1994. text 85.00 (*0-521-24198-7*) Cambridge U Pr.

Pyman, Avril, ed. Bulgakov: The Heart of a Dog (Sobach'e Serdtse) (Bristol Russian Texts Ser.). (RUS.). 132p. 1994. pap. 18.95 (*1-85399-340-9*, Pub. by Brist Class Pr) Focus Pub-R Pullins.

Pyman, Kit. Embroidered Landscapes. 32p. 1989. pap. 8.95 (*0-85532-635-2*, 635-2, Pub. by Srch Pr) A Schwartz & Co.

Pyman, Kit. Every Kind of Smocking. (Illus.). pap. 16.95 (*0-85532-541-0*) Srch Pr.

Pyman, Kit, ed. Every Kind of Smocking. (Illus.). 126p. (YA). 1989. pap. 17.95 (*0-85532-632-8*, 632-8, Pub. by Srch Pr) A Schwartz & Co.

Pyman, Stephen J. Annotated Queensland Building Services Authority Act. 138p. 1993. pap. 39.00 (*0-455-21218-X*, Pub. by LawBk Co) Gaunt.

Pynchon, John. The Pynchon Papers, Vol. 1. Bridenbaugh, Carl, ed. LC 81-70057. (Publications of the Colonial Society of Massachusetts: No. 60-61). 378p. reprint ed. pap. 117.20 (*0-7837-3741-6*, 204342300001) Bks Demand.

— The Pynchon Papers, Vol. 2. Bridenbaugh, Carl, ed. LC 81-70057. (Publications of the Colonial Society of Massachusetts: No. 60-61). 539p. reprint ed. pap. 167.10 (*0-7837-3742-4*, 204342300002) Bks Demand.

Pynchon, Thomas. The Crying of Lot 49. (Perennial Classics Ser.). 160p. 1999. pap. 12.00 (*0-06-093167-1*) HarpC.

— The Crying of Lot 49. 1994. reprint ed. lib. bdg. 32.95 (*1-56849-320-7*) Buccaneer Bks.

— Gravity's Rainbow. 1984. mass mkt. 5.95 (*0-553-24684-4*) Bantam.

— Gravity's Rainbow. (Twentieth-Century Classics Ser.). 528p. 1995. pap. 16.95 (*0-14-018859-2*, Penguin Classics) Viking Penguin.

— Gravity's Rainbow 1973. 784p. 2000. pap. 18.95 (*0-14-028338-2*) Viking Penguin.

— Mason & Dixon. LC 97-6467. 773p. 1995. 27.50 (*0-8050-3758-6*) H Holt & Co.

— Mason & Dixon. 1998. write for info. (*0-8050-5850-8*, Owl) H Holt & Co.

— Slow Learner: Early Stories. 1998. pap. 13.95 (*0-316-19096-9*, Back Bay) Little.

— Slow Learner: Early Stories. LC 84-934. 208p. 1985. reprint ed. pap. 13.95 (*0-316-72443-2*) Little.

— V. 544p. 1999. pap. 14.00 (*0-06-093021-7*) HarpC.

— V. A Novel. 1994. reprint ed. lib. bdg. 49.95 (*1-56849-321-5*) Buccaneer Bks.

— Vineland. 400p. 1997. pap. 13.95 (*0-14-118063-3*) Viking Penguin.

Pynchon, William. The Diary of William Pynchon of Salem. Oliver, Fitch E., ed. LC 75-31131. reprint ed. 52.50 (*0-404-13608-7*) AMS Pr.

Pyne, Frederick W. A Bennett-Faville Genealogy. (Illus.). 128p. (Orig.). 1996. spiral bd. 36.00 (*0-614-13814-0*) F W Pyne.

— Descendants of the Signers of the Declaration of Independence Vol. 1: The New England States. LC 97-68964. 582p. 1997. 49.50 (*0-89725-297-7*, 1801) Picton Pr.

— Descendants of the Signers of the Declaration of Independence Vol. 2: New York State. LC 97-68964. (Illus.). 510p. 1998. 49.50 (*0-89725-339-6*, 1862) Picton Pr.

— Descendants of the Signers of the Declaration of Independence Vol. III: New Jersey. LC 97-68964. (Illus.). 800p. 1998. 59.50 (*0-89725-348-5*, 08/1998) Picton Pr.

— Descendants of the Signers of the Declaration of Independence Vol. 4: Pennsylvania. LC 97-68964. (Illus.). 480p. 1998. text 49.50 (*0-89725-363-9*, 1902) Picton Pr.

***Pyne, Frederick W.** Descendants of the Signers of the Declaration of Independence Vol. 5: Delaware & Maryland. 352p. 1999. 49.50 (*0-89725-379-5*) Picton Pr.

Pyne, Frederick W. The John Pyne Family in America Being the Comprehensive Genealogical Record of the Descendants of John Pyne (1766-1813) of Charleston, South Carolina. LC 92-71301. (Illus.). 224p. 1992. 20.00 (*0-9632539-0-5*) F W Pyne.

Pyne, Henry, tr. England & France in the Fifteenth Century. LC 78-63491. reprint ed. 27.50 (*0-404-17139-7*) AMS Pr.

Pyne, John X. Mind. 408p. 1998. reprint ed. pap. 29.95 (*0-7661-0463-X*) Kessinger Pub.

Pyne, Katherine, jt. auth. see Arnold, Lorna.

Pyne, Kathleen. Art & the Higher Life: Painting & Evolutionary Thought in Late Nineteenth-Century America. (Illus.). 432p. 1996. 50.00 (*0-292-76571-1*) U of Tex Pr.

Pyne, Lynette. Getting Ready for Grade 2. (Home Workbooks Ser.). (Illus.). 64p. (Orig.). (J). (gr. 2). 1996. pap., wbk. ed. 2.49 (*0-88724-361-4*, CD-6858) Carson-Dellos.

— Grade 2 Activities. (Home Workbooks Ser.). (Illus.). 64p. (Orig.). (J). (gr. 2). 1996. pap., wbk. ed. 2.49 (*0-88724-362-2*, CD-6859) Carson-Dellos.

— Numbers 0 to 10. (Basic Skills Ser.). (Illus.). 32p. (J). (gr. k-1). 1997. pap. text 4.95 (*0-88724-387-8*, CD-2122) Carson-Dellos.

Pyne, Lynette & Ruppard, Lynn. Seasonal Activities for 5 Year Olds. Gunzenhauser, Kelly, ed. (Learning for Little Ones Ser.). (Illus.). 64p. (J). (gr. k). 1998. pap. text 8.95 (*0-88724-472-6*, CD-0218) Carson-Dellos.

Pyne, Lynette, jt. auth. see Aemmer, Gail.

Pyne, Lynette, jt. auth. see Schwartz, Mary K.

Pyne, Lynette, ed. see Van Hise, Carol L.

Pyne, Patricia P. The Magic Chopsticks. large type ed. (Illus.). 24p. (J). (gr. 1-8). 1996. lib. bdg. 14.95 (*0-9655465-9-4*) Pelican Pub.

Pyne, R. David, et al. Aquifer Storage Recovery of Treated Drinking Water. LC 96-206548. (Illus.). 195p. 1996. pap. 125.00 (*0-89867-859-5*, 90689) Am Water Wks Assn.

Pyne, R. David, jt. ed. see Johnson, A. Ivan.

Pyne, R. David G. Groundwater Recharge & Wells: A Guide to Aquifer Storage Recovery. 400p. 1995. lib. bdg. 75.00 (*1-56670-097-3*, L1097) Lewis Pubs.

Pyne, Reginald H. Professional Discipline in Nursing, Midwifery, & Health Visiting: Including a Treatise on Professional Regulation. 3rd ed. LC 97-23059. 1997. pap. 34.95 (*0-632-04086-6*) Blackwell Sci.

***Pyne, Robert.** Humanity & Sin. Swindoll, Charles R., ed. LC 98-15089. (Swindoll Leadership Library). 1999. 24.99 (*0-8499-1372-1*) Word Pub.

Pyne, Robert A. Humanity & Sin. (Swindoll Christian Leadership Library). 1999. 19.97 (*0-8499-1570-8*) Word Pub.

Pyne, S. G. Diastereoselective Reactions of Sulfoximines, Vol. 12. (Sulfur Reports). 93p. 1992. pap. text 85.00 (*3-7186-5315-X*, Harwood Acad Pubs) Gordon & Breach.

Pyne, Sandra. Oxford Dictionary of Computing for Learners of English. 400p. 1996. pap. text 13.95 (*0-19-431441-3*) OUP.

Pyne, Stephen J. America's Fires: Management on Wildlands & Forests. LC 97-5304. (Issues Ser.). 1997. pap. 6.95 (*0-89030-053-4*) Forest Hist Soc.

— Burning Bush: A Fire History of Australia. (Illus.). 520p. 1995. pap. 15.95 (*0-8050-2101-9*, Owl) H Holt & Co.

— Burning Bush: A fire history of Australia. (Cycle of Fire). (Illus.). 552p. 1998. pap. 24.95 (*0-295-97677-2*) U of Wash Pr.

— Fire in America: A Cultural History of Wildland & Rural Fire. LC 96-49191. (Illus.). 680p. 1997. reprint ed. pap. 24.95 (*0-295-97592-X*) U of Wash Pr.

— Fire on the Rim: A Firefighter's Season at the Grand Canyon. LC 95-4726. 336p. (C). 1995. pap. 14.95 (*0-295-97483-4*) U of Wash Pr.

— Grove Karl Gilbert: A Great Engine of Research. LC 80-13881. (History of Science Ser.: No. 2). 312p. 1980. text 22.50 (*0-292-72719-4*) U of Tex Pr.

— How the Canyon Became Grand: A Short History. LC 98-20094. (Illus.). 208p. 1998. 24.95 (*0-670-88110-4*) Viking Penguin.

— How the Canyon Became Grand: A Short History. (Illus.). 224p. 1999. pap. 12.95 (*0-14-028056-1*) Viking Penguin.

— The Ice: A Journey to Antarctica. LC 97-45053. (Weyerhaeuser Environmental Classics Ser.). (Illus.). 456p. 1998. pap. 22.50 (*0-295-97678-0*) U of Wash Pr.

— The Ice: A Journey to Antarctica. LC 86-4362. (Illus.). 454p. reprint ed. pap. 140.80 (*0-7837-1624-9*, 204191700024) Bks Demand.

— Vestal Fire: An Environmental History, Told Through Fire, of Europe & Europe's Encounter with the World. LC 97-19032. (Weyerhaeuser Environmental Bks.). (Illus.). 672p. 1997. 45.00 (*0-295-97596-2*) U of Wash Pr.

***Pyne, Stephen J.** Vestal Fire: An Environmental History, Told Through Fire, of Europe & Europe's Encounter with the World. LC 97-19032. (Weyerhaeuser Environmental Book Ser.). (Illus.). 672p. 2000. pap. 24.95 (*0-295-97948-8*) U of Wash Pr.

Pyne, Stephen J. World Fire: The Culture of Fire. 1995. 30.00 (*0-8050-3247-9*) H Holt & Co.

— World Fire: The Culture of Fire on Earth. (Illus.). 408p. 1997. reprint ed. pap. 19.95 (*0-295-97593-8*) U of Wash Pr.

Pyne, Stephen J., et al. Introduction to Wildland Fire. 2nd ed. LC 95-44027. (Illus.). 808p. 1996. 150.00 (*0-471-54913-4*, Wiley-Interscience) Wiley.

Pyne-Timothy, Helen, ed. The Woman, the Writer & Caribbean Society. (CAAS Special Publications: Vol. 11). (Orig.). 1998. pap. text 22.95 (*0-934934-44-4*) CAAS Pubns.

Pyne, W. H. Rustic Vignettes. LC 77-80117. (Illus.). 120p. (Orig.). 1977. pap. 8.95 (*0-486-23547-5*) Dover.

Pyne, William H. Microcosm. LC 68-56512. (Illus.). 1972. reprint ed. 27.95 (*0-405-08872-8*, Pub. by Blom Pubns) Ayer.

Pyne, Zoe K. Giovanni Pierluigi da Palestrina: His Life & Times. 232p. 1990. reprint ed. lib. bdg. 69.00 (*0-7812-9078-3*) Rprt Serv.

— Giovanni Pierluigi da Palestrina, His Life & Times. LC 79-107828. (Select Bibliographies Reprint Ser.). 1977. 23.95 (*0-8369-5159-X*) Ayer.

Pynenburg, W. & De Tollenaere, F., eds. The Second International Round Table Conference on Historical Lexicography: Proceedings. viii, 353p. 1980. pap. 75.00 (*90-70176-21-1*) Mouton.

Pynes, Joan. Human Resources Management for Public & Nonprofit Organizations. LC 96-50184. (Jossey-Bass Nonprofit Sector Ser.). 1997. 34.95 (*0-7879-0808-8*) Jossey-Bass.

Pynes, Joan E. & Lafferty, Joan M. Local Government Labor Relations: A Guide for Public Administrators. LC 92-34943. 256p. 1993. 65.00 (*0-89930-783-3*, PLG, Quorum Bks) Greenwood.

Pynn. American Politics. 4th ed. 1993. teacher ed. 12.50 (*0-697-13982-4*, WCB McGr Hill) McGrw-H Hghr Educ.

— American Politics. 4th ed. 1993. teacher ed. 22.50 (*0-697-20020-5*, WCB McGr Hill) McGrw-H Hghr Educ.

***Pynn, Larry.** Last Stands: A Journey Through North America's Vanishing Ancient Rainforests. 224p. 2000. pap. 17.95 (*0-87071-027-3*) Oreg St U Pr.

Pynn, Roger & Riste, Tormod, eds. Time-Dependent Effects in Disordered Materials. LC 87-28562. (NATO ASI Series B, Physics: Vol. 167). (Illus.). 518p. 1988. 110.00 (*0-306-42782-6*, Plenum Trade) Perseus Pubng.

Pynn, Roger & Skjeltorp, Arne, eds. Scaling Phenomena in Disordered Systems. (NATO ASI Series B, Physics: Vol. 133). 592p. 1986. 120.00 (*0-306-42112-7*, Plenum Trade) Perseus Pubng.

Pynn, Ronald E. American Politics: Changing Expectations. 4th ed. 480p. (C). 1992. text. write for info. (*0-697-12893-8*) Brown & Benchmark.

Pynn, Ronald E. & Shank, Alan. American Politics. (C). 1993. student ed., ring bd. write for info. (*0-697-21028-6*) Brown & Benchmark.

Pynoos, Jon. Breaking the Rules: Bureaucracy & Reform in Public Housing. (Environment, Development, & Public Policy: Public Policy & Social Services Ser.). (Illus.). 236p. (C). 1986. 66.00 (*0-306-42302-2*, Plenum Trade) Perseus Pubng.

Pynoos, Jon & Cohen, Evelyn. Home Safety Guide for Older People: Check It Out Fix It Up. LC 90-60369. (Illus.). 70p. 1990. pap. text 13.95 (*0-914125-01-X*) Serif Pr.

Pynoos, Jon & Liebig, Phoebe S., eds. Housing Frail Elders: International Policies, Perspectives, & Prospects. LC 94-30037. (Illus.). 304p. 1995. text 42.50 (*0-8018-4980-2*) Johns Hopkins.

Pynoos, Jon, et al. Home Modification Resource Guide. 2nd ed. 66p. (C). 1996. pap. 12.00 (*1-881010-01-5*) USC Andrus Geron.

Pynoos, Jon, ed. see Regnier, Victor.

Pynoos, Robert S., jt. auth. see Eth, Spencer.

Pynsent, P. B., et al, eds. Outcome Measures in Trauma. LC 94-9397. (Illus.). 280p. 1994. text 95.00 (*0-7506-1653-9*) Buttrwrth-Heinemann.

Pynsent, P. B., ed. see Carr, A.

Pynsent, Robert B., ed. Literature of Nationalism: Essays on East European Identity. 256p. 1996. text 65.00 (*0-312-16008-9*) St Martin.

— T. G. Masaryk (1850-1937) Vol. 2: Thinker & Critic. 400p. 1989. text 55.00 (*0-312-02680-3*) St Martin.

Pynt, Jenny. Desk Exercises: How to Self Treat Your Pain, Improve Your Shape, & Prevent Chronic Problems. 120p. (Orig.). 1997. pap. 14.95 (*0-86417-804-2*, Pub. by Kangaroo Pr) Seven Hills Bk.

Pyong Gap Min, ed. Asian Americans: Contemporary Perspectives. (Focus Editions Ser.: Vol. 174). 304p. 1994. 59.95 (*0-8039-4335-0*); pap. 26.00 (*0-8039-4336-9*) Sage.

Pyorala, K., et al, eds. Changing Trends in Coronary Heart Disease: Journal: Cardiology, Vol. 72, Nos. 1 & 2. (Illus.). 104p. 1985. pap. 61.00 (*3-8055-4015-9*) S Karger.

Pyper, Andrew. Kiss Me. 136p. 1997. pap. 14.95 (*0-88984-181-0*) Porcup Quill.

***Pyper, Andrew.** Lost Girls. LC 99-47397. 390p. 2000. 23.95 (*0-385-33446-X*) Delacorte.

Pyper, C., jt. auth. see Freeman, M.

Pyper, Diane M. & Angione, Ronald, eds. Optical Astronomy from the Earth & Moon, No. 55. 320p. 1994. 34.00 (*0-937707-74-0*) Astron Soc Pacific.

Pyper, Hugh S. David as Reader: 2 Samuel 12: 1-15 & the Poetics of Fatherhood. LC 96-8398. (Biblical Interpretation Ser.: Vol. 23). xii, 238p. 1996. 87.50 (*90-04-10581-6*) Brill Academic Pubs.

Pyper, Hugh S., ed. The Christian Family: A Concept in Crisis. 146p. (Orig.). 1996. pap. 16.95 (*1-85311-124-4*, 6319, Pub. by Canterbury Press Norwich) Morehouse Pub.

***Pyper, Robert & Robins, L. J.** United Kingdom Governance. LC 99-56734. 2000. write for info. (*0-312-23187-3*) St Martin.

Pyper, Robert & Robins, Lynton, eds. Governing the U. K. in the 1990s. LC 94-43330. 293p. 1995. text 59.95 (*0-312-12552-6*) St Martin.

***Pyper-Smith, Diane.** A Guide to Astronomy. 3rd ed. 216p. (C). 1999. spiral bd. 33.95 (*0-7872-6212-9*, 41621201) Kendall-Hunt.

Pyper-Smith, Diane, jt. auth. see BSCS Staff.

***Pyper, T. R. & Stout, C. A. C.** Dictionary of Cybernyms: Abbreviations & Acronyms Used in Telecommunications, Electronics & Computer Science in English, French, Spanish & German with Some Italian, Portuguese, Swedish, Danish & Finnish. LC 00-37180. 2000. write for info. (*0-444-50478-8*) Elsevier.

Pyper, Terry. French Dictionary of Information Technology. (ENG & FRE.). 800p. 1987. 150.00 (*0-8288-0235-1*, F103160) Fr & Eur.

— French Dictionary of Information Technology. 590p. (C). 1989. 100.00 (*0-415-00244-3*, 07549) Routledge.

Pyrah, Barbara. History of the Yorkshire Museum. (C). 1989. pap. 30.00 (*1-85072-042-8*, Pub. by W Sessions) St Mut.

Pyrah, G. B. Imperial Policy & South Africa, 1902-1910. LC 74-9170. (Illus.). 272p. 1975. reprint ed. lib. bdg. 65.00 (*0-8371-7619-0*, PYIP, Greenwood Pr) Greenwood.

Pyramid Media Staff. Commercial Aircraft: Encyclopedia & Fleets. 1998. pap. 24.95 (*0-944188-50-8*) Pyramid Med Grp.

Pyramis, Alpha. A Dime for Every Minute of Your Time, That It Takes to Finish a Rhyme: And Other Funraising Poems. 30p. 1985. pap. 21.95 (*0-913597-75-9*) Prosperity & Profits.

— Herbal Teas & Their Rhyming Cures. rev. ed. 12p. (Orig.). (C). 1993. pap. text 19.95 (*0-913597-86-4*) Prosperity & Profits.

— Jean or Denim Garments: Recycling Poem Booklet. 4p. (Orig.). 1985. pap. 7.00 (*0-317-00913-3*) Prosperity & Profits.

— Real Estate Poetry to Duplicate & Use, Bk. 1. 20p. 1985. ring bd. 41.95 (*0-913597-82-1*) Prosperity & Profits.

— Recipe Ingredient Substitution Cookbook. 60p. 1992. ring bd. 19.95 (*0-913597-23-6*) Prosperity & Profits.

Pyrcioch, E. J., et al. Production of Pipeline Gas by Hydrogasification of Coal, 1954-1964. (Research Bulletin Ser.: No. 39). iv, 225p. 1972. pap. 50.00 (*1-58222-039-5*) Inst Gas Tech.

***Pyrczak, Fred.** Answer Key: Statistics with a Sense of Humor: A Humorous Workbook & Guide to Study Skills. rev. ed. (Illus.). 64p. (C). 1999. pap. text, wbk. ed. 6.50 (*1-884585-20-5*) Pyrczak Pub.

Pyrczak, Fred. Evaluating Research in Academic Journals: A Practical Guide to Realistic Education. 114p. (C). 1999. pap. text 21.95 (*1-884585-19-1*) Pyrczak Pub.

— Making Sense of Statistics: A Conceptual Overview. 128p. (C). 1995. pap. text 19.95 (*1-884585-00-0*) Pyrczak Pub.

— Research Applications Workbook. 1983. pap. text 15.75 (*0-912736-28-3*) EDITS Pubs.

***Pyrczak, Fred.** Statistics with a Sense of Humor: A Humorous Workbook & Guide to Study Skills. 2nd rev. ed. (Illus.). 136p. (C). 1999. pap. text 19.95 (*1-884585-10-8*) Pyrczak Pub.

***Pyrczak, Fred, ed.** Completing Your Thesis or Dissertation: Professors Share Their Techniques & Strategies. 105p. 2000. pap. text 20.95 (*1-884585-21-3*) Pyrczak Pub.

***Pyrczak, Fred & Bruce, Randall R.** Writing Empirical Research Reports: A Basic Guide for Students of the Social & Behavioral Sciences. 3rd rev. ed. (Illus.). 120p. (C). 1999. pap. text 19.95 (*1-884585-24-8*) Pyrczak Pub.

Pyrczck, Fred. Success at Statistics: A Worktext with Humor. (Illus.). 400p. (Orig.). 1995. pap. text 44.95 (*0-9623744-9-0*) Pyrczak Pub.

Pyre, J. F., jt. ed. see Campbell, Oscar J.

Pyre, James F. The Formation of Tennyson's Style, a Study. (BCL1-PR English Literature Ser.). 252p. 1992. reprint ed. lib. bdg. 79.00 (*0-7812-7698-5*) Rprt Serv.

***Pyrhienen, Heta.** Mayhem & Murder: Narrative & Moral Issues in the Detective Story. 1999. pap. text 21.95 (*0-8020-8267-X*) U of Toronto Pr.

Pyrhonen, Heta. Murder from an Academic Angle: An Introduction to the Study of the Detective Narrative. (COMLIT Ser.). x, 134p. 1994. 60.00 (*1-879751-81-X*) Camden Hse.

Pyritz, Hans, jt. auth. see Deutschen Akademie der Wissenschaften Staff.

Pyrnelle, Louise C. Miss Li'l' Tweetty. LC 72-4705. (Black Heritage Library Collection). 1977. reprint ed. 28.95 (*0-8369-9122-2*) Ayer.

Pyrnelle, Louise-Clarke. Diddie, Dumps & Tot. (Illus.). 240p. (J). (gr. 4-8). 1963. 15.95 (*0-911116-17-6*) Pelican.

Pyroasopoulos, M., ed. see Zurukzoglu, W., et al.

Pyrom, Jay. A Complete Introduction to Frogs & Toads. (Complete Introduction to...Ser.). (Illus.). 128p. (Orig.). 1987. pap. 8.95 (*0-86622-395-9*, CO-041S) TFH Pubns.

Pyron, C. Lee. How to Manage Data with Entity Codes & Data Dictionaries: The Keys to Quality Information Resources & Quality Business Processes. LC 94-92106. (Illus.). 216p. 1994. pap. 45.00 (*0-9641642-1-3*) Pyron Ent.

Pyron, Cherry, ed. see Browning, Bonnie K. & Miller, Phyllis D.

Pyron, Cherry, ed. see Campbell, Patricia B. & Ayars, Mimi.

Pyron, Cherry, jt. ed. see Silitch, Clarissa M.

***Pyron, Darden Asbury.** Liberace: An American Boy. LC 99-89031. (Illus.). 482p. 2000. 27.50 (*0-226-68667-1*) U Ch Pr.

***Pyron, Tim.** Sams Teach Yourself Microsoft Project 2000 in 24 Hours. (Teach Yourself... in 24 Hours Ser.). (Illus.). 592p. 2000. pap. 24.99 (*0-672-31814-8*) Sams.

Pyron, Tim. Sams Teach Yourself Microsoft Project 98 in 24 Hours. LC 98-84400. (Teach Yourself Ser.). 464p. 1998. pap. text 19.99 (*0-672-31258-1*) Sams.

— Using Microsoft Project for Windows. (Illus.). 664p. (Orig.). 1993. 29.95 (*1-56529-151-4*) Que.

— Using Microsoft Project for Windows 95: Special Edition. (Illus.). 742p. 1995. 34.99 (*0-7897-0540-0*) Que.

— Using Microsoft Project 4 for Windows. 780p. 1994. 29.99 (*1-56529-594-3*) Que.

— Using Microsoft Project 98: Special Edition. LC 97-68695. (Illus.). 1032p. 1997. pap. 39.99 (*0-7897-1252-0*) Que.

***Pyron, Tim.** Using Microsoft Project 2000. (Special Edition Using... Que Ser.). (Illus.). 1000p. 2000. pap. 39.99 (*0-7897-2253-4*) Que.

Pyron, Tim. Using Microsoft Project X. 400p. 1997. 24.99 (*0-7897-1258-X*) Que.

Pyros, John. Mike Gold: Dean of Am. Proletarian Literature. 218p. (Orig.). 1980. pap. 3.00 (*0-9604000-0-1*) Dramatika.

Pyrse, Majorie & Spillers, Hortense J. Conjuring: Black Women, Fiction, & Literary Tradition. LC 84-43171. (Everywoman: Studies in History Literature & Culture). (ENG & EWE., Illus.). 274 pgsp. 1985. 29.95 (*0-253-31407-0*) Ind U Pr.

— Conjuring: Black Women, Fiction, & Literary Tradition. LC 84-43171. (Everywoman: Studies in History Literature & Culture). (Illus.). 274p. 1985. pap. text 6.50 (*0-253-20360-0*, MB-360) Ind U Pr.

Pyrus, Victoria, jt. auth. see Robinson, Rachael.

Pyrz, R., ed. see IUTAM Symposium on Microstructure-Property Interac.

P

Pysek, P., et al, eds. Plant Invasions: General Aspects & Special Problems. (Illus.). xi, 263p. 1995. pap. 59.95 (*90-5103-097-5*, Pub. by SPB Acad Pub) Balogh.

***Pyshkin, Alex.** Super Nezh, Chess Assassin. 1999. pap. 20.00 (*0-938650-91-2*) Thinkers Pr.

***Pyskir, Maria Savchyn.** Thousands of Roads: A Memoir of a Young Woman's Life in the Ukrainian Underground During & After World War II. Savage, Ania, tr. (Illus.). 232p. 2000. per. 29.95 (*0-7864-0764-6*) McFarland & Co.

Pysz, Stephen. Team Earth: Advanced ABC Environmental Coloring Book, No. 1. (Illus.). 56p. (J). (gr. k-1). 1991. pap. text 2.95 (*0-9630186-7-1*) Team Earth.

— Team Earth: Show You Care, No. 2. Patton, Sarah, ed. (Illus.). 32p. (J). (gr. 2-5). 1992. pap. text, student ed. 2.95 (*0-9630186-1-2*) Team Earth.

Pyszczynski, T. & Greenberg, J. Hanging on & Letting Go: Understanding the Onset, Progression & Remission of Depression. (Illus.). 225p. 1992. 128.00 (*0-387-97756-2*) Spr-Verlag.

Pyszka, Gloria L., jt. auth. see Merritt, Richard L.

Pytches, David. Child No More. pap. text 6.95 (*0-340-72229-0*, Pub. by Hodder & Stought Ltd) Trafalgar.

Pytches, David. Spiritual Gifts in the Local Church. LC 87-15128. 288p. (Orig.). 1987. pap. 10.99 (*0-87123-984-1*) Bethany Hse.

Pytel. Engineering Mechanics Statics. 2nd ed. (C). 1998. pap. text, teacher ed. write for info. (*0-673-97797-8*) Addison-Wesley.

— Strength of Materials: Solutions Manual. 5th ed. (C). 1996. pap. text, teacher ed. write for info. (*0-673-55580-1*) Addison-Wesley.

Pytel, Andrew. Engineering Mechanics: Dynamics. 2nd ed. (C). 1998. text. write for info. (*0-673-98236-X*) Addison-Wesley.

— Engineering Mechanics: Dynamics & Statics. 2nd ed. (C). 1998. text. write for info. (*0-673-98414-1*) Addison-Wesley.

— Engineering Mechanics: Statics. 2nd ed. (C). 1998. text. write for info. (*0-673-98412-5*) Addison-Wesley.

Pytel, Andrew & Kiulsalaas, Jaan. Engineering Mechanics: Statics & Dynamics SI. (Illus.). 1184p. (C). 1996. text 85.00 (*0-673-99872-X*) Addson-Wesley Educ.

— S/M ENG MECH V2 DYNAM SI. (Illus.). 656p. (C). 1996. pap. text, student ed. 9.00 (*0-673-97246-1*) Addson-Wesley Educ.

Pytel, Andrew & Kiusalaas, Jaan. Engineering Mechanics. 2nd ed. LC 98-37233. 1998. 71.95 (*0-534-95742-0*) Brooks-Cole.

— Engineering Mechanics: Statics. 2nd ed. LC 98-53174. 526p. 1999. 71.95 (*0-534-95741-2*) Brooks-Cole.

Pytel, Andrew & Kiusalaas, Jean. Engineering Mechanics: Dynamics. teacher ed. write for info. (*0-06-501951-2*) HarpC.

— Engineering Mechanics: Dynamics: Solutions Manual. write for info. (*0-06-501952-0*) HarpC.

— Engineering Mechanics: Statics. teacher ed. write for info. (*0-06-501948-2*) HarpC.

— Engineering Mechanics: Statics: Solutions Manuals. write for info. (*0-06-502114-2*) HarpC.

***Pytel, Barbara.** How to Send Your Child to the Right College & Save Thousands: Reveals Secrets Every Parent Should Know about Preparing a Child for College. 86p. 1998. pap. 19.95 (*0-9663840-0-8*) Coll Guidance Servs.

Pythagoras. The Irreconcilable Gnomes: or Continuation to the Comte de Gabalis: Also a Sketch of the Justly Famous Books Known As the Key of Solomon the King & the Grand Grimore. 50p. 1996. reprint ed. pap. 12.00 (*1-56459-588-9*) Kessinger Pub.

Pythagoras & Hierocles. The Golden Verses of Pythagoras. Rowe, N., tr. from GRE. (Sacred Texts Ser.). 93p. (C). 1983. pap. 12.75 (*0-88695-009-0*) Concord Grove.

Python, Monty. Monty Python & the Holy Grail. 1977. pap. 9.95 (*0-458-92970-0*) NAL.

— Monty Python & the Holy Grail. 1977. pap. 17.95 (*0-416-00341-9*) Routledge.

— Monty Python's Flying Circus, Vol. 1. 1989. pap. 15.00 (*0-679-72647-0*) Fodors Travel.

— Monty Python's Flying Circus, Vol. 2. 1989. pap. 16.00 (*0-679-72648-9*) Fodors Travel.

***Pytlak, R.** Numerical Methods for Optimal Control Problems with State Constraints. LC 99-16712. (Lecture Notes in Mathematics Ser.: Vol. 1707). (Illus.). xv, 215p. 1999. pap. 41.00 (*3-540-66214-6*) Spr-Verlag.

***Pytlik, Brenda.** Quilting Workshops. 32p. 2000. pap. 14.95 (*1-885588-32-1*) Chitra Pubns.

Pytlik, Edward C., et al. Technology, Change & Society. 2nd rev. ed. DeVore, Paul, ed. LC 85-72427. (Illus.). 312p. 1985. pap. 21.28 (*0-87192-170-7*) Thomson Learn.

Pytowska, Zofia. The Threshold. 176p. 1982. 18.95 (*0-87073-518-7*); pap. 14.95 (*0-87073-519-5*) Schenkman Bks Inc.

Pywell, Geoff. Staging Real Things: The Performance of Ordinary Events. LC 93-44701. 1994. 32.50 (*0-8387-5274-8*) Bucknell U Pr.

Pywell, Sharon L. Writing That Works. LC 93-9288. (Business Skills Express Ser.). 96p. 1993. text 10.95 (*1-55623-856-8*, Irwn Prfssnl) McGraw-Hill Prof.

Pyx, Martin. Autumn Scandals. (Victorian Era Ser.). 1989. mass mkt. 4.95 (*0-929654-40-4*, 58) Blue Moon Bks.

— Birch Fever. (Orig.). 1994. mass mkt. 5.95 (*1-56201-055-7*) Blue Moon Bks.

— Spring Fevers. 1992. mass mkt. 5.95 (*1-56201-027-1*, 124) Blue Moon Bks.

— Summer Frolics. (Orig.). 1989. mass mkt. 4.50 (*0-929654-14-5*, 52) Blue Moon Bks.

Pyxis Creative Services Staff. Automated Medication Management: Criteria for Evaluating a System. 66p. 1995. pap. text 25.00 (*1-886954-00-3*) Pyxis Pr.

Pyykko, P. Relativistic Theory of Atoms & Molecules. (Lecture Notes in Chemistry Ser.: Vol. 41). ix, 389p. 1986. 62.95 (*0-387-17167-3*) Spr-Verlag.

— Relativistic Theory of Atoms & Molecules 2: A Bibliography, 1986-1992. LC 93-31082. (Lecture Notes in Chemistry Ser.: Vol. 60). 1993. 115.95 (*0-387-57219-8*) Spr-Verlag.

Pyzalski, Leo. The Holy Will of God: Source of Peace & Happiness. LC 90-71554. 163p. 1994. reprint ed. pap. 6.00 (*0-89555-411-9*) TAN Bks Pubs.

Pyzdek, Thomas. CQE Exam Study Guide. 1991. 39.95 (*0-930011-01-5*) Quality Am.

— Pyzdek's Guide to SPC Vol. 1: Fundamentals. (Pyzdek's Guide to SPC Ser.). (Illus.). 154p. (Orig.). 1989. pap. 29.95 (*0-930011-03-1*, H0595) ASQ Qual Pr.

— Pyzdek's Guide to SPC Vol. 1: Fundamentals. (Pyzdek's Guide to SPC Ser.). (Illus.). 88p. (Orig.). 1989. student ed. 14.35 (*0-930011-06-6*) Quality Am.

— Pyzdeks Guide to SPC Vol. II: Applications & Special Topics. (Illus.). 250p. (C). 1991. pap. 34.75 (*0-930011-04-X*) Quality Am.

***Pyzdek, Thomas.** Quality Engineering Handbook. LC 99-52010. (Quality & Reliability Ser.). 1999. write for info. (*0-8247-0365-0*) Dekker.

Pyzdek, Thomas. An SPC Primer: Programmed Introduction to Statistical Process Control Techniques. Orig. Title: Applied Industrial Statistics. 55p. (Orig.). 1984. pap. 19.95 (*0-930011-00-7*, H0657) ASQ Qual Pr.

— WEESKA Quality Control. (What Every Engineer Should Know Ser.: Vol. 26). (Illus.). 272p. 1988. text 65.00 (*0-8247-7966-5*) Dekker.

— What Every Manager Should Know about Quality. (Illus.). 232p. 1990. text 79.75 (*0-8247-8401-4*) Dekker.

Pyzdek, Thomas & Berger, Roger W., eds. Quality Engineering Handbook. (Quality & Reliability Ser.: Vol. 29). (Illus.). 640p. 1991. text 99.75 (*0-8247-8132-5*, H0603) Dekker.

Pyzoha, David S. Implementing a Stormwater Management Program: Practical Guide. 192p. 1993. lib. bdg. 85.00 (*0-87371-470-9*, L470) Lewis Pubs.

Q

Q-Petersen, Ruby. Holiday Journey: Walking on Rainbows. large type ed. LC 97-91888. (Illus.). vii, 97p. (Orig.). 1997. pap. 11.95 (*0-9645451-8-7*) F Swann Pubns.

***Qa, Laura.** The Crown of Affinity. 36p. 2000. pap. 5.00 (*1-891387-04-9*, Pub. by Red Dragon VA) Qa Ent.

Qa, Laura. Tribute to the Hound. LC 95-92588. 64p. (Orig.). 1995. pap. 11.95 (*0-9637704-2-X*) Red Dragon VA.

— The Voice of the Image. LC 92-61605. 64p. (Orig.). 1992. pap. 10.95 (*0-9633497-0-8*) Red Dragon VA.

Qabbani, Nizar. On Entering the Sea: The Erotic & Other Poetry of Nizar Qabbani. Jayyusi, Lena et al, trs. from ARA. 208p. 1996. 22.95 (*1-56656-186-8*) Interlink Pub.

— On Entering the Sea: The Erotic & Other Poetry of Nizar Qabbani. Jayyusi, Lena et al, trs. from ARA. 184p. 1996. pap. 15.00 (*1-56656-193-0*) Interlink Pub.

Qaboos University Staff. Dictionary of Arab Names: Arabic-Arabic, 2 vols., set. (ARA & ENG.). 1990p. 1991. 75.00 (*0-86685-503-3*, LDL5033, Pub. by Librairie du Liban) Intl Bk Ctr.

***Qadar, Sohaid.** Pakistan's Upstream Petroleum Laws & Related Legislation. 211p. 2000. pap. 210.00 (*0-89069-012-X*) Barrows Co.

Qaddafi, Muammar. Escape to Hell & Other Stories. LC 98-161552. 193p. 1998. 19.95 (*2-7604-0613-X*) Stanke.

Qaddumi, Ghada H. Book of Gifts & Rarities. (Middle Eastern Monographs: No. 29). (Illus.). 535p. (Orig.). 1996. pap. 29.95 (*0-932885-13-6*) Harvard CMES.

Qadeer, Mohammad A. Urbanization in the Third World: A Case Study of Lahore, Pakistan. LC 82-15117. 300p. 1983. 69.50 (*0-275-91061-X*, C1061, Praeger Pubs) Greenwood.

Qaderi, M. Taleem-Ul-Islam, 4. (J). 1996. pap. 7.50 (*0-933511-72-8*) Kazi Pubns.

Qadesh La Yahweh Press Editorial Staff, ed. see Clover, Richard.

Qadesh La Yahweh Press Editors, ed. see Clover, R.

***Qadi, Siddiga & Khan, Fareeha, eds.** Hearts Have Changed. Siddigui, Abu Sayeed, tr. from URD. (Stories of the Sahabah Ser.: Vol. 4). 200p. (YA). (gr. 6-8). 2000. pap. text 10.00 (*1-56316-453-1*) Iqra Intl Ed Fdtn.

— Torchbearers of Islam. Siddigui, Abu Sayeed, tr. from URD. (Stories of the Sahabah Ser.: Vol. 5). 200p. (YA). (gr. 6-8). 2000. pap. text 10.00 (*1-56316-454-X*) Iqra Intl Ed Fdtn.

Qadi, Siddiga, ed. see Halman, Hugh Talat.

Qadi, Siddiga, ed. see Yamani, Mohammed Abdu.

Qadir, Asghar. Experimental Gravitation: Proceedings of the International Symposium on Experimental Gravitation, June 26-July 2, 1993, Nathigali, Pakistan. Karim, M., ed. (Illus.). 382p. 1994. 200.00 (*0-7503-0303-4*) IOP Pub.

— Relativity: An Introduction to the Special Theory. 140p. 1989. text 36.00 (*9971-5-0612-2*) World Scientific Pub.

Qadir, Asghar, jt. auth. see Hussain, F.

Qadir, Shahid, jt. ed. see Gills, Barry.

Qadri, A. A. Commentaries on Dissolution of Muslim Marriage Act. 137p. 1961. 40.00 (*0-7855-1351-5*) St Mut.

Qadri, A. Jamil. Intra-Societal Tension & National Integration: Psychological Assessment. 212p. (C). 1988. 27.00 (*81-7022-042-4*, Pub. by Concept) S Asia.

Qadri, Anwar A. Justice in Historical Islam. 144p. 1992. 15.95 (*1-56744-449-0*) Kazi Pubns.

Qadri, Maulana. Translation of the Meanings of Hadith from Muslim & Bukhari (Lu'Lu wa Maarjan), Vols. I & II. 562p. 1985. 69.00 (*1-56744-405-9*) Kazi Pubns.

Qafisheh, Hamdi A. Advanced Gulf Arabic. 356p. 1997. 35.00 (*0-86685-676-5*) Intl Bk Ctr.

Qafisheh, Hamdi A. Arabic Yemeni Reference Grammar. LC 91-77058. 308p. 1992. 65.00 (*0-931745-83-7*) Dunwoody Pr.

— A Basic Course in Gulf Arabic. (ARA.). 482p. 25.00 (*0-86685-048-1*, LDL0481, Pub. by Librairie du Liban) Intl Bk Ctr.

— A Basic Course in Gulf Arabic. 482p. 1975. pap. 25.95 (*0-8165-0483-0*) U of Ariz Pr.

— Gulf Arabic: A Glossary Of. (ARA & ENG.). 1996. 29.95 (*0-86685-670-6*, Pub. by Librairie du Liban) Intl Bk Ctr.

— Gulf Arabic: Intermediate Level. LC 79-18305. 314p. 1979. pap. 97.40 (*0-608-05623-5*, 206607900006) Bks Demand.

— NTC's Gulf Arabic - English Dictionary: A Compact Dictionary of the Contemporary Arabic of the Mideast. (ARA & ENG., Illus.). 672p. 1997. 34.95 (*0-8442-4606-9*, 46069, Natl Textbk Co) NTC Contemp Pub Co.

— NTC's Gulf Arabic-English Dictionary: A Compact Dictionary of the Contemporary Arabic of the Mideast. (ARA & ENG.). 672p. 1999. pap. 27.95 (*0-8442-0299-1*, 02991) NTC Contemp Pub Co.

— NTC's Yemeni Arabic-English Dictionary. 672p. 1999. 34.95 (*0-8442-2597-5*) NTC Contemp Pub Co.

— Yemeni Arabic, Bk. 1. (ARA.). 482p. 1993. 24.95 (*0-86685-665-X*, LDL665X, Pub. by Librairie du Liban) Intl Bk Ctr.

— Yemeni Arabic, Bk. 2. (ARA.). 482p. 24.95 (*0-86685-557-2*, LDL5572, Pub. by Librairie du Liban) Intl Bk Ctr.

Qahl, Bernt. Macromedia Director 5.0 Revealed. 1996. pap. text 50.00 (*1-56830-284-3*) Hayden.

***Qaim, Matin.** Possessing the Impact of Banana Biotechnology in Kenya. (ISAAA Briefs Ser.: Vol. 10). (Illus.). viii, 38p. 1999. pap. 25.00 (*1-892456-12-5*) Agri-Biotech.

Qaim, S. M., ed. Nuclear Data for Science & Technology: Proceedings of an International Conference Held at the Forschungszentrum Julich, FRG, 13-17 May 1991. (Research Reports in Physics). 1100p. 1992. 198.00 (*0-387-55100-X*) Spr-Verlag.

Qaisar, Ahsan J. Building Construction in Mughal India: The Evidence from Painting. (Illus.). 100p. 1989. 35.00 (*0-19-562260-X*) OUP.

Qaisar, Ahsan J. & Verma, Som P., eds. Art & Culture: Endeavours in Interpretation. (C). 1996. 110.00 (*81-7017-315-9*, Pub. by Abhinav) S Asia.

Qaiser, Ahsan J. The Indian Response to European Technology & Culture (A. D. 1498-1707) (Illus.). 242p. 1998. reprint ed. pap. text 26.00 (*0-19-564555-3*) OUP.

Qamar, J. God's Existence & Contemporary Science. 1990. pap. 3.00 (*1-56744-026-6*) Kazi Pubns.

Qamus, Madd A., jt. auth. see Lane, Edward W.

Qarabaghi, Mirza J. A History of Qarabagh: An Annotated Translation of Mirza Jamal Javanshir Qarabaghi's Tarikh-e Qarabagh. Bournoutian, George A., ed. & tr. by. from PER. 206p. (C). 1993. lib. bdg. 24.95 (*1-56859-011-3*) Mazda Pubs.

Qaradawi, Yousaf A. The Lawful & the Prohibited in Islam. 1982. pap. 15.95 (*1-56744-118-1*) Kazi Pubns.

Qaradawi, Yusuf A. Islamic Awakening Between Rejection & Extremism. 1990. pap. 12.95 (*1-56744-090-8*) Kazi Pubns.

— Kayfa Nata'amalu ma'a al Sunnah al Nabawiyah Ma'alim wa Dawabit: Ma'alim wa Dawabit - Outlines & Rules. 3rd ed. (ARA.). 187p. 1991. pap. 7.50 (*0-912463-50-3*) IIIT VA.

Qara'i, Ali Q., tr. see Mughniyyah, Allamah M.

Qara'i, Ali Q., tr. see Mutahhari, Murtaza.

***Qarardewei, Yeusuf.** Fiqh Al Zakah. LC 99-37273. (Islamic Law & Jurisprudence Ser.). 1999. write for info. (*1-56564-270-8*) IIIT VA.

Qasim, Abd A. Rites of Assent: Two Novellas. Theroux, Peter, tr. from EGY. (Border Lines Ser.). 160p. (C). 1995. pap. text 18.95 (*1-56639-354-X*); lib. bdg. 69.95 (*1-56639-353-1*) Temple U Pr.

Qasim, Mir. My Life & Times. (C). 1992. 24.00 (*81-7023-355-0*, Pub. by Allied Pubs) S Asia.

Qasim, Sayed R. & Chiang, W. Walter. Sanitary Landfill Leachate: Generation, Control & Treatment. LC 94-60645. 335p. 1994. pap. 69.95 (*1-56676-129-8*) Technomic.

Qasim, Syed R. Wastewater Treatment Plants: Planning, Design, & Operation. 2nd ed. LC 98-86864. 1140p. 1998. text 149.95 (*1-56676-688-5*) Technomic.

Qasim, Syed R. & Motley, Edward M. Water Works Engineering: Planning, Design & Operations. LC 00-24966. 862p. (C). 2000. 90.00 (*0-13-150211-5*, Macmillan Coll) P-H.

***Qasim, Syed Zahoor.** The Indian Ocean: Images & Realities. 356p. (C). 1999. text 49.50 (*81-204-1380-6*, Pub. by Oxford & IBH Pubng) Enfield Pubs NH.

***Qasimi, Ahmad Nadeem.** The Old Banyan & Other Stories. Memon, Muhammad Umar, ed. Hasan, Faruq, tr. (Pakistan Writers Ser.). 260p. 2000. pap. 9.95 (*0-19-579328-5*) OUP.

Qaukhchishvili, S. The Georgian Chronicle: The Period of Georgi Lasha. Vivian, Katharine, tr. from GEO. xlvii, 198p. 1991. pap. 58.00 (*90-256-0965-1*, Pub. by AM Hakkert) BookLink Distributors.

Qayoumi, Mohammad. Electrical Systems: A Guide for Facility Managers. 250p. 1996. 75.00 (*1-57730-250-8*) UpWord Publng.

Qayoumi, Mohammad H. Electrical Distribution & Maintenance. 272p. 1989. pap. 35.00 (*0-913359-49-1*) APPA VA.

***Qayoumi, Mohammad H.** Electrical Systems: A Guide for Facility Managers 2nd ed. LC 99-35850. 2000. write for info. (*0-88173-324-5*) Fairmont Pr.

Qayyim al-Jawziyya, Ibn. Book of the Spirit. 500p. (C). 1997. pap. 59.95 (*1-871031-66-4*) Kazi Pubns.

Qayyim, Ibn. Handbook of Islamic Prayers. Hamidi, Khalil, ed. Ali, Abid A., tr. 1998. pap. 4.50 (*1-56744-541-1*) Kazi Pubns.

Qayyum, Abdul. On Striving to Be a Muslim. 1992. pap. 14.50 (*0-935782-10-9*) Kazi Pubns.

Qayyum, Abdul, tr. see Al-Ghazali, Muhammad.

Qayyum, Madeenah A. Ramblings from the Heart & Soul of Me, Madeenah. 51p. 1995. pap. 9.98 (*1-888139-06-4*) Y Morris Carib.

***Qazi.** Geography of India: With Special Reference to J&K State. 2000. 39.50 (*81-7648-146-7*, Pub. by BR Pub) S Asia.

***Qazi, Javaid.** Unlikely Stories: Fatal Fantasies & Delusions. LC 99-178404. 156p. 1998. 14.95 (*0-19-577896-0*) OUP.

Qazi, M. A. ABC Islamic Reader. (J). 1982. pap. 3.75 (*0-935782-07-9*) Kazi Pubns.

— Arabic Alphabet Coloring Book. 32p. (J). (ps). 1984. pap. 3.95 (*1-56744-220-X*) Kazi Pubns.

— Arabic for Daily Use. (ARA.). 20p. (Orig.). 1986. pap. 2.50 (*1-56744-221-8*) Kazi Pubns.

— Bilal in Hadith. 1988. pap. 2.00 (*0-935782-50-8*) Kazi Pubns.

— Book of Muslim Names. LC 96-211225. 1989. pap. 3.95 (*0-933511-91-4*) Kazi Pubns.

— Color & Learn Islamic Terms. 143p. 1992. pap. 3.95 (*0-935782-57-5*) Kazi Pubns.

— Glossary of Quran & Hadith. LC 98-27996. 1998. write for info. (*1-881963-64-0*) Al-Saadawi Pubns.

— Short Suras for Prayers. 48p. (Orig.). 1985. pap. 3.95 (*1-56744-384-2*) Kazi Pubns.

Qazi, M. N., ed. Physics & Contemporary Needs: Proceedings of the International Nathiagali Summer College, Islamabad, August 1982, Vol. 7. 312p. (C). 1985. 75.00 (*9971-966-83-2*) World Scientific Pub.

Qazi, Mahmoud A. Quran, Pt. 30. 32p. 1996. pap. 3.50 (*0-614-21040-2*, 1031) Kazi Pubns.

— Quran: Translation & Transliteration, Pt. 30. 1987. pap. 3.95 (*0-934905-07-X*, Library of Islam) Kazi Pubns.

QECD Staff. Agricultural Policies, Markets & Trade in the Central & Eastern European Countries, Selected New Independent States, Mongolia & China: Monitoring & Outlook, 1995. 232p. (Orig.). 1995. pap. 37.00 (*92-64-14434-X*, Pub. by Org for Econ) OECD.

Qesai, C. S., et al, eds. Constitutive Laws for Engineering Materials. 957p. 1991. 200.00 (*0-7918-0024-5*, 800245) ASME Pr.

Qi, Luo. Economic Interests vs. Political Interventions: The Case of Economic Relations Between Mainland China & Taiwan. (EAI Occasional Paper Ser.: No. 8). 42p. 1998. pap. 19.95 (*981-02-3641-7*) World Scientific Pub.

***Qi, Shouhua.** Bridging the Pacific: A Search for Cross-Cultural Understanding Between the United States & China. 214p. 2000. pap. 14.95 (*0-8351-2675-7*) China Bks.

Qi, Wu, jt. auth. see Lindesay, William.

Qi, Yadong, et al. Forestry: A Community Tradition. 3rd rev. ed. Benedict, Linda F., ed. (Illus.). 48p. 1998. write for info. (*0-9662108-0-8*) Urban Forest Prog.

Qian Kan. BBC Mandarin Chinese Phrasebook. (CHI & ENG., Illus.). 288p. 1996. pap. 5.95 (*0-8442-9228-1*, 92281) NTC Contemp Pub Co.

Qian, Ken. Colloquial Chinese: Complete Language Course. (Colloquials Ser.). (C). 1997. audio compact disk 27.99 (*0-415-15530-4*) Routledge.

— Colloquial Chinese: Complete Language Course. (Colloquials Ser.). 1997. audio compact disk 39.99 (*0-415-15531-2*) Routledge.

Qian, Min, jt. auth. see Liu, P. D.

Qian, Min, jt. auth. see Liu, Pei-Dong.

Qian, Mu. Bibliography of Professor Mu Qian. 212p. 1995. pap. text 11.00 (*957-9272-15-8*) World Scientific Pub.

Qian, Shelly, jt. ed. see Lin, T. Y.

Qian, Shie. Joint Time-Frequency Analysis: Methods & Applications. 368p. 1996. 80.00 incl. disk (*0-13-254384-2*) P-H.

Qian, Sima. Historical Records. Dawson, Raymond, tr. & intro. by. LC 93-34053. (World's Classics Ser.). (Illus.). 202p. (C). 1994. pap. 10.95 (*0-19-283115-1*) OUP.

— Records of the Grand Historian: Han Dynasty & Qin Dynasty, 3 vols., Vol. I. rev. ed. Watson, Burton, tr. from CHI. LC 92-34085. (Records of Civilization: Sources & Studies: No. 65). 540p. (C). 1993. text 110.50 (*0-231-08164-2*) Col U Pr.

— Records of the Grand Historian: Han Dynasty & Qin Dynasty, 3 vols., Vol. II. rev. ed. Watson, Burton, tr. from CHI. LC 92-34085. (Records of Civilization: Sources & Studies: No. 65). 520p. (C). 1993. text 110.50 (*0-231-08166-9*) Col U Pr.

— Records of the Grand Historian: Han Dynasty & Qin Dynasty, 3 vols., Vol. III. rev. ed. Watson, Burton, tr. from CHI. LC 92-34085. (Records of Civilization: Sources & Studies: No. 65). 210p. (C). 1993. text 76.00 (*0-231-08168-5*) Col U Pr.

Qian, Wenbao. Rural-Urban Migration & Its Impact on Economic Development in China. 192p. 1996. text 67.95 (*1-85972-456-6*, Pub. by Avebry) Ashgate Pub Co.

***Qian, Yingyi.** Dynamics vs. Tradition in Chinese Foreign Policy Motivation: Beijing's Fifth Column Policy in Hong Kong. LC 99-31602. 265p. 1999. 69.00 (*1-56072-696-2*) Nova Sci Pubs.

Qian, Yingyi, et al. China's Transition to Markets: Market Preserving Federalism Chinese Style. LC 94-42031. (Essays in Public Policy Ser.: No. 55). 46p. (Orig.). 1995. pap. 5.00 (*0-8179-5602-6*) Hoover Inst Pr.

Qian, Zhaoming. Orientalism & Modernism: The Legacy of China in Pound & Williams, 1913-1923. LC 95-6130. (Illus.). 216p. 1995. text 49.95 (*0-8223-1657-9*); pap. text 16.95 (*0-8223-1669-2*) Duke.

Qian Zhong Shu. Emotions. (CHI.). pap. 9.95 (*7-5004-1703-9*, Pub. by China Intl Bk) Distribks Inc.

Qiang, Li, jt. ed. see Tien-tung, Hsueh.

Qiang, Su. Rare Earths Spectroscopy. 388p. (C). 1990. text 101.00 (*981-02-0078-1*) World Scientific Pub.

Qianli, Sun & Rui, Jiang. Two Chinese Treatises on Calligraphy. LC 95-2684. 176p. 1995. 30.00 (*0-300-06118-8*) Yale U Pr.

Qianshen, Wang, et al. Microgravimetry. (Illus.). 158p. 1996. 92.50 (*90-6764-222-3*, Pub. by VSP) Coronet Bks.

Qiao, Chunming, jt. ed. see Senior, John M.

***Qiao, Yuhua.** Interstate Fiscal Disparities in America: A Study of Trends & Causes. LC 99-27909. 1999. write for info. (*0-8153-3393-5*) Garland.

Qibin, Li. Frontiers of Astronomy in, 1990's. 300p. 1993. text 106.00 (*981-02-1514-2*) World Scientific Pub.

Qibrisi, Shaykh N. Mercy Ocean: (Teachings of Abdullah Al Faizi Ad-Daghestani) 1991. pap. 9.95 (*1-56744-136-X*) Kazi Pubns.

Qiguang Zhao. A Study of Dragons, East & West. LC 92-1392. (Asian Thought & Culture Ser.: Vol. 2). (Illus.). X, 237p. 1993. 56.95 (*0-8204-1758-0*) P Lang Pubng.

Qiliang, Wang, tr. see Chengnan, Sun, ed.

Qimao, Chen, jt. ed. see Scalapino, Robert A.

Qiming, Liu, jt. ed. see Jicai, Sha.

Qimron, Elisha & Strugnell, John, eds. Qumran Cave 4 Vol. 4: Miqsat Ma'ase Ha-Torah HQ 394-399. (ENG & HEB., Illus.). 252p. 1994. text 85.00 (*0-19-826344-9*) OUP.

Qimron, Elisha, jt. ed. see Parry, Donald W.

Qin, Duo. The Formation of Econometrics: A Historical Perspective. 234p. 1993. text 49.95 (*0-19-828388-1*) OUP.

***Qin, Q. H.** Fracture Mechanics of Piezoelectric Materials. 280p. 2000. 149.00 (*1-85312-856-2*, Pub. by WIT Pr) Computational Mech MA.

— The Trefftz Finite & Boundary Element Method. (Advances in Boundary Elements Ser.). 272p. 2000. 128.00 (*1-85312-855-4*, Pub. by WIT Pr) Computational Mech MA.

Qin, Zhong, tr. see Wu, Sun.

Qing, Dai. The River Dragon Has Come! The Three Gorges Dam & the Fate of China's Yangtze River. Thibodeau, John G. & Williams, Philip, eds. Yi, Ming, tr. LC 97-23982. 270p. (C). (gr. 13). 1997. 44.95 (*0-7656-0205-9*, East Gate Bk) M E Sharpe.

— The River Dragon Has Come! The Three Gorges Dam & the Fate of China's Yangtze River & Its People. Thibodeau, JOhn G. & Williams, Philip, eds. Yi, Ming, tr. 270p. 1998. pap. 21.95 (*0-7656-0206-7*, East Gate Bk) M E Sharpe.

— Wang Shiwei & 'Wild Lilies' Rectification & Purges in the Chinese Communist Party, 1942-1944. Apter, David E. & Cheek, Timothy, eds. Liu, Nancy & Sullivan, Lawrence R., trs. from CHI. LC 93-34022. 224p. (C). (gr. 13). 1994. pap. text 31.95 (*1-56324-256-7*, East Gate Bk) M E Sharpe.

Qing-Nan, Meng. Land-Based Marine Pollution: International Law Development. 276p. 1987. lib. bdg. 107.00 (*0-86010-909-7*) Kluwer Academic.

Qing, Sihan. Information & Communications Security: Proceedings, 1st International Conference, ICICS '97, Beijing, China, November 11-13, 1997. Han, Yongfei & Okamoto, Tatsuaki, eds. LC 97-45485. (Lecture Notes in Computer Science Ser.: Vol. 1334). x, 484p. 1997. pap. 69.00 (*3-540-63696-X*) Spr-Verlag.

Qing-Zhu, Fu. Fu Qing-Zhu's Gynecology. Shou-Zhong, Yang & Da-Wei, Liu, trs. from CHI. LC 92-71293. 267p. (Orig.). 1992. pap. 23.95 (*0-936185-35-X*) Blue Poppy Pr.

Qingde, Kang. Large Sets of Triple Systems & Related Designs. Du Dingzhu et al, eds. (Descrete Mathematics & Theoretical Computer Science Ser.: Vol. 3). (Illus.). 201p. 1995. 39.95 (*1-880132-13-3*) Sci Pr NY.

Qingkal Zhang. AIDS & Chinese Medicine. 1993. pap. 19.95 (*0-941942-31-7*) Orient Heal Arts.

Qingming, J., jt. ed. see Milliman, John D.

Qingnan, Zeng, jt. auth. see Weiwen, Zhang.

Qingshan, Tan. The Making of U. S. China Policy: From Normalization to the Post-Cold War Era. LC 92-41402. 190p. 1992. pap. text 16.95 (*1-55587-314-6*) L Rienner.

Qingtai, C. Names of Fishes: Chinese/English/Latin. (CHI, ENG & LAT.). 296p. 1992. 49.95 (*0-320-00596-8*) Fr & Eur.

Qingzhao, Hua. From Yalta to Panmunjom: Truman's Diplomacy & the Four Powers, 1945-1953. (Cornell East Asia Ser.: No. 64). 284p. (Orig.). (C). 1993. pap. 14.45 (*0-939657-64-3*) Cornell East Asia Pgm.

Qinlivan, Gary M., jt. ed. see Boxx, T. William.

Qiray, Ann. Prayers from the Flowers. LC 98-72425. (Illus.). 64p. 1998. pap. 11.95 (*0-965301-0-1*) Essa Bks.

Qiu, Haiming, jt. auth. see Rao, Ming.

Qiu, J-W. & Sivers, D., eds. Nuclear Chromodynamics: Topical Conference on Nuclear Chromodynamics, Argonne National Lab., USA, May 19-21, 1988. 312p. 1988. text 84.00 (*9971-5-0652-1*) World Scientific Pub.

Qiu, John. Q's Baccarat: The System. (Q's Baccarat Winning Strategies Ser.: No. 2). 1997. pap. text 26.99 (*0-9651663-0-9*) Gldn Autumn Pubng.

Qiu, Jun. Qiu's Baccarat Winning Strategy. (CHI., Illus.). 200p. (Orig.). 1996. pap. 3.88 (*0-9651663-6-8*) Gldn Autumn Pubng.

Qiu, Li, jt. ed. see Miller, Daniel E.

Qiu Zhong, Grace Y. & Sullivan, Patricia N. Preparation for the TOEFL. 7th ed. 416p. 1995. 12.95 (*0-02-860563-2*, Arco) Macmillan Gen Ref.

— Preparation for the TOEFL. 7th ed. 416p. 1995. 29.95 incl. audio (*0-02-860564-0*, Arco) Macmillan Gen Ref.

Qiu Zhong, Grace Y. & Sullivan, Patricia Noble. TOEFL Supercourse. 3rd ed. LC 95-2445. 672p. 1995. 18.95 (*0-02-860338-9*) Macmillan.

Qiuping Cao. Early Childhood Education in Comparative Perspective: A Select Bibliography. (Special Studies in Comparative Education: No. 28). 40p. (Orig.). 1990. pap. text 10.00 (*0-937033-22-7*) Grad Schl of Educ.

Qjha, J. M. Cultural Communication in India: Role & Impact of Phonograms. (C). 1992. 18.00 (*81-7022-367-9*, Pub. by Concept) S Asia.

QLD Ex-POW Repatriation Committee. Nippon Very Sorry - Many Men Must Die. 123p. (C). 1990. 60.00 (*0-86439-112-9*, Pub. by Boolarong Pubns) St Mut.

Qoyawayma, Elizabeth P., see White, Elizabeth, pseud.

Qoyawayma, Polingaysi, pseud. No Turning Back: A Hopi Indian Woman's Struggle to Live in Two Worlds. LC 64-7652. (Illus.). 187p. 1977. reprint ed. pap. 12.95 (*0-8263-0439-7*) U of NM Pr.

Qsba, G. N. Fungi of Jammu Kashmir. (C). 1991. 122.50 (*81-7136-027-0*, Pub. by Periodical Expert) St Mut.

Qu, F. Q., jt. ed. see Xiao, S. T.

Qu, Rubin, jt. auth. see Agarwal, Ravi P.

Qu-Tb, Sayyid. In the Shade of the Qur An. Salahi, M. A. & Shamis, A. A., trs. from ARA. LC 97-2738. (ARA.). 1997. write for info. (*1-881963-63-2*) Al-Saadawi Pubns.

Qu, Zhihua. Robust Control of Nonlinear Uncertain Systems. LC 97-52402. (Series in Nonlinear Science). 527p. 1998. 98.50 (*0-471-11589-4*, Wiley-Interscience) Wiley.

Qu, Zhihua & Dawson, Darren M. Robust Tracking Control of Robot Manipulators. 256p. 1995. 79.95 (*0-7803-1065-9*, PC4218) Inst Electrical.

Quaak, Peter, et al. Energy from Biomass: A Review of Combustion & Gassification Technologies. LC 98-31271. 78p. 1999. 22.00 (*0-8213-4335-1*) World Bank.

Quaal, Susan J. Comprehensive Intraaortic Balloon Counterpulsation. 2nd ed. LC 92-48411. (Illus.). 581p. (C). (gr. 13). 1993. pap. text 38.95 (*0-8016-6656-2*, 06656) Mosby Inc.

Quaal, Susan J., ed. Cardiac Mechanical Assistance Beyond Balloon Pumping. LC 92-25096. (Illus.). 395p. (C). (gr. 13). 1992. pap. text 43.95 (*0-8016-6442-X*, 06442) Mosby Inc.

Quaal, Ward L. & Brown, James A. Broadcast Management: Radio & Television. 2nd ed. (Illus.). 464p. 1976. pap. text 15.00 (*0-8038-0764-3*) Hastings.

Quaal, Ward L., jt. auth. see Brown, James A.

***Quack, J. F., et al.** Carlsberg Papyri, Vol. 3. 206p. 2000. 87.00 (*87-7289-547-0*, Pub. by Mus Tusculanum) Intl Spec Bk.

Quack, Joachim F. Die Lehren des Ani: Ein Neuagyptischer Weisheitstext in Seinem Kulturellen Umfeld. (Orbis Biblicus et Orientalis Ser.: Vol. 141). (GER.). 338p. 1994. text 68.75 (*3-7278-0984-1*, Pub. by Presses Univ Fribourg) Eisenbrauns.

Quack, Sibylle, ed. Between Sorrow & Strength: Women Refugees of the Nazi Period. (Publications of the German Historical Institute, Washington, D.C.). 390p. (C). 1995. text 85.00 (*0-521-47081-1*) Cambridge U Pr.

***Quack, Sigrid, et al, eds.** National Capitalisms, Global Competition & Economic Performance. 264p. 1999. 45.95 (*3-11-016485-X*); pap. 22.95 (*3-11-016068-4*) De Gruyter.

— National Capitalisms, Global Competition & Economic Performance. LC 99-51376. (Advances in Organization Studies: Vol. 3). xii, 322p. 2000. 44.95 (*1-55619-746-2*) J Benjamins Pubng Co.

Quackenbos, George P., tr. see Mayura.

Quackenbush, Howard, ed. see Rojas, Gonzalo.

Quackenbush, Jan. Inside Out. (Orig.). 1994. pap. 9.95 (*0-7145-0292-8*) Riverrun NY.

— Inside Out & Other Plays. 72p. 1968. 16.95 (*0-910278-41-5*) Boulevard.

Quackenbush, L. Howard, tr. see Samperio, Guillermo.

Quackenbush, Marcia, et al, eds. The AIDS Challenge: Prevention Education for Young People. 526p. 1988. 29.95 (*0-941816-54-0*) ETR Assocs.

— The AIDS Challenge: Prevention Education for Young People. 526p. 1995. pap. 24.95 (*0-941816-53-2*) ETR Assocs.

Quackenbush, Marcia & Sargent, Pamela. Teaching AIDS. rev. ed. 164p. 1988. pap. text 19.95 (*0-941816-41-9*); pap. text 21.95 (*1-56071-029-2*) ETR Assocs.

Quackenbush, Marcia & Schonfeld, David. Teaching Kids about How AIDS Works. (J). (gr. k-3). 1995. 25.00 (*1-56071-377-1*) ETR Assocs.

— Teaching Kids about How AIDS Works. (J). (gr. 4-6). 1995. 25.00 (*1-56071-378-X*) ETR Assocs.

Quackenbush, Marcia & Villarreal, Sylvia. Does AIDS Hurt? Educating Your Children about AIDS. 2nd ed. LC 92-25691. 1992. 17.95 (*1-56071-084-5*) ETR Assocs.

Quackenbush, Marcia, et al. Risk & Recovery: AIDS, HIV, & Alcohol: A Handbook for Providers. LC 92-26635. 256p. 1995. pap. 16.95 (*0-89087-690-8*) Celestial Arts.

Quackenbush, Marian. Air, Sunlight, & a Bit of Land. (Illus.). 1982. 9.95 (*0-87770-275-6*) Ye Galleon.

Quackenbush, Robert. Bat Baby. LC 96-45400. (J). (ps-2). 1997. lib. bdg. 9.99 (*0-679-98541-7*, Pub. by Random Bks Yng Read) Random.

— Bat Baby. LC 96-45400. (Little Dipper Picture Bks.). (Illus.). 32p. (J). 1997. 7.99 (*0-679-88541-2*, Pub. by Random Bks Yng Read) Random.

***Quackenbush, Robert.** Batbaby Finds a Home. (Step into Reading Ser.). 2001. pap. 3.99 (*0-375-80430-7*, Pub. by Random Bks Yng Read) Random.

— Batbaby Finds a Home. (J). 2001. lib. bdg. 9.99 (*0-375-90430-1*) Random Bks Yng Read.

Quackenbush, Robert. Benjamin Franklin & His Friends. (Illus.). 32p. (J). (gr. 2-5). 1991. 14.95 (*0-945912-14-5*) Pippin Pr.

— Clementine. LC 73-13990. (Illus.). 40p. (J). (gr. k-3). 1974. 8.95 (*0-397-31506-6*) HarpC Child Bks.

— Danger in Tibet: A Miss Mallard Mystery. (Illus.). 32p. (J). (gr. 1-4). 1989. 15.95 (*0-945912-03-X*) Pippin Pr.

— Detective Mole & Halloween Mystery. (J). 1989. pap. 3.95 (*0-671-67830-2*) Litle Simon.

— Evil under the Sea: A Miss Mallard Mystery. (Illus.). 32p. (J). (gr. 1-4). 1992. 15.95 (*0-945912-16-1*) Pippin Pr.

— Go Tell Aunt Rhody. LC 72-8711. 32p. (J). (gr. 1-4). 1973. 13.95 (*0-397-31718-2*) HarpC Child Bks.

— Here a Plant, There a Plant, Everywhere a Plant, Plant! A Story of Luther Burbank. LC 94-73390. (Illus.). 36p. (J). (gr. 1-5). 1999. reprint ed. 10.00 (*0-9637883-1-0*) L Burbank Home.

— I Did It with My Hatchet: A Story of George Washington. (Illus.). 32p. (J). (gr. 2-6). 1989. 14.95 (*0-945912-04-8*) Pippin Pr.

— I Don't Want to Go, I Don't Know How to Act. LC 82-48458. (Illus.). 32p. (J). (gr. k-2). 1983. 11.95 (*0-397-32033-7*); lib. bdg. 11.89 (*0-397-32034-5*) HarpC Child Bks.

— James Madison & Dolly Madison & Their Times. (Illus.). 40p. (J). (gr. 2-5). 1992. 14.95 (*0-945912-18-8*) Pippin Pr.

— Lost in the Amazon: A Miss Mallard Mystery. (Illus.). 32p. (J). (gr. 1-4). 1990. lib. bdg. 15.95 (*0-945912-11-0*) Pippin Pr.

— Pass the Quill: I'll Write a Draft: A Story of Thomas Jefferson. (Illus.). 32p. (J). (gr. 2-6). 1989. lib. bdg. 14.95 (*0-945912-07-2*) Pippin Pr.

— Pop! Goes the Weasel & Yankee Doodle: New York in 1776 & Today, with Songs & Pictures. LC 75-28312. (Illus.). 40p. (J). (ps up). 1988. lib. bdg. 13.89 (*0-397-32265-8*) HarpC Child Bks.

— Stairway to Doom. LC 82-21484. (Miss Mallard Mystery Ser.). (Illus.). 48p. (J). (gr. 2-6). 1998. pap. 5.95 (*0-671-67053-0*) S&S Bks Yung.

— Stairway to Doom: A Miss Mallard Mystery. LC 82-21484. (Illus.). 48p. (J). (ps-5). 1983. lib. bdg. 9.95 (*0-13-804595-X*) P-H.

— Too Many Lollipops: A Henry the Duck Coloring Book. 2nd ed. (Illus.). 32p. (J). (gr. k-6). 1990. reprint ed. pap. 3.95 (*0-9612518-8-3*) R Quackenbush.

— Two Miss Mallard Mysteries: Surfboard to Peril & Stage Door to Terror, 2 vols. in 1. rev. ed. (Miss Mallard Mysteries Ser.: Vol. 1). (Illus.). 64p. (J). (gr. 1-5). 1998. reprint ed. pap., per. 4.95 (*0-9612518-9-1*) R Quackenbush.

— Two Slapstick Biographies: Once upon a Time! A Story of the Brothers Grimm & Quick, Annie, Give Me a Catchy Line! A Story of Samuel F. B. Morse. (Two Slapstick Biographies Ser.: Vol. 1). (Illus.). 64p. (YA). (gr. 3 up). 1999. reprint ed. pap. 5.95 (*0-9612518-1-6*) R Quackenbush.

Quackenbush, Robert. It's Raining Cats & Dogs: Cat & Dog Jokes. 40p. (J). (gr. 2-6). 1988. 13.95 (*0-945912-01-3*) Pippin Pr.

Quackenbush, Robert M. Daughter of Liberty: A True Story of the American Revolution. LC 98-12607. 64p. (J). (gr. 2-4). 1999. pap. 3.95 (*0-7868-1286-9*, Pub. by Hyperion); lib. bdg. 14.49 (*0-7868-2355-0*, Pub. by Hyperion) Little.

Quackenbush, Ross & Gastineau, Jerrel. Homework? My Locker Ate It! An Effective Method for Parents to Help Their Student Study at Home & Improve in School. (Illus.). 143p. (Orig.). (J). (gr. 6-12). 1988. pap. 19.95 (*0-9621701-0-0*) CWP.

***Quackenbush, Thomas R.** Better Eyesight: The Complete Magazine of William H. Bates. (Illus.). 500p. (C). 2000. pap. 27.50 (*1-55643-351-4*) North Atlantic.

— Relearning to See: Improve Your Eyesight--Naturally! (Illus.). 515p. 2000. pap. text 27.50 (*1-55643-341-7*) North Atlantic.

Quackenbush, Thomas R. Relearning to See: Naturally & Clearly. LC 96-54600. (Illus.). 521p. (Orig.). 1997. 35.00 (*1-55643-205-4*) North Atlantic.

Quackenbush, Willaim C. & Palefsky, Cliff. Wrongful Employment Termination Practice. 2nd ed. Compton, Linda A. & Johnson, Elizabeth M., eds. LC 97-65688. 1156p. 1997. ring bd. 199.00 (*0-7626-0066-7*, CP-32650) Cont Ed Bar-CA.

***Quackenbush, William A.** Wrongful Employment Termination Practice - 5-99 Update. Johnson, Elizabeth M., ed. LC 97-65688. 718p. 1999. ring bd. 78.00 (*0-7626-0317-8*, CP-32652) Cont Ed Bar-CA.

— Wrongful Employment Termination Practice, 5/98 Update. 2nd ed. Johnson, Elizabeth M., ed. LC 97-65688. 784p. 1998. ring bd. 70.00 (*0-7626-0219-8*, CP-32651) Cont Ed Bar-CA.

***Quackenbush, William C.** Wrongful Employment Termination Practice: June 2000 Update, 2 vols. 2nd ed. LC 97-65688. 1264p. 2000. 119.00 (*0-7626-0449-2*, CP-32653) Cont Ed Bar-CA.

Quadagno, Jill S. Aging. 2nd ed. 574p. 1995. pap. text 39.95 (*0-312-09496-5*) St Martin.

— Aging & the Life Course: An Introduction to Social Gerontology. LC 98-6089. 1998. 57.41 (*0-07-052256-1*) McGraw.

— The Color of Welfare: How Racism Undermined the War on Poverty. (Illus.). 272p. 1996. pap. 14.95 (*0-19-510122-7*) OUP.

— The Transformation of Old Age Security: Class & Politics in the American Welfare State. (Illus.). 270p. 1988. 35.95 (*0-226-69923-4*) U Ch Pr.

Quadagno, Jill S., jt. ed. see Cowart, Marie E.

Quadagno, Jill S., jt. ed. see Peterson, Warren A.

Quade, Edward S. Analysis for Public Decisions. 3rd ed. (C). 1989. text 50.20 (*0-13-052127-2*) P-H.

Quade, Edward S. & Boucher, W. I., eds. Systems Analysis & Policy Planning: Applications in Defense. LC 68-22241. 480p. reprint ed. pap. 148.80 (*0-608-16377-5*, 202627400049) Bks Demand.

Quade, Edward S. & Carter, G. M. Analysis for Public Decisions. 3rd ed. 410p. 1989. 42.75 (*0-444-01471-3*) P-H.

Quade, Edward S., jt. ed. see Miser, Hugh J.

Quade, Kenneth. You Won't Understand If You Have to Ask Why. LC 94-90715. 1995. 16.95 (*0-533-11343-1*) Vantage.

Quade, Quentin. Financing Education: The Struggle Between Governmental Monopoly & Parental Control. LC 96-17333. 176p. 1996. text 34.95 (*1-56000-255-7*) Transaction Pubs.

***Quade, Vicki.** I Remember Bob Collins. (Illus.). 200p. 2000. 22.95 (*1-58261-305-2*, Bannon Multimedia) Sports Pub.

Quade, Vicki. Laughing Eyes. (Illus.). (Orig.). 1979. pap. 5.00 (*0-9602604-0-4*) V Quade.

Quade, Vicki, jt. auth. see MacCready, Jean.

Quadgano, Jill, jt. ed. see Myles, John.

Quadling, Douglas, jt. ed. see Shuard, Hilary.

Quadra Island Child Care Society Staff. Island Cookery: Seafood Specialties & Fovourites from Quadra Island British Columbia, Vol. 1. 214p. 1981. pap. 13.95 (*0-919537-01-4*) Gordon Soules Bk.

Quadri, Franco, et al, jt. ed. Robert Wilson. LC 98-110713. (Illus.). 240p. 1998. 60.00 (*0-8478-2103-X*, Pub. by Rizzoli Intl) St Martin.

***Quadrillion Media Staff.** ABC. (J). 1999. pap. 1.99 (*1-84100-285-2*) Quadrillion Media.

— ABC. 1999. pap. 3.99 (*1-84100-296-8*) Quadrillion Media.

— Ancient Rome (Das Alte Rom) (Start Me Up Ser.: Vol. 8). (Illus.). 48p. (J). (gr. 4-7). 1998. pap. 12.95 (*1-58185-008-5*, Tessloff Publishing) Quadrillion Media.

Quadrillion Media Staff. Castles, 10. (J). 1999. 12.95 (*1-58185-011-5*) Quadrillion Media.

— Celestial Photograph Album. 1999. 36.95 (*1-84100-069-8*) Quadrillion Media.

***Quadrillion Media Staff.** Colors. (J). 1999. pap. 1.99 (*1-84100-286-0*) Quadrillion Media.

— Colors. (Let's Learn Ser.). (J). 1999. pap. 3.99 (*1-84100-299-2*) Quadrillion Pub.

Quadrillion Media Staff. Complete Book of Golf Techniques. 1998. 12.99 (*1-85833-384-9*) Quadrillion Pubng.

— Counting Animals. 1999. 5.95 (*1-58185-216-9*) Quadrillion Media.

— Duckling Peep Swims With The Animals. 1999. 5.95 (*1-58185-219-3*) Quadrillion Media.

***Quadrillion Media Staff.** The Earth (Unsere Erde) (Start Me Up Ser.: Vol. 1). 48p. (J). (gr. 4-7). 1998. pap. 12.95 (*1-58185-000-X*, Tessloff Publishing) Quadrillion Media.

Quadrillion Media Staff. Great World Atlas. 1999. 29.99 (*1-85833-919-7*) Quadrillion Pubng.

***Quadrillion Media Staff.** History No. III. (J). 1999. pap. text 3.95 (*1-58185-100-6*) Quadrillion Media.

Quadrillion Media Staff. International Space Station (Die Internationale Raumstation) A Journey into Space. (Start Me Up Ser.). 64p. (J). (gr. 3-8). 1998. mass mkt. 15.95 (*1-58185-004-2*, Tessloff Publishing) Quadrillion Media.

— Internet (Das Internet) Surfin' the Web. (Start Me Up Ser.). 64p. (J). (gr. 3-8). 1998. pap. 15.95 (*1-58185-023-9*, Tessloff Publishing) Quadrillion Media.

— Mr. Flips Visits The Animals. 1999. 5.95 (*1-58185-217-7*) Quadrillion Media.

— Mysteries of the World (Geklarte u. Ungeklarte Phanomene) (Start Me Up Ser.: Vol. 4). 48p. (J). (gr. 3-8). 1998. mass mkt. 12.95 (*1-58185-003-4*, Tessloff Publishing) Quadrillion Media.

— Nature & Animals. (Start Me Up Ser.). (J). 1999. pap. text 3.95 (*1-58185-101-4*) Quadrillion Media.

***Quadrillion Media Staff.** 123. (J). 1999. pap. 1.99 (*1-84100-284-4*) Quadrillion Media.

— 123. 1999. pap. 3.99 (*1-84100-297-6*) Quadrillion Media.

— Polar Regions, (Start Me Up Ser.: Vol. 13). (Illus.). 2000. 12.95 (*1-58185-017-4*) Quadrillion Media.

Quadrillion Media Staff. Rain Forests (Regenwald) (Start Me Up Ser.: Vol. 6). 48p. (J). (gr. 3-8). 1998. mass mkt. 12.95 (*1-58185-006-9*, Tessloff Publishing) Quadrillion Media.

— Science. (Start Me Up Ser.). (J). 1999. pap. text 3.95 (*1-58185-105-7*) Quadrillion Media.

— Seven Wonders of the Ancient World (Die Sieben Weltwunder) (Start Me Up Ser.: Vol. 3). 48p. (J). (gr. 3-8). 1998. mass mkt. 12.95 (*1-58185-002-6*, Tessloff Publishing) Quadrillion Media.

***Quadrillion Media Staff.** Shapes. (J). 1999. pap. 1.99 (*1-84100-283-6*) Quadrillion Media.

— Shapes. (Let's Learn Ser.). (J). 1999. pap. 3.99 (*1-84100-298-4*) Quadrillion Pub.

— Show Me The Apple! 1999. 3.95 (*1-58185-214-2*) Quadrillion Media.

— Show Me The Ball!, 1. 1999. 3.95 (*1-58185-212-6*) Quadrillion Media.

Quadrillion Media Staff. Show Me the Duck! 1999. 3.95 (*1-58185-215-0*) Quadrillion Media.

***Quadrillion Media Staff.** Show Me The Train! 1999. 3.95 (*1-58185-213-4*) Quadrillion Media.

Q

Quadrillion Media Staff. Sniffer the Rabbit & Friends. 1999. 5.95 (*1-58185-218-5*) Quadrillion Media.
— Space. (Start Me Up Ser.). (J). 1999. pap. text 3.95 (*1-58185-102-2*) Quadrillion Media.
— Technology. (Start Me Up Ser.). (J). 1999. pap. text 3.95 (*1-58185-103-0*) Quadrillion Media.
— Timelines of World History. 1998. 17.99 (*1-85833-854-9*) Quadrillion Pubng.
***Quadrillion Media Staff.** Toby Discovers Opposites. 1999. 3.95 (*1-58185-210-X*) Quadrillion Media.
— Toby Learns Colors. 1999. 3.95 (*1-58185-211-8*) Quadrillion Media.
— Toby Learns How To Count. 1999. 3.95 (*1-58185-208-8*) Quadrillion Media.
— Toby Plays With Shapes. 1999. 3.95 (*1-58185-209-6*) Quadrillion Media.
Quadrillion Media Staff. The Universe (Unser Kosmos) To the Limits of Space & Time. (Start Me Up Ser.: Vol. 7). 48p. (J). (gr. 3-8). 1998. mass mkt. 12.95 (*1-58185-015-8*, Tessloff Publishing) Quadrillion Media.
— Volcanoes (Vulkane) (Start Me Up Ser.: Vol. 9). 48p. (J). (gr. 3-8). 1998. mass mkt. 12.95 (*1-58185-010-7*, Tessloff Publishing) Quadrillion Media.
— Whales & Dolphins (Wale und Delphine) (Start Me Up Ser.: Vol. 5). 48p. (J). (gr. 3-8). 1998. mass mkt. 12.95 (*1-58185-005-0*, Tessloff Publishing) Quadrillion Media.
***Quadrillion Media Staff.** Wild Animals. (Start Me Up Ser.: Vol. 12). (Illus.). (J). 2000. 12.95 (*1-58185-016-6*) Quadrillion Media.
— Wolves. (Start Me Up Ser.: Vol. 11). (Illus.). (J). 2000. 12.95 (*1-58185-013-1*) Quadrillion Media.
Quadrio Curzio, Alberto, et al, eds. Innovation, Resources & Economic Growth. LC 94-8632. (Illus.). viii, 300p. 1994. 107.95 (*0-387-57737-8*) Spr-Verlag.
Quadrio Curzio, Alberto, et al. The Management of Municipal Solid Waste in Europe. LC 95-119991. (Developments in Environmental Economics Ser.: Vol. 5). 262p. 1994. 155.75 (*0-444-81948-7*) Elsevier.
Quadrucci, E., jt. ed. see Walker, R.
***Quadrupani, Charles Joseph.** How to Love God & Keep His Commandments. abr. ed. LC 99-48235. Orig. Title: Light & Peace. 200p. 1999. pap. 14.95 (*1-928832-02-4*) Sophia Inst Pr.
Quadrupani, R. P. Light & Peace. LC 79-67860. 193p. 1980. reprint ed. pap. 7.00 (*0-89555-133-0*) TAN Bks Pubs.
Quafafou, Mohamed, jt. auth. see Zytkow, Jan.
Quagliano, James V. & Vallarino, Lidia M. Chemistry. 3rd ed. (C). 1969. 34.95 (*0-685-03782-7*) P-H.
— Chemistry Answers to Selected Problems. 3rd ed. (C). 1969. 11.95 (*0-685-03783-5*) P-H.
Quagliano, Tony. Feast of Strangers: Selected Essays & Poems of Reuel Denney, 106. Denney, Reuel, ed. LC 98-26417. (Contributions in American Studies: Vol. 106). 272p. 1999. 55.00 (*0-313-30085-2*, Greenwood Pr) Greenwood.
— Fierce Meadows. 24p. 1981. pap. 2.50 (*0-932136-04-4*) Petronium HI.
Quagliarella, D., et al. Genetic Algorithms & Evolution. 404p. 1998. 167.00 (*0-471-97710-1*) Wiley.
Quagliariello, Gaetano. Politics Without Parties. (Avebury Series in Philosophy). 272p. 1996. 69.95 (*1-85972-256-3*, Pub. by Avebry) Ashgate Pub Co.
Quagliati, Paolo. Paolo Quagliati: Libro Primo de'Madrigali a Quattro Voci. Cohen, Judith, ed. (Recent Researches in Music of the Baroque Era Ser.: Vol. RRB79). (Illus.). xxii, 110p. 1996. pap. 45.00 (*0-89579-339-3*) A-R Eds.
Quaglietti, Susan, jt. auth. see Froelicher, Victor F.
Quaglini, Juliana. The Night of the Shepherds: A Christmas Experience. Flanagan, Anne J., tr. from ITA. LC 93-25027. (Illus.). 31p. (Orig.). (J). (gr. 4 up). 1993. pap. 3.95 (*0-8198-5128-0*) Pauline Bks.
Quah, Euston. Economics & Home Production: Theory & Measurement. 256p. 1993. 82.95 (*1-85628-457-3*, Pub. by Avebry) Ashgate Pub Co.
Quah, Euston & Lee, David, eds. Household Economics & the Asian Family. LC 97-945578. 228p. 1996. pap. 22.50 (*981-210-071-7*, Pub. by Times Academic) Intl Spec Bk.
Quah, Jon S. Singapore. LC 90-156512. (World Bibliographical Ser.). 278p. 1989. lib. bdg. 52.50 (*1-85109-071-1*) ABC-CLIO.
Quah, Jon S., ed. In Search of Singapore's National Values. 112p. 1990. pap. write for info. (*981-00-2115-1*, Pub. by Times Academic) Intl Spec Bk.
***Quah, Jon S., ed.** In Search of Singapore's National Values. 128p. 1999. reprint ed. pap. 12.50 (*981-210-137-3*, Pub. by Times Academic) Intl Spec Bk.
Quah, Jon S., jt. auth. see Quah, Stella R.
Quah, Stella R. Family in Singapore: Sociological Perspectives. 2nd ed. LC 98-945732. 314p. 1998. 45.00 (*981-210-133-0*, Pub. by Times Academic); pap. 35.00 (*981-210-116-0*, Pub. by Times Academic) Intl Spec Bk.
Quah, Stella R., ed. The Family As an Asset. 400p. 1990. pap. 25.00 (*981-00-1706-5*, Pub. by Times Academic) Intl Spec Bk.
Quah, Stella R. & Quah, Jon S. Friends in Blue: The Police & the Public in Singapore. (Illus.). 228p. 1987. pap. text 28.00 (*0-19-588854-5*) OUP.
Quaid, Maeve. Job Evaluation: The Myth of Equitable Assessment. LC 93-93041. 283p. 1993. text 45.00 (*0-8020-2904-3*) U of Toronto Pr.
— Job Evaluation: The Myth of Equitable Assessment. 290p. 1996. pap. text 19.95 (*0-8020-7841-9*) U of Toronto Pr.
***Quaide, Rustin.** Al Malik Fiefs. Bridges, Bill, ed. (Illus.). 32p. 1999. pap. 6.95 (*1-888906-17-0*) Holistic Design.
Quaife, Art. Automated Development of Fundamental Mathematical Theories. LC 92-34849. (Automated Reasoning Ser.: Vol. 2). 1992. text 171.00 (*0-7923-2021-2*) Kluwer Academic.
Quaife, Darlene B. Days & Nights on the Amazon. 220p. 1995. pap. 12.95 (*0-88801-183-0*) LPC InBook.
— Death Writes. (Illus.). 144p. (Orig.). 1997. pap. 9.95 (*1-55152-038-9*, Pub. by Arsenal Pulp) LPC InBook.
Quaife, M. M., ed. Early Days of Rock Island (Ill.) & Davenport (Ia.) The Narratives of J. W. Spencer (1872) & J. M. D. Burrows (1888) 315p. 1995. reprint ed. lib. bdg. 37.50 (*0-8328-4670-8*) Higginson Bk Co.
Quaife, Milo M. Lake Michigan. (American Lakes Ser.). lib. bdg. 26.95 (*0-8488-2014-2*) Amereon Ltd.
Quaife, Milo M., ed. Southwestern Expedition of Zebulon M. Pike. LC 70-124252. (Select Bibliographies Reprint Ser.). 1977. 18.95 (*0-8369-5440-8*) Ayer.
Quaife, Milo M., ed. see Brush, Daniel H.
Quaife, Milo M., ed. see Burlend, Rebecca & Burlend, Edward.
Quaife, Milo M., ed. see Davis, Britton.
Quaife, Milo M., ed. see Kelly, Luther S.
Quaife, Milo M., ed. see Leonard, Zenas.
Quaife, Milo M., ed. see Spencer, O. M.
Quaife, Milo M., ed. see Tillson, Christina H.
Quaife, Milo M., ed. see Williams, Alpheus S.
Quaife, Milo M., ed. & intro. see Carson, Kit.
Quaife, Milo M., ed. & intro. see Custer, George A.
Quaife, Milo M., ed. & intro. see Gillett, James B.
Quaife, Milo M., ed. & intro. see Williams, Alpheus S.
Quail, jt. auth. see Diller.
Quail, jt. auth. see Diller, Angela.
Quail, Avrill. Marking Our Times: Aboriginal & Torees Strait Islander Art. LC 95-61182. (Illus.). 100p. (Orig.). 1996. pap. 19.95 (*0-500-97431-4*, Pub. by Thames Hudson) Norton.
Quail, Beverly. Colorado Real Estate Forms & Disk. 190p. 1997. spiral bd., ring bd. 96.00 incl. disk (*0-327-00920-9*, 80324-13, MICHIE) LEXIS Pub.
Quail, Beverly J. Colorado Real Estate Forms, 3 vols. 1660p. 1993. spiral bd. 310.00 (*0-87189-058-5*, 80319-10, MICHIE) LEXIS Pub.
***Quail, Beverly J.** Colorado Real Estate Forms. 2nd ed. LC 99-65062. 2000p. 1999. ring bd. write for info. (*0-327-01480-6*, 8032511) LEXIS Pub.
Quail, Beverly J. Colorado Real Estate Forms, No. 6. 1993. suppl. ed. 80.00 (*0-685-74607-0*, MICHIE) LEXIS Pub.
Quail Botanical Gardens Docents Staff. Cooking with Herbs. LC 97-185450. (Illus.). 128p. (Orig.). 1997. pap. write for info. (*0-9656332-2-5*) Quail Botanical.
Quail, Junius. The Fat Chance Diet Book. LC 82-62878. 64p. 1983. pap. 3.95 (*0-9610764-0-2*) Quail Prods.
Quail, Kenneth J. Arabic Bread Production. LC 96-85018. (Illus.). 148p. 1996. 95.00 (*0-913250-91-0*) Am Assn Cereal Chem.
Quails, Sara H., jt. auth. see Smyer, Michael A.
***Quain, Anthony J.** The Political Reference Almanac. Hershey, Jill E. & Pietropaoli, Edward T., eds. (Illus.). 904p. 1999. pap. 44.95 (*0-9670286-0-4*, Polisci Bks) Keynote Pubng.
Quain, Bill. Guest Services Management, Vol. II. 188p. (C). 1996. pap. text, per. 40.95 (*0-7872-2668-8*, 41266801) Kendall-Hunt.
***Quain, Bill.** Pro Consumer Power! How to Create Wealth by Buying Smarter, Not Cheaper. Price, Steve, ed. 126p. 2000. pap. 11.95 (*1-891279-04-1*) INTI.
Quain, Bill. Reclaiming the American Dream - The Keys to Financial Freedom: Internet Services Corporation Edition. 99p. (Orig.). 1997. pap. 9.95 (*0-9623646-7-3*) Wales Pub.
— Recobrando el Sueno Americano: Claves para Alcanzar la Libertad Financiera. Monterrosa, Ricardo, tr.Tr. of Reclaiming the American Dream. (SPA., Illus.). 124p. (Orig.). 1995. pap. 9.95 (*0-9623646-6-5*) Wales Pub.
Quain, Bill. 10 Rules to Break & 10 Rules to Make Vol. 1: The Do's & Don'ts for Designing Your Destiny. Price, Steve, ed. 168p. 1997. pap. 12.95 (*0-9632667-6-4*) INTI.
***Quain, Bill, ed.** 10 Places Where Money Is Hidden in Your Restaurant: And How to Find It! (Illus.). 88p. 1999. pap. 9.95 (*0-9623646-2-2*) Wales Pub.
Quain, Edwin A. The Medieval Accessus Ad Auctores. LC 86-80646. 60p. reprint ed. pap. 30.00 (*0-7837-5616-X*, 204552500005) Bks Demand.
— Paradosis: Studies in Memory of Edwin A. Quain. LC 76-20905. 240p. reprint ed. pap. 74.40 (*0-7837-5617-8*, 204552600005) Bks Demand.
Quain, Kay D. So Your Daughter Is Engaged: or Why the Mother of the Bride Oughtn't Be in Pictures. LC 89-51256. (Illus.). 64p. (Orig.). 1989. pap. write for info. (*0-9623646-0-6*) Wales Pub.
— Surviving Cancer. LC 88-62065. 126p. 1988. pap. 7.95 (*1-55612-156-3*) Sheed & Ward WI.
Quain, Kevin. The Elvis Reader: Texts & Sources on the King of Rock 'n' Roll. (Illus.). 352p. (Orig.). 1991. pap. 13.95 (*0-312-06966-9*) St Martin.
Quain, William J. Reclaiming the American Dream: The Keys to Financial Freedom. 144p. 1994. pap. 9.95 (*0-9623646-1-4*) Wales Pub.
Quaine, Anthony I. Crime & Riot Control: Index of Modern Authors & Subjects with Guide for Rapid Research. rev. ed. 187p. 1997. 47.50 (*0-7883-1448-3*); pap. 44.50 (*0-7883-1449-1*) ABBE Pubs Assn.
Quaintance, Marilyn K., jt. auth. see Fleishman, Edwin A.
Quakenbush, James, ed. see Sullivan, Joseph R. & Leafgren, Fred.
Quakenbush, John S. & Linguistic Society of the Philippines Staff. Language Use & Proficiency in a Multilingual Setting: A Sociolinguistic Survey of Agutaynen Speakers in Palawan, Philippines LC 90-197329. (Special Monograph Issue/Linguistic Society of the Philippines Ser.). xvi, 158 p. 1989. write for info. (*971-10-5913-4*, Pub. by New Day Pub) S Asia.
Quaker Oat Staff. Bake It Better with Quaker Oats. (Illus.). 96p. 1995. 12.95 (*0-696-20476-2*) Meredith Bks.
Qual-Tech Staff, ed. see Wills, John H.
Qualben, James, ed. see Gilmore, John.
Qualben, James D. Peace in the Parish: How to Use Conflict Redemption Principles & Process. LC 91-214809. 302p. (Orig.). 1992. pap. text 15.95 (*1-880292-00-9*) LangMarc.
Qualben, James D., ed. see Fortin, Noonie.
Qualben, James D., ed. see Foster, Scarlett R.
Qualben, Lois. Christ-Care: Bible Study for Personal & Group Use. 124p. (Orig.). 1991. pap. text 5.95 (*1-880292-01-7*) LangMarc.
— Sand Castles & Fortresses: Christian Relationships. (Illus.). 140p. (Orig.). 1992. pap. text 5.95 (*1-880292-02-5*) LangMarc.
— Values Symphony: How to Harmonize Faith & Choices in Everyday Living. rev. ed. Roberts, R. J., ed. (Illus.). 169p. 1993. pap. 8.95 (*1-880292-17-3*) LangMarc.
Quale, G. Robina. Families in Context: A World History of Population, 35. LC 91-35713. (Contributions to the Study of World History Ser.: No. 35). 480p. 1992. 65.00 (*0-313-27830-X*, QSH/, Greenwood Pr) Greenwood.
— A History of Marriage Systems, 13. LC 87-24957. (Contributions in Family Studies: No. 13). 415p. 1988. 65.00 (*0-313-26010-9*, QHM/, Greenwood Pr) Greenwood.
Quale, Mark E., ed. see Peterson, Charles & Blei, Norbert.
Qualey, Carlton C. Norwegian Settlement in the United States. LC 70-129409. (American Immigration Collection. Series 2). 1978. reprint ed. 23.95 (*0-405-00563-6*) Ayer.
Qualey, Marsha. Close to a Killer. LC 98-19515. 192p. (YA). (gr. 6-12). 1999. 15.95 (*0-385-32597-5*) BDD Bks Young Read.
***Qualey, Marsha.** Close to a Killer. 205p. (YA). (gr. 7). 2000. mass mkt. 4.99 (*0-440-22763-1*, LLL BDD) BDD Bks Young Read.
Qualey, Marsha. Come in from the Cold. LC 93-42064. 208p. (J). 1994. 16.00 (*0-395-68986-4*) HM.
***Qualey, Marsha.** Every Friend a Stranger. LC 00-20934. (Illus.). (J). 2001. write for info. (*0-8037-2602-3*, Dial Yng Read) Peng Put Young Read.
Qualey, Marsha. Hometown. LC 94-49321. 192p. (YA). (gr. 7). 1995. 14.95 (*0-395-72666-2*) HM.
— Hometown. 176p. (YA). 1997. mass mkt. 3.99 (*0-380-72921-0*, Avon Bks) Morrow Avon.
— Hometown. LC 94-49321. (J). 1997. 9.09 (*0-606-11476-9*, Pub. by Turtleback) Demco.
— Revolutions of the Heart. LC 92-24528. 192p. (YA). (gr. 7 up). 1993. 16.00 (*0-395-64168-3*) HM.
— Thin Ice. 272p. (YA). 1999. mass mkt. 4.99 (*0-440-22037-8*) BDD Bks Young Read.
Quality Education Data Staff. Microcomputer & VCR Usage in Schools. (School Trend Ser.). 204p. 1988. pap. 49.95 (*0-88747-217-6*, 2176Q) Quality Ed Data.
— QED's Guide to U. S. School Districts, 1987-88. (School Trend Ser.). 400p. 1988. pap. 79.95 (*0-88747-295-8*, 2958Q) Quality Ed Data.
— Video Purchasing Patterns in Schools. (School Trend Ser.). 204p. 1988. pap. 49.95 (*0-88747-225-7*, 2257Q) Quality Ed Data.
Quality Family Entertainment, Inc. Staff. Shining Time Station: Station House. (Pop-Up Sound-Up Bks.). 2p. (J). (ps-2). 1993. write for info. (*1-883366-10-0*) YES Ent.
Quality Productions Staff, jt. auth. see Biel, Timothy.
Quality Productions Staff, jt. auth. see Wildlife Education, Ltd. Staff.
Qualkinbush, Thomas, jt. auth. see Doane, Bonnie M.
Qualley, Charles. Safety in the Artroom. LC 85-73421. 120p. 1986. pap. text 17.00 (*0-87192-174-X*, 235) Natl Art Ed.
Qualley, Donna. Turns of Thought: Teaching Composition As Reflexive Inquiry. LC 97-2906. (Orig.). (C). 1997. pap. text 24.50 (*0-86709-418-4*, 0418, Pub. by Boynton Cook Pubs) Heinemann.
Qualline, Steven. Practical C Programming. 2nd ed. (Computer Science). (Illus.). 396p. 1993. pap. 29.95 (*1-56592-035-X*) Thomson Learn.
— Windows Programming with Borland C++ 1995. pap. 39.95 incl. disk (*1-55851-313-2*, M&T Bks) IDG Bks.
Qualls, Barry V., ed. see Stevenson, Robert Louis.
Qualls, Barry V., ed. & intro. see Stevenson, Robert Louis.
Qualls, Cathy. The Church at 21 (Centuries) Director's Manual. Sawyer, Kieran, ed. LC 98-103888. (Developing Faith Ser.). 80p. 1997. pap. text, teacher ed. 16.95 (*0-87793-621-8*) Ave Maria.
Qualls, Charles, jt. auth. see Prosser, Bo.
Qualls-Corbett, Nancy. The Sacred Prostitute. (Illus.). 176p. 1995. pap. 18.00 (*0-919123-31-7*, Pub. by Inner City Bks) BookWorld.
Qualls, John R., ed. see Petrie, Bruce I., Jr.
Qualls, Regina M. & Sanchez, L. National Textbook Company Beginner's Spanish & English Dictionary. LC 97-39061. (SPA & ENG., Illus.). 488p. 1995. 12.95 (*0-8442-7698-7*, 76987, Natl Textbk Co) NTC Contemp Pub Co.
Qualls, Regina M. & Sanchez, L., eds. Easy Spanish Bilingual Dictionary, 6 levels. LC 96-24328. (ENG & SPA., Illus.). 496p. 1996. pap. 6.95 (*0-8442-0550-8*, 05508) NTC Contemp Pub Co.
***Qualls, Sarah Honn & Abeles, Norman.** Psychology & the Aging Revolution: How We Adapt to Longer Life. LC 00-36265. 2000. write for info. (*1-55798-707-6*) Am Psychol.
Qualls, William. Mainframe Assembler Programming. LC 97-31763. 576p. 1998. pap. 49.99 incl. disk (*0-471-24993-9*) Wiley.
Qualman, Al. Blood on the Half Shell. LC 82-73152. (Illus.). 168p. 1982. pap. 6.95 (*0-8323-0411-5*) Binford Mort.
Qualman, Jack. The Glamour Photographer Sourcebook. 160p. 1992. pap. text 19.95 (*0-9634137-0-8*) Jax Photo Bks.
Qualman, S., jt. ed. see Dahms, B. B.
Qualset, Calvin O. Appropriate Oversight for Plants with Inherited Traits for Resistance to Pests. (Illus.). 35p. (C). 1998. reprint ed. pap. text 30.00 (*0-7881-4207-0*) DIANE Pub.
Qualset, Calvin O., jt. auth. see Collins, Wanda Williams.
Qualter, Anne. Differentiated Primary Science. LC 95-47949. (Exploring Primary Science & Technology Ser.). 160p. (C). 1996. 80.95 (*0-335-19576-8*) OpUniv Pr.
— Differentiated Primary Science. LC 95-47949. (Exploring Primary Science & Technology Ser.). 160p. (C). 1996. pap. 25.95 (*0-335-19575-X*) OpUniv Pr.
Quam, Jean K., ed. Social Services for Senior Gay Men & Lesbians. LC 96-52129. (Journal of Gay & Lesbian Social Services Ser.: Vol. 6, No. 1). 142p. (C). 1987. pap. text 12.95 (*1-56023-084-3*, Harrington Park) Haworth Pr.
— Social Services for Senior Gay Men & Lesbians. LC 96-52129. (Journal of Gay & Lesbian Social Services Ser.: Vol. 6, No. 1). 142p. (C). 1997. 54.95 (*1-56024-808-4*, Harrington Park) Haworth Pr.
Quam, Kay F. Fundamentals of Teaching & Learning. LC 98-19540. 275p. 1998. 34.00 (*1-56072-585-0*) Nova Sci Pubs.
— Ready, Set, Teach: Learn to Teach, Teach to Learn. LC 98-19540. 277p. 1998. pap. 23.95 (*1-56072-493-5*, Nova Kroshka Bks) Nova Sci Pubs.
Quamme, G. A., ed. Magnesium Homeostasis. (Journal: Mineral & Electrolyte Metabolism Ser.: Vol. 19, Nos. 4-5, 1993). (Illus.). 132p. 1993. pap. 81.00 (*3-8055-5881-3*) S Karger.
***Quammen, David.** Blood Line: Stories of Fathers & Sons. 2000. reprint ed. pap. 14.00 (*1-55566-272-2*) Johnson Bks.
— The Boiler Plate Rhino: Nature in the Eye of the Beholder. LC 99-56894. 288p. 2000. 23.50 (*0-684-83728-5*) Scribner.
Quammen, David. The Flight of the Iguana: A Sidelong View of Science & Nature. LC 97-30332. 320p. 1998. per. 13.00 (*0-684-83626-2*) S&S Trade Pap.
— Natural Acts: A Sidelong View of Science & Nature. 240p. 1996. pap. 12.00 (*0-380-71738-7*, Avon Bks) Morrow Avon.
— The Song of the Dodo: Island Biogeography in an Age of Extinctions. 704p. 1997. per. 17.00 (*0-684-82712-3*) S&S Trade Pap.
— Wild Thoughts from Wild Places. LC 97-29090. 304p. 1998. 23.50 (*0-684-83509-6*) Scribner.
— Wild Thoughts From Wild Places. 304p. 1999. pap. 13.00 (*0-684-85208-X*, Touchstone) S&S Trade Pap.
***Quammen, David & Bilger, Burkhard, eds.** The Best American Science & Nature Writing 2000. 320p. 2000. 27.50 (*0-618-08294-8*); pap. 13.00 (*0-618-08295-6*) HM.
Quan, Cao, jt. auth. see Allen, Virginia F.
***Quan, Holly.** Adventures in Nature: British Columbia. LC 99-44804. (Illus.). 312p. 2000. 18.95 (*1-56261-443-6*) Avalon Travel.
Quan, Judy. Legal Assistant's Guide to Alternative Dispute Resolution. LC 93-49766. (Paralegal Ser.). (C). 1995. ring bd. 52.75 (*0-87632-990-3*) Thomson Learn.
***Quan, Linda & Franklin, Wayne H., eds.** Ventricular Fibrillation: A Pediatric Problem. (Amerrican Heart Association Monograph Ser.). (Illus.). 320p. 2000. 95.00 (*0-87993-452-2*) Futura Pub.
Quan, Robert S. Lotus among the Magnolias: The Mississippi Chinese. LC 81-23991. (Illus.). 180p. reprint ed. pap. 55.80 (*0-7837-1071-2*, 204159400021) Bks Demand.
Quan-Yin, Amorah. Pleiadian Perspectives on Human Evolution. 304p. (Orig.). 1996. pap. 15.00 (*1-879181-33-9*) Bear & Co.
— The Pleiadian Workbook: Awakening Your Divine KA. Vivino, Gail, ed. (Illus.). 352p. (Orig.). 1996. pap. 16.00 (*1-879181-31-2*) Bear & Co.
Quanbeck, Alton H. Strategic Forces: Issues for the Mid-Seventies. LC 73-1088. (Brookings Institution Staff Papers). 104p. reprint ed. pap. 32.30 (*0-608-12467-2*, 202540000043) Bks Demand.
Quanbeck, Alton H. & Wood, Archie L. Modernizing the Strategic Bomber Force: Why & How. LC 75-38890. (Studies in Defense Policy). (Illus.). 128p. reprint ed. pap. 39.70 (*0-608-30816-1*, 202256100028) Bks Demand.
Quanbeck, Maridee, jt. auth. see Kaplan, Jared.
Quance, Frank M. Part-Time Types of Elementary Schools in New York City: A Comparative Study of Pupil Achievement. LC 72-177173. (Columbia University. Teachers College. Contributions to Education Ser.: No. 249). reprint ed. 37.50 (*0-404-55249-8*) AMS Pr.
Quance, Leroy, jt. ed. see Johnson, Glenn L.
Quanchi, Max. Pacific People & Change. (Pacific in the Twentieth Century Ser.). (Illus.). 110p. (C). 1991. pap. text 19.95 (*0-521-37627-0*) Cambridge U Pr.
Quandahl, Ellen, jt. ed. see Donahue, Patricia.
Quandt, Begrundet Von Gottfried, see Von Gottfried Quandt, Begrundet.
***Quandt, James.** Shohei Imamura. 1999. pap. text 16.95 (*0-9682969-0-4*) Ind U Pr.
Quandt, Richard E. The Collected Essays of Richard E. Quandt, 2 vols., Set. (Economists of the Twentieth Century Ser.). 864p. 1992. 230.00 (*1-85278-605-1*) E Elgar.
Quandt, Richard E. & Peston, Maurice H., eds. Prices, Competition & Equilibrium. LC 86-3549. 352p. 1986. 72.50 (*0-389-20626-1*, N8184) B&N Imports.

Q

An Asterisk (*) at the beginning of an entry indicates that the title is appearing for the first time.

Quandt, Richard E. & Rosen, Harvey S. The Conflict Between Equilibrium & Disequilibrium Theories: The Case of the U. S. Labor Market. LC 88-10618. 125p. 1988. text 20.00 (*0-88099-061-9*); pap. text 10.00 (*0-88099-060-0*) W E Upjohn.

Quandt, Richard E., jt. auth. see Asch, Peter.

Quandt, Richard E., jt. auth. see Ekman, Richard.

Quandt, Richard E., jt. auth. see Lasslo, Andrew.

Quandt, Val V., ed. see Scroggins, Ray, et al.

Quandt, William B. Between Ballots & Bullets: Algeria's Transition from Authoritarianism. LC 98-19668. 175p. 1998. pap. 16.95 (*0-8157-7301-3*); text 39.95 (*0-8157-7302-1*) Brookings.

— Camp David: Peacemaking & Politics. LC 85-48174. 426p. 1986. 42.95 (*0-8157-7290-4*); pap. 18.95 (*0-8157-7289-0*) Brookings.

— Peace Process: American Diplomacy & the Arab-Israeli Conflict since 1967. 612p. (C). 1993. 48.00 (*0-520-08388-1*) Brookings.

***Quandt, William B.** Peace Process American Diplomacy & the Arab-Israeli Conflict since 1967. rev. ed. 1999. pap. 19.95 (*0-8157-7275-0*) Brookings.

Quandt, William B. Saudi Arabia in the 1980's: Foreign Policy, Security, & Oil. LC 82-18086. 190p. 1981. 26.95 (*0-8157-7286-6*) Brookings.

— Saudi Arabia's Oil Policy. LC 82-73524. 46p. 1982. pap. 7.95 (*0-8157-7287-4*) Brookings.

— The United States & Egypt: An Essay on Policy for the 1990s. 82p. (C). 1990. pap. 8.95 (*0-8157-7295-5*) Brookings.

Quandt, William B., ed. The Middle East: Ten Years after Camp David. 450p. 1988. 44.95 (*0-8157-7294-7*); pap. 19.95 (*0-8157-7293-9*) Brookings.

Quandt, William B., jt. auth. see Bohi, Douglas R.

Quandt, William B., jt. auth. see Pierre, Andrew J.

Quang Nhuong Huynh. Water Buffalo Days: Growing up in Vietnam. LC 96-35058. (Illus.). 128p. (J). (gr. 2-5). 1997. lib. bdg. 13.89 (*0-06-024958-7*) HarpC Child Bks.

— Water Buffalo Days: Growing up in Vietnam. LC 96-35058. (Illus.). 128p. (J). (gr. 2-5). 1997. 13.95 (*0-06-024957-9*) HarpC Child Bks.

Quang, Pham T. & Chartier-Kastler, C. Merise in Practice. Sumner, F. H., ed. (Computer Science Ser.). (Illus.). 206p. (Orig.). (C). 1991. pap. text 38.00 (*0-333-55020-X*, Pub. by Macmillan Ed) Scholium Intl.

Quanide, Russ. Whos Who among Werewolves: Garou Saga. 96p. 1994. pap., per. 12.00 (*1-56504-140-2*, 3401) White Wolf.

Quann, C. James, et al, eds. Admissions, Academic Records, & Registrar Services. LC 79-88109. (Jossey-Bass Series in Higher Education). (Illus.). 509p. reprint ed. pap. 157.80 (*0-8357-4918-5*, 203784800009) Bks Demand.

Quann, Steve & Satin, Diana. Learning Computers, Speaking English: Comparative Activities for Learning English & Basic Word Processing. (Illus.). 150p. (C). write for info. (*0-472-00302-X*) U of Mich Pr.

— Learning Computers, Speaking English: Comparative Activities for Learning English & Basic Word Processing. (Illus.). 208p. (C). 2000. 19.95 (*0-472-08683-9*, 08683); pap. text 16.95 (*0-472-08655-3*, 08655) U of Mich Pr.

Quanrud, Percy, tr. see Howard, Rick C.

Quansah, George. Explorations in Macroeconomics. 474p. 1998. pap. text 67.10 (*1-56226-416-8*) CAT Pub.

— Explorations in Microeconomics. 530p. 1998. pap. text 68.75 (*1-56226-415-X*) CAT Pub.

Quanstrom, Linda. And Some Are Walked Home: Stories of Grace. LC 94-199950. 68p. 1994. pap. 6.99 (*0-8341-1478-X*) Beacon Hill.

Quant, Mary. Classic Makeup & Beauty Book. LC 96-2373. 120p. 1996. 24.95 (*0-7894-1056-7*) DK Pub Inc.

Quant, Wilhelm, ed. see Orpheus.

Quanten, E. The Polypores of Papua New Guinea: A Preliminary Conspectus. (Opera Botanica Belgica Ser.: Vol. 11). (Illus.). 352p. 1997. 100.00 (*90-72619-34-X*, Pub. by Natl Botanic Grdn Belgium) Balogh.

Quantic, Diane D. The Nature of the Place: A Study of Great Plains Fiction. LC 94-34986. xx, 203p. 1995. text 40.00 (*0-8032-3800-2*) U of Nebr Pr.

— The Nature of the Place: A Study of Great Plains Fiction. LC 94-34986. xx, 203p. 1997. pap. text 17.50 (*0-8032-8850-6*, Bison Books) U of Nebr Pr.

— William Allen White. LC 93-70137. (Western Writers Ser.: No. 109). (Illus.). 52p. 1993. pap. 4.95 (*0-88430-108-7*) Boise St U W Writ Ser.

***Quantick, David.** The Clash. (Kill Your Idols Ser.). (Illus.). 152p. 2000. pap. 13.95 (*1-56025-269-3*, Thunders Mouth) Avalon NY.

***Quantick, R.** Climatology for Airline Pilots LC 99-38977. 2000. write for info. (*0-632-05295-3*) Blackwell Sci.

Quantitative Methods of Investigations in the Clin. Studies on Neuromuscular Diseases: Proceedings of the Quantitative Methods of Investigations in the Clinics of Neuromuscular Diseases International Symposium, Giessen, April 1974. Kunze, K. & Desmedt, J. E., eds. 250p. 1975. 132.25 (*3-8055-1749-1*) S Karger.

Quantrill. Juha Leiviska. pap. write for info. (*0-471-48967-0*) Wiley.

Quantrill, Malcolm. Aalto & After: Finnish Architecture & the Modernist Tradition. (Illus.). 224p. (C). 1998. 70.00 (*0-419-19520-3*, E & FN Spon) Routledge.

— Alvar Aalto: A Critical Study. (Illus.). 307p. (C). 1989. reprint ed. pap. 30.00 (*0-941533-35-2*, NAB) I R Dee.

— The Norman Foster Studio: Consistency Through Diversity. 232p. 1997. 85.00 (*0-419-19750-8*, E & FN Spon) Routledge.

***Quantrill, Malcolm & Frampton, Kenneth.** Latin American Architecture: Six Voices. LC 99-30561. (Studies in Architecture & Culture). (Illus.). 256p. 2000. 60.00 (*0-89096-901-9*) Tex A&M Univ Pr.

Quantrill, Malcolm & Webb, Bruce, eds. The Culture of Silence: Architecture's Fifth Dimension. LC 97-31524. (Studies in Architecture & Culture: No. 4). (Illus.). 320p. 1998. 49.95 (*0-89096-785-7*) Tex A&M Univ Pr.

— Urban Forms, Suburban Dreams. LC 92-43269. (Studies in Architecture & Culture: No. 2). (Illus.). 232p. 1993. 50.00 (*0-89096-535-8*) Tex A&M Univ Pr.

Quantrille, Thomas E. & Liu, Y. A. Artificial Intelligence in Chemical Engineering. (Illus.). 593p. (C). 1992. text 71.00 (*0-12-569550-0*) Acad Pr.

Quantum, Inc. Staff. Development of Copper Organic Gasoline Additives for Improvement of Automotive Engine Combustion Efficiency. 51p. 1962. 7.65 (*0-317-34511-7*, 15) Intl Copper.

Quantz, J. Q. Problems in the Psychology of Reading. (Psychology Monographs General & Applied: Vol. 2). 1974. reprint ed. pap. 55.00 (*0-8115-1401-3*) Periodicals Srv.

Quantz, Johann J. Flute Concerto in G Major: With Piano Cadenzas by Barrere: Centennial Edition. 28p. 1994. pap. 6.95 (*0-7935-3696-0*, 50482222) H Leonard.

Quantz, Vivian D. Foghorns Saved Lives, Too: Lighthouse Living in Michigan's Upper Peninsula. 66p. 1999. pap. write for info. (*0-7392-0157-3*, PO3104) Morris Pubng.

Quanyu, Huang, et al. Business Decision Making in China. LC 96-28274. (Illus.). 316p. (C). 1997. 49.95 (*1-56024-997-8*, Intl Busn Pr); pap. 24.95 (*0-7890-0190-X*, Intl Busn Pr) Haworth Pr.

— A Guide to Successful Business Relations with the Chinese: Opening the Great Wall's Gate. LC 93-19379. 1994. lib. bdg. 59.95 (*1-56024-868-8*) Haworth Pr.

Quapong, Ohene A. True Fasting: A Heart in Anguish in Search of God's Mercy. 1998. pap. write for info. (*0-7392-0036-4*, P02805) Morris Pubng.

Quaraishi, M. Tariq, ed. Some Aspects of Prophet Muhammad's Life. LC 83-71409. 89p. (Orig.). 1985. reprint ed. pap. 4.50 (*0-89259-045-9*) Am Trust Pubns.

Quarantelli, E. L. Chemical Disasters: Preparations & Responses at the Local Level. text. write for info. (*0-8290-1289-3*) Irvington.

— Delivery of Emergency Medical Services in Disasters: Assumptions & Realities. LC 83-13028. 190p. (C). 1985. text 32.50 (*0-8290-0531-5*) Irvington.

— What Is a Disaster? A Dozen Perspectives on the Question. LC 97-30849. 328p. (C). 1998. pap. 27.99 (*0-415-17899-1*) Routledge.

— What Is a Disaster? A Dozen Perspectives on the Question. LC 97-30849. (Illus.). 328p. (C). 1998. 85.00 (*0-415-17898-3*) Routledge.

Quarantelli, E. L., jt. auth. see Helfrich, M. L.

Quarantiello, Laura E. Air-Ways: The Insider's Guide to Air Travel. LC 99-39022. 144p. 2000. pap. 17.95 (*0-936653-85-X*, Limelight Bks) Tiare Pubns.

— Cop Talk! - How to Tune in on Police Radio Communications. 2nd ed. LC 97-35220. 120p. 1999. pap. 14.95 (*0-936653-79-5*) Tiare Pubns.

— Cyber Crime: How to Protect Yourself from Computer Criminals. 144p. (Orig.). 1996. pap. 16.95 (*0-936653-74-4*, Limelight Bks) Tiare Pubns.

— On Guard! How You Can Win the War Against the Bad Guys. LC 93-48851. 128p. 1994. 17.95 (*0-936653-50-7*, Limelight Bks) Tiare Pubns.

— The Root Beer Book: A Celebration of America's Best-Loved Soft Drink. LC 97-3954. (Illus.). 100p. (Orig.). 1997. pap. 14.95 (*0-936653-78-7*) Tiare Pubns.

Quarantotto, Claudio, ed. see Prezzolini, Giuseppe.

Quaratiello, Arlene R. The College Student's Research Companion. LC 97-18811. 125p. 1997. pap. 35.00 (*1-55570-275-9*) Neal-Schuman.

***Quaratiello, Arlene Rodda.** The College Student's Research Companion. 2nd ed. LC 00-28370. 2000. pap. 37.50 (*1-55570-385-2*) Neal-Schuman.

Quaratiello, Elizabeth L., jt. auth. see Collier, George A.

Quarcoopome, Nil O., intro. African Form & Imagery: Detroit Collects. (Illus.). 110p. (Orig.). 1996. pap. 19.95 (*0-89558-145-0*) Det Inst Arts.

Quardt, Robert. Mothers of Priests: True Stories of the "Other Marys" Behind the "Other Christs" Angelus Press Editors, ed. Fisher, Marc S., tr. LC 98-181102. (GER.). 57p. (Orig.). 1995. pap. 4.25 (*0-935952-56-X*) Angelus Pr.

Quark & Behr, Ira S. Star Trek Deep Space Nine: Deep Space Nine: The Ferengi Rules of Acquisition. Ryan, Kevin, ed. 96p. 1995. per. 6.00 (*0-671-52936-6*) PB.

***Quarles, Benjamin.** Allies for Freedom: Blacks on John Brown. 2000. pap. text 18.00 (*0-306-80961-3*) Da Capo.

Quarles, Benjamin. Black Abolitionists. (Quality Paperbacks Ser.). 310p. 1991. reprint ed. pap. 13.95 (*0-306-80425-5*) Da Capo.

— Black Mosaic: Essays in Afro-American History & Historiography. LC 87-13929. 224p. (Orig.). (C). 1988. pap. 16.95 (*0-87023-605-9*) U of Mass Pr.

— Frederick Douglass. 1990. 25.00 (*0-87498-033-X*) Assoc Pubs DC.

— Frederick Douglass. LC 97-15046. (Illus.). 408p. 1997. reprint ed. pap. 15.95 (*0-306-80790-4*) Da Capo.

— Lincoln & the Negro. (Quality Paperbacks Ser.). (Illus.). 275p. 1991. reprint ed. pap. 13.95 (*0-306-80447-6*) Da Capo.

— The Negro in the American Revolution. LC 96-21111. (C). 1996. pap. 15.95 (*0-8078-4603-1*) U of NC Pr.

— The Negro in the American Revolution. LC 61-66795. 250p. 1961. reprint ed. pap. 77.50 (*0-7837-9895-4*, 206062100006) Bks Demand.

— The Negro in the Civil War. (Quality Paperbacks Ser.). (Illus.). 402p. 1989. pap. 13.95 (*0-306-80350-X*) Da Capo.

— The Negro in the Making of America. 400p. 1996. per. 12.00 (*0-684-81888-4*, Touchstone) S&S Trade Pap.

Quarles, Benjamin, ed. Blacks on John Brown. LC 72-188132. (Illus.). 180p. reprint ed. pap. 55.80 (*0-8357-7306-X*, 202022100016) Bks Demand.

Quarles, Benjamin, ed. see Douglass, Frederick.

Quarles, Charles L. Midrash Criticism: Introduction & Appraisal. LC 97-37864. 176p. (C). 1997. 49.00 (*0-7618-0924-4*); pap. 27.50 (*0-7618-0925-2*) U Pr of Amer.

Quarles, Chester, jt. auth. see Kuboviak, Jim.

Quarles, Chester L. The Ku Klux Klan & Related American Racialist & Antisemitic Organizations: A History & Analysis. LC 99-28659. 324p. 1999. lib. bdg. 45.00 (*0-7864-0647-X*) McFarland & Co.

***Quarles, Chester L.** Staying Safe at School. 192p. 2000. pap. 10.99 (*0-8054-2421-0*) Broadman.

Quarles, Chester L. Staying Safe at School. LC 93-6441. (New Survival Skills for Teachers Ser.). 96p. 1993. pap. 16.95 (*0-8039-6086-7*) Corwin Pr.

***Quarles, Chester L.** Terrorism: Avoidance & Survival "Certified Protection Professional" 2nd ed. 264p. 2000. pap. 27.50 (*0-7618-1692-5*) U Pr of Amer.

Quarles, Francis. Argalus & Parthenia. Freeman, David, ed. LC 86-45041. (Renaissance English Text Society Ser.: Series 6, No. 11). (Illus.). 240p. 1987. 30.00 (*0-918016-90-8*) Folger Bks.

— Complete Works in Prose & Verse, 3 vols., Set. (BCL1-PR English Literature Ser.). 1992. reprint ed. lib. bdg. 225.00 (*0-7812-7395-1*) Rprt Serv.

— Emblemes. LC 91-22286. 340p. 1991. 80.00 (*0-8201-1458-8*) Schol Facsimiles.

— Emblemes & Hieroglyphikes of the Life of Man. (GER.). 381p. 1991. reprint ed. write for info. (*3-487-09264-6*) G Olms Pubs.

Quarles, G. J., ed. Solid State Lasers III. 1992. 20.00 (*0-8194-0773-9*, 1627) SPIE.

Quarles, Garland R. Some Worthy Lives. LC 88-51619. (Illus.). 280p. (C). 1988. 23.00 (*0-923198-00-8*) Winchester-Frederick Cty Hist Soc.

***Quarles, Heather.** A Door Near Here. (Illus.). 240p. (YA). 2000. mass mkt. 4.50 (*0-440-22761-5*, LLL BDD) BDD Bks Young Read.

Quarles, Jaime C., jt. auth. see Brown, Jamieson-Fausett.

Quarles, Jaime C., tr. see Brown, Jamieson-Fausett.

Quarles, Jaime C., tr. see Latourette, Kenneth S.

Quarles, Jaime C., tr. see Sullivan, James L.

Quarles, Jim E. Discus As a Hobby: Everything You Need to Know to Get Started. 96p. 1995. pap. text 8.95 (*0-86622-405-X*, TT028) TFH Pubns.

***Quarles, Jim E.** Success with Discus, Vol. 1. (Illus.). 64p. 1999. 24.95 (*0-9673201-0-0*, SWD -1) Creat Aqua Pubg Co.

Quarles, Johnny. Fool's Gold. 368p. 1993. mass mkt. 4.50 (*0-380-76813-5*, Avon Bks) Morrow Avon.

— No Man's Land. 368p. (Orig.). 1993. mass mkt. 4.99 (*0-380-76814-3*, Avon Bks) Morrow Avon.

— Shadow of the Gun. 384p. (Orig.). 1995. mass mkt. 5.50 (*0-380-77657-X*, Avon Bks) Morrow Avon.

— Spirit Trail. 320p. (Orig.). 1995. mass mkt. 4.99 (*0-380-77656-1*, Avon Bks) Morrow Avon.

— Treachery. 1996. mass mkt. 5.99 (*0-380-78325-8*, Avon Bks) Morrow Avon.

Quarles, Lemuel C., tr. see Brown, Jamieson-Fausett.

Quarles, Lemuel C., tr. see Latourette, Kenneth S.

Quarles, Lucille W. Consumer Attitudes & Wishes about Health Care: Index of New Information with Authors, Subjects & Bibliography. rev. ed. 149p. 1995. 47.50 (*0-7883-0701-0*); pap. 44.50 (*0-7883-0702-9*) ABBE Pubs Assn.

— Consumer's Attitudes to Health Care: Index of Modern of Information. rev. ed. LC 88-47542. 155p. 1994. 47.50 (*0-7883-0692-8*); pap. 44.50 (*0-7883-0693-6*) ABBE Pubs Assn.

— Jurisprudence & Rights to Treatment: Index of Modern Information. LC 88-47582. 150p. 1988. 47.50 (*0-88164-762-4*); pap. 44.50 (*0-88164-763-2*) ABBE Pubs Assn.

Quarles, Mary D. & Meyer, Tommye Q. Kirby Kin: From the 16th Century to the Present. LC 89-92785. 496p. (C). 1993. 45.00 (*0-9625367-0-9*) T Q Meyer.

Quarles, Mike. Down & Dirty: Hollywood's Exploitation Filmmakers & Their Movies. LC 92-56683. (Illus.). 208p. 1993. lib. bdg. 32.50 (*0-89950-877-4*) McFarland & Co.

Quarles, Mike, jt. auth. see Anderson, N.

Quarles, Sandra L. The Legal Assistant's Notebook Vol. 1: So. California. 305p. 1992. ring bd. 85.00 (*0-9629697-5-3*) ASAP Pubng.

— The Legal Assistant's Notebook Vol. 2: No. California. 505p. 1992. ring bd. 90.00 (*0-9629697-6-1*) ASAP Pubng.

Quarm, Roger & Wilcox, Scott. Masters of the Sea: British Marine Watercolors, 1650-1930. (Illus.). 96p. 1990. text 29.95 (*0-7148-2490-9*) Phaidon Pr.

***Quarm, Roger & Wyllie, John.** W. L. Wyllie: Marine Artist, 1851-1931. (Illus.). 143p. 1999. 49.50 (*1-871136-01-6*, Pub. by Beetles Ltd) Antique Collect.

Quarmby, F. Banknotes & Banking in the Isle of Man. 1994. 55.00 (*0-907605-51-6*) S J Durst.

Quarmby, Jacqueline, jt. ed. see Clough, Eric.

Quarrell, John, jt. auth. see Nabarro Nathanson Pensions Department Members.

Quarrell, John J. Quarrell: Law of Pension Fund Investment. 230p. 1990. boxed set 134.00 (*0-406-67819-7*, MICHIE) LEXIS Pub.

***Quarrell, Oliver.** Huntington's Disease: The Facts. LC 99-31801. (The Facts Ser.). (Illus.). 160p. 1999. pap. text 19.95 (*0-19-262930-1*) OUP.

Quarrell, W. H., tr. see Lichtenberg, Georg C.

Quarrey, Michael, et al. Taking Stock: Employee Ownership at Work. LC 86-14045. 200p. 1986. 22.50 (*0-88730-131-2*, HarpBusn) HarpInfo.

Quarrie, Bruce. Airborne Assault: Parachute Forces in Action 1940-1990. 1992. 32.95 (*0-85059-807-9*, Pub. by P Stephens) Haynes Manuals.

— Ardennes-Central Sector: V Panzer Army. (Order of Battle Ser.: No. 8). 1999. pap. text 19.95 (*1-85532-857-7*) Ospry.

— Ardennes-Central Sector VII US Corps & VIII US Corps, 9. 1999. pap. text 19.95 (*1-85532-858-5*) Ospry.

— Ardenne's Northern Front, 1944: Allied Forces. (Order of Battle Ser.: Vol. 5). (Illus.). 96p. 1999. pap. 19.95 (*1-85532-854-2*, Pub. by Ospry) Stackpole.

— German Airborne Troops, 1939-45. (Men-at-Arms Ser.: No. 139). (Illus.). 48p. pap. 11.95 (*0-85045-480-8*, 9071, Pub. by Ospry) Stackpole.

— The Waffen-SS Soldier, 1940-45. (Warrior Ser.: No. 2). (Illus.). 64p. pap. 12.95 (*1-85532-288-9*, 9601, Pub. by Ospry) Stackpole.

Quarrie, Gordon M. More Stories of the Old Duck Hunters, Vol. 2. Taylor, Zack, ed. (Illus.). 198p. 1994. 19.50 (*1-57223-004-5*, 1509) Willow Creek Pr.

Quarrie, Paul. Treasures of Eton College Library. (Illus.). 122p. 1990. 24.95 (*0-87598-089-9*) Pierpont Morgan.

Quarrie, Stuart. Navigation, Strategy & Tactics. 1998. pap. text 34.95 (*0-85265-031-0*) Fernhurst Bks.

Quarrier, Ian & Borton, Mark, eds. Embassy's Complete Boating Guide to the Florida Keys & the Dry Tortugas N. Y. P. (Illus.). 450p. 1997. spiral bd. 39.95 (*0-930527-19-4*) Maptech Inc.

Quarrier, Ian, jt. ed. see Caruso, Donna.

***Quarrier Press Staff.** West Virginia Getaways: A Guide to the State's Bed & Breakfast & Country Inns. LC 99-65780. (Illus.). 304p. 1999. pap. 14.95 (*1-891852-08-6*) Quarrier Pr.

Quarrington, Paul. Fishing with My Old Guy: The Hilarious Quest for the Biggest Speckled Trout in North America. Turner, Philip, ed. 176p. 1996. 19.00 (*1-56836-155-6*) Kodansha.

— King Leary. 256p. 1994. pap. 12.95 (*0-385-25484-9*) Doubleday.

***Quarrington, Paul.** The Spirit Cabinet. LC 99-55840. 352p. 2000. 24.00 (*0-87113-805-0*, Pub. by Grove-Atltic) Publishers Group.

— The Spirit Cabinet. 352p. 2000. pap. write for info. (*0-679-31031-2*) Random.

Quarrington, Paul. Whale Music. 224p. 1989. 22.95 (*0-385-25210-2*) Doubleday.

— Whale Music. 240p. 1994. 12.95 (*0-385-25485-7*) Doubleday.

Quarrington, Paul, ed. Original Six: True Stories from Hockey's Classic Era. LC 98-108671. (Illus.). 160p. 21.99 (*0-433-39752-7*) Buttrwrth-Heinemann.

Quarrington, Tom. Logan in Overtime. 224p. 1990. pap. 14.95 (*0-385-25152-1*) Doubleday.

Quarry, Neville. Award Winning Australian Architecture. LC 97-132168. (Illus.). 248p. 1997. text 65.00 (*90-5703-201-5*) Gordon & Breach.

Quarry, W. Edmund. Dictionary of Musical Compositions & Composers. 192p. 1991. reprint ed. 69.00 (*0-7812-9304-9*) Rprt Serv.

***Quarstein, John V.** Battle of the Ironclads. (Civil War History Ser.). (Illus.). 128p. 1999. pap. 18.99 (*0-7385-0113-1*, Pub. by Tempus Pubng) Arcadia Publng.

Quarstein, John V. The Civil War on the Virginia Peninsula. (Images of America Ser.). (Illus.). 128p. 1997. pap. 16.99 (*0-7524-0920-4*) Arcadia Publng.

— Hampton & Newport News in the Civil War: Peninsula at War. (Virginia Civil War Battles & Leaders Ser.). (Illus.). 197p. 1998. 25.00 (*1-56190-109-1*) H E Howard.

— World War I on the Virginia Peninsula. (Images of America Ser.). (Illus.). 128p. 1999. pap. 18.99 (*0-7524-0919-0*) Arcadia Publng.

Quart, Barbara K. Women Directors: The Emergence of a New Cinema. LC 88-1141. 281p. 1988. 55.00 (*0-275-92962-0*, C2962, Praeger Pubs) Greenwood.

— Women Directors: The Emergence of a New Cinema. LC 88-1141. 284p. 1989. pap. 21.95 (*0-275-93477-2*, B3477, Praeger Pubs) Greenwood.

Quart, Irving. Environmental Stress Screening: Facts & Myths. (Illus.). 121p. (C). 1989. student ed. 100.00 (*0-918247-05-5*) Tustin Tech.

Quart, Leonard, jt. auth. see Auster, Albert.

Quart, Leonard, jt. auth. see Carney, Ray.

Quartapelle, L. Numerical Solution of the Incompressible Navier-Stokes Equations. LC 93-28305. (International Series of Numerical Mathematics: Vol. 113). 1993. 100.00 (*3-7643-2935-1*); 118.00 (*0-8176-2935-1*) Birkhauser.

Quartararo, Anne T. Women Teachers & Popular Education in Nineteenth Century France: Social Values & Corporate Identity at the Normal School Institution. LC 94-45047. (Illus.). 232p. 1995. 38.50 (*0-87413-545-1*) U Delaware Pr.

Quartel, Rose. Aqua Lad. 180p. (Orig.). (J). (gr. 8-12). 1996. pap. write for info. (*1-57502-103-X*) Morris Pubng.

***Quarter, Jack.** Beyond the Bottom Line: Socially Innovative Business Owners. LC 00-32815. 254p. 2000. 59.00 (*1-56720-414-7*, Quorum Bks) Greenwood.

Quarter, Jack. Crisis in the Israeli Kibbutz: Meeting the Challenge of Changing Times. Leviatan, Uriel & Oliver, Hugh, eds. LC 97-26902. 208p. 1998. 59.95 (*0-275-95838-8*, Praeger Pubs) Greenwood.

— Crossing the Line: Unionized Employee Ownership & Investment Funds. LC 95-220754. 215p. 29.95 (*1-55028-457-6*, Pub. by J Lorimer); pap. 19.95 (*1-55028-456-8*, Pub. by J Lorimer) Formac Dist Ltd.

Q

Quarter, Jack & Melnyk, George, eds. Partners in Enterprise: The Worker Ownership Phenomenon. 201p. (Orig.). 1989. 45.99 (*0-921689-45-4*, Pub. by Black Rose); pap. 16.99 (*0-921689-44-6*, Pub. by Black Rose) Consort Bk Sales.

— Partners in Enterprise: The Worker Ownership Phenomenon. LC 89-90248. (Black Rose Bks.: Vol. R135). 214p. (Orig.). 1989. reprint ed. pap. 66.40 (*0-608-00460-X*, 206127900007) Bks Demand.

Quarter, Jack, jt. auth. see Wilkinson, Paul.

Quarterly, Cornell. The Essentials of Tableside Cookery. 72p. 8.95 (*0-318-41635-2*, 220) Am Bartenders.

Quarterly Journal Staff. Sourcebook on Asbestos Diseases Case Law Quarterly. 1989. 75.00 (*0-8240-7348-7*, 82414-10, MICHIE) LEXIS Pub.

Quartermain, Peter. Disjunctive Poetics: From Gertrude Stein & Louis Zukofsky to Susan Howe. (Cambridge Studies in American Literature & Culture: No. 59). 254p. (C). 1992. text 59.95 (*0-521-41268-4*) Cambridge U Pr.

Quartermain, Peter, ed. American Poets, 1880-1945: First Series, Vol. 45. (Dictionary of Literary Biography Ser.: Vol. 45). 514p. 1985. text 155.00 (*0-8103-1723-0*) Gale.

— American Poets 1880 to 1945: Third Series, Vol. 54. (Dictionary of Literary Biography Ser.: Vol. 54). (Illus.). 743p. 1986. text 296.00 (*0-8103-1732-X*) Gale.

— American Poets 1880 to 1945: Second Series, Vol. 48. (Dictionary of Literary Biography Ser.: Vol. 48). 350p. 1986. text 155.00 (*0-8103-1726-5*) Gale.

Quartermain, Peter, jt. auth. see DuPlessis, Rachel B.

Quartermain, Peter, jt. ed. see Caddel, Richard.

Quartermain, Peter, jt. ed. see Emony, Elliot.

Quartermaine, L., jt. ed. see Pollard.

Quartermaine, L., ed. see Ramphal.

Quartermaine, Luisa, tr. & intro. see Morandini, Giuliana.

Quartermaine, Peter. Building on the Sea: Form & Meaning in Modern Ship Architecture. (Illus.). 129p. 1996. 50.00 (*1-85490-446-9*, Pub. by Wiley) Wiley.

Quartermaine, Peter. Port Architecture, Academy Edition. (Illus.). 128p. 1999. 45.00 (*0-471-98470-1*) Wiley.

— Thomas Keneally. (Modern Fiction Ser.). 128p. 1991. pap. 10.95 (*0-340-51826-X*, A6318, Pub. by E A) Routldge.

***Quarterman, Corine J.** Killjoy: A Cop's Fight Against Child Sexual Abuse. 288p. 2000. pap. 19.95 (*0-9675443-0-0*) Humming Pr VT.

Quarterman, John P., jt. auth. see Gray, Tom.

Quarterman, John S. E-Mail Companion: Communications Effectively Via the Internet. 336p. (C). 1994. pap. text 19.95 (*0-201-40658-6*) Addison-Wesley.

— The Internet Book: A Complete User & Producer's Guide. (C). 1996. pap. text. write for info. (*0-201-82708-5*) Addison-Wesley.

— The Matrix: Computer Networks & Conferencing Systems Worldwide. (Illus.). 719p. 1989. pap. 64.95 (*1-55558-033-5*, EY C176E-DP, Digital DEC) Buttrwrth-Heinemann.

— UniForum Technology Guide: Network Applications. 34p. pap. text 10.00 (*0-936593-13-X*) UniForum.

— UniForum Technology Guide: Network Substrata. 30p. pap. text 10.00 (*0-936593-14-8*) UniForum.

Quarterman, John S. & Mitchell, Smoot C. The InterNet Connection: System Connectivity & Configuration. (Illus.). 288p. (C). 1993. 39.95 (*0-201-54237-4*) Addison-Wesley.

Quarterman, John S., jt. auth. see Carl-Mitchell, Smoot.

Quartermaster General of the Army Staff. U. S. Army Uniforms & Equipment, 1889: Specifications for Clothing, Camp & Garrison Equipage, & Clothing & Equipage Materials. LC 86-6972. (Illus.). ix, 375p. 1986. reprint ed. pap. 20.00 (*0-8032-9552-9*, Bison Books) U of Nebr Pr.

Quarteroni, A. & Valli, A. Numerical Approximation of Partial Differential Equations. LC 94-21763. (Computational Mathematics Ser.: Vol. 23). 1997. 108.95 (*0-387-57111-6*) Spr-Verlag.

Quarteroni, Alfio & Valli, A. Numerical Approximation of Partial Differential Equations 2nd ed. LC 97-160884. (Series in Computational Mathematics). xvi, 543p. 1997. write for info. (*3-540-57111-6*) Spr-Verlag.

Quarteroni, Alfio & Valli, Alberto. Domain Decomposition Methods for Partial Differential Equations. LC 99-17650. (Numerical Mathematics & Scientific Computation Ser.). (Illus.). 376p. 1999. text 95.00 (*0-19-850178-1*) OUP.

***Quarteroni, Alfio, et al.** Numerical Mathematics. LC 99-59414. (Texts in Applied Mathematics Ser.). 677p. 2000. 59.95 (*0-387-98959-5*) Spr-Verlag.

Quarteroni, Alfio, ed. see Sixth International Conference on Domain Decomposi.

Quartey. Critical Analysis of Contributions. 59.95 (*1-84014-147-6*) Ashgate Pub Co.

Quartim, Joao. Dictatorship & Armed Struggle in Brazil. Fernbach, David, tr. LC 71-178711. 250p. reprint ed. pap. 77.50 (*0-8357-6093-6*, 203434800089) Bks Demand.

Quartly, Marian, et al, eds. Freedom Bound Vol. 1: Documents on Women in Colonial Australia. 240p. 1995. pap. 22.95 (*1-86373-735-9*) Paul & Co Pubs.

Quarto Books Staff. How to Make Your Own Doll & Doll's Clothes. 1993. 12.98 (*1-55521-920-9*) Bk Sales Inc.

— How to Make Your Own Doll Furniture. 1993. 12.98 (*1-55521-923-3*) Bk Sales Inc.

— How to Make Your Own Doll House. 1993. 12.98 (*1-55521-921-7*) Bk Sales Inc.

Quarto, P. Encyclopedia of Model Making Techniques. 192p. 1996. 14.98 (*0-7858-0614-8*) Bk Sales Inc.

— Furniture: The Decorative Arts Library. 160p. 1996. 17.98 (*0-7858-0617-2*) Bk Sales Inc.

— Illustrated Encyclopedia of Tractors. 192p. 1996. 19.98 (*0-7858-0608-3*) Bk Sales Inc.

— Jewelry: The Decorative Arts Library. 160p. 1996. 17.98 (*0-7858-0616-4*) Bk Sales Inc.

— Krafts for Kids: Make It with Models. 96p. 1996. 12.98 (*0-7858-0622-9*) Bk Sales Inc.

— Krafts for Kids: Make It with Paint. 96p. 1996. 12.98 (*0-7858-0621-0*) Bk Sales Inc.

— Krafts for Kids: Origami. 1996. 12.98 (*0-7858-0620-2*) Bk Sales Inc.

— Pickups: Trucking in Style. 192p. 1996. 19.98 (*0-7858-0615-6*) Bk Sales Inc.

— Practical Print Making. 160p. 1996. 15.98 (*0-7858-0655-5*) Bk Sales Inc.

— Real Chili Cookbook. 128p. 1996. pap. text 12.98 (*0-7858-0624-5*) Bk Sales Inc.

— Recreational Railroads. 192p. 1996. 19.98 (*0-7858-0654-7*) Bk Sales Inc.

Quarton, Barbara A., ed. see Reynolds, Ray.

Quarton, Bill, jt. auth. see Barnard, Phil.

Quarton, Marjorie. Corporal Jack. large type ed. 512p. 1988. 27.99 (*0-7089-1840-9*) Ulverscroft.

— The Cow Watched the Battle. 100p. (J). (gr. 3-7). 1990. pap. 6.95 (*1-85371-084-9*, Pub. by Poolbeg Pr) Dufour.

— No Harp Like My Own. large type ed. 1990. 27.99 (*0-7089-2177-9*) Ulverscroft.

— One Dog, His Man & His Trials. (Illus.). 176p. 1993. pap. 12.95 (*0-85236-253-6*, Pub. by Farming Pr) Diamond Farm Bk.

— One Dog, His Man & His Trials. large type ed. 166p. 1995. 19.95 (*1-85695-337-8*, Pub. by ISIS Lrg Prnt) Transaction Pubs.

Quarton, Marjorie & Presberg, Carole. The Working Border Collie: AKC Rank #83. (Illus.). 256p. 1998. 35.95 (*0-7938-0496-5*, TS-287) TFH Pubns.

Quartro, James. The Stewards of South Beach. LC 99-229042. 272p. 1999. 25.00 (*0-9668975-0-1*) C James Pubg.

Quartz, Bob, ed. Return Engagement. (Illus.). 304p. spiral bd. 10.00 (*0-9621733-0-4*) JBQCS.

Quartz, Karen H., jt. ed. see Oakes, Jeannie.

Quartz, Steven R. Who We Are. 2000. write for info. (*0-688-16218-5*, Wm Morrow) Morrow Avon.

Quarve-Peterson, Julee, jt. auth. see Salmen, John P.

***Quas, Jodi A., et al, eds.** Memory & Suggestibility in the Forensic Interview. (A Volume in the Personality & Clinical Psychology Series). 400p. 2000. write for info. (*0-8058-3080-4*) L Erlbaum Assocs.

Quas, Vince. The Lean Body Promise: An Owner's Manual. LC 89-4162. (Illus.). 288p. (Orig.). 1990. pap. 15.95 (*0-925572-36-5*) Synesis Pr.

Quasem, Mohammad A. The Ethics of Al-Ghazali. LC 78-15259. (Monographs in Islamic Religion & Theology). 276p. 1978. 35.00 (*0-88206-021-X*) Caravan Bks.

Quasem, Muhammad A. Al-Ghazali on Islamic Guidance. 1979. 12.00 (*0-318-00409-7*) Quasem.

— The Ethics of Al-Ghazali: A Composite Ethics in Islam. 1975. 17.85 (*0-686-18952-3*); pap. 9.00 (*0-686-18953-1*) Quasem.

— The Jewels of the Qur'an: Al-Ghazali's Theory. 1977. 12.00 (*0-686-23467-7*) Quasem.

— The Jewels of the Qur'an: Al-Ghazali's Theory. 240p. 1982. pap. 14.95 (*0-7103-0034-4*) Routledge.

— The Recitation & Interpretation of the Qur'an. 1979. 12.00 (*0-318-00410-0*) Quasem.

— The Recitation & Interpretation of the Qur'an: Al-Gharzali's Theory. 124p. (Orig.). 1982. pap. 14.95 (*0-7103-0035-2*) Routledge.

— Salvation of the Soul & Islamic Devotion. 1981. 19.95 (*0-318-00411-9*) Quasem.

— Salvation of the Soul & Islamic Devotion. 200p. 1982. pap. 14.95 (*0-7103-0033-6*) Routledge.

Quasha, George. Ainu Dreams: Poems from the Dreams of Buun: Poems from the Dreams of Buun. LC 99-23226. 112p. 1999. pap. text 13.95 (*1-58177-053-7*, Pub. by Barrytown Ltd) Consort Bk Sales.

— Gary Hill: Hand Heard/Liminal Objects. 56p. 1996. pap. text 15.00 (*1-886449-39-2*) Barrytown Ltd.

— Giving the Lily Back Her Hands. LC 79-64920. 64p. 1980. pap. write for info. (*0-930794-10-9*) Station Hill Pr.

— In No Time. (Illus.). 144p. 2000. pap. 7.95 (*0-88268-033-1*) Station Hill Pr.

— Monarch Notes on Beowulf. (Orig.). (C). 3.95 (*0-671-00550-2*, Arco) Macmillan Gen Ref.

— Monarch Notes on Joyce's Portrait of the Artist As a Young Man & Dubliners. (Orig.). (C). 3.95 (*0-671-00563-4*, Arco) Macmillan Gen Ref.

***Quasha, George.** Preverbs of Tell: News Torqued from Undertime. 150p. 2001. pap. 14.95 (*1-58177-070-7*) Barrytown Ltd.

Quasha, George. Raquel Rabinovich: The Dark Is the Source of the Light. 50p. 1997. pap. text 15.00 (*1-886449-38-4*) Barrytown Ltd.

Quasha, George & Rothenberg, Jerome, eds. America a Prophecy: A New Reading of American Poetry from Pre-Columbian Times to the Present. 642p. 1999. pap. text 26.95 (*1-886449-55-4*, P9554, Pub. by Barrytown Ltd) Consort Bk Sales.

Quasha, George & Stein, Charles. Viewer, Vol. 3. (Gary Hill's Projective Installations Ser.). 64p. 1997. pap. text 15.00 (*1-886449-50-3*) Barrytown Ltd.

Quasha, George, et al. Tall Ships. LC 97-12548. (Gary Hill's Projective Installations Ser.). 64p. 1997. 15.00 (*1-886449-54-6*) Barrytown Ltd.

Quasha, George, ed. see Beaulieu, John.

Quasha, George, ed. see Blanchot, Maurice.

Quasha, George, ed. see Chester, Laura.

Quasha, George, ed. see Henderson, Julie.

Quasha, George, ed. see Jahan, Dean.

Quasha, George, ed. see Kelly, Robert.

Quasha, George, ed. see Padmasambhava.

Quasha, George, ed. see Phipps, Frances.

Quasha, George, ed. see Sondheim, Alan.

Quasha, George, ed. see Trager, Milton & Guadagno, Cathy.

***Quasha, Jennifer.** The Manx: The Cat with No Tail. LC 98-53562. 1999. write for info. (*0-8239-5512-5*, PowerKids) Rosen Group.

Quasha, Jennifer. American Shorthair Cats: Everything about Purchase, Care, Nutrition, Health Care, Behavior, & Showing. LC 98-53561. (Kid's Cat Library). 24p. (J). 1999. 18.60 (*0-8239-5513-3*) Rosen Group.

***Quasha, Jennifer.** The Birth & Growth of a Nation: Hands-On Projects about Symbols of American Liberty. LC 00-29809. (Great Social Studies Projects Ser.). (Illus.). (J). 2001. write for info. (*0-8239-5703-9*, PowerKids) Rosen Group.

— Covered Wagons: Hands-On Projects about America's Westward Expansion. LC 00-29855. (Illus.). 2001. write for info. (*0-8239-5704-7*, PowerKids) Rosen Group.

— Gold Rush: Hands-On Projects about Mining the Riches of California. LC 00-27752. 2001. write for info. (*0-8239-5705-5*, PowerKids) Rosen Group.

— Jamestown: Hands-On Projects about One of America's First Communities. LC 00-24315. (Great Social Studies Projects Ser.). (Illus.). (J). 2000. pap. write for info. (*0-8239-5701-2*, PowerKids) Rosen Group.

— Maine Coon Cats: Everything about Purchase, Care, Nutrition, Reproduction, Diseases & Behavior. LC 99-53565. (Kid's Cat Library). 24p. (J). 1999. 18.60 (*0-8239-5510-9*, PowerKids) Rosen Group.

Quasha, Jennifer. Persian Cats. LC 98-53564. (Kid's Cat Library). 24p. (J). 1999. 18.60 (*0-8239-5508-7*, PowerKids) Rosen Group.

***Quasha, Jennifer.** The Pony Express: Hands-On Projects about Early Communication. LC 00-26676. (Great Social Studies Projects). (Illus.). (J). 2000. write for info. (*0-8239-5702-0*, PowerKids) Rosen Group.

Quasha, Jennifer. Siamese Cats. LC 98-46361. (Pets Throughout History Ser.). 24p. (J). 1999. lib. bdg. 18.60 (*0-8239-5509-5*, PowerKids) Rosen Group.

— The Sphynx: The Hairless Cat. LC 98-53563. (A Kid's Cat Library). 24p. 1999. 18.60 (*0-8239-5511-7*, PowerKids) Rosen Group.

***Quasha, Jennifer.** The Story of the Dachshund. LC 99-11606. (Dogs Throughout History Ser.). 24p. (J). 1999. lib. bdg. 18.60 (*0-8239-5516-8*) Rosen Group.

— Story of the Dalmatian. LC 98-49409. (Dogs Throughout History Ser.). 24p. (J). 2000. lib. bdg. 18.60 (*0-8239-5515-X*, PowerKids) Rosen Group.

Quasha, Jennifer. The Story of the Saint Bernard. LC 98-49450. (Dogs Throughout History Ser.). 24p. (J). 1999. lib. bdg. 18.60 (*0-8239-5517-6*, PowerKids) Rosen Group.

***Quashie, Kevin, et al.** New Bones: Contemporary Black Writers in America. LC 00-22516. 1088p. 2000. pap. 44.00 (*0-13-014127-5*) P-H.

Quasney. Qbasic Using Subprograms. 2nd ed. (Programming Ser.). (C). 1997. pap. 56.95 (*0-7600-5099-6*) Course Tech.

***Quasney, James.** Microsoft Excel 2000 Complete Concepts & Techniques. 440p. (C). 1999. 38.95 (*0-7895-4675-2*) Course Tech.

Quasney, James. Programming in QuickBASIC. (Shelly Cashman Ser.). (C). 1991. pap., teacher ed. 18.50 (*0-87835-798-X*) Course Tech.

***Quasney, James.** Qbasic, Fundamentals & Style with introduction to MS Visual Basic. 2nd ed. (Programming Ser.). (C). 2000. pap. 42.50 (*0-619-01625-6*) Course Tech.

Quasney, James, et al. QBASIC Fundamentals & Style with an Introduction to Microsoft Visual Basic for Windows. (Shelly Cashman Ser.). 608p. (C). 1995. pap. 40.00 incl. disk (*0-87709-896-4*) Course Tech.

Quasney, James S. Programming in QuickBASIC. (Shelly Cashman Ser.). 128p. (C). 1991. pap., teacher ed. 10.50 (*0-87835-777-7*) Course Tech.

Quasney, James S. & Maniotes, John. Complete BASIC: For the Short Course. (Illus.). 196p. 1985. teacher ed. write for info. (*0-87835-158-2*) Course Tech.

Quasney, James S. & Waggoner, Gloria A. Complete Computer Concepts & Programming in Microsoft BASIC. (Shelly Cashman Ser.). (Illus.). 450p. (C). 1992. mass mkt. 39.00 (*0-87835-784-X*) Course Tech.

Quasney, James S., et al. Microsoft Excel for Windows 95. LC 96-35075. 432p. 1996. pap. 38.95 (*0-7895-0734-X*) Course Tech.

— QBASIC Fundamentals & Style with an Introduction to Microsoft Visual Basic for Windows, Incl. instr. manual. 608p. (C). 1995. text 57.95 incl. 3.5 ld (*0-7895-0021-3*) Course Tech.

Quassowski, Hans, ed. see Kompanie LAH Veterans.

Quast, Barbara. Making Miniature Flowers with Polymer Clay. LC 98-10111. (Illus.). 128p. 1998. pap. 22.99 (*0-89134-821-2*, North Lght Bks) F & W Pubns Inc.

Quast, Kevin. Reading the Corinthian Correspondence: An Introduction. LC 94-15074. 288p. 1994. pap. 14.95 (*0-8091-3481-0*) Paulist Pr.

— Reading the Gospel of John: An Introduction. LC 91-32111. 176p. 1992. pap. 11.95 (*0-8091-3297-4*) Paulist Pr.

Quast, Kevin B. Peter & the Beloved Disciple: Figures for a Community in Crisis. (JSNT Supplement Ser.: No. 32). 232p. 1989. 70.00 (*1-85075-217-6*, Pub. by Sheffield Acad) CUP Services.

Quast, Otto. Der Begriff des Belief Bei David Hume. (Abhandlungen Zur Philosophie und Ihrer Geschichte Ser.: Bd. 17). (GER.). viii, 122p. 1980. reprint ed. write for info. (*3-487-06776-5*) G Olms Pubs.

Quasten, J. Music & Worship in Pagan & Christian Antiquity. 1983. 14.95 (*0-9602378-7-9*, Pastoral Press) OR Catholic.

Quasten, J., et al, eds. Poems of St. Paulinus of Nola. Walsh, P. G., tr. (Ancient Christian Writers Ser.: No. 40). 1975. 29.95 (*0-8091-0197-1*) Paulist Pr.

Quasten, J. & Paulinus, Nola. Letters of Saint Paulinus of Nola, Vol. 1. (Ancient Christian Writers Ser.: Nos. 35-36). 1966. 18.95 (*0-8091-0088-6*) Paulist Pr.

— Letters of Saint Paulinus of Nola, Vol. 2. (Ancient Christian Writers Ser.: Nos. 35-36). 1967. 24.95 (*0-8091-0089-4*) Paulist Pr.

Quasten, J., jt. auth. see Plumpe, J.

Quasten, J., ed. see Augustine, Saint.

Quasten, J., ed. see Jerome.

Quasten, Johannes. Patrology, Vol. 1. LC 83-72018. 608p. 1994. pap. 32.95 (*0-87061-084-8*) Chr Classics.

Quasten, Johannes. Patrology, Vol. 3. LC 83-72018. Vol. 3. 350p. 1994. pap. 41.95 (*0-87061-086-4*) Chr Classics.

Quasten, Johannes. Patrology, Vol. 4. LC 83-72018. 667p. 1994. pap. 52.95 (*0-87061-127-5*) Chr Classics.

Quasten, Johannes. Patrology, 4 vols., Vol. 4. LC 83-72018. 668p. 1994. pap. 149.95 (*0-87061-141-0*) Chr Classics.

Quasten, Johannes, ed. Patrology, Vol. 2. LC 83-72018. Vol. 2. 452p. 1994. pap. 36.95 (*0-87061-085-6*, 6912) Chr Classics.

Quasthoff, Uta M., ed. Aspects of Oral Communication. LC 94-45206. (Research in Text Theory Ser.: No. 21). vi, 493p. (C). 1995. lib. bdg. 192.35 (*3-11-014465-4*) De Gruyter.

Quastler, I. E. Missouri Pacific Northwest: A History of the Kansas City Northwestern Railroad. (Illus.). 136p. 1994. pap. 31.95 (*0-942035-30-5*) South Platte.

— The Railroads of Lawrence, Kansas, 1854-1900. (Illus.). 1979. pap. 25.00 (*0-87291-094-6*) Coronado Pr.

***Quastler, I. E.** Union Pacific West from Leavenworth: A History of the Leavenworth, Kansas & Western Railway. (Illus.). 88p. 1999. pap. 22.95 (*0-942035-53-4*) South Platte.

Quastler, I. E., jt. auth. see Davies, R. E.

Quastler, Imre E. Kansas Central Narrow Gauge: Slim Rails Across the Midlands. (Illus.). 104p. 1999. pap. 25.95 (*0-942035-48-8*) South Platte.

Quataert, Donald. Home, Workshop & Factory in the Ottoman Middle East, 1800-1914. (Middle East Library). (Illus.). 244p. (C). 1993. text 64.95 (*0-521-42017-2*) Cambridge U Pr.

***Quataert, Donald.** The Ottoman Empire, 1700 - 1922. (New Approaches to European History Ser.: Vol. 17). (Illus.). 232p. 2000. 54.95 (*0-521-63328-1*); pap. 19.95 (*0-521-63360-5*) Cambridge U Pr.

Quataert, Donald, ed. Consumption Studies & the History of the Ottoman Empire, 1550-1992: An Introduction. LC 99-24669. (SUNY Series in the Social & Economic History of the Middle East). 320p. (C). 1999. pap. text 23.95 (*0-7914-4432-5*, Suny Pr) State U NY Pr.

— Manufacturing in the Ottoman Empire & Turkey, 1500-1950. LC 93-36571. (SUNY Series in the Social & Economic History of the Middle East). 175p. (C). 1994. pap. text 19.95 (*0-7914-2016-7*) State U NY Pr.

— Manufacturing in the Ottoman Empire & Turkey, 1500-1950. LC 93-36571. (SUNY Series in the Social & Economic History of the Middle East). 175p. (C). 1994. text 59.50 (*0-7914-2015-9*) State U NY Pr.

Quataert, Donald & Zurcher, Erik J., eds. Workers & Working Class in the Ottoman Empire & the Turkish Republic, 1839-1950. 224p. 1995. text 65.00 (*1-85043-875-7*) St Martin.

Quataert, Donald, jt. ed. see Antoun, Richard T.

Quataert, Donald, ed. see Spivey, Diane M.

Quataert, Jean H. Reluctant Feminists in German Social Democracy, 1885-1917. LC 79-84011. 327p. reprint ed. pap. 101.40 (*0-8357-3850-7*, 203658300004) Bks Demand.

Quataert, Jean H. Staging Philanthropy: Dynastic Women & the National Imagination in Dynastic Germany, 1813-1916. (Illus.). 360p. (C). text 59.50 (*0-472-11171-X*, 11171) U of Mich Pr.

Quataert, Jean H., jt. auth. see Boxer, Marilyn J.

Quataert, Jean H., jt. ed. see Boxer, Marilyn J.

Quatannens, Jo Anne McCormick. Senators of the United States: Historical Bibliography, a Compilation of Works by & About Members of the United States Senate, 1789-1995. 368p. 1995. per. 36.00 (*0-16-063266-8*) USGPO.

Quate, Calvin F., jt. ed. see Khuri-Yakub, Butrus T.

Quaterman, John. The Matrix: Computer Networks & Conferencing Systems Worldwide. 400p. 1999. pap. 39.95 (*1-55558-137-4*, Digital DEC) Buttrwrth-Heinemann.

Quatieri, Thomas F. Principles of Discrete-Time Speech Processing. (C). 1999. 65.00 (*0-13-242942-X*, Macmillan Coll) P-H.

Quatieri, Thomas F. & McAulay, Robert J. Sinusoidal Speech Processing. (C). 2001. 48.00 (*0-13-827015-5*, Macmillan Coll) P-H.

Quatmann, Gail R. & Ewen, Patricia B. Building Blocks: An Infant-Toddler Handbook. rev. ed. LC 92-93262. (Illus.). 85p. (C). 1992. pap. text. write for info. (*0-9631122-8-7*) G R Quatmann.

— Building Blocks: An Infant Toddler Handbook. rev. ed. LC 92-93262. (Illus.). 85p. 1993. pap. write for info. (*0-9631122-9-5*) G R Quatmann.

***Quatrani, Terry.** Visual Modeling with Rational Rose & UML 2000. 2nd ed. LC 99-44733. (Object Technology Ser.). (Illus.). 256p. 1999. pap. 39.95 (*0-201-69961-3*) Addison-Wesley.

Quatremere, M. Prolegomenes D'ebn-Khaldoun, 3 vols., Set. (ARA.). 105.00 (*0-86685-165-8*) Intl Bk Ctr.

Quatriglio, Giuseppe. A Thousand Years in Sicily: From the Arabs to the Bourbons. Vitiello, Justin, tr. (Sicilian Studies). (Illus.). 228p. 1997. pap. 16.00 (*0-921252-17-X*) LEGAS.

An Asterisk (*) at the beginning of an entry indicates that the title is appearing for the first time.

Quatroche, Vincent. Another Rubber Eden. LC 98-85979. 325p. 1998. 25.00 (*0-7388-0015-5*); pap. 15.00 (*0-7388-0031-7*) Xlibris Corp.

Quatrochi, Kathlyn. The Skin Care Book: Simple Herbal Recipes. LC 96-29747. (Illus.). 96p. 1997. pap. 10.95 (*1-883010-24-1*) Interweave.

Quattebaum, Neil. A Year on My Street. (J). 1996. 19.95 (*0-385-44700-0*) Doubleday.

Quattlebaum, Bryan. Managed Care in Dentistry. LC 94-23729. 1994. 44.95 (*0-87814-432-3*) PennWell Bks.

Quattlebaum, M. M. Quattlebaum Family History. 280p. 1994. reprint ed. pap. 48.50 (*0-8328-4079-3*); reprint ed. lib. bdg. 58.50 (*0-8328-4078-5*) Higginson Bk Co.

***Quattlebaum, Mary.** Aunt Ceecee, Aunt Belle & Mama's Surprise. (Illus.). (J). 2000. pap. 5.99 (*0-440-41276-5*) Dell.

Quattlebaum, Mary. Aunt Ceecee, Aunt Belle & Mama's Surprise. LC 97-40357. (Illus.). 32p. (J). 1999. 15.95 (*0-385-32275-5*) Doubleday.

***Quattlebaum, Mary.** Grover G. Graham & Me. 2001. mass mkt. 14.95 (*0-385-32277-1*, Pub. by Random Bks Yng Read) Random.

Quattlebaum, Mary. Jackson Jones & the Puddle of Thorns. LC 93-11433. (Illus.). 128p. (J). (gr. 4-7). 1995. pap. 3.99 (*0-440-41066-5*) Dell.

— Jackson Jones & the Puddle of Thorns. (J). 1995. 9.09 (*0-606-07725-1*, Pub. by Turtleback) Demco.

Quattlebaum, Mary. Jazz, Pizzazz, & the Silver Threads. LC 95-21107. (J). 1997. 9.09 (*0-606-11519-6*, Pub. by Turtleback) Demco.

Quattlebaum, Mary. The Magic Squad & the Dog of Great Potential. (Illus.). 128p. (J). (gr. 2-5). 1998. pap. 3.99 (*0-440-41279-X*, YB BDD) BDD Bks Young Read.

***Quattlebaum, Mary.** Magic Squad & the Dog of Great Potential. 1998. 9.09 (*0-606-13592-8*, Pub. by Turtleback) Demco.

Quattlebaum, Mary. Underground Train. LC 96-30507. (Illus.). 32p. (J). (gr. k-3). 1997. 14.95 (*0-385-32204-6*, DD Bks Yng Read) BDD Bks Young Read.

***Quattlebaum, Mary.** Underground Train. 32p. (J). (gr. k-3). 1999. pap. 5.99 (*0-440-41325-7*) BDD Bks Young Read.

Quattlebaum, Mary. A Year on My Street. (J). 1996. 9.19 (*0-606-12120-X*, Pub. by Turtleback) Demco.

Quattlebaum, Mary A. Adam & Eve. Crawford, Jean B., ed. LC 96-15331. (Family Time Bible Stories Ser.). (Illus.). 28p. (J). 1999. 4.95 (*0-7835-4633-5*) Time-Life.

— The Easter Story. Daniels, Patricia, ed. LC 95-26752. (Family Time Bible Stories Ser.). (Illus.). 32p. (J). (ps-2). 1997. write for info. (*0-7835-4629-7*) Time-Life.

— In the Beginning. Daniels, Patricia, ed. LC 95-25283. (Family Time Bible Stories Ser.). (Illus.). 28p. (J). (ps-2). 1999. 4.95 (*0-7835-4627-0*) Time-Life.

***Quattlebaum, Mary A.** Jesus & the Children. Daniels, Patricia, ed. LC 95-25282. (Family Time Bible Stories Ser.). (Illus.). 32p. (J). (ps-2). 1999. 4.95 (*0-7835-4628-9*) Time-Life.

***Quattlebaum, Patricia D. & Nalty, Lily N.** A Practical Guide to Augmentative & Alternative Communication: Assessment & Intervention Strategies. (Illus.). 48p. (J). 1998. spiral bd., wbk. ed. 14.95 (*1-58650-071-6*, BK-269) Super Duper.

Quattrin, Joseph A., jt. auth. see Purves, Alan C.

Quattrin, Kevin. Living in a Psychic's World: A True-Life Experience. LC 95-131073. 170p. (Orig.). 1994. pap. 9.95 (*1-878901-94-X*) Hampton Roads Pub Co.

Quattrini, Joseph A. Successful Business Presentations. (Illus.). 264p. 1989. 19.95 (*0-8306-0335-2*) McGraw-Hill Prof.

— Successful Business Presentations. 1990. pap. 15.95 (*0-8306-3055-4*) McGraw-Hill Prof.

Quattrini, Joseph A., jt. auth. see Purves, Alan C.

Quattrocchi, Paul B. A Life for Unity: Sister Maria Gabriella. Jeremiah, Mary, tr. from ITA. 184p. 1990. pap. 9.95 (*0-911782-77-X*) New City.

Quattrocchi, Umberto. Guide to Hardy Tropical Plants. Eustacc, Peter, tr. from ITA. LC 97-30258. 1998. 15.00 (*0-684-84499-0*) S&S Trade.

— World Dictionary of Plant Names: Common Names, Scientific Names, Vol. 1. LC 99-31919. 728p. 1999. boxed set 189.95 (*0-8493-2675-3*) CRC Pr.

— World Dictionary of Plant Names: Common Names, Scientific Names, Vol. 2. LC 99-31919. 864p. 1999. boxed set 189.95 (*0-8493-2676-1*) CRC Pr.

— World Dictionary of Plant Names: Common Names, Scientific Names, Vol. 3. 696p. 1999. boxed set 189.95 (*0-8493-2677-X*) CRC Pr.

— World Dictionary of Plant Names: Common Names, Scientific Names, Vol. 4. LC 99-31919. 640p. 1999. boxed set 189.95 (*0-8493-2678-8*) CRC Pr.

Quattrochi, Angelo & Nairn, Tom. The Beginning of the End: France, May, 1968. LC 98-24039. 175p. 1998. pap. 15.00 (*1-85984-290-9*, Pub. by Verso) Norton.

Quattrochi, Dale A. & Goodchild, Michael F. Scale in Remote Sensing & GIS. LC 96-27156. 432p. 1997. lib. bdg. 75.00 (*1-56670-104-X*) Lewis Pubs.

Quattrocki, Carolyn. Santa Claus Is Coming to Town. (Favorite Christmas Tales Ser.). (Illus.). 24p. (J). (ps-4). 1992. lib. bdg. 11.95 (*1-56674-026-6*, HTS Bks) Forest Hse.

— 'Twas the Night Before Christmas. (Favorite Christmas Tales Ser.). (Illus.). 24p. (J). (ps-4). 1992. lib. bdg. 11.95 (*1-56674-027-4*, HTS Bks) Forest Hse.

Quay, Herbert C., ed. Handbook of Juvenile Delinquency. LC 86-34008. (Personality Processes Ser.). 480p. 1987. 175.00 (*0-471-81707-4*) Wiley.

Quay, Herbert C. & Hogan, A. E., eds. Handbook of Disruptive Behavior Disorders. LC 98-56517. (Illus.). 695p. (C). 1999. 125.00 (*0-306-45974-4*, Kluwer Plenum) Kluwer Academic.

Quay, Herbert C. & Werry, John S., eds. Psychopathological Disorders of Childhood. 3rd ed. LC 86-11105. 704p. 1986. text 89.95 (*0-471-88974-1*) Wiley.

Quay, Joyce C. Early Promise, Late Reward: A Biography of Helen Hooven Santmyer. (Illus.). 155p. (Orig.). 1995. pap. 14.95 (*1-879198-15-0*) Knwldg Ideas & Trnds.

Quay, Paul M. The Christian Meaning of Human Sexuality. LC 88-81092. 121p. reprint ed. pap. 14.95 incl. audio (*0-89870-212-7*, 123) Ignatius Pr.

— The Mystery Hidden for Ages in God. LC 93-17286. (American University Studies VII: Vol. 161). XVI, 438p. (C). 1995. text 63.95 (*0-8204-2221-5*) P Lang Pubng.

***Quay, Paul M.** The Mystery Hidden for Ages in God, 161. 2nd ed. (American University Studies: Ser.). XVI, 438p. 1998. pap. 35.95 (*0-8204-4039-6*) P Lang Pubng.

Quay, Ray, jt. auth. see McClendon, Bruce W.

Quay, Richard H., compiled by. Index to Anthologies on Postsecondary Education, 1960-1978. LC 79-8286. 342p. 1980. lib. bdg. 55.00 (*0-313-21272-4*, QPE/, Greenwood Pr) Greenwood.

Quay, Suzanne, jt. auth. see Deuchar, Margaret.

Quay, Thomas L., et al, eds. The Seaside Sparrow, Its Biology & Management. (Occasional Papers of the North Carolina Biological Survey). (Illus.). 174p. 1983. pap. 15.00 (*0-917134-05-2*) NC Natl Sci.

Quayd, Muhammad Y. War in the Land of Egypt. Kenny, Olive E. et al, trs. from ARA. LC 97-21922. 192p. 1998. pap. 12.95 (*1-56656-227-9*) Interlink Pub.

Quaye, Christopher O. Liberation Struggles in International Law. 358p. 1991. 69.95 (*0-87722-712-8*) Temple U Pr.

Quaye, Randolph. Underdevelopment & Health Care in Africa: The Ghanaian Experience. LC 95-687. 188p. 1996. text 79.95 (*0-7734-2254-4*) E Mellen.

Quayle, A., ed. Advances in Mass Spectrometry: Proceedings of a Conference Held in Brussels, September, 1970, Vol. 5. LC QC0454.I64. 798p. reprint ed. pap. 200.00 (*0-8357-5173-2*, 202399500005) Bks Demand.

Quayle, A., ed. see Institute of Petroleum Staff.

Quayle, Amil. Pebble Creek. 80p. 1993. pap. 12.00 (*0-9635559-0-1*) Slow Tempo.

***Quayle, Dan.** Moments that Matter, Vol. 1. 144p. 1999. 12.99 (*0-8499-5529-7*) CDI.

— Worth Fighting For. LC 99-29541. 224p. 1999. 21.99 (*0-8499-1606-2*) Word Pub.

— Worth Fighting For. (Illus.). 2000. pap. 12.99 (*0-8499-3786-8*) Word Pub.

— Worth Fighting For, Set. LC 99-29541. 1999. audio 16.99 (*0-8499-6300-1*) Word Pub.

Quayle, Dan & Medved, Diane. The American Family: Discovering Values That Makes Us Strong. (Illus.). 304p. 1997. pap. 14.00 (*0-06-092810-7*) Zondervan.

— Family Values. 1995. 25.00 (*0-614-15929-6*) HarpC.

***Quayle, Eric.** The Shining Princess: And Other Japanese Legends. (Illus.). 112p. (YA). (gr. 5 up). 2000. reprint ed. pap. 14.95 (*0-86264-883-1*, Pub. by Andersen Pr) Trafalgar.

Quayle, Eric. The Shining Princess & Other Japanese Legends. (Illus.). 112p. (J). (gr. 4-6). 15.95 (*0-316-72865-9*) Little.

Quayle, Margaret S. A Study of Some Aspects of Satisfaction in the Vocation of Stenography. LC 76-177174. (Columbia University. Teachers College. Contributions to Education Ser.: No. 659). reprint ed. 37.50 (*0-404-55659-0*) AMS Pr.

Quayle, Thomas. Poetic Diction: A Study of Eighteenth Century Verse. (BCL1-PR English Literature Ser.). 212p. 1992. reprint ed. lib. bdg. 79.00 (*0-685-54571-7*) Rprt Serv.

Quayle, Thomas E., ed. Jose' el Diablo: The World's Most Traveled Dog. (Illus.). 95p. (Orig.). (YA). 1985. pap. 3.00 (*0-9623144-0-4*) Vilate Pub.

Quayle, Thomas E., jt. auth. see Baker, Beatrice V.

Quayle, William A. Recovered Yesterdays in Literature. LC 74-117829. (Essay Index Reprint Ser.). 1977. 21.95 (*0-8369-1678-6*) Ayer.

Quayson, Ato. Postcolonialism: Theory, Practice of Process? LC 99-25741. 208p. (C). 2000. text 54.95 (*0-7456-1712-3*, Pub. by Polity Pr) Blackwell Pubs.

— Postcolonialism: Theory, Practice or Process? LC 99-25741. 208p. (C). 2000. pap. text 22.95 (*0-7456-1713-1*, Pub. by Polity Pr) Blackwell Pubs.

— Strategic Transformations in Nigerian Writing: Orality & History in the Work of Rev. Samuel Johnson, Amos Tutuola, Wole Soyinka & Ben Okri. LC 97-10960. 1997. 39.95 (*0-253-33343-1*); pap. 19.95 (*0-253-21148-4*) Ind U Pr.

Quayson, Ato, jt. auth. see Gbadamosi, Gabriel.

Quay2 Multimedia Staff. Excel 5: Training on CD. 1995. pap. 49.95 incl. cd-rom (*0-201-88416-X*) Peachpit Pr.

— FreeHand 5.5: Training on CD. 1996. pap. 69.95 incl. cd-rom (*0-201-88412-7*) Peachpit Pr.

— Illustrator 5.5: Training on CD. 1995. 99.95 incl. cd-rom (*0-201-88411-9*) Peachpit Pr.

— Illustrator 6: Training on CD. 1996. pap. 69.95 incl. cd-rom (*0-201-88657-X*) Peachpit Pr.

— Internet & HTML: Training on CD. 1995. pap. 49.95 incl. cd-rom (*0-201-88418-6*) Peachpit Pr.

— Microsoft Office: Training on CD. 1995. pap. 99.95 incl. cd-rom (*0-201-88413-5*) Peachpit Pr.

Quay2 Multimedia Staff. PageMaker 6: Training on CD. 1996. pap. 69.95 incl. cd-rom (*0-201-88410-0*) Peachpit Pr.

Quay2 Multimedia Staff. Photoshop 3: Training on CD. 1995. pap. 99.95 incl. cd-rom (*0-201-88409-7*) Peachpit Pr.

— QuarkXPress 3.3: Training on CD. 1995. pap. 99.95 incl. cd-rom (*0-201-88408-9*) Peachpit Pr.

— Word 6: Training on CD. 1995. pap. 49.95 incl. cd-rom (*0-201-88414-3*) Peachpit Pr.

Quban, Fahim I. Education & Science in the Arab World. 1979. 36.95 (*0-405-10622-X*) Ayer.

Qubayya, Mohammed. Dictionary Grammatical Analysis Holy Qur'an. (ARA.). 830p. 1995. 65.00 (*0-86685-645-5*) Intl Bk Ctr.

Qubein, Nido & Lanning, J. Stephen. How to Sell Professional Services. 34p. 1998. write for info. (*1-891558-03-X*) New Ventures Pub.

Qubein, Nido R. Achieving Peak Performance: A Step by Step System to Grow a Well Trained, Educated & Motivated Team for the 21st Century. (Illus.). 244p. 1996. 29.95 (*0-9636268-5-X*) Exec Pr NC.

— Get the Best from Yourself. 100p. 1986. mass mkt. 5.99 (*0-425-08537-6*) Berkley Pub.

— How to Be a Great Communicator: In Person, on Paper, & at the Podium. (Illus.). 292p. 1997. 29.95 (*0-939975-10-6*) Exec Pr NC.

— How to Be a Great Communicator: In Person, on Paper & on the Podium. LC 96-21829. 272p. 1996. pap. 16.95 (*0-471-16314-7*) Wiley.

— How to Be a Great Sales Professional. 187p. 1998. 29.95 (*0-939975-13-0*) Exec Pr NC.

— How to Get Anything You Want. 175p. 1998. 29.95 (*0-939975-15-7*) Exec Pr NC.

— Stairway to Success: How to Achieve & Enjoy Success, Wealth & Happiness at Work & at Home. (Illus.). 351p. 1996. 29.95 (*0-939975-09-2*) Exec Pr NC.

— Stairway to Success: The Complete Blueprint for Personal & Professional Achievement. LC 97-7567. 229p. 1997. pap. 16.95 (*0-471-15494-6*) Wiley.

— The Time Is Now, the Person Is You. 81p. 1997. 29.95 (*0-939975-12-2*) Exec Pr NC.

Qudamas, Ibn. Censure of Speculative Theology: An Edition & Translation of Ibn Qudamas Tahrim An-Nazar Fi Kutub Ahl Al-Kalam. Makdisi, ed. (Gibb Memorial New Ser.: Vol. 23 Introduction & Notes). 1992. 39.00 (*0-906094-16-X*, Pub. by Aris & Phillips) David Brown.

Que College Staff. dBASE V for Windows Essentials. 1995. 23.00 (*0-7897-0521-4*); teacher ed. 39.99 (*0-7897-0522-2*) Que.

Que College Staff & Hefferin, Linda. WordPerfect 6.1 for Windows Essentials. LC 94-69258. 181p. 1995. pap. text 22.99 (*0-7897-0104-9*) Que Educ & Trng.

***Que Corporation Staff.** Complete Idiot's Guide to MP3: Music on the Internet. (Complete Idiot's Guides (Computers) Ser.). 1999. pap. 49.99 (*0-7897-2317-4*) Que.

— Complete Idiot's Guide to Online Personal Finance. 384p. 2000. 18.95 (*0-7897-2332-8*) Que.

— Dictionary Dalton Version. pap. text 9.95 (*0-88022-586-6*) Que.

— Imagine It! 1.0, 110,000 Premium Graphic Images. 1999. pap. text 49.99 (*0-7897-2287-9*) Que.

— Linux Administration by Example. 550p. 2000. 24.99 (*0-7897-2313-1*) Que.

Que Corporation Staff. Microsoft Office 2000 User Manual. (Illus.). 869p. 1999. pap. 19.99 (*0-7897-1930-4*) Que.

Que Corporation Staff. PowerPoint 4 for Windows SmartStart. LC 94-68012. 278p. 1994. 29.99 (*1-56529-795-4*) Que.

— Practical Linux. 704p. 2000. 29.99 (*0-7897-2251-8*) Que.

— Red Hat Linux 6.0, 6 vols. 1999. pap. text 79.99 (*0-7897-2286-0*) Que.

— Using Microsoft FrontPage 2000 Power Tool Kit. 1999. pap. text 49.99 (*0-7897-2285-2*) Que.

— Windows Nt Server 4 Enterprise MCSE Examgear. 1999. 75.00 (*0-7357-0857-6*) Que.

Que Corporation Staff, ed. Ciyf UK. 1995. teacher ed. 100.00 (*1-57576-130-0*) Que Educ & Trng.

Que Development Group. Reengineering Your Web Site. 600p. 1997. 39.99 (*0-7897-1216-4*) Que.

Que Development Group Staff. The Big Basics Book of Excel for Windows 95. (Illus.). 576p. 1995. 19.99 (*0-7897-0459-5*) Que.

— The Big Basics Book of Windows 95. (Illus.). 598p. (Orig.). 1995. 19.99 (*0-7897-0403-X*) Que.

— The Big Basics Book of Word for Windows 95. LC 95-72554. (Illus.). 590p. 1995. 19.99 (*0-7897-0460-9*) Que.

— The Complete Idiot's Guide to "Madrid" 384p. 1995. pap. 21.99 (*0-7897-0406-4*) Que.

— Corel Office for Java 6 in 1. 600p. 1998. 29.99 (*0-7897-1314-4*) Que.

— CorelDRAW! VisiRef. LC 94-66716. (Illus.). 168p. (Orig.). 1994. 12.99 (*1-56529-861-6*) Que.

— Creating Your Own VRML Web Pages. 250p. 1996. 29.99 incl. cd-rom (*0-7897-0731-4*) Que.

— Easy Ami Pro. 2nd ed. 256p. 1994. 19.99 (*1-56529-624-9*) Que.

— Easy Freelance Graphics 2.0 for Windows. LC 94-65892. 197p. 1994. 19.99 (*1-56529-768-7*) Que.

— Easy Macintosh. 2nd ed. LC 94-65336. (Orig.). 1994. 19.99 (*1-56529-738-5*) Que.

— Easy PCs. 2nd ed. (Illus.). 204p. (Orig.). 1993. 19.95 (*1-56529-276-6*) Que.

— Easy PowerPoint 4 for Windows. LC 94-65337. 214p. 1994. 19.99 (*1-56529-737-7*) Que.

— Extranet Technical Overview. 1997. pap. text 29.99 (*0-7897-1344-6*) Que.

— The HitchHiker's Guide to Internet. (Illus.). 1188p. (Orig.). 1994. 39.95 (*1-56529-353-3*) Que.

— HTML by Example. 576p. 1996. pap. text 34.99 incl. cd-rom (*0-7897-0812-4*) Que.

— I Hate PCs: A Friendly Guide for the Frustrated User. (I Hate! Ser.). (Illus.). 370p. (Orig.). 1993. 16.95 (*1-56529-254-5*) Que.

— Introduction to NC Network Computer Technology. 1997. 29.99 (*0-7897-1278-4*) Que.

— Lotus SmartSuite Notes Bundle. 1994. pap. 100.00 (*1-56529-951-5*) Que.

— Lotus SmartSuite 6-in-1 for Windows 95. (Illus.). (Orig.). 1996. 26.99 (*0-7897-0636-9*) Que.

— Macintosh VisiRef. LC 94-67593. (Illus.). 146p. (Orig.). 1994. 12.99 (*1-56529-831-4*) Que.

Que Development Group, Staff. Microsoft Access 97 Quick Reference. LC 97-66486. 307p. 1997. 16.99 (*0-7897-1212-1*) Que.

Que Development Group Staff. Microsoft Office Bundle with Access. 2nd ed. 1994. pap. 105.00 (*1-56529-852-7*) Que.

— Monster.Tools.Net. (Illus.). 1200p. (Orig.). 1996. 49.99 (*0-7897-0361-0*) Que.

— Office Max - Using Microsoft Office. 1994. student ed. 29.99 (*0-7897-0705-5*) Que.

— Paradox for Windows Power Programming. 2nd ed. (Illus.). 550p. 1994. pap. 29.99 (*0-614-06068-0*) Que.

— PowerPoint97 Quick Reference. 300p. 1997. 16.99 (*0-7897-1268-7*) Que.

— Que's First Look at Chicago. 1994. 14.99 (*0-7897-0074-3*) Que.

— Real Time Web Broadcasting. 400p. 1997. pap. text 39.99 incl. cd-rom (*0-7897-0948-1*) Que.

— Running a Perfect Internet Site with LINUX. LC 95-72569. (Illus.). 500p. (Orig.). 1995. 49.99 (*0-7897-0514-1*) Que.

— Running a Perfect Web Site. (Illus.). 456p. (Orig.). 1995. 39.99 (*0-7897-0210-X*) Que.

— Special Edition Using CompuServe. (Illus.). 1000p. (Orig.). 1995. pap. 39.99 (*0-614-07263-8*) Que.

— Special Edition Using Lotus Notes, New Edition. (Illus.). 1008p. (Orig.). 1995. 49.99 (*0-7897-0368-8*) Que.

— Special Edition Using Microsoft Office Pro for Windows 95 Bundle. 1995. pap. text 110.00 (*0-7897-0657-1*) Que.

— Special Edition Using NaviServer & NaviPress: Special Edition. deluxe ed. (Illus.). 768p. (Orig.). 1995. 39.99 (*0-7897-0407-2*) Que.

— Special Edition Using Quarterdeck Normandy. (Illus.). 600p. (Orig.). 1998. 34.99 (*0-7897-0360-2*) Que.

— Special Edition Using SGML: Special Edition. deluxe ed. LC 95-72571. (Illus.). 600p. (Orig.). 1995. 49.99 (*0-7897-0414-5*) Que.

— Special Edition Using the Internet with Your Mac. (Illus.). 927p. (Orig.). 1995. 39.99 (*0-7897-0212-6*) Que.

— Special Edition Using V R M L: Special Edition. LC 95-72570. (Illus.). 700p. (Orig.). 1996. 49.99 (*0-7897-0494-3*) Que.

— Special Edition Using Windows NT 4.0. LC 95-73277. (Illus.). 1100p. (Orig.). 1995. 49.99 (*0-7897-0251-7*) Que.

— Ten Minute Guide Microsoft Office Bundle. 1993. 39.42 (*1-56761-231-8*, Alpha Ref) Macmillan Gen Ref.

— 10 Minute Guide to Microsoft Mail for Windows 95. 2nd ed. (Illus.). 192p. (Orig.). 1995. pap. 12.99 (*0-7897-0553-2*) Que.

— 10 Minute Guide to WordPerfect for Windows 95. LC 95-72558. (Illus.). 208p. (Orig.). 1995. 14.99 (*0-7897-0454-4*) Que.

— Using ActiveX Special Edition. LC 96-69954. 408p. 1996. pap. text 39.99 incl. cd-rom (*0-7897-0886-8*) Que.

— Using AutoCAD for Windows. 1281p. 1995. 39.99 (*1-56529-887-X*) Que.

— Using CA-Unicenter, Special Edition. 800p. 1996. 59.99 incl. cd-rom (*0-7897-0691-1*) Que.

— Using Chicago Multimedia Special Edition. 1996. 39.99 incl. cd-rom (*0-7897-0058-1*) Que.

— Using ClarisWorks. (Illus.). 676p. (Orig.). 1992. 24.95 (*1-56529-003-8*) Que.

— Using Eudora. 2nd ed. LC 97-65539. 306p. 1997. 24.99 (*0-7897-1166-4*) Que.

— Using Inferno. 500p. 1997. pap. text 34.99 (*0-7897-0966-X*) Que.

— Using Internet Works. (Illus.). 416p. (Orig.). 1995. 19.99 (*0-7897-0283-5*) Que.

— Using Java NC Server. 1997. pap. text 49.99 (*0-7897-1279-2*) Que.

— Using Jigsaw. 300p. 1996. pap. text 34.99 (*0-7897-0968-6*) Que.

— Using Latte. 400p. 1996. pap. text 29.99 (*0-7897-0880-9*) Que.

— Using Macromedia Director. 700p. 1995. 49.99 incl. cd-rom (*1-56529-781-4*) Que.

— Using Microsoft Outlooks 97. 320p. 1997. pap. 19.99 (*0-7897-1257-1*) Que.

— Using Microsoft System Management Server. 744p. 1996. pap. text 59.99 incl. cd-rom (*0-7897-0820-5*) Que.

— Using MS-DOS 6: Special Edition. 1993. pap. 29.95 (*1-56539-020-2*) Color Cnty.

— NetShow 2.0. 400p. 1997. 39.99 (*0-7897-1410-8*) Que.

— Using Netscape 2: Special Edition, Vol. 2. LC 95-71751. (Illus.). 992p. (Orig.). 1995. 49.99 (*0-7897-0612-1*) Que.

— Using Netscape 2 for Macs. 350p. 1996. 24.99 (*0-7897-0729-2*) Que.

— Using Novell PerfectOffice for Windows 95. 1996. 34.99 (*0-7897-0463-3*) Que.

— Using 1-2-3 for Windows. LC 94-66718. 1190p. 1994. 34.99 (*1-56529-743-1*) Que.

— Using 1-2-3 Release X for DOS, Special Edition. LC 94-66724. 1099p. 1994. 29.99 (*1-56529-629-X*) Que.

— Using Paradox for DOS: Special Edition. (Illus.). 1000p. 1994. 29.99 (*1-56529-867-5*) Que.

— Using Powerpoint for Windows. 2nd ed. LC 94-65143. 698p. 1994. 29.99 (*1-56529-651-6*) Que.

— Using Solstice Workshop: Special Edition. 600p. 1996. pap. text 49.99 incl. cd-rom (*0-7897-0967-8*) Que.

— Using VRML. 350p. 1996. 24.99 (*0-7897-0730-6*) Que.

— Using Windows 3.11 Edition, Special Edition. 3rd ed. LC 94-66720. 1101p. 1994. 34.99 (*1-56529-807-1*) Que.

— Using WordPerfect 6 for Windows: Special Edition. (Using... Ser.). (Illus.). 1102p. (Orig.). 1993. 29.95 (*1-56529-138-7*) Que.

Q

— Windows NT 4.O Quick Reference. 1997. pap. text 19.99 (*0-7897-1299-7*) Que.
— Windows 3.11 QuickStart. (Illus.). 246p. (Orig.). 1994. pap. 19.99 (*0-614-06067-2*) Que.
— Windows VisiRef. LC 94-66542. 157p. 1994. 12.99 (*1-56529-805-5*) Que.
— WordPerfect for Windows 95 Visual Quick Reference. (Illus.). 224p. (Orig.). 1995. 12.99 (*0-7897-0461-7*) Que.
— WordPerfect 6 for Windows Quickstart. (Illus.). 608p. (Orig.). 1993. 21.95 (*1-56529-463-7*) Que.
Que Development Group Staff & Flanders, Linda. Using Quicken for Windows: New Edition. (Illus.). (Orig.). 1994. 19.99 (*1-56529-933-7*) Que.
Que Development Group Staff & Gastieger, Dan. Special Edition Using Lotus SmartSuite for Windows 95: Special Edition. (Illus.). 1024p. (Orig.). 1995. pap. 34.99 (*0-7897-0187-1*) Que.
Que Development Group Staff & Grace, Rich. Word for Windows Quick Reference. 2nd ed. 224p. 1993. 10.99 (*1-56529-468-8*) Que.
Que Development Group Staff & Kenney, Cathy. Using Lotus Organizer for Windows. (Illus.). (Orig.). 1995. 24.99 (*1-56529-891-8*) Que.
Que Development Group Staff & Shafran, Andy. Using Lotus SmartSuite, Special Edition. (Illus.). (Orig.). 1994. 34.99 (*1-56529-747-4*) Que.
Que Development Group Staff, jt. see Kent.
Que Development Group Staff, jt. auth. see Doherty, Donald.
Que Development Group Staff, jt. auth. see Person, Ron.
Que Development Group Staff, jt. auth. see Stover, Susan.
Que Development Group Staff, jt. auth. see Wempen, Faithe.
Que Development Group Staff, jt. auth. see Wyatt, Allen L.
Que Development Staff. Professional Developer's Guide to Visual C++ 1998. 49.99 (*0-7897-1457-4*) Que.
— Using HTML 3.2. 3rd ed. LC 98-154529. 416p. 1997. 19.99 (*0-7897-1450-7*) Que.
— Using Red Hat Linux: Special Edition. 560p. 2000. 39.99 (*0-7897-1458-2*) Que.
— Using Slackwave Linux: Special Edition. 560p. 1999. 39.99 (*0-7897-1459-0*) Que.
— Using VB X for Database Programming. 1998. 49.99 (*0-7897-1475-2*) Que.
Que Development Staff, et al. Excel 5 for Windows. 1995. pap. text 39.99 incl. disk (*1-56529-815-2*) Que.
Que E & T Staff. Practice Using MS-DOS 6.2. (C). 1994. 35.33 (*1-56529-718-0*) Que.
Que Editors. 1-2-3 for Windows 95. (Essentials Ser.). 1995. pap. 39.99 (*0-7897-0119-7*) Que.
— 1-2-3 for Windows Release 5 Essentials. LC 94-69257. (Essentials Ser.). 195p. 1995. 22.99 (*0-7897-0105-7*) Que.
Que Education & Training. Explorer 4 Essentials. 1997. 22.99 (*1-57576-828-3*) Que Educ & Trng.
— Netscape Communicator Essentials. 1997. 22.99 (*1-57576-827-5*) Que Educ & Trng.
***Que Education & Training.** 1-2-3 for Windows Release 5 Smartstart. LC 94-68907. 275p. 1999. pap. text 21.33 (*0-7897-0009-3*) Que.
Que Education & Training Experts Staff. Excel 97 Essentials: Annoted Instructor's Edition. annot. ed. 1997. 39.99 (*1-57576-871-2*) Que Educ & Trng.
Que Education & Training Staff. Access for Windows 95 Smartstart. Date not set. text, teacher ed. 39.99 incl. disk (*1-57576-031-2*) Que Educ & Trng.
— Access for Windows 95 Virtual Tutor. 1996. pap. text 49.99 incl. cd-rom (*1-57576-105-X*) Que Educ & Trng.
Que Education & Training Staff. Access 97: Level 1. (Essentials Ser.). 1997. pap. text, teacher ed. 49.99 (*1-57576-789-9*) Que Educ & Trng.
Que Education & Training Staff. Access 2 Virtual Tutor. 1996. pap. text 49.99 incl. cd-rom (*1-57576-093-2*) Que Educ & Trng.
— Access 2000 Complete. 1997. 39.99 (*1-57576-879-8*) Que Educ & Trng.
— Access 97 Essentials (Academic) 1997. teacher ed. 39.99 (*1-57576-869-0*) Que Educ & Trng.
— Access 97 Smartstart Plus. 1997. 39.99 (*1-57576-878-X*) Que Educ & Trng.
— Applications Development Using Access, IM. 1997. text, teacher ed. 39.99 incl. disk (*1-57576-069-X*) Que Educ & Trng.
— Computer Training Personal Training Guide. 1995. pap. text 49.99 (*1-57576-253-6*) Que Educ & Trng.
— Computers in Your Future. 2nd ed. 1997. pap. text, teacher ed. write for info. (*1-57576-708-2*) Que Educ & Trng.
— DOS Basics. 1995. 16.99 (*1-57576-279-X*) Que Educ & Trng.
— Easy Access 97. (Learn Ser.). 247p. 1997. pap., teacher ed. 39.99 (*1-57576-890-9*) Que Educ & Trng.
— Easy Excel 97. 1997. teacher ed. 29.99 (*1-57576-889-5*) Que Educ & Trng.
— Easy Excel 97. 1997. teacher ed. 39.99 (*1-57576-888-7*) Que Educ & Trng.
— Easy Office 97. 1997. 49.99 (*1-57576-887-9*) Que Educ & Trng.
— Easy Office 97. 1997. teacher ed. 39.99 (*1-57576-886-0*) Que Educ & Trng.
Que Education & Training Staff. Easy Windows 95. LC 97-68882. 165p. 1997. 29.99 (*1-57576-969-7*) Que Educ & Trng.
— Excel for Windows 95: Essentials & Level III. LC 96-68608. (Essentials Ser.). 172p. 1997. pap. text 22.99 incl. disk (*1-57576-393-1*) Que Educ & Trng.
— Excel for Windows 95: Level III. 1997. pap. text, teacher ed. 49.99 incl. disk (*1-57576-394-X*) Que Educ & Trng.

Q

Que Education & Training Staff. Excel 2000 Complete. 1997. teacher ed. 39.99 (*1-57576-880-1*) Que Educ & Trng.
— Excel 5 Virtual Tutor. 1996. pap. text 35.00 incl. cd-rom (*1-57576-091-6*) Que Educ & Trng.
— Explorer 4 Essentials. 1997. 39.99 (*1-57576-874-7*) Que Educ & Trng.
— Interacting with Your Computer 2.0 Windows. 1997. pap. text 20.00 (*1-57576-371-0*) Que Educ & Trng.
— An Interactive Guide to Multimedia. LC 95-71651. 239p. 1996. pap. text 85.00 (*1-57576-066-5*) Que Educ & Trng.
— An Interactive Guide to Pagemaker. LC 96-67772. 1996. pap. text 62.00 (*1-57576-065-7*) Que Educ & Trng.
Que Education & Training Staff. Learn Windows 95. 2nd annot. ed. (Learn Ser.). (Illus.). 192p. 1997. pap., teacher ed. 39.99 incl. cd-rom (*1-57576-970-0*) Que Educ & Trng.
— Learn Word 97. 2nd ed. (Illus.). 237p. 1997. teacher ed. 39.99 incl. cd-rom (*1-57576-882-8*) Que Educ & Trng.
Que Education & Training Staff. Lotus 1-2-3 for Windows 95 Essentials. Date not set. 22.99 (*1-57576-598-5*) Que Educ & Trng.
— Lotus 1-2-3 for Windows 95 Essentials, Level 3. Date not set. 22.99 (*1-57576-601-9*) Que Educ & Trng.
— Lotus 1-2-3 Release 5 for Windows Virtual Tutor. (Essentials Ser.). 1997. pap. text 25.00 (*1-57576-112-2*) Que Educ & Trng.
— Lotus 1-2-3 Release 5 Virtual Tutor. Date not set. pap. text 35.00 incl. cd-rom (*1-57576-099-1*) Que Educ & Trng.
— Microsoft Office Virtual Tutor. 1996. pap. text 50.00 incl. cd-rom (*1-57576-107-6*) Que Educ & Trng.
— MS Office 97 Professional Essentials: Essentials Level 1. LC 97-68154. 1997. 49.99 (*1-57576-787-2*) Que Educ & Trng.
Que Education & Training Staff. Netscape Essentials. LC 96-68603. (Essentials Ser.). 181p. 1997. pap. text 22.99 (*1-57576-367-2*) Que Educ & Trng.
Que Education & Training Staff. Netscape 4 Essentials. 1997. 39.99 (*1-57576-875-5*) Que Educ & Trng.
— Netware 4.1 SmartStart. LC 96-68607. (Smartstart Ser.). 330p. 1997. pap. text 29.99 (*1-57576-382-6*) Que Educ & Trng.
— Office Virtual Tutor. Date not set. pap. text 68.00 (*1-57576-095-9*) Que Educ & Trng.
Que Education & Training Staff. PowerPoint for Windows 95 Smartstart. LC 95-74886. 332p. 1996. pap. text 29.99 (*1-57576-038-X*) Que Educ & Trng.
Que Education & Training Staff. PowerPoint for Windows 95 Virtual Tutor. 1997. pap. text 25.00 (*1-57576-491-1*) Que Educ & Trng.
— PowerPoint 97 Essentials (Academic) Imperative Programming Languages, Ii. 1997. teacher ed. 39.99 (*1-57576-870-4*) Que Educ & Trng.
— PowerPoint 97 Smartstart. 1997. teacher ed. 39.99 (*1-57576-821-6*) Que Educ & Trng.
— Upgrading & Repairing PCs. 6th ed. 1997. pap. text, wbk. ed. 30.00 (*1-57576-687-6*) Que Educ & Trng.
— Upgrading & Repairing PCs: Academic Edition. 5th ed. 1996. pap. text 72.00 (*1-57576-063-0*) Que Educ & Trng.
— Visual Basic 5 SmartStart. 1997. teacher ed. 39.99 (*1-57576-873-9*) Que Educ & Trng.
— Virtual Tutor for Microsoft Access 97. Date not set. 25.00 (*1-57576-947-6*) Que Educ & Trng.
— Virtual Tutor For Microsoft Excel 97. Date not set. 25.00 (*1-57576-948-4*) Que Educ & Trng.
— Virtual Tutor for Microsoft Office 97. Date not set. 50.00 (*1-57576-949-2*) Que Educ & Trng.
— Virtual Tutor for Microsoft Powerpoint 97. Date not set. 25.00 (*1-57576-950-6*) Que Educ & Trng.
— Virtual Tutor for Microsoft Word 97. 1997. 25.00 (*1-57576-951-4*) Que Educ & Trng.
— Visual Basic 4 Smartstart. 1996. pap. text 29.99 (*1-57576-010-X*) Que Educ & Trng.
— Windows 95 Virtual Tutor. 1996. pap. text 35.00 incl. cd-rom (*1-57576-083-5*) Que Educ & Trng.
— Windows 95 Basics. 1996. 16.99 (*1-57576-280-3*) Que Educ & Trng.
— Windows 3.11 Virtual Tutor. Date not set. 49.99 incl. cd-rom (*1-57576-087-8*) Que Educ & Trng.
— Windows 3.1 Basics. 1995. 16.99 (*1-57576-282-X*) Que Educ & Trng.
— Word for Windows 95 Essentials, Level 3. LC 96-68610. (Essentials Ser.). 194p. 1997. pap. text 22.99 (*1-57576-383-4*) Que Educ & Trng.
— Word for Windows 95 Virtual Tutor. 1996. pap. text 49.99 (*1-57576-085-1*) Que Educ & Trng.
— Word 97 Essentials (Academic) (Illus.). 215p. 1997. 39.99 (*1-57576-872-0*) Que Educ & Trng.
— Word 6 Virtual Tutor. 1996. pap. text 49.99 incl. cd-rom (*1-57576-089-4*) Que Educ & Trng.
— Word 6 Windows Virtual Tutor. (Essentials Ser.). 1997. pap. text 25.00 (*1-57576-090-8*) Que Educ & Trng.
— Wordperfect 7 for Windows Essentials, Level II. LC 96-68612. (Essentials Ser.). 1997. pap. text 22.99 incl. disk (*1-57576-389-3*) Que Educ & Trng.
— WordPerfect 6.1 Virtual Tutor. 1996. text 49.99 incl. cd-rom (*1-57576-097-5*) Que Educ & Trng.
— Works for Windows 95 Essentials. 2nd ed. 1997. teacher ed. 39.99 (*1-57576-876-3*) Que Educ & Trng.
— Works for Windows 95 Virtual Tutor. 1996. pap. text 49.99 (*1-57576-113-0*) Que Educ & Trng.
— WP for Windows 95 Virtual Tutor. 1996. 49.99 incl. cd-rom (*1-57576-109-2*) Que Educ & Trng.
Que Education & Training Staff & Mueller, Scott. Upgrading & Repairing PCs: Academic Edition. 6th ed. (C). 1997. pap. text, teacher ed. 39.99 incl. disk (*1-57576-697-3*) Que Educ & Trng.

Que Education & Training Staff & Wood, Dawn. Learn PowerPoint 97. (Illus.). 201p. 1997. teacher ed. 39.99 incl. cd-rom (*1-57576-884-4*) Que Educ & Trng.
Que Education & Training Staff, et al. Easy Powerpoint 97. LC 97-68880. (Illus.). 178p. 1997. 29.99 (*1-57576-885-2*) Que Educ & Trng.
— Easy Word 97. LC 97-68880. (Illus.). 207p. 1997. 29.99 (*1-57576-883-6*) Que Educ & Trng.
— Learn Access 97. LC 97-68884. 224p. (C). 1998. pap. text 32.00 (*1-57576-891-7*) Que Educ & Trng.
Que Educational & Training Staff. MS Office 97 Suite Essentials. 1997. 39.99 (*1-57576-972-7*) Que Educ & Trng.
Que Et Staff & Mitchell, Carolyn B. Works 3 for Windows Essentials. LC 94-69265. 423p. 1995. 49.99 (*0-7897-0130-8*) Que.
Que Eudcation & Training Staff. Access for Windows 95 & Windows NT Essentials: Level III. LC 96-69175. (Essentials Ser.). 162p. 1997. pap. text 22.99 (*1-57576-478-4*) Que Educ & Trng.
***Que Hee, Shane S.** Hazardous Waste Analysis. LC 98-43722. 832p. 1999. 99.00 (*0-86587-609-6*, 609) Gov Insts.
Que Hee, Shane S. & Sutherland, Ronald G. The Phenoxyalkanoic Herbicides: Chemistry, Analysis & Environmental Pollution, Vol. I. 321p. 1981. 187.00 (*0-8493-5851-5*, SB952, CRC Reprint) Franklin.
Que Hee, Shayne, ed. Biological Monitoring: An Introduction. 672p. 1993. 110.00 (*0-471-29083-1*, VNR) Wiley.
Que, Lawrence, Jr Metal Clusters in Proteins. LC 88-14504. (ACS Symposium Ser.: Vol. 372). 424p. 1988. reprint ed. pap. 131.50 (*0-608-03292-1*, 206381000007) Bks Demand.
Que, Lawrence, Jr., ed. Metal Clusters in Proteins. LC 88-14504. (ACS Symposium Ser.: No. 372). (Illus.). ix, 413p. 1988. 84.95 (*0-8412-1487-5*) Am Chemical.
— Physical Methods in Bioinorganic Chemistry: Spectroscopy & Magnetism. LC 99-51651. (Illus.). 504p. (C). 2000. text 72.00 (*1-891389-02-5*) Univ Sci Bks.
Que Publishing Staff. Excel Version 5 Para Windows: (Excel 5 Quickstart for Windows) 1995. pap. text 23.99 (*968-880-419-3*) Que.
— Internet Facil: (Complete Idiot's Guide to the Internet. 1995. pap. text 21.99 (*968-880-470-3*) Que.
— 10 Minute Guide to Office Pro Windows 97 with Outlook Bundle. 1998. pap. text 59.00 (*0-7897-1243-1*) Que.
— World Wide Web Business Start-Up Kit. 1995. pap. 99.99 (*0-7897-0721-7*) Que.
Que Staff. Big Basics Book of Windows 98. LC 97-75464. 600p. 1998. 19.99 (*0-7897-1513-9*) Que.
— Easy Lotus Smartsuite Bundle. 1994. pap. 60.00 (*0-7897-0042-5*) Que.
— Easy Microsoft Office 4.2 Bundle. 1994. pap. 54.00 (*0-7897-0041-7*) Que.
— Easy Prodigy. 1996. 19.99 (*0-7897-0558-3*) Que.
— Easy Quicken 99. LC 98-235198. (Easy Ser.). 197p. 1998. pap. 19.99 (*0-7897-1724-7*) Que.
— Easy Works for Windows 95. (Illus.). 249p. (Orig.). 1995. 19.99 (*0-7897-0456-0*) Que.
— Linux User Manual: The Manual You Should Have Received with Linux. 1998. pap. text 19.99 (*0-7897-1877-4*) Que.
— Lotus SmartSuite Quickstart Bundle. 1994. pap. 75.00 (*1-56529-969-8*) Que.
— Microsoft Office VisiRef Bundle. 1994. pap. 39.00 (*0-7897-0043-3*) Que.
— Using CompuServe Special Edition. 875p. 1995. 29.99 incl. cd-rom (*0-7897-0280-0*) Que.
***Que Staff.** Using the Internet. fac. ed. (Using ... / Que Ser.). 1300p. (Orig.). 1999. pap. 60.00 (*0-7897-1140-0*) Que.
Que Staff. Using Visual Basic 3: Special Edition. 1335p. 1995. 39.99 (*0-7897-0326-2*) Que.
***Que Staff, ed.** Complete Idiot's Guide to Online Health & Fitness. 380p. 1999. pap. 18.95 (*0-7897-2208-9*) Que.
— Migrating to Office 2000. 250p. 2000. pap. 17.99 (*0-7897-2224-0*) Que.
Que Staff, ed. Windows 98 Hints & Hacks. LC 98-85720. 1998. pap. 19.99 (*0-7897-1750-6*) Que.
Que Staff, jt. auth. see Eager, Bill.
Que Staff, jt. auth. see Pivovarnick, John.
Que Staff, jt. auth. see Steinberg, Gene.
Que Staff, ed. see Rutledge, Patrice-Anne, et al.
Quebec (Province) Staff. A Fair Price for Health Services: Opinion to the Ministre de la Sante et des Services Sociaux. LC 96-181721. 48p. 1996. write for info. (*2-550-25732-4*) Gvt Quebec.
Quebec Brewers Association Staff. English - French Lexicon of Brewing. (ENG & FRE.). 101p. 1986. pap. 29.95 (*0-8288-9396-9*) Fr & Eur.
Quebec Province Ministere des Finances Staff & Landry, Bernard. The Distribution of Financial Products to The Public: Taking up The Challenge of Change : Quinquennial Report on The Implementation of The Act Respecting Market Intermediaries. LC 96-193636. 38 p. 1996. write for info. (*2-550-30090-4*) Gvt Quebec.
Quebedeaux, Richard. Prime Sources of California & Nevada Local History: 151 Rare & Important City, County & State Directories, 1850-1906. LC 91-74139. (Illus.). 238p. 1992. 65.00 (*0-87062-213-7*) A H Clark.
***Quee, Wong-Toon.** Marketing Research. 3rd ed. 360p. 2000. pap. 39.95 (*0-7506-4707-8*) Buttrwrth-Heinemann.
Queen. Best of Queen - Guitar Signature Picks. 88p. 1997. pap. 19.95 (*0-7935-6697-5*) H Leonard.
Queen. Elem Curric for 21st Century. LC 98-29176. 320p. 1998. 58.00 (*0-02-397051-0*, Prentice Hall) P-H.
— Made in Heaven. 60p. 1996. pap. 15.95 (*0-7935-6475-1*) H Leonard.
— Planning For Instruction. 2000. pap. text 13.27 (*0-13-021996-7*) S&S Trade.

Queen, jt. auth. see Edwards.
Queen, Betty, ed. see Queen, H. L.
Queen, Betty A., jt. auth. see Queen, H. L.
Queen, Carol. Exhibitionism for the Shy: Show off, Dress up & Talk Hot. LC 95-68995. 248p. (Orig.). 1995. pap. 12.50 (*0-940208-16-4*) Down There Pr.
— The Leather Daddy & the Femme. LC 98-6197. 180p. 1998. pap. 14.00 (*1-57344-037-X*) Cleis Pr.
— PoMoSexuals: Challenging Assumptions about Gender & Sexuality. LC 97-37703. 180p. 1997. pap. text 14.95 (*1-57344-074-4*) Cleis Pr.
— Real Live Nude Girl: Chronicles of Sex-Positive Culture. LC 96-50998. 200p. (Orig.). 1997. pap. 14.95 (*1-57344-073-6*) Cleis Pr.
Queen, Carol & Davis, Jack, eds. Sex Spoken Here: Good Vibrations Erotic Reading Circle Selections. LC 97-44294. 216p. 1998. pap. 14.50 (*0-940208-19-9*) Down There Pr.
Queen, Carol & Schimel, Lawrence, eds. Switch Hitters: Lesbians Write Gay Male Erotica & Gay Men Write Lesbian Erotica. 200p. 1996. pap. 12.95 (*1-57344-021-3*) Cleis Pr.
Queen, Carol, jt. ed. see Brent, Bill.
Queen, Charles S. Shadows of Infantrymen Vol. 5000: A 90th Infantry Division Platoon Sergeant's World War II Photographic Collection. LC 98-65084. (Illus.). vi, 63p. 1998. pap. 23.85 (*0-9663259-0-7*, 001) Queen Publ.
Queen, Christopher, jt. ed. see Williams, Duncan R.
Queen, Christopher S., ed. Engaged Buddhism in the West. LC 99-36870. (Illus.). 512p. 1999. pap. 24.95 (*0-86171-159-9*) Wisdom MA.
Queen, Christopher S. & King, Sallie B., eds. Engaged Buddhism: Buddhist Liberation Movements in Asia. LC 95-17232. 446p. (C). 1996. text 74.50 (*0-7914-2843-5*); pap. text 24.95 (*0-7914-2844-3*) State U NY Pr.
Queen, Daniel R. Fruit of the Spirit. 158p. 1997. pap. write for info. (*1-881328-02-3*) Queens Palace.
— Wake up Call: (Final Call) (Illus.). 163p. 1994. pap. 11.95 (*1-881328-01-5*) Queens Palace.
— Wings of the Whirlwind: (A Tribute to Marcus M. Garvey) rev. ed. 86p. 1992. pap. 10.00 (*1-881328-00-7*) Queens Palace.
***Queen, Edward L., II.** Serving Those in Need: A Handbook for Managing Faith-Based Human Services Organizations. 352p. 2000. text 35.00 (*0-7879-4296-0*) Jossey-Bass.
Queen, Edward L., II, et al. Encyclopedia of American Religious History. LC 95-2487. 816p. 1995. 110.00 (*0-8160-2406-5*) Facts on File.
Queen, Ellery. American Gun Mystery: Death at the Rodeo. lib. bdg. 21.95 (*0-8488-1869-5*) Amereon Ltd.
— Cat of Many Tails. LC 88-82351. 247p. 1988. reprint ed. pap. 4.95 (*0-930330-94-3*, Lib Crime Classics) Intl Polygonics.
— The Chinese Orange Mystery. 1983. mass mkt. 2.95 (*0-451-12341-7*, Sig) NAL.
— Chinese Orange Mystery. lib. bdg. 21.95 (*0-8488-1874-1*) Amereon Ltd.
— Cop Out. 1982. mass mkt. 2.50 (*0-451-11562-7*, AE1562, Sig) NAL.
— The Door Between. 400p. 1983. mass mkt. 2.50 (*0-451-12486-3*, Sig) NAL.
Queen, Ellery. The Dragon's Teeth. 1980. mass mkt. 2.50 (*0-451-11310-1*, AE1310, Sig) NAL.
Queen, Ellery. Drury Lane's Last Case. LC 87-82441. 232p. 1987. reprint ed. pap. 4.95 (*0-930330-70-6*) Intl Polygonics.
— The Dutch Shoe Mystery. large type ed. LC 97-51185. 375p. 1998. write for info. (*0-7540-3405-4*, G K Hall Lrg Type) Mac Lib Ref.
— The Dutch Shoe Mystery. large type ed. LC 97-51185. 372p. 1998. 22.95 (*0-7838-8429-X*, G K Hall & Co) Mac Lib Ref.
— The Dutch Shoe Mystery: An Ellery Queen Mystery. lib. bdg. 21.95 (*0-8488-1873-3*) Amereon Ltd.
— The Dutch Shoe Mystery: An Ellery Queen Mystery. 324p. 1995. reprint ed. pap. 6.95 (*1-883402-12-3*) S&S Trade.
— The Ellery Queen Omnibus. LC 88-82352. 700p. 1988. reprint ed. pap. 9.95 (*1-55882-001-9*, Lib Crime Classics) Intl Polygonics.
— Ellery Queen's Mini Mysteries. lib. bdg. 22.95 (*0-8488-1744-3*) Amereon Ltd.
— Ellery Queen's Poetic Justice. 23.95 (*0-8488-0615-8*) Amereon Ltd.
— Ellery Queen's Searches & Seizures. 320p. Date not set. 24.95 (*0-8488-2379-6*) Amereon Ltd.
— Ellerys Queen's Masters of Mystery. 1993. 11.98 (*0-88365-822-4*) Galahad Bks.
***Queen, Ellery.** Face to Face. large type ed. 290p. 2000. pap. 23.95 (*0-7838-9037-0*) Mac Lib Ref.
Queen, Ellery. The Finishing Stroke. large type ed. LC 99-15668. 1999. 30.00 (*0-7838-8667-5*) Mac Lib Ref.
— The Fourth Side of the Triangle. 192p. 1983. mass mkt. 1.95 (*0-345-31743-2*, Ballantine) Ballantine Pub Grp.
— French Powder Mystery. lib. bdg. 21.95 (*0-8488-1870-9*) Amereon Ltd.
— The Greek Coffin Mystery. lib. bdg. 21.95 (*0-8488-1872-5*) Amereon Ltd.
***Queen, Ellery.** The Hollywood Murders: The Devil to Pay, The Four of Hearts, The Origin of Evil. 525p. 2000. pap. 17.00 (*1-56858-173-4*, Pub. by FWEW) Publishers Group.
Queen, Ellery. In the Queens' Parlor & Other Leaves from the Editors' Notebook. LC 70-79516. 1969. reprint ed. 30.00 (*0-8196-0238-8*) Biblo.
— Masters of Suspense. 1992. 9.98 (*0-88365-787-2*) Galahad Bks.
— Queen's Quorum. Date not set. lib. bdg. 18.95 (*0-8488-2133-5*) Amereon Ltd.

An Asterisk (*) at the beginning of an entry indicates that the title is appearing for the first time.

— Queen's Quorum. LC 68-56450. 146p. 1969. 30.00 (*0-8196-0229-9*) Biblo.
— The Roman Hat Mystery. lib. bdg. 21.95 (*0-8488-1871-7*) Amereon Ltd.
— The Roman Hat Mystery. 340p. 1994. reprint ed. 35.00 (*1-883402-19-0*) S&S Trade.
— The Scarlet Letters. 1984. mass mkt. 3.50 (*0-451-12887-7*, E9675, Sig) NAL.
Queen, Ellery. The Siamese Twin Mystery. LC 93-8120. 1993. pap. 6.95 (*1-883402-11-5*) S&S Trade.
Queen, Ellery. The Spanish Cape Mystery. lib. bdg. 25.95 (*0-8488-1868-7*) Amereon Ltd.
— Spanish Cape Mystery. 1995. per. 7.00 (*1-57283-006-9*) S&S Trade.
— Ten Days' Wonder. 416p. 1984. mass mkt. 3.50 (*0-451-12774-9*, AE2774, Sig) NAL.
— Ten Days Wonder. 1999. write for info. (*0-316-72894-2*) Little.
— Ten Days' Wonder. large type ed. LC 97-51187. 1998. 22.95 (*0-7838-8430-3*, G K Hall Lrg Type) Mac Lib Ref.
— There Was an Old Woman. 1984. mass mkt. 3.50 (*0-451-12683-1*, AE2683, Sig) NAL.
***Queen, Ellery.** The Tragedy of Errors & Others. 224p. 1999. pap. 16.00 (*1-885941-36-6*) Crippen & Landru.
— The Tragedy of Errors & Others. 1999. text 15.95 (*0-312-00060-X*) St Martin.
Queen, Ellery. The Tragedy of X. 256p. 1986. pap. 5.95 (*0-930330-43-9*) Intl Polygonics.
— The Tragedy of Z. (Library of Crime Classics). 192p. 1987. pap. 4.95 (*0-930330-58-7*) Intl Polygonics.
Queen, Ellery, ed. Ellery Queen's a Multitude of Sins. 23.95 (*0-89190-794-7*) Amereon Ltd.
— Ellery Queen's Circumstantial Evidence. 23.95 (*0-89190-790-4*) Amereon Ltd.
— Ellery Queen's Masks of Mystery. 23.95 (*0-89190-793-9*) Amereon Ltd.
— Ellery Queen's Secrets of Mystery. 23.95 (*0-89190-791-2*) Amereon Ltd.
— Ellery Queen's The Golden Thirteen. 26.95 (*0-89190-792-0*) Amereon Ltd.
— Ellery Queen's Veils of Mystery. 23.95 (*0-89190-795-5*) Amereon Ltd.
— Ellery Queen's Wings of Mystery. 23.95 (*0-89190-796-3*) Amereon Ltd.
— Great Sports Detective Stories. 1999. lib. bdg. 27.95 (*1-56723-137-3*, 146) Yestermorrow.
***Queen, Ellery, ed.** Nanuk. LC 97-26670. (Illus.). 32p. (J). (gr. k-4). 1998. 15.99 (*0-8037-2194-3*, Dial Yng Read) Peng Put Young Read.
Queen, Ellery, ed. Redbird at Rockefeller Center. LC 96-45728. (Illus.). 32p. (J). (ps-3). 1997. 14.99 (*0-8037-2256-7*, Dial Yng Read) Peng Put Young Read.
***Queen, Erika V.** Johnny Starlight. (Illus.). 30p. (J). (gr. 1-6). 1999. 6.95 (*0-9674878-0-3*) Goldwing Pub.
Queen, George S. The United States & the Materials Advance in Russia, 1881-1906. Bruchey, Stuart & Bruchey, Eleanor, eds. LC 76-5030. (American Business Abroad Ser.). (Illus.). 1976. lib. bdg. 24.95 (*0-405-09297-0*) Ayer.
Queen, H. L. Chronic Mercury Toxicity: New Hope Against an Endemic Disease. (Doctor's Guide for Lifestyle Counseling Ser.: Vol. 1). (Illus.). 302p. (C). 1988. text 45.00 (*0-9620479-1-0*) Queen Co Hlth Comns.
— Your Personal Health Guide: The Secret to Gaining & Maintaining Health. Queen, Betty, ed. 119p. 1997. pap. 14.95 (*0-9620479-4-5*) Queen Co Hlth Comns.
Queen, H. L. & Queen, Betty A. The IV-C Mercury Tox Program: A Guide for the Doctor. (Doctor's Guide for Lifestyle Counseling Ser.). 76p. (Orig.). 1991. pap. text 11.95 (*0-9620479-0-2*) Queen Co Hlth Comns.
— The IV-C Mercury Tox Program: A Guide for the Patient. (Doctor's Guide for Lifestyle Counseling Ser.). 72p. (Orig.). 1991. pap. text 8.95 (*0-9620479-2-9*) Queen Co Hlth Comns.
Queen, J. Allen. Complete Karate. LC 93-24831. (Illus.). 192p. (YA). (gr. 10-12). 1993. 19.95 (*0-8069-8678-6*) Sterling.
— Complete Karate. (Illus.). 192p. 1994. pap. 12.95 (*0-8069-8679-4*) Sterling.
— Geography Smart Junior. LC 97-208526. 1996. pap. 12.00 (*0-679-77522-6*) Random.
— Geography Smart Junior, Vol. 2. (Princeton Review Ser.). 1999. pap. 10.00 (*0-679-77539-0*) Random.
— Karate for Kids. (Illus.). 96p. (J). (gr. 4-7). 1995. pap. 5.95 (*0-8069-0615-4*) Sterling.
Queen, J. Allen. Karate for Kids. 1995. 11.15 (*0-606-12749-6*, Pub. by Turtleback) Demco.
Queen, J. Allen. Responsible Classroom Management. 195p. (C). 1996. pap. text 43.00 (*0-13-442336-4*) P-H.
— Secrets of the Karate Masters. LC 98-26367. (Illus.). 80p. 1996. 17.95 (*0-8069-8136-9*) Sterling.
— Start Karate! LC 96-50442. (Illus.). 96p. (J). 1997. pap 5.95 (*0-8069-9306-5*) Sterling.
— Total Karate. LC 89-49313. (Illus.). 128p. (J). (gr. 4 up). 1991. pap. 8.95 (*0-8069-6715-3*) Sterling.
Queen, J. Allen & Gaskey-Isenhour, Kimberly. The 4 X 4 Block Schedule. LC 98-10667. 1998. 35.95 (*1-883001-56-0*) Eye On Educ.
Queen, James W., & Company Staff. Queen Catalogues, 2 vols., Set. (Illus.). 1665p. 1993. reprint ed. 245.00 (*0-930405-30-7*) Norman SF.
Queen, Jedda. Fibroid Tumors, Where Do They Come From? 41p. 1997. pap. 10.95 (*0-9672544-0-X*) Queens Pubg.
Queen Latifah & Hunter, Karen. Ladies First: Revelations from a Strong Woman. LC 98-41533. (Illus.). 173p. 1999. 22.00 (*0-688-15623-1*, Wm Morrow) Morrow Avon.
Queen Liliuokalani. Hawaii's Story by Hawaii's Queen. LC 63-23301. (Illus.). 432p. 1964. pap. 10.95 (*0-8048-1066-4*) Tuttle Pubng.
Queen, Linda M. To Inspire You: An Inspiring Work of Poetry Filled with Spiritual Messages of Hope. Adejom, Myrna, ed. 72p. 1998. pap. 9.95 (*0-9636042-2-8*) Clark Assoc Busn.
Queen, Margaret M. So You're off to Summer Camp: A Trunk Load of Tips for a Fun-Filled Camp Adventure. LC 93-77129. (Illus.). 136p. (J). (gr. 2-12). 1993. 14.95 (*1-882959-55-8*); per. 6.95 (*1-882959-50-7*) Foxglove TN.
Queen, N. M., tr. see Prudnikov, A. P., et al.
Queen, N. M., tr. see Sibgatullin, N. R.
Queen, Phillip L. Fighting Fire in the Wildland/Urban Interface. Brooks, Carol C., ed. (Illus.). 115p. (Orig.). 1994. pap. text 19.95 (*0-941943-05-4*, 35718) Fire Pubns.
***Queen, Randy.** Darkchylde. 144p. 1999. mass mkt. 19.95 (*1-56389-558-7*) Warner Bks.
Queen, Sandy. Wellness Activities for Youth, Vol. 1. 160p. 1994. pap. 21.95 (*1-57025-026-X*) Whole Person.
— Wellness Activities for Youth, Vol. 2. 160p. 1994. pap. 21.95 (*0-938586-98-X*) Whole Person.
Queen, Sarah A. From Chronicle to Canon: The Hermeneutics of the Spring & Autumn Annals, According to Tung Chung-shu. (Studies in Chinese History, Literature & Institutions). (Illus.). 287p. (C). 1996. text 52.95 (*0-521-48226-7*) Cambridge U Pr.
Queen, Stephanie. Libra, Angel or Vampire. 304p. 1997. 21.95 (*1-57087-336-4*) Prof Pr NC.
Queen, Stuart A. The American City. LC 73-138175. (Illus.). 383p. 1972. reprint ed. lib. bdg. 79.50 (*0-8371-5632-7*, QUAC, Greenwood Pr) Greenwood.
Queen, Stuart A., jt. auth. see Chapin, Francis S.
Queen, W. Patrick. Bent . . . but Not Broken. (Illus.). 46p. 1997. pap. 10.00 (*1-885729-16-2*) Toccoa Falls.
Queenan, Carrie N., jt. ed. see Queenan, John T.
Queenan, Charles F., jt. auth. see Combs-Moore, Wanda.
Queenan, James F., Jr., et al, eds. Chapter Eleven Theory & Practice: A Guide to Reorganization Includes Supplement for October 1994. LC 93-49092. (Bankruptcy Law Ser.). 6000p. 1994. ring bd. 775.00 (*0-934753-99-7*) LRP Pubns.
Queenan, Joe. Confessions of a Cineplex Heckler. LC 98-34695. 256p. (J). 1999. 22.45 (*0-7868-6508-3*) Hyperion.
— Confessions of a Cineplex Heckler: Celluloid Tirades & Escapades. 272p. 2000. pap. 12.95 (*0-7868-8464-9*, Pub. by Hyperion) Time Warner.
— If You're Talking to Me, Your Career Must Be in Trouble: Movies, Mayhem & Malice. 288p. 1999. pap. 14.95 (*0-7868-8460-6*, Pub. by Hyperion) Time Warner.
— Red Lobster, White Trash, & the Blue Lagoon: Joe Queenan's America. LC 98-10821. 320p. 1998. 21.95 (*0-7868-6332-3*, Pub. by Hyperion) Time Warner.
— Red Lobster, White Trash & the Blue Lagoon: Joe Queenan's America. 208p. 1999. reprint ed. pap. 12.95 (*0-7868-8408-8*, Pub. by Hyperion) Time Warner.
Queenan, John T. Management of High-Risk Pregnancy. 3rd ed. (Illus.). 632p. 1993. 89.95 (*0-86542-187-0*) Blackwell Sci.
— Management of High-Risk Pregnancy. 4th ed. LC 99-24041. (Illus.). 14p. 1999. 99.00 (*0-632-04332-6*) Blackwell Sci.
Queenan, John T. & Queenan, Carrie N., eds. A New Life: Pregnancy, Birth & Your Child's First Year. 1986. 24.95 (*0-316-72892-6*) Little.
— A New Life: Pregnancy, Birth, & Your Child's First Year - A Comprehensive Guide. 2nd rev. ed. (Illus.). 240p. 1992. 29.45 (*0-316-72878-0*) Lppncott W & W.
Queenan, John T., et al. Protocols for High-Risk Pregnancies. 3rd ed. (Protocols in Obstetrics & Gynecology Ser.). 512p. 1995. pap. 49.95 (*0-86542-444-6*) Blackwell Sci.
Queenan, Joseph. If You're Talking to Me, Your Career Must Be in Trouble: Movies, Mayhem & Malice. 288p. 1995. pap. 12.45 (*0-7868-8067-8*, Pub. by Hyperion) Time Warner.
— The Unkindest Cut: How a Hatchet-Man Critic Made His Own $7,000 Movie & Put It All on His Credit Card. (Illus.). 304p. (J). 1996. 22.45 (*0-7868-6090-1*, Pub. by Hyperion) Time Warner.
— The Unkindest Cut: How a Hatchet-Man Critic Made His Own $7,000 Movie & Put It All on His Credit Card. (Illus.). 320p. (J). 1997. pap. 11.45 (*0-7868-8198-4*, Pub. by Hyperion) Time Warner.
Queenborough, Lady. Occult Theocracy, 2 vols. 1972. 500.00 (*0-8490-0751-8*) Gordon Pr.
Queenborough, Lady & Miller, Edith Starr. Occult Theocrasy. 741p. 1995. 25.00 (*0-944379-15-X*) CPA Bk Pub.
Queener, Sherry F., jt. auth. see Clark, Julia F.
Queeney, Donna S. Assessing Needs in Continuing Education: An Essential Tool for Quality Improvement. LC 94-37102. (Higher & Adult Education Ser.). 295p. 1995. text 34.45 (*0-7879-0059-1*) Jossey-Bass.
Queeney, Richard. Experiments in the Determination of Mechanical Behavior of Engineering Materials. 156p. (C). 1995. pap. text 20.95 (*0-7872-1850-2*) Kendall-Hunt.
— Mechanical Engineering. 6th ed. 154p. (C). 1998. per. 21.95 (*0-7872-4737-5*) Kendall-Hunt.
Queens College Staff (New York, N.Y.), jt. auth. see Mantsios, Gregory.
Queens Library Foundation Staff, jt. auth. see Kroessler, Jeffrey A.
Queen's Own Hussars Editors, ed. The Queen's Own Hussars: Tercentenary Edition. (Illus.). 96p. 1985. pap. 16.50 (*0-08-033595-0*, P110, T120, Pergamon Pr) Elsevier.
Queen's University (Kingston, Ont.) Staff, jt. auth. see Watts, Ronald L.
Queen's University at Kingston Staff. Discontinuous Solidification of an Aluminum-Copper Alloy. 81p. 1965. 12.15 (*0-317-34515-X*, 66) Intl Copper.
Queen's University Faculty of the Arts Staff. Philosophical Essays Presented to John Watson. LC 70-156704. (Essay Index Reprint Ser.). 1977. reprint ed. 23.95 (*0-8369-2291-3*) Ayer.
Queensboro, Lady, see Miller, Edith S., pseud.
Queenship Publishing Company Staff. I Will Restore You Vol. III: In Faith, Hope & Love. 1999. pap. text 6.95 (*1-57918-110-4*) Queenship Pub.
***Queenship Publishing Company Staff & Leary, John.** Prepare for The Great Tribulation & The Era Of Peace, 13. 1999. pap. text 3.95 (*1-57918-113-9*) Queenship Pub.
Queensland Nurses' Union Staff, jt. auth. see Strachan, Glenda.
Queensland University of Technology Staff, jt. auth. see Horrigan, Bryan.
Queeny, Edgar M. Prairie Wings. (Illus.). 256p. 1979. reprint ed. 50.00 (*0-916838-21-8*) Schiffer.
Queffelec, Henri. Un Homme d'Ouessant. (FRE.). 224p. 1974. pap. 8.95 (*0-7859-4026-X*, 2070365417) Fr & Eur.
— Tempete sur Douarnenez. (FRE.). 1973. pap. 10.95 (*0-7859-4006-5*) Fr & Eur.
Queffelec, M. Substitution Dynamical Systems - Spectral Analysis. (Lecture Notes in Mathematics Ser.: Vol. 1294). 240p. 1987. 44.95 (*0-387-18692-1*) Spr-Verlag.
Queffelec, Yann. Charme Noir. (Folio Ser.: No. 1665). (FRE.). pap. 9.95 (*2-07-037665-6*) Schoenhof.
— Le Charme Noir. (FRE.). 1985. pap. 11.95 (*0-7859-4225-4*) Fr & Eur.
— Noces Barbares. (Folio Ser.: No. 1856). (FRE.). 308p. 1985. pap. 9.95 (*2-07-037856-X*) Schoenhof.
Quegan, Shaun, jt. auth. see Kingsley, Simon.
Quegan, Shaun, jt. auth. see Oliver, Chris J.
Quehl, Gary H., ed. see Chickering, Arthur W., et al.
Quehl, Gary H., jt. ed. see Fisher, James L.
Queinnec, Christian. LISP in Small Pieces. 534p. (C). 1996. text 64.95 (*0-521-56247-3*) Cambridge U Pr.
Queinnec, Christian, jt. ed. see Chailloux, J.
Queiros, Eca de, see de Queiros, Eca.
Queiros, Jose M. De, see De Queiros, Jose M.
Queiros Mattoso, Katia M. De, see De Queiros Mattoso, Katia M.
Queiroz, Edison. La Iglesia Local y las Misiones.Tr. of Local Church & the Missions. (SPA.). 160p. 1994. 5.99 (*1-56063-763-3*, 498560) Editorial Unilit.
Queiroz, Juan P., ed. see De Elia, Tomas.
Queiroz, Kevin De, see De Queiroz, Kevin.
Queiroz, M. S. de, see de Queiroz, M. S.
Queiroz, Rachel De, see De Queiroz, Rachel.
Queiruga, Andres T. Die Offenbarung Gottes in der Verwirklichung des Menschen. (GER.). 420p. 1996. 63.95 (*3-631-43862-1*) P Lang Pubng.
Queisser, H. J., ed. X-Ray Optics: Applications to Solids. (Topics in Applied Physics Ser.: Vol. 22). (Illus.). 1977. 56.95 (*0-387-08462-2*) Spr-Verlag.
Queisser, H. J., et al, eds. Proceedings of the Symposium on the Degradation of Electronic Devices Due to Device Operation As Well As Crystalline & Process-Induced Defects. LC 93-72866. (Proceedings Ser.: Vol. 94-01). 328p. 1994. 37.00 (*1-56677-037-8*) Electrochem Soc.
Queisser, H. J., ed. see Graff, K.
Queisser, H. J., ed. see Seeger, Karlheinz.
Queisser, H. J., ed. see Slichter, Charles P.
Queisser, Hans. The Conquest of the Microchip. LC 87-2440. (Illus.). 272p. 1988. 34.50 (*0-674-16296-X*) HUP.
Queisser, Monika. The Second Generation Pension Reforms in Latin America. LC 98-222354. 144p. 1998. pap. 25.00 (*92-64-16129-5*, 41199811P) OECD.
Queisser, Monika, jt. ed. see Brooks, Douglas H.
Queisser, W., ed. Aktiv Gegen den Krebs Vol. 18, Suppl. 3: Frueherkennung & Vorbeugung. (Journal Ser.: Vol. 18, Suppl. 3, 1995). (GER., Illus.). iv, 72p. 1996. pap. 33.25 (*3-8055-6251-9*) S Karger.
Queisser, W. & Fiebig, H. H., eds. New Drugs in Oncology. (Beitraege Zur Onkologie, Contributions to Oncology Ser.: Vol. 37). (Illus.). 302p. 1989. 68.75 (*3-8055-5047-2*) S Karger.
Queizan, Maria-Xose. The Likeness. Spitzmesser, Ana M., tr. from SPA. LC 98-32075. 119p. (C). 1999. text 32.95 (*0-8204-4177-5*) P Lang Pubng.
Quekett, John. Practical Treatise on the Use of the Microscope. (History of Microscopy Ser.). 512p. 1987. reprint ed. 72.00 (*0-940095-05-X*) Sci Heritage Ltd.
QUELCH. Instructors Manual. 3rd ed. (C). 1995. pap. text. write for info. (*0-201-53973-X*) Addison-Wesley.
***Quelch, Gary.** Feng Shui Almanac 2000: A Daily Guide Based on The Ancient Tung Shu Almanac. 192p. 1999. pap. text 7.95 (*0-572-02550-5*) Foulsham UK.
— T'Ung Shu Almanac 2001. 224p. 2000. pap. 9.95 (*0-572-02616-1*) Foulsham UK.
Quelch, H., tr. see Marx, Karl.
Quelch, John A. Business Strategies in the Middle East. LC 00-20496. 220p. (C). 2001. pap. text. write for info. (*0-201-47154-X*) Addison-Wesley.
— Cases in Marketing Management & Strategy: An Asia-Pacific Perspective. LC 96-26548. 507p. (C). 1997. pap. text 52.00 (*0-13-577057-2*) P-H.
— Cases in Product Management. 450p. (C). 1994. text 52.99 (*0-256-16347-2*, Irwn McGrw-H) McGrw-H Hghr Educ.
— Cases in Strategic Marketing & Management: A Latin-American Perspective. LC 99-86112. 352p. (C). 2001. pap. 60.00 (*0-201-33879-3*) Addison-Wesley.
***Quelch, John A.** Cases in Strategic Marketing Management: Business Strategies in Muslim Countries. 226p. 2000. pap. text 33.33 (*0-13-028357-6*) P-H.
Quelch, John A. Global Marketing Management. 4th ed. LC 98-40715. 720p. (C). 1998. pap. 84.00 (*0-201-35062-9*, Prentice Hall) P-H.
Quelch, John A., et al. Cases in European Marketing Management. LC 93-41069. (Series in Marketing). 544p. (C). 1994. text 52.99 (*0-256-15722-7*, Irwn McGrw-H) McGrw-H Hghr Educ.
— The Marketing Challenge of 1992. (Illus.). 350p. (C). 1989. pap. text 21.50 (*0-201-51562-8*) Addison-Wesley.
— Marketing Management: Text & Cases. LC 92-31499. (Series in Marketing). (Illus.). 960p. (C). 1993. text 70.95 (*0-256-10955-9*, Irwn McGrw-H) McGrw-H Hghr Educ.
Quelch, John A., jt. auth. see D'Andrea, Guillermo.
Quelch, John A., jt. auth. see Farris, Paul W.
Quelch, John A., jt. auth. see Smith, Craig N.
Quelch, John A., jt. auth. see Smith, N. Craig.
Quelet, Lucien. Flore Mycologique de la France & des Pays Limitrophes. 1962. reprint ed. 40.00 (*90-6123-123-X*) Lubrecht & Cramer.
Quell, E., jt. auth. see Finger, J. H.
Quell, Lawrence A. Awaken Your Twelve Personal Powers. Patterson-Oriel, Patricia, ed. (Illus.). (Orig.). 1989. pap. write for info. (*0-318-65233-1*) DC Enterprises.
Quelle, Henri. Tertullianus - Concordance Verbale du "De Exhortatione Castitatis" de Tertullien. (Alpha-Omega, Reihe A Ser.: Bd. CXXXI). (GER.). vi, 226p. 1993. write for info. (*3-487-09501-7*) G Olms Pubs.
Quellen, Verlag. In Praise of Beauty. (Springs Books Ser.). (Illus.). 22p. 1996. spiral bd. 4.95 (*3-85788-325-1*, Pub. by Quellen Verlag) Assoc Pubs Grp.
Quellen Verlag Staff. Springs Book: Joys of Life. (Illus.). 22p. 1995. 4.95 (*3-85788-327-8*, Pub. by Quellen Verlag) Assoc Pubs Grp.
— Springs of Comfort. (Illus.). 22p. 1985. 4.95 (*3-85788-319-7*, Pub. by Quellen Verlag) Assoc Pubs Grp.
— Springs of Friendship. (Illus.). 22p. 1985. 4.95 (*3-85788-310-3*, Pub. by Quellen Verlag) Assoc Pubs Grp.
— Springs of Roman Wisdom. (Illus.). 22p. 1988. 4.95 (*3-85788-307-3*, Pub. by Quellen Verlag) Assoc Pubs Grp.
***Queller, Donald E.** Fourth Crusade: The Conquest of Constantinople. 2nd ed. 1999. pap. 19.95 (*0-8122-1713-6*) U of Pa Pr.
Queller, Donald E. The Venetian Patriciate: Reality vs. Myth. LC 84-28041. 398p. 1985. text 34.95 (*0-252-01144-9*) U of Ill Pr.
Queller, Donald E. & Madden, Thomas F. The Fourth Crusade: The Conquest of Constantinople. 2nd ed. LC 96-39139. 368p. 1997. text 47.50 (*0-8122-3387-5*) U of Pa Pr.
Quellet, Henri. Bibliographia Indicum, Lexicorum et Concordantiarum Auctorum Latinorum. ix, 262p. 1980. write for info. (*3-487-07014-6*) G Olms Pubs.
— Le Gitagovinda de Jayadeva: Texte, Concordance et Index. 570p. 1978. write for info. (*3-487-06515-0*) G Olms Pubs.
— Tertullianus - Concordance Verbale du de Cultu Feminarum de Tertullien. (Alpha-Omega, Reihe A Ser.: Vol. LX). (GER.). iv, 382p. 1986. write for info. (*3-487-07769-8*) G Olms Pubs.
Quellet, Henri, ed. Tertullianus - Concordance Verbale du "De Corona" de Tertullien. (Alpha-Omega, Reihe A Ser.: Vol. XXIII). (GER.). 434p. 1975. write for info. (*3-487-05763-8*) G Olms Pubs.
— Tertullianus - Concordance Verbale du "De Patientia" de Tertullien. (Alpha-Omega, Reihe A Ser.: Vol. XCVII). (GER.). iv, 346p. 1988. write for info. (*3-487-07994-1*) G Olms Pubs.
Quellet, Jean-Claude. Repertoire des Naisances et Baptemes No. 6: L'Isle Vere (1783-1984) (FRE.). 361p. 1994. 33.00 (*2-9803120-5-3*) SGEQ.
Quellette, Edward, jt. auth. see Schmidt, William J.
Quellhorst, E., et al, eds. Trace Elements in Renal Insufficiency. (Contributions to Nephrology Ser.: Vol. 38). (Illus.). x, 206p. 1984. 29.75 (*3-8055-3676-3*) S Karger.
Quellmalz, Werner, jt. auth. see Beeger, Dieter.
***Quema, Anne.** Agony of Modernism: Wyndham Lewis's Allegories, Aesthetics & Politics. LC 98-44002. 240p. 1999. 38.50 (*0-8387-5392-2*) Bucknell U Pr.
Quemada, B. Dictionnaire Academie Francaise Lexicographic Institutions Europeen. (FRE.). 1998. 195.00 (*0-320-00351-5*) Fr & Eur.
Quen, Jacques M., ed. The Psychiatrist in the Courtroom: Selected Papers of Bernard L. Diamond, M.D. 376p. 1994. 47.50 (*0-88163-160-4*) Analytic Pr.
Quenan, Carlos, jt. ed. see Berthelemy, Jean-Claude.
Quencer, Robert M. MRI of the Spine. (MRI Teaching File Ser.). 242p. 1991. text 76.00 (*0-88167-703-5*) Lppncott W & W.
Quendo, Rene. Creativity in Education: The Waldorf Approach. 1982. pap. 9.95 (*0-930420-05-5*) H S Dakin.
Queneau, Joan, ed. see Miro, Joan.
Queneau, P. E., jt. ed. see Anderson, J. N.
Queneau, Paul E. International Symposium Staff. Extractive Metallurgy of Copper, Nickel & Cobalt Vol. 1: Proceedings of the Paul E. Queneau International Symposium, Sponsored by the Extraction & Processing Division of TMS & the Metallurgical Society of the Canadian Institute of Mining, Metallurgy, & Petroleum (CIM), Denver, CO, 1993. Reddy, R. G., ed. LC 92-63261. 1337p. 1993. reprint ed. pap. 200.00 (*0-608-03827-X*, 206278900001) Bks Demand.

Q

Queneau, Paul E. International Symposium Staff. Extractive Metallurgy of Copper, Nickel & Cobalt Vol. 2: Proceedings of the Paul E. Queneau International Symposium, Sponsored by the Extraction & Processing Division of TMS & the Metallurgical Society of the Canadian Institute of Mining, Metallurgy, & Petroleum (CIM), Denver, CO, 1993. LC 92-63261. 444p. 1993. reprint ed. pap. 137.70 (*0-608-03947-0*, 206278900002) Bks Demand.

Queneau, R. Le Chiendent. (FRE.). 1974. pap. 13.95 (*0-8288-3767-8*, M3944) Fr & Eur.

Queneau, Raymond. Bark Tree. 1991. pap. 11.95 (*0-7145-0108-5*) Riverrun NY.

Queneau, Raymond. Batons, Chiffres et Lettres. (Idees Ser.). (FRE.). 384p. 1965. 9.95 (*2-07-035070-3*) Schoenhof.

— Battre la Campagne. (FRE.). 216p. 1968. pap. 10.95 (*0-7859-1336-X*, 2070272974) Fr & Eur.

— The Blue Flowers. Wright, Barbara, tr. from FRE. LC 84-25544. (New Directions Classics Ser.: Vol. 595). 224p. 1985. reprint ed. pap. 8.95 (*0-8112-0945-8*, NDP595, Pub. by New Directions) Norton.

— Bords: Mathematiciens, Precurseurs, Encyclopedistes. (FRE.). 144p. 1978. pap. 24.95 (*0-7859-1607-5*, 270565402X) Fr & Eur.

— Cent Mille Milliards de Poemes. (Gallimard Ser.). (FRE.). 38p. 1965. 59.95 (*2-07-010467-2*) Schoenhof.

— Chene et Chien & Petite Cosmongonie Portative, le Chant du Styrene. (Poesie Ser.). (FRE.). 192p. 1969. pap. 9.95 (*2-07-030231-8*) Schoenhof.

— Chene et Chien, Petite Cosmogonie Portative. (FRE.). 1969. pap. 10.95 (*0-8288-3866-6*, F120250) Fr & Eur.

— Chiendent. (Folio Ser.: No. 588). (FRE.). 431p. 1933. pap. 10.95 (*2-07-036588-3*) Schoenhof.

— Children of Clay. Valguth, Madeline, tr. from FRE. & intro. by. (Classics Ser.: No. 92).Tr. of Les Enfants du Limon. 420p. (Orig.). 1997. pap. 14.95 (*1-55713-286-0*) Sun & Moon CA.

— Contes et Propos. (FRE.). 1990. pap. 12.95 (*0-7859-2920-7*) Fr & Eur.

— Contes et Propos. (Folio Ser.: No. 2127). (FRE.). pap. 9.95 (*2-07-038220-6*) Schoenhof.

— Courir les Rues. 200p. 1967. 5.95 (*0-686-54665-2*) Fr & Eur.

— Courir les Rues. Battre la Campagne. Fendre les Flots. (Poesie Ser.). (FRE.). 1981. pap. 16.95 (*2-07-032204-1*) Schoenhof.

— Courir les Rues, Battre le Compagne, Fendre Flots. (FRE.). 1981. pap. 10.95 (*0-8288-3867-4*, F120280) Fr & Eur.

— Les Derniers Jours: Roman. (FRE.). 232p. 1977. pap. 24.95 (*0-7859-1590-7*, 207010916X) Fr & Eur.

— Le Dimanche de la Vie. (FRE.). 1973. pap. 10.95 (*0-8288-3768-6*, M3945) Fr & Eur.

— Dimanche de la Vie. (Folio Ser.: No. 442). (FRE.). pap. 8.95 (*2-07-036442-9*) Schoenhof.

— Exercices de Style. (FRE.). 1982. pap. 10.95 (*0-8288-3770-8*, M1261) Fr & Eur.

— Exercices de Style. (Folio Ser.: No. 1363). (FRE.). 200p. 1970. pap. 6.95 (*2-07-037363-0*) Schoenhof.

— Exercises in Style. 2nd ed. Wright, Barbara, tr. from FRE. LC 80-26102. (Illus.). 208p. 1981. pap. 10.95 (*0-8112-0789-7*, ND513, Pub. by New Directions) Norton.

— Les Fleurs Bleues. (FRE.). 1978. pap. 10.95 (*0-8288-3771-6*, M11325) Fr & Eur.

— Les Fleurs Bleues. (Folio Ser.: No. 1000). (FRE.). 280p. 1965. 8.95 (*2-07-037000-3*) Schoenhof.

— The Flight of Icarus. Wright, Barbara, tr. from FRE. LC 73-76900. Orig. Title: Le Vol D'Icare. 192p. 1973. pap. 6.95 (*0-8112-0483-9*, NDP358, Pub. by New Directions) Norton.

— Histoire des Litteratures: Litteratures Anciennes, Orientales et Orales, Vol. 1. (Historique Ser.). 2024p. 82.50 (*0-686-56447-2*) Fr & Eur.

— Histoire des Litteratures: Litteratures Francaises, Vol. 3. (Historique Ser.). 2128p. 82.50 (*0-686-56449-9*) Fr & Eur.

— Histoire des Litteratures: Litteratures Occidentales, Vol. 2. (Historique Ser.). 2156p. 53.95 (*0-686-56448-0*) Fr & Eur.

— Une Histoire Modele. 124p. 1966. 4.95 (*0-686-54674-1*); pap. 16.95 (*0-7859-1301-7*, 2070253236) Fr & Eur.

— Histoires des Litteratures, Vol. 1: Anciennes, Orientales, Orales. (FRE.). 1978. lib. bdg. 145.00 (*0-7859-3836-2*) Fr & Eur.

— Histoires des Litteratures, Vol. 2: Etrangers d'Europe. (FRE.). 2150p. 1956. lib. bdg. 140.00 (*0-7859-3774-9*, 2070104079) Fr & Eur.

— Histoires des Litteratures, Vol. 3: Francaises, Connexes et Marginales. (FRE.). 1978. lib. bdg. 140.00 (*0-7859-3837-0*) Fr & Eur.

— L' Instant Fatal & les Ziaux. (FRE.). 1966. pap. 10.95 (*0-8288-3868-2*, F120340) Fr & Eur.

— L' Instant Fatal & les Ziaux. (Poesie Ser.). (FRE.). 224p. 1966. 9.95 (*2-07-030229-6*) Schoenhof.

— Lascaux (Elie) Paintings, 1921-1959. (FRE., Illus.). 52p. 1959. pap. 35.00 (*1-55660-267-7*) A Wofsy Fine Arts.

— The Last Days. 2nd ed. Wright, Barbara, tr. from FRE. LC 90-3075. 237p. 1996. reprint ed. pap. 11.95 (*1-56478-140-2*) Dalkey Arch.

— Loin de Rueil. (FRE.). 1976. pap. 10.95 (*0-8288-3772-4*, F107610) Fr & Eur.

— Loin de Rueil. (Folio Ser.: No. 849). (FRE.). 211p. 1976. 8.95 (*2-07-036849-1*) Schoenhof.

— Morale Elementaire. (FRE.). 152p. 1975. pap. 17.95 (*0-7859-1345-9*, 2070293505) Fr & Eur.

— Odile. (FRE.). 196p. 1992. pap. 14.95 (*0-686-54679-2*, 2070725472) Fr & Eur.

— Odile. (Imaginaire Ser.). (FRE.). 1992. pap. 13.95 (*2-07-072547-2*) Schoenhof.

— Odile. Sanders, Carol, tr. from FRE. & intro. by. LC 88-25051. 128p. 1999. reprint ed. pap. 10.95 (*1-56478-209-3*) Dalkey Arch.

— Oeuvres Completes, Tome 1. deluxe ed. (Pleiade Ser.). (FRE.). 109.95 (*2-07-011168-7*) Schoenhof.

— Oeuvres Completes, Vol. 1. Debon, Claude, ed. (FRE.). 1989. lib. bdg. 165.00 (*0-7859-3887-7*) Fr & Eur.

— Les Oeuvres Completes de Sally Mara. (FRE.). 364p. 1979. pap. 17.95 (*0-7859-1341-6*, 2070287521) Fr & Eur.

— On Est Toujours Trop Bon avec les Femmes. (FRE.). 1981. pap. 10.95 (*0-8288-3773-2*) Fr & Eur.

— On Est Toujours Trop Bon avec les Femmes: Un Roman Irlandais De Sally Mara. (Folio Ser.: No. 1312). (FRE.). 200p. 1971. pap. 8.95 (*2-07-037312-6*) Schoenhof.

— Pierrot Mon Ami. Wright, Barbara, tr. from FRE. LC 87-72849. 160p. 1989. pap. 9.95 (*0-916583-40-6*) Dalkey Arch.

— Pierrot Mon Ami. (Folio Ser.: No. 226). (FRE.). 224p. 1972. pap. 8.95 (*2-07-036226-4*) Schoenhof.

— Pierrot, Mon Ami. (FRE.). 1989. pap. 10.95 (*0-8288-3774-0*, F120390) Fr & Eur.

— Raymond Queneau's Chene et Chien: A Translation with Commentary. Velguth, Madeleine, tr. LC 93-32269. 102p. (C). 1995. text 33.95 (*0-8204-2311-4*) P Lang Pubng.

— Un Rude Hiver. (Imaginaire Ser.). (FRE.). 174p. 1977. 11.95 (*2-07-029648-2*) Schoenhof.

— Saint-Glinglin. (Imaginaire Ser.). (FRE.). 272p. 1948. 12.95 (*2-07-029151-0*) Schoenhof.

***Queneau, Raymond.** Saint Glinglin. Sallis, James, tr. from FRE. & illus. by. 184p. 2000. pap. 11.95 (*1-56478-230-1*, Pub. by Dalkey Arch) Chicago Distribution Ctr.

— Stories & Remarks. Lowenthal, Marc, tr. LC 99-462111. (French Modernist Library). (FRE.). 160p. 2000. 45.00 (*0-8032-3801-0*); pap. 15.00 (*0-8032-8852-2*, Bison Books) U of Nebr Pr.

Queneau, Raymond. The Sunday of Life. Wright, Barbara, tr. from FRE. LC 76-49628. 180p. 1977. 5.95 (*0-8112-0645-9*, Pub. by New Directions) Norton.

— Le Vol d'Icare. (FRE.). 260p. 1968. pap. 17.95 (*0-7859-1277-0*, 2070104699) Fr & Eur.

— Le Vol D'Icare. (Gallimard Ser.). (FRE.). pap. 29.95 (*2-07-027298-2*) Schoenhof.

— Zazie dans le Metro. (FRE.). 1972. pap. 10.95 (*0-8288-3725-2*, F120461) Fr & Eur.

— Zazie dans le Metro. (Folio Ser.: No. 108). (FRE.). 1972. pap. 6.95 (*2-07-036103-9*) Schoenhof.

Queneau, Raymond, et al. Miro's Lithographs, 1953 to 1972, 4 Vols. (Illus.). 1000p. 1981. 2950.00 (*0-915346-83-4*) A Wofsy Fine Arts.

Quenell, Midge. Hist Everyday Things, Vol. 1. 17.50 (*0-7134-1650-5*) B T B.

Quenk, Alex T. & Quenk, Naomi L. Dream Thinking: The Logic, Magic & Meaning of Your Dreams. LC 95-8816. 256p. (Orig.). 1995. pap. 15.95 (*0-89106-076-6*, 7114, Davies-Black Pub) Consulting Psychol.

— True Loves: Finding the Soul in Love Relationships. LC 97-15324. 344p. 1997. pap. 16.95 (*0-89106-107-X*, 7760, Davies-Black Pub) Consulting Psychol.

Quenk, Naomi L. Beside Ourselves: Our Hidden Personality in Everyday Life. LC 93-4373. 304p. 1993. pap. 16.95 (*0-89106-062-6*, 7378, Davies-Black Pub) Consulting Psychol.

***Quenk, Naomi L.** Essentials of Myers-Briggs Type Indicator Assessment. LC 99-32552. (Essentials of Psychological Assessment Ser.). 198p. 1999. pap. 29.95 (*0-471-33239-9*) Wiley.

Quenk, Naomi L., jt. auth. see Quenk, Alex T.

Quenk, Rachel. The Spirit That Moves Us Vol. II: A Literature-Based Resource Guide, Teaching about the Holocaust & Human Rights, Grades 5-8. (Illus.). 224p. (Orig.). 1997. pap. 19.95 (*0-88448-187-5*) Tilbury Hse.

Quennell, C. H., jt. auth. see Quennell, Marjorie.

***Quennell, Marjorie & Quennell, C. H.** Everyday Things in Archaic Greece. 146p. (YA). 1999. pap. 20.00 (*0-8196-0395-3*) Biblo.

— Everyday Things in Homeric Greece. 140p. (YA). 1999. pap. 20.00 (*0-8196-0396-1*) Biblo.

Quennell, Peter. Baudelaire & the Symbolists. LC 72-142689. (Essay Index Reprint Ser.). 1977. reprint ed. 18.95 (*0-8369-2423-1*) Ayer.

— Byron. LC 73-21772. (Studies in Byron: No. 5). 1974. lib. bdg. 75.00 (*0-8383-1784-7*) M S G Haskell Hse.

— Byron in Italy. 1977. 18.95 (*0-8369-7147-7*, 7979) Ayer.

— Caroline of England: An Augustan Portrait. 1977. 21.95 (*0-8369-7148-5*, 7980) Ayer.

— Hogarth's Progress. 1977. text 24.95 (*0-8369-8145-6*, 8285) Ayer.

Quennell, Peter & Johnson, Hamish. Who's Who in Shakespeare. (Who's Who Ser.). 240p. 1995. pap. 14.95 (*0-19-521081-6*) OUP.

— Who's Who in Shakespeare. LC 94-26058. (Who's Who Ser.). 240p. (gr. 13). 1995. pap. 17.99 (*0-415-11883-2*, B4951) Routledge.

Quennell, Peter, ed. see Baudelaire, Charles.

Quennell, Peter, ed. see Connolly, Cyril.

Quenon, Paul. Terrors of Paradise. 54p. 1996. pap. text 14.95 (*0-88753-278-0*) Black Moss.

Quenot, Michael. The Icon: Window on the Kingdom. (Illus.). (Orig.). 1991. pap. 16.95 (*0-88141-098-5*) St Vladimirs.

Quenot, Michel. The Resurrection & the Icon. Breck, Michael, tr. from FRE. LC 97-5312. 1997. pap. 29.95 (*0-88141-149-3*) St Vladimirs.

Quenouille, M. H. Rapid Statistical Calculations: A Collection of Distributions-Free & Easy Methods of Estimation & Testing. 2nd ed. 1972. 12.50 (*0-85264-214-8*) Lubrecht & Cramer.

Quensel, Warren P. Handbook for Learning to Drive. 2nd ed. (Illus.). 92p. 1997. lab manual ed. 2.50 (*0-9636134-2-1*) Safety Ent.

— How to Be a More Perceptive Driver. unabridged ed. (Illus.). 91p. 1997. pap. 9.50 (*0-9636134-1-3*) Safety Ent.

— Parent-Teen Manual for Learning to Drive. (Illus.). 96p. (Orig.). 1994. pap. 9.50 (*0-9636134-0-5*) Safety Ent.

Quenstedt, F. A. Die Ammoniten des Schwaebischen Jura. 1974. 441.00 (*3-510-65041-7*, Pub. by E Schweizerbartsche) Balogh.

Quenstedt, Friedrich A. Handbuch der Petrefaktenkunde: Handbook for the Study of Fossile, 1. Gould, Stephen Jay, ed. LC 79-8345. (History of Paleontology Ser.). (GER., Illus.). 1980. reprint ed. lib. bdg. 68.95 (*0-405-12745-6*) Ayer.

— Handbuch der Petrefaktenkunde: Handbook for the Study of Fossile, Set. Gould, Stephen Jay, ed. LC 79-8345. (History of Paleontology Ser.). (GER., Illus.). 1980. reprint ed. lib. bdg. 136.95 (*0-405-12739-1*) Ayer.

— Handbuch der Petrefaktenkunde: Handbook for the Study of Fossile, Vol. 2. Gould, Stephen Jay, ed. LC 79-8345. (History of Paleontology Ser.). (GER., Illus.). 1980. reprint ed. lib. bdg. 68.95 (*0-405-12749-9*) Ayer.

Quenstedt, W. A., jt. auth. see Lambrecht, K.

Quentin-Baxendale, Marion. Collecting Carnival Glass. (Illus.). 164p. pap. 19.95 (*1-870703-71-5*, Pub. by Francis Jos Pubns) Krause Pubns.

Quentin, Patrick. Black Widow. 218p. 1992. pap. 8.95 (*1-55882-111-2*) Intl Polygonics.

— Puzzle for Players. 250p. 1989. reprint ed. pap. 5.95 (*1-55882-008-6*, Lib Crime Classics) Intl Polygonics.

— Puzzle for Puppets. LC 89-85719. 206p. 1989. pap. 7.95 (*1-55882-020-5*, Lib Crime Classics) Intl Polygonics.

— Puzzle for Wantons. LC 90-80764. 229p. 1990. reprint ed. pap. 7.95 (*1-55882-063-9*) Intl Polygonics.

— Run to Death. LC 91-70602. 192p. 1991. reprint ed. pap. 5.95 (*1-55882-095-7*, Lib Crime Classics) Intl Polygonics.

Quenzer, Ronald W., jt. auth. see Brillman, Judith C.

Quenzer, Ronald W., jt. ed. see Brillman, Judith C.

Quer, Pio F. Diccionario de Botanica. (SPA.). 1284p. 1989. 105.00 (*0-7859-5923-8*, 8433558048) Fr & Eur.

Quera, Vicenc, jt. auth. see Bakeman, Roger.

Queral, Maria V. Violeta. LC 91-71263. (Coleccion Espejo de Paciencia). (SPA., Illus.). 56p. (Orig.). 1992. pap. 9.95 (*0-89729-602-8*) Ediciones.

Queralt, Magaly. The Social Environment & Human Behavior: A Multicultural Perspective. LC 95-11989. 448p. 1995. 82.00 (*0-02-397191-6*, Macmillan Coll) P-H.

Queralt, Rosa, ed. see Pijuan, Hernandez.

Querard, Joseph-Marie. La France Litteraire ou Dictionanaire Bibliographique des Savants, Historiens et Gens de Lettres de la France, 12 tomes, Set. 350.00 (*0-685-35981-6*) Fr & Eur.

— Litterature Francaise Contemporaine. (FRE.). 3150p. 1965. 1095.00 (*0-7859-5223-3*) Fr & Eur.

— La Litterature Francaise Contemporaine, 6 tomes, Set. 262.50 (*0-685-35980-8*) Fr & Eur.

— Les Supercheries Litteraires Devoilees, 3 vols. rev. ed. xiv, 66p. 1965. reprint ed. suppl. ed. write for info. (*0-318-71394-2*) G Olms Pubs.

— Les Supercheries Litteraires Devoilees, 3 vols., Set. 2nd ed. 1965. reprint ed. write for info. (*0-318-71859-6*) G Olms Pubs.

— Les Supercheries Litteraires Devoilees, 3 vols., Set. 2nd rev. ed. xii, 1947p. 1965. reprint ed. write for info. (*0-318-71393-4*) G Olms Pubs.

— Les Supercheries Litteraires Devoiles, 3 tomes, Set. 150.00 (*0-685-35983-2*) Fr & Eur.

Quercia, Valerie. Internet in a Nutshell. Mui, Linda, ed. LC 98-154131. 450p. 1997. pap. 24.95 (*1-56592-323-5*) OReilly & Assocs.

Quercia, Valerie & O'Reilly, Tim. X Window System User's Guide: Motif Edition, Vol. 3M. 2nd ed. (X Window System Ser.). (Illus.). 956p. (Orig.). 1993. pap. 34.95 (*1-56592-015-5*) Thomson Learn.

Quercia, Valerie, jt. auth. see Mui, Linda.

Querciolo, Valter. Pulse Width Modulated (PWM) Power Supplies. LC 93-7123. (Studies in Electrical & Electronic Engineering). 324p. 1993. 190.75 (*0-444-89790-9*) Elsevier.

Quere, Y. Physics of Materials. 496p. 1998. text 38.00 (*90-5699-118-3*, ECU55, Harwood Acad Pubs); pap. text 16.00 (*90-5699-119-1*, ECU22, Harwood Acad Pubs) Gordon & Breach.

Queree, Anne. Realising Multimedia Potential. LC 98-197556. 60 p. 1997. write for info. (*92-828-2606-6*) Intl Pubns Serv.

Querejazu, Pedro & Ferrer, Elizabeth. Potosi: Colonial Treasures & the Bolivian City of Silver. LC 97-74730. (Illus.). 152p. Date not set. pap. 29.95 (*1-879128-16-0*) Americas Soc.

Quereshi, H. Outcomes Comm Care for Serv U. S. A Social Services Perspective. LC 95-49669. 192p. 1996. pap. 34.95 (*0-335-19668-3*) OpUniv Pr.

Quereshi, Ishtiaq H. The Administration of the Moghul Empire. 1990. reprint ed. 11.50 (*81-85418-00-4*, Pub. by Low Price) S Asia.

Querexeta Gallostequi, Jaime. Diccionario Onomastico y Heraldico Vasco, Vol. 5. (SPA.). 288p. 1974. 79.95 (*0-8288-5998-1*, S50375) Fr & Eur.

Querido, A., et al. The Discipline of Medicine: Proceedings of the Symposium, May 25 & 26, 1993. LC 94-27792. 206p. pap. 48.75 (*0-444-85772-9*, North Holland) Elsevier.

Querido, R. M., ed. & intro. see Steiner, Rudolf.

Querido, R. M., tr. see Steiner, Rudolf.

Querido, Rene. The Mystery of the Holy Grail - A Modern Path of Initiation. 1991. pap. 14.95 (*0-945803-12-5*) R Steiner Col.

— Questions & Answers on Reincarnation & Karma. 1977. pap. 5.50 (*0-916786-18-8*, Saint George Pubns) R Steiner Col.

— The Wonder of Childhood - Stepping into Life. 1991. pap. 5.95 (*0-945803-08-7*) R Steiner Col.

Querido, Rene & Moore, Hilmar. Behold, I Make All Things New. 1990. 10.95 (*0-945803-07-9*) R Steiner Col.

Querido, Rene, tr. see Lusseyran, Jacques.

Querido, Rene M. The Esoteric Background of Waldorf Education: The Cosmic Christ Impulse. xx, 108p. (Orig.). 1996. pap. 16.95 (*0-945803-25-7*, 00181) R Steiner Col.

— The Golden Age of Chartres: The Teachings of the Mystery School & the Eternal Feminine. 2nd ed. (Illus.). 157p. 1996. reprint ed. pap. 18.95 (*0-945803-26-5*, 00180) R Steiner Col.

Querido, Rene M., tr. see Steiner, Rudolf.

Querin, S. Dictionnaire des Difficultes du Francais Medical. (FRE.). 1998. 69.95 (*0-320-00212-8*) Fr & Eur.

Querioz, Eca De, see De Querioz, Eca.

Querleu, Dennis, et al. Laparoscopic Surgery in Gynecological Oncology. LC 98-36147. (Illus.). 240p. 1999. 110.00 (*0-86542-692-9*) Blackwell Sci.

Quermonne, Jean-Louis, et al. Adjusting to Europe: The Impact of the European Union on National Institutions & Policies. LC 96-19654. (European Public Policy Ser.). (Illus.). 200p. (C). 1996. 85.00 (*0-415-14410-8*) Routledge.

Quern, Jacqueline. Tools for the Carpenter. LC 94-70024. 1994. pap. 8.95 (*1-55673-897-8*) CSS OH.

Quernemoen, Bruce, jt. auth. see Quernemoen, Lynn.

Quernemoen, Lynn & Quernemoen, Bruce. KARE in the Church, Vol. I. 192p. (Orig.). 1996. per. 5.95 (*1-56383-057-4*, 9300) G & R Pub.

— KARE in the Family, Vol. I. 192p. (Orig.). 1996. pap., per. 5.95 (*1-56383-059-0*, 9302) G & R Pub.

— KARE in the Workplace, Vol. I. 192p. (Orig.). 1996. per. 5.95 (*1-56383-058-2*, 9301) G & R Pub.

Querns, W. International Guide to Total Cost Management. (Total Cost Management Ser.). Date not set. write for info. (*0-8247-9952-6*) Dekker.

Querol, Daniel. Genetic Resources: A Practical Guide to their Conservation. LC 92-35019. (C). 1993. text 55.00 (*1-85649-203-6*, Pub. by Zed Books) St Martin.

Querry, Ron. Bad Medicine. 336p. 1999. reprint ed. pap. 10.95 (*0-553-37799-X*) Bantam.

— The Death of Bernadette Lefthand: A Novel. LC 94-37264. 224p. 1995. pap. 10.95 (*0-553-37536-9*) Bantam.

— The Death of Bernadette Lefthand: A Novel. LC 92-53886. (Illus.). 232p. 1993. 23.95 (*1-878610-25-2*) Red Crane Bks.

— Native American Struggle for Equality. LC 92-7474. (Discrimination Ser.). 112p. (J). 1992. lib. bdg. 18.95 (*0-86593-179-8*) Rourke Corp.

— Native American Struggle for Equality. LC 92-7474. (YA). 1992. 16.95 (*0-685-59320-7*) Rourke Corp.

Querry, Ronald B. I See by My Get-up. LC 93-38190. (Illus.). 176p. 1994. pap. 13.95 (*0-8061-2638-8*) U of Okla Pr.

Quertermous, ed. see Woods, B. J.

Quertermous, Russell & Quertermous, Steve. Modern Guns: Identification & Values. 12th ed. LC 98-221639. 504p. 1998. 12.95 (*1-57432-087-4*) Collector Bks.

***Quertermous, Russell & Quertermous, Steve.** Modern Guns: Identification & Values. 13th ed. (Illus.). 516p. 2000. pap. 14.95 (*1-57432-199-4*) Collector Bks.

Quertermous, Steve, jt. auth. see Quertermous, Russell.

Querubin, Perfecto. E-Z Reader. LC 93-15850. (Illus.). 208p. 1994. pap. 14.95 (*0-942963-34-2*) Distinctive Pub.

Query, Roy D. & Automobile Quarterly Staff. Corvette: An American Legend. LC 86-70357. (Bloomington Gold Corvettes Ser.: Vol. 1). (Illus.). 184p. 1986. 49.95 (*0-915038-51-X*, 3-AQ-0046) Auto Quarterly.

Query, Sharon L. & Hausafus, Cheryl O. Promoting Literacy in At-Risk Youth: Protective Factors & Academic Achievements. rev. ed. LC 98-29806. (Children of Poverty Ser.). (Illus.). 97p. 1998. 35.00 (*0-8153-3226-2*) Garland.

Quesada de Rodriguez, Pura. Componentes de un Sistema de Practica Docente Renovada. LC 78-3641. 119p. 1978. pap. 3.20 (*0-8477-2742-4*) U of PR Pr.

Quesada, Fernando. Argentine Anarchism & La Protesta. 1975. lib. bdg. 250.00 (*0-87968-657-X*) Gordon Pr.

— Sacco & Vanzetti. 1976. lib. bdg. 250.00 (*0-8490-0984-7*) Gordon Pr.

Quesada, Gonzalo De, see De Quesada, Gonzalo.

Quesada, Maria S. Estancias: Las Grandes Haciendas de Argentina. (SPA., Illus.). 204p. 1992. 67.50 (*1-55859-398-5*) Abbeville Pr.

— Estancias: The Great Houses & Ranches of Argentina. Di Giovanni, Norman T., tr. from SPA. LC 92-16213. (Illus.). 204p. 1992. 67.50 (*1-55859-270-9*) Abbeville Pr.

Quesada, Roberto. The Big Banana. Krochmal, Walter, tr. LC 98-28333. 304p. 1999. pap. 12.95 (*1-55885-255-7*) Arte Publico.

— The Ships. St. Martin, Hardie, tr. LC 92-7988. 184p. 1992. 17.95 (*0-941423-65-4*) FWEW.

— When the Road Is Long, Even Slippers Feel Tight: A Collection of Latin American Proverbs. (Little Bks.). (Illus.). 80p. 1998. 4.95 (*0-8362-6790-7*) Andrews & McMeel.

Quesenberry, Charles P. SPC Methods for Quality Improvement. LC 96-44726. 694p. 1997. 125.00 (*0-471-13087-7*) Wiley.

Quesenberry, K. H., jt. auth. see Taylor, N. L.

Quesenberry, Katherine, jt. auth. see Hillyer, Elizabeth V.

Q

An Asterisk (*) at the beginning of an entry indicates that the title is appearing for the first time.

Quesenberry, Peter, jt. ed. see Birmingham, Maureen.

Quesenberry, Peter J., et al, eds. Stem Cell Biology & Gene Therapy. LC 97-48252. 566p. 1998. 109.95 (*0-471-14656-0*, Wiley-Liss) Wiley.

Quesenbery, William D. Direct Current Generators. 16p. 1992. pap., wbk. ed. 7.00 (*0-8064-1115-5*, E51) Bergwall.

Quesenbery, William H. Fluid Power. 20p. (YA). (gr. 10 up). 1995. pap., wbk. ed. 7.00 (*0-8064-0609-7*, H10) Bergwall.

Quesenbury, Pat. What's a Girl to Do? rev. ed. Wright, Bobby J., ed. (Illus.). 133p. (Orig.). (YA). (gr. 7 up). 1981. pap. 8.99 (*0-89114-245-2*) Baptist Pub Hse.

Quesnay, Francois. Economical Table (Tableau Economique). 1973. 250.00 (*0-87968-052-0*) Gordon Pr.

Quesne, P. W. Le, see Atta-Ur-Rahman.

***Quesnel, Annabel M.** Ghosts & Echoes. 242p. 1999. pap. 9.95 (*0-7392-0479-3*, PO3816) Morris Pubng.

Quesnel, Colette, jt. ed. see Hillman, Richard.

Quesnell, Quentin. The Authority for Authority. (Pere Marquette Lectures). 54p. 1969. 15.00 (*0-87462-517-3*) Marquette.

***Quesnell, Quentin.** The Strange Disappearance of Sophia Smith. 250p. 1999. 35.00 (*0-87391-048-6*) Smith Coll.

Quesney, L. Felipe, et al. Electrocorticography: Current Trends & Future Perspectives. LC 98-21791. (Electroencephalography & Clinical Neurophysiology Ser.). 158p. 1998. 161.00 (*0-444-82509-6*) Elsevier.

Quesson, Noel. Spirit of the Psalms. 1990. pap. 14.95 (*0-8091-3199-4*) Paulist Pr.

Quest, Barry & Morris, A. I. Design: The Modern Law & Practice. 2nd ed. 1995. ring bd. write for info. (*0-406-01359-4*, UK, MICHIE) LEXIS Pub.

Quest, Barry, jt. auth. see Morris, A. I.

Quest, Caroline, ed. Liberating Women from Modern Feminism. (Choice in Welfare Ser.: No. 19). 101p. 1994. pap. 19.95 (*0-255-36353-2*, Pub. by Inst Economic Affairs) Coronet Bks.

Quest Editorial Development Staff. Choices. rev. ed. LC 96-117842. (Orig.). 1991. pap., teacher ed. 10.55 (*0-8092-3363-0*) NTC Contemp Pub Co.

— Choices: Consumer Sense. LC 91-9015. 1991. pap. 9.60 (*0-8092-4047-5*) NTC Contemp Pub Co.

— Choices: Discovering Your Community. 1991. pap. 9.60 (*0-8092-4042-4*) NTC Contemp Pub Co.

— Choices: Families & Schools. 1991. pap. 9.60 (*0-8092-4046-7*) NTC Contemp Pub Co.

— Choices: Housing. 1992. pap. 9.60 (*0-8092-4044-0*) NTC Contemp Pub Co.

— Choices: In Good Health. LC 91-14416. 1991. pap. 9.60 (*0-8092-4048-3*) NTC Contemp Pub Co.

— Choices: It's Your Right. 1991. pap. 9.60 (*0-8092-4043-2*) NTC Contemp Pub Co.

Quest, Erica. Cold Coffin. large type ed. (General Ser.). 432p. 1993. 27.99 (*0-7089-2830-7*) Ulverscroft.

— Death Walk. large type ed. (Mystery-Romance Ser.). 384p. 1992. 27.99 (*0-7089-2698-3*) Ulverscroft.

Quest, Marta, ed. see Shubin, David.

***Quest, Peter.** Luminous. 142p. 1999. pap. 13.95 (*0-7414-0201-7*) Buy Books.

Quest-Ritson, Charles. The Garden Lover's Guide to Germany. (Illus.). 144p. 1998. pap. 19.95 (*1-56898-131-7*) Princeton Arch.

— House & Garden Book of Country Gardens. LC 98-18372. 1998. text 40.00 (*0-86565-153-1*) Vendome.

Quest-Ritson, Charles & Blair, Christopher. The RHS Gardener's Yearbook, 1997. (Illus.). 576p. (Orig.). 1997. pap. 36.50 (*0-333-67218-6*, Pub. by Macmillan) Trans-Atl Phila.

Questa, Giorgio S. Fixed Income Analysis for the Global Financial Market: Money Market, Foreign Exchange, & Derivative Securities. LC 98-44947. 351p. 1999. 69.95 (*0-471-24653-0*) Wiley.

Questech Staff. Advanced Robotic Assembly. (Illus.). 120p. 1997. text 99.95 (*1-58100-019-7*) Beckley Cardy.

— Aerodynamics. (Illus.). 120p. 1997. text 99.95 (*1-58100-024-3*) Beckley Cardy.

— Computer Aided Design (CAD) (Illus.). 120p. 1997. text 99.95 (*1-58100-008-1*) Beckley Cardy.

— Desktop Publishing. (Illus.). 120p. 1997. text 99.95 (*1-58100-004-9*) Beckley Cardy.

— Electronic Components & Assembly. (Illus.). 120p. 1997. text 99.95 (*1-58100-010-3*) Beckley Cardy.

— Engineering Materials & Structures. (Illus.). 120p. 1997. text 99.95 (*1-58100-020-0*) Beckley Cardy.

— Flight Simulation. (Illus.). 120p. 1997. text 99.95 (*1-58100-025-1*) Beckley Cardy.

— Health & Wellness. (Illus.). 120p. 1997. text 99.95 (*1-58100-022-7*) Beckley Cardy.

— Hydraulics. (Illus.). 120p. 1997. text 99.95 (*1-58100-011-1*) Beckley Cardy.

— Introductory Robotics. (Illus.). 120p. 1997. text 99.95 (*1-58100-018-9*) Beckley Cardy.

— Marine Transportation. (Illus.). 120p. 1997. text 99.95 (*1-58100-026-X*) Beckley Cardy.

— Plastics. (Illus.). 120p. 1997. text 99.95 (*1-58100-021-9*) Beckley Cardy.

— Pneumatics. (Illus.). 120p. 1997. text 99.95 (*1-58100-012-X*) Beckley Cardy.

— Power Mechanics/Small Engines. (Illus.). 120p. (J). 1997. text 99.95 (*1-58100-013-8*) Beckley Cardy.

— Radio Broadcasting. (Illus.). 120p. 1997. text 99.95 (*1-58100-005-7*) Beckley Cardy.

— Video Editing Module. (Illus.). 120p. 1997. text 99.95 (*1-58100-007-3*) Beckley Cardy.

— Video Production Module. (Illus.). 120p. 1997. text 99.95 (*1-58100-006-5*) Beckley Cardy.

— Weather Information Station. (Illus.). 120p. 1997. text 99.95 (*1-58100-015-4*) Beckley Cardy.

Questel, Lynn K. Federal Laws Prohibiting Employment Discrimination - for State & Local Officials. 104p. 1989. pap. 11.95 (*0-89854-136-0*) U of GA Inst Govt.

Quester, George H. Brazil & Latin-American Nuclear Proliferation: An Optimistic View. (CISA Working Papers: No. 17). 36p. (Orig.). 1979. pap. 15.00 (*0-86682-016-7*) Ctr Intl Relations.

— Deterrence Before Hiroshima. 214p. 1986. 39.95 (*0-88738-087-5*) Transaction Pubs.

— The Falklands & the Malvinas: Strategy & Arms Control. (CISA Working Papers: No. 46). 51p. (Orig.). 1984. pap. 15.00 (*0-86682-059-0*) Ctr Intl Relations.

***Quester, George H.** Nuclear Monopoly. 234p. 2000. 44.95 (*0-7658-0022-5*) Transaction Pubs.

Quester, George H. Offense & Defense in the International System. 239p. 1987. 39.95 (*0-88738-156-1*) Transaction Pubs.

— Peaceful P. A. L. (CISA Working Papers: No. 9). 23p. (Orig.). 1977. pap. 15.00 (*0-86682-008-6*) Ctr Intl Relations.

— The Politics of Nuclear Proliferation. LC 73-8119. 264p. reprint ed. pap. 81.90 (*0-608-11992-X*, 202300200030) Bks Demand.

Quester, George H., ed. Nuclear Proliferation: Breaking the Chain. LC 80-53960. 255p. 1981. reprint ed. pap. 79.10 (*0-608-01972-0*, 206262700003) Bks Demand.

Quester, George H., ed. see Shultz, Richard.

Quester-Neal. Consumer Behavior: Implications. 1993. text 52.76 (*0-256-13178-3*, Irwn McGrw-H) McGrw-H Hghr Educ.

***Questier, M. C., ed.** Newsletters from the Archpresbyterate of George Birkhead. (Camden Fifth Ser.: No. 12). 321p. (C). 2000. 64.95 (*0-521-65260-X*) Cambridge U Pr.

Questier, Michael C. Conversion, Politics & Religion in England, 1580-1625. (Cambridge Studies in Early Modern British History). 254p. (C). 1996. text 59.95 (*0-521-44214-1*) Cambridge U Pr.

Questier, Michael C., jt. ed. see Lake, Peter.

Questron Staff. Princeton Review SAT: Math. 1986. pap. 4.95 (*0-394-88624-0*) Random.

***Quetchenbach, Bernard W.** Back from the Far Field: American Nature Poetry in the Late Twentieth Century. LC 99-89089. 224p. 2000. 49.50 (*0-8139-1953-3*); pap. 18.50 (*0-8139-1954-1*) U Pr of Va.

Quetel, Claude. The History of Syphilis. Braddock, Judith & Pike, Brian, trs. from FRE. (Illus.). 342p. 1992. reprint ed. pap. text 16.95 (*0-8018-4392-8*) Johns Hopkins.

Quetelet, Adolphe J. Letters Addressed to H. R. H. the Grand Duke of Saxe Coburg & Gotha, on the Theory of Probabilities. Cohen, I. Bernard, ed. LC 80-2143. (Development of Science Ser.). (Illus.). 1981. lib. bdg. 33.95 (*0-405-13950-0*) Ayer.

Quetelet, Lambert A. Treatise on Man & the Development of His Faculties, 1842. LC 77-81364. (History of Psychology Ser.). (Illus.). 150p. 1969. 50.00 (*0-8201-1061-2*) Schol Facsimiles.

***Quetglas, Josep.** Fear of Glass: Mies Van Der Rohe's Pavillion in Barcelona. (Illus.). 200p. 2000. pap. 24.95 (*3-7643-6339-8*) Birkhauser.

Quette, Constance Du, see Du Quette, Lon & Du Quette, Constance.

Quette, Lon Du, see Du Quette, Lon.

Queux, William T. Le, see Le Queux, William T.

Queval, Jean. Lexique de la Musique. (FRE.). 130p. 1968. 19.95 (*0-7859-0774-2*, F-11890) Fr & Eur.

— Marcel Carne. (Film Ser.). 1979. lib. bdg. 59.95 (*0-8490-2970-8*) Gordon Pr.

***Queval, Marie-Helene.** Les Paradoxes d'Eros Ou l'Amour dans l'Oeuvre de Johann Christoph Gottsched. (Contacts Ser.: Vol. 48). xiii, 479p. 1999. 62.95 (*3-906763-63-3*, Pub. by P Lang) P Lang Pubng.

Quevauviller, P. & Maier, E. A. Interlaboratory Studies & Certified Reference Materials. (Techniques & Instrumentation in Analytical Chemistry Ser.: Vol. 20). 1999. write for info. (*0-444-82389-1*) Elsevier.

Quevauviller, P., jt. auth. see Colin, F.

Quevauviller, P. L. Method Performance Studies for Speciation Analysis. 290p. 1998. 125.00 (*0-85404-467-1*, Pub. by Royal Soc Chem) Spr-Verlag.

Quevauviller, Philippe H., ed. Quality Assurance in Environmental Monitoring: Sampling & Sample Pretreatment. 2 vols. (Illus.). 306p. 1995. 178.00 (*3-527-28724-8*, Wiley-VCH) Wiley.

Quevauvilliers, J. & Perlemuter, Leon. Dictionnaire Medical de l'Infirmiere. 4th rev. ed. (FRE.). 1344p. 1992. 130.00 (*0-7859-4749-3*, M1900) Fr & Eur.

Quevedo. Los Suenos. unabridged ed. (SPA.). pap. 5.95 (*84-410-0047-6*, Pub. by Bookking Intl) Distribks Inc.

***Quevedo, Et Al.** Posia Borroca. (SPA.). 1999. 13.00 (*84-481-0621-0*, McGrw-H College) McGrw-H Hghr Educ.

Quevedo, Francisco de. Antologia Poetica. Jauralde Pou, Pablo, ed. (Nueva Austral Ser.: Vol. 186). (SPA.). pap. 14.95 (*84-239-1986-2*) Elliots Bks.

Quevedo, Francisco De, see De Quevedo, Francisco.

Quevedo Villegas, Francisco de. El Buscon. pap. 12.95 (*84-376-0237-8*, Pub. by Ediciones Catedra) Continental Bk.

— Historia de la Vida el Buscon: Llamado Don Pablos. unabridged ed. (SPA.). 158p. 1999. pap. 5.95 (*84-410-0003-4*, Pub. by Bookking Intl) Distribks Inc.

Quevedo Y Villegas, Francisco De, see De Quevedo Y Villegas, Francisco.

Queyroz, Fernao De, see De Queyroz, Fernao.

Quezada, Adolfo. Heart Peace: Embracing Life's Adversities. 160p. 1999. pap. 9.95 (*1-878718-52-5*, Resurrection Pr) Catholic Bk Pub.

— Loving Yourself for God's Sake. LC 96-72288. 96p. 1997. pap. 5.95 (*1-878718-35-5*, Resurrection Pr) Catholic Bk Pub.

— Walking with God: Reflections on Life's Meaning. LC 90-60305. 96p. (Orig.). 1990. pap. 3.50 (*0-89243-320-5*) Liguori Pubns.

Quezada, Alfredo, tr. see Leavell, Ronald Q.

***Quezada, Greta.** Maybe I'll Be (Tal Vez Sere) (SPA & ENG., Illus.). 22p. (J). (ps-5). 1998. pap. 14.95 incl. audio (*0-9677193-0-5*) Ninos Del Mundo.

Quezada, J. Gilberto. Border Boss: Manuel B. Bravo & Zapata County. LC 98-42635. (Canseco-Keck History Ser.: Vol. 1). (Illus.). 320p. 1999. 29.95 (*0-89096-865-9*) Tex A&M Univ Pr.

***Quezada, Louise M.** Love's Destiny. 1999. pap. text 8.95 (*1-885478-68-2*, Pub. by Genesis Press) BookWorld.

Quezada, M. Louise. Hearts Remember. LC 99-172631. (Tango Ser.). 183p. 1998. 15.95 (*1-885478-38-0*, Pub. by Genesis Press) BookWorld.

Quezada, Noemi. Los Matlatzincas: Epoca Prehispanica y Epoca Colonial Hasta 1650. (SPA., Illus.). 143p. 1996. pap. 18.50 (*968-36-4665-4*, UN057, Pub. by Instit de Invest) UPLAAP.

— Religion y Sexualidad en Mexico. (SPA.). 126p. 1997. pap. 18.50 (*968-36-6323-0*, UN054, Pub. by Instit de Invest) UPLAAP.

— Sexualidad, Amor y Erotismo: Mexico Prehispanico y Mexico Colonial. (SPA.). 304p. 1996. pap. 18.50 (*968-856-467-2*, UN059) UPLAAP.

Quezada, Sergio A., jt. ed. see Bagley, Bruce M.

Quezada, Shelley. Developing Literacy Programs in Small & Medium-Sized Libraries. LC 96-4327. (LAMA Small Library Publications: 22). 25p. 1996. pap. 5.00 (*0-8389-0682-6*, 0682-6-2045) ALA.

Quezada, Shelley & Nickse, Ruth S. Community Collaborations for Family Literacy Handbook. LC 93-21017. 150p. 1993. pap. 38.50 (*1-55570-164-7*) Neal-Schuman.

Quezada, Victor A., tr. see Coleman, Lucien E., Jr.

Quezon, Manuel L. Good Fight. LC 76-161779. reprint ed. 49.50 (*0-404-09036-2*) AMS Pr.

Quiatt, Duane & Itani, Junichiro, eds. Hominid Culture in Primate Perspecitve. (Illus.). 320p. 1994. 42.50 (*0-87081-313-7*) Univ Pr Colo.

Quiatt, Duane & Reynolds, Vernon. Primate Behaviour: Information, Social Knowledge, & the Evolution of Culture. (Studies in Biological Anthropology: No. 12). (Illus.). 330p. (C). 1995. pap. text 26.95 (*0-521-49832-5*) Cambridge U Pr.

Quible, Zane K. Administrative & Office Management. 6th ed. 1995. pap. text, student ed. 23.00 (*0-13-374844-8*) P-H.

— Administrative Office Management. 6th ed. LC 95-22506. 594p. 1995. 72.00 (*0-13-349457-8*) P-H.

***Quible, Zane K.** Administrative Office Management: An Introduction. 7th ed. 592p. 2000. pap. 52.00 (*0-13-085957-5*, Prentice Hall) P-H.

Quible, Zane K. Writing Improvement for Business Communication. 1995. pap. text 29.33 (*0-13-367574-2*) P-H.

Quible, Zane K., et al. Business Communication: Principles & Applications. LC 95-9246. 575p. 1995. pap. text 68.00 (*0-13-304429-7*) P-H.

— Records Management Manual for Michigan Municipalities. LC 81-620018. 71p. 1998. 10.00 (*0-941872-32-7*) MSU Dept Res Dev.

Quibria, M. G., ed. The Bangladesh Economy in Transition. LC 96-912043. (Illus.). 384p. (C). 1997. text 42.00 (*0-19-564011-X*) OUP.

— Critical Issues in Asian Development: Theories, Experiences & Policies. (Illus.). 280p. 1995. text 60.00 (*0-19-586606-1*) OUP.

— Critical Issues in Asian Development: Theories, Experiences & Policies. (Asian Development Bank Bk.). (Illus.). 280p. 1997. reprint ed. pap. text 21.00 (*0-19-587838-8*) OUP.

— Rural Poverty in Asia: Priority Issues & Policy Options. (Illus.). 456p. 1994. text 75.00 (*0-19-586003-9*); pap. text 26.00 (*0-19-586004-7*) OUP.

Quibria, M. G. & Dowling, J. M., Jr., eds. Current Issues in Economic Development: An Asian Perspective. (Illus.). 428p. 1997. text 65.00 (*0-19-587759-4*) OUP.

***Quiche, Johnny.** Gourmet Cooking - The Easy Way. (Illus.). 186p. 1998. 9.95 (*0-7541-0037-5*, Pub. by Minerva Pr) Unity Dist.

Quicherat, Louis. Dictionnaire Francais-Latin. (FRE & LAT.). 1967. write for info. (*0-7859-7600-0*, 2010041844) Fr & Eur.

— Thesaurus Poeticus Linguae Latinae Ou Dictionnaire Prosodique et Poetique de la Langue Latine. xx, 1251p. 1967. reprint ed. write for info. (*0-318-72070-1*) G Olms Pubs.

— Thesaurus Poeticus Linguae Latine Ou Dictionnaire Prosodique et Poetique de la Langue Latine. xx, 1251p. 1967. reprint ed. write for info. (*0-318-71206-7*) G Olms Pubs.

— Thesaurus Poeticus Linguae Latine Ou Dictionnaire Prosodique et Poetique De la Langue Latine. xx, 1251p. 1922. reprint ed. write for info. (*0-318-71395-0*) G Olms Pubs.

Quick, jt. auth. see Nelson.

Quick & Easy Staff. Greek Quick & Easy. pap. 16.95 incl. audio (*0-88729-905-9*) Langenscheidt.

— Japanese Quick & Easy. pap. 16.95 incl. audio (*0-88729-906-7*) Langenscheidt.

Quick, Amanda, pseud. Affair. 416p. 1998. mass mkt. 6.99 (*0-553-57407-8*) Bantam.

— Affair. large type ed. LC 97-29521. (Large Print Book Ser.). 1997. 26.95 (*1-56895-475-1*) Wheeler Pub.

— Dangerous. 352p. 1993. mass mkt. 6.99 (*0-553-29317-6*) Bantam.

— Dangerous. large type ed. LC 93-13495. 540p. 1993. lib. bdg. 23.95 (*1-56054-726-X*) Thorndike Pr.

— Deception. 432p. 1994. mass mkt. 6.99 (*0-553-56506-0*) Bantam.

— Desire. 400p. 1993. mass mkt. 6.99 (*0-553-56153-7*, Fanfare) Bantam.

— I Thee Wed. large type ed. LC 99-14363. 569p. 1999. 29.95 (*0-7862-1940-8*) Thorndike Pr.

— I Thee Wed. large type ed. LC 99-14363. (Paperback Bestsellers Ser.). 503p. 2000. pap. 27.95 (*0-7862-1941-6*) Thorndike Pr.

***Quick, Amanda, pseud.** I Thee Wed. 384p. 2000. reprint ed. mass mkt. 7.50 (*0-553-57410-8*) Bantam.

Quick, Amanda, pseud. Mischief. 384p. 1997. mass mkt. 6.50 (*0-553-57190-7*) Bantam.

— Mischief. large type ed. LC 96-20873. 1996. lib. bdg. 20.00 (*0-7862-0781-7*) Thorndike Pr.

— Mischief. large type ed. LC 96-20873. 1997. pap. 24.95 (*0-7862-0782-5*) Thorndike Pr.

— Mistress. 384p. 1995. mass mkt. 6.99 (*0-553-56940-6*) Bantam.

— Mystique. 352p. 1996. mass mkt. 6.99 (*0-553-57159-1*) Bantam.

— Mystique. large type ed. 1995. 25.95 (*0-7838-1630-8*, G K Hall Lrg Type) Mac Lib Ref.

— Ravished. 416p. 1992. mass mkt. 6.99 (*0-553-29316-8*) Bantam.

— Ravished. large type ed. LC 92-27922. 538p. 1993. reprint ed. lib. bdg. 20.95 (*1-56054-429-5*) Thorndike Pr.

— Reckless. 400p. 1992. mass mkt. 6.99 (*0-553-29315-X*) Bantam.

— Reckless. large type ed. LC 92-42499. (Romance Ser.). 528p. 1993. reprint ed. lib. bdg. 21.95 (*1-56054-657-3*) Thorndike Pr.

— Reckless. large type ed. 528p. 1993. reprint ed. pap. 13.95 (*1-56054-882-7*) Thorndike Pr.

— Rendezvous. 384p. 1991. mass mkt. 6.99 (*0-553-29325-7*) Bantam.

— Rendezvous. large type ed. LC 92-18581. (General Ser.). 463p. 1992. pap. 16.95 (*0-8161-5454-6*, G K Hall Lrg Type); lib. bdg. 20.95 (*0-8161-5453-8*, G K Hall Lrg Type) Mac Lib Ref.

— Scandal. 352p. 1991. mass mkt. 6.99 (*0-553-28932-2*) Bantam.

— Scandal. large type ed. 564p. 1991. reprint ed. lib. bdg. 21.95 (*1-56054-176-8*) Thorndike Pr.

— Seduction. 352p. 1990. mass mkt. 6.99 (*0-553-28354-5*) Bantam.

— Seduction. large type ed. LC 94-12082. 581p. 1994. lib. bdg. 23.95 (*0-7862-0259-9*) Thorndike Pr.

— Surrender. 384p. 1990. mass mkt. 6.99 (*0-553-28594-7*) Bantam.

— Surrender. large type ed. LC 94-17375. 1994. 25.95 (*1-56895-103-5*) Wheeler Pub.

***Quick, Amanda, pseud.** Wicked Widow. LC 99-59194. 304p. 2000. 23.95 (*0-553-10087-4*) Bantam.

— The Wicked Widow. large type ed. (Basic Ser.). 413p. 2000. write for info. (*0-7862-2596-3*) Thorndike Pr.

— With This Ring. large type ed. LC 98-11020. (Basic Ser.). 1998. 28.95 (*0-7862-1409-0*) Thorndike Pr.

Quick, Amanda, pseud. With This Ring. large type ed. LC 98-11020. (Basic Ser.). 2001. pap. 26.95 (*0-7862-1410-4*) Thorndike Pr.

— With This Ring. 384p. 1999. reprint ed. mass mkt. 6.99 (*0-553-57409-4*) Bantam.

Quick, Anne, jt. ed. see Leyerle, John.

Quick, Barbara. Still Friends: Living Happily Ever After... Even If Your Marriage Falls Apart. LC 99-38533. 192p. 2000. pap. 12.95 (*1-885171-36-6*) Wldcat Canyon.

***Quick, Barbara.** Under Her Wing: The Mentors Who Have Changed Our Lives. 172p. 2000. pap. 13.95 (*1-57224-197-7*) New Harbinger.

***Quick, C. R.** Surgery. (Illus.). 656p. 2000. text 165.00 (*0-19-262230-7*) OUP.

Quick, Charles W., ed. see Hopkins, Ezekiel.

Quick, Charles W., jt. ed. see King, Donald B.

Quick, Daniel L. The Kenai Canoe Trails: Alaska's Premier Hiking & Canoeing System. LC 95-92484. (Illus.). 176p. (Orig.). 1995. pap. 18.95 (*0-9647804-0-2*) Northlite Bks.

Quick, Daryl E. The Healing Journey for Adult Children of Alcoholics. LC 90-39684. 216p. 1990. pap. 11.99 (*0-8308-1328-4*, 1328) InterVarsity.

Quick, Donna. A Place Called Antelope: The Rajneesh Story. 152p. 1995. pap. text 11.50 (*0-9643118-0-1*) August Press.

Quick, E., jt. ed. see Tuson, P.

Quick, Ellen K. Doing What Works in Brief Therapy: A Strategic Solution Focused Approach. (Illus.). 244p. 1996. pap. text 44.95 (*0-12-569660-4*) Acad Pr.

Quick, Emma, jt. auth. see Twining, William.

Quick, Graeme R. & Buchele, Wesley F. The Grain Harvesters. LC 78-65524. (Illus.). 280p. 1978. reprint ed. pap. 17.95 (*0-916150-13-5*, H1278) Am Soc Ag Eng.

Quick, Harriet. Catwalking: A History of the Fashion Model. 1999. 19.99 (*0-7858-1093-5*) Bk Sales Inc.

Quick, James. Fishing the Nymph. LC 60-7610. 144p. reprint ed. pap. 44.70 (*0-608-13663-8*, 20551740001l) Bks Demand.

Quick, James, ed. Career Stress in Changing Times. LC 90-35840. (Prevention in Human Services Ser.: Vol. 8, No. 1). 261p. 1990. text 49.95 (*0-86656-956-1*) Haworth Pr.

Quick, James C., et al, eds. Stress & Well-Being at Work: Assessments & Interventions for Occupational Mental Health. 372p. 1992. pap. text 19.95 (*1-55798-175-2*) Am Psychol.

— Work Stress: Health Care Systems in the Workplace. LC 86-30636. 346p. 1987. 65.00 (*0-275-92329-0*, C2329, Praeger Pubs) Greenwood.

Q

Quick, James C., et al. Preventive Stress Management in Organizations. 2nd ed. LC 97-12689. (Illus.). 368p. 1997. text 39.95 (1-55798-432-8, 431-7920) Am Psychol.

Quick, James C., jt. auth. see Nelson, Debra L.

Quick, Jennifer & O'Neal, Alexandra. Promoting Communication in Infants & Young Children: 500 Ways to Succeed. (Illus.). 40p. (Orig.). 1997. pap. 14.95 (0-937857-72-6, 1512) Speech Bin.

Quick, John. Fool's Hill: A Kid's Life in an Oregon Coastal Town. LC 95-15839. 320p. 1995. 24.95 (0-87071-385-X) Oreg St U Pr.

— Fool's Hill: A Kid's Life in an Oregon Coastal Town. LC 95-15839. (Illus.). 320p. 1997. reprint ed. pap. 15.95 (0-87071-399-X) Oreg St U Pr.

Quick, Jonathan. Modern Fiction & the Art of Subversion. LC 98-18025. (American University Studies III: Vol. 60). 170p. 1999. text 38.95 (0-8204-4097-3, 40973) P Lang Pubng.

Quick, L. M., et al, eds. Materials & Processes for Environmental Protection Vol. 344: Materials Research Society Symposium Proceedings. LC 94-36857. 343p. 1994. text 62.00 (1-55899-244-8) Materials Res.

Quick, Lawrence. A Management Guide to Retrofitting Wastewater Treatment Plants. LC 97-61845. 120p. 1997. pap. text 39.95 (1-56676-594-3) Technomic.

Quick, M., jt. auth. see Croser, J.

Quick, Michael, jt. auth. see Fort, Ilene S.

Quick, Paul, jt. ed. see Foyer, Christine.

Quick, Robert H. Essays on Educational Reformers. reprint ed. lib. bdg. 14.00 (0-7812-0786-X) Rprt Serv.

— Essays on Educational Reformers. Harris, W. T., ed. LC 78-129348. 1971. reprint ed. 14.00 (0-403-00485-3) Scholarly.

***Quick Source Staff.** GroupWise 5.5 Quick Source Guide. (Illus.). 6p. 1999. pap. 4.95 (1-930674-06-6) Quick Source.

— Lotus Freelance Millennium Edition 9.0 Quick Source Guide. (Illus.). 6p. 2000. pap. 4.95 (1-930674-00-7) Quick Source.

— Lotus Notes 5.0 Quick Source Guide. (Illus.). 6p. 1999. pap. 4.95 (1-930674-04-X) Quick Source.

— Lotus Notes 4.6 Quick Source Guide. (Illus.). 6p. 1999. pap. 4.95 (1-930674-05-8) Quick Source.

— Lotus 1-2-3 Millennium Edition 9.0 Quick Source Guide. (Illus.). 6p. 1999. pap. 4.95 (1-930674-03-1) Quick Source.

— Lotus Word Pro Millennium Edition 9.0 Quick Source Guide. (Illus.). 6p. 2000. pap. 4.95 (1-930674-02-3) Quick Source.

— Microsoft Access 97 Quick Source Guide. (Illus.). 6p. 1998. pap. 4.95 (1-930674-20-1) Quick Source.

— Microsoft Access 2000 Quick Source Guide. (Illus.). 6p. 1999. pap. 4.95 (1-930674-15-5) Quick Source.

— Microsoft Excel 97 Quick Source Guide. (Illus.). 6p. 1998. pap. 4.95 (1-930674-18-X) Quick Source.

— Microsoft Excel 2000 Quick Source Guide. (Illus.). 6p. 1999. pap. 4.95 (1-930674-13-9) Quick Source.

— Microsoft Internet Explorer 5.0 Quick Source Guide. (Illus.). 6p. 1999. pap. 4.95 (1-930674-25-2) Quick Source.

— Microsoft Internet Explorer 4.0 Quick Source Guide. (Illus.). 6p. 1997. pap. 4.95 (1-930674-24-4) Quick Source.

— Microsoft Outlook 98 Quick Source Guide. (Illus.). 6p. 1998. pap. 4.95 (1-930674-16-3) Quick Source.

— Microsoft Outlook 2000 Quick Source Guide. (Illus.). 6p. 1999. pap. 4.95 (1-930674-11-2) Quick Source.

— Microsoft PowerPoint 97 Quick Source Guide. (Illus.). 6p. 1998. pap. 4.95 (1-930674-19-8) Quick Source.

— Microsoft PowerPoint 2000 Quick Source Guide. (Illus.). 6p. 1999. pap. 4.95 (1-930674-14-7) Quick Source.

— Microsoft Windows 98 Quick Source Guide. (Illus.). 6p. 1999. pap. 4.95 (1-930674-22-8) Quick Source.

— Microsoft Windows 95 Quick Source Guide. (Illus.). 6p. 1998. pap. 4.95 (1-930674-21-X) Quick Source.

— Microsoft Windows NT-4 Quick Source Guide. (Illus.). 6p. 1998. pap. 4.95 (1-930674-23-6) Quick Source.

— Microsoft Word 97 Quick Source Guide. (Illus.). 6p. 1998. pap. 4.95 (1-930674-17-1) Quick Source.

— Microsoft Word 2000 Quick Source Guide. (Illus.). 6p. 1999. pap. 4.95 (1-930674-12-0) Quick Source.

Quick, Susan. Go Bananas! LC 99-59694. (Illus.). 288p. 2000. pap. 16.00 (0-7679-0403-6) Broadway BDD.

Quick, Thomas, jt. auth. see Barbour, James.

Quick, Thomas L. Getting Good Results from Problem Employees. 1990. pap. 29.95 (1-55840-669-7) Exec Ent Pubns.

— How People Work Best. 1988. pap. 39.95 (0-88057-824-6) Exec Ent Pubns.

— Making Your Sales Team Number 1. 192p. 1992. pap. 19.95 (0-8144-7741-0) AMACOM.

— Manager's Guide to Lawful Terminations. 2nd ed. 1990. pap. 29.95 (1-55840-516-X) Exec Ent Pubns.

— Mastering the Power of Persuasion. 1990. pap. 29.95 (0-685-59307-X) Exec Ent Pubns.

— The Persuasive Manager: How to Sell Yourself & Your Ideas. LC 80-70254. 204p. reprint ed. pap. 63.30 (0-608-15472-5, 202938900060) Bks Demand.

— Power, Influence, & Your Effectiveness in Human Resources. 1988. 18.95 (0-201-06649-1) Addison-Wesley.

— Successful Team Building. LC 92-3224. (AMA Worksmart Ser.). 112p. (Orig.). 1992. pap. 10.95 (0-8144-7794-1) AMACOM.

Quick, Thomas L., jt. auth. see Higginson, Margaret V.

Quick, Tim, jt. auth. see Watts, Andrew.

Quick, W. T. Dreams of Gods & Men. 304p. 1989. pap. 3.95 (0-318-39985-7, Sig) NAL.

— Star Control: Interbellum: A Novel. 288p. 1996. mass mkt. 5.99 (0-7615-0196-7) Prima Pub.

Quick, William D., jt. auth. see Wright, Mildred S.

Quick, William K. Good News from Detroit: Sermons Preached from the City Pulpit. LC 98-169798. 97p. 1998. pap. 6.95 (1-57502-840-9, PO2306) Morris Pubng.

— Take Five! 5 Minutes with Bill Quick. Levack, Mary I., ed. LC 96-92122. 90p. (Orig.). 1996. pap. write for info. (1-57502-159-5, PO755) Morris Pubng.

Quicke, Andrew & Quicke, Juliet. Hidden Agendas: The Politics of Religious Broadcasting in Britain 1987-1991. 276p. (C). 1993. pap. 14.99 (0-9635509-0-X) Dominion Kings.

Quicke, Andrew, jt. auth. see Laszlo, Andrew.

Quicke, Donald L. J. Parasitic Wasps. 2nd ed. LC 96-71731. (Illus.). 488p. 1997. write for info. (0-412-58350-X) Kluwer Academic.

Quicke, John. A Curriculum for Life: Schools for a Democratic Learning Society. LC 98-33198. 184p. 1999. 29.95 (0-335-20297-7) OpUniv Pr.

— Disability in Modern Children's Fiction. LC 84-19844. 176p. 1985. text 15.00 (0-914797-09-3) Brookline Bks.

Quicke, John C. The Cautious Expert. 192p. 1982. 91.00 (0-335-10110-0) OpUniv Pr.

Quicke, Juliet, jt. auth. see Quicke, Andrew.

Quickmire, Carolyn, jt. ed. see Moore, Alex.

Quicksilver Associates Staff. The Mercury in Your Mouth Vol. 1: The Truth about Silver Dental Fillings. rev. ed. LC 95-67129. 208p. (Orig.). 1994. pap. 14.95 (0-9643870-0-X) Quicksilv Pr.

Quida. The Massarenes. LC 79-8186. reprint ed. 44.50 (0-404-62087-6) AMS Pr.

Quidnones, B., jt. auth. see Remenyi, Joe.

Quie, Paul G., et al. Infectious Diseases: Beyond Antibiotics. (C). pap. text. write for info. (1-878294-07-5) Health Dimensions.

Quie, Paul G., jt. ed. see Gallin, John I.

Quie, Sarah. The Myths & Civilizations of the Ancient Egyptians. (Myths & Civilization Ser.). (Illus.). 48p. (J). (gr. 3-7). 1999. lib. bdg. 16.95 (0-87226-282-0, 62820B, P Bedrick Books) NTC Contemp Pub Co.

Quiel, John M., jt. auth. see Gill, James H.

***Quien-Schutz, Friederike.** Revealing Love, Beauty & Personality Tests. 2000. pap. 9.95 (0-8069-2885-9) Sterling.

Quiesser, Hans. The Conquest of the Microchip. 288p. 1990. pap. text 9.95 (0-674-16297-8) HUP.

Quieti, R., ed. Piling & Deep Foundations: Proceedings of the 4th International Conference, Stresa, Italy, April 1991, 2 vols. (Illus.). 1000p. (C). 1991. text 304.00 (90-6191-185-0, Pub. by A A Balkema) Ashgate Pub Co.

Quigel, James P., jt. auth. see Hunsinger, Louis, Jr.

Quigg, Brooke & Wisner, Bern. Selling the Right Way. LC 98-2510. 526p. 1998. pap. text 54.00 (0-13-613654-0) P-H.

Quigg, Chris. Gauge Theories of Strong, Weak & Electromagnetic Interactions. LC 97-43362. 1997. pap. 35.00 (0-201-32832-1) Addison-Wesley.

— Gauge Theories of the Strong, Weak & Electromagnetic Interactions. (Frontiers in Physics Ser.). 334p. (C). 1983. 51.75 (0-8053-6020-4, Health Sci) Addison-Wesley.

— Gauge Theories of the Strong, Weak & Electromagnetic Interactions. (Frontiers in Physics Ser.). 334p. (C). 1983. pap. 45.95 (0-8053-6021-2) Benjamin-Cummings.

Quigg, Chris, ed. Annual Review of Nuclear & Particle Science, Vol. 45. LC 53-995. 1995. text 62.00 (0-8243-1545-6) Annual Reviews.

— Annual Review of Nuclear & Particle Science, Vol. 46. LC 53-995. 1996. text 67.00 (0-8243-1546-4) Annual Reviews.

— Annual Review of Nuclear & Particle Science, Vol. 47. LC 53-995. 1997. text 70.00 (0-8243-1547-2) Annual Reviews.

***Quigg, Chris, ed.** Annual Review of Nuclear & Particle Science, Vol. 49. LC 53-995. 700p. 1999. 140.00 (0-8243-1549-9) Annual Reviews.

Quigg, Chris, et al, eds. Annual Review of Nuclear & Particle Science, 1994, Vol. 44. LC 53-995. (Illus.). 1994. text 62.00 (0-8243-1544-8) Annual Reviews.

Quigg, Chris, ed. see American Institute of Physics.

***Quigg, Claudia.** Read for Joy!, No. 2. 2nd rev. ed. (Illus.). 40p. 1999. pap. write for info. (0-9674061-1-0) Baby Talk.

Quigg, Claudia & Rodriguez, Pedro G. Proceedings/ Memoria Conference on Books in Spanish for Young Readers, Fifth Annual. Schon, Isabel, ed. (SPA.). 23p. (Orig.). (C). 1995. pap. 5.00 (0-9639354-4-5) Ctr Bks Spanish.

Quigg, H. Gerald, ed. Successful Capital Campaign: From Planning to Victory Celebration. 188p. 1986. 41.50 (0-89964-248-9, 29701) Coun Adv & Supp Ed.

Quigg, Mary R. Health & Beauty Tips. (Select Pocket Library). 96p. 1997. 4.98 (0-7858-0445-5) Bk Sales Inc.

— Household Hints. (Select Pocket Library). 96p. 1997. 4.98 (0-7858-0447-1) Bk Sales Inc.

Quigg, Philip W. Antarctica: The Continuing Experiment. LC 85-81558. (Headline Ser.: No. 273). (Illus.). 64p. (Orig.). 1985. pap. 5.95 (0-87124-100-5) Foreign Policy.

Quigg, Philip W., ed. Africa: A Foreign Affairs Reader. LC 75-40999. 346p. 1977. reprint ed. lib. bdg. 65.00 (0-8371-8713-3, QUAF, Greenwood Pr) Greenwood.

Quiggin, Alison H. A Survey of Primitive Money: The Beginnings of Currency. LC 76-44779. reprint ed. 47.50 (0-404-15964-8) AMS Pr.

Quiggin, E. C. Prolegomena to the Study of the Later Irish Bards, 1200-1500. (Studies in Irish Literature). 1970. reprint ed. pap. 19.95 (0-8383-0064-2) M S G Haskell Hse.

Quiggin, E. C., ed. Essays & Studies Presented to William Ridgeway on His Sixtieth Birthday, 6 August 1913. LC 67-22093. (Essay Index Reprint Ser.). 1977. 42.95 (0-8369-0421-4) Ayer.

Quiggin, John. Generalized Expected Utility Theory: The Rank Dependent Model. 224p. (C). Date not set. lib. bdg. 109.00 (0-7923-9302-3) Kluwer Academic.

— Great Expectations: Microeconomic Reform & Australia. 264p. 1997. pap. 29.95 (1-86448-236-2, Pub. by Allen & Unwin Pty) Paul & Co Pubs.

— Taxing Times: A Guide to Australia's Tax Debate. 64p. 1998. pap. 9.95 (0-86840-441-1, Pub. by New South Wales Univ Pr) Intl Spec Bk.

Quiggin, John, jt. auth. see Chambers, Robert G.

Quiggin, John, jt. auth. see Langmore, John.

Quiggin, John, jt. auth. see Van Well, Claire.

***Quiggle, Adam.** BCRAN: Building Cisco Remote Access Networks. (Illus.). 756p. 2000. 70.00 (0-07-212480-6) Osborne-McGraw.

Quiggle, James W. & Redman, Lipman. Procedure Before the IRS. 6th ed. LC 84-72251. (Illus.). 269p. 1987. suppl. ed. 96.00 (0-8318-0449-1, B449/B533) Am Law Inst.

— Procedure Before the IRS - Pocket Supplement. 15p. 1987. pap. text 11.00 (0-8318-0533-1, B533) Am Law Inst.

Quiggle, Kevin. COMAL Library of Functions & Procedures. (Amazing Adventures of Captain COMAL Ser.). (Illus.). 71p. (Orig.). (J). (gr. 6 up). 1984. pap. 14.95 (0-928411-03-6) COMAL Users.

Quigley. Database Design & Development. (DC - Introduction to Computing Ser.). 1994. text 18.95 (0-87709-058-0) Course Tech.

Quigley, A. A. Green Is My Sky. 1983. 9.95 (0-8159-5625-8) Devin.

Quigley, April, ed. Kentucky 1998 Cumulative Supplement, 30 vols. Incl. Vol. 1. Kentucky Revised Statutes, 1998 Cumulative Supplement: 1998 Edition. 1998. pap. (0-327-06028-X, 52501-12, MICHIE); Vol. 2. Kentucky Revised Statutes, 1998 Cumulative Supplement: 1998 Edition. 1998. pap. (0-327-06029-8, 50502-12, MICHIE); Vol. 2A. Kentucky Revised Statutes, 1998 Cumulative Supplement: 1998 Edition. 1998. pap. (0-327-06030-1, 52503-12, MICHIE); Vol. 3. Kentucky Revised Statutes, 1998 Cumulative Supplement: 1998 Edition. 1998. pap. (0-327-06031-X, 52504-12, MICHIE); Vol. 3A. Kentucky Revised Statutes, 1998 Cumulative Supplement: 1998 Edition. 1998. pap. (0-327-06032-8, 52530-12, MICHIE); Vol. 4. Kentucky Revised Statutes, 1998 Cumulative Supplement: 1998 Edition. 1998. pap. (0-327-06033-6, 52505-12, MICHIE); Vol. 4A. Kentucky Revised Statutes, 1998 Cumulative Supplement: 1998 Edition. 1998. pap. (0-327-06034-4, 52506-12, MICHIE); Vol. 5. Kentucky Revised Statutes, 1998 Cumulative Supplement: 1998 Edition. 1998. pap. (0-327-06035-2, 52507-12, MICHIE); Vol. 5A. Kentucky Revised Statutes, 1998 Cumulative Supplement: 1998 Edition. 1998. pap. (0-327-06036-0, 52508-12, MICHIE); Vol. 6. Kentucky Revised Statutes, 1998 Cumulative Supplement: 1998 Edition. 1998. pap. (0-327-06037-9, 52509-12, MICHIE); Vol. 7. Kentucky Revised Statutes, 1998 Cumulative Supplement: 1998 Edition. 1998. pap. (0-327-06038-7, 52510-12, MICHIE); Vol. 7A. Kentucky Revised Statutes, 1998 Cumulative Supplement: 1998 Edition. 1998. pap. (0-327-06039-5, 52511-12, MICHIE); Vol. 8. Kentucky Revised Statutes, 1998 Cumulative Supplement: 1998 Edition. 1998. pap. (0-327-06040-9, 52512-12, MICHIE); Vol. 8A. Kentucky Revised Statutes, 1998 Cumulative Supplement: 1998 Edition. 1998. pap. (0-327-06041-7, 52513-12, MICHIE); Vol. 9. Kentucky Revised Statutes, 1998 Cumulative Supplement: 1998 Edition. 1998. pap. (0-327-06042-5, 52514-12, MICHIE); Vol. 9A. Kentucky Revised Statutes, 1998 Cumulative Supplement: 1998 Edition. 1998. pap. (0-327-06043-3, 52515-12, MICHIE); Vol. 10. Kentucky Revised Statutes, 1998 Cumulative Supplement: 1998 Edition. 1998. pap. (0-327-06044-1, 52516-12, MICHIE); Vol. 10A. Kentucky Revised Statutes, 1998 Cumulative Supplement: 1998 Edition. 1998. pap. (0-327-06045-X, 52517-12, MICHIE); Vol. 11. Kentucky Revised Statutes, 1998 Cumulative Supplement: 1998 Edition. 1998. pap. (0-327-06046-8, 52518-12, MICHIE); Vol. 11A. Kentucky Revised Statutes, 1998 Cumulative Supplement: 1998 Edition. 1998. pap. (0-327-06047-6, 52519-12, MICHIE); Vol. 12. Kentucky Revised Statutes, 1998 Cumulative Supplement: 1998 Edition. 1998. pap. (0-327-06048-4, 52520-12, MICHIE); Vol. 12A. Kentucky Revised Statutes, 1998 Cumulative Supplement: 1998 Edition. 1998. pap. (0-327-06049-2, 52521-12, MICHIE); Vol. 13, Pt. 1. Kentucky Revised Statutes, 1998 Cumulative Supplement: 1998 Edition. 1998. pap. (0-327-06050-6, 52522-12, MICHIE); Vol. 13, Pt.2. Kentucky Revised Statutes, 1998 Cumulative Supplement: 1998 Edition. 1998. pap. (0-327-06051-4, 52523-12, MICHIE); Vol. 14. Kentucky Revised Statutes, 1998 Cumulative Supplement: 1998 Edition. 1998. pap. (0-327-06052-2, 52524-12, MICHIE); Vol. 15. Kentucky Revised Statutes, 1998 Cumulative Supplement: 1998 Edition. 1998. pap. (0-327-06053-0, 52525-12, MICHIE); Vol. 15A. Kentucky Revised Statutes, 1998 Cumulative Supplement: 1998 Edition. 1998. pap. (0-327-06054-9, 52526-12, MICHIE); Vol. 16. Kentucky Revised Statutes, 1998 Cumulative Supplement: 1998 Edition. 1998. pap. (0-327-06055-7, 52527-12, MICHIE); Vol. 17. Kentucky Revised Statutes, 1998 Cumulative Supplement: 1998 Edition. 1998. pap. (0-327-06056-5, 52528-12, MICHIE); Vol. 18A. Kentucky Revised Statutes, 1998 Cumulative Supplement: 1998 Edition. 1998. pap. (0-327-06057-3, 52529-12, MICHIE); Vol. 19. Kentucky Revised Statutes, 1998 Cumulative Supplement: 1998 Edition. 1998. pap. (0-327-06058-1, 43332-13, MICHIE); Vol. 20. Kentucky Revised Statutes, 1998 Cumulative Supplement: 1998 Edition. 1998. pap. (0-327-06059-X, 43333-13, MICHIE); write for info. (0-327-06027-1, MICHIE) LEXIS Pub.

Quigley, Audrey. Chinese Landscape Painting for Beginners: A Practical Course. LC 93-14078. (Illus.). 64p. 1993. reprint ed. pap. 7.95 (0-8069-0500-X) Sterling.

Quigley, Austin E. The Modern Stage & Other Worlds. 352p. 1986. 42.50 (0-416-39310-1, 9273); pap. 13.95 (0-416-39320-9, 9274) Routledge.

Quigley, B. Allan. Rethinking Literacy Education: The Critical Need for Practice-Based Change. LC 96-21258. (Jossey-Bass Higher & Adult Education Ser.). 1996. 32.95 (0-7879-0287-X) Jossey-Bass.

Quigley, B. Allan, ed. Fulfilling the Promise of Adult & Continuing Education. LC 85-644750. (New Directions for Adult & Continuing Education Ser.: No. ACE 44). 1989. pap. 22.00 (1-55542-841-X) Jossey-Bass.

Quigley, Barbara, jt. auth. see Ojea, Patricia.

Quigley, Beth, jt. ed. see Baxter, Judith.

Quigley, Betty. Our Master's Prayers: A Brief Story of Jesus' Life Based on His Prayers. (Illus.). 160p. (YA). 1991. 15.95 (0-9626735-1-X); pap. 8.95 (0-9626735-3-6) Rabeth Pub Co.

Quigley, Betty, ed. see James, I. M.

Quigley, Carroll. The Anglo-American Establishment: From Rhodes to Cliveden. 359p. 1981. reprint ed. pap. 15.00 (0-945001-01-0) GSG & Assocs.

— The Evolution of Civilizations. LC 79-4091. 1979. reprint ed. pap. 7.00 (0-913966-57-6) Liberty Fund.

— The Evolution of Civilizations: An Introduction to Historical Analysis. LC 79-4091. 1979. reprint ed. 14.00 (0-913966-56-8) Liberty Fund.

— Tragedy & Hope: A History of the World in Our Time. unabridged ed. 1348p. 1966. reprint ed. text 40.00 (0-945001-10-X) GSG & Assocs.

Quigley, Charles N., et al, eds. Civitas: A Framework for Civic Education. 665p. (Orig.). 1991. pap. 25.00 (0-89818-124-0) Ctr for Civic Educ.

Quigley, Christine. The Corpse: A History. LC 96-30366. (Illus.). 368p. 1996. lib. bdg. 39.95 (0-7864-0170-2) McFarland & Co.

— Modern Mummies: The Preservation of the Human Body in the Twentieth Century. LC 97-43888. (Illus.). 271p. 1998. boxed set 39.95 (0-7864-0492-2) McFarland & Co.

Quigley, Christine, ed. Death Dictionary: Over 5,500 Clinical, Legal, Literary & Vernacular Terms. LC 93-28817. 207p. 1993. lib. bdg. 32.50 (0-89950-869-3) McFarland & Co.

Quigley, Colin. Music from the Heart: Compositions of a Folk Fiddler. LC 93-39721. (Illus.). 288p. 1995. 35.00 (0-8203-1637-7) U of Ga Pr.

***Quigley, Conor.** Droit Communautaire des Contrats: L'Effet du Droit Communautaire sur les Obligations Contractuelles. 560p. 1998. 149.00 (90-411-9681-1) Kluwer Law Intl.

Quigley, Conor. European Community Contract Law, Vol. 1. LC 98-137767. 1168p. 1997. text 400.00 (90-411-0720-7) Kluwer Law Intl.

Quigley, Conor, jt. auth. see Brealey, Mark.

Quigley, Conor, jt. ed. see Brealey, Mark.

Quigley, David R. The Essential Pocket Book of Emergency Chemical Management. LC 95-51495. 144p. 1996. lib. bdg. 29.95 (0-8493-8989-5, 8989) Lewis Pubs.

— Handbook of Emergency Chemical Management. 752p. 1994. boxed set 141.95 (0-8493-8908-9) CRC Pr.

Quigley, Declan. The Interpretation of Caste. (Oxford Studies in Social & Cultural Anthropology). (Illus.). 244p. 1995. pap. text 24.95 (0-19-828027-0) OUP.

Quigley, Declan, jt. ed. see Gellner, David N.

Quigley, Delia & Pitchford, Polly. Starting Over: Learning to Cook with Natural Foods. LC 87-33007. (Illus.). 144p. (Orig.). 1988. pap. 10.95 (0-913990-55-8) Book Pub Co.

Quigley, Delia, jt. auth. see Pitchford, Polly.

Quigley, Don. Managing Your Kitchen & Bathroom Firm's Finances for Profit. (Illus.). 207p. (Orig.). 1997. pap. text 30.00 (1-887127-10-0, 5302) Natl Kit Bath.

Quigley, Eamonn M. & Sorrell, Michael F. The Gastrointestinal Surgical Patient: Preoperative & Postoperative Care. (Illus.). 583p. 1994. 85.00 (0-683-07001-0) Lppncott W & W.

Quigley, Elaine, jt. auth. see Buchter, Carol.

***Quigley, Ellie.** Complete Perl Training Course. 1998. pap., student ed. 71.93 (0-13-083039-9, Prentice Hall) P-H.

— Linux Shells by Example. LC 00-24614. (Illus.). 784p. 2000. pap. text 44.99 incl. cd-rom (0-13-014711-7) P-H.

Quigley, Ellie. Perl By Example. 2nd ed. LC 97-30316. 576p. (C). 1997. pap. text 39.95 (0-13-655689-2) P-H.

— The UNIX Shells by Example. 2nd ed. LC 99-24947. 654p. 1999. 44.99 (0-13-021222-9) S&S Trade.

Quigley, Harold S. China's Politics in Perspective. LC 72-14000. (Illus.). 266p. 1973. reprint ed. lib. bdg. 69.50 (0-8371-6745-0, QUCP, Greenwood Pr) Greenwood.

— 1937-1941. LC 73-3017. (Illus.). 369p. 1973. reprint ed. lib. bdg. 65.00 (0-8371-6835-X, QUFE, Greenwood Pr) Greenwood.

Quigley, Harold S. & Turner, John E. The New Japan: Government & Politics. LC 74-10473. (Illus.). 456p. 1974. reprint ed. lib. bdg. 79.50 (0-8371-7689-1, QUNJ, Greenwood Pr) Greenwood.

Quigley, Harry A. Diagnosing Early Glaucoma with Nerve Fiber Layer Examination. LC 95-644. (Illus.). 192p. 1996. pap. text, spiral bd. 58.95 (0-89640-295-9) Igaku-Shoin.

Quigley, Hugh. The Cross & the Shamrock: An Irish-American Tale. LC 79-104546. reprint ed. lib. bdg. 22.50 (0-8398-1650-2) Irvington.

An Asterisk (*) at the beginning of an entry indicates that the title is appearing for the first time.

Quigley, Hugh & Clark, R. J. Republican Germany: A Political & Economic Study, 1919-1928. 1976. lib. bdg. 69.95 (*0-8490-2518-4*) Gordon Pr.

Quigley, Isabel, tr. see Fellini, Federico.

Quigley, James. Johnny Germ Head. LC 97-11294. (Illus.). 72p. (J). (gr. 3-4). 1997. 14.95 (*0-8050-5395-6*) H Holt & Co.

Quigley, James F., jt. auth. see McGonigle, Thomas D.

***Quigley, Jean.** The Grammar of Autobiography: A Developmental Account. LC 99-87293. 2000. write for info. (*0-8058-3483-4*) L Erlbaum Assocs.

Quigley, Joan. What Does Joan Say? My Seven Years as White House Astrologer to Nancy & Ronald Reagan. 1990. 17.95 (*1-55972-032-8*, Birch Ln Pr) Carol Pub Group.

Quigley, John. Flight into the Maelstrom: Immigration to Israel & Middle East Peace. 224p. 1997. 40.00 (*0-86372-219-9*, Pub. by Garnet-Ithaca) LPC InBook.

— Palestine & Israel: A Challenge to Justice. LC 89-39218. 345p. (Orig.). (C). 1990. text 54.95 (*0-8223-1011-2*); pap. text 22.95 (*0-8223-1023-6*) Duke.

— The Ruses for War: American Interventionism Since World War II. LC 92-19288. 310p. (C). 1992. 28.95 (*0-87975-767-1*) Prometheus Bks.

Quigley, John J., ed. see Jenks, Jeremiah W. & Clark, Walter E.

***Quigley, John M.** Modern Public Finance. 128p. 2000. pap. 18.95 (*0-674-00420-5*) HUP.

— The Superhuman of Nazareth: A Fusion Theory of Religion. (Illus.). 240p. 2000. 29.50 (*1-85776-464-1*, Pub. by Book Guild Ltd) Trans-Atl Phila.

Quigley, John M., ed. The Economics of Housing, 2 vols., set. LC 97-31130. (International Library of Critical Writings in Economics: Vol. 85). 1320p. (C). 1998. 470.00 (*1-85278-754-6*) E Elgar.

— Perspectives on Local Public Finance & Public Policy, Vol. 3. 196p. 1987. 73.25 (*0-89232-648-4*) Jai Pr.

Quigley, John M. & Rubinfeld, Daniel L., eds. American Domestic Priorities: An Economic Appraisal. LC 84-28013. (California Series in Real Estate Economics & Finance: No. 2). 398p. 1985. pap. 20.00 (*0-520-05522-5*, Pub. by U CA Pr) Cal Prin Full Svc.

Quigley, John M. & Smolensky, Eugene, eds. Modern Public Finance. LC 93-23838. (Illus.). 368p. 1994. 45.95 (*0-674-58054-0*) HUP.

Quigley, John M. & Stinson, Debra. Levels of Property Tax Exemption: Part I, Sources of Basic Data & Part II, Tax Exemption in Central Cities & Suburbs, a Comparison Across States, No. 840. 1975. 6.00 (*0-686-20363-1*, Sage Prdcls Pr) Sage.

Quigley, John M., jt. auth. see Kain, John F.

Quigley, Joseph V. Vision: How Leaders Develop It, Share It, & Sustain It. LC 93-9582. 1993. 24.95 (*0-07-051084-9*) McGraw.

Quigley, Kathy. Tika the Tiger. (Friends of the Forest Adventure Bks.). (Illus.). (J). (ps-8). 1995. 16.95 (*0-9641742-8-6*) Pequot Pubng.

Quigley, Kevin F. For Democracy's Sake: Foundations & Democracy Assistance in Central Europe. LC 97-1541. (Woodrow Wilson Center Press Ser.). 216p. 1997. text 38.00 (*0-943875-80-3*); pap. text 15.95 (*0-943875-81-1*) Johns Hopkins.

Quigley, Kevin F., ed. Comics Underground Japan: A Manga Anthology. (Illus.). 208p. 1995. pap. text 14.95 (*0-922233-16-0*) Blast Bks.

Quigley, Kevin F., jt. ed. see Nau, Henry R.

Quigley, Lydia. Quilting up a Storm: New Ways to Interpret a Classic Block Design. (Illus.). 80p. 1996. pap. 19.95 (*1-56477-138-5*, B255) Martingale & Co.

***Quigley, Martha.** Hazard, Perry County, Kentucky. (Images of America Ser.). (Illus.). 128p. 2000. pap. 18.99 (*0-7385-0575-7*) Arcadia Publng.

Quigley, Martin & Monush, Barry, eds. First Century of Film. (Illus.). 432p. 1995. 49.50 (*0-900610-54-9*) Quigley Pub Co.

Quigley, Martin M., jt. ed. see Wolf, Don P.

Quigley, Martin P., jt. auth. see Higbe, Kirby.

Quigley, Martin S. Peace Without Hiroshima: Secret Action at the Vatican in Spring, 1945. 300p. 1991. 22.95 (*0-8191-8056-4*) Madison Bks UPA.

Quigley, Mary A., jt. auth. see Kaufman, Loretta.

Quigley, Pat. Creative Writing I: A Handbook for Teaching Classes Wherever Adults Gather. (Illus.). 98p. (Orig.). 1982. pap. 4.95 (*0-932910-40-8*) Potentials Development.

— Creative Writing II: A Handbook of Techniques for Effective Writing, Vol. II. 145p. (Orig.). 1983. pap. text 4.95 (*0-932910-45-9*) Potentials Development.

Quigley, Paxton. Armed & Female: Twelve Million American Women Own Guns, Should You? 1993. mass mkt. 5.99 (*0-312-95150-7*) St Martin.

Quigley, Peter, ed. Coyote in the Maze: Tracking Edward Abbey in a World of Words. LC 98-11872. vi, 343p. 1998. pap. 19.95 (*0-87480-563-5*) U of Utah Pr.

***Quigley Publishing Co. Staff.** International Motion Pictures Almanac 2000. 71st ed. Stevens, Tracy, ed. (Illus.). 911p. 2000. lib. bdg. 119.00 (*0-900610-65-4*) Quigley Pub Co.

Quigley, Raymond, ed. see James, I. M.

Quigley, Robert D. Civil War Spoken Here: A Dictionary of Mispronounced People, Places & Things of the 1860s. 216p. 1993. pap. 12.00 (*0-9637745-0-6*) C W Hist.

Quigley, Sarah & Shroyer, Marilyn. Facing Fear, Finding Courage: Your Path to Peace of Mind. 165p. (Orig.). 1996. pap. 12.95 (*0-943233-72-0*) Conari Press.

Quigley, Sebastian & Pickering, Mel. All about Space. LC 97-29790. (Scholastic First Encyclopedia Ser.). (J). 1998. pap. write for info. (*0-590-10472-1*) Scholastic Inc.

Quigley, Stephen P., jt. auth. see King, C. M.

Quigley, Stephen P., jt. auth. see King, Cynthia M.

Quigley, Stephen P., jt. auth. see Paul, Peter V.

Quigley, T. Henry. Killing Time, 1968: Mystery. (Herstam Ser.). 170p. 1995. pap. text 10.99 (*1-887755-01-2*) Prop Micro-Pub.

Quigley, Theresia M. The Child Hero in the Canadian Novel. 192p. (Orig.). 1991. pap. 17.95 (*1-55021-069-6*, Pub. by NC Ltd) U of Toronto Pr.

Quigley, Thomas. Johannes Brahms: An Annotated Bibliography of the Literature Through 1982. LC 89-48412. (Illus.). 763p. 1990. 83.50 (*0-8108-2196-6*) Scarecrow.

Quigley, Thomas & Ingraham, Mary I. Johannes Brahms: An Annotated Bibliography of the Literature from 1982-1996 with an Appendix on Brahms & the Internet, in Collaboration with Mary I. Ingraham. LC 97-41925. (Illus.). 720p. 1998. 85.00 (*0-8108-3439-1*) Scarecrow.

Quigley, Thomas E., ed. American Catholics & Vietnam. LC 68-54102. 197p. reprint ed. pap. 61.10 (*0-8357-5357-3*, 201281400083) Bks Demand.

Quigley, Thomas M. Forest Health in the Blue Mountains: Social & Economic Perspectives. (Illus.). 24p. 1997. reprint ed. pap. 2.50 (*0-89904-636-3*, Ecosytems Resrch) Crumb Elbow Pub.

— Forest Health in the Blue Mountains: The Influence of Insects & Disease. (Illus.). 20p. 1997. reprint ed. pap. 3.50 (*0-89904-637-1*, Ecosytems Resrch) Crumb Elbow Pub.

Quigley, Thomas M., et al, eds. Integrated Scientific Assessment for Ecosystem Management in the Interior Columbia Basin & Portions of the Klamath & Great Basins. (Illus.). 318p. 1997. reprint ed. 40.00 (*0-89904-563-4*, Bear Meadows Resrch Grp); reprint ed. pap. 34.00 (*0-89904-564-2*, Bear Meadows Resrch Grp) Crumb Elbow Pub.

***Quigley, Thomas M., et al, eds.** Integrated Scientific Assessment for Ecosystem Management in the Interior Columbia Basin & Portions of the Klamath & Great Basins. (Illus.). 303p. 2000. reprint ed. pap. text 50.00 (*0-7567-0074-4*) DIANE Pub.

Quigley, Thomas M. & Arbelbide, Sylvia J., eds. An Assessment of Ecosystem Components in the Interior Columbia Basin & Portions of the Klamath & Great Basins, Vol. I. (Illus.). 354p. 1998. reprint ed. 43.00 (*0-89904-750-5*, Bear Meadows Resrch Grp); reprint ed. pap. 38.00 (*0-89904-751-3*, Bear Meadows Resrch Grp) Crumb Elbow Pub.

— An Assessment of Ecosystem Components in the Interior Columbia Basin & Portions of the Klamath & Great Basins, Vol. II. (Illus.). 732p. 1998. reprint ed. 80.00 (*0-89904-752-1*, Bear Meadows Resrch Grp); reprint ed. pap. 75.00 (*0-89904-753-X*, Bear Meadows Resrch Grp) Crumb Elbow Pub.

— An Assessment of Ecosystem Components in the Interior Columbia Basin & Portions of the Klamath & Great Basins, Vol. III. (Illus.). 670p. 1998. reprint ed. 73.00 (*0-89904-754-8*, Bear Meadows Resrch Grp); reprint ed. pap. 68.00 (*0-89904-755-6*, Bear Meadows Resrch Grp) Crumb Elbow Pub.

— An Assessment of Ecosystem Components in the Interior Columbia Basin & Portions of the Klamath & Great Basins, Vol. IV. (Illus.). 360p. 1998. reprint ed. 42.00 (*0-89904-756-4*, Bear Meadows Resrch Grp); reprint ed. pap. 37.00 (*0-89904-757-2*, Bear Meadows Resrch Grp) Crumb Elbow Pub.

— Evaluation of Environmental Impact Statement Alternatives by the Science Integration Team, Vol. II. 1098p. 1998. reprint ed. 115.80 (*0-89904-719-X*, Ecosytems Resrch); reprint ed. pap. 110.80 (*0-89904-720-3*, Ecosytems Resrch) Crumb Elbow Pub.

Quigley, Thomas M. & Cole, Heidi B. Highlighted Scientific Findings of the Interior Columbia Basin Ecosystem Management Project. (Illus.). 50p. 1997. reprint ed. 13.40 (*0-89904-639-8*, Bear Meadows Resrch Grp); reprint ed. pap. 9.40 (*0-89904-640-1*, Bear Meadows Resrch Grp) Crumb Elbow Pub.

Quigley, Tom, jt. auth. see Chamberlain, R. H.

Quigley, Tom, ed. see Allen, Stewart.

Quigley's Village Staff. A Christmas Story: Joy of Giving. (Quigley's Village Ser.: Vol. 5). (J). (ps-2). 12.99 incl. VHS (*0-310-58249-0*, V5155) Zondervan.

— Spike & the Big Blue Bubble Babble Balloon Machine: Sharing. (Quigley's Village Ser.: Vol. 6). (J). (ps-2). 12.99 incl. VHS (*0-310-58179-6*, V6757) Zondervan.

— The Wonder Kids' Colossal Caper: Courage. (Quigley's Village Ser.: Vol. 7). (J). (ps-2). 12.99 incl. VHS (*0-310-58309-8*) Zondervan.

Quigly, Ellie. The Complete PERLl Training Course. 550p. (C). 1998. pap. text 99.95 (*0-13-079980-7*, Macmillan Coll) P-H.

Quigly, Isabel, ed. see Kipling, Rudyard.

Quigly, Isabel, tr. see Parise, Goffredo.

Quigly, Isabel, tr. see Svevo, Livia V.

Quignard, Pascal. Albucius. (FRE.). 1992. pap. 10.95 (*0-7859-3169-4*, 2253059560) Fr & Eur.

— All the World's Mornings: A Novel. Kirkup, James, tr. from FRE. LC 93-2161.Tr. of Tous les Matins du Monde. 96p. 1993. pap. 9.00 (*1-55597-203-9*) Graywolf.

— Carus. (FRE.). 1990. pap. 13.95 (*0-7859-2923-1*) Fr & Eur.

— Carus. (Folio Ser.: No. 2211). (FRE.). pap. 10.95 (*2-07-038301-6*) Schoenhof.

— Escaliers de Chambord. (Folio Ser.: No. 2301). (FRE.). 1971. pap. 9.95 (*2-07-038415-2*) Schoenhof.

— Les Escaliers de Chambord. (FRE.). 1991. pap. 12.95 (*0-7859-2927-4*) Fr & Eur.

— Salon du Wurtemberg. (Folio Ser.: No. 1928). (FRE.). 432p. 1986. pap. 10.96 (*2-07-037928-0*) Schoenhof.

— Le Salon du Wurtemburg. (FRE.). 1988. pap. 13.95 (*0-7859-2915-0*) Fr & Eur.

— Sarx: Poems. Waldrop, Keith, tr. from FRE. (Serie d'Ecriture Ser.: Suppl. 2). 40p. (C). 1997. pap. 5.00 (*1-886224-20-X*) Burning Deck.

— Les Tablettes de Buis d'Apronenia Avtia. (FRE.). 1989. pap. 15.95 (*0-7859-2940-1*) Fr & Eur.

Quigstau, Jan F., jt. ed. see Christiansen, Anne B.

Quijano, Anibal. Nationalism & Capitalism in Peru: A Study in Neo-Imperialism. Lane, Helen R., tr. LC 78-163117. 128p. reprint ed. pap. 39.70 (*0-608-13927-0*, 201925500011) Bks Demand.

Quilan, Hamid, ed. see Sabiq, As-Sayyed.

Quilan, Hamid, ed. see Sabiq, As-Sayyid.

Quiler's Newsletter Magazine Editors, jt. auth. see Townswick, Jane.

Quilici, Alexander E., jt. auth. see Miller, Larry.

Quilici, Alexander E., jt. auth. see Miller, Lawrence H.

Quilici, Folco. Italy from the Air. (Illus.). 160p. 1987. 49.50 (*0-8109-1117-5*, Pub. by Abrams) Time Warner.

Quilici, Gina. Defending the Sword. 352p. mass mkt. 4.99 (*1-55197-120-8*) Picasso Publ.

Quilici-Timmcke, Judi. New Nutrients Against Cancer. LC 99-185182. 48p. 1998. pap. 3.95 (*0-87983-890-6*, Keats Publng) NTC Contemp Pub Co.

Quilici-Timmcke, Judi, jt. auth. see Sinatra, Stephen T.

Quilis, Antonio & Hernandez Alonso, C. Linguistica Aplicada a la Terapia Del Lenguaje. (SPA.). 552p. 1993. 125.00 (*84-249-1427-9*) Elliots Bks.

Quilis, Antonio, jt. auth. see Niederehe, Hans-Josef.

***Quill, Kathleen Ann.** Do-Watch-Listen-Say: Social & Communication Intervention for Children with Autism. LC 99-86525. 2000. write for info. (*1-55766-453-6*) P H Brookes.

Quill, Kathleen Ann. Teaching Children with Autism: Strategies to Enhance Communication & Socialization. 336p. (C). 1995. mass mkt. 45.95 (*0-8273-6269-2*) Delmar.

Quill, Lawrence L., ed. see AEC Technical Information Center Staff.

Quill, Michael, jt. auth. see Mosley, Oswald.

Quill, Monica. Half Past Nun: A Sister Mary Teresa Mystery. LC 97-1182. 1997. 20.95 (*0-312-15541-7*) St Martin.

— Nun Plussed: A Sister Mary Teresa Mystery. LC 95-2321. 250p. 1995. per. 3.99 (*0-373-26187-X*, Wrldwide Lib) Harlequin Bks.

***Quill, Sarah & Windsor.** Ruskins Venice: The Stones Revisited. abr. ed. (Illus.). 206p. 2000. 49.95 (*1-84014-697-4*) Ashgate Pub Co.

Quill, Timothy C. The Impact of the Liturgical Movement on American Lutheranism. LC 97-19273. (Drew Studies in Liturgy: No. 3). 1997. 45.00 (*0-8108-3365-4*) Scarecrow.

Quill, Timothy E. Death & Dignity: Making Choices & Taking Charge. 1994. pap. 10.95 (*0-393-31140-6*) Norton.

— A Midwife Through the Dying Process: Stories of Healing & Hard Choices at the End of Life. LC 96-26475. 208p. 1996. 24.95 (*0-8018-5516-0*) Johns Hopkins.

Quillard. Deux Pieces Symbolistes. (Exeter French Texts Ser.: Vol. 22). (FRE.). 100p. Date not set. pap. text 19.95 (*0-85989-086-4*, Pub. by Univ Exeter Pr) Northwestern U Pr.

Quille, Dan De, see De Quille, Dan.

Quillec, Maurice, ed. Materials for Optoelectronics. LC 95-25831. (International Series in Engineering & Computer Science, Natural Language Processing & Machine Translation: No. 346). 392p. (C). 1996. text 169.50 (*0-7923-9665-0*) Kluwer Academic.

Quillen. Francis Petrarch the Secret. 2000. pap. text 10.95 (*0-312-15438-0*) St Martin.

— Fundamentals in Musculoskeletal Radiology. 1997. pap. text. write for info. (*0-7216-6087-8*, W B Saunders Co) Harcrt Hlth Sci Grp.

— Laboratory Manual T-A Therapeutic Modalities. 3rd ed. 192p. (C). 1994. text, lab manual ed. 19.95 (*0-8016-7921-4*) Mosby Inc.

— Therapeutic Modalities. 4th ed. 160p. 1998. pap., lab manual ed. 25.00 (*0-07-092116-4*) McGraw.

Quillen, jt. auth. see Hirsch.

Quillen, Carol E. Rereading the Renaissance: Petrarch, Augustine, & the Language of Humanism. LC 97-50191. 264p. (C). 1998. text 47.50 (*0-472-10735-6*, 10735) U of Mich Pr.

Quillen, D. G., et al. The Interface of Mathematics & Particle Physics. (Institute of Mathematics & Its Applications Conference Series, New Ser.: New Series 24). (Illus.). 240p. 1990. 59.00 (*0-19-853626-7*) OUP.

Quillen, Ed. Deep in the Heart of the Rockies: Selected Columns from the Denver Post, 1986-1997. Porter, Mary J., ed. (Western Opinion Ser.: Vol. 1). 185p. 1998. pap. 12.95 (*0-9656126-7-8*) Music Mtn Pr.

Quillen, Elisabeth. L' Angleterre et l'Amerique dans la Vie et la Poesie d'Andre Chenier. (American University Studies: Romance Languages & Literature: Ser. II, Vol. 1). (FRE.). 139p. (Orig.). 1982. pap. text 23.00 (*3-261-04987-1*) P Lang Pubng.

***Quillen, Jacqueline L. & Boynton, George, Sr.** The Magic of Wine: A Book of Quotations. LC 99-55747. 2000. 16.95 (*0-87833-173-5*) Taylor Pub.

Quillen, Jim. Alcatraz from Inside: The Hard Years, 1942-1952. (Illus.). 164p. (Orig.). 1992. pap. 11.95 (*0-9625206-1-6*) Gldn Gate Natl Parks Assoc.

Quillen, Maureen, jt. ed. see Anderson, Marc.

Quillen, Rita. Looking for Native Ground: Contemporary Appalachian Poetry. LC 89-83315. 1989. pap. 9.95 (*0-913239-58-5*) Appalach Consortium.

Quillen, Rita, ed. see Agee, James, et al.

Quillen, Rita S. Counting the Sums. 64p. (Orig.). 1995. 20.00 (*1-885912-07-2*); pap. 11.00 (*1-885912-04-8*) Sows Ear Pr.

Quillen, Roger K., jt. auth. see Hirsch, Jeffrey L.

Quiller-Couch, Arthur, ed. The Oxford Book of Ballads, 2 vols in 1. 800p. reprint ed. 55.00 (*0-403-08625-6*) Somerset Pub.

Quiller-Couch, Arthur & Du Maurier, Daphne. Castle D'Or. reprint ed. lib. bdg. 23.95 (*0-88411-148-2*) Amereon Ltd.

Quiller-Couch, Arthur T. Adventures in Criticism. (BCL1-PR English Literature Ser.). 408p. 1992. reprint ed. lib. bdg. 99.00 (*0-7812-7017-0*) Rprt Serv.

— Adventures in Criticism. LC 12-37963. 1969. reprint ed. 9.00 (*0-403-00064-5*) Scholarly.

— The Age of Chaucer. LC 75-155616. xiii, 158p. 1972. reprint ed. 29.00 (*0-404-05201-0*) AMS Pr.

— Cambridge Lectures. LC 72-4723. (Essay Index Reprint Ser.). 1977. reprint ed. 20.95 (*0-8369-2970-5*) Ayer.

— Charles Dickens & Other Victorians. (BCL1-PR English Literature Ser.). 240p. 1992. reprint ed. lib. bdg. 79.00 (*0-7812-7121-5*) Rprt Serv.

— Delectable Duchy: Stories, Studies & Sketches. LC 78-125235. (Short Story Index Reprint Ser.). 1977. 19.95 (*0-8369-3602-7*) Ayer.

— I Saw Three Ships, & Other Winter's Tales. LC 77-103527. (Short Story Index Reprint Ser.). 1977. reprint ed. 21.95 (*0-8369-4023-7*) Ayer.

— Laird's Luck: And Other Fireside Tales. LC 72-10767. (Short Story Index Reprint Ser.). 1977. reprint ed. 29.95 (*0-8369-4223-X*) Ayer.

— A Lecture on Lectures. LC 74-7042. (English Literature Ser.: No. 33). 1974. lib. bdg. 75.00 (*0-8383-1994-7*) M S G Haskell Hse.

— Noughts & Crosses. LC 77-103527. (Short Story Index Reprint Ser.). 1977. 19.95 (*0-8369-3269-2*) Ayer.

— Old Fires & Profitable Ghosts: A Book of Stories. LC 72-10813. (Short Story Index Reprint Ser.). 1977. reprint ed. 24.95 (*0-8369-4224-8*) Ayer.

— The Poet As a Citizen, & Other Papers. LC 75-41219. reprint ed. 27.50 (*0-404-14585-X*) AMS Pr.

— Studies in Literature. (BCL1-PR English Literature Ser.). 324p. 1992. reprint ed. lib. bdg. 89.00 (*0-7812-7018-9*) Rprt Serv.

— Studies in Literature - Second Series, Second Series. (BCL1-PR English Literature Ser.). 301p. 1992. reprint ed. lib. bdg. 89.00 (*0-7812-7019-7*) Rprt Serv.

Quiller-Couch, Arthur T., ed. English Sonnets. LC 68-58821. (Granger Index Reprint Ser.). 1977. 15.95 (*0-8369-6038-6*) Ayer.

Quiller, Stephen. Acrylic Painting Techniques: How to Master the Medium of Our Age. LC 94-17459. (Illus.). 144p. 1994. 29.95 (*0-8230-0105-9*) Watsn-Guptill.

— Color Choices. (Illus.). 144p. 1989. 29.95 (*0-8230-0696-4*) Watsn-Guptill.

— Painter's Guide to Color. LC 99-26870. (Illus.). 144p. 1999. pap. 24.95 (*0-8230-3913-7*) Watsn-Guptill.

Quillet Staff. Dictionnaire Encylopedique Quillet, 10 vols., Set. (FRE.). 1977. 1295.00 (*0-8288-5387-8*, M6139) Fr & Eur.

— Dictionnaire Quillet de la Langue Francais, 4 vols., Set. (FRE.). 2132p. 495.00 (*0-7859-0390-9*, M6153) Fr & Eur.

— Encyclopedie Illustree du Monde Animal. 175.00 (*0-8288-8147-2*, M6210) Fr & Eur.

— Encyclopedie Illustree du Monde Animal. (FRE., Illus.). 600p. 29.95 (*0-7859-0395-X*, M6218) Fr & Eur.

— Encyclopedie Pratique de la Construction du Batiment et des Travaux Publics, 3 vols., Set. (FRE.). 3587p. 350.00 (*0-7859-0396-8*, M6232) Fr & Eur.

— Nouvelle Encyclopedie Autodidactique Quillet, 6 vols., Set. (FRE.). 668p. 1977. 695.00 (*0-8288-5504-8*, M6434) Fr & Eur.

Quillia. Body Language Secrets. 1998. pap. 10.00 (*0-7225-3533-3*) Thorsons PA.

***Quilliam, Neil.** Syria. rev. ed. (World Bibliographical Ser.: No. 73). 376p. 1999. lib. bdg. 87.00 (*1-85109-317-6*) ABC-CLIO.

Quilliam, Sue, ed. see Matthews, Julia.

***Quilliam, Susan.** Love Coach: You Have Never Been Taught How to Make Love Work, until Now. 2000. pap. 12.95 (*0-7225-3986-X*) Thorsons PA.

Quilliam, Susan. Sexual Body Talk. (Illus.). 128p. 1992. pap. 15.95 (*0-88184-757-7*) Carroll & Graf.

— Sexual Body Talk: Understanding the Body Language of Attraction from First Glance to Sexual Happiness. (Illus.). 128p. 1998. pap. text 20.00 (*0-7881-5647-0*) DIANE Pub.

— Women on Sex. LC 94-25589. 256p. 1994. pap. 14.95 (*1-56980-025-1*) Barricade Bks.

***Quillian, Lincoln.** Migration Patterns & the Growth of High Poverty Neighborhoods, 1970-1990. 49p. (C). 1999. pap. text 20.00 (*0-7881-8361-3*) DIANE Pub.

Quillian, Thelma B. A Branch of Quillians from Ireland: Through Georgia to the Texas Lineage. (Illus.). 1984. write for info. (*0-318-58984-2*) Myriad.

Quilligan, Edward J. & Zuspan, Frederick P. Current Therapy in Obstetrics & Gynecology. 5th ed. Schmitt, William et al, eds. LC 99-16181. (Illus.). 525p. 1999. text. write for info. (*0-7216-7579-4*, W B Saunders Co) Harcrt Hlth Sci Grp.

Quilligan, Edward J., jt. auth. see Zuspan, Frederick P.

Quilligan, Edward J., jt. ed. see Flamm, Bruce L.

Quilligan, Edward J., jt. ed. see Zuspan, Frederick P.

Quilligan, Maureen. The Allegory of Female Authority: Christine de Pizan's Cite des Dames. LC 91-55069. 304p. 1992. 45.00 (*0-8014-2552-2*); pap. text 17.95 (*0-8014-9788-4*) Cornell U Pr.

— The Language of Allegory: Defining the Genre. LC 78-74216. 312p. 1992. pap. text 16.95 (*0-8014-8051-5*) Cornell U Pr.

— Milton's Spenser: The Politics of Reading. LC 83-45149. 256p. 1983. 37.50 (*0-8014-1590-X*) Cornell U Pr.

Quillin. The Wisdom of Amish Folk Medicine. 1996. per. write for info. (*0-671-52812-2*) S&S Trade.

Quillin, Noreen, jt. auth. see Quillin, Patrick.

Q

An Asterisk (*) at the beginning of an entry indicates that the title is appearing for the first time.

Quillin, Patrick. Amazing Honey, Garlic & Vinegar Home Remedies: A Doctor's Guide to Using These Natural Remedies. (Illus.). 250p. 1996. pap. 14.95 (*1-886898-03-0*) Leader OH.

Quillin, Patrick. Amish Folk Medicine. 1995. pap. write for info. (*1-886898-00-6*) Leader OH.

Quillin, Patrick. Amish Folk Medicine: Home Remedies Using Foods, Herbs, & Vitamins. (Illus.). 248p. 1995. pap. 14.95 (*1-886898-01-4*) Leader OH.

— Healing Nutrients. 449p. 1989. pap. 14.00 (*0-679-72187-8*) Vin Bks.

— Healing Power of Cayenne Pepper: Complete Handbook of Cayenne Home Remedies. 1999. pap. text. write for info. (*1-886898-05-7*) Leader OH.

— Healing Secrets from the Bible. 1996. pap. text 14.95 (*0-9638372-1-4*) Nutrit Times.

— Healing Secrets from the Bible: God Wants Us to Be Healthy & the Bible Tells Us How. LC 96-140888. (Illus.). 172p. 1995. 14.95 (*1-886898-02-2*) Leader OH.

***Quillin, Patrick.** Immunopower: Harnessing Incredible Healing. 1999. pap. text 14.95 (*0-9638372-6-5*) Nutrit Times.

Quillin, Patrick, ed. Adjuvant Nutrition in Cancer Treatment. (Illus.). 400p. (C). 1993. write for info. (*0-9638263-0-1*) Cancer Treatment.

Quillin, Patrick & Quillin, Noreen. Beating Cancer with Nutrition: Clinically Proven & Easy-to-Follow Strategies to Dramatically Improve Your Quality & Quantity of Life & Chances for a Complete Remission. rev. ed. (Illus.). 286p. 1998. pap. 16.95 (*0-9638372-4-9*) Nutrit Times.

— Immunopower. rev. ed. (Illus.). 110p. 1998. pap. 9.95 (*0-9638372-5-7*) Nutrit Times.

Quillin, Patrick, jt. auth. see Smith, R. Philip.

Quillin, Viv. Pussyfooting: Essential Dance Procedures for Cats. (Illus.). 96p. 1995. 10.00 (*1-56836-078-9*) Kodansha.

Quillinan, Carol, see Sample, Capper, pseud.

Quillinan, Edward. Consolation: A Poem Addressed to Lady Brydges. LC 75-31249. (Romantic Context: Poetry 1789-1830 Ser.: Vol. 98). 1978. reprint ed. lib. bdg. 57.00 (*0-8240-2197-5*) Garland.

Quilliot, Claude, ed. see Camus, Albert.

Quilliot, Roger, ed. see Camus, Albert.

Quillman, Catherine, jt. auth. see Biggs, Michael.

Quillman, Susan M. Nutrition & Diet Therapy. 2nd ed. (Notes Ser.). 208p. 1993. pap. 18.95 (*0-87434-612-6*) Springhouse Corp.

Quillo, Ronald. Catholic Answers to Questions about the New Age Movement. LC 94-79998. 64p. 1995. pap. 2.95 (*0-89243-764-2*) Liguori Pubns.

— Companions in Consciousness: The Bible & the New Age Movement. LC 93-33422. 192p. 1995. reprint ed. pap. 12.95 (*0-89243-824-X*, Liguori Triumph) Liguori Pubns.

— The Psalms, Prayers of Many Moods: Spiritual Enrichment through the Psalms. LC 98-47843. 176p. 1999. pap. 19.95 (*0-8091-3843-3*) Paulist Pr.

— Two Cultures of Belief: The Fallacy of Christian Certitude. LC 95-12690. 176p. (Orig.). 1995. pap. 14.95 (*0-89243-819-3*, Liguori Triumph) Liguori Pubns.

Quillot, Claire & Quillot, Roger. L' Homme sur le Pavois. (FRE.). 1982. pap. 13.95 (*0-7859-4178-9*) Fr & Eur.

Quillot, Roger, jt. auth. see Quillot, Claire.

Quilt National Staff. Fiber Expressions: The Contemporary Quilt. LC 86-63763. (Illus.). 88p. 1987. pap. 12.95 (*0-88740-093-0*) Schiffer.

— The Quilt: New Directions for an American Tradition. LC 83-50843. (Illus.). 80p. 1983. pap. 10.95 (*0-916838-92-7*) Schiffer.

Quilter. Spanish - Analysis for Advanced Students. (C). 1993. pap. text 32.00 (*0-07-051389-9*) McGraw.

Quilter, Daniel, ed. see De Cervantes Saavedra, Miguel.

Quilter, Deborah, jt. auth. see Pascarelli, Emil.

Quilter, E. S. Searoom Handbook with Radar Anti-Collision Tables. LC 76-240. 177p. 1976. spiral bd. 15.00 (*0-87033-221-X*) Cornell Maritime.

Quilter, Jeffrey. Life & Death at Paloma: Society & Mortuary Practices in a Preceramic Peruvian Village. LC 88-31276. (Illus.). 203p. 1989. text 29.95 (*0-87745-194-X*) U of Iowa Pr.

Quilter's Newsletter Magazine Editors & Leman, Bonnie. Choice Scrap Quilts. (Illus.). 120p. (Orig.). 1994. pap. 19.95 (*0-943721-14-8*) Leman Pubns.

— Star Spangled Sampler Quilts: The Art of the States. (Illus.). 64p. (Orig.). 1993. pap. 16.95 (*0-943721-12-1*) Leman Pubns.

Quiltmakers of Georgia Staff. The Olympic Games Quilts: America's Welcome to the World. 144p. 1996. pap. 19.95 (*0-8487-1505-5*) Oxmoor Hse.

Quilty, Deena A., ed. see Kleinschmidt, Linda.

Quilty, Mary. Textual Empires. LC 98-217935. 148p. 1998. pap. 21.95 (*0-7326-1166-0*, Pub. by Monash Asia Inst) Intl Spec Bk.

Quilty, Mary, jt. ed. see Milner, Anthony.

Quimby, Edith H. Radioactive Nuclides in Medicine & Biology. 3rd ed. LC 68-18868. 402p. reprint ed. pap. 124.70 (*0-608-12419-2*, 205570100030) Bks Demand.

Quimby, Fred W., jt. auth. see Loeb, Walter F.

Quimby, George I. The Bayou Goula Site, Iberville Parish, Louisiana. LC 57-2154. (Chicago Natural History Museum, Publication 814, Fieldiana, Anthropology Ser.: Vol. 47, No. 2). 83p. 1957. reprint ed. pap. 30.00 (*0-608-02117-2*, 206276600004) Bks Demand.

— The Dumaw Creek Site: A Seventeenth Century Prehistoric Indian Village & Cemetery in Oceana County, Michigan. LC 66-28392. (Field Museum of Natural History, Publication 1014, Anthropological Ser.: Vol. 56, No. 1). 93p. reprint ed. pap. 30.00 (*0-608-02115-6*, 206276400004) Bks Demand.

— Indian Culture & European Trade Goods: The Archaeology of the Historic Period in the Western Great Lakes Region. LC 78-4995. 217p. 1978. reprint ed. lib. bdg. 35.00 (*0-313-20379-2*, QUIC, Greenwood Pr) Greenwood.

— Indian Life in the Upper Great Lakes 11,000 B. C. to A. D. 1800. LC 60-11799. (Illus.). 197p. pap. 61.10 (*0-8357-8919-5*, 205676800085) Bks Demand.

— Pottery from the Aleutian Islands. LC 46-2911. (Chicago Natural History Museum Anthropology Ser.: Vol. 36, No. 1, September 19, 1945). (Illus.). 13p. 1945. reprint ed. pap. 30.00 (*0-608-02730-8*, 206339500004) Bks Demand.

Quimby, George I., jt. auth. see Ritzenthaler, Robert E.

Quimby, George I., jt. ed. see Casteel, Richard W.

Quimby, H. C. Genealogical History of the Quinby (Quimby) Family in England & America. (Illus.). 604p. 1993. reprint ed. pap. 94.00 (*0-8328-3052-6*); reprint ed. lib. bdg. 104.00 (*0-8328-3051-8*) Higginson Bk Co.

Quimby, Ian M. Winterthur Portfolio, No. 9. Doud, Richard K., ed. (Winterthur Bk.: Vol. 9). (Illus.). 248p. 1978. lib. bdg. 24.00 (*0-226-92135-2*) U Ch Pr.

Quimby, Ian M., ed. American Painting to 1776: A Reappraisal. rev. ed. LC 75-173917. (Winterthur Conference Reports). (Illus.). 396p. 1971. reprint ed. pap. 22.50 (*0-8139-0378-5*) Winterthur.

— American Silver at Winterthur. LC 95-14228. (Illus.). 1995p. (C). 1995. 80.00 (*0-912724-32-3*) Winterthur.

— Arts of the Anglo-American Community in the Seventeen Century. LC 74-22098. (Winterthur Conference Reports). (Illus.). 309p. 1975. pap. 22.50 (*0-8139-0612-1*) Winterthur.

— Ceramics in America: Winterthur Conference Report 1972. LC 72-96715. (Winterthur Conference Reports). (Illus.). 386p. 1973. reprint ed. pap. 22.50 (*0-8139-0476-5*) Winterthur.

— A Winterthur Bk., No. 7. (Winterthur Bk.: Vol. 7). (Illus.). 256p. 1978. lib. bdg. 24.00 (*0-226-92133-6*) U Ch Pr.

— Winterthur Portfolio, No. 11. (Winterthur Bk.). (Illus.). 256p. 1978. lib. bdg. 24.00 (*0-226-92137-9*) U Ch Pr.

— Winterthur Portfolio, No. 12. (Winterthur Bk.). (Illus.). 248p. 1978. lib. bdg. 24.00 (*0-226-92138-7*) U Ch Pr.

— Winterthur Portfolio No. 8: Thematic Issue on Religion in America. (Winterthur Bk.). (Illus.). 256p. 1978. lib. bdg. 24.00 (*0-226-92134-4*) U Ch Pr.

Quimby, Ian M., jt. auth. see Doud, Richard K.

Quimby, Maureen. Eleutherian Mills. (Illus.). 92p. 1985. pap. 5.95 (*0-914650-04-1*) Hagley Museum.

Quimby, Phineas P. Immanuel. 109p. 1997. reprint ed. spiral bd. 11.00 (*0-7873-0687-8*) Hlth Research.

— Phineas Parkhurst Quimby: The Complete Writings, 3 vols., Vol. 1. LC 80-70090. 436p. 1988. pap. 25.00 (*0-87516-600-8*) DeVorss.

— Phineas Parkhurst Quimby: The Complete Writings, 3 vols., Vol. 2. LC 80-70090. 417p. 1988. pap. 25.00 (*0-87516-601-6*) DeVorss.

— Phineas Parkhurst Quimby: The Complete Writings, 3 vols., Vol. 3. LC 80-70090. 436p. 1988. pap. 25.00 (*0-87516-602-4*) DeVorss.

Quimby, Robert S. The U. S. Army in the War of 1812: An Operational & Command Study, 2 vols. LC 97-29481. (Illus.). 1054p. 1998. 85.95 (*0-87013-441-8*) Mich St U Pr.

Quimby, Stuart & Kittner, Cary. The Globe Project. unabridged ed. (Illus.). 68p. 1995. pap. write for info. (*0-9651870-0-4*) Dsgn Sci Toys.

Quimby, Thomas H. Recycling: The Alternative to Disposal: A Case Study of the Potential for Increased Recycling of Newspapers & Corrugated Containers in the Washington Metropolitan Area. LC 74-6836. 144p. reprint ed. pap. 44.70 (*0-608-18668-6*, 202094900020) Bks Demand.

Quin-Hamlin, Janet. Trade Winds. Creative Media Applications Staff, ed. 256p. (Orig.). 1993. pap. text. write for info. (*1-884066-00-3*) NBC Inc.

Quin-Harkin, Janet. All Rapped Up. (Sister, Sister Ser.: No. 1). (J). (gr. 3-6). 1997. pap. 3.99 (*0-671-00288-0*) PB.

— The Boy Next Door. (Love Stories Ser.). 192p. (YA). (gr. 7-12). 1995. mass mkt. 4.50 (*0-553-56663-6*) Bantam.

— The Boyfriend Wars. (Boyfriend Club Special Edition Ser.: No. 2). (J). (gr. 3-7). 1995. pap. 3.95 (*0-8167-3710-X*) Troll Communs.

— Cool in School. (Sister, Sister Ser.: No. 2). (J). (gr. 3-6). 1996. pap. 3.99 (*0-671-00176-0*) PB.

***Quin-Harkin, Janet.** Enchanted Hearts: Love Potion, Vol. 4. (Enchanted Hearts Ser.: No. 4). (Illus.). 192p. (YA). (gr. 7 up). 1999. mass mkt. 4.50 (*0-380-80122-1*, Avon Bks) Morrow Avon.

Quin-Harkin, Janet. Flamingo Revenge. (Full House Club Stephanie Ser.: Vol. 3). 144p. (J). (gr. 3-6). 1997. per. 3.99 (*0-671-00828-5*, Archway) PB.

— Forever Friday. (TGIF Ser.: No. 4). 128p. (J). (gr. 3-6). 1995. pap. 3.50 (*0-671-51020-7*) PB.

— Four's a Crowd. (TGIF Ser.: No. 3). (J). (gr. 3-6). 1995. pap. 3.50 (*0-671-51019-3*) PB.

— Getting Personal: Becky. 1994. per. 3.50 (*0-373-20204-0*, 1-20204-3) Harlequin Bks.

— Ginger's New Crush. LC 94-21666. (Boysie Bks.: No. 5). (Illus.). 176p. (J). (gr. 3-6). 1997. pap. 2.95 (*0-8167-3418-6*, Rainbow NJ) Troll Communs.

— He's All That. (Sister, Sister Ser.: No. 3). (J). (gr. 3-6). 1997. pap. 3.99 (*0-671-00286-4*, Minstrel Bks) PB.

— Homegirl on the Range. (Sister, Sister Ser.: No. 4). (J). (gr. 3-6). 1997. pap. 3.99 (*0-671-00284-8*, Minstrel Bks) PB.

— Justine's Baby-Sitting Nightmare. (YA). 1997. pap. 2.95 (*0-8167-3690-1*) Troll Communs.

— King & I: Junior Novelization. 1999. pap. 3.99 (*0-590-68065-X*) Scholastic Inc.

***Quin-Harkin, Janet.** Love Potion. (Enchanted Hearts Ser.). (Illus.). (J). 1999. 9.85 (*0-606-17966-6*) Turtleback.

Quin-Harkin, Janet. Lovebirds: International Edition. (YA). 1994. pap. 3.50 (*0-553-24181-8*) Bantam.

— No More Boys. (J). 1997. pap. 3.50 (*0-8167-3675-8*) Troll Communs.

— One Crazy Christmas. (Sister, Sister Ser.: No. 5). 144p. (J). (gr. 5-7). 1996. pap. 3.99 (*0-671-00283-X*) PB.

— Queen Justine. LC 94-12252. (Boyfriend Club Ser.: Vol. 4). 176p. (J). (gr. 3-6). 1997. pap. 2.95 (*0-8167-3417-8*) Troll Communs.

— Roni's Dream Boy. LC 93-50680. (Boyfriend Club Ser.: No. 2). (Illus.). 176p. (J). (gr. 3-6). 1997. pap. 2.95 (*0-8167-3415-1*) Troll Communs.

— Roni's Sweet Fifteen. (YA). 1997. pap. 2.95 (*0-8167-3687-1*) Troll Communs.

— Secret Valentine. (TGIF Ser.: No. 6). (J). (gr. 3-6). 1996. pap. 3.50 (*0-671-51022-3*) PB.

— Secrets of Lake Success. 1993. mass mkt. 4.99 (*0-87086-014-3*, Pub. by Tor Bks) St Martin.

— Sister Sister: You Read My Mind. (J). (gr. 3-6). 1996. per. 3.99 (*0-671-00177-9*) PB.

— Sleepover Madness. (TGIF Ser.: No. 1). (J). (gr. 3-6). 1995. pap. 3.50 (*0-671-51017-7*) PB.

— Star Quality. (Sister, Sister Ser.). (J). (gr. 3-6). 1997. pap. 3.99 (*0-671-00285-6*, Minstrel Bks) PB.

— Summer Daze. (Sister, Sister Ser.: No. 6). (J). (gr. 3-7). 1997. pap. 3.99 (*0-671-00287-2*) PB.

— Ten-Boy Summer. (J). 1988. mass mkt. 3.95 (*0-553-19559-X*) BDD Bks Young Read.

— Toe Shoe Trouble. (TGIF Ser.: No. 5). (J). (gr. 3-6). 1996. pap. 3.50 (*0-671-51021-5*, Pocket Books) PB.

— Torn Apart. (Love Stories Ser.). 192p. (YA). (gr. 7-12). 1999. mass mkt. 3.99 (*0-553-49289-6*) BDD Bks Young Read.

— Who Do You Love? (Love Stories Ser.). 192p. (YA). (gr. 7-12). 1996. mass mkt. 4.50 (*0-553-57043-9*) Bantam.

Quin-Harkin, Janet, jt. auth. see Taaffe, Thomas P.

Quin, John J. Urushi: The Technology of Japanese Lacquer. Thompson, Jack C., ed. & intro. by. LC 95-71506. (Illus.). v, 53p. (C). 1995. reprint ed. pap. 8.95 (*1-887719-01-6*) Caber Pr.

Quin, L. D. & Verkade, J. G., eds. Phosphorus-31 NMR Spectral Properties in Compund: Charaterization & Structural Analysis. (Methods in Stereochemical Analysis Ser.). 472p. 1994. 199.00 (*0-471-18587-6*, Wiley-VCH) Wiley.

Quin, Louis D. A Guide to Organophosphorus Chemistry. LC 99-43429. 408p. 2000. 94.95 (*0-471-31824-8*, Wiley-Interscience) Wiley.

Quin, Louis D. & Verkade, John G., eds. Phosphorus Chemistry. LC 81-14956. (ACS Symposium Ser.: No. 171). (Illus.). 656p. 1981. reprint ed. pap. 200.00 (*0-608-03250-6*, 206376900007) Bks Demand.

— Phosphorus Chemistry: Proceedings of the International Conference, 1981. LC 81-14956. (ACS Symposium Ser.: No. 171). 1981. 65.95 (*0-8412-0663-5*) Am Chemical.

— Phosphorus 31 NMR Spectral Properties in Compound Characterization & Structural Analysis. LC 94-13378. (Methods in Stereochemical Analysis Ser.). 455p. 1994. 150.00 (*1-56081-637-6*, Wiley-VCH) Wiley.

Quin, Louis D., jt. ed. see Verkade, John G.

Quin, Mike. The Big Strike. LC 79-14101. 1991. reprint ed. pap. 7.50 (*0-7178-0504-2*) Intl Pubs Co.

Quin, Patricia, jt. auth. see Quin, Suzanne.

Quin, Suzanne. Uncertain Lives, Untimely Deaths: Experiences & Psychological Needs of the Young Adult with Serious Chronic Illness. (Developments in Nursing & Health Care Ser.). 176p. 1996. text 63.95 (*1-85972-497-3*, Pub. by Avebry) Ashgate Pub Co.

***Quin, Suzanne & Quin, Patricia.** Contemporary Irish Social Policy. LC 99-491003. 352p. 2000. pap. 29.95 (*1-900621-24-X*, Pub. by Univ Coll Dublin Pr) Dufour.

Quina, Kathryn & Carlson, Nancy. Rape, Incest, & Sexual Harassment: A Guide for Helping Survivors. LC 89-16160. 275p. 1989. 59.95 (*0-275-92533-1*, C2533, Praeger Pubs) Greenwood.

Quina, Kathryn, jt. ed. see Bronstein, Phyllis.

Quinalt, R. & Langenscheidt Editorial Staff. Tausend Redensarten Deutsch. 248p. 1981. 20.00 (*3-468-43112-0*) Langenscheidt.

Quinan, Jack. Frank Lloyd Wright's Larkin Building: Myth & Fact. (Illus.). 204p. 1989. reprint ed. pap. text 17.95 (*0-262-67003-8*) MIT Pr.

Quinault. Astrate. (Exeter French Texts Ser.: No. 36). (FRE.). 109p. Date not set. pap. text 19.95 (*0-85989-195-X*) Univ Exeter Pr.

— Stratonice. Dubois, ed. (Exeter French Texts Ser.: Vol. 63). (FRE.). 117p. Date not set. pap. text 19.95 (*0-85989-203-4*, Pub. by Univ Exeter Pr) Northwestern U Pr.

Quinault, Roland, jt. ed. see McKitterick, Rosamond.

Quinault, Roland E., jt. auth. see Leventhal, F. M.

Quinault, Roland E., jt. ed. see O'Brien, Patrick K.

Quinby, E. J. Ida Was a Tramp. (Illus.). 277p. 1975. 12.00 (*0-911868-78-X*, C78) Carstens Pubns.

Quinby, Henry C., ed. New England Family History. (Illus.). 866p. 1992. reprint ed. lib. bdg. 88.00 (*0-8328-2436-4*) Higginson Bk Co.

Quinby, Jane & Stevenson, Allan, compiled by. Catalogue of Botanical Books in the Collection of Rachel McMasters Miller Hunt, 2 vols. (Illus.). 1502p. 1991. reprint ed. 150.00 (*1-878598-028-3*) Martino Pubng.

Quinby, Lee. Anti-Apocalypse: Exercises in Genealogical Criticism. LC 93-28600. 1994. pap. 17.95 (*0-8166-2279-5*); text 44.95 (*0-8166-2278-7*) U of Minn Pr.

— Millennial Seduction: A Skeptic Confronts Apocalyptic Culture. LC 98-46230. 1999. 39.95 (*0-8014-3592-7*); pap. 16.95 (*0-8014-8601-7*) Cornell U Pr.

Quinby, Lee, ed. Genealogy & Literature. LC 95-739. 1995. pap. 19.95 (*0-8166-2561-1*); text 49.95 (*0-8166-2560-3*) U of Minn Pr.

Quinby, Lee, jt. ed. see Diamond, Irene.

Quinby, Marge M. I Found My Family: An Orphan's Search. Pappas, Irene, ed. LC 93-87456. (Illus.). 160p. (Orig.). 1994. pap. write for info. (*0-9627478-3-1*) Oceanside Pr.

— Simple Steps to U. S. Citizenship: Bilingual Spanish & English. Sowers, Marjorie, ed. Contreras, Olga, tr. from ENG. LC 93-87459. (Illus.). 112p. 1994. pap. text 16.95 (*0-9627478-2-3*) Oceanside Pr.

— Simple Steps to U. S. Citizenship: Complete Information Needed to Obtain U. S. Citizenship. Gallery, Lee, ed. LC 90-62900. (Illus.). 102p. (Orig.). 1990. pap. text 12.95 (*0-9627478-0-7*) Oceanside Pr.

— Simple Steps to U. S. Citizenship: Complete Information Needed to Obtain U. S. Citizenship. rev. ed. Gallery, Lee, ed. LC 92-83769. (Illus.). 100p. (Orig.). 1993. pap. 14.95 (*0-9627478-1-5*) Oceanside Pr.

Quincannon, Alan, ed. Lifestyles of Colonial America. (Learning & Coloring Bks.). (Illus.). 24p. (YA). (gr. k up). 1992. pap. 3.95 (*1-878452-10-X*, Tory Corner) Quincannon.

— More Soldiers of Colonial America. (Learning & Coloring Bks.). (Illus.). 24p. (YA). (gr. k up). 1992. pap. 3.95 (*1-878452-12-6*, Tory Corner) Quincannon.

— People of Colonial America. (Learning & Coloring Bks.). (Illus.). 20p. (YA). (gr. k up). 1992. pap. 3.95 (*1-878452-09-6*, Tory Corner) Quincannon.

— Soldiers of Colonial America. (Learning & Coloring Bks.). (Illus.). 24p. (YA). (gr. k up). 1992. pap. 3.95 (*1-878452-11-8*, Tory Corner) Quincannon.

Quince, Pamela-Denise & Blake, Tonya M. The Retirement Startup Kit: Your Complete Guide to a Worry-Free Retirement. 2nd rev. ed. 1997. ring bd., wbk. ed. 19.95 (*0-9661597-0-5*) Doulos MI.

***Quincey, Emma.** Forgotten Sins. large type ed. 496p. 1999. 31.99 (*0-7505-1362-4*, Pub. by Mgna Lrg Print) Ulverscroft.

— Her Mother's Sins. large type ed. 496p. 1999. 31.99 (*0-7505-1361-6*, Pub. by Mgna Lrg Print) Ulverscroft.

Quinchon, Jean & Tranchant, Jean. Nitrocelluloses: The Materials & Their Applications in Propellants, Explosives & Other Industries. (Physical Chemistry Ser.). 1989. text 84.95 (*0-470-21542-9*) P-H.

Quincy, Joseph. The History of Harvard University, 2 vols., Set. Metzger, Walter P., ed. LC 76-55188. (Academic Profession Ser.). (Illus.). 1977. reprint ed. lib. bdg. 111.95 (*0-405-10015-9*) Ayer.

— The History of Harvard University, 2 vols., Vol. 1. Metzger, Walter P., ed. LC 76-55188. (Academic Profession Ser.). (Illus.). 1977. reprint ed. lib. bdg. 56.95 (*0-405-10016-7*) Ayer.

— The History of Harvard University, 2 vols., Vol. 2. Metzger, Walter P., ed. LC 76-55188. (Academic Profession Ser.). (Illus.). 1977. reprint ed. lib. bdg. 56.95 (*0-405-10017-5*) Ayer.

Quincy, Josiah, Jr. Memoir of the Life of Josiah Quincy, Jr. (American Biography Ser.). 498p. 1991. reprint ed. lib. bdg. 89.00 (*0-7812-8319-1*) Rprt Serv.

***Quincy, Keith.** Harvesting Pa Chay's Wheat: The Hmong & America's Secret War in Laos. LC 99-59813. 512p. 2000. 29.95 (*0-910055-61-0*, Pub. by East Wash Univ) U of Wash Pr.

— Harvesting Pa Chay's Wheat: The Hmong & America's Secret War in Laos. LC 99-59813. (Illus.). 512p. 2000. pap. 18.95 (*0-910055-60-2*, Pub. by East Wash Univ) U of Wash Pr.

Quincy, Keith. Hmong: History of a People. 2nd ed. LC 95-41342. (Illus.). 224p. 1995. 27.50 (*0-910055-24-6*) East Wash Univ.

— Samuel. 255p. (Orig.). 1991. pap. 5.95 (*0-9628648-0-3*) Smidgen Bks.

Quincy, William S. The Three-Masted Schooner James Miller: A History & Model Maker's Source Book. (Illus.). 48p. 1986. pap. 9.95 (*0-913372-37-4*) Mystic Seaport.

***Quindlen, Anna.** Black & Blue. 336p. 2000. pap. 12.95 (*0-385-33313-7*, Delta Trade) Dell.

Quindlen, Anna. Black & Blue, Set. abr. ed. 1998. pap. text 24.00 incl. audio (*0-375-40190-3*) Random AudioBks.

— Black & Blue: A Novel. 369p. 1999. mass mkt. 7.50 (*0-440-22610-4*) Dell.

— Black & Blue: A Novel. 296p. 1998. 23.00 (*0-375-50051-0*) Random.

— Black & Blue: A Novel. LC 98-24002. 1998. 26.95 (*1-56895-565-0*) Wheeler Pub.

— Happily Ever After. 80p. (gr. 2-5). 1999. pap. 3.99 (*0-14-038706-4*, PuffinBks) Peng Put Young Read.

— Happily Ever After. LC 96-36084. (Illus.). 43p. (J). (gr. k-4). 1997. 13.99 (*0-670-86961-9*) Viking Penguin.

— How Reading Changed My Life. LC 98-30191. 112p. 1998. pap. 8.95 (*0-345-42278-3*) Ballantine Pub Grp.

— Living Out Loud. 272p. 1994. pap. 12.00 (*0-449-90912-3*, Columbine) Fawcett.

— Living Out Loud. 272p. 1989. mass mkt. 5.99 (*0-8041-0527-8*) Ivy Books.

— Object Lessons. 1997. pap. 12.00 (*0-449-00101-6*) Fawcett.

— Object Lessons. 336p. 1992. mass mkt. 6.99 (*0-8041-0946-X*) Ivy Books.

— Object Lessons. 1998. pap. 6.99 (*0-8041-9727-X*) Ivy Books.

— One True Thing. 400p. 1995. mass mkt. 6.99 (*0-440-22103-X*) Dell.

— One True Thing. 304p. 1997. pap. 11.95 (*0-385-31920-7*) Doubleday.

— One True Thing. abr. ed. 1998. 25.00 incl. audio (*0-671-04333-1*, Audioworks) S&S Trade.

— One True Thing. large type ed. LC 94-24046. (Large Print Bks.). 1995. 25.95 (*1-56895-168-X*) Wheeler Pub.

***Quindlen, Anna.** A Short Guide to a Happy Life. LC 00-25894. (Illus.). 112p. 2000. 19.95 (*0-375-50461-3*) Random.

An Asterisk (*) at the beginning of an entry indicates that the title is appearing for the first time.

Quindlen, Anna. Siblings. LC 98-30507. (Illus.). 112p. 1998. 24.95 (*0-670-87882-0*) Viking Penguin.

***Quindlen, Anna.** Thinking Out Loud. 1999. pap. 5.98 (*0-671-04451-6*) PB.

Quindlen, Anna. Thinking Out Loud: On the Personal, the Political, the Public & the Private. 320p. 1994. pap. 12.00 (*0-449-90905-0*, Columbine) Fawcett.

Quindlen, Anna, jt. auth. see Kelsh, Nick.

***Quindlen, Ruthann.** Confessions of a Venture Capitalist: Inside the High-Stakes World of Start-Up Financing. LC 99-49010. 240p. 2000. 25.95 (*0-446-52680-0*, Pub. by Warner Bks) Little.

Quindry, Kenneth E. & Schoening, Niles. State & Local Tax Performance, 1978. rev. ed. 1980. pap. 3.00 (*0-686-29037-2*) S Regional Ed.

Quine, David. Answers for Difficult Days: Surviving the Storm of Secularism. 48p. (YA). (gr. 7 up). 1998. pap. 5.95 (*0-9656512-1-5*) Cmrstone Curriculum.

— St. Kilda. (Colin Baxter Island Guides Ser.). (Illus.). 160p. 1995. 19.95 (*0-948661-58-5*, Pub. by Colin Baxter Ltd) Voyageur Pr.

Quine, David & Quine, Shirley. Let Us Highly Resolve: Preparing Families to Enter the 21st Century. 128p. 1997. pap. text. write for info. (*0-9656512-0-7*) Cmrstone Curriculum.

Quine, Hector. Guitar Technique. (Illus.). 112p. 1990. pap. text 31.95 (*0-19-322323-6*) OUP.

Quine, J. R. & Sarnak, Peter. Extremal Riemann Surfaces, Vol. 201. LC 96-45737. (Contemporary Mathematics Ser.). 243p. 1996. pap. 49.00 (*0-8218-0514-2*, CONM/201) Am Math.

Quine, Judith B. The Bridesmaids. Rubenstein, Julie, ed. 576p. 1990. mass mkt. 5.95 (*0-671-70770-1*) PB.

Quine, Ken. Living Proof: Is There Life after Death? 131p. 1996. pap. 16.50 (*1-85776-064-6*, Pub. by Book Guild Ltd) Trans-Atl Phila.

Quine, Lyn, jt. auth. see Rutter, D. R.

Quine, Maria S. Population Politics in Twentieth Century Europe: Fascist Dictatorships & Liberal Democracies. LC 95-8636. (Historical Connections Ser.). 160p. (C). 1995. pap. 17.99 (*0-415-08069-X*) Routledge.

***Quine, Roger.** Susie Follows Orders. 272p. 2000. pap. 9.95 (*1-901388-56-5*, Pub. by Chimera Pubns) Firebird Dist.

Quine, Rohan. Hallucinations. 184p. (Orig.). 1996. pap. 10.00 (*0-9648700-7-X*) Demon Angel.

Quine, Shirley, jt. auth. see Quine, David.

Quine, Timothy, jt. auth. see Brown, Antony.

Quine, Willard V. Algebraic Logic & Predicate Functors. LC 71-157092. 1971. reprint ed. pap. text 6.95 (*0-672-61267-4*) Irvington.

— Elementary Logic. rev. ed. LC 80-81978. 144p. (C). 1981. pap. 13.50 (*0-674-24451-6*) HUP.

— Elementary Logic. rev. ed. LC 80-81978. 144p. (C). 1981. 25.95 (*0-674-24450-8*) HUP.

— From a Logical Point of View: Nine Logico-Philosophical Essays. 2nd rev. ed. LC 61-15277. 200p. 1980. 26.50 (*0-674-32350-5*) HUP.

— From a Logical Point of View: Nine Logico-Philosophical Essays. 2nd rev. ed. LC 61-15277. 200p. 1980. pap. 15.00 (*0-674-32351-3*) HUP.

— From Stimulus to Science. LC 95-14062. 128p. (C). 1995. 25.95 (*0-674-32635-0*) HUP.

— From Stimulus to Science. 1998. pap. text 12.95 (*0-674-32636-9*) HUP.

— Mathematical Logic. rev. ed. LC 51-7541. 358p. 1979. pap. 16.95 (*0-674-55451-5*) HUP.

— Methods of Logic. 4th ed. (Illus.). 344p. 1982. pap. 19.50 (*0-674-57176-2*) HUP.

— Ontological Relativity & Other Essays. LC 72-91121. (John Dewey Lectures: No. 1). 1977. pap. text 19.50 (*0-231-08357-2*) Col U Pr.

— Philosophical Problems Today, Vol. 1. Flistad, Guttorm, ed. LC 93-38219. 224p. (C). 1994. lib. bdg. 166.50 (*0-7923-2564-8*, Pub. by Kluwer Academic) Kluwer Academic.

— Philosophy of Logic. 2nd ed. 128p. 1986. pap. 14.50 (*0-674-66563-5*) HUP.

— Pursuit of Truth. 128p. 1990. 24.95 (*0-674-73950-7*) HUP.

— Pursuit of Truth. rev. ed. LC 92-5606. 128p. (C). 1992. pap. text 14.50 (*0-674-73951-5*) HUP.

— Quiddities: An Intermittently Philosophical Dictionary. LC 87-11974. 288p. 1987. 32.00 (*0-674-74351-2*) HUP.

— Quiddities: An Intermittently Philosophical Dictionary. 288p. 1987. reprint ed. pap. text 12.50 (*0-674-74352-0*) HUP.

— Selected Logic Papers. enl. ed. LC 94-28372. 320p. 1995. text 48.95 (*0-674-79836-8*, QUISEL); pap. text 19.50 (*0-674-79837-6*, QUISEY) HUP.

— Set Theory & Its Logic. rev. ed. LC 68-14271. 378p. 1969. pap. 16.50 (*0-674-80207-1*) Belknap Pr.

— Theories & Things. 225p. 1986. pap. 12.95 (*0-674-87926-0*) Belknap Pr.

— The Ways of Paradox & Other Essays. enl. rev. ed. LC 75-19554. 364p. 1976. pap. 17.00 (*0-674-94837-8*) HUP.

— Word & Object. 310p. 1964. pap. text 18.50 (*0-262-67001-1*) MIT Pr.

Quine, Willard V. & Carnap, Rudolf. Dear Carnap, Dear Van: The Quine-Carnap Correspondence & Related Work. 499p. 1990. 58.00 (*0-520-06847-5*, Pub. by U CA Pr) Cal Prin Full Svc.

Quine, Willard V., jt. auth. see Ullian, J. S.

Quine, Willard Van Orman, see Van Orman Quine, Willard.

Quiner, Krista. Dominique Moceanu: A Gymnastics Sensation. LC 96-41525. (Illus.). 191p. (Orig.). 1997. pap. 12.95 (*0-9643460-3-6*) Bradford Bk.

— Kim Zmeskal: Determination to Win. LC 94-79473. (Illus.). 200p. (Orig.). (YA). (gr. 5-12). 1995. pap. 9.95 (*0-9643460-0-1*) Bradford Bk.

— Shannon Miller: America's Most Decorated Gymnast. 2nd rev. ed. LC 96-36316. (Illus.). 244p. (Orig.). 1997. pap. 11.95 (*0-9643460-5-2*) Bradford Bk.

Quinet, Bart. Cooked: Dope Poems. 32p. 1992. pap. 5.00 (*1-885710-09-7*) Geekspeak Unique.

— Trammeled. 20p. 1992. pap. 5.00 (*1-885710-07-0*) Geekspeak Unique.

Quinet, Bart, illus. see Andis, Kitrell, et al.

Quiney. Panoramas of English Villages. 1993. 29.95 (*0-297-83126-7*, Pub. by Weidenfeld & Nicolson) Trafalgar.

Quiney, Anthony. John Loughborough Pearson. LC 79-9832. 306p. 1979. 85.00 (*0-300-02253-0*) Yale U Pr.

— Kent Houses: Kent Houses. (Illus.). 288p. 1993. 69.50 (*1-85149-153-8*) Antique Collect.

— The Traditional Buildings of England. LC 89-51819. (Illus.). 224p. 1990. 29.95 (*0-500-34110-9*, Pub. by Thames Hudson) Norton.

Quiney, Anthony. The Traditional Buildings of England. LC 89-51819. (Illus.). 224p. 1995. pap., per. 18.95 (*0-500-27661-7*, Pub. by Thames Hudson) Norton.

Quing, Lao T., ed. Las Mejores Curas Naturales. (SPA., Illus.). 202p. 1996. pap. 7.95 (*0-939193-43-4*) Edit Concepts.

Quinger, H. Pirna: Kunstgeschichtliche Wurdigung Alten Sachsischen Stadt. (GER., Illus.). 64p. 1993. pap. text 7.00 (*3-364-00290-8*) Gordon & Breach.

***Quinian, Kathryn A.** Photographer. LC 98-45192. (Careers Without College Ser.). (Illus.). 48p. (YA). (gr. 4-7). 1999. 21.26 (*0-7368-0176-6*) Capstone Pr.

— Real Estate Sales Agent. LC 98-46142. (Illus.). 48p. 21.26 (*0-7368-0177-4*) Capstone Pr.

Quinion, D. W. & Quinion, G. R. Control of Groundwater. 50p. 1987. 10.00 (*0-7277-0362-5*, Pub. by T Telford) RCH.

Quinion, G. R., jt. auth. see Quinion, D. W.

Quinion, Michael B. Cidermaking. (Album Ser.: No. 95). (Illus.). 32p. 1989. pap. 5.25 (*0-85263-614-8*, Pub. by Shire Pubns) Parkwest Pubns.

Quinitchette, Lucille. Where Do Bumblebees Live? (Illus.). 13p. (Orig.). (J). (gr. 4). 1994. pap. 5.95 (*0-9640122-1-9*) Pen & Pr United.

Quinkert, G., et al. Aspects of Organic Chemistry: Structure. (Illus.). 489p. (C). 1996. 135.00 (*3-906390-15-2*, Wiley-VCH) Wiley.

Quinlan. Food Service Manager. LC 98-22672. (Careers Without College Ser.). (Illus.). 48p. (J). (gr. 4-7). 1998. 19.00 (*0-7368-0034-4*) Capstone Pr.

— Nurse Assistant. LC 98-17782. (Careers Without College Ser.). (Illus.). 48p. (J). (gr. 4-7). 1998. 19.00 (*0-7368-0036-0*) Capstone Pr.

— Paralegal. LC 97-35254. (Careers Without College Ser.). (Illus.). 48p. (YA). (gr. 4-7). 1998. 19.00 (*1-56065-706-5*) Capstone Pr.

— Physical Therapy Assistant. LC 97-32102. (Careers Without College Ser.). (YA). 1998. 19.00 (*1-56065-707-3*) Capstone Pr.

— Working with Words. (EC - HS Communication/English Ser.). 1991. mass mkt. 15.95 (*0-538-61494-3*) S-W Pub.

Quinlan. Working with Words Audiocassette. (Business Communications Ser.). 1991. audio 39.00 (*0-538-61495-1*) Sth-Wstrn College.

Quinlan, Beverly A., jt. auth. see Letts, Marceil F.

Quinlan, Charles. Orthographic Projection Simplified. 4th ed. 128p. 1986. text 11.59 (*0-02-668490-X*) Glencoe.

— Orthographic Projection Simplified. 5th ed. (Illus.). 128p. (YA). (gr. 6-12). 1999. pap., student ed. 11.48 (*0-02-677320-1*) Glencoe.

Quinlan, D. Quinlan's Film Directors. (Illus.). 396p. 1999. 29.95 (*0-7134-7753-9*) B T B.

— The Times TV & Video Guide. 1999. pap. text 11.95 (*0-7134-8443-8*) B T Burch.

Quinlan, Daniel A. & Prasad, Marehalli G., eds. Noise-Con, '91 - Twenty Years of Progress & Future Trends: Proceedings of Noise-Con, '91. (Noise-Con Ser.). xviii, 766p. 1991. pap. 75.00 (*0-931784-22-0*) Noise Control.

Quinlan, David. The Illustrated Guide to Film Directors. LC 83-10572. (Illus.). 336p. 1983. 44.00 (*0-389-20408-0*, N7293) B&N Imports.

***Quinlan, David.** Quinlan's Film Stars. 2000. 34.95 (*1-57488-318-6*) Brasseys.

Quinlan, David. Quinlan's Illustrated Registry of Film Stars. (Illus.). 496p. 1995. 39.95 (*0-8050-1839-5*) H Holt & Co.

— Tom Hanks: A Career in Orbit. LC 98-145269. 1998. pap. text 16.95 (*0-7134-8073-4*, Pub. by B T B) Branford.

Quinlan, David, ed. The Film Lover's Companion: An A to Z Guide to 2,000 Stars & the Movies They Made. LC 96-54734. (Illus.). 510p. 1997. 32.00 (*0-8065-1892-8*, Citadel Pr) Carol Pub Group.

— The Film Lover's Companion: An A to Z Guide to 2000 Stars & the Movies They Made. (Illus.). 510p. 1999. pap. 24.95 (*0-8065-2114-7*, Citadel Pr) Carol Pub Group.

Quinlan, David A., jt. auth. see Dunham, George R.

Quinlan, Donald M., jt. auth. see Harrow, Martin.

Quinlan, Edwin G. Flight Instructor's Lesson Plan Handbook: Airline Pilot Training for Private-Commercial Practical Instrument Certificates-Rating, Based on the FAA Practical Test Standards. LC 94-94272. (Illus.). 300p. 1997. spiral bd. 49.95 (*0-9641188-0-7*) Aviators Pub.

Quinlan, George P. Agility Course Notebook. (Illus.). 1994. ring bd. 22.95 (*1-888994-02-9*) Howln Moon.

***Quinlan, Gudrun.** Dusty Dreams. 1999. pap. write for info. (*1-58235-208-9*) Watermrk Pr.

Quinlan, Hamid, ed. see Abdul Fattah Rashid Hamid.

Quinlan, Hamid, ed. see Abdulhamid Jodah Al Sahhar.

Quinlan, Hamid, ed. see Abu-Saud, Mahmoud.

Quinlan, Hamid, ed. see Choudhury, Masudul A.

Quinlan, Hamid, ed. see El Liwaru, Saidi J. & El Liwaru, Maisha Z.

Quinlan, Hamid, ed. see Kishta, Leila.

Quinlan, Hamid, jt. tr. see Campbell, Charles A.

Quinlan, J. Ross. Applications of Expert Systems, Vol. 1. 224p. (C). 1987. text 26.95 (*0-201-17449-9*) Addison-Wesley.

— Applications of Expert Systems, Vol. 2. 1989. text 36.75 (*0-201-41655-7*) Addison-Wesley.

— C4.5: Programs for Machine Learning. LC 92-32653. (Representation & Reasoning Ser.). 302p. 1993. 53.95 (*1-55860-238-0*); 77.95 incl. disk (*1-55860-240-2*) Morgan Kaufmann.

Quinlan, James E. History of Sullivan County. rev. ed. Gold, David M., ed. & intro. by. LC 93-83400. xi, 239p. (Orig.). 1993. reprint ed. pap. 19.95 (*0-9636097-0-X*) Marielle Pr.

***Quinlan, Jane.** Karibu Means Welcome. Bland, Linda, ed. (Illus.). 36p. (J). (gr. 3-6). 1999. pap. text 10.00 (*0-9678688-0-7*) Ursuline Sisters.

Quinlan, John. God Is with You: Hospital Notes & Prayers. 55p. (Orig.). 1986. pap. 1.95 (*0-86217-252-7*, Pub. by Veritas Pubns) St Mut.

— Loved & Lost: The Journey Through Dying, Death, & Bereavement. LC 96-8727. 108p. (Orig.). 1997. pap. text 9.95 (*0-8146-2439-1*, Liturg Pr Bks) Liturgical Pr.

***Quinlan, Joseph P.** Global Engagement: How American Companies Really Compete in the Global Economy. LC 00-31532. 256p. 2000. 24.95 (*0-8092-2670-7*, Contemporary Bks) NTC Contemp Pub Co.

Quinlan, Joseph P. Vietnam: Business Opportunities & Risks. LC 94-67837. 178p. (Orig.). 1994. pap. 19.95 (*1-881896-10-2*) Pacific View Pr.

Quinlan, Joseph P. & Stevens, Kathryn L. 101 Trends Every Investor Should Know about the Global Economy. LC 97-46461. 240p. 1998. pap. 17.95 (*0-8092-2976-5*, 297650, Contemporary Bks) NTC Contemp Pub Co.

Quinlan, Kathryn A. Actor. LC 97-35228. (Careers Without College Ser.). (YA). (gr. 3 up). 1998. 19.00 (*1-56065-699-9*) Capstone Pr.

— Actor. (Careers Without College Ser.). (Illus.). 48p. (J). (gr. 3-7). 1998. 19.00 (*0-516-21278-8*) Childrens.

— Child Care Worker. LC 98-7185. (Careers Without College Ser.). (J). 1999. 19.00 (*0-7368-0032-8*, Cpstone High Low) Capstone Pr.

— Child Care Worker. (Careers Without College Ser.). 1998. 19.00 (*0-516-21394-6*) Childrens.

— Customer Service Representative. LC 98-31593. (Careers Without College Ser.). (J). (gr. 3-4). 1999. 19.00 (*0-7368-0174-X*, Cpstone High Low) Capstone Pr.

***Quinlan, Kathryn A.** Customer Service Representative. 1999. 19.93 (*0-516-21771-2*) Capstone Pr.

— Food Service Manager. (Careers Without College Ser.). (J). 1998. 19.00 (*0-516-21396-2*) Childrens.

Quinlan, Kathryn A. Makeup Artist. LC 98-45187. (Careers Without College Ser.). (J). (gr. 3-4). 1999. write for info. (*0-7368-0175-8*) Capstone Pr.

***Quinlan, Kathryn A.** Makeup Artist. 1999. 19.93 (*0-516-21773-9*) Capstone Pr.

— Nurse Assistant. (Careers Without College Ser.). (J). 1998. 19.00 (*0-516-21398-9*) Childrens.

Quinlan, Kathryn A. Occupational Therapy Aide. LC 98-7184. (Careers Without College Ser.). (J). 1998. 19.00 (*0-7368-0037-9*, Cpstone High Low) Capstone Pr.

— Occupational Therapy Aide. (Careers Without College Ser.). (J). 1998. 19.00 (*0-516-21399-7*) Childrens.

— Paralegal. (Careers Without College Ser.). (Illus.). 48p. (J). (gr. 3-7). 1998. 19.00 (*0-516-21285-0*) Childrens.

***Quinlan, Kathryn A.** Photographer. 1999. 19.93 (*0-516-21774-7*) Capstone Pr.

Quinlan, Kathryn A. Physical Therapist Assistant. (Careers Without College Ser.). (Illus.). 48p. (J). (gr. 3-7). 1998. 19.00 (*0-516-21286-9*) Childrens.

***Quinlan, Kathryn A.** Real Estate Sales Agent. 1999. 19.93 (*0-516-21776-3*) Capstone Pr.

Quinlan, Kathryn A., jt. auth. see Kent, Deborah.

Quinlan, Kieran. Walker Percy, the Last Catholic Novelist. 1998. pap. text 11.95 (*0-8071-2298-X*) La State U Pr.

Quinlan, Lilith, et al, eds. This Is Where I Love: A Journal by Appalachian Women. (Common Ground Ser.: Vol. IX). (Illus.). 110p. (Orig.). 1997. pap. 10.00 (*1-884478-08-5*) Common Grnd.

Quinlan, Maurice J. Samuel Johnson: A Layman's Religion. LC 64-10260. 256p. 1964. reprint ed. pap. 79.40 (*0-608-01975-5*, 206263000003) Bks Demand.

— William Cowper: A Critical Life. LC 79-106670. 251p. 1970. reprint ed. lib. bdg. 55.00 (*0-8371-3425-0*, QUWC, Greenwood Pr) Greenwood.

Quinlan, Michael. Little Lost Angel. Zion, Claire, ed. 320p. (Orig.). 1995. per. 6.99 (*0-671-88468-9*) PB.

Quinlan, Michael & Royal United Services Institute for Defense Studies. Thinking about Nuclear Weapons: Analyses & Prescriptions. LC 98-146479. (RUSI Whitehall Paper Ser.). iv, 84 p. 1997. write for info. (*0-85516-170-1*) Royal United Services Inst for Defence Studies.

Quinlan, Michael, jt. auth. see Bohle, Philip.

Quinlan, Michael, jt. ed. see Woolsey, R. James.

Quinlan, Michael J. & Sims, B. J. Sergeant & Sims on Stamp Duty. 1996. write for info. (*0-406-06813-5*, SSSD11, MICHIE) LEXIS Pub.

Quinlan, Michael P. & Minogue, Colene M. Guide to the New England Irish. 3rd ed. LC 94-18891. 188p. pap. 13.95 (*0-934665-11-7*) Quinlin C Pubs.

***Quinlan, Patricia.** Brush Them Bright. (Illus.). 64p. (J). (gr. k-3). 1998. pap. 8.95 (*0-921051-65-4*) Somerville Hse.

— On the Phone, Incl. bandages. (Life Skills for Little Ones Ser.). (Illus.). 24p. (J). (ps-k). 1998. pap. 12.95 (*1-895897-24-6*) Somerville Hse.

Quinlan, Patricia. The Real World of Engineering: Case History, No. 65. (Illus.). 24p. 3.50 (*0-614-05234-3*, CHN06503943.5M) ASFE.

Quinlan, Patricia, jt. auth. see Barnes, Lilly.

Quinlan, Patricia M. Baby's Feet. (Illus.). 16p. (J). (ps). 1996. bds. 4.95 (*1-55037-471-0*, Pub. by Annick) Firefly Bks Ltd.

— Baby's Hands. (Illus.). 16p. (J). (ps). 1996. bds. 4.95 (*1-55037-470-2*, Pub. by Annick) Firefly Bks Ltd.

— Emma's Sea Journey. (Illus.). 24p. (J). (ps-3). 1991. pap. 5.95 (*1-55037-177-0*, Pub. by Annick) Firefly Bks Ltd.

— Espanol Rapido. (SPA.). 170p. 1976. 30.00 (*0-249-38828-6*) St Mut.

— My Dad Takes Care of Me. (Illus.). 24p. (J). (ps-3). 1987. pap. 4.95 (*0-920303-76-5*, Pub. by Annick); lib. bdg. 15.95 (*0-920303-79-X*, Pub. by Annick) Firefly Bks Ltd.

— Night Fun. (Illus.). 24p. (J). (ps-2). 1997. 16.95 (*1-55037-487-7*, Pub. by Annick) Firefly Bks Ltd.

— Willy the Champion Ant. (Illus.). 24p. (J). (ps up). 1996. pap. write for info. (*0-88753-240-3*) Black Moss.

Quinlan, Patrick. The Devil & Johnny Dog Food. 180p. (Orig.). 1996. pap. 9.95 (*1-57502-371-7*, P01191) Morris Pubng.

***Quinlan, Paul & DeLuca, Anthony.** Romania, Culture, & Nationalism: A Tribute to Radu Florescu. 160p. 1998. text 22.50 (*0-88033-417-7*, Pub. by East Eur Monographs) Col U Pr.

Quinlan, Paul D. The Playboy King: Carol II of Romania, 52. LC 94-46945. (Contributions to the Study of World History Ser.: No. 52). 288p. 1995. 59.95 (*0-313-29519-0*, Greenwood Pr) Greenwood.

Quinlan, Philip T. Connectionism & Psychology: A Psychological Perspective on New Connectionist Research. 320p. 1991. pap. text 28.95 (*0-226-69961-7*); lib. bdg. 57.50 (*0-226-69960-9*) U Ch Pr.

Quinlan, Ray. Canal Walks of England & Wales. (Illus.). 576p. 1994. boxed set 44.95 (*0-7509-0608-1*, Pub. by Sutton Pub Ltd) Intl Pubs Mktg.

Quinlan, Raymond A., jt. auth. see Cooper, William B.

***Quinlan, Susan C.** Alaska's Ecology: Alaska Wildlife Curriculum Teacher's Guide K-12. rev. ed. Matt, Colleen, ed. (Illus.). 162p. 2000. reprint ed. pap. text 30.00 (*0-7881-8605-1*) DIANE Pub.

Quinlan, Susan C. The Female Voice in Contemporary Brazilian Narrative. LC 91-27454. (American University Studies: Latin American Literature: Ser. XXII, Vol. 7). 205p. (C). 1992. text 40.95 (*0-8204-1281-3*) P Lang Pubng.

Quinlan, Susan E. Case of Mummified Pigs: And Other Mysteries in Nature. LC 94-71027. (Illus.). 128p. (J). (gr. 4-6). 1995. 15.95 (*1-878093-82-7*) Boyds Mills Pr.

— The Case of the Mummified Pigs: And Other Mysteries in Nature. LC 94-71027. (Illus.). 128p. (YA). (gr. 5-9). 1999. pap. 9.95 (*1-56397-783-4*) Boyds Mills Pr.

— Puffins. LC 97-38983. (Illus.). (J). (gr. 2-6). 1998. 19.93 (*1-57505-090-0*, Carolrhoda) Lerner Pub.

Quinlan, Tom. Who Are You Today? A Survivors Handbook for Substitute Teachers. (Illus.). vi, 82p. 1985. pap. 6.95 (*0-9615691-0-7*) Queue Prodns.

***Quinlen, John, Jr.** Bastard Son of D.A. 2000. 18.00 (*0-7388-2065-2*) Xlibris Corp.

Quinley, Eva D. Immunohematology: Principles & Practice. 2nd ed. LC 97-42728. 496p. 1998. text 49.95 (*0-397-55469-9*) Lppncott W & W.

Quinley, Harold E. & Glock, Charles Y. Anti-Semitism In America. LC 83-4956. 259p. 1983. reprint ed. pap. 24.95 (*0-87855-940-X*) Transaction Pubs.

Quinley, Kevin M. Claims Management: How to Select, Manage, & Save Money on Adjusting Services. LC 92-18594. 252p. 1992. 46.50 (*0-934753-67-9*) LRP Pubns.

— Litigation Management. 221p. (C). 1995. pap. 49.99 (*1-886813-00-0*) Intl Risk Mgt.

— The Quality Plan: Practical Advice to Keep Claims Clients Coming Back. 204p. 1992. 19.95 (*0-9634957-0-4*) Insuranceweek.

— Time Management for Claims Professionals. rev. ed. 176p. 1997. reprint ed. 21.95 (*0-9634957-1-2*) Insuranceweek.

— Winning Strategies for Negotiating Claims. 256p. (Orig.). 1995. pap. 39.95 (*1-56842-045-5*) Marshall & Swift.

Quinley, Mary. 52 Ohio Weekends. LC 97-10053. (Fifty-Two... Weekends Ser.). (Illus.). 288p. (Orig.). 1997. pap. 14.95 (*1-56626-184-8*, 61848, Cntry Rds Pr) NTC Contemp Pub Co.

Quinlin, Michael P. Guide to the Boston Irish. (Illus.). 96p. (Orig.). 1985. pap. 4.50 (*0-934665-00-1*) Quinlin C Pubs.

— Guide to the New England Irish. (Illus.). 184p. 1987. pap. 7.95 (*0-934665-08-7*) Quinlin C Pubs.

***Quinlivan, Gary M. & Surkan, Brian.** For the Sake of Freedom & Prosperity: Philip M. McKenna & the Gold Standard League LC 99-25096. 1999. write for info. (*1-885851-14-6*) St Vincent Coll.

Quinlivan, Gary M., jt. auth. see Boxx, T. William.

Quinlivan, Gary M., jt. ed. see Boxx, T. William.

Quinlivan-Hall, David, jt. auth. see Renner, Peter F.

Quinly, Cariel. Crop Circle Cards: The Living Oracle. (Illus.). 134p. 1997. pap. 35.00 (*0-9645416-1-0*) Cosmic Connect.

Quinn. Becoming a Master Manager: A Compentency Framework. 3rd ed. 2000. pap. text. write for info. (*0-471-36178-X*) Wiley.

***Quinn.** Discourse of Western Painting 1584. 1998. 166.95 (*0-904180-35-2*) Ashgate Pub Co.

Quinn. Engineering. 2nd ed. 1998. pap. text 38.00 (*0-471-32417-5*) Wiley.

***Quinn.** English New England Voyages 1602-1608. 1998. 52.95 (*0-904180-14-X*) Ashgate Pub Co.

Quinn. The Gp Receptionist's Handbook. (C). 1996. pap. text 28.00 (*0-7020-1834-1*) Harcourt.

— Parallel Computing: Theory & Practice. 2nd ed. 1993. 15.93 (*0-07-051295-7*) McGraw.

— Practical Guide to Veterinary Microbiology. 1993. 112.00 (*0-8151-6975-2*) Mosby Inc.

— Quinn Math in Context Prelim. Date not set. pap. text 42.27 (*0-395-88806-9*) HM.

— Quinn Math in Context Ssm Prel. Date not set. pap. text 18.57 (*0-395-88807-7*) HM.

— Reclaim Your Power. 1992. 15.00 (*1-85274-102-3*, Pub. by Crucible Pr) Cavendish Bks.

— Secrets of Successful Low-Budget Advertising. 242p. 1988. pap. text 34.95 (*0-434-91614-5*) Buttrwrth-Heinemann.

***Quinn.** Shadow & Light, Vol. 2. (Illus.). 48p. 1999. pap. 10.95 (*1-56163-227-9*, Amerotica) NBM.

— Shadow & Light, Vol. 3. 48p. 2000. pap. 10.95 (*1-56163-254-6*, Amerotica) NBM.

Quinn, jt. auth. see Donahue.

Quinn, jt. auth. see Hoffman.

Quinn, Aine. Line Dancing. 1997. pap. 14.00 (*0-00-472149-7*) Collins.

Quinn, Al. Movies That Inspire: A Discussion Guide for Families & Groups. 112p. 1994. 9.95 (*0-89944-318-4*) Salesiana Pubs.

Quinn, Alan B., jt. auth. see Kolitz, David.

Quinn, Alexandra, tr. see Redonnet, Marie.

Quinn, Alfred O. Iron Rails to Alaskan Copper: The Epic Triumph of Erastus Corning Hawkins. LC 95-72053. (Illus.). 275p. (Orig.). 1995. pap. 24.95 (*0-9646669-0-1*) DAloquin Pub.

Quinn, Alfred O., jt. auth. see Church, Earl.

Quinn, Alima R. The Wings of My Soul. LC 98-93813. 72p. 1999. pap. 8.95 (*0-9628783-1-6*) Emerald Siam.

Quinn, Alison M., jt. ed. see Quinn, David B.

Quinn-Andry, Terri. Designing Campus Network. LC 97-81037. 400p. 1998. pap. 55.00 (*1-57870-030-2*) Cisco Press.

Quinn, Anna, ed. see Breeden, Terri & Egan, Emalie.

Quinn, Anna, ed. see Brisson, Lynn.

Quinn, Anna, ed. see Cochran, Judith.

Quinn, Anna, ed. see Cook, Shirley.

Quinn, Anna, ed. see Forte, Imogene & Frank, Marjorie.

Quinn, Anna, ed. see Forte, Imogene & Schurr, Sandra.

Quinn, Anna, ed. see Frank, Marjorie & Forte, Imogene.

Quinn, Anna, ed. see Frank, Marjorie & Poulos, Charlotte.

Quinn, Anna, ed. see Frank, Marjorie & Preskenis, Sheri.

Quinn, Anna, ed. see Frank, Marjorie & Standing, Diana.

Quinn, Anna, ed. see Graham, Leland & McCoy, Isabelle.

Quinn, Anna, ed. see Michener, Dorothy.

Quinn, Anna, ed. see Newton, Cathy.

Quinn, Anthony & Paisner, Daniel. One Man Tango. 1996. mass mkt. write for info. (*0-614-18003-1*, Harp PBks) HarpC.

Quinn, Antoinette. Patrick Kavanagh: A Critical Study. LC 91-4284. (Irish Studies). 493p. 1991. reprint ed. pap. 152.90 (*0-608-07622-8*, 205993700010) Bks Demand.

Quinn, Arthur. Figures of Speech: Sixty Ways to Turn a Phrase. 103p. 1993. pap. 9.95 (*1-880393-02-6*, Hermagoras) L Erlbaum Assocs.

— Hell with the Fire Out: A History of the Modoc War. 240p. 1998. pap. 14.95 (*0-571-19937-2*) Faber & Faber.

— A New World: An Epic of Colonial America from the Founding of Jamestown to the Fall of Quebec. 544p. 1995. pap. 15.95 (*0-425-14956-0*) Berkley Pub.

— The Rivals: William Gwin, David Broderick, & the Birth of California. LC 97-17728. xii, 320p. 1997. pap. 16.00 (*0-8032-8851-4*, Bison Books) U of Nebr Pr.

Quinn, Arthur, jt. auth. see Nathan, Leonard.

Quinn, Arthur H. Edgar Allan Poe: A Critical Biography. LC 97-18240. (Illus.). 830p. 1997. pap. 18.95 (*0-8018-5730-9*) Johns Hopkins.

— A History of the American Drama: From the Beginning to the Civil War. 2nd ed. (Illus.). (C). 1982. reprint ed. 44.50 (*0-89197-218-8*) Irvington.

— A History of the American Drama: From the Civil War to the Present Day. rev. ed. (Illus.). (C). 1982. reprint ed. 44.50 (*0-89197-219-6*) Irvington.

— Literature of the American People. 1177p. 1989. reprint ed. text 137.50 (*0-8290-2464-6*) Irvington.

— Pennsylvania Stories. 1993. reprint ed. lib. bdg. 89.00 (*0-7812-5820-0*) Rprt Serv.

***Quinn, Barbara.** Shared Services: Mining for Corporate Gold. 256p. 2000. 35.00 (*0-273-64455-6*) F T P-H.

***Quinn, Barney.** Mathnotes: Every Student's Handy Homework Notebook. (Panterra Notes Ser.). 220p. (YA). 1999. pap. 18.95 (*1-892680-00-9*) Panterra Pubng.

Quinn, Bernard. The Small Rural Parish. LC 79-56508. (Orig.). 1980. pap. 5.00 (*0-914422-11-1*) Glenmary Res Ctr.

Quinn, Bernetta. Dancing in Stillness. 90p. (Orig.). 1983. pap. 5.00 (*0-932662-44-7*) St Andrews NC.

— Metamorphic Tradition in Modern Poetry: Essay on the Work of Ezra Pound & Other Poets. LC 66-19365. 263p. 1966. reprint ed. 50.00 (*0-87752-089-5*) Gordian.

Quinn, Betty N., jt. auth. see Lawall, Gilbert.

Quinn, Betty N., jt. ed. see Lawall, Gilbert.

Quinn, Beverly C. Experts Speaking to NonExperts: Closing the Communication Gap. rev. ed. (Illus.). 200p. Date not set. 29.95 (*0-9628765-3-4*) Typhoon Pr.

— Technical Speaker's Guide: Designing & Delivering Business & Professional Presentations. (Illus.). 200p. 1998. 29.95 (*0-9628765-2-6*) Typhoon Pr.

Quinn, Bill. Concealed Carry: A Practical Guide. Quinn, Ele, ed. 160p. (Orig.). 1995. pap. 14.00 (*0-9649373-0-1*) B Quinn.

— How Wal-Mart Is Destroying America. LC 97-45767. 104p. 1998. pap. 9.95 (*0-89815-973-3*) Ten Speed Pr.

***Quinn, Bill.** How Wal-Mart Is Destroying the World: And What You Can Do about It. rev. ed. 144p. 2000. pap. 11.95 (*1-58008-231-9*) Ten Speed Pr.

— PBR: The Making of a Warrior. 310p. 1999. 16.95 (*0-7414-0229-7*) Buy Books.

Quinn, Bob. Windows Sockets Network Programming. 2nd ed. 640p. (C). 2001. pap. 54.95 (*0-201-18394-3*) Addison-Wesley.

Quinn, Bob & Shute, David K. Network Programming with WinSock. LC 95-35247. 656p. (C). 1995. 49.95 (*0-201-63372-8*) Addison-Wesley.

— Windows Sockets Network Programming. (Advanced Windows Ser.). 656p. 1996. pap. text. write for info. (*0-201-92457-9*) Addison-Wesley.

Quinn, Brenda, jt. auth. see Yancey, Philip.

Quinn, Brennan, jt. auth. see Ballard, Jimmy.

Quinn, Brian, ed. World Travel Guide, 1998-99. (Illus.). 1120p. 1998. 159.00 (*0-946393-92-3*) SF Comns.

— World Travel Guide, 1997-98. 16th ed. (Illus.). 1100p. 1997. 159.00 (*0-946393-81-8*) SF Comns.

— World Travel Guide, 1996-97. (Illus.). 1200p. 1996. 159.00 (*0-946393-62-1*) SF Comns.

Quinn, Brian & Mott, Helen, eds. World Travel Guide, 1995-96. 14th ed. (Illus.). 1350p. 1995. 159.00 (*0-946393-47-8*) SF Comns.

— World Travel Guide, 1994-95. 13th ed. (Illus.). 1300p. 1994. 159.00 (*0-946393-35-4*, Pub. by Columbus Pr Ltd) SF Comns.

— World Travel Guide, 1993-94. 12th ed. (Illus.). 1400p. 1993. 139.00 (*0-946393-23-0*, Pub. by Columbus Pr Ltd) SF Comns.

Quinn, Brian P. The Depression Sourcebook. 280p. 1998. pap. 16.00 (*1-56565-856-6*) Lowell Hse.

Quinn, C. Edward. Signers of the Constitution. (Bicentennial of U. S. Constitution Ser.). (Illus.). 112p. 1986. 20.00 (*0-941980-18-9*) Bronx County.

— Signers of the Declaration of Independence. Hermalyn, Gary D. & Ultan, LLoyd, eds. (Bicentennial of U. S. Constitution Ser.). (Illus.). 132p. 1988. reprint ed. 20.00 (*0-941980-29-4*) Bronx County.

Quinn, Campion, jt. auth. see Maldonado, Denise.

Quinn, Carroll A. & Smith, Michael D. The Professional Commitment: Issues & Ethics in Nursing. 208p. 1987. pap. text 32.00 (*0-7216-1098-6*, W B Saunders Co) Harcrt Hlth Sci Grp.

Quinn, Charles J., Jr., jt. ed. see Bachnik, Jane M.

Quinn, Charles U., tr. see Bouyer, Louis.

Quinn, Charlotte A. Mandingo Kingdoms of the Senegambia: Traditionalism, Islam & European Expansion. LC 77-154831. 235p. reprint ed. 72.90 (*0-8357-9463-6*, 201530700093) Bks Demand.

Quinn, Cheri L., jt. auth. see Moore, Kenneth D.

Quinn, Christopher. The Adventures of Jason. Coy, Stanley C., ed. (Illus.). 36p. (Orig.). (J). (gr. 3-5). 1994. pap. 5.95 (*1-881459-13-6*) Eagle Pr SC.

Quinn, D. I. & Day, R. O. Drug Interaction Alert. 44p. pap. text 14.95 (*0-86471-040-2*, Pub. by Adis Intl) Lppncott W & W.

Quinn, D. Michael. Early Mormonism & the Magic World View. 2nd rev. ed. LC 96-24658. (Illus.). 700p. 1998. pap. 19.95 (*1-56085-089-2*) Signature Bks.

— The Mormon Hierarchy: Extensions of Power. LC 95-7798. Vol. 2. (Illus.). 960p. 1997. 44.95 (*1-56085-060-4*) Signature Bks.

— The Mormon Hierarchy: Origins of Power, No. 1. LC 94-14854. Vol. 1. (Illus.). 720p. 1994. 29.95 (*1-56085-056-6*) Signature Bks.

— Same-Sex Dynamics among Nineteenth Century Americans: A Mormon Example. LC 95-32473. (Illus.). 416p. 1996. 29.95 (*0-252-02205-X*) U of Ill Pr.

Quinn, D. Michael, ed. The New Mormon History: Revisionist Essays on the Past. LC 91-21224. (Essays on Mormonism Ser.: No. 4). 310p. (Orig.). 1991. pap. 18.95 (*1-56085-011-6*) Signature Bks.

Quinn, Daniel. Beyond Civilization: Humanity's Next Great Adventure. LC 99-22636. 208p. 1999. 21.95 (*0-609-60490-2*) Harmony Bks.

***Quinn, Daniel.** Beyond Civilization: Humanity's Next Great Adventure. 224p. 2000. reprint ed. pap. 12.95 (*0-609-80536-3*, Three Riv Pr) Crown Pub Group.

Quinn, Daniel. Ishmael. 272p. 1995. pap. 13.95 (*0-553-37540-7*) Bantam.

— My Ishmael. 288p. 1998. pap. 13.95 (*0-553-37965-8*) Bantam.

— Providence: The Story of a Fifty-Year Vision Quest. 192p. (Orig.). 1996. pap. 13.95 (*0-553-37549-0*) Bantam.

— The Spirit Within. 150p. 1993. pap. 11.95 (*1-882421-00-0*) Insite Pub.

— The Story of B. LC 96-21664. 325p. 1997. reprint ed. pap. 13.95 (*0-553-37901-1*) Bantam.

***Quinn, Daniel.** The Story of B: An Adventure of the Mind & Spirit. 325p. 1999. reprint ed. text 23.00 (*0-7881-6603-4*) DIANE Pub.

Quinn, Daniel & Davis, Larry. Multiplication Memorization Made Fun & Easy. 128p. (J). (gr. 1-3). 1993. teacher ed. 9.95 (*0-9629746-1-7*) Texas Trends.

***Quinn, Daniel & Whalen, Tom.** A Newcomer's Guide to the Afterlife: On the Other Side Known Commonly As "The Little Book" (Illus.). 160p. 1998. pap. 13.95 (*0-553-37979-8*) Bantam.

Quinn, Daniel M., et al, eds. Enzymes of the Cholinesterase Family: Proceedings of the Fifth International Meeting on Cholinesterases Held in Madras, India, September 24-28, 1994. LC 95-39179. (Illus.). 552p. 1995. 139.50 (*0-306-45135-2*, Kluwer Plenum) Kluwer Academic.

Quinn, Daniel P. I Am Buddhist, 8 vols., Set. LC 96-6978. (Religions of the World Ser.). (Illus.). 24p. (J). (gr. k-4). 1996. lib. bdg. 13.95 (*0-8239-2379-7*, PowerKids) Rosen Group.

Quinn, David, jt. auth. see Boyd, Frances.

Quinn, David, jt. auth. see Harrap, Simon.

***Quinn, David B.** European Approaches to North America, 1450-1640. LC 98-35583. (Variorum Collected Studies Ser.: Vol. CS630). (Illus.). 350p. 1999. text 101.95 (*0-86078-769-9*, Pub. by Variorum) Ashgate Pub Co.

Quinn, David B. Explorers & Colonies: America, 1500-1625. 464p. 1990. 60.00 (*1-85285-024-8*) Hambledon Press.

— The Lost Colonists: Their Fortune & Probable Fate. (America's 400th Anniversary Ser.). (Illus.). xviii, 53p. 1999. reprint ed. pap. 8.00 (*0-86526-204-7*) NC Archives.

— The Roanoke Voyages, 1584-1590: Documents to Illustrate the English Voyages to North American under. 1990. pap. 14.95 (*0-486-26512-9*) Dover.

— The Roanoke Voyages, 1854-1590. 1990. pap. 14.95 (*0-486-26513-7*) Dover.

Quinn, David B., ed. New American World, 5 vols., Set. (Individual Publications). 1978. lib. bdg. 299.50 (*0-405-10759-5*) Ayer.

Quinn, David B., ed. The Extension of Settlement in Florida, Virginia & the Spanish Southwest. (Illus.). 572p. 1979. 65.95 (*0-405-10764-1*) Arno Press.

— Major Spanish Searches in Eastern North America. (Illus.). xxiv, 594p. 1979. 65.95 (*0-405-10761-7*) Arno Press.

— Newfoundland from Fishery to Colony. xxvi, 454p. 1979. 65.95 (*0-405-10763-3*) Arno Press.

Quinn, David B. & Quinn, Alison M., eds. The First Colonists: Documents on the Planting of the First English Settlements in North America, 1584-1590. (Illus.). xlvi, 199p. 1996. reprint ed. pap. 12.00 (*0-86526-195-4*) NC Archives.

Quinn, David B., ed. see Cavendish, Thomas.

Quinn, Dawn & Malachowski, Cindy. Faithful Followers: Celebrating a Decade of Bon Jovi. Mendel, Kathleen L., ed. LC 94-60066. (Illus.). 64p. (Orig.). 1994. pap. 14.95 (*1-878142-33-X*) Telstar MI.

Quinn, Deborah A. Conquering the Darkness: One Woman's Story of Recovering from Brain Injury. LC 98-14373. 1998. pap. 15.95 (*1-55778-763-8*) Paragon Hse.

***Quinn, Dennis.** Edmund Spenser's Faerie Queene & the Monomyth of Joseph Campbell: Essays in Interpretation. LC 00-32434. (Studies Comparative Literature: Vol. 35). 220p. 2000. 89.95 (*0-7734-7720-9*) E Mellen.

Quinn, Dennis J. Goldwater - Nichols: A 10-Year Retrospective. LC 97-38932. 1997. write for info. (*1-57906-007-2*) Natl Defense.

Quinn, Dennis P. An Examination of Kant's Treatment of Transcendental Freedom. LC 88-9600. 100p. (Orig.). (C). 1988. pap. text 17.00 (*0-8191-6969-2*); lib. bdg. 28.50 (*0-8191-6968-4*) U Pr of Amer.

Quinn, Dermot. Patronage & Piety: The Politics of English Roman Catholicism, 1850-1900. LC 91-75051. 320p. (C). 1993. 45.00 (*0-8047-1996-9*) Stanford U Pr.

Quinn, Dick, et al. Death by Deception: Unmasking Heart Failure. (Illus.). 225p. (Orig.). 1996. pap. 12.95 (*0-9653346-0-0*) R F Quinn.

— Left for Dead. (Illus.). 200p. (Orig.). 1992. pap. 12.95 (*0-9632839-0-1*) R F Quinn.

Quinn, E. V. & Prest, J. M., eds. Dear Miss Nightingale: A Selection of Benjamin Jowett's Letters to Florence Nightingale, 1860-1893. 398p. 1987. 79.00 (*0-19-822953-4*) OUP.

Quinn, Edward. Cote d'Azur Album. (Illus.). 1994. 39.95 (*1-881616-27-4*, Pub. by Scalo Pubs) Dist Art Pubs.

***Quinn, Edward.** A Dictionary of Literary & Thematic Terms. LC 99-21449. 368p. 1999. 45.00 (*0-8160-3232-7*, Checkmark) Facts on File.

— A Dictionary of Literary & Thematic Terms. (Writer's Library Ser.). 368p. 2000. pap. 18.95 (*0-8160-4394-9*, Checkmark) Facts on File.

Quinn, Edward. Max Ernst. (Art & Architecture Ser.). (Illus.). 444p. 1997. boxed set 39.95 (*3-89508-930-3*, 880035) Konemann.

Quinn, Edward, photos by. A Cote d'Azur Album. (Illus.). 45.00 (*3-905080-50-8*, Pub. by Scalo Pubs) Dist Art Pubs.

— Stars, Stars, Stars: Off the Screen. (Illus.). 336p. 1996. 75.00 (*3-931141-28-4*, 620041, Pub. by Scalo Pubs) Dist Art Pubs.

Quinn, Ele, ed. see Quinn, Bill.

Quinn, Elizabeth. Alliances. 392p. 1987. mass mkt. 3.95 (*0-373-97035-8*) Harlequin Bks.

— Killer Whale. 1997. per. 5.99 (*0-671-52770-3*, Pocket Books) PB.

— Lamb to the Slaughter. 1996. mass mkt. 5.99 (*0-671-52765-7*) PB.

— Murder Most Grizzly. Marrow, Linda, ed. 224p. (Orig.). 1993. mass mkt. 4.99 (*0-671-74990-0*) PB.

— A Wolf in Death's Clothing. 1995. mass mkt. 5.50 (*0-671-74991-9*, Pocket Books) PB.

Quinn, Elizabeth, jt. auth. see Moore, Lola.

Quinn, Eric, jt. auth. see Dennis, Craig.

Quinn, Esther C. The Penitence of Adam: (A Study of the Andrius MS.) Dufau, Micheline, tr. LC 79-19056. (Romance Monographs: No. 36). 192p. 1980. 25.00 (*84-499-3367-6*) Romance.

Quinn, Evie, jt. auth. see Young, Mary.

Quinn, F., jt. ed. see Humphreys, J.

***Quinn, F. M.** Principles & Practice of Nurse Education. 3rd ed. 496p. 1999. pap. (*0-7487-3170-9*) S Thornes Pubs.

— Principles & Practice of Nurse Education. 4th ed. (Illus.). 656p. 2000. pap. 42.50 (*0-7487-3895-9*, Pub. by S Thornes Pubs) Intl Spec Bk.

Quinn, F. X., jt. auth. see Hatakeyama, T.

***Quinn, Fawcett.** Scottish Ploy. 2000. text. write for info. (*0-312-87313-1*) St Martin.

Quinn, Flargal. Crowning the Customer. 159p. 1992. 19.95 (*0-9624808-2-7*) Raphel Mktg.

Quinn, Fran. The Goblet Crying for Wine. 73p. (Orig.). 1995. pap. 10.00 (*0-9638722-1-4*) Blue Sofa.

Quinn, Frances, jt. auth. see Elliott, Catherine.

Quinn, Francis M. Principles & Practice of Nurse Education. 3rd ed. (Illus.). 496p. 1994. pap. text 47.50 (*1-56593-295-1*, 0619) Singular Publishing.

Quinn, Frank, ed. Prospects in Topology: Proceedings of a Conference in Honor of William Browder. LC 95-25751. (Annals of Mathematics Studies: No. 138). 340p. 1996. pap. text 29.95 (*0-691-02728-5*, Pub. by Princeton U Pr) Cal Prin Full Svc.

Quinn, Frank & Humphreys, John, eds. Professional Development in Nursing: A Handbook for Practice. 1998. pap. 28.95 (*0-7487-3333-7*, Pub. by S Thornes Pubs) Trans-Atl Phila.

Quinn, Frank, jt. auth. see Freedman, Michael.

Quinn, Frederick. Democracy at Dawn: Notes from Poland & Points East. LC 97-29954. (Eastern European Studies: No. 5). (Illus.). 256p. 1997. 29.95 (*0-89096-786-5*) Tex A&M Univ Pr.

***Quinn, Frederick.** The French Overseas Empire. LC 99-46409. 336p. 2000. 65.00 (*0-275-96799-9*, Praeger Pubs) Greenwood.

Quinn, Frederick. To Heal the Earth. 1994. pap. 9.95 (*0-687-61154-7*) Abingdon.

— To Heal the Earth. 160p. 1994. pap. 10.00 (*0-8358-0702-9*) Upper Room Bks.

Quinn, Frederick, ed. The Federalist Paper's Reader. LC 92-36944. 223p. 1993. pap. 14.95 (*0-929765-35-4*) Seven Locks Pr.

— The Federalist Papers Reader & Historical Documents of Our American Heritage. LC 97-28854. 162p. 1997. reprint ed. 18.95 (*0-929765-58-3*) Seven Locks Pr.

Quinn, French. A Short, Short Story of Adams County. (Illus.). 142p. 1997. reprint ed. lib. bdg. 24.00 (*0-8328-6645-8*) Higginson Bk Co.

***Quinn, George.** The Learner's Dictionary of Today's Indonesian. 480p. 2000. 29.95 (*1-86448-543-4*, Pub. by Allen & Unwin Pty) Paul & Co Pubs.

Quinn, George. The Novel in Japanese: Aspects of Its Social & Literary Character. (KITLV Verhandelingen Ser.: No. 148). (Illus.). 330p. (Orig.). 1992. pap. 33.50 (*90-6718-033-5*, Pub. by KITLV Pr) Cellar.

Quinn, George, jt. ed. see Campbell, Oscar.

Quinn, George V. The Catskills: A Cross-Country Skiing Guide. LC 97-40020. (Illus.). 112p. 1997. pap. 12.50 (*0-935796-89-4*) Purple Mnt Pr.

Quinn, Gerald M., jt. auth. see Hansen, Hardy.

Quinn, Gerald V. The Camcorder Handbook. 1991. 2.30 (*0-8306-5305-8*) McGraw-Hill Prof.

— The Fax Handbook. (Illus.). 144p. 1989. 16.95 (*0-8306-4341-9*); pap. 8.95 (*0-8306-3341-3*) McGraw-Hill Prof.

Quinn, Greg. Tiger Woods: An American Master. (J). (gr. 4-7). 1997. pap. text 3.99 (*0-590-76777-1*) Scholastic Inc.

Quinn, Greg H. Crystals. 32p. (J). (gr. 4-6). 1995. pap. 4.95 (*0-590-48484-2*) Scholastic Inc.

— The Garden in Our Yard. (Read with Me Paperback Ser.). (Illus.). 32p. (J). (ps-2). 1995. pap. 2.50 (*0-590-48536-9*, Cartwheel) Scholastic Inc.

— Gemstones. 32p. (J). (gr. 4-6). 1995. pap. 4.95 (*0-590-48490-7*) Scholastic Inc.

— Gift of a Tree: Book & Starter Kit. LC 94-198800. 32p. (J). (ps-3). 1994. pap. 5.95 (*0-590-48092-8*) Scholastic Inc.

— Minerals. 32p. (J). (gr. 4-6). 1995. pap. 4.95 (*0-590-48487-7*) Scholastic Inc.

— Seashells: The Natural Treasures Collector's Kit. 32p. (gr. 4-6). 1995. pap. 4.95 (*0-590-48486-9*) Scholastic Inc.

— Three Hundred & Sixty-Five Meditations for Teachers. 384p. 1995. pap. 4.95 (*0-590-25508-8*) Scholastic Inc.

Quinn, Greg Henry. The Garden in Our Yard. (J). 1995. 7.70 (*0-606-07556-9*, Pub. by Turtleback) Demco.

Quinn, Herbert F. The Union Nationale: Quebec Nationalism from Duplessis to Levesque. 2nd enl. ed. LC 80-472454. 356p. reprint ed. pap. 110.40 (*0-8357-8359-6*, 203398100088) Bks Demand.

***Quinn, J.** Jungle Tales. 1999. pap. text 17.95 (*1-84018-094-3*, Pub. by Mainstream Pubng) Trafalgar.

Quinn, J., jt. auth. see Nadler, Sam B., Jr.

Quinn, Jack. Digital Data Communication. LC 93-47974. (Illus.). 416p. (C). 1994. 98.00 (*0-02-397240-8*, Macmillan Coll) P-H.

Quinn, Jack. Electronic Communication Systems. 528p. (C). 2001. 57.00 (*0-02-397231-9*, Macmillan Coll) P-H.

Quinn, James. The Handicapper's Stakes Festival: Class Evaluation, Simulcasting, Cross-Track Betting, & the Nation's New Stakes Menagerie. 314p. 1995. 25.00 (*0-688-12790-8*, Wm Morrow) Morrow Avon.

— On Track/Off Track: Playing the Horses in Troubled Times. LC 96-33872. 320p. 1996. 25.00 (*0-688-07512-6*, Wm Morrow) Morrow Avon.

— Praises for All Seasons: The Hymns of James Quinn, SJ. 124p. 1995. pap. text 12.00 (*0-9622553-8-6*, 125-408) Selah Pub Co.

Quinn, James, jt. auth. see Ertmer, Peggy A.

Quinn, James B. Intelligent Enterprise: A Knowledge & Service Based Paradigm for Industry. 224p. 1992. 35.00 (*0-02-925615-1*) Free Pr.

Quinn, James B., et al. Innovation Explosion: Using Intellect & Software to Revolutionize Growth Strategies. LC 97-22960. (Illus.). 448p. 1997. 35.00 (*0-684-83394-8*) Free Pr.

Quinn, James B., jt. auth. see Mintzberg, Henry.

Quinn, James B., jt. ed. see Guile, Bruce R.

Quinn, James B., ed. see National Academy of Engineering Staff.

Quinn, James F. Corrections: A Concise Introduction. 390p. (C). 1999. pap. 27.95 (*1-57766-050-1*) Waveland Pr.

— Criminal Justice. Date not set. pap. text, teacher ed. write for info. (*0-314-06216-5*) West Pub.

Quinn, James F., jt. auth. see Holman, John E.

Q

An Asterisk (*) at the beginning of an entry indicates that the title is appearing for the first time.

Quinn, James P. Grandpa Was No Saint: Poems. 112p. (Orig.). 1995. pap. 8.95 (*1-56474-136-2*) Fithian Pr.
Quinn, James V. Tissue Adhesives in Wound Care. 88p. 1998. boxed set 42.95 incl. cd-rom (*1-55009-067-4*) DEKR.
Quinn, Jane, ed. see Carnegie Council on Adolescent Development Staff.
Quinn, Jane Bryant. Making the Most of Your Money: Completely Revised & Updated for the Twenty-First Century. LC 97-23183. 944p. 1997. 29.50 (*0-684-81176-6*) Simon & Schuster.
Quinn, Janet. I Am a Woman Finding My Voice: Celebrating The Extraordinary Blessings Of Being A Woman. LC 98-49835. 160p. 1999. pap. 15.00 (*0-688-16743-8*, Wm Morrow) Morrow Avon.
— Yesteryear's Love, 1 vol. (Time Passages Ser.). 1999. mass mkt. 5.99 (*0-515-12535-0*, Jove) Berkley Pub.
***Quinn, Janie.** Essential Eating, A Cookbook: Discover How to Eat, Not Diet. LC 00-101942. (Illus.). 352p. 2000. pap. 24.95 (*0-9679843-5-1*) Azure Moon.
***Quinn, Jay.** The Mentor: A Memoir of Friendship & Gay Identity. LC 99-56495. 200p. (C). 2000. pap. 19.95 (*1-56023-937-9*, Harrington Park); lib. bdg. 49.95 (*0-7890-0496-8*, Harrington Park) Haworth Pr.
Quinn, Jennifer W. Medical Biology of Grief-Reactions & Management: Index of New Information. 150p. 1997. 47.50 (*0-7883-1384-3*); pap. 44.50 (*0-7883-1385-1*) ABBE Pubs Assn.
Quinn, Jerome D. Letter to Titus: A New Translation with Notes & Commentary, Vol. 35. 384p. 1990. 28.00 (*0-385-05900-0*) Doubleday.
Quinn, Jerome D. & Wacker, William C. The First & Second Letters to Timothy. LC 97-25597. (Critical Commentary Ser.). 923p. 1999. 65.00 (*0-8028-2443-9*) Eerdmans.
Quinn, Jim & Cohen, Barry. Rock One Hundred. 3rd ed. (Illus.). 1981. pap. text 6.00 (*0-917190-09-2*) Chartmasters.
— Rock One Hundred. 3rd ed. (Illus.). 1982. suppl. ed. write for info. (*0-917190-10-6*) Chartmasters.
Quinn, Jim, jt. auth. see Heartney, Eleanor.
Quinn, Joan. Successful Case Management in Long-Term Care. LC 92-49033. (Illus.). 176p. 1993. 32.95 (*0-8261-7750-6*) Springer Pub.
Quinn, Jocey, et al, eds. Changing the Subject: Women in Higher Education. 240p. 1994. 95.00 (*0-7484-0281-0*); pap. 27.95 (*0-7484-0282-9*) Taylor & Francis.
Quinn, John. Astrological Techniques, Vol. 1: Fundamental Considerations & Natal Astrology. LC 87-90722. (Illus.). 159p. (Orig.). 1988. pap. 19.95 (*0-944189-01-6*) Quinn TX.
— Duck & Swan. 142p. (J). (gr. 5-9). 1994. pap. 7.95 (*1-85371-317-1*, Pub. by Poolbeg Pr) Dufour.
— Generations of the Moon. 368p. 1995. 32.00 (*1-85371-309-0*) Dufour.
— Generations of the Moon. 524p. 1996. pap. 10.95 (*1-85371-552-2*, Pub. by Poolbeg Pr) Dufour.
— The Gold Cross of Killadoo. 106p. (YA). (gr. 5 up). 1993. pap. 9.95 (*1-85371-220-5*, Pub. by Poolbeg Pr) Dufour.
— The Historical Constitution of St. Bonaventure's Philosophy. 981p. text 72.57 (*0-88844-023-5*) Brill Academic Pubs.
— Jungle Tales: Celtic Memories of an Epic Stand. (Illus.). 188p. 1995. 22.95 (*1-85158-673-3*, Pub. by Mainstream Pubng) Trafalgar.
— The Letters of John Quinn to William Butler Yeats. Himber, Alan, ed. LC 83-9207. (Studies in Modern Literature: No. 28). 316p. reprint ed. pap. 98.00 (*0-8357-1464-0*, 207055300001) Bks Demand.
— The Summer of Lily & Esme. 190p. (Orig.). (J). (gr. 6 up). 1992. pap. 8.95 (*1-85371-208-6*, Pub. by Poolbeg Pr) Dufour.
Quinn, John & Crawford, J. M. The Christian Foundation of Criminal Responsibility: Historical-Comparative Approach to the Roots of Theological & Civil Law. LC 90-5638. (Toronto Studies in Theology: Vol. 40). 640p. 1991. lib. bdg. 129.95 (*0-88946-979-2*) E Mellen.
Quinn, John, jt. auth. see Barton, Peggy.
Quinn, John F., jt. auth. see Petrick, Joseph A.
Quinn, John J. I Wish I Had Said That... 161p. 1999. pap. 13.95 (*0-7414-0026-X*) Buy Books.
Quinn, John J., ed. Flannery O'Connor: A Memorial. 136p. (C). 1995. pap. 17.00 (*0-940866-43-9*) U Scranton Pr.
Quinn, John J. & Davies, Peter W. Ethics & Empowerment. LC 99-28642. 1999. 54.95 (*1-55753-173-0*, Ichor Busn Bks) Purdue U Pr.
Quinn, John M. Praise in St. Augustine: Readings & Reflections. 220p. 1987. pap. 8.95 (*0-8158-0430-X*) Chris Mass.
Quinn, John P. Gambling & Gambling Devices. LC 69-14942. (Criminology, Law Enforcement, & Social Problems Ser.: No. 48). (Illus.). 1969. reprint ed. 20.00 (*0-87585-048-0*) Patterson Smith.
— Law Firm Accounting. 340p. 1986. boxed set 65.00 (*0-318-22527-1*, 00602) Law Journal.
Quinn, John R. The Fascinating Freshwater Fish Book: How to Catch Keep & Observe Your Own Native Fish. 122p. (J). 1994. pap. 10.95 (*0-471-58601-3*) Wiley.
— Fields of Sun & Grass: An Artist's Journal of the New Jersey Meadowlands. LC 96-37700. (Illus.). 304p. (C). 1997. pap. 22.50 (*0-8135-2444-X*); text 50.00 (*0-8135-2443-1*) Rutgers U Pr.
— Nature's World Records. LC 97-39476. (Illus.). 224p. (J). (gr. 3-7). 1997. pap. 12.95 (*0-07-052658-3*, Lrning Triangle) McGraw.
— One Square Mile on the Atlantic Coast: An Artist's Journal of the New Jersey Shore. LC 92-38190. (America in Microcosm Ser.). (Illus.). 224p. 1993. pap. 17.95 (*0-8027-7395-8*) Walker & Co.
— Piranhas: Fact & Fiction. (Illus.). 128p. 1992. 23.95 (*0-86622-172-7*, TS-172) TFH Pubns.
— Reform of the Papacy. LC 99-38951. 1999. pap. 19.95 (*0-8245-1826-8*) Crossroad NY.
— The Summer Woodlands. (Illus.). 1980. 9.95 (*0-85699-140-6*) Chatham Pr.
— Wildlife Survivors: The Flora & Fauna of Tomorrow. (Illus.). 208p. 1993. 21.95 (*0-8306-4346-X*); pap. 12.95 (*0-8306-4345-1*, TAB Elctrncs) McGraw-Hill Prof.
— The Winter Woods. LC 76-18486. (Illus.). 1976. 9.95 (*0-85699-138-4*) Chatham Pr.
Quinn, John T. Marine Communications in Desert Shield & Desert Storm. 136p. 1996. per. 14.00 (*0-16-048749-8*) USGPO.
Quinn, Joseph F., et al. Passing the Torch: The Influence of Economic Incentives on Work & Retirement. LC 90-12352. 240p. 1990. text 25.00 (*0-88099-091-0*); pap. text 15.00 (*0-88099-092-9*) W E Upjohn.
Quinn, Julia. Birthright. (Silhouette Romance Ser.). 1996. 19.95 (*0-373-59670-7*) Mac Lib Ref.
— Birthright. (Intimate Moments Ser.). 1993. per. 3.50 (*0-373-07540-5*, 5-07540-3) Silhouette.
— Brighter Than Sun. 384p. 1997. mass mkt. 5.99 (*0-380-78934-5*, Avon Bks) Morrow Avon.
Quinn, Julia. Dancing at Midnight. 384p. (Orig.). 1995. mass mkt. 5.99 (*0-380-78075-5*, Avon Bks) Morrow Avon.
— The Duke & I. LC 99-95337. 384p. 2000. mass mkt. 5.99 (*0-380-80082-9*, Avon Bks) Morrow Avon.
Quinn, Julia. Everything & the Moon. 384p. (Orig.). 1997. mass mkt. 5.99 (*0-380-78933-7*, Avon Bks) Morrow Avon.
***Quinn, Julia.** How to Marry a Marquis. LC 98-93786. (Avon Romantic Treasure Ser.). 384p. 1999. mass mkt. 5.99 (*0-380-80081-0*, Avon Bks) Morrow Avon.
Quinn, Julia. Minx. LC 96-96077. 352p. 1996. mass mkt. 5.99 (*0-380-78562-5*, Avon Bks) Morrow Avon.
Quinn, Julia. Splendid. 400p. (Orig.). 1995. mass mkt. 5.99 (*0-380-78074-7*, Avon Bks) Morrow Avon.
Quinn, Julia. To Catch an Heiress. LC 97-94930. 384p. 1998. mass mkt. 5.99 (*0-380-78935-3*, Avon Bks) Morrow Avon.
***Quinn, Julia.** The Viscount Who Loved Me. 384p. 2000. mass mkt. 6.50 (*0-380-81557-5*) HarpC.
Quinn, Justin. The O o'a'a Bird. 64p. 1995. pap. 14.95 (*1-85754-125-1*, Pub. by Carcanet Pr) Paul & Co Pubs.
Quinn, K., ed. Horace: The Odes. 352p. 1996. pap. text 33.95 (*1-85399-513-4*, Pub. by Brist Class Pr) Focus Pub-R Pullins.
Quinn, Karen, jt. auth. see Peters, Lisa N.
Quinn, Kaye. Cars, Trucks, Trains, & Planes. (Hidden Pictures Coloring Bks.). (Illus.). 48p. (Orig.). (J). (gr. k-2). 1989. pap. 3.99 (*0-8431-2727-9*, Price Stern) Peng Put Young Read.
— Creatures of the Deep. (Hidden Pictures Coloring Bks.). (Illus.). 48p. (Orig.). (J). (gr. k-2). 1989. pap. 3.99 (*0-8431-2726-0*, Price Stern) Peng Put Young Read.
Quinn, Kenneth, ed. see Catullus, Gaius Valerius.
Quinn, Kerker & Shattuck, Charles, eds. Accent Anthology: Selections from Accent, a Quarterly of New Literature, 1940-1945. LC 70-156601. (Essay Index Reprint Ser.). 1977. reprint ed. 38.95 (*0-8369-2302-2*) Ayer.
Quinn, Khaleghl. Chi Kung: Reclaim Your Power. (Illus.). 176p. 1996. pap. 12.00 (*1-85538-503-1*) Thorsons PA.
— Stand Your Ground: The Self-Defence Guide for Women. 1994. pap. 14.00 (*0-04-440894-3*, Pub. by Rivers Oram) NYU Pr.
Quinn, Larry. A History of Magic Valley. (Illus.). 215p. (Orig.). 1996. pap. 10.00 (*0-9651074-0-X*) Magic Valley Hist.
Quinn, Lee D. Challenging Mazes. LC 75-2822. (Illus.). 64p. 1975. reprint ed. pap. 3.50 (*0-486-21177-0*) Dover.
— Perplexing Mazes. (Illus.). 64p. (Orig.). 1992. pap. 3.95 (*0-486-26945-0*) Dover.
— Puzzling Mazes. (Illus.). (J). (gr. k-3). 1994. pap. 1.00 (*0-486-27980-4*) Dover.
Quinn, Lee Daniel. Baffling Mazes. (Illus.). (J). 1995. pap. 3.95 (*0-486-28613-4*) Dover.
— Bewildering Mazes. (Illus.). (J). 1993. pap. 3.50 (*0-486-27616-3*) Dover.
Quinn, Liam. Fast Ethernet. LC 97-8720. 417p. 1997. pap. 34.95 (*0-471-16998-6*) Wiley.
***Quinn, Liam.** XML Database Toolkit: Resources & Techniques for Improved Development. 432p. 2000. pap. text 44.99 (*0-471-37522-5*) Wiley.
Quinn, Lucinda S. Jamaican Cooking: 150 Roadside & Homestyle Recipes. LC 97-1001. 288p. 1997. 15.00 (*0-02-861001-6*) Macmillan.
Quinn, Malcolm. The Swastika: Constructing the Symbol. LC 94-4683. (Material Cultures Ser.). (Illus.). 192p. (C). (gr. 13). 1994. 50.00 (*0-415-10095-X*, B4879) Routledge.
***Quinn, Marc.** Incarnate. (Illus.). 208p. 2000. 75.00 (*1-86154-048-5*) Booth-Clibborn.
***Quinn, Mark & Scott, Mark.** Step by Step Through Scripture: Reproducible Worksheets on the Old & New Testaments. 168p. 1999. pap. 19.95 (*0-87793-692-7*) Ave Maria.
Quinn, Martha, ed. see Francez, James.
Quinn, Mary. So Far from the Bamboo Grove: A Study Guide. Friedland, J. & Kessler, R., eds. (Novel-Ties Ser.). (J). (gr. 5-7). 1996. pap. text 15.95 (*1-56982-654-4*) Lrn Links.
Quinn, Mary A., ed. & intro. see Shelley, Percy Bysshe.
Quinn, Mary E., ed. Reference Books Bulletin, 1996 to 1997. 144p. 1998. pap. 27.95 (*0-8389-7936-X*) ALA.
***Quinn, Mary E., ed.** Reference Books Bulletin, 1997-1998. 144p. 1999. 28.50 (*0-8389-8009-0*) ALA.
Quinn, Mary J. & Tomita, Susan K. Elder Abuse & Neglect: Causes, Diagnosis & Intervention Strategies. 2nd ed. LC 97-2104. (Series on Social Work). 384p. 1997. pap. 32.95 (*0-8261-5122-1*) Springer Pub.
— Elder Abuse & Neglect: Causes, Diagnosis, & Intervention Strategies. 2nd ed. LC 97-2104. (Illus.). 384p. 1997. 48.95 (*0-8261-5121-3*) Springer Pub.
Quinn, Mary L. & Schleh, Eugene P., eds. Consumable Goods No. II: Papers from the North East Popular Culture Association Meeting, 1987. 343p. 1988. pap. 9.95 (*0-943373-01-8*) Natl Poet Foun.
Quinn, Mary M. & Rutherford, Robert B., Jr. Alternative Programs for Students with Social, Emotional, or Behavioral Problems. 56p. 1997. pap. text 11.40 (*0-86586-304-0*) Coun Exc Child.
***Quinn, Meg.** Wildflowers of the Desert Southwest. 80p. 2000. pap. 8.95 (*1-887896-25-2*, Rio Nuevo) Treas Chest Bks.
Quinn, Meredith, jt. ed. see Colette, John.
Quinn, Michael, ed. & illus. see Thorne, Angelo.
Quinn, Michael A., et al. Lead Paint Poisoning in Urban Children: An Annotated Bibliography, No. 1130. 1976. 6.50 (*0-686-20406-9*, Sage Prdcls Pr) Sage.
Quinn, Michael J. Parallel Computing: Theory & Practice. 2nd ed. LC 93-29813. (C). 1993. 93.13 (*0-07-051294-9*) McGraw.
Quinn, Michael J., et al. Writing Inside Out. LC 96-1364. 350p. (C). 1997. pap. 50.00 (*0-673-46988-3*) Addson-Wesley Educ.
Quinn, Michael J., jt. auth. see Hatcher, Philip J.
Quinn, Michael L. The Semiotic Stage: Prague School Theatre Theory. LC 92-37227. (Pittsburgh Studies in Theatre & Culture: Vol. 1). (Illus.). 166p. (C). 1995. text 42.95 (*0-8204-1877-3*) P Lang Pubng.
Quinn, Michael L., jt. auth. see Wolcott, John R.
Quinn, Michelle. Katherine Gibb's Handbook of Business English. 288p. 1987. pap. 5.95 (*0-02-047440-7*) Macmillan.
Quinn, Mickey & Quinn, Terri. How to Pray with Your Children. 1989. pap. 45.00 (*0-905092-91-0*, Pub. by Veritas Pubns) St Mut.
— How to Talk to Your Child about Sex. 1989. pap. 22.00 (*0-86217-057-5*, Pub. by Veritas Pubns) St Mut.
Quinn-Musgrove, Sandra L. & Kanter, Sanford. America's Royalty: All the President's Children. expanded rev. ed. LC 95-7545. 320p. 1995. lib. bdg. 65.00 (*0-313-29535-2*, Greenwood Pr) Greenwood.
Quinn-Musgrove, Sandra L., jt. auth. see Doherty, Edward J.
Quinn, N. & Wenning, Gregor. Multiple System Atrophy. 256p. 1999. text 85.00 (*0-7506-2359-4*) Buttrwrth-Heinemann.
Quinn, Nancy D., jt. auth. see Quinn, Robert J.
Quinn, Naomi, jt. auth. see Strauss, Claudia.
Quinn, Naomi, jt. ed. see Holland, Dorothy.
Quinn, Niall. Stolen Air. LC 89-50973. (Illus.). 116p. 1989. 19.95 (*0-86327-157-X*); pap. 8.95 (*0-86327-158-8*) Dufour.
Quinn, Niall & Jenner, Peter, eds. Disorders of Movement: Clinical, Pharmacological & Physiological Aspects. 567p. 1989. text 178.00 (*0-12-569685-X*) Acad Pr.
Quinn, Noelle, jt. auth. see West, Kari.
Quinn, P. E. Radical Departure. 186p. 1999. pap. 13.95 (*0-7414-0035-9*) Buy Books.
Quinn, P. J., et al, eds. Microbiological & Parasitic Diseases of the Dog & Cat. (Illus.). 500p. 1997. text 90.00 (*0-7020-1985-2*, Pub. by W B Saunders) Saunders.
Quinn, P. J. & Cherry, R. J., eds. Structural & Dynamic Properties of Lipids & Membranes. (Portland Press Research Monographs: Vol. 3). 250p. (C). 1992. text 85.00 (*1-85578-014-3*, Pub. by Portland Pr Ltd) Ashgate Pub Co.
Quinn, P. J. & Harwood, J., eds. Plant Lipid Biochemistry, Structure & Utilization. 483p. (C). 1991. text 80.75 (*1-85578-003-8*, Pub. by Portland Pr Ltd) Ashgate Pub Co.
Quinn, P. J. & Kagan, V. Subcellular Biochemistry Vol. 30: Fat-Soluble Vitamins. (Illus.). 560p. (C). 1998. text 139.50 (*0-306-45846-2*, Kluwer Plenum) Kluwer Academic.
Quinn, Paris. Shadow & Light, Vol. 1. (Illus.). 48p. 1998. pap. 10.95 (*1-56163-199-X*, Amerotica) NBM.
Quinn, Patricia. Discover Nutritional Therapy: A First-Step Handbook to Better Health. LC 98-84067. (Discover Ser.). (Illus.). 120p. 1998. pap. 8.95 (*1-56975-135-8*) Ulysses Pr.
Quinn, Patricia O. Adolescents & ADD: Gaining the Advantage. 128p. (YA). (gr. 8-12). 1995. pap. 12.95 (*0-945354-70-3*) Am Psychol.
— Attention Deficit Disorder: Diagnosis & Treatment from Infancy to Adulthood. LC 96-35535. (Basic Principles into Practice Ser.: No. 13). 240p. 1996. pap. 23.95 (*0-87630-811-6*) Brunner-Mazel.
Quinn, Patricia O., ed. ADD & the College Student: A Guide for High School & College Students with Attention Deficit Disorder. LC 93-36668. 128p. 1994. pap. 13.95 (*0-945354-58-4*) Am Psychol.
Quinn, Patricia O. & McCormick, Anne E., eds. Re-Think AD-HD: A Guide for Fostering Success in Students at the College Level. LC 98-38161. 112p. 1998. pap. text 23.95 (*0-9660366-3-8*) Advantage Books.
Quinn, Patricia O. & Stern, Judith M. The "Putting on the Brakes" Activity Book for Young People with ADHD. (Illus.). 88p. (J). (gr. 3-8). 1993. pap. 14.95 (*0-945354-57-6*) Am Psychol.
***Quinn, Patricia O. & Stern, Judith M., eds.** The Best of "Brakes" An Activity Book for Kids with ADD. LC 99-57770. (Illus.). 96p. (J). (gr. 2-8). 2000. pap. 14.95 (*1-55798-661-4*, 441-6614, Magination Press) Am Psychol.
***Quinn, Patricia O., et al.** Coaching College Students with AD-HD: Issues & Answers. 168p. 2000. pap. 12.95 (*0-9660366-7-0*) Advantage Books.
Quinn, Patricia O., jt. auth. see Kilcarr, Patrick.
Quinn, Patrick. Aquinas, Platonism & the Knowledge of God. (Avebury Series in Philosophy). 112p. 1996. 58.95 (*1-85972-242-3*, Pub. by Avebury) Ashgate Pub Co.
— Thick As Thieves. 288p. 1996. reprint ed. mass mkt. 5.99 (*0-425-15259-6*) Berkley Pub.
***Quinn, Patrick, ed.** THe Centenary Selected Poems. 1999. (*1-85754-126-X*, Pub. by Carcanet Pr) Paul & Co Pubs.
Quinn, Patrick & Bakke, Timothy O., eds. Quick Guide: Wiring. 3rd rev. ed. LC 96-84212. (Quick Guide Ser.). (Illus.). 80p. 1998. pap. 7.95 (*1-880029-83-9*) Creative Homeowner.
Quinn, Patrick, ed. see Feirer, Mark.
Quinn, Patrick, ed. see Germer, Jerry.
Quinn, Patrick F., ed. see Poe, Edgar Allan.
Quinn, Patrick J. The Great War & the Missing Muse: The Early Writings of Robert Graves & Siefried Sassoon. LC 92-56915. 1994. 45.00 (*0-945636-49-0*) Susquehanna U Pr.
— Recharting the Thirties. LC 96-3539. 304p. 1996. 43.50 (*0-945636-90-3*) Susquehanna U Pr.
Quinn, Patrick J., ed. New Perspectives on Robert Graves. LC 99-19629. 232p. 1999. 39.50 (*1-57591-020-9*) Susquehanna U Pr.
Quinn, Paul J. Dusk to Dawn: Survivor Accounts of the Last Night on the Titanic. LC 98-74247. (Illus.). 288p. 1999. 29.95 (*0-9655209-9-4*) Fantail.
— Titanic at Two A. M. An Illustrated Narrative with Survivor Accounts. LC 96-61655. (Illus.). 128p. 1997. 39.95 (*0-9655209-3-5*) Fantail.
Quinn, Paula M. Shadow on My Soul: Overcoming Addiction to Suicide. 188p. (Orig.). 1995. pap. 14.95 (*1-879198-13-4*) Knwldg Ideas & Trnds.
Quinn, Peggy. Understanding Disability: A Lifespan Approach. LC 97-4852. (Sourcebooks for the Human Services Ser.). 232p. 1997. 56.00 (*0-7619-0526-X*); pap. 21.95 (*0-7619-0527-8*) Sage.
Quinn, Peter J., ed. Observatory Operations to Optimize Scientific Return. LC 99-192205. (Proceedings of SPIE Ser.: Vol. 3349). 490p. 1998. 107.00 (*0-8194-2796-9*) SPIE.
Quinn, Peter J., jt. auth. see Kagan, Valerian E.
Quinn, Peyton. A Bouncer's Guide to Barroom Brawling: Dealing with the Sucker Puncher, Streetfighter & Ambusher. (Illus.). 264p. 1990. pap. 21.95 (*0-87364-586-3*) Paladin Pr.
— Real Fighting: Adrenaline Stress Conditioning Through Scenario-Based Training. (Illus.). 192p. 1996. pap. 19.95 (*0-87364-893-5*) Paladin Pr.
Quinn, Phil E. Cry Out! 1988. pap. 12.95 (*0-687-10014-3*) Abingdon.
— From Victim to Victory: Prescriptions from a Survivor of Child Abuse. LC 94-79240. 240p. (Orig.). 1994. pap. 12.95 (*0-687-13655-5*) Abingdon.
— The Golden Rule of Parenting: Using Discipline Wisely. LC 88-34138. 1989. pap. 11.95 (*0-687-15515-0*) Abingdon.
— Renegade Saint: A Story of Hope by a Child Abuse Survivor. 1989. pap. 12.95 (*0-687-36131-1*) Abingdon.
***Quinn, Philip L. & Meeker, Kevin.** The Philosophical Challenge of Religious Diversity. LC 98-33341. 256p. (C). 1999. text 45.00 (*0-19-512154-6*); pap. text 24.95 (*0-19-512155-4*) OUP.
Quinn, Philip L. & Taliaferro, Charles, eds. A Companion to Philosophy of Religion. (Blackwell Companions to Philosophy Ser.). 672p. 1996. reprint ed. pap. 34.95 (*0-631-21328-7*) Blackwell Pubs.
Quinn, Philip L. & Taliafesso, Charles, eds. A Companion to the Philosophy of Religion. LC 96-11495. 700p. 1997. 99.95 (*0-631-19153-4*) Blackwell Pubs.
Quinn, Phillip. Double. 1999. pap. text 12.95 (*1-55082-244-6*) Quarry Pr.
Quinn, Ravadi L. Joy of Thai Cooking. (Illus.). (Orig.). 1990. pap. 15.95 (*0-9628783-0-8*) Emerald Siam.
Quinn, Richard & Landess, Thomas. Jesse Jackson & the Politics of Race. 269p. 1985. 17.95 (*0-915463-08-3*) Jameson Bks.
Quinn, Richard W., ed. see Davis, Whitney.
Quinn, Robert E. Beyond Rational Management: Mastering the Paradoxes & Competing Demands of High Performance. LC 87-46339. (Management Ser.). 221p. 1988. text 30.95 (*1-55542-075-3*) Jossey-Bass.
— Beyond Rational Management: Mastering the Paradoxes & Competing Demands of High Performance. LC 87-46339. (Management Ser.). 223p. 1991. pap. 24.95 (*1-55542-377-9*) Jossey-Bass.
***Quinn, Robert E.** Change the World: How Ordinary People Can Accomplish Extraordinary Things. LC 99-50826. 336p. 2000. 27.00 (*0-7879-5193-5*, Pfffr & Co) Jossey-Bass.
Quinn, Robert E. Deep Change: Discovering the Leader Within. LC 96-22674. 1996. 25.00 (*0-7879-0244-6*) Jossey-Bass.
Quinn, Robert E. & Cameron, Kim S., eds. Paradox & Transformation: Toward a Theory of Change in Organization & Management. 352p. 1988. text 29.95 (*0-88730-156-8*, HarpBusn) HarpInfo.
Quinn, Robert E., et al. Becoming a Master Manager: A Competency Framework. 2nd ed. LC 95-36769. 432p. 1995. pap. 61.95 (*0-471-00744-7*) Wiley.
***Quinn, Robert E., et al.** Pressing Problems in Modern Organizations (That Keep Us Up at Night) Transforming Agendas for Research & Practice. LC 99-32844. (Illus.). 290p. 1999. 34.95 (*0-8144-7052-1*) AMACOM.
Quinn, Robert E., jt. auth. see Cameron, Kim S.
Quinn, Robert E., jt. auth. see Prism Staff.
Quinn, Robert E., jt. ed. see Hall, Richard H.
***Quinn, Robert J.** Oscar de La Hoya. (Latinos in the Limelight Ser.). (Illus.). 2000. 17.95 (*0-7910-6098-5*) Chelsea Hse.

Quinn, Robert J. & Quinn, Nancy D. Figure Skating Pins. LC 87-60429. (Illus.). 152p. (Orig.). (J). (gr. 7-12). 1987. pap. 15.00 (*0-9618349-1-9*) Quin Tel Prodns.

Quinn, Robert M. Beginner's Vietnamese. 513p. 1995. pap. 19.95 (*0-7818-0411-6*) Hippocrene Bks.

— An Intermediate Vietnamese Reader. LC PL4375.Q84. (ENG & VIE.). 214p. reprint ed. pap. 66.40 (*0-7837-1665-6*, 204196400024) Bks Demand.

Quinn, Robert P., et al. The Chosen Few: A Study of Discrimination in Executive Selection. LC 68-64118. 55p. reprint ed. pap. 30.00 (*0-608-17901-9*, 202913400058) Bks Demand.

— The Decision to Discriminate: A Study of Executive Selection. LC 68-65536. 170p. reprint ed. pap. 52.70 (*0-7837-5272-5*, 204501000005) Bks Demand.

Quinn Roberts, Donna, jt. auth. see Morse, Sarah.

Quinn, Robin, ed. see Boog, Bob.

Quinn, Robin, ed. see Camas, Nick.

Quinn, Ruth-Blandina M. Public Policy & the Arts: A Comparative Study of Great Britain & Ireland. LC 97-78099. (Illus.). 352p. 1998. text 72.95 (*1-84014-174-3*, Pub. by Ashgate Pub) Ashgate Pub Co.

Quinn, Sally. The Party: A Guide to Adventurous Entertaining. LC 97-29874. 224p. 1997. 23.50 (*0-684-81144-8*) S&S Trade.

— The Party: A Guide to Adventurous Entertaining. (Illus.). 224p. 1998. pap. 12.00 (*0-684-84960-7*) S&S Trade.

Quinn, Sandra L. & Kantner, Sanford. The Lowdown on Higher Education: Straight Talk to Returning Students. 125p. (C). 1988. pap. 9.95 (*0-8290-1437-3*); text 19.50 (*0-8290-1436-5*) Irvington.

Quinn, Seabury. Weird Crimes & Servants of Satan. 1997. 22.00 (*1-55246-020-7*); pap. 12.00 (*1-55246-021-5*) Battered Silicon.

Quinn, Shelley M. The Historical Development of Surrealism & the Relationships Between Hemispheric Specializations of the Brain. LC 91-28392. (Studies in Comparative Literature: Vol. 16). 224p. 1991. lib. bdg. 89.95 (*0-7734-9738-2*) E Mellen.

Quinn, Shirley & Irvings, Susan. Active Reading in the Arts & Sciences. 3rd ed. 482p. (C). 1997. pap. text, teacher ed. write for info. (*0-205-26465-4*, T6465-3) Allyn.

Quinn, Shirley & Irvings, Susan F. Active Reading in the Arts & Sciences. 3rd ed. LC 96-20704. 482p. 1996. pap. text 40.00 (*0-205-20047-8*, T6046-1) Allyn.

***Quinn, Sholeh Alysia.** Historical Writing During the Reign of Shah 0abbas: Ideology, Imitation & Legitimacy in Safavid Chronicles. LC 00-23477. 176p. 2000. 32.50 (*0-87480-643-7*) U of Utah Pr.

Quinn-Smith, Kara. God's Promises for a Healthy Baby: Speaking Words of Life into Your Unborn Child. (Illus.). 134p. (Orig.). 1997. pap. 11.98 (*1-888246-07-3*) Covenant IL.

— God's Promises for Your Baby. 1999. pap. 12.99 (*0-7852-0028-2*) Nelson.

Quinn, Stephanie, ed. Why Vergil? A Collection of Interpretations. LC 99-51845. 451p. 1999. 80.00 (*0-86516-435-5*) Bolchazy-Carducci.

— Why Vergil? A Collection of Interpretations. LC 99-51845. 1999. pap. 40.00 (*0-86516-418-5*) Bolchazy-Carducci.

***Quinn, Stephen C.** Newsgathering on the Net: An Internet Guide for Australian Journalists. 250p. 1999. pap. 29.95 (*0-7329-5599-8*, Pub. by Macmill Educ) Paul & Co Pubs.

Quinn, Sunny. Morning Mosh: Morning Radio Show Prep. 216p. 1998. pap. 29.95 (*0-9660531-1-7*) Airwave Pub.

— Put Your Mouth Where the Money Is: Get Your Voice on Radio & TV Commercials. LC 97-94503. 176p. 1998. pap. 49.95 (*0-9660531-0-9*) Airwave Pub.

***Quinn, Sunny.** Tales of the American Band: Grand Funk Railroad. LC 99-94698. (Illus.). 575p. 1999. pap. 29.95 (*0-9660531-2-5*) Airwave Pub.

Quinn, Susan. Marie Curie. 512p. 1996. pap. 17.50 (*0-201-88794-0*) Addison-Wesley.

Quinn, T. Anthony. Carving up California: A History of Redistricting, 1951-1984. 334p. 1985. pap. text 40.00 (*1-883638-03-8*) Rose Inst.

— Into the Political Thicket: California's 1951 Reapportionment. 57p. 1980. pap. text 13.50 (*1-883638-06-2*) Rose Inst.

— The Political Geography of California. 132p. 1981. pap. text 23.75 (*1-883638-18-6*) Rose Inst.

— Power Unbridled: The Nineteen Sixty-One Redistricting of California. 50p. 1980. pap. text 12.50 (*1-883638-05-4*) Rose Inst.

Quinn, T. F. Physical Analysis for Tribology. (Illus.). 506p. (C). 1991. text 150.00 (*0-521-32602-8*) Cambridge U Pr.

Quinn, T. J. & McNamara, T. F. Issues in Second Language Learning, General & Particular. 132p. (C). 1988. 51.00 (*0-7300-0550-X*, Pub. by Deakin Univ) St Mut.

Quinn, T. J., et al. The Healthy Lifestyle. (Illus.). 220p. 1987. pap. 24.95 (*0-685-18371-8*) Mouvement Pubns.

Quinn, T. J., jt. ed. see Crovini, L.

Quinn, Tara T. L' Amour Bafoue. (FRE.). 1998. mass mkt. 4.99 (*0-373-38305-3*, 1-38305-8) Harlequin Bks.

— Another Man's Child. (Superromance Ser.). 1997. per. 3.99 (*0-373-70729-0*, 1-70729-8) Harlequin Bks.

— The Birth Mother. (Superromance Ser.). 1996. per. 3.99 (*0-373-70696-0*, 1-70696-9) Harlequin Bks.

— Dare to Love. 1994. per. 3.50 (*0-373-70600-6*, 1-70600-1) Harlequin Bks.

— Father: Unknown: 9 Months Later. (Superromance Ser.). 1998. per. 4.25 (*0-373-70784-3*, 1-70784-3) Harlequin Bks.

— Jacob's Girls. (Superromance Ser.). 1995. per. 3.75 (*0-373-70661-8*, 1-70661-3) Harlequin Bks.

— My Babies & Me: By the Year 2000: Baby. (Superromance Ser.: No. 864). 1999. per. 4.25 (*0-373-70864-5*, 1-70864-3) Harlequin Bks.

— No Cure for Love. (Superromance Ser.). 1994. per. 3.50 (*0-373-70624-3*, 1-70624-1) Harlequin Bks.

— Shotgun Baby. 1997. per. 3.99 (*0-373-70750-9*, 1-70750-4) Harlequin Bks.

— Yesterday's Secrets. (Superromance Ser.). 1993. per. 3.50 (*0-373-70567-0*, 1-70567-2) Harlequin Bks.

Quinn, Tara Taylor. L' Amant Oublie. (Amours d'Aujourd'Hui Ser.). 1999. mass mkt. 4.99 (*0-373-38329-0*, 1-38329-8) Harlequin Bks.

***Quinn, Tara Taylor.** Becca's Baby. (Superromance Ser.: Bk. 943). 2000. mass mkt. 4.50 (*0-373-70943-9*, 1-70943-5) Harlequin Bks.

— Cassidy's Kids. (Maitland Maternity Ser.: Vol. 2). 256p. 2000. mass mkt. 4.50 (*0-373-65063-9*, 1-65063-9) Harlequin Bks.

Quinn, Tara Taylor. Heart of Christmas. (Harlequin Super Romance Ser.). 1998. per. 4.25 (*0-373-70817-3*) Silhouette.

— Her Secret, His Child, 836. (Harlequin Super Romance Ser.). 1999. per. 4.25 (*0-373-70836-X*) Harlequin Bks.

***Quinn, Tara Taylor.** Le Noel de l'Espoir. (Amours d'Aujourd'Hui Ser.: No. 349). (FRE.). 2000. mass mkt. 5.50 (*0-373-38349-5*, 1-38349-6, Harlequin French) Harlequin Bks.

— White Picket Fences. (Superromance Ser.). 2000. mass mkt. 4.50 (*0-373-70954-4*, 1709542) Harlequin Bks.

Quinn, Tara Taylor, jt. auth. see Macomber, Debbie.

Quinn, Terence, ed. see International Congress of Applied Linguistics Staf.

Quinn, Terrance J. & Deriso, Richard B. Quantitative Fish Dynamics. LC 97-35538. (Biological Resource Management Ser.). (Illus.). 560p. 1999. text 95.00 (*0-19-507631-1*) OUP.

Quinn, Terrence M., jt. auth. see Vacher, H. Leonard.

Quinn, Terri, jt. auth. see Quinn, Mickey.

Quinn, Terry. A Death in Brooklyn. LC 99-60445. 411p. 1999. 24.00 (*1-892323-16-8*) Vivisphere.

***Quinn, Terry.** Mad about NewYorkTown. 140p. 2000. pap. 16.00 (*1-892323-22-2*) Vivisphere.

— Mad for Newyorktown. LC 00-101732. 98p. 2000. pap. 12.00 (*1-58776-031-2*, Straw Hse Pr) Vivisphere.

Quinn, Thelma. Broken Pieces of Beauty, Vol. 1. 394p. 1998. pap. 24.95 (*1-892861-01-1*) Vision Pubg Grp.

Quinn, Thomas. The Working Retrievers: The Classic Book for Training, Care, & Handling of Retrievers for Hunting & Field Trials. 2nd ed. (Illus.). 272p. 1998. reprint ed. 40.00 (*1-55821-767-3*) Lyons Pr.

Quinn, Thomas C., ed. Sexually Transmitted Diseases. LC 91-45508. (Advances in Host Defense Mechanisms Ser.: No. 8). (Illus.). 350p. 1992. reprint ed. pap. 108.50 (*0-608-05805-X*, 205977000007) Bks Demand.

Quinn, Thomas Gene. Quinn's Dictionary & Thesaurus. LC 97-74034. xviii, 1201 p. 1997. write for info. (*1-57745-050-7*) Artex Pub.

Quinn, Thomas H., et al. Anatomy for Attorneys. LC 99-10719. 2000. 295.00 (*1-57626-030-5*) Quality Med Pub.

Quinn, Thomas M. Quinn's UCC Forms & Practice, 2 vols. 1986. 210.00 (*0-88712-369-4*) Warren Gorham & Lamont.

— Quinn's UCC Forms & Practice, 2 vols., 1. 1986. write for info. (*0-88712-507-7*) Warren Gorham & Lamont.

— Quinn's UCC Forms & Practice, 2 vols., 2. 1986. write for info. (*0-88712-508-5*) Warren Gorham & Lamont.

— Quinn's Uniform Commercial Code Commentary & Law Digest. (Commercial Law Ser.). 2100p. 1991. suppl. ed. 175.00 (*0-7913-0889-8*, 78-50306) Warren Gorham & Lamont.

Quinn, Thomas P., et al. Seminar on Intelligence, Command, & Control: Guest Presentations, Spring 1994. unabridged ed. (Illus.). 267p. (Orig.). 1995. pap. text. write for info. (*1-879716-23-2*, I-95-3) Ctr Info Policy.

Quinn, Thomas R. Old-Fashioned Homemade Ice Cream: With 58 Original Recipes. (Illus.). 48p. (Orig.). 1983. pap. 2.95 (*0-486-24495-4*) Dover.

Quinn, Tom. Collecting Fishing Tackle: A Beginner's Guide. (Illus.). 80p. 1994. pap. 19.95 (*0-948253-68-1*, Pub. by Sportmans Pr) Trafalgar.

— Grandma's Pet Wildebeest Ate My Homework (And Other Suspect Stories) A Practical Guide for Parenting & Teaching ADHD Kids. LC 98-92488. 260p. 1998. pap. 16.95 (*0-9662590-0-9*) Dunvegan Pub.

— Irish Dancing. LC 97-201080. (Collins Pocket Reference Ser.). 1998. pap. 12.95 (*0-00-472069-5*) Collins SF.

— Tales of the Old Soldiers: Nine Veterans of the First World War Remember Life & Death in the Trenches. 174p. 1995. 20.95 (*1-85695-022-0*, Pub. by ISIS Lrg Prnt) Transaction Pubs.

— Tales of the Old Soldiers: Ten Veterans of the First World War Remember Life & Death in the Trenches. LC 93-2959. (Illus.). 192p. 1993. 26.95 (*0-7509-0090-3*, Pub. by Sutton Pub Ltd) Intl Pubs Mktg.

Quinn, Tom, ed. Fish Tales: A Collection of Angling Stories. (Illus.). 189p. (YA). (gr. 8-12). 1992. 24.95 (*0-7509-0091-1*, Pub. by Sutton Pub Ltd) Intl Pubs Mktg.

Quinn, Tracy, ed. Quotable Women of the Twentieth Century. LC 99-211200. 288p. 1999. 20.00 (*0-688-15991-5*, Wm Morrow) Morrow Avon.

— Through Irish Eyes: Irish-Americans Share Their Wit & Wisdom. LC 98-45425. 160p. 1999. pap. 12.00 (*0-380-79711-9*, Avon Bks) Morrow Avon.

Quinn, V. Beautiful Mexico. 1976. lib. bdg. 69.95 (*0-8490-1481-6*) Gordon Pr.

***Quinn, Vickey L.** Teach Yourself Microsoft Project 2000. LC 99-49484. 384p. 2000. 19.99 (*0-7645-3400-9*) IDG Bks.

Quinn, Victor. Critical Thinking in Young Minds. 160p. 1997. pap. 24.95 (*1-85346-388-4*, Pub. by David Fulton) Taylor & Francis.

Quinn, Victoria, jt. auth. see CFNPP Staff.

Quinn, Vincent. Hilda Doolittle (H. D.) LC 67-28856. (Twayne's United States Authors Ser.). 1967. lib. bdg. 17.95 (*0-8057-0356-X*) Irvington.

Quinn, Virginia N. Applying Psychology. 3rd ed. LC 94-33045. 546p. (C). 1994. pap. 61.56 (*0-07-051339-2*) McGraw.

— Applying Psychology IBM 3.5. 3rd ed. (C). 1994. pap., pap. text 51.50 incl. disk (*0-07-912026-1*) McGraw.

— Applying Psychology IBM 5.25. 3rd ed. (C). 1994. pap., pap. text 51.50 incl. disk (*0-07-912025-3*) McGraw.

Quinn, Warren. Morality & Action. LC 93-2769. (Studies in Philosophy). 271p. (C). 1994. text 69.95 (*0-521-44164-1*); pap. text 21.95 (*0-521-44696-1*) Cambridge U Pr.

Quinn, William. The Saltworks of Historic Cape Cod. LC 92-83913. (Illus.). 256p. 1993. 29.95 (*0-940160-56-0*) Parnassus Imprints.

Quinn, William, tr. see Maillefer, Francois-Elie & D'Auge, Bernard.

Quinn, William A. Chaucer's Rehersynges: The Performability of the Legend of Good Women. LC 93-31914. 253p. 1994. 55.95 (*0-8132-0791-6*) Cath U Pr.

***Quinn, William A., ed.** Chaucer's Dream Visions & Shorter Poems. LC 99-35726. (Basic Readings in Chaucer & His Time Ser.: Vol. 2). 492p. 1999. 75.00 (*0-8153-3100-2*, H2105) Garland.

Quinn, William D., ed. see Krishnamurti, Jiddu.

Quinn, William G., ed. see Westmoreland, Kathy.

Quinn, William P. Cape Cod Maritime Disasters. LC 90-91663. 240p. 1990. 35.00 (*0-936972-13-0*) Lower Cape.

— Shipwrecks along the Atlantic Coast. 240p. 1988. 34.95 (*0-940160-40-4*) Parnassus Imprints.

— Shipwrecks Around Boston. LC 96-70036. (Illus.). 240p. 1997. 45.00 (*0-940160-67-6*) Parnassus Imprints.

— Shipwrecks Around Cape Cod. LC 73-92326. (Illus.). 240p. 1973. pap. 30.00 (*0-936972-01-7*) Lower Cape.

— Shipwrecks Around Maine. 1983. pap. 30.00 (*0-936972-11-4*) Lower Cape.

— Shipwrecks Around New England. LC 79-88076. (Illus.). 240p. 1979. pap. 30.00 (*0-936972-05-X*) Lower Cape.

Quinn, William P., jt. auth. see Morris, Paul C.

Quinn, William W. Buffalo Bill Remembers: Truth & Courage. LC 91-5063. (Illus.). 450p. 1991. boxed set 18.95 (*0-923568-23-9*) Wilderness Adventure Bks.

Quinn, William W., Jr. The Only Tradition. LC 96-42957. (SUNY Series in Western Esoteric Traditions). 384p. (C). 1997. text 74.50 (*0-7914-3213-0*); pap. text 24.95 (*0-7914-3214-9*) State U NY Pr.

Quinnan, Timothy W. Adult Students 'At-Risk' Culture Bias in Higher Education. LC 97-216. (Critical Studies in Education & Culture Ser.). 184p. 1997. 55.00 (*0-89789-521-5*, Bergin & Garvey); pap. 19.95 (*0-89789-522-3*, Bergin & Garvey) Greenwood.

Quinnell, A. J. Blood Ties. large type ed. (Adventure Suspense Ser.). 416p. 1985. 27.99 (*0-7089-8286-7*, Charnwood) Ulverscroft.

— The Mahdi. large type ed. (Adventure Suspense Ser.). 416p. 1982. 27.99 (*0-7089-8081-3*, Charnwood) Ulverscroft.

— Man on Fire. large type ed. (Adventure Suspense Ser.). 422p. 1982. 11.50 (*0-7089-8045-7*, Charnwood) Ulverscroft.

— The Perfect Kill. large type ed. (Charnwood Ser.). 448p. 1994. 27.99 (*0-7089-8744-3*, Charnwood) Ulverscroft.

— Snapshot. large type ed. (Adventure Suspense Ser.). 432p. 1984. 27.99 (*0-7089-8178-X*) Ulverscroft.

Quinnett, Paul G. Darwin's Bass: The Evolutionary Psychology of Fishing Man. LC 98-17664. 256p. 1998. pap. 12.95 (*0-8362-6838-5*) Andrews & McMeel.

— Fishing Lessons: Insights, Fun & Philosophy from a Passionate Angler. LC 98-3986. xiv, 313p. 1998. 21.95 (*0-8362-6839-3*) Andrews & McMeel.

— Pavlov's Trout: The Incompleat Psychology of Everyday Fishing. LC 98-18117. 224p. 1998. pap. 12.95 (*0-8362-6840-7*) Andrews & McMeel.

— Suicide: The Forever Decision: For Those Thinking about Suicide, & For Those Who Know, Love, & Counsel Them. 144p. 1987. pap. 12.95 (*0-8245-1352-5*, Pub. by Crossroad NY) Natl Bk Netwk.

Quinney. Laboratory Workbook for Multimedia Calculus. 136p. 1995. pap. 25.95 (*0-471-02111-3*) Wiley.

Quinney, Douglas A., jt. auth. see Harding, R. D.

Quinney, H. Arthur, et al, eds. Toward Active Living: Proceedings of the International Conference on Physical Activity, Fitness & Health. LC 93-29972. (Illus.). 312p. 1994. pap. text 26.00 (*0-87322-523-6*, BQUI0523) Human Kinetics.

Quinney, Laura. Literary Power & the Criteria of Truth. LC 94-42895. 192p. (C). 1995. 49.95 (*0-8130-1345-3*) U Press Fla.

***Quinney, Laura.** The Poetics of Disappointment: Wordsworth to Ashbery. LC 98-55128. 1999. 30.00 (*0-8139-1858-8*) U Pr of Va.

***Quinney, Richard.** Bearing Witness to Crime & Social Justice. LC 00-. (C). 2000. pap. text 18.95 (*0-7914-4760-X*) State U NY Pr.

— Bearing Witness to Crime & Social Justice. LC 00-. (C). 2000. text 57.50 (*0-7914-4759-6*) State U NY Pr.

Quinney, Richard. For the Time Being: Ethnography of Everyday Life. LC 98-25981. (Illus.). (C). 1998. pap. text 20.95 (*0-7914-3852-X*) State U NY Pr.

— For the Time Being: Ethnography of Everyday Life. LC 98-25981. (SUNY Series in Deviance & Social Control). (Illus.). 256p. (C). 1998. text 62.50 (*0-7914-3851-1*) State U NY Pr.

— Journey to a Far Place. (Visual Studies). (Illus.). 152p. 1991. 29.95 (*0-87722-725-X*) Temple U Pr.

***Quinney, Richard & Trevino, A. Javier.** The Social Reality of Crime. 339p. 2000. pap. 29.95 (*0-7658-0678-9*) Transaction Pubs.

Quinney, Richard, jt. ed. see Pepinsky, Harold E.

Quinn's Staff. Handbook Deschutes River Canyon. 184p. 1993. pap. 24.95 (*1-878175-35-1*) F Amato Pubns.

— Handbook Illinois River Canyon. 164p. 1983. pap. 24.95 (*1-878175-42-4*) F Amato Pubns.

— Handbook Middle Fork Salmon River. 186p. 1993. pap. 24.95 (*0-944664-03-2*) F Amato Pubns.

— Handbook Rogue River Canyon. 1978. pap. 24.95 (*1-878175-50-5*) F Amato Pubns.

— Handbook to the Klamath River Canyon. (Illus.). 1983. pap. 24.95 (*1-878175-49-1*) F Amato Pubns.

Quinodoz, Danielle. Emotional Vertigo: Between Anxiety & Pleasure. Pomerans, Arnold, tr. from FRE. LC 97-12260. (New Library of Psychoanalysis Ser.). 216p. (C). 1997. 85.00 (*0-415-14835-9*); pap. 29.99 (*0-415-14836-7*) Routledge.

Quinodoz, Jean-Michel. The Taming of Solitude: Separation Anxiety in Psychoanalysis. LC 93-9866. (New Library of Psychoanalysis Ser.: Vol. 20). 208p. (C). 1993. 85.00 (*0-415-09153-5*); pap. 29.99 (*0-415-09154-3*) Routledge.

Quinones. Dante Alighieri Updated. 202p. 1998. 32.00 (*0-8057-1636-X*) S&S Trade.

Quinones-Aponte, Vicente, jt. ed. see Gomez-Gomez, Fernando.

Quinones, Arcadio D. Luis Llorens Torres: Antologia Verso y Prosa. LC 86-83002. (Clasicos Ser.). (SPA.). 168p. 1996. pap. 8.75 (*0-940238-87-X*) Ediciones Huracan.

Quinones, Armida. Espanol Vivo: Curso Programado Para Espanol Basico. 6th ed. (SPA.). 260p. (Orig.). (C). 1991. reprint ed. pap. text 13.95 (*1-56328-010-8*) Edit Plaza Mayor.

Quinones, Brunilda. Virgen de Medugorje. (SPA.). 212p. 1993. pap. write for info. (*0-929441-55-9*) Pubns Puertorriquenas.

Quinones De Benavente, Luis. Joco Seria. (Textos y Estudios Clasicos De las Literaturas Hispanicas Ser.). 243p. 1985. reprint ed. write for info. (*3-487-06723-4*) G Olms Pubs.

Quinones, Ferdinand, ed. see International Symposium on Tropical Hydrology Staf.

Quinones, Magali. Suenos de Papel. (Aqui y Ahora Ser.). 126p. 1996. pap. 6.95 (*0-8477-0261-8*) U of PR Pr.

Quinones, Manny, jt. ed. see Cuellar, Carol.

Quinones, Miguel A. & Ehrenstein, Addie, eds. Training for a Rapidly Changing Workplace: Applications of Psychological Research. LC 96-29550. 345p. 1996. pap. 29.95 (*1-55798-386-0*) Am Psychol.

***Quinones Miller, Karen E.** Satin Doll. 288p. 2000. pap. 12.95 (*0-9676028-0-7*) Oshun Pubg Co.

Quinones, Nathan, ed. see Silverstein, Ruth J. & Wald, Heywood.

Quinones, Nathan, ed. see Silverstein, Ruth J., et al.

Quinones, Ricardo J. The Changes of Cain: Violence & the Lost Brother in Cain & Abel Literature. 304p. 1991. text 39.50 (*0-691-06883-6*, Pub. by Princeton U Pr) Cal Prin Full Svc.

— Dante Alighieri. LC 98-21550. (World Authors Ser.: No. 563). 216p. 1979. 32.00 (*0-8057-6405-4*, Twyne) Mac Lib Ref.

— Foundation Sacrifice in Dante's Commedia. (Penn State Studies). 176p. (C). 1994. 35.00 (*0-271-01309-5*) Pa St U Pr.

— Mapping Literary Modernism: Time & Development. LC 84-42899. 314p. 1985. reprint ed. pap. 97.40 (*0-608-02905-X*, 206396900008) Bks Demand.

***Quinones, Sherri & Kirshstein, Rita.** An Educator's Guide to Evaluating the Use of Technology in Schools & Classrooms 1998. Loy, Nancy, ed. 112p. (C). 2000. reprint ed. pap. text 25.00 (*0-7881-8866-6*) DIANE Pub.

Quinones, Wanda M., tr. see Fassler, David & McQueen, Kelly.

Quinonesk, Eloise. Codex Telleriano-Remensis: Ritual, Divination, & History in a Pictorial Aztec Manuscript. LC 93-46481. (Illus.). 382p. (C). 1995. text 75.00 (*0-292-76901-6*) U of Tex Pr.

Quinonez, Ernesto. Bodega Dreams. LC 99-33380. 224p. 2000. pap. 12.00 (*0-375-70589-9*, Vin) Random.

Quinonez, G., ed. Electron Microscopy for the Fine Needle Aspiration of Tumors: A Primer: Vademecum. LC 97-34984. (Karger Landes Systems Publication Ser.). (Illus.). vi, 192p. 1997. 98.00 (*3-8055-6604-2*) S Karger.

***Quinonez, Gilberto & Rodriguez, Sonia.** Dinamicas: Actividades para el Proceso Ensenanza Aprendizaje. 2nd ed.Tr. of Dynamics. (SPA.). 88p. 1999. pap. 8.50 (*0-311-11601-9*, Edit Mundo) Casa Bautista.

Quinonez, Lora A. & Turner, Mary D. The Transformation of American Catholic Sisters. (Women in the Political Economy Ser.). (C). 1991. 49.95 (*0-87722-865-5*) Temple U Pr.

— The Transformation of American Catholic Sisters. 224p. 1993. pap. 19.95 (*1-56639-074-5*) Temple U Pr.

Quinonez, Naomi. Smoking Mirror. 1997. pap. text 8.95 (*0-931122-89-9*) West End.

Quinsey, Katherine M., ed. Broken Boundaries: Women & Feminism in Restoration Drama. LC 96-5329. 256p. 1996. 39.95 (*0-8131-1945-6*) U Pr of Ky.

— Broken Boundaries: Women & Feminism in Restoration Drama. LC 96-5329. (Illus.). 256p. 1996. pap. text 17.95 (*0-8131-0871-3*) U Pr of Ky.

Quinsey, Mary B. Why Does That Man Have Such a Big Nose? LC 85-63760. (Illus.). 32p. (Orig.). (J). (ps-1). 1986. pap. 5.95 (*0-943990-24-6*); lib. bdg. 16.95 (*0-943990-25-4*) Parenting Pr.

An Asterisk (*) at the beginning of an entry indicates that the title is appearing for the first time.

Quinsey, Vernon L. & Lalumiere, Martin L. The Assessment of Sexual Offenders Against Children. (APSAC Study Guides Ser.: Vol. 1). 98p. 1995. pap. 99.95 (0-7619-0110-8) Sage.

Quinsey, Vernon L., et al. Violent Offenders: Appraising & Managing Risk. LC 98-4013. (Law & Public Policy Ser.). 356p. 1998. text 39.95 (1-55798-495-6, 431-604A) Am Psychol.

Quinsey, Vernon L., jt. auth. see Zamble, Edward.

Quint-Abrial. Dictionary French to Cap Verdien (Cabo Verdiano) (FRE.). 75p. 1997. 35.00 (0-320-00472-4) Fr & Eur.

Quint, Alonzo H. Civil War Infantry, the Record of the 2nd Massachusetts Infantry, 1861-1865. (Illus.). 528p. 1995. reprint ed. lib. bdg. 55.00 (0-8328-4633-3) Higginson Bk Co.

Quint, B. G. Arco's Clear & Simple Guide to Bookkeeping. (Clear & Simple Study Guides Ser.). (Illus.). 128p. (C). 1981. 8.00 (0-671-42108-5, Arco) Macmillan Gen Ref.

Quint, Barbara. Wall Street Talk: How to Understand Your Broker. (Illus.). 1983. 11.95 (0-8027-0754-8); pap. 5.95 (0-8027-7232-3) Walker & Co.

Quint, Bruce, jt. auth. see Lindsey, William H.

Quint, David. Epic & Empire: Politics & Generic Form from Virgil to Milton. LC 92-21709. (Literature in History Ser.). 432p. (C). 1993. text 65.00 (0-691-06942-5, Pub. by Princeton U Pr); pap. text 19.95 (0-691-01520-1, Pub. by Princeton U Pr) Cal Prin Full Svc.

— Montaigne & the Quality of Mercy: Ethical & Political Themes in the Essais. LC 97-36185. 200p. 1998. text 35.00 (0-691-04836-3, Pub. by Princeton U Pr) Cal Prin Full Svc.

— Origin & Originality in Renaissance Literature: Versions of the Source. LC 82-24789. 275p. reprint ed. pap. 85.30 (0-7837-4528-1, 208019100003) Bks Demand.

Quint, David, et al, eds. Creative Imitation: New Essays on Renaissance Literature in Honor of Thomas M. Greene. (Medieval & Renaissance Texts & Studies: Vol. 95). 456p. 1992. 36.00 (0-86698-109-8, MR95) MRTS.

Quint, David, tr. from ITA. The Stanze of Angelo Poliziano. LC 92-35532. 128p. (C). 1993. reprint ed. pap. 16.95 (0-271-00937-3) Pa St U Pr.

Quint, David, jt. ed. see Parker, Patricia.

Quint, David, tr. see Ariosto, Ludovico.

Quint, Douglas J., jt. ed. see Silverman, Paul M.

*__Quint, Emanuel.__ A Restatement of Rabbinic Civil Law, Vol. IX. 1999. write for info. (0-7657-6138-6) Aronson.

Quint, Emanuel. A Restatement of Rabbinic Civil Law: Laws of Collection of Debts, Laws of Collection from Heirs, Laws of Mortgages, Laws of Agency, Laws of Guarantee, Laws of Presumption of Ownership of Personality, Chapters 97-139, Vol. 4. LC 89-18546. 384p. 1993. 50.00 (0-87668-197-6) Aronson.

— A Restatement of Rabbinic Civil Law: Laws of Judges & Laws of Evidence, Chapters 1-38, Vol. 1. LC 89-18546. 336p. 1990. 50.00 (0-87668-799-0) Aronson.

— A Restatement of Rabbinic Civil Law: Laws of Loans, Chapters 39-74. LC 89-18546. 352p. 1991. 50.00 (0-87668-678-1) Aronson.

— A Restatement of Rabbinic Civil Law: Laws of Partnerships, Laws of Agents, Laws of Sales, Acquisition of Personality, Vol. 6, Chapters 176-226. LC 89-18546. 416p. 1995. 50.00 (1-56821-319-0) Aronson.

— A Restatement of Rabbinic Civil Law: Laws of Pleading, Chapters 75-96. LC 89-18546. 288p. 1993. 50.00 (0-87668-396-0) Aronson.

— A Restatement of Rabbinic Civil Law: Laws of Presumption of Ownership of Realty, Laws of Injuries to Neighbors, Laws of Joint Ownership of Realty, Laws of Partition of Realty, Chapters 140-175, Vol. 5. LC 89-18546. 336p. 1994. 50.00 (1-56821-167-8) Aronson.

— A Restatement of Rabbinic Civil Law Vol. VII: Discrepancies in Sales, Gifts of a Healthy Person, Gifts Causa Mortis. 304p. 1997. 50.00 (1-56821-907-5) Aronson.

— A Restatement of Rabbinic Civil Law Vol. VIII: Laws of Lost & Found Objects, Laws of Inheritance, Laws of the Unpaid Bai. 344p. 1998. 50.00 (0-7657-9969-3) Aronson.

Quint, Emanuel B. & Hecht, Neil S. Jewish Jurisprudence: Its Sources & Modern Applications, Vol. 2. xviii, 283p. 1986. text 137.00 (3-7186-0064-1); pap. text 44.00 (3-7186-0293-8) Gordon & Breach.

Quint, Emanuel B., jt. auth. see Hecht, Neil S.

Quint, Howard H., et al, eds. Main Problems in American History, Vol. 1. 4th ed. 367p. (C). 1978. pap. text. write for info. (0-534-11247-1) Wadsworth Pub.

Quint, M. Preschool Readiness Book. (J). 1993. pap. 19.50 (1-58095-988-1) Alpha AZ.

Quint, Marie. Progressive Shorthand Passages, Bk. 1. LC 80-42139. (Longman Secretarial Studies). 30p. 1981. reprint ed. pap. 30.00 (0-608-09990-2, 202522600043) Bks Demand.

— Progressive Shorthand Passages, Bk. 2. LC 80-42139. (Longman Secretarial Studies). 32p. 1981. reprint ed. pap. 30.00 (0-608-09991-0, 202522600002) Bks Demand.

— Progressive Shorthand Passages, Bk. 3. LC 80-42139. (Longman Secretarial Studies). 35p. 1982. reprint ed. pap. 30.00 (0-608-09992-9, 202522600003) Bks Demand.

— Progressive Shorthand Passages, Bk. 4. LC 80-42139. (Longman Secretarial Studies). 30p. 1982. reprint ed. pap. 30.00 (0-608-09993-7, 202522600004) Bks Demand.

Quint, Peter E. The Imperfect Union: Constitutional Structures of German Unification. LC 96-39367. 496p. 1997. text 75.00 (0-691-08656-7, Pub. by Princeton U Pr) Cal Prin Full Svc.

Quint, Sharon. Schooling Homeless Children: A Qualitative Study of One Urban School. LC 94-28783. 176p. (C). 1994. pap. 15.95 (0-8077-3391-1); text 30.00 (0-8077-3392-X) Tchrs Coll.

Quintal, Claire, ed. La Femme Franco-Americaine: Franco-American Woman. (ENG & FRE.). 216p. 1994. pap. 14.95 (1-880261-02-2) FI Assump Coll.

— Steeples & Smokestacks: A Collection of Essays on the Franco-American Experience in New England. 683p. 1996. pap. 24.95 (1-880261-03-0) FI Assump Coll.

Quintal, Claire, intro. La Litterature Franco-Americaine Ecrivains et Ecritures: Franco-American Literature Writers & Their Writings. (ENG & FRE.). 193p. (Orig.). (C). 1992. pap. text 10.95 (1-880261-00-6) FI Assump Coll.

— Religion Catholique et Appartenance Franco-Americaine: Franco-Americans & Religion: Impact & Influence. (ENG & FRE.). 202p. (Orig.). (C). 1993. pap. text 11.95 (1-880261-01-4) FI Assump Coll.

Quintal, Claire, ed. see Chartier, Armand.

Quintal, Claire, ed. & tr. see Bonier, Marie L.

Quintana, Alvina E. Home Girls: Chicana Literary Voices. (C). 1996. pap. text 19.95 (1-56639-373-6); lib. bdg. 69.95 (1-56639-372-8) Temple U Pr.

Quintana, Anton. The Baboon King. Nieuwenhuizen, John, tr. LC 99-18322. (DUT.). 192p. (YA). (gr. 7-12). 1999. 16.95 (0-8027-8711-8) Walker & Co.

Quintana, Arturo O. Pablo Casals in Puerto Rico. (Puerto Rico Ser.). 1979. lib. bdg. 59.95 (0-8490-2981-3) Gordon Pr.

Quintana, Bertha B. & Floyd, Lois G. Que Gitano! Gypsies of Southern Spain. Spindler, Louise S. & Spindler, George D., eds. (Case Studies in Cultural Anthropology). (Illus.). 137p. (C). 1983. reprint ed. pap. text 9.95 (0-8290-0582-X) Irvington.

— Que Gitano! Gypsies of Southern Spain. (Illus.). 126p. (C). 1986. reprint ed. pap. text 9.95 (0-88133-217-8) Waveland Pr.

Quintana, Debra. 100 Jobs in the Environment. (100 Jobs Ser.). 1996. 14.95 (0-02-861429-1) Macmillan.

Quintana, Francisco. Una Cita Con el Diablo. LC 90-83578. 159p. 1991. 16.00 (0-89729-576-5) Ediciones.

Quintana, Hilda, et al. Personalidad y Literatura Puertorriquenas. rev. ed. (SPA.). 384p. (C). 1996. pap. text 16.95 (1-56328-102-3) Edit Plaza Mayor.

Quintana, Kathy & Miller, Danny. G-d, Israel, the Future & You: From the Fall of Jordan to the Rapture of the Church. 200p. (Orig.). 1988. pap. 10.00 (0-9621155-0-9) Shalom Colorado.

*__Quintana, Leroy V.__ The Great Whirl of Exile. LC 99-17698. xii, 59p. 1999. pap. 12.95 (1-880684-60-8, Pub. by Curbstone) SPD-Small Pr Dist.

Quintana, Leroy V. The History of Home. LC 93-10204. 96p. 1993. pap. 9.00 (0-927534-36-3) Biling Rev-Pr.

— Interrogations. (Vietnam Generation Ser.). 104p. (Orig.). (C). 1990. pap. 10.00 (0-9628524-5-7) Burning Cities Pr.

— My Hair Turning Gray among Strangers. LC 95-31049. 88p. (Orig.). (C). 1996. pap. 9.00 (0-927534-57-6) Biling Rev-Pr.

Quintana, Marlou J., jt. auth. see Sherman, Lisa.

Quintana, Patricia. Cuisine of the Water Gods: Mexican Seafood & Vegetable Cookery. (Illus.). 352p. 1994. 25.00 (0-671-74898-X) S&S Trade.

— El Sabor de Mexico. LC 98-25889. (SPA., Illus.). 303p. 1998. pap. text 30.00 (1-55670-870-X) Stewart Tabori & Chang.

— The Taste of Mexico. LC 86-5817. (Illus.). 304p. 1986. pap. 27.50 (1-55670-326-0) Stewart Tabori & Chang.

— The Taste of Mexico. Wilkinson, Marilyn, ed. LC 86-5817. (Illus.). 304p. 1986. 50.00 (0-941434-89-3) Stewart Tabori & Chang.

Quintana, Ricardo. Eighteenth Century Plays. (Modern Library College Editions). 484p. (C). 1966. pap. 8.44 (0-07-553659-5) McGraw.

— Swift: An Introduction. LC 79-17607. 204p. 1980. reprint ed. lib. bdg. 55.00 (0-313-22052-2, QUST, Greenwood Pr) Greenwood.

— Two Augustans: John Locke, Jonathan Swift. LC 77-91059. 157p. 1978. reprint ed. pap. 48.70 (0-608-01909-7, 206256100003) Bks Demand.

Quintana, Ricardo, ed. Two Hundred Poems. LC 74-80377. (Granger Index Reprint Ser.). 1977. 23.95 (0-8369-6058-0) Ayer.

Quintana, Ricardo, ed. see Swift, Jonathan.

Quintana, Richardo. The Mind & Art of Jonathan Swift. 1990. 16.50 (0-8446-1370-3) Peter Smith.

Quintanar, Derek, ed. see Ackerman, David, et al.

Quintanar, Derek, ed. see MacLimore, Guy.

Quintanar, Derek, ed. see Pondsmith, Michael, et al.

Quintanilha, A. La Probleme de la Sexualite Chez les Champignons: Recherches sur le Genre Coprinus. (Illus.). 1968. reprint ed. pap. 32.00 (3-7682-0556-8) Lubrecht & Cramer.

Quintanilha, A., ed. Reactive Oxygen Species in Chemistry, Biology, & Medicine. LC 87-38498. (Illus.). 240p. 1988. 75.00 (0-306-42808-3, Plenum Trade) Perseus Pubng.

Quintanilla, Efren. Aventuras de Bartolillo. (SPA.). 7.95 (84-241-5634-X) E Torres & Sons.

Quintanilla Fisac, Miguel A. Diccionario de Filosofia. (SPA.). 300p. 1991. pap. 39.95 (0-7859-6145-3, 8471517094) Fr & Eur.

Quintanilla, Jaime, jt. auth. see Philippe, Jorge.

Quintanilla, Quadalupe C., tr. see Wade, Mary D.

Quintas, Alfonso L. The Knowledge of Values: A Methodological Introduction. LC 89-5597. (Cultural Heritage & Contemporary Life Series I. Culture & Values: Vol. 2). 116p. (Orig.). 1989. 45.00 (0-8191-7418-1); pap. 17.50 (0-8191-7419-X) Coun Res Values.

Quintavalle, David T. The Carl Chronicles. 22p. 1999. pap. 5.00 (1-893068-05-6) P & Q Pr.

— Inky Star: Poems. 28p. 1998. pap. 5.00 (1-893068-01-3, 102) P & Q Pr.

Quintavalle, David T., jt. auth. see Garrison, Peggy.

Quintela, Helen W. Out of Ashes. LC 91-10447. 160p. 1991. pap. 8.99 (0-8361-3554-7) Herald Pr.

Quintella, Rogerio H. The Strategic Management of Technology in the Chemical & Petrochemical Industries. LC 93-21542. 1994. 69.00 (1-85567-146-8) St Martin.

Quintelli-Neary, Marguerite. Folklore & the Fantastic in Twelve Modern Irish Novels, 76. LC 97-13714. 176p. 1997. 52.95 (0-313-30490-4, GM0490) Greenwood.

Quintent, E. Classic Chinese Cooking. 1996. 6.98 (0-7858-0644-X) Bk Sales Inc.

Quintere, J. G., jt. ed. see Cho, P.

Quintern, J. & Riener, R. Neuroprosthetics: From Basic Research to Clinical Applications:Biomedical & Health Research Program (Biomed) of the European Union, Concerted Action:Restoration of Muscle Activity Through Fes & Associated Technology (Raft) LC 96-20390. 670p. 1996. 141.00 (3-540-61084-7) Spr-Verlag.

Quintero. Alexander Pope. 1998. 23.95 (0-8057-7827-6, Twayne) Mac Lib Ref.

Quintero, Alvarez G. Genio Alegre - Amores Yamorios - Muela del Rey Farfan - La Reja. (SPA.). 297p. 1964. 7.95 (0-8288-7177-9) Fr & Eur.

— Genio Alegre - las de Cain. (SPA.). 286p. 1963. 1.50 (0-8288-7144-2) Fr & Eur.

— Puebla de las Mujeres - Genio Alegre. (SPA.). 142p. 1979. 5.95 (0-8288-7101-9) Fr & Eur.

Quintero, Ana H. Hacia la Escuela Que Sonamos. (SPA.). 170p. 1996. pap. write for info. (0-8477-0253-7) U of PR Pr.

— Que Me Pasa con las Matematicas? LC 85-24617. (Illus.). 119p. 1989. pap. 11.50 (0-8477-2749-1) U of PR Pr.

— Representaciones en la Ensenanza de las Matematicas. LC 87-25573. 240p. 1988. pap. 16.00 (0-8477-2750-5) U of PR Pr.

Quintero, Ana H. & Costa, Nancy. Geometria. (SPA., Illus.). 512p. 1994. pap. 19.95 (0-8477-2345-3) U of PR Pr.

Quintero, Angel G. Conflictos de Clase y Politica en PR. (Cuadernos CEREP Ser.). 168p. 1981. pap. 7.25 (0-940238-09-8) Ediciones Huracan.

*__Quintero, Carlos.__ Building a World Class Selling Organization: Criteria for Sales Excellence. (Illus.). 70p. 2000. pap. 24.95 (0-9676255-0-5) Sales Effective.

Quintero, Diomedes & Aiello, Annette, eds. Insects of Panama & Mesoamerica: Selected Studies. (Illus.). 714p. 1992. text 205.00 (0-19-854018-3) OUP.

Quintero, Elizabeth & Rummel, Mary K. American Voices. LC 97-28119. 252p. 1997. pap. text 41.00 (0-13-517807-X) P-H.

Quintero, Elizabeth, jt. ed. see Weinstein-Shr, Gail.

Quintero, Elizabeth P., jt. auth. see Rummel, Mary K.

Quintero, Joaquin Alvarez, see Alvarez Quintero, Serafin & Alvarez Quintero, Joaquin.

Quintero, Jorge A. Acid Base Balance: A Manuel for Clinicians. 2nd ed. LC 77-81798. (Illus.). 138p. 1981. 12.50 (0-87527-148-0) Green.

— Laws, Theories & Values: Biological Approaches to Understanding. 2nd ed. LC 79-50190. (Illus.). 144p. 1980. 10.50 (0-87527-147-2) Green.

Quintero-Joyce, Julie & Joyce, Jonathan E. How to Go to College - Cost Free! 80p. (Orig.). 1996. pap. 9.95 (0-9656808-0-0, 96-1) Dynamic Pub IL.

— What Every Investor Needs to Know: Ideas to Help You Protect Your Money from Bad Advice, Sales Tricks, & Fraud. 88p. (Orig.). 1996. pap. 19.95 (0-9656808-1-9, 96-2) Dynamic Pub IL.

Quintero, Maria C. Poetry As Play: "Gongorismo" & the "Comedia" LC 91-40886. (Purdue University Monographs in Romance Languages: No. 38). xviii, 260p. 1991. 80.00 (1-55619-304-1); pap. 27.95 (1-55619-305-X) J Benjamins Pubng Co.

Quintero Rivera, Angel. Workers' Struggle in Puerto Rico: A Documentary History. Belfrage, Cedric, tr. LC 76-40343. 236p. 1976. reprint ed. pap. 73.20 (0-7837-9615-3, 206037200005) Bks Demand.

Quintero-Rivera, Angel G. Patricios & Plebeyos: Burgueses, Hacendados, Artesanos & Obreros: Las Relaciones de Clase en el Puerto Rico de Cambio de Siglo. LC 87-82379. (Nave y el Puerto Ser.). (SPA.). 332p. 1988. pap. 10.50 (0-940238-93-4) Ediciones Huracan.

Quintero, Roberto, ed. see Cornish, Patty Jo.

Quintero, Ronald G. The CPA's Basic Guide to Mergers & Acquisitions. 144p. 1999. pap. 45.00 (0-87051-253-6, 029872) Am Inst CPA.

Quintero, Ruben. Literate Culture: Pope's Rhetorical Art. LC 90-50939. 192p. 1992. 36.50 (0-87413-433-1) U Delaware Pr.

Quintero, Serafin Alvarez, see Alvarez Quintero, Serafin.

Quintero, Serafin Y. El Genio Alegre. Puebla de las Mujeres. Nebrera, Gregorio T., ed. (Nueva Austral Ser.: Vol. 78). (SPA.). 1991. pap. text 14.95 (84-239-1878-5) Elliots Bks.

Quintero Vega, Esquerdo. Datos y Estadistica Descriptiva. (SPA.). 150p. 1997. pap. write for info. (0-929441-98-2) Pubns Puertorriquenas.

Quinteros, Alvarez. Malvaloca - Dona Clarines. (SPA.). 148p. 1966. 9.95 (0-8288-7106-X) Fr & Eur.

Quintet Books Staff. Floral Needlepoint. 1993. 12.98 (1-55521-969-1) Bk Sales Inc.

— Natural Health Cat Care Manual. 1993. 12.98 (1-55521-970-5) Bk Sales Inc.

— Who Built That? 1993. 12.98 (1-55521-927-6) Bk Sales Inc.

Quintiere. Principles of Fire Phenomena. (Career Education Ser.). 1997. teacher ed. 18.95 (0-8273-7733-9) Delmar.

Quintiere, J. G., et al, eds. Fire Dynamics & Heat Transfer. (Heat Transfer Ser.: Vol. 25). 138p. 1983. pap. text 34.00 (0-317-02619-4, H00269) ASME.

Quintiere, James G. Principles of Fire Behavior. LC 97-11199. (Career Education Ser.). 288p. (C). 1997. mass mkt. 55.95 (0-8273-7732-0) Delmar.

Quintiere, James G., jt. auth. see Karlsson, Bjhorn.

Quintieri, Beniamino. Patterns of Trade, Competition & Trade Policies. 192p. 1995. reprint ed. text 66.95 (1-85972-066-8, Pub. by Avebry) Ashgate Pub Co.

Quintiliani, Patricia S. My Treasury of Chaplets. 3rd ed. LC 97-102611. (Illus.). 240p. 1992. pap. 7.95 (0-911218-25-4) Ravengate Pr.

Quintilianu. De Institutione Oratoria Libri Duodecim, 6 vols., Set. ccxxxvi, 4175p. 1968. reprint ed. write for info. incl. 3.5 hd (0-318-71207-5) G Olms Pubs.

— De Institutione Oratoria Libri Duodecim, Vol. 6: Lexicon Quintilianeum. Bonell, E., ed. lxxxiv, 1044p. 1962. reprint ed. write for info. (0-318-71208-3) G Olms Pubs.

— Training of an Orator, 4 vols. No. 124-127. write for info. (0-318-53200-X) HUP.

Quintilianus. Institutionis Oratoriae Liber I. Colson, Francis H., ed. xcviii, 208p. 1973. reprint ed. write for info. (3-487-04611-3) G Olms Pubs.

— Institutionis Oratoriae Liber X. Peterson, W., ed. lxxx, 227p. 1967. reprint ed. 50.70 (0-685-66507-0, 05101664) G Olms Pubs.

Quintillan, Manuel A. Diccionario Economia General y Empresa, 4 vols., Set. (SPA.). 112p. 1991. pap. write for info. (0-7859-5993-9, 8436806522) Fr & Eur.

— Diccionario Economia General y Empresa, Vol. 1. (SPA.). 112p. 1991. pap. write for info. (0-7859-5994-7, 8436806530) Fr & Eur.

— Diccionario Economia General y Empresa, Vol. 2. (SPA.). 112p. 1991. pap. write for info. (0-7859-5995-5, 8436806549) Fr & Eur.

— Diccionario Economia General y Empresa, Vol. 3. (SPA.). 112p. 1991. pap. write for info. (0-7859-5996-3, M2818) Fr & Eur.

— Diccionario Economia General y Empressa, 4 vols., Set. (SPA.). 448p. 1991. pap. write for info. (0-7859-5992-0, 8436806514) Fr & Eur.

— Diccionario Tematico de Antropologia. (SPA.). 316p. 1985. 49.95 (0-8288-1285-3, S60822) Fr & Eur.

Quintin, Jonathan. Geometric Coloring Book for Adults. (Illus.). 64p. 1991. pap. 5.00 (1-56170-038-X, 142) Hay House.

— Mandala Coloring Book. (Illus.). 140p. 1998. pap. 10.00 (1-56170-542-X, 569) Hay House.

Quintin, Jonathan, des. Geometric Coloring Book, Vol. 2. (Illus.). 64p. (Orig.). 1993. pap. 5.00 (1-56170-066-5, 1422) Hay House.

Quintin, Robert J. An Address Guide to the Catholic Parishes on Ontario. 55p. 1994. pap. 7.50 (1-886560-10-2) Quintin Pub RI.

Quintin, Robert J. The "Dit" Name: French-Canadian Surnames: Aliases, Adulterations, Anglicizations. 171p. 1993. pap. 20.95 (1-58211-070-0, 09303) Quintin Pub RI.

Quintin, Robert J. French Marriages Recorded in the Central Falls, RI City Hall (1850-1950) 50p. 1979. pap. 10.00 (1-886560-15-3) Quintin Pub RI.

Quintin, Robert J. A Genealogical Guide to the Catholic Churches of the Province of Quebec. rev. ed. 88p. 1994. pap. 10.00 (1-58211-069-7, 09304) Quintin Pub RI.

Quintin, Robert J. Guide to the Catholic Parishes on Ontario. 65p. 1994. pap. 10.00 (1-886560-09-9) Quintin Pub RI.

— Marriages of Notre Dame de la Consolation RC Church (1895-1978), Pawtucket, RI. 200p. 1978. pap. 20.00 (1-886560-16-1) Quintin Pub RI.

— Marriages of St. Anne's RC Church 1869-1930, Fall River, Massachusetts. 300p. 1980. pap. 25.00 (1-886560-11-0) Quintin Pub RI.

Quintin, Robert J. The Notaries of French-Canada: 1626-1900: Alphabetical, Chronologically by Area Served. rev. ed. 93p. 1994. pap. 15.00 (1-886560-01-3, 09401) Quintin Pub RI.

Quintin, Robert J., ed. Marriage Records of Notre Dame RC Church 1873-1879, Central Falls, RI. 350p. 1982. pap. 25.00 (1-886560-13-7) Quintin Pub RI.

— Marriages of St. Jean Baptist Church (1901-1979), Fall River, Massachusetts. 85p. 1980. pap. 15.00 (1-886560-12-9) Quintin Pub RI.

Quinting, Gerd. Hesitation Phenomena in Adult Aphasic & Normal Speech. LC 75-170008. (Janua Linguarum, Series Minor: No. 126). 73p. 1971. pap. text 16.95 (90-279-1842-2) Mouton.

Quinto, Carol. The Duke Who Came to Visit. 224p. 1996. mass mkt. 4.50 (0-8217-5429-7, Zebra Kensgtn) Kensgtn Pub Corp.

— Sister of the Bride. 224p. 1997. mass mkt. 4.99 (0-8217-5673-7, Zebra Kensgtn) Kensgtn Pub Corp.

Quinto, Eric T., et al, eds. Tomography, Impedence Imaging & Integral Geometry: Proceedings of the 1993 AMS-SIAM Seminar in Applied Mathematics on Tomography, Impedance Imaging & Integral Geometry, June 7-18, 1993, Mt. Holyoke College, Massachusetts. LC 94-28800. (Lectures in Applied Mathematics: Vol. 30). 287p. 1994. pap. 51.00 (0-8218-0337-9, LAM/30) Am Math.

Quinto, Eric T., jt. ed. see Grinberg, Eric.

Quinton. From Wodehouse Wittgenstein. LC 97-40491. 360p. 1998. text 49.95 (0-312-21161-9) St Martin.

Quinton, Ann. Put Out the Light. 224p. 26.00 (0-7278-5523-9) Severn Hse.

Quinton, Ann. The Ragusa Theme. large type ed. (Romance Suspense Ser.). 416p. 1988. 27.99 (0-7089-1777-1) Ulverscroft.

Quinton, Ann. This Mortal Coil. large type ed. 416p. 31.99 (0-7089-4040-4) Ulverscroft.

Q

An Asterisk (*) at the beginning of an entry indicates that the title is appearing for the first time.

***Quinton, Anthony.** Hume: Great Philosophers. LC 99-22645. 64p. 1999. pap. 6.00 (*0-415-92393-X*) Routledge.

Quinton, Anthony. The Nature of Things. 1978. reprint ed. pap. 19.95 (*0-7100-8903-1*, Routledge Thoemms) Routledge.

— Thoughts & Thinkers. LC 81-13372. 350p. 1982. 54.50 (*0-8419-0772-2*); pap. 29.50 (*0-8419-0773-0*) Holmes & Meier.

— Utilitarian Ethics. 2nd ed. 123p. 1988. pap. 14.95 (*0-8126-9052-4*) Open Court.

Quinton, Anthony, ed. Political Philosophy. (Oxford Readings in Philosophy Ser.). 208p. (Orig.). 1978. pap. 18.95 (*0-19-875002-1*) OUP.

Quinton, David. Joining New Families: Adoption & Fostering in Middle Childhood. LC 98-28949. (Child Care & Protection Ser.). 282p. 1998. pap. 54.95 (*0-471-97837-X*) Wiley.

Quinton, Michael S. The Goshawk Vol. 1: Phantom Hunter of the North. (Illus.). 64p. 1999. pap. 12.95 (*0-88839-423-3*) Hancock House.

— The Mountain Grizzly, Vol. 1. (Illus.). 64p. (YA). (gr. 3 up). 1999. pap. text 12.95 (*0-88839-417-9*) Hancock House.

Quinton, P. M., et al, eds. Fluid & Electrolyte Abnormalities in Exocrine Glands in Cystic Fibrosis. (Illus.). 1982. 15.00 (*0-911302-45-X*) San Francisco Pr.

Quinton, P. M., jt. ed. see Mastella, G.

Quintrell, Brian. Charles I Seminar Studies. LC 92-28086. (Seminar Studies in History). 136p. (C). 1995. pap. 15.93 (*0-582-00354-7*) Longman.

Quintus, Curtius. History of Alexander, 2 vols., 1. (Loeb Classical Library: No. 368-369). 15.50 (*0-674-99405-1*) HUP.

— History of Alexander, 2 vols., 2. (Loeb Classical Library: No. 368-369). 636p. 1946. 18.95 (*0-674-99407-8*) HUP.

Quintus, Harold Von, see Leahy, Rita B. & Von Quintus, Harold.

Quintus Smyrnaeus. Fall of Troy. Way, A. S., tr. (Loeb Classical Library: No. 19). 640p. 1913. 18.95 (*0-674-99022-6*) HUP.

Quintus, Smyrnaeus. The War at Troy: What Homer Didn't Tell. Combellack, Frederick M., tr. & intro. by. LC 67-24612. 288p. reprint ed. pap. 89.30 (*0-7837-1988-4*, 204226200002) Bks Demand.

Quinzii, Martine. Increasing Returns & Economic Efficiency. (Illus.). 176p. 1993. text 55.00 (*0-19-506553-0*) OUP.

Quinzii, Martine, jt. auth. see Magill, Michael.

***Quiram, Jacquelyn, et al, eds.** Alcohol & Tobacco: America's Drugs of Choice. rev. ed. (Information Plus Reference Ser.). (Illus.). 124p. 1999. pap. text 25.95 (*1-57302-096-6*) Info Plus TX.

Quiram, Jacquelyn, et al, eds. Education: Reflecting Our Society. 10th rev. ed. (Information Plus Reference Ser.). (Illus.). 164p. 1998. pap. text 25.95 (*1-57302-062-1*) Info Plus TX.

Quiram, Jacquelyn F., et al, eds. Crime: A Serious American Problem. 10th rev. ed. (Information Plus Reference Ser.). (Illus.). 168p. 1998. pap. text 26.95 (*1-57302-073-7*) Info Plus TX.

Quirarte. How To Look At a Masterpiece. 5th ed. 1998. pap. 20.30 (*0-07-229182-6*) McGraw.

Quiray, David R. Fun with Dick & Jana. 140p. (Orig.). (C). 1996. pap. 9.95 (*0-9647795-0-1*) Kawika Pubng.

Quirchmayr, G., et al, eds. Database & Expert Systems Applications: 9th International Conference, DEXA'98, Vienna, Austria, August 24-28, 1998, Proceedings, Vol. 146. LC 98-39438. (Lecture Notes in Computer Science Ser.: Vol. 1460). xvi, 905p. 1998. pap. 99.00 (*3-540-64950-6*) Spr-Verlag.

Quirey, Belinda. May I Have the Pleasure? 124p. 1976. reprint ed. pap. 17.95 (*1-85273-000-5*, Pub. by Dance Bks) Princeton Bk Co.

Quiri, Patricia R. The Algonquians. LC 91-29111. (First Bks.). (Illus.). 64p. (J). (gr. 4-6). 1992. lib. bdg. 22.00 (*0-531-20065-5*) Watts.

— The Algonquians. (First Bks.). 64p. (J). (gr. 4-6). 1992. pap. 6.95 (*0-531-15633-8*) Watts.

— The American Flag. LC 97-5179. (True Bks.). 48p. (J). (gr. 2-4). 1998. lib. bdg. 21.00 (*0-516-20617-6*) Childrens.

— The American Flag. Joffe, Shari, ed. LC 97-5179. (True Bks.). (Illus.). 48p. (J). 1998. pap. 6.95 (*0-516-26370-6*) Childrens.

— The Bald Eagle. LC 97-12217. (True Bks.). 48p. (J). 1998. lib. bdg. 21.00 (*0-516-20621-4*) Childrens.

— The Bald Eagle. Joffe, Shari, ed. (True Bks.). (Illus.). 48p. (J). 1998. pap. 6.95 (*0-516-26373-0*) Childrens.

— The Bill of Rights. (True Bks.). (Illus.). 48p. (J). (gr. 2-4). 1999. pap. text 6.95 (*0-516-26427-3*) Childrens.

— The Congress. LC 97-50484. (True Bks.). (J). 1998. lib. bdg. 21.00 (*0-516-20662-1*) Childrens.

— Congress. (True Books: Government Ser.). (Illus.). 48p. (J). (gr. 2-4). 1999. pap. text 6.95 (*0-516-26428-1*) Childrens.

— The Constitution. LC 97-48965. (True Bks.). 47 p. (J). 1998. pap. 21.00 (*0-516-20663-X*) Childrens.

— The Constitution. (True Bks.). (Illus.). 48p. (J). (gr. 2-4). 1999. pap. text 6.95 (*0-516-26429-X*) Childrens.

— The Declaration of Independence. LC 97-48966. (True Bks.). 47 p. (J). 1998. lib. bdg. 21.00 (*0-516-20664-8*) Childrens.

— The Declaration of Independence. (True Bks.). (Illus.). 48p. (J). (gr. 2-4). 1999. pap. text 6.95 (*0-516-26430-3*) Childrens.

— Ellis Island. Joffe, Shari, ed. (True Bks.). (Illus.). 48p. (J). 1998. pap. 6.95 (*0-516-26374-9*) Childrens.

— Ellis Island: A True Book. LC 97-9356. (True Bks.). (Illus.). 48p. (J). (gr. 2-4). 1998. 20.00 (*0-516-20622-2*) Childrens.

— The National Anthem. LC 97-10970. (True Bks.). (Illus.). 48p. (J). (gr. k-4). 1998. lib. bdg. 21.00 (*0-516-20625-7*) Childrens.

— The National Anthem. Joffe, Shari, ed. (True Bks.). (Illus.). 48p. (J). 1998. pap. 6.95 (*0-516-26382-X*) Childrens.

— The Presidency. LC 97-48964. (True Bks.). (J). 1998. 21.00 (*0-516-20674-5*) Childrens.

— The Presidency. (True Bks.). (Illus.). 48p. (J). (gr. 3-5). 1999. pap. text 6.95 (*0-516-26438-9*) Childrens.

— The Statue of Liberty. LC 97-12216. (True Bks.). (Illus.). 48p. (J). (gr. 2-4). 1998. 21.00 (*0-516-20628-1*) Childrens.

— The Statue of Liberty. Joffe, Shari, ed. (True Bks.). (Illus.). 48p. (J). (gr. 3-5). 1998. pap. 6.95 (*0-516-26385-4*) Childrens.

— The Supreme Court. LC 97-48950. (True Bks.). (Illus.). 48p. (J). (gr. 2-4). 1998. pap. text 6.95 (*0-516-26441-9*) Childrens.

— The Supreme Court. LC 97-48950. (True Bks.). (J). (gr. 3-5). 1998. 21.00 (*0-516-20679-6*) Childrens.

— The White House. LC 95-44444. (First Bks.). (Illus.). 64p. (J). (gr. 4-7). 1996. lib. bdg. 22.00 (*0-531-20221-6*) Watts.

***Quiri, Patricia Ryon.** Chefs. (Community Workers Ser.). (Illus.). 32p. (J). (gr. 1-2). 2000. write for info. (*0-7565-0007-9*) Compass Point.

— The Lewis & Clark Expedition. (We the People Ser.). (Illus.). 48p. (J). 2000. write for info. (*0-7565-0044-3*) Compass Point.

— Seasons. (Simply Science Ser.). (Illus.). 32p. (J). (gr. 1-2). 2000. write for info. (*0-7565-0034-6*) Compass Point.

Quirin, Bill. Golf Clubs of the MGA: A Centennial History of Golf in the New York Metropolitan Area. (Illus.). 304p. 1997. 39.95 (*1-57243-191-1*) Triumph Bks.

Quirin, H., et al, eds. Historischer Handatlas von Brandenburg und Berlin: 1962-79. Incl. Facsimile 1-6. Facsimile 1 - 6. 72.00 (*3-11-000493-3*); Facsimile 7-12. Facsimile 7 - 12. 78.00 (*3-11-000499-2*); Facsimile 13-18. Facsimile 13 - 18. 78.00 Facsimile 19-24. Facsimile 19 - 24. 78.00 (*3-11-000511-5*); Facsimile 27-30. Facsimile 27 - 30. 52.00 (*3-11-002697-X*); Facsimile 31-34. Facsimile 31 - 34. 52.00 (*3-11-003887-0*); Facsimile 35-36. Facsimile 35 - 36. 26.00 (*3-11-004323-8*); Facsimile 37-41. Facsimile 37 - 41. 93.50 (*3-11-004336-X*); Facsimile 42-46. Facsimile 42 - 46. 100.00 (*3-11-004866-3*); Facsimile 47-49. Facsimile 47 - 49. 60.00 (*3-11-005963-0*); Facsimile 50-52. Facsimile 50 - 52. 64.00 (*3-11-006924-5*); Facsimile 53-56. Facsimile 53 - 56. 90.75 (*3-11-007472-9*); Facsimile 57-60. Facsimile 57 - 60. 90.75 (*3-11-007490-7*); write for info. (*0-318-59219-3*) De Gruyter.

Quirin, Heinz, ed. Historischer Handatlas von Brandenburg und Berlin: 1962-79. 1962. 1224.30 (*3-11-008424-4*) De Gruyter.

Quirin, James. The Evolution of the Ethiopian Jews: A History of the Beta Israel (Falasha) to 1920. LC 91-47665. (Ethnohistory Ser.). (Illus.). 360p. (C). 1992. text 39.95 (*0-8122-3116-3*) U of Pa Pr.

Quirin, Jim, jt. auth. see Cohen, Barry.

Quirin, William, et al. The Greenwich Country Club, 1892-1992. LC 93-16831. 1993. write for info. (*0-89865-862-4*) Donning Co.

Quirin, William L. The Creek: A Pause along the Way, 1923-1998. LC 98-33739. 1998. write for info. (*0-9665228-0-X*) Q Pubng VA.

— Deal Golf & Country Club, 1898-1998. LC 98-39171. 1998. write for info. (*1-57864-051-2*) Donning Co.

— Hollywood Golf Club: The First Hundred Years. LC 98-13478. 1998. write for info. (*1-57864-031-8*) Donning Co.

— The Knollwood Spirit, 1894-1994. LC 94-25156. 1994. text. write for info. (*0-89865-920-5*) Donning Co.

— Morris County Golf Club, 1894-1994. LC 94-24079. 1995. write for info. (*0-89865-928-0*) Donning Co.

— North Jersey Country Club: Celebrating 100 Years. LC 94-47356. 1995. write for info. (*0-89865-929-9*) Donning Co.

— Scarsdale Golf Club: The First Hundred Years, 1898-1998. LC 97-52246. 1998. write for info. (*1-57864-028-8*) Donning Co.

— The Story of the Lesley Cup Matches. LC 97-3176. 1997. write for info. (*0-89865-998-1*) Donning Co.

Quirin, William L., jt. auth. see Cataldo, Joseph.

Quiring, Ethel F., jt. auth. see Savage, Hugh W.

Quiring, Isaac. Strangled Roots, Vol. 1. 186p. (Orig.). 1982. pap. 8.95 (*0-920490-26-3*) Temeron Bks.

Quiring, James P. In Pictures Mount St. Helens: The Continuing Story. LC 91-60040. 48p. (Orig.). 1991. pap. 7.95 (*0-88714-055-6*) KC Pubns.

— In Pictures Mount St. Helens: The Continuing Story. Morales, Brigitte, tr. (GER., Illus.). 48p. (Orig.). 1991. pap. 8.95 (*0-88714-743-7*) KC Pubns.

— In Pictures Mount St. Helens: The Continuing Story. Petzinger, Saori, tr. (JPN., Illus.). 48p. (Orig.). 1991. pap. 8.95 (*0-88714-745-3*) KC Pubns.

Quiring, James P. & Le Bras, Yvon. In Pictures Mount St. Helens: The Continuing Story. (FRE., Illus.). 48p. (Orig.). 1991. pap. 8.95 (*0-88714-744-5*) KC Pubns.

Quiring, Virginia M., ed. The Milton S. Eisenhower Years at Kansas State University. 120p. 1986. 25.00 (*0-685-18353-X*) Friends Lib KSU.

— The Milton S. Eisenhower Years at Kansas State University. limited ed. 120p. 1986. 50.00 (*0-9616658-0-7*) Friends Lib KSU.

Quirino, Carlos. Amang: The Life & Times of Eulogio Rodriguez, Sr. (Illus.). 302p. (Orig.). 1984. pap. 16.50 (*971-10-0141-1*, Pub. by New Day Pub) Cellar.

— Chick Parsons: America's Master Spy in the Philippines. (Illus.). 168p. (Orig.). 1984. pap. 15.00 (*971-10-0198-5*, Pub. by New Day Pub) Cellar.

Quirino, Raffaele. Ani DiFranco: Righteous Babe. (Illus.). 256p. 1999. pap. 16.95 (*1-55082-253-5*) LPC InBook.

***Quirion, R., et al, eds.** Peptide Receptors. 1999. write for info. (*0-444-82972-5*, Excerpta Medica) Elsevier.

Quirion, Remi, jt. ed. see Samson, Willis K.

Quirk. The Employee Handbook. 443p. 1990. 79.95 (*0-88730-474-5*, S74, HarpBusn) HarpInfo.

— Universal Grammar of English. Date not set. pap. text. write for info. (*0-582-55207-9*, Pub. by Addison-Wesley) Longman.

Quirk, Charles E. Sports & the Law: Major Legal Cases. LC 98-47218. 305p. 1999. pap. 29.95 (*0-8153-3324-2*) Garland.

Quirk, Charles E., ed. Sports & the Law: Major Legal Cases. LC 94-35594. (American Law & Society Ser.: Vol. 04). 336p. 1996. text 61.00 (*0-8153-0220-7*, SS765) Garland.

Quirk, Dantia. Q's Who in Pay-per-View. 80p. 1988. 24.95 (*0-910767-17-3*) QV Pub.

— Q's Who in Television Sports. 130p. 1987. 19.95 (*0-910767-20-3*) QV Pub.

Quirk, Dantia & Whitestone, Patricia. The Shrinking Library Dollar. 170p. 1982. 27.95 (*0-685-47122-5*, G K Hall Lrg Type) Mac Lib Ref.

— The Shrinking Library Dollar. LC 81-12319. (Communications Library). 170p. 1982. 27.95 (*0-685-02844-5*, G K Hall & Co) Mac Lib Ref.

Quirk, James. Pay Dirt: The Business of Professional Team Sports. 576p. 1932. pap. text 19.95 (*0-691-01574-0*, Pub. by Princeton U Pr) Cal Prin Full Svc.

Quirk, James, et al, eds. Coal Models & Their Use in Government Planning. LC 81-21153. 261p. 1982. 59.95 (*0-275-90880-1*, C0880, Praeger Pubs) Greenwood.

Quirk, James & Fort, Rodney D. Pay Dirt: The Business of Professional Team Sports. (Illus.). 400p. 1932. text 55.00 (*0-691-04255-1*, Pub. by Princeton U Pr) Cal Prin Full Svc.

***Quirk, James P.** Nonparametric Comparative Statics & Stability. LC 98-35511. 256p. 1999. 55.00 (*0-691-00690-3*, Pub. by Princeton U Pr) Cal Prin Full Svc.

Quirk, James P. & Fort, Rodney D. Hard Ball: The Perilous Future of Pro Team Sports. LC 98-38409. 1999. 22.95 (*0-691-05817-2*, Pub. by Princeton U Pr) Cal Prin Full Svc.

Quirk, James P., jt. ed. see Horwich, George.

Quirk, Joe. The Ultimate Rush. LC 97-29702. 320p. 1998. 23.00 (*0-688-15270-8*, Wm Morrow) Morrow Avon.

***Quirk, Joe.** The Ultimate Rush. abr. ed. 1998. audio. write for info. (*0-671-57896-0*, Pub. by S&S Audio) Lndmrk Audiobks.

Quirk, John. CIA Entrance Examination. (Arco Professional Test Preparation Ser.). 1988. pap. 14.95 (*0-317-66872-2*, Arco) Macmillan Gen Ref.

Quirk, John E. No Red Ribbons. 1965. 10.00 (*0-8159-6306-8*) Devin.

Quirk, Kent, jt. auth. see Kovel, Jeff.

Quirk, Kent J. The More Things Change... 252p. 1998. pap. text 20.00 (*0-9641681-1-1*) Polestar CT.

Quirk, Kevin. Not Now Honey I'm Watching the Game: What to Do When Sports Come Between You & Your Mate. LC 97-19429. 256p. 1997. pap. 12.00 (*0-684-83447-2*) S&S Trade.

***Quirk, Lawrence J.** Bob Hope: The Road Well-Traveled. 400p. 1998. 26.95 (*1-55783-353-2*) Applause Theatre Bk Pubs.

— Bob Hope: The Road Well-Traveled. 2000. pap. 14.95 (*1-55783-450-4*) Applause Theatre Bk Pubs.

Quirk, Lawrence J. The Complete Films of Ingrid Bergman. (Illus.). 1989. pap. 14.95 (*0-8065-0972-4*, Citadel Pr) Carol Pub Group.

— The Complete Films of Joan Crawford. rev. ed. (Illus.). 224p. 1988. pap. 14.95 (*0-8065-1078-1*, Citadel Pr) Carol Pub Group.

— The Complete Films of William Holden. rev. ed. (Illus.). 288p. 1986. pap. 12.95 (*0-8065-0987-2*, Citadel Pr) Carol Pub Group.

— The Complete Films of William Powell. (Illus.). 288p. (Orig.). 1986. pap. 15.95 (*0-8065-0998-8*, Citadel Pr) Carol Pub Group.

— The Films of Gloria Swanson. LC 83-20859. 256p. 19.95 (*0-8065-0874-4*, Citadel Pr) Carol Pub Group.

— The Films of Gloria Swanson. (Illus.). 256p. 1988. reprint ed. pap. 14.95 (*0-8065-1077-3*, Citadel Pr) Carol Pub Group.

— The Films of Myrna Loy. 1980. 16.95 (*0-8065-0735-7*, Citadel Pr) Carol Pub Group.

— The Films of Robert Taylor. (Illus.). 256p. 1975. pap. 7.95 (*0-8065-0667-9*, Citadel Pr) Carol Pub Group.

— The Films of Ronald Colman. (Illus.). 1977. pap. 7.95 (*0-8065-0668-7*, Citadel Pr) Carol Pub Group.

— The Films of Warren Beatty. 1990. pap. 15.95 (*0-8065-1194-X*, Citadel Pr) Carol Pub Group.

— The Films of William Holden. 256p. 1973. pap. 12.95 (*0-8065-0517-6*, Citadel Pr) Carol Pub Group.

— The Great Romantic Films. (Illus.). 256p. 1974. pap. 9.95 (*0-8065-0539-7*, Citadel Pr) Carol Pub Group.

— The Great War Films: From the Birth of the Nation to Today. LC 94-20343. (Illus.). 256p. 1994. pap. 17.95 (*0-8065-1529-5*, Citadel Pr) Carol Pub Group.

— James Stewart: Behind the Scenes of a Wonderful Life. (Illus.). 342p. 1997. 24.95 (*1-55783-329-X*) Applause Theatre Bk Pubs.

— James Stewart: Behind the Scenes of a Wonderful Life. (Legends Ser.). (Illus.). 342p. 1999. pap. 16.95 (*1-55783-416-4*) Applause Theatre Bk Pubs.

— The Kennedys in Hollywood. (Illus.). 400p. 1996. 24.00 (*0-87833-934-5*) Taylor Pub.

— Lauren Bacall: Her Films & Career. (Illus.). 224p. 1986. 19.95 (*0-8065-0935-X*, Citadel Pr) Carol Pub Group.

— Paul Newman: The Man Behind the Steel Blue Eyes. LC 97-5906. (Illus.). 400p. 1997. 24.95 (*0-87833-962-0*) Taylor Pub.

— Some Lovely Image. 1989. pap. 9.95 (*0-8216-2007-X*, Univ Books) Carol Pub Group.

***Quirk, Lawrence J. & Schoell, William.** The Rat Pack: Neon Nights with the Kings of Cool. 368p. 1999. pap. 13.50 (*0-380-73222-X*, Avon Bks) Morrow Avon.

Quirk, Lawrence J. & Schoell, William. The Rat Pack: The Hey-Hey Days of Frank & the Boys. LC 98-10808. 357p. 1998. 23.95 (*0-87833-992-2*) Taylor Pub.

Quirk, Lawrence J., ed. see Dickens, Homer.

Quirk, Mark E. How to Learn & Teach in Medical School: A Learner-Centered Approach. LC 94-21620. 224p. 1994. pap. 36.95 (*0-398-06512-8*) C C Thomas.

— How to Learn & Teach in Medical School: A Learner-Centered Approach. LC 94-21620. (Illus.). 224p. (C). 1994. text 51.95 (*0-398-05925-X*) C C Thomas.

Quirk, Michael. Manufacturing, Teams & Improvement: The Human Art of Manufacturing. LC 98-28547. 322p. 1998. 71.00 (*0-13-924226-0*) P-H.

***Quirk, Michael & Serda, Julian.** Semiconductor Manufacturing Technology. LC 00-41653. 2001. write for info. (*0-13-081520-9*) P-H.

***Quirk, Michael P. & Fandt, Patricia M.** The 2nd Language of Leadership. LC 99-88672. 2000. pap. write for info. (*0-8058-3357-9*) L Erlbaum Assocs.

Quirk, Paul J. Industry Influence in Federal Regulatory Agencies. LC 80-8571. 272p. 1981. reprint ed. pap. 84.40 (*0-7837-9427-4*, 206016800004) Bks Demand.

Quirk, Paul J., jt. auth. see Derthick, Martha.

Quirk, Peter J., et al. Floating Exchange Rates in Developing Countries: Experience with Auction & Interbank Markets. (Occasional Papers: No. 53). vi, 43p. 1987. pap. 7.50 (*0-939934-89-2*) Intl Monetary.

— Policies for Developing Forward Foreign Exchange Markets. (Occasional Papers: No. 60). 51p. 1988. pap. 7.50 (*1-55775-017-3*) Intl Monetary.

Quirk, R. P., ed. Transition Metal Catalyzed Polymerizations-Alkenes & Dienes: Papers Presented at Eleventh Midland Macromolecular Meeting, Midland, Michigan, August 1981, Vol. 4. (MMI Press Symposium Ser.). x, 1349p. 1983. text 598.00 (*3-7186-0143-5*, Harwood Acad Pubs) Gordon & Breach.

Quirk, Randolph. Grammatical & Lexical Variance In English. LC 94-46562. 1998. text 46.50 (*0-582-25359-4*) Addison-Wesley.

Quirk, Randolph & Greenbaum, Sidney. A Concise Grammar of Contemporary English. 484p. (C). 1973. text 59.00 (*0-15-512930-9*, Pub. by Harcourt Coll Pubs) Harcourt.

Quirk, Randolph & Stein, Gabriele. English in Use. 272p. (C). 1990. pap. text 34.50 (*0-582-06613-1*, 78923) Longman.

Quirk, Randolph & Svartvik, Jan. Investigating Linguistic Acceptability. (Janua Linguarum, Ser. Minor: No. 54). (Orig.). 1966. pap. text 30.75 (*90-279-0585-1*) Mouton.

Quirk, Randolph & Wren, C. L. An Old English Grammar. LC 93-39877. 186p. (C). 1994. reprint ed. pap. text 15.00 (*0-87580-560-4*) N Ill U Pr.

Quirk, Randolph, et al. A Comprehensive Grammar of the English Language. 1779p. (C). 1989. text 167.99 (*0-582-51734-6*, 73723) Longman.

Quirk, Randolph, jt. auth. see Crystal, David.

Quirk, Randolph, jt. auth. see Greenbaum, Sidney.

Quirk, Robert E. Fidel Castro. LC 92-39300. (Illus.). 928p. 1995. pap. 18.95 (*0-393-31327-1*, Norton Paperbks) Norton.

— The Mexican Revolution & the Catholic Church, 1910-1929. LC 85-30209. 276p. 1986. reprint ed. lib. bdg. 69.50 (*0-313-25121-5*, QUMC, Greenwood Pr) Greenwood.

Quirk, Roderic P., ed. Applications of Anionic Polymerization Research. LC 98-18647. (Symposium Ser.: No. 696). (Illus.). 352p. 1998. text 120.95 (*0-8412-3565-1*, Pub. by Am Chemical) OUP.

— Transition Metal Catalyzed Polymerizations: Ziegler-Natta & Metathesis Polymerizations. (Illus.). 880p. (C). 1989. text 110.00 (*0-521-33289-3*) Cambridge U Pr.

Quirk, Roderic P., jt. auth. see Hsieh, Henry L.

Quirk, Ronald J. Literature As Introspection: Spain Confronts Trafalgar, Vol. 57. LC 97-15055. (Currents in Comparative Romance Languages & Literatures Ser.). 89p. (C). 1998. text 36.95 (*0-8204-3754-9*) P Lang Pubng.

— Serafin Estebanez Calderon: Bajo la Corteza de su Obra. LC 91-42499. (American University Studies: Romance Languages & Literature: Ser. II, Vol. 187). 223p. (C). 1992. text 38.95 (*0-8204-1748-3*) P Lang Pubng.

Quirk, Rory F. Wars & Peace: The Memoir of an American Family. LC 99-20095. (Illus.). 264p. 1999. 24.95 (*0-89141-683-8*) Presidio Pr.

Quirk, Thomas, jt. auth. see Barbour, James.

Quirk, Thomas C. Reptiles & Amphibians Coloring Book. (Illus.). (J). (gr. k-3). 1981. pap. 2.95 (*0-486-24111-4*) Dover.

Quirk, Tom. Bergson & American Culture: The Worlds of Willa Cather & Wallace Stevens. LC 89-32355. 318p. 1990. pap. 98.60 (*0-608-05205-1*, 206574200001) Bks Demand.

— Coming to Grips with Huckleberry Finn: Essays on a Book, a Boy, & a Man. LC 93-25042. 184p. (C). 1993. text 24.95 (*0-8262-0920-3*) U of Mo Pr.

— Coming to Grips with Huckleberry Finn: Essays on a Book, a Boy, & a Man. 184p. (C). 1995. pap. text 14.95 (*0-8262-1033-3*) U of Mo Pr.

An Asterisk (*) at the beginning of an entry indicates that the title is appearing for the first time.

Quirk, Tom, ed. Mark Twain: A Study of the Short Fiction. LC 97-3445. Vol. 66. 1997. 29.00 (*0-8057-0867-7*, Twyne) Mac Lib Ref.

Quirk, Tom & Scharnhorst, Gary, eds. American Realism & the Canon. LC 94-11782. 1994. 37.50 (*0-87413-524-9*) U Delaware Pr.

Quirk, Tom, jt. auth. see Barbour, James.

Quirk, Tom, jt. ed. see Barbour, James.

Quirk, Tom, jt. ed. see Nagel, James.

Quirk, Tom, ed. & intro. see Twain, Mark, pseud.

Quirk, William, jt. auth. see Bridwell, R.

Quirk, William J. A Company Policy Manual. Haffeman, JoAnne S., ed. 77p. 1991. pap. 34.95 (*0-916592-96-0*) Panel Pubs.

— A Company Policy Manual: Special Report - Critical Company Policy Issues. Haffeman, JoAnne S., ed. 80p. 1991. pap. text 34.95 (*1-878375-81-4*) Panel Pubs.

— Hiring Handbook: Special Report - Critical Hiring Issues. Haffeman, JoAnne S., ed. 80p. 1991. pap. text 45.00 (*1-878375-80-6*) Panel Pubs.

Quirk, William J. & Bridwell, R. Randall. Abandoned: The Betrayal of the American Middle Class since World War II. 468p. 1992. 21.95 (*0-8191-8459-4*) Madison Bks UPA.

— Abandoned: The Betrayal of the American Middle Class since World War II. 468p. 1993. pap. 16.95 (*1-56833-022-7*) Madison Bks UPA.

— Judicial Dictatorship. LC 95-821. 143p. 1995. 34.95 (*1-56000-225-5*) Transaction Pubs.

***Quirke, Bill.** Making the Conncections: Using Internal Communications to Turn Strategy into Action. LC 99-46262. 320p. 2000. 79.95 (*0-566-08175-X*, Pub. by Ashgate Pub) Ashgate Pub Co.

Quirke, N. Challenges in Molecular Simulation. 90p. 1990. pap. text 179.00 (*2-88124-786-5*) Gordon & Breach.

Quirke, N., jt. ed. see Gubbins, K. E.

Quirke, N., ed. see Haile, J. M.

Quirke, Philip, ed. The Molecular Biology of Digestive Diseases. 128p. 1994. pap. text 10.00 (*0-7279-0827-8*, Pub. by BMJ Pub) Login Brothers Bk Co.

Quirke, Philip, jt. auth. see Dixon, Michael F.

Quirke, Ruth M., compiled by. Joyce Mabel (Carter) Allan: Her Antecedents, Descendants & Relatives Including the Carter, Shattock, Calvert, Wilson, Yapp, Parker, Jones & Nott Lines. 128p. (Orig.). 1994. pap. 25.00 (*0-944113-03-6*) Quirke Quirke Assocs.

Quirke, Stephen. Ancient Egyptian Religion. 192p. 1993. pap. 15.95 (*0-486-27427-6*) Dover.

— Hieroglyphs & the Afterlife in Ancient Egypt. LC 95-45424. (Illus.). 192p. 1996. 39.95 (*0-8061-2751-1*) U of Okla Pr.

— Who Were the Pharaohs? A History of Their Names. (Illus.). 80p. 1991. pap. 8.95 (*0-486-26586-2*) Dover.

Quirke, Stephen & Spencer, Jeffrey, eds. The British Museum Book of Ancient Egypt. (Illus.). 240p. 1996. 24.95 (*0-500-27902-0*, Pub. by Thames Hudson) Norton.

Quirke, Stephen, jt. auth. see Parkinson, Richard.

Quirke, Terence T., Jr., compiled by. Alexander Foster McIlraith (1858-1945) Genealogy: Including the Foster, Charland, Gavin & Love Lines; Ontario, North Dakota, Washington, Quebec, Manitoba & Alberta. LC 87-60962. (Illus.). 275p. (Orig.). 1987. pap. 20.00 (*0-944113-00-1*) Quirke Quirke Assocs.

— Goble Genealogy & Family History: Rolvenden & Adjacent Parishes, Kent, England. LC 94-65860. 91p. (Orig.). 1994. 25.00 (*0-944113-02-8*) Quirke Quirke Assocs.

— Grace Genealogy & Family History: East Sussex, England. LC 94-65861. 83p. (Orig.). 1994. 25.00 (*0-944113-01-X*) Quirke Quirke Assocs.

Quiroga, Horacio. Cuentos. (SPA.). pap. 9.95 (*968-432-077-9*, Pub. by Porrua) Continental Bk.

— Cuentos de Amor Locu. LC 96-54877. (SPA.). 160p. 1997. pap. 11.95 (*0-14-026631-3*) Viking Penguin.

— The Decapitated Chicken & Other Stories. Peden, Margaret Sayers, tr. LC 75-40167. (Texas Pan American Ser.). (Illus.). 213p. (C). 1976. pap. 14.95 (*0-292-71541-2*) U of Tex Pr.

— The Exiles & Other Stories. Danielson, J. David & Gambarini, Elsa K., trs. LC 86-30722. (Texas Pan American Ser.). 168p. reprint ed. 52.10 (*0-608-08703-3*, 206922600003) Bks Demand.

— Todos los Cuentos. (Coleccion Archivos de Ediciones Criticas). (SPA.). 37.99 (*84-88344-01-5*, Pub. by Fondo) Continental Bk.

Quiroga, Jose. Tropics of Desire. text 55.00 (*0-8147-6952-7*); pap. text 18.50 (*0-8147-6953-5*) NYU Pr.

Quiroga, Jose. Understanding Octavio Paz. LC 98-25445. (Understanding Modern European & Latin American Literature Ser.). 194p. 1999. 29.95 (*1-57003-263-7*) U of SC Pr.

Quiroga, Roberto, tr. see Albornoz, Fernando, ed.

Quiroga, Robin M., ed. see Romero, John S.

Quiroga, Virginia A. Occupational Therapy: The First 30 Years 1900 to 1930. LC 95-161107. 290p. (C). 1995. pap. 25.00 (*1-56900-025-5*) Am Occup Therapy.

***Quiros, Armando.** Spiritual Homecoming: A Catholic Priest's Journey to Judaism. 256p. 2001. pap. 14.95 (*1-56474-356-X*) Fithian Pr.

Quiros, M., jt. auth. see Tenreiro, R. Dominguez.

Quiroz. Social & Cultural History. 1998. 19.25 (*0-07-428933-0*) McGraw.

Quiroz, Consuelo, tr. see Warr, Michael.

***Quiroz, Gustavo, et al, texts.** Les Unites Discursives dans l'Analyse Semiotique: La Segmentation du Discours. (Tausch Ser: Bd. 12). 184p. 1998. 30.95 (*3-906762-23-8*, Pub. by P Lang) P Lang Pubng.

Quiroz, Julia T. Together in Our Differences: How Newcomers & Established Residents Are Rebuilding American Communities. 100p. 1995. pap. text 12.95 (*0-9645220-0-4*) Nat Immig Forum.

Quiroz-Mercado, Hugo, et al. Macular Surgery. 400p. text 135.00 (*0-7817-1531-8*) Lppncott W & W.

Quiroz, R. S., ed. Meteorological Investigations of the Upper Atmosphere: Proceedings of the AMS Symposium on Meteorological Investigations above 70 Kilometers, Miami, Florida, May 31-June 2, 1967. (Meteorological Monograph: Vol. 9, No. 31). (Illus.). 231p. 1968. 23.00 (*0-933876-29-7*) Am Meteorological.

Quiroz, Roderick S., jt. ed. see Rose, Ingrid.

Quisenaerts, Luc. Hidden Gems of South-West France. (Illus.). 192p. 1999. 34.95 (*90-76124-16-7*, Pub. by D Pubns) Seven Hills Bk.

— Hidden Gems of the Provence: Hotels. 1999. 34.95 (*90-76124-10-8*, Pub. by D Pubns) Seven Hills Bk.

— Hotel Gems of France. (Illus.). 196p. 1997. 59.95 (*90-75658-01-X*, Pub. by Portfolio) Seven Hills Bk.

— Hotel Gems of Great Britain & Ireland. (Hotel Gems Ser.). (Illus.). 210p. 1997. 59.95 (*90-76124-01-9*) Seven Hills Bk.

Quisenaerts, Luc. Hotel Gems of Italy. 59.95 (*90-76124-06-X*, Pub. by D Pubns) Seven Hills Bk.

Quisenaerts, Luc. Hotel Gems of Spain. (Illus.). 192p. 1999. 59.95 (*90-76124-21-3*, Pub. by D Pubns) Seven Hills Bk.

Quisenberry, Anderson C. Kentucky in the War of 1812. (Illus.). 242p. 1996. reprint ed. pap. 25.00 (*0-8063-0282-8*, 4730) Clearfield Co.

— Revolutionary Soldiers in Kentucky. xix, 206p. 1985. reprint ed. lib. bdg. 39.00 (*0-685-10517-2*) Rprt Serv.

Quisenberry, Anderson C., ed. Revolutionary Soldiers in Kentucky. 278p. 1994. reprint ed. pap. 29.50 (*0-8328-4013-0*) Higginson Bk Co.

Quisenberry, Anderson Chenault. Revolutionary Soldiers in Kentucky: Also a Roster of the Virginia Navy. 206p. 1999. reprint ed. pap. 22.50 (*0-8063-0283-6*, 4735, Pub. by Clearfield Co) ACCESS Pubs Network.

Quisenberry, Dan. On Days Like This: Poems. LC 98-12832. 90p. 1998. pap. 12.95 (*1-884235-24-7*) Helicon Nine Eds.

Quisenberry, J. B. The Final Triumph. 1991. pap. 3.75 (*1-55673-395-X*, 9211) CSS OH.

— A Service of Shadows. 1991. pap. 3.75 (*1-55673-390-9*, 9208) CSS OH.

— Voices: Six Dialogues & Orders of Service for Lent. LC 92-34836. 1992. pap. 6.75 (*1-55673-572-3*, 9318) CSS OH.

Quisenberry, J. D. IRS Me The "Beast" from Within rom Within. large type ed. LC 94-234600. 229p. 1995. pap. 10.00 (*0-9670119-0-6*) Wolfridge.

Quisenberry, James D., ed. Changing Family Lifestyles: Their Effect on Children. LC 82-20628. (Illus.). 64p. (C). 1982. reprint ed. pap. 7.50 (*0-87173-100-2*) ACEI.

Quisenberry, James D., et al, eds. Readings from Childhood Education. Vol. II. LC 91-23454. (Illus.). 390p. 1991. 24.50 (*0-87173-121-5*) ACEI.

Quisenberry, Nancy L. & McIntyre, John, eds. Educators Healing Racism. LC 98-47981. 1999. pap. text 18.00 (*0-87173-147-9*) ACEI.

Quisenberry, Nancy L., jt. auth. see Isenberg, Joan.

Quisenberry, Richard. A Message for All in a World So Small. 42p. 1997. 8.00 (*1-885092-01-6*) Forging Pathways.

Quisenberry, Sharron S. & Peairs, Frank B., eds. Response Model for an Introduced Pest - The Russian Wheat Aphid. (Proceedings, Thomas Say Publications in Entomology Ser.). (Illus.). 442p. 1998. pap. 35.00 (*0-938522-68-X*) Entomol Soc.

Quisenberry, Sharron S., jt. auth. see Clement, Stephen L.

Quisenberry, V., jt. auth. see Smith, B.

Quishenberry, Mary, jt. auth. see Linde, Lavaun.

Quisling, Erick. The Angry Clam. LC 98-24401. (Illus.). 96p. 1998. mass mkt. 8.99 (*0-446-67410-9*, Pub. by Warner Bks) Little.

Quisling, Ronald G., jt. auth. see Mancuso, Anthony A.

Quispel, A., ed. see Eijsackers, Herman.

Quisquater, J. J. Computer Security - ESORICS 98: 5th European Symposium on Research in Computer Security, Louvain-la-Neuve, Belgium, September 16-18, 1998, Proceedings, Vol. 148. Deswarte, Y. et al, eds. LC 98-38916. (Lecture Notes in Computer Science Ser.: Vol. 1485). x, 377p. 1998. pap. 59.00 (*3-540-65004-0*) Spr-Verlag.

Quisquater, J. J. & Vandewalle, J., eds. Advances in Cryptology - EUROCRYPT '89: Proceedings of the Workshop on the Theory & Application of Cryptographic Techniques Houthalen, Belgium, April 10-13, 1989. (Lecture Notes in Computer Science Ser.: Vol. 434). x, 710p. 1990. 84.00 (*0-387-53433-4*) Spr-Verlag.

Quist, D., et al. Readings in Principles & Curriculum of Secondary Education. 1971. pap. text 7.75 (*0-8422-0178-5*) Irvington.

Quist, Gerdi, jt. auth. see Gilbert, Lesley.

Quist, John W. Restless Visionaries: The Social Roots of Antebellum Reform in Alabama & Michigan. LC 97-43640. (Illus.). 584p. 1998. text 57.50 (*0-8071-2133-9*) La State U Pr.

Quist, Wim. Museum Beelden aan Zee. (Illus.). 128p. 1999. 21.50 (*90-5662-097-5*, 910712, Pub. by NAi Uitgevers) Dist Art Pubs.

Quistberg, Brian. Winning Rugby: Great Drills to Enhance Your Players' Training & Skills. LC 98-3016. (Illus.). 160p. 1998. pap. 16.95 (*1-57028-181-5*, 81815H, Mstrs Pr) NTC Contemp Pub Co.

Quistorp, Heinrich. Calvin's Doctrine of the Last Things. Knight, Harold, tr. LC 83-45629. reprint ed. 37.50 (*0-404-19846-5*) AMS Pr.

Quitregard, David. Arabic Key Words: The Basic Two Thousand-Word Vocabulary Transliterated & Arranged by Frequency in a Hundred Units. (Language & Literature Ser.: Vol. 16). 144p. (Orig.). 1993. pap. 14.95 (*0-906672-27-9*) Oleander Pr.

Quitt, Andrea, ed. see Varga, Margaret H.

Quitt, Martin H. Virginia House of Burgesses, 1660-1706: The Social, Educational & Economic Bases of Political Power. (Outstanding Studies in Early American History). 388p. 1989. reprint ed. 25.00 (*0-8240-6194-2*) Garland.

Quitter, Deborah. The Repetitive Strain Injury Recovery Book. LC 97-36007. 240p. (Orig.). 1998. pap. 14.95 (*0-8027-7514-4*) Walker & Co.

Quittner, Josh & Slatalla, Michelle. Flame War: A Cyberthriller. LC 97-737. 384p. 1997. 24.00 (*0-688-14366-0*, Wm Morrow) Morrow Avon.

— Speeding the Net: The Inside Story of Netscape & How It Challenged Microsoft & Changed the World. LC 98-9805. 336p. 1998. 25.00 (*0-87113-709-7*, Atlntc Mnthly) Grove-Atltic.

Quittner, Joshua & Slatalla, Michelle. Flame War. 304p. 1998. pap. 12.00 (*0-380-72586-X*, Avon Bks) Morrow Avon.

Quittner, Joshua, jt. auth. see Slatalla, Michelle.

Quittner, Marvin, jt. auth. see Schachner, Robert W.

Quittner, Pal. A Practical Approach to Database Systems. LC 94-181853. 291p. 1994. pap. 90.00 (*963-05-6636-2*, Pub. by Akade Kiado) St Mut.

— Problems, Programs, Processing, Results: Software Techniques for Sci-Tech Programs. LC 78-310575. 381p. 1977. write for info. (*963-05-0949-0*, Pub. by Akade Kiado) Intl Spec Bk.

Quivey, Charles. What If. 191p. 1994. 16.00 (*0-9641135-0-3*) C Quivey.

Quizar, Robin O. My Turn to Weep: Salvadoran Refugee Women in Costa Rica. LC 97-40996. 216p. 1998. 55.00 (*0-89789-540-1*, Bergin & Garvey) Greenwood.

Qumsiyeh, Mazin B. The Bats of Egypt. (Special Publications: No. 23). (Illus.). 102p. 1985. 40.00 (*0-89672-138-8*); pap. 18.00 (*0-89672-137-X*) Tex Tech Univ Pr.

— Mammals of the Holy Land. LC 96-33969. 352p. 1996. 35.00 (*0-89672-364-X*) Tex Tech Univ Pr.

***Qun Wang.** An In-Depth Study of the Major Plays of African American Playwright August Wilson: Vernacularizing the Blues on Stage. LC 99-36642. (Black Studies: Vol. 6). 204p. 1999. text 89.95 (*0-7734-7942-2*) E Mellen.

Qunbos, Abdullhalim M. A Dictionary of Arabic Homonyms: Arabic - Arabic. (ARA & ENG.). 118p. 1991. 29.95 (*0-86685-437-1*, LDL4371, Pub. by Librairie du Liban) Intl Bk Ctr.

Qunin, Petr D. Vegetation Dynamics of Mongolia. LC 98-55182. (Geobotany Ser.). 1999. write for info. (*0-7923-5582-2*) Kluwer Academic.

Quntanna, Beatrex. Tarot: A Universal Language. (Illus.). 96p. (Orig.). 1989. pap. 14.95 (*0-9625292-0-6*) Art Ala Carte Pub.

Quo, F. Q., ed. Politics of the Pacific Nations. (Replica Edition Ser.). 275p. (C). 1984. pap. text 10.00 (*0-86531-951-0*) Westview.

Quo, James C. Concise Chinese - English Dictionary Romanized. LC 60-14372. (CHI & ENG.). 226p. 1961. pap. 8.95 (*0-8048-0116-9*) Tuttle Pubng.

— Concise Chinese-English Dictionary. (CHI & ENG.). 225p. 1980. pap. 9.95 (*0-8288-1607-7*, M14144) Fr & Eur.

— Concise English-Chinese Dictionary Romanized. LC 55-11585. (CHI & ENG.). 324p. 1960. pap. 8.95 (*0-8048-0117-7*) Tuttle Pubng.

— English-Chinese Dictionary, Romanized. (CHI & ENG.). 323p. 37.50 (*0-87557-008-9*) Saphrograph.

— English-Chinese Dictionary Romanized. (CHI & ENG.). 323p. 1964. pap. 6.95 (*0-8288-6772-0*, M-9591) Fr & Eur.

Quoirez, Jacques, jt. auth. see Sagan, Francoise.

Quoist, Michel. New Prayers. 160p. 1990. pap. 12.95 (*0-8245-0983-8*, Pub. by Crossroad NY) Natl Bk Netwk.

— Prayers. LC 63-17141. 190p. 1985. reprint ed. pap. 8.95 (*0-934134-46-4*) Sheed & Ward WI.

***Quokka Sports Staff.** WWW.Whitbread.Org/Book: The 1997 - 98 Whitbread Round the World Race for the Volvo Trophy. (Illus.). 208p. 2000. 35.00 (*0-7893-0287-X*, Pub. by Universe) St Martin.

Quon, Ethel. A Hundred Feelings. 1991. pap. 12.95 (*0-944870-04-X*) Pacific Writers Pr.

Quon-Warner, Maryanna, jt. auth. see Rodecker, Stephen B.

***Quong, Terry.** Values Based Strategic Planning: A Dynamic Approach for Schools. 240p. 1999. pap. 33.40 (*0-13-081926-3*) P-H.

Quontamatteo, Tom. Emptiness That Plays So Rough. LC 93-74142. 56p. 1995. pap. 10.00 (*0-9636156-0-2*) Broken Shadow.

Quortrup. Childhood Matters. 412p. 1994. pap. 44.95 (*1-85628-856-0*) Ashgate Pub Co.

Quorum Health Resources Staff. Reengineering Manual for Healthcare Organizations. 112p. 1996. text 175.00 (*0-7863-1126-6*, Irwn Prfssnl) McGraw-Hill Prof.

Quraeshi, Samina. Lahore: The City Within. (Illus.). 292p. 1989. 75.00 (*0-7103-0335-1*) Routledge.

Quraishi-Ahmed, Huda, ed. Juz Three: Tilka Ar-Rusul: A Textbook for the Classroom, Senior Level. Ghazi, Abidullah et al, trs. from ARA. LC 97-94515. 94p. (YA). (gr. 10-12). 1998. pap. text 6.00 (*1-56316-120-6*) Iqra Intl Ed Fdtn.

Quraishi-Ahmed, Huda, ed. see Akhtar, Hina Naseem.

Quraishi-Ahmed, Huda, ed. see Durkee, Noura.

Quraishi-Ahmed, Huda, ed. see Ghazi, Abidullah.

Quraishi-Ahmed, Huda, jt. ed. see Ghazi, Abidullah.

Quraishi-Ahmed, Huda, ed. see Lemu, B. A.

Quraishi-Ahmed, Huda, ed. see Sadi, Shaikh Muslihuddin.

Quraishi-Ahmed, Huda, ed. see Ur-Rahman, Mushtaq & Rahman, Guljan.

Quraishi-Ahmed, Hudu, ed. see Abiva, Husryin.

Quraishi, Huda, jt. ed. see Akhtar, Hina.

Quraishi, Huda, ed. see El-Amin, Mildred.

Quraishi, Huda, ed. see Ghazi, Abidullah.

Quraishi, Huda, ed. see Ghazi, Suhaib & El-Amin, Mildred.

Quraishi, M. A. Drought Strategy. (C). 1989. 21.50 (*81-7018-562-9*, Pub. by BR Pub) S Asia.

Quraishi, M. Tariq, ed. Islam: A Way of Life & a Movement. LC 83-71408. 221p. (Orig.). 1986. reprint ed. pap. 9.50 (*0-89259-055-6*) Am Trust Pubns.

Quraishi, Mohammed S. Biochemical Insect Control: Its Impact on Economy, Environment, & Natural Selection. LC 76-29701. 288p. reprint ed. pap. 89.30 (*0-8357-7216-0*, 205630400056) Bks Demand.

Quraishi, Salim A., jt. auth. see Burke, S. M.

Quraishi, Salim A. Din, see Burke, Samuel M. & Din Quraishi, Salim A.

QURASHI, AL & Abdallah, Hasan. Spectres of Exile & other Poems: (Bilingual) 1991. text 45.00 (*1-873395-36-1*) St Martin.

Qureshi, A. H., jt. ed. see Sood, Arun K.

Qureshi, A. I. Fiscal System of Islam. 1981. pap. 10.50 (*1-56744-010-X*) Kazi Pubns.

— Islam & the Theory of Interest. 230p. 1984. 15.50 (*1-56744-073-8*) Kazi Pubns.

Qureshi, Abdul Saleem. Jinnah - The Founder of Pakistan: Through the Eyes of His Contemporaries & His Documentary Records at Lincoln's Inn. LC 99-188034. (Illus.). 134p. 1999. text 15.95 (*0-19-577851-0*) OUP.

Qureshi, Ahmed, tr. see Prophet of Islam.

Qureshi, Asif. World Trade Organization: Implementing International Trade Norms. 272p. 1998. pap. 29.95 (*0-7190-5433-8*, Pub. by Manchester Univ Pr) St Martin.

Qureshi, Asif H., ed. The Public International Law of Taxation: Text, Cases & Materials. LC 93-33344. 640p. (C). 1994. lib. bdg. 221.00 (*1-85333-950-4*, Pub. by Graham & Trotman) Kluwer Academic.

Qureshi, Asif H., et al. The Legal & Moral Aspects of International Trade: Freedom & Trade, Vol. 3. LC 97-30853. 272p. (C). 1998. 85.00 (*0-415-15526-6*) Routledge.

Qureshi, B. Transcultural Medicine: Principles & Practice. (C). 1989. text 84.00 (*0-85200-938-0*) Kluwer Academic.

Qureshi, Donna I. Rape: Social Facts from England & America. 293p. 1979. pap. text 8.60 (*0-87563-178-9*) Stipes.

Qureshi, Hazel, et al. Helpers in Case-Managed Community Care. (Illus.). 245p. 1989. text 64.95 (*0-566-05809-X*, Pub. by Arena) Ashgate Pub Co.

Qureshi, Hazel, jt. auth. see Nocon, Andrew.

Qureshi, Hazel, jt. auth. see Walker, Alan.

Qureshi, I. Administration of the Sultanate of Delhi. 5th ed. 1971. 28.50 (*0-317-89899-X*) Coronet Bks.

Qureshi, M. A. WAQFS in India: A Study of Administration & Statutory Control. 1990. 78.50 (*81-212-0282-5*, Pub. by Gian Publng Hse) S Asia.

— WAQFS in India: A Study of Administrative & Legislative Control. (C). 1990. 280.00 (*0-89771-239-0*) St Mut.

Qureshi, M. A., ed. WAQFS in India: A Study of Administrative & Statutory Control. (C). 1990. 275.00 (*0-89771-141-6*) St Mut.

Qureshi, M. A., jt. auth. see Gopa, D.

***Qureshi, M. Naeem.** Pan-Islam in British Indian Politics. LC 99-196668. (Social, Economic & Political Studies of the Middle East & Asia). 1999. write for info. (*90-04-11371-1*) Brill Academic Pubs.

Qureshi, Moeen & von Weizsacker, Richard, eds. The United Nations in Its Second Half-Century. 53p. (C). 1999. pap. text 20.00 (*0-7881-7130-5*) DIANE Pub.

Qureshi, Mohsin. Inorganic Ion Exchangers in Chemical Analysis. (Illus.). 296p. 1991. lib. bdg. 239.00 (*0-8493-5526-5*, QD562) CRC Pr.

Qureshi, Moshin, ed. Handbook of Chromatography: Inorganics, Vol. I. 384p. 1987. lib. bdg. 149.00 (*0-8493-3049-1*) CRC Pr.

Qureshi, Muhammad T., jt. auth. see Gajic, Zoran.

Qureshi, Regula B. Sufi Music of India & Pakistan: Sound, Context & Meaning in Qawwali. 266p. 1996. pap. 24.95 (*0-614-21357-6*, 1381); pap. 24.95 (*0-614-21590-0*, 1381) Kazi Pubns.

— Sufi Music of India & Pakistan: Sound, Context & Meaning in Qawwali. 284p. 1995. pap. text 24.95 (*0-226-70092-5*) U Ch Pr.

Qureshi, Salahudin. Regional Perspective on Dry Farming. (C). 1989. 34.00 (*81-7033-072-6*, Pub. by Rawat Pubns) S Asia.

Qureshi, Z. H. Arabic Writing for Beginners: Part One. 32p. 1992. pap. 3.50 (*0-935782-06-0*) Kazi Pubns.

— Arabic Writing for Beginners: Part Three. 32p. 1989. pap. 3.50 (*0-935782-18-4*) Kazi Pubns.

— Arabic Writing for Beginners: Part Two. 32p. 1991. pap. 3.50 (*0-935782-11-7*) Kazi Pubns.

Qureshi, Zia. Global Capital Supply & Demand: Is There Enough to Go Around? LC 96-13145. (Directions in Development Ser.). 32p. 1996. pap. 22.00 (*0-8213-3627-4*, 13627) World Bank.

Qureshi, Zia, jt. auth. see Shah, Anwar.

Qurik, jt. auth. see Lunsford, Andrea.

Qusar, Namgyal & Sergen, Jean. Tibetan Medicine & Healing. 320p. Date not set. pap. 15.00 (*0-465-08481-8*) Basic.

Qushayri, Abul Q. Sufi Book of Spiritual Ascent. Harris, Rabia, tr. 376p. 1997. pap. 19.95 (*1-871031-53-2*) Kazi Pubns.

Qutb, Muhammad. Islam: The Misunderstood Religion. 199p. 1977. pap. 5.95 (*0-939830-05-1*, Pub. by IIFSO KW) New Era Publns MI.
— Islam: The Misunderstood Religion. 1990. pap. 10.50 (*1-56744-084-3*) Kazi Pubns.
Qutb, Sayyid. Basic Principles of Islamic World View. Mizan Press Staff, tr. from ARA. LC 93-4677.Tr. of Khasais al-tasawwur al-Islami wa-muqawwimatuh. 1993. write for info. (*0-933782-25-X*) Mizan Pr.
— In the Shade of the Quran. Salahi, M. A. & Shamis, A. A., trs. 366p. pap. write for info. (*1-882837-18-5*) W A M Y Intl.
— Islam: The Misunderstood Religion. 200p. 1996. pap. 7.50 (*0-614-21429-7*, 597) Kazi Pubns.
— Islam & the Religion of the Future. 140p. 1996. pap. 19.95 (*0-614-21422-X*, 556); pap. 4.50 (*0-614-21423-8*, 561) Kazi Pubns.
— Islam & the Universal Peace. 82p. 1996. pap. 6.95 (*0-614-21424-6*, 564) Kazi Pubns.
— Islam & Universal Peace. LC 77-89635. 1977. pap. 4.50 (*0-89259-007-6*) Am Trust Pubns.
— Islamic Concept & Its Characteristics. Siddiqui, Mohammed M., tr. from ARA. 217p. (Orig.). (C). 1991. pap. 12.00 (*0-89259-119-6*) Am Trust Pubns.
— Milestone. 1981. pap. 8.50 (*0-934905-14-2*) Kazi Pubns.
— Milestones.Tr. of Ma alim fi at-Tariq. 303p. (Orig.). 1978. pap. 5.95 (*0-939830-07-8*, Pub. by IIFSO KW) New Era Publns MI.
— Milestones. rev. ed.Tr. of Ma alim fi at-Tariq. (Orig.). 1991. pap. 9.00 (*0-89259-076-9*) Am Trust Pubns.
— Social Justice in Islam. 1993. pap. 12.50 (*0-915597-87-X*) Amana Bks.
— Social Justice in Islam. rev. ed. Hardie, John B. & Algar, Hamid, trs. from ARA. LC 99-76692. 350p. 1999. 29.95 (*1-889999-12-1*); pap. 19.95 (*1-889999-11-3*) Islam Pubns Int.
— This Religion of Islam.Tr. of Hadha ad-Din. 104p. (Orig.). 1977. pap. 2.95 (*0-939830-08-6*, Pub. by IIFSO KW) New Era Publns MI.
— This Religion of Islam.Tr. of Hadha ad-Din. 110p. (Orig.). 1996. pap. 4.00 (*0-614-21450-5*, 1231) Kazi Pubns.
Quye, Anita, ed. see Charlesworth, Kate.
Quyen, Nguyen Van, see Hung, Nguyen M. & Van Quyen, Nguyen.
Quynh Dao. Canh Nhan Co Don. Lieu Quoc Nhi, tr. from CHI. (Illus.). 278p. (Orig.). 1994. pap. 13.00 (*1-886535-00-0*) Dong Van.
— Em La Canhhoa Roi. Lieu Quoc Nhi, tr. from CHI. 260p. (Orig.). (YA). 1994. pap. 13.00 (*1-886535-03-5*) Dong Van.
Qvarnstrom, Olle. Hindu Philosophy in Buddhist Perspective. (Lund Studies in African & Asian Religions: No. 4). 170p. (Orig.). 1989. pap. 66.50 (*91-86668-30-7*) Coronet Bks.
Qvist, Per Olov & Von Bagh, Peter. Guide to the Cinema of Sweden & Finland. LC 99-10110. (Reference Guides to World Cinema Ser.). 320p. 2000. lib. bdg. 85.00 (*0-313-30377-0*) Greenwood.
Qvortrup, Lars. The Social Significance of Telematics: An Essay on the Information Society. Edmonds, Philip, tr. LC 85-7493. (Pragmatics & Beyond Ser.: Vol. V:7). xviii, 228p. 1985. pap. 78.00 (*0-915027-04-6*) J Benjamins Pubng Co.
*__Qvortrup, Lars.__ Virtual Interaction: Interaction in Virtual Inhabited 3D Worlds. LC 00-34425. (Illus.). 2000. write for info. (*1-85233-331-6*) Spr-Verlag.
Qvortrup, Lars, et al, eds. Social Experiments with Information Technology & the Challenges of Innovation. (C). 1987. text 184.00 (*90-277-2488-1*) Kluwer Academic.
Qwizinc. Staff. Qwized-Spreadsheet, Student Activities. (DF - Computer Applications Ser.). 1995. mass mkt. 8.50 (*0-538-65635-2*) S-W Pub.
— Qwized Word Processing, Student Activities. (DF - Computer Applications Ser.). 1995. mass mkt., wbk. ed. 8.50 (*0-538-65632-8*) S-W Pub.
Qyqja, Ira, tr. see McIntyre, Sally.

R

R & B Enterprises Engineering Staff & Goldblum, Robert D. EMP Testing Handbook: Per MIL-STD-461C & MIL-STD-462, Notice 5. (Illus.). 201p. (Orig.). 1986. pap. 150.00 (*0-940499-00-2*) R & B Enter.
R. & R. Newkirk Staff & Mitchell, Carolyn B. Business Insurance. 6th ed. LC 95-16210. 310p. 1995. pap. 49.95 (*0-7931-1403-9*, 5412-0606, R & R Newkirk) Dearborn.
— Understanding Personal Umbrella Insurance. LC 95-16211. 100p. 1995. 22.95 (*0-7931-1400-4*, 5731-0101, R & R Newkirk) Dearborn.
— Variable Contracts. 120p. 1995. pap. 25.95 (*0-7931-1355-5*, 5444-0101, R & R Newkirk) Dearborn.
R & R Newkirk Staff, jt. see Dearborn Staff.
R. Bin Wong, jt. auth. see Will, Pierre-Etienne.
R. C. C. Pilotage Foundation Staff. The Atlantic Islands: Azores, Canaries, Madeira & Cape Verde Islands. 2nd ed. (Illus.). 230p. 1994. 125.00 (*0-85288-267-X*, Pub. by Laurie Norie & Wilson Ltd) St Mut.
— The Baltic Sea: Germany, Poland, the Baltic States, Russia, Finland, Sweden, Denmark. Robinson, Oz, ed. (Illus.). 230p. (C). 1992. 125.00 (*0-85288-175-4*, Pub. by Laurie Norie & Wilson Ltd) St Mut.
— Faeroe, Iceland & Greenland: Pilotage for the Arctic Fringe. (Illus.). 90p. 1995. pap. 125.00 (*0-85288-268-8*, Pub. by Laurie Norie & Wilson Ltd) St Mut.
— North Africa: Strait of Gibraltar to Tunisia. (Illus.). 198p. (C). 1995. 125.00 (*0-85288-155-X*, Pub. by Laurie Norie & Wilson Ltd) St Mut.
R. C. C. Pilotage Foundation/SHOM Staff. The Lesser Antilles: Barbados & Grenada to the Virgin Islands. Robinson, O., ed. (Illus.). 256p. 1991. 125.00 (*0-85288-153-3*, Pub. by Laurie Norie & Wilson Ltd) St Mut.
R C Publications Staff. Print's Best Letterheads & Business Cards, No. 3. 192p. 1994. 34.95 (*0-915734-84-2*, 30579) RC Pubns.
— Print's Best Logos & Symbols, No. 3. 192p. 1994. 34.95 (*0-915734-85-0*, 30580) RC Pubns.
R C Publications Staff, ed. Print's Best Illustration & Photography. 192p. 1994. 34.95 (*0-915734-82-6*, 30581) RC Pubns.
R, Joe. Do Yu Know - What Distortion - Sowndz Like: An Urban Legend. 198p. 1998. pap. 16.00 (*1-891408-07-0*, GBP-8) Green Bean.
— The Jeff Book. 224p. 1996. pap. 15.00 (*1-891408-04-6*, GBP-5) Green Bean.
— No Mattrr What. 42p. 1999. pap. 4.00 (*1-891408-09-7*, GBP-10) Green Bean.
R. K. A. L. Conference on Compact Heat Exchangers & Shah. Compact Heat Exchangers for the Process Industries: Proceedings of an International Conference on Compact Heat Exhangers for the Process Industries, Held at the Cliff Lodge & Conference Center, Snowbird, Utah During June 22-27, 1997. LC 97-19023. 1997. write for info. (*1-56700-090-8*) Begell Hse.
R, LAL. Pesticides & Nitrogen Cycle, Vol. 3. LC 87-7985. 184p. 1987. 106.00 (*0-8493-4353-4*, CRC Reprint) Franklin.
R, M. Emiko. My Life Was Like the Storm at Sea. (Illus.). 72p. 1997. pap. 10.00 (*0-8059-4074-X*) Dorrance.
R. M. University of Quigley Staff, ed. see Rowe, R. K.
R., Mark & L., Mary. Stepping Stones to Recovery from Cocaine-Crack Addiction. LC 90-20336. 128p. (Orig.). pap. 7.95 (*0-934125-10-4*) Hazelden.
R. Ram Mohan Rao & Simhadri, S. Development Dynamics in Command Areas of Major Irrigation Project. (C). 1989. 36.50 (*81-210-0236-2*, Pub. by Inter-India Pubns) S Asia.
*__R. S. Means Company Staff.__ Assemblies Cost Data: 2000 Edition. 25th ed. (Assemblies Cost Data Ser.). (Illus.). 570p. 2000. pap. 139.95 (*0-87629-541-3*) R S Means.
— Building Construction Cost Data: 2000 Edition. 58th ed. LC 97-38006. Vol. 58. (Illus.). 694p. 1999. pap. text 85.95 (*0-87629-540-5*) R S Means.
— Building Construction Cost Data 2000. 58th ed. 2000. pap. 109.95 (*0-87629-567-7*) R S Means.
— Building Construction Cost Data 2000: Metric. 58th ed. 2000. pap. 89.95 (*0-87629-551-0*) R S Means.
— Building Construction Cost Data 2000: Western Edition. 13th ed. 2000. pap. 89.95 (*0-87629-561-8*) R S Means.
— Electrical Change Order Cost Data: Professional Estimating Service 2000. 12th ed. 450p. 1999. pap. 89.95 (*0-87629-545-6*) R S Means.
— Electrical Cost Data, 2000. 23rd ed. (Illus.). 2000. pap. 89.95 (*0-87629-543-X*) R S Means.
— Environmental Remediation Cost Data 2000: Assemblies. 6th ed. 2000. 149.95 (*0-87629-565-0*) R S Means.
— Environmental Remediation Cost Data 2000: Unit Price. 6th ed. 2000. pap. 99.95 (*0-87629-564-2*) R S Means.
— Facilities Construction Cost Data 2000. 15th ed. (Illus.). 1150p. 2000. pap. 209.95 (*0-87629-552-9*) R S Means.
— Facilities Maintenance & Repair Cost 2000. 7th ed. 2000. pap. 199.95 (*0-87629-557-X*) R S Means.
R. S. Means Company Staff. Hanscomb's Yardsticks for Costing: Cost Data for the Canadian Construction Industry/Metric & I. 1998. pap. text 86.00 (*0-87629-495-6*) R S Means Co.
*__R. S. Means Company Staff.__ Heavy Construction Cost Data 2000. 14th ed. 1999. pap. 89.95 (*0-87629-553-7*) R S Means.
— Heavy Construction Cost Data 2000. 14th ed. (Illus.). 450p. 2000. pap. 89.95 (*0-87629-555-3*) R S Means.
— Historic Preservation: Project Planning & Estimating. 450p. 2000. 99.95 (*0-87629-573-1*, 67323) R S Means.
— How to Estimate with Means Data & Cost Works. 2000. pap. text 59.95 (*0-87629-539-1*) R S Means.
— Labor Rules for the Construction Industry 2000. 27th ed. 326p. 1999. pap. 189.95 (*0-87629-563-4*) R S Means.
— Light Commercial Cost Data 2000. 19th ed. 1999. pap. 76.95 (*0-87629-562-6*) R S Means.
— Mean Illustrated Construction Dictionary. 3rd ed. (Illus.). 2000. 99.95 (*0-87629-574-X*) R S Means.
— Means Concrete & Masonry Cost Data 2000. 18th ed. 1999. pap. 79.95 (*0-87629-554-5*) R S Means.
— Means Interior Cost Data 2000. 17th ed. 1999. pap. 89.95 (*0-87629-548-0*) R S Means.
— Means Repair & Remodeling Cost Data 2000. 23rd ed. LC 88-641537. 650p. 1999. pap. 79.95 (*0-87629-544-8*) R S Means.
— Mechanical Cost Data: 2000 Edition. 23rd ed. 1999. pap. text 89.95 (*0-87629-542-1*) R S Means.
— Open Shop Building Construction Cost Data 2000. 16th ed. 2000. pap. 89.95 (*0-87629-549-9*) R S Means.
— Plumbing Cost Data: 2000 Edition. 23rd ed. (Illus.). 540p. 1999. pap. text 89.95 (*0-87629-546-4*) R S Means.
— Residential Cost Data 2000. 19th ed. (Illus.). 580p. 1999. pap. 74.95 (*0-87629-556-1*) R S Means.
— Site Work & Landscape Cost Data 2000. 19th ed. 600p. 2000. pap. 89.95 (*0-87629-547-2*) R S Means.
— Square Foot Costs: 2000 Edition. 21st ed. 1999. pap. text 99.95 (*0-87629-550-2*) R S Means.
*__R. S. Means Company Staff & Fee, Sylvia H.__ Landscape Estimating Methods. 3rd rev. exp. ed. LC 99-462613. Orig. Title: Landscape Estimating. 300p. 1998. 62.95 (*0-87629-534-0*, 67295A) R S Means.
*__R S Means Staff.__ Contractor's Pricing Guide: Framing & Rough Carpentry. 300p. (C). 2000. 36.95 (*0-87629-560-X*) R S Means.
— Contractors Pricing Guide: Residential Detailed Costs 2000. 300p. (C). 2000. pap. 36.95 (*0-87629-558-8*) R S Means.
— Contractors Pricing Guide: Residential Square Foot Costs 2000. 300p. (C). 2000. pap. 39.95 (*0-87629-559-6*) R S Means.
*__R S Means Staff, ed.__ Means Illustrated Construction Dictionary. 3rd ed. (Illus.). 2000. 99.95 (*0-87629-538-3*) R S Means.
R&R Newkirk Staff, jt. auth. see Dearborn Staff.
Ra, Carol, jt. auth. see Smith, William J.
Ra, David, tr. see Klaus, Sandra.
Ra, Jong Oh. Labor at the Polls: Union Voting in Presidential Elections, 1952-1976. LC 77-90729. (Illus.). 192p. 1978. 27.50 (*0-87023-026-3*) U of Mass Pr.
Ra, Star. Adonai I Am That I Am, Vol. 1. (Illus.). 180p. (Orig.). (C). 1996. pap. 14.99 (*0-9654549-8-3*) EHYEH.
Ra Un Nefer Amen. Tree of Life Meditation System: General Principles of Holistic Meditation. 280p. pap. 13.95 (*1-877662-13-5*) Kamit Pubns.
Ra Un Nefer Amen I. The Ausar Auset Nutrition Handbook. 54p. (Orig.). 1988. pap. 6.00 (*0-317-93991-2*) Kamit Pubns.
— Metu Neter Vol. 1: The Great Oracle of Tehuti & the Egyptian System of Spiritual Cultivation. 439p. 1990. pap. 16.95 (*1-877662-03-8*) Kamit Pubns.
— Netu Neter Vol. 2: Anuk Ausar: The Kamitic Initiation System. (Illus.). 350p. pap. 14.95 (*1-877662-08-9*) Kamit Pubns.
— A Nutritional, Herbal, & Homeopathic Guide to Healing. 52p. (Orig.). 1988. pap. 6.00 (*0-317-93992-0*) Kamit Pubns.
— The Ritual Systems of Ancient Black Civilizations Vol. 1: Introduction to Meditation. 66p. (Orig.). pap., spiral bd. 15.00 (*1-877662-00-3*) Kamit Pubns.
— The Ritual Systems of Ancient Black Civilizations Vol. 1: Introduction to Meditation. 51p. (Orig.). 1988. pap. 14.95 (*0-317-93993-9*) Kamit Pubns.
— The Ritual Systems of Ancient Black Civilizations Vol. 2: Auset, Mother of the Living. 42p. pap., spiral bd. 15.00 incl. audio (*1-877662-01-1*) Kamit Pubns.
— The Ritual Systems of Ancient Black Civilizations Vol. 3: The Opening of the Way. 40p. pap., spiral bd. 13.00 incl. audio (*1-877662-02-X*) Kamit Pubns.
*__Ra, Young K.__ Probleme Der Literaturgeschichtsschreibung: Uberlegungen Zur Osterreichischen Literatur In Deutschen Literaturgeschichten, Am Beispiel Von Johann Nestroy, Adalbert Stifter Und Karl Kraus Dargestellt. 252p. 1999. 45.95 (*3-631-34586-0*) P Lang Pubng.
Raab, Birgitta & Vedin, Haldo, eds. Climate, Lakes & Rivers. (National Atlas of Sweden Ser.). (Illus.). 176p. 1998. 99.50 (*91-87760-32-0*, Pub. by Almqvist Wiksell) Coronet Bks.
Raab, Charles, jt. auth. see McPherson, Andrew.
Raab, Charles D., jt. auth. see Arnott, Margaret A.
*__Raab, Diana.__ Getting Pregnant & Staying Pregnant: Overcoming Infertility & Managing Your High-Risk Pregnancy. 3rd ed. LC 99-26874. (Illus.). 320p. 1999. 24.95 (*0-89793-238-2*) Hunter Hse.
— Getting Pregnant & Staying Pregnant: Overcoming Infertility & Managing Your High-Risk Pregnancy. 3rd rev. ed. (Illus.). 320p. 1999. 24.95 (*0-89793-274-9*) Hunter Hse.
Raab, Earl, jt. auth. see Lipset, Seymour M.
Raab, Elisabeth M. And Peace Never Came. LC 97-141738. (Illus.). 152p. 1996. pap. 24.95 (*0-88920-292-3*) W Laurier U Pr.
Raab, Evelyn. Clueless in the Kitchen: A Cookbook for Teens. LC 97-932380. (Illus.). 216p. (YA). (gr. 7 up). 1998. pap. 12.95 (*1-55209-224-0*) Firefly Bks Ltd.
*__Raab, Evelyn.__ The Clueless Vegetarian: A Cookbook for the Aspiring Vegetarian. (Illus.). 216p. 2000. pap. 12.95 (*1-55209-497-9*) Firefly Bks Ltd.
Raab, Fred, ed. see Bonsteel, Alan.
Raab, James W. America's Daredevil Balloonist: W. H. Donaldson, 1840-1875. (Illus.). 175p. 1999. 25.95 (*0-89745-238-0*); pap. 17.95 (*0-89745-231-3*) Sunflower U Pr.
— W. W. Loring: Florida's Forgotten General. (Illus.). 260p. 1996. 35.95 (*0-89745-210-0*); pap. 21.95 (*0-89745-205-4*) Sunflower U Pr.
— W. W. Loring - A Biography, Vols. 1 & 2. LC 97-216663. 946p. 1997. 117.00 (*0-89126-198-2*) MA-AH Pub.
Raab, Jonathan. Using Consensus Building to Improve Utility Regulation. LC 94-15737. 317p. (Orig.). (C). 1994. pap. 31.00 (*0-918249-19-8*) Am Coun Energy.
*__Raab, Kelley A.__ When the Priest Is a Woman: A Psychoanalytic Perspective on the Catholic Women's Ordination Debate. LC 99-49657. 2000. pap. 19.50 (*0-231-11335-8*) Col U Pr.
— When Women Became Priests: The Catholic Women's Ordination Debate. 2000. 49.50 (*0-231-11334-X*) Col U Pr.
Raab, Lawrence. The Collector of Cold Weather. LC 76-3301. (American Poetry Ser.: Vol.9). 1977. pap. 2.95 (*0-912946-45-8*, Ecco Press) HarperTrade.
— Other Children. LC 86-70208. (Poetry Ser.). 80p. (C). 1987. 20.95 (*0-88748-028-4*); pap. 11.95 (*0-88748-029-2*) Carnegie-Mellon.
*__Raab, Lawrence.__ The Probable World. LC 99-55293. 96p. 2000. pap. 15.95 (*0-14-058921-X*) Penguin Putnam.
Raab, Lawrence. What We Don't Know about Each Other. LC 93-2664. 96p. (Orig.). 1993. pap. 12.00 (*0-14-058701-2*, Penguin Bks) Viking Penguin.
Raab, Patricia B., ed. see Moynihan, Patricia M.
Raab, R. E., jt. auth. see De Lange, O. L.
Raab, Reginald, tr. see Wachsmuth, Guenther.
Raab, Rex, et al. Eloquent Concrete: How Rudolf Steiner Employed Reinforced Concrete. (Illus.). 141p. 1979. pap. 24.00 (*0-85440-354-X*, Pub. by R Steiner Pr) Anthroposophic.
Raab, Robert A. Coping with Death. rev. ed. Rosen, Ruth C., ed. (Coping Ser.). (YA). (gr. 7-12). 1989. lib. bdg. 17.95 (*0-8239-0960-3*) Rosen Group.
Raab, Rudi, jt. auth. see Freestone, Julie.
Raab, Scott. Reasonable Doubt. 1998. write for info. (*0-679-45772-0*) Villard Books.
Raab, Selwyn, jt. auth. see Ragano, Frank.
Raab, Steve. 1998 Year Book of Pathology & Laboratory Medicine. 2nd ed. (Illus.). 568p. (C). (gr. 13). 1998. text 83.00 (*0-8151-9722-5*, 25009) Mosby Inc.
*__Raab, Steven S.__ With the 3-D Wisconsin Badgers: The Living Experience of the Civil War Through the Journals of Va. LC 99-36030. 286p. 1999. 29.95 (*0-8117-0002-X*) Stackpole.
Raab, Steven S. & Matusky, Gregory. Blueprint for Franchising a Business. LC 87-15932. 256p. 1987. 45.00 (*0-471-85617-7*) Wiley.
Raab, Susan S. & Bierwirth, Johanna. An Author's Guide to Children's Book Promotion. rev. ed. 76p. 1998. pap. 12.95 (*0-9621211-3-4*) Raab Assocs.
Raab, Theodore. Renaissance Lives: Portraits of an Age. 272p. 2001. pap. 18.00 (*0-465-06800-6*, Pub. by Basic) HarpC.
Raabe. 1996 Multistate Corporate Tax Guide Mid-Year Supplement. 1996. 106.00 (*1-56706-311-X*) Panel Pubs.
— Stopfkuchen. unabridged ed. (World Classic Literature Ser.). (GER.). pap. 5.95 (*3-89507-021-1*, Pub. by Bookking Intl) Distribks Inc.
Raabe & Whittenburg. West's Fed Tax Research. 5th ed. LC 98-46491. (SWC-Taxation). 1999. pap. 87.95 (*0-324-00491-5*) Thomson Learn.
Raabe, jt. auth. see Hoffman.
*__Raabe, Anne.__ Das Wort Stammt von Kierkegaard: Alfred Andersch und Soren Kierkegaard. (Beitrage zur Literatur und Literaturwissenschaft des 20. Jahrhunderts Ser.). 236p. 1999. 37.95 (*3-631-35449-5*) P Lang Pubng.
Raabe, C. Dictionnaire E l'Informatique, Internet. (FRE.). 722p. 1997. 69.95 (*0-320-00485-6*) Fr & Eur.
Raabe, D. Computational Materials Science: The Simulation of Materials, Microstructures & Properties. LC 99-163380. (Illus.). 400p. 1998. 185.00 (*3-527-29541-0*) Wiley.
Raabe, Kenneth A., et al. Income Shifting after Tax Return. LC 88-61005. 1200p. 1989. pap. 38.00 (*0-13-454372-6*, Busn) P-H.
Raabe, M. Recent Developments in Insect Neurohormones. (Illus.). 484p. (C). 1989. text 130.00 (*0-306-43175-0*, Kluwer Plenum) Kluwer Academic.
Raabe, Marie. Insect Neurohormones. Marshall, Nissim, tr. from FRE. LC 82-7535. (Illus.). 366p. 1982. 75.00 (*0-306-40782-5*, Plenum Trade) Perseus Pubng.
Raabe, Mechthild, compiled by. Leser und Lekture des 18: Jahrnunderts Die Ausleibucher der Herzog August Bibliothek Wolfenbuttel, 1715-1800, 4 vols. (GER.). 400p. 1987. write for info. (*0-318-61906-7*); write for info. (*0-318-61907-5*); write for info. (*0-318-61908-3*) K G Saur Verlag.
— Leser und Lekture des 18: Jahrnunderts Die Ausleibucher der Herzog August Bibliothek Wolfenbuttel, 1715-1800, 4 vols., Band 1: Einleitung-Alphabetischer Katalog. (GER.). 400p. 1987. lib. bdg. 160.00 (*3-598-10651-3*) K G Saur Verlag.
Raabe, Otto, ed. Internal Radiation Dosimentry: 1994 Health Physics Summer School. LC 94-76682. (Illus.). 667p. (C). 1994. pap. text 48.95 (*0-944838-47-2*) Med Physics Pub.
Raabe, Paul. The Era of German Expressionism. (German Expressionist Ser.). 1980. pap. 13.95 (*0-7145-0699-0*) Riverrun NY.
Raabe, Paul, ed. The Era of German Expressionism. Ritchie, J. M., tr. from GER. LC 72-97580. 424p. 1986. 26.95 (*0-87951-010-2*, Pub. by Overlook Pr); pap. 16.95 (*0-87951-233-4*, Pub. by Overlook Pr) Penguin Putnam.
Raabe, Paul & August, Herzog, eds. Acta Eruditorum, 117 vols. fiche. write for info. (*0-318-70648-2*) G Olms Pubs.
— Acta Eruditorum, 117 vols. fiche. write for info. (*0-318-70649-0*) Lubrecht & Cramer.
— Acta Eruditorum, 117 vols., Vols. 1-10. write for info. (*0-318-70647-4*) G Olms Pubs.
Raabe, Paul, ed. see Kloth, Karen.
Raabe, Paul, ed. see Muller-Jerina, Alwin.
Raabe, Paul R. Obadiah: A New Translation with Introduction & Commentary. LC 95-36913. (Anchor Bible Ser.). (Illus.). 336p. 1996. 34.95 (*0-385-41268-1*, Anchor NY) Doubleday.
Raabe, Paul R. Psalm-Structures: A Study of Psalms with Refrains. (JSOT Supplement Ser.: No. 104). 219p. 1990. 60.00 (*1-85075-262-1*, Pub. by Sheffield Acad) CUP Services.
*__Raabe, Peter B.__ Philosophical Counseling: Theory & Practice. 240p. 2000. 59.00 (*0-275-97056-6*, Praeger Pubs) Greenwood.
Raabe, Rainald. Der Imaginierte Betrachter. (Studien Zur Kunstgeschichte Ser.: Vol. 72). (GER.). 164p. 1996. write for info. (*3-487-10042-8*) G Olms Pubs.
Raabe, Susanne M. Der Wortschatz in den deutschen Schriften Thomas Murners: Band 1: Untersuchengen - Band 2: Worterbuch. (Studia Linguistica Germanica: Band 29). xviii, 358p. (C). 1990. lib. bdg. 275.40 (*3-11-012456-4*) De Gruyter.
Raabe, Tom. Biblioholism: The Literary Addiction. aut. limited num. ed. (Illus.). 192p. 1995. 100.00 (*1-55591-378-4*) Fulcrum Pub.
— Biblioholism: The Literary Addiction. rev. ed. LC 91-7260. (Illus.). 192p. 1995. pap. 10.95 (*1-55591-080-7*) Fulcrum Pub.

An Asterisk (*) at the beginning of an entry indicates that the title is appearing for the first time.

— Sports for the Athletically Impaired. LC 92-54764. (Illus.). 256p. (Orig.). 1993. pap. 10.95 (*1-55591-133-1*) Fulcrum Pub.

— Sports in the Twentieth Century. Baron, Bob, ed. LC 95-8767. (Millennium 2000 Ser.). 144p. 1995. 8.95 (*1-55591-276-1*) Fulcrum Pub.

— The Ultimate Church. 176p. 1991. pap. 8.99 (*0-310-54191-3*) Zondervan.

Raabe, Wilhelm. Novels. Sander, Volkmar, ed. LC 82-22097. (German Library: Vol. 45). 320p. 1992. 39.50 (*0-8264-0280-1*) Continuum.

— Novels. Sander, Volkmar, ed. LC 66-28139. (German Library: Vol. 45). 320p. (C). 1992. 19.95 (*0-8264-0281-X*) Continuum.

Raabe, William A. & Boucher, Karen J. 1997 Multistate Corporate Tax Guide, 2 vols. 1248p. pap. 238.00 (*1-56706-405-1*, S78) Panel Pubs.

Raabe, William A. & Johnson, Ranae. Winters Flower. 261p. 1992. pap. 12.95 (*0-9631506-0-X*) Raintree.

Raabe, William A., et al. Multistate Corporate Tax Guide Vols. I & II: 1992 Edition, 1. Kaiser, Laura B., ed. 950p. 1991. write for info. (*1-878375-57-1*) Panel Pubs.

— Multistate Corporate Tax Guide Vols. I & II: 1992 Edition, 2. Kaiser, Laura B., ed. 950p. 1991. write for info. (*1-878375-58-X*) Panel Pubs.

— Multistate Corporate Tax Guide Vols. I & II: 1992 Edition, Set. Kaiser, Laura B., ed. 950p. 1991. pap. text 185.00 (*1-878375-59-8*) Panel Pubs.

— Multistate S Corporation Tax Guide. 641p. 1990. pap. text 96.00 (*1-878375-08-3*) Panel Pubs.

— West's Federal Tax Research. 4th ed. LC 96-36715. 1997. mass mkt. 60.00 (*0-314-20182-3*) West Pub.

— Wft Research 3rd Edition. 3rd ed. LC 93-24109. (SWC-Taxation). 650p. (C). 1993. mass mkt. 61.50 (*0-314-02650-9*) West Pub.

***Raabenstein.** Leib. (Illus.). 48p. 2000. 24.95 (*3-9803212-3-1*, Pub. by Vice Versa Verlag) Nazraeli Press.

Raack, Richard C. Fall of Stein. LC 65-19828. (Historical Monographs: No. 58). 228p. 1965. 20.00 (*0-674-29200-6*) HUP.

— Stalin's Drive to the West, 1938-1945: The Origins of the Cold War. LC 95-4990. xii, 265p. 1995. 45.00 (*0-8047-2415-6*) Stanford U Pr.

Raad, Boele De, see De Raad, Boele.

Raad, C. Van, see Doernberg, Richard L. & Van Raad, C.

Raad, Kees Van, see Van Raad, Kees.

Raad van het Pluralistisch Onderwijs Staff, jt. auth. see Neve, D. De.

Raad, Virginia. The Piano Sonority of Claude Debussy. LC 93-50847. (Studies in the History & Interpretation of Music: Vol. 34). 92p. 1993. 49.95 (*0-7734-9138-4*) E Mellen.

Raadschelders, J. C. Handbook of Administrative History. LC 97-26144. 274p. 1997. text 39.95 (*1-56000-315-4*) Transaction Pubs.

Raadt, J. D. De, see De Raadt, J. D.

Raaen, Aagot. Grass of the Earth: Immigrant Life in the Dakota Country. LC 93-44859. xxxiv, 238p. 1994. pap. 12.95 (*0-87351-295-2*, Borealis Book) Minn Hist.

Raaf Central Photographic Establishment Staff. Canvas to Carbon Fibre: A Selection of Fine Paintings Depicting the History of the Australian Flying Corps & the Royal Australian Air Force. unabridged ed. LC 94-3141. (Illus.). 80p. 1995. 49.95 (*0-644-42804-X*, 943141X, Pub. by AGPS Pr) Intl Spec Bk.

Raaf, Hermann. Chemie Des Alltags A-Z: Ein Lexikon der Praktischen Chemie. 28th ed. (GER.). 310p. 1992. 59.95 (*0-7859-8375-9*, 3451218534) Fr & Eur.

Raaf, John, jt. ed. see Andrews, Jullie S.

RAAF Public Relations Section Staff. Wings for Warriors: A Photographic History of the Australian Flying Corps & the Royal Australian Air Force. unabridged ed. LC 94-30385. (Illus.). 80p. 1995. 39.95 (*0-644-42702-7*, 9430385, Pub. by AGPS Pr) Intl Spec Bk.

Raafat, H. Machinery Safety: The Risk Based Approach. 1996. pap. 129.00 (*1-85953-006-0*, Pub. by Tech Comm) St Mut.

Raaflaub. Discovery of Freedom. 1994. lib. bdg. 34.95 (*0-226-70101-8*) U Ch Pr.

***Raaflaub, Kurt A. & Rosenstein, Nathan S.** War & Society in the Ancient & Medieval Worlds: Asia, the Mediterranean, Europe & Mesoamerica. LC 99-16656. (Center for Hellenic Studies Colloquia Ser.). 544p. 1999. 50.00 (*0-674-94660-X*) HUP.

Raaflaub, Kurt A. & Tober, Mark, eds. Between Republic & Empire: Interpretations of Augustus & His Principate. 1990. pap. 29.95 (*0-520-08447-0*, Pub. by U CA Pr) Cal Prin Full Svc.

Raaflaub, Kurt A., jt. auth. see Boedeker, Deborah D.

Raag, Virve. The Effects of Planned Change on Estonian Morphology. LC 98-192650. (Studia Uralica Upsaliensia Ser.: Vol. 29). 156p. 1998. pap. 46.50 (*91-554-4204-8*) Coronet Bks.

Raah-ne-ah. May the Light & Love Flow. 160p. (C). 1988. pap. write for info. (*0-7212-0767-7*, Pub. by Regency Pr GBR) St Mut.

Raaij, Fred Van, see Basmossy, Gary & Van Raaij, Fred, eds.

Raaij, W. F. van. The Consumption of Time & the Timing of Consumption: Toward a New Behavioral & Socioeconomics. Antonides, G. & Arts, W., eds. (Verhandelingen der Koninklijke Nederlandse Akademie van Wetenschappen, Afd. Letterkunde, Nieuwe Reeks Ser.: No. 146). vii, 286p. 1991. pap. text 61.25 (*0-444-85733-8*) Elsevier.

Raaimakers, D. Growth of Tropical Rain Forest Trees As Dependent on Phosphorus Supply: Tree Saplings Different in Regeneration Strategy & Their Adaptations to a Low Phosphorus Environment in Guyana. (Tropenbos Technical Ser.: No. 11). (Illus.). 107p. 1994. pap. 30.00 (*90-5113-023-6*, Pub. by Backhuys Pubs) Balogh.

Raal, J. D., jt. auth. see Muhlbauer, Andre.

Raalte, Judy L. Van, see Van Raalte, Judy L.

Raalte, Marlein Van, see Van Ophuijsen, Johannes M. & Van Raalte, Marlein, eds.

Raalte, Susan D. Van, see Van Raalte, Susan D.

Raam, Shanthi, ed. Immunology of Steroid Hormone Receptors, Vol. I. 176p. 1988. 100.00 (*0-8493-4983-4*, QP572, CRC Reprint) Franklin.

Raan, A. F. Van, see Van Raan, A. F., ed.

Ra'anan, Uri, ed. Ethnic Resurgence in Modern Democratic States: A Multidisciplinary Approach to Human Resources & Conflict. (Policy Studies). 1980. 88.00 (*0-08-024647-8*, Pergamon Pr) Elsevier.

— The Soviet Empire & the Challenge of National & Democratic Movements. 272p. 1990. pap. 24.95 (*0-669-24676-X*) Free Pr.

Ra'anan, Uri, et al, eds. Russian Pluralism, Now Irreversible? LC 92-28597. 224p. 1993. text 39.95 (*0-312-08648-2*) St Martin.

Ra'anan, Uri & Martin, Kate, eds. Russia: A Return to Imperialism? 199p. 1996. text 49.95 (*0-312-12927-0*) St Martin.

Raaphorst, Donna Van, see Van Raaphorst, Donna.

Raasch, Maynard S., jt. auth. see Springer, Victor G.

***Raaschelders, Jos C. N.** Handbook of Administrative History. 2000. pap. 29.95 (*0-7658-0726-2*) Transaction Pubs.

Raask, Erich. Mineral Impurities in Coal Combustion: Behavior, Problems, & Remedial Measures. LC 83-26400. (Illus.). 467p. 1985. 132.00 (*0-89116-362-X*) Hemisp Pub.

***Raat.** American Orb. 2000. mass mkt. 20.00 (*0-8133-3522-1*, Pub. by Westview) HarpC.

Raat, W. Dirk. Mexico & the United States: Ambivalent Vistas. 2nd ed. LC 96-18124. 1996. pap. 20.00 (*0-8203-1812-4*) U of Ga Pr.

Raat, W. Dirk & Beezley, William H., eds. Twentieth-Century Mexico. LC 85-14109. (Illus.). xviii, 318p. 1986. pap. text 18.00 (*0-8032-8914-6*, Bison Books) U of Nebr Pr.

Raat, W. Dirk & Janecek, George R. Mexico's Sierra Tarahumara: A Photohistory of the People of the Edge. LC 95-50961. (Illus.). 136p. 1996. 49.95 (*0-8061-2815-1*) U of Okla Pr.

***Raatma, Lucia.** Abraham Lincoln. (Early Biographies Ser.). (Illus.). 32p. (J). (gr. 1-2). 2000. write for info. (*0-7565-0012-5*) Compass Point.

— Bill Gates: Computer Programmer & Entrepreneur. LC 00-37592. (Career Biographies Ser.). (Illus.). 2000. write for info. (*0-89434-335-1*) Ferguson.

Raatma, Lucia. Caring. LC 99-31306. (Character Education Ser.). 24p. (J). 1999. 14.60 (*0-7368-0366-1*, Bridgestone Bks) Capstone Pr.

***Raatma, Lucia.** Caring. (Character Education Ser.). 24p. (J). (gr. k-3). 1999. 14.60 (*0-516-21854-9*, Bridgestone Bks) Capstone Pr.

— Character Education. (Illus.). 24p. 167.30 (*0-7368-0557-5*, Bridgestone Bks) Capstone Pr.

— Charles Lindbergh. (Early Biographies Ser.). (Illus.). 32p. (J). (gr. 1-2). 2000. write for info. (*0-7565-0013-3*) Compass Point.

Raatma, Lucia. Consideration. LC 99-31307. (Character Education Ser.). 24p. (J). 1999. 14.60 (*0-7368-0367-X*, Bridgestone Bks) Capstone Pr.

***Raatma, Lucia.** Consideration. (Character Education Ser.). 24p. (J). (gr. k-3). 1999. 14.60 (*0-516-21855-7*, Bridgestone Bks) Capstone Pr.

— Cooperation. LC 99-47924. (Character Education Ser.). 24p. (J). (ps-3). 2000. lib. bdg. 15.93 (*0-7368-0506-0*, Bridgestone Bks) Capstone Pr.

— Courage. LC 99-48738. (Character Education Ser.). 24p. (J). (ps-3). 2000. lib. bdg. 15.93 (*0-7368-0507-9*, Bridgestone Bks) Capstone Pr.

— Fire Fighters. (Community Workers Ser.). (Illus.). 32p. (J). (gr. 1-2). 2000. write for info. (*0-7565-0009-5*) Compass Point.

— Fire Safety. (Illus.). 24p. 47.80 (*0-7368-0297-5*) Capstone Pr.

Raatma, Lucia. Friendliness. LC 99-31308. (Character Education Ser.). 24p. (J). 1999. 14.60 (*0-7368-0368-8*, Bridgestone Bks) Capstone Pr.

***Raatma, Lucia.** Friendliness. 24p. (J). (gr. k-3). 1999. 14.60 (*0-516-21856-5*) Childrens.

Raatma, Lucia. Honesty. LC 99-23766. (Character Education Ser.). 24p. (J). 1999. 14.60 (*0-7368-0369-6*, Bridgestone Bks) Capstone Pr.

***Raatma, Lucia.** Honesty. 24p. (J). (gr. k-3). 1999. pap. 14.60 (*0-516-21857-3*, Bridgestone Bks) Capstone Pr.

Raatma, Lucia. How Books Are Made. LC 97-26103. (A True Book). 48p. (gr. 2-3). 1998. 21.00 (*0-516-20671-0*) Childrens.

— How Books Are Made. (True Bks.). (Illus.). 48p. (J). 1998. pap. 6.95 (*0-516-26379-X*) Childrens.

***Raatma, Lucia.** Jackie Robinson. (Early Biographies Ser.). (Illus.). 32p. (J). (gr. 1-2). 2000. write for info. (*0-7565-0016-8*) Compass Point.

Raatma, Lucia. Libraries. LC 97-18052. (True Bks.). (Illus.). 48p. (J). (gr. 2-4). 1998. 21.00 (*0-516-20672-9*) Childrens.

— Libraries. Joffe, Shari, ed. (True Bks.). (Illus.). 48p. (J). 1998. pap. 6.95 (*0-516-26380-3*) Childrens.

***Raatma, Lucia.** Maya Angelou: Writer & Documentary Filmmaker. LC 00-37582. (Career Biographies Ser.). (Illus.). 2000. write for info. (*0-89434-336-X*) Ferguson.

— Patience. LC 99-47923. (Character Education Ser.). 24p. (J). (ps-3). 2000. lib. bdg. 15.93 (*0-7368-0508-7*, Bridgestone Bks) Capstone Pr.

— Patriotism. LC 99-48335. (Character Education Ser.). 24p. (J). (ps-3). 2000. lib. bdg. 15.93 (*0-7368-0509-5*, Bridgestone Bks) Capstone Pr.

— Peacefulness. (Character Education Ser.). 24p. (gr. k-3). 1999. 14.60 (*0-516-21858-1*, Bridgestone Bks) Capstone Pr.

Raatma, Lucia. Peacefulness: Teacher & Parent Handbook. LC 99-29181. (Character Education Ser.). 24p. (J). 1999. 14.60 (*0-7368-0370-X*, Bridgestone Bks) Capstone Pr.

***Raatma, Lucia.** Prudence. LC 99-48334. (Character Education Ser.). 24p. (J). (ps-3). 2000. lib. bdg. 15.93 (*0-7368-0510-9*, Bridgestone Bks) Capstone Pr.

Raatma, Lucia. Respect. LC 99-29178. (Character Education Ser.). 24p. (J). 1999. 14.60 (*0-7368-0371-8*, Bridgestone Bks) Capstone Pr.

***Raatma, Lucia.** Respect. (Character Education Ser.). 24p. (gr. k-3). 1999. 14.60 (*0-516-21859-X*, Bridgestone Bks) Capstone Pr.

Raatma, Lucia. Responsibility. LC 99-29182. (Character Education Ser.). 24p. (J). 1999. 14.60 (*0-7368-0372-6*, Bridgestone Bks) Capstone Pr.

***Raatma, Lucia.** Responsibility. (Character Education Ser.). 24p. (gr. k-3). 1999. 14.60 (*0-516-21860-3*, Bridgestone Bks) Capstone Pr.

Raatma, Lucia. Safety. (J). 1998. 116.80 (*0-516-29770-8*) Childrens.

— Safety Around Fire. LC 98-44689. (Safety First! Ser.). (J). (gr. 3-4). 1999. 14.00 (*0-7368-0190-1*, Bridgestone Bks) Capstone Pr.

***Raatma, Lucia.** Safety Around Fires. 1999. 14.60 (*0-516-21766-6*) Capstone Pr.

Raatma, Lucia. Safety Around Strangers. LC 98-22394. (Safety First! Ser.). (J). 1998. 14.00 (*0-7368-0060-3*, Bridgestone Bks) Capstone Pr.

— Safety Around Strangers, 1 vol. (Safety Town Ser.). (J). 1998. 14.00 (*0-516-21358-X*) Childrens.

— Safety at Home. LC 98-18425. (Safety First Ser.). (J). 1998. 14.00 (*0-7368-0061-1*) Capstone Pr.

— Safety at Home. (Safety Town Ser.). (J). 1998. 14.00 (*0-516-21359-8*) Childrens.

Raatma, Lucia. Safety at the Swimming Pool. LC 98-45319. (Illus.). 24p. 15.93 (*0-7368-0191-X*) Capstone Pr.

— Safety at the Swimming Pool. 1999. 14.60 (*0-516-21767-4*) Capstone Pr.

— Safety First Manual. (Illus.). 24p. 95.60 (*0-7368-0268-1*, Bridgestone Bks) Capstone Pr.

— Safety on the Internet. LC 98-45325. (Illus.). 24p. 15.93 (*0-7368-0192-8*, Bridgestone Bks) Capstone Pr.

Raatma, Lucia. Safety on the Internet-Library. 1999. 14.00 (*0-516-21769-0*) Capstone Pr.

— Safety on the Playground. LC 98-19592. (Safety First Ser.). (J). 1998. 14.00 (*0-7368-0063-8*, Bridgestone Bks) Capstone Pr.

— Safety on the Playground. (Safety Town Ser.). (J). 1998. 14.00 (*0-516-21360-1*) Childrens.

— Safety on the School Bus. LC 98-18585. (Safety First Ser.). (J). 1998. 14.00 (*0-7368-0062-X*, Bridgestone Bks) Capstone Pr.

— Safety on the School Bus. (Safety Town Ser.). (J). 1998. 14.00 (*0-516-21361-X*) Childrens.

Raatma, Lucia. Safety on Your Bicycle. LC 98-46239. (Illus.). 24p. 15.93 (*0-7368-0193-6*) Capstone Pr.

— Safety on Your Bicycle. 1999. 14.60 (*0-516-21768-2*) Capstone Pr.

— Self-Discipline. LC 99-48336. (Character Education Ser.). 24p. (J). (ps-3). 2000. lib. bdg. 15.93 (*0-7368-0511-7*, Bridgestone Bks) Capstone Pr.

— Tolerance. LC 99-29180. (Character Education Ser.). 24p. (J). 1999. 14.60 (*0-7368-0373-4*, Bridgestone Bks) Capstone Pr.

***Raatma, Lucia.** Tolerance. (Character Education Ser.). 24p. (gr. k-3). 1999. 14.60 (*0-516-21861-1*, Bridgestone Bks) Capstone Pr.

Raatma, Lucia, jt. auth. see Dahl, Michael.

***Raatz, Kathleen.** Musikermigrationen Im Deutschen Ostseeraum in der Ersten Halfte des 19. Jahrhunderts: Die Kleinstadt Greifswald - Ein Schnittpunkt Zahlreicher Reiserouten. (Europaische Hochschulschriften, Reihe 36). Viii, 387p. 1999. 56.95 (*3-631-34756-1*) P Lang Pubng.

Raatz, S. Graph-Based Proof Procedures for Horn Clauses. (Progress in Computer Science & Applied Logic Ser.: Vol. 10). viii, 147p. 1990. 43.50 (*0-8176-3530-0*) Birkhauser.

Raay, Stefan Van, see Spalding, Julian & Van Raay, Stefan.

Rab, M. A., jt. auth. see Gupta, M. V.

Rab, Victoria Y. & Wood, Karren. Child Care & the ADA: A Handbook for Inclusive Programs. 208p. 1995. pap. 25.95 (*1-55766-185-5*) P H Brookes.

Raba, Joel. Between Remembrance & Denial: The Fate of Jews in the Wars of the Polish Commonwealth During the Mid-Seventeenth Century, as Shown in Contemporary Writings & Historical Research. LC 95-78706. 320p. 1995. 45.00 (*0-88033-325-1*, 428, Pub. by East Eur Monographs) Col U Pr.

Rabadan, Luis Escala, tr. see Milkman, Ruth & Wong, Kent.

Rabaey, Jan M. Digital Integrated Circuits: A Design Perspective. LC 95-22672. (Series in Electronics & VLSI). 702p. (C). 1995. 100.00 (*0-13-178609-1*, Pub. by P-H) S&S Trade.

Rabaey, Jan M. & Pedram, Massoud. Low Power Design Methodologies. LC 95-37557. (Kluwer International Series in Engineering & Computer Science). 367p. (C). 1995. text 127.00 (*0-7923-9630-8*) Kluwer Academic.

Rabalais, J. Wayne. Principles of Ultraviolet Photoelectron Spectroscopy. LC 76-28413. (Wiley-Interscience Monographs in Chemical Physics). 472p. reprint ed. pap. 146.40 (*0-608-16148-9*, 205571000032) Bks Demand.

Rabalais, J. Wayne, ed. Low Energy Ion-Surface Interactions. LC 93-21244. (Current Topics in Ion Chemistry & Physics Ser.). 610p. 1994. 375.00 (*0-471-93891-2*) Wiley.

Rabalais, Nancy N., jt. ed. see Boesch, D. F.

Rabalais, Raphael J., Jr. International Regulation of Finance & Investment, 7 vols. LC 92-61611. 1992. ring bd. 625.00 (*0-379-01267-7*) Oceana.

Raban, Avner & Holum, Kenneth G., eds. Caesarea Maritima: A Retrospective after Two Millenia. LC 96-17561. (Documenta et Monumenta Orientis Antiqui Ser.: Vol. 21). 1996. 260.50 (*90-04-10378-3*) Brill Academic Pubs.

Raban, Bridie, jt. auth. see Moon, Cliff.

Raban, Colin, jt. auth. see Lee, Phil.

Raban, Colin, jt. ed. see Lawless, Paul.

Raban, Jonathan. Bad Land: An American Romance. 324p. 1996. 25.00 (*0-679-44254-5*) Pantheon.

— Bad Land: An American Romance. 1997. pap. 14.00 (*0-679-75906-9*) Vin Bks.

— Bad Land: An American Romance. large type ed. (Americana Series). 1998. 26.95 (*0-7862-1428-7*) Thorndike Pr.

— Foreign Land. large type ed. 512p. 1986. 27.99 (*0-7089-8347-2*, Charnwood) Ulverscroft.

— Hunting Mister Heartbreak. large type ed. 653p. 1991. reprint ed. lib. bdg. 25.95 (*1-56054-224-1*) Thorndike Pr.

— Hunting Mr. Heartbreak: A Discovery of America. LC 98-26450. 384p. 1998. pap. 13.00 (*0-375-70101-X*) Vin Bks.

— Old Glory. LC 98-11006. 544p. 1998. pap. 14.00 (*0-375-70100-1*) Vin Bks.

***Raban, Jonathan.** Passage to Juneau: A Sea & Its Meanings. 2000. pap. 15.00 (*0-679-77614-1*) Knopf.

— Passage to Juneau: A Sea & Its Meanings. LC 99-28777. 448p. 1999. 26.50 (*0-679-44262-6*) Pantheon.

Raban, Jonathan. Soft City: A Documentary Exploration of Metropolitan Life. (Illus.). 256p. 1998. pap. 11.00 (*1-86046-107-7*, Pub. by Harvill Press) FS&G.

Raban, Jonathan, ed. The Oxford Book of the Sea. LC 92-41179. 542p. (Orig.). 1993. pap. 16.95 (*0-19-283148-8*) OUP.

Rabanne, Paco. The Dawn of the Golden Age: A Spiritual Design for Living. 256p. 1999. pap. 14.95 (*1-86204-371-X*, Pub. by Element MA) Penguin Putnam.

— Journey: From One Life to Another. 276p. 1999. pap. 14.95 (*1-86204-473-2*, Pub. by Element MA) Penguin Putnam.

— Journey: From One Life to the Other. LC 96-47784. 192p. 1997. pap. 24.95 (*1-86204-005-2*, Pub. by Element MA) Penguin Putnam.

Rabas, Deb, ed. see Siro.

Rabas, Debra, ed. see Gimenez, Juan & Dal Pra, Roberto.

Rabas, T. J. & Bogart, J. E., eds. Advances in Enhanced Heat Transfer 1994: Proceedings: International Mechanical Engineering Congress & Exposition (1994: Chicago, IL) LC 79-53411. (HTD Ser.: Vol. 287). 71p. 1995. pap. 40.00 (*0-7918-1396-7*, 00891) ASME Pr.

Rabas, T. J. & Webb, R. L., eds. Turbulent Enhanced Heat Transfer. (HTD Ser.: Vol. 239). 72p. 1993. 30.00 (*0-7918-1152-2*, G00796) ASME.

Rabas, T. J., jt. ed. see Sohal, M. S.

Rabasa, George. Floating Kingdom. LC 97-15993. 278p. 1997. 21.95 (*1-56689-063-2*) Coffee Hse.

— Glass Houses: Stories. LC 96-17292. 192p. 1996. pap. 12.95 (*1-56689-051-9*) Coffee Hse.

***Rabasa, Josbe.** Writing Violence on the Northern Frontier: The Historiography of Sixteenth Century New Mexico & Florida & the Legacy of Conquest. LC 00-29403. (Illus.). 344p. 2000. pap. write for info. (*0-8223-2567-5*) Duke.

Rabasa, Jose. Inventing America: Spanish Historiography & the Formation of Eurocentrism. LC 92-34510. (Project for Discourse & Theory Ser.: Vol. 11). 1994. pap. 18.95 (*0-8061-2539-X*) U of Okla Pr.

***Rabasa, Jose.** Writing Violence on the Northern Frontier: The Historiography of Sixteenth Century New Mexico & Florida & the Legacy of Conquest. LC 00-29403. (Illus.). 344p. 2000. lib. bdg. 59.95 (*0-8223-2535-7*) Duke.

Rabassa, Clementine C. Demetrio Aguilera-Malta & Social Justice: The Tertiary Phase of Epic Tradition in Latin American Literature. LC 78-75193. 304p. 1970. 32.50 (*0-8386-2079-5*) Fairleigh Dickinson.

Rabassa, Gregory. Cloudy Day in Gray Minor. Barkan, Stanley H., ed. (Review Chapbook Ser.: No. 35: American Poetry 8). 48p. 1989. 15.00 (*0-89304-870-4*); pap. 5.00 (*0-89304-871-2*) Cross-Cultrl NY.

Rabassa, Gregory, intro. The World of Translation. vii, 382p. 1987. 10.95 (*0-934638-06-3*) PEN Am Ctr.

Rabassa, Gregory, jt. auth. see Ribeiro, Darcy.

Rabassa, Gregory, jt. auth. see Sanchez, Luis Rafael.

Rabassa, Gregory, tr. see Aguilera-Malta, Demetrio.

Rabassa, Gregory, tr. see Amado, Jorge.

Rabassa, Gregory, tr. see Antunes, Antonio L.

Rabassa, Gregory, tr. see Benet, Juan.

Rabassa, Gregory, tr. see Cortazar, Julio.

Rabassa, Gregory, tr. see De Carvalho, Mario.

Rabassa, Gregory, tr. see De Moraes, Vinicius.

Rabassa, Gregory, tr. see Garcia Marquez, Gabriel.

Rabassa, Gregory, tr. see Lezama Lima, Jose.

Rabassa, Gregory, tr. see Lins, Osman.

Rabassa, Gregory, tr. see Machado de Assis, Joaquim Maria.

Rabassa, Gregory, tr. see Pires, Fernando T.

Rabassa, Gregory, tr. see Torres, Ana T.

Rabassa, Gregory, tr. see Valenzuela, Luisa.

Rabassa, Gregory, tr. see Vargas Llosa, Mario.

Rabassa, Gregory, tr. see Vilar, Irene.

R

Rabassa, Jorge, ed. Quaternary of South America & Antarctic Peninsula, Vol. 1. 166p. (C). 1982. text 76.00 (*90-6191-513-9*, Pub. by A A Balkema) Ashgate Pub Co.
— Quaternary of South America & Antarctic Peninsula, Vol. 2. 224p. 1984. text 91.00 (*90-6191-542-2*, Pub. by A A Balkema) Ashgate Pub Co.
— Quaternary of South America & Antarctic Peninsula, Vol. 6. 318p. (C). 1990. text 76.00 (*90-6191-995-9*, Pub. by A A Balkema) Ashgate Pub Co.
— Quaternary of South America & Antarctic Peninsula, Vol. 7. 384p. (C). 1990. text 76.00 (*90-6191-784-0*, Pub. by A A Balkema) Ashgate Pub Co.
— The Quaternary of South America & Antarctic Peninsula, Vol. 9. (Illus.). 225p. (C). 1995. text 70.00 (*90-5410-615-8*, Pub. by A A Balkema) Ashgate Pub Co.
— The Quaternary of South America & Antarctic Peninsula: With Selected Papers of the International Symposium on Late Quaternary Sea-Level Changes & Coastal Evolution, Mar del Plata, 30 Sept. - 3 October 1984, Vol. 3. 232p. (C). 1986. text 76.00 (*90-6191-591-0*, Pub. by A A Balkema) Ashgate Pub Co.
— The Quaternary of South America & Antarctic Peninsula: With Selected Papers of the International Symposium on Sea-Level Changes Quaternary Shorelines, Sao Paulo, 7-14 July 1986, Vol. 4. 344p. 1987. text 76.00 (*90-6191-732-8*, Pub. by A A Balkema) Ashgate Pub Co.
— The Quaternary of South America & Antarctic Peninsula: With Selected Papers of the XIIth INQUA Congress, Ottawa, 1987 on the Quaternary of South America, Vol. 5. 250p. (C). 1987. text 76.00 (*90-6191-733-6*, Pub. by A A Balkema) Ashgate Pub Co.
Rabassa, Jorge & Salemme, Monica, eds. The Quaternary of South America & Antarctic Peninsula. (Illus.). 332p. (C). 1997. text 76.00 (*90-5410-664-6*, Pub. by A A Balkema) Ashgate Pub Co.
— Quaternary of South America & Antarctic Peninsula, Vol. 11. 328p. (C). 1998. text 76.00 (*90-5410-453-8*, Pub. by A A Balkema) Ashgate Pub Co.
— The Quaternary of South America & Antarctic Peninsula Vol. 8: With Selected Papers of the International Symposium on Quarterrary Climates of South America, International Geological Correlation Program UNESCO, Project 281, Medellin, Colombia, 3-6 May 1990. (Illus.). 224p. 1993. text 76.00 (*90-5410-140-7*, Pub. by A A Balkema) Ashgate Pub Co.
***Rabassa, Jorge & Salemme, Monica, eds.** Quaternary of South America & Antarctic Peninsula, 1996-1997 Vol. 12: Special Volume: Quaternary Vertebrate Palaeontology in Southern South America. (Illus.). 320p. 1999. text 76.00 (*90-5410-479-1*) A A Balkema.
Rabasse, Maurice. Du Regime Des Fiefs En Normandie Au Moyen Age. LC 80-2006. reprint ed. 29.50 (*0-404-18588-6*) AMS Pr.
***Rabatbe, Jean-Michel.** Jacques Lacan/The Last Word: Psychoanalysis & the Subject of Literature. LC 00-33296. 2000. pap. write for info. (*0-312-23805-3*) St Martin.
— Lacan in America. LC 00-35629. 2000. pap. write for info. (*1-892746-63-8*) Other Pr.
Rabate, Jean M. Language, Sexuality, & Ideology in Ezra Pound's Cantos. LC 84-23926. 339p. (C). 1986. text 21.50 (*0-88706-036-6*) State U NY Pr.
Rabate, Jean-Michel. The Ghosts of Modernity. Gontarski, S. E., ed. & frwd. by. (Crosscurrents Ser.). 288p. (C). 1996. 49.95 (*0-8130-1440-9*) U Press Fla.
— James Joyce, Authorized Reader. LC 90-49032. 256p. 1991. text 35.00 (*0-8018-4140-2*) Johns Hopkins.
— Writing the Image after Roland Barthes. LC 97-9579. (New Cultural Studies). (C). (gr. 13). 1997. text 37.50 (*0-8122-3369-7*); pap. text 17.50 (*0-8122-1596-6*) U of Pa Pr.
Rabatin, Diana L., jt. auth. see Mayers, Lise B.
Rabatin, June, ed. Count the Ties to Manassas. 85p. 1984. pap. 6.00 (*1-886826-03-X*) Manassas Mus.
Rabaut, Antionette, ed. see Stephen, Shay.
Rabavilas, Andreas, jt. ed. see Vaslamatzis, Grigoris.
Rabb, jt. auth. see Apple, David J.
Rabb, Antonia P. Quiverings in the Net. 100p. 1994. pap. text 10.00 (*0-9644280-0-8*) A P Rabb.
Rabb, George B., jt. auth. see Marx, Hymen.
Rabb, Hamid, jt. auth. see Sanders, Helen.
Rabb, Jane M. The Short Story & Photography, 1880's-1980's. LC 97-40355. 269p. 1998. pap. 19.95 (*0-8263-1871-1*) U of NM Pr.
Rabb, Jane M., ed. Literature & Photography: Interactions, 1840-1990: A Critical Anthology. LC 95-4369. (Illus.). 634p. 1995. pap. 24.95 (*0-8263-1663-8*) U of NM Pr.
Rabb, Jonathan. The Overseer: A Novel. LC 97-44624. 400p. 1998. 24.00 (*0-609-60253-5*, Crown) Crown Pub Group.
— The Overseer: A Novel. 1999. reprint ed. mass mkt. 6.99 (*0-515-12558-X*, Jove) Berkley Pub.
Rabb, Kate M. National Epics. LC 76-84355. (Granger Index Reprint Ser.). 1977. 21.95 (*0-8369-6059-9*) Ayer.
***Rabb, Lauren W.** Walking Through Time. Weinberger, Caspar, Jr., ed. LC 98-60229. iii, 245 p. 1998. pap. 12.00 (*1-883650-48-8*) Windswept Hse.
Rabb, Margaret. Figments of the Firmament. (Harperprints Chapbook Ser.). 28p. 1998. pap. 5.00 (*1-883314-09-7*) NC Writers Network.
***Rabb, Margaret.** Granite Dives. 64p. 2000. pap. 12.00 (*0-932826-88-1*) WMU Poetry & Prose.
Rabb, Theodore, jt. ed. see Rotberg, Robert I.
Rabb, Theodore K. Enterprise & Empire: Merchant & Gentry Investment in the Expansion of England, 1575-1630. LC 67-29629. 434p. reprint ed. pap. 134.60 (*0-7837-4126-X*, 205794900011) Bks Demand.
— Jacobean Gentleman: Sir Edwin Sandys, 1561-1629. LC 97-44316. 384p. 1998. text 55.00 (*0-691-02694-7*, Pub. by Princeton U Pr) Cal Prin Full Svc.
— Origins of the Modern West: Essays & Sources in Early Modern European History to Accompany a Series of Fims Entitled Renaissance. Marshall, Sherrin D., ed. LC 92-43374. 320p. (C). 1993. pap. 36.25 (*0-07-041231-6*) McGraw.
— Origins of the Modern West: Essays & Sources in Early Modern European History to Accompany a Series of Fims Entitled Renaissance. Marshall, Sherrin D., ed. LC 92-43374. (C). 1994. pap., student ed. 10.31 (*0-07-041232-4*) McGraw.
— The Struggle for Stability in Early Modern Europe. (Illus.). 186p. 1976. pap. text 20.95 (*0-19-501956-3*) OUP.
Rabb, Theodore K., ed. The Thirty Years' War. 2nd ed. LC 80-6215. (Illus.). 190p. 1981. reprint ed. pap. text 16.50 (*0-8191-1747-1*) U Pr of Amer.
Rabb, Theodore K. & Rotberg, Robert I., eds. Industrialization & Urbanization: Studies in Interdisciplinary History. LC 80-8675. 336p. 1981. reprint ed. pap. 104.20 (*0-608-04629-9*, 206531600003) Bks Demand.
Rabb, Theodore K. & Seigel, Jerrold E., eds. Action & Conviction in Early Modern Europe: Essays in Memory of E. H. Harbison. LC 68-27407. 487p. reprint ed. pap. 151.00 (*0-8357-3388-2*, 203964400013) Bks Demand.
Rabb, Theodore K., jt. ed. see Rotberg, Robert I.
Rabban, David M. Free Speech in Its Forgotten Years, 1870-1920. (Historical Studies in American Law & Society). 404p. (C). 1997. 36.95 (*0-521-62013-9*) Cambridge U Pr.
— Free Speech in Its Forgotten Years, 1870-1920. (Cambridge Historical Studies in American Law & Society). 416p. (C). 1999. pap. text 18.95 (*0-521-65537-4*) Cambridge U Pr.
Rabbani, Leroy E. Applications of Antisense Therapies to Restenosis. LC 98-51825. 1999. write for info. (*0-7923-8423-7*) Kluwer Academic.
Rabbani, Majid, ed. Image Coding & Compression. LC 92-5748. (Milestone Ser.: Vol. 48). 702p. 1992. pap. 50.00 (*0-8194-0889-1*) SPIE.
— Image Coding & Compression. LC 92-5748. (Milestone Ser.: Vol. 48/HC). 702p. 1992. 65.00 (*0-8194-0888-3*) SPIE.
Rabbani, Majid & Jones, Paul W. Digital Image Compression Techniques. 221p. 1991. pap. 42.00 (*0-8194-0648-1*, VOL. TT07) SPIE.
Rabbani, Majid, jt. ed. see Rajala, Sarah A.
Rabbani, Mian A. I Was the Quaid's Aide-de-Camp. (Illus.). 210p. 1998. pap. 26.95 (*0-19-577659-3*) OUP.
Rabbani, Ruhiyyih. The Guardian of the Baha'i Faith. 251p. 1988. 33.00 (*0-900125-59-4*) Bahai.
— Poems of the Passing. 136p. (Orig.). 1996. pap. 29.95 (*0-85398-410-7*) G Ronald Pub.
Rabbat, Basile G., ed. see Portland Cement Association Staff.
Rabbat, Nasser O. The Citadel of Cairo: A New Interpretation of Royal Mamluk Architecture. 1995. 114.50 (*90-04-10124-1*) Brill Academic Pubs.
Rabbath, Antoine. Documents Inedits pour Servir a l'Histoire du Christianisme en Orient, 2 vols. LC 72-174293. reprint ed. lib. bdg. 125.00 (*0-404-05202-9*) AMS Pr.
Rabbe Nachman. Likutey Moharan, Vol. 3. Mykoff, Moshe, ed. & tr. by. from HEB. Bergman, Ozer, ed. Kramer, Chaim, tr. from HEB. 360p. 1990. 20.00 (*0-930213-78-5*) Breslov Res Inst.
Rabbel, Wolfgang, jt. auth. see Gajewski, Dirk.
Rabben, Linda. Unnatural Selection: The Yanomami, the Kayapo & the Onslaught of Civilisation. LC 98-16768. 1998. write for info. (*0-7453-1249-7*, Pub. by Pluto GBR) Stylus Pub VA.
— Unnatural Selection: The Yanomami, the Kayapo & the Onslaught of Civilisation. LC 98-16768. (Illus.). 250p. 1998. pap. 18.95 (*0-295-97745-0*) U of Wash Pr.
Rabben, Linda, jt. ed. see Fiedler, Maureen.
Rabbetts, John. From Hardy to Faulkner: Wessex to Yoknapatawpha. LC 88-26358. 256p. 1989. text 45.00 (*0-312-02510-6*) St Martin.
Rabbetts, Ronald B., jt. auth. see Bennett, A. G.
Rabbetts, Ronald B., jt. auth. see Bennett, Arthur G.
Rabbi Aryeh Kaplan. Until the Mashiach: The Life of Rabbi Nachman. Shapiro, Dovid, ed. 379p. 1986. text 16.00 (*0-930213-08-4*) Breslov Res Inst.
Rabbi Dalfin. Time & Transcendence: The Deeper Insight of the Jewish Calender. (Illus.). 100p. (Orig.). 1996. pap. 12.95 (*1-880880-13-X*) Israeli Trad.
Rabbi Dr. Joseph Breuer Foundation Staff, ed. The Book of Yechezkel. LC 93-25424. (ENG & HEB.). 1993. 22.95 (*0-87306-956-0*) Feldheim.
Rabbi Ezriel Tauber. I Shall Not Want: The Torah Outlook on Working for a Living. Astor, Yaakov, ed. (Hashkafa Dialogue Ser.). 112p. (Orig.). 1990. pap. 6.00 (*1-878999-00-1*) Shelheves.
Rabbi Nachman of Breslov. The Aleph-Bet Book. Mykoff, Moshe, tr. from HEB. & intro. by.Tr. of Sefer HaMiddot. 268p. 1986. text 16.00 (*0-930213-15-7*) Breslov Res Inst.
— The Fixer. Mykoff, Moshe, ed. (Illus.). 52p. (J). (gr. 1-4). 1996. 8.00 (*0-930213-64-5*) Breslov Res Inst.
— Likutey Moharan, Vol. 1. 2nd rev. ed. Mykoff, Moshe, ed. & tr. by. from HEB. Bergman, Simchah, tr. from HEB. 390p. 1995. 20.00 (*0-930213-92-0*) Breslov Res Inst.
— Likutey Moharan, Vol. 2. 2nd rev. ed. Mykoff, Moshe, ed. & tr. by. from HEB. Bergman, Ozer, ed. 385p. 1993. 20.00 (*0-930213-93-9*) Breslov Res Inst.
— Likutey Moharan, Vol. 5. Mykoff, Moshe, ed. Bergman, Ozer, ed. & tr. by. from HEB. 400p. 1997. 20.00 (*0-930213-80-7*) Breslov Res Inst.
— The Lost Princess. Mykoff, Moshe, ed. (Illus.). 64p. (J). (gr. 1-4). 1996. 8.00 (*0-930213-66-1*) Breslov Res Inst.
— Never Lose Hope. Mykoff, Moshe, ed. (Illus.). 36p. (J). (gr. 1-4). 1996. 8.00 (*0-930213-65-3*) Breslov Res Inst.
— Rabbi Nachman's Tikun: The Tikun Haklali. Greenbaum, Avraham, tr. from HEB. 128p. 1982. pap. 5.00 (*0-930213-07-6*) Breslov Res Inst.
— The Reward for Loyalty. Mykoff, Moshe, ed. (Illus.). 36p. (J). (gr. 1-4). 1996. 8.00 (*0-930213-63-7*) Breslov Res Inst.
— Le Tikoun Haklali. Dimermanas, Alon, tr. from HEB. (FRE.). 125p. 1986. pap. text 3.00 (*0-930213-24-6*) Breslov Res Inst.
— Tsohar. Greenbaum, Avraham, tr. from HEB. 64p. (Orig.). 1986. pap. text 3.00 (*0-930213-26-2*) Breslov Res Inst.
Rabbi Nachman of Breslov, et al. Rabbi Nachman De Breslov. (Illus.). 442p. 1986. pap. 15.00 (*0-930213-20-3*) Breslov Res Inst.
Rabbi Noson of Breslov. Eternally Yours: The Collected Letters of Reb Noson of Breslov. Schorr, Moshe, ed. Gabel, Yaakov, tr. from HEB. 380p. 1993. 16.00 (*0-930213-46-7*) Breslov Res Inst.
— Eternally Yours Vol. 2: The Collected Letters of Reb Noson of Breslov. Schorr, Moshe, ed. Gabel, Yaakov, tr. from HEB. 376p. 1993. 16.00 (*0-930213-47-5*) Breslov Res Inst.
— Eternally Yours Vol. 3: The Collected Letters of Reb Noson of Breslov. Schoff, Moshe, ed. Gabel, Yaakov, tr. from HEB. 320p. 1993. 16.00 (*0-930213-48-3*) Breslov Res Inst.
— Eternally Yours Vol. 4: The Collected Letters of Reb Noson of Breslov. Schorr, Moshe, ed. Gabel, Yaakov, tr. from HEB. 350p. 1993. 16.00 (*0-930213-58-0*) Breslov Res Inst.
— The Fiftieth Gate Vol. 2: Likutey Tefilot - Reb Noson's Prayers (Prayers 21-40) Greenbaum, Avraham, tr. from HEB. 600p. 1993. pap. 13.00 (*0-930213-68-8*) Breslov Res Inst.
Rabbi Obadiah of Bartenura. Pathway to Jerusalem. 96p. 1992. 9.95 (*1-56062-130-3*); pap. 6.95 (*1-56062-131-1*) CIS Comm.
Rabbi Reuven P. Bulka. Jewish Divorce Ethics: The Right Way to Say Goodbye. LC 92-70080. 290p. (Orig.). 1992. pap. text 12.95 (*0-918921-03-1*) Ivy League Pr.
Rabbi Yehoshja Y. Neuwirth. Shemirath Shabbath, Vol. 1. Grangewood, W., tr. from HEB.Tr. of Shemirath Shabbath Kehilchathah. 360p. 1984. 21.95 (*0-87306-298-1*) Feldheim.
Rabbie, Edwin, ed. see Nellen, Henk J.
***Rabbin, Robert.** Echoes of Silence: Awakening the Meditative Spirit. LC 00-130215. (Illus.). 120p. 2000. pap. 15.95 (*1-878019-09-0*) Inner Drctns.
Rabbin, Robert. Invisible Leadership: Igniting the Soul at Work. LC 98-24772. 185p. 1998. pap. 14.95 (*1-889051-35-7*) Acrpls Bks CO.
— Mentored in Silence: The Heart of Meditation. LC 99-13330. 1999. pap. 15.95 (*1-889051-46-2*) Acrpls Bks CO.
— The Sacred Hub: Living in Our Real Self. LC 95-69828. 114p. (Orig.). 1996. pap. text 12.00 (*0-9630390-8-3*) New Leaders.
— The Sacred Hub: Living in Your Real Self. LC 96-22343. 160p. 1996. 16.00 (*1-878019-06-6*) Inner Drctns.
Rabbin, Robert, jt. auth. see Hillyard, Jo.
Rabbinge, R. Simulation & Systems Management in Crop Protection. 434p. (C). 1976. pap. 335.00 (*81-7089-135-3*, Pub. by Intl Bk Distr) St Mut.
— Theoritical Production Ecology Reflections & Prospects. 302p. 1992. pap. 163.00 (*81-7089-183-3*, Pub. by Intl Bks & Periodicals) St Mut.
Rabbinge, R., et al. Foundation Symposium 210 - Precision Agriculture: Spatial & Temporal Variability of Environmental Quality, Vol. 210. LC 97-25663. (CIBA Foundation Symposium Ser.). 260p. 1997. 140.00 (*0-471-97455-2*) Wiley.
Rabbinical Assembly Staff. Siddur Sim Shalom for Shabbat & Festivals. rev. ed. Cahan, Leonard, ed. 800p. 1998. 25.00 (*0-916219-13-5*) Rabbinical Assembly.
Rabbinical Council of America, ed. Traditional Prayerbook for Shabbath & Festivals. rev. ed. De Sola Poole, David, tr. 879p. 1960. 15.00 (*0-87441-118-1*) Behrman.
Rabbinowitz, Joseph, ed. see Marmorstein, Arthur.
Rabbit. Daniel in the Lion's Den. (J). 2000. 10.95 (*0-689-80239-0*) Aladdin.
— Moses the Lawgiver. LC 95-12494. 1999. per. 10.95 (*0-689-80228-5*) Aladdin.
— Parables That Jesus Told. (J). pap. 19.95 (*0-689-80229-3*) Aladdin.
— Ruth in Canaan. (J). 2000. 10.95 (*0-689-80232-3*) Aladdin.
— Tom Thumb. 1999. per. 19.95 (*0-689-80219-6*) Aladdin.
— The White Cat. LC 99-45328. (J). 2000. per. 19.95 (*0-689-80140-8*, Rabbit Ears) Litle Simon.
Rabbit, Daddy, jt. auth. see Fowler Companies, Inc. Staff.
Rabbit Ears Books. Creation. 1999. per. 19.95 (*0-689-80238-2*) Macmillan.
— Five Chinese Brothers. LC 96-22671. (J). 1999. per. 19.95 (*0-689-80241-2*) Macmillan.
— Jonah & the Whale. (J). 1999. per. 10.95 (*0-689-80243-9*) Macmillan.
— The Song of Sacajawea. 1999. per. 19.95 (*0-689-80233-1*) Macmillan.
— Tobias & the Angel. 1999. per. 19.95 (*0-689-80237-4*) Macmillan.
Rabbit, Hardy C. Wanted Female. (Illus.). 64p. 1998. pap. 7.00 (*1-886895-15-5*, Fat Chance Pr) Poetry Harbor.
Rabbit, John T. & Bergh, Peter A. The QS-9000 Miniguide. 88p. 1997. pap. 4.50 (*0-527-76323-3*) Productivity Inc.
— The QS-9000 Book: The Fast Track to Compliance. LC 97-27673. 224p. 1998. 32.95 (*0-8144-7982-0*) AMACOM.
Rabbit, Patrick, ed. Methodology of Frontal & Executive Function. LC 98-128198. 264p. 1997. 54.95 (*0-86377-485-7*, Pub. by Psychol Pr) Taylor & Francis.
Rabbit, Peter. Ornithology. (Illus.). 57p. (Orig.). 1983. pap. 12.00 (*0-9615914-0-4*) Minor Heron.
***Rabbitt, John T.** QS-9000 Miniguide. 1999. pap. 5.25 (*0-527-76356-X*) Productivity Inc.
Rabbitt, John T. & Bergh, Peter. The ISO 9000 Book: A Global Competitor's Guide to Compliance & Certification. 2nd ed. 166p. 1994. 26.95 (*0-8144-0267-4*) AMACOM.
Rabbitt, John T. & Bergh, Peter A. The ISO 9000 Book: A Global Competitor's Guide to Compliance & Certification. LC 93-14904. (Illus.). 176p. 1993. pap. 54.60 (*0-7837-8359-0*, 204914900010) Bks Demand.
— The ISO 9000 Book: A Global Competitor's Guide to Compliance & Certification. 2nd ed. LC 94-15521. (Illus.). 211p. 1994. text 29.95 (*0-527-76258-X*) Productivity Inc.
— The Miniguide to ISO 9000. 59p. 1995. pap. 4.50 (*0-527-76302-0*) Productivity Inc.
— The QS-9000 Book: The Fast Track to Compliance. (Illus.). 240p. 1997. 32.95 (*0-527-76334-9*, 763349) Productivity Inc.
Rabbitt, Thomas. The Abandoned Country. LC 87-71454. (Poetry Ser.). 1988. pap. 11.95 (*0-88748-063-2*) Carnegie-Mellon.
— The Abandoned Country. LC 87-71454. (Poetry Ser.). 1988. 20.95 (*0-88748-062-4*) Carnegie-Mellon.
***Rabbitt, Thomas.** Enemies of the State: Poems. 96p. 2000. 15.95 (*1-57966-022-3*, Black Belt) Black Belt Communs.
Rabboh, Bob & Bartson, Ronald J. Principles of Microeconomics. 4th ed. LC 96-144242. 472p. (C). 1996. pap. text 52.00 (*0-536-59294-2*, HB172) Pearson Custom.
***Rabboh, Bob & Bartson, Ronald J.** Principles of Microeconomics. 5th ed. 436p. 1999. pap. text 50.00 (*0-536-02794-3*) Pearson Custom.
Rabboh, Bob, jt. auth. see Bartson, Ronald J.
Rabboh, Bob A & Bartson, Ronald J. Principles of Macroeconomics. 2nd ed. 552p. (C). 1991. text 65.00 (*0-536-58029-4*) Pearson Custom.
Rabboh, Bob A. & Bartson, Ronald J. Principles Of Macroeconomics. 3rd ed. (C). 1991. text 56.00 (*0-536-58105-3*) Pearson Custom.
Rabboh, Bob A & Bartson, Ronald J. Principles of Microeconomics. 3rd ed. (C). 1991. 56.00 (*0-536-58081-2*) Pearson Custom.
Rabbow, Arnold. Wie Sah das Erste Sternenbanner Aus? What Did the First U. S. Flag Look Like? 1980. 1.50 (*0-934021-36-8*) Natl Flag Foun.
Rabby, Glenda A. The Pain & the Promise: The Struggle for Civil Rights in Tallahassee, Florida. LC 98-44087. (Illus.). 330p. 1999. 40.00 (*0-8203-2051-X*) U of Ga Pr.
Rabby, Rami & Croft, Diane. Take Charge: A Strategic Guide for Blind Job Seekers. 336p. (Orig.). 1990. pap. text 13.95 (*0-939173-16-6*); audio 9.95 (*0-939173-18-2*); disk 9.95 (*0-939173-19-0*) Natl Braille Pr.
— Take Charge: A Strategic Guide for Blind Job Seekers. braille ed. 336p. (Orig.). 1990. 9.95 (*0-939173-17-4*) Natl Braille Pr.
Rabe. Pave the Way. 1997. pap. 5.00 (*0-15-201329-6*) Harcourt.
Rabe, ed. Rhetores Graeci: Prolegomenon Sylloge. (GRE.). 1995. reprint ed. 120.00 (*3-519-01935-3*, T1935, Pub. by B G Teubner) U of Mich Pr.
Rabe, Alan. Be in Health. 288p. (C). 1993. pap. text 21.95 (*0-8403-8387-8*) Kendall-Hunt.
***Rabe-Azoory, Vera.** They Love You, They Love Me Not: The Truth about the Family Favorite & Sibling Rivalry. 224p. 1999. reprint ed. text 20.00 (*0-7881-6238-1*) DIANE Pub.
Rabe, Barry, ed. see Audley, John J.
Rabe, Barry, ed. see Foster, Kathryn A.
Rabe, Barry, ed. see Lowry, William R.
Rabe, Barry, ed. see MacRae, Duncan, Jr. & Whittington, Dale.
Rabe, Barry, ed. see Posner, Paul L.
Rabe, Barry, ed. see Scheberle, Denise.
Rabe, Barry, ed. see Wallin, Bruce A.
Rabe, Barry G. Beyond NIMBY: Hazardous Waste Siting in Canada & the United States. LC 94-19039. 199p. (C). 1994. 34.95 (*0-8157-7308-0*); pap. 14.95 (*0-8157-7307-2*) Brookings.
Rabe, Berniece. Hiding Mr. McMulty. LC 96-49144. 256p. (YA). (gr. 6-8). 1997. 18.00 (*0-15-201330-X*) Harcourt.
— A Smooth Move. Tucker, Kathleen, ed. LC 87-2099. (Albert Whitman Concept Bks.). (Illus.). (J). (gr. 1-4). 1987. lib. bdg. 13.95 (*0-8075-7486-4*) A Whitman.
— Where's Chimpy? Tucker, Kathleen, ed. LC 87-37259. (Illus.). 32p. (J). (ps-2). 1988. lib. bdg. 14.95 (*0-8075-8928-4*) A Whitman.
— Where's Chimpy? Tucker, Kathleen, ed. LC 87-37259. (Illus.). 32p. (J). (ps-3). 1988. pap. 6.95 (*0-8075-8927-6*) A Whitman.
Rabe, David. The Crossing Guard. LC 94-35012. 301p. (J). 1995. 22.45 (*0-7868-6119-3*, Pub. by Hyperion) Time Warner.
Rabe, David. Goose & Tomtom. LC 86-29432. 136p. 1987. pap. 7.95 (*0-8021-5193-0*) Grove-Atltic.
— Hurlyburly & Those the River Keeps: Two Plays. LC 95-39497. 384p. 1995. pap. 14.00 (*0-8021-3351-7*, Grove) Grove-Atltic.
— In the Boom Boom Room. LC 86-45235. 112p. 1986. pap. 9.95 (*0-8021-5194-9*, Grove) Grove-Atltic.
— A Question of Mercy. LC 99-213854. 1998. pap. 5.25 (*0-8222-1643-4*) Dramatists Play.
***Rabe, David.** Recital of the Dog. 320p. 2000. pap. 13.00 (*0-8021-3658-3*, Grove) Grove-Atltic.
Rabe, David. Streamers. 1995. reprint ed. lib. bdg. 24.95 (*1-56849-633-8*) Buccaneer Bks.

An Asterisk (*) at the beginning of an entry indicates that the title is appearing for the first time.

— The Vietnam Plays Vol. 1: The Basic Training at Paulo Hummel & Sticks & Bones. LC 92-37145. 208p. 1993. pap. 12.95 (*0-8021-3313-4*, Grove) Grove-Atltic.

— Vietnam Plays Vol. 2: Streamers & the Orphan. LC 92-37145. 208p. 1993. pap. 12.95 (*0-8021-3345-2*, Grove) Grove-Atltic.

Rabe, David & Selzer, Richard. A Question of Mercy: A Play. LC 97-40046. 128p. 1998. pap. 12.00 (*0-8021-3549-8*, Grove) Grove-Atltic.

Rabe, Gerhard, ed. Safecomp '95: The 14th International Conference on Computer Safety, Reliability & Security. LC 95-37874. 528p. 1995. pap. 115.00 (*3-540-19962-4*) Spr-Verlag.

Rabe, Heidi. Christmas in Beardtown. LC 98-131250. (Illus.). 1997. pap. write for info. (*0-7880-0941-9*) CSS OH.

***Rabe-Hesketh, S. & Everitt, Brian.** A Handbook of Statistical Analyses Using Stata. 2nd ed. LC 00-27322. 2000. 39.95 (*1-58488-201-8*, Chap & Hall CRC) CRC Pr.

Rabe-Hesketh, S., jt. auth. see Everitt, B. S.

Rabe-Hesketh, Sophia & Everitt, Brian. Handbook of Statistical Analysis Using Stata. LC 98-44800. 232p. 1999. per. 39.95 (*0-8493-0387-7*, QA276, Chap & Hall CRC) CRC Pr.

Rabe, Hugo, ed. see Philoponus, Ioannes.

***Rabe, Inge Fernback.** Obstacles, Miracles & Love. 191p. 1999. per. 25.00 (*1-893365-03-4*) Barefooted Friar.

Rabe, Jean. The Dawning of a New Age. (DragonLance Dawning of a New Age Ser.). 1996. pap. 5.99 (*0-7869-0616-2*, Pub. by TSR Inc) Random.

— The Day of the Tempest. (DragonLance Dawning of a New Age Ser.). 1997. pap. 5.99 (*0-7869-0668-5*, Pub. by TSR Inc) Random.

***Rabe, Jean.** Downfall Vol. 1: The Dhamon Saga, 1. (DragonLance Ser.). 384p. 2000. 21.95 (*0-7869-1572-2*) TSR Inc.

Rabe, Jean. Naval Battle System. 1996. 10.95 (*0-7869-0628-6*, Pub. by TSR Inc) Random.

Rabe, John. The Good Man of Nanking: The Diaries of John Rabe. Wickert, Erwin, ed. Woods, John E., tr. from GER. LC 98-15885. (Illus.). 384p. 1998. 26.00 (*0-375-40211-X*) Knopf.

— The Good Man of Nanking: The Diaries of John Rabe. 2000. pap. 14.00 (*0-375-70197-4*) Vin Bks.

Rabe, Monica. Culture Shock! Living & Working Abroad: A Practical Guide. LC 96-77214. (Culture Shock Ser.). 1997. pap. 12.95 (*1-55868-304-6*) Gr Arts Ctr Pub.

Rabe, N. Criminal Courts: Structure, Process & Issues. (C). 1999. text 56.00 (*0-13-780388-5*, Macmillan Coll) P-H.

***Rabe, Peter.** My Lovely Executioner. large type ed. (Star Mystery Ser.). 1999. 19.95 (*0-7862-2024-4*) Five Star.

Rabe, Sheila. The Accidental Bride. 224p. 1994. mass mkt. 3.99 (*0-8217-4597-2*, Zebra Kensgtn) Kensgtn Pub Corp.

— The Adventuress. 256p. 1996. mass mkt. 4.50 (*0-8217-5196-4*, Zebra Kensgtn) Kensgtn Pub Corp.

***Rabe, Sheila.** All I Want for Christmas. 2000. mass mkt. 6.99 (*0-515-12925-9*) Berkley Pub.

Rabe, Sheila. Ghostly Charade. 1991. mass mkt. 3.95 (*0-8217-3545-4*, Zebra Kensgtn) Kensgtn Pub Corp.

— I Hate Whining Except When I'm Doing It: Lessons I Learned at My Children's Knees. 200p. 1996. pap. 10.99 (*0-87509-645-X*) Chr Pubns.

— An Innocent Imposter. 224p. 1995. mass mkt. 4.50 (*0-8217-4944-7*, Pinncle Kensgtn) Kensgtn Pub Corp.

— It's a Wonderful Mid-Life? Finding the Positives in Aging. 157p. 1999. pap. 10.99 (*0-88965-162-0*) Chr Pubns.

— Miss Plympton's Peril. 208p. (Orig.). 1994. mass mkt. 3.99 (*0-515-11453-7*, Jove) Berkley Pub.

Rabe, Sheila & Schneider, Eric S. Interactive Parties & Games: Fun for All Ages. Lent, Penny, ed. LC 94-79465. (Illus.). 150p. (Orig.). pap. text, per. 9.95 (*1-885371-08-X*) Kldoscope Pr.

Rabe, Stephen G. Eisenhower & Latin America: The Foreign Policy of Anticommunism. LC 87-12493. x, 238p. (C). 1988. 49.95 (*0-8078-1761-9*); pap. 18.95 (*0-8078-4204-4*) U of NC Pr.

— The Most Dangerous Area in the World: John F. Kennedy Confronts Communist Revolution in Latin America. LC 98-23112. 272p. 1999. pap. 17.95 (*0-8078-4764-X*); lib. bdg. 39.95 (*0-8078-2461-5*) U of NC Pr.

— The Road to OPEC: United States Relations with Venezuela, 1919-1976. (Texas Pan American Ser.). 272p. (C). 1982. text 27.50 (*0-292-76020-5*) U of Tex Pr.

Rabe, Stephen G., jt. ed. see Paterson, Thomas G.

Rabe, Susan A. Faith, Art & Politics at Saint-Riquier: The Symbolic Vision of Angilbert. (Middle Age Ser.). (Illus.). 256p. (C). 1995. text 37.95 (*0-8122-3208-9*) U of Pa Pr.

Rabe, T. & Runnebaum, B., eds. Fertility Control: Update & Trends. LC 98-33842. (Illus.). 232p. 1998. 99.00 (*3-540-64763-5*) Spr-Verlag.

Rabe, T., et al. Manual on Assisted Reproduction. LC 96-30572. (Illus.). 300p. 1996. 159.00 (*3-540-61134-7*) Spr-Verlag.

***Rabe, T., et al.** Manual on Assisted Reproduction. 2nd ed. LC 00-38608. 2000. pap. write for info. (*3-540-67299-0*) Spr-Verlag.

Rabe, T., jt. auth. see Runnebaum, B.

Rabe, Thomas. Memorix Gynecology. (Memorix Ser.). 288p. (J). 1996. pap. text 17.95 (*0-412-56060-7*, Pub. by E A) OUP.

— Memorix Obstetrics. Davis, A. & Davis, R., trs. LC 94-72653. (Illus.). 304p. (gr. 13). 1996. pap. text 16.50 (*0-412-56080-1*, Pub. by E A) OUP.

Rabe, Tish. Fine Feathered Friends: All about Birds. 1998. lib. bdg. 11.99 (*0-679-98362-7*, Pub. by Random Bks Yng Read) Random.

— Fine Feathered Friends: All about Birds. LC 97-53103. (J). (gr. k-3). 1998. 7.99 (*0-679-88362-2*, Pub. by Random Bks Yng Read) Random.

— Jack. LC 99-162317. 1998. 4.99 (*0-679-89242-7*, Pub. by Random Bks Yng Read) Random.

— Lump. LC 99-162318. 1998. 4.99 (*0-679-89243-5*, Pub. by Random Bks Yng Read) Random.

— Oh Baby, the Places You'll Go. 1997. 6.99 (*0-679-88975-2*) Random.

— Pigs of a Feather. LC 97-38411. (J). 1998. 0.07 (*0-679-89089-0*, Pub. by Random Bks Yng Read) Random.

— Where is Bear? LC 98-40773. (Bear in the Big Blue House Ser.). (Illus.). 48p. (J). (ps-3). 1999. lib. bdg. 11.99 (*0-375-90044-6*) Random.

Rabe, Tish. Where is Bear? LC 98-40773. (Bright & Early Bks.). (Illus.). 48p. (J). (ps-3). 1999. 7.99 (*0-375-80044-1*, Pub. by Random Bks Yng Read) Random.

Rabe, Tish & Seuss, Dr. The King's Beard. LC 96-39839. (Illus.). 1997. 14.00 (*0-679-88633-8*, Pub. by Random Bks Yng Read) Random.

Rabe, Tish, jt. auth. see Seuss, Dr., pseud.

Rabe, Valentin H. The Home Base of American China Missions, 1880-1920. (East Asian Monographs: No. 75). 300p. 1978. 30.00 (*0-674-40581-1*) HUP.

Rabeeya, David. A Guide to Understanding Judaism & Islam: More Similarities Than Differences. 95p. 1992. pap. 14.95 (*0-9631746-1-4*) Maimuna Pr.

Rabeeya, David & Rueveni, Roni. Sephardic Recipes: Delicacies from Baghdad. (Illus.). 52p. 1992. pap. 14.95 (*0-9631746-0-6*) Maimuna Pr.

Rabek, J. F. Experimental Methods in Photochemistry & Photophysics, 2 pts, Pt. 1. LC 81-14787. (Illus.). 612p. 1982. reprint ed. pap. 189.80 (*0-608-08220-1*, 203309000001) Bks Demand.

— Experimental Methods in Photochemistry & Photophysics, 2 pts, Pt. 2. LC 81-14787. (Illus.). 527p. 1982. reprint ed. pap. 163.40 (*0-608-08221-X*, 203309000002) Bks Demand.

— Mechanisms of Photophysical Processes & Photochemical Reactions in Polymers: Theory & Applications. LC 86-15693. (Illus.). 776p. reprint ed. pap. 200.00 (*0-8357-4627-5*, 203755600008) Bks Demand.

— Photodegradation of Polymers: Physical Characteristics & Applications. LC 96-19743. 250p. 1996. 117.00 (*3-540-60716-1*) Spr-Verlag.

Rabek, J. F., jt. auth. see Ranby, Bengt G.

Rabek, J. F., jt. ed. see Ranby, Bengt G.

Rabek, Jan F. Experimental Methods in Polymer Chemistry: Physical Principles & Applications. LC 79-40511. 887p. reprint ed. pap. 200.00 (*0-608-15408-3*, 202926400059) Bks Demand.

— Photochemistry & Photophysics, Vol. IV. 320p. 1991. lib. bdg. 218.00 (*0-8493-4044-6*, QD714) CRC Pr.

— Progress in Photochemistry & Photophysics, Vol. V. 208p. 1992. lib. bdg. 169.00 (*0-8493-4045-4*, QD714) CRC Pr.

— Progress in Photochemistry & Photophysics, Vol. VI. 256p. 1992. lib. bdg. 199.00 (*0-8493-4046-2*) CRC Pr.

Rabek, Jan F. & Scott, Gary W., eds. Photochemistry & Photophysics, Vol. I. 208p. 1989. lib. bdg. 179.00 (*0-8493-4041-1*, QD714) CRC Pr.

— Photochemistry & Photophysics, Vol. II. 192p. 1989. lib. bdg. 180.00 (*0-8493-4042-X*, QD714) CRC Pr.

Rabek, Jan F., jt. ed. see Fouassier, Jean-Pierre.

Rabel, Carmen R. Lope de Vega: El Arte Nuevo de Hacer "Novellas" (Monografias A Ser.: No. A 150). 94p. (C). 1992. 54.00 (*1-85566-016-4*, Pub. by Tamesis Bks Ltd) Boydell & Brewer.

Rabel, Heidi. The What to Fix for Dinner Cookbook. LC 95-79402. 356p. 1995. pap. 21.95 (*1-883697-91-3*) Hara Pub.

Rabel, Lili. Khasi: A Language of Assam. LC 61-15485. (Louisiana State University Studies, Humanities Ser.: No. 10). (Illus.). 273p. reprint ed. pap. 84.70 (*0-608-11046-9*, 205165700004) Bks Demand.

Rabel, Robert J. Plot & Point of View in the Iliad. LC 96-51313. 264p. 1997. text 44.50 (*0-472-10768-2*, 10768) U of Mich Pr.

Rabel, Roberto G. Between East & West: Trieste, the United States & the Cold War, 1941-1954. LC 87-31775. xvii, 222p. (C). 1988. text 45.95 (*0-8223-0831-2*) Duke.

Rabelais, Francois. L' Abbaye de Theleme. 2nd ed. (FRE.). 40p. 1949. pap. 14.95 (*0-7859-5376-0*, F31160) Fr & Eur.

— Le Cinquieme et Dernier Livre des Faits et Dicts Heroiques Du bon Pantagruel. (FRE.). 219p. 1977. pap. 180.00 (*0-7859-5377-9*) Fr & Eur.

— The Complete Works of Francois Rabelais. Frame, Donald M., tr. (FRE.). 992p. 1992. 95.00 (*0-520-06400-3*, Pub. by U CA Pr) Cal Prin Full Svc.

— The Complete Works of Frangois Rabelais. Frame, Donald M., tr. 992p. 1999. pap. text 29.95 (*0-520-06401-1*, Pub. by U CA Pr) Cal Prin Full Svc.

— Gargantua. Screech, M. A., ed. (Illus.). 458p. 1970. 17.50 (*0-686-54693-8*) Fr & Eur.

— Gargantua. (FRE.). 190p. 1987. pap. 10.95 (*0-7859-1270-3*, 2040166998) Fr & Eur.

— Gargantua. (Folio Ser.: No. 773). (FRE.). pap. 10.95 (*2-07-036773-8*) Schoenhof.

— Gargantua & Pantagruel. 1994. 23.00 (*0-679-43137-3*) Everymns Lib.

— Gargantua & Pantagruel. Raffel, Burton, tr. 640p. 1991. pap. 18.95 (*0-393-30806-5*) Norton.

— Gargantua & Pantagruel. Cohen, J. M., tr. (Classics Ser.). 720p. 1955. pap. 13.95 (*0-14-044047-X*, Penguin Classics) Viking Penguin.

— Gargantua & Pantagruel, 3 vols. LC 01-8984. (Tudor Translations, First Ser.: Nos. 24-26). reprint ed. 172.50 (*0-404-51920-2*) AMS Pr.

— Gargantua & Pantagruel: Selections. Gray, Floyd F., ed. & tr. by. (Crofts Classics). 160p. 1966. pap. text 4.95 (*0-88295-068-1*) Harlan Davidson.

Rabelais, Francois. Gargantua Pantagruel. abr. ed. Cohe, J. M., tr. LC 81-740220. 1982. audio 14.00 (*0-694-50349-5*, SWC 1675, Caedmon) HarperAudio.

Rabelais, Francois. Oeuvres, 6 vols. (FRE., Illus.). 400.00 (*0-686-54699-7*) Fr & Eur.

— Oeuvres: Avec: Le Cinquieme Livre, Vol. 5. Plattard, Jean, ed. (FRE.). 400p. 1948. pap. 12.95 (*0-7859-1459-5*, 2251360859) Fr & Eur.

— Oeuvres: Avec: Le Quart-Livre, Vol. 4. Plattard, Jean, ed. (FRE.). 338p. 1959. pap. 17.95 (*0-7859-1458-7*, 2251360840) Fr & Eur.

— Oeuvres: Avec: Le Tiers-Livre, Vol. 3. Plattard, Jean, ed. (FRE.). 78p. 1961. pap. 17.95 (*0-7859-1457-9*, 2251360832) Fr & Eur.

— Oeuvres: Pantagruel, Vol. 2. Plattard, Jean, ed. (FRE.). 220p. 1959. pap. 17.95 (*0-7859-1456-0*, 2251360824) Fr & Eur.

— Oeuvres Completes. Boulanger, Jacques, ed. (FRE.). 1072p. 1978. lib. bdg. 100.00 (*0-7859-3780-3*, 2070104702) Fr & Eur.

— Oeuvres Completes. deluxe ed. Boulenger & Scheler, eds. (Pleiade Ser.). (FRE.). 1934. 63.95 (*2-07-010470-2*) Schoenhof.

— Pantagruel. (FRE.). 1964. pap. 4.50 (*0-685-11475-9*, 1240) Fr & Eur.

— Pantagruel. Saulnier, V. L., ed. (FRE.). 448p. 1973. pap. 13.95 (*0-7859-4556-3*) Fr & Eur.

— Pantagruel. (Folio Ser.: No. 387). (FRE.). pap. 11.95 (*2-07-036387-2*) Schoenhof.

— Pantagrueline Prognostication Pour l'An 1533: Avec les Almanachs pour les Ans 1533, 1535 et 1541. la Grande et Vraye Pronostication Nouvelle De 1544. (FRE., Illus.). 180p. 1975. pap. 24.95 (*0-7859-5378-7*) Fr & Eur.

— Le Quart Livre. (FRE.). 256p. 1990. pap. 10.95 (*0-7859-1425-0*, 2080702408) Fr & Eur.

— Le Quart Livre: Des Faicts et Dicts Heroiques du Bon Pantagruel. Heath, Michael J., ed. (FRE.). 309p. 1990. pap. 6.95 (*1-870725-06-9*, PR2, Pub. by Runnymede) Pegasus Pr.

— Le Tiers Livre. Michel, Pierre, ed. (FRE.). 1973. 4.95 (*0-686-54704-7*) Fr & Eur.

— Le Tiers Livre. Screech, A. M., ed. (FRE.). 474p. 1991. pap. 11.95 (*0-7859-4557-1*) Fr & Eur.

— Le Tiers Livre: Original. (Folio Ser.: No. 462). (FRE.). pap. 9.25 (*2-07-036462-3*) Schoenhof.

— La Vie Tres Honorifique du Grand Gargantua, Vol. 1. (FRE.). 233p. 1973. pap. 180.00 (*0-7859-5379-5*) Fr & Eur.

— La Vie Tres Horrificque du Grand Gargantua. (FRE.). 248p. 1968. 14.95 (*0-8288-7423-9*) Fr & Eur.

Rabeler, Richard K. Gleason's Plants of Michigan. expanded rev. ed. Armentrout, Vivienne N., ed. LC 98-67416. (Illus.). 398p. 1998. pap. 21.95 (*0-9663251-0-9*) Oakleaf Pr.

Rabell, Edda, ed. & tr. see Ronnholm, Ursula O.

Rabello, Camilla, ed. see Reif, Joe & Shahmanesh, Nargess.

Rabellotti, Roberta. External Economies & Cooperation in Industrial Districts: A Comparison of Italy & Mexico. LC 97-9326. 1997. text 69.95 (*0-312-17580-9*) St Martin.

Rabellotti, Roberta, jt. ed. see Pieter van Dijk, Meine.

Raben, Estelle M. Major Strategies in Twentieth-Century Drama: Apocalyptic Vision, Allegory & Open Form. (American University Studies: English Language & Literature: Ser. IV, Vol. 67). 164p. (C). 1989. text 21.50 (*0-8204-0567-1*) P Lang Pubng.

***Raben, Remco.** Representing the Japanese Occupation of Indonesia: Personal Testimonies & Public Images in Indonesia. LC 00-309393. (Illus.). 240p. 2000. pap. 50.00 (*90-400-9346-6*) U of Wash Pr.

Rabenalt, Arthur M. Schriften zum Musiktheater der 20er und 30er Jahre - Opernregie I. (Rabenalt, Arthur Maria, Gesammelte Schriften Ser.: Bd. 1). (GER.). xxxiv, 222p. 1999. 50.00 (*3-487-10864-X*) G Olms Verlag.

Rabenau, Merten. Studien Zum Buch Tobit. (Beiheft zur Zeitschrift fuer die Alttestamentliche Wissenschaft Ser.). (GER.). viii, 249p. (C). 1994. lib. bdg. 106.15 (*3-11-014125-6*) De Gruyter.

Rabeneck, Malvern, et al. F. Kroeber Clock Co. Identification & Price Guide. 36p. 1983. spiral bd. 20.00 (*0-913902-49-7*) Heart Am Pr.

Rabeneck, Malvern, jt. auth. see Ehrhardt, Roy.

Rabeneck, Malvern, jt. auth. see Erhardt, Roy.

Rabenold, Diana. Love, Politics, & "Rescue" in Lesbian Relationships. (Lesbian-Feminist Essay Ser.), 24p. (Orig.). 1987. pap. 3.50 (*0-939821-29-X*) HerBooks.

Rabenort, William L. Spinoza As Educator. LC 70-177175. (Columbia University. Teachers College. Contributions to Education Ser.: No. 38). reprint ed. 37.50 (*0-404-55038-X*) AMS Pr.

Rabenstein, Albert L. Elementary Differential Equations with Lin. 4th ed. (C). 1992. pap. text, teacher ed. 20.75 (*0-03-092732-3*) Harcourt Coll Pubs.

— Elementary Differential Equations with Linear Algebra. 4th ed. 650p. (C). 1992. text 94.50 (*0-15-520984-1*) SCP.

Rabenstein, Rudiger. Radsport und Gesellschaft. (GER.). vi, 333p. 1995. 39.80 (*3-615-00066-8*, Pub. by Weidmann) Lubrecht & Cramer.

Rabeony, Ernest. Fanorona: The Classic Game of Tactical Skill from Madagascar. Fox, Leonard, tr. 1990. 20.00 (*0-932329-02-0*) Intl Fanorona.

Raber. Organic Chemistry. Date not set. pap. text, teacher ed. write for info. (*0-314-35233-3*) West Pub.

Raber, Ann, ed. A Life of Wholeness: Reflections on Abundant Living. rev. ed. LC 93-19617. 160p. 1993. pap. 9.99 (*0-8361-3646-2*) Herald Pr.

Raber, Chester, jt. auth. see Stoesz, Edgar.

Raber, Douglas. Librarianship & Legitimacy: The Ideology of the Public Library Inquiry, 90. LC 97-9376. (Contributions in Librarianship & Information Science: Vol. 90). 184p. 1997. 52.95 (*0-313-30234-0*, Greenwood Pr) Greenwood.

Raber, Douglas & Raber, Nancy. Organic Chemistry. (Chemistry). 1445p. (C). 1988. mass mkt. 69.50 (*0-314-28508-3*) West Pub.

Raber, Merill F. & Dyck, George. Managing Stress for Mental Fitness. 2nd rev. ed. Crisp, Michael, ed. LC 92-74205. (Fifty-Minute Ser.). 85p. 1993. pap. 10.95 (*1-56052-200-3*) Crisp Pubns.

Raber, Nancy, jt. auth. see Raber, Douglas.

Raber, Robert R., ed. Fluid Filtration: Gas, Vol. 1. LC 86-22237. (Special Technical Publication Ser.: No. 975). (Illus.). 430p. 1986. text 39.00 (*0-8031-0945-8*, \) ASTM.

Raber, Robert R., et al, eds. Fluid Filtration, 2 vols., Set. LC 86-22237. (Special Technical Publication Ser.: No. 975). (Illus.). 624p. 1986. text 55.00 (*0-8031-0926-1*, STP975) ASTM.

Raber, Suzanne & Roach, Virginia. The Push & Pull of Standards-Based Reform: How Does It Affect Local School Districts & Students with Disabilities? 2nd ed. 48p. 1998. pap. 12.00 (*1-58434-036-3*) NASBE.

Raber, Thomas R. Bo Jackson: Pro Sports Superstar. (Sports Achievers Biographies Ser.). (Illus.). 64p. (J). (gr. 4-9). 1991. lib. bdg. 18.60 (*0-8225-0487-1*, Lerner Publctns) Lerner Pub.

— Joe Montana: Comeback Quarterback. (Sports Achievers Ser.). (Illus.). 64p. (J). (gr. 4-9). 1989. lib. bdg. 18.60 (*0-8225-0486-3*, Lerner Publctns) Lerner Pub.

— Joe Montana: Comeback Quarterback. (Illus.). 64p. (J). (gr. 4-9). 1990. pap. 4.95 (*0-8225-9572-9*, Lerner Publctns) Lerner Pub.

— Michael Jordan: Basketball Skywalker. 3rd ed. LC 96-33510. (Sports Achievers Biographies Ser.). 80p. (YA). (gr. 4-9). 1997. lib. bdg. 19.93 (*0-8225-3654-4*, LernerSports) Lerner Pub.

***Raber, Thomas R.** Michael Jordan, 3rd Revised & Expanded ed. 3rd ed. (Lerner Sports Achievers Ser.). 80p. 1999. pap. text 5.95 (*0-8225-9846-9*) Lerner Pub.

Raber, Thomas R. Presidential Campaign. (American Politics Ser.). (Illus.). 88p. (J). (gr. 4-8). 1988. lib. bdg. 9.50 (*0-8225-1750-7*, Lerner Publctns) Lerner Pub.

— Wayne Gretzky: Hockey Great. (Sports Achievers Ser.). (Illus.). 64p. (J). (gr. 4-9). 1991. lib. bdg. 19.95 (*0-8225-0539-8*, Lerner Publctns) Lerner Pub.

— Wayne Gretzky: Hockey Great. (Illus.). 64p. (YA). 1992. pap. 4.95 (*0-8225-9601-6*, Lerner Publctns) Lerner Pub.

— Wayne Gretzky: Hockey Great. rev. ed. LC 99-32258. (Sports Achievers Biographies Ser.). 80p. (YA). (gr. 4-9). 1999. 21.27 (*0-8225-3677-3*, LernerSports) Lerner Pub.

Raberg, Per G. The Life Region: The Social & Cultural Ecology of Sustainable Development. LC 96-32983. 464p. (C). 1997. 95.00 (*0-415-15905-9*) Routledge.

***Rabert, Willard, Jr., et al.** The Littlest Christmas Tree: A Children's Christmas Play. 8p. 1999. pap. 3.50 (*0-7880-1515-X*) CSS OH.

Rabes, H., et al, eds. Metastasis: Basic Research & Its Clinical Application. (Beitraege Zur Onkologie, Contributions to Oncology Ser.: Vol. 44). x, 394p. 1992. 68.75 (*3-8055-5610-1*) S Karger.

Rabesa, Arthur. Explosive Karate: Understanding Karate Mechanics. Mattson, George E., ed. (Illus.). 109p. 1993. pap. 15.00 (*0-930559-08-8*) Peabody Pub.

— Kumite: The Complete Fighting Text. LC 84-16609. (Illus.). 133p. (Orig.). 1984. pap. text 10.00 (*0-930559-00-2*) Peabody Pub.

Rabey, David I. David Rudkin: Sacred Disobedience: An Expository Study of His Drama, 1959-1994. (Contemporary Theatre Studies). (Illus.). 228p. 1997. text 41.00 (*90-5702-126-9*, Harwood Acad Pubs); pap. text 16.00 (*90-5702-127-7*, Harwood Acad Pubs) Gordon & Breach.

Rabey, Ed A., jt. auth. see Beyer, Beverly.

Rabey, J. M., jt. ed. see Bonuccelli, U.

Rabey, Lois Mowday. Growing Young: Embracing the Joy & Challenges of Mid-Life. 192p. 1999. 13.95 (*1-57856-143-4*) Waterbrook Pr.

***Rabey, Lois Mowday.** When Your Soul Aches: Hope & Help for Women Who Have Lost Their Husbands. LC 00-35941. 160p. 2000. 12.95 (*1-57856-144-2*) Waterbrook Pr.

Rabey, Lois Mowday. Women of a Generous Spirit: Touching Others with Life-Giving Love. 240p. 1998. 16.95 (*1-57856-050-0*) Waterbrook Pr.

***Rabey, Steve.** Celtic Journeys: A Traveler's Guide to Ireland's Spiritual Legacy. 2000. pap. text 12.95 (*0-8065-2161-9*, Citadel Pr) Carol Pub Group.

Rabey, Steve. Celtic Spirit: Ancient Wisdom for Everyday Life. LC 98-8116. (Illus.). 286p. 1998. 22.95 (*0-525-94409-5*) NAL.

— In the House of Memory: Ancient Celtic Wisdom for Everyday Life. 304p. 1999. pap. 12.95 (*0-452-27953-4*, Plume) Dutton Plume.

***Rabey, Steve.** Revival in Brownsville: Pensacola Pentacostalism & Power of American Revivalism. 1999. pap. text 12.99 (*0-7852-6942-8*) Nelson.

Rabey, Steve. Rock Devotional. 128p. 1989. pap. 7.99 (*0-310-39781-2*, 11789P) Zondervan.

Rabey, Steve, jt. auth. see Key, Dana.

Rabey, Steve, jt. auth. see Talbot, John M.

Rabgay, Lobsang, tr. see Donden, Yeshi.

***Rabhi, Fethi, et al.** Algorithms: A Functional Programming Approach. 2nd ed. LC 99-10106. 320p. (C). 1999. pap. text 48.00 (*0-201-59604-0*) Addison-Wesley.

Rabi, Ibrahim M. Intellectual Origins of Islamic Resurgence in the Modern Arab World. 370p. 1996. pap. 19.95 (*0-614-21226-X*, 1484) Kazi Pubns.

***Rabi Reddy, T.** Rural-Urban Migration: An Economic Interpretation LC 98-903585. xi, 212 p. 1998. write for info. (*81-85972-94-X*, Pub. by Reliance Pub Hse) S Asia.

Rabi, Robert J., et al. Labor & Employment: Problems, Cases & Materials. 2nd ed. LC 95-3407. (American Casebook Ser.). 946p. (C). 1995. 60.00 (*0-314-05458-8*) West Pub.

Rabia, H. Oilwell Drilling Engineering: Principles & Practice. 334p. 1986. pap. text 152.00 (*0-86010-661-6*) G & T Inc.

Rabianski, Joseph, jt. auth. see Epley, Donald R.

Rabianski, Joseph S., jt. auth. see Epley, Donald R.

Rabianski, Joseph S., jt. auth. see Vernor, James D.

Rabideau, Clyde. The Robidous: A Breed Apart. LC 98-65066. (Illus.). 352p. 1998. 23.00 (*0-9662895-0-1*) C M Rabideau.

Rabideau, Clyde M. Robidous in North America: Three Hundred Fifty Years (1643-1993) 608p. 1993. 20.00 (*0-9636684-0-4*) C M Rabideau.

Rabideau, Clyde M., compiled by. Headstone Inscriptions: Clinton County, New York. LC 99-60559. iii, 402p. 1999. 30.00 (*0-9662895-2-8*) C M Rabideau.

— 1998 Vital Statistics: Clinton, Franklin & Essex County, New York. LC 99-60840. iv, 503p. 1999. write for info. (*0-9662895-3-6*) C M Rabideau.

Rabideau, P., ed. The Conformational Analysis of Cyclohexenes, Cyclohexadienes & Related Hydroaromatic Compounds. (Methods in Stereochemical Analysis Ser.). 323p. 1989. 165.00 (*0-471-18708-9*, Wiley-VCH) Wiley.

Rabideau, Peter W., ed. The Conformational Analysis of Cyclohexenes, Cyclohexadienes, & Related Hydroaromatic Compounds. LC 88-33970. (Methods in Stereochemical Analysis Ser.). 323p. 1989. lib. bdg. 100.00 (*0-89573-702-7*, Wiley-VCH) Wiley.

Rabie, A. B. & Urist, Marshall R. Bone Formation & Repair: Proceedings of the International Symposium on Formation & Repair of Mineralized Extracellular Matrix, Hong Kong, 10-19 October, 1996. LC 97-39183. (International Congress Ser.). 232p. 1997. 182.25 (*0-444-82652-1*) Elsevier.

Rabie-Azoory, Vera. Sibling Rivalry: The Truth about the Family Favorite. LC 99-28330. 1998. pap. 14.95 (*1-56980-131-2*) Barricade Bks.

Rabie, M. A., jt. auth. see Fuggle, R. F.

Rabie, Mohamed. Conflict: Resolution & Ethnicity. LC 94-6381. 240p. 1994. 59.95 (*0-275-94598-7*, Praeger Pubs) Greenwood.

— The Politics of Foreign Aid: U. S. Foreign Assistance & Aid to Israel. LC 88-3096. 200p. 1988. 55.00 (*0-275-93000-9*, C3000, Praeger Pubs) Greenwood.

— U. S. - PLO Dialogue: Secret Diplomacy & Conflict Resolution. LC 94-5294. 224p. 1995. 49.95 (*0-8130-1326-7*) U Press Fla.

Rabie, P. J. The Law of Estoppel in South Africa. 130p. 1992. pap. 49.00 (*0-409-05000-8*, SA, MICHIE); boxed set 85.00 (*0-409-05001-6*, SA, MICHIE) LEXIS Pub.

Rabier, J., et al, eds. Dislocations 93. (Solid State Phenomena Ser.: Vol. 35-36). (Illus.). 631p. (C). 1994. 208.00 (*3-908450-02-0*, Pub. by Trans T Pub) Enfield Pubs NH.

Rabier, Jacques-Rene. Euro-Barometer 4: Consumer Attitudes in Europe, October November 1975. LC 79-83752. 1979. write for info. (*0-89138-988-1*) ICPSR.

Rabier, Jacques-Rene & Inglehart, Ronald. Euro-Barometer 10: National Priorities & the Institutions of Europe, October-November 1978. LC 80-84080. 1980. write for info. (*0-89138-955-5*) ICPSR.

— Euro-Barometer 10-A: Scientific Priorities in the European Community, October-November 1978. LC 81-84734. 1981. write for info. (*0-89138-944-X*) ICPSR.

— Euro-Barometer 11: The Year of the Child in Europe, April 1979. LC 81-84735. 1981. write for info. (*0-89138-943-1*) ICPSR.

— Euro-Barometer 12: European Parliamentary Elections, October-November 1979. LC 81-84736. 1981. write for info. (*0-89138-942-3*) ICPSR.

— Euro-Barometer 3: European Men & Women, May 1975. LC 79-83750. 1979. write for info. (*0-89138-989-X*) ICPSR.

— Euro-Barometer 5: Revenues, Satisfaction, & Poverty, May 1976. LC 79-83756. 1979. write for info. (*0-89138-987-3*) ICPSR.

— Euro-Barometer 6: Twenty Years of the Common Market, October-November 1976. LC 79-83757. 1979. write for info. (*0-89138-986-5*) ICPSR.

— Euro-Barometer 7: Science & Technology in the European Community, April 1977. LC 80-84077. 1980. write for info. (*0-89138-952-0*) ICPSR.

— Euro-Barometer 8: Men, Women, & Work Roles in Europe, October-November 1977. LC 80-84078. 1980. write for info. (*0-89138-953-9*) ICPSR.

— Euro-Barometer 9: Employment & Unemployment in Europe, April 1978. LC 80-84079. 1980. write for info. (*0-89138-954-7*) ICPSR.

Rabier, Jacques-Rene, et al. Candidates for the European Parliament, April-May 1979. LC 84-62936. 1985. write for info. (*0-89138-893-1*) ICPSR.

— Euro-Barometer No. 26: Energy Problems, November 1986. LC 89-83656. 240p. 1989. write for info. (*0-89138-876-1*) ICPSR.

— Euro-Barometer 13: Regional Development & Integration, April 1980. LC 82-81760. 1982. write for info. (*0-89138-937-7*, ICPSR 7957) ICPSR.

— Euro-Barometer 14: Trust in the European Community, October 1980. LC 82-81761. 1982. write for info. (*0-89138-936-9*, ICPSR 7958) ICPSR.

— Euro-Barometer 15: Membership in the European Community, April 1981. LC 82-81762. 1982. write for info. (*0-89138-935-0*, ICPSR 7959) ICPSR.

— Euro-Barometer 16: Noise & Other Social Problems, October 1981. LC 83-83374. 1984. write for info. (*0-89138-906-7*) ICPSR.

— Euro-Barometer 17: Energy & the Future, April 1982. LC 83-83375. 1984. write for info. (*0-89138-905-9*) ICPSR.

— Euro-Barometer 18: Ecological Issues, October 1982. LC 83-83376. 1984. write for info. (*0-89138-904-0*) ICPSR.

— Euro-Barometer 19: Gender Roles in the European Community, April 1983. LC 84-80216. 1984. write for info. (*0-89138-903-2*) ICPSR.

— Euro-Barometer 20: Aid to Developing Nations, October 1983. LC 84-62937. 1985. write for info. (*0-89138-894-X*) ICPSR.

— Euro-Barometer 21: Political Cleavages in the European Community, April 1984. LC 85-80716. 1985. write for info. (*0-89138-889-3*) ICPSR.

— Euro-Barometer 22: Energy Problems & the Atlantic Alliance, October 1984. LC 86-82557. (Euro-Barometers Ser.). 174p. 1986. write for info. (*0-89138-884-2*) ICPSR.

— Euro-Barometer 23: The European Currency Unit & Working Conditions, April 1985. LC 86-82556. (Euro-Barometers Ser.). 168p. 1986. write for info. (*0-89138-883-4*) ICPSR.

— Euro-Barometer 25: Holiday Travel & Environmental Problems, April 1986. LC 88-81973. (Euro-Barometers Ser.). 288p. 1988. write for info. (*0-89138-877-X*) ICPSR.

— Euro-Barometer 28: Relations with Third World Countries & Energy Problems, November 1987. LC 89-81140. (Euro-Barometers Ser.). 438p. 1989. write for info. (*0-89138-873-7*) ICPSR.

Rabier, Jacques-Rene, jt. auth. see Inglehart, Ronald.

Rabier, P. J. Topics in One-Parameter Bifurcation Problems. (Tata Institute Lectures on Mathematics). vi, 290p. 1985. 42.95 (*0-387-13907-9*) Spr-Verlag.

Rabier, P. J. & Oden, J. Tinsley. Bifurcation in Rotating Bodies. Ciarlet, P. G. & Lions, J. L., eds. (Recherches en Mathematiques Appliquees Ser.: Vol. 11). vii, 150p. 1990. 44.95 (*0-387-51551-8*) Spr-Verlag.

***Rabier, Patrick J. & Rheinboldt, Werner C.** Nonholonomic Motion of Rigid Mechanical Systems from a DAE Viewpoint. LC 99-53790. (Miscellaneous Titles in Applied Mathematics Ser.: No. 68). (Illus.). 140p. 2000. pap. 36.00 (*0-89871-446-X*, OT0068) Soc Indus-Appl Math.

***Rabiger, Michael.** Developing Story Ideas. LC 99-55120. (Illus.). 192p. 2000. pap. 17.95 (*0-240-80398-1*, Focal) Buttrwrth-Heinemann.

Rabiger, Michael. Directing: Film Techniques & Aesthetics. 2nd ed. (Illus.). 512p. 1996. pap. 39.95 (*0-240-80223-3*, Focal) Buttrwrth-Heinemann.

— Directing the Documentary. 3rd ed. LC 97-6582. 432p. 1997. pap. 39.95 (*0-240-80270-5*, Focal) Buttrwrth-Heinemann.

Rabii, Shahriar & Wooley, Bruce A. The Design of Low-Voltage, Low-Power, Sigma-Delta Modulators. LC 98-44228. (Series in Engineering & Computer Science). 1999. write for info. (*0-7923-8361-3*) Kluwer Academic.

Rabil, Albert, Jr Erasmus & the New Testament: The Mind of a Christian Humanist. LC 93-4903. 208p. (C). 1993. reprint ed. pap. text 26.50 (*0-8191-9217-1*) U Pr of Amer.

Rabil, Albert. Erasmus & the New Testament: The Mind of a Christian Humanist. LC 71-184768. (Trinity University Monograph Series in Religion). 206p. reprint ed. pap. 58.50 (*0-608-30590-1*, 2022565) Bks Demand.

— Erasmus & the New Testament: The Mind of a Christian Humanist. LC 71-184768. (Trinity University Monograph Series in Religion: Vol. 1). 206p. reprint ed. pap. 63.90 (*0-608-10676-3*, 202256500028) Bks Demand.

Rabil, Albert, Jr., ed. Renaissance Humanism: Foundations, Forms & Legacy, Vol. 3. LC 87-13928. (Illus.). 508p. 1988. pap. 36.95 (*0-8122-1374-2*) U of Pa Pr.

Rabil, Albert, Jr., ed. Knowledge, Goodness, & Power: The Debate over Nobility among Quattrocento Italian Humanists. (Medieval & Renaissance Texts & Studies: Vol. 88). 432p. 1991. 36.00 (*0-86698-100-4*, MR88) MRTS.

Rabil, Albert, Jr., jt. ed. see King, Margaret L.

Rabil, Albert, Jr., ed. & tr. see Agrippa, Henry Cornelius.

Rabil, Dick, tr. see National Conference of Catholic Bishops.

Rabillard, Sheila, ed. Essays on Caryl Churchill: Contemporary Representations. 224p. 1997. pap. 24.95 (*0-921368-77-1*) Blizzard Publ.

Rabilloud, Guy. High-Performance Polymers: Chemistry & Applications , 2 vols. LC 97-193983. (Institut Franpcais du Pbetrole Publications). 1997. write for info. (*2-7108-0719-X*); write for info. (*2-7108-0716-5*) Edits Technip.

Rabilloud, Guy. High Performance Polymers Chemistry & Applications. 376p. 1997. pap. 680.00 (*2-7108-0717-3*, Pub. by Edits Technip) Enfield Pubs NH.

***Rabilloud, T. H., ed.** Proteome Research: Two-Dimensional Gel Electrophoresis & Detection Methods. LC 99-15544. (Principles & Practice Ser.). (Illus.). 250p. 1999. 109.00 (*3-540-65689-8*); pap. 62.00 (*3-540-65792-4*) Spr-Verlag.

Rabin. Casey over There. (J). 1997. pap. 5.00 (*0-15-201553-1*, Harcourt Child Bks) Harcourt.

Rabin, Alan A. & Yeager, Leland B. Monetary Approaches to the Balance of Payments & Exchange Rates. LC 82-15587. (Essays in International Finance Ser.: No. 148). 30p. 1982. pap. text 10.00 (*0-88165-055-2*) Princeton U Int Finan Econ.

Rabin, Albert I. Assessment with Projective Techniques: A Concise Introduction. LC 80-26229. 352p. 1981. 46.95 (*0-8261-3550-1*) Springer Pub.

— Projective Techniques for Adolescents & Children. (Illus.). 384p. 1986. 44.95 (*0-8261-4920-0*) Springer Pub.

— Psychological Issues in Biblical Lore: Explorations in the Old Testament. LC 98-17874. (Series on Social Work). 1998. 34.95 (*0-8261-1212-9*) Springer Pub.

Rabin, Arnold. The Outing: Playscript. 53p. (YA). 1992. pap. 6.00 (*0-87602-303-0*) Anchorage.

— The Rat & the Rose. unabridged ed. 175p. (Orig.). 1996. pap. 12.95 (*0-930773-43-8*); lib. bdg. 20.95 (*0-930773-42-X*) Black Heron Pr.

Rabin-Bisby, Bridie & Geekie, Peter. Learning to Read & Write Through Classroom Talk. 96p. 1993. pap. 9.00 (*0-948080-82-5*, Trentham Bks) Stylus Pub VA.

Rabin-Bisby, Bridie, et al. Developing Language & Literacy. 268p. 1995. pap. 22.00 (*1-85856-036-5*, Trentham Bks) Stylus Pub VA.

Rabin, Bruce S. Stress, Immune Function & Health: The Connection. LC 98-30128. 341p. 1999. 94.95 (*0-471-24181-4*) Wiley.

Rabin, C., et al, eds. The Book of Jeremiah. (Hebrew University Bible Ser.). (HEB.). 382p. 1997. text 98.00 (*965-223-933-X*, Pub. by Magnes Pr) Eisenbrauns.

Rabin, Chaim. The Development of the Syntax of Post-Biblical Hebrew. LC 99-20718. (Studies in Semitic Languages & Linguistics Ser.). 1999. write for info. (*90-04-11433-5*) Brill Academic Pubs.

— Qumran Studies, No. 2--2. LC 76-40116. (Scripta Judaica Ser.: No. 2). 135p. 1977. reprint ed. lib. bdg. 35.00 (*0-8371-9060-6*, RAQS, Greenwood Pr) Greenwood.

Rabin, Chaim, tr. see Maimonides.

Rabin, Claire. Equal Partners - Good Friends: Empowering Couples Through Therapy. LC 95-42247. (Illus.). 296p. (C). 1996. 85.00 (*0-415-11614-7*); pap. 25.99 (*0-415-11615-5*) Routledge.

Rabin, D. M., ed. Infrared Solar Physics: Proceedings of the 154th Symposium of the International Astronomical Union, Held in Tucson, Arizona, U. S. A., March 2-6, 1992. LC 93-33129. 628p. (C). 1993. pap. text 107.50 (*0-7923-2523-0*); lib. bdg. 214.50 (*0-7923-2522-2*) Kluwer Academic.

Rabin, Dan & Forget, Carl, eds. The Dictionary of Beer & Brewing. 2nd expanded rev. ed. 315p. 1998. lib. bdg. 45.00 (*1-57958-078-5*) Fitzroy Dearborn.

Rabin, Dan, jt. auth. see Forget, Carl.

Rabin, David. Long-Term Care for the Elderly: A Factbook. (Illus.). 269p. 1986. pap. text 19.95 (*0-19-504106-2*) OUP.

Rabin, Edward H. & Kwall, Roberta R. Modern Real Property, Fundamentals Of. 3rd ed. (University Casebook Ser.). 1092p. 1992. text 45.95 (*0-88277-962-1*) Foundation Pr.

— Teacher's Manual for Fundamentals of Modern Real Property Law. 3rd ed. (University Casebook Ser.). 1992. pap. text. write for info. (*1-56662-002-3*) Foundation Pr.

Rabin, Edwin H. & Kwall, Roberta R. Fundamentals of Modern Real Property Law: 1996 Supplement. 3rd ed. (University Casebook Ser.). 86p. 1996. pap. text, teacher ed. write for info. (*1-56662-416-9*) Foundation Pr.

— Fundamentals of Modern Real Property Law To: 1996 Supplement. 3rd ed. (University Casebook Ser.). 108p. 1996. pap. text. write for info. (*1-56662-391-X*) Foundation Pr.

Rabin, H. M. & Rosenbaum, Max, eds. How to Begin a Psychotherapy Group: Six Approaches. iv, 140p. 1976. text 80.00 (*0-677-15800-9*) Gordon & Breach.

Rabin, Jack, ed. Handbook of Public Budgeting. (Public Administration & Public Policy Ser.: Vol. 46). (Illus.). 760p. 1992. text 250.00 (*0-8247-8592-4*) Dekker.

Rabin, Jack, et al, eds. Handbook of Public Administration. 2nd ed. LC 97-31057. (Public Administration & Public Policy Ser.: Vol. 65). (Illus.). 1272p. 1997. text 265.00 (*0-8247-0086-4*) Dekker.

— Handbook of Public Personnel Administration. (Public Administration & Public Policy Ser.: Vol. 58). (Illus.). 744p. 1994. text 215.00 (*0-8247-9231-9*) Dekker.

— Handbook of Public Sector Labor Relations, LC 94-13202. (Public Administration & Public Policy Ser.: Vol. 56). (Illus.). 440p. 1994. text 190.00 (*0-8247-9235-1*) Dekker.

Rabin, Jack & Bowman, James. Politics & Administration: Woodrow Wilson & American Public Administration. (Public Administration & Public Policy Ser.: Vol. 22). (Illus.). 344p. 1984. text 95.00 (*0-8247-7068-4*) Dekker.

Rabin, Jack & Dodd, Don. State & Local Government Administration. (Public Administration & Public Policy Ser.: Vol. 28). (Illus.). 464p. 1985. text 69.75 (*0-8247-7355-1*) Dekker.

Rabin, Jack, et al. Deborah Budgeting & Financial Management: An Annotated Bibliography. LC 91-11176. (Public Affairs & Administration Ser.: Vol. 25). 180p. 1991. text 15.00 (*0-8240-7595-1*) Garland.

***Rabin, Jack, et al.** Handbook of Strategic Management. 2nd rev. expanded ed. LC 00-24054. (Public Administration & Public Policy Ser.). 2000. write for info. (*0-8247-0339-1*) Dekker.

Rabin, Jack, et al. Handbook on Public Personnel Administration & Labor Relations. fac. ed. LC 83-1468. (Public Administration & Public Policy Ser.: No. 15). 687p. 1983. pap. 200.00 (*0-7837-8334-5*, 204912100010) Bks Demand.

— Public Budgets Lab: Student Workbook. LC 97-171602. (Public Budgeting Laboratory Ser.). 118p. 1996. pap., student ed. 12.95 (*0-89854-183-2*) U of GA Inst Govt.

Rabin, Jack, jt. auth. see Jackowski.

Rabin, Jack, jt. ed. see Golembiewski, Robert T.

Rabin, Jack, jt. ed. see Steinhauer, Marcia B.

Rabin, M. Automata on Infinite Objects & Church's Problem. LC 72-6749. (CBMS Regional Conference Series in Mathematics: No. 13). 22p. 1973. reprint ed. pap. 18.00 (*0-8218-1663-2*, CBMS/13) Am Math.

Rabin, Rhoda. At the Beginning: Teaching Piano to the Very Young Child. 304p. 1995. 30.00 (*0-02-872066-0*, Schirmer Books) Mac Lib Ref.

Rabin, Robert J., et al. Labor & Employment Law: Problems, Cases & Materials in the Law of Work. (American Casebook Ser.). 1014p. 1988. text 44.50 (*0-314-39695-0*); pap. text, teacher ed. write for info. (*0-314-46970-2*) West Pub.

— Labor & Employment Law: Problems, Cases & Materials in the Law of Work 1995 Statutory Supplement. 2nd ed. (American Casebook Ser.). 946p. (C). 1995. pap. 20.00 (*0-314-07069-9*) West Pub.

— Labor & Employment Law Problems, Cases & Materials in the Law of Work, Teacher's Manual to Accompany. 2nd ed. (American Casebook Ser.). 96p. 1995. pap. text, teacher ed. write for info. (*0-314-07549-6*) West Pub.

Rabin, Robert L. Perspectives on Tort Law. 2nd ed. 352p. (C). 1983. 12.00 (*0-316-73003-3*, Aspen Law & Bus) Aspen Pub.

— Tort Law. 4th ed. 448p. 1995. pap. text 28.95 (*0-316-73007-6*, Aspen Law & Bus) Aspen Pub.

Rabin, Robert L. & Sugarman, Stephen D., eds. Smoking Policy: Law, Politics & Culture. LC 92-33045. 256p. 1993. text 55.00 (*0-19-507231-6*) OUP.

Rabin, Robert L., jt. auth. see Franklin, Marc A.

Rabin, Staton. Casey over There. LC 92-30322. (Illus.). 32p. (J). (ps-3). 1994. 14.95 (*0-15-253186-6*) Harcourt.

Rabin, Sue. 101 Ways to Flirt. LC 96-43265. 1997. pap. 9.95 (*0-452-27685-3*, Plume) Dutton Plume.

— Polymer Flow Interaction, No. 137. LC 85-73915. 302p. 1986. lib. bdg. 53.75 (*0-88318-336-6*) Am Inst Physics.

Rabin, Susan & Lagowski, Barbara. Cyberflirt: How to Attract Anyone, Anywhere on the World Wide Web. LC 98-51390. 160p. 1999. pap. 11.95 (*0-452-28054-0*, Plume) Dutton Plume.

Rabin, Susan & Lagowski, Barbara J. How to Attract Anyone, Anytime, Anyplace: The Smart Single's Guide to Flirting in the '90s. LC 93-10133. 144p. (Orig.). 1993. pap. 10.95 (*0-452-27086-3*, Plume) Dutton Plume.

Rabin, Y. & Bruinsma, R. Soft Order in Physical Systems. (NATO ASI Ser.: Vol. 323). (Illus.). 248p. (C). 1994. text 85.00 (*0-306-44678-2*, Kluwer Plenum) Kluwer Academic.

Rabin, Yitzak. The Rabin Memoirs: An Expanded Edition with Recent Speeches, New Photographs, & an Afterword. (Illus.). 416p. (C). 1996. 45.00 (*0-520-20776-9*, Pub. by U CA Pr) Cal Prin Full Svc.

— The Rabin Memoirs: An Expanded Edition with Recent Speeches, New Photographs, & an Afterword. (Illus.). 416p. (C). 1996. pap. 17.95 (*0-520-20766-1*, Pub. by U CA Pr) Cal Prin Full Svc.

Rabinbach, Anson. The Crisis of Austrian Socialism: From Red Vienna to Civil War, 1927-1934. LC 82-10919. (Illus.). 312p. (C). 1994. 22.00 (*0-226-70121-2*) U Ch Pr.

— The Crisis of Austrian Socialism: From Red Vienna to Civil War, 1927-1934. LC 82-10919. (Illus.). 308p. reprint ed. pap. 95.50 (*0-608-09504-4*, 205430500005) Bks Demand.

— In the Shadow of Catastrophe: German Intellectuals Between Apocalypse & Enlightenment. LC 96-39459. (Weimar & Now Ser.). 252p. 1997. 35.00 (*0-520-20744-0*, Pub. by U CA Pr) Cal Prin Full Svc.

***Rabinbach, Anson.** In the Shadow of Catastrophe: German Intellectuals Between Apocalypse & Enlightenment. (Weimar & Now Ser.: Vol. 14). (Illus.). 252p. 2001. pap. 18.95 (*0-520-22690-9*, Pub. by U CA Pr) Cal Prin Full Svc.

Rabinbach, Anson. Marxism. 1998. 26.95 (*0-8057-8620-1*, Twyne); per. 14.95 (*0-8057-8621-X*, Twyne) Mac Lib Ref.

Rabinbach, Anson & Zipes, Jack D., eds. Germans & Jews since the Holocaust: The Changing Situation in West Germany. LC 85-14036. 300p. 1986. 45.00 (*0-8419-0924-5*); pap. 20.00 (*0-8419-0925-3*) Holmes & Meier.

Rabinback, Anson. Human Motor: Energy, Fatigue, & the Origins of Modernity. 1992. pap. 19.95 (*0-520-07827-6*, Pub. by U CA Pr) Cal Prin Full Svc.

Rabinda Kumar Panda. Anandabodha Yati Life & Philosophy. xxiii, 267p. (C). 1997. 27.00 (*81-86339-38-8*, Pub. by Eastern Bk Linkers) Nataraj Bks.

Rabindranath Tagore Festival Committee. Tagore, Rabindranath, a Collection of His Life & Work. (Illus.). 80p. 1986. pap. 40.00 (*0-905836-56-1*, Pub. by Museum Modern Art) St Mut.

Rabine, Leslie W. Reading the Romantic Heroine: Text, History, Ideology. LC 85-13955. (Women & Culture Ser.). 238p. 1985. reprint ed. pap. 73.80 (*0-7837-5653-4*, 205907800005) Bks Demand.

Rabine, Leslie W., jt. auth. see Moses, Claire G.

Rabineau, Phyllis. Feather Arts: Beauty, Wealth & Spirit from Five Continents. 2nd ed. Williams, Patricia, ed. LC 78-74595. (Illus.). 88p. 1980. pap. 7.95 (*0-914868-08-X*) Field Mus.

Rabiner, David L., ed. see Thomas, James H.

Rabiner, Donald, ed. see Brown, Claudia & Chou, Ju-Hsi.

Rabiner, Lawrence R. & Juang, B. H. Fundamentals of Speech Recognition. 496p. 1993. 88.00 (*0-13-015157-2*) P-H.

Rabiner, Lawrence R. & Schafer, Ronald W. Digital Processing of Speech Signals. LC 78-8555. (Signal Processing Ser.). 1978. 105.00 (*0-13-213603-1*) P-H.

Rabiner, Lawrence R., jt. auth. see Crochiere, Ronald E.

Rabiner, S. Thinking Like Your Editor. Date not set. write for info. (*0-393-03892-0*) Norton.

Rabiner, Yakov. Antisemitism in America. 150p. 1995. pap. 7.00 (*0-9649562-0-9*) Kovcheg.

Rabiner, Yakov. Feast Around the Red Table. (Illus.). 180p. Date not set. pap. 5.00 (*0-9649562-1-7*) Kovcheg.

Rabinnovitch, M. & Goldwurm, Hersh. Mishnah-Zeraim: Sheviis. Danziger, Y., ed. (ArtScroll Mishnah Ser.). (Illus.). 254p. 1987. 22.99 (*0-89906-326-8*) Mesorah Pubns.

Rabino di Borhamaie, H. L. Coins, Medals & Seals of the Shahs of Iran 1500-1941. 123p. 1973. reprint ed. pap. 6.00 (*1-889172-01-4*) Numismatic Intl.

Rabinovic, M. I., jt. auth. see Abarbanel, H. D.

Rabinovich, Abraham. The Battle for Jerusalem: June 5-7, 1967. (Illus.). 429p. 1999. reprint ed. pap. text 15.00 (*0-7881-6116-4*) DIANE Pub.

— The Boats of Cherbourg. LC 96-53436. (Bluejacket Bks.). (Illus.). 336p. 1997. pap. 16.95 (*1-55750-714-7*) Naval Inst Pr.

— Teddy Kollek: Builder of Jerusalem. LC 95-15871. (Young Biography Ser.). (J). 1995. 13.95 (*0-8276-0559-5*) JPS Phila.

— Teddy Kollek: Builder of Jerusalem. LC 95-15871. 130p. (J). (gr. 3-8). 1996. pap. 9.95 (*0-8276-0561-7*) JPS Phila.

***Rabinovich, Adriana.** The Little Red Barn Baking Book: Small Treats with Big Flavor. LC 00-21583. (Illus.). 144p. 2000. pap. 22.50 (*0-609-80630-0*) C Potter.

Rabinovich, Boris I., et al. Vortex Processes & Solid Body Dynamics: Spacecraft & Magnetic Levitation Systems Dynamics Problems. LC 94-30833. 1994. text 186.50 (*0-7923-3092-7*) Kluwer Academic.

Rabinovich, Dalia. Flora's Suitcase. LC 98-16837. 256p. 1998. 23.00 (*0-06-019137-6*, HarperFlamingo) HarpC.

— Flora's Suitcase: A Novel. LC 98-16837. 256p. 1999. pap. 13.00 (*0-06-093249-X*) HarpC.

Rabinovich, F. N. Concretes with Dispersed Reinforcement. Rao, P. M., tr. from RUS. LC 99-227204. (Russian Translation Ser.: No. 113). (Illus.). 224p. (C). 1995. text 104.00 (*90-5410-262-4*, Pub. by A A Balkema) Ashgate Pub Co.

Rabinovich, I. B. Thermochemical & Thermodynamic Properties of Organometallic Compounds. LC 98-44458. 181p. 1998. 139.50 (*1-56700-124-6*) Begell Hse.

Rabinovich, Isaiah. Major Trends in Modern Hebrew Fiction. Roston, M., tr. from HEB. LC 68-15035. 300p. reprint ed. pap. 93.00 (*0-608-11050-7*, 202014900016) Bks Demand.

Rabinovich, Itamar. The Brink of Peace: The Israeli-Syrian Negotiations. LC 98-14418. 288p. 1998. 27.95 (*0-691-05868-7*, Pub. by Princeton U Pr) Cal Prin Full Svc.

— The Brink of Peace: The Israeli-Syrian Negotiations. LC 98-14418. 283p. 1999. pap. 15.95 (*0-691-01023-4*, Pub. by Princeton U Pr) Cal Prin Full Svc.

— Waging Peace: Israel & the Arabs at the End of the Century. LC 99-17464. 288p. 1999. text 23.00 (*0-374-10576-6*) FS&G.

***Rabinovich, Itamar.** The War for Lebanon: 1970-1985. rev. ed. 262p. 2000. reprint ed. pap. text 25.00 (*0-7881-9003-2*) DIANE Pub.

Rabinovich, Itamar. The War for Lebanon: 1970-1985. rev. ed. LC 83-45935. 243p. (C). 1984. 39.95 (*0-8014-1870-4*); pap. text 15.95 (*0-8014-9313-7*) Cornell U Pr.

Rabinovich, Itamar & Shaked, Haim, eds. From June to October: The Middle East Between 1967 & 1973. LC 76-45942. 550p. (C). 1977. text 49.95 (*0-87855-230-8*) Transaction Pubs.

Rabinovich, Itamar, jt. ed. see Esman, Milton J.

Rabinovich, Itamar, jt. ed. see Fry, Michael G.

Rabinovich, Itamar, jt. ed. see Shaked, Haim.

Rabinovich, Izrail, jt. auth. see Harris, David A.

Rabinovich, Izrail B. Influence of Isotopy on the Physicochemical Properties of Liquids. LC 69-17695. (RUS., Illus.). 316p. reprint ed. pap. 98.00 (*0-608-30041-1*, 202068100018) Bks Demand.

Rabinovich, M. I. & Trubetskov, D. I. Oscillations & Waves. (C). 1989. text 382.50 (*0-7923-0445-4*) Kluwer Academic.

***Rabinovich, M. I., et al.** The Dynamical Theory of Pattern Formation. 350p. 1999. 82.00 (*981-02-4055-4*); pap. 42.00 (*981-02-4056-2*) World Scientific Pub.

Rabinovich, M. I., jt. auth. see Gaponov-Grekhov, A. V.

Rabinovich, Moysey. Soviet Conventional Arms Transfers to the Third World: Main Missile & Artillery Directorate (1966-1990) (Foreign Technology Assessment Ser.). ix, 49p. (Orig.). 1994. pap. 45.00 (*1-881874-09-5*) Global Cnslts.

Rabinovich, S. G. Measurement Errors & Uncertainties: Theory & Practice. 2nd ed. LC 99-20534. 312p. 1999. pap. 44.95 (*0-387-98835-1*) Spr-Verlag.

Rabinovich, Semyon. Measurement Errors: Theory & Practice. Alferieff, M. E., tr. from RUS. LC 92-28122.Tr. of Pogreshnosti Izmerenii. 1992. 109.00 (*0-88318-866-X*) Spr-Verlag.

— Measurement Errors: Theory & Practice. Alferieff, M. E., tr. from RUS. LC 92-28122.Tr. of Pogreshnosti Izmerenii. (Illus.). 271p. (C). 1994. pap. text 44.95 (*1-56396-323-X*, AIP Pr) Spr-Verlag.

Rabinovich, V. A. & Beketov, V. G. Moist Gases: Thermodynamic Properties. 176p. 1995. 117.50 (*1-56700-033-9*) Begell Hse.

Rabinovich, V. A. & Sheludyak, Yu E. Thermodynamics of Critical Phenomena: New Analysis of the Evaluation of Properties. LC 98-2594. 162p. 1998. write for info. (*1-56700-103-3*) Begell Hse.

Rabinovich, Viktor A. Thermophysical Properties of Gases & Liquids. LC QC0145.4.T5. (Physical Constants & Properties of Substances Ser.: No. 1). 215p. reprint ed. pap. 66.70 (*0-608-30402-6*, 200460500044) Bks Demand.

***Rabinovici, Doron.** The Search for M. LC 00-25928. (Studies in Austrian Literature, Culture, & Thought Ser.).Tr. of Suche nach M. 192p. 2000. pap. 19.50 (*1-57241-088-4*) Ariadne CA.

***Rabinovici, Schoschana.** Thanks to My Mother: An Unforgettable True Story. (YA). 2000. pap. 7.99 (*0-14-130596-7*, PuffinBks) Peng Put Young Read.

Rabinovici, Schoschana & Pressler, Mirjam. Thanks to My Mother. Skofield, James, tr. from GER. LC 97-14407. 242p. (YA). (gr. 8 up). 1998. 17.99 (*0-8037-2235-4*, Dial Yng Read) Peng Put Young Read.

Rabinovitch. Managerial Economics. (C). 1997. 54.95 (*1-55786-814-X*) Blackwell Pubs.

Rabinovitch, B. S., et al, eds. Annual Review of Physical Chemistry, Vol. 29. LC 51-1658. (Illus.). 1978. text 44.00 (*0-8243-1029-2*) Annual Reviews.

— Annual Review of Physical Chemistry, Vol. 30. LC 51-1658. (Illus.). 1979. text 44.00 (*0-8243-1030-6*) Annual Reviews.

— Annual Review of Physical Chemistry, Vol. 31. LC 51-1658. (Illus.). 1980. text 44.00 (*0-8243-1031-4*) Annual Reviews.

— Annual Review of Physical Chemistry, Vol. 32. LC 51-1658. (Illus.). 1981. text 44.00 (*0-8243-1032-2*) Annual Reviews.

— Annual Review of Physical Chemistry, Vol. 33. LC 51-1658. (Illus.). 1982. text 44.00 (*0-8243-1033-0*) Annual Reviews.

— Annual Review of Physical Chemistry, Vol. 34. LC 51-1658. (Illus.). 1983. text 44.00 (*0-8243-1034-9*) Annual Reviews.

— Annual Review of Physical Chemistry, Vol. 35. LC 51-1658. (Illus.). 1984. text 44.00 (*0-8243-1035-7*) Annual Reviews.

— Annual Review of Physical Chemistry, Vol. 36. LC 51-1658. (Illus.). (C). 1985. text 44.00 (*0-8243-1036-5*) Annual Reviews.

***Rabinovitch, B. Seymore.** Contemporary Silver: Commissioning, Designing, Collecting. (Illus.). 160p. 2000. 45.00 (*1-85894-104-0*) Merrell Holberton.

***Rabinovitch, Daphna.** Canadian Living Cooks Step-by-Step. 1999. 33.96 (*0-679-30924-1*) Random.

Rabinovitch, Itamar. Syria under the Ba'th, 1963-1966: Army-Party Symbiosis. 276p. 1972. boxed set 44.95 (*0-87855-163-8*) Transaction Pubs.

Rabinovitch, Judith N., jt. tr. see Bradstock, Timothy R.

***Rabinovitch, Leon & Carson, Steven.** Alaska Zoo Activity & Guide Book. (ENG.). 68p. (J). 1999. pap. 6.00 (*1-57833-120-X*) Todd Commns.

Rabinovitch, M. Mishnah-Nashim: Nedarim. Arem, T. Z., ed. (ArtScroll Mishnah Ser.). (Illus.). 238p. 1985. 22.99 (*0-89906-279-2*) Mesorah Pubns.

Rabinovitch, M. & Kalatsky, Y. Mishnah-Nashim: Nazir-Sotah. Danziger, Y., ed. (ArtScroll Mishnah Ser.). (Illus.). 400p. 1985. 22.99 (*0-89906-281-4*) Mesorah Pubns.

Rabinovitch, Nachum L. Probability & Statistical Inference in Ancient & Medieval Jewish Literature. LC 79-187394. 219p. reprint ed. pap. 67.90 (*0-608-30884-6*, 201434900091) Bks Demand.

Rabinovitch, Sacha, tr. see Lefebvre, Henri.

Rabinovitz, Frances F., jt. auth. see Fried, Robert C.

Rabinovitz, Francine F. & Trueblood, Felicity M., eds. Latin American Urban Research, Vol. 1. LC 78-103483. 314p. reprint ed. pap. 97.40 (*0-608-14194-1*, 202194200026) Bks Demand.

— National-Local Linkages: The Interrelationship of Urban & National Polities in Latin America. LC 72-98042. (Latin American Urban Research Ser.: Vol. 3). 312p. reprint ed. pap. 96.80 (*0-608-14198-4*, 202194100026) Bks Demand.

Rabinovitz, Lauren. For the Love of Pleasure: Women, Movies, & Culture in Turn-of-the-Century Chicago. LC 97-45724. (Illus.). 208p. (C). 1998. text 49.00 (*0-8135-2533-0*); pap. text 19.00 (*0-8135-2534-9*) Rutgers U Pr.

— Points of Resistance: Women, Power, & Politics in the New York Avant-Garde Cinema, 1943-71. (Illus.). 264p. 1991. text 34.95 (*0-252-01744-7*); pap. text 14.95 (*0-252-06139-X*) U of Ill Pr.

***Rabinovitz, Lauren & Havalovich, Mary Beth.** Television, History & American Culture: Feminist Critical Essays LC 99-22693. (Console-Ing Passions Ser.). 1999. 17.95 (*0-8223-2394-X*) Duke.

Rabinovitz, Lauren, jt. ed. see Haralovich, Mary B.

Rabinovitz, Lauren, jt. ed. see Jeffords, Susan.

Rabinovitz, Rubin. The Development of Samuel Beckett's Fiction. LC 83-4850. 248p. 1984. text 24.95 (*0-252-01095-7*) U of Ill Pr.

— Innovation in Samuel Beckett's Fiction. 200p. (C). 1992. text 34.95 (*0-252-01941-5*) U of Ill Pr.

— Iris Murdoch. LC 68-19756. (Columbia Essays on Modern Writers Ser.: No. 34). (Orig.). 1968. pap. text 12.00 (*0-231-03000-2*) Col U Pr.

— Samna: Luxury Word Processing. (Illus.). 288p. 1986. 24.95 (*0-8306-0634-3*); pap. 16.95 (*0-8306-2734-0*, NO. 2734) McGraw-Hill Prof.

Rabinovitz, Rubin, jt. auth. see Barale, Michele A.

Rabinovitz, Rubin, jt. ed. see Barale, Michele A.

Rabinow, Jacob. Inventing for Fun & Profit. (Illus.). 1990. 18.75 (*0-911302-64-6*) San Francisco Pr.

Rabinow, Paul. Essays on the Anthropology of Reason. LC 96-9075. (Princeton Studies in Culture, Power & History). 210p. 1997. text 49.50 (*0-691-01159-1*, Pub. by Princeton U Pr) Cal Prin Full Svc.

— Essays on the Anthropology of Reason. LC 96-9075. (Princeton Studies in Culture, Power & History). 210p. 1997. pap. text 14.95 (*0-691-01158-3*, Pub. by Princeton U Pr) Cal Prin Full Svc.

***Rabinow, Paul.** French DNA: Trouble in Purgatory. LC 99-12162. 200p. 1999. 25.00 (*0-226-70150-6*) U Ch Pr.

Rabinow, Paul. French Modern: Norms & Forms of the Social Environment. 448p. 1989. 49.50 (*0-262-18134-7*) MIT Pr.

— French Modern: Norms & Forms of the Social Environment. LC 95-35465. x, 464p. 1995. pap. text 16.95 (*0-226-70174-3*) U Ch Pr.

— French Modern: Norms & Forms of the Social Environment. 460p. 1991. reprint ed. pap. text 18.95 (*0-262-68066-1*) MIT Pr.

— Making PCR: A Story of Biotechnology. LC 95-49103. (Illus.). 208p. (C). 1996. 22.50 (*0-226-70146-8*) U Ch Pr.

— Making PCR: A Story of Biotechnology. LC 95-49103. 200p. (C). 1997. pap. 13.00 (*0-226-70147-6*) U Ch Pr.

— Reflections on Fieldwork in Morocco. LC 77-71066. (Quantum Bks.: No. 11). 1977. pap. 15.95 (*0-520-03529-1*, Pub. by U CA Pr) Cal Prin Full Svc.

Rabinow, Paul, ed. Ethics: Subjectivity & Truth, Michel Foucault on Truth, Beauty, & Power 1954-1984. 1997. 25.00 (*0-614-20388-0*) New Press NY.

Rabinow, Paul & Sullivan, William M., eds. Interpretive Social Science: A Second Look. 1988. pap. 17.95 (*0-520-05838-0*, Pub. by U CA Pr) Cal Prin Full Svc.

Rabinow, Paul, jt. auth. see Dreyfus, Hubert L.

Rabinow, Paul, ed. see Foucault, Michel.

Rabinowich, Nosson D., tr. from HEB. The Iggeres of Rav Sherira Gaon: The Epistle of Rav Sherira Gaon. 175p. (C). 1992. 18.00 (*0-940118-60-2*) Moznaim.

Rabinowicz, Wlodzimierz. Universalizability. (Synthese Library: No. 141). 190p. 1979. text 78.50 (*90-277-1020-1*, D Reidel) Kluwer Academic.

Rabinowicz. Lithuanian Hasidism. 1970. 27.50 (*0-85303-021-9*, Pub. by M Vallentine & Co) Intl Spec Bk.

Rabinowicz, Ernest. Friction & Wear of Materials. 2nd ed. LC 94-32860. 336p. 1995. 110.00 (*0-471-83084-4*) Wiley.

Rabinowicz, Harry. A World Apart: The Story of the Chasidim in England. LC 95-5666. (Illus.). 320p. 1997. 49.50 (*0-85303-261-0*, Pub. by M Vallentine & Co); pap. 27.50 (*0-85303-278-5*, Pub. by M Vallentine & Co) Intl Spec Bk.

Rabinowicz, Harry M. Hasidism: The Movement & Its Masters. LC 87-37427. 472p. 1990. 45.00 (*0-87668-998-5*) Aronson.

— Hasidism & the State of Israel. (Littman Library of Jewish Civilization). 346p. 1985. 24.95 (*0-19-710049-X*) OUP.

Rabinowicz, Oscar K. Winston Churchill on Jewish Problems. LC 74-43. 231p. (C). 1974. reprint ed. lib. bdg. 65.00 (*0-8371-7357-4*, RAWC, Greenwood Pr) Greenwood.

Rabinowicz, Tzvi M. A Guide to Life: Jewish Laws & Customs of Mourning. LC 89-35085. 256p. 1994. pap. 30.00 (*1-56821-143-0*) Aronson.

— Hasidism in Israel: A History of the Hasidic Movement & its Masters in the Holy Land. LC 98-46952. (Illus.). 344p. 2000. 30.00 (*0-7657-6068-1*) Aronson.

— The Prince Who Turned into a Rooster: One Hundred Tales from Hasidic Tradition. LC 93-31396. 280p. 1994. pap. 30.00 (*0-87668-685-4*) Aronson.

Rabinowicz, Tzvi M., ed. Encylopedia of Hasidism. LC 94-3140. 608p. 1996. 75.00 (*1-56821-123-6*) Aronson.

Rabinowitch, Alexander. Prelude to Revolution: The Petrograd Bolsheviks & the July, 1917, Uprising. LC 68-10278. 315p. reprint ed. 97.70 (*0-8357-9236-6*, 205522400011) Bks Demand.

— Prelude to Revolution: The Petrograd Bolsheviks & the July 1917 Uprising. LC 91-8422. (Illus.). 314p. 1991. reprint ed. 36.95 (*0-253-34768-8*); reprint ed. pap. 6.95 (*0-253-20661-8*, MB-661) Ind U Pr.

Rabinowitch, Alexander, et al, eds. Revolution & Politics in Russia: Essays in Memory of B. I. Nicolaevsky. LC 75-183608. (Russian & East European Studies: No. 41). (Illus.). 430p. reprint ed. pap. 133.30 (*0-608-17411-4*, 205643500067) Bks Demand.

Rabinowitch, David. The Collinasca Cycle. (Illus.). 56p. 1993. pap. 35.00 (*0-935875-11-5*) P Blum Edit.

***Rabinowitch, David.** Construction of Vision: Color Property Drawings, 1972-1975. (Illus.). 2000. pap. 30.00 (*3-928762-96-6*) Richter Verlag.

Rabinowitch, David. David Rabinowitch: Work 1967-1976. (Illus.). 200p. 1992. 60.00 (*3-89322-462-9*, Pub. by Edition Cantz) Dist Art Pubs.

Rabinowitch, Haim D. & Brewster, James L., eds. Onions & Allied Crops, 3 vols., Vol. I. 288p. 1989. boxed set 240.95 (*0-8493-6300-4*, SB341) CRC Pr.

— Onions & Allied Crops, 3 vols., Vol. II. 320p. 1989. lib. bdg. 229.00 (*0-8493-6301-2*, SB341) CRC Pr.

— Onions & Allied Crops, 3 vols., Vol. III. 272p. 1989. lib. bdg. 229.00 (*0-8493-6302-0*, SB341) CRC Pr.

Rabinowitch, Z. E. & Lupandin, K. K. English-Russian Textile Dictionary. (ENG & RUS.). 640p. 1961. 49.95 (*0-685-57824-0*, M-9111) Fr & Eur.

***Rabinowitz.** Encyclopedia of Jewish Folklore. 1999. text 50.00 (*0-8050-5152-X*) St Martin.

Rabinowitz, Aaron. Judaism & Psychology: Meeting Points. LC 98-40643. 1999. 30.00 (*0-7657-6060-6*) Aronson.

Rabinowitz, Abraham H. Israel: The Christian Dilemma. 82p. 1992. pap. 7.95 (*965-229-017-3*, Pub. by Gefen Pub Hse) Gefen Bks.

— The Study of Talmud: Understanding the Halachic Mind. LC 96-13496. 240p. 1996. 40.00 (*1-56821-946-6*) Aronson.

— Taryag: A Study of the Tradition That the Written Torah Contains 613 Mitzvot. LC 96-22408. 240p. 1996. 40.00 (*1-56821-449-9*) Aronson.

***Rabinowitz, Alan.** Jaguar: One Man's Struggle to Establish the World's First Jaguar. LC 99-88301. (Illus.). 416p. 2000. pap. 16.95 (*1-55963-802-8*, Shearwater Bks) Island Pr.

Rabinowitz, Alan. Land Investment & the Predevelopment Process: A Guide for Finance & Real Estate Professionals. LC 87-32594. 239p. 1988. 67.95 (*0-89930-326-9*, RZP/, Quorum Bks) Greenwood.

— Municipal Bond Finance & Administration: A Practical Guide to the Analysis of Tax-Exempt Securities. LC 71-81325. (Illus.). 272p. reprint ed. pap. 84.40 (*0-608-30030-6*, 205157400089) Bks Demand.

— The Real Estate Gamble: Lessons from Fifty Years of Boom & Bust. LC 80-65706. 320p. reprint ed. pap. 99.20 (*0-608-12685-3*, 202350800033) Bks Demand.

— Social Change Philanthropy in America. LC 89-24362. 248p. 1990. 59.95 (*0-89930-536-9*, RSD/, Greenwood Pr) Greenwood.

— Wildlife Field Research & Conservation Training Manual. (Illus.). 282p. (Orig.). 1993. pap. text 25.00 (*0-9642787-0-7*) Paul-Art Pr.

Rabinowitz, Anna. At the Site of Inside Out. LC 96-48655. 88p. 1997. pap. 10.95 (*1-55849-093-0*) U of Mass Pr.

Rabinowitz, C. D. A Teacher's Guide & Syllabus for the Teaching of the Weekly Haftorah. (HEB.). 1997. pap., teacher ed. 4.00 (*0-914131-70-2*, A440) Torah Umesorah.

— A Teacher's Guide for the Teaching of Prayer. (HEB.). 1997. pap., teacher ed. 3.50 (*0-914131-71-0*, A430) Torah Umesorah.

— Teacher's Guides for the Teaching of Nach: Melachim I-II. (HEB.). 1997. pap., teacher ed. 5.00 (*0-914131-66-4*, A415) Torah Umesorah.

— Teacher's Guides for the Teaching of Nach: Shmuel I-II. (HEB.). 1997. pap., teacher ed. 5.00 (*0-914131-69-9*, A410) Torah Umesorah.

— Teacher's Guides for the Teaching of Nach: Shoftim. (HEB.). 1997. pap., teacher ed. 5.00 (*0-914131-67-2*, A405) Torah Umesorah.

— Teacher's Guides for the Teaching of Nach: Yehoshua. (HEB.). 1997. pap., teacher ed. 4.50 (*0-914131-68-0*, A400) Torah Umesorah.

Rabinowitz, Carla B. & Coughlin, Robert E. Analysis of Landscape Characteristics Relevant to Preference. (Discussion Papers: No. 38). 1970. pap. 10.00 (*1-55869-009-3*) Regional Sci Res Inst.

— Some Experiments in Quantitative Measurement of Landscape Quality. (Discussion Papers: No. 43). 1971. pap. 10.00 (*1-55869-116-2*) Regional Sci Res Inst.

Rabinowitz, Chaim D. History Text: Tamtzis Divrei Y'Mei Yisrael. (HEB.). 370p. 1997. pap. 12.00 (*0-914131-18-4*, A280) Torah Umesorah.

Rabinowitz, Clara, jt. ed. see Wortis, Helen.

Rabinowitz, Dan. Overlooking Nazareth: The Ethnography of Exclusion in a Mixed Town in Galilee, Vol. 105. LC 96-11922. (Cambridge Studies in Social & Cultural Anthropology: No. 105). (Illus.). 236p. 1997. text 59.95 (*0-521-56361-5*); pap. text 20.95 (*0-521-56495-6*) Cambridge U Pr.

Rabinowitz, Dorothy. About the Holocaust: What We Know & How We Know It. LC 79-51801. (Illus.). 48p. 1979. pap. 1.50 (*0-87495-014-7*) Am Jewish Comm.

— The Other Jews: Portraits in Poverty. LC 77-183251. (Institute of Human Relations Press Paperback Ser). 64p. (Orig.). 1972. 1.25 (*0-87495-015-5*) Am Jewish Comm.

Rabinowitz, Dorothy, et al. Dimensions of the Holocaust. 2nd ed. 90p. 1990. pap. 9.95 (*0-8101-0908-5*) Northwestern U Pr.

Rabinowitz, H. Building Economics the Development Process: The Development Process. (Architecture Ser.). 1983. text. write for info. (*0-442-27754-7*, VNR) Wiley.

Rabinowitz, Harold. Black Hats - White Hats: Heroes & Villans of the West. 192p. 1996. 24.98 (*1-56799-377-X*, MetroBooks) M Friedman Pub Grp Inc.

— Classic Planes: Twenty-Two Aircraft That Made History. LC 96-37613. 1997. 19.98 (*1-56799-430-X*) M Friedman Pub Grp Inc.

— Conquer the Sky: Great Moments in Aviation. 208p. 1996. 24.98 (*1-56799-381-8*, MetroBooks) M Friedman Pub Grp Inc.

— Pushing the Envelope: Airplanes of the Jet Age. LC 98-4132. 1998. 24.98 (*1-56799-596-9*, MetroBooks) M Friedman Pub Grp Inc.

Rabinowitz, Harold & Kaplan, Rob, eds. A Passion for Books: A Book Lover's Treasury of Stories, Essays, Humor, Lore & Lists on Collecting, Reading, Borrowing, Lending, Caring for & Appreciating Books. LC 99-25583. (Illus.). 384p. 1999. 27.50 (*0-8129-3112-2*, Times Bks) Crown Pub Group.

***Rabinowitz, Harold & Kaplan, Rob, eds.** A Passion for Books: A Book Lover's Treasury of Stories, Essays, Humor, Lore & Lists on Collecting, Reading, Borrowing, Lending, Caring for & Appreciating Books. 2001. pap. 16.00 (*0-8129-3113-0*, Three Riv Pr) Crown Pub Group.

Rabinowitz, Harvey Z. Buildings in Use Study: Part 1: Technical Factors; Part 2: Functional Factors; Appendix: Field Tests Manual, 2 pts. (Publications in Architecture & Urban Planning: No. R75-1). (Illus.). v, 258p. 1985. reprint ed. 22.00 (*0-938744-37-2*) U of Wis Ctr Arch-Urban.

Rabinowitz, Henry & Schaap, Chaim. Portable C. 288p. (C). 1990. pap. 29.95 (*0-13-685967-4*) P-H.

Rabinowitz, Howard N. First New South, 1865-1920. Eisenstadt, A. S. & Franklin, John H., eds. (American History Ser.). 150p. 1992. pap. text 12.95 (*0-88295-883-6*) Harlan Davidson.

— Race, Ethnicity, & Urbanization: Selected Essays. 376p. 1993. text 42.50 (*0-8262-0930-0*) U of Mo Pr.

— Race Relations in the Urban South, 1865-1890. LC 96-19848. 1996. pap. 24.95 (*0-8203-1880-9*) U of Ga Pr.

Rabinowitz, Ilana. Inside Therapy: Illuminating Writings about Therapists, Patients & Psychotherapy. LC 98-5922. xxv, 291p. 1998. text 24.95 (*0-312-18671-1*) St Martin.

R

R

*Rabinowitz, Ilana. Inside Therapy: Illuminating Writings about Therapists, Patients & Psychotherapy. LC 98-5922. 291p. 2000. pap. 13.95 (0-312-26342-2) St Martin.

— Mountains Are Mountains & Rivers Are Rivers: Applying Eastern Techniques to Everyday Life. LC 98-56644. 336p. 1999. 22.95 (0-7868-6476-1, Pub. by Hyperion) Time Warner.

*Rabinowitz, Ilana. Mountains Are Mountains & Rivers Are Rivers: Applying Eastern Techniques to Everyday Life. 304p. 2000. pap. 12.95 (0-7868-8544-0, Pub. by Hyperion) Time Warner.

Rabinowitz, Isaac. A Witness Forever: Ancient Israel's Perception of Literature & the Resultant Hebrew Bible. Owen, David I., ed. (Occasional Publications of the Department of Near Eastern Studies & the Program of Jewish Studies, Cornell U.: 1). 165p. (C). 1994. 20.00 (1-883053-02-1) CDL Pr.

Rabinowitz, Isaac, ed. The Book of the Honeycomb's Flow: Sepher Nopheth Suphim by Judah Messer Leon. LC 81-15273. (Critical Edition & Translation Ser.). 604p. 1983. text 87.50 (0-8014-0870-9) Cornell U Pr.

Rabinowitz, Jacob. The Faces of God. LC 98-22427. 1998. pap. 12.00 (0-88214-117-1) Spring Pubns.

— The Unholy Bible: Hebrew Literature of the Early Kingdom Period. 156p. 1995. pap. 7.00 (1-57027-015-5) Autonomedia.

Rabinowitz, Jacob, ed. The Rotting Goddess: The Origin of the Witch in Classical Antiquity. (Illus.). 160p. (C). 1998. pap. 12.00 (1-57027-035-X) Autonomedia.

Rabinowitz, Jacob, tr. & anno. see Catullus, Gaius Valerius.

Rabinowitz, Jacob J. Jewish Law: Its Influence on the Development of Legal Institutions. 1956. 20.00 (0-8197-0173-4) Bloch.

Rabinowitz, Jan. The Tzedakah Workbook. (Illus.). 32p. (Orig.). (J). (gr. 4-5). 1986. pap. text 4.95 (0-933873-07-7) Torah Aura.

Rabinowitz, Jonathan, ed. see Barnes, Susan.

Rabinowitz, Joseph L., jt. auth. see Chase, Grafton D.

Rabinowitz, Max. The Day They Scrambled My Brains at the Funny Factory. 1978. mass mkt. 1.95 (0-89083-344-3, Zebra Kensgtn) Kensgtn Pub Corp.

Rabinowitz, Mitchell, ed. Cognitive Science Foundations of Instruction. 248p. 1993. text 59.95 (0-8058-1279-2) L Erlbaum Assocs.

Rabinowitz, Nancy S. Anxiety Veiled: Euripides & the Traffic in Women. LC 93-17257. 264p. 1993. text 42.50 (0-8014-2845-9); pap. text 16.95 (0-8014-8091-4) Cornell U Pr.

Rabinowitz, Nancy S. & Richlin, Amy, eds. Feminist Theory & the Classics. LC 92-40745. (Thinking Gender Ser.). 320p. (C). 1993. pap. 20.99 (0-415-90646-6, A7585) Routledge.

Rabinowitz, Nitzan, jt. auth. see Thurber, Clifford H.

Rabinowitz, Noel. Shockwave Power Techniques. LC 96-23739. 528p. 1996. pap. text 44.99 (1-56205-646-8) New Riders Pub.

Rabinowitz, Oskar K. Arnold Toynbee on Judaism & Zionism: A Critique. 372p. 1975. 25.00 (0-8464-0149-5) Beekman Pubs.

Rabinowitz, P. Minimax Methods in Critical Point Theory with Applications to Differential Equations. LC 86-7847. (CBMS Regional Conference Series in Mathematics: No. 65). 110p. 1986. reprint ed. pap. 19.00 (0-8218-0715-3, CBMS/65) Am Math.

Rabinowitz, Paula. Labor & Desire: Women's Revolutionary Fiction in Depression America. LC 91-50259. (Gender & American Culture Ser.). xiv, 212p. (C). 1991. 39.95 (0-8078-1994-8); pap. 16.95 (0-8078-4332-6) U of NC Pr.

— They Must Be Represented: The Politics of Documentary. (Haymarket Ser.). (Illus.). 288p. (J). 1994. pap. 20.00 (1-85984-025-6, B4647, Pub. by Verso) Norton.

— They Must Be Represented: The Politics of Documentary. (Haymarket Ser.). (Illus.). 288p. (C). (gr. 13). 1994. 65.00 (1-85984-925-3, B4643, Pub. by Verso) Norton.

Rabinowitz, Paula, jt. ed. see Nekola, Charlotte.

Rabinowitz, Peter J. Before Reading: Narrative Conventions & the Politics of Interpretation. LC 87-47602. 272p. (C). 1987. pap. 13.95 (0-8014-9472-9) Cornell U Pr.

— Before Reading: Narrative Conventions & the Politics of Interpretation. LC 97-31011. 278p. 1997. pap. text 18.95 (0-8142-0759-6) Ohio St U Pr.

Rabinowitz, Peter J. & Smith, Michael W. Authorizing Readers: Resistance & Respect in the Teaching of Literature. 174p. (YA). (gr. 7 up). 1997. pap. 22.95 (0-8141-4089-0) NCTE.

Rabinowitz, Peter J. & Smith, Michael W. Authorizing Readers: Resistance & Respect in the Teaching of Literature. LC 97-31022. (Language & Literacy Ser.). 1997. 45.00 (0-8077-3690-2); pap. 21.95 (0-8077-3689-9) Tchrs Coll.

Rabinowitz, Peter J., jt. ed. see Phelan, James.

Rabinowitz, Philip, ed. Numerical Methods for Nonlinear Algebraic Equations. LC 78-115963. (Illus.). xii, 200p. 1970. pap. text 77.00 (0-677-14235-8) Gordon & Breach.

Rabinowitz, Philip, jt. auth. see Ralston, Anthony.

Rabinowitz, Philip D. & Schouten, Hans. Ocean Margin Drilling Program Atlases, Vol. 11. (Regional Atlas Ser.). 1986. pap. 295.00 (0-86720-261-0) Jones & Bartlett.

Rabinowitz, Philip D., jt. auth. see Coffin, Millard F.

Rabinowitz, Philip D., jt. auth. see Ewing, John I.

Rabinowitz, Philip D., jt. ed. see Hayes, Dennis E.

*Rabinowitz, Randy S., ed. Occupational Safety & Health Law, 1999 Cumulative Supplement. 684p. 1999. 105.00 (1-57018-147-0, 1147-PR9) BNA Books.

Rabinowitz, Richard. The Spiritual Self in Everyday Life: The Transformation of Personal Religious Experience in Nineteenth-Century New England. (New England Studies). 315p. 1989. text 47.50 (1-55553-022-2) NE U Pr.

Rabinowitz, Samson. Jubilee of Watching. 246p. 1994. 16.95 (0-87306-689-8) Feldheim.

Rabinowitz, Sandy & Keiffer, Christa. Treasured Horses Collection, 14 bks. large type ed. Incl. Changing Times. large type ed. Felder, Deborah. LC 98-44735. (Illus.). 128p. (YA). (gr. 4 up). 1999. lib. bdg. 21.27 (0-8368-2276-5); Christmas in Silver Lake. large type ed. Hubbard, Coleen. LC 99-11768. (Illus.). 128p. (J). (gr. 4 up). 1999. lib. bdg. 21.27 (0-8368-2400-8); Colorado Summer. large type ed. Bograd, Larry & Hubbard, Coleen. LC 98-46294. (Illus.). 128p. (YA). (gr. 4 up). 1999. lib. bdg. 21.27 (0-8368-2277-3); Flying Angels. large type ed. Hubbard, Coleen. LC 99-11745. (Illus.). 128p. (YA). (gr. 4 up). 1999. lib. bdg. 21.27 (0-8368-2401-6); Horse for Hannah. large type ed. Hubbard, Coleen. LC 99-12115. (Illus.). 128p. (J). (gr. 4 up). 1999. lib. bdg. 21.27 (0-8368-2402-4); Kate's Secret Plan. large type ed. Saunders, Susan. LC 98-46295. (Illus.). 128p. (YA). (gr. 4 up). 1999. lib. bdg. 21.27 (0-8368-2278-1); Louisiana Blue. large type ed. Hubbard, Coleen. LC 99-11708. (Illus.). 128p. (J). (gr. 4 up). 1999. lib. bdg. 21.27 (0-8368-2403-2); Pretty Lady of Saratoga. large type ed. Felder, Deborah G. LC 99-11739. (Illus.). 128p. (J). (gr. 4 up). 1999. lib. bdg. 21.27 (0-8368-2404-0); Pride of the Green Mountains. large type ed. Baker, Carin Greenberg. LC 98-46301. (Illus.). 128p. (YA). (gr. 4 up). 1999. lib. bdg. 21.27 (0-8368-2279-X); Ride of Courage. large type ed. Felder, Deborah. LC 98-46304. (Illus.). 128p. (YA). (gr. 4 up). 1999. lib. bdg. 21.27 (0-8368-2280-3); Riding School Rivals. large type ed. Saunders, Susan. LC 98-46305. (Illus.). 128p. (YA). (gr. 4 up). 1999. lib. bdg. 21.27 (0-8368-2281-1); Rush for Gold. large type ed. Hubbard, Coleen. LC 99-11707. (Illus.). 128p. (J). (gr. 4 up). 1999. lib. bdg. 21.27 (0-8368-2405-9); Spirit of the West. large type ed. Malcolm, Jahnna N. LC 98-46303. (Illus.). 122 p. (YA). (gr. 4 up). 1999. lib. bdg. 21.27 (0-8368-2282-X); Stallion of Box Canyon. large type ed. Malcolm, Jahnna N. LC 98-44734. (Illus.). 122 p. (YA). (gr. 4 up). 1999. lib. bdg. 21.27 (0-8368-2283-8); (Illus.). (YA). (gr. 4 up). Set lib. bdg. 159.47 (0-8368-2471-7) Gareth Stevens Inc.

Rabinowitz, Stanley, ed. Index to Mathematical Problems 1980-1984. LC 91-66461. (Indexes to Mathematical Problems Ser.: Vol. 1). 532p. 1992. 49.95 (0-9626401-1-5, QA43) MathPro Pr.

— Problems & Solutions from the Mathematical Visitor, 1877-1896. LC 94-77754. (Classic Problems Collections: No. 1). 272p. (Orig.). (YA). (gr. 9-12). 1996. pap. 24.00 (0-9626401-5-8) MathPro Pr.

Rabinowitz, Stanley, tr. from RUS. The Noise of Change: Russian Literature & the Critics (1891-1917) 244p. (C). 1986. pap. 14.95 (0-88233-526-X) Ardis Pubs.

Rabinowitz, Stanley J. Sologub's Literary Children: Keys to a Symbolist's Prose. (Illus.). 176p. 1980. pap. 18.95 (0-89357-069-9) Slavica.

Rabinowitz, Stanley J., jt. auth. see Griffiths, Frederick T.

Rabinowitz, Victor. Memoirs of an Unrepetant Leftist. LC 95-50239. (C). 1996. text. write for info. (0-614-95870-9) U of Ill Pr.

— Unrepentant Leftist: A Lawyer's Memoir. (Illus.). 352p. 1996. 29.95 (0-252-02253-X) U of Ill Pr.

Rabinowitz, Y. Mishnah-Nashim: Yevamos. Danziger, Y., ed. (ArtScroll Mishnah Ser.). (Illus.). 364p. 1984. 22.99 (0-89906-275-X) Mesorah Pubns.

Rabinowitz, Yaron S., et al. Color Atlas of Corneal Topography: Interpreting Videokeratography. LC 93-208. (Illus.). 96p. 1993. 125.00 (0-89640-235-5) Igaku-Shoin.

Rabinowitz, Yosef. Ezra-The Book of Ezra. (ArtScroll Tanach Ser.). 208p. 1984. 18.99 (0-89906-089-7); pap. 15.99 (0-89906-090-0) Mesorah Pubns.

— Nechemiah. 18.99 (0-89906-095-1, NECH); pap. 15.99 (0-89906-096-X, NECP) Mesorah Pubns.

Rabins, Peter V., et al. Practical Dementia Care. LC 98-49715. (Illus.). 304p. 1999. text 34.95 (0-19-510625-3) OUP.

Rabins, Peter V., jt. auth. see Mace, Nancy L.

Rabins, Peter V., jt. ed. see Billig, Nathan.

Rabins, Peter V., jt. frwd. see Honel, Rosalie W.

Rabinyan, Dorit. Persian Brides. Lotan, Yael, tr. from HEB. LC 97-45493. 240p. 1998. 22.50 (0-8076-1430-0) Braziller.

*Rabinyan, Dorit. Persian Brides. 2000. pap. 15.95 (0-8076-1461-0) Braziller.

Rabior, William. A Healing Place in a Hurting World: Prayers of Solace & Hope. (Illus.). 48p. 1997. pap. 3.95 (0-7648-0108-2) Liguori Pubns.

Rabior, William & Bedard, Vicki W. Catholics Experiencing Divorce: Grieving, Healing, & Learning to Live Again. LC 91-60945. 80p. 1991. pap. text 5.95 (0-89243-347-7) Liguori Pubns.

— Prayers for Catholics Experiencing Divorce: Prayers for Healing. LC 93-78434. 96p. 1993. pap. 4.95 (0-89243-528-3) Liguori Pubns.

Rabjam, G. & Abbot of Rumtek Monastery. Three Vehicles of Buddhist Practice. Holmes, Ken, tr. LC 95-903827. (C). 1995. 15.00 (81-7030-457-1, Pub. by Sri Satguru Pubns) S Asia.

Rabjohn, N. Organic Syntheses Collective Volumes, Vol. 4, Vols. 30-39, Vol. 4, Vols. 30-39. Noland, Wayland E., ed. 1056p. 1963. 145.00 (0-471-70470-9, 2-203) Wiley.

Rabkin, Anna, jt. auth. see Rabkin, Marty.

Rabkin, Eric. Stories. (C). 1997. text, teacher ed. 24.00 (0-06-365306-0) Addison-Wesley.

Rabkin, Eric S. Arthur C. Clarke. 2nd ed. Schlobin, Roger C., ed. LC 79-84709. (Starmont Reader's Guide Ser.: Vol. 1). 80p. 1980. pap. 13.00 (0-916732-21-5) Millefleurs.

Rabkin, Eric S. Stories. 1500p. (C). 1997. pap. text 56.00 (0-06-045327-3) Addson-Wesley Educ.

Rabkin, Eric S., ed. Fantastic Worlds: Myths, Tales, & Stories. 496p. 1979. pap. text 16.95 (0-19-502541-5) OUP.

— Science Fiction: An Historical Anthology. 540p. 1983. pap. text 15.95 (0-19-503272-1) OUP.

Rabkin, Eric S., et al, eds. The End of the World. LC 82-19365. (Alternatives Ser.). 240p. 1983. 21.95 (0-8093-1033-3) S Ill U Pr.

— No Place Else: Exploration in Utopian & Dystopian Fiction. LC 83-4265. (Alternatives Ser.). 288p. 1983. 21.95 (0-8093-1113-5) S Ill U Pr.

— Science Fiction Market Realities. LC 94-23971. 1996. 45.00 (0-8203-1726-8) U of Ga Pr.

Rabkin, Eric S. & Silverman, Eugene M. It's a Gas: A Study of Flatulence. (Illus.). 164p. (Orig.). 1991. pap. 9.95 (1-879378-03-5) Rabkin-Silverman.

Rabkin, Eric S. & Slusser, George E., eds. Fights of Fancy: Armed Conflict in Science Fiction & Fantasy. LC 91-40085. 224p. 1993. pap. 20.00 (0-8203-1533-8) U of Ga Pr.

— Styles of Creation: Aesthetic Technique & the Creation of Fictional Worlds. LC 91-40086. (Proceedings of the J. Lloyd Eaton Conference of Science Fiction & Fantasy Literature Ser.). 304p. 1993. 45.00 (0-8203-1455-2) U of Ga Pr.

Rabkin, Eric S., jt. auth. see Glaspell, Susan.

Rabkin, Eric S., jt. ed. see Slusser, George E.

Rabkin, Gerald. Drama & Commitment. LC 72-6866. (Studies in Drama: No. 39). (C). 1972. reprint ed. lib. bdg. 75.00 (0-8383-1659-X) M S G Haskell Hse.

— Richard Foreman. LC 98-49863. 1999. 38.00 (0-8018-6113-6); pap. 19.95 (0-8018-6114-4) Johns Hopkins.

Rabkin, Jacob. Current Law Forms with Tax Analysis, Looseleaf Updates Avail. 1948. 1850.00 (0-8205-1240-0) Bender.

Rabkin, Jacob & Johnson, Mark H. Federal Income, Gift & Estate Taxation, 9 vols., Set. 1942. ring bd. 1070.00 (0-8205-1590-6) Bender.

*Rabkin, Jeremy. Why Sovereignty Matters. LC 99-185342. (Studies on Global Environmental Policy: Vol. 4). (Orig.). 1998. pap. 14.95 (0-8447-7117-1, Pub. by Am Enterprise) Pub Resources Inc.

*Rabkin, Jeremy & Sheehan, James. Global Greens, Global Governance. (IEA Environmental Working Paper: No. 4). 100p. 1999. pap. 19.95 (0-255-36472-5, Pub. by Inst Economic Affairs) Coronet Bks.

Rabkin, Judith G., et al. Good Doctors, Good Patients: Partners in HIV Treatment. 212p. 1995. pap. 15.00 (0-9643884-0-5) NCM Pubs.

Rabkin, Leslie Y. The Celluloid Couch: An Annotated International Filmography of the Mental Health Professional in the Movies & Television, from the Beginning to 1990. LC 98-5028. 656p. 1998. 85.00 (0-8108-3462-6) Scarecrow.

Rabkin, Marty & Rabkin, Anna. Public Libraries: Travel Treasures of the West. LC 93-34680. (Illus.). 352p. 1993. pap. 19.95 (1-55591-915-4) Fulcrum Pub.

Rabkin, Norman. Shakespeare & the Common Understanding. LC 83-18153. xii, 268p. (Orig.). 1994. pap. text 9.95 (0-226-70180-8) U Ch Pr.

— Shakespeare & the Problem of Meaning. LC 80-18538. 1981. lib. bdg. 16.00 (0-226-70177-8) U Ch Pr.

— Shakespeare & the Problem of Meaning. LC 80-18538. 176p. 1982. pap. text 9.95 (0-226-70178-6) U Ch Pr.

Rabkin, Norman, jt. auth. see Fraser, Russell A.

*Rabkin, Norman J., ed. Drug Control: DEA's Strategies & Operations in the 1990s. (Illus.). 172p. (C). 2000. pap. text 30.00 (0-7881-8483-0) DIANE Pub.

Rabkin, Norman J., et al. Navy Carrier Battle Groups: The Structure & Affordability of the Future Force. (Illus.). 148p. (C). 1997. reprint ed. pap. text 40.00 (0-7881-4134-1) DIANE Pub.

Rabkin, Peggy A. Fathers to Daughters: The Legal Foundations of Female Emancipation, 11. LC 79-6830. (Contributions in Legal Studies: No. 11). 214p. 1980. 55.00 (0-313-20670-8, RFD/, Greenwood Pr) Greenwood.

Rabkin, Yakov M. Science Between the Superpowers: A Twentieth Century Fund Paper. 119p. 1988. 18.95 (0-87078-223-1); pap. 8.95 (0-87078-222-3) Century Foundation.

Rabkin, Yakov M., ed. Diffusion of New Technologies in The Post-Communist World. LC 97-3774. 188p. 1997. lib. bdg. 104.00 (0-7923-4456-1) Kluwer Academic.

Rabkin, Yakov M., jt. ed. see Robinson, Ira.

Rabking, Rhoda P. Cuban Politics: The Revolutionary Experiment. LC 90-38808. (Politics in Latin America Ser.). 256p. 1990. 55.00 (0-275-93739-9, C3739, Praeger Pubs) Greenwood.

Rabl, Ari. Active Solar Collectors & Their Applications. LC 84-14861. (Illus.). 518p. 1985. text 65.00 (0-19-503546-1) OUP.

Rabl, Ari, jt. auth. see Kreider, Jan F.

Rabl, S. S. Boatbuilding in Your Own Backyard. 2nd ed. LC 57-11361. (Illus.). 239p. 1958. 34.95 (0-87033-009-8) Cornell Maritime.

— Ship & Aircraft Fairing & Development for Draftsman & Loftsmen & Sheet Metal Workers. LC 41-51932. (Illus.). 109p. 1941. pap., spiral bd. 19.95 (0-87033-096-9) Cornell Maritime.

Rabl, Veronika, ed. see Electric Power Research Institute Staff.

Rabl, Walter. Walter Rabl: Complete Instrumental Chamber Works. Strauss, John F. & Strauss, Virginia F., eds. (Recent Researches in Music of the Nineteenth & Early Twentieth Centuries Ser.: Vol. RRN24). (Illus.). xiv, 179p. 1978. pap. 65.00 (0-89579-332-6) A-R Eds.

Rable, Baroness Von, see Crawford, Anne & Von Rable, Baroness.

Rable, George C. Civil Wars: Women & the Crisis of Southern Nationalism. (Women in American History Ser.). 416p. 1991. pap. text 16.95 (0-252-06212-4) U of Ill Pr.

— The Confederate Republic: A Revolution Against Politics. LC 93-36491. (Civil War America Ser.). (Illus.). xii, 428p. (C). 1994. 19.95 (0-8078-2144-6) U of NC Pr.

Rabley. April in Moscow. Date not set. pap. text. write for info. (0-582-06073-7, Pub. by Addison-Wesley) Longman.

— Barcelona Game. 1992. pap. text. write for info. (0-582-06416-3, Pub. by Addison-Wesley) Longman.

— Between Two Worlds. Date not set. pap. text. write for info. (0-582-06074-5, Pub. by Addison-Wesley) Longman.

— Billy & the Queen. (Easystarts Ser.). (J). 1996. pap. text. write for info. (0-582-09694-4, Pub. by Addison-Wesley) Longman.

— Dino's Day in London. Date not set. pap. text. write for info. (0-582-03146-X, Pub. by Addison-Wesley) Longman.

— The Fireboy. Date not set. pap. text. write for info. (0-582-06072-9, Pub. by Addison-Wesley) Longman.

— Maisie & the Dolphin. Date not set. pap. text. write for info. (0-582-03148-6, Pub. by Addison-Wesley) Longman.

— Marcel & Mona Lisa. Date not set. pap. text. write for info. (0-582-06075-3, Pub. by Addison-Wesley) Longman.

— Marcel & the Shakespeare Letters. 1996. pap. text. write for info. (0-582-08136-X, Pub. by Addison-Wesley) Longman.

— Marcel Goes Hollywood. 1992. pap. text. write for info. (0-582-06252-7, Pub. by Addison-Wesley) Longman.

Rabley, Stephen. The Eyes of Montezuma. (Illus.). 24p. 1996. pap. text 4.95 (0-19-421935-6) OUP.

— Gold Lasso, 2. (Longman Originals Ser.). 1992. pap. text 5.51 (0-582-07497-5) Addison-Wesley.

— Marcel & White Star. 1990. pap. text. write for info. (0-582-04610-6, Pub. by Addison-Wesley) Longman.

— Tinkers Farm. 1998. pap. text 7.00 (0-582-40289-1) Addison-Wesley.

— Troy Stone. 1990. pap. text. write for info. (0-582-04598-3, Pub. by Addison-Wesley) Longman.

Rabnovitch, S., ed. Annual Review of Physical Chemistry, Vol. 27. LC 51-1658. (Illus.). 1976. 42.00 (0-8243-1027-6) Annual Reviews.

Rabnovitch, S. & Eyring, Henry, eds. Annual Review of Physical Chemistry. LC 51-1658. (Illus.). 1975. 42.00 (0-8243-1026-8) Annual Reviews.

Rabo, Annika. Change on the Euphrates: Villagers, Townsmen & Employees in Northeast Syria. (Illus.). 222p. (Orig.). 1986. pap. text 47.50 (91-85284-26-2) Coronet Bks.

Rabo, Jule A., ed. Zeolite Chemistry & Catalysis. LC 76-17864. (ACS Monograph: No. 171). 1976. 87.95 (0-8412-0276-1) Am Chemical.

— Zeolite Chemistry & Catalysis. LC 76-17864. (ACS Monograph Ser.: Vol. 171). (Illus.). 804p. 1976. reprint ed. pap. 200.00 (0-608-07554-X, 205265400009) Bks Demand.

Raboff, Adeline, tr. see Peter, Katherine.

Raboff, Fran, jt. auth. see Shepherd, Renee.

Raboff, Paul & Greenfield, Yitzchak. From Baal to Ashtoreth: Poetry. LC 98-10739. (Illus.). 136p. 1998. 16.95 (965-229-188-9, Pub. by Gefen Pub Hse) Gefen Bks.

Rabolt, J. F., jt. ed. see Chase, D. B.

Rabolt, Nancy & Miler, Judy K., eds. Concepts & Cases in Retail & Merchandise Management. 360p. 1997. 49.00 (1-56367-086-0) Fairchild.

Rabon, Don. Interviewing & Interrogation. LC 92-81207. 212p. (C). 1992. pap. 17.50 (0-89089-488-4) Carolina Acad Pr.

— Investigative Discourse Analysis: Statements, Letters, & Transcripts. LC 94-70062. 188p. (Orig.). (C). 1994. pap. text 14.95 (0-89089-569-4) Carolina Acad Pr.

Rabone, David. Haynes Norton 500, 600, 650 & 750 Twins Owners Workshop Manual, No. 187: '57-'70. 1979. 23.95 (0-85696-187-6) Haynes Manuals.

Raboni, Giovanni. The Coldest Year of Grace: Selected Poems of Giovanni Raboni. Friebert, Stuart & Rossi, Vinio, trs. from ITA. LC 84-7363. (Wesleyan Poetry in Translation Ser.). 104p. 1985. 12.95 (0-8195-5114-7, Wesleyan Univ Pr) U Pr of New Eng.

Raborg, Frederick A., Jr. Hakata. (Amelia Chapbooks Ser.). (Illus.). 24p. (Orig.). 1992. pap. 5.95 (0-936545-13-5) Amelia.

— Posing Nude. (Amelia Chapbooks Ser.). 64p. (Orig.). 1990. pap. 10.95 (0-936545-14-3) Amelia.

— The Transient Nativity: A Christmas Story. (Amelia Chapbooks Ser.). 8p. 1987. pap. 4.00 (0-936545-07-0) Amelia.

— Tule. (Amelia Chapbooks Ser.). (Illus.). 24p. (Orig.). 1986. pap. 6.95 (0-936545-01-1) Amelia.

Raboteau, Albert J. A Fire in the Bones: Reflections on African-American Religious History. 240p. 1996. pap. 13.00 (0-8070-0933-4) Beacon Pr.

— Slave Religion: The Invisible Institution in the Antebellum South. (Illus.). 400p. 1980. pap. text 15.95 (0-19-502705-1) OUP.

Raboteau, Albert J., jt. ed. see Fulop, Timothy E.

An Asterisk (*) at the beginning of an entry indicates that the title is appearing for the first time.

R

***Raboteau, Albert Jordy.** African-American Religion. LC 98-33669. (Religion in American Life Ser.). 144p. 1999. 22.00 (0-19-510680-6) OUP.

Rabow, Gerald. Peace Through Agreement: Replacing War with Non-Violent Dispute-Resolution Methods. LC 89-71110. 200p. 1990. 52.95 (0-275-93505-1, C3505, Greenwood Pr) Greenwood.

Rabow, Jerome, et al. Advances in Psychoanalytic Sociology: A Text & Reader. LC 83-86. 379p. (C). 1987. text 37.50 (0-89874-608-6) Krieger.

— Learning Through Discussion. LC 93-40761. (C). 1994. text 26.00 (0-8039-5411-5) Sage.

— Learning Through Discussion. 3rd ed. LC 93-40761. (C). 1994. pap. text 10.50 (0-8039-5412-3) Sage.

— Tutoring Matters: Everything You Always Wanted to Know about How to Tutor. LC 98-33360. 240p. 1999. 49.50 (1-56639-695-6); pap. 14.95 (1-56639-696-4) Temple U Pr.

***Rabow, Jerome, et al.** William Fawcett Hill's Learning Through Discussion. 3rd ed. 70p. (C). 2000. pap. 8.95 (1-57766-111-7) Waveland Pr.

Rabow, Jerome, jt. auth. see Empey, LaMar T.

Rabow, Steve. 1998 Official Guide Book to Sarasota, Bradenton & Venice, FL: Steve Rabow's Guide Book. 7th rev. ed. (Illus.). 360p. 1997. pap. 12.95 (0-9639551-4-4) Primitive Pr.

— 1997 Official Guide Book to Sarasota, Bradenton & Venice, FL. 5th rev. ed. (Illus.). 342p. 1997. pap. 12.95 (0-9639551-3-6, Rabow) Primitive Pr.

— Official 1999 Guide Book to Sarasota, Bradenton & Venice, Florida: Steve Rabow's Guide Book. 8th rev. ed. West, Bill, tr. (Illus.). 1999. pap. 14.95 (0-9639551-5-2) Primitive Pr.

Raboy, David G., ed. Essays in Supply Side Economics. 172p. 1982. pap. 0.95 (0-614-04370-0) IRET.

Raboy, Marc. Missed Opportunities: The Story of Canada's Broadcasting Policy. 488p. (C). 1990. pap. 27.95 (0-7735-0775-2, Pub. by McG-Queens Univ Pr); lib. bdg. 65.00 (0-7735-0743-4, Pub. by McG-Queens Univ Pr) CUP Services.

Raboy, Marc & Bruck, Peter A., eds. Communication: For & Against Democracy. 248p. (Orig.). 1989. 48.99 (0-921689-47-0, Pub. by Black Rose); pap. 19.99 (0-921689-46-2, Pub. by Black Rose) Consort Bk Sales.

Raboy, Marc & Dagenais, Bernard. Media, Crisis & Democracy: Mass Communication & the Disruption of Social Order. (Media, Culture & Society Ser.). 224p. (C). 1992. text 55.00 (0-8039-8639-4); pap. text 25.95 (0-8039-8640-8) Sage.

Rabrenovic, Gordana. Community Builders: A Tale of Neighborhood Mobilization in Two Cities. LC 95-33292. (Conflicts in Urban & Regional Development Ser.). 256p. (C). 1996. 69.95 (1-56639-409-0); pap. 24.95 (1-56639-410-4) Temple U Pr.

***Rabson, Arthur & Roitt, Ivan.** Really Essential Medical Immunology. (Illus.). 192p. (C). 2000. pap. 25.95 (0-632-05506-5) Blackwell Sci.

Rabson, Caroline, ed. see McClelland, Elizabeth.

Rabson, Carolyn. Orchestral Excerpts: A Comprehensive Index. LC 92-46475. (Reference Books in Music: No. 25). xi, 221p. 1993. 35.00 (0-914913-26-3, Fallen Lef Pr) Scarecrow.

Rabson, Carolyn, ed. Songs of Oberlin. LC 83-8152. (Illus.). 120p. 1983. reprint ed. 8.50 (0-9611434-0-1); reprint ed. pap. 5.00 (0-9611434-1-X) Oberlin Con Lib.

Rabson, Carolyn, et al. George Whitfield Andrews: A Catalog of His Compositions. LC 86-8591. vii, 27p. 1986. pap. 8.50 (0-9611434-2-8) Oberlin Con Lib.

Rabson, Steve. Righteous Cause of Tragic Folly: Changing Views of War in Modern Japanese Poetry. LC 96-48385. (Michigan Monograph Series in Japanese Studies: No. 17). ix, 287p. 1998. 36.95 (0-939512-77-7) U MI Japan.

Rabson, Steve, jt. ed. see Molasky, Michael.

Rabson, Steve, tr. & contrib. by see Tatsuhiro, Oshiro & Mineo, Higashi.

Rabten, Geshe. Echoes of Voidness. 2nd ed. Batchelor, Stephen, ed. & tr. by. from TIB. (Intermediate Book). (Illus.). 148p. (C). 1986. pap. 8.95 (0-86171-010-X) Wisdom MA.

— The Essential Nectar: Meditations on the Buddhist Path. Willson, Martin, ed. & tr. by. from TIB. 312p. 1992. pap. 14.00 (0-86171-013-4) Wisdom MA.

— Song of the Profound View. Batchelor, Stephen, tr. 96p. 1989. pap. 10.95 (0-86171-086-X) Wisdom MA.

Rabten, Geshe & Dhargyey, Geshe. Advice from a Spiritual Friend. 3rd rev. ed. Beresford, Brian, tr. LC 95-47077. Orig. Title: Advice from a Spiritual Friend: Buddhist Thought Transformation. 176p. 1996. pap. 14.95 (0-86171-107-6) Wisdom MA.

Rabuazzo, Agata M., jt. auth. see Belfiore, F.

Rabuilas, Andreas D., jt. auth. see Stefanis, Costas N.

Rabun, H. P. & Cheely, W. W. Back-Trailing on the Old Frontiers. (Illus.). 1986. reprint ed. 8.50 (0-913150-55-X) Pioneer Pr.

Rabun, J. Stanley. Structural Analysis of Historic Buildings: Restoration, Preservation & Adaptive Reuse Applications for Architects & Engineers. LC 99-36214. 512p. 2000. 80.00 (0-471-31545-1) Wiley.

Rabura, Horst M., et al. Mosaik: Deutsche Kultur und Literatur. 3rd ed. 312p. (C). 1992. pap. 41.25 (0-07-003963-1) McGraw.

Rabura, Horst M., jt. auth. see Barrack, Charles M.

Raburn, Robert. Lonely Planet New Orleans. (Illus.). 312p. 1997. pap. 11.95 (0-86442-430-2) Lonely Planet.

Raburn, Terry. Starting Blocks: Running the Race A-G Style. LC 88-80813. (Radiant Life Ser.). 128p. (YA). (gr. 7 up). 1988. pap. 3.95 (0-88243-860-3, 02-0860) Gospel Pub.

— Starting Blocks: Running the Race A-G Style. LC 88-80813. (Radiant Life Ser.). (YA). (gr. 7 up). 1988. pap., teacher ed. 5.50 (0-88243-200-1, 32-0200) Gospel Pub.

Rabushka, Alvin. A Compelling Case for a Constitutional Amendment to Balance the Budget & Limit Taxes. 29p. 1984. pap. 2.50 (0-911415-05-X) Natl Taxpayers Union Found.

— Freedom's Fall in Hong Kong. LC 97-19861. (Essays in Public Policy Ser.: No. 79). 1997. pap. 5.00 (0-8179-5842-8) Hoover Inst Pr.

— From Adam Smith to the Wealth of America. (Illus.). 364p. (C). 1985. 44.95 (0-88738-029-8); pap. 24.95 (0-88738-645-8) Transaction Pubs.

— Hong Kong. 1993. 10.00 (0-226-70187-5) U Ch Pr.

— Scorecard on the Israeli Economy: A Review of 1989. xvi, 73p. (Orig.). 1990. pap. write for info. (0-923791-01-9) IASPS.

— A Simplified Tax System: The Option for Mexico. LC 92-46379. (Essays in Public Policy Ser.: No. 38). 1993. pap. 5.00 (0-8179-5432-5) Hoover Inst Pr.

— Ten Myths about Higher Taxes. LC 93-30446. (Essays in Public Policy Ser.: No. 43). 1993. pap. 5.00 (0-8179-5482-1) Hoover Inst Pr.

Rabushka, Alvin & Hanke, Steve H., eds. Toward Growth: A Blueprint for Economic Rebirth in Israel. 110p. 1988. pap. 19.00 (0-923791-00-0) IASPS.

Rabushka, Alvin & Ryan, Pauline. The Tax Revolt. (Publication Ser.: No. 270). 272p. 1982. 6.78 (0-8179-7701-5) Hoover Inst Pr.

Rabushka, Alvin, jt. auth. see Bernstam, Michael S.

Rabushka, Alvin, jt. auth. see Hall, Robert E.

Rabushka, Alvin, jt. auth. see Newman, David.

Rabushka, Alvin, jt. ed. see Duignan, Peter.

Rabuzzi, Daniel D., et al. Diagnosis & Management of Deep Neck Infections. 3rd ed. (Self-Instructional Package Ser.). (Illus.). 61p. 1993. pap. text 25.00 (1-56772-006-4) AAO-HNS.

Rabuzzi, Kathryn A. Mother with Child: Transformation Through Children. LC 92-45765. 192p. 1994. 31.95 (0-253-34769-6) Ind U Pr.

Rabwin, Marcella. Yes, Mr. Selznick: Recollections of Hollywood's Golden Era. (Illus.). 184p. 1999. 19.95 (0-8059-4715-9) Dorrance.

Raby, Burgess J., jt. auth. see Raby, William L.

Raby, Elizabeth. The Hard Scent of Peonies. 24p. (Orig.). 1990. pap. 5.00 (0-9625348-2-X) P Goodrich.

Raby, Frederick J., ed. Oxford Book of Medieval Latin Verse. 1959. 59.00 (0-19-812119-9) OUP.

Raby, Geoffrey. Making Rural Australia: An Economic History of Technical & Institutional Creativity, 1788-1860. (Illus.). 240p. 1997. pap. text 38.00 (0-19-553420-4) OUP.

Raby, Julian. The Art of Syria & the Jazira 1100-1250 AD. (Illus.). 174p. 1986. text 49.95 (0-19-728002-1); pap. text 35.00 (0-19-728001-3) OUP.

Raby, Julian. Venice, Durer & the Oriental Mode. (Hans Huth Memorial Studies: No. 1). (Illus.). 104p. 1983. text 45.00 (0-85667-162-2) Sothebys Pubns.

Raby, Julian & Johns, Jeremy. Bayt-al-Maqdis Pt. I: Abd al-Malik's Jerusalem. (Studies in Islamic Art: Vol. IX). (Illus.). 170p. 1993. text 75.00 (0-19-728017-X) OUP.

Raby, Julian, jt. auth. see Atasoy, Nurhan.

Raby, Julian, ed. see Soudavar, Abolala, et al.

Raby, Margaret, jt. auth. see Jevon, Philip.

Raby, Michel J., ed. Le "Huon de Bordeaux" en Prose du XVeme Siecle. (Studies in Humanities: Vol. 27). CLVIII, 300p. 1998. 64.95 (0-8204-3301-2) P Lang Pubng.

Raby, Namika. Kachcheri Bureaucracy in Sri Lanka: The Culture & Politics of Accessibility. (Foreign & Comparative Studies Program, South Asian Ser.: No. 10). (Orig.). 1985. pap. text 10.50 (0-915984-88-1) Syracuse U Foreign Comp.

Raby, Nigel, et al. Accident & Emergency Radiology: A Survival Guide. (Illus.). 262p. 1995. pap. text 33.00 (0-7020-1905-4, Pub. by W B Saunders) Saunders.

Raby, Peter. Aubrey Beardsley: And the Nineties. (Illus.). 1999. 22.95 (1-85585-495-3, Pub. by Collins & Br) Trafalgar.

— Bright Paradise: Victorian Scientific Travellers. LC 97-20228. 276p. 1997. pap. 14.95 (0-691-04843-6, Pub. by Princeton U Pr) Cal Prin Full Svc.

— Importance of Being Ernest: A Reader's Companion. (Masterwork Studies: No. 144). 144p. 1994. 25.95 (0-8057-8587-6, Twyne); mass mkt. 14.95 (0-8057-8588-4, Twyne) Mac Lib Ref.

— Samuel Butler: A Biography. LC 90-71600. (Illus.). 358p. 1991. text 37.95 (0-87745-331-4) U of Iowa Pr.

Raby, Peter, ed. The Cambridge Companion to Oscar Wilde. LC 96-37705. (Cambridge Companions to Literature Ser.). (Illus.). 320p. (C). 1997. text 59.95 (0-521-47471-X); pap. text 18.95 (0-521-47987-8) Cambridge U Pr.

Raby, Peter, ed. see Gogol, Nikolai Vasilevich.

Raby, Peter, ed. see Wilde, Oscar.

Raby, Peter, ed. & intro. see Wilde, Oscar.

Raby, Philip. Complete Canon EOS IX User's Guide: Advanced Photo System SLR Camera. (Illus.). 180p. 1998. pap. 19.95 (1-874031-69-X, Pub. by Hove Foto) Watsn-Guptill.

— Racing Cars. LC 98-49065. (Need for Speed Ser.). 32p. (J). (gr. 5-8). 1999. 23.93 (0-8225-2487-2, LernerSports) Lerner Pub.

— Racing Cars. (Need for Speed Ser.). 32p. (YA). (gr. 5-8). 1999. pap. 7.95 (0-8225-9853-1, LernerSports) Lerner Pub.

Raby, Philip & Nix, Simon. Motorbikes. LC 98-48685. (Need for Speed Ser.). 32p. (J). (gr. 3-9). 1999. 18.60 (0-8225-2486-4, Lerner Publctns) Lerner Pub.

— Motorbikes. (Need for Speed Ser.). 32p. (YA). (gr. 5-10). 1999. pap. 23.93 (0-8225-9854-X, LernerSports) Lerner Pub.

Raby, Rosaline L., et al, eds. Dimensions of the Community College: International, Intercultural, & Multicultural Perspectives. LC 96-3231. (Studies in Higher Education: Vol. 6). (Illus.). 368p. 1996. text 44.00 (0-8153-1343-8, SS1075) Garland.

Raby, S. & Walker, T. The Building Blocks of Creation-from Microfermis to Megaparsecs: Proceedings of 93 Theology Advanced Study Institute. 628p. 1994. text 121.00 (981-02-1592-4) World Scientific Pub.

Raby, William L. & Raby, Burgess J. Tax Practice Management: Client Servicing. ring bd. write for info. (0-318-61973-3) P-H.

Raby, William L. & Tidwell, Victor H. Introduction to Federal Taxation, 1984. (Illus.). 528p. 1983. text 29.95 (0-685-06826-9); student ed. 12.95 (0-685-42582-7) P-H.

— Introduction to Federal Taxation, 1986. (Illus.). 560p. (C). 1985. text. write for info. (0-318-59728-4) P-H.

— Introduction to Federal Taxation, 1987. 528p. (C). 1986. text 29.95 (0-317-45977-5) P-H.

Raby, William L., et al. A Guide to Successful Tax Practice, 3 vols. Incl. Vol. 3. Guide to Successful Tax Practice. 1997. ring bd. (0-7646-0133-4); Vol. 1. 1997. ring bd. (0-7646-0131-8); Vol. 2. 1997. ring bd. (0-7646-0132-6); 170.00 (0-7646-0130-X) Prctnrs Pub Co.

Racagni, G., et al, eds. Critical Issues in the Treatment of Schizophrenia. (International Academy for Biomedical & Drug Research Ser.: Vol. 10). (Illus.). vi, 206p. 1996. 198.25 (3-8055-6199-7) S Karger.

— New Pharmacological Approaches to the Therapy of Depressive Disorders. (International Academy for Biomedical & Drug Research Ser.: Vol. 5). (Illus.). vi, 196p. 1993. 194.00 (3-8055-5746-9) S Karger.

Racagni, G., ed. see Brunello, N., et al.

Racagni, Giorgio, et al, eds. Treatment of Age-Related Cognitive Dysfunction: Pharmacological & Clinical Evaluation. (International Academy for Biomedical & Drug Research Ser.: Vol. 2). (Illus.). vi, 154p. 1992. 121.00 (3-8055-5551-2) S Karger.

Racagni, Giorgio & Mendlewicz, Julien. Serotonin Receptor Subtypes: Pharmacological Significance & Clinical Implications. (International Academy for Biomedical & Drug Research Ser.: Vol. 1). (Illus.). x, 146p. 1992. 117.50 (3-8055-5550-4) S Karger.

Racagni, Giorgio & Smeraldi, Enrico, eds. Anxious Depression: Assessment & Treatment. LC 87-9792. 256p. 1987. reprint ed. pap. 79.40 (0-608-04714-7, 206543500004) Bks Demand.

Racagni, Giorgio, et al. Current Therapeutic Approaches to Panic & Other Anxiety Disorders. (International Academy for Biomedical & Drug Research Ser.: Vol. 8). (Illus.). vi, 206p. 1994. 195.75 (3-8055-5989-5) S Karger.

Racagni, Giorgio, ed. see Collegium Internationale Neuro-Psychopharmacologic.

Racagni, Giorgio, jt. ed. see Costa, E.

Racagni, Giorgio, jt. ed. see Kemali, Dargut.

Racagni, Giorgio, jt. ed. see Mendlewicz, J.

Racanelli, V. M. Crunchy, Munchy Cookies. (Whole-Language Big Bks.). (Illus.). 16p. (Orig.). (J). (ps-2). 1994. pap. 16.95 (1-56784-058-2) Newbridge Educ.

Racaniello, Vincent R., et al. Harvey Lecture Series 1987, 1991-1992. 192p. 1993. 119.95 (0-471-59790-2, B500) Wiley.

Racaut, Luc, tr. see Meynet, Roland.

Race. Teach Yourself Computer Based Systems. (Teach Yourself Ser.). pap. 7.95 (0-685-03265-5) McKay.

Race, A. & Williamson, R., eds. True to This Earth: Global Challenges & Transforming Faith. 200p. 1995. pap. 14.95 (1-85168-099-3, Pub. by Onewrld Pubns) Penguin Putnam.

Race, Bruce & Torma, Carolyn. Youth Planning Charrettes: A Manual for Planners & Teachers. LC 98-73601 (Illus.). 85p. 1998. pap., teacher ed. 19.95 (1-884829-19-8, Planners Press) Am Plan Assn.

***Race, David G.** Social Role Valorization & the English Experience. 256p. 2000. pap. 27.95 (1-86177-027-8, Pub. by Whiting & Birch) Paul & Co Pubs.

Race, Donna. Favorite Mother Goose Songs: A Musical Pop-up Book with Five Different Melodies. (Illus.). 12p. (J). (ps-1). 1993. mass mkt. 12.95 (0-689-71684-2) Aladdin.

— Jolly Old St. Nicholas: A Holiday Book with Lights & Music. LC 91-43087. (Illus.). 12p. (J). (ps up). 1992. mass mkt. 11.95 (0-689-71622-2) Aladdin.

Race, Henrietta V. Improvability: Its Intercorrelations & Its Relations to Initial Ability. LC 73-177176. (Columbia University. Teachers College. Contributions to Education Ser.: No. 124). reprint ed. 37.50 (0-404-55124-6) AMS Pr.

Race-Holmes, Tammy, jt. auth. see Sowers, Jayne.

Race, Jeffrey. War Comes to Long An: Revolutionary Conflict in a Vietnamese Province. LC 79-145793. 1972. pap. 17.95 (0-520-02361-7, Pub. by U CA Pr) Cal Prin Full Svc.

Race, Lynda. Afghan Hounds. 1999. 39.95 (1-85279-101-2) TFH Pubns.

Race, Phil. Five Hundred Tips for Students. 128p. 1996. pap. 24.95 (0-631-18851-7) Blackwell Pubs.

— 500 Tips on Open & Flexible Learning. 192p. 1998. pap. 25.00 (0-7494-2410-9, Kogan Pg Educ) Stylus Pub VA.

***Race, Phil.** 2000 Tips for Lecturers. 306p. 2000. pap. 33.00 (0-7494-3046-X, Kogan Pg Educ) Stylus Pub VA.

Race, Phil & Brown, Sally. 500 Tips for Tutors. 128p. 1993. pap. 19.95 (0-7494-0987-8, Kogan Pg Educ) Stylus Pub VA.

***Race, Phil & Brown, Sally.** 500 Tips on Group Learning. 160p. 1999. pap. 25.00 (0-7494-2884-8, Kogan Pg Educ) Stylus Pub VA.

Race, Phil & Brown, Sally. The Lecturer's Toolkit: A Practical Guide to Teaching, Learning & Assessment. 224p. 1998. ring bd. 125.00 (0-7494-2496-6, Kogan Pg Educ) Stylus Pub VA.

Race, Phil & McDowell, Steve. 500 Computing Tips for Teachers & Lecturers. 160p. 1997. pap., teacher ed. 19.95 (0-7494-1931-8, Kogan Pg Educ) Stylus Pub VA.

***Race, Phil & McDowell, Steve.** 500 Computing Tips for Teachers & Lecturers. 2nd ed. 160p. 2000. pap. 22.50 (0-7494-3150-4, Kogan Pg Educ) Stylus Pub VA.

Race, Phil & Smith, Brenda. 500 Tips for Trainers. LC 95-43405. 132p. 1996. pap. 21.95 (0-88415-288-X, 5288) Gulf Pub.

***Race, Phil, et al.** 500 Tips for Developing a Learning Organization. 160p. 1999. pap. 25.00 (0-7494-2912-7, Kogan Pg Educ) Stylus Pub VA.

Race, Phil, jt. auth. see McDowell, Steve.

Race, Phil, jt. auth. see Packard, Nick.

Race, Phil, jt. auth. see Saunders, Danny.

Race, Phil, jt. auth. see Wharton, Sue.

Race, Philip. How to Get a Good Degree: Making the Most of Your Time at University. LC 98-7254. 258p. 1998. 79.95 (0-335-20025-7); pap. 23.95 (0-335-20024-9) OpUniv Pr.

***Race, Philip.** Tackling Your Final Year at University: Essays, Exams & Employment. LC 99-50030. 160p. 2000. 22.95 (0-335-20511-9) OpUniv Pr.

Race, Steve. The Two Worlds of Joseph Race. large type ed. (Illus.). 1990. 27.99 (0-7089-2143-4) Ulverscroft.

***Race, Susan E.** Succeeding in the Workplace: Critical Skills for a Rewarding Career & Life You Love. Regan, Mary Beth, ed. (Illus.). 263p. (C). 1999. per. 15.95 (0-9673542-7-7) P Growth Syst.

Race, W. H. The Classical Priamel from Homer to Boethius. 1982. pap. 25.00 (90-04-06515-6, MNS, 74) Brill Academic Pubs.

Race, William H. Classical Genres & English Poetry. 240p. 1988. lib. bdg. 59.95 (0-415-00326-1, A1774) Routledge.

— Plato's Lysis. (Greek Commentaries Ser.). 59p. (Orig.). (C). 1983. pap. text 6.00 (0-929524-29-2) Bryn Mawr Commentaries.

— Style & Rhetoric in Pindar's Odes. 229p. 1990. pap. 21.00 (1-55540-491-X, 400424) OUP.

Race, William H., ed. from GRE. Pindar, Vol. I. LC 95-42927. (Loeb Classical Library: Vol. 56 & 485). 400p. 1997. 19.95 (0-674-99564-3) HUP.

— Pindar, Vol. II. (Loeb Classical Library: No. 56 & 485). 416p. 1996. 19.95 (0-674-99534-1) HUP.

Raceanu, Mircea, jt. auth. see Kirk, Roger.

Racek, Jaroslav. Cell-Based Biosensors. 110p. 1994. text 39.95 (1-56676-190-5) Technomic.

Racette, Dorothee, ed. see Cornette, James C., Jr.

Racevskis. Critical Essays on Michael Foucault. large type ed. LC 98-52728. 1p. 1998. 47.00 (0-7838-0071-1, G K Hall Lrg Type) Mac Lib Ref.

Racevskis, Karlis. Modernity's Pretenses: Making Reality Fit Reason from Candide to the Gulag. LC 97-43903. (Series in Postmodern Culture). 192p. (C). 1998. pap. text 18.95 (0-7914-3954-2) State U NY Pr.

— Modernity's Pretenses: Making Reality Fit Reason from Candide to the Gulag. LC 97-43903. (Series in Postmodern Culture). 192p. (C). 1998. text 56.50 (0-7914-3953-4) State U NY Pr.

— Postmodernism & the Search for Enlightenment. LC 93-7338. 172p. reprint ed. pap. 53.40 (0-608-20052-2, 207132400011) Bks Demand.

Racey, P. A., jt. ed. see Loudon, A. S.

Racey, Paul A. & Swift, Susan M., eds. Ecology, Evolution, & Behavior of Bats. (Symposia of the Zoological Society of London Ser.: No. 67). (Illus.). 444p. 1995. text 140.00 (0-19-854945-8) OUP.

Racey, Paul A., jt. ed. see Kunz, Thomas H.

Rach, Dennis. Dear Daddy. 64p. 1999. 10.99 (0-570-05363-3, 12-3414GJ) Concordia.

Rach, Julie. The Budgie: An Owner's Guide to a Happy, Healthy Pet. LC 96-43525. 128p. 1997. 12.95 (0-87605-500-5) Howell Bks.

— The Cockatiel: An Owner's Guide to a Happy, Healthy Pet. LC 97-7624. 128p. 1997. 12.95 (0-87605-526-9) Howell Bks.

— Why Does My Bird Do That? LC 98-23439. 224p. (J). 1998. 22.95 (0-87605-011-9) Howell Bks.

Rach, Julie & Critter Press Staff. Budgies in Your Life. LC 97-31104. 1997. write for info. (0-87605-434-3) Howell Bks.

Rach, Julie A. The Conure: An Owner's Guide to a Happy Healthy Pet. LC 98-6585. (Owner's Guide to a Happy, Healthy Pet Ser.). 128p. 1998. 12.95 (0-87605-226-X) Howell Bks.

— Pets for Fun & Profit. large type ed. (For Fun & Profit Ser.). (Illus.). 300p. Date not set. pap. 24.95 (1-56559-912-8) HGI-Over Fifty.

Rach, Nikki. Dear Mommy. 64p. 1999. 10.99 (0-570-05364-1, 12-3415GJ) Concordia.

Rach, Ruth. Improve Your German. (Improve Your...Ser.). (GER.). 1995. pap. 79.95 incl. audio (0-8442-2572-X, Natl Textbk Co) NTC Contemp Pub Co.

— Practice & Improve Your German. (Practice & Improve Ser.). 1995. pap. 39.95 incl. audio (0-8442-2555-X, Natl Textbk Co) NTC Contemp Pub Co.

— Practice & Improve Your German Plus. (Practice & Improve Ser.). 1995. pap. 39.95 incl. audio (0-8442-2569-X, Natl Textbk Co) NTC Contemp Pub Co.

Rachal, Patricia. Federal Narcotics Enforcement: Reorganization & Reform. LC 82-1722. 183p. (C). 1982. 49.95 (0-86569-089-8, Auburn Hse) Greenwood.

Rachal, Sharon. Rustic Charms, Vol. 1. 100p. 1987. pap. text 6.50 (1-56770-175-2) S Scheewe Pubns.

An Asterisk (*) at the beginning of an entry indicates that the title is appearing for the first time.

R

Rachals, Richard H. On Your Own As a Computer Professional: How to Get Started & Succeed As an Independent. 2nd ed. LC 94-90130. 180p. (Orig.). 1997. pap. 19.95 (*0-9641054-1-1*) Turner Hse Pubns.

Rachamanov. German-Russian Dictionary of Synonyms: Deutsch-Russiches Synonymwoerterbuch. (GER & RUS.). 704p. 1983. 75.00 (*0-8288-1235-7*, F52790) Fr & Eur.

Rachbauer, M. A. Wolfram von Eschenbach. LC 73-140041. (Catholic University Studies in German: No. 4). reprint ed. 37.50 (*0-404-50224-5*) AMS Pr.

Rachel, M. Ayres & Mara, D. Duncan. Analysis of Wastewater for Use in Agriculture: A Laboratory Manual of Parasitological & Bacteriological Techniques. LC 97-108416. (FRE & SPA., Illus.). 35p. (Orig.). (C). 1996. pap. 10.80 (*92-4-154484-8*, 1150432) World Health.

Rachel, Samuel. De Jure Naturae & Gentium Dissertationes. LC 95-77191. (Classics in International Law Reprint Ser.: No.5, Vol.1). (8) 335p. 1995. reprint ed. 100.00 (*1-57588-509-3*) W S Hein.

Rachele, Sal. Life on the Cutting Edge. 352p. 1994. pap. 14.95 (*0-9640535-0-0*) Liv Awareness.

***Rachele, Warren.** Learn C++ in Three Days. 350p. 2000. 29.95 incl. audio compact disk (*1-55622-707-8*) Wordware Pub.

— Learn Object Pascal. (Illus.). 2000. pap. text 32.95 (*1-55622-719-1*) Wordware Pub.

Rachels, David, ed. Augustus Baldwin Longstreet's Georgia Scenes Completed. LC 97-47775. 392p. (C). 1998. pap. 19.95 (*0-8203-2019-6*); text 50.00 (*0-8203-1978-3*) U of Ga Pr.

Rachels, James. Can Ethics Provide Answers? And Other Essays in Moral Philosophy. LC 96-29130. (Studies in Social, Political, & Legal Philosophy: No. 70). 240p. 1997. 60.50 (*0-8476-8347-8*); pap. 20.95 (*0-8476-8348-6*) Rowman.

— Created from Animals: The Moral Implications of Darwinism. 256p. 1999. reprint ed. pap. 14.95 (*0-19-286129-8*, 12291) OUP.

— The Elements of Moral Philosophy. 158p. (C). 1986. pap. text. write for info. (*0-07-553939-X*) McGraw.

— The Elements of Moral Philosophy. 2nd ed. (Heritage Series in Philosophy). 208p. (C). 1992. pap. text 12.75 (*0-07-051098-9*) McGraw.

— The Elements of Moral Philosophy. 3rd ed. LC 98-19786. 256p. 1998. pap. 19.38 (*0-07-052560-9*) McGraw.

— The Right Thing to Do. 2nd ed. LC 98-21045. 336p. 1998. pap. 28.44 (*0-07-051090-3*) McGraw.

— The Right Thing to Do: Basic Readings in Moral Philosophy. (C). 1989. pap. text 26.25 (*0-07-557002-5*) McGraw.

Rachels, James, ed. Ethical Theory: Part 1: The Question of Objectivity; Part 2: Theories about How We Should Live, 2 vols., Vol. 1-2. (Oxford Readings in Philosophy). 586p. 1998. text 39.95 (*0-19-875193-1*) OUP.

***Rachels, James, ed.** Ethical Theory 1: The Question of Objectivity. LC 97-42646. (Oxford Readings in Philosophy Ser.). 256p. 1998. pap. text 19.95 (*0-19-875192-3*) OUP.

— Ethical Theory 2: Theories about How We Should Live. (Oxford Readings in Philosophy Ser.). 330p. 1998. pap. text 19.95 (*0-19-875186-9*) OUP.

Racheotes, Nicholas S., jt. auth. see Jarnis, George M.

Rachet, G. Dictionnaire de la Civilisation Egyptienne. (FRE.). 1998. 49.95 (*0-320-00279-9*) Fr & Eur.

Rachet, Guy. Dictionnaire de la Civilisation. (FRE.). 256p. 1992. 59.95 (*0-8288-7354-2*) Fr & Eur.

— Dictionnaire de la Civilisation Grecque. (FRE.). 272p. 1992. 59.95 (*0-8288-7353-4*) Fr & Eur.

— Dictionnaire de l'Archaeologie. (ENG & FRE.). 1060p. 1982. pap. 49.95 (*0-7859-7814-3*, 2221503228) Fr & Eur.

— Petite Encyclopedie Larousse. (FRE.). 1496p. 1977. 49.95 (*0-7859-0764-5*, M-6473) Fr & Eur.

Racheter, Donald P., et al, eds. Limiting Leviathan. LC 99-17052. 288p. 1999. 95.00 (*1-84064-024-3*) E Elgar.

Racheter, Richard G. Collector's Guide to Homer Laughlin's Virginia Rose: Identification & Values. LC 97-190247. (Collector's Guide to Ser.). 144p. 1997. pap. 18.95 (*0-89145-772-0*, 4860) Collector Bks.

***Racheter, Richard G.** Post '86 Fiesta: Identification & Value Guide. (Illus.). 176p. 2000. pap. 19.95 (*1-57432-203-6*) Collector Bks.

Rachev, S., jt. auth. see Mittnik, Stefan.

Rachev, S. T. & Rhschendorf, Ludger. Mass Transportation Problems Pt. I: Theory. LC 97-34593. (Probability & Its Applications Ser.). 516p. 1998. 79.95 (*0-387-98350-3*) Spr-Verlag.

— Mass Transportation Problems Pt. II: Applications. LC 97-34593. (Probability & Its Applications Ser.). 516p. 1998. 79.95 (*0-387-98352-X*) Spr-Verlag.

Rachev, S. T., jt. auth. see Anastassiou, G.

Rachev, S. T., jt. auth. see Kalashnikov, Vladimir V.

Rachewiltz, I. de, see de Rachewiltz, I.

Rachewiltz, Mary D. Ezra Pound, Father & Teacher: Discretions. LC 73-143717. (Illus.). 336p. 1975. pap. 4.75 (*0-8112-0589-4*, NDP405, Pub. by New Directions) Norton.

Rachfalski, Jane, jt. auth. see Miller, Melinda J.

***Rachia, I. M., ed.** Youth Violence: A Selective Bibliography with Abstracts. (Social Issues Bibliography Series I). 207p. 1999. lib. bdg. 49.00 (*1-56072-713-6*) Nova Sci Pubs.

Rachie, K. O., jt. ed. see Singh, S. R.

Rachilde. The Juggler. Hawthorne, Melanie, tr. & intro. by. LC 90-8070. (Illus.). 232p. (Orig.). (C). 1990. text 37.00 (*0-8135-1594-7*) Rutgers U Pr.

— The Marquise de Sarde. 2nd ed. Heron, Liz, tr. from FRE. & abr. by. LC 96-120965. (Decadence Ser.). 279p. 1999. reprint ed. pap. 14.95 (*1-873982-06-2*, Pub. by Dedalus) Hippocrene Bks.

— Monsieur Venus. 2nd ed. Barres, Mavora & Johnston, Madeleine, eds. Heron, Liz, tr. from FRE. LC 96-120963. (Decadence Ser.). 149p. 1999. reprint ed. pap. 10.95 (*1-873982-20-8*, Pub. by Dedalus) Hippocrene Bks.

***Rachilde, et al.** Madame La Mort & Other Plays. Gounaridou, Kiki & Lively, Frazer, eds. & trs. by. from FRE. LC 97-26493. (PAJ Bks.). 136p. 1998. text 35.00 (*0-8018-5761-9*); pap. text 15.95 (*0-8018-5762-7*) Johns Hopkins.

Rachko, Marina. Cherez Ne Mogu. LC 90-4521. (RUS.). 101p. (Orig.). 1990. pap. 7.00 (*1-55779-032-9*) Hermitage Pubs.

Rachleff, Owen S. Exploring the Bible. (Illus.). 364p. 1981. 39.95 (*0-89659-008-9*) Abbeville Pr.

Rachleff, Peter. Black Labor in Richmond, 1865-1890. LC 88-29432. 264p. 1989. reprint ed. pap. text 11.95 (*0-252-06026-1*) U of Ill Pr.

— Hard-Pressed in the Heartland: The Hormel Strike & the Future of the Labor Movement. 135p. 1993. 30.00 (*0-89608-451-5*); pap. 12.00 (*0-89608-450-7*) South End Pr.

— Marxism & Council Communism: Modern Revolutionary Thought. 312p. 1974. 250.00 (*0-87700-227-4*) Revisionist Pr.

Rachlin. Foreigner. 1999. reprint ed. pap. 12.00 (*0-393-31908-3*) Norton.

Rachlin, Allan. News As Hegemonic Reality: American Political Culture & the Framing of New Accounts. LC 88-12009. 168p. 1988. 52.95 (*0-275-92534-X*, C2534, Praeger Pubs) Greenwood.

Rachlin, Ann. Bach. LC 92-9520. (Famous Children Ser.). (Illus.). 24p. (J). (gr. k-3). 1992. pap. 5.95 (*0-8120-4991-8*) Barron.

— Bach. (Famous Children Ser.). (Illus.). 24p. (J). 1993. 10.95 (*0-8120-6365-1*) Barron.

— Beethoven. (Famous Children Ser.). (Illus.). 24p. (J). (gr. k-3). 1994. pap. 5.95 (*0-8120-1996-2*) Barron.

— Brahms. (Famous Children Ser.). (Illus.). 24p. (J). (gr. k-3). 1993. pap. 5.95 (*0-8120-1542-8*) Barron.

— Chopin. (Famous Children Ser.). (Illus.). 24p. (J). (gr. k-3). 1993. pap. 5.95 (*0-8120-1543-6*) Barron.

— Handel. LC 92-11497. (Illus.). 24p. (J). (gr. k-3). 1992. pap. 5.95 (*0-8120-4992-6*) Barron.

— Handel. (Famous Children Ser.). (Illus.). 24p. (J). 1993. 10.95 (*0-8120-6364-3*) Barron.

— Haydn. LC 92-9521. (Famous Children Ser.). (Illus.). 24p. (J). (gr. k-3). 1992. pap. 5.95 (*0-8120-4988-8*) Barron.

— Haydn. (Famous Children Ser.). (Illus.). 24p. (J). 1993. 10.95 (*0-8120-6363-5*) Barron.

— Mozart. LC 92-10302. (Famous Children Ser.). (Illus.). 24p. (J). (gr. k-3). 1992. 5.95 (*0-8120-4989-6*) Barron.

— Mozart. (Famous Children Ser.). (Illus.). 24p. (J). 1993. 10.95 (*0-8120-6362-7*) Barron.

— Schubert. (Famous Children Ser.). (Illus.). 24p. (J). (gr. k-3). 1994. pap. 5.95 (*0-8120-1995-4*) Barron.

— Schumann. LC 92-26965. (Famous Children Ser.). (Illus.). 24p. (J). (gr. k-3). 1993. pap. 5.95 (*0-8120-1544-4*) Barron.

— Tchaikovsky. (Famous Children Ser.). (Illus.). 24p. (J). (gr. k-3). 1993. pap. 5.95 (*0-8120-1545-2*) Barron.

Rachlin, Edward S., ed. Diagnosis & Comprehensive Management of Myofascial Pain. LC 93-36499. (Illus.). 552p. (C). (gr. 13). 1993. text 85.00 (*0-8016-6817-4*, 06817) Mosby Inc.

Rachlin, Harvey. Extraordinary Artifacts. LC 92-53660. 1993. 18.00 (*0-394-58013-3*) Villard Books.

***Rachlin, Harvey.** Jumbo's Hide, Elvis's Ride & the Tooth of Buddha: More Marvelous Tales of Historical Artifacts. LC 99-39456. (Illus.). 352p. 2000. 25.00 (*0-8050-5683-1*) H Holt & Co.

Rachlin, Harvey. Jumbo's Hide, Elvis's Ride & the Tooth of Buddha: More Marvelous Tales of Historical Artifacts. (Illus.). 384p. 2001. pap. 15.00 (*0-8050-5684-X*, Owl) H Holt & Co.

***Rachlin, Harvey.** Lucy's Bones, Sacred Stones & Einstein's Brain. 2000. pap. 15.00 (*0-8050-6406-0*) St Martin.

Rachlin, Harvey. Lucy's Bones, Sacred Stones & Einstein's Brain: The Remarkable Stories Behind the Great Objects. (Illus.). 416p. 1995. pap. 16.95 (*0-8050-3965-1*, Owl) H Holt & Co.

— Lucy's Bones, Sacred Stones & Einstein's Brain: The Remarkable Stories Behind the Great Objects & Artifacts of History, From Antiquity to the Modern Era. LC 95-19935. (Reference Bks.). (Illus.). 416p. 1995. 27.50 (*0-8050-3964-3*) H Holt & Co.

— The Making of a Cop. Pfefferblit, Elaine, ed. 320p. (Orig.). 1991. reprint ed. mass mkt. 4.99 (*0-671-74740-1*) PB.

Rachlin, Howard. Introduction to Modern Behaviorism. 3rd ed. 302p. (C). 1990. pap. 22.95 (*0-7167-2176-7*) W H Freeman.

***Rachlin, Howard.** Science of Self-Control. LC 99-45204. 2000. text 35.00 (*0-674-00093-5*) HUP.

Rachlin, Nahid. The Heart's Desire. 208p. (Orig.). 1995. 18.95 (*0-87286-304-2*); pap. 9.95 (*0-87286-305-0*) City Lights.

— Married to a Stranger. 232p. (Orig.). 1993. pap. 12.95 (*0-87286-276-3*) City Lights.

— Veils: Short Stories. 180p. (Orig.). 1992. pap. 8.95 (*0-87286-267-4*) City Lights.

Rachlin, Robert. Profit Strategies for Business. LC 79-88674. 127p. 1980. 14.95 (*0-938712-01-2*) Marr Pubns.

— Return on Investment: Strategies for Profit. LC 75-44668. 124p. 1976. 14.95 (*0-938712-00-4*) Marr Pubns.

— Return on Investment Manual: Tools & Applications for Managing Financial Results. LC 97-12691. (Illus.). 416p. 1997. text 62.95 (*0-7656-0014-5*, Sharpe Prof) M E Sharpe.

— Successful Techniques for Higher Profits. LC 80-85150. 260p. 1981. 16.95 (*0-938712-02-0*) Marr Pubns.

***Rachlin, Robert.** Total Business Budgeting: A Step-by-Step Guide with Forms. 2nd ed. LC 99-30106. 321p. 1999. text 69.95 (*0-471-35103-2*) Wiley.

***Rachlin, Robert, ed.** Handbook of Budgeting: March 2000 Supplement. 4th ed. 96p. 2000. pap. 60.00 (*0-471-36139-9*) Wiley.

Rachlin, Robert & Sweeny, H. W. Allen. Handbook of Budgeting. 4th ed. LC 98-2520. 976p. 1998. 160.00 (*0-471-18350-4*) Wiley.

Rachlin, Sidney L., et al. First Steps to Math: A Guide to Beginning Mathematics Activities for Parents & Primary Teachers. (Illus.). 110p. 1993. pap., teacher ed. 13.00 (*1-895411-47-5*) Peguis Pubs Ltd.

***Rachlis, Eric.** Dog Shows, 1930-1949. LC 99-52978. (Illus.). 176p. 2000. pap. 18.95 (*0-8118-2687-2*) Chronicle Bks.

Rachlis, Eugene, jt. ed. see Levine, Mark L.

Rachlis, Michael. Strong Medicine: How to Save Canada's Health-Care System. LC 94-189706. 396p. 1994. write for info. (*0-00-255281-7*, R0122) HarpCollins.

— Strong Medicine: How To Save Canada'S Health-Care System. 448p. 1995. reprint ed. pap. 22.00 (*0-00-638061-1*, R0549) HarpCollins.

Rachman. Advances in Behaviour Research & Therapy, Vols. 3 & 4. pap. 35.00 (*0-08-030465-6*, Pergamon Pr) Elsevier.

— Complete Songs for Voice & Piano. 1998. pap. text 14.95 (*0-486-40195-2*) Dover.

— A Favorite Son: The Legacy of Sandor Ferenczi. (Psychoanalytic Inquiry Ser.: Vol. 17, No. 4). 1998. pap. 20.00 (*0-88163-933-8*) Analytic Pr.

Rachman & Mescon. Business Today. 9th ed. (C). 1998. pap. text, student ed. 20.00 (*0-13-096229-5*, Pub. by P-H) S&S Trade.

Rachman, Arnold W. Identity Group Psychotherapy with Adolescents. LC 95-22840. 340p. 1995. 50.00 (*1-56821-658-0*) Aronson.

— Sandor Ferenczi: The Psychotherapist of Tenderness & Passion. LC 94-32540. 488p. 1997. 60.00 (*1-56821-100-7*) Aronson.

Rachman, Carla. Monet. (Illus.). 352p. 1997. pap. 19.95 (*0-7148-3500-5*, Pub. by Phaidon Press) Phaidon Pr.

Rachman, D. Standard & Poor's How to Invest: A Guide for Buying Stocks, Bonds & Mutual Funds. (C). 1992. text 13.25 (*0-07-051337-6*) McGraw.

Rachman, David. Marketing Today. 3rd ed. (C). 1994. text 30.25 (*0-03-000559-0*) Harcourt Coll Pubs.

Rachman, David J. & Mescon, Michael H. Business Today: Guide for Non-Native Speakers. 8th ed. 1996. pap. text. write for info. (*0-07-037210-1*) McGraw.

Rachman, David J., et al. Business Today. 8th ed. LC 95-19806. (C). 1995. text. write for info. (*0-07-051756-8*); pap. text, student ed. write for info. (*0-07-052159-X*) McGraw.

— Business Today. 8th ed. LC 92-17433. 1996. pap. text, student ed. write for info. (*0-07-051758-4*) McGraw.

— Business Today Vol. 1: Creative Lectures, 1. 8th ed. 1996. pap. text. write for info. (*0-07-052174-3*) McGraw.

— Business Today Vol. 2: Creative Lectures, 2. 8th ed. 1996. pap. text. write for info. (*0-07-052175-1*) McGraw.

Rachman, Jack. The Best of Behaviour Research & Therapy. LC 97-37215. 1997. text 64.00 (*0-08-043078-3*, Pergamon Pr) Elsevier.

Rachman, S. Anxiety. (Clinical Psychology Ser.). 1998. pap. 19.95 (*0-86377-802-X*) L Erlbaum Assocs.

— Anxiety. (Clinical Psychology: a Modular Course Ser.). 192p. 1998. write for info. (*0-86377-801-1*, Pub. by Psychol Pr) Taylor & Francis.

Rachman, Stanley, jt. auth. see De Silva, Padmal.

Rachman, Stanley J. Panic Disorder: The Facts. De Silva, W. P., ed. LC 96-2511. (Facts Ser.). (Illus.). 108p. 1996. pap. 19.95 (*0-19-262738-4*) OUP.

Rachman, Stanley J., ed. Advances in Behavior Research & Therapy, Vol. 2. (Illus.). 186p. 1980. 100.00 (*0-08-027110-3*, Pergamon Pr) Elsevier.

— Contributions to Medical Psychology, 3 vols. 1984. 110.00 (*0-08-030855-4*, Pergamon Pr) Elsevier.

Rachman, Stanley J. & Wilson, T., eds. Advances in Behavior Research & Therapy, Vol. 3. (Illus.). 206p. 1982. 125.00 (*0-08-029671-8*, Pergamon Pr) Elsevier.

— Advances in Behavior Research & Therapy, Vol. 4. (Illus.). 282p. 1984. 125.00 (*0-08-031502-X*, Pergamon Pr) Elsevier.

— Advances in Behavior Research & Therapy, Vol. 5. (Illus.). 258p. 1985. 145.00 (*0-08-032327-8*, Pergamon Pr) Elsevier.

— Advances in Behavior Research & Therapy, Vol. 6. (Illus.). 270p. 1986. 132.00 (*0-08-034143-8*, Pub. by PPL) Elsevier.

Rachman, Stanley J., jt. auth. see Philips, H. Clare.

Rachman, Stanley J., jt. ed. see Eysenck, Hans J.

Rachman, Stanley J., jt. ed. see Maser, Jack D.

Rachman, Stephen, jt. ed. see Rosenheim, Shawn.

Rachmaninoff, Sergei. Singer's Rachmaninoff. 1989. 45.00 (*0-8239-0672-8*) Rosen Group.

Rachmaninoff, Sergey. Album for the Piano. 64p. 1986. pap. 7.95 (*0-7935-5260-5*, 50327300) H Leonard.

Rachmaninoff, Sergey. Complete Preludes & Etudes-Tableaux. 208p. 1999. pap. 10.95 (*0-486-25696-0*) Dover.

— Complete Rachmaninoff Preludes for Piano OP3, OP23, OP32: Centennial Edition. 112p. 1994. 10.95 (*0-7935-3306-6*) H Leonard.

Rachmaninoff, Sergey. Concerto No. 2 Opus 18: 2 Pianos 4 Hands. 64p. 1986. pap. 8.95 (*0-7935-0500-3*, 50260230) H Leonard.

Rachmaninoff, Sergey. Piano Concertos, No. 1, 2 & 3. 400p. 1990. pap. 18.95 (*0-486-26350-9*) Dover.

— Rachmaninoff's Recollections Told to Oskar Von Riesemann. LC 74-111100. (Select Bibliographies Reprint Ser.). 1977. 31.95 (*0-8369-5232-4*) Ayer.

— Sonatas & Other Works for Piano. 176p. pap. 9.95 (*0-486-27307-5*) Dover.

— Symphony No. 2 in E Minor, Op. 27, in Full Score. 1999. pap. text 15.95 (*0-486-40629-6*) Dover.

— Tableaux Etudes, Opus 33 & 39. 104p. 1985. pap. 12.95 (*0-7935-3164-0*, 00123087) H Leonard.

Rachmaninoff, Sergey, jt. auth. see Tchaikovsky, Peter Illich.

Rachmaninov. Prelude in C# Minor Op3 No2. 12p. 1997. per. 4.95 (*0-7935-8319-5*) H Leonard.

Rachmann, Hinrich, jt. auth. see Anken, Ralf H.

Rachmanov, I. V. German-Russian Dictionary of Synonyms. (GER & RUS.). 704p. 1983. 59.95 (*0-8288-1241-1*, M 15173) Fr & Eur.

Rachmilewitz, D. Inflammatory Bowel Disease. 1982. text 155.50 (*90-247-2612-3*) Kluwer Academic.

Rachmilewitz, D., ed. Fifth International Symposium on Inflammatory Bowel Diseases. (Falk Symposium Ser.). 256p. 1998. 146.00 (*0-7923-8743-0*) Kluwer Academic.

— Inflammatory Bowel Diseases 1986. (Development in Gastroenterology Ser.). 1986. lib. bdg. 179.50 (*0-89838-796-5*) Kluwer Academic.

— Inflammatory Bowel Diseases, 1994: Proceedings of the 72nd Falk Symposium Held in Strasbourg, France, September 6-8, 1993. LC 93-44397. 320p. (C). 1994. text 140.00 (*0-7923-8845-3*) Kluwer Academic.

Rachmilewitz, D. & Zimmerman, J., eds. Inflammatory Bowel Diseases, 1990: Proceedings of the Third International Symposium on Inflammatory Bowel Diseases. (Developments in Gastroenterology Ser.). (C). 1990. text 175.00 (*0-7923-0657-0*) Kluwer Academic.

***Rachna, Gilmore.** A Group of One. 2001. text 16.95 (*0-8050-6475-3*) St Martin.

Rachner, Mary J. Anita, Enemy of the People: Let's Take the Communism Out of Womynism. 102p. (Orig.). 1991. pap. 9.95 (*0-9623133-3-5*) Oxner Inst.

— Kerry's Thirteenth Birthday: Everything Your Parents & Their Friends Know about Sex but Are Too Polite to Talk about. rev. ed. LC 93-84599. 80p. (YA). (gr. 8 up). 1993. pap. text 9.95 (*0-9623133-4-3*) Oxner Inst.

— Satanic Reverses. LC 89-61567. (Illus.). 153p. (Orig.). 1989. pap. 9.95 (*0-9623133-0-0*) Oxner Inst.

Rachocki, A. H. Geomorphology for Students. 300p. 1990. pap. 39.95 (*0-471-96978-8*) Wiley.

Rachocki, Andrzej H. Alluvial Fans: An Attempt at an Empirical Approach. LC 80-42061. (Illus.). 171p. reprint ed. pap. 53.10 (*0-8357-3081-6*, 203933800012) Bks Demand.

Rachor, JoAnn. Of These Ye May Freely Eat: A Vegetarian Cookbook. rev. ed. 96p. 1999. pap. 2.95 (*1-878726-02-1*) Fam Hlth Pubns.

Rachow, Louis A., ed. Theatre & Performing Arts Collections. LC 81-6567. (Special Collections: Vol. 1, No. 1). 166p. 1981. text 49.95 (*0-917724-47-X*) Haworth Pr.

Rachowiecki, Rob. Costa Rica. 3rd ed. (Lonely Planet Travel Guides Ser.). (Illus.). 568p. 1997. pap. 17.95 (*0-86442-366-7*) Lonely Planet.

— Lonely Planet Ecuador & the Galapagos. 4th ed. (Illus.). 512p. 1997. pap. 19.95 (*0-86442-348-9*) Lonely Planet.

***Rachowiecki, Rob.** Lonely Planet Peru. 4th ed. (Illus.). 512p. 2000. pap. 17.95 (*0-86442-710-7*) Lonely Planet.

Rachowiecki, Rob. Lonely Planet Southwest. 2nd ed. (Lonely Planet Travel Guides Ser.). (Illus.). 992p. 1999. pap. text 24.95 (*0-86442-539-2*) Lonely Planet.

— Peru: Travel Guide. 4th ed. (Illus.). 512p. 1996. pap. 17.95 (*0-86442-332-2*) Lonely Planet.

Rachowiecki, Rob & Wagenhauser, Betsy. Climbing & Hiking in Ecuador. 4th rev. ed. (Bradt Guides Ser.). (Illus.). 278p. (Orig.). 1997. pap. 17.95 (*1-898323-54-2*, Pub. by Bradt Pubns) Globe Pequot.

Rachui, Scott, jt. auth. see Dummies Press Staff.

Rachum, Ilan. The Illustrated Encyclopedia of the Renaissance. LC 95-33600. (Illustrated Encyclopedia Series). (Illus.). 736p. (Orig.). 1995. 50.00 (*0-8050-4652-6*) H Holt & Co.

***Rachum, Ilan.** Revolution: The Entrance of a New Word into Western Political Discourse. LC 99-41524. 312p. 1999. 57.00 (*0-7618-1503-1*); pap. 39.50 (*0-7618-1504-X*) U Pr of Amer.

Rachunas, Joseph. A New Owner's Guide to Chinese Crested: AKC Rank #72. (New Owner's Guide to Ser.). (Illus.). 160p. 1998. 12.95 (*0-7938-2773-6*, JG-124) TFH Pubns.

Rachveli, N. N., ed. Black Americans: Issues & Concerns. LC 94-1779. 221p. 1995. text 95.00 (*1-56072-173-1*) Nova Sci Pubs.

Rachwal, Tadeusz, jt. ed. see Kalaga, Wojciech H.

Rachwald, Arthur R. In Search of Poland: The Superpowers' Response to Solidarity, 1980-1989. (Publication Ser.: No. 396). 161p. (C). 1990. text 7.98 (*0-8179-8961-7*); pap. text 5.98 (*0-8179-8962-5*) Hoover Inst Pr.

Rachwald, Arthur R., jt. ed. see Mattox, Gale A.

***Rachwiecki, Rob & Thompson, John.** Costa Rica. 4th ed. (Illus.). 572p. 1999. pap. 17.95 (*0-86442-760-3*) Lonely Planet.

Raciborski, M. Parasitische Algen und Pilze Javas, 3 pts. in 1. 1973. reprint ed. 40.00 (*3-7682-0855-9*) Lubrecht & Cramer.

Racicot, Joni. QuickSteps to Learning: Excel 7.0 for Windows Beginners. (Quicksteps to Learning Ser.). 1996. spiral bd. 22.95 (*1-56951-032-6*) Sftware Trng.

An Asterisk (*) at the beginning of an entry indicates that the title is appearing for the first time.

— QuickSteps to Learning: Word 7.0 for Windows Beginners. (Quicksteps to Learning Ser.). (Illus.). (Orig.). 1994. spiral bd. 22.95 (*1-56951-031-8*) Sftware Trng.

— Windows 95 Beginning. (Quicksteps to Learning Ser.). 1995. spiral bd. 22.95 (*1-56951-029-6*) Sftware Trng.

— Windows 95 Upgrade. (Quicksteps to Learning Ser.). 1995. spiral bd. 22.95 (*1-56951-030-X*) Sftware Trng.

Racin, John, ed. & tr. see Chekhov, Anton & Suvorin, Alexei.

***Racina, John.** Supplementary Jazz Studies: Blues Riffs, 4 vols., Vol. 1. 65p. 2000. pap. text 12.95 (*0-9676338-1-8*) J Racina Music Prod.

***Racina, Thom.** Hidden Agenda. 400p. 1999. reprint ed. mass mkt. 6.99 (*0-451-18600-1*) NAL.

Racina, Thomas. Secret Weekend. 1999. mass mkt. 6.99 (*0-451-19705-4*, Onyx) NAL.

***Racine, Bruno.** Living in Rome. (Illus.). 216p. 2000. text 50.00 (*2-08-013675-5*, Pub. by Flammarion) Abbeville Pr.

Racine, David. Floating in a Most Peculiar Way. LC 98-23879. 230p. 1999. 24.00 (*0-9657639-3-5*) Van Neste.

Racine, Drew, ed. Managing Technical Services in the 90's. LC 91-24386. (Journal of Library Administration: Vol. 15, Nos. 1-2). (Illus.). 150p. 1991. lib. bdg. 39.95 (*1-56024-166-7*) Haworth Pr.

Racine, Jean. Alexandre le Grand. Hawcroft, Michael & Worth, Valerie, eds. (Exeter French Texts Ser.: No. 86). (FRE.). 51p. Date not set. pap. text 19.95 (*0-85989-350-2*, Pub. by Univ Exeter Pr) Northwestern U Pr.

— Andromache. Korn, Eric, tr. from FRE. (Old Vic Theatre Collection Ser.: Vol. 1). 116p. 1988. pap. 7.95 (*1-55783-021-5*) Applause Theatre Bk Pubs.

— Andromache. Briffault, tr. 1977. pap. 4.95 (*0-8120-0028-5*) Barron.

— Andromache. Wilbur, Richard, tr. 1982. pap. 5.25 (*0-8222-0048-1*) Dramatists Play.

Racine, Jean. Andromaque. (Illus.). 1965. pap. 4.95 (*0-685-10999-2*, F41504) Fr & Eur.

Racine, Jean. Andromaque. (FRE.). (C). 1961. pap. 7.95 (*0-8442-1993-2*, VF1993-2) NTC Contemp Pub Co.

Racine, Jean. Andromaque. Knight, R. C. & Barnwell, H. T., eds. 210p. 1977. 33.95 (*0-686-54708-X*, FC1729) Fr & Eur.

Racine, Jean. Andromaque, Iphigenie, Britannicus. unabridged ed. (FRE.). 1999. pap. 6.95 (*2-87714-140-3*, Pub. by Bookking Intl) Distribks Inc.

— Athalie. (FRE., Illus.). 128p. 1985. pap. 10.95 (*0-7859-1587-7*, 204016071X) Fr & Eur.

— Bajazet. (FRE.). 128p. 1984. pap. 10.95 (*0-7859-1263-0*, 2040160728) Fr & Eur.

— Berenice. (FRE.). 224p. 1991. pap. 10.95 (*0-7859-1259-2*, 2038714037) Fr & Eur.

— Berenice, Phedre, Athalie. unabridged ed. (FRE.). pap. 5.95 (*2-87714-164-0*, Pub. by Bookking Intl) Distribks Inc.

— Britannicus. (FRE., Illus.). 1991. pap. 10.95 (*0-7859-1260-6*, 2038714045) Fr & Eur.

— Britannicus. (FRE.). (C). pap. 7.95 (*0-8442-1929-0*, VF1929-0) NTC Contemp Pub Co.

— Britannicus. MacDonald, Robert D., tr. 96p. 1999. pap. 12.95 (*1-84002-083-0*, Pub. by Theatre Comm) Consort Bk Sales.

— Esther. (FRE.). 1985. pap. 10.95 (*0-7859-1588-5*, 204016099X) Fr & Eur.

— Iphigenia, Phaedra, Athaliah. Cairncross, John, tr. Incl. Athaliah. 1964. pap. Iphigenia. 1964. pap. (Classics Ser.). 320p. 1964. Set pap. 10.95 (*0-14-044122-0*, Penguin Classics) Viking Penguin.

— Iphigenie. (FRE., Illus.). 128p. 1985. pap. 10.95 (*0-7859-1264-9*, 2040160752) Fr & Eur.

— Jules Cesar. 40p. 1962. 12.50 (*0-686-54709-8*) Fr & Eur.

— Lettres d'Uzes. (FRE., Illus.). 118p. 1991. pap. 24.95 (*0-7859-1557-5*, 2869713746) Fr & Eur.

— Mithridate. (FRE., Illus.). 146p. 1992. pap. 10.95 (*0-7859-1255-X*, 2038701474) Fr & Eur.

— Oeuvres, 3 vols., Set. (FRE., Illus.). 450.00 (*0-686-54711-X*) Fr & Eur.

— Oeuvres, 8 vols., Set. (FRE.). cxliv, 616p. 1973. reprint ed. write for info. (*3-487-05000-5*) G Olms Pubs.

— Oeuvres Completes, Vol. 1. Picard, Jacques, ed. (FRE.). 1216p. 1951. lib. bdg. 100.00 (*0-7859-3781-1*, 2070104710) Fr & Eur.

— Oeuvres Completes, Vol. 2. deluxe ed. Ricard, Raymond, ed. (FRE.). 1168p. 1952. 105.00 (*0-7859-3782-X*, 2070104729) Fr & Eur.

***Racine, Jean.** Phaedra. Morgan, Edwin, tr. 128p. 2000. 18.95 (*1-85754-464-1*, Pub. by Carcanet Pr) Paul & Co Pubs.

Racine, Jean. Phaedra. Wilbur, Richard, tr. 1986. pap. 5.25 (*0-8222-0890-3*) Dramatists Play.

— Phaedra. (FRE., Illus.). 208p. 1990. pap. 10.95 (*0-685-73320-3*, 2038714088) Fr & Eur.

— Phaedra. Wilbur, Richard, tr. (Illus.). 132p. (C). 1987. pap. 10.00 (*0-15-675780-X*, Harvest Bks) Harcourt.

— Phaedra. Pucciani, Oreste F., ed. & tr. by. (Crofts Classics). 96p. 1959. pap. text 4.95 (*0-88295-069-X*) Harlan Davidson.

— Phaedra. Landes, William-Alan, ed. Boswell, Robert B., tr. LC 93-16950. 1993. pap. 7.00 (*0-88734-266-3*) Players Pr.

— Phaedra. Rawlings, Margaret, tr. (ENG & FRE.). 192p. 1992. pap. 11.95 (*0-14-044591-9*, Penguin Classics) Viking Penguin.

— Phaedra: One-Act Adaptation. (Illus.). 35p. 1966. pap. 3.25 (*0-88680-151-6*) I E Clark.

— Phaedra: One-Act Adaptation (Director's Script) (Illus.). 35p. 1966. pap. 10.00 (*0-88680-152-4*) I E Clark.

***Racine, Jean.** Phedre. Hughes, Ted, tr. from FRE. 96p. 2000. pap. 12.00 (*0-374-52616-8*) FS&G.

Racine, Jean. Phedre. (FRE.). (C). 1963. pap. 7.95 (*0-8442-1994-0*, VF1994-0) NTC Contemp Pub Co.

***Racine, Jean.** Phedre. 1999. pap. 7.95 (*1-85459-094-4*, Pub. by Theatre Comm) Consort Bk Sales.

Racine, Jean. Les Plaideurs. (FRE., Illus.). 128p. 1984. pap. 10.95 (*0-7859-1265-7*, 2040160779) Fr & Eur.

— Les Plaideurs. (FRE.). 1987. pap. 10.95 (*0-7859-3138-4*) Fr & Eur.

— Racine: Mithridate. Rudler, Gustave, ed. (Bristol French Texts Ser.). (FRE.). 150p. 1979. pap. 15.95 (*0-631-00440-8*) Blackwell Pubs.

— Racine's Phaedra. Mahon, Derek, tr. LC 96-132803. 66p. 1996. pap. 12.95 (*1-85235-165-9*) Dufour.

— Theatre Complet, 3 vols. (Illus.). 200.00 (*0-686-54715-2*) Fr & Eur.

— Theatre Complet, Tome 1. (Folio Ser.: No. 1412). (FRE.). pap. 15.95 (*2-07-037412-2*) Schoenhof.

— Theatre Complet, Tome 2. (Folio Ser.: No. 1495). (FRE.). pap. 15.95 (*2-07-037495-5*) Schoenhof.

— Theatre Complet, Vol. 1. (FRE.). 1982. pap. 19.95 (*0-7859-2901-0*) Fr & Eur.

— Theatre Complet: Avec Bajazet, Mithridate, Iphigenie, Phedre, Esther, Athalie, Vol. 2. Stegmann, Andre, ed. 378p. 1983. pap. 19.95 (*0-7859-2905-3*) Fr & Eur.

— Theatre Complet: Avec: La Thebaide, Alexandre le Grand, Andromaque, Les Plaideurs, Britannicus, Berenice, Vol. 1. Stegmann, Andre, ed. 436p. 5.95 (*0-686-54713-6*) Fr & Eur.

— Three Plays: Phaedra, Andromache, Britannicus. Dillon, George, tr. LC 61-15938. 199p. 1961. pap. text 11.95 (*0-226-15077-1*, P76) U Ch Pr.

Racine, Jean-Luc, ed. Peasant Moorings: Village Ties & Mobility Rationales in South India. LC 96-34882. 1996. 49.95 (*0-8039-9349-8*) Sage.

Racine, Jean-Luc, et al. Viramma. Hobson, Will, tr. LC 97-39447. (C). 1998. 65.00 (*1-85984-817-6*, Pub. by Verso) Norton.

— Viramma: Life of an Untouchable. Hobson, Will, tr. LC 97-39447. (Illus.). 312p. 1998. pap. 20.00 (*1-85984-148-1*, Pub. by Verso) Norton.

Racine, Karen, jt. ed. see Fey, Ingrid E.

Racine, Michel L. The Arithmetics of Quadratic Jordan Algebras. LC 73-17270. (Memoirs Ser.: No. 1/136). 125p. 1973. pap. 17.00 (*0-8218-1836-8*, MEMO/1/136) Am Math.

***Racine, Philip N.** Seeing Spartanburg: A History in Images. (Illus.). 376p. 1999. pap. 19.95 (*1-891885-10-3*) Hub City Writers.

Racine, Philip N., ed. Unspoiled Heart: The Journal of Charles Mattocks of the 17th Maine. LC 93-21274. (Voices of the Civil War Ser.). (Illus.). 480p. (C). 1994. 38.50 (*0-87049-834-7*) U of Tenn Pr.

Racine, Philip N., jt. ed. see Harwell, Richard B.

Racine, Robert, ed. see Carey, James.

Racine, Robert, ed. see Haines, Stephen G.

Racine, Robert, ed. see Karlson, David & Pettit, Jane.

Racine, Robert, ed. see Minor, Marianne.

Racine, Robert, ed. see Thornton, Virden.

Racine, Wade & Hatch, Robert. Vampire: The Dark Ages Storytellers Secrets. (Vampire Ser.). (Illus.). 128p. (Orig.). 1996. pap. 15.00 (*1-56504-277-8*, 2802) White Wolf.

Racinet. Full-Color Picture Sourcebook of Historic Ornament: All 120 Plates from "L'Ornement Polychrome;" Series II. (Illus.). 128p. pap. 17.95 (*0-486-26096-8*) Dover.

— Racinet's Historic Ornament in Full Color. (Illus.). 112p. pap. 17.95 (*0-486-25787-8*) Dover.

Racinet, Albert. The Historical Encyclopedia of Costumes. (Illus.). 320p. 1988. 45.00 (*0-8160-1976-2*) Facts on File.

Racinet, Auguste. Racinet's Full-Color Pictorial History of Western Costume: With 92 Plates Showing Over 950 Authentic Costumes from the Middle Ages to 1800. (Fine Arts Ser.). (Illus.). iv, 92p. (Orig.). 1987. reprint ed. pap. 16.95 (*0-486-25464-X*) Dover.

***Racino, Julie Ann.** Personnel Preparation in Disability & Community Life: Toward Universal Approaches to Support. LC 00-37737. 2000. pap. write for info. (*0-398-07078-4*) C C Thomas.

— Policy, Program Evaluation & Research in Disability: Community Support for All. LC 99-17248. 473p. 1999. 69.95 (*0-7890-0597-2*) Haworth Pr.

***Racino, Julie Ann.** Policy, Program Evaluation & Research in Disability: Community Support for All. LC 99-17248. 473p. 1999. pap. 39.95 (*0-7890-0598-0*) Haworth Pr.

RACIONERO, LUIS. La Carcel del Amor. 1998. pap. text 9.95 (*84-08-02241-5*) Planeta.

Racioppi, Linda. Soviet Policy Towards South Asia since 1970. (Cambridge Russian, Soviet & Post-Soviet Studies: No. 91). (Illus.). 249p. (C). 1994. text 69.95 (*0-521-41457-1*) Cambridge U Pr.

Racioppi, Linda & O'Sullivan See, Katherine. Women's Activism in Contemporary Russia. LC 96-36093. 264p. 1997. 59.95 (*1-56639-520-8*); pap. 22.95 (*1-56639-521-6*) Temple U Pr.

Racioppo, Lianne. A Winter's Knight. (Orig.). (YA). 1995. pap. 9.99 (*0-88092-289-3*) Royal Fireworks.

Racite, Joseph. The Perfect Marriage: Yes, One Really Does Exist! It's God's Divine Plan. 326p. (YA). 1999. pap. 19.95 (*1-892878-01-1*) You Deserve It.

***Raciti, Richard.** Taking It Literally. 58p. 2000. pap. 7.99 (*0-8059-4673-X*) Dorrance.

Rack, Henry D. Reasonable Enthusiast: John Wesley & the Rise of Methodism. LC 93-15360. 658p. (C). 1993. pap. text 29.95 (*0-687-35625-3*) Abingdon.

Rack, Lynette Ranni. Creative Serging for the Home & Other Quick Decorating Ideas. 1999. pap. text 19.95 (*0-935278-52-4*) Palmer-Pletsch.

Rack, Philip. Race, Culture, & Mental Disorder. 300p. 1982. 33.00 (*0-422-78160-6*, NO. 3801, Pub. by Tavistock) Routldge.

Rackauskas, A., jt. auth. see Paulauskas, V.

Rackauskas, Jonas, ed. Aleksandras Stulginskis: Reminiscences. LC 80-80852.Tr. of Aleksandras Stuiginski; Atsiminimai. (Illus.). 295p. 1980. 12.00 (*0-936694-41-6*) Lith Inst Educ.

Rackauskas, Jonas, jt. auth. see Peckus, Kestutis.

Racke, Kenneth D. & Coats, Joel R., eds. Enhanced Biodegradation of Pesticides in the Environment. LC 90-34194. (ACS Symposium Ser.: No. 426). (Illus.). 296p. 1990. text 75.00 (*0-8412-1784-X*, Pub. by Am Chemical) OUP.

Racke, Kenneth D. & Leslie, Anne R., eds. Pesticides in Urban Environments: Fate & Significance. LC 92-42060. (Symposium Ser.: Vol. 522). (Illus.). 385p. 1993. 94.95 (*0-8412-2627-X*) Am Chemical.

— Pesticides in Urban Environments: Fate & Significance. LC 92-42060. (ACS Symposium Ser.: Vol. 522). 392p. 1993. reprint ed. pap. 121.60 (*0-608-02980-7*, 205255600006) Bks Demand.

Racke, Reinhard, jt. auth. see Jiang, Song.

Racker, Efraim. Science & the Cure of Diseases: Letters to Members of Congress. LC 79-84012. 121p. reprint ed. pap. 34.50 (*0-8357-7014-1*, 2033403) Bks Demand.

Racker, Heinrich. Transference & Countertransference. 216p. 1968. 33.00 (*0-8236-6640-9*) Intl Univs Pr.

Rackerby, Frank & Whelan, James. Contributions to the Archaeology of Southern San Francisco Bay. fac. ed. (San Francisco State College, Anthropology Museum Occasional Papers: No. 3). (Illus.). 136p. 1967. reprint ed. pap. text 15.00 (*1-55567-576-X*) Coyote Press.

Rackerby, Frank, ed. see Pearson, Charles E., et al.

Rackham. From Sight to Insight. 4th ed. (C). 1991. pap. text, teacher ed. 34.00 (*0-03-052209-9*) Harcourt Coll Pubs.

— From Sight to Insight. 5th ed. LC 94-76681. (C). 1994. pap. text 38.50 (*0-15-501099-9*) Harcourt Coll Pubs.

— From Sight to Insight. 5th ed. (C). 1994. teacher ed. 33.75 (*0-15-501230-4*) Harcourt Coll Pubs.

— From Sight to Insight. 6th ed. (C). 1998. pap., teacher ed. write for info. (*0-15-508319-8*) Harcourt Coll Pubs.

— From Sight to Insight. 6th ed. LC 98-85616. (C). 1998. pap. 32.50 (*0-15-508318-X*, Pub. by Harcourt Coll Pubs) Harcourt.

— The Rinehart Reader, Vol. II. 2nd ed. (C). 1994. teacher ed. 33.75 (*0-15-501638-5*) Harcourt Coll Pubs.

Rackham, D. James, et al. Environment & Economy in Anglo-Saxon England: A Review of Recent Work on the Environmental Archaeology of Rural & Urban Anglo-Saxon Settlements in England : Proceedings of a Conference Held at the Museum of London, 9-10 April 1990. LC 95-109071. (ENG & FRE.). vi, 151 p. 1994. write for info. (*1-872414-33-8*) Council for British Archeology.

Rackham, Arthur. Mother Goose. (Children's Library). 176p. (J). 1998. pap. 3.95 (*1-85326-146-7*, 1467WW, Pub. by Wrdsworth Edits) NTC Contemp Pub Co.

Rackham, Arthur. The Fairy Tales of the Brothers Grimm. 176p. 1984. lib. bdg. 35.00 (*0-89835-247-9*) Abaris Bks.

— Mother Goose, the Old Nursery Rhymes. (J). (ps-6). 1978. reprint ed. lib. bdg. 13.00 (*0-932106-02-1*, Pub. by Marathon Press) S J Durst.

— Sleeping Beauty. 110p. (J). (gr. k-4). 1920. pap. 4.95 (*0-486-22756-1*) Dover.

Rackham, Arthur & Spero, James. Rackham's Color Illustrations for Wagner's Ring. LC 78-73985. 72p. 1979. pap. 11.95 (*0-486-23779-6*) Dover.

Rackham, H., tr. Athenian Constitution. (Loeb Classical Library: No. 285). 18.95 (*0-674-99315-2*) HUP.

— Natural History, 9. (Loeb Classical Library: No. 392-394, 418-419). 430p. 1952. text 18.95 (*0-674-99433-7*) HUP.

Rackham, H. & Hett, W. S., trs. Problems, Bks. 22-38. (Loeb Classical Library: No. 317). 15.50 (*0-674-99350-0*) HUP.

Rackham, H., tr. see Aristotle.

Rackham, James. Animal Bones. LC 93-45789. 1994. pap. 13.95 (*0-520-08833-6*, Pub. by U CA Pr) Cal Prin Full Svc.

Rackham, Jeff & Bertagnolli, Olivia. Windows: Exploring Human Values Through Reading & Writing. LC 92-11049. 748p. (C). 1997. pap. text 48.00 (*0-06-043808-8*) Addson-Wesley Educ.

Rackham, Jeff & Slaughter, Beverly J. The Rinehart Reader Vol. II, Vol. I. 2nd ed. LC 94-75161. (Illus.). 740p. (C). 1994. pap. text 39.00 (*0-15-501621-0*) Harcourt Coll Pubs.

Rackham, Jeff, jt. ed. see Bertagnolli, Olivia.

Rackham, Neil. Major Account Sales Strategy. 218p. 1989. 24.95 (*0-07-051114-4*) McGraw.

— Rethinking the Sales Force: Redefining Selling to Create & Capture Customer Value. LC 98-47875. 308p. 1999. 24.95 (*0-07-134253-2*) McGraw.

— SPIN Selling. (Illus.). 197p. 1988. 24.95 (*0-07-051113-6*) McGraw.

— The Spin Selling Fieldbook. (Illus.). 208p. 1996. pap. 18.95 (*0-07-052235-9*) McGraw.

Rackham, Neil & Ruff, Richard. Managing Major Sales: Practical Strategies for Improving Sales Effectiveness. 224p. 1991. 28.00 (*0-88730-508-3*, HarpBusn) HarpInfo.

Rackham, Neil, et al. Getting Partnering Right: How Market Leaders Are Creating Long-Term Competitive Advantage. LC 95-20680. (Illus.). 237p. 1995. 22.95 (*0-07-051782-7*) McGraw.

***Rackham, Oliver.** The Illustrated History of the Countryside. (Illus.). 2000. pap. 24.95 (*1-85799-953-3*) Phoenix Hse.

— The Illustrated History of the Countryside. (Illus.). 2000. pap. 24.95 (*1-84188-104-X*) Seven Dials.

Rackham, Oliver & Moody, Jennifer. The Making of the Cretan Landscape. LC 93-49016. 272p. 1997. text 79.95 (*0-7190-3646-1*); text 29.95 (*0-7190-3647-X*) Manchester Univ Pr.

Rackham, Oliver, jt. auth. see Grove, A. T.

Rackham, Peter. Jane's C41 Systems, 98-99. 1998. 350.00 (*0-7106-1793-3*) Janes Info Group.

— Jane's C4I Systems: Examine the World's Command Systems. 9th ed. (Illus.). 1997. 320.00 (*0-7106-1531-0*) Janes Info Group.

Rackham, T. W., ed. see Rukl, Antonin.

Rackin, Donald. Alice's Adventures in Wonderland & Through the Looking Glass: Nonsense, Sense & Meaning. LC 91-20134. (Twayne's Masterwork Studies: No. 81). 176p. 1991. 29.00 (*0-8057-9430-1*, Twyne) Mac Lib Ref.

Rackin, Phyllis. Stages of History: Shakespeare's English Chronicles. LC 90-55196. 264p. 1990. text 39.95 (*0-8014-2430-5*); pap. text 15.95 (*0-8014-9698-5*) Cornell U Pr.

Rackin, Phyllis & Howard, Jean. Engendering a Nation: A Feminist Account of Shakespeare's English Histories. LC 96-31661. (Feminist Readings of Shakespeare Ser.). 272p. (C). 1997. pap. 24.99 (*0-415-04749-8*) Routledge.

Rackin, Phyllis, jt. auth. see Howard, Jean.

Rackleff, Owen S. Escoffier: King of Chefs. (Illus.). 40p. (Orig.). 1983. pap. 6.95 (*0-88145-000-6*) Broadway Play.

Rackley, Geneva M. Words from the Heart. 35p. 1994. pap. 10.95 (*0-9642363-0-3*) Joan White.

— Words from the Heart. pap. 10.95 (*0-9623630-3-0*) Rainbow Nursery.

Rackley, Lurma, ed. see Caldwell, Earl.

Rackley, Lurma, ed. see Ferrell, Pamela.

Rackley, R. Robert. Accounting & Finance (For CPCU 8) rev. ed. (CPCU Ser.). 1999. 160.00 (*1-57195-125-3*) Insurance Achiev.

— Commercial Liability, Insurance & Risk Management (For CPCU 4) rev. ed. 1998. 160.00 (*1-57195-160-1*) Insurance Achiev.

***Rackley, R. Robert.** Commercial Property Insurance & Risk Management (For CPCU 3) rev. ed. (CPCU Ser.). 1999. 160.00 (*1-57195-191-1*) Insurance Achiev.

Rackley, R. Robert. Economics (For CPCU 9) 2nd rev. ed. (CPCU Ser.). 1997. 160.00 (*1-57195-123-7*) Insurance Achiev.

— Economics (For 322) 2nd rev. ed. (CLU Ser.). 1999. 160.00 (*1-57195-099-0*) Insurance Achiev.

***Rackley, R. Robert.** Essentials of Risk Control (For RM 55) rev. ed. 1999. 16.00 (*1-57195-183-0*) Insurance Achiev.

Rackley, R. Robert. Essentials of Risk Management (For RM 54) rev. ed. (ARM Ser.). 1998. 160.00 (*1-57195-161-X*) Insurance Achiev.

***Rackley, R. Robert.** Ethics, Insurance Perspectives & Insurance Contract Analysis (For CPCU 1) rev. ed. (CPCU Ser.). 1999. write for info. (*1-57195-185-7*) Insurance Achiev.

Rackley, R. Robert. Financial Planning Applications (For 332) rev. ed. 1998. 160.00 (*1-57195-152-0*) Insurance Achiev.

— Group Benefits (For 325) rev. ed. (CLU Ser.). 1998. 160.00 (*1-57195-151-2*) Insurance Achiev.

— Individual Life Insurance (For 323) rev. ed. (CLU Ser.). 1998. 160.00 (*1-57195-150-4*) Insurance Achiev.

— Insurance Operations (For CPCU 5) (CPCU Ser.). 1997. 160.00 (*1-57195-126-1*) Insurance Achiev.

— The Legal Environment of Insurance (For CPCU 6) rev. ed. (CPCU Ser.). 1998. 160.00 (*1-57195-167-9*) Insurance Achiev.

— Life Insurance Law (For 324) 2nd rev. ed. (CLU Ser.). 1999. 160.00 (*1-57195-102-4*) Insurance Achiev.

***Rackley, R. Robert.** Management (For CPCU 7) rev. ed. (CPCU Ser.). 1999. 160.00 (*1-57195-190-3*) Insurance Achiev.

— Personal Risk Management & Insurance (For CPCU 2) rev. ed. (CPCU Ser.). 1999. 160.00 (*1-57195-192-X*) Insurance Achiev.

Rackley, R. Robert. Wealth Accumulation Planning (For 329) 3rd rev. ed. (ChFC Ser.). 1997. 160.00 (*1-57195-116-4*) Insurance Achiev.

Rackliffe, G., jt. auth. see Willis, H. Lee.

***Rackliffe, Karen S.** Wild Days: Creating Discovery Journals. (Illus.). 128p. 1999. pap. text 9.95 (*1-57636-073-3*) SunRise Pbl.

Rackman, Arthur, et al. Rackman's Fairy Tales Coloring Book. (Illus.). (J). (gr. k-3). 1980. pap. 3.50 (*0-486-23844-X*) Dover.

Rackman, Emanuel. Modern Halakhah for Our Time. LC 93-35397. 1993. 29.50 (*0-88125-295-6*) Ktav.

Rackstraw, Anthony J., tr. see Henke, Hans.

Rackwitz, R., et al, eds. Reliability & Optimization of Structural Systems: Proceedings of the Fourth IFIP WG 7.5 Conference, Munich, Germany, September 11-13, 1991. LC 92-16815. (Lecture Notes in Engineering Ser.: Vol. 76). (Illus.). vii, 485p. 1992. 137.95 (*0-387-55403-3*) Spr-Verlag.

Racosky, Rico. Dreams+Action=Reality: A Step-by-Step Guide to Lifelong Success for Youth. LC 97-157333. (Illus.). 148p. (J). (gr. 1-7). 1996. pap. 14.95 (*0-945445-97-0*) ActionGraphics Intl.

Racster, Olga. Chats on Violoncellos. (Illus.). 227p. 1988. reprint ed. pap. 25.00 (*0-87556-363-5*) Saifer.

— The Master of the Russian Ballet: The Memoirs of Cav. Enrico Cecchetti. LC 78-18777. (Series in Dance). (Illus.). 1978. reprint ed. lib. bdg. 35.00 (*0-306-77589-1*) Da Capo.

Racusen, Lorraine C., jt. ed. see Solez, Kim.

Racuya-Robbins, Ann. Collated Narrative: An Emerging Sense of the World. (Sesquin Frontier Ser.). (Illus.). 350p. (Orig.). 1999. pap. 16.95 (*1-884434-09-6*) Images For Media.

— InEvolution of Grace: A Way to the Pond. (Sesquin Americas Ser.). (Illus.). 250p. 2000. pap. write for info. (*1-884434-08-8*) Images For Media.

Racuya-Robbins, Ann, ed. see Berne, Stanley, et al.

Racy, John C., jt. auth. see Chaleby, Kutaiba S.

Racz, Attila J. Courts & Tribunals: A Comparative Study. 246p. (C). 1980. 75.00 (*963-05-1799-X*, Pub. by Akade Kiado) St Mut.

— Problems of Constitutional Development: Essays in Memory of Professor Istvan Kovacs. (FRE & GER.). 225p. 1993. pap. 90.00 (*963-05-6543-9*, Pub. by Akade Kiado) St Mut.

Racz, Attila J., et al. Quantitative Analyses of Law: A Comparative Empirical Study. (Sources of Law in Eastern & Western Europe Ser.). (Illus.). 404p. (C). 1990. 120.00 (*963-05-5673-1*, Pub. by Akade Kiado) St Mut.

Racz, Attila J., jt. ed. see Porter, James.

Racz, Barnabas, jt. ed. see Bukowski, Charles J.

Racz, Endre. Pannonhalma. (Illus.). 95p. (C). 1989. 80.00 (*0-7855-5210-3*, Pub. by Collets) St Mut.

— Pannonhalma. (Illus.). 96p. 1999. 21.00 (*963-13-2868-6*, Pub. by Corvina Bks) St Mut.

Racz, G. J., tr. see Galdos, Benito Perez.

Racz, I., jt. auth. see Daroczy, J.

Racz, Istvan. Drug Formulation. 416p. (C). 1989. 150.00 (*963-05-4676-0*, Pub. by Akade Kiado) St Mut.

Racz, Justin. J. Crewd: A Parody. LC 98-4160. (Illus.). 64p. 1998. pap. 11.95 (*0-385-49280-4*) Bantam.

Racz, P., et al, eds. Accessory Cells in HIV & Other Retroviral Infections. (Illus.). viii, 212p. 1991. 172.25 (*3-8055-5323-4*) S Karger.

— Animal Models of HIV & Other Retroviral Infections. (Illus.). viii, 200p. 1993. 172.25 (*3-8055-5677-2*) S Karger.

— Cytotoxic T Cells in HIV & Other Retroviral Infections. (Illus.). 178p. 1992. 167.00 (*3-8055-5469-9*) S Karger.

Racz, Twyla & Tammany, Rosina, eds. Management & Organization of the Acquisitions Department. LC 94-28265. (Acquisitions Librarian Ser.). (Illus.). 131p. 1994. lib. bdg. 39.95 (*1-56024-583-2*) Haworth Pr.

Raczek, Linda T. The Night the Grandfathers Danced. (Illus.). 32p. (J). (gr. k-3). 1998. pap. 7.95 (*0-87358-720-0*, Rising Moon Bks) Northland AZ.

***Raczek, Linda T. & Hook, Richard.** Stories from Native North America. LC 99-48317. (Multicultural Stories Ser.). 2000. 7.95 (*0-7398-2033-8*) Raintree Steck-V.

Raczek, Linda Theresa. Rainy's Powwow. LC 98-46830. (Illus.). 32p. 1999. 15.95 (*0-87358-686-7*, Rising Moon Bks) Northland AZ.

***Raczek, Linda Theresa.** Stories from Native North America. (Multicultural Stories Ser.). 48p. (J). 2000. lib. bdg. 25.69 (*0-7398-1336-6*) Raintree Steck-V.

Raczka, R., jt. auth. see Barut, Asim O.

Raczka, R., jt. ed. see Maurin, Krzysztof.

Raczka, R., jt. ed. see Pawlowski, M.

Raczkowski, George. Principles of Machine Dynamics. fac. ed. LC 78-72995. (Illus.). 111p. pap. 34.50 (*0-7837-7413-3*, 204720800006) Bks Demand.

Raczymow, Henri. Writing the Book of Esther. Katz, Dori, tr. from FRE. (French Expressions Ser.). 220p. 1995. 24.00 (*0-8419-1335-8*) Holmes & Meier.

Raczynski, Dagmar. Strategies to Combat Poverty in Latin America. LC 95-76280. 225p. (Orig.). 1995. pap. text 18.50 (*0-940602-95-4*) IADB.

Raczynski, Dagmar, ed. Estrategias para Combatir la Pobreza en America Latina: Programas, Instituciones y Recursos. 274p. 1995. 18.50 (*956-204-030-5*, Pub. by CIEPLAN) IADB.

***Raczynski, James M. & DiClemente, Ralph J., eds.** Handbook of Health Promotion & Disease Prevention. LC 99-37316. (Behavioral Psychophysiology & Medicine Ser.). 669p. 1999. 125.00 (*0-306-46140-4*, Kluwer Plenum) Kluwer Academic.

Rad-Grunwald, Stefan Von, see Wilhoyte, Rebecca.

Rad, Philip. E. J. Dent: A Centenary Memoir. 30p. 1976. pap. 5.85 (*0-902070-18-5*) Theodore.

Rad, U. Von, see Von Rad, U.

Rad, U. Von, jt. ed. see Stackelberg, U. Von.

Rada, Alejandro, jt. auth. see Allen, George.

Rada, Georgene. Rada's Guide to Health & Fitness Getaways in the Southwest. LC 91-60053. 192p. (Orig.). 1991. pap. 12.95 (*0-9628203-0-X*) Rada Pubns.

Rada, Jamis. Frida Hahlo. 1997. pap. text 23.98 (*968-13-1743-2*) Libros Fronteras.

***Rada Manufacturing Company Staff.** Desserts. 192p. 1998. 5.95 (*1-56383-079-5*, 8000, Pub. by G & R Pub) CQ Products.

— Holiday Favorites. 192p. 1999. spiral bd. 5.95 (*1-56383-088-4*, 8400, Pub. by G & R Pub) CQ Products.

— Household Hints: Tips to Remedy This or That in the Household. (Illus.). 192p. 1998. spiral bd. 5.95 (*1-56383-081-7*, 8200) G & R Pub.

Rada, R. & Tochtermann, K., eds. Expertmedia, Expert Systems & Hypermedia. LC 95-37188. 200p. 1995. text 54.00 (*981-02-2328-5*) World Scientific Pub.

Rada, Roy. Developing Educational Hypermedia: Coordination & Reuse. (Tutorial Monographs in Artificial Intelligence). 189p. 1995. pap. 39.50 (*1-56750-216-4*); text 73.25 (*1-56750-215-6*) Ablx Pub.

— Interactive Media. LC 95-3759. (Illus.). 256p. 1995. 36.95 (*0-387-94485-0*) Spr-Verlag.

***Rada, Roy.** Re-Engineering Software: How to Re-Use Programming to Build New, State-of-the-Art Software. 300p. 1999. 67.50 (*1-57958-183-8*) Fitzroy Dearborn.

Rada, Roy. Reengineering Software: How to Reuse Programming to Build New, State-of-the-Art Software. 296p. 1999. 55.00 (*0-8144-0509-6*) AMACOM.

***Rada, Roy.** Reengineering Software: How to Reuse Programming to Build New, State-of-the-Art Software. 296p. 2000. 55.00 (*1-888998-61-X*, 98-61-X) Glenlake Pub.

Rada, Roy. Software Reuse. 167p. 1995. 73.25 (*1-56750-188-5*) Ablx Pub.

— Software Reuse. 224p. 1994. pap. text 29.95 (*1-871516-53-6*, Pub. by Intellect) Cromland.

Rada, Roy, jt. auth. see Forsyth, Richard.

Rada, Staefan E., jt. auth. see Harrison, Babs S.

Radabaugh, Arlene, ed. see Radabaugh, Marjorie.

Radabaugh, Joseph. Heaven's Flame: A Guide to Solar Cookers. 2nd rev. ed. Root, Benjamin M., ed. & illus. by. 160p. (YA). (gr. 8-12). 1998. pap. 10.00 (*0-9629588-2-4*) Home Power.

***Radabaugh, Marjorie.** The Farmers Wife. Radabaugh, Arlene, ed. (Illus.). 120p. 1999. pap. write for info. (*1-57579-169-2*, Pub. by Pine Hill Pr) Penmarch Pub.

***Radacsi, Geri.** Ancient Music. 44p. 2000. pap. (*1-877603-67-8*) Pecan Grove.

Radaelli, Claudio Maria. The Politics of Corporate Taxation in the European Union: Knowledge & International Policy Agendas. LC 97-9647. 272p. (C). 1997. 85.00 (*0-415-14999-1*) Routledge.

— Technocracy in the European Union. LC 98-54459. 1999. pap. text 21.95 (*0-582-30493-8*) Addison-Wesley.

Radaj & Sonino. Fatigue Strength Assessment of Welded Structures Using Local Approaches. 1998. boxed set 243.00 (*1-85573-403-6*, Pub. by Woodhead Pubng) Am Educ Systs.

Radaj, D. & Sonsino, C. M., eds. Fatigue Assessment of Welded Joints by Local Approaches. 456p. 1999. 225.00 (*1-884207-79-0*) William Andrew.

Radaj, Dieter. Design & Analysis of Fatigue Resistant Welded Structures. (Illus.). 378p. 1990. boxed set 170.00 (*1-85573-004-9*, Pub. by Woodhead Pubng) Am Educ Systs.

— Heat Effects of Welding: Temperature Field, Residual Stress & Distortion. (Illus.). 344p. 1992. 126.95 (*0-387-54820-3*) Spr-Verlag.

Radak, Zsolt. Free Radicals in Exercise & Aging. Date not set. write for info. (*0-88011-881-4*) Human Kinetics.

Radakovich, Anka. The Wild Girls Club: Tales from below the Belt. 240p. 1995. pap. 10.00 (*0-449-90985-9*) Fawcett.

Radall, Joyce S. Understanding Electricity. LC 98-224437. 96p. 1998. 12.50 (*0-89606-346-1*, 303) Am Assn Voc Materials.

Radan, G. T., jt. ed. see Lengyel, A.

Radan, George T. The Sons of Zebulon: Jewish Maritime History. LC 78-54621. 85p. (Orig.). (C). 1978. pap. 9.95 (*0-935982-24-8*, GTR-01) Spertus Coll.

Radan, Peter & Pavkovic, Aleksandar, eds. The Serbs & Their Leaders in the Twentieth Century. LC 97-16726. 272p. 1997. text 72.95 (*1-85521-891-7*, Pub. by Ashgate Pub) Ashgate Pub Co.

***Radano, Ronald M.** Lying up a Nation. 1998. pap. text 13.95 (*0-226-70198-0*); lib. bdg. 39.95 (*0-226-70197-2*) U Ch Pr.

— Music & Racial Imagination. 1999. lib. bdg. 70.00 (*0-226-70199-9*) U Ch Pr.

Radano, Ronald M. New Musical Figurations: Anthony Braxton's Cultural Critique. LC 93-1878. (Illus.). 336p. 1993. pap. 16.95 (*0-226-70196-4*); lib. bdg. 55.00 (*0-226-70195-6*) U Ch Pr.

***Radano, Ronald M. & Bohlman, Philip V.** Music & the Racial Imagination. LC 00-23672. 1999. pap. text 32.00 (*0-226-70200-6*) U Ch Pr.

Radanovich, Sophie. Sophie's Memoirs. (Illus.). 44p. (Orig.). 1996. pap. 5.95 (*0-9652906-1-1*) Blazin Bks.

Radant, Chris. Home for the Holidays. LC 96-162939. 1995. pap., mass mkt. 5.99 (*0-671-56866-3*, PB Trade Paper) PB.

Radashkevich, Aleksandr. Shpalera. LC 84-60082. (Russica Poetry Ser.: No. 5). (RUS.). 90p. (Orig.). 1986. pap. 8.95 (*0-89830-073-8*) Russica Pubs.

Radau, Hugo. Ninib, the Determiner of Fates. (Publications of the Babylonian Section: Series D, Vol. V/2). (Illus.). x, 73p. 1910. pap. 10.00 (*0-686-11919-3*) U Museum Pubns.

Radauskas, Henrikas. Chimeras in the Tower: Selected Poems of Henrikas Radauskas. LC 84-20984. (Wesleyan Poetry in Translation Ser.): 72p. reprint ed. pap. 30.00 (*0-7837-0219-1*, 204052700017) Bks Demand.

Radautsan, Sergei, ed. Scientific & Technological Achievements Related to the Development of European Cities: Proceedings of the NATO Advanced Research Workshop Held in Kishinev, Republic of Moldova, May 22-24, 1996. LC 96-49531. (NATO ASI Series Partnership Sub-Series 4: Vol. 9). 352p. (C). 1996. lib. bdg. 209.50 (*0-7923-4340-9*) Kluwer Academic.

Radavich, David. By the Way: Poems over the Years. LC 97-72801. 104p. 1998. 20.00 (*0-9658045-1-8*); pap. 12.00 (*0-9658045-0-X*) Buttonwood Press.

Raday, Frances. Adjudication of Interest Disputes: The Compulsory Arbitration Model. 217p. 1986. pap. 25.00 (*1-57588-225-6*, 304430) W S Hein.

Radberg, Manfred W. & Rijal, Minendra P. Location, Scheduling, Design & Integer Programming. (International Series in Operations Research & Management Science: Vol. 3). 232p. (C). 1996. lib. bdg. 115.00 (*0-7923-9715-0*) Kluwer Academic.

Radbertus, Paschasius. Charlemagne's Cousins: Contemporary Lives of Adalard & Wala. Cabaniss, Allen, tr. & intro. by. LC 67-26919. 233p. 1967. reprint ed. pap. 72.30 (*0-608-07601-5*, 205991600010) Bks Demand.

Radbourne, Jennifer & Fraser, Margaret. Arts Management: A Practical Guide. LC 97-206884. 296p. 1997. pap. 39.95 (*1-86448-048-3*, Pub. by Allen & Unwin Pty) Paul & Co Pubs.

***Radbruch, A.** Flow Cytometry & Cell Storing. 2nd ed. LC 99-40869. (Lab Manual Ser.). 300p. 1999. ring bd., lab manual ed. 89.95 (*3-540-65630-8*) Spr-Verlag.

Radbruch, A., ed. Flow Cytometry & Cell Sorting. (Illus.). 208p. 1996. 79.95 (*0-387-55594-3*) Spr-Verlag.

Radbruch, A., jt. auth. see Recktenwald, Diether.

Radbruch, Don. Roaring Roadsters: Track Roadsters from 1924-1956. (Illus.). 200p. 1994. pap. 22.95 (*1-884089-06-2*) CarTech.

Radbruch, Gustav & Klenner, Herman. Literatur- Und Kunsthistorische Schriften. LC 98-166620. x, 454 p. 1997. write for info. (*3-8114-2896-9*) C F Mueller.

Radcliff, jt. auth. see Pevsner, Nikolaus.

Radcliff, Amy, jt. auth. see Radcliff, Benjamin.

Radcliff, Anthony, et al. The Pharmer's Almanac II. rev. ed. (Illus.). 1993. pap. 12.95 (*0-910223-19-X*) MAC Pub.

Radcliff, Benjamin & Radcliff, Amy. Understanding Zen. LC 92-42624. 192p. (Orig.). 1993. pap. 14.95 (*0-8048-1808-8*) Tuttle Pubng.

Radcliff, David. Does God Fight? Violence in the Bible. (Generation Why: Vol. 2:1). 44p. (YA). (gr. 9-12). 1996. pap. 14.95 (*0-87303-265-9*) Faith & Life.

Radcliff, Jennifer L., ed. Heritage: A Pictorial History of Independence Township & the Village of Clarkston. (Illus.). 100p. 1989. 15.00 (*0-685-24269-2*) Clarkston CHS.

— In Remembrance. (Illus.). 150p. 1989. 25.00 (*0-685-29045-X*) White Lk Twnship.

Radcliff, Joni R., tr. see Pena, Jose A.

Radcliff, Pamela B. From Mobilization to Civil War: The Politics of Polarization in the Spanish City of Gijon, 1900-1937. 372p. (C). 1997. text 59.95 (*0-521-56213-9*) Cambridge U Pr.

Radcliff, Pamela B., jt. ed. see Enders, Victoria L.

Radcliff, R. Bruce. Small Engines. LC 96-45663. 1997. 47.96 (*0-8269-0008-9*) Am Technical.

Radcliff-Umstead, Douglas. Birth of Modern Comedy in Renaissance Italy. LC 69-16904. 295p. reprint ed. 91.50 (*0-8357-9642-6*, 201698500005) Bks Demand.

— The Exile into Eternity: A Study of the Narrative Writings of Giorgio Bassani. LC 86-45739. 176p. 1987. 29.50 (*0-8386-3296-3*) Fairleigh Dickinson.

— Wait for Me, Little Girl! 165p. 1989. 25.00 (*0-9624254-0-0*) DeSoto Pr Inc.

Radcliff-Umstead, Douglas, jt. auth. see Rossi, Patrizio.

Radcliff-Unstead, Douglas. The Mirror of Our Anguish: A Study of Luigi Pirandello's Narrative Works. 329p. 1978. 39.50 (*0-8386-1930-4*) Fairleigh Dickinson.

Radcliff, William. Sherman Minton: Hoosier Justice. LC 96-75160. 300p. 1996. 29.95 (*1-878208-81-0*) Guild Pr IN.

Radcliffe. On Hume. (Philosophy Ser.). 1999. pap. text 13.95 (*0-534-57605-2*) Brooks-Cole.

Radcliffe, ed. Investments. 3rd ed. (C). 1990. pap. text, student ed. 25.00 (*0-673-46207-2*) Addson-Wesley Educ.

Radcliffe, Alexander. Works of Captain Alexander Radcliffe. LC 81-9003. 304p. 1981. reprint ed. 50.00 (*0-8201-1365-4*) Schol Facsimiles.

Radcliffe, Ann. Castles of Athlin & Dunbayne: A Highland Story. LC 78-131336. (Gothic Novels Ser.). 1974. reprint ed. 51.95 (*0-405-00808-2*) Ayer.

— The Female Advocate. 173p. reprint ed. lib. bdg. 32.37 (*3-487-06724-2*) G Olms Pubs.

— Gaston de Blondeville. Keeping Festival in Ardenne. St. Alban's Abbey: With Some Poetical Pieces, 4 vols. in 2, Set. (Anglistica & Americana Ser.: No. 160). 1976. reprint ed. 174.20 (*3-487-05903-7*) G Olms Pubs.

— Gaston De Blondeville, Or, the Court of Henry 3rd, Keeping Festival in Ardenne, 2 vols., Set. LC 71-131337. (Gothic Novels Ser.). 1979. reprint ed. 53.95 (*0-405-00815-5*) Ayer.

— The Italian. lib. bdg. 28.95 (*0-8488-2022-3*) Amereon Ltd.

— The Italian. 2nd ed. Garber, Frederick, ed. LC 99-186629. 464p. 1998. pap. 9.95 (*0-19-283254-9*) OUP.

— A Journey Made in the Summer of 1794 Through Holland & the Western Frontier of Germany. (Anglistica & Americana Ser.: No. 121). 507p. 1975. reprint ed. 115.70 (*3-487-05753-0*) G Olms Pubs.

— The Mysteries of Udolpho. 2nd ed. Dobree, Bonamy, ed. (Oxford World's Classics Ser.). 736p. 1998. pap. 11.95 (*0-19-282523-2*) OUP.

— The Poetical Works of Ann Radcliffe, 2 vols. LC 70-37714. reprint ed. 85.00 (*0-404-56805-X*) AMS Pr.

— The Romance of the Forest. lib. bdg. 27.95 (*0-8488-2023-1*) Amereon Ltd.

— The Romance of the Forest. (Oxford World's Classics Ser.). 429p. 1999. pap. 9.95 (*0-19-283713-3*) OUP.

— The Romance of the Forest: Interspersed with Some Pieces of Poetry, 3 Vols. LC 73-22770. 794p. 1979. reprint ed. 94.95 (*0-405-06020-3*) Ayer.

— A Sicilian Romance. Milbank, Alison, ed. (Oxford World's Classics Ser.). 256p. 1999. pap. 9.95 (*0-19-283666-8*) OUP.

— A Sicilian Romance. LC 75-131338. (Gothic Novels Ser.). 1972. reprint ed. 46.95 (*0-405-00809-0*) Ayer.

— A Sicilian Romance, 1792, 2 vols. in 1. LC 94-29214. (Revolution & Romanticism Ser.). 498p. 1995. 65.00 (*1-85477-190-6*) Continuum.

Radcliffe, Anthony. Bronzes 1500-1650: The Robert H. Smith Collection. (Illus.). 160p. 1994. 50.00 (*0-302-00636-2*, Pub. by P Wilson) Hoovers TX.

Radcliffe, Anthony, et al. Renaissance & Later Sculpture: The Thyssen-Bornemisza Collection. (Illus.). 400p. 1992. 250.00 (*0-85667-401-X*) Sothebys Pubns.

Radcliffe-Brown, A. R. On the Concept of Function in Social Science. (Reprint Series in Sociology). (C). 1993. reprint ed. pap. text 5.00 (*0-8290-3815-9*, S-227) Irvington.

Radcliffe-Brown, A. R. & Forde, Daryll, eds. African Systems of Kinship & Marriage. (Illus.). 400p. 1994. pap. text 25.50 (*0-7103-0234-7*, 02347) Routledge.

Radcliffe-Brown, Alfred R. Structure & Function in Primitive Society. 1965. pap. 17.95 (*0-02-925620-8*) Free Pr.

Radcliffe, C. J., et al, eds. Active Control of Noise & Vibration - 1992. (DSC Ser.: Vol. 38). 372p. 1992. 65.00 (*0-7918-2093-9*, G00737) ASME.

Radcliffe College Editors. Catalog of the Arthur & Elizabeth Schlesinger Library on the History of Women in America: The Manuscript Inventories & the Catalogs of Manuscripts, Books, & Periodicals, 10 vols. 2nd ed. 7500p. 1983. 2620.00 (*0-8161-0425-5*, G K Hall & Co) Mac Lib Ref.

Radcliffe, David H. Edmund Spenser: A Reception History. (LCENG Ser.). xiv, 239p. (C). 1996. 65.00 (*1-57113-073-X*) Camden Hse.

— Forms of Reflection: Genre & Culture in Meditational Writing. LC 92-31654. 248p. 1993. text 38.50 (*0-8018-4500-9*) Johns Hopkins.

Radcliffe, Donnie. Hillary Rodham Clinton: A First Lady for Our Time. 272p. 1994. mass mkt. 5.50 (*0-446-60063-6*, Pub. by Warner Bks) Little.

***Radcliffe, Donnie.** Hillary Rodham Clinton: A First Lady for Our Time, 1 vol. 352p. 1999. mass mkt. 14.00 (*0-446-67594-6*, Pub. by Warner Bks) Little.

Radcliffe, Donnie. Simply Barbara Bush: A Portrait of America's Candid First Lady. 256p. 1990. mass mkt. 4.95 (*0-446-36024-4*, Pub. by Warner Bks) Little.

***Radcliffe, Doug.** FreeSpace 2 Official Strategies & Secrets. 256p. 1999. pap. 19.99 (*0-7821-2672-3*) Sybex.

***Radcliffe, Doug, et al.** Star Trek: Star Fleet Command Official Strategies & Secrets. 304p. 1999. 19.99 (*0-7821-2601-4*) Sybex.

Radcliffe, Doug, jt. auth. see Jensen, Chris.

Radcliffe, Duane & Ross, Marcus. The Precepts & Doctrines of Men. LC 97-91301. 1998. pap. 18.95 (*0-533-12622-3*) Vantage.

Radcliffe, Elizabeth S. & White, Carol J., eds. Faith in Theory & Practice: Essays on the Justification of Religious Belief. LC 93-33067. 254p. 1993. 34.95 (*0-8126-9246-2*); pap. 18.95 (*0-8126-9247-0*) Open Court.

Radcliffe, Elsa J. Gothic Novels of the Twentieth Century: An Annotated Bibliography. LC 78-24357. 291p. 1979. lib. bdg. 35.00 (*0-8108-1190-1*) Scarecrow.

Radcliffe, Graham. Cosmic Messenger. 160p. (C). 1990. 90.00 (*0-86439-140-4*, Pub. by Boolarong Pubns) St Mut.

Radcliffe, James. The Reorganisation of British Central Government. 236p. 1991. text 61.95 (*1-85521-176-9*, Pub. by Dartmth Pub) Ashgate Pub Co.

***Radcliffe, James & Campling, Jo.** Green Politics: Dictatorship or Democracy? LC 99-53562. 2000. text 65.00 (*0-312-23138-5*) St Martin.

Radcliffe, James C. & Farentinos, Robert C. High-Powered Plyometrics. LC 99-52761. (Illus.). 184p. 1999. pap. 19.95 (*0-88011-784-2*, PRAD0784) Human Kinetics.

Radcliffe, Jane. Lima Rooftops. 1978. 7.25 (*0-941490-09-2*) Solo Pr.

Radcliffe, Joel, ed. see Walker, John H.

***Radcliffe, Loralyn.** Big & Easy Patterns: Holidays & Seasons. Guckian, Mary Ellen, ed. (Illus.). 224p. 1999. pap., teacher ed. 16.95 (*1-57690-602-7*, TCM2602) Tchr Create Mat.

— Big & Easy Patterns: Themes. Guckian, Mary Ellen, ed. (Illus.). 224p. 1999. pap., teacher ed. 16.95 (*1-57690-592-6*, TCM2592) Tchr Create Mat.

Radcliffe, Loralyn. Creative Crafts for Clever Kids. LC 95-62417. 1997. pap. text 12.95 (*1-55734-678-X*) Tchr Create Mat.

***Radcliffe, Loralyn.** Hooray for the U. S. A.! Creative Kids. LC 98-61565. (Illus.). 160p. 1999. pap., teacher ed. 14.95 (*1-57690-361-3*, TCM2361) Tchr Create Mat.

Radcliffe, Mark F., jt. auth. see Brinson, J. Dianne.

Radcliffe, Mary A. The Female Advocate. LC 93-46509. (Revolution & Romanticism, 1789-1834 Ser.). 1994. reprint ed. 48.00 (*1-85477-172-8*) Continuum.

Radcliffe, Mary-Anne. Manfrone: or The One-Handed Monk, 2 vols., Set. LC 79-131339. (Gothic Novels Ser.). 1979. reprint ed. 53.95 (*0-405-00818-X*) Ayer.

Radcliffe, Nicholas J., jt. auth. see Clayton, Anthony M.

Radcliffe, Rebecca R. About to Burst: Handling Stress & Ending Violence--A Message for Youth. LC 98-93934. (Illus.). 208p. (YA). (gr. 7-12). 1999. pap. 15.00 (*0-9636607-4-8*) EASE.

***Radcliffe, Rebecca R.** Body Prayers: Finding Body Peace--A Journey of Self Acceptance. LC 98-94897. 152p. 1999. pap. 15.00 (*0-9636607-2-1*) EASE.

Radcliffe, Robert C. Investments. 4th ed. 826p. (C). 1994. text 66.87 (*0-673-46657-4*) Addson-Wesley Educ.

— Investments Concepts. 256p. (C). 1997. pap. text, student ed. 24.40 (*0-673-46697-3*) Addson-Wesley Educ.

Radcliffe, Robert J. Effective Ministry As an Associate Pastor: Making Beautiful Music As a Ministry Team. LC 98-25984. 208p. 1998. pap. 11.99 (*0-8254-3629-X*) Kregel.

***Radcliffe, Robert J.** Spiritual Fitness: A Guide to Shaping Up. LC 99-69438. 2000. 25.00 (*0-7388-1272-2*); pap. 18.00 (*0-7388-1273-0*) Xlibris Corp.

Radcliffe-Rogers, B. Adventure Guide to Canada's Atlantic Provinces. (Adventure Guides Ser.). 672p. 1999. pap. text 19.95 (*1-55650-819-0*) Hunter NJ.

Radcliffe-Rogers, Barbara, ed. see Shaw, Lisa.

Radcliffe, Samuel J., jt. auth. see Sedjo, Roger A.

An Asterisk (*) at the beginning of an entry indicates that the title is appearing for the first time.

Radcliffe, Sarah & Westwood, Sallie. Remaking the Nation: Identity & Politics in Latin America. LC 95-26840. (Illus.). 216p. (C). 1996. 85.00 (*0-415-12336-4*); pap. 24.99 (*0-415-12337-2*) Routledge.

Radcliffe, Sarah A. & Westwood, Sallie. Viva: Women & Popular Protest in Latin America. LC 92-20274. (International Studies of Women & Places). 240p. (C). 1993. pap. 25.99 (*0-415-07313-8*, A7383) Routledge.

Radcliffe, Sarah C. Aizer Knegdo: Jewish Woman's Guide to Happiness in Marriage. 254p. 1989. 19.95 (*0-944070-08-6*) Targum Pr.

— Smooth Sailing: Navigating Life's Challenges. (Illus.). 191p. 1994. 18.95 (*1-56871-039-9*, Pub. by Targum Pr) Feldheim.

Radcliffe-Smith, A. Three-Language List of Botanical Name Components. (Illus.). 143p. 1998. pap. 20.00 (*1-900347-50-4*, Pub. by Royal Botnic Grdns) Balogh.

Radcliffe, Stanley, tr. see Fontane, Theodor.

Radcliffe, Theresa. Bashi Elephant Baby. LC 98-124556. 32p. (J). (ps-2). 1998. 15.99 (*0-670-87054-4*) Viking Penguin.

— Cirmu Seal. 32p. 1999. pap. 4.99 (*0-14-055699-0*) Viking Penguin.

***Radcliffe, Theresa.** Maya, Tiger Cub. 32p. (J). 1999. 14.99 (*0-670-87894-4*, Viking Child) Peng Put Young Read.

***Radcliffe, Timothy.** Sing a New Song: The Christian Vocation. unabridged ed. LC 99-75717. (Illus.). 302p. 1999. pap. 15.95 (*0-87243-247-5*) Templegate.

Radcliffe, Walter. Milestones in Midwifery & the Secret Instrument: The Birth of the Midwifery Forceps. (Illus.). 193p. 1989. reprint ed. 75.00 (*0-930405-20-X*) Norman SF.

Radcure '84 (Atlanta, Ga.) Staff. RADCURE '84: Conference Proceedings, September 10-13, 1984, Atlanta, GA. LC 84-51496. (Illus.). 681p. reprint ed. pap. 200.00 (*0-8357-6500-8*, 203587100097) Bks Demand.

Radd, Tommie R. The Children's Affect Needs Assessment. 2nd rev. ed. (Grow with Guidance System Ser.). 1996. write for info. (*1-878317-42-3*) Grow With Guidance.

— The FUN Game (Future U Now) (Grow with Guidance System Ser.). 1996. write for info. (*1-878317-32-6*) Grow With Guidance.

***Radd, Tommie R.** Getting from Here to There... Education for the New Millenium. (Illus.). (C). 2000. pap. write for info. (*1-878317-44-X*) Grow With Guidance.

Radd, Tommie R. The Grow with Guidance System. (Grow with Guidance System Ser.). 1996. text. write for info. (*1-878317-34-2*); disk. write for info. (*1-878317-26-1*) Grow With Guidance.

— The Grow with Guidance System, Level 1. 2nd rev. ed. 1996. text. write for info. (*1-878317-35-0*) Grow With Guidance.

— The Grow with Guidance System, Level 2. 2nd rev. ed. 1996. text. write for info. (*1-878317-36-9*) Grow With Guidance.

— The Grow with Guidance System, Level 3. 2nd rev. ed. 1996. text. write for info. (*1-878317-37-7*) Grow With Guidance.

— The Grow with Guidance System, Level 4. 2nd rev. ed. 1996. text. write for info. (*1-878317-38-5*) Grow With Guidance.

— The Grow with Guidance System, Level 5. 2nd rev. ed. 1996. text. write for info. (*1-878317-39-3*) Grow With Guidance.

— The Grow with Guidance System, Level 6. 2nd rev. ed. 1996. text. write for info. (*1-878317-40-7*) Grow With Guidance.

— The Grow with Guidance System, Level 7. 2nd rev. ed. 1996. text. write for info. (*1-878317-41-5*) Grow With Guidance.

— The Grow with Guidance System, Level 8. 2nd rev. ed. 1996. text. write for info. (*1-878317-30-X*) Grow With Guidance.

— The Grow with Guidance System, Level 9. 2nd rev. ed. 1996. text. write for info. (*1-878317-31-8*) Grow With Guidance.

— The Grow with Guidance System, 6 vols., Set, Levels 1-6. 2nd rev. ed. 1996. text. write for info. (*1-878317-28-8*) Grow With Guidance.

— The Grow with Guidance System, 7 vols., Set, Levels 1-7. 2nd rev. ed. 1996. text. write for info. (*1-878317-27-X*) Grow With Guidance.

— The Grow with Guidance System, 9 vols., Set, Levels 1-9. 2nd rev. ed. 1996. text. write for info. (*1-878317-33-4*) Grow With Guidance.

— The Invitational Teaching Survey Primary & Intermediate. 2nd rev. ed. (Grow with Guidance System Ser.). 1996. write for info. (*1-878317-43-1*) Grow With Guidance.

Radd, Tommie R. & Brightman, Becky. The Grow with Guidance Classroom Activities File. 2nd ed. Date not set. write for info. (*1-878317-29-6*) Grow With Guidance.

Raddatz, Fritz. The Survivor. Manheim, Ralph, tr. 1989. 15.95 (*0-316-73213-3*) Little.

Raddatz, Fritz J., et al. Paul Wunderlich und Karin Szekessy: Correspondenzen. (GER., Illus.). 128p. 1977. 75.00 (*3-7630-1661-9*) Christian Belser.

Radday, Yehuda T. An Analytical Linguistic Concordance to the Book of Isaiah. (Computer Bible Ser.: Vol. 2). 1975. pap. 89.95 (*0-935106-15-4*) E Mellen.

Radday, Yehuda T. & Brenner, Athalya. On Humour & the Comic in the Hebrew Bible. (JSOTS Ser.: Vol. 92). 328p. 1990. pap. 28.50 (*1-85075-701-1*, Pub. by Sheffield Acad) CUP Services.

Radday, Yehuda T. & Levi, Yaakov. An Analytical Linguistic Key-Word-in-Context Concordance to the Book of Exodus. Baird, Arthur J. & Freedman, David, eds. (Computer Bible Ser.: Vol. 28). 1985. pap. 109.95 (*0-935106-23-5*) E Mellen.

Radde, Bruce. The Merritt Parkway. (Illus.). 176p. 1996. pap. 19.95 (*0-300-06877-8*) Yale U Pr.

***Radde, Gerd.** Fritz Karsen: Ein Berliner Schulreformer der Weimarer Zeit Erweiterte Neuausgabe. (GER.). 426p. 1999. 56.95 (*3-631-34896-7*) P Lang Pubng.

Radde, Karl H. Technical Dictionary Applied Sciences, German to Spanish. (GER & SPA.). 1088p. 1994. 350.00 (*0-320-00585-2*) Fr & Eur.

Radde, Karl-Heinz. Oekonomisches Woerterbuch: Spanish-German. (GER & SPA.). 640p. 1989. 105.00 (*0-7859-7034-7*) Fr & Eur.

— Woerterbuch der Technik, Vol. 2. 5th ed. (GER & SPA.). 812p. 1989. 175.00 (*0-8288-5565-X*, S40501) Fr & Eur.

— Woerterbuch der Technik: Spanish-German. 716p. 1977. 95.00 (*0-7859-8467-4*, 3773655304) Fr & Eur.

— Woerterbuch der Technik Spanisch - Deutsch. 6th ed. (GER & SPA.). 960p. 1992. 195.00 (*0-8288-2116-X*, S39877) Fr & Eur.

Radde, Paul O. The Supervision Transition! An Employee Guide to Choosing & Moving into a Supervisory Position. Davis, Larry N., ed. (Illus.). (Orig.). 1990. pap. 17.95 (*0-9625872-0-6*) Thriving Pubns.

— Thrival! - a Guide to Soaring with Your Spirit: Six Essential Steps to Thriving. 21.95 (*0-9625872-1-4*) Thriving Pubns.

Raddeker, Helene B. Treacherous Women of Imperial Japan: Patriarchal Fictions, Patricidal Fantasies. LC 97-23328. (Nissan Institute/Routledge Japanese Studies Ser.). 272p. (C). 1997. 90.00 (*0-415-17112-1*) Routledge.

Radden, Gunter, jt. ed. see Uwe Panther, Klaus.

Radden, Jennifer. Divided Minds & Successive Selves: Ethical Issues in Disorders of Identity & Personality. 325p. 1996. 45.00 (*0-262-18175-4*, Bradford Bks) MIT Pr.

— Madness & Reason. (Studies in Applied Philosophy). 176p. 1985. text 55.00 (*0-04-170034-1*); pap. text 16.95 (*0-04-170035-X*) Routledge.

***Radden, Jennifer, ed.** The Nature of Melancholy: From Aristotle to Kristeva. LC 99-16828. (Illus.). 352p. 2000. 35.00 (*0-19-512962-8*) OUP.

Radder, Hans. In & about the World: Philosophical Studies of Science & Technology. LC 95-46205. (SUNY Series in Science, Technology, & Society). 240p. (C). 1996. text 65.50 (*0-7914-3049-9*); pap. text 21.95 (*0-7914-3050-2*) State U NY Pr.

Radder, J. K., et al. Pathogenesis & Treatment of Diabetes Mellitus. 1986. text 139.00 (*0-89838-828-7*) Kluwer Academic.

Radding, Allan. Knowledge Management: Succeeding in the Information-Based Global Economy. LC 98-22237. (Illus.). 175p. 1998. pap. 295.00 (*1-56607-059-7*) Comput Tech Res.

Radding, Charles M. The Origins of Medieval Jurisprudence: Pavia & Bologna, 850-1150. LC 87-14237. 272p. reprint ed. pap. 84.40 (*0-7837-4539-7*, 208028600004) Bks Demand.

— A World Made by Men: Cognition & Society, 400-1200. LC 85-1111. xi, 286p. 1985. text 39.95 (*0-8078-1664-7*) U of NC Pr.

— A World Made by Men: Cognition & Society, 400-1200. LC 85-1111. (Illus.). 298p. 1985. reprint ed. pap. 92.40 (*0-7837-9036-8*, 204978700003) Bks Demand.

Radding, Charles M. & Clark, William W. Medieval Architecture, Medieval Learning: Builders & Masters in the Age of Romanesque & Gothic. (Illus.). 184p. 1994. pap. 20.00 (*0-300-06130-7*) Yale U Pr.

Radding, Charles M., ed. & tr. see Petrucci, Armando.

Radding, Cynthia R. Wandering Peoples: Colonialism, Ethnic Spaces, & Ecological Frontiers in Northwestern Mexico, 1700-1850. LC 96-35147. (Latin America Otherwise Ser.). (Illus.). 368p. 1997. pap. text 19.95 (*0-8223-1899-7*); lib. bdg. 59.95 (*0-8223-1907-1*) Duke.

Radding, Shirley B., jt. ed. see Jones, Jerry L.

Raddock, David M. Political Behavior of Adolescents in China: The Cultural Revolution in Kwangchow. LC 76-19640. (Monographs: No. 32). vii, 242p. 1977. 22.00 (*0-8165-0607-8*) Assn Asian Studies.

Raddock, David M., ed. Navigating New Markets Abroad: Charting a Course for International Business. 272p. (C). 1993. lib. bdg. 62.50 (*0-8476-7843-1*) Rowman.

Raddon, Alan J. How to Make Rope Soled Footwear. (C). 1982. pap. 45.00 (*0-9508937-0-6*, Pub. by Aberarth Pub) St Mut.

Raddon, Charlene. Forever Mine. 400p. 1996. mass mkt. 4.99 (*0-8217-5193-X*, Zebra Kensgtn) Kensgtn Pub Corp.

— Taming Jenna. 416p. 1994. mass mkt. 4.50 (*0-8217-4604-9*, Zebra Kensgtn) Kensgtn Pub Corp.

— To Have & to Hold. 448p. 1997. mass mkt. 4.99 (*0-8217-5643-5*, Zebra Kensgtn) Kensgtn Pub Corp.

Raddon, Charlotte. Forever Mine. 448p. 1995. mass mkt. 4.99 (*0-8217-4938-2*) NAL.

Raddon, Ethel, jt. auth. see Sluyter, E. H.

Raddon, Rosemary. Information Dynamics. LC 96-8938. 196p. 1996. text 74.95 (*0-566-07568-7*, Pub. by Gower) Ashgate Pub Co.

Raddon, Rosemary, ed. People & Work: Human & Industrial Relations in Library & Information Work. LC 93-104155. 189p. reprint ed. pap. 58.60 (*0-608-08884-6*, 206952100004) Bks Demand.

Raddy, Yehuda T. An Analytical, Linguistic, Key-Work-in-Context Concordance to the Book of Judges. (Computer Bible Ser.: Vol. 11). 1996. 89.95 (*0-935106-10-3*) E Mellen.

Rade, L. & Westergren, B. Mathematics Handbook for Science & Engineering. 4th ed. LC 99-26578. 540p. 1999. 49.95 (*3-540-65569-7*) Spr-Verlag.

Rade, Lennart & Westergren, Bertil. Mathematics Handbook for Science & Engineering. 531p. 1995. 45.00 (*0-8176-3858-X*, QA1) Birkhauser.

Radebaugh. International Accounting. 5th ed. 624p. text. write for info. (*0-471-31949-X*) Wiley.

Radebaugh, Lee H. International Accounting. 4th ed. text. write for info. (*0-471-37198-X*) Wiley.

Radebaugh, Lee H. & Gray, Sidney J. International Accounting & Multinational Enterprises. 4th ed. LC 96-46081. 712p. 1996. text 106.95 (*0-471-05601-4*) Wiley.

Radebaugh, Lee H., jt. auth. see Daniels, John D.

Radebaugh, Teresa S., jt. ed. see Khachaturian, Zaven S.

Radecke, Mark W. God in Flesh Made Manifest: Sermons for Advent, Christmas, & Epiphany: Cycle A, Gospel Texts. LC 95-13428. 1995. 9.50 (*0-7880-0485-9*) CSS OH.

— In Christ: A New Creation. Sherer, Michael L., ed. (Orig.). 1986. pap. 6.75 (*0-89536-821-8*, 6830) CSS OH.

— In Many & Various Ways. 1985. 6.00 (*0-89536-721-1*, 5806) CSS OH.

Radecki, Peter P. Emerging Separation & Separative Reaction Technologies for Process Waste Reduction: Adsorption & Membrane Systems. LC 98-33101. 21p. 1998. 75.00 (*0-8169-0789-7*) Am Inst Chem Eng.

Radek, Karl. Portraits & Pamphlets. LC 67-22113. (Essay Index Reprint Ser.). 1977. 21.95 (*0-8369-0804-X*) Ayer.

Radel. Lab Mnl Qualitatative Analys Chemistry. (Chemistry). 1991. lab manual ed. 12.75 (*0-314-90347-X*) Brooks-Cole.

***Radel, Cliff.** Cincinnati Moments: A Celebration of Photographs from the Cincinnati Enquirer. Lancaster, Sue & Dufour, Liz, eds. LC 99-96177. (Illus.). 148p. 1999. 26.95 (*0-9630442-2-2*) Cinc Equirer.

Radel, Jutta. Zu Gast in Israel: Eine Kulinarische Reise. 3rd ed. (GER., Illus.). 198p. (C). 1994. 40.00 (*3-8170-0004-9*, Pub. by Knstvrlag Weingrtn) Intl Bk Import.

Radel, Rose. The Miniature Pinscher. LC 98-37225. (Owner's Guide to a Happy, Healthy Pet Ser.). (Illus.). 160p. 1998. 9.95 (*0-87605-229-4*) Howell Bks.

Radeleff, Rudolph D. Veterinary Toxicology. 2nd ed. LC 74-85846. 365p. reprint ed. pap. 113.20 (*0-608-14005-8*, 205544000022) Bks Demand.

Radelet, Louis A., jt. auth. see Carter, David L.

Radelet, Michael L., ed. Facing the Death Penalty. 264p. 1990. pap. 22.95 (*0-87722-721-7*) Temple U Pr.

Radelet, Michael L., ed. Final Exposure: Portraits from Death Row. (Illus.). 128p. 1996. pap. text 40.00 (*1-55553-277-2*) NE U Pr.

Radelet, Michael L., et al. In Spite of Innocence: Erroneous Convictions in Capital Cases. 400p. 1992. text 45.00 (*1-55553-142-3*) NE U Pr.

— In Spite of Innocence: Erroneous Convictions in Capital Cases. 416p. 1994. reprint ed. pap. text 17.95 (*1-55553-197-0*) NE U Pr.

Radelet, Michael L., jt. auth. see Miller, Kent S.

Radelet, Steven C., jt. ed. see McPherson, Malcolm F.

Radell, Karen & Tury, Louis J. Season of the Eel. 231p. mass mkt. 4.99 (*1-55197-177-1*) Picasso Publ.

Radeloff, Deanna J., jt. auth. see Charlesworth, Rosalind.

Radeloff, Roger L., jt. auth. see Watlington, Amanda G.

Rademacher, Hans. Collected Papers of Hans Rademacher, 2 vols., 2. Grosswald, Emil, ed. (Mathematicians of Our Time Ser.: Vols. 1 & 2). 659p. 1975. 70.00 (*0-262-07055-3*) MIT Pr.

— Collected Papers of Hans Rademacher, 2 vols., Set. Grosswald, Emil, ed. (Mathematicians of Our Time Ser.: Vols. 1 & 2). 1356p. 1975. 135.00 (*0-262-07173-8*) MIT Pr.

— Collected Papers of Hans Rademacher, 2 vols., Vol. 1. Grosswald, Emil, ed. (Mathematicians of Our Time Ser.: Vols. 1 & 2). 712p. 1975. 70.00 (*0-262-07054-5*) MIT Pr.

— Enjoyment of Mathematics. 208p. 1990. pap. 7.95 (*0-486-26242-1*) Dover.

— Lectures on Elementary Number Theory. LC 76-30495. 156p. 1977. reprint ed. lib. bdg. 18.50 (*0-88275-499-8*) Krieger.

Rademacher, Johannes. Music. LC 96-83723. (Crash Course Ser.). (Illus.). 192p. 1996. 12.95 (*0-8120-9773-4*) Barron.

— Musical Instruments. Jeffers-Brown, Ann & Schreiber, Sally, trs. LC 96-78858. (Crash Course Ser.). (Illus.). 192p. 1997. pap. text 12.95 (*0-7641-0052-1*) Barron.

Rademacher, Susan C., jt. auth. see Klem, Joan R.

Rademacher, T. W., jt. ed. see Isenberg, D. A.

Rademacher, Uwe. Die Bildkunst Des Tacitus. (Spudasmata Ser.: Bd. 29). (GER.). xi, 298p. 1975. write for info. (*3-487-05754-9*) G Olms Pubs.

Rademacher, Verle L. The Drive of '89. (Illus.). 200p. (Orig.). 1993. pap. write for info. (*1-882317-00-9*) Wagon Box Pub.

Rademacher, William J. Lay Ministry: A Theological, Spiritual, & Pastoral Handbook. 288p. (C). 1996. pap. 39.95 (*0-85439-378-1*, Pub. by St Paul Pubns) St Mut.

Rademacher, William J. & Rogers, Marliss. The New Practical Guide for Parish Councils. LC 88-50662. 264p. (Orig.). 1988. pap. 12.95 (*0-89622-371-X*) Twenty-Third.

Raden, Adjeng K. Letters of a Javanese Princess. Geertz, Hildred, ed. Symmers, Agnes L., tr. from DUT. 246p. 1985. reprint ed. pap. text 22.00 (*0-8191-4758-3*) U Pr of Amer.

Radencich, Marguerite C. Administration & Supervision of the Reading - Writing Program. 352p. (C). 1994. 37.00 (*0-205-15217-1*, Longwood Div) Allyn.

Radencich, Marguerite C., ed. Adult Literacy: A Compendium of Articles from the Journal of Reading. 304p. 1994. pap. 24.95 (*0-87207-122-7*) Intl Reading.

— Adult Literacy: A Compendium of Articles from the Journal of Reading. LC 94-12295. 303p. Date not set. reprint ed. pap. 94.00 (*0-608-20629-6*, 207206500003) Bks Demand.

Radencich, Marguerite C. & McKay, Lyn J. Flexible Grouping for Literacy in the Elementary Grades. 208p. (C). 1995. pap. text 33.00 (*0-205-16226-6*, Longwood Div) Allyn.

Radencich, Marguerite C. & Oropallo, Kathy. The Young Author Festival Handbook: What Every Planner Needs to Know. (Beeline Ser.). 1999. pap. 9.95 (*0-325-00020-4*) Heinemann.

Radencich, Marguerite C., et al. A Handbook for the K to Twelve Reading Resource Specialist. LC 93-2920. 253p. (C). 1993. pap. text 50.00 (*0-205-14081-5*, Longwood Div) Allyn.

Radencich, Marguerite C., jt. auth. see Schumm, Jeanne S.

Radencich, Marguerite C., jt. auth. see Schumm, Jeanne Shay.

Radencich, Michael D. Tying the Classic Salmon Fly: A Modern Approach to Traditional Techniques. LC 96-54306. (Illus.). 256p. 1997. 50.00 (*0-8117-0331-2*) Stackpole.

Rader. American Ways. (C). 1999. pap. text 23.50 (*0-15-503689-0*, Pub. by Harcourt Coll Pubs) Harcourt.

— Santa's New Suit. LC 00-100306. 40p. (J). (ps-3). 2000. 4.95 (*0-06-443580-6*) HarpC Child Bks.

Rader, Barbara A. & Zettler, Howard G., eds. The Sleuth & the Scholar: Origins, Evolution, & Current Trends in Detective Fiction, 19. LC 87-24958. (Contributions to the Study of Popular Culture Ser.: No. 19). 151p. 1988. 45.00 (*0-313-26036-2*, ZSS/) Greenwood.

Rader, Benjamin G. American Sports: From the Age of Folk Games to the Age of Televised Sports. 4th ed. LC 98-3784. 344p. (C). 1998. pap. text 39.80 (*0-13-080112-7*) P-H.

— Baseball: A History of America's Game. (Illinois History of Sports Ser.: Vol. 2). (Illus.). 272p. (C). 1993. 24.95 (*0-252-01737-4*); 14.95 (*0-252-06395-3*) U of Ill Pr.

Rader, Benzion, pref. To Touch the Divine: A Jewish Mysticism Primer. 144p. 1989. reprint ed. 17.00 (*0-8266-0494-3*) Kehot Pubn Soc.

Rader, Billie T., ed. see Multi-Amp Institute Staff.

Rader, Carl. Fundamentals of Electronics Mathematics. LC 84-17051. 200p. (C). 1985. pap. 33.50 (*0-8273-2321-2*) Delmar.

— Fundamentals of Electronics Mathematics. LC 84-17051. 200p. (C). 1985. teacher ed. 12.00 (*0-8273-2322-0*) Delmar.

Rader, Charles, jt. auth. see Zoubek, Leslie.

Rader, Charles P., ed. Plastics, Rubber, & Paper Recycling: A Pragmatic Approach. LC 95-37097. (Symposium Ser.: Vol. 609). 1995. 119.95 (*0-614-09700-2*) Am Chemical.

Rader, Charles P., et al. Plastics, Rubber, & Paper Recycling: A Pragmatic Approach. (ACS Symposium Ser.: No. 609). (Illus.). 544p. 1995. text 130.00 (*0-8412-3325-X*, Pub. by Am Chemical) OUP.

Rader, David J. From Tip to Tail: The Layman's Guide to Basic Alpine Ski Tuning. 2nd ed. (Illus.). 65p. 1995. pap. 11.95 (*0-9645550-1-8*) Cornerstne Pub.

Rader, Dick A. Christian Ethics in an African Context: A Focus on Urban Zambia. LC 90-21429. (American University Studies: Theology & Religion: Ser. VII, Vol. 128). XII, 201p. (C). 1991. text 36.95 (*0-8204-1453-0*) P Lang Pubng.

Rader, Dick A., ed. The Fibers of Our Faith: The Herschel H. & Frances J. Hobbs Lectureship in Baptist Faith & Heritage at Oklahoma Baptist University. LC 95-71971. 224p. 1995. pap. 15.95 (*1-881576-76-0*) Providence Hse.

Rader, Hannelore B., ed. Academic Library Instruction: Objectives, Programs, & Faculty Involvement. LC 75-678. (Library Orientation Ser.: No. 5). 1975. 25.00 (*0-87650-063-7*) Pierian.

— Faculty Involvement in Library Instruction. LC 76-21914. (Library Orientation Ser.: No. 6). 119p. 1976. 25.00 (*0-87650-070-X*) Pierian.

— Library Instruction in the '70s: State of the Art. LC 77-75678. (Library Orientation Ser.: No. 7). 135p. 1977. 25.00 (*0-87650-078-5*) Pierian.

Rader, Ilde, ed. see Swanson, Janice M. & Nies, Mary.

Rader, Ilza, ed. see Asperheim, Mary K.

Rader, Ilze, ed. see Ashwill, Jean W. & Droske, Susan C.

Rader, Ilze, ed. see Burns, Catherine E., et al.

Rader, Ilze, ed. see Burroughs, Arlene.

Rader, Ilze, ed. see Curley, Martha A., et al.

Rader, Ilze, ed. see DeWit, Susan C.

Rader, Ilze, ed. see Eckler, Jody A. & Fair, Judy M.

Rader, Ilze, ed. see Eckler, Jody A., et al.

Rader, Ilze, ed. see Hill, Signe S. & Howlett, Helen A.

Rader, Ilze, ed. see Kenner, Carole A., et al.

Rader, Ilze, ed. see Matteson, Mary A., et al.

Rader, Ilze, ed. see Nichols, Francine H. & Zwelling, Elaine.

Rader, Ilze, ed. see Schulte, Elizabeth, et al.

Rader, Ilze, ed. see Varcarolis, Elizabeth M.

Rader, Ilze, ed. see Zerwekh, JoAnn & Claborn, Jo Carol.

Rader, J. Trout. Economics with No Special Technology: Posthumous Essays & Selected Articles. LC 96-75877. xvi, 239p. 1996. lib. bdg. 84.00 (*0-904870-27-8*, Pub. by Input-Output Pub) UH Pr.

Rader, Jack S., jt. auth. see Logue, Dennis E.

Rader, James. Penetrating the U. S. Auto Market: German & Japanese Strategies, 1965-1976. Dufey, Gunter, ed. LC 80-15530. (Research for Business Decisions Ser.: No. 22). 210p. 1980. reprint ed. pap. 65.10 (*0-8357-1106-4*, 207014300064) Bks Demand.

***Rader, Jan & Wiburg, Karen.** Microsoft Excel for Terrified Teachers. (Illus.). 304p. 1999. pap., teacher ed. 24.95 (*1-57690-442-3*, TCM 2442) Tchr Create Mat.

Rader, Janet S. & Rosenhein, Neil B., eds. Ultrasonic Surgical Techniques for the Pelvic Surgeon. LC 94-21216. (Illus.). 112p. 1994. 79.00 (*0-387-94244-0*) Spr-Verlag.

Rader, Jennifer. The Rainy Day Activity Book: How to Make Play Dough, Bubbles, Monster Repellent & More. (Illus.). 112p. (J). 1995. pap. 9.95 (*0-385-48127-6*, Main St Bks) Doubleday.

Rader, Joanne, jt. ed. see Tornquist, Elizabeth M.

***Rader, John R.** Warwick China. (Illus.). 144p. 1999. 34.95 (*0-7643-1016-X*) Schiffer.

Rader, Laura. A Child's Story of Thanksgiving. LC 98-16611. 1998. 6.95 (*1-57102-134-5*, Ideals Child) Hambleton-Hill.

***Rader, Laura.** Hey Diddle, Diddle. (Getting Ready to Read with Mother Goose). 8p. (J). (gr. k). 1999. 18.89 (*0-8215-6963-5*) Sadlier.

— Hey Diddle, Diddle. large type ed. (Getting Ready to Read with Mother Goose). (Illus.). 8p. (J). (gr. k). 1999. 39.00 (*0-8215-6978-3*) Sadlier.

Rader, Laura. My First Christmas Carols. LC 94-17170. (Illus.). 32p. 1994. lib. bdg. 16.65 (*0-8167-3596-4*) Troll Communs.

— My First Christmas Carols. LC 94-17170. (Illus.). 32p. (J). (gr. k-2). 1996. pap. 2.95 (*0-8167-3513-1*) Troll Communs.

— Santa's New Suit. LC 00-100306. 32p. (J). (ps-3). 2000. 12.95 (*0-06-028439-0*) HarpC Child Bks.

***Rader, Laura.** Santa's New suit. 32p. (J). 2000. lib. bdg. 12.89 (*0-06-029284-9*) HarpC Child Bks.

Rader, Laura. Chicken Little. LC 96-42345. 24p. (J). (ps-k). 1998. 9.95 (*0-694-01034-0*) HarpC.

— The First Noel. (Little Angels Ser.). 6p. (J). (ps). 1997. bds. 2.99 (*0-7847-0636-0*, 03746) Standard Pub.

— Joy to the World. (Little Angels Ornament Bks.). 6p. (J). 1997. bds. 2.99 (*0-7847-0635-2*, 24-03745) Standard Pub.

— The Pudgy Where Is Your Nose? Book. (Pudgy Board Bks.). 18p. (J). (ps). 1989. bds. 3.99 (*0-448-02258-3*, G & D) Peng Put Young Read.

— Silent Night. (Little Angels Ornament Bks.). 6p. (J). (ps). 1997. bds. 2.99 (*0-7847-0633-6*, 03743) Standard Pub.

— We Three Kings. (Little Angels Ornament Bks.). 6p. (J). (ps). 1997. bds. 2.99 (*0-7847-0634-4*, 03744) Standard Pub.

Rader, Lyell M. Romance & Dynamite: Essays on Science & the Nature of Faith. LC 98-74550. (Illus.). 232p. 1998. pap. 6.00 (*0-9657601-5-4*, Crest Books) SANP.

Rader, Mamie. Parsley & Paisley: Vegetarian Cooking 101. Morales, Lucy, ed. (Illus.). 407p. (Orig.). 1996. pap. write for info. (*0-9652221-0-1*) Veggies Plus.

***Rader, Marc.** Scanscape. 2000. 29.95 (*84-89698-66-X*) Actar.

Rader, Marth H. & Kurth, Linda A. Business Communication with Contemporary Issues & Microcomputer Applications. 2nd ed. LC 92-17795. (C). 1909. pap. 56.50 (*0-538-70665-1*) S-W Pub.

Rader, Melvin. False Witness. LC 97-32719. (Illus.). 264p. 1998. reprint ed. pap. 12.95 (*0-295-97702-7*) U of Wash Pr.

— A Modern Book of Esthetics. 5th ed. 563p. (C). 1979. text 65.00 (*0-03-019331-1*, Pub. by Harcourt Coll Pubs) Harcourt.

— The Right to Hope: Crisis & Community. LC 81-51284. 148p. 1981. 25.00 (*0-295-95836-7*) U of Wash Pr.

Rader, Melvin M. Presiding Ideas in Wordsworth's Poetry. LC 68-8341. 94p. (C). 1968. reprint ed. 40.00 (*0-87752-090-9*) Gordian.

Rader, Melvin M. & Gill, Jerry H. The Enduring Questions: Main Problems of Philosophy. 5th ed. (C). 1991. pap. text 57.50 (*0-03-032949-3*, Pub. by Harcourt Coll Pubs) Harcourt.

Rader, Norma S. A Road Beyond the Suffering: An Experiential Journey Through the Book of Job. LC 97-68561. (Illus.). 160p. 1997. pap. 14.95 (*1-57736-056-7*) Providence Hse.

Rader, Randy W. S-He. 20p. 1983. pap. 2.00 (*0-913719-65-X*, High Coo Pr) Brooks Books.

Rader, Richard. Entelek Computer-Based Physics Lab. 133p. pap. text 14.95 (*0-87567-035-0*) Entelek.

Rader, Robert J. Advanced Software Design Techniques. (Illus.). 172p. 1979. text 19.95 (*0-89433-046-2*) Petrocelli.

***Rader, Ronald A.** BIOPHARMA 2000: Biopharmaceutical Products in the U. S. Market. 400p. 2000. pap. write for info. (*0-9639573-1-7*) Biotech Info.

Rader, Ronald A., jt. auth. see Young, Sally A.

Rader, Trout. The Economics of Feudalism. Lieberman, Bernhardt, ed. LC 77-132148. (Monographs & Texts in the Behavioral Sciences). (Illus.). xii, 134p. (C). 1971. text 131.00 (*0-677-03280-3*) Gordon & Breach.

Rader, William. The Church & Racial Hostility: A History of Interpretation of Ephesians 2, 11-22. 282p. 1978. 72.50 (*3-16-140112-3*, Pub. by JCB Mohr) Coronet Bks.

Radermacher & Buchheit, eds. Quintiliani, M. Fabii Pt. I: Libri I-VI. (LAT.). 1971. 43.50 (*3-322-00146-6*, T1751, Pub. by B G Teubner) U of Mich Pr.

Radermacher, jt. ed. see Usener.

Radermacher, reinhard, jt. auth. see Alefeld, Georg.

Radermacher, Reinhard, jt. auth. see Herold, Keith E.

Radeschi, Loretta. This Business of Glass: The Complete Guide for Artists, Craftspeople & Retailers. Porcelli, Joe, ed. (Illus.). 320p. 1993. pap. 19.95 (*0-9629053-3-X*) Glass Pr.

Radest, Howard. Felix Adler: An Ethical Culture. LC 96-42927. (American Liberal Religious Thought Ser.: Vol. 5). XII, 181p. (C). 1998. text 43.95 (*0-8204-3682-8*) P Lang Pubng.

Radest, Howard B. Can We Teach Ethics? LC 88-27512. 162p. 1989. 35.95 (*0-275-92857-8*, C2857, Praeger Pubs) Greenwood.

— Community Service: Encounter with Strangers. LC 93-17116. 216p. 1993. 55.00 (*0-275-94186-8*, C4186, Praeger Pubs) Greenwood.

— The Devil & Secular Humanism: The Children of the Enlightenment. LC 90-38843. 184p. 1990. 49.95 (*0-275-93442-X*, C3442, Praeger Pubs) Greenwood.

***Radest, Howard B.** From Clinic to Classroom: Medical Ethics & Moral Education. LC 99-37525. 224p. 2000. write for info. (*0-275-96194-X*) Greenwood.

Radest, Howard B. Humanism with a Human Face: Intimacy & the Enlightenment. LC 95-43764. 224p. 1996. 62.95 (*0-275-94969-9*, Praeger Pubs) Greenwood.

Radetski, Marian. Polish Coal & European Energy Market Integration. 137p. 1995. 56.95 (*1-85972-140-0*, Pub. by Avebry) Ashgate Pub Co.

Radetsky, Peter. Invisible Invaders: The Story of the Emerging Age of Viruses. 1991. 22.95 (*0-316-73216-8*) Little.

Radetsky, Peter, jt. auth. see Garrick, James G.

Radetzki, Marian. Aid & Development: A Handbook for Small Donors. LC 72-92892. (Special Studies in International Economics & Development). 1973. 42.50 (*0-275-28694-0*) Irvington.

— State Mineral Enterprises: An Investigation into Their Impact on International Mineral Markets. LC 85-2346. 150p. 1985. pap. text 15.00 (*0-915707-16-0*) Resources Future.

Radev, Dragomir, jt. ed. see Hovy, Eduard.

Radevsky, Anthony. A Practical Guide to Drafting Pleading. 214p. 1991. 70.00 (*1-85190-141-8*, Pub. by Tolley Pubng) St Mut.

Radevsky, Anthony & Edwards, Quentin. A Practical Guide to Drafting Pleading. (Lawyers Practice & Procedure Ser.). 227p. 1995. pap. 195.00 (*0-85459-948-7*, Pub. by Tolley Pubng) St Mut.

Radford & Haigh. Turbo Pascal for the IBM PC. (C). 1986. pap. 56.95 (*0-534-06426-4*) PWS Pubs.

Radford & Vavra, Anthony. Technical Math with Calculus. (Physics Ser.). 1986. text 62.50 (*0-8273-3870-8*) Delmar.

Radford, A. S. Teach Yourself Computer Programming: FORTRAN. (Teach Yourself Ser.). 1975. pap. 5.95 (*0-685-03266-3*) McKay.

Radford, Albert E., et al. Manual of the Vascular Flora of the Carolinas. LC 68-28264. (Illus.). lxii, 1183p. 1968. 45.00 (*0-8078-1087-8*) U of NC Pr.

— Natural Heritage: Classification, Inventory, & Information. LC 80-23087. xxi, 485p. 1981. 59.95 (*0-8078-1463-6*) U of NC Pr.

Radford, Andrew. Syntactic Theory & the Structure of English: A Minimalist Approach. (Cambridge Textbooks in Linguistics Ser.). 570p. (C). 1997. text 69.95 (*0-521-47125-7*); pap. text 24.95 (*0-521-47707-7*) Cambridge U Pr.

— Syntax: A Minimalist Introduction. 294p. (C). 1997. text 54.95 (*0-521-58122-2*); pap. text 17.95 (*0-521-58914-2*) Cambridge U Pr.

— Transformational Grammar: A First Course. (Cambridge Textbooks in Linguistics Ser.). 640p. 1988. pap. text 29.95 (*0-521-34750-5*) Cambridge U Pr.

Radford, Andrew, et al. Language & Linguistics: An Introduction. LC 98-44358. (Illus.). 368p. (C). 1999. text 59.95 (*0-521-47261-X*); pap. text 22.95 (*0-521-47854-5*) Cambridge U Pr.

Radford, Anne. Managing People in Professional Practices. 160p. 1995. pap. 90.00 (*0-85292-571-9*, Pub. by IPM Hse) St Mut.

Radford Architectural Co. Staff. Radford's Artistic Bungalows: The Complete 1908 Catalog. LC 96-53259. (Illus.). 222p. 1997. reprint ed. pap. text 14.95 (*0-486-29678-4*) Dover.

Radford, Carole M. Hearts Go Home for the Holidays: A Collection of Holiday Recipes. 184p. 1994. spiral bd. 17.95 (*1-886300-00-3*) Heirlooms by Radford.

Radford, Carole M., ed. Hospitality Southern Style: A Collection of Treasured Southern Recipes. 164p. 1994. spiral bd. 17.95 (*1-886300-01-1*) Heirlooms by Radford.

Radford, Colin. Driving to California: An Unconventional Introduction to Philosophy. 336p. 1996. pap. 20.00 (*0-7486-0819-2*, Pub. by Edinburgh U Pr) Col U Pr.

Radford, Darrel. New Castle: A Pictorial History. (Indiana Pictorial History Ser.). (Illus.). 1994. reprint ed. write for info. (*0-943963-28-1*) G Bradley.

Radford, David E., jt. auth. see Lambe, Larry A.

Radford, Derek. Building Machines & What They Do. LC 91-71860. (Illus.). 32p. (J). (ps-3). 1994. pap. 4.99 (*1-56402-364-8*) Candlewick Pr.

— Cargo Machines & What They Do. LC 91-71823. (Illus.). 32p. (J). (ps up). 1992. 8.95 (*1-56402-005-3*) Candlewick Pr.

— Harry at the Garage. LC 94-25699. (Illus.). 32p. (J). (ps up). 1995. 12.99 (*1-56402-564-0*) Candlewick Pr.

— Harry at the Garage. LC 94-25699. (Illus.). 32p. (J). (ps-2). 1997. reprint ed. pap. 6.99 (*0-7636-0157-8*) Candlewick Pr.

Radford, E. & Radford, M. A. Death of a Frightened Editor. large type ed. (Linford Mystery Library). 480p. 1996. pap. 16.99 (*0-7089-7945-9*, Linford) Ulverscroft.

— Death of a Peculiar Rabbit. large type ed. (Linford Mystery Library). 320p. 1996. pap. 16.99 (*0-7089-7908-4*) Ulverscroft.

— Death Takes the Wheel. large type ed. (Linford Mystery Library). 384p. 1996. pap. 16.99 (*0-7089-7937-8*) Ulverscroft.

— Death's Inheritance. large type ed. (Linford Mystery Library). 416p. 1996. pap. 16.99 (*0-7089-7871-1*, Linford) Ulverscroft.

— Jones's Little Murders. large type ed. (Linford Mystery Large Print Ser.). 352p. 1998. pap. 17.99 (*0-7089-5291-7*, Linford) Ulverscroft.

— Married to Murder. large type ed. (Linford Mystery Library). 416p. 1995. pap. 16.99 (*0-7089-7734-0*, Linford) Ulverscroft.

Radford, E. & Radford, M. A. Mask of Murder. large type ed. 320p. pap. 18.99 (*0-7089-5447-2*) Ulverscroft.

— Murder Is Ruby Red. large type ed. 288p. 1999. pap. 18.99 (*0-7089-5465-0*, Linford) Ulverscroft.

Radford, E. & Radford, M. A. Murder Magnified. large type ed. (Mystery Library). 368p. 1995. pap. 16.99 (*0-7089-7655-7*, Linford) Ulverscroft.

— No Reason for Murder. large type ed. (Linford Mystery Library). 400p. 1995. pap. 16.99 (*0-7089-7715-4*, Linford) Ulverscroft.

— The Six Men. 184p. 1995. 19.50 (*0-7451-8657-2*, Black Dagger) Chivers N Amer.

— Two Ways to Murder. large type ed. (Linford Mystery Library). 320p. 1995. pap. 16.99 (*0-7089-7711-1*, Linford) Ulverscroft.

Radford, Edwin & Radford, Mona A. The Encyclopedia of Superstitions. LC 70-88993. 269p. 1969. reprint ed. lib. bdg. 65.00 (*0-8371-2115-9*, RASU, Greenwood Pr) Greenwood.

— The Encyclopedia of Superstitions. rev. ed. Hole, Christina, ed. & rev. by. 384p. 1996. write for info. (*0-7607-0228-4*) Barnes & Noble Inc.

Radford, Elaine. A Complete Introduction to Cockatiels. (Illus.). 128p. 1987. pap. 8.95 (*0-86622-284-7*, CO012S) TFH Pubns.

— Parakeets Today. (Illus.). 64p. 1996. 12.95 (*0-7938-0106-0*, WW008) TFH Pubns.

— A Step-by-Step Book about Finches. (Illus.). 64p. 1989. 9.95 (*0-86622-911-6*, SK-010X); pap. 5.95 (*0-86622-466-1*; SK-010) TFH Pubns.

— A Step-by-Step Book about Parrots. (Step-by-Step Ser.). (Illus.). 64p. (YA). (gr. 9-12). 1988. 9.95 (*0-86622-907-8*, SK-031X); pap. 5.95 (*0-86622-484-X*, SK-031) TFH Pubns.

— A Step-by-Step Book about Training Cockatiels. (Step-by-Step Ser.). (Illus.). 64p. 1989. pap. 5.95 (*0-86622-964-7*, SK-026) TFH Pubns.

— A Step-by-Step Book about Training Parakeets. (Illus.). 64p. 1989. pap. 5.95 (*0-86622-970-1*, SK-028) TFH Pubns.

Radford, Elaine & American Society for the Prevention of Cruelty to. Parakeets Today: A Complete & Up-to-Date Guide. LC 97-3625. (Basic Domestic Pet Library). 76p. (J). (gr. 3 up). 1997. 19.95 (*0-7910-4615-X*) Chelsea Hse.

Radford, Elaine R. & Becker, Gary D. Diagnosis & Management of Inhalant Allergy. 3rd ed. (Self-Instructional Package Ser.). (Illus.). 93p. (Orig.). 1993. pap. text 25.00 (*1-56772-004-8*) AAO-HNS.

— Introduction to the Diagnosis & Treatment of Food Sensitivities. 2nd ed. (Self-Instructional Package Ser.). (Illus.). 65p. (Orig.). 1993. pap. text 25.00 (*1-56772-005-6*) AAO-HNS.

Radford, Elizabeth, ed. New Villagers: Urban Pressure on Rural Areas in Worchester. (Illus.). 76p. 1970. 25.00 (*0-7146-1585-4*, Pub. by F Cass Pubs) Intl Spec Bk.

Radford, Evelyn Morris. The Bridge & the Building: The Art of Government & the Government of Art 2nd ed. LC 98-68185. 1998. write for info. (*0-912133-15-5*) Hilltop Pub Co.

Radford, G. H. Shylock & Others: Eight Studies. LC 72-13311. (Essay Index Reprint Ser.). 1977. reprint ed. 18.95 (*0-8369-8172-3*) Ayer.

Radford, Gail. Modern Housing for America: Policy Struggles in the New Deal Era. LC 96-21155. (Illus.). 240p. 1996. pap. text 17.95 (*0-226-70223-5*, Chicago Visual Lib); lib. bdg. 45.00 (*0-226-70222-7*) U Ch Pr.

Radford, Gary P., jt. ed. see Huspek, Michael.

***Radford-Hill, Sheila.** Further to Fly: Black Women & the Politics of Empowerment. LC 00-9073. 2000. pap. 17.95 (*0-8166-3475-0*) U of Minn Pr.

Radford, Irene. Dragon's Touchstone. Vol. 1. 384p. 1997. pap. 5.99 (*0-88677-744-5*, Pub. by DAW Bks) Penguin Putnam.

— The Glass Dragon. (Dragon Nimbus Ser.). 352p. (Orig.). 1994. mass mkt. 5.99 (*0-88677-634-1*, Pub. by DAW Bks) Penguin Putnam.

— Guardian of the Balance. LC 99-215584. 544p. 1999. text 23.95 (*0-88677-826-3*, Pub. by DAW Bks) Penguin Putnam.

***Radford, Irene.** Guardian of the Balance. (Merlin's Descendants Ser.: Vol. 1). 2000. mass mkt. 6.99 (*0-88677-875-1*, Pub. by DAW Bks) Penguin Putnam.

— Guardian of the Trust. (Merlin's Descendants Ser.: Vol. 2). 544p. 2000. 23.95 (*0-88677-874-3*, Pub. by DAW Bks) Penguin Putnam.

Radford, Irene. The Last Battlemage. (Dragon Nimbus Ser.: No. 2). 352p. 1998. mass mkt. 6.99 (*0-88677-774-7*, Pub. by DAW Bks) Penguin Putnam.

— The Loneliest Magician. 352p. 1996. pap. 5.99 (*0-88677-709-7*, Pub. by DAW Bks) Penguin Putnam.

— The Perfect Princess. (Dragon Nimbus Ser.: No. 2). 352p. 1995. mass mkt. 5.99 (*0-88677-678-3*, Pub. by DAW Bks) Penguin Putnam.

***Radford, Irene.** The Renegade Dragon. (Dragon Nimbus Ser.: Vol. 3). 384p. (J). 1999. mass mkt. 6.99 (*0-88677-855-7*, Pub. by DAW Bks) Penguin Putnam.

— Wizard's Treasure. (Dragon Nimbus Ser.: Vol. 4). 2000. mass mkt. 6.99 (*0-88677-913-8*) DAW Bks.

Radford, Jan. Delightful Beaded Earring Designs. Knight, Denise, ed. LC 93-70574. (Illus.). 72p. (Orig.). 1994. pap., per. 9.95 (*0-943604-37-0*, BOO/27) Eagles View.

Radford, Jean, ed. The Progress of Romance: The Politics of Popular Fiction. 224p. 1987. 32.50 (*0-7102-0717-4*, 07174, Routledge Thoemms); pap. 12.95 (*0-7102-0963-0*, 09630, Routledge Thoemms) Routledge.

Radford, Jeff. The Chaco Coal Scandal. (Illus.). 257p. (Orig.). (C). 1986. pap. 8.00 (*0-936455-01-2*) Rhombus Pub.

Radford, Jill, et al, eds. Women, Policing & Male Violence: An Internation Perspective. 240p. 1988. text 52.50 (*0-415-00692-9*) Routledge.

Radford, Jill & Russell, Diana E. Femicide: The Politics of Woman Killing. 300p. 1992. pap. 20.00 (*0-8057-9028-4*); text 29.95 (*0-8057-9026-8*) Macmillan.

Radford, Jill & Russell, Diana E., eds. Femicide: The Politics of Woman Killing. 400p. 1992. pap. 9.00 (*0-335-15178-7*) OpUniv Pr.

***Radford, Jill, et al.** Women, Violence & Strategies for Action. LC 99-29673. 2000. 25.95 (*0-335-20369-8*) Taylor & Francis.

Radford, Jim, jt. ed. see Eden, Colin.

Radford, Joan. The Complete Book of Family Aromatherapy. 192p. 1993. pap. 19.95 (*0-572-01622-0*, Pub. by W Foulsham) Trans-Atl Phila.

Radford, John. Gender & Choice in Education & Occupation. LC 97-37180. (Illus.). 208p. (C). 1998. 75.00 (*0-415-15394-8*); pap. 24.99 (*0-415-15395-6*) Routledge.

— The New Spain: The First Complete Guide to Contemporary Spanish Wine. LC 99-236908. (Illus.). 224p. 1998. 40.00 (*1-85732-254-1*, Pub. by Mitchell Beazley) Antique Collect.

— Quantity & Quality in Higher Education. LC 96-36549. (Higher Education Policy Ser.). 1996. pap. write for info. (*1-85302-433-3*, Pub. by Jessica Kingsley) Taylor & Francis.

Radford, John, ed. An Indian Journal. 224p. 1994. text 39.50 (*1-85043-776-9*, Pub. by I B T) St Martin.

— Talent, Teaching & Achievement. 160p. 1991. pap. 29.95 (*1-85302-111-3*) Taylor & Francis.

***Radford, John & Brook, Stephen.** Pocket Guide to Fortified & Sweet Wines. 204p. 2000. 14.95 (*1-84000-248-4*, Pub. by Mitchell Beazley) Antique Collect.

Radford, John & Rose, David, eds. The Teaching of Psychology: Method, Content, & Context. LC 79-40824. 380p. reprint ed. pap. 117.80 (*0-8357-7046-X*, 203362100086) Bks Demand.

Radford, K. J. Individual & Small Group Decisions. xiv, 174p. 1989. 90.95 (*0-387-97156-4*) Spr-Verlag.

— Strategic & Tactical Decisions. 2nd ed. (Illus.). 215p. 1988. 94.95 (*0-387-96819-9*) Spr-Verlag.

Radford, M. A., jt. auth. see Radford, E.

Radford, Marie L. The Reference Encounter: Interpersonal Communication in the Academic Library. LC 98-47242. (Publications in Librarianship: No. 52). 256p. 1999. 30.00 (*0-8389-7951-3*) Assn Coll & Res Libs.

Radford, Michael. How to Create a Championship Vision. 176p. 1994. per. 25.00 (*0-8403-9390-3*) Kendall-Hunt.

Radford, Mona A., jt. auth. see Radford, Edwin.

***Radford, Rhonda B.** The Dream Maker. (Illus.). 112p. 2000. pap. 7.99 (*0-9679421-0-1*) Dream Maker.

Radford, Robert. Art for a Purpose: The Artists' International Association 1933-1953. 205p. 1991. 17.95 (*0-9506783-7-6*, Pub. by Winchester Schl Art Pr) Paul & Co Pubs.

— Dali. LC 99-203167. (Art & Ideas Ser.). (Illus.). 352p. 1997. pap. 19.95 (*0-7148-3411-4*, Pub. by Phaidon Press) Phaidon Pr.

Radford, Robert, jt. auth. see Morris, Lynda.

Radford, Russell, jt. auth. see Bean, Roger.

Radford, Russell, jt. auth. see Noori, Hamid.

Radford, T. S., ed. see Institute of Petroleum, London Staff.

Radford, Tom S. What Makes a Project "Marginal?" 1989. 140.00 (*90-6314-862-3*, Pub. by Lorne & MacLean Marine) St Mut.

— What Makes a Project "Marginal?" (C). 1989. 140.00 (*0-89771-730-9*, Pub. by Lorne & MacLean Marine) St Mut.

Radford, Vicki, et al, eds. Light for the Day. 368p. 1989. spiral bd. 6.50 (*0-9624991-0-2*) NWestern Prods.

Radford, Victoria, ed. Meeting Mr. Lincoln. LC 98-24074. (Illus.). 128p. 1998. 18.95 (*1-56663-199-8*, Pub. by I R Dee) Natl Bk Netwk.

Radford, William A. Old House Measured & Scaled Drawings for Builders & Carpenters: An Early 20th Century Pictorial Sourcebook, with 183 Detailed Plates. 2nd ed. (Illus.). 200p. 1983. reprint ed. pap. 12.95 (*0-486-24438-5*) Dover.

Radforth, Ian. Bushworkers & Bosses: Logging in Northern Ontario, 1900-1980. 367p. 1987. pap. 20.95 (*0-8020-6653-4*); text 45.00 (*0-8020-2639-7*) U of Toronto Pr.

Radforth, Ian, jt. ed. see Greer, Allan.

Radforth, N. W., ed. see Muskeg Research Conference Staff.

Radha Krishna, Hari C., jt. ed. see Boldy, Adrian P.

Radha, Sivananda. The Divine Light Invocation. 2nd ed. LC 90-31896. (Illus.). 104p. 1990. pap. 10.95 (*0-931454-17-4*) Timeless Bks.

— From the Mating Dance to the Cosmic Dance: Sex, Love, & Marriage from a Yogic Viewpoint. Foran, Rita & MacKenzie, Ian, eds. LC 92-13848. (Illus.). 208p. 1992. 14.95 (*0-931454-31-X*); pap. 14.95 (*0-931454-32-8*) Timeless Bks.

— Hatha Yoga: The Hidden Language: Symbols, Secrets, & Metaphor. LC 94-45215. (Illus.). 320p. 1995. pap. 19.95 (*0-931454-74-3*) Timeless Bks.

— Hatha Yoga - The Hidden Language: Symbols, Secrets & Metaphor. LC 87-9955. (Illus.). 320p. (Orig.). 1987. 19.95 (*0-931454-12-3*) Timeless Bks.

— In the Company of the Wise: Remembering My Teachers, Reflecting the Light. McKay, Julie, ed. LC 91-7431. (Illus.). 242p. 1991. 14.95 (*0-931454-23-9*) Timeless Bks.

— In the Company of the Wise: Remembering My Teachers, Reflecting the Light. LC 91-7431. (Illus.). 242p. 1993. pap. 14.95 (*0-931454-24-7*) Timeless Bks.

— Kundalini Yoga for the West: A Foundation for Character

An Asterisk (*) at the beginning of an entry indicates that the title is appearing for the first time.

Building, Courage & Awareness. (Illus.). 373p. 1993. reprint ed. 24.95 (*0-931454-37-9*); reprint ed. pap. 18.95 (*0-931454-38-7*) Timeless Bks.

— Mantras: Words of Power. 1998. pap. write for info. (*81-207-1677-9*) Sterling Pubs.

— Mantras: Words of Power. rev. ed. Lenman, Karin, ed. LC 93-46477. (Illus.). 208p. 1994. pap. 14.95 (*0-931454-66-2*) Timeless Bks.

— Radha: Diary of a Woman's Search. 2nd ed. Foran, Rita, ed. LC 90-32272. (Illus.). 242p. (Orig.). 1990. pap. 13.95 (*0-931454-19-0*) Timeless Bks.

— Realities of the Dreaming Mind. LC 94-16766. (Illus.). 384p. 1994. 18.95 (*0-931454-68-9*); pap. 18.95 (*0-931454-69-7*) Timeless Bks.

— The Rose Ceremony. LC 98-107149. (Illus.). viii, 72p. 1997. 9.95 (*0-931454-86-7*) Timeless Bks.

— Seeds of Light. LC 90-49580. (Illus.). 116p. 1991. pap. 7.95 (*0-931454-22-0*) Timeless Bks.

— Time to Be Holy: Reflecting on Daily Life. LC 96-14329. (Illus.). 320p. 1996. 22.95 (*0-931454-84-0*); pap. 19.95 (*0-931454-81-6*) Timeless Bks.

Radhakrishna, Aruna, et al. Identifying the Intersection: Adolescent Unwanted Pregnancy, HIV/AIDS, & Unsafe Abortion. LC 97-36830. (Issues in Abortion Care Ser.). 1997. write for info. (*1-882220-12-9*) IPAS.

Radhakrishna, Rokkam, et al. India's Public Distribution System: A National & International Perspective. (World Bank Discussion Papers: No. 380). 112p. 1997. pap. 22.00 (*0-8213-4090-5*, 14090) World Bank.

Radhakrishna, S., et al, eds. Solid State Materials. 400p. 1992. 75.95 (*0-387-54229-9*) Spr-Verlag.

— Technology for Rural Development: Proceedings of the Second Asia Conference, Kuala Lumpur, Malaysia, December 4-7, 1985. 728p. 1988. text 93.00 (*9971-5-0285-2*) World Scientific Pub.

Radhakrishna, S. & Jain, S. C., eds. Physics of Semiconductor Devices: Proceedings of the Third International Workshop on Physics of Semiconductor Devices, Madras, India, Nov 27 - Dec 2, 1985. 500p. 1985. 78.00 (*9971-5-0082-5*) World Scientific Pub.

Radhakrishna, S. & Srinivasan, K., eds. Physics of Materials: Proceedings of the Fourth & Fifth International Courses. 476p. (C). 1988. text 117.00 (*9971-5-0398-0*) World Scientific Pub.

Radhakrishna, S. & Tan, B. C., eds. Laser Spectroscopy & Nonlinear Optics of Solids: Proceedings of the International Workshop Organized by the Institute for Advanced Studies, University of Malaya, & the Malaysian Institute of Physics (Kuala Lumpur, Malaysia) 500p. 1991. 64.95 (*0-387-52943-8*) Spr-Verlag.

Radhakrishna, S., jt. ed. see Chowdari, B. V.

Radhakrishna, S., jt. ed. see Jain, S. C.

Radhakrishnan, C., jt. auth. see Gopinathan-Nair, P. R.

Radhakrishnan, N., ed. Gandhian Perspective of Nation Building for World Peace. 166p. (C). 1992. text 25.00 (*81-220-0272-2*, Pub. by Konark Pubs Pvt Ltd) Advent Bks Div.

Radhakrishnan, P. Computer Numerical Control (CNC) Machine. (C). 1989. 75.00 (*0-89771-389-3*, Pub. by Current Dist) St Mut.

— Peasant Struggles, Land Reforms & Social Change: Malabar, 1836-1982. 290p. (C). 1989. text 24.00 (*0-8039-9593-8*) Sage.

Radhakrishnan, R. Diasporic Mediations: Between Home & Location. LC 95-46541. (C). 1996. pap. 21.95 (*0-8166-2641-3*); text 54.95 (*0-8166-2640-5*) U of Minn Pr.

Radhakrishnan, Sarvepalli. Eastern Religions & Western Thought. (Oxford India Paperbacks Ser.). 410p. 1990. pap. text 13.95 (*0-19-562456-4*) OUP.

— An Idealist View of Life. LC 77-27145. (Hibbert Lectures: 1929). 352p. reprint ed. 47.50 (*0-404-60425-0*) AMS Pr.

— An Idealist View of Life. (Unwin Paperbacks Ser.). 288p. 1988. reprint ed. pap. 12.95 (*0-04-141009-2*) Routledge.

— Indian Philosophy, Vol. I. 740p. 1989. 49.95 (*0-04-181009-0*) Routledge.

— Indian Philosophy: Centenary Edition, Vol. 1. 2nd ed. 738p. 1996. pap. text 14.95 (*0-19-563819-0*) OUP.

— Indian Philosophy: Centenary Edition, Vol. 2. 2nd ed. 826p. 1996. pap. text 17.95 (*0-19-563820-4*) OUP.

— The Principal Upanishads. 958p. (C). 1995. pap. 12.00 (*81-7223-124-5*, Pub. by Harper SF) HarpC.

— Recovery of Faith. 1968. reprint ed. lib. bdg. 65.00 (*0-8371-0197-2*, RARF, Greenwood Pr) Greenwood.

— Religion & Society. (C). 1995. 9.50 (*81-7223-163-6*, Pub. by Indus Pub) S Asia.

Radhakrishnan, Sarvepalli, ed. The Dhammapada: With Introductory Essays, Pali Text, English Translation & Notes. (Oxford India Paperbacks Ser.). 202p. 1997. pap. 11.95 (*0-19-564080-2*) OUP.

Radhakrishnan, Sarvepalli, ed. The Principal Upanisads. LC 91-47550. (Humanities Paperback Library). 960p. (C). 1992. pap. 32.50 (*0-391-03479-0*) Humanities.

Radhakrishnan, Sarvepalli & Kumari, Ranjana. Higher Education & Scheduled Tribe Youth: From Integration to Alienation. 1989. text 18.95 (*81-7027-117-7*, Pub. by Radiant Pubs) S Asia.

Radhakrishnan, Sarvepalli & Moore, Charles A., eds. Sourcebook in Indian Philosophy. 720p. 1957. pap. text 22.95 (*0-691-01958-4*, Pub. by Princeton U Pr) Cal Prin Full Svc.

Radhakrishnan, Sarvepalli & Raju, P. T., eds. The Concept of Man: A Study in Comparative Philosophy. 546p. (C). 1992. 24.95 (*1-881338-16-9*) Nataraj Bks.

— The Concept of Man: A Study in Comparative Philosophy. (C). 1995. reprint ed. 12.50 (*81-7223-146-6*, Pub. by Indus Pub) S Asia.

Radhakrishnan, Sarvepalli & Ranjana, Kumari. Higher Education & Scheduled Caste Youth in India. 125p. 1989. text 15.95 (*81-7027-118-5*, Pub. by Radiant Pubs) S Asia.

Radhakrishnan, Sarvepalli, tr. see Badarayana.

Radhakrishnan, T., jt. auth. see Mukherjee, R. R.

Radharamanan, R., ed. Robotics & Factories of the Future '87. (Illus.). xvii, 878p. 1988. 150.95 (*0-387-50025-1*) Spr-Verlag.

Radharkrishnan, Sarvepalli. The Bhagavadgita: With an Introductory Essay, Sanskrit Text, English Translation, & Notes. 388p. 1994. pap. 7.00 (*81-7223-087-7*, Pub. by Harper SF) HarpC.

Radhayrapetian, Juliet. Iranian Folk Narrative: A Survey of Scholarship. LC 89-274158. (Folklore Library: Vol. 1). 212p. 1990. text 10.00 (*0-8240-7145-X*, 1285) Garland.

Radhoff, Sandra. The Kyrian Letters: Transformative Messages for Higher Vision. 249p. (Orig.). 1992. pap. 12.00 (*1-882545-00-1*) Herit Pubns.

Radhu, Abdul W. Islam in Tibet: And the Illustrative Narrative Tibetan Caravans. Henry, Gray, ed. Casewit, Jane, tr. (Illus.). 311p. 1997. pap. 24.95 (*1-887752-03-X*) Fons Vitae.

Radhuber, Stanley. Flying over Greenland. Gale, Vi, ed. LC 77-83287. (First Bk.). (Illus.). 1977. pap. 5.00 (*0-915986-06-X*) Prescott St Pr.

— Flying over Greenland. limited ed. Gale, Vi, ed. LC 77-83287. (First Bk.). (Illus.). 1977. 20.00 (*0-915986-05-1*) Prescott St Pr.

Radi, David A. Intelligence Inside the White House: The Influences of Executive Style & Technology, Vol. I-97-3. unabridged ed. LC 98-129575. (Illus.). 27p. 1997. pap. text. write for info. (*1-879716-42-9*) Ctr Info Policy.

Radian, Alex. Resource Mobilization in Poor Countries: Implementing Tax Policies. LC 79-66440. 226p. 1980. text 34.95 (*0-87855-304-5*) Transaction Pubs.

Radian Corp. Staff. Municipal Waste Combustion Study: Assessment of Health Risks Associated with Municipal Waste Combustion Emissions. 248p. 1989. 78.95 (*0-89116-071-X*) Hemisp Pub.

Radic, S., ed. Technological Engineering Dictionary German-Serbocroatian. (CRO, GER & SER.). 495p. 1981. 95.00 (*0-8288-4678-2*, M9687) Fr & Eur.

Radic, S., jt. auth. see Vekaric, Stjepan.

Radic, Therese. Melba, the Voice of Australia. 214p. 1986. 14.95 (*0-918812-45-3*, SB 0005) MMB Music.

Radical History Review Collective Staff, ed. Liberalism & the Left. (Radical History Review Ser.: Vol. 71). 250p. (C). 1999. pap. text 21.95 (*0-521-64470-4*) Cambridge U Pr.

Radican. Ezauto Advance Engine Performance. (IT-Automotive Technology Ser.). (C). 1998. pap. text, wbk. ed. 13.50 (*0-8273-8106-9*) Delmar.

— Ezauto Brakes. (IT-Automotive Technology Ser.). (C). 1998. pap. text, wbk. ed. 13.50 (*0-8273-8109-3*) Delmar.

— Ezauto Brakes. (IT-Automotive Technology Ser.). (C). 2001. mass mkt. 39.00 (*0-8273-8108-5*) Delmar.

— Ezauto Diesel Engines. (IT-Automotive Technology Ser.). (C). 2000. pap. text, wbk. ed. 13.50 (*0-8273-8103-4*) Delmar.

Radice, B., jt. auth. see Branzi, Muschamp A.

Radice, Barbara. Memphis: Research, Experiences, Failures, & Successes of New Design. LC 94-60789. (Illus.). 208p. 1995. pap. 29.95 (*0-500-27377-4*, Pub. by Thames Hudson) Norton.

Radice, Betty. The Letters of the Younger Pliny. (Classics Ser.). 320p. 1963. pap. 11.95 (*0-14-044127-1*, Penguin Classics) Viking Penguin.

— Terence: The Comedies. (Classics Ser.). 400p. 1976. pap. 12.95 (*0-14-044324-X*, Penguin Classics) Viking Penguin.

— Who's Who in the Ancient World. (Reference Ser.). 336p. (Orig.). 1973. pap. 13.95 (*0-14-051055-9*, Penguin Bks) Viking Penguin.

Radice, Betty, ed. Letters, 2 vols., 1. (Loeb Classical Library: No. 55, 59). 596p. 1969. text 18.95 (*0-674-99061-7*) HUP.

Radice, Betty, tr. Letters, 2 vols., 2. (Loeb Classical Library: No. 55, 59). 592p. 1969. text 18.95 (*0-674-99066-8*) HUP.

Radice, Betty, et al. The Letters of Abelard & Heloise. LC 74-177112. (Classics Ser.). 312p. 1998. pap. text 6.67 (*0-14-044297-9*) Addson-Wesley Educ.

Radice, Betty, jt. auth. see Terence.

Radice, Betty, ed. & intro. see Gibbon, Edward.

Radice, Betty, tr. see Erasmus, Desiderius.

Radice, Betty, tr. & anno. see Livy.

*__Radice, Dennis.__ The Home Builder's Sales Management Tool Kit: Working with Agents, Brokers & On-Site Associates. Smith, Carol, ed. LC 99-56037. (Carol Smith's Customer Relations Ser.). 145p. 1999. pap. write for info. (*0-86718-510-4*) Home Builder.

Radice, E. A., jt. auth. see Kaser, Michael C.

Radice, Giles. Offshore: Britain & the European Idea, March 1992. 256p. 1992. text 22.95 (*1-85043-529-4*, Pub. by I B T) St Martin.

Radice, Giles, jt. auth. see Lapping, Brian.

Radice, Judi. Menu Design 5. (Illus.). 240p. 1993. 60.00 (*0-86636-180-4*) PBC Intl Inc.

Radice, Lisanne. Prelude to Appeasement: East European Central Diplomacy in the Early 1930's. (East European Monographs: No. 80). 218p. 1981. text 55.00 (*0-914710-74-5*, Pub. by East Eur Monographs) Col U Pr.

Radice, Mark A., ed. Opera in Context: Essays on Historical Staging from the Late Renaissance to the Time of Puccini. LC 97-2712. (Illus.). 450p. 1998. 44.95 (*1-57467-032-8*, Amadeus Pr) Timber.

Radice, Roberto & Davies, Richard. Aristotle's Metaphysics: An Annotated Bibliography of the Twentieth-Century Literature. LC 97-22097. (Annotated Bibliographies Ser.). (Illus.). xxiv, 904p. 1997. 324.00 (*90-04-10895-5*) Brill Academic Pubs.

Radice, Roberto & Runia, David T. Philo of Alexandria: An Annotated Bibliography, 1937-1986. LC 88-26242. (Supplements to Vigiliae Christianae Ser.: Vol. 8). (Illus.). xli, 469p. 1992. reprint ed. 160.00 (*90-04-08986-1*) Brill Academic Pubs.

Radice, Ronald A. ISO 9001 Interpreted for Software Organizations. Pollack, William, ed. LC 95-11173. 352p. (C). 1995. 39.95 (*0-9645913-0-8*) Paradoxicon Pub.

Radice, William. Louring Skies. 72p. 1985. pap. 14.95 (*0-85646-153-9*, Pub. by Anvil Press) Dufour.

— Strivings: Poems, 1972-1976. 56p. 1980. pap. 14.95 (*0-85646-056-7*, Pub. by Anvil Press) Dufour.

— Teach Yourself Bengali. (BEN & ENG.). 1993. pap. 18.95 (*0-7859-1052-2*, 0-340-552573); pap. 29.95 incl. audio (*0-7859-1058-1*, 0-340-56489X) Fr & Eur.

— Teach Yourself Bengali Complete. (BEN., Illus.). 336p. 1995. pap. 19.95 (*0-8442-3752-3*, Teach Yrslf) NTC Contemp Pub Co.

— Teach Yourself Bengali Complete Course. (BEN.). 336p. 1995. pap. 29.95 incl. audio (*0-8442-3851-1*, Teach Yrslf) NTC Contemp Pub Co.

Radice, William, ed. & tr. see Tagore, Rabindranath.

Radich, Anthony. Economic Impact of the Arts: A Sourcebook. 252p. 1991. pap. 15.00 (*1-55516-216-9*, 2106) Natl Conf State Legis.

Radicke, Jan, jt. ed. see Schepens, G.

Radigan, C. Raymond & Turano, Margaret V. New York Estate Administration, 1998 Supplement. 200p. 1998. write for info. (*0-327-00855-5*, 6890511) LEXIS Pub.

*__Radigan, C. Raymond & Turano, Margaret Valentine.__ New York Estate Administration: 1999 Edition. 900p. 1999. write for info. (*0-327-04987-1*, 6890011) LEXIS Pub.

Radigan, C. Raymond, jt. auth. see Turano, Margaret V.

Radigan, Emily N., ed. see Lyon, Henry C.

Radiguet. Radiguet: Le Diable au corps. Griffiths, ed. (Bristol French Texts Ser.). (FRE.). 158p. 1992. pap. 18.95 (*1-85399-325-5*, Pub. by Brist Class Pr) Focus Pub-R Pullins.

Radiguet, Raymond. Le Bal du Comte d'Orgel. (Folio Ser.: No. 1176). 208p. 1924. 8.95 (*2-07-037476-9*) Schoenhof.

— Le Bal du Comte d'Orgel. unabridged ed. (FRE.). pap. 5.95 (*2-87714-222-1*, Pub. by Bookking Intl) Distribks Inc.

— Cheeks on Fire. Stone, Alan, tr. from FRE. (ENG & FRE.). 112p. 1986. 13.95 (*0-7145-3513-3*) Riverrun NY.

— Count D'Orgel's Ball. Cancogni, Annapaola, tr. from FRE. LC 88-83032. 174p. 1989. reprint ed. pap. 11.00 (*0-941419-30-4*, Eridanos Library) Marsilio Pubs.

— Devil in the Flesh. Smith, A. M., tr. from FRE. (Fiction Ser.).Tr. of Le Diable au Corps. 128p. (YA). 1993. reprint ed. pap. 12.95 (*0-7145-0193-X*) M Boyars Pubs.

— Le Diable au Corps. (Coll. Diamant). (FRE.). 118p. 1991. pap. 6.95 (*0-7859-1492-7*, 2277229695) Fr & Eur.

— Le Diable au Corps. (Folio Ser.: No. 1391). (FRE.). 192p. 1955. pap. 8.95 (*2-07-037391-6*) Schoenhof.

— Le Diable au Corps. unabridged ed. (FRE.). pap. 5.95 (*2-87714-159-4*, Pub. by Bookking Intl) Distribks Inc.

— Oeuvres Completes. 1978. 75.00 (*0-686-54719-5*) Fr & Eur.

Radimersky, George W. German Science Reader: An Analytical Approach to Translation Problems. LC 50-8071. 253p. reprint ed. pap. 78.50 (*0-608-30032-2*, 201253300081) Bks Demand.

Radin. Using the Caldera Desktop: Linux with Graphics. 1996. pap. write for info. (*1-56592-164-X*) Thomson Learn.

Radin, Alexander. Miniature Bearing Technologies in the U. S. S. R. (The Institute VNIPP & NIIChasprom) Tamberg, Andreas, ed. 151p. (Orig.). 1986. pap. text 75.00 (*1-55831-038-X*) Delphic Associates.

Radin, Barbara. Decision Dramas: Real Language for Real Life. 98p. 1992. pap. 10.95 (*0-943327-12-1*) JAG Pubns.

*__Radin, Beryl A.__ Beyond Machiavelli: Policy Analysis Comes of Age. LC 99-36841. 160p. 2000. text 45.00 (*0-87840-772-3*); pap. text 17.95 (*0-87840-773-1*) Georgetown U Pr.

Radin, Beryl A. Federal Policies for Equal Educational Opportunity: Conflict & Confusion. (Policy Research Project Report: No. 23). 147p. 1977. pap. 3.50 (*0-89940-616-5*) LBJ Sch Pub Aff.

— Implementation, Change, & the Federal Bureaucracy: School Desegregation Policy in HEW, 1964-1968. LC 76-58320. (Policy Analysis & Education Ser.). 255p. reprint ed. pap. 79.10 (*0-8357-3007-7*, 203927500011) Bks Demand.

Radin, Beryl A. & Howley, W. D. The Politics of Federal Reorganization: Creating the U. S. Department of Education. LC 87-6972. (Illus.). 250p. 1988. 40.00 (*0-08-033978-6*, Pergamon Pr); pap. 18.95 (*0-08-033977-8*, Pergamon Pr) Elsevier.

Radin, Beryl A. & Purvis, Hoyt H. Women in Public Life. (Symposia Ser.). 56p. 1976. pap. 3.50 (*0-89940-404-9*) LBJ Sch Pub Aff.

Radin, Beryl A., et al. New Goverance for Rural America: Creating Intergovernmental Partnerships. LC 95-46677. (Rural America Ser.). 240p. (C). 1996. 29.95 (*0-7006-0770-6*); pap. 17.95 (*0-7006-0771-4*) U Pr of KS.

Radin, Betty. Dreamdance. 15p. 1997. pap. 5.00 (*1-57141-031-7*) Runaway Spoon.

— Hot Taters & Razzmatazz. 10p. 1997. pap. 5.00 (*1-57141-032-5*) Runaway Spoon.

Radin, Bill. Career Development Reports: Candidate Training in Your Office or on Your Web Site. 56p. 1996. 49.95 (*0-9626147-8-5*) Innovative Consulting.

*__Radin, Bill.__ How to Market & Sell Your Recruiting Services, Set. 12p. 1999. pap. 79.95 incl. audio (*1-929836-00-7*) Innovative Consulting.

— How to Write High Profit Job Orders, Set. 12p. 1999. pap., wbk. ed. 79.95 incl. audio (*1-929836-01-5*) Innovative Consulting.

Radin, Bill. The Recruiter's Almanac of Scripts, Rebuttals & Closes. 2nd rev. ed. Scott, Lou, ed. 1998. pap. 49.95 (*0-9626147-7-7*) Innovative Consulting.

*__Radin, Bill.__ Time Management Secrets of Top-Producing Recruiters, Set. 12p. 1999. pap. 79.95 incl. audio (*1-929836-02-3*) Innovative Consulting.

Radin, Carolyn. The Smart Shopper in Hong Kong: Your Guide to Factory Outlets & Other Useful Information. (Illus.). 130p. (Orig.). 1996. mass mkt. 10.95 (*0-9655110-0-6*) Black Hawk Prods.

*__Radin, Charles A.__ Miles of Tiles. LC 99-20662. (Student Mathematical Library). 120p. 1999. pap. 16.00 (*0-8218-1933-X*) Am Math.

Radin, Dave. Building a Successful Software Business. Loukides, Mike, ed. (Illus.). 394p. (Orig.). 1994. pap. 21.95 (*1-56592-064-3*) Thomson Learn.

Radin, Dean. The Conscious Universe: The Scientific Truth of Psychic Phenomena. LC 97-8602. 384p. 1997. 25.00 (*0-06-251502-0*, Pub. by Harper SF) HarpC.

Radin, Doris. There Are Talismans. LC 91-16268. (Eileen W. Barnes Award Ser.). (Illus.). 64p. (Orig.). 1991. pap. 7.00 (*0-938158-12-0*) Saturday Pr.

Radin, Dorothea P., tr. see Kochanowski, Jan.

Radin, Eric L., et al. Practical Biomechanics for the Orthopaedic Surgeon. 2nd ed. (Illus.). 216p. 1991. text 62.00 (*0-443-08702-4*) Church.

Radin, Eric L., ed. see Wright, Verna.

Radin-Fox, Barbara, jt. auth. see Fox, Larry.

Radin, Grace. Virginia Woolf's "The Years" The Evolution of a Novel. LC 80-22590. 212p. 1981. 31.00 (*0-87049-307-8*) U of Tenn Pr.

Radin, Judi, jt. auth. see Wei, Katherine.

Radin, Judi, jt. auth. see Wei, Kathie.

Radin, M. Judith, jt. auth. see Wellman, Maxey L.

Radin, Margaret J. Contested Commodities. 288p. 1996. 37.95 (*0-674-16697-3*) HUP.

— Reinterpreting Property. LC 93-4908. 278p. 1994. 29.95 (*0-226-70227-8*) U Ch Pr.

— Reinterpreting Property. LC 93-4908. 278p. 1996. reprint ed. pap. text 15.95 (*0-226-70228-6*) U Ch Pr.

Radin, Margaret J., jt. ed. see Gordon, Robert W.

Radin, Max. Handbook of Anglo-American Legal History. LC 93-78454. 638p. 1993. reprint ed. 145.00 (*1-56169-039-2*) Gaunt.

— The Jews among the Greeks & Romans. 1915. pap. 25.00 (*0-8196-2074-2*) Biblo.

— The Jews among the Greeks & Romans. LC 73-2224. (Jewish People; History, Religion, Literature Ser.). 1973. reprint ed. 36.95 (*0-405-05286-3*) Ayer.

— Law as Logic & Experience. 1940. LC 99-30670. 2000. reprint ed. 55.00 (*1-58477-008-2*) Lawbk Exchange.

— The Lawful Pursuit of Gain. LC 75-39268. (Getting & Spending: The Consumer's Dilemma Ser.). 1976. reprint ed. 19.95 (*0-405-08041-7*) Ayer.

Radin, Max, jt. auth. see Schiffer, Walter.

*__Radin, Paul.__ The Story of the American Indian. (LC History-America-E). 391p. 1999. reprint ed. lib. bdg. 89.00 (*0-7812-4272-X*) Rprt Serv.

*__Radin, Paul, ed.__ Crashing Thunder: The Autobiography of an American Indian. LC 99-23924. (Illus.). 256p. (C). 1999. pap. text 17.95 (*0-472-08632-4*, 08632) U of Mich Pr.

Radin, Paul, ed. see Blowsnake, Sam.

Radin, Paul, tr. see Ginzberg, Louis.

Radin, Paul A. African Folktales. LC 74-106800. (Bollingen Ser., Vol. 32). 338p. (Orig.). reprint ed. 104.80 (*0-8357-9491-1*, 201303400083) Bks Demand.

— Autobiography of a Winnebago Indian. 91p. 1920. pap. 4.95 (*0-486-20096-5*) Dover.

— The Genetic Relationship of the North American Indian Languages. fac. ed. (University of California Publications in American Archaeology & Ethnology: Vol. 14: 5). 13p. (C). 1919. reprint ed. pap. text 1.88 (*1-55567-220-5*) Coyote Press.

— A Grammar of the Wappo Language. fac. ed. Lowie, Robert H. & Kroeber, A. L., eds. (University of California Publications in American Archaeology & Ethnology: Vol. 27). 202p. (C). 1920. reprint ed. pap. text 21.88 (*1-55567-275-2*) Coyote Press.

— The Italians of San Francisco. LC 74-17945. (Italian American Experience Ser.). (Illus.). 200p. 1975. reprint ed. 18.95 (*0-405-06415-2*) Ayer.

— The Method & Theory of Ethnology. LC 86-29921. 388p. 1987. pap. 21.95 (*0-89789-118-X*, Bergin & Garvey) Greenwood.

— The Trickster: A Study in American Indian Mythology. LC 74-88986. 212p. 1987. pap. 13.00 (*0-8052-0351-6*) Schocken.

— The Trickster: A Study in American Indian Mythology. LC 74-88986. 211p. 1969. reprint ed. lib. bdg. 38.50 (*0-8371-2112-4*, RATT, Greenwood Pr) Greenwood.

— Wappo Texts - First Series. fac. ed. (University of California Publications in American Archaeology & Ethnology: Vol. 19: 1). 152p. (C). 1924. reprint ed. pap. text 16.88 (*1-55567-235-3*) Coyote Press.

— The Winnebago Tribe. LC 64-63594. (Illus.). xvi, 573p. 1990. reprint ed. pap. 25.00 (*0-8032-5710-4*, Bison Books) U of Nebr Pr.

Radin, Paul A., ed. African Folktales. LC 82-10475. 322p. (Orig.). 1987. reprint ed. pap. 14.95 (*0-8052-0732-5*) Schocken.

R

An Asterisk (*) at the beginning of an entry indicates that the title is appearing for the first time.

Radin, Paul A. & Espinoza, A. M. Folklore de Oaxaca. LC 78-63215. (Folktale Ser.). reprint ed. 37.50 (0-404-16299-1) AMS Pr.

Radin, Ruth. From the Wooded Hill: Reading Level 1-3 & Above. LC 92-42219. (Illus.). 1992. 4.75 (0-88336-039-X) New Readers.

— Morning Streets: Reading Level 1-3 & Above. LC 92-42220. (Illus.). 1993. 4.75 (0-88336-040-3) New Readers.

— Sky Bridges & Other Poems. LC 92-46291. (Illus.). (J). (gr. 1-3). 1993. 3.50 (0-88336-038-1) New Readers.

— Sky Bridges & Other Poems: Reading Level 1-3 & Above. LC 92-46291. 1993. audio 9.95 (0-88336-620-7) New Readers.

Radin, Ruth Y. All Joseph Wanted. LC 91-12643. (Illus.). 80p. (J). (gr. 3-7). 1991. text, lib. bdg. 14.00 (0-02-775641-6, Mac Bks Young Read) S&S Childrens.

— Escape to the Forest. LC 99-26426. (Illus.). 96p. (J). (gr. 4 up). 2001. pap. 4.25 (0-06-440822-1) HarpC Child Bks.

***Radin, Ruth Y.** Escape to the Forest: Based on a True Story of the Holocaust. LC 99-26426. (Illus.). 96p. (YA). (gr. 4 up). 2000. 13.95 (0-06-028520-6); lib. bdg. 13.89 (0-06-028521-4) HarpC Child Bks.

Radin, Ruth Y. Tac's Island. 80p. (J). (gr. 2-9). 1997. reprint ed. pap. 2.95 (0-8167-1320-0) Troll Communs.

Radin, Shelden & Folk, Robert. Physics for Scientists & Engineers. 2nd ed. 832p. (C). 1992. pap. text 93.00 (0-536-58178-9) Pearson Custom.

Radin, Stephen & Greenberg, Harold. Computers in the Doctor's Office. LC 84-8378. 151p. 1984. 47.95 (0-275-91245-0, C1245, Praeger Pubs) Greenwood.

Radin, Victoria. Even So, Come Lord Jesus! A Jewish Perspective of End-Time Prophecy Spanning Genesis to Revelation. (Illus.). 220p. (Orig.). 1996. pap. 15.95 (0-9654763-0-8) Victory Pub NY.

Radin, William G. Billing Power! The Recruiter's Guide to Peak Performance. expanded rev. ed. Smith, Betsy, ed. (Illus.). 224p. (Orig.). 1995. reprint ed. pap. 49.95 (0-9626147-4-2) Innovative Consulting.

Radin, William G. Recruiting & the Art of Control: How to Fill More Jobs in a Candidate-Driven Market. Smith, Betsy, ed. 60p. 1996. text, wbk. ed. 195.00 incl. audio (0-9626147-6-9) Innovative Consulting.

Radin, William G. Shut up & Make More Money: The Recruiter's Guide to Talking Less & Billing More. Smith, Betsy, ed. (Illus.). 224p. 1995. pap. 49.95 (0-9626147-3-4) Innovative Consulting.

Radine, Lawrence B. The Taming of the Troops: Social Control in the United States Army, 22. LC 76-5262. (Contributions in Sociology Ser.: No. 22). 276p. (Orig.). 1977. 65.00 (0-8371-8911-X, RTT/, Greenwood Pr) Greenwood.

***Radinger, Willy & Otto, Wolfgang.** Messerschmitt BF 109 F-K: Development/Testing/Production. (Illus.). 160p. 2000. 35.00 (0-7643-1023-2) Schiffer.

Radinger, Willy & Schick, Walter. Messerschmitt BF109 A-E: Development/Testing/Production. (Illus.). 136p. 1999. 35.00 (0-7643-0951-X) Schiffer.

— Messerschmitt Me 262: Development - Testing - Production. (Illus.). 112p. 1993. 24.95 (0-88740-516-9) Schiffer.

— Secret Messerschmitt Projects.Tr. of Messerschmitt Gehetmeprojerte. (ENG & GER., Illus.). 208p. (C). (gr. 13). 1996. 35.00 (0-88740-926-1) Schiffer.

Radinsky, Leonard B. The Evolution of Vertebrate Design. LC 87-5959. (Illus.). xii, 208p. 1987. pap. text 15.00 (0-226-70236-7) U Ch Pr.

Radio Broadcasting Research Project Staff. Studies in the Control of Radio, Nos. 1[00ad]6. LC 79-161174. (History of Broadcasting: Radio to Television Ser.). 1977. reprint ed. 31.95 (0-405-03581-0) Ayer.

Radio Control Car Action Editors. Radio Control Car How-To's, Vol. 2. Howell, John, ed. (Illus.). 98p. (Orig.). 1994. pap. 14.95 (0-911295-32-1) Air Age.

Radio-Electronics Editors. Radio-Electronics: From "Drawing Board" to Finished Project. (Illus.). 160p. 1989. 15.95 (0-8306-9133-2, 3133); pap. 9.95 (0-8306-3133-X, 3133) McGraw-Hill Prof.

— Radio-Electronics' Guide to Computer Circuits. (Illus.). 170p. 1988. 14.95 (0-8306-0333-6); pap. 9.95 (0-8306-9333-5, 3033P) McGraw-Hill Prof.

Radio Free Europe-Radio Liberty Staff. The Bosnia Crisis & International Broadcasting: A Conference Sponsored by the Radio Free Europe/Radio Liberty Fund. LC 88-30186. (Illus.). 34p. (C). 1997. pap. text 22.50 (0-929849-01-9) RFE-RL Inc.

— Glasnost & Empire: National Aspirations in the U. S. S. R. LC 88-30186. (Illus.). 60p. (Orig.). (C). 1989. pap. text 11.50 (0-929849-00-0) RFE-RL Inc.

Radio Free Europe Staff. Scaling the Wall: Talking to Eastern Europe: The Best of Radio Free Europe. Urban, George R., ed. LC 64-18955. 303p. reprint ed. pap. 94.00 (0-7837-3801-3, 204362100010) Bks Demand.

Radio Ink Magazine Staff Writers. The Radio Book, 3 vols. Incl. Bk. 1. Programming & Promotion. LC 95-67239. 1995. pap. 19.99 (1-886745-00-5); Bk. 2. Management. LC 95-67240. 784p. 1995. pap. 19.99 (1-886745-01-3); Bk. 3. Sales & Marketing. LC 95-67241. 784p. 1995. pap. 19.99 (1-886745-02-1); 1995. Set pap. 49.00 (1-886745-03-X) Streamlne Pr.

Radio Ink Staff Writers. Proven Radio Copy, 3 vols. 651p. (Orig.). 1997. pap. text 197.00 (1-886745-10-2) Streamlne Pr.

— Proven Radio Copy, Vol. 1. 235p. (Orig.). 1997. pap. text 77.00 (1-886745-07-2) Streamlne Pr.

— Proven Radio Copy: Automotive, Professional Services, Vol. 3. 224p. (Orig.). 1997. pap. text 77.00 (1-886745-09-9) Streamlne Pr.

— Proven Radio Copy: Entertainment, Food, Restaurants, Vol. 2. 192p. (Orig.). 1997. pap. text 77.00 (1-886745-08-0) Streamlne Pr.

Radio Magazine Editors. Audio Anthology Vol. 5: When Audio Was Young. (Illus.). 144p. (Orig.). 1993. reprint ed. pap. 16.95 (1-882580-01-X) Audio Amateur.

Radioisotopes & Radiation Effects Committee E-10. Space Radiation Effects on Materials. LC 62-20905. No. 330. 71p. reprint ed. pap. 25.00 (0-317-09203-0, 2000123) Bks Demand.

Radiological Society of North America-RadioGraphic. RSNA, 1992: Selected Scientific Exhibits. 1994. vdisk 500.00 (1-56815-024-5, 10024) Mosby Inc.

Radiquet, Raymond. Bal du Comte d'Orgel. 208p. 1924. write for info. (0-318-63432-5) Fr & Eur.

— Bal du Comte d'Orgel. (FRE.). 256p. 1984. pap. 10.95 (0-7859-1646-6, 2080704060) Fr & Eur.

— Count D'Orgel. Schiff, Violet, tr. from FRE. 160p. 2000. pap. 12.95 (1-885586-02-7, Pub. by Turtle Point Pr) Dist Art Pubs.

Radiquet, Raymond, jt. auth. see Cocteau, Jean.

Radish, Kris. Run, Bambi, Run: The Beautiful Ex-Cop Convicted of Murder Who Escaped to Freedom & Won America's Heart. (Illus.). 1992. 18.95 (1-55972-103-0, Birch Ln Pr) Carol Pub Group.

Radishchev. Journey from Petersburg to Moscow. unabridged ed. (World Classic Literature Ser.). (RUS.). pap. 6.95 (2-87714-258-2, Pub. by Bookking Intl) Distribks Inc.

Radisich, Paula R. Hubert Robert: Painted Spaces of the Enlightenment. LC 97-30194. (Illus.). 224p. (C). 1998. 70.00 (0-521-59351-4) Cambridge U Pr.

Radisson, Pierre E. Voyages of Peter Esprit Radisson, Being an Account of His Travels & Experiences among the North American Indians, from 1652 to 1684: Transcribed from Original Messages in the Bodleian Library & British Museum. (American Biography Ser.). 385p. 1991. reprint ed. lib. bdg. 79.00 (0-7812-8320-5) Rprt Serv.

Raditsa, Leo. Prisoners of a Dream: The South African Mirage. 500p. (Orig.). 1989. pap. 25.00 (0-927104-00-8) Prince Grg St.

Raditsa, Leo, tr. see Kessel, Joseph.

Radivilova, Serafima. Translating from English into Russian: Reference Grammar for Students of Russian. LC 98-22783. 488p. 1998. pap. 38.50 (0-7618-1156-7) U Pr of Amer.

Radjavi, H. & Rosenthal, P. Invariant Subspaces. LC 73-77570. (Ergebnisse der Mathematik und Ihrer Grenzgebiete Ser.: Vol. 77). (Illus.). 230p. 1973. 65.00 (0-387-06217-3) Spr-Verlag.

— Simultaneous Triangularization. LC 99-23772. (Universitext Ser.). 200p. (C). 1998. 54.95 (0-387-98467-4); pap. 29.95 (0-387-98466-6) Spr-Verlag.

Radka, Larry B. Astronomical Revelations on 666: A Scientific & Historical Study of Asteroids & Comets with Respect to the Apocalypse. LC 97-90309. (Illus.). 336p. 1997. pap. 19.95 (0-9657545-4-5) Einhorn Pr.

— Historical Evidence for Unicorns. (Illus.). Date not set. pap. 15.00 (0-614-09533-6) Artex Pub.

— Historical Evidence for Unicorns. limited ed. LC 95-60630. (Illus.). 152p. Date not set. 35.00 (0-930401-81-6) Artex Pub.

Radke. Peoples Choice. 2nd ed. 1998. 13.75 (0-07-233197-6) McGraw.

Radke, Barbara R. & Stein, Barbara L. Creating Newsletters, Brochures, & Pamphlets: A How-to-Do-It Manual for School & Public Librarians. (How-to-Do-It Ser.). 139p. 1992. 39.95 (1-55570-107-8) Neal-Schuman.

Radke, Detlef. The German Social Market Economy: An Option for the Transforming & Developing Countries? (GDI Bks.: Vol. 4). 1994. pap. 22.50 (0-7146-4153-7) Intl Spec Bk.

Radke, Gary M. Viterbo: Profile of a Thirteenth-Century Papal Palace. LC 95-47503. (Illus.). 376p. (C). 1996. text 85.00 (0-521-48200-3) Cambridge U Pr.

Radke, Gary M., jt. auth. see Paletti, John T.

Radke, Gary M., jt. auth. see Paoletti, John T.

Radke, Judith, tr. see Chedid, Andree.

Radke, Ken. But Grace Is Enough. 161p. 1991. pap. text 5.95 (0-87508-459-1) Chr Lit.

Radke, Linda F. The Economical Guide to Self-Publishing: How to Produce & Market Your Book on a Budget. Hawkins, Mary E., ed. 1996. pap. 19.95 (1-877749-16-8) Five Star AZ.

***Radke, Linda F.** Linda Radke's Promote Like a Pro - Small Budget, Big Show: A Step-by-Step Guide to Promoting Anything from Books to Businesses. Caputo, Sal & DeFabis, Sue, eds. LC 99-54903. (Illus.). 182p. 2000. pap. 19.95 (1-877749-36-2) Five Star AZ.

Radke, Linda F. Nannies, Maids, & More: The Complete Guide for Hiring Household Help. Hawkins, Mary E., ed. LC 89-80249. (Illus.). 113p. 1989. pap. 14.95 (0-9619853-2-1) Five Star AZ.

— Options Vol. II: A Directory of Child & Senior Services (Arizona Edition) 1989. pap. 9.95 (0-9619853-4-8) Five Star AZ.

— Options - A Directory of Child & Senior Services. 1987. pap. 6.00 (0-9619853-1-3) Five Star AZ.

— That Hungarian's in My Kitchen: 125 Hungarian - American - Kosher Recipes. Hawkins, Mary E., ed. 179p. 1997. reprint ed. pap. 14.95 (1-877749-28-1) Five Star AZ.

Radke, Martha E. The Cat Who Conducted with His Tail. LC 81-90803. (Illus.). 28p. (Orig.). (J). (ps-3). 1982. pap. 1.95 (0-9607994-0-0) G E Radke.

Radke, William J., jt. auth. see Chiasson, Robert B.

Radke-Yarrow, Marian, et al. Children of Depressed Mothers: From Early Childhood to Maturity. Ronsaville, Donna, ed. LC 98-17213. (Illus.). 200p. (C). 1998. 49.95 (0-521-55131-5) Cambridge U Pr.

Radkevich, V., jt. auth. see Krapivnvi, A.

Radkey, Oliver H. Russia Goes to the Polls: The Election to the All-Russian Constituent Assembly, 1917. LC 89-42884. (Cornell Studies in Soviet History & Society - Studies of the Harriman Institute). 192p. 1989. 35.00 (0-8014-2360-0) Cornell U Pr.

— Russia Goes to the Polls: The Election to the All-Russian Constituent Assembly, 1917. LC 89-42884. (Studies in Soviet History & Society). 197p. reprint ed. pap. 61.10 (0-608-20935-X, 207203400003) Bks Demand.

Radko, Christopher. Christopher Radko - The First Decade. LC 98-121490. (Illus.). 208p. Date not set. 65.00 (0-9647556-0-2) Starad.

— Christopher Radko's Ornaments. LC 99-14443. 1999. 22.50 (0-609-60476-7) Crown Pub Group.

Radko, Christopher, jt. auth. see Kantor, Pamela.

Radko, Michael A. Spatially Linking Basin Wide Stream Inventories to Arcs Representing Streams in a Geographic Information System. (Illus.). 28p. 1997. reprint ed. 9.00 (0-89904-688-6, Bear Meadows Resrch Grp); reprint ed. pap. 4.00 (0-89904-575-8, Bear Meadows Resrch Grp) Crumb Elbow Pub.

Radl, Emanuel. The History of Biological Theories. 1988. reprint ed. lib. bdg. 75.00 (0-7812-0068-7) Rprt Serv.

— The History of Biological Theories. LC 30-28974. 498p. 1930. reprint ed. 69.00 (0-403-01791-2) Scholarly.

Radl, Shirley, jt. auth. see Zimbardo, Philip G.

Radlanski, Ralf J. Contributions to the Development of Human Deciduous Tooth Primordia. LC 92-48439.Tr. of Beitrage zur Gestaltentwicklung Menschlicher Zahnanlagen der Ersten Dentition. 1993. pap. text 58.00 (0-86715-261-3) Quint Pub Co.

Radlauer, Edward. Bears, Bears & More Bears. (Ed Radlauer Bks.). (Illus.). 32p. (J). (ps-4). 1991. lib. bdg. 12.95 (1-878363-34-4) Forest Hse.

— Cats, Cats, & More Cats. (Ed Radlauer Bks.). (Illus.). 32p. (J). (ps-4). 1991. lib. bdg. 12.95 (1-878363-35-2) Forest Hse.

— Ed Radlauer "More" Readers, 3 vols., Set. (Ed Radlauer Bks.). (Illus.). 96p. (J). (ps-5). 1991. lib. bdg. 38.85 (1-56674-922-0) Forest Hse.

— Wheels, Wheels, & More Wheels. (Ed Radlauer Bks.). (Illus.). 32p. (J). (ps-4). 1991. lib. bdg. 12.95 (1-878363-36-0) Forest Hse.

Radlauer, Ruth S. Honor the Flag: A Guide to Its Care & Display. rev. ed. (United States & Its Flag Ser.). (Illus.). 48p. (J). (gr. 2 up). 1996. lib. bdg. 14.95 (1-878363-61-1, JC346) Forest Hse.

— Honor the Flag: A Guide to Its Care & Display. rev. ed. (United States & Its Flag Ser.). (Illus.). 48p. (J). (gr. 3 up). 1996. pap. 8.95 (1-56674-700-7) Forest Hse.

— Molly Goes Hiking. LC 86-18761. (Illus.). 32p. (J). (ps-3). 1987. pap. 10.95 (0-671-66860-9) S&S Trade.

Radle, Gail. Skies. LC 97-27623. (Vanishing from Ser.). (J). 1998. lib. bdg. write for info. (0-8225-1938-0) Lerner Pub.

Radler, Albert J., jt. tr. see Ault, Hugh J.

Radler, K-H., jt. auth. see Krause, F.

Radlett, Marty, jt. ed. see Mirsky, Judith.

Radley, Alan. The Body & Social Psychology. (Social Psychology Ser.). xi, 213p. 1991. 96.95 (0-387-97584-5) Spr-Verlag.

— In Social Relationships: An Introduction to the Social Psychology of Membership & Intimacy. 192p. 1991. 113.00 (0-335-15197-3); pap. 36.95 (0-335-15196-5) OpUniv Pr.

— Making Sense of Illness: The Social Psychology of Health & Disease. 256p. 1995. text 45.00 (0-8039-8908-3); pap. text 15.99 (0-8039-8909-1) Sage.

— Prospects of Heart Surgery. (Contributions to Psychology & Medicine Ser.). (Illus.). 250p. 1988. 105.95 (0-387-96721-4) Spr-Verlag.

Radley, Alan, ed. Worlds of Illness: Biographical & Cultural Perspectives on Health & Disease. 224p. (C). 1995. pap. 27.99 (0-415-13152-9) Routledge.

Radley, Chip. Workout. 1997. pap., student ed. write for info. (0-17-556519-8, Pub. by ITP Nelson) Thomson Learn.

Radley, Gail. Dear Gabby, Things Are Getting Out of Hand . . . 112p. 1998. pap. 3.99 (0-380-78357-6, Avon Bks) Morrow Avon.

— Dear Gabby, Things Are Getting Out of Hand . . . 1998. 9.09 (0-606-13325-9, Pub. by Turtleback) Demco.

— A Feast of ABCs. large type ed. (Illus.). 32p. (Orig.). (J). (gr. 1-2). 1996. pap. 9.50 (0-85398-409-3) G Ronald Pub.

— Forests & Jungles. LC 97-27614. (Vanishing from Ser.). (J). 1998. lib. bdg. write for info. (0-8225-1937-2) Lerner Pub.

— Grasslands & Deserts. LC 97-28627. (Vanishing from Ser.). (J). 1998. lib. bdg. write for info. (0-8225-1936-4) Lerner Pub.

— Old Man Out. LC 94-10858. 144p. (J). (gr. 3-7). 1995. mass mkt. 14.00 (0-02-775792-7, Mac Bks Young Read) S&S Childrens.

— Second Birth: The Goal of Life. (Illus.). 28p. (J). (gr. 1-6). 1984. 8.00 (0-900125-55-1) Bahai.

— Waterways. LC 97-28628. (Vanishing from Ser.). (J). 1998. lib. bdg. write for info. (0-8225-1939-9) Lerner Pub.

Radley, Gail & Sherlock, Jean. Waterways. LC 97-28628. (Vanishing From Ser.). 1999. lib. bdg. write for info. (1-57505-408-6, Carolrhoda) Lerner Pub.

Radley, Gail & Sherlock, Jean. Forests & Jungles. LC 97-27614. (Vanishing from Ser.). (J). 1999. lib. bdg. write for info. (1-57505-405-1, Carolrhoda) Lerner Pub.

— Grasslands & Deserts. LC 97-28627. (Vanishing From Ser.). 1999. lib. bdg. write for info. (1-57505-406-X, Carolrhoda) Lerner Pub.

— Skies. LC 97-27623. (Vanishing from Ser.). 1999. lib. bdg. write for info. (1-57505-407-8, Carolrhoda) Lerner Pub.

Radley, J. A., ed. Industrial Uses of Starch & Its Derivatives. 268p. 1976. 88.25 (0-85334-691-7, Pub. by Elsevier) Elsevier.

Radley, Kenneth. Rebel Watchdog: The Confederate States Army Provost Guard. (Illus.). 360p. 1997. pap. 16.95 (0-8071-2173-8) La State U Pr.

Radley, Paul J. Jack Rivers & Me. 1986. 14.45 (0-89919-429-X, Pub. by Ticknor & Fields); pap. 7.95 (0-89919-433-8, Pub. by Ticknor & Fields) HM.

Radley, Paul J. My Blue-Checker Corker & Me. 1986. 15.45 (0-89919-432-X, Pub. by Ticknor & Fields) HM.

Radley, Sheila. Blood on the Happy Highway. large type ed. 1985. 16.95 (0-7089-1316-4) Ulverscroft.

— The Chief Inspector's Daughter. large type ed. 1982. 27.99 (0-7089-1033-5) Ulverscroft.

— Cross My Heart & Hope to Die: An Inspector Quantrill Mystery. (Quantrill Ser.: No. 8). 288p. 1992. text 19.00 (0-684-19410-4, Scribners Ref) Mac Lib Ref.

— Cross My Heart & Hope to Die: An Inspector Quantrill Mystery. large type ed. 416p. 1998. 29.99 (0-7089-3956-2) Ulverscroft.

Radley, Sheila. Fair Game. large type ed. 416p. 31.99 (0-7089-4028-5) Ulverscroft.

— New Blood From Old Bones. large type ed. 352p. 2000. 31.99 (0-7089-4199-0) Ulverscroft.

Radley, Virginia L. Elizabeth Barrett Browning. (English Authors Ser.: No. 136). 160p. 1972. 32.00 (0-8057-1064-7) Macmillan.

***Radliff, Debbie.** Developing Life Skills. (Illus.). 96p. 1999. pap. text 10.95 (1-58037-115-9, Pub. by M Twain Media) Carson-Dellos.

Radlk, Cupaniopsis, jt. auth. see Adema, F.

Radloff, Bernhard. Cosmopolis & Truth: Melville's Critique of Modernity. (Studies on Themes & Motifs in Literature: Vol. 16). X, 254p. (C). 1996. text 51.95 (0-8204-2716-0) P Lang Pubng.

— Will & Representation: The Philosophical Foundations of Melville's Theatrum Mundi. (Studies on Themes & Motifs in Literature: Vol. 17). XIII, 348p. (C). 1996. text 62.95 (0-8204-2717-9) P Lang Pubng.

Radloff, Carla. Sentence Repetition Testing for Studies of Community Bilingualism. LC 91-68075. (Publications in Linguistics: No. 104). xvi, 214p. (Orig.). 1992. pap. 15.00 (0-88312-667-2) S I L Intl.

Radloff, Roland & Helmreich, Robert. Groups under Stress: Psychological Research in Sealab 2. LC 68-19962. (Century Psychology Ser.). (Illus.). (C). 1968. 30.50 (0-89197-191-2) Irvington.

Radloff, S. E., jt. auth. see Hepburn, H. R.

Radloff, V. V. South-Siberian Oral Literature Turkic Texts, Vol. 1. LC 66-64926. (Uralic & Altaic Ser.: Vol. 79, Bk. 1). 419p. 1967. pap. text. write for info. (0-87750-075-4) Curzon Pr Ltd.

Radlow, James. Understanding Finite Math. (Mathematics Ser.). 1981. pap. text 28.00 (0-87150-328-X) PWS Pubs.

Radmacher, ed. Nelson's New Illustrated Bible Commentary. LC 99-11281. (Illus.). 1200p. 1999. 39.99 (0-7852-1438-0) Nelson.

Radmacher, Earl & Hodges, Zane C. The NIV Reconsidered: A Fresh Look at a Popular Translation. 155p. (Orig.). 1991. pap. 8.95 (0-9607576-9-4) Redencion Viva.

Radmacher, Earl D. Salvation. 1. LC 99-48664. (Swindoll Leadership Library). 1999. 24.99 (0-8499-1374-8) Word Pub.

— Salvation: Supersaver Edition. 1999. 19.97 (0-8499-1597-X) Word Pub.

— You & Your Thoughts - Chinese Edition: The Power of Right Thinking. Tso, Thomas & Huang, Tony, trs. (CHI.). 135p. 1983. pap. 5.00 (1-56582-093-2) Christ Renew Min.

Radmacher, Sally A., jt. auth. see Sheridan, Charles L.

Radman Assoc. Staff. The Radman Guide to the Ionising Radiations Regulations, 1985. (Handbook Ser.: No. 1). (C). 1986. 54.00 (0-948237-00-7, Pub. by H&H Sci Cnslts) St Mut.

Radman, Zdravko. Metaphors: Figures of the Mind. LC 96-50080. (Library of Rhetorics). 204p. (C). 1996. text 147.00 (0-7923-4356-5) Kluwer Academic.

Radman, Zdravko, ed. From a Metaphorical Point of View: A Multidisciplinary Approach to the Cognitive Content of Metaphor. LC 95-11399. (Philosophie & Wissenschaft - Transdisziplinaere Studien: Vol. 7). xi, 460p. (C). 1995. pap. text 44.60 (3-11-014554-5) De Gruyter.

— Horizons of Humanity: Essays in Honour of Ivan Supek. LC 97-20089. (Illus.). xv, 298p. 1997. 63.95 (3-631-30741-1) P Lang Pubng.

— Horizons of Humanity: Essays in Honour of Ivan Supek. LC 97-20089. (Illus.). XV, 298p. 1997. 63.95 (0-8204-3215-6) P Lang Pubng.

Radmer, Ethel E. The Cheshire Cat Syndrome: My Adventures with Arthritis. (Illus.). 240p. (Orig.). 1996. pap. 14.95 (0-9651182-0-7) Euphonia Pub.

Radmore, P. M., jt. auth. see Stephenson, G.

Radmore, Paul M., jt. auth. see Barnett, Stephen M.

Radnboti, Miklbos, jt. auth. see Ozsvbath, Zsuzsanna.

***Radnedge, Keir.** Complete Encyclopedia of Soccer. 1999. text 39.95 (1-85868-487-0, Pub. by Carlton Bks Ltd) Natl Bk Netwk.

— The Complete Encyclopedia of Soccer 2000-2001: The Ultimate Guide to the World's #1 Sport. rev. ed. (Illus.). 648p. 2000. 50.00 (1-84222-058-6) Carlton Bks Ltd.

Radnedge, Keir. The Ultimate Encyclopedia of Soccer: The Definitive Illustrated Guide to World Soccer. LC 94-34097. (Illus.). 608p. 1994. 29.95 (1-55958-702-4) Prima Pub.

Radner, Barbara, ed. see Nero, Ann B.

Radner, Daisie & Radner, Michael. Animal Consciousness. LC 96-29007. 253p. 1996. pap. 17.95 (1-57392-114-9) Prometheus Bks.

Radner, Ephraim, jt. ed. see Sumner, George.

An Asterisk (*) at the beginning of an entry indicates that the title is appearing for the first time.

Radner, Ephriam. The End of the Church: A Pneumatology of Christian Division in the West. LC 98-11281. 360p. 1998. pap. 36.00 (*0-8028-4461-8*) Eerdmans.
Radner, Gilda. It's Always Something. 288p. 1990. mass mkt. 6.99 (*0-380-71072-2*, Avon Bks) Morrow Avon.
***Radner, Gilda.** It's Always Something. LC 00-27610. 256p. 2000. pap. 13.00 (*0-380-81322-X*, HarpEntertain) Morrow Avon.
— It's Always Something. 1989. 11.60 (*0-606-04439-6*, Pub. by Turtleback) Demco.
Radner, Gilda. It's Always Something. abr. ed. 1989. write for info. incl. audio (*0-671-68361-6*, Pub. by S&S Audio) Lndmrk Audiobks.
Radner, Hilary. Shopping Around: Feminine Culture & the Pursuit of Pleasure. 224p. (C). 1994. pap. 19.99 (*0-415-90540-0*, A6797) Routledge.
Radner, Hilary, et al, eds. Film Theory Goes to the Movies: Cultural Analysis of Contemporary Film. (AFI Film Readers Ser.). 320p. (gr. 13). 1992. pap. 22.99 (*0-415-90576-1*, A7159) Routledge.
Radner, Hilary & Luckett, Moya, eds. Swinging Single: Representing Sexuality in the 1960s. LC 99-34136. 320p. 1999. pap. 19.95 (*0-8166-3352-5*, Pub. by U of Minn Pr); lib. bdg. 49.95 (*0-8166-3351-7*, Pub. by U of Minn Pr) Chicago Distribution Ctr.
Radner, Joan N., ed. Feminist Messages: Coding in Women's Folk Culture. LC 92-15701. (Illus.). 344p. (C). 1993. text 39.95 (*0-252-01957-1*); pap. text 18.95 (*0-252-06267-1*) U of Ill Pr.
Radner, Joan N., jt. ed. see Owens, Coilin D.
Radner, Karen. Die Neuassyrischen Privatrechtsurkunden als Quelle fur Mensch und Umwelt. (State Archives of Assyria Studies). (GER.). xlii, 428p. 1997. pap. text 39.50 (*951-45-7783-3*, Pub. by Neo-Assyrian Text) Eisenbrauns.
***Radner, Karen, ed.** The Prosopography of the Neo-Assyrian Empire: B-G, Vol. 1, Pt. 2. 241p. 1999. pap. text 50.00 (*951-45-8645-X*, Pub. by Neo-Assyrian Text) Eisenbrauns.
Radner, Michael, jt. auth. see Radner, Daisie.
Radner, Raymond J. The Cat's Paw. 413p. mass mkt. 4.99 (*1-55197-129-1*) Picasso Publ.
Radner, Ronni. Ghouls: Fatal Addiction. 1997. pap. text 15.00 (*1-56504-230-1*) White Wolf.
Radner, Ronni & Bates, Andrew. Mediums: Speakers with the Dead. (Illus.). (Orig.). 1997. pap. 15.00 (*1-56504-619-6*, 6102) White Wolf.
Radner, Roy, jt. auth. see Marschak, Jacob.
Radnitz, Cynthia, ed. Cognitive-Behavioral Therapy for Persons with Disabilities. LC 99-41432. (Illus.). 9336p. 1999. pap. write for info. (*0-7657-0238-X*) Aronson.
Radnitzky, Gerard, ed. Centripetal Forces in the Sciences, Vol. 1. LC 86-25343. 429p. 1989. 22.95 (*0-89226-047-5*) ICUS.
— Centripetal Forces in the Sciences, Vol. 2. LC 86-30389. 358p. 1989. 29.95 (*0-89226-048-3*) ICUS.
— Universal Economics: Assessing the Achievements of the Economic Approach. 448p. 1992. 34.95 (*0-89226-102-1*) Paragon Hse.
— Values & the Social Order Vol. 3: Voluntary vs. Coercive Orders. (Series in Philosophy). 544p. 1997. 101.95 (*1-85972-399-3*, Pub. by Avebry) Ashgate Pub Co.
Radnitzky, Gerard & Anderson, Gunnar, eds. The Structure & Development of Science. (Boston Studies in the Philosophy of Science: No. 136). 291p. 1979. lib. bdg. 104.50 (*90-277-0994-7*, D Reidel) Kluwer Academic.
Radnitzky, Gerard & Bouillon, Hardy. Values & the Social Order: Society & Order, Vol. 2. 216p. 1995. 69.95 (*1-85628-900-1*, Pub. by Avebry) Ashgate Pub Co.
— Values & the Social Order: Values & Society, Vol. 1. 268p. 1995. 69.95 (*1-85628-899-4*, Pub. by Avebry) Ashgate Pub Co.
Radnitzky, Gerard, jt. ed. see Bernholz, Peter.
***Radnor, Alan T.** Cross-Examining Doctors: A Practical Approach. LC 99-65068. 224p. 1999. 87.75 (*0-8318-0795-4*, B795) Am Law Inst.
Radnor, Hilary. Across the Curriculum. LC 93-42673. (Education Matters Ser.). 176p. 1994. 100.00 (*0-304-32832-4*) Continuum.
Radnor, Hilary A. Assessment & Control at Parkview School: A Qualitative Case Study of Implementing Assessment Change in a Secondary School. LC 96-3849. (Understanding Education & Policy Ser.). 240p. 1996. text 49.50 (*1-57273-034-X*); pap. text 22.95 (*1-57273-035-8*) Hampton Pr NJ.
Radnoti, Miklos. Foamy Sky: The Major Poems of Miklos Radnoti. Ozsvath, Zsuzsanna & Turner, Frederick, trs. LC 91-42350. (Lockert Library of Poetry in Translation). 180p. 1992. reprint ed. pap. 55.80 (*0-608-07125-0*, 2067351) Bks Demand.
Radnoti, Sandor. The Fake. 256p. 1999. pap. 18.95 (*0-8476-9206-X*); text 57.95 (*0-8476-9205-1*) Rowman.
Rado, Erin H., ed. The New Age Resources Directory. 225p. (Orig.). 1994. pap. 15.95 (*1-886329-00-1*) Goddess Pr.
Rado, Ivan J., ed. see Chooluck, Leon.
Rado, Leonard G. Crate Art: Heraldry & History. (Illus.). 125p. 1999. pap. 25.00 (*0-9663607-3-7*) Jurad Assocs.
Rado, Leonard G. & Drakeford, Elaine D. Growing up in Revolutionary Times: A Young Lady's Memories of China, 1910-1930. 2nd rev. ed. (Illus.). 168p. 1998. 24.00 (*0-9663607-1-0*) Jurad Assocs.
***Rado, Lisa.** The Modern Androgyne Imagination: A Failed Sublime. LC 00-28103. 256p. 2000. 57.50 (*0-8139-1979-7*); pap. 18.50 (*0-8139-1980-0*) U Pr of Va.
Rado, Lisa & Cain, William, eds. Modernism, Gender, & Culture: A Cultural Studies Approach. LC 96-46542. (Wellesley Studies in Critical Theory, Literary History & Culture: Vol. 11). (Illus.). 400p. 1997. text 95.00 (*0-8153-1786-7*) Garland.
Rado, Sandor, et al, eds. Adaptational Psychodynamics. LC 70-82528. 306p. 1995. reprint ed. pap. 45.00 (*1-56821-505-3*) Aronson.
Rado, Tibor. Length & Area. LC QA0461.R3. (American Mathematical Society, Colloquium Publications: Vol. 30). 579p. reprint ed. pap. 179.50 (*0-608-30949-4*, 200493600048) Bks Demand.
Radocy, Rudolf E. & Boyle, J. David. Psychological Foundations of Musical Behavior. 3rd ed. LC 96-31867. (Illus.). 408p. 1997. text 61.95 (*0-398-06720-1*); pap. text 44.95 (*0-398-06721-X*) C C Thomas.
Radocy, Rudolf E., jt. auth. see Boyle, David J.
Radoev, Ivan. My Children Are Words. Wilson, Don D., tr. from BUL. 56p. 1994. pap. 7.50 (*1-880286-32-7*) Singular Speech Pr.
***Radoisevibc, Slavo.** International Technology Transfer & Catch-Up in Economic Development. LC 98-50847. 296p. 1999. 95.00 (*1-85898-717-2*) E Elgar.
Radoisevic, Slavo, jt. auth. see Dyker, David A.
Radojcic, Riko, jt. auth. see Pecht, Michael G.
Radojcic, Svetozar. Geschichte der Serbischen Kunst von den Anfaengen bis zum Ende des Mittelalters. (GER., Illus.). (C). 1969. 86.95 (*3-11-000267-1*) De Gruyter.
Radojevic, M. & Bashkin, V. Practical Environmental Analysis. 480p. 1999. pap. 65.00 (*0-85404-594-5*, Pub. by Royal Soc Chem) Spr-Verlag.
Radojevic, V., tr. see Vrhovac, Duska.
Radok, R., tr. see Bliev, N.
Radom, Sandra. Messages from the Journey. (Illus.). 81p. 1995. text 24.95 (*0-9645441-0-5*) Pr of Journey.
***Radomile, Leon J.** Heritage Italian-American Style. 238p. 1999. pap. 14.92 (*0-9675329-0-6*) Vincero.
Radoms, jt. auth. see Dougherty, Pamela M.
Radomski, Wojciech. Bridge Rehabilitation. 300p. 1999. 58.00 (*1-86094-122-2*) World Scientific Pub.
***Radomski, James.** Manuel Garcia, 1775-1832: Chronicle of the Life of a Bel Canto Tenor at the Dawn of Romanticism. LC 99-48687. 384p. 2000. write for info. (*0-19-816373-8*) OUP.
Radomski, Mary V., jt. auth. see Dougherty, Pamela M.
Radomsky, Nellie A. Lost Voices: Women, Chronic Pain, & Abuse. LC 94-29611. 1995. pap. 14.95 (*1-56023-864-X*) Haworth Pr.
— Lost Voices: Women, Chronic Pain & Abuse. LC 94-29611. 172p. 1995. lib. bdg. 54.95 (*1-56024-921-8*, Harrington Park) Haworth Pr.
Radon, Lisa. It's All Fun & Games until Somebody Loses an Eye: Selected Poems, 1990-1998. 36p. 1998. pap. 4.50 (*0-9654684-0-2*) Big Star.
— Now Hear This. 20p. (Orig.). 1994. pap. 3.00 (*0-916397-36-X*) Manic D Pr.
— The Super Deluxe with Everything & Other Poems. 36p. (Orig.). 1996. pap. 6.95 (*0-9654684-8-8*) Big Star.
Rados, David L. Marketing for Non-Profit Organizations. 2nd ed. LC 95-13609. 480p. 1996. text 59.95 (*0-86569-254-8*, Auburn Hse) Greenwood.
— Pushing the Numbers in Marketing: A Real-World Guide to Essential Financial Analysis. LC 91-47643. 200p. 1992. 49.95 (*0-89930-736-1*, RPH, Quorum Bks) Greenwood.
Radosevich, G. E., et al. Evolution & Administration of Colorado Water Law: 1876-1976. LC 76-17952. 1976. reprint ed. 35.00 (*0-918334-12-8*) WRP.
Radosevich, H. R., jt. auth. see Kassicieh, S. K.
Radosevich, Steven R., et al. Weed Ecology: Implications for Vegetation Management. 2nd ed. LC 96-19470. 608p. 1997. 140.00 (*0-471-11606-8*) Wiley.
Radosh, Ronald. The Center Did Not Hold. 1996. 23.00 (*0-02-925701-8*) Free Pr.
— Commies: A Journey Through the Old Left, the New Left & the Leftover Left. 250p. 2000. 24.95 (*1-893554-05-8*) Encounter Bks.
Radosh, Ronald & Milton, Joyce. The Rosenberg File. 2nd rev. ed. LC 97-60012. 640p. 1997. pap. 18.00 (*0-300-07205-8*) Yale U Pr.
Radosh, Ronald, jt. auth. see Klehr, Harvey E.
***Radostits, O. M.** Veterinary Medicine. 9th ed. (C). 1999. text 139.00 (*0-7020-2409-0*, Pub. by Harcourt Coll Pubs) Harcourt.
Radostits, O. M., et al, eds. Veterinary Medicine: A Textbook of the Diseases of Cattle, Sheep, Pigs, Goats & Horses. 8th ed. (Illus.). 1787p. 1994. text 92.00 (*0-7020-1592-X*, Pub. by W B Saunders) Saunders.
Radostits, O. M., et al. Herd Health: Food Animal, Production, Medicine. 2nd ed. LC 92-43548. (Illus.). 640p. 1993. text 110.00 (*0-7216-3655-1*, W B Saunders Co) Harcrt Hlth Sci Grp.
Radouco-Thomas, C. & Garcin, F., eds. Progress in Neuropsychopharmacology, Vol. 4, No. 6. (Illus.). 110p. 1981. pap. 31.00 (*0-08-027157-X*, Pergamon Pr) Elsevier.
Radoui, Nicolas. My Journey. 544p. 1991. 22.95 (*0-8187-0134-X*) Harlo Press.
Radovanovic, D., jt. auth. see Reljic, L.
Radovanovic, Ivana. The Iron Gates Mesolithic. LC 96-49023. (Archaeological Ser.: Vol. 11). (Illus.). viii, 382p. 1997. pap. 48.50 (*1-879621-24-X*); lib. bdg. 89.00 (*1-879621-25-8*) Intl Mono Prehstry.
Radovanovic, M., ed. Fluidized Bed Combustion. (Proceedings of the International Center for Heat & Mass Transfer Ser.). 350p. (C). 1986. 155.00 (*0-89116-409-X*) Hemisp Pub.
Radovanovic, Milorad, ed. Yugoslav General Linguistics. LC 88-7614. (Linguistic & Literary Studies in Eastern Europe: Vol. 26). viii, 381p. (C). 1989. 148.00 (*90-272-1531-6*) J Benjamins Pubng Co.
Radovanovic, Milorad, jt. ed. see Tomic, Olga Miseska.
Radovic, Branislav, jt. auth. see Haselgrove, Michael J.
Radovic, Ljubisa R., jt. ed. see Thrower, Peter A.
Radovich, Don. Tony Richardson: A Bio-Bibliography, 69. LC 95-32990. (Bio-Bibliographies in the Performing Arts Ser.: No. 69). 304p. 1995. lib. bdg. 59.95 (*0-313-28981-6*, Greenwood Pr) Greenwood.
Radowich, Jeffery. Family Limited Partnerships. 1997. 99.00 incl. audio PA Bar Inst.
Radoz, J., jt. auth. see De Gennes, P. G.
Radpour, F., et al, eds. Long Wavelength Infrared Detectors & Arrays: Physics & Applications/State-of-the-Art Program on Compound Semiconductors XIX. LC 93-72863. (Proceedings Ser.: Vol. 94-5). (Illus.). 384p. 1995. 40.00 (*1-56677-034-3*) Electrochem Soc.
***Radrobe & Meredith.** Differential Diagnosis Small Mammals. 2001. 63.00 (*0-7506-4250-5*) Buttrwrth-Heinemann.
Radsdale. A Thinking Person's Guide Racqetball. 1998. 15.00 (*0-07-230261-5*) McGraw.
***Radstone, Susannah, ed.** Memory & Methodology. (Illus.). 256p. 2000. 55.00 (*1-85973-296-8*, Pub. by Berg Pubs); pap. 19.50 (*1-85973-202-X*, Pub. by Berg Pubs) NYU Pr.
Radstone, Susannah, ed. Sweet Dreams: Sexuality, Gender & Popular Fiction. (C). 1988. pap. 19.50 (*0-85315-672-7*, Pub. by Lawrence & Wishart) NYU Pr.
Radszuweit, S. & Spalier, M. Kanurs Lexikon der Sinnverwandten Woerter. (GER.). 560p. 1982. 49.95 (*0-8288-1981-5*, F59970) Fr & Eur.
Radt, S. L. The Importance of the Context. (Mededelingen der Koninklijke Nederlandse Akademie van Wetenschappen, Afd. Letterkunde Ser.: No. 51(9)). 1988. pap. text 12.50 (*0-444-85697-8*) Elsevier.
***Radt, Wolfgang.** Pergamon. 2000. pap. 75.00 (*0-226-70244-8*) U Ch Pr.
Radt, Wolfgang, jt. auth. see Nohlen, Klaus.
Radtchenko, Konstantiu. Developments in Soviet Metal Rolling. Gallant, Jonathan, ed. Squires, Elizabeth, tr. from RUS. (Illus.). 125p. (Orig.). 1989. pap. text 75.00 (*1-55831-094-0*) Delphic Associates.
Radtke, Becky. Circus Fun. (Illus.). 32p. (J). pap. 1.00 (*0-486-40052-2*) Dover.
Radtke, Becky. Circus Mazes. (Illus.). (J). 1995. pap. 1.00 (*0-486-28567-7*) Dover.
Radtke, Becky. Litle Tot Bible Mazes. (Illus.). (J). 1997. pap. text 2.29 (*0-7647-0082-0*) Schaffer Pubns.
— Little Tot Dot-to-Dot: Activity Book. (Illus.). (J). 1997. pap. text 2.29 (*0-7647-0081-2*) Schaffer Pubns.
— Little Tot Hidden Pictures. (Illus.). (J). 1997. pap. text 2.29 (*0-7647-0084-7*) Schaffer Pubns.
— Sports Activity Book. (Illus.). 64p. (J). 1998. pap. 1.00 (*0-486-40303-3*) Dover.
Radtke, Becky J. Easy Hidden Picture Coloring Book. (Illus.). (J). (gr. k-3). 1993. pap. 1.00 (*0-486-27675-9*) Dover.
— Fun Tastic Bulletin Boards for Basic Classroom Curriculum. 224p. teacher ed. 12.99 (*0-86653-722-8*, GA1441) Good Apple.
— Little Farm Activity Book. (Illus.). (J). pap. text 1.00 (*0-486-29423-4*) Dover.
— Little Zoo Activity Book. (Illus.). 1998. pap. text 1.00 (*0-486-28845-5*) Dover.
— Sun Sational Bulletin Boards for Holidays & Special Occasions. (Illus.). 224p. teacher ed. 12.99 (*0-86653-685-X*, GA1419) Good Apple.
Radtke, Becky J., jt. auth. see Whitacre, Deborah.
***Radtke, Bernd, ed.** Fritz Meier: Essays on Islamic Piety & Mysticism. O'Kane, John, tr. from GER. LC 99-31636. 30. xx, 750p. 1999. text 350.00 (*90-04-10865-3*) Brill Academic Pubs.
Radtke, Bernd & O'Kane, John, trs. The Concept of Sainthood in Early Islamic Mysticism: Two Works by Al-Hakim al-Tirmidhi. LC 96-166676. (Curzon Sufi Series). 296p. 1996. pap. 29.95 (*0-7007-0413-2*) Humanities.
— The Concept of Sainthood in Early Islamic Mysticism: Two Works by Al-Hakim al-Tirmidhi. annot. ed. LC 96-166676. (Curzon Sufi Series). 296p. 1996. 65.00 (*0-7007-0452-3*, Pub. by Curzon Pr Ltd) Humanities.
Radtke, Bernd, jt. auth. see De Jong, F. A.
Radtke, Bernd, jt. ed. see Thomassen, Einor.
Radtke, Dawn D., jt. auth. see Morrison, Ruth.
Radtke, Edgar, jt. ed. see Mattheier, Klaus J.
Radtke, Frank, jt. ed. see Hasselberg, Erwin.
Radtke, George A. Budgerigars. Orig. Title: Wellensittiche-Mein Hobby. (Illus.). 96p. 1979. 9.95 (*0-87666-984-4*, KW-011) TFH Pubns.
— A Step-by-Step Book about Budgerigars. (Step-by-Step Ser.). (Illus.). 63p. (Orig.). 1987. pap. 5.95 (*0-86622-463-7*, SK-002) TFH Pubns.
***Radtke, Janel M.** Strategic Communications for Nonprofit Organizations: Seven Steps to Creating a Successful Plan. LC 97-32850. (Nonprofit Law, Finance, & Management Ser.). 234p. 1998. pap. 49.95 (*0-471-17464-5*) Wiley.
Radtke, Kurt & Stam, Joop. Dynamics in Pacific Asia: Conflict, Competition & Cooperation. LC 97-31320. 280p. 1997. 110.00 (*0-7103-0598-2*, Pub. by Kegan Paul Intl) Col U Pr.
***Radtke, Kurt W. & Feddema, Raymond.** Comprehensive Security in Asia: Views from Asia & the West on a Changing Security Environment. LC 99-86420. 2000. write for info. (*90-04-11202-2*) Brill Academic Pubs.
Radtke, Kurt W., tr. see Yoda, Yoshiie.
Radtke, Lorraine & Stam, Henderikus J., eds. Power & Gender: Social Relations in Theory & Practice. LC 93-86424. 328p. (C). 1994. text 45.00 (*0-8039-8674-2*); pap. text 14.99 (*0-8039-8675-0*) Sage.
Radtke, Mick, jt. auth. see Lampton, Christopher.
Radtke, Robert W. Taiwan's Role in the East Asian Economy: Implications for the U. S.-Asia Relations. LC 98-125110. 56p. (Orig.). 1997. 5.00 (*0-87848-519-8*, X88465) Asia Soc.
Radu-Clee, Violeta, jt. auth. see Clee, Paul.
Radu, Kenneth. Letter to a Distant Father. 1987. pap. 9.95 (*0-919626-32-7*, Pub. by Brick Bks) Genl Dist Srvs.
— Romanian Suite. 72p. 1996. pap. 12.95 (*0-919626-89-0*, Pub. by Brick Bks) Genl Dist Srvs.
— Snow over Judaea. 212p. (Orig.). 1994. pap. 13.95 (*1-55065-056-4*, Pub. by Vehicule Pr) Genl Dist Srvs.
Radu, Michael. Eastern Europe & the Third World: East vs. South. LC 80-27494. 356p. 1981. 69.50 (*0-275-90708-2*, C0708, Praeger Pubs) Greenwood.
— The New Insurgencies: Anti-Communist Guerrillas in the Third World. 300p. 1990. 44.95 (*0-88738-307-6*) Transaction Pubs.
Radu, Michael, ed. Violence & the Latin American Revolutionaries. 246p. 1988. 39.95 (*0-88738-195-2*) Transaction Pubs.
Radu, Michael & Klinghoffer, Arthur J. The Dynamics of Soviet Policy in Sub-Saharan Africa. LC 89-34604. x, 160p. 1991. 24.50 (*0-8419-1226-2*) Holmes & Meier.
Radu, Michael & Tismaneanu, Vladimir. Latin American Revolutionaries: Groups, Goals, Methods. 386p. 1998. text 50.00 (*0-7881-5730-2*) DIANE Pub.
Radu, Michael, jt. auth. see Allen, Chris.
Radu, Michael, jt. ed. see Bissell, Richard E.
Radu, R. & Tismaneanu, W. Vladimir. Latin American Revolutionaries: Groups, Goals, Methods. 400p. 1989. 60.00 (*0-08-037429-8*, 3715M) Brasseys.
Radulescu, C., jt. auth. see Dinescu, T. A.
Radulescu, Domnica. Andre Malraux: The "Farfelu" As Expression of the Feminine & the Erotic. LC 93-23079. (American University Studies, II, Romance Language & Literature: Vol. 209). XI, 216p. (C). 1994. text 55.95 (*0-8204-2296-7*) P Lang Pubng.
Radulescu, Florin. The Gamma-Equivariant Form of the Berezin Quantization of the Upper Half Plane. LC 98-2681. (Memoirs of the American Mathematical Society Ser.). 70p. 1998. pap. 38.00 (*0-8218-0752-8*) Am Math.
Radulescu, Stella V. Blood & White Apples. LC 93-29557. 64p. 1993. pap. 14.95 (*0-7734-2769-4*, Mellen Poetry Pr) E Mellen.
***Radulescu, Stella V.** My Dream Has Red Fingers. LC 99-65225. 64p. 2000. pap. 9.95 (*1-58501-050-2*, Pub. by CeShore Pubg) Natl Bk Netwk.
Radulovic, Marjorie. Rage of the Serbs. 531p. 1998. 33.50 (*1-85776-327-0*, Pub. by Book Guild Ltd) Trans-Atl Phila.
Radulovic, Sigrid, ed. see Stafford, Peter.
Radulovich & Belloit. Elementary Algebra for College Students. 4th ed. 1995. pap. text, student ed. 29.33 (*0-13-399221-7*) P-H.
Radulski, John P. Pleasure Paradises: International Clubs & Resorts. LC 96-5730. 1999. pap. text 34.95 (*0-86636-536-2*) PBC Intl Inc.
Radulski, John P. & Weathersby, William. Pleasure Paradises. LC 96-5730. (Illus.). 184p. 1997. text 42.50 (*0-86636-496-X*) St Martin.
Radunski, Peter, et al. West German Political Parties: CDU, CSU, FDP, SPD, the Greens. Livingston, Robert G. & Kielmannsegg, Peter G., eds. LC 86-73191. (German Issues Ser.: No. 4). 102p. 1986. pap. 7.50 (*0-941441-00-8*) Am Inst Contemp Ger Studies.
Radunsky, Eugenia. Yucka Drucka Droni. LC 97-14750. (Illus.). 40p. (J). (ps-1). 1998. 15.95 (*0-590-09837-3*) Scholastic Inc.
Radunzel, Claudia. Das Wortfeld "Behinderter" im Deutschen und Seine Russischen Entsprechungen. (Europaische Hochschulschriften Ser.: Series 16, Band 59). (GER.). 204p. 1998. 39.95 (*3-631-33178-9*) P Lang Pubng.
Radushev, Evgenity, jt. ed. see Velkov, Asparuch.
Raduta, A., ed. Symmetries & Semiclassical Features of Nuclear Dynamics. (Lecture Notes in Physics Ser.: Vol. 279). 1987. 50.95 (*0-387-17926-7*) Spr-Verlag.
Raduta, A. A. Structure & Stability of Nucleon & Nuclear Systems. 600p. 1999. 166.00 (*981-02-3774-X*) World Scientific Pub.
Raduta, A. A., et al. New Trends in Theoretical & Experimental Nuclear Physics: Predeal International Summer School. 600p. 1992. text 106.00 (*981-02-0906-1*) World Scientific Pub.
Radvany, Ruth, et al. Intermediate Algebra Study Aid. (J). 1974. pap. 2.50 (*0-87738-038-4*) Youth Ed.
Radvanyi, Janos. Psychological Operations & Political Warfare in Long-Term Strategic Planning. LC 90-31183. 168p. 1990. 47.95 (*0-275-93623-6*, C3623, Praeger Pubs) Greenwood.
Radvanyi, Janos, ed. The Pacific in the Nineteen Nineties: Economic & Strategic Change. 166p. (C). 1990. pap. text 22.50 (*0-8191-7901-9*); lib. bdg. 47.50 (*0-8191-7900-0*) U Pr of Amer.
Radwan, Lutfi. Mu'jizat Wa-Khawariq Al-Duktur Dahesh Yarwyha Al-Sahafi Lutfi Radwan. 2nd rev. ed. (ARA & ENG., Illus.). 279p. 1997. 15.00 (*0-935359-44-3*) Daheshist.
Radwan, Samir, jt. auth. see Hansen, Bent.
Radwan, Samir, jt. ed. see Mafeje, Archie.
Radwanski, George & Luttrell, Julia. The Will of a Nation: Awakening the Canadian Spirit. 208p. 1992. 22.95 (*0-7737-2637-3*) Genl Dist Srvs.
Radway, Janice, jt. auth. see Grossberg, Lawrence.
Radway, Janice, jt. ed. see Grossberg, Lawrence.
Radway, Janice, jt. ed. see Moi, Toril.
Radway, Janice A. A Feeling for Books: The Book-Of-The-Month Club, Literary Taste, & Middle-Class Desire. LC 96-52037. (Illus.). 448p. (C). (gr. 13). 1997. 37.50 (*0-8078-2357-0*) U of NC Pr.
— A Feeling for Books: The Book-of-the-Month Club, Literary Taste & Middle-Class Desire. LC 96-52037. (Illus.). 448p. 1999. pap. 16.95 (*0-8078-4830-1*) U of NC Pr.

An Asterisk (*) at the beginning of an entry indicates that the title is appearing for the first time.

R

— Reading the Romance: Women, Patriarchy & Popular Literature. 2nd ed. LC 91-50284. x, 296p. (C). 1991. reprint ed. pap. 15.95 (*0-8078-4349-0*) U of NC Pr.

Radwin, George E. & D'Attilio, Anthony. Murex Shells of the World: An Illustrated Guide to the Muricidae. LC 75-7485. (Illus.). 328p. 1976. reprint ed. pap. 30.00 (*0-7837-2164-1*, 204247000004) Bks Demand.

Rady, Martin. Romania in Turmoil. 256p. 1992. text 22.50 (*1-85043-500-6*, Pub. by I B T) St Martin.

Rady, Martyn C. Collapse of Communism in Eastern Europe. LC 95-11728. (Causes & Consequences Ser.). (Illus.). 80p. (J). (gr. 7-8). 1995. lib. bdg. 27.11 (*0-8172-4052-7*) Raintree Steck-V.

— Medieval Buda. 1985. text 68.50 (*0-88033-074-0*, Pub. by East Eur Monographs) Col U Pr.

***Rady, Martyn C.** Nobility, Land & Service in Medieval Hungary. London University College Staff, ed. LC 00-41491. (Studies in Russia & East Europe). 2000. write for info. (*0-312-23582-8*) St Martin.

Rady, Virginia B., jt. auth. see Swanson, Faith H.

Radyke, George A. A Complete Introduction to Lovebirds. (Complete Introduction to...Ser.). (Illus.). 128p. (Orig.). 1987. pap. 8.95 (*0-86622-382-7*, CO-030S) TFH Pubns.

Radzialowski, Frederick M., ed. Hypertension Research: Methods & Models. LC 81-17462. (Modern Pharmacology-Toxicology Ser.: No. 19). (Illus.). 464p. reprint ed. pap. 143.90 (*0-7837-0757-6*, 204107100019) Bks Demand.

Radziemski, Leon J. & Cremers, David A. Lasers-Induced Plasmas & Applications. (Optical Engineering Ser.: Vol. 21). (Illus.). 464p. 1989. text 175.00 (*0-8247-8078-7*) Dekker.

Radziemski, Leon J. & Solarz, Richard W., eds. Laser Spectroscopy & Its Applications. (Optical Engineering Ser.: Vol. 11). (Illus.). 712p. 1986. text 215.00 (*0-8247-7525-2*) Dekker.

Radziewicz, Christine, jt. auth. see Tiegerman, Ellenmorris.

Radziewicz, John, ed. Swift As a Shadow. LC 99-18095. (Illus.). 160p. 1999. pap. 20.00 (*0-395-89228-7*) HM.

Radziewicz-Winnicki, Andrzej. Tradition & Reality in Educational Ethnography of Post-Communist Poland: Essays in Sociology of Education & Social Pedagogy. 168p. 1998. pap. 34.95 (*3-631-32691-2*) P Lang Pubng.

— Tradition & Reality in Educational Ethnography of Post-Communist Poland: Essays in Sociology of Education & Social Pedagogy. LC 98-20727. 168p. (C). 1998. pap. text 34.95 (*0-8204-3547-3*) P Lang Pubng.

Radzig, A. A. & Smirnov, Boris M. Reference Data on Atoms, Molecules & Ions. (Chemical Physics Ser.: Vol. 31). (Illus.). 430p. 1985. 99.00 (*0-387-12415-2*) Spr-Verlag.

Radzik, Donna M., jt. auth. see Lunte, Susan M.

Radzik-Marsh, Kelly & Strutchens, Marilyn, eds. Multicultural Education: Inclusion of All. (Illus.). 298p. (Orig.). pap. write for info. (*0-9624818-2-3*) U GA Coll Ed.

Radzilowski, John. Out on the Winds: Poles & Danes in Lincoln County, Minnesota, 1880-1905. (Illus.). 128p. 1992. pap. 11.95 (*0-9614119-4-5*) Crossings Pr.

Radzilowski, John, jt. auth. see Amato, Joseph.

Radzilowski, Thaddeus C. Feudalism, Revolution & the Meaning of Russian History: An Intellectual Biography of N.P. Pavlov-Silvanskii. LC 94-67904. 320p. (C). 1994. text 47.50 (*0-88033-258-1*, 361, Pub. by East Eur Monographs) Col U Pr.

Radzinowics, Mary Ann, ed. see Milton, John.

Radzinowicz, Leon. Adventures in Criminology. LC 98-35440. 12p. 1999. write for info. (*0-415-19875-5*) Routledge.

Radzinowicz, Leon & Hood, Roger G. Criminology & the Administration of Criminal Justice: A Bibliography. LC 76-24998. 400p. (Orig.). 1977. lib. bdg. 49.95 (*0-8371-9068-1*, RCA/, Greenwood Pr) Greenwood.

— A History of English Law & Its Administration from 1750 Vol. 5: Victorian & Edwardian England: The Emergence of Penal Policy. 864p. 1991. pap. 48.00 (*0-19-825663-9*) OUP.

Radzinowicz, Mary A. Milton's Epics & the Book of Psalms. LC 88-34383. 245p. 1989. reprint ed. pap. 76.00 (*0-608-07122-6*, 206734800009) Bks Demand.

— Toward Samson Agonistes: The Growth of Milton's Mind. LC 77-85559. (Illus.). 461p. 1978. reprint ed. pap. 143.00 (*0-7837-8180-6*, 204788500008) Bks Demand.

Radzinski, Kandy. The Twelve Cats of Christmas. 26p. (J). 1992. 9.95 (*0-8118-0102-0*) Chronicle Bks.

Radzinsky, Charles L. Churches & Synagogues of Middletown & Nearby Communities. (Illus.). 64p. 1993. reprint ed. pap. 15.00 (*0-9666270-1-6*) Stiles Studio.

Radzinsky, Edvard. The Last Tsar: The Life & Death of Nicholas II. Schwartz, Marian, tr. from RUS. LC 93-16757. 496p. 1993. reprint ed. pap. 16.95 (*0-385-46962-4*, Anchor NY) Doubleday.

— The Rasputin Files: The Final Word. Rosengram, Judson, tr. from RUS. LC 99-47637. 512p. 2000. 29.95 (*0-385-48909-9*, N A Talese) Doubleday.

— Stalin: The First In-Depth Biography Based on Explosive New Documents from Russia's Secret Archives. (Illus.). 624p. 1997. pap. 16.95 (*0-385-47954-9*, Anchor NY) Doubleday.

Radzinsky, Jose E. You, God & Me, Vol. I. Veuz, Carlotta, ed. (Illus.). 100p. 1996. 11.00 (*0-9653748-7-4*) Enigma Publng.

Radzio, Renate. Heterologe Gene Expression in Dem Cephalosporin C Produzierenden Hyphenpilz Acremonium Chrysogenum. (Bibliotheca Mycologica: Vol. 164). (Illus.). xiv, 113p. 1997. 48.00 (*3-443-59066-7*, Pub. by Gebruder Borntraeger) Balogh.

Radziuk, B., jt. auth. see Schlemmer, G.

Radziunas, Eileen. Lupus: My Search for a Diagnosis. LC 89-24683. 144p. 1989. pap. 9.95 (*0-89793-065-7*) Hunter Hse.

Rae, Alastair. Quantum Physics: Illusion or Reality? (Canto Book Ser.). (Illus.). 135p. (C). 1994. pap. 10.95 (*0-521-46716-0*) Cambridge U Pr.

Rae, Alastair I. Quantum Mechanics. 3rd ed. (Illus.). 280p. 1992. pap. 30.00 (*0-7503-0217-8*) IOP Pub.

***Rae, Alexander.** The Bluffer's Guide to Astrology & Fortune Telling: Bluff Your Way in Astrology & Fortune Telling. (Bluffer's Guides Ser.). 64p. 2000. pap. 5.95 (*1-903096-20-0*) Oval Bks.

— The Bluffer's Guide to Rugby: Bluff Your Way in Rugby. (Bluffer's Guides Ser.). 64p. 1999. pap. 5.95 (*1-902825-96-9*) Oval Bks.

Rae, Alexander C., jt. auth. see Ainsley, Robert.

Rae, Allan N. Agricultural Management Economics: Activity Analysis & Decision Making. LC 95-106793. (Illus.). 480p. 1994. pap. text 50.00 (*0-85198-768-0*) OUP.

Rae, Andrew, et al, eds. Software Evaluation for Certification: Principles, Practice, & Legal Liability. LC 94-29412. (Software Assurance Ser.). 1994. write for info. (*0-07-709042-X*) McGraw.

Rae, Catherine M. Afterward. large type ed. LC 92-11681. 273p. 1992. reprint ed. 19.95 (*1-56054-422-8*) Thorndike Pr.

— Brownstone Facade. large type ed. 240p. 1990. reprint ed. lib. bdg. 16.95 (*1-56054-027-3*) Thorndike Pr.

— Flight from Fifth Avenue. large type ed. LC 95-14547. 291p. 1995. 21.95 (*0-7862-0493-1*) Thorndike Pr.

***Rae, Catherine M.** The Hidden Cove. large type ed. 229p. 2000. lib. bdg. 27.95 (*1-58547-035-X*) Ctr Point Pubg.

— The Hidden Cove. 183p. 1999. reprint ed. text 20.00 (*0-7881-6634-4*) DIANE Pub.

— Marikes World. 2000. text 21.95 (*0-312-26199-3*) St Martin.

Rae, Catherine M. Sarah Cobb. large type ed. LC 90-29874. 267p. 1991. reprint ed. lib. bdg. 17.95 (*1-56054-125-3*) Thorndike Pr.

— The Ship's Clock: A Family Chronicle. large type ed. LC 93-22972. 310p. 1993. lib. bdg. 21.95 (*0-7862-0000-6*) Thorndike Pr.

— Sunlight on a Broken Column. large type ed. LC 97-43484. (Basic Ser.). 1998. 25.95 (*0-7862-1316-7*) Thorndike Pr.

Rae, Charles B. The Music of Lutoslawski. 3rd ed. (Illus.). 318p. 1999. pap. 22.95 (*0-7119-6910-8*, OP48072) Omnibus NY.

Rae, Cheri. Mojave National Preserve: A Visitor's Guide. 1. 1999. pap. text 12.95 (*0-934161-18-6*) Olympus Pr.

— The Santa Barbara Bargain Book. 94p. (Orig.). 1993. pap. 7.95 (*0-945092-33-4*) EZ Nature.

Rae, Colleen M. Movies in the Mind: How to Build a Short Story. 142p. (Orig.). 1996. pap. 14.95 (*0-9644196-5-3*) Sherman Asher Pub.

Rae, Debra. ABC's of Globalism. LC 96-79608. 368p. 1999. pap. 18.99 (*1-56384-140-1*, Pub. by Huntington Hse) BookWorld.

Rae, Donna. Glow. Kearns, Gail, ed. LC 98-92618. (Illus.). 200p. 1998. pap. 14.95 (*0-9663286-3-9*) Earth Time.

— Glow: Body Brush Your Way to Utterly Gorgeous Skin. Kearns, Gail, ed. (Illus.). 200p. 1998. 19.95 (*0-9663286-2-0*) Earth Time.

Rae, Douglas. Equalities. (Illus.). 224p. 1981. pap. 15.00 (*0-674-25981-5*) HUP.

— Equalities. LC 81-4157. (Illus.). 224p. (C). 1981. 37.95 (*0-674-25980-7*) HUP.

Rae, E. The Country of the Moors. 368p. 1985. 250.00 (*1-85077-030-1*, Pub. by Darf Pubs Ltd) St Mut.

Rae, Eleanor. Women, the Earth, the Divine. LC 93-47614. (Ecology & Justice Ser.). 150p. (Orig.). 1994. pap. 15.00 (*0-88344-952-8*) Orbis Bks.

Rae-Ellis, Vivienne. Black Robinson: Protector of Aborigines. (Illus.). 328p. 1996. pap. 19.95 (*0-522-84744-7*, Pub. by Melbourne Univ Pr) Paul & Co Pubs.

Rae, Gail. Money for College. LC 97-66287. 96p. 1998. pap. 11.95 (*0-87891-072-7*) Res & Educ.

— REA's Guide to Literary Terms. LC 97-67180. 140p. 1998. pap. 3.95 (*0-87891-097-2*) Res & Educ.

Rae-Grant, Quentin, ed. Images in Psychiatry: Canada. LC 96-22436. (Illus.). 317p. 1996. pap. text 29.95 (*0-88048-900-6*, 8900) Am Psychiatric.

Rae, Howard K., ed. Separation of Hydrogen Isotopes: A Symposium Co-Sponsored by the Physical Chemistry Division of the Chemical Institute of Canada, & the Canadian Society for Chemical Engineering at the 2nd Joint Conference of the Chemical Institute of Canada & the American Chemical Society, Montreal, May 30-June 1, 1977. LC 78-760. (ACS Symposium Ser.: No. 68). (Illus.). 192p. 1978. reprint ed. pap. 59.60 (*0-608-07872-7*, 205985400011) Bks Demand.

Rae, Ian F., jt. auth. see Harrison, Maureen A.

Rae, J. E., jt. ed. see Parker, A.

Rae, Jennifer. Dog Tales. LC 99-14279. 32p. (J). (gr. 1-3). 1999. 14.95 (*1-58246-011-6*) Tricycle Pr.

— Gilbert de la Frogponde: A Swamp Story. LC 97-19638. (Illus.). 32p. (J). (gr. 1-5). 1997. 15.95 (*1-56145-163-0*) Peachtree Pubs.

Rae, John. Life of Adam Smith. LC 63-23522. (Reprints of Economic Classics Ser.). xv, 449p. 1965. reprint ed. 57.50 (*0-678-00101-4*) Kelley.

***Rae, John.** Picatinny Arsenal. (Images of America Ser.). 128p. 1999. pap. 18.99 (*0-7385-0196-4*) Arcadia Publng.

Rae, John. Statement of Some New Principles on the Subject of Political Economy: Exposing the Fallacies of the System of Free Trade. LC 65-10366. (Reprints of Economic Classics Ser.). xvi, 414p. 1964. 49.50 (*0-678-00065-4*) Kelley.

***Rae, John & East Hampton Library Staff.** East Hampton. LC 00-101922. (Images of America Ser.). (Illus.). 128p. 2000. pap. 18.99 (*0-7385-0401-7*) Arcadia Publng.

***Rae, John & Volti, Rudi.** The Engineer in History. 2nd ed. VII, 267p. 1999. 32.95 (*0-8204-4478-2*) P Lang Pubng.

Rae, John, et al. The Economics of John Rae. LC 97-29040. 336p. (C). 1998. 90.00 (*0-415-15867-2*) Routledge.

Rae, John, jt. ed. see Moss, Scott.

Rae, John B. American Automobile: A Brief History. LC 65-24981. (Chicago History of American Civilization Ser.). (Illus.). 1967. reprint ed. pap. text 9.00 (*0-226-70264-2*, CHAC23) U Ch Pr.

— The American Automobile: A Brief History. LC 65-24981. (Chicago History of American Civilization Ser.). (Illus.). 297p. reprint ed. pap. 92.10 (*0-608-09505-2*, 205430600005) Bks Demand.

— Development of Railway Land Subsidy in the United States. Bouchey, Stuart, ed. LC 78-53564. (Development of Public Land Law in the U. S. Ser.). 1979. lib. bdg. 26.95 (*0-405-11366-8*) Ayer.

***Rae, John W.** Mansions of Morris County. (Images of America Ser.). 1999. pap. 18.99 (*0-7385-0064-X*) Arcadia Publng.

Rae, John W. The Mendhams. LC 98-87448. (Images of America Ser.). (Illus.). 128p. 1998. pap. 16.99 (*0-7524-1265-5*) Arcadia Publng.

Rae, Joy, jt. ed. see Jickells, Tim D.

Rae, Judy. Bye, Bye Boogieman. rev. ed. LC 83-70412. (Illus.). 42p. (Orig.). (J). (ps-3). 1984. pap. 3.95 (*0-939728-09-5*) Steppingstone Ent.

Rae, L. Manual de Formacion de Personal. Orig. Title: Skills of Training. (SPA.). 263p. 1994. pap. 25.00 (*84-7978-121-1*, Pub. by Ediciones Diaz) IBD Ltd.

Rae-Lee, Kong. The Sources of Capital Goods Innovation: The Role of User Firms in Japan & Korea. LC 99-458424. (Studies in Global Competition: Vol. 4). 200p. 1998. text 30.00 (*90-5702-256-7*, ECU38, Harwood Acad Pubs) Gordon & Breach.

Rae, Leila, ed. see Christiansen, L. A., et al.

Rae, Leslie. Assessing Trainer Effectiveness. 218p. 1991. 78.95 (*0-566-07264-5*, Pub. by Gower) Ashgate Pub Co.

— Evaluating Trainer Effectiveness. LC 92-37513. 300p. 1993. 35.00 (*1-55623-881-9*, Irwn Prfssnl) McGraw-Hill Prof.

Rae, Leslie. Evaluation Approaches for Training & Development. (Illus.). 254p. 1997. pap. 79.95 (*0-7494-2046-4*, Kogan Pg Educ) Stylus Pub VA.

Rae, Leslie. Fifty Activities for Developing Management Skills, Vol. 1. 352p. 1988. ring bd. 229.95 (*0-566-02768-2*, Pub. by Gower) Ashgate Pub Co.

Rae, Leslie. How to Design & Introduce Trainer Development Programmes. 192p. 1994. pap. 25.00 (*0-7494-1400-6*, Kogan Pg Educ) Stylus Pub VA.

Rae, Leslie. How to Measure Training Effectiveness. 3rd ed. LC 96-8091. 200p. 1996. 74.95 (*0-566-07815-5*, Pub. by Gower) Ashgate Pub Co.

— How to Train the Trainer: 23 Complete Lesson Plans for Teaching Basic Skills to New Trainers. LC 96-32845. 377p. 1996. 149.95 (*0-07-913050-X*) McGraw.

— Let's Have a Meeting: A Comprehensive Guide to Making Your Meetings Work. LC 93-43264. 1994. 19.95 (*0-07-707628-1*) McGraw.

— Meetings Management: A Manual of Effective Training Material. LC 92-46124. (McGraw-Hill Training Ser.). 1993. 75.00 (*0-07-707782-2*) McGraw.

— Planning & Designing Training Programmes. LC 97-11021. 244p. 1997. 69.95 (*0-566-07929-1*, Pub. by Gower) Ashgate Pub Co.

— The Skills of Training. 2nd ed. 220p. 1990. text 49.95 (*0-566-02902-2*, Pub. by Gower) Ashgate Pub Co.

— Techniques of Training. 3rd rev. ed. LC 94-47426. 1995. pap. 43.95 (*0-566-07629-2*, Pub. by Gower) Ashgate Pub Co.

***Rae, Leslie.** Using Activities in Training & Development. 2nd ed. 224p. 2000. 29.95 (*0-7494-3102-4*, Pub. by Kogan Page Ltd) Stylus Pub VA.

Rae, Leslie. Using Presentations: In Training & Development. 240p. 1998. pap. 24.95 (*0-7494-2423-0*, Kogan Pg Educ) Stylus Pub VA.

Rae, Maggie, et al. First Rights: New Edition. 1986. 40.00 (*0-946088-15-2*, Pub. by NCCL) St Mut.

Rae, Maggie, jt. auth. see Ellison, Robin.

Rae, Maggie, jt. auth. see Goodman, Leo.

Rae, Malcolm, jt. auth. see Tansley, David V.

Rae, Mary, tr. from SPA. St. John of the Cross: Selected Poems. LC 90-19808. 94p. (C). 1991. text 14.95 (*0-89341-644-4*, Longwood Academic) Hollowbrook.

Rae, Mary M. Over in the Meadow: A Counting-Out Rhyme. (Picture Puffin Ser.). (Illus.). 32p. (J). (ps). 1986. pap. 3.95 (*0-685-14199-3*, Penguin Bks) Viking Penguin.

Rae, Murray, et al. Science & Theology: Questions at the Interface. 272p. (Orig.). pap. 29.95 (*0-567-29265-7*, Pub. by T & T Clark) Bks Intl VA.

Rae, Murray A. Kierkegaard's Vision of the Incarnation: By Faith Transformed. LC 97-25131. 284p. 1998. text 72.00 (*0-19-826940-4*) OUP.

Rae, Nicol C. Conservative Reformers: The Republican Freshman & the Lessons of the 104th Congress. LC 98-13252. (Illus.). 272p. (gr. 13). 1998. pap. text 27.95 (*0-7656-0129-X*) M E Sharpe.

— Conservative Reformers: The Republican Freshmen & the Lessons of the 104th Congress. LC 98-13252. 272p. (C). (gr. 13). 1998. text 70.95 (*0-7656-0128-1*) M E Sharpe.

— Southern Democrats. LC 93-32876. 224p. 1994. pap. text 18.95 (*0-19-508709-7*) OUP.

Rae, Nicol C., jt. auth. see Hames, Tim.

Rae, Nicol C., jt. ed. see Campbell, Colton C.

Rae, Norman, ed. see Baldwin, Edward A.

Rae, Norman, ed. see Lang, Susan.

Rae, Ollie M. Encyclopedia of Line Dances Vol. 1: The Steps That Came & Stayed-Country-Western: Country & Western Line Dances Encyclopedia. ix, 191p. 1997. pap. 21.95 (*0-9659397-1-5*) Siddall & Ray.

Rae, Patricia. Emergency Nurse. (Orig.). 1982. mass mkt. 2.95 (*0-8217-1045-1*, Zebra Kensgtn) Kensgtn Pub Corp.

— The Practical Muse: Pragmatist Poetics in Hulme, Pound, & Stevens. LC 97-11896. 320p. 1997. 46.50 (*0-8387-5352-3*) Bucknell U Pr.

— Storm Tide. 1983. mass mkt. 3.75 (*0-685-07867-1*, Zebra Kensgtn) Kensgtn Pub Corp.

Rae, Robert W. For Hospital Days. 16p. 1976. pap. text 2.99 (*0-8361-1307-1*) Herald Pr.

— Into Thy Hands. (Visitation Pamphlet Ser.). 16p. 1988. pap. 2.99 (*0-8361-3483-4*) Herald Pr.

— Just in for Tests. 16p. 1973. pap. text 2.99 (*0-8361-1710-7*) Herald Pr.

Rae, S. J., jt. auth. see Chamberlain, D. F.

Rae, Saul F., jt. auth. see Gallup, George H.

Rae, Scott & Cox, Paul. Bioethics: A Critical Approach in a Pluralistic Age. LC 99-15037. (Critical Issues in Bioethics Ser.). 336p. 1999. pap. 24.00 (*0-8028-4595-9*) Eerdmans.

Rae, Scott B. The Ethics of Commercial Surrogate Motherhood: Brave New Families? LC 93-17667. 200p. 1993. 57.95 (*0-275-94679-7*, Praeger Pubs) Greenwood.

— Moral Choices: An Introduction to Ethics. 320p. 1995. 24.99 (*0-310-20013-X*) Zondervan.

— Moral Choices: An Introduction to Ethics. 2nd ed. 2000. 27.99 (*0-310-23015-2*) Zondervan.

Rae, Scott B. & Wong, Kenman L. Beyond Integrity: A Judeo-Christian Approach to Business Ethics. 224p. 1996. boxed set 34.99 (*0-310-20173-X*) Zondervan.

Rae, Scott B., jt. auth. see Moreland, James P.

Rae, Simon. Breath Becomes the Wind: Old & New in Karo Religion. 306p. 1994. pap. 39.95 (*0-908569-61-0*, Pub. by Univ Otago Pr) Intl Spec Bk.

Rae, Simon & Rushton, Willie. Soft Targets: From the Weekend Guardian. 96p. 1991. pap. 15.95 (*1-85224-165-9*) Dufour.

***Rae, Tara.** Taraisms: Words of Wisdom. Guire, Cindy, ed. 102p. 1999. pap. 5.95 (*0-9671872-1-4*) Angel Heart.

Rae, Tara A. Universe on the Move: Be All You Can Be Without Joining the Army. Guire, Cindy, ed. (More Universe on the Move Ser.). 180p. (YA). 1999. per. 15.95 (*0-9671872-0-6*) Angel Heart.

Rae, Thomas H. John Dury & the Royal Road to Piety. LC 98-6110. (Studia Irenica Ser.: Vol. 37). (Illus.). 365p. (C). 1998. pap. text 56.95 (*0-8204-3519-8*) P Lang Pubng.

— John Dury & the Royal Road to Piety. Swinne, Axel H., ed. (Studia Irenica: Vol. 37). (Illus.). 365p. 1998. pap. 56.95 (*3-631-32378-6*) P Lang Pubng.

Rae, Wesley D. Thomas Lodge. LC 67-25185. (Twayne's English Authors Ser.). 1967. pap. text 8.95 (*0-8290-2007-1*); lib. bdg. 20.95 (*0-89197-964-6*) Irvington.

Rae, William. The Edinburgh New Official Guide: Scotland's Capital City. (Illus.). 176p. 1994. pap. 9.95 (*1-85158-605-9*, Pub. by Mainstream Pubng) Trafalgar.

Rae, William F. Westward by Rail: The New Route to the East. LC 72-9465. (Far Western Frontier Ser.). 412p. 1973. reprint ed. 25.95 (*0-405-04993-5*) Ayer.

Rae, William H. & Pope, Alan, Jr. Low-Speed Wind Tunnel Testing. 2nd ed. LC 84-3700. 552p. 1984. 150.00 (*0-471-87402-7*) Wiley.

Raebeck, Barry. Transforming Middle Schools: A Guide to Whole School Change. 2nd ed. LC 98-60045. 245p. 1998. pap. text 34.95 (*1-56676-645-1*) Scarecrow.

Raeber, John A. Clear Water Repellent Treatments for Concrete Masonry. 62p. 1993. pap. 10.00 (*0-940116-25-1*) Masonry Inst Am.

Raeburn. History of the International Association of Agricultural Economy. 1990. 66.95 (*1-85521-090-8*) Ashgate Pub Co.

Raeburn, Ben, ed. Treasury for the Free World. LC 72-5771. (Essay Index Reprint Ser.). 1977. reprint ed. 27.95 (*0-8369-7293-7*) Ayer.

Raeburn, Ben, ed. see Green, Aaron G. & DeNevi, Donald P.

Raeburn, Buren Van, see Capp, Al & Van Buren, Raeburn.

Raeburn, D. & Giembycz, Mark A. Rhinitis: Immunopathology & Pharmacotherapy. LC 96-37785. (Respiratory Pharmacology & Pharmacotherapy Ser.). 1997. write for info. (*3-7643-5301-5*) Birkhauser.

Raeburn, D. & Giembycz, Mark A., eds. Airways Smooth Muscle: Development, & Regulation of Contractility. LC 94-8800. (Respiratory Pharmacology & Pharmacotherapy Ser.). 1994. 199.50 (*0-8176-5011-3*, Pub. by Birkhauser) Princeton Arch.

Raeburn, D., ed. see Giembycz, Mark A.

Raeburn, David & Giembycz, Mark A. Airways Smooth Muscle: Peptide Receptors, Ion Channels & Signal Transduction. LC 94-48621. (Respiratory Pharmacology & Pharmacotherapy Ser.). (Illus.). 288p. 1995. 169.00 (*0-8176-5140-3*) Birkhauser.

— Airways Smooth Muscle: Structure, Innervation & Neurotransmission. LC 94-11899. (Respiratory Pharmacology & Pharmacotherapy Ser.). 336p. 1994. 176.00 (*0-8176-5010-5*) Birkhauser.

Raeburn, David & Giembycz, Mark A., eds. Airways Smooth Muscle: Biochemical Control of Contraction & Relaxation. LC 94-20775. (Respiratory Pharmacology & Pharmacotherapy Ser.). viii, 351p. 1994. 207.00 (*0-8176-5043-1*) Birkhauser.

— Airways Smooth Muscle: Neurotransmitters, Amines, Lipid Mediators, & Signal Transduction. LC 95-19812. (Respiratory Pharmacology & Pharmacotherapy Ser.). 1995. 209.00 (*0-8176-5141-1*) Birkhauser.

— Airways Smooth Muscle: Neurotransmitters, Amines, Lipid Mediators, & Signal Transduction. LC 95-19812. (Respiratory Pharmacology & Pharmacotherapy Ser.). 351p. 1996. 209.00 (*3-7643-5141-1*) Birkhauser.

An Asterisk (*) at the beginning of an entry indicates that the title is appearing for the first time.

Raeburn, David, ed. see Giembycz, Mark A.

Raeburn, H. A., jt. auth. see Raeburn, Janet K.

Raeburn, Iain & William, Dana P. Morita Equivalence & Continuous-Trace C*-Algebras. LC 98-25838. (Mathematical Surveys & Monographs: Vol. 60). 327p. 1998. 65.00 (*0-8218-0860-5*) Am Math.

Raeburn, J. R. Agriculture: Foundations, Principles & Development. fac. ed. LC 84-3619. 345p. 1984. reprint ed. pap. 107.00 (*0-7837-8270-5*, 204905100009) Bks Demand.

Raeburn, Janet K. & Raeburn, H. A. Anatomy, Physiology & Hygiene. 4th ed. 1975. pap. text 7.95 (*0-7195-3213-2*) Transatl Arts.

Raeburn, John. Fame Became of Him: Hemingway as Public Writer. LC 83-48831. 248p. 1984. 27.50 (*0-253-12690-8*) Ind U Pr.

— Fame Became of Him: Hemingway as Public Writer. LC 83-48831. 244p. Date not set. reprint ed. pap. 75.70 (*0-608-20568-0*, 205448200002) Bks Demand.

Raeburn, John & Rootman, I. People-Centred Health Promotion. LC 97-22463. 246p. 1997. pap. 54.95 (*0-471-97137-5*) Wiley.

Raeburn, Michael. The Chronicle of Opera. LC 98-60251. (Illus.). 256p. 1998. 45.00 (*0-500-01867-7*, Pub. by Thames Hudson) Norton.

— Green Frog Service. (Illus.). 424p. 1998. 295.00 (*0-9526584-0-2*) Antique Collect.

— Vision: Fifty Years of Visual Culture, 1949-1998. LC 98-61509. (Illus.). 300p. 1999. 40.00 (*0-500-01906-1*, Pub. by Thames Hudson) Norton.

Raeburn, Michael & Kendall, Alan, eds. Heritage of Music: Classical Music & Its Origins, Vol. I. (Illus.). 322p. 1992. text 60.00 (*0-19-505370-2*) OUP.

— Heritage of Music: Classical Music & Its Origins; The Romantic Era; The Nineteenth-Century Legacy; Music in the Twentieth Century, 4 vols., Set. LC 85-21429. (Illus.). 1294p. 1989. text 225.00 (*0-19-520493-X*) OUP.

— Heritage of Music: Music in the Twentieth Century, Vol. IV. (Illus.). 322p. 1992. text 60.00 (*0-19-505373-7*) OUP.

— Heritage of Music: The Nineteenth-Century Legacy, Vol. III. (Illus.). 322p. 1992. text 60.00 (*0-19-505372-9*) OUP.

— Heritage of Music: The Romantic Era, Vol. II. (Illus.). 322p. 1992. text 60.00 (*0-19-505371-0*) OUP.

Raeburn, Michael, jt. auth. see Whitfield, Sarah.

Raeburn, Paul. The Last Harvest: The Genetic Gamble That Threatens to Destroy American Agriculture. 269p. 1995. 23.50 (*0-684-80365-8*) S&S Trade.

— The Last Harvest: The Genetic Gamble That Threatens to Destroy American Agriculture. LC 96-24071. ix, 262p. 1996. pap. 12.00 (*0-8032-8962-6*, Bison Books) U of Nebr Pr.

— Mars: Uncovering the Secrets of the Red Planet. LC 98-13991. 232p. 1998. 40.50 (*0-7922-7373-7*) Natl Geog.

***Raeburn, Paul.** Mars: Uncovering the Secrets of the Red Planet. 232p. 2000. per. 25.00 (*0-7922-7614-0*) Natl Geog.

Raedels, Alan R. Value-Focused Supply Management: Getting the Most out of the Supply Function. LC 94-24842. (NAPM Professional Development Ser.: 3). 192p. 1994. text 45.00 (*0-7863-0237-2*, Irwn Prfssnl) McGraw-Hill Prof.

***Raeder, Erich.** My Life. 2000. pap. text 18.00 (*0-306-80962-1*) Da Capo.

Raeder, Erich. My Life. Drexel, Henry W., tr. LC 79-6121. (Navies & Men Ser.). (Illus.). 1980. reprint ed. lib. bdg. 44.95 (*0-405-13075-9*) Ayer.

Raeder, Hans. Platons' Philosophische Entwicklung. LC 75-13288. (History of Ideas in Ancient Greece Ser.). (GER.). 1976. reprint ed. 29.95 (*0-405-07331-3*) Ayer.

Raeder, Jurgen, et al. Controlled Nuclear Fusion: Fundamentals of Its Utilization for Energy Supply. LC 85-12384. (Wiley-Interscience Publications). 328p. reprint ed. pap. 101.70 (*0-7837-4519-2*, 204429800001) Bks Demand.

Raeder, Myrna S. Federal Pretrial Practice. 2nd ed. 1003p. 105.00 (*0-327-12335-4*) LEXIS Pub.

Raeder, Myrna S. Federal Pretrial Practice. 2nd ed. 1003p. 1995. 105.00 (*1-55834-232-X*, MICHIE) LEXIS Pub.

— Federal Pretrial Practice, 1998 Cumulative Supplement. 300p. 1998. pap. write for info. (*0-327-00606-4*, 6647912) LEXIS Pub.

Raedle, Fidel, ed. Lateinische Ordensdramen des XV-XVIII: Jahrhunderts Mit Deutschen Uebersetzungen. (Ausgaben Deutscher Literatur des XV bis XVIII Jahrhunderts Ser.). (C). 1979. 484.65 (*3-11-003383-6*) De Gruyter.

Raedler, A. & Raedler, Elisabeth. Modulation von Zelloberflaechenstrukturen. (Bibliotheca Anatomica Ser.: No. 25). (Illus.). vi, 82p. 1984. 41.75 (*3-8055-3755-7*) S Karger.

Raedler, Elisabeth, jt. auth. see Raedler, A.

Raedt, Luc, jt. ed. see Bergadano, Francesco.

Raedts, Peter. Richard Rufus of Cornwall & the Tradition of Oxford Theology. (Oxford Historical Monographs). 288p. 1987. text 59.00 (*0-19-822941-0*) OUP.

Raeff, Marc. Origins of the Russian Intelligensia: The Eighteenth-Century Nobility. LC 66-19152. 256p. (Orig.). (C). 1966. pap. 8.95 (*0-15-670150-2*, Harvest Bks) Harcourt.

— Understanding Imperial Russia: State & Society in the Old Regime. Goldhammer, Arthur, tr. LC 83-26241. 240p. 1986. pap. text 21.00 (*0-231-05843-8*) Col U Pr.

Raeff, Marc, ed. Peter the Great Changes Russia. 2nd ed. (Problems in European Civilization Ser.). 228p. (C). 1972. pap. text 18.36 (*0-669-82701-0*) HM Trade Div.

— Russian Intellectual History: An Anthology. 416p. (C). 1978. reprint ed. pap. 25.00 (*0-391-00905-2*) Humanities.

Raeff, Marc & Columbia University Staff. Russian Intellectual History: An Anthology. LC 98-50380. 1998. write for info. (*1-57392-294-3*) Prometheus Bks.

Raeithel, Gert. Awful America: A Dictionary of 200 Years of European Abuse. Aman, Reinhold, ed. Zohn, Harry, tr. from FRE. LC 76-5698. (Maledicta Press Publications: Vol.7). 15.00 (*0-916500-07-1*) Maledicta.

Raeke, Carolyn. Guide to Adopting an Ex-Racing Greyhound. (Illus.). 64p. 1997. pap. 6.95 (*0-7938-1887-7*, RE-337) TFH Pubns.

Raekel, Hans-Herbert S. Die Musikalische Erscheinungsform der Trouverepoesie. 391p. 1977. pap. 35.00 (*3-258-01149-4*) Theodore Front.

***Rael, Elsa O.** What Zeesie Saw on Delancey Street. (Illus.). (J). 2000. per. 5.99 (*0-689-83535-3*) Aladdin.

Rael, Elsa O. What Zeesie Saw on Delancey Street. LC 95-11321. (Illus.). 40p. (J). (gr. k-3). 1996. 16.00 (*0-689-80549-7*) S&S Bks Yung.

— When Zaydeh Danced on Eldridge Street. LC 96-35045. (Illus.). 40p. (J). (gr. k-3). 1997. 16.00 (*0-689-80451-2*) S&S Childrens.

Rael, Joseph. Being & Vibration. LC 92-72320. (Illus.). 185p. 1993. pap. 14.95 (*0-933031-72-6*) Coun Oak Bks.

— Ceremonies of the Living Spirit. LC 97-27077. (Illus.). 150p. (Orig.). (C). 1997. pap. 14.95 (*1-57178-055-6*) Coun Oak Bks.

— The Way of Inspiration: Teachings of Native American Elder Joseph Rael. (Illus.). 64p. 1996. 12.95 (*1-57178-034-3*) Coun Oak Bks.

Rael, Joseph E. Beautiful Painted Arrow: Stories & Teachings from the Native American Tradition. LC 92-1133. 108p. 1992. pap. 12.95 (*1-85230-310-7*, Pub. by Element MA) Penguin Putnam.

Rael, Joseph E. & Sutton, Lindsay. Tracks of Dancing Light: A Native American Approach to Understanding Your Name. LC 93-41375. (Earth Quest Ser.). 1994. pap. 12.95 (*1-85230-434-0*, Pub. by Element MA) Penguin Putnam.

Rael, Juan B. Cuentos Espanoles De Colorado y Nuevo Mejico: Spanish Tales from Colorado & New Mexico, 2 vols., Set. Dorson, Richard M., ed. LC 77-70617. (International Folklore Ser.). 1977. lib. bdg. 116.95 (*0-405-10119-8*) Ayer.

— Cuentos Espanoles De Colorado y Nuevo Mejico: Spanish Tales from Colorado & New Mexico, 2 vols., Vol. 1. Dorson, Richard M., ed. LC 77-70617. (International Folklore Ser.). 1977. lib. bdg. 58.95 (*0-405-10120-1*) Ayer.

— Cuentos Espanoles De Colorado y Nuevo Mejico: Spanish Tales from Colorado & New Mexico, 2 vols., Vol. 2. Dorson, Richard M., ed. LC 77-70617. (International Folklore Ser.). 1977. lib. bdg. 58.95 (*0-405-10121-X*) Ayer.

Rael, Juan B., jt. auth. see Tully, Marjorie F.

Rael, Leyla & Rudhyar, Dane. Astrological Aspects. 244p. 1980. pap. 14.00 (*0-943358-00-0*) Aurora Press.

Raelin, Joseph A. Building a Career: The Effect of Initial Job Experiences & Related Work Attitudes on Later Employment. LC 80-24848. 178p. 1980. pap. 4.00 (*0-911558-73-X*) W E Upjohn.

— The Clash of Cultures: Managers Managing Professionals. 274p. 1991. pap. 12.95 (*0-87584-305-0*) Harvard Busn.

— The Salaried Professional: How to Make the Most of Your Career. LC 83-24796. 304p. 1984. 69.50 (*0-275-91246-9*, C1246, Praeger Pubs) Greenwood.

***Raelin, Joseph A.** Work-Based Learning: The New Frontier of Management Development. LC 98-55917. 281p. (C). 1999. pap. text 40.00 (*0-201-43388-5*, Prentice Hall) P-H.

Raelin, Joseph A., ed. The Clash of Cultures Industries. 299p. 1986. 35.00 (*0-07-103264-9*) McGraw.

***Raelly, L. D.** The God of Daniel. Fowler, John, ed. 63p. 1998. pap. 5.95 (*1-57847-050-1*) Genl Conf Svnth-day.

***Raemaekers, D. C. M.** The Articulation of a 'New Neolithic' The Meaning of the Swifterbant Culture for the Process of Neolithisation in the Western Part of the North European Plain (4900-3400 BC) (Archaeological Studies : No. 3). 224p. 1999. pap. 54.00 (*90-76368-03-1*, Pub. by Leiden Univ Pr) David Brown.

Raemer, Harlod R. Radar Systems Principles. LC 96-8565. (Illus.). 544p. 1996. boxed set 104.95 (*0-8493-9481-3*) CRC Pr.

***Raemer, Jillian.** Whispers Beyond the Rainbow: A Spiritual Quest. Chadwick, Gloria, ed. LC 99-74445. 78p. 1999. pap. 11.00 (*1-883717-47-7*) Myst Mndscapes.

Raemsch, Dorothy C. House of Light: Poems. 32p. (Orig.). 1990. pap. 5.00 (*0-9605398-1-6*) D C Raemsch.

— October Dawn: Poems. 32p. (Orig.). 1980. pap. 5.00 (*0-9605398-0-8*) D C Raemsch.

— Spinning with Gold: Poems for Young & Old. (Illus.). 32p. (Orig.). 1991. pap. 6.00 (*0-9605398-2-4*) D C Raemsch.

— Three Poems by W. H. Davies: Song Set. (Illus.). 12p. (Orig.). 1994. pap. 4.00 (*0-9605398-3-2*) D C Raemsch.

Raeper, William, ed. The Gold Thread: Essays on George MacDonald. 220p. 1991. 68.00 (*0-7486-0166-X*, Pub. by Edinburgh U Pr) Col U Pr.

— The Gold Thread: Essays on George MacDonald. 224p. 1992. pap. 28.00 (*0-7486-0208-9*, Pub. by Edinburgh U Pr) Col U Pr.

Raes, D. & Feyen, J. Practical Guide to Irrigation Systems. 1994. pap. 150.00 (*0-7855-2751-6*, Pub. by Scientific Pubs) St Mut.

Raes, S., jt. ed. see Lemmens, P.

Raes, Stefaan, jt. ed. see Taelman, Piet.

Raeschild, Sheila. Lessons in Leaving. 1974. pap. 2.50 (*0-912786-30-2*) Know Inc.

Raese, Jon W., ed. Oil Shale Symposium Proceedings Index, 1964-82. LC 82-19839. 110p. 1982. pap. text 30.00 (*0-918062-52-7*) Colo Sch Mines.

Raese, Jon W., et al, eds. Subsurface Geology: Petroleum, Mining, Construction. 5th ed. LC 86-18806. (Illus.). 1081p. (C). 1987. 50.00 (*0-918062-68-3*) Colo Sch Mines.

Raese, Jon W. & Goldberg, J. H., eds. Algal Limestones Within the Minturn Formation, Meeker to Dotsero Area, Western Colorado. (Colorado School of Mines Quarterly Ser.: Vol. 78, No. 2). (Illus.). 14p. 1983. pap. 10.00 (*0-686-45171-6*) Colo Sch Mines.

Raese, Jon W., ed. see Agapito, J. F.

Raese, Jon W., ed. see Blackstone, Sandra L.

Raese, Jon W., ed. see Bugbee, Edward E.

Raese, Jon W., ed. see Clark, George B.

Raese, Jon W., ed. see Davis, T. L., et al.

Raese, Jon W., ed. see Huber, G. C.

Raese, Jon W., ed. see Li, Itunda Y.

Raese, Jon W., ed. see McCalpin, James P.

Raese, Jon W., ed. see Parker, Joni M. & Maurer, Ruth A.

Raese, Jon W., ed. see Sonnenberg, Stephen A., et al.

Raese, Jon W., ed. see Wayman, Cooper H. & Genasci, Gail A.

Raese, Jon W., ed. see Willard, Beatrice L.

Raese, Jon W., ed. see Yenge, Li I.

Raese, Robert H. Internet.edu: A Sourcebook for Educators. LC 97-70566. 220p. (Orig.). 1997. pap. 27.95 (*1-57517-072-8*, 1443) SkyLght.

Raeside, Adrain. Dennis the Dragon. 32p. 1994. pap. 4.95 (*0-385-25513-6*) Doubleday.

Raeside, Adrian. The Demented Decade. 144p. 1993. pap. 12.95 (*0-385-25453-9*) Doubleday.

— Jesus of the Apocalypse. 480p. 1996. 34.95 (*0-385-25566-7*) Doubleday.

— There Goes the Neighborhood. 176p. 1992. pap. 15.95 (*0-385-25392-3*) Doubleday.

Raeside, Fiona, ed. see Walker, Eric.

Raeside, James, tr. see Hiroshi, Noma.

Raess, Beat U. & Tunnicliff, G., eds. The Red Cell Membrane: A Model for Solute Transport. LC 89-15438. (Contemporary Biomedicine Ser.: Vol. 10). (Illus.). 495p. 1990. 119.50 (*0-89603-158-6*) Humana.

Raethel, Heinz-Siqurd. The New Duck Handbook. (Illus.). 1989. pap. 9.95 (*0-8120-4088-0*) Barron.

Raether, H. Surface Plasmons. (Tracts in Modern Physics Ser.: Vol. 111). (Illus.). 150p. 1988. 71.95 (*0-387-17363-3*) Spr-Verlag.

Raether, Manfred, jt. auth. see Lazarus, David.

Raevens, John. An Understanding & Enjoyment Music. LC 97-125357. 102p. (C). 1996. text 32.80 (*0-536-59836-3*) Pearson Custom.

Raevsky-Hughes, Olga, jt. ed. see Gasparov, Boris.

Raevsky-Hughes, Olga, ed. see Remizov, Aleksei.

Rafael, Anita. La Survivance: A Companion to the Exhibit at the Museum of Work & Culture, Woonsocket, Rhode Island. (Illus.). 44p. 1998. pap. 5.00 (*0-932840-13-2*) RI Hist Soc.

Rafael, Janis. Playing It Safe with Mr. See-More Safety: Let's Learn about Bicycle Safety, Vol. 2. (Illus.). 24p. (Orig.). (J). (ps-8). Date not set. write for info. (*0-9655604-1-4*) Safewrld Pub.

— Playing It Safe with Mr. See-More Safety: Let's Rap & Rhyme. large type ed. LC 96-71670. (Illus.). 84p. (Orig.). (J). (gr. k-6). 1997. pap. 14.95 (*0-9655604-0-6*) Safewrld Pub.

***Rafael, Jody.** Saving Bernice: Battered Women, Welfare & Poverty. LC 99-88074. (Series on Gender, Crime & Law). 184p. 2000. text 45.00 (*1-55553-439-2*); pap. text 16.95 (*1-55553-438-4*) NE U Pr.

Rafael Rosa, Portada De, see Agramonte, Roberto D. & De Rafael Rosa, Portada.

Rafael, Ruth K. The Western Jewish History Center: Guide to Archival & Oral History Collections. LC 86-50102. (Illus.). 1987. pap. 24.95 (*0-943376-35-1*) Magnes Mus.

Rafael, Vicente L. Contracting Colonialism: Translation & Christian Conversion in Tagalog Society under Early Spanish Rule. LC 87-23937. xiii, 230 p. 1988. 36.50 (*0-8014-2065-2*) Cornell U Pr.

— Contracting Colonialism: Translation & Christian Conversion in Tagalog Society under Early Spanish Rule. LC 92-32739. (Illus.). 256p. 1993. pap. text 17.95 (*0-8223-1341-3*) Duke.

— Contracting Colonialism: Translation & Christian Conversion in Tagalog Society under Early Spanish Rule. LC 87-23937. (Illus.). 247p. reprint ed. pap. 76.60 (*0-608-20936-8*, 207203500003) Bks Demand.

***Rafael, Vicente L.** White Love & Other Events in Filipino History. LC 99-50790. (Illus.). 288p. 2000. pap. 18.95 (*0-8223-2542-X*) Duke.

— White Love & Other Events in Filipino History. LC 99-50790. (Illus.). 288p. 2000. lib. bdg. 54.95 (*0-8223-2505-5*) Duke.

Rafael, Vicente L., ed. Discrepant Histories: Translocal Essays on Filipino Cultures. (Asian American History & Culture Ser.). 240p. (Orig.). (C). 1995. pap. text 18.95 (*1-56639-356-6*); lib. bdg. 69.95 (*1-56639-355-8*) Temple U Pr.

— Figures of Criminality in Indonesia, the Philippines & Colonial Vietnam. (Studies on Southeast Asia: Vol. 25). 259p. 1999. pap. 18.00 (*0-87727-724-9*) Cornell SE Asia.

Rafaela, Judith. Poems along the Path: Ad Adventure in Poetry. 48p. 1994. pap. 7.50 (*0-9644196-0-2*) Sherman Asher Pub.

Rafaela, Judith & Fay, Nancy, eds. The Practice of Peace. LC 98-21101. 208p. 1998. pap. 15.00 (*0-9644196-7-X*) Sherman Asher Pub.

Rafaela, Judith, jt. ed. see Fay, Nancy.

Rafaella. The House of Gabriel. (Black Lace Ser.). 288p. (Orig.). 1996. mass mkt. 5.95 (*0-352-33063-5*, Pub. by Virgin Bks) London Bridge.

Rafaelsen, Lise, jt. ed. see Pines, Malcolm.

Rafai, P., jt. auth. see Kovacs, F.

Rafal, Richard B. Radiologic Oral Examination: Questions & Guide. LC 93-26566. 464p. 1994. pap. 59.50 (*0-89640-246-0*) Igaku-Shoin.

Rafalovich, Danita & Pellman, Kathryn A. Backart: On the Flip Side. (Illus.). 80p. 1991. pap. text 19.95 (*0-942786-10-6*) Eddies Q Bee.

Rafanelli, M., et al, eds. Statistical & Scientific Database Management. (Lecture Notes in Computer Science Ser.: Vol. 339). ix, 454p. 1989. 55.00 (*0-387-50575-X*) Spr-Verlag.

Rafat, Taufiq. A Selection. LC 97-930926. 1997. write for info. (*0-19-577811-1*) OUP.

Rafaty, Laura, jt. auth. see Hopcke, Robert H.

Rafe, Kathleen B., jt. auth. see Rafe, Stephen C.

Rafe-Lawyer, Lyn. Keep Your Pecker Up. unabridged ed. 261p. 1998. pap. write for info. (*1-86106-806-9*, Pub. by Minerva Pr) Unity Dist.

Rafe, Stephen C. Be Prepared: How To Think on Your Feet & Make the Best Business Presentations of Your Life. 1990. 18.95 (*0-88730-437-0*, HarpBusn) HarpInfo.

— Mastering the News Media Interview: How to Do Successful Television, Radio & Print Interviews. 204p. 1991. 24.95 (*0-88730-439-7*, HarpBusn) HarpInfo.

— Mastering the Power Dynamics of Career Interviewing: How to Be in the Best Form, Ask the Right Questions, & Get the Job You Want. 224p. 1990. 18.95 (*0-88730-438-9*, HarpBusn) HarpInfo.

Rafe, Stephen C. & Rafe, Kathleen B. The Jack Russell Terrier. Anderson, Mark, ed. (Pure Breds Ser.). (Illus.). 320p. 2000. 28.50 (*0-944875-57-2*) Doral Pub.

Rafelski, J., jt. auth. see Gutbrod, H. H.

Rafelski, Johann, ed. Strangeness in Hadronic Matter, Proceedings: Conference on Strangeness in Hadronic Matter, 1995, Tucson, AZ. LC 95-77477. (AIP Conference Proceedings Ser.: Vol. 340). 500p. 1995. 135.00 (*1-56396-489-9*) Am Inst Physics.

Rafelski, Johann, jt. ed. see Carruthers, P. A.

Rafelson, Max E. Metal Metabolism & Disease. (Journal: Clinical Physiology & Biochemistry: Vol. 4, No. 1, 1986). (Illus.). 112p. 1986. pap. 36.75 (*3-8055-4264-X*) S Karger.

Rafelson, Max E., ed. Cellular & Humoral Defense against Disease. (Journal: Clinical Physiology & Biochemistry: Vol. 1, No. 2-5, 1983). (Illus.). 228p. 1983. pap. 113.25 (*3-8055-3693-3*) S Karger.

Rafelson, Max E., ed. see Dubin, A.

Rafert, John A., jt. auth. see Long, Bruce W.

Rafert, Stewart. The Miami Indians of Indiana: A Persistent People, 1654-1994. (Illus.). xxvii, 358p. 1996. 29.95 (*0-87195-111-8*) Ind Hist Soc.

***Rafert, Stewart.** The Miami Indians of Indiana: A Persistent People, 1654-1994. (Illus.). xxvii, 358p. 1999. pap. 14.95 (*0-87195-132-0*) Ind Hist Soc.

Raferty, Margaret M. Mary of Nemmegen. (Medieval & Renaissance Texts Ser.: No. 5). 85p. 1991. 42.00 (*90-04-09252-8*) Brill Academic Pubs.

Rafes, Yulian. Dorogami Moei Sud'by: Life in Eastern Europe in the Twentieth Century As Seen Through the Eyes of a Jewish Doctor. LC 97-90942. (RUS., Illus.). 433p. 1997. pap. 25.00 (*1-885563-07-8*) VIA Press MD.

Rafes, Yulian I. Doctor Tsemakh Shabad: A Great Citizen of the Jewish Diaspora. Epstein, Lisa & Sedlis, Steven, eds. LC 99-71195. (Illus.). 228p. 1999. pap. 19.00 (*1-885563-17-5*) VIA Press MD.

— The Way We Were Before Our Destruction: Lives of Jewish Students from Vilna, Who Perished During the Holocaust. Glasser, Paul, ed. LC 97-60290. (Illus.). 220p. (Orig.). 1997. pap. 16.00 (*1-885563-06-X*) VIA Press MD.

Raff, Beverly S. & Anderson, Gene C., eds. Newborn Behavioral Organization Nursing Research & Implications. LC 79-2597. (Alan R. Liss Ser.: Vol. 15, No. 7). 1979. 29.00 (*0-685-03294-9*) March of Dimes.

Raff, Beverly S., ed. see Ramer, Leah.

Raff, Beverly S., ed. see Weiner, Susan M.

Raff, Daniel M., jt. ed. see Lamoreaux, Naomi R.

Raff, Ellison S., ed. Computers & Operations Research: Environmental Applications. 1977. pap. 42.00 (*0-08-021348-0*, Pergamon Pr) Elsevier.

Raff, Gilbert L. Trading the Regression Channel: Defining & Predicting Stock Price Trends. Achelis, Steven B. & Slauson, John C., eds. (University Ser.). (Illus.). 145p. 1996. 39.95 (*1-885439-01-6*) Equis International.

Raff, Hershel. Physiology Secrets. LC 98-29331. (Secrets Ser.). (Illus.). 350p. 1998. pap. text 35.00 (*1-56053-255-6*) Hanley & Belfus.

Raff, Howard B., ed. see Wexler, Linda R.

Raff, Jason, jt. auth. see Lieberman, Janice.

***Raff, Jeffrey.** Jung & the Alchemical Imagination. (Illus.). 288p. 2000. pap. 18.95 (*0-89254-045-1*, Pub. by Nicolas-Hays) Weiser.

***Raff, Lionel M.** Principles of Physical Chemistry. LC 00-41687. 2000. write for info. (*0-13-027805-X*) P-H.

Raff, Rudolf A. The Shape of Life: Genes, Development, & the Evolution of Animal Form. LC 95-49224. 520p. 1996. pap. text 29.95 (*0-226-70266-9*); lib. bdg. 55.00 (*0-226-70265-0*) U Ch Pr.

Raff, Rudolf A. & Kaufman, Thomas C. Embryos, Genes & Evolution: The Developmental-Genetic Basis of Evolutionary Change. LC 90-5351. (Illus.). 421p. reprint ed. pap. 130.60 (*0-608-09358-0*, 205410400002) Bks Demand.

Raff, Stephen, jt. auth. see Clott, Jami.

Raffa, Frederick A. Personal Injury Valuation. 1992. write for info. (*0-8205-1678-3*) Bender.

— Pharmacology: Modern Medical. 2001. text 65.00 (*0-07-135444-1*) McGraw.

— Pharmacology set: Modern Medicine. 2001. text. write for info. (*0-07-135445-X*) McGraw.

R

An Asterisk (*) at the beginning of an entry indicates that the title is appearing for the first time.

R

Raffa, Frederick A., et al, compiled by. United States Employment & Training Programs: A Selected Annotated Bibliography. LC 82-25108. 152p. 1983. lib. bdg. 47.95 (*0-313-23872-3*, RUE/, Greenwood Pr) Greenwood.

Raffa, Jean B. The Bridge to Wholeness: A Feminine Alternative to the Hero Myth. LC 92-10643. 208p. (Orig.). 1992. pap. 14.95 (*0-931055-88-1*) Innisfree Pr.

— Dream Theatres of the Soul: Empowering the Feminine Through Jungian Dreamwork. LC 93-36669. 224p. 1994. pap. 15.95 (*1-880913-10-0*) Innisfree Pr.

Raffa, Kenneth F., jt. ed. see Wagner, Michael.

Raffa, Robert B. Pharmacology. 1999. pap. text 19.95 (*1-889325-38-4*) Fence Crk Pubng.

— Thermodynamics of the Drug-Recreation. text. write for info. (*0-471-72042-9*) Wiley.

Raffa, Robert B. & Porreca, Frank, eds. Antisense Strategies for the Study of Receptor Mechanisms. LC 96-17121. (Molecular Biology Intelligence Unit Ser.). 222p. 1996. 99.00 (*1-57059-345-0*) Landes Bioscience.

Raffael, Theresa H. Pearl at a Great Price LC 96-110902. xii, 238p. 1995. write for info. (*1-56043-559-3*) Destiny Image.

Raffaele, Herbert A. Una Guia a las Aves de Puerto Rico y las Islas Virgenes. rev. ed. (SPA., Illus.). 358p. 1991. pap. 24.95 (*0-89825-000-5*) Pub Resces PR.

Raffaele, Herbert A. Guide to Birds in West Indies. (Illus.). pap. 0.00 (*0-691-02519-3*) Princeton U Pr.

Raffaele, Herbert A. A Guide to the Birds of Puerto Rico & the Virgin Islands. (Illus.). 220p. (C). 1989. pap. 27.50 (*0-691-02424-3*, Pub. by Princeton U Pr); text 55.00 (*0-691-08554-4*, Pub. by Princeton U Pr) Cal Prin Full Svc.

— Princeton Guide to the Birds of the West Indies. LC 97-41790. 512p. 1998. 49.50 (*0-691-08736-9*, Pub. by Princeton U Pr) Cal Prin Full Svc.

Raffaele, Joseph A. The Management of Technology: Change in a Society of Organized Advocacies. rev. ed. LC 79-63752. 1979. pap. text 27.00 (*0-8191-0739-5*) U Pr of Amer.

— System & Unsystem: How American Society Works. 388p. 1974. 18.95 (*0-470-70274-5*) Schenkman Bks Inc.

Raffaeli, Tiziano, ed. Alfred Marshall's Lectures to Women: Some Economic Questions Directly Connected to the Welfare of the Laborer. LC 95-30785. 224p. 1995. 80.00 (*1-85898-310-X*) E Elgar.

Raffaelli, Marcelo. Rise & Demise of Commodity Agreements: An Investigation into the Breakdown of International Commodity Agreements. 256p. 1995. 180.00 (*1-85573-179-7*, Pub. by Woodhead Pubng) Am Educ Systs.

Raffalli, Bernard, jt. auth. see Dumas, Alexandre.

Raffalovich, Isaiah. Our Inheritance: A Collection of Sermons & Addresses for All the Sabbaths & Festivals. 272p. 32.50 (*0-87559-146-9*) Shalom.

***Raffan, James.** Bark, Skin & Cedar: Exploring the Canoe in Canadian Experience. (Phyllis Bruce Bks.). 274p. 2000. pap. 15.00 (*0-00-638653-9*) HarpC.

— Bark, Skin & Cedar: Exploring the Canoe in the Canadian Experience. LC 99-492062. 274p. 2000. 29.95 (*0-00-255730-4*) HarpC.

— Fire in the Bones: Bill Mason & the Canadian Canoeing Tradition. (Phyllis Bruce Bks.). 1999. pap. 19.95 (*0-00-638514-1*) HarpC.

Raffan, John, tr. see Burkert, Walter.

Raffan, Richard. Turned-Bowl Design. LC 87-72008. (Illus.). 176p. 1987. pap. 21.95 (*0-918804-82-5*, 70358) Taunton.

— Turning Boxes with Richard Raffan. LC 97-38035. (Illus.). 176p. 1998. pap. 24.95 (*1-56158-224-7*, 070358) Taunton.

— Turning Projects. LC 90-49026. (Illus.). 176p. 1991. pap. 21.95 (*0-942391-38-1*) Taunton.

— Turning Wood with Richard Raffan. LC 84-52130. (Illus.). 176p. 1985. pap. 21.95 (*0-918804-24-8*, 70039) Taunton.

Raffauf, Robert F. A Handbook of Alkaloids & Alkaloid-containing Plants. LC 73-113713. 1230p. reprint ed. pap. 200.00 (*0-608-13444-9*, 202019000016) Bks Demand.

— Plant Alkaloids: A Guide to Their Discovery & Distribution. LC 96-5319. 298p. 1996. 69.95 (*1-56022-860-1*) Haworth Pr.

Raffauf, Robert F., jt. auth. see Schultes, Richard E.

Raffe, David. Education & the Youth Labour Market: Schooling & Scheming. 225p. 1988. pap. 44.95 (*1-85000-421-8*, Falmer Pr) Taylor & Francis.

Raffe, David, ed. Fourteen to Eighteen: The Changing Pattern of Schooling in Scotland. 276p. 1984. pap. text 17.50 (*0-08-030374-9*, Pergamon Pr) Elsevier.

Raffel. How to Fix a Leak. (Home Care Guides Ser.). (Illus.). 1981. pap. 2.50 (*0-671-42307-X*) S&S Trade.

— U. S. Health System Origins & Functions. 5th ed. (C). 2001. pap. text 36.75 (*0-7668-0714-2*) Delmar.

Raffel, Burton. American Victorians: Explorations in Emotional History. LC 84-3067. xvii, 191p. (C). 1984. lib. bdg. 29.50 (*0-208-02044-6*, Archon Bks) Shoe String.

— The Art of Translating Prose. LC 93-20439. 184p. (C). 1994. 35.00 (*0-271-01080-0*) Pa St U Pr.

— Artists All: Creativity, the University, & the World. 160p. 1991. 33.50 (*0-271-00760-5*) Pa St U Pr.

***Raffel, Burton.** Beethoven in Denver & Other Poems. LC 99-75271. 96p. 1999. 18.00 (*0-9657159-6-5*, Pub. by Conundrum Pr); pap. 13.00 (*0-9657159-4-9*, Pub. by Conundrum Pr) Books West CO.

Raffel, Burton. Beowulf, a New Translation with an Introduction. 1963. 10.09 (*0-606-10140-3*, Pub. by Turtleback) Demco.

— The Forked Tongue: A Study of the Translation Process. LC 79-154530. (De Proprietatibus Litterarum, Ser. Major: No. 14). 181p. 1971. text 29.25 (*3-10-800272-4*) Mouton.

— From Stress to Stress: An Autobiography of English Prosody. LC 92-10538. xxi, 185p. (C). 1992. lib. bdg. 29.50 (*0-208-02330-5*, Archon Bks) Shoe String.

— From the Vietnamese: Ten Centuries of Poetry. 1968. 6.95 (*0-8079-0052-4*); pap. 4.25 (*0-8079-0053-2*) October.

— How to Read a Poem. 1984. pap. 11.95 (*0-452-01033-0*, Plume) Dutton Plume.

— Mia Poems. 1968. 6.95 (*0-8079-0082-6*); pap. 4.25 (*0-8079-0083-4*) October.

— The Origins of Graphic Design in America, 1870-1920. LC 96-52342. 1997. 27.50 (*0-300-06835-2*) Yale U Pr.

— Politicians, Poets, & Con Men: Emotional History in Late Victorian America. LC 86-1178. xi, 220p. (C). 1986. lib. bdg. 32.00 (*0-208-02067-5*, Archon Bks) Shoe String.

Raffel, Burton, ed. Possum & Ole Ez in the Public Eye: Contemporaries & Peers on T. S. Eliot & Ezra Pound. LC 84-24593. 143p. (C). 1985. lib. bdg. 26.00 (*0-208-02057-8*, Archon Bks) Shoe String.

Raffel, Burton, ed. The Signet Classic Book of American Short Stories. 1985. mass mkt. 6.95 (*0-451-52279-6*, Sig Classics) NAL.

Raffel, Burton, tr. Sir Gawain & the Green Knight. (Orig.). 1970. mass mkt. 5.99 (*0-451-62823-3*) NAL.

Raffel, Burton & Olsen, Alexandra Hennessey. Poems & Prose from the Old English. LC 97-22556. 273p. 1998. pap. 15.00 (*0-300-06995-2*) Yale U Pr.

Raffel, Burton, jt. auth. see Chr Etien.

Raffel, Burton, jt. ed. see Zuxin, Ding.

Raffel, Burton, tr. see Anwar, Chairil.

Raffel, Burton, tr. see Balzac, Honore de & Brooks, Peter.

Raffel, Burton, tr. see Chretien.

Raffel, Burton, tr. see De Cervantes Saavedra, Miguel.

Raffel, Burton, tr. see De Troyes, Chretien.

Raffel, Burton, tr. see Espriu, Salvador.

Raffel, Burton, tr. see Olsen, Alexandra Hennessey, ed.

Raffel, Burton, tr. see Rabelais, Francois.

Raffel, Corey & Harsh, Griffith R. The Molecular Basis of Neurosurgical Disease Vol. 8: Concepts in Neurosurgery. (Illus.). 393p. 1997. write for info. (*0-683-18312-5*) Lppncott W & W.

Raffel, Jeffrey A. Historical Dictionary of School Segregation & Desegregation: The American Experience. LC 98-11102. 376p. 1998. lib. bdg. 75.00 (*0-313-29502-6*, Greenwood Pr) Greenwood.

Raffel, Jeffrey A., jt. auth. see Varady, David P.

Raffel, Lee. Should I Stay or Go? LC 98-16841. 304p. 1998. 22.95 (*0-8092-2997-8*, 299780, Contemporary Bks) NTC Contemp Pub Co.

— Should I Stay or Go? How Controlled Separation Can Save Your Marriage. 304p. 1999. pap. 14.95 (*0-8092-2513-1*, 251310, Contemporary Bks) NTC Contemp Pub Co.

Raffel, Lisa, jt. ed. see Olsen, Laurie.

Raffel, M. Particle Image Velocimetry: A Practical Guide. 2000. text. write for info. (*0-471-72027-5*) Wiley.

Raffel, M., et al. Particle Image Velocimetry: A Practical Guide. LC 97-51315. (Experimental Fluid Mechanics Ser.). (Illus.). xvi, 253p. 1998. 79.95 (*3-540-63683-8*) Spr-Verlag.

Raffel, Marshal W. & Raffel, Norma K. The U. S. Health System: Origins & Function. 3rd ed. 1989. pap. text 41.95 (*0-8273-4336-1*) Delmar.

Raffel, Marshall M., ed. Comparative Health Systems: Descriptive Analyses of Fourteen National Health Systems. LC 83-43032. (Illus.). 480p. 1984. 45.00 (*0-271-00363-4*) Pa St U Pr.

Raffel, Marshall M. & Raffel, Norma K., eds. Perspectives on Health Policy: Australia, New Zealand, United States. LC 87-2168. (Wiley-Medical Publication). 296p. reprint ed. pap. 91.80 (*0-8357-3477-3*, 203973600013) Bks Demand.

Raffel, Marshall W., ed. Health Care & Reform in Industrialized Countries. LC 97-16895. (Illus.). xviii, 303p. 1997. 50.00 (*0-271-01620-5*); pap. 19.95 (*0-271-01644-2*) Pa St U Pr.

Raffel, Marshall W. & Raffel, Norma K. The U. S. Health System: Origins & Functions. 4th ed. LC 93-11931. 302p. (C). 1993. mass mkt. 42.25 (*0-8273-5408-8*) Delmar.

Raffel, Norma K., jt. auth. see Raffel, Marshal W.

Raffel, Norma K., jt. auth. see Raffel, Marshall W.

Raffel, Norma K., jt. ed. see Raffel, Marshall M.

Raffel, Stanley. Habermas, Lyotard & the Concept of Justice. 176p. (C). 1992. text 65.00 (*0-333-47323-X*) St Martin.

Raffeld, David. Into the World of Men. limited ed. LC 97-210288. 42p. 1997. 40.00 (*0-938566-74-1*); pap. 10.00 (*0-938566-75-X*) Adastra Pr.

Raffell, Burton. Complete & Annotated Milton. 720p. 1999. mass mkt. 6.95 (*0-553-58110-4*) Bantam.

Raffelt, Albert, ed. see Rahner, Karl.

Raffelt, Georg G. Stars as Laboratories for Fundamental Physics: The Astrophysics of Neutrinos, Axions, & Other Weakly Interacting Particles. LC 95-39684. (Theoretical Astrophysics Ser.). 1996. pap. text 42.00 (*0-226-70272-3*) U Ch Pr.

— Stars as Laboratories for Fundamental Physics: The Astrophysics of Neutrinos, Axions, & Other Weakly Interacting Particles. LC 95-39684. (Theoretical Astrophysics Ser.). 648p. 1997. lib. bdg. 77.00 (*0-226-70271-5*) U Ch Pr.

Raffensperger, Carolyn & Tickner, Joel, eds. Protecting Public Health & the Environment: Implementing the Precautionary Principle. LC 99-19514. (Illus.). 350p. (C). 1999. pap. 30.00 (*1-55963-688-2*) Island Pr.

***Raffensperger, Jeffrey P.** Fattitudes. 256p. 2000. text 22.95 (*0-312-25191-2*) St Martin.

Raffensperger, John. Swenson's Pediatric Surgery. 5th ed. (Illus.). 994p. (C). 1992. pap. text 195.00 (*0-8385-8757-7*, A8757-5, Apple Lange Med) McGraw.

Raffensperger, John, ed. The Old Lady on Harrison Street: Cook County International Hospital, 1833-1995. LC 96-36391. (International Healthcare Ethics Ser.: Vol. 3). X, 455p. (C). 1997. text 65.95 (*0-8204-3461-2*) P Lang Pubng.

Raffensperger, John G., jt. auth. see Beal, John M.

Raffer, Kunibert & Singer, Hans W. The Foreign Aid Business: Economic Assistance & Development Co-operation. LC 95-49829. (Illus.). 256p. 1996. 95.00 (*1-85898-406-8*) E Elgar.

Raffer, Kunibert & Swinger, H. W. The Foreign Aid Business: Economic Assistance & Development Co-Operation. LC 95-49829. 256p. (C). 1997. pap. text 25.00 (*1-85898-446-7*) E Elgar.

Raffer, Kunibert, jt. ed. see Murshed, S. Mansoob.

***Rafferty.** Church Street & Fenian Threat 1861. LC 98-49491. 1999. text 69.95 (*0-312-22063-4*) St Martin.

Rafferty, Anne M., et al. Nursing History & the Politics of Welfare. LC 96-19933. 296p. (C). 1997. 80.00 (*0-415-13835-3*); pap. 25.99 (*0-415-13836-1*) Routledge.

Rafferty, Anne M., jt. ed. see Marland, Hilary.

***Rafferty, Bob & Reynolds, Loys.** Irresistible Overnights in Florida. 2000. pap. 12.99 (*1-55853-818-6*) Rutledge Hill Pr.

Rafferty, Carin. Even Cowboys Get the Blues. (Temptation Ser.). 1994. per. 2.99 (*0-373-25605-1*, 1-25605-6) Harlequin Bks.

— The Hood. (Temptation Ser.: No. 381). 1992. per. 2.99 (*0-373-25481-4*, 1-25481-2) Harlequin Bks.

Rafferty, Cathleen D., et al. Examining Scholarship: A Case Study in Redefining the Role of the Professoriate. 77p. 1999. pap. 23.95 (*0-89333-173-2*) AACTE.

Rafferty, Charles. The Man on the Tower. LC 94-37208. (Poetry Award Ser.). 64p. 1995. pap. 12.00 (*1-55728-340-0*) U of Ark Pr.

Rafferty, Charles. The Man on the Tower. LC 94-37208. (Poetry Award Ser.). 64p. 1995. 18.00 (*1-55728-339-7*) U of Ark Pr.

Rafferty, Charles. The Wave That Will Beach Us Both. Warren, Shirley, ed. 28p. 1994. pap. 5.00 (*1-877801-26-7*) Still Waters.

Rafferty, Denise, ed. see Crawford, Karen & Heaton, Alan.

Rafferty, Ellen, ed. Putu Wijaya in Performance: A Script & Study of Indonesian Literature. LC 89-52201. (Monographs: No. 5). 163p. (C). lib. bdg. 24.95 (*0-614-24178-2*) U Wisc Ctr SE Asian.

***Rafferty, J. Desmond.** Beauty Sleeps. LC 99-93987. 2000. pap. 15.95 (*0-533-13211-8*) Vantage.

Rafferty, Jackie, ed. see Steyaert, Jan & Colombi, David.

Rafferty, Kathleen, ed. The Dell Crossword Dictionary. 448p. 1995. reprint ed. pap. 9.95 (*0-385-31515-5*, Delta Trade) Dell.

Rafferty, Kathleen & Moore, Rosalind, eds. The Dell Crossword Dictionary. large type ed. LC 94-44579. 422p. 1995. 22.95 (*0-7838-1227-2*, G K Hall Lrg Type) Mac Lib Ref.

— The Dell Crossword Dictionary. large type ed. LC 94-44579. 422p. 1995. pap. 23.95 (*0-7838-1228-0*, G K Hall Lrg Type) Mac Lib Ref.

Rafferty, Keen A. Methods in Experimental Embryology of the Mouse. LC 70-101642. (Illus.). 109p. reprint ed. pap. 33.80 (*0-608-06188-3*, 206652000008) Bks Demand.

Rafferty, Kevin, jt. auth. see Kavanaugh, Stephen.

Rafferty, Michael, jt. auth. see Bryan, Dick.

Rafferty, Milton D. Historical Atlas of Missouri. LC 81-675048. (Illus.). 256p. 1982. 29.95 (*0-8061-1663-3*) U of Okla Pr.

— The Ouachita Mountains: A Guide for Fishermen, Hunters, & Travelers. LC 90-50695. 1993. pap. 19.95 (*0-8061-2360-5*) U of Okla Pr.

— The Ozarks Outdoors: A Guide for Fishermen, Hunters, & Tourists. LC 85-40478. (Illus.). 408p. 1988. 29.95 (*0-8061-1554-8*); pap. 19.95 (*0-8061-2088-6*) U of Okla Pr.

Rafferty, Milton D., contrib. by. Rude Pursuits & Rugged Peaks: Schoolcraft's Ozark Journal, 1818-1819. (Illus.). 1996. pap. 18.00 (*1-55728-466-0*) U of Ark Pr.

Rafferty, Oliver P. Catholicism in Ulster, 1603-1983: An Interpretive History. LC 94-11849. 320p. 1994. text 39.95 (*1-57003-025-1*) U of SC Pr.

Rafferty, Patrick J., ed. The Industrial Hygienist's Guide to Indoor Air Quality Investigations. 76p. (C). 1993. pap. 25.00 (*0-932627-49-8*, 144-EQ-93) Am Indus Hygiene.

***Rafferty, Pierce & Wilton-Ely, John.** Guardian of the Sound: A Pictorial History of Fort H. G. Wright, Fishers Island, N. Y. (Illus.). 256p. 1998. 55.00i (*0-9664192-0-0*) Mount Mercer.

Rafferty, R. C., jt. auth. see Mihelick, J. R.

Rafferty, Renata J. Don't Just Give It Away: How to Make the Most of Your Charitable Giving. 224p. 1999. pap. 17.95 (*1-886284-32-6*, Pub. by Chandler Hse) Natl Bk Netwk.

Rafferty, Robert. Dallas FT Worth Metroplex. LC 99-13312. (Lone Star Guides Ser.). 412p. 1999. pap. 15.95 (*0-89123-028-9*, 3028) Gulf Pub.

— Frommer's America's 100 Best Loved State Parks: For Anyone in Search of an Inexpensive Outdoor. 304p. 1995. 16.95 (*0-02-860462-8*) Macmillan.

— Frommer's America's 100 Best State Parks. 1994. pap. 15.95 (*0-671-84895-X*) S&S Trade.

Rafferty, S. S. Cork of the Colonies: The First American Detective. LC 84-80232. 314p. 1984. pap. 4.95 (*0-930330-11-0*) Intl Polygonics.

— Die Laughing. 200p. 1992. pap. 4.95 (*0-930330-16-1*) Intl Polygonics.

***Rafferty, Sean.** Poems. 173p. 1999. pap. 13.50 (*1-901538-15-X*, Pub. by etruscan bks) SPD-Small Pr Dist.

Rafferty, Terence. Video Seminars on Transesphageal Echocardiography: NTSC format. 2nd ed. (Illus.). 132p. 1999. 542.00 incl. VHS (*1-893508-00-5*) Echocardio.

— Video Seminars on Transesphageal Echocardiography: PAL format. 2nd ed. (Illus.). 1999. 542.00 incl. VHS (*1-893508-01-3*) Echocardio.

Rafferty, Terence D. Basics of Transesophageal Echocardiography. LC 95-2999. 1995. text 99.00 (*0-443-08922-1*) Church.

***Rafferty, Tod.** Complete Illustrated Encyclopedia of American Motorcycles. (Illus.). 256p. 1999. 24.98 (*0-7624-0528-7*) Running Pr.

— Ducati. LC 99-89138. (Illus.). 156p. 2000. 29.95 (*0-7603-0663-X*, Pub. by MBI Pubg) Motorbooks Intl.

— Harley: The Ultimate Machine. 1999. 19.99 (*1-84100-307-7*) Quadrillion Pub.

Rafferty, Tod. Harley Memorabilia. 144p. 1997. 17.98 (*0-7858-0821-3*) Bk Sales Inc.

— The Indian. 144p. 1998. 19.99 (*1-85833-843-3*) Quadrillion Pubng.

— 100 Harleys: Tod Rafferty's 100 Hottest Harleys. (Style Ser.). 1999. pap. text 9.99 (*1-84100-136-8*) Quadrillion Media.

Rafferty, Todd. Complete Harley Davidson: A Model by Model History of the American Legend. LC 97-5615. (Illus.). 160p. 1997. 24.98 (*0-7603-0326-6*) MBI Pubg.

Raffery, Jeanne. Stepping Stones to Hell: A Love Story. Merit Group Staff, ed. (Orig.). 1989. pap. text 14.95 (*0-685-30397-7*) Merit Group.

Raffi. Baby Beluga. LC 97-196460. (Raffi Songs to Read Ser.). (Illus.). 30p. (J). (ps-3). 1997. bds. 6.99 (*0-517-70977-5*, Pub. by Crown Bks Yng Read) Random.

— Baby Beluga Dummy. (Raffi Songs to Read Ser.). (J). 1998. pap. 5.99 (*0-517-88570-0*) Crown Bks Yng Read.

— Down by the Bay. 32p. (J). 1999. 6.99 (*0-517-80058-6*) Crown Pub Group.

— Down by the Bay Dummy. (Raffi Songs to Read Ser.). (J). 1998. pap. 5.99 (*0-517-88571-9*) Crown Pub Group.

— Five Little Ducks. (J). 1999. 6.99 (*0-517-80057-8*) Crown Pub Group.

— Raffi: Children's Favorites. (Illus.). 172p. 1993. pap. 21.95 (*0-8256-1362-0*, AM90163) Omnibus NY.

— Raffi: Evergreen, Everblue. (Illus.). 56p. 1992. pap. 14.95 (*0-8256-1340-X*, AM90036) Music Sales.

— Songs - Read-Premium. 1995. 39.92 (*0-517-88300-7*) Random.

— Wheels on the Bus. (Raffi Songs to Read Ser.). (Illus.). 29p. (J). 1998. bds. 6.99 (*0-517-70998-8*, Pub. by Crown Bks Yng Read) Random.

Raffill, Thomas, jt. auth. see Dong, Paul.

Raffin, Deborah. Sharing Christmas: A Treasure Trove of Special Memories. 1990. 9.95 (*0-446-51550-7*) Warner Bks.

Raffin, P. Michele. The Good Nanny Book: How to Find, Hire, & Keep the Perfect Nanny for Your Child. 1996. pap. 12.00 (*0-425-15133-6*) Berkley Pub.

Raffini, Christine. Marsilio Ficino, Pietro Bembo, Baldassare Castiglione: Philosophical, Aesthetic, & Political Approaches in Renaissance Platonism. LC 95-37316. (Renaissance & Baroque Ser.: Vol. 21). (Illus.). XII, 173p. (C). 1998. text 41.95 (*0-8204-3023-4*) P Lang Pubng.

— The Second Sequence in Maurice Sceve's Delie: A Study of Numerological Composition in the Renaissance. LC 88-61803. (ENG & FRE., Illus.). 167p. 1989. lib. bdg. 24.95 (*0-917786-62-9*) Summa Pubns.

Raffini, James P. 150 Ways to Increase Intrinsic Motivation in the Classroom. LC 95-18933. 304p. (C). 1995. pap. text 47.50 (*0-205-16566-4*); pap. text 34.00 (*0-205-16567-2*) Allyn.

— Winners Without Losers: Structures & Strategies for Increasing Student Motivation to Learn. 304p. (C). 1992. pap. text 65.50 (*0-205-14008-4*, H40082) Allyn.

Raffinot, Jean-Paul, tr. see Seely, Contee & Romijn, Elizabeth.

Raffle, Andrew, ed. see Hunter, Donald.

Raffle, David L. A Grain of Salt: Getting A's in College in Ten Easy Lessons. 140p. (Orig.). (C). 1994. pap. text 7.95 (*0-9643534-0-7*) Thumbprnt Pr.

Raffle, P. A., et al, eds. Hunter's Diseases of Occupations, Bk. 1. 8th ed. LC 93-46316. 1994. write for info. (*0-340-57173-X*, Pub. by E A) Routldge.

Raffler-Engel, Walburga von. The Perception of Nonverbal Behavior in the Career Interview. (Pragmatics & Beyond Ser.: Vol:). viii, 148p. 1983. pap. 41.00 (*90-272-2517-6*) J Benjamins Pubng Co.

Raffler-Engel, Walburga von, ed. Doctor-Patient Interaction. LC 89-17883. (Pragmatics & Beyond New Ser.: No. 4). xxxvii, 294p. 1989. 89.00 (*1-55619-079-4*); pap. 29.00 (*1-55619-080-8*) J Benjamins Pubng Co.

Raffles, Rachel T., jt. auth. see Towner, Lawrence W.

Raffles, Sophia. Memoir of the Life & Public Services of Sir Thomas Stamford Raffles. LC 77-87000. reprint ed. 89.00 (*0-404-16774-8*) AMS Pr.

Raffles, Thomas S. The History of Java, 2 vols., Set. LC 77-87509. (Illus.). reprint ed. 95.00 (*0-404-16770-5*) AMS Pr.

Raffman, Diana. Language, Music, & Mind. (Illus.). 180p. 1993. 24.50 (*0-262-18150-9*, Bradford Bks) MIT Pr.

Raffo, Dave. Football. 48p. (J). (gr. 4-7). 1995. pap. 5.95 (*0-8114-6344-3*) Raintree Steck-V.

Raffo, Lynne. Sacristan's Manual. 4th rev. ed. 55p. (C). 1988. pap. text 4.00 (*1-878268-03-1*) Lit Comm Pubs.

Raffo, Susan, ed. Queerly Classed: Gay Men & Lesbians Write about Class. LC 96-43838. 268p. 1997. 40.00 (*0-89608-562-7*); pap. 17.00 (*0-89608-561-9*) South End Pr.

Raffo, Susan, jt. ed. see Brownworth, Victoria A.

An Asterisk (*) at the beginning of an entry indicates that the title is appearing for the first time.

Raffoul, Francois. Heidegger & the Subject. Pettigrew, David & Recco, Gregory, trs. from FRE. LC 99-10399. (Contemporary Studies in Philosophy & Human Sciences Ser.). 335p. 1999. 74.95 (*1-57392-618-3*, Humanity Bks) Prometheus Bks.

Raffoul, Francois. Heidegger & the Subject: Contemporary Studies in Philosophy & the Human Sciences. Pettigrew, David E. & Recco, Gregory, trs. LC 96-48463. (Contemporary Studies in Philosophy & the Human Sciences Ser.). 312p. (C). 1997. text 75.00 (*0-391-04023-5*) Humanities.

Raffoul, Francois, jt. ed. see Pettigrew, David.

Raffoul, Francois, tr. see Dastur, Francoise.

Raffoul, Francois, tr. see Nancy, Jean-Luc & Lacoue-Labarthe, Philippe.

Raffoul, Francois, tr. see Nasio, Juan-David.

Raffoul, Paul R. & McNeece, C. Aaron, eds. Future Issues for Social Work Practice. LC 95-25264. 352p. 1995. pap. text 35.00 (*0-205-17429-9*) Allyn.

Raffucci de Garcia, Carmen I. El Gobierno Civil y la Ley Foraker (Antecedentes Historicos) LC 79-16454. Orig. Title: Las Instituciones de Gobierno Civil en la Elaboracion de la Ley Foraker y Sus Antecedentes Historicos. (SPA.). xi, 145p. 1981. pap. 5.60 (*0-8477-0864-0*) U of PR Pr.

Raffucci de Lockwood, Alicia M. Cuatro Poetas de la "Generacion del 36" Miguel Hernandez, Serrano Plajo, Rosales y Panero. (UPREX, Estudios Literarios Ser.: No. 28). (C). 1974. pap. 1.50 (*0-8477-0028-3*) U of PR Pr.

Raffy, Sabine. Sarraute Romanciere: Espaces Intimes. (American University Studies: Romance Languages & Literature: Ser. II, Vol. 60). X, 269p. (C). 1988. text 47.00 (*0-8204-0479-9*) P Lang Pubng.

Rafi, Aaron. A Seed in the Pocket of Their Blood. 95p. 1998. 29.95 (*0-9682665-0-9*, Pub. by Amph Pubns) Assoc Pubs Grp.

***Rafik, Amal.** Passion Masters: Sex Secrets of a Forbidden Love Cult. 2000. mass mkt. 7.95 (*1-56201-200-2*) Blue Moon Bks.

Rafilson, Fred. The Firefighter. 13th ed. 352p. 1999. pap. text 13.95 (*0-02-863537-X*, Arco) Macmillan Gen Ref.

***Rafilson, Fred.** Police Officer. 15th ed. 480p. 2000. pap. text 13.95 (*0-02-863741-0*) Macmillan Gen Ref.

Rafinesque, C. S. Atlantic Journal & Friend of Knowledge. (Illus.). 1946. pap. 20.00 (*0-685-42244-5*) Lubrecht & Cramer.

— Flora Telluriana, 4 pts. in 1. 1946. pap. 20.00 (*0-934454-33-7*) Lubrecht & Cramer.

— New Flora & Botany of North America, 4 pts. in 1 vol. 1946. reprint ed. pap. 20.00 (*0-934454-66-3*) Lubrecht & Cramer.

Rafinesque, C. S., jt. auth. see Clifford, John D.

Rafinesque, Constantine S. Ichthyologia Ohiensis, or, Natural History of the Fishes Inhabiting the River Ohio & Its Tributary Streams. LC 72-125760. (American Environmental Studies). 1977. reprint ed. 20.95 (*0-405-02686-2*) Ayer.

— Medical Flora: or Manual of the Medical Botany of the United States of North America, 2 vols., Set. LC 75-23755. (Illus.). reprint ed. 60.00 (*0-404-13191-3*) AMS Pr.

Rafiq, Fauzia, ed. Aurat Durbar: Writings by Women of South Asian Origin. (Illus.). 240p. 1995. pap. 14.95 (*0-929005-70-8*, Pub. by Sec Story Pr) LPC InBook.

Rafique, M. Sri Aurobindo's Ideal of Human Life. 127p. (C). 1987. 17.50 (*81-7024-074-3*, Pub. by Ashish Pub Hse) S Asia.

Rafiquzzaman, Mohamed. Fundamentals of Digital Logic & Microcomputer Design. LC 98-91636. (Illus.). 600p. 1998. 69.95 (*0-9664980-0-3*) Rafi Syst.

***Rafiquzzaman, Mohamed.** Fundamentals of Digital Logic & Microcomputer Design. rev. ed. LC 99-93010. (Illus.). 828p. (C). 1999. 84.95 (*0-9664980-1-1*) Rafi Syst.

— Fundamentals of Digital Logic & Microcomputer Design. 3rd ed. (Illus.). 889p. 2000. text 99.00 (*0-9664980-3-8*) Rafi Syst.

Rafiquzzaman, Mohamed. Introduction to Microprocessors & Microcomputer-Based Applications. 2nd ed. LC 95-7374. 800p. 1995. boxed set 99.95 (*0-8493-4475-1*, 4475) CRC Pr.

— Microcomputer Theory & Application. 2nd ed. (C). 1989. text 61.51 (*0-13-583691-3*) P-H.

— Microcomputer Theory & Applications with the Intel SDK-85. 2nd ed. LC 86-15972. 761p. 1987. text 47.95 (*0-471-80040-6*) P-H.

— Microprocessors & Microcomputer-Based System Design. (C). 1990. lib. bdg. 53.95 (*0-8493-4275-9*, QA76) CRC Pr.

— Microprocessors & Microcomputer-Based Systems Design. 2nd ed. 189p. 1995. per. write for info. (*0-8493-2642-7*) CRC Pr.

— Modern Computer Architecture. (West Engineering Ser.). 1988. pap., student ed. 9.00 (*0-534-93842-6*); text 71.95 (*0-534-93841-8*) PWS Pubs.

***Rafiy, Dariusch.** Politische und Soziale Implikationen des Zarathustrismus: Eine Untersuchung von Den Ursprungen Bis Zur Gegenwart. (Europaische Hochschulschriften Ser.: Vol. 31). XI, 313p. 1999. 48.95 (*3-631-35483-5*) P Lang Pubng.

Rafkin, Alan. Cue the Bunny on the Rainbow: Tales from TV's Most Prolific Sitcom Director. LC 98-20443. 182p. 1998. 26.95 (*0-8156-0542-0*) Syracuse U Pr.

Rafkin, Louise. Other People's Dirt: A Housecleaner's Curious Adventures. LC 97-43673. 210p. 1998. 17.95 (*1-56512-162-7*, 72162) Algonquin Bks.

***Rafkin, Louise.** Other People's Dirt: A Housecleaner's Curious Adventures. 208p. 1999. pap. 11.95 (*0-452-28081-8*, Plume) Dutton Plume.

Rafkin, Louise. The Tiger's Eye, the Bird's Fist: A Beginner's Guide to the Martial Arts. (Illus.). (YA). (gr. 3 up). 1997. 12.95 (*0-614-28844-4*) Little.

— What Do Cats Dream? LC 99-208055. 1999. 6.95 (*0-8362-7872-0*) Andrews & McMeel.

— What Do Dogs Dream? LC 98-215710. (Illus.). 48p. 1998. 6.95 (*0-8362-6774-5*) Andrews & McMeel.

Rafkin, Louise, ed. Different Daughters: A Book by Mothers of Lesbians. 2nd rev. ed. 160p. 1996. pap. 12.95 (*1-57344-050-7*) Cleis Pr.

Rafkin, Louise & McGrath, Leslie. Martial Arts: Mastering the Self. LC 96-35407. 1997. write for info. (*0-316-73450-0*) Little.

Rafkin, Louise & Mcgrath, Leslie. The Tiger's Eye, the Bird's Fist: Mastering the Self. LC 96-35407. (Illus.). 144p. (J). 1997. pap. 12.95 (*0-316-73464-0*) Little.

Raflik, M., et al, eds. CAD-I Database: An Approach to an Engineering Database, Version 4.0. (Research Reports ESPRIT, Project 322, CAD Interfaces: Vol. 5). x, 147p. 1990. 29.00 (*0-387-53383-4*) Spr-Verlag.

Raflo, Diane, jt. auth. see Lugar, Richard G.

Rafols-Casamada, Albert. Estrats. limited ed. (Ediciones Especiales y de Bibliofilo Ser.). (CAT., Illus.). 1993. 1750.00 (*84-343-0451-1*); 150.00 (*0-614-00142-0*) Elliots Bks.

— Rafols-Casamada: El Passeig Del Poeta. limited ed. (Ediciones Especiales y de Bibliofilo Ser.). (CAT., Illus.). 88p. 1993. 2750.00 (*0-614-00242-7*); 600.00 (*0-614-00243-5*); 600.00 (*0-614-00138-2*) Elliots Bks.

Rafool, Amanda & Loyacono, Laura L. Creative Solutions for Funding the Arts. 40p. 1995. 25.00 (*1-55516-222-3*, 2112) Natl Conf State Legis.

Rafool, Mandy. State Tax & Expenditure Limits. (Legislative Finance Papers). 30p. 1996. pap. 20.00 (*1-55516-558-3*, 5104-0104) Natl Conf State Legis.

***Rafoth, Bennett A., ed.** A Tutor's Guide: Helping Writer's One to One. LC 99-87604. 186p. 2000. pap. text 17.00 (*0-86709-495-8*, Pub. by Boynton Cook Pubs) Heinemann.

Rafoth, Bennett A., et al, eds. The Social Construction of Written Communication. LC 88-22347. (Writing Research Ser.: Vol. 17). 336p. (C). 1988. text 73.25 (*0-89391-436-3*) Ablx Pub.

Rafoth, Bennett A., et al, eds. The Social Construction of Written Communication. LC 88-22347. (Writing Research Ser.: Vol. 17). 336p. (C). 1988. pap. 39.50 (*0-89391-549-1*) Ablx Pub.

Rafoth, Mary A. Inspiring Independent Learning: Successful Classroom Strategies. LC 99-24013. (Inspired Classroom Ser.). 1999. 12.95 (*0-8106-2954-2*) NEA.

Rafoth, Mary A., et al. Strategies for Learning & Remembering: Study Skills Across the Curriculum. LC 93-589. (Analysis & Action Ser.). 152p. 1993. pap. 14.95 (*0-8106-3048-6*) NEA.

Rafoth, Mary Ann. Inspiring Independent Learning: Successful Classroom Strategies. (Inspired Classroom Ser.). 1998. pap. 12.95 (*0-614-30865-8*) NEA.

Rafoth, Richard. High-Performance Bicycling Nutrition. LC 98-22666. 128p. 1998. pap. 9.95 (*0-933201-92-3*, Bicycle Bks) MBI Pubg.

Rafroidi, Patrick. Irish Literature in English: Romantic Period, 1789-1850, 2 vols., 1. 364p. 1980. 50.00 (*0-86140-272-3*) Dufour.

— Irish Literature in English: Romantic Period, 1789-1850, 2 vols., 2. 392p. 1980. 50.00 (*0-86140-273-1*) Dufour.

Rafson, Harold J. Brownfields: Redeveloping Distressed Properties. 592p. 1999. 79.95 (*0-07-052768-7*) McGraw.

Rafson, Harold J., ed. Odor & VOC Handbook. LC 98-4211. (Illus.). 800p. 1998. 105.00 (*0-07-052523-4*) McGraw.

***Raft, Drake, et al.** Jollyroger.com: Navigating an American Renaissance. 420p. 2000. pap. 18.95 (*1-930151-04-7*) Clasical jolly.

Raftelis, George A. Comprehensive Guide to Financing & Pricing at Water & Wastewater Treatment Plants. 2nd ed. 336p. 1992. lib. bdg. 85.00 (*0-87371-904-2*, L904) Lewis Pubs.

— The Ernst & Young Guide to Water & Wastewater Finance & Pricing. (Illus.). 220p. 1989. boxed set 84.95 (*0-87371-181-5*, L181) Lewis Pubs.

Rafter, B. B., tr. see Breuil, Henri & Lantier, Raymond.

Rafter, Kevin. The Clann: The story of Clann Na Poblachta. LC 96-219381. 208p. 1997. pap. 15.95 (*1-85635-141-6*, Pub. by Mercier Pr) Irish Amer Bk.

***Rafter, Nicole.** Shots in the Mirror: Crime Films & Society. 192p. 2000. pap. 15.95 (*0-19-512983-0*); text 45.00 (*0-19-512982-2*) OUP.

Rafter, Nicole H. Creating Born Criminals. 1998. pap. text 17.95 (*0-252-06741-X*) U of Ill Pr.

— Partial Justice: Women in State Prisons, 1800-1935. LC 84-7990. (Illus.). 295p. 1985. text 47.50 (*0-930350-63-4*) NE U Pr.

— Partial Justice: Women, Prisons & Social Control. 2nd ed. 342p. (C). 1990. pap. 24.95 (*0-88738-826-4*) Transaction Pubs.

Rafter, Nicole H., ed. White Trash: The Eugenics Family Studies, 1877-1919. 428p. 1988. text 55.00 (*1-55553-030-3*) NE U Pr.

Rafter, Nicole H. & Heidensohn, Frances M., eds. International Feminist Perspectives in Criminology: Engendering a Discipline. LC 95-10580. 244p. 1995. 114.95 (*0-335-19389-7*); pap. 31.95 (*0-335-19388-9*) OpUniv Pr.

***Rafter, Nicole H. & Stanley, Debra L.** Prisons in America: A Reference Handbook. LC 99-35719. (Contemporary World Issues Ser.). 200p. 1999. lib. bdg. 45.00 (*1-57607-102-2*) ABC-CLIO.

***Rafter, Nicole Hahn, ed.** Encyclopedia of Women & Crime. (Illus.). 372p. 2000. boxed set 65.00 (*1-57356-214-9*) Oryx Pr.

***Rafter, Patrick.** Rocket to the Top: On the Road with Pat Rafter. (Illus.). 224p. 2000. pap. 24.95 (*0-7322-6459-6*) HarpC.

Rafter, Rosalie, ed. The Potter's Wheel: Change in English Language Arts Classrooms. 109p. (C). 1996. pap. text 10.00 (*0-930348-20-6*) NY St Eng Coun.

Raftery. Churchill's Pocketbook of Surgery. 1996. pap. text 28.00 (*0-443-05057-0*, W B Saunders Co) Harcrt Hlth Sci Grp.

Raftery, Adrian, ed. Sociological Methodology, Vol. 27. 244p. (C). 1996. text 94.95 (*1-57718-109-3*) Blackwell Pubs.

— Sociological Methodology, Vol. 27. 450p. 1997. 89.95 (*0-631-20792-9*) Blackwell Pubs.

Raftery, Adrian E., ed. Sociological Methodology, Vol. 28. 448p. 1998. 70.95 (*0-631-21208-6*) Blackwell Pubs.

***Raftery, Andrew T.** Applied Basic Science for Basic Surgical Training. LC 99-38215. 2000. text. write for info. (*0-443-06144-0*) Church.

Raftery, Anthony & O'Flynn, Criostoir. Blind Raftery. LC 98-167592. 252p. 1998. pap. 16.95 (*1-900693-24-0*, Pub. by Clo Iar-Chonnachta) Dufour.

Raftery, Barry. Pagan Celtic Ireland: The Enigma of the Irish Iron Age. LC 93-61274. (Illus.). 240p. 1998. pap. 29.95 (*0-500-27983-7*, Pub. by Thames Hudson) Norton.

Raftery, Barry, et al, eds. Sites & Sights of the Iron Age. (Monographs in Archaeology: Vol. 56). (Illus.). 180p. 1996. pap. 48.00 (*1-900188-00-7*, Pub. by Oxbow Bks) David Brown.

Raftery, Francis. The Teacher in the Catholic School. 2nd ed. 61p. 1988. 3.00 (*1-55833-014-3*) Natl Cath Educ.

Raftery, James, jt. ed. see Stevens, Andrew.

Raftery, John. Risk Analysis in Project Management. LC 93-32191. (Illus.). 160p. (C). 1993. pap. 39.99 (*0-419-18420-1*, E & FN Spon) Routledge.

Raftery, Judith R. Land of Fair Promise: Politics & Reform in Los Angeles Schools, 1885-1941. LC 91-26888. (Illus.). 312p. (C). 1992. 14.95 (*0-8047-1930-5*) Stanford U Pr.

Raftery, Kevin & Raftery, Kim G. KidsGardening: A Kid's Guide to Messing Around in the Dirt. (Illus.). 92p. (Orig.). (J). 1989. spiral bd. 13.95 (*0-932592-25-2*) Klutz.

Raftery, Kim G., jt. auth. see Raftery, Kevin.

***Raftery, Mary.** States of Fear. 350p. 2000. pap. 19.95 (*1-874597-83-9*, Pub. by New Island Books) Dufour.

Raftery, Susan R., jt. auth. see Halasz, Ida M.

Raftery, William J. Government Accounting & Financial Reporting Manual. 1993. ring bd. 160.00 (*0-685-69613-8*, GARM) Warren Gorham & Lamont.

Raftis, Alkis. The World of Greek Dance. Doumas, Alexandra, tr. from GRE. (Illus.). 249p. 1987. 63.70 (*3-487-09131-3*) G Olms Pubs.

Raftis, J. A. Peasant Economic Development within the English Manorial System. LC 97-193250. 256p. 1996. 55.00 (*0-7735-1403-1*, Pub. by McG-Queens Univ Pr) CUP Services.

Raftis, J. Ambrose. Assart Data & Land Values: Two Studies in the East Midlands, 1200-1350. 169p. 22.29 (*0-88844-352-8*) Brill Academic Pubs.

— A Small Town in Late Medieval England: Godmanchester, 1278-1400. xiv, 479p. pap. text 44.57 (*0-88844-053-7*) Brill Academic Pubs.

Raftis, J. Ambrose. Tenure & Mobility: Studies in the Social History of the Mediaeval English Village. 309p. pap. text 33.14 (*0-88844-008-1*) Brill Academic Pubs.

Raftis, J. Ambrose. Warboys: Two Hundred Years in the Life of an English Medieval Village. x, 267p. 36.00 (*0-88844-029-4*) Brill Academic Pubs.

Raftis, J. Ambrose & Hogan, Mary P. Early Huntingdonshire Lay Subsidy Rolls. 301p. pap. text 38.29 (*0-88844-357-9*) Brill Academic Pubs.

Raftopoulos, Evangelos. The Barcelona Convention & Protocols. 381p. 1993. 85.00 (*1-898029-01-6*, Pub. by Simmonds & Hill Pubng) Gaunt.

Raftoyiannis, John, jt. auth. see Spyrokos, Constantine C.

Raga, A. C., jt. ed. see Millar, T. J.

Ragab, Abdel-Rahman A. & Bayoumi, Salah E. Engineering Solid Mechanics Fundamentals & Applications. LC 98-7492. 944p. 1998. boxed set 84.95 (*0-8493-1607-3*) CRC Pr.

Ragab, S. A. & Piomelli, U., eds. Engineering Applications & Large Eddy Simulations. 1993. LC 93-71644. (FED Ser.: Vol. 162). 155p. 1993. pap. 37.50 (*0-7918-0970-6*, H00802) ASME.

Ragacs, Ursula. Mit Zaum und Zugel Mub Man Ihr Ungestum Bandigen - Ps 32,9: Ein Beitrag zur Christlichen Hebraistik und Antijudischen Polemik im Mittelalter. (Judentum und Umwelt Ser.: Bd. 65). (GER.). 202p. 1997. 44.95 (*3-631-31916-9*) P Lang Pubng.

Ragaglia, Brad, ed. see Levine, Norman G.

Ragahavan, V., et al, trs. The Wondrous Crest-Jewel in Performance: Text & Translation of the Ascaryacudamani of Saktibhadra. (Illus.). 272p. 1985. text 16.95 (*0-19-561714-2*) OUP.

Ragain, Maj. Burley One Dark Sucker Fired. (Working Lives Ser.). 78p. 1998. pap. 9.95 (*0-933087-45-4*) Bottom Dog Pr.

Ragaini, R. C., jt. ed. see Avogadro, A.

Ragan, Andrew & Cummings, Cherilyn, eds. The Southern California Anthology, Vol. V. 144p. (Orig.). 1987. pap. 5.95 (*0-9615108-2-X*) Scanthology.

Ragan, Andy. Dino Files. LC 97-80158. (Disney Adventures Ser.). 96p. (J). (gr. 3-7). 1998. pap. 3.95 (*0-7868-4207-5*, Pub. by Disney Pr) Time Warner.

Ragan, Bryant T., Jr. & Williams, Elizabeth A., eds. Recreating Authority in Revolutionary France. LC 91-45492. 260p. (C). 1992. text 40.00 (*0-8135-1841-5*); pap. text 17.00 (*0-8135-1842-3*) Rutgers U Pr.

Ragan, Bryant T., Jr., jt. ed. see Merrick, Jeffrey.

Ragan, David P. Who's Who in Hollywood: The Largest Cast of Film Personalities Ever Assembled, Set, 1400p ea. 1920p. 1991. 195.00 (*0-8160-2011-6*) Facts on File.

— William Faulkner's "Absalom, Absalom!" A Critical Study. Litz, A. Walton, ed. LC 87-23300. (Studies in Modern Literature: No. 85). 244p. reprint ed. 66.70 (*0-8357-1840-9*, 2070755) Bks Demand.

Ragan, Donal M. Structural Geology: An Introduction to Geometrical Techniques. 3rd ed. LC 84-19658. 416p. 1985. pap. 64.95 (*0-471-08043-8*) Wiley.

Ragan, Gale. Teardrops & Lemonade. (Illus.). 32p. (J). (gr. k-3). 1998. pap. 7.00 (*0-8059-4484-2*) Dorrance.

Ragan, Genie. Beads, The Art of Stringing. (Illus.). 58p. (Orig.). 1986. pap. text 4.95 (*0-935182-44-6*) Gem Guides Bk.

Ragan, J. Anglicko-Slovensky Slovnik Vypoctovej Techniky (English-Slovak Dictionary of Computing) (ENG & SLO.). 320p. 1997. pap. write for info. (*80-08-01117-3*, Pub. by Slov Pegagog Naklad) IBD Ltd.

Ragan, James. The Hunger Wall. LC 95-23561. 128p. 1995. 17.00 (*0-8021-1576-4*, Grove) Grove-Atltic.

— The Hunger Wall. 128p. 1996. reprint ed. pap. 11.00 (*0-8021-3478-5*, Grove) Grove-Atltic.

***Ragan, James.** In the Talking Hours. 2nd ed. 88p. 2000. pap. 15.00 (*1-928746-09-8*) Herodias.

Ragan, James. Lusions. LC 96-35090. 96p. 1997. 20.00 (*0-8021-1603-5*, Grove) Grove-Atltic.

— Womb Weary. 1990. 14.95 (*1-55972-053-0*, Birch Ln Pr) Carol Pub Group.

Ragan, James, ed. see Yevteshenko, Yevgeny.

Ragan, James F., Jr. & Thomas, Lloyd B., Jr. Principles of Economics. 2nd ed. LC 92-81302. 1584p. (C). 1993. text, student ed. 100.50 (*0-03-096632-9*) Dryden Pr.

Ragan, Kathleen. Fearless Girls, Wise Women, & Beloved Sisters: Heroines in Folktales from Around the World. LC 97-30438. 352p. 1998. 29.95 (*0-393-04598-6*) Norton.

***Ragan, Kathleen.** Fearless Girls, Wise Women & Beloved Sisters: Heroines in Folktales from Around the World. 480p. 2000. pap. text 15.95 (*0-393-32046-4*) Norton.

Ragan, Larry. True Tales of Birmingham. (Illus.). 64p. (Orig.). 1992. pap. 6.95 (*0-943994-19-5*) Birmingham Hist Soc.

Ragan, Lise B., ed. see Blosser, Betsy J.

Ragan, Lise B., ed. see Garcia, Mary H. & Gonzalez-Mena, Janet.

***Ragan, Mac.** Diecast Cars of the 1960s: Matchbox, Hot Wheels & Other Great Toy Vehicles of the 1960s. LC 99-87345. (Enthusiast Color Ser.). (Illus.). 96p. 2000. pap. 13.95 (*0-7603-0719-9*, 129804AP, Pub. by MBI Pubg) Motorbooks Intl.

Ragan, Mark A., jt. ed. see Bird, Carolyn J.

Ragan, Mark K. The Hunley: Submarines, Sacrifice, & Success in the Civil War. LC 95-69553. (Illus.). 240p. 1995. 49.95 (*1-886391-04-1*) Narwhal Pr.

***Ragan, Mark K.** Hunley: Submarines, Sacrifice, & Success in the Civil War. 2nd rev. ed. 1999. pap. 19.95 (*1-886391-43-2*) Narwhal Pr.

Ragan, Mark K. Union & Confederate Submarine Warfare in the Civil War. (Illus.). 288p. (C). 1998. 29.95 (*1-882810-32-5*) Savas Pub.

Ragan, Robert C. Step-by-Step Bookkeeping: The Complete Handbook for the Small Business. rev. ed. LC 74-7814. (Illus.). 144p. (YA). (gr. 10-12). 1982. pap. 8.95 (*0-8069-8690-5*) Sterling.

Ragan, Ruth M. Voiceprints of Lincoln: Memories of an Old Massachusetts Town & Its Unique Response to Industrial America. 292p. 1991. text 29.95 (*0-944856-03-9*) Lincoln Hist Soc.

Ragan, Sam. Collected Poems of Sam Ragan: Poet Laureate of North Carolina. Warren, Marsha W., ed. LC 91-60872. 286p. 1990. 20.00 (*0-932662-94-3*); pap. 15.00 (*0-932662-95-1*) St Andrews NC.

— Walk into April. 1986. 10.00 (*0-932662-62-5*) St Andrews NC.

Ragan, Sam, ed. see Bell, Mae Woods.

Ragan, Samuel T. Weymouth. (Illus.). 152p. (Orig.). 1987. 14.00 (*0-932662-71-4*) St Andrews Pr.

Ragan, Sandra. Interior Color by Design-Commercial: A Design Tool for Architects, Interior Designers, & Facility Managers. 160p. 1995. pap. 29.99 (*1-56496-119-2*) Rockport Pubs.

Ragan, Sandra, ed. see Pilaroscia, Jill.

Ragan, Sandra, ed. see Pugh, Jennie L.

Ragan, Sandra L., et al, eds. The Lynching of Language: Gender, Politics, & Power in the Hill-Thomas Hearings. LC 95-32458. 304p. (C). 1996. text 39.95 (*0-252-02126-6*); pap. text 18.95 (*0-252-06517-4*) U of Ill Pr.

Ragan, Sandra L., jt. auth. see Pagano, Michael P.

Ragano, Frank & Raab, Selwyn. Mob Lawyer: Including the Inside Account of Who Killed Jimmy Hoffa & JFK. Grossman, Barbara & Pileggi, Nicholas, eds. (Illus.). 320p. 1994. text 22.00 (*0-684-19568-2*, Scribners Ref) Mac Lib Ref.

Ragans, Rosalind. ArtTalk: Teacher's Wraparound Edition. 1995. teacher ed. 59.25 (*0-02-640296-3*) Glencoe.

— Exploring Art. 1991. 40.99 (*0-02-662281-5*) Glencoe.

— Understanding Art. 1991. 40.99 (*0-02-662286-6*) Glencoe.

Ragans, Rosalind, jt. auth. see Mittler, Gene.

Ragas, A. M., ed. see Nienhuis, P. H.

Ragas, Meg Cohen & Kozlowski, Karen. Read My Lips: The Cultural History of Lipstick. LC 97-46747. (Illus.). 120p. 1998. 14.95 (*0-8118-2011-4*) Chronicle Bks.

***Ragatz, Joseph L.** A Guide for the Study of British Caribbean History. 725p. 2000. reprint ed. 85.00 (*1-57898-226-X*) Martino Pubng.

Ragatz, L. J. Guide for the Study of British Caribbean History, 1763-1834, Including the Abolitions & Emancipation Movements. LC 71-75275. (Law, Politics & History Ser.). 1970. reprint ed. lib. bdg. 75.00 (*0-306-71308-X*) Da Capo.

R

Ragavan, Vanaja V. & Jones, Judith. Drug Development for Life Cycle Management in Women. LC 97-42810. 496p. 1998. 185.00 (*0-471-96850-1*) Wiley.

Ragay. F-102 Delta Dagger in Europe. (Specials Ser.). (Illus.). 64p. 1991. pap. 10.95 (*0-89747-220-9*, 6050) Squad Sig Pubns.

Ragaz, J., et al, eds. Preoperative (Neoadjuvant) Chemotherapy. (Recent Results in Cancer Research Ser.: Vol. 103). (Illus.). 196p. 1986. 76.00 (*0-387-16129-5*) Spr-Verlag.

Ragaz, J. & Ariel, I. M., eds. High-Risk Breast Cancer: Therapy. (Illus.). 536p. 1991. 218.00 (*0-387-51092-3*) Spr-Verlag.

Ragazzi, Maurizio. The Concept of International Obligations Erga Omnes. LC 97-8003. (Oxford Monographs in International Law). 304p. 1998. text 98.00 (*0-19-826480-1*) OUP.

***Ragazzi, Maurizio.** The Concept of International Obligations Erga Omnes. LC 99-45247. (Oxford Monographs in International Law). 304p. 2000. pap. text 35.00 (*0-19-829870-6*) OUP.

Ragazzini, G. Italian-English - English-Italian Dictionary with a Glossary of Terms on Finance, Economy & Business Organizations. 2nd ed. 2320p. 1968. 145.00 (*88-08-04862-4*, Pub. by Zanichelli) IBD Ltd.

— Italian-English/English-Italian Dictionary. (ENG & ITA.). 1996. 105.00 (*0-7859-9687-7*) Fr & Eur.

— Italian-English/English-Italian Dictionary (Il Ragazzini) 3rd ed. (ENG & ITA.). 2400p. 1996. 105.00 (*88-08-09960-1*, Pub. by Zanichelli) IBD Ltd.

Ragazzini, G., et al. Italian-English - English-Italian Concise Dictionary (Il Nuovo Ragazzini) (ENG & ITA.). 1187p. 1994. pap. 40.00 (*88-08-03630-8*, Pub. by Zanichelli) IBD Ltd.

Ragazzini, Giuseppe. English - Italian, Italian - English Commercial Dictionary: Concise Edition. 1991. 75.00 (*0-8288-8476-5*) Fr & Eur.

— Italian & English Commercial Dictionary: Dizionario Commerciale. (ENG & ITA.). 672p. 1984. 39.95 (*0-8288-0108-8*, M7808) Fr & Eur.

— Italian-English - English-Italian Commercial Dictionary: Dizionario Commerciale Italiano-Inglese-Italiano. (ENG & ITA.). 813p. 1981. 150.00 (*0-8288-0109-6*, M8457) Fr & Eur.

— The New Ragazzini English-Italian, Italian-English Dictionary: Il Nuovo Ragazzini Dizionario Inglese-Italiano: Italiano-Inglese. 2nd ed. (ENG & ITA.). 2144p. 1989. lib. bdg. 150.00 (*0-8288-3331-1*, F9072) Fr & Eur.

— Il Nuovo Ragazzini - Biagi Concise Dizionario Inglese e Italiano: Italian English. 2nd ed. 1991. 85.00 (*0-685-49364-4*, F10010) Fr & Eur.

— Il Nuovo Ragazzini Dizionario Inglese-Italiano Italiano-Inglese. 2nd ed. (ENG & ITA.). 2144p. 1989. lib. bdg. 150.00 (*0-685-48307-X*, F9072) Fr & Eur.

— Nuovo Ragazzini Gigante. 2nd ed. (ITA.). 2128p. 250.00 (*0-8288-9420-5*, F9073) Fr & Eur.

— Nuovo Ragazzini Rossi. 2nd ed. (ENG & ITA.). 2352p. 195.00 (*0-8288-9424-8*) Fr & Eur.

Ragazzini, Giuseppe, et al, eds. Oxford Concise Italian Dictionary. 3rd ed. (Illus.). 1,248p. 1998. 27.95 (*0-19-860243-X*) OUP.

Ragazzini, Giuseppe & Biagi, Adele. The New Ragazzini, Biagi Concise Italian-English, English-Italian Dictionary: Il Nuovo Ragazzini - Biagi Concise Dizionario Inglese-Italiano Italiano-Inglese. 2nd ed. (ENG & ITA.). 1200p. 1986. lib. bdg. 85.00 (*0-8288-3332-X*, F10010) Fr & Eur.

Ragazzo, Ernesto, tr. see Babich, Pete.

Rage Against the Machine. Evil Empire. 64p. 1997. otabind 19.95 (*0-7935-6757-2*) H Leonard.

Rage, J. D. Dear Grim Reaper. 80p. 1993. pap., per. 5.00 (*1-886206-06-6*) Venom Pr.

***Rage, J. D.** Devotions & Desecrations, Bk. 1. 62p. 1999. pap. 5.00 (*1-886206-19-8*) Venom Pr.

Rage, J. D. Man Trouble. 73p. 1989. pap., per. 5.00 (*1-886206-01-5*) Venom Pr.

— Rage. 58p. 1989. pap., per. 4.00 (*1-886206-02-3*) Venom Pr.

— Relentless. (Illus.). 51p. (Orig.). 1994. pap. 4.00 (*1-886206-13-9*) Venom Pr.

Rage, J. D., et al. Flashes of Dreams: A Poetry Anthology. 49p. 1988. pap., per. 4.00 (*1-886206-00-7*) Venom Pr.

Rage, Jean-Claude. Serpentes. (Encyclopedia of Paleoherpetology Ser.: Pt. 11). (Illus.). 80p. 1984. pap. text 77.00 (*3-437-30448-8*) Lubrecht & Cramer.

Rageau, Jean-Pierre, jt. auth. see Chaliand, Gerard.

Ragelis, Edward P., ed. Seafood Toxins. LC 84-18551. (ACS Symposium Ser.: No. 262). (Illus.). 472p. 1984. reprint ed. pap. 146.40 (*0-608-03254-9*, 206377300007) Bks Demand.

Ragels. Gnostic Gospels. 1989. pap. 7.95 (*0-07-051097-0*) McGraw.

Ragen, Naomi. The Ghost of Hannah Mendes. (Reading Group Guide Ser.). pap. write for info. (*0-684-00740-1*) S&S Trade.

— The Ghost of Hannah Mendes: A Novel. LC 98-13061. 384p. 1998. 23.50 (*0-684-83393-X*) S&S Trade.

— Jephte's Daughter. LC 88-40183. 416p. 1990. mass mkt. 5.99 (*0-446-35862-2*) Warner Bks.

Ragep, F. J. & Ragep, S. P. Tradition, Transmission, Transformation: Proceedings of Two Conferences on Premodern Science Held at the University of Oklahoma. 1996. 205.50 (*90-04-10119-5*) Brill Academic Pubs.

Ragep, S. P., jt. auth. see Ragep, F. J.

Rager, John C. The Political Philosophy of St. Robert Bellarmine. 2nd unabridged ed. Orig. Title: The Political Philosophy of Blessed Robert Bellarmine. 96p. 1995. reprint ed. pap. 5.95 (*1-888516-00-3*) Apostlte Our Lady.

Rager, Mike. Automotive Rebuilders Hazardous Materials Program Employee Training Manual. (Illus.). (Orig.). (C). 1989. pap. write for info. (*0-318-65936-0*) Amer Hazmat.

— Automotive Repair Shop Hazardous Materials Program Employee Training Manual. (Illus.). (Orig.). (C). 1989. pap. write for info. (*0-318-65934-4*) Amer Hazmat.

— Body Shop Hazardous Materials Program Employee Training Manual. (Illus.). (Orig.). (C). 1989. pap. write for info. (*0-318-65935-2*) Amer Hazmat.

— Business-Industry Hazardous Materials Program Employee Training Manual. (Illus.). (Orig.). (C). 1989. pap. write for info. (*0-318-65930-1*) Amer Hazmat.

— Dryclean-Laundry Managers Manual: Hazardous Materials Program. (Illus.). (Orig.). (C). 1989. pap. write for info. (*0-318-65929-8*) Amer Hazmat.

— Hazardous Materials Program Employee Training Manual. (Illus.). (Orig.). (C). 1989. pap. write for info. (*0-318-65933-6*) Amer Hazmat.

— Photofinishing Hazardous Materials Employee Training Manual. (Illus.). (C). 1989. pap. write for info. (*0-318-65932-8*) Amer Hazmat.

— Vehicle Maintenance Repair Shop Hazardous Materials Program Employee Training Manual. (Illus.). (Orig.). (C). 1989. pap. write for info. (*0-318-65931-X*) Amer Hazmat.

Ragette, Friedrich. Architecture in Lebanon. (Illus.). 200p. 1975. 50.00 (*0-8156-6044-8*, Pub. by Am U Beirut) Syracuse U Pr.

— Architecture in Lebanon: The Lebanese House During the 18th & 19th Centuries. LC 80-14121. 224p. 1980. reprint ed. 50.00 (*0-88206-041-4*) Caravan Bks.

Ragette, Friedrich, ed. Beirut of Tomorrow: Planning for Reconstruction. (Illus.). 142p. 1983. pap. text 9.95 (*0-8156-6069-3*, Pub. by Am U Beirut) Syracuse U Pr.

— Engineering & Architecture & the Future Environment of Man. 1968. pap. 14.95 (*0-8156-6013-8*, Pub. by Am U Beirut) Syracuse U Pr.

Ragg-Kirby, Helena. Adalbert Stifter's Late Prose: The Mania for Moderation. 156p. 2000. 55.00 (*1-57113-043-8*) Camden Hse.

Ragg, Laura, jt. ed. see Ragg, Lonsdale.

Ragg, Lonsdale. Dante & His Italy. LC 72-2129. (Studies in Dante: No. 9). (Illus.). 1972. lib. bdg. 75.00 (*0-8383-1462-7*) M S G Haskell Hse.

Ragg, Lonsdale & Ragg, Laura, eds. The Gospel of Barnabas. LC 98-18467. 273p. 1993. pap. text 9.95 (*1-881316-15-7*) A&B Bks.

Ragg, Mark. Body & Soul: Children, Teenagers & Cancer. 350p. (Orig.). 1995. pap. 18.95 (*0-85572-252-5*, Pub. by Hill Content Pubng) Seven Hills Bk.

Raggatt, Peter, et al, eds. The Learning Society Vol. 2: Challenges & Trends. LC 95-443. (Open University Set Bks.). (Illus.). 312p. (C). 1995. pap. 22.99 (*0-415-13615-6*) Routledge.

Raggatt, Peter & Unwin, Lorna, eds. Change & Intervention: Vocational Education & Training. 224p. 1991. pap. 29.95 (*1-85000-695-4*, Falmer Pr) Taylor & Francis.

***Raggatt, Peter & Williams, Steve.** Government, Markets & Vocational Qualifications: An Anatomy of Policy. LC 99-28029. 240p. 1999. 82.00 (*0-7507-0917-0*, Pub. by Falmer Pr UK); pap. 27.95 (*0-7507-0916-2*, Pub. by Falmer Pr UK) Taylor & Francis.

Ragge, Ken. The Real AA: Beyond the Myth of 12-Step Recovery. rev. ed. 232p. 1997. pap. 12.95 (*1-884365-14-0*) See Sharp Pr.

Ragge, Nicola. Immediate Eye Care. (Illus.). 208p. (C). (gr. 13). 1991. text 115.00 (*0-8151-7008-4*, 21260) Mosby Inc.

Raggett, Dave. Definitive Guide to HTML 3.0: Electronic Publishing on the World Wide Web. LC 96-223622. 416p. (C). 1996. pap. 39.95 (*0-201-87693-0*) Addison-Wesley.

Raggett, Dave, et al. HTML Version X: Electronic Publishing on the World Wide Web. 2nd ed. LC 98-132846. 464p. (C). 1997. pap. text 29.95 (*0-201-17805-2*) Addison-Wesley.

Raggett, G., tr. see Maspero, Gaston C. & Brugsch, Emile.

***Raggio, Olga, et al.** Federico da Montefeltro's Palace at Gubbio & Its Studiolo Vols. 1 & 2: Italian Renaissance Intarsia & the Conservation of the Gubbio Studiolo. (Illus.). 504p. 2000. 125.00 (*0-300-08516-8*) Yale U Pr.

— The Gubbio Studiolo in the Metropolitan Museum of Art, 2 vols. LC 99-612636. (Illus.). 1999. write for info. (*0-87099-925-7*) Metro Mus Art.

Raghariah, Jaiprakash. Basel Mission Industries in Malabar & South Canara, 1834-1914: A Study of Its Social & Economic Impact. 1990. 16.50 (*81-212-0324-4*, Pub. by Gian Publng Hse) S Asia.

Raghava, Sulochana R. Sociology of Indian Literature. (C). 1987. lib. bdg. 26.00 (*81-7033-011-4*, Pub. by Rawat Pubns) S Asia.

Raghavachari, V. T. Appellate Remedies under Excise & Customs. (C). 1990. 65.00 (*0-89771-222-6*) St Mut.

Raghavaiyangar, S. Srinivasa. Memorandum on the Progress of the Madras Presidency During the Last Forty Years of British Administration. (C). 1988. reprint ed. 54.00 (*81-206-0384-2*, Pub. by Asian Educ Servs) S Asia.

Raghavan. Phase Diagrams of Ternary Iron Alloys. 1989. 145.00 (*81-85307-04-0*) Institute of Management Consultants.

***Raghavan, D.** Textbook of Uncommon Cancer. 2nd ed. LC 98-40588. 776p. (C). 1999. 395.00 (*0-471-92921-2*) Wiley.

Raghavan, Derek. Principles & Practice of Genitourinary Oncology. LC 96-8893. 1104p. 1996. text 158.00 (*0-397-51458-1*) Lppncott W & W.

Raghavan, G. N. Introducing India. 130p. 1983. 10.95 (*0-318-37002-6*) Asia Bk Corp.

— The Making of Modern India: Rammohun Roy to Gandhi & Nehru. (C). 1988. 24.00 (*81-212-0112-8*, Pub. by Gian Publng Hse) S Asia.

— New Era in the Indian Polity: A Study of Atal Bihari Vajpayee & the BJP. LC 96-906294. (C). 1996. 48.00 (*81-212-0539-5*, Pub. by Gian Publng Hse) S Asia.

Raghavan, G. N., jt. auth. see Rao, N. Bhaskara.

Raghavan, Prabhakar, jt. auth. see Motwani, Rajeev.

Raghavan, R. K. Indian Police: Problems, Planning & Perspectives. (C). 1989. 31.00 (*81-85054-60-6*, Pub. by Manohar) S Asia.

Raghavan, S., jt. ed. see Ali, I.

Raghavan, S., ed. see Husemoller, Dale.

Raghavan, S., ed. see Ivic, A.

Raghavan, S. V. & Tripathi, Satish K. Networked Multimedia Systems: Concepts, Architecture & Design. LC 97-27377. 397p. 1997. 71.00 (*0-13-210642-6*) P-H.

Raghavan, T. E., ed. Stochastic Games & Related Topics: In Honor of Professor L. S. Shapley. (Theory & Decision Library: Vol. C). (C). 1991. lib. bdg. 155.00 (*0-7923-1016-0*) Kluwer Academic.

Raghavan, T. E., jt. auth. see Bapat, R. B.

***Raghavan, V.** Developmental Biology of Flowering Plants. LC 99-10027. 400p. 1999. 79.95 (*0-387-98781-9*) Spr-Verlag.

Raghavan, V. Molecular Embryology of Flowering Plants. LC 96-44410. (Illus.). 712p. (C). 1997. text 155.00 (*0-521-55246-X*) Cambridge U Pr.

Raghavan, V., ed. The Ramayana Tradition in Asia. 1982. 18.00 (*0-8364-0899-3*, Pub. by National Sahitya Akademi) S Asia.

Raghavan, V., ed. Phase Diagrams of Ternary Iron Alloys, Pt. 1. (Monograph Series on Alloy Phase Diagrams). (Illus.). 219p. (C). 1987. reprint ed. text 197.00 (*0-87170-230-4*, 57702G) ASM.

Raghavan, V., ed. see Bhoja.

Raghavarao, D. Exploring Statistics. (Statistics: Textbooks & Monographs: Vol. 92). (Illus.). 296p. 1988. text 75.00 (*0-8247-7952-5*) Dekker.

Raghavarao, Damaraju. Constructions & Combinatorial Problems in Design of Experiments. 416p. 1988. reprint ed. pap. 10.95 (*0-486-65685-3*) Dover.

Raghaven, G. N. The Press in India: A New History. (C). 1994. 28.50 (*81-212-0482-8*, Pub. by Gian Publng Hse) S Asia.

Raghaven, V. Developmental Biology of Fern Gametophytes. (Illus.). 384p. (C). 1989. text 90.00 (*0-521-33022-X*) Cambridge U Pr.

Raghavendra, A. S. Physiology of Trees. LC 91-7494. 528p. 1991. 220.00 (*0-471-50110-7*) Wiley.

Raghavendra, A. S., ed. Photosynthesis: A Comprehensive Treatise. LC 97-4035. (Illus.). 394p. (C). 1998. text 120.00 (*0-521-57000-X*) Cambridge U Pr.

***Raghavendra, A. S., ed.** Photosynthesis: A Comprehensive Treatise. (Illus.). 394p. (C). 2000. pap. text 49.95 (*0-521-78444-1*) Cambridge U Pr.

Raghavendra, C. S., jt. auth. see Varma, Anujan.

Raghavulu, C. V., jt. ed. see Arora, Ramesh K.

Ragheb, H. S., jt. auth. see Katz, S. E.

***Ragheb, J. Fiona, ed.** Dan Flavin: The Architecture of Light. (Illus.). 96p. 2000. 35.00 (*0-8109-6926-2*, Pub. by Abrams) Time Warner.

Ragheb, Mounir, et al. Free Time Boredom: Manual & Testing Tool. 68p. (Orig.). (C). 1995. pap. 20.00 (*1-882883-19-5*, 114) Idyll Arbor.

Ragheb, Sanaa, tr. see Ezeldin, Ahmed G.

Raghu, Dorairaja, jt. auth. see Hsieh, Hsin N.

Raghu, R. Palat. Tax Planning for the Salaried Employees. (C). 1990. 55.00 (*0-89771-259-5*) St Mut.

***Raghunandan, S.** A Silent Journey. 1998. pap. 100.00 (*81-86982-95-7*, Pub. by Business Pubns) St Mut.

Raghunathan, Anand, et al. High-Level Power Analysis & Optimization. LC 97-42068. 200p. 1997. text 108.00 (*0-7923-8073-8*, D Reidel) Kluwer Academic.

Raghunathan, M. S. Discrete Subgroups of Lie Groups. LC 71-189389. (Ergebnisse der Mathematik und Ihrer Grenzgebiete Ser.: Vol. 68). 240p. 1972. 42.00 (*0-387-05749-8*) Spr-Verlag.

Raghunathan, R. Work Manual for Administrative & Personnel Managers. 1994. write for info. (*81-224-0649-1*, Pub. by Wiley Estrn) Franklin.

Raghupathy, Raj, jt. ed. see Talwar, Gursaran P.

Raghuramaiah, K. Lakshmi. Hurricane: Autobiography of a Woman. LC 94-900448. (C). 1994. 28.00 (*81-7001-100-0*, Pub. by Chanakya) S Asia.

— Night Birds: Indian Prostitutes from Devadasis to Call Girls. (C). 1991. text 19.50 (*81-7001-084-5*, Pub. by Chanakya) S Asia.

Raghuvanshi, G. S., jt. auth. see Sisodia, M. L.

Raghuveer, M. R., jt. auth. see Krishnamurthy, K. A.

***Raghuvira, R. & Chandra, Lokesh.** Gilgit Buddhist Manuscripts: (Bibliotheca Indo-Buddhica, 150-152), 3 vols. 1998. pap. 3750.00 (*81-7030-445-8*, Pub. by Print Hse) St Mut.

Raghvan, G. S. Warning of Kashmir. (C). 1993. reprint ed. 14.00 (*81-7041-824-0*, Pub. by Anmol) S Asia.

Ragin, Bryant T., Jr., tr. see Calvi, Giulia.

Ragin, Charles C. The Comparative Method: Moving Beyond Qualitative & Quantitative Strategies. LC 86-30800. 218p. 1987. pap. 15.95 (*0-520-06618-9*, Pub. by U CA Pr) Cal Prin Full Svc.

— The Comparative Method: Moving Beyond Qualitative & Quantitative Strategies. LC 86-30800. 203p. reprint ed. pap. 63.00 (*0-7837-4698-9*, 204444500003) Bks Demand.

— Constructing Social Research. (Sociology for a New Century Ser.). 208p. 1994. pap. 18.95 (*0-8039-9021-9*) Pine Forge.

Ragin, Charles C. Fuzzy-Set Social Science. LC 99-86553. 1997. pap. text 20.00 (*0-226-70277-4*); lib. bdg. 48.00 (*0-226-70276-6*) U Ch Pr.

Ragin, Charles C. & Becker, Howard S., eds. What Is a Case? Exploring the Foundations of Social Inquiry. (Illus.). 252p. (C). 1992. pap. text 19.95 (*0-521-42188-8*) Cambridge U Pr.

— What Is a Case? Exploring the Foundations of Social Inquiry. (Illus.). 252p. (C). 1992. text 74.95 (*0-521-42050-4*) Cambridge U Pr.

Raginhart, L. America Liberata Bks. 9 & 10: With Ballads. LC 97-92303. (Illus.). viii, 228p. 1997. 19.95 (*0-9659095-0-6*) Conewago Hse.

***Raginhart, L.** Novecento Americano: The Ballad. 32p. 1999. pap. 6.00 (*0-9659095-1-4*) Conewago Hse.

Ragini, Sri. Hindu Dances (Nrityanjali) 84p. 1982. 14.95 (*0-318-36310-0*) Asia Bk Corp.

Ragins, Marianne. Making the Most of Your College Education. 88p. (Orig.). 1995. pap. 10.95 (*0-8050-4404-3*, Owl) H Holt & Co.

— Winning Scholarships for College: An Insider's Guide. 1995. pap. 10.95 (*0-8050-3072-7*) H Holt & Co.

— Winning Scholarships for College: An Insider's Guide. rev. ed. LC 98-53591. 192p. 1999. pap. 12.95 (*0-8050-5969-5*, Pub. by H Holt & Co) VHPS.

Ragins, Sanford. Jewish Responses to Anti-Semitism in Germany, 1870-1914: A Study in the History of Ideas. LC 80-13202. (Alumni Series of the Hebrew Union College Press). 240p. reprint ed. pap. 74.40 (*0-8357-3455-2*, 203971600013) Bks Demand.

Ragir, S., et al. Miscellaneous Papers on Archaeology. (Contributions of the University of California Archaeological Research Facility: No. 14). 125p. (C). 1972. reprint ed. pap. text 13.75 (*1-55567-590-5*) Coyote Press.

Ragir, Sonia. The Early Horizon in Central California Prehistory. (Publications of University of California Archaeological Research Facility: No. 15). (Illus.). 332p. (C). 1972. reprint ed. pap. text 35.00 (*1-55567-414-3*) Coyote Press.

Ragir, Sonia, et al. Notes on Western Nevada Archaeology & Ethnology. fac. ed. (Reports of the University of California Archaeological Survey: No. 66). (Illus.). 138p. 1966. reprint ed. pap. 15.00 (*1-55567-380-5*) Coyote Press.

Raglan, FitzRoy. The Hero: A Study in Tradition, Myth, & Drama. LC 75-23424. 296p. 1975. reprint ed. lib. bdg. 65.00 (*0-8371-8138-0*, RATH, Greenwood Pr) Greenwood.

Ragland. Critical Essays on Jacques Lacan. 1999. 47.00 (*0-7838-0054-1*) Mac Lib Ref.

Ragland, Bryce. The Year 2000 Problem Solver: A Five Step Disaster Prevention Plan. LC 96-47076. (Illus.). 300p. 1997. pap. 29.95 (*0-07-052517-X*) McGraw.

Ragland, Ellie. Essays on the Pleasures of Death: From Freud to Lacan. 240p. (C). (gr. 13). 1994. pap. 19.99 (*0-415-90722-5*, A9909) Routledge.

Ragland, Gaye. Instant Teaching Treasures for Patient Education. LC 96-29271. (Illus.). 300p. (C). (gr. 13). 1996. pap. text 37.95 (*0-8151-4699-X*, 29697) Mosby Inc.

Ragland, Joyce C., jt. auth. see Hill, Marie S.

Ragland, Kay. All About Hamsters. 32p. 2.29 (*0-87666-201-7*) TFH Pubns.

— Guinea Pigs. (Illus.). 128p. 1988. 9.95 (*0-86622-830-6*, KW-016) TFH Pubns.

— Kittens. (Illus.). 96p. 1988. 9.95 (*0-87666-857-0*, KW-019) TFH Pubns.

Ragland, Kenneth W., jt. auth. see Borman, Gary L.

Ragland, Margaret. Full of Joy. 1980. pap. 6.95 (*0-89137-415-9*) Quality Pubns.

— What's It Worth? Probing Our Values with Questions Jesus Asked. 1977. pap. 6.95 (*0-89137-409-4*) Quality Pubns.

Ragland, Mary. Sequel to Crossroads & Byways of the World. 160p. 1998. pap. 13.00 (*0-8059-4321-8*) Dorrance.

Ragland, Mary L. & Williams, Jane J. Warren County, Mississippi, Probate Index. 242p. (Orig.). 1993. pap. text 21.00 (*0-685-70624-9*) Heritage Bk.

Ragland, P. C., jt. ed. see Puffer, J. H.

Ragland, Paul C. Basic Analytical Petrology. (Illus.). 296p. (C). 1989. pap. text 27.95 (*0-19-504535-1*) OUP.

Ragland, Sheila, ed. see Shirley, Anita G.

Ragland-Sullivan, Ellie. Jacques Lacan & the Philosophy of Psychoanalysis. LC 84-16125. 384p. 1987. pap. text 16.95 (*0-252-01465-0*) U of Ill Pr.

Ragland, Teresa & Brown, J. Aaron. Baby Days & Lullabye Nights. (Illus.). 48p. (J). 1993. boxed set 24.95 incl. audio (*0-8249-7629-0*, Ideals Child) Hambleton-Hill.

Ragland, Teresa B. Cooking in the Kitchen with Santa. 32p. (J). (ps up). 1991. lib. bdg. 12.95 (*1-56674-028-2*, HTS Bks) Forest Hse.

— Cooking in the Kitchen with Santa. 32p. (J). (gr. 1-5). 1992. pap. 4.95 (*0-8249-3096-7*, Ideals Child) Hambleton-Hill.

Ragland, Thomas E. The Faces of Fear: An Inside Look at Fear Itself. Libb, Melva, ed. (Illus.). 240p. (Orig.). 1988. pap. text 6.95 (*0-936369-15-9*) Son-Rise Pubns.

Ragle, Larry. Crime Scene: From Fingerprints to Autopsies to DNA Testing-A Fascinating, IN-Depth Introduction to the World of Forensic Investigation. LC 95-90095. (Orig.). 1995. mass mkt. 6.99 (*0-380-77379-1*, Avon Bks) Morrow Avon.

Ragle, Nina S. Even Monkeys Fall Out of Trees: John Naka's Collection of Japanese Proverbs. LC 87-60655. (Illus.). 256p. 1987. 13.95 (*0-9618475-0-6*) Nippon Art Frms.

Raglin, Tim. Pecos Bill. LC 88-11581. 36p. (J). (ps up). 1991. 14.95 (*0-88708-081-2*, Rabbit Ears) Litle Simon.

An Asterisk (*) at the beginning of an entry indicates that the title is appearing for the first time.

Ragman Rolls Staff. Instrumenta Publica Sive Processus Super Fidelitatibus et Homagiis Scotorum Domino Regi Angliae Factis A.D. MCCXCI MCCXCVI. Thomson, Thomas, ed. LC 76-174294. (Bannatyne Club, Edinburgh. Publications: No. 47). reprint ed. 37.50 (*0-404-52757-4*) AMS Pr.

Ragnarsson, Huggy. Elite Street: The Elite Model Look: A Fashion & Style Manual. (Illus.). 160p. 2000. 20.00 (*0-7893-0136-9*, Pub. by Universe) St Martin.

Ragnarsson, Ingemar & Nilsson, Sven G. Shapes & Shells in Nuclear Structure. (Illus.). 422p. (C). 1995. text 105.00 (*0-521-37377-8*) Cambridge U Pr.

Ragner, Claes Lykke, jt. auth. see Northern Sea Route User Conference Staff.

Ragnes, Per. John Ugelated: The Man Behind the Beads. 225p. (C). 1997. 41.00 (*82-00-37673-7*, Pub. by Scand Univ Pr) IBD Ltd.

Ragnisco, O., jt. ed. see Levi, D.

Ragnubs, Nima D., jt. auth. see Lipton, Barbara.

Rago, David. American Art Pottery. 1997. 45.00 (*1-57715-014-7*) Knckerbocker.

Rago, David, ed. see Montgomery, Susan J.

Rago, Henry. Sky of Late Summer: Poems. LC 78-92464. (Phoenix Poets Ser.). 1970. reprint ed. pap. 1.95 (*0-226-70309-6*, PP13) U Ch Pr.

Rago, James J. Career Rx: How to Read Your Career's Vital Signs. 81p. (Orig.). 1997. pap., wbk. ed. write for info. (*0-9653992-1-4*) Wrk Smart Pr.

— Upgrade Your Job: How to Market Your Services Profitably. 116p. 1996. wbk. ed. 34.95 (*0-9653992-0-6*) Wrk Smart Pr.

Rago, Linda O. A Dooryard Herb Cookbook. LC 88-60522. (Illus.). 128p. 1988. pap. 8.95 (*0-933126-92-1*) Pictorial Hist.

— Dooryard Herbs. Knott, Susan, ed. LC 83-62799. (Illus.). 144p. (Orig.). 1984. pap. 12.95 (*0-938634-04-6*) Carabelle.

— Dooryard Herbs. rev. ed. (Illus.). 140p. (Orig.). 1995. pap. 12.95 (*0-9648489-0-2*) Camp Hill.

— Herbal Almanac. (Illus.). 80p. 1992. 12.95 (*0-912347-99-6*) Fulcrum Pub.

— Mugworts in May: A Folklore of Herbs. (Illus.). 121p. (Orig.). 1995. pap. 14.95 (*0-9646197-0-9*) Quarrier Pr.

***Rago, Linda Ours.** Blackberry Cove Herbal: Magic & Healing with Common Wayside Plants in the Appalachian Wise Woman Tradition. (Illus.). 176p. 2000. 18.95 (*1-892123-20-7*) Capital VA.

Rago, Stephen A. UNIX System V Network Programming. LC 92-45276. (Professional Computing Ser.). 800p. (C). 1993. 39.95 (*0-201-56318-5*) Addison-Wesley.

Ragon, Michel. The Space of Death: A Study of Funerary Architecture, Decoration, & Urbanism. Sheridan, Alan, tr. LC 83-5958. (Illus.). 336p. reprint ed. pap. 104.20 (*0-8357-3129-4*, 203939100012) Bks Demand.

***Ragonbe, Helena & Twine, France Winddance.** Ideologies & Technologies of Motherhood: Race, Class, Sexuality & Nationalism. LC 99-54216. 352p. 2000. pap. write for info. (*0-415-92110-4*) Routledge.

Ragone, David A. Thermodynamics of Materials, 2 vols., Vol. 1. 336p. 1994. text 95.95 (*0-471-30885-4*) Wiley.

— Thermodynamics of Materials, 2 vols., Vol. 2. LC 94-25647. 256p. 1994. text 95.95 (*0-471-30886-2*) Wiley.

Ragone, Helena. Surrogate Motherhood: Conception in the Heart. (C). 1994. pap. 25.00 (*0-8133-1979-X*, Pub. by Westview) HarpC.

***Ragone, Helena & Twine, France Winddance, eds.** Ideologies & Technologies of Motherhood: Race Class Sexuality & Nationalism. LC 99-54216. 352p. (C). 2000. text 85.00 (*0-415-92109-0*) Routledge.

Ragone, Helena, jt. ed. see Franklin, Sarah.

Ragonese, Roger R. & Dipierro, Joseph. Principles of Biology. 6th ed. 508p. (C). 1995. pap. text, spiral bd. 45.95 (*0-7872-0619-9*) Kendall-Hunt.

Ragoonath, Aldwin. How Shall They Hear? The Art of Effective Biblical Preaching. LC 96-84852. 122p. (Orig.). 1996. pap. 7.99 (*0-88270-689-6*) Bridge-Logos.

Ragosta, Marjorie, et al. Computer-Assisted Instruction & Compensatory Education: The ETS-Los Angeles Unified School District Study. 35.00 (*0-317-67869-8*) Educ Testing Serv.

Ragosta, Millie, ed. see Baker, Chester E.

Ragosta, Millie J. King John's Treasure. large type ed. LC 98-49032. 1999. 20.95 (*0-7862-1761-8*) Thorndike Pr.

Ragosta, Ray. The Act Proves Untenable. Kaplan, Peter, ed. 1976. 3.00 (*0-915176-18-1*) Pourboire.

— From the Varieties of Religious Experience, Bk. 2. 24p. 1996. pap. 4.00 (*0-945926-31-6*, Pub. by Paradigm RI) SPD-Small Pr Dist.

— Grondines Espisode. (Isthmus Project Ser.). 44p. 1999. pap. 5.00 (*0-945926-53-7*) Paradigm RI.

— Sherds: Poems. limited ed. (Burning Deck Poetry Chapbooks Ser.). 32p. 1982. pap. 15.00 (*0-930901-08-8*) Burning Deck.

— Varieties of Religious Experience: Poems. (Burning Deck Poetry Ser.). 80p. 1993. pap. 8.00 (*0-930901-83-5*) Burning Deck.

— Varieties of Religious Experience: Poems. limited ed. (Burning Deck Poetry Ser.). 80p. 1993. pap. 15.00 (*0-930901-84-3*) Burning Deck.

Ragotzkie, Robert A., ed. Man & the Marine Environment. 200p. 1983. 112.00 (*0-8493-5759-4*, GC21, CRC Reprint) Franklin.

Ragout de Spencer, Alicia L., jt. ed. see Spencer, J. F. T.

Ragozin, Len, et al. The Odds Must Be Crazy. LC 96-37632. 320p. (gr. 8). 1997. 23.95 (*0-316-60497-6*) Little.

Ragozin, Zenaide A., tr. see Leroy-Beaulieu, Anatole.

Ragsdale. Ragsdale Presidential Politics. (C). 1992. pap. text 35.16 (*0-395-51554-8*) HM.

— Spreadsheet Modeling & Decision Analysis. (C). 1996. pap. 53.25 (*0-538-87049-4*) Thomson Learn.

— Spreadsheet Modeling & Decision Analysis. 2nd ed. (Miscellaneous/Catalogs Ser.). 1997. pap. 90.95 (*0-538-86756-6*) S-W Pub.

Ragsdale, Bruce A. A Planter's Republic: The Search for Economic Independence in Revolutionary Virginia. LC 95-18435. (Illus.). 320p. (C). 1996. text 34.95 (*0-945612-40-0*) Madison Hse.

Ragsdale, Bruce A. & Treese, Joel D. Black Americans in Congress, 1870-1989. (Illus.). 164p. (Orig.). 1996. pap. text 35.00 (*0-7881-2797-7*) DIANE Pub.

— Black Americans in Congress, 1870-1989. LC 89-600409. (Illus.). (Orig.). 1990. pap. 16.00 (*0-16-018476-2*, S/N052071008918) USGPO.

Ragsdale, C. S. Living Longer Than Hate: A Story of Survival & Success. (Illus.). 1997. lib. bdg. 25.00 (*0-9659781-0-9*) Holcaust Mus.

***Ragsdale, C. S.** Snoop School Vol. 1: Research Tips & More for Writers, Students, Teacher & all Other Snoops. LC 00-91420. 200p. (YA). 2000. pap. 19.95 (*0-9700257-0-X*) ChessDale.

Ragsdale, Cliff T. Spreadsheet Modeling & Decision Analysis: A Practical Introduction to Management Science. 2nd ed. LC 97-26622. 1997. write for info. (*0-538-88130-5*) S-W Pub.

***Ragsdale, Cliff T.** Spreadsheet Modeling & Decison Analysis. 3rd ed. LC 00-32963. 2000. 86.95 (*0-324-02122-4*) Sth-Wstrn College.

Ragsdale, Crystal S. The Women & Children of the Alamo. LC 93-41998. (Illus.). 128p. (J). 1994. pap. 14.95 (*1-880510-12-X*) State House Pr.

Ragsdale, Crystal S., jt. auth. see Crawford, Ann F.

Ragsdale, Crystal Sasse, jt. auth. see Crawford, Ann Fears.

Ragsdale, Elizabeth. Poetic Notions. 16p. 1993. pap. text 6.00 (*0-9641217-0-0*) Sea-Lark Print.

Ragsdale, Elizabeth S., jt. auth. see Moss, John R.

Ragsdale, Hugh. The Russian Tragedy: The Burden of History. LC 95-39310. 328p. (C). (gr. 13). 1996. pap. text 39.95 (*1-56324-756-9*) M E Sharpe.

— Tsar Paul & the Question of Madness: An Essay in History & Psychology, 13. LC 88-24677. (Contributions to the Study of World History Ser.: No. 13). 284p. 1988. 65.00 (*0-313-26608-5*, RTS/, Greenwood Pr) Greenwood.

Ragsdale, Hugh & Ponomarev, Valerii N., eds. Imperial Russian Foreign Policy. (Woodrow Wilson Center Press Ser.). 471p. (C). 1993. text 80.00 (*0-521-44229-X*) Cambridge U Pr.

Ragsdale, Hugh & Tucker, Robert C. The Russian Tragedy: The Burden of History. LC 95-39310. 328p. (C). (gr. 13). 1996. text 77.95 (*1-56324-755-0*) M E Sharpe.

Ragsdale, Hugh, ed. & tr. see Zubkova, Elena.

Ragsdale, James G., jt. auth. see Karam, Thomas J.

Ragsdale, John. Camper's Guide to Outdoor Cooking: Tips, Techniques, & Delicious Eats. 2nd ed. LC 98-40395. (Camper's Guide Ser.). 192p. 1999. pap. 9.95 (*0-88415-603-6*, 5603) Gulf Pub.

Ragsdale, John G. Dutch Oven Cooking. 3rd ed. LC 97-4079. (Illus.). 80p. 1997. pap. 5.95 (*0-88415-222-7*, 5222) Gulf Pub.

— Dutch Ovens Chronicled: Their Use in the United States. (Illus.). 104p. 1991. 18.00 (*1-55728-220-X*) U of Ark Pr.

Ragsdale, John P. Protestant Mission Education in Zambia, 1880-1954. LC 85-40505. 192p. 1987. 36.50 (*0-941664-09-0*) Susquehanna U Pr.

Ragsdale, Katherine H., ed. Boundary Wars: Intimacy & Distance in Healing Relationships. LC 95-52520. 264p. (Orig.). 1996. pap. 15.95 (*0-8298-1118-4*) Pilgrim OH.

Ragsdale, Kenneth B. Big Bend Country: Land of the Unexpected. LC 97-49196. (Centennial Series of the Association of Former Students, Texas A&M University). (Illus.). 336p. 1998. 24.95 (*0-89096-811-X*) Tex A&M Univ Pr.

— Quicksilver: Terlingua & the Chisos Mining Company. LC 75-4081. (Illus.). 366p. 1995. pap. 14.95 (*0-89096-188-3*) Tex A&M Univ Pr.

— Wings over the Mexican Border: Pioneer Military Aviation in the Big Bend. LC 97-209265. (Illus.). 294p. 1997. pap. 16.95 (*0-292-77081-2*) U of Tex Pr.

Ragsdale, Kenneth B., et al. History Is My Home: A Survey of Texas Architectural Styles. 1981. 10.00 incl. audio, flmstrp (*0-87611-054-5*) Tex St Hist Assn.

Ragsdale, Lisa, jt. auth. see Vettrus, Linda.

Ragsdale, Lyn. Vital Statistics on the Presidency. 2nd rev. ed. LC 98-24915. 500p. 1998. text 50.95 (*1-56802-393-6*); pap. text 39.95 (*1-56802-427-4*) Congr Quarterly.

— Vital Statistics on the Presidency: Washington to Clinton. LC 95-33031. (Illus.). 455p. (YA). (gr. 11). 1995. pap. text 35.95 (*1-56802-049-X*) Congr Quarterly.

— Vital Statistics on the Presidency: Washington to Clinton. LC 95-33031. (Illus.). 455p. (C). (gr. 11). 1996. text 50.95 (*1-56802-050-3*) Congr Quarterly.

Ragsdale, Nancy N., et al, eds. Eight International Congress of Pesticide Chemistry: Options 2000. LC 94-42675. (ACS Conference Proceedings Ser.). 460p. 1995. text 120.00 (*0-8412-2995-3*, Pub. by Am Chemical) OUP.

Ragsdale, Nancy N. & Kuhr, Ronald J., eds. Pesticides: Minimizing the Risks. LC 87-1842. (ACS Symposium Ser.: No. 336). (Illus.). vii, 186p. 1987. 34.95 (*0-8412-1022-5*) Am Chemical.

— Pesticides: Minimizing the Risks. LC 87-1842. (ACS Symposium Ser.: Vol. 336). 194p. 1987. reprint ed. pap. 60.20 (*0-608-03548-3*, 206426700008) Bks Demand.

Ragsdale, Nancy N. & Menzer, Robert E., eds. Carcinogenicity & Pesticides: Principles, Issues, & Relationships. LC 89-18052. (Symposium Ser.: No. 414). (Illus.). 237p. 1989. text 59.95 (*0-8412-1703-3*, Pub. by Am Chemical) OUP.

***Ragsdale, Nancy N. & Seiber, James N.** Pesticides: Managing Risks & Optimizing Benefits. LC 99-14981. (ACS Symposium Ser.: No. 734). (Illus.). 288p. 1999. text 100.00 (*0-8412-3616-X*, Pub. by Am Chemical) OUP.

Ragsdale, Ronald G. Permissible Computing in Education: Values, Assumptions, & Needs. LC 87-35964. 292p. 1988. 59.95 (*0-275-92894-2*, C2894, Praeger Pubs) Greenwood.

Ragsdale, Tod A. Once a Hermit Kingdom: Ethnicity & Education & National Integration in Nepal. 1989. 75.00 (*0-7855-0232-7*, Pub. by Ratna Pustak Bhandar) St Mut.

— Once a Hermit Kingdom: Ethnicity & Education & National Integration in Nepal. 252p. (C). 1989. 300.00 (*0-89771-043-6*, Pub. by Ratna Pustak Bhandar) St Mut.

— Once a Hermit Kingdom: Ethnicity, Education & National Integration in Nepal. (C). 1989. 34.00 (*81-85054-75-4*, Pub. by Manohar) S Asia.

Ragsdale, Usa C. Your Child Doesn't Have to Die! How You Can Help Your Child Overcome Cancer Using Nutritional Therapy. (Orig.). 1996. pap. 12.00 (*0-9654714-0-3*) Abundant Living.

Ragsdale, William O. They Sought a Land: A Settlement in the Arkansas River Valley, 1840-1870. LC 97-17937. (Illus.). 128p. 1997. 24.00 (*1-55728-498-9*) U of Ark Pr.

Ragsdale, Winifred, ed. A Sea of Upturned Faces: Proceedings of the Third Pacific Rim Conference on Children's Literature. LC 88-26534. 306p. 1989. 37.00 (*0-8108-2108-7*) Scarecrow.

Ragsdell, K. M., ed. see American Society of Mechanical Engineers Staff.

Ragubir, Kevin. Misty Dreamer. LC 97-90464. 72p. 2000. pap. 8.95 (*0-533-12414-X*) Vantage.

Ragucci. Voces de Hispanoamerica. 49.95 (*0-686-56674-2*, S-33067); 55.00 (*0-8288-7948-6*, S33067) Fr & Eur.

Raguet, Condy. The Principles of Free Trade: Illustrated in a Series of Short & Familiar Essays. 2nd ed. LC 68-56569. (Reprints of Economic Classics Ser.). xix, 439p. 1969. reprint ed. 49.50 (*0-678-00529-X*) Kelley.

— A Treatise on Currency & Banking. 2nd ed. LC 65-26375. (Library of Money & Banking History). xiv, 323p. 1967. reprint ed. 45.00 (*0-678-00215-0*) Kelley.

Raguin, Virginia & Zakin, Helen. Corpus Vitrearum U. S. A. Stained Glass Before 1700 in the Collections of the Mid-West States, 2 vols. (Illus.). 500p. 1999. 225.00 (*1-872501-00-1*) Gordon & Breach.

Raguin, Virginia C., ed. Conservation & Restoration of Stained Glass: An Owner's Guide. (Illus.). 40p. (Orig.). 1988. pap. 43.00 (*0-317-93881-9*) Census Stained.

— 1994 International Seminar on Stained Glass: Proceedings. (Illus.). 240p. 1994. 25.00 (*0-614-14262-8*) Census Stained.

Raguin, Yves. Paths to Contemplation. 6th ed. Orig. Title: Chemins de la Contemplation. 154p. 1996. reprint ed. pap. 8.95 (*0-940147-04-1*) Source Bks CA.

Ragulskis, K. M. & Yurkauskas, A. Y. Vibration of Bearings. (Applications of Vibration Ser.). (Illus.). 120p. 1989. 95.00 (*0-89116-829-X*) Hemisp Pub.

Ragulskis, K. M., et al. Vibromotors for Precision Microrobots. (Applications of Vibration Ser.). 400p. 1988. 145.00 (*0-89116-549-5*) Hemisp Pub.

Ragusa, James, jt. auth. see Liebowitz, Jay.

Ragusa, Maria & Wolf, Juliette, compiled by. The Alternative Pick, 1997. (Illus.). 500p. 1997. 50.00 (*0-9632606-5-0*, Alternative Pick) Storm Music.

Ragusa, Maria & Wolf, Juliette, contrib. by. The Alternative Pick, 1998. 7th ed. (Illus.). 500p. 1998. 60.00 (*0-9632606-6-9*, Alternative Pick) Storm Music.

Ragusa, Maria & Wolf, Juliette, eds. The Alternative Pick, 1999. 2000. 60.00 (*0-9632606-7-7*) Storm Music.

***Ragusa, Maria & Wolf, Juliette, eds.** Alternative Pick's Multi-Media Directory. (Illus.). 80p. 2000. 60.00 (*0-9679625-0-1*) Storm Music.

Ragusa, Olga. Comparative Perspectives on Manzoni. 38p. 1986. pap. 4.95 (*0-913298-78-6*) S F Vanni.

— Essential Italian Grammar. 111p. (Orig.). 1963. pap. 4.95 (*0-486-20779-X*) Dover.

— First Readings in Italian Literature - Letture Facili. (C). 1990. pap. 10.95 (*0-913298-06-9*) S F Vanni.

— Italian Verbs - Regular & Irregular. 1984. pap. 4.50 (*0-913298-27-1*) S F Vanni.

— Lorenzo Da Ponte in American Perspective: Two Lectures & a Review. 77p. 1998. pap. 10.00 (*0-913298-88-3*) S F Vanni.

— Mallarme in Italy: Literary Influence & Critical Response. 1957. 15.00 (*0-913298-34-4*) S F Vanni.

— Say It in Italian. 1958. pap. 3.95 (*0-486-20806-0*) Dover.

— Teach Yourself Italian: Essential Grammar. (Teach Yourself Ser.). 1992. 14.95 (*0-8288-8364-5*) Fr & Eur.

— Verga's Milanese Tales. 1964. 15.00 (*0-913298-33-6*) S F Vanni.

Ragusa, Shirley, jt. auth. see Billac, Pete.

Ragusso, Viola M. Olympian Plays: A Comprehensive Introduction to Greek Mythology Written in Television Script Form. LC 87-91373. (Illus.). 646p. (YA). (gr. 9-12). 1987. reprint ed. text 11.95 (*0-9619674-0-4*) Olympian Plays.

Ragussis, Michael. Acts of Naming: The Family Plot in Fiction. 278p. 1987. text 75.00 (*0-19-504070-8*) OUP.

— Figures of Conversion: The Jewish Question & English National Identity. LC 94-38191. (Post-Contemporary Interventions Ser.). (Illus.). 352p. 1995. text 54.95 (*0-8223-1559-9*); pap. text 17.95 (*0-8223-1570-X*) Duke.

— The Subterfuge of Art: Language & the Romantic Tradition. LC 78-5845. 256p. reprint ed. pap. 79.40 (*0-8357-6623-3*, 203526900094) Bks Demand.

Ragvald, Lars, jt. auth. see Lang, Graeme.

Ragz, M. M. Eyeballs for Breakfast. MacDonald, Patricia, ed. 128p. (Orig.). (J). (gr. 4-7). 1990. pap. 2.99 (*0-671-68567-8*, Minstrel Bks) PB.

— Eyeballs for Lunch. MacDonald, Patricia, ed. 114p. (J). 1992. pap. 3.50 (*0-671-75882-9*, Minstrel Bks) PB.

— Eyeballs for Lunch. 1992. 8.60 (*0-606-02051-9*, Pub. by Turtleback) Demco.

— Eyeballs for Midnight Snack. MacDonald, Pat, ed. 144p. (Orig.). (J). 1994. pap. 3.50 (*0-671-88411-5*, Minstrel Bks) PB.

— French Fries up Your Nose. MacDonald, Pat, ed. LC 94-148205. 160p. 1994. pap. 2.99 (*0-671-88410-7*, Minstrel Bks) PB.

— French Fries up Your Nose. (J). 1994. 8.09 (*0-606-05836-2*, Pub. by Turtleback) Demco.

— Gotcha! (J). 1995. pap. 3.50 (*0-671-88412-3*) PB.

— Gotcha! 1995. 8.60 (*0-606-09345-1*, Pub. by Turtleback) Demco.

— Lost Little Angel. LC 96-44989. (Illus.). 32p. (J). (ps-2). 1999. 16.00 (*0-689-81067-9*) S&S Bks Yung.

— Sewer Soup. MacDonald, Patricia, ed. 128p. (Orig.). (J). 1992. pap. 3.50 (*0-671-75881-0*) PB.

Raha, M. K. & Ghosh, A. K., eds. North-East India: The Human Interface. LC 98-900829. 469p. 1998. 43.00 (*81-212-0573-5*, Pub. by Gyan Publishing Hse) Nataraj Bks.

Raha, Manis K. Matriliny to Patriliny: A Study of the Rabha Society. (C). 1989. 49.00 (*81-212-0244-2*, Pub. by Gian Publng Hse) S Asia.

— Polyandry in India. (C). 1987. 61.00 (*81-212-0105-5*, Pub. by Gian Publng Hse) S Asia.

— Tribal Situation in West Bengal. (C). 1990. 47.50 (*0-8364-2648-7*, Pub. by Firma KLM) S Asia.

Raha, Manis K. & Commar, P. C., eds. Tribal India: Problem Development Prospect, 2 vols. 400p. 1989. write for info. (*81-212-0273-6*, Pub. by Gian Publng Hse) S Asia.

Raha, Manis K. & Khan, Iar A., eds. Polity, Political Process & Social Control in South Asia: The Tribal & Rural Perspectives. (C). 1993. 32.00 (*81-212-0413-5*, Pub. by Gian Publng Hse) S Asia.

Raha, S., et al, eds. Quark-Gluon Plasma: Lectures. (Research Reports in Physics). (Illus.). 384p. 1991. 53.95 (*0-387-51984-X*) Spr-Verlag.

Raha, S., jt. auth. see Sinha, Bikas K.

Raha, Stephanie, jt. ed. see McSweeney, Thomas J.

Rahaee, Farhang, ed. The Iran-Iraq War: The Politics of Aggression. LC 92-33379. 256p. 1993. 49.95 (*0-8130-1176-0*); pap. 19.95 (*0-8130-1177-9*) U Press Fla.

***Raham, Gary, et al.** The Deep Time Diaries. (Illus.). 96p. 2000. pap. 17.95 (*1-55591-415-2*) Fulcrum Pub.

Raham, R. Gary. Dinosaurs in the Garden: An Evolutionary Guide to Backyard Biology. (Illus.). 280p. 1988. 22.95 (*0-937548-10-3*) Plexus Pub.

— Explorations in Backyard Biology: Drawing on Nature in the Classroom, Grades 4-6. (Illus.). 250p. (J). 1996. pap. text 25.00 (*1-56308-254-3*) Teacher Ideas Pr.

— Sillysaurs: Dinosaurs That Could Have Been. (Illus.). 16p. (Orig.). (J). (gr. k-4). 1990. 2.95 (*0-9626301-0-1*) Biostration.

Rahaman, M. N. Ceramic Processing & Sintering. LC 95-32195. (Materials Engineering Ser.: Vol. 10). (Illus.). 784p. 1995. text 215.00 (*0-8247-9573-3*) Dekker.

Rahaman, Vashanti. O Christmas Tree. LC 95-83193. (Illus.). 32p. (J). (ps-3). 1996. 14.95 (*1-56397-237-9*) Boyds Mills Pr.

— Read for Me, Mama. LC 95-77784. (Illus.). 32p. (J). (gr. 1-5). 1997. 14.95 (*1-56397-313-8*) Boyds Mills Pr.

Rahamimoff, Rami & Katz, Bernard, eds. Calcium Neuronal Function & Transmitter Release. 1986. text 183.50 (*0-89838-791-4*) Kluwer Academic.

Rahardjo, Haianto, jt. auth. see Fredlund, Delwyn G.

Rahardjo, Julfita, jt. auth. see Jones, Gavin W.

Rahat, Naveedi. Male Out Migration & Matri-Weighted Households: A Case Study of a Junjab Village in Pakistan. (C). 1990. text 26.00 (*81-7075-015-6*, Pub. by Hindustan) S Asia.

Rahawi, Steve A. Abraham the Friend of God: The Spiritual Journey of a Great Prophet & the Three Women in His Life. LC 96-92172. (Illus.). 197p. (Orig.). 1996. pap. 14.95 (*0-9652565-1-0*) World Novels.

— No More Strangers: One American & Two Russians in a Race Around the World. LC 96-90370. (Illus.). vii, 275p. (Orig.). 1997. pap. 14.95 (*0-9652565-2-9*) World Novels.

Rahbar, Daud & Schimmel, Annemarie, eds. Urdu Letters of Mirza Asadu'llah Khan Ghalib. LC 87-6447. 628p. 1987. text 29.50 (*0-88706-412-4*) State U NY Pr.

Rahden, Wolfert Von, see Gessinger, Joachim & Von Rahden, Wolfert, eds.

Rahdert, jt. auth. see Roth.

Rahdert, Elizabeth. Adolescent Drug Abuse: Clinical Assessment & Therapeutic Interventions. 378p. 1995. pap. text 15.00 (*0-16-048335-2*) USGPO.

Rahdert, George K. & Roth, Larry M. Appeals to the Eleventh Circuit, 1984-1994, 3 vols. 1000p. 1994. suppl. ed. 42.50 (*0-685-43647-0*, MICHIE) LEXIS Pub.

— Appeals to the Eleventh Circuit, 1984-1994. 32p. 1994. ring bd., suppl. ed. 47.00 (*0-614-03174-5*, MICHIE) LEXIS Pub.

— Appeals to the Fifth Circuit, 2 vols., Issue 23. 151p. 1998. ring bd. 175.00 (*0-327-00794-X*, 8016018) LEXIS Pub.

— Appeals to the Fifth Circuit Manual, 2 vols., Set. 1000p. Date not set. ring bd. 175.00 (*0-409-26070-3*, 80156, MICHIE) LEXIS Pub.

— Appeals to the Fifth Circuit, 1977-1994, 2 vols. 1000p. 1994. suppl. ed. 50.00 (*0-685-73809-4*, MICHIE) LEXIS Pub.

Rahdert, George K., jt. auth. see Roth, Larry M.

Rahdert, Mark C. Covering Accident Costs: Insurance, Liability & Tort Reforms. LC 94-830. 288p. (C). 1995. text 69.95 (*1-56639-232-2*); pap. text 34.95 (*1-56639-233-0*) Temple U Pr.

R

Rahe, Harves. Index to Doctoral Dissertations. 107p. (C). 1975. pap. text 10.00 (0-9603064-1-2) Delta Pi Epsilon.
— Index to Doctoral Dissertations in Business Education, Supplement, 1975-1980. 2nd ed. 71p. (C). 1981. pap. text 10.00 (1-881530-07-8) Delta Pi Epsilon.
Rahe, Jurgen H., et al, eds. Comets in the Post-Halley Era, 2 vols., Set. (C). 1991. pap. text 76.50 (0-7923-1165-5); lib. bdg. 242.00 (0-7923-1164-7) Kluwer Academic.
— Comparative Planetology with an Earth Perspective: Proceedings of the First International Conference, Held in Pasadena, California on June 6-8, 1994. LC 95-40175. 236p. (C). 1995. text 184.00 (0-7923-3790-5) Kluwer Academic.
Rahe, Jurgen H., et al. The International Halley Watch Atlas of Large-Scale Phenomena. (Illus.). 734p. 1992. lib. bdg. write for info. (1-880768-00-3) U Colo Lab Atmos.
Rahe, Jurgen H., jt. auth. see Kopal, Zdenek.
Rahe, Paul A. Republics Ancient & Modern Vol. I: The Ancient Regime in Classical Greece. LC 94-5728. 380p. 1994. pap. text 27.50 (0-8078-4473-X) U of NC Pr.
— Republics Ancient & Modern Vol. II: New Modes & Orders in Early Modern Political Thought. LC 94-5728. 490p. (C). 1994. pap. text 29.95 (0-8078-4474-8) U of NC Pr.
— Republics Ancient & Modern Vol. III: Inventions of Prudence: Constituting the American Regime. LC 94-5728. 380p. (C). 1994. pap. text 24.95 (0-8078-4475-6) U of NC Pr.
Raheb, Mitri. I Am a Palestinian Christian. Gritsch, Ruth C., tr. LC 95-5483. 144p. 1995. pap. 16.00 (0-8006-2663-X, 1-2663, Fortress Pr) Augsburg Fortress.
Raheel, Mastura, ed. Modern Textile Characterization Methods. (International Fiber Science & Technology Ser.: Vol. 13). (Illus.). 576p. 1996. text 225.00 (0-8247-9473-7) Dekker.
— Protective Clothing Systems & Materials. (Occupational Safety & Health Ser.: Vol. 25). (Illus.). 272p. 1994. text 155.00 (0-8247-9118-5) Dekker.
Raheja, Gloria G. The Poison in the Gift: Ritual, Prestation, & the Dominant Caste in North Indian Village. (Illus.). xiv, 300p. 1988. lib. bdg. 51.00 (0-226-70728-8) U Ch Pr.
Raheja, Gloria G. & Gold, Ann G. Listen to the Heron's Words: Reimagining Gender & Kinship in North India. LC 93-12586. 1994. 50.00 (0-520-08370-9, Pub. by U CA Pr); pap. 19.95 (0-520-08371-7, Pub. by U CA Pr) Cal Prin Full Svc.
Rahgozar, Reza, jt. auth. see Pinola, Rudy.
***Rahi, Chuck.** Genetic Witness. LC 99-65731. 312p. 2000. pap. 16.50 (0-88739-312-8) Creat Arts Bk.
***Rahi, Hakim S.** Sri Guru Granth Sahib Discovered: A Reference Book of Quotations from the Adi Cranth. LC 99-931100. xv, 208p. 1999. 58.00 (81-208-1613-7, Pub. by Motilal Bnarsidass) S Asia.
Rahier, Jean Muteba, ed. Representations of Blackness & the Performance of Identities. LC 98-41382. 288p. 1999. 65.00 (0-89789-606-8, Bergin & Garvey); pap. 24.95 (0-89789-607-6, Bergin & Garvey) Greenwood.
Rahilly, Joan, jt. auth. see Ball, Martin J.
Rahim, Afzalur M., et al. Current Topics in Management, Vol. 3. 1998. 78.50 (0-7623-0448-0) Jai Pr.
Rahim, Enayetur. Scholar's Guide to Washington, D. C. for South Asian Studies: Afghanistan, Bangladesh, Bhutan, India, Maldives, Nepal, Pakistan, & Sri Lanka. LC 81-607847. (Scholar's Guide to Washington D.C. Ser.: No. 8). 438p. 1991. pap. 12.95 (0-87474-777-5); text 29.95 (0-87474-778-3) W Wilson Ctr Pr.
***Rahim, Jennifer.** Between the Fence & the Forest. 88p. 1999. pap. (1-900715-27-9, Pub. by VU Univ Pr) Paul & Co Pubs.
Rahim, Lily Z. The Singapore Dilemma: The Political & Educational Marginality of the Malay Community. LC 98-21652. (South-East Asian Social Science Monographs). (Illus.). 320p. 1999. text 49.95 (983-56-0032-5) OUP.
Rahim, M. A. Jesus the Prophet of Islam. 1990. pap. 14.95 (1-56744-500-4) Kazi Pubns.
Rahim, M. A., jt. auth. see Al-Sultan, Khaled S.
Rahim, M. Afzalur. Managing Conflict in Organizations. 2nd ed. LC 92-7479. 248p. 1992. 57.95 (0-275-93680-5, C3680, Praeger Pubs) Greenwood.
***Rahim, M. Afzalur.** Managing Conflict in Organizations. 3rd ed. LC 00-37271. 225p. 2000. 67.00 (1-56720-262-4, Q262, Quorum Bks) Greenwood.
Rahim, M. Afzalur, ed. Managing Conflict: An Interdisciplinary Approach. LC 88-14104. 348p. 1989. 65.00 (0-275-92683-4, C2683, Praeger Pubs) Greenwood.
— Theory & Research in Conflict Management. LC 90-31212. 264p. 1990. 59.95 (0-275-93173-0, C3173, Praeger Pubs) Greenwood.
Rahim, M. Afzalur, et al, eds. Current Topics in Management, Vol. 2. 1997. 78.50 (0-7623-0122-8) Jai Pr.
Rahim, M. Afzalur & Blum, Albert A., eds. Global Perspectives on Organizational Conflict. LC 93-11874. 168p. 1994. 57.95 (0-275-93828-X, Praeger Pubs) Greenwood.
Rahim, Omar, jt. auth. see Chatrath, Paul.
Rahim, Rend, jt. auth. see Fuller, Graham.
Rahimi, Mansour & Karwowski, Waldemar, eds. Human-Robot Interaction. 400p. 1992. 110.00 (0-85066-809-3, Pub. by Tay Francis Ltd) Taylor & Francis.
Rahimieh, Nasrin. Oriental Responses to the West: Comparative Essays in Select Writers from the Muslim World. x, 124p. 1990. pap. 49.50 (90-04-09177-7) Brill Academic Pubs.
Rahimov, Ibrahim. Random Sums & Branching Stochastic Processes. LC 95-2595. (Lecture Notes in Statistics Ser.: Vol. 96). 1995. 48.95 (0-387-94446-X) Spr-Verlag.
Rahimtoola, Shahbudin, jt. auth. see McCall, David.
Rahimtoola, Shahbudin H., jt. auth. see Gersh, Bernard.
Rahimtoola, Shahbudin H., jt. auth. see Yellon, Derek M.
Rahimtoola, Shahbudin H., jt. ed. see Braunwald, Eugene.
Rahimuddin, Muhammad, tr. see Salik, S. A.
Rahina, Rustam N. A Manual of English-Gujarati Dictionary. 1981. write for info. (0-8288-1769-3) Fr & Eur.
Rahinantti, K. Finnish-Portuguese-Finnish Dictionary. (FIN & POR.). 359p. 1975. pap. 69.95 (0-8288-5889-6, M9649) Fr & Eur.
Rahir, Edouard. Catalogue D'une Collection Unique de Volumes Imprimes Par les Elsevier et Divers Typographes Hollandais du XVII Siecle. (FRE.). 491p. 1998. reprint ed. 65.00 (1-57898-113-1) Martino Pubng.
Rahkonen, Carl. Film & Video Resources in Ethnomusicology: An Annotated Filmography. Porter, James, ed. (Garland Library of Music Ethnologies). 200p. Date not set. 30.00 (0-8153-0394-7) Garland.
Rahkonen, Carl John, jt. see Hartsock, Ralph.
Rahl, Inder, jt. ed. see Fisher, Dennis G.
Rahlens, Holly-Jane. Becky Bernstein Goes Berlin. LC 97-9453. 256p. 1997. 22.45 (1-55970-381-4, Pub. by Arcade Pub Inc) Time Warner.
Rahm, Debra L., jt. auth. see Burger, Leslie.
Rahm, Dianne, ed. The Politics of Toxic Waste. (Policy Studies Journal: Vol. 26:4). 1998. pap. write for info. (0-944285-57-0) Pol Studies.
Rahm, Dianne & Lambright, W. Henry, eds. Technology & American Competitiveness. (Orig.). 1989. pap. 15.00 (0-944285-12-0) Pol Studies.
***Rahm, Dianne, et al.** University-Industry R&D Collaboration in the United States, the United Kingdom & Japan. LC 99-51946. (Library of Public Policy & Public Administration). 1999. write for info. (0-7923-6073-7) Kluwer Academic.
Rahm, Dianne, jt. ed. see Lambright, W. Henry.
Rahm, Dick, jt. auth. see Tamburin, Henry J.
Rahmaan, Fred K. The Eye Opener: The African American in the Bible. 42p. 1995. write for info. (0-9627663-2-1) Designer Comns.
Rahman, A. History of Indian Science, Technology & Culture: Ad 1000-1800. LC 99-935800. (Project of History of Indian Science, Philosophy & Culture Ser.). (Illus.). 466p. 1999. text 42.00 (0-19-564652-5) OUP.
— The Mojo & the Sayso. 1990. pap. 6.95 (0-88145-086-3) Broadway Play.
— Studies in Natural Products Chemistry: Stereoselective Synthesis, Pt. E. (Studies in Natural Products Chemistry: Vol. 8). 500p. 1991. 270.50 (0-444-88967-1) Elsevier.
Rahman, A., ed. Studies in Natural Products Chemistry: Stereoselective Synthesis, Vol. 6, Pt. D. 606p. 1990. 299.50 (0-444-88566-8) Elsevier.
— Studies in Natural Products Chemistry: Structure & Chemistry. (Studies & Natural Products Chemistry: Vol. 7). 528p. 1990. 284.00 (0-444-88829-2) Elsevier.
Rahman, A. U. Handbook of Natural Products Data Vol. 3: Isoquinoline Alkaloids. 784p. 1994. 490.75 (0-444-81888-X) Elsevier.
— Studies in Natural Products Chemistry: Stereoselective Synthesis, Vol. 1. 718p. 1992. 382.25 (0-444-89558-2) Elsevier.
— Studies in Natural Products Chemistry: Stereoselective Synthesis, Vol. 1. 528p. 1993. 312.50 (0-444-89366-0) Elsevier.
— Studies in Natural Products Chemistry: Structure & Chemistry, Vol. 9. 632p. 1991. 332.25 (0-444-89165-X) Elsevier.
— Studies in Natural Products Chemistry Vol. 11, Pt. G: Stereoselective Synthesis. 504p. 1992. 294.00 (0-444-89744-5) Elsevier.
Rahman, A. U., ed. Diterpenoid & Steroidal Alkaloids. (Handbook of Natural Products Data Ser.: Vol. 1). 970p. 559.25 (0-444-88173-5) Elsevier.
— Studies in Natural Products Chemistry: Stereoselective Synthesis, Pt. J. 772p. 1995. 484.00 (0-444-82264-X) Elsevier.
— Studies in Natural Products Chemistry: Stereoselective Synthesis, Vol. 14, Pt. 1. 938p. 1994. 507.50 (0-444-81780-8) Elsevier.
Rahman, A. U. & Basha, F. Z. Studies in Natural Products Chemistry Vol. 13: Bioactive Natural Products, Pt. A. 694p. 1993. 395.25 (0-444-89937-5) Elsevier.
Rahman, A. U., jt. auth. see Ahmad, Viqar U.
Rahman, Afzalur. Encyclopaedia of Seerah 1-8. 1989. 65.00 (0-907052-14-2) Kazi Pubns.
— Encyclopaedia of Seerah 1-8. 1989. 65.00 (0-907052-16-9) Kazi Pubns.
— Encyclopaedia of Seerah 1-8. 1989. 65.00 (0-907052-17-7) Kazi Pubns.
— Encyclopaedia of Seerah 1-8. 1989. 65.00 (0-907052-22-3) Kazi Pubns.
— Encyclopaedia of Seerah 1-8. 1991. 65.00 (0-907052-24-X) Kazi Pubns.
— Encyclopaedia of Seerah 1-8. 1991. 65.00 (0-907052-32-0) Kazi Pubns.
— Encyclopaedia of Seerah 1-8. 1991. 65.00 (0-907052-34-7) Kazi Pubns.
— Encyclopaedia of Seerah 1-8. 1991. 65.00 (0-935782-95-8) Kazi Pubns.
— Essentials of Islam: The Faith & Worship. 166p. 1982. pap. 6.50 (0-935782-97-4) Kazi Pubns.
— Muhammad: Encyclopedia of Seerah, Vols. 1-7. 1000p. 1996. 55.00 (0-614-21091-7, 815) Kazi Pubns.
— Muhammad As a Military Leader. 1993. pap. 16.50 (1-56744-146-7) Kazi Pubns.
— Subject Index of Holy Quran. 1992. 19.95 (0-933511-68-X) Kazi Pubns.
— Utility of Prayers. 1994. pap. 4.50 (0-933511-84-1) Kazi Pubns.
Rahman, Afzulur. Islam Ideology & a Way of Life. 1991. pap. 18.95 (0-907052-04-5) Kazi Pubns.
***Rahman, Aminur.** Women & Microcredit in Rural Bangladesh: Anthropological Study of the Rhetoric & Realities of Grameen Bank Lending. LC 99-38235. 188p. 1999. 59.00 (0-8133-3713-5) Westview.
***Rahman, Anika.** Female Genital Mutilation. 2000. pap. 25.00 (1-85649-773-9, Pub. by Zed Books); text 65.00 (1-85649-772-0, Pub. by Zed Books) St Martin.
Rahman, Anika, ed. see Boland, Reed.
Rahman, Anika, jt. ed. see Waisman, Viviana.
Rahman, Anisur. East & West Pakistan: A Problem in the Political Economy of Regional Planning. LC 74-38766. (Harvard University. Center for International Affairs. Occasional Papers in International Affairs: No. 20). reprint ed. 27.50 (0-404-54620-X) AMS Pr.
— Expressive Form in the Poetry of Kamala Das. 1981. 10.00 (0-8364-0730-X, Pub. by Abhinav) S Asia.
— Form & Value in the Poetry of Nissim Ezekiel. 1981. 10.00 (0-8364-0731-8, Pub. by Abhinav) S Asia.
— People's Self Development: Perspectives on Participatory Action Research. LC 93-37607. 256p. (C). 1993. text 65.00 (1-85649-079-3, Pub. by Zed Books); text 25.00 (1-85649-080-7, Pub. by Zed Books) St Martin.
Rahman, Atiur. Peasants & Classes: A Study in Differentiation in Bangladesh. 272p. (C). 1987. pap. 17.50 (0-86232-346-0, Pub. by Zed Books); text 49.95 (0-86232-345-2, Pub. by Zed Books) St Martin.
Rahman, Atta-ur, ed. Advances in Natural Product Chemistry. LC 92-23126. 498p. 1992. text 205.00 (3-7186-5319-2) Gordon & Breach.
Rahman, Attaur & Choudhary, M. Iqbal. New Trends in Natural Product Chemistry. 288p. 1998. text 44.00 (90-5702-287-7, Harwood Acad Pubs) Gordon & Breach.
Rahman, D. H. Making of the Gulf War: Origins of Kuwait's Long-Standing Territorial Dispute with Iraq. 1998. 45.00 (0-86372-207-5, Pub. by Garnet-Ithaca) LPC InBook.
Rahman, Fazlur. Health & Medicine in the Islamic Tradition: Change & Identity. LC 99-216697. 156p. (C). 1997. pap. 15.95 (1-871031-64-8) Kazi Pubns.
— Islam. 285p. 1996. pap. 14.50 (0-614-21416-5, 532) Kazi Pubns.
— Islam. 2nd ed. LC 78-68547. 296p. 1979. pap. text 12.00 (0-226-70281-2) U Ch Pr.
— Islam & Modernity: Transformation of an Intellectual Tradition. LC 82-2720. (Publications of the Center for Middle Eastern Studies: No. 15). 182p. 1984. pap. text 13.95 (0-226-70284-7) U Ch Pr.
— Major Themes of the Qur'an. 190p. 1996. pap. 19.95 (0-614-21060-7, 1534) Kazi Pubns.
— Major Themes of the Qur'an. 2nd ed. LC 79-54189. 1994. 25.00 (0-88297-051-8); pap. 16.00 (0-88297-046-1) Bibliotheca.
— The Philosophy of Mulla Sadra Shirazi. LC 75-31693. 277p. (C). 1976. text 24.50 (0-87395-300-2) State U NY Pr.
— Prophecy in Islam: Philosophy & Orthodoxy. LC 78-66082. (Midway Reprint Ser.). 1992. pap. text 9.00 (0-226-70282-0) U Ch Pr.
— Prophecy in Islam: Philosophy & Orthodoxy. LC 78-66082. (Midway Reprint Ser.). 118p. reprint ed. pap. 36.60 (0-608-09506-0, 205430700005) Bks Demand.
***Rahman, Fazlur.** Revival & the Reform of Islam: A Study of Islamic Fundamentalism. Moosa, Ebrahim, ed. & intro. by. 224p. 1999. pap. 23.95 (1-85168-204-X, Pub. by Element MA) Penguin Putnam.
Rahman, G. Arthur. Sea of Mystery. (Illus.). 1981. 5.95 (0-940244-14-4) Flying Buffalo.
Rahman, Guljan, jt. auth. see Ur-Rahman, Mushtaq.
Rahman, Habib U. Chronology of Islamic History. 256p. (C). 1989. 50.00 (0-8161-9067-4, Hall Reference) Macmillan.
Rahman, Hossain Z. & Hossain, Mahabub, eds. Rethinking Rural Poverty: Bangladesh As a Case Study. LC 94-23400. 292p. 1995. 25.95 (0-8039-9205-X) Sage.
Rahman, Leila B., ed. Singapore Property Tax Cases (1959-1986) xxii, 413p. 1987. 99.00 (9971-70-057-3, MICHIE) LEXIS Pub.
Rahman, M. Agriculture in Pakistan. 150p. 1988. 75.00 (963-05-4608-6, Pub. by Akade Kiado) St Mut.
— Applied Differential Equations for Scientists & Engineers, 2 vols., Set. LC 91-76270. 1991. text 178.00 (1-56252-056-3, 0952) Computational Mech MA.
Rahman, M. Applied Differential Equations for Scientists & Engineers Vol. 1: Ordinary Differential Equations. 656p. 1997. 130.00 (1-85312-124-X) Computational Mech MA.
Rahman, M. Applied Differential Equations for Scientists & Engineers Vol. 2: Partial Differential Equations. LC 91-76270. 356p. 1991. text 69.00 (1-56252-058-X, 1258) Computational Mech MA.
Rahman, M. Applied Differential Equations for Scientists & Engineers Vol. 2: Partial Differential Equations. 356p. 1994. reprint ed. 69.00 (1-85312-125-8) Computational Mech MA.
— Mathematical Methods: With Applications. 450p. 2000. 155.00 (1-85312-847-3, Pub. by WIT Pr) Computational Mech MA.
Rahman, M. Water Waves: Relating Modern Theory to Advanced Engineering Practice, 3. (Institute of Mathematics & Its Applications Monograph). (Illus.). 356p. 1995. text 85.00 (0-19-853478-7) OUP.
Rahman, M., ed. Ocean Waves Engineering. 240p. 1994. 117.00 (1-85312-285-8) Computational Mech MA.
Rahman, M., ed. Ocean Waves Engineering. LC 94-70414. (Advances in Fluid Mechanics Ser.: Vol. 2). 240p. 1994. 117.00 (1-56252-209-4, 2858) Computational Mech MA.
Rahman, M., ed. Potential Flow of Fluids. 264p. 1995. 121.00 (1-85312-356-0) Computational Mech MA.
Rahman, M., et al, eds. Advances in Fluid Mechanics II. LC 98-84063. (Advances in Fluid Mechanics Ser.: Vol. 21). 392p. 1998. 196.00 (1-85312-589-X, 589X) Computational Mech MA.
Rahman, M. & Brebbia, Carlos A., eds. Advances in Fluid Mechanics III, Vol. 26. 744p. 2000. 355.00 (1-85312-813-9, 8139) Computational Mech MA.
Rahman, M., jt. auth. see Gasper, G.
Rahman, M. A., ed. Potential Flow of Fluids. LC 95-68891. (Advances in Fluid Mechanics Ser.: Vol. 6). 264p. 1995. text 121.00 (1-56252-279-5, 3560) Computational Mech MA.
Rahman, M. D. & Rahman, Shafiur, eds. Food Properties Handbook. LC 95-17493. (Contemporary Food Science Ser.). 528p. 1995. boxed set 169.95 (0-8493-8005-7, 8005C2W) CRC Pr.
***Rahman, M. Golam.** Communication Issues in Bangladesh LC 99-934560. 177p. 1999. 0.00 (81-241-0603-7, Pub. by Har-Anand Pubns) S Asia.
Rahman, M. M., et al, eds. Amorphous & Crystalline Silicon Carbide II. (Proceedings in Physics Ser.: Vol. 43). (Illus.). x, 232p. 1989. 65.00 (0-387-51656-5, 3515) Spr-Verlag.
Rahman, M. Samsur. Administrative Elite in Bangladesh. (Illus.). vii, 361p. 1991. 27.00 (81-85445-02-8, Pub. by Manak Pubns Pvt Ltd) Nataraj Bks.
Rahman, M. Shafiur, ed. Handbook of Food Preservation. LC 98-49271. (Food Science & Technology Ser.). (Illus.). 824p. 1999. text 195.00 (0-8247-0209-3) Dekker.
Rahman, Matiur. Applied Differential Equations for Scientists & Engineers Vol. 1: Ordinary Differential Equations. LC 91-76270. 656p. 1991. text 130.00 (1-56252-057-1, 124X) Computational Mech MA.
Rahman, Matiur. Complex Variables & Transform Calculus. LC 96-86041. 344p. 1997. text 152.00 (1-85312-491-5, 4915) Computational Mech MA.
Rahman, Michael & Reinhold, Michael. Why Rush Limbaugh Is Wrong: or The Demise of Traditionalism & the Rise of Progressive Sensibility. LC 95-77891. 160p. 1998. 16.00 (0-9647470-0-6) Mighty Pen.
Rahman, Mohammad A. Guide to ATM Systems & Technlogy: Communications Systems Engineering. LC 98-36741. 1998. 73.00 (0-89006-306-0) Artech Hse.
Rahman, Mohammed M. Betrayal of Intellect in Higher Education. LC 97-218605. 174p. 1998. pap. text. write for info. (0-9682479-0-3) Omniview Pub.
***Rahman, Momin.** Sexuality & Democracy: Identities & Strategies in Lesbian & Gay Politics. 224p. 2000. pap. text 23.00 (0-7486-0958-X) Col U Pr.
Rahman, Muhammad A., jt. ed. see Fals-Borda, Orlando.
Rahman, Mushtaqur. Divided Kashmir: Old Problems, New Opportunities for India, Pakistan, & the Kashmiri People. 219p. 1996. 47.00 (1-55587-589-0) L Rienner.
Rahman, Mushtaqur, ed. Muslim World: Geography & Development. LC 87-14087. (Illus.). 202p. (Orig.). (C). 1987. pap. text 21.50 (0-8191-6559-X); lib. bdg. 38.00 (0-8191-6558-1) U Pr of Amer.
Rahman, Mustafizur. Biological Nitrogen Fixation Associated With Rice Production. LC 96-31600. (Developments in Plant & Soil Sciences Ser.). 1996. text 132.50 (0-7923-4197-X) Kluwer Academic.
Rahman, N. From Molecular Dynamics to Combustion Chemistry: Proceedings of the Conference. 368p. 1992. text 105.00 (981-02-1146-5) World Scientific Pub.
Rahman, N. A. A Course in Theoretical Statistics. 542p. 1968. text 26.95 (0-85264-068-4) Lubrecht & Cramer.
— Practical Exercises in Probability & Statistics: With Answers & Hints on Solutions. 1972. 30.00 (0-85264-217-2) Lubrecht & Cramer.
Rahman, N. K. & Guidotti, C., eds. Collisions & Half-Collisions with Lasers. xiv, 420p. 1984. text 332.00 (3-7186-0192-3) Gordon & Breach.
— Photon-Assisted Collisions & Related Topics. 355p. 1982. text 274.00 (3-7186-0130-3) Gordon & Breach.
Rahman, Philip J., ed. see Wandrei, Donald.
Rahman, Philip J., ed. see Wandrel, Donald.
Rahman, S. S. & Chilingarian, G. V. Casing Design: Theory & Practice. LC 94-39740. (Developments in Petroleum Science Ser.: Vol. 42). 388p. 1994. 211.25 (0-444-81743-3) Elsevier.
Rahman, Shafiur, jt. ed. see Rahman, M. D.
Rahman, Sharif, ed. Fatigue, Fracture & Residual Stresses: Proceedings, A=SME/JSME Joint Pressure Vessels & Piping Conference (1998, San Diego, CA) LC 98-208926. 373. 530p. 1998. pap. 120.00 (0-7918-1869-1) ASME.
Rahman, Sharif, et al, eds. Fatigue & Fracture, 1997: Proceedings ASME Pressure Vessels & Piping Conference (1997, Orlando, FL), Vol. 2. LC 97-72852. (PVP Ser.: Vol. 346). 325p. 1997. pap. 120.00 (0-7918-1562-5) ASME.
Rahman, Sultan H. Macroeconomic Performance, Stabilization & Adjustment: The Experience of Bangladesh in the 1980s. (C). 1992. 12.00 (81-85182-74-4, Pub. by Indus Pub) S Asia.
***Rahman, Syed M. & Raisinghani, Mahesh, eds.** Electronic Commerce: Opportunity & Challenge. LC 99-59766. (Illus.). 418p. (C). 2000. pap. 74.95 (1-878289-76-4) Idea Group Pub.
Rahman, Syedur, jt. auth. see Baxter, Craig.
Rahman, Tariq. Language & Politics in Pakistan. LC 97-930020. (Illus.). 340p. 1997. text 32.00 (0-19-577692-5) OUP.
— Language, Education & Culture. LC 99-921800. 336p. 1999. 26.95 (0-19-579146-0) OUP.
— The Legacy & Other Short Stories. Narang, Harish, ed. (C). 1989. 29.00 (0-8364-2472-7) S Asia.
Rahmani, Bijan M., jt. auth. see Hogan, William W.
Rahmani, Levy. Soviet Psychology: Philosophical, Theoretical & Experimental Issues. LC 72-182041. 560p. 1973. 65.00 (0-8236-6110-5) Intl Univs Pr.

An Asterisk (*) at the beginning of an entry indicates that the title is appearing for the first time.

Rahmani, M. & Strutt, J. E. Hydrodynamic Modeling of Corrosion of Carbon Steels & Cast Irons in Sulfuric Acid. LC 92-80991. (MTI Publication Ser.: No. T-2). (Illus.). 269p. 1992. reprint ed. pap. 83.40 (*0-608-06735-0*, 2066932) Bks Demand.
— Hydrodynamic Modelling of Corrosion of Carbon Steels & Cast Irons in Sulphuric Acid. LC TN0757.. 212p. reprint ed. pap. 65.80 (*0-8357-6992-5*, 203756500010) Bks Demand.
Rahmani, Ray A. & Flores, Romeo M., eds. Sedimentology of Coal & Coal-Bearing Sequences. 396p. 1985. pap. 75.00 (*0-632-01286-2*) Blackwell Sci.
Rahmann, H., ed. Gangliosides & Modulation of Neuronal Functions. (NATO ASI Series H: Vol. 7). xvi, 647p. 1987. 153.00 (*0-387-17587-3*) Spr-Verlag.
Rahmann, H. & Rahmann, M. The Neurobiological Basis of Memory & Behavior. (Illus.). 272p. 1992. 125.00 (*0-387-97545-4*) Spr-Verlag.
Rahmann, Heinrich, ed. Fundamentals of Memory Formation: Neuronal Plasticity & Brain Function. (Progress in Zoology/Fortschritte der Zoologie Ser.: Vol. 37). 431p. 1990. 195.00 (*0-89574-297-7*, Pub. by Gustav Fischer) Balogh.
Rahmann, M., jt. auth. see Rahmann, H.
Rahmas, Sigrid. Mother Sun & Her Planet Children. (Illus.). 32p. (Orig.). (J). (ps-3). 1991. 6.25 (*0-87157-099-8*); pap. 2.95 (*0-87157-599-X*) Story Hse Corp.
Rahmat-Samii, Yahya & Michielssen, Eric, eds. Electromagnetic System Design Using Evolutionary Optimization. LC 98-38414. 480p. 1999. 89.95 (*0-471-29545-0*) Wiley.
Rahmat-Samii, Yahya, jt. auth. see Hoppe, Daniel J.
Rahmatian, Sassan. Management Information Systems: Learning Exercises & Applications. LC 94-32648. (William R. King Series in Information Management). 304p. 1994. pap. text 38.60 (*0-13-172702-8*) P-H.
Rahmato, Dessalegn. Agrarian Reform in Ethiopia. 105p. 1984. 17.95 (*91-7106-226-2*, Pub. by Nordic Africa) Transaction Pubs.
— Agrarian Reform in Ethiopia. per. 7.95 (*0-932415-07-5*) Red Sea Pr.
— Agrarian Reform in Ethiopia. 106p. 1985. 19.95 (*0-932415-06-7*) Red Sea Pr.
— Faminie & Survival Strategies: A Case Study of Northeast Ethiopia. 256p. 1991. pap. text 24.95 (*91-7106-314-5*) Transaction Pubs.
Rahmatullah Khan. The Iran-United States Claims Tribunal: Controversies, Cases & Contribution. (C). 1990. lib. bdg. 136.00 (*0-7923-0633-3*) Kluwer Academic.
Rahmberg-Walsh, Elizabeth, jt. auth. see Cohen, Fred.
Rahme, Lotta & Hartman, Dag. Leather: Preparation & Tanning by Traditional Methods. Thompson, Jack C., ed. Greenebaum, David, tr. from SWE. LC 95-71505. (Illus.). 100p. (C). 1996. text 24.95 (*1-887719-00-8*) Caber Pr.
***Rahmel, Dan.** Building Web Database Applications. 860p. 1999. pap. 44.99 (*0-07-212094-0*) McGraw.
— MSDE Developer's Guide. (Illus.). 600p. 2000. pap. text 39.95 (*0-7645-4698-8*) IDG Bks.
Rahmel, Dan. Sams' Teach Yourself Database Programming with Visual Basic 6 in 24 Hours. LC 98-86256. (Sams' Teach Yourself Ser.). 400p. 1998. 19.99 (*0-672-31409-6*, Pub. by Macmillan) S&S Trade.
— Server Scripts with Visual Java Script. LC 98-29951. 508p. 1998. pap. 39.95 incl. cd-rom (*0-07-913694-X*) McGraw.
— Visual Basic Programmer's Reference. LC 98-136324. (Programmer's Reference Ser.). 448p. 1997. pap. 16.99 (*0-07-882458-3*) Osborne-McGraw.
— Visual Basic 6: Programmer's Reference. 2nd ed. LC 99-162556. (Programmer's Reference Ser.). 416p. 1998. pap. 16.99 (*0-07-882576-8*) Osborne-McGraw.
Rahming, D'Arcy. The College Student's Complete Guide to Self-Protection. Baarman, Jenifer H., ed. (Illus.). 160p. (Orig.). 1992. pap. 14.95 (*0-9627898-2-8*) Mdrn Bu-Jutsu.
— Secrets of Advanced Combat Ju-Jutsu. 2nd ed. Baarman, Jenifer H., ed. Orig. Title: Advanced Combat Ju-Jutsu - Entrance to Secrets. (Illus.). 228p. 1994. pap. 24.95 (*0-9627898-8-7*) Mdrn Bu-Jutsu.
— Secrets of Black Belt Combat Ju-Jitsu. Couper, Benita, ed. (Illus.). 256p. 1996. pap. 28.95 (*1-886219-01-X*) Mdrn Bu-Jutsu.
— Secrets of Miyama Ryu Combat: Combat Ju-Jutsu - The Lost Art. 2nd ed. Orig. Title: Combat Ju-Jutsu - The Lost Art. 160p. 1995. pap. 18.95 (*1-886219-00-1*) Mdrn Bu-Jutsu.
Rahming, D'Arcy, jt. auth. see Hinton, William.
Rahmings, Keith. Printouts. 36p. (Orig.). 1981. pap. 5.50 (*0-937013-06-4*) Potes Poets.
Rahmlow, Harold F. The Teaching-Learning Unit. Langdon, Danny G., ed. LC 77-25107. (Instructional Design Library). (Illus.). 88p. 1978. 27.95 (*0-87778-122-2*) Educ Tech Pubns.
Rahmlow, Harold F., et al. Plato. Langdon, Danny G., ed. LC 79-26395. (Instructional Design Library). 112p. 1980. 27.95 (*0-87778-150-8*) Educ Tech Pubns.
Rahmlow, Lavina. Granny Glee & the Bear-Off Bear. LC 97-91040. (Illus.). 61p. (J). 1998. 13.95 (*0-533-12535-9*) Vantage.
Rahmy, M., jt. auth. see Droz, R.
Rahn. The Wizard of Oz. 1998. pap. 13.95 (*0-8057-8644-9*) Mac Lib Ref.
— The Wizard of Oz: Shaping an Imaginary World. LC 98-6751. 158p. 1998. 29.00 (*0-8057-8623-6*) Mac Lib Ref.
Rahn, Armin. The Basics of Soldering. LC 92-36407. 400p. 1993. 145.00 (*0-471-58471-1*) Wiley.
Rahn, Arthur & Heartwell, Charles M., Jr. Textbook of Complete Dentures. 5th ed. (Illus.). 541p. 1993. text 65.95 (*0-8121-1523-6*) Lppncott W & W.
Rahn, B. J., ed. Ngaio Marsh: The Woman & Her Work. LC 95-5785. (Illus.). 274p. 1995. 34.50 (*0-8108-3023-X*) Scarecrow.
Rahn, Bob. Tempting Fate: An Experimental Test Pilot's Story. 1997. 9.95 (*0-933424-81-7*) Specialty Pr.
Rahn, Carl. The Relation of Sensation to Other Categories in Contemporary Psychology. (Psychology Monographs General & Applied: Vol. 16). 1974. reprint ed. pap. 55.00 (*0-8115-1415-3*) Periodicals Srv.
Rahn, Claude J. Hornberger: Genealogical Information Regarding the Families of Hornberger & Yingling, & Related Families of Eckert, Lenhart, Steffy, Gerwig & Rahn. 164p. 1992. reprint ed. pap. 26.00 (*0-8328-2671-5*) Higginson Bk Co.
— Hornberger: Genealogical Information Regarding the Families of Hornberger & Yingling, & Related Families of Eckert, Lenhart, Steffy, Gerwig & Rahn. 164p. 1995. reprint ed. lib. bdg. 36.00 (*0-8328-2670-7*) Higginson Bk Co.
Rahn, Daniel & Evans, Janine, eds. Lyme Disease. 5th ed. LC 97-3304. (Key Diseases Ser.). 254p. (Orig.). (C). 1998. pap. text 35.00 (*0-943126-58-4*) Amer Coll Phys.
Rahn, Frank J., et al. A Guide to Nuclear Power Technology: A Resource for Decision Making. LC 91-22459. 1000p. (C). 1992. reprint ed. lib. bdg. 145.00 (*0-89464-652-4*) Krieger.
Rahn, Herman & Prakash, Omar, eds. Acid-Base Regulation & Body Temperature. (Developments in Critical Care, Medicine, & Anesthesiology Ser.). 1985. text 154.00 (*0-89838-708-6*) Kluwer Academic.
Rahn, Herman, jt. ed. see Fenn, Wallace O.
Rahn, John. Basic Atonal Theory. 168p. 1987. 22.00 (*0-02-873160-3*, Schirmer Books) Mac Lib Ref.
Rahn, John, ed. Perspectives on Musical Aesthetics. (C). 1995. pap. 18.95 (*0-393-96508-2*) Norton.
Rahn, K. A., ed. Arctic Air Chemistry: Proceedings of the Second Symposium, Graduate School of Oceanography, University of Rhode Island, 6-8 May, 1980. (Atmospheric Environment Ser.: Vol. 15, No. 8). iv, 172p. 1981. pap. 36.00 (*0-08-026288-0*, Pergamon Pr) Elsevier.
Rahn, K. H., jt. auth. see Bonner, Gerd.
Rahn, Melanie. The Write Connection: Love a Child by Mail. (Illus.). (Orig.). (J). (gr. k-8). 1989. pap., ring bd. 16.85 (*0-614-30250-1*) Write Connect.
Rahn, Mikala L. & Hoachlander, E. Gareth. Getting to Work: A Guide for Better Schools. (Practitioner's Guide Ser.). (Illus.). 1087p. 1995. ring bd. 275.00 (*0-9662883-3-5*); ring bd. 65.00 (*0-9662883-5-1*); ring bd. 65.00 (*0-9662883-6-X*); ring bd. 65.00 (*0-9662883-7-8*); ring bd. 65.00 (*0-9662883-8-6*); ring bd. 65.00 (*0-9662883-9-4*) MPR Assocs.
— Getting to Work - Supplements: A Guide for Better Schools. (Illus.). 80p. 1995. ring bd. 12.00 (*0-9662883-1-9*) MPR Assocs.
Rahn, Perry H. Engineering Geology. 2nd ed. 657p. (C). 1996. 95.00 (*0-13-177403-4*) P-H.
— Engineering Geology: An Environmental Approach. 608p. 1986. 60.25 (*0-444-00942-6*) P-H.
Rahn, Richard. Evolve Yourself: Conscious Personal Evolution; An Introduction. LC 99-207932. 1999. pap. text. write for info. (*0-9665593-0-4*) DUH Bks.
Rahn, Richard W. The End of Money: And the Struggle for Financial Privacy. 223p. 1999. 25.00 (*0-9638654-2-0*, Pub. by Discov Inst) Herveys Bklink.
Rahn, Suzanne. Rediscoveries in Children's Literature. LC 94-39594. (Studies in Children's Literature: Vol. 2). (Illus.). 224p. 1995. text 44.00 (*0-8153-0930-9*, SS862) Garland.
Rahnama-Moghadam, Mashaalah, et al. Doing Business in Less Developed Countries: Financial Opportunities & Risks. LC 94-24986. 224p. 1995. 62.95 (*0-89930-854-6*, Quorum Bks) Greenwood.
Rahnejat, Homer. Multi-Body Dynamics: Vehicles, Machines & Mechanisms. LC 98-85951. 368p. 1998. 69.00 (*0-7680-0269-9*, R-238) Soc Auto Engineers.
Rahnema. An Islamic Utopian. 418p. 2000. text 59.50 (*1-86064-118-0*, Pub. by I B T) St Martin.
***Rahnema, Ali.** An Islamic Utopian: A Political Biography of Ali Shariati. 2000. pap. 22.50 (*1-86064-552-6*, Pub. by I B T) St Martin.
Rahnema, Ali, ed. Pioneers of Islamic Revival. (Studies in Islamic Society). 272p. (C). 1994. text 65.00 (*1-85649-253-2*, Pub. by Zed Books); text 25.00 (*1-85649-254-0*, Pub. by Zed Books) St Martin.
Rahnema, Majid & Bawtree, Victoria, compiled by. The Post-Development Reader. LC 96-25685. 384p. 1997. pap. 25.00 (*1-85649-474-8*, Pub. by Zed Books); text 65.00 (*1-85649-473-X*, Pub. by Zed Books) St Martin.
Rahnema, Saeed & Behdad, Sohrab, eds. Iran after the Revolution: Crisis of an Islamic State. 256p. 1996. pap. 19.95 (*1-86064-128-8*) St Martin.
Rahner, Hugo. Church & State in Early Christianity. Davis, Leo D., tr. from GER. LC 91-76752. 342p. 1992. pap. 16.95 (*0-89870-377-8*) Ignatius Pr.
— Greek Myths & Christian Mystery. LC 79-156736. (Illus.). 1971. reprint ed. 32.00 (*0-8196-0270-1*) Biblo.
— Ignatius the Theologian. 2nd ed. LC 90-60756. 246p. 1990. pap. text 15.95 (*0-89870-290-9*) Ignatius Pr.
Rahner, Karl. Anointing of the Sick. 1979. pap. 4.95 (*0-87193-108-7*) Dimension Bks.
— Baptism. 1979. pap. 4.95 (*0-87193-120-6*) Dimension Bks.
— The Church & the Sacraments. 188p. 1994. pap. 30.00 (*0-86012-005-8*, Pub. by Srch Pr) St Mut.
— Confirmation. 1979. pap. 4.95 (*0-87193-123-0*) Dimension Bks.
— Encounters with Silence. 94p. 1994. pap. 21.00 (*0-86012-018-X*, Pub. by Srch Pr) St Mut.
— Encounters with Silence. Demske, James M., tr. from GER. LC 99-19018. 96p. 1999. reprint ed. pap. 9.00 (*1-890318-22-1*) St Augustines Pr.
— Eternal Yes. 1979. pap. 4.95 (*0-87193-119-2*) Dimension Bks.
— Eucharist. 1970. pap. 4.95 (*0-87193-106-0*) Dimension Bks.
— Foundations of Christian Faith: An Introduction to the Idea of Christianity. LC 82-4663. Vol. 1. 470p. 1982. pap. 37.50 (*0-8245-0523-9*) Crossroad NY.
— The Great Church Year: The Best of Karl Rahner's Homilies, Sermons, & Meditations. Raffelt, Albert & Egan, Harvey D., eds. LC 93-3930.Tr. of Grossenkirchenjahr. 384p. 1994. reprint ed. 29.95 (*0-8245-1228-6*); reprint ed. pap. 19.95 (*0-8245-1430-0*) Crossroad NY.
— Hearer of the Word. Donceel, Joseph, tr. from GER. LC 93-38427.Tr. of Horer des Wortes. 192p. 1994. pap. 24.95 (*0-8264-0647-5*) Continuum.
— Herder Theological Lexicon: Herder Theologisches Taschenlexikon. 9th ed. (GER.). 460p. 1983. 225.00 (*0-8288-2309-X*, M7463) Fr & Eur.
— Is Christian Life Possible Today? 1984. pap. 9.95 (*0-87193-210-5*) Dimension Bks.
— Kleines Theologisches Woerterbuch. (GER.). 29.95 (*0-7859-8372-4*, 3451088339) Fr & Eur.
— The Love of Jesus & the Love of Neighbor. (C). 1988. 39.00 (*0-85439-224-6*, Pub. by St Paul Pubns) St Mut.
— Marriage. 1970. pap. 4.95 (*0-87193-118-4*) Dimension Bks.
— Meditations on Freedom & the Spirit. 118p. 1994. pap. 21.00 (*0-86012-047-3*, Pub. by Srch Pr) St Mut.
— The Need & the Blessing of Prayer. Gilette, Bruce W., tr. LC 97-7368. 1997. pap. 9.95 (*0-8146-2453-7*) Liturgical Pr.
— Penance. 1998. pap. 4.95 (*0-87193-109-5*) Dimension Bks.
— Petit Dictionnaire de Theologie Catholique. (FRE.). 512p. 1970. 85.00 (*0-7859-7622-1*, 2020032392) Fr & Eur.
— Prayers for a Lifetime. 1994. pap. 24.95 (*0-567-29132-4*, Pub. by T & T Clark) Bks Intl VA.
— A Priest Forever. 1998. pap. 4.95 (*0-87193-115-X*) Dimension Bks.
***Rahner, Karl.** Samtliche Werke, Vol. 2. (GER.). 1998. 98.00 (*0-8245-2186-2*) Crossroad NY.
— Samtliche Werke, Vol. 3. Vol. 3. (GER.). 1998. 98.00 (*0-8245-2187-0*) Crossroad NY.
— Samtliche Werke, Vol. 8. (GER.). 1998. 98.00 (*0-8245-2192-7*) Crossroad NY.
— Samtliche Werke, Vol. 19. Vol. 19. (GER.). 1998. 98.00 (*0-8245-2228-1*) Crossroad NY.
Rahner, Karl. The Spirit in the Church. 3.95 (*0-8164-2189-7*) Crossroad NY.
— Theological Investigations, Vols. 1-17, 20. Incl. Vol. 2. Man & the Church. 1973. 29.50 (*0-8245-0378-3*); Vol. 7. Further Theology of the Spiritual Life I. 1973. 13.95 (*0-8245-0383-X*); Vol. 17. Jesus, Man & the Church. 1975. 29.50 (*0-8245-0026-1*); 1975. write for info. (*0-318-51489-3*) Crossroad NY.
— Theological Investigations Vol. 22: Humane Society & the Church of Tomorrow, Vol. 22. 288p. 1987. 29.50 (*0-8245-0924-2*) Crossroad NY.
— Theological Investigations Vol. 23: Final Writings, Vol. 23. 240p. 1992. 29.50 (*0-8245-1165-4*) Crossroad NY.
— Theology Investment. (Theological Investigations Ser.: Vol. 21). 352p. 1988. 29.50 (*0-8245-0888-2*) Crossroad NY.
— The Trinity. Doncell, Joseph, tr. LC 96-51964. 144p. 1997. pap. 18.95 (*0-8245-1627-3*, Herdr & Herdr) Crossroad NY.
— The Trinity. 140p. 1994. pap. 24.00 (*0-86012-015-5*, Pub. by Srch Pr) St Mut.
***Rahner, Karl.** Watch & Pray with Me: The Seven Last Words of Jesus Christ. LC 00-265445. 64p. 2000. pap. 9.95 (*0-8245-1840-3*) Crossroad NY.
Rahner, Karl, ed. Encyclopedia of Theology: A Concise Sacramental Mundi. 1850p. 1994. pap. 120.00 (*0-86012-228-X*, Pub. by Srch Pr) St Mut.
Rahner, Karl & Thusing, Wilhelm. A New Christology. 250p. 1994. 27.00 (*0-86012-081-3*, Pub. by Srch Pr) St Mut.
Rahner, Karl & Vorgrimler, Herbert. Small Theological Dictionary: Kleines Theologisches Woerterbuch. 15th ed. (GER.). 460p. 1985. pap. 24.95 (*0-8288-2310-3*, M7508) Fr & Eur.
Rahr, Alexander G., jt. auth. see Azrael, Jeremy R.
Rahr, Richard R. Appleton & Lange's Quick Review: Physician Assistant. 3rd ed. 325p. (C). 1996. pap. text 29.95 (*0-8385-8094-7*, A8094-3, Apple Lange Med) McGraw.
Rahrer, J. Stuart. Challenging How They Think: Intervention & Resolution of Adolescent Delinquent Behaviors & Conduct Problems. (Illus.). 66p. 1998. pap. 11.95 (*1-890897-17-5*) Pharos Consult.
— Fail-Safe Parenting: A Personalized, Foolproof Plan to Prevent or Stop Your Child's Alcohol-Drug Abuse . . . Now! LC 97-68306. (Illus.). 192p. (Orig.). 1998. pap. 24.95 (*1-890897-15-9*) Pharos Consult.
— The First Move: Determining If Your Child Is at Risk for Alcohol-Drug Abuse & What to Do About It. LC 97-69512. (New Parent Awareness Ser.: No. 1). (Illus.). 88p. (Orig.). 1997. pap. 14.95 (*1-890897-03-5*) Pharos Consult.
— The Goals for Recovery: How to Design an Individualized Addiction-Recovery Plan. (Addiction Recovery Ser.). (Illus.). 58p. 1998. pap. 9.95 (*1-890897-16-7*) Pharos Consult.
— Pinpointing: How to Detect Child or Teen Alcohol-Drug Use & What to Do about It. LC 97-92446. (New Parent Awareness Ser.: No. 3). (Illus.). 86p. (Orig.). 1997. pap. 14.95 (*1-890897-05-1*) Pharos Consult.
— Preparing for Tomorrow . . . Today! Designing a Personalized Plan to Prevent Your Child's Alcohol-Drug Abuse. LC 97-69513. (New Parent Awareness Ser.: No. 2). (Illus.). 88p. (Orig.). 1997. pap. 14.95 (*1-890897-01-9*) Pharos Consult.
— Seven Sensible Strategies for Drug-Free Kids. LC 99-28331. 1999. 24.95 (*0-87868-749-1*) Child Welfare.
— Solving the Dilemma: Intervention & Treatment of the Adult Offender with Chemical Dependency. LC 99-70148. (Illus.). 152p. 1999. pap. 19.95 (*1-890897-33-7*) Pharos Consult.
— Stop Before Start: Early Identification & Prevention of Child Delinquent Behaviors & Conduct Problems. LC 99-70147. (Illus.). 92p. 1999. pap. 14.95 (*1-890897-34-5*) Pharos Consult.
Rahrer, J. Stuart, 2nd. The Stop Book: Dealing Effectively with Child or Teen Alcohol-Drug Abuse. LC 97-69511. (New Parent Awareness Ser.: No. 4). (Illus.). 108p. (Orig.). 1997. pap. 16.95 (*1-890897-13-2*) Pharos Consult.
Rahrig, Charlotte. Faith Guarding Kids. 117p. 1996. 8.99 (*0-89274-976-8*, HH-976) Harrison Hse.
Rahrig, Charlotte A. The Glory of God. LC 97-92575. (Illus.). xviii, 158p. 1997. pap. 6.95 (*0-9660646-0-7*) C Rahrig Minist.
Raht, Carlysle G. Romance of Davis Mountains & Big Bend Country. 1993. reprint ed. lib. bdg. 75.00 (*0-7812-5896-0*) Rprt Serv.
Rahtjen, Bruce D. Biblical Truth & Today's World. 1995. pap. 12.95 (*0-9647079-1-8*) Trefoil Pr.
Rahtore, N. S. & Sukhadia, M. L., eds. Natural Resource Base Development. (C). 1991. 250.00 (*0-7855-6761-5*, Pub. by Scientific Pubs) St Mut.
Rahtz, P. Little Ouseburn Barrow, 1958. 127p. 1989. 13.95 (*0-614-21851-9*, Pub. by U York Dept Archaeol) David Brown.
Rahtz, P., et al. Two Roman Villas at Wharram Street. (Wharram Ser.: Vol. IV). 88p. 1986. 10.00 (*0-946722-07-2*, Pub. by U York Dept Archaeol) David Brown.
Rahtz, P., jt. ed. see Watts, L.
Rahtz, Philip. Invitation to Archaeology. 1985. pap. 19.95 (*0-85520-709-4*) Blackwell Pubs.
Rahtz, Philip, et al, eds. St. Mary's Church, Deerhurst, Gloucestershire: Fieldwork, Excavations & Structural Analysis, 1971-1984. LC 96-19670. (Report Research Committee Ser.: Vol. 55). (Illus.). 272p. 1997. 130.00 (*0-85115-687-8*) Boydell & Brewer.
Rahtz, Philip & Watts, L. Wharram Percy: The Memorial Stones of the Churchyard. (Wharram Ser.: Vol. II). 38p. 1983. 14.00 (*0-946722-00-5*, Pub. by U York Dept Archaeol) David Brown.
Rahtz, S. P. Information Technology in the Humanities: Tools, Techniques & Applications. (Computers & Their Applications Ser.). 210p. 1987. text 45.95 (*0-470-20852-X*) P-H.
***Rahul, Ram.** Central Asia: A Textbook History. (Illus.). 2000. 29.50 (*81-215-0888-6*, Pub. by M Manoharial) S Asia.
Rahul, Ram. Dalai Lama: The Institution. (C). 1995. 17.00 (*0-7069-8788-8*, Pub. by Vikas) S Asia.
— Modern Tibet. (C). 1992. 12.00 (*0-8364-2800-5*, Pub. by M Manoharial) S Asia.
— Mongolia: Between China & the U. S. S. R. 1989. 16.00 (*0-685-37831-4*, Pub. by M Manoharial) S Asia.
— Royal Nepal: A Political History. 1996. 14.00 (*81-259-0070-5*, Pub. by Vikas) S Asia.
Rahula, Bhikku T. A Critical Study of the Mahavastu. 1978. 16.95 (*0-89684-018-2*, Pub. by Motilal Bnarsidass) S Asia.
Rahula, Walpola. What the Buddha Taught. rev. ed. LC 73-21017. (Illus.). 192p. 1987. pap. 12.00 (*0-8021-3031-3*, Grove) Grove-Atltic.
Rahuler, M. New Problems in Differential Geometry. (Series on Soviet & East European Mathematics: Vol. 8). 200p. (C). 1993. text 44.00 (*981-02-0819-7*) World Scientific Pub.
Rahv, Philip. Image & Idea: Fourteen Essays on Literary Themes. LC 77-26061. 164p. 1978. reprint ed. lib. bdg. 48.50 (*0-313-20082-3*, RAII, Greenwood Pr) Greenwood.
— Literature in America: An Anthology of Literary Criticism. 1993. 18.75 (*0-8446-2776-3*) Peter Smith.
Rahv, Philip, ed. The Great Short Novels of Henry James. 800p. 1996. pap. 17.95 (*0-7867-0265-6*) Carroll & Graf.
Rahwan, Ralf G. & Witiak, Donald T. Calcium Regulation by Calcium Antagonists. LC 82-16451. (ACS Symposium Ser.: No. 201). 210p. 1982. lib. bdg. 38.95 (*0-8412-0744-5*) Am Chemical.
Rahwan, Ralf G. & Witiak, Donald T., eds. Calcium Regulation by Calcium Antagonists. LC 82-16451. (ACS Symposium Ser.: No. 201). (Illus.). 218p. 1982. reprint ed. pap. 67.60 (*0-608-03214-X*, 206373300007) Bks Demand.
Rai, A. K., ed. Cyanobacterial Nitrogen Metabolism & Environmental Biotechnology. (Illus.). 300p. 1997. 119.00 (*3-540-61305-6*) Spr-Verlag.
Rai, Alok, tr. see Premchand.
Rai, Amar N., ed. Handbook of Symbiotic Cyanobacteria. 272p. 1989. lib. bdg. 220.00 (*0-8493-3275-3*, QR99) CRC Pr.
Rai, B. C. History of Indian Education. 413p. 1981. 9.95 (*0-318-36823-4*) Asia Bk Corp.
Rai-Choudhary, P., et al. Diagnostic Techniques for Semiconductor Materials & Devices. LC 94-61185. (Proceedings Ser.: Vol. 94-33). 400p. 1994. 58.00 (*1-56677-092-0*) Electrochem Soc.
Rai-Choudhury, P. Handbook of Microlithography, Micromaching & Microfabrication. LC 96-40237. 1997. 110.00 (*0-8194-2378-5*) SPIE.
Rai-Choudhury, P., ed. Handbook of Microlithography, Vol. 1. (Materials & Devices Ser.: No. 12). 776p. 1997. 110.00 (*0-85296-906-6*, ED012A) INSPEC Inc.
— Handbook of Microlithography, Micromachining &

R

Microfabrication, 2 vols., Set. (Materials & Devices Ser.: No. 12). 1997. 195.00 (*0-85296-910-4*, ED012, Pub. by INSPEC Inc) Whitehurst & Clark.

— Handbook of Microlithography, Micromachining & Microfabrication Vol. 2: Micromachining & Microfabrication. LC 96-40237. 692p. 1997. 110.00 (*0-8194-2379-3*) SPIE.

— Handbook of Micromachining & Microfabrication, Vol. 2. (Materials & Devices Ser.: No. 12). 702p. 1997. 110.00 (*0-85296-911-2*, ED012B) INSPEC Inc.

Rai-Choudhury, P., et al, eds. Diagnostic Techniques for Semiconductor Materials & Devices. LC 98-158684. (Proceedings Ser.: Vol. 97-12). 478p. 1997. 68.00 (*1-56677-139-0*) Electrochem Soc.

— Diagnostic Techniques for Semiconductor Materials & Devices, Vol. 3322. 478p. 1997. 68.00 (*0-8194-2765-9*) SPIE.

Rai, D., ed. Atomic & Molecular Physics: Proceedings of the Sixth National Workshop on Atomic & Molecular Physics, Varanasi, India 8-13 December 1986. 608p. 1988. text 138.00 (*9971-5-0341-7*) World Scientific Pub.

Rai, Dhanwant K. Developments in Training in Social Services. 1994. pap. 23.00 (*0-902789-91-0*, Pub. by Natl Inst Soc Work) St Mut.

Rai, Dinesh, tr. see Meyer, Kurt W.

***Rai, Gurcharan S., ed.** Medical Ethics & the Elderly: Practical Guide. 132p. 1999. text 54.00 (*90-5702-402-0*, Harwood Acad Pubs); pap. text 22.00 (*90-5702-403-9*, Harwood Acad Pubs) Gordon & Breach.

Rai, Hakumat, ed. The Measurement of Photosynthetic Pigments in Freshwaters & Standardization of Methods: Proceedings of the Workshop Held at Ploen, West Germany, July 28-29, 1978, Vol. 1. (Advances in Limnology Ser.: Vol. 14). (GER., Illus.). 106p. (Orig.). 1980. 33.00 (*3-510-47012-5*, Pub. by E Schweizerbartsche) Balogh.

Rai, Hakumat & Marker, A. F., eds. The Measurement of Photosynthetic Pigments in Freshwaters & Standardization of Methods: Proceedings of the 2nd Workshop Held at Plon, July 17-18, 1980, Vol. 2. (Advances in Limnology Ser.: Vol. 16). (GER., Illus.). 130p. (Orig.). 1982. 36.00 (*3-510-47014-1*, Pub. by E Schweizerbartsche) Balogh.

Rai, Karanjit Singh. Four Decades of Vector Biology at the University of Notre Dame. LC 99-14432. 128p. 1999. pap. 25.00 (*0-268-02853-2*, Pub. by U of Notre Dame Pr) Chicago Distribution Ctr.

Rai, Kul B., et al, eds. America in the 21st Century: Challenges & Opportunities in Domestic Politics. LC 97-13590. 262p. 1997. pap. text 23.80 (*0-13-570946-6*) P-H.

Rai, Kul B. & Critzer, John W. Affirmative Action & the University: Race, Ethnicity & Gender in Higher Education Employment. LC 99-30467. 320p. 2000. text 45.00 (*0-8032-3934-3*) U of Nebr Pr.

Rai, L. B. Human Rights in the Hindu Buddhist Tradition. 1995. pap. 60.00 (*0-7855-0413-3*, Pub. by Ratna Pustak Bhandar) St Mut.

Rai, L. C., et al, eds. Algae & Water Pollution. (Advances in Limnology Ser.: Vol. 42). (GER., Illus.). viii, 302p. 1994. pap. text 70.00 (*3-510-47043-5*, Pub. by E Schweizerbartsche) Balogh.

Rai, Lajpat. History of the Arya Samaj: An Account of Its Origin, Doctrines & Activities with a Biographical Sketch of the Founder. (C). 1992. reprint ed. text 20.00 (*81-215-0578-X*, Pub. by M Manoharial) Coronet Bks.

Rai, Lal D. Human Rights in the Hindu Buddhist Tradition. xii, 192p. 1995. 20.00 (*81-85693-46-3*, Pub. by Nirala Pubns) Nataraj Bks.

Rai, Lala Lajpat, see Lajpat Rai, Lala.

Rai, Lalitkumar, jt. auth. see Rai, Topdhan.

***Rai, M. K.** The Genus Phoma: Identity & Taxonomy. 157p. 1998. pap. 130.00 (*0-7855-7665-7*) St Mut.

Rai, M. K. Herbal Medicines Biodiversity. 1996. pap. 90.00 (*81-7089-221-X*, Pub. by Intl Bk Distr) St Mut.

Rai, Milan. Chomsky's Politics. 160p. (C). 1995. pap. 20.00 (*1-85984-011-6*, C0497, Pub. by Verso) Norton.

Rai, Navin K. Living in a Lean-To: Philippine Negrito Foragers in Transition. LC 89-12557. (Anthropological Papers Ser.: No. 80). xi, 184p. (Orig.). 1990. pap. 12.00 (*0-915703-17-3*) U Mich Mus Anthro.

Rai, P. & Shankar, Vinod. Stylos for Tropical Pastures. 1996. pap. 45.00 (*81-7233-124-X*, Pub. by Scientific Pubs) St Mut.

Rai, Priya M., compiled by. Sikhism & the Sikhs: An Annotated Bibliography, 13. LC 88-38308. (Bibliographies & Indexes in Religious Studies: No. 13). 272p. 1989. lib. bdg. 79.50 (*0-313-26130-X*, RSI/, Greenwood Pr) Greenwood.

Rai, R. K. Along the Kali Gandaki, the Ancient Salt Route in Western Nepal. 1994. pap. 228.00 (*0-7855-0425-7*, Pub. by Ratna Pustak Bhandar) St Mut.

Rai, R. K., ed. Environmental Management: Physio-Ecological Facets, 2 vols., I. (C). 1992. write for info. (*81-7033-152-8*, Pub. by Rawat Pubns) S Asia.

— Environmental Management: Physio-Ecological Facets, 2 vols., II. (C). 1992. write for info. (*81-7033-153-6*, Pub. by Rawat Pubns) S Asia.

— Environmental Management: Physio-Ecological Facets, 2 vols., Set. (C). 1992. 72.00 (*81-7033-154-4*, Pub. by Rawat Pubns) S Asia.

Rai, R. Mohan. Satya Sai Avatar: Glimpses of Divinity. (C). 1995. reprint ed. write for info. (*81-207-1849-6*) Sterling Pubs.

Rai, R. N. Theory of Drama: A Comparative Study of Aristotle & Bharata. (C). 1992. 29.50 (*81-7054-155-7*, Pub. by Classical Pubng) S Asia.

Rai, R. P., jt. auth. see Pant, Niranjan.

Rai, Raghu, ed. A Day in the Life of India. LC 96-33731. (Illus.). 224p. 1996. 45.00 (*0-00-225104-3*) Collins SF.

Rai, Raghu, photos by. Delhi. (Illus.). 1994. 65.00 (*81-7223-092-3*) Harper SF.

Rai, Raghu & Chawla, Navin. Faith & Compassion: The Life & Work of Mother Teresa. (Illus.). 160p. 1996. pap. 30.00 (*1-85230-912-1*, Pub. by Element MA) Penguin Putnam.

***Rai, Ranjit B.** Indians: Why We Are, What We Are. 1998. 22.00 (*81-7049-080-4*) Manas Pubns.

Rai, S. S. Red Star & the Lotus: The Political Dynamics of Indo-Soviet Relations. 400p. 1990. text 37.50 (*81-220-0177-7*, Pub. by Konark Pubs Pvt Ltd) Advent Bks Div.

Rai, Shirin, jt. auth. see Cohen, Robin.

Rai, Shirin, jt. ed. see Fine, Robert.

***Rai, Shirin M.** International Perspectives on Gender & Democratization. LC 99-59235. 240p. 2000. text 65.00 (*0-312-23210-1*) St Martin.

Rai, Shirin M. & Lievesley, Geraldine, eds. Women & the State: International Perspectives. LC 95-48108. (Gender, Change & Society Ser.: Vol. 2). 208p. 1996. 79.95 (*0-7484-0360-4*); pap. 27.95 (*0-7484-0361-2*) Taylor & Francis.

Rai, Topdhan & Rai, Lalitkumar. Trees of the Sikkism Himalaya. (C). 1994. 78.00 (*81-7387-001-2*, Pub. by Indus Pub) S Asia.

Rai, Usha. Taj Mahal. LC 87-14739. (Illus.). 160p. 1997. text 75.00 (*0-86565-078-0*) Vendome.

Rai, V. T. S. Eliot's "The Waste Land" A Critical Study. 1974. lib. bdg. 69.95 (*0-8490-1173-6*) Gordon Pr.

Raia, Susan P., jt. auth. see Burke, Cathryn B.

Raia, William A. Milwaukee Road in Color, Vol. 1. (Illus.). 1995. 49.95 (*1-878887-46-7*) Morning NJ.

Raibert, Marc. Legged Robots That Balance. (Artificial Intelligence Ser.). (Illus.). 256p. 1986. 35.00 (*0-262-18117-7*) MIT Pr.

***Raibert, Marc.** Legged Robots That Balance. (Illus.). 233p. 2000. pap. 35.00 (*0-262-68119-6*) MIT Pr.

Raible, Erwin. Fin de Siecle Prints, Posters & Prose: The Collection of Erwin Raible & Robert Hoskins. LC 90-62623. (Illus.). 44p. (Orig.). 1990. pap. 10.00 (*0-915577-21-6*) Taft Museum.

Raible, Wolfgang. Christliches Ethos und Gottesdienstliche Verkundigung: Unberlegungen Zum Selbstverstandnis Ethischer Predigt. (Europaische Hochschulschriften Ser.: Reihe 23, Bd. 377). (GER.). 448p. 1990. 74.80 (*3-631-42319-5*) P Lang Pubng.

Raiborn & Barfield, Jesse T. Managerial Accounting. 3rd ed. LC 98-28158. (Aq - Managerial Accounting Ser.). (C). 1998. pap. 93.95 (*0-538-88512-2*) S-W Pub.

— Managerial Accounting. 3rd ed. (AQ - Managerial Accounting Ser.). (C). 1998. pap., student ed. 21.95 (*0-538-88513-0*); pap., student ed. 23.95 (*0-538-88515-7*) S-W Pub.

Raiborn, et al. Penn Containers:act Based Cstgcase. 3rd ed. 1998. pap. text 11.00 (*0-538-88522-X*) Thomson Learn.

***Raiborn, et al.** Web Tutor on Webct to Accompany Managerial Accounting. 3rd ed. 1999. pap. 33.00 (*0-534-76352-9*) Wadsworth Pub.

Raiborn, jt. auth. see Barfield, Jesse T.

Raiborn, Cecily A. Accounting: Tutor Demo. 2nd ed. Date not set. write for info. (*0-314-09356-7*) West Pub.

— Llf Mngrl Accntg, 2e. 2nd ed. (SWC-Accounting). 1995. ring bd. 46.50 (*0-314-07591-7*) West Pub.

— Managerial Accounting. Date not set. pap. text. write for info. (*0-314-01757-7*); pap. text, student ed. 21.00 (*0-314-01613-9*) West Pub.

— Managerial Accounting. 2nd ed. Date not set. pap. text, teacher ed. write for info. (*0-314-06403-6*) West Pub.

— Managerial Accounting. 2nd annot. ed. Date not set. text, teacher ed. write for info. (*0-314-07014-1*) West Pub.

— Managerial Accounting Library. Date not set. pap. text. write for info. (*0-314-01756-9*) West Pub.

— Media Guide. Date not set. write for info. (*0-314-08704-4*) West Pub.

Raiborn, Cecily A., et al. Managerial Accounting. 2nd ed. LC 95-33105. 800p. (C). 1995. mass mkt. 72.50 (*0-314-05826-5*) West Pub.

— Txt Managerial Accounting 1e. Leyh, ed. LC 92-29592. (SWC-Accounting). 900p. (C). 1992. mass mkt. 69.25 (*0-314-01169-2*) West Pub.

Raiborn, Cecily A., jt. auth. see Barfield.

Raica-Klotz, Helen. Empower Me! 12 Sessions for Building Self-Esteem in Girls. 64p. 1999. pap. text 34.95 (*0-89390-448-1*) Resource Pubns.

— Journal Me! A Pocketbook for Girls. 96p. 1999. pap. text 9.95 (*0-89390-449-X*) Resource Pubns.

Raica-Klotz, Helen, ed. see Ankney, Patricia A.

Raiche, Annabelle & Biermaier, Ann M., contrib. by. They Came to Teach. 300p. 1994. pap. 19.95 (*0-87839-088-X*) North Star.

Raiche, Diana D., et al. Confirmation: Anointed & Sealed with the Spirit: A Journal for Younger Candidates, Vol. 2. LC 98-103140. (Illus.). 88p. (J). (gr. 1-6). 1997. 5.95 (*1-889108-30-8*) Liv Good News.

***Raichel, Daniel R.** The Science & Applications of Acoustics. LC 99-39801. (Modern Acoustics & Signal Processing Ser.). (Illus.). 450p. 2000. 69.00 (*0-387-98907-2*, AIP Pr) Spr-Verlag.

Raichelson, Richard, ed. see Doran, James M.

***Raichelson, Richard M.** Beale Street Talks: A Walking Tour down the Home of the Blues. 2nd rev. ed. LC 98-73840. (Illus.). 112p. 1999. 16.95 (*0-9647545-1-7*) Arcadia Recs.

Raichert, Lane. D.C. Hopper, the First Starbunny. LC 91-23055. (Illus.). 32p. (J). (gr. 2-6). 1992. 15.95 (*1-880009-81-1*, DC-P1) Blue Zero Pub.

Raichle, Donald R. From a Normal Beginning: The Origins of Kean College of New Jersey. (Illus.). 432p. 1980. 30.00 (*0-8386-4500-3*) Fairleigh Dickinson.

— New Jersey's Union College. LC 83-45027. (Illus.). 272p. 1983. 25.00 (*0-8386-3198-3*) Fairleigh Dickinson.

Raichle, Marcus E., jt. auth. see Posner, Michael I.

Raichle, Marcus E., jt. ed. see Powers, William J.

Raichlen, Steven. The Barbecue Bible. LC 98-17053. 512p. 1998. 27.95 (*0-7611-1317-7*); pap. 227.40 (*0-7611-1179-4*); pap. 18.95 (*1-56305-866-9*) Workman Pub.

***Raichlen, Steven.** Barbecue Sauces, Rubs & Marinades, Bastes, Butters & Glazes: A Barbecue Bible Cookbook. LC 00-26060. (Illus.). 356p. 2000. 22.95 (*0-7611-2013-0*); pap. 14.95 (*0-7611-1979-5*) Workman Pub.

Raichlen, Steven. The Caribbean Pantry Cookbook: Condiments & Seasonings from the Land of Spice & Sun. LC 95-17489. (Illus.). 144p. 1995. 25.00 (*1-885183-10-0*) Artisan.

***Raichlen, Steven.** Healthy Jewish Cooking. (High-Flavor, Low-Fat Cookbook Ser.). (Illus.). 272p. 2000. 29.95 (*0-670-89312-9*, Viking) Viking Penguin.

Raichlen, Steven. High-Flavor, Low-Fat Cooking. (Illus.). 256p. 1994. reprint ed. pap. 18.95 (*0-14-024123-X*, Penguin Bks) Viking Penguin.

— High-Flavor, Low-Fat Vegetarian Cooking. (Illus.). 304p. 1997. pap. 18.95 (*0-14-024124-8*) Viking Penguin.

— Mexican Cooking. LC 99-12872. (High-Flavor, Low-Fat Cookbook Ser.). 272p. 1999. 29.95 (*0-670-88388-3*, Viking) Viking Penguin.

— Miami Spice: The New Florida Cuisine. LC 93-25446. (Illus.). 352p. (Orig.). 1993. pap. 12.95 (*1-56305-346-2*, 3346) Workman Pub.

***Raichlen, Steven.** Steven Raichlen's Healthy Latin Cooking: 200 Sizzling Recipes from Mexico, Cuba, Carribean & Brazil. (Illus.). 416p. 2000. pap. 19.95 (*0-87596-498-2*) Rodale Pr Inc.

Raichlen, Steven. Steven Raichlen's Healthy Latin Cooking: 200 Sizzling Recipes from Mexico, Cuba, the Caribbean, Brazil, & Beyond. LC 98-22947. (SPA., Illus.). 368p. 1998. text 29.95 (*0-87596-497-4*) Rodale Pr Inc.

— Steven Raichlen's Healthy Latin Cooking/Spanish: 200 Sizzling Recipes from Mexico, Cuba, the Caribbean, Brazil, & Beyond. (SPA., Illus.). 368p. 1998. text 29.95 (*0-87596-474-5*) Rodale Pr Inc.

Raichler, Joseph L. The Baseball Encyclopedia. 29.95 (*0-02-578970-8*) Macmillan.

Raichur, Pratima. Absolute Beauty. LC 97-1908. 448p. 1997. 27.50 (*0-06-270172-X*) HarpC.

Raichur, Pratima & Cohn, Maria. Absolute Beauty: Radiant Skin & Inner Harmony Through the Ancient Secrets of Ayurveda. 448p. 1999. 17.00 (*0-06-092910-3*, Perennial) HarperTrade.

Raichyk, J. H. Token Woman: The One That Got Away. LC 97-69622. (Illus.). 160p. 1999. pap. 11.95 (*0-9661022-5-8*) Dectire Pub.

Raico, Ralph, tr. see Von Mises, Ludwig.

Raicu, Irina L. & Grewell, Gregory. Transitions: Lives in America. LC 97-12825. xxvi, 644p. 1997. pap. text 32.95 (*1-55934-958-1*, 1958) Mayfield Pub.

— Transitions Instructor's Manual. vi, 123p. (C). 1997. pap. text, teacher ed. write for info. (*0-7674-0027-5*, 0027-5) Mayfield Pub.

Raidchaudhuri, S. P., ed. Recent Advances in Medicinal, Aromatic & Spice Crops Vol. 1: International Conference Held at New Delhi, India, Jan. 1989. (Illus.). 272p. 1991. text 59.00 (*81-7019-372-9*, Pub. by Today Tomorrow) Lubrecht & Cramer.

Raider, Mark A. The Emergence of American Zionism. LC 98-23089. 250p. 1998. text 60.00 (*0-8147-7498-9*); pap. text 20.00 (*0-8147-7499-7*) NYU Pr.

Raider, Mark A., et al, eds. Abba Hillel Silver & American Zionism. LC 97-26840. 136p. 1997. 45.00 (*0-7146-4824-8*, Pub. by F Cass Pubs); pap. 19.50 (*0-7146-4377-7*, Pub. by F Cass Pubs) Intl Spec Bk.

Raider, Melvyn & Pauline-Morand, Mary B. Social Work Practice with Low-Income, Urban, African-American Families. LC 98-8627. 172p. 1998. text 79.95 (*0-7734-8306-3*) E Mellen.

Raider, Melvyn, jt. auth. see Steele, William.

Raider, S. I., et al, eds. Proceedings of the Symposium on Low Temperature Electronics & High Temperature Superconductivity. LC 93-70073. (Proceedings Ser.: Vol. 93-22). 600p. 1993. 58.00 (*1-56677-071-8*) Electrochem Soc.

Raidl, Stefan. Studien Zur Ontogenie an Rhizomorphen Von Ektomykorrhizen. (Bibliotheca Mycologica: Vol. 169). (GER., Illus.). 184p. 1997. 53.00 (*3-443-59071-3*, Pub. by Gebruder Borntraeger) Balogh.

Ra'Ifa, Mansa K. Love Dipped in Blackness. 48p. 1999. pap. 8.00 (*0-8059-4718-3*) Dorrance.

Raife, Alexandra. Belonging. 1999. mass mkt. 5.99 (*0-451-19818-2*, Sig) NAL.

***Raife, Alexandra.** Belonging. LC 99-48202. 1999. 24.95 (*1-57490-218-0*, Beeler LP Bks) T T Beeler.

— Grianan. large type ed. 448p. 31.99 (*0-7089-4041-2*) Ulverscroft.

— The Larach. large type unabridged ed. 2000. 26.95 (*0-7531-5940-6*, 159406, Pub. by ISIS Lrg Prnt) ISIS Pub.

— Until the Spring. 2000. mass mkt. 5.99 (*0-451-40914-0*, Onyx) NAL.

Raifeld, Y. E. Asymmetric Epoxidation: Mech Tech. & Synthetic App. 1995. 89.95 (*0-8493-8929-1*) CRC Pr.

Raiff, Angela M. Daydreaming Daze: Silly Summer Poems. LC 98-93944. (Illus.). 32p. (J). (gr. k-6). 1999. text 15.95 (*0-9661132-1-7*) Bear Lake Pub.

Raiff, Angela M. & Chinlund, Gregory J. A-Zenith of Creatures. LC 97-92688. (Illus.). 32p. (J). (ps-3). 1997. text 15.95 (*0-9661132-0-9*) Bear Lake Pub.

Raiff, Norma R. & Shore, Barbara K. Advanced Case Management: New Strategies for the Nineties. (Human Services Guides Ser.: Vol. 66). (Illus.). 180p. (C). 1993. text 42.00 (*0-8039-5308-9*); pap. text 18.95 (*0-8039-3872-1*) Sage.

Raiffa, Howard. Analysis for Decision Making, 10 notebks. 821p. (C). reprint ed. ring bd. 995.00 incl. audio (*1-55678-012-5*, 1431) Learn Inc.

Raiffa, Howard. Analysis for Decision Making, Module 1: Decision Trees. 83p. (C). 1987. reprint ed. ring bd. 89.95 incl. audio (*1-55678-013-3*) Learn Inc.

— Analysis for Decision Making, Module 10: Case Analysis: Caroline Development & the Stephen Douglas. 104p. (C). 1987. reprint ed. ring bd. 89.95 incl. audio (*1-55678-022-2*) Learn Inc.

— Analysis for Decision Making, Module 2: New Information: Effect on Uncertainties. 73p. (C). 1987. reprint ed. ring bd. 89.95 incl. audio (*1-55678-014-1*) Learn Inc.

— Analysis for Decision Making, Module 3: Strategies & the Value of Information. 79p. (C). 1987. reprint ed. ring bd. 89.95 incl. audio (*1-55678-015-X*) Learn Inc.

— Analysis for Decision Making, Module 4: Case Analysis: The Rositex Company. 89p. (C). 1987. reprint ed. ring bd. 89.95 incl. audio (*1-55678-016-8*) Learn Inc.

— Analysis for Decision Making, Module 5: Utility Theory: Basic Concepts. 81p. (C). 1987. reprint ed. ring bd. 89.95 incl. audio (*1-55678-017-6*) Learn Inc.

— Analysis for Decision Making, Module 6: Utility Theory: The Assessment Problem. 80p. (C). 1987. reprint ed. ring bd. 89.95 incl. audio (*1-55678-018-4*) Learn Inc.

— Analysis for Decision Making, Module 7: Case Analysis: Edgartown Fisheries & J. B. Robinson. 55p. (C). 1987. reprint ed. ring bd. 89.95 incl. audio (*1-55678-019-2*) Learn Inc.

— Analysis for Decision Making, Module 8: Subjective Probability. 60p. (C). 1987. reprint ed. ring bd. 89.95 incl. audio (*1-55678-020-6*) Learn Inc.

— Analysis for Decision Making, Module 9: The Atr & Science of Probability Assessment. 117p. (C). 1987. reprint ed. ring bd. 89.95 incl. audio (*1-55678-021-4*) Learn Inc.

— The Art & Science of Negotiation. 384p. 1985. pap. text 18.95 (*0-674-04813-X*) Belknap Pr.

— Decision Analysis. (C). 1996. pap. text 40.00 (*0-07-052579-X*) McGraw.

— Lectures on Negotiation Analysis. LC 97-1106. 160p. (Orig.). (C). 1996. pap. 10.00 (*1-880711-09-5*) Prog Negot HLS.

***Raiffa, Howard & Schlaifer, Robert.** Applied Statistical Decision Theory. 384p. 2000. pap. 64.95 (*0-471-38349-X*) Wiley.

Raiffa, Howard & Schlaifer, Robert. Applied Statistical Decision Theory. 1968. reprint ed. pap. text 7.95 (*0-262-68010-6*) MIT Pr.

Raiffa, Howard, jt. auth. see Keeney, Ralph L.

Raiford. The Mainstream: Test Manual. 6th ed. (C). 1994. pap. text, teacher ed., suppl. ed. 40.00 (*0-15-501565-6*, Pub. by Harcourt Coll Pubs) Harcourt.

Raign. Reasons for Writing. (C). 1997. pap. text, teacher ed. 26.75 (*0-15-508264-7*) Harcourt Coll Pubs.

***Raiguel, Jill.** Life Skills: Keys to Effective Living. 1999. pap. 14.95 (*1-893897-00-1*) Marshall Edu.

Raiguel, Jill. The Next Step: A Life Skills Workbook for Adult Survivors of Emotional Abuse. 288p. (Orig.). 1991. pap. 12.95 (*0-944256-08-2*) ACCESS Pubs Network.

Raiha, Niels C., ed. Protein Metabolism During Infancy. LC 94-1490. (Nestle Nutrition Workshop Ser.: Vol. 33). 272p. 1994. text 65.00 (*0-7817-0215-1*) Lppncott W & W.

Raihall, Richard. The Winner's Edge: The Inside Guide to Betting Pro Football. (Guides to Sports Betting Ser.). 180p. (Orig.). 1984. write for info. (*0-915643-09-X*) Santa Barb Pr.

Raijan, A. New Technology & Employment in Insurance, Banking & Building Societies. (C). 1984. 25.00 (*0-7855-4070-9*, Pub. by Witherby & Co) St Mut.

Raikes, Philip. Livestock Development & Policy in East Africa. (Centre for Development Research Publications: No. 6). 254p. 1981. 18.95 (*91-7106-182-7*, Pub. by Nordic Africa) Transaction Pubs.

Raikes, Philip L. Modernising Hunger: Famine, Food Surplus & Farm Policy in the EEC & Africa. LC 90-26661. 280p. (C). 1989. text 40.00 (*0-435-08030-X*, 08030) Heinemann.

— Modernising Hunger: Famine, Food Surplus & Farm Policy in the EEC & Africa. LC 90-26661. 280p. (C). 1991. pap. text 27.50 (*0-435-08058-X*, 08058) Heinemann.

Raikov, I. B. The Protozoan Nucleus: Morphology & Evolution. Bobrov, Nicholas & Verkhovsteva, M., trs. (Cell Biology Monographs: Vol. 9). (Illus.). 450p. 1982. 216.95 (*0-387-81678-X*) Spr-Verlag.

Raikow, Robert J. Hindlimb Myology & Evolution of Old World Suboscine Passerine Birds (Acanthisittidae, Pittidae, Philepihidae, Eurylaimidae) (Ornithological Monographs: Vol. 41). (Illus.). 81p. 1987. pap. 5.00 (*0-943610-51-6*) Am Ornithologists.

Rail, Axel. Mexico. Nobles, Pat, ed. & illus. by. 224p. (Orig.). 1986. write for info. (*0-938105-00-0*) Seabird Pub.

***Rail, Chester D.** Contamination, Sources & Hydrology. LC 00-100621. (Groundwater Contamination Ser.: Vol. 1). 184p. 2000. text 99.95 (*1-56676-870-5*) Technomic.

Rail, Chester D. Groundwater Contamination: Sources, Control, & Preventive Measures. LC 88-51817. 158p. 1989. 34.95 (*0-87762-594-8*) Technomic.

***Rail, Chester D.** Management, Containment, Risk Assessment. LC 00-101718. (Groundwater Contamination Ser.: Vol. 2). 192p. 2000. text 99.95 (*1-56676-897-7*) Technomic.

Rail, Genevieve, ed. Sport & Postmodern Times. LC 97-50231. 352p. (C). 1998. text 65.50 (*0-7914-3925-9*); pap. text 21.95 (*0-7914-3926-7*) State U NY Pr.

An Asterisk (*) at the beginning of an entry indicates that the title is appearing for the first time.

Rail, Robert. Defense Without Damage: A Photo-Illustrated Guide to Low Liability Arrest & Control Skills. 2nd ed. (Illus.). 210p. (Orig.). 1996. pap. text 30.00 (*0-7881-2140-5*) DIANE Pub.

Raileanu, Lia, tr. see Seely, Contee & Romijn, Elizabeth.

Railey, Douglas. Exacta Expose. (Orig.). 1992. 29.95 (*0-9614168-6-6*) Cynthia Pub Co.

Railey, Jay M., jt. auth. see Gallant, Robert W.

Railey, Jim H. & Railey Tschauner, Peggy. Managing Physical Education, Fitness, & Sports Programs. 2nd ed. x, 340p. (C). 1993. text 52.95 (*1-55934-173-4*, 1173) Mayfield Pub.

— Managing Physical Education, Fitness, & Sports Programs: Instructor's Manual. 2nd ed. (C). 1993. pap. text, teacher ed. write for info. (*1-55934-174-2*, 1174) Mayfield Pub.

Railey, Kevin. Natural Aristocracy: History, Ideology, & the Production of William Faulkner. LC 98-58100. 213p. 1999. 29.95 (*0-8173-0956-X*) U of Ala Pr.

Railey Tschauner, Peggy, jt. auth. see Railey, Jim H.

Railfan Magazine Staff. Stephans' Railroad Directory: Railroad Magazine, 1929-1927, Vol. 3. 600p. pap. 43.00 (*0-685-35153-X*) Tioga Pubns.

Railing, John. Ten Awesome Card Tricks: Learn Ten Amazing Card Tricks from a Professional Master Magician!, Incl. cards. (Illus.). 24p. (J). (gr. 3-9). 1998. pap., boxed set 8.95 (*0-8167-4821-7*) Troll Communs.

Raillard, Hanni, tr. see Furtwangler, Elisabeth.

Raillard, Hans, tr. see Furtwangler, Elisabeth.

***Raillard, Matthieu P.** Castles in the Sky. LC 00-191045. 2000. 25.00 (*0-7388-2219-1*); pap. 18.00 (*0-7388-2220-5*) Xlibris Corp.

Raillery, Bonnie, ed. The Reader's Guide to Unavailable Literature & Other Omitted Media. LC 94-76412. 96p. (Orig.). 1994. per. 6.50 (*0-9641544-0-4*, RGB-1) Monitor Pubns.

Railo, Eilo. The Haunted Castle: A Study of the Elements of the English Romanticism. 1973. 300.00 (*0-87968-072-5*) Gordon Pr.

Rails-to-Trails Conservancy Staff. Acquiring Rail Corridors, a How to Manual. Allen, Jeff & Iurino, Tom, eds. LC 96-220056. 138p. (Orig.). (C). 1996. pap. text 17.95 (*0-925794-13-9*) Rails Trails.

***Rails-to-Trails Conservancy Staff.** 1000 Great Rail-Trails. LC 99-45628. (Illus.). 256p. 1999. pap. text 14.95 (*0-7627-0598-1*) Globe Pequot.

Railsback, Brian E. Parallel Expeditions: Charles Darwin & the Art of John Steinbeck. 168p. 1995. lib. bdg. 24.95 (*0-89301-177-0*) U of Idaho Pr.

***Railton, N. M.** No North Sea, the Anglo-German Evangelical Network in the Middle of the 19th Century. (Studies in Christian Mission). 1999. 100.00 (*90-04-11573-0*) Brill Academic Pubs.

Railton, Nicholas. The German Evangelical Alliance & the Third Reich: An Analysis of the "Evangelisches Allianzblatt" LC 98-5777. (German Linguistic & Cultural Studies: Vol. 2). 265p. (C). 1998. pap. text 43.95 (*0-8204-3412-4*) P Lang Pubng.

— The German Evangelical Alliance & the Third Reich: An Analysis of the Evangelisches Allianzblatt, Vol. 2. Lutzeier, Peter, ed. (German Linguistic & Cultural Studies). 265p. 1998. 43.95 (*3-906757-67-6*) P Lang Pubng.

Railton, Stephen. Authorship & Audience: Literary Performance in the American Renaissance. LC 91-607. 250p. 1991. reprint ed. pap. 77.50 (*0-608-02566-6*, 206321100004) Bks Demand.

Raimbault, G. Dictionnaire de l'Euro (Monnaie) (FRE.). 272p. 1997. 65.00 (*0-320-00473-2*) Fr & Eur.

Raimbaut de Vaqueiras. The Poems of the Troubadour Raimbaut de Vaqueiras. Linskill, Joseph, ed. LC 80-2190. reprint ed. 45.00 (*0-404-19014-6*) AMS Pr.

Raimer, David A. The Joseph Principle. (Illus.). (Orig.). 1989. pap. write for info. (*0-9623058-0-4*) Trinity Pub & Mktg.

Raimes. Houghton Handbook. 1998. pap. write for info. (*0-395-90142-1*) HM.

— Keys for Writing Exercises. 2nd ed. 1998. pap. text 5.97 (*0-395-92643-2*) HM.

Raimes, Ann. Electronic Handbook. (C). Date not set. write for info. (*0-395-82455-9*) HM.

— Exploring Through Writing: A Process Approach to ESL Composition. 2nd ed. 414p. (C). 1992. pap. text 24.95 (*0-521-65761-X*) Cambridge U Pr.

— Exploring Through Writing: A Process Approach to ESL Composition: Instructor's Manual. 2nd ed. 40p. (C). 1992. pap., teacher ed. 6.00 (*0-521-65760-1*) Cambridge U Pr.

— Focus on Composition. (Illus.). 214p. 1978. pap. text 12.95 (*0-19-502238-6*) OUP.

— Grammar Troublespots: An Editing Guide for Students. 2nd ed. 176p. (C). 1992. pap. 12.95 (*0-521-65759-8*) Cambridge U Pr.

— How English Works: A Grammar Handbook with Readings. 414p. (C). 1990. pap. text 23.95 (*0-521-65758-X*) Cambridge U Pr.

— How English Works: A Grammar Handbook with Readings: Instructor's Manual. 76p. (C). 1990. pap., teacher ed. 6.00 (*0-521-65757-1*) Cambridge U Pr.

— Identities: Readings from Contemporary Culture. 500p. (C). 1996. pap. text 30.36 (*0-395-70107-4*) HM.

— Identities: Readings from Contemporary Culture. (C). 1996. text, teacher ed. 11.96 (*0-395-77063-7*) HM.

— Keys for Writers. (C). Date not set. pap. 24.36 (*0-395-76499-8*) HM.

— Keys for Writers: A Brief Handbook. 384p. (C). 1995. pap. text 24.36 (*0-395-70111-2*) HM.

— Keys for Writers: A Brief Handbook. 2nd ed. LC 98-72075. xiii, 453 p. 1999. pap. text 21.27 (*0-395-92064-7*) HM.

— Problems & Teaching Strategies in ESL Composition. (Language in Education Ser.: No. 14). 24p. (C). 1986. pap. text 3.67 (*0-13-711987-9*) P-H.

— Techniques in Teaching Writing. (Techniques in Teaching English As a Second Language Ser.). (Illus.). 176p. (Orig.). (C). 1983. pap. text 13.50 (*0-19-434131-3*) OUP.

Raimes, Ann, tr. see Ball, Hugo.

Raimes, James. The Columbia Quiz Book. 1993. pap. 11.50 (*0-231-08079-4*) Col U Pr.

Raimes, S. Wave Mechanics of Electronics in Metals. 1. 500p. 1999. pap. 79.00 (*0-444-10037-7*) Elsevier.

Raimes, Stephen, jt. ed. see Griffin, Michael.

Raimey, Michael. Car Selling 101: Work Book: Buying Styles. Raimey, Ro Derick, ed. (Illus.). 9p. 1998. wbk. ed. 5.95 (*0-9657902-2-3*) Me Me Bks.

— Carselling 101: Sales Training Work Book. Raimey, Ro Derick, ed. (Illus.). 73p. 1998. wbk. ed. 9.95 (*0-9657902-1-5*) Me Me Bks.

Raimey, Michael D. Car Selling 101: The Basics. Raimey, Ro'Derick R., ed. (Illus.). 229p. (Orig.). Date not set. pap. 17.75 (*0-9657902-0-7*) Me Me Bks.

Raimey, Ro Derick, ed. see Raimey, Michael.

Raimey, Ro'Derick R., ed. see Raimey, Michael D.

Raimi, Ralph A. The Philomathic Debating Club. xii, 153p. (Orig.). 1991. pap. 25.00 (*0-9609370-1-3*) Raimi.

— Vested Interests. xiv, 209p. 1982. 14.95 (*0-9609370-0-5*) Raimi.

Raimo, John W., ed. Biographical Directory of American Colonial & Revolutionary Governors, 1607-1789. LC 80-13279. 536p. 1980. lib. bdg. 125.00 (*0-313-28133-5*, RAK/, Greenwood Pr) Greenwood.

— Biographical Directory of the Governors of the United States, 1978-1983. LC 84-20717. 400p. 1985. lib. bdg. 82.95 (*0-313-28098-3*, RBM/, Greenwood Pr) Greenwood.

— A Guide to Manuscripts Relating to America in Great Britain & Ireland. LC 78-12672. 488p. 1979. lib. bdg. 175.00 (*0-313-28135-1*, RMR/, Greenwood Pr) Greenwood.

Raimon, Peire. Le Poesie Di Peire Raimon De Tolosa. Cavaliere, Alfredo, ed. LC 80-2181. reprint ed. 29.50 (*0-404-19010-3*) AMS Pr.

Raimond, Ernst & Genee, Ren E. The Westerbork Observatory, Continuing Adventure in Radio Astronomy. (Astrophysics & Space Science Library). 1996. text 107.00 (*0-7923-4150-3*) Kluwer Academic.

Raimond, Paul. Management Projects: Design, Research, & Presentation. LC 93-14820. 208p. 1993. mass mkt. 29.95 (*0-412-46810-7*) Chapman & Hall.

***Raimond, Susan.** Making Music for Folk Harp: Beginning Level. 32p. 1999. pap. 14.95 incl. audio compact disk (*0-7866-2967-3*, 96704BCD) Mel Bay.

Raimondi, A. J., jt. auth. see Schawlow, A. L.

Raimondi, Anthony J. Pediatric Neurosurgery. (Illus.). 550p. 1987. 479.00 (*0-387-96408-8*) Spr-Verlag.

Raimondi, Anthony J., ed. Concepts in Pediatric Neurosurgery, No. 3. (Illus.). xxii, 226p. 1983. 172.25 (*3-8055-3580-5*) S Karger.

Raimondi, Anthony J., et al, eds. Cerebrovascular Diseases in Children. (Principles of Pediatric Neurosurgery Ser.). (Illus.). xi, 256p. 1992. 138.00 (*0-387-97626-4*) Spr-Verlag.

— Head Injuries in the Newborn & Infant. (Principles of Pediatric Neurosurgery Ser.). (Illus.). 270p. 1986. 115.00 (*0-387-96208-5*) Spr-Verlag.

— Intracranial Cyst Lesions. LC 92-2314. (Principles of Pediatric Neurosurgery Ser.). (Illus.). 256p. 1993. 195.00 (*0-387-97869-0*) Spr-Verlag.

— The Pediatric Spine, Vol. 1. (Principles of Pediatric Neurosurgery Ser.). (Illus.). 220p. 1989. 195.00 (*0-387-96835-0*) Spr-Verlag.

— The Pediatric Spine, Vol. 2. (Principles of Pediatric Neurosurgery Ser.). (Illus.). 255p. 1989. 210.00 (*0-387-96861-X*) Spr-Verlag.

— The Pediatric Spine, Vol. 3. (Principles of Pediatric Neurosurgery Ser.). (Illus.). 205p. 1989. 165.00 (*0-387-96804-0*) Spr-Verlag.

— Posterior Fossa Tumors. LC 92-49986. (Principles of Pediatric Neurosurgery Ser.). 1993. 198.00 (*0-387-97915-8*) Spr-Verlag.

Raimondi, Anthony J., et al. The Dandy-Walker Syndrome. (Illus.). viii, 84p. 1983. 50.50 (*3-8055-1722-X*) S Karger.

Raimondi, Georgia. The Passionate Gardener. LC 98-4833. 1999. 26.95 (*0-7621-0074-5*, Pub. by RD Assn) Penguin Putnam.

Raimondi, Pietro. Il Ventaglio: Libretto by Domenico Gilardoni, after Carlo Goldoni Music by Pietro First Performance Naples, Teatro, Nuovo, 19 April 1831. LC 89-753856. (Italian Opera 1810-1840 Ser.: Vol. 40). 368p. 1990. text 35.00 (*0-8240-6589-1*) Garland.

Raimondi, Steve, ed. Fabio Fitness. xviii, 247 p. 1995. 19.95 (*1-56530-171-4*) Summit TX.

Raimondo, Joyce. Art Safari: An Adventure in Looking for Children & Parents at the Museum of Modern Art. LC 97-70263. (Family Guide Ser.). (Illus.). 32p. (J). 1997. pap. 5.95 (*0-87070-059-6*) Mus of Modern Art.

Raimondo, Henry J. Economics of State & Local Government. LC 91-7783. 288p. 1991. 65.00 (*0-275-93122-6*, C3122, Praeger Pubs); pap. 24.95 (*0-275-93937-5*, B3937, Praeger Pubs) Greenwood.

***Raimondo, Justin.** An Enemy of the State: The Life of Murray N. Rothbard. LC 00-24195. 360p. 2000. 34.95 (*1-57392-809-7*) Prometheus Bks.

Raimondo, Lois. The Little Lama of Tibet. LC 93-13627. (Illus.). 40p. (J). (ps-4). 1994. 15.95 (*0-590-46167-2*) Scholastic Inc.

Raimund, Ferdinand. The Barometer-Maker on the Magic Island & the Diamond of the Spirit King. Kimbell, Edmund, ed. (Austrian Culture Ser.: Vol. 23). 110p. 1996. text 35.95 (*0-8204-3018-8*) P Lang Pubng.

Raimundo, Daniel E. Habla el Coronel Orlando Piedra. LC 94-70900. (Coleccion Cuba y sus Jueces). (SPA., Illus.). 230p. (Orig.). 1994. pap. 19.95 (*0-89729-479-3*) Ediciones.

Raimy, Victor. Misunderstandings of the Self. LC 74-28917. (Jossey-Bass Behavioral Science Ser.). 232p. reprint ed. pap. 72.00 (*0-8357-6884-8*, 203793600009) Bks Demand.

Rain. Quick Reference Guide for Microsoft Office 97. (Quick Reference Guide Ser.). spiral bd. 15.00 (*1-56243-469-1*, G-25HC) DDC Pub.

Rain & the Crew Publishers Staff, ed. see Blue & the Crew Publishers Staff.

***Rain, Blue & the Crew Publishers Staff.** My Name Is Blue, from Me to You, All about PTSD. 16p. 1999. pap. text 6.00 (*1-929396-00-7*) Rain Blue.

Rain, D. A. The Water Book. (Illus.). 1993. 29.95 (*0-8283-1956-1*) Branden Bks.

***Rain, David.** Eaters of the Dry Season: Circular Labor Migration in the West African Sahel. LC 99-21974. 208p. 1999. pap. 60.00 (*0-8133-3616-3*, Pub. by Westview) HarpC.

Rain, Diana. Microsoft Office 97. LC 97-170224. (Quick Reference Guide Ser.). pap., spiral bd. 27.00 (*1-56243-454-3*, G-25) DDC Pub.

Rain, Diana. Microsoft Outlook. LC 97-174137. (New Visual Reference Ser.). spiral bd. 17.00 (*1-56243-438-1*, G-23) DDC Pub.

— Visual Reference for the Internet. 1997. 17.00 (*1-56243-550-7*, G33HC); pap. text 15.00 (*1-56243-544-2*, G33) DDC Pub.

Rain, Jennifer, pseud. Your Husband, My Lover. rev. ed. Frost, Anne, ed. (Illus.). 469p. (Orig.). 1999. pap. 12.95 (*0-9614624-6-9*) Frost Pub.

Rain, Joachim. Die Einwilligung des Sportlers Beim Doping. XV, 217p. 1998. 45.95 (*3-631-34158-X*) P Lang Pubng.

Rain, Mary S. Ancient Echoes: The Anasazi Book of Chants. (Illus.). 216p. 1993. pap. 10.95 (*1-878901-87-7*) Hampton Roads Pub Co.

— Daybreak: The Dawning Ember. 624p. 1991. pap. 14.95 (*1-878901-14-1*) Hampton Roads Pub Co.

Rain, Mary S. Dreamwalker: The Path of Sacred Power. 240p. 1993. 11.95 (*1-878901-63-X*) Hampton Roads Pub Co.

Rain, Mary S. Mountains, Meadows & Moonbeams: A Child's Spiritual Reader. (Illus.). 240p. 1992. pap. 11.95 (*1-878901-39-7*) Hampton Roads Pub Co.

— Phantoms Afoot: Helping the Spirits among Us. 336p. 1993. pap. 12.95 (*1-878901-64-8*) Hampton Roads Pub Co.

— Phoenix Rising: No-Eyes' Vision of the Changes to Come. 176p. 1993. pap. 11.95 (*1-878901-62-1*) Hampton Roads Pub Co.

— The Seventh Mesa: A Novel. LC 95-143348. 272p. 1994. text 19.95 (*1-57174-012-0*) Hampton Roads Pub Co.

— The Seventh Mesa: A Novel. 272p. 1997. reprint ed. pap. 12.95 (*1-57174-061-9*) Hampton Roads Pub Co.

— Soul Sounds: Mourning the Tears of Truth. LC 93-231218. 472p. 1992. pap. 12.95 (*1-878901-33-8*) Hampton Roads Pub Co.

— Spirit Song: The Introduction of No-Eyes. annuals LC 85-15894. 160p. 1993. pap. 10.95 (*1-878901-61-3*) Hampton Roads Pub Co.

— Star Babies. LC 98-146089. (Illus.). 48p. (J). (gr. k-6). 1997. bds. 12.95 (*1-57174-069-4*) Hampton Roads Pub Co.

— Whispered Wisdom: Portraits of Grandmother Earth. 148p. 1992. pap. 18.95 (*1-878901-49-4*) Hampton Roads Pub Co.

Rain, Mary S. & Greystone, Alex. Mary Summer Rain's Guide to Dream Symbols. 608p. 1997. pap. 18.95 (*1-57174-100-3*) Hampton Roads Pub Co.

***Rain, Mary Summer.** Beyond Earthway: A Comprehensive Question & Answer Guide to Total Mind, Body & Spirit Health. LC 99-55446. 400p. 2000. 13.95 (*0-671-03862-1*) PB.

Rain, Mary Summer. Earthway: A Native American Visionary's Path to Total Mind, Body, & Spirit Health. Zion, Claire, ed. 464p. 1992. per. 16.00 (*0-671-70667-5*) PB.

***Rain, Mary Summer.** Eclipse. 335p. 1999. pap. 14.95 (*1-57174-121-6*) Hampton Roads Pub Co.

Rain, Mary Summer. Fireside. LC 98-71579. 212p. 1998. pap. 13.95 (*1-57174-094-5*) Hampton Roads Pub Co.

***Rain, Mary Summer.** Trained in Twilight. 2000. pap. 14.95 (*1-57174-197-6*) Hampton Roads Pub Co.

Rain, Patricia, jt. auth. see Riedner, Ulrich.

Rain, Thomas. Browning for Beginners. LC 72-3194. (Studies in Browning: No. 4). 1972. reprint ed. lib. bdg. 75.00 (*0-8383-1518-6*) M S G Haskell Hse.

Raina, Ashok, jt. auth. see Bobb, Dilip.

Raina, Ashok, jt. auth. see Kac, Victor G.

Raina, B. L. Health Science in Ancient India. (C). 1990. 44.00 (*81-7169-089-0*, Commonwealth) S Asia.

— Introduction to Malaria Problems in India: Prevedic Times to Early 1950's. (C). 1991. 23.00 (*81-7169-108-0*, Pub. by Commonwealth) S Asia.

— Planning Family in India Prevedic Times to Early 1950's. 1990. 42.00 (*81-7169-060-2*, Commonwealth) S Asia.

— Population Challenge. LC 94-900581. (C). 1994. 21.50 (*81-7018-763-X*, Pub. by BR Pub) S Asia.

— Quest for a Small Family. (C). 1991. 44.00 (*81-7169-125-0*, Pub. by Commonwealth) S Asia.

— Social Situation in India. 1990. 55.00 (*81-7169-054-8*, Commonwealth) S Asia.

Raina, Badri. Dickens & the Dialectic of Growth. LC 85-40767. 208p. 1986. text 27.50 (*0-299-10610-1*) U of Wis Pr.

Raina, Dhruv & Habib, S. Irfan, eds. Situating the History of Science: Dialogues with Joseph Needham. LC 99-935798. 376p. 1999. text 35.00 (*0-19-564639-8*) OUP.

Raina, J. L. Structural & Functional Changes in the Joint Family System: A Study Based on D. O. M. Workers. (C). 1989. 25.00 (*81-7022-237-0*, Pub. by Concept) S Asia.

Raina, J. P., ed. see International Conference on Fiber Optics and Photonics Staff, et al.

Raina, K. L. Dictionary of Electrical Engineering. 1989. 33.50 (*81-7041-162-9*, Pub. by Anmol) S Asia.

Raina, M. K. The Creativity Passion: E. Paul Torrance's Voyages of Discovering Creativity. LC 99-89136. 300p. 1998. 73.25 (*1-56750-388-8*); pap. 39.50 (*1-56750-389-6*) Ablx Pub.

***Raina, M. K.** The Creativity Passion: E. Paul Torrance's Voyages of Discovering Creativity. LC 99-89136. (Publications in Creativity Research Ser.). 2000. pap. write for info. (*1-56750-511-2*) Ablx Pub.

Raina, M. K., ed. Creativity Research: International Perspective. 332p. 1980. 18.95 (*0-318-37231-2*) Asia Bk Corp.

Raina, Sadri N. Dickens & the Dialectic of Growth. LC 85-40767. 187p. reprint ed. pap. 58.00 (*0-608-20467-6*, 207171900002) Bks Demand.

***Raina, Trilokinath & Sahitya Akademi Staff.** Dina Nath Nadim LC 98-905193. (Makers of Indian Literature Ser.). 95 p. 1998. write for info. (*81-260-0441-X*) S Asia.

Raina, V. K. Concrete Bridges: Inspection, Repair, Strengthening, Testing & Load Capacity Evaluation. 493p. 1996. 80.00 (*0-07-462349-4*) McGraw.

Rainbird, Ariadne & Rankine, David. Magick Without Peers. (Orig.). 1997. pap. 22.95 (*1-898307-99-7*, Pub. by Capall Bann Pubng) Holmes Pub.

***Rainbird, Helen.** Training in the Workplace. LC 00-30583. (Illus.). 2000. write for info. (*0-312-23551-8*) St Martin.

Rainbird, Helen & Syben, Gerd, eds. Restructuring a Traditional Society: Construction Employment & Skills in Europe. 296p. 1991. 19.50 (*0-85496-585-8*) Berg Pubs.

Rainbird, Helen, jt. auth. see Ainley, Patrick.

Rainbird, Sean, jt. auth. see Beudert, Monique.

Rainboldt, Jo, jt. auth. see Gingras, Louie.

Rainbolt, Jo & Brumback, Dorothy. History of Missoula, Montana. (Illus.). 554p. 1991. 64.50 (*0-88107-178-1*) Curtis Media.

Rainbolt, Jo & Triplett, Bonnie J. Singing Is Natural Vol. 1: How to Learn at Any Age & Have Fun Doing It. LC 98-118720. (Illus.). 150p. 1997. pap. 20.00 (*0-9661184-0-5*) Askinelf Pr.

Rainbolt, Martha & Fleetwood, Janet, eds. On the Contrary: Essays by Men & Women. LC 82-19421. 340p. (C). 1984. pap. text 14.95 (*0-87395-720-2*) State U NY Pr.

Rainbolt, Richard. The Plan to Heal the World. 98p. (Orig.). 1989. pap. 10.00 (*0-317-93650-6*) Peace Curriculum.

Rainbolt, Ricky, contrib. by. Internal Power Tapes. (Illus.). 32p. 1997. pap. 49.95 incl. audio (*1-884350-63-1*) Alpha Pubng.

Rainboth, Walter J. The Taxonomy, Systematics, & Zoogeography of Hypsibarbus, a New Genus of Large Barbs (Pisces, Cyprinidae) from the Rivers of Southeastern Asia. LC 96-13759. (Publications in Zoology: Vol. 129). (Illus.). 214p. (C). 1996. pap. 23.00 (*0-520-09809-9*, Pub. by U CA Pr) Cal Prin Full Svc.

Rainbow. Forecasting Envionmental Fate. text. write for info. (*0-471-49179-9*) Wiley.

Rainbow, A. K. Why Recycle? Proceedings of the Recycling Council Annual Seminar, Birmingham, U. K., February 1994. (Illus.). (C). 1994. text 123.00 (*90-5410-367-1*, Pub. by A A Balkema) Ashgate Pub Co.

Rainbow, A. K., ed. Reclamation, Treatment & Utilization of Coal Mining Wastes: Proceedings of the Third International Symposium, Glasgow, 3-7 September 1990. (Illus.). 544p. (C). 1990. text 168.00 (*90-6191-154-0*, Pub. by A A Balkema) Ashgate Pub Co.

Rainbow, Amy, jt. auth. see Dewey, Mora.

Rainbow Creative Concepts, jt. auth. see Coffey, Judith.

Rainbow, Edward L. & Froehlich, Hildegard C. Research in Music Education: An Introduction to Systematic Inquiry. (Illus.). 330p. (C). 1987. 47.00 (*0-02-870320-0*, Schirmer Books) Mac Lib Ref.

Rainbow, Izo M., jt. auth. see Fleming, Hilary.

Rainbow, Jane. Beginner's Guide to Crewel Embroidery. (Illus.). 48p. 1999. pap. 14.95 (*0-85532-869-X*, Pub. by Srch Pr) A Schwartz & Co.

Rainbow, Jonathan H. The Will of God & the Cross: John Calvin & the Doctrine of Limited Redemption. LC 90-30695. (Princeton Theological Monographs: No. 22). 217p. (Orig.). 1990. pap. 24.00 (*1-55635-005-8*) Pickwick.

***Rainbow Kennedy, Susan Ariel.** Transformation Soup: Healing for the Splendidly Imperfect. Simon & Schuster Staff, ed. 208p. 2000. per. 16.00 (*0-684-85976-9*, Fireside) S&S Trade Pap.

Rainbow, Philip S., jt. ed. see Fincham, A. A.

***Rainbow Publishing Staff.** Bible Workers. 2000. pap. 11.95 (*1-885358-82-2*) Rainbow CA.

— God's Creatures. (Illus.). 2000. pap. 11.95 (*1-885358-81-4*) Rainbow CA.

***Rainbow Spirit Elders Staff.** The Rainbow Spirit in Creation: A Reading of Genesis 1. Habel, Norman, tr. (Illus.). 2000. 14.95 (*0-8146-2716-1*) Liturgical Pr.

Rainbow, Stephen. Green Politics. (Critical Issues in New Zealand Society). 122p. 1994. pap. text 29.95 (*0-19-558272-1*) OUP.

***Rainbow Studies Publishing Staff.** Jesucristo Mi Amigo Fiel: Recuento Personales Descritos por Aquellos Que Jesucristo Toco. (SPA.). 1998. 7.99 (*1-58170-020-2*) Rainbow Studies.

R

Rainbow-Vigourt, Marielle. Listening Comprehension Skills for Intermediate & Advanced Students. 1994. text 24.92 (*0-8013-1085-7*) Addison-Wesley.

Raincoast Books Staff. A Wine Lover's Journal. 128p. 1998. 13.95 (*1-55192-196-0*) Raincoast Bk.

Raincoawst Books Staff. Cruise Memories: A Companion for Travellers by Sea. 160p. 1998. 13.95 (*1-55192-193-6*) Raincoast Bk.

Raindog, ed. Last Call: A Legacy of Madness. 1994. pap. 20.00 (*1-888662-08-5*) Vinegar Hill.

Raine, A. E., ed. Advances in Renal Medicine. LC 92-49499. (Oxford Medical Publications). 504p. 1993. 69.50 (*0-19-262102-5*) OUP.

Raine, Adrian. The Psychopathology of Crime: Criminal Behavior As a Clinical Disorder. LC 93-911. (Illus.). 377p. 1993. text 69.95 (*0-12-576160-0*) Acad Pr.

— The Psychopathology of Crime: Criminal Behavior As a Clinical Disorder. (Illus.). 377p. 1997. reprint ed. pap. text 44.95 (*0-12-576155-4*) Morgan Kaufmann.

Raine, Adrian, et al, eds. Biosocial Bases of Violence: Proceedings of a NATO ASI Held in Rhodes, Greece, May 12-21, 1996. LC 97-13920. (NATO ASI Series A: Vol. 292). 372p. 1997. 115.00 (*0-306-45601-X*) Plenum.

— Schizotypal Personality. (Illus.). 528p. (C). 1995. text 105.00 (*0-521-45422-0*) Cambridge U Pr.

***Raine, Allison.** Sweet Sixteen. (Love Stories Super Edition Ser.). 224p. (YA). (gr. 7-12). 2000. mass mkt. 4.99 (*0-553-49325-6*) BDD Bks Young Read.

Raine, Andy & Skinner, John. Celtic Night Prayer: A Northumbrian Office. 320p. 1996. pap. 16.00 (*0-551-02974-9*, Pub. by M Pickering) Harper SF.

Raine, Andy, jt. auth. see Skinner, John.

Raine, Carolyn. A Woodland Feast: Native American Foodways of the 17th & 18th Centuries. LC 97-67327. (Illus.). 90p. 1997. pap. 15.00 (*0-89725-309-4*, 1831, Penobscot Pr) Picton Pr.

Raine, Cedric S. Multiple Sclerosis: Clinical & Pathogenetic Basis. (Illus.). 448p. 1996. text 125.00 (*0-412-30890-8*, Pub. by E A) OUP.

Raine, Craig. A Martian Sends a Postcard Home. 54p. 1980. pap. 9.95 (*0-19-211896-X*) OUP.

Raine, D. J. The Isotropic Universe. (Monographs on Astronomical Subjects: No. 7). (Illus.). 267p. 1981. 30.00 (*0-85274-370-X*) IOP Pub.

— The Isotropic Universe. 1999. 50.00 (*0-7503-0405-7*) IOP Pub.

Raine, David F., jt. auth. see Boulthee, Paul G.

Raine, David S. Plays in Ten. 1995. 5.50 (*0-87129-588-1*, P95) Dramatic Pub.

— Ten-Minute Theatre. 57p. 1994. pap. 5.50 (*0-87129-431-1*, T17) Dramatic Pub.

Raine, Derek J. & Heller, Michael. The Science of Space-Time. (Astronomy & Astrophysics Ser.: Vol. 9). (Illus.). 256p. 1981. text 38.00 (*0-912918-12-8*, 0012) Pachart Pub Hse.

Raine, Harmony. The Baroness Orczy Collector Guide. (Orig.). (C). 1984. pap. 4.95 (*0-89966-502-0*) Buccaneer Bks.

— The Dorothy Dunnett Collector Guide. (Orig.). (C). 1984. pap. 4.95 (*0-89966-504-7*) Buccaneer Bks.

— The Dorothy Emily Stevenson Collector Guide. (Orig.). (C). 1984. pap. 4.95 (*0-89966-500-4*) Buccaneer Bks.

— The Georgette Heyer Compendium. 95p. (Orig.). 1984. pap. 5.95 (*0-89966-325-7*) Buccaneer Bks.

— The Harold Bell Wright Collector Guide. (Orig.). 1984. pap. 3.95 (*0-89966-498-9*) Buccaneer Bks.

— The Joseph Altsheler Collector Guide. (Orig.). (C). 1984. pap. 4.95 (*0-89966-503-9*) Buccaneer Bks.

— The Martha Finley Collector Guide. (Orig.). (C). 1984. pap. 4.95 (*0-89966-499-7*) Buccaneer Bks.

Raine, Harmony & Heyer, Georgette. The Georgette Heyer Compendium. (Orig.). 1979. 5.95 (*0-89967-000-8*, Harmony Rain) Buccaneer Bks.

Raine, James, ed. The Historians of the Church of York & Its Archbishops, 3 vols. (Rolls Ser.: No. 71). 1969. reprint ed. 210.00 (*0-8115-1139-1*) Periodicals Srv.

— Historical Papers & Letters from the Northern Registers. (Rolls Ser.: No. 61). 1969. reprint ed. 70.00 (*0-8115-1129-4*) Periodicals Srv.

Raine, James W. The Land of Saddle-Bags: A Study of the Mountain People of Appalachia. LC 96-49955. (Illus.). 272p. 1997. pap. 21.00 (*0-8131-0929-9*) U Pr of Ky.

— The Land of Saddle-Bags: A Study of the Mountain People of Appalachia. 2000. reprint ed. 35.00 (*1-55888-378-9*) Omnigraphics Inc.

Raine, Jerry. Smalltime. LC 97-129136. (Bloodlines Ser.). 184p. 1997. pap. 12.95 (*1-899344-13-6*) Dufour.

Raine, Kathleen. Defending Ancient Springs. 198p. 1985. reprint ed. pap. 8.95 (*0-940262-13-4*, Lindisfarne) Anthroposophic.

— Golgonooza - City of Imagination: Last Studies in William Blake. 182p. 1991. pap. 14.95 (*0-940262-42-8*, Lindisfarne) Anthroposophic.

— India Seen Afar. 294p. 1991. 22.95 (*0-8076-1268-5*) Braziller.

— The Inner Journey of the Poet. LC 81-21675. 208p. 1982. 20.00 (*0-8076-1039-9*) Braziller.

— The Presence: Poems, 1984-87. 80p. 1987. 14.95 (*0-940262-20-7*, Lindisfarne) Anthroposophic.

— Selected Poems. 160p. 1988. pap. 12.95 (*0-940262-19-3*, Lindisfarne) Anthroposophic.

— William Blake. (World of Art Ser.). (Illus.). 216p. 1985. pap. 14.95 (*0-500-20107-2*, Pub. by Thames Hudson) Norton.

— Yeats, the Tarot & the Golden Dawn. LC 73-166426. (New Yeats Papers Ser.). 60p. 1972. write for info. (*0-85105-195-2*) Smyth.

— Yeats, the Tarot & the Golden Dawn 2nd rev. ed. LC 76-367856. (New Yeats Papers Ser.). 78 p. 1976. 2.75 (*0-85105-284-3*) Smyth.

Raine, Kathleen & Keeble, Brian, eds. Temenos: A Review Devoted to the Arts of the Imagination, Vol. 4. (Illus.). 216p. (Orig.). 1983. pap. 22.95 (*0-900588-90-X*, Pub. by Temenos) S Perennis.

— Temenos: A Review Devoted to the Arts of the Imagination, Vol. 5. (Illus.). 296p. (Orig.). 1984. pap. 22.95 (*0-900588-91-8*, Pub. by Temenos) S Perennis.

— Temenos: A Review Devoted to the Arts of the Imagination, Vol. 6. (Illus.). 304p. (Orig.). 1985. pap. 22.95 (*0-900588-92-6*, Pub. by Temenos) S Perennis.

— Temenos: A Review Devoted to the Arts of the Imagination, Vol. 7. (Illus.). 335p. (Orig.). 1986. pap. 22.95 (*0-900588-93-4*, Pub. by Temenos) S Perennis.

— Temenos: A Review Devoted to the Arts of the Imagination, Vol. 8. (Illus.). 294p. (Orig.). 1987. pap. 22.95 (*0-900588-94-2*, Pub. by Temenos) S Perennis.

— Temenos: A Review Devoted to the Arts of the Imagination, Vol. 9. (Illus.). 308p. (Orig.). 1988. pap. 22.95 (*0-900588-95-0*, Pub. by Temenos) S Perennis.

— Temenos: A Review Devoted to the Arts of the Imagination, Vol. 10. (Illus.). 306p. (Orig.). 1989. pap. 22.95 (*0-900588-96-9*, Pub. by Temenos) S Perennis.

— Temenos: A Review Devoted to the Arts of the Imagination, Vol. 11. (Illus.). 304p. (Orig.). 1990. pap. 22.95 (*0-900588-97-7*, Pub. by Temenos) S Perennis.

— Temenos: A Review Devoted to the Arts of the Imagination, Vol. 12. (Illus.). 267p. (Orig.). 1991. pap. 22.95 (*0-900588-98-5*, Pub. by Temenos) S Perennis.

— Temenos: A Review Devoted to the Arts of the Imagination, Vol. 13. (Illus.). 296p. (Orig.). 1992. pap. 22.95 (*0-900588-99-3*, Pub. by Temenos) S Perennis.

Raine, Kathleen, tr. see Balzac, Honore de.

Raine, Kathleen, tr. see Calderon de la Barca, Pedro.

Raine, Linnea P., jt. ed. see Cilluffo, Frank J.

***Raine, Nancy Venable.** After Silence: Rape & My Journey Back. 1999. pap. 14.00 (*0-609-80419-7*, Three Riv Pr) Crown Pub Group.

Raine, Norman R. Tugboat Annie. 17.95 (*0-89387-010-2*) Amereon Ltd.

Raine, P. A., jt. ed. see Morton, N. S.

Raine, Patricia, jt. auth. see Gheissari, Nick.

Raine, Peter A., et al, eds. Surgical Emergencies in Children: A Practical Guide. LC 94-27819. (Illus.). 416p. 1994. text 150.00 (*0-7506-1389-0*) Buttrwrth-Heinemann.

Raine, W. M. The Last Shot. 1976. reprint ed. lib. bdg. 20.95 (*0-88411-553-4*) Amereon Ltd.

Raine, William M. Bonanza. 1976. reprint ed. lib. bdg. 25.95 (*0-88411-551-8*) Amereon Ltd.

— Bucky Follows a Cold Trail. large type ed. LC 91-19656. 376p. 1991. reprint ed. lib. bdg. 17.95 (*1-56054-214-4*) Thorndike Pr.

— Colorado. 1976. reprint ed. lib. bdg. 24.95 (*0-88411-557-7*) Amereon Ltd.

— Famous Sheriffs & Western Outlaws. 21.95 (*0-89190-544-8*) Amereon Ltd.

— The Fighting Edge. large type ed. LC 90-11285. 376p. 1990. reprint ed. lib. bdg. 16.95 (*1-56054-077-X*) Thorndike Pr.

— Gunsight Pass. large type ed. 400p. 1991. reprint ed. lib. bdg. 16.95 (*1-56054-213-6*) Thorndike Pr.

— High Grass Valley. large type ed. LC 90-25147. 263p. 1991. reprint ed. lib. bdg. 15.95 (*1-56054-108-3*) Thorndike Pr.

— King of the Bush. 1976. reprint ed. lib. bdg. 27.95 (*0-88411-552-6*) Amereon Ltd.

— Man-Size. large type ed. LC 93-21817. 363p. 1993. lib. bdg. 18.95 (*1-56054-582-8*) Thorndike Pr.

— Powdersmoke Feud. 1980. mass mkt. 1.75 (*0-451-09076-4*, E9076, Sig) NAL.

— Run of the Brush. 1976. reprint ed. lib. bdg. 23.95 (*0-88411-554-2*) Amereon Ltd.

— Square Shooter. 1976. reprint ed. lib. bdg. 23.95 (*0-88411-555-0*) Amereon Ltd.

— Steve Yeager. 1976. reprint ed. lib. bdg. 23.95 (*0-88411-556-9*) Amereon Ltd.

Rainer, Dachine. Giornale di Venezia. 110p. 1996. pap. 12.95 (*3-7052-0964-7*, Pub. by Poetry Salzburg) Intl Spec Bk.

***Rainer, Franz, et al.** Wirtschaftssprache: Anglistische, Germanistische, Romanistische Und Slavistische Beitrage Gewidmet Peter Schifko Zum 60. Geburtstag. (Illus.). 329p. 1998. 51.95 (*3-631-33236-X*) P Lang Pubng.

Rainer, George. Understanding Infrastructure: A Guide for Architects & Planners. LC 89-36569. 304p. 1990. 99.00 (*0-471-50546-3*) Wiley.

Rainer, H., jt. ed. see Jakesz, R.

Rainer, Haselier. Word fur Windows Version. 2nd ed. (GER.). (C). 1991. text. write for info. (*0-201-55990-0*) Addison-Wesley.

Rainer, Howard. A Song for Mother Earth. LC 95-23009. (Illus.). 192p. 1996. pap. 34.95 (*0-89802-661-X*) Beautiful Am.

Rainer, Iris. The Boys in the Mailroom. 1987. mass mkt. 4.95 (*0-446-35002-8*) Warner Bks.

Rainer, John D., et al, eds. Genetic Disease: The Unwanted Inheritance. LC 89-20100. (Loss, Grief & Care Ser.: Vol. 3, Nos. 3 & 4). (Illus.). 213p. 1989. text 6.95 (*0-86656-953-7*) Haworth Pr.

***Rainer, Kathleen.** Outrageous Seas: Shipwreck & Survival in the Waters off Newfoundland, 1583-1893. Baehre, Rainer K., ed. (Illus.). 152p. 1999. text. write for info. (*0-88629-358-8*, Pub. by McG-Queens Univ Pr) CUP Services.

Rainer, Kathleen. Yeats the Initiate: Essays on Certain Themes in the Work of W. B. Yeats. (Illus.). 449p. (C). 1990. text 83.00 (*0-389-20951-1*) B&N Imports.

Rainer, M. & Schmidt, H. J., eds. Current Topics in Mathematical Cosmology: Proceedings of the International Seminar Potsdam, Germany, 30 March-4 April 1998. 450p. 1999. 88.00 (*981-02-3627-1*) World Scientific Pub.

***Rainer, Marilyn.** FTCE Educational Media Specialist. 125p. (C). 2000. per. 22.50 (*1-58197-079-X*) XAM.

***Rainer, Marilyn, et al.** PRAXIS English Middle School. (Praxis Ser.). (C). 2000. per. 22.50 (*1-58197-055-2*) XAM.

Rainer, Peter, ed. Love & Hisses: The National Society of Film Critics Sound off on the Hottest Movie Controversies. LC 92-11175. 560p. 1992. pap. 16.95 (*1-56279-031-5*) Mercury Hse Inc.

Rainer, Pineas. Monarch Notes on Shakespeare's As You Like It. (Orig.). (C). 3.95 (*0-671-00631-2*, Arco) Macmillan Gen Ref.

Rainer, Thom. Closing the Back Door, Set. pap. 54.95 incl. audio Chrch Grwth VA.

Rainer, Thom. Closing the Back Door: How to Stop the Exodus of Members from Your Church. Spear, Cindy G., ed. 18p. 1998. wbk. ed. 54.95 incl. audio (*1-57052-095-X*) Chrch Grwth VA.

— High-Expectations: The Remarkable Secret of Keeping People in Your Church. LC 98-27122. (Illus.). 256p. 1999. pap. 13.99 (*0-8054-1266-2*) Broadman.

Rainer, Thom S. The Book of Church Growth: History, Theology, & Principles. 1998. pap. 19.99 (*0-8054-1872-5*) Broadman.

— Eating the Elephant: Bite-Sized Steps to Achieve Long-Term Growth in Your Church. 1999. pap. text 11.99 (*0-8054-2058-4*) Broadman.

— Effective Evangelistic Churches. 256p. 1996. 13.99 (*0-8054-5402-0*, 4254-02) Broadman.

Rainer, Thom S. & Silva, Michael. Experiencing Personal Revival: A Guide to Renewing Your Relationship & Enlightening Your Walk with God. Spear, Cindy G., ed. 60p. (Orig.). 1996. pap. 10.95 (*1-57052-057-7*) Chrch Grwth VA.

— Experiencing Revival: A Guide to Personal Renewal & Evangelistic Revival in Your Church. Spear, Cindy G., ed. 91p. 1996. ring bd. 109.95 incl. VHS (*1-57052-058-5*) Chrch Grwth VA.

Rainer, Tom. Piano in the Rhythm Section. Cavalier, Debbie, ed. (Contemporary Rhythm Section Ser.). 36p. (Orig.). (YA). 1997. pap. text 24.95 (*1-57623-994-2*, 0051B) Wrner Bros.

Rainer, Tristine. The New Diary: How to Use a Journal for Self-Guidance & Expanded Creativity. LC 76-62677. 324p. 1979. reprint ed. pap. 13.95 (*0-87477-150-1*, Tarcher Putnam) Putnam Pub Group.

— Your Life As Story: Discovering the "New Autobiography" & Writing Memoir As Literature. LC 98-10091. 368p. 1998. reprint ed. pap. 14.95 (*0-87477-922-7*, Tarcher Putnam) Putnam Pub Group.

Rainer, Werner, jt. auth. see De Catanzaro, Christine D.

Rainer, Yvonne. The Films of Yvonne Rainer. LC 88-46035. (Theories of Representation & Difference Ser.). (Illus.). 226p. 1989. 14.00 (*0-253-34906-0*); pap. 5.25 (*0-253-20542-5*) Ind U Pr.

— A Women Who... Essays, Interviews, Scripts. LC 99-20799. 440p. 1999. pap. 45.00 (*0-8018-6078-4*) Johns Hopkins.

***Rainer, Yvonne.** A Women Who... Essays, Interviews, Scripts. LC 99-20799. 440p. 1999. pap. 19.95 (*0-8018-6079-2*) Johns Hopkins.

Raineri, A., et al. The State & Future Directions of Acute Myocardial Infarction. xii, 484p. 1988. text 348.00 (*3-7186-4808-3*) Gordon & Breach.

Raineri, Angelo A., jt. ed. see Leachman, R. D.

Raineri, Deanna, jt. auth. see Blackwell Science Inc., Publishing Staff.

Raineri, Ellen. Wisdom in the Workplace: On the Job Training for the Soul. Sommer, Eleanor K., ed. LC 96-96975. (Illus.). 215p. (Orig.). 1997. pap. 14.95 (*0-9654035-0-5*) Braino.

Raineri, Vivian M. The Red Angel: The Life & Times of Elaine Black Yoneda, 1906-1988. LC 91-15038. (Illus.). xiv, 332p. 1991. 19.00 (*0-7178-0688-X*); pap. 9.95 (*0-7178-0686-3*) Intl Pubs Co.

Raines. Education at Northern Arizona University. 1996. pap. text. write for info. (*0-205-26583-9*) Allyn.

— Education JIT Northern Arizona University. 1996. pap. text. write for info. (*0-205-26706-8*) Allyn.

Raines, et al. Mac Tutorial Software-Mechanics. 1992. text 410.25 (*0-534-93076-X*) PWS Pubs.

Raines, Barbara, ed. see Ireland, Patricia, et al.

Raines, C. W. A Bibliography of Texas. 284p. 1997. reprint ed. 60.00 (*1-57898-017-8*) Martino Pubng.

Raines, Cadwell W. Analytical Index to the Laws of Texas, 1823-1905 (Both Dates Inclusive) 559p. 1987. reprint ed. 52.50 (*0-8377-2534-8*, Rothman) W S Hein.

Raines, Charlie & Wilderness Society Staff. Visitor's Guide to Ancient Forests of Washington. 2nd ed. LC 96-27000. (Illus.). 88p. 1996. pap. 7.95 (*0-89886-473-9*) Mountaineers.

Raines, Claire. Beyond Generation X: A Bridge-Building Guide for Managers. LC 97-65866. (Professional Ser.). (Illus.). 146p. (Orig.). 1997. pap. 12.95 (*1-56052-449-9*) Crisp Pubns.

Raines, Claire & Bradford, Lawrence. Twentysomething. 208p. 1992. 12.95 (*0-942361-62-8*) MasterMedia Pub.

***Raines, Claire & Hunt, Jim.** X'ers & the Boomers. 128p. 2000. pap. 14.95 (*1-56052-587-8*) Crisp Pubns.

Raines, Claire & Williamson, Linda. Using Visual Aids. rev. ed. Hicks, Tony, ed. LC 94-80034. (Fifty-Minute Ser.). (Illus.). 84p. (Orig.). 1995. pap. 10.95 (*1-56052-326-3*) Crisp Pubns.

Raines, Howell. Fly Fishing Through the Midlife Crisis. LC 94-18465. 352p. 1994. pap. 14.00 (*0-385-47519-5*, Anchor NY) Doubleday.

— My Soul Is Rested: Movement Days in the Deep South Remembered. 472p. 1983. pap. 14.95 (*0-14-006753-1*, Penguin Bks) Viking Penguin.

***Raines, Howell.** Whiskey Man. 2000. pap. 16.95 (*0-8173-1067-3*) U of Ala Pr.

Raines, Jeff. The Big Island. 224p. 1989. pap. 3.95 (*0-380-70552-4*, Avon Bks) Morrow Avon.

— Unbalanced Acts. 272p. 1990. mass mkt. 4.50 (*0-380-76008-8*, Avon Bks) Morrow Avon.

Raines, Jocelyn. Romance, Inc. 1996. mass mkt. 5.99 (*0-671-89953-8*) PB.

Raines, John, jt. ed. see Efroymson, Daniel P.

***Raines, John C. & Maguire, Daniel C., eds.** What Men Owe to Women: Men's Voices from World Religions. LC 00-27494. (C). 2000. pap. text 19.95 (*0-7914-4786-3*) State U NY Pr.

— What Men Owe to Women: Men's Voices from World Religions. LC 00-27494. (C). 2001. text 59.50 (*0-7914-4785-5*) State U NY Pr.

***Raines, Kimberley.** Darkest Fantasies. 256p. 2000. pap. 9.95 (*1-901388-52-2*, Pub. by Chimera Pubns) Firebird Dist.

Raines, Lizz. Widowmaker: A Mystery Thriller. 1994. pap. 5.95 (*0-9625632-4-2*) NUVENTURES Pub.

Raines, Paul. TCL/TK Pocket Reference. (Illus.). 96p. 1998. pap. 7.95 (*1-56592-498-3*) OReilly & Assocs.

***Raines, Paul & Tranter, Jeff.** TCL/TK in a Nutshell. Oram, Andy, ed. (In a Nutshell Ser.). (Illus.). 440p. 1999. pap. 24.95 (*1-56592-433-9*) OReilly & Assocs.

Raines, Philip & Brown, Ross, eds. Policy Competition & Foreign Direct Investment in Europe. LC 98-74932. 7p. 1999. 61.95 (*1-84014-768-7*, Pub. by Ashgate Pub) Ashgate Pub Co.

Raines, Rebecca Robbins. Getting the Message Through (Clothbound) A Branch History of the United States Army Signal Corps. 484p. 1996. text 36.00 (*0-16-045351-8*) USGPO.

***Raines, Richard C. & Marchiano, James J.** Handling Depositions: Action Guide - Winter 1999, 2 vols. Compton, Linda, ed. 120p. 1999. ring bd. 58.00 (*0-7626-0293-7*, CP-11056) Cont Ed Bar-CA.

Raines, Robert. A Time to Live: Seven Steps of Creative Aging. 224p. 1998. pap. 12.95 (*0-452-27805-8*, Plume) Dutton Plume.

Raines, Robert A. A Time To Live: Seven Tasks Of Creative Aging / large type ed. LC 98-54117. 1999. 26.95 (*0-7862-1776-6*) Thorndike Pr.

***Raines, Shirley & Isbell, Rebecca.** Tell It Again! Easy to Tell Stories with Activities for Young Children. LC 99-13675. (Illus.). 192p. (J). (ps-3). 1999. pap. 14.95 (*0-87659-200-0*, Pub. by Gryphon Hse) Consort Bk Sales.

Raines, Shirley, jt. auth. see Isbell, Rebecca.

Raines, Shirley C. Four Hundred Fifty More Story Stretchers for the Primary Grades: Activities to Expand Children's Favorite Books. LC 94-9450. 254p. 1994. 19.95 (*0-87659-167-5*) Gryphon Hse.

— More Story Stretchers. 254p. 1991. pap. 19.95 (*0-87659-153-5*) Gryphon Hse.

— Never, Ever, Serve Sugary Snacks on Rainy Days: The Official Little Instruction Book for Teachers of Young Children. LC 95-12515. 96p. (Orig.). 1995. pap. 6.95 (*0-87659-175-6*) Gryphon Hse.

Raines, Shirley C., ed. Whole Language Across the Curriculum. 240p. 1995. pap. text 19.95 (*0-8077-3446-2*) Tchrs Coll.

Raines, Shirley C. & Canady, Robert J. Story S-t-r-e-t-c-h-e-r-s: Activities to Expand Children's Favorite Books. Charner, Kathleen, ed. 251p. 1989. pap. 19.95 (*0-87659-119-5*) Gryphon Hse.

— Story S-t-r-e-t-c-h-e-r-s for the Primary Grades: Activities to Expand Children's Favorite Books. 256p. 1992. pap. 19.95 (*0-87659-157-8*) Gryphon Hse.

— The Whole Language Kindergarten. (Early Childhood Education Ser.: No. 30). 304p. (C). 1990. pap. text 19.95 (*0-8077-3049-1*) Tchrs Coll.

Raines, Shirley C. & Isbell, Rebecca T. Stories: Children's Literature in Early Education. LC 93-28119. 640p. (C). 1994. mass mkt. 64.95 (*0-8273-5509-2*) Delmar.

— Stories: Children's Literature in Early Education. 31p. 1994. teacher ed. 14.95 (*0-8273-5510-6*) Delmar.

***Raines, Theron.** Bruno Bettelheim. 1999. write for info. (*0-679-40196-2*) Knopf.

Rainey. Stressed Out? A Special Unit, Foundation. (HA - Social Studies). (C). 1997. mass mkt. 16.95 (*0-314-22523-4*) S-W Pub.

Rainey, jt. auth. see Massie.

Rainey, A. F., ed. Kinattutu sa Darati: Raphael Kutscher Memorial. (Journal of the Institute of Archaeology of Tel Aviv University - Occasional Publications: Vol. 1). (Illus.). xix, 245p. 1993. text 20.00 (*965-440-002-2*, Pub. by Friends Archeol Inst) Eisenbrauns.

Rainey, Anson F. Canaanite in the Amarns Tablets: A Linguistics Analysis of the Mixed Dialect Used by Scribes from Canaan, 4 vols. LC 95-49131. (Handbuch Der Orientalistik Ser.). 1995. 437.50 (*90-04-10503-4*) Brill Academic Pubs.

Rainey, Anson F., ed. Egypt, Israel, Sinai: Archaeological & Historical Relationships in the Biblical Period. (Books from the American University of Beirut Press). (Illus.). 174p. (C). 1988. pap. text 9.95 (*0-8156-7054-0*) Syracuse U Pr.

***Rainey, Barbara & Escue, Ashley, compiled by.** A Mother's Legacy: Wisdom from Mothers to Daughters. LC 99-85984. 144p. 2000. 12.99 (*0-7852-7007-8*) Nelson.

Rainey, Barbara, jt. auth. see Rainey, Dennis.

Rainey, Barbara, jt. ed. see Rainey, Dennis.

Rainey, Buck. The Life & Films of Buck Jones: The Silent Era. (Illus.). 263p. 1988. pap. 14.95 (*0-936505-07-9*) World Yesterday.

— The Life & Films of Buck Jones: The Sound Era. (Illus.). 388p. (Orig.). 1992. pap. 24.95 (0-936505-08-7) World Yesterday.

— The Reel Cowboy: Essays on the Myth in Movies & Literature. LC 96-3191. (Illus.). 319p. 1996. lib. bdg. 42.50 (0-7864-0106-0) McFarland & Co.

— Serials & Series: A World Filmography, 1912-1956. LC 98-25107. (Illus.). 331p. 1999. lib. bdg. 95.00 (0-7864-0449-3) McFarland & Co.

— The Shoot-Em-Ups Ride Again: A Supplement to Shoot-Em-Ups. LC 90-34151. (Illus.). 319p. 1990. 66.00 (0-8108-2132-X) Scarecrow.

— The Shoot-Em-Ups Ride Again: A Supplement to Shoot-Em-Ups. LC 90-34151. (Illus.). 309p. 1990. pap. 19.95 (0-936505-12-5) World Yesterday.

— Sweethearts of the Sage: Biographies & Filmographies of 258 Actresses Appearing in Western Movies. LC 91-52639. (Illus.). 652p. 1992. lib. bdg. 99.50 (0-89950-565-1) McFarland & Co.

— Those Fabulous Serial Heroines. LC 88-11369. (Illus.). 523p. 1990. pap. text 29.95 (0-936505-10-9) World Yesterday.

— Those Fabulous Serial Heroines: Their Lives & Films. LC 88-11369. (Illus.). 537p. 1990. 66.00 (0-8108-1911-2) Scarecrow.

— Western Gunslingers in Fact & on Film: Hollywood's Famous Lawmen & Outlaws. LC 98-41807. 349p. 1998. pap. 38.50 (0-7864-0396-9) McFarland & Co.

Rainey, Chuck. The Complete Bass Player Bk. 1: The Method. LC 86-119413. (Illus.). 192p. 1985. pap. 22.95 (0-8256-2425-8, AM 37250) Omnibus NY.

— The Complete Electric Bass Player Bk. 2: Playing Concepts & Dexterity. (Illus.). 80p. 1985. pap. 14.95 (0-8256-2426-6, AM37268) Music Sales.

— The Complete Electric Bass Player Bk. 3: Electric Bass Improvisation. (Illus.). 64p. 1985. pap. 14.95 (0-8256-2427-4, AM37284) Music Sales.

— The Complete Electric Bass Player Bk. 4: Slapping Techniques. (Illus.). 64p. 1985. pap. 14.95 (0-8256-2428-2, AM37276) Music Sales.

— The Complete Electric Bass Player Bk. 5: Bass Chording. Vol. 5. (Illus.). 48p. 1985. pap. 14.95 (0-8256-2429-0, AM39405) Music Sales.

Rainey, Clarice H. Mountain of Death. LC 97-92202. 238p. 1998. pap. 12.95 (0-9659622-0-2) C H Rainey.

***Rainey, Dennis.** Building Your Marriage. (Homebuiders Couples Ser.). 230p. 2000. pap. text 10.99 (0-7644-2237-5) Group Pub.

Rainey, Dennis. Familylife Today Marriage Projects Manual. abr. ed. 30p. (Orig.). (C). 1.95 (1-57229-003-X) FamilyLife.

— Fear Not. 16p. (Orig.). (C). 1.95 (1-57229-006-4) FamilyLife.

— One Home at a Time: Restoring the Soul of America Through God's Plan for Your Marriage & Family. LC 97-10893. 267p. 1997. 16.99 (1-56179-545-3) Focus Family.

Rainey, Dennis. Preparing for Marriage Couples Pack. 1997. pap. 16.99 (0-8307-2157-6) Gospel Lght.

Rainey, Dennis. Staying Close. 1992. pap. 12.99 (0-8499-3343-9) Word Pub.

Rainey, Dennis & Boehi, Dave. The Tribute & the Promise. LC 97-20345. 304p. 1997. pap. 12.99 (0-7852-7175-9) Nelson.

Rainey, Dennis & Rainey, Barbara. Familylife Today Parenting Projects Manual. abr. ed. 32p. (Orig.). (C). 1994. 1.95 (1-57229-002-1) FamilyLife.

— Moments Together for Couples: Devotionals for Drawing Near to God & One Another. 385p. 1995. pap. 12.99 (0-8307-1808-7, 5422691, Regal Bks) Gospel Lght.

— New Building Your Mate's Self-Esteem. expanded ed. 312p. 1995. pap. 12.99 (0-7852-7824-9) Nelson.

— Putting the Thanks Back in Thanksgiving. 16p. (Orig.). 1.95 (1-57229-007-2) FamilyLife.

— The Questions Book for Marriage Intimacy. 80p. reprint ed. 9.95 (0-9619022-0-5) Family Ministry.

— The Questions Book for Marriage Intimacy. 3rd ed. Denker, Julie, ed. (Illus.). 84p. pap. text 9.95 (1-57229-001-3) FamilyLife.

***Rainey, Dennis & Rainey, Barbara.** Simply Romantic Ideas: Ways to Romance Your Husband. 2000. pap. 6.99 (1-56292-928-3) Honor Bks OK.

— Simply Romantic Ideas: Ways to Romance Your Wife. 2000. pap. 6.99 (1-56292-929-1) Honor Bks OK.

Rainey, Dennis & Rainey, Barbara. Simply Romantic Ideas: 150 Fun & Creative Ways to Romance Your Husband. LC 98-170118. 160p. 1998. pap. 6.99 (1-56292-448-6) Honor Bks OK.

— Simply Romantic Ideas: 150 Fun & Creative Ways to Romance Your Wife. 160p. 1998. pap. 6.99 (1-56292-449-4) Honor Bks OK.

— Standing Together When Life's Falling Apart. abr. ed. Denker, Julie, ed. 20p. (Orig.). (C). 1994. 1.95 (1-57229-000-5) FamilyLife.

***Rainey, Dennis & Rainey, Barbara.** Starting Your Marriage Right: What You Need to Know in the Early Years to Make It Last a Lifetime. LC 00-37981. 288p. 2000. 19.99 (0-7852-6803-0) Nelson.

Rainey, Dennis & Rainey, Barbara, eds. School Choice: Making Your Decision & Making It Work. 73p. 14.95 (1-57229-056-0) FamilyLife.

Rainey, Dennis, et al. Parenting Today's Adolescent. LC 98-29878. 320p. 1998. 19.99 (0-7852-7084-1) Nelson.

Rainey, Don, jt. auth. see Murray, Tinker D.

Rainey, Froelich. Reflections of a Digger: Fifty Years of World Archaeology. LC 92-12150. (Illus.). xx, 324p. 1992. 22.50 (0-924171-15-4) U Museum Pubns.

Rainey, Froelich G. Excavations in the Ft. Liberte Region, Haiti. LC 76-44780. reprint ed. 37.50 (0-404-15965-6) AMS Pr.

Rainey, Hal G. Understanding & Managing Public Organizations. LC 90-28985. (Public Administration - Management Ser.). 359p. 1991. 40.95 (1-55542-344-2) Jossey-Bass.

— Understanding & Managing Public Organizations. 2nd ed. LC 96-2538. (Public Administration Ser.). 1996. 37.95 (0-7879-0251-9) Jossey-Bass.

Rainey, Homer P., et al. How Fare American Youth? LC 74-1700. (Children & Youth Ser.). 186p. 1974. reprint ed. 21.95 (0-405-05977-9) Ayer.

Rainey, John C. The Thang That Ate My Grandaddy's Dog. LC 97-4447. 368p. 1997. 18.95 (1-56164-130-8) Pineapple Pr.

Rainey, Kaitlin, jt. auth. see Hegedus, Alannah.

***Rainey, Kenneth P. W.** American & Country Music Tune Book. 136p. 2000. pap. 17.95 (0-7866-3190-2, 96796) Mel Bay.

Rainey, Lawrence. Institutions of Modernism: Literary Elites & Public Culture. LC 98-8300. (Illus.). 256p. 1998. 25.00 (0-300-07050-0) Yale U Pr.

Rainey, Lawrence S. Ezra Pound & the Monument of Culture: Text, History & the Malatesta Cantos. LC 90-44410. (Illus.). 368p. 1991. 35.95 (0-226-70316-9) U Ch Pr.

Rainey, Lawrence S., ed. A Poem Containing History: Textual Studies in "The Cantos" LC 96-41212. 288p. (C). 1997. text 57.50 (0-472-10232-X, 10232) U of Mich Pr.

Rainey, Penelope. Medieval Latin Lyric, No. 2. (Latin Commentaries Ser.). 67p. (Orig.). (C). 1993. pap. text 6.00 (0-929524-78-0) Bryn Mawr Commentaries.

— Medieval Latin Lyric, No. 3. (Latin Commentaries Ser.). 75p. (Orig.). (C). 1993. pap. text 6.00 (0-929524-79-9) Bryn Mawr Commentaries.

— Medieval Latin Lyric, Vol. 1. (Latin Commentaries Ser.). 75p. (Orig.). (C). 1993. pap. text 6.00 (0-929524-76-4) Bryn Mawr Commentaries.

— Plato: Laches. 1985. pap. text 6.00 (0-929524-28-4) Bryn Mawr Commentaries.

Rainey, R., jt. auth. see Atkins, K.

Rainey, R. C. Migration & Meteorology: Flight Behaviour & the Atmospheric Environment of Migrant Pests. (Illus.). 344p. 1990. 150.00 (0-19-854541-X) OUP.

Rainey, R. L. Portraits from Paul's Pen. 1994. pap. text 6.25 (0-937396-96-6) Walterick Pubs.

Rainey, R. Randall & Magill, Gerard, eds. Abortion & Public Policy: An Interdisciplinary Investigation Within the Catholic Tradition. xii, 254p. 1996. 24.95 (1-881871-17-7); pap. 16.95 (1-881871-18-5) Creighton U Pr.

Rainey, Ralph E. Wallace A. Rainey & Jessie I. Ringer: Their Ancestors, Descendants & Allied Families. LC 85-90199. (Illus.). 402p. 1985. 35.00 (0-9615061-0-5) Rainey R.

Rainey, Reuben M. Freud As Student of Religion: Perspectives on the Background & Development of His Thought. LC 75-17536. (American Academy of Religion. Dissertation Ser.: No. 7). 184p. reprint ed. pap. 57.10 (0-608-30591-X, 201754800007) Bks Demand.

Rainey, Rhonda. Decorating with Paper & Paint: Combining Decoupage & Faux Finish Techniques. LC 98-3372. (Illus.). 128p. 1998. 27.95 (0-8069-8171-7) Sterling.

***Rainey, Rhonda.** Decorating with Paper & Paint: Combining Decoupage & Faux Finish Techniques. (Illus.). 128p. 1999. pap. 14.95 (0-8069-8172-5, Chapelle) Sterling.

— Faux Finishing for the First Time. 2000. 19.95 (0-8069-4483-8) Sterling.

Rainey, Rhonda. Heartfelt Ways to Say Good-Bye. LC 97-41083. (Illus.). 80p. 1997. 7.95 (0-8069-0835-1) Sterling.

Rainey, Rich. Haunted History. (Orig.). 1992. mass mkt. 4.99 (0-446-36179-8, Pub. by Warner Bks) Little.

Rainey, Richard. The Monster Factory. LC 92-26191. (Illus.). 128p. (YA). (gr. 6 up). 1993. lib. bdg. 19.00 (0-02-775663-7, Mac Bks Young Read) S&S Childrens.

Rainey, Ross. Capsule Comments on the Cults. 1988. pap. 2.50 (0-937396-72-9) Walterick Pubs.

Rainey, Sue. Creating Picturesque America, 1870-1874: Monument to the Natural & Cultural Landscape. LC 94-33484. (Illus.). xvii, 383p. (C). 1994. 34.95 (0-8265-1257-7) Vanderbilt U Pr.

Rainey, Sue, et al. Shaping the Landscape Image, 1865-1910: John Douglas Woodward. LC 97-6008. (Illus.). 1997. pap. 25.00 (0-8139-1768-9) U Pr of Va.

Rainey, Thomas E., Jr. The Flute Manual. (Illus.). 240p. 1991. pap. 12.95 (0-936369-28-0) Son-Rise Pubns.

***Rainey, Todd J.** Money Talk: A Gay & Lesbian Guide to Financial Success. 160p. 1999. pap. 18.95 (1-891689-75-4) Gabriel Pubns.

Rainey, Virginia, jt. auth. see Carroll, John P.

Rainey, William, jt. auth. see Mulcrone, Patricia.

***Rainford, Laura, et al.** Health in England, 1998: Investigating the Links Between Social Inequalities & Health: A Survey of Adults Aged 16 & over in England Carried Out by the Social Survey Division of ONS on Behalf of the Health Education Authority. Mason, Val, ed. (Illus.). viii, 295p. 2000. 65.00 (0-11-621357-4, Pub. by Statnry Office) Balogh.

Rainford, Swainston, jt. auth. see Coad.

Rainforth, Beverly. Collaborative Teams for Students with Severe Disabilities: Integrating Therapy & Educational Services. 2nd ed. LC 97-207. 1997. pap. text 37.00 (1-55766-291-6) P H Brookes.

Rainger, Amanda, jt. auth. see O'Connor, Niobe.

Rainger, Ronald. An Agenda for Antiquity: Henry Fairfield Osborn & Vertebrate Paleontology at the American Museum of Natural History, 1890-1935. LC 90-25167. (History of American Science & Technology Ser.). 376p. (C). 1991. text 44.95 (0-8173-0536-X) U of Ala Pr.

Rainger, Ronald, et al, eds. The American Development of Biology. 380p. (C). 1991. pap. text 20.00 (0-8135-1702-8) Rutgers U Pr.

— The Expansion of American Biology. LC 90-48070. 400p. (C). 1991. text 45.00 (0-8135-1650-1); pap. text 18.00 (0-8135-1651-X) Rutgers U Pr.

***Rainger, Tim.** Surfing. (Extreme Sports Ser.). (Illus.). 32p. (YA). (gr. 5-9). 1999. pap. 6.95 (0-7641-0799-2) Barron.

Raingruber, Bob & Maser, Lou. The King's Gambit As White. 3rd ed. Long, Robert B., ed. (Illus.). 205p. 1995. pap. 22.95 (0-938650-47-5) Thinkers Pr.

Raingruber, Bob, ed. see Christiansen, Larry, et al.

Rainham, David C. Beat Stress, Exercise! (Illus.). 8p. (Orig.). 1996. pap. 2.50 (1-884241-49-2, EHO560) Energeia Pub.

— High School Stress. (Illus.). 12p. (Orig.). (YA). 1996. pap. 2.50 (1-884241-60-3, SPSO315) Energeia Pub.

— How to Relax. (Illus.). 8p. (Orig.). 1995. pap. 2.50 (1-884241-61-1, EHO590) Energeia Pub.

— How to Worry. (Illus.). 16p. (Orig.). 1996. pap. 3.00 (1-884241-64-6, EHO530) Energeia Pub.

— Money Stress. (Illus.). 12p. (Orig.). 1996. pap. 3.00 (1-884241-59-X, EHO570) Energeia Pub.

— Reduce Stress - Communicate. (Orig.). 1996. pap. 3.00 (1-884241-36-0, EHO550) Energeia Pub.

— Self-Esteem: How to Feel Better about Yourself. (Illus.). 8p. (Orig.). 1995. pap. 2.50 (1-884241-58-1, EHO600) Energeia Pub.

— The Stress of Parenting Infants. (Illus.). 24p. (Orig.). 1996. pap. 3.50 (1-884241-48-4, EHO5TO) Energeia Pub.

— The Stress of Teaching, Relieving the Pressure. 48p. (Orig.). Date not set. 7.00 (1-884241-37-9, ETMO020) Energeia Pub.

— The Stress of Unemployment. (Illus.). 24p. (Orig.). 1996. pap. 3.50 (1-884241-46-8, CEO010) Energeia Pub.

— Stress Reducing Attitudes. (Illus.). (Orig.). 1996. pap. 3.00 (1-884241-63-8, EHO520) Energeia Pub.

— Stress Reducing Habits. (Illus.). 8p. (Orig.). 1996. pap. 2.50 (1-884241-65-4, EHO580) Energeia Pub.

— The Stresses of Parenting Teenagers. (Illus.). 24p. (Orig.). 1996. pap. 3.50 (1-884241-47-6, EHO500) Energeia Pub.

— Time Stress. (Illus.). 16p. (Orig.). 1997. pap. 3.00 (1-884241-67-0, EHO540) Energeia Pub.

— University & College Stress. (Illus.). 16p. (Orig.). 1996. pap. 3.00 (1-884241-32-8, SPSO314) Energeia Pub.

Rainich, Gabrielle & Kuipers, A. H., eds. Russian-English Vocabulary with Grammatical Sketch. (ENG & RUS.). 66p. 1990. reprint ed. pap. 17.00 (0-8218-0037-X, REV) Am Math.

Rainier, Chris. Where Masks Still Dance: New Guinea. LC 96-7327. (Illus.). 132p. 1996. 60.00 (0-8212-2261-9, Pub. by Bulfinch Pr) Little.

***Rainis, Kenneth G.** Crime-Solving Science Projects: Forensic Science Experiments. LC 99-50546. (Science Fair Success Ser.). (Illus.). 128p. (YA). (gr. 6 up). 2000. lib. bdg. 20.95 (0-7660-1289-1) Enslow Pubs.

Rainis, Kenneth G. Exploring with a Magnifying Glass. LC 91-18329. (Venture Bks.). (Illus.). 128p. (YA). (gr. 7-12). 1991. lib. bdg. 24.00 (0-531-12508-4) Watts.

— Nature Projects for Young Scientists. (Projects for Young Scientists Ser.). (J). 1989. pap. 6.95 (0-531-15135-2) Watts.

Rainis, Kenneth G. & Nassis, George. Biotechnology Projects for Young Scientists. LC 97-20536. (Projects for Young Scientists Ser.). 160p. (gr. 9 up). 1998. 24.00 (0-531-11419-8) Watts.

— Biotechnology Projects for Young Scientists. (Projects for Young Scientists Ser.). (Illus.). 1998. pap. 6.95 (0-531-15913-2) Watts.

Rainis, Kenneth G. & Russell, Bruce J. Guide to Microlife. LC 95-44973. 288p. (YA). (gr. 9 up). 1996. pap. 40.00 (0-531-11266-7) Watts.

Rainnie, Al, jt. auth. see Hardy, Jane.

Rainolde, Richard. A Booke Called the Foundacion of Rhetorike. LC 78-6210. (English Experience Ser.: No. 91). 1969. reprint ed. 30.00 (90-221-0091-X) Walter J Johnson.

Rains, A. J. 1001 Multiple Choice Questions & Answers in Surgery: A Companion to Surgical Study Based on "Bailey & Love's Short Practice of Surgery" 4th ed. 240p. 1996. pap. 17.99 (0-412-55560-3, Pub. by E A) OUP.

Rains, Alvin L. & Palmer, Michael J. Local Area Networking with Novell Software. 2nd ed. 392p. (C). 1994. mass mkt., teacher ed. 49.95 (0-87709-042-4) Course Tech.

Rains, Darell L. Major Home Appliances: A Common Sense Repair Manual. (Illus.). 160p. (Orig.). 1987. pap. 15.95 (0-8306-2747-2) McGraw-Hill Prof.

Rains, H., ed. 1001 Multiple Choice Questions & Answers in Surgery. 3rd ed. (Illus.). 200p. (Orig.). (C). (gr. 13). 1991. pap. text 27.00 (0-412-40010-3, Chap & Hall NY) Chapman & Hall.

Rains, John. Cruising Ports: Florida to California Via Panama. rev. ed. LC 82-10855. (Illus.). 208p. 1994. pap. 19.95 (0-930030-27-3) ProStar Pubns.

— MexWX (Weather-Radio for Boaters in Mexico) 2nd ed. 1998. 19.95 (0-9638470-1-5) Pt Loma Pubng.

Rains, John & Miller, Patricia. Boating in Spanish (Lexicon for Adventurers) 2000. 22.95 (0-9638470-5-8) Pt Loma Pubng.

***Rains, John & Rains, Pat Miller.** Cruising Ports: Florida to California via Panama (Guidebook) 4th ed. (Illus.). 320p. 1999. pap. text 34.95 (0-9638470-7-4, Pub. by Pt Loma Pubng) R Hale & Co.

Rains, Pat Miller, jt. auth. see Rains, John.

Rains, Prue & Teram, Eli. Normal Bad Boys: Public Policies, Institutions & the Politics of Client Recruitment. 200p. 1992. 60.00 (0-7735-0906-2, Pub. by McG-Queens Univ Pr) CUP Services.

Rains, Rob. The Cardinals Fan's Little Book of Wisdom. LC 94-23542. 1994. pap. 6.95 (0-912083-77-8) Diamond Communications.

***Rains, Rob.** Craig Biggio: Astro All-Star. (Illus.). 96p. (J). 2000. pap. 4.95 (1-58261-253-6) Sports Pub.

Rains, Rob. Mark McGwire. 1999. mass mkt. 5.99 (0-312-97109-5) St Martin.

— Mark McGwire: Home Run Hero. LC 98-38326. (Illus.). 227p. 1998. 22.95 (0-312-20162-1) St Martin.

— Mark McGwire: "Mac Attack!" (SuperStar Ser.). 96p. (YA). (gr. 7-10). 1998. pap. 5.95 (1-58261-004-5) Sprts Pubng.

— Mark McGwire: Slugger! Sporting News Staff, ed. (Illus.). 50p. (J). (gr. k-5). 1998. 15.95 (1-58261-005-3) Sprts Pubng.

***Rains, Rob.** Marshall Faulk. (Illus.). 1999. pap. 4.95 (1-58261-167-X) Sprts Pubng.

— Marshall Faulk: Rushing to Glory. (SuperStar Series: Vol. 8). 96p. (J). 1999. pap. 4.95 (1-58261-191-2, Pub. by Sprts Pubng) Partners-West.

Rains, Rob, jt. auth. see Schoendienst, Red.

Rains, Rob, ed. see Bloom, Barry.

Rains, Rob, ed. see Castle, George.

Rains, Rob, ed. see DeMarco, Tony.

Rains, Rob, ed. see Edwards, Sarah.

Rains, Rob, ed. see Grant, Evan.

Rains, Rob, ed. see Hagen, Paul.

Rains, Rob, ed. see Kernan, Kevin.

Rains, Rob, ed. see Manoloff, Dennis.

Rains, Rob, ed. see Noble, Marty.

Rains, Rob, ed. see O'Connell, Jack.

Rains, Rob, ed. see Rozner, Barry.

Rains, Rob, ed. see Shalin, Michael.

Rains, Rob, ed. see Stone, Larry.

Rains, Rob, ed. see Stuper, John.

Rains, Sally T., jt. auth. see Dever-Boaz, Carie.

Rains, Sally T., jt. auth. see Grawer, Rich.

Rains, Sally T., jt. auth. see Kim, Wendell.

Rains, Sally T., ed. see Stuper, John.

Rains, Sally Tippett, jt. auth. see Jordan, Tim.

Rains, Theodore C., jt. ed. see Dean, John A.

Rainsberger, Richard. FERPA Secondary Education: Guidelines for Implementation of the Family Educational Rights & Privacy Act 1974 As Amended, & the Student. rev. ed. 127p. 1997. pap. 40.00 (1-57858-003-X) Am Assn Coll Registrars.

— FERPA Update, 1998: Guidelines to the Family Educational Rights & Privacy Act of 1974 As Amended. LC 98-19897. 128p. 1998. ring bd. 42.00 (1-57858-016-1, 1279) Am Assn Coll Registrars.

Rainsbery, F. B. A History of Children's Television in English Canada, 1952-1986. LC 87-28773. (Illus.). 320p. 1988. 36.00 (0-8108-2079-X) Scarecrow.

Rainsbury, Julie. The Seventh Seal. 2nd ed. 86p. (J). (gr. 4). 1996. reprint ed. pap. 10.95 (0-8464-4842-4) Beekman Pubs.

Rainsbury, Paul A. & Viniker, D. A., eds. Practical Guide to Reproductive Medicine. LC 96-38763. (Illus.). 542p. 1997. text 85.00 (1-85070-727-8) Prthnon Pub.

Rainsbury, Robert. Written English: An Introduction for Beginning Students of English As a Second Language. (C). 1977. pap. text 21.20 (0-13-970673-9) P-H.

Rainsford. Ethics Philosophy Rhetoric. LC 98-15289. 284p. 1999. text 55.00 (0-312-17533-7) St Martin.

Rainsford, Christina. Authorship Ethics & the Reader. LC 96-27678. 264p. 1997. text 45.00 (0-312-16544-7) St Martin.

Rainsford, K. D. Ibuprofen: A Critical Bibliographic Review. 1999. 165.00 (0-7484-0694-8) Taylor & Francis.

Rainsford, K. D., ed. Side Effects of Anti-Inflammatory Drugs IV. LC 97-180927. 384p. 1997. text 234.00 (0-7923-8713-9) Kluwer Academic.

Rainsford, K. D., et al, eds. Copper & Zinc in Inflammatory & Degenerative Diseases. LC 97-41393. 197p. 1998. 137.00 (0-7923-4827-3, D Reidel) Kluwer Academic.

Rainsford, K. D. & Powanda, M. C., eds. Safety & Efficacy of Non-Prescription (OTC) Analgesics & Nsaids: Proceedings of the International Conference, San Francisco, CA. LC 98-134906. 160p. 1998. text 100.50 (0-7923-8737-6) Kluwer Academic.

Rainsford, Kim D., ed. Advances in Anti-Rheumatic Therapy. 252p. 1995. boxed set 149.95 (0-8493-4937-0, 4937) CRC Pr.

— Anti-Inflammatory & Anti-Rheumatic Drugs: Anti-Rheumatic Drugs, Experimental Agents, & Clinical Aspects of Drug Use, Vol. III. 264p. 1985. 148.00 (0-8493-6232-6, RB405, CRC Reprint) Franklin.

— Anti-Inflammatory & Anti-Rheumatic Drugs Vol. 1: Inflammation Mechanisms & Actions of Traditional Drugs. 208p. 1985. 119.00 (0-8493-6230-X, RM405, CRC Reprint) Franklin.

— Anti-Inflammatory & Anti-Rheumatic Drugs Vol. 2: Newer Anti-Inflammatory Drugs. 296p. 1985. 167.00 (0-8493-6231-8, RM405, CRC Reprint) Franklin.

— Azapropazone: Twenty Years of Clinical Use. 256p. 1990. text 141.50 (0-7923-8911-5) Kluwer Academic.

Rainsford, Kim D., et al, eds. Copper & Zinc in Inflammation. (Inflammation & Drug Therapy Ser.). 160p. (C). 1989. text 106.00 (0-7462-0079-X) Kluwer Academic.

Rainsford, Kim D. & Ford-Hutchinson, A., eds. Prostaglandins & Inflammation. (Agents & Actions Supplements Ser.: No. 6). (Illus.). 242p. 1980. 63.00 (0-8176-1132-0) Birkhauser.

Rainsford, Kim D. & Velo, G. P., eds. New Developments in Anti-Rheumatic Drugs, 2 vols. (Inflammation & Drug Therapy Ser.). 272p. (C). 1989. text 154.00 (*0-7462-0080-3*) Kluwer Academic.
— Side-Effects of Anti-Inflamatory Drugs 3. (Inflammation & Drug Therapy Ser.). (C). 1992. text 223.00 (*0-7923-8966-2*) Kluwer Academic.
— Side-Effects of Anti-Inflammatory Analgesic Drugs. LC 83-13940. (Advances in Inflammation Research Ser.: Vol. 6). 320p. 1984. reprint ed. pap. 99.20 (*0-608-00436-7*, 206115100007) Bks Demand.
Rainsford, Kim D., jt. ed. see Morley, John.
Rainsford, Marcus. Our Lord Prays for His Own: Thoughts on John 17. LC 85-8095. 480p. 1985. pap. 17.99 (*0-8254-3617-6*, Kregel Class) Kregel.
Rainsford, Peter & Bangs, David H., Jr. Restaurant Planning Guide. 176p. 1992. pap. 19.95 (*0-936894-35-0*) Dearborn.
— Restaurant Planning Guide. 2nd ed. 175p. 1996. pap. 22.95 (*1-57410-026-2*, 6100-2302) Dearborn.
— The Restaurant Start-Up Guide. LC 97-13871. 224p. 1997. pap. 22.95 (*1-57410-071-8*, 5614-4901) Dearborn.
***Rainsford, Peter & Bangs, David H., Jr.** The Restaurant Start-Up Guide. 2nd ed. 2000. pap. 22.95 (*1-57410-137-4*) Dearborn.
Rainsford, W. S. Story of a Varied Life. LC 70-126249. (Select Bibliographies Reprint Ser.). (Illus.). 1977. 25.95 (*0-8369-5476-9*) Ayer.
Rainsley, Glen E. Hear Our Prayer: Resources for Worship & Devotions. LC 96-28739. 208p. (Orig.). 1996. pap. 14.95 (*0-8298-1145-1*) Pilgrim OH.
— Small Wonders: Sermons for Children. LC 97-46837. (Illus.). 120p. (Orig.). 1998. pap. 12.95 (*0-8298-1252-0*) Pilgrim OH.
— Words of Worship: Resources for Church & Home. LC 91-17439. 184p. (Orig.). 1991. pap. 12.95 (*0-8298-0899-X*) Pilgrim OH.
***Raintree.** Development Through Life. 7th ed. 1998. mass mkt. 15.00 (*0-534-35963-9*) Brooks-Cole.
Raintree. Minipets. 1999. 95.88 (*0-8172-5591-5*) Raintree Steck-V.
— Science Starters! Over One Thousand Ready-to-Use Attention-Grabbers That Make Science Fun. 1999. 127.84 (*0-8172-5334-3*) Raintree Steck-V.
Raintree, Diane. The Household Book of Hints & Tips. 216p. 1986. pap. 8.95 (*0-8246-0304-4*) Jonathan David.
Raintree, John B., ed. Land, Trees & Tenure: Proceedings of an International Workshop on Tenure Issues in Agroforestry, Nairobi, May 27-31, 1985. (Illus.). 435p. 1987. 15.00 (*0-934519-01-3*) U of Wis Land.
Raintree Staff. Atlas of the World. (Illus.). 64p. (J). (gr. 3-7). 1995. pap. text 7.95 (*0-8114-6389-3*) Raintree Steck-V.
— How We Came to the Fifth World. (ENG & SPA.). 1992. lib. bdg. 5.00 (*0-8172-6724-7*) Raintree Steck-V.
— People Shall Continue. 1992. lib. bdg. 5.00 (*0-8172-6741-7*) Raintree Steck-V.
— The River That Gave Gifts. 1992. 5.00 (*0-8172-6727-1*) Raintree Steck-V.
Raintree Steck-Vaughn Publishers Staff. The Ancient World, 6 vols. (Ancient World Ser.). (J). (gr. 5-10). 1998. 113.88 (*0-8172-5059-X*) Raintree Steck-V.
— Environment Starts Here. 1998. 63.92 (*0-8172-5354-8*) Raintree Steck-V.
— Families Around the World. (Families Around the World Ser.). 1998. 159.80 (*0-8172-4913-3*) Raintree Steck-V.
— History of Warfare, 5 vols. (YA). (gr. 7 up). 1998. 94.90 (*0-8172-5447-1*) Raintree Steck-V.
***Raintree Steck-Vaughn Publishers Staff.** Indian Nations. 1999. write for info. (*0-7398-1713-2*) Raintree Steck-V.
— Indian Nations. (Illus.). 2000. write for info. (*0-8172-5462-5*); write for info. (*0-8172-5541-9*) Raintree Steck-V.
— Multicultural Stories Series. (Illus.). 2000. write for info. (*0-7398-1338-2*) Raintree Steck-V.
— Natural World Book Set. (Illus.). 2000. write for info. (*0-7398-1059-6*) Raintree Steck-V.
Raintree Steck-Vaughn Publishers Staff. New Perspectives. (New Perspectives Ser.). 1998. 151.84 (*0-8172-5022-0*) Raintree Steck-V.
***Raintree Steck-Vaughn Publishers Staff.** Pre-GED Reading. 1999. pap. text 11.94 (*0-7398-0982-2*) Raintree Steck-V.
— Pre-GED Science. 1999. pap. text 11.94 (*0-7398-0984-9*) Raintree Steck-V.
— Pre-GED Writing. 2000. pap. 11.94 (*0-7398-0981-4*) Raintree Steck-V.
— Primary Bilingual Literature Collection. 2000. 86.95 (*0-8172-6189-3*) Raintree Steck-V.
Raintree Steck-Vaughn Publishers Staff. Raintree Rhymers. 1990. pap., boxed set 13.31 (*0-8172-2455-6*) Raintree.
***Raintree Steck-Vaughn Publishers Staff.** Restless Planet. (Illus.). 2000. write for info. (*0-7398-1331-5*) Raintree Steck-V.
Raintree Steck-Vaughn Publishers Staff. Science Projects. (Science Projects Ser.). 1998. 169.80 (*0-8172-4965-6*) Raintree Steck-V.
— Twentieth Century Inventions. (20th Century Inventions Ser.). 1998. 135.84 (*0-8172-4819-6*) Raintree Steck-V.
Raintree Steck-Vaughn Publishers Staff, jt. auth. see Brewer, Paul.
Raintree Steck-Vaughn Publishers Staff, jt. auth. see Sharp.
Raintree Steck-Vaughn Publishers Staff, jt. auth. see Sommerville, Donald.
Raintree Steck-Vaughn Publishers Staff, jt. auth. see Westwell, Ian.
***Raintree Steck-Vaughn Publishing Staff.** Aesop's Fox. 2000. 24.26 (*0-7398-1364-1*) Raintree Steck-V.
— Art from Paper. (Salvaged Ser.). (Illus.). 2000. 21.40 (*0-8172-5275-4*) Raintree Steck-V.
— Carpenter. LC 99-57363. (Workers You Know Ser.). (Illus.). 32p. 2000. lib. bdg. 22.83 (*0-8172-5596-6*) Raintree Steck-V.
— Encyclopedia of Mammals. (J). 1999. 57.07 (*0-7398-0682-3*) Raintree Steck-V.
— Grizzly Bears. LC 96-2834. (Untamed World Ser.). (Illus.). 64p. (J). (gr. 5-9). 2000. pap. 8.95 (*0-7398-1682-9*) Raintree Steck-V.
— Habitats Wetlands. (Illus.). (gr. 4-7). 2000. 24.26 (*0-7398-1409-5*) Raintree Steck-V.
— Japan. (Food & Festivals Ser.). (Illus.). 32p. 2000. lib. bdg. 22.83 (*0-7398-1407-9*) Raintree Steck-V.
— King's Dream. (Illus.). (J). (ps-3). 2000. pap. 6.24 (*0-8114-2193-7*) Raintree Steck-V.
— Lives of The.... 1999. 104.90 (*0-7398-0666-1*) Raintree Steck-V.
Raintree Steck-Vaughn Publishing Staff. Magnet Magic. (Read All about It - Science & Social Studies). (Illus.). 32p. (J). (gr. k-3). 1997. pap. 4.95 (*0-8114-3770-1*) Raintree Steck-V.
***Raintree Steck-Vaughn Publishing Staff.** Nations of the World. 2000. 31.40 (*0-8172-5787-X*) Raintree Steck-V.
— Natural World. (Illus.). (J). 2000. 154.14 (*0-7398-2776-6*) Raintree Steck-V.
— Picnic in October. 2000. 24.26 (*0-7398-1367-6*) Raintree Steck-V.
— Playground Supervisor. LC 99-57362. (Workers You Know Ser.). (Illus.). 32p. 2000. lib. bdg. 22.83 (*0-8172-5593-1*) Raintree Steck-V.
— Pre-GED Mathematics. 2000. pap. 11.94 (*0-7398-0983-0*) Raintree Steck-V.
— Pre-GED Social Studies. 2000. pap. 11.94 (*0-7398-0985-7*) Raintree Steck-V.
— Remarkable Women: Past & Present. 2000. 171.30 (*0-8172-5731-4*) Raintree Steck-V.
— Remarkable Women: Past & Present. (Illus.). (J). 2000. 171.30 (*0-7398-2791-X*) Raintree Steck-V.
— Science World. (Illus.). (J). 2000. 91.32 (*0-7398-1326-9*) Raintree Steck-V.
— Veterinarian. LC 99-54427. (Workers You Know Ser.). (Illus.). 32p. 2000. lib. bdg. 22.83 (*0-8172-5592-3*) Raintree Steck-V.
***Raintree Steck-Vaughn Publishing Staff, ed.** Artisans Around the World. (Illus.). (J). 2000. 107.88 (*0-7398-0123-6*) Raintree Steck-V.
— Cumulative Index. (Remarkable Women Ser.). (Illus.). 2000. 27.12 (*0-7398-2789-8*) Raintree Steck-V.
— Food & Festivals. (Illus.). 2000. 191.76 (*0-8172-5761-6*) Raintree Steck-V.
— History Beneath Your Feet. 2000. pap. 102.76 (*0-8172-5754-3*) Raintree Steck-V.
— House Divided: The Civil War. (Illus.). 2000. pap. 79.92 (*0-8172-5584-2*) Raintree Steck-V.
— I Want to Be... 2000. 81.36 (*0-7398-2826-6*) Raintree Steck-V.
— I Want to Be... (Illus.). (J). 2000. 51.38 (*0-7398-1708-6*) Raintree Steck-V.
— Making of America. (Illus.). 2000. 114.20 (*0-7398-2814-2*) Raintree Steck-V.
— Natural World. (Illus.). (J). 2000. 102.76 (*0-7398-2772-3*) Raintree Steck-V.
— Nature on the Rampage. (Illus.). 2000. 136.98 (*0-7398-1799-X*) Raintree Steck-V.
— New Perspectives. 2000. 244.08 (*0-7398-2793-6*) Raintree Steck-V.
— Ocean Explorer, 4 vols. (Illus.). 2000. pap. 75.92 (*0-7398-1711-6*) Raintree Steck-V.
— Ocean Pilot, 4 vols. (Illus.). 2000. pap. 71.92 (*0-7398-1712-4*) Raintree Steck-V.
— Science Encyclopedia. (Illus.). (J). 2000. 415.00 (*0-7398-1843-0*) Raintree Steck-V.
— Talking Points. 2000. pap. 189.90 (*0-8172-5323-8*) Raintree Steck-V.
— Toms Van. (Illus.). (J). 1998. pap. 11.70 (*0-8172-8512-1*) Raintree Steck-V.
— 20th Century Issues. 2000. pap. 113.88 (*0-8172-5571-0*) Raintree Steck-V.
— We Come From... (Illus.). 2000. 63.92 (*0-7398-2685-9*) Raintree Steck-V.
— We Come From... (Illus.). (J). 2000. 159.80 (*0-8172-5222-3*) Raintree Steck-V.
***Raintree Steck-Vaughn Staff.** All by Herself. 40p. (J). (ps-3). 2000. 24.26 (*0-7398-1378-1*) Raintree Steck-V.
— Egypt. (Economically Developing Countries Ser.). (Illus.). (gr. 4-7). 1996. 24.26 (*0-8172-4533-2*) Raintree Steck-V.
— Encyclopedia of Birds. (Illus.). (J). (gr. 4-7). 1999. 57.07 (*0-7398-0684-X*) Raintree Steck-V.
— Encyclopedia of Fishes. (Illus.). (J). (gr. 4-7). 1999. 57.07 (*0-7398-0683-1*) Raintree Steck-V.
— Encyclopedia of Reptiles & Amphibians. (Illus.). (J). (gr. 4-7). 1999. 57.07 (*0-7398-0685-8*) Raintree Steck-V.
— Light & Dark. (Science Starters Ser.). (Illus.). (J). (ps-3). 2000. 22.83 (*0-8172-5331-9*) Raintree Steck-V.
— Super Materials. (Science Starters Ser.). (ps-3). 2000. 22.83 (*0-8172-5330-0*) Raintree Steck-V.
— Terrorism. (Global Issues Ser.). (Illus.). (gr. 4-7). 2000. 25.69 (*0-8172-4862-5*) Raintree Steck-V.
Raintree Steck-Vaughn Staff. Wide World. 1998. 107.88 (*0-8172-5066-2*) Raintree Steck-V.
***Raintree Steck-Vaughn Staff.** Wilma Unlimited. (Illus.). 40p. (J). (ps-3). 2000. 24.26 (*0-7398-1321-8*) Raintree Steck-V.
Raintree Steck-Vaughn Staff. A World of Holidays! Family Festivities All over the World. (World of Holidays Ser.). 1998. 206.70 (*0-8172-4618-5*) Raintree Steck-V.
Rainville, Earl D. Elementary Differential Equations. 8th ed. 1997. pap. text, student ed. 28.00 (*0-13-592783-8*) P-H.
— Special Functions. LC 70-172380. (Illus.). xii, 365p. 1972. reprint ed. text 27.50 (*0-8284-0258-2*) Chelsea Pub.
Rainville, Earl D., et al. Elementary Differential Equations. 8th ed. LC 96-31777. 530p. (C). 1996. 93.33 (*0-13-508011-8*) P-H.
Rainville, Raymond E. Dreams Across the Lifespan. 234p. (C). 1988. pap. text 22.95 (*0-89641-177-X*) American Pr.
Rainville, Rita. Alone at Last. (Romance Ser.: No. 873). 1992. pap. 2.69 (*0-373-08873-6*, 5-08873-7) Silhouette.
— Bedazzled. (Desire Ser.). 1995. per. 3.25 (*0-373-05918-3*, 1-05918-7) Silhouette.
— City Girls Need Not Apply. (Desire Ser.). 1997. per. 3.50 (*0-373-76056-6*, 1-76056-0) Silhouette.
— Desir Sauvage. (Rouge Passion Ser.). (FRE.). 1997. pap. 3.50 (*0-373-37438-0*, 1-37438-8) Harlequin Bks.
— High Spirits. (Desire Ser.). 1993. per. 2.99 (*0-373-05792-X*, 5-05792-2) Silhouette.
— Hot Property: (Centerfolds) (Desire Ser.). 1994. per. 2.99 (*0-373-05874-8*, 1-05874-2) Harlequin Bks.
— Husband Material. (Desire Ser.). 1996. per. 3.50 (*0-373-05984-1*, 1-05984-9) Silhouette.
— Una Mujer de Ciudad (A City Woman) (Deseo Ser.: No. 222). (SPA.). 1998. per. 3.50 (*0-373-35222-0*) Harlequin Bks.
— Siempre Unidos. (SPA.). 1997. per. 3.50 (*0-373-35184-4*, 1-35184-0) Harlequin Bks.
— Soltero Empedernido: Husband Material. (Deseo Ser.). (SPA.). 1996. per. 3.50 (*0-373-35156-9*, 1-35156-8) Harlequin Bks.
— Tumbleweed & Gibraltar. (Desire Ser.). 1993. per. 2.99 (*0-373-05828-4*, 5-05828-4) Silhouette.
Rainwater, Agnes B. Therapeutic Recreation for Chemically Dependent Adolescents & Adults: Programming & Activities. (Illus.). 196p. (Orig.). 1992. pap. text 28.00 (*0-88314-523-5*, A5235) AAHPERD.
Rainwater, Brenda, jt. auth. see Swanson, Thomas G.
Rainwater, Catherine. Dreams of Fiery Stars The Transformations of Native American Fiction. LC 98-49977. 1998. 39.95 (*0-8122-3481-2*) U of Pa Pr.
— Dreams of Fiery Stars: The Transformations of Native American Fiction LC 98-49977. (Studies in Contemporary Fiction). 1998. 18.50 (*0-8122-1682-2*) U of Pa Pr.
Rainwater, Catherine & Scheick, William J., eds. Contemporary American Women Writers: Narrative Strategies. LC 85-9116. (Illus.). 240p. 1985. pap. 18.00 (*0-8131-0168-9*) U Pr of Ky.
Rainwater, Claren E. The Play Movement. LC 76-143068. 1982. 30.95 (*0-8434-0430-2*, Pub. by McGrath NH) Ayer.
Rainwater, Dorothy T. American Jewelry Manufacturers. LC 87-63485. (Illus.). 280p. 1988. pap. 49.95 (*0-88740-120-1*) Schiffer.
***Rainwater, Dorothy T. & Felger, Donna.** American Silverplate. 3rd rev. ed. (Illus.). 480p. 2000. 37.50 (*0-7643-0901-3*) Schiffer.
Rainwater, Dorothy T. & Felger, Donna H. Spoons from Around the World. LC 92-60628. (Illus.). 288p. 1992. text 59.95 (*0-88740-425-1*) Schiffer.
Rainwater, Dorothy T. & Frank, Beryl. Silver Curios. (Illus.). 160p. 1999. 39.95 (*0-7643-0845-9*) Schiffer.
Rainwater, Dorothy T. & Rainwater, H. Ivan. American Silverplate. enl. rev. ed. LC 72-7998. (Illus.). 480p. 1988. 37.50 (*0-88740-128-7*) Schiffer.
Rainwater, Dorothy T. & Redfield, Judy. Encyclopedia of American Silver Manufacturers. 4th rev. ed. LC 98-24606. 258p. 1998. pap. 19.95 (*0-7643-0602-2*) Schiffer.
Rainwater, Dorothy T., jt. auth. see Felger, Donna H.
Rainwater, H. Ivan, jt. auth. see Rainwater, Dorothy T.
Rainwater, Harold. Two Wheels & a Pair of Nuts. LC 95-60238. 304p. (Orig.). 1995. pap. 10.95 (*0-9645385-0-4*) Wiregrass Pubs.
Rainwater, Holly. Ergonomics - How to Make Your Workstation Work for You. Rhoades-Baum, Patrice et al, eds. (Illus.). 38p. (Orig.). pap. write for info. (*1-57125-050-6*) Help Desk Inst.
Rainwater, Janette. You're in Charge: A Guide to Becoming Your Own Therapist. LC 82-9104. 221p. 1985. reprint ed. pap. 11.00 (*0-87516-552-4*) DeVorss.
Rainwater, Judy. Nutrition for the 90s. 1992. pap., spiral bd. 13.50 (*0-9622066-1-X*) Ranrai Pub.
Rainwater, Lee. And the Poor Get Children: Sex, Contraception, & Family Planning in the Working Class. LC 84-12770. 202p. 1984. reprint ed. lib. bdg. 55.00 (*0-313-24452-9*, RAPG, Greenwood Pr) Greenwood.
Rainwater, Lee, ed. Black Experience: Soul. LC 72-87669. 266p. 1973. reprint ed. pap. text 19.95 (*0-87855-561-7*) Transaction Pubs.
Rainwater, Lee, et al. Workingman's Wife: Her Personality, World & Life Style. Coser, Lewis A. & Powell, Walter W., eds. LC 79-7014. (Perennial Works in Sociology). 1980. reprint ed. lib. bdg. 21.95 (*0-405-12113-X*) Ayer.
Rainwater, Lee, jt. ed. see Rein, Martin.
Rainwater, Lee, jt. ed. see Rein, martin.
Rainwater, Mara, jt. ed. see Kearney, Richard.
Rainwater, Nancy, jt. auth. see Grant, Joseph.
Rainwater, Pearl. Grandma Speaks. LC 94-67905. (Illus.). 141p. (Orig.). 1995. pap. 8.99 (*0-8100-0535-2*, 06N0706) Northwest Pub.
Rainwater, Percy L. Mississippi: Storm Center of Secession, 1856-1861. LC 72-84188. (American Scene, Comments & Commentators Ser.). 1969. reprint ed. lib. bdg. 29.50 (*0-306-71614-3*) Da Capo.
Rainy, Charlotte A., jt. tr. see Behman, Jacob.
Rainy, Charlotte A., tr. see Boehme, Jacob.
Raioahadur, R., jt. auth. see Dey, K. L.
Rairkar, Hema, jt. auth. see Poitevin, Guy.
Rais, Gilles De, see De Rais, Gilles.
Rais, Kathleen. Albert Payson Terhune: A Bibliography of Primary Works. LC 98-174821. (Illus.). 130p. 1997. 50.00 (*0-9660065-1-8*) Kathleen Rais.
Rais, Rasul B. The Indian Ocean & the Superpowers. LC 86-22306. 270p. (C). 1987. 57.00 (*0-389-20695-4*, N8253) B&N Imports.
— War Without Winners: Afghanistan's Uncertain Transition after the Cold War. (Illus.). 298p. 1994. text 32.00 (*0-19-577535-X*) OUP.
Rais, Rasul B., ed. State, Society & Democratic Change in Pakistan. LC 97-930631. 308p. 1997. 75.00 (*0-19-577759-X*) OUP.
Rais, Sarwar, jt. auth. see Ahmad, Naseeruddin.
Raisanen, Heikki. Beyond New Testament Theology. LC 89-48393. 224p. (Orig.). (C). 1990. pap. 15.00 (*0-334-01907-9*) TPI PA.
— Jesus, Paul & Torah: Collected Essays. Orton, David E., tr. from GER. (JSNT Supplement Ser.: No. 43). 286p. (C). 1992. 80.00 (*1-85075-237-0*, Pub. by Sheffield Acad) CUP Services.
Raisanen, Heikki. Marcion, Muhammad & the Mahatma: Exegetical Perspectives on the Encounter of Cultures & Faith. (Illus.). 1997. pap. 27.00 (*0-334-02693-8*) TPI PA.
Raisanen, Heikki. The Messianic Secret in Mark's Gospel. Tuckett, Christopher, tr. from FIN. 320p. 1994. pap. text 31.95 (*0-567-29253-3*, Pub. by T & T Clark) Bks Intl VA.
— Paul & the Law. 2nd ed. (Wissenschaftliche Untersuchungen Zum Neuen Testament Ser.: No. 29). 351p. 1987. 67.50 (*3-16-145198-8*, Pub. by JCB Mohr) Coronet Bks.
Raisbeck, B. L., ed. Evidence. 260p. (C). 1990. pap. 60.00 (*1-85352-790-4*, Pub. by HLT Pubns) St Mut.
Raisch, Marilyn J. & Shaffer, Roberta I., eds. Introduction to Transnational Legal Transactions. LC 95-31699. 363p. 1995. text 85.00 (*0-379-21352-4*) Oceana.
Raischl, Josef, jt. ed. see Cirino, Andre.
Raise, Lawrence. Directory of Business Information. LC 94-40077. 612p. 1995. 162.95 (*0-471-59816-X*) Wiley.
Raiselle, Naomi, ed. see Casarjian, Robin.
Raiser, Martin. Soft Budget Constraints & the Fate of Economic Reforms in Transition Economies & Developing Countries. 290p. (C). 1997. text 92.50 (*3-16-146708-6*, 10878) U of Mich Pr.
Raisglid, Ron & Cubias, Daniel. Buying & Selling Real Estate on the Internet. (Illus.). 224p. 1999. pap. 15.95 (*1-58063-063-4*, Pub. by Renaissance) St Martin.
Raisglid, Ron & Turner, Cheri. Buying & Leasing Cars on the Internet. 224p. 1998. pap. 15.95 (*1-58063-030-8*) Renaissance.
Raish. Benefit Tax Exemptions. 1995. 125.00 (*0-316-73319-9*) Little.
Raish, Carol, jt. auth. see Jemison, Roy.
Raish, Martin & Ensor, Pat, eds. Key Guide to Electronic Resources: Art & Art History. LC 95-51746. (Key Guide Ser.). 120p. 1996. pap. 39.50 (*1-57387-022-6*) Info Today Inc.
Raish, Martin H., jt. auth. see Sorenson, John L.
Raish, Peggy & Klaus, Billie J., eds. Every Nurses Guide to Physical Assessment: A Primary Care Focus. LC 86-34007. (Red Bks.). 500p. 1989. pap. text 33.95 (*0-8273-4213-6*) Delmar.
Raisin, Max. Great Jews I Have Known. LC 71-117331. (Biography Index Reprint Ser.). 1977. 24.95 (*0-8369-8023-9*) Ayer.
Raisinghani, Mahesh, jt. ed. see Rahman, Syed M.
Raiskin. Placing Womens' Studies. Date not set. write for info. (*0-07-230406-5*) McGraw.
Raiskin, Judith. Snow on the Cane Fields: Women's Writing & Creole Subjectivity. 368p. 1995. pap. 19.95 (*0-8166-2301-5*); text 49.95 (*0-8166-2300-7*) U of Minn Pr.
Raiskin, Judith L., ed. see Rhys, Jean & Bronte, Charlotte.
Raisman, Neal A., ed. Directing General Education Outcomes. LC 85-644753. (New Directions for Community Colleges Ser.: No. CC 81). 107p. (Orig.). 1993. pap. 22.00 (*1-55542-686-7*) Jossey-Bass.
Raisman, Vivien. Canopic Equipment in the Petrie Collection. 1984. pap. 39.95 (*0-85668-268-3*, Pub. by Aris & Phillips) David Brown.
Raisner, Debra. Couples A "To Do" List for Life, 1. 1999. 12.95 (*0-7407-0048-0*) Andrews & McMeel.
Raisner, Debra, et al. What Would You Do? LC 97-73840. (Illus.). 374p. (Orig.). 1997. pap. 5.95 (*0-8362-5076-1*) Andrews & McMeel.
Raison, Jennifer & Goldie, Michael. Caraboo: The Servant Girl Princess: The Real Story of the Grand Hoax. LC 94-42794. (Illus.). 220p. 1995. pap. 13.95 (*1-56656-179-5*) Interlink Pub.
Raison, Laura. Florence & Tuscany. (Regional Guides of Italy Ser.). (Illus.). 240p. 1994. pap. 16.95 (*0-8442-9961-8*, 99618, Passprt Bks) NTC Contemp Pub Co.
Raisor, Gary. Less Than Human. Hinchberger, Lauri, ed. (Illus.). 256p. (C). 1992. 29.95 (*0-9633397-0-2*) Overlook Connect.
— Less Than Human. aut. limited ed. Hinchberger, Lauri, ed. (Illus.). 256p. (C). 1992. boxed set 45.00 (*0-9633397-1-0*) Overlook Connect.
Raisor, Philip, ed. Tuned & under Tension: The Recent Poetry of W. D. Snodgrass. LC 98-18956. (Illus.). 176p. 1998. 35.00 (*0-87413-659-8*) U Delaware Pr.
***Raisor, Steven C.** Twentieth-Century Techniques in Selected Works for Solo Guitar: Serialism. LC 99-31633. (Studies in History & Interpretation of Music: Vol. 63). 136p. 1999. text 69.95 (*0-7734-7914-7*) E Mellen.
Raissiguier, Catherine. Becoming Women - Becoming Workers: Identity Formation in a French Vocational School. LC 93-40597. (SUNY Series, Power, Social Identity, & Education). 211p. (C). 1994. text 57.50 (*0-7914-2085-X*) State U NY Pr.
— Becoming Women Becoming Workers: Identity Formation

An Asterisk (*) at the beginning of an entry indicates that the title is appearing for the first time.

in a French Vocational School. LC 93-40597. (SUNY Series, Power, Social Identity, & Education). 211p. (C). 1994. pap. text 18.95 (*0-7914-2086-8*) State U NY Pr.

Raissman, Bob, jt. auth. see Montana, Joe.

***Raisson, Elisabeth.** 60-Second French Grammar Workout: 140 Speed Tests to Boost Your Fluency. (60 Second Ser.). 144p. 2000. pap. 9.06 (*0-658-00413-1*, 004131) NTC Contemp Pub Co.

— 60-second French Vocabulary Workouts: 140 Speed Tests to Boost Your Fluency. (60 Second Ser.). 144p. 2000. pap. 9.06 (*0-658-00440-9*, 004409) NTC Contemp Pub Co.

Raistrick. Alcoholism & Drug Addiction. 1986. text 53.00 (*0-443-03092-8*, W B Saunders Co) Harcrt Hlth Sci Grp.

Raistrick, Arthur. Dynasty of Iron Founders. (Illus.). 347p. (C). 1988. 105.00 (*0-7855-5031-3*, Pub. by W Sessions) St Mut.

— Dynasty of Iron Founders. rev. ed. 1999. pap. 27.00 (*1-85072-058-4*, Pub. by W Sessions) St Mut.

***Raistrick, Arthur.** Quakers in Science & Industry. 1999. pap. 30.00 (*1-85072-106-8*, Pub. by W Sessions) St Mut.

Raistrick, Donald. Index to Legal Citations & Abbreviations. 2nd ed. LC 94-141395. 497p. 1993. lib. bdg. 100.00 (*1-85739-061-X*) Bowker-Saur.

— Lawyers' Law Books. 3rd rev. ed. LC 96-47981. 600p. 1996. 125.00 (*1-85739-087-3*) Bowker-Saur.

Raisz, Erwin J. Principles of Cartography. (Geography Ser.). (C). 1962. text 33.00 (*0-07-051151-9*) McGraw.

Raiten, Daniel J., ed. Vitamin B-6 Metabolism in Pregnancy, Lactation & Infancy. LC 94-32693. 212p. 1995. boxed set 199.95 (*0-8493-4594-4*) CRC Pr.

Raiter, Franklin R., jt. auth. see Carroll, Francis M.

Raithel, Michael A. Tuning SAS Applications in the MVS Environment. 316p. (C). 1995. pap. 39.95 (*1-55544-278-1*, BR55231) SAS Publ.

Raithelhuber, J. Flora Mycologica Argentina, Hongos I. (SPA., Illus.). 371p. (C). 1987. pap. text 42.00 (*3-9801550-1-3*) Lubrecht & Cramer.

— Flora Mycologica Argentina: Hongos II (Fungi II) (SPA., Illus.). 287p. 1988. pap. 35.00 (*3-9801550-2-1*) Lubrecht & Cramer.

Raiti, Salvatore & Tolman, Robert A., eds. Human Growth Hormone. LC 86-3288. (Illus.). 676p. (C). 1986. text 174.00 (*0-306-42053-8*, Kluwer Plenum) Kluwer Academic.

Raitport, Eli. 1980's the United States in Crisis: United States in Crisis. Duplantier, F. R., ed. (United States in Crises Ser.). (Illus.). 214p. (Orig.). (C). 1989. reprint ed. pap. 19.50 (*0-944182-01-1*) Raitport Co.

— The United States - Vulnerable. 2nd ed. Duplantier, F. R., ed. (United States in Crises Ser.). (Illus.). 221p. (Orig.). (C). 1989. reprint ed. pap. 19.50 (*0-944182-02-X*) Raitport Co.

Raitt. Medieval Mysticism. 1996. 24.95 (*0-8057-8614-7*, Twyne) Mac Lib Ref.

Raitt, A. W. The Life of Villiers de l'Isle-Adam. (Illus.). 470p. 1981. text 64.00 (*0-19-815771-1*) OUP.

Raitt, Alan, ed. Pour Louis Bouilhet - Gustave Flauvert. (Exeter French Texts Ser.: Vol. 87). 141p. 1995. pap. text 19.95 (*0-85989-441-X*, Pub. by Univ Exeter Pr) Northwestern U Pr.

Raitt, Alan, ed. see Wright, Barbara.

***Raitt, Alan W.** Flaubert et le Theatre, Vol. 1. 2nd ed. 198p. 1999. 32.95 (*3-906763-19-6*, Pub. by P Lang) P Lang Pubng.

Raitt, Allan W., ed. see Orr, Mary.

Raitt, David I. Libraries for the New Millennium: Implications for Managers. LC 98-161128. 288p. 1997. 75.00 (*1-85604-257-X*, Pub. by Library Association) Bernan Associates.

Raitt, David I., jt. ed. see Ching-Chih, Chen.

***Raitt, Fiona E. & Zeedyk, M. Suzanne.** The Implicit Relation of Psychology & Law: Women & Syndrome Evidence. LC 00-28088. 2000. write for info. (*0-415-14783-2*) Routledge.

Raitt, George D., et al. Masonic History of Unadilla, N. Y. Goerlich, Shirley B., ed. (Illus.). 59p. 1995. reprint ed. pap. 14.00 (*1-887530-00-2*) RSG Pub.

Raitt, Jill. Christian Spirituality, Vol. 2. 528p. 1987. 49.50 (*0-8245-0765-7*) Crossroad NY.

— The Colloquy of Montbeliard: Religion & Politics in the Sixteenth Century. 240p. 1993. text 65.00 (*0-19-507566-8*) OUP.

— The Eucharistic Theology of Theodore Beza: Development of the Reformed Doctrine. LC 74-188907. (American Academy of Religion. Studies in Religion: No. 4). 91p. reprint ed. pap. 30.00 (*0-7837-5490-6*, 204525500005) Bks Demand.

Raitt, Jill, ed. Shapers of Religious Traditions in Germany, Switzerland, & Poland, Fifteen Sixty to Sixteen Hundred. LC 80-23287. 256p. (C). 1981. 42.50 (*0-300-02457-6*) Yale U Pr.

Raitt, Jill, et al, eds. Christian Spirituality: High Middle & Reformation, Vol. 2. (World Spirituality Ser.: Vol. 17). (Illus.). 528p. 1989. pap. 24.95 (*0-8245-0967-6*) Crossroad NY.

Raitt, Jill, ed. see Mallarme, Stephane.

Raitt, Lia C., jt. compiled by see Whitlam, John.

Raitt, Lia Correia, jt. auth. see Whitlam, John.

Raitt, Lia N. Garrett & the English Muse. (Monografias A Ser.: Vol. XCIV). 146p. (C). 1983. 41.00 (*0-7293-0145-1*, Pub. by Tamesis Bks Ltd) Boydell & Brewer.

Raitt, Robert L. Campus on the Hill, a History of Santa Paula High School: And Century of Community Yesterdays. (Illus.). 280p. (C). 1988. 21.50 (*0-9620212-8-8*) Santa Paula HS Alumni.

***Raitt, Suzanne.** May Sinclair: A Modern Victorian. LC 99-55119. 320p. 2000. write for info. (*0-19-812298-5*) OUP.

Raitt, Suzanne. Vita & Virginia: The Work & Friendship of V. Sackville-West & Virginia Woolf. 210p. 1993. pap. text 16.95 (*0-19-812277-2*) OUP.

Raitt, Suzanne, ed. Volcanoes & Pearl Divers: Essays in Lesbian Feminist Studies. 292p. 1996. pap. text 22.95 (*1-56023-880-1*) Haworth Pr.

Raitt, Suzanne & Tate, Trudi, eds. Women's Fiction & the Great War. LC 97-931. (Illus.). 300p. 1997. pap. text 19.95 (*0-19-818278-3*) OUP.

— Women's Fiction & the Great War. LC 97-931. (Illus.). 300p. (C). 1997. text 75.00 (*0-19-818283-X*) OUP.

Raitt, Suzanne, ed. see Mansfield, Katherine.

Raitt, Suzanne, ed. see Woolf, Virginia.

Raitta, C., jt. ed. see Greve, Erik L.

Raitz, Karl B., ed. A Guide to the National Road. LC 95-44726. (Road & American Culture Ser.). (Illus.). 400p. (C). 1996. 34.95 (*0-8018-5156-4*) Johns Hopkins.

— The Theater of Sport. (Illus.). 384p. 1995. pap. 19.95 (*0-8018-4909-8*); text 49.95 (*0-8018-4908-X*) Johns Hopkins.

Raitz, Karl B., jt. auth. see Murray-Wooley, Carolyn.

Raitz, Karl B., jt. ed. see Thompson, George F.

Raitz, Misako, tr. see McIntyre, Sally.

Raitz, Vladimir, jt. auth. see Bray, Roger.

***Raitz von Frentz, Christian.** A Lesson Forgotten: Minority Protection under the League of Nations: The Case of the German Minority in Poland, 1920-1934. LC 99-52701. 2000. text 65.00 (*0-312-23111-3*) St Martin.

Raivio, Kari O., et al, eds. Respiratory Distress Syndrome. 1984. text 125.00 (*0-12-576180-5*) Acad Pr.

Raiz, Carmela. Blue Star Over Red Square. LC 94-39654. 1994. 19.95 (*0-87306-616-2*); pap. text 16.95 (*0-87306-617-0*) Feldheim.

Raizada, M. B. Flora of Mussoorie, Vol. 1. 645p. (C). 1978. 195.00 (*0-7855-3118-1*, Pub. by Intl Bk Distr); text 250.00 (*0-89771-646-9*, Pub. by Intl Bk Distr) St Mut.

— Grasses of Upper Gangetic Plaint, Pt. 3. (C). 1988. text 50.00 (*0-7855-6003-3*, Pub. by Scientific) St Mut.

— Orchids of Mussorie. (C). 1988. 250.00 (*0-7855-3269-2*, Pub. by Scientific) St Mut.

— Supplement to Duthie's Flora of the Upper Gangetic Plain & of the Adjacent Siwalik & Sub Himalayan Tracks. 355p. (C). 1976. text 75.00 (*0-89771-643-4*, Pub. by Intl Bk Distr) St Mut.

Raizada, M. B., ed. Correction & Nomenclatural Changes to the Forest Flora of the Bombay Presidency & Sind, 2 vols., Set. (C). 1976. text 65.00 (*0-89771-645-0*, Pub. by Intl Bk Distr) St Mut.

— Supplement to Duthie's Flora of the Upper Gangetic Plain & of the Adjacent Siwalik & Sub-Himalayan Tracts. 355p. (C). 1976. 75.00 (*0-7855-3044-4*, Pub. by Intl Bk Distr) St Mut.

Raizada, M. K., jt. auth. see LeRoith, D.

Raizada, Mohan K., et al, eds. Cellular & Molecular Neurobiology of Renin-Angiotensin System. 592p. 1993. lib. bdg. 229.00 (*0-8493-4622-3*, QP572) CRC Pr.

— Insulin, Insulin-Like Growth Factors, & Their Receptors in the Central Nervous System. LC 87-20337. (Illus.). 366p. 1987. 85.00 (*0-306-42666-8*, Plenum Trade) Perseus Pubng.

— Recent Advances in Cellular & Molecular Aspects of Angiotensin Receptors. (Advances in Experimental Medicine & Biology Ser.: Vol. 396). (Illus.). 262p. (C). 1996. text 102.00 (*0-306-45209-X*, Kluwer Plenum) Kluwer Academic.

Raizada, Mohan K. & LeRoith, D., eds. Molecular & Cellular Biology of Insulin-Like Growth Factors. (Illus.). 524p. 1989. 120.00 (*0-306-43254-4*, Plenum Trade) Perseus Pubng.

— Molecular Biology & Physiology of Insulin & Insulin-Like Growth Factors. (Advances in Experimental Medicine & Biology Ser.: Vol. 293). (Illus.). 498p. (C). 1991. text 186.00 (*0-306-43928-X*, Kluwer Plenum) Kluwer Academic.

Raizada, Mohan K., jt. ed. see Mukhopadhyay, Amal K.

Raizada, Prabhakar. The Theory of Typewriting. 200p. 1996. pap. 60.00 (*81-209-0970-4*, Pub. by Pitambar Pub) St Mut.

— Typewriting Practice: A Work Book. 244p. 1997. pap., wbk. ed. 60.00 (*81-209-0995-X*, Pub. by Pitambar Pub) St Mut.

***Raizen, Esther.** Modern Hebrew for Beginners: A Multimedia Program for Students at the Beginning & Intermediate Levels. LC 99-58419. 224p. (C). 2000. pap. 18.95 (*0-292-77104-5*) U of Tex Pr.

Raizen, Esther, tr. from ENG. No Rattling of Sabers: An Anthology of Israeli War Poetry. LC 95-83542. (Modern Middle Eastern Literature in Translation Ser.). 200p. (Orig.). 1996. pap. 13.95 (*0-292-77071-5*) U of Tex Pr.

Raizen, Senta A. Bold Ventures, Vol. 3. 1996. lib. bdg. 140.00 (*0-7923-4233-X*) Kluwer Academic.

Raizen, Senta A., ed. Bold Ventures Vol. 2: Case Studies of U. S. Innovations in Science Education, Vol. 2. LC 96-35729. 624p. (C). 1996. lib. bdg. 240.00 (*0-7923-4232-1*) Kluwer Academic.

Raizen, Senta A. & Britton, Edward D. Bold Ventures. LC 96-35729. 1997. lib. bdg. 430.00 (*0-7923-4234-8*) Kluwer Academic.

Raizen, Senta A. & Jones, Lyle V., eds. Indicators of Precollege Education in Science & Mathematics: A Preliminary Review. LC 85-3028. 210p. reprint ed. pap. 65.10 (*0-7837-1263-4*, 204140200020) Bks Demand.

Raizen, Senta A. & Michelsohn, Arie M., eds. The Future of Science in Elementary Schools: Educating Prospective Teachers. LC 93-41154. (Education-Higher Education Ser.). 206p. 1994. text 30.95 (*1-55542-624-7*) Jossey-Bass.

Raizen, Senta A., et al. Technology Education in the Classroom: Understanding the Designed World. LC 95-33950. (Educational Ser.). 279p. 1995. text 36.45 (*0-7879-0178-4*) Jossey-Bass.

Raizen, Senta A., ed. see National Research Council Staff.

Raizer, I. U., jt. auth. see Bazellan, Eduard M.

Raizer, Iuri P. Laser-Induced Discharge Phenomena. Vlases, George C. & Pietrzyk, Z. Adam, eds. Tybulewicz, Albin, tr. LC 77-21738. (Studies in Soviet Science). (Illus.). 380p. 1977. reprint ed. pap. 117.80 (*0-608-05496-8*, 206596500006) Bks Demand.

Raizer, Victor Y. & Cherny, Igor V., eds. Passive Microwave Remote Sensing of Oceans. LC 97-28549. (Illus.). 204p. 1998. 110.00 (*0-471-97170-7*) Wiley.

Raizer, Yuri P. Gas Discharge Physics. LC 96-53988. 1997. pap. write for info. (*3-540-19462-2*) Spr-Verlag.

— Gas Discharge Physics. (Illus.). xi, 449p. 1997. 65.00 (*0-387-19462-2*) Spr-Verlag.

Raizer, Yuri P., et al, eds. Radio-Frequency Capacitive Discharges. LC 94-48594. 304p. 1995. boxed set 149.95 (*0-8493-8644-6*, 8644) CRC Pr.

Raizis, M. Byron & Papas, A. Greek Revolution & the American Muse: A Collection of Philhellenic Poetry 1821-1828. xx, 168p. (Orig.). 1986. reprint ed. pap. text 32.50 (*0-317-57961-4*, Pub. by AM Hakkert) Coronet Bks.

Raiziss, Sonia. Metaphysical Passion: Seven Modern American Poets & the Seventeenth Century Tradition. LC 73-194227. 327p. 1970. reprint ed. lib. bdg. 65.00 (*0-8371-3343-2*, RAMP, Greenwood Pr) Greenwood.

Raiziss, Sonia, tr. see De Palchi, Alfredo.

Raizman, Marjorie B., jt. auth. see Cross, Thomas B.

Raizman, Richard E. Stones Unfolding from the Gardens of Time. 150p. (Orig.). 1994. pap. 7.95 (*0-9642627-0-3*) Mtn Meadow Pr.

Raizner, Albert E. Topics in Clinical Cardiology: Indications for Diagnostic Procedures. LC 96-30883. (Topics in Clinical Cardiology Ser.). 1996. write for info. (*4-260-14318-2*) Igaku-Shoin.

Raizner, Albert E., ed. Topics in Clinical Cardiology: Indications for Diagnostic Procedures. LC 96-30883. (Topics in Clinical Cardiology Ser.). (Illus.). 176p. 1997. 69.50 (*0-89640-318-1*) Igaku-Shoin.

Raizner, Bernard I. Insult to Injury. 224p. 1989. pap. 3.95 (*0-380-70697-0*, Avon Bks) Morrow Avon.

Raj Adhikari, Prakash, see Adhikari, Prakash Raj.

Raj Anand, Mulk. Untouchable. (Classics Ser.). 160p. 1990. pap. 11.95 (*0-14-018395-7*, Penguin Classics) Viking Penguin.

Raj Anand, Mulk & Rao, S. Balu, eds. Panorama: An Anthology of Modern Indian Short Stories. (C). 1997. pap. write for info. (*81-207-1990-5*) Sterling Pubs.

Raj, Anthony S. A New Hermeneutic of Reality: Raimon Panikkar's Cosmotheandric Vision. LC 98-23702. (Studies in the Intercultural History of Christianity: Vol. 111). 193p. 1998. pap. text 30.95 (*0-8204-3445-0*) P Lang Pubng.

Raj, B., jt. ed. see Boadway, R.

Raj, Baldev, ed. Advances in Econometrics & Modelling. (C). 1989. lib. bdg. 132.50 (*0-7923-0299-0*) Kluwer Academic.

— Henri Theil's Contributions to Economics & Econometrics, 3 vols., Set. LC 96-5141. (Advanced Studies in Theoretical & Applied Econometrics). (C). 1992. lib. bdg. 336.00 (*0-7923-1666-5*) Kluwer Academic.

— Henri Theil's Contributions to Economics & Econometrics, Vol. I: Econometric Theory & Methodology, Vol. 1. (Advanced Studies in Theoretical & Applied Econometrics). 616p. (C). 1992. lib. bdg. 226.50 (*0-7923-1548-0*) Kluwer Academic.

— Henri Theil's Contributions to Economics & Econometrics, Vol. II: Consumer Demand Analysis & Information Theory, Vol. 2. (Advanced Studies in Theoretical & Applied Econometrics). 487p. (C). 1992. lib. bdg. 165.00 (*0-7923-1664-9*) Kluwer Academic.

— Henri Theil's Contributions to Economics & Econometrics, Vol. III: Economic Policy & Forecasts, & Management Science, Vol. 3. 350p. (C). 1992. lib. bdg. 141.50 (*0-7923-1665-7*) Kluwer Academic.

Raj, Baldev, et al, eds. Panel Data Analysis. (Studies in Empirical Economics). (Illus.). viii, 220p. 1992. 99.95 (*0-387-91416-1*) Spr-Verlag.

Raj, Baldev, jt. auth. see Dufour, J. M.

Raj, G. D., jt. ed. see Arnand, S. C.

Raj, Gagan. Dictionary of Literary Terms. 1990. 33.50 (*81-7041-284-6*, Pub. by Anmol) S Asia.

Raj, Gopalan Suresh, jt. auth. see Seshadri, Govind K.

Raj, Gurdeep, ed. Encyclopaedia of Agricultural Sciences, 10 vols. 2895p. 1998. pap. 2500.00 (*81-7488-008-9*, Pub. by Print Hse) St Mut.

Raj, Hans. Encyclopaedia of Indian Parliament, 20 vols. (Continuing Ser.). 1997. 1100.00 (*81-7488-165-4*, Pub. by Anmol) S Asia.

— Protection of Foreign Investment, Property & Nationalisation in India. (C). 1989. 250.00 (*0-7855-3709-0*) St Mut.

Raj, K. N. Organizational Issues in Indian Agriculture. 236p. 1990. 28.00 (*0-19-562520-X*) OUP.

Raj, K. N., ed. Essays on the Commercialization of Indian Agriculture. 375p. 1986. 26.00 (*0-19-561729-0*) OUP.

Raj, K. N., ed. see Narain, Dharm.

Raj, Khatiwada Y. Some Aspects of Monetary Policy in Nepal. 1994. pap. 50.00 (*0-7855-0481-8*, Pub. by Ratna Pustak Bhandar) St Mut.

Raj, Maithreyi K. Women's Studies in India: Some Perspectives. 1986. 28.50 (*0-86132-135-9*, Pub. by Popular Prakashan) S Asia.

Raj, N. Desinga. Development Programmes in Agriculture & the Weaker Sections. 217p. 1987. 26.00 (*81-85076-16-2*, Pub. by Chugh Pubns) S Asia.

Raj, P. A. Road to Kathmandu. 1994. pap. 30.00 (*0-7855-0478-8*, Pub. by Ratna Pustak Bhandar) St Mut.

Raj, P. Prithvi. Pain Management: A Comprehensive Review. (Illus.). 592p. (C). (gr. 13). 1995. pap. text 64.95 (*0-8016-7998-2*, 07998) Mosby Inc.

— Practical Management of Pain. 2nd ed. (Illus.). 1120p. (C). (gr. 13). 1991. text 190.00 (*0-8151-7012-2*, 22126) Mosby Inc.

— Practical Management of Pain, Vol. 3. 3rd ed. (Illus.). 1312p. (C). (gr. 13). 2000. text 190.00 (*0-8151-2569-0*, 31308) Mosby Inc.

Raj, Prakash A. Brahmin's of Nepal. 1996. pap. 22.00 (*0-7855-7366-6*, Pub. by Ratna Pustak Bhandar) St Mut.

***Raj, Prakash A.** Inside Nepal. 1998. pap. 22.00 (*0-7855-7603-7*) St Mut.

Raj, Prakash A. Pokhara: A Valley in the Himalayas. (C). 1993. 30.00 (*0-7855-0203-3*, Pub. by Ratna Pustak Bhandar) St Mut.

— Portraits & Photographs from Nepal. 1994. pap. 40.00 (*0-7855-2760-5*, Pub. by Ratna Pustak Bhandar) St Mut.

***Raj, Priya.** Counter Point. LC 99-937287. 1998. pap. 75.00 (*81-86982-57-4*, Pub. by Business Pubns) St Mut.

Raj, Rishi, ed. see ASM Materials Science Seminar Staff.

Raj Shah, Giri. Encyclopaedia of Womens Studies, 2 vols. (C). 1995. 34.00 (*81-212-0474-7*) S Asia.

Raj, Sheela. Mediaevelism to Modernism: Socio Economic & Cultural History of Hyderabad, 1869-1911. (C). 1987. 36.00 (*0-86132-143-X*, Pub. by Popular Prakashan) S Asia.

Raj, V. Manuel. Santal Theology of Liberation. 1990. 22.00 (*81-85024-81-2*, Pub. by Uppal Pub Hse) S Asia.

Raj, Victor A. The Hindu Connection: Roots of the New Age. LC 94-43623. (Scholarship Today Ser.). 224p. 1995. pap. 17.00 (*0-570-04802-8*, 12-3256) Concordia.

Raja. Living Inspirations. 1994. pap. 11.95 (*1-85230-557-6*, Pub. by Element MA) Penguin Putnam.

Raja, Gopal B., jt. auth. see Subramanyam, S. V.

Raja, Jay & Smith, Stuart T., eds. Proceedings from ASPE Spring Topical Meeting on Advances in Surface Metrology. (Illus.). 89p. 1997. pap. write for info. (*1-887706-17-8*) Am Soc Prec Engr.

Raja, Om Prakash. The Words of Om Raja. LC 89-84563. 127p. (Orig.). 1990. reprint ed. pap. 9.95 (*0-9623163-0-X*) FL Pubs.

Raja, P. Many Worlds of Manoj Das. (Orig.). (C). 1993. 8.50 (*81-7018-761-3*, Pub. by BR Pub) S Asia.

Raja, R. & Yoh, John. The Batavia Meeting: Proceedings of the 1992 Meeting of the Division of Particles & Fields of the APS, 2 vols., Set. 750p. 1993. text 178.00 (*981-02-1323-9*) World Scientific Pub.

Raja, Rajendran & Yoh, John. 10th Topical Workshop on Proton-Antiproton Collider Physics: Fermi National Accelerator Laboratory, Batavia, IL, May 9-13, 1995. (AIP Conference Proceedings Ser.: No. 357). (Illus.). 734p. 1996. 190.00 (*1-56396-543-7*) Am Inst Physics.

Raja, Rajendran & Yoh, John, eds. Proton-Antiproton Collider Physics: Proceedings of the 7th Topical Workshop. 912p. (C). 1989. text 138.00 (*9971-5-0754-4*) World Scientific Pub.

Raja, Rajendran, jt. ed. see Geer, Stephen.

Raja Rammohun Roy Library Foundation Staff, jt. auth. see Thomas, V. K.

Raja, Rao. The Great Indian Way: A Life of Mahatma Gandhi LC 98-909492. 480p. 1998. write for info. (*81-7094-308-6*) Vision.

— Kanthapura. LC 77-3040. 244p. 1977. reprint ed. lib. bdg. 47.50 (*0-8371-9573-X*, RAKA, Greenwood Pr) Greenwood.

Raja, Rao V. Perspectives in Phycology. (Illus.). 500p. 1991. 69.00 (*1-55528-192-3*, Pub. by Today Tomorrow) Scholarly Pubns.

Raja, Taryn La, see La Raja, Taryn.

Raja, Tasneem, jt. auth. see Sarup, Madan.

Rajab, Jehan S. Invasion Kuwait: An English Woman's Tale. (Illus.). 224p. 1994. text 39.50 (*1-85043-775-0*, Pub. by I B T) St Martin.

— Palestinian Folk Costume. 200p. 1988. lib. bdg. 65.00 (*0-7103-0283-5*) Routledge.

— Silver Jewellery of Oman. LC 97-179863. (Illus.). 80p. 1997. text 14.95 (*1-86064-310-8*, Pub. by I B T) St Martin.

Rajabov, Y. U., tr. see Entelis, S. G., et al.

Rajacic, Roy. The Best Poems of Roy Rajacic. Maljkovic-Petkovic, Djuro & Kostic, Katarina, eds. (Illus.). 80p. (Orig.). 1982. 7.95 (*0-943898-00-5*); pap. 6.95 (*0-943898-01-3*) Gospic Realty.

Rajadhyaksha, Ashish & Willemen, Paul. Encyclopaedia of Indian Cinema. 544p. 1995. text 49.95 (*0-85170-455-7*) Ind U Pr.

***Rajadhyaksha, Ashish & Willemen, Paul.** Encyclopaedia of Indian Cinema. LC 99-936950. (Illus.). 1999. write for info. (*0-19-564768-8*) OUP.

Rajadhyaksha, Ashish & Willemen, Paul, eds. Encyclopedia of Indian Cinema. 2nd ed. LC 95-905174. (Illus.). 624p. 1999. pap. 29.95 (*0-85170-669-X*) Ind U Pr.

***Rajadhyaksha, Ashish & Willemen, Paul, eds.** Encyclopedia of the Indian Cinema. 2nd rev. ed. (Illus.). 658p. 1999. 75.00 (*1-57958-146-3*) Fitzroy Dearborn.

***Rajaee, Farhang.** Globalization on Trial: The Human Condition & the Information Civilization. LC 99-89900. 164p. 2000. pap. 16.95 (*1-56549-111-4*) Kumarian Pr.

Rajaee, Farhang, ed. Iranian Perspectives on the Iran-Iraq War. LC 96-5954. 200p. (C). 1997. 49.95 (*0-8130-1476-X*) U Press Fla.

Rajaee, Farhang, ed. & tr. see Alidust, A., et al.

Rajaee, Farhang, tr. see Taleqani, Mahmood.

Rajago. Strategic Supply Management: An Implementation Toolkit. 256p. 1997. pap. text 37.95 (*0-7506-3680-7*) Buttrwrth-Heinemann.

Rajagop. Discrete Math Computer Science. (C). 1992. text. write for info. (*0-03-922853-3*) Harcourt Coll Pubs.

R

Rajagopal. Entrepreneurship & Rural Markets. (C). 1992. text 15.00 (*81-7033-167-6*, Pub. by Rawat Pubns) S Asia.

Rajagopal, et al. Organizing Rural Business: Policy, Planning & Management. LC 94-32848. 180p. (C). 1995. 22.95 (*0-8039-9200-9*) Sage.

Rajagopal, jt. auth. see Sharma, Aruna.

***Rajagopal, Arvind.** Politics after Television: Hindu Nationalism & the Reshaping of the Public in India. 325p. 2001. write for info. (*0-521-64053-9*); pap. write for info. (*0-521-64839-4*) Cambridge U Pr.

Rajagopal, Arvind, jt. auth. see Goldman, Robert.

Rajagopal, D., ed. see Krishnamurti, Jiddu.

Rajagopal, K. P. Mechanics of Mixtures. 250p. 1995. text 53.00 (*981-02-1585-1*) World Scientific Pub.

Rajagopal, K. R., ed. Recent Advances in Elasticity, Viscoelasticity & Inelasticity: Festschrift Volume in Honor of Professor Tse-Chien Woo on the Occasion of His 70th Birthday. LC 94-23839. (Series on Advances in Mathematics for Applied Sciences). 248p. 1995. text 99.00 (*981-02-2103-7*) World Scientific Pub.

Rajagopal, K. R., jt. auth. see Truesdell, C.

Rajagopal, K. R., jt. auth. see Wineman, Alan S.

Rajagopal, K. R., jt. ed. see Massoudi, M.

Rajagopal, L. V. Critique of Vedanta. (C). 1993. text 27.00 (*81-215-0592-5*, Pub. by M Manoharial) Coronet Bks.

Rajagopal, R., ed. Environmental Mediation & Conflict Management: A Selection of Papers Presented at the 5th Annual Conference of the NAEP, Washington Dc, April 21-23 1980. 120p. 1981. pap. 12.00 (*0-08-026261-9*, Pergamon Pr) Elsevier.

Rajagopal, Raj. Handbook of Heterogeneous Computing: Living with Windows NT, UNIX & NetWare 1999. LC 98-42548. 1336p. 1998. boxed set 95.00 (*0-8493-9989-0*) CRC Pr.

***Rajagopal, Raj.** Introduction to Windows NT Cluster Server: Administration & Programming. LC 99-43496. 1999. 59.95 (*0-8493-1866-1*) CRC Pr.

— Multi-Operating System Networking. LC 99-40224. (Best Practices Ser.). 1338p. 1999. boxed set 79.95 (*0-8493-9831-2*) CRC Pr.

Rajagopal, Raj. Windows NT 4 Advanced Programming. LC 98-108280. (Windows NT Professional Library). (Illus.). 848p. (Orig.). 1997. pap. 49.99 incl. cd-rom (*0-07-882357-9*, Oracle Press) Osborne-McGraw.

— Windows NT, UNIX, Netware Migration & Coexistence: A Professional's Guide. LC 97-40478. 272p. 1997. boxed set 79.95 (*0-8493-1669-3*) CRC Pr.

Rajagopala, Rao T. A Historical Sketch of Telugu Literature, Vol. 6. 162p. 1986. reprint ed. 15.00 (*0-8364-1693-7*, Pub. by Manohar) S Asia.

Rajagopalachari, Chakravarti. Mahabharata. 1979. pap. 7.95 (*0-89744-929-0*) Auromere.

— Ramakrishna Upanishad. 1.95 (*0-87481-430-8*, Pub. by Ramakrishna Math) Vedanta Pr.

— Ramayana. 320p. 1979. pap. 7.95 (*0-89744-930-4*) Auromere.

Rajagopalachari, Chakravarti, ed. from TAM. Ramayana. 3rd ed. 320p. 1980. pap. 10.00 (*0-934676-17-8*) Greenlf Bks.

Rajagopalachari, M. The Novels of Bernard Malamud. 222p. 1988. text 27.50 (*81-85218-02-1*, Pub. by Prestige) Advent Bks Div.

— The Novels of Manohar Malgonkar. 104p. 1990. text 18.95 (*81-85218-16-1*, Pub. by Prestige) Advent Bks Div.

Rajagopalachari, Parthasarathi. Heart of the Lion. 196p. 1993. 10.00 (*0-945242-24-7*) Shri Ram Chandra.

— Heart to Heart, Vol. II. 344p. 1991. 15.00 (*0-945242-07-7*) Shri Ram Chandra.

— Heart to Heart Vol. III. 292p. 1994. 15.00 (*0-945242-25-5*) Shri Ram Chandra.

— In His Footsteps, Vol. I. 344p. 1988. pap. 15.00 (*0-945242-03-4*) Shri Ram Chandra.

— In His Footsteps, Vol. 3. 400p. 1995. 18.00 (*0-945242-28-X*) Shri Ram Chandra.

— My Master. 184p. 1989. reprint ed. 10.00 (*0-945242-12-3*) Shri Ram Chandra.

— Role of the Master in Human Evolution. 182p. 1994. 10.00 (*0-945242-29-8*) Shri Ram Chandra.

— What Is Sahaj Marg? rev. ed. 248p. 1994. 12.00 (*0-945242-26-3*) Shri Ram Chandra.

Rajagopalachari, Parthasarathi, jt. auth. see Chandra, Ram.

Rajagopalan, K. Finite Element Buckling Analysis of Stiffened Cylindrical Shells. (Illus.). 175p. 1993. text 97.00 (*90-5410-232-2*, Pub. by A A Balkema) Ashgate Pub Co.

— Storage Structures. (Illus.). 397p. (C). 1990. text 95.00 (*90-6191-947-9*, Pub. by A A Balkema) Ashgate Pub Co.

Rajagopalan, M., jt. ed. see Misra, P. R.

Rajagopalan, R., jt. ed. see Chen, S. H.

Rajagopalan, Raj, jt. auth. see Hiemenez, Paul C.

Rajagopalan, Rukmini, et al. Care Management of Skin Diseases: Life Quality & Economic Impact. LC 97-42815. (Illus.). 485p. 1998. text 150.00 (*0-8247-0128-3*) Dekker.

Rajagopalan, S. Guide to Simple Sanitary Measures for the Control of Enteric Diseases. 1974. pap. text 32.00 (*92-4-154047-8*, 1150058) World Health.

Rajagopalan, Swarna, jt. ed. see Bukowski, Jeanie J.

Rajagopalan, Venkatachari. Computer-Aided Analysis of Power Electronic Systems. (Electrical Engineering & Electronics Ser.: Vol. 40). (Illus.). 552p. 1987. text 195.00 (*0-8247-7706-9*) Dekker.

Rajah, Harry, jt. auth. see Choong, T. C.

Rajak, Harry, et al, eds. European Corporate Insolvency: A Practical Guide. 952p. 1995. 177.00 (*0-471-95239-7*) Wiley.

Rajak, Harry & Davis, Richard. Insolvency: A Business by Business Guide. 352p. 1994. pap. text 99.00 (*0-406-02231-3*, UK, MICHIE) LEXIS Pub.

Rajak, R. L., et al. Plant Parasitic Nematodes - A Check List, 1981-1985. (International Bioscience Monographs: Vol. XVIII). (Illus.). 135p. 1987. 17.00 (*1-55528-143-5*) Scholarly Pubns.

Rajala, Jack. Bringing Back the White Pine. Preece, Kathleen, ed. LC 98-161806. (Illus.). 120p. 1998. pap. 2.00 (*0-9662779-0-2*) J Rajala.

Rajala, Richard A. Clearcutting the Pacific Rain Forest: Production, Science, & Regulation. LC 98-171791. (Illus.). 312p. 1999. pap. 24.95 (*0-7748-0591-9*) U BC Pr.

***Rajala, Sarah A. & Rabbani, Majid, eds.** Visual Communications & Image Processing '98. 1120p. 1998. 141.00 (*0-8194-2749-7*) SPIE.

Rajalakshmi, M., jt. auth. see Ramakrishnan, T. V.

***Rajalakshmi, S.** Tamil Nadu Economy. LC 99-938054. 1998. 298.00 (*81-86982-50-7*, Pub. by Business Pubns) St Mut.

Rajam, V. S. A Reference Grammar of Classical Tamil Poetry. LC 91-76989. (Memoirs Ser.: Vol. 199). 672p. (C). 1992. 25.00 (*0-87169-199-X*, M199-RAV) Am Philos.

Rajamanickam, C., et al, eds. Biological Macro Molecules: Structure & Function: Proceedings of Indo-Soviet Binational Symposium, Madurai. 250p. 1985. 79.00 (*0-685-59946-9*) Scholarly Pubns.

Rajamanickam, C. & Packer, Lester, eds. Biomembranes: Structure, Biogenesis & Transport Proceedings of Biomembrane Symposium. (Current Trends in Life Sciences Ser.: Vol. XIII). (Illus.). 358p. 1987. 95.00 (*1-55528-142-7*) Scholarly Pubns.

Rajan, Amin & Fryatt, J., eds. Create or Abdicate: City's Human Resource Choice for the 1990's. (C). 1988. 250.00 (*0-7855-4189-6*, Pub. by Witherby & Co) St Mut.

Rajan, Amin & Fryatt, Julie, eds. Create or Abdicate: The City's Human Resource Choice for the 90's. 240p. 1988. 250.00 (*0-948691-66-2*, Pub. by Witherby & Co) St Mut.

Rajan, B. T. S. Eliot: A Study of His Writings by Several Hands. LC 65-15865. (Studies in T. S. Eliot: No. 11). 1969. reprint ed. lib. bdg. 75.00 (*0-8383-0545-8*) M S G Haskell Hse.

Rajan, Balachandra. The Form of the Unfinished: English Poetics from Spenser to Pound. LC 84-42900. 327p. 1985. reprint ed. pap. 101.40 (*0-608-02894-0*, 206395800007) Bks Demand.

— The Overwhelming Question: A Study of the Poetry of T. S. Eliot. LC 75-32519. 161p. reprint ed. pap. 50.00 (*0-608-15420-2*, 202934600060) Bks Demand.

— Under Western Eyes: India from Milton to Macaulay. LC 98-30647. (Post-Contemporary Interventions Ser.). 1999. 49.95 (*0-8223-2279-X*); pap. 17.95 (*0-8223-2298-6*) Duke.

Rajan, Balachandra, ed. Paradise Lost: A Tercenenary Tribute. LC 77-429833. 154p. reprint ed. pap. 47.80 (*0-608-12872-4*, 202365900033) Bks Demand.

Rajan, Balachandra & Sauer, Elizabeth, eds. Milton & the Imperial Vision. LC 98-40119. (Medieval & Renaissance Literary Studies). 376p. 1999. 58.00 (*0-8207-0303-6*) Duquesne.

Rajan, Gayatri. The Story of Santoshi Devi. (Illus.). 40p. (Orig.). (J). (gr. k-6). pap. write for info. (*0-9644226-0-3*) Buddhi Pubns.

Rajan, Gita & Mohanram, Radhika, eds. Postcolonial Discourse & Changing Cultural Contexts: Theory & Criticism, 64. LC 95-16019. (Contributions to the Study of World Literature Ser.: Vol. 64). 240p. 1995. 62.95 (*0-313-29693-6*, Greenwood Pr) Greenwood.

Rajan, Gita, jt. ed. see Mohanram, Radhika.

Rajan, Janaki, jt. ed. see Arslan, Mehdi.

Rajan, Jane, jt. auth. see Redmill, Felix.

Rajan, K. V. Indian Temple Styles: The Personality of Hindu Architecture. 1972. reprint ed. 38.50 (*0-8364-2604-5*, Pub. by M Manoharial) S Asia.

— Secularism in Indian Art. (C). 1988. 48.50 (*81-7017-245-4*, Pub. by Abhinav) S Asia.

Rajan, K. V. Soundara. Rock-cut Temple Styles: Early Pandyan Art & the Ellora Shrines. LC 98-909054. xiv, 180 p. 1998. write for info. (*81-7039-218-7*) Somaiya Publns.

Rajan, Krishna, ed. see Metallurgical Society of AIME Staff.

Rajan, M. A. Land Reforms in Karnataka. 178p. 1986. 17.50 (*0-8364-1938-3*, Pub. by Hindustan) S Asia.

Rajan, M. S. The Future of Nonalignment & the Nonaligned Movement: Some Reflective Essays. 136p. 1990. text 18.95 (*81-220-0189-0*, Pub. by Konark Pubs Pvt Ltd) Advent Bks Div.

— India & the Commonwealth: Some Studies. 192p. 1990. text 27.50 (*81-220-0187-4*, Pub. by Konark Pubs Pvt Ltd) Advent Bks Div.

***Rajan, Mannaraswamighala S.** India & International Affairs: A Collection of Essays LC 99-932150. 407p. 1999. write for info. (*81-7095-071-6*) Lancer India.

Rajan, Mohan S. Atoms of Hope. 155p. 1980. 15.95 (*0-940500-39-6*, Pub. by Allied Pubs) Asia Bk Corp.

Rajan, Nalini. Secularism, Democracy, Justice: Implications of Rawlsian Principles in India. LC 97-32075. 1998. write for info. (*0-7619-9214-6*) Sage.

Rajan, P. K. The Growth of the Novel in India. (C). 1989. 22.00 (*81-7017-259-4*, Pub. by Abhinav) S Asia.

— Studies in Mulk Raj Anand. viii, 122p. 1986. 11.00 (*81-7017-207-1*, Pub. by Abhinav) S Asia.

Rajan, R. Sundara. The Primacy of the Political. 224p. 1992. text 18.95 (*0-19-562729-6*) OUP.

Rajan, R. Sundara & Indian Institute of Advanced Study Staff. Beyond the Crisis of the European Sciences. LC 99-931772. 1998. write for info. (*81-85952-59-0*) Indian Inst.

Rajan, Rajeswari S. Real & Imagined Women: Gender, Culture, & Postcolonialism. LC 93-6923. (Illus.). 176p. (C). 1993. pap. 20.99 (*0-415-08504-7*, B2281) Routledge.

Rajan, Rajeswari S., ed. The Lie of the Land: English Literary Studies in India. 320p. (C). 1992. 24.95 (*0-19-562829-2*) OUP.

— The Lie of the Land: English Literary Studies in India. 320p. 1994. reprint ed. pap. text 12.95 (*0-19-563361-X*) OUP.

Rajan, Rajeswari Sunder & Kali for Women Organization Staff. Signposts: Gender Issues in Post-Independence India. LC 99-931761. 381 p. 1999. 34.00 (*81-86706-12-7*, Pub. by Kali for Women) S Asia.

Rajan, Ramkishen S. & Asher, Mukul G. The Macroeconomics of Financing Government Expenditure: A Survey of the Static Consequences. LC 97-945648. (Illus.). 123p. (Orig.). 1997. pap. 37.50 (*9971-69-200-7*, Pub. by Sngapore Univ Pr) Coronet Bks.

Rajan, Ramkishen S., jt. ed. see Ling, Ooi Giok.

***Rajan, S. D.** Introduction to Structural Analysis & Design. 736p. 2000. write for info. (*0-471-31997-X*) Wiley.

Rajan, S. Irudaya. Catholics in Bombay: A Historical Demographic Study of the Roman Catholic Population in the Archdiocese of Bombay. (C). 1993. 44.00 (*81-85408-08-4*, Pub. by Firma KLM) S Asia.

Rajan, S. Irudaya, ed. India's Demographic Transition: A Reassessment. 279p. 1997. pap. 250.00 (*81-7533-028-7*, Pub. by Print Hse) St Mut.

Rajan, S. Irudaya, jt. auth. see Zachariah, K. C.

Rajan, S. Irudaya, jt. ed. see Zachariah, K. C.

Rajan, Sudhir C. The Enigma of Automobility: Democratic Politics & Pollution Control. LC 96-10049. (Pitt Series in Policy & Institutional). 208p. 1996. pap. 19.95 (*0-8229-5606-3*); text 44.95 (*0-8229-3947-9*) U of Pittsburgh Pr.

Rajan, Sundar. Essential VHDL: RTL Synthesis Done Right. (Illus.). xxiii, 315p. 1998. pap. 49.95 (*0-9669590-0-0*) S & G.

Rajan, Sunder S. MRI: A Conceptual Overview. LC 96-37408. 144p. 1997. pap. 34.95 (*0-387-94911-9*) Spr-Verlag.

Rajan, Tilottama. Dark Interpreter: The Discourse of Romanticism. 288p. 1980. pap. 15.95 (*0-8014-9369-2*) Cornell U Pr.

— Dark Interpreter: The Discourse of Romanticism. LC 80-14476. 285p. reprint ed. pap. 88.40 (*0-608-20937-6*, 207203600003) Bks Demand.

— The Supplement of Reading: Figures of Understanding in Romantic Theory & Practice. LC 90-55122. 368p. 1990. 47.50 (*0-8014-2045-8*); pap. text 18.95 (*0-8014-9749-3*) Cornell U Pr.

Rajan, Tilottama & Clark, David L., eds. Intersections: Nineteenth-Century Philosophy & Contemporary Theory. LC 94-15204. (SUNY Series, The Margins of Literature). 386p. (C). 1995. text 64.50 (*0-7914-2257-7*); pap. text 21.95 (*0-7914-2258-5*) State U NY Pr.

Rajan, Tilottama & Wright, Julia M., eds. Romanticism, History, & the Possibilities of Genre. LC 97-6879. 306p. (C). 1998. text 59.95 (*0-521-58192-3*) Cambridge U Pr.

Rajan, Tilottama, ed. see Shelley, Mary Wollstonecraft.

Rajan, V. N. Victimology in India. 136p. 1981. 16.95 (*0-940500-86-8*, Pub. by Allied Pubs) Asia Bk Corp.

— Victimology in India: Perspectives Beyond Frontiers. LC 95-900465. vi, 268p. (C). 1995. 32.00 (*81-7024-673-3*, Pub. by Ashish Pub Hse) Nataraj Bks.

Rajan, V. R. Globalising Indian Industries: Strategies & Management. 1998. 30.00 (*81-7629-100-5*) Deep & Deep Pubns.

Rajanayagam, M. J. The Law of Negotiable Instruments in Australia. 2nd ed. Conrick, Brian, ed. 280p. (C). 1989. 76.00 (*0-409-49527-1*, AT, MICHIE); pap. 56.00 (*0-409-49528-X*, AT, MICHIE) LEXIS Pub.

Rajanen, Aini & Kilbride, Robert. A Tale for Saint Urho's Tay LC 81-295. 39 p. (J). 1981. write for info. (*0-87518-215-1*) Silver Burdett Pr.

***Rajani, Balvant & AWWA Research Foundation Staff.** Investigation of Grey Cast Iron Water Mains to Develop a Methodology for Estimating Service Life. LC 00-22365. 2000. write for info. (*1-58321-063-6*) Am Water Wks Assn.

Rajani, Shashi, et al. Tolley's Corporate Insolvency Handbook. 2nd ed. 795p. 1994. 195.00 (*0-85459-748-4*, Pub. by Tolley Pubng) St Mut.

Rajaonarimanana, N. Dictionary Malgache-French. 316p. 1996. 52.00 (*0-320-00822-3*) Fr & Eur.

Rajaonarimanana, N. Dictionary Malgache/French/Malgache. 403p. 1996. 140.00 (*0-320-00821-5*) Fr & Eur.

Rajaonarimanana, Narivelo. Dictionnaire Francais-Malgache. (FRE.). 192p. 1993. pap. 39.95 (*0-7859-5666-2*, 2901795544) Fr & Eur.

Rajapakse, Y., jt. auth. see Baizant, Z. P.

Rajapakse, Y., jt. ed. see Achenbach, J. D.

Rajapakse, Y. D., ed. Mechanics of Thick Composites. LC 93-71576. (AMD Ser.: Vol. 162). 267p. 1993. pap. 55.00 (*0-7918-1141-7*, G00785) ASME.

Rajapakse, Y. D., et al, eds. High Strain Rate Effects on Polymer, Metal & Ceramic Matrix Composites & Other Advanced Materials: Proceedings of the ASME International Mechanical Engineering Congress & Exposition, 1995, San Francisco, CA. LC 95-81259. (1995 ASME International Mechanical Engineering Congress & Exposition Ser.: AD-Vol. 48). 200p. 1995. 88.00 (*0-7918-1726-1*, H01008) ASME.

Rajapakse, Y. D., ed. see American Society of Mechanical Engineers Staff.

Rajapakse, Y. D., jt. ed. see Dempsey, J. P.

***Rajapakse, Yapa D. S. & Kar, George A., eds.** Thick Composites for Load Bearing Structures. (AMS Ser.: Vol. 235). 113p. 1999. 70.00 (*0-7918-1652-4*) ASME Pr.

Rajapatirana, Sarath. Trade Policies in Latin America & the Caribbean: Priorities, Progress & Prospects. LC 97-11094. (Illus.). xix, 237p. (Orig.). 1997. pap. 19.95 (*0-9656930-0-7*) Intl Ctr Economic.

Rajapatirana, Sarath, jt. auth. see Athukorala, Prema-Chandra.

Rajapatirana, Sarath, jt. auth. see Holden, Paul.

Rajapatirana, Sarath, jt. ed. see Brugger, Ernst A.

Rajar, R. & Brebbia, C. A., eds. Water Pollution IV: Modelling, Measuring & Prediction. LC 97-66707. 832p. 1997. 366.00 (*1-85312-470-2*, 4702, Pub. by WIT Pr) Computational Mech MA.

***Rajarama Bhat, B. V., et al, eds.** Lectures on Operator Theory. LC 99-52254. (Fields Institute Monographs: Vol. 13). 323p. 2000. 69.00 (*0-8218-0821-4*) Am Math.

Rajaraman, Dharma. Computer: A Child's Play. 120p. (J). 1989. reprint ed. pap. text 12.95 (*0-9615336-9-2*) Silicon Pr.

Rajaraman, R. Solitons & Instantons: An Introduction to Solitons & Instantons in Quantum Field Theory. (North-Holland Personal Library). viii, 410p. 1989. reprint ed. pap. 79.25 (*0-444-87047-4*, North Holland) Elsevier.

Rajaratnam, T. W. A Judiciary in Crisis? The Trial of Zulfikar Ali Bhutto. (C). 1988. 65.00 (*0-7855-4777-0*) St Mut.

Rajasekaran, B. A Framework for Incorporating Indigenous Knowledge Systems into Agricultural Research, Extension, & NGOs for Sustainable Agricultural Development. (Studies in Technology & Social Change: No. 22). 52p. (Orig.). (C). 1994. pap. 7.00 (*0-945271-32-8*) ISU-CIKARD.

***Rajasekaran, Sanguthevar, et al.** Mobile Networks & Computing. (DIMACS Ser.: Vol. 52). 313p. 2000. 99.00 (*0-8218-1547-4*) Am Math.

Rajasekaran, Sanguthevar, jt. auth. see Pardalos, P. M.

Rajasekhara, S. Masterpieces of Vijayanarara Art. (Illus.). 100p. 1983. text 40.00 (*0-86590-115-5*) Apt Bks.

Rajasekharaiah, T. R. The Roots of Whitman's Grass. LC 76-85762. 522p. 1975. 50.00 (*0-8386-7493-3*) Fairleigh Dickinson.

Rajashekara, Kaushik, et al, eds. Sensorless Control of AC Motor Drives: Speed & Position Sensorless Operation. LC 95-47574. 512p. 1996. 99.95 (*0-7803-1046-2*, PC3996) Inst Electrical.

Rajashekarappa, K. G. Engineering Mechanics: Applied Mechanics. Bhavikatti, S. S., ed. 537p. 1994. text 49.95 (*0-470-22054-6*) Halsted Pr.

Rajasingham, Lalita, jt. auth. see Tiffin, John.

Rajasunderam, D. V., jt. auth. see Bessette, Guy.

Rajat, Sanyal. Voluntary Associations & the Urban Public Life in Bengal. 1983. 16.50 (*0-8364-0980-9*, Pub. by RDDHI) S Asia.

***Rajaval, N.** Tourism in Andaman & Nicobar Islands. 1998. 34.00 (*81-7049-087-1*) Manas Pubns.

Rajbahak, R. P. Nepal-India Open Border: A Bond of Shaved Aspirations. (C). 1992. 48.00 (*0-7855-0199-1*, Pub. by Ratna Pustak Bhandar) St Mut.

***Rajbanshi, B. S.** For World Peace & International Understanding. 1998. pap. 60.00 (*0-7855-7661-4*) St Mut.

Rajbhandari, K. R. A Bibliography of the Plant Science of Nepal. 1994. pap. 135.00 (*0-7855-0427-3*, Pub. by Ratna Pustak Bhandar) St Mut.

RajBhandary, T. L., jt. ed. see Soll, Dieter.

Rajchman, John. Constructions. LC 97-35756. (Writing Architecture Ser.). (Illus.). 155p. 1998. pap. text 15.00 (*0-262-68096-3*) MIT Pr.

***Rajchman, John.** The Deleuze Connections. (Illus.). 120p. (C). 2000. 35.00 (*0-262-18205-X*); pap. 14.95 (*0-262-68120-X*) MIT Pr.

Rajchman, John. Identity in Question. LC 94-24832. 224p. (C). (gr. 13). 1995. pap. 18.99 (*0-415-90618-0*, Pub. by Tavistock) Routldge.

— Philosophical Events: Essays of the Eighties. 192p. 1990. text 39.50 (*0-231-07210-4*) Col U Pr.

Rajchman, John & West, Cornel, eds. Post-Analytic Philosophy. LC 85-377. 304p. 1985. pap. text 22.50 (*0-231-06067-X*) Col U Pr.

Rajcsanyi, Elisabeth, jt. auth. see Rajcsanyi, Peter M.

Rajcsanyi, Peter M. & Rajcsanyi, Elisabeth. High-Speed Liquid Chromatography. LC 75-29922. (Chromatographic Science Ser.: No. 6). 211p. reprint ed. pap. 65.50 (*0-7837-3894-3*, 204374200010) Bks Demand.

Raje, R. K. Shalom, Israel: An Indian Reporter in Holy Land. LC 99-931327. 81 p. 1993. write for info. (*81-85148-47-3*) Advent Bks Div.

***Raje, R. R. & Wong, P. D.** Iatrogenic Diseases. LC 99-10525. (Textbooks for Students Ser.). 144p. 1999. 23.95 (*0-915340-22-4*) PJD Pubns.

Rajecki, D. W. Comparing Behavior: Studying Man Studying Animals. 304p. (C). 1983. 69.95 (*0-89859-259-3*) L Erlbaum Assocs.

***Rajeev, P. V.** Planning for Social Reforms: The Key to Economic Progress. 1999. 20.00 (*81-7629-189-7*, Pub. by Deep & Deep Pubns) S Asia.

Rajeev, S., jt. auth. see Krishnamoorthy, C. S.

Rajeeva, R., ed. An Introduction to the Tribal Development in India. 150p. 1989. 65.00 (*81-7089-109-4*, Pub. by Intl Bk Distr) St Mut.

Rajendra, jt. auth. see Lower.

Rajendra, Cecil. Dove on Fire: Poems on Peace, Justice & Ecology. (Risk Bks.: No. 33). (Illus.). 92p. (Orig.). 1987. pap. 5.75 (*2-8254-0899-9*) Wrld Coun Churches.

Rajendra, Srivastava K. Industrial Marketing. (C). 1997. text. write for info. (*0-201-50579-7*) Addison-Wesley.

An Asterisk (*) at the beginning of an entry indicates that the title is appearing for the first time.

R

*__Rajer, Anton & Style, Christine.__ Public Sculpture in Wisconsin: An Atlas of Outdoor Monuments, Memorials & Masterpieces in the Badger State. (Illus.). 160p. (Orig.). 1999. pap. text 27.95 (*0-9664180-2-6*) U of Wis Pr.

*__Rajesh, M. N.__ Buddhist Monastery. LC 98-909488. 1999. 19.95 (*81-7436-054-9*) Heian Intl.

Rajeshwar, K., et al, eds. Photoelectrochemistry. LC 97-211116. (Proceedings Ser.: Vol. 97-20). 420p. 1997. 85.00 (*1-56677-148-X*) Electrochem Soc.

Rajeshwar, Krishnan & Ibanez, Jorge. Environmental Electrochemistry. LC 96-10927. (Illus.). 776p. 1997. text 95.00 (*0-12-576260-7*) Acad Pr.

Rajeshwar, M. The Novels of Wole Soyinka. 96p. 1990. text 17.95 (*81-85218-21-8*, Pub. by Prestige) Advent Bks Div.

Rajeshwari, D. R. Sakti Iconography. (C). 1988. 65.00 (*81-7076-015-1*, Pub. by Intellectual) S Asia.

Rajfer, Jacob. Urologic Endocrinology. (Illus.). 448p. 1986. text 115.00 (*0-7216-7426-7*, W B Saunders Co) Harcrt Hlth Sci Grp.

Rajgopal, P. R. Communal Violence in India. 141p. 1987. 24.95 (*0-318-37208-8*) Asia Bk Corp.

— Communal Violence in India. (C). 1987. 24.00 (*81-85024-14-6*, Pub. by Uppal Pub Hse) S Asia.

— Social Change & Violence: The Indian Experience. 227p. (C). 1987. 35.00 (*81-85024-27-8*, Pub. by Uppal Pub Hse) S Asia.

Rajhans, Gyan S., jt. auth. see Blackwell, David S.

Rajhathy, Judit. Free to Fly: A Journey Toward Wellness. 2nd ed. Mitchell, Francis, ed. (Illus.). 352p. (Orig.). 1996. reprint ed. pap. 19.95 (*1-895814-04-9*) NewWorld Pub.

Rajiv, Sudhi. Forms of Black Consciousness. 189p. 1992. text 25.00 (*0-89891-062-5*) Advent Bks Div.

Rajka, G. Essential Aspects of Atopic Dermatitis. (Illus.). xvi, 261p. 1989. 133.00 (*0-387-51165-2*) Spr-Verlag.

Rajkowski, Pamela. Linden Girl: A Story of Outlawed Lives. LC 95-213632. 304p. (C). 1995. pap. 24.95 (*1-875560-25-4*, Pub. by Univ of West Aust Pr) Intl Spec Bk.

*__Rajkumar, Ragunathan.__ Operating Systems & Services LC 99-28475. 1999. write for info. (*0-7923-8548-9*, Kluwer Plenum) Kluwer Academic.

Rajkumar, Ragunathan, ed. Synchronization in Real-Time Systems: A Priority Inheritance Approach. 208p. (C). 1991. text 98.00 (*0-7923-9211-6*) Kluwer Academic.

Rajkumar, S. & Toback, C. Principles & Practice of Ambulatory Pediatrics. (Illus.). 856p. (C). 1988. text 210.00 (*0-306-42500-9*, Kluwer Plenum) Kluwer Academic.

Rajmani Tigunait, Pandit. Swami Rama of the Himalayas: His Life & Mission. LC 97-74548. (Illus.). 208p. 1997. 59.95 (*0-89389-147-2*); pap. 39.95 (*0-89389-149-5*) Himalayan Inst.

Rajnavolgyi, Eva. Synthetic Peptides in the Search for T & B Cell Epitopes. LC 94-38447. (Molecular Biology Intelligence Unit Ser.). 200p. 1994. 99.00 (*1-57059-160-1*) Landes Bioscience.

Rajneesh Academy Staff, ed. see Osho.

Rajneesh Foundation International Staff, ed. see Osho.

Rajogopal, Shan, jt. auth. see Chadwick, Tom.

Rajoppi, Joanne. Women in Office: Getting There & Staying There. LC 93-18135. 200p. 1993. 52.95 (*0-89789-343-3*, H343, Bergin & Garvey) Greenwood.

Rajotte, Pierre. Belgian Ale. (Classic Beer Style Ser.). (Illus.). 176p. 1992. pap. 14.95 (*0-937381-31-4*) Brewers Pubns.

Rajput, Pam & Swarup, Hem L., eds. Women & Globalisation: Reflections, Options & Strategies. xxxiv, 393p. (C). 1994. 49.00 (*81-7024-669-5*, Pub. by Ashish Pub Hse) Nataraj Bks.

*__Rajput, Wasim.__ E-Commerce Systems: Architecture, Design & Implementation. LC 00-35553. (Illus.). 428p. 2000. write for info. (*1-58053-085-0*) Artech Hse.

Rajs, Jake. America. (Illus.). 192p. 1996. pap. 22.50 (*0-7893-0027-3*, Pub. by Universe) St Martin.

— The Hudson River: From Tear of the Clouds to Manhattan. Adams, Arthur G., ed. LC 95-30605. (Illus.). 272p. 1995. 60.00 (*1-885254-10-5*, Pub. by Monacelli Pr) Penguin Putnam.

— The Hudson River: From Tear of the Clouds to Manhattan, 4 vols., Set. Adams, Arthur G., ed. LC 95-30605. (Illus.). 272p. 1995. 240.00 (*1-885254-17-2*) Monacelli Pr.

— New York: City of Islands. LC 98-30246. 272p. 1998. 60.00 (*1-58093-009-3*, Pub. by Monacelli Pr) Penguin Putnam.

Rajs, Jake, photos by. Manhattan: An Island in Focus. LC 85-43056. (Illus.). 256p. 1991. 55.00 (*0-8478-0670-7*, Pub. by Rizzoli Intl) St Martin.

Rajshekar, V. T. Dalit: The Black Untouchables of India. LC 87-71663. 100p. (Orig.). 1995. pap. 12.95 (*0-932863-05-1*) Clarity Pr.

Rajski, Janusz & Tyszer, Jerzy. Arithmetic Built-In Self-Test for Embedded Systems. LC 97-30395. 288p. (C). 1997. 89.00 (*0-13-756438-4*) P-H.

*__Rajskina, M. E.__ Ventricular Vibrillation & Sudden Coronary Death. LC 99-33619. (Developments in Cardiovascular Medicine Ser.). 240p. 1999. 140.00 (*0-7923-8570-5*) Kluwer Academic.

Rajskub, MaryLynn. The Big Picture. 10p. 1993. pap. 1.00 (*1-884047-51-3*) Mass Extinct.

*__Rajsuman, R. & Wike, T. R., eds.__ Memory Technology, Design & Testing: Proceedings IEEE International Workshop on Memory Technology, Design & Testing, 7th, San Jose, California, 1999. 131p. 1999. 100.00 (*0-7695-0259-8*) IEEE Comp Soc.

Rajsuman, Rochit. IDDQ Testing for CMOS & VLSI. LC 94-21066. 1994. 85.00 (*0-89006-726-0*) Artech Hse.

*__Rajsuman, Rochit.__ System-on-a-Chip: Design & Test. (Solid-State Technology Library). (Illus.). 303p. 2000. write for info. (*1-58053-107-5*) Artech Hse.

Rajsuman, Rochit, ed. Digital Hardware Testing: Transistor-Level Fault Modeling & Testing. LC 92-8800. (Telecommunications Engineering Library). (Illus.). 371p. 1992. text 87.00 (*0-89006-580-2*) Artech Hse.

Rajtar, Steve. Hiking Trails, Eastern United States: Address, Phone Number & Distances for 5,000 Trails, with Indexing of over 200 Guidebooks. LC 95-17296. 351p. 1995. pap. 39.95 (*0-7864-0142-7*) McFarland & Co.

— Hiking Trails, Western United States: Address, Phone Number & Distances for 4300 Trails, with Indexing of over 200 Guidebooks. LC 96-28493. 284p. 1996. pap. 39.95 (*0-7864-0245-8*) McFarland & Co.

*__Rajtar, Steve.__ Indian War Sites: A Guidebook to Battlefields, Monuments & Memorials, State by State with Canada & Mexico. LC 99-25893. (Illus.). 336p. 1999. pap. 39.95 (*0-7864-0710-7*) McFarland & Co.

Raju, jt. auth. see Narasaiah, P. V.

Raju, Ashish, jt. auth. see Yanofski, Jason.

Raju, B. R. Developmental Migration: A Processual Analysis of Inter State Rural-Rural Migration. (C). 1989. 22.50 (*81-7022-205-2*, Pub. by Concept) S Asia.

Raju, C. K. Time: Towards a Consistent-Theory, 65. LC 94-32856. (Fundamental Theories of Physics Ser.). 272p. (C). 1994. lib. bdg. 156.00 (*0-7923-3103-6*, Pub. by Kluwer Academic) Kluwer Academic.

Raju, K. V., jt. auth. see Maloney, Clarence.

Raju, M. K. W. H. Auden - The Commissar & the Yogi: A Study of His Plays & Longer Poems. 200p. 1991. text 30.00 (*81-85218-25-0*, Pub. by Prestige) Advent Bks Div.

*__Raju, Nambury S., et al.__ Grading the Nation's Report Card: Research from the Evaluation of NAEP. LC 00-8316. (Illus.). 276p. 2000. pap. 43.00 (*0-309-06844-4*) Natl Acad Pr.

Raju, P. K. Integrating Theory & Practice for Engineers: A Case Study Approach. (C). 2001. text. write for info. (*0-201-43660-4*) Addison-Wesley.

Raju, P. K., ed. Vibro-Acoustic Characterization of Materials & Structures. (NCA Ser.: Vol. 14). 242p. 1992. 57.50 (*0-7918-1125-5*, G00769) ASME.

Raju, P. K. & Gibson, R. F., eds. Dynamic Characterization of Advanced Materials. LC 93-73264. 215p. pap. 60.00 (*0-7918-1028-3*) ASME.

Raju, P. T. Introduction to Comparative Philosophy. xii, 364p. (C). 1992. 19.95 (*1-881338-17-7*) Nataraj Bks.

— The Philosophical Traditions of India. 256p. (C). 1992. 19.95 (*1-881338-18-5*) Nataraj Bks.

— Spirit, Being, & Self. (Studies in Indian & Western Philosophy). 285p. 1982. 29.95 (*0-940500-98-1*, Pub. by S Asian Pubs) Asia Bk Corp.

— Spirit, Being, & Self: Studies in Indian & Western Philosophy. 285p. 1982. 29.95 (*0-318-37031-X*) Asia Bk Corp.

— Spirit, Being, & Self: Studies in Indian & Western Philosophy. 284p. 1986. 20.00 (*0-8364-1853-0*, Pub. by S Asia Pubs) S Asia.

— Structural Depths of Indian Thought. (SUNY Series in Philosophy). 599p. (C). 1985. text 64.50 (*0-88706-139-7*) State U NY Pr.

— Structural Depths of Indian Thought. (SUNY Series in Philosophy). 599p. (C). 1989. pap. text 21.95 (*0-88706-140-0*) State U NY Pr.

Raju, P. T., jt. ed. see Radhakrishnan, Sarvepalli.

Raju, R., jt. auth. see Jhala, J.

Raju, R. K. A Mystic Link with India: Life Story of Two Pilgrims Painters of Hungary. (C). 1991. 22.00 (*81-7023-317-8*, Pub. by Allied Pubs) S Asia.

*__Raju, Saraswati, et al.__ Atlas of Women & Men in India. 130p. 1999. 49.00 (*90-5727-024-2*, Pub. by Intl Bks) Paul & Co Pubs.

Raju, Satyanarayana. Fingers Calculator. (Illus.). 200p. (YA). (gr. 7-12). 1996. pap. text 29.95 (*0-9650901-0-8*) Inst of Vedic

Raju, Seshardi & Villavicencio, L. Leonel. Surgical Management of Venous Disease. LC 96-31993. (Illus.). 420p. 1997. 99.00 (*0-683-07111-4*) Lppncott W & W.

Raju, T. Satyanarayana. Play with Numbers. (Illus.). v, 190p. (Orig.). (YA). (gr. 7-12). 1996. pap. 29.95 (*0-9650901-2-4*) Inst of Vedic.

— Recreational Mathematics, Vol. 1. (Illus.). vi, 189p. (Orig.). (YA). (gr. 7-12). 1996. pap. 29.95 (*0-9650901-1-6*) Inst of Vedic.

— Vedic Mathematics, 4 vols., Vol. 1. iv, 190p. (Orig.). (YA). (gr. 7-12). 1996. pap. 29.95 (*0-9650901-3-2*) Inst of Vedic.

Raju, V. B. Commentaries on Evidence Act. 4th ed. (C). 1991. 110.00 (*0-7855-5566-8*) St Mut.

— Commentaries on the Constitution of India. 992p. 1973. 120.00 (*0-7855-1347-7*) St Mut.

— Indian Penal Code. (C). 1990. 100.00 (*0-7855-5337-1*) St Mut.

— Indian Penal Code, Eighteen-Sixty: Nineteen Eighty-Two Bound in One Book W-S 1986, 2 vols., Set. 4th ed. (C). 1986. 200.00 (*0-7855-4699-5*) St Mut.

— Indian Penal Code, 1860, Set. 4th ed. 1982. 660.00 (*0-7855-1345-0*) St Mut.

— Indian Penal Code, 1860, 1982 Edition. 4th ed. (C). 1990. 200.00 (*0-7855-5452-1*) St Mut.

Raju, V. Rajendra. Role of Women in India's Freedom Struggle. (C) 1994. text 20.00 (*81-7141-238-6*, Pub. by Discovery Pub Hse) S Asia.

Rajusuman, Rochit & Mazumder, Pinaki, eds. Semiconductor Memories: Testing & Reliability. 400p. 1997. pap. 45.00 (*0-8186-7797-X*, BP07797) IEEE Comp Soc.

Rajwade, A. R. Squares. (London Mathematical Society Lecture Note Ser.: No. 171). 298p. (C). 1993. pap. text 44.95 (*0-521-42668-5*) Cambridge U Pr.

Rajwar, G. S. Advances in Himalayan Ecology. (Recent Researches in Ecology, Environment & Pollution Ser.: Vol. 6). (Illus.). 360p. 1991. 72.00 (*1-55528-241-5*) Scholarly Pubns.

Rajwar, G. S., ed. Garhwal Himalaya: Ecology & Environment. (Illus.). xii, 263p. 1993. 32.00 (*81-7024-559-1*, Pub. by Ashish Pub Hse) Nataraj Bks.

Rajyalakshmi, P. V. Tribal Food Habits. (C). 1991. 18.50 (*81-212-0337-6*, Pub. by Gian Publng Hse) S Asia.

Rak. Financial Management in Canada. 1997. pap. text. write for info. (*0-201-58875-7*) Addison-Wesley.

Rak, Mary K. Cowman's Wife. 352p. 1993. 29.95 (*0-87611-126-6*); pap. 19.95 (*0-87611-127-4*) Tex St Hist Assn.

— A Cowman's Wife. limited ed. (Illus.). 352p. 1993. boxed set 85.00 (*0-87611-128-2*) Tex St Hist Assn.

*__Rak, Stepan.__ The Guitar Music of Stepan Pak. Yates, Stanley, ed. 72p. 1999. 14.95 (*0-7866-3519-3*, 96730) Mel Bay.

Rakadazan. Rakadazanism or the Exalted Life (1912) 225p. 1998. reprint ed. pap. 18.95 (*0-7661-0189-4*) Kessinger Pub.

Rakas, Frank G. Italian for the Business Traveler. 2nd ed. LC 93-30810. (Foreign Language Business Dictionaries Ser.). (ENG & ITA.). 600p. 1994. pap. 9.95 (*0-8120-1771-4*) Barron.

Rakauski, Casimir. Computer Aided Design Explained. (Series 860). 1981. pap., student ed. 7.00 (*0-8064-0345-4*, 860) Bergwall.

Rake, Alan. One Hundred Great Africans. LC 94-25934. (Illus.). 441p. 1994. text 62.50 (*0-8108-2929-0*) Scarecrow.

— Who's Who in Africa: Leaders for the 1990s. LC 92-8166. 456p. 1992. 62.50 (*0-8108-2557-0*) Scarecrow.

*__Rake, Katherine, ed.__ Women's Incomes over the Lifetime: A Report to the Women's Unit, Cabinet Office. xii, 212p. 2000. 40.00 (*0-11-430162-X*, Pub. by Statnry Office) Balogh.

Rakeffet, ed. The Rav Vol. 1: The World of Rabbi Joseph B. Soloveitchick - Biography. LC 99-37285. (Illus.). 296p. 1998. 35.00 (*0-88125-614-5*) Ktav.

— The Rav Vol. 2: The World of Rabbi Joseph B. Soloveitchik - Insights. LC 99-37285. 300p. 1999. 35.00 (*0-88125-615-3*) Ktav.

Rakel, Robert E. Conn's Current Therapy 1999. 99th ed. Kersey, Ray, ed. 1310p. (C). 1998. text 59.00 (*0-7216-7224-8*, W B Saunders Co) Harcrt Hlth Sci Grp.

Rakel, Robert E. Conn's Current Therapy 2000. (Illus.). 1350p. text 59.00 (*0-7216-7225-6*, W B Saunders Co) Harcrt Hlth Sci Grp.

Rakel, Robert E. Conn's Current Therapy, 1998: Latest Approved Methods of Treatment for the Practicing Physician. 98th ed. Kersey, Ray, ed. (Illus.). 1312p. 1998. text 59.00 (*0-7216-7223-X*, W B Saunders Co) Harcrt Hlth Sci Grp.

— Essentials of Family Practice. 2nd ed. Kersey, Ray, ed. LC 97-34009. (Illus.). 576p. (C). 1998. pap. text 49.95 (*0-7216-5868-7*, W B Saunders Co) Harcrt Hlth Sci Grp.

— Saunders Manual of Medical Practice. Pedersen, Darlene, ed. LC 95-6354. (Illus.). 1287p. 1996. text 105.00 (*0-7216-5192-5*, W B Saunders Co) Harcrt Hlth Sci Grp.

— Saunders Manual of Medical Practice. 2nd ed. Kersey, Ray, ed. (Illus.). 1340p. 1999. text. write for info. (*0-7216-8002-X*, W B Saunders Co) Harcrt Hlth Sci Grp.

— Textbook of Family Practice. 5th ed. (Illus.). 1772p. 1995. text 125.00 (*0-7216-4053-2*, W B Saunders Co) Harcrt Hlth Sci Grp.

Rakel, Robert E. & Bope, Edward T. Conn's Current Therapy 2001. (Illus.). 1310p. Date not set. text. write for info. (*0-7216-8743-1*, W B Saunders Co) Harcrt Hlth Sci Grp.

Rakel, Robert E. & Schuckit, Marc A., eds. Fulfilling the Promises: Desyrel - A Five-Year Review. (Journal: Psychopathology: Vol. 20, Suppl. 1, 1987). (Illus.). vi, 146p. 1987. pap. 47.00 (*3-8055-4653-X*) S Karger.

Rakel, Robert E., jt. auth. see Driscoll, Charles E.

Rakes, Charles D. Alarms: Fifty-Five Electronic Projects & Circuits. (Illus.). 160p. 1988. 19.95 (*0-8306-2096-6*, 2996) McGraw-Hill Prof.

Rakes, Thomas A., jt. auth. see Choate, Joyce S.

Rakesh, Hooja. Administrative Interventions in Rural Development. 1987. 10.95 (*0-8364-2237-6*, Pub. by Rawat Pubns) S Asia.

Rakesh, Ram D. Cultural Heritage of Nepal Terai. xiv, 221p. 1994. 20.00 (*81-85693-26-9*, Pub. by Nirala Pubns) Nataraj Bks.

Rakesh, Ram D., ed. Cultural Heritage of Nepal Terai. 1994. pap. 60.00 (*0-7855-0434-6*, Pub. by Ratna Pustak Bhandar) St Mut.

— Law of Sexual Offences. (C). 1988. 180.00 (*0-7855-6031-9*) St Mut.

Rakesh, Virendra P. Sir William Wedderburn & Indian Freedom Movement. 1989. 26.00 (*0-8364-2538-3*, Commonwealth) S Asia.

Rakestraw, Donald A. For Honor or Destiny: The Anglo-American Crisis over the Oregon Territory. LC 93-46250. (American University Studies: Vol. 160). 256p. (C). 1995. text 58.95 (*0-8204-2454-4*) P Lang Pubng.

Rakestraw, Donald A., jt. ed. see Jones, Howard.

Rakestraw, Lawrence. A History of Forest Conservation in the Pacific Northwest, 1891-1913. Bruchey, Stuart, ed. LC 78-56660. (Management in Public Lands in the U. S. Ser.). 1979. lib. bdg. 18.95 (*0-405-11351-X*) Ayer.

Rakestraw, Robert V., jt. ed. see Clark, David K.

Rakha, Alla, jt. auth. see Feldman, Jeffrey M.

Rakhe, S. M. Education in Ancient India. (Sri Garib Dass Oriental Ser.: No. 135). (C). 1992. text 16.00 (*81-7030-312-5*) S Asia.

Rakhit, A. Development of an Epicyclic Gearbox for Reduced Sub-Synchronous Vibrations in Gas Turbo-Generator Sets. (Technical Papers: Vol. 95FTM6). (Illus.). 7p. 1995. pap. text 30.00 (*1-55589-655-3*) AGMA.

*__Rakhit, A. K.__ Effect of Uncontrolled Heat Treat Distortion on the Pitting Life of Ground, Carburized & Hardened Gears. (Technical Papers: Vol. 98FTM4). 5p. 1998. pap. 30.00 (*1-55589-722-3*) AGMA.

— Performance Study of Nitrided Gears in High Speed Epicyclic Gearbox Used in Gas Turbogenerators - A Case Study. (Technical Papers: Vol. 99FTM11). 4p. 1999. pap. 30.00 (*1-55589-749-5*) AGMA.

Rakic, Bogdan, tr. see Andric, Ivo.

Rakic, Bogdan, tr. see Selimovic, Mesa.

*__Rakic, Svetlana.__ Serbian Icons from Bosnia - Herzegovina: Sixteenth to Seventeenth Century, (Illus.). 280p. 2000. 100.00 (*0-9672101-2-7*) A Pankovich.

Rakich, Jonathon S., et al, eds. Cases in Health Services Management. 3rd ed. LC 94-21117. 368p. 1995. pap. text 32.95 (*1-878812-19-X*) Hlth Prof Pr.

— Instructor's Manual for Cases in Health Services. 3rd ed. 192p. 1995. pap., teacher ed. 22.00 (*1-878812-20-3*, 0203) Hlth Prof Pr.

Rakich, Jonathon S., et al. Instructor's Manual for Managing Health Services Organizations. 3rd ed. 176p. 1992. pap. text 22.00 (*1-878812-13-0*) Hlth Prof Pr.

— Managing Health Services Organizations. 3rd ed. LC 92-1466. 768p. 1992. 58.00 (*1-878812-09-2*) Hlth Prof Pr.

Rakipov, N. G. & Geyer, B., compiled by. Elsevier's Dictionary of Agriculture & Food Production. LC 93-48591. (ENG & RUS.). 910p. 1994. 247.00 (*0-444-89929-4*) Elsevier.

Rakipov, N. G. & Rakipova, A. N. Elsevier's Dictionary of Economics, Business & Finance. 1150p. 1995. write for info. (*0-444-82158-9*) Elsevier.

Rakipova, A. N., jt. auth. see Rakipov, N. G.

Rakita, Gordon F. M., jt. ed. see Hurt, Teresa D.

Rakita, Philip E., jt. ed. see Silverman, Gary S.

Rakitin, Steven R. Software Verification & Validation: A Practitioner's Guide. LC 96-47264. 271p. 1997. 69.00 (*0-89006-889-5*) Artech Hse.

Rakkar, J. S. Muslim Politics in the Punjab. 1986. 36.00 (*0-8364-1904-9*, Pub. by Deep & Deep Pubns) S Asia.

Raknes, Ola, jt. auth. see Grondahl, Illit.

*__Rakness, Tom, ed.__ Chicago: The Best of Images of America. (Images of America Ser.). (Illus.). 128p. 2000. 19.99 (*0-7385-0723-7*) Arcadia Publng.

Rako, Susan. The Hormone of Desire: The Truth About Sexuality, Menopause & Testosterone. LC 95-174598. 144p. 1996. 21.00 (*0-517-70342-4*) Harmony Bks.

Rako, Susan & Mazer, Harvey, eds. Semrad: The Heart of a Therapist. LC 84-45091. 208p. 1983. 40.00 (*0-87668-684-6*) Aronson.

Rakocy, James E., jt. ed. see Costa-Pierce, Barry A.

*__Rakoczy, Piroska Elizabeth, ed.__ Ocular Molecular Biology Protocols. (Methods in Molecular Medicine Ser.: Vol. 47). 350p. 2000. 99.50 (*0-89603-837-8*) Humana.

Rakodi, Carole, ed. The Urban Challenge in Africa: Growth & Management of Its Large Cities. LC 97-4603. (Illus.). 642p. (Orig.). 1997. pap. 40.00 (*92-808-0952-0*, UNUP-0952, Pub. by UN Univ Pr) Brookings.

Rakoff, Dena O. Choosing a Career in the Law. rev. ed. 88p. 1991. pap. 13.00 (*0-943747-15-5*) Harvard OCS.

Rakoff, I. Inside the Prisoner. (Illus.). 192p. 1999. pap. text 17.95 (*0-7134-8413-6*) B T B.

Rakoff, Jed S., et al, eds. Organizational Sentencing Guidelines: Compliance & Mitigation. 1993. ring bd. 85.00 (*0-317-05401-5*, 00619) NY Law Pub.

Rakoff, Jed S. & Goldstein, Howard W., eds. Rico: Civil & Criminal, Law & Strategy. 650p. 1989. ring bd. 110.00 (*0-317-05402-3*, 00609) NY Law Pub.

Rakolta, Terry, et al. Monster in a Box: Television Violence, the First Amendment, & the Case for Government Regulation. (Law & Violence Ser.: No. 2). 160p. (Orig.). 1996. pap. 14.00 (*1-880831-15-5*) Aletheia Pr.

Rakos, John. Software Project Management for Small to Medium Sized Projects. 1990. text 57.00 (*0-13-826173-3*) P-H.

Rakos, Sandor. Catullan Games. Korosy, Maria, tr. from HUN. LC 89-60942. (Illus.). 80p. (Orig.). 1989. pap. 9.00 (*0-910395-53-5*) Marlboro Pr.

Rakosi, Carl. Amulet. 88p. 1967. pap. 1.50 (*0-87685-248-7*) Black Sparrow.

— Collected Poems. LC 84-62266. (Poets Ser.). 550p. (Orig.). 1986. 40.00 (*0-915032-35-X*); pap. 19.95 (*0-915032-36-8*) Natl Poet Foun.

— Collected Prose of Carl Rakosi. LC 83-62144. 150p. 1984. pap. 13.95 (*0-915032-21-X*) Natl Poet Foun.

— Ere-Voice. LC 75-159737. 92p. 1971. 4.50 (*0-87685-251-7*); pap. 2.45 (*0-87685-250-9*) Black Sparrow.

*__Rakosi, Carl.__ The Old Poet's Tale: Collected Works of Carl Rakosi, Vol. 1. 261p. 1999. 49.95 (*1-901538-21-4*, Pub. by etruscan bks); pap. 27.95 (*1-901538-14-1*, Pub. by etruscan bks) SPD-Small Pr Dist.

Rakosi, Carl. Poems, 1923-1941. Crozier, Andrew, ed. (Sun & Moon Classics Ser.: No. 64). 180p. (Orig.). 1995. pap. 12.95 (*1-55713-185-6*) Sun & Moon CA.

Rakosi, Carl, et al. Quarterly Review of Literature: The 1970s, Poetry, Vol. XVII, Nos. 1-2. 1970. pap. 15.00 (*1-888545-13-5*) Quarterly Rev.

Rakosi, Thomas & Jonas, Irmtrud. Orthodontic Diagnosis. LC 92-49147. (Color Atlas of Dental Medicine Ser.). 1993. 179.00 (*0-86577-450-1*) Thieme Med Pubs.

Rakosi, Thomas, jt. auth. see Graber, Thomas M.

Rakosnik, J., jt. auth. see Tichy, M.

Rakova, Alfia A., jt. auth. see Parrott, Ray J., Jr.

***Rakove.** The Constitution Marbury: Origins of Judicial Review. 2001. pap. text 11.95 (*0-312-24733-8*) St Martin.

Rakove. Declaring Rights, Vol. 1. LC 97-72375. 220p. 1997. pap. text 11.95 (*0-312-13734-6*) St Martin.

***RAKOVE.** Federalist: The Essential Essay. 2001. pap. text 11.95 (*0-312-24732-X*) St Martin.

Rakove, Jack N. Dilemma of Declaring Rights. LC 97-72375. 220p. 1997. text 35.00 (*0-312-17768-2*) St Martin.

— James Madison Creation. LC 89-24350. 201p. (C). 1997. pap. 20.20 (*0-673-39994-X*) Addson-Wesley Educ.

***Rakove, Jack N.** Original Meanings: Politics & Ideas in the Making of the Constitution. 439p. 2000. pap. text 17.00 (*0-7881-9199-3*) DIANE Pub.

Rakove, Jack N. Original Meanings: Politics & Ideas in the Making of the Constitution. 448p. 1996. 35.00 (*0-394-57858-9*) Knopf.

— Original Meanings: Politics & Ideas in the Making of the Constitution. 1997. pap. 17.00 (*0-679-78121-8*) Vin Bks.

Rakove, Jack N., ed. Interpreting the Constitution: The Debate over Original Intent. 1990. pap. text 20.00 (*1-55553-081-8*) NE U Pr.

Rakove, Jack N., ed. see Madison, James.

Rakove, Milton L. Don't Make No Waves--Don't Back No Losers: An Insider's Analysis of the Daley Machine. LC 75-1939. 318p. reprint ed. pap. 90.70 (*0-7837-3724-6*, 2057902) Bks Demand.

***Rakovsky, S. K. & Zaikov, G. E.** Kinetics & Mechanism of Ozone Reactions with Organic & Polymeric Compounds in Liquid Phase. 1999. 79.00 (*1-56072-642-3*) Nova Sci Pubs.

Rakow, Bob, jt. auth. see Rakow, Thomas C.

Rakow, Donald A. Gardens of Fabulous Flowers. (Four-H Ser.). (Illus.). 36p. (J). (gr. 9-11). 1992. pap. 5.25 (*1-57753-201-5*, 141L9) Corn Coop Ext.

Rakow, Donald A. & Weir, Richard, 3rd. Pruning: An Illustrated Guide to Pruning Ornamental Trees & Shrubs. 3rd rev. ed. (Information Bulletin Ser.). (Illus.). 28p. (Orig.). 1996. pap. 5.25 (*1-57753-013-6*, 1411B23) Corn Coop Ext.

Rakow, Donald A., et al. Grow with the Flow. (Four-H Ser.). (Illus.). 44p. (J). (gr. 5-7). 1993. pap. 7.75 (*1-57753-218-X*, 141M 7) Corn Coop Ext.

Rakow, Lana, ed. see Bowen, Sheryl P. & Wyatt, Nancy.

Rakow, Lana F. Gender on the Line: Women, the Telephone, & Community Life. (Illinois Studies in Communications). 184p. 1992. text 24.95 (*0-252-01807-9*) U of Ill Pr.

Rakow, Steven J., ed. NSTA Pathways to the Science Standards: Guidelines for Moving the Vision into Practice, Middle School Edition. LC 98-170616. (Illus.). 1998. pap. text 29.95 (*0-87355-166-4*, PB125X) Natl Sci Tchrs.

***Rakow, Steven J., ed.** K-8 Science & Mathematics Education: The Formula for Success. (Illus.). 72p. (C). 2000. pap. text. write for info. (*0-7881-8828-3*) DIANE Pub.

Rakow, Sue F. & Carpenter, Carol B. Signs of Sharing: An Elementary Sign Language & Deaf Awareness Curriculum. LC 92-46219. (Illus.). 380p. (Orig.). 1993. pap., spiral bd. 52.95 (*0-398-05851-2*) C C Thomas.

Rakow, Thomas C. "Copy Me!" Bible Quizzes Vol. 1: A Bible Quiz Collection for Almost Any Occasion. (Illus.). viii, 48p. 1997. pap. 19.95 (*1-891147-78-1*) Rock Dove.

— Hunting & the Bible: A Scripture Safari. (Biblical Art of Hunting Ser.). ii, 20p. 1997. pap. 3.95 (*1-891147-63-3*) Rock Dove.

Rakow, Thomas C. & Rakow, Bob. Raccoon Hunting Basics. iv, 20p. 1998. pap. 3.95 (*1-891147-40-4*) Rock Dove.

***Rakow, Tom C.** The Story of the Prodigal Pooch. 4p. 1998. pap. 4.95 (*1-891147-33-1*) Rock Dove.

Rakowicz-Szulczynska, Ewa M., ed. Nuclear Localization of Growth Factors & of Monoclonal Antibodies. LC 93-12471. 224p. 1993. lib. bdg. 179.00 (*0-8493-4713-0*, QP552) CRC Pr.

Rakowitz, Susan. Social Psychology. 2nd ed. (C). 1995. pap., teacher ed., suppl. ed. write for info. (*0-393-96668-2*) Norton.

Rakowska-Harmstone, Teresa. Communism in Eastern Europe. 2nd ed. LC 83-49501. (Illus.). 400p. 1984. 35.00 (*0-253-31391-0*); pap. text 14.95 (*0-253-20328-7*, MB-328) Ind U Pr.

— Russia & Nationalism in Central Asia: The Case of Tadzhikistan. Published in Cooperation with the Institute for Sino-Soviet Studies, the George Washington University. LC 69-13722. 342p. reprint ed. pap. 106.10 (*0-608-14762-1*, 202586600046) Bks Demand.

Rakowski, Cathy A., ed. Contrapunto: The Informal Sector Debate in Latin America. LC 93-26767. (SUNY Series in Power & Political Economy). 336p. (C). 1994. text 64.50 (*0-7914-1905-3*); pap. text 21.95 (*0-7914-1906-1*) State U NY Pr.

Rakowski, David, jt. auth. see Duemer, Joseph.

Rakowski, Eric. Equal Justice. 398p. 1993. reprint ed. pap. text 28.00 (*0-19-824079-1*) OUP.

Rakowski, John. Cooking on the Road. LC 78-65977. (Illus.). 176p. 1980. pap. 5.95 (*0-89037-200-4*) Anderson World.

***Rakowski, Richard.** Sell. 2000. 22.95 (*0-670-88917-2*) Viking Penguin.

Rakowski, Ronald J. WorkWords: The Book on Understanding the Language of the Workplace. Kovach, John, ed. LC 96-92633. iv, 248p. (Orig.). 1996. pap. 18.95 (*0-9654051-0-9*) R J Rakowski.

Rakowski, Z., ed. Geomechanics '96: Proceedings of an International Conference, Roznov P. R., Czech Republic, 3-6 September 1996. LC 99-496421. (Illus.). 412p. (C). 1997. text 110.00 (*90-5410-921-1*, Pub. by A A Balkema) Ashgate Pub Co.

Rakowski, Zikmund. Geomechanics 93 - Water Jet Cutting: Proceedings of the International Conference, Hradec-Ostrava, Czechia, September 1993. (Illus.). 480p. (C). 1994. text 123.00 (*90-5410-354-X*, Pub. by A A Balkema) Ashgate Pub Co.

Rakowski, Zikmund, ed. Geomechanics 1991: Proceedings of the International Conference on Geomechanics 1991, Hradec, Ostrava, Czecho-Slovakia, 24-26 September 1991. (Illus.). 384p. (C). 1992. text 97.00 (*90-5410-039-7*, Pub. by A A Balkema) Ashgate Pub Co.

Rakshit, Mihir, ed. Studies in Macroeconmics of Developing Countries. LC 98-232316. (Illus.). 198p. 1998. reprint ed. pap. text 6.95 (*0-19-564275-9*) OUP.

— Studies in the Macroeconomics of Developing Countries. (Illus.). 200p. 1989. 17.95 (*0-19-562340-1*) OUP.

Rakshit, Mihir & Chakrabarti, Dilip K. The Archaeology of Ancient Indian Cities. (Oxford India Paperbacks Ser.). (Illus.). 310p. 1997. reprint ed. pap. text 15.95 (*0-19-564174-4*) OUP.

Rakshit, Mihir, ed. see Chakravarty, Sukhamoy.

Rakshit, P. C. Elementary Physical Chemistry. 1985. 100.00 (*0-7855-0728-0*, Pub. by Current Dist) St Mut.

— Thermodynamics. 1985. 100.00 (*0-7855-0755-8*, Pub. by Current Dist) St Mut.

Rakshit, R., jt. auth. see Chattopadhyay, C.

Rakshit, S. C. Molecular Symmetry Groups & Chemistry. 1985. 79.00 (*0-7855-0743-4*, Pub. by Current Dist) St Mut.

Raktoe, B. L. & Hubert, J. J. Basic Applied Statistics. LC 79-727. (Statistics, Textbooks & Monographs: No. 27). (Illus.). 440p. reprint ed. pap. 136.40 (*0-7837-5982-7*, 204578800007) Bks Demand.

Rakusa, Ilma. Steppe: Stories. Emerson, Solveig, tr. from GER. LC 98-104091. (Dichten=Ser.: Vol. 3). 96p. 1997. pap. 10.00 (*1-886224-27-7*) Burning Deck.

Rakusan, Jaromira, jt. ed. see Cowan, William.

Rakusan, Jeromira, jt. auth. see Cowan, William.

Rakusan, K., et al, eds. Oxygen Transport to Tissue, No. XI. (Advances in Experimental Medicine & Biology Ser.: Vol. 247). (Illus.). 812p. 1989. 165.00 (*0-306-43156-4*, Plenum Trade) Perseus Pubng.

Rakusan, Karel, ed. Advances in Organ Biology Vol. 7: Coronary Angiogenesis. 1999. 128.50 (*0-7623-0392-1*) Jai Pr.

Rakusen, Michael L., et al. Distribution of Matrimonial Assets on Divorce. 3rd ed. 1989. boxed set 122.00 (*0-406-51021-0*, UK, MICHIE) LEXIS Pub.

Rakusin. Florida Construction Lien Manual, No. 98-3. 226p. 1998. ring bd. write for info. (*0-327-00704-4*, 8055226) LEXIS Pub.

— Florida Creditors' Rights Manual 99-1, 5 vols. 232p. 1999. ring bd. 48.00 (*0-327-01164-5*, 8059229) LEXIS Pub.

— Florida Creditors' Rights Manual 98-3, 5 vols. 236p. 1998. write for info. (*0-327-00824-5*, 8095228) LEXIS Pub.

— Florida Creditors' Rights Manual 99-2, 5 vols., Set. 212p. 1999. ring bd. write for info. (*0-327-01509-8*, 8059230) LEXIS Pub.

Rakusin, Stephen. Florida Construction Lien Law, 5 vols., Set. 2000p. Date not set. ring bd., suppl. ed. 350.00 (*0-409-26052-5*, 80545-10, MICHIE) LEXIS Pub.

— Florida Construction Lien Manual, 5 vols. 1974. ring bd. 350.00 (*0-327-00933-0*, 80545, MICHIE) LEXIS Pub.

Rakusin, Stephen B. Florida Construction Lien Law, 5 vols. 1994. ring bd., suppl. ed. 45.00 (*0-685-43657-8*, MICHIE) LEXIS Pub.

***Rakusin, Stephen B.** Florida Construction Lien Manual 99-2, 5 vols., Set. 170p. 1999. ring bd. write for info. (*0-327-01653-1*, 8055229) LEXIS Pub.

Rakusin, Stephen B. Florida Creditors' Rights Manual. 1994. ring bd., suppl. ed. 51.00 (*0-685-43215-7*, MICHIE) LEXIS Pub.

— Florida Creditors' Rights Manual, 5 vols., Set. 2000p. Date not set. ring bd. 350.00 (*0-409-26093-2*, 80585-10, MICHIE) LEXIS Pub.

Ralbovsky. Today's Technician: Heavy Duty Truck Electric. (Automotive Technology Ser.). 2000. 62.95 (*0-8273-7006-7*) Thomson Learn.

— Today's Technician: Heavy Duty Truck Electric. (Automotive Technology Ser.). 1997. teacher ed. 16.00 (*0-8273-7007-5*, VNR) Wiley.

— Today's Technology: Heavy Duty Truck Electronics. (Automotive Technology Ser.). 1997. teacher ed. 134.95 (*0-8273-7008-3*) Delmar.

Ralbovsky, Edward. Automotive Diesels. LC 84-19956. (Illus.). 202p. (C). 1985. mass mkt., teacher ed. 55.95 (*0-8273-2217-8*) Delmar.

— Introduction to Compact & Automotive Diesels. (Automotive Technology Ser.). 304p. 1996. teacher ed. 15.50 (*0-8273-6940-9*) Delmar.

Ralbovsky, Edward & Treichler, Fran. Automotive Computer Systems & Circuits. (Illus.). 176p. (C). 1988. pap. text 22.00 (*0-13-054230-X*) P-H.

Rald, Jergen & Rald, Karen. Rural Organization in Bukoba District, Tanzania. 122p. 1975. write for info. (*91-7106-082-0*, Pub. by Nordic Africa) Transaction Pubs.

Rald, Karen, jt. auth. see Rald, Jergen.

Raleigh, jt. auth. see Bowden.

Raleigh, A. S. Hermetic Fundamentals Revealed. 57p. 1996. reprint ed. spiral bd. 9.00 (*0-7873-1178-2*) Hlth Research.

— Hermetic Fundamentals Revealed. 127p. 1993. reprint ed. pap. 8.95 (*1-56459-370-3*) Kessinger Pub.

— Hermetic Science of Motion & Number. 68p. 1993. reprint ed. spiral bd. 9.50 (*0-7873-0688-6*) Hlth Research.

— Metaphysical Healing, Vols. 1 & 2. 87p. 1996. reprint ed. spiral bd. 21.00 (*0-7873-1204-5*) Hlth Research.

— Occult Geometry & Hermetic Science of Motion & Number. 208p. 1991. reprint ed. pap. 11.95 (*0-87516-639-3*) DeVorss.

— Philosophia Hermetica: A Course of Ten Lessons, Being an Introduction to the Philosophy of Alchemy. 127p. 1996. reprint ed. pap. 16.95 (*1-56459-521-8*) Kessinger Pub.

— Science of Alchemy. 172p. 1992. reprint ed. pap. 16.95 (*1-56459-007-0*) Kessinger Pub.

— Scientifica Hermetica: An Introduciton to the Science of Alchemy. 109p. 1996. reprint ed. spiral bd. 13.00 (*0-7873-1049-2*) Hlth Research.

— Scientifica Hermetica: An Introduction to the Science of Alchemy. 115p. 1995. reprint ed. pap. 12.95 (*1-56459-492-0*) Kessinger Pub.

— The Shepherd of Men: An Official Commentary on the Sermon of Hermes Trismegistos. 145p. 1995. reprint ed. pap. 16.95 (*1-56459-493-9*) Kessinger Pub.

— Speculative Art of Alchemy. 191p. 1992. reprint ed. pap. 16.95 (*1-56459-006-2*) Kessinger Pub.

— The Stanzas of Dzjn Theogenesis. 194p. 1997. reprint ed. pap. 24.95 (*0-7661-0055-3*) Kessinger Pub.

Raleigh, C. B., jt. ed. see Behr, H. J.

***Raleigh, Debbie.** Lord Carlton's Courtship. (Zebra Regency Romance Ser.). 256p. 2000. mass mkt. 4.99 (*0-8217-6463-2*, Zebra Kensgtn) Kensgtn Pub Corp.

— Lord Mumford's Minx. 2000. mass mkt. 4.99 (*0-8217-6673-2*) Kensgtn Pub Corp.

Raleigh, Donald J. Revolution on the Volga: 1917 in Saratov. LC 85-12792. (Cornell Studies in Soviet History & Science). (Illus.). 376p. 1986. 45.00 (*0-8014-1790-2*) Cornell U Pr.

— Revolution on the Volga: 1917 in Saratov. LC 85-12792. (Illus.). 375p. reprint ed. pap. 116.30 (*0-608-20938-4*, 207203700003) Bks Demand.

Raleigh, Donald J., ed. A Russian Civil War Diary: Alexis V. Babine in Saratov, 1917-1922. LC 88-3967. (Illus.). xxiv, 264p. 1988. text 37.95 (*0-8223-0835-5*) Duke.

— Soviet Historians & Perstroika: The First Phase. LC 89-10724. 300p. (gr. 13). 1990. text 65.95 (*0-87332-554-0*) M E Sharpe.

Raleigh, Donald J., ed. The Emperors & Empresses of Russia: Rediscovering the Romanovs. LC 95-41894. (The New Russian History Ser.). 432p. (C). (gr. 13). 1996. pap. text 30.95 (*1-56324-760-7*) M E Sharpe.

— The Emperors & Empresses of Russia: Rediscovering the Romanovs. LC 95-41894. (The New Russian History Ser.). 432p. (C). (gr. 13-13). 1996. text 75.95 (*1-56324-759-3*) M E Sharpe.

Raleigh, Donald J., ed. see Ivanova, Galina Mikhailovna.

Raleigh, Donald J., ed. see Khlevniuk, Oleg V.

Raleigh, Donald J., ed. & tr. see Burdzhalov, E. N.

Raleigh, Duane. Ice: Tools & Technique. 2nd ed. LC 95-61190. (Illus.). 128p. (Orig.). 1997. reprint ed. pap. text 11.95 (*1-887216-00-6*, 97003) Elk Mtn Pr.

— Knots & Ropes for Climbers: Knots, Ropes, Cordage & Slings for Climbers. LC 97-22467. (Illus.). 80p. 1998. pap. 7.95 (*0-8117-2871-4*) Stackpole.

Raleigh, Duane, jt. auth. see Benge, Michael.

Raleigh, Duane, jt. auth. see Long, John.

Raleigh, Eugene, jt. auth. see Pasternak, Grigory I.

Raleigh, Eve, jt. auth. see Gonzalez, Jovita.

***Raleigh, Lori E. & Roginsky, Rachel J.** Hotel Investments: Issues & Perspectives. 2nd ed. LC 99-24981. 20p. 1999. 71.95 (*0-86612-193-5*) Educ Inst Am Hotel.

Raleigh, Lori E. & Roginsky, Rachel J., eds. Hotel Investments: Issues & Perspectives. LC 94-39455. 1994. pap. write for info. (*0-86612-088-2*) Educ Inst Am Hotel.

Raleigh, Robert, ed. In Our Lovely Desert: Mormon Fictions. LC 98-6727. 300p. 1998. pap. 17.95 (*1-56085-119-8*) Signature Bks.

Raleigh, Walter. A Declaration of the Demeanor & Cariage of Sir W. Raleigh As Well in His Voyage, As in His Returne. LC 71-25674. (English Experience Ser.: No. 288). 68p. 1970. reprint ed. 20.00 (*90-221-0288-2*) Walter J Johnson.

— England & the War: Being Sundry Addresses Delivered During the War. LC 67-30228. (Essay Index Reprint Ser.). 1977. 17.95 (*0-8369-0805-8*) Ayer.

— English Novel: Being a Short Sketch of Its History from Earliest Times... 1988. reprint ed. lib. bdg. 59.00 (*0-7812-0200-0*) Rprt Serv.

— English Novel: Being a Short Sketch of Its History from the Earliest Times to the Appearance of Waverly. LC 72-131810. 1970. reprint ed. 29.00 (*0-403-00697-X*) Scholarly.

— Milton. LC 67-13336. 1972. reprint ed. 19.95 (*0-405-08873-6*) Ayer.

— Milton. (BCL1-PR English Literature Ser.). 286p. 1992. reprint ed. lib. bdg. 79.00 (*0-7812-7389-7*) Rprt Serv.

— The Ocean to Cynthia: Poems. (Illus.). 1984p. 20.00 (*0-317-40774-0*) Abattoir.

— On Writing & Writers: Being Extracts from His Notebooks. Gordon, G., ed. LC 68-22939. (Essay Index Reprint Ser.). 1977. 19.95 (*0-8369-0806-6*) Ayer.

— The Prerogative of Parliaments in England: Proved in a Dialogue. LC 74-80207. (English Experience Ser.: No. 686). 68p. 1974. reprint ed. 15.00 (*90-221-0686-1*) Walter J Johnson.

— A Report of the Truth of the Fight about the Iles of Acores. LC 72-26280. (English Experience Ser.: No. 183). 32p. 1969. reprint ed. 30.00 (*90-221-0183-5*) Walter J Johnson.

— Selections from His Historie of the World, His Letters, Etc. (BCL1-PR English Literature Ser.). 212p. 1992. reprint ed. lib. bdg. 79.00 (*0-7812-7218-1*) Rprt Serv.

— Shakespeare. LC 74-182702. (English Men of Letters Ser.). reprint ed. 32.50 (*0-404-05206-1*) AMS Pr.

— Shakespeare. (BCL1-PR English Literature Ser.). 233p. 1992. reprint ed. lib. bdg. 79.00 (*0-7812-7283-1*) Rprt Serv.

— Sir Walter Raleigh's Speech from the Scaffold: A Translation of the 1619 Dutch Edition, & Comparison with English Texts. Parker, John & Johnson, Carol A., eds. & trs. by. (Illus.). 80p. (C). 1995. text 15.00 (*0-9601798-5-2*) Assocs James Bell.

— Six Essays on Johnson. (BCL1-PR English Literature Ser.). 184p. 1992. reprint ed. lib. bdg. 69.00 (*0-7812-7368-4*) Rprt Serv.

— Some Authors. LC 68-55855. (Essay Index Reprint Ser.). 1977. 23.95 (*0-8369-0807-4*) Ayer.

— Wordsworth. (BCL1-PR English Literature Ser.). 232p. 1992. reprint ed. lib. bdg. 79.00 (*0-7812-7682-9*) Rprt Serv.

— Wordsworth. LC 76-131811. 1970. reprint ed. 29.00 (*0-403-00698-8*) Scholarly.

***Raleigh, Walter & Rudick, Michael.** The Poems of Sir Walter Ralegh: A Historical Edition. LC 99-54887. (Renaissance English Text Society Ser.: Vol. 209). 1999. write for info. (*0-86698-251-5*) MRTS.

Raleigh, Walter & Whitehead, Neil L. The Discoverie of the Large, Rich, & Bewitful Empyre of Guiana. LC 97-34557. (American Exploration & Travel Ser.: Vol. 77). (Illus.). 240p. 1998. 37.95 (*0-8061-3019-9*); pap. 19.95 (*0-8061-3020-2*) U of Okla Pr.

***Ralescu, A. L. & Shanahan, J. G., eds.** Fuzzy Logic in Artificial Intelligence: IJCAI'97 Workshop, Nagoya, Japan, August 23-24, 1997, Selected & Invited Papers. LC 99-42970. (Lecture Notes in Computer Science Ser.: Vol. 1566). x, 245p. 1999. pap. 52.00 (*3-540-66374-6*) Spr-Verlag.

Ralescu, Anca L., ed. Applied Research in Fuzzy Technology: Results of the Laboratory for International Fuzzy Engineering (LIFE) LC 94-34459. (International Series in Intelligent Technologies). 480p. (C). 1994. text 169.00 (*0-7923-9496-8*) Kluwer Academic.

— Fuzzy Logic in Artificial Intelligence: Proceedings of the IJCAI '93 Workshop, Chambery, France, August 28, 1993. LC 94-33308. (Lecture Notes in Computer Science, Vol. 810; Lecture Notes in Artificial Intelligence: 847). 1994. 29.95 (*3-540-58409-9*) Spr-Verlag.

Ralescu, Anca L. & Martin, Trevor. Fuzzy Logic in Artificial Intelligence: Towards Intelligent Systems: IJCAI '95 Workshop, Montreal, Canada, August 1995, Selected Papers, Vol. 118. LC 97-1011. (Lecture Notes in Artificial Intelligence). viii, 272p. 1997. 49.00 (*3-540-62474-0*) Spr-Verlag.

Ralescu, Anca L., ed. see International Joint Conference on Artificial Intel.

Ralevic, Simo. The Tongue - Our Measure. 62p. 1987. pap. 4.99 (*0-85151-507-X*) Banner of Truth.

***Raley, Charles W.** Life... In the Blood of Jesus. Mason-Raley, Dorothy, ed. 209p. 1999. spiral bd. 15.00 (*1-930479-00-X*) C R Pubs.

Raley, Harold. Responsible Vision: The Philosophy of Julian Marfas. 1980. 20.00 (*0-89217-004-2*); pap. 8.95 (*0-89217-005-0*) American Hispanist.

— A Watch over Mortality: The Philosophical Story of Julian Marias. LC 96-3773. (SUNY Series in Latin American & Iberian Thought & Culture). 320p. (C). 1996. text 65.50 (*0-7914-3153-3*); pap. text 21.95 (*0-7914-3154-1*) State U NY Pr.

Raley, Harold C., tr. see Marias, Julian.

Raley, Mike, jt. auth. see Bloodworth, Trey.

Raley, Nancy, ed. see Sevier, Robert.

Raley, Nancy, ed. see Shoemaker, Donna.

Raley, Nancy S. & Carter, Laura, eds. New Guide to Effective Media Relations. 101p. 1988. 20.00 (*0-89964-255-1*, 24402) Coun Adv & Supp Ed.

Raley, Patricia E. Making Love: How to Be Your Own Sex Therapist. 288p. 1980. pap. 12.95 (*0-380-48819-1*, Avon Bks) Morrow Avon.

Raley, Tom. Country! Cowboys, Rodeo, Women Like Never Before. (Illus.). 170p. (Orig.). 1993. pap. 9.95 (*0-935752-03-X*) Latigo Pr.

***Ralf, Kirsten.** Business Cycles: Market Structure & Market Interaction. LC 99-54021. (Contributions to Economics Ser.). (Illus.). viii, 191p. 2000. pap. 56.00 (*3-7908-1245-5*, Pub. by Physica-Verlag) Spr-Verlag.

Ralf, Sube & Eisenreich, Gunther. Dictionary of Physics: English-German. (ENG & GER.). 1008p. 1987. 225.00 (*0-7859-7072-X*) Fr & Eur.

— Dictionary of Physics: English-German-French-Russian. 2nd ed. (ENG, FRE, GER & RUS.). 2896p. 1984. 750.00 (*0-7859-7069-X*) Fr & Eur.

Ralfe, James. The Naval Biography of Great Britain: Consisting of Historical Memoirs of Those Officers of the British Navy Who Distinguished Themselves During the Reign of His Majesty George III, 4 vols., Set. LC 72-20833. (American Revolutionary Ser.). (Illus.). reprint ed. lib. bdg. 313.00 (*0-8398-1773-8*) Irvington.

— The Naval Biography of Great Britain: Consisting of Historical Memoirs of Those Officers of the British Navy Who Distinguished Themselves During the Reign of His Majesty George III, 4 vols., Vol. 1. LC 72-20833. (American Revolutionary Ser.). (Illus.). 456p. reprint ed. lib. bdg. 75.00 (*0-8290-1850-6*) Irvington.

— The Naval Biography of Great Britain: Consisting of Historical Memoirs of Those Officers of the British Navy Who Distinguished Themselves During the Reign of His Majesty George III, 4 vols., Vol. 2. LC 72-20833. (American Revolutionary Ser.). (Illus.). 534p. reprint ed. lib. bdg. 80.00 (*0-8290-1851-4*) Irvington.

— The Naval Biography of Great Britain: Consisting of Historical Memoirs of Those Officers of the British Navy Who Distinguished Themselves During the Reign of His Majesty George III, 4 vols., Vol. 3. LC 72-20833. (American Revolutionary Ser.). (Illus.). 406p. reprint ed. lib. bdg. 75.00 (*0-685-02674-4*) Irvington.

An Asterisk (*) at the beginning of an entry indicates that the title is appearing for the first time.

— The Naval Biography of Great Britain: Consisting of Historical Memoirs of Those Officers of the British Navy Who Distinguished Themselves During the Reign of His Majesty George III, 4 vols., Vol. 4. LC 72-20833. (American Revolutionary Ser.). (Illus.). 551p. reprint ed. lib. bdg. 83.00 (*0-8290-1853-0*) Irvington.

Ralfel, B. Evenly Distributed Rubble. write for info. (*0-943216-05-2*) MoonsQuilt Pr.

Ralfs, J. British Desmidieae. (Illus.). 1962. 52.00 (*3-7682-0144-9*) Lubrecht & Cramer.

Ralhan, O. P. Encyclopaedia of Political Parties: India, Pakistan, Bangladesh, 32 vols. 1997. 525.00 (*81-7488-287-1*, Pub. by Print Hse) St Mut.

— Encyclopaedia of Sikhism, Religion & Culture, 2 vols. (C). 1996. 140.00 (*81-7488-449-1*, Pub. by Anmol) S Asia.

— Guru Angad Dev. (Great Gurus of the Sikhs Ser.). (C). 1998. 52.00 (*81-7488-671-0*, Pub. by Anmol) S Asia.

— Indian National Movement-Punjabi Martyrs of Freedom, Set. (C). 1995. 225.00 (*81-7041-923-9*, Pub. by Anmol) S Asia.

Ralhan, O. P., ed. All India National Congress. 1998. write for info. (*81-7488-460-2*) Anmol.

— Guru Arjun Dev. (Great Gurus of the Sikhs Ser.). (C). 1998. 52.00 (*81-7488-672-9*, Pub. by Anmol) S Asia.

— Guru Nanak Dev. (Great Gurus of the Sikhs Ser.). 1998. 52.00 (*81-7488-670-2*, Pub. by Anmol) S Asia.

— Guru Tegh Bahadur & Govind Singh. (Great Gurus of the Sikhs Ser.). (C). 1998. 52.00 (*81-7488-696-6*, Pub. by Anmol) S Asia.

— Indian Women Through the Ages, 5 vols. (C). 1995. 170.00 (*81-7488-143-3*, Pub. by Anmol) S Asia.

— Sant Kabir, Mira Bai, Shaikh Farid, Bhikan & Sur Das. (Great Gurus of the Sikhs Ser.). (C). 1998. 48.50 (*81-7488-698-2*, Pub. by Anmol) S Asia.

— Shiromani Akali Dal. 1998. 56.00 (*81-7488-475-0*) Anmol.

Ralhan, O. P. & Sharma, S. K. Life & Times of Indira Gandhi. 1994. pap. 250.00 (*81-7451-003-6*, Pub. by Print Hse) St Mut.

***Ralko, Joe.** Regina, Ready for the New Millennium. LC 99-31369. (Canadian Enterprise Ser.). (Illus.). 104p. 1999. 55.00 (*1-885352-79-4*) Community Comm.

Rall, David, jt. ed. see Bingham, Eula.

Rall, David P., ed. see Institute of Medicine Staff.

Rall, I. B. Automatic Differentiation: Techniques & Applications. (Lecture Notes in Computer Science Ser.: Vol. 120). 165p. 1981. 23.00 (*0-387-10861-0*) Spr-Verlag.

Rall, Louis B. Computational Solution of Nonlinear Operator Equations. LC 78-2378. 236p. (Orig.). 1980. reprint ed. 21.50 (*0-88275-667-2*) Krieger.

Rall, Marlene. Sprachbruecke: Handbuch Fuer Den Unterricht. (GER.). 296p. (C). 1990. pap. text 25.25 (*3-12-557130-8*, Pub. by Klett Edition) Intl Bk Import.

Rall, Medee & Van Rijssen, Bill. Spirits of Our Ancestors. LC 98-134468. (Illus.). 28p. 1998. pap. 9.95 (*0-7021-4144-5*, Pub. by Juta & Co) Intl Spec Bk.

Rall, Ted. All the Rules Have Changed: More Cartoons by Ted Rall. LC 95-71390. (Illus.). 96p. 1995. pap. 9.95 (*0-89620-119-8*) Rip Off.

— My War with Brian. (Illus.). 80p. (YA). 1998. pap. 8.95 (*1-56163-215-5*, Comics Lit) NBM.

— Revenge of the Latchkey Kids: An Illustrated Manifesto for Surviving the 90s & Beyond. LC 97-23163. (Illus.). 256p. 1997. pap. 10.95 (*0-7611-0745-2*) Workman Pub.

— Revenge of the Latchkey Kids: An Illustrated Manifesto for Surviving the 90s & Beyond. LC 97-40927. (Illus.). 256p. 1997. 18.95 (*0-7611-1040-2*) Workman Pub.

— The Worst Thing I've Ever Done. (Illus.). 64p. (Orig.). 1996. pap. 8.95 (*1-56163-157-4*, Comics Lit) NBM.

Rall, Theodore W. Goodman & Gilman's Essentials of Pharmacology. 8th ed. (Illus.). 800p. 1994. pap. 37.00 (*0-07-105430-8*) McGraw.

Rall, W. Anatomy & Function. 1990. 75.00 (*0-8176-3502-5*) Birkhauser.

Ralle, Annette & Ralle, Roger. Shellcraft. (Illus.). 64p. 2000. pap. 17.95 (*0-85532-894-0*, Pub. by Srch Pr) A Schwartz & Co.

Ralle, Roger, jt. auth. see Ralle, Annette.

Ralley, Thomas G., jt. auth. see Dudewicz, Edward J.

Ralli, Angela, jt. ed. see Rivero, Maria-Luisa.

Ralli, Augustus. Guide to Carlyle, 3 vols. LC 74-92979. (Reference Ser.: No. 44). 1970. reprint ed. lib. bdg. 150.00 (*0-8383-0999-2*) M S G Haskell Hse.

Ralli, Augustus J. Critiques. LC 67-22114. (Essay Index Reprint Ser.). 1977. 20.95 (*0-8369-0808-2*) Ayer.

— Later Critiques. LC 68-26469. (Essay Index Reprint Ser.). 1977. reprint ed. 18.95 (*0-8369-0809-0*) Ayer.

Ralli, Mary P., jt. auth. see Ordman, Kathryn A.

Ralling, Christopher. The Kon-Tiki Man: Thor Heyerdahl. large type ed. 312p. 1991. 24.95 (*1-85089-297-0*, Pub. by ISIS Lrg Prnt) Transaction Pubs.

Rallings, Colin, et al, eds. British Elections & Parties Yearbook 1995. 248p. (Orig.). (C). 1996. 60.00 (*0-7146-4705-5*, Pub. by F Cass Pubs); pap. 30.00 (*0-7146-4243-6*, Pub. by F Cass Pubs) Intl Spec Bk.

Rallings, Colin & Thrasher, Michael. Britain Votes 5. (Parliamentary Research Services Ser.). 214p. 1993. text 61.95 (*0-900178-36-1*, Pub. by Dartmth Pub) Ashgate Pub Co.

— British Parliamentary Election Results, 1983-1997. LC 98-47623. 8p. 1999. text 113.95 (*1-84014-058-5*) Ashgate Pub Co.

Rallings, Colin & Thrasher, Michael, eds. Britain Votes 6: British Parliamentary Election Results, 1997. (Illus.). 229p. 1998. text 68.95 (*1-84014-054-2*, Pub. by Ashgate Pub) Ashgate Pub Co.

Rallis, S. L-Functions & the Oscillator Representation. (Lecture Notes in Mathematics Ser.: Vol. 1245). xv, 239p. 1987. 42.95 (*0-387-17694-2*) Spr-Verlag.

***Rallis, Sharon F. & Goldring, Ellen B.** Principals of Dynamic Schools: Taking Charge of Change. 2nd ed. LC 99-50782. (One-Off Ser.). 212p. 2000. pap. 24.95 (*0-7619-7610-8*); lib. bdg. 55.95 (*0-7619-7609-4*) Corwin Pr.

Rallis, Sharon F., et al. Dynamic Teachers: Leaders of Change. LC 95-15691. (Illus.). 176p. 1995. pap. 22.95 (*0-8039-6236-3*) Corwin Pr.

Rallis, Sharon F., jt. auth. see Goldring, Ellen B.

Rallis, Sharon F., jt. auth. see Rossman, Gretchen B.

Rallis, Sharon F., jt. ed. see Reichardt, Charles S.

Rallis, Stephen & Schiffmann, Gerard. Weil Representation I: Intertwining Distributions & Discrete Spectrum. LC 80-12191. (Memoirs of the American Mathematical Society Ser.: No. 25/231). 203p. 1980. pap. 17.00 (*0-8218-2231-4*, MEMO/25/231) Am Math.

Rallison, Janette. Deep Blue Eyes & Other Lies. LC 96-2762. 272p. (Orig.). (J). (gr. 7-12). 1996. mass mkt. 6.95 (*1-57345-191-6*) Deseret Bk.

Rallo, John A., jt. auth. see Mas, Marina.

Ralls, J. Garrett. The Nature of Chaos in Business: Using Complexity to Foster Successful Global Alliances. LC 99-20622. (Illus.). 197p. 1999. 21.95 (*0-88415-504-8*, Cashman Dud) Gulf Pub.

***Ralls, J. Garrett & Webb, Kimberly A.** Mastering the Chaos of Mergers & Acquisitions. LC 99-36244. 1999. 24.95 (*0-87719-365-7*, 9365, Cashman Dud) Gulf Pub.

Ralls, Kenneth M., et al. Introduction to Materials Science & Engineering. 665p. (C). 1976. text 109.95 (*0-471-70665-5*) Wiley.

***Ralls-MacLeod, Karen.** Music & the Celtic Otherworld: From Ireland to Iona. LC 99-58858. 244p. 2000. 49.95 (*0-312-23241-1*) St Martin.

Ralls, Philip W. & Yassa, Nabil A. Ultrasound Companion. 352p. pap. text 59.95 (*0-7817-2623-9*) Lppncott W & W.

Ralls, Philip W., jt. auth. see Jeffrey, Brooke.

Ralls, Philip W., jt. auth. see Jeffrey, R. Brooke, Jr.

Ralls, Scott. Integrating Technology with Workers in the New American Workplace. 81p. 1995. pap. 5.50 (*0-16-045421-2*) USGPO.

RaLonde, R. & Paust, Brian C. Developing a Mariculture Business in Alaska: Information & Resources. (Aquaculture Note Ser.: No. 15). 40p. (Orig.). 1993. pap. 4.00 (*1-56612-020-9*) AK Sea Grant CP.

RaLonde, Raymond, jt. auth. see Paust, Brian C.

Ralov, Kirsten, ed. The Bournonville School, Pt. 4: Labanotation. LC 78-9554. (Dance Program Ser.: Vol. 12). 137p. reprint ed. pap. 42.50 (*0-8357-7370-1*, 202707400054) Bks Demand.

Ralovich, B. Listeriosis Research: Present Situation & Perspective. 222p. (C). 1984. 90.00 (*963-05-3657-9*, Pub. by Akade Kiado) St Mut.

Ralovich, Rudy R. Memory - Short Term & Recall Ability: Index of New Information. 160p. 1998. 47.50 (*0-7883-1914-0*); pap. 44.50 (*0-7883-1915-9*) ABBE Pubs Assn.

Ralovsky, Edward. Introduction to Compact & Automotive Diesels. (Automotive Technology Ser.). 304p. (C). 1996. mass mkt. 46.95 (*0-8273-6939-5*) Delmar.

Ralph. William Macgillivray. 45.00 (*1-85894-088-5*, Pub. by Merrell Holberton) U of Wash Pr.

— World Civilization Study with Study Guide, Vol. 1. 9th ed. 1999. pap. text 22.00 (*0-393-97448-0*) Norton.

Ralph Applebaum Association Staff. Innovations in Glass. LC 89-17779. (Illus.). 64p. 1999. pap. 9.95 (*0-87290-146-7*) Corning.

Ralph, Brian. Cave-In. 1999. pap. text 12.95 (*0-9665363-3-9*) Highwater Bks.

***Ralph, Brian.** Fireball. 1999. pap. text 9.95 (*0-9665363-7-1*) Highwater Bks.

Ralph, Brian, jt. auth. see Kurzydlowski, Krzysztof J.

Ralph, C. John, ed. Handbook of Field Methods for Monitoring Landbirds. (Illus.). 41p. (C). 1999. pap. text 20.00 (*0-7881-7234-4*) DIANE Pub.

Ralph, C. John, et al, eds. Monitoring Bird Populations by Point Counts. (Illus.). 192p. 1998. reprint ed. 26.40 (*0-89904-651-7*, Wildlife Resrch Grp) Crumb Elbow Pub.

— Monitoring Bird Populations by Point Counts. (Illus.). 181p. (C). 1998. reprint ed. pap. text 35.00 (*0-7881-4344-1*) DIANE Pub.

Ralph, C. John, et al. Ecology & Conservation of the Marbled Murrelet. (Illus.). 420p. (C). 1997. reprint ed. pap. text 50.00 (*0-7881-4162-7*) DIANE Pub.

— Manual de Metodos de Campo para el Monitoreo de Aves Terrestres. (SPA., Illus.). 52p. 1997. reprint ed. 11.50 (*0-89904-677-0*, Wildlife Resrch Grp); reprint ed. pap. 6.20 (*0-89904-675-4*, Wildlife Resrch Grp) Crumb Elbow Pub.

Ralph, Diana. Work & Madness: The Rise of Community Psychiatry. 206p. 1983. 38.99 (*0-919619-07-X*, Pub. by Black Rose); pap. 9.99 (*0-919619-04-5*, Pub. by Black Rose) Consort Bk Sales.

Ralph, Edwin G. Developing Practitioners: A Handbook of Contextual Supervision. 127p. 1998. pap. 16.95 (*0-913507-97-0*) New Forums.

— Motivating Teaching in Higher Education: A Manual for Faculty Development. (Illus.). 236p. (C). 1998. pap. 20.95 (*0-913507-96-2*) New Forums.

Ralph, James. Case of Authors by Profession or Trade, 1758, Champion 1739. LC 66-10008. 224p. 1966. 50.00 (*0-8201-1037-X*) Schol Facsimiles.

— Case of Our Present Theatrical Disputes Fairly Stated. LC 70-174295. reprint ed. lib. bdg. 39.50 (*0-404-05208-8*) AMS Pr.

— Northern Protest: Martin Luther King, Jr., Chicago, & the Civil Rights Movement. LC 92-45231. 352p. 1993. text 27.95 (*0-674-62687-7*) HUP.

Ralph, Judy & Gompf, Ray. The Peanut Butter Cookbook for Kids. LC 94-37852. (Illus.). 96p. (J). (gr. 3 up). 1995. lib. bdg. 14.89 (*0-7868-2110-8*, Pub. by Hyprn Child) Little.

— The Peanut Butter Cookbook for Kids. LC 94-37852. (Illus.). 96p. (YA). (gr. 3 up). 1995. pap. 10.45 (*0-7868-1028-9*, Pub. by Hyprn Ppbks) Little.

Ralph, Julian. Alone in China & Other Stories. LC 70-101819. (Short Story Index Reprint Ser.). 1977. 30.95 (*0-8369-3207-2*) Ayer.

— Our Great West. LC 75-126250. (Select Bibliographies Reprint Ser.). 1977. 30.95 (*0-8369-5477-7*) Ayer.

— Prince of Georgia, & Other Tales. LC 74-142274. (Short Story Index Reprint Ser.). 1977. 19.95 (*0-8369-3758-9*) Ayer.

Ralph, Kathleen S., jt. auth. see Eddowes, E. Anne.

Ralph, Margaret N. And God Said What? An Introduction to Biblical Literary Forms for Bible Lovers. 1986. pap. 14.95 (*0-8091-2780-6*) Paulist Pr.

— The Bible & the End of the World: Should We Be Afraid? LC 97-37543. 192p. 1998. pap. 11.95 (*0-8091-3756-9*, 3756-9) Paulist Pr.

— Discovering Old Testament Origins: The Books of Genesis, Exodus, & Samuel. LC 92-8494. (Discovering the Living Word Ser.). 1992. pap. 12.95 (*0-8091-3322-9*) Paulist Pr.

— Discovering Prophecy & Wisdom: The Books of Isaiah, Job, Proverbs & Psalms. LC 93-10245. (Discovering the Living Word Ser.: Vol. IV). 336p. 1993. pap. 12.95 (*0-8091-3402-0*) Paulist Pr.

— Discovering the First Century Church: The Acts of the Apostles, Letters of Paul & the Book of Revelation. (Discovering the Living Word Ser.). 1991. pap. 12.95 (*0-8091-3254-0*) Paulist Pr.

— Discovering the Gospels: Four Accounts of the Good News. (Discovering the Living Word Ser.). 1990. pap. 11.95 (*0-8091-3200-1*) Paulist Pr.

— Plain Word about Biblical Images: Growing in Our Faith Through the Scriptures. 1989. pap. 10.95 (*0-8091-3045-9*) Paulist Pr.

Ralph, Philip L. Study Guide, 1. pap. 17.00 (*0-393-97201-1*) Norton.

— Study Guide, Vol. 2. pap. 17.00 (*0-393-97221-6*) Norton.

***Ralph, Phillips.** World Civilizations, Vols. 1-2. 9th ed. (C). 1999. pap. text 67.50 (*0-393-98216-5*) Norton.

Ralph, Phyllis C. Victorian Transformations: Fairy Tales, Adolescence, & the Novel of Female Development. (American University Studies: English Language & Literature: Ser. IV, Vol. 96). IX, 176p. (C). 1989. text 31.95 (*0-8204-1039-X*) P Lang Pubng.

Ralph, Richard. The Life & Works of John Weaver. LC 82-83649. (Illus.). 1075p. 1985. 125.00 (*0-87127-139-7*, Dance Horizons) Princeton Bk Co.

Ralph, Robert, jt. auth. see MacGillivray, William.

Ralph, Sharon. The Alphabet Book: An ABC Book of AA, Rhymes, Patterns, & Activities. Britt, Leslie, ed. LC 95-179898. (Illus.). 96p. (Orig.). (J). (gr. k-2). 1995. pap. text 10.95 (*0-86530-307-X*, 1P307-0) Incentive Pubns.

Ralph, Sharon, jt. auth. see Breeden, Terri.

Ralph, Wayne. Barker, V. C. The Life, Death & Legend of Canada's Most Decorated War Hero. (Illus.). 320p. 1997. 34.95 (*1-898697-59-0*, Pub. by Grub St) Seven Hills Bk.

— Barker VC: The Classic Story of a Legendary First World War Hero. (Illus.). 336p. 1999. pap. 18.95 (*1-902304-31-4*, Pub. by Grub St) Seven Hills Bk.

Ralphael, Frederic, tr. see Euripides.

Ralphs, J. D., ed. Principles & Practice of Multi-Frequency Telegraphy. (Telecommunications Ser.: No. 11). 206p. 1985. boxed set 109.00 (*0-86341-022-7*, TE011) INSPEC Inc.

Ralphs, Lady & Norman, Geoffrey. The Magistrate As Chairman. 2nd ed. 234p. 1992. pap. 24.00 (*0-406-00118-9*, UK, MICHIE) LEXIS Pub.

Ralphs, Lenny. Organization Development: A Practitioner's Tool Kit. LC 95-83114. (Fifty-Minute Ser.). 114p. (Orig.). 1996. pap. 10.95 (*1-56052-359-X*) Crisp Pubns.

Ralsey, Alicia. Poetic Justice. 320p. 1994. mass mkt. 3.99 (*0-8217-4599-9*, Zebra Kensgtn) Kensgtn Pub Corp.

Ralson, N. Great Rhubarb Recipes. 1991. pap. 2.95 (*0-88266-655-X*, Storey Pub) Storey Bks.

Ralston. How to Do Well in Class & Still Have Fun. (Psychology Ser.). 1996. mass mkt. 6.75 (*0-534-49754-3*) Brooks-Cole.

Ralston & Reilly. Encyclopedia Of Computer Science. 4th ed. (ITBP Reference Ser.). 1998. 149.95 (*1-86152-385-8*, Pub. by ITBP) Thomson Learn.

Ralston, A. & Young, Gail S., eds. The Future of College Mathematics: Proceedings. (Illus.). 278p. 1983. 65.95 (*0-387-90813-7*) Spr-Verlag.

Ralston, Anthony. The Encyclopedia of Computer Science. 4th ed. (C). 1997. text 160.99 (*1-85032-814-5*, VNR) Wiley.

— Introduction to Programming & Computer Science. LC 78-136182. (Mcgraw-hill Computer Science Ser.). xxiii, 513p. 1971. write for info. (*0-07-051161-6*) McGraw.

***Ralston, Anthony, et al, eds.** Encyclopedia of Computer Science. 4th ed. 1600p. 2000. 150.00 (*1-56159-251-X*) Groves Dictionaries.

— Encyclopedia of Computer Science. 4th ed. (Illus.). 1600p. 2000. 150.00 (*1-56159-248-X*) Groves Dictionaries.

Ralston, Anthony & Neill, Hugh. Teach Yourself Algorithms. (Teach Yourself Study Guides Ser.). (Illus.). 192p. 1997. pap. 12.95 (*0-8442-3074-X*) NTC Contemp Pub Co.

Ralston, Anthony & Rabinowitz, Philip. First Course in Numerical Analysis. (International Series in Pure & Applied Mathematics). (C). 1978. pap. text, teacher ed. 56.25 (*0-07-051168-3*) McGraw.

Ralston, Anthony & Reilly, Edwin D., Jr. Encyclopedia of Computer Science & Engineering. 2nd ed. (Illus.). 1678p. 1982. pap. 101.95 (*0-442-24496-7*) Thomson Learn.

Ralston, Anthony & Reilly, Edwin D., eds. Encyclopedia of Computer Science. 3rd ed. 1664p. 1992. text 154.00 (*1-85032-800-5*) ITCP.

Ralston, Anthony & Reilly, Edwin D., Jr., eds. Encyclopedia of Computer Science & Engineering. 3rd rev. ed. (Illus.). 2000p. 1992. pap. 125.00 (*0-442-27679-6*) Thomson Learn.

Ralston, Anthony & Wilf, Herbert S., eds. Mathematical Methods for Digital Computers, Vol. 1. LC QA0076.5.R34. 305p. 1960. reprint ed. pap. 94.60 (*0-608-08272-4*, 205566900030) Bks Demand.

Ralston, Anthony & Wilf, Herberts, eds. Mathematical Methods for Digital Computers, Vol. 3. LC 60-6509. 464p. reprint ed. pap. 143.90 (*0-608-08273-2*, 205655400003) Bks Demand.

Ralston, Anthony, jt. auth. see Maurer, Stephen B.

Ralston, Birgitta. Sisters: Photographic Portraits - An Exhibition. LC 88-51842. 32p. (Orig.). 1989. pap. 7.00 (*0-9621886-0-3*) Univ WI Art Gal.

Ralston, Charles W., jt. ed. see Convery, Frank J.

Ralston, David B. Importing the European Army: The Introduction of European Military Techniques. 198p. (C). 1995. reprint ed. pap. text 14.95 (*0-226-70319-3*) U Ch Pr.

— Importing the European Army: The Introduction of European Military Techniques & Institutions into the Extra-European World, 1600-1914. 210p. 1997. 37.50 (*0-226-70318-5*) U Ch Pr.

Ralston, Dorothy. Sweet Pea Reflections. 98p. 1983. pap. 4.00 (*0-87012-459-5*) McClain.

Ralston, Elizabeth W., jt. auth. see MacKay, Louise L.

Ralston, Elizabeth Welch, jt. auth. see Mackay, Louise Layne.

Ralston, Esther. Some Day We'll Laugh: An Autobiography. LC 85-2482. (Filmmakers Ser.: No. 11). (Illus.). 244p. 1985. 25.00 (*0-8108-1814-0*) Scarecrow.

Ralston, Faith. Hidden Dynamics: How Emotions Affect Business Performance & How You Can Harness Their Power for Positive Results. LC 95-3940. 192p. 1995. 19.95 (*0-8144-0272-0*) AMACOM.

Ralston, Helen. The Christian Ashrams: A New Religious Movement in Contemporary India. LC 87-21019. (Studies in Religion & Society: Vol. 20). 150p. 1987. lib. bdg. 69.95 (*0-88946-854-0*) E Mellen.

— The Lived Experience of South Asian Immigrant Women in Atlantic Canada: The Interconnections of Race, Class & Gender. LC 96-46146. (Women's Studies: Vol. 14). 194p. 1997. text 79.95 (*0-7734-8761-1*) E Mellen.

Ralston, Ian, jt. auth. see Edwards, Kevin J.

Ralston, Ian, jt. ed. see Hunter, John.

Ralston, Ian B. & Hunter, John, eds. Archaeology of Britain: Introduction. LC 98-24844. (Illus.). 360p. (C). 1999. 100.00 (*0-415-13587-7*); pap. 32.99 (*0-415-13588-5*) Routledge.

Ralston, J. K., jt. auth. see Laskowski, J. S.

Ralston, James. The Choice of Emptiness. 2nd ed. LC 87-63357. 170p. 1988. pap. 10.99 (*0-945073-00-3*) Nightsun MD.

— The Night After. 2nd ed. 100p. 1986. pap. text 6.00 (*0-945073-01-1*) Nightsun MD.

— The Poet's Car: Poems. LC 91-62670. 60p. (Orig.). 1992. pap. 7.00 (*0-945073-15-1*) Nightsun MD.

***Ralston, Jim.** Appalachian Grammer Shop. (Upper Potomacs Ser.: Vol. 12). (Illus.). 70p. 2000. mass mkt. 10.00 (*0-945073-22-4*) Nightsun MD.

Ralston, Jim. Long Fall: Screenplay. Bramann, Jorn K., ed. & intro. by. LC 95-70028. (Upper Potomacs Ser.). 120p. 1995. pap. 5.00 (*0-945073-18-6*) Nightsun MD.

Ralston, Margaret C. Fashion Outlines: Dress Cutting by the Block Pattern System. Kliot, Jules & Kliot, Kaethe, eds. (Illus.). 80p. (C). 1990. reprint ed. pap. 12.00 (*0-916896-32-3*) Lacis Pubns.

Ralston, Marion. An Exchange of Gifts: A Storyteller's Handbook. (Pippin Teacher's Library Ser.). 88p. (C). 1993. pap. 13.50 (*0-88751-040-X*, 00737) Heinemann.

Ralston, Meredith L. "Nobody Wants to Hear Our Truth" Homeless Women & Theories of the Welfare State, 153. LC 95-19319. (Contributions in Women's Studies: Vol. 153). 224p. 1996. 57.95 (*0-313-29292-2*, Greenwood Pr) Greenwood.

Ralston, Nancy C. & Jordan, Marynor. The Brown County Cookbook. LC 83-47917. (Illus.). 96p. (Orig.). 1983. pap. 7.95 (*0-253-21250-2*) Ind U Pr.

— The New Zucchini Cookbook: And Other Squash. LC 89-46018. (Illus.). 176p. 1990. pap. 12.95 (*0-88266-589-8*, Garden Way Pub) Storey Bks.

— The New Zucchini Cookbook: And Other Squash. LC 89-46018. (Illus.). 176p. 1990. 16.95 (*0-88266-590-1*, Garden Way Pub) Storey Bks.

Ralston, Norman & Jack, Gale. Raising Healthy Pets: Insights of a Holistic Veterinarian. LC 97-158266. 128p. (Orig.). 1996. pap. 10.95 (*1-882984-22-6*) One Peaceful World.

Ralston, Patricia R., jt. auth. see Sheda, Constance H.

Ralston, Penny, et al, eds. The Decision to Parent: A Teaching Guide. LC HQ0755.7.D43. (Illus.). 176p. reprint ed. pap. 54.60 (*0-608-00120-1*, 206088500006) Bks Demand.

***Ralston, Penny A., et al, eds.** Social Change, Public Policy & Community Collaborations: Training Human Development Professionals for the 21st Century. LC 99-46690. (Outreach Scholarship Ser.). 184p. 1999. 95.00 (*0-7923-8659-0*) Kluwer Academic.

Ralston, Peter. Ancient Wisdom, New Spirit: Investigations into Being Alive. LC 94-25348. 238p. 1994. pap. 12.95 (*1-883319-21-8*) Frog Ltd CA.

R

— Cheng Hsin: Principles of Effortless Power. 2nd ed. LC 98-38443. 1999. pap. text 14.95 (*1-55643-302-6*) North Atlantic.
— Cheng Hsin Tui Shou: The Art of Effortless Power. (Illus.). 380p. 1990. 30.00 (*1-55643-115-5*); pap. 18.95 (*1-55643-094-9*) North Atlantic.
— Reflections of Being. 80p. 1991. pap. 9.95 (*1-55643-119-8*) North Atlantic.
— Sightings: A Maine Coast Odyssey. LC 97-7742. (Illus.). 160p. 1997. 50.00 (*0-89272-408-0*) Down East.
Ralston, Richard E., ed. see Rand, Ayn & Peikoff, Leonard.
Ralston, Richard W., jt. ed. see Weinstock, Harold.
Ralston, Rick. Cast Iron Floor Trains: An Encyclopedia with Rarity & Price Guide. Engebretson, George, ed. LC 93-92799. (Illus.). 336p. 1994. 89.95 (*0-9638315-0-X*) Ralston Pubng.
Ralston, Robert. Principles of the Law Relating to the Discharge of Contracts. LC 97-3620. viii, 68p. 1997. reprint ed. 25.00 (*0-8377-2579-8*, Rothman) W S Hein.
Ralston, Tommy. My Captains. 112p. 1990. pap. 21.00 (*1-898218-27-7*) St Mut.
Ralston, Trudy, jt. auth. see Foster, Eric.
Ralston, Veronica, tr. see Bergman, Margareta.
Ralston, W. R. Songs of the Russian People: As Illustrative of Slavonic Mythology & Russian Social Life. LC 77-132444. (Studies in Music: No. 42). 1970. reprint ed. lib. bdg. 75.00 (*0-8383-1224-1*) M S G Haskell Hse.
— Tibetan Tales: Derived from Indian Sources. 368p. 1989. reprint ed. pap. 30.00 (*957-9482-21-7*) Oriental Bk Store.
Ralston, W. R., jt. tr. see Von Schiefner, F. Anton.
Ralston, William S. Russian Folk-Tales. Dorson, Richard M., ed. LC 77-70619. (International Folklore Ser.). 1977. reprint ed. lib. bdg. 33.95 (*0-405-10122-8*) Ayer.
Ralten, Daniel J., et al, eds. Analysis of Adverse Reactions to Monosodium Glutamate (MSG) 256p. 1995. pap. 65.00 (*0-943029-03-1*) Am Soc Nutr Sci.
Raluy, Poudevida A. Porrua Dictionary of the Spanish Language: Diccionario Porrua de la Lengua Espanola. 26th ed. (SPA.). 849p. 1985. 10.95 (*0-8288-2057-0*, S12281) Fr & Eur.
Raluy, Poudevila A. Diccionario Porrua de la Lengua Espanola. Monterde, Francisco, ed. (SPA.). pap. 10.95 (*0-686-56694-7*, S-12281) Fr & Eur.
— Diccionario Porrua de la Lengua Espanola Para Escuelas Primarias. Monterde, Francisco, ed. (SPA.). 461p. pap. 8.95 (*0-7859-0712-2*, S-12282) Fr & Eur.
***Ram.** Immunology: Clinical, Fundamental & Therapeutic Aspects. 364p. 1998. 110.00 (*0-471-19058-6*) Wiley.
Ram, et al. Conceptual Change: A Special Issue of the "Journal of the Learning Sciences", Vol. 6, No. 1, 1997. 1997. pap. 20.00 (*0-8058-9883-2*) L Erlbaum Assocs.
***Ram, A.** Fundamentals of Polymer Engineering. LC 97-41616. 317p. (C). 1998. 49.50 (*0-306-45726-1*, Plenum Trade) Perseus Pubng.
Ram, Akrishan, jt. auth. see Shah, Amit.
Ram, Alur J., jt. ed. see Bennett, Bruce.
Ram, Ashwin & Eiselt, Kurt, eds. Proceedings of the Sixteenth Annual Conference of the Cognitive Science Society: Atlanta, Georgia, 1994. 1016p. 1994. pap. 180.00 (*0-8058-1803-0*) L Erlbaum Assocs.
Ram, Ashwin & Leake, David B., eds. Goal-Driven Learning. (Illus.). 529p. 1995. 65.00 (*0-262-18165-7*, Bradford Bks) MIT Pr.
Ram, Ashwin & Moorman, Kenneth, eds. Understanding Language Understanding: Computational Models of Reading. LC 98-39141. (Language, Speech & Communication Ser.). (Illus.). 475p. 1999. 50.00 (*0-262-18192-4*) MIT Pr.
Ram, Ashwin, jt. ed. see Aha, David W.
Ram, Ashwin, jt. ed. see DesJardins, Marie.
Ram, Atma. Perspectives on Arthur Miller. (C). 1988. 14.50 (*81-7017-240-3*, Pub. by Abhinav) S Asia.
Ram, Atvar A. Social & Political Study of Modern Hindi Cinema. 1990. 48.50 (*81-7169-049-1*, Commonwealth) S Asia.
Ram, Avtar V. Learn to Play on Sitar. (Illus.). 56p. 1989. 12.95 (*0-940500-41-8*) Asia Bk Corp.
Ram, Bhanu, ed. see Tyle, Praveen.
Ram, Bhanu P., et al, eds. Immunology: Clinical, Fundamental & Therapeutic Aspects. LC 89-24846. (Immunology, Biochemistry & Biotechnology: Vol. 1). 364p. 1990. text 85.00 (*0-89573-763-9*, Wiley-VCH) Wiley.
Ram, Bindeshwar. Land & Society in India: Agrarian Relations in Colonial North Bihar LC 98-901711. xii, 274 p. 1997. write for info. (*81-250-0643-5*, Pub. by Orient Longman Ltd) S Asia.
Ram, D. Sundar. Role of Opposition Parties in Indian Politics: The Andhra Pradesh Experience. (C). 1992. 29.50 (*81-7100-412-1*, Pub. by Deep & Deep Pubns) S Asia.
Ram, D. Sundar, jt. ed. see Easwara Reddi, Agarala.
Ram, Eric, ed. Transforming Health: Christian Approaches to Healing & Wholeness. 356p. 1995. 21.95 (*0-912552-89-1*) MARC.
Ram, Haggay. Myth & Mobilization in Revolutionary Iran: The Use of the Friday Congregational Sermon. LC 94-20284. 278p. (C). 1994. lib. bdg. 65.50 (*1-879383-21-7*) Am Univ Pr.
Ram Irez De La O., Rogelio, jt. auth. see Mazarr, Michael J.
Ram, James. Science of Legal Judgment: A Treatise Designed to Show the Materials Whereof, & the Process by Which, Courts Construct Their Judgments; & Adapted to Practical & General Use in the Discussion & Determination of Questions of Law. 456p. 1988. reprint ed. 48.50 (*0-8377-2539-9*, Rothman) W S Hein.
Ram, James & Townshend, John. Treatise on Facts As Subjects of Inquiry by a Jury. 3rd ed. 486p. 1982. reprint ed. 35.00 (*0-8377-1033-2*, Rothman) W S Hein.
Ram, Janaki. V. K. Krishna Menon: A Personal Memoir. LC 97-906441. (Illus.). 164p. (C). 1997. text 22.00 (*0-19-564228-7*) OUP.
Ram, Kalpana & Jolly, Margaret, eds. Maternities & Modernities: Colonial & Postcolonial Experiences in Asia & the Pacific. LC 97-6813. (Illus.). 320p. (C). 1998. text 64.95 (*0-521-58428-0*); pap. text 23.95 (*0-521-58614-3*) Cambridge U Pr.
Ram, Kalpana, jt. ed. see Jolly, Margaret.
Ram, M. D., ed. Surgery Review: A Self-Assessment Study Manual. LC 87-14466. 225p. 1987. pap. 32.50 (*0-941022-09-9*) Davies Pubng.
Ram, Mahabal. High Yielding Varieties of Crops. 2nd ed. (C). 1986. 18.00 (*81-204-0095-X*, Pub. by Oxford IBH) S Asia.
Ram, Manatha, jt. auth. see Murthy, T. K.
Ram-Mar, pseud. Romances del Alma. LC 93-74228. (Coleccion Espejo de Paciencia). (SPA.). 112p. (Orig.). 1993. pap. 9.95 (*0-89729-714-8*) Ediciones.
***Ram, Michael.** Fragments of Science Festschrift for Mendel Sachs. 1999. 112.00 (*981-02-3884-3*) World Scientific Pub.
Ram, Monder. Managing to Survive: Working Lives in Small Firms. (Warwick Studies in Industrial Relations). 256p. (C). 1994. 64.95 (*0-631-19109-7*) Blackwell Pubs.
Ram, Nandu. Beyond Ambedkar: Essays on Dalits in India. (C). 1995. 44.00 (*81-241-0239-2*, Pub. by Har-Anand Pubns) S Asia.
Ram, Neil M., et al, eds. Significance & Treatment of VOCs in Water Supplies. (Illus.). 576p. 1990. lib. bdg. 99.95 (*0-87371-123-8*, L123) Lewis Pubs.
Ram, Paras. Rep.-Additional Advance & Impex Pass Book Licences. (C). 1989. 125.00 (*0-7855-3710-4*) St Mut.
Ram, Raja. Agricultural Development: Command Area Approach. (C). 1993. 32.00 (*81-7017-299-3*, Pub. by Abhinav) S Asia.
Ram, S., jt. auth. see Ling, W.
Ram Sharma, Sita, jt. auth. see Bakshi, S. R.
Ram Sharma, Sitaram, jt. auth. see Bakshi, S. R.
Ram, Sodhi. Indian Immigrants in Great Britain. 1989. 80.00 (*81-210-0242-7*, Pub. by Inter-India Pubns) S Asia.
RAM Staff. William Lesch: Expansions. Kawaii, K., ed. (ENG & JPN., Illus.). 102p. 1992. 29.95 (*4-8457-0667-9*) RAM Publications.
RAM Staff. My Crystal Glass: A Poetic Journey Through Recovery. iii, 23p. 1992. pap. 5.00 (*1-893035-00-X*) Encircle Pubns.
— My Crystal Glass: A Poetic Journey Through Recovery. rev. ed. iii, 23p. 1998. pap. 6.45 (*1-893035-04-2*) Encircle Pubns.
Ram, Sudha. Database Management Systems. (Illus.). 608p. 1999. pap. text 36.00 (*0-07-050825-9*) McGraw.
Ram, Uri. The Changing Agenda of Israeli Sociology: Theory, Ideology, & Identity. LC 94-33402. (SUNY Series in Israeli Studies). 232p. (C). 1995. text 59.50 (*0-7914-2301-8*); pap. text 19.95 (*0-7914-2302-6*) State U NY Pr.
Ram, Venkata S., jt. ed. see Kaplan, Norman M.
Ram, Y. M., jt. auth. see Caldwell, J.
Rama, Angel. La Ciudad Letrada. (Rama Ser.). (SPA.). 176p. 1984. pap. 13.00 (*0-910061-19-X*, 1502) Ediciones Norte.
— The Lettered City. LC 96-13996. (Post-Contemporary Interventions Ser.). 176p. 1996. text 39.95 (*0-8223-1757-5*); pap. text 14.95 (*0-8223-1766-4*) Duke.
Rama, C., et al. Stress Analysis of Spiral Bevel Gear: A Novel Approach to Tooth Modelling. (Nineteen Ninety-Three Fall Technical Meeting Ser.: Vol. 93FTM4). (Illus.). 14p. 1993. pap. text 30.00 (*1-55589-597-2*) AGMA.
Rama, Carol. Carol Rama. LC 98-155336. (Illus.). 160p. 1999. pap. 35.00 (*88-8158-148-5*, Pub. by Charta) Dist Art Pubs.
Rama, Dasaratha V., jt. ed. see Zlotkowski, Edward.
Rama, Jager. Hemorrhoids: A Book for Silent Sufferers. 164p. 1990. pap. 8.95 (*0-9625295-0-8*) Colon & Rectal Care.
Rama, K. Buddhist Art of Nagarjunakonda. LC 95-900602. (C). 1995. 88.00 (*81-85067-90-2*, Pub. by Sundeep Prak) S Asia.
Rama, Mani. The Physically Handicapped in India: Policy & Programme. 223p. (C). 1988. 26.50 (*81-7024-164-2*, Pub. by Ashish Pub Hse) S Asia.
***Rama, Marie.** Cooking for Dummies. 2nd rev. ed. (For Dummies Ser.). 524p. 2000. pap. 19.99 (*0-7645-5250-3*) IDG Bks.
***Rama, Marie & Mariani, John.** Grilling for Dummies. LC 98-84960. (For Dummies Ser.). (Illus.). 400p. 1998. pap. 19.99 (*0-7645-5076-4*) IDG Bks.
Rama, Marie, jt. auth. see Miller, Bryan.
Rama Rao, P., jt. auth. see Puligandla, R.
Rama, Swami. Freedom from the Bondage of Karma. 2nd ed. 92p. 1977. pap. 10.95 (*0-89389-031-6*) Himalayan Inst.
— Living with the Himalayan Masters. rev. ed. LC 80-82974. (Illus.). 486p. 1999. pap. 18.95 (*0-89389-156-8*) Himalayan Inst.
— Love & Family Life. LC 92-37512. 130p. (Orig.). 1992. pap. 12.95 (*0-89389-133-9*) Himalayan Inst.
***Rama, Swami.** Love Whispers. 120p. 2000. pap. 13.95 (*0-89389-178-9*) Himalayan Inst.
Rama, Swami. Meditation & Its Practice. rev. ed. (Illus.). 110p. 1998. pap. 12.95 (*0-89389-153-3*) Himalayan Inst.
— Path of Fire & Light Vol. 2: A Practical Companion to Volume One. LC 86-7586. 226p. (Orig.). 1988. pap. 14.95 (*0-89389-112-6*) Himalayan Inst.
— Perennial Psychology of the Bhagavad Gita. LC 84-25137. 480p. (C). 1982. pap. 16.95 (*0-89389-090-1*) Himalayan Inst.
— Practical Guide to Holistic Health. rev. ed. LC 80-81598. 110p. 1999. pap. 14.95 (*0-89389-174-6*) Himalayan Inst.
— The Royal Path: Practical Lessons on Yoga. LC 99-13220. Orig. Title: Lectures on Yoga. (Illus.). 138p. 1998. reprint ed. pap. 14.95 (*0-89389-152-5*) Himalayan Inst.
***Rama, Swami.** Spirituality: Transformation Within & Without. rev. ed. Orig. Title: A Call to Humanity. 151p. 1998. pap. 12.95 (*0-89389-150-9*) Himalayan Inst.
Rama, Swami. Wisdom of the Ancient Sages: Mundaka Upanishad. LC 90-48615. 181p. (Orig.). 1990. pap. 12.95 (*0-89389-120-7*) Himalayan Inst.
Rama, Swami, retold by. The Valmiki Ramayana, 2 vols., Vol. 1. LC 93-26312. (Illus.). 520p. 1993. pap. 24.95 (*0-89389-137-1*) Himalayan Inst.
— The Valmiki Ramayana, 2 vols., Vol. 2. LC 93-26312. (Illus.). 520p. 1993. pap. 24.95 (*0-89389-139-8*) Himalayan Inst.
Rama, Swami, tr. from PAN. Japji: Meditation in Sikhism. LC 87-26865. 90p. 1987. pap. 8.95 (*0-89389-107-X*) Himalayan Inst.
Rama, Swami, et al. Meditation in Christianity. rev. ed. LC 79-92042. 130p. 1983. pap. 12.95 (*0-89389-085-5*) Himalayan Inst.
— Science of Breath: A Practical Guide. rev. ed. LC 99-14317. (Illus.). 119p. 1999. pap. 12.95 (*0-89389-151-7*) Himalayan Inst.
Ramabadran, K., jt. auth. see Szekely, J.
Ramacaraka, Yogi. Science of Breath: A Complete Manual of the Oriental Breathing Philosophy, Mental, Psychic & Spiritual Development. 88p. 1996. reprint ed. pap. 11.95 (*1-56459-744-X*) Kessinger Pub.
Ramacciotti, Mary D. Syntax of Il Fiore & of Dante's Inferno As Evidence in the Question of the Authorship of Il Fiore. LC 72-115356. (Catholic University of America: No. 12). reprint ed. 37.50 (*0-404-50312-8*) AMS Pr.
Ramachandra, Dikshitar. Encyclopedia of Human Behavior. 1994. text 165.00 (*0-12-226922-5*); text 165.00 (*0-12-226923-3*); text 165.00 (*0-12-226924-1*) Acad Pr.
— War in Ancient India. (C). 1987. reprint ed. 26.00 (*81-208-0382-5*, Pub. by Motilal Bnarsidass) S Asia.
Ramachandra, K. Lectures on the Mean-Value & Omega Theorems for the Riemann Zeta-Function: Tata Institute Lectures on Mathematics & Physics. 180p. 1996. pap. 35.00 (*3-540-58437-4*) Spr-Verlag.
Ramachandra, Vande M. Satyartha Prakash in English with Comments: Spot Light on Truth. xii, 328p. 1988. text 25.00 (*0-614-00504-3*, Pub. by Sarvadeshik Arya) Nataraj Bks.
***Ramachandra, Vinoth.** Faiths in Conflict? Christian Integrity in a Multicultural World. 192p. 2000. pap. 19.99 (*0-8308-1558-9*) InterVarsity.
Ramachandra, Vinoth. Gods That Fail: Modern Idolatry & Christian Mission. LC 97-12922. 220p. 1997. pap. 14.99 (*0-8308-1896-0*, 1896) InterVarsity.
Ramachandra, Vinoth. The Recovery of Mission: Beyond the Pluralist Paradigm. 293p. 1996. reprint ed. pap. 19.99 (*0-85364-739-9*, Pub. by Paternoster Pub) OM Literature.
Ramachandran. The Economics of Fire Protection. LC 99-161888. (Illus.). 256p. (C). 1998. pap. 90.00 (*0-419-20780-5*) Thomson Learn.
— Pharmacology Recall. LC 99-20847. 1999. 24.95 (*0-683-30285-X*) Lppncott W & W.
— Sri Sankara Vijayam. 1977. pap. 1.50 (*0-89744-123-0*) Auromere.
Ramachandran & Mahadevan, eds. Gandhi: His Relevance for Our Times. 408p. 1983. 20.00 (*0-934676-32-1*) Greenlf Bks.
Ramachandran, C. N. Self-Conscious Structure: A Study of the British Theatre from Buchingham Through Fielding & Sheridan. 210p. 1987. 17.50 (*81-202-0183-3*, Pub. by Ajanta) S Asia.
Ramachandran, H., ed. Environmental Issues in Agricultural Development. 1990. 26.00 (*81-7022-294-X*, Pub. by Concept) S Asia.
Ramachandran, H., ed. see De Campos Guimaraes, J. P.
Ramachandran, K., jt. auth. see Baker, Selwyn J.
Ramachandran, K. S. Gulf War & Environmental Problems. (C). 1991. text 32.00 (*81-7024-399-8*, Pub. by Ashish Pub Hse) S Asia.
— Inflation: The Critical Issues. viii, 204p. (C). 1992. 27.95 (*0-7069-5693-1*, Pub. by Vikas) S Asia.
Ramachandran, K. S., ed. Development Perspectives. 1990. pap. 17.50 (*0-7069-9076-5*, Pub. by Vikas) S Asia.
Ramachandran, K. S., ed. Development Perspectives. 1991. text 25.00 (*0-7069-5332-0*, Pub. by Vikas) S Asia.
Ramachandran, L. Constipation & Indigestion: Prevention & Cure. 284p. 1985. 14.95 (*0-318-36360-7*) Asia Bk Corp.
— Food Planning: Some Vital Aspects. 392p. 1982. 14.95 (*0-940500-68-X*, Pub. by Allied Pubs) Asia Bk Corp.
— Handbook of Management for Primary Health Care Centre Personnel. 1993. 15.95 (*0-7069-6820-4*, Pub. by Vikas) S Asia.
Ramachandran, Narayanan, ed. Materials Research in Low Gravity. LC 98-125244. 23p. 1997. pap. 69.00 (*0-8194-2545-1*) SPIE.
— Space Processing of Materials, Vol. 2809. 412p. 1996. 85.00 (*0-8194-2197-9*) SPIE.
Ramachandran, P. & Oommen, M. A., eds. Some Issues in Development Administration. 223p. (C). 1987. 18.00 (*0-317-89537-0*, Pub. by Oxford IBH) S Asia.
Ramachandran, P. A. Boundary Element Methods in Transport Phenomena. LC 93-72570. (Computational Engineering Ser.). 424p. 1993. text 170.00 incl. disk (*1-56252-184-5*, 2602) Computational Mech MA.
— Boundary Element Methods in Transport Phenomena. 400p. 1993. 160.00 (*1-85861-026-5*, Pergamon Pr) Elsevier.
Ramachandran, P. V. Asymmetric Fluoroorganic Chemistry: Synthesis, Applications & Future Directions. LC 99-48380. (ACS Symposium Ser.: No. 748). (Illus.). 464p. 1999. text 125.00 (*0-8412-3639-9*, Pub. by Am Chemical) OUP.
Ramachandran, R., ed. Recent Advances in Theoretical Physics: Proceedings of the Silver Jubille Workshop, ITT, Kanpur, 5-16 December, 1984. 464p. 1985. 78.00 (*9971-5-0014-0*) World Scientific Pub.
Ramachandran, R. & Mani, H. S., eds. Particle Physics: Superstring Theory. 592p. (C). 1988. text 135.00 (*9971-5-0592-4*) World Scientific Pub.
Ramachandran, Rama V., jt. auth. see Sato, Ryuzo.
Ramachandran, Ravi P. & Mammone, Richard J., eds. Modern Methods of Speech Processing. (International Series in Engineering & Computer Science, Natural Language Processing & Machine Translation). 488p. (C). 1995. text 145.00 (*0-7923-9607-3*) Kluwer Academic.
Ramachandran, S. Biotechnology in Agriculture. Natesh, S. et al, eds. (Indian Edition Ser.: No. 17). 328p. 1988. 91.00 (*90-6191-904-5*, Pub. by A A Balkema) Ashgate Pub Co.
Ramachandran, Suguna, ed. Krishna Chaitanya: A Profile & Selected Papers. xii, 284p. 1991. 30.00 (*81-220-0230-7*) Advent Bks Div.
Ramachandran, Swetha. Top 10 Guide to London. (Top Ten Travel Guides Ser.). (Illus.). 200p. 1999. pap. 14.95 (*1-891382-25-X*) Intrntnlst.
Ramachandran, V. & Nesbitt, C. C., eds. Second International Symposium on Extraction & Processing for the Treatment & Minimization of Wastes. (Illus.). 866p. 1996. 148.00 (*0-87339-369-4*, 3694) Minerals Metals.
Ramachandran, V., jt. auth. see Lindsay, J. F.
Ramachandran, V., ed. see Dutrizac, J. E. & Ji, J.
Ramachandran, V. G. Administrative Law. 1100p. 1984. 600.00 (*0-7855-1344-2*) St Mut.
— Administrative Law. 2nd ed. (C). 1984. 200.00 (*0-7855-4698-7*) St Mut.
— Contempt of Court. (C). 1992. 170.00 (*81-7012-483-2*, Pub. by Eastern Book) St Mut.
— Fundamental Rights & Constitutional Remedies, Set. 2nd ed. 2452p. 1982. 315.00 (*0-7855-1335-3*) St Mut.
— Fundamental Rights & Constitutional Remedies, 2 vols., Set. 2nd ed. (C). 1982. 150.00 (*0-7855-5552-8*) St Mut.
— Law of Agency. (C). 1985. 175.00 (*0-7855-5614-1*) St Mut.
— Law of Contract, 3 vols., Set. 2nd ed. (C). 1989. suppl. ed. 500.00 (*0-7855-4697-9*) St Mut.
— Law of Contract in Three Volumes. (C). 1989. 500.00 (*0-89771-776-7*, Pub. by Eastern Book); pap. 300.00 (*0-7855-6805-0*, Pub. by Eastern Book) St Mut.
— Law of Land: Acquisition & Compensation. 1995. 120.00 (*81-7012-560-X*, Pub. by Eastern Book) St Mut.
— Law of Land Acquisition & Compensation. 7th ed. 1985. 65.00 (*0-7855-1482-1*) St Mut.
— Law of Land Acquisition & Compensation, 2 vols., Set. 7th ed. (C). 1990. suppl. ed. 425.00 (*0-7855-4714-2*) St Mut.
— Law of Land Acquisition & Compensation, with Supplement, 2 vols. 7th ed. (C). 1990. text 450.00 (*0-89771-504-7*) St Mut.
— Law of Limitation in Three Volumes. (C). 1989. 500.00 (*0-89771-788-0*, Pub. by Eastern Book); pap. 300.00 (*0-7855-6804-2*, Pub. by Eastern Book) St Mut.
— The Law of Parliamentary Privileges in India. 912p. 1972. 135.00 (*0-7855-1329-9*) St Mut.
— Law of Writs. 5th rev. ed. (C). 1993. 225.00 (*81-7012-504-9*, Pub. by Eastern Book) St Mut.
Ramachandran, V. G. & Gopalan. Contempt of Court. 5th ed. 1146p. 1983. 420.00 (*0-7855-1343-4*) St Mut.
— Contempt of Court. 6th ed. (C). 1991. 115.00 (*0-7855-5617-6*) St Mut.
Ramachandran, V. K. Wage Labour & Unfreedom in Agriculture: An Indian Case Study. (WIDER Studies in Development Economics). (Illus.). 352p. 1991. text 85.00 (*0-19-828647-3*) OUP.
Ramachandran, V. S. & Blakeslee, Sandra. Phantoms in the Brain: Probing the Mysteries of the Human Mind. LC 98-3953. (Illus.). 320p. 1998. 27.00 (*0-688-15247-3*, Wm Morrow) Morrow Avon.
— Phantoms in the Brain: Probing the Mysteries of the Human Mind. 352p. 1999. reprint ed. pap. 16.00 (*0-688-17217-2*, Quil) HarperTrade.
Ramachandran, Vangipuram S., ed. Concrete Admixtures Handbook: Properties, Science, & Technology. 2nd ed. LC 95-22676. (Illus.). 1153p. 1995. 125.00 (*0-8155-1373-9*) Noyes.
— Encyclopedia of Human Behavior, 4 vols. LC 93-34371. (Illus.). 2765p. 1994. text 685.00 (*0-12-226920-9*) Acad Pr.
— Encyclopedia of Human Behavior, 4 vols., 1. LC 93-34371. (Illus.). 1994. text 165.00 (*0-12-226921-7*) Acad Pr.
Ramachandran, Vangipuram S., et al. Condensed Silica Fume in Concrete. 256p. 1987. lib. bdg. 239.00 (*0-8493-5657-1*, TP884) CRC Pr.
***Ramachandran, Vijaya.** Investing in Africa: Strategies for Private Sector Development. (Overseas Development Council Ser.). 112p. (Orig.). 1999. pap. text 13.95 (*1-56517-031-8*) Overseas Dev Council.
Ramachandran, V.S. & Beaudoin, J.J. Handbook of Analytic Techniques in Concrete. LC 99-29616. 985p. 1999. 225.00 (*0-8155-1437-9*) Noyes.
Ramachondran, C. M. Problems of Higher Education in India. 1987. 27.50 (*0-8364-2218-X*, Pub. by Mittal Pubs Dist) S Asia.

An Asterisk (*) at the beginning of an entry indicates that the title is appearing for the first time.

Ramachandrudu, G., ed. Health Planning in India. LC 97-905307. (Illus.). xiv, 178p. (C). 1997. 23.00 (*81-7024-876-0*, Pub. by APH Pubng) Nataraj Bks.

Ramacharaka. Advanced Course in Yogi Philosophy & Oriental Occultism (1904) 340p. 1998. reprint ed. pap. 24.95 (*0-7661-0169-X*) Kessinger Pub.

— Hatha Yoga or the Yogi Philosophy of Well-Being (1904) 244p. 1998. reprint ed. pap. 19.95 (*0-7661-0187-8*) Kessinger Pub.

— The Philosophies & Religions of India. 360p. 1998. reprint ed. pap. 24.95 (*0-7661-0364-1*) Kessinger Pub.

— A Series of Lessons in Gnani Yogi. 290p. 1998. reprint ed. pap. 12.95 (*0-7661-0225-4*) Kessinger Pub.

— A Series of Lessons in Raja Yoga (1906) 300p. 1998. reprint ed. pap. 19.95 (*0-7661-0140-1*) Kessinger Pub.

Ramacharaka, Yogi. Advanced Course in Yogi Philosophy. reprint ed. 15.00 (*0-911662-02-2*) Yoga.

— The Bhagavad Gita. 184p. 1978. 6.00 (*0-318-37175-8*) Asia Bk Corp.

— Bhagavad Gita. reprint ed. 11.00 (*0-911662-10-3*) Yoga.

— Bhagavad Gita: or The Message of the Master. rev. ed. 184p. 1998. pap. 16.95 (*0-7661-0731-0*) Kessinger Pub.

— Fourteen Lessons in Yoga Philosophy. reprint ed. 15.00 (*0-911662-01-4*) Yoga.

— Gnani Yoga. reprint ed. 15.00 (*0-911662-04-9*) Yoga.

— Hatha Yoga. reprint ed. 15.00 (*0-911662-06-5*) Yoga.

— Hindu-Yogi Breathing Exercises. 1976. reprint ed. 11.00 (*0-911662-62-6*) Yoga.

— Hindu-Yogi Practical Water Cure. reprint ed. pap. text 7.50 (*0-911662-12-X*) Yoga.

— Life Beyond Death. reprint ed. 15.00 (*0-911662-09-X*) Yoga.

— Mystic Christianity. reprint ed. 15.00 (*0-911662-08-1*) Yoga.

— Mystic Christianity or the Inner Teachings of the Master. 274p. 1998. reprint ed. pap. 19.95 (*0-7661-0168-1*) Kessinger Pub.

— The Philosophies & Religions of India. 212p. 1980. 7.95 (*0-318-37149-9*) Asia Bk Corp.

— The Philosophies & Religions of India. reprint ed. 15.00 (*0-911662-05-7*) Yoga.

— Psychic Healing. reprint ed. 15.00 (*0-911662-07-3*) Yoga.

— Raja Yoga. reprint ed. 15.00 (*0-911662-03-0*) Yoga.

— Science of Breath. 88p. 1996. reprint ed. pap. 12.00 (*0-7873-0691-6*) Hlth Research.

— Science of Breath. reprint ed. 11.00 (*0-911662-00-6*) Yoga.

— Spirit of the Upanishads. reprint ed. 11.00 (*0-911662-11-1*) Yoga.

— Yogi Philosophy & Oriental Occultism: Correspondence Class Course, Lessons 1 Through VII. (Yogi Bks.). 139p. 1996. reprint ed. spiral bd. 16.00 (*0-7873-0690-8*) Hlth Research.

Ramacitti, David F. Do-It-Yourself Marketing. 192p. 1994. pap. 18.95 (*0-8144-7800-X*) AMACOM.

Ramadan al-Booti, Muhammad S. Jihad in Islam: How to Understand & Practice It. 188p. (Orig.). 1995. pap. 6.95 (*1-57547-222-8*) Dar Al-Fikr.

Ramadan, Sar. Impressions. Watkins, Colleen, ed. (ReMar Ser.: Vol. 1). (Illus.). 150p. 1997. 20.00 (*0-9659111-0-1*) RaMar OR.

Ramadas, S. R., et al. Methods of Synthesis of Thia Analogues of Gonasteroids: Review of Some Recent Syntheses, Reactions & Bioactivities of Pyridyl Sulfides, Vol. 7. Senning, Alexander, ed. (Sulfer Reports: Vol. 7, No. 4). 70p. 1987. pap. text 72.00 (*3-7186-0442-6*) Gordon & Breach.

Ramade, F. Encyclopedic Dictionary of Ecology & Environmental Sciences, French-English/English-French. (FRE & ENG.). 838p. 1993. pap. 320.00 (*0-320-03064-4*) Fr & Eur.

Ramade, Francois. Dictionnaire Encyclopedique de l'Ecologie et des Sciences De. (FRE.). 1993. write for info. (*0-7859-8052-0*, 2-84074-037-0) Fr & Eur.

— Ecology of Natural Resources. Duffin, W. J., tr. from FRE. LC 84-3678. 245p. reprint ed. pap. 76.00 (*0-7837-0115-2*, 204039200016) Bks Demand.

— Ecotoxicology. Hodgson, L. J., tr. LC 84-26999. 272p. reprint ed. pap. 84.40 (*0-7837-3214-7*, 204323200007) Bks Demand.

Ramadevi, N. The Novels of V.S. Naipaul: Quest for Order & Identity. LC 96-905450. 152p. 1996. write for info. (*81-7551-006-4*, Pub. by Prestige) Advent Bks Div.

Ramadhan, S. Islam & Nationalism. 1989. pap. 3.00 (*1-56744-067-3*) Kazi Pubns.

Ramadhyani, Rachel, jt. compiled by see Cooke, Sarah E.

Ramadier, Cedric, jt. ed. see Houssin, Frederic.

Ramadori, G., jt. ed. see Gressner, A. M.

Ramadori, R. Biological Phosphate Removal from Wastewaters. (Advances in Water Pollution Control Ser.: Vol. 4). 440p. 1987. 105.75 (*0-08-035592-7*, Pergamon Pr) Elsevier.

— Biological Phosphate Removal from Wastewaters: Proceedings of the IAWPRC Specialized Conference Held in Rome, Italy, 28-30 September 1987. (Advances in Water Pollution Control Ser.). 440p. 1987. 90.00 (*0-317-66313-5*, Pergamon Pr) Elsevier.

Ramadurai, S., jt. auth. see Biswas.

Ramadurai, S., jt. ed. see O'Sullivan, D.

***Ramaekers, Dirk.** Effects of Melanocortins & N-Terminal Proopiomelanocortin on Cardiovascular Function & Autonomic Dynamics. (Acta Biomedica Lovaniensia Ser.: Vol. 194). (Illus.). 144p. 1999. pap. 49.50 (*90-6186-958-7*, Pub. by Leuven Univ) Coronet Bks.

Ramage. Writing Arguments. (C). 1998. pap. text 30.71 (*0-536-01342-X*) Pearson Custom.

Ramage & Bean. The Allyn & Bacon Guide to Writing. 2nd ed. LC 99-22480. 743p. 1999. 47.00 (*0-205-29791-9*) Allyn.

— Writing Arguments. LC 98-21160. 264p. 1998. pap. text 26.00 (*0-205-26906-0*) Allyn.

***RAMAGE & BEAN.** The Allyn & Bacon Guide to Writing. 2nd ed. LC 99-22446. 704p. 1999. pap. text 44.00 (*0-205-29792-7*) Allyn.

***RAMAGE & BEAN, ed.** Writing Arguments. 2nd ed. 296p. 1999. pap. text 20.95 (*0-536-02617-3*) P-H.

Ramage, Andrew. Lydian Houses & Architectural Terracottas. LC 78-15507. (Archaeological Exploration of Sardis, Monograph Ser.: No. 5). 104p. 1978. reprint ed. pap. 32.30 (*0-7837-2317-2*, 205740500004) Bks Demand.

***Ramage, Andrew & Craddock, P. T., contrib. by.** King Croesus' Gold: Excavations at Sardis & the History of Gold Refining. LC 99-47954. (Archaeological Exploration of Sardis Monograph). 2000. write for info. (*0-674-50370-8*) HUP.

Ramage, Andrew, jt. auth. see Ramage, Nancy H.

Ramage, Angela. Windows to the Heart of God. LC 95-13224. 144p. 1996. 10.99 (*0-7852-7912-1*) Nelson.

Ramage, Craufurd T. Ramage in South Italy. Clay, Edith, ed. (Illus.). 232p. 1986. reprint ed. pap. 10.00 (*0-89733-216-4*) Academy Chi Pubs.

Ramage, Douglas E. Politics in Indonesia: Democracy Islam & the Ideology of Tolerance. (Politics in Asia Ser.). 296p. (C). 1997. pap. 27.99 (*0-415-16467-2*) Routledge.

Ramage, Edwin S., ed. Atlantis, Fact or Fiction? LC 77-23624. 224p. reprint ed. pap. 69.50 (*0-8357-5836-2*, 205624800056) Bks Demand.

Ramage, James A. Gray Ghost: The Life of Colonel John Singleton Mosby. LC 99-13688. (Illus.). 432p. 1999. 30.00 (*0-8131-2135-3*) U Pr of Ky.

— John Wesley Hunt: Pioneer Merchant, Manufacturer, & Financier. LC 74-7881. (Kentucky Bicentennial Bookshelf Ser.). 115p. reprint ed. pap. 35.70 (*0-7837-2422-5*, 204256800005) Bks Demand.

— Rebel Raider: The Life of General John Hunt Morgan. 336p. 1995. pap. 18.95 (*0-8131-0839-X*) U Pr of Ky.

Ramage, Janet. Energy: A Guidebook. 2nd ed. LC 96-52364. (Illus.). 416p. 1997. pap. 18.95 (*0-19-288022-5*) OUP.

Ramage, Jesse. War Toys. LC 81-84846. 1982. 8.95 (*0-87212-160-7*) Libra.

Ramage, John. National Conference on Bulk Materials Handling, 1996. (National Conference Proceedings Ser.: Vol. 96/12). (Illus.). 417p. 1996. pap. 108.00 (*0-85825-660-6*, Pub. by Inst Engrs Aust-EA Bks) Accents Pubns.

Ramage, John D. Writing Arguments: A Rhetoric with Readings. 4th abr. ed. LC 97-15605. 463p. 1997. pap. text 36.00 (*0-205-26918-4*) Allyn.

Ramage, John D. & Bean, John C. Writing Arguments. 4th ed. LC 97-18531. 721p. 1997. pap. text 42.00 (*0-205-26917-6*) P-H.

***Ramage, John D. & Bean, John C.** Writing Arguments: A Rhetoric with Readings. 2nd ed. 288p. 2000. pap. text 26.00 (*0-205-31747-2*) Allyn.

Ramage, John D. & Bean, John C. Writing Arguments: A Rhetoric with Readings. 4th ed. 192p. (C). 1997. pap. text, teacher ed. write for info. (*0-205-27246-0*, T7246-6) Allyn.

***Ramage, John D. & Bean, John C.** Writing Arguments: A Rhetoric with Readings. 5th ed. 464p. 2000. pap. text 36.00 (*0-205-31746-4*) Allyn.

***Ramage, John D., et al.** Writing Arguments: A Rhetoric with Readings. 5th ed. LC 00-21662. 752p. 2000. pap. text 42.00 (*0-205-31745-6*) Allyn.

***Ramage, Ken.** Guns Illustrated 2001. 33rd rev. ed. LC 69-11342. (Illus.). 352p. 2000. pap. 22.95 (*0-87341-926-X*, GI2001) Krause Pubns.

— Handguns 2001. 13th rev. ed. LC 88-72115. (Illus.). 352p. 2000. pap. 22.95 (*0-87341-927-8*, H2001) Krause Pubns.

Ramage, Nancy H. Roman Art: Romulus to Constantine. 2nd ed. 320p. (C). 1995. pap. text 54.67 (*0-13-440702-4*) P-H.

***Ramage, Nancy H. & Ramage, Andrew.** Roman Art. 3rd ed. 352p. 2000. pap. 54.67 (*0-13-027883-1*, Prentice Hall) P-H.

Ramage, Nancy H. & Ramage, Andrew. Roman Art: Romulus to Constantine. (Illus.). 304p. 1991. 49.50 (*0-8109-3755-7*) Abrams.

Ramage, R. W. The Companies Acts - Table A, 1856-1986. 2nd ed. 220p. 1985. boxed set 70.00 (*0-406-35124-4*, U.K., MICHIE) LEXIS Pub.

Ramage, Roger L. Steps of Love: A History of an Enduring Relationship. 150p. 1999. pap. 7.95 (*0-7392-0053-4*, PO2854) Morris Pubng.

***Ramage, Sean.** And Those Left Behind. LC 00-190382. 296p. 2000. 25.00 (*0-7388-1760-0*); pap. 18.00 (*0-7388-1761-9*) Xlibris Corp.

Ramage, Timothy G., ed. see Stoner, Michael W. & Reichow, Alan W.

Ramaglia, Judith A. & MacDonald, Diane B. Personal Finance: Tools for Decision Making. LC 98-20640. 1998. pap. 87.95 (*0-538-89040-1*) Sth-Wstrn College.

Ramagnoli, Maureen. 1998 Summer Programs Guide. 106p. 1998. ring bd. 6.98 (*1-891486-02-0*) Romagnoli.

***Ramagos, Tonya.** Deceptions. 110p. (J). 1999. 4.50 (*1-928670-67-9*, Byte Me Book) Awe Struck E Bks.

***Ramagos, Tonya Taylor.** The Feud. 148p. (YA). (gr. 9 up). 2000. pap. 10.00 (*1-58345-399-7*) Domhan Bks.

Ramahlo, Enio. Gramatica da Lingua Inglesa. (ENG & POR.). 208p. 1995. 24.95 (*0-7859-9770-9*) Fr & Eur.

Ramahlo, Jose. Learn SQL. LC 99-12468. 1999. pap. text 39.95 (*1-55622-639-X*) Wordware Pub.

***Ramahlo, Jose A.** Data Warehousing with MS SQL 7.0. (Illus.). 2000. pap. 59.95 (*1-55622-718-3*) Wordware Pub.

— Learn Oracle 8i. (Illus.). 2000. pap. write for info. (*1-55622-731-0*) Wordware Pub.

Ramaiah, L. S. The Art of Chinese Cuisine. (Illus.). 208p. 1996. pap. 16.95 (*0-8048-3089-4*) Tuttle Pubng.

— Communicative Language Teaching: A Bibliographical Survey of Resourses. 1986. 17.50 (*0-8364-1556-6*, Pub. by Indian Doc Serv) S Asia.

— Documentation & Bibliographic Control of the Humanities in India. (C). 1992. 32.00 (*81-85689-06-7*, Pub. by Aditya Prakashan) S Asia.

— Gentling the Bull: The Ten Bull Pictures; a Spiritual Journey. (Illus.). 152p. (Orig.). 1996. pap. 12.95 (*0-8048-3088-6*) Tuttle Pubng.

— He's Leaving Home: My Young Son Becomes a Zen Monk. Shore, Jeff, tr. from JPN. 108p. 1995. pap. 8.95 (*0-8048-2060-0*) Tuttle Pubng.

— Linear Analysis of Competitive Economies. LC 94-31582. (L. S. E. Handbooks in Economics Ser.). 184p. (C). 1995. pap. 42.00 (*0-13-342973-3*, Pub. by Wheatsheaf Bks) P-H.

— Roman Italy, 338 BC - AD 200. LC 96-24878. (Illus.). 256p. 1996. text 59.95 (*0-312-16072-0*) St Martin.

Ramaiah, L. S., et al, eds. Artists of Chinese Origin in North America Directory. 2nd ed. (Illus.). 233p. 1995. 75.00 (*1-885594-02-X*) Pt Fine Arts.

Ramaiah, L. S. & Chou. Electrocardiography in Clinical Practice. 4th ed. Zorab, Richard, ed. (Illus.). 736p. 1996. text 104.00 (*0-7216-5647-1*, W B Saunders Co) Harcrt Hlth Sci Grp.

Ramaiah, L. S., jt. auth. see Pathak, Vijay.

Ramaix, Isabelle De, see De Ramaix, Isabelle, ed.

Ramaiya, A. Guide to Companies Act. (C). 1988. 340.00 (*0-7855-3547-0*) St Mut.

— Guide to Companies Act. 11th ed. (C). 1988. 440.00 (*0-7855-4812-2*) St Mut.

— Guide to the Companies Act. (C). 1990. 220.00 (*0-89771-220-X*) St Mut.

Ramaiya, R. Company Law Digest, 1956-1990. (C). 1990. 400.00 (*0-89771-221-8*) St Mut.

Ramakant, Ditors & Misra, Ramesh C. Bhutan: Society & Policy. 1996. 36.00 (*0-614-25271-7*, Pub. by Indus Pub) S Asia.

— Bhutan: Society & Policy. LC 96-906368. (C). 1996. 36.00 (*81-7387-044-6*, Pub. by Indus Pub) S Asia.

Ramakant, M. A. & Phil, D. China & South Asia. 1988. 17.50 (*81-7003-092-7*) South Asia Pubns.

Ramakant, R. Indo-Nepal Relations. (C). 1991. text 60.00 (*0-7855-0143-6*, Pub. by Ratna Pustak Bhandar) St Mut.

— Indo-Nepalese Relations. 1968. text 35.00 (*0-685-14080-6*) Coronet Bks.

Ramakers, Micha. The Art of Tom of Finland. (Photo & Sexy Bks.). (Illus.). 1998. 69.69 (*3-8228-8598-3*) Taschen Amer.

***Ramakers, Micha.** Dirty Pictures: Tom of Finland, Masculinity & Homosexuality. LC 99-43148. (Illus.). 288p. 2000. text 27.95 (*0-312-20526-0*) St Martin.

Ramakrihna, P., ed. Proceedings of the International Conference Advances in Composite Materials. (C). 1991. 74.00 (*81-204-0572-2*, Pub. by Oxford IBH) S Asia.

Ramakrishna. God & Divine Incarnations. 1947. pap. 3.00 (*0-87481-445-6*, Pub. by Ramakrishna Math) Vedanta Pr.

Ramakrishna Math Staff, jt. auth. see Mbhartrta, Anna.

Ramakrishna, P. S., ed. Conservation & Management of Biological Resources in Himalaya. (Illus.). 620p. (C). 1997. 85.00 (*1-886106-88-6*) Science Pubs.

Ramakrishna, Shantha. Translation & Multilingualism: Post Colonial Context. LC 97-905481. 262 p. 1997. write for info. (*81-85753-18-0*) Advent Bks Div.

Ramakrishna, Sri. Sayings of Sri Ramakrishna. pap. 4.95 (*81-7120-377-9*, Pub. by Ramakrishna Math) Vedanta Pr.

— Teachings of Sri Ramakrishna. 344p. (C). 1934. pap. 4.95 (*0-87481-133-3*, Pub. by Advaita Ashrama) Vedanta Pr.

— Words of the Master. Brahmananda, Swami, ed. 1932. pap. 2.00 (*0-87481-135-X*, Pub. by Advaita Ashrama) Vedanta Pr.

Ramakrishnam, K. Introducing India. 88p. 1982. 10.95 (*0-940500-95-7*, Pub. by Pubns Div) Asia Bk Corp.

***Ramakrishnan.** Database Management Systems. 2nd ed. LC 99-37109. 936p. 1999. 68.75 (*0-07-232206-3*) McGraw.

Ramakrishnan, Alladi, ed. see Institute of Mathematical Sciences (India).

Ramakrishnan, D. & Valenza, R. J. Fourier Analysis on Number Fields. LC 98-16715. (Graduate Texts in Mathematics Ser.: Vol. 186). 372p. 1998. 39.00 (*0-387-98436-4*) Spr-Verlag.

***Ramakrishnan, E. V.** The Tree of Tongues: An Anthology of Modern Indian Poetry. LC 99-938121. 1999. 29.50 (*81-85952-70-1*, Pub. by Manohar) S Asia.

***Ramakrishnan, Malayattoor & Viswanathan, R.** Five Cents of Land. LC 98-902448. 1998. write for info. (*0-14-027218-6*) Penguin Books.

Ramakrishnan, P., ed. Powder Metallurgy Alloys: Proceedings of the Symposium on Powder Metallurgy Alloys Held at I. I. T. Bombay on 11th October, 1980. 124p. (C). 1982. text 91.00 (*90-6191-406-X*, Pub. by A A Balkema) Ashgate Pub Co.

— Powder Metallurgy & Related High Temperature Materials. 500p. 1988. text 316.00 (*0-87849-577-0*, Pub. by Trans T Pub) Enfield Pubs NH.

Ramakrishnan, P. & Indian Institute of Technology Staff, eds. Powder Metallurgy in Automotive Applications. (Illus.). 318p. 1998. 85.00 (*1-57808-025-8*) Science Pubs.

Ramakrishnan, P. S. Shifting Agriculture & Sustainable Development. (Man & the Biosphere Ser.: Vol. 10). (Illus.). 424p. (C). 1992. 85.00 (*1-85070-383-3*) Prthnon Pub.

Ramakrishnan, P. S., et al, eds. Conserving the Sacred: For Biodiversity Management. (Illus.). 480p. 1998. 69.00 (*1-57808-036-3*) Science Pubs.

Ramakrishnan, Raghu. Database Management Systems. LC 97-23748. 768p. 1997. 76.25 (*0-07-050775-9*) McGraw.

Ramakrishnan, Raghu, ed. Applications of Logic Databases. (International Series in Engineering & Computer Science, Natural Language Processing & Machine Translation). 304p. (C). 1994. text 133.50 (*0-7923-9533-6*) Kluwer Academic.

Ramakrishnan, Raghu & Stuckey, Peter, eds. Constraints & Databases. LC 97-41579. 192p. 1997. text 121.00 (*0-7923-8045-2*, D Reidel) Kluwer Academic.

Ramakrishnan, T. V. & Rajalakshmi, M. Non-Debye Relaxation in Condensed Matter: Proceedings of a Discussion Meeting, Bangalore, India. 416p. (C). 1987. text 100.00 (*9971-5-0381-6*) World Scientific Pub.

Ramakrishna's Disciples Staff. Message of Our Master. 1936. pap. 1.95 (*0-87481-102-3*) Vedanta Pr.

— Spiritual Talks. 1936. pap. 4.50 (*0-87481-103-1*, Pub. by Advaita Ashrama) Vedanta Pr.

Ramakrisnananda, Swami. Life of Sri Ramuja. 1979. pap. 5.95 (*81-7120-433-3*) Vedanta Pr.

Ramakrisnnan. Database Management Systems: Pre. Pub. Cu. 1996. pap. text 40.00 (*0-07-052522-6*) McGraw.

Ramakrshna, Kilaparti & Woodwell, George M., eds. World Forests for the Future: Their Use & Conservation. LC 92-34492. 208p. (C). 1993. 26.50 (*0-300-05749-0*) Yale U Pr.

Ramakumar, R. Engineering Reliability: Fundamentals & Applications. 496p. (C). 1992. text 64.60 (*0-13-276759-7*) P-H.

Ramaley, Judith, et al. Molecular & Biochemical Aspects of Progesterone Function. 173p. 1972. text 29.75 (*0-8290-2380-1*) Irvington.

Ramaley, William C. Functional Calculus: Brief Calculus for Management, Life, & Social Sciences. 592p. (C). 1995. text. write for info. (*0-697-32992-5*, WCB McGr Hill) McGrw-H Hghr Educ.

Ramaley, William C. & Foard, Pat. Student's Solutions Manual to Accompany Functional Calculus & Applied Calculus. 128p. (C). 1995. text 16.88 (*0-697-21629-2*, WCB McGr Hill) McGrw-H Hghr Educ.

Ramalho de Sousa Santos, Maria I., jt. ed. see Materassi, Mario.

***Ramalho, Josbe Antonio.** Learn SQL. LC 99-46367. 1999. pap. 49.95 (*1-55622-661-6*) Wordware Pub.

***Ramalho, Jose.** Developer's Guide to Oracle Tools. (Illus.). 2000. pap. 59.95 (*1-55622-717-5*) Wordware Pub.

Ramalho, Jose. Learn Advanced HTML 4.0. LC 98-26338. 1998. pap. text 39.95 (*1-55622-586-5*) Wordware Pub.

— Learn Personal Oracle 8.0 with Power Objects 2.0. LC 98-14500. (Illus.). 433p. 1998. pap. 49.95 (*1-55622-546-6*) Wordware Pub.

Ramalho, R. S. Introduction to Wastewater Treatment Processes. 2nd ed. 1983. text 94.00 (*0-12-576560-6*) Acad Pr.

Ramalingam, G. Bounded: Incremental Computation, Vol. 108. LC 96-19066. (Lecture Notes in Computer Science Ser.). 189p. 1996. pap. 36.00 (*3-540-61320-X*) Spr-Verlag.

Ramalingam, M. L., et al, eds. 1997 International Mechanical Engineering Congress & Exposition: Proceedings of the ASME Advanced Energy Systems Division, Dallas, Texas, November 16-21, 1997. LC 97-77360. (AES Ser.: Vol. 37). 504p. 1997. 170.00 (*0-7918-1845-4*, H01126) ASME Pr.

Ramalingam, T., jt. auth. see Goel, Prem K.

Ramalingam, Vimala, et al. Medicinal Plants, Vol. 1. Singh, N. & Mital, H. C., eds. 161p. 1974. text 25.50 (*0-8422-7240-2*) Irvington.

Ramalingham, R., jt. ed. see Kops, L.

Ramambason, Laurent W. Missiology - Its Subject-Matter & Method: A Study of Mission-Doers in Madagascar. LC 99-15095. (Studies in the Intercultural History of Christianity: Vol. 116). 208p. 1999. pap. text 37.95 (*0-8204-4320-4*) P Lang Pubng.

***Ramambason, Laurent W.** Missiology: Its Subject-Matter & Method: A Study of Mission-Doers in Madagascar. 208p. 1999. pap. 37.95 (*3-631-34602-6*) P Lang Pubng.

Ramamoorthy, S., jt. auth. see Moore, J. W.

Ramamoorthy, Sita. Chlorinated Organic Compounds in the Environment: Regulatory & Monitoring Assessment. LC 97-6799. 368p. 1997. lib. bdg. 69.95 (*1-56670-041-8*) Lewis Pubs.

Ramamoorthy, Sub. Handbook of Chemical Toxicity Profiles Biological Species Vol. 2: Avian. 416p. 1995. lib. bdg. 120.00 (*1-56670-014-0*, L1014) Lewis Pubs.

Ramamoorthy, Sub & Baddaloo, E. G. Handbook of Chemical Toxicity Profiles of Biological Species Vol. 1: Aquatic Species, Vol. 1. LC 94-41896. 400p. 1995. lib. bdg. 120.00 (*1-56670-013-2*, L1013) Lewis Pubs.

Ramamoorthy, T. P., et al, eds. Biological Diversity of Mexico: Origins & Distributions. (Illus.). 856p. 1993. text 110.00 (*0-19-506674-X*) OUP.

***Ramamoorti, Sridhar, et al.** Using Neural Networks for Risk Assessment in Internal Auditing: A Feasibility Study. Campbell, Lee A., ed. LC 99-181410. xiv, 130 p. 1998. write for info. (*0-89413-420-5*) Inst Inter Aud.

Ramamoorty, M. Computer-Aided Design of Electrical Equipment. 138p. 1988. text 41.95 (*0-470-21210-1*) P-H.

***Ramamoorty, M.** Harnessing Hydropower: The Story of Hydropower Development in India. LC 99-939750. (Illus.). 1998. write for info. (*0-07-463182-9*) McGrw-H Hghr Educ.

Ramamoorty, M., ed. Automation & Instrumentation for Power Plants: Proceedings of the IFAC Symposium, December 15-17, 1986, Bangalore, India. (IFPS Proceedings Ser.: No. 8700). 280p. 1989. 140.00 (*0-08-034197-7*, Pergamon Pr) Elsevier.

Ramamritham, Krithi & Chrysanthis, Panos K. Advances in Concurrency Control & Transaction Processing. LC 96-29058. 120p. 1996. pap. 24.00 (*0-8186-7405-9*) IEEE Comp Soc.

An Asterisk (*) at the beginning of an entry indicates that the title is appearing for the first time.

Ramamurthy, A. Advaita: A Conceptual Analysis. LC 96-904808. (C). 1996. text 24.00 (81-246-0067-8, Pub. by DK Pubs Ind) S Asia.

Ramamurthy, Bhargavi, jt. ed. see Ronnas, Per.

Ramamurthy, K. G. Coherent Structures. 1990. text 144.00 (0-7923-0869-7) Kluwer Academic.

Ramamurthy, V. Photochemistry in Organized & Constrained Media. 875p. 1991. 210.00 (0-471-18744-5, Wiley-VCH) Wiley.

***Ramamurthy, V. & Schanze, Kirk S.** Organic, Physical & Materials Photochemistry. LC 00-40476. (Molecular & Supramolecular Photochemistry Ser.). 2000. write for info. (0-8247-0404-5) Dekker.

***Ramamurthy, V. & Schanze, Kirk S., eds.** Multimetallic & Macromolecular Inorganic Photochemistry. (Molecular & Supramolecular Photochemistry Ser.: Vol. 4). (Illus.). 360p. 1999. text 175.00 (0-8247-7392-6) Dekker.

— Organic & Inorganic Photochemsitry. LC 98-35550. (Molecular & Supramolecular Photochemistry Ser.). (Illus.). 368p. 1998. text 175.00 (0-8247-0174-7) Dekker.

Ramamurthy, Vaidhyanathan, ed. Photochemistry in Organized & Constrained Media. 526p. 1991. 135.00 (0-89573-775-2, Wiley-VCH) Wiley.

Ramamurti, G. Grammar of the Sora (Savora) Language. 254p. 1931. 59.95 (0-7859-9820-9) Fr & Eur.

Ramamurti, Ravi, ed. Privatizing Monopolies: Lessons from the Telecommunications & Transport Sectors in Latin America. LC 95-18040. (Illus.). 401p. (C). 1996. text 55.00 (0-8018-5135-1) Johns Hopkins.

Ramamurti, Ravi & Vernon, Raymond. Privatization & Control of State-Owned Enterprises. (EDI Development Studies). 344p. 1991. pap. 30.00 (0-8213-1863-2, 11863) World Bank.

Ramamurti, V. Computer Aided Mechanical Design & Analysis. 3rd ed. LC 98-208917. (Illus.). 416p. 1998. 64.95 (0-07-060036-8) McGraw.

Ramamurty, A. The Central Philosophy of the Rig-Veda. (C). 1991. 32.00 (81-202-0306-2, Pub. by Ajanta) S Asia.

Ramamyya, N. Venkata. Studies in the History of the Third Dynasty of Vijayanagara. 568p. 1986. 30.00 (81-212-0066-0, Pub. by Gian Publng Hse) S Asia.

Raman. Probate & Administration in Singapore & Malaysia - Law & Practice. 201p. 1991. boxed set 135.00 (0-409-99602-5, MICHIE) LEXIS Pub.

Raman, A. & Labine, P., eds. Reviews on Corrosion Inhibitor Science & Technology, Vol. 2. (Illus.). 350p. (Orig.). 1996. pap. text 95.00 (1-57590-005-X) NACE Intl.

— Reviews on Corrosion Inhibitors Science & Technology. LC 92-61226. 716p. 1993. pap. 78.00 (1-877914-42-8) NACE Intl.

Raman, A., jt. auth. see Ananthakrishnan, T. N.

Raman, Anantanarayanan, ed. Ecology & Evolution of Plant-Feeding Insects in Natural & Man-Made Environments. 1997. 75.00 (90-73348-71-4, Pub. by Backhuys Pubs) Balogh.

Raman, Bangalore V. Ashtakavarga System of Prediction. (C). 1993. text 6.50 (81-85674-25-6, Pub. by UBS Pubs Dist) S Asia.

— Female Horoscopy: Strijataka. rev. ed. (C). 1992. pap. 5.00 (81-85674-40-X, Pub. by UBS Pubs Dist) S Asia.

— Hindu Astrology & the West. (BVR Astrology Ser.). (C). 1992. pap. 6.00 (81-85273-97-9, Pub. by UBS Pubs Dist) S Asia.

— Hindu Predictive Astrology. (C). 1992. 6.00 (81-85273-93-6, Pub. by Ranjan Pubs) S Asia.

— Hindu Predictive Astrology. (C). 1993. 6.50 (81-85273-54-5, Pub. by UBS Pubs Dist) S Asia.

— How to Judge a Horoscope, 2 vols., 1. 1991. reprint ed. pap. 12.50 (81-208-0847-9) S Asia.

— How to Judge a Horoscope, 2 vols., 2. 1991. reprint ed. pap. 12.50 (81-208-0845-2) S Asia.

— How to Judge a Horoscope, 2 vols., Set. 1991. reprint ed. pap. 24.00 (81-208-0849-5) S Asia.

— Manual of Hindu Astrology: Correct Casting of Horoscopes. (BVR Astrology Ser.). (C). 1992. pap. 4.50 (81-85674-29-9, Pub. by UBS Pubs Dist) S Asia.

— Muhurtha (Electional Astrology) (C). 1993. 6.50 (81-85674-68-X, Pub. by UBS Pubs Dist) S Asia.

— My Experiences in Astrology. (BVR Astrology Ser.). (C). 1992. 6.00 (81-85273-73-1, Pub. by UBS Pubs Dist) S Asia.

— Notable Horoscopes. (C). 1991. reprint ed. 14.00 (81-208-0900-9, Pub. by Motilal Bnarsidass) S Asia.

— Planetary Influences on Human Affairs. (C). 1992. 4.50 (81-85273-90-1, Pub. by Ranjan Pubs) S Asia.

— Prasna Marga, Pt. 2. (ENG & SAN.). (C). 1992. text 17.50 (81-208-1034-1, Pub. by Motilal Bnarsidass); pap. text 11.50 (81-208-1035-X, Pub. by Motilal Bnarsidass) S Asia.

— Prasna Marga, Part 1: English Translation with Original Text in Devanagri & Notes. (C). 1991. reprint ed. 12.50 (81-208-0918-1, Pub. by Motilal Bnarsidass); reprint ed. 12.52 (81-208-0914-9, Pub. by Motilal Bnarsidass) S Asia.

— Raman's One Hundred Ten Year Ephemeris of Planetary Positions (1891-2000 AD) (BVR Astrology Ser.). (C). 1992. pap. 6.00 (81-85273-92-8, Pub. by UBS Pubs Dist) S Asia.

— Sri Neelakanta's Prasna Tantra: Horary Astrology. Astrological Magazine Staff, ed. (Orig.). (C). 1993. pap. text 6.50 (81-85674-66-3, Pub. by UBS Pubs Dist) S Asia.

— Studies in Jaimini Astrology. 1996. reprint ed. 6.00 (81-208-1397-9, Pub. by Motilal Bnarsidass) S Asia.

— Three Hundred Important Combinations: Indian Astrology. (C). 1991. reprint ed. 14.00 (81-208-0843-6, Pub. by Motilal Bnarsidass) S Asia.

— Varshaphal: or The Hindu Progressed Horoscope. (BVR Astrology Ser.). (C). 1992. pap. 5.00 (81-85674-24-8, Pub. by UBS Pubs Dist) S Asia.

Raman, Chandrasekhara V. New Physics. LC 73-128292. (Essay Index Reprint Ser.). 1977. 19.95 (0-8369-2020-1) Ayer.

— Scientific Papers of C. V. Raman Vol. 1: Scattering of Light. Ramaseshan, S., ed. (Illus.). 608p. 1989. 55.00 (81-85324-01-8) OUP.

— Scientific Papers of C. V. Raman Vol. 2: Acoustics. Ramaseshan, S., ed. (Illus.). 668p. 1989. 55.00 (81-85324-02-6) OUP.

— Scientific Papers of C. V. Raman Vol. 3: Optics. Ramaseshan, S., ed. (Illus.). 576p. 1989. 55.00 (81-85324-03-4) OUP.

— Scientific Papers of C. V. Raman Vol. 4: Optics of Minerals & Diamond. Ramaseshan, S., ed. (Illus.). 766p. 1989. 55.00 (81-85324-04-2) OUP.

— Scientific Papers of C. V. Raman Vol. 5: Physics of Crystals. Ramaseshan, S., ed. (Illus.). 874p. 1989. 55.00 (81-85324-05-0) OUP.

— Scientific Papers of C. V. Raman Vol. 6: Floral Colors & Visual Perception. Ramaseshan, S., ed. (Illus.). 636p. 1989. 55.00 (81-85324-06-9) OUP.

Raman, G., et al, eds. High-Speed Jet Flows - 1995. LC 95-78827. (1995 ASME/JSME Fluids Engineering Conference Ser.: FED-Vol. 214). 184p. 1995. 96.00 (0-7918-1469-6, G00964) ASME.

Raman, G. Venkat. Clinical Nephrology. (Illus.). 300p. 1997. text 75.00 (0-412-45700-8, Pub. by E A) OUP.

Raman, G. Venkat, jt. auth. see Lee, H. A.

Raman, Lakshmi & Raman, Lakshmi. Fundamentals of Telecommunications Network Management. LC 98-47636. (IEEE Series on Network Management). 368p. 1999. 69.95 (0-7803-3466-3) Inst Electrical.

Raman, Lakshmi, jt. auth. see Raman, Lakshimi.

Raman, N., jt. auth. see Natarajan, K.

Raman, N. S. Shri Varadrajswamy Temple-Kanchi. (Illus.). 206p. 1975. 29.95 (0-318-36252-X) Asia Bk Corp.

Raman, N. S. & Indian Institute of Advanced Study Staff. Methodological Studies in the History of Religions: With Special Reference to Hinduism & Buddhism LC 99-931770. x, 255p. 1998. write for info. (81-85952-54-X) Indian Inst.

Raman, Narayan. Real Time Scheduling Problems in a General Flexible Manufacturing System. LC 93-49427. (Studies on Industrial Productivity). 136p. 1994. text 15.00 (0-8153-1672-0) Garland.

Raman, Papri S., jt. auth. see Sen, Abhijit.

Raman, Parvathi. Kalulu the Hare & Other Zambian Folk-Tales LC 84-237123. 107p. 1979. write for info. (0-7223-1219-9, Pub. by A H S Ltd) St Mut.

Raman, Rajeswari. Hatha Yoga for All. (C). 1991. reprint ed. 5.00 (81-208-0937-8, Pub. by Motilal Bnarsidass) S Asia.

Raman, S. Capture Gamma-Ray Spectroscopy & Related Topics 1984: International Symposium, Knoxville, Tennessee. LC 84-73303. (AIP Conference Proceedings Ser.: No. 125). 984p. 1985. lib. bdg. 65.50 (0-88318-324-2) Am Inst Physics.

Raman, S., jt. ed. see Singh, M. P.

Raman, Sunder. Constitutional Amendments in India, 1950-1989. (C). 1990. 85.00 (0-89771-198-X) St Mut.

Raman, T. V. Audio System for Technical Readings. LC 99-10038. (Lecture Notes in Computer Science Ser.: Vol. 1410). xvi, 121p. 1999. pap. 31.00 (3-540-65515-8) Spr-Verlag.

— Auditory User Interfaces: Toward the Speaking Computer. LC 97-25860. 1997. text 104.50 (0-7923-9984-6) Kluwer Academic.

Raman, V. Glimpses of Indian Heritage. 1989. 31.00 (0-86132-181-2, Pub. by Popular Prakashan) S Asia.

***Raman, V. V.** Glimpses of Ancient Science & Scientists. LC 99-91900. 359p. 1999. 25.00 (0-7388-1362-1); pap. 18.00 (0-7388-1363-X) Xlibris Corp.

— Scientific Perspectives: Essays & Reflections of a Physicist - Humanist. LC 99-91484. 2000. 25.00 (0-7388-0822-9); pap. 18.00 (0-7388-0823-7) Xlibris Corp.

Raman, Varadaraja V. Bealakearnrda: Reameayarna as Literature & Cultural History. LC 98-907002. xxviii, 350 p. 1998. write for info. (81-7154-746-X) Popular Prakashan.

Ramana, A. The Handbook to Perpetual Happiness. 446p. 1997. 24.95 (1-888599-10-3); pap. write for info. (1-888599-11-1) AHAM Pubns.

— There Is Neither "I" nor "Other" Than I - There Is Only. 216p. 1999. 19.95 (1-888599-12-X); pap. write for info. (1-888599-13-8) AHAM Pubns.

***Ramana, A., ed.** What's Happening: A Daily Diary or Personal Journal. 398p. 2000. 12.95 (1-888599-19-7) AHAM Pubns.

Ramana, D. V. Economics of Sericulture & Silk Industry in India. (C). 1987. 21.00 (81-7100-034-7, Pub. by Deep & Deep Pubns) S Asia.

Ramana, Rao D., jt. auth. see Reddy, G. Narayana.

Ramanadham, V. V. Privatisation in the U. K. 256p. (C). 1988. lib. bdg. 69.50 (0-415-00150-1) Routledge.

— Studies in Public Enterprise. 275p. 1986. 42.00 (0-7146-3267-8, Pub. by F Cass Pubs) Intl Spec Bk.

Ramanadham, V. V. & Bennett, Anthony. How Does Privatization Work? Essays on Privatization in Honour of Professor V. V. Ramanadham. LC 97-6814. 352p. (C). 1997. 90.00 (0-415-17023-0) Routledge.

Ramanamma, A. Women in Indian Industry. 232p. 1987. 27.50 (0-8364-2085-3, Pub. by Mittal Pubs Dist) S Asia.

Ramanamurty, Y. V., jt. ed. see Rawer, Karl.

Ramanan, K. Venkata. Nagarjuna's Philosophy. 409p. (C). 1987. reprint ed. 18.00 (81-208-0159-8, Pub. by Motilal Bnarsidass) S Asia.

Ramanan, S., ed. Proceedings of the Hyderabad Conference on Algebraic Groups. 546p. 1991. 60.00 (81-231-0090-6, HCAG/1C) Am Math.

Ramanan, S., jt. auth. see Adler, Alan.

Ramanan, S., ed. see Van der Kallen, W. L.

Ramanarayanan, R., ed. Particle Design Via Crystallization. LC 91-29216. (AIChE Symposium Ser.: Vol. 87, No. 284). 203p. 1991. pap. text 35.00 (0-8169-0553-3) Am Inst Chem Eng.

Ramanarayanan, T. A., et al, eds. Proceedings of the International Symposium on Ionic & Mixed Conducting Ceramics, 2nd. LC 94-70844. (Proceedings Ser.: Vol. 94-12). 622p. 1994. 68.00 (1-56677-044-0) Electrochem Soc.

Ramanarayanan, T. A., ed. see International Symposium on Ionic & Mixed Conductin.

Ramanathan. Intro Econometrics 4e+esl Sfwr. 4th ed. 1997. 105.50 (0-03-023568-5) Dryden Pr.

Ramanathan & Link. All Our Futures: Principals & Research for School Work Practice in a Global Era. LC 98-24882. (Social Work Ser.). 1998. pap. 37.95 (0-534-35587-0) Brooks-Cole.

Ramanathan, Geetha. Sexual Politics & the Male Playwright: The Portrayal of Women in 10 Contemporary Plays. LC 95-45246. 200p. 1996. lib. bdg. 35.00 (0-7864-0063-3) McFarland & Co.

Ramanathan, Hema, tr. see Chaudhary.

Ramanathan, Indira. China & the Ethnic Chinese in Malaysia & Indonesia 1949-1992. (C). 1994. 18.50 (81-7027-196-7, Pub. by Radiant Pubs) S Asia.

Ramanathan, J. Methods & Applied Fourier Analysis. LC 98-4738. (Applied & Numerical Harmonic Analysis Ser.). 385p. 1998. 65.00 (0-8176-3963-2) Spr-Verlag.

Ramanathan, Ramu. Introductory Econometrics with Applications. 614p. (C). 1988. teacher ed. 1.25 (0-15-546486-8) Harcourt Coll Pubs.

— Introductory Econometrics with Applications. 4th ed. 816p. (C). 1997. text 105.50 (0-03-024616-4) Dryden Pr.

— Statistical Methods in Econometrics. (Illus.). 405p. 1993. text 59.95 (0-12-576830-3) Acad Pr.

Ramanathan, S., jt. auth. see Indian Institute of Public Administration Staff.

Ramanathan, Sivam. Obstetric Anesthesia. LC 87-17293. 432p. reprint ed. pap. 134.00 (0-7837-2742-9, 204312200006) Bks Demand.

Ramanathan, Suguna. The Novels of C. P. Snow: A Critical Introduction. LC 79-300490. xi, 125p. 1978. write for info. (0-333-23480-4) Macmillan.

Ramanathan, V., jt. ed. see Crutzen, P.

Ramanathan, Vai. Alzheimer Discourse: Some Sociolinguistic Dimensions. (LEA's Communication Ser.). 192p. 1997. 36.00 (0-8058-2354-9); pap. 18.00 (0-8058-2355-7) L Erlbaum Assocs.

Ramanayya, N. Venkata. Vijayanagara Origin of the City & the Empire. (C). 1990. 19.00 (81-206-0545-4, Pub. by Asian Educ Servs) S Asia.

Ramanayyan, Venkata. An Essay on the Origin of the South Indian Temples. (Illus.). 92p. 1986. reprint ed. 15.00 (0-8364-1725-9, Pub. by Manohar) S Asia.

Ramand, Pierre, ed. Yukawa Couplings & the Origins of Mass. (Series in Physics). 350p. (C). 1996. 42.00 (1-57146-025-X) Intl Pr Boston.

Ramani, K., jt. ed. see Saigal, A.

Ramani, P. S. Stop Worrying about Backache. 102p. 1983. 8.95 (0-318-36400-X) Asia Bk Corp.

Ramani, R. V., ed. Longwall-Shortwall Mining, State of the Art. fac. ed. LC 81-67436. (Illus.). 306p. 1981. reprint ed. pap. 94.90 (0-7837-7849-X, 204760800007) Bks Demand.

— Proceedings of the 26th International Symposium on Application of Computers & Operations Research in the Mineral Industry. LC 96-69563. (Illus.). 548p. 1996. 95.00 (0-87335-137-1) SMM&E Inc.

Ramani, R. V., et al. Computers in Mineral Industry. (Illus.). 366p. (C). 1994. text 71.00 (90-5410-242-X, Pub. by A A Balkema) Ashgate Pub Co.

Ramani, R. V., jt. ed. see Frantz, R. L.

Ramani, R. V., ed. see International Symposium on the Application of Comp.

Ramani, Raja V., ed. Proceedings of the 6th International Mine Ventilation Symposium. LC 96-72548. (Illus.). 568p. 1997. text 95.00 (0-87335-146-0, 146-0) SMM&E Inc.

Ramani, Raja V. & Ghose, Ajoy K., eds. Longwall Thick Seam Mining: Proceedings of the Indo-U. S. Seminar on Longwall Mining Systems for Thick Seam Mining - Assessment of Progress & Needs, Indian School of Mines, Dhanbad, 11-13 January 1986. 270p. (C). 1988. text 136.00 (90-6191-901-0, Pub. by A A Balkema) Ashgate Pub Co.

Ramani, S., et al, eds. Knowledge Based Computer Systems: International Conference KBCS, '89, Bombay, India, December 11-13, 1989 Proceedings. (Lecture Notes in Artificial Intelligence Ser.: Vol. 444). x, 546p. 1990. 53.95 (0-387-52850-4) Spr-Verlag.

— Proceedings of the International Conference on Computer Communication, 10th, New Delhi, 4-9 November 1990. 800p. 1991. 142.95 (0-387-53449-0) Spr-Verlag.

Ramani, S. & Verma, Pramode K., eds. The Computer Communication Revolution: Multi-Disciplinary Retrospective & Prospective. (Illus.). 230p. 1997. 45.00 (1-891365-01-0) ICCC Pr.

Ramaniah, J. Temples of South India: A Study of Hindu, Jain & Buddhist Monuments of the Deccan. (C). 1989. 52.00 (81-7022-223-0, Pub. by Concept) S Asia.

Ramankutty, Ramesh, jt. auth. see Brandon, Carter.

Ramano, et al. Biology Laboratory: An Inquiry Approach. 2nd ed. 304p. (C). 1997. spiral bd. 45.95 (0-7872-3908-9) Kendall-Hunt.

Ramanthan, Jayakumar. Methods of Applied Fourier Analysis. LC 98-4738. (Applied & Numerical Harmonic Analysis Ser.). 1998. write for info. (3-7643-3963-2) Birkhauser.

Ramanujachari, C., tr. see Tyagaraja.

Ramanujachary, N. C. A Lonely Disciple: Monograph on T. Subba Row 1856-90. 1993. pap. 5.95 (81-7059-215-1, 7606, Quest) Theos Pub Hse.

Ramanujam, P. Renga. Marxism, Ideology & Literary Criticism. ix, 199p. 1996. 20.00 (81-85445-96-6, Pub. by Manak Pubns Pvt Ltd) Nataraj Bks.

— Reflections on Distance Education for India. (Illus.). 181p. 1995. 20.00 (81-85445-93-1, Pub. by Manak Pubns Pvt Ltd) Nataraj Bks.

Ramanujan, A. K. The Collected Essays of A. K. Ramanujan. Dharwadker, Vinay, ed. 656p. 2000. text 45.00 (0-19-563937-5) OUP.

— The Collected Poems of A. K. Ramanujan. 328p. 1999. reprint ed. pap. text 12.95 (0-19-564068-3) OUP.

— Flowering Tree & Other Indian Oral Tales. Blackburn, Stuart H. & Dundes, Alan, eds. LC 95-43422. 276p. (C). 1997. pap. 17.95 (0-520-20399-2, Pub. by U CA Pr) Cal Prin Full Svc.

— Flowering Tree & Other Indian Oral Tales. Blackburn, Stuart H., ed. & pref. by. Dundes, Alan, pref. LC 95-43422. 276p. 1997. 48.00 (0-520-20398-4, Pub. by U CA Pr) Cal Prin Full Svc.

— Poems of Love & War: From the 8 Anthologies & the 10 Songs of Classical Tamil. LC 84-12182. 320p. 1985. pap. text 23.50 (0-231-05107-7) Col U Pr.

— Second Sight. 88p. 1986. pap. text 11.95 (0-19-561874-2) OUP.

— Selected Poems. (Three Crowns Bks.). 1977. pap. 2.95 (0-19-560689-2) OUP.

Ramanujan, A. K., ed. Folktales from India. (Fairy Tale & Folklore Library). (Illus.). 384p. 1994. reprint ed. pap. 17.00 (0-679-74832-6) Pantheon.

Ramanujan, A. K., et al, eds. When God Is a Customer: Telugu Courtesan Songs by Ksetrayya & Others. LC 93-28264. (C). 1994. pap. 13.95 (0-520-08069-6, Pub. by U CA Pr) Cal Prin Full Svc.

Ramanujan, A. K., tr. The Interior Landscape: Love Poems from a Classical Tamil Anthology. (India Paperbacks Ser.). 126p. 1994. pap. 7.95 (0-19-563501-9) OUP.

Ramanujan, A. K., jt. ed. see Dharwadker, Vinay.

***Ramanujan Aiyangar, Srinivasa & Yogananda, C. S.** Collected Papers Of Srinivasa Ramanujan. LC 00-20455. 2000. write for info. (1-56881-118-7) AK Peters.

***Ramanujan Aiyangar, Srinivasa, et al.** Collected Papers of Srinivasa Ramanujan. LC 99-43778. 2000. write for info. (0-8218-2076-1) Am Math.

Ramanujan, M. S., jt. auth. see Dubinsky, Ed.

Ramanujan, M. S., tr. see Meise, Reinhold & Vogt, Dietmar.

Ramanujan, R. V., jt. ed. see Banerjee, S.

Ramanujan, S. R. The Lost Notebook. xxvi, 419p. 1988. 69.00 (0-387-18726-X) Spr-Verlag.

Ramanujian, A. K., tr. & intro. see Wyatt, Thomas.

Ramasami, T. Education & Personality Development. (Illus.). x, 159p. 1993. 18.00 (81-7024-515-X, Pub. by Ashish Pub Hse) Nataraj Bks.

Ramasamy, C., jt. ed. see Hazell, Peter B.

Ramasamy, P. Plantation Labour, Unions, Capital, & the State in Peninsular Malaysia. LC 93-26972. (South-East Asian Social Science Monographs). (Illus.). 220p. 1994. 55.00 (967-65-3031-X) OUP.

Ramasarma, T., jt. auth. see Singhal, G. S.

***Ramasastri, A. S.** Quantitative Methods for Valuation of Financial Assets: 100 Questions & Answers. LC 99-51499. 2000. pap. write for info. (0-7619-9408-4) Sage.

Ramasay, John. Dog Tales. LC 87-80984. (Illus.). 107p. (Orig.). 1987. pap. 5.95 (0-935680-35-7) Kentucke Imprints.

Ramaseder, Josef, tr. see Ricard, Rene.

Ramaseshan, S., ed. see Raman, Chandrasekhara V.

Ramashray, Roy. Democracy in Two Nations - U. S. A. & India. 403p. 1982. 29.95 (0-318-37232-0) Asia Bk Corp.

— Gandhi: Soundings in Political Philosophy. 1984. 16.00 (0-8364-1104-8, Pub. by Chanakya) S Asia.

Ramasubramanian, R., jt. auth. see Nickalls, R. W.

Ramasut, Arlene, ed. Whole-School Approaches: Meeting the Special Educational Needs of All Children - A Guide to Teachers. 280p. 1989. 85.00 (1-85000-569-9, Falmer Pr) Taylor & Francis.

Ramaswami, Murali & Institute of Chartered Financial Analysts Staff. Active Currency Management LC 99-207588. viii, 56 p. 1993. write for info. (0-943205-19-0) RFICFA.

Ramaswami, Murali & Moeller, Susan E. Investing in Financially Distressed Firms: A Guide to Pre- & Post-Bankruptcy Opportunities. LC 89-10749. 183p. 1990. 59.95 (0-89930-404-4, RRO/, Greenwood Pr) Greenwood.

Ramaswami, N. S. Indian Monuments. 1986. 16.00 (0-8364-1843-3, Pub. by Abhinav) S Asia.

— Political History of Carnatic under the Nawabs. 1985. 40.00 (0-8364-1262-1, Pub. by Abhinav) S Asia.

Ramaswami, R., jt. auth. see Latouche, G.

Ramaswami, Rajiv & Sivarajan, Kumar. Optical Networks. LC 97-46057. 600p. 1998. text 72.95 (1-55860-445-6) Morgan Kaufmann.

***Ramaswami, Srivatsa.** Yoga for the Three Stages of Life: Developing Your Practice as an Art Form, a Physical Therapy & a Guiding Philosophy. (Illus.). 272p. 2000. pap. 19.95 (0-89281-820-4) Inner Tradit.

Ramaswami, Uma. Work, Union & Community: Industrial Man in South India. 1983. 16.95 (0-19-561503-4) OUP.

An Asterisk (*) at the beginning of an entry indicates that the title is appearing for the first time.

Ramaswami, V. & Wirth, P. E., eds. Teletraffic Contributions for the Information Age: Proceedings of the 15th International Teletraffic Congress-ITC-15, Washington, D. C., U. S. A., 22-27 June, 1977, Vols. 2A & 2B. LC 97-20195. (Teletraffic Science & Engineering Ser.). 1528p. 1997. 468.75 (*0-444-82598-3*, North Holland) Elsevier.
Ramaswamy, A. E. The Rayon Spinners: The Strategic Management of Industrial Relations. 196p. (C). 1995. 27.00 (*0-19-563537-X*) OUP.
Ramaswamy, E. A. A Question of Balance: Labour, Management, & Society. 280p. 1997. text 23.95 (*0-19-564168-X*) OUP.
Ramaswamy, G. S. Modern Prestressed Concrete Design. (Illus.). 1976. pap. 29.95 (*0-8464-0639-X*); pap. 29.95 (*0-686-77190-7*) Beekman Pubs.
Ramaswamy, G. S. & Rao, V. V. S I Units: A Source Book. 1973. text 15.00 (*0-07-096575-7*) McGraw.
Ramaswamy, N. S. Indian Monuments. 187p. 1979. 31.95 (*0-318-37001-8*) Asia Bk Corp.
Ramaswamy, P., jt. ed. see Nayyar, Harish.
Ramaswamy, Ramu V., jt. ed. see Park, Yoon-Soo.
Ramaswamy, Rohit. Design & Management of Service Processes. (Engineering Process Improvement Ser.). 464p. (C). 1996. 52.00 (*0-201-63383-3*) Addison-Wesley.
Ramaswamy, Suchila, jt. ed. see Mukherjee, Subrata.
Ramaswamy, Sumathi. Passions of the Tongue: Language Devotion In Tamil India, 1891-1970. LC 96-52441. (Studies on the History of Society & Culture). 343p. 1997. 50.00 (*0-520-20804-8*, Pub. by U CA Pr) Cal Prin Full Svc.
— Passions of the Tongue: Language Devotion in Tamil India, 1891-1970. LC 96-52441. (Studies on the History of Society & Culture). 343p. 1997. pap. 20.00 (*0-520-20805-6*, Pub. by U CA Pr) Cal Prin Full Svc.
Ramaswamy, Sundar, jt. auth. see Ramaswamy, Sunita.
Ramaswamy, Sunita & Ramaswamy, Sundar. Vedic Heritage Teaching Program, Vol. III. Schleicher, Irene, ed. 280p. (Orig.). (C). 1994. pap. text. write for info. (*1-882325-05-2*) Arsha Vidya.
— Vedic Heritage Teaching Program Teaching Manual, Vol. I. Schleicher, Irene, ed. (Illus.). 294p. (Orig.). 1992. pap. text. write for info. (*1-882325-00-1*) Arsha Vidya.
— Vedic Heritage Teaching Program Teaching Manual, Vol. II. Schleicher, Irene, ed. 236p. (Orig.). (C). 1993. pap. text. write for info. (*1-882325-03-6*) Arsha Vidya.
Ramaswamy, Sushila, jt. auth. see Mukherjee, Subrata.
Ramaswamy, Sushila, jt. ed. see Mukherjee, Subrata.
Ramaswamy, T. N. Essentials of Indian Statecraft: Kautilya's Arthasastra for Contemporary Readers. (C). 1994. text 20.00 (*81-215-0655-7*, Pub. by M Manoharial) Coronet Bks.
Ramaswamy, T. N., jt. ed. see Mukherjee.
Ramat. The Indo-European Languages. LC 96-40341. (Illus.). 640p. (C). 1998. 130.00 (*0-415-06449-X*) Routledge.
Ramat, Anna G., et al, eds. Papers from the Seventh International Conference on Historical Linguistics. LC 87-8100. (Current Issues in Linguistic Theory Ser.: Vol. 48). xvi, 672p. (C). 1987. 139.00 (*90-272-3542-2*) J Benjamins Pubng Co.
Ramat, Anna G. & Hopper, Paul J., eds. The Limits of Grammaticalization. LC 98-21202. (Typological Studies in Linguistics: Vol. 37). vi, 307p. 1998. 79.00 (*1-55619-649-0*); pap. text 29.95 (*1-55619-650-4*) J Benjamins Pubng Co.
Ramat, Paolo. Linguistic Typology. (Empirical Approaches to Language Typology Ser.: No. 1). (Illus.). xii, 244p. (C). 1987. lib. bdg. 89.25 (*0-89925-085-8*) Mouton.
Ramat, Paolo, et al, eds. The History of Linguistics in Italy. LC 86-17407. (Studies in the History of Linguistics: Vol. 33). x, 364p. 1986. 84.00 (*90-272-4515-0*) J Benjamins Pubng Co.
— Linguistic Reconstruction & Indo-European Syntax: Proceedings of the Colloquium of the "Indogermanische Gesellschaft", University of Pavia, 6-7 September 1979. (Current Issues in Linguistic Theory Ser.: No 19). viii, 263p. 1980. 59.00 (*90-272-3512-0*) J Benjamins Pubng Co.
Ramat, Paolo, jt. auth. see Bernini, Giuliano.
Ramat, Paolo, jt. ed. see Harris, Martin.
Ramaurthy, V. & Schanze, Kirk S., eds. Organic Photochemistry Vol. 1: Molecular & Supramolecular Photochemistry. LC 97-186938. 608p. 1997. text 195.00 (*0-8247-0012-0*) Dekker.
Ramaurti, Ravi. State-Owned Enterprises in High Technology Industries: Studies in India & Brazil. LC 85-30751. 319p. 1987. 69.50 (*0-275-92156-5*, C2156, Praeger Pubs) Greenwood.
Ramawat, K. G. & Merillon, J. M., eds. Biotechnology: Secondary Metabolites. LC 99-40283. (Illus.). 390p. 1999. text 49.50 (*1-57808-057-6*) Science Pubs.
Ramaya, Shona. Flute. 1999. pap. 7.95 (*0-14-012394-6*, Viking) Viking Penguin.
Ramayya, A. V. & Greiner, Walter. Nuclear Physics of Our Times. 584p. 1993. text 114.00 (*981-02-1358-1*) World Scientific Pub.
Ramayya, N. Narasimha. Linguistic Entropy in Othello of Shakespeare. LC 93-910449. 95p. (C). 1998. pap. 63.00 (*81-85880-22-0*, Pub. by Print Hse) St Mut.
Ramazani, Jahan. Poetry of Mourning: The Modern Elegy from Hardy to Heaney. LC 93-31581. 436p. 1994. pap. text 16.95 (*0-226-70340-1*) U Ch Pr.
— Poetry of Mourning: The Modern Elegy from Hardy to Heaney. LC 93-31581. 419p. 1995. lib. bdg. 42.00 (*0-226-70339-8*) U Ch Pr.
Ramazani, Mohammad. 600 Mulla Nasreddin Tales: 600 Dastan-E Mulla Nasreddin. LC 97-2753. (Popular Persian Texts Ser.: Vol. 1). (PER.). 1997. reprint ed. pap. 16.00 (*0-936347-09-0*) IBEX.
Ramazani, Mwanvuwa A. African Names: Claiming Your True Heritage. LC 96-90344. (Illus.). 72p. (Orig.). 1995. pap. 9.95 (*0-9647075-0-0*) Montecom Pubng.
Ramazani, Nesta. Persian Cooking: A Table of Exotic Delights. LC 96-45556. (Illus.). 320p. 1997. reprint ed. pap. 17.95 (*0-936347-77-5*) IBEX.
Ramazani, Rouhollah K. Beyond the Arab-Israeli Settlement: New Directions for U. S. Policy in the Middle East. LC 77-87564. (Foreign Policy Reports). 69p. 1977. 11.95 (*0-89549-006-4*) Inst Foreign Policy Anal.
— The Foreign Policy of Iran: A Developing Nation in World Affairs, 1500-1941. LC 66-12469. 349p. 1966. reprint ed. pap. 108.20 (*0-608-05906-4*, 206624100007) Bks Demand.
— Iran's Foreign Policy, 1941-1973: A Study of Foreign Policy in Modernizing Nations. LC 74-16467. 523p. 1975. reprint ed. pap. 162.20 (*0-608-05907-2*, 206624200007) Bks Demand.
— Middle East & the European Common Market. LC 64-13718. 175p. reprint ed. 54.30 (*0-8357-9810-0*, 201365800086) Bks Demand.
— The Persian Gulf: Iran's Role. LC 72-77262. (Illus.). 175p. reprint ed. pap. 54.30 (*0-608-30879-X*, 200229100012) Bks Demand.
— The Persian Gulf & the Strait of Hormuz. (International Straits of the World Ser.: No. 3). 200p. 1979. 35.00 (*0-685-04604-4*) Kluwer Academic.
— Revolutionary Iran: Challenge & Response in the Middle East. LC 86-45440. 327p. 1986. reprint ed. pap. 101.40 (*0-608-07388-1*, 206761500009) Bks Demand.
Ramazani, Rouhollah K., ed. Iran's Revolution: The Search for Consensus. LC 89-7516. (Illus.). 160p. 1990. 29.95 (*0-253-34796-3*); pap. 9.95 (*0-253-20548-4*, MB-548) Ind U Pr.
Ramazani, Rouhollah K., et al. The Gulf Cooperation Council: Record & Analysis. LC 87-37170. (Illus.). 256p. 1988. text 45.00 (*0-8139-1148-6*) U Pr of Va.
Ramazanoglu, Caroline. Feminism & the Contradictions of Oppression. 196p. 1989. 49.95 (*0-415-02835-3*) Routledge.
— Feminism & the Contradictions of Oppression. 178p. (C). 1989. pap. 22.99 (*0-415-02836-1*) Routledge.
Ramazanoglu, Caroline, ed. Up Against Foucault: Explorations of Some Tensions Between Foucault & Feminism. LC 93-9861. 304p. (C). (gr. 13). 1993. pap. 24.99 (*0-415-05011-1*) Routledge.
Ramazanoglu, Gulseren. Turkish Embroidery. 2nd ed. (Illus.). 104p. 1987. reprint ed. pap. 13.95 (*0-442-26799-1*, Pub. by Ramazanoglu Yayinlari) Bosphorus Bks.
Ramazanoglu, Huseyin, ed. Turkey in the World Capitalist System: A Study of Industrialisation, Power & Class. 300p. 1985. text 79.95 (*0-566-05049-8*, Pub. by Dartmth Pub) Ashgate Pub Co.
Ramazanov, Zakir, et al. New Secret of Effective Natural Stress Weight Management: Using Rhodiola Rosea & Rhododendron Caucasirum. LC 99-71262. (Illus.). 88p. 1999. pap. 8.95 (*1-884820-45-X*) SAFE GOODS.
Rambachan, Anantanand. Bharata: Love & Justice in the Ramayana. 76p. (Orig.). 1993. pap. 5.00 (*0-9634164-3-X*) Vijnana Pubns.
— Gitamrtam: The Essential Teachings of Bhagavadgita. (C). 1993. pap. 9.50 (*81-208-1167-4*, Pub. by Motilal Bnarsidass) S Asia.
***Rambachan, Anantanand.** Gitanidarsana: Similes of the Bhagavadgita. 75p. 1999. pap. 100.00 (*81-208-1695-1*, Pub. by Motilal Bnarsidass) St Mut.
Rambachan, Anantanand. Hanuman: The Devotee of God. 85p. 1991. pap. 5.00 (*0-9634164-2-1*) Vijnana Pubns.
— Hanuman: The Messenger of God. 94p. 1990. pap. 5.00 (*0-9634164-1-3*) Vijnana Pubns.
— The Hindu Vision. (C). 1992. text 7.00 (*81-208-1059-7*, Pub. by Motilal Bnarsidass) S Asia.
— The Limits of Scripture: Vivekananda's Reinterpretation of the Authority of the Vedas. LC 93-44277. 186p. 1993. text 31.00 (*0-8248-1542-4*) UH Pr.
— Love & Truth in the Ramayana of Tulsidas. 72p. 1989. pap. 5.00 (*0-9634164-0-5*) Vijnana Pubns.
— Rama Darshan: The Valmiki - Rama Dialogue. (Ramayana Ser.). 94p. (Orig.). 1995. pap. write for info. (*0-9634164-5-6*) Vijnana Pubns.
— Rama Gita: The Dialogues of Rama. 100p. 1994. pap. 5.00 (*0-9634164-4-8*) Vijnana Pubns.
Rambali, Paul. Boulangerie: The Craft & Culture of Baking in France. (Illus.). 180p. 1998. text 20.00 (*0-7881-5272-6*) DIANE Pub.
— In the Cities & Jungles of Brazil. LC 93-30666. 1995. 23.00 (*0-8050-3079-4*); pap. 12.95 (*0-8050-3078-6*) H Holt & Co.
Rambaud, Alfred N. History of Russia from the Earliest Time to 1882, 3 vols. enl. ed. Dole, Nathan H., ed. Lang, Leonora B., tr. LC 73-124766. (Illus.). reprint ed. 205.00 (*0-404-05230-4*) AMS Pr.
Rambaud, J. P. & LaMont, J. T., eds. Updates on Clostridium Difficile. (Illus.). 145p. 1996. 80.00 (*2-287-59639-9*, Pub. by Spl France Editions) Spr-Verlag.
***Rambaud, Patrick.** The Battle: A Novel. Hobson, Will, tr. LC 99-86344. 320p. 2000. 25.00 (*0-8021-1662-0*, Pub. by Grove-Atltic) Publishers Group.
Rambeau. The Morgan Bay Mysteries: Low Vocabulary, High Interest Level. large type ed. Incl. Mystery of the Midnight Visitor. (gr. 3-10). (*0-89064-084-X*); Mystery of the Morgan Castle. (gr. 2-9). (*0-89064-083-1*); (J). reprint ed. write for info. (*0-318-66044-X*) NAVH.
Rambeau, John & Rambeau, Nancy. The Mystery of Morgan Castle. (Morgan Bay Mysteries Ser.). 10.00 (*0-614-30535-7*) NAVH.
— The Mystery of the Marble Angle. (Morgan Bay Mysteries Ser.). 10.00 (*0-614-30532-2*) NAVH.
— The Mystery of the Midnight Visiter. (Morgan Bay Mysteries Ser.). 10.00 (*0-614-30533-0*) NAVH.
— The Mystery of the Missing Marlin. (Morgan Bay Mysteries Ser.). 10.00 (*0-614-30534-9*) NAVH.
Rambeau, Nancy, jt. auth. see Rambeau, John.
Rambeaud, J. J. & Vincent, F., eds. Local Prostatic Carcinoma. (Contributions to Oncology Ser.: Vol. 47). (Illus.). viii, 146p. 1995. 121.75 (*3-8055-5973-9*) S Karger.
Rambeck, Richard. Anfernee (Penny) Hardaway. LC 96-14497. (Sports Superstars Ser.). (Illus.). 24p. (J). (gr. 2-6). 1996. lib. bdg. 21.36 (*1-56766-315-X*) Childs World.
— Babe Ruth. (Superstrellas Deportes Ser.). (SPA., Illus.). 32p. (J). (gr. 2-6). 1992. lib. bdg. 21.36 (*1-56766-054-1*) Childs World.
— Barry Bonds. LC 95-6460. (Sports Superstars Ser.). (Illus.). 24p. (J). (gr. 2-6). 1995. lib. bdg. 21.36 (*1-56766-201-3*) Childs World.
— Bonnie Blair. LC 95-6464. (Sports Superstars Ser.). (Illus.). 24p. (J). (gr. 2-6). 1995. lib. bdg. 21.36 (*1-56766-186-6*) Childs World.
— Brett Favre. LC 97-11613. (Sports Superstars Ser.). (Illus.). 24p. (J). (gr. 2-6). 1997. lib. bdg. 21.36 (*1-56766-458-X*) Childs World.
— Cal Ripken, Jr. (Sports Superstars Ser.). (Illus.). 32p. (J). (gr. 2-6). 1992. lib. bdg. 21.36 (*0-89565-867-4*) Childs World.
— Dan Marino. LC 96-7670. (Sports Superstars Ser.). (Illus.). 24p. (J). (gr. 2-6). 1996. lib. bdg. 21.36 (*1-56766-313-3*) Childs World.
— Emmitt Smith. LC 97-9221. (Sports Superstars Ser.). (Illus.). 24p. (J). (gr. 2-6). 1997. lib. bdg. 21.36 (*1-56766-408-3*) Childs World.
— Grant Hill. LC 97-2520. (Sports Superstars Ser.). (Illus.). 24p. (J). (gr. 2-6). 1997. lib. bdg. 21.36 (*1-56766-409-1*) Childs World.
— Greg Maddux. LC 96-14644. (Sports Superstars Ser.). (Illus.). 24p. (J). (gr. 2-6). 1996. lib. bdg. 21.36 (*1-56766-314-1*) Childs World.
— Hakeem Olajuwon. LC 95-5625. (Sports Superstars Ser.). (Illus.). 24p. (J). (gr. 2-6). 1995. lib. bdg. 21.36 (*1-56766-200-5*) Childs World.
— The History of the Anaheim Angels. (Baseball Ser.). (Illus.). 32p. (YA). (gr. 3-12). 1998. lib. bdg. 21.30 (*0-88682-901-1*, Creat Educ) Creative Co.
— The History of the Baltimore Orioles. (Baseball Ser.). (Illus.). 32p. (YA). (gr. 3 up). 1998. lib. bdg. 21.30 (*0-88682-899-6*, Creat Educ) Creative Co.
— The History of the Boston Red Sox. (Baseball Ser.). (Illus.). 32p. (YA). (gr. 3 up). 1998. lib. bdg. 21.30 (*0-88682-900-3*, Creat Educ) Creative Co.
— The History of the Chicago White Sox. (Baseball Ser.). (Illus.). 32p. (YA). (gr. 3 up). 1998. lib. bdg. 21.30 (*0-88682-904-6*, Creat Educ) Creative Co.
— The History of the Cleveland Indians. (Baseball Ser.). (Illus.). 32p. (YA). (gr. 3 up). 1998. lib. bdg. 21.30 (*0-88682-906-2*, Creat Educ) Creative Co.
— The History of the Detroit Tigers. (Baseball Ser.). (Illus.). 32p. (YA). (gr. 3 up). 1998. lib. bdg. 21.30 (*0-88682-908-9*, Creat Educ) Creative Co.
— The History of the Kansas City Royals. (Baseball Ser.). (Illus.). 32p. (YA). (gr. 3 up). 1998. lib. bdg. 21.30 (*0-88682-911-9*, Creat Educ) Creative Co.
— The History of the Milwaukee Brewers. (Baseball Ser.). (Illus.). 32p. (YA). (gr. 3 up). 1998. lib. bdg. 21.30 (*0-88682-913-5*, Creat Educ) Creative Co.
— The History of the Minnesota Twins. (Baseball Ser.). (Illus.). 32p. (YA). (gr. 3 up). 1998. lib. bdg. 21.30 (*0-88682-914-3*, Creat Educ) Creative Co.
***Rambeck, Richard.** The History of the New York Yankees. (Baseball Ser.). (Illus.). 32p. (YA). (gr. 3 up). 1998. lib. bdg. 21.30 (*0-88682-918-6*, Creat Educ) Creative Co.
Rambeck, Richard. The History of the Oakland Athletics. (Baseball Ser.). (Illus.). 32p. (YA). (gr. 3 up). 1998. lib. bdg. 21.30 (*0-88682-919-4*, Creat Educ) Creative Co.
— The History of the Texas Rangers. (Baseball Ser.). (Illus.). 32p. (YA). (gr. 3 up). 1998. lib. bdg. 21.30 (*0-88682-927-5*, Creat Educ) Creative Co.
— The History of the Toronto Blue Jays. (Baseball Ser.). (Illus.). 32p. (YA). (gr. 3 up). 1998. lib. bdg. 21.30 (*0-88682-928-3*, Creat Educ) Creative Co.
— Jackie Joyner-Kersee. (Sports Superstars Ser.). (Illus.). 24p. (J). (gr. 2-6). 1996. lib. bdg. 21.36 (*1-56766-271-4*) Childs World.
— Jerry Rice. LC 95-6463. (Sports Superstars Ser.). (Illus.). 24p. (J). (gr. 2-6). 1995. lib. bdg. 21.36 (*1-56766-204-8*) Childs World.
— Jim Abbott. LC 92-43044. (Sports Superstars Ser.). (Illus.). 32p. (J). (gr. 2-6). 1994. lib. bdg. 21.36 (*1-56766-072-X*) Childs World.
— Karl Malone. (Superstrellas Deportes Ser.). (SPA., Illus.). 32p. (J). (gr. 2-6). 1992. lib. bdg. 21.36 (*1-56766-055-X*) Childs World.
— Kirby Puckett. (Superstrellas Deportes Ser.). (SPA., Illus.). 32p. (J). (gr. 2-6). 1993. lib. bdg. 21.36 (*1-56766-053-3*) Childs World.
— Kirby Puckett. (Sports Superstars Ser.). (Illus.). 32p. (J). (gr. 2-6). 1993. lib. bdg. 21.36 (*0-89565-960-3*) Childs World.
— Kristi Yamaguchi. LC 97-12961. (Sports Superstars Ser.). (Illus.). 24p. (J). 1997. lib. bdg. 21.36 (*1-56766-411-3*) Childs World.
— Lou Gehrig. LC 92-40673. (Sports Superstars Ser.). (Illus.). 32p. (J). (gr. 2-6). 1994. lib. bdg. 21.36 (*1-56766-073-8*) Childs World.
— Martina Hingis. LC 97-44094. (Illus.). (J). 1998. lib. bdg. 21.36 (*1-56766-519-5*) Childs World.
— Mia Hamm. LC 97-42443. 24P32p. (J). 1998. lib. bdg. 21.36 (*1-56766-523-3*) Childs World.
— Michael Johnson. LC 97-5466. (Sports Superstars Ser.). 24p. (J). (gr. 2-6). 1997. lib. bdg. 21.36 (*1-56766-460-1*) Childs World.
— Michael Johnson. (Sports Superstars Ser.). (Illus.). 24p. (J). 1997. lib. bdg. 21.36 (*1-56766-413-X*, 6413X) Childs World.
— Michael Jordan. LC 97-44096. (Illus.). 24[00d0]32p. (J). 1998. lib. bdg. 21.36 (*1-56766-520-9*) Childs World.
— Michelle Kwan. LC 97-12956. (Sports Superstars Ser.). 24p. (J). (gr. 2-6). 1997. lib. bdg. 21.36 (*1-56766-461-X*) Childs World.
— Michelle Kwan. (Illus.). 24p. 1997. lib. bdg. 21.36 (*1-56766-412-1*) Childs World.
— Monica Seles. LC 96-14171. (Illus.). 24p. (J). (gr. 2-6). 1996. lib. bdg. 21.36 (*1-56766-312-5*) Childs World.
— Patrick Ewing. LC 92-11508. (Sports Superstars Ser.). (Illus.). 32p. (J). (gr. 2-6). 1994. lib. bdg. 21.36 (*0-89565-967-0*); lib. bdg. 21.36 (*1-56766-112-2*) Childs World.
— Pete Sampras. LC 95-42610. (Sports Superstars Ser.). (Illus.). 24p. (J). (gr. 2-6). 1996. lib. bdg. 21.36 (*1-56766-262-5*) Childs World.
— Rebecca Lobo. LC 97-52771. (Illus.). (J). 1998. lib. bdg. 21.36 (*1-56766-524-1*) Childs World.
— Shaquille O'Neal. LC 95-6462. (Sports Superstars Ser.). (Illus.). 24p. (J). (gr. 2-6). 1995. lib. bdg. 21.36 (*1-56766-199-8*) Childs World.
— Steve Young. (Sports Superstars Ser.). (Illus.). 24p. (J). (gr. 2-6). 1996. lib. bdg. 21.36 (*1-56766-264-1*) Childs World.
— Tara Lipinski. LC 98-6785. (Illus.). 24[00d0]32p. (J). 1998. lib. bdg. 21.36 (*1-56766-522-5*) Childs World.
— Tiger Woods. LC 98-26368. (Sports Superstars Ser.). (Illus.). (J). 1998. lib. bdg. 21.36 (*1-56766-521-7*, 65217) Childs World.
— The U. S. Women's Gymnastics Team. LC 97-9040. (Sports Superstars Ser.). (Illus.). 24p. (J). (gr. 2-6). 1997. lib. bdg. 21.36 (*1-56766-410-5*) Childs World.
— Wayne Gretsky. LC 95-5624. (Sports Superstars Ser.). (Illus.). 24p. (J). (gr. 2-6). 1995. lib. bdg. 21.36 (*1-56766-203-X*) Childs World.
Ramberg, Bennett. Nuclear Energy at War: The Implications of Israel's Reactor Strike. (CISA Working Papers: No. 34). 34p. (Orig.). 1992. pap. 15.00 (*0-86682-045-0*) Ctr Intl Relations.
Ramberg, Bennett, ed. Arms Control Without Negotiation: From the Cold War to the New World Order. LC 93-9339. 285p. 1993. lib. bdg. 48.00 (*1-55587-376-6*) L Rienner.
Ramberg, Bennett, jt. auth. see Intriligator, Michael D.
Ramberg, Bennett, jt. ed. see Thomas, Raju G.
Ramberg, Christina. Christina Ramberg: A Retrospective: 1968-1988. (Illus.). 32p. 1988. pap. 15.00 (*0-941548-13-9*) Ren Soc U Chi.
Ramberg, Ivar B. & Neumann, Else-Ragnhild, eds. Tectonics & Geophysics of Continental Rifts. (NATO Advanced Study Institute Ser.: No. 37). 1978. text 135.00 (*90-277-0867-3*) Kluwer Academic.
Ramberg, Ivar B., jt. ed. see Neumann, Else-Ragnhild.
Ramberg, Jan. Incoterms in the Era of Electronic Data Interchange. (Forum Internationale Ser.: No. 13). 1989. 24.00 (*90-6544-430-0*) Kluwer Law Intl.
Ramberg, Jan. International Commercial Transactions. 512p. 1998. pap. 167.50 (*91-39-20062-0*, Pub. by Almqvist Wiksell) Coronet Bks.
— International Commercial Transactions. 512p. 1998. pap. text 149.95 (*92-842-1245-6*, 588) ICC Pub.
***Ramberg, Jan.** International Commercial Transactions. 512p. 1998. pap. 105.00 (*90-411-9656-0*) Kluwer Law Intl.
Rambert, Francis. Claude Vasconi: Buildings & Projects 1980-1997. LC 98-123441. (GER., Illus.). 176p. 1998. pap. 45.00 (*3-7643-5632-4*, Pub. by Birkhauser) Princeton Arch.
Rambert, Judy. All New Beautiful Braids. (Illus.). 64p. 1993. spiral bd. 5.98 (*1-56173-231-1*, 3612102) Pubns Intl Ltd.
— Beautiful Braids. 1990. pap. 5.98 (*0-88176-925-8*) Pubns Intl Ltd.
***Rambirez Cordova, Antonio.** Renovada Penumbra. LC 00-23315. (Coleccibon Sinsonte Ser.). 2000. pap. write for info. (*0-8477-0097-6*) U of PR Pr.
***Rambirez Kidd, Josbe E.** Alterity & Identity in Israel: The [Ger] in the Old Testament. LC 99-36918. (Beihefte Zur Zeitschrift Fhur Die Alttestamentliche Wissenschaft Ser.). 1999. 82.60 (*3-11-016625-9*) De Gruyter.
Rambisoon, Amar. The Essentials of Successful Evangelism. LC 98-91409. 78p. 1998. pap. 10.00 (*1-57502-792-5*, PO2190) Morris Pubng.
— Jumping Jehoshaphat: The Ups & Downs in Leadership. 116p. 1998. pap. 5.00 (*1-57502-901-4*, PO2474) Morris Pubng.
Rambisoon, Amar B. The Unfinished Man. 163p. 1998. pap. 8.00 (*1-55630-888-4*) Brentwood Comm.
Ramble, Charles, jt. ed. see Rustomji, N. K.
Rambler. Guide to Florida. LC 64-66300. (Floridiana Facsimile & Reprint Ser.). (Illus.). 197p. 1964. reprint ed. 19.95 (*0-8130-0193-5*) U Press Fla.
Rambler, Mitchell B., et al, eds. Global Ecology: Towards a Science of the Biosphere. 204p. 1989. text 52.00 (*0-12-576890-7*) Acad Pr.
Rambler's Assn. Staff. The Ramblers Yearbook & Accommodation Guide, 1996. 219p. 1996. pap. text 19.95 (*0-900613-79-3*, Pub. by W Foulsham) Trans-Atl Phila.
Rambo, A. Terry. Primitive Polluters: Semang Impact on the Malaysian Tropical Rain Forest Ecosystem. (Anthropological Papers Ser.: No. 76). (Illus.). 104p. (Orig.). 1985. pap. 8.00 (*0-915703-04-1*) U Mich Mus Anthro.

Rambo, A. Terry, et al, eds. The Challenges of Highland Development in Vietnam. LC 95-41204. 1995. write for info. (*0-86638-176-7*) EW Ctr HI.

— Ethnic Diversity & the Control of Natural Resources in Southeast Asia. LC 87-62020. (Michigan Papers on South & Southeast Asia: No. 32). (Illus.). 320p. 1987. 31.95 (*0-89148-043-9*); pap. 17.95 (*0-89148-044-7*) Ctr S&SE Asian.

Rambo, A. Terry & Gillogly, Kathleen, eds. Profiles in Cultural Evolution: Papers from a Conference in Honor of Elman R. Service. LC 90-25676. (Anthropological Papers Ser.: No. 85). xviii, 450p. (Orig.). 1991. pap. 20.00 (*0-915703-23-8*) U Mich Mus Anthro.

Rambo, A. Terry, jt. ed. see Le, Trong Cuc.

Rambo, Anne H., et al. Practicing Therapy: Exercises for Growing Therapists. 180p. (C). 1993. pap. 14.95 (*0-393-70161-1*) Norton.

Rambo, Beverly J. Adaptation Nursing: Assessment & Intervention. (Illus.). 1984. teacher ed. write for info. (*0-7216-2031-0*, W B Saunders Co) Harcrt Hlth Sci Grp.

— Adaptation Nursing: Assessment & Intervention. (Illus.). 432p. 1984. pap. text 52.00 (*0-7216-1048-X*, W B Saunders Co) Harcrt Hlth Sci Grp.

Rambo, David R. Our Hope for the Future. (Christian Living Ser.). 1996. pap. 1.59 (*0-87509-670-0*) Chr Pubns.

Rambo, Dorothy, ed. see Ceasor, Ebraska D.

Rambo, Elizabeth L. Colonial Ireland in Medieval English Literature. LC 93-46784. 1995. 35.00 (*0-945636-61-X*) Susquehanna U Pr.

Rambo, Karen. Tacos y Mas. Haralson, Carol, ed. (Y Mas Ser.). (Illus.). 80p. (Orig.). 1999. pap. 12.95 (*1-891795-04-X*) Resort Gifts.

Rambo, Karen & Haralson, Carol. Asada: Flavors from a Southwestern Grill. LC 99-64719. (Y Mas Ser.). (Illus.). 96p. 2000. pap. 13.95 (*1-891795-05-8*) Resort Gifts.

Rambo, Karl, jt. auth. see Nunley, Michael.

Rambo, Lewis R. Understanding Religious Conversion. 1995. pap. 16.00 (*0-300-06515-9*) Yale U Pr.

Rambo, Marge. Granny's Pearls: Poetry, Prose & Prayer. (Illus.). 122p. (Orig.). 1997. pap. 14.50 (*0-9657852-0-3*) Whispering Pines.

Rambo, Mary E., jt. auth. see Rambo, Simmeon B.

Rambo, Ralph. Pen & Inklings: Nostalgic Views of Santa Clara County. Muller, Kathleen & Jamison, Roberta, eds. (Illus.). 192p. 1984. 22.95 (*0-914139-01-0*) Hist San Jose.

Rambo, Sarah. Private Pilot - Airplane. LC 82-21299. (Illus.). 194p. 1983. pap. 24.95 (*0-8138-1382-4*) Iowa St U Pr.

Rambo, Simmeon B. & Rambo, Mary E. The Rambo Heritage. (Illus.). 188p. 1983. 25.00 (*0-89308-385-2*, BFH 17) Southern Hist Pr.

Rambo, William M. The Student's Textbook of Surgery. (Illus.). 400p. 1995. pap. 22.95 (*0-86542-485-3*) Blackwell Sci.

— The Student's Textbook of Surgery. LC 95-12316. (Medical Bks.). 1995. pap. write for info. (*0-393-71032-7*) Norton.

Rambold, Gerhard. A Monograph of the Saxicolous Lecideoid Lichens of Australia: Excl. Tasmania. Wirth, Volkmar et al, eds. (Bibliotheca Lichenologica: Vol. 34). (GER., Illus.). 345p. 1989. pap. 77.00 (*3-443-58013-0*, Pub. by Gebruder Borntraeger) Balogh.

Rambold, Gerhard & Triebel, Dagmar. The Interlecanoralean Associations. Wirth, Volkmar et al, eds. (Bibliotheca Lichenologica: Vol. 48). (GER., Illus.). 201p. 1992. pap. 53.00 (*3-443-58027-0*, Pub. by Gebruder Borntraeger) Balogh.

Rambon, Sheppard. School Dropouts: Everybody's Problem. Lewis, Anne & Usdan, Michael D., eds. 58p. (Orig.). 1986. pap. 7.50 (*0-937846-91-0*) Inst Educ Lead.

Rambousek, Walter H. Indian Agriculture Between Isolation & Integration: A Theoretical Review & an Analysis of the Economic & Social Geography of Four Villages in South India. (European University Studies: Asian & African Studies: Ser. 27, Vol. 3). 120p. 1977. pap. 28.00 (*3-261-02981-1*) P Lang Pubng.

Rambova, N., jt. ed. see Piankoff, A.

Rambow, Gunter. Gunther Rambow Students. 1998. 45.00 (*3-89322-345-2*, Pub. by Edition Cantz) Dist Art Pubs.

Rambow, Owen, jt. ed. see Abeille, Anne.

Ramboz, Ina W. Christmas Songs in Spanish. (SPA.). 32p. (J). (gr. 6-9). 1992. pap. 7.95 (*0-8442-7097-0*, Passprt Bks) NTC Contemp Pub Co.

— Christmas Songs in Spanish. (SPA.). 1985. 13.15 (*0-606-01253-2*, Pub. by Turtleback) Demco.

Ramboz, Ina W., ed. Spanish Verbs & Essentials of Grammar. LC 98-54289. 136p. (C). 1988. pap. 7.95 (*0-8442-7214-0*, 72140, Pub. by S Thomes Pubs) St Mut.

Rambsel, Yacov. His Name Is Jesus. LC 98-50159. 283p. 1999. pap. 6.99 (*0-8499-4096-6*) Word Pub.

— His Name Is Jesus: The Mysterious Yeshua Codes. 278p. 1997. pap. 12.99 (*0-921714-42-4*, Pub. by Fon3tier Res) Spring Arbor Dist.

— Su Nombre es Jesus.Tr. of His Name is Jesus. (SPA.). 261p. 1999. pap. 10.99 (*0-88368-522-1*) Whitaker Hse.

— Yeshua: The Name of Jesus Revealed in the Old Testament. 173p. pap. 11.95 (*0-921714-34-3*, Pub. by Fon3tier Res) Spring Arbor Dist.

Rambsel, Yacov A. Yeshua. LC 97-11905. (SPA.). 171p. 1997. pap. 10.99 (*0-88368-491-8*) Whitaker Hse.

***Rambsel, Yacov A.** Yeshua. LC 97-47662. 1998. mass mkt. 6.99 (*0-8499-4097-4*) Word Pub.

Rambsel, Yacov A. Yeshua: The Hebrew Factor LC 97-121591. xxi, 173 p. 1996. write for info. (*1-56043-582-8*) Destiny Image.

Rambusch, Viggo B. Lighting the Liturgy. (Meeting House Essays Ser.: No. 7). 62p. (Orig.). 1994. pap. 6.00 (*1-56854-061-2*, LITLIT) Liturgy Tr Pubns.

Rambuss, Richard. Closet Devotions. LC 98-19598. 1998. 49.95 (*0-8223-2180-7*) Duke.

— Closet Devotions. LC 98-19598. (Illus.). 1998. pap. 17.95 (*0-8223-2197-1*) Duke.

— Spenser's Secret Career. LC 92-8539. (Cambridge Studies in Renaissance Literature & Culture: No. 3). (Illus.). 180p. (C). 1993. text 54.95 (*0-521-41663-9*) Cambridge U Pr.

***Ramc, Gerardus.** Octopus Magnus: An Allegoric Play. 2000. pap. text 14.95 (*1-889534-42-0*) Jay St Pubs.

Ramchand, Gillian C. Aspect & Predication: The Semantics of Argument Structure. LC 97-164757. (Illus.). 260p. 1997. text 55.00 (*0-19-823651-4*) OUP.

Ramchandani, R. R., ed. India Africa Economic Relations, in the Context of Economic Co-Operation among Developing Countries, Vol. 2. (Illus.). xii, 380p. 1990. 33.00 (*81-85163-12-X*, Pub. by Kalinga) Nataraj Bks.

— India Africa Relations, Vol. 1: Issues & Policy Options. vi, 405p. 1990. 37.00 (*81-85163-11-1*, Pub. by Kalinga) Nataraj Bks.

Ramchandani, R. R., jt. auth. see Ali, Shanti S.

Ramchandani, R. R., jt. ed. see Ali, Shanti S.

Ramchandani, Vijit, jt. auth. see Gilbertsen, Beth.

Ramcharan, B. G. The Concept & Present Status of the International Protection of Human Rights. (C). 1989. lib. bdg. 223.50 (*90-247-3759-1*) Kluwer Academic.

— Humanitarian Good Offices in International Law. 1983. lib. bdg. 111.00 (*90-247-2805-3*) Kluwer Academic.

— The International Conference on the Former Yugoslavia: Official Papers, 2 vols. LC 97-19437. 1736p. 1997. 541.00 (*90-411-0437-2*) Kluwer Law Intl.

— The International Conference on the Former Yugoslavia: Official Papers. LC 97-19437. 1997. write for info. (*90-411-0436-4*); write for info. (*90-411-0429-1*) Kluwer Law Intl.

— International Law & Fact-Finding in the Field of Human Rights. 1982. lib. bdg. 119.00 (*90-247-3042-2*) Kluwer Academic.

— The International Law & Practice of Early-Warning & Preventive Diplomacy: The Emerging Global Watch. (C). 1991. lib. bdg. 93.00 (*0-7923-1338-0*) Kluwer Academic.

— The International Law Commission. 1977. pap. text 75.50 (*90-247-1984-4*) Kluwer Academic.

— Keeping Faith with the United Nations. 354p. (C). 62.50 (*90-247-3516-5*) UN.

Ramcharan, B. G., ed. The Principle of Legality in International Human Rights Institutions: Selected Legal Opinions, Vol. RAWA 3. LC 97-12116. (Raoul Wallenberg Institute Human Rights Guides Ser.). 1997. 225.00 (*90-411-0299-X*) Kluwer Law Intl.

— The Right to Life in International Law. 1985. lib. bdg. 153.00 (*90-247-3074-0*) Kluwer Academic.

Ramcharan, Paul, et al, eds. Empowerment in Everyday Life: Learning Disability. LC 97-118540. 280p. 1996. pap. 29.95 (*1-85302-382-5*, Pub. by Jessica Kingsley) Taylor & Francis.

Ramcharan, R. G., ed. Human Rights: Thirty Years After the Universal Declaration. 1979. lib. bdg. 101.00 (*90-247-2145-8*) Kluwer Academic.

Ramdahl, jt. auth. see Bjorseth, Alf.

Ramdas, Swami. In Quest of God: The Saga of an Extraordinary Pilgrimage. LC 94-12042. (Swami Ramdas Pilgrimage Ser.: Vol. 1). 170p. 1994. reprint ed. pap. 14.00 (*1-884997-01-5*) Blue Dove Pr.

— In the Vision of God Vol. I: The Continuing Saga of an Extraordinary Pilgrimage. LC 94-17493. 273p. 1995. pap. 14.95 (*1-884997-03-1*) Blue Dove Pr.

— In the Vision of God Vol. 2: The Conclusion to the Saga of an Extraordinary Pilgrimage, Vol. II. LC 94-17493. 262p. (Orig.). 1995. reprint ed. pap. 14.95 (*1-884997-05-8*) Blue Dove Pr.

Ramdass, jt. ed. see Gopalakrishnan, K. C.

Ramdeo, Radha. Xandria. LC 98-89511. 375p. 1998. text 25.00 (*0-7388-0221-2*); pap. text 15.00 (*0-7388-0222-0*) Xlibris Corp.

***Ramdin, Ron.** Arising from Bondage: A History of the Indo-Caribbean People. LC 99-89313. 1999. text 40.00 (*0-8147-7548-9*) NYU Pr.

— Reimaging Britain: Five Hundred Years of Black & Asian History. LC 99-34705. 352p. 2000. 69.95 (*0-7453-1600-X*); pap. 22.50 (*0-7453-1599-2*, Pub. by Pluto GBR) Stylus Pub VA.

Ramdohr, Paul. Ore Minerals & Intergrowth. 1980. 97.00 (*0-08-011635-3*, Pergamon Pr) Elsevier.

Ramdohr, Paul & Ingerson, D. Ore Minerals & Their Inter-Growths Vol. 1: English Translation of 4th Edition, 2 vols., Set. 2nd ed. LC 79-40745. (International Series in Earth Science: Vol. 35). (Illus.). 1269p. 1980. 203.00 (*0-08-023801-7*, Pub. by Pergamon Repr) Franklin.

Rame, Franca & Fo, Dario. A Woman Alone & Other Plays. Hood, Stuart, ed. Hanna, Gillian et al, trs. (Methuen Modern Plays Ser.). 206p. (Orig.). (C). 1991. pap. 16.95 (*0-413-64030-2*, AO562, Methuen Drama) Methn.

***Rame, Franca, et al.** Franca Rame: A Woman on Stage. Valeri, Walter, ed. Jenkins, Ron, tr. (Crossings Ser.: Vol. 6).Tr. of Sesso? Grazie Tanto per Gradire. 175p. 1999. pap. 15.00 (*1-884419-25-9*) Bordighera.

Rameau-Collman, Marthamarie. Ballads & Other Island Things. (Illus.). 100p. (Orig.). (YA). (gr. 5 up). 1992. pap. 6.00 (*0-9631903-0-X*) M R Collman.

Rameau, Jean-Philippe. Code de Musique Pratique. fac. ed. (Monuments of Music & Music Literature in Facsimile, II Ser.: Vol. 5). 1965. lib. bdg. 50.00 (*0-8450-2205-9*) Broude.

— Complete Works for Solo Keyboard. 144p. pap. 10.95 (*0-486-27847-6*) Dover.

— Demonstration du Principe de L'Harmonie. fac. ed. (Monuments of Music & Music Literature in Facsimile Ser., Series II: Vol. 4). (Illus.). 1965. lib. bdg. 35.00 (*0-8450-2204-0*) Broude.

— Erreurs sur la Musique Dans l'Encyclpedie. fac. ed. (Monuments of Music & Music Literature in Facsimile, II Ser.: Vol. 137). (FRE., Illus.). 1969. lib. bdg. 32.50 (*0-8450-2337-3*) Broude.

— Generation Harmonique. fac. ed. (Monuments of Music & Music Literature in Facsimile, II Ser.: Vol. 6). (Illus.). 1966. lib. bdg. 40.00 (*0-8450-2206-7*) Broude.

— Nouveau Systeme de Musique Theorique. fac. ed. (Monuments of Music & Music Literature in Facsimile, II Ser.: Vol. 7). (Illus.). 1965. lib. bdg. 35.00 (*0-8450-2207-5*) Broude.

— Nouvelles Reflexions sur sa demonstration du principe de l'harmonie. fac. ed. (Monuments of Music & Music Literature in Facsimile, II Ser.: Vol. 138). (Illus.). 1969. lib. bdg. 35.00 (*0-8450-2338-1*) Broude.

Rameau, Jean-Philippe. Nouvelles Suites de Pieces de Clavecin. fac. ed. (Monuments of Music & Music Literature in Facsimile, I Ser.: Vol. 13). (Illus.). 1967. lib. bdg. 35.00 (*0-8450-2013-7*) Broude.

Rameau, Jean-Philippe. Observations sur Notre Instinct pour la Musique. fac. ed. (Monuments of Music & Music Literature in Facsimile, II Ser.: Vol. 54). (Illus.). 1967. lib. bdg. 35.00 (*0-8450-2254-7*) Broude.

— Traite de l'Harmonie Reduite A Ses Principes Naturels. fac. ed. (Monuments of Music & Music Literature in Facsimile Ser., Series II: Vol. 3). 1965. lib. bdg. 60.00 (*0-8450-2203-2*) Broude.

— A Treatise on Harmony. Gossett, Philip, tr. 491p. 1971. 13.95 (*0-486-22461-9*) Dover.

Rameau, Jean-Phillipe. Les Paladins: Comedie Lyrique, Vol. 44. Wolf, R. Peter, ed. LC 85-753846. (French Opera in the 17th & 18th Centuries Ser.: No. 3). (Illus.). 402p. 1987. lib. bdg. 94.00 (*0-918728-63-0*) Pendragon NY.

Rameau, Pierre. Le Maitre a Danser. fac. ed. (Monuments of Music & Music Literature in Facsimile, II Ser.: Vol. 45). (Illus.). 1967. lib. bdg. 45.00 (*0-8450-2245-8*) Broude.

Ramee, Louise De La, see De La Ramee, Louise.

Ramee, Pierre D. La, see La Ramee, Pierre D.

Ramee, Stephen R., jt. ed. see White, Christopher J.

Rameh, Clea, jt. auth. see Abreu, Maria I.

Rameh, Clea, ed. see Georgetown University Round Table on Languages & L.

Ramek, M., jt. auth. see Gruber, B.

Ramek, Michael, jt. ed. see Gruber, Bruno.

Ramel, Michael. One of the Guise. 1998. pap. write for info. (*1-57553-781-8*) Watermrk Pr.

***Ramelet, A. A. & Montilla, M. Robert.** Phlebology: The Guide. 448p. 1999. pap. 30.00 (*2-84299-147-8*, Pub. by ESME) Elsevier.

Ramella, Franco, jt. ed. see Baily, Samuel L.

Ramelli, Agostino. The Various & Ingenious Machines of Agostino Ramelli: A Classic Sixteenth-Century Illustrated Treatise on Technology. (Illus.). 608p. 1994. pap. text 24.95 (*0-486-28180-9*) Dover.

Ramelmeier, R. Andrew, jt. ed. see Kelley, Brian D.

Ramelow, Tilman. Gott, Freiheit, Weltenwahl: Der Ursprung des Begriffes der Besten Aller Moglichen Welten in der Metaphysik der Willensfreiheit Zwischen Antonio Perez S. J. (1599-1649) & G. W. Leibniz (1646-1716) (Studies in Intellectual History: Vol. 72). (GER.). 512p. 1997. text 159.00 (*90-04-10641-3*, NLG255) Brill Academic Pubs.

Ramenofsky, Ann F. Unit Issues in Archaeology: Measuring Time, Space & Material. LC 97-36485. 1997. 55.00 (*0-87480-547-3*); pap. text 25.00 (*0-87480-548-1*) U of Utah Pr.

— Vectors of Death: The Archaeology of European Contact. LC 87-19232. (Illus.). 316p. 1987. reprint ed. pap. 98.00 (*0-608-04148-3*, 206488100011) Bks Demand.

***Rameny, Fred.** Hermann Goering: Hitler's Second in Command. LC 00-8568. (Holocaust Biographies Ser.). 2000. 19.95 (*0-8239-3307-5*) Rosen Group.

— Influenza. LC 00-9380. (Epidemics! Ser.). (Illus.). (J). 2000. lib. bdg. write for info. (*0-8239-3347-4*, PowerKids) Rosen Group.

Rameny, Fred, ed. see Kobza, Kim P.

Ramer, Andrew. Angel Answers: A Joyful Guide to Creating Heaven on Earth. Bestler, Emily, ed. 192p. (Orig.). 1995. per. 12.00 (*0-671-52589-1*) PB.

— Revelations for a New Millenium: Saintly & Celestial Prophecies of Joy & Renewal. LC 96-36515. 192p. 1997. pap. 13.00 (*0-06-251470-9*, Pub. by Harper SF) HarpC.

— Two Flutes Playing: A Spiritual Journeybook for Gay Men. LC 97-71665. (Illus.). 160p. (Orig.). 1997. pap. 12.95 (*1-886360-05-7*) Alamo Sq Pr.

Ramer, Andrew, jt. auth. see Cunningham, Donna.

Ramer, Jeanette C., jt. ed. see Miller, Geoffrey.

Ramer, Leah. Culturally Sensitive Caregiving & Childbearing Families. Raff, Beverly S. & Fiore, Ellen, eds. LC 92-13293. (Nursing Issues for the Twenty-First Century Ser.: No. 4, Module 1). 1992. pap. write for info. (*0-86525-054-5*) March of Dimes.

Ramer, Maurer. Flapdragon Dreams. 32p. (Orig.). 1995. pap. 3.95 (*0-933990-11-1*) Canterbury Pr.

— Kaleidoscope Ride. 32p. 1996. pap. 3.95 (*0-933990-14-6*) Canterbury Pr.

Ramer, Samuel. Sensuous Trekker: How to Enhance Your Relationship with a Star Trek Fan. 208p. 1997. pap. text 10.95 (*0-8065-1919-3*, Citadel Pr) Carol Pub Group.

Ramer, Samuel C., tr. see Kochina, Elena I.

Ramerez, loAnne. Back Yard Play Vol. 2: Pen & Ben. large type ed. (Illus.). 24p. (J). (gr. k-2). 1999. pap. 3.95 (*1-929078-01-3*, APB02) Gods Kids.

Rames, Stephen R., jt. ed. see White, Christopher J.

Ramesey, William. Astrologia Restaurata: Astrology Restored, 4 vols. Wiggers, Carol A., ed. Cochran, Kathleen R., tr. Incl. Vol. 1.Tr. of Astrology Restored. (Illus.). 39p. 1996. pap. 15.00 (*1-878935-30-5*); Vol. 2.Tr. of Astrology Restored. (Illus.). 72p. 1996. pap. 15.00 (*1-878935-31-3*); Vol. 3.Tr. of Astrology Restored. (Illus.). 90p. 1996. pap. 15.00 (*1-878935-32-1*); Vol. 4.Tr. of Astrology Restored. (Illus.). 141p. 1996. pap. 30.00 (*1-878935-33-X*); 75.00 (*1-878935-34-8*) JustUs & Assocs.

Ramesh, jt. auth. see Pratt, Jamie.

Ramesh, A., ed. Contributions to Indian Geography Vol. 5: Resource Geography. 1985. 38.50 (*0-8364-1303-2*, Pub. by Heritage IA) S Asia.

Ramesh, A., jt. auth. see Misra, R. P.

Ramesh, Jairam. Mobilizing Technology for World Development. LC 79-53493. 234p. 1979. 69.50 (*0-275-90410-5*, C0410, Praeger Pubs) Greenwood.

Ramesh, Jairam & Weiss, Charles, Jr., eds. Mobilizing Technology for World Development. LC 79-5349. 240p. 1979. pap. 6.95 (*0-03-055451-9*) Overseas Dev Council.

***Ramesh, K.** Digital Photoelasticity: Advanced Techniques & Applications. LC 00-22973. 415p. 2000. 116.00 incl. cd-rom (*3-540-66795-4*) Spr-Verlag.

Ramesh, K. Human Relations in an Indian University: An Organizational Perspective. LC 99-938913. (C). 1991. 21.00 (*81-202-0304-6*, Pub. by Ajanta) S Asia.

Ramesh, K. S., et al, eds. Catalyst Materials for High-Temperature Processes: Proceedings, Catalyst Materical for High-Temperature Processes Symposium, Indianapolis, IN, 1996. (Ceramic Transactions Ser.: Vol. 73). 180p. 1997. 95.00 (*1-57498-036-X*, CT073) Am Ceramic.

Ramesh, K. T., ed. Experimental Techniques in the Dynamics of Deformable Solids. LC 93-71579. (AMD Ser.: Vol. 165). 1993. pap. 35.00 (*0-7918-1144-1*, G00788) ASME.

Ramesh, K. V., ed. Indian History & Epigraphy. 1990. 125.00 (*0-8364-2597-9*, Pub. by Agam) S Asia.

***Ramesh, M. & Asher, Mukul G.** Welfare Capitalism in Southeast Asia: Social Security, Health & Education Policies. LC 99-49745. (International Political Economy Ser.). 2000. text 65.00 (*0-312-23016-8*) St Martin.

Ramesh, M., jt. auth. see Howlett, Michael.

Ramesh, R., ed. Thin Film Ferroelectric Materials & Devices. LC 97-26415. (Electronic Materials Ser.: No. 3). 249p. 1997. text 135.00 (*0-7923-9993-5*) Kluwer Academic.

Ramesh, R., et al, eds. Epitaxial Oxide Thin Films & Heterostructures Vol. 341: Materials Research Society Symposium Proceedings. LC 94-22184. 407p. 1994. text 30.00 (*1-55899-241-3*) Materials Res.

Ramesh, R., et al, eds. Ferroelectric Thin Films IV. (MRS Symposium Proceedings Ser.: Vol. 361). 623p. 1995. 77.00 (*1-55899-262-6*) Materials Res.

***Ramesh, Ram.** Financial Analyst's Indispensable Pocketguide. 2000. pap. 16.95 (*0-07-136156-1*) McGraw.

Ramesh, S. & Sivakumar, G., eds. Foundations of Software Technology & Theoretical Computer Science: Proceedings of the 17th Conference, Kharagpur, India, December 18-20, 1997. (Lecture Notes in Computer Science Ser.: Vol. 1346). xi, 343p. 1997. pap. 59.00 (*3-540-63876-8*) Spr-Verlag.

Ramesh, Srinivasan & Gupta, Arun. Venture Capital & the Indian Financial Sector. (Illus.). 210p. 1995. text 27.00 (*0-19-563633-3*) OUP.

Rameshray, Roy. Perspectives on Indian Politics. 489p. 1987. 48.50 (*0-8364-2014-4*, Pub. by Usha) S Asia.

Rameshwar, Sinha P. & Surya, Dandekar. South East Asia: People's Struggle & Political Identity. 1998. 36.00 (*81-7391-238-6*) Kaniska Pubs Dist.

Ramet. Balkan Babel. 3rd ed. LC 99-28670. 1999. pap. 26.00 (*0-8133-9034-6*, Pub. by Westview) HarpC.

***Ramet, Adele.** Creating a Twist in the Tale: Write Winning Twist Stories for Popular Magazines. 2nd ed. (Successful Writing Ser.). (Illus.). 144p. 2000. pap. 19.95 (*1-85703-558-5*, Pub. by How To Bks) Midpt Trade.

— Creative Writing: How to Develop Successful Writing Skills for Fiction & Non-Fiction Publication. 2nd ed. (Successful Writing Ser.). (Illus.). 136p. 1999. pap. 19.95 (*1-85703-398-1*, Pub. by How To Bks) Trans-Atl Phila.

Ramet, Adele. Creative Writing: How to Develop Your Writing Skills for Successful Fiction & Non-Fiction Work. (Successful Writing Ser.). 135p. 1997. pap. 19.95 (*1-85703-451-1*, Pub. by How To Bks) Trans-Atl Phila.

***Ramet, Carlos.** Ken Follett: The Transformation of a Writer. LC 99-21431. 1999. 20.95 (*0-87972-798-5*) Bowling Green Univ Popular Press.

Ramet, Carlos. Ken Follett: The Transformation of a Writer. LC 99-21431. 155p. 1999. 40.95 (*0-87972-797-7*) Bowling Green Univ Popular Press.

Ramet, Pedro. Cross & Commissar: The Politics of Religion in Eastern Europe & the U. S. S. R. LC 86-46165. (Illus.). 256p. (C). 1987. 35.00 (*0-253-31575-1*) Ind U Pr.

— Eastern Christianity & Politics in the Twentieth Century. LC 87-27029. (Christianity under Stress Ser.). vii, 471p. (C). 1988. text 59.95 (*0-8223-0827-4*) Duke.

— Nationalism & Federalism in Yugoslavia, 1963-1983. LC 83-49055. 319p. reprint ed. pap. 98.90 (*0-8357-6685-3*, 205686400094) Bks Demand.

Ramet, Pedro, ed. Catholicism & Politics in Communist Societies. LC 89-39178. 463p. (Orig.). (C). 1990. text 59.95 (*0-8223-1010-4*); pap. text 24.95 (*0-8223-1047-3*) Duke.

— Religion & Nationalism in Soviet & East European Politics. enl. rev. ed. LC 88-21132. 560p. (C). 1988. text 74.95 (*0-8223-0854-1*); pap. text 29.95 (*0-8223-0891-6*) Duke.

An Asterisk (*) at the beginning of an entry indicates that the title is appearing for the first time.

Ramet, Sabrina P. Balkan Babel: The Disintegration of Yugoslavia from the Death of Tito to Ethnic War. 2nd ed. LC 95-25078. 356p. (C). 1996. pap. 22.00 (*0-8133-2559-5*, Pub. by Westview) HarpC.
— Nationalism & Federalism in Yugoslavia, 1962-1991. 2nd ed. LC 91-23623. 365p. 1992. reprint ed. pap. 113.20 (*0-608-01072-3*, 205938000001) Bks Demand.
— Nihil Obstat: Religion, Politics & Social Change in East-Central Europe & Russia. LC 97-23350. ix, 425p. 1998. text 69.95 (*0-8223-2056-8*); pap. text 23.95 (*0-8223-2070-3*) Duke.
*__Ramet, Sabrina P.__ The Radical Right in Central & Eastern Europe since 1989. LC 98-20764. (Post-Communist Cultural Studies). 1999. 65.00 (*0-271-01810-0*); pap. 22.50 (*0-271-01811-9*) Pa St U Pr.
Ramet, Sabrina P. Social Currents in Eastern Europe: The Sources & Consequences of the Great Transformation. 2nd ed. LC 94-28352. 624p. 1994. text 69.95 (*0-8223-1551-3*); pap. text 29.95 (*0-8223-1548-3*) Duke.
— Whose Democracy? Nationalism, Religion, & the Doctrine of Collective Rights in Post-1989 Eastern Europe. LC 97-7819. 224p. (Orig.). 1997. 62.50 (*0-8476-8323-0*) Rowman.
— Whose Democracy? Nationalism, Religion, & the Doctrine of Collective Rights in Post-1989 Eastern Europe. LC 97-7819. 224p. (Orig.). 1997. pap. 20.95 (*0-8476-8324-9*) Rowman.
Ramet, Sabrina P., ed. Beyond Yugoslavia: Politics, Economics & Culture in a Shattered Community. (Eastern Europe after Communism Ser.). 484p. (C). 1995. text 85.00 (*0-8133-7953-9*, Pub. by Westview) HarpC.
— Eastern Europe: Politics, Culture, & Society since 1939. LC 98-26834. (Illus.). 448p. 1998. 39.95 (*0-253-33470-5*) Ind U Pr.
— Eastern Europe: Politics, Culture & Society since 1939. LC 98-26834. (Illus.). 448p. 1998. pap. 19.95 (*0-253-21256-1*) Ind U Pr.
— Gender Politics in the Western Balkans: Women, Society & Politics in Yugoslavia & the Yugoslav Successor States. LC 98-20732. (Post-Communist Cultural Studies Ser.). 320p. 1998. 55.00 (*0-271-01801-1*); pap. 18.95 (*0-271-01802-X*) Pa St U Pr.
— Gender Reversals & Gender Cultures: Anthropological & Historical Perspectives. LC 95-26198. (Illus.). 256p. (C). 1996. 85.00 (*0-415-11482-9*); pap. 27.99 (*0-415-11483-7*) Routledge.
— Protestantism & Politics in Eastern Europe & Russia: The Communist & Post-Communist Eras. LC 92-9418. (Christianity under Stress Ser.: Vol. 3). 408p. 1993. text 46.95 (*0-8223-1241-7*) Duke.
— Religious Policy in the Soviet Union. 381p. (C). 1993. text 80.00 (*0-521-41643-4*) Cambridge U Pr.
Ramet, Sabrina P. & Treadgold, Donald W., eds. Render unto Caesar: The Religious Sphere in World Politics. 500p. (C). 1995. 77.00 (*1-879383-43-8*); pap. 33.50 (*1-879383-44-6*) Am Univ Pr.
Ramette, Peggy L. & Sternberg, Dick. America's Favorite Fish Recipes. LC 92-6416. (Hunting & Fishing Library). (Illus.). 160p. 1992. 19.95 (*0-86573-039-3*) Creat Pub Intl.
Ramette, Richard W. Chemical Equilibrium & Analysis. (Chemistry Ser.). (Illus.). 672p. (C). 1981. text. write for info. (*0-201-06107-4*) Addison-Wesley.
Ramey, Alan A., ed. A Glimpse Beyond the Veil: The Art of Matthew Brooks. (Illus.). 80p. 1998. pap. 24.95 (*0-9666636-0-8*, 0001) ACR Pub.
Ramey, Ardella. Company Policy & Personnel Workbook. 4th ed. LC 99-30673. 336p. 1999. pap., wbk. ed. 29.95 (*1-55571-486-2*, Oasis Pr) PSI Resch.
Ramey, Bern C. The Great Wine Grapes & the Wines They Make. (Illus.). 49.95 (*0-8436-2257-1*) Great Wine Grapes.
*__Ramey, Craig T. & Ramey, Sharon L.__ Going to School: How to Help Your Child Succeed. LC 99-61457. (Parenting Guides Ser.). (Illus.). 256p. 1999. pap. 19.95 (*0-9666397-3-1*, Pub. by Goddard Pr) Natl Bk Netwk.
Ramey, Craig T. & Ramey, Sharon L. Right from Birth: Building Your Child's Foundation for Life. LC 98-96648. 288p. 1999. pap. 19.95 (*0-9666397-1-5*) Goddard Pr.
Ramey, Craig T., jt. auth. see Ramey, Sharon L.
Ramey, David A. Empowering Leaders. LC 91-35001. 256p. (Orig.). (C). 1991. pap. 14.95 (*1-55612-372-8*) Sheed & Ward WI.
Ramey, David W. Anatomy of a Horse. 1997. 29.95 (*0-87605-685-0*) Macmillan.
— Concise Guide to Alternative Therapies in the Horse. (Illus.). 224p. 1999. pap. 16.95 (*1-58245-062-5*) Howell Bks.
— Concise Guide to Arthritis in the Horse. 128p. 1998. pap. text 16.95 (*0-87605-091-7*) Howell Bks.
— Concise Guide to Colic in the Horse. (Concise Guide Ser.). 128p. 1996. 14.95 (*0-87605-911-6*) Howell Bks.
— Concise Guide to Medications & Supplements for the Horse. LC 95-25006. (Concise Guide Ser.). (Illus.). 192p. (Orig.). 1996. 16.95 (*0-87605-916-7*) Howell Bks.
— Concise Guide to Navicular Syndrome in the Horse. LC 96-8496. 1996. 14.95 (*0-87605-913-2*) Howell Bks.
— Concise Guide to Tendon & Ligament Injuries in the Horse. LC 95-25005. (Concise Guide Ser.). (Illus.). 144p. (Orig.). 1996. 14.95 (*0-87605-912-4*) Howell Bks.
*__Ramey, David W.__ Horse Sense: A Veterinarian's Collection of Common Knowledge. 1999. pap. 12.95 (*1-58245-002-1*) Howell Bks.
Ramey, David W. Horsefeathers: Facts vs. Myths about Your Horse's Health. (Illus.). 192p. 1995. 25.00 (*0-87605-986-8*) Howell Bks.
Ramey, David W. & Duren, Stephen E. Concise Guide to Nutrition in the Horse. LC 98-5054. 160p. 1998. 16.95 (*0-87605-089-5*) Howell Bks.
*__Ramey, Denny L., et al.__ OSBA Desk Manual. LC 99-64023. 329p. 1999. ring bd. 49.95 (*0-9664544-2-1*) OSBACLE Institute.
Ramey, Emily G. & Gott, John K. The Years of Anguish: Fauquier County, Virginia, 1861-1865. (Illus.). 230p. 1998. pap. 24.00 (*0-7884-0963-8*, G577) Heritage Bk.
Ramey, Gladys Q., jt. auth. see Claypoole, Richard L.
Ramey, Henry J., et al. Gas Well Test Analysis Under Water-Drive Conditions. 312p. 1973. 12.00 (*0-318-12634-6*, L00311) Am Gas Assn.
Ramey, Jerry & Stewart, Ed. How to Go to Work on Your Faith. 132p. 1992. pap. 8.99 (*0-8341-1430-5*) Beacon Hill.
Ramey, Judith, ed. see Wilson, Karen, et al.
Ramey, Judith, jt. ed. see Wixon, Dennis.
Ramey, Lester L. Biking the Trails of Rabun. (Illus.). 186p. (Orig.). 1996. pap. 9.95 (*0-9653236-0-9*) Ramco Inc.
Ramey, Mary. Adult Children, Adult Choices: Outgrowing Codependency. LC 92-12728. 176p. (Orig.). 1992. pap. 10.95 (*1-55612-406-6*, LL1406) Sheed & Ward WI.
Ramey, Mary L., jt. auth. see Thomas, M. Angele.
Ramey, Nan. Adults Who Don't Discipline Children: And How to Work with Them. Hall, Dot, ed. 50p. (Orig.). 1996. pap. 6.95 (*1-57502-111-0*) Morris Pubng.
Ramey, Phillip & Thomas, Virgil. Paul Bowles: Music. limited ed. Swan, Claudia, ed. (EOS Ser.: Vol. 1). (Illus.). 152p. 1995. 35.00 (*0-9648083-0-7*) Eos Music.
Ramey, R. Intro to Physics Laboratory. 2nd ed. 268p. (C). 1999. spiral bd. 27.95 (*0-7872-5701-X*, 41570101) Kendall-Hunt.
Ramey, Ralph. 50 Hikes in Ohio: Day Hikes & Backpacking Trips in the Buckeye State. 2nd ed. LC 97-18838. (50 Hikes Ser.). (Illus.). 256p. 1997. pap. 15.00 (*0-88150-401-7*, Pub. by Countryman) Norton.
— Walks & Rambles in Southwestern Ohio: From the Stillwater to the Ohio River. LC 94-13657. (Walks & Rambles Ser.). (Illus.). 192p. (Orig.). 1994. pap. 12.00 (*0-88150-250-2*, Pub. by Countryman) Norton.
Ramey, Robert H., Jr. The Dynamic Congregation: A Manual for Energizing Your Church. LC 99-29736. 1999. pap. 15.99 (*0-8272-0626-7*) Chalice Pr.
— 52 Devotions for Church Leaders. LC 98-43549. 144p. 1999. pap. 14.99 (*0-8272-1023-X*) Chalice Pr.
— Growing Church Leaders: New Skills for New Tasks. 104p. 1995. pap. 7.95 (*1-885121-13-X*) CTS Press.
— The Pastor's Start-Up Manual: Beginning a New Pastorate. Miller, Herb, ed. (Leadership Insight Ser.). 144p. (Orig.). 1995. pap. 12.95 (*0-687-01486-7*) Abingdon.
*__Ramey, Robert H.__ Thriving in Ministry. 2000. pap. 18.99 (*0-8272-3652-2*) Chalice Pr.
Ramey, Robert H., Jr. & Johnson, Ben C. Living the Christian Life: A Guide to Reformed Spirituality. 208p. (Orig.). 1992. pap. 17.95 (*0-664-25286-9*) Westminster John Knox.
Ramey, Sharon L. & Ramey, Craig T. Going to School: How to Help Your Child Succeed. (Illus.). 256p. 1999. 24.95 (*0-9666397-2-3*, Pub. by Goddard Pr) Natl Bk Netwk.
Ramey, Sharon L., jt. auth. see Ramey, Craig T.
Ramey, Timothy & Project Air Force Staff. Lean Logistics: High-Velocity Logistics Infrastructure & the C-5 Galaxy. LC 98-54431. (Illus.). 135p. 1999. pap. 15.00 (*0-8330-2697-6*, MR-581-AF) Rand Corp.
Ramezzana, Warren, ed. Quick Guide: Plumbing. 2nd ed. LC 92-81624. (Quick Guide Ser.). (Illus.). 80p. 1998. pap. 7.95 (*1-880029-12-X*) Creative Homeowner.
Ramfjord, Sigurd P. & Ash, M., Jr. Periodontology & Periodontics: Modern Theory & Practice. (Illus.). 370p. 1989. 59.50 (*0-912791-40-3*, Ishiyaku EuroAmerica) Med Dent Media.
Ramfjord, Sigurd P. & Ash, Major M. Occlusion. 4th ed. LC 94-7653. 1994. text 75.00 (*0-7216-5591-2*, W B Saunders Co) Harcrt Hlth Sci Grp.
*__Ramfos, Stelios & Russell, Norman.__ Like a Pelican in the Wilderness: Reflections on the Sayings of the Desert Fathers. LC 99-59976. 2000. pap. write for info. (*1-885652-40-2*) Holy Cross Orthodox.
Ramgulam, P. Mauritius. LC 93-180475. (World Bibliographical Ser.). 179p. 1992. lib. bdg. 70.00 (*1-85109-153-X*) ABC-CLIO.
Ramiah, B. K. & Chickanagappa, L. L., eds. Handbook of Soil Mechanics & Foundation Engineering. 594p. 1990. 60.00 (*90-6191-143-5*, Pub. by A A Balkema) Ashgate Pub Co.
Ramie, Alain. Bethsaida & Biblical. 1999. pap. text 8.95 (*0-941037-76-2*) D & F Scott.
— Picasso's Complete Ceramics. (Illus.). 315p. 1988. 325.00 (*1-55660-067-4*) A Wofsy Fine Arts.
Ramierez, Gonzalo, Jr. & Ramierez, Jan L. Multiethnic Children's Literature. LC 93-39662. 158p. (C). 1994. pap. 28.25 (*0-8273-5433-9*) Delmar.
Ramierez, Jan L., jt. auth. see Ramierez, Gonzalo, Jr.
Ramig, Joyce, et al. Teaching Science Process Skills. 192p. teacher ed. 15.99 (*0-86653-835-6*, GA1526) Good Apple.
Ramig, Lorraine O. Voice Treatment for Parkinson's Disease & Other Neurological Disorders. 1998. 65.00 incl. audio, VHS (*1-58041-019-7*, 0112096) Am Speech Lang Hearing.
Ramig, Lorraine O., et al. Voice Treatment for Parkinson Disease & Other Neurological Disorders. 2nd ed. 250p. 2000. pap. 45.00 (*1-56593-906-9*, 1794) Thomson Learn.
Ramig, R. F., ed. Current Topics in Microbiology & Immunology: Rotaviruses. 330p. 1994. 143.95 (*0-387-56761-5*) Spr-Verlag.
Ramiksson, Harold, ed. IUTAM Symposium on Lubricated Transport of Viscous Materials: Proceedings of the IUTAM Symposium Held in Tobago, West Indies, 7-10 January, 1997. LC 97-45957. (Fluid Mechanics & Its Applications Ser.). 239p. 1998. text 133.50 (*0-7923-4897-4*) Kluwer Academic.
Ramin, Jonathan. Power Windows 96. 600p. 1995. pap. 29.95 incl. disk (*1-55828-380-3*, MIS Pr) IDG Bks.
Ramin, Terese. A Certain Slant of Light. (Intimate Moments Ser.). 1995. per. 3.75 (*0-373-07634-7*, 1-07634-8) Silhouette.
*__Ramin, Terese.__ A Drive-By Wedding. (Intimate Moments Ser.: No. 981). 2000. per. 4.50 (*0-373-07981-8*, 1-07981-3) Harlequin Bks.
Ramin, Terese. Five Kids, One Christmas. 1995. per. 3.75 (*0-373-07680-0*, 1-07680-1) Silhouette.
— Mary's Child. (Intimate Moments Ser.). 1998. per. 4.25 (*0-373-07881-1*, 1-07881-5) Silhouette.
— An Unexpected Addition. (Intimate Moments Ser.: No. 793). 1997. per. 3.99 (*0-373-07793-9*, 1-07793-2) Silhouette.
— Winter Beach. 2000. mass mkt. 4.50 (*0-373-82230-8*, 1-82230-3) Harlequin Bks.
Ramin, Terese. Winter Beach. (Intimate Moments Ser.). 1993. mass mkt. 3.39 (*0-373-07477-8*, 5-07477-8) Silhouette.
Raminsky, Judy Sklar, jt. auth. see Kaiser, Barbara.
Ramio, Christian, jt. auth. see Mention, Philippe.
Ramiorez, J. Yankee Duchess. 304p. mass mkt. 4.50 (*0-06-108075-6*, Harp PBks) HarpC.
*__Ramirez.__ Florida Evidence Manual 99-3. 356p. 1999. ring bd. write for info. (*0-327-01476-8*, 8063730) LEXIS Pub.
— Florida Evidence Manual 99-4, 5 vols., Set. 250p. 1999. ring bd. write for info. (*0-327-01651-5*, 8063731) LEXIS Pub.
Ramirez. Florida Evidence Manual 99-2, 5 vols. 160p. 1999. ring bd. 48.00 (*0-327-01166-1*, 8063729) LEXIS Pub.
— Florida Evidence Manual 99-1, 5 vols. 602p. 1999. lib. bdg. write for info. (*0-327-01048-7*, 8063728) LEXIS Pub.
— Introduction to Program Design with BASIC, Custom Pub. 2nd ed. (C). 1994. pap. text 20.50 (*0-07-051819-X*) McGraw.
*__Ramirez.__ Prime Movers: Define Your Business or Have Someone Define It Against You. 350p. 2000. 34.95 (*0-471-89944-5*, Wiley Heyden) Wiley.
Ramirez, Alex O. Tjatjakiymatchan (Coyote) A Legend from Carmel Valley. (Illus.). 16p. (Orig.). (J). 1995. pap. 6.00 (*0-9625175-3-4*) Oyate.
Ramirez, Alfonso R., ed. Four Generations of Velas. (Illus.). 96p. 1986. 15.00 (*0-935071-01-6*) New Santander.
Ramirez, Anthony. The Best of Latin American Short Stories - A Bilingual Edition: Los Mejores Cuentos Hispanoamericanos. Hamel, Bernard H., ed. 114p. (Orig.). 1995. pap., per. 10.95 (*1-886835-02-0*) Bilingual Bk Pr.
Ramirez, Anthony, Jr. Romualdo Pacheco: Governor of California. (Illus.). 1974. 10.00 (*0-911302-26-3*, PS3-6) San Francisco Pr.
Ramirez, Anthony. Two Holiday Folktales from Mexico. Hamel, Bernard H., ed. (ENG & SPA., Illus.). 36p. (YA). 1996. pap. 8.95 (*1-886835-04-7*) Bilingual Bk Pr.
Ramirez, Arnulfo G. Bilingualism Through Schooling: Cross-Cultural Education for Minority & Majority Students. LC 83-24246. 275p. (C). 1985. text 64.50 (*0-87395-891-8*); pap. text 21.95 (*0-87395-892-6*) State U NY Pr.
— Creating Contexts for Second Language Acquisition: Theory & Methods. LC 94-6628. 395p. (C). 1995. pap. text 47.81 (*0-8013-0480-6*, 78313) Longman.
Ramirez, Arturo, jt. auth. see Villarino, Jose.
Ramirez-Baez, Ramon A. Los Hijos de Machepa. (SPA.). 240p. 1997. pap. 18.95 (*0-9658743-1-1*) Edit Silet.
Ramirez, Bernardo & Lastiri, Santiago, eds. Casos en Administracion de Servicios de Salud: Un Enfoque para la Solucion de Problemas. (SPA., Illus.). 180p. (Orig.). (C). 1989. pap. text 14.55 (*0-910591-23-7*) AUPHA Pr.
Ramirez, Bernardo & Parra-Elliott, Ligia, eds. Educacion en Administracion de Salud en America Latina y El Caribe. LC 87-72570. 140p. (Orig.). 1987. pap. text 8.00 (*0-910591-06-7*) AUPHA Pr.
Ramirez, Blandina C., jt. auth. see Cardenas, Jose A.
Ramirez, Bruno. When Workers Fight: The Politics of Industrial Relations in the Progressive Era, 1898-1916, 2. LC 77-83895. (Contributions in Labor History Ser.: No. 2). 241p. 1978. 55.00 (*0-8371-9826-7*, RAW/, Greenwood Pr) Greenwood.
Ramirez, Bruno, jt. auth. see Tana, Paul.
Ramirez, Carl & Richardson, Delois. Electronic Banking: Experiences Reported by Banks in Implementing On-Line Banking. (Illus.). 53p. 1999. pap. text 20.00 (*0-7881-7965-9*) DIANE Pub.
Ramirez, Cecillee, ed. see Brookshire, Wanda S.
Ramirez-Christensen, Esperanza. Heart's Flower: The Life & Poetry of Shinkei. LC 93-17305. xiv, 475p. 1994. 60.00 (*0-8047-2253-6*) Stanford U Pr.
Ramirez de Arellano, Annette B. & Seipp, Conrad. Colonialism, Catholicism, & Contraception: A History of Birth Control in Puerto Rico. LC 82-13646. 231p. 1983. reprint ed. pap. 71.70 (*0-7837-9029-5*, 204978000003) Bks Demand.
Ramirez de Arellano, E., ed. Algebraic Geometry & Complex Analysis. (Lecture Notes in Mathematics Ser.: Vol. 1414). vi, 180p. 1990. 30.60 (*0-387-52175-5*, 3875) Spr-Verlag.
*__Ramirez de Arellano, E., et al.__ Complex Analysis & Related Topics. LC 99-51336. (Operator Theory Ser.: Vol. 114). 296p. 2000. 105.00 (*3-7643-6228-6*, Pub. by Birkhauser) Spr-Verlag.
Ramirez De Arellano, Rafael. Folklore Portoriqueno. LC 78-63213. (Folktale Ser.). reprint ed. 37.50 (*0-404-16154-5*) AMS Pr.
Ramirez, Donald E., jt. auth. see Dunkl, Charles F.
Ramirez, Doreen, jt. auth. see Manuel, Ted.
Ramirez, Doreen, ed. see Manuel, Ted.
Ramirez, Eduardo & Ramirez, Elvira, trs. Milagros Inagotables para Cristianos Agotados. (Nineteen Ninety-Eight Fifty-Day Spiritual Adventure Ser.). (SPA.). 1996. wbk. ed. 6.00 (*1-57849-039-1*) Mainstay Church.
Ramirez, Eduardo, tr. see Chapel of the Air Ministries, Inc. Staff.
*__Ramirez, Elizabeth C.__ Chicanas/Latinas in American Theatre: A History of Performance. (Illus.). 224p. 2000. pap. 16.95 (*0-253-21371-1*); lib. bdg. 39.95 (*0-253-33714-3*) Ind U Pr.
Ramirez, Elizabeth C. Footlights across the Border: A History of Spanish-Language Professional Theatre on the Texas Stage. (American University Studies: Theatre Arts: Ser. XXVI, Vol. 1). (Illus.). 206p. (C). 1990. text 43.95 (*0-8204-1035-7*) P Lang Pubng.
*__Ramirez, Elvira, tr.__ Promesas Dignas de Cumplirse: Spanish Journal. (Nineteen Ninety-Nine 50-Day Spiritual Adventure Ser.). 64p. 1998. 7.00 (*1-57849-106-1*) Mainstay Church.
Ramirez, Elvira, tr. see Chapel of the Air Ministries, Inc. Staff.
Ramirez, Elvira, jt. tr. see Ramirez, Eduardo.
Ramirez-Faria, C. Origins of Economic Inequality Between Nations: Critique of Western Theories & Underdevelopement. 334p. (C). 1990. pap. text 22.50 (*0-04-445843-6*) Routledge.
Ramirez, Felipe, jt. auth. see Perez Taylor, Rafael.
Ramirez, Francisco O., ed. Rethinking the Nineteenth Century: Contradictions & Movements, 76. LC 87-17791. (Contributions in Economics & Economic History Ser.: No. 76). 241p. 1988. 59.95 (*0-313-25997-6*, RRK/, Greenwood Pr) Greenwood.
*__Ramirez, Frank.__ Apocalypse When? Daniel & Revelation. (Generation Why Ser.: No. 4, Pt. 1). 40p. (YA). (gr. 9-12). 1998. pap. 12.95 (*0-87303-281-0*) Faith & Life.
— Choosing Sides: Faithfulness in the Book of Joshua. (Good Ground Ser.: Vol. 1:6). 53p. 1999. pap. 5.95 (*0-87303-356-6*) Faith & Life.
Ramirez, Frank. Coming Home: Advent Christmas Sermons from the Book of Haggai. LC 98-9764. 78p. 1998. pap. 7.75 (*0-7880-1281-9*) CSS OH.
— Daniel. LC 97-35842. (Covenant Bible Studies). 111p. 1998. pap. 5.95 (*0-87178-012-7*, FaithQuest) Brethren.
— The Gospel of Mark. LC 95-42590. (Covenant Bible Studies). 86p. (Orig.). 1996. pap. 5.95 (*0-87178-321-5*, FaithQuest) Brethren.
*__Ramirez, Frank.__ He Took a Towel: Sermons & Services for Communion & Feet Washing. 2000. pap. 7.50 (*0-7880-1554-0*) CSS OH.
Ramirez, Frank. Take Two Tablets: The Ten Commandments. (Generation Why Ser.: Vol. 3:1). 48p. (YA). (gr. 9-12). 1997. pap. 14.95 (*0-87303-274-8*) Faith & Life.
*__Ramirez-Gelpi, Ana Sofia & Hammarstrand, Robert E.__ Advanced Spanish. (Advanced Courses Ser.). (SPA & ENG.). 1999. pap. 29.95 incl. audio (*0-609-60487-2*) Liv Lang.
Ramirez-Gelpi, Ana Sofia & Hammarstrand, Robert E. Advanced Spanish Coursebook, 1. 1999. pap. 6.95 (*0-609-80450-2*) Liv Lang.
Ramirez, Gloria, tr. see Mann, Peggy.
Ramirez, Heredia Rafael. Con M de Marilyn. 1998. pap. 19.95 (*968-19-0336-6*) Santillana.
Ramirez, Ivan D., ed. see Flores, Sergio.
Ramirez, Ivan D., ed. see List, Gloria.
*__Ramirez, Jan Seidler, et al.__ Painting the Town: Cityscapes of New York, Paintings from the Museum of the City of New York. LC 99-54934. (Illus.). 320p. 2000. 45.00 (*0-300-08199-5*) Yale U Pr.
Ramirez, Jose, III. Things about the Guitar. Teresita, tr. (Illus.). 230p. 1994. pap. 34.95 (*0-933224-88-5*, ST401, Pub. by Soneto Ediciones) Bold Strummer Ltd.
Ramirez, Juan. Florida Civil Procedure, 2 vols. 2nd ed. LC 97-73641. 1397p. 1997. text. write for info. (*1-55834-565-5*, 80522-11, MICHIE); text. write for info. (*0-327-00991-8*, 80523-11, MICHIE) LEXIS Pub.
Ramirez, Juan, Jr. Florida Civil Procedure, 2 vols., Vols. 1 & 2. 2nd ed. 1997. 160.00 (*0-327-00961-6*, 80520-11, MICHIE) LEXIS Pub.
— Florida Civil Procedure: Spring 1999 Cumulative Supplement, 2 vols. 2nd ed. LC 97-73641. 350p. 1999. suppl. ed. 49.00 (*0-327-01273-0*, 8049712) LEXIS Pub.
— Florida Civil Procedure: 1998 Supplement, Vols. 1 & 2. 2nd ed. LC 97-73641. 200p. 1998. suppl. ed. 50.00 (*0-327-00140-2*, 80497-10) LEXIS Pub.
— Florida Civil Procedure Vol. 1: Spring 1999 Cumulative Supplement. 2nd ed. LC 97-73641. 1999. suppl. ed. write for info. (*0-327-01274-9*, 8049812) LEXIS Pub.
— Florida Civil Procedure Vol. 2: Spring 1999 Cumulative Supplement. 2nd ed. LC 97-73641. 1999. suppl. ed. write for info. (*0-327-01275-7*, 8049912) LEXIS Pub.
— Florida Civil Procedure, Fall 1998 Cumulative Supplement, 2 vols. 2nd ed. 250p. 1998. pap. write for info. (*0-327-00593-9*, 8049711) LEXIS Pub.
— Florida Civil Procedure, Fall 1998 Cumulative Supplement, Vol. 1. 2nd ed. 1998. write for info. (*0-327-00656-0*, 8049811) LEXIS Pub.
— Florida Civil Procedure, Fall 1998 Cumulative Supplement, Vol. 2. 2nd ed. 1998. write for info. (*0-327-00657-9*, 8049911) LEXIS Pub.
Ramirez, Juan. A Patriot after All: The Story of a Chicano Vietnam Vet. LC 98-46679. 180p. 1999. pap. 15.95 (*0-8263-1959-9*) U of NM Pr.
— A Patriot after All: The Story of a Chicano Vietnam Vet. LC 98-46679. (Illus.). 180p. 1999. 29.95 (*0-8263-1958-0*) U of NM Pr.

R

An Asterisk (*) at the beginning of an entry indicates that the title is appearing for the first time.

R

Ramirez, Juan A. Duchamp: Love & Death, Even. Tulloch, Alexander R., tr. from SPA. (Illus.). 296p. 1999. 45.00 (*1-86189-027-3*) Reaktion Bks.

***Ramirez, Juan Antonio.** The Beehive Metaphor: From Gaudi to le Corbusier. (Essays in Art & Culture Ser.). (Illus.). 304p. 2000. pap. 24.95 (*1-86189-056-7*, Pub. by Reaktion Bks) Consort Bk Sales.

Ramirez-Krodel, Aurora, jt. auth. see Smith, Iva A.

Ramirez, Laureana, tr. see Holden, Dwight L.

Ramirez, LoAnne. Birthday Surprise Vol. 10: Pen & Ben. large type ed. (Illus.). 24p. (J). (gr. 2-3). 1999. pap. 3.95 (*1-929078-10-2*, APB10) Gods Kids.

— Riding Bikes Vol. 6: Pen & Ben. large type ed. (Illus.). 24p. (J). (gr. k-2). 1999. pap. 3.95 (*1-929078-05-6*, APB06) Gods Kids.

— Scout Knots Vol. 12: Pen & Ben. large type ed. (Illus.). 24p. (J). (gr. 2-3). 1999. pap. 3.95 (*1-929078-09-9*, APB12) Gods Kids.

Ramirez, LoAnne, jt. auth. see Storm, Jill.

Ramirez-Lopez, Heladio. La Sindicalizacion de Trabajadores Agricolas en Mexico: La Experiencia de la Confederacion Nacional Campesina (CNC) (Research Reports: No. 26).Tr. of Unionization of Agricultural Workers in Mexico: The Experience of the National Peasant Confederation. 16p. (Orig.). (C). 1981. pap. 5.00 (*0-935391-25-8*, RR-26) UCSD Ctr US-Mex.

Ramirez, Lynette, ed. see Miller, P. B.

Ramirez, Lynette, ed. see Wallach, Paul.

Ramirez, Magda. Manual de Adoracion: Worship Manual. (SPA.). 56p. 1996. pap. 7.95 (*0-88177-184-8*, DR184) Discipleship Res.

Ramirez, Manuel, III. Multicultural Psychotherapy: An Approach to Individual & Cultural Differences. 2nd ed. 236p. (C). 1998. 42.00 (*0-205-28904-5*) Allyn.

Ramirez, Mari C. Cantos Paralelos: La Parodia Plastica en el Arte Argentino Contemporaneo (Visual Parody in Contemporary Argentinean Art) (ENG & SPA., Illus.). 312p. 1999. pap. 50.00 (*0-935213-14-7*) J S Blanton Mus.

Ramirez, Mari C., et al, contrib. by. Encounters - Displacements: Luis Camnitzer, Alfredo Jarr, Cildo Meireles. (Illus.). 77p. 1992. pap. 24.00 (*0-935213-23-6*) J S Blanton Mus.

Ramirez, Mari C., ed. El Taller Torres-Garcia: The School of the South & Its Legacy. LC 91-20731. (Illus.). 411p. 1992. pap. 29.95 (*0-292-78122-9*) U of Tex Pr.

Ramirez, Mari C., et al. Re-Aligning Vision: Alternative Currents in South American Drawing. LC 97-71055. (Illus.). 238p. (C). 1997. pap. 35.00 (*0-935213-07-4*) J S Blanton Mus.

Ramirez Mattei, Aida E. Carmelina Vizcarrondo: Vida, Obra y Antologia. (UPREX, Estudios Literarios Ser.: No. 8). 261p. (C). 1972. pap. 1.50 (*0-8477-0008-9*) U of PR Pr.

Ramirez-Mattei, Aida E. La Narrativa de Carlos Fuentes: Afan por la Armonia en la Multiplicidad Antagonica del Mundo. LC 83-1322. (SPA.). xv, 437p. (Orig.). (C). 1983. pap. 8.50 (*0-8477-3507-9*) U of PR Pr.

Ramirez, Michael R. Gingerbread Sleepover. (Chana! Ser.: No. 3). 96p. (J). (gr. 1-4). 1997. pap. 3.99 (*0-380-79019-X*, Avon Bks) Morrow Avon.

— Hola, California! (Chana! Ser.: No. 1). (J). (gr. 3-5). 1997. pap. 3.99 (*0-380-79017-3*, Avon Bks) Morrow Avon.

— Hoppin' Halloween! (Chana! Ser.: No. 2). (J). 1997. pap. 3.99 (*0-380-79018-1*, Avon Bks) Morrow Avon.

— The Legend of the Hummingbird: A Tale from Puerto Rico. LC 96-38004. (Illus.). 32p. (J). (gr. k-4). 1998. pap. 4.95 (*1-57255-232-8*) Mondo Pubng.

Ramirez, Michael R. & Sawaya, Linda. The Little Ant - La Hormiga Chiquita. LC 95-10282.Tr. of La Hormiga Chiquita. (ENG & SPA., Illus.). 32p. (J). 1995. 12.95 (*0-8478-1922-1*, Pub. by Rizzoli Intl) St Martin.

Ramirez, Michael Rose. Gingerbread Sleepover, 3. (Chana! Ser.). (J). 1997. 9.09 (*0-606-12652-X*, Pub. by Turtleback) Demco.

Ramirez, Michael Rose. Hola, California! (Chana! Ser.). 1997. 9.09 (*0-606-11199-9*, Pub. by Turtleback) Demco.

— Hoppin' Halloween!, 2. (Chana! Ser.). 1997. 9.09 (*0-606-11200-6*, Pub. by Turtleback) Demco.

Ramirez, Miguel D. Development Banking in Mexico: The Case of the Nacional Financiera, S. A. LC 85-16700. 252p. 1985. 59.95 (*0-275-92032-1*, C2032, Praeger Pubs) Greenwood.

— Mexico's Economic Crisis: Its Origins & Consequences. LC 88-30738. 164p. 1989. 52.95 (*0-275-92867-5*, C2867, Praeger Pubs) Greenwood.

Ramirez, Noel, jt. auth. see Lindenberg, Marc M.

Ramirez, Noemi, jt. auth. see Eoff, Sherman H.

Ramirez, O. T., jt. ed. see Galindo, E.

Ramirez, Oscar M. & Daniel, R. K. Endoscopic Aesthetic Surgery: A Video Manual, PAL Version. (Illus.). 80p. 1995. 225.00 (*3-540-92626-7*) Spr-Verlag.

Ramirez, Oscar M. & Daniel, Rollin K. Manual of Endoscopic Aesthetic Surgery. LC 94-30008. 1994. 245.00 (*0-387-92623-2*) Spr-Verlag.

Ramirez, Oscar M. & Daniel, Rollin K., eds. Endoscopic Techniques in Plastic & Aesthetic Surgery. LC 95-16149. (Illus.). 424p. 1995. 269.00 (*0-387-94466-4*) Spr-Verlag.

Ramirez, P. C., jt. ed. see Colburn, I. P.

Ramirez-Pekarsky, Anna, ed. see Esparza, June F.

Ramirez, Rafael, jt. auth. see Delano, Poli.

Ramirez, Rafael, jt. auth. see Normann, Richard.

Ramirez, Rafael, jt. auth. see Normann, Richard A.

Ramirez, Rafael E. El Arrabal y la Politica. Lopez-Chiclana, Margarita, tr. from ENG. LC 76-40124. (Centro de Investigaciones Sociales Ser.). (Orig.). Title: Politics & the Urban Poor. (SPA., Illus.). (Orig.). 1977. 4.80 (*0-8477-2484-0*) U of PR Pr.

Ramirez, Rafael L. Dime Capitan: Raflexiones Sobre la Masculinidad. LC 93-74310. 133p. (Orig.). 1993. pap. 8.50 (*0-929157-18-4*) Ediciones Huracan.

— What It Means to Be a Man: Reflections on Puerto Rican Masculinity. Casper, Rosa E., tr. from SPA. LC 98-49682. 144p. (C). 1999. text 48.00 (*0-8135-2660-4*); pap. text 17.00 (*0-8135-2661-2*) Rutgers U Pr.

Ramirez, Rafael L. & Deliz, Wenceslao S., eds. Crisis y Critica de las Ciencias Sociales en Puerto Rico. 310p. 1980. pap. 5.95 (*0-8477-2465-4*) U of PR Pr.

Ramirez, Rafael L., jt. auth. see Rivera-Medina, Eduardo.

***Ramirez, Raul.** Signposts Language Arts Activities for Grade 3. Barbe, Walter B., ed. 64p. (J). (gr. 3-4). 2000. wbk. ed. 2.95 (*1-56762-120-1*) Modern Learn Pr.

***Ramirez, Raul C., Jr.** Signposts Language Arts Activities for Grade 3 Teacher's Manual. Barbe, Walter B., ed. 80p. 2000. teacher ed. 16.95 (*1-56762-124-4*) Modern Learn Pr.

Ramirez, Ricardo. Fiesta, Worship & Family. anniversary ed. 56p. 1981. write for info. (*0-614-04868-0*) Mex Am Cult.

Ramirez-Rivera, Jose, tr. see Coll Y Toste, Cayetano.

Ramirez, Robert W. The FFT: Fundamentals & Concepts. LC 84-8284. (Illus.). 192p. (C). 1985. 86.00 (*0-13-314386-4*) P-H.

Ramirez, Ron & Prosise, Michael. Philco Radio, 1928-1942. LC 93-85275. (Illus.). 160p. 1993. pap. 29.95 (*0-88740-547-9*) Schiffer.

Ramirez, Sabet, tr. see Serbin, Andres.

Ramirez, Santiago & Cohen, Robert S., eds. Mexican Studies in the History & Philosophy of Science. LC 95-13783. (Boston Studies in the Philosophy of Science: Vol. 172). 1995. lib. bdg. 144.00 (*0-7923-3462-0*, Pub. by Kluwer Academic) Kluwer Academic.

Ramirez, Sergio. Hatful of Tigers: Reflections on Art, Culture & Politics. Flakoll, Darwin J., tr. from SPA. LC 94-23592. 136p. 1995. 15.00 (*0-915306-98-0*) Curbstone.

— Stories from Nicaragua. Caistor, Nick, tr. from SPA. (Readers International Ser.). (Illus.). 120p. (C). 1987. pap. 7.95 (*0-930523-29-6*) Readers Intl.

— To Bury Our Fathers: A Novel of Nicaragua. Caistor, Nick, tr. from SPA. LC 84-61849. (Illus.). 257p. (C). 1985. pap. 11.95 (*0-930523-03-2*) Readers Intl.

Ramirez, Sergio & Conrad, Robert E., eds. Sandino, the Testimony of a Nicaraguan Patriot, 1921-1934. LC 89-48567. (Illus.). 465p. 1990. reprint ed. pap. 144.20 (*0-608-02578-X*, 206322400004) Bks Demand.

Ramirez, Sharon. Brinktown. 150p. (Orig.). 1981. pap. 5.00 (*0-932112-12-9*) Carolina Wren.

Ramirez, Sharon & Scheie, David. Cops & Neighbors: An Evaluation of the Whittier Community-Based Policing Project. 70p. (Orig.). (C). 1994. pap. text 30.00 (*0-7881-0753-4*) DIANE Pub.

Ramirez, Sharon, et al. Better Together: Religious Institutions As Partners in Community Based Development. (Illus.). 80p. (Orig.). 1994. pap. 8.00 (*0-9624428-5-2*) Rainbow Research.

Ramirez, Sixto. The Church of God at Corinth. (Know Your Bible Ser.). 204p. (Orig.). 1997. pap. 5.95 (*1-889505-08-0*) White Wing Pub.

— El Sermon del Monte - The Sermon on the Mount. (Serie Conozca Su Biblia - Know Your Bible Ser.). (SPA.). 149p. 1996. pap. text 5.95 (*1-889505-02-1*) White Wing Pub.

Ramirez, Stephen. Health Promotion for All: Strategies for Reaching Diverse Populations at the Workplace. LC 94-232169. 128p. (Orig.). 1994. pap. 25.00 (*0-9628334-3-6*) WELCOA.

Ramirez, Steven A., ed. Kansas Corporation Law & Practice: Including Tax Aspects. 4th rev. ed. LC 98-65371. 800p. 1998. ring bd. write for info. (*1-890452-04-1*) KS Bar.

Ramirez, Susan Berry Brill de, see Brill de Ramirez, Susan Berry.

Ramirez, Susan E. The World Upside Down: Cross-Cultural Contact & Conflict in Sixteenth-Century Peru. (Illus.). 250p. 1998. pap. 18.95 (*0-8047-3520-4*) Stanford U Pr.

Ramirez, Susan E., ed. see MacLeod, Murdo J., et al.

Ramirez Villareal, Humberto. Diccionario Ilustrado de Electronica. (SPA.). 192p. 24.95 (*0-7859-0708-4*, S-25248) Fr & Eur.

Ramirez, W. F. Computational Methods in Process Simulation. 2nd ed. LC 98-149714. (Illus.). 512p. 1998. text 70.00 (*0-7506-3541-X*) Buttrwrth-Heinemann.

Ramirez, W. Fred. Computational Methods for Process Simulation. (Illus.). 501p. 1989. 79.95 (*0-409-90184-9*) Buttrwrth-Heinemann.

— Process Control & Identification. (Illus.). 424p. 1993. text 73.00 (*0-12-577240-8*) Acad Pr.

***Ramirez, Yasmin & Estrada, Henry.** Pressing the Point: Parallel Expressions in the Graphic Arts of the Chicano & Puerto Rican Movement. (ENG & SPA., Illus.). 56p. 1999. pap. write for info. (*1-882454-09-X*) El Museo Barrio.

Ramirez, Yasmin, jt. auth. see Cullen, Deborah.

***Ramiro, J. M. Santamaria & Aisa, P. A. Brana.** Risk Analysis & Reduction in the Chemical Process Industry. Hutchinson, J. S. M., tr. LC 97-61082. (Illus.). 384p. 1998. write for info. (*0-7514-0374-1*) Kluwer Academic.

Ramis, Guillermo, jt. auth. see Cerda, Victor.

Ramis, J. P., jt. ed. see Gerard, R.

Ramis, Jean-Pierre. Theoremes d'Indices Gevrey pour les Equations Differentielles Ordinaires. LC 83-27157. (Memoirs Ser.: No. 48/296). 95p. 1984. pap. 17.00 (*0-8218-2296-9*, MEMO/48/296) Am Math.

Ramis, Magali G. Happy Days, Uncle Sergio. Esteves, Carmen C., tr. from SPA. (Secret Weapons Ser.: Vol. 8). 176p. (Orig.). 1995. pap. 12.00 (*1-877727-52-0*) White Pine.

Ramis, Magali G. & Chesler, Phyllis. Las Noches del Riel de Oro. LC 94-21995. 204p. 1996. pap. text. write for info. (*1-56758-039-4*) Edit Cultl.

***Ramjerdi, Jan E.** Re.La.Vir. LC 99-47452. 125p. 1999. pap. 9.95 (*1-57366-082-5*) Northwestern U Pr.

Ramjhun, Ahmad F. Implementing the Code of Practice for Children with Special Educational Needs: A Practical Guide. 128p. 1995. pap. 19.95 (*1-85346-416-3*, Pub. by David Fulton) Taylor & Francis.

Ramji, D., jt. auth. see Gacesa, P.

Ramji, Dipak P., jt. auth. see Gacesa, Peter.

Ramjohn, M. Opinion Writing & Drafting in Equity & Trusts. 250p. 1996. pap. write for info. (*1-85941-033-2*, Pub. by Cavendish Pubng) Gaunt.

— Revenue Law. (Questions & Answers Ser.). 320p. 1996. 18.00 (*1-874241-35-X*, Pub. by Cavendish Pubng) Gaunt.

Ramjohn, Mohammed. Sourcebook on Law of Trusts. (Sourcebook Ser.). 790p. 1995. pap. 36.00 (*1-85941-102-9*, Pub. by Cavendish Pubng) Gaunt.

— Sourcebook on Trusts Law. 2nd ed. (Cavendish Publishing Sourcebook Ser.). 976p. 1998. pap. 40.00 (*1-85941-186-X*) Gaunt.

Ramke, Bin. The Erotic Light of Gardens. LC 88-28070. (Wesleyan Poetry Ser.). 71p. 1989. pap. 12.95 (*0-8195-1174-9*, Wesleyan Univ Pr); text 25.00 (*0-8195-2171-X*, Wesleyan Univ Pr) U Pr of New Eng.

— The Language Student: Poems. LC 86-7439. 64p. 1986. reprint ed. pap. 30.00 (*0-608-00870-2*, 206166200010) Bks Demand.

— The Language Student. Poems. LC 86-7439. 58p. 1986. text 15.95 (*0-8071-1344-1*) La State U Pr.

— Massacre of the Innocents. LC 94-37407. (Iowa Poetry Prize Ser.). 95p. (Orig.). 1995. pap. 11.95 (*0-87745-492-2*) U of Iowa Pr.

— Wake. LC 98-47406. (Iowa Poetry Prize Ser.). 130p. 1999. pap. 10.95 (*0-87745-658-5*) U of Iowa Pr.

Ramker. New York. (Discover America Ser.). 1979. 6.99 (*0-8442-7469-0*) NTC Contemp Pub Co.

Ramkinshina, D., ed. Neal R. Amundson: A Special Issue in His Honor - A Special Issue of the Journal Chemical Engineering Communications. 486p. 1987. pap. text 757.00 (*2-88124-256-1*) Gordon & Breach.

***Ramkrishna, Doraiswami.** Population Balances: Theory & Applications to Particulate Systems in Engineering. 400p. 2000. 115.00 (*0-12-576970-9*) Acad Pr.

Ramkrishnan, E. V. Making It New: Modernism in Malahalam, Marathi & Hindi Poetry. (C). 1995. 29.50 (*81-85952-26-4*, Pub. by M Manoharial) S Asia.

Ramkumar, Usha, jt. auth. see Tara, S. Nayana.

***Ramljak, Suzanne, et al.** Turning Wood into Art: The Jane & Arthur Mason Collection. LC 99-41228. (Illus.). 224p. 2000. 49.50 (*0-8109-4483-9*, Pub. by Abrams) Time Warner.

Ramlu, M. A. Mine Disasters & Mine Rescue. (Illus.). 408p. (C). 1991. text 123.00 (*90-6191-964-9*, Pub. by A A Balkema) Ashgate Pub Co.

— Mine Hoisting. LC 99-227028. (Illus.). 586p. (C). 1996. text 149.00 (*90-5410-298-5*, Pub. by A A Balkema) Ashgate Pub Co.

Ramly, Anita. Malay: Language Survival Kit. (Illus.). 130p. 1996. pap. 5.95 (*0-86442-463-9*) Lonely Planet.

Ramm, A. G. Iterative Methods of Calculating Static Fields & Wave Scattering by Small Bodies. (Illus.). 124p. 1982. 79.95 (*0-387-90682-7*) Spr-Verlag.

— Multidimensional Inverse Scattering Problems. 392p. 1992. 155.00 (*0-582-05665-9*, LM5665, Chap & Hall CRC) CRC Pr.

— Scattering by Obstacles. 1986. text 248.00 (*90-277-2103-3*) Kluwer Academic.

— Theory & Applications of Some New Classes of Integral Equations. 344p. 1980. pap. 31.50 (*0-685-04732-6*) Spr-Verlag.

***Ramm, A. G., et al, eds.** Operator Theory & Its Applications. (FIC Ser.: Vol. 25). 574p. 2000. 130.00 (*0-8218-1990-9*) Am Math.

Ramm, Agatha, ed. Beloved & Darling Child: Last Letters Between Queen Victoria & Her Eldest Daughter, 1886-1901. (Illus.). 304p. 1998. pap. 27.95 (*0-7509-1825-X*, Pub. by Sutton Pub Ltd) Intl Pubs Mktg.

— The Gladstone-Granville Correspondence. (Camden Classic Reprints Ser.: No. 5). 416p. (C). 1998. text 64.95 (*0-521-64208-6*); pap. text 24.95 (*0-521-64559-X*) Cambridge U Pr.

Ramm, Alexander G. Random Fields Estimation Theory. LC 89-33272. (Pitman Monographs & Surveys in Pure & Applied Mathematics: No. 48). 282p. 1990. pap. 87.50 (*0-608-05239-6*, 206577600001) Bks Demand.

Ramm, Alexander G., ed. Inverse Problems, Tomography & Image Processing: Proceedings of Mathematics; Theoretical & Mathematical Physics; Biomedical Engineering. LC 98-18144. (Illus.). 268p. (C). 1998. text 95.00 (*0-306-45828-4*, Kluwer Plenum) Kluwer Academic.

— Spectral & Scattering Theory: Proceedings of Sessions from the 1st Congress of the International Society for Analysis, Applications, & Computing Held in Newark, Delaware, June 2-6, 1997. LC 98-15605. (Illus.). 216p. (C). 1998. text 79.50 (*0-306-45829-2*, Kluwer Plenum) Kluwer Academic.

Ramm, Alexander G. & Katsevich, Alexander I. The Radon Transform & Local Tomography. LC 96-2194. (Illus.). 485p. 1996. lib. bdg. 94.95 (*0-8493-9492-9*) CRC Pr.

***Ramm, Bernard.** The Evangelical Heritage: A Study in Historical Theology. 192p. (C). 2000. reprint ed. pap. 15.99 (*0-8010-2238-X*) Baker Bks.

Ramm, Bernard. Protestant Biblical Interpretation: A Textbook of Hermeneutics. 3rd ed. 328p. 1999. pap. 14.99 (*0-8010-2083-2*) Baker Bks.

Ramm, Bernard L. Offense to Reason: A Theology of Sin. 187p. 1992. reprint ed. ring bd. 12.95 (*1-57383-001-1*) Regent College.

— Protestant Biblical Interpretation. Chan, Silas, tr. from ENG. (CHI.). (C). 1984. pap. write for info. (*0-941598-10-1*) Living Spring Pubns.

Ramm, Charles A. Meditations on the Mystery of Christmas. Lilly, Catherine M., ed. LC 59-15709. (Illus.). 76p. 1959. 12.95 (*0-87015-092-8*) Pacific Bks.

Ramm, Hartmut. The Marxism of Regis Debray: Between Lenin & Guevara. LC 77-17915. xii, 240p. 1978. 25.00 (*0-7006-0170-8*) U Pr of KS.

Ramm, Heinrich J. Fluid Dynamics for the Study of Transonic Flow. (Oxford Engineering Science Ser.: No. 23). (Illus.). 216p. 1990. text 65.00 (*0-19-506097-0*) OUP.

Ramm, Herman. Roman York from A. D. 71: A Pictorial Guide with Map & Suggested Roman Walk. (C). 1990. 40.00 (*1-85072-001-0*, Pub. by W Sessions) St Mut.

— Roman York from AD 71. 6th rev. ed. 1999. pap. 21.00 (*1-85072-084-3*, Pub. by W Sessions) St Mut.

Rammage, Linda A., jt. auth. see Koschkee, Danna L.

Rammel, Hal. Aero into the Aether: Surrealist Comics & Poems. (Illus.). 28p. 1980. pap. 12.00 (*0-941194-14-0*) Black Swan Pr.

— Nowhere in America: The Big Rock Candy Mountain & Other Comic Utopias. (Folklore & Society Ser.). (Illus.). 184p. 1990. text 25.95 (*0-252-01717-X*) U of Ill Pr.

***Rammelkamp, Charles.** I Don't Think God's That Cruel (Poems by Charles Rammelkamp) 33p. 2000. pap. 46.00 (*1-882983-46-7*) March Street Pr.

Rammeloo, J., ed. Mexique: Des Plantes pour les Hommes. (FRE., Illus.). 143p. 1993. pap. 45.00 (*1-878762-81-8*, Pub. by Natl Botanic Grdn Belgium) Balogh.

— Mousses, Bonkei, Bonsai: Un Secret Seculaire du Jardinier Japonais. (FRE., Illus.). 137p. 1989. pap. 40.00 (*1-878762-82-6*, Pub. by Natl Botanic Grdn Belgium) Balogh.

Rammeloo, J. & Walleyn, R. The Edible Fungi of Africa South of the Sahara: A Literature Survey. (Scripta Botanica Belgica Ser.: Vol. 5). (Illus.). 63p. 1993. 21.00 (*90-72619-12-9*, Pub. by Natl Botanic Grdn Belgium) Balogh.

Rammeloo, J., jt. auth. see Walleyn, R.

Rammensee, Hans-Georg & Bachmann, Jutta. MHC Ligands & Peptide Motifs. LC 97-18997. (Molecular Biology Intelligence Unit Ser.). 1997. text 99.00 (*1-57059-460-0*) Landes Bioscience.

Rammer. Quantum Transport Theory. (C). 1998. write for info. (*0-201-48320-3*) Addison-Wesley.

Rammer, Jorgen. Quantum Transport Theory. LC 98-86414. (Frontiers in Physics Ser.). 528p. 1998. text 55.00 (*0-7382-0048-4*) Perseus Pubng.

Rammerstorfer, F. G., ed. Nonlinear Analysis of Shells by Finite Elements. (CISM International Centre for Mechanical Sciences Ser.: Vol. 328). (Illus.). v, 283p. 1992. 86.95 (*0-387-82416-2*) Spr-Verlag.

Rammerstorfer, F. G., jt. auth. see Hult, J.

Rammey, Austin, jt. auth. see Butler, David.

Ramminger, Johann, ed. see Avitus, Alcimus E.

Rammohun Roy, R. The English Works of Raja Ramohun Roy. Ghose, Jogendra C., ed. LC 75-41220. reprint ed. 72.50 (*0-404-14738-0*) AMS Pr.

***Rammstein.** Rammstein. 1999. pap. 29.95 (*3-931126-32-3*) Die Gestalten.

An Asterisk (*) at the beginning of an entry indicates that the title is appearing for the first time.

— Rammstein. (Illus.). 160p. 1999. 39.99 (*3-931126-19-6*, Pub. by Die Gestalten) Consort Bk Sales.

Rammuny, Raji M. Advanced Business Arabic. (ARA.). 320p. 1994. pap. 24.95 (*0-86685-416-9*, IBC4169) Intl Bk Ctr.

— Advanced Standard Arabic: Through Authentic Texts & Audiovisual Materials, Pt. 2. 128p. 1994. pap. text 24.95 (*0-472-08262-0*, 08262) U of Mich Pr.

— Advanced Standard Arabic: Through Authentic Texts & Audiovisual Materials, Pt. 1. 344p. 1994. pap. text 29.95 (*0-472-08261-2*, 08261) U of Mich Pr.

— Arabic Sounds & Letters: A Programmed Course Text. (ARA.). 104p. 1999. pap. text 15.95 (*0-916798-18-6*) UM Dept NES.

— Business Arabic, Advanced Level: Authentic Texts & Audiovisual Materials. (Illus.). 408p. 1999. pap. text 29.95 (*0-472-08511-5*, 08511) U of Mich Pr.

— Business Arabic, Intermediate Level: Language, Culture, & Communication. (Illus.). 344p. 1999. pap. text 34.50 (*0-472-08510-7*, 08510) U of Mich Pr.

— Programmed Arabic-Islamic Reader, Bk. I. 1991. audio 65.00 (*0-86685-545-9*) Intl Bk Ctr.

Rammuny, Raji M. Programmed Arabic-Islamic Reader II. 320p. 1994. pap., teacher ed. 5.95 (*0-86685-747-8*) Intl Bk Ctr.

Rammuny, Raji M. Programmed Arabic-Islamic Reader II, Bk. 2. (ARA & ENG.). 1988. teacher ed. 5.95 (*0-86685-635-8*); pap. 24.95 (*0-86685-431-2*); audio 99.95 (*0-86685-546-7*) Intl Bk Ctr.

Rammuny, Raji M. Programmed Arabic-Islamic Reader I. (Illus.). 206p. 1987. pap., teacher ed. 5.95 (*0-86685-746-X*) Intl Bk Ctr.

Rammuny, Raji M. Programmed Arabic-Islamic Reader I. 1991. pap. 19.95 (*0-86685-412-6*) Intl Bk Ctr.

— Standard Achievement Tests. 118p. 1994. pap. text 11.00 (*1-57074-141-7*) Greyden Pr.

— Supplementary Enrichment Vocabulary: Preliminary Edition, Lessons 1-40. 82p. (C). 1994. pap. text 9.00 (*1-57074-145-X*) Greyden Pr.

Rammuny, Raji M. & McCarus, Ernest N. A Programmed Course in Modern Literary Arabic Phonology & Script. 1995. 14.95 (*0-86685-384-7*, UM02X) Intl Bk Ctr.

Rammuny, Raji M. & Parkinson, Dilworth B., eds. Investigating Arabic: Linguistic, Pedagogical & Literary Studies in Honor of Ernest N. McCarus. 310p. (C). 1994. pap. text 21.95 (*1-57074-108-5*) Greyden Pr.

Rammuny, Raji M., et al. Course in Levantine Arabic. 335p. 1979. 24.95 (*0-86685-385-5*, UM070, Pub. by Librairie du Liban) Intl Bk Ctr.

— First Lessons in Literary Arabic. 1972. 13.95 (*0-86685-383-9*) Intl Bk Ctr.

Ramnarayan, Gowri. Past Forward: 6 Artists in Search of Their Childhood. LC 97-906438. (Illus.). 82p. (C). 1997. 17.95 (*0-19-563939-1*) OUP.

Ramnarayan, Gowri, tr. see Tendulkar, Vijay.

Ramnarayan, S., et al. Organization Development: Interventions & Strategies. LC 97-41760. 1998. write for info. (*0-7619-9223-5*); pap. write for info. (*0-7619-9224-3*) Sage.

Ramni, K. V. Readings in Personnel Management Vols. 1-4: Dynamics of Personnel Management; Personnel Management & Industrial Relations; Sociology of Personnel Management & Rural Relations; & Personnel Management Technology for Productivity, 4 vols. 1270p. 1995. 1050.00 (*81-7099-622-8*, Pub. by Print Hse) St Mut.

Ramnujan, A. K., tr. see Murthy, U. R.

Ramo, Roberta C., frwd. Lawyer's Guide to the Internet. LC 95-75479. 368p. 1995. pap. 29.95 (*1-57073-149-7*) ABA Prof Educ Pubns.

Ramo, Simon. America's Technology Slip. LC 80-21525. 304p. reprint ed. pap. 94.30 (*0-8357-5410-3*, 202150300021) Bks Demand.

Ramo, Simon, et al, eds. Peacetime Uses of Outer Space. LC 76-52430. (Illus.). 279p. 1977. reprint ed. lib. bdg. 38.50 (*0-8371-9368-0*, RAPU, Greenwood Pr) Greenwood.

Ramo, Simon, et al. Fields & Waves in Communication Electronics. 3rd ed. 864p. 1994. text 100.95 (*0-471-58551-3*) Wiley.

— Fields & Waves in Communication Electronics. 3rd ed. 251p. 1994. pap. text 20.95 (*0-471-30846-3*) Wiley.

Ramogale, Marcus, ed. To Kill a Man's Pride & Other Stories from Southern Africa. 2nd rev. ed. LC 97-182824. 272p. 1996. pap. text 14.95 (*0-86975-460-2*, Pub. by Ravan Pr) Ohio U Pr.

Ramoleko. Information Technology & the Developing World. 69.95 (*1-85972-057-9*) Ashgate Pub Co.

***Ramon.** My Questions - God's Questions. LC 99-56443. 160p. Date not set. 16.00 (*1-57312-294-7*) Smyth & Helwys.

Ramon. Psychiatry in Transition. (C). pap. 18.95 (*0-7453-0470-2*, Pub. by Pluto GBR) Stylus Pub VA.

— Psychiatry in Transition: The British & Italian Experiences. 288p. (C). 49.95 (*0-7453-0177-0*, Pub. by Pluto GBR) Stylus Pub VA.

Ramon, Alberto. On Both Sides of the River. 1998. pap. 16.95 (*1-878208-84-5*) Guild Pr IN.

***Ramon, Brother.** Seven Days of Solitude: A Guidebook for a Personal Retreat. LC 99-88234. 192p. 2000. pap. 13.95 (*0-7648-0501-0*) Liguori Pubns.

Ramon, J. Motivando a Nuestra Gente.Tr. of Motivating Our People. (SPA.). 1995. pap. 6.99 (*0-8297-1863-X*) Vida Pubs.

Ramon-Medrano, M., jt. ed. see Julve, J.

Ramon, Pitarch. Ch'ulel: Una Etnografia de las Almas Tzeltales (An Ethnography of the Tzeltal Souls) (SPA.). 274p. 1996. pap. 14.99 (*968-16-4818-8*, Pub. by Fondo) Continental Bk.

Ramon, Shulamit. Mental Health in Europe: Ends, Beginnings, & Rediscoveries. 224p. 1996. text 59.95 (*0-312-16066-6*) St Martin.

— Psychiatric Hospital Closure: Myths & Realities. 224p. 1992. pap. 47.75 (*1-56593-048-7*, 0296) Thomson Learn.

Ramon Y Cajal, Santiago. Advice for a Young Investigator. LC 98-26036. (Illus.). 120p. 1999. 22.50 (*0-262-18191-6*, Bradford Bks) MIT Pr.

— New Ideas on the Structure of the Nervous System in Man & Vertebrates. Swanson, Larry W. & Swanson, Neely, trs. from FRE. 200p. 1990. 37.95 (*0-262-18141-X*) MIT Pr.

— Reglas y Consejos Sobre Investigacion Cientifica. (Nueva Austral Ser.: Vol. 232). (SPA.). 1991. pap. text 24.95 (*84-239-7232-1*) Elliots Bks.

Ramona. Thirty-Four Years & Counting: A Journal of My Struggle with Leukemia. 205p. 1998. pap. write for info. (*1-893250-00-8*) Mariah Pr Inc.

Ramond, Pierre. Beyond the Standard Model. (C). 1998. write for info. (*0-201-56978-7*) Addison-Wesley.

— Field Theory. 2nd ed. (C). 1990. pap. 50.00 (*0-201-30450-3*) Addison-Wesley.

— Field Theory: A Modern Primer. 2nd ed. (Frontiers in Physics Ser.). (Illus.). 352p. 1988. text 43.25 (*0-201-15772-1*) Addison-Wesley.

***Ramond, Pierre.** Journeys Beyond the Standard Model. 304p. 1999. 60.00 (*0-7382-0116-2*, Pub. by Perseus Pubng) HarpC.

— Marquetry. (Illus.). 238p. 1998. 110.00 (*2-85101-005-0*) Antique Collect.

Ramond, Pierre. Marquetry. Derenne, Jackqueline et al, trs. from FRE. LC 88-51885. (Illus.). 240p. 1995. 75.00 (*0-942391-19-5*, 70098) Taunton.

***Ramond, Pierre.** Masterpieces of Marquetry, Vols. 1-3. LC 99-86492. 2000. write for info. (*0-89236-594-3*, J P Getty Museum) J P Getty Trust.

Ramonda, Robert, jt. auth. see Smith, Lonna.

Ramondetta, P. J. Facies & Stratigraphy of the San Andres Formation, Northern & Northwestern Shelves of the Midland Basin, Texas & New Mexico. (Reports of Investigations: RI 128). (Illus.). 56p. 1982. pap. 2.50 (*0-318-03277-5*) Bur Econ Geology.

Ramondino, Salvatore. Spanish-English Dictionary. rev. ed. (SPA.). 1996. mass mkt. 6.99 (*0-451-18168-9*, Sig) NAL.

Ramondino, Salvatore, jt. auth. see Madrigal, M.

Ramondino, Salvatore, jt. auth. see Morehead, Andrew.

Ramone, Dee Dee. Poison Heart: Surviving the Ramones. (Illus.). 192p. 1998. pap. 16.95 (*0-946719-19-5*, Pub. by Helter Skelter) Interlink Pub.

***Ramone, Dee Dee, et al.** Lobotomy: Surviving the Ramones. LC 99-42130. Orig. Title: Poison Heart: Surviving the Ramones. 256p. 2000. pap. 14.95 (*1-56025-252-9*, Thunders Mouth) Avalon NY.

Ramoniene, Meilute, jt. auth. see Press, Ian.

Ramos. Developing As a Democracy. LC 98-40746. 2000. text 30.00 (*0-312-20204-0*) St Martin.

— The Last Client of Luis Montez, Vol. 1. 1997. mass mkt. write for info. (*0-312-96105-7*) St Martin.

Ramos, jt. auth. see Kaiser.

Ramos, A. Diccionario de la Naturaleza. (SPA.). 976p. 1987. lib. bdg. 49.95 (*0-7859-5016-8*, 8423969495) Fr & Eur.

— Diccionario de la Naturaleza: Hombre, Ecologia, Paisaje. (SPA.). 1032p. 1989. 225.00 (*0-7859-9236-7*) Fr & Eur.

Ramos, Aaron G., ed. Las Ideas Anexionistas en Puerto Rico Bajo la Dominacion Norteamericana. LC 87-82378. (Clasicos Huracan Ser.). (SPA.). 183p. 1987. pap. 8.25 (*0-940238-92-6*) Ediciones Huracan.

Ramos, Abiud R. Vocabulario Tecnico de Contabilidad Moderna. 159p. 1992. pap. 8.95 (*0-8477-2645-2*) U of PR Pr.

Ramos, Adam & Ramos, Joseph R. California Brandy: The Wine Drinker's Spirit. (Illus.). 160p. 1990. 14.95 (*0-929935-08-X*) Countrywomans Pr.

— Mixed Wine Drinks: 700 Recipes for Punches, Hot Drinks, Coolers & Cocktails. 2nd ed. LC 74-25080. (Illus.). 160p. 1990. pap. 9.95 (*0-02-003504-7*) Macmillan.

Ramos, Alberto G. The New Science of Organizations: A Reconceptualization of the Wealth of Nations. 224p. 1984. pap. 17.95 (*0-8020-6561-9*) U of Toronto Pr.

— The New Science of Organizations: A Reconceptualization of the Wealth of Nations. LC 81-178962. 224p. reprint ed. pap. 69.50 (*0-608-16236-1*, 202646900049) Bks Demand.

Ramos, Alcida R. Indigenism: Ethnic Politics in Brazil. LC 98-15472. 1998. 55.00 (*0-299-16040-8*); pap. 21.95 (*0-299-16044-0*) U of Wis Pr.

— Sanuma Memories: Yanomani Ethnography in Times of Crisis. LC 94-39614. (New Directions in Anthropological Writing Ser.). (Illus.). 320p. 1995. pap. text 19.95 (*0-299-14654-5*); lib. bdg. 50.00 (*0-299-14650-2*) U of Wis Pr.

***Ramos, Alice.** Beauty, Art & the Polis. LC 00-21847. 2000. write for info. (*0-9669226-2-X*) Am Maritain.

Ramos, Angel, ed. Diccionario de la Naturaleza: Hombre, Ecologio, Paisaje. (SPA., Illus.). 1032p. 1989. 239.50 (*84-239-6949-5*) Elliots Bks.

Ramos-Arizpe, Miguel. Report That Dr. Miguel Ramos de Arizpe, Priest of Borbon, & Deputy in the Present General & Special Cortes of Spain for the Province of Coahuila, One of the Four Eastern Interior Provinces of the Kingdom of Mexico, Presents to the August Congress, 11--11. Benson, Nettie L., tr. & intro. by. LC 69-19011. 61p. 1970. reprint ed. lib. bdg. 55.00 (*0-8371-1036-X*, TLRR) Greenwood.

Ramos, Artur. The Negro in Brazil. Pattee, Richard, tr. LC 80-25342. (Perspectives in Latin American History Ser.: No. 3). xx, 203p. 1980. reprint ed. lib. bdg. 35.00 (*0-87991-604-4*) Porcupine Pr.

Ramos-Bossini, Francisco. Legal Dictionary, Spanish-English/English-Spanish. (ENG & SPA.). 568p. 1997. 150.00 (*0-7859-9643-5*) Fr & Eur.

Ramos, Carey R, & Practising Law Institute Staff. Handling Intellectual Property Issues in Business Transactions: Strategies for the Business Lawyer. LC 98-170057. (Patents, Copyrights, Trademarks, & Literary Property Course Handbook Ser.). 344p. 1998. 129.00 (*0-87224-461-X*) PLI.

Ramos, Christine, ed. see Gustafson, Marilyne.

Ramos, David E., ed. Walnut Production Manual. LC 95-62443. (Illus.). viii, 320p. 1997. 50.00 (*1-879906-33-3*, 3373-H); pap. 35.00 (*1-879906-27-9*, 3373) ANR Pubns CA.

Ramos, Diane P., jt. auth. see Matejka, Ken.

Ramos, Efren Rivera, see Rivera Ramos, Efren.

Ramos, Elias T. Dualistic Unionism & Industrial Relations. 250p. (Orig.). (C). 1990. pap. 16.50 (*971-10-0415-1*, Pub. by New Day Pub) Cellar.

Ramos-Elorduy, Julieta & Menzel, Peter. Creepy Crawly Cuisine: The Gourmet Guide to Edible Insects. LC 97-48506. (Illus.). 128p. 1998. pap. 16.00 (*0-89281-747-X*, Park St Pr) Inner Tradit.

Ramos, Emilio, et al. Computer Networking Concepts. LC 95-18636. 358p. 1995. 111.00 (*0-02-408031-4*, Macmillan Coll) P-H.

Ramos, Emilio, et al. Data Communications & Networking Fundamentals Using Novell Netware. (Illus.). 473p. (Orig.). (C). 1992. teacher ed. write for info. (*0-318-69336-4*) Macmillan.

— Data Communications & Networking Fundamentals Using Novell Netware. (Illus.). 496p. (Orig.). (C). 1992. pap. text 77.00 (*0-02-407791-7*, Macmillan Coll) P-H.

— Data Communications & Networking Fundamentals Using Novell NetWare 3.11. LC 93-8780. 475p. (C). 1993. pap. text 97.00 (*0-02-407766-6*, Macmillan Coll) P-H.

Ramos, Emilio, et al. Data Communications & Networking Fundamentals Using Novell NetWare 3.12. LC 95-37992. 485p. (C). 1995. pap. text 111.00 (*0-13-502246-0*) P-H.

Ramos, Emilio, et al. Networking Using Novell NetWare 3.12. LC 95-38018. 274p. (C). 1995. pap. text 93.00 (*0-13-236035-7*) P-H.

— Networking Using Novell 3.11: Release 3.11. LC 93-30153. (Illus.). 268p. (Orig.). (C). 1993. pap. text 88.00 (*0-02-408025-X*, Macmillan Coll) P-H.

— Visual Basic: A Beginner's Approach. Cote, Lynne D., ed. LC 95-8094. (Illus.). 350p. (C). 1995. pap. text 24.95 (*0-201-80884-6*) Addison-Wesley.

Ramos, Emilio, jt. auth. see Schroeder, Al.

Ramos Escobar, Jose L. El Olor del Popcorn. 1996. pap. text. write for info. (*1-56758-043-2*) Edit Cultl.

Ramos, Fernando, et al, eds. INDC'98: 7th IFIP - ICCC Conference on Information Networks & Data Communications. LC 99-185540. (Illus.). 330p. 1998. 30.00 (*1-891365-03-7*) ICCC Pr.

Ramos, Francisco J. Hacer: Pensar. 1994. 22.95 (*0-8477-0184-0*) U of PR Pr.

Ramos-Garcia, Luis A., ed. A Bilingual Anthology of Contemporary Spanish Poetry: The Generation of 1970. Oliphant, Dave, tr. LC 97-32323. (Hispanic Literature Ser.: Vol. 43). 364p. 1997. 99.95 (*0-7734-8435-3*) E Mellen.

— A South American Trilogy: Osman Lins, Felisberto Hernandez & Luis Fernando Vidal. (ENG, POR & SPA.). 1982. 5.95 (*0-934840-04-0*) Studia Hispanica.

— Southwest Graduate Symposium of Spanish & Portuguese, Literature & Language at the University of Texas. 1980. 5.00 (*0-934840-03-2*) Studia Hispanica.

— Tales from Austin. 1980. 5.95 (*0-934840-02-4*) Studia Hispanica.

Ramos-Garcia, Luis A. & Lugones, Nestor, eds. Studia Hispanica I in Honor of Rodolfo Cardona. 1982. 12.95 (*0-934840-01-6*) Studia Hispanica.

Ramos-Garcia, Luis A. & O'Hara, Edgar, eds. The Newest Peruvian Poetry in Translation. 1979. 4.95 (*0-934840-00-8*) Studia Hispanica.

Ramos-Garcia, Luis A., ed. see Colaizzi, Giuliana.

Ramos-Garcia, Luis A., jt. ed. see Klee, Carol A.

Ramos-Garcia, Luis A., ed. see Montengon, Pedro.

Ramos-Garcia, Luis A., ed. see Talens, Jenaro.

Ramos-Garcia, Luis A., ed. see Talens, Jenaro & Nerlich, Michael.

Ramos-Gomez, F., ed. Statistical Physics. 160p. (C). 1991. text 59.00 (*981-02-0584-8*) World Scientific Pub.

Ramos, Graciliano. Barren Lives. Dimmick, Ralph E., tr. from SPA. LC 65-16468. (Texas Pan American Ser.). (Illus.). 165p. 1965. pap. 12.95 (*0-292-70133-0*) U of Tex Pr.

Ramos, Guillem. Technique of Icon Painting. (Illus.). 80p. 1997. pap. 17.95 (*0-85532-687-5*) A Schwartz & Co.

Ramos, H. M. & Almorza, D., eds. Applied Sciences & the Environment. LC 99-219512. (Environmental Engineering Ser.: Vol. 4). 20p. 1998. 184.00 (*1-85312-603-9*, 6039, Pub. by WIT Pr) Computational Mech MA.

Ramos, Henry A. A People Forgotten, a Dream Pursued: The American GI Forum. LC 98-8679. 224p. 1998. 24.95 (*1-55885-261-1*); pap. 14.95 (*1-55885-262-X*) Arte Publico.

Ramos, Humerto, jt. auth. see Augustyn, Brian.

Ramos, I., jt. ed. see Diaz, J.

Ramos, I., jt. ed. see Tjoa, A. M.

Ramos, Isabel. Aleph-Alfa-Alfa. LC 98-90373. (J). (gr. 3-5). 1998. pap. 7.95 (*0-533-12774-2*) Vantage.

Ramos, J. I. Internal Combustion Engine Modeling. (Illus.). 460p. 1989. 100.00 (*0-89116-157-0*) Hemisp Pub.

Ramos, J. M. Combat Raceguns: The World's Best Custom Pistols. (Illus.). 168p. 1993. pap. 25.00 (*0-87364-750-5*) Paladin Pr.

— The CZ-75 Family: The Ultimate Combat Handgun. (Illus.). 1990. pap. 21.00 (*0-87364-566-9*) Paladin Pr.

Ramos, J. R. California Land Use Procedure. 1050p. 1991. ring bd. 175.00 (*0-685-70496-3*) Shepards.

***Ramos, Jan C.** Answers for Airline Passengers. Casanova, Cynthia, ed. (Illus.). 86p. 1999. pap. text. write for info. (*0-9672645-0-2*) J C Ramos.

— Answers for Airline Passengers. LC 99-97534. 2000. pap. 8.95 (*0-533-13411-0*) Vantage.

Ramos, Joseph R. Neoconservative Economics in the Southern Cone of Latin America, 1973-1983. LC 86-165. (Johns Hopkins Studies in Development). (Illus.). 223p. reprint ed. pap. 69.20 (*0-608-06189-1*, 206652100008) Bks Demand.

Ramos, Joseph R., jt. auth. see Ramos, Adam.

Ramos, Juan A. En Casa de Guillermo Tell. (Biblioteca de Autores de Puerto Rico Ser.). (SPA.). 104p. (Orig.). 1991. pap. text 5.95 (*1-56328-004-3*) Edit Plaza Mayor.

— El Manual Del Buen Modal y Otras Ocurrencias "Light" 1993. 7.95 (*0-8477-0185-9*) U of PR Pr.

***Ramos, Julio.** Divergent Modernities: Culture & Politics in Nineteenth-Century Latin America. Blanco, John D., tr. from SPA. LC 99-33997. 376p. 1999. 59.95 (*0-8223-1981-0*) Duke.

Ramos, Julio, ed. Amor y Anarquia: Los Escritos de Luisa Capetillo. LC 91-78121. (Clasicos Huracan Ser.). (SPA.). 222p. 1992. pap. 8.95 (*0-929157-15-X*) Ediciones Huracan.

Ramos, Lindsey. Four Chinese Children's Stories. (Illus.). 24p. (J). 1991. 14.95 (*0-9628563-0-4*) Lttle Peop Pr.

Ramos, Luciana L., jt. auth. see Garcia, Sarah S.

Ramos, Luis A. Within These Walls. Zimmerman, Samuel A., tr. from SPA. LC 97-17340. (Discoveries Ser.). 192p. 1997. pap. 13.95 (*0-935480-89-7*) Lat Am Lit Rev Pr.

Ramos, Luis A. & Armas, Jose, eds. Angela de Hoyos: A Critical Look. (Illus.). 53p. 1979. pap. 3.50 (*0-918358-08-6*) Pajarito Pubns.

Ramos, M. La Obra del Espiritu Santo. (Serie Creciendo - Growing Ser.).Tr. of Work of the Holy Spirit. (SPA.). 39p. 2.50 (*1-56063-961-X*, 493035) Editorial Unilit.

Ramos, M. Los Privilegios del Cristiano.Tr. of Christian Privileges. (SPA.). 2.50 (*1-56063-391-3*, 493038) Editorial Unilit.

Ramos, M. Relaciones Humanas, Sanas y Positivas. (Serie Realidades - Realities Ser.).Tr. of Safe & Positive Human Relations. (SPA.). 31p. 1995. pap. 1.99 (*1-56063-125-2*, 498137) Editorial Unilit.

Ramos, Manuel. Ballad of Gato Guerrero. 1996. mass mkt. 4.99 (*0-312-95720-3*, Pub. by Tor Bks) St Martin.

Ramos, Marcos A. Nuevo Diccionario de Religiones, Denominaciones y Sectas.Tr. of New Dictionary of Religions, Denominations & Cults. (SPA.). 1997. 12.99 (*0-89922-284-6*, C100-315X) Caribe Betania.

— Protestantism & Revolution in Cuba. 168p. (C). 1989. pap. text 16.95 (*0-614-11068-8*) Transaction Pubs.

Ramos, Mary A. Greek Orthodox Faith in Poetry: Poems on the Major Themes of the Orthodox Faith. 200p. 1994. pap. 9.95 (*1-880971-02-X*) Light&Life Pub Co MN.

Ramos, Mary G., ed. Texas Almanac, 1998-99. 100p. 1997. pap. 9.95 (*0-914511-27-0*) Dallas Morning.

— Texas Almanac, 1998-99: State Industrial Guide. (Illus.). 672p. 1997. 19.95 (*0-914511-26-2*) Dallas Morning.

— Texas Almanac 1998-99: State Industrial Guide. (Illus.). 672p. 1997. pap. 12.95 (*0-914511-25-4*) Dallas Morning.

***Ramos-Mattei, Carlos J.** Annotations on the Philosophy of Values. LC 98-46452. (American University Studies V: Vol. 185). VI, 244p. (C). 1999. text 49.00 (*0-8204-4019-1*) P Lang Pubng.

Ramos, Michael. Many Mountains Moving, Vol. 2 No. 3. (Illus.). 170p. 1996. pap. 6.50 (*1-886976-05-8*) Many Mntns.

Ramos, Michael J. Auditing Estimates & Other Soft Accounting Information. Delahanty, Linda C., ed. 107p. 1998. pap. 56.25 (*0-87051-199-8*, 010010) Am Inst CPA.

***Ramos, Michael J.** A CPA's Guide to Accounting, Auditing, & Tax for Construction Contractors. 252p. 2000. pap. 45.00 (*0-87051-296-X*, 091000) Am Inst CPA.

Ramos, Miguel W. Seminario de Religion Yoruba: Santeria. (SPA.). 54p. (Orig.). (C). 1988. pap. 16.99 (*1-877845-05-1*) M W Ramos.

Ramos, Mimoso A. Vida & Poesia en Jose Antonio Davila. (UPREX, Estudios Literarios Ser.: No. 71). 409p. 1986. pap. 6.00 (*0-8477-0071-2*) U of PR Pr.

Ramos, Moises. Los Acontecimientos del Fin. (Serie Realidades - Realities Ser.).Tr. of Ending Events. (SPA.). 29p. 1991. pap. 1.99 (*1-56063-120-1*, 498143) Editorial Unilit.

— Los Acontecimientos del Principio. (Serie Realidades - Realities Ser.).Tr. of Beginning Events: How It All Began. (SPA.). 34p. 1992. pap. 1.99 (*1-56063-318-2*, 498157) Editorial Unilit.

Ramos, Moises. Problemas de Familia. (Serie Enriquezca a la Familia - Enriching the Family Ser.).Tr. of Family Problems: Tragedies & Opportunities. (SPA.). 1.99 (*1-56063-884-2*, 498206) Editorial Unilit.

Ramos, Moises. Problemas de Familia.Tr. of Family Problems: Tragedies & Opportunities. (SPA.). 100p. 1995. pap. write for info. (*0-614-27116-9*) Editorial Unilit.

— Problemas de Familia - Family Problems: Tragedies & Opportunities. (SPA.). 100p. 1995. write for info. (*0-614-24398-X*) Editorial Unilit.

Ramos, Myra B., tr. see Freire, Paulo.

Ramos, O. Diezmo y Bindicione.Tr. of Diezmo y Bendiciones. (SPA.). 1996. pap. 4.99 (*0-8297-0478-7*) Vida Pubs.

Ramos, Oliveira A. Politics, Economics & Men of Modern Spain, 1808-1946. Hall, Teener, tr. LC 72-4285. (World Affairs Ser.: National & International Viewpoints). 720p. 1972. reprint ed. 41.95 (*0-405-04578-6*) Ayer.

R

An Asterisk (*) at the beginning of an entry indicates that the title is appearing for the first time.

Ramos-Poqui, Guillem. The Technique of Icon Painting. (Illus.). 80p. 1994. pap. 18.95 (*0-8192-1624-0*) Morehouse Pub.

Ramos-Ramos, Abiud. Stocks & Bonds. LC 80-20002. (Illus.). 30p. (C). 1980. pap. 2.80 (*0-8477-2637-1*) U of PR Pr.

Ramos, Raul. Harrap's Gramatic Inglesa. 1995. per. 5.00 (*0-671-52081-4*) S&S Trade.

— Harrap's Verbos Ingleses. 1995. per. 5.00 (*0-671-52079-2*) S&S Trade.

Ramos, Ricardo. Flipping. LC 97-60105. 176p. (Orig.). 1998. pap. 12.95 (*0-942777-14-X*) Floating Lotus.

Ramos, Roberto. Bibliografia de la Revolucion Mexicana, 3 vols. 1976. lib. bdg. 300.00 (*0-8490-1494-8*) Gordon Pr.

Ramos, Shroeder, jt. auth. see Emilio, Al.

Ramos, Teresita V. Conversational Tagalog: A Functional-Situational Approach. LC 84-8612. 358p. 1985. pap. text 17.00 (*0-8248-0944-0*) UH Pr.

— Tagalog Dictionary. LC 71-152471. (PALI Language Texts, Philippines Ser.). (TAG.). 374p. (Orig.). (C). 1971. pap. text 15.00 (*0-87022-676-2*) UH Pr.

— Tagalog Structures. LC 75-152472. (PALI Language Texts, Philippines Ser.). 186p. (Orig.). (C). 1971. pap. text 14.00 (*0-87022-677-0*) UH Pr.

Ramos, Teresita V. & Bautista, Maria. Handbook of Tagalog Verbs: Inflections, Modes, & Aspects. LC 86-6983. 306p. 1986. pap. text 16.00 (*0-8248-1018-X*) UH Pr.

Ramos, Teresita V. & Cena, Resty M. Modern Tagalog: Grammatical Explanations & Exercises for Non-Native Speakers. LC 90-15577. 184p. (C). 1990. pap. text 14.00 (*0-8248-1332-4*) UH Pr.

Ramos, Teresita V. & Clausen, Josie. Filipino Word Book. (ILO & TAG., Illus.). 128p. (J). (gr. k-6). 1993. 19.95 (*1-880188-54-6*); pap. 11.95 (*1-880188-44-9*) Bess Pr.

— Filipino Word Book. (Rainbow International Word Book Ser.). (Illus.). 128p. 1993. pap., text 19.95 incl. audio (*1-880188-63-5*) Bess Pr.

Ramos, Teresita V. & De Guzman, Videa P. Tagalog for Beginners. LC 77-148651. (Pacific & Asian Linguistics Institute. PALI Language Texts: Philippines Ser.). 875p. reprint ed. pap. 200.00 (*0-608-18676-7*, 202958400061) Bks Demand.

Ramos, Teresita V. & Goulet, Rosalina M. Intermediate Tagalog: Developing Cultural Awareness Through Language. LC 81-16037. 542p. (C). 1981. pap. text 21.00 (*0-8248-0776-6*) UH Pr.

***Ramos, Victor A. & Keppie, J. Duncan.** Laurentia-Gondwana Connections Before Pangea. LC 99-47508. (Special Papers). 1999. write for info. (*0-8137-2336-1*) Geol Soc.

***Ramos, Violet.** Pedro & Donkeeta. Wright, Catherine & Elwood, Krissy, eds. (Illus.). 31p. (J). (ps-4). 2000. 17.95 (*0-9658334-2-9*) VR Pubns.

Ramos, Violet. Young at Heart: The Step-by-Step Way of Writing Children's Stories. LC 98-91058. 80p. 1999. pap. text 12.95 (*0-9658334-1-0*) VR Pubns.

Ramos, Violet M. Sara & Grandmother Rose. (Illus.). 32p. (Orig.). (J). (ps-6). 1997. mass mkt. 3.95 (*0-9658334-0-2*) VR Pubns.

Ramotti, Ottavio C. The Nostradamus Code: The Lost Manuscript That Unlocks the Secrets of the Master Prophet. Calliope, Tami, tr. from ITA. LC 98-16398. (Illus.). 192p. 1998. 25.00 (*0-89281-666-X*, Inner Trad) Inner Tradit.

Ramounachou Moon, Germaine L. Barstow Depots & Harvey Houses. LC 80-80936. (Illus.). 42p. (Orig.). (C). 1980. pap. text 3.50 (*0-918614-02-3*) Mojave Riv Val.

Ramp & Cox. Biology 101, Humankind Biotics. 2nd ed. 98p. 1998. pap. text 14.95 (*0-536-01372-1*) Pearson Custom.

***Ramp & Cox.** Biology 102: Human Biotic. 2nd ed. 112p. 1998. pap. text 18.60 (*0-536-01896-0*) Pearson Custom.

Ramp, Philip, tr. see Kazantzakis, Nikos.

Rampa, T. Lobsang. Candlelight. 1994. lib. bdg. 25.95 (*1-56849-438-6*) Buccaneer Bks.

— Chapters of Life. 1994. lib. bdg. 31.95 (*1-56849-436-X*) Buccaneer Bks.

— Feeding the Flame. 190p. 1990. pap. 15.00 (*0-938294-89-X*) Inner Light.

— Hermit. 160p. 1990. pap. 15.00 (*0-938294-96-2*) Inner Light.

— My Visit to Venus. 75p. 1992. 10.00 (*0-938294-61-X*) Inner Light.

— The Third Eye. 1986. mass mkt. 5.99 (*0-345-34038-8*) Ballantine Pub Grp.

— Thirteenth Candle. 1994. lib. bdg. 29.95 (*1-56849-437-8*) Buccaneer Bks.

— Wisdom of the Ancients. 192p. 1991. reprint ed. lib. bdg. 27.95 (*0-89966-776-7*) Buccaneer Bks.

— You Forever. LC 90-40257. 282p. (Orig.). 1990. pap. 9.95 (*0-87728-717-1*) Weiser.

— You-Forever. 224p. 1991. reprint ed. lib. bdg. 28.95 (*0-89966-775-9*) Buccaneer Bks.

Rampage, John, intro. International Coal Engineering Conference, 1990. (Illus.). 326p. (Orig.). 1990. pap. 81.75 (*0-85825-499-9*, Pub. by Inst Engrs Aust-EA Bks) Accents Pubns.

Rampage, Roger. The Tallahassee Experience. LC 97-92267. 80p. 1997. pap. 5.95 (*1-57502-538-8*, PO1579) Morris Pubng.

***Rampal, Jang B., ed.** Oligonucleotide Array: Methods & Protocols. (Methods in Molecular Biology Ser.). 350p. 2000. 99.50 (*0-89603-822-X*) Humana.

Rampal, Jean-Pierre & Wise, Deborah. Music My Love: An Autobiography. 1989. 18.95 (*0-318-42516-5*) Random.

Rampal, Krishna G., jt. auth. see Sadhra, Stephen.

Rampal, P., jt. ed. see Scarpignato, C.

Rampal, S. N. Indian Women & Sex. 192p. 1978. 14.95 (*0-318-37064-6*) Asia Bk Corp.

Rampal, V. V. & Mehta, P. C. Lasers & Holography. 450p. 1993. text 99.00 (*981-02-1214-3*) World Scientific Pub.

Rampani, Robert M. The Eagle's Nest. 1998. pap. write for info. (*1-57553-700-1*) Watermrk Pr.

Rampaul, Hoobasar. Pipe Welding Procedures. LC 73-7849. (Illus.). 238p. 1973. 28.50 (*0-8311-1100-3*) Indus Pr.

Rampelmann, Katja, jt. compiled by see Pumroy, Eric L.

***Rampersad, Arnold.** Jackie Robinson. 1998. pap. 16.00 (*0-345-42655-X*) Ballantine Pub Grp.

Rampersad, Arnold. Langston Hughes: The Man, His Art, & His Continuing Influence. Trotman, C. James, ed. LC 95-15708. (Critical Studies in Black Life & Culture: Vol. 29). (Illus.). 200p. 1995. text 45.00 (*0-8153-1763-8*, H1872) Garland.

Rampersad, Arnold. The Life of Langston Hughes, 1902-1941 Vol. I: I, Too, Sing America. (Illus.). 448p. (C). 1986. text 39.95 (*0-19-504011-2*) OUP.

Rampersad, Arnold. The Life of Langston Hughes, 1902-1941 Vol. I: I, Too, Sing America. (Illus.). 480p. 1988. pap. 17.95 (*0-19-505426-1*) OUP.

— The Life of Langston Hughes, Vol. I, 1902-1941: I, Too, Sing America. (Illus.). 448p. 1986. pap. 9.95 (*0-685-13534-9*) OUP.

— The Life of Langston Hughes, Vol. II, 1941-1967: I Dream a World. (Illus.). 526p. 1988. reprint ed. text 39.95 (*0-19-504519-X*) OUP.

— The Life of Langston Hughes, Vol. II, 1941-1967: I Dream a World. (Illus.). 528p. 1989. reprint ed. pap. 17.95 (*0-19-506169-1*) OUP.

— Selected Stories & Poems: Langston Hughes. (Riverside Editions Ser.). 416p. 1999. pap. 12.00 (*0-395-98076-3*) HM.

Rampersad, Arnold, ed. Richard Wright: A Collection of Critical Essays. LC 94-19515. 211p. (C). 1994. pap. text 9.80 (*0-13-036120-8*) P-H.

Rampersad, Arnold, jt. auth. see Ashe, Arthur.

Rampersad, Arnold, ed. see Hughes, Langston.

Rampersad, Arnold, ed. see Wright, Richard.

Rampersad, Arnold, ed. see Wright, Richard A.

Rampersad, Garvin. The End of Existence: Membership & Metaphysics. LC 98-70122. (Avebury Series in Philosophy). 174p. 1998. text 59.95 (*1-84014-372-X*, Pub. by Ashgate Pub) Ashgate Pub Co.

Rampersad, Hubert K. Integrated & Simultaneous Design for Robotic Assembly. 226p. 1995. pap. 70.00 (*0-471-95466-7*, EM15) Wiley.

Rampersad, Pradeep. Love the Essence of Life. 1997. pap. write for info. (*1-57553-454-1*) Watermrk Pr.

Ramphal. The Commonwealth: A Common Culture. Maltby, Richard & Quartermaine, L., eds. 126p. 1989. pap. text 17.95 (*0-85989-318-9*, Pub. by Univ Exeter Pr) Northwestern U Pr.

Ramphal, Shridath, frwd. Banking on Apartheid: Prepared for Commonwealth Committee of Foreign Minister on S.AFt. 96p. (C). 1990. pap. text 15.00 (*0-435-08044-X*, 08044) Heinemann.

Ramphele, Mamphela. Across Boundaries: The Journey of a South African Woman Leader. LC 96-35474. 272p. 1997. 19.95 (*1-55861-165-7*) Feminist Pr.

— Across Boundaries: The Journey of a South African Woman Leader. (Women Writing Africa Ser.). 256p. 1999. pap. 14.95 (*1-55861-166-5*, Pub. by Feminist Pr) Consort Bk Sales.

— A Bed Called Home: Life in the Migrant Labor Hostels of Cape Town. LC 93-19117. (Illus.). 160p. (Orig.). (C). 1993. pap. text 21.95 (*0-8214-1063-6*) Ohio U Pr.

Rampini, Charles J. Letters from Jamaica the Lands of Streams & Woods. 1977. text 17.95 (*0-8369-9246-6*, 9100) Ayer.

Rampley, Matthew. Nietzsche, Aesthetics & Modernity. LC 99-19420. 336p. (C). 1999. 59.95 (*0-521-65155-7*) Cambridge U Pr.

Rampling, Anne, pseud. Belinda. 512p. 1988. mass mkt. 7.99 (*0-515-09355-6*, Jove) Berkley Pub.

— Exit to Eden. 384p. 1996. pap. 14.00 (*0-345-40196-4*) Ballantine Pub Grp.

Rampnal, Shridath & Sinding, Steven W., eds. Population Growth & Environmental Issues. LC 96-16279. (Environmental Literacy Ser.). 216p. 1996. 57.95 (*0-275-95371-8*, Praeger Pubs) Greenwood.

Rampo, Edogawa. Japanese Tales of Mystery & Imagination. Harris, James B., tr. LC 56-6804. (Illus.). 232p. (YA). (gr. 9 up). 1956. pap. 12.95 (*0-8048-0319-6*) Tuttle Pubng.

***Rampolla, Mary Lynn.** Pocket Guide to Writing History. LC 97-74969. 85p. 1998. pap. text 8.95 (*0-312-18006-3*) St Martin.

— Pocket Guide to Writing History. 3rd ed. 2000. pap. text, student ed. write for info. (*0-312-24766-4*) St Martin.

Rampp, Lary C., jt. auth. see Anderson, Craig.

Ramprogus. Deconstruction of Nursing. 208p. 1995. 77.95 (*1-85972-101-X*) Ashgate Pub Co.

Rampton, Ben. Crossing: Language & Ethnicity among Adolescents. LC 94-29266. (Real Language Ser.). 400p. (C). 1995. pap. text 35.64 (*0-582-21791-1*, 77023, Pub. by Addison-Wesley) Longman.

Rampton, Glenn M., jt. ed. see Wiskoff, Martin F.

Rampton, Richard & Sharp, Victoria. Duncan & Neill: Defamation. 3rd ed. Neill, Brian, ed. 1995. write for info. (*0-406-17831-3*, U.K., MICHIE) LEXIS Pub.

Rampton, Sheldon & Stauber, John. Mad Cow U. S. A. Could the Nightmare Happen Here? LC 97-22500. 224p. 1997. 24.95 (*1-56751-111-2*) Common Courage.

Rampton, Sheldon, jt. auth. see Chilsen, Liz.

Rampton, Sheldon, jt. auth. see Stauber, John.

Rampton, Thomas G. Arkansas River Guide: Granite to Canon City, Colorado. LC 96-84647. (Illus.). 96p. (Orig.). 1996. pap. 13.75 (*0-9634799-1-1*) Blacktail Ent.

— River Guide to Desolation & Gray Canyons: On the Green River, Utah. LC 92-97528. (Illus.). 72p. (Orig.). 1992. pap. 9.95 (*0-9634799-0-3*) Blacktail Ent.

***Rampton, Thomas G.** Vietnam in the Absence of War. (Illus.). 304p. 2000. pap. write for info. (*0-9634799-2-X*) Blacktail Ent.

Rampulla, Ciro, et al, eds. Cardiopulmonary Rehabilitation. LC 93-13742. (Current Topics in Rehabilitation Ser.). 1995. 69.00 (*0-387-19836-9*) Spr-Verlag.

Rampulla, Leo. There's No Escaping: Tony's Tale. 104p. 1998. pap. 10.00 (*0-8059-4313-7*) Dorrance.

Ramquist, Grace. Christmas Programs for All Ages. 1991. pap. write for info. (*0-00-528702-2*) Lillenas.

— Four Dramas for Christmas. 37p. 1978. pap. 4.99 (*0-8341-9376-0*) Lillenas.

— Four Dramas for Christmas. 1991. pap. write for info. (*0-00-528430-9*) Lillenas.

— Four Services for Easter. 36p. 1974. 4.99 (*0-8341-9594-1*, ME-20) Lillenas.

Ramquist, Grace, compiled by. Children's Day Program Builder No. 7. 32p. 1974. pap. 4.50 (*0-8341-9556-9*) Nazarene.

— Christmas Program Builder, No. 23. 32p. 1970. 4.99 (*0-8341-9138-5*, MC-123) Lillenas.

— Christmas Program Builder, No. 25. 32p. 1972. 4.99 (*0-8341-9139-3*, MC-125) Lillenas.

— Christmas Program Builder, No. 27. 32p. 1974. 4.99 (*0-8341-9140-7*, MC-127) Lillenas.

— Christmas Program Builder, No. 28. 32p. 1975. 4.99 (*0-8341-9141-5*, MC-128) Lillenas.

— Easter Program Builder, No. 11. 1965. 4.99 (*0-8341-9200-4*, ME-111) Lillenas.

— Easter Program Builder, No. 12. 32p. 1967. 4.99 (*0-8341-9593-3*, ME-112) Lillenas.

— Easter Program Builder, No. 13. 32p. 1969. 4.99 (*0-8341-9592-5*, ME-113) Lillenas.

— Easter Program Builder, No. 14. 32p. 1975. 4.99 (*0-8341-9201-2*, ME-114) Lillenas.

Ramraj, Victor J., ed. Concert of Voices: An Anthology of World Writing in English. 400p. (C). 1994. pap. 24.95 (*1-55111-025-3*) Broadview Pr.

Ramrakha, Punit s. & Moore, Kevin P. Oxford Handbook of Acute Medicine. LC 97-26292. (Illus.). 892p. 1998. pap. 34.50 (*0-19-262682-5*) OUP.

Ramras-Rauch, Gila. Aharon Appelfeld: The Holocaust & Beyond. LC 93-5016. 228p. 1994. 39.95 (*0-253-34831-5*) Ind U Pr.

— The Arab in Israeli Literature. LC 88-46017. (Jewish Literature & Culture Ser.). 256p. 1989. 39.95 (*0-253-34832-3*) Ind U Pr.

Ramsaier, Yves, jt. auth. see Bronkhorst, Johannes.

Ramsar Convention Bureau Staff. A Directory of Wetlands of International Importance. 796p. 1990. 51.00 (*2-8317-0014-0*, Pub. by IUCN) Island Pr.

Ramsaran, Ramesh F. The Challenge of Structural Adjustment in the Commonwealth Caribbean. LC 91-37505. 224p. 1992. 65.00 (*0-275-94209-0*, C4209, Praeger Pubs) Greenwood.

Ramsaran, Rollin A. Liberating Words: Paul's Use of Rhetorical Maxims in First Corinthians 1-10. LC 96-24733. 176p. 1996. pap. 17.00 (*1-56338-164-8*) TPI PA.

Ramsauer, Gottfried, ed. & comment see Aristotle.

Ramsay. Consumer Protection. xxvi, 561p. 1989. 70.00 (*0-297-79498-1*) W S Hein.

Ramsay. New Ideas Efforting School Improvement. 250p. 1990. pap. 39.95 (*1-85000-697-0*, Falmer Pr) Taylor & Francis.

— Normal Values in Pregnancy. (C). 1996. pap. text 38.00 (*0-7020-2021-4*) Harcourt.

— Ramsay: Hawaii Landmark Collection. LC 88-83768. (Illus.). 64p. (Orig.). 1989. pap. 25.00 (*0-317-93360-4*) In Black Inc.

Ramsay, Angela. Handmade Paper Book: The Ultimate Guide to Making & Using Handmade Paper. LC 98-49730. (Illus.). 80p. 1999. 22.95 (*1-58017-174-5*) Storey Bks.

Ramsay, A. T. Oceanic Micropalaeontology, Vol. 1. 1977. text 209.00 (*0-12-577301-3*) Acad Pr.

Ramsay, Agnes D. Everyday Life in Turkey. LC 77-87636. reprint ed. 32.50 (*0-404-16461-7*) AMS Pr.

Ramsay, Alan & Ramsay, Leslie. The MAX: A Personal Financial Management System. 72p. 1983. vinyl bd. 15.00 (*0-932925-00-6*) Cactus Max.

***Ramsay, Alex.** Touring Guide to Scotland. (Collins Pocket Guides). (Illus.). 112p. 1998. pap. 12.95 (*0-00-412973-3*) Collins SF.

Ramsay, Alistair J., jt. auth. see Ada, G. L.

Ramsay, Allan. Ever Green, 2 vols. LC 74-144532. reprint ed. 47.50 (*0-404-08684-5*) AMS Pr.

— Poems of Allan Ramsay, 2 vols. LC 71-144498. reprint ed. 110.00 (*0-404-08584-9*) AMS Pr.

— Tea-Table Miscellany: Or, a Collection of Choice Songs, Scots & English. 12th ed. LC 73-144572. reprint ed. 41.50 (*0-404-08687-X*) AMS Pr.

Ramsay, Anna. The Legend of Dr. Markland. large type ed. 257p. 1992. 11.50 (*0-7505-0391-2*) Ulverscroft.

Ramsay, Anna A. Sir Robert Peel. LC 72-95076. (Select Bibliographies Reprint Ser.). 1977. 24.95 (*0-8369-5076-3*) Ayer.

— Sir Robert Peel. LC 72-95076. (Select Bibliographies Reprint Ser.). 1982. reprint ed. lib. bdg. 24.50 (*0-8290-0839-X*) Irvington.

Ramsay, Ansil & Mungkandi, Wiwat, eds. Thailand - U. S. Relations: Changing Political, Strategic, & Economic Factors. LC 88-8027. (Research Papers & Policy: No. 23). 330p. (Orig.). 1988. pap. 20.00 (*1-55729-001-6*) IEAS.

Ramsay, Arlan & Richtmyer, Robert D. Introduction to Hyperbolic Geometry. LC 94-25789. (Universitext Ser.). 1994. 42.95 (*0-387-94339-0*) Spr-Verlag.

Ramsay, Burt. Alien Bodies: Representations of Modernity, "Race" & Nation in Early Modern Dance. LC 97-23360. 240p. (C). 1998. 75.00 (*0-415-14594-5*); pap. 22.99 (*0-415-14595-3*) Routledge.

Ramsay, C. A. Tino. (Illus.). 188p. 1996. write for info. (*0-9650882-0-0*) Ramsay Property.

Ramsay, Caroline C. International Directory of Resources for Artisans, 1992. 2nd ed. Mooney, Sheilia A., ed. 181p. 1991. 49.95 (*0-9625480-0-6*) Crafts Ctr.

Ramsay, Caroline C. & Mooney, Sheila A. International Directory of Resources for Artisans. 1990. 100.00 (*0-318-50018-3*) Crafts Ctr.

Ramsay, Clay. The Ideology of the Great Fear: The Soissonnais in 1789. LC 91-17676. (Studies in Historical & Political Science: 109th Series, No. 2 (1991)). (Illus.). 352p. 1991. text 49.95 (*0-8018-4197-6*) Johns Hopkins.

Ramsay, Craig, ed. U. S. Health Policy Groups: Institutional Profiles. LC 94-27942. 488p. 1995. lib. bdg. 85.00 (*0-313-28618-3*) Greenwood.

Ramsay, D. A., ed. see Mulliken, Robert S.

Ramsay, D. J. & Booth, D. A., eds. Thirst. (Illus.). 509p. 1991. 75.00 (*3-540-19641-2*, 196412) Spr-Verlag.

Ramsay, David. Eulogium upon Benjamin Rush, M. D. (Notable American Authors Ser.). 1999. reprint ed. lib. bdg. 125.00 (*0-7812-8778-2*) Rprt Serv.

— The History of the American Revolution, 2 vols. LC 89-14583. (Illus.). (C). 1990. reprint ed. pap. 15.00 (*0-86597-081-5*); reprint ed. text 25.00 (*0-86597-078-5*) Liberty Fund.

— History of the American Revolution. (Notable American Authors Ser.). 1999. reprint ed. lib. bdg. 125.00 (*0-7812-8775-8*) Rprt Serv.

— History of the Revolution of South Carolina. (Notable American Authors Ser.). 1999. reprint ed. lib. bdg. 125.00 (*0-7812-8774-X*) Rprt Serv.

— History of the United States. (Notable American Authors Ser.). 1999. reprint ed. lib. bdg. 125.00 (*0-7812-8779-0*) Rprt Serv.

— Life of George Washington. (Notable American Authors Ser.). 1999. reprint ed. lib. bdg. 125.00 (*0-7812-8776-6*) Rprt Serv.

***Ramsay, David.** The Life of George Washington: Commander in Chief of the Armies of the United States of America Throughout the War Which Established Their Independence & First President of the United States. annot. anniversary ed. Phillips, John T., II, ed. & illus. by. Snyder, Wade C., illus. (Compleat George Washington Ser.: Vol. 2). 368p. 2000. reprint ed. lthr. 39.95 (*0-9656758-2-3*) Goose Creek.

Ramsay, David. Memoirs of the Life of Martha Laurens Ramsay. (Notable American Authors Ser.). 1999. reprint ed. lib. bdg. 125.00 (*0-7812-8777-4*) Rprt Serv.

— Universal History Americanized. (Notable American Authors Ser.). 1999. reprint ed. lib. bdg. 125.00 (*0-7812-8780-4*) Rprt Serv.

Ramsay, Diana. Four Steps to Death. large type ed. LC 90-40508. 290p. 1990. reprint ed. lib. bdg. 7.95 (*1-56054-037-0*) Thorndike Pr.

Ramsay, Diane P. Voyage to Discovery: An Activity Guide to the Age of Exploration. (Illus.). xiii, 346p. (Orig.). 1992. pap. text 25.00 (*1-56308-063-X*) Teacher Ideas Pr.

Ramsay, Douglas. Principles of Engineering Instrumentation. 216p. 1996. pap. text 44.95 (*0-470-23616-7*) Halsted Pr.

Ramsay, Douglas, jt. ed. see Lewis, Michael.

Ramsay, E. Mary. Christian Science & Its Discoverer. (Twentieth-Century Biographers Ser.). 123p. 1983. 26.95 (*0-87510-346-4*) Writings of Mary Baker.

Ramsay, Elisabeth. Cold Silver. large type ed. (Linford Romance Library). 256p. 1996. pap. 16.99 (*0-7089-7929-7*) Ulverscroft.

Ramsay, Freda, anno. The Day Book of Daniel Campbell of Shawfield 1767: With Relevant Papers Concerning the Estate of Islay. 1991. 39.90 (*0-08-040933-4*, Pub. by Aberdeen U Pr) Macmillan.

Ramsay, G. D. Wiltshire Woollen Industry in the Sixteenth & Seventeenth Centuries. 2nd rev. ed. 165p. 1965. reprint ed. 35.00 (*0-7146-1355-X*, Pub. by F Cass Pubs) Intl Spec Bk.

Ramsay, G. G., tr. see Goold, G. P.

***Ramsay, Gordan.** A Chef for All Seasons. 224p. 2000. 35.00 (*1-58008-234-3*) Ten Speed Pr.

Ramsay, Graham. Commercial Biosensors: Applications to Clinical, Bioprocess, & Environmental Samples. LC 97-28054. (Chemistry Analysis). 304p. 1998. 79.95 (*0-471-58505-X*, Wiley-Interscience) Wiley.

— Soccer for Girls: An Introdutory, Step by Step Guide, 1. 1999. pap. 12.95 (*1-56649-143-6*) Welcome Rain.

Ramsay, Gregg. The Complete Guide to Networking Your Home Computers. 1999. pap. 24.95 (*0-9652502-5-3*) Williams Hill.

Ramsay, Gregg & Rogak, Lisa. The 100 Best Businesses for the 21st Century. 224p. 1999. pap. 15.95 (*0-9652502-3-7*) Williams Hill.

Ramsay, Harvie, jt. ed. see Beirne, Martin.

***Ramsay, Heather.** Who Will My Lover Be? 1999. 9.95 (*0-8118-2372-5*) Chronicle Bks.

Ramsay, Helena. Hot & Cold. LC 98-9170. (Step-by-Step Science Ser.). (Illus.). (J). 1998. 18.00 (*0-516-20957-4*) Childrens.

— Sound. LC 97-51970. (Step-by-Step Science Ser.). (Illus.). (J). (gr. 2-5). 1998. 18.00 (*0-516-20958-2*) Childrens.

— Water. LC 98-6563. (Step-by-Step Science Ser.). (Illus.). (J). 1998. 18.00 (*0-516-20959-0*) Childrens.

Ramsay, Helena, et al. Color. LC 98-15041. (Step-by-Step Science Ser.). (Illus.). (J). 1998. 18.00 (*0-516-20956-6*) Childrens.

Ramsay, I. M., jt. auth. see Ford, H. A.

Ramsay, Iain, ed. Consumer Law. (International Library of Essays in Law & Legal Theory). 500p. (C). 1992. lib. bdg. 150.00 (*0-8147-7423-7*) NYU Pr.

An Asterisk (*) at the beginning of an entry indicates that the title is appearing for the first time.

— Consumer Law in the Global Economy: National & International Dimensions. LC 96-39606. 400p. 1997. text 82.95 (*1-85521-843-7*, Pub. by Dartmth Pub) Ashgate Pub Co.

Ramsay, J. O. & Silverman, B. W. Functional Data Analysis. LC 96-54729. (Springer Series in Statistics). (Illus.). 320p. 1997. 49.95 (*0-387-94956-9*) Spr-Verlag.

Ramsay, Jack C., Jr. Jean Laffite: Prince of Pirates. LC 95-5782. (Illus.). 224p. 1996. 21.95 (*1-57168-029-2*, Eakin Pr) Sunbelt Media.

–Photographer...Under Fire: The Story of George S. Cook, 1819-1902. LC 94-79971. (Illus.). 192p. 1994. 34.95 (*0-9642511-0-8*) Hist Res Pr.
Today daguerreotypes & unfaded portraits by George S. Cook PHOTOGRAPHER, ex-associate of Mathew Brady, prove he could "find beauty in any face." From within Fort Sumter, George S. Cook, CIVIL WAR HISTORIAN, captured ironclads in action & the burst of an exploding shell. PHOTOGRAPHER...UNDER FIRE "is a fascinating trip through American photography with one of the earliest 'forgotten practitioners'...While Cook made his name in Charleston, Richmond forged Cook's destiny."--(RICHMOND-TIMES DISPATCH). "Text in this fascinating work is comprehensive & thoroughly researched, yet flows with a graceful, highly readable style. Representative photos demonstrate Cook's mastery of his craft. Cook's diary is an intriguing primary document. Recipes included. Readers of diverse interest should make this book a welcomed edition to their library."--(THE CIVIL WAR COURIER). "...this interesting book offers a fascinating look at military life during the war...Rare views of South Carolina volunteer companies."--(MILITARY IMAGES). Endnotes, bibliography, index & Cook's photographs, some never before published. $29.95 plus shipping. Will invoice. Tel. 940-321-1066, 2104 POST OAK COURT, CORINTH, TX 76205, website: WWW.ABOOK4U.COM, e-mail: historybuffs@worldnet.att.net. *Publisher Paid Annotation.*

— Sunshine on the Prairie: The Story of Cynthia Ann Parker. Eakin, Edwin M., ed. (Illus.). 224p. 1990. 16.95 (*0-89015-686-7*) Sunbelt Media.

Ramsay, James H. The Angevin Empire: Or The Three Reigns of Henry II, Richard I, & John, 1154-1216. LC 76-29840. (Illus.). reprint ed. 72.50 (*0-404-15426-3*) AMS Pr.

— The Foundations of England: Or, Twelve Centuries of British History, 2 vols., Set. LC 80-2215. reprint ed. 125.00 (*0-404-18780-3*) AMS Pr.

Ramsay, James W. Basic Skills for Academic Reading. (Illus.). 272p. (C). 1997. pap. text 27.60 (*0-13-066036-1*) P-H.

Ramsay, Jay. Kingdom of the Edge: Poems for the Spirit. LC 98-31817. (Illus.). 160p. 1999. pap. 13.95 (*1-86204-510-0*, Pub. by Element MA) Penguin Putnam.

— Meditations on the Unknown God. 143p. 1997. pap. 14.95 (*3-7052-0052-6*, Pub. by Poetry Salzburg) Intl Spec Bk.

— Raw Spiritual: Selected Poems, 1980-1985. (C). 1986. pap. 38.00 (*0-947612-20-3*, Pub. by Rivelin Grapheme Pr) St Mut.

Ramsay, Jay, ed. The White Poem. (Illus.). 48p. (C). 1988. 60.00 (*0-947612-29-7*, Pub. by Rivelin Grapheme Pr); pap. 39.00 (*0-947612-30-0*, Pub. by Rivelin Grapheme Pr) St Mut.

Ramsay, Jay & Palmer, Martin, trs. Illustrated Tao Te Ching: The New Translation. (Sacred Arts Ser.). (Illus.). 192p. 1993. pap. 24.95 (*1-85230-322-0*, Pub. by Element MA) Penguin Putnam.

Ramsay, Jeff, et al. Historical Dictionary of Botswana. 3rd ed. Woronoff, Jon, ed. LC 96-5457. (African Historical Dictionaries Ser.: No. 70). 320p. 1996. 64.00 (*0-8108-3143-0*) Scarecrow.

Ramsay, Jo, jt. auth. see Jordan, Louise.

Ramsay, Joan, jt. auth. see Moules, Tina.

Ramsay, John. American Potters & Pottery. LC 76-22944. (Illus.). 1976. reprint ed. 37.95 (*0-89344-006-X*) Ars Ceramica.

— Scotland & Scotsmen in the Eighteenth Century, 2 vols., Set. Allerdyce, Alexander, ed. (Contemporary Memoirs Ser.: Ser. 5 & 6). 578p. 1996. 200.00 (*1-85506-400-6*) Bks Intl VA.

— Scotland & Scotsmen in the Eighteenth Century: From the Memoirs of John Ramsay Esq. of Ochtertyre, 2 vols. Allardyce, Alexander, ed. LC 78-67537. reprint ed. 97.50 (*0-404-17520-1*) AMS Pr.

Ramsay, John G. & Huber, Martin. The Techniques of Modern Structural Geology, Vol. 1. 1984. text 128.00 (*0-12-576901-6*); pap. text 58.00 (*0-12-576921-0*) Acad Pr.

— Techniques of Modern Structural Geology: Folds & Fractures, Vol. 2. 400p. 1987. pap. text 58.00 (*0-12-576922-9*) Acad Pr.

***Ramsay, John G. & Lisle, Richard J.** Modern Structural Geology: Applications of Continuum Mechanics in Structural Geology. (Techniques of Modern Structural Geology Ser.: Vol. 3). 608p. 2000. pap. 65.00 (*0-12-576923-7*) Acad Pr.

Ramsay, John R., jt. ed. see Jackson, Michael B.

Ramsay, Laurie. Laurie's Indispensable Babysitter's Guide. (Illus.). 35p. (YA). (gr. 5 up). 1997. pap. 8.95 (*0-9659146-0-7*) Pascal Inc.

Ramsay, Leslie, jt. auth. see Ramsay, Alan.

Ramsay, Linda M. Secrets of Success for Today's Interior Designers & Decorators: Easily Sell the Job, Plan It Correctly & Keep the Customer Coming Back for Repeat Sales. 3rd rev. ed. Bachelis, Faren, ed. LC 91-91011. (Illus.). 336p. 1996. reprint ed. pap. text 39.99 (*0-9629918-3-X*) Touch Design.

— Start Your Own Interior Design Business & Keep It Growing! Your Guide to Business Success. Bachelis, Faren, ed. LC 93-93833. 384p. (Orig.). (C). 1994. pap. text 39.99 (*0-9629918-0-5*) Touch Design.

***Ramsay, Lynne.** Ratcatcher. (Screenplays Ser.). (Illus.). 128p. 2000. pap. 14.00 (*0-571-20349-3*) Faber & Faber.

Ramsay, M. A. The Worst Paid Labourer in England: Minor Tactics in the British Army, 1870-1918. LC 98-56634. (Praeger Studies in Diplomacy & Strategic Thought). 2000. write for info. (*0-275-96326-8*, Praeger Pubs) Greenwood.

Ramsay, Maggie. Light Pasta Sauces. (Illus.). 64p. 1999. 17.50 (*0-8478-2188-9*) Rizzoli Intl.

Ramsay, Maggy. Magic Motif Crochet. LC 87-5381. (Illus.). 160p. 1987. 16.95 (*0-87131-519-X*) M Evans.

Ramsay, Margaret H. The Grand Union (1970-1976) An Improvisational Performance Group. LC 91-17013. (Artists & Issues in the Theatre Ser.). (Illus.). 195p. (C). 1992. text 41.95 (*0-8204-1547-2*) P Lang Pubng.

Ramsay, Marina, tr. from RUS. Notes on Russian America Pts. II-V: Kad'iak, Unalashka, Atkha, Pribylov Islands, No. 42. LC 96-30255. (Alaska History Ser.). (Illus.). 1994. 30.00 (*1-895901-02-2*) Limestone Pr.

Ramsay, Marina, tr. see Alekseev, Aleksandr I.

Ramsay, Marina, tr. see Shelikhov, Grigorii I.

Ramsay, Marjorie B. Golden Prince. LC 77-79266. (Illus.). 1977. 4.95 (*0-917182-04-9*) Triumph Pub.

— Nyra. (Illus.). (J). (gr. 4-7). 1979. 4.95 (*0-917182-10-3*) Triumph Pub.

Ramsay, Maureen. Human Needs & the Market. 229p. 1992. 77.95 (*1-85628-258-9*, Pub. by Avebry) Ashgate Pub Co.

— What's Wrong with Liberalism: A Critique of Key Concepts. LC 96-34461. (Critical Political Studies). 224p. (C). 1997. pap. text 21.95 (*0-7185-1811-X*) Bks Intl VA.

— What's Wrong with Liberalism: A Critique of Key Concepts. LC 96-34461. (Critical Political Studies). 224p. (C). 1998. 75.00 (*0-7185-1808-X*) Bks Intl VA.

Ramsay, Meredith. Community, Culture, & Economic Development: The Social Roots of Local Action. LC 95-4241. (SUNY Series, Democracy in American Politics). 163p. (C). 1995. text 49.50 (*0-7914-2749-8*); pap. text 18.95 (*0-7914-2750-1*) State U NY Pr.

Ramsay, Nancy J. Pastoral Diagnosis: A Resource for Ministries of Care & Counseling. 112p. 1998. pap. 18.00 (*0-8006-2629-X*, 1-2629) Augsburg Fortress.

Ramsay, Nancy J., jt. ed. see McClure, John S.

Ramsay, Nigel, et al, eds. St. Dunstan: His Life, Times & Cult. (Illus.). 360p. (C). 1992. 125.00 (*0-85115-301-1*) Boydell & Brewer.

Ramsay, Nigel, jt. ed. see Blair, John.

Ramsay, O. Bertrand & Nicholson, Elva M. Estimating the Optimum pH & Temperature for Digestive Enzyme Activity. Neidig, H. Anthony, ed. (Modular Laboratory Program in Chemistry Ser.). 12p. (C). 1994. pap. text 1.50 (*0-87540-444-8*, REAC 444-8) Chem Educ Res.

Ramsay, Ogden B., ed. Van't Hoff - LeBel Centennial: A Symposium Sponsored by the Division of the History of Chemistry at the 168th Meeting of the American Chemical Society, Atlantic City, NJ, September 11-12, 1974. LC 75-9656. (ACS Symposium Ser.: No. 12). (Illus.). 208p. reprint ed. pap. 64.50 (*0-8357-4123-0*, 205233400005) Bks Demand.

Ramsay, Pamela. Early Childhood Planner: Year-Round Activities & Planning Tips. 1992. pap. 18.70 (*0-201-81784-5*) Addison-Wesley.

Ramsay, Patricia C., et al. Multicultural Education: A Source Book. LC 88-31061. (Source Books on Education: Vol. 18). 190p. 1989. text 35.00 (*0-8240-8558-2*) Garland.

Ramsay, Paul. Lochs & Glens of Scotland. (Illus.). 160p. 1994. 29.95 (*1-55859-867-7*) Abbeville Pr.

Ramsay, R. Cuan Bueno Debo Ser?Tr. of How Good Should I Be?. 6.99 (*0-7899-0353-9*, 497487) Editorial Unilit.

Ramsay, R. M. & Rowe, G. C. Environmental Law & Policy in Australia - Text & Materials. LC 96-123067. 920p. 1995. pap. write for info. (*0-409-30682-7*, MICHIE) LEXIS Pub.

Ramsay, Raylene L. The French New Autobiographies: Sarraute, Duras, & Robbe-Grillet. LC 95-49495. (Crosscurrents Ser.). (Illus.). 216p. (C). 1996. 49.95 (*0-8130-1397-6*) U Press Fla.

— Robbe-Grillet & Modernity: Science, Sexuality, & Subversion. LC 92-12415. (University of Florida Humanities Monographs: No. 66). (Illus.). 336p. 1992. 49.95 (*0-8130-1145-0*) U Press Fla.

Ramsay, Richard, jt. auth. see Bagley, Christopher.

Ramsay, Richard B. Que Tan Bueno Debo Ser? Estudios Biblicos Acerca de la Gracia de Dios.Tr. of Am I Good Enough? Learning to Live by God's Grace. (ENG & SPA., Illus.). 102p. 1992. pap. 4.99 (*0-87552-396-X*) P & R Pubng.

Ramsay, Robert L. Our Storehouse of Missouri Place Names. LC 73-79512. 160p. 1973. pap. 10.95 (*0-8262-0586-0*) U of Mo Pr.

Ramsay, T. S., ed. Oceanic Micropalaeontology, Vol. 2. 1978. text 209.00 (*0-12-577302-1*) Acad Pr.

Ramsay, Verna, ed. see Academy of Motion Picture Arts & Sciences Staff.

Ramsay, W. M. The Letters to the Seven Churches. rev. ed. Wilson, Mark W., ed. LC 94-33869. (Illus.). 320p. 1994. pap. 19.95 (*1-56563-059-9*) Hendrickson MA.

Ramsay, W. M. & Bell, Gertrude L. The Thousand & One Churches. (Illus.). xvi, 580p. reprint ed. lib. bdg. 100.00 (*0-89241-121-X*) Caratzas.

Ramsay, William. Unpaid Costs of Electrical Energy: Health & Environmental Impacts from Coal & Nuclear Power. LC 78-15668. 180p. 1978. pap. 14.95 (*0-8018-2230-0*) Resources Future.

Ramsay, William M. Asianic Elements in Greek Civilisation. Gifford Lecture in the University of Edinburgh, 1915-1916. LC 77-97894. reprint ed. 35.00 (*0-404-05209-6*) AMS Pr.

— Asianic Elements in Greek Civilization. 303p. 1976. pap. 25.00 (*0-89005-173-9*) Ares.

— The Cities & Bishoprics of Phrygia. LC 75-7336. (Roman History Ser.). (Illus.). 1975. reprint ed. 63.95 (*0-405-07055-1*) Ayer.

***Ramsay, William M.** The Education of Christ. 151p. 1998. pap. 14.00 (*1-57910-188-7*) Wipf & Stock.

Ramsay, William M. Historical Commentary on First Corinthians. 176p. 1996. pap. 10.99 (*0-8254-3637-0*) Kregel.

— Historical Commentary on Galatians. Wilson, Mark, ed. LC 96-52010. 368p. 1997. reprint ed. pap. 14.99 (*0-8254-3638-9*) Kregel.

— Historical Commentary on the Pastoral Epistles. 160p. 1996. pap. 10.99 (*0-8254-3636-2*) Kregel.

— The Westminster Guide to the Books of the Bible. 608p. 1994. 34.95 (*0-664-22061-4*) Westminster John Knox.

Ramsay, Young S. & Davis, Deborah. Flavors of Korea. LC 98-18396. (Illus.). 192p. 1998. pap. 12.95 (*1-57067-053-6*) Book Pub Co.

Ramsberger, Jack. The Battle History of the Four Hundred Seventy-Third U. S. Infantry in World War Two. 22p. 1981. reprint ed. 4.95 (*0-932572-08-1*) Phillips Pubns.

Ramsberger, Peter F., jt. auth. see Laurence, Janice H.

Ramsbotham, Oliver. Humanitarian Intervention in Contemporary Conflict: A Reconceptualizton. Woodhouse, Tom, ed. 254p. 1996. 60.95 (*0-7456-1510-4*) Blackwell Pubs.

Ramsbotham, Oliver & Woodhouse, Tom. Encyclopedia of International Peacekeeping Operations. LC 98-49834. 356p. (YA). (gr. 10). 1999. lib. bdg. 75.00 (*0-87436-892-8*) ABC-CLIO.

— Humanitarian Intervention in Contemporary Conflict: A Reconceptualization. 254p. 1996. pap. 28.95 (*0-7456-1511-2*) Blackwell Pubs.

Ramsbotham, Oliver, jt. auth. see Woodhouse, Tom.

Ramsbottom, A. E. Depth Charts of the Cumbrian Lakes. 1976. 30.00 (*0-900386-25-8*) St Mut.

Ramsdale, David A. & Ramsdale, Ellen J. Sexual Energy Ecstasy: A Practical Guide to Lovemaking Secrets of the East & West. LC 93-10329. (Illus.). 384p. 1993. pap. 17.95 (*0-553-37231-9*) Bantam.

— Sexual Energy Ecstasy: A Practical Guide to Lovemaking Secrets of the East & West. 2nd rev. ed. (Illus.). 384p. 1991. 24.95 (*0-917879-04-X*) Peak Skill.

Ramsdale, Ellen J., jt. auth. see Ramsdale, David A.

Ramsdale, Jeanne. Long-Haired Cats. 80p. pap. 6.95 (*0-86622-174-3*) TFH Pubns.

Ramsdale, Jeanne. Long-Haired Cats. (Illus.). 80p. 1984. pap. text 6.95 (*0-86622-231-6*, PB-116) TFH Pubns.

— Persian Cats & Other Longhairs. (Illus.). 271p. 1964. 23.95 (*0-86622-718-0*, H-918) TFH Pubns.

Ramsdale, P. A. & Slade, M. G. Command, Control & Communication. (Brassey's Battlefield Weapons Systems & Technology Ser.: Vol. 6). 160p. 1983. text 30.00 (*0-08-028332-2*, Pergamon Pr); pap. text 14.95 (*0-08-028333-0*, Pergamon Pr) Elsevier.

Ramsdell, Charles W. Behind the Lines in the Southern Confederacy. Stephenson, Wendell H., ed. LC 96-45592. (Walter Lynwood Fleming Lectures in Southern History). (Illus.). 160p. 1997. pap. 11.95 (*0-8071-2186-X*) La State U Pr.

— Reconstruction in Texas. 1993. reprint ed. lib. bdg. 75.00 (*0-7812-5897-9*) Rprt Serv.

Ramsdell, Daniel B. The Japanese Diet: Stability & Change in the Japanese House of Representatives, 1890-1990. 256p. (C). 1992. lib. bdg. 48.50 (*0-8191-8494-2*) U Pr of Amer.

Ramsdell, Donald C., jt. ed. see Caruso, Frank L.

Ramsdell, Heather. Lost Wax: Poems. LC 97-33774. (National Poetry Ser.). 80p. 1998. pap. 11.95 (*0-252-06706-1*) Univ of Illinois at Chicago.

Ramsdell, J. V. Atmospheric Relative Concentrations in Building Wakes. 147p. 1997. per. 15.00 (*0-16-062843-1*) USGPO.

Ramsdell, James V., et al. Siting Handbook for Small Wind Energy Conversion Systems. rev. ed. Wegley, Harry L., ed. (Illus.). 100p. 2000. pap. 39.95 (*0-88016-003-9*) WindBks.

Ramsdell, Kristin. Romance Fiction: A Guide to the Genre. LC 99-10207. (Illus.). 435p. 1999. 45.00 (*1-56308-335-3*) Libs Unl.

— What Do I Read Next? 2nd ed. 1991. 110.00 (*0-8103-5405-5*) Gale.

— What Do I Read Next? 3rd ed. 1992. 110.00 (*0-8103-5406-3*) Gale.

Ramsdell, Marcia, jt. auth. see Lord, Linda A.

Ramsdell, Melissa S., ed. My First Year As a Doctor: Real World Stories from America's M. D.s. LC 94-4990. (First Year Career Ser.). 144p. 1994. 19.95 (*0-8027-1290-8*); pap. 9.95 (*0-8027-7418-0*) Walker & Co.

***Ramsdell, William.** Ramsdell Family: William Ramsdell Genealogy. 68p. 2000. 23.50 (*0-7404-0890-9*) Higginson Bk Co.

Ramsdell, William. Ramsdell Family: William Ramsdell Genealogy. rev. ed. 60p. 1994. reprint ed. pap. 12.00 (*0-8328-4184-6*) Higginson Bk Co.

Ramsden. Psychosocial Issues in Health. (C). 1999. text 31.00 (*0-7020-2230-6*, Pub. by W B Saunders) Saunders.

Ramsden, Anne, et al. Elinor: Electronic Library Project. LC 97-41679. 167p. 1997. write for info. (*1-85739-255-8*) Bowker-Saur.

Ramsden, Caroline. Racing Without Tears: Horses. (Illus.). 1978. pap. 10.00 (*0-87556-247-7*) Saifer.

Ramsden, E. C., tr. see Undset, Sigrid.

Ramsden, E. H., tr. Letters of Michelangelo, Vols. 1 & 2. (Illus.). 1963. 125.00 (*0-8047-0183-0*) Stanford U Pr.

Ramsden, E. H. & Eates, Margot, eds. Eidos: A Journal of Painting, Sculpture & Design, Set, Nos. 1[00ad]3. LC 68-9237. (Contemporary Art Ser.). (Illus.). 1968. reprint ed. 24.95 (*0-405-00718-3*) Ayer.

Ramsden, E. N. A-Level Chemistry. 3rd ed. 820p. 1994. pap. 59.50 (*0-7487-1688-2*) Trans-Atl Phila.

***Ramsden, E. N.** A-Level Chemistry. 4th ed. (Illus.). 825p. (YA). 2000. pap. 79.50 (*0-7487-5299-4*, Pub. by S Thornes Pubs) Trans-Atl Phila.

Ramsden, E. N. Calculations for A-Level Chemistry. 3rd ed. 298p. 1995. pap. 32.50 (*0-7487-1594-0*, Pub. by S Thornes Pubs) Trans-Atl Phila.

— A Level Chemistry. 2nd ed. (C). 1990. text 97.50 (*0-7487-0154-0*, Pub. by S Thornes Pubs) Trans-Atl Phila.

— A New First Chemistry Course. 192p. (C). 1994. pap. 19.95 (*0-85950-758-0*, Pub. by S Thornes Pubs) Trans-Atl Phila.

Ramsden, Eileen. Calculations for GCSE Chemistry. 96p. (YA). (gr. 9-11). 1998. pap. 23.00 (*0-7487-1738-2*) St Mut.

— Key Science: Chemistry. (Teacher's Guide ser.). (Illus.). 384p. 1994. teacher ed. 33.00 (*0-7487-1721-8*, Pub. by S Thornes Pubs); pap. 33.00 (*0-7487-1675-0*, Pub. by S Thornes Pubs) Trans-Atl Phila.

— Key Science: Chemistry Extension File. 256p. 1998. pap. 130.00 (*0-7487-3006-0*, Pub. by S Thornes Pubs) Trans-Atl Phila.

— Key Science - Chemistry. 2nd ed. (Illus.). 383p. (YA). (gr. 9-11). 1998. pap. 29.50 (*0-7487-3009-5*, Pub. by S Thornes Pubs) Trans-Atl Phila.

Ramsden, Eileen, et al. Key Science 4, Bk. 1. 428p. (YA). (gr. 9-11). 1998. pap. 48.00 (*0-7487-0492-2*) St Mut.

— Key Science 4, Bk. 2. 480p. (YA). (gr. 9-11). 1998. pap. 48.00 (*0-7487-0494-9*) St Mut.

Ramsden, Francis, ed. see O'Dell, Jennifer.

Ramsden, Gayanne. Beowulf. 42p. (Orig.). (YA). (gr. 7-12). 1992. pap. 3.50 (*1-57514-149-3*, 1117) Encore Perform Pub.

Ramsden, H., ed. & intro. see Garcia Lorca, Federico.

Ramsden, John. The Age of Churchill & Eden: A History of the Conservative Party, 1940-1957. LC 95-9778. 368p. (C). 1995. 106.00 (*0-582-50463-5*) Longman.

***Ramsden, John.** An Appetite for Power: Buthelezi's Inkatha & South Africa. 1999. pap. 15.95 (*0-00-638757-8*, Pub. by HarpC) Trafalgar.

Ramsden, John. Winds Change. (History of the Conservative Party Ser.). 528p. (C). 1995. text 100.31 (*0-582-27570-9*) Longman.

Ramsden, John, jt. auth. see Williams, Glyn.

Ramsden, John, jt. ed. see Cook, Chris.

Ramsden, Mark. The Dark Magus & the Sacred Whore. 160p. 1999. pap. 12.99 (*1-85242-598-9*) Serpents Tail.

***Ramsden, Mark.** The Dungeonmaster's Apprentice. LC 99-63333. 176p. 1999. pap. 13.00 (*1-85242-623-3*, Pub. by Serpents Tail) Consort Bk Sales.

— Radical Desire. (Illus.). 120p. 2001. pap. 25.00 (*1-85242-653-5*) Serpents Tail.

Ramsden, Pamela & Zacharias, Joan. Action Profiling. 386p. 1994. 88.95 (*0-566-02727-5*, Pub. by Gower) Ashgate Pub Co.

Ramsden, Paul. Learning to Lead in Higher Education. LC 97-24258. 288p. (C). 1998. pap. 24.99 (*0-415-15200-3*) Routledge.

— Learning to Lead in Higher Education. LC 97-24258. 304p. (C). 1998. 75.00 (*0-415-15199-6*) Routledge.

— Learning to Teach in Higher Education. LC 91-20971. 288p. (Orig.). (C). 1991. pap. 24.99 (*0-415-06415-5*, A6590) Routledge.

Ramsden, Paul, jt. auth. see Percy, Keith.

Ramsden, Philip. The Cash Flow Challenge. 160p. 1997. pap. text 26.95 (*0-566-07807-4*, Pub. by Gower) Ashgate Pub Co.

— The Essentials of Management Ratios. LC 97-42342. 272p. 1998. pap. 61.95 (*0-566-07953-4*, Pub. by Gower) Ashgate Pub Co.

***Ramsden, Wayne S.** The Mountains Were Not Found. LC 98-91118. 1999. pap. 7.95 (*0-533-13050-6*) Vantage.

Ramsell, John. Questions & Answers. 128p. pap. 13.95 (*0-8464-4277-9*) Beekman Pubs.

— Questions & Answers. 110p. 1992. pap. 7.00 (*0-85207-240-6*, Pub. by C W Daniel) Natl Bk Netwk.

Ramsell, John, jt. auth. see Howard, Judy.

***Ramsey.** Commercial Nuclear Power Assuring Safety for the Future. 600p. 1998. pap. 525.00 (*0-471-29286-9*) Wiley.

Ramsey. Earth Science 1986. 1986. 52.50 (*0-03-001904-4*) Harcourt Schl Pubs.

— Exercise & Inv for Holt General Science. 1988. pap. text, student ed. 18.50 (*0-03-010118-2*) Holt R&W.

— Exercises & Investigations for Holt General Science. 1988. pap. text, teacher ed. 21.75 (*0-03-010119-0*) Holt R&W.

— Images. 1987. pap. text. write for info. (*0-582-74407-5*, Pub. by Addison-Wesley) Longman.

— Physical Science, 1988. 1987. 52.50 (*0-03-014394-2*) H Holt & Co.

R

An Asterisk (*) at the beginning of an entry indicates that the title is appearing for the first time.

Ramsey. Plenty to Say. Date not set. pap. text. write for info. (*0-582-00299-0*, Pub. by Addison-Wesley) Longman.

Ramsey. Statistics for Economy. 2001. 60.00 (*0-534-37111-6*) Wadsworth Pub.

— Teaching Atlas of Spine Imaging. (Illus.). 912p. 1998. 149.00 (*0-86577-778-0*) Thieme Med Pubs.

— Well Spoken. Date not set. pap. text. write for info. (*0-582-02090-5*, Pub. by Addison-Wesley) Longman.

Ramsey & Schafer. Student Solutions Manual for the Statistical Sleuth: A Course in Methods of Data Analysis. (Statistics Ser). 1997. pap. 18.75 (*0-534-25381-4*) Brooks-Cole.

Ramsey, jt. auth. see O'Neill.

Ramsey, A. H. The Nameless War. 1978. pap. 5.00 (*0-911038-38-8*, 0309, Noontide Pr) Legion Survival. .

Ramsey, A. H. M. The Nameless War. unabridged ed. 112p. 1952. reprint ed. pap. 10.00 (*0-945001-85-1*) GSG & Assocs.

Ramsey, A. T. & Baldauf, J. G., eds. A Reassessment of the Southern Ocean Biochronology. (Geological Society Memoir Ser.: No. 18). 112p. 1999. 75.00 (*1-86239-027-4*, Pub. by Geol Soc Pub Hse) AAPG.

Ramsey, Alex & Atlee, Helena. Italian Gardens: A Guide. 600p. 1998. pap. 17.95 (*1-899858-53-9*) Watsn-Guptill.

Ramsey, Allan & Barrett, Rosalind. AI in Practice: Examples in POP-11. (Artificial Intelligence Ser.). 316p. 1987. pap. text 23.95 (*0-470-20770-1*) P-H.

Ramsey, Ann L. Angels in Poetry. (Illus.). 24p. (Orig.). 1994. pap. write for info. (*0-9645663-0-3*) Crown Peak Pubns.

— Behind the Gate. (Illus.). 28p. (Orig.). 1996. pap. write for info. (*0-9645663-1-1*) Crown Peak Pubns.

— Love, God & You. (Illus.). 28p. 1999. pap. write for info. (*0-9645663-3-8*) Crown Peak Pubns.

— More Than a Memory: A Tribute to John Denver. (Illus.). 24p. 1997. pap. write for info. (*0-9645663-2-X*) Crown Peak Pubns.

Ramsey, Ann W. Liturgy, Politics & Salvation: The Catholic League in Paris & the Nature of Catholic Reform, 1540-1630. LC 99-17827. (Illus.). 512p. 1999. 99.00 (*1-58046-031-3*, Pub. by Univ Rochester Pr) Boydell & Brewer.

Ramsey, Anthony. Owner's Guide to Successful Restaurant & Retail Business. 175p. (Orig.). 1997. pap. 17.95 (*0-9646898-3-9*) Silent Comn.

Ramsey, Arthur S. An Introduction to the Theory of Newtonian Attraction. LC 41-15935. 194p. reprint ed. pap. 55.30 (*0-608-30447-6*, 2051354) Bks Demand.

Ramsey, Bennett. Submitting to Freedom: The Religious Vision of William James. (Religion in America Ser.). 192p. 1993. text 45.00 (*0-19-507426-2*) OUP.

Ramsey, Bets. Old & New Quilt Patterns in the Southern Tradition. LC 87-25182. 132p. 1987. 19.95 (*0-934395-92-6*); pap. 9.95 (*0-934395-63-2*) Rutledge Hill Pr.

Ramsey, Bets & Waldrogel, Merikay. Southern Quilts: Surviving Relics of the Civil War. LC 98-2846. (Illus.). 144p. 1998. pap. 19.95 (*1-55853-598-5*) Rutledge Hill Pr.

Ramsey, Bets & Waldvogel, Merikay. The Quilts of Tennessee: Images of Domestic Life Prior to 1930. (Illus.). 128p. 1998. pap. 19.95 (*1-55853-613-2*) Rutledge Hill Pr.

Ramsey, Boniface. Ambrose. LC 97-224345. (Early Church Fathers Ser.). 256p. (C). 1997. pap. 24.99 (*0-415-11842-5*) Routledge.

— Ambrose. LC 97-224345. (Early Church Fathers Ser.). 256p. (C). 1997. 75.00 (*0-415-11841-7*) Routledge.

— Beginning to Read the Fathers. 288p. (Orig.). 1985. pap. 19.95 (*0-8091-2691-5*) Paulist Pr.

Ramsey, Boniface, ed. John Cassian: The Conferences. LC 97-6523. (Ancient Christian Writers Ser.: No. 57). 912p. 1997. 39.95 (*0-8091-0484-9*) Paulist Pr.

***Ramsey, Boniface, tr.** John Cassian: The Institutes. (Ancient Christian Writers Ser.: No. 58). 288p. 2000. 34.95 (*0-8091-0522-5*) Paulist Pr.

Ramsey, Boniface, tr. The Sermons of St. Maximus of Turin. (Ancient Christian Writers Ser.: No. 50). 1989. 22.95 (*0-8091-0423-7*) Paulist Pr.

Ramsey, Boniface, tr. see Kasper, Walter.

Ramsey, Brian, ed. The Fiber Optic LAN Handbook. 3rd ed. (Illus.). 467p. (C). 1991. pap. text 17.95 (*0-9626933-3-2*) Codenoll Tech.

Ramsey, Brian & Zack, Tim, eds. The Fiber Optic LAN Handbook. 4th ed. (Illus.). 449p. 1991. pap. 17.95 (*0-9626933-4-0*) Codenoll Tech.

Ramsey, Brian D. & Parnell, Thomas A., eds. Gamma-Ray & Cosmic-Ray Detectors, Techniques & Missions. 646p. 1996. 102.00 (*0-8194-2194-4*) SPIE.

Ramsey, Caroline C. International Directory of Resources for Artisans. 3rd ed. 1994. lib. bdg. 100.00 (*0-9625480-1-4*) Crafts Ctr.

Ramsey, Charles. Architectural Graphic Standards. 248p. 1998. pap. 49.95 (*0-471-24762-6*) Wiley.

Ramsey, Charles B. Accident Prevention & Investigation. LC 97-38062. (Illus.). 368p. 1998. 69.95 (*0-442-01839-8*, VNR) Wiley.

Ramsey, Charles B. & Modarres, Mohammad. Commercial Nuclear Power: Assuring Safety for the Future. LC 97-38062. 508p. 1998. 84.95 (*0-471-29186-2*) Wiley.

***Ramsey, Charles G.** Traditional Details for Building Restoration, Renovation & Rehabilitation. 304p. 1998. pap. 49.95 (*0-471-24761-8*) Wiley.

Ramsey, Charles G., et al, eds. Construction Details from Architectural Graphic Standards. LC 91-25165. (Ramsey-Sleeper Architectural Graphic Standards Ser.: No. 1955). 408p. 1991. 150.00 (*0-471-54899-5*) Wiley.

Ramsey, Charles G. & Sleeper, Harold R. Architectural Graphic Standards Facsimile. LC 89-22431. 233p. 1990. 275.00 (*0-471-51556-6*) Wiley.

— Architectural Graphic Standards for Architects, Engineers, Decorators, Builders,& Draftsmen. deluxe ed. 248p. 1990. 200.00 (*0-471-51940-5*) Wiley.

— Residential & Light Construction from Architectural Graphic Standards. LC 90-29318. 480p. 1991. 150.00 (*0-471-54371-3*) Wiley.

— Site Details from Architectural Graphic Standards. LC 91-43622. (Ramsey-Sleeper Architectural Graphic Standards Ser.: No. 1955). 336p. 1992. 150.00 (*0-471-57060-5*) Wiley.

***Ramsey, Charles George & Sleeper, Harold Reeve.** Architectural Graphic Standards CD-Rom. 3rd ed. Hoke, John Ray, Jr., ed. 2000. 425.00 (*0-471-36932-2*) Wiley.

— Ramsey/Sleeper Architectural Graphics: Standards. 10th ed. 1088p. 2000. 225.00 (*0-471-34816-3*) Wiley.

***Ramsey, Charles George, et al.** Architectural Graphic Standards. 2000. 600.00 (*0-471-39186-7*) Wiley.

— Ramsey/Sleeper Architectural Graphics Standards. LC 00-38203. 2000. student ed. write for info. (*0-471-34817-1*) Wiley.

Ramsey, Christian N., Jr., ed. Family Systems in Medicine. LC 88-24477. (Family Therapy Ser.). (Illus.). 615p. 1989. lib. bdg. 79.95 (*0-89862-103-8*) Guilford Pubns.

Ramsey, Christopher, ed. see Martins, Peter.

Ramsey, Claire L. Deaf Children in Public Schools Vol. 3: Placement, Context & Consequences. (Sociolinguistics in Deaf Communities Ser.: Vol. 3). 125p. 1997. 39.95 (*1-56368-062-9*, DCPS-TXT) Sign Enhancers.

Ramsey, Dan. Budget Flying: A Private Pilot's Guide. 2nd ed. (Illus.). 192p. 1989. 24.95 (*0-8306-9448-X*) McGraw-Hill Prof.

— Builder's Guide to Barriers: Doors, Windows, & Trim. (Illus.). 249p. 1998. pap. text 30.00 (*0-7881-5509-1*) DIANE Pub.

— Builder's Guide to Foundations & Floor Framing. (Builder's Guide Ser.). (Illus.). 294p. 1997. pap. 24.95 (*0-07-052552-8*) McGraw.

— Builder's Guide to Foundations & Framing. LC 94-48314. 320p. 1995. 44.00 (*0-07-051814-9*) McGraw.

— Building a Log Home from Scratch or Kit. 2nd ed. (Illus.). 302p. (Orig.). 1987. pap. 16.95 (*0-8306-2858-4*) McGraw-Hill Prof.

— Building a Log Home from Scratch or Kit. 2nd ed. 302p. 1987. pap. 19.95 (*0-07-155212-X*) McGraw.

— The Complete Foundation & Floor Framing Book. (Illus.). 220p. 1987. pap. 15.95 (*0-8306-2878-9*) McGraw-Hill Prof.

— Complete Idiot's Guide to Smart Moving. LC 97-80978. (Complete Idiot's Guide Ser.). 309p. 1998. 16.95 (*0-02-862126-3*) Macmillan Gen Ref.

— Complete Idiot's Guide to Trouble - Free Car Care. 256p. 1996. 16.95 (*0-02-861041-5*) Macmillan Gen Ref.

***Ramsey, Dan.** The Complete Idiot's Guide to Trouble-Free Car Repair. 2nd ed. LC 99-65262. (Complete Idiot's Guides (Lifestyle) Ser.). (Illus.). 265p. 1999. pap. 16.95 (*0-02-863583-3*, Alpha Ref) Macmillan Gen Ref.

Ramsey, Dan. Doors, Windows & Skylights. 2nd ed. (Illus.). 240p. 1990. 14.95 (*0-8306-8248-1*, 3248); pap. 14.95 (*0-8306-3248-4*) McGraw-Hill Prof.

— Electrical Contractor: Start & Run a Money-Making Business. 323p. 1994. pap. 21.95 (*0-07-051289-2*) McGraw.

— Electrical Contractor: Start & Run a Money-Making Business. LC 93-23867. 1993. pap. text 17.95 (*0-8306-4467-9*) McGraw-Hill Prof.

— Fences, Decks & Other Backyard Projects. 2nd ed. (Illus.). 304p. 1988. 22.95 (*0-8306-0478-2*); pap. 15.95 (*0-8306-2778-2*) McGraw-Hill Prof.

— Fences, Decks & Other Backyard Projects. 3rd ed. 288p. 1992. 24.95 (*0-8306-3494-0*, 4071) McGraw-Hill Prof.

— Hardwood Floors. 2nd ed. (Illus.). 160p. 1991. pap. 14.95 (*0-8306-3529-7*) McGraw-Hill Prof.

— Home Improvements. 1991. 23.95 (*0-8306-5315-5*) McGraw-Hill Prof.

— 101 Best Home Businesses. LC 96-37685. 192p. (Orig.). 1997. pap. 14.99 (*1-56414-263-9*) Career Pr Inc.

— 101 Best Weekend Businesses. 192p. (Orig.). 1996. pap. 14.99 (*1-56414-257-4*) Career Pr Inc.

— The Pocket Idiot's Guide to Car Repair. (Pocket Idiot's Guides Ser.). (Illus.). 192p. 1997. pap. 9.95 (*0-02-862014-3*) Macmillan Gen Ref.

— Tile Floors. 2nd ed. (Illus.). 164p. 1991. pap. 13.95 (*0-8306-3535-1*) McGraw-Hill Prof.

— Weather Forecasting: A Young Meteorologist's Guide. (Illus.). 144p. (YA). 1990. 19.95 (*0-8306-8338-0*, 3338); pap. 10.95 (*0-8306-3338-3*) McGraw-Hill Prof.

— Woodworker's Guide to Pricing Your Work. LC 94-33313. 160p. 1995. pap. 18.99 (*1-55870-372-1*, Betrwy Bks) F & W Pubns Inc.

Ramsey, Dave. Financial Peace: Restoring Financial Hope to You & Your Family. LC 96-32569. 244p. 1997. 22.95 (*0-670-87361-6*) Viking Penguin.

— The Financial Peace Planner: A Step-By-Step Guide to Restoring Your Family's Financial Health. LC 98-107795. (Illus.). 273p. 1998. pap. 14.95 (*0-14-026468-X*) Viking Penguin.

***Ramsey, Dave.** How to Have More Than Enough: A Step-by-Step Guide to Creating Abundance. 288p. 2000. pap. 14.95 (*0-14-028193-2*) Penguin Putnam.

Ramsey, Dave. More Than Enough: Proven Keys to Building Your Family & Financial Peace. LC 98-31590. 330p. 1999. 22.95 (*0-670-88253-4*) Viking Penguin.

Ramsey, Dennis A., jt. auth. see Nowicki, Edward J.

Ramsey, Donald E. The Planet, Humanity & the Albino - Aryan - European World Order. LC 98-91355. 266p. 1998. 18.00 (*0-9663137-0-4*) Olmec Pub.

Ramsey, Donald O. Your Tax Return: How to Organize & Prepare It. 140p. 1991. student ed. 15.95 (*0-9630667-0-6*) KISS Enter.

Ramsey, Doug. Jazz Matters: Reflections on the Music & Some of Its Makers. LC 88-26165. 336p. 1989. pap. 18.00 (*1-55728-061-4*) U of Ark Pr.

Ramsey, Doug, ed. see Lowe, Deborah, et al.

Ramsey, Doug, ed. see Wartenberg, Daniel.

Ramsey, Douglas L. & Skroch, Larry E. The Raging Red: The 1950 Red River Valley Flood. 300p. 1995. pap. 9.95 (*0-9635253-0-1*) Valley Heritage.

***Ramsey, E. D., ed.** Analytical Supercritical Fluid Extraction Techniques. 1998. write for info. (*0-7514-0446-2*) Kluwer Academic.

Ramsey, Edwin P. & Rivele, Stephen. Lieutenant Ramsey's War: From Horse Soldier to Guerrilla Commander. (World War II Commemorative Ser.). (Illus.). 336p. 1996. reprint ed. pap. 17.95 (*1-57488-052-7*) Brasseys.

Ramsey, Elizabeth M. The Placenta: Human & Animal. LC 81-23372. 187p. 1982. 65.00 (*0-275-91378-3*, C1378, Praeger Pubs) Greenwood.

Ramsey, Erica, ed. see McDonald, Trevy.

Ramsey, F. Jeffress. Global Studies: Africa. 7th ed. 224p. (C). 1997. text. write for info. (*0-697-37422-X*) Brown & Benchmark.

Ramsey, Frances M., ed. English Episcopal Acta Vol. X: Bath & Wells, 1061-1205. (British Academy Ser.). (Illus.). 352p. 1995. text 85.00 (*0-19-726131-0*) OUP.

Ramsey, Frank P. On Truth: Original Manuscript Materials from the Ramsey Collection at the University of Pittsburgh (1927-1929) (Episteme Ser.). 160p. (C). 1991. lib. bdg. 107.50 (*0-7923-0857-3*, Pub. by Kluwer Academic) Kluwer Academic.

Ramsey, Fred L. & Schafer, Daniel W. The Statistical Sleuth: A Course in Methods of Data Analysis. LC 96-35423. (C). 1996. pap. 98.95 (*0-534-25380-6*) Wadsworth Pub.

***Ramsey, Frederic.** Been Here & Gone. LC 99-38538. 1999. pap. 19.95 (*0-8203-2195-8*) U of Ga Pr.

Ramsey, Frederic, Jr. A Guide to Longplay Jazz Records. LC 77-9065. (Roots of Jazz Ser.). (Illus.). 1977. reprint ed. lib. bdg. 32.50 (*0-306-70891-4*) Da Capo.

Ramsey, Frederic & Frederic, Harold. Jazzmen. 1988. reprint ed. lib. bdg. 75.00 (*0-317-90916-9*) Rprt Serv.

Ramsey, Frederic & Smith, Charles E., eds. Jazzmen. LC 78-181233. 360p. 1939. reprint ed. 39.00 (*0-403-01654-1*) Scholarly.

***Ramsey, G. Lee.** Care-Full Preaching: From Sermon to Caring Community. 224p. 2000. pap. 21.99 (*0-8272-0480-9*) Chalice Pr.

***Ramsey, George W.** The Quest for the Historical Israel. 208p. 1999. pap. 20.00 (*1-57910-271-9*) Wipf & Stock.

Ramsey, Gerald. Transsexuals: Candid Answers to Private Questions. (Illus.). 192p. (Orig.). 1996. 24.95 (*0-89594-790-0*) Crossing Pr.

***Ramsey, Gordon.** Gordon Ramsay's Passion for Flavour: Recipes from the Aubergine. (Illus.). 192p. 2000. 45.00 (*1-85029-841-6*, Pub. by Conran Octopus) Antique Collect.

Ramsey, Greg. The Red Ribbon: A Story of Hope. LC 94-68021. 35p. (J). (gr. k-5). 1994. 19.95 (*0-9642815-0-3*); 19.95 (*0-9642815-9-7*) Natl Fmly Prtnship.

— The Red Ribbon: A Story of Hope. (J). (ps-5). 1994. teacher ed. 2.95 (*0-9642815-1-1*) Natl Fmly Prtnship.

— The Red Ribbon: A Story of Hope. deluxe ed. 35p. (J). (gr. k-5). 1994. 100.00 (*0-9642815-2-X*) Natl Fmly Prtnship.

Ramsey, Guy R. Postmarked Washington: Pierce County. LC 81-620032. (Illus.). 123p. 1981. pap. 8.50 (*0-917048-54-7*) Wash St Hist Soc.

Ramsey Head Pr. Staff. Eating & Drinking in Edinburgh. 1987. 50.00 (*0-902859-90-0*) St Mut.

Ramsey, I. T., ed. see Locke, John.

Ramsey, Iain. Debtors & Creditors - A Socio-Legal Perspective. 1986. text 56.00 (*0-86205-101-0*, UK, MICHIE) LEXIS Pub.

Ramsey, Ian T., ed. Prospect for Metaphysics: Essays of Metaphysical Exploration. LC 72-97318. 240p. 1970. reprint ed. lib. bdg. 59.50 (*0-8371-2557-X*, RAME, Greenwood Pr) Greenwood.

Ramsey, Ida T. Ida's in the Kitchen. (Illus.). 174p. (Orig.). 1994. pap. text 9.95 (*0-9646860-0-7*) Viola Hilltop Pub.

Ramsey, J. G. Annals of Tennessee to the End of the Eighteenth Century. LC 77-146413. (First American Frontier Ser.). (Illus.). 1971. reprint ed. 55.95 (*0-405-02877-6*) Ayer.

— Annals of Tennessee to the End of the 18th Century. (Illus.). 743p. 1995. reprint ed. lib. bdg. 77.50 (*0-8328-5040-3*) Higginson Bk Co.

Ramsey, J. G., jt. auth. see Thomas, Jane H.

***Ramsey, J. G. M.** Annals of Tennessee. 821p. 1999. 47.50 (*1-57072-091-6*) Overmountain Pr.

Ramsey, J. T. Sallust's Bellum Catilinae. LC 81-21281. (American Philological Association Textbook Ser.). 262p. (C). 1984. pap. 15.00 (*0-89130-560-2*, 40 03 09) OUP.

Ramsey, Jackson E. Research & Development: Project Selection Criteria. rev. ed. Farmer, Richard, ed. LC 86-16085. (Research for Business Decisions Ser.: No. 80). 221p. reprint ed. pap. 68.60 (*0-8357-1708-9*, 207041200088) Bks Demand.

***Ramsey, James.** Deploying & Supporting Internetworking Services in Windows 2000. 700p. 2000. pap. 39.99 incl. cd-rom (*0-7897-2230-5*) Que.

Ramsey, James. Objections to the Abolition of the Slave Trade with Answers. LC 73-83873. (Black Heritage Library Collection). 1977. 14.95 (*0-8369-8644-X*) Ayer.

— Winter Watch. (Illus.). 154p. (Orig.). (YA). (gr. 10). 1989. pap. 9.95 (*0-88240-329-X*, Alaska NW Bks) Gr Arts Ctr Pub.

Ramsey, James B. Economic Forecasting - Models or Markets? LC 80-21911. (Cato Papers: No. 15). 112p. 1980. pap. 1.00 (*0-932790-28-3*) Cato Inst.

— Revelation: An Exposition of the First Eleven Chapters. (Geneva Commentaries Ser.). 1977. 26.99 (*0-85151-256-9*) Banner of Truth.

Ramsey, James B., et al, eds. The Economics of Exploration for Energy Resources. LC 82-477. (Contemporary Studies in Economic & Financial Analysis: Vol. 26). 365p. 1981. 78.50 (*0-89232-159-8*) Jai Pr.

Ramsey, James B. & Walter, Ingo I. Bidding & Oil Leases. LC 79-3169. (Contemporary Studies in Economic & Financial Analysis: Vol. 25). 181p. 1980. 78.50 (*0-89232-148-2*) Jai Pr.

Ramsey, James G. Autobiography & Letters. Hesseltine, William B., ed. LC 54-63080. 385p. reprint ed. pap. 119.40 (*0-8357-5906-7*, 202221600025) Bks Demand.

Ramsey, James L. Who Am I Now That I Am Alone? 3rd ed. (Orig.). 1994. pap. 49.95 (*0-614-04768-4*); pap. 10.95 (*0-614-04769-2*) ABT Inc.

Ramsey, James L., jt. auth. see Bommarito, Patricia S.

Ramsey, James P., jt. auth. see MacBrayne, Lewis.

Ramsey, James R. Architectural, Building, & Mechanical System Acoustics: A Guide to Technical Literature, Volume I Applications. LC 86-63348. viii, 95p. 1986. pap. 28.00 (*0-940737-00-0*) RT Books.

— Architectural, Building, & Mechanical System Acoustics: A Guide to Technical Literature, Volume II Technology. LC 86-63349. viii, 83p. 1986. pap. 25.00 (*0-940737-01-9*) RT Books.

— Sound & Vibration Engineered Environments - Manufacturers & Fabricators of Architectural, Building & Mechanical System Products. vi, 246p. 1988. pap. 28.00 (*0-940737-03-5*) RT Books.

***Ramsey, Janet L. & Blieszner, Rosemary.** Spiritual Resiliency in Older Women: Models of Strength for Challenges Through the Life Span. LC 98-40299. 180p. 1999. 49.00 (*0-7619-1276-2*) Sage.

Ramsey, Janet L. & Blieszner, Rosemary. Spiritual Resiliency in Older Women: Models of Strength for Challenges Through the Life Span. LC 98-40299. 1999. 25.95 (*0-7619-1277-0*) Sage.

Ramsey, Jarold. Hand-Shadows. (QRL Poetry Bks.: Vols. XXVIII-XXIX). 1989. 20.00 (*0-614-06428-7*) Quarterly Rev.

— Reading the Fire: Essays in the Traditional Indian Literatures of the Far West. LC 82-21775. 272p. 1983. reprint ed. pap. 84.40 (*0-608-03476-2*, 206418600008) Bks Demand.

***Ramsey, Jarold.** Reading the Fire: The Traditional Indian Literatures of America. rev. expanded ed. LC 99-13656. 332p. 1999. pap. text 19.95 (*0-295-97787-6*) U of Wash Pr.

Ramsey, Jarold, ed. Coyote Was Going There: Indian Literature of the Oregon Country. LC 76-49158. (Illus.). 336p. 1978. pap. 18.95 (*0-295-95731-X*) U of Wash Pr.

Ramsey, Jarold, jt. ed. see Jones, Suzi.

Ramsey, John. Clarity. LC 83-91303. (Illus.). 160p. (Orig.). 1985. pap. 10.00 (*0-9613286-1-4*) Brainchild Bks.

— Clarity, 3 cass., Set. LC 83-91303. (Illus.). 160p. (Orig.). 1985. audio 22.00 (*0-317-14112-0*) Brainchild Bks.

***Ramsey, John & Ramsey, Patsy.** Death of Innocence: The Untold Story of JonBenet's Murder & How Its Exploitation Compromised the Pursuit of Truth. 288p. 2000. 24.99 (*0-7852-6816-2*) Nelson.

Ramsey, John, et al. Municipal Solid Waste: A STS Case Study. 140p. (C). 1996. spiral bd. 10.80 (*0-87563-647-0*) Stipes.

Ramsey, John F. Love to Be Loved: A Collection of Poetry in Emotion. 64p. 1998. pap. 14.95 (*0-9647940-7-1*) Adventura Pubng.

Ramsey, John T. & Licht, A. Lewis. The Comet of 44 B. C. & Caesar's Funeral Games. LC 96-17535. (APA American Classical Studies). 236p. 1997. pap. 17.95 (*0-7885-0274-3*, 400439) OUP.

Ramsey, John T., jt. auth. see Barnes, E. J.

Ramsey, Jonathan, jt. ed. see Hall, Spencer.

Ramsey, Kamau. "No" Means Find Another Way to Do It: And Other Mental Morsels. (Illus.). 296p. 1998. per. 12.95 (*0-9668786-3-9*) Quiet Warrior.

Ramsey, Karen. Everything You Know about Money Is Wrong. 224p. 2000. pap. 12.00 (*0-06-098741-3*) HarpC.

— Everything You Know About Money Is Wrong: Overcome the Financial Myths Keeping You From the Life You Want. LC 99-18727. 224p. 1999. 17.95 (*0-06-039273-8*) HarpC.

Ramsey, Katherine D., jt. auth. see Close, Elizabeth.

***Ramsey, Kwasi.** Notes from the New Chitlin Circuit. iv, 124p. 1999. pap. 11.95 (*0-9671082-1-7*, Division of Wrds) Black Alchemist.

Ramsey, Lee C. Chivalric Romances: Popular Literature in Medieval England. LC 83-47659. 255p. 1983. reprint ed. pap. 79.10 (*0-7837-9664-1*, 205929800005) Bks Demand.

Ramsey, Leslie A., ed. The School Administrator's Handbook of Internet Sites. 186p. 1996. spiral bd. 54.00 (*1-56925-045-6*, NET) Capitol Publns.

Ramsey, Leslie A., jt. auth. see Hale, Phale.

Ramsey, Lester B. Medical Surveillance of Populations for Health & Disease with Global Watch for Transmission & Infections: Index of New Information. rev. ed. 149p. 1997. 47.50 (*0-7883-1628-1*); pap. 44.50 (*0-7883-1629-X*) ABBE Pubs Assn.

Ramsey, Linda, jt. auth. see Wilson, Ed.

***Ramsey, Lydia.** Manners That Sell: Adding the Polish That Builds Profits. (Illus.). 2000. pap. 19.95 (*0-9670012-0-X*) L Ramsey.

Ramsey, Marcy Dunn. Rosie's Posies. LC 96-105686. (Illus.). 34p. (J). (ps-3). 1995. 14.95 (*0-87033-472-7*, Tidewtr Pubs) Cornell Maritime.

Ramsey, Marcy Dunn. Danger: Twins at Work! (Sweet Valley Kids Ser.: No. 76). 96p. (J). (gr. 1-3). 1998. pap. 3.50 (*0-553-48615-2*, Sweet Valley) BDD Bks Young Read.

R

— Little Drummer Girls. (Sweet Valley Kids Ser.: No. 75). 96p. (J). (gr. 1-3). 1998. pap. 3.50 (*0-553-48614-4*, Sweet Valley) BDD Bks Young Read.

Ramsey, Marcy Dunn, jt. auth. see Luke, Melinda.

Ramsey, Marjorie E., ed. It's Music! LC 84-435. (Illus.). 56p. (J). (ps-9). 1984. 7.50 (*0-87173-104-5*) ACEI.

Ramsey, Marjorie E., jt. ed. see Dittmann, Laura L.

Ramsey, Martha. Blood Stories. (CSU Poetry Ser.: Vol. XLIX). 75p. (Orig.). 1996. pap. 10.00 (*1-880834-19-7*) Cleveland St Univ Poetry Ctr.

— Where I Stopped: Remembering Rape at Thirteen. LC 96-47488. (Harvest Book Ser.). 368p. 1997. pap. 13.00 (*0-15-600493-3*) Harcourt.

***Ramsey, Mason L.** Bodies in the Bay. Fisher, Randi Elizabeth & Bartel, An, eds. (Illus.). 307p. 2000. 23.95 (*0-9666390-0-6*, Pub. by Arrow Hunt) ACCESS Pubs Network.

Ramsey, Michael. Be Still & Know: A Study in the Life of Prayer. 128p. (Orig.). 1984. 6.95 (*0-8164-2473-X*) Harper SF.

— Be Still & Know: A Study in the Life of Prayer. LC 83-4765. 108p. (Orig.). 1993. reprint ed. pap. 9.95 (*1-56101-083-9*) Cowley Pubns.

— The Christian Priest Today. rev. ed. 112p. 1994. pap. 9.95 (*1-56101-106-1*) Cowley Pubns.

— Modern Spirituality Series. 96p. 1990. pap. 4.95 (*0-87243-178-9*) Templegate.

Ramsey, Michael & Griffiss, James E., prefs. Holy Spirit: A Biblical Study. LC 92-25733. (Cowley Classic Ser.). 140p. 1992. pap. 9.95 (*1-56101-069-3*) Cowley Pubns.

***Ramsey, Michelle.** Phonics Games Kids Can't Resist! 25 Lively Learning Games That Make Teaching Phonics Easy & Fun. (Illus.). 64p. (J). (gr. k-2). 2000. pap. 15.99 (*0-439-10796-2*) Scholastic Inc.

Ramsey, Nancy, jt. auth. see McCorduck, Pamela.

Ramsey, Norman, jt. auth. see Kleppner, Daniel.

Ramsey, Norman F. Spectroscopy with Coherent Radiation: Selected Papers of Norman F. Ramsey. LC 98-16290. (World Scientific Series in 20th Century Physics: Vol. 21). 400p. 1997. 78.00 (*981-02-3250-0*) World Scientific Pub.

Ramsey, Paige. In the Middle of Muddle. (Illus.). 95p. (Orig.). 1991. pap. 5.95 (*1-879366-05-3*) Hearthstone OK.

Ramsey-Palmer, Paige. Young Troopers: Stories of Army Children on the Frontier. LC 96-35089. (Illus.). 64p. (J). 1997. pap. 9.95 (*1-877856-68-1*) SW Pks Mnmts.

Ramsey, Patricia. Making Friends in School: Promoting Peer Relationships in Early Childhood. (Early Childhood Education Ser.: Vol. 32). 256p. 1991. text 42.00 (*0-8077-3128-5*) Tchrs Coll.

Ramsey, Patricia G. A Killin' 18p. 1990. pap. 3.50 (*0-87129-011-1*, K22) Dramatic Pub.

— Making Friends in School: Promoting Peer Relationships in Early Childhood. (Early Childhood Education Ser.: Vol. 32). 256p. 1991. pap. text 18.95 (*0-8077-3127-7*) Tchrs Coll.

— Teaching & Learning in a Diverse World: Multicultural Education for Young Children. (Early Childhood Education Ser.). 224p. 1986. pap. text 17.95 (*0-8077-2828-4*) Tchrs Coll.

— Teaching & Learning in a Diverse World: Multicultural Education for Young Children. 2nd ed. LC 97-47502. (Early Childhood Education Ser.). 240p. 1998. 46.00 (*0-8077-3723-2*); pap. 21.95 (*0-8077-3722-4*) Tchrs Coll.

Ramsey, Patricia G., et al. Multicultural Education: A Source Book. 2nd ed. (Source Books on Education). 300p. 1998. text 45.00 (*0-8153-1744-1*) Garland.

Ramsey, Patsy, jt. auth. see Ramsey, John.

Ramsey, Paul. The Art of John Dryden. LC 70-80088. (South Atlantic Modern Language Association Award Study). 224p. reprint ed. pap. 69.50 (*0-8357-5762-5*, 203005500067) Bks Demand.

— Basic Christian Ethics. LC 78-56925. 424p. 1980. pap. text 14.00 (*0-226-70383-5*) U Ch Pr.

— Basic Christian Ethics. (Library of Theological Ethics). 416p. 1993. pap. 19.00 (*0-664-25324-5*) Westminster John Knox.

— The Essential Paul Ramsey: A Collection. Werpehowski, William & Crocco, Stephen, eds. LC 93-35449. 320p. (C). 1994. 37.50 (*0-300-05815-2*) Yale U Pr.

— Fabricated Man: The Ethics of Genetic Control. LC 78-123395. (Yale Fastback Ser.: No. 6). 182p. reprint ed. pap. 56.50 (*0-7837-2783-6*, 204317500006) Bks Demand.

— The Fickle Glass: A Study of Shakespeare's Sonnets. LC 77-15910. (Studies in the Renaissance: No. 4). 1979. 34.50 (*0-404-16032-8*) AMS Pr.

— The Just War: Force & Political Responsibility. 524p. (C). 1991. pap. text 19.95 (*0-8226-3014-1*) Littlefield.

— The Patient As Person: Explorations in Medical Ethics. LC 77-118737. (Lyman Beecher Lectures at Yale University). 305p. reprint ed. pap. 94.60 (*0-8357-8260-3*, 203386300087) Bks Demand.

— Speak up for Just War or Pacifism: A Critique of the United Methodist Bishop's Pastoral Letter "In Defense of Creation" LC 87-21295. 256p. 1988. pap. 16.95 (*0-271-00639-0*); lib. bdg. 30.00 (*0-271-00619-6*) Pa St U Pr.

— War & the Christian Conscience: How Shall Modern War Be Conducted Justly? LC 61-10666. xxiv, 331p. 1961. reprint ed. pap. text 18.95 (*0-8223-0361-2*) Duke.

— War & the Christian Conscience: How Shall Modern War be Conducted Justly? LC 61-10666. 353p. reprint ed. pap. 109.50 (*0-608-12308-0*, 202376600033) Bks Demand.

Ramsey, Paul & Wilson, John F., eds. The Study of Religion in Colleges & Universities. LC 70-90957. 365p. 1970. reprint ed. pap. 113.20 (*0-7837-9429-0*, 206017000004) Bks Demand.

Ramsey, Paul, ed. see Edwards, Jonathan.

Ramsey, Paul G., jt. auth. see Larson, Eric B.

Ramsey, Paula. A Lady's Day Out in Fredericksburg. 200p. 1992. write for info. (*0-9633537-0-5*) Ladys Day Out.

Ramsey, Phil. Frankl's "Big Itch" Fieldbook. (Illus.). 32p. 1998. pap., wbk. ed. 12.95 (*1-883823-29-3*, BB004) Pegasus Comm.

— Frankl's "Thorn Patch" Fieldbook. (Illus.). 32p. 1997. pap., wbk. ed. 12.95 (*1-883823-21-8*, BB002) Pegasus Comm.

Ramsey, Philip. Billibonk & the Big Itch. LC 97-24972. (Illus.). 83p. 1997. pap. 19.95 (*1-883823-17-X*) Pegasus Comm.

— Billibonk & the Thorn Patch. LC 96-39253. (Illus.). 64p. (Orig.). 1996. pap. 19.95 (*1-883823-09-9*) Pegasus Comm.

Ramsey, R. D. Mother's Wisdom. 288p. 1995. 12.00 (*0-8092-3433-5*, 343350, Contemporary Bks) NTC Contemp Pub Co.

Ramsey, Ramsey E. The Long Path to Nearness: A Contribution to a Corporeal Philosophy of Communication & the Groundwork for an Ethics of Relief. LC 97-9253. 160p. 1997. 49.95 (*0-391-04048-0*) Humanities.

— The Long Path to Nearness: A Contribution to a Corporeal Philosophy of Communication & the Groundwork for an Ethics of Relief. 160p. 1999. 49.95 (*1-57392-450-4*, Humanity Bks) Prometheus Bks.

Ramsey, Rick. All about Administering NIS+ 2nd ed. 480p. 1994. pap. 59.00 (*0-13-309576-2*) P-H.

Ramsey, Robert. 501 Tips for Teachers. LC 97-18252. 224p. 1997. pap. 12.00 (*0-8092-3042-9*, 304290, Contemporary Bks) NTC Contemp Pub Co.

Ramsey, Robert, ed. English for International Business. 1997. text 19.47 (*0-673-19190-7*) Addison-Wesley.

Ramsey, Robert C. Texas Family Law Evidence. 1998. 99.00 (*1-58012-020-2*) James Pub Santa Ana.

Ramsey, Robert D. Administrator's Complete School Discipline Guide: Creating an Environment Where All Kids Can Learn. LC 94-31881. 272p. (C). 1994. text 34.95 (*0-13-079401-5*) P-H.

— Educator's Discipline Handbook. LC 81-38402. 284p. 1981. text 24.95 (*0-13-240788-4*, Parker Publishing Co) P-H.

***Ramsey, Robert D.** Fiscal Fitness for School Administrators: How to Stretch Resources & Do Even More with Less. LC 00-9509. 2000. pap. write for info. (*0-7619-7608-6*) Corwin Pr.

— 501 Ways to Boost Your Child's Success in School. LC 99-53466. 192p. 2000. pap. 12.95 (*0-8092-2548-4*, 254840, Contemporary Bks) NTC Contemp Pub Co.

Ramsey, Robert D. 501 Ways to Boost Your Child's Self-Esteem. 128p. 1995. pap. 7.95 (*0-8092-3391-6*, 339160, Contemporary Bks) NTC Contemp Pub Co.

— Five Hundred One Ways to Boost Your Child's Self-Esteem. LC 93-38723. 1994. pap. 5.95 (*1-56943-037-3*) NTC Contemp Pub Co.

— Lead, Follow, or Get Out of the Way: How to Be a More Effective Leader in Today's Schools. 232p. 1999. 61.95 (*0-8039-6770-5*); pap. 24.95 (*0-8039-6771-3*) Corwin Pr.

— The Principal's Book of Lists. LC 96-28871. 402p. (C). 1996. pap. text 34.95 (*0-13-447749-9*) P-H.

— Relapse Traps: How to Avoid or Escape Them. LC 98-65294. 207p. 1999. per. 15.95 (*1-879899-00-0*) Newjoy Pr.

Ramsey, Robert L. The Place Names of Boone County, Missouri. (Publications of the American Dialect Society: No. 18). (Illus.). 52p. 1952. pap. text 5.35 (*0-8173-0618-8*) U of Ala Pr.

Ramsey, Robert Lee, jt. auth. see Head, John W.

Ramsey, Robert W. Carolina Cradle: Settlement of the Northwest Carolina Frontier, 1747-1762. LC 64-22530. xvii, 251p. 1987. reprint ed. pap. 18.95 (*0-8078-4189-7*) U of NC Pr.

***Ramsey, Roberta.** Excet Elementary Sample Questions. (ExCet Teacher Certification Ser.). (C). 1999. pap. 22.50 (*1-58197-103-6*) XAM.

— ExCet Special Education. (ExCet Teacher Certification Ser.). (C). 1999. pap. 40.00 (*1-58197-100-1*) XAM.

— FTCE Specific Learning Disabilities. rev. ed. Orig. Title: Special Education Teacher Competency Tests-Revised. 328p. (C). 2000. per. 40.00 (*1-58197-060-9*) XAM.

— FTCE Varying Exceptionalities. rev. ed. Orig. Title: Special Education Teacher Competency Tests-Revised. 328p. (C). 2000. per. 40.00 (*1-58197-061-7*) XAM.

Ramsey, Roberta. FTCE Elementary Education. (Praxis Ser.). (C). 1998. per. 22.50 (*1-58197-064-1*) XAM.

***Ramsey, Roberta.** PRAXIS Elementary Education & Middle Grade Teacher Certification. (Praxis Ser.). (C). 2000. per. 40.00 (*1-58197-009-9*); per. 30.00 (*1-58197-008-0*) XAM.

— PRAXIS Special Education. (Praxis Ser.: Vol. 2). Orig. Title: Special Education Teacher Competency Tests - Revised. (Illus.). 328p. (C). 2000. per. 50.00 (*1-58197-001-3*) XAM.

— PRAXIS Special Education. rev. ed. (Praxis Ser.). Orig. Title: Special Education Teacher Competency Tests - Revised. (Illus.). 328p. (C). 2000. spiral bd. 40.00 (*1-58197-000-5*, 569-245-6080) XAM.

***Ramsey, Ron.** Childhoods Past: Children's Art of the Twentieth Century. (Illus.). 48p. (J). 2000. pap. text 19.95 (*0-642-54134-5*, AusInfo) Aust Gov Pub.

Ramsey, Roy V. The Manly-Rickert Text of the Canterbury Tales. LC 93-50809. 716p. 1994. 139.95 (*0-7734-9128-7*) E Mellen.

Ramsey, Russell W. God's Joyful Runner: The Story of Eric Liddell. LC 87-71167. 225p. 1987. pap. 9.99 (*0-88270-624-1*) Bridge-Logos.

— Guardians of the Other Americas: Essays on the Military Forces of Latin America. LC 96-48624. 290p. 1997. pap. 32.50 (*0-7618-0637-7*) U Pr of Amer.

— On Law & Country: The Biography & Speeches of Russell Archibald Ramsey. (Illus.). 200p. 1993. pap. 12.95 (*0-8283-1970-7*) Branden Bks.

***Ramsey, Russell W., ed.** Economics of National Security: Proceedings of the 5th Conference on Latin America. (Illus.). 172p. (C). 1999. reprint ed. pap. text 35.00 (*0-7881-8198-X*) DIANE Pub.

Ramsey, Russell W., ed. see Holley, Joseph W.

Ramsey, Ruth G. Diagnostic Radiology of the Brain: CT, DSA, NMR. 2nd ed. (Advanced Exercises in Diagnostic Radiology Ser.: Vol. 9). (Illus.). 320p. 1984. pap. text 65.00 (*0-7216-1177-X*, W B Saunders Co) Harcrt Hlth Sci Grp.

— Neuroradiology. 3rd ed. LC 93-26474. (Illus.). 1056p. 1994. text 175.00 (*0-7216-3657-8*, W B Saunders Co) Harcrt Hlth Sci Grp.

— A Teaching Atlas of Spine Imaging. LC 98-27857. 1998. 149.00 (*3-13-115791-7*) Thieme Med Pubs.

Ramsey, S., jt. auth. see MacBeth, A.

Ramsey, S. Robert. The Languages of China. (Illus.). 353p. 1986. pap. text 21.95 (*0-691-01468-X*, Pub. by Princeton U Pr) Cal Prin Full Svc.

Ramsey, S. Robert, jt. auth. see Lee, Iksop.

***Ramsey, Sally.** Quick & Easy Study Guide for the U. S. Constitution. 79p. 2000. 39.95 (*1-58532-092-7*) Basic Ed Materials.

Ramsey, Samuel. English Language & English Grammar: An Historical Study. LC 68-24968. (Studies in Language: No. 41). 1969. reprint ed. lib. bdg. 75.00 (*0-8383-0231-9*) M S G Haskell Hse.

Ramsey, Shirley L., jt. auth. see Harris, Edie G.

Ramsey, T. Upton. George Washington Ate Here: A Frolic Through History with Food & Famous Folks. Ware, Don, ed. (Illus.). 210p. 1997. 24.95 (*0-614-30915-8*) T Ramsey.

— George Washington Ate Here! A Frolic Through History with Food & Famous Folks! 1997. 29.95 (*0-9658000-0-8*) T Ramsey.

Ramsey, Theresa, ed. Healthy Children--Toxic Environments: Acting on the Unique Vulnerability of Children Who Dwell Near Hazardous Waste Sites. 39p. 1998. pap. text 15.00 (*0-7881-7534-3*) DIANE Pub.

Ramsey, V. Jean, jt. auth. see Gallos, Joan V.

Ramsey, Verna, ed. see Academy of Motion Picture Arts & Sciences Staff.

Ramsey, W. General Science. 1988. text 60.00 (*0-03-010114-X*); pap. text, teacher ed. 81.00 (*0-03-010117-4*) Holt R&W.

— Modern Earth Science. 1989. text 61.00 (*0-03-004449-9*) Holt R&W.

— Modern Earth Science. 98th ed. 1998. text 62.25 (*0-03-050609-3*) Holt R&W.

Ramsey, Wes, jt. auth. see McClure, Carol A.

Ramsey, Willard A. Facing Eternity: How to Know Where You Will Go When You Die. 121p. 1999. pap. 8.95 (*0-9625220-4-X*) Millennium Three Pubs.

— Zion's Glad Morning. (Illus.). 320p. (Orig.). 1990. 15.95 (*0-9625220-0-7*); pap. 9.95 (*0-9625220-1-5*) Millennium Three Pubs.

Ramsey, William, et al, eds. Philosophy & Connectionist Theory. 336p. (C). 1991. pap. 36.00 (*0-8058-0883-3*); text 69.95 (*0-8058-0592-3*) L Erlbaum Assocs.

Ramsey, William, jt. ed. see DePaul, Michael R.

Ramsey-Woodward, Maureen, ed. see Woodward, Dan.

Ramseyer, jt. auth. see Klein.

Ramseyer, Alice R., jt. auth. see Ramseyer, Robert.

Ramseyer, J. Mark. Japanese Law. LC 98-23875. (Illus.). 308p. 1999. 45.00 (*0-226-70384-3*) U Ch Pr.

***Ramseyer, J. Mark.** Japanese Law: Readings in the Political Economy of Japanese Law. LC 00-29957. (International Library of Essays in Law & Legal Theory). 2000. write for info. (*0-7546-2083-2*, Pub. by Ashgate Pub) Ashgate Pub Co.

Ramseyer, J. Mark. Japan's Political Marketplace. (Illus.). 272p. 1997. pap. text 18.00 (*0-674-47281-0*) HUP.

— Odd Markets in Japanese History: Law & Economic Growth. (Political Economy of Institutions & Decisions Ser.). (Illus.). 205p. (C). 1996. text 54.95 (*0-521-56386-0*) Cambridge U Pr.

Ramseyer, J. Mark & Rosenbluth, Frances M. Japan's Political Marketplace. LC 92-33647. (Illus.). 288p. 1993. 44.00 (*0-674-47280-2*) HUP.

— The Politics of Oligarchy: Institutional Choice in Imperial Japan. (Political Economy of Institutions & Decisions Ser.). (Illus.). 224p. (C). 1995. text 54.95 (*0-521-47397-7*) Cambridge U Pr.

— The Politics of Oligarchy: Institutional Choice in Imperial Japan. (Political Economy of Institutions & Decisions Ser.). (Illus.). 224p. (C). 1998. pap. text 19.95 (*0-521-63649-3*) Cambridge U Pr.

Ramseyer, J. Mark, et al. Law & Investment in Japan: Cases & Materials. (East Asian Legal Studies Project, Harvard Law School). 766p. 1995. text 55.00 (*0-674-51375-4*, YANLAW) HUP.

Ramseyer, J. Mark, jt. auth. see Klein, William A.

Ramseyer, Robert & Ramseyer, Alice R. Mennonites in China. rev. ed. Funk, Herta & Kelsey, Betty, eds. (Illus.). 114p. 1989. reprint ed. pap. 6.00 (*1-877736-02-3*) MB Missions.

Ramseyer, William L. Jellyfish Mask. 64p. 1992. pap. 9.95 (*1-882620-01-1*) Buy Yourself.

Ramsfield, Jill J., jt. auth. see Ray, Mary B.

Ramshaw, Elaine. The Godparent Book. LC 93-29858. 96p. 1994. pap. 8.95 (*1-56854-015-9*, GPBOOK) Liturgy Tr Pubns.

— Ritual & Pastoral Care. LC 85-45487. (Theology & Pastoral Care Ser.). 128p. 1987. pap. 14.00 (*0-8006-1738-X*, 1-1738, Fortress Pr) Augsburg Fortress.

Ramshaw, G., ed. Hawaii Revised Statutes Annotated. Cycle B. write for info. (*0-614-05834-1*, MICHIE) LEXIS Pub.

Ramshaw, Gail. Between Sundays: Daily Bible Readings Based on the Revised Common Lectionary. LC 97-21553. 1997. 12.00 (*0-8066-3590-8*, 3-401) Augsburg Fortress.

— Every Day & Sunday, Too. LC 96-21178. (Illus.). 44p. 1996. pap. 15.99 (*0-8066-2334-9*, 10-23349) Augsburg Fortress.

— God beyond Gender: Feminist Christian God-Language. LC 94-17695. 152p. 1995. pap. 15.99 (*0-8006-2774-1*, 1-2774, Fortress Pr) Augsburg Fortress.

— Liturgical Language: Keeping It Metaphoric, Making It Inclusive. LC 95-33193. (American Essays in Liturgy Ser.). 64p. (Orig.). 1996. pap. 5.95 (*0-8146-2408-1*, Liturg Pr Bks) Liturgical Pr.

— A Metaphorical God: An Abecedary of Images for God. (Illus.). 133p. 1995. 13.00 (*1-56854-128-7*, C/MGOD) Liturgy Tr Pubns.

— A Metaphorical God: An Abecedary of Images for God. rev. ed. LC 95-812. (Illus.). 133p. 1995. pap. 8.00 (*1-56854-071-X*, P/MGOD) Liturgy Tr Pubns.

— 1-2-3 Church. LC 96-35443. (Illus.). 36p. 1996. 15.99 (*0-8066-2335-7*, 10-23357, Augsburg) Augsburg Fortress.

***Ramshaw, Gail.** Reviving Sacred Speech: The Meaning of Liturgical Language. Orig. Title: Christ in Sacred Speech. 178p. 1999. pap. 14.95 (*1-878009-36-2*) Order St Luke Pubns.

Ramshaw, Gail. Sunday Morning. (Illus.). 46p. 1993. 16.00 (*1-56854-005-1*, SUN/AM) Liturgy Tr Pubns.

— Sunday Morning. (Illus.). 48p. (J). (gr. 2-5). 1994. pap. 9.00 (*1-56854-081-7*, PSUNAM) Liturgy Tr Pubns.

— Under the Tree of Life: The Religion of a Feminist Christian. 156p. 1998. pap. 17.95 (*0-8264-1110-X*) Continuum.

— Words Around the Fire. (Illus.). 77p. 1994. pap. 6.95 (*0-929650-14-X*, WORDS) Liturgy Tr Pubns.

— Words Around the Font. LC 94-24022. (Illus.). 124p. 1995. pap. 8.95 (*1-56854-063-9*, WFONT) Liturgy Tr Pubns.

Ramshaw, Gail. Words Around the Table. (Illus.). 122p. (Orig.). 1991. pap. 10.00 (*0-929650-28-X*, WORDST) Liturgy Tr Pubns.

Ramshaw, Gail. Words That Sing. 167p. (Orig.). 1992. pap. 9.95 (*0-929650-42-5*, WOSING) Liturgy Tr Pubns.

Ramshaw, Gail, ed. Homilies for the Christian People, Cycles A, B, C. 572p. 1992. pap. 25.00 (*0-8146-6092-4*, Pueblo Bks) Liturgical Pr.

— Intercessions for the Christian People, Cycles A, B, C. 216p. 1992. pap. 19.95 (*0-8146-6091-6*, Pueblo Bks) Liturgical Pr.

Ramshaw, Gail & Lathrop, Gordon W. Psalter for the Christian People: An Inclusive Language Revision of the Psalter of the Book of Common Prayer 1979. 208p. (Orig.). 1993. pap. text 14.95 (*0-8146-6134-3*, Pueblo Bks) Liturgical Pr.

Ramshaw, Gail, jt. ed. see Lathrop, Gordon.

Ramshaw, Paul, et al, eds. Intervention on Trial: The New York War Crimes Tribunal on Central America & the Caribbean. LC 86-30342. 218p. 1987. 57.95 (*0-275-92188-3*, C2189, Praeger Pubs); pap. 14.95 (*0-275-92189-1*, B2189, Praeger Pubs) Greenwood.

Ramshaw, Raymond S. & Van Heeswijk, R. G. Energy Conversion: Electric Motors & Generators. (Illus.). 224p. (C). 1995. teacher ed. write for info. (*0-03-003402-7*) OUP.

Ramshaw-Schmidt, Gail. Letters for God's Name. (Illus.). 1986. 5.95 (*0-86683-880-5*, 7458) Harper SF.

Ramshaw-Schmitt, Gail. Searching for Language. (Worship Ser.). 213p. 1988. pap. 11.95 (*0-912405-49-X*, Pastoral Press) OR Catholic.

***Ramshaw, Wendy & Watkins, David.** The Paper Jewelry Collection. LC 00-101181. (Illus.). 40p. 2000. 25.95 (*0-500-51019-9*, Pub. by Thames Hudson) Norton.

Ramshorst, J. D. Van, see Van Ramshorst, J. D.

***Ramsics, Ignac.** Hungary in the Twentieth Century. 624p. 1999. pap. 82.00 (*963-13-4830-X*, Pub. by Corvina Bks) St Mut.

Ramsier. Physics 291. 284p. (C). 1998. pap. text 35.75 (*0-536-01493-0*) Pearson Custom.

Ramsing, Nick, jt. auth. see Waterfield, Charles W.

Ramsland, Clement, jt. ed. see Bowditch, John.

Ramsland, J. Children of the Back Lanes. (Illus.). 250p. 1994. 29.95 (*0-86840-369-5*, Pub. by New South Wales Univ Pr) Intl Spec Bk.

Ramsland, Karen. Piercing the Darkness. 2000. pap. 14.00 (*0-06-107322-9*) HarpC.

— Piercing the Darkness: Undercover with Vampires in America Today. 560p. 1999. mass mkt. 6.99 (*0-06-105945-5*, HarperPrism) HarpC.

***Ramsland, Katherine.** Bliss: Writing to Find Your True Self. 192p. 2000. pap. 14.99 (*0-89879-975-9*, Walking Stick Pr) F & W Pubns Inc.

Ramsland, Katherine M. The Art of Learning: A Self-Help Manual for Students. LC 91-15155. 236p. (C). 1992. text 21.50 (*0-7914-0921-X*) State U NY Pr.

— Dean Koontz: A Writer's Biography. 528p. 1998. pap. 16.00 (*0-06-105351-1*, HarperPrism) HarpC.

— Engaging the Immediate: Kierkegaard's Indirect Communication & Psychotherapy. LC 87-46432. 136p. 1989. 29.50 (*0-8387-5152-0*) Bucknell U Pr.

— Piercing the Darkness: Undercover with Vampires in America Today. LC 98-7784. (Illus.). 384p. 1998. 24.00 (*0-06-105062-8*, HarperPrism) HarpC.

— Prism of Night: A Biography of Anne Rice. 432p. 1994. pap. 13.95 (*0-452-27331-5*, Plume) Dutton Plume.

— The Vampire Companion: The Official Guide to Anne Rice's the Vampire Chronicles. (Illus.). 640p. 1995. pap. 17.95 (*0-345-39739-8*) Ballantine Pub Grp.

Ramsland, Katherine M., ed. The Vampire's Almanac, 1998-1999 Edition. (Illus.). 80p. 1998. pap. 13.00 (*0-9669169-0-5*) Endless Night.

Ramsland, Katherine M., jt. auth. see Ramsland, Steve.

Ramsland, Marie, ed. Variete, Prespectives in French Literature, Society & Culture: Studies in Honour of Kenneth Raymond Dutton, Emeritus Professor, the University of Newcastle, Australia. LC 98-56002. (Illus.). 349p. (C). 1999. pap. text 51.95 (*0-8204-3614-3*) P Lang Pubng.

***Ramsland, Marie, ed.** Variety: Perspectives in French Literature, Society & Culture. 349p. 1999. 51.95 (*3-631-33630-6*) P Lang Pubng.

Ramsland, Steve & Ramsland, Katherine M. Quesadillas over 100 Fast, Fresh & Festive Recipes. LC 96-15833. 192p. 1997. pap. 12.00 (*0-7615-0544-X*) Prima Pub.

***Ramsley, Kenneth R.** Absence Absorbed: A Public Journal. 208p. 1999. pap. 16.00 (*0-9674007-0-8*) Design Network.

Ramslove. The Magical Circle. rev. ed. (Illus.). 96p. 1985. pap., spiral bd. 24.95 (*0-9614605-0-4*) Trout Gulch Pr.

Ramson, jt. auth. see Hughes.

Ramson, Ronald. Praying with Frederic Ozanam. Koch, Carl, ed. LC 98-234036. (Companions for the Journey Ser.). (Illus.). 128p. 1998. pap. 8.95 (*0-88489-504-1*) St Marys.

Ramson, W. S., ed. The Australian Concise Oxford Dictionary. 2nd ed. 1424p. 1993. text 39.95 (*0-19-553442-5*) OUP.

— The Australian National Dictionary: A Dictionary of Australianisms on Historical Principles. 830p. 1989. text 85.00 (*0-19-554736-5*) OUP.

Ramsower, Reagan M. Telecommuting: The Organizational & Behavioral Effects of Working at Home. Farmer, Richard, ed. LC 84-28095. (Research for Business Decisions Ser.: No. 75). 207p. reprint ed. 64.20 (*0-8357-1628-7*, 207041300088) Bks Demand.

Ramstad, C. J. Legend: Arctic Cat's First Four Decades. 2nd rev. ed. LC 99-60936. (Illus.). 1999. 49.95 (*0-9603786-3-4*) PPM Bks.

Ramstad, C. J. & Satran, Bob. Of Ice & Engines: Twenty-Five Years of Eagle River World's Championship Snowmobile Derby Racing. (Illus.). 146p. (Orig.). 1988. pap. text 19.95 (*0-9603786-2-6*) PPM Bks.

Ramstad, P. E., jt. ed. see Watson, S. A.

Ramstad, T. A., et al. Subband Compression of Images: Principals & Examples. LC 95-17786. (Advances in Image Communication Ser.: Vol. 6). 394p. 1995. 376.00 (*0-444-89431-4*) Elsevier.

Ramstedt, Gustav J. Seven Journeys Eastward, 1898-1912. Krueger, John R., tr. from SWE. (Mongolia Society Occasional Papers: No. 9). Orig. Title: Seitseman Retkea Itaan. 1978. pap. 15.00 (*0-910980-19-5*) Mongolia.

Ramstetter, Charles & Ramstetter, Mary. John Gregory Country: Place Names, Ralston Buttes Quadrangle. LC 96-96350. (Orig.). 1999. per. 25.00 (*0-9643283-2-1*) C Lazy Three.

Ramstetter, Mary. Down the Valley of the Shadow Vol. 1: An American Novel. (Orig.). 1999. per. 14.00 (*0-9643283-1-3*) C Lazy Three.

— Over the Mountains of the Moon: An American Novel. LC 94-93954. 458p. (Orig.). 1998. reprint ed. pap. 14.00 (*0-9643283-0-5*) C Lazy Three.

Ramstetter, Mary, jt. auth. see Ramstetter, Charles.

Ramsurrun, Pahlad. Folk Tales of Mauritius. 120p. 1988. text 15.95 (*81-207-0733-8*, Pub. by Sterling Pubs) Apt Bks.

***Ramteke.** Networks. 2nd ed. 720p. 2000. 95.00 (*0-13-901265-6*) P-H.

Ramteke, Timothy. Introduction to C & C++ for Technical Students: A Skill-Building Approach. LC 97-39999. 488p. (C). 1998. pap. 87.00 (*0-13-249608-9*) P-H.

— Networks. LC 93-41893. 482p. 1993. 106.00 (*0-13-958059-X*) P-H.

***Ramteke, Timothy.** Unix by Experimentation. (Illus.). 208p. (C). 1999. pap. text 51.00 (*0-13-020944-9*) P-H.

Ramtha. L' Ame Soeur. 1991. 19.95 (*2-920083-56-2*) Edns Roseau.

— A Beginner's Guide to Creating Reality: An Introduction to Ramtha & His Teachings. 1997. 14.95 (*1-57873-025-2*) JZK Inc.

— Children's View of Destiny & Purpose, 1. 1998. 14.95 (*1-57873-005-8*) JZK Inc.

***Ramtha.** Guia Del Iniciado para Crear la Realidad. Castro, Juan M., tr.Tr. of A Beginner's Guide to Creating Reality. (SPA., Illus.). 159p. 1999. pap. 15.00 (*0-9632573-9-0*) Sin Limites.

Ramtha. I Am Ramtha. 136p. 1987. 24.95 (*0-941831-11-6*) Beyond Words Pub.

— Independencia Financiera, Vol. 1. Zion, Judi P., ed. Castro, Juan M., tr.Tr. of Financial Freedom. (SPA.). 148p. 1996. pap. 12.00 (*0-9632573-3-1*) Sin Limites.

Ramtha. Las Antiguas Escuelas de Sabiduria. Munoz-Smith, Diane, ed. Castro, Juan M., tr. Orig. Title: Ancient Schools of Wisdom. (SPA.). 196p. 1997. pap. 17.00 (*0-9632573-6-6*) Sin Limites.

Ramtha. The Plane of Bliss: On Earth as It Is in Heaven. 1997. pap. text 10.95 (*1-57873-026-0*) JZK Inc.

Ramtha, jt. contrib. by see Knight, J. Z.

***Ramthun, Bonnie.** Earthquake Games. 304p. 2000. 24.95 (*0-399-14666-0*) Putnam Pub Group.

— Ground Zero. 2000. mass mkt. 6.99 (*0-425-17632-0*) Berkley Pub.

Ramthun, Bonnie. Ground Zero: Novel. 304p. 1999. 24.95 (*0-399-14509-5*, G P Putnam) Peng Put Young Read.

Ramtin. Capitalism & Automation: Revolution in Technology & Capitalist Breakdown. 211p. (C). 49.95 (*0-7453-0370-6*, Pub. by Pluto GBR) Stylus Pub VA.

Ramu, G. N. Family Structure & Fertility: Emerging Patterns in an Indian City. 188p. (C). 1988. text 20.00 (*0-8039-9547-4*) Sage.

— Women, Work & Marriage in Urban India: A Study of Dual- & Single-Earner Couples. 200p. (C). 1990. text 24.00 (*0-8039-9626-8*) Sage.

Ramu, G. N. & Govitrikar, Vishwas P., eds. Liberalization: India & Canadian Perspectives. (C). 1995. 17.50 (*81-7023-446-8*, Pub. by Allied Pubs) S Asia.

Ramu, S. Shiva. International Licensing: Managing Intangible Resources. LC 96-3335. 256p. 1997. text 36.00 (*0-8039-9345-5*) Sage.

— Strategic Alliances: Building Network Relationships for Mutual Gain. LC 96-3336. (Response Bks.). 192p. 1997. 33.50 (*0-8039-9343-9*) Sage.

***Ramulu, G. Sree.** Voyage into Consciousness: The Fiction of Anita Desai & Virginia Woolf. 2000. 26.00 (*81-207-2252-3*, Pub. by Sterling Pubs) S Asia.

Ramulu, M., jt. ed. see Jahanmir, Said.

Ramulu, R. & Komanduri, R., eds. Machining of Advanced Composites. LC 93-73268. 227p. pap. 60.00 (*0-7918-1033-X*) ASME.

Ramundo, Bernard A. The Bargaining Manager: Enhancing Organizational Results Through Effective Negotiation. LC 93-32881. 176p. 1994. 55.00 (*0-89930-805-8*, Quorum Bks) Greenwood.

— Effective Negotiation: A Guide to Dialogue Management & Control. LC 91-40961. 216p. 1992. 57.95 (*0-89930-727-2*, REM, Quorum Bks) Greenwood.

— Peaceful Coexistence: International Law in the Building of Communism. LC 67-12421. 176p. reprint ed. pap. 54.60 (*0-608-06190-5*, 206652200008) Bks Demand.

Ramundo, Michael. Complete Book on Customer Service. LC 97-10669. 384p. (C). 1997. text 32.95 (*0-13-399882-7*) P-H.

Ramundo, Peggy, jt. auth. see Kelly, Kate.

Ramunny, Murkot. World of Nagas. 1993. reprint ed. 30.00 (*81-7211-035-9*) S Asia.

Ramus, Charles, ed. see Daumier, Honore.

Ramus, Daniel. New England Who, What, When & Where Book. 1994. 9.98 (*0-88365-855-0*) Galahad Bks.

Ramus, David. The Gravity of Shadows. LC 98-10175. 304p. 1998. 24.00 (*0-06-018779-4*) HarpC.

— The Gravity of Shadows: A Novel. 432p. 1999. mass mkt. 6.50 (*0-06-109626-1*, Harp PBks) HarpC.

***Ramus, David.** On Ice: A Thriller. LC 99-89929. 321p. 2000. 24.95 (*0-671-04184-3*, Pocket Books) PB.

Ramus, David. Thief of Light. large type ed. 1996. pap. 22.95 (*1-56895-304-6*) Wheeler Pub.

Ramus, Erica, jt. auth. see Frank, Norman.

Ramus, Jack & Birchall, Simon. Contract Practice for Surveyors. 3rd ed. LC 97-170910. 288p. 1997. pap. 42.95 (*0-7506-2661-5*, Pub. by Laxtons) Buttrwrth-Heinemann.

Ramus, Petrus. Grammatica. 119p. 1991. reprint ed. write for info. (*0-318-71466-3*) G Olms Pubs.

— Scholae in Liberales Artes. (GER.). xvi, 1166p. 1970. reprint ed. write for info. (*0-318-70504-4*); reprint ed. write for info. (*0-318-71467-1*) G Olms Pubs.

— Scholae in Liberales Artes. Ong, Walter J., ed. xvi, 1166p. 1970. reprint ed. write for info. (*0-318-71275-X*) G Olms Pubs.

— Scholarum Mathematicarum Libri Unus et Triginta. 314p. reprint ed. write for info. (*0-318-71468-X*) G Olms Pubs.

Ramus, Petrus & Talaeus, Audomarus. Collectaneae Praefationes, Epistolae, Orationes. xxviii, 625p. 1969. reprint ed. write for info. incl. 3.5 hd (*0-318-71465-5*) G Olms Pubs.

Ramusack, Barbara N. & Sievers, Sharon. Women in Asia. LC 99-21719. (Restoring Women to History Ser.). (Illus.). 216p. 1999. text 35.00 (*0-253-33481-0*) Ind U Pr.

***Ramusack, Barbara N. & Sievers, Sharon.** Women in Asia. LC 99-21719. (Restoring Women to History Ser.). (Illus.). 216p. 1999. pap. 14.95 (*0-253-21267-7*) Ind U Pr.

Ramutkowski, Barbara, et al. Glencoe Administrative Procedures for Medical Assisting: A Patient-Centered Approach,Study Guide. (Illus.). 368p. (YA). (gr. 6-12). student ed. 14.31 (*0-02-804864-4*) Glencoe.

— Glencoe Clinical Procedures for Medical Assisting: A Patient-Centered Approach. 608p. 39.00 (*0-02-802443-5*) Glencoe.

— Glencoe Medical Assisting: A Patient-Centered Approach to Administrative & Clinical Competencies. 944p. write for info. (*0-02-802422-2*); write for info. (*0-02-802442-7*) McGraw-Hill HPD.

Ramuz, C. F. Cezanne: Form. (Rhythem & Color Two Ser.). 1970. 9.95 (*0-8288-9515-5*) Fr & Eur.

Ramuz, Mark. Birdhouses: 20 Unique Woodworking Projects for Houses & Feeders. LC 95-33263. (Illus.). 128p. (Orig.). 1996. pap. 18.95 (*0-88266-917-6*, 917-6, Storey Pub) Storey Bks.

Ramuz, Mark, jt. auth. see Summers, James.

Ramwell, P., et al, eds. Sex Steroids & the Cardiovascular System. LC 92-49749. (Schering Foundation Workshop Ser.: Vol. 5). (Illus.). xii, 201p. 1993. 59.00 (*3-540-55728-8*); 64.95 (*0-387-55728-8*) Spr-Verlag.

Ramwell, Peter W., jt. ed. see O'Flaherty, Joseph T.

***Ramy, Herbert N. & Moppett, Samantha A.** Navigating the Internet: Legal Research on the World Wide Web. LC 99-50143. 1999. write for info. (*0-8377-1077-4*, Rothman) W S Hein.

Ramy, Kamala. Losing Gravity. LC 97-60120. 270p. (Orig.). 1997. pap. 12.95 (*0-9656598-0-1*) Word Wrap.

Ramzaev, P. V., ed. Medical Consequences of the Chernobyl Nuclear Accident. 237p. 1994. lib. bdg. 145.00 (*1-56072-111-1*) Nova Sci Pubs.

Ramzy, Ashraf. How to Advertise Your Hotel to Success: The Marketing Guide to Hotel Advertising. LC 91-65993. 174p. (Orig.). (C). 1991. pap. 39.95 (*0-9630095-0-8*) Townhouse FL.

Ramzy, Ibrahim. Clinical Cytopathology & Aspir Biology. 2nd ed. (Illus.). 608p. 1999. 195.00 (*0-8385-1069-8*) McGraw.

— Clinical Cytopathology & Aspiration Biopsy. (Illus.). 427p. (C). 1992. pap. text 110.00 (*0-8385-1279-8*, A1279-7, Apple Lange Med) McGraw.

Ran, Bin & Boyce, David E. Dynamic Urban Transportation Network Models: Theory & Implications for Intelligent Vehicle-Highway Systems. LC 94-22844. 1994. write for info. (*0-387-58360-2*) Spr-Verlag.

— Modeling Dynamic Transportation Networks: An Intelligent Transportation System Oriented Approach. LC 96-18806. 356p. 1996. 99.50 (*3-540-61139-8*) Spr-Verlag.

Ran-Moseley, Faye. The Tragicomic Passion: Clowns, Fools & Madmen in Drama, Film & Literature. LC 92-27556. (American University Studies: Comparative Literature: Ser. III, Vol. 40). 208p. (C). 1994. text 43.95 (*0-8204-1551-0*) P Lang Pubng.

Rana & Dhungel. Contemporary Nepal. 1998. pap. 84.00 (*0-7855-7372-0*, Pub. by Ratna Pustak Bhandar) St Mut.

Rana, P. S. Jung Bahadur Rana - The Sloving of His Rise & Glory. 1998. pap. 67.00 (*0-7855-7423-9*, Pub. by Ratna Pustak Bhandar) St Mut.

Rana, A. P., ed. Four Decades of Indo - U. S. Relations: A Commemorative Retrospective. (C). 1994. 36.00 (*81-241-0156-6*, Pub. by Har-Anand Pubns) S Asia.

Rana, B. C., ed. Damaged Ecosystems & Restoration. LC 98-198485. 350p. 1998. 58.00 (*981-02-3174-1*) World Scientific Pub.

***Rana, Binni.** How BabyKrishna Got His Blue. LC 99-91356. (Illus.). 12p. (J). 1999. write for info. (*1-929981-00-7*) kahani com.

Rana, I. M. Economic System under Umer the Great. 1986. 14.50 (*0-935782-86-9*) Kazi Pubns.

Rana, Inder K. An Introduction to Measure & Integration. 380p. 1997. text 49.00 (*81-7319-120-4*) Am Math.

— Number Systems: Constructions & Properties. LC 97-52724. 370p. 1998. 36.00 (*981-02-3304-3*) World Scientific Pub.

Rana, Indi. The Roller Birds of Rampur. 304p. (YA). (gr. 7 up). 1995. 15.95 (*0-8050-2670-3*, Bks Young Read) H Holt & Co.

***Rana, Kranti.** Modern Working Women & the Development Debate. 1998. 36.00 (*81-7391-248-3*, Pub. by Kaniska Pubs Dist) S Asia.

Rana, M. S. India Votes: Lok Sabha & Vidhan Sabha Elections 1998. LC 98-908958. 1998. 74.00 (*81-7646-026-5*, Pub. by BR Pub) S Asia.

— Writings on Indian Constitution, 1861-1985. 548p. (C). 1987. 57.50 (*0-8364-2093-4*, Pub. by Usha) S Asia.

Rana, M. Waheed. Human Embryology Made Easy. 376p. 1998. spiral bd. 50.00 (*90-5702-545-0*, Harwood Acad Pubs) Gordon & Breach.

Rana, Margo. Barbie Doll Exclusively for Timeless Creations. LC 95-141684. (Illus.). 160p. 1997. 24.95 (*0-87588-474-1*, 5296) Hobby Hse.

— Barbie Exclusives Bk. II: Identification & Values. 176p. 1996. pap. 18.95 (*0-89145-687-2*, 4632) Collector Bks.

— Barbie Exclusives, Identification & Values. 160p. 1995. pap. 18.95 (*0-89145-632-5*, 3957) Collector Bks.

— Collectibly Yours Barbie Doll, 1980-1990. LC 98-185500. (Illus.). 160p. 1998. 29.95 (*0-87588-511-X*, H5454) Hobby Hse.

— Disney Dolls Identification & Price Guide. (Illus.). 156p. 1999. 24.95 (*0-87588-541-1*) Hobby Hse.

Rana, Padma J. Life of Maharaja Sir Jung Bahadur of Nepal. 1980. 75.00 (*0-7855-0317-X*, Pub. by Ratna Pustak Bhandar) St Mut.

Rana, Pradumna B. & Hamid, Naved, eds. From Centrally Planned to Market Economies: The Asian Approach. LC 93-47050. (C). 1994. pap. write for info. (*0-19-586621-5*) OUP.

— From Centrally Planned to Market Economies: The Asian Approach, Vol. 1. LC 93-47050. 272p. (C). 1994. 55.00 (*0-19-586620-7*) OUP.

— From Centrally Planned to Market Economies: The Asian Approach: Lao PDR, Myanamar, & Viet Nam, Vol. III. (Illus.). 512p. 1996. text 80.00 (*0-19-586604-5*) OUP.

— From Centrally Planned to Market Economies: The Asian Approach: People's Republic of China & Mongolia, Vol. 2. 474p. 1996. text 75.00 (*0-19-586603-7*) OUP.

— From Centrally Planned to Market Economies Vol. 1: The Asian Approach: An Overview. (Illus.). 270p. 1995. text 65.00 (*0-19-586602-9*) OUP.

Rana, Pudma J. Life of Maharaja Sir Jung Bahadur of Nepal. 1980. 75.00 (*0-7855-0259-9*, Pub. by Ratna Pustak Bhandar) St Mut.

— Life of Maharaja Sir Jung Bahadur of Nepal. 314p. (C). 1980. 100.00 (*0-89771-064-9*, Pub. by Ratna Pustak Bhandar); 100.00 (*0-89771-112-2*, Pub. by Ratna Pustak Bhandar) St Mut.

Rana, S. S. Study of Skanda Cult. 1995. 28.00 (*81-7081-303-4*, Pub. by Nag Pubs) S Asia.

Rana, V. V., et al, eds. Advanced Metallization for ULSI Applications. (Materials Research Society Conference Proceedings Ser.: Vol. V-7). 577p. 1992. text 62.00 (*1-55899-152-2*) Materials Res.

Ranabhumi, R. The Bending Reed. (C). 1993. 30.00 (*0-7855-0173-8*, Pub. by Ratna Pustak Bhandar) St Mut.

Ranada, Julie G. The Economic Impact of Rising Oil Prices: A Survey of Theory & Methodology. LC HD9576.A689. (Working Papers: No. 82-15). 76p. reprint ed. pap. 30.00 (*0-608-14945-4*, 202597300047) Bks Demand.

***Ranade, Ashok D.** ASAP Implementations for SAP R/3. (Professional - Reference Ser.). (Illus.). 2000. pap. 39.99 (*0-672-31847-4*) Sams.

Ranade, Ashok D. Essays in Indian Ethnomusicology. 1998. 36.00 (*81-215-0807-X*, Pub. by M Manoharial) Coronet Bks.

— Indology & Ethnomusicology: Conturs of the Indo-British Relationship. 93p. 1992. 8.95 (*1-881338-01-0*) Nataraj Bks.

Ranade, Jay. DB2: Concepts, Programming & Design. 432p. 1991. 52.95 (*0-07-051265-5*) McGraw.

— Elements of C Programming Style. 1993. pap. 29.95 (*0-07-051278-7*) McGraw.

Ranade, Jay & Sackett, George C. Advanced SNA Networking: A Guide to Using VTAM-NCP. (Ranade Ser.). (Illus.). 256p. 1991. 49.00 (*0-07-051143-8*) McGraw.

Ranade, Jay, ed. see Dawson, Mike.

Ranade, Prabha S. Population Dynamics in India. 1990. 32.50 (*81-7024-307-6*, Pub. by Ashish Pub Hse) S Asia.

Ranade, R. D. Mysticism in India: The Poet-Saints of Maharashtra. LC 82-10458. (Illus.). 494p. (C). 1983. reprint ed. text 23.50 (*0-87395-669-9*) State U NY Pr.

— Mysticism in Maharashtra (Indian Mysticism) (C). 1988. 31.00 (*81-208-0575-5*, Pub. by Motilal Bnarsidass) S Asia.

— Tukaram. 231p. (C). 1994. pap. text 9.95 (*0-7914-2092-2*) State U NY Pr.

Ranade, Subhash. Natural Healing Through Ayurveda. 238p. 1993. pap. 14.95 (*1-878423-13-4*) Morson Pub.

Ranade, Vasant V. & Hollinger, Mannfred A. Drug Delivery Systems. LC 95-17154. (CRC Pharmacology & Toxicology). 384p. 1995. boxed set 139.95 (*0-8493-8542-3*, 8542) CRC Pr.

Ranade, Wendy. A Future for the NHS? Health Care in the 1990s. LC 93-14037. 1994. pap. text. write for info. (*0-582-05978-X*) Longman.

— Markets & Health Care: A Comparative Analysis. LC 97-37202. 272p. (C). 1998. pap. text 25.75 (*0-582-28985-8*) Longman.

***Ranadive, Vivek.** Power of Now: How Winning Companies Sense & Respond to Change Using Real-Time Technology. LC 00-271759. 214p. 1999. 29.99 (*0-07-135684-3*) McGraw.

***Ranaghan, Denise.** Institutional - Eyes. LC 99-96861. 2000. pap. 11.95 (*0-533-13364-5*) Vantage.

Ranaghan, Dorothy G. A Closer Look at the Enneagram. LC 89-83732. 42p. (Orig.). 1989. pap. 2.95 (*0-937779-10-5*) Greenlawn Pr.

Ranaghan, Kevin. In the Power of the Spirit: Effective Catholic Evangelization. LC 91-61640. 96p. (Orig.). 1991. pap. 6.95 (*1-878718-05-3*, Resurrection Pr) Catholic Bk Pub.

Ranai, K. & Srinivasan, B., eds. Visual Editing on UNIX. 200p. (C). 1989. text 55.00 (*9971-5-0770-6*) World Scientific Pub.

Ranai, K., jt. ed. see Srinivasan, B.

Ranaivo, Flavien. The Poetic Works of Flavien Ranaivo: L'Ombre et le Vent, Mes Chansons de Toujours, Le Retour au Bercail. (B. E. Ser.: No. 29). 1962. 25.00 (*0-8115-2980-0*) Periodicals Srv.

Ranald, Joseph. Pens & Personalities. 25.95 (*0-685-01130-5*) NCUP.

Ranald, Margaret L. The Eugene O'Neill Companion. LC 83-22671. 827p. 1984. lib. bdg. 110.00 (*0-313-22551-6*, REO/, Greenwood Pr) Greenwood.

— John Webster. (English Authors Ser.: No. 465). 197p. 1989. text 25.95 (*0-8057-6976-5*, TEAS 465) Macmillan.

— Monarch Notes on Shakespeare's Selected Comedies. (Orig.). (C). 4.25 (*0-671-00629-0*, Arco) Macmillan Gen Ref.

— Monarch Notes on Shakespeare's Taming of the Shrew. (Orig.). (C). 3.95 (*0-671-00654-1*, Arco) Macmillan Gen Ref.

— Monarch Notes on Shakespeare's Winter's Tale. (Orig.). (C). 3.95 (*0-671-00656-8*, Arco) Macmillan Gen Ref.

— Shakespeare & His Social Context: Essays in Osmotic Knowledge & Literary Interpretation. LC 83-45279. (Studies in the Renaissance: No. 10). 1987. 42.50 (*0-404-62280-1*) AMS Pr.

Ranald, Margaret L., et al. A Style Manual for College Students: A Guide to Written Assignments & Papers. rev. ed. 1982. reprint ed. pap. 1.00 (*0-930146-07-7*) Queens Coll Pr.

Ranald, Ralph. Animal Farm. (C). 3.95 (*0-671-00718-1*, Arco) Macmillan Gen Ref.

— Permanent Remissions. LC 97-34766. 320p. 1997. 25.00 (*0-671-00776-9*) PB.

Ranald, Ralph A. Monarch Notes on James' Washington Square. (Orig.). (C). 3.95 (*0-671-00846-3*, Arco) Macmillan Gen Ref.

— George Orwell's 1984. (C). 3.95 (*0-671-00719-X*, Arco) Macmillan Gen Ref.

— Monarch Notes on Shakespeare's The Tempest. (Orig.). (C). 3.95 (*0-671-00644-4*, Arco) Macmillan Gen Ref.

Ranaldo, Jim, ed. Cooking with Beth & Bill Cookbook. (Illus.). 104p. 1998. pap. 12.00 (*1-893048-01-2*) Phoenix Magazine.

Ranaldo, Lee. Bookstore & Others. (Illus.). 90p. (Orig.). 1995. pap. 7.00 (*1-885175-06-X*) Hozomeen Pr.

— Journals 80s: The Tour Diaries of Lee Ranaldo, from the Early Days of Sonic Youth. 1999. 24.00 (*1-887128-32-8*) Soft Skull Pr.

— JRNLS 80s: Poems, Lyrics, Letters Observations, Wordplay, & Postcards from the Early Days of Sonic Youth. 144p. 1998. pap. 15.00 (*1-887128-31-X*) Soft Skull Pr.

— Road Movies. 90p. 1994. pap. 8.00 (*1-887128-07-7*) Soft Skull Pr.

Ranalli, Giorgio. Rheology of the Earth: Deformation & Flow Processes in Geophysics & Geodynamics. LC 86-17311. 388p. 1987. text 100.00 (*0-04-551110-1*); pap. text 39.95 (*0-04-551111-X*) Routledge.

Ranalli, Paolo, ed. Advances in Hemp Research. LC 98-12986. (Illus.). 270p. 1998. lib. bdg. 69.95 (*1-56022-872-5*, Food Products) Haworth Pr.

An Asterisk (*) at the beginning of an entry indicates that the title is appearing for the first time.

Ranallo, Frank, jt. auth. see Smith, Hans J.

Ranallo, Ryan T., jt. auth. see Farrell, Shawn O.

Ranande, Rekha. Sir Bartle Frere & His Times. (C). 1990. text 18.50 (*81-7099-222-2*, Pub. by Mittal Pubs Dist) S Asia.

Ranard, Donald A. & Pfleger, Margot, eds. From the Classroom to the Community: A Fifteen Year Experiment in Refugee Education. LC 95-7785. (Language in Education Ser.: Vol. 86). (Illus.). 144p. (Orig.). 1995. pap. text 14.95 (*0-937354-55-4*) Delta Systems.

Ranard, John. Forty Pounds of Salt. (Illus.). (Orig.). 1995. pap. 15.00 (*0-9639585-5-0*) Fly by Nght.

***Ranasinghe, Nalin.** The Soul of Socrates. 2000. 35.00 (*0-8014-3746-6*) Cornell U Pr.

Ranaudot, Eusebius, tr. Ancient Accounts of India & China by Two Mohammedan Travellers: Who Went to Those Parts in the 9th Century. (C). 1995. reprint ed. 44.00 (*81-206-1021-0*, Pub. by Asian Educ Servs) S Asia.

***Ranawake, Silvia & Jackson, Harry, eds.** Arthur of the Germans: The Arthurian Legend in Medieval German Literature & Life. 256p. 2000. 65.00 (*0-7083-1595-X*, Pub. by U Wales Pr) Paul & Co Pubs.

Ranawake, Silvia, jt. auth. see James, Dorothy.

Ranawat, C. S., ed. Total-Condylar Knee Arthroplasty. (Illus.). 250p. 1985. 160.00 (*0-387-96043-0*) Spr-Verlag.

Ranby, B., et al, eds. Macromolecular Concept & Strategy for Humanity in Science, Technology & Industry. 160p. 1996. 117.00 (*3-540-60315-8*) Spr-Verlag.

Ranby, Bengt G. & Rabek, J. F. Photodegradation, Photo-Oxidation, & Photostabilization of Polymers: Principles & Applications. LC 74-2498. 585p. reprint ed. pap. 181.40 (*0-608-10152-4*, 201618300001) Bks Demand.

Ranby, Bengt G. & Rabek, J. F., eds. Singlet Oxygen: Reactions with Organic Compounds & Polymers. LC 77-2793. 341p. reprint ed. pap. 105.80 (*0-608-18822-0*, 203047500069) Bks Demand.

Rancan, Janet. How to Draw Cats. LC 81-52121. (Illus.). 32p. (J). (gr. 2-6). 1982. pap. 2.95 (*0-89375-680-6*) Troll Communs.

— How to Draw Cats. LC 81-52121. (Illus.). 32p. (J). (gr. 2-6). 1997. lib. bdg. 17.25 (*0-89375-679-2*) Troll Communs.

— How to Draw Cats. 1982. 7.70 (*0-606-01056-4*, Pub. by Turtleback) Demco.

Rance, Adrian. Fast Boats & Flying Boats: A Biography of Hubert Scott-Paine. (C). 1989. 39.00 (*1-85455-026-8*, Pub. by Ensign Pubns & Print) St Mut.

Rance, Brian, jt. auth. see Muir, Tom.

Rance, Eva. Eva's Story: Memoirs of 90 Years in Buckinghamshire. large type ed. (Reminiscence Ser.). 23.95 (*1-85695-126-X*, Pub. by ISIS Lrg Prnt) Transaction Pubs.

Rance, Nicholas. Wilkie Collins & Other Sensation Novelists: Walking the Moral Hospital. LC 90-48390. 1991. 36.50 (*0-8386-3444-3*) Fairleigh Dickinson.

Rance, Sheila. Heron's Reach. large type ed. (Linford Romance Library). 240p. 1992. pap. 16.99 (*0-7089-7201-2*) Ulverscroft.

Rances, Atilano. Diccionario Ilustrado de la Lengua Espanola. (SPA.). 480p. 1983. pap. 14.95 (*0-7859-5108-3*) Fr & Eur.

Ranchan, Rahul. Night Sea Journey. vii, 46p. 1989. text 12.50 (*81-220-0157-2*, Pub. by Konark Pubs Pvt Ltd) Advent Bks Div.

Ranchan, Som P. An Adventure in Vedanta: J. D. Salingers The Glass Family. 1989. 14.50 (*81-202-0245-7*, Pub. by Ajanta) S Asia.

— America with Love: An Epic Tantric Poem. 120p. 1989. text 18.95 (*81-220-0048-7*, Pub. by Konark Pubs Pvt Ltd) Advent Bks Div.

— Anteros - Poems: Opus Alchymicum on Friendship. 90p. 1992. text 15.95 (*81-220-0266-8*, Pub. by Konark Pubs Pvt Ltd) Advent Bks Div.

— Aurobindran Yoga: A Revisioning. 1993. 12.95 (*81-220-0308-7*, Pub. by Konark Pubs Pvt Ltd) Advent Bks Div.

— Jawaharlal Nehru: Puer Aeternus. 109p. 1992. text 15.95 (*81-220-0256-0*, Pub. by Konark Pubs Pvt Ltd) Advent Bks Div.

— New Sights on the Gita. (C). 1987. 11.00 (*81-202-0184-1*, Pub. by Ajanta) S Asia.

— Nigamas: For the Age. 93p. 1989. text 15.95 (*81-220-0156-4*, Pub. by Konark Pubs Pvt Ltd) Advent Bks Div.

— Revisioning Gita. 200p. 1991. text 27.50 (*81-220-0216-1*, Pub. by Konark Pubs Pvt Ltd) Advent Bks Div.

Ranchan, Som P. & Gupta, K. D. Sri Aurobindo As a Political Thinker: An Interdisciplinary Study. 113p. 1989. text 15.95 (*81-220-0111-4*, Pub. by Konark Pubs Pvt Ltd) Advent Bks Div.

Rancho Park Publishing Staff, tr. see Beierle, Marlene & Sylvan, Anne.

Rancho Park Publishing Staff, tr. see De la Garza, Velda.

Rancho Park Publishing Staff, tr. see Fries, Marcia.

Rancho Park Publishing Staff, tr. see Keeler, Renee.

Rancho Park Publishing Staff, tr. see Williams, Rozanne L.

***Ranchod-Nilsson, Sita & Tetreault, Mary Ann.** Women, States & Nationalism: At Home in the Nation? LC 99-88061. 2000. pap. write for info. (*0-415-22173-0*) Routledge.

Ranciere, Jacques. Disagreement: Politics & Philosophy. Rose, Julie, tr. LC 98-42205. 160p. 1998. 29.95 (*0-8166-2844-0*) U of Minn Pr.

— The Ignorant Schoolmaster: Five Lessons in Intellectual Emancipation. Ross, Kristin, tr. from FRE. 176p. 1991. 39.50 (*0-8047-1874-1*) Stanford U Pr.

— The Names of History: On the Poetics of Knowledge. Melehy, Hassan, tr. LC 94-7212. (ENG & FRE.). 1994. pap. 16.95 (*0-8166-2403-8*); text 42.95 (*0-8166-2401-1*) U of Minn Pr.

— The Nights of Labor: The Workers' Dream in Nineteenth-Century France. Drury, John, tr. from FRE. 448p. (C). 1989. 49.95 (*0-87722-625-3*) Temple U Pr.

— The Nights of Labor: The Worker's Dream in Nineteenth-Century France. Drury, John, tr. 448p. 1991. pap. 22.95 (*0-87722-833-7*) Temple U Pr.

— On the Shores of Politics. Heron, Liz, tr. (Phronesis Ser.). 256p. (C). 1995. pap. 18.00 (*0-86091-637-5*, B3632, Pub. by Verso) Norton.

— On the Shores of Politics. Heron, Liz, tr. (Phronesis Ser.). 256p. (C). (gr. 13). 1995. 60.00 (*0-86091-467-4*, B3628, Pub. by Verso) Norton.

Ranck, Dawn J. Deliciously Easy Breads with Herbs. LC 98-41850. (Deliciously Easy . . . With Herbs Ser.). 32p. 1998. pap. 3.50 (*1-56148-254-4*) Good Bks PA.

— Soups with Herbs. LC 98-41885. (Deliciously Easy Ser.). 32p. 1998. pap. 3.50 (*1-56148-255-2*) Good Bks PA.

***Ranck, Dawn J. & Good, Merle.** Ideas for Small Groups. 256p. 2000. pap. 9.95 (*1-56148-303-6*) Good Bks PA.

Ranck, Dawn J. & Good, Phyllis Pellman. Deliciously Easy Appetizers & Snacks with Herbs. LC 98-41851. (Deliciously Easy . . . With Herbs Ser.). 32p. 1998. pap. 3.50 (*1-56148-261-7*) Good Bks PA.

— Deliciously Easy Breakfasts, Brunches, & Pastas with Herbs. LC 98-41886. (Deliciously Easy . . . With Herbs Ser.). 32p. 1998. pap. 3.50 (*1-56148-260-9*) Good Bks PA.

— Deliciously Easy Desserts & Refreshments with Herbs. LC 98-41887. (Deliciously Easy . . . With Herbs Ser.). 32p. 1998. pap. 3.50 (*1-56148-259-5*) Good Bks PA.

— Deliciously Easy Main Dishes with Herbs. LC 98-41501. (Deliciously Easy . . . With Herbs Ser.). 32p. 1998. pap. 3.50 (*1-56148-258-7*) Good Bks PA.

— Deliciously Easy Salads & Sauces with Herbs. LC 98-41502. (Deliciously Easy . . . With Herbs Ser.). 32p. 1998. pap. 3.50 (*1-56148-256-0*) Good Bks PA.

— Deliciously Easy Vegetables with Herbs. LC 98-41852. (Deliciously Easy . . . With Herbs Ser.). 32p. 1998. pap. 3.50 (*1-56148-257-9*) Good Bks PA.

— Favorite Recipes with Herbs. LC 97-42052. (Illus.). 284p. 1997. pap. 14.95 (*1-56148-225-0*) Good Bks PA.

***Ranck, Dawn J. & Good, Phyllis Pellman.** Fix-It & Forget-It Cookbook: Feasting with Your Slow Cooker. 188p. 2000. pap. 13.95 (*1-56148-317-6*) Good Bks PA.

Ranck, Dawn J., jt. auth. see Stoltzfus, Louise.

Ranck, George W. Boonesborough: Its Founding, Pioneer Struggles, Indian Experiences, Transylvania Days, & Revolutionary Annals. LC 70-146414. (First American Frontier Ser.). (Illus.). 1971. reprint ed. 37.18 (*0-405-02878-4*) Ayer.

— Boonesborough: Its Founding, Pioneer Struggles, Indian Experiences, Transylvania Days & Revolutionary Annals, with Full Historical Notes & Appendix. (Illus.). 286p. 1997. reprint ed. lib. bdg. 34.00 (*0-8328-6729-2*) Higginson Bk Co.

— History of Lexington: Its Early Annals & Recent Progress, Including Biographical Sketches & Personal Reminiscences of the Pioneer Settlers, Notices of Prominent Citizens, Etc. (Illus.). 428p. 1997. reprint ed. lib. bdg. 45.00 (*0-8328-6735-7*) Higginson Bk Co.

Ranck, Glenn N. Pictures from Northwest History. (Shorey Historical Ser.). (Illus.). 36p. 1982. reprint ed. pap. 10.00 (*0-8466-0115-X*, S-115) Shoreys Bkstore.

Ranck, James B. Albert Gallatin Brown: Radical Southern Nationalist. LC 73-16349. (Perspectives in American History Ser.: No. 20). (Illus.). xiv, 320p. 1974. reprint ed. lib. bdg. 45.00 (*0-87991-347-9*) Porcupine Pr.

Ranck, Joanne, jt. auth. see Pellman, Rachel T.

Ranck, Katherine H., jt. auth. see Cavan, Ruth S.

Ranck, Katherine Q. Portrait of Dona Elena. LC 82-83842. 1982. pap. 2.95 (*0-89229-012-9*) TQS Pubns.

Ranck, Sarah. Wheat, Barley, Rice, Rye & Oat Genome Mapping: Sponsored CRIS/ICAR Projects & Bibliography. 72p. (Orig.). (C). 1996. pap. text 35.00 (*0-7881-2728-4*) DIANE Pub.

Ranck, Sarah, jt. auth. see Kalinski, Andrew.

Ranck, Shirley A. Cakes for the Queen of Heaven. 232p. (Orig.). 1995. pap. 13.95 (*1-878980-10-6*) Delphi IL.

Rancour-Laferriere, Daniel. Signs of the Flesh: An Essay on the Evolution of Homonid Sexuality. (Approaches to Semiotics Ser.: No. 71). x, 473p. 1986. 161.55 (*0-89925-121-8*) Mouton.

— The Slave Soul of Russia: Moral Masochism & the Cult of Suffering. 330p. (C). 1995. text 50.00 (*0-8147-7458-X*) NYU Pr.

— The Slave Soul of Russia: Moral Masochism & the Cult of Suffering. 330p. (C). 1996. pap. text 20.00 (*0-8147-7482-2*) NYU Pr.

— Tolstoy on the Couch: Misogyny, Masochism, & the Absent Mother. LC 98-6757. 256p. 1998. text 40.00 (*0-8147-7509-8*) NYU Pr.

Rancour-Laferriere, Daniel, ed. Russian Literature & Psychoanalysis. LC 89-280. (Linguistic & Literary Studies in Eastern Europe: Vol. 31). x, 485p. 1989. 130.00 (*90-272-1536-7*); pap. 32.95 (*90-272-1540-5*) J Benjamins Pubng Co.

— Self-Analysis in Literary Study: Exploring Hidden Agendas. (Literature & Psychoanalysis Ser.). 240p. (C). 1994. text 45.00 (*0-8147-7439-3*) NYU Pr.

Rancourt, Jacques & Deane, John F. The Distribution of Bodies. LC 96-102153. 88p. 1995. pap. 13.95 (*1-873790-81-3*) Dufour.

Rancourt, James D. Optical Thin Films: Users Handbook. LC 96-28046. 289p. 1996. 60.00 (*0-8194-2285-1*) SPIE.

Rancourt, Judie & Teuber, Peter. The Illustrated Guidebook to Residential Airparks (U. S. A.-East) LC 95-79804. (Illus.). 240p. 1995. pap. 29.65 (*0-9649303-0-7*) HPT Aero.

Rancourt, Judie, jt. auth. see Teuber, Peter.

Rancourt, Karen L. Yeah but, Children Need . . . 144p. 1978. 18.95 (*0-87073-959-X*) Schenkman Bks Inc.

Rancourt, Sylvie. Melody Bk. 1: The Orgies of Abitibi. Schreiner, Dave, ed. Boivin, Jacques, tr. & illus. by. (Melody; the True Stories of a Nude Dancer Ser.). 128p. 1991. 29.95 (*0-87816-140-6*); pap. 14.95 (*0-87816-141-4*) Kitchen Sink.

Rand & Colangelo, Shelton. Voices of Student Teachers: Cases from the Field. LC 98-37354. 192p. (C). 1998. pap. text 26.00 (*0-13-674268-8*) P-H.

Rand, et al. Batteries for Electric Vehicles. LC 97-80676. 572p. 1997. 55.00 (*0-7680-0127-7*) Soc Auto Engineers.

Rand, jt. auth. see Kozulin, Alex.

Rand, A. Stanley. Iguanas of the World: Their Behavior, Ecology & Conservation. Burghardt, Gordon M., ed. LC 82-7932. (Animal Behavior, Ecology, Conservation & Management Ser.). (Illus.). 472p. 1983. 79.00 (*0-8155-0917-0*) Noyes.

Rand, Andrew. Explore Seattle: A Guide Book. 192p. 1992. pap. 8.95 (*0-9631315-0-8*) Silver Pen.

— Explore Seattle, 1993: The Local's Guide Book. 1992. pap. 9.95 (*0-9631315-2-4*) Silver Pen.

Rand, Austin L. Social Feeding Behavior of Birds. LC 54-1522. (Chicago Natural History Museum, Publication 720: Vol. 36, No. 1). 71p. 1954. reprint ed. pap. 30.00 (*0-608-03785-0*, 206463900009) Bks Demand.

Rand, Austin L., jt. auth. see Archbold, Richard.

Rand, Ayn. Anthem. LC 52-5216. 1953. 12.95 (*0-87004-124-X*) Caxton.

— Anthem. anniversary ed. LC 95-9854. 1995. 23.95 (*0-525-94015-4*, Dutt) Dutton Plume.

— Anthem. 50th ed. 1995. 12.09 (*0-606-00353-3*, Pub. by Turtleback) Demco.

— Anthem. 50th anniversary ed. Peikoff, Leonard, ed. & intro. by. 256p. 1999. pap. 13.95 (*0-452-28125-3*, Plume) Dutton Plume.

— Anthem. 50th anniversary ed. 128p. 1996. mass mkt. 7.99 (*0-451-19113-7*, Sig) NAL.

***Rand, Ayn.** Atlas Shrugged. 1192p. 1999. pap. 17.95 (*0-452-01187-6*, Plume) Dutton Plume.

Rand, Ayn. Atlas Shrugged. 1992. 13.09 (*0-606-00473-4*, Pub. by Turtleback) Demco.

— Atlas Shrugged. 35th anniversary ed. 1088p. 1992. 39.95 (*0-525-93418-9*, Dutt) Dutton Plume.

— Atlas Shrugged. 35th anniversary ed. 1088p. 1996. mass mkt. 8.99 (*0-451-19114-5*, Sig) NAL.

Rand, Ayn. Ayn Rand: Atlas Shrugged, the Fountainhead, 2 vols. 1997. mass mkt. 17.98 (*0-451-93560-8*, Sig) NAL.

Rand, Ayn. The Ayn Rand Column: Written for the Los Angeles Times. 2nd rev. ed. Schwartz, Peter, ed. LC 98-7897. 136p. 1998. pap. 14.95 (*1-56114-292-1*) Second Renaissance.

— The Ayn Rand Letter: 1971-1976, Vols. 1-4. 5th ed. LC 90-616721. 400p. 1993. reprint ed. lib. bdg. 44.95 (*1-56114-147-X*) Second Renaissance.

— The Ayn Rand Lexicon. Binswanger, Harry, ed. 1988. pap. 17.95 (*0-452-01051-9*, Mer) NAL.

— The Ayn Rand Reader. Hull, Gary & Peikoff, Leonard, eds. LC 98-26698. 512p. 1999. pap. 16.95 (*0-452-28040-0*, Plume) Dutton Plume.

— Ayn Rand's Marginalia: Her Critical Comments on the Writings of over 20 Authors. Mayhew, Robert, ed. & intro. by. LC 95-25776. 240p. (Orig.). 1995. pap. 14.95 (*1-56114-250-6*, CM02B) Second Renaissance.

— Capitalism: The Unknown Ideal. 1986. mass mkt. 7.99 (*0-451-14795-2*, Sig) NAL.

— The Early Ayn Rand. 448p. 1986. mass mkt. 6.99 (*0-451-14607-7*, Sig) NAL.

— For the New Intellectual. LC 97-133393. 1963. mass mkt. 7.99 (*0-451-16308-7*) NAL.

— The Fountainhead. 752p. 1994. pap. 18.95 (*0-452-27333-1*, Plume) Dutton Plume.

— The Fountainhead. 727p. 1985. 45.00 (*0-02-600910-2*) Macmillan.

— The Fountainhead. 704p. 1996. mass mkt. 8.99 (*0-451-19115-3*, Sig) NAL.

***Rand, Ayn.** The Fountainhead. LC 86-8760. 752p. 2000. 50.00 (*0-684-86971-3*) S&S Trade.

Rand, Ayn. The Fountainhead. Date not set. 15.00 (*0-672-50669-6*) Sams.

Rand, Ayn. The Fountainhead. 1993. 14.09 (*0-606-01752-6*, Pub. by Turtleback) Demco.

Rand, Ayn. An Introduction to Objectivist Epistemology. Peikoff, Leonard & Binswanger, Harry, eds. LC 89-39565. 314p. 1990. pap. 17.95 (*0-452-01030-6*, Mer) NAL.

— Journals of Ayn Rand, 1 vol. 752p. 1999. pap. 18.95 (*0-452-27887-2*) NAL.

— The Letters of Ayn Rand. 720p. 1997. pap. 17.95 (*0-452-27404-4*, Plume) Dutton Plume.

— The Night of January 16th. 17.95 (*0-89190-772-6*) Amereon Ltd.

— The Night of January 16th. 1971. pap. 10.95 (*0-452-26486-3*, Plume) Dutton Plume.

— The Night of January 16th: A Play Book. 1979. pap. 10.00 (*0-679-39100-2*) McKay.

— The Night of January 16th: A Play Book. 1980. pap. 10.00 (*0-679-39051-0*) McKay.

— The Objectivist Newsletter, 1962-1966, Vols. 1-4. 4th ed. LC 90-61904. 224p. 1994. reprint ed. lib. bdg. 39.95 (*1-56114-149-6*) Second Renaissance.

— The Objectivist, 1966-1971, Vols. 5-10. 4th ed. LC 90-61907. 400p. 1994. reprint ed. lib. bdg. 54.95 (*1-56114-148-8*) Second Renaissance.

— Philosophy: Who Needs It? LC 82-4320. 288p. 1984. write for info. (*0-672-52725-1*); pap. write for info. (*0-672-52795-2*) Macmillan.

— Philosophy: Who Needs It? 1984. pap. 4.99 (*0-451-17394-5*, Sig); mass mkt. 7.99 (*0-451-13893-7*, Sig) NAL.

— Return of the Primitive: The Anti-Industrial Revolution. Schwartz, Peter, ed. & intro. by. LC 98-24523. 304p. 1999. pap. 14.95 (*0-452-01184-1*, Plume) Dutton Plume.

— The Romantic Manifesto. 1971. mass mkt. 6.99 (*0-451-14916-5*, AE2374, Sig) NAL.

— Russian Writings on Hollywood. Berliner, Michael S., ed. LC 99-196372. (Illus.). 224p. 1999. pap. 19.95 (*0-9625336-3-7*) Ayn Rand Inst.

— The Virtue of Selfishness. 1964. mass mkt. 7.99 (*0-451-16393-1*) NAL.

— We the Living. 1999. audio 16.95 (*0-14-086311-7*) Viking Penguin.

— We the Living: 60th Anniversary Edition. anniversary ed. 448p. 1996. mass mkt. 7.99 (*0-451-18784-9*, Sig) NAL.

***Rand, Ayn & Boeckmann, Tore.** The Art of Fiction: A Guide for Writers & Readers. LC 99-35588. 2000. pap. 12.95 (*0-452-28154-7*, Plume) Dutton Plume.

Rand, Ayn & Peikoff, Leonard. The Voice of Reason: Essays in Objectivist Thought. (Ayn Rand Library Ser.: Vol. V). 372p. 1990. pap. 15.95 (*0-452-01046-2*, Mer) NAL.

— Why Businessmen Need Philosphy. Ralston, Richard E., ed. 203p. 1999. pap. 19.95 (*0-9625336-2-9*) Ayn Rand Inst.

***Rand, Ben, et al.** Microsoft FrontPage 2000: A Hands-On Guide. 192p. 1999. spiral bd. 26.60 (*1-57426-139-8*) Computer Lit Pr.

Rand, Benjamin. Berkeley's American Sojourn. LC 75-3329. reprint ed. 32.50 (*0-404-59323-2*) AMS Pr.

Rand, Benjamin, ed. The Life, Unpublished Letters, & Philosophical Regimen of Anthony, Earl of Shaftesbury: 1900 Edition. 567p. 1996. reprint ed. 100.00 (*1-85506-129-5*) Bks Intl VA.

— Second Characters or the Language of Forms: 1914 Editions. 210p. 1996. reprint ed. 56.00 (*1-85506-426-X*) Bks Intl VA.

Rand, Benjamin, ed. see Shaftesbury, Anthony Ashley Cooper.

Rand, Clayton. Sons of the South. LC 97-42468. (Illus.). 224p. Date not set. pap. 19.95 (*1-56554-674-1*) Pelican.

— Sons of the South. LC 97-42468. (Illus.). 224p. 1998. 19.95 (*0-911116-76-1*) Pelican.

Rand Corp., Communications Consulting Group Staff & Rand Corp., Publications Department Staff. Guidelines for Preparing Briefings. 26p. 1996. pap. text 6.00 (*0-8330-2445-0*, CP-269) Rand Corp.

Rand Corp., Publications Department Staff, jt. auth. see Rand Corp., Communications Consulting Group Staff.

Rand Corp. Staff & Peterson, Mark A. Compensation of Injuries: Civil Jury Verdicts in Cook County. LC 84-13473. 1984. pap. text 7.50 (*0-8330-0590-1*, R-3011-ICJ) Rand Corp.

Rand Corp. Staff & Raymer, Daniel P. Next Generation Attack Fighter: Design Tradeoffs & Notional System Concepts. LC 96-23122. 1996. pap. text 13.00 (*0-8330-2406-X*, MR-595-AF) Rand Corp.

Rand Corp. Staff, et al. Government Contracting Options: A Model & Application. LC 96-28078. 65p. 1996. pap. text 9.00 (*0-8330-2422-1*, MR-693-A) Rand Corp.

— Relating Resources to Personnel Readiness: Use of Army Strength Management Models. LC 96-39448. (Illus.). xix, 91p. 1997. pap. 15.00 (*0-8330-2458-2*, 790-OSD) Rand Corp.

— The Search for Equity in School Finance. LC 82-11510. 200p. 1983. text 29.95 (*0-88410-840-6*, HarpBusn) HarpInfo.

Rand Corporation Staff, jt. auth. see Hoffman, Bruce.

Rand, D. A., et al, eds. Progress in Electrochemistry. (Studies in Physical & Theoretical Chemistry). 470p. 1981. reprint ed. 141.00 (*0-444-41955-1*) Elsevier.

***Rand, Donna & Parker, Toni Trent.** Black Books Galore! Guide to Great African American Children's Books for Boys. 256p. 2000. pap. 15.95 (*0-471-37527-6*) Wiley.

— Black Books Galore! Guide to Great African American Children's Books for Girls. 256p. Date not set. pap. 15.95 (*0-471-37526-8*) Wiley.

Rand, Donna, et al. Black Books Galore! Guide to Great African American Children's Books. LC 98-10680. (Illus.). 256p. 1998. pap. 15.95 (*0-471-19353-4*) Wiley.

Rand Drug Policy Research Center Staff, jt. auth. see Burnham, Audrey.

Rand, E. K. & Jones, L. W. Earliest Book of Tours. (Mediaeval Academy of America Publications: Vol. 20). 1934. 140.00 (*0-527-01692-6*) Periodicals Srv.

Rand, E. K. & Tester, S. J., trs. Theological Tractates. (Loeb Classical Library: No. 74). 1973. 15.50 (*0-674-99083-8*) HUP.

Rand, E. K., et al. Serviani in Aeneidem Commentarii Vol. 3: Editio Harvardiana - Aeneid III-V. (American Philological Association Special Publications Ser.). 590p. 1974. 39.50 (*0-89130-718-4*, 40 05 01) OUP.

Rand, Earl. The Syntax of Mandarin Interrogatives. LC 78-626766. (University of California Publications in Social Welfare: Vol. 55). (Illus.). 123p. reprint ed. pap. 38.20 (*0-608-10992-4*, 201178800080) Bks Demand.

Rand, Edward A. The Tent in the Notch. LC 72-2040. (Black Heritage Library Collection). 1977. reprint ed. 24.95 (*0-8369-9054-4*) Ayer.

Rand, Edward K. Cicero in the Courtroom of Saint Thomas Aquinas. (Aquinas Lectures). 1945. 15.00 (*0-87462-109-7*) Marquette.

An Asterisk (*) at the beginning of an entry indicates that the title is appearing for the first time.

Rand, Erica. Barbie's Queer Accessories. Barale, Michele A. et al, eds. LC 94-38509. (Series Q). (Illus.). 256p. 1995. pap. 16.95 (*0-8223-1620-X*); text 49.95 (*0-8223-1604-8*) Duke.

Rand, Erika. Lying Eyes. (Intrigue Ser.). 1994. per. 2.99 (*0-373-22259-9*, 1-22259-5) Harlequin Bks.

Rand, Frank P. The Story of David Grayson. 160p. 1963. 9.95 (*0-686-31118-3*) Jones Lib.

Rand, G. K. & Eglese, R. W., eds. Further Developments in Operational Research. 1985. text 63.00 (*0-08-033361-3*, Pub. by PPL) Franklin.

Rand, G. K., jt. auth. see Chambers, Andrew D.

Rand, G. K., jt. ed. see Eglese, R. W.

Rand, Gary M. & Petrocelli, Sam R., eds. Fundamentals of Aquatic Toxic: Effects, Environmental Fate & Risk Assessment. 2nd ed. LC 84-4529. (Illus.). 1150p. (C). 1995. 168.00 (*1-56032-090-7*); pap. 79.95 (*1-56032-091-5*) Hemisp Pub.

Rand, Gertrude. The Factors That Influence the Sensitivity of the Retina to Color. (Psychology Monographs General & Applied: Vol. 15). 1972. reprint ed. 55.00 (*0-8115-1414-5*) Periodicals Srv.

Rand, Glenn M. & Litschel, David R. Black & White Photography. Jucha, ed. LC 93-14290. 300p. (C). 1994. pap. 28.25 (*0-314-02460-3*) West Pub.

***Rand, Glenn M. & Litschel, David R.** Black & White Photography. 2nd ed. (C). 2000. pap. 32.00 (*0-7668-1817-9*) Thomson Learn.

Rand, Gloria. Baby in a Basket. LC 96-33805. (Illus.). (J). 1997. write for info. (*0-614-13391-2*, Dutton Child) Peng Put Young Read.

— Baby in a Basket. LC 96-33805. (Illus.). 32p. (J). (ps-3). 1997. 15.99 (*0-525-65233-7*, Dutton Child) Peng Put Young Read.

— Baby in a Basket. 32p. (J). 1999. pap. 5.99 (*0-14-056623-6*, PuffinBks) Peng Put Young Read.

— The Cabin Key. LC 93-10398. (Illus.). 32p. (J). (ps-3). 1994. 15.00 (*0-15-213884-6*) Harcourt.

— Fighting for the Forest. LC 98-6610. (Illus.). (J). (gr. k-2). 1999. 15.95 (*0-8050-5466-9*) H Holt & Co.

***Rand, Gloria.** Little Flower. 2001. text 15.95 (*0-8050-6480-X*) H Holt & Co.

Rand, Gloria. Prince William. LC 91-25180. (J). (ps-3). 1995. pap. 5.95 (*0-8050-3384-X*) H Holt & Co.

— Prince William. LC 91-25180. (Illus.). 32p. (J). (gr. 1-3). 1995. 14.95 (*0-8050-1841-7*, Bks Young Read) H Holt & Co.

— Salty Dog. LC 88-13453. (Illus.). 32p. (J). (ps-2). 1995. pap. 4.95 (*0-8050-1847-6*, Bks Young Read) H Holt & Co.

— Salty Sails North. LC 89-39063. (Illus.). 89p. (J). (ps-3). 1995. pap. 4.95 (*0-8050-2188-4*, Owlet BYR) H Holt & Co.

— Salty Takes Off. LC 90-46371. (Salty Ser.). (Illus.). 32p. (J). (ps-2). 1995. 14.95 (*0-8050-1159-5*, Bks Young Read) H Holt & Co.

— Willie Takes a Hike. LC 95-13698. (Illus.). 32p. (J). (ps-3). 1996. 15.00 (*0-15-200272-3*) Harcourt.

Rand, Harry. Arshile Gorky: The Implications of Symbols. LC 90-47360. (Illus.). 270p. 1991. 65.00 (*0-520-06371-6*, Pub. by U CA Pr); pap. 29.95 (*0-520-06345-7*, Pub. by U CA Pr) Cal Prin Full Svc.

— The Beginning of Things: Translations from Genesis. (Illus.). 1983. pap. 9.95 (*0-931848-53-9*) Dryad Pr.

— The Clouds. limited ed. (Illus.). 50p. 1996. 1500.00 (*0-9638014-1-4*) Dov Press.

— Color: Suite in Four Parts. deluxe limited ed. (Illus.). 56p. 1993. ring bd. 3000.00 (*0-9638014-0-6*) Dov Press.

— Hundertwasser. (SPA.). 1996. pap. text 19.99 (*3-8228-9560-1*) Taschen Amer.

— Hundertwasser. (Big Art Ser.). 1998. 19.99 (*3-8228-7212-1*) Taschen Amer.

— Louis Ribak, the Late Paintings. 36p. 1984. pap. 10.00 (*0-914983-00-8*) Roswell Mus.

— Manet's Contemplation at the Gare Saint-Lazare. LC 86-25077. (Illus.). 168p. 1987. 48.00 (*0-520-05967-0*, Pub. by U CA Pr) Cal Prin Full Svc.

Rand, Howard B. Behold, He Cometh. 1955. 5.00 (*0-685-08798-0*) Destiny.

— Digest of the Divine Law. 1943. 8.00 (*0-685-08802-2*) Destiny.

— Documentary Studies, 3 vols. Incl. Vol. 1. 1947. 12.00 Vol. 2. 1950. 12.00 write for info. (*0-318-51710-8*) Destiny.

— Hour Cometh. 1966. 5.00 (*0-685-08805-7*) Destiny.

— Marvels of Prophecy. 1959. 5.00 (*0-685-08810-3*) Destiny.

Rand, Ingersoll, jt. auth. see Rand, Melroe.

Rand, James A., ed. Total Knee Arthroplasty. LC 92-12132. 480p. 1992. text 136.50 (*0-88167-930-5*) Lppncott W & W.

Rand, James R. Fire Department Management: Scope & Method Study Guide. Davis, Stewart, ed. 188p. 1972. reprint ed. pap. 10.95 (*0-945250-03-7*) Davis Pub Co.

Rand, Jonathan, jt. auth. see Donaldson, Lee.

Rand, Joyce. A Hippo with Feathers. LC 92-9952. (Illus.). 32p. (J). 1992. pap. 5.49 (*0-89084-627-8*, 058545) Bob Jones Univ.

Rand, Kathleen G. Marianne's Magical Journey. (Illus.). 15p. (J). (ps-8). 1998. pap. 6.95 (*1-880710-18-8*) Monterey Pacific.

Rand, Kristen. Lawyers, Guns & Money: The Impact of Tort Restriction on Firearms Safety & Gun Control. 76p. (Orig.). Date not set. pap. 10.00 (*0-927291-06-1*) Violence Policy Ctr.

Rand, Laurance B. High Stakes: The Life & Times of Leigh S. J. Hunt. (American University Studies: History: Ser. IX, Vol. 76). 352p. (C). 1989. text 51.00 (*0-8204-0992-8*) P Lang Pubng.

Rand, Le Clanche Du, see Du Rand, Le Clanche.

Rand, Lydia, tr. see Bomani, Asake & Rooks, Belvie, eds.

Rand, Margaret. The Red Wines of France. Simon, Joanna, ed. (Illus.). 161p. 1997. reprint ed. text 25.00 (*0-7881-5035-9*) DIANE Pub.

Rand, Marguerite C. Ramon Perez de Ayala. (Twayne's World Authors Ser.). 175p. (C). 1971. lib. bdg. 20.95 (*0-8290-1734-8*) Irvington.

Rand, Maria. A. K. A. Ruby Brooklyn. (Illus.). 390p. (Orig.). 1994. pap. 13.95 (*0-9642457-3-6*) Goddesses We Aint.

Rand, Mary E. & Burger, Irene T. The Dog Owner's Guide to Washington. LC 92-97113. 224p. (Orig.). 1992. pap. 14.95 (*0-9628685-1-5*) Edington-Rand.

Rand McNall & Company Staff. Children's Atlas of the Environment. (Environmental Bks.). (Illus.). 80p. (J). (gr. 2-6). 1994. lib. bdg. 18.95 (*1-878363-74-3*) Forest Hse.

***Rand McNally Fact Books Staff.** Portland, Oregon. 1999. 3.95 (*0-528-98009-2*) Rand McNally.

***Rand McNally Facts Books Staff & Muster, Bill.** World Facts & Maps 2000. (Illus.). 1999. pap. text 10.95 (*0-528-84176-9*) Rand McNally.

Rand McNally Staff. Alabama. 1997. pap. 5.95 (*0-528-96879-3*) Rand McNally.

— Alaska. 1997. pap. 5.95 (*0-528-96695-2*) Rand McNally.

— Albuquerque, New Mexico. 1998. pap. 5.95 (*0-528-96746-0*) Rand McNally.

Rand McNally Staff. Alphabet Travels. 1998. pap. text 3.95 (*0-528-83976-4*) Rand McNally.

***Rand McNally Staff.** America: A Celebration of the United States. LC 99-14258. 1999. 39.95 (*0-528-84174-2*) Rand McNally.

— Amsterdam. pap. 6.95 (*0-528-95147-5*) Rand McNally.

Rand McNally Staff. Answer Atlas. (Illus.). 176p. 1996. pap. text 12.95 (*0-528-83872-5*) Rand McNally.

— Are We There Yet? Backseat Book. (Illus.). 64p. (J). 1996. pap. 3.95 (*0-528-83817-2*) Rand McNally.

Rand McNally Staff. Arkansas/Mississippi. 1997. pap. 5.95 (*0-528-97000-3*) Rand McNally.

— Arlington, Texas. 1999. 5.95 (*0-528-97838-1*) Rand McNally.

— Athens. pap. 14.95 (*0-528-91496-0*) Rand McNally.

— Atlanta, Georgia. 1998. pap. 5.95 (*0-528-96750-9*) Rand McNally.

— Atlas of American History. 1998. pap. 9.25 (*0-528-84500-4*) Rand McNally.

Rand McNally Staff. Atlas of the World: Masterpiece Edition. LC 94-22280. 1994. write for info. (*0-528-83715-X*) Rand McNally.

— Atlas of World History. LC 95-6576. 192p. 1995. pap. 24.95 (*0-528-83779-6*) Rand McNally.

— Atlas of World Regional Geography. (C). 1996. pap. text 13.00 (*0-528-17790-7*) Rand McNally.

— Atlas Pack. 1998. 9.95 (*0-528-83989-6*) Rand McNally.

***Rand McNally Staff.** Austin, Texas. 1998. pap. 5.95 (*0-528-96748-7*) Rand McNally.

— Baltimore, Maryland. 1998. pap. 5.95 (*0-528-97256-1*) Rand McNally.

— Barcelona. pap. 14.95 (*0-528-91497-9*) Rand McNally.

Rand McNally Staff. Baton Rouge Louisiana, 1. 1999. 5.95 (*0-528-97607-9*) Rand McNally.

— Beaumont/Port Arthur. 1998. 5.95 (*0-528-97807-1*) Rand McNally.

Rand McNally Staff. Belgium. pap. 16.95 (*0-528-91408-1*) Rand McNally.

— Benelux. pap. 16.95 (*0-528-91466-9*) Rand McNally.

— Berlin. pap. 6.95 (*0-528-95954-9*) Rand McNally.

— Berlin: West & East. pap. 14.95 (*0-528-91498-7*) Rand McNally.

— Bern. pap. 14.95 (*0-528-91502-9*) Rand McNally.

Rand McNally Staff. Best Travel Activity Book Ever! (Backseat Bks.). (Illus.). 320p. (J). (gr. 1-6). 1994. pap. 3.95 (*0-528-81410-9*) Rand McNally.

— Best Travel Activity Book Ever! Backseat Book. (Illus.). 256p. (J). 1996. pap. 3.95 (*0-528-83819-9*) Rand McNally.

***Rand McNally Staff.** Boca Raton Florida. 1999. 5.95 (*0-528-97840-3*) Rand McNally.

— Boston. pap. 6.95 (*0-528-95146-7*) Rand McNally.

— Boston, Massachusetts. 1998. pap. 5.95 (*0-528-96752-5*) Rand McNally.

Rand McNally Staff. Boulder. 1998. 5.95 (*0-528-97808-X*) Rand McNally.

Rand McNally Staff. Budapest. pap. 14.95 (*0-528-91503-7*) Rand McNally.

Rand McNally Staff. Buffalo. 1998. 5.95 (*0-528-94502-5*) Rand McNally.

***Rand McNally Staff.** Business Travelers Road Atlas. 1998. pap. 9.95 (*0-528-84038-X*) Rand McNally.

— Business Traveler's Road Atlas, 1997. (Illus.). 208p. 1996. pap. text 9.95 (*0-528-81523-7*) Rand McNally.

— Canada, 1. 1999. 3.95 (*0-88640-234-4*) Rand McNally.

Rand McNally Staff. Canada Road Atlas & Vacation Guide 1996. (Illus.). 1995. pap. text 7.95 (*0-528-81510-5*) Rand McNally.

— Castle. (Story Scenes Ser.). (Illus.). 6p. (J). 1997. 6.95 (*0-528-83839-3*) Rand McNally.

Rand McNally Staff. Central America. pap. 16.95 (*0-528-91459-6*) Rand McNally.

Rand McNally Staff. Chicago & Cook County. (Streetfinder Ser.). 1996. pap. text 15.95 (*0-528-96901-3*) Rand McNally.

***Rand McNally Staff.** Chicago & Cook County Streetfinder. 1998. 15.95 (*0-528-97874-8*) Rand McNally.

Rand McNally Staff. Children's Atlas of Earth Through Time. Fagan, Elizabeth G., ed. (Illus.). 80p. (J). 1990. 14.95 (*0-528-83415-0*) Rand McNally.

— Children's Atlas of the Environment. 80p. (J). (gr. 4-7). 1991. 14.95 (*0-528-83438-X*) Rand McNally.

— Childrens Deluxe Atlas Set: Childrens Atlas of the World & Childrens Atlas of the U. S. 1998. pap. text 14.95 (*0-528-84075-4*) Rand McNally.

***Rand McNally Staff.** Children's Millennium Atlas of the U. S. (Illus.). (J). 2000. pap. 9.95 (*0-528-84606-X*) Rand McNally.

— Children's Millennium Atlas of the United States. (Illus.). (J). (gr. 3-7). 1999. 16.95 (*0-528-84204-8*) Rand McNally.

— Children's Millennium Atlas of the World. (J). (gr. 3-7). 1999. 16.95 (*0-528-84205-6*) Rand McNally.

Rand McNally Staff. Circus. (Story Scenes Ser.). (Illus.). 6p. 1997. 6.95 (*0-528-83838-5*) Rand McNally.

Rand McNally Staff. Cityflash: Paris. pap. 6.95 (*0-528-91376-X*) Rand McNally.

Rand McNally Staff. Classic World Atlas. 1996. 24.95 (*0-528-83870-9*) Rand McNally.

***Rand McNally Staff.** Cleveland, Ohio. 1998. 5.95 (*0-528-94510-6*) Rand McNally.

Rand McNally Staff. Coast-to-Coast Games. 80p. 1996. pap. text 3.95 (*0-528-83818-0*) Rand McNally.

— Collier/Lee County Florida, 1. (Rand McNally Streetfinder Ser.). 1999. pap. text 16.95 (*0-528-97880-2*) Rand McNally.

***Rand McNally Staff.** Colorado Springs, Colorado. 1998. 5.95 (*0-528-94512-2*) Rand McNally.

— Columbus, Ohio. 1998. 5.95 (*0-528-94508-4*) Rand McNally.

Rand McNally Staff. Commercial Atlas & Marketing Guide. 1999. 395.00 (*0-528-83992-6*) Rand McNally.

— Compact Road Atlas. 1998. pap. 7.95 (*0-528-84040-1*) Rand McNally.

Rand McNally Staff. Compact Road Atlas, 1996: United States, Canada, Mexico. (Illus.). 224p. 1995. pap. 6.95 (*0-528-81489-3*) Rand McNally.

Rand McNally Staff. Conozco: Las Banderas. 1995. pap. 2.50 (*0-528-83739-7*) Rand McNally.

Rand McNally Staff. Copenhagen. pap. 14.95 (*0-528-91504-5*) Rand McNally.

Rand McNally Staff. Corpus Christi. 1998. pap. 5.95 (*0-528-94514-9*) Rand McNally.

— Cosmopolitan World Atlas. 1997. 49.95 (*0-528-83963-2*) Rand McNally.

— Cosmopolitan World Atlas. rev. ed. LC 94-15785. 340p. 1994. 70.00 (*0-528-83674-9*) Rand McNally.

— Dallas, Ft. Worth & Vicinity. (Rand McNally Streetfinder Ser.). 1996. pap. text 24.95 (*0-528-96921-8*) Rand McNally.

Rand McNally Staff. Dallas, Texas. 1996. pap. 5.95 (*0-528-94516-5*) Rand McNally.

— Delaware/maryland. 1997. 5.95 (*0-528-96654-5*) Rand McNally.

— Deluxe Motor Carrier Rd Atlas 2000, (Illus.). 158p. 1999. pap. 79.95 (*0-528-84130-0*) Rand McNally.

Rand McNally Staff. Deluxe Motor Carriers Road Atlas. 1998. pap. 79.95 (*0-528-84031-2*) Rand McNally.

— Deluxe Road Atlas & Travel Guide: United States, Canada & Mexico. (Rand McNally Ser.). (Illus.). 176p. 1998. pap. 7.95 (*0-528-84036-3*) Rand McNally.

Rand McNally Staff. Denver, Colorado. 1997. 5.95 (*0-528-94518-1*) Rand McNally.

— Denver Streetfinder: Regional & Vicinity. (Rand Mcnally Streetfinder Ser.). 1998. pap. text 34.95 (*0-528-95329-X*) Rand McNally.

— Des Moines/ames, Iowa. 1998. pap. 5.95 (*0-528-97257-X*) Rand McNally.

— Detroit, Michigan. 1997. 5.95 (*0-528-94520-3*) Rand McNally.

— Detroit Tri-Counties (Streetfinder Ser.). 1997. 24.95 (*0-528-96947-1*) Rand McNally.

Rand McNally Staff. Discovery Atlas of Animals. LC 93-7252. 64p. (J). 1993. 4.95 (*0-528-83579-3*) Rand McNally.

— Discovery Atlas of Native Americans. LC 93-39472. 64p. (J). 1994. pap. 4.95 (*0-528-83678-1*) Rand McNally.

— Discovery Atlas of Planets & Stars. LC 93-16805. 64p. (J). 1993. 4.95 (*0-528-83580-7*) Rand McNally.

— Discovery Atlas of the World. LC 93-12560. 64p. (J). 1993. 4.95 (*0-528-83577-7*) Rand McNally.

— Dist-O-Map. 1995. 7.95 (*0-528-88369-0*) Rand McNally.

— Eastern U.S.-Map. 1993. 2.95 (*0-528-96052-0*) Rand McNally.

***Rand McNally Staff.** Easy to Read Road Atlas 2000, 1999. pap. 10.95 (*0-528-84127-0*) Rand McNally.

Rand McNally Staff. Easy-To-Read Travel Atlas: United States, Canada, Mexico. 1999th ed. (Illus.). 88p. 1998. pap. 9.95 (*0-528-84021-5*) Rand McNally.

Rand McNally Staff. Easy to Read Travel Atlas, 1997. rev. ed. (Illus.). 96p. 1996. pap. text 9.95 (*0-528-81521-0*) Rand McNally.

— El Paso. LC 97-684052. (Easy Finder Plus Ser.). 1996. 9.95 (*0-528-97180-8*) Rand McNally.

Rand McNally Staff. Exploring America's National Parks. 1998. pap. text 4.95 (*0-528-84047-9*) Rand McNally.

— Family World Atlas. LC 93-48823. 200p. (J). 1995. 11.95 (*0-528-83782-6*) Rand McNally.

— Family World Atlas. (Illus.). 200p. 1996. pap. text 15.95 (*0-528-83810-5*) Rand McNally.

Rand McNally Staff. Finland. pap. 16.95 (*0-528-91410-3*) Rand McNally.

Rand McNally Staff. First Atlas. LC 93-37528. (Illus.). 24p. (J). 1994. 9.95 (*0-528-83679-X*) Rand McNally.

Rand McNally Staff. Florence. pap. 14.95 (*0-528-91505-3*) Rand McNally.

Rand McNally Staff. The Fort Wayne. LC 98-677684. (Easy Finder Plus Ser.). 1997. pap. 9.95 (*0-528-96998-6*) Rand McNally.

***Rand McNally Staff.** Fort Worth, Texas. 1998. pap. 5.95 (*0-528-94522-X*) Rand McNally.

Rand McNally Staff. Ft. Lauderdale. (Easy Finder Plus Ser.). 1996. pap. 5.95 (*0-528-97121-2*) Rand McNally.

— Game-Funfinder II Anytime Anyplace. 1997. pap. 4.95 (*0-528-83845-8*) Rand McNally.

— Giant Childrens World Atlas. 1989. 27.95 (*0-528-17731-1*) Rand McNally.

— Globe Trotting Games. (J). 1997. pap. 4.95 (*0-528-83866-0*) Rand McNally.

— Goode's World Atlas. 19th ed. (Illus.). 384p. 1996. 34.95 (*0-528-83130-5*) Rand McNally.

— Great Highways of the World: Ancient & Modern Routes. 192p. 1996. 29.95 (*0-528-83798-2*) Rand McNally.

— Greater Charleston South Carolina, 1. (Rand McNally Streetfinder Ser.). 1999. pap. text 9.95 (*0-528-95336-2*) Rand McNally.

— Greater Columbia/Richland South Carolina, 1. (Rand McNally Streetfinder Ser.). 1999. pap. text 9.95 (*0-528-95338-9*) Rand McNally.

Rand McNally Staff. Guide to Wine Country. pap. 5.95 (*0-528-96111-X*) Rand McNally.

— Hawaiian Islands, 1. (Mapguide Ser.). 1998. 5.95 (*0-528-94946-2*) Rand McNally.

Rand McNally Staff. Historical Atlas & Guide. LC 93-11581. 1993. 14.95 (*0-528-83624-2*) Rand McNally.

— Historical Atlas & Guide. LC 93-11581. 1993. pap. 9.95 (*0-528-83623-4*) Rand McNally.

Rand McNally Staff. Hong Kong. pap. 6.95 (*0-528-95970-0*) Rand McNally.

— Houston, Texas. 1997. pap. 5.95 (*0-528-94524-6*) Rand McNally.

— Hungary. pap. 16.95 (*0-528-91415-4*) Rand McNally.

Rand McNally Staff. Illustrated Atlas of the World: 1993 Edition. rev. ed. LC 93-504. (Illus.). 390p. 1994. 99.95 (*0-528-83696-X*) Rand McNally.

— International Geographic Atlas. rev. ed. 1993. 19.95 (*0-528-83629-3*) Rand McNally.

— Irving/Carroll Texas, 1. 1999. 5.95 (*0-528-97842-X*) Rand McNally.

Rand McNally Staff. Istanbul. pap. 14.95 (*0-528-91512-6*) Rand McNally.

Rand McNally Staff. Jacksonville/Duval County Florida, 1. (Rand McNally Streetfinder Ser.). 1999. pap. text 16.95 (*0-528-97887-X*) Rand McNally.

— The Jungle. (Story Scenes Ser.). (Illus.). 6p. (J). 1997. 6.95 (*0-528-83840-7*) Rand McNally.

— Kids' U. S. Road Atlas. 80p. (J). 1996. pap. text 3.95 (*0-528-83816-4*) Rand McNally.

***Rand McNally Staff.** Knoxville Easy Finder Plus. 1998. 9.95 (*0-528-97085-2*) Rand McNally.

— Lexington, Kentucky, 1. 1998. pap. 5.95 (*0-528-96762-2*) Rand McNally.

Rand McNally Staff. Little Rock Arkansas, 1. (Rand McNally Streetfinder Ser.). 1999. pap. text 17.95 (*0-528-97883-7*) Rand McNally.

— London. 1998. pap. 5.95 (*0-528-94651-X*) Rand McNally.

Rand McNally Staff. London. pap. 6.95 (*0-528-95955-7*) Rand McNally.

— Louisiana. 1998. pap. 5.95 (*0-528-96666-9*) Rand McNally.

Rand McNally Staff. Louisville Easy Finder Plus. LC 98-681876. (Easy Finder Plus Ser.). 1998. 9.95 (*0-528-97214-6*) Rand McNally.

— Luminous Star Finder: Glow-In-The-Dark with Zodiac Dial. (Illus.). 1989. pap. 5.95 (*0-528-83374-X*) Rand McNally.

— Madison. LC 98-682865. (Easy Finder Plus Ser.). 1996. 9.95 (*0-528-97091-7*) Rand McNally.

— Miami/Dade/Broward/Palm Beach Counties Florida. (Rand McNally Streetfinder Ser.). 1999. pap. text 35.00 (*0-528-97889-6*) Rand McNally.

Rand McNally Staff. Minneapolis/st. Paul Minnesota. 1997. pap. 5.95 (*0-528-97152-2*) Rand McNally.

Rand McNally Staff. Missouri: State Map. 1998. write for info. (*0-528-97405-X*) Rand McNally.

***Rand McNally Staff.** Motor Carrier Road Atlas 2000, 1999. pap. 19.95 (*0-528-84129-7*) Rand McNally.

Rand McNally Staff. Motor Carriers Road Atlas. 1998. pap. 19.95 (*0-528-84028-2*) Rand McNally.

— Motor Carrier's Road Atlas, 1997. rev. ed. (Illus.). 216p. 1996. pap. text 19.95 (*0-528-81525-3*) Rand McNally.

Rand McNally Staff. Munich. pap. 6.95 (*0-528-95971-9*) Rand McNally.

Rand McNally Staff. My First Backseat Books: See the U. S. A. 64p. (J). 1997. pap. text 3.95 (*0-528-83849-0*) Rand McNally.

— My First Backseat Books Travel Time. (Illus.). 64p. (J). 1997. pap. text 3.95 (*0-528-83846-6*) Rand McNally.

— Nashville. 1998. 5.95 (*0-528-97567-6*) Rand McNally.

Rand McNally Staff. Nashville, Tennessee. 1997. pap. 5.95 (*0-528-97223-5*) Rand McNally.

— Netherlands. pap. 16.95 (*0-528-91430-8*) Rand McNally.

Rand McNally Staff. The New International Atlas. 25th deluxe ed. (Illus.). 560p. 1994. 200.00 (*0-528-83694-3*) Rand McNally.

— The New International Atlas: Twenty-Fifth Anniversary Edition. 25th anniversary ed. LC 94-15784. 560p. 1994. 150.00 (*0-528-83693-5*) Rand McNally.

— New International World Atlas. 25th anniversary ed. (Illus.). 560p. 1996. 150.00 (*0-528-83808-3*) Rand McNally.

Rand McNally Staff. New Mexico. 1997. pap. 5.95 (*0-528-97208-1*) Rand McNally.

— New Orleans, Louisiana. 1997. pap. 5.95 (*0-528-97200-6*) Rand McNally.

Rand McNally Staff. New York Quik-Finder. 1991. pap. 4.95 (*0-88433-005-2*) Geographia.

Rand McNally Staff. 1991 Road Atlas. (Illus.). pap. 190.80 (*0-528-80502-9*) Rand McNally.

— Road Altas 96. annuals (Illus.). 160p. pap. 13.95 (*0-528-81494-X*) Rand McNally.

Rand McNally Staff. Noah's Ark. (Story Scenes Ser.). (Illus.). 6p. 1997. 6.95 (*0-528-83841-5*) Rand McNally.

An Asterisk (*) at the beginning of an entry indicates that the title is appearing for the first time.

— Northeast Connecticut, 1. (Rand McNally Streetfinder Ser.). 1999. pap. text 15.95 (*0-528-97885-3*) Rand McNally.

Rand McNally Staff. Northern Europe. pap. 16.95 (*0-528-91490-1*) Rand McNally.

— North/south Carolina. 1997. pap. 5.95 (*0-528-96676-6*) Rand McNally.

— North/south Dakota. 1997. pap. 5.95 (*0-528-96699-5*) Rand McNally.

— Omaha/Council Bluffs, New England, 1. 1999. 3.95 (*0-528-98005-X*) Rand McNally.

— Oregon. 1997. pap. 5.95 (*0-528-96682-0*) Rand McNally.

— Orlando, Florida. 1999. pap. text 19.95 (*0-528-97875-6*) Rand McNally.

— Our Magnificent Earth. pap. 53.95 (*0-528-83088-0*) Rand McNally.

— Panorama Austria. pap. 19.95 (*0-528-91386-7*) Rand McNally.

— Panorama Swiss. pap. 19.95 (*0-528-91385-9*) Rand McNally.

Rand McNally Staff. Passport Atlas. (Illus.). 128p. 1996. pap. text 5.95 (*0-528-83883-0*) Rand McNally.

***Rand McNally Staff.** Peninsula Cities, California, 1. 1999. 3.95 (*0-528-97759-8*) Rand McNally.

— Pennsylvania. 1997. pap. 5.95 (*0-528-96684-7*) Rand McNally.

Rand McNally Staff. Pensacola Florida, 1. (Rand McNally Streetfinder Ser.). 1999. pap. text 16.95 (*0-528-97878-0*) Rand McNally.

— Philadelphia. LC 98-689710. 1997. 5.95 (*0-528-96527-1*) Rand McNally.

***Rand McNally Staff.** Phoenix Arizona. 1999. pap. text 17.95 (*0-528-97719-9*) Rand McNally.

— Phoenix, Arizona. 1997. 5.95 (*0-528-94532-7*) Rand McNally.

— Pittsburgh. 1998. pap. 5.95 (*0-528-94534-3*) Rand McNally.

Rand McNally Staff. Pittsburgh, 1. 1998. pap. 15.95 (*0-528-97254-5*) Rand McNally.

— Pocket Road Atlas. 1998. pap. 2.95 (*0-528-84042-8*) Rand McNally.

***Rand McNally Staff.** Pocket Road Atlas. (Illus.). 64p. 1999. pap. 2.95 (*0-528-84134-3*) Rand McNally.

Rand McNally Staff. Pocket Road Atlas, 1997. 64p. 1996. pap. text 2.95 (*0-528-81562-8*) Rand McNally.

— Pocket World Atlas. 1992. pap. 2.50 (*0-528-83517-3*) Rand McNally.

***Rand McNally Staff.** Portland, Oregon. 1998. 5.95 (*0-528-94536-X*) Rand McNally.

— Portland West Suburban, Oregon, 1. 1999. 3.95 (*0-528-98011-4*) Rand McNally.

— Prague. pap. 6.95 (*0-528-95972-7*) Rand McNally.

Rand McNally Staff. Quick Reference Atlas. (Illus.). 1995. audio compact disk 20.36 (*0-528-52018-0*) Rand McNally.

— Quick Reference World Atlas. 1p. (C). 1990. pap. text 7.93 (*0-13-749532-3*) P-H.

— Quick Reference World Atlas. 64p. 1993. pap. 4.95 (*0-528-83622-6*) Rand McNally.

— Quick Reference World Atlas. LC 95-675139. (Illus.). 64p. 1996. pap. 5.95 (*0-528-83733-8*) Rand McNally.

— Quick Reference World Atlas with Map. 1995. pap. 5.95 (*0-528-83765-6*) Rand McNally.

— Quick Reference World U. S. Atlas. 1995. pap. 7.95 (*0-528-83764-8*) Rand McNally.

— Rand McNally Animal Sticker Atlas. (Illus.). 16p. (J). (ps-3). 1993. pap. 4.95 (*0-528-83586-6*) Rand McNally.

— Rand McNally Business Traveler's Road Atlas. (Rand McNally Ser.). (Illus.). 208p. 1997. pap. text 9.95 (*0-528-83909-8*) Rand McNally.

— Rand McNally Children's Atlas of the United States. (Illus.). 112p. (J). (gr. 3-6). 1991. reprint ed. lib. bdg. 18.95 (*1-878363-37-9*) Forest Hse.

— Rand McNally Children's Atlas of the World. rev. ed. LC 92-24028. (Illus.). 96p. (J). (gr. 4-7). 1992. pap. 7.95 (*0-528-83541-6*) Rand McNally.

— Rand McNally Commercial Atlas & Marketing Guide: United States. (Rand McNally Ser.). 576p. 1997. 395.00 (*0-528-83903-9*) Rand McNally.

— Rand McNally Compact Road Atlas: United States-Canada-Mexico. (Illus.). 224p. 1994. pap. 5.95 (*0-528-81428-1*) Rand McNally.

— Rand McNally Dinosaur Sticker Atlas. (Illus.). 16p. (J). (ps-3). 1993. pap. 4.95 (*0-528-83585-8*) Rand McNally.

***Rand McNally Staff.** Rand McNally Easyfinder Ft. Myers, Florida. (Easyfinder Ser.). 1999. pap. 5.95 (*0-528-98161-7*) Rand McNally.

Rand McNally Staff. Rand McNally Great National Park Vacations, 1988. 224p. 1988. pap. 12.95 (*0-528-88256-2*) S&S Trade.

***Rand McNally Staff.** Rand Mcnally International Austrailia, 1999 Ed. 1999. pap. 9.95 (*0-528-97693-1*) Rand McNally.

— Rand Mcnally International England/ireland/scotland, 1999 Ed. 1999. pap. 9.95 (*0-528-97697-4*) Rand McNally.

— Rand Mcnally International Europe, 1999 Ed. 1999. pap. 9.95 (*0-528-97694-X*) Rand McNally.

— Rand Mcnally International France, 1999 Ed. 1999. pap. 9.95 (*0-528-97695-8*) Rand McNally.

— Rand Mcnally International Germany, 1999 Ed. 1999. pap. 9.95 (*0-528-97696-6*) Rand McNally.

— Rand Mcnally International Italy, 1999 Ed. 1999. pap. 9.95 (*0-528-97698-2*) Rand McNally.

— Rand Mcnally International South America, 1999 Ed. 1999. pap. 9.95 (*0-528-97699-0*) Rand McNally.

Rand McNally Staff. Rand Mcnally New International Atlas. anniversary ed. 1998. 99.00 (*0-528-83961-6*) Rand McNally.

— Rand McNally New Universal World Atlas. LC 94-3532. 1994. 49.95 (*0-528-83717-6*) Rand McNally.

— Rand McNally 1998 Road Atlas: United States, Canada, Mexico. (Illus.). 144p. 1997. pap. text 9.95 (*0-528-81587-3*) Rand McNally.

— Rand McNally 1998 Ultimate Road Atlas & Vacation Guide: United States, Canada, Mexico. (Illus.). 224p. 1997. pap. text 19.95 (*0-528-81578-4*) Rand McNally.

— Rand McNally 1998 Road Atlas & Trip Planner: United States, Canada, Mexico. (Rand McNally Ser.). (Illus.). 96p. 1997. pap. text 5.95 (*0-528-83929-2*) Rand McNally.

***Rand McNally Staff.** Rand Mcnally Omaho & Vicinity Streetfinder. 1998. pap. 14.95 (*0-528-91155-4*) Rand McNally.

Rand McNally Staff. Rand McNally Premier World Atlas. LC 97-11900. (Illus.). 248p. 1997. pap. 15.95 (*0-528-83894-6*) Rand McNally.

— Rand McNally Premier World Atlas. 248p. 1997. 24.95 (*0-528-83893-8*) Rand McNally.

— Rand McNally Road Atlas: United States, Canada & Mexico. 1991. 8.95 (*0-685-83176-0*) Wehman.

***Rand McNally Staff.** Rand McNally Road Atlas: United States, Canada & Mexico 2000. 138p. (Orig.). 1999. pap. 10.95 (*0-528-84125-4*) Rand McNally.

Rand McNally Staff. Rand McNally Road Atlas: United States, Canada, Mexico. 1p. 1995. pap. 10.95 (*0-395-78327-5*) HM.

***Rand McNally Staff.** Rand Mcnally Road Atlas 2000. 1999. pap. 10.95 (*0-375-71941-5*) Random.

— Rand Mcnally Spain/portugal, 1999 Ed. 1999. pap. 9.95 (*0-528-97700-8*) Rand McNally.

Rand McNally Staff. Rand McNally Streetfinder: Atlanta & Vicinity, GA. (Streetfinder Ser.). 1996. pap. text 15.95 (*0-528-96918-8*) Rand McNally.

— Rand McNally Streetfinder: Dallas & Vicinity, TX. 1996. pap. text 15.95 (*0-528-96919-6*) Rand McNally.

— Rand McNally Streetfinder: Los Angeles. 1994. pap. 17.95 (*0-528-91323-9*) Rand McNally.

— Rand McNally Streetfinder: Minneapolis/St. Paul. 1996. pap. text 15.95 (*0-528-96935-8*) Rand McNally.

— Rand McNally Streetfinder: Nashville. 1994. pap. 14.95 (*0-528-91321-2*) Rand McNally.

— Rand McNally Streetfinder: Nashville. 1997. pap. text 15.95 (*0-528-96953-6*) Rand McNally.

— Rand McNally Streetfinder: San Diego, CA. (Streetfinder Ser.). 1996. pap. text 12.95 (*0-528-96930-7*) Rand McNally.

— Rand McNally Streetfinder: West Palm Beach, FL. (Streetfinder Ser.). 1996. pap. text 15.95 (*0-528-96910-2*) Rand McNally.

***Rand McNally Staff.** Rand McNally Streetfinder Chicago Six-County, IL. (Streetfinder Ser.). 1998. pap. text 35.95 (*0-528-97863-2*) Rand McNally.

Rand McNally Staff. Rand McNally Streetfinder, Jacksonville, Florida. pap. 15.95 (*0-528-96939-0*, 682888Q) Rand McNally.

***Rand McNally Staff.** Rand McNally Streetfinder New Orleans. (Streetfinder Ser.). (Illus.). 1999. pap. 15.95 (*0-528-97876-4*) Rand McNally.

— Rand Mcnally Switzerland, 1999 Ed. 1999. pap. 9.95 (*0-528-97701-6*) Rand McNally.

Rand McNally Staff. Rand McNally World Atlas. (Illus.). 256p. 1995. pap. 15.95 (*0-528-83697-8*) Rand McNally.

— Rand McNally World Atlas. rev. ed. (Illus.). 256p. 1995. 22.95 (*0-528-83698-6*) Rand McNally.

— Rand McNally World Sticker Atlas. 16p. 1992. pap. 4.95 (*0-528-83490-8*) Rand McNally.

— Rand McNally Zip Code Finder. (Rand McNally Ser.). 1997. pap. text 7.95 (*0-528-83904-7*) Rand McNally.

***Rand McNally Staff.** Rand McNally Zip Code Finder, 2000. 432p. 1999. pap. 7.95 (*0-528-84177-7*) Rand McNally Bk.

— Rand McNally Zip Code Finder, 2000. 1999. pap. 7.95 (*0-375-71940-7*) Random Ref & Info.

Rand McNally Staff. Rand McNally Zip Finder. 1p. 1995. pap. 7.95 (*0-395-78328-3*) HM.

— Rand McNally's America. 1998. write for info. (*0-528-83984-5*) Rand McNally.

***Rand McNally Staff.** Rand McNally's Quick Pack, 2 vols. 2000. pap. 5.95 (*0-528-84751-1*) Rand McNally.

Rand McNally Staff. Road Atlas: United States, Canada, Mexico. gif. ed. (Rand McNally Ser.). (Illus.). 136p. 1998. pap. 13.95 (*0-528-84020-7*) Rand McNally.

Rand McNally Staff. Road Atlas & Travel Guide, 1997. deluxe ed. 176p. 1996. pap. text 7.95 (*0-528-81529-6*) Rand McNally.

— Road Atlas & Trip Planner: BIPAD 2000. (Illus.). 1999. pap. 6.95 (*0-528-84234-X*) Rand McNally.

Rand McNally Staff. Road Atlas & Trip Planner: United States, Canada, Mexico. 1999th ed. 88p. 1998. pap. 5.95 (*0-528-84032-0*) Rand McNally.

Rand McNally Staff. Road Atlas & Trip Planner, 1997. (Illus.). 95p. 1996. pap. text 5.95 (*0-528-81560-1*) Rand McNally.

Rand McNally Staff. Road Atlas Deluxe Wirebound. deluxe ed. LC 00-553132. 144p. 1998. spiral bd. 14.95 (*0-528-84050-9*) Rand McNally.

— Road Atlas, 1997. (Illus.). 144p. 1996. pap. text 9.95 (*0-528-81517-2*) Rand McNally.

— Road Atlas, 1997: Deluxe. 144p. 1996. pap. 13.95 (*0-528-81558-X*) Rand McNally.

— Road Atlas, 1997, Gift Edition. 1996. pap. text 13.95 (*0-528-81559-8*) Rand McNally.

Rand McNally Staff. Road Atlas 95: United States - Canada - Mexico. 160p. pap. 12.95 (*0-528-81458-3*) Rand McNally.

— Road Atlas 2000 Deluxe, (Illus.). 136p. 1999. pap. 16.95 (*0-528-84147-5*) Rand McNally.

— Road Atlas/Trip Plan Deluxe, LC 73-2433. (Illus.). 176p. 1999. pap. 8.95 (*0-528-84132-7*) Rand McNally.

— Rocky Mountain National Park. 1997. pap. 5.95 (*0-528-96662-6*) Rand McNally.

— Romania: Bulgaria. pap. 16.95 (*0-528-91432-4*) Rand McNally.

— Rome. pap. 15.95 (*0-528-91525-8*) Rand McNally.

Rand McNally Staff. Saint Louis Streetfinder. 1998. pap. text 5.95 (*0-528-97230-8*) Rand McNally.

***Rand McNally Staff.** Salem, Oregon, 1. 1999. 3.95 (*0-528-98010-6*) Rand McNally.

Rand McNally Staff. Salt Lake City, UT Mapguide. (Illus.). 1999. 5.95 (*0-528-97579-X*) Rand McNally.

***Rand McNally Staff.** Salt Lake City Utah. 1999. 5.95 (*0-528-96711-8*) Rand McNally.

— San Francisco. pap. 6.95 (*0-528-93685-9*) Rand McNally.

— San Francisco, California. 1997. 5.95 (*0-528-94549-1*) Rand McNally.

Rand McNally Staff. Sarasota/Bradenton Florida, 1. 1999. 5.95 (*0-528-97605-2*) Rand McNally.

***Rand McNally Staff.** Sarsota/Bandenton Florida. (Rand McNally Streetfinder Ser.). 1999. pap. text 16.95 (*0-528-97888-8*) Rand McNally.

— Seattle, Washington. 1997. pap. 5.95 (*0-528-94551-3*) Rand McNally.

— See the U. S. A. 1998. pap. text 47.40 (*0-528-83854-7*) Rand McNally.

— South Carolina. (Rand McNally Streetfinder Ser.). 1999. 18.95 (*0-528-97411-4*) Rand McNally.

— South Germany. pap. 16.95 (*0-528-91493-6*) Rand McNally.

Rand McNally Staff. South Orange County. 1996. pap. 9.95 (*0-528-97089-5*) Rand McNally.

***Rand McNally Staff.** Southeast Connecticut. 1999. pap. text 15.95 (*0-528-97879-9*) Rand McNally.

— Southern Italy. pap. 16.95 (*0-528-91494-4*) Rand McNally.

— Southern Scandinavia. pap. 16.95 (*0-528-91448-0*) Rand McNally.

— Soviet Union & Baltic Nations. pap. 7.95 (*0-528-83504-1*) Rand McNally.

Rand McNally Staff. Spokane. LC 98-684186. (Easy Finder Plus Ser.). 1997. 9.95 (*0-528-96673-1*) Rand McNally.

***Rand McNally Staff.** Springfield Massachusetts. 1999. 5.95 (*0-528-97834-9*) Rand McNally.

— St. Charles County, Missouri, 1. 1999. 3.95 (*0-528-98004-1*) Rand McNally.

Rand McNally Staff. St. Louis. 1998. 5.95 (*0-528-97569-2*) Rand McNally.

— Streetfinder, 1998 ed. (Streetfinder Ser.). 1997. pap. 38.95 (*0-528-52076-8*) Rand McNally.

— Student's World Atlas. 19th rev. ed. LC 93-41312. 96p. (J). 1994. 7.95 (*0-528-83699-4*) Rand McNally.

— Tacoma Washington, 1. (Rand McNally Streetfinder Ser.). 1999. pap. text 15.95 (*0-528-97882-9*) Rand McNally.

— Tallahassee Florida, 1. 1999. 5.95 (*0-528-97844-6*); pap. text 16.95 (*0-528-97881-0*) Rand McNally.

Rand McNally Staff. Tampa, Florida. 1997. pap. 5.95 (*0-528-96828-9*) Rand McNally.

— Texas, 1. (Mapguide Ser.). 1998. 5.95 (*0-528-94628-5*) Rand McNally.

Rand McNally Staff. Things on the Go. 1998. pap. text 3.95 (*0-528-83977-2*) Rand McNally.

— Today's World. 1998. 29.95 (*0-528-83985-3*) Rand McNally.

— Today's World. rev. ed. 200p. 1997. pap. 29.95 (*0-528-83871-7*) Rand McNally.

— Today's World: A New World Atlas from the Cartographers of Rand McNally. rev. ed. LC 92-16250. (Illus.). 200p. 1995. 29.95 (*0-528-83778-8*) Rand McNally.

— Travel Games. 1998. pap. text 3.95 (*0-528-83978-0*) Rand McNally.

— Travel Games II. 1998. pap. text 3.95 (*0-528-83979-9*) Rand McNally.

— Traveler's World Atlas & Guide. LC 93-11580. 1993 14.95 (*0-528-83626-9*); pap. 9.95 (*0-528-83625-0*) Rand McNally.

— Traveler's World Atlas & Guide. 240p. 1996. 14.95 (*0-528-83719-2*) Rand McNally.

— Traveler's World Atlas & Guide. (Illus.). 240p. 1995. pap. text 9.95 (*0-528-83781-8*) Rand McNally.

***Rand McNally Staff.** Travels with Santa. (Illus.). (J). 1998. pap. 53.10 (*0-528-83862-8*, Rand McNally for Kids) Rand McNally.

Rand McNally Staff. Travels with Santa. 1998. pap. 2.95 (*0-528-83868-7*) Rand McNally.

— Trip Tracker. 1998. pap. text 12.95 (*0-528-84058-4*) Rand McNally.

— Tripmaker. (Tripmaker Ser.). 1997. pap. 38.95 (*0-528-52070-9*) Rand McNally.

— Tripmaker, 1999 Edtion. 1998. pap. text 44.95 (*0-528-52099-7*) Rand McNally.

***Rand McNally Staff.** Tuscaloosa: City Map, 1. 1999. 2.50 (*0-528-96085-7*) Rand McNally.

— 2000 Business Traveler's Briefcase Atlas. 1999. pap. 14.95 (*0-528-84133-5*) Rand McNally.

— 2000 Large Scale Road Atlas. 1999. pap. 19.95 (*0-528-84236-6*) Rand McNally.

— 2000 Road Atlas, gif. ed. 1999. pap. 14.95 (*0-528-84126-2*) Rand McNally.

— 2000 Road Atlas & Trip Planner. (Illus.). 1999. pap. 6.95 (*0-528-84131-9*) Rand McNally.

— 2000 Ultimate Road Atlas & Vacation Planner. (Illus.). 1999. pap. 19.95 (*0-528-84128-9*) Rand McNally.

Rand McNally Staff. Ultimate Road Atlas & Vacation Guide. 1998. pap. 19.95 (*0-528-84024-X*) Rand McNally.

— Ultimate Road Atlas & Vacation Guide, 1997. 1996. pap. text 19.95 (*0-528-81574-1*) Rand McNally.

— United States/Canada/Mexico Sticker Atlas. 16p. 1995. pap. text 4.95 (*0-528-83721-4*) Rand McNally.

— U.S Laminated Refill. 1998. 179.40 (*0-528-84162-9*) Rand McNally.

— Vacation America. (Illus.). 232p. 1996. pap. text 14.95 (*0-528-81520-2*) Rand McNally.

— Vacation Fun Pack. 1998. pap. text 5.25 (*0-528-83975-6*) Rand McNally.

Rand McNally Staff. Vienna. pap. 14.95 (*0-528-91528-2*); pap. 6.95 (*0-528-95957-3*) Rand McNally.

— Virginia. 1997. pap. 5.95 (*0-528-96688-X*) Rand McNally.

— Washington. 1997. pap. 5.95 (*0-528-96888-2*) Rand McNally.

Rand McNally Staff. West Palm Beach & Vincinity, 1. (Rand McNally Streetfinder Ser.). 1999. pap. text 16.95 (*0-528-97877-2*) Rand McNally.

Rand McNally Staff. West Palm Beach, Florida, 1. 1997. pap. 5.95 (*0-528-97154-9*) Rand McNally.

— West Virginia. 1997. pap. 5.95 (*0-528-96701-0*) Rand McNally.

— World. pap. 16.95 (*0-528-91464-2*) Rand McNally.

Rand McNally Staff. The World Afghanistan to Zimbabwe. LC 95-74681. (Illus.). 272p. (J). 1995. 49.95 (*0-528-83773-7*) Rand McNally.

— World Atlas. LC 98-676271. (Notebook Ser.). (Illus.). 32p. 1996. pap. 2.95 (*0-528-83807-5*) Rand McNally.

— World Facts & Maps. 1998. pap. 10.95 (*0-528-83994-2*) Rand McNally.

— World Facts & Maps, 1997. (Illus.). 208p. 1996. pap. text 10.95 (*0-528-83881-4*) Rand McNally.

— World Geography Atlas. 1998. 9.06 (*0-07-366116-3*) McGraw.

— World Laminated Cosmopolitan 2-Sided Map Refill. 1998. 179.40 (*0-528-84161-0*) Rand McNally.

Rand McNally Staff. Wyoming. 1997. pap. 5.95 (*0-528-96705-3*) Rand McNally.

— Yellowstone National Park. 1996. pap. 4.95 (*0-528-97149-2*) Rand McNally.

Rand McNally Staff. Zip Code Finder. 1999th ed. 432p. 1998. pap. 7.95 (*0-528-83991-8*) Rand McNally.

— Zip Code Finder, 1997. 1996. pap. text 7.95 (*0-528-81516-4*) Rand McNally.

Rand McNally Staff. Zurich. pap. 6.95 (*0-528-95974-3*) Rand McNally.

Rand McNally Staff, ed. Fishing Hotspots: Wisconsin. (Illus.). 104p. (Orig.). 1988. pap. 2.95 (*0-528-88272-4*) S&S Trade.

— 1999 Exploring America's National Parks. LC 98-226172. 1998. pap. 4.95 (*0-528-84052-5*) Rand McNally.

***Rand McNally Staff, ed.** Pocket City Atlas. (Illus.). 64p. 1999. pap. 2.95 (*0-528-84135-1*) Rand McNally.

— Rand McNally Streetfinder Cape Cod & Southern Masschusetts 2000-2001. (Illus.). 2000. pap. 15.95 (*0-528-97907-8*) Rand McNally.

— Rand McNally Streetfinder Fairfield County. (Illus.). 2000. pap. 15.95 (*0-528-97904-3*) Rand McNally.

Rand McNally Staff & Cunningham, David. The Rand McNally Children's Atlas of Native Americans: Native Cultures of North & South America. Adelman, Elizabeth, ed. (United States & Its Flag Ser.). (Illus.). 78p. (J). (gr. 3-6). 1996. 15.95 (*1-878363-99-9*) Forest Hse.

Rand McNally Staff & Harris, Nicholas. Oceans. LC 96-8342. (Fold-Out Book Ser.). (Illus.). 16p. (J). 1996. 14.95 (*0-528-83835-0*) Penguin Putnam.

— Rand McNally Rainforest Fold-Out Book. LC 96-8343. (Illus.). 16p. (J). 1996. 14.95 (*0-528-83834-2*) Rand McNally.

Rand McNally Staff & Zapenski, David, eds. Commercial Atlas & Marketing Guide, 1998. (Illus.). 568p. 1997. 395.00 (*0-528-81602-0*) Rand McNally.

Rand McNally Staff, jt. auth. see Encyclopaedia Britannica Staff.

Rand, Melroe & Rand, Ingersoll. Bobby & Minny We Can Do Anything. Couch, Dennis et al, eds. LC 97-69526. (Illus.). 28p. (J). (ps-6). 1997. write for info. (*1-882370-01-5*) Melroe.

Rand, Michael R., jt. auth. see Greenfield, Lawerence A.

Rand, Miriam, jt. auth. see Porter, Ona L.

***Rand, Muriel K.** Giving It Some Thought: Cases for Early Childhood Practice. LC 00-102450. 182p. 2000. pap. 9.00 (*0-935989-94-3*) Natl Assn Child Ed.

Rand, Naomi. Silko, Morrison, & Roth: Studies in Survival. LC 97-32320. (Studies on Themes & Motifs in Literature: Vol. 37). 118p. (C). 1999. pap., pap. text 23.95 (*0-8204-3949-5*) P Lang Pubng.

Rand, Nicholas. Questions for Freud: The Secret History of Psychoanalysis. LC 97-15084. 240p. 1997. 24.95 (*0-674-74325-3*) HUP.

***Rand, Nicholas.** Questions for Freud: The Secret History of Psychoanalysis. 256p. 2000. pap. 16.95 (*0-674-00421-3*) HUP.

Rand, Nicholas T., tr. see Abraham, Nicolas & Torok, Maria.

Rand, Pamela. English for Kids: And the Whole Family. unabridged ed. 38p. (J). (ps-6). 1997. pap. 14.95 incl. audio (*1-878245-03-1*) OptimaLearning.

— French for Kids: And the Whole Family. unabridged ed. Orig. Title: French for Tots. (Illus.). 35p. (J). (ps-6). 1988. pap. 19.95 incl. digital audio (*1-878245-02-3*) OptimaLearning.

— Spanish for Kids: And the Whole Family. unabridged ed. (Illus.). 31p. (J). (ps-6). 1990. pap. 19.95 incl. digital audio (*1-878245-01-5*) OptimaLearning.

Rand, Paul. Design, Form, & Chaos. LC 92-62277. (Illus.). 224p. (C). 1993. 50.00 (*0-300-05553-6*) Yale U Pr.

— From Lascaux to Brooklyn. (C). 1996. 50.00 (*0-614-95685-4*) Yale U Pr.

— From Lascaux to Brooklyn. LC 95-61920. (Illus.). 187p. (C). 1996. 55.00 (*0-300-06676-7*) Yale U Pr.

***Rand, Paul.** Paul Rand: A Designer's Art. (Illus.). 242p. 2000. pap. 30.00 (*0-300-08282-7*) Yale U Pr.

An Asterisk (*) at the beginning of an entry indicates that the title is appearing for the first time.

R

Rand, Paul, et al. The Basel School of Design & Its Philosophy: The Armin Hofmann Years, 1946-1986, an Exhibition of Posters. Longhauser, Elsa, ed. (Illus.). 48p. 1986. pap. 25.00 (*1-58442-003-0*) Galleries at Moore.

Rand, R. H. & Armbruster, D. Perturbation Methods, Bifurcation Theory & Computer Algebra. (Applied Mathematical Sciences Ser.: Vol. 65). (Illus.). 255p. 1987. 58.95 (*0-387-96589-0*) Spr-Verlag.

Rand, Richard. Topics in Nonlinear Dynamics with Computer Algebra. LC 94-2869. (Computers in Education Ser.: Vol. 1). ix, 229p. 1994. text 59.00 (*2-88449-113-9*); pap. text 27.00 (*2-88449-114-7*) Gordon & Breach.

Rand, Richard, ed. Logomachia: The Conflict of the Faculties Today. LC 92-6977. xii, 219p. 1992. pap. text 15.00 (*0-8032-8940-5*, Bison Books) U of Nebr Pr.

Rand, Richard & Bianco, Juliette M. Intimate Encounters: Love & Domesticity in Eighteenth-Century France. LC 97-172. 232p. 1997. pap. text 35.00 (*0-691-01662-3*, Pub. by Princeton U Pr) Cal Prin Full Svc.

— Intimate Encounters: Love & Domesticity in Eighteenth-Century France. LC 97-172. (Illus.). 232p. 1997. text 65.00 (*0-691-01663-1*, Pub. by Princeton U Pr) Cal Prin Full Svc.

Rand, Richard, tr. see Derrida, Jacques.

Rand-Riley, Candy. Fifty Ways to Please Your Lover: A Woman's Guide to a Mutually Pleasurable Love Relationship. 173p. (Orig.). 1990. pap. 14.95 (*0-9625452-0-1*) Persimmon CA.

Rand, Ritch, jt. auth. see Reynolds, William.

Rand, Robert. Strange Sins. 1995. 22.00 (*0-671-78689-X*) S&S Trade.

Rand, Roberta. Playing the Tuba at Midnight: The Joys & Challenges of Singleness. LC 95-20348. 180p. (Orig.). 1995. pap. 9.99 (*0-8308-1690-9*, 1690) InterVarsity.

Rand, Roy E. Recirculating Electron Acclerators. (Nuclear Physics Ser.: Vol. 3). xviii, 236p. 1984. text 271.00 (*3-7186-0183-4*) Gordon & Breach.

Rand, Sharon R. The French Imparfait & Passe Simple in Discourse. LC 93-60371. (Publications in Linguistics Ser.: Vol. 116). xii, 136p. 1993. pap. 15.00 (*0-88312-822-5*) S I L Intl.

Rand, Silas. English-Micmac Dictionary. 1994. 62.50 (*0-7859-9682-6*) Fr & Eur.

Rand, Suzanne. Three Cheers: International Edition. (YA). 1994. pap. 3.50 (*0-553-24385-3*) Bantam.

Rand, Ted. Here Are My Hands Board Book. LC 99-193723. (J). (ps-1). 1998. 6.95 (*0-8050-5911-3*) H Holt & Co.

— A Home for Spooky. LC 97-18573. 32p. (J). 1995. 15.95 (*0-8050-4611-9*) H Holt & Co.

Rand, Theodore H. Treasury of Canadian Verse. LC 76-75717. (Granger Index Reprint Ser.). 1977. 23.95 (*0-8369-6039-4*) Ayer.

Rand, Toby, jt. auth. see Schasre, June.

Rand, W. & Lee, Z. Teach Yourself Czech. (Teach Yourself Ser.). 1992. 19.95 (*0-8288-8310-6*) Fr & Eur.

Rand, W. W. Diccionario de la Santa Biblia. (SPA., Illus.). 768p. 1969. reprint ed. pap. 14.99 (*0-89922-003-7*) Caribe Betania.

Rand, Walter. Paddles Flashing in the Sun. (Illus.). 314p. (Orig.). 1995. pap. 22.95 (*0-9649728-0-8*) Pathfndr CT.

Rand, William L. The Reiki Class. 1994. pap. Price not set. incl. audio (*1-886785-01-5*) Vision Pub.

— Reiki the Healing Touch: First & Second Degree Manual. 44p. 1992. 12.95 (*0-9631567-0-5*) Vision Pub.

— Spiritual Protection & Healing. pap. Price not set. incl. audio (*1-886785-00-7*) Vision Pub.

***Randa, Ernest W.** Salt Lake Community College: A College on the Move, 1948-1998. (Illus.). 176p. 2000. 25.00 (*1-888106-46-8*) Agreka Bks.

Randa, Laura E., ed. Society's Final Solution: A History & Discussion of the Death Penalty. LC 97-1663. 288p. 1997. 44.50 (*0-7618-0713-6*) U Pr of Amer.

***Randal, Jonathan.** After Such Knowledge, What Forgiveness? My Encounters with Kurdistan. LC 98-27709. 356p. 2000. pap. 16.00 (*0-8133-3580-9*, Pub. by Westview) HarpC.

Randal, Jonathan C. After Such Knowledge, What Forgiveness? My Encounters with Kurdistan. LC 96-48612. 326p. 1997. text 25.00 (*0-374-10200-7*) FS&G.

Randal, Jude. A Miracle for Bryan. (Romance Ser.). 1994. pap. 2.75 (*0-373-08986-4*, 5-08986-7) Silhouette.

Randall. Color Atlas of Avian Histol/Histpathology. 1995. text 155.00 (*0-7234-2087-4*) Wolfe Pubng AZ.

***Randall.** ECG Interpretation. (Quicklook Medicine Ser.). 2000. 19.95 (*1-889325-79-1*, Pub. by Fence Crk Pubng) Blackwell Sci.

Randall. The Mind of Thomas Jefferson. 1999. text 25.00 (*0-8050-3795-0*) St Martin.

Randall. Principles Marketing. 1993. pap. write for info. (*1-86152-344-0*, Pub. by ITBP) Thomson Learn.

Randall. Universal Journalist. LC 96-8113. 216p. 1996. 95.95 (*0-7453-1108-3*) Pluto GBR.

— Universal Journalist. 216p. 1996. pap. 28.95 (*0-7453-1109-1*, Pub. by Pluto GBR) Stylus Pub VA.

Randall, ed. We the People: The Story of America. (C). 1998. text, student ed. write for info. (*0-673-99216-0*) Addison-Wesley.

— We the People: The Story of America, Vol. 1. (C). 1998. text. write for info. (*0-673-99217-9*) Addison-Wesley.

— We the People: The Story of America, Vol. 2. (C). 1998. text. write for info. (*0-673-99218-7*) Addison-Wesley.

Randall, jt. auth. see Huang.

Randall, jt. compiled by see Mitchell.

Randall, Richard L. & Overdorf, Scot W., eds. Ways & Means: Maximize the Value of Your Retirement Savings. LC 98-74337. 494p. 1999. 39.95 (*0-922943-07-9*) Esperti Petrsn.

***Randall, Adrian & Charlesworth, Andrew.** Moral Economy & Popular Protest. LC 99-15312. 1999. text 69.95 (*0-312-22592-X*) St Martin.

***Randall, Alan.** Making the Environment Count: Selected Essays of Alan Randall. LC 99-17604. (New Horizons in Environmental Economics Ser.). 256p. (C). 1999. 90.00 (*1-84064-086-3*) E Elgar.

Randall, Alan. Resource Economics: An Economic Approach to Natural Resource & Environmental Policy. 2nd ed. LC 87-4988. 448p. 1987. text 93.95 (*0-471-87468-X*) Wiley.

Randall, Albert B. The Mystery of Hope in the Philosophy of Gabriel Marcel, 1888-1973: Hope & "Homo Viator" LC 92-26572. (Problems in Contemporary Philosophy Ser.: Vol. 33). 420p. 1992. text 109.95 (*0-7734-9160-0*) E Mellen.

— Theologies of War & Peace among Jews, Christians & Muslims. LC 98-40015. (Toronto Studies in Theology: Vol. 77). 500p. 1998. text 109.95 (*0-7734-8254-7*) E Mellen.

Randall, Alice E. The Sources of Spenser's Classical Mythology. 1972. 35.00 (*0-8490-1092-6*) Gordon Pr.

— The Sources of Spenser's Classical Mythology. LC 72-115364. reprint ed. 21.50 (*0-404-05223-1*) AMS Pr.

Randall, Allan D. & Johnson, A. Ivan, eds. The Northeast Glacial Aquifers: Papers Presented at AWRA Symposium on Monitoring, Modeling, & Mediating Water Quality, May 17-20, 1987, Syracuse, New York. LC TD0223.A1A87. (AWRA Monograph Ser.: Vol. 11). 160p. 1988. reprint ed. pap. 49.60 (*0-7837-9277-8*, 206001500005) Bks Demand.

Randall, Ann M. Free from Secrets: Healing Meditations of an Abuse Survivor. LC 96-92426. 96p. (Orig.). 1998. pap. 10.00 (*0-9652361-0-2*, 101) Pathway Possibilites.

Randall, Anthony G. The Time Museum Catalogue of Chronometers. Chandler, Bruce, ed. (Illus.). x, 366p. 1992. 139.00 (*0-912947-03-9*) Time Museum.

Randall, Arthur. Laura. limited unabridged ed. 228p. 1998. 95.00 (*1-881119-04-1*) Pyncheon Hse.

— Laura. unabridged ed. 228p. 1998. 65.00 (*1-881119-17-3*) Pyncheon Hse.

Randall, Belle. Drop Dead Beautiful. (Illus.). 32p. 1998. 28.00 (*1-890654-11-6*); pap. 8.00 (*1-890654-10-8*) Wood Work.

Randall, Bernice. When Is a Pig a Hog? A Guide to Confoundingly Related English Words. 336p. 1997. 9.99 (*0-88365-977-8*) Galahad Bks.

Randall, Bernice, tr. see Ada, Alma Flor.

Randall, Bob. The Fan. mass mkt. 2.50 (*0-446-91887-3*, Pub. by Warner Bks) Little.

Randall, Bonnie. Garden Tours of England: London to the Lake District. LC 98-92338. (Illus.). 150p. 1999. pap. 14.95 (*0-9656510-2-9*) Windsor Hill.

— Garden Tours of England: The Cotswolds. (Illus.). 155p. (Orig.). 1997. pap. 14.95 (*0-9656510-0-2*) Windsor Hill.

— Garden Tours of England: The Southern Region. (Illus.). 152p. 1998. pap. 14.95 (*0-9656510-1-0*) Windsor Hill.

***Randall, Bonnie.** Noddy's Busy Counting Day. (Cuddly Tale Ser.). (Illus.). 10p. (J). (ps-k). 2000. bds. 6.99 (*1-57584-685-3*, Pub. by Rdrs Digest) S&S Trade.

Randall, Brad. Death Investigation: The Basics. LC 97-2185. (Illus.). 150p. (Orig.). 1997. pap. 24.95 (*1-883620-24-4*) Galen AZ.

Randall, Brian. The B Book. LC 93-40927. 96p. 1994. 22.95 (*0-446-51801-8*) Warner Bks.

Randall, Bruce C. The Name. 168p. mass mkt. 4.99 (*1-55197-281-6*) Picasso Publ.

Randall, C. & Clepper, Henry. Famous & Historic Trees. 4.50 (*0-686-26725-7*, 21) Am Forests.

Randall, C., jt. auth. see Youngman, Wilbur H.

Randall, C. J. Diseases of Domestic Fowl & Turkey. 2nd ed. 1996. 92.95 (*0-7234-1628-1*) Iowa St U Pr.

Randall, Catharine. Building Codes: The Aesthetics of Calvinism in Early Modern Europe. LC 99-17838. 1999. 36.50 (*0-8122-3490-1*) U of Pa Pr.

Randall, Charles A., Jr., ed. Extra-Terrestrial Matter. LC 69-15447. (Illus.). 331p. 1969. 30.00 (*0-87580-009-2*) N Ill U Pr.

Randall, Charles E. & Clepper, Henry. Famous & Historic Trees. rev. ed. LC 76-39710. (Illus.). 90p. 1977. pap. 4.50 (*0-685-46351-6*) Am Forests.

Randall, Charles E. & Clipper, Henry. American Forests Famous & Historic Trees: Make History Plant a Tree. (Illus.). 44p. 1994. pap. text 2.00 (*0-9642811-0-4*) Famous & Hist.

Randall, Charles H. & Bushnell, Joan L. Hisses, Boos & Cheers. 1986. 12.95 (*0-87129-421-4*, H49) Dramatic Pub.

— Trapped by a Treacherous Twin. 1982. 5.25 (*0-87129-498-2*, T56) Dramatic Pub.

Randall, Charles T. The Encyclopedia of Window Fashions: America's Favorite Window Decorating Book. 4th rev. ed. (Illus.). 158p. 1997. pap. 19.95 (*0-9624736-9-3*, EWF4P); spiral bd. 39.95 (*0-9624736-8-5*, EWF4S) Randall Intl.

Randall, Clarence B. Folklore of Management. rev. ed. 204p. 1997. pap. 14.95 (*0-471-18511-6*) Wiley.

Randall, Clifford W., et al, eds. Design & Retrofit of Wastewater Treatment Plants for Biological Nutrient Removal. LC 92-53521. (Water Quality Management Library: Vol. 5). 375p. 1992. text 104.95 (*0-87762-922-6*) Technomic.

Randall, Clyde L., jt. auth. see Nicholas, David H.

Randall, Clyde L., jt. auth. see Nichols, David H.

***Randall, Coleman Thomas.** Macbeth & King John & Timon of Athens: The Shakespeare Novels, Vol. IV, Vol. 4. LC 00-190576. 2000. 25.00 (*0-7388-1414-8*); pap. 18.00 (*0-7388-1415-6*) Xlibris Corp.

— The Shakespeare Novels Vol. 1: Hamlet - The Novel & All's Well That Ends Well. LC 99-91597. 2000. 25.00 (*0-7388-0928-4*); pap. 18.00 (*0-7388-0929-2*) Xlibris Corp.

— The Shakespeare Novels Vol. 3: King Lear - A Tale of Ruin & Redemption & Cymbeline-Imogen: The Princess Who Followed Her Heart. LC 99-91769. 2000. 25.00 (*0-7388-1250-1*); pap. 18.00 (*0-7388-1251-X*) Xlibris Corp.

Randall, Curt, jt. auth. see Tavella, Domingo.

Randall, D. D., et al, eds. Current Topics in Plant Biochemistry & Physiology, Vol. 6. (Illus.). 190p. (Orig.). 1987. 12.00 (*0-936463-05-8*) U MO Plant Bio.

— Current Topics in Plant Biochemistry & Physiology, Vol. 7. (Illus.). 258p. (Orig.). 1988. 12.00 (*0-685-35120-3*) U MO Plant Bio.

— Current Topics in Plant Biochemistry & Physiology, Vol. 8. (Illus.). 316p. (Orig.). 1989. 15.00 (*0-936463-07-4*) U MO Plant Bio.

— Current Topics in Plant Biochemistry & Physiology, Vol. 9. (Illus.). (Orig.). 1990. 17.50 (*0-936463-08-2*) U MO Plant Bio.

— Current Topics in Plant Biochemistry & Physiology: Symposium Proceedings, Vol. 5. (Illus.). 216p. (Orig.). 1986. 12.00 (*0-936463-04-X*) U MO Plant Bio.

Randall, D. J. Type A Personality: Index of Authors & Subjects with Guide for Rapid Research. rev. ed. 1994. 47.50 (*0-7883-0182-9*); pap. 44.50 (*0-7883-0183-7*) ABBE Pubs Assn.

Randall, D. J., jt. ed. see Hoar, W. S.

Randall, D. V. Once upon the Eighth Day. 325p. 1993. write for info. (*0-9636838-0-2*) D V Randall.

Randall, Dale B. Gentle Flame: The Life & Verse of Dudley, Fourth Lord North. LC 82-21143. xviii, 255p. (C). 1983. text 54.95 (*0-8223-0491-0*) Duke.

— The Golden Tapestry: A Critical Survey of Non-Chivalric Spanish Fiction in English Translation, 1543-1657. LC 63-13313. 272p. reprint ed. pap. 84.40 (*0-608-11973-3*, 202343800033) Bks Demand.

— Joseph Conrad & Warrington Dawson: The Record of a Friendship. LC 68-56068. 258p. reprint ed. pap. 80.00 (*0-608-11972-5*, 202343900033) Bks Demand.

— Winter Fruit: English Drama, 1642-1660. LC 95-7634. (Illus.). 472p. 1995. 44.95 (*0-8131-1925-1*) U Pr of Ky.

Randall, Dale B., ed. see Perrin, Anne Elliott.

Randall, Dale B., ed. see Perrin, Annie Elliott.

Randall, Dale B., ed. see Southeastern Renaissance Conference Staff.

Randall, Daniel R. A Puritan Colony in Maryland. LC 78-63763. (Johns Hopkins University. Studies in the Social Sciences. Thirtieth Ser. 1912: 6). reprint ed. 29.50 (*0-404-61031-5*) AMS Pr.

***Randall, David.** The Universal Journalist. 2nd ed. LC 00-8411. 2000. write for info. (*0-7453-1642-5*, Pub. by Pluto GBR) Stylus Pub VA.

Randall, David & Shoraka-Blair, Suzanne, eds. An Evaluation of the Cost of Incinerating Wastes Containing PVC. 85p. 1994. 35.00 (*0-7918-1214-6*) ASME.

Randall, David A., jt. ed. see Snow, Patrick R.

***Randall, David J.** General Circulation Model Development. 742p. 2000. 99.95 (*0-12-578010-9*) Acad Pr.

Randall, David J. & Farrell, Anthony P., eds. Deep Sea Fishes. (Fish Physiology Ser.: Vol. 16). (Illus.). 388p. 1997. text 89.95 (*0-12-350440-6*) Morgan Kaufmann.

Randall, David J., et al. Eckert Animal Physiology: Mechanisms & Adaptations. 4th ed. LC 96-31713. 768p. 1997. text 78.95 (*0-7167-2414-6*) W H Freeman.

Randall, Deborah. The Sin-Eater. 1989. pap. 11.95 (*1-85224-041-5*, Pub. by Bloodaxe Bks) Dufour.

— White Eyes, Dark Ages. (Illus.). 64p. 1994. pap. 12.95 (*1-85224-222-1*, Pub. by Bloodaxe Bks) Dufour.

Randall, Deborah A., ed. see American Academy of Healthcare Attorneys of the Am.

Randall, Denise J. Management of Personnel in Health Sciences: Index of New Information with Authors & Subjects. 180p. 1993. 47.50 (*1-55914-858-6*); pap. 44.50 (*1-55914-859-4*) ABBE Pubs Assn.

— Psychological Adaptations in Life & Work: Subject Analysis Index with Reference Bibliography. LC 85-47866. 150p. 1987. 47.50 (*0-88164-406-4*); pap. 44.50 (*0-88164-407-2*) ABBE Pubs Assn.

Randall, Doanda, compiled by. Buddhist & Hindu Art in the Collection of John H. Mann. (Illus.). 285p. (Orig.). 1981. 65.00 (*0-940492-01-6*) Asian Conserv Lab.

***Randall, Don.** Kipling's Imperial Boy: Adolescence & Cultural Hybridity. LC 00-41494. 2000. write for info. (*0-312-23787-1*) St Martin.

***Randall, Doug, et al.** 2005 - Scenarios for Credit Unions: An Executive Report. 69p. 1999. pap. 179.00 (*1-889394-48-3*) Credit Union Execs.

Randall, Dudley. Black Poets. 1971. 12.09 (*0-606-03732-2*, Pub. by Turtleback) Demco.

— Cities Burning. LC 68-18623. 1966. pap. 5.00 (*0-910296-64-2*) Broadside Pr.

— A Litany of Friends: New & Selected Poems. 2nd ed. LC 83-82770. 103p. (YA). (gr. 9-12). 1983. per. 6.00 (*0-916418-50-2*) Lotus.

Randall, Dudley, ed. The Black Poets. (Illus.). 384p. 1985. mass mkt. 7.50 (*0-553-27563-1*, Bantam Classics) Bantam.

— Homage to Hoyt Fuller. LC 84-72587. 356p. (YA). (gr. 12 up). 1984. 20.00 (*0-910296-22-7*); pap. 15.00 (*0-910296-24-3*) Broadside Pr.

Randall, E. O. The Separatist Society of Zoar: An Experiment in Communism - from Its Commencement to Its Conclusion. (Ohio History, Communism Ser.). (Illus.). 128p. 1990. reprint ed. pap. 14.80 (*1-56651-019-8*); reprint ed. lib. bdg. 31.80 (*1-56651-020-1*) A W McGraw.

— Serpent Mound - Adams County, Ohio: Mystery of the Mound & History of the Serpent. (Ohio History, Prehistoric Indians, Serpent Worship Ser.). (Illus.). 56p. (C). 1993. reprint ed. pap. 7.55 (*1-56651-087-2*); reprint ed. lib. bdg. 25.65 (*1-56651-088-0*) A W McGraw.

Randall, E. Vance. Private Schools & Public Power: A Case for Pluralism. 240p. (C). 1994. text 34.00 (*0-8077-3344-X*) Tchrs Coll.

Randall, E. Vance, jt. auth. see Cooper, Bruce S.

***Randall, Ed.** The European Union & Health Policy. LC 00-34490. 2000. write for info. (*0-312-23583-6*) St Martin.

Randall, Edith L., jt. auth. see Campbell, Florence.

Randall, Edith M., jt. auth. see Stillwell, Susan B.

Randall, Edward C. Frontiers of the Afterlife (1923) 212p. 1998. reprint ed. pap. 17.95 (*0-7661-0614-4*) Kessinger Pub.

Randall, Elinor, tr. see Marti, Jose.

Randall, Elinor, tr. see Zamora, Daisy.

Randall, Emilius O. History of Ohio, 5 vols., Set. 1993. reprint ed. lib. bdg. 450.00 (*0-7812-5397-7*) Rprt Serv.

— History of the Zoar Society. 1993. reprint ed. lib. bdg. 89.00 (*0-7812-5396-9*) Rprt Serv.

— History of the Zoar Society. 3rd ed. LC 75-134427. 1972. reprint ed. 31.50 (*0-404-08467-2*) AMS Pr.

Randall, Esther. Esther Randall's Embellishing with Silk Ribbon Embroidery. Johnston, Becky, ed. (Illus.). 144p. 1996. 26.95 (*0-9646870-2-X*); pap. 24.95 (*0-9646870-1-1*) Landauer Bks IA.

Randall, Everett. Introduction to Underwriting. LC 94-79892. 224p. 1994. pap. text 22.00 (*0-89462-084-3*, 6002) IIA.

Randall, Everett D. Premium Auditing Applications, Vols. 1 & 2. 4th ed. LC 97-77730. 673p. 1997. pap. text 41.00 (*0-89462-119-X*, 9202) IIA.

— Principles of Premium Auditing. 3rd rev. ed. LC 95-81903. (Associate in Premium Auditing Ser.: Vol. 2). (Illus.). 317p. (C). 1995. pap. text 41.00 (*0-89462-097-5*, 9102/9103) IIA.

Randall, F. A. Randall & Allied Families: William Randall, 1609-1693 of Scituate & His Descendants with Ancestral Families. (Illus.). 596p. 1993. reprint ed. pap. 89.00 (*0-8328-3733-4*); reprint ed. lib. bdg. 99.00 (*0-8328-3732-6*) Higginson Bk Co.

Randall, Fiona & Downie, Robin S. Palliative Care Ethics: A Companion for All Specialties. 2nd ed. LC 99-20410. 332p. 1999. pap. text 34.95 (*0-19-263068-7*) OUP.

Randall, Frances. Denali Diary: Letters from McKinley. (Illus.). 160p. 1987. pap. 9.95 (*0-938567-01-2*) Mountaineers.

Randall, Francis B. N. G. Chernyshevskii. LC 67-19353. (Twayne's World Authors Ser.). 1967. lib. bdg. 20.95 (*0-8057-2212-2*) Irvington.

Randall, Frank A. History of the Development of Building Construction in Chicago. LC 72-5070. (Technology & Society Ser.). (Illus.). 400p. 1978. reprint ed. 33.95 (*0-405-04720-7*) Ayer.

Randall, Frank A. & Randall, John D. History of the Development of Building Construction in Chicago. 2nd ed. LC 98-8927. 512p. 1999. 44.95 (*0-252-02416-8*) U of Ill Pr.

Randall, Frank H. Psychology: The Cultivation & Development of Mind & Will by Positive & Negative Processes, the Primacy of Will Power. 193p. 1996. reprint ed. spiral bd. 14.50 (*0-7873-0692-4*) Hlth Research.

— Your Mesmeric Forces & How to Develop Them. 151p. 1996. reprint ed. spiral bd. 12.00 (*0-7873-0693-2*) Hlth Research.

***Randall, Gary W.** Tales Out of Life. 123p. 2000. pap. 18.00 (*0-7388-2119-5*) Xlibris Corp.

Randall, Geoffrey. Effective Marketing. LC 94-2995. (Self-Development for Managers Ser.). 128p. (C). 1994. pap. 14.99 (*0-415-10236-7*, B4119) Thomson Learn.

— The Principles of Marketing. LC 92-45846. (Series in the Principles of Management). 256p. (C). 1993. pap. 21.95 (*0-415-07266-2*) Thomson Learn.

— Trade Marketing Strategies: The Partnership Between Manufacturers, Brands & Retailers. 2nd ed. (Professional Development Ser.). 183p. 2000. pap. text 41.95 (*0-7506-2012-9*) Buttrwrth-Heinemann.

Randall, George I. Haskell. Genealogy of Roger Haskell of Salem, Massachusetts, to November 1925. (Illus.). 99p. 1997. reprint ed. pap. 18.00 (*0-8328-9032-4*); reprint ed. lib. bdg. 28.00 (*0-8328-9031-6*) Higginson Bk Co.

Randall, Glenn. Cold Comfort: Keeping Warm in the Outdoors. (Illus.). 144p. (Orig.). 1987. pap. 10.95 (*0-941130-46-0*) Lyons Pr.

— Modern Backpacker's Handbook. LC 93-37444. (Illus.). 288p. 1994. pap. 14.95 (*1-55821-248-5*) Lyons Pr.

— Mount McKinley Climber's Handbook. (Illus.). 120p. (Orig.). 1992. pap. 18.00 (*0-934641-55-2*) Falcon Pub Inc.

— The Outward Bound Map & Compass Handbook. 2nd rev. ed. LC 98-18603. (Illus.). 128p. 1998. pap. 10.95 (*1-55821-747-9*) Lyons Pr.

***Randall, Glenn.** Outward Bound Staying Warm in the Outdoors Handbook. 2000. 14.95 (*1-58574-089-6*) Lyons Pr.

Randall, Glenn R. & Lutz, Ellen L. Serving Survivors of Torture. 218p. 1991. 18.00 (*0-87168-433-0*, 91-42S) AAAS.

Randall, Gregory C. America's Original GI Town: Park Forest, Illinois. LC 99-26762. (Creating the North American Landscape Ser.). 1999. 42.50 (*0-8018-6207-8*) Johns Hopkins.

Randall, H. Advanced Level Accounting. 464p. (C). 1990. 65.00 (*1-870941-36-5*) St Mut.

Randall, Harriet H., ed. The Backstretch. 120p. 1989. write for info. (*0-318-16780-8*) United Thoroughbred Trnrs.

Randall, Heather, ed. see Schiavone, Giuseppe.

An Asterisk (*) at the beginning of an entry indicates that the title is appearing for the first time.

Randall, Henry S. The Life of Thomas Jefferson, 3 vols. LC 79-172011. (American Scene Ser.). (Illus.). 1972. reprint ed. lib. bdg. 175.00 (*0-306-70250-9*) Da Capo.

— The Life of Thomas Jefferson, 3 Vols, Set. LC 72-117890. (Select Bibliographies Reprint Ser.). 1977. 108.95 (*0-8369-5343-6*) Ayer.

Randall, Herbert, jt. auth. see Tusa, Bobs M.

***Randall, Ian M.** Evangelical Experiences: A Study in the Spirituality of English Evangelicalism, 1918-1939. (Biblical & Theological Monographs). xii, 309p. 1999. reprint ed. pap. 40.00 (*0-85364-919-7*, Pub. by Paternoster Pub) OM Literature.

Randall, J. Personal Defense Weapons. LC 92-72813. 102p. (Orig.). 1992. pap. 12.00 (*1-55950-087-5*, 19188) Loompanics.

— Uncertainties in Nist Noise-Temperature Measurements. 50p. 1998. pap. 4.25 (*0-16-056687-8*) USGPO.

***Randall, J. G. & Current, Richard N.** Lincoln the President. LC 99-39598. 2000. pap. 19.95 (*0-252-06872-6*) U of Ill Pr.

Randall, J. Herman. The Power of Suggestion. 71p. 1996. reprint ed. spiral bd. 9.00 (*0-7873-1066-2*) Hlth Research.

Randall, J. K. Something Medieval. LC 80-80808. (Illus.). 48p. 1988. 14.50 (*0-939044-24-2*) Lingua Pr.

Randall, J. K., jt. auth. see Boretz, Benjamin.

Randall, Jack. Sensor Sensibility. 140p. (YA). (gr. 9-12). 1997. pap. text 18.95 (*1-55953-287-4*) Key Curr Pr.

Randall, James. California Personal Injury Forms, 1987-1990, 2 vols. annuals suppl. ed. 130.00 (*0-8321-0004-8*) West Group.

Randall, James C., ed. NMR & Macromolecules: Sequence, Dynamic, & Domain Structure. LC 84-366. (ACS Symposium Ser.: No. 247). 181p. 1984. lib. bdg. 43.95 (*0-8412-0829-8*) Am Chemical.

Randall, James C., Jr., ed. NMR & Macromolecules: Sequence, Dynamic, & Domain Structure. LC 84-366. (ACS Symposium Ser.: Vol. 247). 297p. 1984. reprint ed. pap. 92.10 (*0-608-03127-5*, 206358000007) Bks Demand.

Randall, James E. Microcomputers & Physiological Simulation. 1980. pap. write for info. (*0-201-06128-7*) Addison-Wesley.

— Microcomputers & Physiological Simulation. LC 86-26275. 303p. 1987. reprint ed. pap. 94.00 (*0-608-03438-X*, 206413900008) Bks Demand.

Randall, James G. Constitutional Problems under Lincoln. 632p. 1996. text 75.00 (*0-252-02288-2*) U of Ill Pr.

— Lincoln & the South. LC 80-22084. (Walter Lynwood Fleming Lectures in Southern History). (Illus.). 161p. 1980. reprint ed. lib. bdg. 55.00 (*0-313-22843-4*, RALS, Greenwood Pr) Greenwood.

Randall, James G., jt. auth. see Current, Richard N.

Randall, Joe & Tipton-Martin, Toni. Taste of Heritage: The New African-American Cuisine. LC 97-43736. 352p. 1998. 27.50 (*0-02-860382-6*) Macmillan.

Randall, Joel. Essence. 219p. 1994. pap. write for info. (*1-882400-10-0*) Featherweed.

Randall, Joel & Randall, Mark. Cowboy or Farmer? Sometimes Its Hard to Tell. 2nd rev. ed. (Illus.). 67p. 1996. pap. 9.95 (*0-9661865-0-8*) Heartld Pub.

Randall, John. Feature Films on a Low Budget. (Illus.). 152p. 1991. pap. 34.95 (*0-240-80097-4*, Focal) Buttrwrth-Heinemann.

— Monkey & the Moon. (Illus.). 32p. (J). 1996. pap., bds. 12.95 (*0-7892-0211-5*, Abbeville Kids) Abbeville Pr.

— Plato: Dramatist of the Life of Reason. LC 71-106565. 288p. reprint ed. pap. 89.30 (*0-608-14583-1*, 202482600038) Bks Demand.

— Wattle Hurdles & Leather Gaiters. (Illus.). 202p. 1995. pap. 13.95 (*0-85236-306-0*, Pub. by Farming Pr) Diamond Farm Bk.

Randall, John C. How to Save Time ... & Worry Less. LC 79-92477. (Illus.). 65p. (Orig.). 1980. pap. 24.95 (*0-935864-01-6*, 804) Hotline Multi-Ent.

Randall, John D., jt. auth. see Petrie, Ted.

Randall, John D., jt. auth. see Randall, Frank A.

Randall, John E. Coastal Fishes of Oman. (Illus.). 432p. 1995. text 85.00 (*0-8248-1808-3*) UH Pr.

— Diver's Guide to Fishes of the Maldives. (Illus.). 192p. (C). 1995. pap. 72.00 (*0-907151-53-1*, Pub. by IMMEL Pubng) St Mut.

— The Diver's Guide to Red Sea Reef Fishes. (Illus.). 96p. 1995. pap. 66.00 (*0-907151-05-1*, Pub. by IMMEL Pubng) St Mut.

— Guide to Hawaiian Reef Fishes. LC 85-24551. (Illus.). 84p. 1985. 21.95 (*0-915180-07-3*); pap. 18.95 (*0-915180-29-4*) Harrowood Bks.

— Red Sea Reef Fishes. (Illus.). 192p. 1995. pap. 85.00 (*0-907151-87-6*, Pub. by IMMEL Pubng) St Mut.

— Red Sea Reef Fishes. (Illus.). 192p. (C). 1995. 110.00 (*0-907151-04-3*, Pub. by IMMEL Pubng) St Mut.

— Sharks of Arabia. 148p. (C). 1990. 125.00 (*0-907151-09-4*, Pub. by IMMEL Pubng) St Mut.

— Sharks of Arabia. (Illus.). 148p. 1995. 81.00 (*0-7855-2701-X*, Pub. by IMMEL Pubng) St Mut.

— Shore Fishes of Hawaii. (Illus.). 216p. (Orig.). 1996. pap. 14.95 (*0-939560-21-6*) Natural World.

— Shore Fishes of Hawai'i. LC 96-30157. (Illus.). 216p. 1998. reprint ed. pap. 19.95 (*0-8248-2182-3*) UH Pr.

— The Underwater Guide to Hawaiian Reef Fishes. LC 79-27625. (Illus.). 72p. 1980. spiral bd. 18.95 (*0-915180-02-2*) Harrowood Bks.

Randall, John E., et al. Fishes of the Great Barrier Reef & Coral Sea. expanded rev. ed. (Illus.). 564p. 1997. 85.00 (*0-8248-1895-4*) UH Pr.

Randall, John H. Aristotle. LC 60-6030. (C). 1960. text 64.50 (*0-231-02359-6*) Col U Pr.

— The Career of Philosophy Vol. 2: From the German Enlightenment to the Age of Darwin. LC 62-10454. 687p. reprint ed. pap. 200.00 (*0-8357-6048-0*, 203419100002) Bks Demand.

— How Philosophy Uses Its Past. LC 63-20464. (Matchette Lectures: No. 14). 120p. reprint ed. pap. 37.20 (*0-608-10322-5*, 200720300062) Bks Demand.

— How Philosophy Uses Its Past. LC 83-12754. 106p. 1983. reprint ed. lib. bdg. 49.50 (*0-313-24127-9*, RAH0, Greenwood Pr) Greenwood.

Randall, John H., 3rd. The Landscape & the Looking Glass: Willa Cather's Search for Value. LC 72-6207. (Illus.). 425p. 1973. reprint ed. lib. bdg. 35.00 (*0-8371-6466-4*, RALG, Greenwood Pr) Greenwood.

Randall, John H., Jr. The Making of the Modern Mind: A Survey of the Intellectual Background of the Present Age. LC 76-20740. 720p. 1976. reprint ed. pap. text 34.50 (*0-231-04143-8*) Col U Pr.

Randall, John H. Nature & Historical Experience: Essays in Naturalism & the Theory of History. LC 57-11694. (C). 1962. pap. text 25.50 (*0-231-08537-0*) Col U Pr.

Randall, John H., Jr. Philosophy after Darwin: Chapters for the Career of Philosophy & Other Essays, Vol. 3. Singer, Beth J., ed. LC 62-10454. 1977. text 64.50 (*0-231-04114-4*) Col U Pr.

— Problem of Group Responsibility to Society. LC 72-89760. (American Labor, from Conspiracy to Collective Bargaining Ser., No. 1). 296p. 1974. reprint ed. 19.95 (*0-405-02145-3*) Ayer.

Randall, John H., Jr., ed. see Woodbridge, Frederick J.

Randall, John M. & Marinelli, Janet, eds. Invasive Plants: Weeds of the Global Garden. LC 98-104097. (Twenty-First Century Gardening Ser.). (Illus.). (Orig.). 1997. pap. 9.95 (*0-945352-95-6*) Bklyn Botanic.

Randall, Judson, ed. see Hagen, Susan, et al.

Randall, Julia. Moving in Memory. Poems. LC 86-27623. 51p. 1987. pap. 6.95 (*0-8071-1388-3*) La State U Pr.

— The Path to Fairview: New & Selected Poems. LC 92-19003. 224p. 1992. pap. 14.95 (*0-8071-1783-8*); text 24.95 (*0-8071-1782-X*) La State U Pr.

Randall, Karen. The 12 Truths, about Surviving & Succeeding in the Office, & Some of Them Aren't Very Nice. LC 97-156062. 192p. 1999. pap. 12.00 (*0-425-15621-4*) Berkley Pub.

Randall, Kenneth A. Only the Echoes: The Life of Howard Bass Cushing. LC 95-61957. (Illus.). 120p. 1995. 25.00 (*1-881325-17-2*); pap. text 12.95 (*1-881325-19-9*) Yucca Tree Pr.

Randall, Laura. The Political Economy of Brazilian Oil. LC 92-15781. 328p. 1993. 69.50 (*0-275-94091-8*, C4091, Praeger Pubs) Greenwood.

— The Political Economy of Mexican Oil. LC 89-16099. 238p. 1989. 59.95 (*0-275-93372-5*, C3372, Praeger Pubs) Greenwood.

— The Politics Economoy of Venezuelan Oil. LC 87-15848. 260p. 1987. 65.00 (*0-275-92823-3*, C2823, Praeger Pubs) Greenwood.

Randall, Laura, ed. Changing Structure of Mexico: Political, Social & Economic Prospects. LC 95-25404. (Columbia University Seminars Ser.). 430p. (C). 1996. text 81.95 (*1-56324-641-4*) M E Sharpe.

— Changing Structure of Mexico: Political, Social & Economic Prospects. LC 95-25404. (Columbia University Seminars Ser.). (Illus.). 430p. (C). (gr. 13). 1996. pap. text 34.95 (*1-56324-642-2*) M E Sharpe.

— The Political Economy of Latin American in the Postwar Period. LC 97-34275. (Critical Reflections on Latin America Ser.). (Illus.). 288p. 1997. 30.00 (*0-292-77086-3*); pap. 15.95 (*0-292-77083-9*) U of Tex Pr.

— Reforming Mexico's Agrarian Reform. LC 95-25771. (Columbia University Seminars Ser.). 360p. 1996. pap. text 34.95 (*1-56324-644-9*) M E Sharpe.

— Reforming Mexico's Agrarian Reform. LC 95-25771. (Columbia's University Seminars Ser.). 360p. (gr. 13). 1996. text 81.95 (*1-56324-643-0*) M E Sharpe.

***Randall, Laura & Anderson, Joan B., eds.** Schooling for Success: Preventing Repetition & Dropout in Latin American Primary Schools. LC 98-46625. (Columbia University Seminar Ser.). 352p. 1999. pap. text 25.95 (*0-7656-0239-3*) M E Sharpe.

Randall, Laura & Anderson, Joan B., eds. Schooling for Success: Preventing Repetition & Dropout in Latin American Primary Schools. LC 98-46625. (Columbia University Seminar Ser.). 352p. (C). (gr. 13). 1999. text 66.95 (*0-7656-0238-5*) M E Sharpe.

Randall, Laveta, jt. ed. see Evans, Robert L.

Randall, Lawanda. Nelson Jackson - Cowboy. (Illus.). (Orig.). (J). (gr. 3-7). 1997. 10.95 (*0-9656838-1-8*) DPSI.

Randall, Lee. A Day in the Life of a Baby Dinosaur. LC 96-225908. (Illus.). 32p. (Orig.). (J). (ps-3). 1996. pap. 3.50 (*0-8167-4112-3*, Whistlstop) Troll Communs.

— The Garth Brooks Scrapbook. (Illus.). 240p. 1992. pap. 18.95 (*0-8065-1300-4*, Citadel Pr) Carol Pub Group.

— The Madonna Scrapbook. (Illus.). 224p. 1992. pap. 15.95 (*0-8065-1297-0*, Citadel Pr) Carol Pub Group.

— The Madonna Scrapbook. (Illus.). 224p. 1998. pap. text 16.00 (*0-7881-5568-7*) DIANE Pub.

Randall, Lilian M., et al. Medieval & Renaissance Manuscripts in the Walters Art Gallery Vol. 3: Belgium, 1250-1530. (Illus.). 704p. 1997. text 149.95 (*0-8018-5317-6*) Johns Hopkins.

Randall, Lillian M. Medieval & Renaissance Manuscripts in the Walters Art Gallery Vol. 1: France, 875-1420. LC 88-45410. (Illus.). 432p. 1989. text 85.00 (*0-8018-2869-4*) Johns Hopkins.

— Medieval & Renaissance Manuscripts in the Walters Art Gallery, Vol. II: France, 1420-1540, 2 vols. LC 88-45410. (Illus.). 832p. 1993. text 135.95 (*0-8018-2870-8*) Johns Hopkins.

Randall, Lindsay. Dangerous Courtship. 224p. 1999. mass mkt. 4.99 (*0-8217-6184-6*, Zebra Kensgtn) Kensgtn Pub Corp.

— Lady Lissa's Liaison. 224p. 1998. pap. 4.99 (*0-8217-5957-4*) Kensgtn Pub Corp.

— Miss Marcie's Mischief. 224p. 1995. mass mkt. 3.99 (*0-8217-4814-9*, Zebra Kensgtn) Kensgtn Pub Corp.

— Miss Meredith's Marriage. 288p. 1995. mass mkt. 3.99 (*0-8217-5051-8*, Zebra Kensgtn) Kensgtn Pub Corp.

Randall, Lonnie O. And Ye Shall Know the Truth: Answers from the Bible. (Illus.). iv, 145p. Date not set. pap. 10.00 (*0-9677302-0-1*) Joy Enterp.

Randall, Louise A. Bible Heroes: Stories for Children Ages One to Six. LC 87-82112. (Illus.). 56p. (J). (ps). 1988. pap. 5.98 (*0-88290-316-0*) Horizon Utah.

— Scripture Stories for Tiny Tots: Read-Aloud Stories from the Bible for Children 1 to 6. LC 83-83429. 38p. (Orig.). (J). (gr. k-3). 1983. pap. 5.98 (*0-88290-209-1*) Horizon Utah.

Randall, Lucian, jt. auth. see Welch, Chris.

Randall, Lyman K. Notes from Midlife & Other Poems. LC 86-800088. 70p. 1986. pap. 5.95 (*0-317-52124-1*) Freeman Farms.

***Randall, Mac.** Exit Music: The Radiohead Story. LC 00-29037. 288p. 2000. pap. 13.95 (*0-385-33393-5*, Delta Trade) Dell.

Randall-Maciver, David & Wilkin. Libyan Notes: Essentially a Study of the Berber Tribes. 176p. 1990. 125.00 (*1-85077-169-3*, Pub. by Darf Pubs Ltd) St Mut.

***Randall, Marga L.** How Beautiful We Once Were: A Rememberance of the Holocaust & Beyond. 2nd ed. Del Prete, Tony, ed. (Illus.). 93p. 1998. reprint ed. pap. 13.99 (*0-9675921-0-0*) M L Randall.

Randall, Margaret. Coming Home: Peace without Complacency. (Illus.). 52p. (Orig.). 1990. pap. 5.95 (*0-931122-57-0*) West End.

— Dancing with the Doe: New & Selected Poems, 1986-91. 73p. (Orig.). 1992. pap. 9.95 (*0-931122-70-8*) West End.

— Gathering Rage: The Failure of Twentieth Century Revolutions to Develop a Feminist Agenda. LC 92-29712. 224p. (C). 1992. text 30.00 (*0-85345-860-X*, Pub. by Monthly Rev); pap. text 15.00 (*0-85345-861-8*, Pub. by Monthly Rev) NYU Pr.

— Hunger's Table: Women, Food & Politics. LC 96-30599. (Illus.). 128p. (Orig.). 1997. pap. 10.00 (*1-57601-000-7*) M Randall.

— Memory Says Yes. LC 87-73442. 80p. 1988. pap. 7.95 (*0-915306-77-8*) Curbstone.

— The Old Cedar Bar. (Fine Art Ser.). (Illus.). 100p. 1992. 350.00 (*0-89556-092-5*) Gateways Bks & Tapes.

— Our Voices Our Lives: Stories of Women from Central America & the Caribbean. 200p. 1995. text 29.95 (*1-56751-047-7*); pap. text 12.95 (*1-56751-046-9*) Common Courage.

— Part of the Solution: Portrait of a Revolutionary. LC 72-93974. 1973. pap. 2.95 (*0-8112-0471-5*, NDP350, Pub. by New Directions) Norton.

— The Price You Pay: The Hidden Cost of Women's Relationship to Money. LC 95-50497. 223p. (C). 1996. 65.00 (*0-415-91203-2*); pap. 17.99 (*0-415-91204-0*) Routledge.

— Risking a Somersault in the Air: Conversations with Nicaraguan Writers. Alexander, Floyce, ed. Mills, Christina, tr. from SPA. LC 86-10052. (Illus.). 215p. 1990. reprint ed. pap. 9.95 (*0-915306-92-1*) Curbstone.

— Sandino's Daughters Revisited: Feminism in Nicaragua. LC 93-10819. (Illus.). 311p. (C). 1994. pap. 16.95 (*0-8135-2025-8*); text 47.00 (*0-8135-2024-X*) Rutgers U Pr.

— This Is about Incest. LC 87-412. (Illus.). 72p. (Orig.). 1987. pap. 8.95 (*0-932379-29-X*); lib. bdg. 18.95 (*0-932379-30-3*) Firebrand Bks.

— Walking to the Edge: Essays of Resistance. 207p. 1991. 25.00 (*0-89608-398-5*); pap. 12.00 (*0-89608-397-7*) South End Pr.

— We. 1978. pap. 1.50 (*0-918266-10-6*) Smyrna.

— Women in Cuba-Twenty Years Later. LC 80-54055. (Illus.). 182p. (C). 1981. 19.95 (*0-918266-15-7*); pap. 8.95 (*0-918266-14-9*) Smyrna.

Randall, Margaret, tr. see Borge, Tomas.

Randall, Margaret, tr. see Castillo, Otto R.

Randall, Margaret, tr. see Zamora, Daisy.

Randall, Mark, jt. auth. see Randall, Joel.

Randall, Marta. John F. Kennedy. (World Leaders Past & Present Ser.). (Illus.). 120p. (YA). (gr. 5 up). 1987. lib. bdg. 19.95 (*0-87754-586-3*) Chelsea Hse.

— John F. Kennedy. (World Leaders Past & Present Ser.). (Illus.). 112p. (YA). (gr. 5 up). 1989. pap. 8.95 (*0-7910-0580-1*) Chelsea Hse.

— John F. Kennedy. (World Leaders Past & Present Ser.). (J). 1988. 13.15 (*0-606-04454-X*, Pub. by Turtleback) Demco.

— The Sword of Winter. LC 83-4830. 271p. 1983. 25.00 (*0-89366-160-0*) Ultramarine Pub.

Randall, Marta, ed. New Dimensions, No. 13. (Orig.). 1982. pap. 3.50 (*0-671-44227-9*) PB.

Randall, Mary Ella. Their Eyes Were Watching, Notes. (Cliffs Notes Ser.). (Illus.). 88p. 1995. pap. 4.95 (*0-8220-1275-8*, Cliff) IDG Bks.

***Randall-May, Cay.** Pray Together Now: How to Find or Form a Prayer Group. LC 99-36500. 208p. 1999. text 16.95 (*1-86204-497-X*, Pub. by Element MA) Penguin Putnam.

Randall-McIver, David. Mediaeval Rhodesia. 106p. 1971. reprint ed. 45.00 (*0-7146-1885-3*, Pub. by F Cass Pubs) Intl Spec Bk.

Randall, Mercedes M. Improper Bostonian: Emily Greene Balch. LC 64-25058. (Illus.). 475p. 1964. 32.50 (*0-8290-0178-6*) Irvington.

Randall, Michael. Building Resemblance: Analogical Imagery in the Early French Renaissance. LC 96-2251. 256p. 1996. text 40.00 (*0-8018-5298-6*) Johns Hopkins.

Randall, Monica. The Mansions of Long Island's Gold Coast. LC 86-31558. (Illus.). 256p. 1988. reprint ed. pap. 35.00 (*0-8478-0821-1*, Pub. by Rizzoli Intl) St Martin.

— Phantoms of the Hudson Valley: The Glorious Estates of a Lost Era. (Illus.). 224p. 1997. 55.00 (*0-87951-617-8*, Pub. by Overlook Pr) Penguin Putnam.

Randall, Neil. The Soul of the Internet: Net Gods, Netizens & the Wiring of the World. (Illus.). 320p. 1996. text 25.00 (*1-85032-191-4*) ITCP.

— Using Microsoft Frontpage 98: Special Edition. 960p. 1997. 49.99 (*0-7897-1343-8*) Que.

Randall, Neil & December, John. The World Wide Web Unleashed, 1996. (Illus.). 1440p. (Orig.). 1995. pap. 49.99 (*1-57521-040-1*) Sams.

Randall, Neil & Jones, Dennis. Using Microsoft FrontPage 2000: Special Edition. (Using ... / Que Ser.). 1213p. 1999. pap. 39.99 (*0-7897-1910-X*) Que.

Randall, Neil, et al. Netscape 2 Unleashed. LC 95-70176. (Illus.). 922p. 1995. 49.99 (*1-57521-007-X*) Sams.

Randall, Neil, jt. auth. see Zelazny, Roger.

Randall, Oran E. History of Chesterfield, New Hampshire, from 1776 to 1881, with Family Histories. 525p. 1988. reprint ed. lib. bdg. 53.00 (*0-8328-0047-3*) Higginson Bk Co.

Randall, P. J., et al, eds. Genetic Aspects of Plant Mineral Nutrition: The Fourth International Symposium on Genetic Aspects of Plant Mineral Nutrition, Canberra, Australia, 30 September - 4 October 1991, Vol. 50. LC 92-43811. 400p. (C). 1993. text 289.50 (*0-7923-2118-9*) Kluwer Academic.

Randall, P. K. Genealogy of a Branch of the Randall Family, 1666 to 1879. 389p. 1989. reprint ed. pap. 43.00 (*0-8328-1001-0*); reprint ed. lib. bdg. 51.00 (*0-8328-1000-2*) Higginson Bk Co.

Randall, Pamela. Aikido. LC 97-49274. (Martial Arts Ser.). 24p. (J). 1999. 17.26 (*0-8239-5234-7*, PowerKids) Rosen Group.

— Jiu Jitsu. LC 97-49269. (Martial Arts Ser.). 24p. (J). 1999. 17.26 (*0-8239-5235-5*, PowerKids) Rosen Group.

***Randall, Pamela.** Judo. LC 97-49270. (Martial Arts Ser.). 24p. (J). 1999. 17.26 (*0-8239-5238-X*, PowerKids) Rosen Group.

Randall, Pamela. Karate. LC 97-49273. (Martial Arts Ser.). 24p. (J). 1999. 17.26 (*0-8239-5236-3*, PowerKids) Rosen Group.

— Kung Fu. LC 97-49272. (Martial Arts Ser.). 24p. (J). 1999. 17.26 (*0-8239-5237-1*, PowerKids) Rosen Group.

— Tae Kwon Do. LC 97-49271. (Martial Arts Ser.). 24p. (J). 1999. 17.26 (*0-8239-5233-9*, PowerKids) Rosen Group.

Randall, Paul. Baby Photos of the Country Stars. (Illus.). 200p. (Orig.). 1987. pap. 12.95 (*0-911679-01-4*) Union & Confed Inc.

Randall, Paul, jt. auth. see Williams, Douglas.

Randall, Paul M., ed. Engineers' Guide to Cleaner Production Technologies. LC 96-60866. 236p. 1997. pap. text 104.95 (*1-56676-423-8*) Technomic.

Randall, Paula. Art Works! Prevention Programs for Youth & Communities. (Illus.). 96p. 1998. pap. text 20.00 (*0-7881-4349-2*) DIANE Pub.

Randall, Peg. Little Shiner. (Illus.). 32p. 1995. 13.95 (*0-9644372-0-1*) Elder Magic.

Randall, Peter. Adult Bullying: Perpetrators & Victims. LC 96-1856. 192p. (C). 1997. 75.00 (*0-415-12672-X*); pap. 22.99 (*0-415-12673-8*) Routledge.

Randall, Peter. A Community Approach to Bullying. 224p. 1996. pap. 22.00 (*1-85856-060-8*, Trentham Bks) Stylus Pub VA.

Randall, Peter & Parker, Jonathan. Supporting the Families of Children with Autism LC 98-55962. 252p. 1999. pap. 34.95 (*0-471-98218-0*) Wiley.

***Randall, Peter & Parker, Jonathan.** Supporting the Families of Children with Autism. 252p. 1999. 82.95 (*0-471-97484-6*) Wiley.

Randall, Peter, tr. see Boesak, Allan A.

Randall, Peter E. Out on the Shoals: Twenty Years of Photography on the Isles of Shoals. (Illus.). 64p. 1995. pap. 16.50 (*0-914339-52-4*, Pub. by P E Randall Pub) U Pr of New Eng.

Randall, Peter E., photos by. New Hampshire: A Living Landscape. (Illus.). 96p. 1996. 35.00 (*0-914339-56-7*, Pub. by P E Randall Pub) U Pr of New Eng.

Randall, Peter E. & Burke, Maryellen, eds. Gosport Remembered: The Last Village at the Isles of Shoals. LC 97-19948. (Portsmouth Marine Society Ser.: No. 23). (Illus.). 180p. 1997. 35.00 (*0-915819-22-8*) Portsmouth Marine Soc.

Randall, Peter G. Lotus Guide to 1-2-3: Release 2.2. 1990. pap. 24.95 (*0-13-539529-1*) P-H.

Randall, Peter G. & Bennett. Laser Jet Companion. 3rd ed. 1991. pap. 5.00 incl. 3.5 hd (*0-13-524786-1*) Macmillan USA.

— Laser Jet Handbook. 2nd ed. 1990. pap. 5.00 incl. 3.5 hd (*0-13-523747-5*) Macmillan USA.

Randall, Richard C. Practical Guide to ISO 9000: Implementation, Registration, & Beyond. (Engineering Process Improvement Ser.). 464p. (C). 1995. 47.00 (*0-201-63379-5*) Addison-Wesley.

Randall, Richard C., ed. Marijuana, Medicine & the Law: Direct Testimony of Witnesses on Marijuana's Medical Use. LC 88-80330. 502p. (Orig.). 1988. pap. 29.95 (*0-936485-02-7*, Galen Pr DC) Lkng Glass Pubns.

— Marijuana, Medicine & the Law Vol. II: The Legal Argument. LC 88-80330. 484p. (Orig.). pap. 25.95 (*0-936485-04-3*, Galen Pr DC) Lkng Glass Pubns.

Randall, Richard E., jt. auth. see Khan, Hashim.

R

An Asterisk (*) at the beginning of an entry indicates that the title is appearing for the first time.

R

Randall, Richard H., Jr. The Golden Age of Ivory: Gothic Carvings in North American Collections. LC 93-19466. (Illus.). 160p. 1993. 75.00 (*1-55595-076-0*) Hudson Hills.

Randall, Richard S. The American Constitution: Development, Politics, Cases. (C). 2000. text. write for info. (*0-8013-2017-8*) Longman.

— The American Constitution: Development, Politics, Cases, 001. (C). 2000. pap. text. write for info. (*0-8013-2019-4*) Longman.

— The American Constitution: Development, Politics, Cases, Vol. 2. (C). 2000. pap. text. write for info. (*0-8013-2021-6*) Longman.

— Censorship of the Movies: The Social & Political Control of a Mass Medium. LC 68-14035. 296p. reprint ed. pap. 91.80 (*0-608-20468-4*, 207172000002) Bks Demand.

— Freedom & Taboo: Pornography & the Politics of a Self Divided. 1992. pap. 15.95 (*0-520-08034-3*, Pub. by U CA Pr) Cal Prin Full Svc.

Randall, Rick, jt. auth. see Hagee, John.

Randall, Robert. Residential Structures & Framing: Practical Engineering & Advanced Framing Techniques for Builders. Bliss, Steven & Masterson-Glen, Josie, eds. (Illus.). 264p. 1999. reprint ed. pap. 34.95 (*0-9632268-8-6*, Jrnl Lght) Builderburg Grp.

— What People Expect from Church: Why Meeting the Needs of People Is More Important Than Church Meetings. Shaller, Lyle E., ed. LC 92-33162. (Ministry for the Third Millennium Ser.). 128p. (Orig.). 1993. pap. 12.95 (*0-687-13387-4*) Abingdon.

Randall, Robert, jt. auth. see Fahey, Liam.

Randall, Robert, jt. ed. see Fahey, Liam.

Randall, Robert C. Marijuana & AIDS: Pot, Politics & PWAs in America. LC 91-77140. 183p. (Orig.). 1991. pap. 12.95 (*0-936485-07-8*, Galen Pr DC) Lkng Glass Pubns.

Randall, Robert C., ed. Cancer Treatment & Marijuana Therapy: Marijuana's Use in the Reduction of Nausea & Vomiting & for Appetite Stimulation in Cancer Patients. Testimony from Historic Federal Hearings. LC 90-81972. (Marijuana, Medicine & the Law Ser.). 365p. (Orig.). 1990. pap. 23.95 (*0-936485-05-1*, Galen Pr DC) Lkng Glass Pubns.

— Muscle Spasm, Pain & Marijuana Therapy: Testimony from Federal & State Court Proceedings on Marijuana's Medical Use. LC 91-71175. (Marijuana, Medicine & the Law Ser.). 237p. 1991. pap. 14.95 (*0-936485-06-X*, Galen Pr DC) Lkng Glass Pubns.

Randall, Robert C. & O'Leary, Alice M. Marijuana Rx: The Patients' Fight for Medicinal Pot. LC 98-27499. 528p. 1999. pap. 14.95 (*1-56025-166-2*, Thunders Mouth) Avalon NY.

Randall, Robert E. Elements of Ocean Engineering. LC 97-5912. (Illus.). 350p. 1997. 65.00 (*0-939773-24-4*) Soc Naval Arch.

Randall, Robert L. Let's Talk: Helping Couples, Groups & Individuals Communicate. LC 97-25732. 112p. (Orig.). 1997. pap. 12.95 (*0-8298-1214-8*) Pilgrim OH.

— Pastor & Parish: The Psychological Care of Ecclesiastical Conflicts. LC 86-27176. 172p. 1987. 38.95 (*0-89885-348-6*, Kluwer Acad Hman Sci) Kluwer Academic.

— The Time of Your Life: Self-Time Management for Pastors. LC 93-45856. 144p. (Orig.). 1994. pap. 8.37 (*0-687-37137-6*) Abingdon.

— Walking Through the Valley: Understanding & Emerging from Clergy Depression. LC 97-42421. 144p. 1998. pap. 14.95 (*0-687-01463-8*) Abingdon.

Randall, Robert M., jt. auth. see Fahey, Liam.

***Randall, Rod.** Along Came a Spider, Vol. 7. LC 99-42992. (Heebie Jeebies Ser.: Vol. 7). 144p. (J). (gr. 3-7). 2000. pap. 5.99 (*0-8054-1981-0*) Broadman.

— I Scream the Truck. (Heebie Jeebies Ser.: Bk. 5). 1999. pap. 5.99 (*0-8054-1974-8*) Broadman.

— The Mysterious Treasure of the Slimy Sea Cave. LC 98-37534. (Heebie Jeebies Ser.: Vol. 3). 144p. (YA). 1999. pap. 5.99 (*0-8054-1000-7*) Broadman.

Randall, Rod. Welcome to Camp Creeps, Vol. 2. LC 98-14295. (Heebie Jeebies Ser.). 144p. (J). (gr. 1-6). 1998. pap. 5.99 (*0-8054-1195-X*) Broadman.

Randall, Rod, jt. auth. see Buchanan, Paul.

Randall, Ron, jt. auth. see Verheiden, Mark.

Randall, Rona. Arrogant Duke. large type ed. (Romance Ser.). 416p. 1993. 27.99 (*0-7089-2918-4*) Ulverscroft.

— Dragonmede. large type ed. (Ulverscroft Large Print Ser.). 528p. 1997. 27.99 (*0-7089-3782-9*) Ulverscroft.

— The Eagle at the Gate. large type ed. 608p. 1995. 27.99 (*0-7089-3420-X*) Ulverscroft.

***Randall, Rona.** The Frozen Ceiling. large type ed. 272p. 1999. 31.99 (*0-7089-4062-5*) Ulverscroft.

Randall, Rona. Knight's Keep. large type ed. (Romance Suspense Ser.). 432p. 1993. 27.99 (*0-7089-2973-7*) Ulverscroft.

— The Ladies of Hanover Square. large type ed. (Charnwood Large Print Ser.). 1994. 27.99 (*0-7089-8795-8*) Ulverscroft.

— Lyonhurst. large type ed. (Ulverscroft Large Print Ser.). 448p. 1997. 27.99 (*0-7089-3831-0*) Ulverscroft.

— Mountain of Fear. 1989. 18.00 (*0-7278-1760-4*) Severn Hse.

— Mountain of Fear. large type ed. 1995. 27.99 (*0-7089-3381-5*) Ulverscroft.

— The Potter's Niece. large type ed. 1990. 18.95 (*0-7089-2130-2*) Ulverscroft.

— Seven Days from Midnight. large type ed. (Large Print Ser.). 304p. 1997. 27.99 (*0-7089-3673-3*) Ulverscroft.

— The Watchman's Stone. large type ed. 464p. 1995. 27.99 (*0-7089-3280-0*) Ulverscroft.

— Writing Popular Fiction. 1998. pap. 18.95 (*0-7136-4731-0*, Pub. by A & C Blk) Midpt Trade.

Randall, Ronne. Baby Bunny's Book of Bedtime Dreams. (Illus.). 12p. (J). 1996. boxed set 15.95 (*1-884628-45-1*, Flyng Frog) Allied Pub MD.

— Daniel in the Lion's Den. (Illus.). 32p. (J). 1996. pap. 3.99 (*1-884628-27-3*, Flyng Frog) Allied Pub MD.

— David & Goliath. (Illus.). 32p. (J). 1996. pap. 3.99 (*1-884628-18-4*, Flyng Frog) Allied Pub MD.

— Disney's Pooh: Thank You, Pooh! (Illus.). 24p. (J). 1996. pap. text 1.29 (*0-307-98756-6*, Goldn Books) Gldn Bks Pub Co.

***Randall, Ronne.** Israel. LC 98-45756. 32p. (J). 1999. lib. bdg. 22.83 (*0-8172-5759-4*) Raintree Steck-V.

Randall, Ronne. Moses in the Bulrushes. (Illus.). 32p. (J). 1996. pap. 3.99 (*1-884628-26-5*, Flyng Frog) Allied Pub MD.

— Noah's Ark. (Illus.). 32p. (J). 1996. pap. 3.99 (*1-884628-17-6*, Flyng Frog) Allied Pub MD.

Randall, Ronne P. Baby Forest Animals. (Happytime Storybks.). (Illus.). 24p. (J). (ps). 1987. pap. 1.25 (*0-7214-9546-X*, S871-2, Ladybrd) Penguin Putnam.

— Gingerbread Man. (First Fairy Tales Ser.: No. S852-9). (J). 1988. boxed set 3.95 (*0-7214-5102-0*, Ladybrd) Penguin Putnam.

— The Little Red Hen. (Favorite Tales Ser.). (Illus.). 28p. (J). 1994. 2.99 (*0-7214-5394-5*, Ladybrd) Penguin Putnam.

— Marcus & Lionel. (Teddy Bear Tales Ser.: No. S897-5). (J). 1989. pap. 3.95 (*0-7214-5228-0*, Ladybrd) Penguin Putnam.

— One to Ten. (Happytime Ser.). (Illus.). 24p. (J). (ps). 1987. pap. 1.25 (*0-7214-9554-0*, S871-10, Ladybrd) Penguin Putnam.

— Opposites. (Happytime Ser.). (Illus.). 24p. (J). (ps). 1987. pap. 1.25 (*0-7214-9556-7*, S871, Ladybrd) Penguin Putnam.

Randall, Ronnie. Israel. (Food & Festivals Ser.). 32p. (J). (gr. 2-5). 1999. pap. 6.95 (*0-7398-0959-8*) Raintree Steck-V.

— Optical Illusions Lab: The Ultimate Optical Illusions Pack. (Science Lab Ser.). (Illus.). 32p. (J). (gr. 3-7). 1999. 19.95 (*1-57145-383-0*, Silver Dolph) Advantage Pubs.

— Sleeping Beauty. (First Fairy Tales Ser.: No. S852-7). (Illus.). (J). (ps-2). pap. 3.95 (*0-7214-5100-4*, Ladybrd) Penguin Putnam.

Randall, Ruth & Geiger, Keith. School Choice: Issues & Answers. LC 98-160764. 228p. (Orig.). 1991. pap. 21.95 (*1-879639-02-5*) Natl Educ Serv.

Randall, Sara L. & State Library of Iowa Staff. Up & Running: Implementing Z39.50: Proceedings of a Symposium Sponsored by the State Library of Iowa, November 26, 1996, Ames, Iowa. LC 98-10255. (National Information Standards Ser.). 54p. 1998. pap. 39.00 (*1-880124-33-5*) NISO.

Randall, Sidney. ABC of the Old Science of Astrology for Beginners. (Illus.). 114p. 1998. reprint ed. pap. 14.95 (*0-7661-0437-0*) Kessinger Pub.

Randall, Stephen J. Colombia & the United States: Hegemony & Interdependence. LC 91-17739. (United States & the Americas Ser.). (Illus.). 344p. 1992. 40.00 (*0-8203-1401-3*); pap. 20.00 (*0-8203-1402-1*) U of Ga Pr.

— The Diplomacy of Modernization: Colombian-American Relations 1920-1940. LC 77-4480. 251p. reprint ed. pap. 77.90 (*0-608-18378-4*, 202644000049) Bks Demand.

— United States Foreign Oil Policy, 1919-1948: For Profits & Security. 320p. 1985. 60.00 (*0-7735-0449-4*, Pub. by McG-Queens Univ Pr) CUP Services.

Randall, Stephen J. & Mount, Graeme S. The Caribbean Basin: An International History. LC 97-40734. (New International History Ser.). 224p. (C). 1998. 65.00 (*0-415-08998-0*); pap. 22.99 (*0-415-08999-9*) Routledge.

Randall, Stephen J., jt. auth. see Thompson, John H.

Randall, Steve, ed. see Tulku, Tarthang.

Randall, Steven, tr. see Le Goff, Jacques.

***Randall, Susan.** Thomas Food Industry Register Buying Guide. 2400p. 2000. 75.00 (*1-882554-51-5*) Thomas Pub NY.

Randall, T. E. History of the Chippewa Valley: Faithful Record of All Important Events, Incidents & Circumstances That Have Transpired in the Valley of the Chippewa from Its Earliest Settlement by White People...; Also of the Counties Embracing the Valley...; Also a Brief Biographical Sketch of the... (Illus.). 207p. 1997. reprint ed. lib. bdg. 29.00 (*0-8328-6964-3*) Higginson Bk Co.

Randall, Tom, jt. auth. see Culbertson, Judi.

Randall, V. A., jt. auth. see Van Neste, D.

Randall, Veronica, jt. auth. see Spears, Grady.

***Randall, Vicky.** The Politics of Child Daycare in Britain. 260p. 2000. text 65.00 (*0-19-828048-3*) OUP.

Randall, Vicky. Women & Politics: An International Perspective. xii, 362p. 1997. pap. text 15.95 (*0-226-70332-4*) U Ch Pr.

— Women & Politics: An International Perspective. 2nd ed. xii, 374p. 1988. lib. bdg. 39.00 (*0-226-70391-6*) U Ch Pr.

Randall, Vicky, ed. Democratization & the Media. LC 98-6865. 258p. 1998. 42.50 (*0-7146-4894-9*, Pub. by F Cass Pubs); pap. 19.50 (*0-7146-4446-3*, Pub. by F Cass Pubs) Intl Spec Bk.

— Political Parties in the Third World. 256p. (C). 1988. text 69.95 (*0-8039-8143-0*); pap. text 16.95 (*0-8039-8144-9*) Sage.

Randall, Vicky & Theobald, Robin. Political Change & Underdevelopment: A Critical Introduction to Third World Politics. LC 85-10176. ix, 215p. 1985. text 49.95 (*0-8223-0564-X*); pap. text 18.95 (*0-8223-0662-X*) Duke.

— Political Change & Underdevelopment: A Critical Introduction to Third World Politics. 2nd ed. LC 97-52380. 1998. write for info. (*0-8223-2079-7*) Duke.

— Political Change & Underdevelopment: A Critical Introduction To Third World Politics. 2nd ed. LC 97-52380. 1998. pap. 18.95 (*0-8223-2093-2*) Duke.

Randall, Vicky & Waylen, Georgina, eds. Gender Politics & the State. LC 98-9382. 224p. (C). 1998. 85.00 (*0-415-16401-X*); pap. 24.99 (*0-415-16402-8*) Routledge.

Randall, Vicky, ed. see Deegan, Heather.

Randall, Vicky, ed. see Haynes, Jeff.

Randall, Vicky, ed. see Pinkney, Robert.

Randall, Vicky, ed. see Waylen, Georgina.

Randall, Warren, jt. auth. see Brodie, Robert.

Randall, Whiffer. Sir Gordon: Pig of Pigs. (Illus.). 76p. (J). 1996. pap. write for info. (*1-57579-051-3*) Pine Hill Pr.

Randall, Willard. George Washington. 512p. 1998. pap. 15.95 (*0-8050-5992-X*, Owl) H Holt & Co.

Randall, Willard S. Alexander Hamilton: A Life. 528p. 2000. 35.00 (*0-8050-5897-4*) H Holt & Co.

— American Lives, Vol. 2. LC 96-11929. Vol. 2. 320p. (C). 1997. pap. text 39.06 (*0-673-46987-5*, GoodYrBooks) Addson-Wesley Educ.

— George Washington. LC 97-19125. 512p. 1995. 35.00 (*0-8050-2779-3*) H Holt & Co.

— Thomas Jefferson: A Life. 736p. 1995. 35.00 (*0-8050-1577-9*, J Macrae Bks) H Holt & Co.

— Thomas Jefferson: A Life. LC 94-14363. 736p. 1994. pap. 20.00 (*0-06-097617-9*) HarpC.

Randall, Willard S. & Nahra, Nancy. American Lives, Vol. 1. LC 96-11929. Vol. 1. 320p. (C). 1997. pap. text 39.06 (*0-673-46986-7*) Addson-Wesley Educ.

— Forgotten Americans: Footnote Figures Who Changed American History. 288p. 1999. pap. text 15.00 (*0-7382-0150-2*, Pub. by Perseus Pubng) HarpC.

Randall, William L. The Stories We Are: An Essay on Self-Creation. 288p. 1995. text 45.00 (*0-8020-0564-0*); pap. text 19.95 (*0-8020-6986-X*) U of Toronto Pr.

***Randall, William L. & Kenyon, Gary M.** Ordinary Wisdom: Biographical Aging & the Journey of Life. LC 00-22889. 240p. 2000. 59.00 (*0-275-96556-2*, C6556, Praeger Pubs) Greenwood.

Randall, William L., jt. auth. see Kenyon, Gary M.

***Randa's Road Trips Staff.** Randa's Road Trips: To Monterey & Carmel with Map. 1998. audio 15.95 (*1-893402-00-2*) Randa Road.

Randau, Karen, ed. Country Profile - Bangladesh: A Social Studies/Mission Unit. (Teaching Your Child God's Love for the World - Uganda Ser.). Date not set. 9.99 (*0-939989-10-7*) Food for Hungry Inc.

— Country Profile - Bolivia: A Social Studies/Mission Unit - Bolivia. (Teaching Your Child God's Love for the World - Uganda Ser.: Vol. 3). 1996. 9.99 (*0-939989-02-6*) Food for Hungry Inc.

— Country Profile - Dominican Republic: A Social Studies/Mission Unit. (Teaching Your Child God's Love for the World - Uganda Ser.). Date not set. 9.99 (*0-939989-08-5*) Food for Hungry Inc.

— Country Profile - Guatemala: A Social Studies/Mission Unit. (Teaching Your Child God's Love for the World - Uganda Ser.). Date not set. 9.99 (*0-939989-04-2*) Food for Hungry Inc.

— Country Profile - Kenya: A Social Studies/Mission Unit. (Teaching Your Child God's Love for the World - Uganda Ser.). Date not set. 9.99 (*0-939989-05-0*) Food for Hungry Inc.

— Country Profile - Mozambique: A Social Studies/Mission Unit. (Teaching Your Child God's Love for the World - Uganda Ser.). Date not set. 9.99 (*0-939989-09-3*) Food for Hungry Inc.

— Country Profile - Peru: A Social Studies/Mission Unit. (Teaching Your Child God's Love for the World - Uganda Ser.). Date not set. 9.99 (*0-939989-07-7*) Food for Hungry Inc.

— Country Profile - Philippines: A Social Studies/Mission Unit - Philippines. (Teaching Your Child Gods Love for the World Ser.: Vol. 4). 1996. 9.99 (*0-939989-03-4*) Food for Hungry Inc.

— Country Profile - Thailand: A Social Studies/Mission Unit. (Teaching Your Child God's Love for the World - Uganda Ser.). Date not set. 9.99 (*0-939989-06-9*) Food for Hungry Inc.

— Country Profile - Uganda: A Social Studies/Mission Unity-Uganda. (Teaching Your Child God's Love for the World - Uganda Ser.: Vol. 2). 1996. 9.99 (*0-939989-01-8*) Food for Hungry Inc.

— Teaching Your Child God's Love for the World Vol. 1: A Social Studies/Mission Unit Study Guide. (Illus.). 160p. 1996. ring bd. 29.99 (*0-939989-00-X*) Food for Hungry Inc.

Randazzo, Angela. Bats in the Belfry. 1975. pap. 5.50 (*0-87129-360-9*, B12) Dramatic Pub.

***Randazzo, Angela.** The Tiger Turned Pink. 35p. 1999. pap. 3.50 (*0-87129-944-5*, TB8) Dramatic Pub.

Randazzo, Anthony F. & Jones, Douglas S., eds. The Geology of Florida. LC 96-28022. (Illus.). 400p. 1997. 39.95 (*0-8130-1496-4*) U Press Fla.

Randazzo, Deborah, et al. Activities for Everyone: Children of All Abilities in a Regular Physical Activity Program. Seaman, Janet A., ed. (Illus.). 210p. 1997. pap. 25.00 (*0-88314-650-9*, 302-10094) AAHPERD.

Randazzo, Sela W. I Am Rock-Medicine. 102p. 1996. pap. 20.00 (*0-9653352-1-6*) Lifeforce Publns.

Rande, Wallace. Bar & Beverage Management. 400p. (C). 2000. 59.33 (*0-13-375924-5*, Macmillan Coll) P-H.

Rande, Wallace L. Introduction to Professional Foodservice. 352p. 1995. pap. text, teacher ed. write for info. (*0-471-30620-7*) Wiley.

— Introduction to Professional Foodservice. LC 95-13388. 296p. 1995. student ed., wbk. ed. 54.95 (*0-471-57746-4*) Wiley.

Randel, Don M. Harvard Concise Dictionary of Music. LC 78-5948. (Illus.). 584p. 1978. text 22.50 (*0-674-37471-1*); pap. text 16.50 (*0-674-37470-3*) Belknap Pr.

— Harvard Dictionary of Music: Diccionario Harvard de Musica. (SPA.). 559p. 1984. 49.95 (*0-8288-2184-4*, F138171) Fr & Eur.

— An Index to the Chant of the Mozarabic Rite. LC 72-5384. (Princeton Studies in Music: No. 6). 692p. reprint ed. pap. 200.00 (*0-608-10868-5*, 201140000075) Bks Demand.

Randel, Don M., ed. The Harvard Biographical Dictionary of Music. LC 96-16456. (Illus.). 1128p. 1996. 39.95 (*0-674-37299-9*) Belknap Pr.

— The Harvard Concise Dictionary of Music & Musicians. LC 99-40644. (Illus.). 800p. 1999. 35.00 (*0-674-00084-6*) HUP.

— The New Harvard Dictionary of Music. LC 86-4780. (Illus.). 1024p. 1986. text 39.95 (*0-674-61525-5*) Belknap Pr.

Randel, Judith, jt. auth. see German, Tony.

Randel, Mary G. The Historical Prose of Fernando de Herrera. (Monografias A Ser.: Vol. XX). 206p. (Orig.). (C). 1970. pap. 51.00 (*0-900411-16-3*, Pub. by Tamesis Bks Ltd) Boydell & Brewer.

Randel, William P., ed. see Eggleston, Edward.

Randell, Brian, ed. The Origins of Digital Computers. 3rd ed. (Texts & Monographs in Computer Science). (Illus.). 598p. 1982. 87.00 (*0-387-11319-3*) Spr-Verlag.

Randell, Geoff. Branding. (Marketing & Sales Ser.). 1997. pap. 24.95 (*0-7494-2126-6*) Kogan Page Ltd.

Randell, Gerry, et al. Staff Appraisal: A First Step to Effective Leadership. rev. ed. 128p. (C). 1984. 48.00 (*0-85292-333-3*, Pub. by IPM Hse) St Mut.

Randell, J., jt. ed. see Hardy, Lammers.

***Randell, Janet.** In Him We Move: Creative Dancing in Worship. (Illus.). 240p. 1999. reprint ed. pap. 30.00 (*1-900507-83-8*, Pub. by Solway) OM Literature.

Randell, Joan. Crystal Clear. 176p. 1995. boxed set 39.95 (*0-7872-1001-3*) Kendall-Hunt.

Randell, Kimberly. In the Midnight Hour. (A Haunting Hearts Romance Ser.). 304p. 1999. 5.99 (*0-515-12483-4*, Jove) Berkley Pub.

Randell, R. Singularities. LC 89-6662. (Contemporary Mathematics Ser.: Vol. 90). 359p. 1989. pap. 50.00 (*0-8218-5096-2*, CONM/90) Am Math.

Randell, Roscoe. Radiation Curing/Polymers, II, No. 89. 1991. 128.00 (*0-85186-377-9*) CRC Pr.

Randell, Roscoe & Neagel. Surface Analysis Techniques & Applications, No. 84. 1990. 109.00 (*0-85186-597-6*) CRC Pr.

RanDelle, B. J. & Marshbum, Sandra. Lessons in Love. LC 24-476. (Illus.). 64p. (J). (gr. k-4). 1982. text 5.95 (*0-910445-00-1*) Randelle Pubns.

Randelli, M. R. Surgical Techniques for the Shoulder. 224p. 1995. text 108.00 (*88-7744-006-6*) Gordon & Breach.

Randelman, Mary U. Memories of a Cuban Kitchen. 352p. 1996. 16.95 (*0-02-860998-0*, Pub. by Macmillan) S&S Trade.

Randelzhofer, Albrecht & Tomuschat, Christian. State Responsibility & the Individual: Reparation in Instances of Grave Violation of Human Rights. LC 98-54614. xiii, 296p. 1999. 105.00 (*90-411-1147-6*) Kluwer Law Intl.

Randeraad, Nico. Authority in Search of Liberty: The Prefects in Liberal Italy. (Scrinium VII). 220p. 1993. 53.00 (*90-5170-218-3*, Pub. by Thesis Pubs) D Brown Bk Co.

Randeria, Jer D. The Parsi Mind: A Zoroastrian Asset to Culture. 175p. (C). 1993. 33.50 (*81-215-0560-7*, Pub. by M Manoharial) Coronet Bks.

Randers, Jorgen, ed. Elements of the System Dynamics Method. LC 79-20019. (Illus.). 320p. 1980. pap. text 50.00 (*1-883823-44-7*, XELEM) Pegasus Comm.

— Elements of the System Dynamics Method. LC 79-20019. 344p. (C). 1979. reprint ed. pap. text 50.00 (*0-915299-39-9*) Productivity Inc.

Randers-Pehrson, Justine D. Barbarians & Romans: The Birth Struggle of Europe A. D. 400-700. LC 82-20025. 400p. 1993. pap. 16.95 (*0-8061-2511-X*) U of Okla Pr.

***Randers-Pehrson, Justine D.** Germans & the Revolution of 1848-1849. LC 98-29251. (New German-American Studies - Neue Deutsch-Amerikanische Studien: Vol. 18). (Illus.). XIII, 585p. (C). 1999. text 69.95 (*0-8204-4118-X*) P Lang Pubng.

Randerson, Jane, jt. auth. see Gress, Susan.

Randey, Pajendra. Social Inequality: Features, Forms & Functions. 317p. 1982. 34.95 (*0-317-13625-9*, Pub. by Anuja) Asia Bk Corp.

Randhawa, Bikkar S., jt. ed. see Leong, Che K.

Randhawa, Bikki K., jt. auth. see Sacay, Orlando J.

Randhawa, D. S., jt. auth. see Randhawa, M. S.

Randhawa, G. S. Ornamental Horticulture in India. (Illus.). 144p. 1973. 8.00 (*1-55528-089-7*, Pub. by Today Tomorrow) Scholarly Pubns.

An Asterisk (*) at the beginning of an entry indicates that the title is appearing for the first time.

Randhawa, G. S. & Mukhopadhyay, A. Floriculture in India. 1986. 38.00 (*81-7023-057-8*, Pub. by Allied Pubs) S Asia.

Randhawa, G. S. & Srivastava, K. C. Citriculture in India. (C). 1986. 62.00 (*0-8364-2420-4*, Pub. by Hindustan) S Asia.

Randhawa, M. S. Basohli Painting. 116p. 1981. 49.95 (*0-940500-92-2*, Pub. by Pubns Div) Asia Bk Corp.

— Kangra Paintings of the Bihari Sat Sai. (Illus.). 87p. 1982. 49.95 (*0-318-36339-9*) Asia Bk Corp.

— Kangra Paintings of the Gita Govinda. (Illus.). 132p. 1982. 85.00 (*0-318-36340-2*) Asia Bk Corp.

— Kangra Valley Painting. (Illus.). 68p. 1982. 34.95 (*0-318-36341-0*) Asia Bk Corp.

— Paintings of the Babur Nama. 139p. 1983. 80.00 (*0-318-36345-3*) Asia Bk Corp.

Randhawa, M. S. & Randhawa, D. S. Guler Paintings. (Illus.). 60p. 1982. 32.95 (*0-318-36336-4*) Asia Bk Corp.

— Kishangarh Painting. (Illus.). 46p. 1980. 32.95 (*0-318-36342-9*) Asia Bk Corp.

Randhawa, Maninder S. The Rural & Urban Aged. (C). 1991. 28.00 (*81-85135-55-X*, Pub. by Natl Bk Orgn) S Asia.

Randhawa, Simran P. Eurofashion... Unleashing the Designer in You. LC 92-70333. (Illus.). 180p. (Orig.). 1992. pap. 24.95 (*0-9631974-9-5*) Immis Pub.

Randhawa, T. S. The Last Wanderers: Nomads & Gypsies of India. 227p. 1996. 65.00 (*81-85822-16-6*, Pub. by Mapin Pubng) Antique Collect.

Randhofer, Regina. Psalmen in Einstimmigen Vokalen Uberlieferungen: Eine Vergleichende Untersuchung Judischer und Christlicher Traditionen, 2 vols. (Europaische Hochschulschriften Ser.: Reihe 36, Bd. 131). (GER., Illus.). XII, 286p. 1995. 68.95 (*3-631-48037-7*) P Lang Pubng.

Randi, James. Conjuring. (Illus.). 336p. 1993. pap. 19.95 (*0-312-09771-9*) St Martin.

— Encyclopedia of Claims, Frauds, & Hoaxes. LC 96-47870. 336p. 1997. pap. 14.95 (*0-312-15119-5*) St Martin.

— The Faith Healers. rev. ed. LC 87-17241. (Illus.). 324p. 1987. 20.95 (*0-87975-369-2*) Prometheus Bks.

— The Faith Healers. rev. ed. LC 87-17241. (Illus.). 328p. 1989. pap. 19.95 (*0-87975-535-0*) Prometheus Bks.

— Flim-Flam! The Truth about Unicorns, Parapsychology, & Other Delusions. LC 82-60953. (Illus.). 358p. 1982. reprint ed. pap. 18.95 (*0-87975-198-3*) Prometheus Bks.

— Magic World of Amazing Randi. 168p. 1989. pap. 10.95 (*1-55850-982-8*) Adams Media.

— The Mask of Nostradamus: The Prophecies of the World's Most Famous Seer. LC 92-41554. (Illus.). 270p. (C). 1993. reprint ed. pap. 19.95 (*0-87975-830-9*) Prometheus Bks.

— The Truth about Uri Geller. rev. ed. LC 82-60951. (Illus.). 242p. 1982. pap. 20.95 (*0-87975-199-1*) Prometheus Bks.

Randic, M. & Trinajstic, Nenad. On the Relative Stabilities of Conjugated Heterocycles Containing Divalent Sulfur (SR) 48p. 1986. pap. text 53.00 (*3-7186-0372-1*) Gordon & Breach.

Randich, Keith. Carving the Little Guys: An Introductory Text by Keith Randich. LC 91-91341. (Illus.). 60p. (Orig.). 1991. pap. 9.95 (*0-9642327-0-7*) K Randich Pubng.

— Carving the Little Sailors: An Introductory Text by Keith Randich. LC 93-92743. (Illus.). 80p. (Orig.). 1993. pap. 10.95 (*0-9642327-1-5*) K Randich Pubng.

— Old Time Whittling: An Introductory Text by Keith Randich. LC 94-92208. (Illus.). 60p. (Orig.). 1994. pap. 9.95 (*0-9642327-2-3*) K Randich Pubng.

Randisi, Jennifer L. On Her Way Rejoicing: The Fiction of Muriel Spark. LC 90-32628. (Contexts & Literature Ser.: Vol. 3). 129p. 1991. text 29.95 (*0-8132-0730-4*) Cath U Pr.

— A Tissue of Lies: Eudora Welty & the Southern Romance. LC 82-45042. 198p. (Orig.). (C). 1982. pap. text 24.00 (*0-8191-2452-4*); lib. bdg. 55.00 (*0-8191-2451-6*) U Pr of Amer.

***Randisi, Robert J.** Alone with the Dead. 368p. 1999. reprint ed. 5.50 (*0-8439-4641-5*, Pub. by Dorchester Pub Co) CMG.

Randisi, Robert J. Blood on the Arch: A Joe Keough Mystery. 256p. 2000. text 22.95 (*0-312-24179-8*) St Martin.

— Full Contact: A Miles Jacoby Mystery. 2000. mass mkt. 2.95 (*0-380-69984-2*, Avon Bks) Morrow Avon.

***Randisi, Robert J.** The Ghost with Blue Eyes. 224p. 1999. mass mkt. 4.50 (*0-8439-4571-0*, Pub. by Dorchester Pub Co) CMG.

— In the Shadow of the Arch. (Joe Keough Mysteries Ser.). 368p. 2000. pap. 4.99 (*0-8439-4761-6*, Leisure Bks) Dorchester Pub Co.

Randisi, Robert J. In the Shadow of the Arch. LC 97-34708. 368p. 1997. text 24.95 (*0-312-18115-9*) St Martin.

***Randisi, Robert J.** New & Classic Tales of Detection, Vol. 3. (First Cases Ser.). 288p. 1999. mass mkt. write for info. (*0-451-19892-1*, Sig) NAL.

Randisi, Robert J. Separate Cases. 192p. 1990. 18.95 (*0-8027-5723-5*) Walker & Co.

***Randisi, Robert J.** Shamus Game. 2000. mass mkt. 6.50 (*0-451-20129-9*, Sig) NAL.

— The Sixth Phase. 400p. 1999. mass mkt. 5.99 (*0-8439-4651-2*, Leisure Bks) Dorchester Pub Co.

Randisi, Robert J. Stand-Up: A Miles Jacoby Mystery. LC 94-18377. 246p. 1994. 20.95 (*0-8027-3196-1*) Walker & Co.

— Targett. 176p. 1997. reprint ed. mass mkt. 3.99 (*0-8439-4337-8*, Leisure Bks) Dorchester Pub Co.

Randisi, Robert J., ed. An Eye for Justice. 224p. 1989. 9.95 (*0-89296-979-2*); pap. 9.95 (*0-685-67688-9*) Mysterious Pr.

— The Eyes Have It: The First Private Eye Writers of America Anthology. 336p. 1987. 8.95 (*0-89296-906-7*) Mysterious Pr.

— Justice for Hire: The Fourth Private Eye Writers of American Anthology. 256p. 1990. 18.45 (*0-89296-371-9*, Pub. by Mysterious Pr) Little.

— Justice for Hire: The Fourth Private Eye Writers of American Anthology. deluxe limited ed. 256p. 1990. 75.00 (*0-89296-425-1*) Mysterious Pr.

***Randisi, Robert J., ed.** Tin Star. 2000. mass mkt. 5.99 (*0-425-17405-0*) Berkley Pub.

Randisi, Robert J., ed. Writing the Private Eye Novel: A Handbook by the Private Eye Writers of America. LC 97-13699. 240p. 1997. 18.99 (*0-89879-767-5*, Wrtrs Digest Bks) F & W Pubns Inc.

Randisi, Robert J., et al. Legend. 400p. 1999. mass mkt. 5.99 (*0-8439-4496-X*) Dorchester Pub Co.

Randisi, Robert J., jt. auth. see Matthews, Christine.

Randjbar-Dacmi, S., et al, eds. Recent Developments in Conformal Field Theories: Trieste Conference. 320p. (C). 1990. pap. text 37.00 (*981-02-0280-6*); text 101.00 (*981-02-0279-2*) World Scientific Pub.

Randjbar-Daemi, S. & Lu, Yu. Quantum Field Theory & Condensed Matter Physics: Proceedings of the 4th Trieste Conference on Quantum Field. 148p. 1994. text 53.00 (*981-02-1622-X*) World Scientific Pub.

Randklev, James. Florida: A Book of 30 Postcards. 1995. pap. text 8.95 (*1-56313-774-7*) BrownTrout Pubs Inc.

— Georgia Images of Wildness. 128p. 1992. pap. 19.95 (*1-56579-008-1*) Westcliffe Pubs.

Randklev, James, photos by. Wild & Scenic Florida. LC 95-35810. (Illus.). 128p. 1995. write for info. (*1-56313-702-X*) BrownTrout Pubs Inc.

Randle, Damian. Natural Resources. LC 93-25195. (Young Geographer Ser.). (Illus.). 32p. (J). 1993. lib. bdg. 21.40 (*1-56847-056-8*) Raintree Steck-V.

Randle, Dave. Baby Fiats. 1999. pap. text 19.95 (*0-7509-2211-7*) A Sutton.

Randle, Deatrice. Transitional Guide to College. 1998. pap. 30.00 (*0-938609-25-4*) Graduate Group.

Randle, Guy, jt. auth. see Payne, Marvin.

Randle, Kevin. Faces of the Visitors: An Illustrated Reference to Alien Contact. LC 97-30932. (Illus.). 320p. 1997. pap. 12.00 (*0-684-83973-3*, Fireside) S&S Trade Pap.

— Galactic MI. 208p. (Orig.). 1993. mass mkt. 4.50 (*0-441-27238-X*) Ace Bks.

— Lost Gold & Buried Treasure: A Treasure Hunter's Guide to 250 Fortunes Waiting to Be Found. LC 95-34592. (Illus.). 288p. 1995. 19.95 (*0-87131-792-3*) M Evans.

— Project Blue Book Exposed. 288p. 1998. pap. 14.95 (*1-56924-691-2*) Marlowe & Co.

— The Randle Report. (Illus.). 256p. 1998. pap. 14.95 (*0-87131-859-8*) M Evans.

— The Randle Report: UFOs in the '90s. LC 96-29946. (Illus.). 256p. 1997. 19.95 (*0-87131-820-2*) M Evans.

— The Rat Trap. (Galactic MI Ser.: No. 2). 1993. pap. 4.50 (*0-441-27243-6*) Ace Bks.

***Randle, Kevin.** Spaceships of the Visitors: An Illustrated Guide to Alien Spacecraft. 352p. 2000. per. 14.00 (*0-684-85739-1*) S&S Trade.

***Randle, Kevin D.** Abduction Enigma. 2000. mass mkt. 5.99 (*0-8125-8030-3*) Tor Bks.

Randle, Kevin D. Conspiracy of Silence: From Roswell to Project Blue Book--What the Government Doesn't Want You to Know about UFOs. LC 96-40863. 336p. 1997. pap. 12.50 (*0-380-72691-2*, Avon Bks) Morrow Avon.

— Conspiracy of Silence: From Roswell to Project Blue Book--What the Government Doesn't Want You to Know about UFOs. 384p. 1998. mass mkt. 6.99 (*0-380-79918-9*, Avon Bks) Morrow Avon.

— History of Ufo Crashes. LC 94-96569. 296p. 1995. mass mkt. 5.99 (*0-380-77666-9*, Avon Bks) Morrow Avon.

— The October Scenario. LC 88-1669. (Illus.). 176p. (Orig.). pap. 9.95 (*0-934523-35-5*) Middle Coast Pub.

— Project Moon Dust: Beyond Roswell--Exposing the Government's Continuing Covert UFO Investigation. 328p. 1999. mass mkt. 6.99 (*0-380-80603-7*, Avon Bks) Morrow Avon.

***Randle, Kevin D.** The Roswell Encyclopedia. (Illus.). 448p. 2000. pap. 15.00 (*0-380-79853-0*, Quil) HarperTrade.

Randle, Kevin D. Roswell UFO Crash Update: Exposing the Military Coverup of the Century. 15.00 (*0-938294-41-5*) Inner Light.

— Scientific Ufology: How the Application of Scientific Methodology Can Analyze, Illuminate & Prove the Reality of UFO's. 256p. 1999. pap. 12.50 (*0-380-79852-2*, Avon Bks) Morrow Avon.

***Randle, Kevin D.** Scientific Ufology: Roswell & Beyond--How Scientific Methodology Can Prove the Reality of Ufos. (Illus.). 256p. 2000. mass mkt. 6.99 (*0-380-81383-1*, HarpTorch) Morrow Avon.

Randle, Kevin D. To Touch the Light. 320p. 1994. mass mkt. 4.99 (*0-7860-0047-3*, Pinncle Kensgtn) Kensgtn Pub Corp.

— The UFO Casebook. 256p. (Orig.). 1989. mass mkt. 5.99 (*0-446-35715-4*, Pub. by Warner Bks) Little.

***Randle, Kevin D. & Cone, William P.** The Abduction Enigma. 2000. pap. 16.95 (*0-312-87270-4*) St Martin.

Randle, Kevin D. & Cornett, Robert. Remember the Alamo! large type ed. LC 97-42239. 1997. 21.95 (*0-7838-8351-X*, G K Hall Lrg Type) Mac Lib Ref.

Randle, Kevin D. & Schmitt, Donald R. The Truth about the UFO Crash at Roswell. 336p. 1994. mass mkt. 6.99 (*0-380-77803-3*, Avon Bks) Morrow Avon.

— UFO Crash at Roswell. 352p. (Orig.). 1991. mass mkt. 6.99 (*0-380-76196-3*, Avon Bks) Morrow Avon.

Randle, Kevin D., et al. Alien Rape: An Investigation of the Alien Abduction Phenomenon. LC 99-23888. 416p. 1999. 25.95 (*0-312-86708-5*, Pub. by Forge NYC) St Martin.

Randle, Kristen D. Breaking Rank. (gr. 7 up). pap. 4.95 (*0-380-73281-5*) Morrow Avon.

Randle, Kristen D. Breaking Rank. (J). 1999. lib. bdg. write for info. (*0-688-16244-4*, Wm Morrow) Morrow Avon.

***Randle, Kristen D.** Breaking Rank. LC 98-27867. 208p. (J). 1999. 15.95 (*0-688-16243-6*, Wm Morrow) Morrow Avon.

Randle, Kristen D. Breaking Rank. 1998. pap. 16.99 (*0-525-67570-1*, Dutton Child) Peng Put Young Read.

— The Only Alien on the Planet. LC 93-34594. 228p. (J). (gr. 8 up). 1996. pap. 4.99 (*0-590-46310-1*) Scholastic Inc.

Randle, Kristen D. The Only Alien on the Planet. LC 93-34594. (J). 1995. 10.09 (*0-606-11710-5*, Pub. by Turtleback) Demco.

Randle, Kristen D. Why Did Grandma Have to Die? (J). 1987. pap. 5.95 (*0-88494-621-5*) Bookcraft Inc.

Randle, Michael. People Power: The Building of a New European Home. (Conflict & Peacemaking Ser.). (Illus.). 256p. 1991. 16.95 (*1-869890-29-9*, Pub. by Hawthorn Press) Anthroposophic.

Randle, Michael & Rogers, Paul. Alternatives in European Security. (Illus.). 175p. 1990. 61.95 (*1-85521-050-9*, Pub. by Dartmth Pub) Ashgate Pub Co.

Randle, Michael C., ed. Birmingham's Best. (Illus.). 125p. (Orig.). 1989. pap. 4.95 (*1-878225-01-4*) First Pub Inc.

Randle, Michael C. & McWhorter, Mitzi, eds. Birmingham's Commercial Real Estate - Review & Forecast. (Illus.). 1989. pap. 2.95 (*0-685-29149-9*) First Pub Inc.

Randle, Michael C. & White, Colleen, eds. Birmingham's Health Care - Review & Forecast. (Illus.). 1989. pap. 2.95 (*0-685-29150-2*) First Pub Inc.

Randle, Robert. Making Peace with Germany, 1918: The Pre-Armistice Negotiations. (Pew Case Studies in International Affairs). 50p. (C). 1993. pap. text 3.50 (*1-56927-435-5*) Geo U Inst Dplmcy.

Randle, Robert F. Issues in the History of International Relations: The Role of Issues in the Evolution of the State System. LC 87-14614. 320p. 1987. 75.00 (*0-275-92700-8*, C2700, Praeger Pubs) Greenwood.

Randle, Sonja, et al, eds. The Heritage of Cleburne County, Alabama. (Heritage of Alabama Ser.: No. 15). (Illus.). 540p. 1998. 55.00 (*1-891647-03-2*) Herit Pub Consult.

Randle, V. The Measurement of Grain Boundary Geometry. (Electron Microscopy in Materials Science Ser.). (Illus.). 184p. 1993. 147.00 (*0-7503-0235-6*) IOP Pub.

Randle, Valerie. Microtexture Determination & Its Application. 192p. 1992. 80.00 (*0-901716-35-9*, Pub. by Inst Materials) Ashgate Pub Co.

— The Role of the Coincidence Site Lattice in Grain Boundary Engineering. (Illus.). 128p. 1996. 70.00 (*1-86125-006-1*, Pub. by Inst Materials) Ashgate Pub Co.

***Randle, Valerie & Engler, Olaf.** Introduction to Texture Analysis: Macrotexture, Microtexture & Orientation Mapping. 280p. 2000. text 95.00 (*90-5699-224-4*, G & B Science) Gordon & Breach.

Randle, Yvonne, jt. auth. see Flamholtz, Eric G.

Randler, Ted. The Guessing Game. 200p. 1999. 24.00 (*1-928662-00-5*) Palari Pubg.

Randles. Mind Monsters. 1990. pap. 9.95 (*0-85030-829-1*, Pub. by Aqrn Pr) Harper SF.

Randles, Bill. Making War in the Heavenlies: A Different Look at Spiritual Warfare. (Illus.). 193p. (Orig.). 1994. pap. 10.00 (*0-9646626-0-4*) B Randles.

— Weighed & Found Wanting: Putting the Toronto Blessing in Context. (Illus.). 249p. (Orig.). 1995. pap. 10.00 (*0-9646626-1-2*) B Randles.

***Randles, Bill, et al, eds.** The Midnight Ride. (Illus.). 288p. 2000. pap. 14.99 (*1-885831-08-0*) Proclaim Pubng.

Randles, Harry E. Stories for Tight Places. LC 89-91744. 156p. (Orig.). 1990. pap. 1.95 (*0-9623219-0-7*) H Randles.

Randles, Jenny. Alien Contact: The First Fifty Years. LC 97-13332. (Illus.). 144p. 1997. pap. text 12.95 (*0-8069-0476-3*) Sterling.

— Alien Contacts & Abductions: The Real Story from the Other Side. LC 94-20750. (Illus.). 196p. 1994. pap. 9.95 (*0-8069-0751-7*) Sterling.

***Randles, Jenny.** Complete Book of Alien Abductions. (Illus.). 192p. 2000. 29.95 (*0-7499-1956-6*, Pub. by Piatkus Bks) London Brdge.

Randles, Jenny. Life after Death & the World Beyond: Investing Heaven & Sporotual Dimension. 1998. text 24.95 (*0-7499-1681-8*, Pub. by Piatkus Bks) London Brdge.

***Randles, Jenny.** The Little Giant Encyclopedia of UFOs. (Illus.). 512p. 2000. pap. 9.95 (*0-8069-1891-8*) Sterling.

— Looking for the Aliens. (UFO Files Ser.). (Illus.). 241p. 2000. pap. 9.95 (*0-7137-2800-0*) Blandford Pr.

Randles, Jenny. The Paranormal Source Book: The Comprehensive Guide to Strange Phenomena Worldwide. (Illus.). 256p. 1997. pap. 14.95 (*0-7499-1411-4*, Pub. by Piatkus Bks) London Brdge.

***Randles, Jenny.** The Paranormal Source Book: The Comprehensive Guide to Strange Phenomena Worldwide. (Illus.). 1998. pap. 14.95 (*0-7499-1884-5*, Pub. by Piatkus Bks) London Brdge.

Randles, Jenny. The Sixth Sense: Psychic Powers & Your Five Senses. 240p. (C). 1987. 75.00 (*0-7090-2802-4*) St Mut.

— Something in the Air. 192p. 1997. 19.95 (*0-7090-5974-4*) Parkwest Pubns.

— Star Children: The True Story of Alien Offspring among Us. LC 95-30212. 224p. 1995. pap. 10.95 (*0-8069-3856-0*) Sterling.

— Strange & Unexplained Mysteries of the 20th Century. LC 93-45608. Orig. Title: The Unexplained. (Illus.). 144p. 1994. pap. 14.95 (*0-8069-0768-1*) Sterling.

— Truly Weird: Real-Life Cases of the Paranormal. (Illus.). 144p. 1999. pap. 12.95 (*1-85585-442-2*, Pub. by Collins & Br) Sterling.

— The Truth Behind Men in Black. LC 98-158677. 1997. mass mkt. 5.99 (*0-312-96521-4*) St Martin.

— UFO Crash Landing: Friend or Foe? LC 98-177423. (Illus.). 232p. 1998. 12.95 (*0-7137-2655-5*, Pub. by Blandford Pr) Sterling.

— UFO! Danger in the Air. LC 98-50987. 192p. 1999. pap. 9.95 (*0-8069-8713-8*) Sterling.

— UFO Retrievals: The Recovery of Alien Spacecraft. (Illus.). 200p. 1995. pap. 10.95 (*0-7137-2493-5*, Pub. by Blandford Pr) Sterling.

— UFOs & How to See Them. (Illus.). 144p. 1993. pap. 14.95 (*0-8069-0297-3*) Sterling.

Randles, Jenny & Hough, Peter. The Complete Book of UFOs: An Investigation into Alien Contacts & Encounters. LC 96-26161. (Illus.). 304p. 1996. pap. 14.95 (*0-8069-8132-6*) Sterling.

— Life after Death & the World Beyond. LC 98-176844. (Illus.). 160p. 1998. 12.95 (*0-8069-0719-3*) Sterling.

— Strange but True. (Illus.). 192p. (Orig.). 1996. pap. 16.95 (*0-7499-1459-9*, Pub. by Piatkus Bks) London Brdge.

***Randles, Jenny & Hough, Peter.** Supernatural Causes: Case Studies of Mysterious Death & Injury. 2000. 26.95 (*1-902809-34-3*, London House) Allison & Busby.

Randles, Jenny & Hough, Peter. World's Best "True" UFO Stories. LC 94-19807. (Illus.). 96p. 1994. 14.95 (*0-8069-1258-8*) Sterling.

***Randles, Jenny, et al.** UFO's That Never Were. (Illus.). 2000. 26.95 (*1-902809-35-1*, London House) Allison & Busby.

***Randles, Kevin, Jr.** A Black Man's Love for a Black Princess. 1999. pap. write for info. (*1-57553-848-2*) Watermrk Pr.

Randles, Ronald H. & Wolfe, Douglas A. Introduction to the Theory of Nonparametric Statistics. 464p. (C). 1991. reprint ed. lib. bdg. 59.95 (*0-89464-543-9*) Krieger.

Randles, Slim. Raven's Prey. 1999. 24.95 (*0-9632596-9-5*); pap. 16.95 (*0-9632596-8-7*) McRoy & Blackburn.

Randles, Susan, et al. Guide to Lighthouses of Nova Scotia. 112p. 1999. pap. text 10.95 (*1-55109-246-8*) Nimbus Publ.

Randles, W. G. The Unmaking of the Medieval Christian Cosmos, 1500-1760: From Solid Heavens to Boundless Aether. LC 98-39359. (Illus.). 340p. 1999. text 86.95 (*1-84014-624-9*, Pub. by Ashgate Pub) Ashgate Pub Co.

Randlesome, Colin. The Business Culture in Germany. 288p. 1994. pap. text 39.95 (*0-7506-1833-7*) Buttrwrth-Heinemann.

— Business Cultures in Europe. 2nd ed. 320p. 1993. pap. text 39.95 (*0-7506-0872-2*) Buttrwrth-Heinemann.

Randlev, Karen. Light Runner. (New Alaskan Poets Ser.). 128p. 1987. pap. 5.95 (*0-914221-08-6*) Fireweed Pr AK.

Randloph, J., tr. see Trismegistus, Hermes M.

Rando, Caterina. Words of Women: Quotations for Success. (Orig.). 1995. pap., spiral bd. 6.95 (*0-9644906-0-9*) PowerDynamics.

Rando, Caterina, compiled by. Words of Women: Quotations for Success. (Illus.). 18p. (Orig.). 1996. 19.95 incl. disk (*0-9644906-1-7*) PowerDynamics.

Rando, Ciaetuno, tr. from ITA. Blue Whale. (Picas Ser.: Vol. 14). 168p. pap. 13.00 (*1-55071-118-0*, Pub. by Guernica Editions) Paul & Co Pubs.

Rando, Emily N., jt. auth. see Napoli, Donna J.

Rando, Emily N., jt. ed. see Napoli, Donna J.

Rando, Gaetano, tr. see Cappiello, Rose.

Rando, Guy L., jt. auth. see Jones, Rees L.

Rando, Guy L., jt. auth. see Muirhead, Desmond.

Rando, Therese A. Grief, Dying, & Death: Clinical Interventions for Caregivers. LC 84-60903. 488p. (Orig.). 1984. pap. text 22.95 (*0-87822-232-4*, 2324) Res Press.

— How to Go on Living When Someone You Love Dies. 352p. 1991. pap. 14.95 (*0-553-35269-5*) Bantam.

— Treatment of Complicated Mourning. LC 90-64044. 768p. 1992. text 39.95 (*0-87822-329-0*, 4428) Res Press.

Rando, Therese A., ed. Clinical Dimensions of Anticipatory Mourning: Theory & Practice in Working with the Dying, Their Loved Ones & Their Caregivers. 612p. 2000. pap. text 29.95 (*0-87822-380-0*) Res Press.

— Parental Loss of a Child. LC 86-61549. 570p. (Orig.). 1986. pap. text 22.95 (*0-87822-281-2*, 2812) Res Press.

Randoll, Wilma V. Back Pain & Spinal Problems: Index of New Information with Authors, Subjects & References. rev. ed. LC 96-185. 149p. 1996. 47.50 (*0-7883-1028-3*); pap. 44.50 (*0-7883-1029-1*) ABBE Pubs Assn.

Randolph, A. Philip, et al. The Papers of A. Philip Randolph. LC 91-11920. (Black Studies Research Sources). 35p. 1990. write for info. (*1-55655-024-3*) U Pubns Amer.

Randolph, Alan & Posner, Barry Z. Getting the Job Done! Managing Project Teams & Task Forces for Success. (Illus.). 192p. (C). 1991. 32.95 (*0-13-616285-1*) P-H.

Randolph, Alan, jt. auth. see Posner, Barry Z.

Randolph, Barbara. Gifts from the Kitchen. 72p. 1991. 15.00 (*0-385-25332-X*) Doubleday.

— Potpourri. 72p. 1991. 15.00 (*0-385-25334-6*) Doubleday.

Randolph, Barbara, jt. auth. see Vaillant, Janet.

Randolph, Benjamin, ed. The Unger Brothers 1904 Catalogue. (Historical Catalogue Ser.: Vol. 7). (Illus.). 210p. 1998. reprint ed. pap. 59.95 (*0-9656139-3-3*) Eden Sterling.

Randolph, Benjamin, ed. see Tilton, George P.

Randolph, Benjamin A., ed. Whiting Manufacturing Company, 1896. (Historical Catalogue Ser.: Vol. 6). (Illus.). 60p. 1998. pap. 24.95 (*0-9656139-2-5*) Eden Sterling.

Randolph, Benjamin A., ed. see Dietz, Ulysses G.

Randolph, Betty L. Achieve Excellence. Success Education Institute International, ed. (Success Ser.). 1989. 14.98 incl. audio (*1-55909-229-7*, 180P); 14.98 incl. audio (*1-55909-230-0*, 180PM) Randolph Tapes.

— Creative Thinking. Success Education Institute International Staff, ed. 1990. 9.98 incl. audio (*1-55909-274-2*, 46B) Randolph Tapes.

— Easy Visualization. Success Education Institute International Staff, ed. 1990. 9.98 incl. audio (*1-55909-276-9*, 105B) Randolph Tapes.

— Effective Communication. Success Education Institute International Staff, ed. (Educational Ser.). 1989. 14.98 incl. audio (*1-55909-254-8*, 420P); Price not set. incl. audio Randolph Tapes.

— Good Decisions. Success Education Institute International Staff, ed. (Educational Ser.). 1989. 14.98 incl. audio (*1-55909-258-0*, 460P); Price not set. incl. audio Randolph Tapes.

— I Can (Pre-Birth-2 Yrs.) Success Education Institute International Staff, ed. (I Can Ser.). 1989. 9.98 incl. audio (*1-55909-112-6*, 92S) Randolph Tapes.

— Mega Learning. Success Education Institute International Staff, ed. (Educational Ser.). 1989. 14.98 incl. audio (*1-55909-242-4*, 310P); Price not set. incl. audio Randolph Tapes.

— Mind Your Health. Success Education Institute International Staff, ed. (Health Ser.). 1989. 14.98 incl. audio (*1-55909-250-5*, 380P); Price not set. incl. audio Randolph Tapes.

— Passing Exams. Success Education Institute International Staff, ed. 1990. 9.98 incl. audio (*1-55909-275-0*, 53B) Randolph Tapes.

— Power of Persuasion. Success Education Institute International, ed. (Success Ser.). 1989. 14.98 incl. audio (*1-55909-231-9*, 190P); 14.98 incl. audio (*1-55909-232-7*, 190PM) Randolph Tapes.

— Power Weight Loss. Success Education Institute International, ed. (Health Ser.). 1989. 14.98 incl. audio (*1-55909-209-2*, 2P); 14.98 incl. audio (*1-55909-210-6*, 2PM); 14.98 incl. audio (*1-55909-207-6*, 1P); 35.00 incl. audio (*1-55909-208-4*, 1PM) Randolph Tapes.

— Profit from Real Estate. Success Education Institute International Staff, ed. (Specialized Sales Ser.). 1989. 14.98 incl. audio (*1-55909-214-9*, 80PM) Randolph Tapes.

— Resolving Problems. Success Education Institute International Staff, ed. (Success Ser.). 1989. 14.98 incl. audio (*1-55909-259-9*, 470P) Randolph Tapes.

— Sales Power. Success Education Institute International, ed. (Success Ser.). 1989. 14.98 incl. audio (*1-55909-240-8*, 300P); 14.98 incl. audio (*1-55909-241-6*, 300PM) Randolph Tapes.

— Self-Esteem. Success Education Institute International Staff, ed. (Success Ser.). 1989. 14.98 incl. audio (*1-55909-249-1*, 370P) Randolph Tapes.

— Smoke No More. Success Education Institute International, ed. (Health Ser.). 1989. 14.98 incl. audio (*1-55909-260-2*, 500P); 14.98 incl. audio (*1-55909-261-0*, 500PM) Randolph Tapes.

— Speak Effectively. Success Education Institute International Staff, ed. (Educational Ser.). 1989. 14.98 incl. audio (*1-55909-251-3*, 390P) Randolph Tapes.

— Stop Procrastination. Success Education Institute International Staff, ed. (Success Ser.). 1989. 14.98 incl. audio (*1-55909-255-6*, 430P) Randolph Tapes.

— Stress for Success. Success Education Institute International Staff, ed. (Success Ser.). 1989. 14.98 incl. audio (*1-55909-244-0*, 330P) Randolph Tapes.

— Successful Marriage. Success Education Institute International Staff, ed. (Relationship Ser.). 1989. 9.98 incl. audio (*1-55909-099-5*, 83X) Randolph Tapes.

— Take Care (For Care Givers) Success Education Institute International, ed. (Health Ser.). 1989. 14.98 incl. audio (*1-55909-238-6*, 230P); 14.98 incl. audio (*1-55909-239-4*, 230PM) Randolph Tapes.

— Taking Control (Alzheimer's) Success Education Institute International Staff, ed. (Health Ser.). 1989. 14.98 incl. audio (*1-55909-237-8*, 220PM) Randolph Tapes.

— Taking Control of Illness. Success Education Institute International Staff, ed. (Health Ser.). 1989. 14.98 incl. audio (*1-55909-228-9*) Randolph Tapes.

— Winning Bowling. Success Education Institute International Staff, ed. 1989. 9.98 incl. audio (*1-55909-128-2*, 104X) Randolph Tapes.

— Winning Leadership. Success Education Institute International Staff, ed. (Success Ser.). 1989. 14.98 incl. audio (*1-55909-248-3*, 360P) Randolph Tapes.

— Winning Self-Image. Success Education Institute International Staff, ed. (Success Ser.). 1989. 14.98 incl. audio (*1-55909-247-5*, 350P) Randolph Tapes.

— Yes, I Can. Success Education Institute International, ed. (I Can Ser.). 1989. 14.98 incl. audio (*1-55909-245-9*, 340P); 14.98 incl. audio (*1-55909-246-7*, 340PM) Randolph Tapes.

Randolph, Bob. I Am Writing of Hand Grenades, Butterflies & Kisses. (Illus.). 214p. (Orig.). 1991. pap. 10.00 (*1-881969-25-8*) Randolph Hse.

Randolph, Boris. Bible Verses in Verse. LC 80-67992. 144p. 1980. pap. 3.95 (*0-87516-424-2*) DeVorss.

Randolph, Brenda, jt. auth. see Vaillant, Janet.

Randolph, Carman F. Law of Eminent Domain in the United States. cxxv, 462p. 1991. reprint ed. 55.00 (*0-8377-2545-3*, Rothman) W S Hein.

Randolph, Corliss F. A History of Seventh Day Baptists in West Virginia: Woodbrighton, Salemville Churches in PA, Shrewsbury Church in NJ. LC 98-128779. (Illus.). 504p. 1998. pap. 41.50 (*0-7884-0778-3*, R052) Heritage Bk.

Randolph, David. This Is Music: A Guide to the Pleasures of Listening. rev. ed. 236p. 1997. pap. 12.50 (*0-88739-110-9*) Creat Arts Bk.

Randolph, David J. Power That Heals: Love Healing & the Trinity. LC 93-31888. 160p. (Orig.). 1994. pap. 3.29 (*0-687-33207-9*) Abingdon.

Randolph, David J., et al. God's Party: Dynamic Worship for the 21st Century. Holmes, Bill & Holmes, Joan, eds. (Illus.). 78p. 1997. pap. 10.00 (*1-891217-01-1*) Hanging Grdns.

Randolph, Dennis A. Civil Engineering for the Community. LC 93-12282. 96p. 1993. 22.00 (*0-87262-845-0*) Am Soc Civil Eng.

***Randolph, Diana.** In the Heart of the Forest: Poetry & Pastel Paintings. (Illus.). 28p. 1999. pap. 7.95 (*1-886028-38-9*, Pub. by Savage Pr) Bookmen Inc.

Randolph, Eleanor. Waking the Tempests: Ordinary Life in the New Russia. 448p. 1996. 25.50 (*0-684-80912-5*) S&S Trade.

Randolph, Elizabeth. Guide to Your Cat's Symptoms. 1999. write for info. (*0-375-50078-2*) Villard Books.

— Guide to Your Dog's Symptoms. 1999. write for info. (*0-375-50079-0*) Villard Books.

— How to Help Your Puppy Grow Up To Be a Wonderful Dog. 288p. 1988. reprint ed. mass mkt. 5.99 (*0-449-21503-2*, Crest) Fawcett.

Randolph, Elizabeth, jt. auth. see Dibra, Bash.

Randolph, Elizabeth, jt. auth. see Dibra, Bashkim.

Randolph, Ellen. Threads of Love. large type ed. (Romance Ser.). 288p. 1993. 27.99 (*0-7089-2993-1*) Ulverscroft.

Randolph, Francis. Know Him in the Breaking of the Bread: A Guide to the Mass. LC 98-72284. 1998. pap. 10.95 (*0-89870-701-3*) Ignatius Pr.

Randolph, Francis L. Studies for a Byron Bibliography. LC 79-13752. 144p. 1979. 25.00 (*0-915010-26-7*) Sutter House.

Randolph, Gretchen L. & Appleton, Wanda H. Jackie Meets the Anger Monster.Tr. of Jackie Conoce al Monstrun de Enojo. (ENG & SPA., Illus.). 28p. (Orig.). (J). (ps-6). 1996. pap. 26.95 incl. audio (*1-890239-52-6*) Healthy Assn.

— Jackie Meets the Anger Monster: Jackie Conoce al Monstrun de Enojo. (ENG & SPA., Illus.). 28p. (J). (ps-6). 1997. pap. 19.95 incl. audio (*1-890239-53-4*) Healthy Assn.

Randolph, Howard S. Funsten-Meade. Ancestors & Descendants of Colonel David Funsten & His Wife Susan Everard Meade. (Illus.). 93p. 1997. reprint ed. pap. 18.00 (*0-8328-8676-9*); reprint ed. lib. bdg. 28.00 (*0-8328-8675-0*) Higginson Bk Co.

Randolph, Howard S. & Rankin, Russell B., eds. Paramus, Bergen County, New Jersey, Reformed Dutch Church Baptisms, 1740-1850: Together with Records from the Gravestones in the Church Yard & a List of Church Members. Versteeg, Dingman, tr. 224p. 1992. reprint ed. lib. bdg. 41.00 (*1-56012-124-6*, 120) Kinship Rhinebeck.

Randolph, I. & Clokey, J. The Grasshopper: A Tragic Tale. 20p. 1965. 3.95 (*0-87487-708-3*) Summy-Birchard.

Randolph, J. A. Science Tools. (Thinking Like a Scientist Ser.). (Illus.). 20p. (J). Date not set. pap. 16.95 (*1-58273-113-6*) Newbridge Educ.

Randolph, J. Thornton. Cabin & Parlor: Or, Slaves & Masters. LC 77-149876. (Black Heritage Library Collection). 1977. 28.95 (*0-8369-8756-X*) Ayer.

Randolph, Jacob. Memoirs of the Life & Character of Philip Syng Physick. 1993. reprint ed. lib. bdg. 89.00 (*0-7812-5821-9*) Rprt Serv.

Randolph, James C., jt. ed. see Randolph, Polley A.

***Randolph, Jeanne.** Psychoanalysis & Synchronized Swimming & Other Writings on Art. (Illus.). 184p. 1999. reprint ed. pap. 15.00 (*0-7881-6365-5*) DIANE Pub.

Randolph, Jewell, jt. ed. see Cox, Margie.

Randolph, Joan. True Stories by Three Men of the Sea. Sappey, Maureen, ed. 192p. (Orig.). 1990. pap. 10.95 (*0-9627510-0-6*) Island Harbor Pr.

Randolph, John. Sir John Randolph's King's Bench Reports. Bryson, W. Hamilton, ed. LC 96-35586. 104p. 1996. 45.00 (*1-57588-125-X*, 310720) W S Hein.

Randolph, John, ed. Championship Track & Field Vol. 1: Track Events. LC 79-92134. (Illus.). 192p. 1982. reprint ed. pap. 59.60 (*0-608-06467-X*, 206177100001) Bks Demand.

Randolph, Judson G., ed. The Injured Child: Surgical Management. LC 79-21432. (Illus.). 434p. reprint ed. pap. 134.60 (*0-8357-7599-2*, 205692100096) Bks Demand.

Randolph, K. B. Lover's Handbook. 154p. (Orig.). 1995. pap. 12.00 (*0-9643139-0-1*) Hawkins Kelly Pub.

Randolph, Keith. The Truth about Astral Projection. (Llewellyn's Truth about Ser.). 64p. (Orig.). 1999. mass mkt. 1.99 (*0-87542-350-7*) Llewellyn Pubns.

Randolph, L. Child Abuse & Neglect: ECE 112 Course. 286p. (C). 1994. write for info. (*0-933195-66-4*) CA College Health Sci.

Randolph, L. F. Basics of Radio Control Airplanes. Uravitch, Richard, ed. (Illus.). 84p. 1990. pap. 15.95 (*0-911295-10-0*) Air Age.

Randolph, L. V. Fitz Randolph Traditions: A Story of a Thousand Years. (Illus.). 134p. 1993. reprint ed. pap. 24.00 (*0-8328-3313-4*); reprint ed. lib. bdg. 34.00 (*0-8328-3312-6*) Higginson Bk Co.

Randolph, Lamar P. Forecasting: Index of Modern Information. LC 88-47564. 150p. 1990. 47.50 (*1-55914-160-3*); pap. 44.50 (*1-55914-161-1*) ABBE Pubs Assn.

Randolph, Larry. The Crosspatch. 1973. pap. 3.50 (*0-87129-080-4*, C36) Dramatic Pub.

— User Friendly Prophecy. LC 99-166681. 208p. 1998. pap. 10.99 (*1-56043-695-6*) Destiny Image.

Randolph, Laura B., jt. auth. see LaBelle, Patti.

Randolph, Laura B., jt. auth. see Labelle, Patti.

***Randolph, Lauri Ann.** Lauri's Low-Carb Cookbook: Rapid Weight Loss with Satisfying Meals! 2nd ed. 256p. 1999. pap. 19.95 (*0-9667963-1-4*) Avalon Ent.

Randolph, Leonard. Scar Tissue. (Hollow Spring Poetry Ser.). (Illus.). 64p. (C). 1984. pap. text 5.00 (*0-318-00815-7*) Hollow Spring Pr.

— Wind over Ashes: Selected Poems. (Illus.). 174p. (Orig.). 1982. pap. 7.00 (*0-932112-15-3*) Carolina Wren.

Randolph, Lillian. The Fundamental Laws of Governmental Organization. 1971. pap. 15.95 (*0-8084-0141-6*) NCUP.

Randolph, Linda B., jt. auth. see Thompson, Charles L.

Randolph Macon Woman's College Staff. Masterpieces of American Painting from Randolph-Macon Woman's College. 1990. pap. 3.95 (*0-486-26384-3*) Dover.

Randolph, Mark A., ed. see Institute of Medicine, Committee on Addressing Car.

Randolph, Mary. Dog Law 3. 3rd rev. ed. Warner, Ralph E. & Repa, Barbara K., eds. LC 97-12409. (Illus.). 336p. 1997. pap. 14.95 (*0-87337-392-8*) Nolo com.

— 8 Ways to Avoid Probate 2nd ed. LC 99-24442. (Quick & Legal Series). 216p. 1999. pap. 16.95 (*0-87337-528-9*) Nolo com.

Randolph, Mary. Eight Ways to Avoid Probate 1.2. 2nd ed. LC 96-41179. (Quick & Legal Ser.). (Illus.). 216p. 1997. pap. 15.95 (*0-87337-353-7*) Nolo com.

Randolph, Mary. The Virginia Housewife. Hess, Karen, ed. LC 83-19869. 417p. 1984. 24.95 (*0-87249-423-3*) U of SC Pr.

— The Virginia Housewife: or Methodical Cook: A Facsimile of an Authentic Early American Cookbook. LC 93-32924. 192p. 1993. reprint ed. pap. text 5.95 (*0-486-27772-0*) Dover.

Randolph, Mary, jt. auth. see Clifford, Denis.

Randolph, Mary, jt. auth. see Jordan, Cora.

Randolph, Mary, jt. auth. see Zagone, Frank.

Randolph, Mary, ed. see Clifford, Denis.

Randolph, Mary, ed. see Clifford, Denis & Jordan, Cora.

Randolph, Mary, ed. see Jordan, Cora.

Randolph, Melanie. Heart Full of Rainbows. LC 98-8708. 1998. 23.95 (*0-7862-1597-6*) Five Star.

Randolph, Nancy S. American Nursing Review for Psychiatric & Mental Health Nursing Certification. 2nd ed. LC 97-46587. 256p. 1998. pap. text 32.95 (*0-87434-907-9*) Springhouse Corp.

Randolph, Norman. Gangs, My Town & the Nation. LC 96-144930. 1996. pap. 19.95 (*1-55691-119-X*, 19X) Learning Pubns.

Randolph, P. B. The Tobacco Habit. 16p. 1972. pap. 3.00 (*0-916285-57-X*) Humanitarian.

Randolph, Paschal B. After Death: The Disembodiment of Man. 1996. reprint ed. spiral bd. 13.00 (*0-7873-0701-7*) Hlth Research.

— After Death: The Immortality of Man. Clymer, Emerson M., ed. 272p. 1970. 9.95 (*0-932785-00-X*) Philos Pub.

— Beyond the Veil: Posthumous Work of Paschal Beverly Randolph. 1996. reprint ed. pap. 16.50 (*0-7873-0696-7*) Hlth Research.

— Dealings with the Dead: The Human Soul, Its Migrations & Its Transmigrations. 156p. 1959. spiral bd. 11.00 (*0-7873-0694-0*) Hlth Research.

— Eulis: History of Love. 2nd ed. 1996. reprint ed. 12.00 (*0-7873-1321-1*) Hlth Research.

— Hermes Mercurius Trismegistus: His Divine Pymander. 1996. reprint ed. pap. 12.00 (*0-7873-0700-9*) Hlth Research.

— The Immortality of Love (Eulis) Clymer, Emerson M. et al, eds. 290p. 1979. 9.95 (*0-932785-17-4*) Philos Pub.

— The Immortality of Love (Eulis) deluxe ed. Clymer, Emerson M., ed. 290p. 1979. 15.00 (*0-932785-82-4*) Philos Pub.

— Pre-Adamite Man: Demonstrating the Existence of the Human Race. 6th ed. 408p. 1996. reprint ed. spiral bd. 21.50 (*0-7873-0695-9*) Hlth Research.

— Pre-Adamite Man: Demonstrating the Existence of the Human Race upon This Earth 100,000 Thousand Years Ago! (1888) 408p. 1996. reprint ed. pap. 19.95 (*1-56459-825-X*) Kessinger Pub.

— Ravalette: The Rosicrucian's Story. 283p. 1940. 9.95 (*0-932785-40-9*) Philos Pub.

— Ravalette: The Rosicrucian's Story. 1996. reprint ed. spiral bd. 13.00 (*0-7873-0698-3*) Hlth Research.

— Seership: Guide to Soul Sight. xv, 153p. 1930. 10.95 (*1-891485-06-7*) Philos Pub.

— Seership: Soul Sight. 1996. reprint ed. spiral bd. 10.00 (*0-7873-0697-5*) Hlth Research.

— Soul! The Soul World! Clymer, R. Swinburne, ed. 246p. 1932. 15.00 (*0-932785-45-X*) Philos Pub.

— The Soul World: The Home of the Dead. 1996. reprint ed. spiral bd. 15.50 (*0-7873-0699-1*) Hlth Research.

***Randolph, Patrick A. & Jianbo, Lou.** Chinese Real Estate Law. LC 99-43186. 1999. write for info. (*90-411-9432-0*) Kluwer Law Intl.

Randolph, Paul B. One-Third of What Is Known about Natural Philosophy. 103p. (C). 1989. pap. text 4.50 (*0-317-93248-9*) Randolph Dallas.

Randolph, Polley A. & Randolph, James C., eds. Readings in Ecology. (Illus.). (C). 1973. text 39.50 (*0-8422-5085-9*) Irvington.

Randolph, Priscilla S. Lifehunter: Selected Stories, Poems & Essays. 326p. 1994. text 19.95 (*0-9642113-0-0*) Beecher Pr.

Randolph, R. I., jt. auth. see Carter, R. R.

Randolph, R. Sean. The United States & Thailand: Alliance Dynamics, 1950-1985. LC 86-82389. (Research Papers & Policy: No. 12). (Illus.). x, 246p. (Orig.). 1987. pap. 15.00 (*0-912966-92-0*) IEAS.

Randolph, Randy. R-C Airplane Building Techniques. (Illus.). 146p. 1991. 17.95 (*0-911295-13-5*) Air Age.

Randolph, Robert. R. Cory in Winter. 32p. (YA). (gr. 9 up). 1998. pap. 5.00 (*1-890767-00-X*) Bacchae Pr.

Randolph, Robert P. & McCafferty, W. Patrick. Diversity & Distribution of the Mayflies (Ephemeroptera) of Illinois, Indiana, Kentucky, Michigan, Ohio, & Wisconsin. LC 98-66938. (Bulletin New Ser.: Vol. 13, No. 1). (Illus.). 188p. 1998. pap. text 30.00 (*0-86727-131-0*) Ohio Bio Survey.

Randolph, Ruth E., jt. auth. see Roses, Lorraine E.

Randolph, Ruth E., jt. ed. see Roses, Lorraine E.

Randolph, Sallie. Gerald R. Ford: President. LC 86-16333. 128p. (J). (gr. 5 up). 1987. 12.95 (*0-8027-6666-8*); lib. bdg. 13.85 (*0-8027-6667-6*) Walker & Co.

— Richard M. Nixon, President. (Presidential Biography Ser.). 128p. (J). (gr. 5 up). 1989. 13.95 (*0-8027-6848-2*); lib. bdg. 14.85 (*0-8027-6849-0*) Walker & Co.

— Woodrow Wilson. (Presidential Biography Ser.). 128p. (J). (gr. 6-9). 1992. 14.95 (*0-8027-8143-8*); lib. bdg. 15.85 (*0-8027-8144-6*) Walker & Co.

Randolph, Sallie & Bolick, Nancy O. Shaker Inventions. (Illus.). (J). (gr. 4-7). 1990. 12.95 (*0-8027-6933-0*); lib. bdg. 13.85 (*0-8027-6934-9*) Walker & Co.

Randolph, Sallie G., jt. auth. see Bolick, Nancy O.

Randolph, Sarah E., jt. ed. see Hay, Simon I.

Randolph, Sarah N. The Domestic Life of Thomas Jefferson. LC 78-14312. (Illus.). 452p. 1979. pap. 16.95 (*0-8139-0718-7*) U Pr of Va.

Randolph, Shirley L. & Heiniger, Margot C. Kids Learn from the Inside Out: How to Enhance the Human Matrix. 2nd ed. Terra, Jean, ed. (Illus.). 256p. 1998. pap. 18.95 (*1-887747-19-2*) Legendary Pub.

Randolph, Shirley L., et al. Kids Learn from the Inside Out: How to Enhance the Human Matrix. rev. ed. Terra, Jean, ed. LC 93-80615. (Illus.). 282p. 1998. pap. 18.95 (*0-9625040-4-1*, 297-231-X) Legendary Pub.

Randolph, Spring. Seafood List: FDA's Guide to Acceptable Market Names for Seafood Sold in Interstate Commerce, 1993. 85p. 1994. pap. 8.00 (*0-16-042999-4*) USGPO.

Randolph, Spring & Snyder, Mary. The Seafood List: FDA's Guide to Acceptable Market Names for Seafood Sold in Interstate Commerce (1993) 67p. (Orig.). (C). 1994. pap. text 30.00 (*0-7881-1324-0*) DIANE Pub.

Randolph, Susan, jt. auth. see Harik, Iliya.

Randolph, Theron G. Human Ecology & Susceptibility to the Chemical Environment. (Illus.). 160p. 1981. 33.95 (*0-398-01548-1*); pap. 23.95 (*0-398-06335-4*) C C Thomas.

Randolph, Theron G. & Moss, Ralph W. An Alternative Approach to Allergies: The New Field of Clinical Ecology Unravels the Environmental Causes of Mental & Physical Ills. rev. ed. LC 88-45902. 352p. 1990. reprint ed. pap. 14.00 (*0-06-091693-1*, Perennial) HarperTrade.

Randolph, Thomas. Poetical & Dramatic Works of Thomas Randolph, 2 vols. Hazlitt, William C., ed. LC 68-57192. 1972. reprint ed. 48.95 (*0-405-08874-4*) Ayer.

Randolph, Timothy. How to Invent, Protect & Sell! Insider's Guide to Inventing Product Development & Marketing. LC T339.R361996. 108p. (Orig.). 1996. per. 12.95 (*0-9651527-1-5*) T T Randolph.

Randolph, Vance. Blow the Candle Out Vol. II: "Unprintable" Ozark Folksongs & Folklore: Folk Rhymes & Other Lore. LC 91-17685. 392p. 1992. text 60.00 (*1-55728-237-4*) U of Ark Pr.

— Ozark Magic & Folklore. Orig. Title: Ozark Superstition. 367p. 1947. pap. 7.95 (*0-486-21181-9*) Dover.

— Pissing in the Snow & Other Ozark Folktales. LC 76-18181. 192p. 1976. 8.95 (*0-252-01364-6*) U of Ill Pr.

— Roll Me in Your Arms Vol. 1: "Unprintable" Ozark Folksongs & Folklore: Folksongs & Music. Legman, G., ed. LC 91-17685. 582p. 1992. text 60.00 (*1-55728-231-5*) U of Ark Pr.

— We Always Lie to Strangers. LC 74-12852. (Illus.). 309p. 1974. reprint ed. lib. bdg. 35.00 (*0-8371-7765-0*, RAAL, Greenwood Pr) Greenwood.

Randolph, W. Alan, et al. Organization Game: A Simulation Participant's Manual. 3rd ed. 120p. (C). 1997. pap. text 42.00 (*0-673-46861-5*) Addson-Wesley Educ.

Randolph, W. Alan, jt. auth. see Miles, Robert H.

Randolph, Wassell. Archer. George Archer I, or the Umberland Archers of Henrico Co., Va., & His Descendants. 83p. 1996. reprint ed. pap. 17.00 (*0-8328-5364-X*); reprint ed. lib. bdg. 27.00 (*0-8328-5363-1*) Higginson Bk Co.

***Random Acts of Kindness Foundation Staff.** Christian Acts of Kindness. LC 99-23771. 160p. 1999. pap. 11.95 (*1-57324-173-3*) Conari Press.

Random, Candice F. Jimmy Crack Corn. LC 93-16657. (Illus.). (J). (gr. 2-5). 1994. lib. bdg. 19.95 (*0-87614-786-4*, Carolrhoda) Lerner Pub.

Random Fields and Applications Seminar on Stochastic Analysis Staff, et al. Seminar on Stochastic Analysis, Random Fields & Applications: Centro Stefano Franscini, Ascona, September 1996. LC 99-14457. (Progress in Probability Ser.). 1999. 125.00 (*0-8176-6106-9*) Birkhauser.

Random, Henry. Tell Leonidas by Henry Random: A Play in Three Acts. 96p. 1975. pap. 10.00 (*0-9631753-1-9*) C-C OGrady.

Random House Books for Young Readers Staff. Birthday Bear. (J). 1999. pap. 2.99 (*0-375-80060-3*, Pub. by Random Bks Yng Read) Random.

— Brought to You by the Letter A. (ps-3). 1999. pap. 1.99 (*0-375-80379-3*, Pub. by Random Bks Yng Read) Random.

***Random House Books for Young Readers Staff.** Brought to You by the Letter B. (ps-3). 1999. pap. 1.99 (*0-375-80380-7*, Pub. by Random Bks Yng Read) Random.

— Brought to You by the Letter C. (ps-3). 1999. pap. 1.99 (*0-375-80381-5*, Pub. by Random Bks Yng Read) Random.

An Asterisk (*) at the beginning of an entry indicates that the title is appearing for the first time.

— Diesels & Engines. (Illus.). 80p. (J). (ps-1). 2000. pap. 2.99 (*0-375-80554-0*, Pub. by Random Bks Yng Read) Random.
— Fun in the Sun!, Vol. 1. (Sticker Time Ser.). (Illus.). 16p. (J). (ps-3). 2000. pap. 2.99 (*0-375-80487-0*, Pub. by Random Bks Yng Read) Random.
— Happy Halloween! (Illus.). 80p. (ps-3). 1999. pap. 2.99 (*0-375-80377-7*, Pub. by Random Bks Yng Read) Random.

Random House Books for Young Readers Staff. Happy Holidays. (ps-3). 1999. pap. 2.99 (*0-375-80375-0*, Pub. by Random Bks Yng Read) Random.

***Random House Books for Young Readers Staff.** Merry Christmas. (ps-3). 1999. pap. 2.99 (*0-375-80376-9*, Pub. by Random Bks Yng Read) Random.
— Winter Walk. (ps-3). 1999. pap. 2.99 (*0-375-80374-2*, Pub. by Random Bks Yng Read) Random.

Random House Books for Young Readers Staff, ed. Elmo's Christmas. (ps-3). 1999. pap. 1.99 (*0-375-80373-4*, Pub. by Random Bks Yng Read) Random.
— Hawaiian Shirt. (J). 1998. pap. 3.25 (*0-679-89413-6*, Pub. by Random Bks Yng Read) Random.
— Journey to Otherwhere. LC 99-54382. (Voyage of the Basset Ser.: Vol. 3). (Illus.). 224p. (J). (gr. 5-8). 2000. pap. 3.99 (*0-375-80051-4*, Pub. by Random Bks Yng Read) Random.

Random House College Dictionary Staff. The Random House College Dictionary. rev. ed. 1982. 14.95 (*0-394-52762-3*) Random.

***Random House College Dictionary Staff.** Webster's Deluxe College Dictionary. 2nd ed. (Illus.). 1600p. 2000. 32.00 (*0-375-42561-6*) Random Ref & Info.

***Random House Dictionary Staff.** Latin American Spanish Dictionary. 2nd ed. 736p. 1999. pap. 12.95 (*0-375-70736-0*) Random Ref & Info.
— Random House Webster's Dictionary. 1999. mass mkt. 5.99 (*0-345-91597-6*, Ballantine) Ballantine Pub Grp.
— Random House Webster's Dictionary: Classic Edition. abr. ed. LC 99-11296. 832p. 1999. 16.95 (*0-375-40703-0*) Random.
— Webster's College Dictionary. rev. ed. (Illus.). 1600p. 2000. 24.95 (*0-375-42560-8*) Random Ref & Info.
— Webster's Handy Spanish Dictionary. LC 99-31112. 384p. 1999. pap. 3.99 (*0-375-70701-8*) Random Ref & Info.
— Webster's Mini American Dictionary. LC 99-23570. 384p. 1999. pap. 3.99 (*0-375-70702-6*) Random Ref & Info.

Random House Editors. Random House Webster's Medical Dictionary. 1997. mass mkt. write for info. (*0-345-41442-X*) Ballantine Pub Grp.

***Random House Large Print Publishing Staff.** Webster's Large Print Spanish Dictionary. 880p. 2000. 40.00 (*0-375-41048-1*); pap. text 26.00 (*0-375-70926-6*) Random Hse Lrg Prnt.

***Random House Reference Staff.** Random House Handy Diet & Nutrition Guide. (Illus.). 1999. pap. 3.99 (*0-375-70826-X*) Random.

Random House Reference Staff. Webster's Concise Dictionary. LC 98-36736. 1999. 4.99 (*0-517-20545-9*) Random Hse Value.

***Random House Reference Staff.** Webster's Student Notebook Writers' Guide. 96p. 2000. pap. 4.99 (*0-375-71951-2*) Random Ref & Info.

***Random House Staff.** Animals. (Play It Smart Workbks.). 32p. (J). 2001. pap. 2.99 (*0-375-80463-3*) Random Bks Yng Read.
— Are We There Yet? (Pictureback Ser.). 24p. (J). 2000. pap. 3.25 (*0-375-80436-6*, Pub. by Random Bks Yng Read) Random.

Random House Staff. At the Playground. (Board Bks.). (J). 1997. 2.50 (*0-679-88885-3*, Pub. by Random Bks Yng Read) Random.

***Random House Staff.** Babe the Brave. (Illus.). (J). 1999. 9.44 (*0-606-18482-1*) Turtleback.

Random House Staff. Babe 2: Pig in the City Movie Storybook. LC 98-66576. 1998. pap. 5.99 (*0-679-89154-4*) Random.
— Bear's House. 1999. pap. 2.99 (*0-375-80059-X*, Pub. by Random Bks Yng Read) Random.

***Random House Staff.** A Beary Merry Christmas. (Painting Time Ser.). (Illus.). 32p. (J). (ps-3). 2000. pap. 3.99 (*0-375-80650-4*, Pub. by Random Bks Yng Read) Random.

Random House Staff. Best Friends. LC 96-71575. (Life Favors Ser.). 1997. 6.99 (*0-679-88409-2*, Pub. by Random Bks Yng Read) Random.
— Big Bird Takes a Walk. (Chunky Book with Legs Ser.). (J). 1999. 5.99 (*0-679-89090-4*, Pub. by Random Bks Yng Read) Random.

***Random House Staff.** Brought to You by the Number 1. (Illus.). 32p. (J). (gr. k-3). 2000. pap. 1.99 (*0-375-80455-2*) Random.
— Brought to You by the Number 3. (Illus.). 32p. (J). (gr. k-3). 2000. pap. 1.99 (*0-375-80457-9*, Pub. by Random Bks Yng Read) Random.
— Brought to You by the Number 2. (Illus.). 32p. (J). (gr. k-3). 2000. pap. 1.99 (*0-375-80456-0*) Random.
— The Bunny Hop. LC 99-60941. (Illus.). 24p. (J). (ps-1). 2000. 2.99 (*0-375-80386-6*, Pub. by Random Bks Yng Read) Random.
— Calling All Boats. (Baby Fingers Book Ser.). (Illus.). (J). 2000. 4.99 (*0-375-80345-9*) Random.
— Cassie's Babysitting Surprise. (Sticker Time Ser.). (Illus.). 16p. (J). (ps-3). 2000. pap. 2.99 (*0-375-81065-X*) Random.

Random House Staff. Children: In Their Own Words. 1997. 6.99 (*0-679-88410-6*) Random Bks Yng Read.
— Christmas Poems, Stories & Carols. 112p. 1995. 5.99 (*0-517-12439-4*) Random.

***Random House Staff.** Cookies & Milk. (Sticker Time Ser.). (Illus.). 16p. (J). (ps-3). 2000. pap. 2.99 (*0-375-80640-7*, Pub. by Random Bks Yng Read) Random.
— Counting Numbers 1 to 20. (Star Wars). 16p. (J). (ps-2). 1999. pap. 4.99 (*0-375-80172-3*, Pub. by Random Bks Yng Read) Random.

Random House Staff. Crayon Box. (Great Big Flap Bks.). (Illus.). (J). 1998. 11.99 (*0-679-89289-3*, Pub. by Random Bks Yng Read) Random.

***Random House Staff.** Diesel 10 Means Trouble. LC 99-87627. (Illus.). 24p. (J). (ps-1). 2000. pap. 3.25 (*0-375-80552-4*, Pub. by Random Bks Yng Read) Random.
— Dragon Doodles. (Super Coloring Time Ser.). (Illus.). 80p. (J). (ps-3). 2000. pap. 2.99 (*0-375-80636-9*, Pub. by Random Bks Yng Read) Random.
— Drive You Crazy. (J). 2001. mass mkt. 4.99 (*0-375-81159-1*, Pub. by Random Bks Yng Read) Random.
— Droids, Creatures & Vehicles. (Star Wars). (Illus.). 80p. (J). (ps-3). 1999. pap. 2.99 (*0-375-80015-8*, Pub. by Random Bks Yng Read) Random.
— Elmo & Zoe's Alphabet. (Super Coloring Time Ser.). (Illus.). 80p. (J). (ps-3). 2000. pap. 2.99 (*0-375-80490-0*, Pub. by Random Bks Yng Read) Random.
— Elmo Can Quack Like a Duck. 24p. (J). 2000. 1.99 (*0-375-80444-7*, Pub. by Random Bks Yng Read) Random.

Random House Staff. Elmo Jumps. (Chunky Book with Legs Ser.). (J). 1999. 5.99 (*0-679-88981-7*, Pub. by Random Bks Yng Read) Random.

***Random House Staff.** Elmo Likes... (Great Big Board Bks.). (Illus.). (J). 2000. 7.99 (*0-375-81051-X*, Pub. by Random Bks Yng Read) Random.
— Elmo Loves You. (Illus.). 24p. (J). 2000. 2.99 (*0-375-80320-3*, Pub. by Random Bks Yng Read) Random.
— Elmo Says... (Illus.). 24p. (J). 2000. 1.99 (*0-375-80442-0*, Pub. by Random Bks Yng Read) Random.
— Emmy's Dream House. (Dragon Tales Ser.). (Illus.). 24p. (ps). 2000. 2.99 (*0-375-80324-6*) Random.

Random House Staff. The F Word. 2nd ed. LC 99-20049. 288p. 1999. pap. 14.00 (*0-375-70634-8*) Random.

***Random House Staff.** First Steps. 24p. (J). 2000. 1.99 (*0-375-80451-X*, Pub. by Random Bks Yng Read) Random.
— Fiske Interactive Guide to Colleges 1996. 1995. cd-rom 32.00 (*0-8129-2744-3*, Times Bks) Crown Pub Group.

Random House Staff. Fodor's World Weather Guide. 1998. pap. 17.95 (*0-375-70349-7*) Random Ref & Info.

***Random House Staff.** Friends Forever. (Sticker Time Ser.). (Illus.). 16p. (J). (ps-3). 2000. pap. 2.99 (*0-375-80639-3*, Pub. by Random Bks Yng Read) Random.
— Fun with ABC: Letters. (Sesame Seeds Workbks.). (Illus.). 32p. (J). (ps). 2000. pap. 2.99 (*0-375-80458-7*, Pub. by Random Bks Yng Read) Random.
— Fun with 1, 2, 3: Numbers. (Sesame Seeds Workbks.). (Illus.). 32p. (J). (ps). 2000. pap. 2.99 (*0-375-80459-5*) Random.
— Fun with Opposites: Sesame Seeds Workbooks. (Illus.). 32p. (J). (ps). 2000. pap. 2.99 (*0-375-80460-9*, Pub. by Random Bks Yng Read) Random.
— Fun with Shapes & Colors: Play It Smart Workbooks. (Illus.). 32p. (J). (ps). 2000. pap. 2.99 (*0-375-80462-5*, Pub. by Random Bks Yng Read) Random.
— Funny Food Faces. (Illus.). (J). 2000. 7.99 (*0-375-81054-4*, Pub. by Random Bks Yng Read) Random.

Random House Staff. Good Morning, Little Bert. (Board Bks.). (J). 1997. 2.50 (*0-679-88886-1*, Pub. by Random Bks Yng Read) Random.
— Good Night, Little Grover. (Board Bks.). (J). 1997. 2.50 (*0-679-88882-9*, Pub. by Random Bks Yng Read) Random.
— Grover Dances. (Chunky Book with Legs Ser.). (J). 1999. 5.99 (*0-679-88980-9*, Pub. by Random Bks Yng Read) Random.

***Random House Staff.** Happy Birthday, Elmo! (Super Coloring Time Ser.). (Illus.). 80p. (J). (ps-3). 2000. pap. 2.99 (*0-375-80495-1*, Pub. by Random Bks Yng Read) Random.
— Happy Easter. (J). 2000. pap. 2.99 (*0-375-80454-4*, Pub. by Random Bks Yng Read) Random.
— How the Grinch Stole Christmas! Happy Who-Liday, Mr. Grinch. (Super Coloring Time Ser.). (Illus.). (J). 2000. pap. 2.99 (*0-375-80693-8*) Random.
— How the Grinch Stole Christmas! Ornament Punch & Play Book. (Illus.). (J). 2000. pap. 3.99 (*0-375-81011-0*) Random.
— How the Grinch Stole Christmas! Who's Who in Who-Ville? (Super Coloring Time Ser.). (Illus.). (J). 2000. pap. 2.99 (*0-375-81013-7*) Random.
— How the Grinch Stole Christmas! Grinch & Bear It: Life According to the Supreme Green Meany. (Life Favors Ser.). (Illus.). (J). 2000. 6.99 (*0-375-81012-9*, Pub. by Random Bks Yng Read) Random.
— I Am a Bird. (Great Big Board Bks.). (Illus.). (J). 2000. 7.99 (*0-375-81050-1*, Pub. by Random Bks Yng Read) Random.

Random House Staff. Irish Wonders. LC 96-2346. 240p. 1996. 7.99 (*0-517-12396-7*) Random.
— Large Print Assortment. 1998. pap. text 26.00 (*0-676-59839-0*) Random.

***Random House Staff.** Latin American Spanish Dictionary. 2nd ed. 736p. 1999. 24.95 (*0-375-40720-0*) Random Ref & Info.
— Learning Shapes. (Star Wars). 16p. (ps-2). 1999. pap. 4.99 (*0-375-80004-2*, Pub. by Random Bks Yng Read) Random.
— Learning the Ropes. (J). 2001. mass mkt. 3.99 (*0-375-81160-5*) Random Bks Yng Read.
— Let's Eat. (Pictureback Ser.). 24p. (J). 2000. pap. 3.25 (*0-375-80435-8*, Pub. by Random Bks Yng Read) Random.
— Let's Go to Rainbow Canyon. (Painting Time Ser.). (Illus.). 32p. (J). (ps-3). 2000. pap. 3.99 (*0-375-80638-5*, Pub. by Random Bks Yng Read) Random.
— Let's Go to School with Thomas. (Toddler Bks.). (Illus.). 12p. (J). (ps). 2000. bds. 2.99 (*0-375-80279-7*, Pub. by Random Bks Yng Read) Random.
— Let's Pretend. (Sticker Time Ser.). (Illus.). 16p. (J). (ps-3). 2000. pap. 2.99 (*0-375-81064-1*) Random.
— Little Engines Can Do Big Things. (Illus.). 24p. (J). (ps-1). 2000. pap. 3.25 (*0-375-80553-2*, Pub. by Random Bks Yng Read) Random.

Random House Staff. Little Ernie's Animal Friends. (Board Bks.). (J). 1997. 2.50 (*0-679-88884-5*, Pub. by Random Bks Yng Read) Random.

***Random House Staff.** Mary's Story. 176p. (J). (gr. 4-7). 1999. pap. 4.99 (*0-375-80332-7*, Pub. by Random Bks Yng Read) Random.
— Matt's Story. 176p. (J). (gr. 4-7). 1999. pap. 4.99 (*0-375-80333-5*) Random Hse Chldrns.
— My Name Is Grover. 24p. (J). 2000. 1.99 (*0-375-80446-3*, Pub. by Random Bks Yng Read) Random.

Random House Staff. New York Times Film Reviews, Vol. 10: 1975-1976. 1988. text 180.00 (*0-8240-7584-6*) Garland.
— New York Times Film Reviews, Vol. 11: 1977-1978. 1988. text 180.00 (*0-8240-7585-4*) Garland.
— New York Times Film Reviews, Vol. 12: 1979-1980. 1988. text 180.00 (*0-8240-7586-2*) Garland.
— New York Times Film Reviews, Vol. 13: 1981-1982. 350p. 1989. text 180.00 (*0-8240-7587-0*) Garland.
— New York Times Film Reviews, Vol. 14: 1983-1984. 1988. text 180.00 (*0-8240-7588-9*) Garland.
— New York Times Theater Reviews, Vol. 20: 1977-1978. 1988. text 80.00 (*0-8240-7568-4*) Garland.
— New York Times Theater Reviews, Vol. 22: 1981-1982. 1988. text 80.00 (*0-8240-7570-6*) Garland.
— New York Times Theater Reviews, Vol. 24: 1985-1986. 550p. 1989. text 80.00 (*0-8240-7572-2*) Garland.
— New York Times Theater Reviews, Vol. 25: 1987-1988. 500p. 1990. text 80.00 (*0-8240-7573-0*) Garland.
— New York Times Theatre Review, Vol. 1: 1870-1885. 550p. 1990. text 80.00 (*0-8240-7549-8*) Garland.
— New York Times Theatre Review, Vol. 2: 1886-1895. 1988. text 80.00 (*0-8240-7550-1*) Garland.
— New York Times Theatre Reviews, Vol. 3: 1896-1903. 550p. 1990. text 80.00 (*0-8240-7551-X*) Garland.
— New York Times Theatre Reviews, Vol. 4: 1904-1911. 1988. text 80.00 (*0-8240-7552-8*) Garland.
— New York Times Theatre Reviews, Vol. 5: 1912-1919. 1988. text 80.00 (*0-8240-7553-6*) Garland.
— New York Times Theatre Reviews, Vol. 6: Index 1870-1919. 550p. 1991. text 195.00 (*0-8240-7554-4*) Garland.
— New York Times Theatre Reviews, Vol. 15: Index 1920-1970. 550p. 1990. text 195.00 (*0-8240-7563-3*) Garland.
— The New York Times Theatre Reviews, 1991-92. (New York Times Theater Reviews Ser.: Vol. 27). 1994. text 180.00 (*0-8153-0643-1*) Garland.
— Nursery Rhymes from Mother Goose. LC 94-11973. (Illus.). 96p. (J). (gr. 2-8). 1994. 8.99 (*0-517-11857-2*) Random Hse Value.

***Random House Staff.** Oh, the Things You Can Say from A-Z. (Dr. Seuss Beginner Fun Ser.). (J). 1998. pap. 2.99 (*0-679-89278-8*) Random.
— On the Farm. (J). 2000. pap. 2.99 (*0-375-80501-X*, Pub. by Random Bks Yng Read) Random.
— On the Go. (J). 2000. pap. 2.99 (*0-375-80502-8*, Pub. by Random Bks Yng Read) Random.

Random House Staff. Pillsbury Best Assortment, 3. 1999. 19.95 (*0-676-58496-9*) Random.

***Random House Staff.** Play It Smart Workbooks: Human Body. (J). 2001. pap. 2.99 (*0-375-80461-7*) Random Bks Yng Read.

Random House Staff. Playtime with Big Bird. (Board Bks.). (J). 1997. 2.50 (*0-679-88881-0*, Pub. by Random Bks Yng Read) Random.

***Random House Staff.** Rain or Shine. (Painting Time Ser.). (Illus.). 32p. (J). (ps-3). 2000. pap. 3.99 (*0-375-80504-4*, Pub. by Random Bks Yng Read) Random.

Random House Staff. Random House Compact World Atlas. 2nd ed. 1997. pap. 15.95 (*0-679-77712-1*) Random.
— Random House Easy Learning French Dictionary. (FRE.). 1999. pap. write for info. (*0-375-70596-1*) Random Ref & Info.
— Random House Easy Learning Spanish Dictionary. 1999. pap. write for info. (*0-375-70597-X*, spa) Random Ref & Info.
— Random House French-English Dictionary. (ENG & FRE.). 1998. pap. 12.95 (*0-375-70086-2*) Random Ref & Info.
— Random House French-English, English-French Dictionary. 1997. mass mkt. 5.99 (*0-345-41438-1*) Ballantine Pub Grp.
— Random House Health & Medicine Dictionary. 1997. pap. 5.99 (*0-679-77709-1*) Random Ref & Info.
— Random House Japanese Dictionary. 1996. pap. 7.99 (*0-679-77373-8*) Random.

***Random House Staff.** Random House Roget's College Thesaurus. 2000. write for info. (*0-375-40946-7*) Random Ref & Info.
— Random House Roget's Handy American Thesaurus. 2000. pap. 3.99 (*0-375-70744-1*) Random.

Random House Staff. Random House Roget's Thesaurus. 2nd ed. LC 96-96204. (Illus.). 717p. (Orig.). 1996. mass mkt. 4.99 (*0-345-40094-1*) Ballantine Pub Grp.
— Random House School & Office Thesaurus. 1998. pap., student ed. 9.38 (*0-07-366071-X*) McGraw.
— Random, House Spanish-English English-Spanish Dictionary. Raventos, Margaret H., ed. (SPA & ENG.). 825p. 1996. mass mkt. 5.99 (*0-345-40547-1*) Ballantine Pub Grp.
— Random House Spanish to English & English to Spanish Dictionary. LC 99-10228. 1999. 20.00 (*0-375-40483-X*); pap. 12.95 (*0-375-70436-1*) Random Ref & Info.
— Random House Student Notebook Thesaurus. 1998. pap., student ed. 4.95 (*0-375-70246-6*) Random Ref & Info.

***Random House Staff.** The Random House Treasury of Favorite Love Poems. 384p. 1999. pap. 10.00 (*0-375-70768-9*) Random Ref & Info.

Random House Staff. Random House Treasury of Love Poems. 1999. write for info. (*0-375-40514-3*) Random Ref & Info.
— The Random House Unabridged Dictionary. 2nd unabridged ed. 1993. 100.00 (*0-679-42441-5*) Random Ref & Info.
— Random House Webster's Biographical Dictionary of Scientists. LC 97-25159. 608p. 1997. pap. 18.00 (*0-375-70057-9*) Random Ref & Info.
— Random House Webster's Build Your Power Vocabulary. LC 98-7914. 1998. pap. 10.95 (*0-375-70247-4*) Random Ref & Info.
— Random House Webster's College Dictionary. 1992. 20.00 (*0-685-56462-2*) Random.
— Random House Webster's College Dictionary. 2nd ed. LC 97-903. (Illus.). 1568p. 1997. 23.95 (*0-679-45570-1*) Random Ref & Info.
— Random House Webster's College Dictionary. 2nd deluxe ed. LC 97-903. 1568p. 1997. 30.00 (*0-679-45858-1*) Random.
— Random House Webster's College Thesaurus. 1997. pap. 12.95 (*0-375-70065-X*) Random Ref & Info.
— Random House Webster's College Thesaurus. rev. ed. 800p. 1997. 20.00 (*0-375-40066-4*) Random Ref & Info.
— Random House Webster's Concise Dictionary. 1996. text. write for info. (*0-07-052199-9*) McGraw.
— Random House Webster's English Language Desk Reference. LC 96-49233. 1997. pap. 14.95 (*0-679-78000-9*) Random Ref & Info.
— Random House Webster's French-English, English-French Dictionary. LC 97-245. 1997. 22.00 (*0-679-44851-9*) Random Ref & Info.
— Random House Webster's Large Print Dictionary. large type ed. 880p. 1998. 40.00 (*0-375-40114-8*) Random Ref & Info.
— Random House Webster's Pocket American Dictionary. 3rd ed. LC 98-67042. 376p. 1998. pap. 6.99 (*0-375-70353-5*) Random Ref & Info.
— Random House Webster's Pocket Business Dictionary. 2nd ed. 336p. 1997. pap. 6.99 (*0-375-70059-5*) Random Ref & Info.
— Random House Webster's Pocket French Dictionary. 1997. pap. 6.99 (*0-375-70156-7*) Random Ref & Info.
— Random House Webster's Pocket Grammar, Usage & Punctuation. 1998. pap. 6.99 (*0-375-70283-0*) Random Ref & Info.
— Random House Webster's Pocket Power Vocabulary. 1997. pap. 6.99 (*0-375-70191-5*) Random Ref & Info.
— Random House Webster's Quick & Easy American English Dictionary. LC 99-23573. 1999. pap. 5.99 (*0-375-70625-9*) Random.
— Random House Webster's School & Office Dictionary. 2nd rev. ed. LC 99-25970. 576p. 1997. pap. 11.95 (*0-679-78008-4*) Random Ref & Info.
— Random House Webster's School & Office Thesaurus. 624p. 1995. pap. 10.95 (*0-679-76157-8*) Random Ref & Info.
— Random House Webster's School & Office Thesaurus. 2nd ed. LC 99-215465. 624p. 1997. pap. 11.95 (*0-679-78009-2*) Random Ref & Info.
— Random House Webster's Spell Checker. 2nd ed. LC 98-28868. 1998. 8.95 (*0-375-40390-6*) Random Ref & Info.
— Random House Webster's Student Notebook Spanish Dictionary. LC 99-29298. 128p. 1999. pap. 4.95 (*0-375-70359-4*) Knopf.
— Random House Webster's Unabridged Dictionary. 2nd unabridged ed. LC 97-17702. 2256p. 1997. 59.95 incl. cd-rom (*0-679-45854-9*) Random Ref & Info.
— Random House Webster's Unabridged Dictionary & CD-ROM Version 3.0, Vol. 3. 1999. 75.00 incl. cd-rom (*0-375-40383-3*) Random.

***Random House Staff.** Random House Webster's Visual Dictionary of Everyday American English. 1999. pap. 14.95 (*0-375-70532-5*) Random Hse Value.

Random House Staff. Remember When. LC 96-71574. (Life Favors Ser.). 1997. 6.99 (*0-679-88407-6*, Pub. by Random Bks Yng Read) Random.

***Random House Staff.** Rise & Shine. (Sesame Street Pop-up Ser.). 1999. pap. 3.25 (*0-375-80408-0*) Random.
— Roget's Handy American Thesaurus. 2000. 39.95 (*0-375-70860-X*) Random Ref & Info.

Random House Staff. Roget's Pocket American Thesaurus. 400p. 2000. pap. 6.99 (*0-375-70354-3*) Random Ref & Info.
— Russian-English Dictionary. 640p. 1999. pap. 16.95 (*0-375-70250-4*) Random Ref & Info.
— Songs & Games for Young Children. (Illus.). 96p. (J). (gr. 2-8). 1994. 4.99 (*0-517-10191-2*) Random Hse Value.

***Random House Staff.** Surviving in American English: A Guide to Words, Phrases & Cultural Practices Unique to the USA. LC 00-29069. 160p. 2000. pap. 7.95 (*0-375-70468-X*) Random Ref & Info.
— Taco Bell Chihuahua 1-2-3. (Illus.). 24p. (J). (ps-3). 2000. pap. 8.99 (*0-375-80684-9*) Random.
— Taco Bell Chihuahua Paper Dog Book. (Illus.). 8p. (J). (ps-3). 2000. mass mkt. 5.99 (*0-375-80683-0*) Random.
— Taco Bell Chihuahua Sticker Book. (Illus.). 4p. (J). (ps-3). 2000. pap. 5.99 (*0-375-80682-2*) Random.

R

Random House Staff. Taking Care: Self-Care for 100 Common Symptoms & 25 Long-Term Ailments. LC 96-41153. 1997. pap. 12.00 (*0-679-77794-6*) Random.

***Random House Staff.** Theodore's Birthday Surprise. 24p. (J). 2000. 2.99 (*0-375-80249-5*, Pub. by Random Bks Yng Read) Random.

Random House Staff. Theodore's Whistle. LC 98-15464. (J). 1998. pap. 3.25 (*0-679-89419-5*) Random.

— These Things I Love. 1997. 6.99 (*0-679-88408-4*, Pub. by Random Bks Yng Read) Random.

***Random House Staff.** Thomas & the Magic Railroad. (Thomas the Tank Engine Ser.). (Illus.). 80p. (J). (gr. k-1). 2000. pap. 2.99 (*0-375-80555-9*, Pub. by Random Bks Yng Read) Random.

— Thomas & the Magic Railroad. LC 99-85990. (Illus.). 32p. (J). (ps-1). 2000. 10.99 (*0-375-80551-6*, Pub. by Random Bks Yng Read) Random.

— Thomas' Railway Word Book. (Thomas the Tank Engine Ser.). (Illus.). (J). 2000. pap. 3.25 (*0-375-80281-9*) Random.

Random House Staff. Thomas the Tank Engine Colors. (Board Bks.). (J). 1997. 2.50 (*0-679-88888-8*, Pub. by Random Bks Yng Read) Random.

— Thomas the Tank Engine Coming & Going. (Board Bks.). (J). 1997. 2.50 (*0-679-88880-2*, Pub. by Random Bks Yng Read) Random.

— Thomas the Tank Engine Counts to Ten. (Board Bks.). (Illus.). (J). 1997. 2.50 (*0-679-88879-9*, Pub. by Random Bks Yng Read) Random.

— Thomas the Tank Engine Shapes & Sizes. (Board Bks.). (J). 1997. 2.50 (*0-679-88887-X*, Pub. by Random Bks Yng Read) Random.

***Random House Staff.** Thomas the Tank Engine's Sounds. (Toddler Bks.). (Illus.). 12p. (J). (ps). 2000. bds. 2.99 (*0-375-80302-5*, Pub. by Random Bks Yng Read) Random.

— Time for Bed, Elmo. (J). 2000. 8.99 (*0-375-80322-X*, Pub. by Random Bks Yng Read) Random.

Random House Staff. Trucks,]. LC 98-65566. (J). 1998. lib. bdg. 7.99 (*0-679-99185-9*, Pub. by Random Bks Yng Read) Random.

— Tubby Time for Little Ernie. (Board Bks.). (J). 1997. 2.50 (*0-679-88883-7*, Pub. by Random Bks Yng Read) Random.

***Random House Staff.** A Very Grouchy Christmas. (Super Coloring Time Ser.). (Illus.). 80p. (J). (ps-3). 2000. pap. 2.99 (*0-375-80648-2*, Pub. by Random Bks Yng Read) Random.

— Web American Dictionary: College Edition. 2nd ed. 960p. 2000. 11.95 (*0-375-42555-1*) Random.

Random House Staff. Webster's American Family Concise Dictionary. 1998. pap. 11.95 (*0-375-70360-8*) Random Ref & Info.

— Webster's College Dictionary. rev. ed. LC 99-12620. 1999. 24.95 (*0-375-40741-3*) Random Ref & Info.

— Webster's College Thesaurus. 1998. 11.25 (*0-07-366070-1*) McGraw.

— Webster's Compact Crossword. 2000. write for info. (*0-375-40547-X*) Random.

— Webster's Concise American Family Dictionary. LC 98-48027. 1999. 14.95 (*0-375-40507-0*) Random Ref & Info.

— Webster's Dictionary: Random House. 2nd rev. ed. LC 96-96192. (Illus.). 896p. (Orig.). 1996. mass mkt. 5.99 (*0-345-40095-X*) Ballantine Pub Grp.

— Webster's Dictionary of American English. 1998. pap. 20.00 (*0-679-78007-6*) Random Ref & Info.

— Webster's Medical Spell Checker. 1998. 8.95 (*0-375-40152-0*) Random Ref & Info.

— Webster's Pocket American Learner's Dictionary. 400p. 1999. pap. 7.99 (*0-375-70699-2*) Random Ref & Info.

— Webster's Pocket Bad Speller Dictionary. 1997. pap. 6.99 (*0-375-70212-1*) Random Ref & Info.

— Webster's Pocket Reference. 1998. pap. 19.95 (*0-375-70327-6*) Random Ref & Info.

— Webster's Pocket Rhyming Dictionary. rev. ed. 1999. pap. 6.99 (*0-375-70514-7*) Random Ref & Info.

— Webster's Pocket Russian Dictionary. 2000. pap. 8.99 (*0-375-70467-1*) Random Ref & Info.

— Webster's Pocket Spanish Dictionary. 3rd ed. 400p. 2000. pap. 6.99 (*0-375-70566-X*) Random Ref & Info.

— Webster's School & Office Dictionary. 1999. pap. 0.00 (*0-375-70601-1*) Random.

— Webster's Student Notebook Dictionary. 1998. pap. 4.95 (*0-375-70165-6*) Random Ref & Info.

***Random House Staff.** Websters Unabreviated English Language Dictionary. 3rd ed. 2000. write for info. (*0-375-40656-5*) Random Ref & Info.

— Wings & Tales & Dragon Scales. (Super Coloring Time Ser.). (Illus.). 80p. (J). (ps-3). 2000. pap. 2.99 (*0-375-80637-7*, Pub. by Random Bks Yng Read) Random.

Random House Staff. The World According to Babe & Friends. LC 98-67198. (J). 1998. 7.99 (*0-679-89447-0*, Pub. by Random Bks Yng Read) Random.

Random House Staff, compiled by. Botanica's Annuals & Perennials. LC 99-41152. (Illus.). 1008p. 1999. pap. 19.95 (*1-57145-648-1*, Laurel Glen Pub) Advantage Pubs.

— Botanica's Trees & Shrubs. LC 99-41602. (Illus.). 1008p. 1999. pap. 19.95 (*1-57145-649-X*, Laurel Glen Pub) Advantage Pubs.

Random House Staff, contrib. by. White Butcher Block. 1989. 120.00 (*0-394-58542-9*) Random.

Random House Staff, ed. Alligator King. (J). 1998. 3.25 (*0-679-89412-8*, Pub. by Random Bks Yng Read); lib. bdg. 8.99 (*0-679-99412-2*, Pub. by Random Bks Yng Read) Random.

— Babe & Friends: The Complete Scrapbook. LC 98-66575. (Illus.). 48p. (ps-3). 1998. pap. 6.99 (*0-679-89386-5*) Random.

— Getting Ready to Read. (J). 1986. pap. 9.95 incl. VHS (*0-394-88317-9*, Pub. by Random Bks Yng Read) Random.

— Hawaiian Shirt. (J). 1998. lib. bdg. 8.99 (*0-679-99413-0*, Pub. by Random Bks Yng Read) Random.

— Interview with Anne Rice. 1997. 90.00 (*0-679-45830-1*) Random.

Random House Staff, ed. Knee Hight Books. 4.99 (*5-559-37088-6*) Random.

— Learning about Letters. (J). (gr. k up). 1986. pap. 19.95 incl. VHS (*0-394-88319-5*, Pub. by Random Bks Yng Read) Random.

Random House Staff, ed. Learning about Numbers. (J). 1986. pap. 9.95 incl. VHS (*0-394-88315-2*, Pub. by Random Bks Yng Read) Random.

— Random House Webster's Concise Thesaurus. 1998. 11.95 (*0-375-40197-0*) Random Ref & Info.

— Random House Webster's Dictionary. unabridged ed. 1998. write for info. (*0-375-40479-1*) Random Ref & Info.

— Random House Webster's Large Print Dictionary. large type ed. LC 96-47193. 873p. 1998. pap. 26.00 (*0-375-70106-0*) Random Ref & Info.

— Random House Webster's Large Print Thesaurus. large type ed. 640p. 1998. 40.00 (*0-375-40220-9*); pap. 26.00 (*0-375-70211-3*) Random Ref & Info.

— Random House Webster's Modern Office Dictionary. LC 99-26279. 800p. 1999. 16.95 (*0-375-40517-8*) Random Ref & Info.

— Random House Webster's Pocket German Dictionary. 2nd ed. (GER.). 320p. 1998. pap. 6.99 (*0-375-70160-5*) Random Ref & Info.

— Random House Webster's Pocket Italian Dictionary. 2nd ed. (ITA.). 352p. 1997. pap. 6.99 (*0-375-70159-1*) Random Ref & Info.

— Requiem. deluxe ed. 1997. 175.00 (*0-679-46197-3*) Random.

— RH Webster's Smart Learner's. (J). 2000. pap. 12.95 (*0-375-70484-1*, Pub. by Random Bks Yng Read) Random.

— Sir Cumference. (J). 1998. pap. 3.99 (*0-679-88378-9*); lib. bdg. 11.99 (*0-679-98378-3*) Random.

— The Smallest Elf. 1999. lib. bdg. 7.99 (*0-375-90101-9*) Random.

— Special Coloring No. 4, 4. 1999. pap. 2.99 (*0-375-80024-7*) Random.

— Thomas Getting Ready for School. 1999. pap. 3.99 (*0-375-80081-6*, Pub. by Random Bks Yng Read) Random.

— Untitle Truck. (J). 1999. 7.99 (*0-375-80083-2*, Pub. by Random Bks Yng Read) Random.

— Webster's American College Dictionary. LC 98-53044. 1999. 10.95 (*0-375-40529-1*) Random Ref & Info.

— Webster's Basic Dictionary. 1998. 12.50 (*0-07-228678-4*) McGraw.

— Webster's Basic Dictionary of American English. LC 98-2885. 608p. 1998. pap. 10.95 (*0-679-78005-X*) Random Ref & Info.

— Webster's English Language Dictionary. 1999. write for info. (*0-375-40518-6*) Random Ref & Info.

— Webster's English Language Dictionary. 2nd ed. LC PE1112.R28 1999. 640p. 1999. pap. 15.95 (*0-375-70464-7*) Random Ref & Info.

Random House Staff, ed. Webster's Family Dictionary. LC 97-14176. 960p. 1997. 5.00 (*0-517-18361-7*) Random Hse Value.

Random House Staff, ed. World Explorers Series. (J). 1994. 75.00 (*0-679-87014-8*) Random.

— Writing Numbers to 10: Pre-School-Kindergarten, No. 3. (Star Wars). 16p. (J). (ps-2). 1999. pap., wbk. ed. 4.99 (*0-375-80007-7*, Pub. by Random Bks Yng Read) Random.

Random House Staff, jt. auth. see New York Times Staff.

Random House Staff, jt. creator see Lucas Books.

Random House Staff, ed. see Mathieu, Joseph.

***Random House Thesaurus Staff.** Random House Roget's Thesaurus. 1999. mass mkt. 4.99 (*0-345-91598-4*, Ballantine) Ballantine Pub Grp.

— Roget's College Thesaurus. rev. ed. 832p. 2000. 20.00 (*0-375-42559-4*) Random.

***Random House U. K. Ltd.** Batman Beyond:Gene Splicers. 24p. (J). 2001. mass mkt. 3.25 (*0-375-80655-5*, Pub. by Random Bks Yng Read) Random.

— Bear Bakes a Cake. (J). 2001. mass mkt. 2.99 (*0-375-81139-7*, Pub. by Random Bks Yng Read) Random.

Random House U. K. Ltd. Big Head. LC 97-39009. 1998. lib. bdg. 26.00 (*0-679-99018-6*, Pub. by Random Bks Yng Read) Random.

***Random House U. K. Ltd.** Casual Friday Paper Doll Book. (YA). 2001. mass mkt. 5.99 (*0-375-80660-1*, Pub. by Random Bks Yng Read) Random.

— Cute Adorable Baby Animals. 80p. (J). 2001. mass mkt. 2.99 (*0-375-81142-7*, Pub. by Random Bks Yng Read) Random.

— Elmo's World: Hair. 16p. (J). 2001. mass mkt. 2.99 (*0-375-81141-9*) Random Bks Yng Read.

— Elmo's World: Sports. 80p. (J). 2001. mass mkt. 2.99 (*0-375-81143-5*, Pub. by Random Bks Yng Read) Random.

— Fairy Tales & Nursery Rhymes. 80p. (J). 2001. mass mkt. 2.99 (*0-375-81144-3*, Pub. by Random Bks Yng Read) Random.

— Let's Go to the Firehouse. (J). 2001. mass mkt. 4.99 (*0-375-80312-2*, Pub. by Random Bks Yng Read) Random.

— Let's Make Music. 80p. (J). 2001. mass mkt. 2.99 (*0-375-81145-1*) Random Bks Yng Read.

— Lift the Lid, Use the Potty. (J). 2001. mass mkt. 7.99 (*0-375-81146-X*, Pub. by Random Bks Yng Read) Random.

— Museum of Monster Art. 16p. (J). 2001. mass mkt. 2.99 (*0-375-81140-0*, Pub. by Random Bks Yng Read) Random.

— Races, Rescues & Runways. (J). 2001. mass mkt. 2.99 (*0-375-81138-9*, Pub. by Random Bks Yng Read) Random.

***Random House Value Publishing Staff.** Ain't I a Woman. 1999. 7.99 (*0-517-20504-1*) Random Hse Value.

Random House Value Publishing Staff. Alien Presence. 1997. 12.99 (*0-517-15973-2*) Random Hse Value.

— Alternative Healing Secrets. LC 97-52140. 176p. 1999. 7.99 (*0-517-16047-1*) Random Hse Value.

— American Indian Fairy Tales. LC 97-50637. 128p. (J). 1998. 6.99 (*0-517-20300-6*) Random Hse Value.

— Ansel Adams. 1999. 9.99 (*0-517-16119-2*) Random Hse Value.

— Anybody Designer Series on Antiques. 1998. 5.99 (*0-517-20240-9*) Random Hse Value.

— Anybody Designer Series on Grape Folliage. 1998. 5.99 (*0-517-20244-1*) Random Hse Value.

— Anybody Novelty Series on Hearts. 1998. 5.99 (*0-517-20258-1*) Random Hse Value.

— Anybody Novelty Series on Tee Time. 1998. 5.99 (*0-517-20257-3*) Random Hse Value.

— Anything Book, 3. 1999. 5.99 (*0-517-20510-6*) Crown Pub Group.

***Random House Value Publishing Staff.** Anything Book, Vol. 7. 1999. 5.99 (*0-517-20520-3*) Random Hse Value.

— Anything Book Novelty, Vol. 1. 1999. 5.99 (*0-517-20523-8*) Random Hse Value.

— Anything Book Novelty, Vol. 2. 1999. 5.99 (*0-517-20524-6*) Random Hse Value.

Random House Value Publishing Staff. Art of Aromatherapy. Date not set. write for info. (*0-517-20323-5*) Random Hse Value.

— Audubon. 1999. 9.99 (*0-517-16117-6*) Random Hse Value.

— Black Beauty. 240p. 1998. 5.99 (*0-517-18958-5*) Random Hse Value.

— Cassatt. 80p. 1998. 9.99 (*0-517-16065-X*) Random Hse Value.

— Cat Spells. LC 98-46601. 1999. 4.99 (*0-517-16125-7*) Random Hse Value.

— Cezanne. 80p. 1998. 9.99 (*0-517-16064-1*) Random Hse Value.

— Child's Book of Stories. 480p. 1998. 5.99 (*0-517-18961-5*) Random Hse Value.

— The Complete Book of Fortune. LC 97-52030. 624p. 1998. 9.99 (*0-517-20262-X*) Random Hse Value.

— Degas. 80p. 1998. 9.99 (*0-517-16066-8*) Random Hse Value.

— Dictionary of the Arts. LC 99-19354. 1999. 9.99 (*0-517-20347-2*) Random Hse Value.

— Dos, Don'ts & Maybes of English Usage. 1999. 6.99 (*0-517-20340-5*) Random Hse Value.

— Dream Spells. LC 98-49666. 1999. 4.99 (*0-517-16124-9*) Random Hse Value.

***Random House Value Publishing Staff.** Ellis Island. LC 99-27774. (Illus.). 2000. 9.99 (*0-517-20879-2*) Random Hse Value.

Random House Value Publishing Staff. Elvis: The King of Rock 'n' Roll. 1998. 12.99 (*0-517-16053-6*) Random Hse Value.

— 50 Years of Chrysler's Hottest. 1999. 19.99 (*0-517-18734-5*) Random Hse Value.

— First Christmas. LC 99-17617. 1999. 6.99 (*0-517-20634-X*) Random Hse Value.

— Five Language Dictionary. Date not set. write for info. (*0-517-20137-2*) Random Hse Value.

***Random House Value Publishing Staff.** Forgotten Ireland. 80p. 2000. 9.99 (*0-517-16159-1*) Random Hse Value.

Random House Value Publishing Staff. Frank Lloyd Wright. 1999. 9.99 (*0-517-16115-X*) Random Hse Value.

— A Garden of Virtues. LC 97-48812. 272p. 1998. 5.99 (*0-517-20282-4*) Random Hse Value.

— Garden Spells. LC 98-49665. 1999. 4.99 (*0-517-16126-5*) Random Hse Value.

— Georgia O'Keeffe. 1999. 9.99 (*0-517-16123-0*) Random Hse Value.

— Ghost. 1997. 12.99 (*0-517-15970-8*) Random Hse Value.

— Great Tales of the Mountains & Plains. 1996. 11.99 (*0-517-15069-7*) Random Hse Value.

***Random House Value Publishing Staff.** Green. 1998. 5.99 (*0-517-20314-6*) Random Hse Value.

Random House Value Publishing Staff. Half Hours with Best Poets. LC 99-35646. 1999. 7.99 (*0-517-20431-2*) Random Hse Value.

— Half Hours with the Best Thinkers. LC 99-31718. 1999. 7.99 (*0-517-20432-0*) Random Hse Value.

— Harley-Davidson: A Love Affair. 128p. 1998. 12.99 (*0-517-16051-X*) Random Hse Value.

— Heidi. 352p. 1998. 5.99 (*0-517-18967-4*) Random Hse Value.

— Katherine Hepburn. LC 98-18840. 1998. 20.00 (*0-517-20097-X*) Random Hse Value.

— Hudson River School. 1999. 9.99 (*0-517-16120-6*) Random Hse Value.

— Illustrated Library for Children Poems for Children. (Illus.). 1999. 5.99 (*0-517-20326-X*) Random Hse Value.

— Illustrated Library for Children Songs & Games. (Illus.). 1999. 5.99 (*0-517-20331-6*) Random Hse Value.

— Irish Coats of Arms. 1997. 9.99 (*0-517-15072-7*) Random Hse Value.

— Irish Spirit. 288p. 1998. 7.99 (*0-517-20168-2*) Random Hse Value.

— Jacqueline Kennedy Onassis. LC 96-36064. 1997. 20.00 (*0-517-20077-5*) Random Hse Value.

— John Paul II: A Tribute. 80p. 1998. 9.99 (*0-517-16076-5*) Random Hse Value.

— The Jumbo Quiz Book. 1999. 7.99 (*0-517-20502-5*) Random Hse Value.

— King Arthur & His Knights. 400p. 1998. 5.99 (*0-517-18969-0*) Random Hse Value.

— Leonardo Da Vinci. 80p. 1998. 9.99 (*0-517-16062-5*) Random Hse Value.

***Random House Value Publishing Staff.** Lincoln. 1999. pap. 5.00 (*0-517-20742-7*) Random Hse Value.

— London. (Illus.). 128p. 2000. 12.99 (*0-517-16174-5*) Random Hse Value.

Random House Value Publishing Staff. Maxfield Parrish. 1999. 9.99 (*0-517-16122-2*) Random Hse Value.

— McClane's Fishing Encyclopedia. LC 98-6833. 1168p. 1998. 29.99 (*0-517-20336-7*) Random Hse Value.

— Michelangelo. 80p. 1998. 9.99 (*0-517-16058-7*) Random Hse Value.

— Monet. 80p. 1998. 9.99 (*0-517-16055-2*) Random Hse Value.

— Muhammed Ali. LC 96-36218. 1997. 20.00 (*0-517-20080-5*) Random Hse Value.

— My Book of Favorite Fairy Tales. LC 97-51198. 128p. (J). 1998. 6.99 (*0-517-20302-2*) Random Hse Value.

— My Sticker Dictionary. (J). 1998. 3.99 (*0-517-16040-4*) Random Hse Value.

— Natural Healing Secrets: An A to Z Guide to the Best Home Remedies. 176p. 1998. 7.99 (*0-517-16046-3*) Random Hse Value.

— Norman Rockwell. 1999. 9.99 (*0-517-16121-4*) Random Hse Value.

— Nursery Rhymes: A Collection from Mother Goose. (c). (Illus.). 1999. 5.99 (*0-517-20330-8*) Random Hse Value.

***Random House Value Publishing Staff.** Our Family History. deluxe ed. 160p. 2000. 14.99 (*0-517-43636-1*) Random Hse Value.

— Paris. (Illus.). 128p. 2000. 12.99 (*0-517-16175-3*) Random Hse Value.

Random House Value Publishing Staff. Personality of the Horse. LC 96-215516. 352p. 1988. 9.99 (*0-517-03785-8*) Random Hse Value.

— Peter Pan. 1999. 5.99 (*0-517-20577-7*) Random Hse Value.

***Random House Value Publishing Staff.** Pictorial Historic Presidents of the United States. 128p. 2001. 12.99 (*0-517-16160-5*) Random Hse Value.

Random House Value Publishing Staff. Practical Art of Aromatherapy. Date not set. write for info. (*0-517-20325-1*) Random Hse Value.

— Prayers & Graces. (Illus.). 1999. 5.99 (*0-517-20327-8*) Random Hse Value.

— Pre-Raphaelites. 1999. 9.99 (*0-517-16116-8*) Random Hse Value.

— The Recipe Encyclopedia: A Complete A-Z of Good Food & Cooking. Tomnay, Susan, ed. LC 97-17176. (Illus.). 496p. 1997. 19.99 (*0-517-18442-7*) Random Hse Value.

— Renoir. 80p. 1998. 9.99 (*0-517-16067-6*) Random Hse Value.

— Robert Burns: The Scottish Bard. LC 98-41113. 1999. 7.99 (*0-517-16100-1*) Random Hse Value.

***Random House Value Publishing Staff.** Rome. (Illus.). 128p. 2000. 12.99 (*0-517-16176-1*) Random Hse Value.

Random House Value Publishing Staff. Ronald Reagan. LC 96-36063. 1997. 20.00 (*0-517-20078-3*) Random Hse Value.

— The Secret Garden. (Children's Classics Ser.). 288p. 1998. 5.99 (*0-517-18960-7*) Random Hse Value.

— Sex on the Beach & Other Wild Drinks. (Illus.). 96p. 1997. 5.99 (*0-517-18501-6*) Random Hse Value.

— Sonnets from the Portuguese. (Illus.). 64p. 1997. 4.99 (*0-517-18721-3*) Random Hse Value.

— The Soul of Michael Jordan & Company. 1998. 12.99 (*0-517-20455-X*) Random Hse Value.

— The Soul of Tiger Woods. 1998. 12.99 (*0-517-20458-4*) Random Hse Value.

— The Story of Hanukkah. Finamore, Frank J., ed. 64p. 1997. 4.99 (*0-517-18360-9*) Random Hse Value.

— Tan. 1998. 5.99 (*0-517-20313-8*) Random Hse Value.

— Test Your Bible IQ. LC 98-56181. 1999. 6.99 (*0-517-16097-8*) Random Hse Value.

— 365 Ways to Love Your Cat. LC 99-47468. 2000. 6.99 (*0-517-18275-0*) Random Hse Value.

— 365 Bible Stories. Date not set. pap. write for info. (*0-517-20434-7*) Random Hse Value.

— 365 Bible Stories. LC 97-34904. 192p. 1998. 5.99 (*0-517-18820-1*) Random Hse Value.

— Travels with Elvis. LC 98-35933. 1999. 5.99 (*0-517-20309-X*) Random Hse Value.

— Treasure Island. (Children's Classics Ser.). 272p. 1998. 5.99 (*0-517-18963-1*) Random Hse Value.

— Words of Wisdom. LC 97-27888. 224p. 1998. 7.99 (*0-517-18837-6*) Random Hse Value.

— Ultimate Yankee Baseball Quiz Book. LC 97-47066. 228p. (J). 1998. 7.99 (*0-517-18738-8*) Random Hse Value.

— Van Gogh. 80p. 1998. 9.99 (*0-517-16054-4*) Random Hse Value.

— Webster's Concise Encyclopedia. LC 98-16355. 728p. 1998. 9.99 (*0-517-20320-0*) Random Hse Value.

Random House Value Publishing Staff. Webster's Encyclopedic Unabridged Dictionary. rev. ed. 1704p. 1994. 12.00 (*0-517-15141-3*) Random Hse Value.

Random House Value Publishing Staff. Wind in the Willows. (J). 1996. 9.99 (*0-517-16023-4*) Random Hse Value.

— The World of Butterflies. 1999. 12.99 (*0-517-16133-8*) Random Hse Value.

— The World of Seashells. 1999. 12.99 (*0-517-16132-X*) Random Hse Value.

— The World's Best Guns. 2000. 7.99 (*0-517-19461-9*) Random Hse Value.

***Random House Value Publishing Staff.** World's Greatest Military Leader. (Illus.). 256p. 2000. 14.99 (*0-517-16161-3*) Random Hse Value.

An Asterisk (*) at the beginning of an entry indicates that the title is appearing for the first time.

Random House Value Publishing Staff, ed. Ali Baba, Illustrated Stories for Children. 1999. 6.99 (*0-517-20425-8*) Random Hse Value.

***Random House Value Publishing Staff, ed.** Bible Promises. (Illus.). 16p. 2000. 5.99 (*0-517-19453-8*) Random Hse Value.

Random House Value Publishing Staff, ed. Caring for Cats. 2000. 9.99 (*0-517-16141-9*) Random Hse Value.

— Caring for Dogs. 2000. 9.99 (*0-517-16140-0*) Random Hse Value.

— England the Beautiful Land. 1999. 14.99 (*0-517-44100-4*) Random Hse Value.

Random House Value Publishing Staff, ed. From America's Favorite Kitchen: All New Treasury of Christmas Recipes. 1991. 6.99 (*0-517-06235-6*) Random Hse Value.

Random House Value Publishing Staff, ed. The Good Luck Book. 192p. 1999. 5.99 (*0-517-16096-X*) Random Hse Value.

***Random House Value Publishing Staff, ed.** Handguns & Rifles. (Illus.). 128p. 1999. 12.99 (*0-517-16142-7*) Random Hse Value.

Random House Value Publishing Staff, ed. How to Tell Your Fortunes. 1999. 3.99 (*0-517-42907-1*) Random Hse Value.

— Kitchen Klips. 1992. 12.99 (*0-517-08468-6*) Random Hse Value.

***Random House Value Publishing Staff, ed.** Natural Disasters. (Illus.). 128p. 1999. 12.99 (*0-517-16144-3*) Random Hse Value.

Random House Value Publishing Staff, ed. Rip Van Winkle, Illustrated Stories for Children. 1999. 6.99 (*0-517-20426-6*) Random Hse Value.

— Shakespeare, Illustrated Stories for Children. 1999. 6.99 (*0-517-20430-4*) Random Hse Value.

Random House Value Publishing Staff, ed. Thirty Minute Menus. 1992. spiral bd. 6.99 (*0-517-05671-2*) Random Hse Value.

Random House Value Publishing Staff, ed. Visions of Nostradamus & Others. LC 98-34972. 1999. 5.99 (*0-517-16094-3*) Random Hse Value.

— Warplanes of World War I. 1999. 3.99 (*0-517-21962-X*) Random Hse Value.

— Who's Who in the New Testament. 1998. 17.99 (*0-517-15934-1*) Random Hse Value.

— Witness to an Era: The Civil War Western Photographs of Alexander Gardner. 1998. 19.99 (*0-517-18344-7*) Random Hse Value.

Random House Value Publishing Staff & Dickens, Charles. Children Stories from Dickens. LC 97-51199. 128p. (J). 1998. 6.99 (*0-517-20301-4*) Random Hse Value.

Random House Value Publishing Staff & Finamore, Frank J. Devilish Doings. LC 96-5820. 336p. 1997. 7.99 (*0-517-18504-0*) Random Hse Value.

Random House Value Publishing Staff & Irving, Washington. The Legend of Sleepy Hollow. LC 97-51194. 112p. (J). 1998. 6.99 (*0-517-20303-0*) Random Hse Value.

Random House Value Publishing Staff & Miller, David. A Century of War. 112p. 1997. 12.99 (*0-517-18440-0*) Random Hse Value.

***Random House Value Publishing Staff & Wilde, Oscar.** Wit & Wisdom of Oscar Wilde: A Treasury of Quotations, Anecdotes & Observations. LC 99-14881. 1999. 6.99 (*0-517-19460-0*) Random Hse Value.

Random House Value Publishing Staff & Wordsworth, William. Wordsworth: The Eternal Romantic. LC 98-41110. 1999. 7.99 (*0-517-16109-5*) Random Hse Value.

Random House Value Publishing Staff, ed. see Aesop.

Random, Melanie, jt. auth. see Fried, Katrina.

Randon, Anita, jt. auth. see Perri 6.

Randon, R. K. & Sudarshan, K. N. Child Prostitution. (C). 1997. 62.00 (*81-7024-909-0*, Pub. by Ashish Pub Hse) S Asia.

Randorf, Gary. Beside the Stilled Waters. Jerry, Jocelyn & Beamish, Richard J., eds. (Acid Rain Ser.: No. 1). (Illus.). 24p. 1989. pap. 5.00 (*0-614-14002-1*) Adirondack Council.

***Randour, Mary Lou.** Animal Grace: Entering a Spiritual Relationship with Our Fellow Creatures. LC 99-49172. 224p. 2000. 20.00 (*1-57731-104-3*, Pub. by New Wrld Lib) Publishers Group.

Randour, Mary Lou, et al, eds. Exploring Sacred Landscapes: Religious & Spiritual Experiences in Psychotherapy. 216p. (C). 1993. text 49.50 (*0-231-07000-4*) Col U Pr.

Randow, R. Von, see Von Randow, R., ed.

***Randreas.** Carvaka Caritra: Tale of a Hindu Hedonist-Materialist. 382p. 1999. pap. 18.95 (*0-7414-0170-3*) Buy Books.

Randrianarivelo, Lucien & Jedele, Tom. Malagasy Newspaper Reader. LC 96-84386. 250p. 1997. write for info. (*1-881265-31-5*) Dunwoody Pr.

Rands, Jeffrey. Seattle Style Guide: Cultural Imperatives of the Hot Seattle Scene. 125p. (Orig.). 1993. pap. 9.95 (*0-9636753-0-3*) J Rands.

Rands, William B., see Browne, Matthew, pseud.

Randsborg, Klavs. Archaeology & the Man-Made Material Reality. (Illus.). 104p. (Orig.). (C). 1992. pap. 15.95 (*87-7288-412-6*, Pub. by Aarhus Univ Pr) David Brown.

— Hjortspring: Warfare & Sacrifice in Early Europe. LC 96-204887. (Illus.). 256p. (C). 1996. text 33.00 (*87-7288-545-9*, Pub. by Aarhus Univ Pr) David Brown.

Randsford, Tessa. A Dancing Innocence. (C). 1993. pap. 28.00 (*0-86334-063-6*, Pub. by Saltire Soc) St Mut.

***Randy, Lady.** Lord & Lady of Heat: The Poem. 1999. pap. 14.00 (*0-9674838-0-8*, LLH-1) LadyRandy.

Randy, Rieffeld. Joey Lawrence. 192p. (YA). 1993. per. 3.99 (*0-671-88719-X*) PB.

Rane, Bill. Talfulano. LC 75-27249. 104p. 1976. pap. 10.00 (*0-912292-39-3*) Smith.

Ranelagh, E. L. The Past We Share: The Near Eastern Ancestry of Western Folk Literature. (Illus.). 288p. 1981. 21.95 (*0-7043-2234-X*, Pub. by Quartet) Charles River Bks.

Ranelagh, John O'Beirne. A Short History of Ireland. 2nd rev. ed. 315p. 2000. pap. text 22.95 (*0-521-46944-9*) Cambridge U Pr.

Ranes, Barbara. From Baba to Tovarishch: The Bolshevik Revolution & Soviet Women's Struggle for Liberation. (Illus.). 128p. 1994. pap., per. 15.00 (*0-86714-027-5*) Marxist-Leninist.

Ranew, Nathanael. Solitude Improved by Divine Meditation. 341p. 1995. reprint ed. 24.95 (*1-57358-012-0*) Soli Deo Gloria.

Raney, Charles. If You Are Born Again: You Can Not Think Evil. 28p. 1983. pap. 2.00 (*0-9610842-0-0*) Lve Chrch Mins.

Raney, Deborah. In the Still of Night. LC 96-45850. 24p. 1997. pap. 8.99 (*1-55661-667-8*) Bethany Hse.

— In the Still of Night. large type ed. LC 97-35679. (Christian Fiction Ser.). 331p. 1997. 22.95 (*0-7862-1235-7*) Thorndike Pr.

— Kindred Bond. LC 97-45450. (Portraits Ser.). 288p. 1998. pap. 8.99 (*1-55661-999-5*) Bethany Hse.

***Raney, Deborah.** Kindred Bond. large type ed. 2000. 22.95 (*0-7862-2257-3*) Thorndike Pr.

— Vow to Cherish: Love Remembers. LC 95-45105. 240p. 1999. pap. 9.99 (*0-7642-2335-6*) Bethany Hse.

Raney, Deborah & Miller, Vicky. Children's Sermons to Go: 52 Take-Home Lessons about God. LC 98-35784. 112p. 1998. pap. 10.00 (*0-687-05257-2*) Abingdon.

Raney, Donald C., jt. auth. see Gillette, M. L.

Raney, James O., ed. Listening & Interpreting: The Challenge of the Work of Robert Langs. LC 83-8816. 544p. 1984. 50.00 (*0-87668-624-2*) Aronson.

Raney, Laura, jt. auth. see Subbarao, K.

Raney, Mardell Jefferson, ed. see Ohler, Jason.

Raney, Mark. Believing in the Wind. 235p. 1981. 10.00 (*0-933272-02-2*) Hurricane Co.

— Breathe All Seasons. (Illus.). 241p. 1977. 10.00 (*0-933272-00-6*) Hurricane Co.

— This Soil of Sand. (Illus.). 26p. 1978. 20.00 (*0-933272-01-4*) Hurricane Co.

Raney, R. Beverly. Pediatric Tumor Boards on CD-ROM, No. 1.1. 1997. cd-rom 89.95 (*0-412-14411-5*, Pub. by E A) OUP.

Raney, Richard B., jt. auth. see Brashear, H. Robert, Jr.

Ranfagni, A. Trajectories & Rays: The Path - Summation in Quantum Mechanics & Optics. Mugnai, D. et al, eds. 240p. (C). 1990. text 70.00 (*9971-5-0781-1*) World Scientific Pub.

Ranfft, Erich & Hughes, Anthony, eds. Sculpture & Its Reproductions. (Critical Views Ser.). (Illus.). 224p. 1997. pap. 24.95 (*1-86189-002-8*, Pub. by Reaktion Bks) Consort Bk Sales.

Ranft. A Womans Way to Perfection. LC 99-59605. 1999. text 39.95 (*0-312-21712-9*) St Martin.

Ranft, Bryan & Till, Geoffrey. The Sea in Soviet Strategy. 2nd ed. LC 88-61128. (Illus.). 275p. 1988. 32.95 (*0-87021-992-8*) Naval Inst Pr.

Ranft, Bryan M. The Beatty Papers: Selections from the Private & Official Correspondence of Admiral of the Fleet Earl Beatty, Vol. I: 1902-1918. 600p. 1989. text 69.95 (*0-85967-807-5*, Pub. by Scolar Pr) Ashgate Pub Co.

— The Beatty Papers, Vol. II: 1916-1927. (Navy Records Ser.). 1993. 104.95 (*0-85967-964-0*, Pub. by Scolar Pr) Ashgate Pub Co.

Ranft, Bryan M., ed. Ironclad to Trident: 100 Years of Defence Commentary, Brassey's 1886-1986. 272p. 1986. 65.00 (*0-08-031191-1*, Pergamon Pr) Elsevier.

Ranft, Patricia. Women & Spiritual Equality in Christian Tradition. pap. 18.95 (*0-312-22966-6*) St Martin.

Ranft, Patricia. Women & Spirtual Equality in the Christian Tradition. LC 97-50397. 288p. 1998. text 39.95 (*0-312-15911-0*) St Martin.

— Women & the Religious Life in Pre-Modern Europe. 176p. 1996. text 45.00 (*0-312-12434-1*) St Martin.

— Women & the Religious Life in Premodern Europe. 159p. (C). 1998. text 24.00 (*0-7881-5609-8*) DIANE Pub.

— Women & the Religious Life in Premodern Europe. 176p. 1997. pap. 17.95 (*0-312-17679-1*) St Martin.

Ranfurly, C. War with Whitaker. 15.95 (*0-7493-1954-2*, Pub. by Random) Trafalgar.

Rang, H. P. Pharmacology. 4th ed. LC 98-31756. 1999. write for info. (*0-443-05974-8*) Church.

Rang, H. P. & Dale, M. M. Pharmacology. 2nd ed. (Illus.). 955p. 1991. pap. text 55.00 (*0-443-04110-5*) Church.

Rang, H. P., et al. Pharmacology. 3rd ed. LC 94-47182. 1995. pap. text 38.00 (*0-443-07560-3*) Church.

Rang, Jack C. How to Read the Bible Aloud: Oral Interpretation of Scripture. 224p. 1994. pap. 10.95 (*0-8091-3493-4*) Paulist Pr.

Rang, Mary L. Manual of Newborn Care Plans. (Spiral Manual Ser.). 1981. 14.00 (*0-316-73380-6*, Little Brwn Med Div) Lppncott W & W.

Rang, Mercer. A New Anthology of Orthopaedics. 2000. text 79.00 (*0-7216-7141-1*) Harcrt Hlth Sci Grp.

Rang, Mercer, jt. auth. see Wenger, Dennis R.

Rang, William R. It Began with a Parachute. (Illus.). 93p. (Orig.). (J). 1992. pap. 7.90 (*0-921100-38-8*) Inhtce Pubns.

— Salt in His Blood: The Life of Michael de Ruyter. LC 96-39179. (J). 1996. 9.90 (*0-921100-59-0*) Inhtce Pubns.

Rangachari, K., jt. auth. see Thurston, Edgar.

Rangacharya, Adya. Introduction to Bharata's Natyasastra. 1998. 12.50 (*81-215-0829-0*, Pub. by M Manoharial) Coronet Bks.

— Natyasastra: English Translation with Critical Notes. LC 97-901591. (C). 1997. 45.00 (*81-215-0680-8*, Pub. by M Manoharial) Coronet Bks.

— Quest for Wisdom: Thoughts on the Bhagawadgita. (C). 1993. 22.00 (*81-7154-709-5*, Pub. by Popular Prakashan) S Asia.

Rangacharya, K., jt. auth. see Mahadeva, A.

Rangacharya, M. Hindu Philosophy of Conduct, Vol. 3. (C). 1991. 35.00 (*0-685-50021-7*, Pub. by M Manoharial) S Asia.

— The Hindu Philosophy of Conduct-Lectures on the Bhagavadgita, Vol. 1. (C). 1989. 58.50 (*0-685-30709-3*, Pub. by M Manoharial) S Asia.

Rangacharya, M. & Aiyangar, M. B., trs. The Vedantasutras with the Sribhasya of Ramanujacarya, Vol. 1. (C). 1988. 36.00 (*81-215-0091-5*, Pub. by M Manoharial) Coronet Bks.

Rangan. Cases in Marketing Management. 9th ed. 1997. text. write for info. (*0-256-22942-2*, Irwn McGrw-H) McGrw-H Hghr Educ.

— Large Concrete Buildings. 320p. (C). 1996. 99.95 (*0-582-10130-1*) Addison-Wesley.

***Rangan, C. Pandu, et al, eds.** Foundations of Software Technology & Theoretical Computer Science: Proceedings of the 19th Conference, Chennai, India, December 13-15, 1999. LC 99-58792. (Lecture Notes in Computer Science Ser.: Vol. 1738). xii, 452p. 1999. pap. 73.00 (*3-540-66836-5*) Spr-Verlag.

***Rangan, Haripriya.** Of Myths & Movements: Rewriting Chipko into Himalayan History. 256p. 2000. 60.00 (*1-85984-783-8*, Pub. by Verso); pap. 20.00 (*1-85984-305-0*, Pub. by Verso) Norton.

Rangan, Ravi, jt. ed. see Busnaina, Ahmed A.

Rangan, Subramanian. Prism on Globalization Corporate Responses to the Dollar LC 99-6415. 1999. 36.95 (*0-8157-7360-9*) Brookings.

— Prism on Globalization: Corporate Responses to the Dollar. LC 99-6415. 1999. pap. text. write for info. (*0-8157-7359-5*) Brookings.

Rangan, U. Srinivasa, jt. auth. see Yoshino, Michael Y.

Rangan, Venkat P., ed. Network & Operating System Support for Digital Audio & Video: Third International Workshop, La Jolla, California, U. S. A., November 1992, Proceedings. LC 93-11825. (Lecture Notes in Computer Science Ser.: Vol. 712). 1993. 61.95 (*0-387-57183-3*) Spr-Verlag.

Ranganathan. Planning & Manage African Power, Vol. 1. 302p. 1998. pap. text 65.00 (*1-85649-551-5*, Pub. by Zed Books); pap. text 27.50 (*1-85649-552-3*, Pub. by Zed Books) St Martin.

Ranganathan, Janet, jt. auth. see Ditz, Daryl.

Ranganathan, K. S., jt. auth. see Balakrishnan, R.

Ranganathan, N. VLSI & Parallel Computing for Pattern Recognition & Artificial Intelligence. (Series in Machine Perception & Artificial Intelligence: Vol. 18). 250p. 1995. text 64.00 (*981-02-2312-9*) World Scientific Pub.

Ranganathan, S., et al, eds. Interfaces - Structure & Properties. 400p. 1993. text 133.00 (*0-87849-613-0*, Pub. by Trans T Pub) Enfield Pubs NH.

Ranganathan, S. R. Cataloguing Practice. 2nd ed. 517p. reprint ed. text 50.00 (*81-85273-14-6*, Pub. by Sarada Ranganathan Endowment for Library Science) Advent Bks Div.

— Classification & Communication. 291p. 1990. pap. 13.95 (*81-85273-27-8*, Pub. by Sarada Ranganathan Endowment for Library Science) Advent Bks Div.

— Classified Catalogue Code: With Additional Rules for Dictionary Catalogue Code. 5th ed. 844p. (C). 1988. reprint ed. text 50.00 (*81-85273-06-5*, Pub. by Sarada Ranganathan Endowment for Library Science) Advent Bks Div.

— Colon Classification. rev. ed. 400p. (C). 1988. reprint ed. pap. text 50.00 (*81-85273-11-1*, Pub. by Sarada Ranganathan Endowment for Library Science) Advent Bks Div.

— Elements of Library Classification. 108p. 1990. reprint ed. text 20.00 (*81-85273-30-8*, Pub. by Sarada Ranganathan Endowment for Library Science) Advent Bks Div.

— The Five Laws of Library Science. 2nd ed. 449p. (C). 1988. reprint ed. pap. 18.95 (*81-85273-07-3*, Pub. by Sarada Ranganathan Endowment for Library Science) Advent Bks Div.

— Library Administration. 678p. 1990. reprint ed. pap. 25.00 (*81-85273-22-7*, Pub. by Sarada Ranganathan Endowment for Library Science) Advent Bks Div.

— Library Book Selection. 436p. 1990. reprint ed. text 50.00 (*81-85273-26-X*, Pub. by Sarada Ranganathan Endowment for Library Science) Advent Bks Div.

— Library Catalogue: Fundamentals & Procedures. (Library Science Ser.). 1980. lib. bdg. 75.00 (*0-8490-3168-0*) Gordon Pr.

— Library Manual: For Library Authorities, Librarians & Library Workers. rev. ed. 414p. (C). 1990. reprint ed. pap. 18.95 (*81-85273-03-0*, Pub. by Sarada Ranganathan Endowment for Library Science) Advent Bks Div.

— Philosophy of Library Classification. 133p. 1990. pap. 5.95 (*81-85273-33-2*, Pub. by Sarada Ranganathan Endowment for Library Science) Advent Bks Div.

— Prolegomena to Library Classification, Vol. I. 640p. 1990. reprint ed. pap. 30.00 (*81-85273-16-2*, Pub. by Sarada Ranganathan Endowment for Library Science) Advent Bks Div.

Ranganathan, S. R. Ramanujan: The Man & the Mathematician. 1997. reprint ed. 22.00 (*81-85273-37-5*, Pub. by UBS Pubs) S Asia.

Ranganathan, S. R. Reference Service. 432p. 1990. reprint ed. pap. 18.95 (*81-85273-20-0*, Pub. by Sarada Ranganathan Endowment for Library Science) Advent Bks Div.

Ranganathan, Sarala. Women & Social Order: A Profile of Major Indicators & Determinants. 1998. 34.00 (*81-7391-272-6*) Kaniska Pubs Dist.

Ranganathan, V., ed. see AFREPREN Staff.

Ranganathananda, Swami. Human Being in Depth: A Scientific Approach to Religion. Nelson, Elva L., ed. LC 90-43594. 159p. (C). 1991. pap. text 16.95 (*0-7914-0680-6*) State U NY Pr.

— Science & Religion. 1979. pap. 4.95 (*0-87481-190-2*, Pub. by Advaita Ashrama) Vedanta Pr.

***Rangarajan, C.** Indian Economy: Essays on Money & Finance. LC 98-906198. 1999. reprint ed. 28.00 (*81-7476-211-6*, Pub. by UBS Pubs) S Asia.

Rangarajan, G. Word-Formation in Sanskrit: With Special Reference to Taddhita-Formation. LC 99-931368. xii, 168 p. 1999. write for info. (*81-85616-55-8*) S Asia.

Rangarajan, Haripriya. Spread of Vaisnavism in Gujarat up to 1600 AD: A Study with Special Reference to the Iconic Forms of Visnu. (C). 1991. 72.00 (*81-7039-192-X*, Pub. by Somaiya) S Asia.

Rangarajan, Mahesh. Fencing the Forest: Conservation & Ecological Change in India's Central Provinces 1860-1914. LC 96-900513. (Studies in Social Ecology & Environment History). (Illus.). 258p. (C). 1996. text 27.00 (*0-19-563712-7*) OUP.

Rangarajan, Mahesh, ed. The Oxford Anthology of Indian Wildlife Hunting & Shooting, 1. 456p. 2000. 19.95 (*0-19-564592-8*) OUP.

— The Oxford Anthology of Indian Wildlife Watching & Conserving, 2. 320p. 2000. 19.95 (*0-19-564593-6*) OUP.

Rangarao, B. V. & Chaubey, N. P., eds. Social Perspective of Development of Science & Technology in India. 1983. 22.00 (*0-8364-0931-0*, Pub. by Heritage IA) S Asia.

Rangarao, Madhavan, jt. auth. see Vogel, Andreas.

Rangarao, S. Good Food from India. 284p. 1985. 9.95 (*0-318-36291-0*) Asia Bk Corp.

Rangaswami, Vanaja. Story of Integration: A New Interpretation of Princely States in India. 1982. 34.00 (*0-8364-0876-4*, Pub. by Manohar) S Asia.

Rangaswamy, K. M., jt. auth. see Arnold, David M.

Rangaswamy, N. S., jt. auth. see Shivanna, K. R.

***Rangaswamy, Padma.** Namaste America: Indian Immmigrants in an American Metropolis. LC 99-30458. 2000. 20.00 (*0-271-01981-6*) Pa St U Pr.

Rangaswamy, R. Textbook of Agricultural Statistics. 1995. write for info. (*81-224-0758-7*, Pub. by Wiley Estrn) Franklin.

Rangaswamy, R., jt. ed. see Martin, J. Paul.

Rangdrol, Tsele N. Empowerment. 128p. 1996. pap. 14.00 (*962-7341-15-0*) Bookpeople.

— The Heart of the Matter. 108p. 1996. pap. 11.00 (*962-7341-26-6*, Pub. by Rang Jung Yshe) Bookpeople.

— Lamp of Mahamudra. LC 88-34344. 128p. (Orig.). 1989. pap. 9.95 (*0-87773-487-9*, Pub. by Shambhala Pubns) Random.

— Mirror of Mindfulness. 144p. 1996. pap. 14.00 (*962-7341-18-5*, Pub. by Rang Jung Yshe) Bookpeople.

Range, Diane, ed. see Martinson, L. Keith & Range, Fritz.

Range, Fritz, jt. auth. see Martinson, L. Keith.

Range, Maggie, jt. auth. see Kindervatter, Suzanne.

Range, R. M. Holomorphic Functions & Integral Representations in Several Complex Variables. (Graduate Texts in Mathematics Ser.: Vol. 108). (Illus.). 375p. 1986. 59.95 (*0-387-96259-X*) Spr-Verlag.

***Range, Thomas E. & Smith, Sean P.** The Penn State Blue Band: A Century of Pride & Precision. LC 99-24468. 1999. 30.00 (*0-271-01960-3*) Pa St U Pr.

Range, Willard. Jawaharlal Nehru's World View: A Theory of International Relations. LC 61-15570. 149p. reprint ed. pap. 46.20 (*0-608-15793-7*, 203103800073) Bks Demand.

— The Rise & Progress of Negro Colleges in Georgia, 1865-1949. LC 51-14571. (University of Georgia Phelps-Stokes Fellowship Studies: No. 15). 264p. reprint ed. pap. 81.90 (*0-608-15805-4*, 203108800073) Bks Demand.

Rangel, Carlos. The Latin Americans: Their Love-Hate Relationship with the United States. rev. ed. 322p. 1987. pap. 24.95 (*0-88738-692-X*) Transaction Pubs.

— Third World Ideology & Western Reality: Manufacturing Political Myth. 180p. 1986. pap. 24.95 (*0-88738-601-6*) Transaction Pubs.

Rangel, Doris. Mountain Man. (Special Edition Ser.: No. 1140). 1997. per. 3.99 (*0-373-24140-2*, 1-24140-5) Silhouette.

— Prenuptial Agreement. 1998. per. 4.25 (*0-373-24224-7*, 1-24224-7, Mira Bks) Harlequin Bks.

Rangel-Guerrero, Daniel. Gil Vicente: Comedia Sobre a Divisa da Cidade de Coimbra. LC 79-24434. (Romance Monographs: No. 38). 84p. 1980. 15.00 (*84-499-3496-6*) Romance.

Rangel, Kimberly. The Homecoming. 368p. (Orig.). 1998. mass mkt. 5.50 (*0-8439-4352-1*, Leisure Bks) Dorchester Pub Co.

— Shadows. 368p. (Orig.). 1996. mass mkt. 4.99 (*0-8439-4054-9*, Leisure Bks) Dorchester Pub Co.

Rangel Nafaile, Carlos E. Los Materiales de la Civilizacion. (Ciencia para Todos Ser.). (SPA.). pap. 6.99 (*968-16-2567-6*, Pub. by Fondo) Continental Bk.

Rangel-Ribeiro, Lea. Time, Measurement, & Money. Evento, Susan, ed. (Macmillan Early Skills Program - Conversion Ser.). 64p. 1995. pap. 9.95 (*1-56784-509-6*) Newbridge Educ.

Rangel-Ribeiro, Lea & Rangel-Ribeiro, Victor. Wonderful World. Evento, Susan, ed. (Macmillan Early Skills Program - Conversion Ser.). 64p. 1995. pap. 9.95 (*1-56784-514-2*) Newbridge Educ.

Rangel-Ribeiro, Victor. Tivolem. LC 97-43264. 370p. 1998. 24.00 (*1-57131-019-3*) Milkweed Ed.

Rangel-Ribeiro, Victor, jt. auth. see Rangel-Ribeiro, Lea.

R

An Asterisk (*) at the beginning of an entry indicates that the title is appearing for the first time.

R

Rangeley, Robert & Kirmani, Syed S. International Inland Waters: Concepts for a More Active World Bank Role. LC 94-4996. (Technical Papers: No. 239). 31p. 1994. pap. 22.00 (*0-8213-2799-2*, 12799) World Bank.
Rangeley, Robert, et al. International River Basin Organizations in Sub-Saharan Africa. LC 94-12868. 90p. 1994. pap. 22.00 (*0-8213-2871-9*) World Bank.
Rangell, Leo. The Human Core: The Intrapsychic Base of Behavior, Vol. 1. x, 468p. 1990. 70.00 (*0-8236-2365-3*) Intl Univs Pr.
— The Human Core: The Intrapsychic Base of Behavior, Vol. 2. 500p. 1990. 72.50 (*0-8236-2366-1*) Intl Univs Pr.
Rangell, Leo & Moses-Hrushovski, Rena, eds. Psychoanalysis at the Political Border: Essays in Honor of Rafael Moses. 336p. 1996. 50.00 (*0-8236-5110-X*, BN 05110) Intl Univs Pr.
Rangelovska, Lidija, ed. see Vaknin, Samuel.
Ranger, jt. see Bhebe.
Ranger, G., ed. Eurojet: European Jetliner Directory. 125p. (C). 1993. text 195.00 (*0-9516105-0-3*, Pub. by Euravia Bks) St Mut.
Ranger, Jeff, jt. auth. see Lucas, Andrew J.
Ranger, Laurel A. High Mid-Volume Competitive Analysis, Pt. 2. (Copier Productivity Ser.). 50p. 1996. pap. 48.00 (*0-9629936-4-6*) Minnella Ent.
— High Mid-Volume Competitive Analysis, Pt. 3. (Copier Productivity Ser.: No. II). 52p. 1996. pap. 48.00 (*0-9629936-5-4*) Minnella Ent.
— Low Mid-Volume Competitive Analysis. Kasper, Juneann, ed. (Copier Productivity Ser.). 50p. (Orig.). 1994. pap. 45.00 (*0-9629936-2-X*) Minnella Ent.
Ranger, Laurel A. McKee, see McKee Ranger, Laurel A.
Ranger, Lucie, tr. see Peloquin, Claude.
Ranger, Mike, jt. auth. see Daise, Natalie E.
Ranger, P. Performance: Practical Examinations in Speech & Drama. 200p. 1990. pap. 22.95 (*0-419-14460-9*, A3884, E & FN Spon) Routledge.
Ranger, Robin. Arms & Politics, 1958-1978. (Illus.). 280p. (Orig.). 1982. pap. text 34.00 (*0-7715-5677-2*) Westview.
Ranger, T. O., jt. auth. see Bhebe, Ngwabi.
Ranger, Terence. Chingaira Makoni's Head: Myth, History & the Colonial Experience. (Hans Wolff Memorial Lectures). 27p. 1988. 5.00 (*0-941934-52-7*) Indiana Africa.
— Voices from the Rocks: Nature, Culture & History in the Matopos Hills of Zimbabwe. LC 98-40424. (Illus.). 320p. 1999. 49.95 (*0-253-33527-2*); pap. 19.95 (*0-253-21288-X*) Ind U Pr.
Ranger, Terence, et al, eds. Culture, Identity & Politics. (Research in Ethnic Relations Ser.). 176p. 1996. 68.95 (*1-85628-571-5*, Pub. by Avebry) Ashgate Pub Co.
Ranger, Terence & Slack, Paul A., eds. Epidemics & Ideas: Essays on the Historical Perception of Pestilence. (Past & Present Publications). 357p. (C). 1996. pap. text 19.95 (*0-521-55831-X*) Cambridge U Pr.
Ranger, Terence, jt. ed. see Hobsbawm, Eric J.
Ranger, Terence, jt. ed. see Werbner, Richard P.
Ranger, Terence, jt. ed. see Werbner, Richard.
Ranger, Terence O. Are We Not Also Men? The Samkange Family & African Politics in Zimbabwe 1920-1964. LC 95-21484. (Social History of Africa Ser.). 211p. 1995. 60.00 (*0-435-08975-7*, 08975); pap. 24.95 (*0-435-08977-3*, 08977) Heinemann.
— Peasant Consciousness & Guerilla War in Zimbabwe: A Comparative Study. LC 85-40286. (Perspectives on Southern Africa Ser.: No. 37). 399p. reprint ed. pap. 123.70 (*0-7837-4693-8*, 204444000003) Bks Demand.
Ranger, Terence O. & Bhebe, Ngwabi, eds. Soldiers in Zimbabwe's Liberation War. LC 95-4003. (Social History of Africa Ser.). 211p. 1995. 60.00 (*0-435-08974-9*, 08974); pap. 24.95 (*0-435-08972-2*) Heinemann.
Ranger, Terence O. & Kimambo, I. N., eds. The Historical Study of African Religion. LC 76-186104. 317p. reprint ed. pap. 98.30 (*0-608-17972-8*, 202906000058) Bks Demand.
Ranger, W.M. Due. UNIX to Microsoft Windows NT Migration. (gr. 8). 1998. pap. 39.95 (*1-57231-353-6*) Little.
Rangert, Bo, jt. auth. see Renouard, Frank.
Rangger, Andrea, jt. auth. see Insam, Heribert.
Rangis, T. V., ed. see Nielsen, E. Schmidt & Edwards, Ed.
Rangl, Deborah. Milady's Standard Hair Coloring Manual & Activities Book: A Level System Approach. 2nd abr. rev. ed. LC 97-10089. (Milady - Cosmetology). 208p. 1997. 27.95 (*1-56253-356-8*) Thomson Learn.
Rangnath, Molly, ed. see Fallon, Joan M.
Rangnekar, Pama, ed. see Rangnekar, Sharu.
***Rangnekar, Sharu.** In the Wonderland of Indian Managers. Rangnekar, Pama, ed. 1998. pap. 9.50 (*0-7069-9977-0*, Pub. by Vikas) S Asia.
Rangnow, Warren. Hut Two. 224p. 1994. text 15.95 (*1-57087-076-4*) Prof Pr NC.
Rango, A., jt. ed. see Johnson, Arnold I.
Rangoonwala, Ramzan, jt. auth. see LaScolea, Len J., Jr.
Rangoussis, Steve. Blood & the Imperial Purple. LC 98-89666. 280p. 1999. pap. 9.99 (*0-9668837-0-5*, AD-300) Pantheon Pr.
Rangra, Ranavir. Interviews with Indian Writers. (New World Literature Ser.: No. 48). (C). 1992. 24.00 (*81-7018-699-4*, Pub. by BR Pub) S Asia.
Rangwala, S. S., jt. ed. see Jouaneh, M.
Rani. Feast of India. 256p. (Orig.). 1991. pap. 16.95 (*0-8092-4095-5*, 409550, Contemporary Bks) NTC Contemp Pub Co.
Rani, Bilimoria. Female Criminality. (C). 1989. 50.00 (*0-89771-764-3*, Pub. by Eastern Book) St Mut.
— Female Criminality. 1985. 65.00 (*0-7855-1481-3*) St Mut.
— Female Criminality a Socio-Legal Study, 1987: With Supplement. (C). 1990. 75.00 (*0-7855-5560-9*) St Mut.
Rani, Bilmoria. Female Criminality. (C). 1987. 35.00 (*0-7855-5339-8*) St Mut.
Rani, D. Lalitha. Women Entrepreneurs. (Illus.). xvi, 392p. 1996. 40.00 (*81-7024-773-X*, Pub. by APH Pubng) Nataraj Bks.
Rani Gopal, K. Economics of Health & Nutrition: Some Aspects of Growth & Welfare. (C). 1987. 22.50 (*81-85076-18-9*, Pub. by Chugh Pubns) S Asia.
Rani, Seema & Malviya, Achla. Communication & Rural Women. (Illus.). x, 148p. 1991. 13.00 (*81-85445-15-X*, Pub. by Manak Pubns Pvt Ltd) Nataraj Bks.
Ranice, Teresa K. Baby's First Massage: The Gift of Gentle Massage for Your Newborn. rev. ed. Whipple, Gail, ed. (Illus.). 28p. 1992. spiral bd. 7.95 (*0-9661560-0-5*) Babys First.
Ranicki, A. A. Algebraic L-Theory & Topological Manifolds. (Tracts in Mathematics Ser.: No. 102). 368p. (C). 1993. text 74.95 (*0-521-42024-5*) Cambridge U Pr.
— Lower K & L-Theory. (London Mathematical Society Lecture Note Ser.: No. 178). 182p. (C). 1992. pap. text 39.95 (*0-521-43801-2*) Cambridge U Pr.
Ranicki, A. A., et al, eds. Algebraic & Geometric Topology. (Lecture Notes in Mathematics Ser.: Vol. 1126). v, 423p. 1985. 54.95 (*0-387-15235-0*) Spr-Verlag.
Ranicki, A. A. & Hughes, B. Ends of Complexes. (Tracts in Mathematics Ser.: No. 123). 378p. (C). 1996. text 74.95 (*0-521-57625-3*) Cambridge U Pr.
Ranicki, Andrew. Exact Sequences in the Algebraic Theory of Surgery. LC 80-18277. (Mathematical Notes Ser.: No. 26). (Illus.). 887p. 1981. reprint ed. pap. 200.00 (*0-608-06497-1*, 206679400009) Bks Demand.
— High-Dimensional Knot Theory: Algebraic Surgery in Codimension 2. LC 98-25080. (Springer Monographs in Mathematics). 1998. 79.95 (*3-540-63389-8*) Spr-Verlag.
Ranicki, Andrew, jt. auth. see Wall, C. T.
Ranicki, Andrew A. The Hauptvermntung Book: A Collection of Papers on the Topology of Manifolds. LC 96-30330. (K-Monographs). 196p. (C). 1996. text 121.50 (*0-7923-4174-0*) Kluwer Academic.
***Ranier, Marilyn, et al.** FTCE Elementary Education Competency & Skill. (Praxis Ser.). (C). 2000. per. 40.00 (*1-58197-066-8*) XAM.
— FTCE English Middle School. (C). 2000. per. 22.50 (*1-58197-078-1*) XAM.
— PRAXIS Elementary Competency & Skills. (Praxis Ser.). (C). 2000. per. 40.00 (*1-58197-010-2*) XAM.
— PRAXIS II Elementary Education Competency & Skill. (Praxis Ser.). (C). 2000. per. 40.00 (*1-58197-011-0*) XAM.
***Ranieri Gibellieri.** Steel Industry in the New Millenium, Vol. 2. 354p. 1998. 150.00 (*1-86125-024-X*) Institute of Management Consultants.
Ranieri, Helene. Let's "Unhook" the French Verbs & 77 Quick Grammar, Syntax & Pronunciation "Tips" 2nd rev. ed. LC 77-85156. (Illus.). 1974. 10.50 (*0-686-24866-X*) H Ranieri.
Ranieri, Joe. Diary of the Lord's Place. 128p. (Orig.). 1992. pap. 7.95 (*0-9631517-5-4*) Jeremiah Pr.
Ranieri, John J. Eric Voegelin & the Good Society. 288p. 1995. text 39.95 (*0-8262-1012-0*) U of Mo Pr.
Ranieri, R. & Aylen, J., eds. The Steel Industry in the New Millennium Vol. 1: Technology & the Market. (Illus.). 354p. 1998. 150.00 (*1-86125-019-3*, Pub. by Inst Materials) Ashgate Pub Co.
Ranieri, Ralph F. Meditations from Downtown: A Counselor's Reflections on Life. LC 90-61149. 64p. (Orig.). 1990. pap. 1.95 (*0-89243-326-4*) Liguori Pubns.
Ranina, H. P., ed. Business & Corporate Taxation: A Handbook, with Supplement Containing 7 New Chapters on Tax Planning for Partnership Firms. (C). 1990. 175.00 (*0-89771-265-X*) St Mut.
Ranina, N. English-Gujarati Dictionary. (ENG & GUJ.). 650p. 1997. 59.95 (*0-7859-9488-2*) Fr & Eur.
Ranina Rustam, N. Manual of English Gujarati Dictionary. (ENG & GUJ.). 640p. 1910. 59.95 (*0-7859-9830-6*) Fr & Eur.
Ranis, Gustav. The United States & the Developing Economies. rev. ed. (Problems of Modern Economy Ser.). (C). 1973. pap. write for info. (*0-393-09999-7*) Norton.
— The United States & the Developing Economies. 2nd rev. ed. LC 72-141594. (Problems of Modern Economy Ser.). 350p. (C). 1973. 8.95 (*0-393-05461-6*) Norton.
Ranis, Gustav, ed. En Route to Modern Growth: Latin American in the 1990s - Essays in Honor of Carlos Diaz-Alejandro. 160p. 1994. pap. text 18.50 (*0-940602-85-7*) IADB.
— Government & Economic Development. LC 79-140537. (Economic Growth Center, Yale University Publication Ser.). (Illus.). 581p. reprint ed. pap. 180.20 (*0-8357-8148-8*, 203386400087) Bks Demand.
— Japan & the United States in the Developing World. LC 97-14375. (Illus.). x, 277p. (Orig.). (C). 1997. pap. 15.95 (*0-9656930-1-5*) Intl Ctr Economic.
Ranis, Gustav, et al, eds. The Political Economy of Comparative Development into the 21st Century Vol. 1: Essays in Memory of John C. H. Fei, Vol. 1. LC 98-29702. 416p. 1999. 100.00 (*1-85898-878-0*) E Elgar.
— The Political Economy of Taiwan's Development into the 21st Century Vol. 2: Essays in Memory of John C. H. Fei, Vol. 2. LC 98-49231. 360p. 1999. 95.00 (*1-85898-879-9*) E Elgar.
Ranis, Gustav, et al. Linkages in Developing Economies: A Philippine Study. LC 89-48871. 83p. 1990. pap. 14.95 (*1-55815-049-8*) ICS Pr.
Ranis, Gustav, jt. auth. see Fei, John C.
Ranis, Gustav, jt. auth. see Fei, John C. H.
Ranis, Gustav, ed. & pref. see Barros, Ricardo, et al.
Ranis, Peter. Class, Democracy & Labor in Contemporary Argentina. rev. ed. LC 94-26252. Orig. Title: Argentine Workers. 310p. (C). 1994. pap. 24.95 (*1-56000-775-3*) Transaction Pubs.
Ranish, J. M. & Struck, C. W., eds. Proceedings of the International Symposium on High Temperature Lamp Chemistry, 3rd. LC 93-72869. (Proceedings Ser.: Vol. 93-16). 280p. 1993. 37.00 (*1-56677-040-8*) Electrochem Soc.
Ranjan, A. Hemant. Advancement in Iron Nutrition Research. 1994. pap. 100.00 (*0-7855-2750-8*, Pub. by Scientific Pubs) St Mut.
— Advances in Micro-Nutrient Research. 1994. pap. 120.00 (*81-7233-086-3*, Pub. by Scientific Pubs) St Mut.
Ranjan, Kumud. Women & Modern Occupation in India. (C). 1993. 42.00 (*81-85613-78-8*, Pub. by Chugh Pubns) S Asia.
Ranjana, Kumari, jt. auth. see Radhakrishnan, Sarvepalli.
Ranjeva, R. & Boudet, A. M., eds. Signal Perception & Transduction in Higher Plants. (NATO ASI Series H: Cell Biology: Vol. 47). (Illus.). ix, 344p. 1990. 142.95 (*0-387-51772-3*) Spr-Verlag.
Ranjhan, S. K. Animal Nutrition & Feeding Practices. 5th ed. 1997. pap. 12.00 (*0-7069-7100-0*, Pub. by Vikas) S Asia.
Ranjhan, S. K. Animal Nutrition in Tropics. 446p. 1980. 19.95 (*0-7069-1005-2*) Asia Bk Corp.
Ranjit Singh, D. S. & Sidhu, Jatswan S. Historical Dictionary of Brunei Darussalam. LC 96-52065. (Asian & Oceanian Historical Dictionaries Ser.: No. 25). (Illus.). 232p. 1997. 64.00 (*0-8108-3276-3*) Scarecrow.
Ranjitkar, S. B. Development Efforts in Nepal. 1996. pap. 22.00 (*0-7855-7378-X*, Pub. by Ratna Pustak Bhandar) St Mut.
Rank, Hugh. Persuasion Analysis: A Companion to Composition. LC 88-25696. 160p. (Orig.). 1988. pap. text 10.00 (*0-943468-02-7*) Counter-Prop Pr.
— The Pitch. 2nd rev. ed. (Illus.). 160p. 1991. pap. text 14.95 (*0-943468-03-5*, HF5821.R26) Counter-Prop Pr.
Rank, Hugh, ed. see Wedekind, Frank.
Rank, Kid, jt. auth. see Pop, Snap C.
Rank, Mark R. Living on the Edge: The Realities of Welfare in America. LC 93-22818. 266p. 1994. 35.00 (*0-231-08424-2*) Col U Pr.
— Living on the Edge: The Realities of Welfare in America. LC 93-22818. 266p. 1995. pap. 20.00 (*0-231-08425-0*) Col U Pr.
Rank, Mark R. & Kain, Edward L., eds. Diversity & Change in Families: Patterns, Prospects & Policies. LC 94-28524. 480p. 1994. pap. text 25.00 (*0-13-219668-9*) P-H.
Rank, Maureen. Dealing with the Dad of Your Past. 176p. (Orig.). 1990. pap. 7.99 (*0-87123-622-2*) Bethany Hse.
— Free to Grieve: Coping with the Trauma of Miscarriage. LC 85-11273. 176p. 1985. pap. 8.99 (*0-87123-806-3*) Bethany Hse.
Rank, Maureen, jt. auth. see Chapman, Annie.
Rank, Otto. Art & Artist. 1989. pap. 17.95 (*0-393-30574-0*) Norton.
Rank, Otto. Beyond Psychology. 291p. 1958. pap. text 8.95 (*0-486-20485-5*) Dover.
Rank, Otto. The Double: A Psychoanalytic Study. 112p. 1989. reprint ed. pap. text 24.00 (*0-946439-58-3*, Pub. by H Karnac Bks Ltd) Other Pr LLC.
— The Incest Theme in Literature & Legend. Richter, Gregory C., tr. from GER. LC 91-19651. 672p. 1991. text 65.00 (*0-8018-4176-3*) Johns Hopkins.
— Psychology & the Soul: A Study of Origin, Conceptual Evolution, & Nature of the Soul. Richter, Gergory C. & Lieberman, James, trs. LC 97-30223. 360p. 1998. text 29.95 (*0-8018-5739-2*) Johns Hopkins.
— A Psychology of Difference: The American Lectures. Kramer, Robert, ed. & intro. by. 416p. 1996. text 39.50 (*0-691-04470-8*, Pub. by Princeton U Pr) Cal Prin Full Svc.
— The Trauma of Birth. LC 93-21385. (Illus.). 256p. 1994. reprint ed. pap. 7.95 (*0-486-27974-X*) Dover.
Rank, Otto, et al. In Quest of the Hero. 210p. (C). 1990. pap. text 12.95 (*0-691-02062-0*, Pub. by Princeton U Pr) Cal Prin Full Svc.
Rank, Otto, jt. auth. see Ferenczi, Sandor.
Rank, Richard. Criminal Justice Systems of the Latin-American Nations: A Bibliography of the Primary & Secondary Literature. (New York University Criminal Law Education & Research Center, Publication Ser.: Vol. 11). 576p. 1981. reprint ed. 45.00 (*0-8377-1026-X*, Rothman) W S Hein.
Ranka, S. & Sahni, S. Hypercube Algorithms: With Applications to Image Processing & Pattern Recognition. (Bilkent University Lectures). 256p. 1990. 63.95 (*0-387-97322-2*) Spr-Verlag.
Rankama, K. Isotope Geology. 246.00 (*0-08-009007-9*, Pub. by Pergamon Repr) Franklin.
Ranke, Fredrich. Gottfried von Strassburg: Tristan und Isold. (GER.). iii, 247p. 1978. write for info. (*3-296-20200-5*, Pub. by Weidmann) Lubrecht & Cramer.
Ranke-Heinemann, Uta. Eunuchs for Heaven: The Catholic Church & Sexuality. LC 90-160864. x, 326p. 1990. write for info. (*0-233-98553-0*) Andre Deutsch.
Ranke, Hermann. Die Aegyptischen Personennamen. Incl. Form, Meaning, History of Names. 128.00 List of Components. (GER.). 75.00 List of Names. 90.00 write for info. (*0-318-53734-6*) J J Augustin.
Ranke, Kurt. Folktales of Germany. Baumann, Lotte, tr. LC 66-13884. (Folktales of the World Ser.). 291p. reprint ed. pap. 90.30 (*0-608-09507-9*, 205430800005) Bks Demand.
— Die Welt der einfachen Formen: Studien zur Motiv- Wort- und Quellenkunde. (C). 1978. 176.95 (*3-11-007420-6*) De Gruyter.
Ranke, Kurt, ed. Enzyklopaedie des Maerchens: Handwoerterbuch zur Historischen und vergleichenden Erzaehlforschung, 12 vols., Vol. 1. 703p. (C). 1977. 340.00 (*3-11-006781-1*) De Gruyter.
— Enzyklopaedie des Maerchens: Handwoerterbuch zur Historischen und vergleichenden Erzaehlforschung, 12 vols., Vol. 2. (GER.). 723p. (C). 1981. 340.00 (*3-11-008091-5*) De Gruyter.
— Enzyklopaedie des Maerchens: Handwoerterbuch zur Historischen und vergleichenden Erzaehlforschung, 12 vols., Vol. 3. (GER.). 144p. (C). 1983. 340.00 (*3-11-008201-2*) De Gruyter.
— Enzyklopaedie des Maerchens: Handwoerterbuch zur Historischen und vergleichenden Erzaehlforschung, 12 vols., Vol. 4. (GER.). 720p. (C). 1984. 340.00 (*3-11-009566-1*) De Gruyter.
Ranke, Kurt, et al. Enzyklopadie des Marchens: Handworterbuch Zur Historischen Und Vergleichenden Erzahlforschung. 4400p. 1999. 282.00 (*3-11-016402-7*) De Gruyter.
Ranke, Leopold. Civil Wars & Monarchy in France: In the Sixteenth & Seventeenth Centuries; A History of France Principally During That Period, 2 vols. Garvey, M. A., tr. LC 78-38365. (Select Bibliographies Reprint Ser.). 1977. reprint ed. 57.95 (*0-8369-6782-8*) Ayer.
Ranke, M. B. & Dowie, J., eds. Standardization of Growth Hormone Measurement Evidence-Based Medicine: 3rd KIGS/KIMS Expert Meeting on Growth & Growth Disorders, Sorrento, November 1998. (Hormone Research Ser.: Vol. 51, Suppl. 1 (1999)). (Illus.). iv, 88p. 1999. pap. 34.00 (*3-8055-6898-3*) S Karger.
Ranke, M. B. & Gilli, G., eds. Growth Standards, Bone Maturation & Idiopathic Short Stature. (Journal: Hormone Research Ser.: Vol. 45, Suppl. 2, 1996). (Illus.). iv, 68p. 1996. pap. 28.00 (*3-8055-6324-8*) S Karger.
Ranke, M. B. & Preece, M. A., eds. Growth & Growth Hormone Treatment of Children Born SGA, Body Composition: 2nd KIGS Expert Meeting on Growth & Growth Disorder, Lake Como, November 1996. (Journal: Hormone Research Ser.: Vol. 48, Suppl. 1, 1997). (Illus.). iv, 76p. 1997. pap. 35.00 (*3-8055-6505-4*) S Karger.
Ranke, M. B., jt. ed. see Albertsson-Wikland, K.
Ranke, M. B., jt. ed. see Christiansen, J. S.
Ranki, Gyorgy. Economy & Foreign Policy. (East European Monographs: No. 141). 224p. 1983. text 55.50 (*0-88033-032-5*, Pub. by East Eur Monographs) Col U Pr.
— Hungarian History-World History. (Indiana University Turkish Studies: No. 1). 316p. (C). 1984. 56.00 (*963-05-3997-7*, Pub. by Akade Kiado) St Mut.
Ranki, Gyorgy & Pok, S. Hungary & European Civilization. (Indiana University Studies on Hungary: Vol. 3). 480p. (C). 1989. 150.00 (*963-05-5502-6*, Pub. by Akade Kiado) St Mut.
Ranki, Gyorgy, jt. auth. see Berend, T. I.
Ranki, Vera. The Politics of Inclusion & Exclusion: Jews & Nationalism in Hungary. LC 98-45937. 274p. 1999. pap. 18.95 (*0-8419-1402-8*); text 45.00 (*0-8419-1401-X*) Holmes & Meier.
Rankilor, Peter R. Membranes in Ground Engineering. LC 80-40504. (Illus.). 387p. reprint ed. pap. 120.00 (*0-8357-3827-2*, 203655100004) Bks Demand.
***Rankin.** Antipope. 2000. pap. 8.95 (*0-552-13841-X*, Pub. by Transworld Publishers Ltd) Trafalgar.
— Apocalypso. 2000. pap. 8.95 (*0-552-14589-0*, Pub. by Transworld Publishers Ltd) Trafalgar.
— Armageddon: The Musical. 2000. pap. 10.95 (*0-552-13681-6*, Pub. by Transworld Publishers Ltd) Trafalgar.
— Armageddon: The Remake. 3rd ed. 2000. pap. 8.95 (*0-552-13923-8*, Pub. by Transworld Publishers Ltd) Trafalgar.
— Armageddon 2: The B Movie. 2000. pap. 10.95 (*0-552-13832-0*, Pub. by Transworld Publishers Ltd) Trafalgar.
Rankin. Athletic Training Management. 2nd ed. 336p. 2000. 55.31 (*0-07-092143-1*) McGraw.
***Rankin.** Book of Ultimate Truths. 2000. pap. 10.95 (*0-552-13922-X*, Pub. by Transworld Publishers Ltd) Trafalgar.
— Brentford Chainstore Massacre. 2000. pap. 8.95 (*0-552-14357-X*, Pub. by Transworld Publishers Ltd) Trafalgar.
— Brentford Triangle. 2000. pap. 8.95 (*0-552-13842-8*, Pub. by Transworld Publishers Ltd) Trafalgar.
— Dance of the Vodoo Handbag. 2000. pap. 8.95 (*0-552-14580-7*, Pub. by Transworld Publishers Ltd) Trafalgar.
— A Garden of Unearthly Delights: Bioengineering & the Future of Food. 2000. pap. 10.95 (*0-552-14212-3*, Pub. by Transworld Publishers Ltd) Trafalgar.
— Nostradamus Ate My Hamster. (J). 2000. pap. 8.95 (*0-552-14355-3*, Pub. by Transworld Publishers Ltd) Trafalgar.
— RankinWorks. (Illus.). 240p. 2000. 49.50 (*1-86154-161-9*, Pub. by Booth-Clibborn) Dist Art Pubs.
— Sprout Mask Replica. (J). 2000. 29.95 (*0-385-40706-8*, Pub. by Transworld Publishers Ltd) Trafalgar.
— The Sprouts of Wrath. 2000. pap. 8.95 (*0-552-13844-4*, Pub. by Transworld Publishers Ltd) Trafalgar.
Rankin, jt. auth. see Lightbourne.
Rankin, Andrew, tr. see Nakagami, Kenji.
Rankin, Arthur C. The Poetry of Stevie Smith: "Little Girl Lost" LC 84-16896. (Illus.). 120p. 1985. 43.00 (*0-389-20508-7*, BNB-08066) B&N Imports.

An Asterisk (*) at the beginning of an entry indicates that the title is appearing for the first time.

Rankin, Bob. Dr. Bob's Painless Guide to the Internet & Amazing Things You Can Do with E-Mail. LC 96-12821. 152p. 1996. 12.95 (*1-886411-09-3*) No Starch Pr.
— Juno: Free E-Mail & More. LC 97-33998. (Illus.). 200p. 1998. pap. text 14.95 (*1-886411-23-9*) No Starch Pr.
***Rankin, Bob.** Linux for Kids. LC 00-30741. 2000. pap. 24.95 (*1-886411-39-5*) No Starch Pr.
Rankin, Bob. The No B. S. Guide to Linux: Just What You Need to Know to Install, Optimize, & Use Linux. LC 97-6234. 352p. 1997. pap. text 34.95 incl. cd-rom (*1-886411-04-2*) No Starch Pr.
— The No B. S. Guide to Red Hat Linux 6: Just What You Need to Know to Install, Optimize & Use Red Hat Linux. LC 99-18467. 421p. 1999. pap. 34.95 incl. cd-rom (*1-886411-30-1*) No Starch Pr.
Rankin-Box, D. & Slater, V., eds. Nurse's Handbook of Complementary Therapies: U. S. A. Edition. (Illus.). 190p. 1996. pap. write for info. (*0-443-07791-6*) Church.
Rankin-Box, Denise F., ed. The Nurses' Handbook of Complementary Therapies. LC 94-41151. 1995. pap. text 17.95 (*0-443-05180-1*) Church.
Rankin, Carroll W. Dandelion Cottage. 4th ed. 1982. reprint ed. 8.95 (*0-938746-00-6*) Marquette Cnty.
Rankin, Charles E., ed. Legacy: New Perspectives on the Battle of the Little Bighorn. LC 96-24512. (Illus.). 132p. 1996. 20.00 (*0-917298-41-1*); pap. 19.95 (*0-917298-42-X*) MT Hist Soc.
— Wallace Stegner: Man & Writer. 272p. 1996. pap. 19.95 (*0-8263-1756-1*) U of NM Pr.
— Wallace Stegner: Man & Writer. LC 96-4422. 280p. (C). 1996. 19.95 (*0-8263-1741-3*) U of NM Pr.
Rankin, Chris. Country Decorating with Fabric: More Than Eighty Projects to Add Country Style, Charm & Color to Every Room in Your Home. (Illus.). 160p. 1992. 27.95 (*0-8069-8380-9*) Sterling.
— Country Decorating with Fabric: More Than 80 Projects to Add Country Style, Charm & Color to Every Room in Your Home. (Illus.). 160p. 1993. pap. 14.95 (*0-8069-8381-7*) Sterling.
— Creative Smocking: Contemporary Design, Traditional Techniques. Parks, Carol, ed. LC 97-4054. (Illus.). 112p. 1997. 24.95 (*1-887374-33-7*, Pub. by Lark Books) Random.
— Decorating Table Linens: Sixty Tablecloths, Place Mats, & Napkins to Applique, Paint, Cross-Stitch, Embroider & Sew. (Illus.). 144p. 1993. pap. 14.95 (*0-8069-8599-2*) Sterling.
— The Filet Crochet Book. LC 89-21904. (Illus.). 160p. 1992. pap. 16.95 (*0-8069-5823-5*) Sterling.
— Gorgeous Cross-Stitch: More Than 60 Enchanting Projects to Decorate Every Room. LC 94-24193. (Illus.). 144p. 1995. 27.95 (*0-8069-0974-9*) Sterling.
— Gorgeous Cross-Stitch: More Than 60 Enchanting Projects to Decorate Every Room. (Illus.). 144p. 1997. pap. 14.95 (*0-8069-0967-6*) Sterling.
— Scrap Crafts Year Round. (Illus.). 128p. 1998. 14.95 (*0-8069-8167-9*) Sterling.
— Splendid Silk Ribbon Embroidery: Embellishing Clothing, Linens & Accessories. (Illus.). 128p. 1997. pap. text 14.95 (*0-8069-4881-7*) Sterling.
Rankin, Chris, jt. auth. see Evans, K. Lee.
Rankin, Chris, jt. auth. see Theiss, Nola.
***Rankin, Claire & Phillips, Annelise Tracey.** Employment Tribunal Claims: A Practical Guide. (Legal Guidance Ser.). 200p. 2000. pap. 50.00 (*0-11-702393-0*, Pub. by Statnry Office) Balogh.
Rankin, D. J. A History of the County of Antigonish Nova Scotia. 402p. 1998. reprint ed. pap. 33.95 (*1-58211-060-3*, 097659) Quintin Pub RI.
— History of the County of Antigonish, N.S. 390p. 1996. reprint ed. lib. bdg. 45.00 (*0-8328-5222-8*) Higginson Bk Co.
Rankin, David. Celts & the Classical World. 340p. 1996. pap. 22.99 (*0-415-15090-6*) Routledge.
— Tertullian & the Church. 247p. (C). 1995. text 59.95 (*0-521-48067-1*) Cambridge U Pr.
Rankin, David, jt. auth. see Christensen, Alice.
Rankin, David C., ed. see Houzeau, Jean-Charles.
***Rankin, David L.** Fast Sketching Techniques. LC 99-87547. (Illus.). 144p. 2000. pap. 22.99 (*1-58180-005-3*, North Lght Bks) F & W Pubns Inc.
Rankin, David L., jt. auth. see Wilcox, Earl J.
Rankin, David O. So Great a Cloud of Witnesses. LC 78-2584. (Illus.). 208p. (Orig.). 1978. pap. 6.95 (*0-89407-014-2*) Strawberry Hill.
Rankin, Dorothy. Pestos! Cooking With Herb Pastes. LC 85-17121. (Illus.). 150p. 1985. pap. 8.95 (*0-89594-180-5*) Crossing Pr.
Rankin, Dorothy, jt. auth. see Chesman, Andrea.
Rankin, Dorothy, jt. auth. see Thomas, Shirley.
Rankin, Dorothy, ed. see Thomas, Shirley.
Rankin, Douglas A. Queen Jane's Version: The Holy Bible for Adults Only. LC 98-93134. (Illus.). 1152p. 1998. 29.95 (*0-9665208-6-6*) Dallas Emporia.
Rankin-Eagles, jt. auth. see Flatt.
Rankin Eagles, Heather, jt. auth. see Hult, Michael J.
***Rankin, Elizabeth A.** Quick Reference for Psychopharmacology. LC 99-38317. 558p. 2000. 31.95 (*0-7668-0631-6*) Delmar.
Rankin, Ernest H. The Indians of Gitchi Gumee. (Illus.). 24p. (Orig.). 1975. pap. 2.00 (*0-938746-08-1*) Marquette Cnty.
Rankin, Ernest H., jt. ed. see Carter, James L.
Rankin, Graham. Magnolia! A Care Manual. LC 98-56391. (Care Manual Ser.: Vol. 6). (Illus.). 128p. 1999. 19.95 (*1-57145-638-4*, Laurel Glen Pub) Advantage Pubs.
Rankin, Gwen. Help! I'm a Parent! How to Cope in the First Year. LC 97-109273. 200p. (Orig.). 1996. pap. text 12.95 (*0-7499-1382-7*, Pub. by Piatkus Bks) London Brdge.
Rankin, H. C., jt. auth. see Barbour, Charlotte.
Rankin, H. D. Antisthenes Sokratikos. vi, 210p. 1986. 64.00 (*90-256-0896-5*, Pub. by AM Hakkert) BookLink Distributors.
Rankin, Hattie L. I Saw It Happen to China. 1960. 25.00 (*0-87511-684-1*) Claitors.
Rankin-Hill, Lesley M. A Biohistory of 19th-Century Afro-Americans: The Burial Remains of a Philadelphia Cemetery. LC 96-7172. 224p. 1997. 59.95 (*0-89789-435-9*, Bergin & Garvey) Greenwood.
Rankin, Howard J. Power Talk: The Art of Effective Communication. LC 98-85059. 200p. 1999. pap. 11.95 (*0-9658261-3-9*) Stepwise Pr.
— 7 Steps to Wellness: Control Your Weight, Control Your Life. LC 97-81418. 192p. 1997. pap. 11.95 (*0-9658261-1-2*) Stepwise Pr.
— 10 Steps to a Great Relationship: What Every Couple Should Know about Love. 192p. 1998. pap. 11.95 (*0-9658261-2-0*) Stepwise Pr.
Rankin, Hugh F. The North Carolina Continentials. LC 79-135311. 440p. reprint ed. pap. 136.40 (*0-8357-3866-3*, 203659800004) Bks Demand.
— North Carolina in the American Revolution. (Illus.). vii, 75p. 1996. reprint ed. pap. 8.00 (*0-86526-091-5*) NC Archives.
— Pirates of Colonial North Carolina. (Illus.). viii, 72p. 1998. reprint ed. pap. 8.00 (*0-86526-100-8*) NC Archives.
Rankin, Hugh F., jt. auth. see Scheer, George F.
Rankin, Ian. Black & Blue, Vol. 1. 1999. mass mkt. 5.99 (*0-312-96677-6*, Pub. by Tor Bks) St Martin.
— Black & Blue: An Inspector Rebus Mystery. LC 97-25381. 1997. text 24.95 (*0-312-16783-0*) St Martin.
— Black & Blue: An Inspector Rebus Novel. large type ed. LC 98-9297. (Mystery Ser.). 626p. 1998. 26.95 (*0-7838-8443-5*, G K Hall & Co) Mac Lib Ref.
***Rankin, Ian.** The Black Book. 352p. 2000. mass mkt. 6.50 (*0-312-97675-5*, St Martins Paperbacks) St Martin.
Rankin, Ian. The Black Book: An Inspector Rebus Novel. LC 94-8929. 288p. 1994. reprint ed. 21.00 (*1-883402-77-8*) S&S Trade.
— Dead Souls. LC 99-44276. 320p. 1999. text 24.95 (*0-312-20293-8*) St Martin.
***Rankin, Ian.** Dead Souls. 448p. 2000. mass mkt. 6.50 (*0-312-97420-5*) St Martin.
— Death is not Enough. mass mkt. write for info. (*0-312-97628-3*) St Martin.
— Death is Not the End. LC 00-35272. 80p. 2000. text 11.95 (*0-312-26142-X*, Minotaur) St Martin.
Rankin, Ian. The Hanging Garden. LC 98-12404. 352p. 1998. text 24.95 (*0-312-19278-9*) St Martin.
***Rankin, Ian.** The Hanging Garden. large type ed. 432p. 1999. 31.99 (*0-7089-9124-6*) Ulverscroft.
— The Hanging Garden. 384p. 1999. reprint ed. mass mkt. 5.99 (*0-312-96913-9*, Minotaur) St Martin.
Rankin, Ian. Hide & Seek. (Detective John Rebus Mystery Ser.). 1997. mass mkt. 5.99 (*0-312-96397-1*, St Martins Paperbacks) St Martin.
— Hide & Seek: A John Rebus Mystery. 288p. 1994. reprint ed. 21.00 (*1-883402-74-3*) S&S Trade.
— Let It Bleed. 1996. 20.00 (*1-883402-76-X*) S&S Trade.
— Let It Bleed. LC 96-30535. 288p. 1996. 20.50 (*0-684-83055-8*) S&S Trade.
— Let It Bleed. 320p. 1998. pap. 5.99 (*0-312-96665-2*, Pub. by Tor Bks) St Martin.
***Rankin, Ian.** Let It Bleed: An Inspector Rebus Novel. large type ed. LC 00-37764. 530p. 2000. pap. 26.95 (*0-7862-2677-3*) Thorndike Pr.
Rankin, Ian. Mortal Causes. 1995. 21.50 (*1-883402-75-1*) S&S Trade.
— Mortal Causes. 3rd ed. (Dead Letter Mysteries Ser.). 288p. 1997. mass mkt. 5.99 (*0-312-96094-8*) St Martin.
***Rankin, Ian.** Set in Darkness. 2000. 24.95 (*0-312-20609-7*) St Martin.
Rankin, Ian. Strip Jack, Vol. 1. 272p. 1998. 5.99 (*0-312-96514-1*, Pub. by Tor Bks) St Martin.
***Rankin, Ian.** Strip Jack: An Inspector Rebus Novel. large type ed. LC 99-86628. (General Ser.). 330p. 2000. pap. 23.95 (*0-7862-2474-6*) Thorndike Pr.
Rankin, Ian. Tooth & Nail. 1996. mass mkt. 5.99 (*0-312-95878-1*) St Martin.
Rankin, Jacqueline A. Body Language: First Impressions. 5th ed. LC 86-81321. (Illus.). 133p. 1995. pap. write for info. (*1-887711-02-3*) Rankin File.
— Body Language in Love & Romance: Finding the Love of Your Life. 2nd ed. (Illus.). 80p. 1997. pap. 15.00 (*1-887711-01-5*) Rankin File.
— Body Language in Negotiations & Sales. 2nd ed. 96p. 1995. pap. 15.00 (*1-887711-00-7*) Rankin File.
— Body Language of the Abused Child. 270p. 1999. pap. 25.00 (*1-887711-06-6*) Rankin File.
Rankin, James M. Living the Magic: A Life Changing Journey. (Method Selling Ser.: Vol. II). 128p. 1998. pap. 8.95 (*0-9641729-1-7*) eDreampubng.
Rankin, Jane L. Cookin' up a Storm: The Life & Recipes of Annie Johnson. LC 98-84673. 166p. 1998. 24.95 (*0-9657387-0-1*) Grace Pubs.
Rankin, Jeanne, jt. auth. see Rankin, Paul.
Rankin, Jerry & Rutledge, Don. A Journey of Faith & Sacrifice: Retracing the Steps of Lottie Moon. LC 96-207859. (Illus.). 110p. 1996. per. 39.95 (*1-56309-188-7*, N964152, New Hope) Womans Mission Union.
Rankin, Jimmie R. As Perceived by the Patient: Introduction to the Literature of Patient Response. LC 93-26011. (Literature of Patient Response Ser.: Vol. I). 70p. 1993. pap., per. 12.95 (*1-883938-02-3*) Dry Bones Pr.
— Disability, Stigma, & Recovery: The Patient As Anthropologist. (Literature of a Patient Response Ser.). 75p. 1997. pap. 14.95 (*1-883938-13-9*) Dry Bones Pr.
— Disparate Voices. 30p. 1993. pap. 4.95 (*1-883938-08-2*) Dry Bones Pr.
— Listening with the "Third Ear" Reading What Patients Write - a Basic Course. (Literature of Patient Response Ser.). 100p. 1995. pap. 29.95 incl. VHS (*1-883338-21-2*) Dry Bones Pr.
— The Nursing Diagnosis, "Swallowing Impaired" The Bedside Assessment of Swallowing in Neurologically-Involved Cases. 150p. 1993. pap. 19.95 (*1-883938-06-6*) Dry Bones Pr.
— Nursing with the "Third Ear" Reading What Patients Write - a Basic Course. (Literature of Patient Response Ser.). 100p. 1994. pap. 29.95 (*1-883938-16-3*) Dry Bones Pr.
— Recovery Room! A Nurse's Guide to Care of the Patient, Post Anesthesia. 150p. 1994. pap. 24.95 (*1-883938-15-5*) Dry Bones Pr.
— Talking Head: The Novelist & Gullain-Barre. (Literature of a Patient Response Ser.). 770p. 1994. pap. 14.95 (*1-883938-14-7*) Dry Bones Pr.
— Who's in Charge Here? The Patient As Primary Caregiver. (Literature of Patient Response Ser.: Vol. II). 70p. 1993. pap. 12.95 (*1-883938-05-8*) Dry Bones Pr.
Rankin, Jimmie R., ed. Bill Graham Presents & the Family Dog: Dry Bones Research Database, Numbered Posters, Tickets & Memorabilia. 100p. (Orig.). 1997. pap. 25.00 (*1-883938-20-1*) Dry Bones Pr.
— Dry Bones Anthology. (Dry Bones Anthologies Ser.: Vol. I). (Illus.). 80p. (Orig.). pap. 14.95 (*1-883938-30-9*) Dry Bones Pr.
Rankin, Jimmie R. & Aquino, Marifi. Staff Development: The Director of Staff Development in Long Term Care, a 24 Hour Course. (Illus.). 150p. (Orig.). 1995. ring bd. 49.95 (*1-883938-19-8*) Dry Bones Pr.
Rankin, Jimmie R., ed. see Gandhi, Mohandas Karamchand.
Rankin, Jimmie R., ed. see Neale, John Mason.
Rankin, Jo, jt. ed. see Bishoff, Tonya.
Rankin, Joan. Scaredy Cat. LC 95-47597. (Illus.). 32p. (J). (ps-3). 1996. 16.00 (*0-689-80948-4*) McElderry Bks.
— Scaredy Cat. LC 95-47597. (Illus.). 32p. 1999. per. 5.99 (*0-689-82462-9*) S&S Childrens.
— Wow! It's Great Being a Duck. LC 97-71300. (Illus.). 32p. (J). (ps-3). 1998. per. 16.00 (*0-689-81756-8*) S&S Childrens.
***Rankin, Joan.** You're Somebody Special, Walliwigs!, Vol. 1. LC 98-65820. (Illus.). 32p. (J). (ps-3). 1999. 16.00 (*0-689-82230-8*) McElderry Bks.
Rankin, John. Letters on American Slavery, Addressed to Mister Thomas Rankin, Merchant at Middlebrook, Augusta County, Virginia. LC 73-82214. (Anti-Slavery Crusade in America Ser.). 1970. reprint ed. 13.95 (*0-405-00653-5*) Ayer.
Rankin, John, et al, eds. The Heritage of Madison County, Alabama. (Heritage of Alabama Ser.: No. 45). (Illus.). 280p. 1998. 55.00 (*1-891647-18-0*) Herit Pub Consult.
***Rankin, John C.** First the Gospel, Then Politics..., 3 vols., Set. LC 99-97575. 2200p. 1999. text 96.00 (*0-9677472-0-1*) T E I Pubng.
Rankin, John C. & Jensen, Frank B., eds. Fish Ecophysiology. LC 92-37628. (Fish & Fisheries Ser.: Vol. 9). 448p. (gr. 13). 1993. text 110.95 (*0-412-45920-5*) Chapman & Hall.
Rankin, Jonathan P. & Morris—orris, WadeWade. The Buckaroo Fiddle: The Biography of Chas. E. Morris, Historic Western Photographer, Vol. 3. (From Texas to Montana: Vol. 3). 124p. 1998. pap. 10.00 (*0-9645626-4-2*) Dallywelter Pr.
Rankin, Joyce. Children's Running: An After-School Program for Elementary School Children. Ohlrich, Warren H., ed. LC 94-61609. (Illus.). 88p. 1995. pap. 15.00 (*1-882426-02-9*) W H O Pr.
Rankin, Judy, jt. auth. see McCleery, Peter R.
Rankin, Karl L. China Assignment. LC 64-20488. (Illus.). 363p. 1964. 20.00 (*0-295-73742-5*) U of Wash Pr.
Rankin, Kenneth. The Recovery of the Soul: An Aristotelian Essay on Self-Fulfilment. 320p. 1991. 65.00 (*0-7735-0796-5*, Pub. by McG-Queens Univ Pr) CUP Services.
Rankin, Kim. Cut & Create! ABC: Easy Step-by-Step Projects That Teach Scissor Skills. (Illus.). 80p. (J). (ps-2). 1998. pap., teacher ed. 8.95 (*1-57310-114-1*) Teachng & Lrning Co.
— Cut & Create! Bugs & Other Creatures: Easy Step-by-Step Projects That Teach Scissor Skills. Mitchell, Judy, ed. (Illus.). 80p. (Orig.). (J). (ps-2). 1997. pap., teacher ed. 8.95 (*1-57310-082-X*) Teachng & Lrning Co.
— Cut & Create! Fairy Tales: Easy Step-by-Step Projects That Teach Scissor Skills. (Illus.). 80p. (J). (ps-2). 1998. pap., teacher ed. 8.95 (*1-57310-115-X*) Teachng & Lrning Co.
— Cut & Create! Holidays: Easy Step-by-Step Projects That Teach Scissor Skills. Mitchell, Judy, ed. (Illus.). 80p. (Orig.). (J). (ps-2). 1997. pap., teacher ed. 8.95 (*1-57310-083-8*) Teachng & Lrning Co.
— Cut & Create! Mother Goose: Easy Step-by-Step Projects That Teach Scissor Skills. (Illus.). 80p. (J). (ps-2). 1998. pap., teacher ed. 8.95 (*1-57310-116-8*) Teachng & Lrning Co.
— Cut & Create! Transportation: Easy Step-by-Step Projects That Teach Scissor Skills. Mitchell, Judy, ed. (Illus.). 80p. (Orig.). (J). (ps-2). 1997. pap., teacher ed. 8.95 (*1-57310-084-6*) Teachng & Lrning Co.
Rankin, Laura. The Handmade Alphabet. (J). 1991. 15.99 (*0-8037-0974-9*, Dial Yng Read) Peng Put Young Read.
— The Handmade Alphabet. LC 90-24593. 1996. 10.19 (*0-606-11425-4*, Pub. by Turtleback) Demco.
— The Handmade Alphabet. (Illus.). 32p. (J). 1996. pap. 5.99 (*0-14-055876-4*) Viking Penguin.
— The Handmade Counting Book. LC 97-38463. (J). 1998. 15.89 (*0-8037-2311-3*, Dial Yng Read) Peng Put Young Read.
— The Handmade Counting Book. LC 97-38463. (Illus.). (J). 1998. 15.99 (*0-8037-2309-1*, Dial Yng Read) Peng Put Young Read.
— Merl & Jasper's Supper Caper. (J). 1998. pap. 6.99 (*0-679-89311-3*, Pub. by Random Bks Yng Read) Random.
Rankin, Lee. Como Tener Exito en Su Matrimonio.Tr. of Your Marriage & Making It Work. (SPA.). 176p. 1989. pap. 4.99 (*0-8297-0486-8*) Vida Pubs.
Rankin, Lee, jt. auth. see Martin, Ray.
Rankin, Lois, jt. ed. see Abrahams, Roger D.
Rankin, Lois, ed. see Clifton, James, et al.
Rankin, Louise. Daughter of the Mountains. (J). (gr. 5-9). 1996. 18.75 (*0-8446-6895-8*) Peter Smith.
— Daughter of the Mountains. (Puffin Newbery Library). (J). 1993. 10.09 (*0-606-02585-5*, Pub. by Turtleback) Demco.
Rankin, Marie. Children's Interests in Library Books of Fiction. LC 70-177178. (Columbia University. Teachers College. Contributions to Education Ser.: No. 906). reprint ed. 37.50 (*0-404-55906-9*) AMS Pr.
Rankin, Marjorie. Trends in Educational Occupations. LC 74-177179. (Columbia University. Teachers College. Contributions to Education Ser.: No. 412). reprint ed. 37.50 (*0-404-55412-1*) AMS Pr.
Rankin, Martha, jt. auth. see Whitlock, Sarah.
Rankin, Mary B. Early Chinese Revolutionaries: Radical Intellectuals in Shanghai & Chekiang, 1902-1911. LC 76-115479. 354p. 1971. pap. 16.00 (*0-674-22004-8*) HUP.
— Elite Activism & Political Transformation in China: Zhejiang Province, 1865-1911. LC 86-5875. 448p. 1986. 52.50 (*0-8047-1321-9*) Stanford U Pr.
Rankin, Mary B., jt. ed. see Esherick, Joseph W.
Rankin, Myra. Danger in Paradise. 144p. 1994. pap. 6.95 (*1-57087-102-7*) Prof Pr NC.
Rankin, Neil, jt. ed. see Dixon, Huw.
Rankin, Neil O., jt. auth. see Vadum, Arlene C.
Rankin, Oliver S. Jewish Religious Polemic in Narrative, Poetry, Letters & Debate. rev. ed. 1969. 25.00 (*0-87068-007-2*) Ktav.
Rankin, Paul & Rankin, Jeanne. Gourmet Ireland. LC 97-192. (Illus.). 192p. (Orig.). 1997. pap. 18.95 (*0-912333-15-4*) BB&T Inc.
— Gourmet Ireland II. LC 97-46795. 1998. pap. 18.95 (*0-912333-34-0*) BB&T Inc.
Rankin, Paula. Augers. LC 80-70565. (Poetry Ser.). 1981. pap. 11.95 (*0-915604-46-9*) Carnegie-Mellon.
— By the Wreckmaster's Cottage. LC 77-80343. (Poetry Ser.). 1977. pap. 11.95 (*0-915604-13-2*) Carnegie-Mellon.
— Divorce: A Romance. LC 90-84780. 56p. (Orig.). 1991. pap. 11.95 (*0-88748-111-6*) Carnegie-Mellon.
— To the House Ghost. LC 84-72993. (Poetry Ser.). 56p. 1985. 20.95 (*0-88748-013-6*); pap. 11.95 (*0-88748-014-4*) Carnegie-Mellon.
— Your Rightful Childhood: New & Selected Poems. LC 96-83426. 120p. 1997. 20.95 (*0-88748-245-7*); pap. 11.95 (*0-88748-246-5*) Carnegie-Mellon.
Rankin, Peg. How to Care for the World & Still Take Care of Yourself: A Woman's Complete Guide to Setting Priorities. LC 94-2431. 1994. pap. 9.99 (*0-8054-5370-9*, 4253-70) Broadman.
***Rankin, Peg.** Pasos Dentro de las Aguas. (SPA.). 2000. pap. 9.99 (*0-7899-0569-8*) Spanish Hse Distributors.
Rankin, Richard. North Carolina Nature Writing: Four Centuries of Personal Narratives & Descriptions. LC 96-2640. (Illus.). (Orig.). 1996. pap. 12.95 (*0-89587-151-3*) Blair.
***Rankin, Robert.** A Dog Called Demolition. (J). 2000. 27.95 (*0-385-40516-2*, Pub. by Transworld Publishers Ltd) Trafalgar.
— Dog Called Demolition. (J). 2000. pap. 10.95 (*0-552-14213-1*, Pub. by Transworld Publishers Ltd) Trafalgar.
— East of Ealing. 2000. pap. 8.95 (*0-552-13843-6*, Pub. by Transworld Publishers Ltd) Trafalgar.
— Greatest Show Off Earth. (J). 2000. pap. 10.95 (*0-552-13924-6*, Pub. by Transworld Publishers Ltd) Trafalgar.
— Most Amazing Man Who Ever Lived. 2000. pap. 10.95 (*0-552-14211-5*, Pub. by Transworld Publishers Ltd) Trafalgar.
— Nostradamus Ate My Hamster. 2000. 27.50 (*0-385-40705-X*, Pub. by Transworld Publishers Ltd) Trafalgar.
— Sprout Mask Replica. 2000. pap. 10.95 (*0-552-14356-1*, Pub. by Transworld Publishers Ltd) Trafalgar.
Rankin, Robert S. When Civil Law Fails. LC 39-16186. reprint ed. 29.50 (*0-404-05224-X*) AMS Pr.
Rankin, Robert S. & Dallmayr, Winfried R. Freedom & Emergency Powers in the Cold War. LC 63-21213. (C). 1964. reprint ed. pap. text 17.95 (*0-89197-531-4*) Irvington.
***Rankin, Rush.** The Failure of Grief. LC 00-100565. 50p. 2000. pap. 8.95 (*0-9673030-2-8*, bkrr001) Nettle Pr.
Rankin, Russell B., jt. ed. see Randolph, Howard S.
Rankin, S. C., jt. auth. see Gedroyc, W.
Rankin, Sally H. & Stallings, Karen D. Patient Education: Issues, Principles & Practices. 3rd ed. LC 95-10728. 400p. 1995. pap. text 29.95 (*0-397-55194-0*) Lppncott W & W.
Rankin, Sally H. & Stallings, Karen Duffy. Patient Education: Principles & Practice. 4th ed. 428p. pap. text 32.95 (*0-7817-2022-2*) Lppncott W & W.

R

Rankin, Sheila. The Ultimate German Shepherd Dog. LC 97-46158. (J). 1998. 34.95 (*0-87605-035-6*) Howell Bks.

Rankin, Susan K. & Hiley, David, eds. Music in the Medieval English Liturgy: Plainsong & Mediaeval Music Society Centennial Essays. (Illus.). 422p. 1993. text 105.00 (*0-19-316125-7*) OUP.

Rankin, T. E., et al. Fred Newton Scott Anniversary Papers, Contributed by Former Students & Colleagues of Professor Scott & Presented to Him in Celebration of His Thirty-Eighth Year of Distinguished Service in the University of Michigan, 1888-1926. LC 68-29205. (Essay Index Reprint Ser.). 1977. reprint ed. 21.95 (*0-8369-0459-1*) Ayer.

Rankin, Thomas M. Stonewall Jackson's Romney Campaign, January 1-February 20, 1862. (Virginia Civil War Battles & Leaders Ser.). (Illus.). 192p. 1994. 25.00 (*1-56190-070-2*) H E Howard.

— Thirty-Seventh Virginia Infantry. (Virginia Regimental Histories Ser.). (Illus.). 150p. 1987. 19.95 (*0-930919-44-0*) H E Howard.

***Rankin, Thomas M.** 22nd Battalion Virginia Infantry. (Virginia Regimental Histories Ser.). (Illus.). 113p. 1999. 19.95 (*1-56190-115-6*) H E Howard.

Rankin, Thomas M. Twenty Third Virginia Infantry. (Virginia Regimental Histories Ser.). (Illus.). 141p. 1985. 19.95 (*0-930919-14-9*) H E Howard.

Rankin, Tom. New Forms of Work Organization: The Challenge for North American Unions. 168p. 1990. text 40.00 (*0-8020-2698-2*) U of Toronto Pr.

— New Forms of Work Organization: The Challenge for North American Unions. 168p. 1992. pap. text 17.95 (*0-8020-7398-0*) U of Toronto Pr.

— Sacred Space: Photographs from the Mississippi Delta. LC 93-6973. (Illus.). 96p. 1993. pap. 19.95 (*0-87805-641-6*) U Pr of Miss.

Rankin, Tom, ed. Faulkner's World: The Photographs of Martin J. Dain. LC 97-13772. (Illus.). 112p. 1997. 40.00 (*1-57806-016-8*) U Pr of Miss.

***Rankin, Tom & Stack, Trudy W.** Local Heroes Changing America. (Illus.). 292p. 2000. 29.95 incl. cd-rom (*0-393-05028-9*) Norton.

Rankin, Tom, ed. & intro. see Sayre, Maggie L.

Rankin, Virginia. The Thoughtful Researcher: Teaching the Research Process to Middle School Students. LC 98-55916. 260p. 1999. pap. 27.00 (*1-56308-698-0*) Libs Unl.

Rankin, W. Tarantulas & Scorpions. (Illus.). 96p. 1995. pap. text 9.95 (*0-7938-0259-8*, RE124) TFH Pubns.

Rankin, W. Parkman. The Practice of Newspaper Management. LC 85-28099. 176p. 1986. 55.00 (*0-275-92051-8*, C2051, Praeger Pubs) Greenwood.

Rankin, William. Come Hibernate with Me. (Illus.). 214p. (Orig.). (YA). (gr. 9 up). 1989. 30.00 (*0-9623948-0-7*) M Camphouse.

— Introducing Newton. (Illus.). 176p. 1994. pap. text 9.95 (*1-874166-07-2*, Pub. by Totem Bks) Natl Bk Netwk.

***Rankin, William.** Introducing Newton & Classical Physics. 2000. pap. 11.95 (*1-84046-158-6*) Totem Bks.

Rankin, William J., ed. see Office of Commissioner Federal Judicial Affairs St.

Rankin, William P. & Waggaman, Eugene S., Jr. Business Management of General Consumer Magazines. 2nd ed. LC 84-1908. 236p. 1984. 59.95 (*0-275-91745-2*, C1745, Praeger Pubs) Greenwood.

Rankin, William W. Confidentiality & Clergy: Churches, Ethics & the Law. LC 90-37966. 144p. (Orig.). 1990. pap. 8.95 (*0-8192-1530-9*) Morehouse Pub.

Rankine, Claudia. The End of the Alphabet. LC 98-24717. 128p. 1998. 20.00 (*0-8021-1634-5*, Grove) Grove-Atltic.

— Nothing in Nature Is Private. Archer, Nuala, ed. (CSU Poetry Ser.: Vol. XLIV). 88p. (Orig.). 1994. pap. 10.00 (*1-880834-09-X*) Cleveland St Univ Poetry Ctr.

— Nothing in Nature Is Private. Archer, Nuala, ed. (CSU Poetry Ser.: Vol. XLIV). 88p. (Orig.). 1995. 15.00 (*1-880834-10-3*) Cleveland St Univ Poetry Ctr.

***Rankine, D.** Commercial Due Diligence: A Guide to Reducing Risk in Acquisitions. (Illus.). 1999. pap. 167.50 (*0-273-63971-4*, Pub. by F T P-H) Trans-Atl Phila.

Rankine, David, jt. auth. see Block, Janice.

Rankine, David, jt. auth. see Rainbird, Ariadne.

Rankine, Denzil. A Practical Guide to Acquisitions: How to Make a Success of the Most Risky Business Activity. LC 97-9427. 170p. 1997. pap. 49.95 (*0-471-97598-2*) Wiley.

Rankinen. Digital Courseware. (Electrical Trades Ser.). 1998. 59.95 (*0-8273-7767-3*) Delmar.

Rankins, Solomon. MS SQL Server 6.5 Unleashed MC. 1997. 69.99 (*0-672-31191-7*) Sams.

Rankins, William. A Mirrour of Monsters. (English Stage Ser.: Vol. 9). 1973. lib. bdg. 61.00 (*0-8240-0592-9*) Garland.

Rankins, William H., III & Wilson, David A. Practical Sun Power. 2nd rev. ed. (Illus.). 132p. 1999. pap. 12.00 (*0-934852-13-8*, LH-13) Lorien Hse.

— The Solar Energy Notebook. 2nd rev. ed. (Illus.). 116p. 1999. pap. 12.00 (*0-934852-15-4*, LH-15) Lorien Hse.

Rankka, Kristine M. Women & the Value of Suffering: An Aw(e)ful Rowing Toward God. 240p. 1998. pap. 19.95 (*0-8146-5866-0*) Liturgical Pr.

***Rankl, Wolfgang.** Smart Card Handbook. 2nd ed. 2000. 125.00 (*0-471-98875-8*) Wiley.

Rankl, Wolfgang & Effing, Wolfgang. Smart Card Handbook. Chanterelle Translations Staff, tr. LC 97-1037. 460p. 1997. 135.00 (*0-471-96720-3*) Wiley.

Rankoff, P. Bulgarian-German Pocket Dictionary: Taschenwoerterbuch Bulgarisch-Deutsch. 11th ed. (BUL & GER.). 367p. 1987. 14.95 (*0-8288-0999-2*, F34910) Fr & Eur.

— German-Bulgarian Pocket Dictionary: Taschenwoerterbuch Deutsch-Bulgarisch. 12th ed. (BUL & GER.). 315p. 1987. 14.95 (*0-8288-1000-1*, F34920) Fr & Eur.

Rankonen, Carl, ed. World Music in the Music Library. LC 94-16512. 77p. 1994. 24.00 (*0-914954-49-0*) Music Library Assn.

Rankov, Boris. The Praetorian Guard. (Elite Ser.). (Illus.). 64p. 1994. pap. 12.95 (*1-85532-361-3*, 9465, Pub. by Osprey) Stackpole.

Rankov, N. B., jt. auth. see Austin, N. J.

Rankova, M. English-Bulgarian Dictionary, 2 vols., Set. 1086p. (C). 1987. 295.00 (*0-89771-905-0*, Pub. by Collets) St Mut.

Ranlet, Philip. Enemies of the Bay Colony. LC 93-39513. (American University Studies: Ser. IX, Vol. 157). 344p. (C). 1995. text 59.95 (*0-8204-2439-0*) P Lang Pubng.

— The New York Loyalists. LC 85-29601. 317p. reprint ed. pap. 98.30 (*0-608-08627-4*, 206915000003) Bks Demand.

Ranly, Don. Principles American Journalism. 336p. (C). 1996. pap. text, per. 48.95 (*0-7872-0748-9*) Kendall-Hunt.

— Principles of American Journalism: Introduction. 322p. (C). 1990. 58.00 (*0-536-57827-3*) Pearson Custom.

Ranly, Don. Publication Editing. 300p. (C). 1998. pap. 48.95 (*0-7872-5606-4*, 41560601) Kendall-Hunt.

Rann, D. Z: A Beginner's Guide. 1994. mass mkt. 33.95 (*0-412-55660-X*, Chap & Hall NY) Chapman & Hall.

Rann, W. S., ed. History of Chittendon County, Vermont. (Illus.). 867p. 1993. reprint ed. lib. bdg. 87.50 (*0-8328-3171-9*) Higginson Bk Co.

Rann, W. S., jt. auth. see Smith, H. P.

Rann, W. S., jt. ed. see Smith, H. P.

***Rannefeld, Clarence.** Laminated Designs in Wood: Techniques * Patterns * Projects. Doran, Laura D., ed. LC 97-25656. (Illus.). 144p. 1998. pap. 19.95 (*1-57990-021-6*, Pub. by Lark Books) Random.

Rannells, Jackson. PNG: A Fact Book on Modern Papua New Guinea. 2nd ed. (Illus.). 224p. 1995. pap. 49.95 (*0-19-553679-7*) OUP.

Ranney, Austin. The American Elections of 1980. LC 81-7907. (AEI Studies: No. 327). 408p. reprint ed. pap. 126.50 (*0-8357-4433-7*, 203726700008) Bks Demand.

— The American Elections of 1984. LC 85-24573. (Illus.). 382p. reprint ed. pap. 118.50 (*0-8357-4434-5*, 203726800008) Bks Demand.

— The Doctrine of Responsible Party Government, Its Origins & Present State. LC 82-15517. (Illus.). 176p. 1982. reprint ed. lib. bdg. 35.00 (*0-313-22873-6*, RADR, Greenwood Pr) Greenwood.

— Governing: An Introduction to Political Science. 7th ed. LC 95-22602. 448p. (C). 1995. 61.00 (*0-13-326216-2*) P-H.

***Ranney, Austin.** Governing: An Introduction to Political Science. 8th ed. 528p. 2000. 49.33 (*0-13-018039-4*) P-H.

Ranney, Austin. Pathways to Parliament: Candidate Selection in Britain. LC 65-16364. 314p. 1965. reprint ed. pap. 97.40 (*0-608-01898-8*, 206255000003) Bks Demand.

Ranney, Austin, ed. Britain at the Polls, 1983: A Study of the General Election. LC 84-24646. (At the Polls Ser.). xiv, 227p. 1985. pap. text 16.95 (*0-8223-0620-4*) Duke.

— Britain at the Polls, 1983: A Study of the General Election. LC 84-24646. (At the Polls Ser.). xiv, 227p. 1985. text 46.00 (*0-8223-0619-0*) Duke.

— Britain at the Polls, 1983: A Study of the General Election. LC 84-24646. (Illus.). 239p. reprint ed. pap. 74.10 (*0-8357-4438-8*, 203727200008) Bks Demand.

— Essays on the Behavioral Study of Politics. LC 73-88582. 209p. reprint ed. pap. 64.80 (*0-608-08664-9*, 206918700003) Bks Demand.

— The Referendum Device: A Conference. LC 80-25657. (AEI Symposia Ser.: No. 80G). 208p. reprint ed. pap. 64.50 (*0-7837-1085-2*, 204161700021) Bks Demand.

Ranney, Austin & Penniman, Howard R. Democracy in the Islands: The Micronesian Plebiscites of 1983. LC 85-3895. (AEI Studies: No. 420). (Illus.). 160p. reprint ed. pap. 49.60 (*0-8357-4461-2*, 203730500008) Bks Demand.

Ranney, Austin & Sartori, Giovanni, eds. Eurocommunism: The Italian Case. LC 78-17068. (AEI Symposia Ser.: 78G). (Illus.). 208p. reprint ed. pap. 64.50 (*0-8357-4475-2*, 203732300008) Bks Demand.

Ranney, Austin, et al. Courts & the Political Process: Jack W. Peltason's Contributions to Political Science. LC 96-3748. 139p. 1996. pap. 12.95 (*0-87772-369-9*) UCB IGS.

— Linking the Governors & the Governed. Taylor, Richard W., ed. (Illus.). 238p. 1981. pap. text 9.95 (*0-933522-09-6*) Kent Popular.

Ranney, Austin, jt. ed. see Butler, David E.

Ranney, Brooks. The Odyssey of Thomas Ranny. LC 94-92014. (Illus.). 420p. 1994. 15.00 (*0-9618939-3-1*); pap. 12.00 (*0-9618939-4-X*) B Ranney.

— The Origin & Education of a Doctor. LC 90-92020. (Illus.). 396p. 1990. pap. 12.00 (*0-9618939-2-3*) B Ranney.

— To Cross the River Barriers. LC 87-90553. (Illus.). 450p. 1987. 15.00 (*0-9618939-0-7*) B Ranney.

Ranney, Don. Chronic Musculoskeletal Injuries in the Workplace. Lampert, Richard, ed. 400p. 1996. pap. text 54.00 (*0-7216-6841-0*, W B Saunders Co) Harcrt Hlth Sci Grp.

Ranney, Doug, jt. auth. see Ledoux, Trish.

Ranney, Edward. Prairie Passage: The Illinois & Michigan Canal Corridor. LC 98-8906. 224p. 1998. 24.95 (*0-252-06714-2*); text 49.95 (*0-252-02411-7*) U of Ill Pr.

Ranney, Edward & Mondejar, Publio L., intros. Martin Chambi: Photographs, 1920-1950. LC 92-62314. (Illus.). 115p. (Orig.). 1993. pap. 39.95 (*1-56098-244-6*) Smithsonian.

Ranney, J. T. Pennsylvania Criminal Law & Practice, 3 vols., Set. 2000p. 295.00 (*0-8205-1697-X*, 697) Juris Pubng.

***Ranney, James T.** Pennsylvania Crimes & Defenses. 200p. 1999. spiral bd. 40.00 (*1-57823-056-X*) Juris Pubng.

— Pennsylvania Search & Seizure. 142p. 1999. spiral bd. 40.00 (*1-57823-057-8*) Juris Pubng.

Ranney, Jeffrey M., jt. auth. see Goure, Daniel.

Ranney, Karen. Above All Others. 384p. 1996. mass mkt. 4.99 (*0-8217-5377-0*, Zebra Kensgtn) Kensgtn Pub Corp.

***Ranney, Karen.** After the Kiss. 384p. 2000. mass mkt. 5.99 (*0-380-81298-3*, Avon Bks) Morrow Avon.

Ranney, Karen. Heaven Forbids. 304p. 1998. pap. 4.99 (*0-8217-5867-5*, Zebra Kensgtn) Kensgtn Pub Corp.

***Ranney, Karen.** My Beloved. LC 99-94775. 372p. 1999. mass mkt. 5.99 (*0-380-80590-1*, Avon Bks) Morrow Avon.

— My True Love. 384p. 2000. mass mkt. 5.99 (*0-380-80591-X*, Avon Bks) Morrow Avon.

Ranney, Karen. My Wicked Fantasy. LC 97-94075. 384p. 1998. mass mkt. 5.99 (*0-380-79581-7*, Avon Bks) Morrow Avon.

— A Promise of Love. 384p. 1997. mass mkt. 4.99 (*0-8217-5750-4*, Zebra Kensgtn) Kensgtn Pub Corp.

— Tapestry. 384p. 1996. pap. 2.99 (*0-8217-5485-8*) Kensgtn Pub Corp.

— Upon a Wicked Time. LC 98-93174. 384p. 1998. mass mkt. 5.99 (*0-380-79583-3*, Avon Bks) Morrow Avon.

Ranney-Marinelli, Alesia, jt. auth. see Saggese, Nicholas P.

Ranney, Victoria P., et al, eds. The Papers of Frederick Law Olmsted Vol. 5: The California Frontier, 1863-1865. LC 89-15315. (Illus.). 848p. 1990. text 55.00 (*0-8018-3885-1*) Johns Hopkins.

Ranney, Wayne. Canyon Country. (Plateau Ser.). (Illus.). 34p. 1993. pap. 5.95 (*0-89734-113-9*) Mus Northern Ariz.

— Sedona Through Time: Geology of the Red Rocks. (Illus.). 97p. 1993. pap. 12.95 (*0-9611678-9-0*) Red Lake Bks.

— The Verde Valley: A Geological History. (Plateau Ser.: Vol. 60, No. 3). 32p. 1989. pap. 4.95 (*0-89734-096-5*) Mus Northern Ariz.

Ranniaia, Tom L, tr. see Bulgakov, Mikhail Afanasevich.

Rannie, David W. Scenery in Shakespeare's Plays & Other Studies. LC 70-153346. reprint ed. 45.00 (*0-404-05225-8*) AMS Pr.

— Wordsworth & His Circle. LC 72-3432. (Studies in Wordsworth: No. 29). (Illus.). 1972. reprint ed. lib. bdg. 75.00 (*0-8383-1537-2*) M S G Haskell Hse.

Rannigan, Remley L. Minnesota Multiphasic Personality Inventory (MMPI) Index of Modern Authors & Subjects with Guide for Rapid Research. 200p. 1991. 47.50 (*1-55914-280-4*); pap. 44.50 (*1-55914-281-2*) ABBE Pubs Assn.

— MMPI (Minnesota Multiphasic Personality Inventory) in Testing, Medicine & Psycology: Guidebook for Reference & Research. rev. ed. 150p. 1998. 47.50 (*0-7883-1070-4*); pap. 44.50 (*0-7883-1071-2*) ABBE Pubs Assn.

Rannow, Jerry. Writing Television Comedy. LC 99-59329. 212p. 2000. pap. 14.95 (*1-58115-042-3*) Allworth Pr.

***Ranns, R. H. B.** Site Agent's Handbook: Construction under the Ice Conditions. 216p. (C). (gr. 13). 1998. pap. text 32.99 (*1-85032-041-1*) ITCP.

***Rannveig Traustadbottir & Johnson, Kelley.** Women with Intellectual Disabilities: Finding a Place in the World. LC 99-56737. 2000. pap. 27.95 (*1-85302-846-0*) Jessica Kingsley.

Ranny, M. Thin-Layer Chromatography with Flame Ionization Detection. (C). 1987. text 139.00 (*90-277-1973-X*) Kluwer Academic.

Rano, Balbino. Augustinian Origins, Charism, & Spirituality. LC 94-32757. (The/Augustinian Ser.: Vol. 3). 1994. 32.00 (*0-941491-75-7*); pap. text 19.95 (*0-941491-76-5*) Augustinian Pr.

Ranocchia, Diane D., ed. Rochester Forth Applications Conference, 1984: Proceedings. 1984. pap. 25.00 (*0-914593-05-6*) Inst Appl Forth.

Ranoldi, Adrienne, ed. see Julian, Bob.

Rans, Geoffrey. Cooper's Leather-Stocking Novels: A Secular Reading. LC 91-10607. xxiii, 282p. (C). 1991. 49.95 (*0-8078-1975-1*) U of NC Pr.

Rans, Jon & Eckelman, Mark. Collectors Encyclopedia of Muncie Pottery Identification. 240p. 1999. 24.95 (*1-57432-118-8*) Collector Bks.

Rans, Laurel, jt. auth. see Sturgeon, Susan.

Ransbottom. Budgeting Your Time & Money. (YA - Adult Education Ser.). 1993. pap., wbk. ed. 5.95 (*0-538-70838-7*) S-W Pub.

— Introduction to Personal Banking. (YA - Adult Education Ser.). 1993. pap., wbk. ed. 5.95 (*0-538-70839-5*) S-W Pub.

— Making Major Financial Decisions: Money Management. (YA - Adult Education Ser.). 1993. pap., wbk. ed. 5.95 (*0-538-70841-7*) S-W Pub.

— Money Management. (YA - Adult Education Ser.). 1992. pap. 9.95 (*0-538-70663-5*) S-W Pub.

— Understanding Your Income Taxes: Money Management. (YA - Adult Education Ser.). 1993. pap., wbk. ed. 5.95 (*0-538-70840-9*) S-W Pub.

Ransbottom, jt. auth. see Taylor.

Ransch-Trill, Barbara. Harlekin. (Philosophische Texte und Studien: Vol. 34). (GER.). 222p. 1993. write for info. (*3-487-09689-7*) G Olms Pubs.

Ranschaert, Ryan, jt. auth. see Dobek, Sandra.

***Ransdell, S. E., et al.** Laboratory in Cognition & Perception. 3rd ed. (Illus.). 208p. (C). 1999. pap. 25.00 (*1-892919-00-1*) Psychology SW Inc.

Ransdell, Sarah, jt. ed. see Levy, C. Michael.

Ransel, David L. The Politics of Catherinian Russia: The Panin Party. LC 74-29736. 337p. reprint ed. pap. 104.50 (*0-8357-8276-X*, 203386500087) Bks Demand.

***Ransel, David L.** Village Mothers: Three Generations of Change in Russia & Tataria. LC 00-38908. (Indiana-Michigan Series in Russian & East European Studies). 2000. pap. write for info. (*0-253-33825-5*) Ind U Pr.

Ransel, David L., ed. The Family in Imperial Russia: New Lines of Historical Research. LC 78-17579. 352p. reprint ed. pap. 109.20 (*0-7837-5742-5*, 204540300006) Bks Demand.

Ransel, David L., jt. auth. see Burbank, Jane.

Ransel, David L., ed. & tr. see Semyonova Tian-Shanskaia.

Ransen, Owen. AutoCAD Programming in C/C++ LC 96-43718. 510p. 1997. pap. text 70.00 incl. disk (*0-471-96336-4*) Wiley.

Ransford, H. Edward. Race & Class in American Society. rev. ed. LC 94-13489. 1994. pap. 18.95 (*0-87047-069-8*) Schenkman Bks Inc.

— Race & Class in American Society. 2nd rev. ed. LC 94-13489. 1994. 29.95 (*0-87047-068-X*) Schenkman Bks Inc.

— Race & Class in American Society: Black, Chicano, Anglo. LC 74-84674. 200p. 1977. pap. text 11.95 (*0-87073-041-X*) Schenkman Bks Inc.

Ransford, Ken. Proposed Income Tax Benefits for Charitable Gifts of Social Security & Pension Payments. (Issue Paper #3-97 Ser.). 19p. 1997. pap. text 8.00 (*1-57655-155-5*) Independ Inst.

Ransford, Lynn. Creepy Crawlies for Curious Kids. (Illus.). 48p. (J). 1987. student ed. 7.95 (*1-55734-217-2*) Tchr Create Mat.

Ransford, Rosalind, ed. The Early Charters of the Augustinian Canons of Waltham Abbey, Essex, 1062-1230. (Studies in the History of Medieval Religion: Vol. 2). 608p. (C). 1989. 110.00 (*0-85115-516-2*) Boydell & Brewer.

Ransford, Sandy. Dogs. LC 95-43799. (Pocket Gem Ser.). (Illus.). 64p. (J). (gr. 1 up). 1996. 3.95 (*0-8120-6590-5*) Barron.

— Global Warming: A Pop-up Book of Our Endangered Planet. (J). (ps-3). 1992. pap. 15.00 (*0-671-77080-2*) S&S Bks Yung.

— Master Magician: An Action Book. (Illus.). 18p. (J). (gr. 4-7). 1994. 19.95 (*1-56138-460-7*) Running Pr.

— The Otter. LC 98-40378. (Animal Lives Ser.). (Illus.). 32p. (gr. k-3). 1999. teacher ed. 9.95 (*0-7534-5176-X*) LKC.

***Ransford, Sandy.** 2001: A Joke Odyssey. (Illus.). (J). 2000. pap. 5.99 (*0-330-34988-0*) Mcm Child Bks.

Ransford, Thomas. Potential Theory in the Complex Plane. (London Mathematical Society Student Texts Ser.: No. 28). 242p. (C). 1995. text 69.95 (*0-521-46120-0*); pap. text 24.95 (*0-521-46654-7*) Cambridge U Pr.

Ranshofen-Wertheimer, E. F. The International Secretariat: A Great Experiment in International Administration. (Studies in the Administration of International Law & Organization). 1969. reprint ed. 45.00 (*0-527-00881-8*) Periodicals Srv.

Ransil, M. Michele, jt. auth. see Gruser, Mark.

Ransil, M. Michele, ed. see Gruber, Mark.

Ransmayr, Christoph. Morbus Kitahara. 1999. 24.95 (*3-596-13782-9*) Fischer Taschen.

— Morbus Kitahara. (GER.). 448p. 1995. 39.75 (*3-10-062908-6*, Pub. by S Fischer) Intl Bk Import.

Ransmayr, Christopher. The Dog King. Woods, John, tr. LC 96-39160. 355p. 1997. 4.99 (*0-679-45057-2*) Knopf.

— The Kitahara Syndrome. Woods, John, tr. from GER. LC 96-39160. 1998. pap. 14.00 (*0-679-76860-2*) Vin Bks.

— The Last World. Woods, John E., tr. from GER. 256p. 1996. reprint ed. pap. 12.00 (*0-8021-3458-0*, Grove) Grove-Atltic.

— Last World. Rosenman, Jane, ed. 256p. 1992. reprint ed. per. 10.00 (*0-671-74962-5*, WSP) PB.

— The Terrors of Ice & Darkness. Woods, John E., tr. from GER. 240p. 1996. reprint ed. pap. 12.00 (*0-8021-3459-9*, Grove) Grove-Atltic.

Ransmayr, G., jt. ed. see Poewe, W.

Ransohoff, Daniel J., jt. auth. see Aft, Richard N.

Ransohoff, Richard M. & Benveniste, Etty N., eds. Cytokines & the CNS. LC 95-38135. 368p. 1996. boxed set 129.95 (*0-8493-2452-1*, 2452) CRC Pr.

Ransohoff, Richard M., ed. see Sen, Ganes C.

Ransohoff, Rita M. Venus after Forty: Sexual Myths, Men's Fantasies & Truths about Middle Aged Women. LC 87-12233. 289p. 1990. pap. 11.95 (*0-88282-064-8*) New Horizon NJ.

— Venus after Forty: Sexual Myths, Mens's Fantasies & Truth. LC 87-12233. 289p. 1987. 20.95 (*0-88282-034-6*) New Horizon NJ.

Ransom. Practical Strategies in OB/GYN. LC 99-33413. (C). 1999. text 105.00 (*0-7216-7854-8*, W B Saunders Co) Harcrt Hlth Sci Grp.

— Sabrina. (Orig.). (J). 1993. pap. 2.75 (*0-685-66034-6*) Scholastic Inc.

Ransom, Angela, et al. Improving Higher Education in Developing Countries. LC 92-28785. (EDI Seminar Ser.). 90p. 1993. pap. 22.00 (*0-8213-2216-8*, 12216) World Bank.

Ransom, Arthur. Oscar Wilde: A Critical Study. LC 79-151283. (English Literature Ser.: No. 33). 1971. reprint ed. lib. bdg. 75.00 (*0-8383-1230-6*) M S G Haskell Hse.

An Asterisk (*) at the beginning of an entry indicates that the title is appearing for the first time.

R

*Ransom, Barbara & Wainwright, Sonya.** Recent Advances & Issues in Geology. (Frontiers of Science Ser.). (Illus.). 304p. 2000. 44.95 (*1-57356-356-0*) Oryx Pr.

Ransom, Bill. Burn. LC 95-9747. 320p. 1995. pap. 19.95 (*0-441-00246-3*) Ace Bks.

— Burn. 1996. mass mkt. 5.99 (*0-441-00362-1*) Ace Bks.

— Learning the Ropes: A Creative Autobiography. LC 95-4342. 1995. pap. 5.00 (*0-87421-190-5*) Utah St U Pr.

— Viravax. LC 92-21148. 320p. 1993. pap. 17.95 (*0-441-86476-7*) Ace Bks.

— Viravax. 320p. 1994. mass mkt. 4.99 (*0-441-00083-5*) Ace Bks.

Ransom, Bruce R., jt. auth. see Kettenmann, Helmut.

Ransom, Bruce R., jt. ed. see Kaila, Kai.

Ransom, Candice F. The Big Green Pocketbook. LC 92-29393. (Laura Geringer Bks.). (Illus.). 32p. (J). (ps-3). 1993. lib. bdg. 16.89 (*0-06-020849-X*) HarpC Child Bks.

— The Big Green Pocketbook. LC 92-29393. (Illus.). 32p. (J). (ps-3). 1995. pap. 6.95 (*0-06-443395-1*, HarpTrophy) HarpC Child Bks.

— The Big Green Pocketbook. 1993. 10.15 (*0-606-07285-3*, Pub. by Turtleback) Demco.

— Children of the Civil War. LC 97-32624. (Picture the American Past Ser.). (J). (gr. 3-6). 1998. 22.60 (*1-57505-241-5*, Carolrhoda) Lerner Pub.

— The Christmas Dolls. LC 98-10696. (Illus.). 32p. (J). (gr. k-2). 1998. 15.95 (*0-8027-8659-6*); lib. bdg. 16.85 (*0-8027-8661-8*) Walker & Co.

***Ransom, Candice F.** Danger at Sand Cave. LC 99-21416. (On My Own History Ser.). (Illus.). 56p. (J). (gr. 1-3). 2000. 21.27 (*1-57505-379-9*, Carolrhoda) Lerner Pub.

— Danger at Sand Cove. (On My Own History Ser.). (Illus.). 56p. (J). (gr. 1-3). 2000. pap. 5.95 (*1-57505-454-X*, Carolrhoda) Lerner Pub.

— Fire in the Sky. (Illus.). (J). 1996. lib. bdg. 19.93 (*0-87614-867-4*, Carolrhoda) Lerner Pub.

Ransom, Candice F. Fire in the Sky. (Illus.). 72p. (J). (ps-3). 1997. pap. text 5.95 (*1-57505-079-X*, Carolrhoda) Lerner Pub.

— Listening to Crickets: A Story about Rachel Carson. (Creative Minds Biographies Ser.). (Illus.). (J). (gr. 3-6). 1993. lib. bdg. 19.95 (*0-87614-727-9*, Carolrhoda) Lerner Pub.

— Listening to Crickets: A Story about Rachel Carson. (Illus.). 56p. (J). (gr. 3-6). 1993. pap. 5.95 (*0-87614-615-9*, Carolrhoda) Lerner Pub.

***Ransom, Candice F.** More Than a Name. 115p. (J). (gr. 2-5). 1999. reprint ed. text 14.00 (*0-7881-6609-3*) DIANE Pub.

Ransom, Candice F. One Christmas Dawn. LC 93-39751. (Illus.). 32p. (J). (ps-3). 1996. 15.95 (*0-8167-3384-8*) BrdgeWater.

— One Christmas Dawn. LC 93-39751. (Illus.). 32p. (J). (gr. k-3). 1997. pap. 4.95 (*0-8167-3385-6*) Troll Communs.

— The Promise Quilt. LC 99-13053. (Illus.). 32p. (J). (gr. 2-4). 1999. 15.95 (*0-8027-8694-4*); lib. bdg. 16.85 (*0-8027-8695-2*) Walker & Co.

— So Young to Die: The Story of Hannah Senesh. (J). (gr. 4-7). 1993. pap. 2.95 (*0-685-65620-9*) Scholastic Inc.

— The Spitball Class. MacDonald, Patricia, ed. 160p. (Orig.). 1994. pap. 2.99 (*0-671-72910-1*, Minstrel Bks) PB.

— Teacher's Pest. (Illus.). 64p. (Orig.). (J). (gr. 1-4). 1997. pap. 3.95 (*0-8167-4017-8*) Troll Communs.

— Third Grade Detectives. LC 93-41364. (Tales from Third Grade Ser.). (Illus.). 128p. (J). (gr. 2-4). 1994. lib. bdg. 15.85 (*0-8167-2992-1*) Troll Communs.

— Third Grade Stars: Tales from Third Grade. LC 93-7868. (Illus.). 128p. (J). (gr. 2-4). 1996. pap. 3.95 (*0-8167-2995-6*) Troll Communs.

— Thirteen. (J). 1984. pap. 2.75 (*0-590-43459-4*) Scholastic Inc.

— Thirteen. 192p. (J). (gr. 4-6). 1990. pap. 2.95 (*0-590-43742-9*) Scholastic Inc.

— We're Growing Together. LC 92-7424. (Illus.). 32p. (J). (ps-2). 1993. lib. bdg. 14.95 (*0-02-775666-1*, Bradbury S&S) S&S Childrens.

— When the Whippoorwill Calls. LC 94-41567. (Illus.). 32p. (J). (gr. 2-5). 1995. 16.00 (*0-688-12729-0*, Wm Morrow); lib. bdg. 15.93 (*0-688-12730-4*, Wm Morrow) Morrow Avon.

— Who Needs Third Grade? LC 92-30754. (Tales from Third Grade Ser.). 128p. (J). (gr. 2-4). 1996. pap. 3.95 (*0-8167-2989-1*) Troll Communs.

— Why Are Boys So Weird? LC 93-6222. (Tales from the Third Grade Ser.). (Illus.). 128p. (J). (gr. 2-6). 1994. pap. text 3.95 (*0-8167-2991-3*); lib. bdg. 15.85 (*0-8167-2990-5*) Troll Communs.

Ransom, Dana. Liar's Promise. 1990. mass mkt. 4.25 (*0-8217-2881-4*, Zebra Kensgtn) Kensgtn Pub Corp.

— Lifetime Investment. (Lucky in Love Ser.: No. 27). 288p. 1993. mass mkt. 3.50 (*0-8217-4113-6*, Zebra Kensgtn) Kensgtn Pub Corp.

— Sweet Texas Dreams. 352p. 1996. mass mkt. 4.99 (*0-8217-5517-X*, Zebra Kensgtn) Kensgtn Pub Corp.

— Texas Renegade. 384p. 1996. mass mkt. 4.99 (*0-8217-5267-7*, Zebra Kensgtn) Kensgtn Pub Corp.

— Totally Yours. 320p. 1993. mass mkt. 3.99 (*0-8217-4053-9*, Zebra Kensgtn) Kensgtn Pub Corp.

— Wild Texas Bride. 384p. 1995. mass mkt. 4.99 (*0-8217-4833-5*, Zebra Kensgtn) Kensgtn Pub Corp.

Ransom, Daniel. The Fugitive Stars. 288p. (Orig.). 1995. mass mkt. 4.99 (*0-88677-625-2*, Pub. by DAW Bks) Penguin Putnam.

— Night Screams. 176p. (Orig.). (J). 1996. pap. 3.99 (*0-380-72561-4*, Avon Bks) Morrow Avon.

— Zone Soldiers. 336p. 1996. pap. 5.99 (*0-88677-737-2*, Pub. by DAW Bks) Penguin Putnam.

Ransom, Daniel J. Poets at Play: Irony & Parody in the Harley Lyrics. LC 85-544. 160p. (C). 1985. 29.95 (*0-937664-67-7*) Pilgrim Bks OK.

Ransom, David F. George Keller: Architect. (Illus.). 218p. 1978. pap. 12.00 (*0-917482-14-X*) Stowe-Day.

Ransom, Donald. Nothin' but the 'Boo. (Illus.). 20p. (Orig.). 1981. pap. text 2.50 (*0-686-32817-5*) Skydog OR.

Ransom, Ed. Saints for Our Time. LC 97-62563. 304p. 1998. pap. 14.95 (*0-89622-921-1*) Twenty-Third.

Ransom, Evelyn. Complementation: Its Meaning & Forms. LC 86-3554. (Typological Studies in Language: Vol. 10). xii, 226p. 1986. 59.00 (*0-915027-87-9*); pap. 29.95 (*0-915027-88-7*) J Benjamins Pubng Co.

Ransom, Harry, ed. People's Architects. LC 64-15812. 156p. reprint ed. pap. 48.40 (*0-8357-9652-3*, 201699100005) Bks Demand.

Ransom, Harry H. The Conscience of the University & Other Essays. Ransom, Hazel H., ed. 120p. 1982. text 14.95 (*0-292-71078-X*) U of Tex Pr.

— The Conscience of the University & Other Essays. Ransom, Hazel H., ed. LC 82-4890. 117p. reprint ed. pap. 36.30 (*0-608-08699-1*, 206922200003) Bks Demand.

— The Intelligence Establishment. enl. rev. ed. LC 70-115480. 327p. 1970. reprint ed. pap. 101.40 (*0-7837-2318-0*, 205740600004) Bks Demand.

— The Other Texas Frontier. Ransom, Hazel H., ed. (Illus.). 75p. 1984. 19.95 (*0-292-71101-8*) U of Tex Pr.

Ransom, Hazel H., ed. see Ransom, Harry H.

***Ransom, J.** The Relaxed Home. LC 99-43792. 2000. 30.00 (*0-688-17186-9*, Hearst) Hearst Communs.

***Ransom, Jackie.** Bichon Frise Today. 224p. 1999. 29.95 (*1-58245-126-5*) Howell Bks.

Ransom, Jackie. A Dog Owner's Guide to Standard, Miniature & Toy Poodles. 119p. 1995. 10.95 (*1-56465-130-4*, 16024) Tetra Pr.

— Yorkshire Terriers. (Dog Owner's Guide Ser.). (Illus.). 119p. 1995. 11.95 (*1-56465-138-X*, 16043) Tetra Pr.

Ransom, Jane. Bye-Bye. LC 96-51221. 150p. 1997. 17.95 (*0-8147-7490-3*) NYU Pr.

— Bye-Bye. 208p. 1999. reprint ed. 12.00 (*0-671-02708-5*, WSP) PB.

Ransom, Jane R. Scene of the Crime: Poems. LC 97-17496. 66p. 1997. 11.00 (*1-885266-56-1*) Story Line.

— Without Asking. (Roerich Poetry Prize Winner Ser.). 64p. 1989. pap. 9.95 (*0-934257-29-9*) Story Line.

Ransom, Janet H. & Ortaldo, John R., eds. Leukolysins & Cancer. LC 87-17221. (Contemporary Biomedicine Ser.: Vol. 8). (Illus.). 344p. 1988. 125.00 (*0-89603-125-X*) Humana.

Ransom, Jay Ellis. Companion Field Guide to North American Wildlife West. (J). 1981. 13.50 (*0-690-01971-8*) HarpC Child Bks.

***Ransom, Jeanie Franz.** I Don't Want to Talk about It. (Illus.). 32p. (J). (ps-3). 2000. 14.95 (*1-55798-664-9*, 441-6649, Magination Press); pap. 8.95 (*1-55798-703-3*, 441-7033, Magination Press) Am Psychol.

Ransom, John Crowe. Beating the Bushes: Selected Essays, 1941-1970. LC 79-159758. (New Directions Bks.). 186p. reprint ed. pap. 57.70 (*0-8357-7086-9*, 202617400048) Bks Demand.

— College Primer of Writing. 1943. 20.00 (*0-686-17405-4*) R S Barnes.

— The New Criticism. LC 78-31133. 339p. 1979. reprint ed. lib. bdg. 65.00 (*0-8371-9079-7*, RANC, Greenwood Pr) Greenwood.

— Selected Essays of John Crowe Ransom. fac. ed. Young, Thomas D. & Hindle, John, eds. LC 83-12041. (Southern Literary Studies). 368p. 1984. reprint ed. pap. 114.10 (*0-7837-7816-3*, 204757200007) Bks Demand.

— Selected Essays of John Crowe Ransom. Young, Thomas D. & Hindle, John, eds. LC 83-12041. (Southern Literary Studies). 368p. reprint ed. pap. 114.10 (*0-608-09829-9*, 2069997) Bks Demand.

— Selected Letters of John Crowe Ransom. Young, Thomas D. & Core, George, eds. LC 84-10006. (Southern Literary Studies). 430p. 1985. text 60.00 (*0-8071-1168-6*) La State U Pr.

— Selected Letters of John Crowe Ransom. Young, Thomas D. & Core, George, eds. LC 84-10006. (Southern Literary Studies). 446p. reprint ed. pap. 138.30 (*0-608-09812-4*, 206998000007) Bks Demand.

— The World's Body. fac. ed. LC 68-7658. (Louisiana Paperbacks Ser.: No. L-28). 408p. 1968. reprint ed. pap. 126.50 (*0-7837-7931-3*, 204768700008) Bks Demand.

Ransom, John Crowe, ed. Annual Index, 1990. 524p. 1990. pap. text 29.95 (*0-914899-08-2*) Current Lit Pubns.

Ransom, John Crowe. Twigs Bent under God: New & Selected Poems. 120p. 1996. 8.95 (*0-9636373-2-0*); pap. 19.95 (*0-9636373-3-9*) OverBoard Pr.

Ransom, John L. Andersonville Diary. LC 73-21807. (American History & Americana Ser.: No. 47). 1974. lib. bdg. 75.00 (*0-8383-1783-7*) M S G Haskell Hse.

— John Ransom's Andersonville Diary. Orig. Title: John Ransom's Diary. 304p. 1994. pap. 12.95 (*0-425-14146-2*) Berkley Pub.

Ransom, John S. Foucault's Discipline: The Politics of Subjectivity. LC 96-34130. 280p. 1997. pap. text 16.95 (*0-8223-1869-5*); lib. bdg. 49.95 (*0-8223-1878-4*) Duke.

Ransom, Jon C. Nephrology & Transplantation, 1986. 1986. pap. text 24.95 (*0-914899-04-X*) Current Lit Pubns.

— Nephrology & Transplantation, 1987. 340p. 1987. pap. text 24.95 (*0-914899-05-8*) Current Lit Pubns.

— Nephrology & Transplantation, 1988. 436p. 1988. pap. text 29.95 (*0-914899-06-6*) Current Lit Pubns.

— Nephrology, 1985. 337p. 1985. pap. text 24.95 (*0-914899-03-1*) Current Lit Pubns.

— Nephrology, 1984. 338p. (Orig.). 1984. pap. text 24.95 (*0-914899-01-5*) Current Lit Pubns.

Ransom, Jon C., ed. Annual Index, 1989. 472p. 1989. pap. text 29.95 (*0-914899-07-4*) Current Lit Pubns.

Ransom, Judy G. Courage to Care. 1994. 9.95 (*0-687-60165-7*) Abingdon.

Ransom, Julie, ed. How to Move Your AS/400 Beyond Y2K: The Complete Story. 276p. 1998. pap. 69.00 (*0-9663375-0-6*, 601) AS-Four Hundr Pr.

Ransom, Julie, et al. How to Move Your AS/400 Beyond Y2K. (AS/400 Ser.). 290p. 1998. pap. 54.95 (*1-889671-28-2*) Advice Pr.

Ransom, Katherine. Marriage-Go-Round. (American Romance Ser.: No. 440). 1992. per. 3.39 (*0-373-16440-8*, 1-16440-9) Harlequin Bks.

Ransom, La Tricia, ed. see Ravel, Sally & Wolfe, Lee A.

Ransom, M. A. & Engle, Eloise K. Sea of the Bear. LC 79-6122. (Navies & Men Ser.). (Illus.). 1980. reprint ed. lib. bdg. 24.95 (*0-405-13076-7*) Ayer.

Ransom, Marion, ed. see Ives, James L.

Ransom, McAllister. Fuzzy Mules, Pink Slippers Vol. 1: Came a Clown. LC 88-80849. 883800p. (Orig.). 1992. pap. 5.95 (*0-945969-00-7*) Kohinoor Bks.

***Ransom, P. J.** Scotland's Inland Waterways: Canals, Rivers & Lochs. (Past in Action Ser.). (Illus.). 96p. 1999. pap. 8.95 (*1-901663-22-1*, 3221, Pub. by Natl Mus Scotland) A Schwartz & Co.

Ransom, Patti & Towne, Kathleen. I'm Afraid to Go Home: A Program to Help Students Cope with Violent Families or Violent Neighborhoods. LC 94-77206. (Illus.). 52p. 1994. 10.95 (*1-884063-27-6*) Mar Co Prods.

Ransom, Paul. Job Security & Social Stability: The Impact of Mass Unemployment on Expectations of Work. 188p. 1995. 72.95 (*1-85628-966-4*, Pub. by Avebry) Ashgate Pub Co.

Ransom-Quiones, Maribel. Inspirational Poetry of the Gospel of Jesus Christ. 72p. 1998. pap. 8.00 (*0-8059-4353-6*) Dorrance.

***Ransom, Ray A.** College Degrees through Home Study: A Step-by-Step Guide by One Who's Been There & Earned Them, 1. (Illus.). 350p. (C). 2000. pap. 49.00 (*0-9700062-0-9*, 1101) Palm West.

Ransom, Reverdy. Pilgrimage of Harriet Ransom's Son. (American Autobiography Ser.). 336p. 1995. reprint ed. lib. bdg. 89.00 (*0-7812-8622-0*) Rprt Serv.

Ransom, Richard, jt. auth. see Beattie, Gregory.

Ransom, Robert C. Practical Formation Evaluation. LC 95-11161. (Illus.). 490p. 1995. 140.00 (*0-471-10755-7*) Wiley.

Ransom, Robert J. Computers & Embryos: Models in Developmental Biology. LC 81-197475. 224p. reprint ed. pap. 69.50 (*0-608-15668-X*, 203194100077) Bks Demand.

Ransom, Robert J. & Matela, Ray. Computers in Biology: An Introduction. 160p. 1985. pap. 40.00 (*0-335-15018-7*) OpUniv Pr.

Ransom, Roger L. Conflict & Compromise: The Political Economy of Slavery, Emancipation, & the American Civil War. (Illus.). 334p. (C). 1989. pap. text 18.95 (*0-521-31167-5*) Cambridge U Pr.

Ransom, Roger L., et al, eds. Research in Economic History, Vol. 1. 371p. 1976. 73.25 (*0-89232-001-X*) Jai Pr.

— Research in Economic History, Vol. 4. 356p. 1979. 73.25 (*0-89232-080-X*) Jai Pr.

— Research in Economic History, Vol. 5. 301p. 1980. 73.25 (*0-89232-117-2*) Jai Pr.

— Research in Economic History, Vol. 6. 254p. 1981. 73.25 (*0-89232-119-9*) Jai Pr.

— Research in Economic History, Vol. 7. 361p. 1982. 73.25 (*0-89232-198-9*) Jai Pr.

— Research in Economic History, Vol. 10. 308p. 1986. 73.25 (*0-89232-676-X*) Jai Pr.

— Research in Economic History, Vol. 11. 316p. 1988. 73.25 (*0-89232-677-8*) Jai Pr.

— Research in Economic History, Vol. 12. 239p. 1990. 73.25 (*1-55938-007-1*) Jai Pr.

— Research in Economic History, Vol. 13. 275p. 1992. 73.25 (*1-55938-151-5*) Jai Pr.

— Research in Economic History, Vol. 14. 381p. 1993. 73.25 (*0-614-09933-1*); 73.25 (*1-55938-368-2*) Jai Pr.

— Research in Economic History, Vol. 15. 1995. 73.25 (*1-55938-604-5*) Jai Pr.

— Research in Economic History: An Annual Compilation of Research, Vol. 2. LC 76-13771. 389p. 1978. 73.25 (*0-89232-036-2*) Jai Pr.

— Research in Economic History: Emergence of the Modern Political Economy, Supplement 4, No. 4. 224p. 1985. 73.25 (*0-89232-619-0*) Jai Pr.

— Research in Economic History: Recent Developments in the Study of Economics & Business History: Essays in Memory of Herman E. Kroos. LC 76-13956. (Research in Economic History Ser.: Suppl. 1). 315p. 1977. suppl. ed. 73.25 (*0-89232-035-4*) Jai Pr.

— Research in Economic History Suppl. 2: Variations in Business & Economic History: Essays in Honor of Donald L. Kemmerer. 217p. 1982. suppl. ed. 73.25 (*0-89232-262-4*) Jai Pr.

— Research in Economic History Suppl. 3: Technique, Spirit & Form in the Making of the Modern Economics: Essays in Honor of William N. Parker. 300p. 1984. suppl. ed. 73.25 (*0-89232-414-7*) Jai Pr.

— Research in Economic History Suppl. 5: Agrarian Organization in the Century of Industrialization, 2 vols., Set. 542p. 1989. suppl. ed. 146.50 (*0-89232-855-X*) Jai Pr.

— Research in Economic History Suppl. 6: The Vital One: Essays in Honor of Jonathan Hughes. 348p. 1991. suppl. ed. 73.25 (*1-55938-150-7*) Jai Pr.

***Ransom, Roger L. & Sutch, Richard.** One Kind of Freedom: The Economic Consequences of Emancipation. (Illus.). 450p. 2000. write for info. (*0-521-79169-3*); pap. write for info. (*0-521-79550-8*) Cambridge U Pr.

Ransom, Roger L., ed. see Uselding, Paul.

Ransom, Ron. Angel Carving. LC 88-64157. (Illus.). 80p. 1989. pap. text 12.95 (*0-88740-147-3*) Schiffer.

— Carving Santas with Special Interests. LC 91-65655. (Illus.). 64p. 1991. pap. 12.95 (*0-88740-328-X*) Schiffer.

— Celebration Carvings. LC 97-68171. (Schiffer Book for Woodcarvers Ser.). (Illus.). 64p. 1997. pap. 14.95 (*0-7643-0362-7*) Schiffer.

— Patterns & Carving Tips for Santas, Snowmen, & More. LC 97-80065. (Schiffer Book for Woodcarvers Ser.). (Illus.). 64p. 1997. pap. 14.95 (*0-7643-0361-9*) Schiffer.

— Ron Ransom Carves an Amish Family, Plain & Simple. LC 95-34653. (Schiffer Book for Woodcarvers Ser.). (Illus.). 64p. (gr. 10). 1996. pap. 12.95 (*0-88740-893-1*) Schiffer.

— Santa Carving. (Illus.). 48p. 1987. pap. 8.95 (*0-88740-107-4*) Schiffer.

Ransom, Scott & McNeeley, Gene. Gynecology for the Primary Care Provider. Schmitt, William, ed. LC 96-37235. (Illus.). 288p. 1997. text 49.00 (*0-7216-6433-4*, W B Saunders Co) Harcrt Hlth Sci Grp.

Ransom, Scott B. & Pinsky, William, eds. Clinical Resource & Quality Management. LC 98-86857. 447p. 1999. write for info. (*0-924674-67-9*) Am Coll Phys Execs.

Ransom, Stanley A. History of Hartland: The 69th Town in the Colony of Connecticut. (Illus.). 189p. 1995. reprint ed. pap. 19.00 (*0-8328-4983-9*); reprint ed. lib. bdg. 29.00 (*0-8328-4982-0*) Higginson Bk Co.

Ransom, Susan L., ed. see Nicoll, Jessica F.

Ransom, Susan L., ed. see O'Leary, Daniel E.

Ransom, Susan L., ed. see O'Leary, Daniel E., et al.

Ransom, Teresa. Fanny Trollope. LC 95-17068. 240p. 1995. text 45.00 (*0-312-12618-2*) St Martin.

— The Mysterious Miss Marie Corelli: Queen of Victorian Bestsellers. 1999. 39.95 (*0-7509-1570-6*, Pub. by Sutton Publng) Intl Pubs Mktg.

Ransom, Timothy W. The Beach Troop of the Gombe. LC 77-92573. (Illus.). 319p. 1979. 46.50 (*0-8387-1704-7*) Bucknell U Pr.

Ransom, Victoria & Bernstein, Henrietta. The Crone Oracles: Initiate's Guide to the Ancient Mysteries. LC 93-42843. 176p. (Orig.). 1994. pap. 12.95 (*0-87728-800-3*) Weiser.

Ransom, W. H. Building Failures. 2nd ed. 200p. 1981. text 45.00 (*0-419-14260-6*, E & FN Spon) Routledge.

— Building Failures. 2nd ed. (Illus.). 174p. (C). 1987. pap. 27.99 (*0-419-14270-3*, E & FN Spon) Routledge.

Ransom, Will. Private Presses & Their Books. 493p. 1992. 75.00 (*1-882860-05-5*) J Cummins Bksell.

— Private Presses & Their Books. LC 75-41221. reprint ed. 32.50 (*0-404-14732-1*) AMS Pr.

— Selective Check Lists of Press Books. 420p. 1992. 75.00 (*1-882860-03-9*) J Cummins Bksell.

Ransom, William L. Majority Rule & the Judiciary. LC 78-166099. (American Constitutional & Legal History Ser). 1971. reprint ed. lib. bdg. 22.50 (*0-306-70205-3*) Da Capo.

Ransom, Wyllys C. Ransom Historical Outline of the Ransom Family of America, & Genealogical Records of the Colchester, Ct., Branch. (Illus.). 408p. 1995. lib. bdg. 72.00 (*0-8328-4454-3*) Higginson Bk Co.

— Ransom Historical Outline of the Ransom Family of America, & Genealogical Records of the Colchester, Ct., Branch. (Illus.). 408p. 1995. reprint ed. pap. 62.00 (*0-8328-4455-1*) Higginson Bk Co.

Ransom, Wyllys C., et al. Ransom Family of America: Historical Outline of the Ransom Family of America & Genealogical Record of the Colchester, Connecticut Branch; Including the Descendants of John Noyes. (Illus.). xiii, 495p. 1999. write for info. (*0-944893-20-1*) After Thoughts Inc.

***Ransome, Arthur.** The Big Six. (Swallows & Amazons Ser.). (Illus.). (YA). (gr. 5 up). 2000. reprint ed. pap. 14.95 (*1-56792-119-1*) Godine.

Ransome, Arthur. Coot Club. LC 88-46106. (Swallows & Amazons Ser.). (Illus.). 352p. (J). (gr. 4-6). 1990. reprint ed. pap. 14.95 (*0-87923-787-2*) Godine.

— Edgar Allan Poe: A Critical Study. LC 72-3534. (Studies in Poe: No. 23). 1972. reprint ed. lib. bdg. 75.00 (*0-8383-1548-8*) M S G Haskell Hse.

— Favorite Russian Fairy Tales. LC 94-45619. (Children's Thrift Classics Ser.). (Illus.). 96p. (J). 1998. pap. text 1.00 (*0-486-28632-0*) Dover.

— The Fool of the World & the Flying Ship: A Russian Tale. LC 68-54105. (Illus.). 48p. (J). (ps-3). 1968. 16.00 (*0-374-32442-5*) FS&G.

— The Fool of the World & the Flying Ship: A Russian Tale. (Sunburst Ser.). (Illus.). 48p. (J). (ps up). 1987. pap. 6.95 (*0-374-42438-1*) FS&G.

Ransome, Arthur. Peter Duck. LC 86-46247. (Swallows & Amazons Ser.). (Illus.). 414p. 1987. reprint ed. pap. 14.95 (*0-87923-660-4*) Godine.

Ransome, Arthur. Pigeon Post. (Swallows & Amazons Ser.). (Illus.). 382p. (YA). 1992. pap. 11.95 (*0-87923-864-X*) Godine.

— Secret Water. LC 95-24644. (Swallows & Amazons Ser.). (Illus.). 376p. (J). (gr. 5-8). 1995. pap. 14.95 (*1-56792-064-0*) Godine.

— Swallowdale. LC 84-48802. (Illus.). 448p. 1985. pap. 14.95 (*0-87923-572-1*) Godine.

— Swallowdale. 1995. reprint ed. lib. bdg. 24.95 (*1-56849-673-7*) Buccaneer Bks.

— Swallows & Amazons. LC 84-48803. (Swallows & Amazons Ser.). 352p. 1985. pap. 14.95 (*0-87923-573-X*) Godine.

— Swallows & Amazons. 1995. reprint ed. lib. bdg. 24.95 (*1-56849-672-9*) Buccaneer Bks.

— Tontimundo y el Barco Volador. Negroni, Maria, tr. (Mirasol Ser.). (SPA., Illus.). 48p. (J). (ps-3). 1991. 15.95 (*0-374-32443-3*) FS&G.

An Asterisk (*) at the beginning of an entry indicates that the title is appearing for the first time.

R

— We Didn't Mean to Go to Sea. 352p. 1994. pap. 14.95 (*0-87923-991-3*) Godine.

Ransome, Arthur. Winter Holiday. LC 86-46286. (Swallows & Amazons Ser.: Vol. 4). (Illus.). 352p. (J). (gr. 5-8). 1988. reprint ed. pap. 14.95 (*0-87923-661-2*) Godine.

Ransome, Arthur, jt. auth. see Avery, Gillian.

Ransome, David R., et al, eds. Camden Miscellany XXXIII: Seventeenth Century Parliamentary & Financial Papers. (Royal Historical Society Camden Fifth Ser.: No. 7). 492p. (C). 1996. text 54.95 (*0-521-57395-5*) Cambridge U Pr.

Ransome, F. L. Mines of the Goldfield, Bullfrog & Other Southern Nevada Districts. (Illus.). 144p. 1983. pap. 19.95 (*0-913814-60-1*) Nevada Pubns.

Ransome, Grace G., compiled by. Puppets & Shadows: A Selective Bibliography to 1930. LC 97-26981. (Studies in Puppetry: No. 1). 68p. 1997. text 29.95 (*0-7734-8573-2*) E Mellen.

Ransome, Hilda M. The Sacred Bee in Ancient Times & Folklore. 1976. lib. bdg. 250.00 (*0-8490-2552-4*) Gordon Pr.

Ransome, Ian G., jt. ed. see De Wit, Maarten J.

***Ransome, James.** Jack & Beanstalk. (J). 1999. 16.99 (*0-8037-2248-6*, Dial Yng Read) Peng Put Young Read.

Ransome, James, jt. auth. see Woodson, Jacqueline.

Ransome, Julia. The Book of Sandwiches. (Book of...Ser.). (Illus.). 120p. (Orig.). 1989. pap. 12.00 (*0-89586-789-3*, HP Books) Berkley Pub.

Ransome, Lesa. Satchel Paige. LC 97-13790. (Illus.). 40p. (J). (gr. 1-5). 2000. per. 16.00 (*0-689-81151-9*) S&S Childrens.

Ransome, Mary, jt. ed. see Horn, D. B.

Ransome, Michael, jt. auth. see West, Daphne.

***Ransome, Paul.** Sociology & the Future of Work: Contemporary Discourses & Debates. 298p. 1999. text 74.95 (*0-7546-1159-0*, Pub. by Inst Materials) Ashgate Pub Co.

Ransome, Paul. The Work Paradigm. 224p. 1996. 72.95 (*1-85972-183-4*, Pub. by Avebry) Ashgate Pub Co.

Ransome, Wilson. Number-Cell Challenges: A Collection of Ingenious Number Puzzles. 36p. (YA). (gr. 4 up). 1997. pap. 8.50 (*1-899618-07-4*, Pub. by Tarquin Pubns) Parkwest Pubns.

Ranson, Amy. The Feminine as Fantastic in the Conte Fantastique: Visions of the Other, Vol. 16. (Age of Revolution & Romanticism: Interdisciplinary Studies). 286p. (C). 1995. 51.95 (*0-8204-2785-3*) P Lang Pubng.

Ranson, Charles E. Statesman of Harper's Ferry: Biography. LC 95-68286. 180p. 1995. 14.95 (*0-9636320-3-5*) Nuggets Wisdom.

Ranson, Charles W. A Missionary Pilgrimage. LC 88-7021. (Illus.). 212p. reprint ed. pap. 65.80 (*0-8357-4367-5*, 203719600007) Bks Demand.

Ranson, Daniel. The Forsaken. 1988. pap. 3.50 (*0-318-35176-5*) St Martin.

Ranson, David. Forensic Medicine & the Law: An Introduction. 200p. 1997. pap. 34.95 (*0-522-84469-3*, Pub. by Melbourne Univ Pr) Paul & Co Pubs.

Ranson, David L., jt. ed. see Clement, John G.

Ranson, Nancy R. Wildflowers: Legends, Poems, & Paintings. Laughlin, Harold E., ed. LC 89-80596. (Louise Lindsey Merrick Natural Environment Ser.: No. 24). (Illus.). 102p. (C). 1996. 16.95 (*0-89096-740-7*) Tex A&M Univ Pr.

Ranson, Nancy R. Wildflowers: Legends, Poems, & Paintings. Laughlin, Harold E., ed. LC 89-80596. (Louise Lindsey Merrick Natural Environment Ser.: No. 24). (Illus.). 102p. (C). 1996. 16.95 (*0-89096-702-4*) Tex A&M Univ Pr.

Ranson, Nicholas, jt. ed. see Merrix, Robert P.

Ranson, Rebecca. Elmatha's Apology. (Illus.). 70p. (Orig.). 1985. pap. 5.00 (*0-932112-21-8*) Carolina Wren.

— Ward 5B. 1999. text. write for info. (*0-670-81138-6*) Viking Penguin.

Ranson, Rebecca, ed. Theater in the South. (Southern Exposure Ser.). (Illus.). 120p. (Orig.). 1986. pap. 4.00 (*0-943810-21-3*) Inst Southern Studies.

Ranson, Robert. East Coast Florida Memoirs 1837 to 1886. Martin, Val, ed. (Florida Classics Ser.). (Illus.). 48p. 1989. reprint ed. pap. 4.95 (*0-912451-09-2*) Florida Classics.

Ranson, Ron. Big Brush Watercolor. (Illus.). 128p. 1996. pap. 19.95 (*0-7153-0195-0*, Pub. by D & C Pub) Sterling.

— Learn Watercolor the Edgar Whitney Way. (Illus.). 144p. 1997. pap. 22.99 (*0-89134-808-5*, North Lght Bks) F & W Pubns Inc.

— Ron Ranson on Skies: Techniques in Watercolor & Other Media. (Illus.). 160p. 1997. 27.95 (*0-289-80152-4*, Pub. by SVista Bks) Sterling.

— Ron Ranson on Skies: Techniques in Watercolor & Other Media. (Illus.). 128p. 1998. pap. 19.95 (*0-289-80175-3*, Pub. by SVista Bks) Sterling.

— Watercolor Impressionists. (Illus.). 128p. 1998. pap. 19.95 (*0-7153-0694-4*, Pub. by D & C Pub) Sterling.

— Watercolor Painting from Photographs. LC 97-51379. (Illus.). 128p. 1998. pap. 19.95 (*0-8230-5709-7*) Watsn-Guptill.

Ranson, Stewart. Inside the Learning Society. LC 99-165889. 1998. pap. 24.95 (*0-304-70182-3*) Continuum.

— Towards the Learning Society. (Education Ser.). 224p. 1994. 90.00 (*0-304-32770-0*); pap. 31.95 (*0-304-32769-7*) Continuum.

Ransone, Coleman B., Jr. The American Governorship, 69. LC 81-6653. (Contributions in Political Science Ser.: No. 69). (Illus.). 197p. 1982. 55.00 (*0-313-22977-5*, RAG/, Greenwood Pr) Greenwood.

— Office of Governor in the United States. LC 78-130564. (Select Bibliographies Reprint Ser.). 1977. 26.95 (*0-8369-5537-4*) Ayer.

Ransone, Gary. The Contractor's Legal Kit: The Complete, User-Friendly Legal Guide for Home Builders & Remodelers. 316p. 1996. 59.95 incl. cd-rom (*0-9632268-3-5*) Builderburg Grp.

Ransone, Gary. The Contractor's Legal Kit: The Complete, User-Friendly Legal Guide for Home Builders & Remodelers. 2nd ed. Bliss, Steven & Masterson-Glen, Josie, eds. 348p. 1997. reprint ed. pap. 59.95 (*0-9632268-5-1*, Jrnl Lght) Builderburg Grp.

Ranston, Jackie. Lawyer Manley Vol. 1: First Time Up. 1998. 40.00 (*976-640-049-0*, Pub. by UWI Fac Law); pap. 25.00 (*976-640-050-4*, Pub. by UWI Fac Law) Gaunt.

Ranstorp, Magnus. Hizb'Allah in Lebanon. 272p. 1997. pap. 18.95 (*0-312-16491-2*) St Martin.

Rant. Courts-Martial Handbook. LC 98-30953. (C). 1999. text 133.50 (*0-471-97482-X*) Wiley.

***Rant, Davis.** Elementary Mathematical Modeling. 600p. 2000. text 73.33 (*0-13-096202-3*) P-H.

Rant, Lilian V., jt. auth. see Pounds, V. H.

Ranta, Aarne. Type-Theoretical Grammar. (Indices Ser.: No. 1). (Illus.). 238p. 1995. text 59.00 (*0-19-853857-X*) OUP.

Ranta, Donald E., ed. Applied Mining Geology: Ore Reserve Estimation. LC 86-61399. 212p. (Orig.). reprint ed. pap. 65.80 (*0-8357-3483-8*, 203974200013) Bks Demand.

Ranta, J., ed. Analysis, Design & Evaluation of Man-Machine Systems, 1988: Selected Papers from the Third IFAC-IFIP-IEA-IFORS Conference, Oulu, Finland, 14-16 June, 1988. (IFAC Proceedings Ser.). 456p. 1989. 235.00 (*0-08-036226-5*, Pergamon Pr) Elsevier.

Ranta, Judith A. Women & Children of the Mills: An Annotated Guide to Nineteenth-Century American Textile Factory Literature, 28. LC 99-25507. (Bibliographies & Indexes in American Literature Ser.: No. 28). 352p. 1999. lib. bdg. 69.50 (*0-313-30860-8*, GR860, Greenwood Pr) Greenwood.

Ranta, Rachel & Ward, Elizabeth. Lawndale Live! A Retrospective, 1979-1990. LC 93-80111. (Illus.). 72p. 1993. 15.00 (*1-883754-00-3*) Lawndale Art.

Rantala, Kathryn. Missing Pieces: A Coroner's Companion. LC 98-30614. (Illus.). 128p. 1999. pap. 11.95 (*0-938075-28-4*) Ocean View Bks.

Rantala, M. L. O. J. Unmasked: The Trial, the Truth, & the Media. 286p. 1996. pap. 18.95 (*0-8126-9328-0*) Open Court.

Rantala, M. L., et al. Billy Colias Midwest Master. (Illus.). 190p. (Orig.). 1966. pap. 12.95 (*0-945470-56-8*) Chess Ent.

Rantala, M. L., jt. ed. see Milgram, Arthur J.

Rantala, P. K. & Luonsi, A. A., eds. Anaerobic Treatment of Forest Industry Wastewaters: Proceedings of the First IAWPRC Symposium on Forest Industry Wastewaters, Tampere, Finland, 11-15 June 1984. (Illus.). 348p. 1985. pap. 54.50 (*0-08-032729-X*, Pub. by PPL) Elsevier.

Rantalaiho, Liisa & Heiskanen, Tuula. Gendered Practices in Working Life. LC 96-23689. 228p. 1997. pap. 18.95 (*0-312-16368-1*) St Martin.

Rantanen, Norman W. & Hanser, Michael L., eds. Proceedings of the 1996 Dubai International Equine Symposium: The Equine Athlete: Tendon, Ligament & Soft Tissue Injuries. (Illus.). 448p. 1996. write for info. (*0-9656603-0-3*) M R Rantanen.

— Proceedings of the 1997 Dubai International Equine Symposium: The Diagnosis & Treatment of Respiratory Disease. (Illus.). 460p. 1997. write for info. (*0-9656603-1-1*) M R Rantanen.

Rantanen, Norman W. & McKinnon, Angus O. Equine Diagnostic Ultrasonography. LC 97-33085. (Illus.). 700p. 1997. 129.00 (*0-683-07123-8*) Lppncott W & W.

Rantanen, Tehri, jt. ed. see Boyd-Barrett, Oliver.

Rantanen, Terhi, jt. ed. see Boyd-Barrett, Oliver.

Rantete, Johannes. The African National Congress & the Negotiated Settlement in South Africa. LC 98-173088. 323 p. 1998. write for info. (*0-627-02329-0*, Pub. by J L Van Schaik) BHB Intl.

Rantisi, Audeh & Beebe, Ralph. Blessed Are the Peacemakers: An Arab Christian in the Occupied West Bank. 208p. 1990. pap. 8.99 (*0-310-52591-8*) Zondervan.

Rants-Rodriguez, Deanna, jt. auth. see Stringer, Gayle M.

Rantucci, Giovanni. Geological Disasters in the Philippines: The July 1990 Earthquake & the June 1991 Eruption of Mount Pinatubo. (Illus.). 154p. (Orig.). (C). 1995. pap. text 40.00 (*0-7881-2075-1*) DIANE Pub.

Rantucci, Melanie J. Pharmacists Talking with Patients: A Guide to Patient Counseling. LC 96-15264. (Illus.). 280p. 1997. 28.95 (*0-683-07127-0*) Lppncott W & W.

Rantwijk, F. Van, see Kieboom, A. P. & Van Rantwijk, F.

Rantz, Joanne M., ed. Proceedings of the International Symposium of Nitrogen in Grapes & Wine. 323p. (C). 1991. lib. bdg. 50.00 (*0-963071l-0-6*) Am Soc Enology.

— Proceedings of the International Symposium on Clonal Selection, 1995. 1995. 25.00 (*0-9630711-2-2*) Am Soc Enology.

— Proceedings of the International Symposium on Table Grape Production. LC 95-137769. (Illus.). (C). 1994. pap. text 40.00 (*0-9630711-1-4*) Am Soc Enology.

Rantz, Joanne M. & Waterhouse, Andrew L., eds. Wine in Context: Nutrition, Physiology, Policy: Proceedings of the Symposium on Wine & Health, 1996. LC 97-206427. 89p. 1996. 40.00 (*0-9630711-3-0*) Am Soc Enology.

Rantz, Marilyn & Miller, Tari V. Quality Documentation for Long-Term Care: A Nursing Diagnosis Approach. 250p. ring bd. 120.00 (*0-8342-0384-7*, S75) Aspen Pub.

***Rantz, Marilyn, et al.** The Nursing Homes That Seniors Love. 2000. pap. 14.95 (*1-57749-099-1*) Fairview Press.

Rantz, Marilyn, et al. Outcome-Based Quality Improvement in Long-Term Care. LC 98-35896. 320p. 1998. ring bd. 129.00 (*0-8342-1147-5*, 11475) Aspen Pub.

Rantz, Marilyn, jt. auth. see Miller, Tari Vinz.

Rantz, Marilyn J. Nursing Quality Measurement: A Review of Nursing Studies. 198p. (Orig.). 1995. pap. 33.95 (*1-55810-105-5*, NP-93) Am Nurses Pub.

Rantz, Marilyn J. & Popejoy, Lori L. Using MDS Quality Indicators to Improve Outcomes. LC 97-32677. 200p. 1998. 39.00 (*0-8342-1047-9*, 10479) Aspen Pub.

Rantz, Marilyn J., et al. Classification of Nursing Diagnoses: Proceedings of the Twelfth Conference. LC 97-19692. 1997. write for info. (*0-910478-58-9*) Cum Index Nursing.

Rantz, Marilyn J., ed. see North American Nursing Diagnosis Association Staff.

Ranucci, Ernest R. & Rollins, Wilma E. Curiosities of the Cube. LC 76-1837. (Illus.). (YA). (gr. 7 up). 1977. 11.50 (*0-690-01135-0*) HarpC Child Bks.

Ranucci, Karen & Feldman, Julie, eds. A Guide to Latin American, Caribbean & U.S. Latino Made Film & Video. LC 96-45665. (Illus.). 374p. 1998. 74.50 (*0-8108-3285-2*) Scarecrow.

Ranucci, Michael, jt. auth. see Cunningham, Janet.

Ranucci, Rick, ed. see Sweeney, Jill.

Ranuga, Thomas K. The New South Africa & the Socialist Vision: Positions & Perspectives Toward a Post-Apartheid Society. LC 95-18539. (Revolutionary Studies). 168p. (C). 1995. text 49.95 (*0-391-03926-1*) Humanities.

***Ranuga, Thomas K.** South Africa under Majority Rule: A Study in Power Sharing, Racial Equality & Democracy. LC 00-32450. (African Studies: Vol. 54). 260p. 2000. 89.95 (*0-7734-7716-0*) E Mellen.

Ranulf, Svend. The Jealousy of the Gods & Criminal Law at Athens: A Contribution to the Sociology of Moral Indignation, 2 vols. LC 73-14176. 486p. 1974. reprint ed. 27.95 (*0-405-05519-6*) Ayer.

Ranum, Orest, ed. see Bossuet, Jacques B.

Ranum, Orest, jt. ed. see Forster, Robert.

Ranum, Orest A. Artisans of Glory: Writers & Historical Thought in Seventeenth-Century France. LC 79-19248. (Illus.). xiii, 355p. 1980. 39.95 (*0-8078-1413-X*) U of NC Pr.

Ranum, Orest A., ed. National Consciousness, History, & Political Culture in Early-Modern Europe. LC 74-6837. (Johns Hopkins Symposia in Comparative History Ser.: No. 5). (Illus.). 192p. reprint ed. pap. 59.60 (*0-8357-4328-4*, 203712800007) Bks Demand.

Ranum, Orest A. & Forster, Robert, eds. Deviants & the Abandoned in French Society. LC 77-17253. (Selections from the Annales, Economies, Societies, Civilisations Ser.: Vol. 4). 259p. reprint ed. pap. 80.30 (*0-608-12105-3*, 202414600035) Bks Demand.

— Food & Drink in History. LC 78-21920. 186p. reprint ed. pap. 57.70 (*0-608-13162-8*, 205595700041) Bks Demand.

Ranum, Patricia M. Vers une Chronologie des Oeuvres de Marc-Antoine Charpentier: Les Papiers Employes par le Compositeur: un Outil pour l'Etude de Sa Production et de Sa Vie. (FRE., Illus.). ii, 59p. (C). 1994. pap. text. write for info. (*0-9660997-0-2*) P M Ranum.

Ranum, Patricia M., tr. see Aries, Philippe.

Ranum, Patricia M., tr. see Forster, Robert & Ranum, Orest, eds.

Ranum, Patricia M., tr. see Le Goff, Jacques.

Ranville, Michael. To Strike at a King: The Turning Point in the McCarthy Witch Hunts. (Illus.). 292p. 1996. 29.95 (*1-879094-53-3*) Momentum Bks.

Ranville, Myralene. Tex. (Illus.). 32p. (J). (gr. 1-3). 1999. 16.95 (*1-55209-294-1*) Firefly Bks Ltd.

— Tex. (Illus.). 32p. (J). 1999. pap. 6.95 (*1-55209-291-7*) Firefly Bks Ltd.

Ranweiler, Robert J. A CPA's Guide to Saving Tax Dollars for Farm Clients. 1998. pap. 45.00 (*0-87051-226-9*, 090445) Am Inst CPA.

Ranweiler, Robert J., jt. auth. see Behrenfeld, William H.

Ranweiler, Robert J., jt. auth. see Biebl, Andrew R.

Ranwez, Alain D. Jean-Paul Sartre's "Les Temps Modernes" A Literary History, 1945-1952. LC 80-50077. viii, 157p. 1981. 45.00 (*0-87875-191-2*) Whitston Pub.

Ranyard, Rob, et al. Decision Making: Cognitive Models & Explanations. LC 97-15835. (Frontiers of Cognitive Science Ser.). 272p. (C). 1997. 85.00 (*0-415-15818-4*) Routledge.

Ranz, Charlotte A., ed. see Galbreath, Margaret J.

Ranzani, Ermanno, ed. Mario Bellini, Architecture, 1982-1995. (Illus.). 300p. 1996. 62.00 (*3-7643-5375-9*) Birkhauser.

Ranzato, Gabriele. The Spanish Civil War. (Illus.). 1999. pap. 15.00 (*1-56656-297-X*) Interlink Pub.

Ranzoni, Patricia. Claiming. Hunting, Constance, ed. 65p. (Orig.). 1995. pap. 8.95 (*0-913006-59-9*) Puckerbrush.

***Rao.** Accoustical Perspective on Raga-Rasa Theory. 2000. 27.50 (*81-215-0878-9*, Pub. by Munshiram) S Asia.

Rao. Applied Statistical Methods. (Statistics). 1998. pap., teacher ed. write for info. (*0-534-93439-0*) Brooks-Cole.

— Applied Statistical Methods. (Statistics Ser.). 1998. pap., student ed. 16.00 (*0-534-93437-4*) Wadsworth Pub.

— Early Business Opportunities in Interactive Television. LC 96-125203. 124p. 1995. 2650.00 (*1-56965-062-4*, G154) BCC.

— Flowering Plants of Travencore. 502p. (C). 1976. reprint ed. 300.00 (*0-685-21738-8*, Pub. by Intl Bk Distr) St Mut.

— Linear Statistical Inference & Its Applications. 371p. 1998. pap. text 199.95 (*0-471-13733-2*) Wiley.

Rao. Linear Statistical Inference & Its Applications , Vol. 1. 3rd ed. 640p. write for info. (*0-471-24061-3*) Wiley.

Rao. Physics As a Career. 6th ed. 1998. pap. text, lab manual ed. 24.67 (*0-13-957606-1*) P-H.

***Rao.** Social Movement in India: Studies in Peasant, Backward Classes, Sectarian, Tribal & Women's Movements. 2000. pap. 16.00 (*81-7304-335-3*, Pub. by Manohar) S Asia.

Rao, jt. auth. see Lyon.

Rao, jt. ed. see Greene.

Rao, A. Amruth. Personnel Management & Municipal Administration in India. 1985. 32.50 (*0-8364-1389-X*, Pub. by Ashish Pub Hse) S Asia.

Rao, A. Amruth, jt. ed. see Rao, V. Bhaskara.

Rao, A. G. & Rao, T. V., eds. Fatigue & Fracture in Steel & Concrete Structures: Proceedings of the International Symposium, 19-21 December 1991, Madras, India, 3 vols. (Illus.). 1900p. (C). 1992. text 272.00 (*90-5410-205-5*, Pub. by A A Balkema) Ashgate Pub Co.

Rao, A. G. Madhava, see Dover, W. D. & Madhava Rao, A. G., eds.

Rao, A. K., jt. auth. see Naidu, D. S.

Rao, A. M., jt. ed. see Eklund, P. C.

Rao, A. M., tr. see Kagan, I. K. & Vol, N. E.

Rao, A. N., ed. Food, Agriculture & Education. LC 86-25243. (Science & Technology Education & Future Human Needs Ser.: Vol. 6). (Illus.). 254p. 1987. 120.00 (*0-08-033948-4*, Pub. by Pergamon Repr) Franklin.

Rao, A. P. Distributive Justice: A Third-World Response to Rawls & Nozick. LC 97-7116. 362p. 1997. 74.95 (*1-57309-097-2*); pap. 54.95 (*1-57309-096-4*) Intl Scholars.

— Understanding Principia & Tractatus: Russell & Wittgenstein Revisited. LC 97-7115. 268p. 1997. 69.95 (*1-57309-099-9*); pap. 49.95 (*1-57309-098-0*) Intl Scholars.

***Rao, A. R.** Flood Frequency Analysis. (New Directions in Civil Engineering Ser.). 1999. 79.95 (*1-58488-025-2*, Chap & Hall CRC) CRC Pr.

Rao, A. R. A Taxonomy for Texture Description & Identification. Jain, R. C., ed. (Perception Engineering Ser.). (Illus.). 208p. 1990. 65.95 (*0-387-97302-8*) Spr-Verlag.

Rao, A. R. & Chang, Ning, eds. Machine Vision Applications in Industrial Inspection V, Vol. 3029. LC 97-175319. 206p. 1997. 69.00 (*0-8194-2440-4*) SPIE.

— Machine Vision Applications in Industrial Inspection VI, Vol. 3306. 164p. 1998. 48.00 (*0-8194-2746-2*) SPIE.

Rao, A. R. & Shukla, Priti. Pollen Flora of the Gangetic Plain. (Indian Pollen Spore Flora Ser.: Vol. I). 140p. 1977. 15.00 (*0-88065-179-2*) Scholarly Pubns.

Rao, A. R., jt. ed. see Varma, C. V.

Rao, A. Ramachandra, jt. auth. see Govindaraju, R. S.

***Rao, A. Ramachandro & Hamed, Khaled.** Flood Frequency Analysis. 376p. (C). 1999. boxed set 79.95 (*0-8493-0083-5*) CRC Pr.

Rao, A. Ramakrishna, ed. Comparative Perspectives on Indian Literature. 160p. (C). 1992. 25.00 (*81-85218-64-1*, Pub. by Prestige) Advent Bks Div.

Rao, A. S. Modern Commercial Drafting. (C). 1989. 200.00 (*0-7855-6694-5*) St Mut.

Rao, A. S., ed. Commentaries on Delhi Apartment Ownership Act, 1986: With Supplement. (C). 1989. 90.00 (*0-7855-6520-5*) St Mut.

Rao, Adapa R. & Sivaramkrishna, M., eds. When East Meets West: Indian Thought in Anglo-Indian & Indo-English Fiction. LC 93-910447. (C). 1995. write for info. (*81-207-1513-6*) Sterling Pubs.

Rao, Ammula Sambasiva. Life History of Shirdi Sai Baba. 1997. pap. 10.00 (*81-207-2033-4*, Pub. by Sterling Pubs) S Asia.

Rao, Anand, jt. auth. see Wooldridge, Michael J.

Rao, Anand V. Data Warehousing & Storage: Hardware, Software & Applications. LC 98-120784. 92p. 1997. 2950.00 (*1-56965-086-1*, G-215) BCC.

Rao, Anthony. Dinosaur Coloring Book. (Illus.). (J). (gr. k-3). 1980. pap. 2.95 (*0-486-24022-3*) Dover.

Rao, Aparna. Autonomy: Life Cycle, Gender, & Status among Himalayan Pastoralists. LC 97-15842. (Illus.). 350p. 1997. 78.00 (*1-57181-903-7*) Berghahn Bks.

Rao, Aparna & Boeck, Monika. Culture, Creation & Procreation: Concepts of Kinship in South Asian Practice. LC 97-35432. 2000. 69.95 (*1-57181-911-8*); pap. 25.00 (*1-57181-912-6*) Berghahn Bks.

Rao, Aparna, jt. ed. see Casimir, Michael J.

Rao, Arun. Netscape Internet Foundation Classes Programming. LC 97-68572. 350p. 1997. 34.99 (*0-7897-1251-2*) Que.

Rao, Aruna, ed. Women's Studies International: Nairobi & Beyond. LC 90-48653. 376p. 1991. 35.00 (*1-55861-031-6*); pap. 15.95 (*1-55861-032-4*) Feminist Pr.

Rao, Aruna, et al, eds. Gender Analysis in Development Planning: A Case Book. LC 91-31013. (Library of Management for Development). (Illus.). 103p. (Orig.). 1991. pap. 15.95 (*0-931816-61-0*); pap., teacher ed. 7.95 (*0-931816-62-9*) Kumarian Pr.

Rao, Aruna, et al. Gender at Work: Organizational Change for Equality. LC 99-33624. 272p. 1999. 58.00 (*1-56549-103-3*) Kumarian Pr.

***Rao, Aruna, et al.** Gender at Work: Organizational Change for Equality. LC 99-33624. 272p. 1999. pap. 23.95 (*1-56549-102-5*) Kumarian Pr.

Rao, Ashok. Capacity Management Training Aid. LC 82-72090. 39p. 1982. 35.00 (*0-935406-18-2*) Am Prod & Inventory.

Rao, Ashok, et al. Total Quality Management: A Cross Functional Approach. LC 95-46097. 656p. 1996. text 100.95 (*0-471-10804-9*) Wiley.

Rao, Atam S., et al, eds. International Conference on Nuclear Engineering: 4th: 1996: New Orleans, Louisiana. 3498p. Date not set. pap. 500.00 (*0-7918-1226-X*) ASME.

An Asterisk (*) at the beginning of an entry indicates that the title is appearing for the first time.

Rao, B. Bhaskar. Metamorphic Petrology. 190p. (C). 1986. text 70.00 (*90-6191-483-3*, Pub. by A A Balkema) Ashgate Pub Co.

Rao, B. Bhaskara, jt. auth. see Srivastava, V. K.

Rao, B. D. & Kemple, Marvin D., eds. NMR As a Structural Tool for Macromolecules: Current Status & Future Directions. LC 96-21442. (Illus.). 400p. (C). 1996. text 144.00 (*0-306-45313-4*, Kluwer Plenum) Kluwer Academic.

Rao, B. K., ed. Profitable Condition Monitoring. 330p. 1992. text 279.50 (*0-7923-2098-0*) Kluwer Academic.

Rao, B. K. & Behera, S. N. Novel Materials - Design & Properties. LC 98-21481. 1998. 115.00 (*1-56072-559-1*) Nova Sci Pubs.

Rao, B. L. Prakasa, see Prakasa Rao, B. L. S.

***Rao, B. L. S. Prakasa.** Statistical Inference for Diffusion Type Processes. (Kendall's Library of Statistics: 8). 368p. 1999. text 95.00 (*0-340-74149-X*) OUP.

Rao, B. Narahari. A Semiotic Reconstruction of Ryle's Critique of Cartesianism. LC 94-31008. (Quellen Und Studien Zur Philosophie: Bd. 38). xiv, 165p. (C). 1994. lib. bdg. 96.35 (*3-11-014156-6*) De Gruyter.

Rao, B. Rhaskara. Cointegration: For the Applied Economist. 1995. pap. 21.95 (*0-312-15809-2*) St Martin.

Rao, B. Suryanarain. Sri Sarwarthachintamani, 3 pts. LC 96-903484. 1996. 36.00 (*81-208-1351-0*, Pub. by Motilal Bnarsidass) S Asia.

Rao, Bhaskara K. Theories of Charges: A Study of Finitely Additive Measures. (Pure & Applied Mathematics Ser.). 1983. text 157.00 (*0-12-095780-9*) Acad Pr.

Rao, Bindu R. Object-Oriented Databases: Technology, Applications & Products (McGraw Hill Database Experts') 1994. pap. 40.00 (*0-07-051279-5*) McGraw.

Rao, C. H. Agricultural Growth, Rural Poverty & Environmental Degradation in India. (Illus.). 288p. 1994. text 27.00 (*0-19-563343-1*) OUP.

Rao, C. Hanumantha & Linnemann, Hans, eds. Economic Reforms & Poverty Alleviation in India. (Indo-Dutch Studies on Development Alternatives: Vol. 17). 272p. 1996. 38.00 (*0-8039-9302-1*) Sage.

Rao, C. Hayavadana. Indian Caste System: A Study. (C). 1988. reprint ed. 11.50 (*81-206-0270-6*, Pub. by Asian Educ Servs) S Asia.

Rao, C. M., tr. see Glazovskaya, M. A.

Rao, C. N. Advances in Solid State Chemistry: Proc of the Insa Golden Jubilee Symp. 428p. 1987. 85.00 (*9971-5-0137-6*) World Scientific Pub.

— Chemical & Structural Aspects of High Temperature Superconductors. 248p. (C). 1988. pap. 39.00 (*9971-5-0608-4*); text 84.00 (*9971-5-0607-6*) World Scientific Pub.

— Chemical Approaches to the Synthesis of Inorganic Materials. 102p. 1995. 59.95 (*0-470-23431-8*) Wiley.

Rao, C. N., ed. Bismuth & Thallium Cuprate Superconductors: A Special Issue of the Journal Phase Transitions. 96p. 1989. pap. text 267.00 (*0-677-25930-1*) Gordon & Breach.

— Chemistry of High-Temperature Superconductors. 400p. (C). 1991. text 104.00 (*981-02-0805-7*) World Scientific Pub.

— Solid State Chemistry. LC 73-82705. (Illus.). 923p. 1974. reprint ed. pap. 200.00 (*0-7837-0918-8*, 204122300009) Bks Demand.

Rao, C. N. & Gopalakrishnan, J. New Directions in Solid State Chemistry. 2nd ed. LC 96-37412. (Illus.). 564p. (C). 1997. text 115.00 (*0-521-49559-8*) Cambridge U Pr.

— New Directions in Solid State Chemistry. 2nd ed. LC 96-37412. (Illus.). 608p. (C). 1997. pap. text 47.95 (*0-521-49907-0*) Cambridge U Pr.

Rao, C. N. & Raveau, B., eds. Colossal Magnetoresistance & Related Properties of Metal Oxides. 345p. 1998. 64.00 (*981-02-3276-4*) World Scientific Pub.

Rao, C. N. & Raveau, Bernard. Transition Metal Oxides. LC 95-10717. (Illus.). xii, 340p. 1995. 120.00 (*1-56081-647-3*, Wiley-VCH) Wiley.

Rao, C. N., jt. auth. see Edwards, P. P.

Rao, C. N., jt. auth. see Graziani, M.

Rao, C. N., jt. auth. see Mashelkar, R. A.

Rao, C. Nagaraja. Dr. S. Radhakrishnan: His Life & Work. 1986. 12.50 (*0-8364-2566-9*, Pub. by Mittal Pubs Dist) S Asia.

***Rao, C. P., ed.** Globalization & Its Managerial Implications. LC 99-46052. 2000. write for info. (*1-56720-263-2*, Quorum Bks) Greenwood.

Rao, C. P., ed. Globalization, Privatization & Free Market Economy. LC 97-32994. 296p. 1998. 65.00 (*1-56720-075-3*, Quorum Bks) Greenwood.

***Rao, C. P., ed.** Marketing & Multicultural Diversity. 2001. write for info. (*1-56720-074-5*) Greenwood.

Rao, C. R. Handbook of Statistics 10: Signal Processing & Its Applications. Bose, N. K., ed. LC 93-18104. (Handbook of Statistics Ser.: Vol. 10). 1010p. 1993. 190.00 (*0-444-89205-2*, North Holland) Elsevier.

— Statistics & Truth, Putting Chance to Work. LC 97-10349. 240p. 1997. text 25.00 (*981-02-3111-3*) World Scientific Pub.

Rao, C. R., ed. Computational Statistics. LC 93-7155. (Handbook of Statistics Ser.: Vol. 9). 1066p. 1993. 190.00 (*0-444-88096-8*, North Holland) Elsevier.

— Indian Response to African Literature. 1993. text 15.95 (*81-85218-71-4*, Pub. by Prestige) Advent Bks Div.

— Multivariate Analysis: Future Directions. LC 93-16230. (Series in Statistics & Probability: Vol. 5). 488p. 1993. 184.00 (*0-444-89687-2*, North Holland) Elsevier.

Rao, C. R. & Chakraborty, Ranajit, eds. Handbook of Statistical Methods in Biological & Medical Sciences. (Handbook of Statistics Ser.: No. 8). 554p. 1991. 163.00 (*0-444-88095-X*, North Holland) Elsevier.

Rao, C. R. & Kleffe, J. Estimation of Variance Components & Applications. (North-Holland Series in Statistics & Probability: Vol. 3). 370p. 1988. 140.75 (*0-444-70023-4*) Elsevier.

Rao, C. R. & Rao, M. B. Matrix Algebra & Its Applications to Statistics & Econometrics. LC 98-5596. 600p. 1998. 86.00 (*981-02-3268-3*) World Scientific Pub.

Rao, C. R. & Toutenburg, H. Linear Models. 2nd ed. Bickel, P. et al, eds. LC 99-14735. (Series in Statistics). (Illus.). 464p. 1999. 69.95 (*0-387-98848-3*) Spr-Verlag.

Rao, C. R., jt. auth. see Balakrishnan, N.

Rao, C. R., jt. ed. see Cuadras, C. M.

Rao, C. R., jt. ed. see Ghosh, S.

Rao, C. R., jt. ed. see Krishaiah, P. R.

Rao, C. R., jt. ed. see Krishnaiah, P. R.

Rao, C. R., jt. ed. see Maddala, G. S.

Rao, C. R., jt. ed. see Patil, G. P.

Rao, C. Radhakrishna. Linear Statistical Inference & Its Applications. 2nd ed. (Probability & Mathematical Statistics Ser.). 656p. 1973. 199.95 (*0-471-70823-2*) Wiley.

Rao, C. S. Environmental Pollution Control Engineering. LC 91-10923. 431p. 1992. text 69.95 (*0-470-21763-4*) Halsted Pr.

— Environmental Pollution Control Engineering. (C). 1992. pap. 18.50 (*81-224-0301-8*) S Asia.

Rao, C. Vimala, tr. see Triveni.

Rao, Chinatamani N. & Raveau, Bernard. Transition Metal Oxides: Structure, Properties, & Synthesis of Ceramic Oxides. 2nd ed. LC 97-33008. 392p. 1998. 105.00 (*0-471-18971-5*, Wiley-VCH) Wiley.

Rao, D. N., et al, eds. Perspectives in Environmental Botany, Vol. 2. (Illus.). xiv, 325p. 1988. 69.00 (*1-55528-098-6*, Pub. by Today Tomorrow) Scholarly Pubns.

Rao, D. Panduranga, ed. Dimensions of Rural Transportation. (C). 1989. 78.50 (*81-210-0235-4*, Pub. by Inter-India Pubns) S Asia.

Rao, D. Ratnagiri. Cultural Advancement of Orissa under the Gangas of Kalinga. (C). 1995. 34.00 (*81-85094-80-2*, Pub. by Punthi Pus) S Asia.

Rao, D. V. Blockage 2.5 User's Manual. 135p. 1996. per. 14.00 (*0-16-062796-6*) USGPO.

— Drywell Debris Transport Study: Final Report. 225p. 2000. per. 30.00 (*0-16-050193-8*) USGPO.

Rao, D. V. & Vinay, Mudda. Regional Development. 1990. 20.00 (*81-7001-075-6*, Pub. by Chanakya) S Asia.

Rao, Dandamudi V., et al, eds. Physics of Nuclear Medicine: Recent Advances: Proceedings of the AAPM 1983 Summer School Held at Farleigh Dickinson University, Madison, New Jersey, July 24-29, 1983. (American Association of Physicists in Medicine Symposium Ser.: No. 10). 570p. 1984. 60.00 (*0-88318-440-0*, Pub. by Am Inst Physics) Med Physics Pub.

Rao, Digumarti Bhaskara. Earth Summit, 2 vols. 1998. 110.00 (*81-7141-435-4*) Discovery Pub Hse.

— National Policy on Education: Towards an Enlightened & Humane Society. LC 98-908225. 1998. 62.00 (*81-7141-426-5*, Pub. by Discovery Pub Hse) S Asia.

Rao, Digumarti Bhaskara & Latha, Digumarti Pushpa, eds. International Encyclopedia of Women, 5 vols. 1998. 280.00 (*81-7141-410-9*, Pub. by Discovery Pub Hse) Nataraj Bks.

Rao, Dileep. Development Finance Source Guide. 154p. 1993. pap. write for info. (*1-884147-01-1*) InterFinance.

— Fast Track Business Plans. 250p. 1993. pap. write for info. (*1-884147-02-X*) InterFinance.

***Rao, Dileep.** Financing Business Workbook: How to Structure Your Business Financing. 105p. 1999. pap., wbk. ed. 19.00 (*1-884147-04-6*) InterFinance.

Rao, Dileep. Find Financing Frustration-Free. 1993. pap. write for info. (*1-884147-03-8*) InterFinance.

— Smarter Business Finance. 298p. 1993. pap. write for info. (*1-884147-00-3*) InterFinance.

Rao, Dileep, jt. auth. see Cardozo, Dick.

Rao, Doreen, ed. Choral Music for Children. annot. ed. 176p. (C). 1990. pap. 20.00 (*0-940796-80-5*, 1502) MENC.

Rao, Duggirala K., jt. auth. see Gustafson, Karl E.

Rao, E. Nageswara, ed. John Keats: An Anthology of Recent Criticism. 1993. 32.00 (*81-85753-02-4*, Pub. by Pencraft International) S Asia.

Rao, Eleonora. Strategies for Identity: The Fiction of Margaret Atwood. LC 93-14218. (Writing about Women Ser.: Vol. 9). XXV, 204p. (Orig.). 1994. pap. text 31.95 (*0-8204-2216-9*) P Lang Pubng.

Rao, G. P. Piecewise Constant Orthogonal Functions & Their Application to Systems & Control. (Lecture Notes in Control & Information Sciences: Vol. 55). 254p. 1983. 35.95 (*0-387-12556-6*) Spr-Verlag.

Rao, G. P., et al, eds. Sugarcane Pathology Vol. 1: Fungal Diseases. (Illus.). 320p. 1999. 86.00 (*1-57808-046-0*) Science Pubs.

Rao, G. P., jt. auth. see Saha, D. C.

Rao, G. P., ed. see Bhargava-Festschrift, K. S.

Rao, G. P., jt. ed. see Sinha, Naresh K.

Rao, G. Parthasardhy. Alankaratnakara of Sobhakaramitra: A Study. (C). 1992. text 50.00 (*81-7099-406-3*, Pub. by Mittal Pubs Dist) S Asia.

Rao, G. Stayanarayan. The Telegu Chodas of Kanduru: History, Art & Architecture. 1987. 34.00 (*0-8364-2205-8*) S Asia.

Rao, Ganti P. & Patra, Amit. General Hybrid Orthogonal Functions & Their Applications in Systems & Control. (Lecture Notes in Control & Information Sciences: Vol. 213). 124p. 1996. pap. 43.00 (*3-540-76039-3*) Spr-Verlag.

Rao, Goutham. Primary Care Management: Cases & Discussions. LC 98-25307. 1998. 56.00 (*0-7619-1204-5*); pap. 29.95 (*0-7619-1205-3*) Sage.

Rao, Gundu H. Handbook of Platelet Physiology & Pharmacology LC 99-27962. 1999. write for info. (*0-7923-8538-1*) Kluwer Academic.

Rao, H. P. The Psychology of Music. (Illus.). 80p. 1986. reprint ed. 15.00 (*0-8364-1765-8*, Pub. by Abhinav) S Asia.

Rao, H. S., jt. ed. see Ghose, Ajoy K.

Rao, Hanumantha. Unstable Agriculture & Droughts. 155p. 1988. text 25.00 (*0-7069-4041-5*, Pub. by Vikas) S Asia.

Rao, Hayagriva. Teach Yourself . . . Windows NT. 1995. pap. 21.95 (*1-55828-269-6*, MIS Pr) IDG Bks.

Rao, Hemlata. Federal State Financial Relations: Theories & Principles. LC 94-904460. (Illus.). 228p. 1994. 25.00 (*81-7024-613-X*, Pub. by Ashish Pub Hse) Nataraj Bks.

— Rural Energy Crisis: A Diagnostic Analysis. 1990. 32.50 (*81-7024-275-4*, Pub. by Ashish Pub Hse) S Asia.

— Scheduled Castes & Tribes: Socio-Economic Upliftment Programmes. Babu, M. Devendra, ed. LC 93-907639. (Illus.). vi, 150p. (C). 1994. 16.00 (*81-7024-566-4*, Pub. by Ashish Pub Hse) Nataraj Bks.

***Rao, I. Panduranga.** The Universe That Is God: An Insight into the Thousand Names of Lord Visnu. xvi, 435p. 1999. 38.00 (*81-246-0153-4*, Pub. by D K Printwrld) Nataraj Bks.

Rao, J. R. Extensions of the UNITY Methodology: Compositionality, Fairness & Probability in Parallelism. Goos, G. et al, eds. (Lecture Notes in Computer Science Ser.: Vol. 908). xi, 178p. 1995. 36.00 (*3-540-59173-7*) Spr-Verlag.

Rao, J. S. Advanced Theory of Vibrations: Nonlinear Vibration of One Dimensional Structures. 1992. write for info. (*81-224-0442-1*, Pub. by Wiley Estrn) Franklin.

— Advanced Theory of Vibrations: Nonlinear Vibration, One-Dimensional Machine Members & Structures. LC 92-14502. 431p. 1992. text 69.95 (*0-470-21861-4*) Halsted Pr.

— Turbomachine Unsteady Aerodynamics. 1994. write for info. (*81-224-0653-X*, Pub. by Wiley Estrn) Franklin.

Rao, J. S., ed. see Indian Society of Theoretical & Applied Mechanics,.

Rao, Jagadiswari, jt. auth. see Prakash, Anand.

Rao, John, ed. Consumer Law Pleading, No. 3. 368p. 1997. pap. 90.00 (*1-881793-63-X*) Nat Consumer Law.

— Consumer Law Pleadings, Vol. 4. 370p. 1998. 90.00 (*1-881793-68-0*) Nat Consumer Law.

— Consumer Law Pleadings, Vol. 5. 400p. 1999. 90.00 (*1-881793-80-X*) Nat Consumer Law.

Rao, Josyula R. Extensions of the UNITY Methodology: Compositionality, Fairness & Probability in Parallelism. LC 95-10413. (Lecture Notes in Computer Science Ser.: Vol. 908). 1995. write for info. (*0-387-59173-7*) Spr-Verlag.

Rao, K. Damodar. Novels of Ayi Kwei Armah. 1993. 15.95 (*81-85218-75-7*, Pub. by Prestige) Advent Bks Div.

Rao, K. H. Sivaji, see Philip, A. T. & Sivaji Rao, K. H.

Rao, K. Koteswara. Motivation & Job Satisfaction. (Dynamic Organisational Behaviour Ser.). (C). 1991. 38.00 (*81-7141-153-3*) S Asia.

Rao, K. L. Mahatma Gandhi & Comparative Religion. rev. ed. 1990. 15.00 (*81-208-0755-3*, Pub. by Motilal Bnarsidass) S Asia.

Rao, K. N. Learn Vedic Astrology Without Tears. (C). 1995. 9.00 (*0-8364-2906-0*, Pub. by Ranjan Pubs) S Asia.

— The Rotation & Lorentz Groups & Their Representations for Physicists. (C). 1988. 35.00 (*81-224-0056-6*) S Asia.

Rao, K. N., ed. Textbook of Tuberculosis. 607p. 1981. 24.95 (*0-318-36372-0*) Asia Bk Corp.

Rao, K. N., jt. auth. see Bloomer, O. T.

Rao, K. N., jt. auth. see Guelachvili, G.

Rao, K. Narahari, jt. auth. see Guelachvili, Guy.

Rao, K. P. Deccan Megaliths. 175p. (C). 1988. 48.00 (*81-85067-07-4*, Pub. by Sundeep Prak) S Asia.

Rao, K. R. Digital Image, Audio Coding & International Standards. LC 96-15550. 600p. 1996. 83.00 (*0-13-309907-5*) P-H.

Rao, K. R., ed. Codes & Standards for Quality Engineering: Proceedings of the Pressure Vessels & Piping Conference, Minneapolis, MN, 11994. LC 94-71664. (PVP Ser.: vol. 285). 279p. 1994. pap. 60.00 (*0-7918-1358-4*) ASME.

— Standards & Common Interfaces for Video Information Systems: Proceedings of a Conference Held 25-26 October 1995, Philadelphia, Pennsylvania. (Critical Reviews of Optical Science & Technology Ser.: Vol. CR60). 1995. pap. 66.00 (*0-8194-1983-4*) SPIE.

Rao, K. R. & Asada, Y. International Pressure Vessels & Piping Codes & Standards - Current Applications, Vol. 2. 528p. 1995. pap. 150.00 (*0-614-96398-2*, H0976B) ASME.

Rao, K. R. & Asada, Y., eds. International Pressure Vessels & Piping Codes & Standards, Set, Vols. 1 & 2. 1995. pap. write for info. (*0-614-96752-X*) ASME.

— International Pressure Vessels & Piping Codes & Standards - Current Applications, Vol. 1. 468p. 1995. pap. 140.00 (*0-7918-1344-4*, H0976A) ASME.

— International Pressure Vessels & Piping Codes & Standards - Current Perspectives. 528p. 1995. pap. 150.00 (*0-614-96751-1*, H0976B) ASME.

***Rao, K. R. & Bojkovic, Z. S.** Packet Video Communications over ATM Networks. LC 99-44156. (Illus.). 420p. 1999. 65.00 (*0-13-011518-5*) P-H.

Rao, K. R. & Todd, J. A., eds. Changing Priorities of Codes & Standards: Failure, Fatigue & Creep; Proceedings of the Pressure Vessels & Piping Conference, Minneapolis, MN, 1994. LC 94-71665. (PVP Ser.: Vol. 286). 175p. 1994. pap. 50.00 (*0-7918-1359-2*) ASME.

Rao, K. R., jt. auth. see Bapna, S. L.

Rao, K. R., jt. auth. see Sailaja, P.

Rao, K. R., jt. ed. see Deepak, Adarsh.

Rao, K. Raghavendra. Society, Culture & Population Policy in India. 1989. 19.50 (*81-202-0241-4*, Pub. by Ajanta) S Asia.

Rao, K. Raghavendra, tr. see Bhyrappan, S. L.

Rao, K. Ramakrishna, ed. Cultivating Consciousness: Enhancing Human Potential, Wellness, & Healing. LC 92-43428. 248p. 1993. 62.95 (*0-275-94515-4*, C4515, Praeger Pubs) Greenwood.

Rao, K. Ramamohan. Perspectives of Archeology, Art & Culture in Early Andhra Desa. (C). 1992. text 42.00 (*81-85689-01-6*, Pub. by Aditya Prakashan) S Asia.

Rao, K. Ramamohan, ed. Discrete Transforms & Their Applications. LC 89-48054. 350p. 1990. reprint ed. 54.50 (*0-89464-442-4*) Krieger.

Rao, K. Ramamohan, jt. auth. see Elliott, Douglas F.

Rao, K. S. & Rasjeswari, V. Quantum Theory of Angular Momentum: Selected Topics. xxiii, 315p. 1993. 69.00 (*0-387-56308-3*) Spr-Verlag.

Rao, K. S., jt. auth. see Van Dijck, Pitou.

Rao, K. Srinivasa. Public Sector Banks in India & the Productivity Question. (C). 1989. 34.00 (*81-7024-252-5*, Pub. by Ashish Pub Hse) S Asia.

Rao, K. Strinivasa, jt. ed. see Sudarshan, E. C.

Rao, K. U. A Dictionary of Bharatnatyam. (Illus.). 92p. 1980. 16.95 (*0-318-36307-0*) Asia Bk Corp.

Rao, K. Uma. Kuchipudi Bharatam or Kuchipudi Dance: A South Indian Classical Tradition. (C). 1992. 28.50 (*81-7030-291-9*) S Asia.

Rao, K. V. The Role of the Cell Surface in Development, 2 vols., Vol. II. LC 86-13684. 144p. 1987. 87.00 (*0-8493-4689-4*, QH601, CRC Reprint) Franklin.

Rao, K. V., jt. auth. see Halli, Shivalingappa S.

Rao, K. Vaninadha, jt. auth. see Wicks, Jerry W.

Rao, K. Venkateswara. Leprosy in Rural India. (Illus.). xii, 500p. 1992. 34.00 (*81-85445-43-5*, Pub. by Manak Pubns Pvt Ltd) Nataraj Bks.

Rao, Kala, jt. auth. see Virmani, B. R.

Rao, Krishna, jt. auth. see Hall, David O.

Rao, Krishna C., et al. MRI & CT of the Spine. (Illus.). 608p. 1993. 135.00 (*0-683-07133-5*) Lppncott W & W.

Rao, Krishna P., ed. Weather Satellites: Systems, Data, & Environmental Applications. (Illus.). 518p. 1990. 95.00 (*0-933876-87-4*) Am Meteorological.

Rao, M. & Stetkaer, H. An Invitation to Complex Analysis. 252p. (C). 1991. text 37.00 (*981-02-0375-6*); pap. text 21.00 (*981-02-0376-4*) World Scientific Pub.

Rao, M. A. & Hartel, Richard W. Phase State Transition in Foods: Chemical, Structural & Rheological Changes. LC 98-16714. (IFT Basic Symposium Ser.). (Illus.). 416p. 1998. text 165.00 (*0-8247-0179-8*) Dekker.

***Rao, M. Anandha.** Rheology of Fluids & Semisolid Foods: Principles & Applications. LC 99-20667. 433p. 1999. 125.00 (*0-8342-1264-1*, 12641) Aspen Pub.

Rao, M. B. Integrated Rural Development & Areas Planning in India. (C). 1991. text 24.00 (*81-7041-499-7*, Pub. by Anmol) S Asia.

Rao, M. B., ed. Social Movements in India: Peasant & Backward Classes Movements, Vol. 1. 1980. 17.50 (*0-8364-0199-9*) S Asia.

Rao, M. B., jt. auth. see Rao, C. R.

Rao, M. Gangadhar, et al. Organizational Behaviour: Text & Cases. 584p. 1990. text 40.00 (*81-220-0040-1*, Pub. by Konark Pubs Pvt Ltd) Advent Bks Div.

Rao, M. Govinda, et al. Sales Taxation in Madhya Pradesh. 1990. text 22.50 (*0-7069-5327-4*, Pub. by Vikas) S Asia.

Rao, M. Kodanda. Cultural & Structural Dimensions of Family: A Study of Jalari Fisherman. 1990. 20.00 (*81-7022-270-2*, Pub. by Concept) S Asia.

Rao, M. M. Conditional Measures & Applications. (Pure & Applied Mathematics Ser.: Vol. 177). (Illus.). 424p. 1993. text 165.00 (*0-8247-8884-2*) Dekker.

— Probability Theory with Applications. (Probability & Mathematical Statistics Ser.). (C). 1984. text 74.00 (*0-12-580480-6*) Acad Pr.

— Real & Stochastic Analysis: Recent Advances. LC 97-143. (Probability & Stochastics Ser.). 416p. 1997. lib. bdg. 84.95 (*0-8493-8078-2*) CRC Pr.

— Stochastic Processes: General Theory. (Mathematics & Its Applications Ser.: Vol. 342). 1995. lib. bdg. 259.00 (*0-7923-3725-5*) Kluwer Academic.

***Rao, M. M.** Stochastic Processes: Inference Theory. LC 00-39096. (Mathematics & Its Applications Ser.). 2000. write for info. (*0-7923-6324-8*, Kluwer Plenum) Kluwer Academic.

Rao, M. M. & Ren, Z. D. Theory of Orlicz Spaces. (Pure & Applied Mathematics Ser.: Vol. 146). (Illus.). 472p. 1991. text 199.00 (*0-8247-8478-2*) Dekker.

Rao, M. M. & Rizvi, S. S. H., eds. Engineering Properties of Food. 2nd expanded rev. ed. (Food Science & Technology Ser.: Vol. 63). (Illus.). 544p. 1994. text 185.00 (*0-8247-8943-1*) Dekker.

Rao, M. M., et al. Stochastic Processes & Functional Analysis: In Celebration of M. M. Rao's 65th Birthday. LC 96-48137. (Lecture Notes in Pure & Applied Mathematics Ser.: Vol. 186). (Illus.). 296p. 1997. pap. text 150.00 (*0-8247-9801-5*) Dekker.

Rao, M. M., jt. auth. see Schwartzberg.

Rao, M. R. Flowering Plants of Travancore. 502p. (C). 1976. text 325.00 (*0-89771-647-7*, Pub. by Intl Bk Distr) St Mut.

Rao, M. S. Social Movements & Social Transformation: A Study of Two Backward Class Movements in India. (C). 1987. reprint ed. 27.50 (*0-8364-2133-7*, Pub. by Manohar) S Asia.

— Studies in Migration: Internal & International Migration in India. 410p. 1986. 34.00 (*81-85054-08-8*, Pub. by Manohar) S Asia.

Rao, M. S., ed. Social Movements in India: Tribal, Sectarian & Women's Movements, Vol. 2. 1981. 17.50 (*0-8364-0787-3*, Pub. by Manohar) S Asia.

R

Rao, M. S., ed. Urban Sociology in India. 1992. 18.00 (0-86311-280-3, Pub. by Sangam Bks Ltd) S Asia.

Rao, Mangesh, jt. auth. see Watsa, C.

Rao, Maya, ed. see Brandon, Ruth.

Rao, Maya, ed. see Gercik, Patricia.

Rao, Maya, ed. see Lockridge, Frances & Lockridge, Richard.

Rao, Ming. Integrated System for Intelligent Control. (Lecture Notes in Control & Information Sciences: Vol. 167). (Illus.). 144p. 1992. 41.95 (0-387-54913-7) Spr-Verlag.

Rao, Ming & Qiu, Haiming. Process Control Engineering: A Textbook for Chemical, Mechanical & Electrical Engineers. 410p. 1993. text 81.00 (2-88124-628-1) Gordon & Breach.

Rao, Ming, et al. Integrated Distributed Intelligent Systems for Engineering Design. 344p. 1996. text 39.00 (90-5699-510-3) Gordon & Breach.

— Modeling & Advanced Control for Process Industries: Applications to Paper Making Processes. LC 94-26235. (Advances in Industrial Control Ser.). (Illus.). 297p. 1994. 59.95 (0-387-19881-4) Spr-Verlag.

Rao, Mohini. Teach Yourself Hindi. (Language Bks.). 207p. (C). 1989. pap. 8.95 (0-87052-831-9) Hippocrene Bks.

Rao, Myers & Rao, Raja. Images of India in English Fiction: Studies on Kipling. (C). 1991. 28.00 (81-7018-609-9, Pub. by BR Pub) S Asia.

Rao, N. A. Biopsy Pathology of the Eye & Ocular Adnexa. (Biopsy Pathology Ser.). (Illus.). 424p. 1996. text 99.00 (0-412-56720-2, Pub. by E A) OUP.

Rao, N. B. Family Planning in India. 132p. 1976. 7.95 (0-318-36837-4) Asia Bk Corp.

Rao, N. Bhaskara & Raghavan, G. N. Social Effects of Mass Media in India. 1996. 40.00 (81-212-0521-2, Pub. by Gian Publng Hse) S Asia.

***Rao, N. P.** Ancient & Modern Precepts in Administration: A Probe into the Epics. 247p. 1998. pap. 150.00 (81-7533-084-8, Pub. by Print Hse) St Mut.

Rao, N. P. Terrorism, Violence & Human Destruction: Causes, Effects, & Control Measures. (C). 1992. 15.00 (81-7041-568-3, Pub. by Anmol) S Asia.

Rao, N. S. Soil Microorganisms & Plant Growth. 350p. 1995. text 29.95 (1-886106-18-5) Science Pubs.

***Rao, N. S. Subba.** Soil Microbiology: Fourth Edition of Soil Microorganisms & Plant Growth. LC 99-39259. (Illus.). 424p. 1999. text 37.50 (1-57808-070-3) Science Pubs.

Rao, N. Subba. Fisheries Development & Management in India, 1785-1986: A Bibliography. 1989. 44.00 (81-85119-60-0, Pub. by Northern Bk Ctr) S Asia.

Rao, N. Venkat, tr. see Amurskii, G. I., et al.

Rao, Narasinga. Handbook of Kanarese Proverbs. 1988. reprint ed. 5.50 (81-206-0317-6, Pub. by Asian Educ Servs) S Asia.

Rao, Natti S. Design Formulas for Plastics Engineers. 135p. (C). 1991. text 34.95 (1-56990-084-1) Hanser-Gardner.

***Rao, Natti S. & O'Brien, Keith T.** Design Data for Plastics Engineers. LC 98-37253. x, 207p. 1998. pap. 34.95 (1-56990-264-X) Hanser-Gardner.

Rao, Navalgund Anant Hemant Kumar, jt. auth. see Daly, Charles J.

Rao, Nirmala. The Making & Unmaking of Local Self-Government. 272p. 1994. text 72.95 (1-85521-635-3, Pub. by Dartmth Pub) Ashgate Pub Co.

***Rao, Nirmala.** Representation & Community in Western Democracies. LC 99-52071. 2000. text 68.00 (0-312-22960-7) St Martin.

Rao, Nirmala. Towards Welfare Pluralism: Public Services in a Time of Change. (Illus.). 224p. 1996. 85.95 (1-85521-727-9, Pub. by Dartmth Pub); pap. 28.95 (1-85521-732-5, Pub. by Dartmth Pub) Ashgate Pub Co.

Rao, Nirmala & Young, Ken. Local Government since 1945. LC 97-10418. (Making Contemporary Britain Ser.). 336p. (C). 1997. pap. text 23.95 (0-631-19582-3) Blackwell Pubs.

Rao, Nirmala, jt. auth. see Young, Ken.

Rao, P. Statistical Research Methods in the Life Sciences. LC 97-15435. (Statistics-Probability Ser.). 780p. 1997. mass mkt. 93.95 (0-534-93141-3) Wadsworth Pub.

Rao, P. B., ed. Textbook of Diseases of Nose, Throat & Ear. 340p. (C). 1990. 90.00 (0-7855-6744-5, Pub. by Interprint) St Mut.

Rao, P. Chandrasekhara. The Indian Constitution & International Law. 248p. (C). 1995. lib. bdg. 83.00 (0-7923-2739-X, Pub. by M Nijhoff) Kluwer Academic.

Rao, P. Dharma, ed. Focus on Alaska's Coals '86 - Proceedings of the Conference. (MIRL Reports: No. 72). 396p. 1987. 20.00 (0-911043-00-4) UAKF Min Ind Res Lab.

Rao, P. Dharma, et al. Characterization & Washability Studies of Raw Coal from the Little Tonzona Field, Alaska. (MIRL Reports: No. 88). 120p. (Orig.). 1991. pap. 7.00 (0-911043-11-X) UAKF Min Ind Res Lab.

Rao, P. Dharma, jt. auth. see Lin, H. K.

Rao, P. Dharma, jt. auth. see Walsh, Daniel E.

***Rao, P. K.** The Economics of Global Climatic Change. LC 99-41507. (Illus.). 224p. 1999. text 58.95 (0-7656-0460-4) M E Sharpe.

— The Economics of Global Climatic Change. (Illus.). 224p. 2000. pap. text 22.95 (0-7656-0461-2) M E Sharpe.

Rao, P. K. Professional Crime in India. 256p. 1983. text 27.50 (0-685-14724-X) Coronet Bks.

— Sustainable Development. LC 99-22432. 304p. 1999. pap. 29.95 (0-631-20994-8) Blackwell Pubs.

— Sustainable Development: Economics & Policy. LC 99-22432. 304p. 1999. 59.95 (0-631-20993-X) Blackwell Pubs.

***Rao, P. K.** The World Trade Organization & the Environment. LC 00-33265. 2000. write for info. (0-312-23774-X) St Martin.

Rao, P. M., tr. see Akramkhodzhaev, A. M., et al.

Rao, P. M., tr. see McHedlidze, G. A.

Rao, P. M., tr. see Rabinovich, F. N.

Rao, P. M., tr. see Syroechkovskii, E. E.

Rao, P. N. Fundamentals of Indian Philosophy. 205p. 1981. 16.95 (0-318-37020-4) Asia Bk Corp.

Rao, P. Raghunadha. History of Modern Andhra Pradesh. (C). 1993. pap. write for info. (81-207-1547-0) Sterling Pubs.

Rao, P. Subba. Contemporary Challenges in Management. (Dynamic Organisational Behaviour Ser.). (C). 1991. 34.00 (81-7141-136-3) S Asia.

— Human Resource Management: Environmental Influence. (C). 1989. 44.00 (81-85076-59-6, Pub. by Chugh Pubns) S Asia.

Rao, P. Syamasundar, ed. Transcatheter Therapy in Pediatric Cardiology. 528p. 1993. 235.00 (0-471-58827-X) Wiley.

***Rao, P. V.** Style in Journalism. 1998. pap. 11.00 (81-250-1035-1, Pub. by Orient Longman Ltd) S Asia.

Rao, P. V., jt. auth. see Sood, P.

***Rao, Paul R., et al, eds.** Managing Stroke: A Guide to Living Well After Stroke. 320p. 2000. 27.00 (1-886236-24-0) ABI Prof Pubns.

Rao, Peggy L. & Mahoney, Jean. Japanese Accents in Western Interiors. 168p. 1997. pap. 26.00 (0-87040-988-3) Japan Pubns USA.

— Nature on View: Homes & Gardens Inspired by Japan. (Illus.). 192p. 1993. 29.95 (0-8348-0299-6) Weatherhill.

Rao, Peggy L., jt. auth. see Mahoney, Jean.

Rao, Prakasa, jt. ed. see Basawa, Ishwar V.

Rao, Pratima V., jt. ed. see Ziff, Bruce H.

Rao, Pratima V., jt. ed. see Ziff, Bruce.

Rao, R., jt. ed. see Pappu, S. S.

Rao, R. G. Bhrigu Nandi Nadi. (C). 1991. reprint ed. text 24.00 (0-8364-2878-1, Pub. by Ranjan Pubs) S Asia.

— Your Destiny in Thumb. (Illus.). 1991. write for info. (0-318-68201-X, Pub. by Ranjan Pubs) S Asia.

Rao, R. P., ed. Luminescence: Phenomena, Materials & Devices. (Solid State Physics, Luminescence Ser.). 448p. (C). 1991. text 195.00 (1-56072-013-1) Nova Sci Pubs.

Rao, R. R. & Razi, B. A. A Synoptic Flora of Mysore District. (International Bioscience Monographs: No. 7). 694p. 1981. 65.00 (0-88065-180-6) Scholarly Pubns.

Rao, R. R., jt. auth. see Baishya, A. J.

Rao, R. R., jt. auth. see Baishya, A. K.

Rao, R. R., jt. auth. see Haridasan, K.

Rao, R. R., jt. auth. see Jain, S. K.

Rao, R. Rama. India's Energy Scene: Options for the Future. (Illus.). 120p. 1988. text 20.00 (81-7027-122-3, Pub. by Radiant Pubs) S Asia.

Rao, R. S. Flora of Goa, Div, Daman, Dadra & Nagarhaveli, 1. (C). 1987. text 40.00 (0-7855-3153-X, Pub. by Scientific) St Mut.

— Flora of Goa, Div, Daman, Dadra & Nagarhaveli, 2. (C). 1987. text 50.00 (0-7855-3154-8, Pub. by Scientific) St Mut.

Rao, R. V. Human Resources Development: Experiences, Interventions, Strategies. LC 95-46607. 304p. (C). 1996. 38.00 (0-8039-9273-4) Sage.

***Rao, R. V.** Perspectives on Indian Development: Economy, Polity & Society. 2000. 54.00 (81-207-2253-1, Pub. by Sterling Pubs) S Asia.

Rao, R. V. Rural Industrialisation in India. 1987. reprint ed. 10.50 (0-8364-2258-9, Pub. by Concept) S Asia.

Rao, Radhakrishna & Toutenburg, Helge. Linear Models: Least Squares & Alternative Methods. LC 95-23947. (Springer Series in Statistics). 352p. 1995. 57.95 (0-387-94562-8) Spr-Verlag.

Rao, Raghuveer M. Wavelet Transforms: Introduction to Theory & Applications. LC 98-22332. 336p. (C). 1998. 64.95 (0-201-63463-5, Prentice Hall) P-H.

Rao, Raja. Kanthapura. LC 63-18637. 1967. pap. 10.95 (0-8112-0168-6, NDP224, Pub. by New Directions) Norton.

— The Serpent & the Rope. LC 85-13628. 408p. 1986. 22.50 (0-87951-220-2, Pub. by Overlook Pr) Penguin Putnam.

— The Serpent & the Rope. 408p. 1988. pap. 9.95 (0-87951-243-1, Pub. by Overlook Pr) Penguin Books.

Rao, Raja, jt. auth. see Rao, Myers.

Rao, Rajiv, jt. auth. see Baghdadi, Rafique.

Rao, Ramakrishna. India's Borders: Ecology & Security Perspectives. (C). 1991. 24.00 (81-85515-02-6, Pub. by Promilla) Nataraj Bks.

Rao, Ramesh K. Accounting Principles: Integrative Casebook, Financial Management. 3rd ed. 1995. text 15.95 (0-538-84681-X) S-W Pub.

— Financial Management: Concepts & Applications. 3rd ed. LC 94-22216. 1994. write for info. (0-534-21930-6) S-W Pub.

Rao, Ranga R., jt. auth. see Bhattacharya, R. N.

Rao, Ratna N. Social Organization in an Indian Slum. 1990. 37.50 (81-7099-186-2, Pub. by Mittal Pubs Dist) S Asia.

Rao, Rolla S. Flora of Goa, Diu, Daman, Dadra & Nagarhaveli, Vol. 1. (Flora of India Ser.: No. 2). 198p. 1985. text 35.00 (0-945345-52-6, Pub. by Mahendra Pal Singh) Lubrecht & Cramer.

— Flora of Goa, Diu, Daman, Dadra & Nagarhaveli, Vol. 2. (Flora of India Ser.: No. 2). 546p. 1986. text 35.00 (0-945345-53-4, Pub. by Mahendra Pal Singh) Lubrecht & Cramer.

Rao, S. Interoperability in Broadband Networks. LC 94-75948. 458p. (gr. 12). 1994. 125.00 (90-5199-160-6) IOS Press.

Rao, S., ed. Interworking in Broadband Networks. LC 93-78257. 500p. (gr. 12). 1993. 125.00 (90-5199-135-5, Pub. by IOS Pr) IOS Press.

Rao, S. B., jt. auth. see Schwartz, R. W.

Rao, S. Balu, jt. ed. see Raj Anand, Mulk.

Rao, S. K. Encyclopaedia of Indian Medicine Vol. 1: Historical Perspectives. (C). 1985. 31.00 (0-8364-2322-4, Pub. by Popular Prakashan) S Asia.

— Encyclopaedia of Indian Medicine Vol. 2: Basic Concepts. (C). 1987. 47.50 (0-8364-2323-2, Pub. by Popular Prakashan) S Asia.

— Encyclopaedia of Indian Medicine Vol. 3: Clinical Examination & Diagnostic Methods. (C). 1987. 42.50 (0-8364-2324-0, Pub. by Popular Prakashan) S Asia.

Rao, S. P. & Sinha, V. M., eds. Professionalism in Public Administration. 1990. text 27.50 (0-685-31755-2, Pub. by Assoc Pub Hse) Advent Bks Div.

Rao, S. R. Dawn & Devolution of the Indus Civilization. (C). 1991. 120.00 (81-85179-74-3, Pub. by Aditya Prakashan) S Asia.

— Electrical Gadgets & Their Repairs: A Book That Teaches Not Only What but Also How & Why about Electrical Appliances. 292p. 1994. pap. 75.00 (81-209-0683-7, Pub. by Pitambar Pub) St Mut.

— New Frontiers of Archaeology: Heras Memorial Lectures. LC 95-900334. (C). 1994. 20.00 (81-7154-689-7, Pub. by Popular Prakashan) S Asia.

Rao, S. R., ed. Coal Preparation & Use - A World Review: International Coal Preparation Congress, New Delhi, India, 9th. 1982. 259p. (C). 1982. text 207.00 (90-6191-256-3, Pub. by A A Balkema) Ashgate Pub Co.

Rao, S. Ramachandra. Xanthates & Related Compounds. LC 77-141626. 512p. reprint ed. pap. 158.80 (0-608-17096-8, 202713000054) Bks Demand.

Rao, S. S. Mechanical Vibrations. 3rd ed. (C). 1995. pap. text, student ed. 42.66 (0-201-52687-5) Addison-Wesley.

Rao, S. V., ed. Women's Studies in India: A Directory of Research Institutions. (Illus.). viii, 123p. 1993. 13.00 (81-7024-569-9, Pub. by Ashish Pub Hse) Nataraj Bks.

Rao, S. V., et al. Women at Work in India Vol. 2: An Annotated Bibliography. 324p. 1994. 25.00 (0-8039-9173-8) Sage.

Rao, S. Vasudeva. Status of Women & Children in Slums: A Study of Hyderabad City. (C). 1992. 15.00 (81-7013-094-8, Pub. by Navarang) S Asia.

Rao, S. Venogopal, ed. Perspectives in Criminology. 250p. 1988. text 40.00 (0-7069-4000-8, Pub. by Vikas) S Asia.

Rao, S. Venugopal. Criminal Justice: Problems & Perspectives in India. xiv, 310p. 1991. 35.00 (81-220-0233-1) Advent Bks Div.

Rao, Sadasiva M. Time Domain Electromagnetics. LC 98-52663. (Electrical & Electronic Engineering Ser.). (Illus.). 372p. 1999. 89.95 (0-12-580190-4) Harcourt.

Rao, Salem S. Chemistry of Oxide Superconductors. 1991. 44.00 (0-632-02302-3) CRC Pr.

— Impact Assessment of Hazardous. 1. LC 98-47582. 15p. 1999. lib. bdg. 69.95 (0-8493-4109-4) CRC Pr.

— Role of Cell Surface Development, Vol. I. 152p. 1987. 88.00 (0-8493-4688-6, CRC Reprint) Franklin.

— The Role of the Cell Surface in Development, 2 vols. 1987. 229.95 (0-8493-4687-8, QH601, CRC Reprint) Franklin.

Rao, Salem S., ed. Acid Stress & Aquatic Microbial Interactions. 192p. 1989. lib. bdg. 179.00 (0-8493-5168-5, QR105) CRC Pr.

— Impact Assessment of Hazardous Aquatic Contaminants: Concepts & Approaches. LC 98-47582. 228p. 1999. 75.00 (1-57504-116-2) CRC Pr.

***Rao, Satish S.** Gastrointestinal Motility: Tests & Problem-Oriented Approach. LC 99-16121. 1999. write for info. (0-306-46129-3) Kluwer Academic.

Rao, Sethu, jt. auth. see Bouvier, Leon F.

Rao, Shanta. Stories of Women. LC 97-136336. (Illus.). 136p. 1996. 45.00 (1-899235-30-2, 620353, Pub. by Dewi Lewis) Dist Art Pubs.

***Rao, Shanta R.** Seethu: A Novel. 1998. pap. 5.50 (81-250-1017-3, Pub. by Orient Longman Ltd) S Asia.

***Rao, Singiresu S.** Applied Numerical Methods For Engineers & Scientists. (C). 2000. text. write for info. (0-201-33791-6) Addison-Wesley.

Rao, Singiresu S. Engineering Optimization: Theory & Practice. 3rd ed. LC 96-4982. (Illus.). 920p. 1996. 140.00 (0-471-55034-5) Wiley.

— The Finite Element Method in Engineering. 3rd ed. LC 99-158637. 608p. 1998. pap. 65.00 (0-7506-7072-X) Buttrwrth-Heinemann.

— Mechanical Vibrations. 2nd ed. (C). 1992. pap. text. write for info. (0-201-55693-6) Addison-Wesley.

— Mechanical Vibrations. 3rd ed. LC 93-3311. 920p. (C). 1995. pap. text 105.00 (0-201-52686-7) Addison-Wesley.

Rao, Singiresu S., ed. The Finite Element Method in Engineering. LC 80-40817. 400p. 1981. text 96.00 (0-08-025467-5, Pergamon Pr); pap. text 30.95 (0-08-025466-7, Pergamon Pr) Elsevier.

Rao, Singiresu S., jt. auth. see San Diego State University Staff.

Rao, Srinivasa. Perceptual Error: The Indian Theories. LC 98-20652. (Monographs of the Society for Asian & Comparative Philosophy: Vol. 16). 168p. 1998. pap. text 20.00 (0-8248-1958-6) UH Pr.

Rao, Stephen M., ed. Neurobehavioral Aspects of Multiple Sclerosis. (Illus.). 288p. 1990. text 42.50 (0-19-505400-8) OUP.

Rao, Stephen M., jt. auth. see Fogel, Barry S.

Rao, Subba. Jurisprudence & Legal Theory. (C). 1991. 40.00 (0-89771-798-8, Pub. by Eastern Book) St Mut.

— Shastra Evam Vidhi Ke Sidhant (Jurisprudence & Legal Theory in Hindi) 377p. 1981. 52.50 (0-7855-1325-6) St Mut.

Rao, Sudha V. Education & Rural Development. 320p. (C). 1986. text 25.00 (0-8039-9491-5) Sage.

Rao, Surya P., jt. auth. see Gangadhara, Rao M.

Rao, T. A., jt. auth. see Banerjee, L. K.

Rao, T. A. Gopinatha, see Gopinatha Rao, T. A.

Rao, T. Ananda. Compendium of Foliar Sclerids in Angiosperms: Morphology & Taxonomy. (C). 1991. 62.00 (81-224-0067-1) S Asia.

Rao, T. K., et al, eds. Genotoxicology of N-Nitroso Compounds. LC 83-23716. (Topics in Chemical Mutagenesis Ser.: Vol. 1). 288p. 1984. 75.00 (0-306-41445-7, Plenum Trade) Perseus Pubng.

Rao, T. Nageswara. Inviolable Air: Canadian Poetic-Modernism in Perspective. (C). 1994. 20.00 (81-7018-779-6, Pub. by BR Pub) S Asia.

Rao, T. Subba. Applications of Time Series Analysis in Astronomy & Meteorology. Priestly, M. B. et al, eds. LC 96-70803. (Illus.). 472p. (C). 1997. ring bd. 99.95 (0-412-63800-2, Chap & Hall CRC) CRC Pr.

Rao, T. Subba, see Subba Rao, T.

Rao, T. V. Economic Efficiency of the Organizational Decisions of the Firm. (Illus.). 240p. 1989. 72.95 (0-387-51570-4, 3423) Spr-Verlag.

— Human Resources Development: Experiences, Interventions, Strategies. LC 95-46607. 1996. pap. 18.95 (0-8039-9274-2) Sage.

— Readings in Human Resource Development. (C). 1991. text 29.50 (81-204-0585-4, Pub. by Oxford IBH) S Asia.

Rao, T. V. & Pereira, D. F. Recent Experiences in Human Resources Development. (C). 1986. 18.50 (81-204-0120-4, Pub. by Oxford IBH) S Asia.

Rao, T. V. & Rastogi, Ranjul. Discretionary Managerial Behavior. LC 97-37989. 244p. 1997. 115.50 (0-7923-8016-9) Kluwer Academic.

Rao, T. V., jt. ed. see Rao, A. G.

Rao, Tenneti V. Handbook of Metallurgical Coatings. 1998. 125.00 (0-8493-2945-0) CRC Pr.

Rao, U. R., et al, eds. Perspectives in Communications: Proceedings of the Workshop ICTP, Trieste, Italy, November 14-December 2, 1983, 2 vols. 1504p. 1987. text 291.00 (9971-978-76-8) World Scientific Pub.

Rao, U. R., ed. see Gandhi, M. K.

Rao, U. R., ed. see Gandhi, Mohandas Karamchand.

Rao, U. S. Panorama of Indian Dances. (Raga Nrtya Ser.: No. 6). (C). 1993. 68.50 (81-7030-330-3) S Asia.

Rao, V. Bhaskara. Public Administration in India. (C). 1989. 31.00 (81-202-0233-3, Pub. by Ajanta) S Asia.

Rao, V. Bhaskara & Rao, A. Amruth, eds. Nehru & Administration. (C). 1989. 34.00 (81-202-0231-7, Pub. by Ajanta) S Asia.

Rao, V. G., jt. auth. see Pande, Alaka.

Rao, V. K. Organisational & Financial Management of Religious Institutions. (C). 1992. 34.00 (0-8364-2807-2, Pub. by Deep & Deep Pubns) S Asia.

Rao, V. K. & Reddy, R. S. Readings in Learning Education Vols. 1-5: Contemporary Education; Parent Education; Comparative Education; Secondary Education; & Environmental Education, 5 vols. 1997. 1250.00 (81-7169-441-1, Pub. by Print Hse) St Mut.

Rao, V. L., jt. auth. see Wengel, Jan Ter.

Rao, V. Lakshmana. Essays on Indian Economy. (Illus.). xii, 165p. 1994. 20.00 (81-7024-660-1, Pub. by Ashish Pub Hse) Nataraj Bks.

Rao, V. M., ed. Poor in a Hostile Society: Glimpses of Changing Poverty Scenario in India. LC 98-908691. 1998. 28.00 (81-259-0615-0, Pub. by Vikas) S Asia.

Rao, V. M. & Aziz, Abdul. Poverty Alleviation in India: Programmes & Action. (C). 1989. 30.00 (81-7024-255-X, Pub. by Ashish Pub Hse) S Asia.

Rao, V. R. Selected Doctrines from Indian Philosophy. (C). 1987. 21.50 (81-7099-000-9, Pub. by Mittal Pubs Dist) S Asia.

Rao, V. S. Management in Action. (Dynamic Organisational Behaviour Ser.). (C). 1991. text 30.00 (81-7141-126-6) S Asia.

***Rao, V. S.** Principles of Weed Science. 2nd ed. LC 99-39247. (Illus.). 558p. 2000. text 49.50 (1-57808-069-X) Science Pubs.

Rao, V. S. & Narayana, P. S. Management Concepts & Thoughts. 2nd rev. ed. 556p. 1990. text 45.00 (81-220-0154-8, Pub. by Konark Pubs Pvt Ltd) Advent Bks Div.

Rao, V. S., et al. Conformation of Carbohydrates. (Illus.). 409p. 1998. text 111.00 (90-5702-314-8, Harwood Acad Pubs); pap. text 42.00 (90-5702-315-6, Harwood Acad Pubs) Gordon & Breach.

Rao, V. V., et al. ASEAN External Debt Perspectives. LC 94-944333. 112p. 1994. pap. 14.50 (981-210-050-4, Pub. by Times Academic) Intl Spec Bk.

Rao, V. V., jt. auth. see Ramaswamy, G. S.

Rao, Valluru B. C++ Neural Networks & Fuzzy Logic. 1995. pap. 39.95 (1-55828-298-X, MIS Pr) IDG Bks.

Rao, Vasant, et al. Switch-Level Timing Simulation of MOS VLSI Circuits. (C). 1988. text 110.00 (0-89838-302-1) Kluwer Academic.

Rao, Velcheru N. & Roghair, Gene H., trs. from TEL. Siva's Warriors: The Basava Purana of Palkuriki Somanatha. 325p. 1990. text 57.50 (0-691-05591-2, Pub. by Princeton U Pr) Cal Prin Full Svc.

Rao, Velcheru N., et al. Symbols of Substance: Court & State in Nayaka Period Tamil Nadu. (Illus.). 370p. 1998. reprint ed. pap. text 19.95 (0-19-564399-2) OUP.

— Symbols of Substance: Court & State in Nayaka Period Tamilnadu. (Illus.). 388p. 1993. 55.00 (0-19-563021-1) OUP.

***Rao, Veluri S.** Theories of Knowledge Bk. II: A Critique. 1998. 30.00 (81-7030-575-6, Pub. by Sri Satguru Pubns) S Asia.

Rao, Vepa. Curve in the Hills: Communication & Development. LC 97-913731. 98p. 1997. pap. 9.00 (81-85952-41-8, Pub. by Indian Inst) Nataraj Bks.

Rao, Vijay M., et al. MRI & CT Atlas of Correlative Imaging in Otolaryngology. 383p. (C). 1993. pap. text 165.00 (0-8385-6526-3, A6526-6, Apple Lange Med) McGraw.

Rao, Vithala. Analysis for Strategic Marketing. LC 97-3230. 400p. (C). 1997. pap. 67.00 (0-321-00198-2, Prentice Hall) P-H.

An Asterisk (*) at the beginning of an entry indicates that the title is appearing for the first time.

Rao, Vithala R. & Steckel, Joe H. The New Science of Marketing: State-of-the-Art Tools for Anticipating & Tracking the Market Forces that Will Shape Your Company's Future. LC 96-195518. 250p. 1995. text 42.50 (*1-55738-539-4*, Irwn Prfssnl) McGraw-Hill Prof.

Rao, Vithala R., jt. auth. see McLaughlin, Edward W.

Rao, Vlcheru N. A Poem at the Right Moment: Remembered Verses from Premodern South India. Shulman, David, tr. LC 96-29616. (Voices from Asia Ser.). 195p. 1997. pap. 16.95 (*0-520-20849-8*, Pub. by U CA Pr) Cal Prin Full Svc.

Rao, Y. K. Stoichiometry & Thermodynamics of Metallurgical Processes. 976p. (C). 1996. reprint ed. text 110.00 (*1-878907-92-1*, RAN) TechBooks.

Rao, Y. Kris, jt. ed. see Kudryk, Val.

Rao, Y. V. Communication & Development: A Study of Two Indian Villages. LC 66-21940. 152p. reprint ed. pap. 47.20 (*0-608-15120-3*, 205589800039) Bks Demand.

— Introduction to Thermodynamics. 1993. write for info. (*81-224-0558-4*, Pub. by Wiley Estrn) Franklin.

— Theory & Problems of Thermodynamics. 1994. write for info. (*81-224-0659-9*, Pub. by Wiley Estrn) Franklin.

Raof, Hussein F. Subject, Theme & Agent in Modern Standard Arabic. LC 98-216040. 288p. 1997. 75.00 (*0-7007-0672-0*, Pub. by Curzon Pr Ltd) Paul & Co Pubs.

Ra'Oof, Jum & Ra'Oof, Mae O. Five Friends of Rainbow Forest (Series), Series 2. unabridged ed. (Illus.). 304p. (Orig.). (J). (gr. 3-5). 1995. 44.95 (*1-888527-11-0*) New Wrld Ent.

Ra'Oof, Jum, jt. auth. see Ra'Oof, Mae O.

Ra'Oof, Mae O. & Ra'Oof, Jum. A Bow for Rachel Rabbit. unabridged ed. (Five Friends of Rainbow Forest Ser.). (Illus.). 59p. (Orig.). (J). (gr. 3-5). 1995. pap. 8.95 (*1-888527-07-2*) New Wrld Ent.

— A Bow for Rachel Rabbit. unabridged ed. (Five Friends of Rainbow Forest Ser.). (Illus.). 46p. (Orig.). (J). (ps-2). 1995. pap. 7.95 (*1-888527-01-3*) New Wrld Ent.

— Casper the Ugliest Caterpillar. unabridged ed. (Five Friends of Rainbow Forest Ser.). (Illus.). 49p. (Orig.). (J). (gr. 3-5). 1995. pap. 8.95 (*1-888527-08-0*) New Wrld Ent.

— Casper the Ugliest Caterpillar. unabridged ed. (Five Friends of Rainbow Forest Ser.). (Illus.). 38p. (Orig.). (J). (ps-2). 1995. pap. 7.95 (*1-888527-02-1*) New Wrld Ent.

— Five Friends of Rainbow Forest (Series), Series 1. unabridged ed. (Illus.). 246p. (Orig.). (J). (ps-2). 1995. pap. 39.75 (*1-888527-05-6*) New Wrld Ent.

— Little Ricky Rabbit. unabridged ed. (Five Friends of Rainbow Forest Ser.). (Illus.). 61p. (Orig.). (J). (gr. 3-5). 1995. pap. 8.95 (*1-888527-06-4*) New Wrld Ent.

— Little Ricky Rabbit. unabridged ed. (Five Friends of Rainbow Forest Ser.). (Illus.). 50p. (Orig.). (J). (ps-2). 1995. pap. 7.95 (*1-888527-00-5*) New Wrld Ent.

— Little Stinky Skunk. unabridged ed. (Five Friends of Rainbow Forest Ser.). (Illus.). 69p. (Orig.). (J). (gr. 3-5). 1995. pap. 8.95 (*1-888527-09-9*) New Wrld Ent.

— Little Stinky Skunk. unabridged ed. (Five Friends of Rainbow Forest Ser.). (Illus.). 58p. (Orig.). (J). (ps-2). 1995. pap. 7.95 (*1-888527-03-X*) New Wrld Ent.

— Timmy the Turtle. unabridged ed. (Five Friends of Rainbow Forest Ser.). (Illus.). 65p. (Orig.). (J). (gr. 3-5). 1995. pap. 8.95 (*1-888527-10-2*) New Wrld Ent.

— Timmy the Turtle. unabridged ed. (Five Friends of Rainbow Forest Ser.). (Illus.). 54p. (Orig.). (J). (ps-2). 1995. pap. 7.95 (*1-888527-04-8*) New Wrld Ent.

Ra'Oof, Mae O., jt. auth. see Ra'Oof, Jum.

Raoof, Suhail A. & Khan, Faroque, eds. Mechanical Ventilation: A Practice Approach. LC 97-3305. 186p. (Orig.). (C). 1998. pap. text 40.00 (*0-943126-57-6*) Amer Coll Phys.

Rao's Restaurant Staff, jt. auth. see Pellegrino, Frank W.

Raouf, A. & Ben-Daya, M. Flexible Manufacturing Systems: Recent Developments. LC 94-48220. (Manufacturing Research & Technology Ser.: Vol. 23). 324p. 1995. 171.75 (*0-444-89798-4*) Elsevier.

Raouf, A., jt. auth. see Dhillon, B. S.

Raoul, Bill. Stock Scenery Construction Handbook. 250p. 1991. pap. 12.95 (*0-911747-23-0*) Broadway Pr.

Raoul, Gordon, ed. Puerto Rico: A Guide to the Island of Boriguen. 1976. lib. bdg. 250.00 (*0-8490-1375-5*) Gordon Pr.

Raoul, Valerie. Distinctly Narcissistic: Diary Fiction in Quebec. (Theory - Culture Ser.). 336p. 1993. text 55.00 (*0-8020-2882-9*) U of Toronto Pr.

Raoult, Didier. Antimicrobial Agents & Intracellular Pathogens. LC 93-2668. 400p. 1993. lib. bdg. 210.00 (*0-8493-4924-9*, RM409) CRC Pr.

Raoult, J. C., et al, eds. CAAP '92. (Lecture Notes in Computer Science Ser.: Vol. 581). 361p. 1992. 57.95 (*0-387-55251-0*) Spr-Verlag.

Raous, M., et al. Contact Mechanics: Proceedings of the Second International Symposium Held in Carry-Le-Rouet, France, September 19-23, 1994. LC 95-34062. (Illus.). 482p. (C). 1995. 135.00 (*0-306-45065-8*, Plenum Trade) Perseus Pubng.

Raous, M., jt. ed. see Lagarde, A.

Rap, Le. Bonjour, Mr. McGrue. (Nursery Rhymes Ser.). 15p. (J). (gr. k-2). 1991. pap. text 4.50 (*1-56843-087-6*) EMG Networks.

— Bonjour, Mr. McGrue: Big Book. (Nursery Rhymes Ser.). 15p. (J). (gr. k-2). 1991. pap. text 23.00 (*1-56843-040-X*) EMG Networks.

— Little Betty Blue. (Nursery Rhymes Ser.). 15p. (J). (gr. k-2). 1991. pap. text 23.00 (*1-56843-042-6*); pap. text 4.50 (*1-56843-089-2*) EMG Networks.

— A Lost Little Pig. (Nursery Rhymes Ser.). 15p. (J). (gr. k-2). 1991. pap. text 23.00 (*1-56843-038-8*); pap. text 4.50 (*1-56843-085-X*) EMG Networks.

— The Secret of the Sheep. (Nursery Rhymes Ser.). 15p. (J). (gr. k-2). 1991. pap. text 23.00 (*1-56843-037-X*); pap. text 4.50 (*1-56843-084-1*) EMG Networks.

— Sherman Be Nimble. (Nursery Rhymes Ser.). 15p. (J). (gr. k-2). 1991. pap. text 4.50 (*1-56843-091-4*) EMG Networks.

— Sherman Be Nimble: Big Book. (Nursery Rhymes Ser.). 15p. (J). (gr. k-2). 1991. pap. text 23.00 (*1-56843-044-2*) EMG Networks.

— Who's in the Shoe? (Nursery Rhymes Ser.). 15p. (J). (gr. k-2). 1991. pap. text 23.00 (*1-56843-041-8*); pap. text 4.50 (*1-56843-088-4*) EMG Networks.

Rapaccini, L. Parlo Italiano. (Monnier Ser.). 27.95 (*88-00-85275-0*) Schoenhof.

Rapacki, Lyle J. Satanism: The Not So New Problem. (Illus.). 65p. (Orig.). 1988. pap. 10.00 (*0-9621597-0-0*) Crossroads Ministries.

Rapaczynski, Andrzej. Nature & Politics: Liberalism in the Philosophies of Hobbes, Locke, & Rousseau. LC 87-5451. 312p. (C). 1987. pap. text 16.95 (*0-8014-9606-3*) Cornell U Pr.

Rapaczynski, Andrzej, jt. auth. see Frydman, Roman.

Rapahango, Ana B. & Liller, William. Speak Rapanui! Hable Rapanui! The Language of Easter Island. Liller, Tamara & Drake, Alan, eds. 1996. pap. 12.00 (*1-880636-03-4*) Easter Isl Fnd.

Rapaille, Clotaire. 7 Secrets of Marketing in a Multi-Cultural World. 224p. 1999. 21.95 (*1-890009-74-1*) Exec Excell.

Rapakko, A. Base Company Taxation. 272p. 1990. 83.00 (*90-6544-431-9*) Kluwer Law Intl.

Rapakko, Timo. Unlimited Shareholder Liability in Multinationals. LC 97-38145. 500p. 1997. 135.00 (*90-411-0997-8*) Kluwer Law Intl.

Rapalje, Stewart. Treatise on Contempt: Including Civil & Criminal Contempts of Judicial Tribunals, Justices of the Peace, Legislative Bodies, Municipal Boards, Committees, Notaries, Commisioners, Referees & Other Officers Exercising Judicial & Quasi-Judicial Functions - With Practice & Forms. xliv, 273p. 1981. reprint ed. 42.50 (*0-8377-1030-8*, Rothman) W S Hein.

— Treatise on the Law of Witnesses. LC 97-28842. xc, 573p. 1997. reprint ed. 125.00 (*0-8377-2581-X*, Rothman) W S Hein.

Rapalje, Stewart & Lawrence, Robert L. Dictionary of American & English Law, with Definitions of the Technical Terms of the Canon & Civil Laws: Also Containing a Full Collection of Latin Maxims, & Citations of Upwards of Forty Thousand Reported Cases, in Which Words & Phrases Have Been Judicially Defined or Construed, 2 vols. LC 97-33546. 1416p. 1997. reprint ed. 245.00 (*0-8377-2582-8*, Rothman) W S Hein.

— A Dictionary of American & English Law with Definitions of the Technical Terms of the Canon & Civil Laws: Also, Containing a Full Collection of Latin Maxims, & Citations of Upwards of Forty Thousand Reported Cases, in Which Words & Phrases Have Been Judicially Defined or Construed, 1888. LC 97-38484. xxxviii, 1380p. 1997. 195.00 (*1-886363-33-1*) Lawbk Exchange.

***Rapanarivo, S. H., et al.** Pachypodium (Apocynaceae) Taxonomy, Habitats & Cultivation. (Illus.). 128p. (C). 1999. text 48.50 (*90-5410-485-6*, Pub. by A A Balkema) Ashgate Pub Co.

Rapant, Larry. Collecting the Empties: Poems. LC 92-20423. 64p. 1992. pap. 12.95 (*0-7734-9519-3*) E Mellen.

— Esther's Areolas. LC 98-85387. 325p. 1998. 25.00 (*0-9663501-8-9*); pap. 15.00 (*0-7388-0019-8*) Xlibris Corp.

— Flesh Colors. Schultz, Patricia, ed. LC 89-12171. (Lewiston Poetry Ser.: Vol. 9). 64p. 1989. pap. 14.95 (*0-88946-898-2*) E Mellen.

Rapaport, Al, intro. Buddhism in America: The Offical Record of the Landmark Conference on the Future of Buddhist Meditative Practices in the West. LC 97-19315. (Illus.). 568p. 1996. pap. 24.95 (*0-8048-3152-1*) Tuttle Pubng.

Rapaport, Ben. Collecting Antique Meerschaum Pipes. LC 98-44885. (Illus.). 176p. 1999. 49.95 (*0-7643-0765-7*) Schiffer.

Rapaport, D. C. The Art of Molecular Dynamics Simulation. (Illus.). 414p. (C). 1996. text 80.00 (*0-521-44561-2*) Cambridge U Pr.

— The Art of Molecular Dynamics Simulation. (Illus.). 414p. 1997. pap. text 42.95 (*0-521-59942-3*) Cambridge U Pr.

Rapaport, David. Collected Papers of David Rapaport. 1996. 95.00 (*1-56821-473-1*) Aronson.

— The History of the Concept of Association of Ideas. LC 73-89438. 120p. 1974. 30.00 (*0-8236-2330-0*) Intl Univs Pr.

— No Justice, No Peace: The 1996 OPSEU Strike against the Harris Government in Ontario. 60.00 (*0-7735-1858-4*); pap. 22.95 (*0-7735-1865-7*) McG-Queens Univ Pr.

— Structure of Psychoanalytic Theory: A Systematizing Attempt. (Psychological Issues Monographs: No. 6, Vol. 2, No. 2). 158p. (Orig.). 1967. 27.50 (*0-8236-6180-6*) Intl Univs Pr.

Rapaport, David, et al. Diagnostic Psychological Testing. rev. ed. LC 68-16993. 562p. 1968. 75.95 (*0-8236-1260-0*) Intl Univs Pr.

Rapaport, David, jt. auth. see Shakow, David.

Rapaport, David, tr. see Hartmann, Heinz.

Rapaport, Diane S. How to Make & Sell Your Own Recording: The Complete Guide to Independent Recording. 5th rev. ed. LC 99-21099. 258p. 1999. pap. 29.95 (*0-13-923947-2*, JHP100016, Pub. by Jerome Headlands) Music Sales.

Rapaport, Elizabeth, ed. & intro. see Mill, John Stuart.

Rapaport, Elliot, ed. see Denton, Timothy & Matloff, Jack.

Rapaport, Elliott, ed. Cardiology & Co-Existing Disease. (Illus.). 352p. 1993. text 99.00 (*0-443-08887-X*) Church.

— Early Interventions in Acute Myocardial Infarction. (Developments in Cardiovascular Medicine Ser.). (C). 1989. text 181.00 (*0-7923-0175-7*) Kluwer Academic.

Rapaport, Elliott, ed. see De Busk, Robert.

Rapaport, Elliott, ed. see Kemp, Harvey.

Rapaport, Era. Letters from Tel Mond Prison: An Israeli Settler Defends His Act of Terror. 280p. 1996. 22.50 (*0-684-83180-5*) S&S Trade.

Rapaport, Felix T., jt. auth. see Sheil, A. G.

Rapaport, Herman. Between the Sign & the Gaze. (Illus.). 312p. 1993. 41.50 (*0-8014-2898-X*); pap. text 18.95 (*0-8014-8133-3*) Cornell U Pr.

— Heidegger & Derrida: Reflections on Time & Language. LC 88-4748. x, 293p. 1989. pap. text 15.00 (*0-8032-8927-8*, Bison Books) U of Nebr Pr.

— Is There Truth in Art? LC 96-28088. (Illus.). 248p. 1996. text 45.00 (*0-8014-3275-8*); pap. text 17.95 (*0-8014-8353-0*) Cornell U Pr.

— Milton & the Postmodern. LC 82-21935. 284p. 1983. reprint ed. pap. 88.10 (*0-608-01853-8*, 206250300003) Bks Demand.

***Rapaport, Herman.** The Theory Mess: Deconstruction in Eclipse. 2001. pap. 17.50 (*0-231-12135-0*); text 44.50 (*0-231-12134-2*) Col U Pr.

Rapaport, J., et al, eds. Neutron-Nucleus Collisions: A Probe of Nuclear Structure: Burr Oak State Park, Ohio, 1984. LC 84-73216. (AIP Conference Proceedings Ser.: No. 124). 548p. 1985. lib. bdg. 52.00 (*0-88318-323-4*) Am Inst Physics.

Rapaport, Jacques, et al. Small States & Territories: Status & Problems. LC 72-140128. (UNITAR Studies). 1971. 65.95 (*0-405-02237-9*) Ayer.

Rapaport, Lowell, jt. auth. see Berkel, Bob.

Rapaport, Lynn. Jews in Germany after the Holocaust: Memory, Identity, & Jewish-German Relations. (Cultural Social Studies). 337p. (C). 1997. text 59.95 (*0-521-58219-9*) Cambridge U Pr.

Rapaport, Matthew. Computer Mediated Communications: Bulletin Boards, Computer Conferencing, Electronic Mail & Information Retrieval. LC 91-8668. 373p. 1991. pap. 64.99 (*0-471-51642-2*) Wiley.

Rapaport, Moshe, ed. The Pacific Islands: Environment & Society. (Illus.). 480p. (C). 1999. pap. text 39.95 (*1-57306-042-9*) Bess Pr.

Rapaport, Richard. Graham Gund Architects. (Illus.). 288p. 1993. 50.00 (*1-55835-093-4*) AIA Press.

Rapaport, Ron, jt. auth. see Garrett, Betty.

Rapaport, Samuel I. Introduction to Hematology. 2nd ed. LC 65-10036. (Illus.). 624p. 1987. pap. text 38.00 (*0-397-50838-7*, Lippnctt) Lppncott W & W.

Rapaport, Stanley, ed. see Fenichel, Otto.

Rapaport, Wendy Satin. When Diabetes Hits Home. LC 98-17224. 256p. 1998. pap. 19.95 (*0-945448-88-0*, 00880Q, Pub. by Am Diabetes) NTC Contemp Pub Co.

Raparaz, M. C. & Oosterveld-Egas. Legal Dictionary Dutch - Spanish: With Spanish - Dutch Index. (DUT & SPA.). 371p. 1992. 295.00 (*0-8288-9435-3*) Fr & Eur.

Rapatz, F. & Roll, F. Diccionario Enciclopedico Tecnico: Materiales Siderurgicos. (SPA.). 260p. 1968. 49.95 (*0-8288-6624-4*, S-33724) Fr & Eur.

Rapcewicz, K., jt. auth. see Paszkiewicz, T.

Rapcsak, Tamas. Smooth Nonlinear Optimization Vol. 19: Nonconvex Optimization & Its Applications. LC 97-26091. 374p. 1997. lib. bdg. 169.00 (*0-7923-4680-7*) Kluwer Academic.

Rape & Abuse Crisis Ctr. Staff. Annie. rev. ed. (Illus.). 21p. (J). (ps up). 1985. pap. text 2.50 (*0-914633-03-1*) Rape Abuse Crisis.

— Gente Bandera Roja y Gente Bandera Verde: Red Flag Green Flag People. Peterson, Francisca E., tr. from ENG. (SPA., Illus.). 36p. (J). (gr. k-5). 1987. student ed. 4.00 (*0-914633-13-9*) Rape Abuse Crisis.

— Red Flag Green Flag People. (Illus.). 28p. (J). (gr. k up). 1985. pap., student ed. 4.00 (*0-914633-10-4*) Rape Abuse Crisis.

Rapee, Erno. Encyclopedia of Music for Pictures. LC 77-124034. (Literature of Cinema Ser.). 1978. reprint ed. 27.95 (*0-405-01634-4*) Ayer.

— Motion Picture Moods for Pianists & Organists, a Rapid Reference Collection of Selected Pieces. LC 70-124035. (Literature of Cinema, Ser. 1). 1979. reprint ed. 48.95 (*0-405-01635-2*) Ayer.

Rapee, Ronald M. Overcoming Shyness & Social Phobia: A Step-by-Step Guide. LC 97-27509. 144p. 1998. pap. 25.00 (*0-7657-0120-0*) Aronson.

Rapee, Ronald M., ed. Current Controversies in the Anxiety Disorders. LC 95-24718. 388p. 1995. lib. bdg. 45.00 (*1-57230-023-X*, 0023) Guilford Pubns.

Rapee, Ronald M. & Barlow, David H., eds. Chronic Anxiety: Generalized Anxiety Disorder & Mixed Anxiety-Depression. LC 91-24737. 214p. 1991. lib. bdg. 35.00 (*0-89862-771-0*) Guilford Pubns.

Rapee, Ronald M. & Sanderson, William C. Social Phobia: Clinical Application of Evidence-Based Psychotherapy. LC 97-19446. 184p. 1997. text 35.00 (*0-7657-0004-2*) Aronson.

***Rapee, Ronald M., et al.** Helping Your Anxious Child: A Step-by-Step Guide for Parents. (Illus.). 160p. 2000. pap. 12.95 (*1-57224-191-8*) New Harbinger.

— Treating Anxious Children & Adolescents: An Evidence-Based Approach. (Illus.). 196p. 2000. 49.95 (*1-57224-192-6*) New Harbinger.

Rapela, C. W., jt. auth. see Harmon, R. S.

Rapela, C. W., jt. ed. see Kay, S. M.

Rapela, Carlos W., jt. ed. see Harmon, Russell S.

Raper, Arthur F. Preface to Peasantry: A Tale of Two Black Belt Counties. LC 72-137183. (Poverty U. S. A. Historical Record Ser.). 1971. reprint ed. 33.95 (*0-405-03121-1*) Ayer.

— Tenants of the Almighty. LC 76-137184. (Poverty U. S. A. Historical Record Ser.). 1971. reprint ed. 30.95 (*0-405-03122-X*) Ayer.

— Tragedy of Lynching. LC 72-90191. (Mass Violence in America Ser.). 1969. reprint ed. 19.95 (*0-405-01334-5*) Ayer.

— Tragedy of Lynching. LC 69-14943. (Criminology, Law Enforcement, & Social Problems Ser.: No. 25). 1969. reprint ed. 16.00 (*0-87585-025-1*) Patterson Smith.

— The Tragedy of Lynching. LC 69-16568. (Illus.). 499p. 1969. reprint ed. lib. bdg. 35.00 (*0-8371-1145-5*, RAL&, Greenwood Pr) Greenwood.

Raper, Arthur J., ed. see Shay, Frank.

Raper, Bill & Raper, June. Sail to Freedom: A Handbook for Extended Cruising. 96p. (C). 1939. text 59.00 (*0-906754-91-7*, Pub. by Fernhurst Bks) St Mut.

Raper, Jonathan, ed. Three-Dimensional Applications in G. I. S. 260p. 1989. 89.95 (*0-85066-776-3*) Taylor & Francis.

Raper, Julius R. From the Sunken Garden: The Fiction of Ellen Glasgow, 1916-1945. fac. ed. LC 79-16703. (Southern Literary Studies). 228p. 1980. reprint ed. pap. 70.70 (*0-7837-7817-1*, 204757300007) Bks Demand.

— Narcissus from Rubble: Competing Models of Character in Contemporary British & American Fiction. LC 91-32604. 200p. (C). 1992. text 30.00 (*0-8071-1712-9*) La State U Pr.

Raper, Julius R., et al, eds. Lawrence Durrell: Comprehending the Whole. 224p. 1994. text 39.95 (*0-8262-0982-3*) U of Mo Pr.

Raper, June. The Beaufort Scale Cook Book: Boat Cuisine for All Weathers. (Illus.). 96p. 1989. pap. 12.95 (*0-906754-43-7*) McGraw-Hill Prof.

— Boat Cuisine: The All-Weather Cookbook. 96p. 1998. pap. 15.95 (*1-898660-02-6*) Fernhurst Bks.

Raper, June, jt. auth. see Raper, Bill.

Raper, K. B. & Charlesthom. Manual of the Penicillia. 172p. 1984. pap. 175.00 (*0-7855-0380-3*, Pub. by Intl Bks & Periodicals) St Mut.

Raper, Kenneth B. The Dictyostelids. LC 83-43089. 466p. 1984. reprint ed. pap. 144.50 (*0-608-02912-2*, 206397600008) Bks Demand.

Raper, Richard, compiled by. Consolidated Index to the Oxford History of England. (Oxford History of England Ser.: Vol. 16). 632p. 1991. 65.00 (*0-19-821786-2*) OUP.

Rapf, Joanna E. & Green, Gary L. Buster Keaton: A Bio-Bibliography. LC 94-21062. (Popular Culture Bio-Bibliographies Ser.). 272p. 1995. lib. bdg. 59.95 (*0-313-25148-7*, Greenwood Pr) Greenwood.

***Rapf, Maurice.** All about the Movies: A Textbook for the Movie-Loving Layman. (Illus.). 112p. 2000. 29.95 (*0-8108-3768-4*); pap. 19.95 (*0-8108-3791-9*) Scarecrow.

— Back Lot: Growing up with the Movies. Slide, Anthony, ed. LC 98-34656. (Filmmakers Ser.: No. 64). (Illus.). 240p. 1998. 39.50 (*0-8108-3583-5*) Scarecrow.

Rapgay, Lobsang, jt. auth. see Arpaia, Joseph.

Rapgay, Lopsang. The Tibetan Book of Healing. (Illus.). 208p. (Orig.). 1997. pap., per. 12.95 (*1-878423-21-5*) Morson Pub.

Raph, Alan. The Double Valve Bass Trombone A Method. (Illus.). 64p. 1949. pap. 10.95 (*0-8258-0190-7*, 0-4808) Fischer Inc NY.

Raph, Alan, jt. auth. see Watrous, Bill.

Raph, Theodore, ed. The American Song Treasury: One Hundred Favorites. 416p. 1986. reprint ed. pap. 14.95 (*0-486-25222-1*) Dover.

Raphael. Book of the Stars: A Manual of Astrology. 1996. reprint ed. spiral bd. 15.50 (*0-7873-0706-8*) Hlth Research.

— Drawings of Raphael. Longstreet, Stephen, ed. (Master Draughtsman Ser.). (Illus.). (Orig.). 1962. pap. 4.95 (*0-87505-181-2*) Borden.

— Essence & Purpose of Yoga. 128p. 1996. pap. 12.95 (*1-85230-866-4*, Pub. by Element MA) Penguin Putnam.

— The Guide to Astrology, Vol. 1. 200p. 1996. reprint ed. spiral bd. 14.00 (*0-7873-0705-X*) Hlth Research.

— Guide to Astrology (1926) 134p. 1998. reprint ed. pap. 13.95 (*0-7661-0629-2*) Kessinger Pub.

***Raphael.** Initiation into the Philosophy of Plato. 144p. 2000. pap. 18.95 (*0-85683-179-4*, Pub. by Shepheard-Walwyn Pubs) Paul & Co Pubs.

Raphael. The Key to Astrology. 1996. reprint ed. spiral bd. 11.00 (*0-7873-0704-1*) Hlth Research.

— Necessity Anti-Semitism. LC 97-39682. 1998. text 45.00 (*0-312-21171-6*) St Martin.

— The Pathway of Non-Duality (Advaitavada) An Approach to Some Key-Points of Gaudapada's Asparsavada & Samkara's Advaita Vedanta by Means of a Series of Questions Answered by an Asparsin. xi, 88p. 1992. 10.95 (*1-881338-19-3*) Nataraj Bks.

— Proudhon Marx Picasso. (C). 1979. pap. 18.50 (*0-85315-549-6*, Pub. by Lawrence & Wishart) NYU Pr.

— Raphael: Tables of Houses. 9.95 (*0-685-38474-8*) Wehman.

— Raphael's Astro Ephemeris (Any Year) pap. 9.95 (*0-685-22085-0*) Wehman.

***Raphael.** Raphael's Astronomical Ephemeries 2001. 48p. 2000. pap. 5.95 (*0-572-02548-3*) W Foulsham.

Raphael. Raphael's Guide to Astrology - Containing a Complete System of Genethliacal Astrology. 132p. 1991. pap. 15.00 (*0-89540-189-4*, SB-189, Sun Bks) Sun Pub.

— Raphael's Horary Astrology: By Which Every Question Relating to the Future May be Answered. 4th ed. 1996. reprint ed. spiral bd. 10.50 (*0-7873-0703-3*) Hlth Research.

— Raphael's Key to Astrology. 118p. 1991. pap. 12.00 (*0-89540-142-8*, SB-142, Sun Bks) Sun Pub.

— Raphael's Medical Astrology: or The Effects of the Planets & Signs upon the Human Body. 80p. 1991. reprint ed. pap. 8.00 (*0-89540-180-0*, SB-180, Sun Bks) Sun Pub.

R

— Raphael's Mundane Astrology: or The Effects of the Planets & Signs upon the Nations & Countries of the World. 112p. 1996. pap. 7.00 (*0-89540-231-9*, SB-231, Sun Bks) Sun Pub.
— Self & Non-Self: The Drigdrisyaviveka Attributed to Sankara. 140p. 1990. 35.00 (*0-7103-0377-7*, A4515) Routledge.
— Tat Tvam Asi - That Thou Art: The Path of Fire According to Asparsa-Yoga. xiii, 122p. 1992. 12.95 (*1-881338-20-7*) Nataraj Bks.
Raphael, jt. auth. see Green, H. S.
Raphael, A. Cheirosophy (the Hand) A Scientific Treatise on Palmistry. 1993. reprint ed. spiral bd. 16.50 (*0-7873-0707-6*) Hlth Research.
***Raphael, Adam.** Europe's Wonderful Little Hotels & Inns: Great Britain & Ireland 2001. (Illus.). 2000. pap. 19.95 (*0-09-187853-5*) Ebury Pr.
Raphael, Adam. The Ultimate Risk. 1995. pap. 8.99 (*0-552-13935-1*) Bantam.
— Ultimate Risk: The Inside Story of the Lloyd's Catastrophe. LC 95-11797. (Illus.). 302p. 1995. 24.95 (*1-56858-056-8*) FWEW.
***Raphael, Adam & Raphael, Caroline.** Europe's Wonderful Little Hotels & Inns 2001: Continental Europe. 624p. 2000. pap. 19.95 (*0-09-187171-9*, Pub. by Ebury Pr) IPG Chicago.
***Raphael, Adam & Raphael, Caroline, eds.** Europe's Wonderful Little Hotels & Inns 2001: Great Britain & Ireland. 624p. 2000. pap. 19.95 (*0-09-187170-0*, Pub. by Ebury Pr) IPG Chicago.
Raphael, Alan. Criminal Procedure. rev. ed. 256p. (C). 1999. ring bd. 68.00 (*1-879581-74-4*) Lupus Pubns.
Raphael, Alan J., jt. auth. see Reichenberg, Norman.
Raphael, Albert. Earthology, Humanity Characterized. 223p. 1996. reprint ed. spiral bd. 20.00 (*0-7873-0708-4*) Hlth Research.
Raphael, Alice. Things That Are: Poems. 1969. 4.95 (*0-8079-0155-5*); pap. 1.95 (*0-8079-0156-3*) October.
Raphael, Amy. Girls, Viva Rock Divas. 240p. 1996. pap. 12.95 (*0-312-14109-2*) St Martin.
— Hole: Look Through This. (Illus.). 80p. 1995. pap. 19.95 (*1-873884-42-7*, VX02000) Music Sales.
Raphael, Antoine A. Concern No. 3: Harmony & Contrast. 216p. (Orig.). 1992. text 11.99 (*0-9631764-0-4*); pap. text 9.99 (*0-9631764-1-2*) A A Raphael.
— Le Drame Haitien. rev. ed. (FRE.). 200p. (C). 1992. 24.95 (*0-9631764-2-0*); pap. 19.95 (*0-9631764-3-9*) A A Raphael.
— Fateful Encounters. 2nd ed. 142p. (YA). 1991. 9.05 (*0-9631764-7-1*); text 11.95 (*0-9631764-8-X*); pap. text 8.00 (*0-9631764-9-8*) A A Raphael.
Raphael, B., jt. auth. see Kumar, B.
Raphael, B., jt. ed. see Wilson, J. P.
Raphael, Beverley. The Anatomy of Bereavement. LC 94-66571. 454p. 1995. pap. 40.00 (*1-56821-270-4*) Aronson.
***Raphael, Beverley & Wilson, John P., eds.** Psychological Debriefing: Theory, Practice & Evidence. LC 99-52565. (Illus.). 366p. 2000. text. write for info. (*0-521-64700-2*) Cambridge U Pr.
Raphael, Beverly & Burrows, Graham D., eds. Handbook of Studies on Preventive Psychiatry. 716p. 1995. 246.50 (*0-444-81836-7*) Elsevier.
Raphael, Bishop. Anglican-Orthodox Intercommunion. 1972. pap. 0.25 (*0-89981-004-7*) Eastern Orthodox.
Raphael, Carol, jt. ed. see Fox, Daniel M.
Raphael, Caroline. Europe's Wonderful Little Hotels. 2nd ed. (Europe's Wonderful Little Hotels & Inns Ser.). 1999. pap. 21.95 (*0-312-19875-2*) St Martin.
— Europe's Wonderful Little Hotels & Inns: Great Britain & Ireland. Rubenstein, Hilary, ed. 480p. 1998. pap. 21.95 (*0-312-19451-X*) St Martin.
Raphael, Caroline, jt. auth. see Raphael, Adam.
Raphael, Caroline, jt. ed. see Raphael, Adam.
***Raphael, Cathy.** It's Our Turn to Play!!! (Illus.). 86p. 1999. pap. 14.95 (*0-9675014-5-8*) Its Our.
Raphael, Chaim. The Sephardi Story: A Celebration of Jewish History. 1991. text 27.50 (*0-85303-247-5*, Pub. by M Vallentine & Co); pap. text 15.00 (*0-85303-251-3*, Pub. by M Vallentine & Co) Intl Spec Bk.
Raphael, Chaim, intro. The Jewish Manual: or Practical Information in Jewish & Modern Cookery with a Collection of Valuable Recipes & Hints Relating to the Toilette (Edited by a Lady) LC 83-2405. 288p. 1983. reprint ed. 24.95 (*0-911389-01-6*); reprint ed. pap. 12.95 (*0-911389-00-8*) NightinGale Res.
Raphael, Chaim, tr. Kabbalat Shabbat: The Sabbath Evening Service. pap. 4.95 (*0-87441-418-0*) Behrman.
Raphael, Cherene. Hard Core Dreamer. LC 96-92851. 1997. write for info. (*1-890149-01-2*) Pencil Press.
Raphael, Chester M., ed. see Reich, Wilhelm.
Raphael, D. D. British Moralists, 1650-1800 Vol. II: Hume - Bentham. LC 90-85423. 437p. (C). 1991. reprint ed. pap. 17.95 (*0-87220-117-1*) Hackett Pub.
— Moral Philosophy. 2nd ed. LC 93-3919. 160p. (Orig.). 1994. pap. text 16.95 (*0-19-289246-0*) OUP.
Raphael, D. D., ed. British Moralists, 1650-1800 Vol. I: Hobbes - Gay. LC 90-85423. 431p. (C). 1991. reprint ed. pap. 17.95 (*0-87220-116-3*) Hackett Pub.
Raphael, D. D., intro. British Moralists, 1650-1800, 2 vols., Set. LC 90-85423. 1991. reprint ed. pap. text 30.00 (*0-87220-120-1*); reprint ed. lib. bdg. 75.00 (*0-87220-121-X*) Hackett Pub.
Raphael, D. D., et al. Great Economists. LC 96-36196. (Past Masters Ser.). 392p. 1997. pap. text 15.95 (*0-19-287694-5*) OUP.
Raphael, D. D., ed. see Smith, Adam.
Raphael, Dan. Polymerge. 24p. (Orig.). 1979. pap. text 4.00 (*0-686-35895-3*) Skydog OR.
— Trees Through the Road. 36p. 1997. pap. 7.50 (*1-878888-23-4*) Nine Muses Books.
— Zone du Jour. 28p. (Orig.). 1981. pap. 5.50 (*0-937013-00-5*) Potes Poets.
Raphael, Dana, ed. Being Female: Reproduction, Power, & Change. (World Anthropology Ser.). xvi, 294p. 1975. 30.80 (*90-279-7599-X*) Mouton.
Raphael, Dana & Davis, Flora. Only Mothers Know: Patterns of Infant Feeding in Traditional Cultures, 54. LC 84-15742. (Contributions in Women's Studies: No. 54). (Illus.). 159p. 1985. 49.95 (*0-313-24541-X*, RBR/, Greenwood Pr) Greenwood.
Raphael, Daniel. Sacred Relationships: A Guide to Authentic Loving. LC 98-19126. 192p. 1999. pap. 15.95 (*1-57983-001-3*) Origin Pr CA.
Raphael, David D. Paradox of Tragedy. LC 77-128293. (Essay Index Reprint Ser.). 1977. 18.95 (*0-8369-2021-X*) Ayer.
Raphael, Donna, ed. see McCarthy, Alice R., et al.
Raphael, Edwin. The Complete Book of Dreams. 344p. (Orig.). 1995. pap. 11.95 (*0-572-01714-6*, Pub. by Foulsham UK) Assoc Pubs Grp.
Raphael, Elaine. Ancient Egypt: Drawing History. (Illus.). 32p. (J). (gr. 4-6). 1995. pap. 4.95 (*0-590-48082-0*) Scholastic Inc.
— Ancient Greece: Drawing History. (Illus.). 32p. (gr. 4-6). 1995. pap. 4.95 (*0-590-22729-7*) Scholastic Inc.
— Ancient Rome: Drawing History. (Illus.). 32p. (gr. 4-6). 1995. pap. 4.95 (*0-590-25090-6*) Scholastic Inc.
***Raphael, Elaine.** Rescue in Space. LC 99-51751. (2050, Voyage of the Starseeker Ser.: No. 2). (Illus.). 48p. (J). (ps-3). 2000. write for info. (*0-439-07816-4*, Cartwheel) Scholastic Inc.
***Raphael, Elaine & Bolognese, Don.** Asteroid Alert. LC 99-16495. (2050, Voyage of the Star Seeker Ser.: No. 1). (Illus.). 48p. (J). (ps-3). 2000. 3.99 (*0-439-07815-6*, Cartwheel) Scholastic Inc.
Raphael, Elaine & Bolognese, Don. Daniel Boone, Frontier Hero. LC 95-8465. (Drawing America Ser.). (Illus.). 32p. (J). (gr. 1-3). 1996. 14.95 (*0-590-47900-8*, Cartwheel) Scholastic Inc.
— Pocahontas, Princess of the River Tribes. LC 92-41990. 32p. (J). (gr. 1-3). 1993. 12.95 (*0-590-44371-2*) Scholastic Inc.
— The Story of the First Thanksgiving. 32p. (J). (gr. 1-3). 1992. pap. 3.95 (*0-590-44374-7*, Cartwheel) Scholastic Inc.
Raphael, Ezekiel. The Racist Mind: Portraits of American Neo-Nazis & Klansmen. 368p. 1996. pap. 13.95 (*0-14-023449-7*, Penguin Bks) Viking Penguin.
Raphael, Frederic. Coast to Coast. LC 98-48916. 240p. 1999. 22.95 (*0-945774-42-7*, PR6068.A6C63) Catbird Pr.
— Darling: An Original Screenplay, Directed by Richard Lester. Garrett, George P. et al, eds. LC 71-135273. (Film Scripts Ser.). 1989. pap. text 19.95 (*0-89197-719-8*) Irvington.
***Raphael, Frederic.** A Double Life. LC 99-53507. 374p. 2000. 24.00 (*0-945774-46-X*) Catbird Pr.
Raphael, Frederic. Eyes Wide Open: Working with Stanley Kubrick. LC 99-34690. 1999. pap. 12.00 (*0-345-43776-4*) Ballantine Pub Grp.
— France: The Four Seasons. (Illus.). 144p. 1994. 29.95 (*1-55859-869-3*) Abbeville Pr.
— Popper: Great Philosophers. LC 99-22646. (Great Philosophers Ser.). 64p. 1999. pap. 6.00 (*0-415-92391-3*) Routledge.
Raphael, Frederic, tr. see Aeschylus.
Raphael, Frederic, tr. see Euripides.
Raphael, Harold J. & Olsson, David L. Management of the Packaging Function. LC 76-55109. (American Management Associations. Management Briefing Ser.). 38p. reprint ed. pap. 30.00 (*0-608-11682-3*, 205130500094) Bks Demand.
Raphael, Jacqueline, jt. auth. see Tobias, Sheila.
Raphael, Jesse, jt. auth. see Fox, Ivan.
Raphael, Jesse S. The Uniform Commercial Code Simplified. LC 67-15469. 416p. reprint ed. pap. 129.00 (*0-608-30175-2*, 201237000081) Bks Demand.
Raphael, Lawrence J., et al, eds. Language & Cognition: Essays in Honor of Arthur J. Bronstein. LC 83-22987. (Cognition & Language Ser.). 306p. 1984. 70.00 (*0-306-41433-3*, Plenum Trade) Perseus Pubng.
Raphael, Lawrence J., jt. ed. see Bell-Berti, Fredericka.
Raphael, Lawrence W., ed. Mystery Midrash: An Anthology of Jewish Mystery & Detective Fiction. LC 99-30222. 304p. 1999. pap. 16.95 (*1-58023-055-5*) Jewish Lights.
Raphael-Leff, Joan. Pregnancy: The Inside Story. LC 95-32293. 1995. 40.00 (*1-56821-579-7*) Aronson.
Raphael-Leff, Joan & Perelberg, Rosine J., eds. Female Experience: Three Generations of British Women Psychoanalysts on Work with Women. LC 96-40328. 328p. (C). 1997. 85.00 (*0-415-15769-2*); pap. 29.99 (*0-415-15770-6*) Routledge.
Raphael, Lev. Dancing on Tisha B'av. (Stonewall Inn Editions Ser.). 240p. 1991. pap. 8.95 (*0-312-06326-1*) St Martin.
***Raphael, Lev.** Death of a Constant Lover. LC 98-42836. (Nick Hoffman Mystery Ser.). 288p. 2000. pap. 12.95 (*0-312-26496-8*) St Martin.
Raphael, Lev. Death of a Constant Lover. LC 98-42836. (Nick Hoffman Mystery Ser.). 288p. 1999. 22.95 (*0-8027-3326-3*) Walker & Co.
— The Edith Wharton Murders: A Nick Hoffman Mystery. LC 97-7598. 208p. 1997. text 21.95 (*0-312-15519-0*) St Martin.
— The Edith Wharton Murders: A Nick Hoffman Mystery. LC 98-50898. (Stonewall Inn Mysteries Ser.). 240p. 1998. pap. 11.95 (*0-312-19863-9*) St Martin.
— Let's Get Criminal. 2nd ed. LC 96-48910. 244p. 1997. pap. 11.95 (*0-312-15160-8*) St Martin.
***Raphael, Lev.** Little Miss Evil: A Nick Hoffman Mystery. LC 99-88139. 256p. 2000. 23.95 (*0-8027-3342-5*) Walker & Co.
Raphael, Lev. Winter Eyes. 256p. 1993. pap. 8.95 (*0-312-10576-2*, Stonewall Inn) St Martin.
Raphael, Lev, jt. auth. see Kaufman, Gershen.
Raphael, Lewis. Oh! The Answer. 200p. (Orig.). 1997. pap. text 20.00 (*0-9659190-0-5*) Telinet.
Raphael, Linda S. & Raphael, Marc L., eds. When Night Fell: Short Stories of the Holocaust. LC 98-52808. 336p. (C). 1999. text 50.00 (*0-8135-2662-0*) Rutgers U Pr.
Raphael, Linda Schermer & Raphael, Marc Lee, eds. When Night Fell: An Anthology of Holocaust Short Stories. LC 98-52808. 300p. (C). 1999. pap. 20.00 (*0-8135-2663-9*) Rutgers U Pr.
Raphael, Lisa. O - Becoming One: Transformation Beyond Survival. (Illus.). 127p. 1998. pap. 15.95 (*0-9662582-9-0*) Cadence Pub.
Raphael, Marc L. Abba Hillel Silver: A Profile in American Judaism. LC 89-7581. 282p. 1989. 49.50 (*0-8419-1059-6*) Holmes & Meier.
— Jews & Judaism in a Midwestern Community: Columbus, Ohio, 1840-1975. (Illus.). 296p. 1979. 5.00 (*0-318-00876-9*) Ohio Hist Soc.
— Understanding American Jewish Philanthropy. 25.00 (*0-87068-689-5*) Ktav.
Raphael, Marc L., jt. ed. see Raphael, Linda S.
Raphael, Marc Lee, jt. see Olitzky, Kerry M.
Raphael, Marc Lee, jt. ed. see Raphael, Linda Schermer.
Raphael, Marie. Streets of Gold: A Novel. Sena, Jerry, ed. (Illus.). 216p. (J). (gr. 6-9). 1998. per. 7.95 (*1-883088-05-4*) Source CA.
***Raphael, Marie.** Streets of Gold: A Novel. rev. ed. 224p. (J). 2000. pap. 9.95 (*0-89255-256-5*, Pub. by Persea Bks) Norton.
Raphael, Marty. Spiritual Vampires: The Use & Misuse of Spiritual Power. LC 95-75339. 272p. (Orig.). 1996. pap. 14.95 (*1-57282-006-3*) Message NM.
Raphael, Mary L., jt. ed. see Gorock, Jeffrey S.
***Raphael, Maryanne.** Mother Teresa, Called to Love. 200p. 2000. pap. 14.95 (*0-9679865-0-8*) Writers World.
***Raphael, Matthew J.** Bill W. & Mr. Wilson: The Legend & Life of A. A.'s Cofounder. LC 99-86304. 224p. 2000. 24.95 (*1-55849-245-3*) U of Mass Pr.
Raphael, Max. The Demands of Art: With an Appendix, Toward an Empirical Theory of Art. LC 65-10431. (Bollingen Ser.: No. 78). (Illus.). 293p. reprint ed. pap. 90.90 (*0-608-11101-5*, 205118200083) Bks Demand.
Raphael, Melissa. Introducing Thealogy: Discourse on the Goddess. (Introductions in Feminist Theology Ser.: Vol. 3). 181p. 1999. pap. 19.95 (*1-85075-975-8*, Pub. by Sheffield Acad) CUP Services.
— Rudolf Otto & the Concept of Holiness. LC 97-489. 250p. 1997. text 65.00 (*0-19-826932-3*) OUP.
— Thealogy & Embodiment: The Post-Patriarchal Reconstruction of Female Sacrality. (Feminist Theology Ser.). 319p. 1996. pap. 24.50 (*1-85075-757-7*, Pub. by Sheffield Acad) CUP Services.
Raphael, Monir B. Coptic Language Analysis Pt. 1: Coptic Liturgy of St. Basil for the Faithful. (ARA & ENG.). 160p. (Orig.). 1994. pap. 20.00 (*0-9644158-0-1*) Copts In.
— Coptic Language Analysis Pt. 2: Coptic Liturgy of St. Basil for the Catechumen. (ARA & ENG.). 64p. (Orig.). 1995. pap. 8.00 (*0-9644158-1-X*) Copts In.
— Coptic Language Analysis Pt. 3: Coptic Liturgies Raising of Incense. (ARA & ENG.). 150p. 1996. pap. 10.00 (*0-9644158-2-8*) Copts In.
— Coptic Language Analysis Pt. 4 & 5: Coptic Liturgies of St. Gregory & St. Cyril. 360p. (C). 1998. pap. 20.00 (*0-9644158-3-6*) Copts In.
— Coptic Language Analysis Pt. 6: Gospel According to St. Matthew. (Coptic Language Analysis Ser.: No. 5). (ARA, COP & ENG.). 216p. 1999. pap. 20.00 (*0-9644158-4-4*) Copts In.
***Raphael, Monir B.** Gospel According to St. Mark, Pt. 7. (Coptic Language Analysis Ser.: Vol. 6). (ARA, COP & ENG.). 108p. 2000. pap. 10.00 (*0-9644158-5-2*) Copts In.
Raphael, Morris. The Battle in the Bayou Country. 5th ed. (Illus.). 199p. (YA). (gr. 5-12). 1976. 19.95 (*0-9608866-0-5*) M Raphael.
— A Gunboat Named Diana: And Other Exciting Stories of Civil War Battles Which Raged in South Louisiana. (Illus.). 216p. 1994. 19.95 (*0-9608866-9-9*) M Raphael.
— Halo for a Devil. 120p. (YA). (gr. 9 up). 1989. 14.95 (*0-9608866-6-4*) M Raphael.
— How Do You Know When You're in Acadiana. (Illus.). 32p. (YA). (gr. 5 up). 1984. pap. 3.95 (*0-9608866-3-X*) M Raphael.
— The Loup-Garou of Cote Gelee. (Illus.). 48p. (J). (gr. 3-9). 1990. 19.95 (*0-9608866-7-2*) M Raphael.
— Maria: Goddess of the Teche. (Illus.). 48p. (J). (gr. 4-9). 1991. 19.95 (*0-9608866-8-0*) M Raphael.
— My Natchez Years. (Illus.). 160p. (YA). (gr. 5 up). 1998. 19.95 (*0-8187-0312-1*) M Raphael.
— Mystic Bayou. LC 85-81338. 88p. 1985. 12.95 (*0-9608866-4-8*) M Raphael.
— Weeks Hall: The Master of the Shadows. LC 81-90439. (Illus.). 207p. (J). (gr. 5-12). 1981. 14.95 (*0-9608866-1-3*) M Raphael.
— The Weeks Hall Tapes. LC 83-91286. 90p. (Orig.). 1983. pap. 7.95 (*0-9608866-2-1*) M Raphael.
Raphael, Neil & Raphael, Ray. Comic Cops. 182p. (Orig.). (J). (gr. 4-8). 1992. pap. 6.95 (*1-881102-13-0*) Real Bks.
Raphael, Pierre. God Behind Bars: A Prison Chaplain Reflects on the Lord's Prayer. LC 99-10067. 144p. 1999. pap. 10.95 (*0-8091-3868-9*) Paulist Pr.
— Inside Rikers Island: A Chaplain's Search for God. Maloney, Linda M., tr. LC 90-7632. 159p. 1990. reprint ed. pap. 49.30 (*0-7837-9859-8*, 206058800005) Bks Demand.
Raphael, Ray. Cash Crop: An American Dream. LC 85-8376. (Illus.). 179p. (Orig.). (C). 1985. pap. 8.00 (*0-934203-03-2*) Ridge Times Pr.
— An Everyday History of Somewhere: Being the True Story of Indians, Deer, Homesteaders, Potatoes, Loggers, Trees, Fishermen, Salmon, & Other Living Things in the Backwoods of Northern California. LC 92-8470. (Illus.). 192p. 1992. reprint ed. pap. 15.95 (*1-881102-25-4*) Real Bks.
— Little White Father: Redick McKee on the California Frontier. LC 93-8515. 1993. pap. 15.95 (*1-883254-00-0*) Humboldt Cnty.
— The Men from the Boys: Rites of Passage in Male America. LC 88-17369. 246p. 1988. reprint ed. pap. 76.30 (*0-608-00483-9*, 206130200007) Bks Demand.
Raphael, Ray, jt. auth. see Raphael, Neil.
Raphael, Sandra. An Oak Spring Pomona. LC 90-62575. (Oak Spring Garden Library: Vol. 2). (Illus.). 300p. (C). 1991. 65.00 (*0-300-04936-6*) Yale U Pr.
— An Oak Spring Sylva. LC 89-61800. (Oak Spring Garden Library: Vol. 1). (Illus.). 160p. 1989. text 50.00 (*0-300-04652-9*) Yale U Pr.
Raphael, Sidney. GRE, Psychology. 2nd ed. 304p. 1994. per. 15.95 (*0-671-87462-4*, Arco) Macmillan Gen Ref.
Raphael, Silvia, tr. see Sand, George.
Raphael, Simcha P. Jewish Views of the Afterlife. LC 94-10597. 512p. 1995. 40.00 (*0-87668-583-1*) Aronson.
Raphael, Stanley S. Lynch's Medical Laboratory Technology. 4th ed. (Illus.). 864p. 1983. text 93.00 (*0-7216-7465-8*, W B Saunders Co) Harcrt Hlth Sci Grp.
Raphael, Sylvia, ed. & tr. see Balzac, Honore de.
Raphael, Sylvia, tr. see Balzac, Honore de.
Raphael, Sylvia, tr. see Madame de Stael.
Raphael, Sylvia, tr. see Sand, George.
Raphael, Taffy E. & Au, Kathryn H., eds. Literature Based Instruction: Reshaping the Curriculum. LC 98-106739. 408p. (J). (gr. k-8). 1998. pap. text, teacher ed. 46.95 (*0-926842-70-6*) CG Pubs Inc.
Raphael, Taffy E. & Hiebert, Elfreidah. Creating an Integrated Approach to Literacy Instruction. LC 95-81597. 336p. (C). 1996. pap. text 35.00 (*0-03-051554-8*, Pub. by Harcourt Coll Pubs) Harcourt.
Raphael, Taffy E., et al. Book Club: A Literature-Based Curriculum. LC 97-176959. (Illus.). viii, 296p. 1997. pap., teacher ed. 29.95 (*0-9656211-0-3*) Sm Planet Commns Inc.
Raphael, Taffy E., jt. auth. see Hiebert, Elfrieda H.
Raphael, Taffy E., jt. ed. see Hammond, W. Dorsey.
Raphael, Taffy E., jt. ed. see McMahon, Susan I.
Raphael, Winifred. Patients & Their Hospitals. King Edward's Hospital Fund Staff, ed. 46p. 1977. pap. 19.95 (*0-8464-1297-7*) Beekman Pubs.
***Raphaela.** Living in Christ: Essays on the Christian Life by an Orthodox Nun. LC 99-88452. 2000. write for info. (*0-88141-199-X*) St Vladimirs.
Raphaell, Katrina. Crystal Healing: The Therapeutic Application of Crystals & Stones. 220p. 1987. pap. 16.95 (*0-943358-30-2*) Aurora Press.
— The Crystalline Transmission - A Synthesis of Light, Vol. III. 300p. 1989. pap. 18.95 (*0-943358-33-7*) Aurora Press.
Raphaelson, Arnold H., ed. Restructuring State & Local Services: Ideas, Proposals & Experiments. LC 97-32944. (Privatizing Government Ser.). 160p. 1998. 59.95 (*0-275-94942-7*, Praeger Pubs) Greenwood.
Raphals, Lisa. Knowing Words: Wisdom & Cunning in the Classical Traditions of China & Greece. LC 91-55554. (Myth & Poetics Ser.). 304p. 1992. text 45.00 (*0-8014-2619-7*) Cornell U Pr.
— Sharing the Light: Representations of Women & Virtue in Early China. LC 97-43324. (SUNY Series in Chinese Philosophy & Culture). (Illus.). 352p. (C). 1998. pap. text 21.95 (*0-7914-3856-2*) State U NY Pr.
— Sharing the Light: Representations of Women & Virtue in Early China. LC 97-43324. (SUNY Series in Chinese Philosophy & Culture). (Illus.). 352p. (C). 1998. text 65.50 (*0-7914-3855-4*) State U NY Pr.
***Raphel, Annette.** Math Homework That Counts: Grades 4-6. LC 00-40187. (Illus.). (J). (gr. 4-6). 2000. write for info. (*0-941355-27-6*) Math Solns Pubns.
Raphel, Mary. Money, Emotions & the Recovery Process. 96p. 1993. pap. 10.95 (*0-9639287-0-8*) M Raphel.
Raphel, Murray. Customerization. 117p. 1993. 19.95 (*0-9624808-5-1*) Raphel Mktg.
— Mind Your Own Business: Rules, Guidelines, Examples, Stories & Exhortations. 1992. 19.95 (*0-9624808-4-3*) Raphel Mktg.
Raphel, Murray & Erdman, Ken. The Do-It-Yourself Direct Mail Handbook. LC 86-63913. 1986. 19.95 (*0-939951-01-0*) Marketers Bookshelf.
Raphel, Murray & Raphel, Noil. Tough Selling for Tough Times. 198p. 1992. 19.95 (*0-9624808-1-9*) Raphel Mktg.
Raphel, Murray, jt. auth. see Pellon, Dick.
Raphel, Neil & Raye, Janis. Loyalty Marketing Resource Book. 171p. 1998. pap. 79.95 (*0-9624808-9-4*) Raphel Mktg.
Raphel, Noil, jt. auth. see Raphel, Murray.
Raphelson, Samson. Skylark: Manuscript Edition. 1942. pap. 13.00 (*0-8222-1319-2*) Dramatists Play.
Rapi, Nina & Chowdhry, Maya, eds. Acts of Passion: Sexuality, Gender, & Performance. LC 98-24201. 274p. 1998. 39.95 (*0-7890-0370-8*); pap. 24.95 (*1-56023-108-4*, Harrington Park) Haworth Pr.
Rapi, Nina, jt. auth. see Schramm-Evan, Zoe.

An Asterisk (*) at the beginning of an entry indicates that the title is appearing for the first time.

R

— Deep Cover: Police Intelligence Operations. 136p. 1989. pap. 15.00 (0-87364-507-3) Paladin Pr.
— Homicide Investigation: A Practical Handbook. LC 89-63201. 184p. 1989. pap. text 16.95 (1-55950-020-4) Loompanics.
— Shoplifting & Employee Theft Investigation. LC 88-46126. (Illus.). 172p. 1989. pap. text 14.95 (0-915179-87-3, 40061) Loompanics.
— The Two Eleven Book: Armed Robbery Investigation. 184p. 1989. pap. text 15.95 (1-55950-019-0) Loompanics.
Rapp, Carl. Fleeing the Universal: The Critique of Post-Rational Criticism. LC 97-47021. 297p. (C). 1998. text 65.50 (0-7914-3625-X); pap. text 21.95 (0-7914-3626-8) State U NY Pr.
— William Carlos Williams & Romantic Idealism. LC 83-40561. 175p. 1984. reprint ed. pap. 54.30 (0-608-02294-2, 206293500004) Bks Demand.
***Rapp, Carlton & Rapp, Kati.** Obeah. LC 99-65314. 192p. 2000. pap. 11.95 (1-56315-215-0, Pub. by SterlingHse) Natl Bk Netwk.
Rapp, Catherine. Burgher & Peasant. LC 75-140039. (Catholic University Studies in German: No. 7). reprint ed. 37.50 (0-404-50227-X) AMS Pr.
Rapp, Charles A. The Strengths Model: Case Management with People Suffering from Severe & Persistent Mental Illness. LC 96-50963. (Illus.). 240p. (C). 1997. text 41.95 (0-19-511444-2) OUP.
Rapp, Charles A. & Poertner, John. Social Administration. 308p. (C). 1995. pap. text, teacher ed. 24.00 (0-8013-0450-4, 78262) Longman.
— Social Administration: A Client-Centered Approach. 308p. (C). 1991. pap. 79.00 (0-8013-0435-0, 78244) Longman.
Rapp, Dean. Samuel Whitbread, 1764-1815: A Social & Political Study. (Modern European History Ser.). 512p. 1987. text 15.00 (0-8240-7829-2) Garland.
Rapp, Diane, jt. auth. see Rapp, Laura.
Rapp, Doris J. Allergies & Your Family. 352p. 1990. reprint ed. pap. 12.95 (0-9616318-2-1) Practical Allergy.
— Is This Your Child? Discovering & Treating Unrecognized Allergies in Children & Adults. LC 92-8944. 1992. pap. 13.00 (0-688-11907-7, Quil) HarperTrade.
— El Nino Insoportable. Zaragoza, Lydia J., tr. Orig. Title: The Impossible Child. (SPA., Illus.). 170p. 1988. pap. 12.95 (1-880509-01-6); VHS 16.95 (1-880509-02-4) Practical Allergy.
— Recognize & Manage Your Allergies. (Self-Care Health Library). 32p. (Orig.). 1987. pap. 2.50 (0-87983-396-3, 33963K, Keats Publng) NTC Contemp Pub Co.
Rapp, Doris J. & Bamberg, Dorothy L. The Impossible Child in School, at Home: A Guide for Caring Teachers & Parents. 2nd rev. ed. LC 87-63550. (Illus.). 160p. 1988. pap. 10.95 (0-9616318-1-3) Practical Allergy.
Rapp, Fred, ed. Frontiers in Virology: In Honour of Joseph L. Melnick on the Occasion of His 60th Birthday. (Progress in Medical Virology Ser.: Vol. 21). (Illus.). 250p. 1976. 86.25 (3-8055-2202-9) S Karger.
— On Cogenic Herpesviruses, Vol. 1. 208p. 1980. 120.00 (0-8493-5619-9, QR400, CRC Reprint) Franklin.
— On Cogenic Herpesviruses, Vol. 2. 152p. 1980. 89.00 (0-8493-5620-2, CRC Reprint) Franklin.
Rapp, Friedrich. Analytical Philosophy of Technology. (Boston Studies in the Philosophy of Science: No. 63). 213p. 1981. pap. text 51.50 (90-277-1222-0) Kluwer Academic.
— Gesetz & Determination in der Sowjetphilosophie: Zur Gesetzeskonzeption des Dialectischen Materialismus unter Besonderer Beruecksichtigung der Diskussion ueber Dynamische & Statistiche Gesetzmaeszigkeit in der Zeitgenoessischen Sowjetphilosophie. (Sovietica Ser.: No. 26). (GER.). 174p. 1968. lib. bdg. 129.50 (90-277-0065-6) Kluwer Academic.
Rapp, Friedrich, ed. Contributions to a Philosophy of Technology: Studies in the Structure of Thinking in the Technological Sciences. Trotter, Ian J., tr. LC 74-77969. (Theory & Decision Library: No. 5). 243p. 1974. text 121.50 (90-277-0433-3, D Reidel) Kluwer Academic.
Rapp, Friedrich & Wiehl, Reiner, eds. Whitehead's Metaphysics of Creativity. LC 89-4479. 223p. (C). 1990. pap. text 21.95 (0-7914-0203-7) State U NY Pr.
Rapp, Friedrich, jt. ed. see Durbin, Paul T.
Rapp, G., Jr. & Mulholland, S. C. Phytolith Systematics: Emerging Issues. (Advances in Archaeological & Museum Science Ser.: Vol. 1). (Illus.). 376p. (C). 1992. 75.00 (0-306-44208-6, Plenum Trade) Perseus Pubng.
Rapp, George, Jr. & Gifford, John A., eds. Archaeological Geology. LC 84-40201. 455p. 1985. reprint ed. pap. 141.10 (0-7837-3326-7, 205773200007) Bks Demand.
***Rapp, George, et al.** Determining Geologic Sources of Artifact Copper: Source Characterization Using Trace Element Patterns. 168p. 2000. 37.50 (0-7618-1688-7) U Pr of Amer.
Rapp, George R. & Hill, Christopher L. Geoarchaeology: The Earth-Science Approach to Archaeological Interpretation. LC 97-16880. 280p. 1998. 40.00 (0-300-07075-6); pap. 22.50 (0-300-07076-4) Yale U Pr.
Rapp, George R., Jr., ed. see Minnesota Messenia Expedition Staff.
Rapp-Hunt, Tawney. The Boo Boo Zoo. (First Book Ser.). 36p. (J). 1993. text 11.95 (0-9638882-0-X) Tawney Pubng.
Rapp, Irene, jt. auth. see Groen, Elaine.
Rapp, James. Successful Sales Meetings. 247p. 1990. pap. 29.95 (0-85013-171-5) Dartnell Corp.
Rapp, James A. Education Law, 1 vols. 1984. ring bd. 740.00 (0-8205-1397-0) Bender.
— Illinois Corporations System. 1984. write for info. (0-8205-1447-0) Bender.
Rapp, Joel. Let's Get Growing: Twenty-Five Quick & Easy Gardening Projects for Kids. (J). 1992. pap. 7.00 (0-517-58880-3, Crown) Crown Pub Group.
***Rapp, John A. & Andrew, Anita M.** Autocracy & China's Rebel Founding Emperors: Comparing Chairman Mao & Ming Taizu. LC 99-89975. 464p. 2000. pap. 26.95 (0-8476-9580-8); text 64.00 (0-8476-9579-4) Rowman.
Rapp, Jorg, jt. auth. see Schonwiese, Christian D.
Rapp, Kati, jt. auth. see Rapp, Carlton.
Rapp, Laura & Rapp, Diane. Cruising the Caribbean. 2nd rev. ed. (Illus.). 260p. (Orig.). 1997. pap. 16.95 (1-55650-799-2) Hunter NJ.
Rapp, Lucien, ed. Telecommunications & Space Journal: Law - Economics - Public Policy, 1996, Vol. 3, 1996. 368p. 1996. 69.95 (0-8058-2328-X) L Erlbaum Assocs.
— Telecommunications & Space Journal, 1995. 360p. 1995. 72.00 (0-8058-2327-1) L Erlbaum Assocs.
Rapp, Marrin, jt. auth. see Weaver, Herbert.
Rapp, Marvin A. Canal Water & Whiskey: Tall Tales of the Erie Canal Country. rev. ed. (Illus.). 398p. (C). 1992. pap. 19.95 (1-878097-07-5) Canisius Coll Pr.
Rapp, Michael W. Practicing Safety in the Organic Chemistry Laboratory. Jeffers, J., ed. (Modular Laboratory Program in Chemistry Ser.). 12p. (C). 1997. pap. text 1.75 (0-87540-700-5) Chem Educ Res.
***Rapp, Paul E., ed.** Nonlinear Dynamics & Brain Functioning. 273p. 1999. 95.00 (1-56072-648-2) Nova Sci Pubs.
***Rapp, Peet.** Online Business-to-Business Segments & Case Studies. unabridged ed. Gurney, Margaret, ed. (Illus.). 90p. 1999. 395.00 (1-58637-016-2) ActivMedia.
***Rapp, Peet & Wolhandler, Harry.** Fashion & Style: Building Consumer Loyalty Online, 2 vols. unabridged ed. Gurney, Margaret, ed. (Illus.). 300p. 2000. ring bd. 1295.00 (1-58637-036-7) ActivMedia.
— Real Numbers Behind the Online Business-to-Business Industry. unabridged ed. Gurney, Margaret, ed. (Illus.). 264p. 1999. 1495.00 (1-58637-014-6) ActivMedia.
— Top 100 Consumer E-Commerce Websites of 1999. unabridged ed. Gurney, Margaret, ed. (Illus.). 250p. 2000. ring bd. 1495.00 (1-58637-042-1) ActivMedia.
Rapp, R. & Samso, F., eds. Determination of the Geoid. (International Association of Geodesy Symposia Ser.: Vol. 106). (Illus.). 496p. 1991. 113.00 (0-387-97470-9) Spr-Verlag.
Rapp, R. H., jt. ed. see Grafarend, E. W.
Rapp, Rayna. Testing Women, Testing the Fetus: The Social Impact of Amniocentesis in America. LC 98-45968. 368p. 1999. 30.00 (0-415-91644-5) Routledge.
***Rapp, Rayna.** Testing Women, Testing the Fetus: The Social Impact of Amniocentesis in America. (Anthropology of Everyday Life Ser.). 2000. pap. 19.95 (0-415-91645-3) Routledge.
Rapp, Rayna, jt. ed. see Ginsburg, Faye D.
Rapp, Rayna, jt. ed. see Schneider, Jane.
Rapp, Reinhard. Die Berechnung von Assoziationen. (Sprache und Computer Ser.: Bd. 16). (GER.). iv, 272p. 1996. 45.00 (3-487-10252-8) G Olms Pubs.
Rapp, Richard C., jt. ed. see Siegal, Harvey A.
Rapp, Richard H., et al, eds. Global Gravity Field & Its Temporal Variations: Symposium, 116th, Boulder, CO, July 12, 1995. LC 96-13297. (International Association of Geodesy Symposia Ser.: Vol. 116). 236p. 1996. pap. 99.50 (3-540-60882-6) Spr-Verlag.
Rapp, Richard T. Industry & Economic Decline in Seventeenth Century Venice. (Historical Monographs: No. 69). (Illus.). 224p. 1976. 20.00 (0-674-44545-7) HUP.
Rapp, Robert. The Pill Book Guide to over the Counter Medications. LC 98-105756. 1120p. 1997. mass mkt. 6.99 (0-553-57729-8) Bantam.
Rapp, Rosemary & Twohig, Maureen A. American Paintings from Nature: Flower, Fruit, & Leaf. (Illus.). 36p. (Orig.). 1988. 14.95 (0-9620585-0-5) Cahoon Mus Amer Art.
Rapp, Sandy. God's Country: A Case Against Theocracy. LC 91-7771. (Illus.). 160p. 1991. pap. 14.95 (0-918393-94-9) Haworth Pr.
— God's Country: A Case Against Theocracy. LC 91-7771. (Illus.). 160p. 1991. lib. bdg. 39.95 (1-56024-103-9) Haworth Pr.
Rapp, Scott. Mountain Biking Bend. LC 97-50137. (Illus.). 1998. pap. 10.95 (1-56044-593-9) Falcon Pub Inc.
***Rapp, Stan.** Max e-Marketing for the Net Future: How to Outsmart the Competition in the Battle for the Internet. 2000. 24.95 (0-07-136472-2) McGraw.
Rapp, Stan. Rapp on the New Market. 1996. 22.95 (0-07-052156-5) McGraw.
— Rapp on the New Market. 1996. pap. text 14.95 (0-07-052151-4) McGraw.
Rapp, Stan & Collins, Thomas L. The New Maximarketing: The New Direction in Advertising, Promotion, & Marketing Strategy. 2nd ed. LC 95-37007. (Illus.). 330p. 1995. 24.95 (0-07-052033-X) McGraw.
— Send 'Em One White Sock: 67 Outrageously Simple Ideas from Around the World for Building Your Business or Brand. LC 97-52681. 224p. 1998. 18.00 (0-07-052668-0, BusinessWeek Bks) McGraw.
Rapp, Stephen H. K art lis c xovreba: The Georgian Royal Annals & Their Medieval Armenian Adaptation. LC 98-7832. (Anatolian & Caucasian Studies). 1998. write for info. (0-88206-092-9) Caravan Bks.
Rapp, Valerie. What the River Reveals: Understanding & Restoring Healthy Watersheds. LC 97-27607. (Illus.). 208p. 1997. pap. 14.95 (0-89886-527-1) Mountaineers.
Rapp, William G. Construction of Structural Steel Building Frames. 2nd ed. LC 87-16605. 416p. (C). 1988. reprint ed. lib. bdg. 68.50 (0-89464-241-3) Krieger.
Rappaport. Inside Terrorist Organizations. 42.50 (0-7146-3332-1, Pub. by F Cass Pubs) Intl Spec Bk.
— Menorah. LC 99-33606. 32p. (J). 2000. 14.45 (0-7868-0400-9, Pub. by Hyperion); lib. bdg. 15.49 (0-7868-2352-6, Pub. by Hyperion) Little.
***Rappaport.** Smart Antennas for Wireless Communications: CDMA Applications. LC 99-11800. 528p. 1999. 78.00 (0-13-719287-8) P-H.
Rappaport, Alain, jt. ed. see Schorr, Herbert.
Rappaport, Alain, ed. see Smith, Reid.
Rappaport, Alfred. Creating Shareholder Value: A Guide for Managers & Investors. 272p. 1986. 35.00 (0-02-925720-4) Free Pr.
— Creating Shareholder Value: A Guide for Managers & Investors. 2nd rev. ed. LC 97-38479. 224p. 1997. 34.50 (0-684-84410-9) Free Pr.
Rappaport, Ann. Development & Transfer of Pollution Prevention Technology. LC 93-292. 224p. 1993. 62.95 (0-89930-816-3, Q816, Quorum Bks) Greenwood.
Rappaport, Ann & Flaherty, Margaret F. Corporate Responses to Environmental Challenges: Initiatives by Multinational Management. LC 91-44706. 216p. 1992. 55.00 (0-89930-715-9, RMJ/, Quorum Bks) Greenwood.
Rappaport, Anna M. & Schieber, Sylvester J., eds. Demography & Retirement in the 21st Century. LC 92-46552. 344p. 1993. 62.95 (0-275-94248-1, C4248, Praeger Pubs) Greenwood.
Rappaport, Armin. The British Press & Wilsonian Neutrality. 1951. 16.50 (0-8446-1378-9) Peter Smith.
— The Navy League of the United States. LC 62-8227. 284p. reprint ed. pap. 88.10 (0-7837-3684-3, 204355800009) Bks Demand.
Rappaport, Armin, ed. Monroe Doctrine. LC 64-25181. 128p. 1976. reprint ed. pap. 10.50 (0-03-048705-6) Krieger.
Rappaport, Armin, ed. see Bailey, Thomas A.
Rappaport, Aviva, tr. see Fried, Leah.
Rappaport, Benjamin. The Complete Guide to Collecting Antique Pipes. 2nd rev. ed. LC 79-88253. (Illus.). 256p. 1998. pap. 24.95 (0-7643-0596-4) Schiffer.
Rappaport, Bruce M. Open Adoption Book: A Guide to Making Adoption Work for You. 208p. 1997. 13.95 (0-02-862170-0) Macmillan.
Rappaport Clark, Jamie, ed. National Survey of Fishing, Hunting & Wildlife-Associated Recreation (1996) (Illus.). 169p. (C). 1999. reprint ed. pap. text 25.00 (0-7881-7889-X) DIANE Pub.
Rappaport, Claudia. How to Make & Market Costume Jewelry for Fun or Profit. 24p. 1992. 4.95 (0-9634225-0-2) C Rappaport.
***Rappaport, David.** Snow. 160p. 2000. pap. 10.95 (0-9679780-0-9) Crown-Liquid.
Rappaport, Donald, jt. auth. see Butler, Robert E.
***Rappaport, Doreen.** Arise! Songs & Stories of Slave Resistance. LC 00-29756. (Illus.). (J). 2002. write for info. (0-7636-0984-6) Candlewick Pr.
Rappaport, Doreen. The Boston Coffee Party. LC 87-45301. (I Can Read Bks.). (Illus.). 64p. (J). (ps-3). 1990. pap. 3.95 (0-06-444141-5, HarpTrophy) HarpC Child Bks.
— But She's Still My Grandma! LC 81-20236. (Illus.). 32p. (J). (gr. 1-5). 1982. 16.95 (0-89885-072-X, Kluwer Acad Hman Sci) Kluwer Academic.
— The Dare. 32p. (J). 2000. pap. 4.99 (0-7868-1229-X, Pub. by Hyprn Ppbks) Little.
— Escape From Slavery. LC 90-38170. (Illus.). 128p. (J), (gr. 4-7). 1991. 15.95 (0-06-021631-X) HarpC Child Bks.
— Escape from Slavery: Five Journeys to Freedom. LC 90-38170. (Illus.). 128p. (J). (gr. 4-7). 1999. pap. 4.95 (0-06-446169-6, HarpTrophy) HarpC Child Bks.
— The Flight of Red Bird: The Life of Zitkala-Sa. LC 96-18339. (Illus.). 208p. 1997. pap. 15.99 (0-8037-1438-6, NewStar Pr) NewStar Media.
— The Flight of the Red Bird: The Life of Zitkala-Sa. LC 96-18339. 1999. pap. 14.89 (0-8037-1439-4, NewStar Pr) NewStar Media.
— The Flight of the Red Bird: The Life of Zitkala-Sa. (Illus.). 186p. (YA). (gr. 5-9). 1999. pap. 5.99 (0-14-130465-0, PuffinBks) Peng Put Young Read.
— Freedom River. LC 99-33438. 32p. (J). (ps-3). 2000. lib. bdg. 15.49 (0-7868-2291-0, Jump at the Sun) Hyprn Child.
— Freedom River. LC 99-33438. (Illus.). 32p. (J). 2000. 14.99 (0-7868-0350-9, Pub. by Hyprn Child) Time Warner.
***Rappaport, Doreen.** Martin's Big Words. (Illus.). 40p. (J). 2001. 15.99 (0-7868-0714-8, Pub. by Disney Pr) Time Warner.
— Off to America. 1924. write for info. (0-688-17150-8, Wm Morrow) Morrow Avon.
Rappaport, Doreen. A Scary Day. (J). (ps-1). 1988. audio 9.95 (0-685-25201-9) Jan Prods.
— A Scary Day. unabridged ed. (Happy Enddings Ser.). (J). (ps-1). 1988. pap. 9.95 incl. audio (0-87386-052-7) Jan Prods.
— We Are the Many. (J). 1924. write for info. (0-688-16559-1, Wm Morrow) Morrow Avon.
***Rappaport, Doreen & Callan, Lyndall.** Dirt on Their Skirts: The Story of the Young Women Who Won the World Championship. LC 98-47080. (Illus.). (J). 2000. 16.99 (0-8037-2042-4, Dial Yng Read) Peng Put Young Read.
Rappaport, Doreen & Spirn, Michele S. The Cat Who Couldn't Meow. unabridged ed. (Happy Endings! Ser.). (J). (ps-1). 1988. pap. 9.95 incl. audio (0-87386-050-0) Jan Prods.
***Rappaport, Erika D.** Shopping for Pleasure: Women in the Making of London's West End. LC 99-28152. (Illus.). 328p. 2000. 35.00 (0-691-04477-5, Pub. by Princeton U Pr) Cal Prin Full Svc.
Rappaport, Ernest A. Anti-Judaism: A Psychohistory. LC 75-36297. 312p. 1976. 12.50 (0-9603382-0-9) Perspective Chicago.
Rappaport, George D. Stability & Change in Revolutionary Pennsylvania: Banking, Politics, & Social Structure. 288p. 1996. 37.50 (0-271-01531-4) Pa St U Pr.
Rappaport, Gilbert C. Grammatical Function & Syntactic Structure: The Adverbial Participle of Russian. (UCLA Slavic Studies: Vol. 9). 218p. 1984. pap. 22.95 (0-89357-133-4) Slavica.
Rappaport, Harold M., tr. see Basrani, Enrique.
Rappaport, Harvey M., et al. The Guidebook for Patient Counseling. LC 93-79389. 90p. 1993. pap. text 31.95 (1-56676-089-5) Technomic.
***Rappaport, Helen.** Joseph Stalin: A Biographical Companion. (Biographical Companions Ser.). (Illus.). 300p. 1999. 55.00 (1-57607-084-0) ABC-CLIO.
— Women Social Reformers: A Biographical Dictionary. 2001. lib. bdg. 65.00 (1-57607-101-4) ABC-CLIO.
***Rappaport, Herb.** Holiday Blues. 2000. 17.95 (0-7624-0806-5) Running Pr.
Rappaport, J., jt. auth. see Seidman, E.
Rappaport, Joanne. Cumbe Reborn: An Andean Ethnography of History. LC 93-4909. (Illus.). 262p. 1993. pap. text 15.95 (0-226-70526-9) U Ch Pr.
— Cumbe Reborn: An Andean Ethnography of History. LC 93-4909. (Illus.). 262p. 1993. lib. bdg. 41.95 (0-226-70525-0) U Ch Pr.
Rappaport, Jon, ed. see Cantwell, Alan, Jr.
***Rappaport, Josh.** Algebra Survival Guide: A Conversational Handbook for the Thoroughly Befuddled. LC 99-72866. (Illus.). 288p. 2000. pap. 14.95 (0-9659113-8-1) Singing Turtle Pr.
Rappaport, Josh. Algebra Survival Kit: A Conversational Guide for the Thoroughly Befuddled. unabridged ed. LC 97-68144. (Illus.). 520p. (YA). (gr. 8-12). 1998. pap. 22.95 (0-9659113-5-7) Singing Turtle Pr.
Rappaport, Julian & Hess, Robert, eds. Studies in Empowerment: Steps Toward Understanding & Action. LC 84-4461. (Prevention in Human Services Ser.: Vol. 3, Nos. 2-3). 230p. 1984. text 49.95 (0-86656-283-4) Haworth Pr.
***Rappaport, Julian & Seidman, Edward.** Handbook of Community Psychology. LC 99-49482. 982p. 2000. 170.00 (0-306-46160-9, Kluwer Plenum) Kluwer Academic.
***Rappaport, Karen.** Directory of Schools for Alternative & Complementary Health Care. 2nd ed. LC 99-39050. 352p. 1999. pap. 54.50 (1-57356-294-7) Oryx Pr.
Rappaport, Ken, jt. auth. see Wilner, Barry.
Rappaport, R. Cytokinesis in Animal Cells. (Developmental & Cell Biology Ser.: No. 32). (Illus.). 398p. (C). 1996. text 95.00 (0-521-40173-9) Cambridge U Pr.
Rappaport, Rhoda. When Geologists Were Historians, 1665-1750. LC 97-24040. (Illus.). 336p. 1997. 39.95 (0-8014-3386-X) Cornell U Pr.
Rappaport, Richard. Kaplan McLaughlin Diaz: Innovation & Individualism. (Illus.). 208p. 1998. 39.99 (1-56496-236-9) Rockport Pubs.
— Motivating Clients in Therapy: Values Love & the Real Relationship. LC 97-205912. 352p. (C). 1997. 75.00 (0-415-91265-2); pap. 20.99 (0-415-91266-0) Routledge.
Rappaport, Roy A. Ecology, Meaning, & Religion. 259p. 1988. 25.00 (0-938190-28-8) North Atlantic.
— Ecology, Meaning, & Religion. 284p. 1988. pap. 14.95 (0-938190-27-X) North Atlantic.
***Rappaport, Roy A.** Pigs for the Ancestors: Ritual in the Ecology of a New Guinea People. 501p. (C). 2000. pap. 22.95 (1-57766-101-X) Waveland Pr.
Rappaport, Roy A. Ritual & Religion in the Making of Humanity. LC 98-24494. (Studies in Social & Cultural Anthropology: No. 110). 480p. (C). 1999. text 59.95 (0-521-22873-5); pap. text 19.95 (0-521-29690-0) Cambridge U Pr.
Rappaport, S. Perspectives in Judaism: South Africa. 378p. 1986. 17.95 (0-8197-0523-3) Bloch.
Rappaport, S. A., jt. ed. see Van Den Heuvel, Edward P.
Rappaport, Sheldon. You Can Take it with You. 198p. pap. 8.95 (0-942494-38-5) Coleman Pub.
Rappaport, Sheldon R. Public Education for Children with Brain Dysfunction. LC 69-17693. (Illus.). 257p. reprint ed. pap. 79.70 (0-8357-3983-X, 203668100005) Bks Demand.
Rappaport, Sol R., et al, eds. Child Sexual Abuse Curriculum for the Developmentally Disabled. LC 96-39271. 172p. 1997. text 44.95 (0-398-06733-3); pap. text 32.95 (0-398-06734-1) C C Thomas.
Rappaport, Stephen P. The Affluent Investor: Investment Strategies for All Markets. 1990. 24.95 (0-317-03937-7) NY Inst Finance.
Rappaport, Stephen P., jt. auth. see Lamb, Robert.
Rappaport, Steven. Models & Reality in Economics. LC 97-43551. (Advances in Economic Methodology Ser.). 232p. 1998. 85.00 (1-85898-575-7) E Elgar.
Rappaport, Suki, jt. auth. see Jay, Ira.
Rappaport, Susan S., ed. Traveler's Guide to Museum Exhibitions, 1996: U. S. Edition. (Illus.). 160p. (Orig.). 1995. pap. 12.95 (0-923041-00-1) Mus Guide Pubns Inc.
Rappaport, Theodore. Wireless Communications: Principles & Practice. 656p. 1995. 79.95 (0-7803-1167-1, PC5641) Inst Electrical.
Rappaport, Theodore S. Cellular Radio & Personal Communications Vol. II: Advanced Selected Readings. 550p. 1996. pap. 49.95 (0-7803-2307-6, SR101) Inst Electrical.
— Cellular Radio & Personal Communications Self-Study Course, Incl. (2) course readers, final exam. Zaputowycz, Roman & Bamburak, Michael, eds. 374p. 1995. student ed. 329.00 (0-7803-2315-7, HL5731) Inst Electrical.
***Rappaport, Theodore S.** Smart Antennas. (Illus.). 1998. pap. 69.95 (0-7803-4800-1) IEEE Standards.
Rappaport, Theodore S. Wireless Communications. LC 96-164067. 656p. 1995. 84.00 (0-13-375536-3) P-H.
— Wireless Personal Communications: Improving Capacity,

An Asterisk (*) at the beginning of an entry indicates that the title is appearing for the first time.

Services & Reliability. LC 97-37171. (Kluwer International Series In Engineering & Computer Science). 240p. 1997. text 108.50 (*0-7923-8017-7*) Kluwer Academic.

Rappaport, Theodore S., et al, eds. Wireless Personal Communications: The Evolution of Personal Communications Systems. (International Series in Engineering & Computer Science, Natural Language Processing & Machine Translation: Vol. 349). xi, 216p. (C). 1996. text 107.50 (*0-7923-9676-6*) Kluwer Academic.

— Wireless Personal Communications: Trends & Challenges. LC 93-50913. (International Series in Engineering & Computer Science, VLSI, Computer Architecture, & Digital Screen Processing: Vol. 262). 280p. (C). 1994. text 133.50 (*0-7923-9430-5*) Kluwer Academic.

Rappaport, Theodore S., jt. auth. see Tranter, William.

Rappaport, Theodore S., jt. ed. see Feuerstein, Martin J.

Rappaport, Theodore S., jt. ed. see Gibson, Jerry D.

Rappaport, Uriel, jt. ed. see Dimant, Devorah.

Rappard, H. V., et al. Annals of Theoretical Psychology, Vol. 8. LC 84-644088. (Illus.). 306p. (C). 1993. 95.00 (*0-306-44564-6*, Plenum Trade) Perseus Pubng.

— Annals of Theoretical Psychology, Vol. 9. LC 84-644088. (Illus.). 280p. (C). 1993. 95.00 (*0-306-44624-3*, Plenum Trade) Perseus Pubng.

Rappard, William E. Collective Security in Swiss Experience, 1291-1948. LC 84-10758. 150p. 1984. reprint ed. lib. bdg. 55.00 (*0-313-24381-6*, RACS, Greenwood Pr) Greenwood.

— International Relations As Viewed from Geneva. LC 72-4290. (World Affairs Ser.: National & International Viewpoints). 238p. 1972. reprint ed. 23.95 (*0-405-04582-4*) Ayer.

Rappaz, J., jt. auth. see Crouzeix, M.

Rappe, Anthony K. & Casewit, Carla J. Molecular Mechanics Across Chemistry. LC 96-13315. (Illus.). 444p. 1997. text 58.00 (*0-935702-77-6*) Univ Sci Bks.

Rappe, C., et al, eds. Chlorinated Dioxins & Dibenzofurans in Perspective. (Illus.). 589p. 1986. 318.00 (*0-87371-056-8*, TD196, CRC Reprint) Franklin.

— Environmental Carcinogens: Methods of Analysis & Exposure Measurement, Vol. 11: Oolychlorinated Dioxins & Dibenzofurans, Vol. 11. (IARC Scientific Publications: No. 108). (Illus.). 464p. 1992. 120.00 (*92-832-2108-7*) OUP.

***Rappe, Sara.** Reading Neoplatonism: Non-Discursive Thinking in the Texts of Plotinus, Proclus & Damascius. LC 99-11395. 288p. 2000. 59.95 (*0-521-65158-1*) Cambridge U Pr.

Rappel, Yoel, ed. Yearning for the Holy Land: Hasidic Tales of Israel. Himmelstein, Shmuel, tr. (Illus.). 176p. 1987. reprint ed. 11.95 (*0-915361-27-2*); reprint ed. pap. 9.95 (*0-915361-86-8*) Lambda Pubs.

Rappel, Yoel & Ben-Dov, Meir. Mosaics in the Holy Land: Christian, Moslem & Jewish. Himmelstein, Shmuel, tr. from HEB. (Illus.). 148p. 1987. 15.95 (*0-915361-54-X*) Lambda Pubs.

— Mosaics in the Holy Land: Christian, Moslem & Jewish. (Illus.). 148p. (J). (ps up). 1987. 15.95 (*0-915351-54-4*) Lambda Pubs.

Rappelfeld, Joel. Complete In-Line Skater: Basic & Advanced Techniques, Exercises & Equipment for Fitness. 1996. pap. 9.95 (*0-312-15267-1*) St Martin.

***Rappelfeld, Joel.** Patinaje en Linea. 1998. pap. text 9.95 (*84-8327-005-6*) E Martinez Roca.

***Rappengluck, Michael A.** Eine Himmelskarte Aus der Eiszeit: Ein Beitrag Zur Urgeschichte der Himmelskunde und Zur Palaoastronomischen Methodik Aufgezeigt am Beispiel der Szene in Le Puits, Grotte de Lascaux (Com. Montignac, Dep. Dordogne, Reg. Aquitaine, France) 531p. 1999. 79.95 (*3-631-34847-9*) P Lang Pubng.

Rapping, Elayne. The Culture of Recovery: Making Sense of the Self-Help Movement in Women's Lives. 240p. 1997. pap. 15.00 (*0-8070-2717-0*) Beacon Pr.

— Media-tions: Forays into the Culture & Gender Wars. 286p. (C). 1994. pap. 15.00 (*0-89608-478-7*) South End Pr.

— Media-tions: Forays into the Culture & Gender Wars. 286p. (C). 1994. lib. bdg. 30.00 (*0-89608-479-5*) South End Pr.

— The Movie of the Week: Private Stories - Public Events. (American Culture Ser.: Vol. 5). 208p. (C). 1992. pap. 16.95 (*0-8166-2018-0*); text 42.95 (*0-8166-2017-2*) U of Minn Pr.

Rappisarda, et al. Machine Tool & Manufacturing Technology Workbook. (Machine Tools Ser.). 224p. (C). 1997. text, wbk. ed. 19.50 (*0-8273-7587-5*) Delmar.

Rappleye, Greg. Holding down the Earth. 100p. 1995. pap. 10.00 (*0-9646557-0-5*) Skybooks MI.

***Rappleye, Greg.** A Path Between Houses. 2000. 11.95 (*0-299-17014-4*); 18.95 (*0-299-17010-1*) U of Wis Pr.

Rappleyea, Alan, ed. Federal Fisheries Management Update No. 2: A Guidebook to the Magnuson Fishery Conservation & Management Act. rev. ed. (Illus.). (C). 1989. pap. text 4.50 (*0-945216-02-5*) U OR Ocean & Law Ctr.

Rappold, Edward A. Reflections of Old Cedarburg. 3rd ed. (Illus.). 156p. 1994. pap. 14.95 (*0-9625597-2-5*) Cedarburg Cultural Ctr.

Rappold, Judith. Get Paid to Shop. 120p. 1998. pap. 26.95 (*0-9667580-1-3*) Business Resources.

— Starting Your Secret Shopping Business. 2nd rev. ed. 237p. 1996. pap. 599.00 (*0-9667580-0-5*) Business Resources.

Rappole, John B. The Ecology of Migrant Birds: A Neotropical Perspective. LC 95-10214. 504p. 1995. text 35.00 (*1-56098-514-3*) Smithsonian.

***Rappole, John H.** Birds of the Southwest: Arizona, New Mexico, Southern California & Southern Nevada. LC 00-44315. (Natural History Ser.). (Illus.). 2000. write for info. (*0-89096-958-2*) Tex A&M Univ Pr.

Rappole, John H. The Ecology of Migrant Birds: A Neotropical Perspective. LC 95-10214. 270p. 1997. pap. text 19.95 (*1-56098-513-5*) Smithsonian.

Rappole, John H. & Blacklock, Gene W. Birds of Texas: A Field Guide. LC 93-8448. (W. L. Moody, Jr. Natural History Ser.: Vol. 14). (Illus.). 372p. 1994. 34.95 (*0-89096-544-7*); pap. 16.95 (*0-89096-545-5*) Tex A&M Univ Pr.

— Birds of the Texas Coastal Bend: Abundance & Distribution. LC 84-40567. (W. L. Moody, Jr. Natural History Ser.: No. 7). (Illus.). 184p. 1985. 24.95 (*0-89096-221-9*) Tex A&M Univ Pr.

Rappole, John H., et al. Aves Migratorias Nearticas En los Neotropicos. 348p. 1993. 19.00 (*0-9638408-0-0*) C & RC Nat Zool.

Rappole, John H., jt. auth. see DeGraaf, Richard M.

Rappolt, Hedwig, jt. ed. see Schelbert, Leo.

Rappolt, Hedwig, tr. see Buchner, Georg.

Rappolt, Hedwig, tr. see Mussmann, Linda.

Rappolt, Hedwig, tr. & intro. see Buchner, Georg.

Rappolt, Miriam E. One Paddle, Two Paddle: Hawaiian Teen Age Mystery & Suspense Stories. Pultz, Jane W., ed. LC 82-24048. (Illus.). 190p. (YA). (gr. 7-12). 1993. pap. 10.95 (*0-916630-69-2*) Pr Pacifica.

— Queen Emma: A Woman of Vision. (Illus.). (Orig.). (YA). 1991. pap. 12.95 (*0-916630-68-4*) Pr Pacifica.

Rappoport. The Chemistry of Dienes & Polyenes. 2000. text. write for info. (*0-471-72054-2*) Wiley.

Rappoport, Albert, jt. auth. see Burgess, Ernest M.

Rappoport, Angelo S. The New Gresham Encyclopaedia of the World, 12 vols. 1991. 5500.00 (*81-85484-18-X*, Pub. by Print Hse) St Mut.

Rappoport, Angelo S., jt. auth. see Peretz, Isaac L.

Rappoport, Aviva, ed. see Epstein, Sue.

Rappoport, Chaim. Likkut Dinei U'Minnogei Roshchodesh. (HEB.). 140p. 1990. 8.00 (*0-8266-5210-7*) Kehot Pubn Soc.

Rappoport, David S. Cave Life. 1991. pap. 5.25 (*0-8222-0192-5*) Dramatists Play.

Rappoport-Gelfand, Lidia. Musical Life in Poland. (Musicology: A Book Ser.). xviii, 248p. 1991. text 39.00 (*2-88124-319-3*) Gordon & Breach.

Rappoport, James, et al, eds. Office Planning & Design Desk Reference. LC 91-33863. 352p. 1991. 120.00 (*0-471-50820-9*) Wiley.

Rappoport, Jon. AIDS Inc. Scandal of the Century. LC 88-80560. (Illus.). 275p. 1988. pap. 13.95 (*0-941523-03-9*) Human Energy Pr.

— Madalyn Murray O'Hair: Most Hated Woman in America. 170p. 1998. mass mkt. 6.95 (*0-939040-04-2*, 184) Truth Seeker.

— The Secret Behind Secret Societies. 416p. 1998. text 29.95 (*0-7872-5260-3*, 41526001) Kendall-Hunt.

— The Secret Behind Secret Societies: Liberation of the Planet in the 21st Century. LC 98-61063. 410p. 1998. pap. 24.95 (*0-939040-08-5*) Truth Seeker.

Rappoport, Jon, jt. auth. see Icke, David.

Rappoport, Jon, jt. auth. see Stein, Henry B.

Rappoport, Ken. Bobby Bonilla. LC 92-34583. (Illus.). 144p. (J). (gr. 5 up). 1993. 14.95 (*0-8027-8255-8*); lib. bdg. 15.85 (*0-8027-8256-6*) Walker & Co.

— Grant Hill. LC 96-508. (J). 1996. 15.95 (*0-8027-8455-0*); lib. bdg. 16.85 (*0-8027-8456-9*) Walker & Co.

— Guts & Glory: Making It in the NBA. LC 96-48212. (Illus.). 144p. (J). (gr. 5 up). 1997. 15.95 (*0-8027-8430-5*); lib. bdg. 16.85 (*0-8027-8431-3*) Walker & Co.

— Mario Lemieux: Star Center. LC 97-49431. (Sports Reports Ser.). 104p. (YA). (gr. 4-10). 1998. lib. bdg. 20.95 (*0-89490-932-0*) Enslow Pubs.

— Nolan Ryan: The Ryan Express. LC 92-3244. (Taking Part Ser.). (Illus.). 64p. (J). (gr. 3 up). 1992. lib. bdg. 13.95 (*0-87518-524-X*, Dillon Silver Burdett) Silver Burdett Pr.

— Scottie Pippen: Star Forward. LC 98-35036. (Sports Reports Ser.). (Illus.). 104p. (YA). (gr. 4-10). 1999. lib. bdg. 20.95 (*0-7660-1080-5*) Enslow Pubs.

— Shaquille O'Neal. LC 93-38561. 128p. (YA). 1994. 15.95 (*0-8027-8294-9*); lib. bdg. 16.85 (*0-8027-8295-7*) Walker & Co.

— Sports Great Eric Lindros. LC 96-52884. (Sports Great Bks.). (Illus.). 64p. (J). (gr. 4-10). 1997. lib. bdg. 17.95 (*0-89490-871-5*) Enslow Pubs.

— Sports Great Wayne Gretzky. LC 95-18840. (Sports Great Bks.). (Illus.). 64p. (J). (gr. 4-10). 1996. lib. bdg. 17.95 (*0-89490-757-3*) Enslow Pubs.

— Tar Heel, North Carolina Football. LC 76-19968. (College Sports Bks.). (Illus.). 1980. 10.95 (*0-87397-029-2*, Strode Pubs) Circle Bk Service.

***Rappoport, Ken.** Tim Duncan: Star Forward. LC 99-35721. (Sports Reports Ser.). (Illus.). 112p. (gr. 4-10). 2000. lib. bdg. 20.95 (*0-7660-1334-0*) Enslow Pubs.

Rappoport, Ken. Top 10 Basketball Legends. LC 94-32060. (Sports Top 10 Ser.). (Illus.). 48p. (J). (gr. 4-10). 1995. lib. bdg. 18.95 (*0-89490-610-0*) Enslow Pubs.

— Wake up the Echoes: Notre Dame Football. rev. ed. (College Sports Book Ser.). (Illus.). 464p. 1988. 19.95 (*0-87397-309-7*, Strode Pubs) Circle Bk Service.

Rappoport, Leon H., jt. auth. see Kren, George M.

Rappoport, Lisa, ed. see Jones, Courtney R.

Rappoport, Paul S. Value for Value Psychotherapy: The Economic & Therapeutic Barter. LC 82-16573. 195p. 1983. 52.95 (*0-275-91724-X*, C1724, Praeger Pubs) Greenwood.

Rappoport, Pavela. Building the Churches of Kievan Russia. 256p. 1995. 83.95 (*0-86078-327-8*, Pub. by Variorum) Ashgate Pub Co.

Rappoport, Wendy V. Premenstrual Syndrome: A Self Help Guide. (Illus.). 96p. (Orig.). 1984. pap. 4.95 (*0-936320-19-2*) Compact Books.

Rappoport, Z. & Apeloig, Y., eds. The Chemistry of Organic Silicon Compounds, Vol. 3. (Chemistry of Functional Groups Ser.: Vol. 2, Pts. 1, 2 & 3). 2830p. 1998. 1650.00 (*0-471-96757-2*) Wiley.

Rappoport, Zvi. The Chemistry of the Cyclopropyl Group, Part 1. LC 87-10440. (The Chemistry of Functional Groups Ser.). 822p. 1987. reprint ed. pap. 200.00 (*0-7837-8273-X*, 204905400001) Bks Demand.

— The Chemistry of the Cyclopropyl Group, Pt. 2. LC 87-10440. (The Chemistry of Functional Groups Ser.). 944p. 1987. reprint ed. pap. 200.00 (*0-7837-8274-8*, 204905400002) Bks Demand.

Rappoport, Zvi, ed. The Chemistry of Dienes & Polyenes, Vol. 1, Vol. 1. LC 96-4962. (Chemistry of Functional Groups Ser.). 1074p. 1997. 1015.00 (*0-471-96512-X*) Wiley.

— The Chemistry of Enamines. (Chemistry of Functional Groups Ser.). 1720p. 1994. 1775.00 (*0-471-93339-2*) Wiley.

— The Chemistry of the Cyano Group. LC 70-116165. (Chemistry of Functional Groups Ser.; Vol. 8). (Illus.). 1059p. 1970. reprint ed. pap. 200.00 (*0-608-08133-7*, 205664800078) Bks Demand.

— The Chemistry of the Cyclopropyl Group, Vol. 2. (Chemistry of Functional Groups Ser.: Vol. 3, Pt. 3). 980p. 1996. 1075.00 (*0-471-94074-7*) Wiley.

Rappoport, Zvi & Patai, Saul E., eds. The Chemistry of Halides, Pseudo-Halides, & Azides, Pt. 1. LC 82-23908. (Chemistry of Functional Groups Ser.: Supplement No. D). 945p. reprint ed. pap. 200.00 (*0-8357-5603-3*, 205231200001) Bks Demand.

— The Chemistry of Halides, Pseudo-Halides, & Azides, Pt. 2. LC 82-23908. (Chemistry of Functional Groups Ser.: Supplement No. D). 950p. reprint ed. pap. 200.00 (*0-8357-5604-1*, 205231200002) Bks Demand.

— The Chemistry of the Quinonoid Compounds, Vol. 2, Pt. 1. LC 86-32494. (The Chemistry of Functional Groups Ser.). 892p. 1988. pap. 200.00 (*0-7837-8489-9*, 204929600002) Bks Demand.

— The Chemistry of Triple-Bonded Functional Groups, Pt. 1. LC 82-17355. (Chemistry of Functional Groups Ser.: Supplement C). (Illus.). 750p. reprint ed. pap. 200.00 (*0-608-08140-X*, 203048900001) Bks Demand.

— The Chemistry of Triple-Bonded Functional Groups, Pt. 2. LC 82-17355. (Chemistry of Functional Groups Ser.: Supplement C). (Illus.). 801p. reprint ed. pap. 200.00 (*0-608-08141-8*, 203048900002) Bks Demand.

— Supplement D2 Pts. 1 & 2: The Chemistry of Halides, Pseudo-Halides & Azides. LC 94-18657. (Chemistry of Functional Groups Ser.: Vol. 2). 1818p. 1995. 1825.00 (*0-471-94209-X*) Wiley.

Rappoport, Zvi, jt. auth. see Patai, Saul.

Rappoport, Zvi, ed. see Breuer, Eli, et al.

Rappoport, Zvi, jt. ed. see Patai, Saul E.

Rappoport, Zvi, jt. ed. see Patai, Saul.

Rappoport, Zvi, jt. ed. see Stang, Peter J.

Rapport, David J., et al, eds. Evaluating & Monitoring the Health of Large-Scale Ecosystems: Proceedings of the NATO Advanced Research Workshop, Held at Montebello, Quebec, Canada, October 10-15, 1993. LC 94-43600. (NATO ASI Ser.: Series I, Global Environmental Change: Vol. 28). (Illus.). xi, 454p. 1995. 212.95 (*3-540-58805-1*) Spr-Verlag.

Rapport, David J., et al. Ecosystem Health: Principles & Practice. LC 97-27825. (Illus.). 304p. 1998. pap. 46.95 (*0-632-04368-7*) Blackwell Sci.

Rapport, Leonard & Northwood, Arthur, Jr. Rendezvous with Destiny. (Illus.). 1977. 20.00 (*0-686-26296-4*) One Hund First Air.

Rapport, Maurice M. & Gorio, Alfredo, eds. Gangliosides in Neurological & Neuromuscular Function, Development & Repair. fac. ed. LC 81-48322. (Illus.). 296p. pap. 91.80 (*0-7837-7200-9*, 204709900005) Bks Demand.

***Rapport, Michael.** Nationality & Citizenship in Revolutionary France: The Treatment of Foreigners 1789-1799. 280p. 2000. text 70.00 (*0-19-820845-6*) OUP.

Rapport, Nigel. Diverse World Views in an English Village. 224p. 1994. 60.00 (*0-7486-0417-0*, Pub. by Edinburgh U Pr) Col U Pr.

***Rapport, Nigel.** Social & Cultural Anthropology. 2000. pap. 19.99 (*0-415-18156-9*) Routledge.

— Social & Cultural Anthropology: The Key Concepts. 2000. 65.00 (*0-415-18155-0*) Routledge.

Rapport, Nigel. Transcendent Individual: Essays Toward a Literary & Liberal Anthropology. LC 97-7414. 232p. (C). 1997. 80.00 (*0-415-16966-6*); pap. 24.99 (*0-415-16967-4*) Routledge.

Rapport, Nigel & Dawson, Andrew, eds. Migrants of Identity: Perceptions of 'Home' in a World in Movement. LC 98-230639. (Ethnicity & Identity Ser.). 224p. 1998. 55.00 (*1-85973-994-6*, Pub. by Berg Pubs); pap. 19.50 (*1-85973-999-7*, Pub. by Berg Pubs) NYU Pr.

Rapport, Nigel, jt. ed. see Cohen, Anthony P.

Rapport, Virginia, ed. see Association for Childhood Education International Staff.

Rappuoli, Rino & Montecucco, Cesare, eds. Guidebook to Protein Toxins & Their Use in Cell Biology. LC 96-29554. (The Guidebook Ser.). (Illus.). 274p. 1997. pap. text 50.00 (*0-19-859954-4*) OUP.

— Guidebook to Protein Toxins & Their Use in Cell Biology. LC 96-29554. (The Guidebook Ser.). (Illus.). 274p. (C). 1997. text 105.00 (*0-19-859955-2*) OUP.

Raps, Beth G., tr. see Coquery-Vidrovitch, Catherine.

Raps, Beth G., tr. see Dibango, Manu & Rouard, Danielle.

Raps, Beth G., tr. see Gibbal, Jean-Marie.

Raps, Beth G., tr. see Melonio, Francoise.

Rapsch, Jurgen & Najock, Dietmar, eds. Sallust - Concordantia in Corpus Sallustianum, 2 vols., Set. (Alpha-Omega, Reihe A Ser.: Bd. IX). (GER.). xii, 1472p. 1990. write for info. (*3-487-09384-7*) G Olms Pubs.

Rapske, Brian. The Book of Acts & Paul in Roman Custody. Winter, Bruce W., ed. LC 94-34745. (Book of Acts in Its First Century Setting: Vol. 3). (Illus.). 600p. 1994. text 38.00 (*0-8028-2435-8*) Eerdmans.

Rapsomanikis, Spyridon, jt. ed. see Harrison, Roy M.

Rapson, E. J. Ancient India: From the Earliest Times to the First Century AD. (C). 1995. reprint ed. 14.00 (*81-206-1107-1*, Pub. by Asian Educ Servs) S Asia.

Rapson, Penelope R. A Technique for Indentifying Textual Errors & Its Application to the Sources of Music by Thomas Tallis. 832p. 1989. text 10.00 (*0-8240-2023-5*) Garland.

Rapson, Richard, jt. auth. see Hatfield, Elain.

Rapson, Richard, jt. auth. see Hatfield, Elaine.

Rapson, Richard L. American Yearnings: Love, Money, & Endless Possibility. LC 88-17216. 282p. (Orig.). (C). 1988. pap. text 25.00 (*0-8191-7089-5*) U Pr of Amer.

Rapson, Richard L., ed. Major Interpretations of the American Past. LC 72-149210. (Literature of History Ser.). (Orig.). (C). 1971. 32.50 (*0-89197-284-6*); pap. text 9.95 (*0-89197-285-4*) Irvington.

Rapson, Richard L., jt. auth. see Hatfield, Elaine.

Rapson, Rip, jt. auth. see Proescholdt, Kevin.

Rapsus, Ginger. The United States Clad Coinage. (Illus.). 184p. (Orig.). 1992. pap. text 12.95 (*0-943161-42-8*) Bowers & Merena.

Raptaosh, Diane. Just West of Now, Vol. 1. (Essential Poets Ser.). 64p. 1993. pap. 8.00 (*0-920717-71-3*) Guernica Editions.

Raptis, Leda, ed. SV40 Protocols. (Methods in Molecular Biology Ser.: Vol. 165). 300p. 2000. 89.50 (*0-89603-653-7*) Humana.

Raptosh, Diane. Labor Songs. LC 97-72802. (Essential Poets Ser.: Vol. 78). 80p. 1999. pap. 10.00 (*1-55071-059-1*) Guernica Editions.

***Rapuano, Christopher J., et al.** Requisites in Ophthalmology: The Anterior Segment. LC 99-35199. (Illus.). 425p. (C). 1999. text 89.00 (*0-323-00173-4*) Mosby Inc.

Raqaz, jt. auth. see Ackerman, A. Bernard.

Raquin, Michele, jt. auth. see Bookmaker.

Raraty, ed. Hoffman: Prinzessin Brambilla. (Bristol German Texts Ser.). (GER.). 183p. 1972. pap. 16.95 (*0-631-01880-8*) Blackwell Pubs.

Raraty, Maurice, tr. Erich Von Drygalski: The German South Polar Expedition, 1901-1903. 400p. 1998. pap. 160.00 (*1-85297-031-6*, Pub. by Erskine Press) St Mut.

Rardin. Int Oper Research SM. 1998. write for info. (*0-02-398416-3*) P-H.

***Rardin, Lori Durante.** This Too Shall Pass: A Handbook for the Emotions of Infertility. LC 99-96152. (Illus.). 112p. 1999. 7.95 (*0-9676377-0-8*) Chasing Rainbows.

Rardin, Ronald L. Optimization in Operations Research. LC 97-27030. 919p. (C). 1997. 97.00 (*0-02-398415-5*) P-H.

Rardin, Ronald L., jt. ed. see Parker, R. Gary.

Rardon, James R., jt. auth. see Kroes, Michael J.

Rare Earth Research Conference Staff, et al. The Rare Earths in Modern Science & Technology 1983: Proceedings of the Sixteenth Rare Earth Research Conference, Tallahassee, FL, U. S. A., April 18-21, 1983. LC 83-20666. (Illus.). 1983. write for info. (*0-444-75021-5*) Elsevier.

— Rare Earths 1986: Proceedings of the Seventeenth Rare Earth Research Conference, Hamilton, Ontario, Canada, June 9-12, 1986. LC 87-5399. 1987. write for info. (*0-444-75061-4*) Elsevier.

Rarey, Damon, ed. see Rarey, George.

Rarey, George. Laughter & Tears. Rarey, Damon, ed. LC 96-61847. (Illus.). 192p. 1996. pap. 49.95 (*1-56550-057-1*) Vis Bks Intl.

Rarey, J. S. The Modern Art of Taming Wild Horses. LC 95-36386. (Illus.). 64p. 1996. reprint ed. pap. 7.95 (*1-55709-126-9*) Applewood.

Rarick, Holly M. Progressive Vision: The Planning of Downtown Cleveland 1903-1930. LC 86-12950. 96p. 1986. pap. 16.95 (*0-910386-86-2*) Cleveland Mus Art.

Rarick, Sarah, jt. auth. see Rarick, Troy.

***Rarick, Troy & Rarick, Sarah.** Fruita Fat Tire Guide. (Illus.). 64p. 2000. pap. 9.95 (*0-9700855-0-8*) Fruita Fat Tire Guide.

Rarique, M. Indian & Muslim Philosophy: A Comparative Study. 1988. 13.00 (*81-7024-171-5*, Pub. by Ashish Pub Hse) S Asia.

Raritan Arsenal Staff. Modern Ordnance Materiel, 1943. (Illus.). 216p. 1992. reprint ed. pap. 30.00 (*0-910667-30-6*) Victory WW Two.

Rarity, John, ed. see Weisbuch, Claude.

Rarwood, Hebert, Jr. Baltimore's Light Rail. 1995. pap. 15.95 (*0-915276-55-0*) Quadrant Pr.

Ras, Barbara. Bite Every Sorrow: Poems. LC 97-32675. 88p. 1998. pap. 14.95 (*0-8071-2264-5*); text 19.95 (*0-8071-2263-7*) La State U Pr.

Ras, Barbara, intro. Costa Rica: A Traveler's Literary Companion. LC 93-41735. (Travelers' Literary Companions Ser.: Vol. 1). 256p. (Orig.). 1994. pap. 13.95 (*1-883513-00-6*) Whereabouts.

Ras, J. J. & Robson, S. O., eds. Variation, Transformation & Meaning: Studies on Indonesian Literatures in Honour of A. Teeuw. (KITLV Verhandelingen Ser.: No. 144). 236p. (Orig.). 1992. pap. 26.50 (*90-6718-027-0*, Pub. by KITLV Pr) Cellar.

Ras, Jim. Write TSRs Now with Borland's Turbo Assembler, Turbo C, Turbo Pascal. LC 93-14077. (Popular Applications Ser.). 200p. (Orig.). 1993. pap. 15.95 (*1-55622-335-8*) Wordware Pub.

Ras, Saphan, tr. see Ho, Minfong.

R

Ras, V. Shalapati & Melnick, Joseph L., eds. Human Viruses in Sediments, Sludges, & Soils. LC 87-20942. 272p. 1987. 144.00 (*0-8493-6572-4*, RA644, CRC Reprint) Franklin.

Ras, Z. W., et al, eds. Foundations of Intelligent Systems: 11th International Symposium, ISMIS'99, Warsaw, Poland, June 8-11, 1999, Proceedings. LC 99-30632. (Lecture Notes in Artificial Intelligence Ser.: Vol. 1609). xii, 676p. 1999. pap. 96.00 (*3-540-65965-X*) Spr-Verlag.

Ras, Zbigniew W., et al, eds. Foundations of Intelligent Systems: 10th International Symposium, ISMIS '97, Charlotte, North Carolina, U .S. A., October 15-18, 1997: Proceedings. LC 97-35567. (Lecture Notes in Computer Science Ser.: Vol. 1325). xi, 630p. 1997. pap. 89.00 (*3-540-63614-5*) Spr-Verlag.

Ras, Zbigniew W. & Komorowski, J., eds. Methodologies for Intelligent Systems: Proceedings of the 7th International Symposium, ISMIS '93, Trondheim, Norway, June 15-18, 1993. (Lecture Notes in Artificial Intelligence: Vol. 689). xi, 651p. 1993. 93.95 (*0-387-56804-2*) Spr-Verlag.

Ras, Zbigniew W. & Michalewics, Maciej. Foundations of Intelligent Systems: Proceedings of the 9th International Symposium, ISMIS '96, Zakopane, Poland, June 9-13, 1996, Vol. 107. LC 96-8654. (Lecture Notes in Artificial Intelligence). 664p. 1996. pap. 100.00 (*3-540-61286-6*) Spr-Verlag.

Ras, Zbigniew W. & Zemankova, Maria, eds. Methodologies for Intelligent Systems: Proceedings of the 8th International Symposium, ISMIS '94, Charlotte, North Carolina, USA, October 16-19, 1994. (Lecture Notes in Computer Science: Lecture Notes in Artificial Intelligence: Vol. 869). x, 610p. 1994. 87.95 (*3-540-58495-1*) Spr-Verlag.

Ras, Zbigniew W., ed. see International Symposium on Methodologies for Intel.

***Rasajalanidhi.** Wealth of Indian Alchemy & Its Medicinal Uses, 2 vols. Mukherji, B. C., tr. from SAN. LC 98-907257. 1998. 78.50 (*81-7030-582-9*, Pub. by Sri Satguru Pubns) S Asia.

Rasato, Donald V. Injection Molding Handbook. 2nd ed. 1994. 135.00 (*0-412-98221-8*) Chapman & Hall.

Rasbach, Hubert H. The Dinkywinkies & Snickity Snackety Snort. LC 79-89378. (Illus.). (J). (ps-4). 1982. pap. 6.95 (*0-934822-05-0*) Plus One Pub.

Rasband, Ester. Confronting the Myth of Self-Esteem: Twelve Keys to Finding Peace. LC 98-25905. 1998. pap. 12.95 (*1-57345-381-1*) Deseret Bk.

Rasband, Judith A. Accessory Selection & Coordination, No. 4. (Wardrobe Strategies Ser.: 4). 1996. 128.95 (*0-8273-6165-3*) Delmar.

— Clothing Care: Shop/Value, No. 6. (Wardrobe Strategies Ser.: 6). 1996. 85.00 (*0-8273-6168-8*) Delmar.

— Fabric, Color, Pattern, No. 2. (Wardrobe Strategies Ser.: 2). 1996. 128.95 (*0-8273-6163-7*) Delmar.

— Fabulous Fit. LC 92-73509. (Illus.). 160p. (C). 1994. pap. text 32.00 (*0-87005-739-1*) Fairchild.

— Personal Appearance: Personal Appearance/Style, No. 1. (Wardrobe Strategies Ser.: 1). 1996. 128.95 (*0-8273-6162-9*) Delmar.

— Wardrobe Cluster: Wardrobe Cluster Concept, No. 3. (Wardrobe Strategies Ser.: 3). 1996. 128.95 (*0-8273-6164-5*) Delmar.

— Wardrobe Evaluation, No. 5. (Wardrobe Strategies Ser.: 5). 1996. 128.95 (*0-8273-6166-1*) Delmar.

— Wardrobe Strategies for Women. LC 94-8251. (Illus.). 394p. (Orig.). (C). 1995. mass mkt. 47.95 (*0-8273-6159-9*) Delmar.

— Wardrobe Strategies for Women. (Fashion Merchandising Ser.). (Orig.). 1996. pap., teacher ed. 12.00 (*0-8273-6160-2*) Delmar.

Rasband, S. Neil. Chaotic Dynamics of Nonlinear Systems. LC 89-32903. 230p. 1990. 110.00 (*0-471-63418-2*) Wiley.

— Chaotic Dynamics of Nonlinear Systems. LC 89-32903. 230p. 1997. pap. 54.95 (*0-471-18434-9*, Wiley-Interscience) Wiley.

— Dynamics. 286p. 1990. reprint ed. 43.95 (*0-89464-445-9*) Krieger.

Rasberry, Erin. The Grandparents Book for Grandchildren. unabridged ed. 78p. 1996. pap. 14.95 (*0-9653084-0-5*) Mtn Hse Pub.

Rasberry, Robert W. & Lemoine, Laura F. Effective Managerial Communication. (SWC-Business Communication). 484p. (C). 1986. pap. 61.50 (*0-534-04554-5*) S-W Pub.

Rasberry, Robert W. & Lindsay, Laura L. Effective Managerial Communication. 2nd ed. LC 93-2578. 688p. 1993. mass mkt. 53.00 (*0-534-21468-1*) S-W Pub.

Rasberry, Robert W. & Penrose, John M. Advanced Business Communication. 3rd ed. (EC - HS Communication/English Ser.). 1996. pap. 81.95 (*0-538-86416-8*) S-W Pub.

Rasberry, Robert W., jt. auth. see Flacks, Niki.

Rasberry, Salli, jt. auth. see Phillips, Michael.

Rascal. Socrates. 1992. 12.15 (*0-606-08925-X*, Pub. by Turtleback) Demco.

Rascal, Louis Joos. Oregon's Journey. (J). 1993. 10.15 (*0-606-07976-9*) Turtleback.

Rasch, Arthur R. Manual for SIS Micro-Computer Software System. Ussery, Robert, ed. (Illus.). 101p. (C). 1987. student ed. 45.00 (*0-317-91111-2*, SIS030-M) Summa Info Systs.

Rasch, Bodo, jt. ed. see Rasch, Heinz.

Rasch, D., et al, eds. Elsevier's Dictionary of Biometry. LC 94-1645. (DUT, ENG, FRE, GER & ITA.). 898p. 1994. 227.00 (*0-444-81495-7*) Elsevier.

Rasch, Deborah K. & Webster, Dawn E., eds. Clinical Manual of Pediatric Anesthesia. (Clinical Manual Ser.). (Illus.). 624p. 1993. pap. text 39.00 (*0-07-051119-5*) McGraw-Hill HPD.

Rasch, Dieter. Biometrical Dictionary: English, French, German, Italian, Spanish. 3rd ed. (ENG, FRE, GER, ITA & SPA.). 965p. 1987. 175.00 (*0-7859-9962-0*) Fr & Eur.

Rasch, Dieter & Herrendorfer, Gunter. Experimental Design: Sample Size Determination & Block Designs. LC 85-18285. 1986. text 122.00 (*90-277-1684-6*) Kluwer Academic.

Rasch, Dieter & Tiku, Moti L., eds. Robustness of Statistical Methods & Nonparametric Statistics. 1986. text 164.00 (*90-277-2076-2*) Kluwer Academic.

Rasch, Georg. Probabilistic Models for Some Intelligence & Attainment Tests. LC 80-16546. 208p. 1980. pap. text 9.00 (*0-226-70554-4*) U Ch Pr.

— Probabilistic Models for Some Intelligence & Attainment Tests. expanded ed. LC 80-16546. (Illus.). 224p. reprint ed. pap. 69.50 (*0-608-09508-7*, 205430900005) Bks Demand.

— Probabilistic Models for Some Intelligence & Attainment Tests. LC 80-16546. (Illus.). 222p. (C). 1993. reprint ed. pap. text 20.00 (*0-941938-05-0*) Mesa Pr.

Rasch, Heinz & Rasch, Bodo, eds. Gefesselter Blick. (GER & ENG., Illus.). 112p. 1998. 60.00 (*1-56898-112-0*) Princeton Arch.

Rasch, John D. Rehabilitation of Workers' Compensation & Other Insurance Claimants: Case Management, Forensic, & Business Aspects. (Illus.). 222p. 1985. 44.95 (*0-398-05087-2*) C C Thomas.

Rasch, Joseph. Handling Federal Estate & Gift Taxes, 3 vols., Set. 4th ed. LC 84-81703. 1984. 330.00 (*0-685-59864-0*) West Group.

— New York Landlord & Tenant: Including Summary Proceedings. 4th ed. LC 98-22395. 1998. write for info. (*0-8366-1250-7*) West Group.

— New York Landlord & Tenant: Rent Control & Rent Stabilization. 2nd ed. LC 87-80713. 1987. 95.00 (*0-317-01506-0*) West Group.

— New York Landlord & Tenant: Rent Control & Rent Stabilization. 2nd ed. LC 87-80713. 1993. suppl. ed. 52.50 (*0-317-03311-5*) West Group.

— New York Landlord & Tenant, Summary Proceedings, 3 vols. 3rd ed. LC 71-154362. 1988. 285.00 (*0-317-03188-0*) West Group.

— New York Landlord & Tenant, Summary Proceedings, 3 vols. 3rd ed. LC 71-154362. 1993. suppl. ed. 60.00 (*0-317-03189-9*) West Group.

— New York Law & Practice of Real Property, 3 vols. 2nd ed. LC 62-4443. 285.00 (*0-317-00514-6*) West Group.

— New York Law & Practice of Real Property, 3 vols. 2nd ed. LC 62-4443. 1993. suppl. ed. 50.00 (*0-317-05565-8*) West Group.

Rasch, Matthias. Win95 Game Programming. 1995. 44.95 incl. cd-rom (*1-55755-294-0*) Abacus MI.

Rasch, Philip J. Gunsmoke in Lincoln County. DeArment, Robert K., ed. LC 96-44659. (Outlaw-Lawman Research Ser.: Vol. 2). 315p. 1997. 29.95 (*0-935269-24-X*) Western Pubns.

— Trailing Billy the Kid. DeArment, Robert K., ed. LC 95-12960. (Outlaw-Lawman Research Studies: Vol. 1). 232p. 1995. 29.95 (*0-935269-19-3*) Western Pubns.

— Weight Training. 5th ed. 128p. (C). 1989. text. write for info. (*0-697-10417-6*) Brown & Benchmark.

Rasch, Philip J., ed. Kinesiology & Applied Anatomy. 7th ed. LC 88-26649. (Illus.). 286p. 1989. text 42.00 (*0-8121-1132-X*) Lppncott W & W.

***Rasch, Philip J. & DeArment, Robert K.** Desperadoes of Arizona Territory. LC 99-26945. (Outlaw-Lawman Research Ser.). 1999. write for info. (*0-935269-27-4*) Western Pubns.

Rasch, Philip J. & Dearment, Robert K. Warriors of Lincoln County. LC 98-23137. (Outlaw-Lawman Research Ser.). 1998. 29.95 (*0-935269-26-6*) Western Pubns.

Rasch, Rudolf. Johannes de Garlandia en de Voor-Franconische Notatie. (Wissenschaftliche Abhandlungen-Musicological Studies: Vol. 20). (DUT.). 250p. 1969. lib. bdg. 54.00 (*0-912024-90-9*) Inst Mediaeval Mus.

***Rasch, William.** Observing Complexity: Systems Theory & Postmodernity. 2000. pap. 19.95 (*0-8166-3298-7*) U of Minn Pr.

Raschack, Jason B. The Art & Science of Meeting Women: How to Charm Any Woman with Ease. (Illus.). 224p. 1999. pap. 19.95 (*1-885724-02-0*, 003) Edutainment Media.

— Comic Book Publishing: How to Start a Comic Book Publishing Company. Yronwode, Catherine, ed. (Illus.). 224p. (Orig.). 1999. pap. 24.95 (*1-885724-01-2*, 002) Edutainment Media.

Raschack, Jason B., ed. see Bessey, Vance.

Rasche, Jeffrey. Devotional Companion to the International Lessons, 1999-2000. 112p. 1999. pap. 10.00 (*0-687-02313-0*) Abingdon.

Rasche, Jeffrey A. Devotional Companion to the International Lessons, 1995-1996. 112p. (Orig.). 1995. pap. 8.95 (*0-687-00420-9*) Abingdon.

Rasche, John, jt. auth. see Johnson, K.

Rasche, Robert H. & Johannes, James M. Controlling the Growth of Monetary Aggregates. (C). 1987. lib. bdg. 98.00 (*0-89838-226-2*) Kluwer Academic.

Rasche, Robert H., jt. auth. see Hoffman, Dennis L.

Rasche, Ruth W. The Deaconess Heritage: One Hundred Years of Caring, Healing & Teaching. 350p. 1994. pap. 9.95 (*0-9642849-0-1*) Deaconess Fnd.

Rasche, Stephen M., jt. ed. see Zimmerman, James M.

Raschen, Dan. Wrong Again Dan! Karachi to Krakatoa. 256p. 1984. 40.00 (*0-7212-0638-7*, Pub. by Regency Pr GBR) St Mut.

Rascher, S. M. One Hundred Fifty Eight Saxophone Exercises. 68p. 1986. pap. 10.95 (*0-7935-5431-4*, 50332850) H Leonard.

Raschi, A., et al, eds. Plant Responses to Elevated CO2: Evidence from Natural Springs. LC 97-8030. (Illus.). 280p. (C). 1997. text 69.95 (*0-521-58203-2*) Cambridge U Pr.

Raschka, Chris. Arlene Sardine. LC 98-12018. (Illus.). 40p. (J). 1998. 15.95 (*0-531-30111-7*); lib. bdg. 16.99 (*0-531-33111-3*) Orchard Bks Watts.

— The Blushful Hippopotamus. LC 95-51562. (Illus.). 32p. (J). (ps-1). 1996. 14.95 (*0-531-09532-0*); lib. bdg. 15.99 (*0-531-08882-0*) Orchard Bks Watts.

— Can't Sleep. LC 94-48805. (Illus.). 32p. (J). (ps-1). 1999. 14.95 (*0-531-09479-0*); lib. bdg. 15.99 (*0-531-08779-4*); bds. 6.95 (*0-531-30201-6*) Orchard Bks Watts.

— Charlie Parker Played Be Bop. LC 91-38420. (Illus.). 32p. (J). (ps-1). 1992. 15.95 (*0-531-05999-5*) Orchard Bks Watts.

Raschka, Chris. Charlie Parker Played Be Bop. LC 91-38420. (Illus.). 32p. (J). (ps-3). 1992. lib. bdg. 16.99 (*0-531-08599-6*) Orchard Bks Watts.

Raschka, Chris. Charlie Parker Played Be Bop. LC 91-38420. (Illus.). 32p. (J). (ps-1). 1997. pap. 5.95 (*0-531-07095-6*) Orchard Bks Watts.

***Raschka, Chris.** Doggy Dog. LC 99-51777. (Thingy Things Ser.). (Illus.). 24p. (J). (ps-k). 2000. 3.99 (*0-7868-0642-7*, Pub. by Hyprn Child) Time Warner.

Raschka, Chris. Elizabeth Imagined an Iceberg. LC 93-4875. (Illus.). 32p. (J). (ps-2). 1994. 14.95 (*0-531-06817-X*); lib. bdg. 15.99 (*0-531-08667-4*) Orchard Bks Watts.

***Raschka, Chris.** Goosey Goose. LC 99-51685. (Thingy Things Ser.). (Illus.). 24p. (J). (ps-k). 2000. bds. 3.99 (*0-7868-0641-9*, Pub. by Hyprn Child) Time Warner.

— Lamby Lamb. LC 99-51681. (Thingy Things Ser.). (Illus.). 24p. (J). (ps-k). 2000. bds. 3.99 (*0-7868-0640-0*, Pub. by Hyprn Child) Time Warner.

— Like Likes Like. 32p. 15.95 (*0-7894-4481-X*) DK Pub Inc.

Raschka, Chris. Like Likes Like. LC 98-3659. (Illus.). (J). (ps-k). 1999. 15.95 (*0-7894-2564-5*, D K Ink) DK Pub Inc.

***Raschka, Chris.** Moosey Moose. LC 99-39078. (Illus.). 24p. (J). (ps-1). 2000. 3.99 (*0-7868-0581-1*, Pub. by Disney Pr) Time Warner.

Raschka, Chris. Mysterious Thelonious. LC 97-6994. (Illus.). 32p. (J). (ps up). 1997. 13.95 (*0-531-30057-9*); lib. bdg. 14.99 (*0-531-33057-5*) Orchard Bks Watts.

***Raschka, Chris.** Ring? Yo! LC 99-41080. (Illus.). 40p. (J). (ps-2). 2000. 15.95 (*0-7894-2614-5*, D K Ink) DK Pub Inc.

Raschka, Chris. Simple Gifts: A Shaker Hymn. LC 97-16734. (Illus.). (J). (ps-3). 1998. 15.95 (*0-8050-5143-0*) H Holt & Co.

***Raschka, Chris.** Sluggy Slug. LC 99-39077. (Illus.). 24p. (J). (ps-1). 2000. 3.99 (*0-7868-0584-6*, Pub. by Disney Pr) Time Warner.

— Snaily Snail. LC 99-51689. (Thingy Things Ser.). (Illus.). 24p. (J). (ps-k). 2000. bds. 3.99 (*0-7868-0639-7*, Pub. by Hyprn Child) Time Warner.

— Whaley Whale. LC 99-39076. (Illus.). 24p. (J). (ps-1). 2000. 3.99 (*0-7868-0583-8*, Pub. by Disney Pr) Time Warner.

— Wormy Worm. LC 99-39587. (Illus.). 24p. (J). (ps-1). 2000. 3.99 (*0-7868-0582-X*, Pub. by Disney Pr) Time Warner.

Raschka, Chris. Yo! Yes? LC 92-25644. (Illus.). 32p. (J). (ps-1). 1993. 15.95 (*0-531-05469-1*); lib. bdg. 16.99 (*0-531-08619-4*) Orchard Bks Watts.

— Yo! Yes? LC 92-25644. (Illus.). 32p. (J). (ps-1). 1998. pap. 6.95 (*0-531-07108-1*) Orchard Bks Watts.

Raschke. La Batalla Final.Tr. of Final Battle. (SPA.). 1997. 9.99 (*0-88113-454-6*, B105-4546) Caribe Betania.

Raschke, Carl A. The Alchemy of the Word: Language & the End of Theology. LC 79-15490. (American Academy of Religion. Studies in Religion: No. 20). 106p. reprint ed. pap. 32.90 (*0-7837-5476-0*, 204524100005) Bks Demand.

***Raschke, Carl A.** The End of Theology. rev. ed. LC 00-26998. (Series in Philosophical & Cultural Studies in Religion). 2000. write for info. (*1-888570-53-9*) Davies Grp.

Raschke, Carl A. Fire & Roses: Postmodernity & the Thought of the Body. LC 95-4242. (SUNY Series in Postmodern Culture). 190p. (C). 1995. text 49.50 (*0-7914-2729-3*); pap. text 16.95 (*0-7914-2730-7*) State U NY Pr.

— The Interruption of Eternity: Modern Gnosticism & the Origins of the New Religious Consciousness. LC 79-16460. 280p. 1980. 37.95 (*0-88229-374-5*) Burnham Inc.

Raschke, Carl A. & Raschke, Susan D. The Engendering God: Male & Female Faces of God. 144p. (Orig.). 1996. pap. 19.95 (*0-664-25502-7*) Westminster John Knox.

Raschke, Ehrhard. Radiation & Water in the Climate System: Remote Measurements. LC 96-27902. (NATO ASI Series H: Cell Biology). 616p. 1996. 109.50 (*3-540-61470-2*) Spr-Verlag.

Raschke, Ehrhard, et al, eds. Remote Sensing of Atmospheres & Oceans. (Advances in Space Research Ser.: No. 9). 474p. 1989. pap. 70.00 (*0-08-040149-X*, 2208; 2307; 2309, Pergamon Pr) Elsevier.

— Solar Radiation Atlas of Africa: Global & Diffuse Radiation Fluxes at Ground Level Derived from Imaging Data of the Geostationary Satellite METEOSAT 2. (Illus.). 172p. (C). 1991. text 207.00 (*90-5410-109-1*, Pub. by A A Balkema) Ashgate Pub Co.

Raschke, Linda B., jt. auth. see Connors, Laurence A.

Raschke, Sandy. Female of the Species: A Collection of Speculative Poetry. (Illus.). 12p. 1998. pap. 3.00 (*1-886467-38-2*) WJM Press.

Raschke, Susan D., jt. auth. see Raschke, Carl A.

Raschke, U. Fachwoerterbuch Sozialrecht und Arbeitsschutz. (ENG, FRE & GER.). 195p. 1987. pap. 75.00 (*0-8288-7951-6*) Fr & Eur.

Raschke, Wendy J., ed. The Archaeology of the Olympics: The Olympics & Other Festivals in Antiquity. LC 87-40150. (Wisconsin Studies in Classics). 312p. reprint ed. pap. 96.80 (*0-7837-1984-1*, 204225800002) Bks Demand.

Raschko, Bettyann B. Housing Interiors for the Disabled & Elderly. 1991. pap. 46.95 (*0-442-00983-6*, VNR) Wiley.

Raschue, Carl A. Game Plan for Economic Development in Colorado. (Issue Papers: No. 13-86). 11p. 1986. pap. text 8.00 (*1-57655-010-9*) Independ Inst.

Raschzok, Klaus. Christuserfahrung Und Kunstlerische Existenz: Praktisch-Theologische Studien Zum Christomorphen Kunstlerselbstbildnis. (Illus.). 464p. 1999. 67.95 (*3-631-34003-6*) P Lang Pubng.

Rasco, Jose I. Hispanidad y Cubanidad. LC 87-82479. (Coleccion Cuba y sus Jueces). (SPA.). 42p. (Orig.). 1987. pap. 6.00 (*0-89729-461-0*) Ediciones.

— Jacques Maritain y la Democracia Cristiana. LC 80-68468. (SPA.). 63p. (Orig.). 1980. pap. 4.95 (*0-89729-274-X*) Ediciones.

Rasco, Jose I., intro. Pensadores Hispano-Americans. LC 95-60332. (SPA.). 218p. (Orig.). 1995. pap. 15.00 (*0-89729-770-9*) Ediciones.

Rasco, Jose I., et al. Forjadores de la Conciencia Nacional Cubana. (SPA., Illus.). 108p. (Orig.). 1984. pap. 5.00 (*0-89729-366-5*) Ediciones.

— La Nacion Cubana: Esencia y Existencia. LC 99-60995. (Coleccion Felix Varela Ser.: Vol. 9). (SPA.). 103p. 1999. pap. 9.95 (*0-89729-897-7*) Ediciones.

Rascoe, B. Theodore Dreiser. LC 72-3569. (American Literature Ser.: No. 49). (C). 1972. reprint ed. lib. bdg. 75.00 (*0-8383-1545-3*) M S G Haskell Hse.

Rascoe, Bailey, Jr. & Hyne, Norman J., eds. Petroleum Geology of the Mid-Continent. (Illus.). 162p. (C). 1988. 35.00 (*0-945087-00-4*) Tulsa Geol Soc.

Rascoe, Burton. Prometheans: Ancient & Moderns. LC 70-156707. (Essay Index Reprint Ser.). 1977. reprint ed. 20.95 (*0-8369-2855-5*) Ayer.

— Titans & Prometheans, 2 vols. 1972. 100.00 (*0-8490-1216-3*) Gordon Pr.

— Titans of Literature from Homer to the Present. LC 76-121502. (Essay Index Reprint Ser.). 1977. 23.95 (*0-8369-1775-8*) Ayer.

Rascon, Armando. Xicano Progeny: Investigative Agents, Executive Council, & Other Representatives from the Sovereign State of Aztlan. Lipsett, Suzanne, ed. LC 98-111038. (SPA., Illus.). 56p. (Orig.). 1995. 10.00 (*1-880508-03-6*) Mexican Museum.

Rascon, Art. On Assignment: The Stories Behind the Stories: Inspiring Experiences of an LDS Broadcast Journalist. LC 98-28168. 1998. 15.95 (*1-57734-294-1*, 01113526) Covenant Comms.

Rascon, Bonnie & Levy, Judith. Feasting on an Allergy Diet. (Illus.). 224p. (Orig.). 1985. lib. bdg. 8.95 (*0-9615136-4-0*) Cuissential.

Rascon, Susan, tr. see Gonzalez, Gaspar P.

***Rascon, Susan G. & Penalosa, Fernando, trs.** La Estructura Sociopolitica de Jacaltenango. (SPA.). 120p. 2000. pap. 12.95 (*1-886502-32-3*) Yax Te Found.

Rascon, Susan G., tr. see Bencastro, Mario.

Rascon, Susan G., tr. see Fernandez, Alfredo L.

Rascovsky, Arnaldo. Filicide: The Murder, Humiliation, Mutilation, & Abandonment of Children by Parents. Rogers, Susan H., tr. LC 94-46705.Tr. of Filicidio. 304p. 1995. pap. 45.00 (*1-56821-456-1*) Aronson.

Rase, Eva, et al. Ralph Bell: Art As Life Force. (Illus.). 20p. (Orig.). 1997. mass mkt. write for info. (*1-891122-02-9*) Spfld Mus Art.

Rase, Howard F. Chemical Reactor Design for Process Plants: Principles & Techniques, Vol. 1. LC 77-1285. (Illus.). 784p. 1977. reprint ed. pap. 200.00 (*0-608-18203-6*, 205660700078) Bks Demand.

— Chemical Reactor Design for Process Plants Vol. 2: Case Studies & Design Data. LC 77-1285. 258p. 1977. reprint ed. pap. 80.00 (*0-7837-1462-9*, 205660700079) Bks Demand.

— Fix-Bed Reactor Design & Diagnostics: Gas-Phase Reactions. 376p. 1990. pap. text 74.95 (*0-409-90003-6*) Buttrwrth-Heinemann.

— Handbook of Commercial Catalysts. 520p. 2000. boxed set 139.95 (*0-8493-9417-1*) CRC Pr.

— The Philosophy & Logic of Chemical Engineering. LC 61-18166. (Illus.). 176p. reprint ed. pap. 54.60 (*0-608-18172-2*, 203288200081) Bks Demand.

— Piping Design for Process Plants. LC 89-24404. (Illus.). 312p. 1990. reprint ed. 73.00 (*0-89464-424-6*) Krieger.

Rase, Howard F. & Barrow, M. H. Project Engineering of Process Plants. LC 57-5929. 708p. reprint ed. pap. 200.00 (*0-608-13184-9*, 205594700040) Bks Demand.

Rase, Howard F. & Cunningham, William A. Chemical Engineering at the University of Texas, 1910-1990. (Illus.). 282p. (C). 1990. 40.00 (*0-9627614-0-0*) UTX Austin DCE.

Raser, Harold E. Phoebe Palmer: Her Life & Thought. LC 86-31251. (Studies in Women & Religion: Vol. 22). 392p. 1987. lib. bdg. 99.95 (*0-88946-527-4*) E Mellen.

Raser, Jamie B. Raising Children You Can Live With: A Guide for Frustrated Parents. 2nd ed. LC 98-88660. 160p. (Orig.). 1999. pap. 14.95 (*1-886298-11-4*) Bayou Pubng.

Raser, Lois. Carol Builds a House. LC 92-70674. 96p. (Orig.). 1992. pap. 6.95 (*0-916035-48-4*) Evangel Indiana.

Raser, Timothy B. A Poetics of Art Criticism: The Case of Baudelaire. LC 88-27319. (North Carolina Studies in the Romance Languages & Literatures: Vol. 234). 202p. 1989. reprint ed. pap. 62.70 (*0-608-02060-5*, 206271300003) Bks Demand.

An Asterisk (*) at the beginning of an entry indicates that the title is appearing for the first time.

Rasetti, M. G. Modern Methods in Equilibrium Statistical Mechanics. (Series on Advances in Statistical Mechanics: Vol. 2). 270p. 1986. text 47.00 (*9971-966-27-1*); pap. text 28.00 (*9971-966-29-8*) World Scientific Pub.

Rasetti, M. G., ed. The Hubbard Model: Recent Results. (Advances in Statistical Mechanics Ser.: Vol. 7). 240p. (C). 1991. pap. 43.00 (*981-02-0624-0*); text 83.00 (*981-02-0623-2*) World Scientific Pub.

— New Problems, Methods & Techniques in Quantum Field Theory & Statistical Mechanics. 232p. (C). 1990. text 61.00 (*981-02-0225-3*); pap. text 33.00 (*981-02-0226-1*) World Scientific Pub.

Rasetti, M. G., jt. ed. see Montorsi, A.

Rasevic, Marc, jt. ed. see Druart, Therese-Anne.

Rasey, Marie I., ed. The Nature of Being Human. LC 58-12082. (Franklin Lectures of 1956-1957 Ser.). 129p. reprint ed. pap. 40.00 (*0-7837-3672-X*, 204354600009) Bks Demand.

***Rasey, Midge.** It Doesn't Hurt to Talk about It: A Summer in Europe on Loose Change from a Coffee Can. LC 99-64693. 245p. 1999. pap. 14.95 (*0-9662860-0-6*) Cenografix.

Rasgotra, M. & Chopra, V. D., eds. India's Relations with Russia & China: A New Phase. LC 97-905429. 251p. 1997. 34.00 (*81-212-0559-X*, Pub. by Gyan Publishing Hse) Nataraj Bks.

Rasgotra, M., jt. ed. see Aiyar, Mani S.

Rasgotra, M., jt. ed. see Chopra, V. D.

***Rash, Andy.** The Robots Are Coming & Other Problems. LC 99-86908. (Illus.). 40p. (J). (ps-7). 2000. 15.95 (*0-439-06306-X*, A A Levine) Scholastic Inc.

Rash, Ansley F. The Message of the Minor Prophets. 2nd ed. 48p. 1989. reprint ed. pap. 4.00 (*0-934666-30-X*) Artisan Pubs.

Rash, Felicity. The German Language in Switzerland: Multilingualism, Diglossia & Variation. LC 98-13293. (German Linguistic & Cultural Studies: Vol. 3). 321p. (C). 1998. pap. text 31.95 (*0-8204-3413-2*) P Lang Pubng.

Rash, Felicity J. French & Italian Lexical Influences in German-Speaking Switzerland (1550-1650) (Studia Linguistica Germanica: No. 25). 9xii, 411p. (C). 1989. lib. bdg. 138.50 (*3-11-011862-9*) De Gruyter.

Rash, Francis C., jt. auth. see Block, Robert W.

Rash, James N. Meter & Language in the Lyrics of the Suppliants of Aeschtlus. rev. ed. Connor, W. R., ed. LC 80-2665. (Monographs in Classical Studies). 1981. lib. bdg. 34.95 (*0-405-14049-5*) Ayer.

Rash, Jim, jt. auth. see Scott, Jameson.

Rash, Nancy. The Painting & Politics of George Caleb Bingham. (Illus.). 304p. (C). 1991. 42.50 (*0-300-04731-2*) Yale U Pr.

Rash, Ron. Eureka Mill. LC 97-50381. 64p. 1998. pap. 12.95 (*0-930769-13-9*) Bench Pr SC.

— The Night the New Jesus Fell to Earth & Other Stories from Cliffside, North Carolina. LC 94-18350. 1994. pap. 14.95 (*0-930769-11-2*) Bench Pr SC.

Rash, Wayne, Jr. Politics on the Net: Wiring the Political Process. LC 96-46740. 256p. 1997. pap. text 22.95 (*0-7167-8324-X*) W H Freeman.

Rasha. The Calling. 208p. 1998. pap. 14.95 (*0-9659003-0-4*) Earthstar Pr.

Rashad, Adib. Aspects of Eurocentric Thought. 220p. (C). 1990. pap. text 11.95 (*1-56411-012-5*) Untd Bros & Sis.

— Islam, Black Nationalism, & Slavery: A Detailed History. LC 95-6716. (Illus.). 286p. (Orig.). 1995. pap. 16.00 (*0-9627854-8-2*) Writers Inc.

Rashad, Adib, ed. Elijah Muhammad & the Ideological Foundation of the Nation of Islam. (Illus.). 290p. (Orig.). 1994. pap. 11.00 (*1-56411-065-6*) Untd Bros & Sis.

Rashad, Ahmad. Selected from Rashad: Mikes, Vikes & Something on the Backside. abr. ed. (Writers' Voices Ser.). 64p. (Orig.). 1991. pap. text 3.95 (*0-929631-30-7*, Signal Hill) New Readers.

Rashad, Johari. Steppin' over the Glass: Life Journeys in Poetry & Prose. 80p. (Orig.). 1991. pap. 9.95 (*1-879260-05-0*) Evanston Pub.

Rashad, Mahmoud, jt. ed. see Magen, Ursula.

Rashash, Diana M., et al. Identification & Control of Odorous Algal Metabolites. LC 96-210603. (Illus.). 242p. 1996. pap. 195.00 (*0-89867-855-2*, 90682) Am Water Wks Assn.

Rashba, E. I. & Sturge, M. D., eds. Excitons: Selected Chapters from the Book "Excitons," Volume 2 in the Series Modern Problems in Condensed Matter Sciences. (North-Holland Personal Library: Vol. 2). x, 486p. 1987. pap. 84.75 (*0-444-87052-0*, North Holland) Elsevier.

Rashba, E. I., jt. ed. see Landwehr, G.

Rashbaum, Beth, jt. auth. see Silverstein, Olga.

Rashdall, Hastings. Ideas & Ideals. Major, H. D. & Cross, F. L., eds. LC 68-16970. (Essay Index Reprint Ser.). 1977. reprint ed. 19.95 (*0-8369-0810-4*) Ayer.

— Philosophy & Religion: Six Lectures Delivered at Cambridge. LC 79-98791. 1970. lib. bdg. 39.75 (*0-8371-3025-5*, RAPR, Greenwood Pr) Greenwood.

— The Universities of Europe in the Middle Ages Vol. I: Salerno-Bologna-Paris, Vol. 1. 2nd ed. Powicke, Frederick M. & Emden, A. B., eds. 640p. 1987. text 120.00 (*0-19-822981-X*) OUP.

— The Universities of Europe in the Middle Ages Vol. II: Italy-Spain-France-Germany-Scotland, etc. Powicke, Frederick M. & Emden, A. B., eds. 352p. 1987. 85.00 (*0-19-822982-8*) OUP.

— The Universities of Europe in the Middle Ages Vol. III: English Universities - Student Life, Vol. 3. Powicke, Frederick M. & Emden, A. B., eds. 588p. 1987. 115.00 (*0-19-822983-6*) OUP.

Rashed, Roshdi. The Development of Arabic Mathematics: Between Arithmetic & Algebra. Armstrong, Angela, tr. from FRE. LC 93-39784. (Boston Studies in the Philosophy of Science: Vol. 156).Tr. of Entre Arithmetique et Algebre. 384p. 1994. lib. bdg. 166.50 (*0-7923-2565-6*, Pub. by Kluwer Academic) Kluwer Academic.

— Optique et Mathematiques: Recherches Sur l'Historie de la Pensee Scientifique en Arabe. (Collected Studies: Vol. CS378). 352p. 1992. 124.95 (*0-86078-330-8*, Pub. by Variorum) Ashgate Pub Co.

Rashed, Roshdi, ed. Encyclopedia of the History of Arabic Science, 3 vols., Set. (Illus.). 1264p. (C). 1996. 325.00 (*0-415-02063-8*) Routledge.

Rashed, Roshdi, jt. ed. see Jolivet, Jean.

Rashed, Youssef F. Boundary Element Formulations for Thick Plates. (Topics in Engineering Ser.: Vol. 35). 176p. 1999. 124.00 (*1-85312-628-4*) Computational Mech MA.

Rasheed, Asalia. The Order of the Universe: Who is the Messiah? 52p. (Orig.). (C). 1991. pap. text 10.00 (*0-317-04219-X*) Darby Pub.

Rasheed, Janice M. & Rasheed, Mikal N. Social Work Practice with African American Men: The Invisible Presence. LC 98-40211. (Sourcebooks for the Human Services Ser.). 1999. 22.95 (*0-7619-1117-0*) Sage.

***Rasheed, Janice M. & Rasheed, Mikal N.** Social Work Practice with African American Men: The Invisible Presence. LC 98-40211. (Human Services Guides Ser.: Vol. 39). 201p. 1999. 22.95 (*0-7619-1116-2*) Sage.

Rasheed, Madawi A. Politics in an Arabian Oasis. (Illus.). 300p. 1997. text 19.95 (*1-86064-193-8*, Pub. by I B T) St Martin.

Rasheed, Mikal N., jt. auth. see Rasheed, Janice M.

Rashevsky, Nicolas, ed. see Richardson, Lewis F.

Rashford, Nicholas & Coghlan, David. The Dynamics of Organizational Levels: A Change Framework for Managers & Consultants. (Organization Development Ser.). (Illus.). 156p. (C). 1993. pap. text 40.00 (*0-201-54323-0*) Addison-Wesley.

Rashid. Microelectronic Circuits rev. ed. 1999. pap. text 67.50 (*0-534-37241-4*) Thomson Learn.

Rashid, jt. auth. see Kondrashin.

Rashid, A. Cell Physiology & Genetics of Higher Plant, 2 vols. 184p. 1988. 106.00 (*0-8493-6062-5*, QK725, CRC Reprint); 117.00 (*0-8493-6063-3*, QK725, CRC Reprint) Franklin.

Rashid, Ahmed. The Resurgence of Central Asia: Islam or Nationalism? (Politics in Contemporary Asia Ser.). 160p. (C). 1994. text 59.95 (*1-85649-131-5*, Pub. by Zed Books) St Martin.

— The Resurgence of Central Asia: Islam or Nationalism? (Politics in Contemporary Asia Ser.). 160p. (C). 1995. text 25.00 (*1-85649-132-3*) Zed Books.

***Rashid, Ahmed.** Taliban: Militant Islam, Oil & Fundamentalism in Central Asia. LC 99-68718. (Illus.). 256p. 2000. 27.50 (*0-300-08340-8*) Yale U Pr.

Rashid, Al M. Jordan, the United States & the Middle East Peace Process, 1974-1991. (Middle East Library: No. 28). 301p. (C). 1993. text 69.95 (*0-521-41523-3*) Cambridge U Pr.

***Rashid, Bob, photos by.** Gone Fishing. LC 99-6877. 1999. 34.95 (*0-299-16820-4*) U of Wis Pr.

Rashid, Bob, photos by. Wisconsin's Rustic Roads: A Road Less Travelled. LC 95-14187. (Illus.). 144p. 1996. 35.00 (*1-883755-02-6*) Lost Riv Pr.

Rashid, M. A. Geochemistry of Marine Humic Compounds. LC 85-14692. (Illus.). xii, 300p. 1985. 139.00 (*0-387-96135-6*) Spr-Verlag.

Rashid, M. H. Electronics Circuit Design Using Electronics Workbench. LC 97-24245. (PWS Bookware Companion Ser.). (C). 1998. pap. 24.95 (*0-534-95405-7*) PWS Pubs.

Rashid, Mansoora, jt. auth. see Andrews, Emily S.

Rashid, Mark. Considering the Horse: Tales of Problems Solved & Lessons Learned. LC 93-2522. (Illus.). 224p. (Orig.). 1993. pap. 15.95 (*1-55566-118-1*, Sprng Creek Pr) Johnson Bks.

— A Good Horse Is Never a Bad Color. LC 95-51232. (Illus.). 208p. (Orig.). 1996. pap. 15.95 (*1-55566-142-4*, Sprng Creek Pr) Johnson Bks.

***Rashid, Mark.** Horses Never Lie: The Heart of Passive Leadership. LC 99-86260. (Illus.). 192p. 2000. pap. 16.00 (*1-55566-249-8*) Johnson Bks.

***Rashid, Muhammad.** Microelectronics Laboratory Using Electronics Workbench: Self Study Course. 100p. 2000. 395.00 (*0-7803-4804-4*) Inst Electrical.

Rashid, Muhammad H. Fundamentals of Power Electronics Self-Study Course. 1996. 329.00 (*0-7803-2308-4*, HL5720) Inst Electrical.

— Recent Developments in Power Electronics: Selected Readings. 600p. 1996. pap. text 49.95 (*0-7803-2311-4*, SR102) Inst Electrical.

— SPICE for Circuits & Electronics Using PSpice. 2nd ed. LC 94-17481. 1994. pap. text 44.00 (*0-13-124652-6*) Prntice Hall Bks.

Rashid, Muhammad Ho. Power Electronics Lab Using Spice. Bass, Richard, ed. 1996. lab manual ed. 349.00 (*0-7803-2309-2*, HL5721) Inst Electrical.

Rashid, Muhammed. Culinary Classics: A Guide to Culinary Creation. large type ed. (Culinary Classic Creation Ser.: Vol. 1). Date not set. pap. 18.95 (*0-9663194-0-0*) M Rashid.

Rashid, Muhammed H. Power Electronics: Circuits, Devices, & Applications. 2nd ed. 650p. 1993. text 95.00 (*0-13-678996-X*) P-H.

Rashid, Nasser I. & Shaheen, Esber I. King Fahd & Saudi Arabia's Great Evolution. (Current Events, Historical-Societal Progress Ser.). (Illus.). 342p. 1987. 39.95 (*0-940485-00-1*) Intl Inst Tech.

— Saudi Arabia: All You Need to Know. LC 95-5829. 1995. 39.95 (*0-940485-02-8*) Intl Inst Tech.

— Saudi Arabia & the Gulf War. LC 92-9853. (Illus.). 564p. 1992. 39.95 (*0-940485-01-X*) Intl Inst Tech.

Rashid, Richard F., ed. CMU Computer Science: A Twenty-Fifth Anniversary Commemorative. (ACM Press Anthology Ser.). (Illus.). 560p. (C). 1991. 47.95 (*0-201-52899-1*) Addison-Wesley.

***Rashid, Salim.** Economic Policy for Growth: Economic Development Is Human Development. LC 00-37072. 2000. write for info. (*0-7923-7846-6*) Kluwer Academic.

Rashid, Salim. Economies with Many Agents: An Approach Using Nonstandard Analysis. LC 86-45442. (Illus.). 272p. reprint ed. pap. 84.40 (*0-608-06191-3*, 206652300008) Bks Demand.

***Rashid, Salim.** The Myth of Adam Smith. LC 97-30625. 240p. 1998. 85.00 (*1-85898-532-3*) E Elgar.

Rashid, Salim, ed. The Clash of Civilizations? Asian Responses. LC 98-195816. 172p. 1998. 24.95 (*0-19-577933-9*) OUP.

Rashid, Syed K. & Bharatiya, V. P. Muslim Law: Syed Khalid Rashid's. 1999. pap. 30.00 (*81-7012-562-6*, Pub. by Eastern Book) St Mut.

Rashidd, Amir & Williams, L. V. Breath of Blood & Milk: Dry Long So Poems. LC 88-70764. 64p. (Orig.). 1989. pap. 10.95 (*0-943767-05-9*) Audacious Pr.

***Rashidi, Hooman H. & Buehler, Lukas K.** Introduction to Bioinformatics: Applications in the Biological Sciences & Medicine. LC 99-40191. 200p. 1999. boxed set 69.95 (*0-8493-2375-4*) CRC Pr.

Rashidi, Runoko, ed. see Van Sertima, Ivan.

Rashish, Peter S. Regionalism or Globalism? A Report of the September 1994 Seminar: Transatlantic Trade & Investment: Factors for Stability. 76p. (Orig.). 1995. pap. 15.00 (*0-9628287-0-X*) European Inst.

Rashish, Peter S., ed. Building Blocks for a Transatlantic Economic Area: Final Report of the European Institute 5th Annual Seminar On Trade & Investment. LC 96-85535. 70p. (Orig.). 1996. pap. 15.00 (*1-886607-02-8*) European Inst.

— Developing a New Consensus for the International Treatment of Investment: Report of the European Institute Sixth Transatlantic Seminar on Trade & Investment November 1996. LC 97-60645. 55p. 1997. pap. 15.00 (*1-886607-04-4*) European Inst.

— Partnership for Growth: Reshaping Trade & Investment Patterns: New Approaches to Assisting Central & Eastern Europe. LC 94-71785. 136p. (Orig.). 1994. pap. 15.00 (*0-9628287-7-7*) European Inst.

— Transatlantic & Global Economic Integration: The Role of Investment: Report of the European Institute's 7th Annual Transatlantic Seminar on Trade & Investment. LC 98-70332. 63p. 1997. pap. 15.00 (*1-886607-07-9*) European Inst.

Rashish, Peter S., jt. ed. see Barry, Charles.

Rashke, Richard. Escape from Sobibor. (Illus.). 1987. pap. 3.95 (*0-380-75394-4*, Avon Bks) Morrow Avon.

— Escape from Sobibor. LC 94-47590. 416p. 1995. 16.95 (*0-252-06479-8*) U of Ill Pr.

***Rashke, Richard.** Killing of Karen Silkwood: The Story Behind the Kerr-McGee Plutonium Case. 2000. pap. text 17.95 (*0-8014-8667-X*) Cornell U Pr.

Rashke, Richard. Runaway Father: One Family's Seventeen-Year Search. 271p. 1988. 17.95 (*0-15-179040-X*) Harcourt.

Rashkevich, J. English - Latvian Dictionary. (ENG & LAV.). 1985. 59.95 (*0-8288-2485-1*) Fr & Eur.

***Rashkin, Elissa.** Women Filmmakers in Mexico: The Country of Which We Dream. LC 00-41772. (Illus.). 2001. pap. write for info. (*0-292-77109-6*) U of Tex Pr.

Rashkin, Esther. Family Secrets & the Psychoanalysis of Narrative. 224p. 1992. text 26.95 (*0-691-06951-4*, Pub. by Princeton U Pr) Cal Prin Full Svc.

Rashkind, Alan B. & Gallagher, R. Craig. Virginia Insurance Case Finder: 1998 Cumulative Supplement. 1998. 45.00 (*0-327-00194-1*, 66462-13) LEXIS Pub.

— Virginia Insurance Case Finder, 1999 Cumulative Supplement. 215p. 1999. 50.00 (*0-327-01156-4*, 66464214) LEXIS Pub.

Rashkind, Alan B. & Rowe, Gerard P. Virginia Insurance Case Finder. 805p. 1994. 95.00 (*1-55834-146-3*, 66461-10, MICHIE) LEXIS Pub.

Rashkovich, L. N. KDP-Family Single Crystals. (Optics & Optoelectronics Ser.). (Illus.). 212p. 1991. 130.00 (*0-7503-0105-8*) IOP Pub.

Rashkovsky, Avigail, ed. see Dovlatov, Sergei.

***Rashkow, Ilona N.** Taboo Or Not Taboo: Sexuality & Family in the Hebrew Bible. LC 99-48079. 2000. pap. 22.00 (*0-8006-3085-8*, Fortress Pr) Augsburg Fortress.

— Upon the Dark Places: Anti-Semitism & Sexism in English Renaissance Biblical Translation. (Bible & Literature Ser.: Vol. 28). 180p. 1990. 52.50 (*1-85075-251-6*, Pub. by Sheffield Acad) CUP Services.

Rashotte, Michael E., jt. auth. see Amsel, Abram.

Rashwan, A., jt. auth. see Shawaki, I.

Rashwan, A., jt. ed. see Shawaki, I.

Rasiah, Rajah. Foreign Capital & Industrialization in Malaysia. LC 94-31773. (Studies in the Economies of East & Southeast Asia). 1995. write for info. (*0-312-12440-6*) St Martin.

Rasic, Mirko R. Postal History & Postage Stamps of Serbia, 1841-1921. (Illus.). 276p. 1979. 18.00 (*0-912574-25-9*) Collectors.

Rasico, Philip D. The Minorcans of Florida: Their History, Language, & Culture. LC 90-30600. (Illus.). 200p. (C). 1990. pap. 24.95 (*1-877633-07-0*) Luthers.

Rasiel, Ethan M. The McKinsey Way: Using the Techniques of the World's Top Strategic Consultants to Help You & Your Business. LC 98-51500. 187p. 1999. 21.95 (*0-07-053448-9*) McGraw.

Rasiel, Rosa, jt. auth. see Kalechofsky, Roberta.

Rasing, Thera. Passing on the Rites of Passage: Girls' Initiation Rites in the Context of an Urban Roman Catholic Community on the Zambian Copperbelt. LC 97-136350. (African Studies Center Leiden). 124p. (Orig.). 1996. pap. 43.95 (*1-85972-301-2*, Pub. by Avebry) Ashgate Pub Co.

Rasinski, Tim, jt. auth. see Opitz, Michael F.

***Rasinski, Timothy & Padak, Nancy.** Effective Reading Strategies: Teaching Children who Find Reading Difficult. 2nd ed. LC 99-13910. 343p. (C). 1999. pap. text 34.00 (*0-13-099669-6*) P-H.

Rasinski, Timothy, jt. auth. see Vacca, Richard T.

Rasinski, Timothy V. Parents & Teachers: Helping Children Learn to Read & Write. LC 94-75766. (Illus.). 200p. (Orig.). (C). 1994. pap. text 37.00 (*0-15-501315-7*, Pub. by Harcourt Coll Pubs) Harcourt.

Rasinski, Timothy V. & Gillespie, Cindy. Sensitive Issues: An Annotated Guide to Children's Literature K-6. LC 92-18682. 288p. 1992. pap. 29.95 (*0-89774-777-1*) Oryx Pr.

***Rasinski, Timothy V. & Padak, Nancy.** From Words to Fluency. LC 00-32262. 2000. write for info. (*0-321-04903-9*) Longman.

Rasis, E. P. Technical Reference Handbook. 3rd ed. (Illus.). 220p. 1996. 24.96 (*0-8269-3452-8*) Am Technical.

Rasjeswari, V., jt. auth. see Rao, K. S.

Rask, Mark. American Autobahn: The Road to an Interstate Freeway with No Speed Limit. Register, Cheri & Lindgren, Amy, eds. LC 98-90867. (Illus.). 304p. 1999. 27.95 (*0-9669136-0-4*, VNFB-899-AA1) Vanguard Nonfictn.

Raskas, Bernard S. Heart of Wisdom-One. 1962. 8.50 (*0-8381-2102-0*) USCJE.

— Heart of Wisdom-Two. 1979. 9.50 (*0-8381-2104-7*) USCJE.

Raskevics, J., et al. English-Latvian-Russian Dictionary. (ENG, LAV & RUS.). 718p. 1977. 50.00 (*0-7855-7302-X*) St Mut.

Raskin. First Principles. 1997. 23.50 (*0-02-874107-2*) Free Pr.

— Radiographic Anatomy: A Gallery of Images. (Illus.). 1996. pap. text 24.95 (*0-9655384-0-0*) Scholar Educ Systs.

Raskin, Abram. Petrodvorets: Palaces, Gardens, Fountains, Sculpture. 346p. 1979. 155.00 (*0-7855-1648-4*) St Mut.

Raskin, Allen, ed. see Conference on Depression in Childhood Staff.

Raskin, Allen, jt. ed. see Gershon, Samuel.

Raskin, Arfron L., ed. see Schneerson, Shmuel.

Raskin, Barbara. A List. 1990. 18.95 (*0-685-33569-0*) Random.

Raskin, C., jt. ed. see Hodges-Aeberhard, J.

Raskin, Chuck. Designing with Motion Handbook. 5th ed. 448p. 1997. pap. text. write for info. (*0-7506-9966-3*) Tech Eighty.

Raskin, Chuck. Designing with Motion Handbook: Design, Integration, Software Tips & Techniques. 5th rev. ed. (Illus.). 448p. 1997. pap. (*0-9671554-0-1*, 9004) Tech Eighty.

Raskin, David, ed. Psychological Methods in Criminal Investigation & Evidence. 416p. 1989. 46.95 (*0-8261-6450-1*) Springer Pub.

Raskin, Doma. Vitamin Vitality: Use Nature's Powers to Obtain Optimal Health. Men's Health Books Editors, ed. LC 97-17375. (Illus.). 176p. 1997. pap. 14.95 (*0-87596-408-7*) Rodale Pr Inc.

Raskin, Donald. Broadband Return Systems for Hybrid Fiber/Coax Cable TV Networks. LC 97-47131. 320p. (C). 1997. 63.00 (*0-13-636515-9*) P-H.

Raskin, Donna, et al. Good Loving: Keys to a Lifetime of Passion, Pleasure & Sex. LC 97-44353. (Men's Health Life Improvement Guides Ser.). 176p. 1998. pap. 14.95 (*0-87596-441-9*) Rodale Pr Inc.

Raskin, Ellen. Figgs & Phantoms. (Illus.). 160p. (J). (gr. 5-9). 1989. pap. 5.99 (*0-14-032944-7*, PuffinBks) Peng Put Young Read.

***Raskin, Ellen.** Figgs & Phantoms. (J). (gr. 4-8). 2000. 19.50 (*0-8446-7153-3*) Peter Smith.

Raskin, Ellen. Figgs & Phantoms. (Puffin Newbery Library). (J). 1974. 11.09 (*0-606-04040-4*, Pub. by Turtleback) Demco.

— The Mysterious Disappearance of Leon (I Mean Noel) (Illus.). 160p. (J). (gr. 5-9). 1989. pap. 5.99 (*0-14-032945-5*, PuffinBks) Peng Put Young Read.

— The Mysterious Disappearance of Leon (I Mean Noel) (J). 1971. 10.09 (*0-606-04096-X*, Pub. by Turtleback) Demco.

— The Westing Game. (Illus.). 192p. (YA). (gr. 7 up). 1984. pap. 3.50 (*0-380-67991-4*, Avon Bks) Morrow Avon.

— The Westing Game. (J). (gr. 5-9). 1978. 15.99 (*0-525-42320-6*, Dutton Child) Peng Put Young Read.

— The Westing Game. (Assessment Packs Ser.). 15p. 1998. pap. text 15.95 (*1-58303-069-7*) Pthways Pubng.

— The Westing Game. 1997. 10.09 (*0-606-02442-5*, Pub. by Turtleback) Demco.

Raskin, Eugene. Architecturally Speaking. (Illus.). 1970. reprint ed. pap. 7.95 (*0-8197-0003-7*) Bloch.

— Citronella. 1980. 10.95 (*0-8197-0444-X*); pap. 4.95 (*0-8197-0483-0*) Bloch.

Raskin, Eugene, intro. Jewish Life: Paintings by Saul Raskin in Postcards. (Illus.). 30p. 1999. pap. 11.95 (*1-893262-03-0*) Robern Pubg.

Raskin, Herbert A., jt. auth. see Krystal, Henry.

***Raskin, Ilya & Ensley, Burt D.** Phytoremediation of Toxic Metals: Plants to Clean up the Environment, 1. LC 99-43427. 304p. 1999. 89.95 (*0-471-19254-6*) Wiley.

***Raskin, Jeffrey B.** Humane Interface: An Engineering Guide for Product & Software Developers. (Illus.). 256p. 2000. pap. text 24.95 (*0-201-37937-6*) Addison-Wesley.

Raskin, Jeffrey B., ed. see Raskin, Nord.

R

R

Raskin, Jonah. For the Hell of It: The Life & Times of Abbie Hoffman. LC 95-52181. (Illus.). 315p. (C). 1997. 35.00 (*0-520-20575-8*, Pub. by U CA Pr) Cal Prin Full Svc.

— For the Hell of It: The Life & Times of Abbie Hoffman. 1998. pap. text 17.95 (*0-520-21379-3*, Pub. by U CA Pr) Cal Prin Full Svc.

— James D. Houston. LC 91-55033. (Western Writers Ser.: No. 99). (Illus.). 48p. 1991. 4.95 (*0-88430-098-6*) Boise St U W Writ Ser.

— My Search for B. Traven. LC 80-15834. 249 p. 1980. write for info. (*0-416-00751-1*) Routledge.

Raskin, Jonathan D., jt. ed. see Niemeyer, Robert A.

Raskin, Lawrie & Pearson, Debora. 52 Days by Camel: My Sahara Adventure. (Illus.). 88p. (J). (gr. 3 up). 1998. pap. 14.95 (*1-55037-518-0*, Pub. by Annick) Firefly Bks Ltd.

— 52 Days by Camel: My Sahara Adventure. (Illus.). 88p. (YA). (gr. 5 up). 1998. lib. bdg. 24.95 (*1-55037-519-9*, Pub. by Annick) Firefly Bks Ltd.

Raskin, Linda, jt. auth. see Lawrence, Jan.

Raskin, Linda, ed. see Granet, Roger.

Raskin, Marcus G. Abolishing the War System. 1992. pap. 14.00 (*0-9623718-8-2*); lib. bdg. 30.00 (*0-9623718-9-0*) Aletheia Pr.

— Essays of a Citizen: From National Security State to Democracy. LC 90-9074. 336p. (gr. 13). 1991. text 59.95 (*0-87332-764-0*) M E Sharpe.

— The Politics of National Security. LC 78-55935. (Issues in Contemporary Civilization Ser.). 320p. 1979. 39.95 (*0-87855-239-1*) Transaction Pubs.

— Presidential Disrespect: From Thomas Paine to Rush Limbaugh. (Illus.). 240p. 1996. 19.95 (*1-55972-374-2*, Birch Ln Pr) Carol Pub Group.

— Visions & Revisions: Reflections on Culture & Democracy at the End of the Century. LC 94-25203. (Voices & Visions Ser.). 360p. 1995. pap. 18.95 (*1-56656-172-8*, Olive Branch Pr) Interlink Pub.

— Visions & Revisions: Reflections on Culture & Democracy at the End of the Century. LC 94-25203. (Voices & Visions Ser.). 360p. 1996. 40.00 (*1-56656-171-X*, Olive Branch Pr) Interlink Pub.

Raskin, Marcus G., ed. Next Steps for a New Administration. 48p. 1976. pap. 21.95 (*0-87855-657-5*) Transaction Pubs.

Raskin, Marcus G., et al, eds. New Ways of Knowing: The Sciences, Society & Reconstructive Knowledge. 352p. 1987. pap. 26.50 (*0-8476-7463-0*) Rowman.

Raskin, Marcus G., jt. ed. see Hartman, Chester.

Raskin, Michael M. Comparative Abdominal & Pelvic Anatomy by Computed Tomography & Ultrasound. 304p. 1979. 130.00 (*0-8493-5369-6*, RC944, CRC Reprint) Franklin.

Raskin, Miriam S. Empirical Studies in Field Instruction. LC 88-24670. (Clinical Supervisor Ser.: Vol. 6, Nos. 3 & 4). (Illus.). 399p. 1994. text 49.95 (*0-86656-869-7*) Haworth Pr.

Raskin, Miriam S., jt. ed. see Daley, Dennis C.

Raskin, Neil H. Headache. 2nd ed. LC 88-2848. (Illus.). 406p. reprint ed. pap. 125.90 (*0-7837-2561-2*, 204272000006) Bks Demand.

Raskin, Nord. Colonoscopy: Principles & Techniques. Raskin, Jeffrey B. & Nord, H. Juergen, eds. LC 95-3481. (Illus.). 384p. 1995. 89.50 (*0-89640-277-0*) Igaku-Shoin.

Raskin, Patricia. Success, Your Dream & You: A Personal Success Guide to Marketing. LC 90-52808. 224p. 1991. 19.95 (*0-915677-51-2*) Roundtable Pub.

Raskin, Paul D. Fretboard Vision for Guitar: Attain Complete Mastery of the Fretboard. LC 96-93138. (Illus.). 87p. 1997. pap. 18.95 (*0-9656336-0-8*) Sound Perspective.

— LEAP: A Description of the LDC Energy Alternatives Planning System. (Energy, Environment & Development in Africa Ser.: No. 8). 149p. 1986. write for info. (*91-7106-247-5*, Pub. by Nordic Africa) Transaction Pubs.

Raskin, Philip, jt. ed. see Rifkin, Harold.

Raskin, Richard. Color: An Outline of Terms & Concepts. (Illus.). 32p. (C). 1986. pap. 6.95 (*87-7288-063-5*, Pub. by Aarhus Univ Pr) David Brown.

— Elements of Picture Composition. (Illus.). 64p. (C). 1986. pap. 7.95 (*87-7288-033-3*, Pub. by Aarhus Univ Pr) David Brown.

— Film Terminology. (Illus.). 28p. 1986. pap. 4.95 (*87-7288-017-1*, Pub. by Aarhus Univ Pr) David Brown.

— Gustave Courbet's "Les Casseurs de Pierres" Aspects of a Major Work of Art. (Illus.). 122p. (C). 1989. pap. 21.00 (*87-7288-170-4*, Pub. by Aarhus Univ Pr) David Brown.

— Nuit & Brouillard: On the Making, Reception & Functions of a Major Documentary Film. (Illus.). 186p. (C). 1987. pap. 23.00 (*87-7288-100-3*, Pub. by Aarhus Univ Pr) David Brown.

— Some Procedures for Sound Editing on Videotape. (Illus.). 19p. 1996. pap. 4.95 (*87-7288-151-8*, Pub. by Aarhus Univ Pr) David Brown.

Raskin, Robin, jt. auth. see Christian, Kaare.

Raskin, Sarah & Mateer, Catherine. Treatment of Mild Cognitive & Emotional Sequelae of Neurologic Dysfunction. LC 99-13808. (Illus.). 312p. 1999. text 49.95 (*0-19-508527-2*) OUP.

Raskin, Saul. Hagadah for Passover: Drawings by Saul Raskin. 92p. 1994. 39.95 (*0-8197-0605-1*) Bloch.

— Our Father, Our King: Drawings by Saul Raskin. 96p. 1966. 39.95 (*0-8197-0603-5*) Bloch.

— Pirke Aboth: Sayings of the Fathers: Drawings by Saul Raskin. 136p. 1994. 39.95 (*0-8197-0608-6*) Bloch.

Raskin, Uri. Cracks in the Wall. 15.99 (*0-89906-128-1*); pap. 12.99 (*0-89906-130-3*) Mesorah Pubns.

Raskin, Valerie D. When Words Are Not Enough: The Women's Prescription for Depression & Anxiety. LC 96-38081. 336p. 1997. pap. 16.00 (*0-553-06713-3*) Broadway BDD.

Raskin, Valerie D., jt. auth. see Kleiman, Karen R.

Raskin, Victor & Weiser, Irwin H. Language & Writing: Applications of Linguistics to Rhetoric & Composition. LC 86-17753. 304p. 1987. text 73.25 (*0-89391-405-3*) Ablx Pub.

Raskin, Victor, jt. ed. see Bjarkman, Peter C.

Raskin, Xan, jt. auth. see Weitzman, Allan H.

Raskina, Alexandra, ed. see Alexandra.

Raskind, Leo J., jt. auth. see Gifford, Daniel J.

Raskind, Wayne, ed. see AMS-IMS-SIAM Joint Summer Research Conference Staff.

Raskob, Tony. The Sex Backpack. (Illus.). (YA). (gr. 7-12). 1994. pap. 9.95 (*0-9642469-0-2*) Lrning to Lrn.

— Truth & Consequences. (Orig.). 1989. write for info. (*0-318-65039-8*) YNot Read.

Raskolnikov, F. F. Kronstadt & Petrograd in 1917. (Illus.). 368p. 1982. pap. 18.95 (*0-929087-95-X*) Mehring Bks.

Raskova, H., ed. Pharmacology & Toxicology of Naturally Occurring Toxins. 2 vols. LC 77-130797. 1971. 323.00 (*0-08-016797-7*, Pub. by Pergamon Repr) Franklin.

Raskova, Jana & Mikhail, Nagy. Laboratory Medicine Casebook: Introduction to Clinical Reasoning. 334p. (C). 1996. pap. text 37.95 (*0-8385-5574-8*, A5574-7, Apple Lange Med) McGraw.

***Rasky, Harry.** Tennessee Williams: A Portrait in Laughter & Lamentation. (Illus.). 200p. 1999. pap. 14.00 (*0-88962-703-7*) Mosaic.

Rasler, Karen A. & Thompson, William R. The Great Powers & Global Struggle, 1490-1990. LC 94-31406. 296p. 1994. 37.50 (*0-8131-1889-1*) U Pr of Ky.

— War & State Making: The Shaping of the Global Powers. (Studies in International Conflict: Vol. 2). 272p. (C). (gr. 13). 1989. text 62.95 (*0-04-445097-4*) Routledge.

Rasley, Alicia. A Midsummer's Delight. 320p. 1993. mass mkt. 3.99 (*0-8217-4230-2*, Zebra Kensgtn) Kensgtn Pub Corp.

Rasley, Alicia & Kerstan, Lynn. Gwen's Christmas Ghost. (Zebra Regency Special Ser.). 304p. (Orig.). 1995. mass mkt. 4.50 (*0-8217-5145-X*, Zebra Kensgtn) Kensgtn Pub Corp.

Raslish, Peter S., ed. A New Approach for the Transatlantic Economic Partnership: Report of the European Institute, 8th Annual Transatlantic Seminar on Trade & Investment, November 4-5, 1998. LC 99-72186. 82p. 1999. pap. 15.00 (*1-886607-11-7*) European Inst.

Rasmer, Raymond, ed. see Oscard, Anne.

Rasminsky, Judy S., jt. auth. see Kaiser, Barbara.

Rasmueen, Tina. Diversity: ASTD Trainer's Sourcebook. 294p. 1995. pap. 39.95 (*0-07-053438-1*) McGraw.

***Rasmus, Daniel W.** Building Artificial Knowledge with Objects. LC 98-39478. (Advances in Object Technology Ser.: No. 17). 300p. (C). 1998. pap. 39.95 (*0-521-64549-2*) Cambridge U Pr.

Rasmusen, Eric. Games & Information: An Introduction to Game Theory. 2nd ed. LC 93-40356. (Illus.). 375p. 1994. 47.95 (*1-55786-502-7*) Blackwell Pubs.

***Rasmusen, Eric, ed.** Readings in Games & Information. (Readings for Contemporary Economics Ser.). 400p. 2000. 72.95 (*0-631-21556-5*); pap. 36.95 (*0-631-21557-3*) Blackwell Pubs.

Rasmuson, Mark R., et al. Communication for Child Survival. 144p. 1988. pap. 8.00 (*0-685-59932-9*) Acad Educ Dev.

Rasmusse, Cecilia. L. A. Unconventional: The Men & Women Who Did L. A. Their Way. (Illus.). 192p. 1998. 29.95 (*1-883792-23-1*) LA Times.

Rasmusse, Ken, jt. auth. see Pitsula, James M.

Rasmussen. Major European Governments. 10th ed. (C). Date not set. pap. text. write for info. (*0-15-507864-X*) Harcourt Coll Pubs.

— New Land New Lives: Scandinavian Immigrants to the Pacific Northwest. LC 93-22999. (Illus.). 344p. 1993. 24.95 (*0-295-97288-2*) U of Wash Pr.

— Practical Design & Evaluation of Biomedical Research. Date not set. text. write for info. (*0-397-51660-6*) Lppncott W & W.

— Research & Documentation. 5th ed. 88p. 1998. pap. 7.80 (*0-13-081627-2*) P-H.

Rasmussen, A. W. The Last Chapter. 288p. 1973. mass mkt. 5.99 (*0-88368-021-1*) Whitaker Hse.

Rasmussen, Ann M. Mothers & Daughters in Medieval German Literature. LC 96-19775. 304p. 1996. text 45.00 (*0-8156-2709-2*, RAMD); pap. text 17.95 (*0-8156-0389-4*, RAMDP) Syracuse U Pr.

***Rasmussen, Anne & Nemiroff, Marc.** The Very Lonely Bathtub. LC 99-36790. (Illus.). 32p. (J). (ps-2). 1999. 14.23 (*1-55798-607-X*, 441-6070, Magination Press) Am Psychol.

Rasmussen, Anne & Rasmussen, Matt. Going Places: Adventures in Listening & Thinking. LC 98-90338. (Illus.). 150p. 1998. pap. 14.95 (*0-936110-21-X*, 056) Tin Man Pr.

Rasmussen, Anne K., jt. auth. see Lornell.

Rasmussen, Anne M., tr. see Willumsen, Dorrit.

Rasmussen, B. & Caratti, G. Wind Energy No. 2: Proceedings of the Second Contractor's Meeting, Brussels, November 23-24, 1987, Vol. 2. xiv, 420p. 1988. text 218.00 (*3-7186-4843-1*) Gordon & Breach.

Rasmussen, Barbara. Absentee Landowning & Exploitation in West Virginia, 1760-1920. LC 94-5096. 232p. 1994. 32.50 (*0-8131-1880-8*) U Pr of Ky.

Rasmussen, Bill. Sports Junkies Rejoice! The Birth of ESPN. 256p. 1983. 14.95 (*0-318-00106-3*) QV Pub.

Rasmussen, Brian. Managed Care Survival Manual: The Rehabilitation Therapist's Guide to Capitation & Per-Case Payment. 122p. (Orig.). 1996. pap. 69.95 (*1-887759-02-6*, P-118) Am Phys Therapy Assn.

— Reimbursement Manual for Medical Equipment in Managed Care. LC 97-16282. 1997. 159.00 (*0-8342-0868-7*, S440) Aspen Pub.

Rasmussen, C. A. History of Goodhue County. (Illus.). 336p. 1997. reprint ed. lib. bdg. 39.00 (*0-8328-6803-5*) Higginson Bk Co.

— History of Goodhue County. (Illus.). 336p. 1999. reprint ed. lib. bdg. 39.50 (*0-8328-9790-6*) Higginson Bk Co.

Rasmussen, C. E., jt. auth. see Kozura, J. U.

Rasmussen, Carl G. The NIV Atlas of the Bible. 256p. 1989. 49.99 (*0-310-25160-5*) Zondervan.

Rasmussen, Cecilia. Curbside L. A. An Offbeat Guide to the City of Angels. (Illus.). 224p. 1996. pap. 16.95 (*1-883792-13-4*, Pub. by LA Times) Sunbelt Pubns.

— L. A. Unconventional: The Men & Women Who Did L. A. Their Way. (Illus.). 168p. 1998. 29.95 (*1-883792-48-7*) LA Times.

Rasmussen, Charles & Tilman, Rick. Jacques Loeb: His Science & Social Activism & Their Philosophical Foundations. LC 95-79390. (Memoirs Ser.: No. 229). 260p. 1999. 20.00 (*0-87169-229-5*, M229-rac) Am Philos.

Rasmussen, Charlie O. Where the River Is Wide: Pahquahwong & the Chippewa Flowage. LC 98-86693. (Illus.). 72p. 1998. pap. 12.00 (*0-9665820-0-4*) Grt Lake Indian Fish.

Rasmussen, Christian A. History of Red Wing. (Illus.). 296p. 1999. reprint ed. lib. bdg. 45.00 (*0-8328-9791-4*) Higginson Bk Co.

Rasmussen, D. M. Symbol & Interpretation. 107p. 1975. pap. text 62.50 (*90-247-1579-2*) Kluwer Academic.

Rasmussen, D. Tab & Schopf, eds. The Origin & Evolution of Humans & Humanness. LC 93-6741. 160p. 1993. pap. text 37.50 (*0-86720-857-0*) Jones & Bartlett.

***Rasmussen, David, ed.** Proceedings of the Twentieth World Congress of Philosophy Vol. XI: Social & Political Philosophy. LC 99-66878. 250p. (C). 2000. 45.00 (*1-889680-15-X*) Philos Document.

Rasmussen, David, ed. Universalism vs. Communitarianism: Contemporary Debates in Ethics. 308p. 1990. 36.00 (*0-262-18140-1*); pap. text 18.00 (*0-262-68063-7*) MIT Pr.

Rasmussen, David, jt. auth. see Rasmussen, Steven.

Rasmussen, David, jt. ed. see Bernauer, James W.

Rasmussen, David, jt. ed. see Kemp, T. Peter.

Rasmussen, David M., ed. The Handbook of Critical Theory. LC 95-49861. 500p. (C). 1996. text 82.95 (*0-631-18379-5*) Blackwell Pubs.

— The Handbook of Critical Theory. 432p. (C). 1999. pap. 29.95 (*0-631-18381-7*) Blackwell Pubs.

Rasmussen, David M., jt. ed. see Deflem, Mathieu.

Rasmussen, David W. Agriculture in the U. S. A Documentary History, Vol. 2. (Documentary Reference Collections). 1977. lib. bdg. 95.00 (*0-313-20149-8*, RAAG2, Greenwood Pr) Greenwood.

— Agriculture in the U. S. A Documentary History, Vol. 3. (Documentary Reference Collections). 1977. lib. bdg. 95.00 (*0-313-20150-1*, RAAG3, Greenwood Pr) Greenwood.

— Agriculture in the U. S. A Documentary History, Vol. 4. (Documentary Reference Collections). 1977. lib. bdg. 95.00 (*0-313-20151-X*, RAAG4, Greenwood Pr) Greenwood.

— Agriculture in the United States: A Documentary History, Vol. 1. 1977. lib. bdg. 95.00 (*0-313-20148-X*, RAAG1, Greenwood Pr) Greenwood.

Rasmussen, David W. & Benson, Bruce L. The Economic Anatomy of a Drug War: Criminal Justice in the Commons. 280p. (C). 1994. pap. text 26.95 (*0-8476-7910-1*); lib. bdg. 66.00 (*0-8476-7909-8*) Rowman.

Rasmussen, David W., jt. auth. see Benson, Bruce L.

Rasmussen, Dennis. Poetry & Truth. LC 74-75364. (De Proprietatibus Litterarum, Ser. Minor: No. 20). 123p. 1974. pap. text 20.80 (*90-279-3462-2*) Mouton.

***Rasmussen, Dixie.** Varney's Midwife. (Illus.). 256p. (C). 2000. pap. text, student ed. 37.50 (*0-7637-1082-2*) JB Pubns.

Rasmussen, Donald P. Doing Something for Someone Else: A History of the Wisconsin Lions. Goc, Michael J., ed. 288p. 1995. 25.00 (*0-938627-27-9*) New Past Pr.

Rasmussen, Douglas & Den Uyl, Douglas. Liberty & Nature: An Aristotelian Defense of Order. LC 90-20965. 284p. (C). 1991. 49.95 (*0-8126-9119-9*) Open Court.

Rasmussen, Douglas & Sterba, James. Catholic Bishops & the Economy: A Dialog. 150p. 1987. 34.95 (*0-912051-15-9*); pap. 21.95 (*0-912051-16-7*) Transaction Pubs.

***Rasmussen, Douglas B. & Den Uyl, Douglas J.** Liberalism Defended: The Challenge of Post-Modernity. LC 97-38258. (Shaftesbury Papers: Vol. 9). 96p. (C). 1998. pap. 15.00 (*1-85898-557-9*) E Elgar.

Rasmussen, Douglas B., jt. ed. see Machan, Tibor R.

Rasmussen, Douglas B., jt. intro. see Den Uyl, Douglas J.

Rasmussen, Ellis T. A Latter-Day Saint Commentary on the Old Testament. LC 93-47675. (Illus.). 718p. 1994. 25.95 (*0-87579-712-1*) Deseret Bk.

Rasmussen, Emil F. The Key of Faith. 80p. 1997. pap. write for info. (*1-57579-058-0*) Pine Hill Pr.

***Rasmussen, Emil F.** The Man Who Shot Dan McGrew. LC 99-91970. 2000. 25.00 (*0-7388-1450-4*); pap. 18.00 (*0-7388-1451-2*) Xlibris Corp.

Rasmussen, Eric. A Textual Companion to Doctor Faustus. LC 93-18696. (Revels Plays Companion Library). 1994. text 79.95 (*0-7190-1562-6*) Manchester Univ Pr.

Rasmussen, Eric, jt. ed. see Bevington, David M.

Rasmussen, Eric, ed. see Marlowe, Christopher.

Rasmussen, Erik. Complementarity & Political Science: An Essay on Fundamentals of Political Science Theory & Research Strategy. 137p. (Orig.). 1987. pap. 37.50 (*87-7492-628-4*, Pub. by Odense Universitets Forlag) Coronet Bks.

Rasmussen, Gary. How to Buy Telephone Equipment in the Secondary Market. 1991. 19.95 (*0-936648-58-9*) Telecom Bks.

Rasmussen, Greg. Kayaking in Paradise: Journeys from Alaska Through the Inside Passage. (Illus.). 120p. 1997. text 29.95 (*1-55110-633-7*) Whitecap Bks.

Rasmussen, Greta. Brain Stations: A Center Approach to Thinking Skills. (Illus.). 112p. (Orig.). 1989. pap., teacher ed. 11.95 (*0-936110-07-4*) Tin Man Pr.

— The Great Unbored Blackboard Book. LC 85-51757. 56p. (Orig.). (J). (gr. 2-6). 1985. pap. 6.95 (*0-936110-05-8*) Tin Man Pr.

— The Great Unbored Bulletin Board Book. LC 80-52305. (Illus.). 56p. (Orig.). (J). (gr. 2-6). 1984. pap. 6.95 (*0-936110-01-5*) Tin Man Pr.

— The Great Unbored Bulletin Board Book, Book II. LC 80-52305. (Illus.). (Orig.). (J). (gr. 2-6). 1984. pap. 6.95 (*0-936110-04-X*) Tin Man Pr.

— Is It Friday Already? Learning Centers That Work. LC 79-92710. (Illus.). 230p. (Orig.). (J). (gr. 2-6). 1980. pap. 16.95 (*0-936110-00-7*) Tin Man Pr.

— Nifty Fifty: Five Hundred Thinking Challenges about 50 Familiar Things. LC 87-51619. (Illus.). 112p. 1988. pap. 11.95 (*0-936110-06-6*) Tin Man Pr.

— OPQ: Offbeat Adventures with the Alphabet. rev. ed. LC 81-82798. (Illus.). 64p. (Orig.). (J). (gr. 2-6). 1994. pap. 8.95 (*0-936110-03-1*) Tin Man Pr.

— Play by the Rules: Creative Practice in Direction-Following. LC 89-51969. (Illus.). 112p. 1990. pap. 11.95 (*0-936110-09-0*) Tin Man Pr.

— Waiting for Lunch. LC 81-82797. (Illus.). 64p. (Orig.). (J). (gr. 2-6). 1981. pap. 8.95 (*0-936110-02-3*) Tin Man Pr.

Rasmussen, Greta & Rasmussen, Ted. Are They Thinking? A Thinking - Skills Program for the Elementary Grades. LC 95-62182. (Illus.). 320p. 1996. pap. 21.95 (*0-936110-18-X*, 053) Tin Man Pr.

— Ideas to Go: Fifty Ready-to-Use Thinking Challenges. LC 92-80381. (Illus.). 112p. 1992. pap. 11.95 (*0-936110-14-7*) Tin Man Pr.

— Just Write! Strategies to Build Writing Skill & Confidence. (Illus.). 112p. (gr. 2-6). 1999. pap. 11.95 (*0-936110-22-8*) Tin Man Pr.

— Letter Getters: For Language Development & Thinking Fun. LC 98-90339. (Illus.). 112p. 1998. pap. 11.95 (*0-936110-20-1*; 055) Tin Man Pr.

— Loosen Up! Quick Activities to Build Confidence & Creativity. (Illus.). 64p. (Orig.). (J). (gr. 2-6). 1997. pap. 8.95 (*0-936110-19-8*) Tin Man Pr.

— Smart Snips: Hands-on Adventures in Thinking, Reading & Direction-Following. 112p. 1993. pap. 11.95 (*0-936110-15-5*) Tin Man Pr.

— T Is for Think: Thinking Fun with the Alphabet. LC 94-61645. (Illus.). 64p. 1995. pap. 8.95 (*0-936110-17-1*) Tin Man Pr.

— WakerUppers: A Spirited Collection of Thinking Activities. LC 93-95045. (Illus.). 112p. 1994. pap. 11.95 (*0-936110-16-3*) Tin Man Pr.

Rasmussen, H. On Law & Policy in the European Court of Justice. 1986. lib. bdg. 245.50 (*90-247-3217-4*) Kluwer Academic.

Rasmussen, Hanne N. Terrestrial Orchids: From Seed to Mycotrophic Plant. (Illus.). 456p. (C). 1995. text 74.95 (*0-521-45165-5*) Cambridge U Pr.

***Rasmussen, Hans Korno.** No Entry: Immigration Policy in Europe. LC 98-106367. 1999. 32.00 (*87-16-13358-7*) Mksgaard.

Rasmussen, Henry. D-Day Plus Fifty Years: The Normandy Beaches Revisited. 205p. 1997. 100.00 (*1-86227-004-X*, Pub. by Spellmnt Pubs) St Mut.

Rasmussen, Henry R., photos by. D-Day Plus Fifty Years: The Normandy Beaches Revisited. (Illus.). 192p. 1994. 39.95 (*1-879301-05-9*) Top Ten Pub.

— D-Day plus Fifty Years: The Normandy Beaches Revisited. (Illus.). 192p. 1994. 39.95 (*1-879301-06-7*) Top Ten Pub.

— Ferrari: Salute to the Spyder. (Top Ten Ser.). (Illus.). 132p. 1992. 29.95 (*1-879301-00-8*) Top Ten Pub.

— Porsche: Six Cylinder Supercars. (Top Ten Ser.). (Illus.). 132p. 1992. 29.95 (*1-879301-02-4*) Top Ten Pub.

— Porsche 356 & 550: A Pictorial History. (Illus.). 160p. 1992. 29.95 (*1-879301-03-2*) Top Ten Pub.

***Rasmussen, Hjalte.** European Community Case Law: Summaries of Leading E. C. Court Cases. (Studies in Economics & Management). 1999. 41.00 (*87-16-13221-1*) Mksgaard.

Rasmussen, Howard. Cell Communication in Health & Disease: Readings from Scientific American. (Scientific American Reader Ser.). (Illus.). 144p. (C). 1991. pap. text 16.95 (*0-7167-2224-0*) W H Freeman.

Rasmussen, J. Lewis & Oakley, Robert B. Conflict Resolution in the Middle East: Simulating a Diplomatic Negotiation Between Israel & Syria. LC 92-30410. 1992. pap. text 6.95 (*1-878379-19-4*) US Inst Peace.

Rasmussen, J. Lewis, jt. auth. see Zartman, I. William.

Rasmussen, James, ed. see Cave, George A.

Rasmussen, Jane. Musical Taste As a Religious Question in Nineteenth Century America: The Development of Episcopal Church Hymnody. LC 86-12774. (Studies in American Religion: Vol. 20). 632p. 1986. lib. bdg. 129.95 (*0-88946-664-5*) E Mellen.

Rasmussen, Janet E. New Land, New Lives: Scandinavian Immigrants to the Pacific Northwest. LC 93-22999. (Illus.). 334p. 1998. pap. text 12.95 (*0-295-97711-6*) U of Wash Pr.

Rasmussen, Jens, et al, eds. Distributed Decision Making: Cognitive Models for Cooperative Work. LC 90-12462. (New Technologies & Work Ser.). 416p. 1991. 545.00 (*0-471-92828-3*) Wiley.

Rasmussen, Jens, et al, eds. New Technology & Human Error. fac. ed. LC 86-5607. (New Technologies & Work Ser.). 370p. 1987. reprint ed. pap. 114.70 (*0-7837-8271-3*, 204905200009) Bks Demand.

Rasmussen, Jens & Rouse, William B., eds. Human Detection & Diagnosis of System Failures. LC 81-8699. (NATO Conference Series III, Human Factors: Vol. 15). 726p. 1981. 125.00 (*0-306-40744-2*, Plenum Trade) Perseus Pubng.

Rasmussen, Jens & Zunde, Pranas, eds. Empirical Foundations of Information & Software Science, Vol. 3. LC 87-12275. (Illus.). 280p. 1987. 75.00 (*0-306-42585-8*, Plenum Trade) Perseus Pubng.

Rasmussen, Jens, et al. Cognitive Systems Engineering. (Wiley-Interscience Publication). 396p. 1994. 84.95 (*0-471-01198-3*) Wiley.

***Rasmussen, Jens E.** Selected Papers on Indo-European Linguistic: With a Selection on Comparative Eskimo, 2 vols. 720p. 1999. 70.00 (*87-7289-529-2*, Pub. by Mus Tusculanum) Paul & Co Pubs.

Rasmussen, Jewell J. History of Utah's First Century of Taxation & Public Debt: 1896-1995. 183p. (Orig.). 1996. pap. 15.00 (*0-942486-10-2*) Univ Utah.

Rasmussen, John H., tr. see Grane, Leif, ed.

Rasmussen, Jorg. The Robert Lehman Collection Vol. 10: Italian Majolica. 304p. (C). 1989. text 110.00 (*0-691-04073-7*, Pub. by Princeton U Pr) Cal Prin Full Svc.

Rasmussen, Jorgen S. The British Political Process: Concentrated Power vs. Accountability. 256p. (C). 1993. pap. text 31.00 (*0-534-20064-8*) Harcourt.

Rasmussen, Jorgen S. & Moses, Joel C. Major European Governments. 9th ed. LC 94-17290. 710p. (C). 1995. pap. text 75.00 (*0-534-22212-9*) Harcourt.

Rasmussen, K. B. The School Foundation Workbook. 1993. 72.00 (*1-56925-015-4*, TSFW) Capitol Publns.

Rasmussen, Kent R., ed. The Quotable Mark Twain. LC 97-43653. (Illus.). 416p. 1997. 25.00 (*0-8092-3088-7*, 308870, Contemporary Bks) NTC Contemp Pub Co.

— The Quotable Mark Twain. LC 97-43653. (Illus.). 416p. 1998. pap. 16.95 (*0-8092-2987-0*, 298700, Contemporary Bks) NTC Contemp Pub Co.

Rasmussen, Knud. Alaskan Eskomo Words. 1998. reprint ed. lib. bdg. 99.00 (*0-7812-4787-X*) Rprt Serv.

— Intellectual Culture of the Copper Eskimos. 350p. 1998. reprint ed. lib. bdg. 90.00 (*0-7812-4789-6*) Rprt Serv.

— Netsilk Eskimos. 1998. reprint ed. lib. bdg. 99.00 (*0-7812-4788-8*) Rprt Serv.

Rasmussen, Knud, jt. auth. see Field, Edward.

Rasmussen, Knud J. Across Arctic America, Narrative of the Fifth Thule Expedition. LC 68-55213. 388p. 1970. reprint ed. lib. bdg. 35.00 (*0-8371-1489-6*, RAAA, Greenwood Pr) Greenwood.

— The Alaska Eskimos As Described in the Posthumous Notes of Knud Rasmussen. LC 76-21645. (Thule Expedition, 5th, 1921-1924 Ser.: Vol. 10, No. 3). 1976. reprint ed. 60.00 (*0-404-58327-X*) AMS Pr.

— Alaskan Eskimo Words. LC 76-21784. (Thule Expedition, 5th, 1921-1924 Ser.: Vol. 3 No. 4). reprint ed. 30.00 (*0-404-58314-8*) AMS Pr.

— Greenland by the Polar Sea. LC 74-5867. (Illus.). reprint ed. 67.50 (*0-404-11674-4*) AMS Pr.

— Intellectual Culture of the Copper Eskimos. LC 76-21675. (Thule Expedition, 5th, 1921-1924 Ser.: No. 9). (Illus.). reprint ed. 84.50 (*0-404-58324-5*) AMS Pr.

— Intellectual Culture of the Hudson Bay Eskimos, 3 vols., Set. (Fifth Thule Expedition Ser.: Vol. 7). reprint ed. 189.50 (*0-404-58320-2*) AMS Pr.

— Intellectual Culture of the Iglulik Eskimos. LC 76-22535. (Fifth Thule Expedition Ser.: Vol. 7, No. 1). reprint ed. 105.00 (*0-404-58321-0*) AMS Pr.

— Knud Rasmussen's Posthumous Notes on East Greenland Legends & Myths. Osterman, H., ed. LC 74-19913. reprint ed. 27.00 (*0-404-12296-5*) AMS Pr.

— Knud Rasmussen's Posthumous Notes on the Life & Doings of the East Greenlanders in Olden Times. Osterman, H., ed. LC 74-19915. (Illus.). reprint ed. 37.50 (*0-404-12297-3*) AMS Pr.

— The Mackenzie Eskimos. LC 76-21643. (Thule Expedition, 5th, 1921-1924 Ser.: Vol. 10, No. 2). reprint ed. 42.50 (*0-404-58326-1*) AMS Pr.

— The Netsilik Eskimos. LC 76-21685. (Thule Expedition, 5th, 1921-1924 Ser.: No. 8, Pts. 1-2). reprint ed. 105.00 (*0-404-58323-7*) AMS Pr.

— Observations on the Intellectual Culture of the Caribou Eskimos. LC 76-22536. (Fifth Thule Expedition Ser.: Vol. 7, No. 2 & No. 3). reprint ed. write for info. (*0-404-58322-9*) AMS Pr.

— The People of the Polar North: A Record . . . Herring, G., ed. LC 74-5868. (Illus.). reprint ed. 74.50 (*0-404-11675-2*) AMS Pr.

Rasmussen, Larry L. Earth Community, Earth Ethics. LC 96-26923. 376p. 1998. pap. 20.00 (*1-57075-186-2*) Orbis Bks.

— Moral Fragments & Moral Community: A Proposal for Church in Society. LC 93-18155. (Fry Lectureship Ser.). 176p. 1993. pap. 17.00 (*0-8006-2757-1*, 1-2757, Fortress Pr) Augsburg Fortress.

Rasmussen, Larry L., ed. Reinhold Niebuhr: Theologian of Public Life. LC 91-14239. (Making of Modern Theology Ser.). 312p. 1991. pap. 20.00 (*0-8006-3407-1*, 1-3407) Augsburg Fortress.

Rasmussen, Larry L., jt. auth. see Birch, Bruce C.

Rasmussen, Larry L., jt. auth. see Maguire, Daniel C.

Rasmussen, Lauge & Rauner, Felix, compiled by. Industrial Cultures & Production: Understanding Competitiveness. LC 96-3517. 229p. 1996. pap. 74.95 (*3-540-76029-6*) Spr-Verlag.

Rasmussen, Linda J. Tribal Writes: The Correspondence Guide for Native Americans. 2nd ed. LC 95-68649. vii, 196p. (Orig.). 1995. reprint ed. pap. 22.95 (*0-9657905-0-9*) Native Amer Path.

Rasmussen, Lissi. Christian & Muslim Relations in Africa: The Cases of Northern Nigeria & Tanzania Compared. 200p. 1993. text 59.50 (*1-85043-641-X*) I B T.

Rasmussen, Lore. Miquon Math Lab Series: Complete Home School. rev. ed. Incl. Blue Book. 1977. pap. text 5.95 (*0-913684-52-X*); First Grade Diary. Hightower, Robert. 218p. 1977. 5.95 (*0-913684-67-8*); Green Book. 1977. pap. text 5.95 (*0-913684-53-8*); Lab Sheet Annotations. Rasmussen, Peter & Hightower, Robert. 372p. 1977. 13.95 (*0-913684-64-3*); Notes to Teachers. 53p. 1977. 3.95 (*0-913684-62-7*); Orange Book. 1977. pap. text 5.95 (*0-913684-50-3*); Purple Book. 1977. pap. text 5.95 (*0-913684-55-4*); Red Book. 1977. pap. text 5.95 (*0-913684-51-1*); Yellow Book. 1977. pap. text 5.95 (*0-913684-54-6*); (J). (gr. 1-4). 1977. 53.95 (*1-55953-195-9*) Key Curr Pr.

Rasmussen, Louis J. California Wagon Train Lists, Vol. 1. LC 94-67422. (Ship, Rail & Wagon Train Ser.). 400p. 1994. 29.95 (*0-911792-79-1*) SF Hist Records.

— San Francisco Ship Passenger Lists (1850-1864), Vol. I. LC 78-60799. (Illus.). 289p. 1978. reprint ed. 27.50 (*0-8063-0823-0*) Clearfield Co.

Rasmussen, Lucinda A., jt. auth. see Burton, Jan E.

Rasmussen, Margaret, ed. see Bain, Winifred E.

Rasmussen, Margaret, ed. see Smith, Agnes.

Rasmussen, Matt, jt. auth. see Rasmussen, Anne.

Rasmussen, Maurice. Hypersonic Flow. 639p. 1994. 140.00 (*0-471-51102-1*) Wiley.

Rasmussen, Mike & Gilbert, Tammy H. Beat the Auto Dealers at Their Own Game. LC 98-106537. (Illus.). 90p. (Orig.). 1997. pap. 9.95 (*0-9639984-8-X*) Century Creations.

Rasmussen, Nicolas. Picture Control: The Electron Microscope & the Transformation of Biology in America, 1940-1960. LC 97-1230. (Writing Science Ser.). 424p. 1997. 55.00 (*0-8047-2837-2*) Stanford U Pr.

***Rasmussen, Nicolas.** Picture Control: The Electron Microscope & the Transformation of Biology in America, 1940-1960. 1999. 24.95 (*0-8047-3850-5*) Stanford U Pr.

***Rasmussen, Nils & Eichorn, Christopher J.** Budgeting: Technology, Trends, Software Selection & Implementation. 256p. 2000. 49.95 (*0-471-39207-3*) Wiley.

Rasmussen, Nils, jt. auth. see Schoyen, Christian.

Rasmussen, Norman C., jt. auth. see Oldenberg, Otto.

Rasmussen, P., jt. auth. see Macedo, E. A.

Rasmussen, Paul. Massage Parlor Prostitution. 163p. text. write for info. (*0-8290-1029-7*) Irvington.

***Rasmussen, Peter.** SEC Regulation of Corporate Takeovers. 416p. 2000. pap. text 100.00 (*0-8080-0495-6*) CCH INC.

Rasmussen, Peter, jt. auth. see King, Julie.

Rasmussen, Peter, ed. see Suppes, Patrick C.

Rasmussen, R. Kent. Farewell to Jim Crow: The Rise & Fall of Segregation in America. LC 96-48329. (Library of African-American History Ser.). 176p. (YA). (gr. 7-12). 1997. 19.95 (*0-8160-3248-3*) Facts on File.

— Mark Twain A to Z: The Essential Reference to His Life & Writings. LC 94-39156. (Illus.). 512p. 1995. 45.00 (*0-8160-2845-1*) Facts on File.

— Mark Twain A to Z: The Essential Reference to His Life & Writings. LC 96-26826. (Illus.). 576p. 1996. reprint ed. pap. 21.50 (*0-19-511028-5*) OUP.

— Modern African Political Leaders. LC 97-31162. (Global Profiles Ser.). (Illus.). 130p. (J). (gr. 5-12). 1998. 19.95 (*0-8160-3277-7*) Facts on File.

Rasmussen, R. Kent, ed. The African American Encyclopedia, 10 vols., Set. 2nd rev. ed. (Illus.). 3000p. lib. bdg. 459.95 (*1-76147-208-9*) Marshall Cavendish.

Rasmussen, R. Kent, ed. Mark Twain's Book for Bad Boys & Girls. LC 95-32766. (Illus.). 192p. 1995. 12.95 (*0-8092-3398-3*, 339830, Contemporary Bks) NTC Contemp Pub Co.

Rasmussen, R. Kent & Rubert, Steven C. Historical Dictionary of Zimbabwe. 2nd ed. LC 90-45366. (African Historical Dictionaries Ser.: No. 46). (Illus.). 542p. 1990. 58.00 (*0-8108-2337-3*) Scarecrow.

Rasmussen, R. Kent, jt. auth. see Rubert, Steven C.

Rasmussen, R. Kent, ed. see Schuyler, George S.

Rasmussen, Randy. Children of the Night: The Six Archetypal Characters of Classic Horror Films. LC 97-18383. 277p. 1998. lib. bdg. 38.50 (*0-7864-0337-3*) McFarland & Co.

Rasmussen, Ritva. Ritva's Fairies & Trolls. (Illus.). 1996. pap. 10.95 (*1-883675-16-2*, 116) J Shaw Studio.

— Ritva's Fairyland. (Illus.). 1995. pap. 10.95 (*1-883675-10-3*, 110) J Shaw Studio.

— Ritva's Winter Book. (Illus.). 1997. pap. 10.95 (*1-883675-21-9*, 121) J Shaw Studio.

Rasmussen, Robert. Imagine Meeting Him: Soul-Stirring Encounters with the Son of God. LC 97-36551. (From Casual Acquaintance to Devoted Friend Ser.). 1998. pap. 12.99 (*1-57673-251-7*) Multnomah Pubs.

— Mountain Biking the Coast Range Guide 11: Orange County & Cleveland National Forest. 2nd ed. 1995. pap. 11.95 (*0-938665-37-5*) Fine Edge Prods.

— Safe in His Sanctuary: An Invitation to the Wealth, Warmth & Wonder of Christ. LC 99-13513. 1999. pap. 12.99 (*1-57673-408-0*) Multnomah Pubs.

Rasmussen, Robert R., tr. see Nentvig, Juan.

Rasmussen, Roderick C. Paw Paw Lake, Michigan: A 100 Year Resort History, 1890's-1990's. LC 94-65459. 144p. (Orig.). 1994. pap. 16.70 (*0-9640093-1-5*) SW Mich Pubns.

Rasmussen, Roderick L. A History of Little Paw Paw Lake & Deer Forest, Michigan. LC 98-61721. 88p. 1999. pap. 15.10 (*0-9640093-4-X*) SW Mich Pubns.

— Paw Paw Lake, Michigan: A 100 Year Resort History, 1890's-1990's. LC 94-65459. 144p. (Orig.). 1994. 28.40 (*0-9640093-0-7*) SW Mich Pubns.

— Paw Paw Lake, Michigan: Images of a Lake. LC 95-72991. 128p. (Orig.). 1996. 28.30 (*0-9640093-2-3*); pap. 17.45 (*0-9640093-3-1*) SW Mich Pubns.

Rasmussen, Roy H., ed. Golfers Travel Guide: Great Lakes Edition, Vol. 1, No. 1. 208p. (Orig.). 1987. pap. 12.95 (*0-940703-00-9*) RSG Pub MI.

— Illinois Golfers Travel Guide. 34p. (Orig.). 1992. pap. 6.95 (*0-940703-04-1*) RSG Pub MI.

— Indiana Golfers Travel Guide. 33p. (Orig.). 1992. pap. 6.95 (*0-940703-03-3*) RSG Pub MI.

— Michigan Golfers Travel Guide. 36p. (Orig.). 1992. pap. 6.95 (*0-940703-01-7*) RSG Pub MI.

— Minnesota - Wisconsin Golfers Travel Guide. 40p. (Orig.). 1992. pap. 6.95 (*0-940703-05-X*) RSG Pub MI.

— Ohio Golfers Travel Guide. 35p. (Orig.). 1992. pap. 6.95 (*0-940703-02-5*) RSG Pub MI.

***Rasmussen, Sandra.** Addiction Treatment: Theory & Practice. LC 00-8183. 2000. write for info. (*0-7619-0843-9*) Sage.

Rasmussen, Shelley. An Introduction to Statistics with Data Analysis. 707p. (C). 1992. text 69.95 (*0-534-13578-1*) Wadsworth Pub.

Rasmussen, Sheryl, ed. Pacific Northwest Bookfinder: A Directory of Used Bookshops & Bookdealers in Alaska, British Columbia, Idaho, Oregon & Washington. 6th rev. ed. (Illus.). 80p. (Orig.). 1996. 5.50 (*0-9652864-0-1*) Antiquarian Direct.

Rasmussen, Steen E. Experiencing Architecture. 2nd ed. (Illus.). 246p. 1964. pap. text 12.50 (*0-262-68002-5*) MIT Pr.

— Towns & Buildings. 1969. pap. text 20.00 (*0-262-68011-4*) MIT Pr.

Rasmussen, Steven. Key to Fractions Reproducible Tests. rev. ed. 32p. 1991. pap. 9.95 (*0-913684-96-1*) Key Curr Pr.

— Key to Fractions Series. Incl. Key to Fractions Answer Book. 37p. 1980. pap. 3.25 (*0-913684-97-X*); Bk. 1. Fraction Concepts. 37p. 1980. 2.25 (*0-913684-91-0*); Bk. 2. Multiplying & Dividing. 37p. 1980. 2.25 (*0-913684-92-9*); Bk. 3. Adding & Subtracting. 37p. 1980. 2.25 (*0-913684-93-7*); Bk. 4. Mixed Numbers. 37p. 1980. 2.25 (*0-913684-94-5*); (gr. 4-12). 1980. 12.25 (*1-55953-153-3*) Key Curr Pr.

Rasmussen, Steven & Rasmussen, David. Key to Percents Reproducible Tests. Incl. Bk. 1. Percent Concepts. 45p. 1988. pap. text 2.25 (*0-913684-57-0*); Bk. 2. Percents & Fractions. 45p. 1988. pap. text 2.25 (*0-913684-58-9*); Bk. 3. Answers & Notes. 45p. 1988. 3.25 (*0-913684-61-9*); (J). (gr. 4-12). 1988. 9.95 (*0-913684-95-3*) Key Curr Pr.

— Percents & Decimals, Bk. 3. 45p. 1988. pap. text 2.25 (*0-913684-59-7*) Key Curr Pr.

Rasmussen, Steven & Rosekrans, Spreck. Key to Decimals Reproducible Tests. 32p. 1985. pap. 9.95 (*0-913684-26-0*) Key Curr Pr.

Rasmussen, Steven & Rosekraus, Spreck. Key to Decimals Series. Incl. Answers & Notes. 45p. 1985. pap. 3.25 (*0-913684-25-2*); Bk. 1. Decimal Concepts. 45p. 1985. pap. 2.25 (*0-913684-21-X*); Bk. 2. Adding, Subtracting, Multiplying. 45p. 1985. pap. 2.25 (*0-913684-22-8*); Bk. 3. Dividing. 45p. 1985. pap. 2.25 (*0-913684-23-6*); Bk. 4. Using Decimals. 45p. 1985. pap. 2.25 (*0-913684-24-4*); (gr. 4-12). 1985. 10.80 (*1-55953-152-5*) Key Curr Pr.

Rasmussen, Steven J., jt. auth. see Houpis, Constantine S.

Rasmussen, Susan J. The Poetics & Politics of Tuareg Aging: Life Course & Personal Destiny in Niger. LC 96-43794. 208p. 1997. lib. bdg. 32.00 (*0-87580-220-6*) N Ill U Pr.

— Spirit Possession & Personhood among the Kel Ewey Tuareg. (Cambridge Studies in Social & Cultural Anthropology: No. 94). 193p. (C). 1995. text 54.95 (*0-521-47007-2*) Cambridge U Pr.

Rasmussen, Tarald. Inimici Ecclesiae, Das Ekklesiologische Feinbild in Luther's "Dictata Super Psalterium" (1513-1515) im Horizont der Theologischen Tradition. LC 89-37288. (Studies in Medieval & Reformation Thought: Vol. 44). (GER.). x, 242p. 1989. 94.50 (*90-04-08837-7*) Brill Academic Pubs.

Rasmussen, Ted, jt. auth. see Rasmussen, Greta.

Rasmussen, Theodore & Marino, Raul, Jr., eds. Functional Neurosurgery. fac. ed. LC 77-85871. (Illus.). 288p. pap. 89.30 (*0-7837-7178-9*, 204712100005) Bks Demand.

Rasmussen, Thomas H., jt. auth. see Peterson, Steven A.

Rasmussen, Tom. Bucchero Pottery from Southern Etruria. LC 78-13464. (Cambridge Classical Studies). (Illus.). 248p. 1979. text 65.00 (*0-521-22316-4*) Cambridge U Pr.

Rasmussen, Tom & Spivey, Nigel J., eds. Looking at Greek Vases. (Illus.). 300p. (C). 1991. pap. text 19.95 (*0-521-37679-3*) Cambridge U Pr.

Rasmussen, Tom, jt. auth. see Barker, Graeme.

Rasmussen, Tom, ed. see Nicholls, Richard.

Rasmussen, Wayne D. Agriculture in the United States: A Documentary History, 4 vols., Set. LC 74-9643. (Documentary Reference Collections). 1977. lib. bdg. 295.00 (*0-313-20147-1*, RAAG, Greenwood Pr) Greenwood.

— Taking the University to the People: Seventy-Five Years of Cooperative Extension. LC 88-37672. (Illus.). 310p. 1989. 41.95 (*0-8138-0419-1*) Iowa St U Pr.

Rasmussen, Wendy. Picture Me As Little Bo Peep & Other Nursery Rhymes. 8p. (Orig.). (J). (ps-2). 1999. bds. 6.99 (*1-57151-543-7*) Picture Me Bks.

— Picture Me As Yankee Doodle Dandy & Other Nursery Rhymes. 8p. (Orig.). (J). (ps-2). 1999. bds. 6.99 (*1-57151-544-5*) Picture Me Bks.

Rasmussen, Wendy & Rhinehart, Ric. Tea Basics: A Quick & Easy Guide. LC 98-28198. 208p. 1998. pap. 16.95 (*0-471-18518-3*) Wiley.

Rasmussen, William, jt. auth. see Kelly, James.

Rasmussen, William M. & Tilton, Robert S. George Washington: The Man Behind the Myths. LC 98-31010. (Illus.). 344p. 1999. pap. 24.95 (*0-8139-1900-2*) U Pr of Va.

Rasmussen, William M. S., jt. auth. see Kelly, James C.

Rasmussn, R. Post-Trib, Pre-Wrath Rapture. LC 96-92137. 1998. pap. 12.00 (*0-9651789-0-0*) Post-Trib Res.

Rasmusson, Arne. The Church As Polis: From Political Theology to Theological Politics. LC 94-45054. 418p. (C). 1996. text 18.95 (*0-268-00810-8*) U of Notre Dame Pr.

Rasmusson, Arne, et al. The Church As Polis: From Political Theology to Theological Politics as Exemplified by Jurgen Moltmann & Stanley Hauerwas. LC 94-45054. 1995. text 34.95 (*0-268-00809-4*) U of Notre Dame Pr.

Rasmusson, D. C. Barley. (Agronomy Monograph Ser.: No. 26). 522p. 1985. 40.00 (*0-89118-085-0*) Am Soc Agron.

Rasmusson, Rasmus, jt. auth. see Mbithi, Philip M.

***Rasnake, Eddie.** Following God Bible Study. 192p. 1999. pap., teacher ed. 21.99 (*0-89957-306-1*) AMG Pubs.

Rasnake, Roger N. Domination & Cultural Resistance: Authority & Power among Andean People. LC 87-35834. xi, 323p. (C). 1988. text 49.95 (*0-8223-0809-6*) Duke.

Rasnake, Sam. Necessary Motions: Poems. 72p. 1998. pap. 12.00 (*1-885912-10-2*) Sows Ear Pr.

— Religions of the Blood. 27p. 1998. pap. 7.95 (*0-944754-53-8*) Pudding Hse Pubns.

Rasneo, Mark, ed. see Subotnik, Rena F., et al.

Raso, Anne. Datebook Stars. (Starlog Celebrity Ser.: No. 9). 4.99 (*0-934551-55-3*) Starlog Grp Inc.

***Raso, Anne, ed.** Backstreet & Friends. (Starlog Celebrity Ser.: No. 14). 1999. pap. 4.99 (*0-934551-88-X*, Pub. by Starlog Grp Inc) Kable News Co Inc.

— Backstreet Boys. (Celebrity Ser.: No. 20). (J). 2000. pap. 4.99 (*0-88013-011-3*, Pub. by Starlog Grp Inc) Kable News Co Inc.

— Backstreet Boys. (Teen Girl Power Poster Special Ser.: No. 2). 2000. pap. 3.99 (*0-88013-026-1*, Pub. by Starlog Grp Inc) Kable News Co Inc.

— Backstreet Boys Fall Fling. (Celebrity Ser.: No. 28). 2000. pap. 4.99 (*0-88013-029-6*, Pub. by Starlog Grp Inc) Kable News Co Inc.

Raso, Anne, ed. Battle of the Boys. (Starlog Celebrity Ser.: No. 15). 1999. pap. 4.99 (*0-934551-90-1*, Pub. by Starlog Grp Inc) Kable News Co Inc.

— 'N Sync & Friends. (Starlog Celebrity Ser.: No. 16). 1999. pap. 4.99 (*0-934551-89-8*, Pub. by Starlog Grp Inc) Kable News Co Inc.

***Raso, Anne, ed.** N'Sync. (Celebrity Ser.: No. 22). 2000. pap. 4.99 (*0-88013-014-8*, Pub. by Starlog Grp Inc) Kable News Co Inc.

— N'Sync. (Teen Girl Power Poster Special Ser.: No. 1). 2000. pap. 3.99 (*0-88013-025-3*, Pub. by Starlog Grp Inc) Kable News Co Inc.

— N'Sync Back to School. (Celebrity Ser.: No. 27). 2000. pap. 4.99 (*0-88013-027-X*, Pub. by Starlog Grp Inc) Kable News Co Inc.

— Ricky Martin & Friends. (Starlog Celebrity Ser.: No. 13). 1999. pap. 4.99 (*0-934551-91-X*, Pub. by Starlog Grp Inc) Kable News Co Inc.

— Shockwave. (Celebrity Ser.: No. 17). 1999. pap. 4.99 (*0-934551-92-8*, Pub. by Starlog Grp Inc) Kable News Co Inc.

— Starlog Celebrity Series Presents Vol. 25: TV Cartoons. 2000. pap. 4.99 (*0-88013-018-0*, Pub. by Starlog Grp Inc) Kable News Co Inc.

— Starlog Celebrity Series Presents Vol. 26: Teen Divas, (C). 2000. pap. (*0-88013-024-5*) Starlog Grp Inc.

— Starlog Celebrity Series Presents Vol. 29: Backstreet Boys. 2000. pap. 4.99 (*0-88013-019-9*, Pub. by Starlog Grp Inc) Kable News Co Inc.

— Starlog Celebrity Series Presents Teen Love Match, Vol. 23. 2000. pap. 4.99 (*0-88013-016-4*, Pub. by Starlog Grp Inc) Kable News Co Inc.

— Teen Date Book. (Celebrity Ser.: No. 29). 2000. pap. 4.99 (*0-88013-012-1*, Pub. by Starlog Grp Inc) Kable News Co Inc.

Raso, Anne, ed. Teen Datebook. (Celebrity Ser.: Vol. 18). 1999. pap. 4.99 (*0-934551-83-9*, Pub. by Starlog Grp Inc) Kable News Co Inc.

***Raso, Anne & Walsh, Kimberly.** Backstage Pass: Just Justin. (Illus.). 48p. (J). (gr. 4-7). 2000. pap. 7.99 (*0-439-17450-3*) Scholastic Inc.

Raso, Anne M. Ricky Martin: A Scrapbook in Words & Pictures. LC 99-232440. 32p. 1999. pap. 7.95 (*0-440-22893-X*) Dell.

***Raso, Anne M.** Ricky Martin: A Scrapbook in Words & Pictures. 32p. 1999. pap. 7.95 (*0-440-22825-5*) Dell.

Raso, Jack. Alternative Healthcare: A Comprehensive Guide. LC 93-48260. 275p. (C). 1994. 28.95 (*0-87975-891-0*) Prometheus Bks.

Raso, Jack & Barrett, Stephen. Mystical Diets: Paranormal, Spiritual, & Occult Nutrition & Practices. LC 92-40828. (Consumer Health Ser.). 299p. 1993. 26.95 (*0-87975-761-2*) Prometheus Bks.

***Rasoloson, Janie.** Malagasy-English/English Malagasy Dictionary & Phrasebook. 180p. 2000. pap. 11.95 (*0-7818-0843-X*) Hippocrene Bks.

R

Rasool & Banks. Critical Thinking. (Freshman English/Advanced Writing Ser.). 1993. teacher ed. 21.50 (0-534-12819-X) Wadsworth Pub.

Rasool, Joan. Primer for Diversity in Middle & Secondary School Classrooms. LC 99-56808. (Education). 2000. pap. 52.95 (0-534-50847-2) Wadsworth Pub.

Rasool, Joan, et al. Critical Thinking: Reading & Writing in a Diverse World. 2nd ed. LC 95-23293. 1995. 32.50 (0-534-25692-9) Wadsworth Pub.

Rasool, S. I. Potential of Remote Sensing for the Study of Global Change: COSPAR Report to the International Council of Scientific Unions S. I. Rasool. (Advances in Space Research Ser.: Vol. 7). 1988. pap. 63.00 (0-08-036648-1, Pergamon Pr) Elsevier.

Rasooli, Jay M. & Allen, Cady H. Dr. Sa'eed of Iran: Kurdish Physician to Princes & Peasants, Nobles & Nomads. LC 57-13245. (Illus.). 192p. 1983. reprint ed. pap. 6.95 (0-87808-743-5) William Carey Lib.

***Rasor, Eugene L.** Arthur James Balfour, 1848-1930: Historiography & Annotated Bibliography, Vol. 22. LC 98-27676. (Bibliographies of British Statesmen Ser.: Vol. 22). 144p. 1998. lib. bdg. 65.00 (0-313-28877-1, Greenwood Pr) Greenwood.

Rasor, Eugene L. The Battle of Jutland: A Bibliography, 7. LC 91-24368. (Bibliographies of Battles & Leaders Ser.: No. 7). 192p. 1991. lib. bdg. 49.95 (0-313-28124-6, RJU, Greenwood Pr) Greenwood.

— British Naval History since Eighteen Fifteen: A Guide to Literature. LC 90-3310. (Military History Bibliographies Ser.: Vol. 13). 854p. 1990. text 35.00 (0-8240-7735-0, 1069) Garland.

— The China-Burma-India Campaign, 1931-1945: Historiography & Annotated Bibliography, 22. LC 97-49967. (Bibliographies of Battles & Leaders Ser.). 304p. 1998. lib. bdg. 75.00 (0-313-28872-0, Greenwood Pr) Greenwood.

— Earl Mountbatten of Burma, 1900-1979: Historiography & Annotated Bibliography, 21. LC 97-49964. (Bibliographies of British Statesmen Ser.: Vol. 21). 160p. 1998. lib. bdg. 65.00 (0-313-28876-3, Greenwood Pr) Greenwood.

— The Falklands-Malvinas Campaign: A Bibliography, 6. LC 91-24365. (Bibliographies of Battles & Leaders Ser.: No. 6). 216p. 1991. lib. bdg. 59.95 (0-313-28151-3, RFK, Greenwood Pr) Greenwood.

— The Solomon Islands Campaign, Guadalcanal to Rabaul: Historiography & Annotated Bibliography, 20. LC 96-41333. (Bibliographies of Battles & Leaders Ser.). 168p. 1997. lib. bdg. 65.00 (0-313-30059-3) Greenwood.

— The Southwest Pacific Campaign, 1941-1945: Historiography & Annotated Bibliography, 19. LC 96-5845. (Bibliographies of Battles & Leaders Ser.: No. 19). 304p. 1996. lib. bdg. 79.50 (0-313-28874-7, Greenwood Pr) Greenwood.

— The Spanish Armada of 1588: Historiography & Annotated Bibliography, 10. LC 92-31759. (Bibliographies of Battles & Leaders Ser.: No. 10). 295p. 1992. lib. bdg. 69.50 (0-313-28303-6, RXS, Greenwood Pr) Greenwood.

***Rasor, Eugene L.** Winston S. Churchill, 1874-1965: A Comprehensive Historiography & Annotated Bibliography, Vol. 6. annot. ed. LC 00-30883. (Bibliographies of World Leaders Ser.: Vol. 6). 2000. lib. bdg. write for info. (0-313-30546-3, Greenwood Pr) Greenwood.

Rasor, Eugene L., ed. General Douglas MacArthur, 1880-1964: Historiography & Annotated Bibliography, Vol. 12. LC 93-43711. (Bibliographies of Battles & Leaders Ser.: Vol. 12). 248p. 1994. lib. bdg. 69.50 (0-313-28873-9, Greenwood Pr) Greenwood.

Rasor, Paul B. Consumer Finance Law. 1985. teacher ed. write for info. (0-8205-0122-0) Bender.

Rasovsky, Yuri, jt. auth. see Adorjan, Carol.

Rasp, Barbara. The Lines of Light: With Prayers for the Heart. LC 95-60621. (Illus.). 128p. (Orig.). 1995. pap. 9.95 (0-9643006-6-4) Equalite Pr.

Rasp, Richard A. In Pictures Hawaii Volcanoes: The Continuing Story. LC 92-71531. (Illus.). 48p. 1992. pap. 7.95 (0-88714-069-6) KC Pubns.

— In Pictures Hawaii Volcanoes: The Continuing Story. Morales, Brigitte, tr. (GER., Illus.). 48p. 1992. pap. 8.95 (0-88714-730-5) KC Pubns.

— In Pictures Hawaii Volcanoes: The Continuing Story. Le Bras, Yvon, tr. (FRE., Illus.). 48p. 1992. pap. 8.95 (0-88714-731-3) KC Pubns.

— In Pictures Hawaii Volcanoes: The Continuing Story. Petzinger, Saori, tr. (JPN., Illus.). 48p. 1992. pap. 8.95 (0-88714-732-1) KC Pubns.

— In Pictures Hawaii Volcanoes: The Continuing Story. (KOR., Illus.). 48p. 1993. pap. 8.95 (0-88714-733-X) KC Pubns.

— In Pictures Hawaii Volcanoes: The Continuing Story. Mehta, Yufen L., tr. (CHI., Illus.). 48p. 1997. pap. 8.95 (0-88714-820-4) KC Pubns.

— Redwood: The Story Behind the Scenery. LC 88-80122. (Illus.). 54p. (Orig.). 1989. pap. 7.95 (0-88714-022-X) KC Pubns.

— Redwood: The Story Behind the Scenery. Morales, Brigitte, tr. (GER., Illus.). 54p. (Orig.). 1997. pap. 8.95 (0-88714-813-1) KC Pubns.

Raspa, Anthony. The Emotive Image: Jesuit Poetics in the English Renaissance. LC 83-502. 185p. 1983. reprint ed. pap. 57.40 (0-608-04107-6, 206483900011) Bks Demand.

Raspa, Anthony, ed. see Donne, John.

***Raspa, Dick & Wardrop, Daneen.** The Collaborative Imperative: Librarians & Faculty Working Together in the Information U. 168p. (C). 2000. pap. 24.00 (0-8389-8085-6) Assn Coll & Res Libs.

Raspa, Richard, jt. auth. see Mathias, Elizabeth.

Raspail, Jean. Blue Island. Leggatt, Jeremy, tr. from FRE. LC 90-49381. 208p. 1991. 17.95 (0-916515-99-0) Mercury Hse Inc.

— The Camp of the Saints. 313p. 1975. pap., student ed. 9.00 (0-936247-06-1) Amer Immigration.

— The Camp of the Saints. Shapiro, Norman R., tr. from FRE. 311p. 1994. pap. 12.95 (1-881780-07-4) Social Contract.

— The Camp of the Saints: The End of the White Race. 1984. lib. bdg. 250.00 (0-87700-584-2) Revisionist Pr.

Raspall de Cahue, Joana. Diccionari Practic de Sinonims Catalans: Mots i Frases. (CAT.). 640p. 1979. 24.95 (0-7859-9861-6) Fr & Eur.

Raspall de Cauhe, Joana, et al. Diccionari Usual de Sinonims Catalans: Mots i Frases. (CAT.). 545p. 1975. 29.95 (0-8288-5801-2, S50048) Fr & Eur.

Raspall Juanola, Joana. Diccionari d'Homonims i Paronims. (CAT.). 256p. 1988. 19.95 (0-7859-6233-6, 8475334334) Fr & Eur.

Raspanti, Celeste. I Never Saw Another Butterfly - Full. 1971. pap. 5.95 (0-87129-276-9, I22) Dramatic Pub.

— I Never Saw Another Butterfly - One Act. 1982. pap. 3.95 (0-87129-319-6, I33) Dramatic Pub.

— No Fading Star. 1979. pap. 3.50 (0-87129-250-5, N24) Dramatic Pub.

Raspberry, William. Looking Backward at Us. LC 91-21565. 1991. 20.00 (0-87805-535-5) U Pr of Miss.

Raspe, Erich R. Baron Munchausen. 3rd ed. Blow, David, ed. (European Classics). (Illus.). 267p. 1999. reprint ed. pap. 11.95 (1-873982-35-6, Pub. by Dedalus) Hippocrene Bks.

Raspe, G., et al, eds. Advances in the Biosciences. Incl. Vol. 2. Schering Symposium on Biodynamics & Mechanism of Action of Steroid Hormones, Berlin 1968. 364p. 1970. 105.00 (0-08-006942-8); Vol. 14. Schering Workshop on Prognostic Factors in Human Acute Leukemia. 520p. 1975. 100.00 (0-08-019621-7); write for info. (0-318-55130-6, Pub. by Pergamon Repr) Franklin.

Raspe, Rudolph E. Baron Munchausen. (Dedalus European Fiction Classics Ser.). (Illus.). 287p. 1989. pap. 11.95 (0-946626-28-6) Hippocrene Bks.

Rasper, Vladimir F. & Preston, Ken R., eds. The Extensigraph Handbook. LC 91-73488. (Illus.). 50p. 1991. 64.00 (0-913250-72-4) Am Assn Cereal Chem.

Raspler, Dan & Hill, Michael C., eds. Lobo's Greatest Hits. (Illus.). 176p. 1992. pap. 12.95 (1-56389-013-5) DC Comics.

Raspler, Dan, ed. see Dixon, C. & Grant, A.

Raspler, Dan, ed. see Grant, Alan.

Rasputin, Valentin. Farewell to Matyora: A Novel. 2nd ed. Bouis, Antonina W., tr. (European Classics Ser.). 227p. 1995. pap. 14.95 (0-8101-1329-5) Northwestern U Pr.

— Live & Remember. Bouis, Antonina W., tr. from RUS. 225p. 1992. reprint ed. pap. 15.95 (0-8101-1053-9) Northwestern U Pr.

— Siberia on Fire: Stories & Essays by Valentin Rasputin. Mikkelson, Gerald & Winchell, Margaret, trs. from RUS. 252p. 1989. 32.00 (0-87580-152-8); pap. 16.00 (0-87580-547-7) N Ill U Pr.

— Siberia, Siberia. Winchell, Margaret & Mikkelson, Gerald, trs. 380p. 1996. 40.00 (0-8101-1287-6) Northwestern U Pr.

— Siberia, Siberia. Winchell, Margaret & Mikkelson, Gerald, trs. (Illus.). 443p. 1997. pap. 17.95 (0-8101-1575-1) Northwestern U Pr.

Rasputin, pseud. Bridge over Troubled Waters. Kelsey, Avonelle, ed. (GER.). 207p. (Orig.). 1994. pap. 9.95 (0-9640610-0-7) Cheval Intl.

Rasputnis, Victor & Tartakosky, Anatole. PowerBuilder 4 Expert Solutions. (Illus.). 1000p. (Orig.). 1995. 60.00 (0-7897-0346-7) Que.

Rasquinha, J. Managerial Issues in the Reformed NHS. Malek, M. et al, eds. 280p. 1993. 175.95 (0-471-94033-X) Wiley.

Rass, Rebecca. The Fairy Tales of My Mind. LC 78-53828. (Illus.). 145p. (Orig.). 1978. 8.00 (0-931642-03-5); pap. 5.00 (0-931642-02-7) Lintel.

— Monarch Notes: Simone De Beauvoir's the Second Sex. 128p. 1988. pap. 4.50 (0-671-67126-X, Arco) Macmillan Gen Ref.

Rassais. Le Francais Depart-Arrivee. 3rd ed. (College French Ser.). (FRE.). (C). 1992. teacher ed. 19.95 (0-8384-3895-4) Heinle & Heinle.

Rassam, A. Yasmine. Women in the Domicile: The Treatment of Women's Work in International Law. LC 93-655022. (MacArthur Scholar Series, Occasional Paper: No. 24). 67p. (Orig.). 1994. pap. 4.00 (1-881157-26-1) In Ctr Global.

Rassam, Amal, jt. auth. see Bates, Daniel.

Rassam, Clive. Design & Corporate Success. 200p. 1995. 59.95 (0-566-07534-2, Pub. by Gower) Ashgate Pub Co.

Rassam, G. N. Multilingual Thesaurus of Geosciences. (ENG, FRE, GER, ITA & RUS.). 516p. 1988. 195.00 (0-8288-7952-4) Fr & Eur.

Rassel, Gary R., jt. auth. see O'Sullivan, Elizabethann.

Rassem, M., jt. ed. see Prat, E. H.

Rassi, Judith A. & McElroy, Margaret D., eds. The Education of Audiologists & Speech-Language Pathologists. LC 92-16758. 496p. 1992. text 49.50 (0-912752-30-0) York Pr.

Rassi, Z. El, see El Rassi, Z., ed.

Rassia, J. M. Lecture Notes on Mixed Type Partial Differential Equations. 152p. (C). 1990. text 43.00 (981-02-0275-X); pap. text 23.00 (981-02-0406-X) World Scientific Pub.

Rassias, G., jt. ed. see Stratopoulos, G.

Rassias, G. M. Differential Topology-Geometry & Related Fields. 376p. (C). 1985. 130.00 (0-7855-4990-0, Pub. by Collets) St Mut.

— The Mathematical Heritage of C. F. Gauss. 550p. (C). 1991. text 118.00 (981-02-0201-6) World Scientific Pub.

Rassias, G. M., ed. Morse Theory & Its Applications. 400p. (C). 1994. text 58.00 (9971-5-0977-6) World Scientific Pub.

Rassias, J. M. Counter-Examples in Differential Equations & Related Topics. 192p. 1991. text 48.00 (981-02-0460-4); pap. text 25.00 (981-02-0461-2) World Scientific Pub.

Rassias, J. M., ed. Geometry, Analysis & Mechanics. 388p. (C). 1995. text 95.00 (981-02-0757-3) World Scientific Pub.

Rassias, John. Mixed Type Equations. 312p. (C). 1986. 160.00 (0-7855-4980-3, Pub. by Collets) St Mut.

Rassias, John A. Le Francais: Depart-Arrivee. 3rd ed. (FRE.). (C). 1992. mass mkt. 57.95 (0-8384-3726-5) Heinle & Heinle.

Rassias, John H. Differential Geometry, Calculus of Variations & Their Applications: Calculus of Variations & Their Applications. (Lecture Notes in Pure & Applied Mathematics Ser.: Vol. 100). (Illus.). 544p. 1985. pap. text 170.00 (0-8247-7267-9) Dekker.

Rassias, John M., ed. Functional Analysis, Approximation Theory & Numerical Analysis. 500p. (C). 1994. text 114.00 (981-02-0737-9) World Scientific Pub.

Rassias, Themistocles M. Constantin Caratheodory: An International Tribute, 2 Vols. 1468p. 1991. text 301.00 (981-02-0544-9) World Scientific Pub.

— Inner Product Spaces & Applications. 1997. pap. 67.95 (0-582-31711-8, Pub. by Addison-Wesley) Longman.

— Topics in Mathematical Analysis. 992p. (C). 1989. pap. 55.00 (9971-5-0801-X); text 147.00 (9971-5-0666-1) World Scientific Pub.

***Rassias, Themistocles M., ed.** Complex Analysis in Several Variables. 195p. (C). 1999. pap. 65.00 (1-57485-043-1) Hadronic Pr Inc.

Rassias, Themistocles M., ed. Constantin Caratheodory: An International Tribute, 2 vols., Set. 1468p. (C). 1991. text 238.00 (0-685-58546-8) World Scientific Pub.

***Rassias, Themistocles M., ed.** New Approaches in Nonlinear Analysis. 240p. 1999. pap. write for info. (1-57485-042-3) Hadronic Pr Inc.

Rassias, Themistocles M., ed. Nonlinear Analysis. 572p. 1988. text 99.00 (9971-5-0140-6) World Scientific Pub.

***Rassias, Themistocles M., ed.** Nonlinear Mathematical Analysis & Applications. 320p. 1999. pap. 75.00 (1-57485-044-X) Hadronic Pr Inc.

Rassias, Themistocles M., ed. The Problem of Plateau: A Tribute to Jesse Douglas & Tibor Rado. 400p. (C). 1992. text 130.00 (981-02-0556-2) World Scientific Pub.

***Rassias, Themistocles M.** Approximation Theory & Applications: Collection of Original & Edited Articles in Advanced Mathematics. 200p. 1999. write for info. (1-57485-041-5) Hadronic Pr Inc.

Rassias, Themistocles M. & Prastaro, A. Geometry in Partial Differential Equations. 500p. 1994. text 121.00 (981-02-1407-3) World Scientific Pub.

Rassias, Themistocles M. & Srivastava, H. M. Analytic & Geometric Inequalities & Applications. LC 99-21369. (Mathematics & Its Applications Ser.). 1999. write for info. (0-7923-5690-X) Kluwer Academic.

Rassias, Themistocles M. & Srivastava, H. M., eds. Analysis, Geometry & Groups: A Riemann Legacy Volume. 712p. 1993. text 180.00 (0-911767-85-1); pap. text 120.00 (0-911767-59-2) Hadronic Pr Inc.

Rassias, Themistocles M. & Tabor, Jozef, eds. Stability of Mappings of Hyers-Ulam Type. 160p. 1994. text 90.00 (0-911767-82-7); pap. text 60.00 (0-911767-64-9) Hadronic Pr Inc.

Rassias, Themistocles M., et al. Topics in Polynomials of One & Several Variables & Their Applications. 500p. (C). 1993. text 127.00 (981-02-0614-3) World Scientific Pub.

Rassieur, Charles L. Pastor, Our Marriage Is in Trouble: A Guide to Short-Term Counseling. 129p. 1992. pap. 10.95 (1-56024-350-3) Haworth Pr.

Rasskazov, L. N., jt. auth. see Goldin, A. L.

***Rassman, William R. & Bernstein, Robert M.** The Patient's Guide to Hair Restoration. (Illus.). 239p. 1999. pap. 5.95 (0-9701405-0-9) New Hair.

Rassmus, Jens. Farmer Enno & His Cow. LC 97-40437. (Illus.). 32p. (J). (gr. 1-5). 1998. pap. 14.95 (0-531-30081-1) Orchard Bks Watts.

Rassmusen, Knud. Across Arctic America: Narrative of the Fifth Thule Expedition. Cole, Terrence, ed. LC 98-32117. (Classic Reprint Ser.: No. 6). (Illus.). 27p. 1999. reprint ed. 35.95 (0-912006-93-5); reprint ed. pap. 24.95 (0-912006-94-3) U of Alaska Pr.

Rassmussen, Richard M. Mysteries of Space: Opposing Viewpoints. LC 93-13592. (Great Mysteries Ser.). 128p. 1994. lib. bdg. 22.45 (1-56510-097-2) Greenhaven.

Rassner, Gernot. Atlas of Dermatology. 3rd ed.Tr. of Atlas der Dermatologie und Venerologie. (Illus.). 382p. 1994. text 89.00 (0-8121-1601-1) Lppncott W & W.

Rasso, Ann, ed. Starlog Celebrity Series Presents: Just Tay. 1998. pap. 3.99 (0-934551-39-1) Starlog Grp Inc.

Rassogianis, John, jt. auth. see Festos, Nicholas.

Rassool, G. Hussein. Substance Use & Misuse: Nature, Context, & Clinical Interventions. LC 98-2838. 282p. 1998. pap. write for info. (0-632-04884-0) Blackwell Sci.

Rassool, Hussein. Addiction Nursing. (Illus.). 240p. (Orig.). 1997. pap. 39.95 (1-56593-824-0, 1618) Singular Publishing.

Rassool, Naz. Literacy for Sustainable Development in the Age of Information. LC 98-44259. (Language & Education Library). 250p. 1999. pap. text 34.95 (1-85359-432-6) Multilingual Matters.

***Rassool, Naz.** Literacy for Sustainable Development in the Age of Information. LC 98-44259. 250p. 1999. 95.00 (1-85359-433-4) Multilingual Matters.

Rassool, Naz, jt. auth. see Morley, Louise.

Rassoull, Abass. The Jacobite Scheme. 76p. (Orig.). 1992. pap. text 6.95 (1-56411-016-8) Untd Bros & Sis.

Rassudova, O. Aspectual Usage in Modern Russian. 200p. (C). 1984. 75.00 (0-7855-4228-0, Pub. by Collets); 70.00 (0-7855-5357-6, Pub. by Collets) St Mut.

Rassuli, Kathleen, jt. ed. see Hollander, Stanley.

Rast, Hubert, jt. auth. see Bruggemann, Aminia.

***Rast, Joel.** Remaking Chicago: The Political Origins of Urban Industrial Change. LC 98-33177. xvi,201p. 1999. 36.00 (0-87580-248-6) N Ill U Pr.

Rast, N. & Delaney, F. M., eds. Profiles of Orogenic Belts. (Geodynamics Ser.: Vol. 10). 310p. 1983. 36.00 (0-87590-510-2) Am Geophysical.

Rast, N., ed. see Nalivkin, Dmitrii V.

Rast, Nicholas, jt. ed. see Horton, J. Wright, Jr.

***Rast, Peter & Stearns, Robert E.** Low Speed Automobile Accidents: Investigation, Documentation & Case Preparation. 144p. 2000. spiral bd. 45.00 (0-913875-87-2, 5872-N) Lawyers & Judges.

Rast, Richard R. Environmental Remediation Estimating Methods. LC 98-106183. (Illus.). 300p. 1997. boxed set 99.95 (0-87629-461-1, 64777) R S Means.

Rast, W., jt. auth. see Thornton, Jeffrey A.

Rast, Walter E. Through the Ages in Palestinian Archaeology: An Introductory Handbook. LC 92-33156. 240p. 1992. pap. 17.00 (1-56338-055-2) TPI PA.

Rast, Walter E. & Zeiger, Marion, eds. Preliminary Reports of ASOR-Sponsored Excavations, 1980-84. (BASOR Supplements Ser.: Vol. 26). (Illus.). 177p. (C). 1990. pap. 15.00 (0-89757-326-9, Pub. by Am Sch Orient Res) David Brown.

Rast, Walter E. & Zeiger, Marion, eds. Preliminary Reports of ASOR-Sponsored Excavations, 1981-83. LC 85-12851. (BASOR Supplements Ser.: No. 23). (Illus.). 135p. 1985. pap. 15.00 (0-89757-323-4, Pub. by Am Sch Orient Res) David Brown.

Rast, Walter E. & Zeiger, Marion, eds. Preliminary Reports of ASOR-Sponsored Excavations, 1982-85. (BASOR Supplements Ser.: Vol. 25). (Illus.). 222p. (C). 1988. pap. 15.00 (0-8018-3697-2, Pub. by Am Sch Orient Res) David Brown.

— Preliminary Reports of ASOR-Sponsored Excavations, 1982-89. (BASOR Supplements Ser.: Vol. 27). (Illus.). 154p. 1991. pap. 15.00 (0-89757-327-7, Pub. by Am Sch Orient Res) David Brown.

Rast, Walter E., jt. auth. see Schaub, R. Thomas.

Rastall, P. R. Empirical Phonology & Cartesian Tables. LC 93-28814. 108p. 1993. text 59.95 (0-7734-9327-1) E Mellen.

— A Functional View of English Grammar. (Studies in Education: Vol. 21). 164p. 1995. write for info. (0-7734-9037-X) E Mellen.

— A Functional View of English Grammar. LC 95-11024. (Studies in Education: Vol. 21). 164p. 1995. 79.95 (0-7734-8922-3) E Mellen.

***Rastall, Paul.** A Linguistic Philosophy of Language. LC 99-58703. (Studies in Linguistics & Semiotics: Vol. 6). 328p. 2000. text 99.95 (0-7734-7778-0) E Mellen.

Rastall, Peter. Postprincipia: Gravitation for Physicists & Astronomers. 300p. (C). 1991. text 48.00 (981-02-0778-6) World Scientific Pub.

***Rastall, Richard.** The Heaven Singing: Music in Early English Religious Drama. (Illus.). 454p. 1999. pap. 35.00 (0-85991-550-6) Boydell & Brewer.

— Minstrels Playing: Music in Early English Religious Drama II. 464p. 2000. 110.00 (0-85991-585-9) Boydell & Brewer.

Rastegar, Sohi, ed. Advances in Bioengineering: Proceedings, ASME International Mechanical Engineering Congress & Exposition, Atlanta, GA, 1996. LC 96-78682. (BED Ser.: Vol. 33). 498p. 1996. pap. 150.00 (0-7918-1540-4, R856) ASME.

Rastell, John. Nature of the Four Elements. LC 71-133725. (Tudor Facsimile Texts. Old English Plays Ser.: No. 7). reprint ed. 59.50 (0-404-53307-8) AMS Pr.

— Les Termes de la Ley: Or, Certain Difficult & Obsure Words & Terms of the Common & Statute Law of England, Now in Use, Expounded & Explained. iv, 392p. 1993. reprint ed. 85.00 (0-8377-2575-5, Rothman) W S Hein.

Rastell/Rayner. William Byrd: Six Part Fantasies in G Minor. 67.95 (1-85928-348-9) Ashgate Pub Co.

Rastetter, J. W., jt. auth. see Begemann, H.

Rastetter, J. W., jt. auth. see Loeffler, H.

Rastier, Francois. Ideologie et Theorie des Signes. (Approaches to Semiotics Ser.). (Illus.). 168p. 1972. text 36.95 (90-279-2114-8) Mouton.

— Meaning & Textuality. LC 98-145906. (Toronto Studies in Semiotics). (Illus.). 352p. 1997. pap. text 24.95 (0-8020-8029-4) U of Toronto Pr.

***Rastogi.** TV Holography. 2000. write for info. (0-471-49052-0) Wiley.

Rastogi, Navjivan. Introduction to Tantraloka: A Study in Structure. 589p. 1987. 36.00 (0-318-32818-6, Pub. by Motilal Bnarsidass) S Asia.

— Introduction to the Tantraloka: A Study in Structure. 589p. 1987. 36.00 (81-208-0180-6, Pub. by Motilal Bnarsidass) S Asia.

— Krama Tantricism of Kashmir. (C). 1996. 28.00 (81-208-1302-2, Pub. by Motilal Bnarsidass) S Asia.

— Krama Tantricism of Kashmir, Vol. 1. 1979. 18.50 (0-89684-048-4, Pub. by Motilal Bnarsidass) S Asia.

Rastogi, Navjivan, ed. see Gupta, Abhina.

***Rastogi, P. K. & Inaudi, Daniele.** Trends in Optical Non-Destructive Testing & Inspection. LC 99-87326. 2000. write for info. (0-08-043020-1) Elsevier.

Rastogi, P. N. Ethnic Tensions in Indian Society. 1986. 38.00 (0-8364-1931-6, Pub. by Mittal Pubs Dist) S Asia.

— Management of Technology & Innovation: Competing Through Technological Excellence. 195p. 1995. 32.00 (0-8039-9263-7) Sage.

An Asterisk (*) at the beginning of an entry indicates that the title is appearing for the first time.

— Policy Analysis & Problem-Solving for Social Systems: Toward Understanding, Monitoring, & Managing Complex Real World Problems. (Illus.). 150p. (C). 1992. 27.50 (0-8039-9425-7) Sage.

— Productivity, Innovation, Management & Development: A Study in the Productivity Cultures of Nations & System Renewal. 273p. (C). 1988. text 28.00 (0-8039-9563-6) Sage.

Rastogi, Pramod K. Holographic Interferometry: Principles & Methods. LC 93-39992. (Series in Optical Sciences: Vol. 68). (Illus.). 410p. 1994. text 65.00 (0-387-57354-2) Spr-Verlag.

Rastogi, Pramod K., ed. Optical Measurement Techniques & Applications. LC 97-12547. 456p. 1997. 103.00 (0-89006-516-0) Artech Hse.

***Rastogi, Pramod K., ed.** Photomechanics. (Topics in Applied Physics Ser.: Vol. 77). (Illus.). 438p. 1999. 165.00 (3-540-65990-0) Spr-Verlag.

Rastogi, Pramod K. & Gyimesi, Ferenc, eds. International Conference on Applied Optical Metrology, Vol. 3407. LC 99-170355. 540p. 1998. 99.00 (0-8194-2859-0) SPIE.

Rastogi, Pramod K., jt. ed. see Tiziani, Hans J.

Rastogi, Ranjul, jt. auth. see Rao, T. V.

Rastogi, T. C. Islamic Mysticism Sufism. 126p. 1982. 23.95 (0-318-37184-7) Asia Bk Corp.

— Muslim World (Islam Breaks Fresh Ground) 1986. 29.00 (81-7024-039-5, Pub. by Ashish Pub Hse) S Asia.

— Western Influence in Iqbal. (C). 1987. 34.00 (81-7024-080-8, Pub. by Ashish Pub Hse) S Asia.

Rastogi, V. B. Modern Biology, Vol. 1. 508p. 1997. pap. 150.00 (81-209-0442-7, Pub. by Pitambar Pub) St Mut.

— Modern Biology, Vol. 2. 782p. 1997. pap. 200.00 (81-209-0496-6, Pub. by Pitambar Pub) St Mut.

Rastogi, V. B. & Kishore, B. A Complete Course in Certificate Biology, Vol. 2. 212p. 1997. pap. 55.00 (81-209-0875-9, Pub. by Pitambar Pub) St Mut.

— A Complete Course in ISC Biology, Vol. 1. 592p. 1997. pap. 175.00 (81-209-0822-8, Pub. by Pitambar Pub) St Mut.

— A Complete Course in ISC Biology, Vol. 2. 412p. 1997. pap. 105.00 (81-209-0823-6, Pub. by Pitambar Pub) St Mut.

***Rastorfer, Darl.** Six Bridges: The Legacy of Othmar H. Ammann. LC 99-39824. (Illus.). 224p. 2000. 39.95 (0-300-08047-6) Yale U Pr.

Rastorgueva, V. S. A Short Sketch of Tajik Grammar. Paper, Herbert H., ed. & tr. by. LC 64-63907. (General Publications). 1992. reprint ed. 19.90 (0-933070-28-4) Res Inst Inner Asian Studies.

Rastovski, A., ed. Storage of Potatoes: Post Harvest Behaviour Store Design, Storage Practice, Handling. 462p. 1989. pap. 425.00 (81-7089-111-6, Pub. by Intl Bk Distr) St Mut.

Rastyannikov, V. G. Food for Developing Countries in Asia & North Africa. Watts, George S., tr. LC 75-26311. (World Food Supply Ser.). (Illus.). 1976. reprint ed. 15.95 (0-405-07789-0) Ayer.

Rasu, Michael. Revolutionary Organizations in Latin America & the Caribbean. (WVSS on Latin America & the Caribbean Ser.). (C). 1996. text 45.00 (0-8133-7292-5) Westview.

Rasul. Love Triangles. 1998. pap. 12.95 (1-890301-05-1) M Bey.

— You Must Inhale to Exhale: A Psychotherapeutic Book on Relational Shortcomings & How to Cope after Shock. 128p. (Orig.). 1996. pap. 12.95 (0-9656137-0-4) M Bey.

Rasul, Chuma W. The Third Eye of a Butterfly. Alaye, Sundiata N., ed. LC 98-67624. 165p. 1998. pap. 15.00 (0-9666802-0-0) Pauline Publishing.

Rasul, Chuma W., ed. & photos by see Tantra.

Rasul, Chuora Whahid, ed. see Fisiwe.

Rasul, Rafique Y. Life-Skills for Living. LC 97-93058. (Life-Skill Book for You Ser.). 336p. (Orig.). 1997. pap. 14.95 (0-9656917-5-6) LifePubns.

Rasula, Jed. The American Poetry Wax Museum: Reality Effects, 1940-1990. LC 95-23878. (Refiguring English Studies). 639p. 1995. pap. 32.95 (0-8141-0138-0) NCTE.

— Tabula Rasula. LC 85-30378. (Illus.). 96p. 1986. pap. 15.00 (0-930794-62-1) Station Hill Pr.

Rasula, Jed & McCaffery, Steve, eds. Imagining Language: An Anthology. LC 97-40632. (Illus.). 638p. 1998. 55.00 (0-262-18186-X) MIT Pr.

Rasuly-Paleczek, Gabriele, ed. Turkish Families in Transition. (Illus.). 215p. 1996. pap. 42.95 (3-631-30085-9) P Lang Pubng.

— Turkish Families in Transition. (Illus.). 215p. 1996. pap. 42.95 (0-8204-3170-2) P Lang Pubng.

Rasuso, John N. Atlantic Wrecks, Bk. 1. Barrett, Linda, ed. (Fisherman Library). (Illus.). 176p. (Orig.). 1992. pap. text 17.95 (0-923155-15-5) Fisherman Lib.

Rasvan, V., jt. auth. see Halanay, A.

***Raswan, Carl.** The Black Tents of Arabia: My Life Amongst the Bedouins. 280p. 2000. text 110.00 (0-7103-0672-5) Col U Pr.

Raswan, Carl & Seydel, R. H. Der Araber und Sein Pferd. (Documenta Hippologica Ser.). (Illus.). 166p. 1990. reprint ed. write for info. (3-487-08234-9) G Olms Pubs.

Raswan, Carl R. Black Tents of Arabia: My Life among the Bedouins. LC 98-70347. 206p. 1998. reprint ed. pap. 14.00 (1-886913-21-8) Ruminator Bks.

— Escape from Baghdad. (Illus.). 278p. 1978. reprint ed. 50.70 (3-487-08158-X) G Olms Pubs.

— Im Land der Schwarzen Zelte. (Illus.). 167p. 1990. reprint ed. write for info. (3-487-08136-9) G Olms Pubs.

— Sohne der Wuste. (Documenta Hippologica Ser.). (Illus.). 132p. 1977. write for info. (3-487-08134-2) G Olms Pubs.

— Trinker der Lufte. (Illus.). 154p. 1990. write for info. (3-487-08140-7) G Olms Pubs.

Rat, ed. see Montaigne, Michel de.

Rat, A. Rusty. Summer's Salmon. (Illus.). 74p. 1997. 50.00 (1-886967-05-9) Meadow Run Pr.

Rat, Maurice. Larousse Dictionnaire des Locutions Francaises. (FRE.). 464p. 1970. 49.95 (0-7859-4628-4) Fr & Eur.

Rat, Maurice, ed. see Montaigne, Michel de.

Rat, Maurice, ed. see Musset, Alfred.

Rata, Elizabeth. A Political Economy of Neotribal Capitalism. LC 99-28297. 288p. 2000. 65.00 (0-7391-0068-8) Lxngtn Bks.

Ratain, Mark J., et al. Oncology Therapeutics: A Quick Reference Guide. (Illus.). 350p. pap. text. write for info. (0-7216-8123-9, W B Saunders Co) Harcrt Hlth Sci Grp.

Ratajczak, H., et al, eds. Molecular Interactions, 3 vols., 1. LC 79-40825. (Illus.). 437p. 1980. reprint ed. pap. 135.50 (0-608-08427-1, 203048000001) Bks Demand.

— Molecular Interactions, 3 vols., 2. LC 79-40825. (Illus.). 651p. 1981. reprint ed. pap. 200.00 (0-608-08428-X, 203048000002) Bks Demand.

— Molecular Interactions, 3 vols., 3. LC 79-40825. (Illus.). 583p. 1982. reprint ed. pap. 180.80 (0-608-08429-8, 203048000003) Bks Demand.

Ratajewicz, Zbigniew, jt. auth. see Tomasik, Piotr.

***Ratan, Anurag, ed.** Encyclopaedia of Practical Management, 6 vols. 1999. 580.00 (81-7020-869-6, Pub. by Cosmo Pubn) S Asia.

Ratan, Jai, ed. Contemporary Urdu Short Stories: An Anthology. (C). 1992. write for info. (81-207-1304-4) Sterling Pubs.

Ratan, Jai, tr. from HIN. Anthology of Hindi Short Stories. (C). 1993. 18.00 (81-7201-527-5, Pub. by Indian Pubs) S Asia.

— Krishan Chander: Selected Short Stories. (C). 1990. 12.50 (0-8364-2618-5, Pub. by Indian Pubs) S Asia.

— Modern Hindi Short Stories. (C). 1991. 24.00 (81-7023-187-6, Pub. by Allied Pubs) S Asia.

— Modern Urdu Short Stories. vi, 200p. 1987. 13.50 (0-8364-2049-7, Pub. by Allied Pubs) S Asia.

Ratan, Rajiv R., jt. auth. see Koliatsos, Vassilis E.

Ratanakul, Pinit, jt. ed. see Coward, Harold G.

Ratanlal, Mishra. Epigraphical Studies of Rajasthan Inscriptions. 1990. 44.50 (81-7018-596-3, Pub. by BR Pub) S Asia.

Ratanov, V. F., jt. auth. see Zakladnoi, G. A.

Ratanova, V. F., jt. auth. see Zakladnoi, G. A.

***Ratasczak, Eric.** Centre County Pennsylvania Street Atlas. (Illus.). 128p. 2000. pap. 15.95 (0-9678952-0-0) Ratajczak Maps.

***Ratay, Robert T.** Forensic Structural Engineering Handbook. (Illus.). 816p. 2000. 99.95 (0-07-052667-2) McGraw-Hill Prof.

Ratay, Robert T. Handbook of Temporary Structures in Construction. 2nd ed. (Illus.). 700p. 1996. 105.00 (0-07-051261-2) McGraw.

Ratay, Robert T., ed. Construction Safety Affected by Codes & Standards. LC 97-36207. (Illus.). 55p. 1997. pap. text 19.00 (0-7844-0280-9, 40280-9) Am Soc Civil Eng.

— Temporary Structures in Construction Operations. 156p. 1987. 18.00 (0-87262-592-3) Am Soc Civil Eng.

Ratch, Jerry. Hot Weather: Poems Selected & New. Peters, Robert B., ed. LC 81-21473. (Poets Now Ser.: No. 3). 202p. 1982. 14.50 (0-8108-1511-7) Scarecrow.

— Light. LC 88-62610. 64p. 1988. 8.00 (0-929022-03-3) O Bks.

Ratcheson, Robert A., jt. auth. see Wirth, Fremont P.

Ratchford, B. U. American State Debts. LC 71-182704. reprint ed. 37.50 (0-404-05226-6) AMS Pr.

Ratchford, James W. & Sieburg, Evelyn. Memoirs of a Confederate Staff Officer: From Bethel to Bentonville. LC 98-20933. (Civil War Heritage Ser.). 1999. 9.95 (1-57249-092-6) White Mane Pub.

Ratchford, Paula G. Instruction in Singlesness. 124p. student ed. 13.00 (0-9641801-1-1); pap. text 8.00 (0-9641801-0-3) P G Ratchford.

Ratchford, Walt. How to Be a Successful Bachelor: A Humorous Guide to Your New Life. LC 93-61870. (Illus.). 198p. 1995. pap. 12.95 (0-9640027-0-1) Virgin Pubng.

Ratchnevsky, Paul. Genghis Khan: His Life & Legacy. 272p. 1993. pap. 25.95 (0-631-18949-1) Blackwell Pubs.

Ratclife, Stephen. Distance. LC 86-71353. 112p. (Orig.). 1986. pap. 6.00 (0-939691-00-0) Avenue B.

Ratcliff, Bob, ed. see Mansell, John S.

Ratcliff, Bryan. Introducing Software Engineering Specification Using Z: A Practical Case Study Approach. LC 93-33831. (International Series in Software Engineering). 1994. 17.95 (0-07-707965-5) McGraw.

Ratcliff, Carter. Alex Katz: Cutouts. (Illus.). 34p. 1979. pap. 5.00 (0-944680-31-3) R Miller Gal.

— Andy Warhol. LC 83-3835. (Modern Masters Ser.). (Illus.). 128p. 1986. 35.00 (0-89659-385-1); pap. 14.95 (1-55859-257-1) Abbeville Pr.

— Bernar Venet. (Illus.). 200p. 1993. 60.00 (1-55859-699-2, Cross Riv Pr) Abbeville Pr.

— Bruce Rosen: A Selection of Paintings. (Illus.). 24p. 1998. pap. 12.00 (0-9662920-0-6) M D Rosen.

— The Fate of a Gesture: Jackson Pollock & Postwar American Art. LC 95-12081. (Illus.). 360p. 1996. text 35.00 (0-374-15381-7) FS&G.

— The Fate of a Gesture: Jackson Pollock & Postwar American Art. 1998. pap. text 20.00 (0-8133-3544-2, Pub. by Westview) HarpC.

— Fever Coast. 7.00 (0-686-09757-2); pap. 3.50 (0-686-09758-0) Kulchur Foun.

***Ratcliff, Carter.** Gary T. Erbe: Paintings. (Illus.). 48p. 1999. 10.00 (0-934306-22-2) Springfield.

Ratcliff, Carter. Give Me Tomorrow. (Illus.). 48p. 1983. text 12.00 (0-931428-03-3) Vehicle Edns.

— John Singer Sargent. LC 82-6779. (Illus.). 256p. 1986. 39.98 (0-89660-014-9, Artabras) Abbeville Pr.

— Jorge Castillo: Dibujo, Pintura, Escultura. (Grandes Monografias). (SPA., Illus.). 412p. 1993. 350.00 (84-343-0476-7) Elliots Bks.

— Komar & Melamid. (Illus.). 208p. 1989. 19.98 (0-89659-891-8) Abbeville Pr.

— Lynda Benglis & Keith Sonnier: A Ten Year Retrospective, 1977-1987. Hammill, Audrey, ed. LC 87-19544. (Illus.). 56p. (Orig.). 1987. pap. text 14.00 (0-944564-00-3) Alex Mus.

— Mia Westerlund Roosen. Blank, Shoshana, ed. (Illus.). 22p. (Orig.). 1989. pap. text 10.00 (0-317-93161-X) Shoshana Wayne Gall.

***Ratcliff, Carter.** Out of the Box: The Reinvention of Art: 1965-1975. (Illus.). 224p. 2000. pap. 19.95 (1-58115-073-3, Pub. by Allworth Pr) Watsn-Guptill.

Ratcliff, Carter. Pressures of the Hand: Expressionist Impulses in Recent American Art. (Illus.). 36p. 1984. pap. 12.50 (0-942746-05-8) SUNYP R Gibson.

Ratcliff, Carter, frwd. Donald Baechler. (Illus.). 88p. 1998. pap. 29.95 (1-891475-08-8, 810891) T Shafrazi.

***Ratcliff, Carter, text.** Paul Georges. (Illus.). 31p. 2000. pap. 20.00 (1-58821-075-8) Salander OReilly.

Ratcliff, Carter, text. Robert Rahway Zakawitch. (Grand Dado Ser.). 36p. 1996. pap. 20.00 (1-879173-28-X) Locks Gallery.

Ratcliff, Carter, et al, texts. Kenny Scharf. (Illus.). 120p. 1998. pap. 39.95 (1-891475-12-6, 810952) T Shafrazi.

Ratcliff, Carter & Reuter, Laurel J. Peter Dean. (Illus.). 68p. (Orig.). 1989. pap. 15.00 (0-943107-02-4) ND Mus Art.

Ratcliff, Carter & Rosenblum, Robert. Gilbert & George: The Singing Sculpture. Wolmer, Bruce, ed. LC 92-82072. (Illus.). 64p. 1993. 35.00 (0-9635649-0-0) A McCall NY.

Ratcliff, Carter & Sobel, Kim. Immediacies of the Hand: Recent Abstract Painting in New York. (Illus.). 20p. 1999. pap. 5.00 (1-885998-18-X) Hunter College.

Ratcliff, Carter, et al. Enzo Cucchi: Simm' Nervosi. (Illus.). 57p. 1998. pap. 35.00 (88-422-0708-X, 810881) T Shafrazi.

— Giorgio Cavallon, 1904-1989 a Retrospective View. (Illus.). 32p. Date not set. 5.00 (0-614-10427-0) W Benton Mus.

Ratcliff, Carter, jt. auth. see Schweizer, Paul D.

Ratcliff, Clarence E. North Carolina Taxpayers, 1701-1786. LC 84-80487. 228p. 1999. reprint ed. 20.00 (0-8063-1079-0) Genealog Pub.

— North Carolina Taxpayers, 1679-1790. 230p. 1996. reprint ed. 25.00 (0-8063-1204-1, 4762) Genealog Pub.

***Ratcliff, Donald.** Christian Views of Sociology. 392p. 1999. pap. text 37.45 (1-56226-429-X) CAT Pub.

Ratcliff, Donald, ed. Handbook of Children's Religious Education. LC 91-43038. 285p. (Orig.). 1992. pap. 24.95 (0-89135-085-3) Religious Educ.

— Handbook of Preschool Religious Education. LC 88-30868. 306p. (Orig.). 1989. pap. 24.95 (0-89135-068-3) Religious Educ.

Ratcliff, Donald & Davies, James A., eds. Handbook of Youth Ministry. 318p. (Orig.). 1990. pap. 24.95 (0-89135-079-9) Religious Educ.

Ratcliff, Donald & Neff, Blake J. A Complete Guide to Religious Education Volunteers. 246p. (Orig.). 1993. pap. 21.95 (0-89135-089-6) Religious Educ.

Ratcliff, Donald, jt. auth. see Meier, Paul.

Ratcliff, Donald, jt. ed. see Neff, Blake J.

Ratcliff, Gerald Lee, ed. see Sophocles.

Ratcliff, Graham, jt. ed. see Farah, Martha.

Ratcliff, J. Timecode: A User's Guide. 3rd ed. LC 99-236028. 276p. 2000. pap. text 56.95 (0-240-51539-0, Focal) Buttrwrth-Heinemann.

Ratcliff, James L., ed. ASHE Reader on Community Colleges. 340p. (C). 1992. pap. text 44.00 (0-536-58226-2) Pearson Custom.

— Community Colleges. 2nd ed. (ASHE Reader Ser.). 504p. (C). 1994. pap. text 51.00 (0-536-58571-7) Pearson Custom.

Ratcliff, James L. & Jones, Elizabeth A., eds. Assessment & Curriculum Reform. LC 85-644752. (New Directions for Higher Education Ser.: No. HE 80). 100p. 1992. pap. 22.00 (1-55542-735-9) Jossey-Bass.

Ratcliff, James L., jt. auth. see Gaff, Jerry G.

Ratcliff, John. Timecode: A User's Guide. 2nd ed. (Illus.). 224p. 1995. pap. 47.95 (0-240-51404-1, Focal) Buttrwrth-Heinemann.

Ratcliff, John D. Lives & Dollars. LC 70-111859. (Essay Index Reprint Ser.). 1977. 21.95 (0-8369-2022-8) Ayer.

— Modern Miracle Men. LC 79-37770. (Essay Index Reprint Ser.). 1977. reprint ed. 26.95 (0-8369-2619-6) Ayer.

Ratcliff, Kathryn S., ed. Healing Technology: Feminist Perspectives. 436p. 1989. pap. text 18.95 (0-472-06395-2, 06395) U of Mich Pr.

Ratcliff, Mel. Keys of Succession: A Guide for Spouses, Children, &-or Successor Trustees. 320p. 1995. boxed set 44.95 (0-9646347-1-6) Possiblts Pr.

Ratcliff, R. E. English-French Dictionary of Naval Terminology. (ENG & FRE.). 168p. 1983. pap. 75.00 (0-8288-1580-1, F25470) Fr & Eur.

Ratcliff, Richard E., jt. auth. see Zeitlin, Maurice.

Ratcliff, Robert D., jt. auth. see Hargrove, William D.

Ratcliff, Roger. How to Meet the Right Man. 224p. 1996. 14.95 (1-55972-375-0, Birch Ln Pr) Carol Pub Group.

— How to Meet the Right Man: A Five-Step Strategy That Really Works. (Illus.). 208p. 1998. pap. 10.95 (0-8065-2016-7) Carol Pub Group.

— How to Meet the Right Man: A Five-Step Strategy That Really Works. 1998. pap. 65.70 (0-8065-9832-8, Citadel Pr) Carol Pub Group.

— How to Meet the Right Woman. 224p. 1996. 14.95 (1-55972-380-7, Birch Ln Pr) Carol Pub Group.

— How to Meet the Right Woman: A Five-Step Strategy That Really Works. 1998. pap. 65.70 (0-8065-9827-1) Carol Pub Group.

— How to Meet the Right Woman: A Five-Step Strategy That Really Works. (Illus.). 208p. 1998. pap. 10.95 (0-8065-2021-3, Citadel Pr) Carol Pub Group.

Ratcliff, Ruth. Scottish Folk Tales. 1977. 50.00 (0-7855-7145-0) St Mut.

Ratcliffe. ADA Yearbook 1995. LC 95-75768. 452p. (gr. 12). 1995. 82.00 (90-5199-218-1) IOS Press.

— Race Ethnicity & Nation: Ethnicity & Nation International Perspectives on Social Conflict. 256p. 1996. pap. 27.50 (1-85728-661-8, Pub. by UCL Pr Ltd) Taylor & Francis.

— Race Ethnicity & Nation: International Perspectives on Social Conflict. LC 94-12567. 1994. 75.00 (1-85728-099-7, Pub. by UCL Pr Ltd) Taylor & Francis.

— Urban Planning & Real Estate. (Natural & Built Environment Ser.: Vol. 8). 512p. 1996. pap. 34.95 (1-85728-564-6, Pub. by UCL Pr Ltd) Taylor & Francis.

— Women & Health. (C). 1999. pap. text 25.00 (0-205-30597-0) Allyn.

Ratcliffe & Richardson. Off the Shelf, Bk. 1. 1993. pap. text. write for info. (0-582-91281-4, Pub. by Addison-Wesley) Longman.

— Off the Shelf, Bk. 2. 1993. pap. text. write for info. (0-582-91282-2, Pub. by Addison-Wesley) Longman.

Ratcliffe, A. The Truth about Hitler & the Roman Catholic Church. 1982. lib. bdg. 59.95 (0-87700-362-9) Revisionist Pr.

Ratcliffe, A., ed. & tr. see Zakhvatkin, A. A.

Ratcliffe, Amy, ed. see Jankowski, Dennis A. & Butler, L. Rick.

Ratcliffe, Ann. Chemistry: The Experience. LC 92-27306. 240p. 1993. pap. 49.95 (0-471-57707-3) Wiley.

Ratcliffe, Betram, jt. auth. see Ysaye, Antoine.

Ratcliffe, Bill. The Art of Senior Golf. LC 94-61584. (Illus.). 124p. (Orig.). 1995. pap. 10.95 (1-884570-20-8) Research Triangle.

***Ratcliffe, David T. & Prouty, L. Fletcher, eds.** Understanding Special Operations: And Their Impact on the Vietnam War Era, 1989 Interview with L. Fletcher Prouty, Colonel USAF (Retired) LC 99-75115. 424p. 1999. pap. 23.00 (0-9673507-0-0) Rat Haus Real Pr.

Ratcliffe, Denis F. Second Chances. 280p. 1996. pap. 16.95 (1-85411-151-5, Pub. by Seren Bks) Dufour.

Ratcliffe, Derek A. Bird Life of Mountain & Upland. (Bird Life Ser.). (Illus.). 268p. (C). 1991. text 47.95 (0-521-33123-4) Cambridge U Pr.

— The Peregrine Falcon. LC 80-65963. (Illus.). 1980. 25.00 (0-931130-05-0) Harrell Bks.

— The Peregrine Falcon. 2nd ed. (Illus.). 454p. 1993. text (0-85661-060-7) Poyser.

— The Raven: A Natural History in Britain & Ireland. (Poyser Birds Ser.). (Illus.). 352p. 1997. text 39.95 (0-85661-090-9) Morgan Kaufmann.

Ratcliffe, Dolores. Women Entrepreneurs, Networking & Sweet Patato Pie: Creating Capital in the 21st Century. (YA). (gr. 10 up). 1997. pap. 16.95 (0-933016-03-4) Corita Comm.

Ratcliffe, Donald J. Party Spirit in a Frontier Republic: Democratic Politics in Ohio, 1793-1821. LC 98-23575. 357p. 1998. text 60.00 (0-8142-0775-8, RATPAR); pap. text 23.95 (0-8142-0776-6, RATPAX) Ohio St U Pr.

***Ratcliffe, Donald J.** The Politics of Long Division: The Birth of the Second Party System in Ohio, 1818-1828. LC 99-50891. (Illus.). 344p. (C). 2000. text 65.00 (0-8142-0849-5) Ohio St U Pr.

Ratcliffe, Elisabeth. A Country Parish Neen Savage in 1981. 112p. (C). 1989. 50.00 (0-86157-140-1, Pub. by S A Baldwin) St Mut.

Ratcliffe, Eric. Anthropos. 112p. pap. write for info. (3-7052-0429-7, Pub. by Poetry Salzburg) Intl Spec Bk.

Ratcliffe, Eric. The Caxton of Her Age: The Career & Family Background of Emily Faithfull (1835-95) (Illus.). 96p. 1997. 11.95 (1-897817-24-X, Pub. by Poetry Salzburg) Intl Spec Bk.

Ratcliffe, Eric. Fire in the Bush: Poems 1955-1992. 178p. pap. write for info. (3-7052-0926-4, Pub. by Poetry Salzburg) Intl Spec Bk.

Ratcliffe, Eric, jt. ed. see Gortschacher, Wolfgang.

Ratcliffe, F. N., jt. auth. see Fenner, Frank.

Ratcliffe, Florence M. Myself When Young. (C). 1989. text 39.00 (1-872795-42-0, Pub. by Pentland Pr) St Mut.

Ratcliffe, James M. Good Samaritan & the Law. 1990. 16.50 (0-8446-2783-6) Peter Smith.

Ratcliffe, John & Stubbs, Michael. Urban Planning & Real Estate. LC 96-223096. (Natural & Built Environment Ser.: Vol. 8). 512p. 1996. 95.00 (1-85728-563-8, Pub. by UCL Pr Ltd) Taylor & Francis.

Ratcliffe, John A. The Magneto-Ionic Theory & Its Applications to the Ionosphere: A Monograph. LC 59-896. 216p. reprint ed. pap. 61.60 (0-608-11666-1, 2050747) Bks Demand.

Ratcliffe, John G. Foundations of Hyperbolic Manifolds. LC 94-8958. (Graduate Texts in Mathematics Ser.). (Illus.). 768p. 1994. 69.95 (0-387-94249-1) Spr-Verlag.

— Foundations of Hyperbolic Manifolds. (Graduate Texts in Mathematics Ser.: Vol. 149). (Illus.). 747p. 1994. pap. text 54.95 (0-387-94348-X) Spr-Verlag.

Ratcliffe, Krista. Anglo-American Feminist Challenges to the Rhetorical Traditions: Virginia Woolf, Mary Daly, & Adrienne Rich. LC 94-40053. 248p. (C). 1995. 31.95 (0-8093-1934-9) S Ill U Pr.

Ratcliffe, Marjorie. Jimena: A Woman in Spanish Literature. 250p. 63.50 (0-916379-94-9) Scripta.

Ratcliffe, Mitch. Newton's Law: The Brave New World of Apple's Personal Digital Assistant. 480p. 1993. pap. 24.00 (0-679-74647-1) Random.

Ratcliffe, Mitch, jt. auth. see Gore, Andrew.

R

R

Ratcliffe, N. A. & Rowley, A. F., eds. Invertebrate Blood Cells: Anthropods to Urchordates Invertebrates & Vertebrates Compared, Vol. 2. LC 80-41248. 1981. text 209.00 (*0-12-582102-6*) Acad Pr.
— Invertebrate Blood Cells: General Aspects, Animals Without True Circulatory Systems to Cephalopods, Vol. 1. LC 80-41248. 1981. text 209.00 (*0-12-582101-8*) Acad Pr.
Ratcliffe, Robert H., ed. Great Cases of the Supreme Court. (Illus.). (gr. 7-8). 1975. teacher ed. 5.56 (*0-685-02291-9*) HM.
***Ratcliffe, Robert R.** The Broken Plural Problem in Arabic & Comparative Semitic: Allomorphy & Analogy in Non-Concatenative Morphology. LC 98-47558. (Amsterdam Studies in the Theory & History of Linguistic Science: Vol. 168). xii, 261p. 1998. 84.00 (*1-55619-884-1*) J Benjamins Pubng Co.
Ratcliffe, Robert R. & Bubenik, Vit. A Historical Syntax of Late Middle Indo-Aryan (Apabhramsa) LC 98-47558. (Current Issues in Linguistic Theory Ser.: Vol. 165). xxiv, 265p. 1998. 89.00 (*1-55619-881-7*) J Benjamins Pubng Co.
Ratcliffe, Robert R., jt. ed. see Eid, Mushira.
Ratcliffe, Ronald. Steinway. (Illus.). 196p. 1989. 45.00 (*0-87701-592-9*) Chronicle Bks.
Ratcliffe, Sam D. Painting Texas History to 1900. LC 92-9752. (American Studies). (Illus.). 190p. 1992. 29.95 (*0-292-78113-X*) U of Tex Pr.
***Ratcliffe, Stephen.** Idea's Mirror. 144p. 1999. 12.50 (*1-893541-22-3*, Pub. by Potes Poets) SPD-Small Pr Dist.
Ratcliffe, Stephen. Listening to Reading. LC 99-88760. (C). 2000. text 59.50 (*0-7914-4503-8*); pap. text 19.95 (*0-7914-4504-6*) State U NY Pr.
— Mallarme: Poem in Prose. LC 98-60130. xii, 100p. 1998. pap. 12.95 (*0-9655497-1-2*) SB Review Pubns.
— New York Notes. 32p. (Orig.). 1983. pap. text 3.50 (*0-939180-22-7*) Tombouctou.
— Present Tense. 104p. (Orig.). 1995. pap. 12.00 (*0-935724-71-0*) Figures.
— Sculpture. 96p. 1996. pap. 10.95 (*1-55713-297-6*) Sun & Moon CA.
— Spaces in the Light Said to Be Where One Comes From. 88p. (Orig.). 1993. pap. 9.50 (*0-937013-42-0*) Potes Poets.
Ratcliffe, Stephen, et al, eds. Family Practice Obstetrics. 2nd rev. ed. (Illus.). 450p. 2000. pap. text 55.00 (*1-56053-359-5*) Hanley & Belfus.
— Handbook of Pregnancy & Perinatal Care in Family Practice. LC 95-39444. (Illus.). 500p. (Orig.). 1996. pap. text 50.95 (*1-56053-113-4*) Hanley & Belfus.
Ratcliffe, Susan, ed. The Little Oxford Dictionary of Quotations. 496p. 1995. 13.95 (*0-19-866207-6*) OUP.
***Ratcliffe, Susan, ed.** The Oxford Dictionary of Thematic Quotations. 576p. 2000. 24.95 (*0-19-860218-9*) OUP.
Ratcliffe, Susan, ed. Oxford Love Quotations. LC 98-39812. 336p. 1999. pap. 7.95 (*0-19-860240-5*) OUP.
Ratcliffe, T. J., Jr., jt. auth. see Vanderdoes, Amanda.
Ratcliffe, Thomas A., jt. auth. see Munter, Paul.
Rateaver, Bargyla & Rateaver, Gylver. Organic Method Primer Basics: The Basics: Special Edition. (Conservation Gardening & Farming Ser.). (Illus.). 100p. 1994. pap. 25.00 (*0-915966-04-2*) Rateavers.
— Organic Method Primer Update: Special Edition. (Conservation Gardening & Farming Ser.). (Illus.). 700p. 1993. 200.00 (*0-915966-01-8*) Rateavers.
Rateaver, Bargyla, ed. see Cotten, Emmi.
Rateaver, Bargyla, ed. see Hills, Lawrence D.
Rateaver, Bargyla, ed. see Turner, F. Newman.
Rateaver, Gylver, jt. auth. see Rateaver, Bargyla.
Rateaver, Gylver, ed. see Corley, Hugh.
Rateaver, Gylver, ed. see Cotten, Emmi.
Rateaver, Gylver, ed. see Hainsworth, P. H.
Rateaver, Gylver, ed. see Hills, Lawrence D.
Rateaver, Gylver, ed. see Leatherbarrow, Margaret.
Rateaver, Gylver, ed. see Stephenson, W. A.
Rateaver, Gylver, ed. see Turner, F. Newman.
Rateitschak, Klaus H., et al. Color Atlas of Periodontology. 2nd rev. ed. Hassell, Thomas, tr. from GER. (Dental Medicine Ser.). (Illus.). 400p. 1989. text 165.00 (*0-86577-318-1*) Thieme Med Pubs.
Rateitschak, Klaus H., ed. see Spiekermann, Hubertus.
Ratel, J. Dictionary of Childhood Health: Diccionario de la Salud Infantil. (SPA.). 480p. 1983. pap. 19.95 (*0-8288-1875-4*, S60549) Fr & Eur.
***Rateliff, John.** TSR Jam, 1999. 64p. 1999. pap. 12.95 (*0-7869-1445-9*, Pub. by TSR Inc) Random.
Rateliff, John, ed. see Cordell, Bruce.
Rateliff, John D. Return to the Keep on the Borderlands. (AD&D Accessory Ser.). 64p. 1999. 12.95 (*0-7869-1327-4*) TSR Inc.
Ratelle, Sylvie, ed. Preventive Medicine & Public Health: PreTest Self-Assessment & Review. 8th ed. LC 97-22240. (Pretest Clinical Science Ser.). (Illus.). 200p. 1997. pap. text 18.95 (*0-07-052534-X*) McGraw-Hill HPD.
Rateman, Herbert J. Charity & Sex & the Young Man. 62p. (YA). (gr. 9 up). 1999. reprint ed. pap. 5.95 (*0-912141-69-7*) Roman Cath Bks.
***Ratermann, Dale.** Baseball by the Numbers. (By the Numbers Ser.). (Illus.). 112p. (J). 2000. pap. 4.95 (*1-58261-186-6*) Sprts Pubng.
— Basketball by the Numbers. 2000. pap. 4.95 (*1-58261-189-0*) Sprts Pubng.
— Basketball Crosswords. 208p. pap. 12.95 (*1-57028-214-5*, 82145H, Mstrs Pr) NTC Contemp Pub Co.
Ratermann, Dale. Basketball Crosswords. rev. ed. 224p. 1996. pap. text 12.95 (*1-57028-101-7*, Mstrs Pr) NTC Contemp Pub Co.
— Big Ten: A Century of Excellence. (Illus.). 456p. 1996. 39.95 (*1-57167-037-8*) Sports Pub.
Ratermann, Dale. Football Crosswords, Vol. 3. 208p. pap. 12.95 (*1-57028-213-7*, 82137H, Mstrs Pr) NTC Contemp Pub Co.
Ratermann, Dale. Golf Crosswords. (Illus.). 208p. 1998. pap. 12.95 (*1-57028-193-9*, 81939H, Mstrs Pr) NTC Contemp Pub Co.
***Ratermann, Dale.** Hockey by the Numbers. 2000. pap. 4.95 (*1-58261-188-2*) Sprts Pubng.
Ratermann, Dale. 101 Little Known Facts about Karl Malone. (One Hundred One Little Known Facts Ser.). (Illus.). 101p. 1997. pap. 6.95 (*1-57167-150-1*) Sports Pub.
***Ratermann, Dale.** Racing by the Numbers. (By the Numbers Ser.). (Illus.). 112p. (J). 2000. pap. 4.95 (*1-58261-185-8*) Sprts Pubng.
Ratermann, Dale & Brosi, Brian. 1001 Basketball Trivia Questions. 184p. 1999. pap. 12.95 (*1-58382-006-X*) Sports Masters.
***Ratermann, Dale & Greenberg, Steve.** Golf Gadgets: Cool Stuff You Never Knew You Needed. 160p. 1999. pap. 12.95 (*1-58382-014-0*) Sports Masters.
Ratermann, Dale & Ociepka, Bob. Basketball Playbook: Plays from the Pros. (Illus.). 128p. 1995. pap. 12.95 (*1-57028-008-8*, 80088H, Mstrs Pr) NTC Contemp Pub Co.
Ratermann, Dale, jt. auth. see Ociepka, Bob.
Ratesh, Nestor. Romania: The Entangled Revolution, 152. Laqueur, Walter, ed. LC 91-18244. (Washington Papers: No. 152). 208p. 1991. 45.00 (*0-275-94145-0*, C4145, Praeger Pubs) Greenwood.
Ratesh, Nestor. Romania: The Entangled Revolution, 152. Laqueur, Walter, ed. LC 91-18244. (The Washington Papers: No. 152). 208p. 1991. pap. 12.95 (*0-275-94144-2*, B4244, Praeger Pubs) Greenwood.
Ratey, John. A User's Guide to the Brain. 1999. pap. write for info. (*0-375-70107-9*) Knopf.
Ratey, John J. Neuropsychiatry of Personality Disorders. (Neuropsychiatry Ser.). (Illus.). 352p. 1994. 69.95 (*0-86542-293-1*) Blackwell Sci.
Ratey, John J., ed. Mental Retardation: Developing Pharmacotherapies. LC 90-14485. (Progress in Psychiatry Ser.: No. 32). 162p. 1991. text 12.95 (*0-88048-452-7*, 8452) Am Psychiatric.
Ratey, John J. & Johnson, Catherine. Shadow Syndromes: The Mild Forms of Major Mental Disorders That Sabotage Us. 400p. 1998. reprint ed. pap. 13.00 (*0-553-37959-3*) Bantam.
Ratey, John J., jt. auth. see Hallowell, Edward M.
Ratey, John J., jt. auth. see Johnson, C.
Rath, ed. Financial Institutions & Capital Markets. (C). 1997. pap. text, student ed. 25.00 (*0-673-99319-1*) Addison-Wesley.
Rath, Alan. Alan Rath: Plants, Animals, People, Machines. (Illus.). 48p. 1995. pap. 20.00 (*0-9646426-2-X*, Pub. by Smart Art Pr) RAM Publications.
Rath, B. B. & Misra, M. S., eds. Role of Interfaces on Material Dumping: Proceedings of an International Symposium Held in Conjunction with ASM's Materials Week & TMS-AIME Fall Meeting, 13-17 October 1985, Toronto, Ontario, Canada. LC 86-71998. (Illus.). 131p. reprint ed. pap. 40.70 (*0-608-16004-0*, 203308100083) Bks Demand.
Rath, Bhakta B., ed. see AIME, Metallurgical Society Staff.
Rath, Daniel D., jt. ed. see Mayers, Marvin K.
Rath, Eric. Container Systems. LC 72-13139. (Materials Handling & Packaging Ser.). 595p. 1973. reprint ed. pap. 184.50 (*0-7837-3464-6*, 205779200008) Bks Demand.
Rath, George. The Black Sea Germans in the Dakotas. LC 76-57046. 1990. 25.00 (*0-614-23870-6*) Am Hist Soc Ger.
Rath, Gustave & Shawchuck, Norman. Benchmarks of Quality in the Church: Twenty-One Ways to Continuously Improve the Content of Your Ministry. 144p. (Orig.). 1994. pap. 15.95 (*0-687-34912-5*) Abingdon.
Rath, H. J., ed. Microgravity Fluid Mechanics: IUTAM Symposium, Bremen, 1991. (International Union of Theoretical & Applied Mechanics Symposia Ser.). xxii, 611p. 1992. 163.95 (*0-387-55122-0*) Spr-Verlag.
Rath, H. J. & Egbers, C., eds. Advances in Fluid Mechanics & Turbomachinery. LC 98-14716. (Illus.). xiv, 181p. 1998. 99.00 (*3-540-64111-4*) Spr-Verlag.
Rath, H. J., ed. see G1 Symposium of COSPAR Scientific Commission.
Rath, H. J., jt. ed. see Kuhlmann, H. C.
***Rath, Jan.** Immigrant Business: The Economic Political Social Environment. LC 99-41120. 2000. text 65.00 (*0-312-22775-2*) St Martin.
***Rath, Jay.** The I-Files: True Reports of Unexplained Phenomena in Illinois. Stoga, Stan, ed. LC 99-72897. (Illus.). 175p. 1999. pap. 14.95 (*0-915024-74-8*) Trails Media.
Rath, Jay. The M-Files: True Reports of Minnesota's Unexplained Phenomena. McBride, Elizabeth & Roerden, Chris, eds. LC 98-61219. (Illus.). 120p. 1998. pap. 14.95 (*0-915024-66-7*) Trails Media.
— The W-Files Vol. 1: True Reports of Wisconsin's Unexplained Phenomena. McBride, Elizabeth, ed. LC 97-61553. 148p. 1997. pap. 14.95 (*0-915024-59-4*) Trails Media.
Rath, Jeffrey O. Photographs. large type ed. 58p. 1999. pap. 4.99 (*1-893151-12-3*) Weavers Old.
Rath, Mary. Dear Jane. 64p. 1997. pap. 8.00 (*0-8059-4222-X*) Dorrance.
Rath, Matthias. America's Most Successful Cardiovascular Health Program: Vitamin Program. 1995. pap. text 12.95 (*0-9638768-2-1*) Health Now.
— Warum Kennen Tiere Keinen Herzinfarkt: Aber Wir Menschen. 255p. 1997. pap. 19.80 (*0-9638768-4-8*) Health Now.
— Why Animals Don't Get Heart Attacks, but People Do. rev. ed. 1997. pap. 12.95 (*0-9638768-5-6*) Health Now.
Rath, Navaneeta. Women in Rural Society: A Quest for Development. 183p. 1996. pap. 150.00 (*81-85880-89-1*, Pub. by Print Hse) St Mut.
Rath, Patricia. Introduction to Fashion Merchandising CTB. (General Business & Business Education Ser.). 1994. 57.95 (*0-8273-5400-2*) Delmar.
Rath, Patricia, et al. Introduction to Fashion Merchandising. LC 92-39192. (C). 1994. mass mkt. 41.75 (*0-8273-4871-1*) Delmar.
Rath, Patricia M., et al. Fashion Forecaster for Introduction to Fashion Merchandising. 277p. 1994. student ed. 27.95 (*0-8273-5065-1*) Delmar.
— Introduction to Fashion Merchandising. 156p. 1993. teacher ed. 15.95 (*0-8273-5064-3*) Delmar.
Rath, R., et al, eds. Diversity & Unity in Cross-Cultural Psychology. vi, 374p. 1982. pap. 56.50 (*90-265-0431-4*) Swets.
Rath, R. K. Fresh Water Aquaculture. (C). 1993. pap. 90.00 (*81-7233-055-3*, Pub. by Scientific Pubs) St Mut.
Rath, Rabindranath, jt. auth. see Das, Hari H.
Rath, Ralph. After Death: Judgment or Recycling? (Get the Facts Ser.: Series I). 30p. (Orig.). 1993. pap. 2.95 (*0-9640167-3-7*) Peter Pubns.
— Christian Community: A Reporter's Inside Look. (Get the Facts Ser.: Series II). 32p. (Orig.). 1994. pap. 2.95 (*0-9640167-6-1*) Peter Pubns.
— The Devil: An Old Fashioned Belief? (Get the Facts Ser.: Series I). 30p. (Orig.). 1992. pap. 2.95 (*0-9640167-0-2*) Peter Pubns.
— Get the Facts Series I, Set. (Orig.). 1993. pap. 11.80 (*0-9640167-8-8*) Peter Pubns.
— Get the Facts Series II, Set. (Orig.). 1995. pap. 11.80 (*0-9640167-9-6*) Peter Pubns.
— Homosexuality: What Are the Issues? (Get the Facts Ser.: Series II). 32p. (Orig.). 1993. pap. 2.95 (*0-9640167-4-5*) Peter Pubns.
— Inner Guides: OK for Catholics? (Get the Facts Ser.: Series I). 30p. (Orig.). 1992. pap. 2.95 (*0-9640167-1-0*) Peter Pubns.
— Jesus: Guru or God? (Get the Facts Ser.: Series II). 32p. (Orig.). 1994. pap. 2.95 (*0-9640167-5-3*) Peter Pubns.
— Mantras: Helpful or Harmful? (Get the Facts Ser.: Series I). 30p. (Orig.). 1993. pap. 2.95 (*0-9640167-2-9*) Peter Pubns.
— The New Age: A Christian Critique. LC 90-80211. viii, 343p. (Orig.). 1990. pap. 6.95 (*0-937779-15-6*) Greenlawn Pr.
Rath, Reuben J. The Provisional Austrian Regime in Lombardy - Venetia, 1814-1815. LC 69-18808. 426p. reprint ed. pap. 132.10 (*0-8357-7756-1*, 203611400002) Bks Demand.
— The Viennese Revolution of 1848. LC 56-11770. 440p. reprint ed. pap. 136.40 (*0-8357-7757-X*, 203611500002) Bks Demand.
***Rath, Sara.** About Cows. 2nd ed. LC 99-87662. (Town Square Bk.). (Illus.). 224p. 2000. pap. 16.95 (*0-89658-465-8*) Voyageur Pr.
Rath, Sara. The Complete Cow. LC 98-11971. (Illus.). 156p. 1998. 29.95 (*0-89658-375-9*) Voyageur Pr.
***Rath, Sara.** The Complete Pig: An Entertaining History of Pigs. LC 99-45618. (Town Square Bks.). (Illus.). 144p. 2000. 29.95 (*0-89658-435-6*) Voyageur Pr.
Rath, Sharada. Women in Public Administration of the American States: A Study of Their Administrative Values. 150p. 1998. pap. 100.00 (*81-7533-065-1*, Pub. by Print Hse) St Mut.
***Rath, Sharada, ed.** Women in India: A Search for Identity. 1999. 34.00 (*81-261-0450-3*, Pub. by Anmol) S Asia.
Rath, Sharada, et al. Role of Elites & Citizens in Rural Development of India. 193p. 1993. pap. 125.00 (*81-85880-18-2*, Pub. by Print Hse) St Mut.
Rath, Sura P. Flannery O'Connor: New Perspectives. LC 94-48867. (C). 1996. pap. text 18.00 (*0-8203-1804-3*) U of Ga Pr.
Rathaur, K. R. The Gurkhas: A History of the Recruitment in the British Indian Army. 1995. pap. 25.00 (*0-7855-0411-7*, Pub. by Ratna Pustak Bhandar) St Mut.
Rathaur, Majula. Unmarried Working Women. 165p. 1988. text 18.95 (*81-7027-134-7*, Pub. by Radiant Pubs) S Asia.
Rathban, Sara, ed. see Jackson, James, Jr.
Rathbone, Andy. Dummies 101: Windows 3.1. LC 95-82325. 256p. 1996. pap. 24.99 incl. 3.5 hd (*1-56884-627-4*) IDG Bks.
— Dummies 101: Windows 98. LC 98-84308. 288p. 1998. pap. 24.99 incl. cd-rom (*0-7645-0208-5*) IDG Bks.
Rathbone, Andy. Dummies 101: Windows 95. 2nd ed. (Illus.). 288p. 1997. pap. 24.99 incl. 3.5 hd (*0-7645-0181-X*) IDG Bks.
— Microsoft's Windows Millennium Edition for Dummies. (For Dummies Ser.). (Illus.). 384p. 2000. pap. 19.99 (*0-7645-0735-4*) IDG Bks.
— More Microsoft's Windows Millennium Edition for Dummies. (For Dummies Ser.). (Illus.). 384p. 2000. pap. 22.99 (*0-7645-0734-6*) IDG Bks.
Rathbone, Andy. More Windows 98 for Dummies. 384p. 1998. pap. 22.99 (*0-7645-0234-4*) IDG Bks.
— More Windows 95 for Dummies. 360p. 1996. pap. 22.99 (*1-56884-607-X*) IDG Bks.
***Rathbone, Andy.** MP3 for Dummies. (For Dummies Ser.). 360p. 1999. pap. 19.99 incl. cd-rom (*0-7645-0585-8*) IDG Bks.
Rathbone, Andy. Multimedia & CD-ROMs. 2nd ed. LC 95-77667. 400p. 1995. pap. 29.99 (*1-56884-909-5*) IDG Bks.
— Multimedia & CD-ROMs for Dummies. LC 94-75906. 350p. 1994. pap. 19.95 (*1-56884-089-6*) IDG Bks.
— Multimedia & CD-ROMs for Dummies. 2nd ed. 384p. 1995. pap. 19.99 (*1-56884-907-9*) IDG Bks.
— Multimedia & CD-ROMs for Dummies: Interactive Multimedia Value Pack. LC 94-76885. 384p. 1994. pap. 29.95 (*1-56884-225-2*) IDG Bks.
— Multimedia & CD-ROMs for Dummies: Interactive Multimedia Value Pack. 2nd ed. LC 95-77667. 372p. 1995. pap. 29.99 (*1-56884-908-7*) IDG Bks.
Rathbone, Andy. OS/2 for Dummies. 375p. 1993. pap. 19.95 (*1-878058-76-2*) IDG Bks.
Rathbone, Andy. OS/2 Warp for Dummies. 2nd ed. 384p. 1995. pap. 19.99 (*1-56884-205-8*) IDG Bks.
— PCs for Dummies. 3rd ed. 432p. 1995. pap. 16.99 (*1-56884-904-4*) IDG Bks.
— Upgrading & Fixing PCs for Dummies. (Illus.). 350p. 1993. pap. 19.95 (*1-56884-002-0*) IDG Bks.
— Upgrading & Fixing PCs for Dummies. 2nd ed. 384p. 1995. pap. 19.99 (*1-56884-903-6*) IDG Bks.
— Upgrading & Fixing PCs for Dummies. 4th ed. LC TK7887.R38 1998. (For Dummies Ser.). 384p. 1998. pap. 19.99 (*0-7645-0418-5*) IDG Bks.
***Rathbone, Andy.** Upgrading & Fixing PCs for Dummies. 5th ed. (For Dummies Ser.). (Illus.). 408p. 2000. pap. 19.99 (*0-7645-0719-2*) IDG Bks.
— Windows for Dummies. (Illus.). 350p. 1992. pap. 16.95 (*1-878058-61-4*) IDG Bks.
Rathbone, Andy. Windows 98 for Dummies. 408p. 1998. pap. 19.99 (*0-7645-0261-1*) IDG Bks.
— Windows 95 pour les Nuls. (FRE.). 332p. 1995. 49.95 (*0-7859-9853-5*) Fr & Eur.
Rathbone, Andy. Windows 95 for Dummies. 2nd ed. LC 96-80286. (Illus.). 408p. 1997. pap. 19.99 (*0-7645-0180-1*) IDG Bks.
Rathbone, Andy. Windows 95 for Dummies. 3rd ed. 408p. 1995. pap. 19.99 (*1-56884-240-6*) IDG Bks.
— Windows NT 5 for Dummies. 432p. 1999. pap. 19.99 (*0-7645-0339-1*) IDG Bks.
— Windows NT for Dummies. 2nd ed. LC 96-232906. 408p. 1996. pap. 19.99 (*1-56884-613-4*) IDG Bks.
***Rathbone, Andy.** Windows NT 4 Workstation for Dummies. 2nd ed. LC QA76.76.O63R39123. (For Dummies Ser.). 432p. 1999. pap. 19.99 (*0-7645-0496-7*) IDG Bks.
Rathbone, Andy. Windows 3.1 pour les Nuls. (FRE.). 350p. 1995. 49.95 (*0-7859-9855-1*) Fr & Eur.
— Windows 3.1 for Dummies. 2nd ed. 384p. 1994. pap. 16.95 (*1-56884-182-5*) IDG Bks.
***Rathbone, Andy.** Windows 2000 Professional for Dummies. (For Dummies Ser.). 432p. 2000. pap. 19.99 (*0-7645-0641-2*) IDG Bks.
Rathbone, Andy & Gookin, Dan. PCs for Dummies. 2nd ed. (For Dummies Ser.). (Illus.). 350p. 1994. pap. 16.95 (*1-56884-078-0*) IDG Bks.
Rathbone, Andy & IDG Books Staff. Windows 3.11 for Dummies. 4th ed. LC 98-84309. (For Dummies Ser.). 448p. 1998. pap. 19.99 (*0-7645-0338-3*) IDG Bks.
Rathbone, Andy & McComb, Gordon. VCRs & Camcorders for Dummies. LC 94-79604. 384p. 1994. pap. 14.99 (*1-56884-229-5*) IDG Bks.
Rathbone, Andy & Rathbone, Tina. Modems for Dummies. 3rd ed. LC 96-78141. (Illus.). 512p. 1997. pap. 19.99 (*0-7645-0069-4*) IDG Bks.
Rathbone, Andy, jt. auth. see Dummies Press Staff.
Rathbone, Andy, jt. auth. see Gookin, Dan.
Rathbone, B. J. & Heatley, Richard V. Helicobacter Pylori & Gastroduodenal Disease. 2nd ed. (Illus.). 312p. 1992. 150.00 (*0-632-03346-0*) Blackwell Sci.
Rathbone, Basil. In & Out of Character. 17.95 (*0-8488-1113-5*) Amereon Ltd.
— In & Out of Character. LC 88-21531. (Illus.). 288p. 1989. reprint ed. pap. 14.95 (*0-87910-119-9*) Limelight Edns.
***Rathbone, Belinda.** Walker Evans: A Biography. (Illus.). 368p. 2000. pap. 15.00 (*0-618-05672-6*) HM.
Rathbone, Belinda, et al, eds. Two Lives - Georgia O'Keeffe & Alfred Stieglitz: A Conversation in Paintings & Photographs. LC 92-36411. (Illus.). 144p. 1992. pap. 28.00 (*0-943044-17-0*) Phillips Coll.
Rathbone, Charles, et al. Multiage Portraits: Teaching & Learning in Mixed-Age Classrooms. 185p. 1993. pap. 19.95 (*0-9627389-7-2*, Crystal Spgs) Soc Dev Educ.
Rathbone, Charles H. It's the Climate. LC 71-134974. (Short Story Index Reprint Ser.). (Illus.). 1977. 18.95 (*0-8369-3705-8*) Ayer.
Rathbone, Charles H., jt. auth. see Hyman, Ronald T.
Rathbone, Cristina. On the Outside Looking In: A Year in an Inner-City High School. 400p. 1999. reprint ed. pap. 14.00 (*0-87113-736-4*, Atlntc Mnthly) Grove-Atltic.
Rathbone, Dominic. Economic Rationalism & Rural Society in Third-Century AD Egypt: The Heroninos Archive & the Appianus Estate. (Cambridge Classical Studies). (Illus.). 509p. (C). 1991. text 90.00 (*0-521-40149-6*) Cambridge U Pr.
Rathbone, Eliza E. Bill Jensen. LC 87-27312. (Illus.). 45p. 1987. pap. 15.00 (*0-943044-10-3*) Phillips Coll.
Rathbone, Irene. We That Were Young. LC 88-31029. 528p. 1989. 35.00 (*1-55861-001-4*); pap. 10.95 (*1-55861-002-2*) Feminist Pr.
Rathbone, Julian. Accidents Will Happen. (Mask Noir Title Ser.). 256p. 1997. pap. text 12.99 (*1-85242-312-9*) Serpents Tail.
***Rathbone, Julian.** Blame Hitler. large type ed. 1998. 27.95 (*0-7531-5582-6*, Pub. by ISIS Lrg Prnt) Transaction Pubs.
Rathbone, Julian. The Brandenburg Concerto. LC 97-61911. (Mask Noir Ser.). 224p. 1998. pap. 13.99 (*1-85242-525-3*) Serpents Tail.
***Rathbone, Julian.** The Last English King. LC 99-55913. 400p. 1999. text 24.95 (*0-312-24213-1*) St Martin.
Rathbone, Julian. Sand Blind. (Masks Ser.). 304p. 1994. pap. 12.99 (*1-85242-281-5*) Serpents Tail.
— A Spy of the Old School. 1984. mass mkt. 2.95 (*0-07-545341-X*) McGraw.
Rathbone, Lee, ed. see Blum, Miriam D.

An Asterisk (*) at the beginning of an entry indicates that the title is appearing for the first time.

Rathbone-McCuan, Eloise & Fabian, Dorothy R., eds. Self-Neglecting Elders: A Clinical Dilemma. LC 91-36343. 216p. 1992. 52.95 (*0-86569-047-2*, T047, Auburn Hse) Greenwood.

Rathbone-McCuan, Eloise & Havens, Betty, eds. North American Elders: United States & Canadian Perspectives, 8. LC 87-15048. (Contributions to the Study of Aging Ser.: No. 8). 312p. 1988. 65.00 (*0-313-25484-2*, REL/, Greenwood Pr) Greenwood.

Rathbone, Michael J. Oral Mucosal Drug Delivery. (Drugs & the Pharmaceutical Sciences Ser.: Vol. 74). (Illus.). 464p. 1996. text 185.00 (*0-8247-9744-2*) Dekker.

***Rathbone, Michael J. & Gurny, Robert.** Controlled Release Veterinary Drug Delivery: Biological & Pharmaceutical Considerations. LC 00-42171. 2000. write for info. (*0-444-82992-X*) Elsevier.

Rathbone, Richard. Ghana, 1941-1952. (British Documents on the End of Empire Series B: Vol. 1, Pt. 1). lxxxviii, 421p. 1992. 120.00 (*0-11-290525-0*, Pub. by Statnry Office) Balogh.

— Murder & Politics in Colonial Ghana. LC 92-44865. (Illus.). 256p. (C). 1993. 40.00 (*0-300-05504-8*) Yale U Pr.

***Rathbone, Richard.** Nkrumah & the Chiefs: The Politics of Chieftaincy in Ghana, 1951-1960. LC 99-46031. (West African Ser.). 200p. 1999. text 44.95 (*0-8214-1305-8*); pap. text 19.95 (*0-8214-1306-6*) Ohio U Pr.

Rathbone, Richard, ed. Ghana, 1952-1957. (British Documents on the End of Empire Series B: Vol. 1, Pt. 2). xxx, 443p. 1992. 120.00 (*0-11-290526-9*, Pub. by Statnry Office) Balogh.

Rathbone, Richard, jt. see Anderson, David.

Rathbone, Richard, jt. auth. see Anderson, David.

Rathbone, Robert R. Communicating Technical Information. LC 66-25632. (Engineering Ser.). (Illus.). (Orig.). 1966. pap. write for info. (*0-201-06305-0*) Addison-Wesley.

Rathbone, Tina. Modems for Dummies. (Illus.). 400p. 1993. pap. 19.95 (*1-56884-001-2*) IDG Bks.

— Modems for Dummies. 2nd ed. LC 94-79833. 512p. 1994. pap. 19.99 (*1-56884-223-6*) IDG Bks.

— More Modems & On-Line Services for Dummies. 416p. 1996. pap. 22.99 (*1-56884-365-8*) IDG Bks.

Rathbone, Tina, jt. auth. see Rathbone, Andy.

Rathbun. Eyelid Surgery. 1990. 200.00 (*0-316-73437-3*, Little Brwn Med Div) Lppncott W & W.

Rathbun, Bill. Whatever Happened to Professor Coyote? A Journey to the Heart of the Handgame. (Illus.). 320p. 1999. 25.00 (*0-9631242-3-4*); pap. 15.00 (*0-9631242-4-2*) Yerba Buena.

Rathbun, Carole. The Village in the Turkish Novel & Short Story, 1920-1955. (Near & Middle East Monographs: No. 2). 192p. 1972. text 56.95 (*90-279-2327-2*) Mouton.

Rathbun, Carolyn. Journey to Joy. LC 97-123165. 144p. (Orig.). 1997. pap. 11.99 (*0-8280-1251-2*) Review & Herald.

Rathbun, Carolyn R. Sara Bear's Surprise. (Land of Pleasant Dreams Ser.). (Illus.). (Orig.). (J). (ps). 1993. 12.95 (*0-9634808-0-4*); pap. 4.50 (*0-9634808-1-2*) Endless Love.

Rathbun, Elizabeth. Exploracion del Sistema Solar. Larios S, Maia & Sanz, Maria L., trs. (Explora y Aprende Ser.). (SPA., Illus.). 96p. (J). (gr. 3-8). 1993. 15.00 (*0-915741-46-6*) C D Stampley Ent.

Rathbun, Galen, jt. auth. see Nicoll, Martin E.

Rathbun, Gilbert. Monarch Notes on Williams' Glass Menagerie. (Orig.). (C). 3.95 (*0-671-00700-9*, Arco) Macmillan Gen Ref.

— Monarch Notes on Williams' Street-Car Named Desire. (Orig.). (C). 3.95 (*0-671-00701-7*, Arco) Macmillan Gen Ref.

Rathbun, John W. & Grecu, Monica M., eds. American Literary Critics & Scholars, 1850-1880. (Dictionary of Literary Biography Ser.: Vol. 64). 450p. 1987. text 155.00 (*0-8103-1742-7*) Gale.

Rathbun, Jonathan. Narrative of Jonathan Rathbun of the Capture of Fort Griswold with Accurate Accounts of the Capture of Groton Fort, the Massacre That Followed, & the Sacking & Burning of New London, September 6, 1781 by the British Forces Under the Command of the Traitor Benedict Arnold. LC 76-140878. (Eyewitness Accounts of the American Revolution Ser.). 1971. reprint ed. 21.95 (*0-405-01217-9*) Ayer.

Rathbun, Katharine C., jt. auth. see Richards, Edward P., III.

Rathbun, Katharine C., jt. auth. see Richards, Edward P., III.

Rathbun, Linda & Ringrose, Linda. Foothills to Mount Evans: West of Denver Trailguide. 6th ed. (Illus.). 80p. (Orig.). 1996. pap. 6.95 (*0-9606108-0-4*) Wordsmiths.

Rathbun, Mary & Peron, Dennis. Brownie Mary's Marijuana Cookbook: Recipes for Social Change. 65p. (Orig.). 1993. pap. 9.95 (*0-9639892-0-0*) Trail of Smoke.

Rathbun, Mary C., jt. auth. see Hayes, Bartlett H., Jr.

Rathbun, Mary J., jt. auth. see Edmondson, C. H.

Rathbun, Robert D., ed. Shopping Centers & Malls, No. 4. (Illus.). 224p. 1992. 49.95 (*0-934590-45-1*) Visual Refer.

— Shopping Centers & Malls, Vol. II. (Illus.). 192p. 1988. 54.95 (*0-934590-25-7*) Visual Refer.

Rathbun, Robert D., intro. Shopping Centers & Malls, Vol. III. 3rd ed. (Illus.). 224p. 1990. 49.95 (*0-934590-34-6*) Visual Refer.

Rathbun, Ron. The Silent Miracle: Awakening Your True Spiritual Nature by Stilling Your Mind. LC 98-235014. 288p. 1999. pap. text 13.00 (*0-425-16678-3*) Berkley Pub.

— The Way Is Within: A Spiritual Journey. 272p. (Orig.). 1997. pap. 13.00 (*0-425-15460-2*) Berkley Pub.

Rathbun, Ted A. & Buikstra, Jane E., eds. Human Identification: Case Studies in Forensic Anthropology. (Illus.). 456p. 1984. pap. 55.95 (*0-398-06337-0*) C C Thomas.

— Human Identification: Case Studies in Forensic Anthropology. (Illus.). 456p. (C). 1984. 87.95 (*0-398-04875-4*) C C Thomas.

Rathbun, W. B., jt. ed. see Hockwin, Otto.

Rathbun, William, et al. Treasures of Asian Art from the Idemitsu Collection. LC 81-52557. (Illus.). 204p. 1981. pap. 13.95 (*0-932216-06-4*) Seattle Art.

Rathbun, William J., ed. Beyond the Tanabata Bridge: Traditional Japanese Textiles. 1994. pap. 35.00 (*0-500-27740-0*) Thames Hudson.

Rathburn, Amy K. Taking Center Stage: Drama in America. 168p. 1997. pap., teacher ed. 14.95 (*0-472-08431-3*, 08431); pap. text 16.95 (*0-472-08393-7*, 08393) U of Mich Pr.

Rathburn, Thomas A., ed. Modeling on Micros & Workstations, 1991. 10th ed. 104p. 1991. pap. 48.00 (*0-911801-84-7*, MSM-91) Soc Computer Sim.

Rathe, Eric J., ed. Inter-Noise '77: Proceedings of the International Conference on Noise Control Engineering Held in Zurich, Switzerland March 1-3, 1977. (Inter-Noise Ser.). 986p. Date not set. 45.00 (*0-614-11280-X*) Noise Control.

Rathe, Gustave. The Wreck of the Barque Stefano off the North West Cape of Australia in 1875. (Illus.). 160p. (YA). 1992. 17.00 (*0-374-38585-8*) FS&G.

Rathe, John C. & Elliott, Paul. Radiologic Tumor Localization. 71p. (C). 1982. pap. 12.50 (*0-87527-249-5*) Green.

Rathe, John F. Bibliography of the Typophile Chap Books, 1935-1992. Lerner, Abe, ed. (Typophile Chap Bks.: No. 60). 94p. 1992. 35.00 (*0-945074-02-6*) Dawsons.

Rathe, Kurt. Die Ausdrucksfunktion Extrem Verkurzter Figren. (Warburg Institute Studies: Vol. 8). 1972. reprint ed. 30.00 (*0-8115-1386-6*) Periodicals Srv.

Rathenau, Ernest G. Oskar Kokoschka: Drawings, 1906-1965. 1993. pap. 22.95 (*0-87024-333-0*) U of Miami Pr.

Rathenau, Walter. Walter Rathenau: Industrialist, Banker, Intellectual, & Politician: Notes & Diaries 1907-1922. Von Strandmann, Hartmut P., ed. Von Strandmann, Hilary & Pinder-Cracraft, Caroline, trs. 360p. 1985. text 98.00 (*0-19-822506-7*) OUP.

***Rather, Dan.** Deadlines & Datelines. LC 99-10754. 240p. 1999. 23.00 (*0-688-16566-4*, Wm Morrow) Morrow Avon.

— Deadlines & Datelines. LC 99-46165. 1999. 25.95 (*1-56895-779-3*, Compass) Wheeler Pub.

— Deadlines & Datelines: Essays at the Turn of the Century. 220p. 2000. 23.00 (*0-7881-9349-X*) DIANE Pub.

— Deadlines & Datelines: Essays at the Turn of the Century. 256p. 2000. pap. 14.00 (*0-688-17905-3*) Morrow Avon.

— The Joy of Fly Fishing. 1924. write for info. (*0-688-17283-0*, Wm Morrow) Morrow Avon.

Rather, Dan & Hebert, Anne L. Austin: Celebrating a Lone Star Millennium. LC 99-33223. (Urban Tapestry Ser.). (Illus.). 1999. 49.95 (*1-881096-71-8*) Towery Pub.

Rather, Dan, ed. see Sullivan, Mark.

Rather, L., ed. see Virchow, Rudolph.

Rather, L. J. Reading Wagner: A Study in the History of Ideas. LC 89-37814. 368p. 1990. text 50.00 (*0-8071-1557-6*) La State U Pr.

Rather, L. J., et al. Johannes Mueller & the Nineteenth-Century Origins of Tumor Cell Theory. LC 86-6616. 1987. 15.00 (*0-88135-080-X*) Watson Pub Intl.

Rather, Lelland J. A Commentary on the Medical Writings of Rudolf Virchow: Based on Schwalbe's Virchow-Bibliographie, 1843-1901. (Bibliography Ser.: No. 3). (Illus.). 236p. 1990. 125.00 (*0-930405-19-6*) Norman SF.

— The Genesis of Cancer: A Study in the History of Ideas. LC 78-2785. 280p. reprint ed. pap. 86.80 (*0-8357-6624-1*, 203527000094) Bks Demand.

Rather, Lois. Bonanza Theater. limited ed. (Illus.). 1977. 35.00 (*0-686-20514-6*) Rather Pr.

— Dunsmuir House. limited ed. (Illus.). 1982. 35.00 (*0-686-37970-5*) Rather Pr.

— Henry George: Printer to Author. limited ed. (Illus.). 1978. 35.00 (*0-686-22963-0*) Rather Pr.

— J. Ross Browne: Adventurer. limited ed. (Illus.). 1978. 35.00 (*0-686-05279-X*) Rather Pr.

— Lotta's Fountain. limited ed. (Illus.). 1979. 35.00 (*0-686-15713-3*) Rather Pr.

— The Man with the Hoe. limited ed. (Illus.). 1977. 35.00 (*0-686-20513-8*) Rather Pr.

— Miss Kate: Kate Douglas Wiggin in San Francisco. limited ed. (Illus.). 1980. 35.00 (*0-686-26424-X*) Rather Pr.

— R. W. Emerson, Tourist. limited ed. (Illus.). 1979. 35.00 (*0-686-26147-X*) Rather Pr.

— Rather a Small Press. limited ed. (Illus.). 1976. 17.50 (*0-686-20625-8*) Rather Pr.

— West Is West: Rudyard Kipling in San Francisco. limited ed. (Illus.). 1976. 35.00 (*0-686-20624-X*) Rather Pr.

Rather, Marsha L., jt. ed. see Dickelmann, Nancy L.

Rather, Petra, jt. auth. see Buhring, Anne.

Rather, Susan. Archaism, Modernism, & the Art of Paul Manship. LC 92-14217. (American Studies Ser.). (Illus.). 284p. (C). 1993. text 42.50 (*0-292-76035-3*) U of Tex Pr.

Rathert, Donna R. Advent is for Waiting. (Illus.). 24p. (J). (ps-k). 1987. pap. 2.99 (*0-570-04140-6*, 56-1569) Concordia.

— Lent Is for Remembering. LC 56-1613. 24p. (Orig.). (J). (ps-1). 1987. pap. 2.99 (*0-570-04147-3*, 56-1613) Concordia.

Rathert, P., et al. Urinary Cytology: Manual & Atlas. 2nd rev. ed. Telger, Terry C., tr. from GER. LC 92-49568. 1992. 158.00 (*0-387-53312-5*) Spr-Verlag.

Rathert-Phillips, Annette, see Uriel, Alexandria, pseud.

Rathgeb. Success Signs. 1999. pap. 13.95 (*0-312-20678-X*) St Martin.

Rathgeb, Marlene M. Sexual Astrology. 304p. (Orig.). 1993. pap. 11.00 (*0-380-76888-7*, Avon Bks) Morrow Avon.

— Success Signs. (Illus.). 224p. 1981. pap. 5.95 (*0-312-77486-9*) St Martin.

Rathgeb, Steven & Lipsky, Michael. Nonprofits for Hire: The Welfare State in the Age of Contracting. (Illus.). 312p. 1995. pap. 19.50 (*0-674-62639-7*, SMINOX) HUP.

Rathgeber, Daniel C. For My Wife with Love at Christmas. 44p. 1996. pap. 9.95 (*0-9635337-6-2*) Realty Res.

Rathgeber, David, jt. auth. see Riggins, Elmer.

Rathgeber, David G. Buying a Home in the Washington, D. C. Metropolitan Area. LC 94-93992. 142p. 1999. pap. 14.95 (*0-9635337-3-8*) Realty Res.

— Selling Your Home in the Washington, D.C. Metropolitan Area. LC 94-93991. 123p. 1998. pap. 9.95 (*0-9635337-4-6*) Realty Res.

***Rathgeber, Eva M. & Adera, Edith Ofwona.** Gender & the Information Revolution in Africa. 300p. 2000. pap. 24.95 (*0-88936-903-8*, Pub. by IDRC Bks) Stylus Pub VA.

Rathgeber, Eva-Maria, jt. auth. see Altbach, Philip G.

Rathi, Manohar L., ed. Current Perinatology. (Illus.). 290p. 1988. 125.00 (*0-387-96758-3*) Spr-Verlag.

— Current Perinatology Two. (Illus.). xii, 230p. 1990. 125.00 (*0-387-97214-5*) Spr-Verlag.

Rathi, Manohar L. & Kumar, Sudhir. Perinatal Medicine, 2 vols. 1982. text 39.50 (*0-07-051208-6*) McGraw.

— Perinatal Medicine, 2 vols., Vol. 1. 1980. text 35.00 (*0-07-051204-3*) McGraw.

Rathje, Linda, et al. ClarisWorks for Students. 4th rev. ed. (Illus.). 416p. (Orig.). 1996. student ed., spiral bd. 39.95 (*0-9644314-3-2*) HRS Pubns.

— ClarisWorks for Students Bk. 2: A Beginner's Guide to Desktop Publishing. (Illus.). 397p. (YA). (gr. 7-12). 1996. student ed., spiral bd. 44.95 (*0-9644314-4-0*) HRS Pubns.

Rathje, William L. Archaeology. 2nd ed. (C). 2000. pap. text 42.00 (*0-15-505177-6*) Harcourt.

Rathje, William L., jt. auth. see Lilienfeld, Robert M.

Rathjen, Dan. Lego Crazy Action Contraptions: A LEGO Inventions Book. Editors of Klutz, ed. (Illus.). 66p. (J). (gr. 4-7). 1998. pap. 19.95 (*1-57054-157-4*) Klutz.

Rathjen, Frederick. Texas Panhandle Frontier. rev. ed. LC 98-8399. (Classic Reissues of the American West Ser.). (Illus.). 288p. 1998. pap. 16.95 (*0-89672-399-2*) Tex Tech Univ Pr.

***Rathjen, Heidi & Montpetit, Charles.** December 6: From the Montreal Massacre to Gun Control: the Inside Story. 211p. 1999. 21.95 (*0-7710-6125-0*) McCland & Stewart.

Rathjen, Joseph E. Locksmithing: From Apprentice to Master. 309p. 1994. pap. 24.95 (*0-07-051645-6*) McGraw.

Rathjens, C., jt. ed. see Muller, P. C.

***Rathkamp, David & Siodlarz, Christopher.** The Pediatric Repair Manual. Vu, Quynh, ed. LC 00-91683. (Illus.). 354p. 2000. pap. 19.95 (*0-9700586-0-8*, Pub. by Rocco) BookMasters.

Rathke, Ann M., jt. ed. see Lysengen, Janet D.

Rathke, David E. & Edwards, Clayton J., eds. A Review of Trends in Lake Erie Water Quality with Emphasis on the 1978-1979 Intensive Survey: Report to the Surveillance Work Group. fac. ed. LC 86-103207. (Illus.). 139p. 1985. pap. 43.10 (*0-7837-8627-1*, 207524100007) Bks Demand.

Rathke, Ewald, jt. ed. see Hering, Karl H.

Rathkopf, Charles A., et al. Rathkopf's Law of Zoning & Planning, 5 vols. 4th ed. LC 56-2013. (Real Property - Zoning Ser.). 1975. ring bd. 550.00 (*0-87632-020-5*) West Group.

Rathlef, Ernst L. Geschichte Jetztlebender Gelehrter, als eine Fortsetzung des Jetztlebenden Gelehrten Europa, 3 vols., Set. 1972. reprint ed. write for info. (*3-487-04384-X*) G Olms Pubs.

Rathlev, Mary & Riley, Martha. Youth & HIV: It's up to You & Me: A Reference Guide for Service Providers. (YA). 1994. pap. 7.95 (*0-9634295-0-7*) Childs Hosp.

Rathlev, Mary, jt. auth. see Parrott, Robert H.

Rathman, Helena R. Yin Deficiency & Yin-Yang: Index of New Information & Research Guide. 150p. 1994. 47.50 (*0-7883-0106-3*); pap. 44.50 (*0-7883-0107-1*) ABBE Pubs Assn.

Rathman, R. Annabel, ed. see Dean, Bob.

Rathman, R. Annabel, ed. see Grossman, Alvin.

Rathman, R. Annabel, ed. see Travis, John W.

Rathman, R. Annabel, ed. see Walkowicz, Chris.

Rathmann, Charles & Crimmins, James. Rockin' Jimmy's Daily Guitar Workout. (Illus.). 36p. 1999. pap. 5.95 (*0-9673686-1-8*) Rathmann Commns.

Rathmann, Peggy. Good Night, Gorilla. LC 92-29020. (Illus.). 40p. (J). (ps-1). 1994. 14.99 (*0-399-22445-9*, G P Putnam) Peng Put Young Read.

— Good Night, Gorilla. LC 92-29020. (Illus.). 32p. (J). (ps). 1996. bds. 6.99 (*0-399-23003-3*, G P Putnam) Peng Put Young Read.

***Rathmann, Peggy.** Good Night, Gorilla. (Illus.). 40p. (J). (ps-3). 2000. pap. 5.99 (*0-698-11649-6*, PuffinBks) Peng Put Young Read.

— Good Night, Gorilla. (Illus.). (J). 2000. 11.44 (*0-606-18837-1*) Turtleback.

Rathmann, Peggy. Ruby, Mono Ve, Mono Hace. 1995. 10.15 (*0-606-08086-4*, Pub. by Turtleback) Demco.

— Ruby, Mono Ve, Mono Hace: Ruby the Copycat. 32p. (J). (ps-k). 1995. pap. 4.95 (*0-590-50211-5*) Scholastic Inc.

— Ruby the Copycat. 32p. (J). (ps-3). 1991. 14.95 (*0-590-43747-X*, Scholastic Hardcover) Scholastic Inc.

Rathmann, Peggy. Ruby the Copycat. 32p. (J). (ps-3). 1993. pap. 4.95 (*0-590-47423-5*) Scholastic Inc.

Rathmann, Peggy. Ruby the Copycat. LC 91-101. (Illus.). 32p. (J). (ps-2). 1997. 9.95 (*0-590-76715-1*) Scholastic Inc.

— Ruby the Copycat. (Blue Ribbon Bks.). (J). 1991. 10.15 (*0-606-05573-8*, Pub. by Turtleback) Demco.

— 10 Minutes till Bedtime. LC 97-51295. (Illus.). 32p. (J). (ps-1). 1998. 16.99 (*0-399-23103-X*, G P Putnam) Peng Put Young Read.

Rathmann, Peggy. Officer Buckle & Gloria. LC 93-43887. 37p. (J). (ps-3). 1995. 15.99 (*0-399-22616-8*, G P Putnam) Peng Put Young Read.

Rathmann, Rodney L., jt. ed. see Bergt, Caolyn S.

Rathmann, Rodney L., jt. ed. see Bergt, Carolyn S.

Rathmayer, H. G. & Saari, K. H., eds. Improvement of Ground: Proceedings of the Eighth European Conference on Soil Mechanics & Foundation Engineering, Helsinki 23-26 May 1983, 3 vols. 1398p. 1983. text 621.00 (*90-6191-240-7*, Pub. by A A Balkema) Ashgate Pub Co.

Rathmell, Andrew. The Changing Military Balance in the Gulf. LC 98-127161. iv, 149 p. 1996. write for info. (*0-85516-145-0*) Royal United Services Inst for Defence Studies.

Rathmell, George. Realms of Gold: Literary Life in San Francisco, 1850-1950. LC 97-67373. (Illus.). 256p. (Orig.). 1998. pap. 14.95 (*0-88739-162-1*) Creat Arts Bk.

Rathmill, K., et al, eds. Robot Technology & Applications. (Illus.). 203p. 1985. 69.00 (*0-387-13960-5*) Spr-Verlag.

Rathmill, K. & Macconaill, P. A., eds. Computer Integrated Manufacturing. (Illus.). 280p. 1988. 123.00 (*0-387-18758-8*) Spr-Verlag.

Rathnaiah, K. Social Change among Malsa: An Ex-Untouchable Caste in South India. (C). 1991. 24.50 (*81-7141-137-1*) S Asia.

***Rathnaswamy, P.** Political Question & Article 356. 1998. 34.00 (*81-7049-083-9*, Pub. by Manas Pubns) S Asia.

Rathner, Donald M., et al, eds. The Classicist, Vol. 1. (Illus.). 96p. 1994. pap. 34.95 (*1-56000-804-0*) Transaction Pubs.

Rathod, Rajendrasinh N., ed. see Chandra, Ram & Rajagopalachari, Parthasarathi.

Rathore, H. C. Management of Distance Education in India. (Illus.). x, 225p. 1993. 26.00 (*81-7024-532-X*, Pub. by Ashish Pub Hse) Nataraj Bks.

Rathore, H. S. Reliability of Metals in Electronics. LC 95-60438. (Proceedings Ser.: Vol. 95-3). 243p. 1995. pap. 42.00 (*1-56677-097-1*) Electrochem Soc.

Rathore, H. S., et al, eds. Interconnect & Contact Metallization: Materials, Processes & Reliability. LC 98-203944. (Proceedings Ser.: Vol. 97-31). 276p. 1998. 54.00 (*1-56677-184-6*) Electrochem Soc.

— Low & High Dielectric Constant Materials: Materials Science, Processing & Reliability Issues. LC 98-100811. (Proceedings Ser.: Vol. 97-8). 262p. 1997. 48.00 (*1-56677-135-8*) Electrochem Soc.

— Reliability of Semiconductor Devices - Interconnections & Laser Processes for Microelectronic Applications. LC 92-70488. (Proceedings Ser.: Vol. 92-4). 340p. 1992. 42.00 (*1-56677-003-3*) Electrochem Soc.

Rathore, Hamir S. Handbook of Chromatography: Liquid Chromatography Polylyclicicl. 432p. 1993. lib. bdg. 200.00 (*0-8493-3005-X*, QD341) CRC Pr.

Rathore, L. S. & Haqqi, S. A. Political Theory & Organization. (C). 1988. 65.00 (*0-7855-3520-9*) St Mut.

— Principles of Political Theory & Organization. (C). 1988. 60.00 (*0-7855-5447-5*) St Mut.

Rathore, N. S. Natural Resources Base Development. (C). 1992. pap. 45.00 (*81-7233-032-4*, Pub. by Scientific Pubs) St Mut.

Rathore, R. & Haqqi, S. A. Political Theory & Organization for Law Students. (C). 1991. text 60.00 (*0-89771-505-5*) St Mut.

Rathore, Sandhya. Kaunda Bhatta's "Vaiyakaranabhusanasara" LC 98-906648. 1998. 26.00 (*81-85636-41-9*, Pub. by I C P R IND) S Asia.

Raths, James. NCATE Accreditation: A Framework for Preparing Section II of the Institutional Report. 1993. 21.00 (*0-89333-106-6*) AACTE.

Raths, James, jt. ed. see Katz, Lilian G.

Raths, Louis E. Meeting the Needs of Children: Creating Trust & Security. LC 98-70460. 166p. (C). 1998. pap. text 21.95 (*0-9658339-7-6*) Educ Intl Pr.

Rathschmidt, Jack & Cronin, Gaynell B. Rituals for Home & Parish: Healing & Celebrating Our Families. 160p. 1996. pap. 17.95 (*0-8091-3650-3*, 3650-3) Paulist Pr.

Rathschmidt, Jack, jt. auth. see Cronin, Gaynell Bordes.

Rathswohl, Eugene, jt. auth. see Beekman, George.

Rathus. Adjustment & Growth. 6th ed. LC 94-77536. (C). 1994. text 72.50 (*0-15-501670-9*) Harcourt Coll Pubs.

— Adjustment & Growth. 6th ed. (C). 1995. pap. text, lab manual ed. 22.50 (*0-15-503126-0*, Pub. by Harcourt Coll Pubs) Harcourt.

— Adjustment & Growth: Challenge. 7th ed. LC 98-88489. (C). 1998. text 72.50 (*0-15-508043-1*, Pub. by Harcourt Coll Pubs) Harcourt.

— Chronological Child Development. (Education Ser.). 1919. pap. 42.00 (*0-534-52785-X*) Wadsworth Pub.

— Essentials of Psychology. 6th ed. (C). 2000. pap. text. write for info. (*0-15-508065-2*) Harcourt Coll Pubs.

— Lifespan Development. 2000. pap. text 42.00 (*0-534-52776-0*) Thomson Learn.

— Oht T/a Psychology New Millenium 7e. 7th ed. (C). 1998. pap. text 441.50 (*0-15-507172-6*) Harcourt Coll Pubs.

***Rathus.** Psychology. (C). 1999. pap. text 15.00 (*0-15-507460-1*) Harcourt Coll Pubs.

R

— Psychology: The Core. (C). 1999. pap. text 22.50 (*0-15-507459-8*); pap. text 57.50 (*0-15-507452-0*) Harcourt.

Rathus. Psychology: The Core. (C). 1999. pap. text 44.50 (*0-15-507454-7*) Harcourt Coll Pubs.

— Psychology in New Millennium. 7th ed. (C). 1998. pap. text, student ed. 28.00 (*0-15-508221-3*) Harcourt.

***Rathus.** Topical Child Development. 2002. 42.00 (*0-534-52794-9*) Wadsworth Pub.

***Rathus & Nevid.** Supplementman Sexuality in a World of Diversity: Human Sexuality in a World of Diversity. 4th ed. 2000. 74.00 incl. cd-rom (*0-205-32528-9*) Allyn.

Rathus, Jill H. & Sanderson, William. Marital Distress: Cognitive Behavioral Interventions for Dysfunctional Couples (A1) LC 98-21980. 1998. 50.00 (*0-7657-0000-X*) Aronson.

***Rathus, Spencer.** Psychology: The Core. (C). 1999. pap. text 22.50 (*0-15-507461-X*) Harcourt.

Rathus, Spencer A. Adjustment & Growth: Challenges of Life. 6th ed. (C). 1994. pap. text, student ed. 27.00 (*0-15-502439-6*) Harcourt Coll Pubs.

— Adjustment & Growth: Challenges of Life. 6th ed. (C). 1994. pap. text, teacher ed., suppl. ed. 41.50 (*0-15-502440-X*, Pub. by Harcourt Coll Pubs) Harcourt.

— Critical Thinking Workbook in Psychology: Critical Thinking. 4th ed. (C). 1990. pap. text, wbk. ed. 28.00 (*0-03-033702-X*, Pub. by Harcourt Coll Pubs) Harcourt.

Rathus, Spencer A. Essentials of Psychology. 5th ed. (Illus.). (C). 1997. pap. text 58.50 (*0-15-507576-4*) Harcourt.

Rathus, Spencer A. Essentials of Psychology. 5th ed. LC 95-82359. 864p. (C). 1996. pap. text 58.50 (*0-15-503731-5*, Pub. by Harcourt Coll Pubs); pap. text 33.50 (*0-15-503732-3*, Pub. by Harcourt Coll Pubs); pap. text, teacher ed. 28.00 (*0-15-503733-1*) Harcourt Coll Pubs.

— Psychology. 4th ed. 768p. (C). 1990. text 74.00 (*0-03-034597-9*, Pub. by Harcourt Coll Pubs) Harcourt.

— Psychology. 6th ed. LC 94-79633. (C). 1995. text 77.50 (*0-15-501699-7*) Harcourt Coll Pubs.

— Psychology: Telecourse Faculty Guide. 6th ed. (C). 1995. pap. text, teacher ed. 44.50 (*0-15-503653-X*, Pub. by Harcourt Coll Pubs) Harcourt.

— Psychology: Telecourse Study Guide. 6th ed. (C). 1995. pap. text, student ed. 28.50 (*0-15-503654-8*) Harcourt Coll Pubs.

— Psychology: Thinking & Writing Workbook. 6th ed. (C). 1995. wbk. ed. 13.50 (*0-15-503220-8*) Harcourt Coll Pubs.

— Psychology in the New Millenium. 6th ed. (C). 1995. pap. text, student ed. 27.00 (*0-15-503218-6*) Harcourt Coll Pubs.

— Psychology in the New Millenium. 6th ed. (C). 1995. pap. text, teacher ed. 35.00 (*0-15-503217-8*) Harcourt Coll Pubs.

— Psychology in the New Millennium. 7th ed. 832p. (C). 1998. text 77.50 (*0-15-508215-9*, Pub. by Harcourt Coll Pubs) Harcourt.

— Think & Writing about Psychology. 2nd ed. 168p. (C). 1996. wbk. ed. 13.50 (*0-15-504141-X*, Pub. by Harcourt Coll Pubs) Harcourt.

— Understanding Child Development. (C). 1988. pap. text, student ed. 28.50 (*0-03-001839-0*) Harcourt Coll Pubs.

— Understanding Child Development. (C). 1988. teacher ed. 409.50 (*0-03-001843-9*) Harcourt Coll Pubs.

Rathus, Spencer A. & Boughn, Susan. AIDS: What Every Student Needs to Know. 2nd ed. LC 93-80577. 106p. (C). 1994. pap. text 23.50 (*0-15-501700-4*) Harcourt.

Rathus, Spencer A. & Favaro, Peter. Understanding Child Development. (Illus.). 688p. (C). 1988. text 69.50 (*0-03-001837-4*) Harcourt Coll Pubs.

Rathus, Spencer A. & Kornblum. Adjustment & Growth: Challenges of Life. 6th ed. (C). 1994. pap. text, teacher ed. 35.00 (*0-15-502438-8*) Harcourt Coll Pubs.

Rathus, Spencer A., et al. Essential Human Sexuality. LC 97-18307. 450p. (C). 1997. pap. text 36.00 (*0-205-27255-X*) P-H.

Rathus, Spencer A., et al. Essentials of Human Sexuality. 208p. (C). 1997. pap. text, teacher ed. write for info. (*0-205-27452-8*, T7452-0) Allyn.

***Rathus, Spencer A., et al.** Essentials of Human Sexuality. LC 97-18307. (Illus.). 450p. 1998. pap. 0.00 (*0-205-30005-7*) Allyn.

Rathus, Spencer A., et al. Essentials of Human Sexuality: Examination Copy. 464p. (C). 1997. pap. text. write for info. (*0-205-27648-2*, T7648-3) Allyn.

— Human Sexuality in a World of Diversity. 4th ed. LC 99-16469. 714p. (C). 1999. 77.00 (*0-205-27949-X*, Macmillan Coll) P-H.

Rathvon, Henry, et al. Boston Globe Sunday Crosswords Vol. 2, Vol. 2. Vol. 2. 1995. pap. 9.00 (*0-8129-2539-4*, Times Bks) Crown Pub Group.

Rathvon, Natalie. Effective School Interventions: Strategies for Enhancing Academic Achievement & Social Competence. LC 98-34856. (School Practitioner Ser.). 366p. 1999. lib. bdg. 36.00 (*1-57230-409-X*) Guilford Pubns.

— The Unmotivated Child. 240p. 1996. per. 12.00 (*0-684-80306-2*) S&S Trade.

Rathwell, Tom, et al, eds. Tipping the Balance Towards Primary Health Care: A Pan-European Analysis. 200p. 1995. 72.95 (*1-85628-941-9*, Pub. by Avebry) Ashgate Pub Co.

Ratigan, Virginia K. & Swidler, Arlene A., eds. A New Phoebe: Perspectives on Roman Catholic Women & the Permanent Diaconate. LC 90-60898. 120p. (Orig.). (C). 1990. pap. 7.95 (*1-55612-357-4*) Sheed & Ward WI.

Ratigan, William. Great Lakes Shipwrecks. (Illus.). 384p. 1994. 10.98 (*0-88365-853-4*) Galahad Bks.

Ratigan, William. Great Lakes Shipwrecks & Survivals. 3rd ed. 384p. 1989. pap. 16.00 (*0-8028-7010-4*) Eerdmans.

Rational Data Systems, Inc. Staff. NetWare for AOS - VS, 5 bks., Set. 1992. pap. 375.00 incl. disk (*1-881378-14-4*) Rational Data.

— NetWare for AOS - VS Concepts. 1992. pap. 75.00 incl. disk (*1-881378-07-1*) Rational Data.

— NetWare for AOS - VS Installation. 1992. pap. 75.00 incl. disk (*1-881378-10-1*) Rational Data.

— NetWare for AOS - VS System Administration. 1992. pap. 75.00 incl. disk (*1-881378-09-8*) Rational Data.

— NetWare for AOS - VS System Messages. 1992. pap. 75.00 incl. disk (*1-881378-11-X*) Rational Data.

— NetWare for AOS - VS Utilities. 1992. pap. 75.00 incl. disk (*1-881378-08-X*) Rational Data.

— PC - Mail User's Guide. 99p. 1992. pap. 3.50 incl. disk (*1-881378-06-3*) Rational Data.

— PC - Remote User's Guide. 192p. 1992. pap. 4.00 incl. disk (*1-881378-01-2*) Rational Data.

— PC - VS System Managers Guide. 84p. 1992. pap. 10.00 incl. disk (*1-881378-03-9*) Rational Data.

— PC - VS System Managers Guide, No. 5. 1992. pap. 10.00 incl. disk (*1-881378-15-2*) Rational Data.

— PC - VS User's Guide. 194p. 1992. pap. 4.00 incl. disk (*0-685-55375-2*) Rational Data.

— PopTerm - NVT for MS-DOS User's Guide. 40p. 1992. pap. 5.50 incl. disk (*1-881378-04-7*) Rational Data.

— PopTerm - NVT for Windows User's Guide. 30p. 1992. pap. 5.50 incl. disk (*1-881378-05-5*) Rational Data.

— PopTerm User's Guide. 84p. 1992. pap. 4.00 incl. disk (*1-881378-00-4*) Rational Data.

— Report on PC Integration, 1992. 136p. 1992. 24.95 (*1-881378-13-6*) Rational Data.

— Report on PC Integration, 1991. 118p. 1992. 5.00 (*1-881378-12-8*) Rational Data.

Rational Software Corporation Staff, jt. auth. see Lockheed Martin Advanced Concepts Center Staff.

Ratisbonne, Theodore. St. Bernard of Clairvaux: Oracle of the 12th Century (1091-1153) Abbot, Confessor & Doctor of the Church. LC 91-67795. Orig. Title: The Life & Times of St. Bernard. 437p. 1991. reprint ed. pap. 18.50 (*0-89555-453-4*) TAN Bks Pubs.

Ratisseau, Elizabeth. Dogs Tell Their Own Stories. 192p. 1999. 19.95 (*1-883211-15-8*, Darling & Comp) Laughing Elephant.

— Fairies. LC 99-168119. (Illus.). 48p. 1998. 16.95 (*1-883211-12-3*) Laughing Elephant.

— Guardian Angels. (Illus.). 48p. 1999. 16.95 (*1-883211-20-4*) Laughing Elephant.

— Mermaids. 48p. 1998. 16.95 (*1-883211-14-X*) Laughing Elephant.

Ratiu, Tudor S., jt. auth. see Marsden, Jerrold E.

Ratke, Lorenz, et al, eds. Materials & Fluids under Low Gravity: Proceedings of the IX European Symposium on Gravity Dependent Phenomena in Physical Sciences, Held at Berlin, Germany, 2-5 May 1995. LC 95-51687. (Lecture Notes in Physics Ser.: Vol. 464). 424p. 1996. 92.00 (*3-540-60677-7*) Spr-Verlag.

Ratkevich, Ronald P., jt. auth. see Casanova, Richard L.

Ratkos, James. Spyro the Dragon: Prima's Official Strategy Guide. LC 98-67669. (Games Ser.). 96p. 1998. per. 12.99 (*0-7615-1860-6*) Prima Pub.

***Ratkos, James M.** Legend of Zelda: Link's Awakening DX: Official Strategy Guide. LC 99-63282. (Illus.). 112p. 1999. pap. 12.99 (*0-7615-2240-9*, Prima Games) Prima Pub.

Ratkos, James M., jt. auth. see Hollinger, Elizabeth M.

Ratkowsky, David A. Handbook of Nonlinear Regression Models. LC 89-27493. (Statistics, Textbooks & Monographs: Vol. 107). (Illus.). 259p. reprint ed. pap. 80.30 (*0-608-10639-9*, 207126100009) Bks Demand.

— Nonlinear Regression Modeling: A Unified Practical Approach. (Statistics: Textbooks & Monographs: Vol. 48). (Illus.). 288p. 1983. text 125.00 (*0-8247-1907-7*) Dekker.

Ratkowsky, David A., et al. Cross-over Experiments: Design, Analysis & Application. (Statistics: Textbooks & Monographs: Vol. 135). (Illus.). 480p. 1992. text 160.00 (*0-8247-8892-3*) Dekker.

Ratledge, Colin, ed. Biochemistry of Microbial Degradation. LC 93-10260. 584p. (C). 1994. text 402.50 (*0-7923-2273-8*) Kluwer Academic.

— Physiology of Biodegradative Microorganisms. 142p. 1991. text 171.00 (*0-7923-1132-9*) Kluwer Academic.

Ratledge, Colin, et al, eds. The Biology of the Mycobacteria Vol. 3: Clinical Aspects of Mycobacterial Disease. 621p. 1989. text 209.00 (*0-12-582303-7*) Acad Pr.

— Biotechnology for the Oils & Fats Industry. 298p. 1984. 40.00 (*0-935315-08-X*) Am Oil Chemists.

***Ratledge, Colin & Dale, Jeremy.** Mycobacteria: Molecular Biology & Virulence. LC 99-24452. (Illus.). 1999. pap. 185.00 (*0-632-05304-6*) Blackwell Sci.

Ratledge, Colin & Stanford, John L., eds. Biology of the Mycobacteria Vol. 2: Immunological & Environmental Aspects. 1983. text 209.00 (*0-12-582302-9*) Acad Pr.

Ratledge, Colin & Wilkinson, S. G., eds. Microbial Lipids, Vol. 1. 450p. 1988. text 209.00 (*0-12-582304-5*) Acad Pr.

— Microbial Lipids, Vol. 2. 726p. 1989. text 209.00 (*0-12-582305-3*) Acad Pr.

Ratledge, Colin, jt. ed. see Kyle, D. J.

***Ratledge, David.** Observing the Caldwell Objects. LC 99-57027. (Illus.). 225p. 2000. 34.95 (*1-85233-628-5*, Pub. by Spr-Verlag) Spr-Verlag.

Ratledge, David. Software & Data for Practical Astronomers: The Best of the Internet. Moore, P., ed. LC 98-29961. (Practical Astronomy Ser.). viii, 184p. 1999. pap. 49.95 incl. cd-rom (*1-85233-055-4*) Spr-Verlag.

Ratledge, David, ed. The Art & Science of CCD Astronomy, Vol. XIV. LC 96-43811. (Practical Astronomy Ser.). 212p. 1996. pap. 39.95 (*3-540-76103-9*) Spr-Verlag.

Ratledge, Edward C. & Jacoby, Joan E. Handbook on Artificial Intelligence & Expert Systems in Law Enforcement. LC 89-7467. (Illus.). 212p. 1989. lib. bdg. 59.95 (*0-313-26461-9*, RHX/, Greenwood Pr) Greenwood.

Ratledge, Marcus W. Hot Cars! An Inside Look at the Auto Theft Industry. (Illus.). 136p. 1982. pap. 15.00 (*0-87364-220-1*) Paladin Pr.

Ratliff, Jack. Texas Courts: Trial & Appeal : Cases & Materials. 3rd ed. LC 97-220114. 566 p. 1997. write for info. (*0-9648201-8-8*) Grail & Tucker.

Ratliff, A. H., et al. Selected References in Elective Orthopaedics. xviii, 204p. 1991. pap. 39.00 (*0-387-19682-X*) Spr-Verlag.

— Selected References in Orthopaedic Trauma. xvii, 124p. 1989. 40.95 (*0-387-19556-4*) Spr-Verlag.

Ratliff, Donald E. Map, Compass, & Campfire: A Handbook for the Outdoorsman. LC 64-8453. (Illus.). 64p. 1993. reprint ed. pap. 7.95 (*0-8323-0129-9*) Binford Mort.

Ratliff, Floyd. Mach Bands: Quantitative Studies on Neural Networks in the Retina. LC 65-10436. 1965. 38.00 (*0-8162-7045-7*) Holden-Day.

— Paul Signac & Color in Neo-Impressionism. (Illus.). 317p. 1992. 49.95 (*0-87470-050-7*) Rockefeller.

Ratliff, Floyd, ed. Studies on Excitation & Inhibition in the Retina. LC 73-89539. (Illus.). 688p. 1974. 17.50 (*0-87470-019-1*) Rockefeller.

Ratliff, Gerald L. Coping with Stage Fright. (Illus.). 119p. (YA). (gr. 7-12). 1985. lib. bdg. 17.95 (*0-8239-0638-8*) Rosen Group.

— Introduction to Readers Theatre: A Guide to Classroom Performance. LC 99-37424. 224p. (YA). (gr. 9-12). 1999. pap. 16.95 (*1-56608-053-3*, U-B234) Meriwether Pub.

— Playing Scenes: A Sourcebook for Performers. Zapel, Theodore O., ed. LC 93-11356. (Illus.). 440p. (Orig.). (YA). (gr. 9 up). 1993. pap. 14.95 (*0-916260-89-5*, B109) Meriwether Pub.

— The Theatre Audition Book: Playing Monologs from Contemporary, Modern, Period, Shakespeare & Classical Plays. Zapel, Ted, ed. LC 98-29131. 288p. 1998. pap. 16.95 (*1-56608-044-4*, B224) Meriwether Pub.

Ratliff, Gerald L. & Zapel, Theodore O., eds. Playing Contemporary Scenes: 31 Famous Scenes & How to Play Them. LC 96-36394. (Illus.). 368p. (YA). (gr. 9 up). 1996. pap. 16.95 (*1-56608-025-8*, B100) Meriwether Pub.

Ratliff, Jack. Texas Courts: Trial & Appeal: Cases & Materials, 1995-1996. LC 96-103335. xii, 668p. 1995. write for info. (*0-9648201-0-2*) Grail & Tucker.

Ratliff, Larry, et al. Some Descendants of John Ratliff & Charlotte White, 1765-1997. LC 98-152421. 718p. 1998. 60.00 (*0-7884-0864-X*, R074) Heritage Bk.

Ratliff, Martha. Meaningful Tone: A Study of Tonal Morphology in Compounds, Form Classes, & Expressive Phrases in White Hmong. (Special Reports: No. 27). 275p. 1992. pap. 19.95 (*1-877979-77-5*) SE Asia.

Ratliff, Martha, jt. auth. see Jaisser, Annie.

Ratliff, R., et al. Internal Auditing: Principles & Techniques. 2nd ed. Campbell, Lee A., ed. 1105p. 1996. text 85.00 (*0-89413-167-2*, A762) Inst Inter Aud.

Ratliff, Randy L. Data Communication: With Network Management. Freeman, Whitney G., ed. (Illus.). (C). 1994. teacher ed., ring bd. 35.00 (*1-884268-05-6*); ring bd. 59.95 (*1-884268-03-X*); ring bd., lab manual ed. 35.00 (*1-884268-04-8*) Marcraft Intl.

— Network Analysis: DC-5510. Hall, Michael R., ed. & illus. by. Boulay, Cathy J., illus. (C). 1997. teacher ed., ring bd. 49.95 (*1-884268-94-3*) Marcraft Intl.

— Network Analysis - ITT Version: DC-5300 ITT. Hall, Michael R., ed. & illus. by. Boulay, Cathy J., illus. (C). 1997. teacher ed., ring bd. 35.00 (*1-884268-81-1*); ring bd. 32.95 (*1-884268-82-X*) Marcraft Intl.

Ratliff, Raymond D. Meadows in the Sierra Nevada of California: State of Knowledge. (Illus.). 64p. 1998. reprint ed. 13.40 (*0-89904-517-0*, Bear Meadows Resrch Grp); reprint ed. pap. 7.40 (*0-89904-518-9*, Bear Meadows Resrch Grp) Crumb Elbow Pub.

Ratliff, Scott, jt. auth. see Flynn, Janet.

Ratliff, Sharon K. Caring for Cambodian Americans: A Mutlidisciplinary Resource for the Helping Professions. LC 97-33180. (Asian Americans Ser.). 408p. 1997. text 89.00 (*0-8153-2989-X*) Garland.

Ratliff, Susan, jt. auth. see Lambeis, Barbara.

Ratliff, T., jt. ed. see Catalona, William J.

Ratliff, Thomas A. The Laboratory Quality Assurance System. 2nd ed. 372p. 1997. 62.95 (*0-442-02511-4*, VNR) Wiley.

Ratliff, Thomas A. The Laboratory Quality Assurance System: A Manual of Quality Procedures with Related Forms. 2nd ed. 256p. 1996. pap. 71.95 (*0-471-28828-4*, VNR) Wiley.

Ratliff, Timothy L. & Catalona, William J., eds. Genitourinary Cancer. (Cancer Treatment & Research Ser.). 1987. text 219.00 (*0-89838-830-9*) Kluwer Academic.

Ratliff, Wayne & Byers, Robert A. Emerald Bay: The Guide to Multi-user Applications. 400p. 1989. pap. 18.95 (*0-318-41956-4*) P-H.

Ratliff, William E. Castroism & Communism in Latin America, 1959-1976: The Varieties of Marxist-Leninist Experience. LC 76-28554. (AEI-Hoover Policy Studies: No. 19). 260p. reprint ed. pap. 80.60 (*0-8357-4444-2*, 203727900008) Bks Demand.

— Following the Leader in the Horn: The Soviet-Cuban Presence in East Africa. 1986. 3.00 (*0-317-90496-5*) Cuban Amer Natl Fndtn.

Ratliff, William E., ed. Yearbook on Latin American Communist Affairs, 1971. (Publication Ser.: No. 112). 194p. 1971. pap. 7.95 (*0-8179-6121-6*) Hoover Inst Pr.

Ratliff, William E. & Miranda, Roger. The Civil War in Nicaragua: Inside the Sandinistas. 298p. (C). 1992. 39.95 (*1-56000-064-3*) Transaction Pubs.

— The Civil War in Nicaragua: Inside the Sandinistas. 298p. (C). 1994. pap. 24.95 (*1-56000-761-3*) Transaction Pubs.

Ratliff, William E., et al. Judicial Reform in Latin America: A Framework for National Development. LC 95-45618. (Essays in Public Policy Ser.: No. 65). 1995. pap. 5.00 (*0-8179-5702-2*) Hoover Inst Pr.

— The Selling of Fidel Castro: The Media & the Cuban Revolution. 193p. 1986. 34.95 (*0-88738-104-9*); pap. 21.95 (*0-88738-649-0*) Transaction Pubs.

Ratliff, William E., jt. auth. see Buscaglia, Edgardo.

Ratliff, William E., jt. auth. see Fontaine, Roger W.

Ratliff, William F., et al. Cara A Cara PB. 2nd ed. (SPA.). 240p. (C). 1982. pap. text 36.00 (*0-03-057597-4*) Harcourt Coll Pubs.

Ratliff, William G. Faithful to the Fatherland: Julius Curtius & Weimar Foreign Policy. (American University Studies: History: Ser. IX, Vol. 62). XII, 216p. (C). 1990. text 43.95 (*0-8204-0948-0*) P Lang Pubng.

Ratliffe. Pediatric Physical Therapy for the Physical Therapist Assistant. LC 97-29089. (Illus.). 464p. (gr. 13). 1997. text 39.00 (*0-8151-7088-2*, 27167) Mosby Inc.

Ratliffe, Colan, intro. C. S. Ironclad Virginia & U. S. Ironclad Monitor. rev. ed. (Illus.). 54p. 1996. pap. 9.95 (*0-917376-44-7*) Mariners Mus.

Ratliffe, Kate. A Culinary Journey in Gascony: Recipes & Stories from My French Canal Boat. (Illus.). 144p. (Orig.). 1995. pap. 16.95 (*0-89815-753-6*) Ten Speed Pr.

Ratliffe, Laraine M., jt. auth. see Ratliffe, Thomas.

Ratliffe, Larraine M., jt. auth. see Ratliffe, Thomas.

Ratliffe, Sharon & Stech, Ernest L. Effective Group Communication. 352p. 1991. pap. 15.95 (*0-8442-5146-1*, NTC Business Bks) NTC Contemp Pub Co.

Ratliffe, Sharon, jt. auth. see Oberhaus, Mary A.

Ratliffe, Sharon A. & Hudson, David D. Communication for Everyday Living. 256p. (C). 1988. pap. text 61.00 (*0-13-154386-5*) P-H.

Ratliffe, Thomas & Ratliffe, Laraine M. Teaching Children Fitness: Becoming a Master Teacher. LC 93-42449. (Illus.). 128p. 1994. pap. text 16.00 (*0-87322-478-7*, BRAT0478) Human Kinetics.

Ratliffe, Thomas & Ratliffe, Larraine M. Teaching Children Fitness. (Becoming a Master Teacher Ser.). 128p. 1994. pap. text 31.95 incl. VHS (*0-87322-707-7*, AMTP0309) Human Kinetics.

Ratna Pustak Bhandar Staff, ed. Ratna Trekker's Pocket-Pal: Nepali Word & Phrase Guide. (C). 1986. 30.00 (*0-89771-081-9*, Pub. by Ratna Pustak Bhandar) St Mut.

Ratna Pustak Bhandar Staff, tr. Cooking in Nepal: A Selection of International & Nepali Recipes. 204p. (C). 1982. 75.00 (*0-89771-094-0*, Pub. by Ratna Pustak Bhandar); pap. 55.00 (*0-7855-6580-9*, Pub. by Ratna Pustak Bhandar) St Mut.

***Ratnaike, R. N., ed.** Diarrhoea & Constipation in Geriatric Practice. LC 98-46889. (Illus.). 212p. (C). 1999. pap. write for info. (*0-521-65388-6*) Cambridge U Pr.

***Ratnaike, Ranjit N., ed.** Small Bowel Disorders. (An Arnold Publication Ser.). 640p. 2000. text 195.00 (*0-340-76008-7*) OUP.

Ratnaker, Pramesh. Hinduism. 1999. 19.95 (*81-7437-048-X*) Heian Intl.

Ratnam, K. J., jt. auth. see Milne, R. S.

Ratnam, Perala. Afghanistan's Uncertain Future. 100p. 1981. 12.95 (*0-940500-18-3*, Pub. by Tulsi Pub Hse) Asia Bk Corp.

— Laos & the Super Powers. 167p. 1980. 15.95 (*0-940500-19-1*, Pub. by Tulsi Pub Hse) Asia Bk Corp.

Ratnam, S. Shan & Landy, Uta, eds. Prevention & Treatment of Contraceptive Failure. LC 86-25318. 256p. 1986. 69.50 (*0-306-42477-0*, Plenum Trade) Perseus Pubng.

Ratnam, S. Shan & Lim, A. S. Ophthalmic Microsurgery: Proceedings of the Workshop on Microsurgery, Singapore, May 1977. (Advances in Ophthalmology Ser.: Vol. 36). (Illus.). 1978. 102.75 (*3-8055-2782-9*) S Karger.

Ratnam, S. Shan, et al. Contributions to Obstetrics & Gynecology, Vol. 1. (Illus.). 258p. 1991. text 95.00 (*0-443-04669-7*) Church.

— Contributions to Obstetrics & Gynecology, Vol. 2. (Illus.). 232p. 1991. text 95.00 (*0-443-04670-0*) Church.

Ratnapala, Nandasena. Buddhist Sociology. (Bibliotheca Indo-Buddhica Ser.: No. 117). 1993. 21.00 (*81-7030-363-X*) S Asia.

— Crime & Punishment in the Buddhist Tradition. (C). 1993. 22.00 (*81-7099-463-2*, Pub. by Mittal Pubs Dist) S Asia.

Ratnapala, Nandasena. The Police of Sri Lanka: Police-Public Relations. (Illus.). 100p. (C). 1988. reprint ed. pap. text 4.95 (*0-942511-13-1*) OICJ.

Ratnapala, S. & Moens, G. A. Jurisprudence of Liberty. LC 97-148494. 300p. 1996. pap. write for info. (*0-409-30785-8*, MICHIE) LEXIS Pub.

Ratnapala, Suri, jt. ed. see Stephenson, M. A.

Ratnatunga, Janek. Ratnatunga Financial. (C). 1993. text. write for info. (*0-201-50987-3*) Addison-Wesley.

***Ratnatunga, Manel.** Best Loved Folk Tales of Sri Lanka: Legends & Folklore. LC 99-933499. 215p. 1999. write for info. (*81-207-2011-3*, Pub. by Sterling Pubs) Cambridge U Pr.

Ratnatunga, P. D. & Davidson, S. S. Pali Text Society Journal Index 1882-1927. (C). 1973. pap. 16.00 (*0-86013-058-4*, Pub. by Pali Text) Elsevier.

***Ratnavira, Natalie Ann.** Even Frogs Care. Gornik, Joe & Albright, Lisa, eds. 20p. (J). (ps-7). 2000. pap. 12.50 (*0-9673036-0-5*) Purple Hse.

***Ratnayake, Ravi.** Trade Liberalism & the Environment. 2000. 55.00 (*981-02-4194-1*) World Scientific Pub.

***Ratnayake, Ravi, ed.** Trade & the Environment: A New Zealand Perspective. 232p. 1999. text 69.95 (*1-84014-524-2*, Pub. by Ashgate Pub) Ashgate Pub Co.

Ratner. Institutional Investors. 1978. text 34.00 (*0-88277-446-8*) Foundation Pr.

***Ratner.** Introduction to Quantum Mechanics in Chemistry. 305p. 2000. 86.00 (*0-13-895491-7*) Pearson Educ.

Ratner. Something to Say: Student Essays for Freshman English. 2nd ed. 172p. (C). 1991. pap. text 18.00 (*0-536-57932-6*) Pearson Custom.

Ratner, Buddy D. & Castner, David G., eds. Surface Modification of Polymeric Biomaterials: Proceedings of the American Chemical Society Division of Polymer Chemistry International Symposium Held in Anaheim, California, April 2-6, 1995. LC 96-40102. (Illus.). 214p. (C). 1997. text 85.00 (*0-306-45512-9*, Kluwer Plenum) Kluwer Academic.

Ratner, Buddy D. & Lemon, Jack E. Biomaterials Science. Scheon, Frederick J., ed. 1997. pap. text 79.95 (*0-12-582461-0*) Acad Pr.

Ratner, Buddy D. & Tsukruk, Vladimir V., eds. Scanning Probe Microscopy of Polymers. LC 98-15684. (Symposium Ser.: No. 694). (Illus.). 384p. 1998. text 120.95 (*0-8412-3562-7*, Pub. by Am Chemical) OUP.

Ratner, C. Vygotsky's Sociohistorical Psychology & Its Contemporary Applications. LC 90-25506. (Psycholinguistics Ser.). (Illus.). 380p. (C). 1991. 57.50 (*0-306-43656-6*, Plenum Trade) Perseus Pubng.

Ratner, Carl. Cultural Psychology & Qualitative Methodology: Theoretical & Empirical Considerations. LC 97-7783. (PATH in Psychology Ser.). (Illus.). 276p. (C). 1997. 45.00 (*0-306-45463-7*, Plenum Trade) Perseus Pubng.

Ratner, David L. Securities Regulation: Cases & Materials 5th Edition. 6th ed. LC 98-11081. (Paralegal). 300p. 1998. pap. text 15.00 (*0-314-23127-7*) West Pub.

— Securities Regulation, Cases & Materials: 1996 Supplement To. Hayen, Thomas L., ed. (American Casebook Ser.). 70p. 1996. pap. text. write for info. (*0-314-20470-9*) West Pub.

— Securities Regulation in a Nutshell. 5th ed. (Nutshell Ser.). 300p. (C). 1996. pap. text 17.50 (*0-314-06591-1*) West Pub.

— Securities Regulation, Selected Statutes, Rules & Forms: 1995 Edition. Hazen, Thomas L., ed. 1246p. 1994. 26.00 (*0-314-04766-2*) West Pub.

Ratner, David L. & Hazen, Thomas L. Securities Regulation: Cases & Materials. 5th ed. LC 96-169801. 991p. (C). 1996. text 45.00 (*0-314-06655-1*) West Pub.

— Securities Regulation: Materials for a Basic Course On. 4th ed. (American Casebook Ser.). 1062p. (C). 1990. text 52.00 (*0-314-79326-7*) West Pub.

— Securities Regulation Cases & Materials: 1998 Supplement. annuals 5th ed. (American Casebook Ser.). 150p. 1997. pap. text, suppl. ed. write for info. (*0-314-22831-4*) West Pub.

— Securities Regulation, Selected Statutes, Rules & Forms: 1997 Edition. 10th ed. 1280p. (C). 1997. pap. text. write for info. (*0-314-21221-3*) West Pub.

— Securities Regulations, Cases & Materials. 4th ed. (American Casebook Ser.). 41p. (C). 1991. pap. text. write for info. (*0-314-92863-4*) West Pub.

Ratner, David L. & Hazen, Thomas L., eds. Securities Regulation, Selected Statutes, Rules & Forms: 1996 Edition. 1315p. 1996. pap. 28.50 (*0-314-07699-9*) West Pub.

Ratner, David L. & Mazen, Thomas L. Securities Regulation: Cases & Materials Containing Problems & New Cases & Materials, 1994 Supplement. 4th ed. (American Casebook Ser.). 62p. 1993. pap. text 8.00 (*0-314-03030-1*) West Pub.

Ratner, David L., jt. auth. see Hazen, Thomas Lee.

Ratner, Elaine. The Feisty Woman's Breast Cancer Book. LC 99-23722. 288p. 1999. 24.95 (*0-89793-270-6*, Pub. by Hunter Hse); pap. 14.95 (*0-89793-269-2*, Pub. by Hunter Hse) Publishers Group.

Ratner, Elaine, ed. see Roman, Sanaya.

Ratner, Elaine, ed. see Roman, Sanaya & Packer, Duane.

Ratner, Ellen. Savory Soups. LC 88-70045. (Allergy Kitchen Ser.: Vol. 1). (Illus.). 128p. 1988. pap. 7.95 (*0-9616708-7-8*) Allergy Pubns.

Ratner, Jonathan. Medicare HMO's: HCFA Can Promptly Eliminate Hundreds of Millions in Excess Payments. (Illus.). 58p. 1998. pap. text 20.00 (*0-7881-4762-5*) DIANE Pub.

— Prescription Drugs: Spending Controls in Four European Countries. (Illus.). 100p. (Orig.). (C). 1994. pap. text 35.00 (*0-7881-1172-8*) DIANE Pub.

Ratner, Joseph, ed. see Dewey, John.

Ratner, Julie, et al, eds. Human Factors & Web Development. LC 97-15656. 300p. 1997. write for info. (*0-8058-2823-0*); pap. write for info. (*0-8058-2824-9*) L Erlbaum Assocs.

Ratner, Laurance. Led Zeppelin - Live Dreams: A Photographer's Visual History of the Led Zeppelin Live Experience. 2nd ed. Wynne, Eric, ed. (Illus.). 208p. Date not set. 74.95 (*0-9637721-0-4*) Margaux Pub.

Ratner, Leonard G. The Beethoven String Quartets: Compositional Strategies & Rhetoric. 360p. (C). 1995. 25.95 (*1-887981-00-4*) Stanford Bookstore.

— Classic Music: Expression, Form & Style. 496p. 1985. pap. 28.00 (*0-02-872690-1*) Mac Lib Ref.

— Romantic Music: Sound & Syntax. 348p. 1992. 45.00 (*0-02-872065-2*, Schirmer Books) Mac Lib Ref.

Ratner, Lorman A. Andrew Jackson & His Tennessee Lieutenants: A Study in Political Culture, 176. LC 96-50292. (Contributions in American History Ser.: Vol. 176). 152p. 1997. 52.95 (*0-313-29958-7*, Greenwood Pr) Greenwood.

— James Kirke Paulding, 146. LC 92-8846. (Contributions in American History Ser.: No. 146). 168p. 1992. 47.95 (*0-313-28550-0*, RJP, Greenwood Pr) Greenwood.

Ratner, Lorman A., jt. ed. see Buenker, John D.

***Ratner, Lynn H.** Contemporary Diagnosis & Management of Breast Cancer. (Illus.). 220p. 2000. pap. 29.99 (*1-884065-55-4*, Hndbks Hlth Care) Assocs in Med.

Ratner, Mark, jt. ed. see Aviram, Ari.

Ratner, Mark A., jt. auth. see Jortner, Joshua.

Ratner, Megan, jt. auth. see Billing, Billie.

Ratner, Michael & Smith, Michael S., eds. Che Guevara & the FBI: The U. S. Political Police Dossier on the Latin American Revolutionary. (Illus.). 225p. 1997. pap. 18.95 (*1-875284-76-1*) Ocean Pr NJ.

Ratner, Michael, jt. auth. see Brody, Reed.

Ratner, Michael, jt. auth. see Stephens, Beth.

Ratner, Michael, jt. ed. see Deutschmann, David.

Ratner, Nan B. & Healey, E. Charles. Stuttering Research & Practice: Bridging the Gap. LC 98-28844. 264p. 1998. 59.95 (*0-8058-2458-8*); pap. 29.95 (*0-8058-2459-6*) L Erlbaum Assocs.

Ratner, Nan B., jt. ed. see Menn, Lise.

***Ratner, Peter.** Mastering 3D Animation. (Illus.). 480p. 2000. pap. 35.00 incl. cd-rom (*1-58115-068-7*, Pub. by Allworth Pr) Watsn-Guptill.

Ratner, Peter. 3-D Human Modeling & Animation. LC 97-29910. (Design & Graphic Design Ser.). 1997. pap. 49.95 (*0-442-02508-4*, VNR) Wiley.

***Ratner, Peter.** 3D Human Modeling & Animation. LC 97-29910. (Illus.). 320p. 1998. pap. 44.95 (*0-471-29229-X*) Wiley.

Ratner, R. S., tr. see Makrinenko, Leonid I. & Bradley, John S., eds.

Ratner, Rochelle. Bobby's Girl. LC 86-20794. 128p. (Orig.). 1986. pap. 9.95 (*0-918273-22-6*) Coffee Hse.

— Combing the Waves. LC 79-2276. (Illus.). 1979. pap. 6.00 (*0-914610-16-3*) Hanging Loose.

— Hide & Seek. (Offset Offshoot Ser.: No. 2). 50p. 1979. pap. 4.00 (*0-317-06438-X*) Ommation Pr.

— The Lion's Share. LC 91-24085. 176p. (Orig.). 1991. pap. 10.95 (*0-918273-87-0*) Coffee Hse.

— Practicing to Be a Woman: New & Selected Poems. Peters, Robert B., ed. LC 81-21472. (Poets Now Ser.: No. 2). 152p. 1982. 14.50 (*0-8108-1510-9*) Scarecrow.

— Someday Songs. LC 92-4608. 64p. 1992. 9.50 (*0-933532-89-X*) BkMk.

— Trying to Understand What It Means to Be a Feminist: Essays on Women Writers. (Chapbook Ser.). 100p. (Orig.). (C). 1983. pap. 5.00 (*0-936556-10-2*) Contact Two.

— Zodiac Arrest. (Orig.). 1995. pap. text 6.00 (*1-56439-047-0*) Ridgeway.

***Ratner, Rochelle, ed.** Bearing Life: Women's Writing on Childlessness. LC 99-41438. 256p. 2000. 23.95 (*1-55861-236-X*) Feminist Pr.

Ratner, Rochelle, ed. see Drachler, Rose.

Ratner, S., ed. Mechanisms of Lymphocyte Extravasation. (Journal: Invasion & Metastasis: Vol. 12, No. 2, 1992). (Illus.). 92p. 1992. pap. 52.25 (*3-8055-5657-8*) S Karger.

***Ratner, Sabina Teller.** Camille Saint-Saens 1835-1921 Vol. I: A Thematic Catalogue of His Complete Works: The Instrumental Works. 592p. 2000. text 120.00 (*0-19-816320-7*) OUP.

Ratner, Sidney, ed. The New American State Papers: Public Finance, 1789-1860 Subject Set, 32 vols., Set. LC 72-95580. 1973. lib. bdg. 1850.00 (*0-8420-1610-4*) Scholarly Res Inc.

Ratner, Sidney, ed. see Bentley, Arthur F.

Ratner, Sidney R., et al. The Evolution of the American Economy: The Growth, Welfare & Decision Making. 2nd ed. LC 92-11088. (Illus.). 599p. (C). 1993. text 69.80 (*0-02-398680-8*, Macmillan Coll) P-H.

Ratner, Steven R. & Abrams, Jason S. Accountability for Human Rights Atrocities in International Law: Beyond the Nuremberg Legacy. LC 97-14441. (Oxford Monographs in International Law). 404p. 1998. text 98.00 (*0-19-826550-6*) OUP.

***Ratner, Steven R. & Abrams, Jason S.** Accountability for Human Rights Atrocities in International Law: Beyond the Nuremberg Legacy. 408p. 2000. pap. 24.95 (*0-19-829871-7*) OUP.

Ratner, Vadim A., et al. Molecular Evolution. 2nd ed. LC 95-24950. (Biomathematics Ser.: Vol. 24). 1995. write for info. (*3-540-57083-7*) Spr-Verlag.

Ratner, Vadim A., jt. ed. see Kolchanov, N. A.

Ratner, Vivienne L. & Harris, Laura R. Understanding Language Disorders: The Impact on Learning. LC 93-23636. 1994. 55.00 (*0-930599-90-X*) Thinking Pubns.

***Ratneshwar, S., et al.** The Why of Comsumption: Contemporary Perspectives on Consumer Motives, Goals & Desires. LC 00-32316. (Studies in Interpretive Marketing Research). 2000. write for info. (*0-415-22095-5*) Routledge.

Ratnett, Michael. Dracula Steps Out. LC 97-76357. (Illus.). 12p. (J). (ps-1). 1998. 15.95 (*0-531-30100-1*) Orchard Bks Watts.

— Horrible Holly's Pet Raptor. LC 97-10050. (Illus.). 32p. (J). (ps-3). 1997. 15.95 (*0-8167-4391-6*) BrdgeWater.

***Ratnett, Michael.** Monster Train. (Illus.). 12p. (J). (gr. k-1). 2000. 15.95 (*0-531-30293-8*) Orchard Bks Watts.

Ratney, Ronald S., ed. Hazard Assessment & Control Technology in Semiconductor Manufacturing, Vol. II. (Illus.). (C). 1993. text 80.00 (*1-882417-02-X*) Am Conf Govt Indus Hygienist.

Ratnoff, Oscar D. & Forbes, Charles D. Disorders of Hemostasis. 3rd ed. Zorab, Richard, ed. LC 95-2349. (Illus.). 576p. 1996. text 154.00 (*0-7216-5273-5*, W B Saunders Co) Harcrt Hlth Sci Grp.

Rato, Khyongla. My Life & Lives: The Story of a Tibetan Incarnation. 2nd rev. ed. 280p. Date not set. reprint ed. pap. 14.95 (*0-9630293-0-4*) Rato Pubns.

Ratoff, Michael. Silver & Shiny. LC 97-80761. (Illus.). 60p. (J). (gr. k-6). 1997. 9.95 (*0-9627986-1-4*) Rebel Butterfly Pr.

Ratrimonimerina. Valin-Kitsaka! La Riposte Merina, Race aux Mpandoro Rova. Andrianarivo, Jonah, ed. LC 99-90331. (FRE.). xx, 204p. 1999. pap. 24.95 (*0-9671137-0-9*, 01) J Andrianarivo.

***Ratsch, Christian.** Marijuana Medicine: A World Tour of the Healing & Visionary Powers of Cannabis. (Illus.). 224p. 2001. pap. 24.95 (*0-89281-933-2*) Inner Tradit.

Ratsch, Christian. Plants of Love: Aphrodisiacs in Myth, History, & the Present. LC 97-7265. (Illus.). 208p. (Orig.). 1997. pap. 19.95 (*0-89815-928-8*) Ten Speed Pr.

Ratsch, Ulrich, et al. Intelligence & Artificial Intelligence: An Interdisciplinary Debate. LC 98-22468. 250p. 1998. 49.95 (*3-540-63780-X*) Spr-Verlag.

Ratschek, Helmut H. & Rokne, J. Computer Methods for the Range of Functions. (Mathematics & Its Applications Ser.). 168p. 1984. text 59.95 (*0-470-20034-0*) P-H.

Ratschiller, Tobias, jt. auth. see Gerken, Till.

Ratschow, Carl H., ed. Paul Tillich Main Works, Vol. 5. (Writings on Religion). xvii, 325p. 1987. lib. bdg. 75.40 (*3-11-011541-7*) De Gruyter.

Ratschow, Carl H., et al, eds. Paul Tillich's Main Works in Six Volumes - Hauptwerke in 6 Banden Vol. 1: Philosophical Writings. (GER.). xiv, 424p. (C). 1989. lib. bdg. 103.10 (*3-11-011533-6*) De Gruyter.

Ratschow, Carl H., ed. see Tillich, Paul Johannes.

Ratsoy, Eugene W., jt. auth. see Richards, Donald M.

Rattalino, Piero. Historia Del Piano. 1999. pap. text 15.95 (*1-58045-903-X*) SpanPr.

Rattalma, Marco Frigessi de, see De Rattalma, Marco Frigessi.

Rattan, Raj. Making Sense of Dental Practice Management: The Business Side of General Dental Practice. LC 95-52760. 237p. 1996. pap. 29.95 (*1-85775-017-9*, Radcliffe Med Pr) Scovill Paterson.

Rattan, Ram. Gandhi's Thought & Action. ix, 348p. 1991. 30.00 (*81-85163-21-9*, Pub. by Kalinga) Nataraj Bks.

Rattan, S. S. Resupinate Aphyllophorales of the Northwestern Himalayas. (Bibliotheca Mycologica Ser.: No. 60). (Illus.). 1977. lib. bdg. 78.00 (*3-7682-1172-X*) Lubrecht & Cramer.

Rattan, Suresh I. & Toussaint, Olivier, eds. Molecular Gerontology: Research Status & Strategies. LC 96-37284. 224p. (C). 1997. text 69.50 (*0-306-45491-2*, Kluwer Plenum) Kluwer Academic.

Rattana. The Destiny of Women Is the Destiny of the World. 310p. 1996. pap. 20.00 (*1-888029-00-5*) Heart Quest.

Rattana & Maxwell, Ann M. Introduction to Kundalini Yoga: With the Kundalini Yoga Sets & Meditations of Yogi Bhajan. (Illus.). 135p. 1995. spiral bd. 20.00 (*1-888029-05-6*) Heart Quest.

— Relax & Renew: With the Kundalina Yoga & Meditations of Yogi Bhajan. (Illus.). 195p. 1995. spiral bd. 25.00 (*1-888029-04-8*) Heart Quest.

— Sexuality & Spirituality: Kundaline Yoga Sets & Meditations of Yogi Bhajan. (Illus.). 200p. 1995. spiral bd. 25.00 (*1-888029-03-X*) Heart Quest.

— Transitions to a Heart-Centered World: Through the Kundaline Yoga & Meditations of Yogi Bhajan. (Illus.). 200p. 1995. spiral bd. 25.00 (*1-888029-02-1*) Heart Quest.

Rattansi, A., ed. Rethinking Radical Education: Essays in Honour of Brian Simon, (C). 1992. pap. 19.50 (*0-85315-717-0*, Pub. by Lawrence & Wishart) NYU Pr.

Rattansi, Ali & Westwood, Sallie, eds. Racism Modernity & Identity on the Western Front. 350p. 1994. pap. 28.95 (*0-7456-0942-2*) Blackwell Pubs.

Rattansi, Ali, jt. auth. see Donald, James.

Rattansi, Ali, jt. ed. see Boyne, Roy.

Rattansi, Piyo, jt. ed. see Clericuzio, Antonio.

Rattay, F. Electrical Nerve Stimulation: Theory, Experiments & Applications. (Illus.). iv, 264p. 1991. 79.95 (*0-387-82247-X*) Spr-Verlag.

Rattay-Prade, Regina. Die Vegetation Auf Strassenbegleitstreifen in Verschiedenen Naturraeumen Suedbadens -ihre Bewertung Fuer Den Naturschutz und Ihre Bedeutung Fuer ein Biotopverbundsystem. (Dissertationes Botanicae Ser.: Band 114). (GER., Illus.). v, 228p. 1988. pap. 77.00 (*3-443-64026-5*, Pub. by Gebruder Borntraeger) Balogh.

Ratte, John, ed. see Peabody, Robert E.

Rattee, Michael. Calling Yourself Home. (CSU Poetry Ser.: Vol. XXI). 67p. (Orig.). 1986. pap. 6.00 (*0-914946-59-5*) Cleveland St Univ Poetry Ctr.

Rattenborg, Christen C., ed. Clinical Use of Mechanical Ventilation. LC 80-25269. (Illus.). 383p. reprint ed. pap. 118.80 (*0-8357-7629-8*, 205695200096) Bks Demand.

Rattenbury, J. Ernest. The Eucharistic Hymns of John & Charles Wesley. 2nd rev. ed. Crouch, Timothy J., ed. 216p. 1996. pap. 19.95 (*1-878009-29-X*, 296) Order St Luke Pubns.

Rattenbury, Jeanne. Understanding Alternative Medicine. LC 98-15669. (Venture Book Ser.). (J). 1999. 24.00 (*0-531-11413-9*) Watts.

***Rattenbury, John.** A Living Architecture: Frank Lloyd Wright & Taliesin Architects. LC 00-37315. (Illus.). 296p. 2000. boxed set 70.00 (*0-7649-1366-2*, A571) Pomegranate Calif.

Rattenbury, Judith. Introduction to the IBM 360 Computer & OS-JCL (Job Control Language) rev. ed. LC 73-620248. 113p. reprint ed. pap. 35.10 (*0-7837-5258-X*, 204499500005) Bks Demand.

Rattenbury, Judith & Pelletier, Paula. Data Processing in the Social Sciences with OSIRIS. LC 74-620138. (Illus.). 253p. reprint ed. pap. 78.50 (*0-7837-5273-3*, 204501100005) Bks Demand.

Rattenbury, Judith, et al. Computer Processing of Social Science Data Using OSIRIS IV. LC 84-2727. 194p. (Orig.). reprint ed. pap. 60.20 (*0-7837-5276-8*, 204501400005) Bks Demand.

Rattenbury, Ken. Duke Ellington, Jazz Composer. LC 89-16544. (Illus.). 384p. (C). 1993. reprint ed. pap. 20.00 (*0-300-05507-2*) Yale U Pr.

Rattenbury, Richard C. Packing Iron: Gunleather of the Frontier West. Begley, Janet, ed. LC 93-17019. (Illus.). 218p. 1993. 45.00 (*0-939549-08-5*) ZON Intl Pub.

Ratter, J. A., jt. auth. see Milliken, William.

Ratter, J. J., jt. auth. see Rimbaud, Penny.

Ratteray, Joan D. & Shujaa, Mwalimu J. Dare to Choose: Parental Choice at Independent Neighborhood Schools. (Illus.). 216p. 1987. pap. text 25.00 (*0-941001-03-2*); pap. text 4.50 (*0-941001-04-0*) Inst Indep Educ.

Ratteray, Oswald M., ed. see Nichols, Edwin J., et al.

Ratterman, P. H. The Emerging Catholic University: With a Commentary on the Joint Statement on the Rights & Freedoms of Students. LC 68-8746. 191p. reprint ed. pap. 59.30 (*0-7837-0464-X*, 204078700018) Bks Demand.

***Rattermann, Mark.** Residential Sales Comparison Approach: Deriving, Documenting & Defending Your Value Opinion. LC 00-44763. (Illus.). 2000. write for info. (*0-922154-61-9*) Appraisal Inst.

Ratterree, John. Lonely Planet Diving & Snorkeling Guide to Red Sea. LC 94-25371. (Pisces Diving & Snorkeling Guides Ser.). 96p. 1994. 14.95 (*1-55992-081-5*, PISCES, Pisces Books) Lonely Planet.

Ratterree, John, jt. auth. see Rosenberg, Steve.

Rattey, Beatrice. Los Hebreos (The Hebrews) 2nd ed. (Breviarios Ser.). (SPA.). 208p. 1984. pap. 7.99 (*968-16-0699-X*, Pub. by Fondo) Continental Bk.

Ratti, Achille, see Pius XI, pseud.

Ratti, Carlo G. & Morassi, Antonio, trs. Alessandro Magnasco. (Illus.). 64p. 1967. pap. 3.00 (*0-912303-03-4*) Michigan Mus.

Ratti, John. Samson's Riddle. 1985. pap. 6.00 (*0-914610-41-4*) Hanging Loose.

Ratti, John T., et al, compiled by. Waterfowl Ecology & Management: Selected Readings. LC 82-70782. (Illus.). xvi, 1328p. (Orig.). (C). 1982. pap. 29.00 (*0-933564-09-0*) Wildlife Soc.

Ratti, Oscar. Secrets of the Samurai: The Martial Arts of Feudal Japan. 1999. pap. text 9.99 (*0-7858-1073-0*) Bk Sales Inc.

Ratti, Oscar & Westbrook, A. Secrets of Samurai. 21.00 (*0-685-47575-1*) Wehman.

Ratti, Oscar & Westbrook, Adele. Secrets of the Samurai: The Martial Arts of Feudal Japan. LC 72-91551. (Illus.). 483p. 1991. pap. 21.95 (*0-8048-1684-0*) Tuttle Pubng.

Ratti, Oscar, jt. auth. see Westbrook, A. M.

Ratti, Oscar, tr. see Arano, Luisa C.

Ratti, Remigio, et al, eds. The Dynamics of Innovative Regions: The GREMI Approach. LC 97-74440. (Illus.). 416p. 1997. text 83.95 (*1-84014-326-6*, Pub. by Ashgate Pub) Ashgate Pub Co.

Rattigan. The Winslow Boy. 1991. pap. text. write for info. (*0-582-06019-2*, Pub. by Addison-Wesley) Longman.

Rattigan, Jama K. Dumpling Soup. (Illus.). 32p. (J). (gr. 4-8). 1993. 16.95 (*0-316-73445-4*) Little.

— Dumpling Soup. (Illus.). 32p. (J). (gr. k-3). 1998. pap. 5.95 (*0-316-73047-5*) Little.

— Truman's Aunt Farm. LC 93-4860. (Illus.). 32p. (J). 1994. 14.95 (*0-395-65661-3*) HM.

— Truman's Aunt Farm. LC 93-4860. (Illus.). 32p. (J). (ps-3). 1996. pap. 5.95 (*0-395-81656-4*) HM.

Rattigan, Jama Kim. Dumpling Soup. (J). 1998. 10.15 (*0-606-13349-6*, Pub. by Turtleback) Demco.

— Truman's Aunt Farm. LC 93-4860. 1994. 11.15 (*0-606-10959-5*, Pub. by Turtleback) Demco.

Rattigan, Neil. Images of Australia: One Hundred Films of the New Australian Cinema. LC 90-52662. (Illus.). 320p. 1991. 24.95 (*0-87074-312-0*); pap. 15.95 (*0-87074-313-9*) SMU Press.

***Rattigan, Neil.** This is England: British Film & the People's War, 1939-1945. LC 00-42956. (Illus.). 2001. write for info. (*0-8386-3862-7*) Fairleigh Dickinson.

Rattigan, Terence. After the Dance. 128p. 1996. pap. text 14.95 (*1-85459-217-3*, Pub. by N Hern Bks) Theatre Comm.

— The Browning Version. 128p. 1994. pap. 13.95 (*1-85459-202-5*, Pub. by N Hern Bks) Theatre Comm.

— French Without Tears. 128p. 1996. pap. text 14.95 (*1-85459-212-2*, Pub. by N Hern Bks) Theatre Comm.

— Man & Boy. 101p. 1964. 16.95 (*0-910278-42-3*) Boulevard.

— O Mistress Mine. 116p. 1949. 16.95 (*0-910278-43-1*) Boulevard.

— The Sleeping Prince. 126p. 1954. 16.95 (*0-910278-44-X*) Boulevard.

— The Winslow Boy. 1950. pap. 5.25 (*0-8222-1264-1*) Dramatists Play.

— The Winslow Boy. 96p. 1995. pap. 13.95 (*1-85459-296-3*, Pub. by N Hern Bks) Theatre Comm.

***Rattigan, Terence.** Winslow Boy. 128p. 2000. pap. 16.95 (*1-85459-467-2*) Theatre Comm.

***Rattigan, Terrence.** Deep Blue Sea. 1999. pap. 16.95 (*1-85459-423-0*, Pub. by Theatre Comm) Consort Bk Sales.

— Separate Tables. 1999. pap. 16.95 (*1-85459-424-9*, Pub. by Theatre Comm) Consort Bk Sales.

Rattigan, William H. Private International Law. LC 96-76320. xv, 267p. 1996. reprint ed. 58.00 (*1-57588-083-0*, 310610) W S Hein.

***Rattiner, Jeffrey H.** Getting Started as a Financial Planner. LC 00-36022. 304p. 2000. 34.95 (*1-57660-035-1*, Pub. by Bloomberg NJ) Norton.

R

R

Rattiner, Susan L., ed. Great Poems by American Women: An Anthology. LC 98-4391. 224p. Date not set. pap. 2.00 (*0-486-40164-2*) Dover.

***Rattiner, Susan L., ed.** Women's Wit & Wisdom: A Book of Quotations. 2000. pap. 1.00 (*0-486-41123-0*) Dover.

Rattingan, W. H. De Jure Personarum or, a Treatise on the Roman Law of Persons. LC 93-79723. 362p. 1994. reprint ed. 85.00 (*1-56169-081-3*) Gaunt.

Rattinger, Hans, jt. ed. see Flynn, Gregory.

Rattkay, Suellen, ed. see Coin World Staff.

Rattlehead, David. The Life & Adventures of an Arkansaw Doctor. McNeil, W. K., ed. LC 89-4692. 200p. 1989. pap. 16.00 (*1-55728-079-7*) U of Ark Pr.

Rattner, Arye & Fishman, Gideon. Justice for All? Jews & Arabs in the Israeli Criminal Justice System. LC 98-10075. 152p. 1998. 55.00 (*0-275-95908-2*, Praeger Pubs) Greenwood.

Rattner, Donald M. & Cameron, Richard W., eds. Modern Classical Architecture & the Problem of Archaeology, Vol. 2. (Classicist Ser.). (Illus.). 123p. (Orig.). (C). 1996. pap. text 34.95 (*1-56000-850-4*) Transaction Pubs.

***Rattner, Joan.** Unbelievably Good Deals & Great Adventures That You Absolutely Can't Get Unless You're over 50. 12th ed. LC 99-59791. 2000. pap. text 12.95 (*0-8092-9903-8*) NTC Contemp Pub Co.

Rattner, Ronald, jt. ed. see Cameron, Richard.

Ratto, Andrea, jt. auth. see Eells, James.

Ratto, C. F. & Solari, G., eds. Wind Energy & Landscape: Proceedings of the International Workshop on Wind Energy & Landscape, Genova, Italy, 26-27 June 1997. LC 99-496420. (Illus.). 162p. (C). 1998. text 66.00 (*90-5410-913-0*, Pub. by A A Balkema) Ashgate Pub Co.

Ratto, Corrado F., jt. ed. see Lalas, Demetri P.

Ratto, Linda L. Coping with a Physically Challenged Brother Or Sister. Rosen, Ruth C., ed. (Coping Ser.). (YA). (gr. 7-12). 1992. lib. bdg. 17.95 (*0-8239-1492-5*) Rosen Group.

— Coping with Being Physically Challenged. Rosen, Ruth C., ed. (Coping Ser.). (YA). (gr. 7-12). 1991. lib. bdg. 17.95 (*0-8239-1344-9*) Rosen Group.

Ratto, R. Aes Grave Italique. (Illus.). 33p. 1974. 15.00 (*0-915018-06-3*) Attic Bks.

Rattok, Lily, jt. ed. see Diament, Carol.

Ratton, Serge, jt. ed. see Desmurs, Jean-Roger.

Rattray, C. & Van Rijsbergen, C. J., eds. Specification & Verification of Concurrent Systems. (Workshops in Computing Ser.). 624p. 1990. 59.00 (*0-387-19581-5*) Spr-Verlag.

Rattray, Charles & Clark, Robert G., eds. The Unified Computation Laboratory: Modelling, Specifications, & Tools. (Institute of Mathematics & Its Applications Conference Series, New Ser.: New Series 34). (Illus.). 480p. 1992. 110.00 (*0-19-853684-4*) OUP.

Rattray, Charles, jt. auth. see Rus, Teodor.

Rattray, David. How I Became One of the Invisible. 1992. pap. 7.00 (*0-936756-98-5*) Autonomedia.

— Opening the Eyelid. deluxe ed. LC 90-84027. 96p. (Orig.). 1991. pap. 9.95 (*0-9627430-1-1*); pap. 500.00 (*0-9627430-2-X*) diwan.

— Opening the Eyelid. limited ed. LC 90-84027. 96p. (Orig.). 1991. 35.00 (*0-9627430-0-3*) diwan.

Rattray, Evelyn C. The Teotihuacan Burials & Offerings: A Commentary & Inventory. Fowler, William et al, eds. (Vanderbilt University Publications in Anthropology: No. 42). 254p. (Orig.). 1992. pap. 23.00 (*0-935462-33-3*) VUPA.

Rattray, Evelyn C., et al, eds. Interaccion Cultural en Mexico Central. 222p. 1981. pap. 2.50 (*1-877812-44-7*, UN021) UPLAAP.

Rattray, Evelyn C., jt. auth. see McClung, Emily.

Rattray, Everett. Jeremiah Dimon: A Novel of Old East Hampton. LC 85-60911. 1985. 17.95 (*0-916366-34-0*, Pub. by Pushcart Pr) Norton.

— Jeremiah Dimon: A Novel of Old East Hampton. LC 85-60911. 1990. pap. 9.95 (*0-916366-51-0*, Pub. by Pushcart Pr) Norton.

— The South Fork. 1989. pap. 15.00 (*0-916366-41-3*, Pub. by Pushcart Pr) Norton.

Rattray, Gregory J., jt. ed. see Larsen, Jeffrey A.

Rattray, James B., ed. Biotechnology of Plant Fats & Oils. 184p. (C). 1991. 70.00 (*0-935315-33-0*) Am Oil Chemists.

Rattray, Jamie, et al. Kids & Alcohol. 200p. 1983. pap. 5.95 (*0-932194-13-3*, 22H93) Health Comm.

— Kids & Drugs. 208p. 1983. pap. text 5.95 (*0-932194-19-2*, 22H98) Health Comm.

— Kids & Smoking. 199p. 1983. pap. text 5.95 (*0-932194-14-1*, 22H49) Health Comm.

Rattray, Robert F. Bernard Shaw: A Chronicle. LC 74-30342. (George Bernard Shaw Ser.: No. 92). 1974. lib. bdg. 75.00 (*0-8383-1892-4*) M S G Haskell Hse.

— Samuel Butler. LC 73-21671. (Literary Biography Ser.: No. 31). 1974. lib. bdg. 59.00 (*0-8383-1782-0*) M S G Haskell Hse.

Rattray, Robert S. Akan-Ashanti Folk-Tales. LC 78-63214. (Folktale Ser.). (Illus.). 320p. 1983. reprint ed. 34.50 (*0-404-16155-3*) AMS Pr.

— Ashanti. LC 73-92759. (Illus.). 348p. 1971. reprint ed. lib. bdg. 35.00 (*0-8371-2201-5*, RAA&) Greenwood.

— Religion & Art in Ashanti. LC 76-44781. reprint ed. 34.50 (*0-404-15878-1*) AMS Pr.

Ratts, J. R. Fiscal Federalism & State-Local Finance: The Scandinavian Perspective. LC 98-27695. 448p. 1998. 100.00 (*1-85898-752-0*) E Elgar.

Rattue, James. The Living Stream: Holy Wells in Historical Context. (Illus.). 191p. 1995. 55.00 (*0-85115-601-0*) Boydell & Brewer.

Raturi. Principles of Operation Management. 6th ed. (SWC-Management Ser.). 2000. pap. text 35.00 (*0-324-00896-1*) Thomson Learn.

Ratushinkaya, Irina. No, I'm Not Afraid. McDuff, David, tr. from RUS. 142p. 1987. reprint ed. 27.00 (*1-85224-057-1*, Pub. by Bloodaxe Bks) Dufour.

— No, I'm Not Afraid. McDuff, David, tr. from RUS. 142p. 1992. reprint ed. pap. 16.95 (*0-906427-95-9*, Pub. by Bloodaxe Bks) Dufour.

Ratushinskay. Pencil Letter. 1988. pap. write for info. (*0-09-173550-5*, Pub. by Random) Random House.

Ratushinskaya, Irina. Beyond the Limit. Brent, Frances P. & Avins, Carol, trs. (ENG & RUS.). 121p. 1987. 24.95 (*0-8101-0748-1*); pap. 12.95 (*0-8101-0749-X*) Northwestern U Pr.

— Dance with a Shadow. McDuff, David, tr. from RUS. 77p. 1992. 28.00 (*1-85224-232-9*, Pub. by Bloodaxe Bks) Dufour.

— Dance with a Shadow. McDuff, David, tr. from RUS. 77p. 1993. pap. 14.95 (*1-85224-233-7*, Pub. by Bloodaxe Bks) Dufour.

***Ratushinskaya, Irina.** Fictions & Lies. Kojevnikova, Aeyona, tr. 288p. 1999. text 28.00 (*0-7195-5685-6*, Pub. by John Murray) Trafalgar.

Ratushinskaya, Irina. Grey Is the Color of Hope. Kojevnikov, Alyona, tr. (Vintage International Ser.). 1989. pap. 8.95 (*0-685-30682-8*) Vin Bks.

— Grey Is the Color of Life. Kojevnikov, Alyona, tr. 1989. pap. 8.95 (*0-685-26532-3*) Vin Bks.

— Stikhi, Poems, Poemes. Devergnas, Meery et al, trs. LC 84-12974. (ENG, FRE & RUS.). 134p. 1984. pap. text 8.50 (*0-938920-54-5*) Hermitage Pubs.

— A Tale of Three Heads. Ignashev, Diane N., tr. & intro. by. LC 86-25623.Tr. of Skazka o Trekh Golovakh. (ENG & RUS.). 128p. 1986. pap. 7.50 (*0-938920-83-9*) Hermitage Pubs.

***Ratushinskaya, Irina.** Wind of the Journey. Stone, Lydia Razran, tr. 138p. 2000. 14.95 (*0-940895-44-7*, Pub. by Cornerstone IL) Midpt Trade.

Raty, Loren, jt. auth. see Spielman, Patricia.

Raty, Loren, jt. auth. see Spielman, Patrick.

Ratych, Joanna M., tr. see Pinthus, Kurt, ed.

Ratz, Jack. Endless Miracles: A Memoir. LC 97-62062. 173 p. 1999. 20.00 (*0-88400-202-0*, Pub. by Schreiber Pub) Natl Bk Netwk.

Ratz, John L., et al, eds. Textbook of Dermatologic Surgery. LC 97-41386. (Illus.). 1000p. 1997. text 185.00 (*0-397-51495-6*) Lppncott W & W.

Ratz, Konrad. Maximilian in Queretaro. Bilddokumentation Ueber Den Untergang Des Zweiten Mexikanischen Kaiserreiches. fac. ed. (GER., Illus.). 424p. 1992. 57.00 (*3-201-01551-2*, Pub. by Akademische Druck-und) Balogh.

— Maximilian in Queretaro. Bilddokumentation Ueber Den Untergang des Zweiten Mexikanischen Kaiserreiches (Maximilian in Queretaro. Pictorial Atlas of the Second Mexican Empire) fac. ed. (GER., Illus.). 424p. 1992. 57.00 (*3-201-01474-5*, Pub. by Akademische Druck-und) Balogh.

— Maximilian und Juarez. Das Zweite Mexikanische Kaiserreich und die Republik (Maximilian & Juarez. The Second Mexican Empire & the Republic); Die Augenblicke der Gefahr ("Queretaro-Chronik") (The Moment of Danger ("Queretaro-Chronicles")), 2 vols. fac. ed. (GER.). 940p. 1998. 47.00 (*3-201-01679-9*, Pub. by Akademische Druck-und) Balogh.

Ratz, O., jt. auth. see Eisenbarth, M. A.

***Ratzabi, Shalom.** Between Zionism & Judaism: The Radical Circle in Brith Shalom, 1925-1933. (Series in Jewish Studies). 435p. 2000. 149.50 (*90-04-11507-2*) Brill Academic Pubs.

Ratzan, Scott C. The Mad Cow Crisis: Health & the Public Good. LC 97-38913. 1998. text 55.00 (*0-8147-7510-1*); pap. text 18.50 (*0-8147-7511-X*) NYU Pr.

— The Mad Cow Crisis: Health & the Public Good. 256p. 1997. pap. text 24.95 (*1-85728-812-2*, Pub. by UCL Pr Ltd) Taylor & Francis.

Ratzan, Scott C., ed. AIDS: Effective Health Communicaton for the 90's. LC 92-17933. 1992. 44.95 (*1-56032-273-X*) Hemisp Pub.

— The Mad Cow Crisis: Health & the Public Good. 256p. 1997. 69.95 (*1-85728-828-9*, Pub. by UCL Pr Ltd) Taylor & Francis.

Ratzel, Friedrich. History of Mankind, 3 vols. 1702p. 1989. 1200.00 (*81-7158-084-X*, Pub. by Scientific Pubs) St Mut.

Ratzenhofer, Gustav. Die Sociologische Erkenntnis: Sociological Knowledge: The Positive Philosophy of Social Life. LC 74-25775. (European Sociology Ser.). 372p. 1975. reprint ed. 31.95 (*0-405-06529-9*) Ayer.

Ratzenhofer, M., ed. see Hoefler, H. & Walter, G. F.

***Ratzer, Beryl.** A Historical Tour of the Holy Land. 2nd rev. ed. LC 99-43809. (Illus.). 156p. 1999. pap. 15.95 (*965-229-218-4*, Pub. by Gefen Pub Hse) Gefen Bks.

Ratzer, Beryl. A Historical Tour of the Holyland. (Illus.). 128p. 1997. pap. 15.00 (*965-229-166-8*) Gefen Bks.

Ratzer, Gerald F. FORTRAN 90 C & Algorithms. LC 97-126570. 450p. (C). 1996. pap. text, per. 33.95 (*0-7872-3235-1*) Kendall-Hunt.

Ratzin-Jackson, Catherine G., ed. Nutrition for the Recreational Athlete. LC 94-19402. (Nutrition in Exercise & Sport Ser.). 272p. 1995. boxed set 94.95 (*0-8493-7914-8*) CRC Pr.

Ratzin-Turner, Rosemary A. Handbook of Nutrition for Vegetarians. (Modern Nutrition Ser.). 620p. 1999. 125.00 (*0-8493-8508-3*) CRC Pr.

Ratzinger, Cardinal J. Seek That Which Is Above. Harrison, Graham, tr. from GER. LC 86-81553.Tr. of Suchen was Droben Ist. 133p. 1986. 9.95 (*0-89870-101-5*) Ignatius Pr.

Ratzinger, Cardinal Joseph. Milestones: Memoirs, 1927-1977. LC 98-71929. 1998. pap. 12.95 (*0-89870-702-1*) Ignatius Pr.

Ratzinger, Joseph & Board of St. Paul Editorial Staff. Ministers of Your Joy: Reflections on Priestly Spirituality. 128p. (C). 1996. pap. 39.95 (*0-85439-287-4*, Pub. by St Paul Pubns) St Mut.

Ratzinger, Joseph & Seewald, Peter. Salt of the Earth: The State of the Church at the End of the Millennium. Ignatius, Adrian W., tr. LC 97-70806. 301p. 1997. pap. text 12.95 (*0-89870-640-8*) Ignatius Pr.

Ratzinger, Joseph C. Behold the Pierced One. LC 86-80103.Tr. of Schauen auf den Durchbohrten. (Illus.). 128p. 1986. pap. 9.95 (*0-89870-087-6*) Ignatius Pr.

— Called to Communion: Understanding the Church Today. LC 95-79953.Tr. of Zur Gemeinschaft Gerufen: Kirche Heute Verstehen. 162p. (Orig.). 1996. pap. 11.95 (*0-89870-578-9*) Ignatius Pr.

— Church, Ecumenism & Politics. (C). 1988. 50.00 (*0-7855-3225-0*, Pub. by St Paul Pubns) St Mut.

— Church, Ecumenism & Politics. 278p. (C). 1996. pap. 39.95 (*0-85439-267-X*, Pub. by St Paul Pubns) St Mut.

— Co-Workers of Truth. McCarthy, Mary F. & Krauth, Lothar, trs. from GER. LC 92-71960. 415p. 1992. pap. 17.95 (*0-89870-409-X*) Ignatius Pr.

— Dogma & Preaching. O'Connell, Matthew J., tr. 135p. 1983. 5.95 (*0-8199-0819-3*, Frncscn Herld) Franciscan Pr.

— Eschatology: Death & Eternal Life. Nichols, Aidan, ed. Waldstein, Michael, tr. LC 87-35107. (Dogmatic Theology Ser.: Vol. 9). 307p. 1988. pap. 14.95 (*0-8132-0633-2*) Cath U Pr.

— The Feast of Faith. Harrison, Graham, tr. from GER. LC 85-82175. Orig. Title: Das Fest des Glaubens. (Illus.). 153p. (Orig.). 1986. pap. 9.95 (*0-89870-056-6*) Ignatius Pr.

— In the Beginning: A Catholic Understanding of the Story of Creation & the Fall. (Ressourcement Ser.). 1995. pap. 13.00 (*0-8028-4106-6*) Eerdmans.

— Introduction to Christianity. Foster, J. R., tr. from GER. LC 90-82991. 280p. 1990. pap. text 15.95 (*0-89870-316-6*) Ignatius Pr.

— Journey Towards Easter. 160p. (C). 1996. pap. 39.95 (*0-85439-258-0*, Pub. by St Paul Pubns) St Mut.

— The Meaning of Christian Brotherhood. 2nd ed. Glen-Doeple, W. A., tr. from GER. LC 92-65064. 115p. 1993. pap. 9.95 (*0-89870-446-4*) Ignatius Pr.

— The Nature & Mission Theology. LC 94-79301. 130p. 1995. pap. 12.95 (*0-89870-538-X*) Ignatius Pr.

— A New Song for the Lord. LC 96-33184. 144p. 1996. pap. 24.95 (*0-8245-1536-6*) Crossroad NY.

— Principles of Catholic Theology: Building Stones for Fundamental Theology. McCarthy, Mary F., tr. from GER. LC 86-83133.Tr. of Theologische Prinzipienlehre. 398p. (Orig.). 1986. 31.95 (*0-89870-133-3*) Ignatius Pr.

— Theology of History According to St. Bonaventure. Hayes, Zachary, tr. from GER. 268p. 1989. pap. 12.50 (*0-8199-0415-5*, Frncscn Herld) Franciscan Pr.

— To Look on Christ: Exercise in Faith, Hope & Love. 120p. (C). 1996. pap. 39.95 (*0-85439-330-7*, Pub. by St Paul Pubns) St Mut.

— Turning Point for Europe. LC 93-78528. 177p. pap. 12.95 (*0-89870-461-8*) Ignatius Pr.

Ratzinger, Joseph C. & Messori, Vittorio. The Ratzinger Report. Attanasio, Salvator & Harrison, Graham, trs. LC 85-81218.Tr. of Rapporto sulla Fede. (GER & ITA.). 197p. (Orig.). 1987. pap. 10.95 (*0-89870-080-9*) Ignatius Pr.

Ratzinger, Joseph C. & Schonborn, Christoph. Introduction to the Catechism of the Catholic Church. LC 94-75081. 97p. pap. 9.95 (*0-89870-485-5*) Ignatius Pr.

Ratzinger, Joseph C., et al. The Church & Women: A Compendium. Krauth, Lothar et al, trs. from GER. LC 88-81309. 277p. (Orig.). 1988. pap. 14.95 (*0-89870-164-3*) Ignatius Pr.

— Principles of Christian Morality. Harrison, Graham, tr. from GER. LC 85-82176. Orig. Title: Prinzipien Chrislicher Moral. (Illus.). 104p. (Orig.). 1986. pap. 7.95 (*0-89870-086-8*) Ignatius Pr.

***Ratzinger, Joseph Cardinal.** The Spirit of the Liturgy. 250p. 2000. pap. 17.95 (*0-89870-784-6*, Pub. by Ignatius Pr) Midpt Trade.

Ratzlaff, Dale. The Cultic Doctrine of Seventh-Day Adventists: An Evangelical Resource, an Appeal to SDA Leadership. LC 96-94063. 388p. (Orig.). 1996. pap. 14.95 (*0-9627546-9-2*) Life Assurance.

— Sabbath in Crisis: The Gospel, the Sabbath, the Old & New Covenants. LC 90-91938. (Illus.). 352p. (Orig.). 1995. pap. 14.95 (*0-9627546-0-9*) Life Assurance.

Ratzlaff, John T. Tesla Said. LC 83-72252. (Illus.). 292p. (Orig.). 1984. pap. text 28.00 (*0-914119-00-1*) Tesla Bk Co.

Ratzlaff, John T., compiled by. Dr. Nikola Tesla - Complete Patents, 2 vols. 2nd ed. LC 79-67722. (Illus.). 500p. lib. bdg. 43.50 (*0-9603536-8-2*); 35.00 (*0-914119-27-3*) Tesla Bk Co.

— Dr. Nikola Tesla - Complete Patents, 2 vols., Vol. I. 2nd ed. LC 79-67722. (Illus.). 500p. write for info. (*0-914119-10-9*) Tesla Bk Co.

— Dr. Nikola Tesla - Complete Patents, 2 vols., Vol. II. 2nd ed. LC 79-67722. (Illus.). 500p. write for info. (*0-914119-11-7*) Tesla Bk Co.

Ratzlaff, John T., compiled by. Nikola Tesla: Complete Patents. unabridged ed. 500p. 1983. reprint ed. 40.00 (*0-945001-70-3*) GSG & Assocs.

Ratzlaff, John T., ed. Tesla: Complete Patents. (Nikola Tesla Ser.). 1986. lib. bdg. 125.00 (*0-8490-3838-3*) Gordon Pr.

Ratzlaff, John T. & Anderson, Leland I. Dr. Nikola Tesla Bibliography. 248p. 1995. reprint ed. spiral bd. 24.95 (*0-9636012-6-1*) Twty Frst Cent.

Ratzlaff, John T. & Jost, Fred A. Dr. Nikola Tesla, 3 pts. LC 79-67377. (Illus.). (Orig.). 1979. pap. 20.00 (*0-9603536-0-7*) Tesla Bk Co.

Ratzlaff, K. L., jt. ed. see Sweedler, J. V.

Ratzlaff, Keith. Across the Known World. 56p. (J). 1997. 22.00 (*0-931209-74-9*, Loess Hills Bks); pap. 12.00 (*0-931209-75-7*, Loess Hills Bks) Mid-Prairie Bks.

— Man under a Pear Tree. LC 97-70025. (Anhinga Prize for Poetry - 1996 Ser.). 96p. (Orig.). 1997. 18.95 (*0-938078-51-8*); pap. 10.00 (*0-938078-50-X*) Anhinga Pr.

Ratzlaff, Kenneth L. Introduction to Computer-Assisted Experimentation. LC 86-19011. 464p. 1987. 150.00 (*0-471-86525-7*) Wiley.

Ratzlaff, Leslie A. Education Regulations Library: A Guide to the Making of Federal Education Laws & Rules. LC 87-110637. 22p. 1986. pap. 9.95 (*0-937925-14-4*) Capitol VA.

Ratzlaff, Leslie A., ed. The Education Evaluator's Workbook: How to Assess Education Programs, Vol. I. 100p. (Orig.). 1987. 32.00 (*0-937925-16-0*, EE) Capitol VA.

— The Education Evaluator's Workbook: How to Assess Education Programs, Vol. II. 145p. (Orig.). 1986. 30.00 (*0-937925-17-9*, EEW) Capitol VA.

— The Education Evaluator's Workbook: How to Assess Education Programs, Vol. III. 120p. (Orig.). 1987. 29.00 (*0-937925-18-7*, EEN) Capitol VA.

Ratzlaff, Patricia, jt. auth. see National Association of Home Builders Staff.

Ratzlaff, Robert K. John Rutledge, Jr. South Carolina Federalist, 1766-1819. 1981. 29.95 (*0-405-14104-1*) Ayer.

Ratzlatf, John T., ed. Dr. Nikola Tesla - Selected Patent Wrappers from the National Archives, 4 vols. LC 80-83299. (Illus.). 940p. 1981. pap. 60.00 (*0-9603536-2-3*) Tesla Bk Co.

Ratzleff, Edith. The Power of the Lamb. 48p. 1988. teacher ed. 1.50 (*0-919797-72-5*) Kindred Prods.

Ratzloff, John. North Cabin Gallery. 1992. pap. 12.95 (*0-934860-87-4*) Adventure Pubns.

Ratzsch, Del. The Battle of Beginnings: Why Neither Side Is Winning the Creation-Evolution Debate. LC 95-48958. 248p. (Orig.). 1996. pap. 15.99 (*0-8308-1529-5*, 1529) InterVarsity.

***Ratzsch, Del.** Nature, Design & Science: The Status of Design in Natural Science. (C). 2001. pap. text 18.95 (*0-7914-4894-0*) State U NY Pr.

— Nature, Design & Science: The Status of Design in Natural Science. (C). 2001. text 57.50 (*0-7914-4893-2*) State U NY Pr.

Ratzsch, Del. Science & Its Limits. 1999. pap. 12.99 (*0-8308-1580-5*) InterVarsity.

Rau, A. Ravi, jt. auth. see Fano, Ugo.

Rau, Albert G. & David, Hans T. Catalogue of Music by American Moravians, 1742-1842. LC 76-134283. reprint ed. 29.50 (*0-404-07206-2*) AMS Pr.

Rau, B. Ramakrishna & Fisher, Joseph A., eds. Instruction-Level Parallelism: A Special Issue of the Journal of Supercomputing. LC 93-10962. (International Series in Engineering & Computer Science, VLSI, Computer Architecture, & Digital Screen Processing: No. 235). 288p. (C). 1993. text 201.50 (*0-7923-9367-8*) Kluwer Academic.

Rau, Bob, jt. auth. see Fisher, Joseph A.

Rau, Dana, jt. auth. see Fowler, Allan.

Rau, Dana, ed. see Brimner, Larry D.

Rau, Dana, ed. see Flanagan, Alice K.

Rau, Dana, ed. see Fowler, Alan.

Rau, Dana, ed. see Fowler, Allan.

Rau, Dana, ed. see McKissack, Frederick & McKissack, Patricia.

Rau, Dana, ed. see Simon, Charnan.

Rau, Dana M. Arctic Adventure: Inuit Life in the 1800s. LC 97-10792. (Smithsonian Odyssey Ser.). (Illus.). 32p. (J). (gr. 1-4). 1997. pap. 5.95 (*1-56899-417-6*) Soundprints.

— Arctic Adventure: Inuit Life in the 1800s. LC 97-10792. (Smithsonian Odyssey Ser.). (Illus.). 32p. (J). (gr. 2-5). 1997. 14.95 (*1-56899-416-8*); 19.95 incl. audio (*1-56899-423-0*, BC6005) Soundprints.

— Arctic Adventure: Inuit Life in the 1800s, Incl. toy. (Smithsonian Odyssey Ser.). (Illus.). (J). (gr. 2-5). 1997. 29.95 (*1-56899-418-4*); 35.95 incl. audio (*1-56899-421-4*); pap. 17.95 (*1-56899-419-2*); pap. 25.95 incl. audio (*1-56899-420-6*) Soundprints.

— Bob's Vacation. LC 98-19037. (Rookie Readers Ser.). 32p. (J). (gr. 1-2). 1999. 17.50 (*0-516-21543-4*) Childrens.

— A Box Can Be Many Things. LC 96-21173. (Rookie Readers Ser.). (Illus.). 32p. (J). (gr. k-2). 1997. lib. bdg. 17.00 (*0-516-20317-7*) Childrens.

***Rau, Dana M.** Feet. LC 99-30169. (Rookie Readers Ser.). (Illus.). (J). 2000. 15.00 (*0-516-22008-X*) Childrens.

Rau, Dana M. One Giant Leap: The First Moon Landing. LC 96-15035. (Smithsonian Odyssey Ser.). (Illus.). 32p. (J). (gr. 2-5). 1996. 14.95 (*1-56899-343-9*); pap. 5.95 (*1-56899-344-7*) Soundprints.

Rau, Dana M. One Giant Leap: The First Moon Landing. (Odyssey Ser.). (Illus.). 32p. (J). (gr. 2-5). 1996. 19.95 incl. audio (*1-56899-360-9*, BC6001) Soundprints.

Rau, Dana M. One Giant Leap: The First Moon Landing, Incl. toy. (Smithsonian Odyssey Ser.). (Illus.). 32p. (J). (gr. 2-5). 1996. 29.95 (*1-56899-345-5*); 35.95 incl. audio (*1-56899-347-1*); pap. 17.95 (*1-56899-346-3*) Soundprints.

— Robin at Hickory Street. (Smithsonian's Backyard Ser.). (Illus.). 32p. (J). (ps-2). 1995. 15.95 (*1-56899-168-1*) Soundprints.

Rau, Dana M. Robin at Hickory Street. (Smithsonian's Backyard Ser.). (Illus.). 32p. (J). (ps-2). 1995. 19.95 incl. audio (*1-56899-172-X*, BC5007) Soundprints.

Rau, Dana M. Robin at Hickory Street, Incl. 10" toy. (Smithsonian's Backyard Ser.). (Illus.). 32p. (J). (ps-2). 1995. 32.95 (*1-56899-170-3*) Soundprints.

An Asterisk (*) at the beginning of an entry indicates that the title is appearing for the first time.

— Robin at Hickory Street, Micro bk. (Smithsonian's Backyard Ser.). (Illus.). 32p. (J). (ps-2). 1995. 4.95 (*1-56899-169-X*) Soundprints.

— Robin at Hickory Street, Micro bk., incl. 6" toy. (Smithsonian's Backyard Ser.). (Illus.). 32p. (J). (ps-3). 1995. 12.95 (*1-56899-171-1*) Soundprints.

— The Secret Code. LC 97-18797. (Illus.). 32p. (J). (gr. k-2). 1998. 17.00 (*0-516-20700-8*) Childrens.

— The Secret Code. (Rookie Readers Ser.). (Illus.). 32p. (J). 1998. pap. 4.95 (*0-516-26362-5*) Childrens.

— Undersea City: A Story of a Caribbean Coral Reef. LC 96-39099. (Habitat Ser.). (Illus.). 36p. (J). (gr. 1-4). 1997. 15.95 (*1-56899-433-8*); pap. 5.95 (*1-56899-434-6*) Soundprints.

— Undersea City: A Story of a Caribbean Coral Reef, Incl. toy. (Illus.). 36p. (J). (gr. 1-4). 1997. 26.95 (*1-56899-436-2*); 31.95 incl. audio (*1-56899-437-0*); pap. 16.95 (*1-56899-438-9*); pap. 19.95 incl. audio (*1-56899-439-7*) Soundprints.

— Undersea City: A Story of a Carribean Coral Reef. (Habitat Ser.). (Illus.). 36p. (J). (gr. 1-4). 1997. 19.95 incl. audio (*1-56899-435-4*, BC7002) Soundprints.

Rau, Dana Meachen. Bob's Vacation. (Rookie Readers Ser.). 1999. lib. bdg. 4.95 (*0-516-26472-9*) Childrens.

***Rau, Dana Meachen.** Chanukah. LC 00-21082. (True Bks.). (J). 2000. 22.00 (*0-516-21514-0*) Childrens.

— Chanukah. (True Bks.). (Illus.). 48p. (J). (gr. 3-5). 2000. pap. 6.95 (*0-516-27059-1*) Childrens.

— Christmas. LC 99-85972. (True Bks.). (Illus.). (J). 2000. 22.00 (*0-516-21513-2*) Childrens.

— Christmas. (True Bks.). (Illus.). 48p. (J). (gr. 3-5). 2000. pap. 6.95 (*0-516-27060-5*) Childrens.

Rau, Dana Meachen. Circle City. LC 98-53055. (Rookie Readers Ser.). 24p. (J). (gr. k-1). 1999. 15.00 (*0-516-21632-5*) Childrens.

***Rau, Dana Meachen.** Circle City. (Rookie Readers Ser.). (J). 2000. pap. text 4.95 (*0-516-26542-3*) Childrens.

Rau, Dana Meachen. Circle City. LC 98-53055. (Rookie Readers Ser.). (J). 2000. write for info. (*0-516-21690-2*) Childrens.

***Rau, Dana Meachen.** Climb up a Mountain. LC 99-86667. (Adventurers Ser.). (Illus.). (J). 2000. write for info. (*1-57103-317-3*) Rourke Pr.

— Explore in a Cave. LC 99-86665. (Adventurers Ser.). (J). 2000. write for info. (*1-57103-318-1*) Rourke Pr.

— Feet. (Rookie Readers Ser.). (Illus.). 24p. (J). (gr. k-1). 2000. pap. 4.95 (*0-516-27042-7*) Childrens.

— George Lucas: Creator of Star Wars. (Illus.). (J). 1999. 12.30 (*0-606-18149-0*) Turtleback.

— Hands. (Rookie Readers Ser.). (Illus.). 24p. (J). (gr. k-1). 2000. pap. 4.95 (*0-516-27043-5*) Childrens.

— Harriet Tubman. (Early Biographies Ser.). (Illus.). 32p. (J). (gr. 1-2). 2000. write for info. (*0-7565-0015-X*) Compass Point.

— Harry Houdini, Master Magician. LC 00-39930. (Book Report Biography Ser.). (Illus.). 2001. write for info. (*0-531-11599-2*) Watts.

— Kwanzaa. LC 99-86741. (True Bks.). (Illus.). (J). 2000. 22.00 (*0-516-21517-5*) Childrens.

— Kwanzaa. (True Bks.). (Illus.). 48p. (J). (gr. 3-5). 2000. pap. 6.95 (*0-516-27061-3*) Childrens.

— Las Manos. (Rookie Espanol Ser.). (SPA., Illus.). (J). 2000. 15.00 (*0-516-22021-7*) Childrens.

— Marie Curie. (Early Biographies Ser.). (Illus.). (J). (gr. 1-2). 2000. write for info. (*0-7565-0017-6*) Compass Point.

— New Year's Day. LC 99-86740. (Illus.). (J). 2000. 22.00 (*0-516-21516-7*) Childrens.

— New Years' Day. (True Bks.). (Illus.). 48p. (J). (gr. 3-5). 2000. pap. 6.95 (*0-516-27062-1*) Childrens.

Rau, Dana Meachen. One Giant Leap, the First Moon Landing. LC 96-15035. (Smithsonian Institution Odyssey Ser.). 1996. 11.15 (*0-606-10276-0*, Pub. by Turtleback) Demco.

— Panama. (True Bks.). (Illus.). 48p. (gr. 2-4). 1999. lib. bdg. 6.95 (*0-516-26497-4*) Childrens.

***Rau, Dana Meachen.** Los Pies. (Rookie Espanol Ser.). (SPA., Illus.). (J). 2000. 15.00 (*0-516-22020-9*) Childrens.

— Purple is Best. (Rookie Readers Ser.). (J). 2000. pap. text 4.95 (*0-516-27001-X*) Childrens.

Rau, Dana Meachen. Purple Is Best. LC 98-53053. (Rookie Readers Ser.). (Illus.). 32p. (J). (gr. 1-2). 1999. 17.50 (*0-516-21638-4*) Childrens.

***Rau, Dana Meachen.** The Solar System. (Simply Science Ser.). (Illus.). 32p. (J). 2000. write for info. (*0-7565-0036-2*) Compass Point.

— Stroll by the Sea. LC 99-86666. (Adventurers Ser.). (J). 2000. write for info. (*1-57103-320-3*) Rourke Pr.

— Thanksgiving. LC 99-85973. (True Bks.). (Illus.). (J). 2000. 22.00 (*0-516-21515-9*) Childrens.

— Thanksgiving. (True Bks.). (Illus.). 48p. (J). (gr. 3-5). 2000. pap. 6.95 (*0-516-27063-X*) Childrens.

— Visit the Desert. LC 99-86669. (Adventurers Ser.). (J). 2000. write for info. (*1-57103-321-1*) Rourke Pr.

***Rau, Dana Meachen & Stromoski, Rick.** Hands. LC 99-15865. (Rookie Readers Ser.). (J). 2000. 15.00 (*0-516-22009-8*) Childrens.

Rau, Deborah. Dearest Anna. (Super Saga Ser.). 252p. 1986. pap. 6.95 (*0-310-47471-X*, 15593P) Zondervan.

Rau, Diantha C. Dear Angels. 61p. (Orig.). 1985. pap. 12.95 (*0-935557-00-8*) D C Rau.

Rau, Edward P., Jr. Wytopitloc: Tales of a Deer Hunter. 200p. 1998. 42.95 (*0-89754-156-1*); pap. 13.95 (*0-89754-150-2*) Dan River Pr.

***Rau-Foster, Mary.** Dealing with Challenging Dialysis Patient Situations: A Resource Guide Designed Specifically for Nephrology Professionals. xiv, 234p. 1999. 100.00 incl. disk (*1-930069-00-6*) F S C Pubng.

Rau, Gustav. Die Deutschen Pferdezuchten. (GER., Illus.). 239p. 1986. write for info. (*3-487-08255-1*) G Olms Pubs.

— Die Reitkunst der Welt an den Olympischen Spielen, 1936.Tr. of Equitation du Monde aux Jeux Olympiques de 1936/The World's Equestrian Sports at the Olympic Games of 1936. (Illus.). 399p. 1978. write for info. (*3-487-08156-3*) G Olms Pubs.

Rau, Gustav & Duerst, Ulrich J. Pferdebeurteilung. (Documenta Hippologica Ser.). (GER., Illus.). 62p. 1996. reprint ed. write for info. (*3-487-08210-1*) G Olms Pubs.

***Rau, Joachim.** Umweltaspekte Eines Umfassenden Qualitatsmanagements: Konzeption, State of the Art Und Umsetzung. (Illus.). XXXI, 465p. 1998. 79.95 (*3-631-33970-4*) P Lang Pubng.

Rau, John. Secrets from the Search Firm Files: What It Really Takes to Get Ahead in Corporate America. LC 97-1469. 224p. 1997. 24.95 (*0-7863-1192-4*) McGraw.

Rau, Joseph L. Respiratory Care Drug Reference. (Illus.). 464p. (C). (gr. 13). 1996. pap. text 19.95 (*0-8151-8456-5*, 28390) Mosby Inc.

— Respiratory Care Pharmacology. 5th ed. LC 97-18095. (Illus.). 432p. (C). (gr. 13). 1997. pap. text 39.00 (*0-8151-2337-X*, 31046) Mosby Inc.

***Rau, Joseph L., Jr.** Respiratory Care Pharmacology: Includes Testbank. 5th ed. 1998. teacher ed. write for info. (*0-323-00358-3*) Mosby Inc.

Rau, Joseph L. Understanding Chest Radiographers. 1985. 23.95 (*0-8016-4026-1*) Mosby Inc.

Rau, Joseph L. & Rau, Mary Y. Fundamental Respiratory Therapy Equipment: Principles of Use & Operation. LC 77-73776. (Illus.). 214p. reprint ed. pap. 66.40 (*0-608-15508-X*, 202973900064) Bks Demand.

Rau, Jospeh L., Jr. Respiratory Therapy Pharmacology. 3rd ed. (Illus.). 316p. 1988. 29.95 (*0-685-34790-7*) Mosby Inc.

Rau, Karl H. Lehrbuch der Politischen Oekonomie. 1997. write for info. (*3-487-10335-4*) G Olms Pubs.

Rau, Lucy, jt. auth. see Postman, Leo J.

Rau, Margaret. Musk Oxen: Bearded Ones of the Arctic. LC 75-26538. (Illus.). 40p. (J). (gr. 3-7). 1976. lib. bdg. 10.89 (*0-690-01040-0*) HarpC Child Bks.

— The Ordeal of Olive Oatman: A True Story of the American West. LC 97-28182. (Illus.). 112p. (YA). (gr. 5 up). 1998. lib. bdg. 18.95 (*1-883846-21-8*) M Reynolds.

Rau, Marie T. Coping with Communication Challenges in Alzheimers Disease. LC 92-41712. (Coping with Aging Ser.). (Illus.). 228p. (C). 1993. pap. 19.95 (*1-879105-76-4*, 0339) Thomson Learn.

Rau, Mary Y., jt. auth. see Rau, Joseph L.

Rau, Nicholas J., jt. ed. see Pearce, David W.

Rau, Pradaeep A., jt. auth. see Ryans, John K., Jr.

Rau, R., ed. Low-Dose Methotrexate-Therapy in Rheumatic Diseases. (Rheumatology Ser.: Vol. 9). (Illus.). xii, 268p. 1986. 155.75 (*3-8055-4236-4*) S Karger.

***Rau, Richard & Higgins, Kathleen, eds.** Forensic Sciences: Review of Status & Needs. 71p. (C). 2000. pap. text 20.00 (*0-7881-8797-X*) DIANE Pub.

Rau, Robert. Copperfield & Co. The Best Tricks of the Greatest Magicians. MagicWeb Staff, tr. from GER. (Illus.). 300p. 1998. 29.99 (*1-890167-31-2*); pap. 19.99 (*1-890167-32-0*) MagicWeb.

Rau, Rudolph, jt. auth. see Rauff, Rebecca.

Rau, Sara S., ed. Woman to Woman: Entrepreneurial Advice for All Week Long from Ash to Zunkel. (Illus.). 55p. (Orig.). 1992. pap. 8.95 (*0-9633089-0-4*) Phillippe-Fenton.

Rau, Zbigniew. Contractarianism vs. Holism: Reinterpreting Locke's Two Treatises of Government. LC 95-6234. 160p. (C). 1995. pap. text 26.50 (*0-8191-9930-3*); lib. bdg. 48.00 (*0-8191-9929-X*) U Pr of Amer.

Raub, John J. Who Told You That You Were Naked? Freedom from Judgement, Guilt & Fear of Punishment. 160p. (C). 1990. 49.00 (*0-85439-423-0*, Pub. by St Paul Pubns) St Mut.

— Who Told You That You Were Naked? Freedom from Judgment, Guilt, & Fear of Punishment. 128p. (Orig.). 1992. pap. 13.95 (*0-8245-1203-0*) Crossroad NY.

Raub, Patricia. Yesterday's Stories: Popular Women's Novels of the Twenties & Thirties, 104. LC 94-4794. (Contributions in American Studies). 160p. 1994. 55.00 (*0-313-29259-0*, Greenwood Pr) Greenwood.

Raub, T. L., jt. auth. see Audus, K. L.

Raube, K. Health & Social Support of the Elderly. 124p. (Orig.). (C). 1994. pap. text 40.00 (*0-7881-1056-X*) DIANE Pub.

Rauber, Diane B., et al. Court Improvement Progress Report, 1998. LC 98-19003. 1998. write for info. (*1-57073-570-0*) Amer Bar Assn.

***Rauber, Diane B., et al.** Court Improvement Progress Report 1999. LC 99-35020. 1999. write for info. (*1-57073-687-1*) Amer Bar Assn.

***Rauber, Diane Boyd, et al.** Court Improvement Progress Report 2000. LC 00-38602. 2000. pap. write for info. (*1-57073-792-4*) ABA Prof Educ Pubns.

— Representing Parents in Child Welfare Cases: A Basic Introduction for Attorneys. LC 00-39367. 2000. write for info. (*1-57073-794-0*) ABA Prof Educ Pubns.

Raubicheck, Walter & Srebnick, Walter, eds. Hitchcock's Rereleased Films: From Rope to Vertigo. LC 90-49240. (Contemporary Film & Television Ser.). (Illus.). 302p. (C). 1991. text 39.95 (*0-8143-2325-1*); pap. text 19.95 (*0-8143-2326-X*) Wayne St U Pr.

Raubitschek, A. E. Supplementum Inscriptionum Atticarum VII: Dedications from the Athenian Acropolis. 637p. 1999. 65.00 (*0-89005-533-5*, SIA07) Ares.

Raubitschek, Isabelle K. The Metal Objects, 1952-1989. (Isthmia: Vol. 7). (Illus.). 200p. (C). 1998. text 150.00 (*0-87661-937-5*) Am Sch Athens.

Raucat, Thomas. L' Honorable Partie de Campagne. (FRE.). 1984. pap. 11.95 (*0-7859-4213-0*) Fr & Eur.

Raucci, Richard. Mosaic for Windows: A Hands-on Configuration & Set-up Guide to Popular Web Browsers. LC 95-11636. (Illus.). 192p. 1995. 21.95 (*0-387-97996-4*) Spr-Verlag.

— Netscape for Macintosh: A Hands-On Configuration & Set-Up Guide for Popular Web Browsers. LC 95-47549. (Illus.). 179p. 1996. pap. text 24.95 (*0-387-94662-4*) Spr-Verlag.

— Netscape for the Macintosh. 1996. pap. 24.95 (*0-614-12617-7*) Spr-Verlag.

— One-a-Day Web Page Wake-Ups! 464p. 1996. 29.99 (*1-56276-490-X*, Ziff-Davis Pr) Que.

— Personal Robotics: Real Robots to Construct, Program & Explore the World. LC 98-51745. (Illus.). 250p. 1999. 25.00 (*1-56881-089-X*) AK Peters.

— A Windows NT Guide to the Web Vol. VI: Covering Browsers, Servers, & Related Software. (Illus.). 130p. 1996. pap. 24.95 (*0-387-94792-2*) Spr-Verlag.

Rauch. Outnation: Searching the Soul of Japan. 200p. 1992. 22.50 (*0-07-103370-X*) McGraw.

Rauch, L. Edwin. The Original Version of Office Copier Humor. (Illus.). 98p. 1996. spiral bd. 9.95 (*0-9668402-0-8*) Spittin Image.

Rauch, A. H., ed. see American Society for Metals Staff.

***Rauch, Angelika.** The Hieroglyph of Tradition: Freud, Benjamin, Gadamer, Novalis, Kant. LC 99-86009. 2000. write for info. (*0-8386-3846-5*) Fairleigh Dickinson.

Rauch, Basil. Roosevelt: From Munich to Pearl Harbor. LC 74-34446. (FDR & the Era of the New Deal Ser.). 527p. 1975. reprint ed. lib. bdg. 45.00 (*0-306-70739-X*) Da Capo.

Rauch, Erich. Diagnostics According to F. X. Mayr: Criteria of Good, Marginal & Ill Health. Fogg, David M., tr. from GER. (Illus.). 129p. (Orig.). 1993. pap. text 25.00 (*2-8043-4004-X*, Pub. by Edits Haug Intl) Medicina Bio.

— Health Through Inner Body Cleansing: The Famous MAYR Intestinal Therapy From Europe. 3rd ed. Peters, Mollie C., tr. from GER. (Illus.). 89p. 1990. pap. 9.95 (*3-7760-1179-3*, Pub. by K F Haug Pubs) Medicina Bio.

— Naturopathic Treatment of Colds & Infectious Diseases. Fogg, David M., tr. from GER. (Illus.). 83p. (Orig.). 1993. pap. 9.95 (*2-8043-4003-1*, Pub. by K F Haug Pubs) Medicina Bio.

***Rauch, Fred D. & Weissich, Paul R.** Plants for Tropical Landscapes: A Gardener's Guide. LC 99-26677. 2000. 39.95 (*0-8248-2034-7*) UH Pr.

Rauch, Friedrich. Psychology: or A View of the Human Soul, Including Anthropology. LC 74-22335. (History of Psychology Ser.). 416p. 1975. 60.00 (*0-8201-1142-2*) Schol Facsimiles.

Rauch, Friedrich, ed. Iconsource. (Illus.). 1990. write for info. incl. cd-rom, disk (*0-318-71805-7*) G Olms Pubs.

Rauch, George V. Conflict in the Southern Cone. LC 98-44597. 248p. 1999. 69.50 (*0-275-96347-0*, Praeger Pubs) Greenwood.

Rauch, Gerry. The One Year Guide to the Catechism of the Catholic Church. LC 98-48280. 266 p. 1999. pap. 11.99 (*1-56955-026-3*) Servant.

Rauch, H. Artificial Intelligence in Real Time Control 1997. LC 98-21862. 558p. 1998. pap. write for info. (*0-08-042927-0*) Elsevier.

Rauch, H., jt. ed. see Bonse, U.

***Rauch, Helmut & Werner, Samuel.** Neutron Interferometry: Lessons in Experimental Quantum Mechanics. (Oxford Series on Neutron Scattering in Condensed Matter: Vol. 12). (Illus.). 416p. 2000. text 120.00 (*0-19-850027-0*) OUP.

Rauch, Irmengard. The Old Saxon Language: Grammar, Epic Narrative, Linguistic Formation. LC 92-20320. (Berkeley Models of Grammar Ser.: Vol. 1). XLIII, 416p. (C). 1992. text 60.95 (*0-8204-1893-5*) P Lang Pubng.

Rauch, Irmengard, et al, eds. On Germanic Linguistics: Issues & Methods. LC 92-21566. (Trends in Linguistics, Studies & Monographs: No. 68). viii, 416p. (C). 1992. lib. bdg. 152.35 (*3-11-013000-9*) Mouton.

Rauch, Irmengard & Carr, Gerald F., eds. Insights in Germanic Linguistics No. 1: Methodology in Transition. (Trends in Linguistics, Studies & Monographs: No. 83). vii, 354p. (C). 1995. lib. bdg. 152.30 (*3-11-014359-3*) Mouton.

— Insights in Germanic Linguistics II: Classic & Contemporary. (Trends in Linguistics Ser.: Vol. 94). x, 354p. (C). 1997. lib. bdg. 162.90 (*3-11-014854-4*) Mouton.

— Language Change. LC 82-48626. 286p. 1983. reprint ed. pap. 88.70 (*0-7837-6106-6*, 205915200008) Bks Demand.

— Linguistic Method: Essays in Honor of Herbert Penzl. (Janua Linguarum, Series Major: No. 79). 1979. text 142.35 (*90-279-7767-4*) Mouton.

***Rauch, Irmengard & Carr, Gerald F., eds.** New Insights in Germanic Linguistics I, Vol. 33. LC 99-23178. 260p. (C). 1999. text 52.95 (*0-8204-3888-X*) P Lang Pubng.

Rauch, Irmengard & Carr, Gerald F., eds. The Semiotic Bridge: Trends from California. (Approaches to Semiotics Ser.: No. 86). x, 428p. (C). 1989. lib. bdg. 142.35 (*0-89925-626-0*) Mouton.

— The Signifying Animal: The Grammar of Language & Experience. LC 79-3624. (Advances in Semiotics Ser.). (Illus.). 304p. reprint ed. pap. 94.30 (*0-8357-6696-9*, 205687600094) Bks Demand.

Rauch, Irmengard & Moore, Cornelia N., eds. Across the Oceans: Studies from East to West in Honor of Richard K. Seymour. LC 95-14377. 208p. (C). 1995. pap. text 25.00 (*0-8248-1693-5*) UH Pr.

Rauch, Irmengard & Scott, Charles T., eds. Approaches in Linguistic Methodology. LC 66-22863. 167p. 1969. reprint ed. pap. 51.80 (*0-608-01900-3*, 206255200003) Bks Demand.

Rauch, J. Partial Differential Equations. Ewing, J. H. et al, eds. (Graduate Texts in Mathematics Ser.: Vol. 128). (Illus.). 256p. 1997. 43.95 (*0-387-97472-5*) Spr-Verlag.

Rauch, J., et al, eds. Quasiclassical Methods. LC 97-26430. (IMA Volumes in Mathematics & Its Applications Ser.: No. 95). (Illus.). 243p. 1997. 54.95 (*0-387-98310-4*) Spr-Verlag.

Rauch, James, ed. Kline Guide to the Ink Industry. LC 81-84941. (Illus.). 140p. 1982. pap. 85.00 (*0-917148-18-5*) Kline.

Rauch, James, jt. ed. see Deitsch, Marian.

Rauch, James A. Rauch Guide to U. S. Adhesives & Sealants Industry. Dykes, Donald & Keimel, Fred, eds. (Illus.). 350p. 1996. spiral bd. 445.00 (*0-932157-05-X*) Impact Mrkting.

Rauch, James E., jt. auth. see Meier, Gerald M.

Rauch, Jeffrey & Taylor, Michael E., eds. Singularities & Oscillations. LC 97-2460. (IMA Volumes in Mathematics & Its Applications Ser.: Vol. 91). (Illus.). 164p. 1997. 49.95 (*0-387-98200-0*) Spr-Verlag.

Rauch, Jennifer. Before You Were Born. LC 97-49253. (Illus.). 36p. (J). (ps-2). 1998. pap. 10.95 (*0-7611-1200-6*) Workman Pub.

***Rauch, Jonathan.** Government's End: Why Washington Stopped Working. LC 99-41893. 288p. 1999. pap. 12.00 (*1-891620-49-5*, Pub. by PublicAffairs NY) HarpC.

Rauch, Jonathan. Kindly Inquisitors: The New Attacks on Free Thought. LC 92-35805. 192p. (C). 1993. 17.95 (*0-226-70575-7*) U Ch Pr.

— Kindly Inquisitors: The New Attacks on Free Thought. 178p. 1995. pap. 9.95 (*0-226-70576-5*) U Ch Pr.

— The Outnation: A Search for the Soul of Japan. LC 91-37946. (Illus.). 182p. 1992. 18.95 (*0-87584-320-4*) Harvard Busn.

Rauch, Jonathan, jt. auth. see Litan, Robert E.

Rauch, Julia B., ed. Assessment: A Sourcebook for Social Work Practice. LC 93-27098. 416p. 1993. pap. 28.95 (*0-87304-267-0*) Manticore Pubs.

Rauch, Julia B., jt. auth. see Eanet, Karen.

Rauch, Karen, jt. auth. see Fessler, Jeff.

Rauch, Kennedy. Shattered Faith. LC 97-52797. 256p. 1998. pap. 12.95 (*0-8050-5828-1*, Owl) H Holt & Co.

Rauch, L. Edwin. The R Rated Version of Office Copier Humor. (Illus.). 97p. 1996. spiral bd. 9.95 (*0-9668402-1-6*) Spittin Image.

— The X Rated Version of Office Copier Humor. (Illus.). 97p. 1996. spiral bd. 12.95 (*0-9668402-2-4*) Spittin Image.

Rauch, Leo & Sherman, David. Hegel's Phenomenology of Self-Consciousness: Text & Commentary. LC 99-19061. (SUNY Series in Hegelian Studies). 236p. (C). 1999. pap. text 17.95 (*0-7914-4158-X*) State U NY Pr.

— Hegel's Phenomenology of Self-Consciousness: Text & Commentary. LC 99-19061. (SUNY Series in Hegelian Studies). 224p. (C). 1999. text 54.50 (*0-7914-4157-1*) State U NY Pr.

Rauch, Leo, tr. see Hegel, Georg Wilhelm Friedrich.

Rauch, Leo, tr. see Kant, Immanuel.

Rauch, Martin & Wurster, Ekkehard. Schulbuchforschung Als Unterrichtsforschung: Vergleichende Schreibtisch- und Praxisevaluation von Unterrichtswerken Fur den Sachunterricht (DFG-Projekt) (Mit Ausfuhrlicher Dokumentation der Meinstrumente) (Freiburger Beitrage Zur Erziehungswissenschaft und Fachdidaktik Ser.: Bd. 3). (GER., Illus.). XVI, 412p. 1997. 56.95 (*3-631-31192-3*) P Lang Pubng.

Rauch, Nicolas. French Artist Books, 1867-1957 - Bibliography: Les Peintres et Livre, 1867-1957. rev. ed. (FRE., Illus.). 228p. 1991. 100.00 (*1-55660-127-1*) A Wofsy Fine Arts.

Rauch-Nolan, Elizabeth, tr. see Verschuur-Basse, Denyse.

Rauch, Paul H. How to Be Your Own Contractor: Remodeling, Additions, Alterations, & Building a New Home. 3rd ed. LC 88-6986. 1994. pap. 9.95 (*0-931790-74-3*) Brick Hse Pub.

Rauch, Rainer, jt. auth. see Herrmann, Reinhild.

Rauch, Robert S. Smile, Be True to Your Teeth & They'll Never Be False to You. 2nd rev. ed. (Illus.). 105p. 1991. pap. 9.95 (*0-9624076-0-7*) R S Rauch.

Rauch, Rufus W. Rauch Book. (Illus.). 89p. 1997. reprint ed. pap. 17.50 (*0-8328-9497-4*); reprint ed. lib. bdg. 27.50 (*0-8328-9496-6*) Higginson Bk Co.

Rauch, Seymour. Legalized Stealing: The American Way of Life. (American University Studies: Economics: Ser. XVI, Vol. 2). X, 334p. (C). 1989. text 43.00 (*0-8204-0625-2*) P Lang Pubng.

Rauch, Sidney J. Barnaby Brown: Home from Erehwon. (Barnaby Brown Bks.: Bk. 5). (Illus.). 80p. (Orig.). (J). (gr. 2-4). 1990. pap. 4.95 (*1-55743-162-0*) Berrent Pubns.

— The Further Adventures of Barnaby Brown. (Barnaby Brown Bks.: Bk. 4). (Illus.). 63p. (Orig.). (J). (gr. 2-4). 1990. pap. 4.95 (*1-55743-159-0*) Berrent Pubns.

— The Return of B. B. (Barnaby Brown Bks.: Bk. 2). (Illus.). 48p. (Orig.). (J). (gr. 2-4). 1989. pap. 4.95 (*1-55743-153-1*) Berrent Pubns.

— A Visit to B. B.'s Planet. (Barnaby Brown Bks.: Bk. 3). (Illus.). 64p. (Orig.). (J). (gr. 2-4). 1989. pap. 4.95 (*1-55743-156-6*) Berrent Pubns.

— The Visitor from Outer Space. (Barnaby Brown Bks.: Bk. 1). (Illus.). 48p. (Orig.). (J). (gr. 2-4). 1989. pap. 4.95 (*1-55743-150-7*) Berrent Pubns.

Rauch, Sidney J. & Sanacore, Joseph, eds. Handbook for the Volunteer Tutor. 2nd ed. LC 84-15723. 147p. (Orig.). reprint ed. pap. 45.60 (*0-7837-4735-7*, 204454300004) Bks Demand.

Rauch, Steffen G. Nachtragliche Werbungskosten - Zu Spate Aufwendungen? (GER.). LXXVI, 132p. 1996. 42.95 (*3-631-30069-7*) P Lang Pubng.

Rauch, Virginia. Fireside Stories. 1995. pap. 7.95 (*0-7880-0603-7*, 6037, Fairway Pr) CSS OH.

R

Rauch, Walter. Real-World Survival! What Has Worked for Me. unabridged ed. LC 98-91247. (Illus.). 160p. 1998. pap. 15.95 (*0-9663260-0-8*) Rauch & Co.

Rauch, Wendy. Open Systems Engineering: How to Plan & Develop Client-Server Systems. LC 95-50773. 400p. 1996. pap. 54.99 incl. cd-rom (*0-471-13038-9*) Wiley.

Rauchbauer, Otto, ed. Ancestral Voices: The Big House in Anglo-Irish Literature. (Illus.). 295p. 1992. 50.70 (*3-487-09531-9*) G Olms Pubs.

— Ancestral Voices: The Big-House in Anglo-Irish Literature. 1996. 49.95 (*0-946640-86-6*, Pub. by Lilliput Pr) Irish Bks Media.

Rauche, G. A. The Abdication of Philosophy, the Abdication of Man: A Critical Study of the Interdependence of Philosophy As Critical Theory & Man As a Free Individual. 168p. 1975. pap. text 65.00 (*90-247-1657-8*, Pub. by M Nijhoff) Kluwer Academic.

— Contemporary Philosophical Alternatives & the Crises of Truth: A Critical Study of Positivism, Existentialism & Marxism. 168p. 1971. pap. text 57.00 (*90-247-5017-2*, Pub. by M Nijhoff) Kluwer Academic.

Raucher, Alan R. Paul G. Hoffman: Architect of Foreign Aid. LC 85-13406. 224p. 1985. 29.95 (*0-8131-1555-8*) U Pr of Ky.

Raucher, Herman. Summer of Forty-Two. 23.95 (*0-8488-0310-8*) Amereon Ltd.

— Summer of Forty-Two. 1991. reprint ed. lib. bdg. 27.95 (*1-56849-079-8*) Buccaneer Bks.

Raucher, Robert S., et al. Estimating the Cost of Compliance with Drinking Water Standards: A User's Guide. LC 96-134104. (Illus.). 380p. 1996. pap. 135.00 (*0-89867-828-5*, 90688) Am Water Wks Assn.

Raucherbaumer, Jon, jt. auth. see Livera, Giovanni.

Rauchfuss, Cynog H. Von, see Von Rauchfuss, Cynog H.

Rauchut, E. A., jt. compiled by see Elton, William R.

***Rauchwerger, Lisa.** Chocolate Chip Challah: Activity Book. (Illus.). (J). 2000. pap. 7.95 (*0-8074-0736-4*) UAHC.

Rauchwerger, Lisa. Chocolate Chip Challah: And Other Twists on the Jewish Holiday Table. LC 99-25976. (Illus.). 96p. (YA). (gr. k-6). 1999. pap. 15.95 (*0-8074-0700-3*, 510606) UAHC.

Raudabaugh, James E., jt. auth. see Heilman, Karl J.

Raudenbush, Brenda. Brilly & the Boot. LC 97-75963. (Illus.). 97p. (J). (gr. 4-6). 1998. pap. 9.95 (*0-9661531-0-3*) Panola Pub.

Raudenbush, Stephen W., jt. auth. see Bryk, Anthony S.

***Raudkivi, Arved J.** Loose Boundary Hydraulics. (Illus.). 512p. (C). 1998. text 100.00 (*90-5410-447-3*, Pub. by A A Balkema); pap. text, student ed. 53.00 (*90-5410-448-1*, Pub. by A A Balkema) Ashgate Pub Co.

Raudkivi, Arved J. Loose Boundary Hydraulics. 3rd ed. (Civil Engineering Ser.). (Illus.). 556p. 1990. pap. text 74.95 (*0-08-034073-3*, Prgamon Press) Buttrwrth-Heinemann.

— Sedimentation: Exclusion & Removal of Sediment from Diverted Water. (Hydraulic Structures Design Manual Ser.: No. 6). (Illus.). 176p. 1993. text 110.00 (*90-5410-132-6*, Pub. by A A Balkema) Ashgate Pub Co.

Raudkivi, Arved J. & Breusers, H. N. Scouring. (Hydraulic Structures Design Manual Ser.: No. 2). (Illus.). 152p. (C). 1991. text 110.00 (*90-6191-983-5*, Pub. by A A Balkema) Ashgate Pub Co.

Raudsepp, Jaanus. Gogol v KGB. LC 91-76741.Tr. of Gogol' in KGB - A Documentary Novel. (RUS.). 141p. (Orig.). 1992. pap. 12.00 (*0-911971-72-6*) Effect Pub.

Raudszus, Gabriele. Die Zeichensprache der Kleidung. (GER.). X, 278p. 1985. write for info. (*3-487-07531-8*) G Olms Pubs.

***Raudzens, George.** Empires: Europe & Globalization, 1492-1788. 1999. 36.95 (*0-7509-1986-8*) A Sutton.

Raue, F., ed. Hypercalcemia of Malignancy. (Recent Results in Cancer Research Ser.: Vol. 137). 170p. 1994. 93.00 (*0-387-57631-2*) Spr-Verlag.

Raue, F., et al, eds. Medullary Thyroid Carcinoma. LC 92-2297. (Recent Results in Cancer Research Ser.: Vol. 125). (Illus.). 232p. 1992. 104.00 (*0-387-55372-X*) Spr-Verlag.

Raueiser, Stefan. Schweigemuster Uber die Rede Vom Heiligen Schweigen: Eine Untersuchung Unter Besonderer Berucksichtigung von Odo Casel, Gustav Mensching, Rudolf Otto, Karl Rahner, Wilhelm Weischedel und Bernhard Welte. (Europaische Hochschulschriften Ser.: Reihe 23, Bd. 582). (GER.). XLVI, 308p. 1996. 57.95 (*3-631-30732-2*) P Lang Pubng.

Rauen, Peter J., jt. auth. see Barchers, Suzanne I.

***Rauen, Sheila.** Sassy Cats: Purr-Fect Craft Projects. (Illus.). 96p. 2000. pap. 19.95 (*1-56477-328-0*) Martingale & Co.

***Rauer, Christine.** Beowulf & the Dragon: Parallels & Analogues. 256p. 2000. 75.00 (*0-85991-592-1*) Boydell & Brewer.

Rauert, W., jt. auth. see Moser, H.

Rauf, A. Ahadith for Children. Bakhtiar, Laleh, ed. 150p. (J). 1990. pap. 10.50 (*0-933511-14-0*) Kazi Pubns.

— Quran for Children. Bakhtiar, Laleh, ed. 1989. pap. 10.50 (*0-935782-08-7*) Kazi Pubns.

— Story of Islamic Culture. Nur, Muhammad, tr. 52p. (C). 1997. pap. 3.50 (*0-933511-65-5*) Kazi Pubns.

Rauf, Abdul. Bilal Ibn Rabah. LC 76-49691. 1977. pap. 3.95 (*0-89259-008-4*) Am Trust Pubns.

Rauf, Bulent. Addresses. 72p. (Orig.). 1986. pap. 9.00 (*0-904975-12-6*, Pub. by Beshara) New Leaf Dist.

Rauf, Bulent, tr. see Burckhardt, Titus.

Rauf, Feisal A. Islam: A Search for Meaning. 132p. (Orig.). 1995. pap. 7.95 (*1-56859-037-7*) Mazda Pubs.

Rauf, M. A. Arabic for English Speaking Students. 1991. 22.95 (*0-935782-21-4*) Kazi Pubns.

Rauf, Muhammad A. Imam Ali Ibn Abi Talib: The First Intellectual Muslim Thinker. LC 96-35053. 124p. (Orig.). 1996. pap. text 6.00 (*1-881963-49-7*) Al-Saadawi Pubns.

— The Islamic View of Women & the Family. 4th ed. LC 96-35054. 159p. 1996. pap. text 6.95 (*1-881963-51-9*) Al-Saadawi Pubns.

— Marriage in Islam: A Manual. 6th ed. LC 96-42977. 87p. 1996. reprint ed. pap. text 5.00 (*1-881963-48-9*) Al-Saadawi Pubns.

Rauf, S. A. Advice to a Friend. 1980. pap. 3.95 (*0-935782-25-7*) Kazi Pubns.

Rauf, S. A., tr. see Amin Ahsan Islahi.

Raufa, Dhyan, tr. see Jones, Proctor.

***Raufaste, Noel J.** Building & Fire Research Laboratory Activities, Accomplishments & Recognitions 1998. 56p. 1999. pap. 15.00 (*0-16-056996-6*) USGPO.

Raufaste, Noel J. Nist Building & Fire Research Laboratory: Project Summaries, 1997. 230p. 1998. per. 20.00 (*0-16-054773-3*) USGPO.

— Wind & Seismic Effects: Proceedings of the 28th Joint Meeting of the United States-Japan Cooperative Program in Natural Resources, Panel on Wind & Seismic Effects. 643p. 1996. per. 49.00 (*0-16-053344-9*) USGPO.

— Wind & Seismic Effects: Proceedings of the 30th Joint Meeting of the United States-Japan Cooperative Program in Natural Resources, Panel on Wind & Seismic Effects. 632p. 1998. per. 49.00 (*0-16-056751-3*) USGPO.

***Raufaste, Noel J., ed.** Wind & Seismic Effects: Proceedings of the 28th Joint Meeting of the U. S. Japan Cooperative Program in Natural Resources Panel on Wind & Seismic Effects. (Illus.). 575p. 1999. reprint ed. pap. text 60.00 (*0-7881-8189-0*) DIANE Pub.

Raufer, Roger K. Pollution Markets in a Green Country Town: Urban Environmental Management in Transition. LC 97-32945. 288p. 1998. 65.00 (*0-275-96174-5*, Praeger Pubs) Greenwood.

Raufer, Roger K. & Feldman, Stephen L. Acid Rain & Emissions Trading: Implementing a Market Approach to Pollution Control. 176p. (C). 1988. 56.00 (*0-8476-7555-6*) Rowman.

Rauff, James V. Math Matters. LC 94-42054. 512p. 1995. pap. 55.95 (*0-471-30452-2*) Wiley.

Rauff, Rebecca & Rau, Rudolph. Everyday Situations for Communicating in English: Advanced Beginning Through Intermediate: Full Color Scenes & Activities. (Illus.). 128p. 1992. teacher ed. 11.95 (*0-8442-0677-6*, Natl Textbk Co) NTC Contemp Pub Co.

— Everyday Situations for Communicating in English: Advanced Beginning Through Intermediate: Full Color Scenes & Activities. (Illus.). 144p. 1994. pap. 19.95 (*0-8442-0676-8*, Natl Textbk Co) NTC Contemp Pub Co.

Rauff, Rebecca, jt. ed. see Schinke-Llano, Linda.

***Raugel, Pierre-Jean.** Rapid Food Analysis & Hygiene Monitoring: Kits, Instruments & Systems: Kits, Instruments & Systems. LC 98-43880. xx, 921p. 1998. 269.00 (*3-540-63253-0*) Spr-Verlag.

Raugh, Harold E., Jr. Wavell in the Middle East, 1939-1941: A Study in Generalship. (Illus.). 348p. 1993. 54.00 (*0-08-040983-0*, Pub. by Brasseys) Brasseys.

Raughton. Colloquial Slovak. 1997. audio 27.99 (*0-415-11541-8*) Routledge.

***Raugust, Karen.** International Licensing: A Status Report, 2000 Edition. (Illus.). 200p. 1999. pap. 2195.00 (*1-885747-25-X*) EPM Communs.

Raugust, Karen. The Licensing Business Handbook. 3rd ed. Mayer, Ira, ed. (Illus.). 216p. 2000. pap. 59.95 (*1-885747-00-4*) EPM Communs.

— Merchandise Licensing in the Television Industry. (Broadcasting & Cable Ser.). 142p. 1995. pap. 34.95 (*0-240-80210-1*, Focal) Buttrwrth-Heinemann.

Rauh, Nicholas K. The Sacred Bonds of Commerce: Religion, Economy, & Trade Society at Hellenistic Roman Delos. 392p. 1993. lib. bdg. 87.00 (*90-5063-156-8*, Pub. by Gieben) J Benjamins Pubng Co.

Rauh, W. Bromelien (Bromeliads) 3rd rev. ed. (GER., Illus.). 458p. 1990. 93.00 (*3-8001-6371-3*, Pub. by Eugen Ulmer) Balogh.

Rauh, Werner. Kakteen an Ihren Standorten. Unter Besonderer Beruecksichtigung Ihrer Morphologie und Systematik (Cacti & Their Species. With Special Regards Towards Their Morphology & Systematics) (Illus.). 230p. 1979. pap. 29.00 (*3-8263-2684-9*, Pub. by Blckwell Wissenschafts) Balogh.

Rauhauser, Bill & Lewis, David L. The Car & the Camera: The Detroit School of Automotive Photography. (Illus.). 96p. (Orig.). 1996. pap. 19.95 (*0-8143-2674-9*) Wayne St U Pr.

Rauhauser, William & McLennan, Ann. America's Schools: Making Them Work. LC 95-74756. 61p. (Orig.). 1995. pap. 9.00 (*0-944337-27-9*, 279) New View Pubns.

Rauhe, Hermann, et al, contrib. by. Kulturmanagement: Theorie und Praxis Einer Professionellen Kunst. x, 594p. 1997. 45.35 (*3-11-015655-5*) De Gruyter.

Rauhut, J. Brent & Darter, Michael I. Early Analyses of LTPP General Pavement Studies Data. 32p. (C). 1993. pap. text 10.00 (*0-309-05774-4*, SHRP-P-392) SHRP.

Rauk, Arvi. Orbital Interaction Theory of Organic Chemistry. 336p. 1994. 82.50 (*0-471-59389-3*) Wiley.

Raul, Arreola. Chistes Manchados. (SPA.). 1997. pap. text 6.98 (*968-403-527-6*) Selector.

Raul, Bonoratt. Guitarra Sin Maestro. (SPA.). 1997. pap. text 10.98 (*968-15-0167-5*) Ed Mex.

Raul, K. B. Naked to the Night. rev. ed. 176p. 1986. reprint ed. pap. 10.00 (*0-917342-20-8*) Gay Sunshine.

Raulerson, John D., jt. auth. see Wong, Martin R.

Raulet. Van Cleef & Arpels. 1998. 18.95 (*0-7893-0201-2*, Pub. by Universe) St Martin.

Raulet, Gerard & Steiner, Uwe, eds. Walter Benjamin: Asthetik und Geschichtphilosophie Esthetique et Philosophie de l'Histoire. 231p. 1998. 41.95 (*3-906757-49-8*) P Lang Pubng.

Raulet, Gerard, jt. auth. see Bialas, Wolfgang.

Raulet, Sylvie. Maharajas' Palaces: European Style in Imperial India. LC 97-5250. (Illus.). 297p. 1997. text 85.00 (*0-86565-989-3*) Vendome.

***Raulet, Sylvie.** Rock Crystal Treasures: From Antiquity to Today. LC 99-26517. 240p. 1999. text 65.00 (*0-86565-211-2*) Vendome.

Raulin, F. & Greenberg, J. Mayo, eds. Life Sciences: Complex Organics in Space. (Advances in Space Research Ser.: Vol. 19, No. 7). 184p. 1997. pap. 108.00 (*0-08-043108-9*, Pergamon Pr) Elsevier.

Raulin, F., jt. auth. see Chelaflores, Julian.

Raulin, F., jt. ed. see Levasseur-Regourd, A. C.

Raulin, Michael L., jt. auth. see Graziano, Anthony M.

Raulston, J. C., jt. auth. see Tripp, Kim E.

Raulston, J. Leonard & Livingood, James W. Sequatchie: A Story of the Southern Cumberlands. LC 73-17360. (Illus.). 313p. 1974. reprint ed. pap. 97.10 (*0-7837-5391-8*, 204515500005) Bks Demand.

Raulston, Ruth N., ed. see Sinks, Charles.

***Rault, Lucie.** Musical Instruments: Traditions & Craftsmanship from Pre-History to the Present. (Illus.). 240p. 2000. 60.00 (*0-8109-4384-0*, Pub. by Abrams) Time Warner.

Raultbee, Paul G., compiled by. Cayman Islands, Vol. 187. LC 96-223556. (World Bibliographical Ser.). 150p. 1996. lib. bdg. 65.00 (*1-85109-240-4*) ABC-CLIO.

Rauluszkiewicz, J., et al, eds. Physics of Magnetic Materials: Proceedings of the 2nd International Conference. 592p. 1985. 100.00 (*9971-978-34-2*) World Scientific Pub.

Raum, Otto F. Chaga Childhood: A Description of Indigenous Education in an East African Tribe. LC 76-44782. reprint ed. 39.50 (*0-404-15966-4*) AMS Pr.

— Chaga Childhood: A Description of Indigenous Education in an East African Tribe. LC 41-12399. 435p. reprint ed. pap. 134.90 (*0-8357-6966-6*, 203902600009) Bks Demand.

— The Social Functions of Avoidances & Taboos among the Zulu. (Illus.). (C). 1973. 211.55 (*3-11-003460-3*) De Gruyter.

Raum, Otto F., tr. see Kecskesi, Maria.

Rauman, Richard. For the Reputation of Truth: Politics, Religion & Conflict Among the Pennsylvanian Quakers, 1750-1800. LC 79-143626. 280p. reprint ed. pap. 86.80 (*0-608-14643-9*, 202582800046) Bks Demand.

Raumer, J. F. Von, see Von Raumer, J. F., ed.

Raun, Alo. Basic Course in Uzbek. LC 66-63899. (Uralic & Altaic Ser.: Vol. 59). 271p. 1969. reprint ed. spiral bd. write for info. (*0-87750-066-5*) Curzon Pr Ltd.

— Essays in Finno-Ugric & Finnic Linguistics. (Uralic & Atlaic Ser.: Vol. 107). 1971. pap. text 12.00 (*0-87750-152-1*) Res Inst Inner Asian Studies.

Raun, R.Roger & Chen, Paul L. Water in Foods & Biological Materials: A Nuclear Magnetic Resonance Approach. LC 97-61860. 305p. 1997. pap. text 159.95 (*1-56676-589-7*) Technomic.

Raun, Toivo U. Estonia & the Estonians. 2nd ed. (Publication Ser.: No. 405). 336p. 1991. pap. 18.95 (*0-8179-9132-8*) Hoover Inst Pr.

Raundalen, Magne, jt. auth. see Dodge, Cole.

Raundelen, Magne, jt. auth. see Dodge, Cole P.

***Rauner, Diana Mendley.** They Still Pick Me up When I Fall: The Role of Caring in Youth Development & Community Life. 224p. 2000. text 49.50 (*0-231-11854-6*) Col U Pr.

— They Still Pick Me up When I Fall: The Role of Caring in Youth Development & Community Life. LC 00-26739. 2000. pap. 21.50 (*0-231-11855-4*) Col U Pr.

Rauner, Felix, ed. Qualification for Computer-Integrated Manufacturing. 240p. 1995. pap. 59.95 (*3-540-19971-3*) Spr-Verlag.

Rauner, Felix, jt. compiled by see Rasmussen, Lauge.

Rauner, Judy A. Helping People Volunteer. LC 80-82556. (Illus.). 96p. (Orig.). 1980. pap. 9.95 (*0-9604594-0-5*) Marlbrgh Pubns.

Rauner, Judy A., jt. auth. see Trost, Arty.

***Rauner, Marion Sabine.** Strategisches Management Von Praventivprogrammen: Ein Umfassendes Entscheidungsunterstutzungssystem Fur die Aids-Epidemie. (Illus.). 279p. 1998. 48.95 (*3-631-32831-1*) P Lang Pubng.

Raunikar, Robert & Huang, Chung-Liang, eds. Food Demand Analysis: Problems, Issues & Empirical Evidence. LC 86-30534. 302p. (C). 1987. text 39.95 (*0-8138-1841-9*) Iowa St U Pr.

Rauniker, Donald F. Choosing God's Best: Wisdom for Lifelong Romance. LC 97-49264. (Wisdom for Lifelong Romance Ser.). 240p. (YA). 1998. 18.99 (*1-57673-328-9*) Multnomah Pubs.

— Choosing God's Best: Wisdom for Lifelong Romance. 2000. pap. text 12.99 (*1-57673-567-2*, Pub. by Multnomah Pubs) GL Services.

Raunio, Anne M., jt. ed. see Gilbert, Scott F.

Raunio, Tapio. The European Perspective: Transnational Party Groups in the 1989-94 European Parliament. LC 97-19090. (Illus.). 232p. 1997. text 73.95 (*1-85521-988-3*, Pub. by Ashgate Pub) Ashgate Pub Co.

Raunkiaer, Christen. The Life Forms of Plants & Statistical Plants Geography. Egerton, Frank N., 3rd, ed. Gilbert-Carter, H. et al, trs. LC 77-74249. (History of Ecology Ser.). (Illus.). 1978. reprint ed. lib. bdg. 56.95 (*0-405-10418-9*) Ayer.

Raup, David M. Extinction: Bad Genes or Bad Luck? 224p. 1992. pap. 12.95 (*0-393-30927-4*) Norton.

— The Nemesis Affair: A Story of the Death of the Dinosaurs & the Ways of Science. 240p. 1999. pap. 13.00 (*0-393-31918-0*) Norton.

Raup, David M. & Stanley, Steven M. Principles of Paleontology. 2nd ed. LC 77-17443. (Illus.). 481p. (C). 1978. text 66.95 (*0-7167-0022-0*) W H Freeman.

Raup, H., jt. auth. see Johnson, F.

Raup, H. F., ed. see Hamy, Ernest T.

Raup, Omer B. Geology Along Trail Ridge Road. LC 96-84363. (Illus.). 52p. 1996. pap. 10.95 (*1-56044-481-9*) Falcon Pub Inc.

Raup, Ruth M. Intergovernmental Relations in Social Welfare. LC 70-168966. 234p. 1972. reprint ed. lib. bdg. 69.50 (*0-8371-6239-4*, RASW, Greenwood Pr) Greenwood.

Raup, Tariq, et al. Inventory of International Nonproliferation Organizations & Regimes. (CNS Working Papers). 68p. 1992. pap. 25.00 (*1-885350-00-7*) Ctr Nonproliferation.

Raupach, Manfred, jt. auth. see Dechert, Hans W.

Raupach, Manfred, jt. ed. see Dechert, Hans W.

Raupach, Manfred, jt. ed. see Dechert, Hans.

Raupp, Magdala, jt. auth. see Yedlin, Jane.

Raupp, Michael J., jt. ed. see Tallamy, Douglas W.

Rauquist, Karen. The EPM Fad Study. Mayer, Ira, ed. 255p. 1998. pap. 295.00 (*1-885747-15-2*) EPM Communs.

Raurell, Lydia. Aria. 12p. (Orig.). 1975. pap. 1.00 (*0-934776-01-6*) Bard Pr.

Raus, J., jt. ed. see Lowenthal, A.

Raus, Jef, jt. auth. see Zhang, Jingwu.

Rausa, Rosario. The Blue Angels: An Illustrated History. (Illus.). 104p. 1979. 14.50 (*0-685-03409-7*) Moran Pub Corp.

Rausa, Rosario, jt. auth. see Mogensen, Allan H.

Rausa, Rosario "zip". R. G. Smith, The Man & his Art: An Autobiography. LC 98-88370. (Illus.). 112p. 1999. 29.95 (*0-7643-0755-X*) Schiffer.

Rausand, Marvin, jt. auth. see Hyland, Arnljot.

Rausch, Alexander, ed. Opusculum de Musica Ex Traditione Iohannis Hollandrini. (Theorists in Translation Ser.: Vol. 15). (ENG, GER & LAT.). 182p. 1997. 48.00 (*1-896926-00-2*) Inst Mediaeval Mus.

Rausch, David A. Arno C. Gaebelein, Eighteen Sixty-One to Nineteen Forty-Five: Irenic Fundamentalist & Scholar. LC 83-9364. (Studies in American Religion: Vol. 10). (Illus.). 318p. 1984. lib. bdg. 99.95 (*0-88946-652-1*) E Mellen.

— Messianic Judaism: Its History, Theology, Polity. LC 82-20382. (Texts & Studies in Religion: Vol. 14). 304p. 1983. lib. bdg. 99.95 (*0-88946-802-8*) E Mellen.

— Zionism Within Early American Fundamentalism, 1878-1918: A Convergence of Two Traditions. LC 79-66371. (Texts & Studies in Religion: Vol. 4). viii, 386p. 1980. lib. bdg. 99.95 (*0-88946-875-3*) E Mellen.

Rausch, David A., jt. auth. see Craig, Russell L.

Rausch, David A., jt. auth. see Voss, Carl H.

Rausch, Deidra T., jt. auth. see Jarrett, John C., 2nd.

Rausch, Don. Nuts, Bolts & Carnations: 3-Act Comedy. 58p. 1977. pap. 4.00 (*0-88680-143-5*) I E Clark.

Rausch, Donald O., et al, eds. Lead Zinc Update. LC 77-83619. (Illus.). 422p. 1977. reprint ed. pap. 130.90 (*0-7837-9179-8*, 204987800003) Bks Demand.

Rausch, Erwin. Balancing Needs of People & Organizations: The Linking Elements Concept. 321p. 1978. 26.50 (*0-87179-274-5*) Didactic Syst.

— Financial Analysis. (Simulation Game Ser.). 1972. pap. 26.25 (*0-89401-026-3*) Didactic Syst.

Rausch, Erwin & Rausch, George. Leading Groups to Better Decisions. (Simulation Game Ser.). (GER.). 1971. pap. 35.00 (*0-89401-048-4*) Didactic Syst.

— Leading Groups to Better Decisions. (Simulation Game Ser.). 1971. pap. 26.25 (*0-89401-046-8*) Didactic Syst.

— Leading Groups to Better Decisions. (Simulation Game Ser.). (FRE.). 1971. pap. 35.00 (*0-89401-047-6*) Didactic Syst.

Rausch, Erwin & Washbush, John B. High Quality Leadership: Practical Guidelines to Becoming a More Effective Manager. LC 98-13521. (Illus.). 292p. 1998. 32.00 (*0-87389-395-6*, H0984) ASQ Qual Pr.

Rausch, Erwin & Wohlking, Wallace. Handling Conflict in Hospital Management: Conflict Among Peers (Game I) (Simulation Game Ser.). 1973. pap. 26.25 (*0-89401-036-0*) Didactic Syst.

— Handling Conflict in Hospital Management: Superior - Subordinate Conflict (Game III) (Simulation Game Ser.). 1974. pap. 26.25 (*0-89401-043-3*) Didactic Syst.

— Handling Conflict in Management: Conflict Among Peers-Game 1. (Simulation Game Ser.). 1969. pap. 26.25 (*0-89401-035-2*) Didactic Syst.

— Handling Conflict in Management: Superior - Subordinate Conflict Game 111. (Simulation Game Ser.). 1969. pap. 26.25 (*0-89401-098-0*); pap. 35.00 (*0-89401-041-7*); pap. 35.00 (*0-89401-042-5*) Didactic Syst.

— Handling Conflict in Management: Superior-Subordinate-Group Conflict Game II. 1969. 26.25 (*0-89401-039-5*) Didactic Syst.

Rausch, Erwin, jt. auth. see Carter, Harry.

Rausch, Erwin, jt. auth. see Lieberman, Harvey.

Rausch, G. Jay, jt. auth. see Mundell, E. H., Jr.

Rausch, George, jt. auth. see Rausch, Erwin.

Rausch, Gerald, jt. auth. see Tonnis, John.

Rausch, Ilka, jt. auth. see Rausch, Rudolf.

Rausch, Jane M. Colombia: Territorial Rule & The Llanos Frontier LC 99-22477. 1999. 49.95 (*0-8130-1718-1*) U Press Fla.

— The Llanos Frontier in Colombian History, 1830-1930. LC 92-480. (Illus.). 413p. 1993. reprint ed. pap. 128.10 (*0-608-04126-2*, 206485900011) Bks Demand.

An Asterisk (*) at the beginning of an entry indicates that the title is appearing for the first time.

***Rausch, Jane M. & Hanke, Lewis, eds.** People & Issues in Latin American History Vol. II: From Independence to the Present. 2nd rev. ed. (Illus.). 380p. 1999. pap. text 22.95 (*1-55876-195-0*) Wiener Pubs Inc.

Rausch, Jane M., jt. auth. see Hanke, Lewis.

Rausch, Jane M., jt. auth. see Mehring, Arndt.

Rausch, Jane M., jt. ed. see Weber, David J.

Rausch, Joseph P. LP-CD Master: Record Album Reference & Price Guide 1940-1987. LC 87-92216. 378p. (Orig.). 1988. pap. 39.95 (*0-9620095-0-4*) Standard Music.

Rausch, R. The Phosphating of Metals. 418p. 1991. 144.00 (*0-904477-11-8*, Pub. by FMJ Intl) St Mut.

Rausch, R., jt. auth. see Kinzelbach, W.

Rausch, Ralph, jt. auth. see Morner, Kathleen.

Rausch, Ronald D., jt. ed. see Culp, Robert D.

Rausch, Rudolf & Rausch, Ilka. Deutsche Phonetik Fur Auslander. 404p. 1991. 38.95 (*3-324-00145-5*) Langenscheidt.

Rausch, Thomas P. Catholicism at the Dawn of the Third Millennium. 272p. (Orig.). 1996. pap. 19.95 (*0-8146-5770-2*, M Glazier) Liturgical Pr.

***Rausch, Thomas P.** Catholics & Evangelicals: Do They Share a Common Future? 160p. 2000. pap. 14.99 (*0-8308-1566-X*) InterVarsity.

Rausch, Thomas P. Priesthood Today: An Appraisal. LC 92-747. 160p. 1992. pap. 9.95 (*0-8091-3326-1*) Paulist Pr.

***Rausch, Thomas P.** Reconciling Faith & Reason: Apologists, Evangelists, & Theologians in a Divided Church. 144p. 2000. 24.95 (*0-8146-5096-1*); pap. 14.95 (*0-8146-5956-X*) Liturgical Pr.

***Rausch, Thomas P., ed.** Catholics & Evangelical: Do They Share a Common Future? 192p. 2000. pap. 12.95 (*0-8091-3986-3*) Paulist Pr.

Rausch, Thomas P., ed. The College Students' Introduction to Theology. 216p. (Orig.). 1993. pap. text 14.95 (*0-8146-5841-5*, M Glazier) Liturgical Pr.

Rauschenbach, Boris V. Hermann Oberth: The Father of Space Flight. deluxe ed. Zavrel, B. John, ed. Kvinnesland, Lynne, tr. from RUS. (Illus.). 256p. (Orig.). 1994. pap. 80.00 (*0-914301-15-2*) West-Art.

Rauschenberg, Christopher. Photographs, 1973-1980. LC 82-81916. (Illus.). 139p. (Orig.). 1982. pap. 10.00 (*0-943446-00-7*) Pair O Dice.

Rauschenberg, Christopher, ed. Drugstore Photographs: A Collection of Anonymous Snapshots. (Illus.). 64p. (Orig.). 1976. pap. 2.95 (*0-943446-01-5*) Pair O Dice.

Rauschenberg, Robert. Robert Rauschenberg: Anagrams (A Pun) Schwartz, Sheila, ed. LC 99-61011. (Illus.). 54p. 1999. write for info. (*1-878283-83-9*) PaceWildenstein.

Rauschenberger, Maria. Shakespeare's Imagery: Versuch einer Definition. (Bochum Studies in English: No. 11). (GER.). x, 731p. (Orig.). 1981. pap. 50.00 (*90-6032-203-7*) J Benjamins Pubng Co.

Rauschenbusch, Walter. Christianity & the Social Crisis. (Library of Theological Ethics). 448p. 1992. reprint ed. pap. 19.00 (*0-664-25321-0*) Westminster John Knox.

— A Theology for the Social Gospel. 289p. 1996. pap. 20.00 (*1-57910-022-8*) Wipf & Stock.

Rauschenbusch, Walter & Stackhouse, Max L. The Righteousness of the Kingdom. LC 99-17044. (Texts & Studies in the Social Gospel: Vol. 2). 352p. 1999. reprint ed. lib. bdg. 89.95 (*0-7734-8149-4*) E Mellen.

Rauschenbush, Walter. A Theology for the Social Gospel. LC 97-1589. (Library of Theological Ethics). 1997. pap. 18.00 (*0-664-25730-5*) Westminster John Knox.

Rauscher, Elizabeth A. Electromagnetic Phenomena in Complex Geometries & Nonlinear Phenomena, Non-Hertzian Waves & Magnetic Monopoles. LC 83-50845. 141p. (Orig.). 1983. pap. text 15.50 (*0-9603536-9-0*) Tesla Bk Co.

Rauscher, Erwin. Religion Im Dialog: Facherverbindung - Projektstruktur - Religionsunterricht. (Europaische Hochschulschriften Ser.: Reihe 23, Bd. 405). (GER.). VIII, 293p. 1991. 64.80 (*3-631-42977-0*) P Lang Pubng.

Rauscher, F. J., III, jt. ed. see Vogt, P. K.

Rauscher, Freya. Cruising Guide to Belize & Mexico's Caribbean Coast, Including Guatemala's Rio Dulce. 2nd ed. LC 96-61079. (Illus.). 304p. 1996. pap. 34.95 (*0-918752-23-X*) Wescott Cove.

— Florida Keys & Everglades Cruising Guide. Wilensky, Julius M., ed. LC 97-60025. (Illus.). 256p. 1997. pap. 32.95 (*0-918752-24-8*) Wescott Cove.

Rauscher, H. Michael, jt. auth. see Schmoldt, Daniel L.

Rauscher, Michael. International Trade, Factor Movements & the Environment. LC 96-19523. (Illus.). 348p. 1997. text 75.00 (*0-19-829050-0*) OUP.

Rauscher, Tom. The Idea Logbook. 240p. 1999. pap. 59.95 (*0-9672613-0-9*) Inventors Place.

Rauscher, Tom. Inserts to the Pocket Journal for Creative Ideas, Thoughts, Notes, Drawings & Inspirations. pap. 5.89 (*0-9672613-2-5*) Inventors Place.

— The Pocket Journal for Creative Ideas, Thoughts, Notes, Drawings & Inspirations. 62p. 2000. pap. 8.95 (*0-9672613-1-7*) Inventors Place.

Rauscher, Tomlinson G. & Ott, Linda M. Software Development & Management for Microprocessor-Based Systems. (Illus.). 256p. 1987. text 32.95 (*0-317-56706-3*) P-H.

Rauschkolb, Roy S. & Hornsby, Arthur G. Nitrogen Management in Irrigated Agriculture. (Illus.). 252p. 1994. text 65.00 (*0-19-507835-7*) OUP.

Rauschmayer, Dennis. ADSL/VDSL Principles. LC 96-80467. 350p. 1998. 44.99 (*1-57870-015-9*) Macmillan Tech.

Rauschning, Dieter, et al, eds. Key Resolutions of the United Nations General Assembly, 1946-1996. LC 97-20462. 620p. (C). 1998. text 135.00 (*0-521-59287-9*); pap. text 64.95 (*0-521-59704-8*) Cambridge U Pr.

Rauschning, Hermann. Men of Chaos. LC 71-167405. (Essay Index Reprint Ser.). 1977. reprint ed. 23.95 (*0-8369-2471-1*) Ayer.

— The Revolution of Nihilism: Warning to the West. Dickes, E. W., tr. LC 72-180666. reprint ed. 34.50 (*0-404-56402-X*) AMS Pr.

— The Revolution of Nihilism: Warning to the West. LC 72-4291. (World Affairs Ser.: National & International Viewpoints). 318p. 1972. reprint ed. 23.95 (*0-405-04583-2*) Ayer.

Rause, Vince. Handy As I Wanna Be. LC 99-25767. 279p. 1999. 22.00 (*0-671-03284-4*) PB.

Rausenberger, Mark. A Somalia Journal. LC 95-77772. 96p. (Orig.). 1995. pap. 12.95 (*1-878044-26-5*) Mayhaven Pub.

Rauser, Wilfid E., et al. Sulfur Nutrition & Assimilation in Higher Plants: Regulatory Agricultural & Environmental Aspects. (Illus.). 1993. 89.00 (*90-5103-084-3*, Pub. by SPB Acad Pub) Balogh.

Raush, Charlotte L., jt. auth. see Raush, Harold L.

Raush, Harold L. Communication, Conflict & Marriage. LC 73-18506. (Jossey-Bass Behavioral Science Ser.). 264p. reprint ed. pap. 81.90 (*0-608-30420-4*, 201375100087) Bks Demand.

Raush, Harold L. & Raush, Charlotte L. Halfway House Movement: A Search for Sanity. LC 68-18037. (Century Psychology Ser.). (C). 1968. 30.50 (*0-89197-197-1*) Irvington.

Raush, Harold L., jt. ed. see Levinger, George.

Raush, Lawrence M. Asis's New High Tech Competitors. (Illus.). 72p. (C). 1997. reprint ed. pap. text 30.00 (*0-7881-4248-8*) DIANE Pub.

Raushenbush, Stephen. March of Fascism. 1939. 69.50 (*0-686-83616-2*) Elliots Bks.

Raushenbush, Winifred. Robert E. Park: Biography of a Sociologist. LC 77-88063. 220p. reprint ed. pap. 68.20 (*0-608-15281-1*, 205221200060) Bks Demand.

Rauss, Erhard & Natzmer, Oldwig. The Anvil of War: German Generalship on the Eastern Front. Tsouras, Peter G., ed. 320p. 1994. 34.95 (*1-85367-181-9*, 5403) Stackpole.

Rauss, Erhard, et al. Fighting in Hell: The German Ordeal on the Eastern Front. Tsouras, Peter G., ed. (Illus.). 288p. 1995. 34.95 (*1-85367-218-1*, Pub. by Greenhill Bks) Stackpole.

***Rausseo, Victoria & Winitz, Harris.** Basic Structures 3: Spanish. 2nd ed. (Basic Structures : Bk. 3). (SPA., Illus.). 260p. 1999. pap. text 25.00 (*1-887371-20-6*) Intl Linguistics.

Rausser. New Directions in Econometric Modelling & Forecasting in U. S. Agriculture. 830p. 1983. 135.00 (*0-444-00736-9*) P-H.

Rausser, G. C., jt. auth. see Gardner, B. L.

Rausser, Gordon C., et al. GATT Negotiations & the Political Economy of Policy Reform. LC 94-33513. 1994. write for info. (*0-387-58470-6*) Spr-Verlag.

Rautarharju, P., jt. auth. see MacFarlane, P. W.

Rautbord, Sugar. The Chameleon. LC 98-37558. 528p. 1999. 24.00 (*0-446-52187-6*, Pub. by Warner Bks) Little.

***Rautbord, Sugar.** The Chameleon. (Illus.). 560p. 2000. mass mkt. 7.50 (*0-446-60815-7*) Warner Bks.

Rautenbach, Frans. Labour Litigation: Practical Guide to Procedure & Tactics. 1993. write for info. (*0-7021-2992-5*, Pub. by Juta & Co) Gaunt.

Rautenbach, Frans, ed. Noter-Up to the Industrial Law Journal. 34p. 1992. pap. write for info. (*0-7021-2813-9*, Pub. by Juta & Co) Gaunt.

Rautenbach, I. M. Algemene Bepalings van die Suid-Afrikaanse Handves van Regte. (AFR.). 188p. 1995. pap. write for info. (*0-409-05043-1*, MICHIE) LEXIS Pub.

— General Provisions of the South African Bill of Rights. LC 95-150877. 180p. 1995. pap. write for info. (*0-409-05044-X*, MICHIE) LEXIS Pub.

***Rautenbach, I.M.** What Does the Constitution Say? LC 98-140181. 74p. 1998. write for info. (*0-627-02335-5*, Pub. by J L Van Schaik) BHB Intl.

Rautenbach, R. & Albrecht, R. Membrane Processes. LC 87-23211. 470p. 1989. 785.00 (*0-471-91110-0*) Wiley.

Rautenberg, Arne. Dislimitation. (Illus.). 34p. (Orig.). 1995. pap. 5.00 (*1-57141-009-0*) Runaway Spoon.

Rautenberg, W., ed. Omega-Bibliography of Mathematical Logic, Vol. 1. (Perspectives in Mathematical Logic Ser.). xxxix, 483p. 1987. 275.00 (*0-387-17321-8*) Spr-Verlag.

— Omega-Bibliography of Mathematical Logic, Vol. II. (Perspectives in Mathematical Logic Ser.). xxxvii, 468p. 1987. 245.00 (*0-387-15521-X*) Spr-Verlag.

Rauter, Peter, jt. auth. see Lander, Hugh.

Rauth, Eric, tr. see Debray, Regis.

***Rauth, Leslie.** Maryland, 5 vols. , Set. LC 98-43960. (Celebrate the States Ser.). (Illus.). 144p. (J). (gr. 4-7). 2000. lib. bdg. 35.64 (*0-7614-0671-9*, Benchmark NY) Marshall Cavendish.

Rauth, Ruth B. Reflections of Mind & Place: Nature Poems & Photographs. unabridged ed. LC 99-163060. (Illus.). v, 96p. 1998. 18.00 (*0-9666400-0-4*, IP0915098) Images in Print.

Rautiainen, Risto, jt. auth. see Donham, Kelly J.

Rautian, S. G., ed. Nonlinear Optics. 537p. (C). 1992. lib. bdg. 225.00 (*1-56072-074-3*) Nova Sci Pubs.

Rautian, Sergei G., ed. Eleventh International Conference on Nonlinear Optics, Vol. 3485. LC 99-208415. 750p. 1998. 124.00 (*0-8194-2943-0*) SPIE.

Rautkallio, Hannu. Finland & the Holocaust: The Finnish Experience. 1987. 20.95 (*0-89604-120-4*, Holocaust Library); pap. 13.95 (*0-89604-121-2*, Holocaust Library) US Holocaust.

***Rautman, Alison E.** Reading the Body: Representations & Remains in the Archaeological Record. LC 99-33513. 1999. pap. text 22.50 (*0-8122-1709-8*) U of Pa Pr.

Rautmenn, R., ed. Approximation Methods for Navier-Stokes Problems: Proceedings. (Lecture Notes in Mathematics Ser.: Vol. 771). 581p. 1980. 59.95 (*0-387-09734-1*) Spr-Verlag.

Rautsi, Inari, jt. auth. see Karsh, Efraim.

***Rauwendaal, Chris.** SPC: Statistical Process Control in Injection Molding & Extrusion. LC 00-39565. 2000. write for info. (*1-56990-285-2*) Hanser-Gardner.

Rauwendaal, Chris. Understanding Extrusion. LC 98-34474. (Hanser Understanding Bks.). 1998. pap. 34.95 (*1-56990-233-X*) Hanser-Gardner.

Rauwendaal, Chris J. Polymer Extrusion. 3rd rev. ed. 1994. 34.50 (*1-56990-140-6*) Hanser-Gardner.

— SPC-Statistical Process Control in Extrusion. 181p. 1992. 69.00 (*1-56990-086-8*) Hanser-Gardner.

Rauwendaal, Chris J., ed. Mixing in Polymer Processing. (Plastics Engineering Ser.: Vol. 23). (Illus.). 488p. 1991. text 225.00 (*0-8247-8521-5*) Dekker.

Rauzduel, Rosan. Dialectique et Savoir Systemique. (Publications Universitaires Europeennes: Serie 22, Vol. 333). viii, 524p. 1999. 55.95 (*3-906762-15-7*, Pub. by P Lang) P Lang Pubng.

Rauzon, Mark. The Sky's the Limit. LC 98-41600. (Illus.). 32p. (J). (gr. 2-4). 1999. lib. bdg. 21.90 (*0-7613-1263-3*, Copper Beech Bks) Millbrook Pr.

Rauzon, Mark J. Catch a Comet by the Tail. (Illus.). 48p. (J). (gr. 5-10). 1985. pap. 6.95 (*0-935181-00-8*) Marine Endeavors.

***Rauzon, Mark J.** Golden Eagles of Devil Mountain LC 99-38208. 2000. 22.50 (*0-531-11787-1*) Watts.

Rauzon, Mark J. Hummingbirds. LC 96-36156. (First Bks.). (J). (gr. 4-6). 1997. lib. bdg. 22.00 (*0-531-20260-7*) Watts.

— Hummingbirds. (First Books). (J). (gr. 4-6). 1997. pap. text 6.95 (*0-531-15849-7*) Watts.

***Rauzon, Mark J.** Isles of Refuge: Wildlife & History of the Northwestern Hawaiian Islands. LC 00-29874. (Illus.). 2001. pap. write for info. (*0-8248-2330-3*) UH Pr.

Rauzon, Mark J. The Last Condor. (Illus.). 24p. (Orig.). (J). (gr. 5 up). 1986. pap. 3.95 (*0-935181-02-4*) Marine Endeavors.

— Parrots. LC 96-33773. (First Books-Animals). 64p. (J). (gr. 4-6). 1996. lib. bdg. 22.00 (*0-531-20244-5*) Watts.

— Parrots. (First Bks.). 64p. 1997. pap. 6.95 (*0-531-15815-2*) Watts.

— Seabirds. LC 96-7185. (First Books-Animals). 64p. (J). (gr. 4-6). 1996. lib. bdg. 22.00 (*0-531-20246-1*) Watts.

— Seabirds. (First Bks.). 64p. (J). 1997. pap. 6.95 (*0-531-15817-9*) Watts.

— Vultures. LC 96-31019. (First Bks.). (J). 1997. lib. bdg. 22.00 (*0-531-20271-2*) Watts.

— Vultures. (First Books). (J). 1997. pap. text 6.95 (*0-531-15853-5*) Watts.

— Water, Water Everywhere. LC 92-34521. 1994. 10.90 (*0-606-10021-0*, Pub. by Turtleback) Demco.

***Rauzon, Mark J., et al.** Chickens & Peacocks: What They Have in Common. LC 99-59419. (Animals in Order Ser.). (J). 2001. write for info. (*0-531-11689-1*) Watts.

Rauzon, Mark J. & Bix, Cynthia O. Water, Water Everywhere. LC 92-34521. (Illus.). 32p. (J). (gr. k-3). 1994. 14.95 (*0-87156-598-6*, Pub. by Sierra Club Childrens) Little.

Rauzon, Mark J., et al. Water, Water Everywhere. LC 92-34521. (Illus.). 32p. (J). (ps-3). 1995. pap. 6.95 (*0-87156-383-5*, Pub. by Sierra Club Childrens) Little.

Ravage, Barbara. George Westinghouse: A Genius for Invention. LC 96-17490. (Innovative Minds Ser.). 112p. (J). 1997. lib. bdg. 27.11 (*0-8172-4402-6*) Raintree Steck-V.

— Rachel Carson, Gentle Crusader. LC 96-20313. (Innovative Minds Ser.). 112p. (J). 1997. lib. bdg. 27.11 (*0-8172-4406-9*) Raintree Steck-V.

Ravage, John W. Black Pioneers: Images of the Black Experience on the North American Frontier. LC 97-33416. (Illus.). 286p. 1997. 24.95 (*0-87480-546-5*) U of Utah Pr.

Ravagnan, G. & Chiesa, C., eds. Yersiniosis: Present & Future. (Contributions to Microbiology & Immunology Ser.: Vol. 13). (Illus.). xii, 340p. 1996. 299.25 (*3-8055-6138-5*) S Karger.

Ravai, Nazanine, jt. auth. see Forestier, Nadege.

Ravaioli, Umberto, jt. auth. see Cancellieri, Giovanni.

Ravaioli, Umberto, ed. see Leburton, Jean-Pierre, et al.

Ravaisson, Felix. Essai sur la Metaphysique D'Aristote. (GER.). xviii, 185p. 1996. reprint ed. 320.00 (*3-487-00404-6*) G Olms Pubs.

— Essai Sur la Metaphysique d'Aristote, 2 vols., Set. (FRE.). xii, 1183p. 1963. reprint ed. write for info. (*0-318-71397-7*) G Olms Pubs.

Raval, Devyani S., ed. see Albritton, Sabra, et al.

Raval, Hasmukh. Bhagavad Gita: A Philosophical System. (Illus.). 112p. 1990. pap. 15.00 (*0-87527-484-6*) Green.

Raval, P. J. Going to the U. S. A. A Newcomer's Practical Reference Book for Travel, Study, Work & Business in America. LC 90-82585. x, 142p. (Orig.). 1990. pap. 9.95 (*0-9628660-0-8*) Crown Apar Ent.

Raval, Suresh. Grounds of Literary Criticism. LC 97-45410. 288p. 1998. text 46.95 (*0-252-02408-7*); text 21.95 (*0-252-06711-8*) U of Ill Pr.

Ravallion, Martin. Markets & Famines. (Illus.). 212p. 1990. reprint ed. pap. text 24.00 (*0-19-828727-5*) OUP.

— Poverty Comparisons. LC 93-14943. 130p. 1994. pap. text 27.00 (*3-7186-5402-4*) Gordon & Breach.

— Poverty Comparisons: A Guide to Concepts & Methods. (Living Standards Measurement Study Ser.: No. 88). 134p. 1992. 22.00 (*0-8213-2036-X*, 12036) World Bank.

Ravallion, Martin. Poverty Comparisons: A Guide to Concepts & Methods. (Living Standards Measurement Study Ser.: No. 122-F). (FRE.). 176p. 1996. 22.00 (*0-8213-3546-4*, 13546) World Bank.

— Poverty Comparisons: A Guide to Concepts & Methods. (Living Standards Measurement Study Ser.: No. 88R). (RUS.). 144p. 1999. 22.00 (*0-8213-4116-2*, 14116) World Bank.

Ravallion, Martin. Poverty Lines in Theory & Practice. LC 98-4023. (Living Standards Measurement Study Ser.: No. 133). 52p. 1998. pap. 22.00 (*0-8213-4226-6*, 14226) World Bank.

Ravallion, Martin, jt. auth. see Datt, Gaurav.

Ravanesi, Bill, et al. Breath Taken: The Landscape & Biography of Asbestos. (Illus.). 50p. 1991. pap. 30.00 (*1-879842-91-2*) Ctr Vis Arts.

Ravango, Miguel, jt. auth. see Tausend, Marilyn.

Ravani, Bahram, ed. CAD Based Programming for Sensory Robots. (NATO Asi Series F: Vol. 50). 580p. 1988. 135.95 (*0-387-50415-X*) Spr-Verlag.

Ravani, Bahram & Merlet, J. P., eds. Computational Kinematics '95: Proceedings: Workshop on Computational Kinematics Held in Sophia Antipolis, France, September 4-6, 1995. LC 95-34596. (Solid Mechanics & Its Applications Ser.: Vol. 40). 310p. (C). 1995. text 144.00 (*0-7923-3673-9*, QA841) Kluwer Academic.

Ravani, Bahram, jt. ed. see Lenarcic, Jadran.

Ravanipur, Moniru. Satan's Stones. Ghanoonparvar, M. R., ed. Moin, Parichehr et al, trs. from PER. 93p. 1996. pap. 9.95 (*0-292-77076-6*) U of Tex Pr.

— Satan's Stones. Ghanoonparvar, Mohammad R., ed. Karim et al, trs. from PER. 93p. 1996. text 25.00 (*0-292-77075-8*) U of Tex Pr.

Ravden, Susannah J. & Hohnson, Graham I. Evaluating Human-Computer Interfaces: A Practical Method for Assessing Usability. 1989. text 37.95 (*0-470-21496-1*) P-H.

Ravdin, Jonathan I., ed. Amebiasis. (Series on Tropical Medicine). 300p. 1999. 46.00 (*1-86094-133-8*) World Scientific Pub.

Rave, Elizabeth S. & Larsen, Carolyn C. Ethical Decision Making in Therapy: Feminist Perspectives. LC 95-18762. 284p. 1995. lib. bdg. 33.00 (*0-89862-089-9*) Guilford Pubns.

Raveau, B., jt. ed. see Rao, C. N.

Raveau, Bernard, et al. Crystal Chemistry of High Tc Superconducting Copper Oxides. Gonser, U. et al, eds. (Materials Science Ser.: Vol. 15). (Illus.). 352p. 1991. 119.95 (*0-387-51545-3*) Spr-Verlag.

Raveau, Bernard, jt. auth. see Rao, C. N.

Raveau, Bernard, jt. auth. see Rao, Chinatamani N.

Raveed, Sion. Joint Ventures Between U. S. Multinational Firms & Host Governments in Selected Developing Countries. Bruchey, Stuart, ed. LC 80-590. (Multinational Corporations Ser.). (Illus.). 1981. lib. bdg. 31.95 (*0-405-13381-2*) Ayer.

Raveed, Sion, jt. auth. see Renforth, William.

***Raveendran, N. V.** Aesthetics of Sensuality: A Stylistic Study of the Poetry of Kamala Das. 2000. 28.50 (*81-7156-874-2*, Pub. by Atlantic Pubs) S Asia.

Raveendran, Paramesran & Simpson, Robert J. Advanced 8-Bit Microprocessor: MC6809. LC 97-16270. (Illus.). 250p. 1998. pap. 20.00 (*981-3083-09-3*) Spr-Verlag.

Raveh, Yael-Anna, jt. auth. see Weinshall, Theodore D.

Raveill, Ken. North Carolina Plantation & Historic Homes Cookbook. 32p. (Orig.). (C). 1992. pap. 4.50 (*0-936672-92-7*) Aerial Photo.

Raveill, Ken, ed. Georgia, Plantation & Historic Homes Cookbook. (Illus.). (Orig.). 1990. pap. 3.95 (*0-936672-80-3*) Aerial Photo.

Ravel. Le Tombeau de Couperin & Other Works. 1998. pap. 9.95 (*0-486-29806-X*) Dover.

Ravel, Anne De, see De Ravel, Anne.

Ravel, Aviva. Women Write for Theatre, Vol. 3. LC 76-17184. 1997. pap. text 7.95 (*0-88754-050-3*) Theatre Comm.

Ravel, Jeffrey S. Contested Parterre: Public Theater & French Political Culture, 1680-1791. LC 99-10072. (Illus.). 256p. 1999. pap. 19.95 (*0-8014-8541-X*) Cornell U Pr.

Ravel, M. La Valse in Full Score. 1997. pap. 11.95 (*0-486-29591-5*, 706121Q) Dover.

Ravel, Maurice. Daphnis & Chloe in Full Score. 320p. reprint ed. pap. 15.95 (*0-486-25826-2*) Dover.

***Ravel, Maurice.** Daphnis et Chloe Suite No. 2. unabridged ed. 128p. 1999. reprint ed. pap. 4.95 (*0-486-40640-7*) Dover.

Ravel, Maurice. Four Orchestral Works in Full Score: Rapsidoe Espagnole, Mother Goose Suite, Valses Nobles et Sentimentales, & Pavane for a Dead Princess. 240p. pap. 12.95 (*0-486-25962-5*) Dover.

— Piano Masterpieces of Maurice Ravel. 128p. 1986. pap. 8.95 (*0-486-25137-3*) Dover.

— Songs, 1895-1914. 160p. 1990. pap. 10.95 (*0-486-26354-1*) Dover.

Ravel, Maurice, jt. auth. see Debussy, Claude.

Ravel, O. E. Numismatique Grecque Falsifications Moyens pour les Reconnaitre. (FRE.). 105p. 1980. reprint ed. 20.00 (*0-916710-71-8*) Obol Intl.

— Les "Poulains" de Corinthe. (Illus.). 1979. text 80.00 (*0-916710-47-5*) Obol Intl.

Ravel, Richard. Clinical Laboratory Medicine: Clinical Application of Laboratory Data. 6th ed. LC 94-30386. (Illus.). 736p. (C). (gr. 13). 1994. pap. text 47.00 (*0-8151-7148-X*, 23833) Mosby Inc.

Ravel, Sally & Wolfe, Lee A. The Best Retirement Residences in California & the West. Ransom, La Tricia, ed. 456p. 1997. pap. 14.95 (*0-9653207-2-3*) San Jose Mercury.

Ravell-Pinto, Thelma, jt. ed. see Makward, Edris.

***Ravelle, Lou.** Gymbiz: Starting & Running Your Own Gym for Profit. 2000. pap. 14.95 (*1-55210-019-7*, 584-020, Pub. by MuscleMag Intl) BookWorld.

Ravelli, Louise, jt. ed. see Davies, Martin.

R

Ravelli, Robert J., ed. Car-Free in New York City: The Regional Public Transit Guide, 1994-1995. LC 92-34898. (Car-Free Ser.). 220p. (Orig.). 1994. pap. 7.95 (*0-940159-17-1*) Camino Bks.
— Car-Free in Philadelphia: The Regional Public Transit Guide, 1993-1994. LC 92-22255. (Car-Free Ser.). (Illus.). 176p. (Orig.). 1993. pap. 6.95 (*0-940159-16-3*) Camino Bks.
Raven. Art Notebook T/A Biology. 3rd ed. 1994. student ed. 16.50 (*0-697-24252-8*, WCB McGr Hill) McGrw-H Hghr Educ.
— Biology. 2nd ed. 1994. 28.12 (*0-697-25442-9*, WCB McGr Hill); teacher ed. 37.18 (*0-697-25441-0*, WCB McGr Hill); teacher ed., lab manual ed. 7.81 (*0-697-25444-5*, WCB McGr Hill) McGrw-H Hghr Educ.
— Biology. 3rd ed. 1994. teacher ed., lab manual ed. 16.87 (*0-697-25255-8*, WCB McGr Hill) McGrw-H Hghr Educ.
— Biology. 6th ed. 2001. pap. 48.00 (*0-07-303120-8*) McGraw.
— Biology Glencoe Version. 5th ed. 1999. text 6275.00 (*0-07-235692-8*) McGraw.
— Biology of Plants. 6th ed. LC 98-60171. 1999. 65.00 (*1-57259-611-2*) Worth.
***Raven.** Biology of Plants Diversity Chapter. 6th ed. 1998. pap. text 37.95 (*0-7167-3594-6*, Pub. by W H Freeman) VHPS.
Raven. Environment. (C). 1993. pap. text, teacher ed., suppl. ed. 34.00 (*0-03-072751-0*) Harcourt Coll Pubs.
— Environment. 2nd ed. (C). 1997. text, teacher ed. 26.75 (*0-03-024963-5*) Harcourt Coll Pubs.
— Environment Canadian. (C). 1993. pap. text, suppl. ed. 17.50 (*0-03-097143-8*, Pub. by Harcourt Coll Pubs) Harcourt.
— Environment Great Lakes. (C). 1993. pap. text, suppl. ed. 17.50 (*0-03-097139-X*, Pub. by Harcourt Coll Pubs) Harcourt.
— Environment Mid Atlantic. (C). 1993. pap. text, suppl. ed. 17.50 (*0-03-097137-3*, Pub. by Harcourt Coll Pubs) Harcourt.
— Environment Northeast. (C). 1993. pap. text, suppl. ed. 17.50 (*0-03-097136-5*, Pub. by Harcourt Coll Pubs) Harcourt.
— Environment Northwest. (C). 1993. pap. text, suppl. ed. 17.50 (*0-03-097142-X*, Pub. by Harcourt Coll Pubs) Harcourt.
— Environment Southeast. (C). 1993. pap. text, suppl. ed. 17.50 (*0-03-097138-1*, Pub. by Harcourt Coll Pubs) Harcourt.
— Environment Southwest. (C). 1993. pap. text, suppl. ed. 17.50 (*0-03-097141-1*, Pub. by Harcourt Coll Pubs) Harcourt.
— Environment 1995: Update. (C). 1995. 322.50 (*0-03-015523-1*, Pub. by Harcourt Coll Pubs) Harcourt.
— Fielding Gray. 1969. pap. 3.75 (*0-586-02768-8*) HarpC.
— Returns Only-saunders Reg Env Iss Samplr. (C). 1993. 8.50 (*0-03-097973-0*) Harcourt.
— Returns Only Saunders Reg Env Sup-canada. (C). 1993. pap. text 8.50 (*0-03-097428-3*) Harcourt.
— Returns Only Saunders Reg Env Sup-grt Lk. (C). 1993. pap. text 8.50 (*0-03-097424-0*) Harcourt.
— Returns Only Saunders Reg Env Sup-midatl. (C). 1993. pap. text 8.50 (*0-03-097422-4*) Harcourt.
— Returns Only Saunders Reg Env Suppl - Nw. (C). 1993. pap. text 8.50 (*0-03-097427-5*) Harcourt.
— Returns Only Saunders Reg Env Suppl - Se. (C). 1993. pap. text 8.50 (*0-03-097423-2*) Harcourt.
— Returns Only Saunders Reg Env Suppl - Sw. (C). 1993. pap. text 8.50 (*0-03-097426-7*) Harcourt.
— Returns Only Saunders Reg Env Suppl-midw. (C). 1993. pap. text 8.50 (*0-03-097425-9*) Harcourt.
— Returns Only Saunders Reg Env Suppl-ne. (C). 1993. pap. text 8.50 (*0-03-097421-6*) Harcourt.
— Understanding Biology. 1994. 12.81 (*0-697-25450-X*, WCB McGr Hill) McGrw-H Hghr Educ.
— Understanding Biology. 2nd ed. 1994. teacher ed. 144.37 (*0-697-23508-4*) McGraw.
— Understanding Biology. 2nd ed. 1994. teacher ed. 450.31 (*0-697-23509-2*, WCB McGr Hill) McGrw-H Hghr Educ.
— Urban Regional Environmental Issues. (C). 1997. pap. text. write for info. (*0-03-004608-4*) Harcourt Coll Pubs.
Raven & Johnson. Biology. 4th ed. 1996. teacher ed. 12.81 (*0-697-22573-9*) McGraw.
— Biology. 4th ed. 1996. teacher ed., lab manual ed. 21.87 (*0-697-22571-2*) McGraw.
— Biology: Test Item File. 4th ed. 1996. 26.87 (*0-697-31286-0*, WCB McGr Hill) McGrw-H Hghr Educ.
— Understanding Biology. 3rd ed. 1995. teacher ed. 16.87 (*0-697-22214-4*, WCB McGr Hill) McGrw-H Hghr Educ.
— Understanding Biology. 3rd ed. 1995. teacher ed., lab manual ed. 9.06 (*0-697-22218-7*, WCB McGr Hill) McGrw-H Hghr Educ.
— Understanding Biology: Student Study Art Notebook. 3rd ed. 1995. 63.25 (*0-697-26489-0*, WCB McGr Hill) McGrw-H Hghr Educ.
Raven, et al. Environment. 2nd ed. LC 97-67174. (Illus.). 688p. (C). 1997. text 77.00 (*0-03-018679-X*, Pub. by SCP) Harcourt.
Raven, Patzi. Behind the Stained-Glass Window. 338p. 1998. pap. write for info. (*0-7541-0249-1*, Pub. by Minerva Pr) Unity Dist.
Raven, Ann. Clinical Trials: An Introduction. 1996. pap. 15.95 (*1-85775-035-7*, Radcliffe Med Pr) Scovill Paterson.
Raven, Arlene. Crossing Over: Feminism & Art of Social Concern. Kuspit, Donald, ed. & pref. by. LC 87-25545. (Contemporary American Art Critics Ser.: No. 10). (Illus.). 240p. 1988. reprint ed. pap. 74.40 (*0-8357-2017-9*, 207067600016) Bks Demand.
***Raven, Arlene.** True Grit. Harrisburg, Halley, ed. (Illus.). 36p. 2000. pap. 20.00 (*1-930416-02-4*) M Rosenfeld.
Raven, Arlene, intro. Art in the Public Interest. LC 89-16719. (Studies in the Fine Arts: Criticism: No. 32). 379p. 1990. pap. 117.50 (*0-8357-1970-7*, 207075600004) Bks Demand.
Raven, Arlene, jt. auth. see Bando, Flavia.
Raven, Bertram H., ed. Policy Studies Review Annual, Vol. 4. 768p. 1980. text 69.95 (*0-8039-1119-X*) Transaction Pubs.
Raven, C. H. God's Sanctuary. 1996. pap. 14.99 (*0-946351-31-7*, Pub. by John Ritchie) Loizeaux.
Raven, Charles. Apollinarianism: An Essay on the Christology of the Early Church. LC 77-84706. reprint ed. 38.00 (*0-404-16113-8*) AMS Pr.
Raven, Charles E. Christian Socialism 1848-1854. LC 68-56058. xii, 396p. 1968. reprint ed. 32.50 (*0-678-05148-8*) Kelley.
— Christian Socialism, 1848-1854. 396p. 1968. reprint ed. 35.00 (*0-7146-2129-3*, Pub. by F Cass Pubs) Intl Spec Bk.
— Natural Religion & Christian Theology: First & Second Series, 2 vols., Set. LC 77-27176. (Gifford Lectures: 1951-52). reprint ed. 37.50 (*0-404-60540-0*) AMS Pr.
***Raven, D. S.** Latin Metre. (Advanced Language Ser.). 124p. (C). 1998. pap. text 27.95 (*1-85399-564-9*, Pub. by Brist Class Pr) Focus Pub-R Pullins.
Raven, Diederick, et al, eds. Cognitive Relativism & Social Science. 150p. (C). 1992. 44.95 (*0-88738-425-0*) Transaction Pubs.
Raven, E. Toussaint. Cattle Footcare & Claw Trimming. (Illus.). 128p. (Orig.). 1985. pap. 32.95 (*0-85236-149-1*, Pub. by Farming Pr) Diamond Farm Bk.
Raven, Ellen M. Gupta Gold Coins with a Garuda-Banner, 2 vols., Set. (Gonda Indological Studies: No. 1). (Illus.). 1994. pap. text 142.00 (*90-6980-065-9*, Pub. by Egbert Forsten) Hodlder & Stoughton.
Raven, Ellen M., et al, eds. Panels of the Seventh World Sanskrit Conference Vol. 10: Indian Art & Archaeology. LC 91-28801. (Illus.). 135p. 1991. 91.00 (*90-04-09553-5*) Brill Academic Pubs.
Raven, Francis H. Automatic Control Engineering. 5th ed. LC 94-10701. (McGraw-Hill Series in Mechanical Engineering). 619p. (C). 1994. 102.19 (*0-07-051341-4*) McGraw.
— Automatic Control Engineering. 5th ed. 1995. pap. text, teacher ed. write for info. (*0-07-051342-2*) McGraw.
***Raven, Francis H.** Journey. (Poetry Chapbks.: No. 4). 64p. 2000. pap. 8.00 (*1-930259-03-4*) Anabasis.
— The Plot of a Strangemaker. (Poetry Chapbks.). 2000. pap. 8.00 (*1-930259-11-5*) Anabasis.
Raven, G. J. & Rodger, N. A. Navies & Armies: The Anglo Dutch Relationship in War & Peace 1688-1988. 128p. (C). 1997. text 50.00 (*0-85976-292-0*, Pub. by J Donald) St Mut.
Raven, Greg. Water-Cooled Volkswagen Performance Handbook. LC 98-51692. (Illus.). 224p. 1999. pap. 21.95 (*0-7603-0491-2*) MBI Pubg.
Raven-Hansen, Peter. First Use of Nuclear Weapons: Under the Constitution, Who Decides?, 38. LC 86-33655. (Contributions in Legal Studies: No. 38). 259p. 1987. 65.00 (*0-313-25520-2*, RVF/, Greenwood Pr) Greenwood.
Raven-Hansen, Peter, jt. auth. see Banks, William.
Raven-Hansen, Peter, jt. auth. see Shreve, Gene R.
Raven, J. E. Pythagoreans & Eleatics. 196p. 1981. 20.00 (*0-89005-367-7*) Ares.
Raven, James. British Fiction, 1750-1770: A Chronological Check-List of Prose Fiction Printed in Britain & Ireland. LC 87-6041. 360p. 1987. 50.00 (*0-87413-324-6*) U Delaware Pr.
Raven, James. Judging New Wealth: Popular Publishing & Responses to Commerce in England 1750-1800. 340p. 1992. text 75.00 (*0-19-820237-7*) OUP.
Raven, James. Subzero: The Adventures of Batman & Robin. (Batman Ser.). (J). (gr. 3-7). 1997. pap. 3.50 (*0-614-28846-0*) Little.
Raven, James, et al, eds. The Practice & Representation of Reading in England. (Illus.). 331p. (C). 1996. text 59.95 (*0-521-48093-0*) Cambridge U Pr.
Raven, John. Competence in Modern America: Its Identification, Development & Release. 268p. 1997. pap. 15.00 (*0-89824-532-X*, 532X) Trillium Pr.
— Managing Education for Effective Schooling. 184p. 1994. pap. 9.99 (*0-89824-531-1*, 5311) Trillium Pr.
— The New Wealth of Nations. 372p. 1995. pap. 20.00 (*0-89824-232-0*, 2320) Trillium Pr.
— Plants & Plant Lore in Ancient Greece. (Illus.). 144p. 2000. 36.95 (*0-904920-40-2*, Pub. by Leopards Head Pr) David Brown.
Raven, John. Tragic Illusion: Educational Testing. 1991. pap. 14.99 (*0-89824-523-0*) Trillium Pr.
Raven, John A. Energetics & Transport in Aquatic Plants. LC 84-12525. (MBL Lectures in Biology Ser.: Vol. 4). 598p. (C). 1984. 110.00 (*0-8451-2203-7*) Krieger.
Raven, John A., jt. auth. see Falkowski, Paul G.
Raven, John E. Plato's Thought in the Making: A Study of the Development of His Metaphysics. LC 85-10074. 256p. 1985. reprint ed. lib. bdg. 65.00 (*0-313-24958-X*, RAPT, Greenwood Pr) Greenwood.
Raven-Johnson. Biology. 4th ed. 1996. pap. text 612.18 (*0-697-22600-X*) McGraw.
— Understanding Biology. 2nd ed. 1994. teacher ed. 20.62 (*0-697-23504-1*, WCB McGr Hill) McGrw-H Hghr Educ.
Raven, Kay, ed. see Chappell, Nancy A.
Raven, Lee. Hands on Spinning. LC 86-83427. (Illus.). 120p. 1987. pap. 12.95 (*0-934026-27-0*) Interweave.
Raven, Margot. Angels in the Dust. LC 95-3627. (Illus.). 32p. (J). (gr. k-3). 1997. 15.95 (*0-8167-3806-8*) BrdgeWater.
Raven, Margot T. Angels in the Dust. (Illus.). 32p. (J). (gr. k-5). 1999. pap. 5.95 (*0-8167-5608-2*) Troll Communs.
Raven, Mark. Barrow. LC 86-82477. (Illus.). 191p. 1987. 18.95 (*0-9617588-0-5*) Huttman Co.
Raven, P. H., jt. auth. see Zardini, E. M.
Raven, P. H., jt. ed. see Polhill, R. M.
***Raven, Peter.** Environment: With Data Sheet. 2nd ed. 1998. 93.00 (*0-03-020804-1*) SCP.
Raven, Peter. Laboratory Topics in Botany: Biology of Plants. 6th ed. (Illus.). (C). 1998. text, lab manual ed. 24.60 (*1-57259-605-8*) Worth.
Raven, Peter H. Biology. 6th ed. 2001. student ed. 19.74 (*0-07-303122-4*) McGraw.
— Biology. 6th ed. 2002. 36.00 (*0-07-303121-6*) McGraw.
— Native Shrubs of Southern California. (California Natural History Guides Ser.: No. 15). (Illus.). 1966. pap. 11.95 (*0-520-01050-7*, Pub. by U CA Pr) Cal Prin Full Svc.
Raven, Peter H., et al, eds. Biogeography of the Tropical Pacific: Proceedings of a Symposium. (Illus.). 228p. 1984. pap. 15.00 (*0-942924-09-6*) Assn Syst Coll.
Raven, Peter H. & Burke, Margaret G. Biology. 4th ed. 416p. (C). 1996. text, student ed. 25.00 (*0-697-22574-7*, WCB McGr Hill) McGrw-H Hghr Educ.
Raven, Peter H. & Johnson, George B. Biology. 2nd ed. 1264p. (C). 1993. text. write for info. (*0-697-25092-X*, WCB McGr Hill); student ed. 25.00 (*0-697-23506-8*, WCB McGr Hill) McGrw-H Hghr Educ.
— Biology. 3rd ed. 1260p. (C). 1993. text. write for info. (*0-697-23494-0*, WCB McGr Hill); text. write for info. (*0-697-23498-3*, WCB McGr Hill) McGrw-H Hghr Educ.
— Biology. 3rd ed. LC 94-198620. 1344p. (C). 1994. text, student ed. write for info. (*0-697-24251-X*, WCB McGr Hill) McGrw-H Hghr Educ.
— Biology. 3rd ed. (C). 1995. text, student ed. write for info. (*0-697-32663-2*, WCB McGr Hill) McGrw-H Hghr Educ.
— Biology. 4th ed. LC 95-81058. 1280p. (C). 1996. text 81.92 (*0-697-22570-4*, WCB McGr Hill) McGrw-H Hghr Educ.
***Raven, Peter H. & Johnson, George B.** Biology 5th ed. LC 97-48875. xxviii, 1284p. 1999. write for info. (*0-07-115511-2*) McGraw.
Raven, Peter H. & Johnson, George B. How Scientists Think. LC 94-73775. 104p. (C). 1995. text. write for info. (*0-697-27875-1*, WCB McGr Hill) McGrw-H Hghr Educ.
— Understanding Biology. 896p. (C). 1994. text. write for info. (*0-697-25448-8*, WCB McGr Hill) McGrw-H Hghr Educ.
— Understanding Biology. 2nd ed. 850p. (C). 1993. text. write for info. (*0-697-23503-3*, WCB McGr Hill); text, student ed. write for info. (*0-697-23505-X*, WCB McGr Hill) McGrw-H Hghr Educ.
— Understanding Biology. 2nd ed. 850p. (C). 1994. text. write for info. (*0-697-25253-1*, WCB McGr Hill) McGrw-H Hghr Educ.
— Understanding Biology. 3rd ed. 64p. (C). 1995. text, student ed. write for info. (*0-697-25031-8*, WCB McGr Hill) McGrw-H Hghr Educ.
— Understanding Biology. 3rd ed. LC 94-72422. 968p. (C). 1995. text. write for info. (*0-697-22213-6*, WCB McGr Hill) McGrw-H Hghr Educ.
— Understanding Biology. 3rd ed. 416p. (C). 1995. text, student ed. 34.00 (*0-697-22217-9*, WCB McGr Hill) McGrw-H Hghr Educ.
— Understanding Biology. 3rd ed. 384p. (C). 1995. text, student ed. 25.00 (*0-697-22216-0*, WCB McGr Hill) McGrw-H Hghr Educ.
— Understanding Biology, Vol. I. 3rd ed. LC 94-72422. 552p. (C). 1995. text. write for info. (*0-697-26327-4*, WCB McGr Hill) McGrw-H Hghr Educ.
— Understanding Biology, Vol. II. 3rd ed. 496p. (C). 1995. text. write for info. (*0-697-26328-2*, WCB McGr Hill) McGrw-H Hghr Educ.
Raven, Peter H., et al. Biology. 2nd ed. 480p. (C). 1994. text, student ed. 25.00 (*0-697-25440-2*, WCB McGr Hill) McGrw-H Hghr Educ.
— Biology. 3rd ed. 240p. (C). 1993. text, student ed. 25.00 (*0-697-23497-5*, WCB McGr Hill) McGrw-H Hghr Educ.
— Biology. 4th ed. 576p. (C). 1996. text, lab manual ed. write for info. (*0-697-22572-0*, WCB McGr Hill) McGrw-H Hghr Educ.
— Biology. 5th ed. 576p. (C). 1998. text, lab manual ed. write for info. (*0-697-35356-7*, WCB McGr Hill) McGrw-H Hghr Educ.
— Biology of Plants. 4th ed. 800p. (C). 1986. text 53.95 (*0-87901-315-X*) Worth.
— Biology of Plants. 4th ed. 800p. (C). 1986. 15.95 (*0-87901-318-4*) Worth.
— Biology of Plants. 5th ed. 791p. 1992. text 63.95 (*0-87901-532-2*) Worth.
— Biology of Plants. 5th ed. 791p. 1992. pap. text 24.60 (*0-87901-521-7*) Worth.
— Biology of Plants. 6th ed. LC 98-60171. 875p. (C). 1998. text 65.00 (*1-57259-041-6*) Worth.
Raven, Peter H., jt. auth. see Iwatsuki, Kunio.
Raven, Peter H., jt. auth. see Johnson, George B.
Raven, Peter H., jt. auth. see Osterbrock, Donald E.
Raven, Peter H., jt. contrib. by see Wu Zhengyi.
Raven, Peter H., jt. ed. see Gilbert, Lawrence E.
Raven, Peter H., ed. see National Academy of Sciences Staff, et al.
Raven Rock Publishing Staff. General Novel Study for Use with Students in Grades 4-8, 23 vols. 1998. pap. 7.95 (*0-9683640-5-5*) Raven Rocks Pr.
Raven, Ronald W. An Atlas of Oncology. (Encyclopedia of Visual Medicine Ser.). (Illus.). 238p. 1994. 85.00 (*1-85070-363-9*) Prthnon Pub.
— The Theory & Practice of Oncology: Historical Evolution & Present Principles. (History of Medicine Ser.). (Illus.). 366p. 1990. 95.00 (*1-85070-179-2*) Prthnon Pub.
Raven, Ronald W., et al. Cancer Care: An International Survey. LC 86-9247. 340p. reprint ed. pap. 105.40 (*0-7837-4506-0*, 204428300001) Bks Demand.
Raven, Sarah. The Cutting Garden. LC 96-15547. (Illus.). 168p. 1996. 32.95 (*0-89577-884-X*, Pub. by RD Assn) Penguin Putnam.
Raven, Sarah & Buckley, Jonathan. The Bold & Brilliant Garden. (Illus.). 168p. 2000. 29.95 (*1-58062-162-7*) Adams Media.
Raven, Simon. The Feathers of Death. 224p. 1998. pap. 14.95 (*0-85449-274-7*, Pub. by Gay Mens Pr) LPC InBook.
Raven, Susan. Rome in Africa. 3rd rev. ed. LC 92-13208. (Illus.). 304p. (C). 1993. pap. 29.99 (*0-415-08150-5*, A9619) Routledge.
Ravenal, Earl C., ed. Peace with China? U. S. Decisions for Asia. LC 71-162433. 1971. pap. 2.95 (*0-87140-257-2*, Pub. by Liveright) Norton.
Ravenal, John B. Sidney Goodman: Paintings & Drawings, 1959-95. LC 95-50783. (Illus.). 104p. 1996. pap. write for info. (*0-87633-099-5*) Phila Mus Art.
***Ravenal, John B.** Vanitas: Meditations on Life & Death in Contemporary Art. West, Rosalie A., ed. LC 00-23320. (Illus.). 64p. 2000. pap. 18.95 (*0-917046-55-2*, Pub. by Va Mus Arts) U of Wash Pr.
Ravenal, John B., et al. Twenty Philadelphia Artists: Celebrating Fleisher Challenge at Twenty. LC 98-23822. 1998. 19.95 (*0-87633-124-X*) Phila Mus Art.
Ravender, Goyal. Monolithic Microwave Integrated Circuits: Technology & Design. (Microwave Library). (Illus.). 842p. 1989. text. write for info. (*0-89006-309-5*) Artech Hse.
Ravenel, D. C., jt. ed. see Miller, H. R.
Ravenel, Douglas C. Nilpotence & Periodicity in Stable Homotopy Theory. LC 92-26785. (Annals of Mathematics Studies: No. 128). 209p. (C). 1993. text 79.50 (*0-691-08792-X*, Pub. by Princeton U Pr); pap. text 29.95 (*0-691-02572-X*, Pub. by Princeton U Pr) Cal Prin Full Svc.
Ravenel, Henry E. Ravenel Records: History & Genealogy of the Huguenot Family of Ravenel, of South Carolina, with Some Incidental Account of the Parish of St. Johns, Berkeley, Which Was Their Principal Location. (Illus.). 279p. 1995. reprint ed. pap. 43.00 (*0-8328-4824-7*); reprint ed. lib. bdg. 53.00 (*0-8328-4823-9*) Higginson Bk Co.
Ravenel, Marion R. Rivers Delivers. (Illus.). 212p. 1995. 19.95 (*0-941711-24-2*) Wyrick & Co.
Ravenel, Mazyck P., ed. Half Century of Public Health: Jubilee Historical Volume of the American Public Health Association in Commemoration of the Fiftieth Anniversary Celebration of Its Foundation, New York City, Vol. 14. LC 74-112569. (Rise of Urban America Ser.). (Illus.). 1976. reprint ed. 35.95 (*0-405-02472-X*) Ayer.
Ravenel, Shannon. New Stories from the South: The Year's Best, 1994. 368p. 1994. pap. 10.95 (*1-56512-088-4*) Algonquin Bks.
— New Stories from the South: The Year's Best 1998. (New Stories from the South Ser.). 324p. 1998. pap. 12.95 (*1-56512-219-4*) Algonquin Bks.
Ravenel, Shannon, ed. New Stories from the South: The Year's Best, 1987. 248p. 1987. pap. 10.95 (*0-912697-73-3*) Algonquin Bks.
— New Stories from the South: The Year's Best, 1993. 374p. 1993. pap. 11.95 (*1-56512-053-1*) Algonquin Bks.
— New Stories from the South: The Year's Best, 1995. (New Stories from the South Ser.). 288p. 1995. pap. 10.95 (*1-56512-123-6*, 72123) Algonquin Bks.
— New Stories from the South: The Year's Best, 1997. 324p. 1997. pap. 12.95 (*1-56512-175-9*, 72175) Algonquin Bks.
***Ravenel, Shannon, ed.** New Stories from the South: The Year's Best 1999. 312p. 1999. pap. 14.95 (*1-56512-247-X*) Algonquin Bks.
— New Stories from the South: The Year's Best, 2000. 320p. 2000. pap. 14.95 (*1-56512-295-X*) Algonquin Bks.
Ravenel, Shannon, ed. New Stories from the South: The Year's Best, 1996. (New Stories from the South Ser.). 286p. 1996. pap. 10.95 (*1-56512-155-4*) Algonquin Bks.
Ravenel, Shannon, intro. The Best American Short Stories, 1980-89. 384p. 1990. pap. 16.00 (*0-395-52223-4*) HM.
— New Stories from the South: The Year's Best, 1991. 256p. 1991. pap. 9.95 (*0-945575-82-3*) Algonquin Bks.
— New Stories from the South: The Year's Best, 1992. 368p. 1992. pap. 10.95 (*1-56512-011-6*) Algonquin Bks.
Ravenel, Shannon, jt. ed. see Ford, Richard.
Ravenel, Shannon, jt. ed. see Tyler, Anne.
Ravenette, Tom. Personal Construct Theory in Educational Psychology: A Practitioner's View. 1999. pap. 34.95 (*1-86156-121-0*) Whurr Pub.
Ravenhill, David. For God's Sake Grow Up! LC 98-132195. 176p. 1997. pap. 10.99 (*1-56043-299-3*) Destiny Image.
***Ravenhill, David.** They Drank from the River & Died in the Wilderness. 160p. 2000. pap. 11.99 (*0-7684-2038-5*) McFarland & Co.
Ravenhill, John. Collective Clientelism: The Lome Conventions & North-South Relations. LC 84-17674. 460p. 1985. text 66.00 (*0-231-05804-7*) Col U Pr.
Ravenhill, John, ed. No Longer an American Lake? Alliance Problems in the South Pacific. LC 89-7612. (Research Ser.: No. 73). (Illus.). 240p. 1989. pap. text 14.95 (*0-87725-173-8*) U of Cal IAS.

An Asterisk (*) at the beginning of an entry indicates that the title is appearing for the first time.

— The Political Economy of East Asia, 6 vols. Incl. Vol. 2. China, Korea & Taiwan., 2 bks. set LC 95-7192. 1995. 400.00 (1-85898-253-7); Vol. 3. Singapore, Indonesia, Malaysia, the Philippines & Thailand., 2 bks. set LC 95-7193. 1120p. 1995. 400.00 (1-85898-254-5); 3444p. 1995. 1150.00 (1-85898-031-3) E Elgar.

Ravenhill, John, jt. ed. see Callaghy, Thomas M.

Ravenhill, John, jt. ed. see Noble, Gregory W.

Ravenhill, Leonard. Revival Gods Way. LC 83-15589. 16p. (Orig.). 1986. pap. 7.99 (0-87123-620-6) Bethany Hse.

— Revival Praying. 176p. 1962. pap. 7.99 (0-87123-482-3) Bethany Hse.

— Sodom Had No Bible. 28p. 1979. reprint ed. pap. 8.99 (0-87123-496-3) Bethany Hse.

— Tried & Transfigured. LC 81-71752. 16p. 1963. pap. 7.99 (0-87123-544-7) Bethany Hse.

— Why Revival Tarries. 176p. 1979. pap. 7.99 (0-87123-607-9) Bethany Hse.

Ravenhill, M. Faust. 1997. pap. 10.95 (0-413-71840-9) Methn.

***Ravenhill, Mark.** Handbag. (Modern Plays Ser.). 2000. pap. 10.95 (0-413-73760-8, Methuen Drama) Methn.

— Shopping & F***ing. 1996. pap. 10.95 (0-413-71240-0) Methn.

— Some Explicit Polaroids. (Modern Plays Ser.). 90p. 2000. pap. 10.95 (0-413-74170-2, Methuen Drama) Methn.

Ravenhill, Philip L. Dreams & Reverie: Images of Otherworld Mates among the Baule, West Africa. (Illus.). 128p. 1996. text 34.95 (1-56098-650-6) Smithsonian.

— The Self & the Other: Personhood & Images among the Baule, Cote d'Ivoire. LC 94-72498. (Monograph Ser.: No. 28). (Illus.). 48p. 1994. pap. 15.00 (0-930741-39-0) UCLA Fowler Mus.

Ravenhill, William, ed. see Jones, Helen.

Ravenhurst, Omar K., intro. Principia Discordia. (Illus.). 120p. 1991. reprint ed. pap. 9.95 (0-9626534-2-X) IllumiNet Pr.

Ravenna, Giovanni Da, see Da Ravenna, Giovanni.

Ravenna, Giovanni Di Conversino da, see Di Conversino da Ravenna, Giovanni.

Ravens, David A. Luke & the Restoration of Israel. (JSNT Supplement Ser.: No. 119). 287p. 1996. 80.00 (1-85075-565-5, Pub. by Sheffield Acad) CUP Services.

Ravenscraft, David J. & Scherer, F. M. Mergers, Sell-Offs, & Economic Efficiency. LC 87-14018. 290p. 1987. 36.95 (0-8157-7348-X); pap. 16.95 (0-8157-7347-1) Brookings.

Ravenscraft, Sue A., jt. auth. see Marini, John J.

Ravenscroft, Donald R. Taxation & Foreign Currency: The Income Tax Consequences of Foreign Exchange Transactions & Exchange Rate Fluctuations. LC 72-81277. (Illus.). 888p. 1973. 50.00 (0-915506-15-7) Harvard Law Intl Tax.

— Taxation & Foreign Currency, 1973-1981, Suppl. 1. LC 81-19391. 233p. 1982. pap. 30.00 (0-915506-25-4) Harvard Law Intl Tax.

Ravenscroft, Donald R., jt. auth. see Ravenscroft, Margaret.

RAVENSCROFT, HELENA. Bound by Contract. 1999. mass mkt. 6.95 (0-352-33447-9) London Brdge.

Ravenscroft, Margaret & Ravenscroft, Donald R. Alternatives To Republican Policies. LC 96-42441. (Illus.). viii, 145p. 1996. pap. 12.00 (0-86663-217-4) Ide Hse.

— Handbook for Voters & Liberal Democratic Candidates. LC 95-6391. viii, 106p. 1995. pap. 8.00 (0-86663-210-7) Ide Hse.

Ravenscroft, Peter J. & Cavanaugh, John. A Guide to Symptom Relief in Advanced Cancer. 160p. 1994. pap. text 19.95 (0-07-470134-7) McGraw-Hill HPD.

Ravenscroft, Raphael. The Complete Saxophone Player, Bk. 1. Vol. 1. (Illus.). 48p. 1987. pap. 12.95 (0-7119-0887-7, AM62712) Music Sales.

Ravenscroft, Raphael. The Complete Saxophone Player, Bk. 2. (Illus.). 48p. 1987. pap. 12.95 (0-7119-0888-5, AM62720) Music Sales.

Ravenscroft, Raphael. The Complete Saxophone Player, Bk. 3. (Illus.). 48p. 1987. pap. 12.95 (0-7119-0889-3, AM62738) Music Sales.

Ravenscroft, Raphael. The Complete Saxophone Player, Bk. 4. (Illus.). 48p. 1987. pap. 12.95 (0-7119-0890-7, AM62746) Music Sales.

Ravenscroft, Thomas. A Brief Discourse of the True (But Neglected) Use of Charact'ring the Degrees... fac. ed. (Monuments of Music & Music Literature in Facsimile, II Ser.: Vol. 22). 1976. lib. bdg. 45.00 (0-8450-2222-9) Broude.

— Four Fantasies A5. Brookes, Virginia, ed. (Viol Consort Ser.: Vol. 35). iii, 32p. 1998. pap. 16.00 (1-56571-154-8, VC035) PRB Prods.

Ravenscroft, Trevor. The Cup of Destiny: The Quest for the Grail. LC 82-60160. 192p. 1982. pap. 11.00 (0-87728-546-2) Weiser.

— The Spear of Destiny. LC 82-60165. 400p. 1982. pap. 12.95 (0-87728-547-0) Weiser.

Ravenscroft, Trevor & Murphy, T. Wallace. The Mark of the Beast: The Continuing Story of the Spear of Destiny. 2nd ed. LC 96-14629. (Illus.). 256p. 1997. reprint ed. pap. 12.95 (0-87728-870-4) Weiser.

Ravenscroft, Trevor & Wallace-Murphy, Tim. The Mark of the Beast. 256p. 1992. pap. 12.95 (0-8065-1322-5, Citadel Pr) Carol Pub Group.

Ravenscroft, W. The Comacines. 120p. 1992. reprint ed. pap. 12.95 (1-56459-054-2) Kessinger Pub.

Ravenshear, Kit. Simplified V-Springs: A Guncraftsmanship Manual. 1991. 4.00 (0-913150-71-1) Pioneer Pr.

Ravenstein, E. G. The Laws of Migration, Nos. 1 & 2. LC 75-38142. (Demography Ser.). (Illus.). 1976. reprint ed. 17.95 (0-405-07995-8) Ayer.

Ravenstein, E. G., ed. The Strange Adventures of Andrew Battell of Leigh in Angola & the Adjoining Regions. (Hakluyt Society Works: No. 2, Vol. 6). (Illus.). 1974. reprint ed. 40.00 (0-8115-0329-1) Periodicals Srv.

Ravenstein Staff. Grosse Reisekarte 1: 2 000 000, Osteuropa. 1993. 11.95 (3-87660-896-1) Ravenstein Vrlg.

— Grosse Reisekarte 1: 600 000. 1993. 11.95 (3-87660-889-9) Ravenstein Vrlg.

— Strassen: Deutschland & Europa. 1996. pap. 14.95 (3-87660-817-1, Pub. by Ravenstein Vrlg) Seven Hills Bk.

Ravenstein Verlag Staff. Benelux Road Atlas. 216p. 1993. pap. text 17.95 (3-87660-799-X, Pub. by Ravenstein Vrlg) Seven Hills Bk.

— New Zealand. 1993. 11.95 (3-87660-862-7) Ravenstein Vrlg.

***Ravenstein Verlag Staff.** Strassen 2000. rev. ed. (Illus.). 264p. 1998. pap. text 14.95 (3-87660-819-8, Pub. by Ravenstein Vrlg) Seven Hills Bk.

Ravenstein Verlag Staff. Super Strassen - Superhighways. 240p. 1993. pap. text 17.95 (3-87660-800-7, Pub. by Ravenstein Vrlg) Seven Hills Bk.

Ravenstone, Piercy. A Few Doubts As to the Correctness of Some Opinions Generally Entertained on the Subjects of Population & Political Economy. LC 64-22243. (Reprints of Economic Classics Ser.). xxiii, 474p. 1966. reprint ed. 57.50 (0-678-00124-3) Kelley.

— Thoughts on the Funding System & Its Effects. LC 66-28961. (Reprints of Economic Classics Ser.). 80p. 1966. reprint ed. 25.00 (0-678-00192-8) Kelley.

Ravenswaay, Charles Van, see Van Ravenswaay, Charles.

Ravenswood, Fritzen. The Witching. 1989. mass mkt. 3.95 (0-8217-2657-9, Zebra Kensgtn) Kensgtn Pub Corp.

Ravenswood, Fritzen, ed. see Bailey, Keith.

Ravenswood, Fritzen, ed. & illus. see Bailey, Keith.

Ravenswood Publ. Ltd. Staff. French Hospitals & European Health Care. (C). 1987. 79.00 (0-901812-15-3) St Mut.

— Hospitals in the EEC. (C). 1987. 115.00 (0-7855-3757-0) St Mut.

— Law on Accidents to Health Service Staff & Volunteers. (C). 1987. 125.00 (0-901812-23-4); pap. 89.00 (0-901812-24-2) St Mut.

— Legal Liability for Claims Arising from Hospital Treatment. (C). 1987. pap. 89.00 (0-7855-3752-X); write for info. (0-901812-14-5) St Mut.

— Occupier's Liability Act, 1957 & Liability of Hospitals. (C). 1957. 135.00 (0-901812-20-X); pap. 110.00 (0-901812-19-6) St Mut.

Ravensworth, Olivia M. Domestic Service. 1998. mass mkt. 6.95 (1-56333-615-4) Masquerade.

Raventon, Edward. A Piece of Paradise: The Story of Custer State Park. LC 96-7949. (Illus.). 104p. 1996. pap. 14.95 (1-56044-499-1) Falcon Pub Inc.

Raventos, Margaret H. Spanish-English English-Spanish Dictionary. (ENG & SPA.). 1998. mass mkt. 5.99 (0-345-91353-1) Ballantine Pub Grp.

Raventos, Margaret H. & Gold, David L., eds. Random House New Spanish-English, English-Spanish Dictionary. (ENG & SPA.). 650p. 1995. 18.00 (0-679-43897-1) Random.

Raventos, Margaret H., ed. see Random House Staff.

RavenWing, Josie. The Return of Spirit: A Woman's Call to Spiritual Action. 240p. 1996. pap. 11.95 (1-55874-385-5) Health Comm.

RavenWolf, Silver. Angels: Companions in Magick. LC 96-27953. (Illus.). 304p. (Orig.). 1996. reprint ed. pap. 14.95 (1-56718-724-2) Llewellyn Pubns.

— Beneath a Mountain Moon. LC 95-11763. (Illus.). 360p. 1995. pap. 15.95 (1-56718-722-6) Llewellyn Pubns.

***RavenWolf, Silver.** Halloween: Customs, Recipes & Spells. LC 99-29146. (Illus.). 264p. 1999. pap. 12.95 (1-56718-719-6) Llewellyn Pubns.

RavenWolf, Silver. HexCraft: Dutch Country Magick. LC 95-2100. (Llewellyn's Practical Magic Ser.). (Illus.). 320p. 1995. pap. 15.95 (1-56718-723-4) Llewellyn Pubns.

***RavenWolf, Silver.** Murder at Witches' Bluff. 2000. pap. 14.95 (1-56718-727-7) Llewellyn Pubns.

— Silver Ravenwolf's Teen Witch Kit: Everything You Need to Make Magick! LC 99-59442. (Illus.). (J). 2000. write for info. (1-56718-554-1) Llewellyn Pubns.

RavenWolf, Silver. Silver's Spells for Prosperity. LC 99-17322. (Silver's Spells For... Ser.). (Illus.). 240p. 1999. pap. 7.95 (1-56718-726-9) Llewellyn Pubns.

***RavenWolf, Silver.** Silver's Spells for Protection. LC 99-58550. (Illus.). 264p. 2000. pap. 7.95 (1-56718-729-3) Llewellyn Pubns.

RavenWolf, Silver. Teen Witch: Wicca for a New Generation. LC 98-26071. (Illus.). 251p. (YA). (gr. 7-12). 1998. pap. 12.95 (1-56718-725-0, K725) Llewellyn Pubns.

— To Light a Sacred Flame: Practical Witchcraft for the Millennium. LC 98-45978. (Illus.). 320p. 1999. 14.95 (1-56718-721-8, K721) Llewellyn Pubns.

— To Ride a Silver Broomstick: New Generation Witchcraft. LC 92-38151. (Illus.). 300p. 1993. pap. 14.95 (0-87542-791-X) Llewellyn Pubns.

— To Stir a Magick Cauldron: A Witch's Guide to Casting & Conjuring. LC 95-45595. (New Generation Witchcraft Ser.). (Illus.). 320p. 1999. pap. 14.95 (1-56718-424-3) Llewellyn Pubns.

***RavenWolf, Silver.** Witches' Night Out. LC 99-462288. (Witches' Chillers Ser.). 240p. (YA). (gr. 7-12). 2000. pap. 4.99 (1-56718-728-5) Llewellyn Pubns.

RavenWolf, Silver, jt. auth. see Jackson, Nigel.

Raver, Anne. Deep in the Green. 1996. pap. 13.00 (0-679-76798-3) Random.

Raver, Mary F. Women's Health Diary: The Essential Health Record for Every Woman Aged 35 to 55. 52p. (Orig.). 1995. pap. 4.95 (1-886245-00-2) Adelante CA.

Raver, Miki. Listen to Her Voice: Women of the Hebrew Bible. LC 97-49312. (Illus.). 176p. 1998. 27.50 (0-8118-1895-0) Chronicle Bks.

Raver, Sharon A. Intervention Strategies for Infants & Toddlers with Special Needs: A Team Approach. 2nd ed. LC 98-16979. 464p. (C). 1998. pap. text 48.00 (0-13-674730-2, Scribners Ref) Mac Lib Ref.

— Strategies for Teaching At-Risk & Handicapped Infants & Toddlers. (C). 1991. text 73.00 (0-675-21202-2, Merrill Coll) P-H.

Ravera, O., jt. auth. see Mislin, Hans.

Raverat, Gwen. Period Piece. (Ann Arbor Paperbacks Ser.). (Illus.). 290p. (C). 1991. reprint ed. pap. 17.95 (0-472-06475-4, 06475) U of Mich Pr.

Raverty, H. C., tr. see Al-din, Minhaj.

Raverty, H. G. A Dictionary of the Puk'hto, Pus'hto, or Language of the Afghans; with Remarks on the Originality of the Language & Its Affinity to the Semitic & Other Oriental Tongues. 1987. reprint ed. 52.00 (81-206-0286-2, Pub. by Asian Educ Servs) S Asia.

— Dictionary of the Pushto Language: Pushto - English Dictionary. (ENG & PUS.). 1140p. 1987. 79.95 (0-8288-8477-3) Fr & Eur.

— A Grammar of the Puk'hto, Pus'hto, or Language of the Afghans. (C). 1987. reprint ed. 36.00 (0-8364-2400-X, Pub. by Asian Educ Servs) S Asia.

— Selection of Poetry of the Afghans. (C). 1988. 135.00 (1-85077-197-9, Pub. by Darf Pubs Ltd) St Mut.

Ravesloot, John C. Mortuary Practices & Social Differentiation at Casas Grandes, Chihuahua, Mexico. LC 88-15385. (Anthropological Papers). 113p. 1988. pap. 27.95 (0-8165-1048-2) U of Ariz Pr.

Ravet, Serge, contrib. by. Technology Based Training: A Comprehensive Guide to All New Digital Training Media for Trainers. 224p. 1996. 59.95 (0-7494-1975-X, Falmer Pr) Taylor & Francis.

Ravet, Serge & Laute, Maureen. Technology-Based Training. LC 97-17796. (Improving Human Performance Ser.). (Illus.). 320p. 1997. 39.95 (0-88415-866-7, 5866) Gulf Pub.

Ravette Books Staff. Bluff Your Way in Advertising. 64p. 1995. pap. text 5.95 (1-85304-090-8, Pub. by Ravette Bks) Assoc Pubs Grp.

— Bluff Your Way in Astrology. 64p. 1995. pap. text 5.95 (1-85304-404-0, Pub. by Ravette Bks) Assoc Pubs Grp.

— Bluff Your Way in Chess. 64p. 1995. pap. text 5.95 (1-85304-654-X, Pub. by Ravette Bks) Assoc Pubs Grp.

— Bluff Your Way in Computers. 64p. 1995. pap. text 5.95 (1-85304-081-9, Pub. by Ravette Bks) Assoc Pubs Grp.

— Bluff Your Way in Consultancy. 64p. 1995. pap. text 5.95 (0-948456-40-X, Pub. by Ravette Bks) Assoc Pubs Grp.

— Bluff Your Way in Golf. 64p. 1995. pap. text 5.95 (0-948456-76-0, Pub. by Ravette Bks) Assoc Pubs Grp.

— Bluff Your Way in Jazz. 64p. 1995. pap. text 5.95 (0-948456-64-7, Pub. by Ravette Bks) Assoc Pubs Grp.

— Bluff Your Way in Literature. 64p. 1995. pap. text 5.95 (0-948456-03-5, Pub. by Ravette Bks) Assoc Pubs Grp.

— Bluff Your Way in Management. 64p. 1995. pap. text 5.95 (0-948456-75-2, Pub. by Ravette Bks) Assoc Pubs Grp.

— Bluff Your Way in Marketing. 64p. 1996. pap. text 5.95 (1-85304-198-X, Pub. by Ravette Bks) Assoc Pubs Grp.

— Bluff Your Way in Modern Art. 64p. 1996. pap. text 5.95 (1-85304-240-4, Pub. by Ravette Bks) Assoc Pubs Grp.

— Bluff Your Way in Music. (Illus.). 64p. 1995. pap. text 5.95 (1-85304-674-4, Pub. by Ravette Bks) Assoc Pubs Grp.

— Bluff Your Way in Music. 64p. 1996. pap. text 5.95 (0-948456-74-4, Pub. by Ravette Bks) Assoc Pubs Grp.

— Bluff Your Way in Opera. 64p. 1995. pap. text 5.95 (1-85304-217-X, Pub. by Ravette Bks) Assoc Pubs Grp.

— Bluff Your Way in Poetry. 64p. 1995. pap. text 5.95 (1-85304-100-9, Pub. by Ravette Bks) Assoc Pubs Grp.

— Bluff Your Way in Public Speaking. 64p. 1995. pap. text 5.95 (1-85304-089-4, Pub. by Ravette Bks) Assoc Pubs Grp.

— Bluff Your Way in Seduction. 64p. 1995. pap. text 5.95 (1-85304-158-0, Pub. by Ravette Bks) Assoc Pubs Grp.

— Bluff Your Way in Skiing. 64p. 1995. pap. text 5.95 (1-85304-296-X, Pub. by Ravette Bks) Assoc Pubs Grp.

— Bluff Your Way in Whiskey. 64p. 1995. pap. text 5.95 (1-85304-364-8, Pub. by Ravette Bks) Assoc Pubs Grp.

— Bluff Your Way on the Flight Deck. 64p. 1995. pap. text 5.95 (1-85304-373-7, Pub. by Ravette Bks) Assoc Pubs Grp.

— Bluff Your Way to Bluffing. 64p. 1995. pap. text 5.95 (1-85304-125-4, Pub. by Ravette Bks) Assoc Pubs Grp.

— Bluff Your Way to Champagne. 64p. 1995. pap. text 5.95 (1-85304-432-6, Pub. by Ravette Bks) Assoc Pubs Grp.

Ravetto, Carlo. Fine-Needle Aspiration Cytodiagnosis: A Color Atlas. (Illus.). 210p. 1984. text 71.00 (88-299-0085-0, Pub. by Piccin Nuova) Gordon & Breach.

Ravetto, Carlo & Boccato, P. Fine-Needle Aspiration Cytodiagnosis: A Color Atlas. 210p. 1984. text 64.00 (1-57235-031-8) Piccin Nuova.

Ravetto, Carlo & Boccato, Paolo. Fine-Needle Aspiration Cytodiagnosis: A Color Atlas. (Illus.). 212p. 1984. text 160.00 (0-407-01054-8) Buttrwrth-Heinemann.

Ravetz, A. & Turkington. The Place of Home: English Domestic Environments, 1914-2000. (Studies in History, Planning & the Environment). (Illus.). 256p. (C). 1995. 80.00 (0-419-17980-1, E & FN Spon) Routledge.

Ravetz, J. R. The Merger of Knowledge with Power: Essays in Critical Science. 352p. 1990. text 104.00 (0-7201-2021-7) Continuum.

Ravetz, J. R., jt. auth. see Fincham, John.

Ravetz, Jerome R. Scientific Knowledge & Its Social Problems. 480p. (C). 1995. pap. text 29.95 (1-56000-851-2) Transaction Pubs.

Ravetz, Jerome R., jt. auth. see Funtowicz, Silvio O.

Ravetz, Jerome R., jt. ed. see Sardar, Ziauddin.

Ravetz, Tom, ed. see Capel, Evelyn F.

Ravi, Jennifer. Notable North Carolina Women. LC 92-70165. (Illus.). 156p. (Orig.). 1992. pap. 9.95 (1-878177-03-6) Bandit Bks.

Ravi, K. V., et al. Diamond Materials: 4th International Symposium. LC 95-60439. (Proceedings Ser.: Vol. 95-4). 729p. 1995. 72.00 (1-56677-098-X) Electrochem Soc.

Ravi, K. V., ed. see Electrochemical Society Staff.

Ravi, P. Agarwal. Inequalities & Applications. 604p. 1994. text 104.00 (981-02-1830-3) World Scientific Pub.

Ravi, Srilata. L' Inde Romancee: L'Inde dans le Genre Romanesque Francais Depuis 1947. (Francophone Cultures & Literatures Ser.: Vol. 19). 206p. (C). 1997. text 46.95 (0-8204-3725-5) P Lang Pubng.

Ravi, V. A., ed. see Minerals, Metals & Materials Society Staff.

Raviart, P. A., jt. auth. see Girault, V.

Ravich, M. G., et al. Geological Structure of Mac. Robertson Land (East Antarctica) Ghosh, S. P., tr. from RUS. (ENG.). 266p. (C). 1985. text 123.00 (90-6191-439-6, Pub. by A A Balkema) Ashgate Pub Co.

Ravich, Rand, jt. auth. see Tine, Robert.

***Ravich, Samantha F.** Marketization & Democracy: East Asian Experiences. (RAND Studies in Policy Analysis). (Illus.). 292p. (C). 2000. 39.95 (0-521-66165-X) Cambridge U Pr.

Ravich, Uri I., et al. Semiconducting Lead Chalcogenides. Stillbans, L. S. & Tybulewicz, Albin, eds. LC 77-107542. (Monographs in Semiconductor Physics: Vol. 5). 393p. reprint ed. pap. 121.90 (0-608-16657-X, 202630800049) Bks Demand.

***Ravichandran, K. S., et al.** Small Fatigue Cracks. LC 99-35694. 510p. 1999. 175.00 (0-08-043011-2) Elsevier.

Ravichandran, N. Stochastic Methods in Reliability Theory. LC 90-34833. 201p. 1991. text 94.95 (0-470-21681-6) Halsted Pr.

Ravicz, Robert. The Japanese Artist's Book: Wood Block Impressions 17th - 20th Centuries. Zangar, Catherine, ed. (Illus.). 20p. (Orig.). (C). 1988. pap. 3.95 (1-880269-04-X) D H Sheehan.

Ravicz, Simone. High on Stress: A Woman's Guide to Optimizing the Stress in Her Life. LC 97-75481. 240p. 1998. pap. 13.95 (1-57224-110-1) New Harbinger.

***Ravicz, Simone.** Thriving with Your Autoimmune Disorder: A Woman's Mind-Body Guide. 350p. 2000. pap. 16.95 (1-57224-189-6) New Harbinger.

Ravid, Benjamin, ed. & tr. see Rawidowicz, Simon.

Ravid, Benjamin C., ed. see Rawidowicz, Simon.

Ravid, Dorit D. Language Change in Child & Adult Hebrew: A Psycholinguistic Perspective. (Oxford Studies in Sociolinguistics). (Illus.). 256p. 1995. pap. text 24.95 (0-19-509036-5) OUP.

Ravid, Katya & Freshney, Ian. DNA Transfer to Cultured Cells. LC 97-50456. (Culture of Specialized Cells Ser.). (Illus.). 312p. 1998. pap. 79.95 (0-471-16572-7, Wiley-Liss) Wiley.

Ravid, Ruth. Practical Statistics for Educators. LC 94-4720. 366p. 1994. lib. bdg. 57.50 (0-8191-9498-0) U Pr of Amer.

***Ravid, Ruth.** Practical Statistics for Educators. 2nd ed. LC 99-57337. 384p. 2000. pap. 37.50 (0-7618-1594-5) U Pr of Amer.

***Ravid, Ruth & Oyer, Elizabeth.** Workbook to Accompany Practical Statistics for Educators. 2nd ed. 120p. 2000. pap. 16.00 (0-7618-1676-3) U Pr of Amer.

Raviele, A. Cardiac Arrhythmias 1995: Proceedings of the 4th International Workshop, Venice, Italy, October 6-8, 1995. 260p. 1995. pap. 102.00 (0-387-75012-6) Spr-Verlag.

Raviele, Antonio. Cardiac Arrhythmias 1997: Proceedings of the 5th International Workshop on Cardiac Arrhythmias, Venice, 7-10 October, 1997. LC 97-36011. 1997. write for info. (88-470-0002-5) Spr-Verlag.

Raviele, Antonio, jt. auth. see International Workshop on Cardiac Arrhythmias Staff.

Ravier, Andre. As a Little Child. Buckley, Cornelius M., tr. from FRE. LC 97-19566. Orig. Title: Comme un Enfant. 138p. (Orig.). 1998. mass mkt. 5.50 (0-8189-0796-7) Alba.

— A Do-It-at-Home Retreat: The Spiritual Exercises of St. Ignatius of Loyola. Buckley, Cornelius, tr. from FRE. LC 90-85500. 233p. (Orig.). 1991. pap. 12.95 (0-89870-363-8) Ignatius Pr.

— Francis de Sales: Sage & Saint. LC 87-83532. 270p. (Orig.). 1988. pap. 12.95 (0-89870-193-7) Ignatius Pr.

— Saint Bruno the Carthusian. LC 94-75668. 197p. (Orig.). 1995. pap. 11.95 (0-89870-562-2) Ignatius Pr.

Ravier, Roger, ed. see Saint Francois de Sales.

Raviez, Marilyn E. Early Colonial Religious Drama in Mexico: From Tzompantli to Golgotha. LC 77-76157. 273p. reprint ed. pap. 84.70 (0-608-18726-7, 202950600061) Bks Demand.

Ravignant, Patrick, jt. auth. see Aubier, Catherine.

Ravikovitch, Dahlia. The Window: New & Selected Poems. Bloch, Chana & Bloch, Ariel, trs. from HEB. LC 88-34896. 133p. 1989. pap. 13.95 (0-935296-82-4, Pub. by Sheep Meadow); text 27.50 (0-935296-81-6, Pub. by Sheep Meadow) U Pr of New Eng.

Ravikumar, Vaidyanathan M. Play the Benko Gambit. (Chess Library). (Illus.). 120p. 1991. write for info. (0-08-029767-6, Pub. by CHES); pap. 19.95 (0-08-029766-8, Pub. by CHES) Macmillan.

Ravila, Paavo. Finnish Literary Reader. LC 65-63019. (Uralic & Altaic Ser.: Vol. 44). (Orig.). 1965. pap. text. write for info. (0-87750-012-6) Curzon Pr Ltd.

Ravilious, Eric. Ravilious & Wedgwood: The Complete Wedgwood Designs of Eric Ravilious. (Illus.). 54p. 1996. 40.00 (0-903685-38-8, Pub. by R Dennis) Antique Collect.

R

An Asterisk (*) at the beginning of an entry indicates that the title is appearing for the first time.

R

Ravin, Abe, et al. Auscultation of the Heart. 3rd ed. LC 76-53227. 297p. reprint ed. pap. 92.10 (0-8357-5886-9, 202650600049) Bks Demand.

Ravin, Carl E., ed. Imaging & Invasive Radiology in the Intensive Care Unit. LC 92-49509. (Illus.). 181p. 1992. text 83.00 (0-443-08868-3) Church.

Ravin, Carl E., jt. auth. see Putman, Charles E.

Ravin, Ed, et al. Using & Managing UUCP. unabridged ed. LC 96-219779. (Illus.). 424p. (Orig.). 1996. pap. 29.95 (1-56592-153-4) Thomson Learn.

Ravin, James G., jt. auth. see Marmor, Michael F.

Ravin, Thomas, jt. auth. see Dorman, Thomas A.

Ravin, Yael. Lexical Semantics Without Thematic Roles. 256p. 1990. 70.00 (0-19-824831-8) OUP.

***Ravin, Yael & Leacock, Claudia, eds.** Polysemy: Theoretical & Computational Approaches. (Illus.). 256p. 2000. text 75.00 (0-19-823842-8) OUP.

Ravina, Mark. Land & Lordship in Early Modern Japan. LC 97-51268. 1998. 45.00 (0-8047-2898-4) Stanford U Pr.

Ravindra, N. M. & Singh, R. K., eds. Transient Thermal Processing Techniques in Electronic Materials. (Illus.). 179p. 1996. 20.00 (0-87339-331-7) Minerals Metals.

Ravindra, Ravi. Christ the Yogi: A Hindu Reflection on the Gospel of John. LC 98-21279. 256p. 1998. pap. 14.95 (0-89281-671-6) Inner Tradit.

— Krishnamurti: Two Birds on One Tree. 90p. 1995. pap. 8.00 (0-8356-0718-6, Quest) Theos Pub Hse.

Ravindra, Ravi & Murray, Priscilla. Yoga & the Teaching of Krishna: Essays on the Indian Spiritual Traditions. LC 98-915899. xi, 390 p. 1998. 18.95 (81-7059-316-6) Theos Pub Hse.

Ravindran, A., et al. Operations Research 2. 2nd ed. LC 86-5561. 656p. 1987. text 99.95 (0-471-08608-8) Wiley.

Ravindran, C., ed. see Conference on Process Control & Reliability Analys.

Ravindran, D. J., ed. A Handbook on Training Paralegals: Report of a Seminar on Training of Paralegals, TagaTay City, Philippines, 5-9 December, 1988. LC KZ0385.. 49p. reprint ed. pap. 30.00 (0-7837-0093-8, 204037000017) Bks Demand.

Ravindran, K. Customized Derivatives: A Step-By-Step Guide to Using Exotic Options, Swaps, & Other Customized Derivatives. LC 97-9623. 1997. 70.00 (0-7863-0556-8, Irwn Prfssnl) McGraw-Hill Prof.

***Ravindran, P. A., ed.** Black Pepper, Piper Nigram. (Medicinal & Aromatic Plants - Industrial Profiles Ser.: Vol. 13). 400p. 2000. text 125.00 (90-5702-453-5, Harwood Acad Pubs) Gordon & Breach.

Ravindran, Sundari. Gender Issues in Health Projects & Programmes. (Oxfam Research Discussion Papers). 28p. (C). 1995. pap. 12.95 (0-85598-295-0, Pub. by Oxfam Pub) Stylus Pub VA.

Ravindran, T. K. On the Other Shore Poems. 104p. 1991. text 10.00 (81-220-0214-5, Pub. by Konark Pubs Pvt Ltd) Advent Bks Div.

Ravindranath, B. Principles & Practice of Chromatography. 1989. text 79.95 (0-470-21328-0) P-H.

Ravindranath, N. H. & Hall, D. O. Biomass, Energy & Environment: A Developing Country Perspective from India. (Illus.). 390p. (C). 1995. text 115.00 (0-19-856436-8) OUP.

Ravindranath, P. K. Sharad Pawar: The Making of a Modern Maratha. (C). 1992. 14.00 (81-85674-46-9, Pub. by UBS Pubs Dist) S Asia.

Ravindranathan, T. R. Bakunin & the Italians. 344p. (C). 1988. text 65.00 (0-7735-0646-2, Pub. by McG-Queens Univ Pr) CUP Services.

Raving Beauties Editors. No Holds Barred. 128p. Date not set. pap. 8.95 (0-7043-3963-3, Pub. by Womens Press) Trafalgar.

Raving Beauties Staff, ed. In the Pink: The Raving Beauties. rev. ed. (Illus.). 128p. pap. 9.95 (0-7043-3920-X, Pub. by Womens Press) Trafalgar.

Raviola, Roberto, see Magnus, pseud.

Ravise, J. Suzanne. Tableaux Culturels de la France. 3rd ed. (FRE.). (C). pap., teacher ed. 5.50 (0-8442-1274-1, VF1274-1); pap., student ed. 26.75 (0-8442-1273-3, VF1273-3) NTC Contemp Pub Co.

Ravishankar, K., jt. auth. see Burton, Dudley J.

***Ravitch, Diane.** The American Reader: Words That Moved a Nation. 2nd ed. LC 00-38279. 400p. 2000. pap. 18.00 (0-06-273733-3, Perennial) HarperTrade.

— Brookings Papers on Education Policy 2000 2000. pap. 19.95 (0-8157-7357-9) Brookings.

Ravitch, Diane. Debating the Future of American Education. 182p. (C). 1995. 16.95 (0-8157-7353-6) Brookings.

***Ravitch, Diane.** The Great School Wars: New York City, 1805-1971: The History of the Public Schools as Battlefield of Social Change. 480p. 2000. pap. 24.95 (0-8018-6471-2) Johns Hopkins.

— Left Back: A Century of Failed School Reforms. LC 00-38067. 560p. 2000. 30.00 (0-684-84417-6) Simon & Schuster.

Ravitch, Diane. National Standards in American Education: A Citizen's Guide. 223p. (C). 1995. 38.95 (0-8157-7352-8) Brookings.

— National Standards in American Education: A Citizen's Guide. 223p. 1996. pap. 16.95 (0-8157-7351-X) Brookings.

— New Schools for a New Century: The Redesign of Urban Education. 336p. 1999. pap. text 15.95 (0-300-07874-9) Yale U Pr.

— The Troubled Crusade: American Education, 1945-1980. 384p. 1985. pap. 22.00 (0-465-08757-4, Pub. by Basic) HarpC.

Ravitch, Diane, ed. American Reader. LC 89-46553. 400p. 1991. reprint ed. pap. 17.00 (0-06-272016-3, Harper Ref) HarpC.

— Brookings Papers on Education Policy, 1999. 300p. 1998. pap. 19.95 (0-8157-7355-2) Brookings.

— Brookings Papers on Education Policy: 1998: 1998. 383p. 1997. pap. 19.95 (0-8157-1183-2) Brookings.

Ravitch, Diane & Vinovskis, Maris A., eds. Learning from the Past: What History Teaches Us about School Reform. LC 94-27015. 440p. 1995. text 48.50 (0-8018-4920-9); pap. text 18.95 (0-8018-4921-7) Johns Hopkins.

***Ravitch, Diane & Viteritti, Joseph, eds.** City Schools: Lessons from New York. LC 99-58542. 416p. 2000. 59.95 (0-8018-6341-4); pap. 21.50 (0-8018-6342-2) Johns Hopkins.

Ravitch, Diane & Viteritti, Joseph P. New Schools for a New Century: The Redesign of Urban Education. LC 96-39929. 320p. 1997. 30.00 (0-300-07046-2) Yale U Pr.

Ravitch, Diane, ed. see Conference on Needs & Opportunities for the Study.

Ravitch, Diane, jt. ed. see Goodenow, Ronald K.

Ravitch, Frank S. School Prayer & Discrimination: The Civil Rights of Religious Minorities & Dissenters. LC 98-48851. 273p. 1999. 50.00 (1-55553-392-2) NE U Pr.

Ravitch, Mark M. A Century of Surgery: The History of the American Surgical Association, Vol. 1. LC 80-21381. (Illus.). 800p. 1981. reprint ed. pap. 200.00 (0-608-05875-0, 205984200001) Bks Demand.

— A Century of Surgery: The History of the American Surgical Association, Vol. 2. LC 80-21381. (Illus.). 800p. 1981. reprint ed. pap. 200.00 (0-608-05876-9, 205984200002) Bks Demand.

Ravitch, Mark M., ed. The Papers of Alfred Blalock, 2 Vols. (Illus.). 1966. 195.00 (0-8018-0544-9) Johns Hopkins.

Ravitch, Mark M. & Steichen, Felician M. Atlas of General Thoracic Surgery. (Illus.). 400p. 1988. text 220.00 (0-7216-7474-7, W B Saunders Co) Harcrt Hlth Sci Grp.

Ravitch, Melech. Night Prayers & Other Poems. Mayne, Seymour & Augenfeld, Rivka, trs. 24p. pap. 5.00 (0-88962-563-8) Mosaic.

Ravitch, Norman. Sword & Mitre: Government & Episcopate in France & England in the Age of Aristocracy. 1966. text 35.40 (3-11-200273-3) Mouton.

Ravitz, Abe C. Alfred Henry Lewis. LC 78-52560. (Western Writers Ser.: No. 32). 46p. 1978. pap. 4.95 (0-88430-056-0) Boise St U W Writ Ser.

— David Graham Phillips. (Twayne's United States Authors Ser.). 1966. pap. text 4.95 (0-685-42217-8); lib. bdg. 20.95 (0-8290-0006-2) Irvington.

— Imitations of Life: Fannie Hurst's Gaslight Sonatas. LC 97-7085. 240p. 1997. 39.95 (0-8093-2142-4) S Ill U Pr.

— Leane Zugsmith: Thunder on the Left. LC 92-16381. 130p. 1992. pap. 6.95 (0-7178-0702-9) Intl Pubs Co.

— Rex Beach. (Western Writers Ser.: No. 113). (Illus.). 52p. 1994. pap. 4.95 (0-88430-112-5) Boise St U W Writ Ser.

***Ravitz, Leonard J.** Electrodynamic Man: Measuring Human Emotions. (Illus.). 276p. 2000. 39.95 (0-8290-5213-5) Ardent Media.

Ravitzky, Aviezer. History & Faith: Studies in Jewish Philosophy. LC 97-161472. (Amsterdam Studies in Jewish Thought: Vol. 2). 325p. 1996. lib. bdg. 80.00 (90-5063-597-0, Pub. by Gieben) J Benjamins Pubng Co.

Ravitzky, Aviezer. Messianism, Zionism, & Jewish Religious Radicalism. 280p. 1996. pap. text 18.00 (0-226-70578-1) U Ch Pr.

— Messianism, Zioinism, & Jewish Religious Radicalism. Swirsky, Michael & Chipman, Jonathan, trs. 280p. 1996. lib. bdg. 48.00 (0-226-70577-3) U Ch Pr.

Raviv, Amiran, ed. see Bar-Tal, Raviv.

Raviv, Dan, jt. auth. see Melman, Yossi.

Raviv, Hana. A House of Memories: The Story of 58 Avenue Road. LC 98-159371. (Illus.). 100p. 1998. 27.50 (0-85303-343-9, Pub. by M Vallentine & Co) Intl Spec Bk.

— A House of Memories: 58 Avenue Road. LC 98-159371. 92p. 1998. pap. write for info. (0-85303-344-7, Pub. by M Vallentine & Co) Intl Spec Bk.

Raviv, Moshe. Israel at Fifty. 1999. 40.00 (0-297-81851-1) Weidenfeld & Nicolson.

Ravizza, Ken, jt. auth. see Hanson, Tom.

Ravizza, Luigi. Psychiatry & Advanced Technologies. Bogetto, Filippo & Zanalda, Enrico, eds. LC 92-48413. (Illus.). 321p. 1993. reprint ed. pap. 99.60 (0-608-05766-5, 205973000007) Bks Demand.

Ravizza, Mark, jt. auth. see Fischer, John M.

Ravizza, Mark, jt. auth. see Fischer, John Martin.

Ravizza, Mark, jt. ed. see Fischer, John M.

Ravizza, Mary A. The Nature of Liturgical Prayer in Catechumenate Team Formation. LC 97-148989. (Pastoral Ministry Ser.). 80p. (Orig.). 1996. pap. 8.95 (1-55612-954-8, LL1954) Sheed & Ward WI.

Ravizza, Richard, jt. auth. see Ray, William J.

Ravn, Anders P. & Rischel, Hans. Formal Techniques in Real-Time & Fault-Tolerant Systems: 5th International Symposium, FTRTFT'98, Lyngby, Denmark, September 14-18, 1998, Proceedings, Vol. 148. Goos, G. et al, eds. LC 98-40041. (Lecture Notes in Computer Science Ser.: Vol. 1486). viii, 339p. 1998. pap. 55.00 (3-540-65003-2) Spr-Verlag.

Ravn, M. K., tr. see Fabricius, Johann C.

Ravn, O. E. A Catalogue of Oriental Cylinder Seals & Impressions in the Danish National Museum. (Publications of the National Museum: No. 1, Pt.8). (Illus.). 135p. (C). 1960. pap. text 25.00 (0-614-12691-6, Pub. by Aarhus Univ Pr) David Brown.

Ravnik, D., jt. auth. see Gadzijev, E. M.

Ravnitzky, Michael. Automotive Textiles. 550p. 1995. 89.00 (1-56091-599-4, PT-51) Soc Auto Engineers.

Ravnitzky, Yehoshua H., jt. ed. see Bialik, Hayim N.

Ravnkilde, Knud. Danish in Three Months. LC 98-48011. (Hugo Ser.). 240p. 1999. pap. 14.95 (0-7894-4425-9) DK Pub Inc.

— Hugo Danish in Three Months: Simplified Language Course. LC 98-48011. (Hugo Ser.). (DAN & ENG.). 1999. pap. 29.95 incl. audio (0-7894-4434-8) DK Pub Inc.

Ravoira, LaWanda & Cherry, Andrew L., Jr. Social Bonds & Teen Pregnancy. LC 92-9821. 200p. 1992. 45.00 (0-275-94179-5, C4179, Praeger Pubs) Greenwood.

Ravoofs, A. A. Meet Mr. Jinnah. 1983. pap. 9.50 (1-56744-135-1) Kazi Pubns.

Ravthon, H., jt. auth. see Cox, E.

Ravve, A. Principles of Polymer Chemistry. (Illus.). 510p. (C). 1995. text 71.00 (0-306-44873-4, Kluwer Plenum) Kluwer Academic.

***Ravve, A.** Principles of Polymer Chemistry. 2nd ed. LC 99-89493. (Illus.). 708p. 2000. 89.00 (0-306-46368-7, Kluwer Plenum) Kluwer Academic.

Ravve, Abe. Organic Chemistry of Macromolecules: An Introductory Textbook. LC 67-17006. (Illus.). 512p. reprint ed. pap. 158.80 (0-7837-0902-1, 204120700019) Bks Demand.

***Ravvin, Norm, ed.** Great Stories of the Sea. 256p. 2000. pap. 16.95 (0-88995-219-1, Pub. by Red Deer) Genl Dist Srvs.

Ravvin, Norman. A House of Words: Jewish Writing, Identity & Memory. LC 98-219968. 192p. 1997. text 55.00 (0-7735-1664-6, Pub. by McG-Queens Univ Pr); pap. text 19.95 (0-7735-1665-4, Pub. by McG-Queens Univ Pr) CUP Services.

Ravy, Gilbert, jt. ed. see Benay, Jeanne.

Raw, Anthony, jt. auth. see O'Toole, Christopher.

Raw, Barbara C. Trinity & Incarnation in Anglo-Saxon Art & Thought. LC 96-23375. (Studies in Anglo-Saxon England: No. 21). (Illus.). 231p. (C). 1997. text 64.95 (0-521-55371-7) Cambridge U Pr.

Raw, Mary-Elizabeth & Parkinson, T. J., eds. The Veterinary Annual, No. 32. (Illus.). 320p. (C). 1992. pap. 178.95 (0-8464-4163-2) Beekman Pubs.

— The Veterinary Annual, No. 34. (Illus.). 256p. 1994. 135.00 (0-86542-809-3) Blackwell Sci.

— The Veterinary Annual, 1994, No. 34. (Illus.). 272p. 1994. 97.95 (0-632-03878-0) Blackwell Sci.

— The Veterinary Annual, 1996, No. 36. (Illus.). 400p. 1996. 120.00 (0-632-04049-1) Blackwell Sci.

***Raw Vision Staff.** Raw Vision #30. 2000. pap. 12.00 (1-56466-075-3) Archer Fields.

Rawady, Ed. Everywhere & Everything: A Spiritual Story about the First Dream. LC 97-91421. (Illus.). 48p. (YA). (gr. 3 up). 1998. 18.95 (0-9662194-0-6) Table Twelve Pubg.

Rawal, Munni. Dadabhai Naoroji: A Prophet of Indian Nationalism. 1989. 21.00 (81-7041-131-9, Pub. by Anmol) S Asia.

Rawal, Narinder, et al, eds. Management of Acute & Chronic Pain. 231p. 1998. pap. text 43.00 (0-7279-1193-7) Login Brothers Bk Co.

Rawal, Narinder & Coombs, Dennis W., eds. Spinal Narcotics. (Current Management of Pain Ser.). (C). 1989. text 131.50 (0-7923-0374-1) Kluwer Academic.

Rawat, Ajay S. History of Forestry in India. (C). 1991. 44.00 (81-85182-57-4, Pub. by Indus Pub) S Asia.

Rawat, Ajay S., ed. Indian Forestry: A Perspective. (C). 1993. 44.00 (81-85182-78-7, Pub. by Indus Pub) S Asia.

Rawat, B. & Zhou Siyong, eds. Recent Advances in Microwave Technology (IAP) Proceedings of the 2nd International Symposium on Recent Advances in Microwave Technology, Beijing, China, 4-8 September 1989. (International Academic Publishers Ser.). xx, 660 p. 1990. 230.00 (0-08-040184-8, Pub. by IAP) Elsevier.

Rawat, Harish & Veliath, Deepak. Professional Java Networking. 1000p. Date not set. pap. 49.99 (1-86100-460-5) Wrox Pr Inc.

Rawcliffe. Environmental Pressure Groups in Transition. 176p. 1998. text 79.95 (0-7190-5212-2, Pub. by Manchester Univ Pr) St Martin.

Rawcliffe, Carole. Medicine & Society in Later Medieval England. (History Paperbacks Ser.). (Illus.). 256p. 1998. pap. 22.95 (0-7509-1497-1, Pub. by Sutton Pub Ltd) Intl Pubs Mktg.

— Medicine for the Soul: The Life & Work of An English Medieval Hospital. 2000. 55.00 (0-7509-2009-2) Sutton Pub Ltd.

Rawcliffe, Carole, tr. Sources for the History of Medicine in Late Medieval England. LC 94-45554. (Documents of Practice Ser.). 1995. pap. 6.00 (1-879288-54-0) Medieval Inst.

***Rawdon, Richard M., Jr., et al.** Kentucky Civil Practice Before Trial. 2nd ed. 790p. 1998. 99.00 (1-58757-021-1) Univ of KY.

Rawe, Richard L. Creating a Worlds Class Airport: Cincinnati/Northern Kentucky International, 1947-1997. (Illus.). 212p. 1997. 34.95 (1-882933-14-1) Cherbo Pub Grp.

Rawer, K., et al, eds. Low & Equatorial Latitudes in the International Reference Ionosphere: Proceedings of the COSPAR International Scientific Symposium Held in New Delhi, India, 9-13 January 1995. (Advances in Space Research Ser.: No. 18). 338p. 1995. pap. text 92.75 (0-08-042673-5, Pergamon Pr) Elsevier.

Rawer, K. & Bilitza, D., eds. Quantitive Description of Ionospheric Storm Effects & Irregularities: Proceedings of the C4.2 Symposium of COSPAR Scientific Commission C Which Was Held During the 31st COSPAR Scientific Assembly, Birmingham, UK, 14-21 July 1996. 162p. 1997. pap. 100.50 (0-08-043306-5, Pergamon Pr) Elsevier.

Rawer, Karl. Wave Propagation in the Ionosphere. LC 92-24066. (Developments in Electromagnetic Theory & Application Ser.: No. 5). 424p. (C). 1993. text 264.50 (0-7923-0775-5) Kluwer Academic.

Rawer, Karl, ed. Geophysics Three. (Encyclopedia of Physics Ser., Gruppe 10-Geophysik: Band 49, Teil 7). (Illus.). 720p. 1985. 385.95 (0-387-11425-4) Spr-Verlag.

Rawer, Karl, et al, eds. Advances in Global - Regional Descriptions of Ionospheric Parameters: Proceedings of URSI - COSPAR Symposium Held in Athens, Greece, 1-4 October, 1991. (Advances in Space Research Ser.: Vol. 13). 144p. 1992. pap. 190.25 (0-08-042188-1, Pergamon Pr) Elsevier.

— Models of the Atmosphere & Ionosphere: Proceedings of Workshops VIII & X of the COSPAR 25th Plenary Meeting held in Graz, Austria, 25 June-7 July 1984. (Illus.). 242p. 1985. pap. 54.00 (0-08-033196-3, Pub. by PPL) Elsevier.

Rawer, Karl & Bradley, P. A., eds. Ionospheric Informatics & Empirical Modelling: Proceedings of Workshop XII of the COSPAR 27th Plenary Meeting Held in Espoo, Finland, 18-29 July, 1988. (Advances in Space Research Ser.: Vol. 10). (Illus.). 144p. 1990. pap. 105.00 (0-08-040165-1, Pergamon Pr) Elsevier.

Rawer, Karl & Piggott, W. R., eds. Development of IRI-90: Proceedings of a Workshop Held in Abingdon, U. K., 7-9 August, 1989. (Advances in Space Research Ser.: Vol. 10). 124p. 1991. pap. 95.75 (0-08-040785-4, Pergamon Pr) Elsevier.

— Enlarged Space & Ground Data Base for Ionospheric Modelling: Proceedings of the Topical Meeting of the COSPAR Interdisciplinary Scientific Commission, 28th Plenary Meeting Held in the Hague, the Netherlands, 25 June-6 July 1990. (Advances in Space Research Ser.: Vol. 11). (Illus.). 216p. 1991. pap. 147.00 (0-08-041166-5, ASR 11, NO. 10, Pergamon Pr) Elsevier.

Rawer, Karl & Ramanamurty, Y. V., eds. International Reference Ionosphere - Status 1985-86: Proceedings of the URSI-COSPAR Workshop on the International Reference Ionosphere Held in Louvain-la-Neuve, Belgium, 25 October - 1st November. 138p. 1986. pap. 52.00 (0-08-034026-1, Pergamon Pr) Elsevier.

Rawer, Karl, et al. Ionospheric Informatics: Proceedings of an International (URSI & COSPAR Sponsored) Workshop Held in Novgorod, USSR, 25-29 May 1987. LC 83-645550. (Advances in Space Research Ser.: No. 8). (Illus.). 254p. 1988. pap. 60.00 (0-08-036868-9, Pergamon Pr) Elsevier.

— Off Median Phenomena & International Reference Ionosphere. (Advances in Space Research Ser.: Vol. 15, No. 2). 216p. 1994. pap. 105.75 (0-08-042537-2, Pergamon Pr) Elsevier.

***Rawes, Alan.** Byron's Poetic Experimentation: Childe Harold, the Tales & the Quest for Comedy. LC 00-42046. (Nineteenth Century Ser.). 2000. write for info. (0-7546-0171-4, Pub. by Ashgate Pub) Ashgate Pub Co.

Rawet, Samuel. The Prophet & Other Stories. Vieira, Nelson, tr. LC 98-23096. (Jewish Latin American Ser.). 86p. 1998. 29.95 (0-8263-1837-1); pap. 12.95 (0-8263-1952-1) U of NM Pr.

Rawick, George P. The American Slave: A Composite Autobiography, 11. LC 71-38591. (Contributions in Afro-American & African Studies: Vol. 11). 1972. lib. bdg. 865.00 (0-8371-3316-5, Greenwood Pr) Greenwood.

Rawick, George P. The American Slave: A Composite Autobiography, Pt. 2. LC 71-38591. (Contributions in Afro-American & African Studies: Vol. 11). 1972. text 695.00 (0-614-25933-9, Greenwood Pr) Greenwood.

— From Sundown to Sunup: The Making of the Black Community, Vol. 11. LC 71-38591. (Contributions in Afro-American & African Studies: No. 11). 208p. 1973. pap. 17.95 (0-8371-6747-7, RSM, Greenwood Pr) Greenwood.

Rawick, George P., ed. The American Slave: A Composite Autobiography, 19 vols., 11. Incl. Vol. 1. LC 71-38591. 208p. 1971. lib. bdg. 75.00 (0-8371-6299-8, RSM&, Greenwood Pr); Vol. 2. LC 71-38591. 1972. lib. bdg. 95.00 (0-8371-6300-5, RSN&, Greenwood Pr); Vol. 3. LC 71-38591. 1972. lib. bdg. 95.00 (0-8371-6301-3, RSO&, Greenwood Pr); Vol. 4. LC 71-38591. 1972. lib. bdg. 75.00 (0-8371-6302-1, RSP&, Greenwood Pr); Vol. 5. LC 71-38591. 1972. lib. bdg. 75.00 (0-8371-6303-X, RSQ&, Greenwood Pr); Vol. 6. LC 71-38591. 1972. lib. bdg. 85.00 (0-8371-6304-8, RSR&, Greenwood Pr); Vol. 7. LC 71-38591. 1971. lib. bdg. 75.00 (0-8371-6305-6, RSS&, Greenwood Pr); Vol. 1. LC 71-38591. 1972. lib. bdg. 75.00 (0-8371-6306-4, RST&, Greenwood Pr); Vol. 2. LC 71-38591. 1972. lib. bdg. 75.00 (0-8371-6307-2, RSU&, Greenwood Pr); Vol. 3. LC 71-38591. 1972. lib. bdg. 75.00 (0-8371-6308-0, RSV&, Greenwood Pr); Vol. 4. LC 71-38591. 1972. lib. bdg. 85.00 (0-8371-6309-9, RSW&, Greenwood Pr); Vol. 5. LC 71-38591. 1972. lib. bdg. 95.00 (0-8371-6310-2, RSX&, Greenwood Pr); Vol. 6. LC 71-38591. 1972. lib. bdg. 95.00 (0-8371-6311-0, RSY&, Greenwood Pr); Vol. 7. LC 71-38591. 1972. lib. bdg. 75.00 (0-8371-6312-9, RSZ&, Greenwood Pr); Vol. 8. LC 71-38591. 1972. lib. bdg. 75.00 (0-8371-6313-7, RSA&, Greenwood Pr); Vol. 9. LC 71-38591. 1972. lib. bdg. 85.00 (0-8371-6314-5, RSB&, Greenwood Pr); Vol. 10. LC 71-38591. 1972. lib. bdg. 85.00 (0-8371-6315-3, RSC&, Greenwood Pr); Vol. 11. LC 71-38591. 1972. lib. bdg. 85.00 (0-8371-6316-1, RSD&, Greenwood Pr); Vol. 12. LC 71-38591. 1972. lib. bdg. 75.00 (0-8371-6317-X, RSE&, Greenwood Pr); LC 71-38591. (Contributions in Afro-American & African Studies: No. 11). 1972. Set lib. bdg. 495.00 (0-8371-3314-9, RSL & RSF, Greenwood Pr) Greenwood.

— The American Slave: A Composite Autobiography, Vols. 1-7, Vols. 1-7. LC 71-38591. (Contributions in Afro-American & African Studies: No. 11). 1972. lib. bdg. 250.00 (0-685-42146-5, Greenwood Pr) Greenwood.

— The American Slave: A Composite Autobiography, Vols. 8-19, Vols. 8-19. LC 71-38591. (Contributions in Afro-American & African Studies: No. 11). 1972. lib. bdg. 445.00 (0-685-42147-3, Greenwood Pr) Greenwood.

An Asterisk (*) at the beginning of an entry indicates that the title is appearing for the first time.

— The American Slave: A Composite Autobiography, Supplement Series 1, 12 vols., 35. Incl. Vol. 1. Alabama Supplement. LC 77-88899. 1978. lib. bdg. 69.50 (0-8371-9761-9, RAA/01, Greenwood Pr); Vol. 2. Arkansas Collected Supplement. LC 77-88899. 1978. lib. bdg. 69.50 (0-8371-9762-7, RAA/02, Greenwood Pr); Vol. 3. Georgia, Supplement 1. LC 77-88899. 1978. lib. bdg. 69.50 (0-8371-9763-5, RAA/03, Greenwood Pr); Vol. 4. Georgia, Supplement 2. LC 77-88899. 1978. lib. bdg. 69.50 (0-8371-9764-3, RAA/04, Greenwood Pr); Vol. 5. Ind-Ohio Supplement. LC 77-88899. 1978. lib. bdg. 69.50 (0-8371-9765-1, RAA/05, Greenwood Pr); Vol. 6. Mississippi. LC 77-88899. 1978. lib. bdg. 69.50 (0-8371-9766-X, RAA/06, Greenwood Pr); Vol. 7. Mississippi. LC 77-88899. 1978. lib. bdg. 69.50 (0-8371-9767-8, RAA/07, Greenwood Pr); Vol. 8. Mississippi. LC 77-88899. 1978. lib. bdg. 69.50 (0-8371-9768-6, RAA/08, Greenwood Pr); Vol. 9. Mississippi. LC 77-88899. 1978. lib. bdg. 69.50 (0-8371-9769-4, RAA/09, Greenwood Pr); Vol. 10. Mississippi. LC 77-88899. 1978. lib. bdg. 69.50 (0-8371-9770-8, RAA/10, Greenwood Pr); Vol. 11. North Carolina-South Carolina Supplement. LC 77-88899. 1978. lib. bdg. 69.50 (0-8371-9771-6, RAA/11, Greenwood Pr); Vol. 12. Oklahoma Supplement. LC 77-88899. 1978. lib. bdg. 69.50 (0-8371-9772-4, RAA/12, Greenwood Pr); LC 77-88899. (Contributions in Afro-American & African Studies: No. 35). 1978. Set lib. bdg. 795.00 (0-8371-9756-2, RAA/, Greenwood Pr) Greenwood.

— The American Slave: A Composite Autobiography, Supplement Series 2, 10 vols., 49. Incl. Vol. 1. LC 79-12456. 1979. lib. bdg. 75.00 (0-313-21979-6, RAB/01, Greenwood Pr); Vol. 2. LC 79-12456. 1979. lib. bdg. 69.50 (0-313-21980-X, RAB/02, Greenwood Pr); Vol. 3. LC 79-12456. 1979. lib. bdg. 69.50 (0-313-21981-8, RAB/03, Greenwood Pr); Vol. 4. LC 79-12456. 1979. lib. bdg. 69.50 (0-313-21982-6, RAB/04, Greenwood Pr); Vol. 5. LC 79-12456. 1979. lib. bdg. 69.50 (0-313-21983-4, RAB/05, Greenwood Pr); Vol. 6. LC 79-12456. 1979. lib. bdg. 69.50 (0-313-21984-2, RAB/06, Greenwood Pr); Vol. 7. LC 79-12456. 1979. lib. bdg. 69.50 (0-313-21985-0, RAB/07, Greenwood Pr); Vol. 8. LC 79-12456. 1979. lib. bdg. 69.50 (0-313-21986-9, RAB/08, Greenwood Pr); Vol. 9. LC 79-12456. 1979. lib. bdg. 69.50 (0-313-21987-7, RAB/09, Greenwood Pr); Vol. 10. LC 79-12456. 1979. lib. bdg. 69.50 (0-313-21988-5, RAB/10, Greenwood Pr); LC 79-12456. (Contributions in Afro-American & African Studies: No. 49). 1980. Set lib. bdg. 675.00 (0-313-21423-9, RAB/, Greenwood Pr) Greenwood.

Rawicz, Leonard, jt. auth. see Nash, Ralph C., Jr.

Rawicz, Slavomir. The Long Walk. 1995. reprint ed. lib. bdg. 27.95 (1-56849-676-1) Buccaneer Bks.

***Rawicz, Slavomir.** The Long Walk. abr. deluxe ed. LC 99-67831. (Adventure Library Ser.: Vol. 20). 268p. 1999. reprint ed. lib. bdg. 32.50 (1-885283-20-2) Advent Library.

Rawicz, Slavomir. The Long Walk: The True Story of a Trek to Freedom. LC 98-107014. 252p. 1997. reprint ed. 25.00 (1-55821-634-0); reprint ed. pap. 12.95 (1-55821-684-7) Lyons Pr.

Rawidowicz, Simon. Israel: The Ever-Dying People & Other Essays. Ravid, Benjamin, ed. & tr. by. LC 84-46115. 248p. 1987. 37.50 (0-8386-3253-X) Fairleigh Dickinson.

— State of Israel, Diaspora, & Jewish Continuity: Essays on the "Ever-Dying People" Ravid, Benjamin C., ed. LC 97-36813. (Tauber Institute Ser.: Vol. 26). 280p. 1998. pap. 25.00 (0-87451-846-6) U Pr of New Eng.

Rawidowicz, Simon, ed. The Chicago Pinkas. (ENG & HEB.). 319p. (C). 1952. 7.95 (0-935982-05-1, SR-01) Spertus Coll.

***Rawl, Miriam F.** From the Ashes of Ruin. LC 99-12716. 371p. 1999. 24.00 (1-887714-39-1) Summerhse Pr.

Rawle, Graham. Diary of Amateur Photographer. LC 99-162330. 128p. 1998. 19.95 (0-670-87775-1) Viking Penguin.

***Rawle, Graham.** Lost Consonants. 2000. pap. 13.95 (1-872180-09-4, Pub. by Fourth Estate) Trafalgar.

— Lost Consonants VI. 2000. pap. 13.95 (1-85702-563-6, Pub. by Fourth Estate) Trafalgar.

— Lost Consonants VII. 2000. pap. 13.95 (1-85702-775-2, Pub. by Fourth Estate) Trafalgar.

Rawle, Graham. Lying Doggo: He Sometimes Tells a Fib. (Illus.). 23p. 1997. pap. 13.95 (0-330-33999-0, Pub. by Macmillan) Trafalgar.

— Wonder Book of Fun. LC 94-228358. 64p. 1994. pap. 11.95 (0-15-600094-6) Harcourt.

Rawle, William. View of the Constitution of the United States of America. LC 70-109548. (American Constitutional & Legal History Ser). 1970. reprint ed. lib. bdg. 39.50 (0-306-71902-9) Da Capo.

Rawle, William H. Practical Treatise on the Law of Covenants for Title. 3rd enl. rev. ed. LC 97-28843. xliii, 832p. 1997. reprint ed. 97.50 (0-8377-2583-6, Rothman) W S Hein.

Rawlence, G. Jane Austen. LC 74-39869. (Jane Austen Ser.: No. 69). 1972. reprint ed. lib. bdg. 75.00 (0-8383-1405-8) M S G Haskell Hse.

Rawles, J. Atrial Fibrillation. (Illus.). xii, 243p. 1991. 129.00 (0-387-19699-4) Spr-Verlag.

***Rawles, James Wesley,.** Patriots: Surviving the Coming Collapse. LC 98-75122. 352p. 1998. pap. 15.99 (1-56384-155-X) Huntington Hse.

Rawles, Jess, ed. The House That Jack Built. (Illus.). 32p. (J). 1994. pap. 3.95 (1-879384-24-8) Cypress Hse.

Rawles, Nancy. Love Like Gumbo. LC 97-31392. (Discoveries Ser.: No. 2). 272p. 1997. pap. 14.00 (0-940242-75-3) Fjord Pr.

Rawles, William A. Centralizing Tendencies in the Administration of Indiana. (Columbia University. Studies in the Social Sciences: No. 44). 1968. reprint ed. 32.50 (0-404-51044-2) AMS Pr.

Rawley, Donald. Duende: Poems. LC 94-22714. 76p. 1994. pap. 13.95 (0-941749-32-0) Black Tie Pr.

— Malibu Stories. LC 91-2465. 68p. (Orig.). 1991. pap. 12.50 (0-941749-23-1) Black Tie Pr.

— Mecca. LC 91-10123. 108p. (Orig.). 1991. pap. 12.50 (0-941749-24-X) Black Tie Pr.

— The Night Bird Cantata. LC 97-44611. 256p. 1998. mass mkt. 23.00 (0-380-97609-9, Avon Bks) Morrow Avon.

— The Night Bird Cantata. 256p. 1999. reprint ed. pap. 12.00 (0-380-79584-1) Morrow Avon.

— Sirens. 76p. (Orig.). 1996. pap. 8.95 (1-882550-21-8) Quiet Lion Pr.

— Slow Dance on Fault Line. LC 98-24480. 240p. 1998. pap. 12.00 (0-380-79959-6, Avon Bks) Morrow Avon.

***Rawley, Donald.** Tina in the Back Seat: Stories, Vol. 1. 160p. 1999. pap. 12.00 (0-380-80723-8, Avon Bks) Morrow Avon.

Rawley, Donald. The View from Babylon: The Notes of a Hollywood Voyeur. LC 98-40034. 224p. 1999. 23.00 (0-446-52411-5, Pub. by Warner Bks) Little.

Rawley, Donald & Ortner, Toni. Steaming. LC 93-19965. 76p. 1993. pap. 12.50 (0-941749-30-4) Black Tie Pr.

Rawley, James A. Abraham Lincoln & a Nation Worth Fighting For. Kraut, Alan M. & Wakelyn, Jon L., eds. (American Biographical History Ser.). 242p. (C). 1996. pap. text 12.95 (0-88295-930-1) Harlan Davidson.

— The Politics of Union: Northern Politics During the Civil War. LC 80-17173. 216p. 1980. reprint ed. pap. 61.60 (0-608-01402-8, 2062165) Bks Demand.

— Secession: The Disruption of the American Republic, 1844-1861. LC 89-2505. (Anvil Ser.). 276p. (Orig.). 1990. pap. 14.50 (0-89464-249-9) Krieger.

— Turning Points of the Civil War (New Edition) LC 89-4873. (Illus.). xvi, 230p. 1989. pap. 9.95 (0-8032-8935-9, Bison Books) U of Nebr Pr.

Rawley, James A., ed. Lincoln & Civil War Politics. LC 77-8812. (American Problem Studies). 136p. 1977. reprint ed. pap. text 10.50 (0-88275-576-5) Krieger.

Rawley, Michael. Book. (Illus.). 128p. 1982. 15.00 (0-938580-00-0) Please Pr.

Rawling, Bill. Surviving Trench Warfare: Technology & the Canadian Corps, 1914-1918. 320p. 1992. text 50.00 (0-8020-5017-4); pap. text 19.95 (0-8020-6002-1) U of Toronto Pr.

Rawling, Eleanor M. & Daugherty, Richard A., eds. Geography into the Twenty-First Century. LC 95-52309. 1996. pap. text 51.00 (0-471-96236-8) Wiley.

Rawlings. Agribusiness & Economics. (Agriculture Ser.). 1997. pap. 48.95 (0-8273-7396-1) Delmar.

Rawlings, C., jt. ed. see Craig, I.

Rawlings, C., jt. ed. see Solomon, E.

Rawlings, C. J., jt. ed. see Bishop, M. J.

Rawlings, Charles A. Electrocardiography: Biophysical Measurements. 129p. (C). 1991. 28.00 (0-9627449-1-3) SpaceLabs.

Rawlings, Chris, jt. ed. see Bishop, Martin.

Rawlings, Christopher, et al, eds. Proceedings of the Third International Conference on Intelligent Systems for Molecular Biology. (Illus.). 512p. (Orig.). 1995. pap. text 50.00 (0-929280-83-0) AAAI Pr.

Rawlings, Douglas E. Biomining: Theory, Microbes & Industrial Processes. LC 97-23624. (Biotechnology Intelligence Unit Ser.). 227p. 1998. 119.00 (1-57059-470-8) Landes Bioscience.

Rawlings, Douglas E., ed. Biomining: Theory, Microbes & Industrial Processes. LC 97-23624. (Biotechnology Intelligence Unit Ser.). (Illus.). 227p. 1997. 112.00 (3-540-63252-2) Spr-Verlag.

Rawlings, Edna I. & Carter, Dianne K. Psychotherapy for Women: Treatment Toward Equality. (Illus.). 500p. 1977. pap. 59.95 (0-398-06338-9); text 74.95 (0-398-03584-9) C C Thomas.

Rawlings, Edna I., et al. Loving to Survive: Sexual Terror, Men's Violence & Women's Lives. LC 94-3057. (Feminist Crosscurrents Ser.). 321p. (C). 1995. pap. text 19.50 (0-8147-3059-0) NYU Pr.

Rawlings, Eleanor H., ed. Audubon's Birds in Color for Decoupage. LC 77-70050. (Pictorial Archive Ser.). (Illus.). 56p. 1977. pap. 4.95 (0-486-23492-4) Dover.

— The Cornucopia of Design & Illustration for Decoupage & Other Arts & Crafts. (Illus.). 160p. (Orig.). 1984. pap. 9.95 (0-486-24486-5) Dover.

— Decoupage: The Big Picture Sourcebook. LC 75-11080. (Pictorial Archive Ser.). (Illus.). 176p. 1975. pap. 11.95 (0-486-23182-8) Dover.

— Godey Costume Plates in Color for Decoupage & Framing. (Illus.). 56p. 1980. pap. 6.95 (0-486-23879-2) Dover.

— One Thousand & One Scrolls, Ornaments & Borders: Ready-to-Use Illustrations for Decoupage & Other Crafts. (Illus.). 128p. 1979. pap. 8.95 (0-486-23795-8) Dover.

Rawlings, Ellen. Deadly Harvest. 1997. mass mkt. 5.99 (0-449-14987-0) Fawcett.

— The Murder Lover. 1997. mass mkt. 5.99 (0-449-14988-9) Fawcett.

Rawlings, Hunter R. The Structure of Thucydides' History. LC 80-8572. 293p. reprint ed. pap. 90.90 (0-8357-7898-3, 203631700002) Bks Demand.

Rawlings, J. Death in the Dark Walk. 1995. mass mkt. 13.95 (0-340-60702-5, Pub. by Hodder & Stought Ltd) Trafalgar.

Rawlings, James B., ed. Dynamics & Control of Chemical Reactors, Distillation Columns & Batch Processes (DYCORD '95) The 4th IFAC Symposium, Copenhagen, Denmark, June 7-9, 1995. (IFAC Postprint Ser.). 512p. 1995. pap. 90.75 (0-08-042368-X, Pergamon Pr) Elsevier.

***Rawlings, John.** Stanford Alpine Club. 200p. 2000. write for info. (1-57586-245-X, Pub. by CSLI) Cambridge U Pr.

Rawlings, John O., et al. Applied Regression Analysis: A Research Tool. 2nd ed. LC 97-48858. (Texts in Statistics Ser.). 672p. (C). 1998. 79.95 (0-387-98454-2) Spr-Verlag.

Rawlings, Kenrick. MCSE Training Guide Internet Explorer 4.0. LC 98-85226. (MCSE Training Guide Ser.). 1998. pap. text 49.99 (1-56205-889-4) New Riders Pub.

Rawlings, Kevin. We Were Marching on Christmas Day: A History & Chronicle of Christmas During the Civil War. LC 96-60897. (Illus.). 167p. 1995. 24.95 (0-9612670-6-2) Toomey Pr.

Rawlings, Louisa. Scarlet Woman. (Historical Ser.). 1993. per. 3.99 (0-373-28794-1, 1-28794-5) Harlequin Bks.

Rawlings, Margaret, tr. see Racine, Jean.

Rawlings, Marjorie Kinnan. Cross Creek. 26.95 (0-8488-0700-6) Amereon Ltd.

— Cross Creek. (Illus.). 384p. 1996. per. 12.00 (0-684-81879-5, Touchstone) S&S Trade Pap.

— Cross Creek Cookery. (Illus.). 256p. 1996. per. 12.00 (0-684-81878-7) S&S Trade.

— Golden Apples. 25.95 (0-8488-0701-4) Amereon Ltd.

— Poems by Marjorie Kinnan Rawlings: Songs of a Housewife. Tarr, Rodger L., ed. LC 96-50245. 288p. 1997. 24.95 (0-8130-1491-3) U Press Fla.

— Short Stories by Marjorie Kinnan Rawlings. Tarr, Rodger L., ed. LC 93-30649. (Illus.). 392p. (C). 1994. 49.95 (0-8130-1252-X); pap. 24.95 (0-8130-1253-8) U Press Fla.

— Sojourner. 24.95 (0-8488-0616-6) Amereon Ltd.

— Sojourner. large type ed. LC 99-10424. 491p. 1999. 25.95 (0-7838-8553-9, G K Hall & Co) Mac Lib Ref.

— The Sojourner. LC 90-27830. 336p. 1991. reprint ed. 34.95 (0-87797-228-1) Cherokee.

— South Moon Under. 25.95 (0-89190-773-4) Amereon Ltd.

— When the Whippoorwill. 23.95 (0-89190-686-X) Amereon Ltd.

— The Yearling. LC 85-40301. (Scribners Illustrated Classics Ser.). (Illus.). 416p. (J). 1985. 27.00 (0-684-18451-3) Scribner.

— The Yearling. 1938. 11.05 (0-606-00109-3, Pub. by Turtleback) Demco.

— The Yearling. annot. ed. LC 86-20743. (Illus.). 428p. (YA). (gr. 7-12). 1988. pap. 5.95 (0-02-044931-3) Aladdin.

— The Yearling. large type ed. LC 94-15061. 559p. 1994. lib. bdg. 22.95 (0-8161-5992-0, G K Hall Lrg Type) Mac Lib Ref.

— The Yearling. 250p. (YA). 1991. reprint ed. lib. bdg. 27.95 (0-89966-841-0) Buccaneer Bks.

Rawlings, Marjorie Kinnan, jt. auth. see Perkins, Maxwell E.

Rawlings, Mary. The Ablemarle of Other Days. (Illus.). 145p. 1997. reprint ed. lib. bdg. 22.50 (0-8328-7180-X) Higginson Bk Co.

Rawlings, Maurice. Life Wish: Reincarnation, Reality or Hoax? LC 81-16763. 157 p. 1981. 4.95 (0-8407-5792-1) Nelson Comm.

Rawlings, Maurice S. Beyond Death's Door. 176p. 1991. mass mkt. 5.99 (0-553-22970-2) Bantam.

— To Hell & Back. 288p. 1996. mass mkt. 5.99 (0-7852-7534-7) Nelson.

Rawlings, Paul. Smoking Gun. 274p. 1998. pap. 14.95 (0-9662562-0-4) Fair Hope Pr.

***Rawlings, Peter.** Americans on Shakespeare, 1776-1914. LC 99-25540. 551p. 1999. text 78.95 (1-84014-644-3, Pub. by Ashgate Pub) Ashgate Pub Co.

Rawlings, Peter, ed. Critical Essays on Henry James. (Critical Thoughts Ser.: Vol. 5). 353p. 1993. 69.95 (0-85967-953-5, Pub. by Scolar Pr) Ashgate Pub Co.

Rawlings, Peter, ed. see James, Henry.

Rawlings, Philip, jt. auth. see Lowry, John.

Rawlings, R. D., jt. auth. see Matthews, F. L.

Rawlings, Richard. Law, Society, & Economy: Centenary Essays for the London School of Economics & Political Science 1895-1995. LC 96-39194. 396p. 1997. text 85.00 (0-19-826228-0) OUP.

Rawlings, Richard, jt. auth. see Harlow, Carol.

Rawlings, Roger. Orphan in the Attic: Photographs by James Baker Hall. (Illus.). 28p. (C). 1995. pap. 12.00 (0-614-13241-X) Univ KY Art Mus.

Rawlings, Romy. Healing Gardens: Aromatherapy - Feng Shui - Holistic Gardening - Herbalism - Color Therapy - Meditation. (Illus.). 176p. 1999. 24.95 (1-57223-208-0, 2080) Willow Creek Pr.

Rawlings, S. G., jt. auth. see Sivia, Deviderjit Singh.

Rawlings, Shirley. Whippets: An Owners Companion. (Illus.). 1992. 39.95 (1-85223-279-X, Pub. by Crowood) Trafalgar.

Rawlings, Stuart, jt. auth. see Wolf, Juri.

Rawlings Sydnor, James, jt. ed. see Batastini, Robert J.

Rawlingson, F. Chinese Ethical Ideals: A Study of the Ethical Values in China's Literary, Social & Religious Life. 1972. lib. bdg. 79.95 (0-87968-551-4) Krishna Pr.

Rawlins. Agribusiness & Economics. (Agriculture Ser.). 1997. teacher ed. 10.00 (0-8273-7397-X) Delmar.

— Broken Country, Vol. 1. 1998. pap. 13.00 (0-8050-3717-9) St Martin.

— Water Slashing on a Rock. 1998. 27.00 (0-8050-5240-2) H Holt & Co.

— Water Splashing on a Rock. 1999. 12.95 (0-8050-5239-9) H Holt & Co.

Rawlins, jt. auth. see Ricketts.

Rawlins, Jack L. Incredible But True. 1998. pap. text 19.95 (0-9664129-0-7) Bell Pub Co.

Rawlins, Bert J. The Parish Churches & Nonconformist Chapels of Wales: Their Records & Where to Find Them Vol. 1: Includes: Cardigan, Carmarthen & Pembroke Counties. (Illus.). 648p. 1987. pap. text 28.95 (0-685-24267-6) Celtic Heritage Pub.

Rawlins, C. L. In Gravity National Park: Poems. LC 98-22256. (Western Literature Ser.). 80p. 1998. pap. 11.00 (0-87417-322-1) U of Nev Pr.

— Sky's Witness. 1995. pap. write for info. (0-8050-3208-8) H Holt & Co.

— Sky's Witness: A Year in Wyoming's Wind River Range. LC 92-8698. 336p. 1995. 23.95 (0-8050-1597-3, J Macrae Bks) H Holt & Co.

Rawlins, C. L., jt. auth. see Dorman, L. S.

Rawlins, Carol. The Colorado River: Lifeline of the Southwest. LC 98-52125. (Watts Library). (Illus.). 63p. (J). (gr. 5-7). 1999. 24.00 (0-531-11738-3) Watts.

— The Grand Canyon. (Wonders of the World Ser.). (Illus.). 64p. (J). (gr. 4-7). 1994. lib. bdg. 25.64 (0-8114-6364-8) Raintree Steck-V.

— The Orinoco River. LC 99-10816. (Watts Library). 1999. 24.00 (0-531-11740-5) Watts.

***Rawlins, Carol.** The Seine River. LC 00-39874. (Illus.). 2001. write for info. (0-531-11853-3) Watts.

***Rawlins, Carol B.** Colorado River. (Watts Library). (Illus.). (J). 2000. pap. 8.95 (0-531-16421-7) Watts.

— Orinoco River. (Watts Library). (Illus.). (J). 2000. pap. 8.95 (0-531-16429-2) Watts.

Rawlins, Clayton. 1472: Active Devices Course Guide. 1998. text 11.41 (1-56870-312-0) RonJon Pub.

***Rawlins, Clive.** William Barclay: The Authorized Biography. (Illus.). 240p. 1998. pap. 16.95 (0-00-628097-8, Pub. by HarpC) Trafalgar.

Rawlins, Debbi. The Bride to Be . . . or Not to Be? (American Romance Ser.). 1998. per. 3.99 (0-373-16730-X, 1-16730-3) Harlequin Bks.

— The Cowboy & the Centerfold. LC 96-3548. (American Romance Ser.). 251p. 1996. per. 3.75 (0-373-16618-4, 1-16618-0) Harlequin Bks.

***Rawlins, Debbi.** Her Mysterious Stranger. (Intrigue Ser.: Bk. 587). 2000. mass mkt. 4.25 (0-373-22587-3, 1-22587-9) Harlequin Bks.

Rawlins, Debbi. His, Hers & Theirs. (American Romance Ser.: Bk. 808). 1999. per. 3.99 (0-373-16808-X, 1-16808-7) Harlequin Bks.

— I Saw Daddy Kissing Santa Claus. (Love & Laughter Ser.: No. 34). 1997. per. 3.50 (0-373-44034-0) Harlequin Bks.

— If Wishes Were . . . Husbands: Three Coins in a Fountain. (American Romance Ser.: Vol. 741). 1998. per. 3.99 (0-373-16741-5, 1-16741-0) Harlequin Bks.

— Love, Marriage & Other Calamities. 1997. per. 3.75 (0-373-16675-3, 1-16675-0) Harlequin Bks.

***Rawlins, Debbi.** Marriage Incorporated. 2000. mass mkt. 4.50 (0-373-82209-X, 1-82209-7) Harlequin Bks.

Rawlins, Debbi. Marriage Incorporated: In Name Only. LC 95-6864. (American Romance Ser.). 249p. 1995. per. 3.50 (0-373-16580-3, 1-16580-3) Harlequin Bks.

— Marry Me, Baby. 1997. per. 3.75 (0-373-16691-5, 1-16691-7) Harlequin Bks.

— The Outlaw & the City Slicker. LC 96-2469. (American Romance Ser.). 249p. 1996. per. 3.75 (0-373-16622-2, 1-16622-2) Harlequin Bks.

— Overnight Father. (American Romance Ser.). 1999. per. 3.99 (0-373-16790-3, 1-16790-7) Harlequin Bks.

— Stud for Hire? (American Romance Ser.: No. 780). 1999. per. 3.99 (0-373-16780-6, 1-16780-8, Harlequin) Harlequin Bks.

Rawlins, Donna, jt. auth. see Snowball, Diane.

Rawlins, Duane. More Than a Father: Breaking down the Barriers to Intimacy. 132p. (Orig.). 1993. pap. 7.99 (1-883002-00-1) Emerald WA.

Rawlins, Duane & Rawlins, LeeAnn. Raising Kids Right in a World Gone Wrong: Helping Your Children Discover & Develop Their Full Potential. 148p. (Orig.). 1995. pap. 7.99 (1-883002-30-3) Emerald WA.

Rawlins, George & Rich, Jillian. Look, Listen & Trust: A Framework for Learning Through Drama. LC 91-51056. 92p. (Orig.). 1992. pap. 17.00 (0-88734-618-9) Players Pr.

Rawlins, Gregory J. Compared to What? An Introduction to the Analysis of Algorithms. LC 91-30850. 536p. (C). 1991. pap. text 59.95 (0-7167-8243-X, Computer Sci Pr) W H Freeman.

— Foundations of Genetic Algorithms. 341p. 1998. text 47.95 (1-55860-170-8) Morgan Kaufmann.

— Moths to the Flame: The Seductions of Computer Technology. LC 96-4729. (Illus.). x, 184p. 1996. 25.00 (0-262-18176-2, Bradford Bks) MIT Pr.

— Moths to the Flame: The Seductions of Computer Technology. (Illus.). 194p. 1997. reprint ed. pap. text 12.50 (0-262-68097-1, Bradford Bks) MIT Pr.

— Slaves of the Machine: The Quickening of Computer Technology. LC 97-4013. (Illus.). 145p. 1997. 25.00 (0-262-18183-5, Bradford Bks) MIT Pr.

— Slaves of the Machine: The Quickening of Computer Technology. (Illus.). 145p. 1998. pap. text 12.00 (0-262-68102-1, Bradford Bks) MIT Pr.

— What? (C). 1993. text 48.00 (0-7167-8279-0) W H Freeman.

Rawlins, Howard. Coming Out of the Fires of Homosexuality & Homophobia. 400p. (Orig.). 1995. pap. 27.95 (0-9648517-0-9) D Richardson.

Rawlins, Jack P. The Writer's Way, 2 vols. 2nd ed. (C). 1991. pap. text, teacher ed. 2.76 (0-395-60157-6) HM.

— The Writer's Way, 3 vols. 3rd ed. (C). 1995. text, teacher ed. 11.96 (0-395-75384-8) HM.

— The Writer's Way, 3 vols. 3rd ed. (C). 1995. pap. text 29.96 (0-395-74533-0) HM.

Rawlins, John C., jt. auth. see Fulton, Stanley R.

R

An Asterisk (*) at the beginning of an entry indicates that the title is appearing for the first time.

***Rawlins, John Clayton & Fulton, Stanley R.** Basic AC Circuits. 2nd ed. LC 00-37957. (Illus.). 2000. pap. 39.95 (0-7506-7173-4, Newnes) Buttrwrth-Heinemann.

***Rawlins, LeeAnn.** Loving for Life: Building a Covenant Marriage. 2nd ed. 1999. pap. 9.95 (1-929125-02-X, Pub. by Loyal Pubng) BookWorld.

Rawlins, LeeAnn, jt. auth. see Rawlins, Duane.

Rawlins, M. D., jt. ed. see Wilkinson, G. R.

***Rawlins, Marla.** Favorite Utah Pioneer Recipes. 128p. 2000. pap. 9.98 (0-88290-684-4) Horizon Utah.

Rawlins, Nancy V. Silent Rain: A Search for the Child Within. 232p. 1993. 14.95 (1-879908-04-2) Milton Pub.

Rawlins, Paul. No Lie Like Love: Stories. LC 96-11960. 1996. 24.95 (0-8203-1868-X) U of Ga Pr.

Rawlins, Richard G. & Kessler, Matt J., eds. The Cayo Santiago Macaques: History, Behavior, & Biology. LC 86-19616. (SUNY Series in Primatology). 306p. (Orig.). (C). 1986. pap. text 24.95 (0-88706-136-2) State U NY Pr.

Rawlins, Ruth P. Comp Package of Rawlins Mental Health-Psychiatric. 3rd ed. 1993. write for info. (0-8016-7359-3) Mosby Inc.

Rawlins, Ruth P., et al, eds. Mental Health - Psychiatric Nursing: A Holistic Life-Cycle Approach. 3rd ed. LC 92-49347. (Illus.). 960p. (C). (gr. 13). 1992. text 57.00 (0-8016-6331-8, 06331) Mosby Inc.

Rawlins, Ruth P. & Heacock, Patricia E. Clinical Manual of Psychiatric Nursing. 2nd ed. LC 92-12910. (Illus.). 416p. (C). (gr. 13). 1992. spiral bd. 35.00 (0-8016-6333-4, 06333) Mosby Inc.

Rawlins, Ruth P., et al. Mental Health-Psychiatric Nursing. 3rd ed. (Illus.). 960p. 1993. teacher ed. write for info. (0-8151-3894-6) Mosby Inc.

Rawlins, Stephen L., ed. see Morgan, Mark & Ess, Dan.

Rawlins, W. H., jt. auth. see Kerruish, C. M.

Rawlins, William K. Friendship Matters: Communication, Dialectics, & the Life Course. (Communication & Social Order Ser.). 320p. 1992. lib. bdg. 51.95 (0-202-30403-5) Aldine de Gruyter.

— Friendship Matters: Communication, Dialectics & the Life Course. (Communication & Social Order Ser.). 320p. 1992. pap. text 25.95 (0-202-30404-3) Aldine de Gruyter.

Rawlins, Winifred. If Flowers of Kindness Bloom: Poems. LC 91-62505. 52p. 1991. pap. 4.50 (0-938875-27-2) Pittenbruach Pr.

— The Inner Islands. (C). 1953. pap. 4.00 (0-87574-073-1) Pendle Hill.

— New Forest of Hope. 45p. 1996. pap. 4.50 (0-938875-35-3) Pittenbruach Pr.

— Occasions for Joy: Poems. LC 95-67768. 49p. 1995. pap. 4.50 (0-938875-34-5) Pittenbruach Pr.

***Rawlinson.** Online Newsgathering. 256p. 2000. 42.95 (0-240-51608-7, Focal) Buttrwrth-Heinemann.

Rawlinson. William Blakes Comic Vision. LC 98-50635. 212p. 1999. text 59.95 (0-312-22064-2) St Martin.

Rawlinson, Andrew, ed. The Book of Enlightened Masters: Western Teachers in Eastern Traditions. LC 97-17135. (Illus.). 670p. (Orig.). 1997. pap. 34.95 (0-8126-9310-8) Open Court.

Rawlinson, David & Tanner, Brian. Financial Management in Local Governments. 2nd ed. (Managing Local Government Ser.). 158p. (Orig.). 1996. pap. 62.50 (0-273-62523-3, Pub. by Pitman Pub) Trans-Atl Phila.

Rawlinson, George. Phoenicia. LC 70-39206. (Select Bibliographies Reprint Ser.). 1977. reprint ed. 30.95 (0-8369-6808-5) Ayer.

— The Religions of the Ancient World. 1996. reprint ed. spiral bd. 15.50 (0-7873-0709-2) Hlth Research.

— The Religions of the Ancient World. 180p. 1996. reprint ed. pap. 14.95 (1-56459-895-0) Kessinger Pub.

Rawlinson, George, tr. Histories. 736p. (Orig.). 1994. reprint ed. pap. text 12.95 (0-460-87170-6, Everyman's Classic Lib) Tuttle Pubng.

Rawlinson, George, tr. see Herodotus.

Rawlinson, H. Site Surveying & Levelling: Level 2. LC 81-8122. (Longman Technician Series, Construction & Civil Engineering). (Illus.). 173p. reprint ed. pap. 53.70 (0-608-17298-7, 203034200068) Bks Demand.

Rawlinson, H. G. Intercourse Between India & the Western World: From the Earliest Times to the Fall of Rome. (C). 1992. 20.00 (81-85565-06-6, Pub. by Uppal Pub Hse) S Asia.

Rawlinson, H. G., ed. see Hall, Basil.

Rawlinson, H. G., ed. see Ovington, J.

Rawlinson, Hugh G. Bactria: The History of a Forgotten Empire. LC 77-93189. reprint ed. 32.50 (0-404-05227-4) AMS Pr.

— Makers of India. LC 77-134126. (Essay Index Reprints - Living Names Ser.). 1977. reprint ed. 15.95 (0-8369-2251-4) Ayer.

Rawlinson, Hugh G., ed. see Hall, Basil.

Rawlinson, Jean, ed. & tr. see Nijinska, Bronislava.

Rawlinson, John L. China's Struggle for Naval Development, 1839-1895. LC 66-10127. (Harvard East Asian Ser.: No. 25). 329p. reprint ed. pap. 102.00 (0-7837-3962-1, 204379100011) Bks Demand.

-Rawlinson, The Recorder & China's Revolution: A Topical Biography of Frank Joseph Rawlinson, 1871-1937, Bk. 1. LC 90-82198. (Church & the World; The West & the Wider World Ser.: Vol. 5 & 6). (Illus.). 350p. 1990. 39.50 (0-940121-12-3, H107) Cross Cultural Pubns.

Of great historical importance to students of the turn-of-the-century events in China, this book was written by the son of one of the most influential missionaries of the time. Editor of a great English-language newspaper intended mostly for missionaries, Frank Joseph Rawlinson was a highly visible & brought significant prominence to his role to the benefit of all the missionaries of the time. The two-book work chronicles his life & work & the effects these had on his two families, both of them committed to the work of the Church in China. Interesting anecdotes from the lives of his several children, both in China & in the United States, make this a delightful & pleasurable work, in spite of its serious nature. It is amply illustrated with photographs of a time & place now surely lost.
Publisher Paid Annotation.

-Rawlinson, The Recorder & China's Revolution: A Topical Biography of Frank Joseph Rawlinson, 1871-1937, Bk. 2. LC 90-82198. (Church & the World; The West & the Wider World Ser.: Vol. 5 & 6). (Illus.). 280p. 1990. pap. 39.50 (0-940121-13-1, H108) Cross Cultural Pubns.

Of great historical importance to students of the turn-of-the-century events in China, this book was written by the son of one of the most influential missionaries of the time. Editor of a great English-language newspaper intended mostly for missionaries, Frank Joseph Rawlinson was a highly visible & brought significant prominence to his role to the benefit of all the missionaries of the time. The two-book work chronicles his life & work & the effects these had on his two families, both of them committed to the work of the Church in China. Interesting anecdotes from the lives of his several children, both in China & in the United States, make this a delightful & pleasurable work, in spite of its serious nature. It is amply illustrated with photographs of a time & place now surely lost.
Publisher Paid Annotation.

Rawlinson, Jon. From Space to Seabed. (Great Adventures Ser.). (Illus.). 32p. (YA). (gr. 4 up). 1988. lib. bdg. 22.60 (0-86592-872-X) Rourke Enter.

— Nuclear Carriers. (Sea Power Library). (Illus.). 48p. (J). (gr. 3-8). 1989. 13.95 (0-685-58646-4) Rourke Corp.

— Titanic. (Great Adventure Ser.). (Illus.). 32p. (J). (gr. 4 up). 1988. lib. bdg. 12.95 (0-685-58290-6) Rourke Corp.

— Titanic. (Great Adventure Ser.). (Illus.). 32p. (J). (gr. 4 up). 1988. lib. bdg. 22.60 (0-86592-873-8) Rourke Enter.

Rawlinson, Jon, jt. auth. see Walmer, Max.

***Rawlinson, Mark.** British Writing of the Second World War. (Oxford English Monographs). 240p. 2000. 60.00 (0-19-818456-5) OUP.

Rawlinson, Michael, jt. auth. see Wells, Peter.

Rawlinson, N. J. F., et al. Tuna Baitfish & the Pole & Line Industry in Kiribati. 1992. pap. 105.00 (1-86320-067-3, Pub. by ACIAR) St Mut.

Rawlinson, Nigel, jt. auth. see Dunn, David C.

Rawlinson, Peter. The Caverel Claim. 224p. 1998. text 21.95 (0-312-19343-2) St Martin.

— Hatred & Contempt. large type ed. 528p. 1995. 27.99 (0-7089-3247-9) Ulverscroft.

— His Brother's Keeper. large type ed. 1995. 27.99 (0-7089-3281-9) Ulverscroft.

***Rawlinson, Peter.** Indictment for Murder: Mystery. LC 99-57114. 256p. 2000. text 22.95 (0-312-25325-7) St Martin.

Rawlinson, Regenia M. From Discipline to Responsibility: Principles for Raising Children Today. LC 97-60034. (Illus.). 112p. 1997. pap. 8.95 (0-932796-79-6) Ed Media Corp.

Rawlinson, Roger. Larzac. 212p. 1999. pap. 30.00 (1-85072-177-7, Pub. by W Sessions) St Mut.

Rawlinson, W. & Cornwell-Kelly, M. P. Essentials of EEC Law. (Waterlow Practitioner's Library). 400p. (Orig.). 1990. pap. 39.95 (0-08-033103-3) Macmillan.

Rawlinson, William & Cornwell-Kelly, M. P. European Community Law. (Waterlow Practitioner's Library). 256p. 1990. 35.95 (0-685-32856-2, Pergamon Pr) Elsevier.

Rawlinson, William & Cornwell-Kelly, Malachy P. European Community Law Vol. 1. 2nd ed. 1994. pap. text 80.00 (0-421-50320-3, Pub. by Sweet & Maxwll) Gaunt.

Rawls, jt. auth. see Madsen, David.

Rawls, Bea O. Drugs & Anger. (Drug Abuse Prevention Library). 64p. (gr. 7-12). 1997. pap. 6.95 (1-56838-173-5, 1765 A) Hazelden.

— Drugs & Anger. LC 94-1906. (Drug Abuse Prevention Library). (Illus.). 64p. (YA). (gr. 7-12). 1994. lib. bdg. 17.95 (0-8239-1706-1) Rosen Group.

Rawls, Bea O. & Johnson, Gwen. Drugs & Where to Turn. Rosen, Ruth C., ed. (Drug Abuse Prevention Library). (Illus.). 64p. (YA). (gr. 7-12). 1993. lib. bdg. 16.95 (0-8239-1466-6) Rosen Group.

Rawls, G. B., ed. Seismic Engineering, 1998: Proceedings, ASME/JSME Joint Pressure Vessels & Piping Conference (1998, San Diego, CA) 364. 468p. 1998. pap. 150.00 (0-7918-1860-8) ASME.

Rawls, G. B., et al, eds. Seismic Engineering, 1997: Proceedings ASME Pressure Vessels & Piping Conference (1997, Orlando, FL) (PVP Ser.: Vol. 345). 269p. 1997. pap. 104.00 (0-7918-1561-7) ASME.

***Rawls, George.** Papa, I Want to Be a Surgeon. LC 99-73385. 140p. 1999. 22.95 (1-57860-032-4) Guild Pr IN.

Rawls, Greg, ed. Computers in Health & Safety. 255p. 1990. 40.00 (0-932627-39-0) Am Indus Hygiene.

Rawls, J. James. California Interpretive History. 6th ed. 544p. (C). 1992. 46.88 (0-07-004269-1) McGraw.

Rawls, James J. California Dreaming: More Stories from Dr. History. (C). 1994. pap. text 19.68 (0-07-052029-1) McGraw.

— Chief Red Fox is Dead. LC 95-80946. (C). 1996. pap. text 21.00 (0-15-501796-9, Pub. by Harcourt Coll Pubs) Harcourt.

— Indians of California: The Changing Image. LC 83-21710. (Illus.). 312p. 1986. pap. 16.95 (0-8061-2020-7) U of Okla Pr.

— Never Turn Back: Father Serra's Mission. Haley, Alex, ed. LC 92-12814. (Stories of America Ser.). (Illus.). 52p. (J). (gr. 2-5). 1993. pap. write for info. (0-8114-8061-5); lib. bdg. 24.26 (0-8114-7221-3) Raintree Steck-V.

— New Directions in California History: A Book of Readings. 399p. (C). 1988. pap. 34.06 (0-07-051253-1) McGraw.

Rawls, James J. & Bean, Walton. California: An Interpretive History. 7th ed. LC 96-40054. 600p. (C). 1997. pap. 45.94 (0-07-052411-4) McGraw.

Rawls, James J., et al. A Golden State: Mining & Economic Development in California. LC 98-26238. (California History Sesquicentennial Ser.). 335p. 1999. 50.00 (0-520-21770-5, Pub. by U CA Pr); pap. 24.95 (0-520-21771-3, Pub. by U CA Pr) Cal Prin Full Svc.

Rawls, James J., ed. see Egger-Bovet, Howard & Smith-Baranzini, Marlene.

Rawls, Jim. Dame Shirley & the Gold Rush. Haley, Alex, ed. LC 92-18083. (Stories of America Ser.). (Illus.). 55p. (J). (gr. 2-5). 1993. lib. bdg. 24.26 (0-8114-7222-1) Raintree Steck-V.

— Dame Shirley & the Gold Rush. Haley, Alex, ed. LC 92-18083. (Stories of America Ser.). (Illus.). 55p. (J). (gr. 4-7). 1993. pap. 4.95 (0-8114-8062-3) Raintree Steck-V.

— Dr. History's Whiz Bang: Favorite Stories of California's Past. LC 91-27640. (Illus.). 118p. (Orig.). 1991. pap. 9.95 (0-935382-77-1) WBE.

— DR History's Sampler: More Stories of California's Past. (C). 1994. pap. text 17.81 (0-07-051482-8) McGraw.

Rawls, John. Collected Papers. LC 98-55932. 1999. 39.95 (0-674-13739-6) HUP.

— Justice As Fairness. (Reprints in Philosophy Ser.). (C). 1991. reprint ed. pap. text 2.50 (0-8290-2600-2, F-174) Irvington.

— The Law of Peoples. LC 99-34785. 180p. 1999. 22.50 (0-674-00079-X) HUP.

***Rawls, John.** Lectures on the History of Moral Philosophy. (Illus.). 416p. 2000. 45.00 (0-674-00296-2); pap. 19.95 (0-674-00442-6) HUP.

Rawls, John. Political Liberalism. 401p. (C). 1993. 46.50 (0-231-05248-0) Col U Pr.

— Political Liberalism. 401p. 1996. pap. 18.00 (0-231-05249-9) Col U Pr.

— Theory of Justice. LC 73-168432. (Illus.). 607p. 1971. 38.00 (0-674-88010-2); pap. text 21.00 (0-674-88014-5) Belknap Pr.

— Theory of Justice. rev. ed. LC 99-29110. 986p. 1999. pap. text 22.00 (0-674-00078-1) HUP.

***Rawls, John.** A Theory of Justice. rev. ed. LC 99-29110. 986p. 1999. 45.00 (0-674-00077-3) HUP.

Rawls, John. Two Concepts of Rules. (Reprints in Philosophy Ser.). (C). 1991. reprint ed. pap. text 5.00 (0-8290-2601-0) Irvington.

Rawls, Joyce. Soul Survival: Poetic Inspirations about Love, Life & Family Values. LC 96-92625. 71p. (Orig.). 1997. pap. 10.00 (0-9652317-0-4) J R Prods.

Rawls, Loyd H. Seeking Succession: How to Continue the Family Business Legacy. 1999. 34.95 (0-9663801-9-3); pap. 19.95 (0-9663801-8-5) Horizon Busn.

Rawls, Lucia, jt. auth. see Long, David E.

Rawls, Rod R. & Hagen, Mark A. AutoLISP Programming: Principles & Techniques. LC 97-13891. 1997. 37.28 (1-56637-417-0) Goodheart.

Rawls, Rod R., jt. auth. see Madsen, David A.

Rawls, S. C. The Redneck Instruction Book. LC 96-16301. (Illus.). 96p. (Orig.). 1996. pap. 4.95 (1-56554-176-6) Pelican.

Rawls, Sam. How to Speak Fishing: or How to Ruin a Perfectly Good Marriage. LC 97-189985. (Illus.). 128p. (Orig.). 1997. pap. 4.95 (1-888952-59-8) Cumberland Hse.

Rawls, Walter C., Jr., jt. auth. see Davis, Albert R.

Rawls, Walton. Disney Dons Dogtags: The Best of Disney Military Insignia from World War II. (Illus.). 96p. 1992. 9.98 (1-55859-401-9) Abbeville Pr.

— The Great Book of Currier & Ives' America. (Illus.). 488p. 1996. 85.00 (0-89659-070-4); pap. 11.95 (1-55859-229-6) Abbeville Pr.

Rawls, Wilson. Summer of the Monkeys. 288p. (J). 1998. pap. 5.50 (0-440-41580-2) BDD Bks Young Read.

— Summer of the Monkeys. 304p. (J). (gr. 4-7). 1992. mass mkt. 5.99 (0-553-29818-6) Bantam.

— Summer of the Monkeys. LC 75-32295. 240p. (YA). 1989. 15.95 (0-385-11450-8) Doubleday.

— Summer of the Monkeys. (Bantam Starfire Bks.). (J). 1992. 10.60 (0-606-00432-7, Pub. by Turtleback) Demco.

— Where the Red Fern Grows. LC 61-9201. 208p. (YA). (gr. 4-7). 1996. 16.95 (0-385-32330-1, Delacorte Pr Bks) BDD Bks Young Read.

— Where the Red Fern Grows. LC 87-14334. 256p. (J). (gr. 4-7). 1984. mass mkt. 5.99 (0-553-27429-5) Bantam.

— Where the Red Fern Grows. LC 87-14334. (Illus.). 208p. (J). (gr. 4-7). 1996. pap. 5.99 (0-440-41267-6) Dell.

Rawls, Wilson. Where the Red Fern Grows. 249p. (YA). (gr. 5 up). pap. 5.99 (0-8072-1467-1); pap. 5.99 (0-8072-1358-6) Listening Lib.

— Where the Red Fern Grows. LC 99-33703. (Masterpiece Series Access Editions). (J). 1999. write for info. (0-8219-1987-3) Paradigm MN.

— Where the Red Fern Grows. (YA). (gr. 4-7). 2000. mass mkt. 2.99 (0-375-80681-4, Pub. by Random Bks Yng Read) Random.

Rawls, Wilson. Where the Red Fern Grows: The Story of Two Dogs & a Boy. (Bantam Starfire Bks.). (J). 1974. 10.60 (0-606-00108-5, Pub. by Turtleback) Demco.

— Where the Red Fern Grows: The Story of Two Dogs & a Boy. (J). 1996. 10.60 (0-606-10972-2, Pub. by Turtleback) Demco.

Rawlyk, G. A. Is Jesus Your Personal Saviour? In Search of Canadian Evangelicalism in the 1990s. 248p. 1996. pap. 22.95 (0-7735-1412-0) McG-Queens Univ Pr.

— Is Jesus Your Personal Saviour? In Search of Canadian Evangelicalism in the 1990s. 248p. 1996. 60.00 (0-7735-1411-2) McG-Queens Univ Pr.

Rawlyk, G. A., ed. Aspects of the Canadian Evangelical Experience. (McGill-Queen's Studies in the History of Religion Ser.). 568p. 1997. 60.00 (0-7735-1547-X, Pub. by McG-Queens Univ Pr) CUP Services.

Rawlyk, G. A., jt. ed. see Scobie, Charles H.

Rawlyk, George, jt. auth. see Downie, Mary A.

Rawlyk, George A. The Canada Fire: Radical Evangelicalism in British North America, 1775-1812. (Illus.). 264p. 1994. 65.00 (0-7735-1221-7, Pub. by McG-Queens Univ Pr); pap. 24.95 (0-7735-1277-2, Pub. by McG-Queens Univ Pr) CUP Services.

— Champions of the Truth: Fundamentalism, Modernism & the Maritime Baptists. 136p. (C). 1990. 60.00 (0-7735-0760-4, Pub. by McG-Queens Univ Pr); pap. 24.95 (0-7735-0783-3, Pub. by McG-Queens Univ Pr) CUP Services.

— Is Jesus Your Personal Saviour? In Search of Canadian Evangelicalism in the 1990s. 239p. 1996. pap. 19.95 (0-614-29718-4, Pub. by McG-Queens Univ Pr) CUP Services.

— Nova Scotia's Massachusetts: A Study of Massachusetts - Nova Scotia Relations, 1630 to 1784. (Illus.). 256p. (C). 1973. 49.95 (0-7735-0142-8, Pub. by McG-Queens Univ Pr) CUP Services.

— Ravished by the Spirit: Religious Revivals, Baptists, & Henry Alline. 192p. 1984. 60.00 (0-7735-0439-7, Pub. by McG-Queens Univ Pr); pap. 24.95 (0-7735-0440-0, Pub. by McG-Queens Univ Pr) CUP Services.

— Wrapped up in God: A Study of Several Canadian Revivals & Revivalists. 184p. 1993. pap. 24.95 (0-7735-1131-8, Pub. by McG-Queens Univ Pr) CUP Services.

Rawlyk, George A., ed. Canadian Baptists & Christian Higher Education. 144p. (C). 1988. text 60.00 (0-7735-0677-2, Pub. by McG-Queens Univ Pr); pap. text 24.95 (0-7735-0684-5, Pub. by McG-Queens Univ Pr) CUP Services.

— The Canadian Protestant Experience, 1760-1990. 256p. 1993. pap. 22.95 (0-7735-1132-6, Pub. by McG-Queens Univ Pr) CUP Services.

— Henry Alline: Selected Writings. (Sources of American Spirituality Ser.: Vol. 8). 384p. 1987. 19.95 (0-8091-0396-6) Paulist Pr.

Rawlyk, George A. & Noll, Mark A., eds. Amazing Grace: Evangelicalism in Australia, Britain, Canada & the United States. (McGill-Queen's Studies in the History of Religion Ser.). 416p. (C). 1994. 65.00 (0-7735-1207-1, Pub. by McG-Queens Univ Pr); pap. text 24.95 (0-7735-1214-4, Pub. by McG-Queens Univ Pr) CUP Services.

Rawn, jt. auth. see Kask.

Rawn, J. David, jt. auth. see Kask, Uno.

Rawn, Melanie. Diviner. 688p. 1998. pap. 24.95 (0-88677-765-8, Pub. by DAW Bks) Penguin Putnam.

— Dragon Prince. (Dragon Prince Ser.: No. 1). 576p. 1988. reprint ed. mass mkt. 6.99 (0-88677-450-0, Pub. by DAW Bks) Penguin Putnam.

— The Dragon Token. (Dragon Star Ser.: Bk. 2). 656p. 1993. mass mkt. 6.99 (0-88677-542-6, Pub. by DAW Bks) Penguin Putnam.

***Rawn, Melanie.** The Golden Key. 2000. mass mkt. 7.99 (0-88677-899-9, Pub. by DAW Bks) Penguin Putnam.

Rawn, Melanie. Knights of the Morningstar. (Quantum Leap Ser.: No. 4). 1996. mass mkt. 5.99 (1-57297-171-1) Blvd Books.

— The Mageborn Traitor. LC 97-143884. 688p. 1997. pap. 23.95 (0-88677-730-5, Pub. by DAW Bks) Penguin Putnam.

— The Mageborn Traitor: Exiles, Vol. 2. Vol. 2. 842p. 1998. pap. 6.99 (0-88677-731-3, Pub. by DAW Bks) Penguin Putnam.

— The Ruins of Ambrai, Vol. 1. 480p. 1994. 20.95 (0-88677-619-8, Pub. by DAW Bks) Penguin Putnam.

— The Ruins of Ambrai, Vol. 1. 656p. 1995. mass mkt. 6.99 (0-88677-668-6, Pub. by DAW Bks) Penguin Putnam.

— Skybowl. (Dragon Star Ser.: Bk. 3). 776p. 1994. mass mkt. 6.99 (0-88677-595-7, Pub. by DAW Bks) Penguin Putnam.

— The Star Scroll. (Dragon Prince Ser.: Bk. 2). 592p. 1989. reprint ed. mass mkt. 6.99 (0-88677-349-0, Pub. by DAW Bks) Penguin Putnam.

— Stronghold. (Dragon Star Ser.: Bk. 1). 592p. 1991. mass mkt. 6.99 (0-88677-482-9, Pub. by DAW Bks) Penguin Putnam.

— Sunrunner's Fire. (Dragon Prince Ser.: Bk. 3). 480p. 1990. mass mkt. 6.99 (0-88677-403-9, Pub. by DAW Bks) Penguin Putnam.

Rawn, Melanie, et al. The Golden Key. LC 96-228052. 688p. 1996. pap. 24.95 (0-88677-691-0, Pub. by DAW Bks) Penguin Putnam.

— The Golden Key. 800p. 1997. mass mkt. 6.99 (*0-88677-746-1*, Pub. by DAW Bks) Penguin Putnam.

Rawnsley, Allan, ed. A Manual of Industrial Marketing Research: Prepared under the Auspices of the Industrial Marketing Research Association. LC 77-7272. (Illus.). 206p. reprint ed. pap. 63.90 (*0-8357-3082-4*, 2039339000l2) Bks Demand.

Rawnsley, Ellis. Roses. (Illus.). 48p. 1984. 22.00 (*0-88014-070-4*) Mosaic Pr OH.

***Rawnsley, Gary D.** Taiwan's Informal Diplomacy & Propoganda. LC 99-43350. (Studies in Diplomacy). 2000. text 65.00 (*0-312-22932-1*) St Martin.

Rawnsley, H. Memories of Tennysons. LC 72-675. (Studies in Tennyson: No. 27). 1972. reprint ed. lib. bdg. 75.00 (*0-8383-1417-1*) M S G Haskell Hse.

Rawnsley, Howard M., jt. auth. see Mitruka, Brij M.

Rawnsley, J., jt. auth. see Robinson, P.

Rawnsley, J. H., jt. auth. see Burstall, F. E.

Raworth, Jenny & Berry, Susan. Decorating with Flowers: Flowers for Every Occasion & Season. (Illus.). 128p. 1999. 24.95 (*1-85585-460-0*, Pub. by Collins & Br) Sterling.

Raworth, Jenny & Bradley, Val. The Complete Guide to Indoor Gardening. (Illus.). 192p. 1998. 29.95 (*0-7892-0349-9*) Abbeville Pr.

Raworth, Philip. The Legislative Process in the European Community. LC 93-7393. 1993. 68.00 (*90-6544-690-7*) Kluwer Law Intl.

Raworth, Philip, ed. Constitutions of Dependencies & Territories, 11 vols. LC 75-21651. 1975. ring bd. 695.00 (*0-379-00278-7*) Oceana.

Raworth, Philip M., ed. European Union Law Guide, 6 vols. 1994. ring bd. 795.00 (*0-379-10175-0*) Oceana.

— International Regulation of Trade in Services, 4 vols. LC 96-89650. 1996. ring bd. 450.00 (*0-379-00842-4*) Oceana.

Raworth, Tom. Clean & Well Lit: Selected Poems 1987-1995. LC 96-67835. (Roof Bks.). (Illus.). 112p. (Orig.). 1996. pap. 10.95 (*0-937804-64-9*) Segue NYC.

— Eternal Sections. (Sun & Moon Classics Ser.: No. 23). 64p. (Orig.). 1992. pap. 9.95 (*1-55713-129-5*) Sun & Moon CA.

— Meadow. LC 99-19058. 41p. 1999. pap. 7.00 (*0-942996-34-8*, Pub. by Post Apollo Pr) SPD-Small Pr Dist.

***Raworth, Tom.** Tottering State: Selected Early Poems 1963-1983. 240p. 2000. pap. 15.00 (*1-882022-38-6*, Pub. by O Bks) SPD-Small Pr Dist.

Raworth, Tom. Visible Shivers. LC 87-90687. 88p. 1987. 8.00 (*0-917585-15-1*) O Bks.

Rawski, Conrad H., tr. see Petrarca, Francesco.

Rawski, Evelyn S. Agricultural Change & the Peasant Economy of South China. LC 77-173407. (Harvard East Asian Ser.: No. 66). 300p. reprint ed. pap. 93.00 (*0-7837-1525-0*, 204180200024) Bks Demand.

Rawski, Evelyn S., jt. auth. see Naquin, Susan.

Rawski, Evelyn S., jt. ed. see MacLeod, Murdo J.

Rawski, Evelyn S., jt. ed. see Watson, James L.

Rawski, Thomas G. China's Transition to Industrialism: Producer Goods & Economic Development in the Twentieth Century. (Studies on China). (Illus.). 226p. 1980. text 37.50 (*0-472-08755-X*, 08755) U of Mich Pr.

Rawski, Thomas G. & Li, Lillian M., eds. Chinese History in Economic Perspective. (Studies on China: Vol. 13). (C). 1992. 55.00 (*0-520-07068-2*, Pub. by U CA Pr) Cal Prin Full Svc.

Rawski, Thomas G., et al. Economics & the Historian. LC 94-24931. (Illus.). 304p. 1996. 50.00 (*0-520-07268-5*, Pub. by U CA Pr); pap. 18.95 (*0-520-07269-3*, Pub. by U CA Pr) Cal Prin Full Svc.

Rawson & Rowan-Kedge. Sporting Cookbook. 29.95 (*0-948253-35-5*) Sportsmans Pr.

Rawson, Barbara E. History of the Town of Cornish, with Genealogical Record, 1910-1960 Vol. III: Supplemental Narrative & Genealogy. (Illus.). 207p. 1998. reprint ed. lib. bdg. 29.50 (*0-8328-9714-0*) Higginson Bk Co.

Rawson, Beryl, ed. The Family in Ancient Rome: New Perspectives. LC 85-18976. 280p. (C). 1986. pap. text 16.95 (*0-8014-9460-5*) Cornell U Pr.

— Marriage, Divorce, & Children in Ancient Rome. (Illus.). 266p. (C). 1996. pap. text 32.00 (*0-19-815045-8*) OUP.

Rawson, Beryl & Weaver, Paul, eds. The Roman Family in Italy: Status, Sentiment, Space. LC 96-45146. (OUP/Humanities Research Centre of the Australian National University Ser.). (Illus.). 394p. (C). 1997. text 85.00 (*0-19-815052-0*) OUP.

— The Roman Family in Italy: Status, Sentiment, Space. 400p. 1999. pap. 35.00 (*0-19-815283-3*) OUP.

Rawson, Christopher. Disguise & Make-Up. (Spy Guides Ser.). (J). (gr. 3-6). 1979. pap. 4.50 (*0-86020-166-X*, Usborne) EDC.

— How Machines Work. (Children's World Ser.). (Illus.). 48p. (J). (gr. 2-5). 1976. pap. 8.95 (*0-86020-197-X*) EDC.

Rawson, Christopher & Hindley, Judy. How Your Body Works. (Children's World Ser.). 48p. (J). (gr. 2 up). 1995. pap. 7.95 (*0-7460-2300-6*, Usborne); lib. bdg. 16.95 (*0-88110-775-1*, Usborne) EDC.

Rawson, Christopher, jt. auth. see Spector, Joanna.

Rawson, Claude. Gulliver & the Gentle Reader: Studies in Swift & Our Time. LC 91-16181. 208p. (C). 1991. pap. 18.50 (*0-391-03710-2*) Humanities.

— Henry Fielding & the Augustan Ideal under Stress. LC 91-16182. 288p. (C). 1991. pap. 19.95 (*0-391-03711-0*) Humanities.

— Order from Confusion Sprung: Studies in Eighteenth-Century Literature from Swift to Cowper. LC 92-5336. 448p. (C). 1992. reprint ed. pap. 25.00 (*0-391-03745-5*) Humanities.

— Order from Confusion Sprung: Studies in 18th Century Literature from Swift to Cowper. 272p. 1985. text 19.95 (*0-04-800019-1*) Routledge.

***Rawson, Claude.** Satire & Sentiment, 1660-1830: Stress Points in the English Augustan Tradition. LC 99-68561. 328p. 2000. pap. 19.00 (*0-300-07916-8*) Yale U Pr.

Rawson, Claude, ed. The Character of Swift's Satire: A Revised Focus. LC 81-72062. 344p. 1983. 45.00 (*0-87413-209-6*) U Delaware Pr.

— Jonathan Swift: A Collections of Critical Essays. LC 94-4782. (New Century Views Ser.). 307p. (C). 1994. pap. text 12.95 (*0-13-091299-9*) P-H.

Rawson, Claude & Lock, F. P., eds. Collected Poems of Thomas Parnell. LC 85-41023. (Illus.). 720p. 1989. 89.50 (*0-87413-154-5*) U Delaware Pr.

Rawson, Claude, ed. see Ashton, Rosemary.

Rawson, Claude, ed. see Batchelor, John Calvin.

Rawson, Claude, ed. see Byrd, Max.

Rawson, Claude, ed. see Dickens, Charles.

Rawson, Claude, ed. see Gray, Richard.

Rawson, Claude, ed. see Makin, Peter.

Rawson, Claude, jt. ed. see Nisbet, H. B.

Rawson, Claude, ed. see Riley, E. C.

Rawson, Claude, ed. see Sutherland, John.

Rawson, Claude, ed. see Turner, Paul D.

Rawson, Claude, ed. see Williams, John R.

Rawson, Clayton. Death from a Top Hat. 288p. 1986. pap. 4.95 (*0-930330-44-7*) Intl Polygonics.

— The Footprints on the Ceiling. 256p. 1987. pap. 4.95 (*0-930330-45-5*) Intl Polygonics.

— The Headless Lady. (Library of Crime Classics). 224p. 1987. pap. 4.95 (*0-930330-60-9*) Intl Polygonics.

— No Coffin for the Corpse. LC 87-82444. 254p. 1987. reprint ed. pap. 4.95 (*0-930330-74-9*) Intl Polygonics.

Rawson, David. Murder on Mount Desert. LC 95-34706. 304p. 1996. pap. 15.95 (*0-89272-363-7*) Down East.

Rawson, Don C. Russian Rightists & the Revolution of Nineteen Hundred Five. LC 94-8850. (Russian, Soviet & Post-Soviet Studies: No. 95). (Illus.). 302p. (C). 1995. text 85.00 (*0-521-46487-0*) Cambridge U Pr.

Rawson, Elizabeth. Intellectual Life in the Late Roman Repulic. LC 85-9819. 365p. 1985. reprint ed. pap. 113.20 (*0-608-03743-5*, 206456800009) Bks Demand.

— Roman Culture & Society: Collected Papers. (Illus.). 626p. 1991. text 175.00 (*0-19-814752-X*, 12235) OUP.

— The Spartan Tradition in European Thought. (Illus.). 400p. 1991. pap. text 39.95 (*0-19-814733-3*) OUP.

Rawson, Elizabeth, ed. Cicero: A Portrait. (Bristol Classical Paperbacks Ser.). 368p. 1994. pap. 31.95 (*0-86292-051-5*, Pub. by Brist Class Pr) Focus Pub-R Pullins.

Rawson, Eric G., ed. Selected Papers on Fiber Optic Local Area Networks. LC 93-42627. (Milestone Ser.: Vol. 91). 1994. pap. 45.00 (*0-8194-1502-2*) SPIE.

— Selected Papers on Fiber Optic Local Area Networks. LC 93-42627. (Milestone Ser.: Vol. 91/HC). 1994. 45.00 (*0-8194-1503-0*) SPIE.

Rawson, F. L. Treatment, or Healing by True Prayer. 353p. 1998. reprint ed. pap. 24.95 (*0-7661-0336-6*) Kessinger Pub.

Rawson, Gertrude E. Strawberries & Rhymes. Kreider, Rayma B. & Irwin, Jane B., eds. (Illus.). 180p. (Orig.). 1996. pap. write for info. (*0-9652212-0-2*) R & J Beebe.

Rawson, Gloria & Callinan, David. The Ten Minute Miracle: The Quick Fix Survival Guide for Mind & Body. 192p. 1999. 8.00 (*0-7225-3658-5*) Thorsons PA.

Rawson, H. Glasses & Their Applications. 174p. 1991. 70.00 (*0-901462-89-6*, Pub. by Inst Materials) Ashgate Pub Co.

Rawson, Hugh. New Signet World Atlas. rev. ed. (C). 1998. mass mkt. 8.99 (*0-451-19732-1*) NAL.

— Unwritten Laws. 304p. 1998. pap. 14.00 (*0-609-80304-2*) Crown Pub Group.

Rawson, Hugh N., ed. The New International Dictionary of Quotations. 2nd ed. 562p. 1994. mass mkt. 6.99 (*0-451-17597-2*, Sig) NAL.

Rawson, Hugh N. & Miner, Margaret, eds. The American Heritage Dictionary of American Quotations. 1999. mass mkt. 7.99 (*0-451-18011-9*, Sig) NAL.

Rawson, J. On Reflection. (C). 1990. 39.00 (*0-7223-2568-1*, Pub. by A H S Ltd) St Mut.

Rawson, J., ed. see Silone, Ignazio.

Rawson, Jessica. Chinese Jade Thru the Ages. (Illus.). 152p. 1975. pap. 25.00 (*0-87556-754-1*) Saifer.

Rawson, Jessica, ed. The British Museum Book of Chinese Art. LC 92-61337. (Illus.). 396p. 1996. reprint ed. pap. 24.95 (*0-500-27903-9*, Pub. by Thames Hudson) Norton.

Rawson, Joanna. Quarry. LC 98-25468. (Pitt Poetry Ser.). 48p. 1998. pap. 12.95 (*0-8229-5681-0*); text 25.00 (*0-8229-4081-7*) U of Pittsburgh Pr.

Rawson-Jones, Keith, jt. ed. see Nazarenko, Alla L.

Rawson, Judie. Fowl Play, 1. 1998. pap. text 9.95 (*0-9665323-3-3*) A Wldn Kent.

Rawson, Judith A., tr. see Machiavelli, Niccolo.

Rawson, Kenneth, ed. Carriage of Bulk Oil & Chemicals at Sea. 116p. 1994. pap. 30.00 (*0-85295-318-6*, 9CH105) Gulf Pub.

***Rawson, M. Jean & Kocal, Annette.** A Manual of Special Education Law for Educators & Parents. 150p. 2000. pap. 17.95 (*0-9676206-0-0*) Morgen Pubg Inc.

Rawson, Margaret B. Many Faces of Dyslexia. 270p. 1992. pap. 18.50 (*0-89214-003-8*) Intl Dyslexia.

Rawson, Marion, tr. see Lussu, Emilio.

Rawson, Martyn, jt. auth. see Clouder, Christopher.

Rawson, P. F., ed. see International Symposium on the Boreal Lower Cretac.

Rawson, P. F., tr. see Cope, J. C., et al, eds.

Rawson, Pam, jt. auth. see Lilburn, Pat.

Rawson, Peter F., jt. ed. see Culver, Stephen J.

Rawson, Philip. Ceramics. LC 83-12480. (Illus.). 203p. 1984. reprint ed. pap. 18.95 (*0-8122-1156-1*) U of Pa Pr.

— Drawing. 2nd ed. LC 87-10929. (Illus.). 336p. 1987. reprint ed. pap. text 21.95 (*0-8122-1251-7*) U of Pa Pr.

— Sacred Tibet. LC 90-70359. (Art & Imagination Ser.). (Illus.). 96p. 1991. pap. 15.95 (*0-500-81032-X*, Pub. by Thames Hudson) Norton.

— Tantra: The Indian Cult of Ecstasy. (Art & Imagination Ser.). (Illus.). 1984. pap. 15.95 (*0-500-81001-X*, Pub. by Thames Hudson) Norton.

Rawson, Philip & Legeza, Laszlo. Tao: The Chinese Philosophy of Time & Change. (Art & Imagination Ser.). (Illus.). 1984. pap. 15.95 (*0-500-81002-8*, Pub. by Thames Hudson) Norton.

Rawson, Philip S. The Art of Southeast Asia: Cambodia, Vietnam, Thailand, Laos, Burma, Java & Bali. LC 89-52204. (World of Art Ser.). (Illus.). 252p. 1990. pap. 14.95 (*0-500-20060-2*, Pub. by Thames Hudson) Norton.

— Art of Tantra. (World of Art Ser.). (Illus.). 216p. 1985. pap. 14.95 (*0-500-20166-8*, Pub. by Thames Hudson) Norton.

— Sculpture. LC 96-28432. (Illus.). 162p. 1997. 29.95 (*0-8122-8258-2*) U of Pa Pr.

***Rawson, Richard A. & Urban, Rose M., eds.** Treatment for Stimulant Use Disorders. 226p. (C). 2000. pap. text 40.00 (*0-7881-8902-6*) DIANE Pub.

Rawson, Ruth. Acting. LC 68-21664. (Theatre Student Ser.). (Illus.). (YA). (gr. 7-12). 1970. lib. bdg. 14.95 (*0-8239-0151-3*) Rosen Group.

Rawson-Wade, Henry W. Towards Administrative Justice. LC 63-9896. (Michigan Legal Publications). vii, 138p. 1985. reprint ed. lib. bdg. 35.00 (*0-89941-390-0*, 303600) W S Hein.

Rawsthorne, A., tr. see Davalo, Eric & Naim, Patrick.

Rawstron, D. D., ed. Rights of Children. (C). 1989. 39.00 (*0-903534-35-5*, Pub. by Brit Ag for Adopt & Fost) St Mut.

Rawstron, D. D. & Cullen, D. Child Care Law: A Summary of the Law in England & Wales. (C). 1989. 60.00 (*0-903534-64-9*, Pub. by Brit Ag for Adopt & Fost) St Mut.

Rawtiu, Tudor S., jt. auth. see Marsden, Jerrold E.

***RawVision Publishing Staff, ed.** Raw Vision, Vol. 29. (Illus.). 2000. pap. 12.00 (*1-56466-074-5*) Archer Fields.

Ray. Alvah & Arvilla. (J). 1997. pap. 6.00 (*0-15-201547-7*, Harcourt Child Bks) Harcourt.

— Communication & Disenfranchisement & Case Studies in Communication & Disenfranchisement. 1996. pap. 49.95 (*0-8058-2507-X*) L Erlbaum Assocs.

— Computer Education Administration. 1991. teacher ed. 37.81 (*0-07-051258-2*) McGraw.

— Cpsq Handbook Public Speaking. 4th ed. 1998. pap. text 8.74 (*0-07-230541-X*) McGraw.

— Drugs. 7th ed. 1996. teacher ed. 28.12 (*0-8151-7301-6*) Mosby Inc.

***Ray.** Drugs & Social Human Behaviour. 8th ed. 1999. 8.00 (*0-07-236102-6*) McGraw.

Ray. Drugs, Society & Human Behavior. 9th ed. 2001. 37.33 (*0-07-231963-1*) McGraw.

— Facilitative Leader. LC 98-40499. 173p. 1998. pap. text 32.20 (*0-13-895228-0*) P-H.

— Focus on Phytochemical Pesticides, Vol. II. 1992. 99.50 (*0-8493-4102-7*, CRC Reprint) Franklin.

— Ghana. (Marxist Regimes Ser.). 212p. 1988. text 49.00 (*0-86187-475-7*); pap. text 17.50 (*0-86187-476-5*) St Martin.

— Methods Toward a Science: Behavior & Experiment. (Psychology Ser.). 1981. 6.25 (*0-534-01012-1*) Brooks-Cole.

— Methods Toward Scientific Behavior & Explanation. 4th ed. (Psychology Ser.). 1992. pap., student ed., wbk. ed. 20.00 (*0-534-17840-5*) Brooks-Cole.

Ray & Lainiotis, Dmitri G., eds. Distributed Parameter Systems: Identification, Estimation & Control. (Control & Systems Theory Ser.: Vol. 6). 616p. 1978. text 220.00 (*0-8247-6601-6*) Dekker.

Ray, et al. Office Automation: A System Approach. 3rd ed. 672p. boxed set 91.95 (*0-538-71048-9*); boxed set 91.95 (*0-538-71049-7*) S-W Pub.

Ray, A. & Velusamy, R., eds. Supernovae & Stellar Evolution: Proceedings of the School & Workshop, Goa, Indian, 10-17 March 1989. 340p. (C). 1991. text 104.00 (*981-02-0657-7*) World Scientific Pub.

Ray, A. B. Students & Politics in India. 232p. 1977. 15.95 (*0-318-36618-5*) Asia Bk Corp.

Ray, A. K. Widows Are Not for Burning. 1985. 24.95 (*0-318-37316-5*) Asia Bk Corp.

Ray, A. K., jt. auth. see Dutt, R.

Ray, A. S. An Outline of Indian Culture. 112p. 1978. 8.95 (*0-318-36962-1*) Asia Bk Corp.

Ray, Acharya P., jt. ed. see Ray, Priyadaranjian.

Ray, Alan, jt. auth. see Butler, Daniel.

Ray, Aletha B. Defining Your Destiny Vol. I: A Spiritual Guide to Wholeness. 80p. 1996. pap. 13.95 (*0-9655114-0-5*); audio 13.95 (*0-9655114-1-3*) Defining Your Destiny.

Ray, Alvin, jt. auth. see Burger, Kenneth.

Ray, Alvin E., jt. auth. see Burger, Kenneth A.

Ray, Amalendu. Calcutta: An Annotated Bibliography. 1990. 17.50 (*0-8364-2626-6*, Pub. by Asiatic Bk Agency) S Asia.

Ray, Amitava, tr. see Sayeed, Ayyub A.

Ray, Anandarup. Cost-Benefit Analysis: Issues & Methodologies. LC 83-49367. 176p. 1984. pap. text 16.95 (*0-8018-3069-9*) Johns Hopkins.

— Cost-Benefit Analysis: Issues & Methodologies. LC 83-49367. 166p. reprint ed. pap. 51.50 (*0-608-16426-7*, 202670700051) Bks Demand.

Ray, Angie. A Knight to Cherish. 314p. 1999. mass mkt. 5.99 (*0-515-12567-9*, Jove) Berkley Pub.

— My Lady in Time. 1998. mass mkt. 5.99 (*0-515-12227-0*, Jove) Berkley Pub.

Ray, Anil. Students & Politics: A Case Study of Benares Hindu University, India. 1978. 14.00 (*0-88386-789-3*) S Asia.

Ray, Animesh. Maritime India: Ports & Shipping. (Illus.). 746p. (C). 1995. reprint ed. 67.50 (*81-215-0691-3*, Pub. by M Manoharial) Coronet Bks.

Ray, Ann, ed. see Hills, Christopher.

Ray, Annada S. Yes, I Saw Gandhi. 215p. 1994. 15.00 (*0-934676-78-X*) Greenlf Bks.

Ray, Anthony. Liverpool Printed Tiles. (Illus.). 72p. 1994. 69.95 (*0-9512140-7-1*, Pub. by J Horne) Antique Collect.

***Ray, Anthony.** Spanish Pottery 1248-1898 1248-1898. 1999. 250.00 (*1-85177-291-X*) Vicariato Augstnian.

Ray, Arabinda. Fifty Years of Indian Management: An Insider's View. 128p. 2000. text 17.95 (*0-19-565123-5*) OUP.

Ray, Aric C., jt. auth. see Ray, Maria L.

***Ray, Arjun.** Kashmir Diary: Psychology of Militancy. LC 97-904589. 1998. 34.00 (*81-7049-089-8*, Pub. by Manas Pubns) S Asia.

Ray, Arthur J. The Canadian Fur Trade in the Industrial Age. 284p. 1990. 40.00 (*0-8020-2699-0*); pap. 19.95 (*0-8020-6743-3*) U of Toronto Pr.

***Ray, Arthur J.** I Have Lived Here since the World Began: An Illustrated History of Canada's Native People. (Illus.). 448p. 1998. pap. 29.95 (*1-55013-986-X*, Pub. by Key Porter) Firefly Bks Ltd.

Ray, Arthur J. Indians in the Fur Trade: Their Role As Trappers, Hunters, & Middle Man in the Lands Southwest of Hudson Bay, 1660-1860. LC 73-89848. (Illus.). 1974. pap. text 16.95 (*0-8020-6226-1*) U of Toronto Pr.

— Indians in the Fur Trade: Their Roles as Trappers, Hunters & Middlemen in the Lands Southwest. rev. ed. LC 98-162603. (Illus.). 320p. 1998. text 50.00 (*0-8020-4133-7*) U of Toronto Pr.

— Indians in the Fur Trade: Their Roles as Trappers, Hunters & Middlemen in the Lands Southwest. 2nd rev. ed. LC 98-162603. (Illus.). 320p. 1998. pap. text 21.95 (*0-8020-7980-6*) U of Toronto Pr.

Ray, Arthur J. & Freeman, Donald B. Give Us Good Measure: An Economic Analysis of Relations Between the Indians & the Hudson's Bay Company Before 1763. LC 79-304038. (Illus.). 316p. reprint ed. pap. 98.00 (*0-8357-8146-1*, 203398700088) Bks Demand.

Ray, Asok, jt. auth. see Nayak, Nitin.

Ray, B. C., ed. Tribals of Orissa: The Changing Socio-Economic Profile. 170p. 1989. 16.00 (*81-212-0270-1*, Pub. by Gian Publng Hse) S Asia.

Ray, Barbara & Ray, Norman H. Life Times: The Life Experiences Journal. deluxe ed. LC 89-92021. 288p. 1990. 49.95 (*1-877810-34-7*, LT) Rayve Prodns.

Ray, Barbara, et al. National Admissions to Substance Abuse Treatment Services: The Treatment Episode Data Set, 1992-1995. (Illus.). 91p. (C). 1998. pap. text 25.00 (*0-7881-4907-5*) DIANE Pub.

Ray, Barbara, tr. see Kadare, Ismail.

***Ray, Barbara L.** President. Alexander, OluFemi, ed. (Divine Weight Loss Formula Ser.). (Illus.). 15p. 1999. spiral bd. write for info. (*0-9673712-0-1*) B Ray.

Ray, Benjamin C. African Religions: Symbol, Ritual & Community. 2nd ed. LC 99-30522. 218p. (C). 1999. pap. text 23.60 (*0-13-082842-4*) P-H.

Ray, Benjamin C., jt. ed. see Patton.

Ray, Beverly, jt. auth. see Ridge, Holly.

Ray, Bharati. From Independence Towards Freedom: Indian Women since 1947. LC 99-933482. (Gender Studies Ser.). (Illus.). 270p. 1999. text 29.95 (*0-19-564575-8*) OUP.

— From the Seams of History: Essays on Indian Women. (Gender-Women's Studies). 316p. 1995. 35.00 (*0-19-563226-5*) OUP.

— Hyderabad & British Paramountcy. (Illus.). 250p. 1989. text 21.00 (*0-19-562231-6*) OUP.

Ray, Bharati, ed. From the Seams of History: Essays on Indian Women. (Oxford India Paperbacks Ser.). (Illus.). 306p. 1998. reprint ed. pap. text 8.95 (*0-19-564438-7*) OUP.

Ray, Bharati, jt. auth. see Basu, Aparna.

Ray, Bibek. Food Biopreservatives of Microbial Origin. 400p. 1992. lib. bdg. 225.00 (*0-8493-4943-5*, QR115) CRC Pr.

— Fundamental Food Microbiology. LC 95-48899. 528p. (C). 1996. boxed set 79.95 (*0-8493-9442-2*) CRC Pr.

Ray, Bibek, ed. Injured Index & Pathogenic Bacteria: Occurrence & Detection in Foods, Water, & Feeds. 224p. 1989. lib. bdg. 210.00 (*0-8493-4928-1*, QR115) CRC Pr.

Ray, Bibek, jt. ed. see Bozoglu, T. Faruk.

Ray, Bidyut L. Jagannatha Cult. LC 98-901401. 1998. 135.00 (*81-86218-07-6*, Pub. by Kant Pubns) S Asia.

— Studies in Jagannatha-Cult. (C). 1993. text 19.50 (*81-7054-176-X*, Pub. by Classical Pubng) S Asia.

Ray, Bijoya, jt. auth. see Ray, Satyajit.

Ray, Bill T. Environmental Engineering. LC 94-26681. (Engineering Ser.). 608p. (C). 1994. pap. 101.95 (*0-534-20652-2*) PWS Pubs.

Ray, Bill T. Wastewater Engineering. (Civil Engineering Ser.). (C). 2001. mass mkt. 76.95 (*0-534-95100-7*) PWS Pubs.

Ray, Binavendranath. Consciousness in Neo-Realism. LC 75-3330. reprint ed. 29.50 (*0-404-59324-0*) AMS Pr.

Ray, Biswanath, ed. West Bengal Today: A Fresh Look. (C). 1993. 28.00 (*81-7099-527-2*, Pub. by Mittal Pubs Dist) S Asia.

Ray, Blaine. Look, I Can Talk! Student Notebook in English. (Illus.). 100p. 1991. pap. text, teacher ed. 12.95 (*1-56018-456-6*) Sky Oaks Prodns.

R

An Asterisk (*) at the beginning of an entry indicates that the title is appearing for the first time.

R

— Look, I Can Talk! Student Notebook in Spanish. 2nd ed. Asher, James J., ed. (SPA., Illus.). 96p. (Orig.). 1997. pap. text, student ed. 12.95 (*1-56018-474-4*) Sky Oaks Prodns.
— Look, I Can Talk! Teacher's Guidebook. 3rd ed. Asher, James J., ed. 52p. 1998. pap. text, teacher ed. 12.00 (*1-56018-008-0*) Sky Oaks Prodns.
— Look, I Can Talk! (Schau, Ich Kann Reden!: Deutsches Schuler Arbeitsbuch) Student Notebook in German. Asher, James J., ed. (GER., Illus.). 96p. 1998. pap. text 14.00 (*1-56018-461-2*) Sky Oaks Prodns.
— Patricia Va a California, Vol. 2. (TPRS First-Year Spanish Novels Ser.). (SPA.). ii, 42p. (YA). (gr. 7-12). 1999. pap. 3.95 (*0-929724-50-X*) Command Performance.
— Pobre Ana. (TPRS First-Year Spanish Novels Ser.). (SPA.). ii, 39p. (gr. 7-12). 1999. pap. 3.95 (*0-929724-47-X*) Command Performance.
Ray, Blaine & Buchan, Greg. Look, I Can Talk! Student Notebook in French. 2nd ed. Asher, James J., ed. (FRE., Illus.). 100p. (Orig.). 1995. pap. text, student ed. 12.95 (*1-56018-497-3*) Sky Oaks Prodns.
Ray, Blaine & Gross, Susan. TPRS Gestures & Mini-Situations: For Look, I Can Talk! First-Year Mini-Stories. iv, 92p. 1998. pap. 12.00 (*0-929724-44-5*) Command Performance.
Ray, Blaine & Neilson, Joe. Look, I'm Still Talking: A Step-by-Step Approach to Communication Through TPR Stories, Vol. 3. (Look, I Can Talk! Ser.). (Illus.). vi, 72p. (Orig.). (YA). (gr. 9-12). 1993. pap. text 12.95 (*0-929724-18-6*, 18-6) Command Performance.
— Mirame, Todavia Estoy Hablando: Look, I'm Still Talking!, Vol. 3. (Look, I Can Talk! Ser.). (SPA., Illus.). vi, 72p. (Orig.). (YA). (gr. 9-12). 1994. pap. text 12.95 (*0-929724-22-4*, 22-4) Command Performance.
— Regardez-moi, Je Continue a Parler! Look, I'm Still Talking, Vol. 3. (Look, I Can Talk! Ser.). (FRE., Illus.). vi, 72p. (Orig.). (YA). (gr. 9-12). 1993. pap. text 12.95 (*0-929724-25-9*, 25-9) Command Performance.
Ray, Blaine & Seely, Contee. Fluency Through TPR Storytelling. 2nd ed. xviii, 222p. (Orig.). 1998. pap. text 14.95 (*0-929724-21-6*, 21-6) Command Performance.
Ray, Blaine, et al. Look, I Can Talk More! In English - Student Textbook. Asher, James J., ed. (Illus.). 120p. (Orig.). 1997. pap. text 13.95 (*1-56018-489-2*) Sky Oaks Prodns.
— Look, I Can Talk More! - Mirame, Puedo Hablar Mas! In Spanish - Student Textbook. (Illus.). 120p. (Orig.). 1995. pap. text 13.95 (*1-56018-490-6*) Sky Oaks Prodns.
— Look, I Can Talk More! - Regardez-Moi, Je Peux Parler Plus! In French - Student Textbook. (Illus.). 120p. 1999. pap. text 13.95 (*1-56018-491-4*, 123) Sky Oaks Prodns.
Ray, Blaine, jt. auth. see Turner, Lisa R.
Ray, Blair. Introduction to Professional Communication. 384p. (C). 1989. pap. text 37.51 (*0-13-493149-1*) P-H.
Ray, Boyd S. Blue Mountains & Green Valleys: Stories from Upper East Tennessee. 110p. (Orig.). 1996. pap. 8.95 (*1-57502-186-2*, P0810) Morris Pubng.
***Ray, Brenda.** The Midwife's Song: A Story of Moses' Birth. LC 00-102602. 256p. 2000. pap. 14.95 (*0-9653966-8-1*, Pub. by Karmichael Pr) Follett Library.
— The Season's Beauty. Laurie, Gloria J., ed. (Illus.). 33p. 2000. pap. 8.00 (*0-9701089-1-5*) Morn Dove Studio.
— Where Is Teddy? (Illus.). 26p. (J). (ps-6). 2000. pap. 8.00 (*0-9701089-0-7*) Morn Dove Studio.
Ray, Brian, jt. ed. see McDowell, Susan.
Ray, Brian D. Strengths of Their Own - Home Schoolers Across America: Academic Achievement, Family Characteristics, & Longitudinal Traits. (Illus.). 160p. 1997. pap. write for info. (*0-9657554-0-1*) Nat Home Educ.
Ray, Bruce. Withhold Not Correction. 1978. pap. 6.99 (*0-87552-400-1*) P & R Pubng.
***Ray, Bruce A.** Celebrating the Sabbath: Finding Rest in a Restless World. LC 99-58578. 140p. 2000. pap. 8.99 (*0-87552-394-3*) P & R Pubng.
Ray, C., ed. AIDS, Stories of Living Longer. 32p. (Orig.). 1991. pap. 3.25 (*0-9616792-9-8*) Taterhill.
Ray, C. & Baum, M. Psychological Aspects of Early Breast Cancer. (Contributions to Psychology & Medicine Ser.). (Illus.). 160p. 1985. 75.95 (*0-387-96122-4*) Spr-Verlag.
Ray, C. Claiborne. The New York Times Book of Science Questions & Answers: Answers by Leading Scientists to the Most Commonly Asked Science Questions. LC 96-36828. 240p. 1997. pap. 12.95 (*0-385-48660-X*) Doubleday.
Ray, Carlton, jt. auth. see Baxter, John.
Ray, Caroline, jt. ed. see Lenderyou, Gill.
Ray, Cecil A. Living the Responsible Life. Hogg, G. A., ed. 160p. 1983. pap. text 12.50 (*0-311-72371-3*) Casa Bautista.
Ray, Charles. Conversations Chinoises Prises sur le Vif, 2 vols. (Asian Folklore & Social Life Monographs: Nos. 47-48). (FRE.). 746p. 1973. 24.00 (*0-89986-045-1*) Oriental Bk Store.
— A Marvellous Ministry. 1985. pap. 6.00 (*1-56186-217-7*) Pilgrim Pubns.
— Mrs. C. H. Spurgeon. 1979. pap. 7.00 (*1-56186-305-X*) Pilgrim Pubns.
Ray, Charles, et al. Charles Ray. LC 98-22452. 1998. 30.00 (*0-914357-59-X*) Los Angeles Mus Contemp.
Ray, Charles, jt. auth. see Adkins, Myrna A.
Ray, Charles L., Jr. How to Start & Operate an Electrical Contracting Business. 2nd ed. LC 97-46919. (Illus.). 256p. 1998. 29.95 (*0-07-052661-3*); pap. 17.95 (*0-07-052621-4*) McGraw.
Ray, Charles M., jt. auth. see Palmer.
Ray-Chaudhuri, D., ed. Relations Between Combinatorics & Other Parts of Mathematics. LC 78-25979. (Proceedings of Symposia in Pure Mathematics Ser.: Vol. 34). 378p. 1979. reprint ed. pap. 44.00 (*0-8218-1434-6*, PSPUM/34) Am Math.
Ray, Christina I. The Bond Market: Trading & Risk Management. 553p. 1992. text 75.00 (*1-55623-289-6*, Irwn Prfssnl) McGraw-Hill Prof.
Ray, Christopher. Time, Space & Philosophy. (Philosophical Issues in Science Ser.). (Illus.). 288p. (C). 1991. 75.00 (*0-415-03221-0*, A5750) Routledge.
Ray, Clayton E., ed. Geology & Paleontology of the Lee Creek Mine, North Carolina, Pt. I. LC 82-600265. (Smithsonian Contributions to Paleobiology Ser.: No. 53). 535p. reprint ed. pap. 165.90 (*0-608-14270-0*, 202220300025) Bks Demand.
Ray, Clyde. Across the Dark River: The Odyssey of the 56th N. C. Infantry in the American Civil War. LC 96-30104. 260p. 1996. pap. 18.95 (*1-887905-04-9*) Pkway Pubs.
Ray, Clyde E. Life's Memory Book. 224p. 1998. 59.50 (*1-889137-06-5*) Genie Pubng.
Ray, Colin H. Background to Children's Books. LC 74-180017. 18p. 1974. write for info. (*0-85353-188-9*) Book Trust.
Ray, Colin H. & National Book League (Great Britain) Staff. Background to Children's Books. LC 76-370147. 21 p. 1975. 0.40 (*0-85353-232-X*) Book Trust.
— Background to Children's Books. LC 77-373980. 28 p. 1977. write for info. (*0-85353-261-3*) Book Trust.
***Ray, Cosmic.** Flagstaff & Sedona: 50 Favorite Hikes. 4th abr. ed. Orig. Title: Favorite Hikes: Flagstaff & Sedona. 110p. 1999. pap. 8.95 (*0-9664769-2-1*, Pub. by Cos Ray Publ) Sunbelt Pubns.
Ray, Cyril. Cyril Ray's Compleat Imbiber, No. 16. 192p. 1992. 24.95 (*1-85732-944-9*, Pub. by Reed Illust Books) Antique Collect.
— Robert Mondavi of the Napa Valley. 192p. 1986. mass mkt. 12.95 (*0-446-38322-8*, Pub. by Warner Bks) Little.
Ray, D. B. Text-Book on Campbellism. 1991. reprint ed. 24.00 (*0-685-40811-6*) Church History.
Ray, Darby K. Deceiving the Devil: Atonement, Abuse & Ransom. LC 97-44077. 176p. 1998. pap. 15.95 (*0-8298-1253-9*) Pilgrim OH.
Ray, Darrell W. & Bronstein, Howard. Teaming Up: Making the Transition to a Self-Directed, Team-Based Organization. LC 94-33604. (Illus.). 272p. 1994. 24.95 (*0-07-051646-4*) McGraw.
Ray, Dauglas. Palmistry & the Inner Self. 1995. pap. 150.00 (*81-208-1350-2*, Pub. by Print Hse) St Mut.
Ray, Dave. Inside Brother's Check-Up. 2nd ed. (Illus.). 112p. 1994. pap. 9.95 (*1-57326-023-1*, 502) Core Ministries.
— The Liberating Devotional: Daily Planner-Compact Pak. 200p. 1993. ring bd. 24.95 (*1-57326-003-7*) Core Ministries.
— The Liberating Devotional: Intro-Pak. 70p. 1994. pap. 6.95 (*1-57326-004-5*) Core Ministries.
— The Liberating Devotional: Soft Cover Pak. 110p. 1993. spiral bd. 24.95 (*1-57326-001-0*) Core Ministries.
— The Liberating Devotional: Standard Version. 200p. 1993. ring bd. 29.95 (*1-57326-000-2*) Core Ministries.
— The Liberating Devotional: The Executive Version. 200p. 1993. ring bd. 79.95 (*1-57326-002-9*) Core Ministries.
— Man's Check-Up. 56p. 1994. 9.95 (*1-57326-015-0*) Core Ministries.
— One Hour Management Check-Up. (Illus.). 61p. (Orig.). 1996. pap., wbk. ed. 6.95 (*1-57326-020-7*, 311) Core Ministries.
— Outside Brother's Check - Up. 2nd ed. LC 99-176502. (Illus.). 166 p. 1998. pap., wbk. ed. 14.95 (*1-57326-026-6*) Core Ministries.
— Pastoral Search Check-Up. 50p. 1997. pap., wbk. ed. 14.95 (*1-57326-025-8*) Core Ministries.
— Pastor's Check-Up. 36p. 1994. pap. 9.95 (*1-57326-016-9*) Core Ministries.
— Teen's Clinic: A First Aid Kit for the Teen Years. 308p. 1996. ring bd., wbk. ed. 49.95 (*1-57326-021-5*) Core Ministries.
Ray, Dave & Schmees, Paul. Job Search Check-Up. 68p. 1994. pap. 10.95 (*1-57326-017-7*) Core Ministries.
***Ray, David.** Demons in the Diner. (Richard Snyder Publication Award Ser.). 82p. 1999. pap. 10.00 (*0-912592-42-7*) Ashland Poetry.
Ray, David. Endless Search. 1999. text 23.95 (*0-525-94107-X*) Viking Penguin.
— The Farm in Calabria & Other Poems. Sklar, Morty, ed. LC 80-123410. (Outstanding Author Ser.: No. 3). (Illus.). 32p. (Orig.). 1980. pap. 5.00 (*0-930370-08-2*) Spirit That Moves.
Ray, David. On Wednesday I Cleaned out My Wallet. 32p. 1985. 11.00 (*0-942908-15-5*) Pancake Pr.
Ray, David. On Wednesday I Cleaned out My Wallet. 32p. (C). 1985. pap. 5.95 (*0-942908-07-4*) Pancake Pr.
— Pumpkin Light. LC 92-25118. (Illus.). 32p. (J). (ps-3). 1993. 15.95 (*0-399-22028-3*, Philomel) Peng Put Young Read.
— Pumpkin Light. LC 92-25118. (Illus.). 32p. (J). (ps-3). 1996. pap. 5.99 (*0-698-11397-7*, PapStar) Peng Put Young Read.
Ray, David. Pumpkin Light. 1996. 11.15 (*0-606-09769-4*, Pub. by Turtleback) Demco.
Ray, David, ed. New Letters: A Book of Translations. (New Letters Ser.). (Illus.). 184p. (Orig.). 1985. pap. 4.00 (*0-938652-09-5*) New Letters MO.
— New Letters, Fall, 1985, Vol. 52, No. 1. (Illus.). 136p. 1985. pap. 4.00 (*0-317-44322-4*) New Letters MO.
— New Letters, Fall, 1984, Vol. 51, No. 1. (Illus.). 1984. pap. 4.00 (*0-317-17179-8*) New Letters MO.
— New Letters Reader I: Reader One. (New Letters Ser.). 288p. (Orig.). 1983. pap. 7.50 (*0-938652-07-9*) New Letters MO.
— New Letters Reader II. (New Letters Ser.). 288p. (Orig.). 1984. pap. 7.50 (*0-938652-08-7*) New Letters MO.
Ray, David. Robin Hood & Little John. 32p. (J). (ps-3). 1998. pap. 5.99 (*0-698-11627-5*, PapStar) Peng Put Young Read.
Ray, David, tr. from SAN. Not Far from the River: Poems from the Gatha-Saptasati. LC 90-81354. 160p. (Orig.). 1990. pap. 10.00 (*1-55659-034-2*) Copper Canyon.
Ray, David & Ray, Judy. Fathers: A Collection of Poems. 272p. 1999. pap. 10.95 (*0-312-20964-9*) St Martin.
Ray, David & Ray, Judy, eds. Fatherhood. LC 96-54504. 1997. text 16.95 (*0-312-15527-1*) St Martin.
— Fathers. 1997. pap. 16.95 (*0-614-29448-7*) St Martin.
Ray, David & Singh, Amritjit, eds. India. (New Letters Ser.). 272p. (Orig.). 1982. pap. 5.00 (*0-938652-05-2*) New Letters MO.
Ray, David, ed. see Mayo, E. L.
Ray, David M., jt. ed. see Johnson, E. Elizabeth.
Ray, David R. The Big Small Church Book. LC 92-30774. 256p. (Orig.). 1992. pap. 15.95 (*0-8298-0936-8*) Pilgrim OH.
***Ray, Deborah.** Hokusai. 2001. text. write for info. (*0-374-33263-0*) FS&G.
— HTML 4 for Dummies Quick Reference. 2nd ed. 224p. 2000. spiral bd. 12.99 (*0-7645-0721-4*) IDG Bks.
— Mastering HTML 4: Premium Edition. (Mastering Ser.). 1216p. 1999. 49.99 (*0-7821-2524-7*) Sybex.
***Ray, Deborah & Ray, Eric J.** Mastering HTML 4. 2nd ed. LC 99-61309. (Mastering Ser.). (Illus.). 960p. 1999. 34.99 (*0-7821-2523-9*) Sybex.
Ray, Deborah, jt. auth. see Ray, Eric.
Ray, Deborah K. The Cloud. LC 83-48438. (Illus.). 48p. (J). (gr. k-3). 1984. 13.95 (*0-06-024846-7*) HarpC Child Bks.
Ray, Deborah K. The Snowchild. LC 94-78861. (Pudgy Pal Board Bks.). 18p. (J). (ps). 1995. bds. 3.95 (*0-448-40883-X*, G & D) Peng Put Young Read.
Ray, Deborah S. HTML for Dummies Quick Reference. 2nd ed. LC 97-209084. 240p. 1997. spiral bd. 14.99 (*0-7645-0248-4*) IDG Bks.
Ray, Deborah S. & Erdos, Dawn. Dummies 101: HTML 4. 2nd ed. LC 98-70133. 288p. 1998. pap. 24.99 incl. cd-rom (*0-7645-0205-0*) IDG Bks.
***Ray, Deborah S. & Ray, Eric J.** Access 2000 for Windows. (Visual QuickStart Guides Ser.). (Illus.). 272p. 1999. pap. text 17.99 (*0-201-35434-9*) Peachpit Pr.
Ray, Deborah S., jt. auth. see Ray, Eric J.
Ray, Deborah W. & Stewart, Gloria P. Loyal to the Land: The History of a Greenwich Connecticut Family. LC 90-46740. (Illus.). 192p. 1990. 45.00 (*0-914659-50-2*) Phoenix Pub.
Ray, Debra & Walley, Patti. James & the Giant Peach: A Study Guide. (Novel-Ties Ser.). (J). (gr. 3-5). 1988. pap. text, teacher ed., student ed. 15.95 (*0-88122-077-9*) Lrn Links.
Ray, Debraj. Development Economics. LC 97-33459. 848p. 1998. text 55.00 (*0-691-01706-9*, Pub. by Princeton U Pr) Cal Prin Full Svc.
Ray, Debraj, jt. auth. see Mookherjee, Dilip.
Ray, Delia. Behind the Blue & Gray: A Soldier's Life in the Civil War. (Illus.). 112p. (YA). (gr. 5 up). 1996. pap. 9.99 (*0-14-038304-2*) Viking Penguin.
Ray, Delia. Behind the Blue & Gray: The Soldier's Life in the Civil War. (Young Readers' History of the Civil War Ser.). 1996. 12.19 (*0-606-10751-7*, Pub. by Turtleback) Demco.
Ray, Delia. A Nation Torn: The Story of How the Civil War Began. (Illus.). 112p. (YA). (gr. 5 up). 1996. pap. 9.99 (*0-14-038105-8*, PuffinBks) Peng Put Young Read.
Ray, Delia. A Nation Torn, the Story of How the Civil War Began. LC 90-5533. (Young Readers' History of the Civil War Ser.). (J). 1996. 12.19 (*0-606-09676-0*, Pub. by Turtleback) Demco.
Ray, Delmas D. Accounting & Business Fluctuations. LC 60-6718. 196p. reprint ed. pap. 60.80 (*0-7837-4925-2*, 204459100004) Bks Demand.
Ray, Deng D. The Politics of Two Sudans: The South & the North, 1821-1969. 183p. 1994. pap. 42.50 (*91-7106-344-7*) Coronet Bks.
Ray, Dennis M., ed. Research on International & Comparative Entrepreneurship, Vol. 1. Date not set. 73.25 (*1-55938-948-6*) Jai Pr.
— Research on International & Comparative Entrepreneurship, Vol. 2. Date not set. 73.25 (*0-7623-0021-3*) Jai Pr.
Ray, Diane T. Fashion Doll Dream Castle. LC 93-86558. 146p. 1994. pap. 14.95 (*0-9638031-3-1*) Needlecrft Shop.
Ray, Diane T., et al, contrib. by. Fashion Doll Dream House. LC 95-72038. (Illus.). 160p. 1996. 19.96 (*1-57367-066-9*) Needlecrft Shop.
Ray, Don. California Investigator's Handbook: A Public Records Primer & Investigator's Handbook. 6th ed. 286p. 1995. pap. 18.95 (*0-9629552-3-X*) ENG Pr.
— Checking out Lawyers. LC 96-44473. 1997. 15.95 (*1-877639-60-5*) Military Information.
***Ray, Don.** The Investigator's Handbook: How to Use Open Sources & Public Records to Locate Information on Anyone. Flowers, James R., ed. 480p. 2000. pap. 19.95 (*1-889150-17-7*, Pub. by Facts on Demand) Natl Bk Netwk.
Ray, Don E., et al. Guide to Dealerships, 2 vols. Incl. Vol. 1. 1997. ring bd. (*0-7646-0110-5*); Vol. 2. 1997. ring bd. (*0-7646-0111-3*); 130.00 (*0-7646-0109-1*) Prctnrs Pub Co.
— Guide To Dealerships, 2 vols. Incl. Vol. 1. 1998. ring bd. 138.00 (*0-7646-0391-4*); Vol. 2. 1998. ring bd. 138.00 (*0-7646-0392-2*); 138.00 (*0-7646-0390-6*) Prctnrs Pub Co.
***Ray, Don E., et al.** Guide to Dealerships, 2 vols. 1999. ring bd. 138.00 (*0-7646-0897-5*) Prctnrs Pub Co.
— Guide to Dealerships, Vol. 1. 1999. ring bd. write for info. (*0-7646-0898-3*) Prctnrs Pub Co.
— Guide to Dealerships, Vol. 2. 1999. ring bd. write for info. (*0-7646-0899-1*) Prctnrs Pub Co.
Ray, Donald I. Dictionary of the African Left: Parties, Movements & Groups. 2nd ed. 290p. 1989. text 91.95 (*1-85521-014-2*, Pub. by Dartmth Pub) Ashgate Pub Co.
***Ray, Doris.** The Ghosts Behind Him: One Family's Battle with Schizophrenia. 218p. 1999. pap. 16.95 (*0-920576-77-X*) Caitlin Pr.
Ray, Dorothy J. The Eskimos of Bering Strait, 1650-1898. LC 91-28577. (Illus.). 360p. 1991. reprint ed. pap. 18.95 (*0-295-97122-3*) U of Wash Pr.
— A Legacy of Arctic Art. LC 95-36452. (Illus.). 208p. 1996. pap. 24.95 (*0-295-97518-0*); text 40.00 (*0-295-97507-5*) U of Wash Pr.
— Setting It Free: An Exhibition of Modern Alaskan Eskimo Ivory Carving. Larsen, Dinah, ed. (Illus.). 110p. (Orig.). 1982. pap. 10.00 (*0-931163-08-0*) U Alaska Museum.
Ray, Douglas. Human Rights Education: International Perspectives. Beauchamp, Edward R., ed. (Reference Books in International Education). 350p. Date not set. text 47.50 (*0-8153-1131-1*) Garland.
Ray, Edward J. U. S. Protectionism & the World Debt Crisis. LC 89-3774. 259p. 1989. 65.00 (*0-89930-367-6*, RUP/, Quorum Bks) Greenwood.
Ray, Eileen B., ed. Case Studies in Communication & Disenfranchisement: Social Health Issues & Implications. (LEA's Communication Ser.). 294p. 1996. text 59.95 (*0-8058-1674-7*); pap. text 29.95 (*0-8058-1675-5*) L Erlbaum Assocs.
— Case Studies in Health Communication. (Communication Textbooks, Applied Communication Subseries). 328p. (C). 1993. pap. 29.95 (*0-8058-1109-5*); text 79.95 (*0-8058-1108-7*) L Erlbaum Assocs.
— Communication & Disenfranchisement: Social Health Issues & Implications. (LEA's Communication Ser.). 504p. 1996. text 89.95 (*0-8058-1530-9*); pap. text 39.95 (*0-8058-1531-7*) L Erlbaum Assocs.
Ray, Eileen B. & Donohew, L., eds. Communication & Health: Systems & Applications. 224p. 1989. 49.95 (*0-8058-0154-5*); pap. 22.50 (*0-8058-0697-0*) L Erlbaum Assocs.
Ray, Eleanor & Marinacci, Barbara. Vineyards in the Sky: The Life of Legendary Vintner Martin Ray. LC 92-74051. (Illus.). 448p. 1993. 28.95 (*0-9623048-4-0*); pap. 18.95 (*0-9623048-5-9*) Heritage West.
Ray, Eric. The AltaVista Search Revolution. 2nd ed. 1998. pap. text 24.99 (*0-07-882435-4*) Osborne-McGraw.
— Sofer: The Story of a Torah Scroll. LC 85-52420. (Illus.). 32p. (Orig.). (J). (gr. 4). 1998. pap. 6.95 (*0-933873-98-0*) Torah Aura.
Ray, Eric & Grishaver, Joel Lurie. Sofer: The Story of a Torah Scroll. (Illus.). 32p. (Orig.). 1988. text 12.95 (*0-933873-24-7*) Torah Aura.
***Ray, Eric & Maden, Chris.** Learning XML. Posner, John, ed. (Illus.). 250p. 2000. 32.95 (*0-596-00046-4*) OReilly & Assocs.
Ray, Eric & Ray, Deborah. Mastering HTML 4.0. 1040p. 1997. pap. text 49.99 (*0-7821-2102-0*) Sybex.
Ray, Eric J. HTML 4 Instant Reference. 1999. pap. text 16.99 (*0-7821-2578-6*) Sybex.
***Ray, Eric J.** Mastering XHTML. 896p. 2000. pap. text 39.99 (*0-7821-2820-3*) Sybex.
Ray, Eric J. & Ray, Deborah S. Quick Reference HTML 4 for Dummies. LC 97-81228. (For Dummies). (Illus.). 240p. 1998. spiral bd. 14.99 (*0-7645-0332-4*) IDG Bks.
— UNIX: Visual QuickStart Guide. (Visual QuickStart Guides Ser.). 368p. (C). 1998. pap. text 17.99 (*0-201-35395-4*, Pub. by Peachpit Pr) Addison-Wesley.
Ray, Eric J., jt. auth. see Ray, Deborah.
Ray, Eric J., jt. auth. see Ray, Deborah S.
Ray, Eunice V., ed. see Reisman, Judith A.
Ray, Francis. Bargain. 1995. mass mkt. 4.99 (*0-7860-0174-7*, Pinncle Kensgtn) Kensgtn Pub Corp.
***Ray, Francis.** Bargain. (Zebra Historical Romance Ser.). 352p. 2000. mass mkt. 5.99 (*0-8217-6616-3*, Zebra Kensgtn) Kensgtn Pub Corp.
Ray, Francis. Break Every Rule. 256p. 1998. pap. 4.99 (*0-7860-0544-0*) Kensgtn Pub Corp.
— Forever Yours. 1994. mass mkt. 4.99 (*0-7860-0025-2*, Pinncle Kensgtn) Kensgtn Pub Corp.
— Heart of the Falcon. 224p. 1998. mass mkt. 4.99 (*0-7860-0483-5*, Pinncle Kensgtn) Kensgtn Pub Corp.
***Ray, Francis.** Incognito. 1999. mass mkt. 4.99 (*1-58314-055-7*) BET Bks.
Ray, Francis. Incognito. 240p. 1997. mass mkt. 4.99 (*0-7860-0364-2*, Pinncle Kensgtn) Kensgtn Pub Corp.
— Only Hers. 1996. pap. 4.99 (*0-7860-0255-7*, Pinncle Kensgtn) Kensgtn Pub Corp.
— Silken Betrayal. 256p. 1997. mass mkt. 4.99 (*0-7860-0426-6*, Pinncle Kensgtn) Kensgtn Pub Corp.
— Undeniable. 256p. 1995. mass mkt. 4.99 (*0-8217-0125-8*, Zebra Kensgtn); mass mkt. 4.99 (*0-7860-0125-9*, Pinncle Kensgtn) Kensgtn Pub Corp.
— Until There Was You. 256p. 1999. mass mkt. 4.99 (*1-58314-028-X*) Kensgtn Pub Corp.
***Ray, Francis.** Winter Nights. 1999. mass mkt. 4.99 (*1-58314-039-5*) BET Bks.
Ray, Francis, et al. Winter Nights. LC 98-65851. 304p. 1998. 22.00 (*1-57566-369-4*) Kensgtn Pub Corp.
Ray, Fred O. The New Poverty Row: Independent Filmmakers As Distributors. LC 91-52743. (Illus.). 240p. 1991. lib. bdg. 39.95 (*0-89950-628-3*) McFarland & Co.
Ray, Frederic. Old Fort Niagara: An Illustrated History. rev. ed. (Illus.). 16p. (J). 1988. reprint ed. pap. 1.75 (*0-941967-06-9*) Old Fort Niagara Assn.
Ray, Frederic E. Our Special Artist: Alfred R. Waud's Civil War. (Illus.). 192p. 1994. 22.95 (*0-8117-1194-3*) Stackpole.
Ray, G., jt. ed. see Nabseth, Lars.
Ray, G. P. Thickness Testing of Electroplated & Related Coatings. 170p. 1997. pap. 180.00 (*0-901150-27-4*) St Mut.

An Asterisk (*) at the beginning of an entry indicates that the title is appearing for the first time.

Ray Garfield Staff. Life & Love. 184p. (Orig.). 1983. pap. 5.95 (*0-9609856-0-3*) Garfield Pubns.

Ray, Gary A., jt. auth. see Blyler, John E.

Ray, Gene, ed. Joseph Beuys at the End of the Twentieth Century: Mapping the Legacy. (Illus.). 224p. 1999. pap. 35.00 (*1-891024-03-5*, 910571) Dist Art Pubs.

Ray, George. Poems of Life & Nature. 1995. pap. 4.95 (*1-57087-048-9*) Prof Pr NC.

Ray, Gordon N. The Buried Life: A Study of the Relation Between Thackeray's Fiction & His Personal History. LC 74-6372. (Thackeray Ser.: No. 91). 1974. lib. bdg. 75.00 (*0-8383-1984-X*) M S G Haskell Hse.

— H. G. Wells & Rebecca West. LC 74-77990. (Illus.). 241p. reprint ed. pap. 74.80 (*0-8357-8161-5*, 203391800087) Bks Demand.

— The Illustrator & the Book in England from 1790 to 1914. (Illus.). 384p. 1992. reprint ed. pap. 29.95 (*0-486-26955-8*) Dover.

Ray, Gordon N., ed. see James, Henry & Wells, H. G.

Ray, Gordon N., ed. see Thackeray, William Makepeace.

Ray, Gordon N., ed. see Wells, H. G.

Ray, Grace, jt. ed. see Vinz, Mark.

Ray H. Bennett Lumber Co., Inc. Staff. Bennett's Small House Catalog, 1920. LC 93-40012. (Illus.). 80p. 1993. reprint ed. pap. text 8.95 (*0-486-27809-3*) Dover.

Ray, H. P. Trade & Diplomacy in India-China Relations: A Study of Bengal During the 15th Century. 1993. text 25.00 (*81-7027-202-5*, Pub. by Radiant Pubs) S Asia.

Ray, H. S. Kinetics of Metallurgical Reactions. 312p. (C). 1993. 29.95 (*1-881570-05-3*) Science Pubs.

Ray, H. S. & Mitra, A. K. Utilisation of Natural Resources: Chemical Engineering Approach. (International Series on Chemical Engineering). 1994. write for info. (*81-7236-099-1*, Pub. by Wiley Estrn) Franklin.

Ray, Harold L., jt. auth. see Palmatier, Robert A.

Ray, Hemen. China & Eastern Europe. 150p. 1988. text 25.00 (*81-7027-115-0*, Pub. by Radiant Pubs) S Asia.

— The Enduring Friendship: Soviet-Indian Relations in Mrs. Gandhi's Days. (C). 1989. 21.50 (*81-7017-249-7*, Pub. by Abhinav) S Asia.

— Sino-Soviet Conflict over India. (C). 1988. 16.00 (*81-7017-206-3*, Pub. by Abhinav) S Asia.

Ray, Himanshu P. The Winds of Change: Buddhism & the Early Maritime Links of South Asia. (Illus.). 256p. 1995. 29.95 (*0-19-563551-5*) OUP.

— The Winds of Change: Buddhism & the Maritime Links of Early South Asia. (Oxford India Paperbacks Ser.). (Illus.). 244p. 1999. reprint ed. pap. text 14.95 (*0-19-564359-3*) OUP.

Ray, Himanshu P. & Salles, J. F., eds. Traditional & Archaeology: Early Maritime Contacts in the Indian Ocean. (C). 1996. 80.00 (*81-7304-145-8*, Pub. by Manohar) S Asia.

Ray, Irene R. & Gupta, Mallika C. Story of Vivekananda. (Illus.). 72p. (J). (gr. 4-7). 1971. pap. 2.00 (*81-85301-65-4*, Pub. by Advaita Ashrama) Vedanta Pr.

Ray, Irv, jt. auth. see Benson, Tony.

Ray, Isaac. Contributions to Mental Pathology (1873). LC 73-9908. (History of Psychology Ser.). 576p. 1973. reprint ed. lib. bdg. 85.00 (*0-8201-1120-1*) Schol Facsimiles.

— A Treatise on the Medical Jurisprudence of Insanity. (Historical Foundations of Forensic Psychiatry & Psychology Ser.). xvi, 480p. 1983. reprint ed. lib. bdg. 45.00 (*0-306-76181-5*) Da Capo.

— A Treatise on the Medical Jurisprudence of Insanity. 5th ed. LC 75-16732. (Classics in Psychiatry Ser.). 1977. reprint ed. 54.95 (*0-405-07453-0*) Ayer.

Ray, Isaac & Earle, Pliny. American Psychiatrists Abroad: An Original Anthology. LC 75-16679. (Classics in Psychiatry Ser.). 1976. 30.95 (*0-405-07411-5*) Ayer.

Ray, J. & Davis, L. Computers in Educational Administration. (C). 1990. text 39.25 (*0-07-051257-4*) McGraw.

Ray, J. P. & Engelhardt, F. R. Produced Water Vol. 1: Technological/Environmental Issues & Solutions. (Environmental Science Research Ser.: Vol. 46). (Illus.). 632p. (C). 1993. 155.00 (*0-306-44358-9*, Plenum Trade) Perseus Pubng.

Ray, Jack H. Casa Blanca: An Early Archaic Upland Base Camp in Southwest Missouri. LC 44-14131. (The Missouri Archaeologist Ser.: Vol. 55). (Illus.). 124p. 1997. pap. 7.50 (*0-943414-84-9*) MO Arch Soc.

Ray, James. Entrepreneur's Handbook: A Complete Guide to Venture Selection & Business Planning. 384p. 1994. per. 50.00 (*0-7863-0326-3*, Irwn Prfssnl) McGraw-Hill Prof.

Ray, James A. The Science of Success: How to Attract Prosperity & Create Life Balance Through Proven Principles. LC 98-87858. (Illus.). 192p. 1998. 22.95 (*0-9667400-0-9*); pap. 14.95 (*0-9667400-1-7*) J Ray Intl.

Ray, James C. The Most Valuable Business Legal Forms You'll Ever Need. 2nd ed. LC 98-3338. (Legal Survival Guides Ser.). 140p. 1998. pap. 19.95 (*1-57071-345-6*) Sourcebks.

— The Most Valuable Corporate Forms You'll Ever Need. 2nd ed. LC 98-6006. (Legal Survival Guides Ser.). 220p. 1998. pap. 24.95 (*1-57071-346-4*) Sourcebks.

Ray, James Earl. Who Killed Martin Luther King? The True Story by the Alleged Assassin. 2nd ed. LC 98-155195. (Illus.). 320p. 1997. pap. text 13.95 (*1-56924-711-0*) Marlowe & Co.

Ray, James L. Democracy & International Conflict: An Evaluation of the Democratic Peace Proposition. Kegley, Charles W., Jr. & Puchala, Donald J., eds. LC 95-4339. (Studies in International Relations). 243p. (C). 1998. pap. 16.95 (*1-57003-241-6*) U of SC Pr.

— The Future of American-Israeli Relations: A Parting of the Ways. LC 85-706. 167p. reprint ed. pap. 51.80 (*0-7837-5813-8*, 204548000006) Bks Demand.

— Global Politics, 6 vols. 6th ed. LC 94-76542. (C). 1994. pap. text 44.76 (*0-395-70848-6*) HM.

Ray, James L., ed. Global Politics, 6 vols. (C). 1994. pap., teacher ed. 11.96 (*0-395-72562-3*) HM.

Ray, James L., jt. ed. see Smith, Dale L.

Ray, James Lee, jt. ed. see Smith, Dale L.

Ray, Jane. Address Book. 96p. 1994. 14.95 (*0-385-25492-X*) Doubleday.

— Creation. 32p. 1992. 19.50 (*0-385-25394-X*) Doubleday.

— Day Book. 96p. 1994. 14.95 (*0-385-25493-8*) Doubleday.

— Let There Be Light. LC 97-29456. (Illus.). 96p. (J). 1997. 19.99 (*0-525-45925-1*, Dutton Child) Peng Put Young Read.

— Story of Christmas: Words from the Gospels of Matthew & Luke. (J). 1998. pap. 7.99 (*0-14-056456-X*, PuffinBks) Peng Put Young Read.

Ray, Jane. Magical Tales from Many Lands. LC 93-12164. 128p. (J). 1993. 22.99 (*0-525-45017-3*, Dutton Child) Peng Put Young Read.

Ray, Jane. Hansel & Gretel. LC 97-6693. 32p. (J). (ps-3). 1997. 15.99 (*0-7636-0358-9*) Candlewick Pr.

***Ray, Janisse.** Ecology of a Cracker Childhood. LC 99-13403. (Illus.). 224p. 1999. 19.95 (*1-57131-234-X*) Milkweed Ed.

— Ecology of a Cracker Childhood. (Illus.). 304p. 2000. pap. 14.95 (*1-57131-247-1*) Milkweed Ed.

Ray, Jayanta K., jt. auth. see Mamoon, Muntassir.

***Ray, Jeanne.** Julie & Romeo. LC 00-23539. 192p. 2000. 21.00 (*0-609-60672-7*) Harmony Bks.

— Juliet & Romeo: A Novel. LC 00-37438. 2000. write for info. (*0-7862-2660-9*) Thorndike Pr.

Ray, Jennie H. Haggard. History of the Haggard Family in England & America, 1433 to 1899 to 1938. (Illus.). 184p. 1998. reprint ed. pap. 25.00 (*0-8328-8886-9*); reprint ed. lib. bdg. 35.00 (*0-8328-8885-0*) Higginson Bk Co.

Ray, Jerry. Away in a Manager. 4p. 1989. pap. 2.50 (*0-7390-0340-2*, 3649) Alfred Pub.

— Christmas with Style: 10 Carol Arrangements for the Piano. 32p. 1986. pap. 6.95 (*0-7390-0399-2*, 659) Alfred Pub.

— Simply Christmas. 32p. 1988. 6.95 (*0-7390-0561-8*, 1188) Alfred Pub.

— World's Greatest Hymns. 144p. 1993. pap. 15.95 (*0-7390-0410-7*, 6662) Alfred Pub.

Ray, Jerry L. Narrative Irony in Luke-Acts: The Paradoxical Interaction of Prophetic Fulfillment & Jewish Rejection. LC 95-12483. (Biblical Press Ser.: Vol. 28). 200p. 1996. 79.95 (*0-7734-2359-1*, Mellen Biblical Pr) E Mellen.

Ray, Joan K. Sams Teach Yourself UNIX System Administration In 21 Days. 800p. 1999. pap. 29.99 (*0-672-31660-9*) Sams.

Ray, Joan K., jt. auth. see Ray, Robert D.

Ray, Jocelyn, intro. N. A. Tink Tinkham: Watchmaker, Music Maker. 126p. 1981. lib. bdg. 34.50 (*1-56475-210-0*); fiche. write for info. (*1-56475-211-9*) U NV Oral Hist.

Ray, Joel, jt. auth. see Marino, Andrew A.

Ray, John. The Correspondence of John Ray. Lankester, Edwin R., ed. LC 74-26287. (History, Philosophy & Sociology of Science Ser.). 1975. reprint ed. 42.95 (*0-405-06613-9*) Ayer.

— Miscellaneous Discourses Concerning the Dissolution & Changes of the World. (Anglistica & Americana Ser.: No. 10). 259p. 1968. reprint ed. 50.70 (*0-685-66508-9*, 05102001) G Olms Pubs.

— The Night Blitz, 1940-41. (Illus.). 224p. 1996. 24.95 (*1-85409-270-7*, Pub. by Arms & Armour) Sterling.

***Ray, John.** Second World War: A Narrative History. (Illus.). 2000. 29.95 (*0-304-35303-5*) Continuum.

Ray, John. Synopsis Methodica Animalium Quadrupedum et Serpentini Generis. Sterling, Keir B., ed. LC 77-81111. (Biologists & Their World Ser.). (LAT.). 1978. reprint ed. lib. bdg. 31.95 (*0-405-10694-7*) Ayer.

— Synopsis Methodica Avium & Piscium. Derham, William & Sterling, Keir B., eds. LC 77-81111. (Biologists & Their World Ser.). (LAT., Illus.). 1978. reprint ed. lib. bdg. 39.95 (*0-405-10695-5*) Ayer.

— Three Physico-Theological Discourses: Primitive Chaos, & Creation of the World, the General Deluge, Its Causes & Effects. Albritton, Claude C., Jr., ed. LC 77-6538. (History of Geology Ser.). 1978. reprint ed. lib. bdg. 37.95 (*0-405-10457-X*) Ayer.

***Ray, John.** Using TCP/IP: Special Edition. LC 98-87538. (Using ... / Macmillan Computer Ser.). 1999. pap. text 29.99 (*0-7897-1897-9*) Que.

Ray, John. The Wisdom of God Manifested in the Works of the Creation. (Anglistica & Americana Ser.: No. 122). 250p. 1974. reprint ed. 50.70 (*3-487-05403-5*) G Olms Pubs.

— The Wisdom of God Manifested in the Works of the Creation: Heavenly Bodies, Elements, Meteors, Fossils, Vegetables, Animals. Egerton, Frank N., 3rd, ed. LC 77-74250. (History of Ecology Ser.). 1978. reprint ed. lib. bdg. 44.95 (*0-405-10419-7*) Ayer.

Ray, John & Warden, Kathleen. Technology, Computers & the Special Needs Learner. LC 94-6812. 240p. 1994. mass mkt. 54.95 (*0-8273-6476-8*) Delmar.

Ray, John D., jt. auth. see Freeman, Charles.

Ray, John R. Computers & the Special Needs Learner. (Special Education Ser.). 1995. text, teacher ed. 14.95 (*0-8273-6477-6*) Delmar.

***Ray, Jonathan.** Everything You Need to Know About Wine. LC 99-16959. (Illus.). 144p. 1999. pap. 14.95 (*1-58080-041-6*) Burford Bks.

Ray, Jordan B., jt. auth. see Gleim, Irvin N.

Ray, Joseph. Ray's Arithmetic Set, 8 vols. 1985. teacher ed. 99.99 (*0-88062-050-1*) Mott Media.

Ray, Judith A. A Single Lady's Guide to Bar Games. 65p. (Orig.). 1989. pap. 4.00 (*0-9622689-0-9*) J A Ray.

Ray, Judy. Pebble Rings. 64p. 1980. pap. 3.00 (*0-912678-42-9*, Greenfld Rev Pr) Greenfld Rev Lit.

— Pigeons in the Chandeliers. (Illus.). 75p. (Orig.). 1993. pap. 10.00 (*0-944048-04-8*) Timberline Missouri.

— Tokens: A Poem. 8p. (Orig.). 1995. pap. 3.00 (*1-884235-15-8*) Helicon Nine Eds.

Ray, Judy, jt. auth. see Ray, David.

Ray, Judy, jt. ed. see Ray, David.

Ray, Juliana. By Grace Alone. 192p. 1987. pap. 6.95 (*0-310-55162-5*, 19016P) Zondervan.

Ray, K. K., et al. An Aid to Radiology for the MRCP. LC 98-51790. (At a Glance Ser.). (Illus.). 370p. 2000. pap. 39.95 (*0-632-04912-X*) Blackwell Sci.

***Ray, Kabita.** History of Public Health: Colonial Bengal, 1921-1947. LC 98-903406. xii, 375 p. 1998. write for info. (*81-7074-200-5*) S Asia.

Ray, Karen. Sleep Song. LC 94-24859. (Illus.). 32p. (J). (ps). 1995. 15.95 (*0-531-06878-1*) Orchard Bks Watts.

— The T. F. Letters. 160p. (J). (gr. 3-5). 1998. 15.95 (*0-7894-2530-0*, D K Ink) DK Pub Inc.

***Ray, Karen.** The T. F. Letters. LC 99-27810. (Illus.). (J). 2000. pap. 4.99 (*0-14-130705-6*) Peng Put Young Read.

Ray, Karen. To Cross a Line. LC 93-11813. 160p. (YA). (gr. 7 up). 1994. 15.95 (*0-531-06831-5*); lib. bdg. 16.99 (*0-531-08681-X*) Orchard Bks Watts.

— To Cross a Line. 160p. (YA). (gr. 7 up). 1995. pap. 4.99 (*0-14-037587-2*, PuffinBks) Peng Put Young Read.

— To Cross a Line. 1995. 9.09 (*0-606-08679-X*, Pub. by Turtleback) Demco.

Ray, Karen, jt. auth. see Winer, Michael.

Ray, Kathleen C., ed. see Curd, Rollin C.

Ray, Kathleen M., ed. Experience Teaches: A Teacher's Journey Through the School Year. 2nd ed. LC 97-41291. (Illus.). 56p. 1997. pap. 11.00 (*0-912099-25-9*, 510) Kappa Delta Pi.

***Ray, Katie W.** Wondrous Words: Learning to Write. LC 99-31886. 317p. 1999. pap. 22.95 (*0-8141-5816-1*) NCTE.

Ray, Keith, jt. auth. see McClary, Cheryl.

Ray, Keka D. Political Upsurges in Post-War India, 1945-6. (C). 1992. 15.00 (*0-685-63242-3*, Pub. by Intellectual) S Asia.

***Ray, Kitty.** A Peculiar Chemistry. large type ed. 480p. 2000. write for info. (*0-7505-1483-3*, Pub. by Mgna Lrg Print) Ulverscroft.

Ray, L. E., jt. ed. see Giam, C. S.

Ray, L. P. Twice Sold, Twice Ransomed. LC 76-173613. (Black Heritage Library Collection). 1977. reprint ed. 28.95 (*0-8369-8905-8*) Ayer.

Ray, Larry. Social Theory & the Crisis of State Socialism. LC 95-42409. (Studies of Communism in Transition). 304p. 1996. 90.00 (*1-85278-688-4*) E Elgar.

Ray, Larry & Reed, Michael. Organizing Modernity: New Weberian Perspectives on Work, Organizations, & Society. LC 94-7259. 320p. (C). 1994. pap. 24.99 (*0-415-08917-4*, B4466) Routledge.

Ray, Larry J. Rethinking Critical Theory: Emancipation in the Age of Global Social Movements. (Illus.). 256p. 1993. 69.95 (*0-8039-8363-8*); pap. 21.95 (*0-8039-8364-6*) Sage.

Ray, Leslie. Oil Spill Prevention & Response: How to Comply with OPA & OSPRA. LC 93-40393. 250p. 1994. 69.95 (*0-87814-389-0*) PennWell Bks.

Ray, Leslie A., tr. see Adrados, Francisco Rodriguez.

Ray, Lisa. Southern Women Artists: From the Collection of the Columbia Museum of Art. 38p. (Orig.). 1990. pap. 3.00 (*0-9627858-0-6*) Columbia Mus Art.

Ray, M. Catherine. I'm Here to Help: A Guide for Caregivers, Hospice Workers & Volunteers. 2nd ed. LC 96-26981. (Illus.). 128p. 1997. pap. 10.95 (*0-553-37797-3*) Bantam.

— I'm Here to Help: A Hospice Worker's Guide to Communicating with Dying People & Their Loved Ones. (Illus.). 72p. 1992. reprint ed. pap. 7.00 (*0-9636311-0-1*) McRay.

— I'm with You Now: A Guide Through Incurable Illness for Patients, Families & Friends. LC 96-41070. 256p. 1997. pap. 10.95 (*0-553-37801-5*) Bantam.

Ray, M. L. Pumpkins. Root, Barry, ed. LC 90-47305. (Gulliver Green Book Ser.). (Illus.). 32p. (J). (ps-3). 1992. 15.00 (*0-15-252252-2*, Gulliver Bks) Harcourt.

Ray, M. S. & Johnston, D. W. Chemical Engineering Design Project: A Case Study Approach, Vol. 6. xxvi, 558p. 1989. 146.00 (*2-88124-712-1*); text 201.00 (*2-88124-713-X*) Gordon & Breach.

Ray, Malibika, ed. Environmental Protection & Afforetions: National Seminar Visva-Bharati, Sanitiniketan. 250p. 1990. 45.00 (*0-685-59954-X*) Scholarly Pubns.

Ray, Man. Man Ray's Celebrity Portrait Photographs. (Illus.). 80p. 1995. reprint ed. pap. text 9.95 (*0-486-28811-0*) Dover.

— Photographs by Man Ray, 1920-1934. LC 79-50461. (Illus.). 128p. 1980. reprint ed. pap. 11.95 (*0-486-23842-3*) Dover.

— Self Portrait. LC 98-44426. 352p. 1999. pap. 29.95 (*0-8212-2474-3*, Pub. by Bulfinch Pr) Little.

Ray, Man & Breton, Andre. Man Ray, 1890-1976. LC 95-5561. (Illus.). 352p. 1995. 65.00 (*0-8109-4277-1*) Abrams.

***Ray, Man & Horst, Horst P.** Chorus of Light: Photographs from the Sir Elton John Collection. (Illus.). 176p. 2000. 60.00 (*0-8478-2313-X*) Rizzoli Intl.

Ray, Manash R., jt. auth. see Gupta, Praveen P.

Ray, Maria L. & Ray, Aric C. Dream Venture: A Spiritual Quest. LC 97-71736. 192p. 1997. 21.95 (*1-878398-07-5*) Blue Note Pubns.

Ray, Marilyn A., jt. ed. see Watson, Jean.

Ray, Mark A. The Eagle Court of Honor Book: The Complete Guide to Scouting's Greatest Moment. 2nd rev. ed. LC 99-61926. (Illus.). x, 182p. (Orig.). 1999. pap. 10.95 (*0-9651207-1-6*) Ray Pubng.

Ray, Martin. Joseph Conrad. LC 93-24481. (Modern Fiction Ser.). 128p. 1995. pap. 16.95 (*0-7131-6559-6*, Pub. by E A) OUP.

— Thomas Hardy: A Textual Study of the Short Stories. LC 97-15585. (Nineteenth Century Ser.). 376p. (C). 1997. text 74.95 (*1-85928-202-4*) Ashgate Pub Co.

Ray, Martin, ed. Joseph Conrad: Interviews & Recollections. LC 89-52160. 254p. 1990. text 34.95 (*0-87745-290-3*) U of Iowa Pr.

Ray Martyn, Martyn S. & Sneesby, Martin G. Chemical Engineering Design Project: A Case Study. 2nd ed. (Illus.). 360p. 1998. text 80.00 (*90-5699-136-1*) Gordon & Breach.

Ray, Martyn S. Chemical Engineering Bibliography, 1967-1988. LC 89-77185. 887p. 1990. 98.00 (*0-8155-1241-4*) Noyes.

— Chemical Process & Plant Design Bibliography, 1959-1989. LC 90-22371. 196p. 1991. 54.00 (*0-8155-1272-4*) Noyes.

— Engineering Experimentation: Ideas, Techniques & Presentation. (C). 1990. text 48.00 (*0-07-084184-5*) McGraw.

Ray, Martyn S. & Sneesby, Martin G. Chemical Engineering Design Project: A Case Study. 2nd ed. (Illus.). 360p. 1998. pap. text 22.00 (*90-5699-137-X*) Gordon & Breach.

Ray, Mary. Cooking for a Crowd: Menus, Recipes, & How-to's For Church Kitchens. LC 94-33297. 128p. (Orig.). 1995. pap. 6.97 (*0-687-00253-2*) Abingdon.

— The Ides of April. LC 98-83214. (Young Adult Bookshelf Ser.). 165p. (YA). (gr. 9 up). 1999. pap. text 11.95 (*1-883937-43-4*, 43-4) Bethlehem Bks.

Ray, Mary, et al, eds. Gloucester, Massachusetts, Town & City Records Guide: Including Other Related Material. 151p. 1992. pap. 19.50 (*0-8328-2582-4*); lib. bdg. 29.50 (*0-8328-2581-6*) Higginson Bk Co.

Ray, Mary-Ann. Seven Partly Underground Rooms for Water, Ice, & Midgets. LC 97-4042. (Pamphlet Architecture Ser.: Vol. 20). (Illus.). 64p. (Orig.). 1997. pap. 12.95 (*1-56898-103-1*) Princeton Arch.

Ray, Mary-Ann, jt. auth. see Mangurian, Robert.

Ray, Mary B. & Cox, Barbara J. Beyond the Basics: A Text for Advanced Legal Writing. 375p. (C). 1993. reprint ed. pap. text, teacher ed. write for info. (*0-314-92269-5*) West Pub.

Ray, Mary B. & Ramsfield, Jill J. Legal Writing: Getting It Right & Getting It Written. 2nd ed. 361p. (C). 1993. pap. 25.50 (*0-314-02255-4*) West Pub.

Ray, Mary F. & Dondi, Beda. Professional Cooking & Baking. (Illus.). 450p. (C). 1981. teacher ed. 14.65 (*0-02-665440-7*); text 31.99 (*0-02-665430-X*); student ed. 7.77 (*0-02-665450-4*) Glencoe.

Ray, Mary F., jt. auth. see Lewis.

Ray, Mary F., jt. auth. see Lewis, Evelyn Jones.

Ray, Mary H. & Nicholls, Robert P., eds. A Guide to Significant & Historic Gardens of America. LC 82-74400. (Illus.). 327p. (Orig.). 1984. pap. 9.95 (*0-9612486-0-2*) Garden GA.

— The Traveler's Guide to American Gardens. rev. ed. (Illus.). xv, 375p. 1988. 19.95 (*0-8078-1787-2*) U of NC Pr.

Ray, Mary L. Angel Baskets: A Little Story about the Shakers. LC 87-50789. (Illus.). 32p. (Orig.). (J). 1987. pap. write for info. (*0-9609384-3-5*) M Wetherbee.

— Mud. LC 94-28711. (Illus.). 32p. (J). (ps-3). 1996. 16.00 (*0-15-256263-X*) Harcourt.

— My Carousel Horse. LC 93-45876. (Illus.). (J). 1994. text 13.95 (*0-15-200023-2*) Harcourt.

— Pianna. LC 91-14609. (Illus.). 32p. (J). (ps-3). 1994. 14.95 (*0-15-261357-9*, Harcourt Child Bks) Harcourt.

— Pumpkins: A Story for a Field. LC 90-47305. (Illus.). 32p. 1996. pap. 6.00 (*0-15-201358-X*) Harcourt.

— Shaker Boy. LC 93-1333. (Illus.). 48p. (J). (gr. k-3). 1994. 15.95 (*0-15-276921-8*, Harcourt Child Bks) Harcourt.

— Shaker Boy. (J). 1997. pap. 6.00 (*0-15-201563-9*, Harcourt Child Bks) Harcourt.

Ray, Mary L., ed. see Wetherbee, Martha & Taylor, Nathan.

Ray, Mary Lyn. Basket Moon. LC 96-49013. (Illus.). 32p. (J). (ps-3). 1999. 15.95 (*0-316-73521-3*) Little.

— Pumpkins, a Story for a Field. 1996. 11.20 (*0-606-11770-9*, Pub. by Turtleback) Demco.

— Red Rubber Boot Day. LC 97-25676. (Illus.). 32p. (J). 2000. 16.00 (*0-15-213756-4*, Harcourt Child Bks) Harcourt.

Ray, Maurice, ed. Recruitment Advertising: A Means of Communication. 240p. (C). 1980. 85.00 (*0-85292-259-0*, Pub. by IPM Hse) St Mut.

Ray, Michael. Setting up Home in Florida: How to Buy, Rent or Timeshare Residential Property in the Sunshine State. (Living & Working Abroad Ser.). 110p. 1996. pap. 19.95 (*1-85703-434-1*, Pub. by How To Bks) Trans-Atl Phila.

Ray, Michael & Rinzler, Alan, eds. The New Paradigm in Business: Emerging Strategies for Leadership & Organizational Change. LC 92-26205. 320p. 1993. pap. 15.95 (*0-87477-726-7*, Tarcher Putnam) Putnam Pub Group.

Ray, Michael, jt. auth. see Catford, Lorna.

Ray, Michael, jt. auth. see Littman, Barbara.

Ray, Michael J. Boeing 757-767 Simulator Checkride Procedures Manual. 8th rev. ed. (Illus.). 288p. 1995. pap. 49.95 (*0-936283-02-5*) U Temecula Pr.

— Rivers of Time: A Graphic Chronology of Man. 280p. (C). write for info. (*0-936283-01-7*) U Temecula Pr.

— Then & Now: Cartoons about Airline Pilots. 96p. (Orig.). 1986. pap. 10.00 (*0-936283-00-9*) U Temecula Pr.

— The Unofficial Boeing 737 Super Guppy Simulator Pt. 1: Checkride Survival Manual. (Illus.). 188p. 1998. pap. 29.92 (*0-936283-04-1*) U Temecula Pr.

R

Ray, Michael L., ed. Measurement Readings for Marketing Research. LC 84-9385. 382p. reprint ed. pap. 118.50 (*0-7837-2492-6*, 204265700005) Bks Demand.

Ray, Michael L. & Meyers, Rochelle. Creativity in Business. 240p. 1988. pap. 12.95 (*0-385-24851-2*) Doubleday.

Ray, Michael L. & Ward, Scott, eds. Communicating with Consumers: The Information Processing Approach. LC 75-32370. (Sage Contemporary Social Science Issues Ser.: No. 21). 142p. reprint ed. pap. 44.10 (*0-608-10914-2*, 202194300026) Bks Demand.

Ray, Muriel, ed. see Martel, Sarah.

Ray, Murphy E., Jr., jt. auth. see Brothers, Al.

Ray, N. Idea & Image in Indian Art. (Illus.). 1973. text 32.50 (*0-685-13741-4*) Coronet Bks.

Ray, N., et al. Normal Structures & Bordism Theory, with Applications to MSP. LC 77-10134. (Memoirs Ser.: No. 12/193). 66p. 1977. pap. 21.00 (*0-8218-2193-8*, MEMO/12/193) Am Math.

Ray, N. R., ed. Dictionary of National Biography, Supplement Vol. 1. (C). 1986. 54.00 (*0-8364-2364-X*) S Asia.

Ray, N. R. & Chakrabarti, P. N., eds. Studies in Cultural Development of India. (C). 1991. 44.00 (*81-85094-43-8*, Pub. by Punthi Pus) S Asia.

Ray, Nicholas. Cambridge Architecture: A Concise Guide. (Illus.). 142p. (C). 1994. pap. text 19.95 (*0-521-45855-2*) Cambridge U Pr.

— Cambridge Architecture: A Concise Guide. (Illus.). 152p. (C). 1994. text 59.95 (*0-521-45222-8*) Cambridge U Pr.

— I Was Interrupted: Nicholas Ray on Making Movies. LC 92-35003. 1993. 40.00 (*0-520-08233-8*, Pub. by U CA Pr) Cal Prin Full Svc.

— I Was Interrupted: Nicholas Ray on Making Movies. Ray, Susan, ed. & intro. by. (Illus.). 243p. 1995. pap. 15.95 (*0-520-20169-8*, Pub. by U CA Pr) Cal Prin Full Svc.

Ray, Nicholas D. Arab Islamic Banking & the Renewal of Islamic Law. LC 95-9842. (Arab & Islamic Laws Ser.). 1995. lib. bdg. 110.00 (*1-85966-104-1*, Pub. by Graham & Trotman) Kluwer Academic.

Ray, Nick. Cambodia. 3rd ed. (Illus.). 224p. 1996. pap. 15.95 (*0-86442-447-7*) Lonely Planet.

***Ray, Nick.** Lonely Planet Cambodia. 3rd ed. (Lonely Planet Travel Guides Ser.). (Illus.). 224p. 1999. pap. 15.95 (*0-86442-670-4*) Lonely Planet.

Ray, Nigel & Walker, Grant, eds. Proceedings of the Adams Memorial Symposium on Algebraic Topology, Vol. 1. (London Mathematical Society Lecture Note Ser.: No. 175). (Illus.). 316p. (C). 1992. pap. text 49.95 (*0-521-42074-1*) Cambridge U Pr.

— Proceedings of the Adams Memorial Symposium on Algebraic Topology, Vol. 2. (London Mathematical Society Lecture Note Ser.: No. 176). (Illus.). 329p. (C). 1992. pap. text 49.95 (*0-521-42153-5*) Cambridge U Pr.

Ray, Nihar-Ranjan. Brahmanical Gods in Burma: A Chapter of Indian Art & Iconography. LC 77-87020. reprint ed. 32.50 (*0-404-16852-3*) AMS Pr.

— An Introduction to the Study of Theravada Buddhism in Burma: A Study of Indo-Burmese Historical & Cultural Relations from the Earliest Times to the British Conquest. LC 77-87021. reprint ed. 32.50 (*0-404-16853-1*) AMS Pr.

— Sanskrit Buddhism in Burma. LC 78-70112. reprint ed. 41.50 (*0-404-17367-5*) AMS Pr.

Ray, Niharranjan. The Sikh Gurus & the Sikh Society. 1975. 14.50 (*0-8364-2615-0*, Pub. by M Manoharial) S Asia.

Ray, Nisith R. Dimensions of National Integration: The Experiences & Lessons of Indian History. (C). 1993. 40.00 (*81-85094-62-4*, Pub. by Punthi Pus) S Asia.

— Growth of Public Opinion in India: 19th & Early 20th Centuries. (C). 1989. 34.00 (*81-85109-94-X*, Pub. by Naya Prokash) S Asia.

— The Urban Experience: Essays in Honour of Professor Nisith R. Ray. 1987. 17.50 (*0-8364-2276-7*, Pub. by RDDHI) S Asia.

Ray, Norm. Easy Financials for Your Home-Based Business: The Friendly Guide to Successful Management Systems for Busy Home Entrepreneurs. LC 92-50682. (Illus.). 184p. (Orig.). 1993. pap. 19.95 (*1-877810-92-4*, EZ) Rayve Prodns.

— Smart Tax Write-Offs: Hundreds of Tax Deduction Ideas for Home-Based Businesses, Independent Contractors, All Entrepreneurs. 2nd ed. LC 98-52102. 1999. 12.95 (*1-877810-19-3*) Rayve Prodns.

***Ray, Norm.** Smart Tax Write-Offs, 1999-2000: Hundreds of Tax Deduction Ideas for Home-Based Businesses, Independent Contractors, All Entrepreneurs. 3rd ed. LC 00-20303. 144p. 2000. pap. 13.95 (*1-877810-18-5*) Rayve Prodns.

Ray, Norman H., jt. auth. see Ray, Barbara.

Ray, Oakley S. & Ksir, Charles. Drugs, Society, & Human Behavior. 8th ed. LC 98-7758. 1998. 39.14 (*0-07-059307-8*) McGraw.

***Ray, Oakley S. & Ksir, Charles.** Drugs, Society & Human Behavior with Annual Editions Online. 8th ed. (Illus.). 512p. 1999. pap., student ed. 55.00 (*0-07-235248-5*) McGraw.

Ray, Olden M., Sr. Black Valentine. 100p. 1988. 6.95 (*0-9616488-4-8*) Alef Bet Comns.

Ray, Ollie M. A Handbook of Novelty, Country & Western Dances: Country & Western Dance. 2nd rev. ed. ix, 140p. (YA). (gr. 9-12). 1993. pap. 19.95 (*0-9659397-0-7*) Siddall & Ray.

Ray, Ollie M., jt. auth. see Howell, Robert.

Ray, Ollie M., jt. auth. see Vincent, Jenny W.

Ray, P. K. Advances in Immunity & Cancer Therapy, Vol. 2. (Illus.). 305p. 1986. 91.00 (*0-387-96258-1*) Spr-Verlag.

— Aquaculture in Sundarban Delta: Its Perspective & Assessment. 212p. 1993. pap. 175.00 (*0-7855-0401-X*, Pub. by Intl Bks & Periodicals) St Mut.

— A Practical Guide to Multi-Risk Crop Insurance for Developing. (C). 1991. text 21.50 (*81-204-0604-4*, Pub. by Oxford IBH) S Asia.

— A Practical Guide to Multi-Risk Crop Insurance for Developing Countries. (Illus.). 180p. 1998. 40.00 (*1-57808-028-2*) Science Pubs.

Ray, P. K., ed. Management & Welfare of Farm Animals: The UFAW Handbook. 3rd ed. 260p. 1994. reprint ed. pap. 175.00 (*0-900767-87-1*, Pub. by Univs Fed Animal Welfare) St Mut.

Ray, Paul C. The Surrealist Movement in England. LC 70-145626. 331p. 1971. 20.00 (*0-685-10518-0*) Lib Soc Sci.

Ray, Paul H. & Anderson, Sherry Ruth. The Cultural Creatives: How 50,000,000 People Are Changing the World. LC 00-38293. (Illus.). 320p. 2000. 25.00 (*0-609-60467-8*) Harmony Bks.

Ray, Pearl J. Beyond Today. 288p. (Orig.). (C). 1986. pap. 6.95 (*0-9616405-0-2*) Harvest Age.

Ray, Peter. Not a Ghost of a Chance: A Mystery. 1997. pap. 3.50 (*1-57514-314-3*, 1177) Encore Perform Pub.

Ray, Peter S., ed. Mesoscale Meteorology & Forecasting. (Illus.). 793p. (C). 1987. reprint ed. text 66.25 (*0-933876-66-1*) Am Meteorological.

***Ray, Pradeep.** Cooperative Management of Enterprise Networks. LC 00-24561. (Network & Systems Management Ser.). 2000. write for info. (*0-306-46276-1*, Kluwer Plenum) Kluwer Academic.

Ray, Prasanta K., ed. Immunobiology & Transplantation, Cancer & Pregnancy. 500p. 1983. 200.00 (*0-08-025994-4*, Pergamon Pr) Elsevier.

Ray, Priyadaranjan & Ray, Acharya P., eds. History of Chemistry in Ancient & Medieval India, Incorporating the History of Hindu Chemistry. LC 79-8619. reprint ed. 42.50 (*0-404-18483-9*) AMS Pr.

Ray, Punya S., et al. Bengali Language Handbook. LC 66-29717. (Language Handbook Ser.). 155p. reprint ed. pap. 48.10 (*0-8357-3357-2*, 203959400013) Bks Demand.

Ray, R., et al. Role & Status of Women in India. 167p. 1978. 11.95 (*0-318-37071-9*) Asia Bk Corp.

Ray, R. Randy, ed. High-Definition Seismic 2-D, 2-D Swath, & 3-D Case Histories. LC 95-74721. (Illus.). 214p. 1995. write for info. (*0-933979-17-7*) Rocky Mtn Assoc Geol.

Ray, Rabindra. The Naxalites & Their Ideology. 262p. 1993. reprint ed. pap. text 10.95 (*0-19-563125-0*) OUP.

***Ray, Rachael.** Rachael Ray's Open House Cookbook: Over 200 Recipes for Easy Entertaining. (Illus.). 2000. pap. 17.95 (*1-891105-04-3*) Lake Isle Pr.

Ray, Rachael. 30-Minute Meals. 1999. pap. 14.95 (*1-891105-03-5*) Lake Isle Pr.

Ray, Rajat. Urban Roots of Indian Nationalism. 246p. 1979. 18.95 (*0-318-36867-6*) Asia Bk Corp.

Ray, Rajat K. Social Conflict & Political Unrest in Bengal, Eighteen Seventy-Five to Nineteen Twenty-Seven. (Illus.). 410p. (C). 1985. text 34.00 (*0-19-561654-5*) OUP.

Ray, Rajat K., ed. Entrepreneurship & Industry in India, 1800-1947. (Oxford in India Readings: Themes in Indian History Ser.). 276p. 1992. 18.95 (*0-19-562806-3*) OUP.

Ray, Rajat K., ed. Mind, Body & Society: Life & Mentality in Colonial Bengal. LC 96-900190. (Illus.). 498p. 1996. text 35.00 (*0-19-563757-7*) OUP.

***Ray, Rajat Kanta.** Exploring Emotional History: Gender, Mentality, & Literature in the Indian Awakening. 400p. 2001. text 29.95 (*0-19-565292-4*) OUP.

Ray, Raka. Fields of Protest: Women's Movements in India. LC 98-30623. (Social Movements, Protest & Contention Ser.: Vol. 8). (Illus.). 224p. 1999. 49.95 (*0-8166-3131-X*); pap. 19.95 (*0-8166-3132-8*) U of Minn Pr.

Ray, Ralph. Wills & Post-Death Tax Planning. 2nd expanded ed. 148p. 1997. pap. 43.00 (*1-85811-122-6*, Pub. by CLT Prof) Gaunt.

Ray, Ralph P. & Redman, John E. Practical Inheritance Tax Planning. 3rd ed. LC 95-135359. 416p. 1994. pap. 45.00 (*0-406-02417-0*, UK, MICHIE) LEXIS Pub.

Ray, Randolph, ed. One Hundred Great Religious Poems. LC 78-80378. (Granger Index Reprint Ser.). 1977. 18.95 (*0-8369-6060-2*) Ayer.

Ray, Randy, jt. ed. see Kearney, Mark.

Ray, Ratnalakha & Sen, S. P. Modern Bengal: A Socio-Economic Survey. (C). 1990. 26.00 (*81-85421-00-5*, Pub. by Naya Prokash) S Asia.

***Ray, Rayburn.** Bible IQ: 1,000 Questions to Rate Your Scriptural Savvy. 256p. 2000. pap. 1.99 (*1-57748-837-7*) Barbour Pub.

Ray, Rayburn, jt. ed. see Knight, George.

Ray, Rayburn W. & Ray, Rose A. Wedding Anniversary Idea Book. 96p. 1985. pap. 9.95 (*0-939298-43-0*, 430) J M Pr.

Ray, Rebecca L. Bridging Both Worlds: The Communication Consultant in Corporate America. LC 93-28996. 194p. (Orig.). (C). 1993. pap. text 28.50 (*0-8191-9279-1*); lib. bdg. 52.50 (*0-8191-9278-3*) U Pr of Amer.

Ray, Reginald A. Buddhist Saints in India: A Study in Buddhist Values & Orientations. 528p. 1999. pap. 25.00 (*0-19-513483-4*) OUP.

***Ray, Reginald A.** Indestructible Truth: The Living Spirituality of Tibetan Buddhism. LC 00-30128. (Illus.). 2000. 29.95 (*1-57062-166-7*, Pub. by Shambhala Pubns) Random.

Ray, Richard. Case Studies in Athletic Training Administration. LC 94-28362. (Illus.). 104p. (Orig.). 1994. pap. text 14.00 (*0-87322-675-5*, BRAY0675) Human Kinetics.

***Ray, Richard.** Management Strategies in Athletic Training. 2nd ed. LC 99-27701. (Athletic Training Education Ser.). (Illus.). 328p. 2000. 45.00 (*0-88011-810-5*) Human Kinetics.

— QR/HTML for Dummies. 224p. 1996. spiral bd. 12.99 (*1-56884-990-7*) IDG Bks.

Ray, Richard & Wiese-Bjornstal, Diane M., eds. Counseling in Sports Medicine. LC 98-40303. (Illus.). 376p. 1998. text 42.00 (*0-88011-527-0*, BRAY0527) Human Kinetics.

Ray, Richard P., jt. ed. see Elton, David J.

Ray, Richard R., Jr. Management Strategies in Athletic Training. LC 93-5167. (Illus.). 280p. 1993. text 33.00 (*0-87322-582-1*, BRAY0582) Human Kinetics.

Ray, Robert B. The Avant-Garde Finds Andy Hardy. LC 95-13646. (Illus.). 272p. (C). 1996. text 44.00 (*0-674-05537-3*); pap. text 20.50 (*0-674-05538-1*) HUP.

— A Certain Tendency of the American Cinema, 1930-1980. LC 84-42901. (Illus.). 405p. 1985. pap. text 23.95 (*0-691-10174-4*, Pub. by Princeton U Pr) Cal Prin Full Svc.

Ray, Robert D. & Ray, Joan K. Integrating Aerospace Science into the Curriculum: K-12. Flack, Jerry D., ed. (Gifted Treasury Ser.). (Illus.). xxi, 191p. 1992. pap. text 21.50 (*0-87287-924-0*) Teacher Ideas Pr.

Ray, Robert H. An Andrew Marvell Companion. LC 97-34073. (Literature Reference Ser.). 224p. 1998. text 45.00 (*0-8240-6248-5*, H1243) Garland.

Ray, Robert H., ed. Approaches to Teaching Shakespeare's King Lear. LC 86-12734. (Approaches to Teaching World Literature Ser.: No. 12). x, 166p. 1986. pap. 18.00 (*0-87352-498-5*, AP12P); lib. bdg. 37.50 (*0-87352-497-7*, AP12C) Modern Lang.

Ray, Roger L. Christian Wisdom for Today: Three Classic Stages of Spirituality. 152p. 1998. pap. 14.99 (*0-8272-0476-0*) Chalice Pr.

Ray, Ronald, jt. auth. see U. S. Government Accounting Staff.

Ray, Rose A., jt. auth. see Ray, Rayburn W.

Ray, Rose M. Superwomen Do It Less . . . A Guide to Having It All: Children, a Career, & a Loving Relationship. Baird, Nelle, ed. LC 91-65759. (Illus.). (Orig.). 1992. pap. 12.95 (*0-9629361-0-3*) Yankee Pub.

***Ray, Ruth E.** Beyond Nostalgia: Aging & Life-Story Writing. LC 99-55852. 256p. 2000. 35.00 (*0-8139-1939-8*) U Pr of Va.

Ray, S., jt. ed. see Kiceniuk, J. W.

Ray, S., jt. ed. see Kiceniuk, Joe W.

Ray, S. Dutta. Psychological Disorders of Young Children. 259p. 1980. 19.95 (*0-318-36940-0*) Asia Bk Corp.

Ray, S. N. Communication & Rural Development in India: The Changing Perceptions & the Search for a New Public Policy. (C). 1992. pap. text 5.00 (*81-7304-030-3*, Pub. by Manohar) S Asia.

Ray, S. S. Reinforced Concrete: Analysis & Design. LC 94-13306. (Illus.). 576p. 1994. 99.95 (*0-632-03724-5*, Pub. by Blckwll Scitfc UK) Blackwell Sci.

— Structural Steelwork: Analysis & Design. LC 97-34497. 1998. 90.00 (*0-632-03857-8*) Blackwell Sci.

Ray, Sally J. Strategic Communication in Crisis Management: Lessons from the Airline Industry. LC 98-41664. 272p. 1999. 65.00 (*1-56720-153-9*, Quorum Bks) Greenwood.

Ray, Sam. Post Cards from Old Kansas City. LC 80-84468. (Illus.). 48p. 1980. pap. 9.50 (*0-685-02273-0*) Hist Kansas City.

Ray, Samuel N. Resumes for the Over-50 Job Hunter. LC 92-22988. 216p. 1993. pap. 16.95 (*0-471-57423-6*) Wiley.

Ray, Sandy. The Lamb. Sytsma, Cheryle, ed. (Illus.). 15p. (Orig.). (J). 1991. pap. write for info. (*1-879068-10-9*) Ray-Ma Natsal.

— The Little Seed. Sytsma, Cheryle, ed. LC 90-63623. (Illus.). 30p. (Orig.). (J). (gr. k-5). 1991. pap. write for info. (*1-879068-01-X*) Ray-Ma Natsal.

— Sir Joshua, Himself. Sytsma, Cheryle, ed. LC 90-63622. (Illus.). 30p. (Orig.). (J). (gr. k-5). 1991. pap. write for info. (*1-879068-02-8*) Ray-Ma Natsal.

— Songs of My Heart. Sytsma, Cheryle, ed. (Illus.). 160p. (Orig.). 1991. pap. 7.98 (*1-879068-07-9*) Ray-Ma Natsal.

— Songs of Sorrow Songs of Praise. Sytsma, Cheryle, ed. LC 90-91937. (Illus.). 160p. (Orig.). 1990. pap. 7.98 (*1-879068-00-1*) Ray-Ma Natsal.

— Words from My Father. Sytsma, Cheryle, ed. (Illus.). 192p. (Orig.). 1991. pap. 8.95 (*1-879068-03-6*) Ray-Ma Natsal.

***Ray, Sangeeta.** En-Gendering India: Woman & Nation in Colonial & Postcolonial Narratives. LC 99-45705. 216p. 2000. pap. 17.95 (*0-8223-2490-3*) Duke.

Ray, Sangeeta & Schwarz, Henry, eds. A Companion to Post Colonial Studies: An Historical Introduction. LC 99-33933. (Blackwell Companions to Literature & Culture Ser.). 500p. 1999. 99.95 (*0-631-20662-0*) Blackwell Pubs.

Ray, Satyajit. Brave Professor Shonku. 108p. 1986. 7.95 (*0-318-36944-3*) Asia Bk Corp.

— Our Films, Their Films. 219p. 1983. 19.95 (*0-86125-637-9*) Asia Bk Corp.

— Our Films, Their Films. 224p. (J). 1994. 22.45 (*0-7868-6122-3*, Pub. by Hyperion) Time Warner.

Ray, Satyajit & Majumdar, Gopa. The House of Death & Other Feluda Stories. LC 97-905477. 339p. 1997. 16.00 (*0-14-026803-0*, Penguin Bks) Viking Penguin.

— The Royal Bengal Mystery & Other Feluda Stories. LC 98-901284. viii, 349 p. 1997. 15.00 (*0-14-027590-8*, PuffinBks) Peng Put Young Read.

***Ray, Satyajit & Ray, Bijoya.** Childhood Days: A Memoir. LC 99-932530. xii, 173 p. 1998. 16.00 (*0-14-025079-4*) Penguin Putnam.

Ray, Sharon. Bass for Beginners. 1996. pap. 17.90 incl. audio compact disk (*0-88284-806-2*); pap. 7.95 (*0-88284-853-4*) Alfred Pub.

Ray, Sheila, jt. ed. see Hunt, Peter.

Ray, Shreela. Night Conversations with None Other. (American Dust Ser.: No. 6). 85p. 1977. 6.95 (*0-913218-32-4*); pap. 2.95 (*0-913218-31-6*) Dustbooks.

Ray, Sibnarayan, ed. For a Revolution from Below. (C). 1989. 17.50 (*81-85195-15-3*, Pub. by Minerva) S Asia.

— Selected Works of M. N. Roy, 1917-1922, Vol I. (Illus.). 596p. 1988. 45.00 (*0-19-562038-0*) OUP.

Ray, Sibnarayan, ed. see Roy, M. N.

Ray, Sidartha. Apoptosis. 83p. 1997. pap. text 30.00 (*90-5699-616-9*) Gordon & Breach.

Ray, Sidney F. Applied Photographic Optics: Lenses & Optical Systems for Photography, Film, Video & Electronic Imaging. 2nd ed. LC 93-44367. (Illus.). 576p. 2000. pap. text 69.95 (*0-240-51499-8*, Focal) Buttrwrth-Heinemann.

— The Photographic Lens: Media Manual. 2nd ed. (Illus.). 355p. 2000. pap. text 37.95 (*0-240-51329-0*, Focal) Buttrwrth-Heinemann.

— Scientific Photography & Applied Imaging. LC 99-25855. (Illus.). 559p. 1999. text 150.00 (*0-240-51323-1*, Focal) Buttrwrth-Heinemann.

Ray, Sidney F., ed. High Speed Photography & Photonics. LC 97-171034. (Illus.). 416p. 1997. text 84.95 (*0-240-51479-3*, Focal) Buttrwrth-Heinemann.

Ray, Sidney H. A Comparative Study of the Melanesian Island Languages. LC 75-35151. reprint ed. 87.50 (*0-404-14166-8*) AMS Pr.

Ray, Sidney H. & Haddon, Alfred C. A Study of the Languages of Torres Straits. LC 75-35153. reprint ed. 31.50 (*0-404-14168-4*) AMS Pr.

Ray, Sidney H. & Riley, E. Baxter. A Grammar of the Kiwai Language, Fly Delta, Papua, with a Kiwai Vocabulary. LC 75-35152. reprint ed. 29.50 (*0-404-14167-6*) AMS Pr.

Ray, Siva P. Turning of the Wheel. Ghosh, A., ed. (Illus.). 132p. (Orig.). 1987. pap. 6.95 (*0-9611614-2-6*) A Ghosh.

Ray, Slim. The Canoe Handbook: Techniques for Mastering the Sport of Canoeing. LC 91-16032. (Illus.). 224p. 1992. pap. 15.95 (*0-8117-3032-8*) Stackpole.

— Swiftwater Animal Rescue: A Handbook for Animal Rescue in Flood & Swiftwater Incidents. (Illus.). 70p. 1999. pap. text 9.95 (*0-9649585-2-X*) CFS Pr.

— Swiftwater Rescue: A Manual for the Rescue Professional. LC 96-84128. (Illus.). 243p. (Orig.). 1997. pap. text 24.95 (*0-9649585-0-3*) CFS Pr.

— Swiftwater Rescue Field Guide. LC 98-92636. (Illus.). 52p. 1998. spiral bd. 14.95 (*0-9649585-1-1*) CFS Pr.

Ray, Slim, jt. auth. see Bechdel, Les.

Ray, Sondra. Celebration of Breath. LC 83-1770. 192p. 1995. pap. 9.95 (*0-89087-355-0*) Celestial Arts.

— Drinking the Divine. LC 84-45361. 256p. (Orig.). 1995. pap. 9.95 (*0-89087-460-3*) Celestial Arts.

— Essays on Creating Sacred Relationships. 192p. 1996. pap. 11.95 (*0-89087-796-3*) Celestial Arts.

— Healing with Sondra Ray. 235p. 1997. pap. 15.00 (*0-9651546-6-1*) Med Bear.

— How to Be Chic, Fabulous & Live Forever. LC 89-85828. 240p. 1995. 18.95 (*0-89087-564-2*) Celestial Arts.

— Ideal Birth. LC 84-71025. 300p. (Orig.). 1995. pap. 8.95 (*0-89087-364-X*) Celestial Arts.

— Inner Communion. LC 90-82187. 144p. (Orig.). 1995. pap. 8.95 (*0-89087-621-5*) Celestial Arts.

Ray, Sondra. Lasting Love Relationships. 142p. 1995. pap. 16.95 incl. audio (*1-879323-23-0*) Sound Horizons AV.

Ray, Sondra. Loving Relationships. LC 79-55633. 192p. 1995. pap. 9.95 (*0-89087-244-9*) Celestial Arts.

— Loving Relationships II. 192p. 1995. pap. 9.95 (*0-89087-661-4*) Celestial Arts.

— The Only Diet There Is. LC 80-70795. 156p. 1995. pap. 8.95 (*0-89087-321-6*) Celestial Arts.

— Pure Joy. LC 86-26911. 216p. 1995. pap. 9.95 (*0-89087-491-3*) Celestial Arts.

Ray, Sondra & Mandel, Bob. Birth & Relationships: How Your Birth Affects Your Relationships. LC 86-28404. 172p. 1995. pap. 8.95 (*0-89087-486-7*) Celestial Arts.

Ray, Sondra, jt. auth. see Orr, Leonard D.

Ray, Stephen & Murdoch, Kathleen. The Ant Nest. LC 92-34254. (Voyages Ser.). (Illus.). (J). 1993. 4.25 (*0-383-03614-3*) SRA McGraw.

— Have You Ever Found a Beetle? LC 92-27265. (Voyages Ser.). (Illus.). (J). 1993. 3.75 (*0-383-03627-5*) SRA McGraw.

— In the Forest. LC 92-27266. (Voyages Ser.). (Illus.). (J). 1993. 3.75 (*0-383-03635-6*) SRA McGraw.

— Just Right for the Night. LC 92-21398. (Illus.). (J). (gr. 4 up). 1993. 4.25 (*0-383-03580-5*) SRA McGraw.

— Snake. LC 92-21453. (Illus.). (J). 1993. 4.25 (*0-383-03653-4*) SRA McGraw.

— Some Snakes. LC 93-113. (Illus.). (J). 1994. pap. write for info. (*0-383-03715-8*) SRA McGraw.

— Tall Stories about Snakes. LC 93-6630. (Illus.). (J). 1994. pap. write for info. (*0-383-03716-6*) SRA McGraw.

Ray, Stephen K. Crossing the Tiber. LC 95-79951. 1997. pap. text 12.95 (*0-89870-577-0*) Ignatius Pr.

Ray, Steven K. Upon This Rock: St. Peter & the Primacy of Rome in Scripture & the Early Church. LC 98-74065. 1999. pap. text 16.95 (*0-89870-723-4*) Ignatius Pr.

Ray, Subhash C., jt. auth. see Lott, William F.

Ray, Sukumar. Folk-Music of Eastern India. (C). 1988. 24.00 (*81-85109-81-8*, Pub. by Naya Prokash) S Asia.

— Music of Eastern India. 1986. 20.00 (*0-8364-1581-7*) S Asia.

— The Select Nonsense of Sukumar Ray. Chaudhuri, Sukanta, tr. (Oxford India Paperbacks Ser.). (Illus.). 80p. (Orig.). 1998. pap. text 5.00 (*0-19-563039-4*) OUP.

Ray, Supryia M., jt. auth. see Murfin, Ross C.

Ray, Susan, ed. Consciously Creating Each Day: A Perpetual Calendar of Spirited Thought from Voices Past & Present. 382p. 1999. spiral bd. 12.95 (*0-9661327-0-X*) Moment Pt Pr.

Ray, Susan, jt. auth. see Isaak, Gudrum.

An Asterisk (*) at the beginning of an entry indicates that the title is appearing for the first time.

Ray, Susan, ed. & intro. see Ray, Nicholas.
Ray, Susan, tr. see Adelsberger, Lucie.
Ray, Susan H., tr. see Kesting, Jurgen.
Ray, Susan H., tr. see Schimmel, Annemarie.
Ray, Susan H., tr. see Schnauber, Cornelius.
Ray, Suzanne S., et al, compiled by. Preliminary Guide to Pre-Nineteen Hundred & Four County Records in the Virginia State Library & Archives. xxv, 331p. 1994. reprint ed. pap. 12.00 (*0-88490-179-3*) Library of VA.
Ray, Syamal K. Indian Bureaucracy at the Crossroads. 407p. 1979. 25.95 (*0-940500-58-2*, Pub. by Sterling) Asia Bk Corp.
Ray, Thomas P. Predoctoral Astrophysics School: 5th: 1992: Berlin, Germany: Star Formation & Techniques in Infrared & mm-Wave Astronomy: Lectures Held at the Predoctoral Astrophysics School V, Organized by the European Astrophysics Doctoral Network (EADN) in Berlin, Germany, 21 Sept.-20 Oct. 1992. Beckwith, S., ed. LC 94-25872. 1994. 72.95 (*0-387-58196-0*) Spr-Verlag.
Ray, Thomas P., jt. ed. see Sandqvist, Aage.
***Ray, Tiernan.** E-Trading Today. (Sams Teach Yourself Ser.). 425p. 2000. 17.99 (*0-672-31821-0*) Sams.
Ray, Tim. The Patient Stones. 54p. (Orig.). 1996. pap. text. write for info. (*1-57579-018-1*) Pine Hill Pr.
Ray, Tina. Through My Eyes - From My Heart. (Orig.). 1996. pap. write for info. (*1-57553-287-5*) Watermrk Pr.
Ray, Todd. Ultimate Skate Guide: To the San Francisco Bay Area. LC 95-61280. 224p. (Orig.). 1995. pap. 17.95 (*1-56550-053-9*) Vis Bks Intl.
Ray, Ujjal. From Diffidence to Reliance: Journey of a Colonial Intellectual 1839-94. (C). 1993. 14.00 (*81-85195-51-X*, Pub. by Minerva) S Asia.
Ray, Uma. Indian Music for English Speaking Singers. (Illus.). 125p. 1995. text 35.00 (*0-89341-736-X*); pap. text 18.50 (*0-89341-737-8*) Hollowbrook.
Ray, Verne F. Cultural Relations in the Plateau of Northwestern America. LC 76-43807. reprint ed. 35.00 (*0-404-15664-9*) AMS Pr.
— Culture Element Distributions No. XXII: Plateau. fac. ed. Kroeber, A. L. et al, eds. (University of California Publications: No. 8:2). (Illus.). 168p. (C). 1942. reprint ed. pap. 18.13 (*1-55567-092-X*) Coyote Press.
— The Sanpoil & Nespelem: Salishan Peoples of Northeastern Washington. LC 76-43809. (Univ. of Washington Publications in Anthropology: Vol. 5). reprint ed. 45.00 (*0-404-15663-0*) AMS Pr.
Ray, Verne F., ed. Cultural Stability & Cultural Change: American Ethnological Society Proceedings, 1957. LC 84-45544. 1988. reprint ed. pap. 35.00 (*0-404-62651-3*) AMS Pr.
— Intermediate Societies, Social Mobility, & Communication: American Ethnological Society Proceedings, 1959. LC 84-45546. 1988. reprint ed. pap. 35.00 (*0-404-62653-X*) AMS Pr.
— Systems of Political Control & Bureaucracy in Human Societies: American Ethnological Society Proceedings, 1958. LC 84-45545. 1988. reprint ed. pap. 35.00 (*0-404-62652-1*) AMS Pr.
Ray, Verne F., ed. see Teicher, Morton I.
Ray, Veronica. Accepting Ourselves. (A Moment to Reflect Ser.). pap. 2.50 (*0-89486-570-6*, 5102 A) Hazelden.
— Choosing Happiness: The Art of Living Unconditionally. 238p. (Orig.). pap. 12.00 (*0-89486-658-3*) Hazelden.
— I Can Make a Differnce. (A Moment to Reflect Ser.). pap. 2.50 (*0-89486-762-8*) Hazelden.
— I Have Choices. (A Moment to Reflect Ser.). pap. 2.50 (*0-89486-760-1*) Hazelden.
— I Know Myself. (A Moment to Reflect Ser.). pap. 2.50 (*0-89486-763-6*) Hazelden.
— I'm Good Enough. (A Moment to Reflect Ser.). pap. 2.50 (*0-89486-761-X*) Hazelden.
— Letting Go. (A Moment to Reflect Ser.). pap. 2.50 (*0-89486-569-2*) Hazelden.
— Living Our Own Lives. (A Moment to Reflect Ser.). pap. 2.50 (*0-89486-571-4*) Hazelden.
— Miracles on Main Street. 1996. mass mkt. 5.50 (*0-312-95700-9*, Pub. by Tor Bks) St Martin.
Ray, Veronica. Personal Evolution: The Art of Living with Purpose. 10.00 incl. audio (*0-89486-825-X*) Hazelden.
Ray, Veronica. Setting Boundaries. (A Moment to Reflect Ser.). pap. 2.50 (*0-89486-585-4*) Hazelden.
— Zen Gardening: A Down-to-Earth Philosophy. LC 96-170031. (Illus.). 192p. 1996. pap. text 11.95 (*0-425-15299-5*) Berkley Pub.
Ray, W. Harmon, jt. auth. see Ogunnaike, Babatunde A.
***Ray, Walter.** Coming Clean: A Tale Told from the Heart. unabridged ed. Click, Sharon & Stewart, Emma, eds. (Illus.). 400p. 1999. 16.95 (*0-9673518-0-4*) Bird In Paradise.
***Ray, Wendel A. & De Shazer, Steve, eds.** Evolving Brief Therapies: In Honor of John Weakland. (C). 1999. pap. text 29.95 (*1-884228-27-5*) Geist & Russell.
Ray, Wendel A. & Keeney, Bradford. Resource-Focused Therapy. (Systemic Thinking & Practice Ser.). 112p. 1993. pap. text 19.50 (*1-85575-049-X*, Pub. by H Karnac Bks Ltd) Other Pr LLC.
Ray, Wendel A. & Weakland, John H., eds. Propagations: Thirty Years of Influence from the Mental Research Institute. LC 94-32743. 310p. (C). 1995. lib. bdg. 49.95 (*1-56024-936-6*) Haworth Pr.
Ray, Wendel A., jt. auth. see Silberman, Bernice S.
Ray, William J. Methods Toward a Science of Behavior & Experience. 4th ed. 1992. pap., teacher ed. write for info. (*0-534-17839-1*) Brooks-Cole.
— Methods Toward a Science of Behavior & Experience. 4th ed. 480p. (C). 1993. text 45.50 (*0-534-17838-3*) Brooks-Cole.
— Methods Toward a Science of Behavior & Experience. 5th ed. LC 96-12020. (Psychology Ser.). 496p. (C). 1996. pap. 52.25 (*0-534-20346-9*) Brooks-Cole.
— Methods Toward a Science of Behavior & Experience. 5th ed. 1996. mass mkt., teacher ed. write for info. (*0-534-34390-2*) Brooks-Cole.
— Methods Toward a Science of Behavior & Experience. 6th ed. LC 99-34371. (Psychology Ser.). 441p. 1999. pap. text 85.95 (*0-534-35721-0*) Brooks-Cole.
— Methods Toward a Science of Behavior & Experience: Methods in Action: Study Guide & Activities Workbook. 4th ed. Date not set. wbk. ed. 125.20 (*0-534-30725-6*) Brooks-Cole.
— Methods Toward a Science of Behavior & Experience: Study Guide & Activities Workbook. 5th ed. (Psychology Ser.). (C). 1996. mass mkt., student ed., wbk. ed. 20.00 (*0-534-34389-9*) Brooks-Cole.
Ray, William J. & Ravizza, Richard. Methods Toward a Science of Behavior & Experience. 2nd ed. (C). 1984. mass mkt. 32.75 (*0-534-04041-1*) Brooks-Cole.
— Methods Toward a Science of Behavior & Experience. 3rd ed. 373p. (C). 1987. mass mkt. 46.75 (*0-534-08778-7*) Brooks-Cole.
Ray, William J., jt. ed. see Michelson, Larry K.
Ray, William W. Graduate Student Research in Planning, Urban Design & Urban Affairs, 1974-76, No. 1176. 1976. 9.50 (*0-686-20418-2*, Sage Prdcls Pr) Sage.
Ray, Willis H. & Szekely, Julian. Process Optimization: With Applications in Metallurgy & Chemical Engineering. LC 73-936. (Wiley-Interscience Publications). (Illus.). 382p. reprint ed. pap. 118.50 (*0-7837-3465-4*, 205779300008) Bks Demand.
Ray, Winifred, tr. see Heiden, Konrad.
Ray, Worth S. Austin (Texas) Colony Pioneers: Including History of Bastrop, Fayette, Grimes, Montgomery & Washington Counties, Texas. LC 95-75023. (Illus.). 378p. 1995. reprint ed. 22.50 (*0-8063-1473-7*) Clearfield Co.
— Lost Tribes of North Carolina: Index & Digest to Hathaway's "North Carolina Historical & Genealogical Register", Pt. 1. 192p. 1997. reprint ed. pap. 22.50 (*0-8063-0479-0*, 4795) Clearfield Co.
— Lost Tribes of North Carolina: Old Albemarle & Its Absentee Landlords, Pt. IV. LC 67-9767. 156p. 1998. reprint ed. pap. 17.50 (*0-8063-0287-9*) Clearfield Co.
— Tennessee Cousins: A History of Tennessee People. LC 68-24685. (Illus.). 819p. 1999. reprint ed. 40.00 (*0-8063-0289-5*, 4800) Genealog Pub.
Raya, Joseph. Abundance of Love: The Incarnation & Byzantine Tradition. (Illus.). 143p. (Orig.). 1989. pap. 8.95 (*1-56125-015-5*) Educ Services.
— Acathist Hymn to the Name of Jesus. Vinck, Jose de, ed. 40p. 1990. reprint ed. pap. 6.75 (*0-911726-46-2*, CODE NJB) Alleluia Pr.
— Byzantine Church & Culture. De Vinck, Jose M., ed. LC 91-77254. (Illus.). 172p. 1992. (*0-911726-54-3*, CODE CCC) Madonna Hse.
Raya, Joseph. Christmas: Birth of Our Lord God & Saviour, Jesus Christ. 156p. 1997. 23.95 (*0-921440-45-6*) Madonna Hse.
— Theophany & Sacraments of Initiation. 200p. 1993. 24.95 (*0-921440-36-7*) Madonna Hse.
— Transfiguration of Our Lord & Saviour Jesus Christ. 120p. 1992. 21.95 (*0-921440-29-4*) Madonna Hse.
Raya, Joseph & De Vinck, Jose. Byzantine Altar Gospel. 350p. 1979. 157.00 (*0-911726-34-9*, CODE AGC) Alleluia Pr.
— Byzantine Daily Worship. 1036p. 1969. 48.75 (*0-911726-07-1*, BDW) Alleluia Pr.
— Byzantine Epistles Lectionary: Apostolos. 550p. 1981. 105.00 (*0-911726-37-3*, AEC) Alleluia Pr.
Raya, Joseph M. The Face of God: Essays in Byzantine Spirituality. 220p. (Orig.). 1984. pap. text 10.00 (*1-887158-00-6*) God With Us.
Raya, Joseph M. Theotokos: Mary Mother of Our Lord God & Saviour Jesus Christ. 150p. 1995. 22.95 (*0-921440-39-1*) Madonna Hse.
Raya-Norman, Faye. Wolf Songs. Carpenter, Christina D., ed. (Illus.). 32p. (YA). (ps-1). 1999. 15.95 (*1-886440-04-2*) Portunus Pubng.
Rayala, Martin. Guide to Curriculum Planning in Art Education. 2nd rev. ed. LC 95-621568. 200p. (C). 1995. pap. text 30.00 (*1-57337-003-7*) WI Dept Pub Instruct.
***Rayala, Martin.** Wisconsin's Model Academic Standards for Art & Design. 32p. 2000. pap. 9.00 (*1-57337-080-0*) WI Dept Pub Instruct.
Rayan, William M., jt. auth. see Boyer, Ralph E.
Rayaprol, Aparna. Negotiating Identities: Women in the Indian Diaspora. LC 97-903275. 180p. 1998. 19.95 (*0-19-564151-5*) OUP.
Rayar, Louise, et al, trs. from DUT. Dutch Penal Code. rev. ed. LC 93-46355. (American Series of Foreign Penal Codes: Vol. 30). xxiii, 277p. 1997. 47.50 (*0-8377-0050-7*, Rothman) W S Hein.
Rayas, Lucia, tr. see Diaz Polanco, Hector.
Rayback, Joseph G. A History of American Labor. LC 59-5344. 1966. pap. 19.95 (*0-02-925850-2*) Free Pr.
Rayback, Joseph G., jt. auth. see Mushkat, Jerome.
Rayback, Robert J. Millard Fillmore: Biography of a President. Speirs, Katherine E., ed. LC 91-78015. (Signature Ser.). (Illus.). 470p. 1992. reprint ed. 32.50 (*0-945707-04-5*) Amer Political.
Rayban, C. Havana to Hollywood. (Illus.). (J). 1997. mass mkt. 7.95 (*0-340-68164-0*, Pub. by Hodder & Stought Ltd) Trafalgar.
— Models Move on to Starring Roles. mass mkt. 8.95 (*0-340-71428-X*, Pub. by Hodder & Stought Ltd) Trafalgar.
— Models One: Screen Kiss. (Illus.). mass mkt. 7.95 (*0-340-68162-4*, Pub. by Hodder & Stought Ltd) Trafalgar.
— Skin Deep. mass mkt. 8.95 (*0-340-71429-8*, Pub. by Hodder & Stought Ltd) Trafalgar.
— Street to Stardom. (Illus.). (J). 1997. mass mkt. 7.95 (*0-340-68165-9*, Pub. by Hodder & Stought Ltd) Trafalgar.
***Raybeck, Douglas.** Looking Down the Road: A Systems Approach to Futures Studies. 131p. (C). 2000. pap. 10.95 (*1-57766-116-8*) Waveland Pr.
Raybeck, Douglas. Mad Dogs, Englishmen, & the Errant Anthropologist: Fieldwork in Malaysia. 20th ed. LC 97-205614. (Illus.). 248p. (C). 1996. pap. text 12.50 (*0-88133-906-7*) Waveland Pr.
***Raybin, David & Holley, Linda Tarte.** Closure in the Canterbury Tales: The Role of The Parson's Tale. LC 99-46313. (Studies in Medieval Culture). 2000. pap. text 20.00 (*1-58044-012-6*) Medieval Inst.
Raybin-Emert, Phyllis. Ghosts, Hauntings & Mysterious Happenings. (Strange Unsolved Mysteries Ser.). (J). 1992. 8.09 (*0-606-11928-0*, Pub. by Turtleback) Demco.
Raybin-Emert, Phyllis. Monsters, Strange Dreams, & UFO's, 2. (Strange Unsolved Mysteries Ser.). (J). 1994. 7.60 (*0-606-11926-4*, Pub. by Turtleback) Demco.
Raybin-Emert, Phyllis. Mysteries of Bizarre Animals & Freaks of Nature. (Strange Unsolved Mysteries Ser.). (J). 1994. 8.09 (*0-606-11929-9*, Pub. by Turtleback) Demco.
Raybin-Emert, Phyllis. Mysteries of People & Places, 3. (Strange Unsolved Mysteries Ser.). (J). 1992. 7.60 (*0-606-11927-2*, Pub. by Turtleback) Demco.
— Mysteries of Ships & Planes. (Strange Unsolved Mysteries Ser.). (J). 1990. 7.60 (*0-606-11925-6*, Pub. by Turtleback) Demco.
— Mysteries of Space & the Universe. (Strange Unsolved Mysteries Ser.). (J). 1994. 8.09 (*0-606-11930-2*, Pub. by Turtleback) Demco.
— Mysteries of the Mind & the Senses No. 8. (Strange Unsolved Mysteries Ser.). (J). 1995. 8.09 (*0-606-11932-9*, Pub. by Turtleback) Demco.
— Strange Appearances from Beyond. (Strange Unsolved Mysteries Ser.). (J). 1995. 8.09 (*0-606-11931-0*, Pub. by Turtleback) Demco.
Raybon, Patricia. My First White Friend. 256p. 1997. pap. 11.95 (*0-14-024436-0*) Viking Penguin.
— My First White Friend: Confessions on Race, Love & Forgiveness. 233p. 1996. 22.95 (*0-670-85956-7*, Viking); 22.95 (*0-614-95763-X*, Viking) Viking Penguin.
Raybould, David M. Comparative Law of Monopolies: 1989 Basic Work & 1989 Supplement Services. (C). 1989. ring bd. 324.00 (*0-86010-941-0*, Pub. by Graham & Trotman) Kluwer Academic.
— Comparative Law of Monopolies: 1991 Basic Work & 1991 Supplement Service. 400p. 1991. 400.00 (*1-85333-515-0*, Pub. by Graham & Trotman) Kluwer Academic.
— Comparative Law of Monopolies Vols. 1-2: 1995 Basic Work, 2 vols., Set. 1000p. 1995. ring bd. 405.00 (*1-85333-826-5*, Pub. by Graham & Trotman) Kluwer Academic.
— Comparative Law of Monopolies, Vols. 1 & 2: 1992 Basic Work & 1992 Supplement Service. 600p. 1992. ring bd. 332.00 (*1-85333-669-6*, Pub. by Graham & Trotman) Kluwer Academic.
Raybould, David M., ed. Comparative Law of Monopolies: Basic Work & Supplement Service, 1990. 1990. ring bd. 350.00 (*1-85333-326-3*, Pub. by Graham & Trotman) Kluwer Academic.
Raybould, David M. & Firth, Alison. Law of Monopolies: Competition Law & Practice in the U. S. A., E. E. C., Germany & the U. K. 592p. (C). 1991. lib. bdg. 177.00 (*1-85333-624-6*, Pub. by Graham & Trotman) Kluwer Academic.
Raybould, Edward, jt. auth. see Solity, Jonathan.
Raybould, Helen, jt. ed. see Mayer, Emeran A.
Raybould, S. Universities, Adult Education & Social Criticism. (Tolley Medal Ser.). 1970. 1.50 (*0-686-52207-9*, WPT 3) Syracuse U Cont Ed.
Rayburn, jt. auth. see Tosh, Dennis.
Rayburn, Alan. Dictionary of Canadian Place Names. LC 98-121014. 480p. 1997. 37.50 (*0-19-541086-6*) OUP.
— Naming Canada: Stories about Place Names from Canadian Geographic. (Illus.). 300p. 1994. pap. 16.95 (*0-8020-6990-8*); text 55.00 (*0-8020-0569-1*) U of Toronto Pr.
— Place Names of Ontario. LC 97-160862. 400p. 1997. pap. 21.95 (*0-8020-7207-0*) U of Toronto Pr.
Rayburn, Cherie. Where's Kitty? Gress, Jonna, ed. (Illus.). 12p. (J). (ps-5). 1994. pap. write for info. (*0-944943-45-4*, 23304-5) Current Inc.
Rayburn, Francis M., jt. auth. see Lindsey, Bonnie J.
***Rayburn, Jim, 3rd.** From Bondage to Liberty: Dance, Children, Dance. (Illus.). 224p. 1999. 17.95 (*0-9673897-4-7*) Morningst Pr.
Rayburn, John. Gregorian Chant: A History of Controversy Concerning Its Rhythm. LC 80-27616. 90p. 1981. reprint ed. lib. bdg. 35.00 (*0-313-22811-6*, RAGR, Greenwood Pr) Greenwood.
Rayburn, John C., et al, eds. Century of Conflict, 1821-1913: Incidents in the Lives of William Neale & William A. Neale, Early Settlers in South Texas. LC 76-1556. (Chicano Heritage Ser.). (Illus.). 1977. reprint ed. 16.95 (*0-405-09520-1*) Ayer.
Rayburn, L. Gayle. Cost Accounting, Chapters 1-14. 5th ed. (C). 1999. text, student ed. 85.95 (*0-256-18865-3*, Irwn McGrw-H) McGrw-H Hghr Educ.
— Cost Accounting, Chapters 1-14. 6th ed. 688p. (C). 1995. text, student ed. 27.50 (*0-256-17481-4*, Irwn McGrw-H) McGrw-H Hghr Educ.
— Cost Accounting, International: Using a Cost Management Approach. 5th ed. 1024p. (C). 1992. text 36.50 (*0-256-10809-9*, Irwn McGrw-H) McGrw-H Hghr Educ.
Rayburn, Letricia G. Cost Accounting: Using a Cost Management Approach. 6th ed. LC 95-23347. (Irwin Series in Undergraduate Accounting). 912p. (C). 1995. text 74.25 (*0-256-17480-6*, Irwn Prfssnl) McGraw-Hill Prof.
Rayburn, Linda. Living (And Loving) the Low-Carb Life! 170p. 1999. pap. 21.95 (*0-9670780-0-8*) Darlin Pubns.
Rayburn, Madison. Rayburn on Condemnation: Texas Eminent Domain Applied with Forms. 1998. write for info. (*1-58012-032-6*) James Pub Santa Ana.
Rayburn, Morris P. I'll Never Forget: A Compendium of Events - 1936 to 1945 China - Burma - India World War II. 614p. 1996. text 34.50 (*0-9656823-0-7*) M P Rayburn.
Rayburn, Richard. Elections. (Illus.). 96p. (Orig.). (J). (gr. 4-8). 1992. student ed. 11.95 (*1-55734-069-2*) Tchr Create Mat.
Rayburn, Richard, jt. auth. see Hale, Janet.
Rayburn, Rosalie & Bush, Kathleen. Living & Working in Saudi Arabia: How to Prepare for a Successful Short or Longterm Stay. (Living & Working Abroad Ser.). 158p. 1997. pap. 28.50 (*1-85703-152-0*, Pub. by How To Bks) Trans-Atl Phila.
Rayburn, S. R. The Foundations of Laboratory Safety. (Contemporary Bioscience Ser.). (Illus.). xiii, 418p. 1989. 92.95 (*0-387-97125-4*) Spr-Verlag.
Rayburn, William B., jt. auth. see Appraisal Institute Staff.
Rayburn, William F., ed. Obstetrics. 2nd ed. (House Officer Ser.). (Illus.). 272p. 1988. pap. text 20.00 (*0-683-07159-9*) Lppncott W & W.
Rayburn, William F. & Carey, J. Christopher. Obstetrics & Gynecology. LC 95-23109. (House Officer Ser.). (Illus.). 512p. 1996. pap. 23.95 (*0-683-07181-5*) Lppncott W & W.
Raychahduri, S. P. & Verma, J. P., eds. Review of Tropical Plant Pathology: Diseases of Fruits, Vol. 2. iv, 406p. 1986. 99.00 (*1-55528-081-1*, Pub. by Today Tomorrow) Scholarly Pubns.
Raychard, Al. Al Raychard's Fly Fishing in Maine: The Complete Guide to the Best Fly Fishing in Maine. rev. ed. LC 80-12126. (Illus.). 184p. 1990. pap. 9.95 (*0-945980-20-5*) Nrth Country Pr.
— Al Raychard's Guide to Remote Trout Ponds in Maine. LC 88-22524. (Illus.). 211p. (Orig.). 1984. pap. 9.95 (*0-945980-06-X*) Nrth Country Pr.
— Bonefish Tarpon Permit: Fly Fishing Guide. (Illus.). 80p. 1996. pap. 14.95 (*1-57188-050-X*) F Amato Pubns.
***Raychard, Al.** Brook Trout Fly Fishing Guide. 2000. pap. 24.95 (*1-57188-192-1*, BRK) F Amato Pubns.
Raychard, Al. Fly Fishing the Salt: A Guide to Saltwater Fly Fishing from Maine to the Chesapeake Bay. LC 89-3084. (Illus.). 169p. (Orig.). 1989. pap. 8.95 (*0-945980-08-6*) Nrth Country Pr.
— Flying-In for Trout: A Guide to Fishing the Remote Waters of Maine, Quebec, & Labrador. LC 87-7844. (Illus.). 168p. (Orig.). 1987. pap. 7.95 (*0-89621-108-8*) Nrth Country Pr.
— Salar Vol. 1: An Angling Guide to Landlocked Salmon. LC 94-20776. (Illus.). 180p. 1994. pap. 14.95 (*0-945980-45-0*) Nrth Country Pr.
— Trout & Salmon Fishing in Northern New England: A Guide to Selected Waters in Maine, New Hampshire, Vermont & Massachusetts. LC 82-5930. (Illus.). 206p. (Orig.). 1982. pap. 9.95 (*0-945980-42-6*) Nrth Country Pr.
Raychaudhuri, A. K. Classical Mechanics: A Course of Lectures. (Illus.). 224p. 1984. pap. text 19.95 (*0-19-561343-0*) OUP.
— Theoretical Cosmology. (Oxford Studies in Physics). (Illus.). 1980. 29.95 (*0-19-851462-X*) OUP.
Raychaudhuri, A. K., et al. General Relativity, Relativistic Astrophysics & Cosmology. Harwit, Martin D. et al, eds. (Astronomy & Astrophysics Library). (Illus.). 320p. 1992. 69.95 (*0-387-97813-5*) Spr-Verlag.
Raychaudhuri, Ajitava, jt. auth. see Marjit, Sugata.
Raychaudhuri, D., jt. auth. see Goodman, D. J.
Raychaudhuri, Hemchandra. Political History of Ancient India. LC 78-174301. reprint ed. 49.50 (*0-404-05228-2*) AMS Pr.
— Political History of Ancient India: From the Accession of Parikshit to the Extinction of the Gupta Dynasty. 8th ed. (Illus.). 885p. 1998. reprint ed. pap. text 14.95 (*0-19-564376-3*) OUP.
Raychaudhuri, S. P. Recent Advances in Medicinal Aromatic & Spice Crops, 2 vols. (Illus.). 1000p. 1991. 150.00 (*1-55528-260-1*, Pub. by Today Tomorrow) Scholarly Pubns.
Raychaudhuri, S. P., ed. Recent Advances in Medicinal, Aromatic & Spice Crops: International Conference Held on 28-31, January 1989, at New Delhi, India, Vol. 1. (Illus.). 280p. 1992. 59.00 (*1-55528-229-6*, Pub. by Today Tomorrow) Scholarly Pubns.
— Recent Advances in Medicinal, Aromatic & Spice Crops: International Conference Held on 28-31, January 1989, at New Delhi, India, Vol. 2. 568p. 1992. 59.00 (*1-55528-266-0*, Pub. by Today Tomorrow) Scholarly Pubns.
Raychaudhuri, S. P. & Maramorosch, Karl, eds. Biotechnology & Plant Protection in Forestry Science. LC 99-14151. 250p. 1999. 78.00 (*1-57808-047-9*) Science Pubs.
Raychaudhuri, S. P. & Mitra, D. K. Mollicute Diseases of Plants. 1993. text 56.00 (*1-881570-13-4*) Science Pubs.
Raychaudhuri, S. P. & Varma, Anupam, eds. Plant Diseases Caused by Fastidious Prokaryotes: Third Regional Workshop on Plant Mycoplasma. viii, 139p. 1989. 59.00 (*1-55528-179-6*) Scholarly Pubns.
Raychaudhuri, S. P. & Verma, J. P. Review of Tropical Plant Pathology: Diseases of Cereals, Maize & Millet, Vol. 1. (Illus.). 564p. 1984. 79.00 (*1-55528-080-3*, Pub. by Today Tomorrow) Scholarly Pubns.
— Review of Tropical Plant Pathology Vol. 5: Diseases of Fibre & Oilseed Crops. (Illus.). vi, 316p. 1989. 95.00 (*1-55528-173-7*) Scholarly Pubns.

An Asterisk (*) at the beginning of an entry indicates that the title is appearing for the first time.

Raychaudhuri, S. P. & Verma, J. P., eds. Hall of Fame. (Review of Tropical Plant Pathology Ser.: Vol. 7). 275p. 1992. 95.00 (*1-55528-232-6*, Pub. by Today Tomorrow) Scholarly Pubns.

— Review of Tropical Plant Pathology: Diseases of Plantation Crops & Forest Trees, Vol. IV. (Illus.). 350p. 1988. 99.00 (*1-55528-092-7*, Pub. by Today Tomorrow) Scholarly Pubns.

— Review of Tropical Plant Pathology: Diseases of Vegetables, Vol. 3. (Illus.). 586p. 1987. 95.00 (*1-55528-144-3*, Pub. by Today Tomorrow) Scholarly Pubns.

Raychaudhuri, S. P., ed. see Maramorosch, Karl.

Raychaudhuri, S. P., jt. ed. see Maramorosch, Karl.

Raychaudhuri, S. P., jt. ed. see Singh, B. P.

Raychaudhuri, Tapan. Bengal under Akbar & Jahangir: An Introductory Study in Social History. 275p. 1969. text 25.00 (*0-685-43637-3*) Coronet Bks.

— Europe Reconsidered: Perceptions of the West in Nineteenth-Century Bengal. 388p. 1989. 35.00 (*0-19-562066-6*) OUP.

— Europe Reconsidered: Perceptions of the West in Nineteenth Century Bengal. 388p. 1990. reprint ed. pap. 14.95 (*0-19-562441-6*) OUP.

— Perceptions, Emotions, Sensibilities: Essays on India's Colonial & Post-Colonial Experiences. 260p. 2000. text 29.95 (*0-19-564863-3*) OUP.

Raycher, Jeanne. Birth Plan Guide. (Illus.). (Orig.). (C). 1988. pap. 9.95 (*0-944252-00-1*) CC Services.

Raycraft, Carol, jt. auth. see Raycraft, Don.

Raycraft, Don & Raycraft, Carol. American Country Store: A Wallace-Homestead Price Guide. LC 94-11628. (Illus.). 160p. 1994. pap. 14.95 (*0-87069-723-4*, Wllce-Homestd) Krause Pubns.

— American Stoneware: A Wallace-Homestead Price Guide. LC 95-12045. (Illus.). 160p. 1995. pap. 16.95 (*0-87069-714-5*, Wllce-Homestd) Krause Pubns.

— Country & Folk Antiques: With Price Guide. LC 95-18997. (Illus.). 176p. (Orig.). 1995. pap. 29.95 (*0-88740-828-1*) Schiffer.

— Wallace-Homestead Price Guide to American Country Antiques. 16th ed. LC 86-640023. 256p. 1999. pap. 19.95 (*0-87341-761-5*) Krause Pubns.

Raycraft, Don, et al. Collectibles-One Hundred & One: Baseball. LC 98-89304. (Illus.). 160p. 1999. pap. 29.95 (*0-7643-0759-2*) Schiffer.

Raycraft, Mary B., tr. see Perdrizet, Marie-Pierre.

***Raycroft, Mark.** White-Tailed Deer. (Illus.). 144p. 1999. pap. 19.95 (*1-55209-375-1*) Firefly Bks Ltd.

Raycroft, Mary. Releasers of Life. LC 99-165744. 1998. pap. 10.99 (*1-56043-198-9*) Destiny Image.

Rayder, Nicholas F. & Fails, Sandy. The Life-Planning Workbook: The Leap of Faith - The Dance of Change. 148p. 1995. write for info. (*0-9648454-0-7*) Paradise CO.

Raydo, Linda, jt. auth. see Eddy, Mary L.

Rayds, John, jt. auth. see Fishel, Kent.

Raye, jt. auth. see Jacobs.

Raye, Helen, jt. auth. see Saunders, Richard.

Raye, Janis, jt. auth. see Raphel, Neil.

Raye, Jodie. Lustful Desires. 112p. (Orig.). 1997. pap. 10.95 (*0-9659250-2-1*) Whte Wlf Pr.

Raye, John. Born to Win: Success & Prosperity Now. 104p. (Orig.). 1990. pap. 8.95 (*0-9650978-2-X*) Creat Ideas Bk.

Raye, John, jt. auth. see Horton, Joseph H.

***Raye, Kimberly.** Breathless: Blaze. 1999. per. 3.75 (*0-373-25828-3*, 1-25828-4, Harlequin) Harlequin Bks.

— Faithless Angel. 368p. 1999. mass mkt. 5.50 (*0-505-52296-9*, Love Spell) Dorchester Pub Co.

Raye, Kimberly. Gettin' Lucky. (Love & Laughter Ser.: Vol. 50). 1998. per. 3.50 (*0-373-44050-2*, 1-44050-2) Harlequin Bks.

***Raye, Kimberly.** Midnight Fantasies. 400p. 2000. pap. 5.99 (*0-505-52392-2*, Love Spell) Dorchester Pub Co.

— Midnight Kisses. (Time of Your Life Ser.). 400p. 2000. mass mkt. 5.99 (*0-505-52361-2*, Love Spell) Dorchester Pub Co.

Raye, Kimberly. Now & Forever, Bk. 65. (Shadows Ser.). 1996. per. 3.50 (*0-373-27065-8*, 1-27065-1) Silhouette.

***Raye, Kimberly.** Restless. (Temptation Ser.). 2000. mass mkt. 3.99 (*0-373-25895-X*) Harlequin Bks.

— Shameless, Vol.791. (Temptation Ser.). 2000. mass mkt. 3.99 (*0-373-25891-7*, 1-25891-2) Harlequin Bks.

Raye, Kimberly. Something Wild. 368p. 1998. mass mkt. 5.50 (*0-505-52272-1*, Love Spell) Dorchester Pub Co.

— Til We Meet Again. (Shadows Ser.). 1996. mass mkt. 3.50 (*0-373-27060-7*, 1-27060-2) Silhouette.

Raye, Kimberly & Riley, Eugenia. How Sweet It Is & Second-Chance Groom. (Duets Ser.: No. 11). 1999. per. 5.99 (*0-373-44077-4*, 1-44077-5) Harlequin Bks.

Raye, Kimberly, jt. auth. see Copeland, Lori.

Raye, Kimberly, jt. auth. see Dale, Ruth J.

Raye, Marina. Do You Have an Owner's Manual for Your Brain? 320p. (Orig.). 1991. pap. 12.95 (*1-878010-00-X*) A Schlossberg.

— Sexuality: The Sacred Journey: An Awakening to Ecstasy. (Illus.). 224p. (Orig.). 1994. pap. 12.95 (*1-878010-01-8*) A Schlossberg.

Rayed, Amal. The Nehru Legacy: An Appraisal. 1991. 28.00 (*81-204-0556-0*, Pub. by Oxford IBH) S Asia.

Rayes, Ammar, jt. auth. see Guizani, Mohsen.

Rayes, Joseph. Living Religious Vows: A Personal Pilgrimage. 69p. (Orig.). 1987. pap. 5.95 (*0-86716-063-2*) St Anthony Mess Pr.

Rayes, Patrick J. & Leathers, Charles G. Economists & the Stock Market: Speculative Theories of Stock Market Fluctuations. LC 98-53753. 192p. 2000. 65.00 (*1-85898-564-1*) E Elgar.

Rayess, George. Art of Lebanese Cooking. 240p. 1992. 19.95 (*0-86685-038-4*, LDL0380, Pub. by Librairie du Liban) Intl Bk Ctr.

Rayevsky, Paulina. Tak Eto Bylo - It Was Like This: One Family Story, Russia - U. S. A., 1950-1990. LC 92-72486. (RUS., Illus.). 370p. (Orig.). 1992. 16.00 (*0-911971-73-4*) Effect Pub.

Rayevsky, Robert. Three Sacks of Truth: A Story from France. 32p. (J). (gr. k-3). 1993. lib. bdg. 15.95 (*0-8234-0921-X*) Holiday.

— A Word to the Wise: And Other Proverbs. LC 93-26836. 40p. (J). (ps up). 1994. 15.00 (*0-688-12065-2*, Wm Morrow) Morrow Avon.

Rayez, Andre. Dictionnaire de Spiritualite, 12 vols., Set.Tr. of Dictionary of Spirituality. (FRE.). 1970. 4995.00 (*0-8288-6518-3*, M-6125) Fr & Eur.

***Rayfiel, Thomas.** Colony Girl. LC 99-20042. 256p. 1999. text 23.00 (*0-374-12644-5*) FS&G.

— Colony Girl. pap. 13.00 (*0-312-26719-3*, Picador USA) St Martin.

Rayfield, D. Action: An Analysis of the Concept. 104p. 1972. pap. text 50.50 (*90-247-1304-8*) Kluwer Academic.

— Chekhov's Uncle Vanya & the Wood Demon: Critical Study. (Critical Studies in Russian Literature Ser.). 128p. 1995. pap. 16.95 (*1-85399-405-7*, Pub. by Brist Class Pr) Focus Pub-R Pullins.

***Rayfield, Donald.** Anton Chekhov: A Life. LC 00-41864. 2000. pap. 22.95 (*0-8101-1795-9*) Northwestern U Pr.

Rayfield, Donald. The Cherry Orchard: Catastrophe & Comedy. LC 93-29455. (Twayne's Masterwork Studies: No. 131). 168p. 1994. 29.00 (*0-8057-8364-4*, Twyne); pap. 18.00 (*0-8057-4451-7*, Twyne) Mac Lib Ref.

***Rayfield, Donald.** The Literature of Georgia: A History. 2nd rev. ed. 288p. 1999. (*0-7007-1163-5*, Pub. by Curzon Pr Ltd) Paul & Co Pubs.

— Understanding Chekhov: A Critical Study of Chekhov's Prose & Drama. LC 99-10704. 1999. pap. 22.95 (*0-299-16314-8*) U of Wis Pr.

Rayfield, Elliot J. & Solimini, Cheryl. Diabetes: Beating the Odds: The Doctor's Guide to Reducing Your Risk. LC 92-14725. (Illus.). 198p. 1992. pap. 13.00 (*0-201-57784-4*) Addison-Wesley.

Rayfield, J. R. Languages of a Bilingual Community. LC 73-106457. (Janua Linguarum, Ser. Practica: No. 77). 1970. pap. text 40.80 (*90-279-0730-7*) Mouton.

Rayfield, Joan R., tr. see Maquet, Jacques P.

Rayfield, Julie K. The Office Interior Design Guide: An Introduction for Facility & Design. LC 93-21638. 264p. 1997. pap. 59.95 (*0-471-18138-2*) Wiley.

***Rayfield, R. Stephen.** Why My Company Needs Integrated Marketing Now! (Illus.). 1999. pap. 14.95 (*0-9683356-0-8*) ESIL Pub.

Rayfield, Susan. More Wildlife Painting: Techniques of Modern Masters. LC 96-2887. (Illus.). 144p. 1996. 29.95 (*0-8230-5747-X*) Watsn-Guptill.

***Rayfield, Susan.** More Wildlife Painting: Techniques of Modern Masters. (Illus.). 144p. 2000. pap. 19.95 (*0-8230-5745-3*) Watsn-Guptill.

Rayfield, Susan. Pierre-Auguste Renoir. LC 98-12988. (First Impressions Ser.). (Illus.). 92p. (J). (gr. k up). 1998. 19.95 (*0-8109-3795-6*, Pub. by Abrams) Time Warner.

— Wildlife Painting: Techniques of Modern Masters. (Illus.). 144p. 1990. pap. 18.95 (*0-8230-5748-8*) Watsn-Guptill.

Rayfield, Sylvia & Manning, Loretta. NCLEX-RN (TM)-RN 101: How to Pass. 2nd ed. 264p. (C). 1996. pap. 24.95 incl. disk (*0-9643622-1-X*) ICAN LA.

— Nursing Made Easy. (Illus.). 304p. 1997. pap. 24.95 (*0-9643622-2-8*) ICAN LA.

Rayford, Arthur. Quality Time: The Thoughts & Observations of an Ex-Con. 144p. (Orig.). 1995. pap. text 15.95 (*1-885066-03-1*) Four-G Pubs.

***Rayford, Curtis.** Black Jack. 1999. pap. 12.00 (*1-878647-61-X*) APU Pub Grp.

Rayford, Julian L. Cottonmouth. LC 90-20351. (Library of Alabama Classics). 424p. 1991. pap. 15.95 (*0-8173-0529-7*) U of Ala Pr.

Rayford, R. J. Consider a Career in Retailing. 1999. pap. 30.00 (*0-938609-37-8*) Graduate Group.

Rayfus, Rosemary, ed. ICSID Reports: (Reports of Cases Decided under the Convention on the Settlement of Investment Disputes Between States & Nationals of Other States, 1965), Vol. 1. 750p. (C). 1993. text 570.00 (*1-85701-009-4*, Pub. by Grotius Pubns Ltd) St Mut.

— ICSID Reports: (Reports of Cases Decided under the Convention on the Settlement of Investment Disputes Between States & Nationals of Other States, 1965), Vol. 2. 350p. (C). 1993. text 456.00 (*1-85701-010-8*, Pub. by Grotius Pubns Ltd) St Mut.

— ICSID Reports Vol. 3. 439p. (C). 1995. text 240.00 (*0-521-47512-0*) Cambridge U Pr.

Raygor. Science of Psychology. (C). Date not set. text. write for info. (*0-15-507244-7*); pap. text, student ed. write for info. (*0-15-507245-5*) Harcourt Coll Pubs.

Raygor, Robin D. & Bateson, Robert N. BASIC Programming for the IBM PC. (Illus.). 318p. (Orig.). (C). 1986. pap. text, teacher ed. write for info. (*0-314-97148-3*) West Pub.

Raygor, Robin D., jt. auth. see Bateson, Robert N.

Raygoza, Mireya C., tr. see Bailey, Mari V.

Rayha, Bonnie J., ed. see Degroodt, Mary P.

Rayhawk, Peggie & Eng, Vincent A. Almanac of the Executive Branch, 1999. 3rd rev. ed. (Illus.). 801p. 1999. pap. 149.00 (*1-886222-16-9*, BPD2169) Bernan Pr.

Rayher, Ed. Alice's Flip Book. (Illus.). 38p. (J). 1982. pap., per. 1.75 (*0-934714-19-3*) Swamp Pr.

— Flight of the Mantas. (Illus.). 12p. 1986. pap. 5.00 (*0-934714-11-8*) Swamp Pr.

Rayhorn, Nancy. Manual of Gastrointestinal Procedures Pediatric Supplement: A Publication of the Society of Gastroenterology Nurses & Associates. 2nd ed. 35p. 1995. pap. write for info. (*0-683-07182-3*) Lppncott W & W.

Rayker, Esfir. Natural Gas Transport in the U. S. S. R. Young, Maureen, ed. 103p. (Orig.). 1983. pap. text 75.00 (*1-55831-039-8*) Delphic Associates.

Raykov, Mariana. Beginner's Bulgarian. (Eurolingua Beginner's Languages Ser.). 207p. 1994. pap. 9.95 (*0-7818-0300-4*) Hippocrene Bks.

Rayl, David C., ed. see Charpentier, Marc-Antoine.

Rayl, Nancy B., ed. More Slices of Orange. 89p. 1996. pap. 14.00 (*1-888574-01-1*) Lightning.

— Slices of Orange. 96p. 1994. pap. 14.00 (*0-9632702-9-X*) Lightning.

Rayl, Nancy B., ed. see Andrews, Mary, et al.

Rayl, Nancy B., ed. see Spear, Catherine.

Rayle, Roy E. Random Shots: Episodes in the Life of a Weapons Developer. 2nd rev. ed. (Military History Monograph: Vol. 317). (Illus.). 122p. 1997. 29.95 (*1-57638-044-0*, M317H); pap. 19.95 (*1-57638-039-4*, M317S) Merriam Pr.

Rayleigh, Robert J. Life of John William Strutt, Third Baron Rayleigh, O. M., F. R. S. LC 68-16063. 467p. reprint ed. pap. 144.80 (*0-608-14658-7*, 202372200033) Bks Demand.

Rayleigh, Strutt. Theory of Sound, 2 vols., 1. 1945. pap. 14.95 (*0-486-60292-3*) Dover.

— Theory of Sound, 2 vols., 2. 1945. pap. 12.95 (*0-486-60293-1*) Dover.

Raylor, R., ed. see Schibsbye, Knud & Kossmann, H.

Raylor, Timothy. Cavaliers, Clubs, & Literary Culture: Sir John Mennes, James Smith, & the Order of the Fancy. LC 93-37277. (C). 1994. 48.50 (*0-87413-523-0*) U Delaware Pr.

— The Essex House Masque of 1621: Viscount Doncaster & the Jacobean Masque. LC 99-6669. (Medieval & Renaissance Literary Studies). (Illus.). 224p. 2000. text 58.00 (*0-8207-0310-9*) Duquesne.

Raylor, Timothy, jt. ed. see Leslie, Michael.

Rayman, Jack R., ed. The Changing Role of Career Services. LC 85-644751. (New Directions for Student Services Ser.: No. SS 62). 114p. (Orig.). 1993. pap. 22.00 (*1-55542-699-9*) Jossey-Bass.

Rayman, Paula, et al. Pathways for Women in the Sciences: The Wellesley Report, Pt. I. (Illus.). 154p. (Orig.). 1997. pap. 42.50 (*0-9641921-0-1*) WC Ctr Res Women.

— Pathways for Women in the Sciences: The Wellesley Report, Pt. II. (Illus.). 154p. (Orig.). 1997. pap. 42.50 (*0-9641921-2-8*) WC Ctr Res Women.

Rayman, Paula, jt. ed. see Bruyn, Severyn T.

***Rayman, Paula M.** Dignity at Work. 1999. text. write for info. (*0-312-22282-3*) St Martin.

Rayman, Paula M. The Kibbutz Community & Nation Building. LC 81-47152. 323p. reprint ed. pap. 100.20 (*0-7837-1414-9*, 204176800023) Bks Demand.

Rayman, R. A. Economics Through the Looking-Glass: Reflections on a Perverted Science. LC 98-3171. 346p. 1998. text 72.95 (*1-84014-419-X*, HB171.R37, Pub. by Ashgate Pub) Ashgate Pub Co.

***Rayman, Rebecca.** Nurse Trivia Calendar 2000. 300p. 1999. boxed set 12.95 (*1-56930-104-2*) Skidmore Roth Pub.

Rayman, Russell B., et al, eds. Occupational Health in Aviation: Maintenance & Support Personnel. LC 94-25272. (Illus.). 238p. 1995. text 63.00 (*0-12-583560-4*) Acad Pr.

Rayment, A. Different Mary. Date not set. pap. 4.99 (*0-906731-95-X*, Pub. by Christian Focus) Spring Arbor Dist.

— Hundred Houses. 1996. pap. 6.99 (*1-871676-77-0*, Pub. by Christian Focus) Spring Arbor Dist.

— Only Children. Date not set. 4.99 (*1-871676-29-0*, Pub. by Christian Focus) Spring Arbor Dist.

— Puzzle Trains in Chinatown & Ancient Rome. Date not set. 4.99 (*1-871676-92-4*, Pub. by Christian Focus) Spring Arbor Dist.

Rayment-Pickard, Hugh, jt. auth. see Burns, Robert.

Raymer, Daniel P. Aircraft Design: A Conceptual Approach. 2nd ed. (Educ Ser.). 729p. 1992. 66.95 (*0-930403-51-7*, 51-7) AIAA.

***Raymer, Daniel P.** Aircraft Design: A Conceptual Approach 3rd ed. LC 99-29325. (Education Ser.). 1999. write for info. (*1-56347-281-3*) AIAA.

Raymer, Daniel P. RDS-Student: Software for Aircraft Design, Sizing, & Performance, Version 3.0. (Educ Ser.). 71p. 1992. student ed. 69.95 incl. disk (*1-56347-047-0*, 47-0) AIAA.

Raymer, Daniel P., jt. auth. see Rand Corp. Staff.

Raymer, Daniel P., jt. auth. see Watman, Kenneth H.

Raymer, Dorothy. Key West Collection. 1999. pap. 11.95 (*0-9641735-4-9*) Ketch & Yawl.

Raymer, Dottie, jt. auth. see Jacobson, Jennifer R.

Raymer, Dottie, jt. auth. see Jacobson, Jennifer Richard.

Raymer, Edward C. Descent into Darkness: Pearl Harbor, 1941: A Navy Diver's Memoir. LC 96-33674. (Illus.). 240p. 1996. 21.95 (*0-89141-589-0*) Presidio Pr.

Raymist, Malkah. The Stiff Necked City. 400p. 1992. pap. 15.95 (*965-229-038-6*, Pub. by Gefen Pub Hse) Gefen Bks.

Raymo, Chet. The Dork of Cork. (Fresh Voices Ser.). 368p. 1994. mass mkt. 11.99 (*0-446-67000-6*, Pub. by Warner Bks) Little.

— Honey from Stone: A Naturalist's Search for God. LC 96-78377. (Illus.). 188p. 1997. reprint ed. pap. 15.00 (*1-886913-12-9*) Ruminator Bks.

— In the Falcon's Claws: A Novel of the Year 1000. 1990. 17.95 (*0-685-31428-6*) Viking Penguin.

— Natural Prayers. LC 99-72103. 212p. 1999. 22.00 (*1-886913-29-3*, Pub. by Ruminator Bks) Consort Bk Sales.

***Raymo, Chet.** Natural Prayers. 2000. pap. 15.00 (*1-886913-45-5*) Ruminator Bks.

Raymo, Chet. Skeptics & True Believers: The Exhilarating Connection Between Science & Religion. 288p. 1999. pap. 12.95 (*0-8027-7564-0*) Walker & Co.

— The Soul of the Night: An Astronomical Pilgrimage. LC 96-76408. (Illus.). 210p. 1996. pap. 15.00 (*1-886913-11-0*) Ruminator Bks.

— 365 Starry Nights: An Introduction to Astronomy for Every Night of the Year. (Illus.). 268p. 1990. pap. 15.00 (*0-671-76606-6*, Fireside) S&S Trade Pap.

Raymo, Jim. Marching to a Different Drummer. (Orig.). 1996. pap. 8.95 (*0-87508-719-1*, 719) Chr Lit.

Raymo, Judith G. Shattering the Myths: Women in Academe. LC 98-49542. 200p. 1999. 38.00 (*0-8018-6120-9*) Johns Hopkins.

Raymon, Loren A. Petrology: The Study of Igneous, Sedimentary & Metamorphic Rocks. 240p. (C). 1995. student ed., spiral bd. write for info. (*0-697-05976-6*, WCB McGr Hill) McGrw-H Hghr Educ.

Raymond. California Criminal Law & Procedure. LC 98-8348. 584p. (C). 1998. 73.95 (*0-8273-7940-4*) Delmar.

***Raymond.** The Complete Handbook of Soccer Conditioning. (Illus.). 370p. 1999. pap. 19.95 (*1-890946-05-2*) Reedswain.

Raymond. Learners with Mild Disabilities. LC 99-48413. 427p. (C). 1999. pap. text 70.00 (*0-205-20064-8*) P-H.

— Moves Writers Make. 2nd ed. 320p. (C). 1998. pap. text 21.70 (*0-536-01270-9*) Pearson Custom.

— Rhetorically Arranging the Reader. LC 98-20021. 312p. 1998. pap. text 34.00 (*0-13-440041-0*) P-H.

— Structures Power Modern France. LC 99-32872. 184p. 2000. text 59.95 (*0-312-22558-X*) St Martin.

Raymond, A. W., et al. Journal of California & Great Basin Anthropology. fac. ed. (Malki Museum, Journal of California & Great Basin Anthropology Ser.: Vol. 12:1). (Illus.). 148p. (C). 1990. reprint ed. pap. text 16.25 (*1-55567-777-0*) Coyote Press.

Raymond, Agnes. Jean Giraudoux: The Theatre of Victory & Defeat. LC 65-26238. 216p. 1966. pap. 16.95 (*0-87023-013-1*) U of Mass Pr.

Raymond, Al. Swinging Big Bands into the Millenium. Orig. Title: Swingng Big Bands into the 90's. 245p. 1999. reprint ed. pap. 20.00 (*0-9634600-0-5*) Harmony Pr PA.

***Raymond, Alan & Raymond, Susan.** Children in War. LC 99-89374. (Illus.). 144p. 2000. 24.00 (*1-57500-098-9*, Pub. by TV Bks) HarpC.

Raymond, Alex. Flash Gordon: The Fall of Ming. Schreiner, Dave, ed. LC 90-549. (Flash Gordon Ser.: Vol. 4). (Illus.). 112p. 1992. 34.95 (*0-87816-167-8*) Kitchen Sink.

— Flash Gordon: "The Tides of Battle" Schreiner, Dave, ed. LC 90-549. (Illus.). 112p. 1992. 34.95 (*0-87816-161-9*) Kitchen Sink.

— Flash Gordon: "Three Against Ming" Schreiner, Dave, ed. LC 90-5049. (Illus.). 112p. 1991. 34.95 (*0-87816-120-1*); pap. 19.95 (*0-87816-139-2*) Kitchen Sink.

— Flash Gordon: 1941-1943 Between Worlds at War, Vol. 5. Poplaski, Peter, ed. 112p. 1993. 34.95 (*0-87816-176-7*) Kitchen Sink.

— Triumph in Tropica. Schreiner, Dave & Poplaski, Peter, eds. LC 90-549. (Flash Gordon Ser.: Vol. 6). (Illus.). 96p. 1993. 34.95 (*0-87816-198-8*) Kitchen Sink.

Raymond, Amos. Sincerely Yours. (Illus.). 76p. 1998. 18.95 (*0-9661260-0-9*) Bob L Pub.

Raymond, Anan S. & Fike, Richard E. Rails East to Promontory, the Utah Stations. 3rd ed. (Illus.). iv, 140p. 1997. reprint ed. pap. 14.95 (*0-9659012-0-3*) Pioneer Ents.

***Raymond, Andre.** Cairo. Wood, Willard, tr. (Illus.). 448p. 2001. 35.00 (*0-674-00316-0*) HUP.

Raymond, Boris & Duffy, Paul. Historical Dictionary of Russia. LC 97-22659. (European Historical Dictionaries Ser.). 448p. 1998. 72.00 (*0-8108-3357-3*) Scarecrow.

***Raymond, Boris & Jones, David R.** The Russian Diaspora, 1917-1941. LC 00-24822. 2000. write for info. (*0-8108-3786-2*) Scarecrow.

Raymond, Boris, jt. auth. see Apostle, Richard A.

Raymond, Bruce C. & Bandy, D. Brent, eds. Business & Managerial Decision-Making Conference. 124p. 1996. pap. 60.00 (*1-56555-085-4*, BUS/MIS96) Soc Computer Sim.

Raymond, Bruce C., jt. ed. see Johnson, George.

Raymond, C. Elizabeth. George Wingfield: Owner & Operator of Nevada. LC 92-17980. (Wilbur S. Shepperson Series in History & Humanities: No. 34). (Illus.). 368p. 1992. 31.95 (*0-87417-197-0*) U of Nev Pr.

Raymond, C. Elizabeth, jt. ed. see James, Ronald M.

Raymond, Carole. Coordinating Physical Education Across the Primary School. LC 98-178657. (Subject Leaders Handbks.). 222p. 1998. pap. 23.95 (*0-7507-0693-7*, Falmer Pr) Taylor & Francis.

— Safety Across the Curriculum: Key Stages 1 & 2. 176p. 1999. pap. 26.95 (*0-7507-0984-7*, Falmer Pr) Taylor & Francis.

— The Student's Vegetarian Cookbook: Quick, Easy, Economical, & Great Tasting. LC 97-8932. 256p. 1997. per. 12.00 (*0-7615-0854-6*) Prima Pub.

Raymond, Cathy, jt. auth. see Dollemore, Doug.

Raymond, Charles D. & Peyser, Joseph L. On the Eve of Conquest: The Chevalier De Raymond's Critique of New France in 1754. LC 97-34837. xii, 181 p. 1998. 39.95 (*0-87013-433-7*) Mich St U Pr.

Raymond, Christopher P., jt. auth. see Silberston, Aubrey.

Raymond, Clarinda H., ed. see Fein, Richard.

Raymond, Clarinda H., ed. see Langille, Carol.

An Asterisk (*) at the beginning of an entry indicates that the title is appearing for the first time.

R

Raymond, D. Wide-Row Planting. 1983. pap. 2.95 (*0-88266-176-0*, Storey Pub) Storey Bks.

Raymond, Dan. Saltwater Flavor Vol. I: Two Short Stories. 48p. 1999. mass mkt. 4.60 (*0-9670339-0-X*, (H) 14193) Rock Reef.

***Raymond, Dan.** Sol Carvings: The History of Surfing in San Diego. 176p. 2000. 19.95 (*0-9670339-1-8*) Rock Reef.

Raymond, Daniel. Elements of Political Economy: In Two Parts with Additions from the 3rd Edition of 1836, 2 vols., Set. 2nd ed. LC 63-22260. (Reprints of Economic Classics Ser.). 1964. reprint ed. 95.00 (*0-678-00067-0*) Kelley.

Raymond, Darrel R., et al. Automata Implementation: First International Workshop on Implementing Automata, WIA '96, London, Ontario, Canada, August 29-31, 1996 : Revised Papers. LC 97-22637. viii, 189p. 1997. pap. write for info. (*3-540-63174-7*) Spr-Verlag.

Raymond, Derek. Crust on Its Uppers. (Masks Ser.). 190p. 1993. pap. 11.99 (*1-85242-268-8*) Serpents Tail.

***Raymond, Derek.** Crust on Its Uppers. 192p. 2000. pap. 12.00 (*1-85242-735-3*) Serpents Tail.

Raymond, Derek. A State of Denmark. (Mask Noir Ser.). 272p. (Orig.). 1995. pap. 12.99 (*1-85242-315-3*) Serpents Tail.

Raymond, Diana. House of the Dolphin. large type ed. 352p. 1987. 27.99 (*0-7089-1646-5*) Ulverscroft.

— Roundabout. large type ed. 368p. 1996. 27.99 (*0-7089-3403-X*) Ulverscroft.

— The Sea Family. large type ed. (Ulverscroft Large Print Ser.). 368p. 1998. 29.99 (*0-7089-3896-5*) Ulverscroft.

Raymond, Diane. Existentialism & the Philosophical Tradition. 432p. (C). 1990. pap. text 26.20 (*0-13-295775-2*) P-H.

Raymond, Diane, ed. Sexual Politics & Popular Culture. LC 90-82104. 249p. (C). 1990. 37.95 (*0-87972-501-X*); pap. 18.95 (*0-87972-502-8*) Bowling Green Univ Popular Press.

Raymond, Diane, jt. auth. see Blumenfeld, Warren J.

Raymond, Dick. Dick Raymond's New Kitchen Garden. LC 96-43306. (Illus.). 112p. (Orig.). 1997. pap. 16.95 (*1-881535-23-1*) New Eng Pr VT.

— Down-to-Earth Gardening Know-How for the '90s: Vegetables & Herbs. rev. ed. Watson, Ben, ed. LC 90-50416. (Illus.). 192p. 1991. 24.95 (*0-88266-658-4*, Garden Way Pub); pap. 14.95 (*0-88266-649-5*, Garden Way Pub) Storey Bks.

— Down-to-Earth Natural Lawn Care. Watson, Ben, ed. LC 92-53950. (Illus.). 176p. 1993. 27.95 (*0-88266-812-9*, Garden Way Pub); pap. 16.95 (*0-88266-810-2*, Garden Way Pub) Storey Bks.

— Garden Way's Joy of Gardening. LC 82-12075. (Illus.). 384p. 1983. 25.00 (*0-88266-320-8*, Garden Way Pub); pap. 19.95 (*0-88266-319-4*, Garden Way Pub) Storey Bks.

Raymond, Dick & Raymond, Jan. Home Gardening Wisdom. LC 82-3050. (Illus.). 320p. (Orig.). 1983. pap. 9.95 (*0-88266-265-1*, Garden Way Pub) Storey Bks.

Raymond, Dora N. British Policy & Opinion During the Franco-Prussian War. LC 21-20208. (Columbia University. Studies in the Social Sciences: No. 227). reprint ed. 32.50 (*0-404-51227-5*) AMS Pr.

— Captain Lee Hall of Texas. LC 73-5131. (Illus.). 384p. 1982. 29.95 (*0-8061-0086-9*) U of Okla Pr.

— Oliver's Secretary. LC 71-174302. reprint ed. 32.50 (*0-404-05229-0*) AMS Pr.

Raymond, Dorothy. What You Can Do with a Word: 300 Classroom Reading Activities. 144p. 1981. pap. 12.00 (*0-87879-269-4*) Acad Therapy.

Raymond, E. The Gem Stones in the Breastplate. (Illus.). 48p. (Orig.). 1987. pap. 4.00 (*0-934666-18-0*) Artisan Pubs.

Raymond, E., ed. see Adams, Andrew.

Raymond, E. Neill. Victorian Viceroy. 346p. 1984. 39.00 (*0-7212-0599-2*, Pub. by Regency Pr GBR) St Mut.

Raymond, E. T. Man of Promise: Lord Rosebery. LC 72-1276. (Select Bibliographies Reprint Ser.). 1977. reprint ed. 18.95 (*0-8369-6834-4*) Ayer.

Raymond, E. T. & Chenoweth, C. C. Aircraft Flight Control Actuation System Design. 325p. 1993. 49.00 (*1-56091-376-2*, R-123) Soc Auto Engineers.

Raymond, Edward L., Jr., ed. see Zunz, Edward A., Jr. & Kraus, Alan E.

Raymond, Eleanor. Early Domestic Architecture of Pennsylvania. LC 77-92980. (Illus.). 158p. 1977. reprint ed. 29.95 (*0-916838-11-0*) Schiffer.

Raymond, Elizabeth, jt. auth. see Jersild, Thomas N.

Raymond, Eric, et al. Learning GNU Emacs. 2nd rev. ed. 533p. (Orig.). 1996. pap. 29.95 (*1-56592-152-6*) Thomson Learn.

***Raymond, Eric S.** Cathedral & the Bazaar: Musings on Linux & Open Source by an Accidental Revolutionary. O'Reilly, Tim, ed. LC 99-45768. 288p. 1999. 19.95 (*1-56592-724-9*) OReilly & Assocs.

Raymond, Eric S. The New Hacker's Dictionary. 3rd ed. (Illus.). 569p. 1996. 39.00 (*0-262-18178-9*); pap. text 19.50 (*0-262-68092-0*) MIT Pr.

Raymond, F. & Waltham, R. W. Forage Conservation & Feeding. 5th ed. (Illus.). 250p. 1996. text 34.95 (*0-85236-350-8*, Pub. by Farming Pr) Diamond Farm Bk.

***Raymond, F. M.** God, a Woman & the Way: Mediator & Mediatrix. 184p. 2000. reprint ed. pap. 12.45 (*0-9639032-5-X*, Pub. by Sarto Hse) Spring Arbor Dist.

Raymond, Florian. Living Can Be Hazardous to Your Health. 1996. 10.95 (*0-943873-43-6*) Elder Bks.

— Surviving Alzheimer's: A Guide for Families. 1994. 10.95 (*0-943873-00-2*) Elder Bks.

Raymond, Frank B., et al, eds. Information Technologies: Teaching to Use - Using to Teach. LC 99-10046. 284p. 1998. 59.95 (*0-7890-0679-0*) Haworth Pr.

Raymond, Frank E. Rowayton on the Half Shell: The History of a Connecticut Coastal Village. LC 90-7392. (Illus.). 240p. 1990. 20.00 (*0-914659-48-0*) Phoenix Pub.

Raymond, Gail & Lau-Dickinson, Aileen C. LILAC: Lessons for Inclusive Language Activities in the Classroom. 192p. (Orig.). (J). (ps-1). 1996. pap. text 18.95 (*0-937857-71-8*) Speech Bin.

Raymond, George L. Fundamentals in Education, Art & Civics: Essays & Addresses. LC 67-23263. (Essay Index Reprint Ser.). 1977. 23.95 (*0-8369-0811-2*) Ayer.

— Memoirs of Robert William Elliston, 2 vols., 1 bk. LC 77-81218. 1048p. 1972. 48.95 (*0-405-08875-2*, Pub. by Blom Pubns) Ayer.

— The Orator's Manual: A Practical & Philosophical Treatise on Vocal Culture, Emphasis & Gesture. rev. ed. LC 72-434. (Granger Index Reprint Ser.). 1977. reprint ed. 23.95 (*0-8369-6368-7*) Ayer.

Raymond, Gerard. New York Scene, 1996-97. (Illus.). 256p. 1996. pap. 10.95 (*0-85449-228-3*, Pub. by Gay Mens Pr) LPC InBook.

Raymond, Gino. Andre Malraux: Politics & the Temptation of Myth. 224p. 1995. 67.95 (*1-85972-132-X*, Pub. by Avebry) Ashgate Pub Co.

Raymond, Gino, tr. see Bourdieu, Pierre.

Raymond, Gino G., ed. France During the Socialist Years. 296p. 1994. 77.95 (*1-85521-518-7*, Pub. by Dartmth Pub) Ashgate Pub Co.

Raymond, Grace. How They Kept the Faith: A Tale of the Huguenots of Languedoc. LC 96-39181. (Huguenot Inheritance Ser.). (J). 1996. 12.90 (*0-921100-64-7*) Inhtce Pubns.

Raymond, Gregory A. Conflict Resolution & the Structure of the State System: An Analysis of Arbitrative Settlements. LC 79-53702. (Illus.). 122p. 1980. text 41.00 (*0-916672-12-3*) Rowman.

— Salvador Allende & the Peaceful Road to Socialism. (Pew Case Studies in International Affairs). 50p. (C). 1992. pap. text 3.50 (*1-56927-451-7*) Geo U Inst Dplmcy.

Raymond, Gregory A., jt. auth. see Kegley, Charles W., Jr.

Raymond, Gregory A., jt. auth. see Kegley, Charles W.

Raymond, Gregory A., jt. ed. see Taylor, Phillip.

Raymond, Hal. America Smiles. LC 97-90806. 129p. 1998. pap. 11.95 (*0-533-12489-1*) Vantage.

Raymond, Hank. Learn in Your Car: Russian, Level 3. (ENG & RUS.). (gr. 7). 1994. pap. 16.95 incl. audio (*1-56015-147-1*) Penton Overseas.

Raymond, Harold R. & Kempshi, Ted. 101 Delaware Wing-T Drills. LC 97-80944. (Illus.). 120p. 1997. pap. 16.95 (*1-57167-162-5*) Coaches Choice.

— 101 Delaware Wing-T Plays. LC 97-80943. (Illus.). 116p. 1997. pap. 16.95 (*1-57167-163-3*) Coaches Choice.

Raymond, Harold R. & Kempski, Ted. The Delaware Wing-T: The Option Game. LC 97-81035. (Illus.). 160p. 1997. pap. 16.95 (*1-57167-164-1*) Coaches Choice.

— The Delaware Wing-T: The Running Game. LC 97-81033. (Illus.). 164p. 1997. pap. 16.95 (*1-57167-166-8*) Coaches Choice.

Raymond, Helen D. Sophie Willard Dana Ripley: Co-Founder of Brook Farm. (Illus.). 124p. 1995. 15.00 (*0-914339-51-6*, Pub. by P E Randall Pub) U Pr of New Eng.

Raymond, Henry N. Apprendre en Voiture: Anglais, Level 1, set.Tr. of Learn in Your Car: English. (ENG & FRE.). 1992. pap. 16.95 incl. audio (*1-56015-150-1*) Penton Overseas.

— Apprendre en Voiture: Anglais, Level 2, set.Tr. of Learn in Your Car: English. (ENG & FRE.). 1992. pap. 16.95 incl. audio (*1-56015-154-4*) Penton Overseas.

— Apprendre en Voiture: Anglais, Level 3, set.Tr. of Learn in Your Car: English. (ENG & FRE.). Date not set. pap. 16.95 incl. audio (*1-56015-158-7*) Penton Overseas.

— Aprenda en su Auto: Ingles, Level 1, set.Tr. of Learn in Your Car: English. (ENG & SPA.). 1992. pap. 16.95 incl. audio (*1-56015-151-X*) Penton Overseas.

Raymond, Henry N. The Civil War Vol. 2: The Fall of New Orleans & the Battle of Shiloh, unabridged ed. (American Heritage Voices from the Front Ser.). 1996. 16.95 incl. audio (*1-882071-78-6*, 394312, Pub. by B&B Audio) Lndmrk Audiobks.

Raymond, Henry N. Learn in Your Car: French, Level 1. unabridged ed. (ENG & FRE.). 1990. pap. 16.95 incl. audio (*1-56015-125-0*) Penton Overseas.

Raymond, Henry N. Learn in Your Car: French, Level 1, set. unabridged ed. (FRE & ENG.). 1990. pap. 34.95 incl. audio compact disk (*1-56015-122-6*) Penton Overseas.

Raymond, Henry N. Learn in Your Car: French, Level 2, set. unabridged ed. LC 84-203565. (FRE & ENG.). 1991. pap. 16.95 incl. audio (*1-56015-129-3*) Penton Overseas.

Raymond, Henry N. Learn in Your Car: French, Level 2, set. unabridged ed. (FRE & ENG.). 1991. pap. 34.95 incl. audio compact disk (*1-56015-119-6*) Penton Overseas.

Raymond, Henry N. Learn in Your Car: French, Level 3, set. LC 84-203565. (FRE & ENG.). 1992. pap. 16.95 incl. audio (*1-56015-133-1*) Penton Overseas.

— Learn in Your Car: French, 3 Levels, Set. (FRE.). 1992. pap. 39.95 incl. audio (*1-56015-138-2*) Penton Overseas.

— Learn in Your Car: French, 2 Levels, Set. unabridged ed. (ENG & FRE.). Date not set. 29.95 incl. audio (*1-56015-121-8*) Penton Overseas.

***Raymond, Henry N.** Learn in Your Car: German, Level 1, set. (GER & ENG.). 1999. 34.95 incl. audio compact disk (*1-56015-117-X*) Penton Overseas.

Raymond, Henry N. Learn in Your Car: German, Level 1, set. unabridged ed. (ENG & GER.). (gr. 7). 1990. pap. 16.95 incl. audio (*1-56015-128-5*) Penton Overseas.

— Learn in Your Car: German, Level 2, set. unabridged ed. LC 84-203565. (GER & ENG.). 1991. pap. 16.95 incl. audio (*1-56015-132-3*) Penton Overseas.

— Learn in Your Car: German, Level 3, set. LC 84-203565. (GER & ENG.). 1992. pap. 16.95 incl. audio (*1-56015-136-6*) Penton Overseas.

— Learn in Your Car: German, 3 Levels, Set. (GER.). 1992. pap. 39.95 incl. audio (*1-56015-139-0*) Penton Overseas.

— Learn in Your Car: Italian, Level 1, set. unabridged ed. LC 84-203565. (ITA & ENG.). 1991. pap. 16.95 incl. audio (*1-56015-127-7*) Penton Overseas.

— Learn in Your Car: Italian, Level 2, set. unabridged ed. (ITA.). 1991. pap. 16.95 incl. audio (*1-56015-131-5*) Penton Overseas.

— Learn in Your Car: Italian, Level 3, set. (ITA & ENG.). 1992. pap. 16.95 incl. audio (*1-56015-135-8*) Penton Overseas.

— Learn in Your Car: Italian, 3 Levels, Set. unabridged ed. (ENG & ITA.). 1992. pap. 39.95 incl. audio (*1-56015-140-4*) Penton Overseas.

— Learn in Your Car: Japanese, Level 1, set. (JPN & ENG.). 1992. pap. 16.95 incl. audio (*1-56015-137-4*) Penton Overseas.

— Learn in Your Car: Japanese, Level 2, set. unabridged ed. (JPN & ENG.). 1993. pap. 16.95 incl. audio (*1-56015-143-9*) Penton Overseas.

— Learn in Your Car: Japanese, Level 3. (JPN & ENG.). 1993. pap. 16.95 incl. audio (*1-56015-145-5*) Penton Overseas.

— Learn in Your Car: Japanese, 3 Levels, Set. unabridged ed. (JPN & ENG.). 1993. pap. 39.95 incl. audio (*1-56015-146-3*) Penton Overseas.

— Learn in Your Car: Russian, Level 1, set. unabridged ed. (RUS & ENG.). 1993. pap. 16.95 incl. audio (*1-56015-142-0*) Penton Overseas.

Raymond, Henry N. Learn in Your Car: Russian, Level 2, set. (RUS & ENG.). 1994. pap. 16.95 incl. audio (*1-56015-144-7*) Penton Overseas.

Raymond, Henry N. Learn in Your Car: Russian, 3 Levels, Set. (ENG & RUS.). 1994. pap. 39.95 incl. audio (*1-56015-148-X*) Penton Overseas.

— Learn in Your Car: Spanish, Level 1, set. unabridged ed. (SPA & ENG.). 1990. pap. 34.95 incl. audio compact disk (*1-56015-149-8*) Penton Overseas.

— Learn in Your Car: Spanish, Level 1, set. unabridged ed. LC 84-203565. (SPA & ENG.). 1990. pap. 16.95 incl. audio (*1-56015-126-9*) Penton Overseas.

— Learn in Your Car: Spanish, Level 2, set. unabridged ed. LC 84-203565. (SPA & ENG.). 1991. pap. 16.95 incl. audio (*1-56015-130-7*) Penton Overseas.

Raymond, Henry N. Learn in Your Car: Spanish, Level 2, set. unabridged ed. (SPA & ENG.). 1991. pap. 34.95 incl. audio compact disk (*1-56015-123-4*) Penton Overseas.

Raymond, Henry N. Learn in Your Car: Spanish, Level 3, set. (SPA & ENG.). 1992. pap. 16.95 incl. audio (*1-56015-134-X*) Penton Overseas.

Raymond, Henry N. Learn in Your Car: Spanish, Level 3, set. (SPA & ENG.). 1992. pap. 34.95 incl. audio compact disk (*1-56015-124-2*) Penton Overseas.

Raymond, Henry N. Learn in Your Car: Spanish, 2 Levels, Set. unabridged ed. (ENG & SPA.). Date not set. pap. 29.95 incl. audio (*1-56015-120-X*) Penton Overseas.

— Lern Im Auto: Englisch, Level 1, set. unabridged ed.Tr. of Learn in Your Car: English. (ENG & GER.). pap. 16.95 incl. audio (*1-56015-153-6*) Penton Overseas.

Raymond, Henry N. World War I: The LaFayette Escadrille & Belleau Wood, Vol. 1. (American Heritage Voices from the Front Ser.). 1996. 16.95 incl. audio (*1-882071-73-5*, 393913 , Pub. by B&B Audio) Lndmrk Audiobks.

Raymond, Irving W. Teaching of the Early Church on the Use of Wine & Strong Drink. LC 79-120207. (Columbia University. Studies in the Social Sciences: No. 286). reprint ed. 20.00 (*0-404-51286-0*) AMS Pr.

Raymond, Irving W., tr. Medieval Trade in the Mediterranean World: Illustrative Documents. 458p. 1990. text 75.00 (*0-231-01865-7*) Col U Pr.

Raymond, J., jt. ed. see Laurie, G.

Raymond, J. Scott, jt. ed. see Oyuela-Caycedo, Augusto.

Raymond, Jack. Robert O. Anderson: Oil Man-Environmentalist & His Leading Role in the International Environmentalist Movement. 64p. (Orig.). (C). 1988. pap. text 10.50 (*0-8191-7043-7*) U Pr of Amer.

— Show Music on Record: The First One Hundred Years. rev. ed. LC 91-23483. 440p. 1992. text 45.00 (*1-56098-151-2*) Smithsonian.

Raymond, Jacque, jt. auth. see Banerji, Dilip.

Raymond, James C. Writing: An Unnatural Act. 464p. (C). 1997. pap. text 47.00 (*0-06-045341-9*) Addson-Wesley Educ.

Raymond, James C., ed. English As a Discipline: or Is There a Plot in This Play? LC 95-26586. 208p. (Orig.). (C). 1996. pap. text 19.95 (*0-8173-0820-2*) U of Ala Pr.

Raymond, James C., ed. see McMillan, James B.

Raymond, Jan, jt. auth. see Raymond, Dick.

Raymond, Janice G. The Transsexual Empire: The Making of the She-Male. LC 93-46771. No. 39. 256p. (C). 1994. pap. text 17.95 (*0-8077-6272-5*) Tchrs Coll.

— Women As Wombs: Reproductive Technologies & the Battle over Women's Freedom. 254p. 1998. text 22.00 (*0-7881-5512-1*) DIANE Pub.

— Women as Wombs: Reproductive Technology & the Battle over Women's Freedom. 288p. 1998. 24.95 (*1-875559-26-4*) LPC InBook.

— Women as Wombs: Reproductive Technology & the Battle over Women's Freedom. 288p. 1998. pap. 14.95 (*1-875559-41-8*, Pub. by SpiniFex Pr) LPC InBook.

Raymond, Janice G., jt. auth. see Leidholdt, Dorchen.

Raymond, Janice G., jt. ed. see Leidholdt, Dorchen.

Raymond, Jehan. Decorative Floral Designs for Needleworkers & Craftspeople. (Pictorial Archive Ser.). 60p. 1986. reprint ed. pap. 5.95 (*0-486-25134-9*) Dover.

Raymond, Jennifer. Fat-Free & Easy: Great Meals in Minutes. LC 96-54488. 152p. (Orig.). 1997. pap. 10.00 (*1-57067-041-2*) Book Pub Co.

— The Peaceful Palate: Vegetarian's Favorite Cookbook. rev. ed. LC 96-3806. (Illus.). 162p. 1996. pap. 15.00 (*1-57067-031-5*) Book Pub Co.

Raymond, Jennifer, jt. auth. see Schumann, Kate.

Raymond, Joad. The Invention of the Newspaper: English Newsbooks, 1641-1649. 392p. 1996. text 90.00 (*0-19-813002-3*) OUP.

Raymond, Joad, ed. Making the News: An Anthology of the Newsbooks of Revolutionary England, 1941-1660. LC 93-1629. 1993. text 49.95 (*0-312-10093-0*) St Martin.

Raymond, Joad, ed. News, Newspapers & Society in Early Modern Britain. LC 98-45230. (Prose Studies). 158p. 1999. pap. 24.50 (*0-7146-8003-6*, Pub. by F Cass Pubs) Intl Spec Bk.

***Raymond, Joad, ed.** News, Newspapers & Society in Early Modern Britain. LC 98-45230. (Prose Studies). 158p. 1999. 52.50 (*0-7146-4944-9*, Pub. by F Cass Pubs) Intl Spec Bk.

Raymond, Jocelyn M. The Nursery World of Dr. Blatz. 280p. 1991. text 35.00 (*0-8020-2793-8*) U of Toronto Pr.

Raymond, John. Catholics on the Internet. LC 97-27233. 448p. 1997. pap. 19.95 (*0-7615-1168-7*) Prima Pub.

— Catholics on the Internet 2000. 480p. 2000. pap. 19.99 (*0-7615-1567-4*) Prima Pub.

***Raymond, Judith.** Simplicity Just in Time for Summer: Spring, Early Summer, Summer. (Illus.). 1999. 15.95 (*0-918178-35-5*) Simplicity.

Raymond, Kathleen Z., jt. auth. see Newman, Jim.

Raymond, Kenneth N., ed. Bioinorganic Chemistry II: A Symposium Co-Sponsored by the Division of Inorganic Chemistry & by the Division of Biological Chemistry at the 171st Meeting of the American Chemical Society, New York, April 7-9, 1976. LC 77-22225. (Advances in Chemistry Ser.: No. 162). (Illus.). 456p. 1977. reprint ed. pap. 141.40 (*0-608-06744-X*, 206694100009) Bks Demand.

Raymond, Kenneth W. General, Organic & Biochemistry. (C). 1999. pap. text, student ed. write for info. (*0-8053-4439-X*) Benjamin-Cummings.

Raymond, L. Douglas. Opinions, Sage-Advise & Words of Wisdom: From Guy Holloway Raymond "Moe" (Illus.). 77p. 1997. pap. 21.95 (*0-9661821-0-3*) L Raymond.

Raymond, Laurie W. & Rosbrow-Reich, Susan. The Inward Eye: Psychoanalysts Reflect on Their Lives & Work. LC 96-12694. 504p. 1997. 55.00 (*0-88163-252-X*) Analytic Pr.

— Psychoanalytic Reflections. 40.00 (*0-87668-513-0*) Aronson.

Raymond, Loren A. Petrology: The Study of Igneous, Sedimentary & Metamorphic Rocks. 672p. (C). 1994. text. write for info. (*0-697-00190-3*, WCB McGr Hill) McGrw-H Hghr Educ.

— Sedimentary Petrology, Vol. II. 320p. (C). 1994. text. write for info. (*0-697-23691-9*, WCB McGr Hill) McGrw-H Hghr Educ.

Raymond, Loren A., ed. Melanges: Their Nature, Origin, & Significance. LC 85-761. (Geological Society of America Ser.: Vol. 198). (Illus.). 182p. 1984. reprint ed. pap. 56.50 (*0-608-07727-5*, 206781500010) Bks Demand.

***Raymond, Louis & American Society for Testing & Materials Staff.** ASTM Standards & Other Documents Related to the Evaluation & Control of Hydrogen Embrittlement with Emphasis on Fasteners. LC 99-85709. 2000. write for info. (*0-8031-2733-2*) ASTM.

Raymond, M. The Family That Overtook Christ. LC 86-19670. 416p. 1995. pap. 7.95 (*0-8198-2625-1*) Pauline Bks.

***Raymond, M.** Spiritual Secrets of a Trappist Monk: The Truth of Who You Are & What God Call You to Be. Orig. Title: You. 432p. 2000. pap. 22.95 (*1-928832-07-5*) Sophia Inst Pr.

Raymond, M. Your Hour. 216p. 1995. reprint ed. text 19.95 (*0-912141-23-9*) Roman Cath Bks.

Raymond, M. D. Gray Genealogy: Being a Genealogical Record & History of the Descendants of John Gray of Beverly, Massachusetts, & Including Sketches of Other Gray Families. 316p. 1994. reprint ed. pap. 47.50 (*0-8328-4094-7*); reprint ed. lib. bdg. 57.50 (*0-8328-4093-9*) Higginson Bk Co.

Raymond, M. Susan. Health & Policymaking in the Arab Middle East. 70p. (Orig.). 1978. pap. text 4.00 (*0-932568-00-9*) GU Ctr CAS.

Raymond, Maria E., ed. see Clinton, Hillary Rodham, et al.

Raymond-Martimbeau, Pauline. Phlebologia Houston, 1991: Proceedings of the Intensive Practical Course in Phlebologia. 438p. 1991. write for info. (*1-880693-00-3*) P Ray-Mart.

Raymond, Mary. Grandma Tyson's Legacy. large type ed. (Romance Ser.). 336p. 1984. 27.99 (*0-7089-1230-3*) Ulverscroft.

— Her Part of the House. large type ed. (General Ser.). 336p. 1993. 27.99 (*0-7089-2866-8*) Ulverscroft.

— Hide My Heart. large type ed. (Linford Romance Library). 304p. 1985. pap. 16.99 (*0-7089-6101-0*) Ulverscroft.

— Island of the Heart. large type ed. (Romance Ser.). 336p. 1985. 27.99 (*0-7089-1393-8*) Ulverscroft.

— The Long Journey Home. large type ed. (Linford Romance Library). 320p. 1985. pap. 16.99 (*0-7089-6071-5*, Linford) Ulverscroft.

— The Pimpernel Project. large type ed. (Linford Romance Library). 288p. 1989. pap. 16.99 (*0-7089-6654-3*, Linford) Ulverscroft.

— Shadow of a Star. large type ed. (Romance Ser.). 304p. 1987. 27.99 (*0-7089-1591-4*) Ulverscroft.

R

— Take-Over. large type ed. 304p. 1986. 27.99 (0-7089-1546-9) Ulverscroft.
— That Summer. large type ed. (Romance Ser.). 288p. 1986. 27.99 (0-7089-1507-8) Ulverscroft.
— Villa of Flowers. large type ed. (Linford Romance Library). 288p. 1985. pap. 16.99 (0-7089-6056-1) Ulverscroft.
Raymond, Michael J. Mild Traumatic Brain Injury: A Clinician's Guide. LC 98-46594. 1999. 37.00 (0-89079-809-5) PRO-ED.
Raymond, Michael J., jt. ed. see Bennett, Thomas L.
Raymond, Mike. The Human Side of Diabetes: Beyond Doctors, Diets & Drugs. LC 91-50644. 288p. (Orig.). 1991. pap. 13.95 (1-879360-09-8) Noble Pr.
***Raymond, Neville.** The Genesis of Genocide: Why the Holocaust Happened. 204p. 2000. 24.95 (0-9679486-0-6, SunBrst Bks) Unltd Resourc Intl.
Raymond, P. A., et al, eds. Systems Approaches to Developmental Neurobiology. (NATO ASI Ser.: Vol. 192). (Illus.). 204p. (C). 1990. text 102.00 (0-306-43594-2, Kluwer Plenum) Kluwer Academic.
Raymond, Percy E. The Appendages, Anatomy, & Relationships of Trilobites. (Connecticut Academy of Arts & Sciences Ser., Trans.: Vol. 7). 1920. pap. 200.00 (0-685-22866-5) Elliots Bks.
Raymond, Richard D. Myth of the Appalachian Brain Drain. LC 72-187762. 78p. 1972. pap. 7.95 (0-937058-06-8) West Va U Pr.
Raymond, Robert. From Bees to Buzz Bombs: Robert Raymond's Boyhood-to-Blitz Memoirs. (Orig.). 1992. pap. 24.95 (0-7022-2449-9, Pub. by Univ Queensland Pr) Intl Spec Bk.
— Out of the Fiery Furnace: The Impact of Metals on the History of Mankind. LC 86-2367. (Illus.). 1986. pap. 10.00 (0-271-00441-X) Pa St U Pr.
Raymond, Robert, jt. ed. see Fair, Donald E.
Raymond, Robert G. Scouting, Cavorting & Other World War II Memories. LC 95-92095. (Illus.). (Orig.). 1995. pap. 12.50 (0-9645021-0-0) R G Raymond.
Raymond, Robert L. At a Dollar a Year: Ripples on the Edge of the Maelstrom. LC 76-157794. (Short Story Index Reprint Ser.). 1977. reprint ed. 19.95 (0-8369-3906-9) Ayer.
Raymond, Ronald R., Jr., et al. Grow Your Roots Anywhere, Anytime. 1980. 12.95 (0-89256-152-1, Rawson Assocs) Macmillan.
Raymond, Rossiter W. Peter Cooper. LC 72-1252. (Select Bibliographies Reprint Ser.). 1977. reprint ed. 15.95 (0-8369-6835-2) Ayer.
***Raymond, Ruth A.** The Day the Earth Went Flat. (Illus.). 58p. (J). (gr. 6-8). 1999. pap. 19.95 (0-9659533-2-7) H L Osmer.
Raymond, S. Forbidden Fruit. 1998. mass mkt. 6.95 (0-352-33306-5) Virgin Isl Bks.
— Genealogy of the Raymond Family of New England 1630 to 1886, with a Historical Sketch of Some of the Raymonds of Early Times. (Illus.). 304p. 1989. reprint ed. pap. 46.00 (0-8328-1007-X); reprint ed. lib. bdg. 54.00 (0-8328-1006-1) Higginson Bk Co.
Raymond, S. & Cunliffe, R. Tomorrow's Office: Creating Effective & Humane Interiors. (Illus.). 208p. 1996. 70.00 (0-419-21240-X, E & FN Spon) Routledge.
***Raymond, Santa & Cunliffe, Roger.** Tomorrow's Office: Creating Effective & Humane Interiors. (Illus.). 208p. 2000. pap. 32.99 (0-419-24400-X, E & FN Spon) Routledge.
***Raymond, Scott E.** Voices Behind the Bricks. (Illus.). xii, 102p. 1999. pap. 16.00 (0-9675107-0-8) S E Raymond.
Raymond, Sharon. Simple Shoemaking: Instructional Patterns for Making Low-Heeled Out-Stitched Shoes, with or Without the Use of Lasts. (Illus.). 75p. 1999. pap. 19.95 (0-9667424-0-0) Barleycorn Pr.
Raymond, Steve. Bowling Madness: Hey Pops, You Hustled Me. LC 88-83761. 278p. (Orig.). 1989. pap. 8.95 (0-927707-16-0) FL Bay Pubs.
— The Estuary Flyfisher. LC 97-102994. (Illus.). 95p. 1996. pap. 19.95 (1-57188-060-7) F Amato Pubns.
— Kamloops: An Angler's Study of the Kamloops Trout. LC 94-214960. (Illus.). 148p. 1994. 25.95 (1-878175-74-2); pap. 19.95 (1-878175-73-4) F Amato Pubns.
— Rivers of the Heart: A Fly-Fishing Memoir. LC 97-43885. (Illus.). 256p. 1998. 25.00 (1-55821-700-2) Lyons Pr.
— Steelhead Country. (Illus.). 224p. 1991. 19.95 (1-55821-126-8) Lyons Pr.
— Steelhead Country: Angling in Northwest Waters. LC 94-12073. (Illus.). 208p. 1994. reprint ed. pap. 9.95 (1-57061-014-2) Sasquatch Bks.
— The Year of the Angler. rev. ed. (Illus.). 256p. 1995. pap. 12.95 (1-57061-023-1) Sasquatch Bks.
— Year of the Angler & Year of the Trout, 2 vols. (Illus.). 256p. 1995. pap., boxed set 25.00 (1-57061-032-0) Sasquatch Bks.
— The Year of the Trout. rev. ed. (Illus.). 288p. 1995. pap. 12.95 (1-57061-022-3) Sasquatch Bks.
Raymond, Steve & Karman, Mal. The Poison River: An Unbelievable True Story of Betrayal & Redemption. (Illus.). 354p. (Orig.). (C). 1994. 19.95 (0-9642533-9-9); pap. 12.95 (0-9642533-8-0) New Amstrdm Pr.
Raymond, Susan. Life Sciences & Health Challenges. (Annals of the New York Academy of Science Ser.). 160p. 1999. pap. 19.95 (0-8018-6300-7) Johns Hopkins.
— Life Sciences & Health Challenges. 160p. 1998. pap. 30.00 (1-57331-148-0) NY Acad Sci.
Raymond, Susan, jt. auth. see Raymond, Alan.
Raymond, Susan G. Aleph Through Tav - Chalkboard Games. Solomon, Richard D. & Solomon, Elaine C., eds. (Illus.). 100p. (C). 1989. pap. text 25.00 (0-9617198-9-3) NIRT Inc.
Raymond, Susan G., et al. Jewish Handbook for Group Discussion. 65p. 1988. pap. text 15.00 (0-9617198-8-5) NIRT Inc.
Raymond, Susan U. Science, Technology, & the Economic Future. 240p. 1998. pap. 30.00 (1-57331-147-2) NY Acad Sci.
***Raymond, Susan U.** Science, Technology & the Economic Future. 240p. 1999. pap. text 22.50 (0-8018-6213-2) Johns Hopkins.
Raymond, Susan U., et al. The Technology Link to Economic Development: Past Lessons & Future Imperatives. LC 96-20393. (Annals of the New York Academy of Sciences Ser.). 1996. write for info. (1-57331-042-5); pap. 110.00 (1-57331-043-3) NY Acad Sci.
Raymond, Susan U., jt. ed. see Greenberg, Henry M.
***Raymond, Susie.** Taking Liberties. (Black Lace Ser.). 1999. pap. 9.99 (0-352-33357-X) Virgin Bks.
Raymond, Valerie. Surviving Proposition Thirteen: Fiscal Crisis in California Counties. LC 88-2766. 96p. (Orig.). reprint ed. pap. 30.00 (0-608-20119-7, 207139100011) Bks Demand.
Raymond, Walter J. The Attitudes of Voters & Planning Commissioners Toward Regional Planning, No. 1088. 1976. 5.50 (0-686-20403-4, Sage Prdcls Pr) Sage.
— Dictionary of Politics: Selected American & Foreign Political & Legal Terms. 7th ed. LC 92-14215. (Illus.). 762p. 1992. 39.50 (1-55618-008-X) Brunswick Pub.
— Substate Regional Planning in Virginia: A Bibliographical Essay, No. 1086. 1976. 5.00 (0-686-20402-6, Sage Prdcls Pr) Sage.
Raymond, Walter J., jt. ed. see Belyakov, Vladimir V.
Raymond, Walter M. Rebels of the New South. LC 72-2027. (Black Heritage Library Collection). (Illus.). 1977. reprint ed. 19.95 (0-8369-9055-2) Ayer.
Raymond, William. The Angel with the Smallest Wings. (Illus.). 32p. (J). 1996. 14.95 (0-9653601-0-5) Genesi.
— Biographical Sketches of Distinguished Men of Columbia County, Including an Account of the Most Important Offices They Have Filled. (Illus.). 119p. 1997. reprint ed. pap. 16.00 (0-8328-6120-0); reprint ed. lib. bdg. 26.00 (0-8328-6119-7) Higginson Bk Co.
Raymond, William O. The Infinite Moment, & Other Essays in Robert Browning. 2nd ed. LC 65-1834. (Canadian University Paperbooks Ser.: No. 32). 272p. reprint ed. pap. 84.40 (0-8357-4167-2, 203694100007) Bks Demand.
Raymondo, Chris. No Justice. Charles, Rodney & Pasco, Elizabeth, eds. LC 96-69531. 500p. 1997. 23.95 (1-887472-14-2) Sunstar Pubng.
Raymondo, James C. Population Estimation & Projection: Methods for Marketing, Demographic, & Planning Personnel. LC 91-45709. 224p. 1992. 59.95 (0-89930-663-2, RPF, Quorum Bks) Greenwood.
— Statistical Analysis in the Behavioral Sciences. LC 98-21046. 480p. 1998. 55.00 (0-07-052283-9) McGraw.
Raymont, Andre, ed. see Rousseau, Jean-Jacques.
Raymont, Henry. Troubled Neighbors: U. S.-Latin American Relations from FDR to Clinton & Beyond. (C). 1998. text 35.00 (0-8147-7474-1) NYU Pr.
Raymont, John E. Plankton & Productivity in the Oceans: Zooplankton, Vol. 2. 2nd ed. (Illus.). 700p. 1983. 368.00 (0-08-024404-1, Pub. by Pergamon Repr) Franklin.
Raymont, Michael E., ed. Sulfur: New Sources & Uses. LC 82-1645. (ACS Symposium Ser.: No. 183). 1982. 37.95 (0-8412-0713-5) Am Chemical.
— Sulfur, New Sources & Uses. LC 82-1645. (ACS Symposium Ser.: Vol. 183). 272p. 1982. reprint ed. pap. 84.40 (0-608-03108-9, 206356100007) Bks Demand.
Raymund, Bernard. Hidden Waters. LC 76-144720. (Yale Series of Younger Poets: No. 13). reprint ed. 18.00 (0-404-53813-4) AMS Pr.
Rayn, Jay. Butch. 194p. (Orig.). 1992. pap. text 10.95 (0-9633031-0-4) RMG Ent.
Rayna, Gerhard. Reduce: Software for Algebraic Computation. LC 87-20535. 335p. 1987. 72.95 (0-387-96598-X) Spr-Verlag.
Raynack, Elton. Not So Free to Choose: The Political Economy of Milton Friedman & Ronald Reagan. LC 86-21276. 224p. 1986. 57.95 (0-275-92363-0, C2363, Praeger Pubs) Greenwood.
***Raynal, Dudley J. & Leopold, Donald J.** Landowners Guide to State-Protected Plants of Forests in New York State. (Illus.). 1999. pap. text 19.95 (0-9670681-0-X, Pub. by State U NY Coll Enviro) Syracuse U Pr.
Raynal, Guillaume T. The Revolution of America. Billias, George A., ed. LC 72-10134. (American Revolutionary Ser.). 1979. reprint ed. lib. bdg. 42.50 (0-8398-1774-6) Irvington.
***Raynal, J. A., et al, eds.** Environmental Engineering & Health Sciences. LC 98-61876. 476p. 2000. pap. 58.00 (1-887201-17-3) WRP.
Raynal, Jose, ed. Hydrology & Water Resources Education Training & Management. 485p. 1992. text 45.00 (0-918334-73-X) WRP.
Raynal, Maurice. Modern French Painters. LC 76-91374. (Contemporary Art Ser.). 1970. reprint ed. 23.95 (0-405-00735-3) Ayer.
Raynal, Michel & Helary, Jean-Michel. Synchronization & Control of Distributed Systems & Programs. LC 90-12210. (Wiley Series in Parallel Computing). (Illus.). 134p. 1990. reprint ed. pap. 41.60 (0-608-05306-6, 206584400001) Bks Demand.
Raynal, Michel, jt. ed. see Bermond, J. C.
Raynaud, C., ed. Nuclear Medicine & Biology Advances: Proceedings of the Third World Congress on Nuclear Medicine & Biology, August 29 - September 2, 1982, Paris, France, 7 vols. 3685p. 1983. 1672.00 (0-08-026405-0, Pub. by Pergamon Repr) Franklin.
Raynaud, Ernest. La Melee Symboliste, 3 vols. in 1. LC 77-11474. reprint ed. 37.50 (0-404-16336-X) AMS Pr.
Raynaud, Fernand. Heureux! (FRE.). 1976. pap. 11.95 (0-7859-4066-9) Fr & Eur.
Raynaud, Gaston. Recueil de Motets Francais des XIIe et XIIIe Siecles. (Bibliotheque Francaise Du Moyen Age Ser.: No. 1-2). liv, 811p. 1972. reprint ed. write for info. (3-487-04274-6) G Olms Pubs.
Raynaud, M. & Shioda, T., eds. Algebraic Geometry. (Lecture Notes in Mathematics Ser.: Vol. 1016). 528p. 1983. 54.95 (0-387-12685-6) Spr-Verlag.
Raynaud, Philippe. Dictionnaire de Philosophie Politique. (FRE.). 800p. 1996. 225.00 (0-7859-9491-2) Fr & Eur.
Raynauld, Andre & Vidal, Jean-Pierre. Labour Standards & International Competitiveness: A Comparative Analysis of Developing & Industrialized Countries. LC 98-21275. 128p. 1999. 70.00 (1-85898-949-3) E Elgar.
Raynaut, Claude & Delville, Philippe L. Societies & Nature in the Sahel: Rethinking Environmental Degradation. Simon, Dominique & Koziol, Hillary, trs. LC 97-162460. (Routledge/Stockholm Environmental Institute Global Ser.: Vol. 1). (Illus.). 376p. (C). 1997. 85.00 (0-415-14102-8) Routledge.
Rayne, E. Catherine, jt. auth. see Stark, Gregor.
Rayne, Josephine E., et al, eds. Register Index Vol. 1: The New England Historical & Genealogical Index Per Persons A-O. LC 88-32255. 1989. 20.00 (0-929539-15-X) Picton Pr.
Rayne, Martha L. What Can a Woman Do?: or Her Position in the Business & Literary World. LC 74-3970. (Women in America Ser.). (Illus.). 584p. 1974. reprint ed. 44.95 (0-405-06118-8) Ayer.
Rayne, Richard C., ed. Neurotransmitter Methods. LC 96-49802. (Methods in Molecular Biology Ser.: Vol. 72). (Illus.). 288p. 1997. 89.50 (0-89603-394-5) Humana.
***Rayner & Rayner-Canham, Geoffrey.** Descriptive Inorganic Chemistry Solutions Manual. 2nd ed. 1999. pap. text 26.95 (0-7167-3759-0) St Martin.
— Descriptive Inorganic Chemistry: Instructors Resource Manual. 2nd ed. 1999. pap. text 30.95 (0-7167-3745-0) W H Freeman.
Rayner & Shoo. Ready Steady Read Cyrils Cats Mouse Practice. (Illus.). 64p. (J). pap. 7.95 (0-14-038086-8, Pub. by Pnguin Bks Ltd) Trafalgar.
Rayner, A. J. & Colman, David, eds. Current Issues in Agricultural Economics. LC 92-30623. (Current Issues in Economics Ser.). 320p. 1993. text 45.00 (0-312-09091-9) St Martin.
Rayner, A. J., jt. auth. see Ingersent, K. A.
Rayner, Alan D. Degrees of Freedom: Living in Dynamic Boundaries. 300p. 1997. 38.00 (1-86094-037-4) World Scientific Pub.
Rayner, Alice. Comic Persuasion: Moral Structure in British Comedy from Shakespeare to Stoppard. LC 86-28281. (Illus.). 181p. reprint ed. pap. 56.20 (0-7837-4699-7, 204444600003) Bks Demand.
— To Act, to Do, to Perform: Drama & the Phenomenology of Action. LC 94-3828. (Theater: Theory - Text - Performance Ser.). 176p. 1994. text 39.50 (0-472-10537-X, 10537) U of Mich Pr.
Rayner, Amanda. Some Mother's Child. 288p. 1998. pap. 19.95 (1-86066-093-2, Pub. by R Cohen Bks) Trafalgar.
Rayner, Ann, jt. auth. see Major, A.
Rayner, Anthony C. & Little, Ian M. Higgledy Piggledy Growth Again: An Investigation of the Predictability of Company Earnings & Dividends in the U. K. 1951-1961. LC 66-73566. (Illus.). 111p. 1966. 27.50 (0-678-06261-7) Kelley.
Rayner-Canham, Geoffrey, jt. auth. see RAYNER.
Rayner-Canham, Geoffrey W. Descriptive Inorganic Chemistry. LC 95-11084. 512p. (C). 1995. pap. text 72.95 (0-7167-2819-2) W H Freeman.
— Descriptive Inorganic Chemistry. 2nd ed. LC 99-34073. (Illus.). 1999. pap. text 82.95 (0-7167-3553-9) St Martin.
Rayner-Canham, Geoffrey W., et al. Foundations of Chemistry. LC 82-18486. (Illus.). 525p. (C). 1983. teacher ed. write for info. (0-201-10414-8); teacher ed., lab manual ed. write for info. (0-201-10416-4); text. write for info. (0-201-10284-6) Addison-Wesley.
Rayner-Canham, Geoffrey W., jt. auth. see Rayner-Canham, Marelene F.
Rayner-Canham, Marelene F. & Rayner-Canham, Geoffrey W. A Devotion to Their Science: Pioneer Women of Radioactivity. LC 98-131383. (Illus.). 280p. 1997. 55.00 (0-941901-16-5); pap. 19.95 (0-941901-15-7) Chem Heritage Fnd.
— A Devotion to Their Science: Pioneer Women of Radioactivity. 320p. 1997. 65.00 (0-7735-1608-5, Pub. by McG-Queens Univ Pr); pap. 24.95 (0-7735-1642-5, Pub. by McG-Queens Univ Pr) CUP Services.
— Harriet Brooks: Pioneer Nuclear Scientist. LC 91-90627. (Illus.). 204p. 1994. pap. 22.95 (0-7735-1254-3, Pub. by McG-Queens Univ Pr) CUP Services.
— Harriet Brooks: Pioneer Nuclear Scientist. LC 91-90627. (Illus.). 192p. 1992. 37.95 (0-7735-0881-3) U of Toronto Pr.
— Women in Chemistry: Their Changing Roles from Alchemical Times to the Mid-20th Century. LC 98-3890. (History of Modern Chemical Sciences Ser.). (Illus.). 240p. 1998. 34.95 (0-8412-3522-8) Am Chemical.
Rayner, Chessy, jt. auth. see Schezen, Roberto.
Rayner, Claire. Bedford Row. large type ed. (Orig.). 1991. 27.99 (0-7089-2557-X) Ulverscroft.
— Charing Cross. large type ed. 672p. 1992. 11.50 (0-7089-2631-2) Ulverscroft.
— Chelsea Reach. large type ed. (General Fiction Ser.). 576p. 1992. 27.99 (0-7089-2700-9) Ulverscroft.
— Dangerous Things. large type ed. (Charnwood Large Print Ser.). 1994. 27.99 (0-7089-8801-6) Ulverscroft.
— First Blood. large type ed. (Charnwood Large Print Ser.). 1995. 27.99 (0-7089-8825-3, Charnwood) Ulverscroft.
— Flanders: The Poppy Chronicles II. large type ed. 466p. 1989. 11.50 (0-7089-8518-1, Charnwood) Ulverscroft.
— Fourth Attempt. large type ed. (Charnwood Large Print Ser.). 496p. 1997. 27.99 (0-7089-8975-6) Ulverscroft.
— The House on the Fen. large type ed. (Linford Mystery Library). 272p. 1989. pap. 11.95 (0-7089-6731-0, Linford) Ulverscroft.
— Jubilee: The Poppy Chronicles I. large type ed. 624p. 1988. 11.50 (0-7089-8479-7, Charnwood) Ulverscroft.
— The Legacy. large type ed. (Charnwood Large Print Ser.). 608p. 1998. 29.99 (0-7089-9006-1, Charnwood) Ulverscroft.
— Life & Love & Everything. (Children's Questions Ser.). (Illus.). 96p. (J). (gr. 2-5). 1995. 9.95 (1-85626-112-3, Pub. by Cathie Kyle) Trafalgar.
— London Lodgings: The Quentin Quartet 1. large type ed. (Charnwood Large Print Ser.). 512p. 1995. 27.99 (0-7089-8847-4, Charnwood) Ulverscroft.
— Long Acre. large type ed. 592p. 1992. 27.99 (0-7089-2593-6) Ulverscroft.
— Paying Guests. large type ed. 1996. 27.99 (0-7089-8882-2, Charnwood) Ulverscroft.
— Piccadilly. large type ed. (General Fiction Ser.). 560p. 1992. 27.99 (0-7089-2776-9) Ulverscroft.
— Second Opinion. large type ed. (Charnwood Large Print Ser.). 528p. 1996. 27.99 (0-7089-8897-0) Ulverscroft.
— Seven Dials. large type ed. (General Ser.). 592p. 1993. 27.99 (0-7089-2812-9) Ulverscroft.
— Shaftesbury Avenue. large type ed. (General Fiction Ser.). 544p. 1992. 27.99 (0-7089-2735-1) Ulverscroft.
— The '60s: (Poppy Chronicles VI) large type ed. (Charnwood Ser.). 432p. 1994. 27.99 (0-7089-8751-6, Charnwood) Ulverscroft.
— The Strand. large type ed. (General Fiction Ser.). 576p. 1992. 27.99 (0-7089-2669-X) Ulverscroft.
Rayner, D. A. Escort: The Battle of the Atlantic. Roskill, S. W., ed. (Classics of Naval Literature Ser.). (Illus.). 256p. 1998. 32.95 (1-55750-696-5) Naval Inst Pr.
Rayner, David. Thyroid Autoimmunity. Champion, B. R., ed. LC 95-24720. (Medical Intelligence Unit Ser.). (Illus.). 238p. 1995. 99.00 (1-57059-301-9) Landes Bioscience.
Rayner, Derek. Road Rollers. 1989. pap. 6.25 (0-7478-0153-3, Pub. by Shire Pubns) St Mut.
Rayner, Desmond. The Dawlish Season. large type ed. (General Ser.). 656p. 1993. 11.50 (0-7089-2792-0) Ulverscroft.
— The Husband. 512p. 1993. lib. bdg. 22.00 (0-7278-4400-8) Severn Hse.
Rayner, Emma. Handicapped among the Free. 1977. text 19.95 (0-8369-9252-0, 9105) Ayer.
Rayner, Eric. The Independent Mind in British Psychoanalysis. LC 91-6403. 360p. 1991. 45.00 (0-87668-560-2) Aronson.
— Unconscious Logic: An Introduction to Matte Blanco's Bi-Logic & Its Uses. LC 94-45146. (New Library of Psychoanalysis Ser.). 176p. (C). 1995. 85.00 (0-415-12725-4, C0565); pap. 27.99 (0-415-12726-2, C0566) Routledge.
Rayner, J. C. & Best, D. J. Smooth Tests of Goodness of Fit. (Oxford Statistical Science Ser.). (Illus.). 176p. 1989. text 65.00 (0-19-505610-8) OUP.
Rayner, John D. Jewish Religious Law: A Progressive Perspective. LC 98-10685. (Progressive Judaism Today Ser.). 224p. 1998. 39.95 (1-57181-975-4); pap. 15.50 (1-57181-976-2) Berghahn Bks.
— A Jewish Understanding of the World. LC 97-49487. (Progressive Judaism Today Ser.). 208p. 1998. 39.95 (1-57181-973-8); pap. 15.50 (1-57181-974-6) Berghahn Bks.
— An Understanding of Judaism. LC 97-38773. 272p. 1998. pap. 19.95 (1-57181-972-X) Berghahn Bks.
— An Understanding of Judaism, 1. LC 97-38773. 272p. 1998. 49.95 (1-57181-971-1) Berghahn Bks.
***Rayner, John N.** Dynamic Climatology: The Basis in Mathematics & Physics. LC 00-37833. (Environmental Systems Ser.). 2000. pap. write for info. (1-57718-016-X) Blackwell Pubs.
Rayner, John N., jt. ed. see Golledge, Reginald G.
Rayner, Jonathan. The Films of Peter Weir. LC 97-45722. 240p. 1999. 89.50 (0-304-70122-X, Pub. by Cassell); pap. 17.95 (0-304-70123-8, Pub. by Cassell) Cassell.
Rayner, Keith & Pollatsek, Alexander. The Psychology of Reading. 536p. 1994. pap. 49.95 (0-8058-1872-3) L Erlbaum Assocs.
Rayner, Keith & Whitaker, H. A., eds. Eye Movements & Visual Cognition: Scene Perception & Reading. (Neuropsychology Ser.). (Illus.). 480p. 1992. 128.00 (0-387-97711-2) Spr-Verlag.
Rayner, Kenneth. Listing Securities in the United States & the United Kingdom: A Comparative Guide to the Regulatory & Accounting Requirements. 288p. 1991. lib. bdg. 146.00 (1-85333-565-7, Pub. by Graham & Trotman) Kluwer Academic.
Rayner, Lois. The Adopted Child Comes of Age. 1980. 40.00 (0-7855-0553-9, Pub. by Natl Inst Soc Work) St Mut.
Rayner, Lynn, jt. auth. see Butler, Kurt.
***Rayner, Manny, et al.** The Spoken Language Translator. LC 99-54619. (Studies in Natural Language Processing). (Illus.). 350p. (C). 2000. text 54.95 (0-521-77077-7) Cambridge U Pr.
Rayner, Mary. Mrs. Pig's Bulk Buy. LC 80-19875. (Illus.). 32p. (J). (gr. k-3). 1981. 14.95 (0-689-30831-0) Atheneum Yung Read.
— Ten Pink Piglets: Garth Pig's Wall Song. (Illus.). 24p. (J). (ps-1). 1994. 5.99 (0-685-70795-4, Dutton Child) Peng Put Young Read.
Rayner, Moira. Rooting Democracy: Growing the Society We Want. LC 97-149284. 304p. 1997. pap. 17.95 (1-86448-132-3, Pub. by Allen & Unwin Pty) Paul & Co Pubs.

An Asterisk (*) at the beginning of an entry indicates that the title is appearing for the first time.

*Rayner, N. A. Copepoda: Calanoida - Diaptomidae: Paradiaptominae. (Guides to the Identification of the Microinvertebrates of the Continental Waters of the World Ser.). (Illus.). 126p. 1999. pap. 45.00 (90-5782-043-9, Pub. by Backhuys Pubs) Balogh.

Rayner, P. J., jt. auth. see Godsill, Simon H.

Rayner, R., tr. see Moser, Meinhard.

Rayner, Ranulf. The Story of the America's Cup, 1851-1995. (Illus.). 96p. 1996. 50.00 (1-895629-65-9) Warwick Publ.

Rayner, Richard. The Blue Suit: A Memoir of Crime. 224p. 1997. pap. 12.00 (0-395-86005-9) HM.

***Rayner, Richard.** The Cloud Sketcher. 2001. write for info. (0-06-019634-3) HarpC.

— The Cloud Sketcher. 2002. pap. write for info. (0-06-095613-5, Perennial) HarperTrade.

Rayner, Richard. Los Angeles Without a Map: A Love Story. LC 97-35013. 192p. 1997. pap. 12.00 (0-395-83809-6, Mariner Bks) HM.

— Murder Book. 432p. 1999. mass mkt. 5.99 (0-06-109737-3) HarpC.

Rayner, S. Dance Apple Dumpling. (Illus.). (J). 1996. mass mkt. 7.95 (0-340-61957-0, Pub. by Hodder & Stought Ltd) Trafalgar.

— Ginger Ninja, Bk. 1. (Illus.). (J). 1995. mass mkt. 7.95 (0-340-61955-4, Pub. by Hodder & Stought Ltd) Trafalgar.

— Ginger Ninja: Three's a Crowd. (Illus.). (J). 1997. mass mkt. 6.95 (0-340-69380-0, Pub. by Hodder & Stought Ltd) Trafalgar.

— Ginger Ninja Return Tiddles, Bk. 2. (Illus.). (J). 1995. mass mkt. 7.95 (0-340-61956-2, Pub. by Hodder & Stought Ltd) Trafalgar.

— Shaggy Ghost Stories. (Illus.). (J). 1997. mass mkt. 8.95 (0-340-69013-5, Pub. by Hodder & Stought Ltd) Trafalgar.

— St. Felix for Cup. (Illus.). (J). 1996. mass mkt. 7.95 (0-340-61958-9, Pub. by Hodder & Stought Ltd) Trafalgar.

***Rayner, Shoo.** Christmas Stocking Joke Book. (Illus.). (J). 1998. pap. 5.95 (0-14-032823-8, Pub. by Pnguin Bks Ltd) Trafalgar.

— Cyril's Cat: Charlie's Night Out. (Illus.). 64p. (J). (ps-3). 1993. pap. 7.95 (0-14-036141-3, Pub. by Pnguin Bks Ltd) Trafalgar.

— Cyril's Cat & the Big Surprise. (Illus.). 64p. (J). (ps-3). 1993. pap. 7.95 (0-14-036142-1, Pub. by Pnguin Bks Ltd) Trafalgar.

Rayner, Shoo. My First Joke Book. 32p. 1999. pap. 3.99 (0-14-054822-X) NAL.

Rayner, Shoo. Noah's ABC. (Illus.). 32p. (J). pap. 9.95 (0-14-054360-0, Pub. by Pnguin Bks Ltd) Trafalgar.

— Pirate Joke & Fun Book. (Illus.). 96p. (J). 1999. pap. 5.95 (0-14-037518-X, Pub. by Pnguin Bks Ltd) Trafalgar.

Rayner, Stephen, ed. Butterworths Privatisation in Central & Eastern Europe. 215p. 1992. pap. 153.00 (0-406-00840-X, UK, MICHIE) LEXIS Pub.

— Butterworths Trade & Finance in Central & Eastern Europe. 200p. 1993. pap. 160.00 (0-406-02088-4, U.K., MICHIE) LEXIS Pub.

Rayner, Stephen R. Team Traps: Survival Stories & Lessons from Team Disasters, Near-Misses, Mishaps & Other Near-Death Experiences. LC 95-49752. 190p. 1996. 24.95 (0-471-13285-3) Wiley.

Rayner, Steve, jt. auth. see Flanagan, James G.

Rayner, Steve, jt. auth. see Gross, Jonathan L.

Rayner, Steven R. Recreating the Workplace: The Pathway to High Performance Work Systems. LC 92-85209. 281p. 1993. 27.50 (0-939246-32-5) Wiley.

— Recreating the Workplace: The Pathway to High Performance Work Systems. 288p. 1995. 29.95 (0-471-13202-0) Wiley.

— Team Traps: Survival Stories & Lessons from Team Disasters, Mishaps & Other Near-Death Experiences. 256p. 1995. 25.00 (0-939246-79-1) Wiley.

Rayner, Victoria. Clinical Cosmetology: A Medical Approach to Esthetics Procedures. (SKIN). (Illus.). 440p. (C). 1993. pap. 41.95 (1-56253-056-9) Thomson Learn.

Rayner, Victoria L. The Survival Guide for Today's Career Woman. 208p. (Orig.). 1994. pap. 19.95 (0-924272-06-6) Info Net Pub.

Rayner, William. Images of History: Twentieth Century British Columbia Through the Front Pages. (Illus.). 224p. 1997. pap. 18.95 (1-55143-089-4) Orca Bk Pubs.

Raynes. Valley So Sweet. 1995. 12.00 (0-9642423-1-1) Whte Willow.

Raynes, Bert. Birds of Grand Teton: And the Surrounding Area. Broadus, Debbie, ed. (Illus.). 90p. 1986. reprint ed. pap. 7.95 (0-931895-00-6) Grand Teton NHA.

Raynes, Harold E. Social Security in Britain: A History-A Greenwood Archival Edition. 2nd ed. LC 76-40057. 264p. 1977. reprint ed. lib. bdg. 79.50 (0-8371-9055-X, RASSB, Greenwood Pr) Greenwood.

***Raynes, John.** Drawing & Painting People. (Illus.). 128p. 2000. pap. 24.99 (1-58180-002-9, North Lght Bks) F & W Pubns Inc.

Raynes, John. A Step-by-Step Guide to Drawing the Figure. (Illus.). 128p. 1997. pap. 24.99 (0-89134-794-1, North Lght Bks) F & W Pubns Inc.

Raynes, Livia, ed. see Stiles, Tom.

Raynes, Norma V., et al. Homes for Mental Handicapped People. 240p. 1988. text 65.00 (0-422-60770-3, Pub. by Tavistock) Routldge.

— Organisational Structure & the Care of the Mentally Retarded. LC 79-83740. (Praeger Special Studies). 240p. 1979. 62.95 (0-275-90411-3, C0411, Praeger Pubs) Greenwood.

Raynes, Norma V., jt. ed. see Hogg, James.

Rayney, Peter, jt. auth. see Hart, Gerry.

Raynham, Doone. Griffon Bruxellois. 2nd ed. 1999. 23.95 (1-85279-072-5) TFH Pubns.

Raynolds, Stone. Halo Effect. 1999. pap. write for info. (0-312-24565-3) St Martin.

— Volunteering. 224p. 1999. pap. 12.95 (1-58238-058-9, Whitman Coin) St Martin.

Raynor, Bill & Bay, Roger R., eds. Proceedings of the Workshop on Research Methodologies & Applications for Pacific Island Agroforestry. (Illus.). 86p. (Orig.). (C). 1994. pap. text 25.00 (0-7881-1073-X) DIANE Pub.

Raynor, G., jt. auth. see Pearson, W.

Raynor, G. V. An Introduction to the Electron Theory of Metals. 96p. 1988. text 20.00 (0-901462-37-3, Pub. by Inst Materials) Ashgate Pub Co.

Raynor, Joel O. & Entin, Elliot E. Motivation, Career Striving & Aging. 1981. text 24.95 (0-07-051274-4) McGraw.

Raynor, Joyce, et al. The Coins of Ancient Meiron. LC 87-19135. (Meiron Excavation Project Ser.: Vol. 4). (Illus.). vii, 140p. 1988. text 35.00 (0-89757-208-4); pap. text 25.00 (0-89757-209-2) Am Sch Orient Res.

Raynor, Lois. The Adopted Child Comes of Age. LC 79-41348. (London. National Institute for Social Work Training. National Institute Social Services Library: No. 36). 176p. reprint ed. pap. 54.60 (0-8357-5117-1, 202318000032) Bks Demand.

Raynor, Louise A. & Kerr, Carolyn H. Church Needlepoint. 2nd ed. (Illus.). 72p. 1989. pap. 10.95 (0-8192-1436-1) Morehouse Pub.

***Raynor, Maggie.** A Bit More Than a Mouth. (Pony Guides Ser.: No. 5). 16p. (J). (gr. 1-5). 1999. pap. 5.95 (1-900667-04-5, Pub. by Compass Equestrian Ltd) Trafalgar.

— Bodywork. (Pony Guides Ser.: No. 3). 16p. (J). (gr. 1-5). 1999. pap. 5.95 (1-900667-02-9, Pub. by Compass Equestrian Ltd) Trafalgar.

— Filling up the Tank. (Pony Guides Ser.: No. 7). 16p. (J). (gr. 1-5). 1999. pap. 5.95 (1-900667-06-1, Pub. by Compass Equestrian Ltd) Trafalgar.

— Forelegs & Four Feet. (Pony Guides Ser.: No. 4). 16p. (J). (gr. 1-5). 1999. pap. 5.95 (1-900667-03-7, Pub. by Compass Equestrian Ltd) Trafalgar.

— Head First. (Pony Guides Ser.: No. 2). 16p. (J). (gr. 1-5). 1999. pap. 5.95 (1-900667-01-0, Pub. by Compass Equestrian Ltd) Trafalgar.

— More Than Just a Pet. (Pony Guides Ser.: No. 1). 16p. (J). (gr. 1-5). 1999. pap. 5.95 (1-900667-00-2, Pub. by Compass Equestrian Ltd) Trafalgar.

— Top, Tail & Overcoat. (Pony Guides Ser.: No. 6). 16p. (J). (gr. 1-5). 1999. pap. 5.95 (1-900667-05-3, Pub. by Compass Equestrian Ltd) Trafalgar.

— Why Does He Do That? (Pony Guides Ser.: No. 8). 16p. (J). (gr. 1-5). 1999. pap. 5.95 (1-900667-07-X, Pub. by Compass Equestrian Ltd) Trafalgar.

Raynor, Mary. Thank You for the Tadpole. LC 87-474. (Share-a-Story Bks.). (J). (gr. k-2). 1988. 8.95 (0-385-29604-5) Delacorte.

Raynor, Sherry & Drouillard, Richard. Get a Wiggle On. Alonso, Lou, ed. (Illus.). 80p. 1978. pap. 6.00 (0-88314-077-2) AAHPERD.

— Move It!!! Alonso, Lou, ed. (Illus.). 96p. 1978. pap. 6.00 (0-88314-132-9) AAHPERD.

Raynor, Shoo. Little Book of New Year's Resolutions. (J). 1994. pap. 5.95 (0-14-036804-3, Pub. by Pnguin Bks Ltd) Trafalgar.

***Raynor, Steve & Malone, Elizabeth, eds.** Human Choice & Climate Change, 4 vols. 1998. 250.00 (1-57477-045-4) Battelle.

Raynor, Steve & Malone, Elizabeth, eds. Human Choice & Climate Change, 4 vols., Set. 1998. pap. 100.00 (1-57477-040-3) Battelle.

— Resources & Technology. (Human Choice & Climate Change Ser.: Vol. 2). 496p. 1998. 75.00 (1-57477-046-2); pap. 34.95 (1-57477-041-1) Battelle.

— The Societal Framework. (Human Choice & Climate Change Ser.: Vol. 1). 536p. 1998. 75.00 (1-57477-049-7); pap. 34.95 (1-57477-044-6) Battelle.

— The Tools for Policy Analysis. (Human Choice & Climate Change Ser.: Vol. 3). 474p. 1998. 75.00 (1-57477-047-0); pap. 34.95 (1-57477-042-X) Battelle.

— What Have We Learned? (Human Choice & Climate Change Ser.: Vol. 4). 208p. 1998. 60.00 (1-57477-048-9); pap. 25.00 (1-57477-043-8) Battelle.

Raynor, Steve, jt. auth. see Ribbins, Peter.

Raynor, Victoria. Clinical Cosmetology: A Medical Approach to Esthetics Procedures. 1993. 41.95 (1-56293-056-7) Phoenix Soc.

Raynor, William. The International Dictionary of Artificial Intelligence. 380p. 1998. 45.00 (0-8144-0444-8) AMACOM.

Raynor, William, ed. International Dictionary of Artificial Intelligence. 250p. 1999. lib. bdg. 45.00 (1-884964-68-0) Fitzroy Dearborn.

Raynouard, F. Dictionary Roman, Langue des Troubadours, 6 vols. (FRE.). 1996. 995.00 (0-320-00877-0) Fr & Eur.

Raynova, Yvanka, jt. auth. see McBride, William L.

Raynovich, William, jt. auth. see Gonsoulin, Sheryl M.

Rayns, Tony. Seoul Stirring: 5 Korean Directors. LC 95-236368. 1996. pap. text 9.95 (0-905263-79-0, Pub. by British Film Inst) Ind U Pr.

Raynus, Joseph. Software Process Improvement with CMM. 1998. 65.00 (0-89006-644-2) Artech Hse.

Rayor, Diane, tr. Sappho's Lyre: Archaic Lyric & Women Poets of Ancient Greece. LC 90-48642. (Illus.). 234p. 1991. 45.00 (0-520-07335-5, Pub. by U CA Pr); pap. 15.95 (0-520-07336-3, Pub. by U CA Pr) Cal Prin Full Svc.

Rayor, Diane, jt. tr. see Lombardo, Stanley.

Rayor, Diane J. & Batstone, William W., eds. Latin Lyric & Elegiac Poetry: An Anthology of New Translations. LC 94-37902. 384p. 1995. text 70.00 (0-8153-0087-5, H1425); pap. text 26.95 (0-8153-1540-6, H1425) Garland.

Raycumi, Magdy A., ed. Parallel Algorithms & Architectures for DSP Applications. 304p. (C). 1991. text 117.00 (0-7923-9209-4) Kluwer Academic.

Rayside, David. On the Fringe: Gays & Lesbians Politics. LC 97-35245. (Illus.). 384p. 1998. pap. 19.95 (0-8014-8374-3, Comstock Pub); text 49.95 (0-8014-3321-5) Cornell U Pr.

Rayside, David M. A Small Town in Modern Times: Alexandria, Ontario. 360p. (C). 1991. text 55.00 (0-7735-0826-0, Pub. by McG-Queens Univ Pr) CUP Services.

Raysman, Richard & Brown, Peter. Computer Law: Drafting & Negotiating Forms & Agreements. 1984. 145.00 (0-318-12028-3) NY Law Pub.

Raysman, Richard, et al. Multimedia Law: Forms & Analysis. (Commercial Law Intellectual Property Ser.). 1994. write for info. (0-614-32425-4) Law Journal.

Raysman, Victor. Say It in Polish. (Orig.). 1954. pap. 3.95 (0-486-20808-7) Dover.

Rayson, Ann, ed. Hawaiian Word Book. (Illus.). 104p. 1982. 19.95 (1-880188-24-4) Bess Pr.

Rayson, Ann & Bauek, Helen. Hawai'i: The Pacific State. Orig. Title: Hawaii: The Aloha State. (Illus.). 144p. (YA). (gr. 4 up). 1997. pap., teacher ed. 9.95 (1-57306-073-9); pap., wbk. ed. 8.95 (1-57306-063-1) Bess Pr.

Rayson, Ann & Bauer, Helen. Hawai'i: The Pacific State. LC 99-163014. Orig. Title: Hawaii: The Aloha State. (Illus.). 144p. (YA). (gr. 4 up). 1997. text 39.95 (1-57306-062-3) Bess Pr.

Rayson, Ann, et al. The Hawaiian Monarchy. LC 82-74176. (Illus.). 256p. (J). (gr. 5-8). 1983. 39.95 (0-935848-17-7); pap., student ed. 8.95 (0-935848-31-2) Bess Pr.

Rayson, Ann, jt. auth. see Wong, Helen.

Rayson, Ann L. Modern Hawaiian History. rev. ed. (Illus.). 304p. (YA). (gr. 9-12). 1996. 8.95 (1-57306-051-8); 34.95 (1-880188-90-2) Bess Pr.

Rayson, Ethel. Polish Music & Chopin, Its Laureate. 64p. 1991. reprint ed. lib. bdg. 59.00 (0-7812-9344-8) Rprt Serv.

Rayson, Hannie. Falling from Grace. 70p. (C). 1994. pap. 14.95 (0-86819-387-9, Pub. by Currency Pr) Accents Pubns.

— Hotel Sorrento. 3rd rev. ed. (Currency Plays Ser.). (Illus.). xvi, 94p. (Orig.). 1995. pap. 16.95 (0-86819-337-2, Pub. by Currency Pr) Accents Pubns.

Rayson, Jane, jt. auth. see Mallender, Paul.

Raysor, Thomas M., ed. see Wordsworth, William & Coleridge, Samuel Taylor.

Raysuni, Ahmad A. Nazariyat al Maqasid 'Inda al Imam al Shatibi: The Theory of the Law's Objectives According to al Shatibi. 2nd ed. LC 92-8243. (Silsilat al Rasa'il al Jami'iyah Ser.: No. 1). (ARA.). 383p. 1993. 18.00 (1-56564-036-5); pap. 12.00 (1-56564-037-3) IIIT VA.

Raytheon E-Systems Staff. How to 2000. LC 97-74336. 656p. 1997. pap. 49.99 (0-7645-3101-8) IDG Bks.

***Rayudu, A. V.** Chaman Nahal's The Ghandi Quartet: Gandhian Ideology & the Indian Novel. 2000. 29.50 (81-7551-075-7, Pub. by Prestige) S Asia.

Rayudu, C. S. Agricultural Credit & Rural Development in Drought Regions: A Study of Cooperative Banks of A. P. (C). 1992. text 21.00 (81-7022-385-7, Pub. by Concept) S Asia.

Rayudu, Garimella V., ed. Radiotracers for Medical Applications, Vol. I. 320p. 1983. 155.00 (0-8493-6015-3, R895) CRC Pr.

— Radiotracers for Medical Applications, Vol. II. 304p. 1983. 154.00 (0-8493-6016-1, R895, CRC Reprint) Franklin.

Rayudu, P. V. How to Read a Horoscope: A Scientific Model of Prediction Bases on Benefic & Malefic Analysis of Planets & Bhayas As per Hindu Astrology. LC 97-902517. (C). 1997. 28.00 (81-208-1458-4, Pub. by Motilal Bnarsidass) S Asia.

Raywalt, James K. Barnhart: The Descendants of John & Mariah (Hiveley) Barnhart: a Genealogy of the Ancestors & Descendants of John Barnhart & Mariah Hively of Eastern Ohio to the Present. (Illus.). 109p. 1992. reprint ed. pap. 19.50 (0-8328-2409-7); reprint ed. lib. bdg. 29.50 (0-8328-2408-9) Higginson Bk Co.

— Lane . . . And a Cast of Thousands: A History of the Lane Family of Canada & the U. S. from Their Arrival in 1819 to the Present. (Illus.). 751p. 1992. reprint ed. pap. 89.50 (0-8328-2407-0); reprint ed. lib. bdg. 99.50 (0-8328-2406-2) Higginson Bk Co.

— Morgan: A History of the Descendants of Henry Oscar Morgan & Ellen Jane Mandigo. (Illus.). 203p. 1992. reprint ed. pap. 29.00 (0-8328-2411-9); reprint ed. lib. bdg. 39.00 (0-8328-2410-0) Higginson Bk Co.

— Shove: An English Ancestry: an Account of the Ancestry of Edward Melvin Shove & His Siblings. (Illus.). 149p. 1992. reprint ed. pap. 21.00 (0-8328-2413-5); reprint ed. lib. bdg. 31.00 (0-8328-2412-7) Higginson Bk Co.

Rayward-Smith, V. Modern Heuristic Search Methods. LC 97-08470. 314p. 1996. 135.00 (0-471-96280-5) Wiley.

Rayward, W. Boyd & Metcalf, John W. Developing a Profession of Librarianship in Australia: Travel Diaries & Other Papers of John Wallace Metcalfe. LC 94-32935. 389p. 1995. 50.00 (0-8108-2944-4) Scarecrow.

Rayward, W. Boyd, ed. see Chicago University, Graduate Library School Staff.

***Raywid, Mary Anne & Arinaga, Esther Kwon, eds.** Allan Saunders: The Man & His Legacy. LC 99-54199. (Illus.). 240p. 2000. pap. text 19.95 (0-8248-2013-4) UH Pr.

Rayworth, Ivan W. Listless. 254p. 1997. pap. text, per. 8.95 (0-9658263-0-9) I W Rayworth.

Rayyan, Omar. Count Silvernose: A Story from Italy. LC 95-30935. 32p. (J). (gr. k-3). 1996. 15.95 (0-8234-1216-4) Holiday.

— Rimonah of the Flashing Sword: A North African Tale. LC 93-40091. 32p. (J). (gr. k-3). 1995. lib. bdg. 15.95 (0-8234-1093-5) Holiday.

Raz. Project Planning & Computer Models. 1995. pap. 32.95 (0-442-01843-6, VNR) Wiley.

Raz, Aviad E. Riding the Black Ship: Japan & Tokyo Disneyland, Vol. 173. LC 98-43028. (Harvard East Asian Monographs). 1999. write for info. (0-674-76893-0); pap. write for info. (0-674-76894-9) HUP.

Raz, E., ed. Gene Vaccination: Theory & Practice. LC 98-22471. (Principles & Practice Ser.). 192p. 1998. 129.00 (3-540-64428-8) Spr-Verlag.

Raz, Hilda. Divine Honors. LC 97-10481. (Wesleyan Poetry Ser.). 117p. 1997. pap. 12.95 (0-8195-2249-X, Wesleyan Univ Pr); text 25.00 (0-8195-2248-1, Wesleyan Univ Pr) U Pr of New Eng.

— Truly Bone. (Illus.). 20p. 1998. pap. 500.00 (1-893125-01-7) Womens Studio Wrkshop.

— What Is Good? 64p. (Orig.). 1988. pap. 5.95 (0-939395-09-6) Thorntree Pr.

Raz, Hilda, ed. Living on the Margins: Women Writers on Breast Cancer. LC 99-32917. 304p. 1999. 25.95 (0-89255-244-1, Pub. by Persea Bks) Norton.

— The "Prairie Schooner" Anthology of Contemporary Jewish American Writing: Fiction & Poetry. LC 97-41201. iv, 293p. 1998. pap. 20.00 (0-8032-8971-5, Bison Books) U of Nebr Pr.

***Raz, Hilda & Flaherty, Kate, eds.** Best of "Prairie Schooner" Personal Essays. LC 99-86691. 224p. 2000. pap. 20.00 (0-8032-8982-0, Bison Books) U of Nebr Pr.

Raz, Joseph. The Authority of Law: Essays on Law & Morality. (Illus.). 304p. 1983. pap. text 35.00 (0-19-825493-8) OUP.

— The Concept of a Legal System: An Introduction to the Theory of a Legal System. 2nd ed. 256p. 1980. pap. text 29.95 (0-19-825363-X) OUP.

— Engaging Reason: On the Theory of Value & Action. LC 99-45063. 344p. 2000. 45.00 (0-19-823829-0) OUP.

— Ethics in the Public Domain: Essays in the Morality of Law & Politics. 390p. 1996. pap. text 35.00 (0-19-826069-5) OUP.

— The Morality of Freedom. 448p. 1988. pap. text 32.00 (0-19-824807-5) OUP.

***Raz, Joseph.** Practical Reason & Norms. 224p. 1999. pap. text 29.95 (0-19-826834-3) OUP.

Raz, Joseph, ed. Authority. (Readings in Social & Political Theory Ser.). 330p. (C). 1990. text 50.00 (0-8147-7414-8); pap. text 20.00 (0-8147-7415-6) NYU Pr.

Raz, Joseph, jt. ed. see Hacker, P. M.

Raz, Mirla G. "Help Me Talk Right" How to Correct a Child's Lisp in 15 Easy Lessons. LC 92-63349. (Illus.). 128p. (Orig.). 1993. pap. 32.00 (0-9635426-0-5) Gersten Weitz.

***Raz, Mirla G.** "Help Me Talk Right" How to Teach a Child to Say the "L" Sound in 15 Easy Lessons. LC 98-75259. 94 p. 1999. pap. 32.00 (0-9635426-4-8) Gersten Weitz.

Raz, Mirla G. "Help Me Talk Right" Teach a Child to Say the "R" Sound in 15 Easy Lessons. LC 96-75526. (Illus.). 110p. (Orig.). 1996. pap. 32.00 (0-9635426-1-3) Gersten Weitz.

Raz, Naftali. The Other Side of the Error Term: Aging & Development As Model Systems in Cognitive Neuroscience, Vol. 125. LC 98-3180. (Advances in Psychology Ser.). 458p. 1998. 135.00 (0-444-82522-3) Elsevier.

Raz, S. Flat Knitting: The New Generation. 1991. 100.00 (3-87525-053-2, Pub. by Textile Inst) St Mut.

— Tigre Grammar & Texts. LC 81-71735. (Afroasiatic Dialects Ser.: Vol. 4). xviii, 145p. (C). 1983. pap. 26.00 (0-89003-097-9) Undena Pubns.

Raz, Shlomo. Atlas of Transvaginal Surgery. 1992. text 175.00 (0-7216-2431-6, W B Saunders Co) Harcrt Hlth Sci Grp.

— Female Urology. 2nd ed. Valkoff, Sandra, ed. LC 95-17714. 656p. 1996. text 180.00 (0-7216-6723-6, W B Saunders Co) Harcrt Hlth Sci Grp.

Raz, Shlomo, jt. ed. see Izre'el, Shlomo.

Raz, Simcha. Hasidic Wisdom: Sayings from the Jewish Sages. Elkins, D. Peretz & Elkins, Jonathan, trs. from HEB. LC 97-19304. 344p. 1997. 35.00 (0-7657-9972-3) Aronson.

— Melodies from My Father's House: Hasidic Wisdom for the Heart & Soul. Elkins, Dov Peretz, ed. & tr. by. from HEB. LC 95-82346. (Illus.). 176p. (Orig.). 1996. pap. 12.00 (0-918834-15-5) Growth Assoc.

— The Sayings of Menahem Mendel of Kotsk. Levin, Edward, tr. LC 94-28313. 224p. 1995. 30.00 (1-56821-297-6) Aronson.

— A Tzaddik in Our Time. Wengrov, Charles V., tr. from HEB. (Illus.). 1976. 22.95 (0-87306-130-6) Feldheim.

Raza, Asmi. Pakistan's Quest for Food Security. (C). 1993. 18.50 incl. cd-rom (81-7024-550-8, Pub. by Ashish Pub Hse) S Asia.

Raza, Hilal A., jt. ed. see Bender, Friedrich K.

Raza, M. Ali & Anderson, A. Janell. Labor Relations & the Law. LC 95-52840. 1996. write for info. (0-614-95869-5) P-H.

Raza, M. Ali, et al. The ups & Downs of Affirmative Action Preferences. LC 99-15395. 224p. 1999. 59.95 (0-275-96713-1) Greenwood.

Raza, Mehdi, jt. auth. see Shafi, Mohammad.

Raza, Mehdi, jt. ed. see Shafi, Mohammad.

An Asterisk (*) at the beginning of an entry indicates that the title is appearing for the first time.

R

Raza, Moonis. Higher Education in India: A Comprehensive Bibliography. (C). 1991. 62.50 (*81-7022-346-6*, Pub. by Concept) S Asia.

Raza, Moonis, ed. Renewable Resources for Regional Development. (C). 1988. 52.00 (*81-7022-229-X*, Pub. by Concept) S Asia.

Raza, Moonis, jt. ed. see Misra, R. P.

Raza, Rafi. Zulfikar Ali Bhutto & Pakistan 1967-1977. (Illus.). 420p. (C). 1997. text 45.00 (*0-19-577697-6*) OUP.

***Raza, Rafi, ed.** Pakistan in Perspective, 1947-1997. LC 97-930910. (The Jubilee Ser.). 354p. 1998. 35.00 (*0-19-577842-1*) OUP.

Razaboni, Rosa M., jt. auth. see Taylor, G. Ian.

Razack, Nasser. Conquering Hair Loss: A Complete Medical Guide to Hair Loss Assessment, Prevention & Restoration. unabridged ed. LC 96-92990. (Illus.). iv, 270p. (Orig.). 1997. pap. 29.95 (*0-9656921-0-8*) Raztec Entrprises.

Razack, Sherene H. Looking White People in the Eye: Gender, Race & Culture in Courtrooms & Classrooms. LC 99-164793. 272p. 1998. text 55.00 (*0-8020-0928-X*); pap. text 21.95 (*0-8020-7898-2*) U of Toronto Pr.

Razak, Achmad. Indonesia. 2nd ed. LC 99-916181. (Illus.). 200p. 1996. 170.00 (*1-85564-374-X*, Pub. by Euromoney) Am Educ Systs.

Razak, Victoria M. Carnival in Aruba. abr. ed. (Illus.). 84p. 1998. mass mkt. 15.00 (*0-9657608-1-2*) Cenda Pub.

Razakis. 81 Fresh & Fun Critical Thinking Environmental Studies. 112p. 1998. pap. 12.95 (*0-590-37526-1*, 893241Q) Scholastic Inc.

Razams, Yum. Refracciones: Guia para el Iniciado. (SPA.). 137p. (Orig.). Date not set. pap. 9.60 (*0-9653347-1-6*) Transpersonal.

Razavi, Ahmad. Continental Shelf Delimination & Related Maritime Issues in the Persian Gulf. LC 96-48894. (Publications on Ocean Development). 1996. lib. bdg. 112.00 (*90-411-0333-3*) Kluwer Academic.

Razavi, Amir H. ArcView GIS-Avenue Developer's Guide. 2nd ed. LC 96-49394. 432p. (C). 1997. pap. 54.95 (*1-56690-118-9*) Thomson Learn.

***Razavi, Amir H.** Arcview GIS Developer's Guide. 4th ed. (Student Material TV Ser.). 2001. pap. 42.75 (*0-7668-2800-X*) Delmar.

Razavi, Amir H. ArcView GIS/Avenue Developer's Guide. 3rd ed. LC 99-59094. (C). 1999. pap. text 54.95 (*1-56690-167-7*) Thomson Learn.

***Razavi, Amir H.** ArcView GIS/Avenue Programmer's Reference: Version 3.1. 3rd ed. (Illus.). (C). 1999. pap. text 56.95 (*1-56690-170-7*) Thomson Learn.

Razavi, Amir H., et al. ArcView GIS-Avenue Programmer's Reference: Class Hierarchy Quick Reference & 101 Scripts. 2nd ed. LC 96-29962. 552p. 1997. pap. 54.95 incl. cd-rom (*1-56690-123-5*, OnWord Pr) High Mtn.

Razavi, B. Trends in Lower Power Electronics. (Current Topics in Electronics & Systems Ser.). 200p. 1994. text 48.00 (*981-02-1863-X*) World Scientific Pub.

Razavi, Behfar. Javastations. 400p. (C). 2002. pap. text 39.95 (*0-13-887423-9*) P-H.

***Razavi, Behzad.** Design of Analog CMOS Integrated Circuits. LC 00-44789. (Illus.). 2001. write for info. (*0-07-238032-2*) McGraw.

Razavi, Behzad. Principles of Data Conversion System Design. LC 94-26694. 272p. 1994. 79.95 (*0-7803-1093-4*, PC4465) Inst Electrical.

Razavi, Behzag B. Monolithic Phase-Locked Loops & Clock Recovery Circuits: Theory & Design. LC 96-6102. 508p. 1996. 89.95 (*0-7803-1149-3*, PC5620) Inst Electrical.

Razavi, Hossein. Financing Energy Projects in Emerging Economies. 285p. 1996. 79.95 (*0-87814-469-2*) PennWell Bks.

Razavi, Hossein & Fesharaki, Fereidun. Fundamentals of Petroleum Trading. LC 91-8072. 232p. 1991. 69.50 (*0-275-93920-0*, C3920, Praeger Pubs) Greenwood.

Razavi, Hossein, et al. Gas & Power in the Developing World: A Systematic Look at Countries & Their Investment Needs. LC 96-44329. 1996. pap. 40.00 (*0-87814-705-5*) PennWell Bks.

Razavi, Mehdi Amin, see Amin Razavi, Mehdi, ed.

***Razavi, Shahra, ed.** Gendered Poverty & Well-Being. 288p. 2000. pap. text 32.95 (*0-631-21793-2*) Blackwell Pubs.

Razavi, Shahra, jt. ed. see Miller, Carol.

Razdan, M. K. & Cocking, E. C., eds. Conservation of Plant Genetic Resources. (Illus.). 314p. 1997. text 88.00 (*1-886106-76-2*) Science Pubs.

— Conservation of Plant Genetic Resources in Vitro Vol. 2: Applications & Limitations. (Illus.). 320p. 1999. text 88.00 (*1-57808-055-X*) Science Pubs.

Razdan, M. N., jt. auth. see Bhojwani, S. S.

Razdolskaya, Vera. Martyros Saryan, 1860-1972. (Great Painters Ser.). (Illus.). 176p. 1997. 40.00 (*1-85995-320-4*) Parkstone Pr.

— Rubens. (Masters of World Painting Ser.). (C). 1983. text 60.00 (*0-569-08768-6*, Pub. by Collets) St Mut.

Razeen, Sally. Classical Liberalism & International Economic Order: Studies in Theory & Intellectual History. LC 98-4867. 240p. (C). 1998. 85.00 (*0-415-16493-1*) Routledge.

Razeghi, M. The MOCVD Challenge Vol. 2: A Study of GaInAsP-GaAs for Photonic & Electronic Device Applications. (Illus.). 443p. 1995. 231.00 (*0-7503-0309-3*) IOP Pub.

Razeghi, M., ed. Optoelectronic Materials & Device Concepts. 1991. pap. 20.00 (*0-8194-0533-7*, PM05) SPIE.

Razeghi, Manijeh, ed. Long Wavelength Infrared Detectors. (Optoelectronic Properties of Semiconductor Ser.). 488p. 1997. text 81.00 (*2-88449-208-9*); pap. text 48.00 (*2-88449-209-7*) Gordon & Breach.

Razeghi, Manijeh, jt. ed. see Brown, Gail J.

Razeghi, Manijeh, jt. ed. see Wong, Ka-Kha.

Razek, et al. Introduction to Managerial Accounting, 1998 Edition. 1998. pap. 54.95 (*0-87393-824-0*) Dame Pubns.

Razek, Joseph R., et al. Introduction to Governmental & Not-for-Profit Accounting. 4th ed. LC 99-27148. (Illus.). 644p. 1999. 70.00 (*0-13-917873-2*) P-H.

***Razek, Rula.** Internet Cool Guide: Online Entertainment: A Savvy Guide to the Hottest Entertainment Sites. 2000. pap. 9.95 (*3-8238-5446-1*) te Neues.

— Internet Cool Guide: Online Shopping: A Savvy Guide to the Hottest Shopping Sites. 2000. pap. 9.95 (*3-8238-5445-3*) te Neues.

Razek, Rula & Tung, James, eds. Internet Cool Guide: A Savvy Guide to the Best Destinations on the Web. (Illus.). 300p. 1999. pap. 14.95 (*3-8238-0997-0*) te Neues.

Razetti, Alezio, et al. Ten Italian Violin Concertos from Fonds Blancheton I. Hirshberg, Jehoash, ed. (Recent Researches in Music of the Classic Era Ser.: Vol. RRC19). (Illus.). 106p. 1984. pap. 40.00 (*0-89579-171-4*) A-R Eds.

***Razgaitis, Richard.** Early-Stage Technologies: Risk Management, Valuation, & Pricing. LC 99-30149. (Intellectual Property Ser.). (Illus.). 291p. 1999. text 65.00 (*0-471-32856-1*) Wiley.

Razgon, Lev. True Stories. Crowfoot, John, tr. from RUS. 1997. 27.95 (*0-87501-108-X*) Ardis Pubs.

Razheghi, M. The MOCVD Challenge Vol. 1: A Survey of GaInAsP-InP for Photonic & Electronic Applications. (Illus.). 340p. 1989. 184.00 (*0-85274-161-8*) IOP Pub.

Razi, B. A., jt. auth. see Rao, R. R.

Razi, F. D. The Modern Persian-Urdu-English Dictionary. (ENG, PER & URD.). 250p. 1981. 29.95 (*0-8288-1454-6*, M14111) Fr & Eur.

Razi, Najm A. The Path of God's Bondsmen: From Origin to Return. Algar, Hamid, tr. from PER. (Persian Heritage Ser.: Vol. 35). 537p. 1982. text 42.00 (*0-88206-052-X*) Bibliotheca Persica.

Razi, Sayyid, ed. see Talib, Ali B. Abi.

Razi, Zvi & Smith, Richard. Medieval Society & the Manor Court. LC 96-2644. (Illus.). 726p. 1996. text 140.00 (*0-19-820190-7*, Clarendon Pr) OUP.

Razia Akter Banu, U. A., ed. Islam in Contemporary Bangladesh. LC 91-19061. (International Studies in Sociology & Social Anthropology: No. 58). xviii, 194p. 1992. pap. 56.50 (*90-04-09497-0*) Brill Academic Pubs.

Razik, Sail I. A History of the Imams & Seyyids of Oman. 592p. 1986. 350.00 (*1-85077-129-4*, Pub. by Darf Pubs Ltd) St Mut.

Razik, Taher A., ed. Bibliography of Programmed Instruction & Computer-Assisted Instruction. LC 76-125875. (Educational Technology Bibliography Ser.: Vol.1). 288p. 1971. 39.95 (*0-87778-013-7*) Educ Tech Pubns.

***Razik, Taher A. & Swanson, Austin D.** Fundamental Concepts of Educational Leadership. 2nd ed. LC 00-36120. 2001. write for info. (*0-13-014491-6*, Merrill Coll) P-H.

Razik, Taher A. & Swanson, Austin D. Fundamental Concepts of Educational Leadership & Management. (Illus.). 740p. 1995. 64.80 (*0-02-398732-4*, Macmillan Coll) P-H.

Razin, Aharon, et al, eds. DNA Methylation. (Molecular Biology Ser.). (Illus.). xiii, 392p. 1984. 175.00 (*0-387-96038-4*) Spr-Verlag.

Razin, Andrew M., et al. Helping Cardiac Patients: Biobehavioral & Psychotherapeutic Approaches. LC 84-47995. (Joint Publication in the Jossey-Bass Social & Behavioral Science Series & the Jossey-Bass Health Ser.). 230p. reprint ed. pap. 71.30 (*0-7837-2533-7*, 204269200006) Bks Demand.

Razin, Assaf & Sadka, Efraim. The Economy of Modern Israel: Malaise & Promise. LC 93-3054. (Illus.). 272p. (C). 1993. 34.95 (*0-226-70589-7*) U Ch Pr.

— Population Economics. LC 94-27773. 285p. 1995. 34.50 (*0-262-18160-6*) MIT Pr.

Razin, Assaf & Sadka, Efraim, eds. The Economics of Globalization: Policy Perspectives from Public Economics. LC 97-52781. (Illus.). 424p. (C). 1999. text 69.95 (*0-521-62268-9*) Cambridge U Pr.

Razin, Assaf & Slemrod, Joel, eds. Taxation in the Global Economy. LC 90-30262. (National Bureau of Economic Research Project Report Ser.). (Illus.). ix, 454p. 1991. pap. text 23.00 (*0-226-70592-7*) U Ch Pr.

— Taxation in the Global Economy. LC 90-30262. (National Bureau of Economic Research Project Report Ser.). (Illus.). x, 444p. 1992. lib. bdg. 58.00 (*0-226-70591-9*) U Ch Pr.

— Taxation in the Global Economy. LC 90-30262. (National Bureau of Economic Research Ser.). (Illus.). 453p. reprint ed. pap. 140.50 (*0-7837-4095-6*, 205791600011) Bks Demand.

Razin, Assaf, et al. Trade & Tax Policy, Inflation & Exchange Rates: A Modern View. LC 97-25728. (Studies in International Economics & Institutions). vi, 296p. 1997. write for info. (*3-540-63120-8*) Spr-Verlag.

Razin, Assaf, jt. auth. see Frenkel, Jacob A.

Razin, Assaf, jt. auth. see Milesi-Ferretti, Gian M.

Razin, Assaf, jt. ed. see Helpman, Elhanan.

Razin, Assaf, jt. ed. see Leiderman, Leonardo.

Razin, Ehud & Rivera, Juan. Signal Transduction in Mast Cells & Basophils. LC 98-30561. 1999. write for info. (*0-387-98625-1*) Spr-Verlag.

Razin, Sergey V. The Nuclear Matrix & Spatial Organization of Chromosomal DNA Domains. LC 96-29884. (Molecular Biology Intelligence Unit Ser.). 198p. 1997. 99.00 (*1-57059-425-2*) Landes Bioscience.

Razin, Shimuel & Tully, Joseph G., eds. Molecular & Diagnostic Procedures in Mycoplasmology Vol. 1: Molecular Characterization. (Illus.). 483p. 1995. text 89.95 (*0-12-583805-0*) Acad Pr.

— Molecular & Diagnostic Procedures in Mycoplasmology Vol. 2: Diagnostic Procedures. LC 95-4586. (Illus.). 466p. 1996. text 89.95 (*0-12-583806-9*) Acad Pr.

Razionale, Janet K. & Kircher, Lisa C. Letters to Parents in Math Grades. (Illus.). 128p. 1997. 11.95 (*0-673-36370-8*, 757192Q, GoodYrBooks) Addson-Wesley Educ.

Razis, Dennis D. Human Predicament. LC 96-3036. 297p. 1996. 32.95 (*1-57392-085-1*) Prometheus Bks.

Razkova, S. & Remesh, T. Early Soviet Photographs. (C). 1990. pap. 100.00 (*0-7855-4424-0*, Pub. by Collets) St Mut.

Razlogov, Kyrill E., jt. ed. see Boutenko, Irene A.

Razmus, Thomas F. & Williamson, Gail F. Current Oral & Maxillofacial Imaging. 1996. text 37.00 (*0-7216-4005-2*, W B Saunders Co) Harcrt Hlth Sci Grp.

Razmyslov, Iurii P. Identities of Algebras & Their Representations. LC 94-20766. (Translations of Mathematical Monographs: Vol. 138).Tr. of Tozhdestva Algebr i ikh Predstavlenii. 318p. 1994. text 120.00 (*0-8218-4608-6*, MMONO/138) Am Math.

Raznick, Barbara, jt. ed. see Schwartz, Howard.

Raznjevic, Kuzman. Handbook of Thermodynamic Tables. 2nd rev. ed. 243p. 1996. 77.50 (*1-56700-046-0*) Begell Hse.

— Physical Quantities & the Units of the International System (SI) 252p. 1996. 65.00 (*1-56700-047-9*) Begell Hse.

Razo, Antonio. Antologia De La Superacion Ii. (SPA.). 1997. pap. text 20.98 (*968-13-3045-5*) Edit Diana.

Razquin, M. C., jt. auth. see Baert, A. E.

Razso, Imre. English-Hungarian Technical Dictionary: Angol Magyar Muszaki Szotar. (ENG & HUN.). 49.50 (*0-87557-041-0*) Saphrograph.

Razumikhin, B. S. Classical Principles & Optimization Problems. (C). 1987. text 300.50 (*90-277-2605-1*) Kluwer Academic.

— Physical Models & Equilibrium Methods in Programming & Economics. (Mathematics & Its Applications, Soviet Ser.). 372p. 1984. text 200.00 (*90-277-1644-7*) Kluwer Academic.

Razumov, Alexander V. & Saveliev, Mikhail V. Lie Algebras, Geometry, & Toda Type Systems. LC 96-46118. (Cambridge Lecture Notes in Physics Ser.: No. 7). (Illus.). 266p. (C). 1997. pap. text 34.95 (*0-521-47923-1*) Cambridge U Pr.

Razumovsky, Maria. Marina Tsvetayeva: A Critical Biography. Gibson, Aleksey, tr. LC 88-70234. (Illus.). 400p. 1995. reprint ed. 65.00 (*1-85224-045-8*, Pub. by Bloodaxe Bks) Dufour.

Razvalyaev, A. V. Continental Rift Formation & Its Prehistory. Chakraverty, R., ed. (Russian Translation Ser.: No. 87). (Illus.). 208p. (C). 1991. text 110.00 (*90-6191-991-6*, Pub. by A A Balkema) Ashgate Pub Co.

Razwy, Sayed A. Salman El-Farsi. 1985. pap. 5.95 (*0-933543-02-6*) Aza Khana.

— Salman El-Farsi. rev. ed. LC 83-50152. 1990. pap. text 5.95 (*0-940368-29-3*; 67) Tahrike Tarsile Quran.

— Salman El-Farsi: Friend of Prophet Muhammad. 124p. 1996. pap. 8.50 (*0-614-21716-4*, 1103) Kazi Pubns.

Razwy, Sayed A., ed. Khadija-Tul-Kubra: The Wife of Prophet Muhammed. LC 89-50010. 120p. 1989. pap. 5.95 (*0-940368-93-5*, 15) Tahrike Tarsile Quran.

Razzaq, Roshi. Low Fat Indian Cookbook. 128p. 1993. 12.98 (*1-55521-898-9*) Bk Sales Inc.

Razzell, Mary. The Secret Code of DNA. (Illus.). 36p. (J). (ps-8). 1986. 7.95 (*0-920806-83-X*, Pub. by Penumbra Pr) U of Toronto Pr.

Razzell, Peter. Victorian Working Class: Selections from the "Morning Chronicle" Wainwright, R. W., ed. (Illus.). 380p. 1973. 37.50 (*0-7146-2957-X*, Pub. by F Cass Pubs) Intl Spec Bk.

Razzi, Jim. Terror in the Mirror. LC 89-5230. (Horror Show Ser.). 96p. (YA). (gr. 7 up). 1990. lib. bdg. 10.50 (*0-8167-1684-6*) Troll Communs.

— Terror in the Mirror. LC 89-5230. (Horror Show Ser.). 96p. (YA). (gr. 7 up). 1996. pap. 2.95 (*0-8167-1685-4*) Troll Communs.

Razzi, Jim, adapted by. Disney's Mickey's Christmas Carol. LC 92-58971. (Junior Novelization Ser.). (Illus.). (J). (gr. 1-4). 1992. pap. 2.75 (*1-56282-239-X*, Pub. by Disney Pr) Time Warner.

Razzolini, Laura, jt. auth. see Shughart, William F.

Rbade Roque, Raquel. Cocina Cubana: Las Mejores Recetas. 205p. 1996. pap. 14.95 (*0-941010-05-8*) Downtown Bk.

Rbe, Elaine F. 101 Secrets to Negotiating Success. LC 98-73721. ix, 203p. 1998. write for info. (*0-9666933-0-2*) Canyon Crest Pubg.

Rbeno, Fred, jt. auth. see Hudson, Robert.

R.B.I. Staff. Exchange Control Facilities for Investment by Non-Resident Indians. (C). 1988. 35.00 (*0-7855-4773-8*) St Mut.

RB43 Staff, et al. Atlas of Microscopic Artifacts & Foreign Materials. LC 96-50067. 1997. write for info. (*4-260-14331-X*) Igaku-Shoin.

RC Pubns. Staff. Print's Best, No. 2: Typography. (Illus.). 192p. 1996. 34.95 (*1-883915-00-7*) RC Pubns.

— Print's Best, No. 4: Letterhead & Business Cards. (Illus.). 192p. 1996. 34.95 (*1-883915-01-5*) RC Pubns.

— Print's Best, No. 4: Logos & Symbols. 4th ed. (Illus.). 192p. 1996. 34.95 (*1-883915-02-3*) RC Pubns.

RCA Service Co. Staff. Electrical Circuits in Gas Appliances. 61p. 1964. pap. 1.50 (*0-318-12605-2*, X55564) Am Gas Assn.

RCA Staff. RCA Electro-Optics Handbook. (Illus.). 1974. 4.95 (*0-913970-11-5*, EOH-11) RCA Solid State.

RCA Symposium Staff. Future Agricultural Technology & Resource Conservation: Proceedings of the RCA Symposium, Future Agricultural Technology & Resource Conservation, Held December 5-9, 1982, in Washington, D.C. LC 84-4502. (Illus.). 618p. 1984. reprint ed. pap. 191.60 (*0-608-00079-5*, 206084200006) Bks Demand.

RCAF Staff. Royal Canadian Air Force Exercise Plans for Physical Fitness. 1990. mass mkt. 5.50 (*0-671-72755-9*) PB.

RCC Pilotage Foundation Staff. Atlantic Crossing Guide. Hammick, Anne, ed. 1996. pap. 125.00 (*0-7136-3599-1*, Pub. by Laurie Norie & Wilson Ltd) St Mut.

— Atlantic Spain & Portugal. 196p. 1996. 150.00 (*0-85288-298-X*, Pub. by Laurie Norie & Wilson Ltd) St Mut.

— Islas Baleares: Ibiza, Formentera, Mallorca & Menorca. Hammick, Anne, ed. 260p. 1997. 125.00 (*0-85288-389-7*, Pub. by Laurie Norie & Wilson Ltd) St Mut.

— The Pacific Crossing Guide. Pocock, Michael, ed. (Illus.). 224p. 1997. 59.50 (*1-57409-036-4*) Sheridan.

RCC Pilotage Foundation Staff, jt. auth. see Jones, Steven.

Rcheulishvili, G. L., ed. Problems in High Energy Physics & Field Theory: Proceedings of the 16th Workshop on Problems on High Energy Physics & Field Theory, 1993, Protvino. 247p. (Orig.). (C). 1995. pap. 30.00 (*1-57485-005-9*) Hadronic Pr Inc.

Rcheulishvili, G. L., jt. ed. see Samokhin, A. P.

Rchowdari, B. V., et al. Solid State Ionic Materials: Proceedings of the 4th Asian Conference on Solid State Ionics. 472p. 1994. text 109.00 (*981-02-1861-3*) World Scientific Pub.

RCI (Olson) Staff. Study Skills: The Parent Connection. 64p. 1996. student ed. 95.00 incl. VHS (*0-7872-2919-9*) Kendall-Hunt.

— Study Skills: The Parent Connection. 3rd rev. ed. (Illus.). 49p. 1995. pap., student ed. 7.50 (*0-7872-2917-2*) Kendall-Hunt.

Rdenour. Como Ser Cristiano Sin Ser Religioso.Tr. of How to Be Christian Without Being Religious. (SPA.). 144p. write for info. (*0-614-27012-X*) Editorial Unilit.

RDI Staff. Decision Making. 1995. 23.50 (*0-256-21297-X*) McGraw.

***Re, A.** Robert Micro Dictionary de la Language. (FRE.). 1999. 22.95 (*2-85036-529-7*) Robert.

Re, Charmaine A. In a Japanese Garden. (Illus.). 48p. 1999. 11.00 (*1-57178-086-6*) Coun Oak Bks.

Re Cruz, Alicia. The Two Milpas of Chan Kom: Scenarios of a Maya Village Life. LC 95-15375. (SUNY Series in the Anthropology of Work). 203p. (C). 1996. text 74.50 (*0-7914-2829-X*); pap. text 24.95 (*0-7914-2830-3*) State U NY Pr.

Re, E. Del, see Del Re, E., ed.

Re, Edward D. Remedies, Cases & Materials On. 4th ed. (University Casebook Ser.). 225p. 1996. pap. text, teacher ed. write for info. (*1-56662-443-6*) Foundation Pr.

Re, Edward D. & Krauss, Stanton D. Remedies, Cases & Materials On. 3rd ed. (University Casebook Ser.). 1296p. (C). 1991. text 44.95 (*0-88277-945-1*) Foundation Pr.

— Remedies, Teacher's Manual to Accompany Cases & Materials On. 3rd ed. (University Casebook Ser.). 126p. 1992. pap. text. write for info. (*0-88277-988-5*) Foundation Pr.

Re, Edward D. & Re, Joseph R. Brief Writing & Oral Argument. 8th ed. LC 99-28469. 312p. 1999. text 55.00 (*0-379-20428-2*) Oceana.

— Brief Writing & Oral Argument. 8th ed. LC 99-28469. 312p. 1999. pap. text 35.00 (*0-379-20427-4*) Oceana.

— Remedies, Cases & Materials On. 4th ed. (University Casebook Ser.). 1336p. (C). 1995. text 49.95 (*1-56662-308-1*) Foundation Pr.

Re, Frank M. Re Views. 80p. 1975. pap. 2.95 (*0-686-14654-9*) F M Re.

Re, Gianmarco Del, see Del Re, Gianmarco.

Re, Joseph M. Earn & Learn: The Complete Guide to Cooperative Education. 1997. pap. text 5.00 (*1-57509-023-6*) Octameron Assocs.

***Re, Joseph M.** Financial Aid Financer: Expert Answers to College Financing Questions. 11th ed. 1999. pap. text 5.00 (*1-57509-051-1*) Octameron Assocs.

Re, Joseph R., jt. auth. see Re, Edward D.

Re, Judith & Schneider, Meg F. Social Savvy. (Illus.). 208p. 1992. per. 12.00 (*0-671-74198-5*) S&S Trade Pap.

Re, Lucia. Calvino & the Age of Neorealism: Fables of Estrangement. LC 89-49547. 432p. 1990. 45.00 (*0-8047-1650-1*) Stanford U Pr.

Re, Patricia Del, see Del Re, Gerard.

Re, Patricia Del, see Del Re, Gerard & Del Re, Patricia.

Re, Patricia Del, see Del Re, Gerard.

Re, Patricia Del, see Del Re, Gerard & Del Re, Patricia.

Re, Paul. The Dance of the Pencil: Serene Art by Paul Re. limited ed. LC 92-91089. (Illus.). 128p. 1993. 88.00 (*0-9634902-0-6*) Paul Re.

Re, Richard N. Bioburst: The Impact of Modern Biology on the Affairs of Man. LC 86-7422. (Illus.). xvi, 254p. 1986. text 35.00 (*0-8071-1289-5*) La State U Pr.

Re Ville, Jack B. & Stephenson, Joe. Safety Training Methods: Practical Solutions for the Next Millenniu, Second Edition. 2nd ed. LC 94-18137. 336p. 1995. 99.00 (*0-471-55230-5*) Wiley.

Rea, Alayna, jt. auth. see Rea, John D.

Rea, Alexander. Monumental Remains of the Dutch East India Company in the Presidency of Madras LC 98-905013. 79 p. 1998. write for info. (*81-206-1316-3*) Asian Educ Servs.

— South Indian Buddhist Antiquities: Including the Stups of Bhattiprolu, Gudivada, & Ghanta Sala & Other Ancient Sites in the Krishna District Madras Presidency; with Notes on Dome Construction; Andhra Numismatics & Marble Sculpture. (C). 1989. reprint ed. 18.00 (*81-206-0512-8*, Pub. by Asian Educ Servs) S Asia.

An Asterisk (*) at the beginning of an entry indicates that the title is appearing for the first time.

Rea, Amadeo M. At the Desert's Green Edge: An Ethnobotany of the Gila River Pima. LC 97-4577. 480p. 1997. text 60.00 (*0-8165-1540-9*) U of Ariz Pr.
— Folk Mammalogy of the Northern Pimans. LC 97-33809. (Illus.). 285p. 1997. 45.00 (*0-8165-1663-4*) U of Ariz Pr.
— Once a River: Bird Life & Habitat Changes on the Middle Gila. LC 82-23815. (Illus.). 285p. 1983. 41.00 (*0-8165-0799-6*) U of Ariz Pr.
Rea, Amadeo M., ed. see Unitt, Philip.
Rea, Ba & Rea, C. J. There Have Always Been Puffins. LC 97-93621. (Illus.). 24p. (Orig.). (J). (gr. 4 up). 1997. pap. 7.95 (*0-9657472-0-4*) Bas Relief.
— A Whale's Tale from the Supper Sea. LC 98-93836. (Illus.). 32p. (J). (gr. k-6). 1999. pap. 10.95 (*0-9657472-1-2*) Bas Relief.
Rea, C. British Basidomysetaceae: A Handbook to the Larger British Fungi. 1968. pap. 120.00 (*3-7682-0561-4*) Lubrecht & Cramer.
Rea, C. J., jt. auth. see Rea, Ba.
Rea, David, jt. ed. see Duncan, Robert.
Rea, Dean. Write Stuff Adventure: Exploring the Art of Writing. 208p. (YA). (gr. 7-10). 1999. pap. 19.99 (*1-883934-04-4*) Grt Expect Bk.
Rea-Dickins, Pauline & Germaine, Kevin. Evaluation. Widdowson, H. G. & Candlin, C. N., eds. (Illus.). 188p. 1992. pap. text 14.95 (*0-19-437138-7*) OUP.
Rea-Dickins, Pauline & Germaine, Kevin P. Managing Evaluation & Innovation in Language Teaching: Building Bridges. LC 98-24975. (Applied Linguistics & Language Study Ser.). 1999. pap. text 35.63 (*0-582-30373-7*) Longman.
Rea, Elizabeth Richbourg. Michael Steiner: Bronze Sculpture. LC 90-60996. 113p. 1990. pap. 40.00 (*1-58821-068-5*) Salander OReilly.
Rea, F. G. A School in South Uist: Reminiscences of a Hebridean Schoolmaster, 1890-1913. Campbell, John L., ed. & intro. by. (Illus.). 240p. 1998. pap. 13.95 (*1-874744-87-4*, Pub. by Birlinn Ltd) Dufour.
Rea, G. Thomas, ed. 6th International Symposium on Vulcanospeleology. (Illus.). 286p. 1991. pap. 11.00 (*1-879961-02-4*, 07-0006) Natl Speleological.
Rea, G. Thomas, ed. see Wefer, Fred L.
Rea, Gavin A., jt. auth. see Jones, Keith E.
Rea, J. E. T.A. Crerar: A Political Life. LC 99-219649. (Illus.). 328p. 1997. text 39.95 (*0-7735-1629-8*, Pub. by McG-Queens Univ Pr) CUP Services.
Rea, Jana. A Spiritual Formation Journal: A Renovare Resource for Spiritual Formation. LC 96-189421. 224p. 1996. pap. 14.00 (*0-06-066757-5*, Pub. by Harper SF) HarpC.
Rea, Jesus Guerrero, see Rohmer, Harriet & Guerrero Rea, Jesus.
Rea, John. Charisma's Bible Handbook on the Holy Spirit. LC 98-28753. 368p. 1998. 24.99 (*0-88419-566-X*) Creation House.
— The Holy Spirit in the Bible. LC 89-80826. 394p. (Orig.). 1989. pap. 19.99 (*0-88419-261-X*) Creation House.
Rea, John D. Patterns of the Whole Vol. 1: Healing & Quartz Crystals (A Journey with our Souls) (Illus.). 376p. (Orig.). 1986. pap. 12.95 (*0-938183-01-X*) Two Trees Pub.
Rea, John D. & Rea, Alayna. The Twelve Days of Christmas: The Twelve Stages of a Soul (The Creation of a Universe) 40p. (Orig.). 1987. pap. 4.95 (*0-938183-04-4*) Two Trees Pub.
Rea, Kathryn, jt. auth. see Lientz, Bennet P.
Rea, Kathryn, jt. ed. see Lientz, Bennet P.
Rea, Kathryn P., jt. auth. see Lientz, Bennet P.
Rea, Kenneth J. The Prosperous Years: The Economic History of Ontario, 1939-1975. (Ontario Historical Studies). 304p. 1985. pap. 14.95 (*0-8020-6592-9*) U of Toronto Pr.
— The Prosperous Years: The Economic History of Ontario, 1939-1975. LC 86-182022. (Ontario Historical Studies). 301p. reprint ed. pap. 93.40 (*0-8357-3771-3*, 203650000003) Bks Demand.
Rea, Lena. A Commentary on the Book of Revelation. 250p. (Orig.). 1996. pap. 14.95 (*1-56794-088-9*, C-2389) Star Bible.
Rea, Leonard O. The Financial History of Baltimore, 1900-1926. LC 78-64132. (Johns Hopkins University. Studies in the Social Sciences. Thirtieth Ser. 1912: 3). 128p. 1983. reprint ed. 39.50 (*0-404-61245-8*) AMS Pr.
Rea, Louis M. & Parker, Richard A. Designing & Conducting Survey Research: A Comprehensive Guide. 2nd ed. LC 97-7969. 254p. 1997. 30.95 (*0-7879-0810-X*) Jossey-Bass.
***Rea, Mark S., ed.** IESNA Lighting Handbook: Reference & Application HB-9-00. 9th rev. ed. LC 99-76610. (Illus.). 1004p. 1999. 425.00 (*0-87995-150-8*, HB-99) Illum Eng.
Rea, Mark S., ed. Selected Papers on Architectural Lighting. LC 92-19412. (Milestone Ser.: Vol. 58). 1992. pap. 45.00 (*0-8194-0992-8*) SPIE.
— Selected Papers on Architectural Lighting. LC 92-19412. (Milestone Ser.: Vol. MS 58/HC). 1992. 55.00 (*0-8194-0991-X*) SPIE.
Rea, Michael, ed. American Story: The Rea Award for the Short Story. 328p. 1996. pap. 17.00 (*0-88001-435-0*) HarpC.
— Material Constitution: A Reader. LC 96-37532. 408p. 1997. 73.00 (*0-8476-8383-4*); pap. 24.95 (*0-8476-8384-2*) Rowman.
Rea, Nicky. Defilers & Preservers of Wizards. 1996. 15.95 (*0-7869-0383-X*, Pub. by TSR Inc) Random.
— A Guide to Transylvania. 1996. 12.95 (*0-7869-0424-0*, Pub. by TSR Inc) Random.
Rea, Nicky & Cassada, Jackie. Renegades. (Wruith Ser.). (Illus.). 1998. pap. 16.00 (*1-56504-636-6*, 6065) White Wolf.
Rea, Nicky, et al. Transylvania by Night. (Vampire Ser.). (Illus.). (Orig.). 1997. pap. 18.00 (*1-56504-287-5*, 2808) White Wolf.
Rea, Nicky, jt. auth. see Campbell, Brian.
Rea, Nicky, jt. auth. see Cassada, Jackie.
Rea, Nicky, jt. auth. see White Wolf Publishing Staff, Wolf.
Rea, Paul W. Canyon Interludes: Between White Water & Red Rock. LC 96-18052. 294p. (Orig.). 1996. pap. 14.95 (*1-56085-054-X*) Signature Bks.
***Rea, Peter & Irving, David K.** Producing & Directing the Short Film & Video. 2nd ed. (Illus.). 384p. 2000. pap. 39.95 (*0-240-80394-9*, Focal) Buttrwrth-Heinemann.
Rea, Peter & Kerzner, Harold. Strategic Planning: A Practical Guide. LC 97-14573. (Industrial Engineering Ser.). 500p. 1997. text 39.95 (*0-442-02271-9*, VNR) Wiley.
Rea, Peter J. & Kerzner, Harold. Strategic Planning: A Practical Guide. 336p. 1997. 69.95 (*0-471-29197-8*, VNR) Wiley.
Rea, Peter W. & Irving, David K. Producing & Directing the Short Film & Video. (Illus.). 304p. 1995. pap. 39.95 (*0-240-80188-1*, Focal) Buttrwrth-Heinemann.
Rea, Phil. How to Become a Millionaire Selling Remodeling: I Did It--& So Can You! Howey, Paul M., ed. LC 97-46827. 178p. 1998. 24.95 (*1-877749-29-X*) Five Star AZ.
Rea, R. Sam. Attorney's Master Guide to Successful Solo Law Practice. LC 83-18652. 288p. 1983. text 49.50 (*0-87624-024-4*, Inst Busn Plan) P-H.
Rea, Richard C., ed. see American Institute of Certified Public Accountants.
Rea, Richard G. & Gray, John W. Parliamentary Procedure: A Programmed Introduction. 2nd ed. 124p. 1993. per. 15.95 (*0-8403-8882-9*) Kendall-Hunt.
Rea, Rober R., jt. ed. see Coker, William S.
Rea, Robert R. Major Robert Farmar of Mobile. LC 90-32562. 200p. 1990. 34.95 (*0-8173-0505-X*) U of Ala Pr.
Rea, Robert R., jt. auth. see Ware, John D.
Rea, Robert R., jt. ed. see Newton, Wesley P.
Rea, Robert R., jt. ed. see Servies, James A.
***Rea-Rossenberger, Sharon.** Workbook for Synonyms, Homonyms, & Antonyms. 248p. 1999. pap. 39.00 (*0-12-784458-9*) Acad Pr.
Rea, Samuel A., jt. auth. see Pesando, James E.
Rea, Sara W. The Koreshan Story. Bigelow, Jo, ed. (Illus.). 72p. (Orig.). 1994. pap. 10.00 (*0-9632676-0-4*) Koreshan Unity.
REA Staff. AP Calculus AB with Software. LC 98-65432. (TESTware Ser.). 1999. pap. 29.95 incl. disk (*0-87891-113-8*) Res & Educ.
— AP Chemistry with Software. (TESTware Ser.). Date not set. pap. 29.95 incl. disk (*0-87891-116-2*) Res & Educ.
— AP Government & Politics with Software. (TESTware Ser.). Date not set. pap. 29.95 incl. disk (*0-87891-119-7*) Res & Educ.
— Careers for the Year 2000 & Beyond. 656p. 1997. pap. 21.95 (*0-87891-477-3*) Res & Educ.
— Essentials of Math Made Nice-n-Easy IV. 150p. 1999. pap. 6.95 (*0-87891-203-7*) Res & Educ.
— Essentials of Math Made Nice-n-Easy I. 150p. 1999. pap. 6.95 (*0-87891-200-2*) Res & Educ.
— Essentials of Math Made Nice-n-Easy III. 150p. 1999. pap. 6.95 (*0-87891-202-9*) Res & Educ.
— Essentials of Math Made Nice-n-Easy II. 150p. 1999. pap. 6.95 (*0-87891-201-0*) Res & Educ.
— How to Cope with Being Downsized. 275p. Date not set. pap. 29.95 (*0-87891-092-1*) Res & Educ.
— Postal Examination - Test Battery 460/470, 2 cass. LC 98-65408. 320p. 1998. pap. 25.95 incl. audio (*0-87891-080-8*) Res & Educ.
— PRAXIS II: NTE with Computer Adaptive Software (CAT) (TESTware Ser.). Date not set. pap. 34.95 incl. disk (*0-87891-134-0*) Res & Educ.
— REA's Authoritative Guide to the Top College Majors. 400p. Date not set. pap. 17.95 (*0-87891-081-6*) Res & Educ.
— REA's Authoritative Guide to the Top Graduate Programs. LC 97-69316. 750p. 1998. pap. 25.95 (*0-87891-079-4*) Res & Educ.
***REA Staff.** REA's Practical Help for Pre-Algebra. LC 97-68647. 226p. 1998. pap. 13.95 (*0-87891-761-6*) Res & Educ.
REA Staff. SAT TestBuster. 250p. 2000. pap. 17.95 (*0-87891-145-6*) Res & Educ.
— STS HSPT - Scholastic Testing Service High School Placement Test. 672p. Date not set. pap. 19.95 (*0-87891-095-6*) Res & Educ.
— Verbal Builder for Admission & Standardized Tests: Test Prep Book. LC 97-75376. (TESTware Ser.). 320p. 2000. pap. 18.95 incl. cd-rom (*0-87891-172-3*) Res & Educ.
***Rea, Stephen.** Stewart Parker Plays: Includes Northern Star, Heavenly Bodies & Pentecost. (Contemporary Dramatists Ser.). 2000. pap. 14.95 (*0-413-74350-0*, Methuen Drama) Methn.
REA Testware Staff. GRE General Test CAT. LC 97-75934. 1998. pap. text 34.95 incl. cd-rom (*0-87891-107-3*) Res & Educ.
Rea, Tom, ed. Caving Basics. LC 82-61922. 128p. 1987. pap. 11.00 (*0-9615093-1-7*, 06-0004) Natl Speleological.
Rea, Val & Martin, Mike. Rural Blacksmith, Rural Businessman: Making & Selling Metal Goods in Malawi. (Orig.). 1991. pap. 42.95 (*1-85339-094-1*, Pub. by Intermed Tech) Stylus Pub VA.
— Stove Maker, Stove User: Fuel-Efficient Stoves in Sri Lanka. (Orig.). 1991. pap. 42.95 (*1-85339-099-2*, Pub. by Intermed Tech) Stylus Pub VA.
Rea, Val, jt. auth. see Martin, Mike.
Rea, Walter T. The White Lie. LC 81-83353. (Illus.). 409p. (Orig.). 1982. 16.95 (*0-9607424-0-9*); pap. 13.95 (*0-9607424-1-7*) M & R Pubns.
Rea, William. African Art. LC 97-143883. (International Encyclopedia of Art Ser.). 64p. 1996. 19.95 (*0-8160-3330-7*) Facts on File.
Rea, William J. Chemical Sensitivity, 4 vols. 1995. write for info. (*1-56670-201-1*) Lewis Pubs.
— Chemical Sensitivity: Tools for Diagnosis & Methods of Treatment, Vol. 4. 928p. 1996. lib. bdg. 99.95 (*0-87371-965-4*, L965) Lewis Pubs.
— Chemical Sensitivity Vol. 1: Principles & Mechanisms. 242p. 1992. lib. bdg. 99.95 (*0-87371-541-1*, L541) Lewis Pubs.
— Chemical Sensitivity Vol. 2: Sources of Total Body Load. 592p. 1994. lib. bdg. 95.00 (*0-87371-963-8*, L963) Lewis Pubs.
— Chemical Sensitivity Vol. 3: Clinical Manifestations of Pollutant Overload. 928p. 1995. lib. bdg. 99.95 (*0-87371-964-6*, L964) Lewis Pubs.
Reaburn, Peter & Jenkins, David. Training for Speed & Endurance. (Illus.). 192p. (Orig.). 1997. pap. 13.95 (*1-86448-120-X*, Pub. by Allen & Unwin Pty) IPG Chicago.
Reaburn, Peter, jt. auth. see Jenkins, David.
Reach, Jim & Schwartz, Bernard. Softball Everyone. 2nd ed. 180p. 1992. pap. text 15.95 (*0-88725-162-5*) Hunter Textbks.
Reach, Russell, ed. Big Road Interstate Exit Guide, 1992: United States Eastern Edition. (Illus.). 300p. (Orig.). 1992. pap. 9.95 (*1-880477-00-9*) Inter Am Pub.
Reachem, Richard G., jt. auth. see Cairncross, Sandy.
Read. Bears Had Chairs. (C). Date not set. pap. write for info. (*0-395-65999-X*); pap. write for info. (*0-395-65998-1*) HM.
Read. Early Days. 1996. pap. 12.95 (*0-14-023895-6*, Pub. by Pnguin Bks Ltd) Trafalgar.
Read. Howards of Caxley. (J). 17.95 (*0-8488-1454-1*) Amereon Ltd.
— Journal of Accounting & Computers. (C). 1993. mass mkt. 9.25 (*0-538-83655-5*) S-W Pub.
— The Lies They Tell. (Sky Bks.). Date not set. pap. text. write for info. (*0-582-08109-2*, Pub. by Addison-Wesley) Longman.
— Miss Read's Christmas. Date not set. lib. bdg. 21.95 (*0-8488-1701-X*) Amereon Ltd.
— My Big Dictionary. 1995. pap. 27.28 (*0-395-76202-2*) HM.
— Over the Gate. Date not set. lib. bdg. 21.95 (*0-8488-1695-1*) Amereon Ltd.
— Psychiatry in Learning Disability. 1997. pap. text 69.00 (*0-7020-2119-9*) Bailliere Tindall.
— Storm in the Village. Date not set. lib. bdg. 22.95 (*0-8488-1691-9*) Amereon Ltd.
— Student Evaluation Portfolio, Level 7. 1991. pap. write for info. (*0-395-55924-3*) HM.
— Student Evaluation Portfolio, Level 8. 1991. pap. write for info. (*0-395-55925-1*) HM.
— Student Evaluation Portfolio, Level ABC. 1991. pap. write for info. (*0-395-55914-6*) HM.
— Student Evaluation Portfolio: Level 1, Level 1. 1991. pap. write for info. (*0-395-55915-4*) HM.
— Student Evaluation Portfolio: Level 1, Level 1. 1993. pap. write for info. (*0-395-64854-8*) HM.
— Student Evaluation Portfolio: Level 1+, Level 1+ 1991. pap. write for info. (*0-395-55916-2*) HM.
— Student Evaluation Portfolio: Level 1+, Level 1+ 1993. pap. write for info. (*0-395-64855-6*) HM.
— Student Evaluation Portfolio: Level 2, Level 2. 1991. pap. write for info. (*0-395-55917-0*) HM.
— Student Evaluation Portfolio: Level 2, Level 2. 1993. pap. write for info. (*0-395-64856-4*) HM.
— Student Evaluation Portfolio: Level 2+, Level 2+ 1991. pap. write for info. (*0-395-55918-9*) HM.
— Student Evaluation Portfolio: Level 2+, Level 2+ 1993. pap. write for info. (*0-395-64857-2*) HM.
— Student Evaluation Portfolio: Level 3, Level 3. 1991. pap. write for info. (*0-395-55919-7*) HM.
— Student Evaluation Portfolio: Level 3, Level 3. 1993. pap. write for info. (*0-395-64858-0*) HM.
— Student Evaluation Portfolio: Level 3+, Level 3+ 1991. pap. write for info. (*0-395-55920-0*) HM.
— Student Evaluation Portfolio: Level 3+, Level 3+ 1993. pap. write for info. (*0-395-64859-9*) HM.
— Student Evaluation Portfolio: Level 4, Level 4. 1991. pap. write for info. (*0-395-55921-9*) HM.
— Student Evaluation Portfolio: Level 4, Level 4. 1993. pap. write for info. (*0-395-64860-2*) HM.
— Student Evaluation Portfolio: Level 5, Level 5. 1991. pap. write for info. (*0-395-55922-7*) HM.
— Student Evaluation Portfolio: Level 5, Level 5. 1993. pap. write for info. (*0-395-64861-0*) HM.
— Student Evaluation Portfolio: Level 6, Level 6. 1991. pap. write for info. (*0-395-55923-5*) HM.
— Student Evaluation Portfolio: Level 6, Level 6. 1993. pap. write for info. (*0-395-64862-9*) HM.
— Teacher's Book Walk Through. 1990. pap. write for info. (*0-395-56840-4*) HM.
— Tyler's Row. Date not set. lib. bdg. 21.95 (*0-8488-1702-8*) Amereon Ltd.
— Village Diary. Date not set. lib. bdg. 22.95 (*0-8488-1690-0*) Amereon Ltd.
— Village School. Date not set. lib. bdg. 21.95 (*0-8488-1689-7*) Amereon Ltd.
Read & Houston. Health Education: Cog Behavior. (Health Science Ser.). 112p. 1996. pap., teacher ed. 10.00 (*0-7637-0351-6*) Jones & Bartlett.
Read & Matthews. Tandem Plus. 1992. pap. text. write for info. (*0-17-555880-9*) Addison-Wesley.
***Read, Martha M.** Tiggy & the Fairacre Festival. large type ed. LC 99-55515. (General Ser.). 2000. pap. 24.95 (*0-7862-2314-6*) Thorndike Pr.
Read, Martha M., tr. see De Tourtoulon, Pierre.
***Read, Alan.** Architecturally Speaking: Practices of Art, Architecture & the Everyday. LC 00-32186. 2000. pap. write for info. (*0-415-23544-8*) Routledge.
Read, Alan. Theatre & Everyday Life. 304p. (C). 1995. pap. 27.99 (*0-415-06941-6*, A7978) Routledge.
— Theatre & Everyday Life: A Theoretical Introduction. LC 92-11913. (Illus.). 244p. (C). (gr. 13). 1993. text 59.95 (*0-415-06940-8*, A7974) Routledge.
Read, Alexander. A Treatise of the First Part of Chirurgerie. LC 76-57411. (English Experience Ser.: No. 826). 1977. reprint ed. lib. bdg. 24.00 (*90-221-0826-0*) Walter J Johnson.
Read, Alice. Read: The Reads & Their Relatives, Being an Account of Col. Clemens & Madam Read of Bushy Forest, Lunenburg County, Virginia, Their Eight Children, Their Descendants, & Allied Families. (Illus.). 688p. 1993. reprint ed. pap. 99.50 (*0-8328-3389-4*); reprint ed. lib. bdg. 109.50 (*0-8328-3388-6*) Higginson Bk Co.
Read, Allen W. Classic American Graffiti: Lexical Evidence from Folk Epigraphy in Western North America; a Glossarial Study of the Low Element in the English Vocabulary. LC 76-5697. (Maledicta Press Publications: Vol. 6). 96p. (C). 1977. reprint ed. pap. 7.50 (*0-916500-06-3*) Maledicta.
Read Alone Books Staff. Let's Be Friends. (Read Alone Bks.). (Illus.). (J). (ps). 1997. pap. 15.95 (*0-395-88090-4*) HM.
Read, Andrew. Porpoises. LC 98-51770. (WorldLife Library). (Illus.). 72p. (YA). (gr. 6 up). 1999. pap. 16.95 (*0-89658-420-8*) Voyageur Pr.
Read, Andrew P., jt. auth. see Strachan, Tom.
Read, Ann, jt. auth. see Garrison, Linda.
Read, Anne. Edgar Cayce on Jesus & His Church. 1988. mass mkt. 3.95 (*0-446-35106-7*, Pub. by Warner Bks) Little.
Read, Anthony & Fisher, David. The Fall of Berlin. 524p. 1993. 29.95 (*0-393-03472-0*) Da Capo.
— The Fall of Berlin. (Illus.). 535p. 1995. reprint ed. pap. 16.95 (*0-306-80619-3*) Da Capo.
— The Proudest Day: India's Long Road to Independence. LC 98-10707. (Illus.). 566p. 1998. 35.00 (*0-393-04594-3*) Norton.
— The Proudest Day: India's Long Road to Independence. (Illus.). 608p. 1999. pap. 17.50 (*0-393-31898-2*) Norton.
Read, Bendict, ed. Pre-Raphaelite Sculpture: Nature & Imagination in British Sculpture 1848-1914. (British Sculptors & Sculpture Ser.). (Illus.). 176p. (C). 1991. 70.00 (*0-85331-609-0*, Pub. by Lund Humphries) Antique Collect.
Read, Benedict. Victorian Sculpture. LC 83-70483. (Paul Mellon Centre for Studies in British Art). (Illus.). 416p. 1984. reprint ed. pap. 35.00 (*0-300-03177-7*) Yale U Pr.
Read, Benedict, ed. Herbert Read: A British Vision of World Art. (Illus.). 160p. (C). 1993. pap. 39.95 (*0-85331-643-0*, Pub. by Lund Humphries) Antique Collect.
Read, Benjamin. History of Swanzey, New Hampshire, from 1734 to 1890. (Illus.). 585p. 1988. reprint ed. lib. bdg. 59.50 (*0-8328-0057-0*, NH0025) Higginson Bk Co.
Read, Benjamin M. Illustrated History of New Mexico. Cortes, Carlos E., ed. LC 76-1562. (Chicano Heritage Ser.). (Illus.). 1977. reprint ed. 58.95 (*0-405-09521-X*) Ayer.
Read, Bernard E. Chinese Materia Medica: Dragon & Snake Drugs. 1979. lib. bdg. 300.00 (*0-8490-3063-3*) Krishna Pr.
Read, Bobbie. Single Adult Journey. 1992. pap. 4.99 (*0-87162-616-0*, D7001) Warner Pr.
— Single Parent Journey. 1992. pap. 4.99 (*0-87162-614-4*, D7000) Warner Pr.
Read, Brendan B., ed. Understanding Regulations on OSHA Design Safety Standards. (Understanding NE Code Rules on Ser.). (Illus.). 164p. 1991. pap. 12.76 (*0-87288-458-9*) Intertec Pub.
— Understanding Regulations on OSHA Electrical Work Rules. LC 98-170570. (Understanding NE Code Rules on Ser.). (Illus.). 139p. 1991. pap. 12.76 (*0-87288-459-7*) Intertec Pub.
Read, Bryan E. & Dean, G. D. The Determination of Dynamic Properties of Polymers & Composites. LC 79-302865. 217p. reprint ed. pap. 67.30 (*0-608-11443-X*, 202256400028) Bks Demand.

the material very strong..."--Literary Agent, ICM, Inc.. "It would take a while to share with you all that I have found to be in common with your story, though they are different, the similarities are undeniable. It's amazing how the Enemy's signature is the same."--A Youth Minister. For ordering information call Toll Free: 1-877-WWENEMY. ***Publisher Paid Annotation.***

R

Read, C. B., jt. ed. see Beaumont, E. C.

Read, C. B., jt. ed. see Johnson, R. B.

Read, C. B., jt. ed. see Northrop, S. A.

Read, Campbell, jt. auth. see Patel, Jagdish K.

Read, Campbell B., jt. auth. see Patel, Jagdish K.

Read, Campbell B., jt. ed. see Kotz, Samuel.

Read, Cathy. Preventing Breast Cancer: The Politics of an Epidemic. 264p. 1995. pap. text 13.00 (*0-04-440909-5*) NYU Pr.

Read, Cedric & Kaufman, Scott. Building Value: The CFO As Corporate Architect. LC 97-26644. 312p. 1997. 39.95 (*0-471-97599-0*) Wiley.

Read, Charles. Children's Creative Spelling. (International Library of Psychology). (Illus.). 192p. (C). 1986. 39.95 (*0-7100-9802-2*, 98022, Routledge Thoemms) Routledge.

Read, Charles, jt. auth. see Kent, Raymond D.

Read, Charles H. & Dalton, Ormonde M. Antiquities from the City of Benin & from Other Parts of West Africa in the British Museum. LC 71-143360. (Illus.). 1973. reprint ed. 150.00 (*0-87817-079-0*) Hacker.

Read, Christopher. From Tsar to Soviets: The Russian People & Their Revolution, 1917-1921. (Illus.). 336p. (C). 1996. text 57.00 (*0-19-521242-8*); pap. text 25.95 (*0-19-521241-X*) OUP.

Read, Clark P. Parasitism & Symbiology: An Introductory Text. LC 75-110390. 326p. reprint ed. 101.10 (*0-8357-9947-6*, 205513900008) Bks Demand.

Read, Colin. The Rising in Western Upper Canada, 1837-38: The Duncombe Revolt & After. LC 82-168779. 339p. reprint ed. pap. 105.10 (*0-8357-6366-8*, 203572000096) Bks Demand.

Read, Conyers. The Government of England under Elizabeth. LC 79-65980. (Folger Guides to the Age of Shakespeare Ser.). 1979. pap. 4.95 (*0-918016-07-X*) Folger Bks.

— Mr. Secretary Walsingham & the Policy of Queen Elizabeth, 3 vols., Set. LC 75-41223. reprint ed. 225.00 (*0-404-13490-4*) AMS Pr.

— Tudors: Personalities & Practical Politics in Sixteenth Century England. LC 68-24854. (Essay Index Reprint Ser.). 1977. 20.95 (*0-8369-0812-0*) Ayer.

Read, Conyers, ed. see Lambarde, William.

Read, Craig. Challenging the Tribe: Sir Winston Churchill's, World Government & World Leadership Government. 402p. 1998. pap. write for info. (*1-86106-607-4*, Pub. by Minerva Pr) Unity Dist.

Read, D. J., et al, eds. Techniques for Mycorrhizal Research. (Methods in Microbiology Ser.: Vols. 23 & 24). (Illus.). 960p. 1994. 67.00 (*0-12-521490-1*) Acad Pr.

Read, D. T. & Reed, R. P., eds. Fracture Mechanics: Eighteenth Symposium. LC 87-30666. (Special Technical Publication Ser.: No. 945). (Illus.). 1135p. 1988. 120.00 (*0-8031-0949-0*, STP945) ASTM.

Read, Daniel. Daniel Read: Collected Works. Kroeger, Karl, ed. (Music of the U. S. A. - Recent Researches in American Music Ser.: Vol. MUSA4). (Illus.). xxxviii, 332p. 1995. pap. 155.00 (*0-89579-319-9*) A-R Eds.

***Read, David.** Temperate Conquests: Spenser & the Spanish New World. LC 99-33276. 258p. 1999. 34.95 (*0-8143-2872-5*) Wayne St U Pr.

Read, David B. The Lives of the Judges of Upper Canada & Ontario: From 1791 to the Present Time, Vol. 1. 486p. 1995. reprint ed. 122.00 (*1-56169-110-0*) Gaunt.

Read, David H. The Christian Faith. large type ed. 1985. pap. 9.95 (*0-8027-2515-5*) Walker & Co.

Read, David J., jt. ed. see Smith, Sally.

Read, David T., jt. ed. see Chen, William T.

Read, Diana, ed. see McLaine, Patricia.

Read, Donald. The Age of Urban Democracy: England 1868-1914. 2nd rev. ed. LC 93-20486. (History of England Ser.). 536p. (C). 1995. pap. 41.40 (*0-582-08921-2*, 76256) Addison-Wesley.

— Power of News: The History of Reuters. 2nd ed. LC 98-36926. (Illus.). 558p. 1999. 49.95 (*0-19-820768-9*) OUP.

— Press & People, 1790-1850: Opinion in Three English Cities. (Modern Revivals in Economic & Social History Ser.). 225p. (C). 1993. text 56.95 (*0-7512-0245-2*, Pub. by Gregg Revivals) Ashgate Pub Co.

Read, Donald A. Health Education: A Cognitive-Behavioral Approach. LC 96-22262. (Series in Health Sciences). 336p. 1996. pap. 41.25 (*0-7637-0147-5*) Jones & Bartlett.

Read, Donald R. ObjectVision Programming for Windows. (Illus.). 352p. 1993. text 34.95 (*0-8306-4194-7*, 4258, Windcrest) TAB Bks.

Read, Edward M. Partners in Change: The 12-Step Referral Handbook for Probation, Parole & Community Corrections. LC 96-136647. 270p. 1996. 17.95 (*1-56838-101-8*) Am Correctional.

Read, Edward M. & Daley, Dennis C. Getting High & Doing Time: What's the Connection?: A Recovery Guide for Alcoholics & Drug Addicts in Trouble with the Law. (Illus.). 80p. (Orig.). 1990. pap. 11.00 (*0-929310-31-4*, 416) Am Correctional.

Read, Elizabeth. Let's Cook It Metric. LC 75-5395. (Illus.). 1975. pap. 5.00 (*0-9600996-1-1*) E Read.

— Twenty-First Century Guide to Building Your Vocabulary. Princeton Language Institute Staff, ed. 224p. 1994. mass mkt. 5.99 (*0-440-21721-0*) Dell.

Read, F. W. Egyptian Religion & Ethics. (African Heritage Classical Research Studies). pap. 25.00 (*0-938818-34-1*) ECA Assoc.

Read, Forrest. Seventy Six: One World & the Cantos of Ezra Pound. LC 80-15892. 488p. reprint ed. pap. 151.30 (*0-8357-4406-X*, 203722600008) Bks Demand.

Read, Frank H. Electromagnetic Radiation. LC 79-41484. (Manchester Physics Ser.). (Illus.). 315p. reprint ed. pap. 97.70 (*0-7837-6392-1*, 204610500010) Bks Demand.

Read, G. Westhill Project - Judaism: Photopack. (C). 1990. text 190.00 (*1-871402-22-0*, Pub. by S Thornes Pubs) Trans-Atl Phila.

Read, Gardner. Compendium of Modern Instrumental Techniques. LC 92-17854. 296p. 1993. lib. bdg. 59.95 (*0-313-28512-8*, RCZ, Greenwood Pr) Greenwood.

— Modern Rhythmic Notation. LC 77-9860. 211p. reprint ed. pap. 65.50 (*0-7837-1506-4*, 205729600024) Bks Demand.

— Music Notation. LC 68-54213. (Illus.). (C). 1979. reprint ed. pap. 23.95 (*0-8008-5453-5*, Crescendo) Taplinger.

— Pictographic Score Notation: A Compendium. LC 97-49480. 296p. 1998. lib. bdg. 65.00 (*0-313-30469-6*, Greenwood Pr) Greenwood.

— Source Book of Proposed Music Notation Reforms, 11. LC 86-14315. (Music Reference Collection: No. 11). 489p. 1987. lib. bdg. 75.00 (*0-313-25446-X*, RHN/, Greenwood Pr) Greenwood.

— Style & Orchestration. LC 77-15884. (Illus.). 320p. 1979. reprint ed. pap. 99.20 (*0-7837-9011-2*, AU0046300004) Bks Demand.

— Thesaurus of Orchestral Devices. LC 53-13253. 653p. 1953. reprint ed. pap. 200.00 (*0-608-00003-5*, AU0046900006) Bks Demand.

— Thesaurus of Orchestral Devices. LC 69-14045. 631p. 1969. reprint ed. lib. bdg. 45.00 (*0-8371-1884-0*, REOD, Greenwood Pr) Greenwood.

— Twentieth-Century Microtonal Notation, 18. LC 90-2782. (Contributions to the Study of Music & Dance Ser.: No. 18). 208p. 1990. 65.00 (*0-313-27398-7*, RCD/, Greenwood Pr) Greenwood.

Read, Geoffrey F. & Vickridge, Ian G., eds. Sewers - Rehabilitation & New Construction Pt. 1: Repair & Renovation. 544p. 1997. text 199.95 (*0-470-23564-0*) Halsted Pr.

Read, George. High Performance Ford Engine Parts Interchange. LC 99-218301. (Illus.). 128p. 1998. pap. 18.95 (*1-884089-33-X*, S-A Design) CarTech.

Read, Grace. Only One Cure. large type ed. (Dales Large Print Ser.). 244p. 1997. pap. 18.99 (*1-85389-730-2*) Ulverscroft.

Read, H. H. & Gribble, Colin D. Rutley's Elements of Minerology. 27th rev. ed. 512p. 1988. text 75.00 (*0-04-549010-4*) Routledge.

— Rutley's Elements of Minerology. 27th rev. ed. 512p. 1989. pap. 42.95 (*0-04-549011-2*) Thomson Learn.

Read, H. H. & Watson, Janet. Introduction & Geology, 2 vols. Incl. Vol. 2., 2 pts. 1975. write for info. (*0-318-52890-8*) Halsted Pr.

Read, Hadley & Andersen, Mary K. Just Be My Friend. (Illus.). 90p. 1989. pap. 6.50 (*0-9617924-0-X*) M K Andersen.

Read, Helen J. Woodland Habitats. LC 98-45288. (Habitat Guides Ser.). 1999. 85.00 (*0-415-18089-9*); pap. 25.99 (*0-415-18090-2*) Routledge.

Read, Helen J., jt. auth. see Hopkin, Stephen P.

Read, Herbert. Coleridge As Critic. LC 65-15891. 40p. (C). 1964. lib. bdg. 75.00 (*0-8383-0613-6*) M S G Haskell Hse.

Read, Herbert & Stangos, Nikos. The Thames & Hudson Dictionary of Art & Artists. 2nd rev. ed. LC 93-61272. (World of Art Ser.). (Illus.). 352p. 1994. pap. 14.95 (*0-500-20274-5*, Pub. by Thames Hudson) Norton.

Read, Herbert E. Ambush. LC 74-7020. (English Literature Ser.: No. 33). 1974. lib. bdg. 75.00 (*0-8383-1996-3*) M S G Haskell Hse.

— Annals of Innocence & Experience. LC 74-7019. (English Literature Ser.: No. 33). 1974. lib. bdg. 75.00 (*0-8383-1993-9*) M S G Haskell Hse.

— Aristotle's Mother. (Dramascripts Ser.: Vol. 1). 1963. pap. 4.95 (*0-900891-03-3*) Oleander Pr.

— Concise History of Modern Painting. LC 84-51313. (World of Art Ser.). (Illus.). 396p. 1985. pap. 16.95 (*0-500-20141-2*, Pub. by Thames Hudson) Norton.

— The Green Child. LC 48-9595. 1966. pap. 11.95 (*0-8112-0172-4*, NDP208, Pub. by New Directions) Norton.

— In Defence of Shelley & Other Essays. LC 68-26470. (Essay Index Reprint Ser.). 1977. reprint ed. 18.95 (*0-8369-0813-9*) Ayer.

— The Limits of Permissiveness in Art. 50p. 1968. pap. 1.00 (*0-8477-2105-1*) U of PR Pr.

— Lord Byron at the Opera. (Dramascripts Ser.: Vol. 3). 1995. 5.95 (*0-900891-02-5*) Oleander Pr.

— Meet Kropotkin, the Master. 1973. 59.95 (*0-8490-0602-3*) Gordon Pr.

— Modern Sculpture. (World of Art Ser.). (Illus.). 310p. 1985. pap. 14.95 (*0-500-20014-9*, Pub. by Thames Hudson) Norton.

— Nature of Literature. LC 74-105034. (Essay Index Reprint Ser.). 1977. 26.95 (*0-8369-1478-3*) Ayer.

— The Philosophy of Modern Art. LC 70-128294. (Essay Index Reprint Ser.). 1977. 24.95 (*0-8369-2023-6*) Ayer.

— Poems, 1911-1931. LC 78-64052. (Des Imagistes: Literature of the Imagist Movement Ser.). reprint ed. 37.50 (*0-404-17092-7*) AMS Pr.

— Poetry & Anarchism. 1972. 59.95 (*0-8490-0857-3*) Gordon Pr.

— Poetry & Anarchism. LC 72-290. (Essay Index Reprint Ser.). 1977. reprint ed. 13.95 (*0-8369-2819-9*) Ayer.

— Reason & Romanticism. LC 72-6856. (English Literature Ser.: No. 33). 1974. lib. bdg. 75.00 (*0-8383-1640-9*) M S G Haskell Hse.

— Sense of Glory: Essays in Criticism. LC 67-26773. (Essay Index Reprint Ser.). 1977. 19.95 (*0-8369-0814-7*) Ayer.

— Tenth Muse. LC 73-99646. (Essay Index Reprint Ser.). 1977. 29.95 (*0-8369-1427-9*) Ayer.

— To Hell with Culture: And Other Essays on Art & Society. LC 72-3370. (Essay Index Reprint Ser.). 1977. reprint ed. 18.95 (*0-8369-2918-7*) Ayer.

— The True Voice of Feeling: Studies in English Romantic Poetry. LC 75-30010. reprint ed. 34.50 (*0-404-14016-5*) AMS Pr.

— Wordsworth. LC 83-1723. 194p. (C). 1983. reprint ed. lib. bdg. 49.75 (*0-313-23321-7*, REWO, Greenwood Pr) Greenwood.

Read, Herbert E. & Stangos, Nikos, eds. The Thames & Hudson Dictionary of Art & Artists. rev. ed. LC 87-50342. (World of Art Ser.). (Illus.). 1988. 19.95 (*0-500-52340-1*) Thames Hudson.

Read, Herbert E., et al. Five European Sculptors. LC 75-86444. (Museum of Modern Art Publications in Reprint). 1969. reprint ed. 26.95 (*0-405-01541-0*) Ayer.

Read, Herbert E., ed. see Orage, Alfred R.

Read, Hollis. Negro Problem Solved: Or, Africa As She Was, As She Is, & As She Shall Be, Her Curse & Her Cure. LC 77-83874. (Black Heritage Library Collection). 1977. 20.95 (*0-8369-8645-8*) Ayer.

Read, Horace E. Recognition & Enforcement of Foreign Judgments in the Common Law Units of the British Commonwealth. LC 38-18887. (Harvard Studies in the Conflict of Laws: Vol. 2). xiv, 371p. 1978. reprint ed. lib. bdg. 47.50 (*0-89941-127-4*, 302790) W S Hein.

Read, Horace E., et al. Materials on Legislation. 4th ed. LC 81-17479. (University Casebook Ser.). 953p. (C). 1981. text 38.00 (*0-88277-045-4*) Foundation Pr.

Read, Howard. Defending the Public: Milo R. Maltbie & Utility Regulation in New York. LC 98-215399. (Illus.). 168p. 1997. 14.00 (*0-8059-4243-2*) Dorrance.

Read, Ian G. Australia's Eastern Outback: An Eco-Touring Drive Guide. (Illus.). 1999. pap. 17.95 (*1-86315-121-4*) Little Hills.

— The Bush: A Guide to the Vegetated Landscapes of Australia. (Illus.). 184p. 1995. pap. 25.95 (*0-86840-254-0*, Pub. by New South Wales Univ Pr); pap. 27.95 (*0-86840-238-9*, Pub. by New South Wales Univ Pr) Intl Spec Bk.

— Continent of Extremes: Recording Australia's Natural Phenomena. (Illus.). 156p. 1998. pap. 14.95 (*0-86840-624-4*, Pub. by New South Wales Univ Pr) Intl Spec Bk.

Read, J. Don & Lindsay, D. Steve, eds. Recollections of Trauma: Scientific Evidence & Clinical Practice: Proceedings of a NATO ASI Held in Port de Bourgenay, France, June 1996. LC 97-17155. (NATO ASI Series A, Life Sciences: Vol. 291). 612p. (C). 1997. 149.50 (*0-306-45618-4*, Plenum Trade) Perseus Pubng.

Read, J. Fred, et al. Milankovitch Sea-Level Changes, Cycles, & Reservoirs on Carbonate: Platforms in Greenhouse & Icehouse Worlds. LC 95-215854. (Short Course Notes Ser.: No. 35). (Illus.). 212p. (Orig.). 1995. pap. 55.00 (*1-56576-020-4*) SEPM.

Read, Jacinda. The New Avengers: Feminism, Feminity & the Rape-revenge Cycle. pap. write for info. (*0-7190-5905-4*, Pub. by Manchester Univ Pr); text. write for info. (*0-7190-5904-6*, Pub. by Manchester Univ Pr) St Martin.

***Read, James H.** Power Versus Liberty: Madison, Hamilton, Wilson, & Jefferson. LC 99-34633. (Illus.). 224p. 2000. 47.50 (*0-8139-1911-8*) U Pr of Va.

Read, James M. Atrocity Propaganda, 1914-1919. LC 72-4676. (International Propaganda & Communications Ser.). 333p. 1977. reprint ed. 20.95 (*0-405-04760-6*) Ayer.

Read, Jan. The Simon & Schuster Guide to the Wines of Spain. (Illus.). 288p. (Orig.). 1997. reprint ed. pap. text 15.00 (*0-7881-5030-8*) DIANE Pub.

— The Wines of Chile. 184p. 1997. 29.95 (*1-85732-330-0*, Pub. by Mitchell Beazley) Antique Collect.

— The Wines of Spain. (Mitchell Beazley Pocket Guides Ser.). 208p. 1998. write for info. (*1-84000-019-8*, Pub. by Mitchell Beazley) Antique Collect.

Read, Jan & Manjon, Maite. Catalonia: Traditions, Places, Wines & Food. (Illus.). 222p. 1992. pap. 19.95 (*1-871569-42-7*, NAB) I R Dee.

Read, Jane. Counselling for Fertility Problems. (Counselling in Practice Ser.). 240p. 1995. text 49.95 (*0-8039-8949-0*); pap. text 21.50 (*0-8039-8950-4*) Sage.

***Read, Janet.** Disability, the Family & Society: Listening to Mothers LC 99-31549. 2000. 29.95 (*0-335-20310-8*) OpUniv Pr.

Read, Jennifer S., jt. auth. see Zeichner, Steven L.

Read, Jesse, jt. auth. see Burkitt, Lemuel.

Read, Joan R. The Norfolk Terrier. (Illus.). 344p. 1989. 29.95 (*0-9623261-0-0*) J R Read.

— The Norfolk Terrier. 2nd rev. ed. LaMar, Nat R., ed. 1994. write for info. (*0-9623261-1-9*) J R Read.

Read, John. The Alchemist in Life, Literature & Art. LC 79-8620. reprint ed. 37.50 (*0-404-18486-3*) AMS Pr.

— The Alchemist in Life, Literature, & Art. (Illus.). 120p. 1992. reprint ed. pap. 17.95 (*1-56459-210-3*) Kessinger Pub.

— From Alchemy to Chemistry. unabridged ed. LC 95-6387. (Illus.). 240p. 1995. reprint ed. pap. text 8.95 (*0-486-28690-8*) Dover.

— Humour & Humanism in Chemistry. LC 79-8621. reprint ed. 42.50 (*0-404-18487-1*) AMS Pr.

— Prelude to Chemistry: An Outline of Alchemy, Its Literature & Relationships. LC 79-8622. (Illus.). reprint ed. 48.00 (*0-404-18488-X*) AMS Pr.

— Prelude to Chemistry: An Outline of Alchemy, its Literature & Relationships. 328p. 1992. reprint ed. pap. 24.95 (*1-56459-015-1*) Kessinger Pub.

— Through Alchemy to Chemistry. 206p. 1992. reprint ed. pap. 19.95 (*1-56459-013-5*) Kessinger Pub.

— Through Alchemy to Chemistry: A Procession of Ideas & Personalities. LC 79-8623. (Illus.). reprint ed. 37.50 (*0-404-18489-8*) AMS Pr.

Read, Karen, jt. auth. see Marrs, Texe W.

Read, Katherine. Early Childhood. 9th ed. (C). 1993. pap. text, teacher ed. 3.75 (*0-03-096889-5*) Harcourt Coll Pubs.

Read, Katherine, et al. Early Childhood Programs: Human Relationships & Learning. 9th ed. 448p. (C). 1993. text 73.50 (*0-03-074166-1*, Pub. by Harcourt Coll Pubs) Harcourt.

***Read, Kay A.** Handbook of Mesoamerican Mythology. (Handbooks of World Mythology Ser.). 325p. 2000. lib. bdg. 55.00 (*0-87436-998-3*) ABC-CLIO.

Read, Kay A. Time & Sacrifice in the Aztec Cosmos: Religion in North America. LC 97-45753. (Religion in North America Ser.). (Illus.). 352p. 1998. 39.95 (*0-253-33400-4*) Ind U Pr.

Read, Ken, ed. Improving Secondary School Management in an Era of Change Special Issue of School Organization, 6.1. 120p. 1986. 14.00 (*0-8002-4177-0*) Taylor & Francis.

Read, Kenneth E. The High Valley. 265p. 1980. reprint ed. pap. text 20.50 (*0-231-05035-6*) Col U Pr.

Read, Lauren. The Financing of Small Business: A Comparative Study of Male & Female Business Owners. LC 97-40388. 256p. (C). 1998. 80.00 (*0-415-16956-9*) Routledge.

Read, Leonard E. Accent on the Right. 124p. 1968. 6.95 (*0-910614-35-0*) Foun Econ Ed.

— Anything That's Peaceful: The Case for the Free Market. 2nd ed. LC 98-73673. 1964. pap. 5.95 (*1-57246-079-2*) Foun Econ Ed.

— Castles in the Air. 187p. 1975. 6.95 (*0-910614-52-0*) Foun Econ Ed.

— Deeper Than You Think. 207p. 1967. 6.95 (*0-910614-38-5*) Foun Econ Ed.

— The Freedom Freeway. 136p. 1979. pap. 3.95 (*0-910614-62-8*) Foun Econ Ed.

— The Freedom Philosophy. 2nd ed. Poirot, Paul L., ed. (Freeman Library Ser.). 146p. 1990. pap. 9.95 (*0-910614-75-X*) Foun Econ Ed.

— Government - An Ideal Concept. 2nd ed. LC 96-61993. 149p. 1997. pap. 5.95 (*1-57246-061-X*) Foun Econ Ed.

— Having My Way. 188p. 1974. pap. 3.95 (*0-910614-49-0*) Foun Econ Ed.

— How Do We Know? 127p. 1981. 6.95 (*0-910614-68-7*) Foun Econ Ed.

— Let Freedom Reign. 167p. 1969. 6.95 (*0-910614-40-7*) Foun Econ Ed.

— The Love of Liberty. 173p. 1975. pap. 3.95 (*0-910614-54-7*) Foun Econ Ed.

— Seeds of Progress. 136p. 1980. pap. 3.95 (*0-910614-66-0*) Foun Econ Ed.

— Then Truth Will Out. 189p. 1971. pap. 3.95 (*0-910614-27-X*) Foun Econ Ed.

— To Free or Freeze. 221p. 1972. 6.95 (*0-910614-44-X*) Foun Econ Ed.

— Vision. 158p. 1978. 6.95 (*0-910614-59-8*) Foun Econ Ed.

— Who's Listening? 222p. 1973. 6.95 (*0-910614-48-2*) Foun Econ Ed.

Read, Lorna. Creepy Crawlies. (Look & Learn Ser.). (Illus.). 12p. (J). (ps). 1996. bds. 4.98 (*1-85854-389-4*) Brimax Bks.

— Dinosaurs. (Look & Learn Ser.). (Illus.). 12p. (J). (ps). 1996. bds. 4.98 (*1-85854-386-X*) Brimax Bks.

— Farm Animals. (Illus.). 12p. (J). (ps). Date not set. bds. 3.98 (*1-85854-560-9*) Brimax Bks.

— Five Little Ducklings. (Illus.). 12p. (J). (ps). 1997. bds. 3.98 (*1-85854-561-7*) Brimax Bks.

— I Can Count. (Illus.). 12p. (J). (ps). Date not set. bds. 3.98 (*1-85854-558-7*) Brimax Bks.

— I See Red Green Blue. (My Big Little Fat Bks.). (Illus.). 20p. (J). (ps). 1996. bds. 3.49 (*1-85854-175-1*) Brimax Bks.

— Look & Listen. (My Big Little Fat Bks.). (Illus.). 20p. (J). (ps). 1996. bds. 3.49 (*1-85854-160-3*) Brimax Bks.

— My ABC. (My Big Little Fat Bks.). (Illus.). 20p. (J). (ps). 1996. bds. 3.49 (*1-85854-173-5*) Brimax Bks.

— One to Ten - Count Again. (My Big Little Fat Bks.). (Illus.). 20p. (J). (ps). 1996. bds. 3.49 (*1-85854-174-3*) Brimax Bks.

— Sea Creatures. (Look & Learn Ser.). (Illus.). 12p. (J). (ps). 1996. bds. 4.98 (*1-85854-388-6*) Brimax Bks.

— The Sky Is Blue. (Illus.). 12p. (J). (ps). 1997. bds. 3.98 (*1-85854-559-5*) Brimax Bks.

— Wild Animals. (Look & Learn Ser.). (Illus.). 12p. (J). (ps). 1996. bds. 4.98 (*1-85854-387-8*) Brimax Bks.

Read, M. D. & Wellby, Diana. A Practical Guide for the Obstetric Team. LC 84-15257. 197p. reprint ed. pap. 61.10 (*0-7837-1879-9*, 204208000001) Bks Demand.

Read, M. M., tr. see De Tourtoulon, Pierre.

***Read Magazine Editorial Staff.** Read in a Different Light: Stories of Loners, Outcasts & Rebels. LC 99-36120. 160p. (J). (gr. 5). 2000. lib. bdg. 22.40 (*0-7613-1615-9*) Millbrook Pr.

Read Magazine Editorial Staff. Read into the Millennium: Stories of the Future. LC 98-8390. (J). 1999. pap. write for info. (*0-7613-0388-X*) Millbrook Pr.

Read Magazine Editors. Read into the Millennium: Stories of the Future. LC 98-8390. 160p. (YA). (gr. 5 up). 1999. lib. bdg. 22.40 (*0-7613-0962-4*, Copper Beech Bks) Millbrook Pr.

An Asterisk (*) at the beginning of an entry indicates that the title is appearing for the first time.

Read Magazine Editors, compiled by. Read for Your Life: Tales of Survival from the Editors of Read Magazine. LC 97-29403. 160p. (YA). (gr. 5 up). 1998. lib. bdg. 22.40 (*0-7613-0362-6*) Millbrook Pr.

***Read, Malcolm.** Practical Guide to Sports Injuries. (Illus.). 336p. 2000. pap. 45.00 (*0-7506-3251-8*) Buttrwrth-Heinemann.

Read, Malcolm & Wade, Paul. Sports Injuries: A Unique Guide to Self-Diagnosis & Rehabilitation. 2nd ed. (Illus.). 192p. 1997. pap. text. write for info. (*0-7506-3112-0*) Buttrwrth-Heinemann.

— What to Do When It Hurts: Self-Diagnosis & Rehabilitation of Common Aches & Pains. LC 96-14912. (Illus.). 192p. (Orig.). 1996. pap. 14.95 (*1-882606-66-3*) Peoples Med Soc.

Read, Malcolm K. Language, Text, Subject: A Critique of Hispanism. LC 92-15636. 244p. 1992. 49.95 (*1-55753-027-0*) Purdue U Pr.

Read, Malcom K. Jorge Luis Borges & His Predecessors: Notes Towards a Materialist Historiography of Linguistic Idealism. LC 92-80589. (Studies in the Romance Languages & Literatures: No. 242). 210p. (C). 1992. pap. 32.50 (*0-8078-9246-7*) U of NC Pr.

— Visions in Exile: The Body in Spanish Literature & Linguistics, 1500-1800. LC 89-17736. (Purdue University Monographs in Romance Languages: Vol. 21). xii, 211p. 1990. 65.00 (*1-55619-071-9*); pap. 27.95 (*1-55619-072-7*) J Benjamins Pubng Co.

Read, Margaret. Children of Their Fathers: Growing up Among the Ngoni of Malawi. Spindler, Louise S. & Spindler, George D., eds. 112p. 1982. reprint ed. pap. text 6.95 (*0-8290-0320-7*) Irvington.

— The Ngoni of Nyasaland. LC 57-994. 220p. reprint ed. pap. 68.20 (*0-8357-3223-1*, 205711700010) Bks Demand.

Read, Margery. The Fortune Cookie Book. LC 96-40239. (Illus.). 112p. 1997. 12.95 (*1-888952-38-5*) Cumberland Hse.

Read, Margery, jt. auth. see Will, Richard.

Read, Marie, jt. auth. see Elliott, Lang.

Read Martin, Jane & Marx, Patricia. Now I Will Never Leave the Dinner Table. LC 94-3209. (Illus.). 32p. (J). (ps-3). 1999. pap. 5.95 (*0-06-443556-3*) HarpC Child Bks.

Read Martin, Jane & Ryan, Pam. Now Everybody Really Hates Me. LC 92-13075. (J). 1993. 10.15 (*0-606-09701-5*, Pub. by Turtleback) Demco.

Read, Maureen H. Earthen Vessel: James Hay, Ordinary Man. 188p. 1993. pap. 7.95 (*1-883294-01-0*) Masthof Pr.

Read, Maureen H. & St. John, Patricia M. The Least One. LC 88-31445. (Illus.). 192p. (Orig.). 1989. pap. 7.99 (*0-8361-3491-5*) Herald Pr.

Read, Melvyn. The Politics of Tobacco: Policy Networks & the Cigarette Industry. LC 96-84592. 215p. 1996. 68.95 (*1-85628-661-4*, Pub. by Avebry) Ashgate Pub Co.

Read, Michael, ed. Ancestral Dialogues: The Photographs of Albert Chong. (Untitled Ser.: No. 57). (Illus.). 64p. 1994. pap. 18.95 (*0-933286-63-5*) Frnds Photography.

Read, Michael, ed. see Solnit, Rebecca, et al.

Read, Michael, ed. see Willis, Deborah.

Read, Michael D. & Mellor, Stuart. Obstetrics in Outline. LC 85-9367. (Illus.). 264p. reprint ed. pap. 81.90 (*0-8357-3828-0*, 203655200004) Bks Demand.

Read, Mike. Forever England: The Life of Rupert Brooke. (Illus.). 256p. 1998. 35.00 (*1-85158-995-3*, Pub. by Mainstream Pubng) Trafalgar.

Read-Miller, Cynthia. Main Street U. S. A., in Early Photographs: 113 Detroit Publishing Co. Views. (Illus.). 128p. 1988. pap. 12.95 (*0-486-25841-6*) Dover.

Read, Miss. Celebrations at Thrush Green. 1993. pap. 11.00 (*0-14-015798-0*, Pub. by Pnguin Bks Ltd) Trafalgar.

— Christmas at Fairacre. 368p. pap. 16.95 (*0-14-012900-6*, Pub. by Pnguin Bks Ltd) Trafalgar.

Read, Miss. Christmas Mouse. (J). lib. bdg. 14.95 (*0-8488-1452-5*) Amereon Ltd.

***Read, Miss.** Country Bunch: An Anthology of the Countryside. large type ed. LC 99-89824. (General Ser.). 2000. pap. 24.95 (*0-7862-2451-7*) Thorndike Pr.

Read, Miss. Country Cooking. large type ed. 296p. 1993. 27.99 (*0-7505-0217-7*) Ulverscroft.

— Emily Davis. Date not set. lib. bdg. 21.95 (*0-8488-1700-1*) Amereon Ltd.

***Read, Miss.** Fairacre Affairs Omnibus. 480p. 1998. pap. 16.95 (*0-14-024945-1*, Pub. by Pnguin Bks Ltd) Trafalgar.

Read, Miss. The Fairacre Festival. Date not set. lib. bdg. 21.95 (*0-8488-1698-6*) Amereon Ltd.

— The Fairacre Festival. (Illus.). 104p. 1990. reprint ed. pap. 8.00 (*0-89733-333-0*) Academy Chi Pubs.

— Fresh from the Country. (J). 21.95 (*0-8488-1453-3*) Amereon Ltd.

— Friends at Thrush Green. large type ed. LC 92-6847. 355p. 1992. reprint ed. pap. 19.95 (*1-56054-310-8*) Thorndike Pr.

— The Market Square. Date not set. lib. bdg. 21.95 (*0-8488-1696-X*) Amereon Ltd.

— Miss Clare Remembers. 1996. 24.95 (*0-614-14677-1*, G K Hall Lrg Type) Mac Lib Ref.

— Miss Clare Remembers. 1996. 24.95 (*0-614-14676-3*, G K Hall Lrg Type) Mac Lib Ref.

— Miss Clare Remembers. large type ed. 276p. 1996. 24.95 (*0-7838-1658-8*, G K Hall Lrg Type) Mac Lib Ref.

— Miss Read's Country Cooking. (Illus.). 248p. 1992. 20.00 (*0-89733-373-X*) Academy Chi Pubs.

— News from Thrush Green. LC 92-40907. lib. bdg. 21.95 (*0-8488-1455-X*) Amereon Ltd.

— News from Thrush Green. large type ed. 1993. 22.00 (*0-8161-5504-6*, G K Hall Lrg Type) Mac Lib Ref.

— News from Thrush Green. large type ed. LC 92-40907. (General Ser.). (Illus.). 325p. 1993. lib. bdg. 21.95 (*0-8161-5503-8*, G K Hall Lrg Type) Mac Lib Ref.

— News from Thrush Green. LC 92-40907. (Illus.). 240p. 1990. reprint ed. pap. 20.00 (*0-89733-334-9*, G K Hall Lrg Type) Mac Lib Ref.

— Over the Gate. large type ed. LC 96-5402. (Illus.). 1996. 25.95 (*0-7838-1656-1*, G K Hall Lrg Type) Mac Lib Ref.

— A Peaceful Retirement, Set. (Fairacre Chronicles Ser.). 1998. audio 24.95 (*0-7540-7522-2*) Chivers N Amer.

— Storm in the Village. large type ed. (Illus.). 1996. 25.95 (*0-7838-1655-3*, G K Hall Lrg Type) Mac Lib Ref.

— Tales from a Village School. LC 95-19637. (Illus.). 176p. 1995. 19.95 (*0-395-71762-0*) HM.

— Tales from a Village School. large type ed. 226p. 1995. 24.95 (*0-7838-1441-0*, G K Hall Lrg Type) Mac Lib Ref.

— Tales from a Village School. large type ed. 226p. 1996. pap. 21.95 (*0-7838-1442-9*, G K Hall Lrg Type) Mac Lib Ref.

— Thrush Green. Date not set. lib. bdg. 21.95 (*0-8488-1692-7*) Amereon Ltd.

— Thrush Green. 1982. reprint ed. lib. bdg. 25.95 (*0-89966-435-0*) Buccaneer Bks.

— Tyler's Row. large type ed. LC 92-30416. (General Ser.). 312p. 1993. lib. bdg. 20.95 (*0-8161-5509-7*, G K Hall Lrg Type) Mac Lib Ref.

— Village Centenary. large type ed. LC 96-5403. (Illus.). 309p. 1996. 24.95 (*0-7838-1657-X*, G K Hall Lrg Type) Mac Lib Ref.

— Village Christmas & the Christmas Mouse. large type ed. LC 93-16779. (Large Print Bks.). 172p. 1993. 23.95 (*0-8161-5501-1*, G K Hall Lrg Type) Mac Lib Ref.

— Village Christmas & The Christmas Mouse. large type ed. LC 93-16779. (Large Print Bks.). 172p. 1994. pap. 17.95 (*0-8161-5502-X*, G K Hall Lrg Type) Mac Lib Ref.

— Winter in Thrush Green. 1982. reprint ed. lib. bdg. 25.95 (*0-89966-436-9*) Buccaneer Bks.

— The World of Thrush Green. large type ed. LC 93-16776. (Illus.). 326p. 1993. 22.95 (*0-8161-5507-0*, G K Hall Lrg Type) Mac Lib Ref.

— The Year at Thrush Green. large type ed. LC 96-42155. (Core Ser.). 349p. 1996. 25.95 (*0-7838-1964-1*) Thorndike Pr.

Read, Miss & Goodall, J. S. Winter in Thrush Green. (J). 1999. 21.95 (*0-8488-1456-8*) Amereon Ltd.

Read, Nicholas. One in a Million. (Illus.). 144p. (Orig.). (J). (gr. 3-6). 1996. pap. write for info. (*1-896095-22-4*) Polstar Bk.

Read, Opie. Confessions of a Negro Preacher. LC 73-18597. reprint ed. 37.50 (*0-404-11408-3*) AMS Pr.

— My Young Master. Novel. LC 86-27443. (Library of Southern Civilization). 352p. 1987. pap. text 18.95 (*0-8071-1395-6*) La State U Pr.

Read, Opie & Pixley, Frank. The Carpetbagger: A Novel. LC 72-2070. (Black Heritage Library Collection). 1977. reprint ed. 27.95 (*0-8369-9056-0*) Ayer.

Read, P. A. Commercial Law. 276p. (C). 1990. pap. 120.00 (*1-85352-782-3*, Pub. by HLT Pubns) St Mut.

Read, P. A., ed. Commercial Law. 556p. 1996. pap. 120.00 (*0-7510-0693-9*, Pub. by HLT Pubns) St Mut.

— Commercial Law Cases. 346p. 1996. pap. 95.00 (*0-7510-0659-9*, Pub. by HLT Pubns) St Mut.

— Commercial Law, Vol. 1: Sale of Goods, Consumer Credit & Agency. 390p. (C). 1991. 76.00 (*1-85352-382-8*, Pub. by HLT Pubns) St Mut.

— Contract Law. 222p. (C). 1990. pap. text 60.00 (*1-85352-755-6*, Pub. by HLT Pubns) St Mut.

— Contract Law. 428p. 1996. pap. 95.00 (*0-7510-0685-8*, Pub. by HLT Pubns) St Mut.

— Contract Law Cases. 416p. 1996. pap. 95.00 (*0-7510-0652-1*, Pub. by HLT Pubns) St Mut.

— General Principles of English Law. 400p. (C). 1991. pap. 400.00 (*1-85352-928-1*, Pub. by HLT Pubns) St Mut.

— Sale of Goods & Credit. 365p. (C). 1991. 110.00 (*1-85352-907-9*, Pub. by HLT Pubns) St Mut.

Read, P. A., jt. ed. see Lichtenstein, E. A.

***Read, Paul.** Restoration of Motion Picture Film. (Illus.). 256p. 2000. 120.00 (*0-7506-2793-X*) Buttrwrth-Heinemann.

Read, Paul, jt. auth. see Preece, John E.

***Read, Peter.** Belonging: Australians, Place & Aboriginal Ownership. (Illus.). 240p. (C). 2000. Price not set. (*0-521-77354-7*); pap. Price not set. (*0-521-77409-8*) Cambridge U Pr.

— A Rape of the Soul So Profound: The Return of the Stolen Generation. (Illus.). 248p. 2000. pap. 19.95 (*1-86448-885-9*, Pub. by Allen & Unwin Pty) Paul & Co Pubs.

Read, Peter. Responding to Global Warming: The Technology, Economics & Politics of Sustainable Energy. LC 93-18986. 256p. (C). 1994. text 65.00 (*1-85649-161-7*, Pub. by Zed Books) St Martin.

— Returning to Nothing: The Meaning of Lost Places. 254p. (C). 1997. text 64.95 (*0-521-57154-5*) Cambridge U Pr.

Read, Peter, ed. Down There with Me on the Cowra: An Oral History of Erambie Aboriginal Reserve Cowra, New South Wales. (Illus.). 144p. 1985. text 22.00 (*0-08-029856-7*, Pergamon Pr) Elsevier.

Read, Peter, jt. ed. see Chapman, Valerie.

Read, Peter B., jt. ed. see Izard, Carroll E.

Read, Peter G. Gemmology. (Illus.). 372p. 1995. pap. 34.95 (*0-7506-2290-3*, Focal) Buttrwrth-Heinemann.

***Read, Peter G.** Gemology. 2nd ed. 384p. 1999. pap. text 39.95 (*0-7506-4411-7*, Newnes) Buttrwrth-Heinemann.

Read, Phyllis J., et al. Strategies for Learning. 2nd ed. 132p. (C). 1996. pap. text, spiral bd. 25.95 (*0-7872-3030-8*, 41303001) Kendall-Hunt.

Read, Piers P. Alive: The Story of the Andes Survivors. LC 73-22269. (Illus.). 318p. 1979. mass mkt. 6.99 (*0-380-00321-X*, Avon Bks) Morrow Avon.

— Alive: The Story of the Andes Survivors. 1975. 12.09 (*0-606-01930-8*, Pub. by Turtleback) Demco.

— Alive: The Story of the Andes Survivors. rev. ed. LC 96-85590. (Adventure Library: Vol. 8). (Illus.). 320p. 1996. lib. bdg. 32.50 (*1-885283-08-3*) Advent Library.

— The Patriot. large type ed. LC 96-23995. 1997. pap. 22.95 (*0-7862-0832-5*) Thorndike Pr.

— A Season in the West. large type ed. (General Fiction Ser.). 496p. 1992. 11.50 (*0-7089-2632-0*) Ulverscroft.

***Read, Piers P.** Templars: The Dramatic History of the Knights Templar, the Most Powerful Military Order of the Catholic Church. (Illus.). 368p. 2000. 27.95 (*0-312-26658-8*) St Martin.

Read, R. Secrets of Art & Nature. 350p. 1992. reprint ed. pap. 27.50 (*1-56459-004-6*) Kessinger Pub.

Read, Ralph H., ed. Younger Churchmen Look at the Church. LC 74-156708. (Essay Index Reprint Ser.). 1977. reprint ed. 23.95 (*0-8369-2330-8*) Ayer.

Read, Ralph R., tr. see Bienek, Horst.

Read, Randy, jt. auth. see Rusk, Tom.

Read, Richard. Essence of Communication Theory. LC 98-6981. (Essence of Engineering Ser.). 208p. (C). 1998. pap. text 19.95 (*0-13-521022-4*, Prentice Hall) P-H.

Read, Richard, jt. auth. see Morse-Cluley, Elizabeth.

Read, Rick, jt. auth. see Miranda, Gary.

Read, Roland H., jt. auth. see Waesche, James F.

Read, Ronald C. Tangrams: Three Hundred & Thirty Puzzles. 1978. pap. 4.95 (*0-486-21483-4*) Dover.

Read, Ronald C. & Wilson, Robin J. Atlas of Graphs. LC 99-206498. (Illus.). 466p. 1999. text 140.00 (*0-19-853289-X*) OUP.

***Read, Rupert J. & Richman, Kenneth.** The New Hume Debate. LC 99-86749. 2000. write for info. (*0-415-23884-6*) Routledge.

Read, Rupert J., jt. ed. see Crary, Alice Marguerite.

Read, Samuel. Political Economy: An Inquiry into the Natural Grounds of Right to Vendible Property. LC 68-56570. (Reprints of Economic Classics Ser.). xxxiv, 398p. 1976. reprint ed. 57.50 (*0-678-00959-7*) Kelley.

Read, Seth A., jt. auth. see Haller, H. Brandon.

Read, Simon. The Illustrated Evolution of the Grand Prix/F1 Car: The First 100 Years. (Illus.). 112p. 1997. pap. 19.95 (*1-874105-91-X*, Pub. by Vivid Publ) Motorbooks Intl.

Read, Stephen. Thinking about Logic: An Introduction to the Philosophy of Logic. 270p. 1995. pap. text 21.00 (*0-19-289238-X*) OUP.

Read, Stephen, ed. see Nineth European Symposium on Medieval Logic & Sema.

Read, Stephen J. & Miller, Lynn C., eds. Connectionist Models of Social Reasoning & Social Behavior. LC 97-44954. 350p. 1997. write for info. (*0-8058-2215-1*); pap. write for info. (*0-8058-2216-X*) L Erlbaum Assocs.

Read, Stuart. The Oracle Edge. LC 99-35387. 256p. 1999. 19.95 (*1-58062-165-1*) Adams Media.

Read, T. R. & Cressie, N. Goodness-of-Fit Statistics for Discrete Multivariate Data. (Series in Statistics). (Illus.). 260p. 1988. 72.95 (*0-387-96682-X*) Spr-Verlag.

Read, Tess. Vietnam. (Illus.). 288p. 1999. pap. 15.95 (*1-873756-31-3*, Pub. by Trailblazer) Seven Hills Bk.

Read, Thomas T., jt. auth. see Bain, Foster H.

Read, W. L., jt. auth. see Chappell, C.

Read, W. L., jt. auth. see Chappell, R. T.

Read, W. S. The Making of Modern New Guinea-with Special Reference to Culture Contact in the Mandated Territory. LC 43-7044. (American Philosophical Society, Memoirs Ser.: Vol. 18). 353p. reprint ed. pap. 109.50 (*0-608-11769-2*, 200036400025) Bks Demand.

Read, William. Look Around You. LC 91-38758. 1992. 13.95 (*0-87949-364-X*) Ashley Bks.

Read, William A. Florida Place-Names of Indian Origin & Seminole Personal Names. LC 32-28107. (Louisiana State University Studies: No. 11). 97p. reprint ed. pap. 30.10 (*0-608-13700-6*, 205531300013) Bks Demand.

— Indian Place Names in Alabama. rev. ed. LC 84-2593. (Library of Alabama Classics). 128p. 1984. reprint ed. pap. 15.95 (*0-8173-0231-X*) U of Ala Pr.

Read, William H. America's Mass Media Merchants. LC 76-17231. 222p. 1976. pap. 68.90 (*0-7837-7457-5*, 204917900010) Bks Demand.

Read, William H. & Youtie, Jan L. Telecommunications Strategy for Economic Development. LC 95-40582. 184p. 1996. 57.95 (*0-275-95415-3*, Praeger Pubs) Greenwood.

Read, William H., jt. auth. see Sapronov, Walter.

Read, William H., jt. ed. see Compaine, Benjamin M.

Read, William J. The Pontmercy's of Paris. (Illus.). 148p. (Orig.). 1996. pap. 12.95 (*1-57502-339-3*, P01127) Morris Pubng.

Readdy, Margaret, tr. see Bergeron, F., et al.

Reade. Assyrian Sculpture. pap. 9.95 (*0-674-05015-0*) HUP.

Reade, Aleyn L. Jervis, Porter & Other Allied Families. (Illus.). 266p. 1997. reprint ed. pap. 39.50 (*0-8328-9333-1*); reprint ed. lib. bdg. 49.50 (*0-8328-9332-3*) Higginson Bk Co.

Reade, Angela. Beyond That Last Blue Mountain - To Sai Baba: A Discovery of Ways of Helping Oneself Towards Keeping 'Awake' (Integrated Awareness) (Illus.). 164p. 1996. pap. 19.95 (*1-85776-057-3*, Pub. by Book Guild Ltd) Trans-Atl Phila.

Reade, Bob. Coaching Football Successfully. LC 93-1272. (Illus.). 192p. 1993. pap. 19.95 (*0-87322-518-X*, PREA0518) Human Kinetics.

Reade, C. Cornewall: The House of Cornewall Family in England. (Illus.). 316p. 1993. reprint ed. pap. 47.50 (*0-8328-3660-5*); reprint ed. lib. bdg. 57.50 (*0-8328-3659-1*) Higginson Bk Co.

— Read. (Illus.). 148p. 1991. reprint ed. pap. 23.50 (*0-8328-2162-4*) Higginson Bk Co.

— Smith Family: Being a Popular Account of Most Branches of the Names - However Spelt. (Illus.). 324p. 1990. reprint ed. pap. 48.00 (*0-8328-1537-3*); reprint ed. lib. bdg. 56.00 (*0-8328-1536-5*) Higginson Bk Co.

Reade, Charles. Peg Woffington & Christie Johnstone. (BCL1-PR English Literature Ser.). 329p. 1992. reprint ed. lib. bdg. 89.00 (*0-7812-7621-7*) Rprt Serv.

— Works of Charles Reade, 17 vols. LC 73-118070. reprint ed. 1487.50 (*0-404-05260-6*) AMS Pr.

Reade, Chris. Elements of Functional Programming. (International Computer Science Ser.). (Illus.). 464p. (C). 1989. 49.00 (*0-201-12915-9*) Addison-Wesley.

Reade, David. The Age of Orion: The Lockheed P-3 Story. (Illus.). 224p. 1998. 49.95 (*0-7643-0478-X*) Schiffer.

Reade, David L. Beyond Buffalo: A Photographic Journey & Guide to the Secret Natural Wonders of Our Region. (Illus.). 112p. 1997. pap. 19.95 (*1-879201-19-4*) WNY Wares.

Reade, Eric. Britain & Sweden: Current Issues in Local Government. xii, 170p. (Orig.). 1989. pap. 53.25 (*91-540-9318-X*) Coronet Bks.

— History & Heartburn: The Saga of Australian Film, 1896-1978. 353p. 1980. 60.00 (*0-8386-3082-0*) Fairleigh Dickinson.

— Practical Work in Planning Education. (C). 1981. 35.00 (*0-7855-3863-1*, Pub. by Oxford Polytechnic) St Mut.

Reade, Eugene W., jt. auth. see Smith, Carl B.

Reade, Eugene W., ed. see Smith, Carl B.

Reade, J. E., jt. ed. see Curtis, J. E.

***Reade, John.** The Literary Faculty of the Native Races of America. (LC History-America-E). 30p. 1999. reprint ed. lib. bdg. 69.00 (*0-7812-4289-4*) Rprt Serv.

Reade, John B. An Introduction to Mathematical Analysis. 140p. 1986. 40.00 (*0-19-853258-X*) OUP.

Reade, Julian. Assyrian Sculpture. LC 99-201175. 1999. pap. text 18.95 (*0-674-05017-7*) HUP.

— Mesopotamia. (British Museum Paperbacks Ser.). (Illus.). 72p. (C). 1991. pap. 14.00 (*0-674-56958-X*) HUP.

Reade, Julian, ed. The Indian Ocean in Antiquity. (Illus.). 535p. 1996. 212.50 (*0-7103-0435-8*, Pub. by Kegan Paul Intl) Col U Pr.

Reade, Julian, ed. see Parpola, Simo.

Reade, Kathleen M. The Plaintiff's Personal Injury Handbook. LC 94-163. (Paralegal Ser.). (C). 1995. ring bd. 52.75 (*0-87632-993-8*) Thomson Learn.

Reade, Marjorie. Historic Buildings, Ann Arbor, Michigan. rev. ed. (Illus.). 96p. 1986. reprint ed. pap. 3.00 (*1-882574-01-X*) Ann Arbor Hist.

Reade, Marjorie & Wineberg, Susan. Historic Buildings, Ann Arbor, Michigan. 2nd ed. 250p. 1992. pap. 14.95 (*1-882574-00-1*) Ann Arbor Hist.

Reade, Simon. Absolute Monologues: European Classics for Men. 124p. 1994. pap. text 14.95 (*0-948230-72-X*, Pub. by N Hern Bks) Theatre Comm.

— Cheek by Jowl: Ten Years of Celebration. 136p. 1997. pap. 21.95 (*0-948230-49-5*, Pub. by Absolute Classics) Theatre Comm.

— Classical Monologues for Women. 140p. 1994. pap. text 14.95 (*0-948230-73-8*, Pub. by N Hern Bks) Theatre Comm.

Reade, W. Winwood. The Martyrdom of Man. 1981. lib. bdg. 300.00 (*0-686-71630-2*) Revisionist Pr.

— The Veil of Isis: Mysteries of the Druids. 1996. reprint ed. spiral bd. 16.00 (*0-7873-0710-6*) Hlth Research.

— The Veil of Isis: or Mysteries of the Druids. 1991. lib. bdg. 79.95 (*0-8490-4960-1*) Gordon Pr.

— The Veil of Isis: or Mysteries of the Druids. 256p. 1992. pap. 9.95 (*0-87877-176-X*) Newcastle Pub.

— The Veil of Isis or Mysteries of the Druids. 250p. 1998. reprint ed. pap. 14.50 (*0-7661-0310-2*) Kessinger Pub.

Reade, W. Winwood, jt. auth. see Hosking, Eric.

Reade, Winwood. The Martydom of Man. 342p. 1995. reprint ed. 36.00 (*1-896032-46-X*) Battered Silicon.

— The Martyrdom of Man. unabridged ed. (Classic Reprint Ser.). (Illus.). 455p. 1997. reprint ed. 45.00 (*0-936128-83-6*) De Young Pr.

Readel, Fred W. All Heavens Ranges. (Orig.). 1986. pap. 4.95 (*0-9616822-3-X*) F W Readel.

Readence, et al. Content Area Literacy: An Integrated Approach. 6th ed. LC 98-65393. 352p. 1998. per. 42.95 (*0-7872-3884-8*, 41388401) Kendall-Hunt.

Readence, jt. auth. see Searfoss.

Readence, jt. auth. see Tierney.

***Readence, John E., et al.** Prereading Activities for Content Area Reading & Learning. 3rd ed. (Orig.). 2000. pap., teacher ed. 15.95 (*0-87207-261-4*, 261) Intl Reading.

Readence, John E., jt. auth. see Searfoss, Lyndon.

Readence, John E., jt. auth. see Searfoss, Lyndon W.

Reader. Regis Debray: The Writing of Commitment. LC 95-14373. (Modern European Thinkers Ser.). 1995. 44.95 (*0-7453-0821-X*, Pub. by Pluto GBR); pap. 13.95 (*0-7453-0822-8*, Pub. by Pluto GBR) Stylus Pub VA.

Reader, Alice, jt. auth. see Morrison, Kathy.

***Reader, Craig D.** My Town Is in Development. (Illus.). 73p. 2000. 14.99 (*0-9678522-0-X*) Zero to One.

Reader, Dennis J. Coming Back Alive. 256p. 1983. pap. 2.25 (*0-380-61416-2*, 61416-2, Avon Bks) Morrow Avon.

Reader, Dennis J., jt. ed. see Hallwas, John E.

Reader, F. S. Some Pioneers of Washington County: A Family History. (Illus.). 154p. 1997. reprint ed. pap. 19.00 (*0-8328-6458-7*) Higginson Bk Co.

Reader, G. T., jt. auth. see Richardson.

Reader, G. T., jt. auth. see Richardson, J.

Reader, Ian. Australia's Central & Western Outback: The Driving Guide. 1998. pap. text 17.95 (*1-86315-061-7*) Little Hills.

— Australia's Northern Outback: The Driving Guide. 1998. pap. text 17.95 (*1-86315-081-1*) Little Hills.

An Asterisk (*) at the beginning of an entry indicates that the title is appearing for the first time.

— Australia's Wet Tropics & North-eastern Outback: The Driving Guide. 1998. pap. text 17.95 (1-86315-110-9) Little Hills.

— A Poisonous Cocktail? Aum Shinrikyo's Path to Violence. 116p. 1998. pap. 19.95 (87-87062-55-0, Pub. by NIAS) Paul & Co Pubs.

— Religion in Contemporary Japan. 320p. 1991. pap. text 18.00 (0-8248-1354-5) UH Pr.

***Reader, Ian.** Religious Violence in Contemporary Japan: The Case of Aum Shinrikyeo. LC 00-23317. 2000. pap. write for info. (0-8248-2340-0) UH Pr.

Reader, Ian. Religious Violence in Contemporary Japan: The Case of Aum Shinrikyo. (NIAS Monographs: Vol. 82). 200p. (C). 1999. text 48.00 (0-7007-1108-2, Pub. by Curzon Pr Ltd); pap. text 22.95 (0-7007-1109-0, Pub. by Curzon Pr Ltd) UH Pr.

Reader, Ian & Tanabe, George J., Jr. Practically Religious: Worldly Benefits & the Common Religion of Japan. LC 98-4192. (Illus.). 328p. 1998. text 45.00 (0-8248-2065-7); pap. text 22.95 (0-8248-2090-8) UH Pr.

Reader, Ian, et al. Japanese Religions: Past & Present. LC 93-2725. (Illus.). 136p. 1993. text 36.00 (0-8248-1545-9); pap. text 16.95 (0-8248-1546-7) UH Pr.

— Simple Guide to Shinto: The Religion of Japan. (Simple Guides Ser.: Series 3). (Illus.). 120p. 1998. pap. 9.95 (1-86034-003-2, Pub. by Global Bks) Midpt Trade.

Reader, Ian, jt. ed. see Soderberg, Marie.

Reader, J. The Divine Mystery. 79p. pap. 4.95 (0-88172-117-4) Believers Bkshelf.

Reader, John. Africa: A Biography of the Continent. LC 97-36892. (Illus.). 802p. (YA). 1998. 45.00 (0-679-40979-3) Knopf.

***Reader, John.** Africa: A Biography of the Continent. (Illus.). 816p. 1999. pap. 17.00 (0-679-73869-X) Knopf.

Reader, John. The Rise of Life: The First 3.5 Billion Years. (Illus.). 192p. 1999. reprint ed. text 27.00 (0-7881-6094-X) DIANE Pub.

Reader, K. S. The Modern British Economy in Historical Perspective. LC 78-423071. xii, 236 p. 1969. write for info. (0-582-41029-0) Longman.

***Reader, Keith.** Robert Bresson. LC 99-54911. 2000. write for info. (0-7190-5365-X, Pub. by Manchester Univ Pr); pap. write for info. (0-7190-5366-8, Pub. by Manchester Univ Pr) St Martin.

Reader, Keith, jt. auth. see Hughes, Alex.

Reader, Lesley & Ridout, Lucy. Bali & Lombok. (Rough Guide Ser.). (Illus.). 448p. (Orig.). 1999. pap. 16.95 (1-85828-352-3) Rough Guides.

— First-Time Asia. (Rough Guide Special Ser.). (Illus.). 272p. 1998. pap. text 9.95 (1-85828-332-9, Pub. by Rough Guides) Penguin Putnam.

Reader, Mary. Book of One-Pot Cooking. LC 96-219629. 120p. 1996. pap. 12.00 (1-55788-252-5, HP Books) Berkley Pub.

Reader, Michele. WordPerfect 7 for Windows 95 SmartStart. LC 95-74891. (Smartstart Ser.). (Illus.). 319p. 1997. pap. 29.99 (1-57576-046-0) Sams.

Reader, Ralph, ed. see Conference on Canberra, 1973.

Reader, Roberta, ed. Russian Folk Lyrics. LC 92-7155. (Illus.). 208p. 1993. 35.00 (0-253-34623-1); pap. text 16.95 (0-253-20749-5, MB-749) Ind U Pr.

***Reader, Ted.** The Complete Idiot's Guide to Grilling with Ted Reader. 2000. pap. 24.95 (0-13-086720-9, Prentice Hall) P-H.

***Reader, Ted & Sloan, Kathleen.** Sticks & Stones: The Art of Grilling on Plank, Vine & Stone. LC 99-18070. (Game & Fish Mastery Library: Vol. 5). (Illus.). 96p. 1999. 19.50 (1-57223-221-8, 2218) Willow Creek Pr.

Reader, Willie. Back Packing. 1975. 1.50 (0-936814-02-0) New Collage.

***Reader's Digest Association South Africa.** Modern Times, 1970-99. LC 99-88341. (Eventful 20th Century Ser.). 2000. write for info. (0-7621-0272-1) RD Assn.

***Reader's Digest Association Staff.** El Asombroso Cuerpo. 2000. 35.00 (84-88746-23-7, Pub. by RD Assn) Penguin Putnam.

— Discover Australia & New Zealand. LC 00-37261. (Discover the World Ser.). (Illus.). 2000. pap. write for info. (0-7621-0310-8) RD Assn.

— Discover Western Europe. LC 00-36916. 2000. write for info. (0-7621-0309-4) RD Assn.

— Forging the Modern Age, 1900-14. LC 00-24209. 2000. write for info. (0-7621-0286-1) RD Assn.

— Health & Happiness. LC 00-20387. (Health & Healing the Natural Way Ser.). 2000. write for info. (0-7621-0281-0) RD Assn.

— Holding Back the Clock. LC 00-20386. (Health & Healing the Natural Way Ser.). (Illus.). 2000. write for info. (0-7621-0280-2) RD Assn.

— How Did It Really Happen? LC 00-31083. 2000. write for info. (0-7621-0277-2) RD Assn.

— The Last Adventure. LC 00-28606. (Eventful 20th Century Ser.). (Illus.). 2001. write for info. (0-7621-0289-6) RD Assn.

— Lost Mysteries World. 2000. pap. 30.00 (1-876689-42-0, Pub. by RD Assn) Penguin Putnam.

— Milestones of Medicine. LC 00-23050. (Eventful 20th Century Ser.). 2000. write for info. (0-7621-0285-3) RD Assn.

— Our Story: A Grandparent's Record Book. 2000. pap. 24.95 (0-7621-0303-5, Pub. by RD Assn) Penguin Putnam.

— Reader's Digest Complete Guide to Pain Relief. LC 00-25468. 2000. write for info. (0-7621-0278-0) RD Assn.

— Secrets of the Seas. 2000. 19.95 (0-7621-0109-1, Pub. by RD Assn) Penguin Putnam.

— Shaping Up. LC 00-20388. (Health & Healing the Natural Way Ser.). (Illus.). 2000. write for info. (0-7621-0282-9) RD Assn.

— The Space Race. LC 00-28089. (Eventful 20th Century Ser.). (Illus.). 2000. write for info. (0-7621-0287-X, Pub. by RD Assn) RD Assn.

Readers Digest Association Staff. The Visual Handbook of Building & Remodeling. (Woodworking Ser.). (Illus.). 594p. 1999. 29.95 (0-7621-0193-8, Pub. by RD Assn) Penguin Putnam.

***Reader's Digest Association Staff.** The War to End Wars, 1914-18. LC 00-28607. 2000. write for info. (0-7621-0288-8) RD Assn.

***Reader's Digest Association Staff, ed.** The Healthy Environment. LC 00-20377. (Health & Healing the Natural Way Ser.). 2001. write for info. (0-7621-0283-7) RD Assn.

***Readers Digest Children Staff.** Book of Amazing Facts: A Children's Guide to the World. (Illus.). (J). 2000. 26.95 (0-276-42434-4) RD Assn.

***Readers Digest Children Staff, ed.** Bug Pokemon: Caterpie, Metapod, Butterfree. (Pokemon Elvolvers Bks.). (Illus.). (J). 2000. pap. 3.99 (1-57584-436-2, RDYF) Rdrs Digest.

— Fighting Pokemon: Machop, Machoke, Machamp. (Pokemon Elvolvers Bks.). (Illus.). (J). 2000. pap. 3.99 (1-57584-438-9, RDYF) Rdrs Digest.

— Fire Pokemon: Charmander, Charmeleon, Charizard. (Pokemon Elvolvers Bks.). (Illus.). (J). (gr. 4-7). 2000. pap. 3.99 (1-57584-434-6, RDYF) Rdrs Digest.

— Ghost Pokemon: Gastly, Haunter, Gengar. (Pokemon Elvolvers Bks.). (Illus.). (J). (gr. 4-7). 2000. pap. 3.99 (1-57584-440-0, RDYF) Rdrs Digest.

— Grass Pokemon: Bulbasaur, Ivysaur, Venusaur. (Pokemon Elvolvers Bks.). (Illus.). (J). (gr. 4-7). 2000. pap. 3.99 (1-57584-433-8, RDYF) Rdrs Digest.

— Psychic Pokemon: Abra, Kadabra, Alakazam. (Pokemon Elvolvers Bks.). (Illus.). (J). (gr. 4-7). 2000. pap. 3.99 (1-57584-437-0, RDYF) Rdrs Digest.

— Rock Pokemon: Geodude, Graveler, Golem. (Pokemon Elvolvers Bks.). (Illus.). (J). 2000. pap. 3.99 (1-57584-439-7, RDYF) Rdrs Digest.

— Water Pokemon: Squirtle, Wartortle, Blastoise. (Pokemon Elvolvers Bks.). (Illus.). (J). 2000. pap. 3.99 (1-57584-435-4, RDYF) Rdrs Digest.

Reader's Digest Editors. The A-Z of Annuals, Biennials & Bulbs. LC 93-37667. (Successful Gardening Ser.). (Illus.). 176p. 1994. 18.98 (0-89577-584-0) RD Assn.

— A-Z of Deciduous Trees & Shrubs. LC 94-13100. (Successful Gardening Ser.). (Illus.). 176p. 1994. 18.98 (0-89577-615-4) RD Assn.

— A-Z of Evergreen Trees & Shrubs. LC 94-47610. (Successful Gardening Ser.). (Illus.). 176p. 1995. 18.98 (0-89577-698-7) RD Assn.

— A-Z of Perennials. LC 93-26149. (Successful Gardening Ser.). (Illus.). 176p. 1993. 18.98 (0-89577-554-9) RD Assn.

— A-Z of Perennials. (Successful Gardening Ser.). 1998. pap. text 19.95 (0-89577-960-9, Pub. by RD Assn) Penguin Putnam.

— Adding on. (Woodworking Ser.). 374p. 1999. pap. 17.95 (0-7621-0147-4, Pub. by RD Assn) Penguin Putnam.

— Advanced Routing. (Workshop Companion Ser.). 128p. 1999. 19.95 (0-7621-0197-0, Pub. by RD Assn) Penguin Putnam.

— America A to Z. LC 96-268. (Illus.). 1997. 30.00 (0-89577-900-5, Pub. by RD Assn) Penguin Putnam.

— America by the Sea. (Explore America Ser.). (Illus.). 144p. 1996. 16.98 (0-89577-864-5) RD Assn.

— America in the '40s: A Sentimental Journey. LC 97-40679. (Illus.). 160p. 1998. 19.95 (0-7621-0010-9, Pub. by RD Assn) Penguin Putnam.

— American Country Furniture. LC 00-23927. (Woodworking Ser.). 328p. 1999. pap. 15.95 (0-7621-0148-2, Pub. by RD Assn) Penguin Putnam.

— American Folk Healing: An A-Z Guide to Traditional American Remedies. LC 97-23574. 1998. write for info. (0-7621-0009-5) RD Assn.

— American Treasures. LC 97-27745. (Explore America Ser.). 1997. write for info. (0-89577-965-X) RD Assn.

— America's Fascinating Indian Heritage: The First Americans: Their Customs, Art, History & How They Lived. LC 78-55614. (Illus.). 416p. 1990. reprint ed. 30.00 (0-89577-372-4, Pub. by RD Assn) Penguin Putnam.

— America's Historic Places: An Illustrated Guide to our Country's Past. LC 87-4757. (Illus.). 352p. 1988. 28.00 (0-89577-265-5, Pub. by RD Assn) Penguin Putnam.

— Ask the Experts: 2500 Great Hints & Smart Tips from the Pros. LC 99-24696. 1999. write for info. (0-7621-0237-3) RD Assn.

— Ask the Family Handy-Man: Fast Answers to More Than 1000 Often Asked Questions about Home Repair. LC 99-24913. (Illus.). 384p. 1999. 30.00 (0-7621-0142-3, Pub. by RD Assn) Penguin Putnam.

— Astronomy. LC 97-46925. (Reader's Digest Explores Ser.). (Illus.). 160p. 1998. 24.95 (0-7621-0042-7, Pub. by RD Assn) Penguin Putnam.

— Baby's First Memories: A Parents' Record Book. (First Bible Collection). (Illus.). 48p. (YA). 1998. bds. 14.99 (1-57584-224-6, Pub. by Rdrs Digest) Random.

— Baby's First Photo Album. (First Bible Collection). (Illus.). 20p. 1998. bds. 14.99 (1-57584-225-4, Pub. by Rdrs Digest) Random.

Reader's Digest Editors. Back Roads & Hidden Corners. LC 93-8254. (Explore America Ser.). (Illus.). 144p. 1993. 16.98 (0-89577-545-X, Pub. by RD Assn) Penguin Putnam.

Reader's Digest Editors. Back to Basics: How to Learn & Enjoy Traditional American Skills. (Illus.). 456p. 1997. 26.95 (0-89577-939-0, Pub. by RD Assn) Penguin Putnam.

— Backyard Builder. LC 99-24916. (Woodworking Ser.). 120p. 1999. pap. 12.95 (0-7621-0180-6, Pub. by RD Assn) Penguin Putnam.

— The Big Book of Small Household Repairs. (Woodworking Ser.). 308p. 1999. pap. 15.95 (0-7621-0162-8, Pub. by RD Assn) Penguin Putnam.

— Book of Dogs. 2nd rev. ed. (Illus.). 432p. 1994. 27.00 (0-88850-205-2, Pub. by RD Assn) Penguin Putnam.

— Book of North American Birds, 3 bks. in 1. LC 89-70261. (Illus.). 576p. 1990. 32.95 (0-89577-351-1, Pub. by RD Assn) Penguin Putnam.

— Book of Skills: A Step-By-Step Guide to Do-It-Yourself Techniques a Homeowner's Encyclopedia of Tools, Hardware & Materials. LC 92-28686. (Illus.). 360p. 1993. 30.00 (0-89577-469-0, Pub. by RD Assn) Penguin Putnam.

— Cabinetry. (Woodworking Ser.). 440p. 1999. 27.95 (0-7621-0165-2, Pub. by RD Assn) Penguin Putnam.

— Caring for Your Plants. (Successful Gardening Ser.). (Illus.). 176p. 1994. 18.98 (0-89577-603-0) RD Assn.

— Changes: An Anthology by New Writers. (New Writers' Voices Ser.). 64p. (Orig.). 1993. pap. text 3.50 (1-56853-006-4, Signal Hill) New Readers.

— Children's Atlas of the Universe. LC 99-36177. (Illus.). 128p. (gr. 3-8). 2000. lib. bdg. 26.99 (1-57584-379-X) Rdrs Digest.

— Children's Atlas of the World. LC 99-26619. (Illus.). 128p. (YA). (gr. 3-8). 2000. 26.99 (1-57584-378-1) Rdrs Digest.

— Children's Atlas of the World. rev. ed. LC 99-26619. (Illus.). 128p. (YA). (gr. 3-8). 2000. 24.99 (1-57584-372-2) Rdrs Digest.

— Color Round the Year. LC 93-45391. (Successful Gardening Ser.). (Illus.). 176p. 1994. 18.98 (0-89577-602-2) RD Assn.

— The Complete Book of Money Secrets. LC 98-49625. 1999. write for info. (0-7621-0131-8) Readrs Digest Pr.

— Complete Guide to Needlework. Colton, Virginia, ed. LC 78-71704. (Illus.). 504p. 1981. 28.00 (0-89577-059-8, Pub. by RD Assn) Penguin Putnam.

— Complete Guide to the Bible. LC 98-6836. 448p. 1998. 29.95 (0-7621-0073-7, Pub. by RD Assn) Penguin Putnam.

— Complete Painters Handbook. (Woodworking Ser.). 150p. 1999. pap. 14.95 (0-7621-0167-9, Pub. by RD Assn) Penguin Putnam.

— Country Accents. (Woodworking Ser.). (Illus.). 124p. 1999. pap. 14.95 (0-7621-0149-0, Pub. by RD Assn) Penguin Putnam.

— Country Furniture. (Reader's Digest Woodworking Ser.). 1999. pap. text 14.95 (0-7621-0151-2, Pub. by RD Assn) Penguin Putnam.

— Country Pine Projects. LC 99-14913. (Woodworking Ser.). 320p. 1999. 27.95 (0-7621-0169-5, Pub. by RD Assn) Penguin Putnam.

— Crafts & Hobbies: A Step-by-Step Guide to Creative Skills. LC 79-63118. (Illus.). 456p. 1981. 24.95 (0-89577-063-6, Pub. by RD Assn) Penguin Putnam.

— Creative Garden Design. LC 94-39325. (Successful Gardening Ser.). (Illus.). 176p. 1995. 18.98 (0-89577-693-6) RD Assn.

— Curing Everyday Ailments the Natural Way. LC 99-21950. 2000. 35.00 (0-7621-0240-3, Pub. by RD Assn) Penguin Putnam.

— Daily Life in Colonial America. LC 93-2719. (Journeys into the Past Ser.). (Illus.). 144p. 1993. 18.98 (0-89577-497-6) RD Assn.

— Desks & Bookcases. (Reader's Digest Woodworking Ser.). 1999. 19.95 (0-7621-0152-0, Pub. by RD Assn); pap. 14.95 (0-7621-0153-9, Pub. by RD Assn) Penguin Putnam.

— Le Dictionnaire Plus. (FRE.). 703p. 1992. 110.00 (0-7859-1004-2, 2709803704) Fr & Eur.

***Reader's Digest Editors.** Diet & Weight Control. LC 98-50535. (Health & Healing the Natural Way Ser.). 1999. write for info. (0-7621-0145-8) RD Assn.

Reader's Digest Editors. Display Cases, Frames & Shelves. (Reader's Digest Woodworking Ser.). 1999. 19.95 (0-7621-0154-7, Pub. by RD Assn); pap. 14.95 (0-7621-0155-5, Pub. by RD Assn) Penguin Putnam.

— Down Home Cooking: The New Healthier Way. LC 94-13511. (Illus.). 384p. 1995. 28.00 (0-89577-646-4, Pub. by RD Assn) Penguin Putnam.

Reader's Digest Editors. The Easy Way to Play 100 Unforgettable Hits. LC 92-773077. (Illus.). 224p. 1991. 30.00 (0-89577-385-6, Pub. by RD Assn) Penguin Putnam.

Reader's Digest Editors. Eat Well, Stay Well: 500 Delicious Recipes Made with Healing Foods. LC 98-28078. (Illus.). 450p. 1998. 29.95 (0-7621-0124-5, Pub. by RD Assn) Penguin Putnam.

***Reader's Digest Editors.** Exercise & Your Health. LC 99-54712. 2000. write for info. (0-7621-0265-9) RD Assn.

Reader's Digest Editors. Eyes, Nose, Ears & Toes! large type ed. (First Blessings Flap Bks.: Vol. 4). (Illus.). 18p. (J). (gr. k-3). 1998. bds. 3.99 (1-57584-082-0, Pub. by Rdrs Digest) Random.

— The Family Handyman: Easy Repair. LC 94-14896. (Illus.). 192p. 1994. 19.95 (0-89577-624-3, Pub. by RD Assn) Penguin Putnam.

— The Family Handyman: Helpful Hints. LC 94-1807. (Illus.). 384p. 1995. 30.00 (0-89577-617-0, Pub. by RD Assn) Penguin Putnam.

— The Family Handyman: Interior Remodeling. LC 95-22069. (Illus.). 192p. 1995. 19.95 (0-89577-791-6, Pub. by RD Assn) Penguin Putnam.

— The Family Handyman: Outdoor Projects. (Illus.). 192p. 1994. 19.95 (0-89577-623-5, Pub. by RD Assn) Penguin Putnam.

— The Family Handyman: Toys, Games & Furniture You Can Make Out of Wood. LC 95-30437. (Illus.). 192p. 1995. 19.95 (0-89577-790-8, Pub. by RD Assn) Penguin Putnam.

— Family Handyman Assortment. Date not set. write for info. (0-676-50864-2) Readrs Digest Pr.

— Family Handyman Decks & Patios. 1996. pap. 19.95 (0-676-51411-1) Readrs Digest Pr.

— The Family Handyman Decks, Patios & Porches: Plans, Projects & Instructions for Expanding Your Outdoor Living Space. LC 95-44744. (Illus.). 192p. 1996. pap. 19.95 (0-89577-852-1, Pub. by RD Assn) Penguin Putnam.

— The Family Handyman Power Tool Techniques & Tips. LC 97-3673. 1997. 19.95 (0-89577-982-X, Pub. by RD Assn) Penguin Putnam.

— The Family Handyman Simple Car Care & Repair. LC 96-47545. 1997. 16.95 (0-89577-930-7, Pub. by RD Assn) Penguin Putnam.

— Family Handyman Updating Home. 1996. pap. 19.95 (0-676-51412-X) Readrs Digest Pr.

— The Family Handyman Updating Your Home: Easy Ways to Make Your Home Look & Work Better. LC 95-44751. (Illus.). 195p. 1996. pap. 19.95 (0-89577-851-3, Pub. by RD Assn) Penguin Putnam.

— Family Medical Dictionary: Diccionario Medico Familiar. (SPA.). 756p. 1981. 95.00 (0-8288-1878-9, S34982) Fr & Eur.

— Family Songbook. LC 70-84403. (Illus.). 252p. 1981. spiral bd. 29.95 (0-89577-002-4, Pub. by RD Assn) Penguin Putnam.

— Family Word Finder. LC 75-18006. 896p. 1975. 27.99 (0-89577-023-7) RD Assn.

***Reader's Digest Editors.** Fighting Allergies. LC 99-47859. (Health & Healing the Natural Way Ser.). 2000. write for info. (0-7621-0264-0) RD Assn.

Reader's Digest Editors. Finish Carpentry. (Workshop Companion Ser.). 128p. 1999. 19.95 (0-7621-0198-9, Pub. by RD Assn) Penguin Putnam.

— Finishing. (Workshop Companion Ser.). 128p. 1999. 19.95 (0-7621-0199-7, Pub. by RD Assn) Penguin Putnam.

— Flower, Arts & Dried Flower Assortments. Date not set. write for info. (0-676-50865-0) Readrs Digest Pr.

— Foods That Harm, Foods That Heal. LC 96-24477. 1997. 30.00 (0-89577-912-9, Pub. by RD Assn) Penguin Putnam.

— For the Weekend Woodworker. (Reader's Digest Woodworking Ser.). 120p. 1999. pap. 12.95 (0-7621-0181-4, Pub. by RD Assn) Penguin Putnam.

***Reader's Digest Editors.** The Fragile Peace, 1919-1939. LC 99-51309. 2000. 19.95 (0-7621-0270-5, Pub. by RD Assn) Penguin Putnam.

Reader's Digest Editors. Fruits & Vegetables. LC 95-12022. (Successful Gardening Ser.). (Illus.). 176p. 1995. 18.98 (0-89577-824-6) RD Assn.

— A Garden for All Seasons. (Illus.). 432p. 1991. 32.95 (0-89577-380-5, Pub. by RD Assn) Penguin Putnam.

— The Garden Problem Solver. LC 94-30615. (Successful Gardening Ser.). (Illus.). 176p. 1994. 18.98 (0-89577-675-8) RD Assn.

***Reader's Digest Editors.** Garden Problem Solver: The Ultimate Guide for Successful Gardening. LC 98-47125. 1999. 35.00 (0-7621-0140-7, Pub. by RD Assn) Penguin Putnam.

Reader's Digest Editors. Get House Smart: The Quick Start Guide to the Workings of Your Home. LC 97-17441. 1997. pap. text 19.95 (0-89577-981-1, Pub. by RD Assn) Penguin Putnam.

— Glass Painting: A Practical Guide with Project Book, Materials & Equipment. 1999. 24.95 (0-276-42388-7) RD Assn.

— Gluing & Clamping. (Workshop Companion Ser.). (Illus.). 128p. 1999. 19,95 (0-7621-0200-4, Pub. by RD Assn) Penguin Putnam.

— Grandparenting Today: Making the Most of Your Grandparenting Skills with Grandchildren of All Ages. LC 97-14157. 288p. 1997. 26.95 (0-89577-954-4, Pub. by RD Assn) Penguin Putnam.

— Great All-American Wooden Toy Book. LC 99-14910. (Woodworking Ser.). 212p. 1999. pap. 14.95 (0-7621-0172-5, Pub. by RD Assn) Penguin Putnam.

Reader's Digest Editors. Great American Homes. LC 97-20746. (Explore America Ser.). 1997. write for info. (0-89577-964-1) RD Assn.

— Great Chicken Dishes: Delicious Recipes from Light Salads to Hearty Stews. LC 99-45682. (Illus.). 1999. 30.00 (0-7621-0238-1, Pub. by RD Assn) Penguin Putnam.

— Greetings Cards: A Practical Guide with Project Book, Materials & Equipment 1999. 24.95 (0-276-42389-5) RD Assn.

Reader's Digest Editors. Growing Your Favorite Plants. LC 93-20907. (Successful Gardening Ser.). (Illus.). 176p. 1993. 18.98 (0-89577-577-8) RD Assn.

— Guide to Medical Cures & Treatments. LC 95-39005. (Illus.). 480p. 1996. 29.97 (0-89577-846-7, Pub. by RD Assn) Penguin Putnam.

— Guide to Places of the World: A Geographical Dictionary of Countries, Cities, Natural & Man-Made Wonders. LC 87-670034. (Illus.). 736p. 1987. 29.95 (0-276-39826-2) RD Assn.

— Guide to the Coast of Victoria, Tasmania & South Australia. (Illus.). 208p. (Orig.). 1987. pap. 16.95 (0-86438-010-0) RD Assn.

***Reader's Digest Editors.** Hands on Health. LC 98-50504. (Health & Healing the Natural Way Ser.). 1999. 19.95 (0-7621-0146-6, Pub. by RD Assn) Penguin Putnam.

An Asterisk (*) at the beginning of an entry indicates that the title is appearing for the first time.

— The Healing Power of Vitamins, Minerals & Herbs: The Better Way to Better Health. LC 98-28049. (Illus.). 416p. 1999. 29.97 (*0-7621-0132-6*, Pub. by RD Assn) Penguin Putnam.

— A Healthy Heart. LC 99-54731. (Health & Healing the Natural Way Ser.). 2000. write for info. (*0-7621-0263-2*) RD Assn.

Reader's Digest Editors. Hints & Tips to Make Life Easier. LC 97-19237. 1997. 29.95 (*0-89577-986-2*, Pub. by RD Assn) Penguin Putnam.

Reader's Digest Editors. Historic Places. LC 93-21872. (Explore America Ser.). (Illus.). 144p. 1993. 16.98 (*0-89577-506-9*, Pub. by RD Assn) Penguin Putnam.

Reader's Digest Editors. Home Made Best Made: Hundreds of Ways to Make All Kinds of Useful Things. LC 97-46894. (Illus.). 352p. 1998. 30.00 (*0-7621-0076-1*, Pub. by RD Assn) Penguin Putnam.

***Reader's Digest Editors.** Householder's Survival Manual. LC 98-49589. (Illus.). 384p. 1999. 29.95 (*0-7621-0135-0*, Pub. by RD Assn) Penguin Putnam.

Reader's Digest Editors. How in the World? A Fascinating Journey Through the World of Human Ingenuity. LC 90-30663. (Illus.). 448p. 1990. 32.00 (*0-89577-353-8*, Pub. by RD Assn) Penguin Putnam.

— The How-to Book of Healthy Cooking: Good Food That's Good For You. LC 95-5940. (Illus.). 352p. 1996. 30.00 (*0-89577-789-4*, Pub. by RD Assn) Penguin Putnam.

***Reader's Digest Editors.** How to Do Just about Anything on a Computer. LC 99-48314. 2000. write for info. (*0-7621-0279-9*) RD Assn.

Reader's Digest Editors. Illustrated Guide to Cabinetmaking. (Woodworking Ser.). 374p. 1999. 29.95 (*0-7621-0183-0*, Pub. by RD Assn) Penguin Putnam.

Reader's Digest Editors. The Indoor Garden. LC 94-35382. (Successful Gardening Ser.). (Illus.). 176p. 1995. 18.98 (*0-89577-684-7*) RD Assn.

Reader's Digest Editors. Intelligence in Animals. LC 97-16348. (The Earth, Its Wonders, Its Secrets Ser.). 1997. 19.95 (*0-89577-913-7*, Pub. by RD Assn) Penguin Putnam.

— Jigs, Fixtures & Shop Furniture. (Reader's Digest Woodworking Ser.). 124p. 1999. 19.95 (*0-7621-0156-3*, Pub. by RD Assn); pap. text 14.95 (*0-7621-0157-1*, Pub. by RD Assn) Penguin Putnam.

— Joining Wood. (Workshop Companion Ser.). 128p. 1999. 19.95 (*0-7621-0201-2*, Pub. by RD Assn) Penguin Putnam.

— Kitchen Secrets: Tips, Tricks, Techniques & Recipes. LC 97-14882. 1997. 30.00 (*0-7621-0008-7*, Pub. by RD Assn) Penguin Putnam.

— Know Your Rights: And How to Make Them Work for You. LC 95-9561. 512p. 1996. 35.00 (*0-89577-831-9*, Pub. by RD Assn) Penguin Putnam.

— Landscape Projects: Planning, Planting & Building for a More Beautiful Yard & Garden. LC 97-27810. (Family Handyman Ser.). 191p. 1998. 19.95 (*0-7621-0047-8*, Pub. by RD Assn) Penguin Putnam.

— Laughter, the Best Medicine: Jokes, Gags & Laugh Lines from America's Most Popular Magazine. LC 97-1844. 1997. pap. 9.95 (*0-89577-977-3*, Pub. by RD Assn) Penguin Putnam.

***Reader's Digest Editors.** Life Before Man. LC 98-48673. (The Earth, Its Wonders, Its Secrets Ser.). 1999. write for info. (*0-7621-0138-5*) RD Assn.

Reader's Digest Editors. Life in These United States: True Stories & Humorous Glimpses from America's Most Popular Magazine. LC 95-49496. (Illus.). 216p. 1996. pap. 9.95 (*0-89577-855-6*, Pub. by RD Assn) Penguin Putnam.

— Like Grandma Used to Make: A Treasury of Fondly Remembered Dishes. 1996. 30.00 (*0-89577-890-4*, Pub. by RD Assn) Penguin Putnam.

— The Living Forest. LC 99-10119. (Earth, Its Wonders, Its Secrets Ser.). 1998. write for info. (*0-7621-0137-7*) RD Assn.

— Magic & Medicine of Plants. LC 85-30101. (Illus.). 464p. 1986. 27.95 (*0-89577-221-3*, Pub. by RD Assn) Penguin Putnam.

— Main Street America. LC 98-5245. (Explore America Ser.). 1998. write for info. (*0-7621-0077-X*) RD Assn.

***Reader's Digest Editors.** Majestic Mountains. LC 99-22010. (Earth, Its Wonders, Its Secrets Ser.). 1999. write for info. (*0-7621-0136-9*) RD Assn.

Reader's Digest Editors. The Make It Yourself Gift Book: Gifts to Make at Home for All Your Family & Friends. LC 97-40456. 1998. 27.95 (*0-7621-0021-4*, Pub. by RD Assn) Penguin Putnam.

— Making Boxes & Chests. (Workshop Companion Ser.). 128p. 1999. pap. text 19.95 (*0-7621-0202-0*, Pub. by RD Assn) Penguin Putnam.

— Making Built-In Cabinets. (Workshop Companion (Reader's Digest) Ser.). (Illus.). 1999. 19.95 (*0-7621-0203-9*, Pub. by RD Assn) Penguin Putnam.

— Making Desks & Bookcases. (Workshop Companion Ser.). 128p. 1999. 19.95 (*0-7621-0204-7*, Pub. by RD Assn) Penguin Putnam.

— Making Flawless Cabinets & Built-Ins. (Woodworking Ser.). 128p. 1999. 19.95 (*0-7621-0186-5*, Pub. by RD Assn) Penguin Putnam.

— Making Joints. (Woodworking Ser.). 120p. 1999. 21.95 (*0-7621-0176-8*, Pub. by RD Assn) Penguin Putnam.

— Making Tables & Chairs. (Workshop Companion (Reader's Digest) Ser.). (Illus.). 1999. 19.95 (*0-7621-0207-1*, Pub. by RD Assn) Penguin Putnam.

***Reader's Digest Editors.** Managing Pain. LC 98-43587. (Health & Healing the Natural Way Ser.). 1999. write for info. (*0-7621-0144-X*) RD Assn.

Reader's Digest Editors. Martin Guitars. (Woodworking Ser.). 264p. 1999. 40.00 (*0-7621-0174-1*, Pub. by RD Assn) Penguin Putnam.

— The Most Scenic Drives in America. LC 95-47306. (Illus.). 400p. 1997. 30.00 (*0-89577-862-9*, Pub. by RD Assn) Penguin Putnam.

— Mysteries of the Rain Forest. LC 98-21012. (Earth, Its Wonders, Its Secrets Ser.). 1998. 19.98 (*0-7621-0110-5*) RD Assn.

Reader's Digest Editors. National Parks. LC 92-35785. (Explore America Ser.). (Illus.). 144p. 1993. 16.98 (*0-89577-447-X*, Pub. by RD Assn) Penguin Putnam.

— Natural Disasters. LC 97-22869. (Earth, Its Wonders, Its Secrets Ser.). 1997. 19.95 (*0-89577-915-3*, Pub. by RD Assn) Penguin Putnam.

Reader's Digest Editors. Natural Wonders. LC 96-38845. (Explore America Ser.). 1997. write for info. (*0-89577-950-1*) RD Assn.

— Never Say Good-Bye: An Anthology by New Writers in Prison. (New Writers' Voices Ser.). 64p. (Orig.). 1993. pap. text 3.50 (*1-56853-005-6*, Signal Hill) New Readers.

— New Baby's Bible. (First Bible Collection). (Illus.). 8p. (J). (ps-3). 1998. text 10.99 (*1-57584-083-9*, Pub. by Rdrs Digest) Random.

Reader's Digest Editors. The New Complete Do-It-Yourself Manual. LC 90-46830. (Reader's Digest Ser.). (Illus.). 528p. 1991. 30.00 (*0-89577-378-3*, Pub. by RD Assn) Penguin Putnam.

Reader's Digest Editors. New Fix-It-Yourself Manual: How to Repair, Clean & Maintain Anything & Everything in & Around Your Home. LC 96-15189. 448p. 1996. 35.00 (*0-89577-871-8*, Pub. by RD Assn) Penguin Putnam.

— Night, Night, God Bless! large type ed. (First Blessings Flap Bks.: Vol. 1). (Illus.). 18p. (J). (gr. k-3). 1998. bds. 3.99 (*1-57584-079-0*, Pub. by Rdrs Digest) Random.

— Noah's Ark. (Little Bible Playbks.: Vol. 1). (Illus.). 18p. (J). (gr. k-3). 1998. bds. 4.99 (*1-57584-260-2*, Pub. by Rdrs Digest) Random.

***Reader's Digest Editors.** North American Wildlife: An Illustrated Guide to 2,000 Plants & Animals. 1998. 28.95 (*0-7621-0020-6*, Pub. by RD Assn) Penguin Putnam.

Reader's Digest Editors. Off the Beaten Path: A Guide to More Than 1,000 Scenic & Interesting Places Still Uncrowded & Inviting. LC 86-11372. (Illus.). 384p. 1987. 28.00 (*0-89577-253-1*, Pub. by RD Assn) Penguin Putnam.

— The Easy Way to Play. LC 97-701256. 224p. 1996. 30.00 (*0-89577-833-5*, Pub. by RD Assn) Penguin Putnam.

— 1001 Hints & Tips for Your Garden. LC 96-179. (Illus.). 416p. 1996. 30.00 (*0-89577-860-2*, Pub. by RD Assn) Penguin Putnam.

— Our Family History: Record Book, Photograph Album & Family Tree. 1999. 24.95 (*0-7621-0232-2*, Readers Digest) Login Bros.

— Our Glorious Century. LC 94-14328. (Illus.). 512p. 1994. 40.00 (*0-89577-616-2*, Pub. by RD Assn) Penguin Putnam.

— Our Living History. LC 96-30610. (Explore America Ser.). 1996. write for info. (*0-89577-945-5*) RD Assn.

— Our National Parks. rev. ed. (Illus.). 352p. 1997. 30.00 (*0-89577-941-2*, Pub. by RD Assn) Penguin Putnam.

— Outdoor Structures. (Woodworking Ser.). 124p. 1999. pap. 14.95 (*0-7621-0158-X*, Pub. by RD Assn) Penguin Putnam.

***Reader's Digest Editors.** Perfect Poultry. LC 99-44148. (Great Healthy Cooking Ser.). (Illus.). 1999. write for info. (*0-7621-0275-6*) RD Assn.

Reader's Digest Editors. The Pioneers: Novels of the American Frontier. LC 85-23236. (Illus.). 640p. 1988. 19.95 (*0-89577-229-9*) RD Assn.

— Places of Folklore & Legend. LC 96-40045. (Explore America Ser.). 1997. write for info. (*0-89577-905-6*) RD Assn.

— Plant Partners. LC 94-13509. (Successful Gardening Ser.). (Illus.). 176p. 1994. 18.98 (*0-89577-614-6*) RD Assn.

— Plant Partners. (Successful Gardening Ser.). (Illus.). 176p. 1998. pap. text 19.95 (*0-89577-961-7*, Pub. by RD Assn) Penguin Putnam.

— The Practical Gardener. LC 93-19529. (Successful Gardening Ser.). (Illus.). 176p. 1993. 18.98 (*0-89577-539-5*) RD Assn.

— Problem Solver. LC 99-27221. (Reader's Digest Woodworking Ser.). 312p. 1999. 29.95 (*0-7621-0225-X*, Pub. by RD Assn) Penguin Putnam.

— Projects for the Home Craftsman. (Woodworking Ser.). 264p. 1999. pap. 14.95 (*0-7621-0196-2*, Pub. by RD Assn) Penguin Putnam.

***Reader's Digest Editors.** Reader's Digest Beginner's Guide to Home Computing: Everything You Need to Know to Set Up & Start. LC 98-41597. (Reader's Digest Learn-As-You-Go Guide Ser.). 1998. 24.93 (*0-7621-0102-4*, Pub. by RD Assn) Penguin Putnam.

Reader's Digest Editors. The Reader's Digest Children's Atlas of World History. LC 93-4320. (Illus.). 128p. (J). (gr. 4-7). 1993. 20.00 (*0-89577-526-3*) RD Assn.

— The Reader's Digest Children's Songbook. LC 86-752834. (Illus.). 252p. (J). (ps up). 1985. 29.95 (*0-89577-214-0*, Pub. by RD Assn) Penguin Putnam.

— Reader's Digest Complete Guide to Sewing: Step-by-Step Techniques for Making Clothes & Home Furnishings. rev. ed. LC 97-175997. (Illus.). 432p. 1995. 30.00 (*0-88850-247-8*, Pub. by RD Assn) Penguin Putnam.

— Reader's Digest Get Online! The Beginner's Guide to the Internet, E-mail & Faxing. LC 99-32240. 1999. pap. text 24.95 (*0-7621-0259-4*, Readers Digest) Login Bros.

— Reader's Digest Guide to Creative Gardening. LC 87-128856. (Illus.). 384p. 1987. 32.95 (*0-276-35223-8*) RD Assn.

— Reader's Digest Guide to Places of the World: A Geographical Dictionary. rev. ed. 732p. 1995. 39.95 (*1-874912-31-9*, Pub. by RD Assn) Penguin Putnam.

— Reader's Digest Home Decorating. LC 98-34016. (Illus.). 192p. 1999. 24.95 (*0-7621-0105-9*, Pub. by RD Assn) Penguin Putnam.

— Reader's Digest Home Do-It-Yourself Projects: Furniture to Build Home Improvements to Make. LC 96-15812. (Illus.). 368p. 1996. pap. 19.95 (*0-89577-893-9*, Pub. by RD Assn) Penguin Putnam.

— Reader's Digest Ideas for Your Garden. LC 96-34354. 1996. 30.00 (*0-89577-919-6*, Pub. by RD Assn) Penguin Putnam.

— Reader's Digest Illustrated Atlas of the World. 3rd rev. ed. (Illus.). 1997. 24.00 (*0-89577-937-4*, Pub. by RD Assn) Penguin Putnam.

— Reader's Digest Illustrated Encyclopedic Dictionary, 2 vols., Set. LC 87-9650. (Illus.). 1920p. 1987. 59.96 (*0-89577-269-8*) RD Assn.

— Readers Digest Illustrated Great World Atlas. 288p. 1997. 40.00 (*0-89577-988-9*, Pub. by RD Assn) Penguin Putnam.

— The Reader's Digest Merry Christmas Songbook. LC 81-51285. (Illus.). 252p. 1981. 29.95 (*0-89577-105-5*, Pub. by RD Assn) Penguin Putnam.

— Readers Digest Mysteries of the Bible: The Unanswered Questions of the Scriptures. 1997. pap. text 18.95 (*0-89577-938-2*, Pub. by RD Assn) Penguin Putnam.

— Reader's Digest North American Wildlife: Birds. LC 97-32723. 1998. 16.95 (*0-7621-0036-2*, Pub. by RD Assn) Penguin Putnam.

— Reader's Digest North American Wildlife: Mammals, Reptiles & Amphibians. LC 97-32724. (Illus.). 204p. 1998. pap. 16.95 (*0-7621-0035-4*, Pub. by RD Assn) Penguin Putnam.

— Reader's Digest North American Wildlife: Trees & Nonflowering Plants. LC 97-32725. 276p. 1998. 16.95 (*0-7621-0037-0*, Pub. by RD Assn) Penguin Putnam.

— Reader's Digest North American Wildlife: Wildflowers. LC 97-32727. 480p. 1998. 24.95 (*0-7621-0034-6*, Pub. by RD Assn) Penguin Putnam.

— Reader's Digest Oxford Complete Wordfinder. LC 96-12309. 1996. write for info. (*0-89577-894-7*) RD Assn.

— Reader's Digest Practical Guide to Home Landscaping: Planning, Planting & Building. 1996. 27.95 (*0-89577-896-3*, Pub. by RD Assn) Penguin Putnam.

— Reader's Digest Quotable Quotes: Wit & Wisdom for All Occasions from America's Most Popular Magazine. LC 96-3456. 1997. 9.95 (*0-89577-925-0*, Pub. by RD Assn) Penguin Putnam.

— The Reader's Digest Word Power Quiz Book: 1,000 Word Challenges from America's Most Popular Magazine. LC 96-2161. 1996. write for info. (*0-89577-901-3*) RD Assn.

— Remembering Yesterday's Hits. (Illus.). 252p. 1986. spiral bd. 29.95 (*0-89577-249-3*, Pub. by RD Assn) Penguin Putnam.

— Reverse Dictionary. (Illus.). 1997. pap. text 16.95 (*0-89577-951-X*, Pub. by RD Assn) Penguin Putnam.

— Right Technique. (Woodworking Ser.). 312p. 1999. 27.95 (*0-7621-0228-4*, Pub. by RD Assn) Penguin Putnam.

— Rob's Shiny Dump Truck, 1. 1999. 5.99 (*1-57584-314-5*, Readers Digest) Login Bros.

— Routing & Shaping. (Workshop Companion Ser.). 128p. 1999. pap. text 19.95 (*0-7621-0209-8*, Pub. by RD Assn) Penguin Putnam.

— Safe, Secure & Streetwise: The/Essential Guide to Protecting Yourself, Your Home & Your Family from Crime. LC 98-139991. 280 p. 1997. write for info. (*1-874912-85-8*) Rdrs Digest.

— Sanding & Planing. (Workshop Companion Ser.). 128p. 1999. 19.95 (*0-7621-0210-1*, Pub. by RD Assn) Penguin Putnam.

— Santa. (J). 1995. 4.99 (*0-89577-813-0*) RD Assn.

— Scenic Highways. LC 97-14290. (Explore America Ser.). 1997. write for info. (*0-89577-906-4*) RD Assn.

— The Secret Life of Animals. LC 98-7852. (Earth, Its Wonders, Its Secrets Ser.). 1998. write for info. (*0-7621-0112-1*) RD Assn.

***Reader's Digest Editors.** 70 Wonders of the Modern World. LC 99-49604. (Eventful 20th Century Ser.). 2000. 19.95 (*0-7621-0271-3*, Pub. by RD Assn) Penguin Putnam.

Reader's Digest Editors. Sharks. LC 97-46928. (Reader's Digest Explores Ser.). (Illus.). 160p. 1998. 24.95 (*0-7621-0041-9*, Pub. by RD Assn) Penguin Putnam.

— Sharks: Silent Hunters of the Deep. LC 87-670009. (Illus.). 208p. 1987. 19.95 (*0-86438-014-3*) RD Assn.

— Sharpening. (Workshop Companion Ser.). 128p. 1999. 19.95 (*0-7621-0211-X*, Pub. by RD Assn) Penguin Putnam.

— Shop Tips. (Woodworking Ser.). 320p. 1999. pap. 14.95 (*0-7621-0189-X*, Pub. by RD Assn) Penguin Putnam.

— Snowman. (J). 1995. 4.99 (*0-89577-814-9*) RD Assn.

— Southern Africa Spectacular World of Wildlife. (Illus.). 272p. 1994. 35.00 (*1-874912-05-X*, Pub. by RD Assn) Penguin Putnam.

— Speaking to One Another: An Anthology by New Writers. (New Writers' Voices Ser.). 64p. 1993. pap. text 3.15 (*1-56853-007-2*, Signal Hill) New Readers.

— The Story of Mankind. LC 98-18899. (Earth, Its Wonders, Its Secrets Ser.). 1998. write for info. (*0-7621-0111-3*) RD Assn.

— Strange Stories, Amazing Facts of America's Past. LC 88-11515. (Illus.). 416p. 1989. 32.95 (*0-89577-307-4*, Pub. by RD Assn) Penguin Putnam.

— Successful Gardening: A-Z of Deciduous Trees & Shrubs. (Illus.). 176p. 1996. pap. 24.95 (*0-89577-870-X*, Pub. by RD Assn) Penguin Putnam.

— Successful Gardening: A-Z of Evergreen Trees & Shrubs. (Successful Gardening Ser.). (Illus.). 176p. 1998. pap. 19.95 (*0-7621-0046-X*, Pub. by RD Assn) Penguin Putnam.

— Successful Gardening: Caring for Your Plants. (Successful Gardening Ser.). (Illus.). 176p. 1998. pap. 19.95 (*0-7621-0045-1*, Pub. by RD Assn) Penguin Putnam.

— Successful Gardening: The Practical Gardener, Vol. 1. (Illus.). 176p. 1996. pap. 24.95 (*0-89577-869-6*, Pub. by RD Assn) Penguin Putnam.

— Successful Gardening Journal: A Seasonal Diary for Your Garden. 144p. 1996. 14.95 (*0-89577-892-0*, Pub. by RD Assn) Penguin Putnam.

***Reader's Digest Editors.** Teaching Your Router New Tricks. (Woodworking Ser.). 128p. 1999. 19.95 (*0-7621-0188-1*, Pub. by RD Assn) Penguin Putnam.

Reader's Digest Editors. Through Indian Eyes: Our Nations Past as Experienced by Native Americans. LC 95-34273. (Illus.). 400p. 1996. 40.00 (*0-89577-819-X*, Pub. by RD Assn) Penguin Putnam.

— Understanding Wood Finishing. LC 99-19181. (Woodworking Ser.). 320p. 1999. pap. 16.95 (*0-7621-0191-1*, Pub. by RD Assn) Penguin Putnam.

— Using Hand Tools. (Workshop Companion Ser.). 128p. 1999. 19.95 (*0-7621-0212-8*, Pub. by RD Assn) Penguin Putnam.

— Using the Bandsaw. (Workshop Companion Ser.). 128p. 1999. 19.95 (*0-7621-0214-4*, Pub. by RD Assn); pap. 12.95 (*0-7621-0215-2*, Pub. by RD Assn) Penguin Putnam.

— Using the Drill Press. (Workshop Companion Ser.). 128p. 1999. 19.95 (*0-7621-0217-9*, Pub. by RD Assn) Penguin Putnam.

— Using the Scroll Saw. (Workshop Companion Ser.). 128p. 1999. 19.95 (*0-7621-0218-7*, Pub. by RD Assn) Penguin Putnam.

— Using the Table Saw. (Workshop Companion Ser.). 128p. 1999. 19.95 (*0-7621-0219-5*, Pub. by RD Assn); pap. 12.95 (*0-7621-0220-9*, Pub. by RD Assn) Penguin Putnam.

— Visual Building & Remodeling. LC 99-25441. (Reader's Digest Woodworking Ser.). (Illus.). 1999. pap. text 19.95 (*0-7621-0194-6*, Pub. by RD Assn) Penguin Putnam.

— Weather. LC 97-3324. (Reader's Digest Explores Ser.). 160p. 1997. 24.95 (*0-89577-975-7*, Pub. by RD Assn) Penguin Putnam.

— The Weather & Its Secrets. LC 97-52721. 1998. write for info. (*0-7621-0084-2*) RD Assn.

— Weekend Projects. (Woodworking Ser.). (Illus.). 124p. 1999. pap. 14.95 (*0-7621-0159-8*, Pub. by RD Assn) Penguin Putnam.

— Weekend Projects, Plus: Complete Step-by-Step Instructions for 40 Woodworking Projects You Can Build in a Weekend. (Woodworking Ser.). 278p. 1999. 29.95 (*0-7621-0177-6*, Pub. by RD Assn) Penguin Putnam.

— Weekend Woodworker: 101 Easy to Build Projects. (Woodworking Ser.). 294p. 1999. pap. 15.95 (*0-7621-0195-4*, Pub. by RD Assn) Penguin Putnam.

— Whales, Dolphins & Porpoises. LC 97-3331. (Reader's Digest Explores Ser.). 1997. 24.95 (*0-89577-976-5*, Pub. by RD Assn) Penguin Putnam.

— The Whale's Tale. (Little Bible Playbks.: Vol. 2). (Illus.). 18p. (J). (gr. k-3). 1998. bds. 4.99 (*1-57584-261-0*, Pub. by Rdrs Digest) Random.

— What to Do in an Emergency: Action Guide. LC 88-18537. (Illus.). 354p. 1988. 24.95 (*0-89577-319-8*, Pub. by RD Assn) Penguin Putnam.

— Where Land & Sea Meet. LC 98-25946. (Earth, Its Wonders, Its Secrets Ser.). 1998. write for info. (*0-7621-0114-8*) RD Assn.

— Who's Who in the Bible: An Illustrated Biographical Dictionary. LC 94-17591. (Illus.). 480p. 1994. 32.00 (*0-89577-618-9*, Pub. by RD Assn) Penguin Putnam.

— Wild Kingdoms. LC 96-1917. (Explore America Ser.). 1996. write for info. (*0-89577-902-1*) RD Assn.

— Wood & Woodworking Materials. (Workshop Companion (Reader's Digest) Ser.). (Illus.). 1999. 19.95 (*0-7621-0221-7*, Pub. by RD Assn) Penguin Putnam.

— The Woodworkers Visual Handbook. (Reader's Digest Woodworking Ser.). 448p. 1999. 29.95 (*0-7621-0226-8*, Pub. by RD Assn) Penguin Putnam.

— Woodworking with the Router. LC 99-14911. (Woodworking Ser.). 344p. 1999. pap. 17.95 (*0-7621-0227-6*, Pub. by RD Assn) Penguin Putnam.

— The Word Power Quiz Book: Over 1,000 Word Challenges from America's Most Popular Magazine. LC 95-21922. (Illus.). 216p. 1995. pap. 9.95 (*0-89577-822-X*, Pub. by RD Assn) Penguin Putnam.

— The World at Arms: The Reader's Digest Illustrated History of World War II. (Illus.). 512p. 1989. 29.95 (*0-89577-333-3*, Pub. by RD Assn) Penguin Putnam.

— The World's Last Mysteries. LC 77-87127. (Illus.). 320p. 1978. 23.97 (*0-89577-044-X*) RD Assn.

Reader's Digest Editors, ed. A-Z of Rock Garden & Water Plants. (Successful Gardening Ser.). 1995. write for info. (*0-89577-836-X*) RD Assn.

— The American Story. LC 96-13262. 1996. write for info. (*0-89577-891-2*) RD Assn.

— Atlas of America: Our Nation in Maps, Facts & Pictures. 256p. 1998. 40.00 (*0-7621-0072-9*, Pub. by RD Assn) Penguin Putnam.

— Best Loved Dog Stories. LC 98-44150. (Illus.). 285p. 1998. 19.95 (*0-7621-0089-3*, Pub. by RD Assn) Penguin Putnam.

— Children's Atlas of the Universe. LC 99-36177. (Illus.). 128p. (J). (gr. 3-8). 2000. 24.99 (*1-57584-373-0*, Pub. by Rdrs Digest) S&S Trade.

***Reader's Digest Editors, ed.** Energize Your Life. LC 99-39192. 1999. write for info. (*0-7621-0262-4*) RD Assn.

— Fruit Dishes & Desserts. LC 99-33599. 1999. write for info. (*0-7621-0274-8*) RD Assn.

R

Reader's Digest Editors, ed. Great American Journeys. LC 95-24913. (Explore America Ser.). (Illus.). 144p. 1996. 16.98 (*0-89577-847-5*, Pub. by RD Assn) Penguin Putnam.

***Reader's Digest Editors, ed.** Great Mysteries of the 20th Century. LC 99-16600. (Illus.). 1999. 19.95 (*0-7621-0267-5*, Pub. by RD Assn) Penguin Putnam.

Reader's Digest Editors, ed. Home Storage Projects: A Room-by-Room Guide to Practical Storage Solutions. LC 96-12462. (Illus.). 1997. 19.95 (*0-89577-889-0*, Pub. by RD Assn) Penguin Putnam.

***Reader's Digest Editors, ed.** Inventions That Changed the World. LC 99-38516. 1999. 19.95 (*0-7621-0269-1*, Pub. by RD Assn) Penguin Putnam.

Reader's Digest Editors, ed. Just off the Interstate. LC 96-17469. (Explore America Ser.). 1996. 19.95 (*0-89577-895-5*, Pub. by RD Assn) Penguin Putnam.

— Mind Mood Foods. LC 98-44148. 1998. 24.95 (*0-7621-0104-0*) Login Bros.

— Natural Wonders. LC 96-38845. (Explore America Ser.). 1997. write for info. (*0-89577-904-8*) RD Assn.

***Reader's Digest Editors, ed.** Nature's Medicine Chest. LC 99-39191. 1999. write for info. (*0-7621-0261-6*) RD Assn.

Reader's Digest Editors, ed. The Only Kid's Party Book You'll Ever Need: Hundreds of Great Ideas Plus a Unique Mix-&-Match Plan. 1998. 24.95 (*0-7621-0090-7*, Pub. by RD Assn) Penguin Putnam.

— Our Living History. LC 96-30610. (Explore America Ser.). 1996. write for info. (*0-89577-903-X*) RD Assn.

— Our Native American Heritage. LC 96-907. (Explore America Ser.). 1996. write for info. (*0-89577-867-X*) RD Assn.

***Reader's Digest Editors, ed.** The Way We Lived. LC 99-16601. 1999. 19.95 (*0-7621-0258-6*, Pub. by RD Assn) Penguin Putnam.

— The World at War, 1939-45. LC 99-16602. 1999. 19.95 (*0-7621-0268-3*, Pub. by RD Assn) Penguin Putnam.

***Reader's Digest Editors.** New Illustrated Guide to Gardening. rev. ed. LC 99-49792. 544p. 2000. 35.00 (*0-7621-0276-4*, Pub. by RD Assn) Penguin Putnam.

Reader's Digest Editors & Attenborough, David. Selected from "Life on Earth" (Our World Ser.). (Illus.). 64p. (Orig.). 1993. pap. text 3.95 (*1-56853-002-1*, Signal Hill) New Readers.

Reader's Digest Editors & Binney, Ruth, eds. Origins of Everyday Things. LC 98-55992. 320p. 1999. 29.95 (*0-276-42320-8*); 29.95 (*0-7621-0141-5*, Pub. by RD Assn) Penguin Putnam.

Reader's Digest Editors & Cobb, Nancy. Letter Writer Starter Set. rev. ed. (Illus.). 64p. (J). (gr. 2-6). 1999. pap. text 8.99 (*1-57584-326-9*, Pub. by Rdrs Digest) Random.

Reader's Digest Editors & Eaglemoss Publications Ltd. Staff. Learn to Draw & Paint. LC 96-52461. 288p. 1997. 29.95 (*0-89577-956-0*, Pub. by RD Assn) Penguin Putnam.

Reader's Digest Editors & Gould, David, eds. How Was It Done? The Story of Human Ingenuity Through the Ages. LC 98-10374. (Illus.). 448p. 1998. 29.95 (*0-7621-0088-5*, Pub. by RD Assn) Penguin Putnam.

Reader's Digest Editors & Heyerdahl, Thor. Selected from "Kon-Tiki" (Our World Ser.). (Illus.). 64p. (Orig.). 1993. pap. text 3.95 (*1-56853-001-3*, Signal Hill) New Readers.

Reader's Digest Editors & Holder, Andre. Fatal Beauty. (New Writers' Voices Ser.). (Illus.). 64p. (Orig.). 1993. pap. text 3.50 (*1-56853-003-X*, Signal Hill) New Readers.

Reader's Digest Editors & Hood, Susan. Match Shapes with Me. (Fisher Price Spin & Learn Bks.). (Illus.). 12p. (J). (gr. k-3). 1999. bds. 6.99 (*1-57584-324-2*, Pub. by Rdrs Digest) Random.

***Reader's Digest Editors & Royston, Angela.** Space. (On the Spot). 16p. (J). (gr. 4-6). 1999. 7.99 (*1-57584-340-4*) Rdrs Digest.

Reader's Digest Editors & Sagan, Carl. Selected from Cosmos. (Our World Ser.). (Illus.). 64p. (Orig.). 1993. pap. text 3.95 (*1-56853-000-5*, Signal Hill) New Readers.

Reader's Digest Editors, et al. Bronco Billy & the Runaway Coach. (Playmobil Play Stables Ser.: Vol. 1). (Illus.). 14p. (J). (gr. k-3). 1998. bds. 14.99 (*1-57584-240-8*, Pub. by Rdrs Digest) Random.

— A Gothic Treasure Trove. LC 85-25734. (Illus.). 640p. 1987. 18.99 (*0-89577-228-0*) RD Assn.

— Snapshots. (New Writers' Voices Ser.). (Illus.). 64p. (Orig.). 1993. pap. text 3.50 (*1-56853-004-8*, Signal Hill) New Readers.

Reader's Digest Editors, jt. auth. see Balducci, Rita.

Reader's Digest Editors, jt. auth. see Goldsack, Gaby.

Reader's Digest Editors, jt. auth. see Hood, Susan.

Reader's Digest Editors, jt. auth. see Packard, Mary.

Reader's Digest Editors, jt. auth. see Singer, Muff.

Reader's Digest Editors, jt. auth. see Smath, Jerry.

Reader's Digest Editors, jt. auth. see Wait, Marianne.

Reader's Digest Editors, ed. see Bright, Michael.

Reader's Digest Editors, ed. see Flemming, Paul.

Reader's Digest Editors, ed. see Hood, Susan.

Reader's Digest Editors, ed. see Maidment, Stella.

Reader's Digest Editors, ed. see Man, John.

Reader's Digest Editors, ed. see Neville, Peter, et al.

Reader's Digest Editors, ed. see Paine, Melanie.

Reader's Digest Editors, ed. see Roddie, Shen & Healey, Tim.

Reader's Digest Editors, ed. see Welford, Heather.

Reader's Digest Editors, ed. see Wise, Debra.

Readett, Alan G., jt. ed. see Herbst, Robert.

Readey, H. & Readey, W. Mathematical Concepts in Nursing: A Workbook. 1980. pap. text 17.56 (*0-201-06166-X*, Health Sci) Addison-Wesley.

Readey, W., jt. auth. see Readey, H.

Readhead, Lloyd. Fantastic Book of Gymnastics. LC 97-10591. (Fantastic Book of . . . Ser.). (Illus.). 32p. (J). (gr. 2-6). 1997. 10.95 (*0-7613-0637-4*, Copper Beech Bks) Millbrook Pr.

— Fantastic Book of Gymnastics. LC 97-10591. (Fantastic Book of...Ser.). (Illus.). 32p. (J). (gr. 2-6). 1997. lib. bdg. 22.40 (*0-7613-0622-6*, Copper Beech Bks) Millbrook Pr.

— Gymnastics. LC 95-39275. (Olympic Library). (Illus.). (J). 1998. 18.50 (*1-57572-036-1*) Heinemann Lib.

— Men's Gymnastics Coaching Manual. (Illus.). 208p. 1997. pap. 29.95 (*1-86126-076-8*, Pub. by Cro1wood) Trafalgar.

Readhead, Paul A., ed. Vacuum Science & Technology: Pioneers of the 20th Century. LC 93-28714. (History of Vacuum Science & Technology Ser.: Vol. 2). (Illus.). 300p. 1993. pap. text 44.95 (*1-56396-248-9*, AIP Pr) Spr-Verlag.

Readicher-Henderson, E., jt. auth. see Readicher-Henderson, L.

Readicher-Henderson, L. & Readicher-Henderson, E. Coastal Alaska & the Inside Passage. 3rd ed. (Adventure Guide Ser.). (Illus.). 260p. 1999. pap. 15.95 (*1-55650-859-X*) Hunter NJ.

Readicker-Henderson, Ed. Alaska Highway. 2nd ed. (Adventure Guide). 390p. 1998. pap. text 15.95 (*1-55650-824-7*) Hunter NJ.

— The Traveler's Guide to Japanese Pilgrimages. (Illus.). 240p. (Orig.). 1994. pap. 14.95 (*0-8348-0291-0*) Weatherhill.

Reading, et al. Microsoft Office 97 Professional Edition: A Second Course. 10th ed. (Illustrated Ser.). (Illus.). 544p. (C). 1997. pap. 50.95 (*0-7600-5135-6*) Course Tech.

Reading, Alison J., et al. Humid Tropical Environments. LC 94-27803. (Natural Environment Ser.). 384p. 1995. 88.95 (*0-631-17287-4*) Blackwell Pubs.

Reading, Anna, jt. auth. see Stokes, Jane C.

Reading, Ben, jt. auth. see McReynolds, Roger.

Reading, Brian. The Fourth Reich. 268p. 1997. 40.00 (*0-297-81453-2*, Pub. by Weidenfeld & Nicolson) Trafalgar.

— In Place of Growth: A Critique of Labour's Economic Strategy. LC 77-528808. (Publications Ser.: No. 452). 48p. 1969. pap. write for info. (*0-85070-452-9*) Conserv Poli Ctr.

— Japan: The Coming Collapse. LC 92-54421. (Illus.). 320p. 1992. reprint ed. 25.00 (*0-88730-607-1*, HarpBusn) HarpInfo.

Reading Catalog of the Library of the American Mus. Research Catalog of the Library of the American Museum of Natural History: Classed Catalog. 1978. 1320.00 (*0-8161-0238-4*, G K Hall & Co) Mac Lib Ref.

Reading, Clive. Strategic Business Planning: An Action Program for Forward-Looking Businesses. 400p. 1993. 29.95 (*0-89397-391-2*) Nichols Pub.

Reading, Gerald R. The South Sea Bubble. LC 73-109972. (Illus.). 176p. 1978. reprint ed. lib. bdg. 55.00 (*0-8371-4480-9*, RESO, Greenwood Pr) Greenwood.

Reading, Joseph H. A Voyage along the Western Coast or Newest Africa, a Description of Newest Africa: or the Africa of Today & the Immediate Future. LC 72-5528. (Black Heritage Library Collection). 1977. reprint ed. 25.95 (*0-8369-9147-8*) Ayer.

Reading Laboratory Staff. Double Your Reading Speed. 1985. mass mkt. 5.99 (*0-449-30022-6*) Fawcett.

— Double Your Reading Speed. 1986. mass mkt. 4.99 (*0-449-44250-0*, Prem) Fawcett.

Reading, Lee & O'Reilly, Gretchen. Wilton Art Programs Student Workbook, 30 bks. 3rd ed. (Illus.). 24p. (J). (gr. 1-5). 1989. reprint ed. wbk. ed. 60.00 (*0-924041-13-7*); reprint ed. wbk. ed. 180.00 (*0-924041-14-5*) Reading & OReilly.

Reading, M. K. Bowne: William Bowne of Yorkshire, England & His Descendants. (Illus.). 47p. 1994. reprint ed. pap. 10.00 (*0-8328-4199-4*) Higginson Bk Co.

Reading, Peter. Collected Poems: Poems 1970-1984. 318p. 1996. 45.00 (*1-85224-320-1*, Pub. by Bloodaxe Bks) Dufour.

— Collected Poems: Poems 1970-1984, I. 318p. 1996. pap. 23.00 (*1-85224-321-X*, Pub. by Bloodaxe Bks) Dufour.

— Collected Poems Vol. 2: Poems 1985-1996. LC 96-101604. 318p. 1997. 42.00 (*1-85224-356-2*, Pub. by Bloodaxe Bks); pap. 21.00 (*1-85224-357-0*, Pub. by Bloodaxe Bks) Dufour.

— Last Poems. 45p. 1995. 15.95 (*0-7011-6100-0*, Pub. by Chatto & Windus) Trafalgar.

***Reading, Peter.** Marfan. 2000. pap. 16.95 (*1-85224-516-6*, Pub. by Bloodaxe Bks) Dufour.

— Ob. 64p. 1999. pap. (*1-85224-490-9*, Pub. by Bloodaxe Bks) Dufour.

Reading, Peter. Ukulele Music - Perduta Gente. 112p. 1994. 26.95 (*0-8101-5030-1*, TriQuart); pap. 11.95 (*0-8101-5005-0*, TriQuart) Northwestern U Pr.

— Work in Regress. LC 98-128333. 62p. 1998. pap. 15.95 (*1-85224-421-6*, Pub. by Bloodaxe Bks) Dufour.

***Reading Public Library Staff.** Reuben Nakian: Centennial Retrospective. 1998. write for info. (*0-9654594-2-X*) Reading Pub Mus.

Reading Research Dept. Staff. Atlantis. (Library: Vol. 22). 480p. 1987. lib. bdg. 24.95 (*0-87604-204-3*, 1122) ARE Pr.

— Egypt Pt. 1: The Story of RaTa. (Library: Vol. 23). 340p. 1989. lib. bdg. 24.95 (*0-87604-220-5*, 1123) ARE Pr.

— Egypt Pt. 2: The Teachings & the Temples. (Library Ser.: Vol. 24). 362p. 1989. lib. bdg. 24.95 (*0-87604-228-0*, 1124) ARE Pr.

***Reading, Richard P. & Miller, Brian.** Endangered Animals: A Reference Guide to Conflicting Issues. LC 99-49149. 416p. 2000. 59.95 (*0-313-30816-0*, Greenwood Pr) Greenwood.

Reading, Susan. Desert Plants. (Plant Life Ser.). 64p. (YA). 1990. 15.95 (*0-8160-2421-9*) Facts on File.

***Reading, Susan.** Desert Plants. (Illus.). 62p. (YA). (gr. 6-12). 1999. reprint ed. text 16.00 (*0-7881-6344-2*) DIANE Pub.

Readings, Bill. Introducing Lyotard: Art & Politics. (Critics of the Twentieth Century Ser.). 224p. (C). 1991. pap. 22.99 (*0-415-05536-9*, A4854) Routledge.

— The University in Ruins. 256p. 1996. 33.50 (*0-674-92952-7*) HUP.

— The University in Ruins. 256p. 1997. reprint ed. 15.95 (*0-674-92953-5*) HUP.

Readings, Bill, jt. ed. see Melville, Stephen.

Readings, Bill, tr. see Lyotard, Jean-Francois.

Readings Research Dept. Staff. Astrology, Pt. 1, Vol. 18. (Library). 611p. 1985. lib. bdg. 24.95 (*0-87604-159-4*, 1118) ARE Pr.

— Mind, Vol. 20. (Library). 346p. 1986. lib. bdg. 22.95 (*0-87604-180-2*, 1120) ARE Pr.

Readings, William & Schaber, Bennet, eds. Postmodernism Across the Ages. 320p. 1993. text 39.95 (*0-8156-2577-4*); pap. text 19.95 (*0-8156-2581-2*) Syracuse U Pr.

Readio, Skip. How to Do Electrical Systems. (Illus.). 125p. 1993. pap. 22.95 (*1-884089-02-X*) CarTech.

Readman, jt. auth. see Mayers.

Readman, Alison, jt. auth. see McCallum, R. B.

Readman, Jo. Muck & Magic: Start Your Own Natural Garden with Colorful, Simple Projects. (Illus.). 48p. (J). (gr. 4-7). 1994. pap. 12.95 (*0-85532-757-X*, 757-X, Pub. by Srch Pr) A Schwartz & Co.

Readman, Mark C. Flexible Joint Robots. 160p. 1994. boxed set 78.95 (*0-8493-2601-X*, 2601) CRC Pr.

Readshaw, Grahame. Keep It Simple System for Water Colour Painting. (C). 1990. 90.00 (*0-86439-144-7*, Pub. by Boolarong Pubns) St Mut.

Readshaw, Grahame R., jt. auth. see Wood, R.

Readus, James H. The Big Hit. 224p. (Orig.). 1983. mass mkt. 2.25 (*0-87067-218-5*, BH218) Holloway.

— Death Merchants. 256p. 1992. mass mkt. 3.95 (*0-87067-323-8*, BH323) Holloway.

Readwell. English - Assamese Dictionary. 1992. reprint ed. 19.95 (*0-8288-8478-1*) Fr & Eur.

Ready, Anna. Mississippi. LC 92-31056. (Hello U. S. A. Ser.). (Illus.). 72p. (J). (gr. 3-6). 1993. lib. bdg. 19.93 (*0-8225-2743-X*, Lerner Publctns) Lerner Pub.

***Ready, Anna.** Mississippi. (Hello U. S. A. Ser.). (Illus.). 72p. (J). (gr. 3-6). 2000. pap. 5.95 (*0-8225-9788-8*, First Ave Edns) Lerner Pub.

Ready, Dee. Bibliotecarios. LC 98-21425. 1999. 19.00 (*1-56065-799-5*) Capstone Pr.

— Bomberos. LC 98-18754. 1999. 14.00 (*1-56065-797-9*, Bridgestone Bks) Capstone Pr.

Ready, Dee. Carteros y Carteras. Schon, Isabel, ed. Ferrer, Martin Luis Guzman, tr. 15.93 (*1-56065-800-2*, Bridgestone Bks) Capstone Pr.

Ready, Dee. Carteros y Carteras. (SPA.). (J). 1998. 14.00 (*0-516-21364-4*) Childrens.

— Dentists (Dentistas) Ferrer, Martin L., tr. (Illus.). 24p. (J). (gr. k-3). 1999. lib. bdg. 10.50 (*1-56065-795-2*, Bridgestone Bks) Capstone Pr.

— Doctores. LC 98-18752. (Servidores Comunitarios Ser.). 1999. 9.95 (*1-56065-796-0*) Capstone Pr.

Ready, Dee. Enfermeras y Enfermeros. 15.93 (*1-56065-801-0*, Bridgestone Bks) Capstone Pr.

— Granjeros y Granjeras. 15.93 (*1-56065-798-7*, Bridgestone Bks) Capstone Pr.

Ready, Dee. Granjeros y Granjeras. (SPA.). (J). 1998. 14.00 (*0-516-21369-5*) Childrens.

— Librarians. (Community Helpers Ser.). (Illus.). 24p. (J). (gr. k-3). 1997. lib. bdg. 14.00 (*0-516-20877-2*) Childrens.

— Mail Carriers. (Community Helpers Ser.). (Illus.). 24p. (J). (gr. k-3). 1997. lib. bdg. 14.00 (*0-516-20878-0*) Childrens.

— Motorcycles. (Early-Reader Science Transportation Ser.). 24p. (J). (gr. k-3). 1997. lib. bdg. 14.00 (*0-516-20904-3*) Childrens.

— Nurses. (Community Helpers Ser.). (J). 1997. lib. bdg. 14.00 (*0-516-20504-8*) Childrens.

— Plumbers. (Community Helpers Ser.). (J). 1998. 14.00 (*0-516-21347-4*) Childrens.

— Police Officers. (Community Helpers Ser.). (Illus.). (J). 1997. lib. bdg. 14.00 (*0-516-20505-6*) Childrens.

Ready, Dee. Policias. 15.93 (*1-56065-802-9*, Bridgestone Bks) Capstone Pr.

Ready, Dee. School Bus Driver. (Community Helpers Ser.). (Illus.). 24p. (J). (gr. k-3). 1997. lib. bdg. 14.00 (*0-516-20875-6*) Childrens.

— School Bus Driver (Choferes de Autobuses Escolares) Ferrer, Martin L., tr. (Illus.). 24p. (J). (gr. k-3). 1999. lib. bdg. 10.50 (*1-56065-803-7*, Bridgestone Bks) Capstone Pr.

— School Buses. (Early-Reader Science Transportation Ser.). 24p. (J). (gr. k-3). 1997. lib. bdg. 14.00 (*0-516-20905-1*) Childrens.

— Servidores Comunitarios, 10 vols. 1999. 140.00 (*0-7368-0147-2*) Capstone Pr.

— Trucks Early. (Early-Reader Science Transportation Ser.). 24p. (J). (gr. k-3). 1997. lib. bdg. 14.00 (*0-516-20906-X*) Childrens.

— Veterinarians. (Community Helpers Ser.). (J). (gr. k-3). 1997. 14.00 (*0-516-20506-4*) Childrens.

Ready, Dee. Veterinarios y Veterinarias. 15.93 (*1-56065-804-5*, Bridgestone Bks) Capstone Pr.

Ready, Dee, jt. auth. see Capstone Press Staff.

Ready, Dolores. Joan, the Brave Soldier: Joan of Arc. LC 77-86597. (Stories About Christian Heroes Ser.). (Illus.). (J). (gr. 1-5). 1983. 0.95 (*0-86683-764-7*) Harper SF.

— Meeting Jesus. Zanzig, Thomas, ed. (Discovering Program Ser.). (Illus.). 42p. 1989. teacher ed. 6.00 (*0-88489-191-7*); text 3.00 (*0-88489-190-9*) St Marys.

— Praying. Zanzig, Thomas, ed. (Discovering Program Ser.). (Illus.). 43p. 1989. teacher ed. 6.00 (*0-88489-195-X*); text 3.00 (*0-88489-194-1*) St Marys.

— Understanding Myself. Zanzig, Thomas, ed. (Discovering Program Ser.). (Illus.). 24p. 1989. 3.00 (*0-88489-196-8*); teacher ed. 6.00 (*0-88489-197-6*) St Marys.

Ready, Dolores, jt. auth. see Riehle, Mary C.

Ready, J. Lee. Arrogance on the Battlefield: A Primary Cause of Defeat, 1775-1991. LC 97-125747. (Illus.). 312p. 1997. 29.95 (*1-85409-319-3*, Pub. by Arms & Armour) Sterling.

Ready, John F. Industrial Applications of Lasers. 2nd ed. LC 96-39078. (Illus.). 599p. 1997. text 99.00 (*0-12-583961-8*) Morgan Kaufmann.

Ready, John F., ed. Lasers in Modern Industry. LC 79-66705. (Illus.). 276p. reprint ed. pap. 85.60 (*0-8357-6489-3*, 203586000097) Bks Demand.

Ready, Kathryn J., jt. ed. see Bognanno, Mario F.

Ready, Keith F., jt. auth. see Burke, Louise L.

***Ready, Ken.** Smashing Out of the Comfort Zone. abr. ed. 1998. 16.95 incl. audio (*0-9670558-0-6*) Life Mgmt Org.

Ready, Kevin. Hybrid HTML Design: A Multi Browser HTML Reference. LC 96-15555. 448p. 1996. pap. text 35.00 (*1-56205-617-4*) New Riders Pub.

Ready, Kevin & Vachier, Paul. Plug-n-Play JavaScript. 450p. 1996. 34.99 (*1-56205-674-3*) New Riders Pub.

Ready, Kevin E. Gaia Weeps: The Crisis of Global Warming. LC 98-86376. 374p. 1998. pap. 12.95 (*0-943039-00-2*) Saint Gaudens.

Ready, Kevin E. & Parlier, Cap. TWA 800: Accident or Incident? LC 98-87155. xv, 414 p. 1998. pap. 12.95 (*0-943039-80-0*) Saint Gaudens.

Ready, Mark, tr. see Johnson, Thomas M.

Ready, Mark, tr. see Wittmann, Thomas T., et al.

Ready, Milton. Asheville: Land of the Sky. LC 86-23368. (Illus.). 136p. 1986. 22.95 (*0-89781-168-2*) Am Historical Pr.

Ready, Milton L. The Castle Builders: Georgia's Economy Under the Trustees, 1732-1754. LC 77-14750. (Dissertations in American Economic History Ser.). 1978. 37.95 (*0-405-11053-7*) Ayer.

Ready, N. P. Ship Registration. 2nd ed. 216p. 1994. 105.00 (*1-85044-824-8*) LLP.

Ready, Nigel, jt. auth. see Karatzas, Theodoros.

Ready, Robert. Hazlitt at Table. LC 79-22811. 126p. 1981. 24.50 (*0-8386-2414-6*) Fairleigh Dickinson.

Ready-Smith, John. Living in Spain. 5th ed. (Illus.). 223p. 1990. 33.50 (*0-7090-4100-4*) Trans-Atl Phila.

Ready, Timothy. Latino Immigrant Youth: Passages from Adolescence to Adulthood. LC 91-19038. (Studies in Education & Culture: Vol. 5). 282p. 1991. text 46.00 (*0-8153-0057-3*, SS728) Garland.

Ready, William B. Files on Parade: A Memoir. LC 81-23310. (Illus.). 274p. 1982. 26.50 (*0-8108-1516-8*) Scarecrow.

Readywriter, True E. Fervent Prayer. 212p. 1999. pap. 14.95 (*0-7414-0060-X*) Buy Books.

Reagan, Charles E. Paul Ricoeur: His Life & His Work. (Illus.). 160p. 1996. 24.95 (*0-226-70602-8*) U Ch Pr.

— Paul Ricoeur: His Life & His Work. (Illus.). 152p. 1998. pap. 13.00 (*0-226-70603-6*) U Ch Pr.

Reagan, Charles E., jt. ed. see Richter, William L.

Reagan, Christopher J., ed. see Seneca, Lucius Annaeus.

Reagan, D. El Plan Supremo.Tr. of Master Plan. (SPA.). 9.99 (*0-7899-0076-9*, 492300) Editorial Unilit.

Reagan, Danial. Where's Bill? Missing in Action. 24p. 1994. pap. 10.95 (*1-886504-00-8*) Funny Bone FL.

Reagan, Daniel, ed. see Melville, Herman.

***Reagan, David R.** Living for Christ in the End Times. 2000. pap. 10.99 (*0-89221-499-6*) New Leaf.

Reagan, David R. Trusting God: Learning to Walk by Faith. 2nd rev. ed. LC 94-79447. 264p. (Orig.). 1995. pap. 9.95 (*0-945593-03-1*) Lamb Lion Minstrs.

***Reagan, Dawn.** Bear Toons Coloring Book. Toon Takes Staff, ed. (Illus.). 32p. (J). (ps-5). 1999. pap. 3.00 (*1-929456-08-5*) Myrtle Seal Pubg.

— Duck Pad: Toon Takes Artist Pad & Pencil. (Illus.). 50p. (J). (gr. 1-7). 1999. pap. 7.95 (*1-929456-11-5*) Myrtle Seal Pubg.

— Duck Toons Coloring Book. Toon Takes Staff, ed. (Illus.). 32p. (J). (ps-5). 1999. pap. 3.00 (*1-929456-07-7*) Myrtle Seal Pubg.

Reagan, Dawn. For Our Baby Scrapbook Kit: Scrapbook Activity Kit for Kids. Takes, Toon, ed. (Illus.). 29p. (J). (gr. k-6). 1999. pap. 15.50 (*1-929456-04-2*) Myrtle Seal Pubg.

— New Testament Bible Adventure Kit: Bible Storyboard Adventures for Kids. Takes, Toon, ed. (Illus.). 16p. (ps-5). 1999. pap. 29.95 (*1-929456-01-8*) Myrtle Seal Pubg.

— Old Testament Bible Adventure Kit: Bible Storyboard Adventures for Kids. Takes, Toon, ed. (Illus.). 16p. 1999. pap. 29.95 (*1-929456-00-X*) Myrtle Seal Pubg.

***Reagan, Dawn.** Toon Takes Turtles: Coloring Book of Turtle Toons. Toon Takes Staff, ed. (Illus.). 32p. (J). (ps-2). 1999. pap. 3.00 (*1-929456-06-9*) Myrtle Seal Pubg.

— Toon Toys Trio: Coloring Book & Toy Kit. deluxe ed. Toon Takes Staff, ed. (Illus.). 15p. (J). (ps-7). 1999. pap. 15.95 (*1-929456-09-3*) Myrtle Seal Pubg.

Reagan, Dian C. Home for the Howl-idays. 128p. (J). (gr. 4-6). 1994. pap. 2.95 (*0-590-48772-8*) Scholastic Inc.

Reagan, Douglas P. & Waide, Robert B., eds. The Food Web of a Tropical Rain Forest. LC 95-50299. (Illus.). 640p. 1996. pap. text 39.95 (*0-226-70600-1*); lib. bdg. 110.00 (*0-226-70599-4*) U Ch Pr.

An Asterisk (*) at the beginning of an entry indicates that the title is appearing for the first time.

Reagan, Gary. The Book of Bourbon & Other Fine American Whiskeys. LC 98-34478. 256p. 1998. pap. 15.00 (*0-395-93522-9*) HM.

Reagan, J. E., ed. see Petroleum Mechanical Engineering Workshop & Confer.

Reagan, James & Smith, Earl. Metal Spinning: Metal Spinning for Craftsman, Instructors & Students. 80p. reprint ed. pap. 9.95 (*0-917914-83-X*) Lindsay Pubns.

Reagan, James, jt. auth. see Smith.

Reagan, Janet T., jt. auth. see Gelman, Sherril B.

Reagan, Jim. Castle King-Four. LC 89-38938. 336p. (Orig.). 1990. pap. 10.95 (*0-931832-37-3*) Fithian Pr.

— The Scene: And Other Stories. LC 94-17947. 176p. 1994. pap. 9.95 (*1-56474-103-6*) Fithian Pr.

Reagan, John H. Memoirs, with Special Reference to Secession & the Civil War. McCaleb, Walter F., ed. LC 79-174304. reprint ed. 29.50 (*0-404-04620-7*) AMS Pr.

Reagan, Leslie J. When Abortion Was a Crime: Women, Medicine & Law in the United States, 1867-1973. LC 96-22568. (Illus.). 384p. (C). 1997. 29.95 (*0-520-08848-4*, Pub. by U CA Pr) Cal Prin Full Svc.

— When Abortion Was a Crime: Women, Medicine & Law in the United States, 1867-1973. 400p. 1998. pap. 17.95 (*0-520-21657-1*, Pub. by U CA Pr) Cal Prin Full Svc.

Reagan, M. Patricia. The Dirty Old Men of Sixty Minutes: Gloving Care in the White House. rev. ed. LC 89-61567. (Adventures in Reverse Pornography Ser.: Vol. 2). 202p. 1995. reprint ed. lib. bdg. 39.95 (*0-9623133-6-X*) Oxner Inst.

***Reagan, Mary Pat.** The Destiny of Eddie Morris: And Other Essays. rev. ed. LC 89-61567. Orig. Title: Satanic Reverses. 152p. 1999. per. 21.95 (*0-9623133-7-8*) Oxner Inst.

Reagan, Maureen & Herrmann, Dorothy. First Father, First Daughter: A Memoir. (Illus.). 288p. 1989. 19.95 (*0-316-73631-7*) Little.

Reagan, Michael. The Common Sense of an Uncommon Man: The Wit, Wisdom, & Eternal Optimism of Ronald Reagan. LC 98-8386. 160p. 1998. 12.99 (*0-7852-7548-7*) Nelson.

— Making Waves: Bold Exposes from Talk Radio's Number One Night Time Host. LC 96-15763. 304p. 1996. 22.99 (*0-7852-7588-6*) Nelson.

Reagan, Michael & Hyams, Joe. On the Outside Looking In. 1988. 17.95 (*0-8217-2392-8*, Zebra Kensgtn) Kensgtn Pub Corp.

Reagan, Michael D. The Accidental System: Health Care Policy in America. LC 98-55763. (Dilemmas in American Politics Ser.). 176p. 1999. pap. 17.00 (*0-8133-9996-3*, Pub. by Westview) HarpC.

***Reagan, Michael D.** The Accidental System: Health Care Policy in America. LC 98-55763. (Dilemmas in American Politics Ser.). 176p. 1999. 59.00 (*0-8133-9997-1*, Pub. by Westview) HarpC.

Reagan, Michael D. The Managed Economy. LC 81-13262. 288p. 1982. reprint ed. lib. bdg. 65.00 (*0-313-23154-0*, REME, Greenwood Pr) Greenwood.

Reagan, Nancy. My Turn. 4.98 (*0-394-68388-9*) Random.

— My Turn, Vol. 1. large type ed. LC 90-41187. 650p. 1990. reprint ed. lib. bdg. 22.95 (*1-56054-056-7*) Thorndike Pr.

Reagan, Nancy & Novak, William. My Turn: The Memoirs of Nancy Reagan. (Illus.). 1989. 21.95 (*0-394-56368-9*) Random.

Reagan, Patricia A. & Brookins-Fisher, Jodi. Community Health in the 21st Century. LC 96-24914. 532p. 1996. pap. text 63.00 (*0-205-19749-3*) Allyn.

Reagan, Patricia A. & Brookins-Fisher, Jodi. Community Health in the 21st Century. (C). 1997. pap., teacher ed. write for info. (*0-205-26492-1*, T6492-7) Allyn.

Reagan, Patrick D. Designing a New America: The Origins of New Deal Planning, 1890-1943. LC 99-30717. (Political Development of the American Nation Ser.). 400p. 2000. 40.00 (*1-55849-230-5*) U of Mass Pr.

Reagan, Patrick D., jt. ed. see Brown, Jerold E.

Reagan, Priscilla, ed. see James, Robert.

Reagan, R. Douglas, et al. Kansas Limited Liability Company Forms & Practice Manual. LC 96-5650. 430p. 1996. ring bd. 219.90 (*1-57400-023-3*) Data Trace Pubng.

Reagan, Ron. Siamese Cats. (Illus.). 96p. 1988. 9.95 (*0-87666-860-0*, KW-062) TFH Pubns.

Reagan, Ronald. An American Life. 1995. reprint ed. lib. bdg. 39.95 (*1-56849-607-9*) Buccaneer Bks.

***Reagan, Ronald.** An American Life: An Autobiography. (Illus.). 1999. per. 17.95 (*0-7434-0025-9*) PB.

— I Love You Ronnie: The Letters of Ronald Reagan to Nancy Reagan. 2000. 24.95 (*0-375-50554-7*) Random.

Reagan, Ronald. Reagan on Cuba: Selected Statements by the President. 1986. 4.00 (*0-317-90497-3*) Cuban Amer Natl Fndtn.

***Reagan, Ronald.** Ronald Reagan: The Great Communicator. 2000. 30.00 (*0-06-019606-8*) HarpC.

Reagan, Ronald. Ronald Reagan Talks to America. 1985. 12.95 (*0-8159-6719-5*) Devin.

— Ronald Reagan Talks to America. 2nd rev. ed. LC 68-26085. 226p. 1982. 12.95 (*0-8159-5222-8*) Devin.

— A Shining City: The Legacy of Ronald Reagan. LC 97-36576. 256p. 1998. 24.50 (*0-684-84678-0*) S&S Trade.

Reagan, Sally B., et al, eds. Writing With: New Directions in Collaborative Teaching, Learning, & Research. LC 93-15365. (SUNY Series, Feminist Theory in Education). 311p. (C). 1994. text 64.50 (*0-7914-1841-3*); pap. text 21.95 (*0-7914-1842-1*) State U NY Pr.

***Reagan, Susan Joy.** Dreamcatcher I: Poetry Companion to Egg-Shell Dancing. 110p. (Orig.). 1999. pap. write for info. (*0-7392-0411-4*, PO3658) Morris Pubng.

— Dreamcatcher II: Poetry Companion to Egg-Shell Dancing. 108p. (Orig.). 1999. pap. write for info. (*0-7392-0412-2*) Morris Pubng.

— Egg-Shell Dancing: One Woman's Journey to a Life She Can Claim As Her Own. 100p. (Orig.). 1999. pap. write for info. (*0-7392-0410-6*, PO3657) Morris Pubng.

***Reagan, Timothy G.** Non-Western Educational Traditions: Alternate Approaches to Educational Thought & Practice. 2nd ed. LC 99-54729. 2000. pap. write for info. (*0-8058-3450-8*) L Erlbaum Assocs.

***Reagan, Timothy G., et al.** Becoming a Reflective Educator: How to Build a Culture of Inquiry in the Schools. 2nd ed. LC 99-6930. 184p. 2000. pap. 24.95 (*0-7619-7553-5*); lib. bdg. 53.95 (*0-7619-7552-7*) Corwin Pr.

Reagan, Wesley C., ed. see Durham, Ron & DeGraffenried, Doug.

Reagan, Wesley C., ed. see Durham, Ron, et al.

Reagan, Wesley C., ed. see Durhan, Ron & De Graffenried, Doug.

Reagan, William J., et al. Veterinary Hematology: Atlas of Common Domestic Species. LC 97-7678. (Illus.). 1997. 39.95 (*0-8138-2664-0*) Iowa St U Pr.

Reagar, Daniel, ed. see Melville, Herman.

Reage, Pauline. Return to the Chateau. 1995. pap. 10.00 (*0-345-39465-8*) Ballantine Pub Grp.

— Story of O. 240p. 1981. mass mkt. 6.99 (*0-345-30111-0*) Ballantine Pub Grp.

— Story of O. Hand, John P., tr. 186p. 1996. mass mkt. 7.95 (*1-56201-035-2*) Blue Moon Bks.

Reagen, James E. Wizardry: The League of the Crimson Crescent--A Novel. 288p. 1995. mass mkt. 5.99 (*1-55958-671-0*) Prima Pub.

Reagen, Michael V. & Chertow, Doris S., eds. The Challenge of Modern Church-Public Relations. LC 72-5637. (Occasional Papers: No. 33). 68p. (Orig.). 1972. pap. 3.00 (*0-87060-056-7*, OCP 33) Syracuse U Cont Ed.

Reagin, Nancy R. Lucrative Differences: Gender, Class & the Work of the Women's Movement in Hanover, 1880-1933. LC 94-39348. 1995. pap. text 19.95 (*0-8078-4525-6*); lib. bdg. 59.95 (*0-8078-2210-8*) U of NC Pr.

***Reagle, Kenn.** Theodore Sterner Christ: Civil War Surgeon from Union County. LC 99-29389. 1999. write for info. (*0-917127-12-9*) Oral Traditions.

Reagle, Merl. Merl Reagle's Sunday Crosswords, 1. Rosen, David, ed. (Merl Reagle's Sunday Crosswords Ser.). (Illus.). 56p. (Orig.). 1991. pap. 7.95 (*0-9630828-0-9*) PuzzleWorks.

— Merl Reagle's Sunday Crosswords, Vol. 2. 56p. (Orig.). 1996. pap. 7.95 (*0-9630828-1-7*) PuzzleWorks.

— Merl Reagle's Sunday Crosswords, Vol. 3. 56p. (Orig.). 1996. pap. 7.95 (*0-9630828-2-5*) PuzzleWorks.

— Merl Reagle's Sunday Crosswords, Vol. 4. 56p. (Orig.). 1996. pap. 7.95 (*0-9630828-3-3*) PuzzleWorks.

— Merl Reagle's Sunday Crosswords, Vol. 5. 56p. (Orig.). 1997. pap. 8.95 (*0-9630828-4-1*) PuzzleWorks.

— Merl Reagle's Sunday Crosswords, Vol. 6. (Illus.). 40p. (Orig.). 1999. pap. 8.95 (*0-9630828-5-X*) PuzzleWorks.

Reagon, Bernice J., ed. Black American Culture & Scholarship: Contemporary Issues. (Illus.). 184p. (Orig.). (C). 1985. pap. text 3.00 (*0-929847-00-8*) Natl Mus Am.

— We'll Understand It Better by & By: Pioneering African American Gospel Composers. LC 91-37954. (Illus.). 432p. 1992. pap. text 24.95 (*1-56098-167-9*) Smithsonian.

***Reagon, Bernice Johnson.** If You Don't Go, Don't Hinder Me: The African American Sacred Song Tradition. (Abraham Lincoln Lecture Ser.). 2000. text 30.00 (*0-8032-3913-0*); pap. text 15.00 (*0-8032-8983-9*) U of Nebr Pr.

Reah, Danuta. The Language of Newspapers. LC 97-17315. 136p. (C). 1998. pap. 14.99 (*0-415-14600-3*) Routledge.

***Reajasekheara.** The Color Guide to Vrndeavana: The City of over 5,000 Temples. LC 00-34336. (Illus.). 2000. write for info. (*1-887089-30-6*) Torchlght Pub.

Reak, Jack. Kanuga - Story of a Gathering Place. Gooch, Albert S., Jr. et al, eds. LC 93-80360. (Illus.). 192p. 1993. 16.95 (*0-9639021-0-5*) Kanuga Confer.

Reaka-Kubla, Marjorie L., et al, eds. Biodiversity II: Understanding & Protecting Our Biological Resources. (Illus.). 560p. (Orig.). 1997. pap. 29.95 (*0-309-05584-9*, Joseph Henry Pr) Natl Acad Pr.

Reaka-Kudla, Marjorie L., et al, eds. Biodiversity II: Understanding & Protecting Our Biological Resources. rev. ed. LC 96-30851. 560p. (Orig.). (C). 1996. 34.95 (*0-309-05227-0*, Joseph Henry Pr) Natl Acad Pr.

Reakes, Lizzie. Ragwork. (New Crafts Ser.). (Illus.). 96p. 1996. 14.95 (*1-85967-238-8*, Lorenz Bks) Anness Pub.

Reakes, Paul. King Arthur. LC 99-165468. 89p. 1997. write for info. (*0-573-06498-9*) S French Trade.

Real. Co-Evolution. pap. text. write for info. (*0-7167-5077-5*) W H Freeman.

***Real Academia Espanola Staff.** Diccionario De La Lengua Espanola. 1999. 198.95 (*84-239-9804-5*) Planeta.

Real Academia Espanola Staff, ed. Diccionario Manual e Ilustrado de la Lengua Espanola. 4th ed. (SPA., Illus.). 1666p. 1989. 275.00 (*84-239-5978-3*) Elliots Bks.

Real Academia De Ciencias Morales Y Politic Staff. Acerca de "Centesimus Annus" (Nueva Austral Ser.: Vol. 245). (SPA.). 1991. pap. text 24.95 (*84-239-7245-3*) Elliots Bks.

Real Academia De Ciencias Staff. Scientific & Technical Vocabulary: Vocabulario Cientifico y Tecnico. (SPA.). 503p. 1983. 175.00 (*0-8288-2145-3*, S60131) Fr & Eur.

Real Academia de la Lengua Espanol Staff. Diccionario de la Lengua Espanol, 2 vols., Set. 19th ed. (SPA.). 1456p. 1986. 295.00 (*0-8288-4402-X*, S12257) Fr & Eur.

— Diccionario Manuel e Ilustrado de la Lengua Espanol, 5 vols., Set. 4th ed. (SPA.). 1666p. 1989. 195.00 (*0-8288-2736-2*, S38002) Fr & Eur.

— Esbozo de una Neuva Gramatica de la Lengua Espanola. 13th ed. (SPA.). 1991. pap. 59.95 (*0-7859-5215-2*) Fr & Eur.

Real Academia Espano. Diccionario Manual. 4th ed. (SPA.). 1668p. 1989. 195.00 (*0-7859-5752-9*) Fr & Eur.

Real Academia Espano Staff. Diccionario de la Lengua Espanola. 21st ed. (SPA.). 1548p. 1992. 295.00 (*0-7859-9232-4*) Fr & Eur.

— Diccionario de la Real Academia Expanola. 2nd ed. 980p. 1991. 275.00 (*0-7859-6048-1*, 8460076059) Fr & Eur.

— Diccionario Historico de la Lengua Espanola: Fascicles 1-10, Bound Together. (SPA.). 1991. 650.00 (*84-600-3782-7*) Elliots Bks.

— Diccionario Historico de la Lengua Espanola (Faciculos) (SPA.). 156p. 1984. pap. 29.95 (*0-7859-6046-5*, 8460037835) Fr & Eur.

— Diccionario Manual e Illustrado de la Lengua Espanola. (SPA.). 1666p. 1989. 195.00 (*0-7859-9231-6*) Fr & Eur.

— Diccionario Manual e Ilustrado de la Lengua Espanola, Vol. 1. (SPA.). 1983. 45.00 (*0-7859-5754-5*) Fr & Eur.

— Diccionario Manual e Ilustrado de la Lengua Espanola, Vol. 2. (SPA.). 1983. 45.00 (*0-7859-5755-3*) Fr & Eur.

— Diccionario Manual e Ilustrado de la Lengua Espanola, Vol. 3. (SPA.). 1983. 45.00 (*0-7859-5756-1*) Fr & Eur.

— Diccionario Manual e Ilustrado de la Lengua Espanola, Vol. 5. (SPA.). 1983. 45.00 (*0-7859-5758-8*) Fr & Eur.

— Diccionario Manual e Ilustrado de la Lengua Espanola, Vol. 6. (SPA.). 1983. 45.00 (*0-7859-5759-6*) Fr & Eur.

— Esbozo de una Nueva Gramatica de la Lengua Espanola. (SPA.). 592p. pap. 59.95 (*84-239-4759-9*) Elliots Bks.

Real Academia Espano Staff, ed. Diccionario de la Lengua Espanol, 2 vols. 21st ed. (SPA.). 2183p. 1995. 95.00 (*0-7859-9780-6*) Fr & Eur.

— Diccionario de la Lengua Espanola. 21st ed. (SPA.). 1548p. 1993. 240.00 (*84-239-4399-2*) Colton Bk.

— Diccionario de la Lengua Espanola, 2 vols. 21st ed. (SPA.). 2133p. 1994. text 85.95 (*84-239-9416-3*) Colton Bk.

— Esbozo de una Nueva Gramatica de la Lengua Espanola. (SPA.). 592p. 1991. 89.50 (*84-239-4762-9*) Elliots Bks.

— Fuero Juzgo. (SPA.). 131p. 1968. 250.00 (*0-614-00126-9*) Elliots Bks.

Real Academia Espano Staff, ed. see Alarcos Llorach, Emilio.

Real Academia Galega Staff. Diccionario da Lingua Galega. (SPA.). 840p. 1990. 69.95 (*0-7859-6047-3*, 8460075095) Fr & Eur.

Real Academia Staff. Diccionario de la Lengua Espanola, 2 vols. 21st ed. (SPA.). 1992. pap. 95.00 (*0-7859-9180-8*) Fr & Eur.

Real, Antony. The Story of the Stick: Folklore & Anthropology. 1977. lib. bdg. 250.00 (*0-8490-2691-1*) Gordon Pr.

Real-Cabello, Gaspar, ed. El Campo Queretano en Transicion. (Transformation of Rural Mexico Ser.). (SPA.). (C). 1996. pap. 12.00 (*1-878367-28-5*) UCSD Ctr US-Mex.

Real Estate Brokerage Council Staff. Real Estate Office Management. 3rd ed. 1996. pap. 52.00 (*0-7931-1530-2*, 19071503, Real Estate Ed) Dearborn.

***Real Estate Educ. Co. Staff.** New York Real Estate Exam Review. 2nd ed. 2000. 21.95 (*0-7931-3724-1*) Dearborn.

Real Estate Educ. Co. Staff, ed. New York Real Estate Exam Review. 142p. 1998. pap. text 19.95 (*0-7931-2678-9*, 1510-3901, Real Estate Ed) Dearborn.

Real Estate Education Co. Staff, ed. Los Bienes Raices y los Numeros. 6th ed.Tr. of Mastering Real Estate Mathematics. (SPA.). 208p. 1997. pap. text 24.95 (*0-7931-2697-5*, 1700-0601, Real Estate Ed) Dearborn.

Real Estate Education Company Staff. Virginia Real Estate: Practice & Law. 5th ed. LC 99-20564. 1999. pap. text 16.95 (*0-7931-3220-7*) Dearborn.

Real Estate Education Company Staff & Huber, Walter R. California Real Estate Economics. 3rd ed. LC 98-11118. 1998. 33.25 (*0-7931-2834-X*) Dearborn.

Real Estate Record Assn. Staff. History of Real Estate, Building & Architecture in New York City. LC 67-23061. (Illus.). 1967. reprint ed. 46.95 (*0-405-00054-5*) Ayer.

Real Estate Research Corp. Staff. Air Rights & Highways. LC 78-97085. (Urban Land Institute, Technical Bulletin Ser.: No. 64). (Illus.). 84p. reprint ed. pap. 30.00 (*0-8357-8014-7*, 203395300087) Bks Demand.

Real Estate Timesharing & the Property Staff. Real Estate Timesharing & the Property Tax. Bloch, Stuart M., ed. LC HJ3241.. (Lincoln Institute Monograph: No. 85-4). 115p. reprint ed. pap. 35.70 (*0-7837-2159-5*, 204246200004) Bks Demand.

Real Estate Valuation Colloquium Staff. Real Estate Valuation Colloquium, 1984: A Redefinition of Real Estate Appraisal Precepts & Processes. Kinnard, William N., Jr., ed. LC 86-1388. (Lincoln Institute of Land Policy Bk.). 415p. reprint ed. pap. 128.70 (*0-7837-3268-6*, 204328700007) Bks Demand.

Real Francia, Pedro J. Del, see Del Real Francia, Pedro J.

Real Goods Co. Staff & Schaeffer, John. Solar Living: The Complete Guide to Renewable Energy Technologies & Sustainable Living. 9th ed. (Real Goods Independent Living Bks.). (Illus.). 700p. (Orig.). 1996. pap. 24.95 (*0-930031-68-7*) Real Goods Pub.

Real, H. G., jt. auth. see Fox, R. M.

Real, Herrman J. Jonathan Swift, the Battle of the Books. (Quellen und Forschungen zur Sprach und Kulturgeschichte der Germanischen Voelker: Vol. 71). (C). 1978. 107.10 (*3-11-006985-7*) De Gruyter.

Real, Lavergne, jt. ed. see Momar-Coumba, Diop.

Real, Leslie A., ed. Behavioral Mechanisms in Evolutionary Biology. LC 94-14131. 480p. 1994. pap. text 29.95 (*0-226-70597-8*); lib. bdg. 80.00 (*0-226-70595-1*) U Ch Pr.

— Ecological Genetics. LC 93-4762. (Illus.). 272p. 1994. pap. text 29.95 (*0-691-00066-2*, Pub. by Princeton U Pr) Cal Prin Full Svc.

Real, Leslie A., jt. ed. see Brown, James H.

Real, Maria E. Del, see Del Real, Maria E.

Real, Michael R. Exploring Media Culture: A Guide. LC 96-10043. (Communication & Human Values Ser.). 405p. 1996. 52.00 (*0-8039-5876-5*); pap. 24.95 (*0-8039-5877-3*) Sage.

— Super Media: A Cultural Studies Approach. (Communication & Human Values Ser.). (Illus.). 282p. (C). 1989. text 52.00 (*0-8039-3313-4*); pap. text 24.95 (*0-8039-3314-2*) Sage.

Real, Palma, ed. see Soler, Elpa.

Real Property Law Institute & Institute of Continuing Legal Education, Georgia S. Program Materials for Real Property Law Institute: May 8-10, 1986, St. Simons, May 22-23, 1986, Atlanta. LC 86-623182. 1986. 23.00 (*0-685-18536-2*) ICLE Georgia.

Real Ramos, Cesar, ed. see Melendez Valdes, Juan.

Real, Sande M. Food for Thought: The Animated Story of an Inspiring Cupcake. LC 95-92437. (Illus.). 224p. (Orig.). 1996. pap. 11.00 (*0-9647708-0-6*) Real Expressions.

Real, Terrence. I Don't Want To Talk About It: Overcoming the Secret Legacy of Male Depression. LC 97-39236. 384p. 1998. per. 13.00 (*0-684-83539-8*) S&S Trade.

— I Don't Want to Talk about It: Overcoming the Secret Legacy of Male Depression. LC 96-41711. 384p. 1997. 23.50 (*0-684-83102-3*) Scribner.

Real, Terry. I Don't Need a Baby to Be Who I Am: Thoughts & Affirmations on a Fulfilling Life. 144p. 1977. 1.50 (*0-671-00980-X*, PB Hardcover) PB.

Real To Reel Productions Staff. User's Guide, Skillbusters: Mystery at Wellsley Manor. (Keyboarding/Typesetting-1st Yr Ser.). 1999. pap. 12.00 (*0-538-68348-1*) S-W Pub.

Real, Willy, ed. see Herzfeld, Hans.

Reale, A., jt. ed. see Lichtlen, P. R.

Reale, D. L., ed. see Thomas-Trautman.

Reale, Giovanni. The Concept of First Philosophy & the Unity of the Metaphysics of Aristotle. Catan, John R., ed. & tr. by. LC 79-13867. 513p. (C). 1980. text 24.50 (*0-87395-385-1*) State U NY Pr.

— A History of Ancient Philosophy Vol. III: Systems of the Hellenistic Age. Catan, John R., ed. & tr. by. LC 79-13867. (Series in Philosophy). 499p. (C). 1985. text 21.50 (*0-88706-027-7*) State U NY Pr.

— A History of Ancient Philosophy Vol. IV: The Schools of the Imperial Age. Catan, John R., ed. & tr. by. LC 84-16310. (SUNY Series in Philosophy). 548p. (C). 1989. pap. text 21.95 (*0-7914-0129-4*) State U NY Pr.

— A History of Ancient Philosophy Vol. IV: The Schools of the Imperial Age. Catan, John R., ed. & tr. by. LC 84-16310. (Series in Philosophy). 548p. (C). 1990. text 64.50 (*0-7914-0128-6*) State U NY Pr.

— Toward a New Interpretation of Plato. Catan, John R. & Davies, Richard, trs. LC 95-34533. 459p. 1997. 44.95 (*0-8132-0847-5*); pap. 29.95 (*0-8132-0854-8*) Cath U Pr.

Reale, Robert, jt. auth. see Reale, Willie.

Reale, Willie. Many Happy Returns & Fast Women: Two One Act Plays. 1983. pap. 3.25 (*0-8222-0729-X*) Dramatists Play.

Reale, Willie. Short & Sweet. Date not set. pap. 5.95 (*0-8222-1770-8*) Dramatists Play.

Reale, Willie, ed. The Bedtime Zone: The 52nd Street Project Plays. 1995. spiral bd. 20.00 (*0-8222-1443-1*) Dramatists Play.

— The Butler Did It! The 52nd Street Project Plays. 1995. spiral bd. 30.00 (*0-8222-1442-3*) Dramatists Play.

— The 52nd Street Project Kid Theater Kit: Plays, Projects & Programs for Young People. 1995. spiral bd. 195.00 (*0-8222-1440-7*) Dramatists Play.

— Plays for Pairs: The 52nd Street Project Plays. 1995. spiral bd. 15.00 (*0-8222-1444-X*) Dramatists Play.

— The Spring Thing: The 52nd Street Project Plays. 1995. spiral bd. 15.00 (*0-8222-1445-8*) Dramatists Play.

Reale, Willie, et al, eds. 52 Pick-Up: A Practical Guide to Doing Theatre with Children from the 52nd Street Project. 1995. spiral bd. 35.00 (*0-8222-1441-5*) Dramatists Play.

Reale, Willie & Reale, Robert. The Dinosaur Musical: The 52nd Street Project, Musical. 1995. spiral bd. 25.00 (*0-8222-1446-6*) Dramatists Play.

— Quark Victory: The 52nd Street Project, Musical. 1995. spiral bd. 25.00 (*0-8222-1447-4*) Dramatists Play.

***Realey, Anne & Koller, Angie.** Cardiopulmonary Workbook & Study Guide. 122p. (C). 1999. spiral bd., wbk. ed. 26.95 (*0-7872-6348-6*, 41634801) Kendall-Hunt.

Realfonzo, Riccardo. Money & Banking: Theory & Debate (1900-1940) LC 98-27885. (ITA.). 208p. 1998. 80.00 (*1-85898-765-2*) E Elgar.

Realize Team Staff. Realize the Internet: An Introduction to the Internet. (Illus.). 180p. 1997. pap. write for info. (*0-9659800-0-6*) Realize Communs.

Reals, Willis H. A Study of the Summer High School. LC 79-177180. (Columbia University. Teachers College. Contributions to Education Ser.: No. 337). reprint ed. 37.50 (*0-404-55337-0*) AMS Pr.

Realuyo, Bino A. The Umbrella Country. LC 98-11668. (Ballantine Reader's Circle Ser.). 298p. 1999. pap. 12.95 (*0-345-42888-9*) Ballantine Pub Grp.

Realuyo, Bino A., et al, eds. The Nuyorasian Anthology: Asian American Writings on New York City. (Illus.). 472p. 1999. pap. 19.95 (*1-889876-07-0*) Asian Am Writers.

Ream, John. Velvet & Steel: Effective Fathering for Christians. LC 97-28453. (Illus.). 160p. 1997. pap. 13.95 (*0-89390-408-2*) Resource Pubns.

Ream, Lanny, jt. auth. see Jackson, Bob.

R

An Asterisk (*) at the beginning of an entry indicates that the title is appearing for the first time.

R

Ream, Lanny R. The Gem, Mineral & Fossil Collector's Guide to Montana, Vol. 1. (Illus.). 40p. (Orig.). 1992. pap. 5.95 (*0-928693-06-6*) L R Ream.

— Gems & Minerals of Washington. (Illus.). 216p. 1996. pap. 9.95 (*0-918499-09-7*) Jackson Mtn.

— Idaho Minerals. (Illus.). 329p. 1989. 34.95 (*0-928693-03-1*) L R Ream.

Ream, Louise, et al. Encyclopedia of Heisey Glassware: Etchings & Carvings. 2nd rev. ed. (Illus.). 298p. 1977. pap. 26.95 (*1-888939-12-5*) Heisey Collectrs.

Ream, S. L., ed. Focus on Laser Materials Processing. (Illus.). 280p. 1988. 182.95 (*0-387-19005-8*) Spr-Verlag.

Ream, Victoria J. Art in Bloom. LC 96-93122. (Illus.). 288p. 1997. 69.95 (*0-9655928-0-4*) Deseret Equity.

Ream, Walt & Field, Katherine G. Molecular Biology Techniques: An Intensive Laboratory Course. (Illus.). 234p. (C). 1998. spiral bd. 39.95 (*0-12-583990-1*) Acad Pr.

Ream, Walt & Gelvin, Stanton B., eds. Crown Gall: Advances in Understanding Interkingdom Gene Transfer. LC 96-86520. 156p. (C). 1996. pap. text 39.00 (*0-89054-222-8*) Am Phytopathol Soc.

Reaman, George E. The Trail of the Black Walnut. (Illus.). 288p. 1993. reprint ed. 25.00 (*0-8063-1394-3*, 4809) Genealog Pub.

Reaman, Micki, et al, eds. Present Tense: Writing & Art by Young Women. LC 96-24820. (Illus.). 176p. (Orig.). (C). 1997. 26.95 (*0-934971-54-4*); pap. 14.95 (*0-934971-53-6*) Calyx Bks.

Reamer, Frederic. Social Work Research & Evaluation: A Case-Based, User-Friendly Approach. LC 97-37983. (Illus.). 488p. 1998. 50.00 (*0-231-10222-4*) Col U Pr.

Reamer, Frederic G. AIDs & Ethics. 1993. pap. 21.00 (*0-231-07359-3*) Col U Pr.

— Ethical Dilemmas in Social Service: A Guide for Social Workers. 2nd ed. 266p. 1993. pap. 26.00 (*0-231-06969-3*) Col U Pr.

— Ethical Standards in Social Work: A Critical Review of the NASW Code of Ethics. LC 98-9666. 307p. 1998. pap. 24.95 (*0-87101-293-6*) Natl Assn Soc Wkrs.

— The Philosophical Foundations of Social Work. 219p. 1995. pap. 20.50 (*0-231-07127-2*) Col U Pr.

— Social Work Malpractice & Liability: Strategies for Prevention. LC 94-7628. 1994. pap. 24.00 (*0-231-08263-0*) Col U Pr.

— Social Work Values & Ethics. LC 94-38229. 217p. 1995. pap. 21.00 (*0-231-09991-6*) Col U Pr.

***Reamer, Frederic G.** Social Work Values & Ethics. 2nd ed. LC 98-46759. 8p. 1999. 49.50 (*0-231-11390-0*) Col U Pr.

— Social Work Values & Ethics. 2nd ed. LC 98-46759. 1999. pap. text 19.50 (*0-231-11391-9*) Col U Pr.

Reamer, Frederic G., ed. AIDS & Ethics. 384p. 1991. text 50.00 (*0-231-07358-5*) Col U Pr.

— The Foundations of Social Work Knowledge. LC 94-7273. (Illus.). 496p. 1994. 50.00 (*0-231-08034-4*) Col U Pr.

Reames, Cheryl. Parenting. (Lifesearch Ser.). 64p. (Orig.). 1994. pap. 4.95 (*0-687-77868-9*) Abingdon.

Reames, Nancy. Scrap Basket Crafts. 1998. pap. 14.95 (*0-87596-969-0*) Rodale Pr Inc.

Reames, Richard & Delbol, Barbara. How to Grow a Chair: The Art of Tree Trunk Topiary. (Illus.). 112p. 1995. pap. 16.00 (*0-9647280-0-1*) Arborsmith Studios.

Reames, Sherry L. The Legenda Aurea: A Reexamination of Its Paradoxical History. LC 84-40502. (Illus.). 336p. 1985. 40.00 (*0-299-10150-9*) U of Wis Pr.

Reames, Stephen, et al. Deep Secrets: The Discovery & Exploration of Lechuguilla Cave. LC 99-21728. (Illus.). 300p. 1999. 32.95 (*0-939748-18-5*); pap. 24.95 (*0-939748-28-2*) Cave Bks MO.

Reams, Bernard D. American International Law Cases, Second Series, 1979-1989, 27 vols., Set. LC 86-33167. 1986. 2025.00 (*0-379-20633-1*) Oceana.

Reams, Bernard D., Jr. Health Care Reform 1993-1994: The American Experience: Clinton & Congress - Law, Policy, & Economics, 31 vols., Set. LC 96-75538. (Federal Health Law Ser.: Part 9). 1996. 4500.00 (*1-57588-073-3*, 308980) W S Hein.

— Index to Update to Internal Revenue Acts. write for info. (*1-57588-302-3*, 306680) W S Hein.

— Insider Trading & Securities Fraud Enforcement: A Legislative History of the Insider Trading & Securities Fraud Enforcement Act of 1988, Pub. Law No. 100-704, 6 vols., Set. LC 89-85648. (Federal Legislative Histories of Economics, Monetary Policy & Stock Market Ser.: Part 5). 7000p. 1989. 460.00 (*0-89941-716-7*, 306100) W S Hein.

Reams, Bernard D. Insider Trading & the Law: A Legislative History of the Insider Trading Sanctions Act of 1984, Pub. Law No. 98-376: Federal Legislative Histories of Laws & Legislation on Economics, Monetary Policy & Stock Market Regulation, Pt. 2. LC 89-7532. Part 3. viii, 590p. 1989. lib. bdg. 82.00 (*0-89941-688-8*, 305860) W S Hein.

Reams, Bernard D., Jr Reader in Law Librarianship. LC 87-82949. xv, 375p. 1987. reprint ed. lib. bdg. 45.00 (*0-89941-589-X*, 305430) W S Hein.

— Reams' Legal Citation-at-a-Glance. 1995. pap. 3.00 (*1-57588-355-4*, 303320) W S Hein.

— The Stock Market Crash of October, 1987: Federal Documents & Materials on the Stock Market & Stock Index Futures Markets, 2 vols. LC 88-81970. Part 1. 2100p. 1988. reprint ed. lib. bdg. 180.00 (*0-89941-656-X*, 305650) W S Hein.

— Tax Equity & Fiscal Responsibility Act of 1982. Date not set. write for info. (*1-57588-381-3*, 311390) W S Hein.

— Technology Transfer Law: The Export Administration Acts of the United States, 1969-1985 Federal Laws, Legislative Histories, &..., 15 vols. in 33 bks. Part 2. 1986. reprint ed. 1750.00 (*0-89941-437-0*, 303790) W S Hein.

— University-Industry Research Partnerships: The Major Legal Issues in Research & Development Agreements. LC 85-9589. (Illus.). 365p. 1986. 75.00 (*0-89930-121-5*, RUI/, Quorum Bks) Greenwood.

Reams, Bernard D., Jr., compiled by. Federal Price & Wage Control Programs, 1917-1979: Legislative Histories, Laws & Administrative Documents, 77 vols, 50 bks., Set. LC 79-93088. 1980. lib. bdg. 2595.00 (*0-89941-052-9*, 301260) W S Hein.

Reams, Bernard D., Jr., ed. American International Law Cases, 1990-1996, 3rd Series, 67 vols. 3rd ed. LC 98-140405. 1993. text 5145.00 (*0-379-21250-1*) Oceana.

— Congress & the Courts: A Legislative History, 1985-1992, the 99th Through the 102d Congresses, Series II, Pt. 2. LC 85-17713. 1994. 1850.00 (*0-89941-868-6*, 308110) W S Hein.

— Economic Recovery Tax Act of 1981. Date not set. write for info. (*1-57588-382-1*, 311380) W S Hein.

— Education of the Handicapped: Laws, Legislative Histories & Administrative Documents, 55 vols., Set. LC 82-81360. (Federal Legislative Histories of the Law of Disabled Persons Ser.: Part 2). 1982. lib. bdg. 2750.00 (*0-89941-157-6*, 302020) W S Hein.

— Federal Laws of the Mentally Handicapped: Laws, Legislative Histories, & Administrative Documents,, 42 vols., Set. LC 81-83898. (Legislative Histories of the Law of Disabled persons Ser.: Part 1). 1981. 2047.50 (*0-89941-106-1*, 302010) W S Hein.

Reams, Bernard D., ed. Federal Legislative Histories: An Annotated Bibliography & Index to Officially Published Sources, 21. LC 93-38809. (Bibliographies & Indexes in Law & Political Science Ser.: No. 21). 624p. 1994. lib. bdg. 115.00 (*0-313-23092-7*, Greenwood Pr) Greenwood.

Reams, Bernard D., Jr., ed. General & Plastic Surgery Devices Panel Breast Implants Transcript of the FDA Panel Meeting on November 12, 13 & 14, 1991. LC 92-49827. (Federal Health Law Ser.: Part 7). 1294p. 1992. reprint ed. 135.00 (*0-89941-806-6*, 307590) W S Hein.

— General & Plastic Surgery Devices Panel Transcript of the FDA Meeting on Silicone Gel-Filled Breast Implants on February 18, 19 & 20, 1992. LC 92-49830. (Federal Health Law Ser.: Part 6). 1390p. 1992. reprint ed. 135.00 (*0-89941-805-8*, 307600) W S Hein.

— Health Care Quality Improvement Act of 1986: A Legislative History of Pub. Law No. 99-660. LC 89-83918. (Federal Health Law Ser.: Part 3). ix, 721p. 1990. lib. bdg. 75.00 (*0-89941-693-4*, 306000) W S Hein.

— Housing & Transportation of the Handicapped: Laws, Legislative Histories & Administrative Documents, Pt. 3. LC 83-81032. Part 3. 30,000p. 1983. reprint ed. 1750.00 incl. mic. form (*0-89941-247-5*, 400430) W S Hein.

— Individuals with Disabilities Education Act: A Legislative History of Public Law 101-476 As Amended by Public Law 102-119, 5 vols., Set. LC 93-29859. (Federal Legislative Histories of the Law of Disabled Persons Ser.: Part 4). 4394p. 1994. 460.00 (*0-89941-849-X*, 307930) W S Hein.

— Internal Revenue Acts of the United States: Revenue Act of 1954 with Legislative Histories & Congressional Documents, 11 vols., Set, Vols. 1-11. LC 82-83005. 8000p. 1982. reprint ed. 995.00 (*0-89941-168-1*, 301980) W S Hein.

— Internal Revenue Acts of the United States: Revenue Acts of 1953-1972 with Legislative Histories, Laws & Congressional Documents, 48 vols., Set. LC 84-82233. 1987. fiche 1735.00 (*0-89941-624-1*, 201681) W S Hein.

— Internal Revenue Acts of the United States: 1950-1951 Legislative Histories, Laws & Administrative Documents, 7 vols. in 9. LC 82-81278. 1982. 468.00 (*0-89941-155-X*, 301970) W S Hein.

— Internal Revenue Acts of the United States: 1950-1951 Legislative Histories, Laws & Administrative Documents, 7 vols. in 9. LC 82-81278. 1986. fiche 298.00 (*0-89941-703-5*, 301971) W S Hein.

— Internal Revenue Acts of the United States, 1909-1950: Legislative Histories & Administrative Documents - Index, 146 bks., Set. rev. ed. LC 78-71405. 176000p. 1978. reprint ed. lib. bdg., student ed. 8950.00 incl. fiche (*0-930342-69-0*, 301270) W S Hein.

— Internal Revenue Code of 1954, 2 vols., Set. LC 92-39056. 2512p. 1993. 195.00 (*0-89941-830-9*, 307580) W S Hein.

— Legislative History of the Financial Institutions Reform, Recovery, & Enforcement Act of 1989, 39 vols. 1998. 4250.00 (*1-57588-416-X*, 310950) W S Hein.

— Market Reform Act of 1990 Legislative History of Public Law No. 101-432: Congressional Response to the Stock Market Crash of October 1987. LC 94-78778. Part 6. 1994. 125.00 (*0-89941-908-9*, 308510) W S Hein.

— Medical Waste Tracking Act of 1988: A Legislative History of Public Law 100-582, 5 vols., Set. LC 93-78606. (Federal Health Law Ser.: Part 8). 4068p. 1993. 395.00 (*0-89941-848-1*, 307940) W S Hein.

— Medicare & Medicaid Patient & Program Protection Act of 1987: A Legislative History of Pub. Law No. 98-507, 3 vols., Set. LC 89-83920. (Federal Health Law Ser.: Part 5). 1932p. 1990. lib. bdg. 185.00 (*0-89941-695-0*, 305960) W S Hein.

— Monopoly Problems in Regulated Industries: Hearings Before the House Committee on the Judiciary, 84th Congress, Serial No. 14, 8 vols., Set. LC 91-72268. (Illus.). 8378p. 1991. reprint ed. lib. bdg. 675.00 (*0-89941-766-3*, 307180) W S Hein.

— Monopoly Problems in Regulated Industries: Hearings Before the House Committee on the Judiciary, 84th Congress, Serial No. 22, 8 vols., Set. LC 91-72318. (Illus.). 6656p. 1991. lib. bdg. 750.00 (*0-89941-765-5*, 307190) W S Hein.

— Monopoly Problems in Regulated Industries: Hearings Before the House Committee on the Judiciary, 87th Congress, Serial No. 10, 2 vols., Set. LC 91-72670. (Illus.). 2004p. 1991. reprint ed. lib. bdg. 195.00 (*0-89941-764-7*, 307150) W S Hein.

— National Organ Transplant Act of 1984: A Legislative History of Pub. Law No. 98-507, 3 vols., Set. LC 89-83919. (Federal Health Law Ser.: Part 1). 2466p. 1990. lib. bdg. 225.00 (*0-89941-691-8*, 305920) W S Hein.

— Omnibus Anti-Crime Act: A Legislative History of the Violent Crime Control & Law Enforcement Act of 1994 Public Law 103-322, 20 vols. LC 97-80048. 1997. 1995.00 (*1-57588-346-5*, 308970) W S Hein.

— Peer Review Improvement Act of 1982: A Legislative History of Pub. Law No. 97-248. LC 89-83917. (Federal Health Law Ser.: Part 2). 564p. 1990. lib. bdg. 58.00 (*0-89941-692-6*, 305930) W S Hein.

— Professional Standards Review Act: A Legislative History of Title Eleven of the Social Securities Amendments of 1972 Pub. Law No. 92-603, 2 vols., Set. LC 89-84259. (Federal Health Law Ser.: Part 4). 1636p. 1990. lib. bdg. 150.00 (*0-89941-694-2*, 305950) W S Hein.

— Revenue Reconciliation Act of 1993: A Legislative History of Title XIII Omnibus Budget Reconciliation Act of 1993, Public Law 103-66, 23 vols., Set. LC 95-75935. 27,408p. 1995. 2500.00 (*0-89941-930-5*, 308280) W S Hein.

— The Safe Medical Devices Act of 1990: A Legislative History of Public Law No. 101-629, 5 vols., Set. LC 96-75096. (Federal Health Law Ser.: Part 10). 1996. 490.00 (*1-57588-093-8*, 309070) W S Hein.

— The Stock Market Crash of October, 1987: Federal Documents & Materials on the Volatility of the Stock Market & Stock Index Futures Markets, 6 vols., Set. LC 88-81970. (Federal Legislative Histories of Law of Economics Ser.: Pt. 2). 1994. suppl. ed. 750.00 (*0-89941-909-7*, 308520) W S Hein.

— Study of Monopoly Power, 12 vols., Set. LC 90-83671. 1990. 1095.00 (*0-89941-748-5*, 306750) W S Hein.

— Tax Reform, 1980: A Legislative History of Public Law 96-613, 3 vols., Set. LC 95-78418. 3464p. 1995. 325.00 (*1-57588-280-9*, 307960) W S Hein.

— Tax Reform, 1988: A Legislative History of the Technical & Miscellaneous Revenue Act of 1988 Public Law No. 100-647, 30 vols., Set. LC 94-79748. 29,000p. 1994. 2695.00 (*0-89941-886-4*, 307310) W S Hein.

— Tax Reform, 1975: A Legislative History of the Tax Reduction Act of 1975 Public Law No. 94-12, 8 vols. LC 95-79411. 9324p. 1995. 895.00 (*0-89941-984-4*, 307390) W S Hein.

— Tax Reform, 1971: A Legislative History of the Revenue Act of 1971, 6 vols., Set. LC 95-80021. 1996. 650.00 (*0-89941-988-7*, 307530) W S Hein.

— Tax Reform, 1969: A Legislative History of the Tax Reform Act of 1969, 25 vols., Set. LC 91-71948. 27000p. 1991. lib. bdg. 2350.00 (*0-89941-762-0*, 306130) W S Hein.

— Tax Reform 1978: A Legislative History of the Revenue Act of 1978. LC 78-72018. 1982. fiche 348.00 (*0-89941-565-2*, 301801) W S Hein.

— Tax Reform 1984: The Law, Reports, Hearings, Debates & Related Documents, 20 vols. LC 85-45437. 1985. fiche 515.00 (*0-89941-669-1*, 303931) W S Hein.

— Trade Agreements Program of the United States: Annual Reports of the President, 9 vols., Set. LC 89-83415. 1989. reprint ed. lib. bdg. 925.00 (*0-89941-711-6*, 306080) W S Hein.

Reams, Bernard D., Jr., et al, eds. Internal Revenue Acts of the United States, 1909-1950: Legislative Histories & Administrative Documents - Guide & Index. LC 78-71405. xii, 400p. 1979. 200.00 (*0-930342-94-1*, 301280) W S Hein.

Reams, Bernard D., Jr. & Couture, Faye, eds. Civil Rights Act of 1991: A Legislative History of Public Law 102-166, 7 vols., Set. LC 93-81348. 1994. 595.00 (*0-89941-869-4*, 308030) W S Hein.

Reams, Bernard D. & Couture, Faye L., eds. Revenue Reconciliation Act of 1990: Title XI Omnibus Budget Reconciliation Act of 1990, Public Law 101-508. LC 94-15648. 8748p. 1994. 760.00 (*0-89941-873-2*, 308180) W S Hein.

Reams, Bernard D., Jr & Gary, Carol J., eds. Government Securities Law: A Legislative History of the Government Securities Act of 1986, Pub Law No. 99-571, 10 vols., Set. LC 89-84148. (Federal Legislative Histories of Laws & Legislation on Trade Law & Economic Policy Ser.: Part 4). 9800p. 1989. lib. bdg. 625.00 (*0-89941-696-9*, 305970) W S Hein.

Reams, Bernard D., Jr & Gray, Carol J. Congressional Impeachment Process & the Judiciary: Documents & Materials on the Removal of Federal District Judge Harry E. Claiborne, 6 vols., Set. LC 87-19801. 1987. 336.00 (*0-89941-556-3*, 305140) W S Hein.

Reams, Bernard D., Jr & Haworth, Charles B., eds. Congress & the Courts: A Legislative History, 1787-1978, 6 vols. in 30, with index & supp. 1. ,1978. LC 78-50643. (Illus.). 1978. lib. bdg. write for info. (*0-930342-56-9*, 301300) W S Hein.

Reams, Bernard D., Jr & House, Emelyn B., eds. Tax Reform, 1976: A Legislative History of the Tax Reform Act of 1976 (Public Law 94-455), 17 vols. LC 91-73158. 1992. 1650.00 (*0-89941-773-6*, 307020) W S Hein.

Reams, Bernard D., Jr & Manz, William H. Federal Telecommunications Law: A Legislative History of the Telecommunications Act of 1996. LC 97-70098. 1997. 1995.00 (*1-57588-279-5*, 310960) W S Hein.

— A Legislative History of the International Antitrust Enforcement Assistance Act of 1994, Pub. L. No. 103-438, 3 vols. LC 97-80026. 1997. 295.00 (*1-57588-392-9*, 310970) W S Hein.

Reams, Bernard D., Jr. & Manz, William H., eds. Federal Bankruptcy Law: A Legislative History of the Bankruptcy Reform Act of 1994 Including the National Bankruptcy Commission Act & Other Bankruptcy Code Amendments, 16 vols. LC 99-172335. No. 4. 1998. 1495.00 (*1-57588-444-5*) W S Hein.

— Legislative History of the Prison Litigation Reform Act of 1996 Public Law 104-134, 2 vols. LC 97-80292. 1997. 195.00 (*1-57588-405-4*, 310980) W S Hein.

Reams, Bernard D., Jr. & McDermott, Margaret H. Deficit Control & the Gramm-Rudman-Hollings Act: History of the Balanced Budget & Emergency Deficit Control Act of 1985 (P.L. 99-177), 5 vols., Set. LC 86-80964. 1986. lib. bdg. 250.00 (*0-89941-484-2*, 304110) W S Hein.

— Tax Reform, 1986: A Legislative History of the Tax Reform Act of 1986, 64 vols. 1987. lib. bdg. 4195.00 (*0-89941-621-7*, 305450) W S Hein.

Reams, Bernard D., Jr. & McDermott, Margaret H., eds. Federal Deficit Control: The Legislative History of the Balanced Budget & Emergency Deficit Control Reaffirmation Act of 1987, 32 vols. in 33 bks., Set. 30000p. 1989. lib. bdg. 1995.00 (*0-89941-672-1*, 305790) W S Hein.

Reams, Bernard D., Jr. & Nelson, Mary A. Trade Reform Legislation, 1988: A Legislative History of the Omnibus Trade & Competitiveness Act of 1988, 10 vols. LC 91-75494. 1991. 995.00 (*0-89941-777-9*, 306760) W S Hein.

Reams, Bernard D., Jr. & Nelson, Mary A., eds. Immigration Reform & the Simpson-Rodino Act: A Legislative History of the Immigration Reform & Control Act of 1986 (P. L. 99-603) with Related Documents. 1986. 1350.00 (*1-57588-301-5*, 305150) W S Hein.

— United States-Canada Free Trade Act: A Legislative History of the US-Canada Free Trade Agreement Implementation Act of 1988, Pub. L. 100-449, 13 vols., Set. LC 89-81792. (Federal Legislative Histories of Laws & Legislation on Trade Law & Economic Policy Ser.: Part 2). 12084p. 1990. lib. bdg. 1150.00 (*0-89941-728-0*, 306450) W S Hein.

Reams, Bernard D., Jr. & Wypyski, Eugene M. Bankruptcy Reform Amendments: A Legislative History of the Bankruptcy Amendments & Federal Judgeship Act of 1984, Public Law 98-353, 10 vols. LC 91-40244. (Federal Legislation on Bankruptcy Reform Ser.: No. 2). 1992. 895.00 (*0-89941-783-3*, 307300) W S Hein.

Reams, Bernard D., Jr., et al. Disability Law in the United States: A Legislative History of the Americans with Disabilities Act of 1990, Public Law 101-336, 6 vols., Set. LC 92-28987. (Federal Disabilities Laws Ser.). 3470p. 1992. 625.00 incl. mic. film (*0-89941-797-3*, 307400) W S Hein.

Reams, Bernard D., Jr., jt. auth. see Gray, Carol J.

Reams, Bernard D., Jr., jt. auth. see Kutten, L. J.

Reams, Bernard D., Jr., jt. auth. see Livermore, Samuel.

Reams, Bernard D., Jr., jt. auth. see Schultz, Jon S.

Reams, Bernard D., Jr., ed. see Ames, James B.

Reams, Bernard D., Jr., ed. see Burge, William.

Reams, Bernard D., Jr., ed. see Choate, George F.

Reams, Bernard D., Jr., ed. see Coke, Edwardo.

Reams, Bernard D., ed. see Duncombe, Giles.

Reams, Bernard D., Jr., jt. ed. see Godan, Jurgen C.

Reams, Bernard D., Jr., ed. see Goffin, R. J.

Reams, Bernard D., Jr., ed. see Gray, John C.

Reams, Bernard D., Jr., ed. see Hoffman, David.

Reams, Bernard D., Jr., ed. see Holdsworth, William S.

Reams, Bernard D., Jr., ed. see Jameson, J. Franklin.

Reams, Bernard D., Jr., jt. ed. see Kavass, Igor I.

Reams, Bernard D., ed. see Keasbey, E. Quinton.

Reams, Bernard D., Jr., ed. see Maine, Henry J.

Reams, Bernard D., Jr., ed. see McClelland, Ralph A.

Reams, Bernard D., Jr., jt. ed. see Nelson, Mary A.

Reams, Bernard D., ed. see Pike, Luke O.

Reams, Bernard D., Jr., ed. see Pomeroy, John N. & Mann, John C.

Reams, Bernard D., Jr., ed. see Reed, Alfred Z.

Reams, Bernard D., Jr., ed. see Reeve, Tapping.

Reams, Bernard D., Jr., ed. see Russell, Elmer B.

Reams, Bernard D., Jr., jt. ed. see Schultz, Jon S.

Reams, Bernard D., Jr., ed. see Street, Thomas A.

Reams, Bernard D., Jr., ed. see Sullivan, James.

Reams, Bernard D., Jr., ed. see Taylor, John N.

Reams, Bernard D., Jr., ed. see Thomas, J. H.

Reams, Bernard D., Jr., ed. see Wood, Horace G.

Reams, Bernard D., Jr., jt. ed. see Wypyski, Eugene M.

Reams, Bernard J., Jr., jt. ed. see Helmholz, R. H.

Reams, William. The Whole Man: Meditations on the Life of Christ. xiv, 242p. (Orig.). 1999. reprint ed. pap. text 10.00 (*0-9669329-0-0*) A R Griffin Graphic.

***Reamsnider, Fred.** Banquets by Men - Anyone Can Do. Spears-Stewart, Reta, ed. (Illus.). 99p. 1999. pap. write for info. (*1-892477-20-3*) Barnabs Pub.

Reamy, Martha & Reamy, William, compiled by. Index to the Roll of Honor: With a Place Index to Burial Sites Compiled by Mark Hughes. LC 95-78115. 1210p. 1995. 75.00 (*0-8063-1483-4*) Genealog Pub.

Reamy, Martha, ed. see Brown, George S.

Reamy, Tom. Blind Voices. LC 78-3817. 254p. 1978. 25.00 (*0-399-12240-0*) Ultramarine Pub.

— San Diego Lightfoot Sue & Other Stories. LC 79-54396. (Illus.). 1979. 19.95 (*0-935128-00-X*) Ursus Imprints.

Reamy, William, jt. compiled by see Reamy, Martha.

Reamy, William, ed. see Brown, George S.

Reaney, James. Alice Through the Looking Glass. LC 95-109895. 160p. 1994. pap. write for info. (*0-88984-147-0*) Porcup Quill.

— The Box Social & Other Stories. LC 96-177432. 160p. 1996. pap. write for info. (*0-88984-173-X*) Porcup Quill.

An Asterisk (*) at the beginning of an entry indicates that the title is appearing for the first time.

— The Boy with an R in His Hand. 112p. 1980. pap. write for info. (0-88984-059-8) Porcup Quill.
— Colours in the Dark. 136p. 1969. pap. 12.95 (0-88922-001-8, Pub. by Talonbks) Genl Dist Srvs.
— Listen to the Wind. 208p. 1972. reprint ed. 12.95 (0-88922-002-6, Pub. by Talonbks) Genl Dist Srvs.
— Take the Big Picture. 176p. 1986. pap. write for info. (0-88984-087-3) Porcup Quill.
Reaney, James & Gervais, C. H. Baldoon. 120p. 1976. pap. write for info. (0-88984-016-4) Porcup Quill.
Reaney, James S. The Plays of James Reaney. 110p. 1977. pap. 7.00 (0-920763-30-8, Pub. by ECW) LPC InBook.
Reaney, P. H. The Origin of English Surnames. 1980. pap. 12.95 (0-7100-0353-6, Routledge Thoemms) Routledge.
Reaney, P. H. & Wilson, M. A Dictionary of English Surnames. 3rd ed. 640p. (C). 1991. 90.00 (0-415-05737-X) Routledge.
Reaney, P. H. & Wilson, R. M. A Dictionary of English Surnames. 2nd rev. ed. LC 97-216995. (Illus.). 590p. 1997. pap. 16.95 (0-19-860092-5) OUP.
Reanney, Darryl. Music of the Mind: An Adventure into Consciousness. (Illus.). 192p. 1997. pap. 14.95 (0-285-63288-4, Pub. by Souvenir Pr Ltd) IPG Chicago.
Reanult, Michael, ed. see Rolliet, D. G.
***Reapsome, James.** Abraham. (Fisherman Bible Studyguides Ser.). 2000. pap. 4.99 (0-87788-003-4, H Shaw Pubs) Waterbrook Pr.
— Exodus. (LifeGuide Bible Studies). 2000. pap. 4.99 (0-8308-3023-5) InterVarsity.
Reapsome, James. Exodus: Learning to Trust God. LC 89-15299. (LifeGuide Bible Studies). 110p. (Orig.). 1989. pap., wbk. ed. 4.99 (0-8308-1023-4, 1023) InterVarsity.
— Growing Through Life's Challenges. (Fisherman Bible Studyguide Ser.). 1995. pap. text 4.99 (0-87788-381-5, H Shaw Pubs) Waterbrook Pr.
— Hebrews: Race to Glory. (LifeGuide Bible Studies). 64p. (Orig.). 1991. pap., wbk. ed. 4.99 (0-8308-1017-X, 1017) InterVarsity.
— Jeremiah: The Man & His Message. 80p. 1998. pap. 4.99 (0-87788-417-X, H Shaw Pubs) Waterbrook Pr.
— Romans: The Christian Story. (Fisherman Bible Studyguide Ser.). 96p. 1989. pap. 4.99 (0-87788-734-9, H Shaw Pubs) Waterbrook Pr.
Reapsome, James & Reapsome, Martha. Discipleship: The Growing Christian's Lifestyle. (Fisherman Bible Studyguide Ser.). 64p. 1984. pap. 4.99 (0-87788-175-8, H Shaw Pubs) Waterbrook Pr.
— Discipleship: The Growing Christian's Lifestyle - Chinese Edition. Ting, Yi-Hsin, tr. (CHI.). 57p. 1995. pap. 5.00 (1-56582-009-6) Christ Renew Min.
— Effective Prayer. (Discipleship Ser.). 48p. 1992. pap. 5.99 (0-310-54731-8) Zondervan.
— Marriage: God's Design for Intimacy. (LifeGuide Bible Studies). 64p. 1986. pap., wbk. ed. 4.99 (0-8308-1056-0, 1056) InterVarsity.
***Reapsome, James & Reapsome, Martha.** Marriage: God's Design for Intimacy. rev. ed. (Life Guide Bible Studies Ser.). 63p. 1999. pap. 4.99 (0-8308-3056-1, 3056) InterVarsity.
Reapsome, James & Reapsome, Martha. Money: How Much Is Enough. LC 93-49885. (Truthseed Ser.). 96p. 1995. pap. 4.99 (1-56476-309-9, 6-3309, Victor Bks) Chariot Victor.
— Spiritual Warfare. (Discipleship Ser.). 48p. 1992. pap. 5.99 (0-310-54771-7) Zondervan.
***Reapsome, James W.** Final Analysis. 240p. 1999. 14.95 (0-9617751-4-9) Evangel Missions.
Reapsome, Jim & Reapsome, Martha. Senior Saints: Growing Older in God's Family. (Fisherman Bible Studyguide Ser.). 80p. (Orig.). 1993. pap. text 4.99 (0-87788-746-2, H Shaw Pubs) Waterbrook Pr.
***Reapsome, Martha.** Colossians & Philemon. (LifeGuide Bible Studies). 2000. pap. 4.99 (0-8308-3014-6) InterVarsity.
Reapsome, Martha. Colossians & Philemon: Finding Fulfillment in Christ. LC 89-15298. (LifeGuide Bible Studies). 63p. (Orig.). 1989. pap. 4.99 (0-8308-1014-5, 1014) InterVarsity.
— Treasures: Discovering God's Riches. 48p. 1998. pap. 5.99 (1-880266-29-6) Neighborhood Bible.
Reapsome, Martha, jt. auth. see Reapsome, James.
Reapsome, Martha, jt. auth. see Reapsome, Jim.
Rearden, Jim. Alaska's Salmon Fisheries. (Alaska Geographic Ser.: Vol. 10, No. 3). (Illus.). 128p. 1983. pap. 19.95 (0-88240-174-2) Alaska Geog Soc.
— Alaska's Wolf Man: The 1915-55 Wilderness Adventures of Frank Glaser. LC 98-66445. (Illus.). 330p. 1998. pap. 17.95 (1-57510-047-9) Pictorial Hist.
— Castner's Cutthroats: Saga of the Alaska Scouts. (Illus.). 380p. 1990. 28.95 (0-935632-93-X) Wolfe Pub Co.
— Tales of Alaska's Big Bears. 238p. (Orig.). 1989. pap. 12.95 (0-935632-83-2) Wolfe Pub Co.
Rearden, Jim, jt. auth. see Conkle, Bud.
Rearden, Nita Prince. Fish Camp in Alaska. 32p. (J). (gr. 1-7). 1993. pap. 6.95 (1-878051-14-8) Circumpolar Pr.
Rearden, Steven L., jt. auth. see Thompson, Kenneth W.
Rearden, Steven L., jt. ed. see Thompson, Kenneth W.
Reardon & Lenz. Career Development & Planning: A Cognitive Approach. LC 99-16354. (Counseling Ser.). 1999. 67.95 (0-534-36472-1) Brooks-Cole.
Reardon, A. A Study of Humor in Greek Tragedy. 1972. 59.95 (0-8490-1153-1) Gordon Pr.
Reardon, Agnes. Personality & Morality: A Developmental Approach. (Illus.). 122p. (Orig.). 1983. pap. 8.95 (0-931474-26-4) TBW Bks.
Reardon-Anderson, James. Pollution, Politics, & Foreign Investment in Taiwan: The Lukang Rebellion. LC 92-29888. (Taiwan in the Modern World). 134p. (C). (gr. 13). 1992. text 53.95 (0-87332-702-0, East Gate Bk) M E Sharpe.
— The Study of Change: Chemistry in China, 1840-1949. (Illus.). 464p. (C). 1991. text 85.00 (0-521-39150-4) Cambridge U Pr.
— Unites States-China Nuclear Cooperative Agreement of 1985. (Pew Case Studies in International Affairs). 50p. (C). 1993. pap. text 3.50 (1-56927-110-0) Geo U Inst Dplmcy.
Reardon, Anne M. & Chambers, Kate. Called to Live Justly: Social Justice Themes in Luke/Acts. (Illus.). 36p. 1984. pap. text 2.95 (0-934134-20-0) Sheed & Ward WI.
— Follow Me: Becoming a Disciple According to Matthew's Gospel. (Illus.). 32p. 1985. pap. text 2.95 (0-934134-81-2, LL0812) Sheed & Ward WI.
Reardon, B. P. The Form of Greek Romance. 223p. 1991. text 39.50 (0-691-06838-0, Pub. by Princeton U Pr) Cal Prin Full Svc.
Reardon, B. P., ed. Collected Ancient Greek Novels. 835p. 1997. pap. 32.50 (0-520-04306-5, Pub. by U CA Pr) Cal Prin Full Svc.
Reardon, B. P., tr. see Lucian.
Reardon, Bernard G. Kant As Philosophical Theologian. 192p. 1987. 50.00 (0-389-20759-4, N8318) B&N Imports.
Reardon, Bernard M. Religion in the Age of Romanticism: Studies in Early Nineteenth Century Thought. 313p. 1985. text 90.00 (0-521-30088-6) Cambridge U Pr.
— Religious Thought in the Reformation. 2nd ed. LC 94-36908. (C). 1995. text 50.95 (0-582-25960-6) Longman.
— Religious Thought in the Reformation. 2nd ed. (C). 1996. pap. text 20.95 (0-582-25959-2) Wiley.
— Religious Thought in the Victorian Age: A Survey from Coleridge to Gore. 2nd ed. LC 95-15347. 400p. (C). 1996. pap. text 36.80 (0-582-26516-9) Addison-Wesley.
— Religious Thought Reform. (C). 1981. pap. text 28.50 (0-582-49031-6, 73448) Longman.
— Religious Thought Victorian Age. 2nd ed. LC 95-15347. 400p. (C). 1996. text 56.25 (0-582-26514-2) Addison-Wesley.
Reardon, Bernard M., ed. Liberal Protestantism. 244p. 1968. 32.50 (0-8047-0647-6) Stanford U Pr.
Reardon, Betty A. Comprehensive Peace Education: Educating for Global Responsibility. 136p. 1988. text 26.00 (0-8077-2886-1); pap. text 13.95 (0-8077-2885-3) Tchrs Coll.
— Educating for Human Dignity: Learning about Rights & Responsibilities. (Pennsylvania Studies in Human Rights). 340p. 1995. text 49.95 (0-8122-3306-9); pap. text 24.95 (0-8122-1524-9) U of Pa Pr.
— Sexism & the War System. 132p. (Orig.). (C). 1996. pap. 17.95 (0-8156-0348-7, RESWP) Syracuse U Pr.
— Women & Peace: Feminist Visions of Global Security. LC 92-9682. (SUNY Series, Global Conflict & Peace Education). 209p. (C). 1993. text 57.50 (0-7914-1399-3); pap. text 19.95 (0-7914-1400-0) State U NY Pr.
Reardon, Betty A., ed. Educating for Global Responsibility: Teacher-Designed Curricula for Peace Education, K-12. 216p. (C). 1987. pap. text 15.95 (0-8077-2879-9) Tchrs Coll.
— Educating for Global Responsibility: Teacher-Designed Curricula for Peace Education, K-12. LC 87-18017. 216p. 1988. reprint ed. pap. 67.00 (0-7837-9601-3, 206035800005) Bks Demand.
Reardon, Betty A. & Nordland, Eva, eds. Learning Peace: The Promise of Ecological & Cooperative Education. LC 93-731. (SUNY Series, Global Conflict & Peace Education). 234p. (C). 1994. text 57.50 (0-7914-1755-7); pap. text 18.95 (0-7914-1756-5) State U NY Pr.
Reardon, Bob, et al, eds. 1996 Olympic Games Cookbook: From Athens to Atlanta. (Illus.). 24p. (Orig.). 1995. pap. 6.95 (1-880970-19-8) Aerial Photo.
Reardon, Carol. Pickett's Charge in History & Memory. LC 97-10965. (Civil War America Ser.). (Illus.). 296p. (gr. 13). 1997. 29.95 (0-8078-2379-1) U of NC Pr.
— Soldiers & Scholars: The U. S. Army & the Uses of Military History, 1865-1920. LC 90-50111. (Modern War Studies). viii, 272p. 1990. 35.00 (0-7006-0466-9) U Pr of KS.
Reardon, Colleen. Agostino Agazzari & Music at Siena Cathedral, 1597-1641. (Oxford Monographs on Music). (Illus.). 224p. 1994. text 65.00 (0-19-816272-3) OUP.
Reardon, David, jt. auth. see Makimaa, Julie.
Reardon, David C. The Jericho Plan: Breaking down the Walls Which Prevent Post-Abortion Healing. LC 96-83667. 120p. (Orig.). 1996. pap. 8.95 (0-9648957-5-7) Acorn Books.
— Making Abortion Rare: A Healing Strategy for a Divided Nation. LC 95-81057. 224p. (Orig.). 1996. 24.95 (0-9648957-7-3) Acorn Books.
Reardon, Geraldine. Power & Process: Gender & Development. LC 96-155018. (Gender & Development Ser.). 280p. (C). 1995. pap. 15.95 (0-85598-297-7, Pub. by Oxfam Pub) Stylus Pub VA.
— Women & Environment: Gender & Development. (Gender & Development Ser.). (Illus.). 64p. (C). 1993. pap. 12.95 (0-85598-221-7, Pub. by Oxfam Pub) Stylus Pub VA.
Reardon, J. Koga's Zero: The Fighter That Changed World War II. (Illus.). 114p. 1995. pap. 12.95 (0-929521-56-0) Pictorial Hist.
Reardon, James. Big Time Tommy Sloane. LC 86-31957. 320p. 1987. 18.95 (0-88191-043-0) Freundlich.
Reardon, James, jt. auth. see Hasty, Ronald W.
Reardon, Jim, tr. see Huntington, Sidney.
***Reardon, Joan.** Oysters: A Culinary Celebration. rev. ed. LC 99-35886. (Illus.). 256p. 2000. 25.00 (1-55821-944-7) Lyons Pr.
Reardon, Joan. Poetry by American Women, 1975-1989: A Bibliography. LC 90-21020. 242p. 1990. 32.50 (0-8108-2366-7) Scarecrow.
Reardon, Joan & Thorsen, Kristine A. Poetry by American Women, 1900-1975: A Bibliography. LC 78-11944. 631p. 1979. 39.50 (0-8108-1173-1) Scarecrow.
Reardon, John. All-Star Dads. 104p. 1997. pap. 9.95 (0-9650315-4-3) Glacier Publng.
Reardon, John J. America & the Multinational Corporation: The History of a Troubled Partnership. LC 92-12211. 194p. 1992. 55.00 (0-275-93918-9, C3918, Praeger Pubs) Greenwood.
— Peyton Randolph, 1721-1775: One Who Presided. LC 81-70431. (Illus.). 112p. 1982. lib. bdg. 12.95 (0-89089-201-6) Carolina Acad Pr.
Reardon, Judy. Criminal Justice Research under the Crime Act, 1995-1996. 85p. (C). 1999. text 20.00 (0-7881-7911-X) DIANE Pub.
Reardon, Kathleen K. Persuasion in Practice. 2nd ed. (Illus.). 232p. 1991. 45.00 (0-8039-3316-9); pap. 19.95 (0-8039-3317-7) Sage.
— Persuasion, Theory, & Context. LC 81-1892. (Sage Library of Social Research: No. 122). 283p. 1981. reprint ed. pap. 87.80 (0-608-01446-X, 205949000001) Bks Demand.
— They Don't Get It, Do They? Communication in the Workplace - Closing the Gap Between Men & Women. 1996. pap. 12.95 (0-316-73634-1) Little.
— They Don't Get It, Do They? Communication in the Workplace - Closing the Gap Between Women & Men. 1996. pap. 12.95 (0-614-12585-5) Little.
***Reardon, Kathleen Kelley.** The Secret Handshake: Mastering the Politics of the Business Inner Circle. 320p. 2000. 24.95 (0-385-49527-7) Doubleday.
Reardon, L. F., jt. auth. see Kleinberg, Howard.
***Reardon, Lisa.** Billy Dead. LC 98-18721. 260p. 2000. pap. 12.95 (0-14-028051-0) Viking Penguin.
Reardon, Lisa. Billy Dead: A Novel. LC 98-18721. 304p. 1998. 22.95 (0-670-88224-0) Viking Penguin.
***Reardon, Lisa.** Blameless. LC 99-55524. 336p. 2000. 24.95 (0-375-50405-2) Random.
Reardon, Madeliene, ed. see York, Norman J. & York, Madeleine.
Reardon, Madeliene, ed. see York, Norman J. & York, Madeleine A.
Reardon, Marge. How to Flatten Your Tush. 1979. 2.00 (0-87980-369-X) Wilshire.
Reardon, Patricia, jt. auth. see Lippman, Helen.
Reardon, Patrick T. Daily Meditations with Scripture for Busy Dads. LC 95-78804. 368p. 1995. pap. 8.95 (0-87946-128-4, 196) ACTA Pubns.
***Reardon, Patrick T.** Starting Out: Reflections for Young People. LC 00-101208. 112p. 2000. pap. 5.95 (0-87946-212-4) ACTA Pubns.
Reardon, Ray. Universal Reflections. 90p. 1993. pap. 120.00 (0-949823-33-3, Pub. by Deakin Univ) St Mut.
Reardon, Robert C. & Lenz, Janet G. The Self-Directed Search & Related Holland Career Materials: A Practitioner's Guide. LC 97-45675. 320p. 1997. pap. text 29.00 (0-911907-28-9) Psych Assess.
Reardon, Roy, ed. see Fallada, Hans.
Reardon, Ruth. Listening to a Teenager. LC 95-184472. (Illus.). 64p. 1995. 8.95 (0-8378-8830-1) Gibson.
— Listening to the Littlest. (Illus.). 48p. 1984. 8.95 (0-8378-1749-8) Gibson.
Reardon, Ruth & Rodegast, Roland. Listen to My Feelings. (Illus.). (J). 1992. 8.95 (0-8378-2499-0) Gibson.
Reardon, Thomas, jt. ed. see Vosti, Stephen A.
***Reardon, Thomas M.** Managed Care Contracting: A Practical Guide for Health Care Executives. LC 98-43360. 1999. 45.95 (0-7879-4581-1) Jossey-Bass.
Reardon, Timothy A., jt. auth. see Baumgold, Sharon.
Reardon, William R. & Pawley, Thomas D. Black Teacher & the Dramatic Arts: A Dialogue, Bibliography & Anthology, 3. LC 73-90789. 487p. 1970. 65.00 (0-8371-1850-6, RET&) Greenwood.
Rearick, Charles. The French in Love & War: Popular Culture in France, 1914-1945. LC 96-50287. (Illus.). 384p. 1997. 37.00 (0-300-06433-0) Yale U Pr.
— Pleasures of the Belle Epoque: Entertainment & Festivity in Turn-of-the-Century France. LC 85-40468. 263p. 1985. pap. 81.60 (0-7837-8653-0, 208236600009) Bks Demand.
— Pleasures of the Belle Epoque: Entertainment & Festivity in Turn-of-the-Century France. LC 85-40468. 240p. (C). 1988. reprint ed. pap. 25.00 (0-300-04381-3) Yale U Pr.
Rearick, Elizabeth C. Dances of the Hungarians. LC 72-177181. (Columbia University. Teachers College. Contributions to Education Ser.: No. 770). reprint ed. 37.50 (0-404-55770-8) AMS Pr.
Rearick, W. R., et al. Jacopo Bassano, 1510-1592. Marini, Paola, ed. & intro. by. Pillsbury, Edmund P. et al, intros. (Illus.). 594p. 1993. 115.00 (0-912804-28-9) Kimbell Art.
Reasbeck, Philip & Smith, James G. Batteries for Automotive Use. LC 97-3760. (Electronic & Electrical Engineering Research Studies). 1997. write for info. (0-86380-176-5) Wiley.
Reasenberg, R. D. & Vessot, R. F., eds. Relativistic Gravitation: Proceedings of Symposium 15 of the CCSPAR Twenty-Seventh Plenary Meeting Held in Espoo, Finland, 18-29 July 1988. (Advances in Space Research Ser.: No. 9). (Illus.). 158p. 1989. pap. 92.75 (0-08-040151-1, 1702; 1709; 2308, Pergamon Pr) Elsevier.
Reasenberg, Robert D., ed. Astronomical Interferometry. (Proceedings of SPIE Ser.: Vol. 3350). 1102p. 1998. 158.00 (0-8194-2797-7) SPIE.
Reaser, Donald. Essentials in Historical Geology. 168p. (C). 1996. pap. text, spiral bd. 38.95 (0-7872-1864-2) Kendall-Hunt.
Reaser, Jamie, jt. auth. see Greenberg, Russell.
Reash, Janice M. Early Vows. 2nd ed. reprint ed. pap. 6.00 (0-9616908-0-1) Piedmont Pr OH.
— Spending the Light. (Illus.). (Orig.). Date not set. pap. text 7.95 (0-9616908-1-X) Piedmont Pr OH.
***Reashid, Rushdei & Vahabzadeh, B.** Khayyam: The Mathematician. LC 00-28814. 2000. write for info. (0-933273-43-6) Bibliotheca Persica.
Reaske, Christopher R. The Compleat Clammer. LC 98-43772. (Illus.). 176p. 1999. reprint ed. pap. 14.95 (1-58080-028-9) Burford Bks.
— The Compleat Crab & Lobster Book. rev. ed. LC 98-43873. (Illus.). 176p. 1999. reprint ed. pap. 14.95 (1-58080-027-0) Burford Bks.
— Separate Peace. (C). 3.95 (0-671-00889-7, Arco) Macmillan Gen Ref.
Reaske, Herbert. Monarch Notes on Tolstoy's Anna Karenina. (Orig.). (C). 3.95 (0-671-00571-5, Arco) Macmillan Gen Ref.
Reasmus, Desiderius. Collected Works of Erasmus Vol. 84: Controversies with Alberto Pio. Minnich, Nelson, ed. Sheerin, Daniel, ed. & tr. by. 792p. 1999. text 175.00 (0-8020-4397-6) U of Toronto Pr.
Reason. Da'akfal. (S. O. R. D. Ser.). (Illus.). 128p. 1998. pap. 21.95 (0-9655070-3-3) Fractal Dimensions.
— Tribal Raids. (Gamelet Ser.: Vol. 3). (Illus.). 16p. 1998. pap. 8.95 (0-9655070-4-1) Fractal Dimensions.
Reason, J. T., jt. ed. see Broadbent, Donald E.
Reason, Jack. Arrowdust. large type ed. (Dales Large Print Ser.). 191p. 1996. pap. 18.99 (1-85389-686-1, Dales) Ulverscroft.
***Reason, Jack.** Roughshod. large type ed. 224p. 1999. pap. 18.99 (0-7089-5543-6, Linford) Ulverscroft.
Reason, Jack. Wild Gold. large type ed. (Dales Western Ser.). 208p. 1998. pap. 19.99 (1-85389-798-1, Dales) Ulverscroft.
Reason, James. Human Error. 316p. (C). 1990. pap. text 26.95 (0-521-31419-4) Cambridge U Pr.
— Managing Risks of Organizational Accidents. LC 97-24648. 200p. 1997. pap. 37.95 (1-84014-105-0, Pub. by Ashgate Pub) Ashgate Pub Co.
Reason, James, jt. auth. see Maurino, Daniel E.
Reason, James T. Managing Risks of Organizational Accidents. LC 97-24648. (Illus.). 252p. 1997. text 78.95 (1-84014-104-2, Pub. by Ashgate Pub) Ashgate Pub Co.
Reason, Joseph H. Inquiry into the Structural Style & Originality of Chrestien's Yvain. LC 79-174304. (Catholic University of America. Studies in Romance Languages & Literatures: No. 57). reprint ed. 37.50 (0-404-50357-8) AMS Pr.
Reason, Peter, ed. Human Inquiry in Action: Developments in New Paradigm Research. 272p. (C). 1989. text 45.00 (0-8039-8089-2); pap. text 17.95 (0-8039-8090-6) Sage.
— Participation in Human Inquiry. 240p. 1995. 69.95 (0-8039-8831-1); pap. 26.95 (0-8039-8832-X) Sage.
Reason, Peter & Rowan, John, eds. Human Inquiry: A Sourcebook of New Paradigm Research. LC 80-41585. 554p. 1981. pap. 94.50 (0-471-27936-6) Wiley.
Reason, Rea & Boote, Rene. Helping Children with Reading & Spelling: A Special Needs Manual. 2nd ed. LC 94-1685. (Illus.). 144p. (C). 1994. pap. 25.99 (0-415-10733-4, B4571) Routledge.
Reason, Ron. Communicating with Type. 1997. 39.99 (1-56830-390-4) Hayden.
Reason, Sharon, ed. see Zakutinsky, Ruth.
Reasoner, Barbara. Becoming Whole in a Half Assed World: A Primer to Lighten up & Balance Your Life. LC 95-80243. 125p. 1995. pap. 14.95 (1-885221-17-7) BookPartners.
Reasoner, Charles. Color Crunch! (Mini Bites Ser.). (Illus.). 32p. (J). (ps-k). 1998. pap. 4.99 (0-8431-7820-5, Price Stern) Peng Put Young Read.
***Reasoner, Charles.** Funny Bones. (Halloween Glow Bks.). (Illus.). 14p. (J). (ps-k). 2000. bds. 4.99 (0-8431-7607-5, Price Stern) Peng Put Young Read.
— Going Batty. (Halloween Glow Bks.). (Illus.). 14p. (J). (ps-k). 2000. bds. 4.99 (0-8431-7605-9, Price Stern) Peng Put Young Read.
Reasoner, Charles. Jack-O'-Lantern. (Halloween Bk.). 14p. 1999. pap. 4.99 (0-8431-7515-X, Price Stern) Peng Put Young Read.
— Lunch Box. (Little Box Bks.). (Illus.). 8p. (J). (ps up). 1995. bds. 8.95 (0-614-03672-0, Price Stern) Peng Put Young Read.
— The Magic Amber. LC 93-43180. (Legends of the World Ser.). (Illus.). 32p. (J). (gr. 2-5). 1994. pap. 4.95 (0-8167-3408-9) Troll Communs.
— The Magic Amber. LC 93-43180. (Legends of the World Ser.). (Illus.). 32p. (J). (gr. 2-5). 1997. lib. bdg. 18.60 (0-8167-3407-0) Troll Communs.
— Magic Amber: A Korean Legend. LC 93-43180. (Legends of the World Ser.). 1994. 9.15 (0-606-06550-4, Pub. by Turtleback) Demco.
***Reasoner, Charles.** Mrs. Broom. (Halloween Glow Bks.). (Illus.). 14p. (J). (ps-k). 2000. bds. 4.99 (0-8431-7606-7, Price Stern) Peng Put Young Read.
Reasoner, Charles. Night Owl & the Rooster: A Haitian Legend. (Legends of the World Ser.). (J). 1995. 9.15 (0-606-07949-1, Pub. by Turtleback) Demco.
— Number Munch! LC 95-122272. (Illus.). 34p. (J). (ps-k). 1993. pap. 9.95 (0-8431-3674-X, Price Stern) Peng Put Young Read.
— Number Munch! (Mini Bites Ser.). (Illus.). 32p. (J). (ps-k). 1998. pap. 4.99 (0-8431-7821-3, Price Stern) Peng Put Young Read.
— Who Drives This? LC 95-68614. (Sliding Surprise Ser.). (J). (ps-k). 1996. pap. 9.95 (0-8431-3939-0, Price Stern) Peng Put Young Read.
— Who Pretends? (Sliding Surprise Ser.). (J). (ps up). 1996. pap. 9.95 (0-8431-3940-4, Price Stern) Peng Put Young Read.

R

— Who's Bugging You? (Sliding Surprise Ser.). (Illus.). 12p. (J). (ps). 1997. pap. 9.99 (0-8431-7989-9, Price Stern) Peng Put Young Read.

*Reasoner, Charles. Who's Got Mail. (Illus.). 14p. (ps-k). 2000. pap. 7.99 (0-8431-7592-3, Price Stern) Peng Put Young Read.

Reasoner, Charles. Who's Hatching? LC 93-87680. (Sliding Surprise Ser.). (Illus.). 12p. (J). (ps). 1994. pap. 9.99 (0-8431-3717-7, Price Stern) Peng Put Young Read.

— Who's Peeking? (Sliding Surprise Ser.). (Illus.). 12p. (J). (ps). 1993. pap. 9.99 (0-8431-3478-X, Price Stern) Peng Put Young Read.

— Who's There? (Sliding Surprise Ser.). (Illus.). 12p. (J). (ps). 1993. pap. 9.99 (0-8431-3479-8, Price Stern) Peng Put Young Read.

— Whose Daddy Does This? LC 96-67354. (Sliding Surprise Ser.). (Illus.). 12p. (J). (ps). 1997. pap. 9.95 (0-8431-7988-0, Price Stern) Peng Put Young Read.

— Whose House Is This? (Sliding Surprise Ser.). (Illus.). 12p. (J). 1995. pap. 9.99 (0-8431-3911-0, Price Stern) Peng Put Young Read.

— Whose Mommy Is This? LC 93-87681. (Sliding Surprise Ser.). (Illus.). 12p. (J). (ps). 1994. pap. 9.99 (0-8431-3718-5, Price Stern) Peng Put Young Read.

Reasoner, Charles, ed. Night Owl & the Rooster: A Haitian Legend. LC 95-9983. 32p. (J). (gr. 2-6). 1995. pap., teacher ed. 4.95 (0-8167-3750-9) Troll Communs.

— Night Owl & the Rooster: A Haitian Legend. LC 95-9983. (Legends of the World Ser.). 32p. (J). (gr. 2-6). 1997. lib. bdg. 18.60 (0-8167-3749-5) Troll Communs.

Reasoner, Charles. The Princess Who Lost Her Hair: An Akamba Legend. LC 92-13273. 32p. (J). (gr. 2-5). 1992. pap. 4.95 (0-8167-2816-X) Troll Communs.

— The Princess Who Lost Her Hair: An Akamba Legend. LC 92-13273. 32p. (J). (gr. 2-5). 1997. lib. bdg. 18.60 (0-8167-2815-1) Troll Communs.

Reasoner, Charles, jt. auth. see Lilly, Melinda.

Reasoner, Charles, jt. auth. see Warren, Vic.

Reasoner, J. L. Healer's Calling. 352p. 1996. mass mkt. 5.99 (0-425-15487-4) Berkley Pub.

— The Healer's Road, Bk. 1. 352p. (Orig.). 1995. mass mkt. 5.99 (0-515-11762-5, Jove) Berkley Pub.

— Rivers of Gold: A Novel of the California Gold Rush. 352p. (Orig.). 1995. mass mkt. 5.50 (0-515-11524-X, Jove) Berkley Pub.

***Reasoner, James.** Antietam: A Novel. 383p. 2000. 22.95 (1-58182-084-4, Cumberland Hearthside) Cumberland Hse.

— Manassas. LC 98-52494. (Civil War Battles Ser.: Vol. 1). 352p. 1999. 22.95 (1-58182-008-9) Cumberland Hse.

— Shiloh. LC 99-46301. (Civil War Battles Ser.: Vol. 2). 352p. 1999. 22.95 (1-58182-048-8, Cumberland Hearthside) Cumberland Hse.

Reasoner, James. Siege on the Belle, 1 vol. 1999. mass mkt. 5.99 (0-425-17112-4) Berkley Pub.

— Stark's Justice: A Judge Earl Stark Western. LC 94-131790. 1994. mass mkt. 3.99 (0-671-87140-4) PB.

— Stark's Justice: A Judge Earl Stark Western. large type ed. LC 94-35471. 1994. 21.95 (1-56895-153-1) Wheeler Pub.

— Under Outlaw Flags: From the Frontier to the Front: An American Story. 1998. mass mkt. 5.99 (0-425-16305-9) Berkley Pub.

— Walker, Texas Ranger: The Novel. (Orig.). 1999. mass mkt. 5.99 (0-425-16815-8) Berkley Pub.

— Walker, Texas Ranger Vol. 2: Hell's Half Acre. 1999. mass mkt. 5.99 (0-425-16972-3) Blvd Books.

Reasoner, James & Reasoner, Livia. Lyron's Lament Bk. 1: Sanctum Trilogy. (Margaret Weis Presents Crusade Ser.). 224p. 1995. pap. 9.95 (0-9647973-0-5) Westvenge.

***Reasoner, James & Washburn, Livia J.** Tie a Black Ribbon. LC 99-56407. 214p. 2000. 21.95 (0-7862-2362-6) Five Star.

Reasoner, James, jt. auth. see Lovisi, Gary.

Reasoner, James M. The Diablo Grant. 240p. (Orig.). 1995. mass mkt. 4.99 (0-671-87142-0) PB.

Reasoner, Livia. Mending Fences. (Our Town Ser.). 1998. mass mkt. 5.99 (0-515-12211-4, Jove) Berkley Pub.

Reasoner, Livia, jt. auth. see Reasoner, James.

Reasoner, Mark. The Strong & the Weak: Romans 14.1-15.13 in Context. LC 98-20168. (Society for New Testament Studies Monograph Ser.: No. 103). (Illus.). 294p. (C). 1999. text 59.95 (0-521-63334-6) Cambridge U Pr.

Reasoner, Robert W. Building Self-Esteem in the Elementary Schools. 2nd rev. ed. 1992. teacher ed., ring bd. 154.00 (0-89106-056-1) Consulting Psychol.

***Reasoner, Vic.** The Hope of the Gospel: An Introduction to Wesleyan Eschatology. 416p. 1999. pap. 29.95 (0-9629383-7-8) Fundmntl Wesleyan.

Reasoner, Vic, ed. see Smith, A. J.

Reasoner, Victor P. The Hole in the Holiness Movement. 149p. (Orig.). 1991. pap. 4.95 (0-9629383-3-5) Fundmntl Wesleyan.

Reasoner, Victor P. & Brush, Robert L., eds. The Wesley Workbook: A Brief Biography Plus a Study Guide to the Standard Sermons. 95p. 1996. spiral bd. 8.95 (0-9629383-5-1) Fundmntl Wesleyan.

Reasonner, James M. The Hawthorne Legacy. Grad, Doug, ed. (Orig.). 1994. mass mkt. 4.99 (0-671-87141-2) PB.

Reat, N. Ross. Buddhism: A History. LC 93-1792. (Religions of the World Ser.). 392p. (C). 1993. pap. 20.00 (0-87573-002-7); text 30.00 (0-87573-001-9) Jain Pub Co.

— Origins of Indian Psychology. LC 90-48484. 400p. (C). 1990. pap. 25.00 (0-89581-924-4); text 30.00 (0-89581-923-6) Asian Humanities.

Reat, N. Ross & Perry, Edmund F. A World Theology: The Central Spiritual Reality of Humankind. 328p. (C). 1991. text 65.00 (0-521-33159-5) Cambridge U Pr.

Reath, Andrews, et al, eds. Reclaiming the History of Ethics: Essays for John Rawls. 422p. 1997. text 64.95 (0-521-47240-7) Cambridge U Pr.

Reati, Angelo, jt. ed. see Michie, Jonathan.

Reato, Danilo. Venice. (Places & History Ser.). (Illus.). 136p. 1997. 24.95 (1-55670-532-8) Stewart Tabori & Chang.

Reatto, L. & Manghi, F. Progress in Computational Physics of Matter: Methods, Software & Applications. LC 96-146973. 300p. 1995. text 76.00 (981-02-2404-4) World Scientific Pub.

Reau, Louis. Dictionnaire Polyglotte des Termes d'Art et d'Archeologie. (ENG, FRE, GER & ITA.). 1977. write for info. (0-7859-8668-5, 3535015502) Fr & Eur.

— Dictionnaire Polyglotte des Termes d'Art et d'Archeologie. (ENG, FRE, GER & ITA.). 961p. 1977. reprint ed. 595.00 (0-8288-9540-6, M6612) Fr & Eur.

— Inconographie de l'Chretien: Paris, 1955-1959, 3. vols. 1969. 780.00 (0-8115-0046-2) Periodicals Srv.

Reaues, Brian A. & Smith, Pheny Z. Felony Defendants in Large Urban Counties (1992) (Illus.). 47p. (Orig.). (C). 1995. pap. text 25.00 (0-7881-2543-5) DIANE Pub.

Reaugh, Frank. Frank Reaugh: Painter to the Longhorns. LC 85-40051. (Joe & Betty Moore Texas Art Ser.: No. 7). (Illus.). 148p. 1985. 34.95 (0-89096-236-7) Tex A&M Univ Pr.

Reaume, Chuck, jt. auth. see Knight, E. Leslie.

***Reaume, Geoffrey.** Remembrance of Patients Past: Patient Life at the Toronto Hospital for the Insane, 1870-1940. (Canadian Social History Ser.). (Illus.). 376p. 2000. pap. 19.95 (0-19-541538-8) OUP.

Reaumur, Rene A. De, see De Reaumur, Rene A.

Reaveley, Mabel. Weathervane Secrets. LC 83-25854. (Illus.). (Orig.). 1984. pap. 8.95 (0-87233-075-3) Bauhan.

Reaven, Gerald M. Clinician's Guide to Non-Insulin-Dependent Diabetes Mellitus Pathogenesis & Treatment. 152p. 1989. text 75.00 (0-8247-8083-3) Dekker.

***Reaven, Gerald M.** Type 2 Diabetes - Questions & Answers. (Questions & Answers Ser.). (Illus.). 2000. pap. text 17.95 (1-873413-17-3) Merit Pub Intl.

Reaven, Gerald M. & Laws, Ami, eds. Insulin Resistance: The Metabolic Syndrome X. LC 98-36840. (Contemporary Endocrinology Ser.: Vol. 12). (Illus.). 374p. 1999. 145.00 (0-89603-588-3) Humana.

Reaven, Gerald M., et al. Syndrome X: Overcoming the Silent Killer That Can Give You a Heart Attack. LC 99-52592. (Illus.). 288p. 2000. 24.50 (0-684-86862-8) S&S Trade.

Reaver, Chap. Bill. LC 93-35491. (J). 1996. 9.09 (0-606-09076-2, Pub. by Turtleback) Demco.

Reaver, Chap. A Little Bit Dead. LC 92-7185. 240p. (YA). (gr. 6 up). 1992. 15.00 (0-385-30801-9) Delacorte.

Reaver, Chap. A Little Bit Dead. LC 92-7185. 1992. 9.09 (0-606-06534-2, Pub. by Turtleback) Demco.

Reaver, Chap. A Little Bit Dead. large type ed. LC 93-42210. (J). 1994. lib. bdg. 15.95 (0-7862-0139-8) Thorndike Pr.

Reaver, J. Russell. Emerson as Mythmaker. LC 54-8431. 116p. reprint ed. pap. 36.00 (0-7837-4997-X, 204466400004) Bks Demand.

Reaves & Roberts. Write Stuff. 198p. 1996. pap. text 19.60 (0-536-59600-X) Pearson Custom.

***Reaves, Ken.** Going Online at Home: How to Make the Internet a Family Activity. (Illus.). 272p. 2000. pap. 14.99 (0-8054-2136-X) Broadman.

Reaves, Bill. Southport Brunswick County North Carolina, a Chronology, 1920-1940, Vol. III. (Illus.). iii, 294p. 1997. pap. 12.00 (1-892444-06-2) Southport Hist.

— Southport (Smithville) a Chronology, 1887-1920, Vol. II. (Illus.). iv, 325p. 1998. reprint ed. pap. 20.00 (1-892444-05-4) Southport Hist.

— Southport (Smithville) a Chronology, 1520-1887, Vol. I. (Illus.). iv, 129p. 1992. reprint ed. pap. 15.00 (1-892444-04-6) Southport Hist.

***Reaves, Bill.** Southport (Smithville) a Chronology, 1941-1970, Vol. IV. (Illus.). vi, 275p. 1999. pap. 16.95 (1-892444-07-0) Southport Hist.

Reaves, Brian A. Local Police Departments (1993) 22p. (Orig.). (C). 1996. pap. text 20.00 (0-7881-3007-2) DIANE Pub.

***Reaves, Brian A. & Goldberg, Andrew L.** Law Enforcement Management & Administrative Statistics 1997: Data for Individual State & Local Agencies with 100 or More Officers. (Illus.). 294p. 1999. pap. text 45.00 (0-7881-8190-4) DIANE Pub.

Reaves, Brian A. & Goldberg, Andrew L., contrib. by. Campus Law Enforcement Agencies (1995) (Illus.). 44p. (C). 1997. reprint ed. pap. text 25.00 (0-7881-4253-4) DIANE Pub.

Reaves, Brian A. & Smith, Pheny Z. Law Enforcement Management & Administrative Statistics, 1993: Data for Individual State & Local Agencies with 100 or More Officers. (Illus.). 296p. (Orig.). (C). 1995. pap. text 50.00 (0-7881-2441-2) DIANE Pub.

***Reaves, Bruce.** Operation Snowfall. 148p. 1999. pap. 13.95 (0-7414-0128-2) Buy Books.

Reaves, Celia C. Quantitative Research for the Behavioral Sciences. LC 91-39997. 400p. (C). 1991. text 81.95 (0-471-61683-4) Wiley.

Reaves, George A., jt. auth. see Frank, Joseph A.

Reaves, J. Graham. A Stranger to Myself: An Adult Guide to Higher Self-Esteem & Creative Living. 120p. 1991. pap. text 8.95 (0-9630046-0-3) Lydian Comm.

Reaves, James N. Black Cops. Wartman, William, ed. (Illus.). 216p. 1991. 21.95 (0-9627161-4-6) QLP CA.

Reaves, Kin W. The Flow System for Winning at Blackjack. 128p. (Orig.). 1996. pap. 25.00 (1-57502-352-0, PO1150) Morris Pubng.

***Reaves, Lucy Marion.** Arkansas Families: Glimpses of Yesterday Columns from the Arkansas Gazette. 2nd ed. 229p. 2000. pap. 28.50 (1-56546-164-9) Arkansas Res.

Reaves, Marilyn & Schulte, Eliza. Brush Lettering: An Instructional Manual of Western Brush Lettering. LC 93-37176. 128p. 1993. pap. 24.95 (1-55821-269-8) Lyons Pr.

***Reaves, Michael.** Hell on Earth. 2000. pap. 12.00 (0-345-42335-6) Ballantine Pub Grp.

Reaves, Michael. Night Hunter. 1997. mass mkt. 5.99 (0-8125-1994-9, Pub. by Tor Bks) St Martin.

— Voodoo Child. LC 97-29847. 352p. 1998. text 25.95 (0-312-85608-3) St Martin.

— Voodoo Child. 352p. 1999. mass mkt. 6.99 (0-8125-1993-0, Pub. by Tor Bks) St Martin.

Reaves, Sam. Bury it Deep. 272p. 1994. mass mkt. 4.99 (0-380-72266-6, Avon Bks) Morrow Avon.

— Fear Will Do It. 352p. 1994. mass mkt. 4.99 (0-380-72034-5, Avon Bks) Morrow Avon.

— A Long Cold Fall. 304p. 1992. mass mkt. 4.50 (0-380-71641-0, Avon Bks) Morrow Avon.

Reaves, Shiela. Wisconsin: Pathways to Prosperity. (Illus.). 336p. (YA). (gr. 7 up). 1988. 32.95 (0-89781-236-0) Am Historical Pr.

Reaves, Verne. Heading South: A Guide to Budget Travel in Latin America. LC 81-52888. 142p. 1982. pap. 6.95 (0-9607036-0-8) Sec Thoughts OR.

Reaves, Verne, ed. see Baehr, Russell.

Reaves, Wendy W. Celebrity Caricature in America. LC 97-46906. (Illus.). 320p. 1998. 45.00 (0-300-07463-8) Yale U Pr.

Reaves, William E., Jr. Texas Art & a Wildcatter's Dream: Edgar B. Davis & the San Antonio Art League. LC 97-24600. (Joe & Betty Moore Texas Art Ser.: Vol. 9). (Illus.). 144p. 1998. pap. 24.95 (0-89096-820-9) Tex A&M Univ Pr.

Reaves, William E. Texas Art & a Wildcatter's Dream: Edgar B. Davis & the San Antonio Art League. LC 97-24600. (Joe & Betty Moore Texas Art Ser.). 114p. 1998. 49.95 (0-89096-812-8) Tex A&M Univ Pr.

Reaves, William M. Strength Through Struggle: The Chronological & Historical Record of the African-American Community in Wilmington, North Carolina, 1865-1950. Teherton, Beverly, ed. (Illus.). 580p. 1998. 30.00 (0-9670410-0-7) New Hanover.

Reavey, Duncan, jt. auth. see Graves, Jonathan.

Reavey, George, ed. New Russian Poets. 1966. 15.00 (0-8079-0095-8); pap. 7.95 (0-8079-0096-6) October.

Reavey, George, ed. The New Russian Poets. 320p. 1981. pap. 9.95 (0-7145-2715-7) M Boyars Pubs.

Reavey, George, tr. see Berdiaev, Nikolai A.

Reavey, George, tr. see Mayakovsky, Vladimir.

Reavey, George, tr. see Turgenev, Ivan Sergeevich.

Reavey, George, tr. see Yevtushenko, Yevgeny.

Reavey, Patrick G. Legal Malpractice No. 24: A Research Guide for Lawyers & Law Students. LC 95-15352. Vol. 24. xix, 94p. 1995. 42.00 (0-89941-933-X, 308680) W S Hein.

Reavill, Gil, jt. auth. see Zimmerman, Jean.

Reavis, Charles. Cooking with Fresh Sausage. 1989. pap. 2.95 (0-88266-530-8, Garden Way Pub) Storey Bks.

— Hardwood Grilling Tips & Recipes. (Country Wisdom Bulletins Ser.: Vol. A-118). 1990. pap. 2.95 (0-88266-627-4) Storey Bks.

— Home Sausage Making. LC 80-39703. (Illus.). 128p. 1983. pap. 12.95 (0-88266-246-5, Garden Way Pub) Storey Bks.

— Home Sausage Making: Healthy Low-Salt, Low-Fat Recipes. rev. ed. Oxley, Constance, tr. LC 87-45094. (Illus.). 176p. (Orig.). 1987. pap. 14.95 (0-88266-477-8, Garden Way Pub) Storey Bks.

Reavis, Cheryl. The Bartered Bride. (Historical Ser.). 1996. per. 4.99 (0-373-28919-7, 1-28919-8) Harlequin Bks.

***Reavis, Cheryl.** The Captive Heart. (Historical Ser.: Vol. 512). 296p. 2000. per. 4.99 (0-373-29112-4) Harlequin Bks.

Reavis, Cheryl. Harrigan's Bride. (Historical Ser.: No. 439). 1998. per. 4.99 (0-373-29039-X, 0-29039-5) Harlequin Bks.

— Little Darlin' 1998. per. 4.25 (0-373-24177-1, 1-24177-7) Silhouette.

— The Long Way Home. (Special Edition Ser.: No. 1245). 1999. per. 4.25 (0-373-24245-X, 1-24245-2) Silhouette.

— Meggie's Baby. (Special Edition Ser.: No. 1039). 1996. per. 3.99 (0-373-24039-2, 1-24039-9) Silhouette.

— Mother to Be. (Family Blessings Ser.). 1997. per. 3.99 (0-373-24102-X, 1-24102-5) Silhouette.

— One of Our Own: (That Special Woman!) (Special Edition Ser.). 1994. per. 3.50 (0-373-09901-0, 1-09901-9) Harlequin Bks.

— The Prisoner. (Historical Ser.: No. 726). 1992. per. 3.99 (0-373-28726-7, 1-28726-7) Harlequin Bks.

***Reavis, Cheryl.** Promise Me a Rainbow. 1999. 25.95 (0-7862-2200-X) Five Star.

Reavis, Cheryl. Tenderly: That Special Woman! (Special Edition Ser.: No. 1147). 1998. per. 3.99 (0-373-24147-X, 1-24147-0) Silhouette.

Reavis, Cheryl, jt. auth. see Eagle, Kathleen.

Reavis, Dick J. Ashes of Waco: An Investigation. LC 95-33125. 320p. 1995. 24.00 (0-684-81132-4) S&S Trade.

— The Ashes of Waco: An Investigation. LC 97-46646. 1998. pap. 19.95 (0-8156-0502-1) Syracuse U Pr.

— Texas. 2nd ed. LC 96-49826. (Compass American Guides Ser.). 336p. 1997. pap. 18.95 (1-878867-98-9, Compass Amrcn) Fodors Travel.

Reavis, Dick J., tr. see Perez, Ramon.

Reavis, Dick J., tr. see Perez, Ramon T.

***Reavis, George H.** The Animal School: The Administration of the School Curriculum with References to Individual Differences. (Illus.). 24p. 2000. reprint ed. pap. 5.95 (1-884548-31-8, 6094, Crystal Spgs) Soc Dev Educ.

Reavis, George H. Factors Controlling Attendance in Rural Schools. LC 76-177182. (Columbia University. Teachers College. Contributions to Education Ser.: No. 108). reprint ed. 37.50 (0-404-55108-4) AMS Pr.

Reavis, George H. & Good, Carter V. An Educational Platform for the Public School. LC 96-70321. 72p. 1996. pap. 13.00 (0-87367-492-8) Phi Delta Kappa.

Reavis, H. Kenton, et al, eds. BEST Practices: Behavioral & Educational Strategies for Teachers. 152p. 1996. pap. text 22.50 (1-57035-052-3, 79BEST) Sopris.

Reavis, Larry. The Master Homeowner. (Illus.). 256p. (Orig.). 1991. pap. 12.98 (0-9617523-1-9) Hathaway Pub.

Reavis, Larry, ed. Certain Carbon Steel Butt-Weld Pipe Fittings from France, Inoia, Israel, Malaysia, the Republic of Korea, Thailand, the United Kingdom, & Venezuela (1994) 56p. (C). 1999. reprint ed. pap. text 25.00 (0-7881-7715-X) DIANE Pub.

Reavis, Marguerite, tr. see Ruckert, Janet.

***Reavis, Tracey.** Stealth Jet Fighter: The F-117a. (High Interest Bks.). (Illus.). (J). 2000. 19.00 (0-516-23341-6) Childrens.

— Stealth Jet Fighter: The F-117A. LC 00-24387. (High Interest Bks.). (Illus.). 48p. (J). (gr. 4-7). 2000. pap. write for info. (0-516-23541-9) Childrens.

***Reavley, Nicola & Holt, Stephen.** The New Encyclopedia of Vitamins, Minerals, Supplements & Herbs: A completely cross-referenced user's guide for optimal health. 794p. 1999. pap. 19.95 (0-87131-897-0, Pub. by M Evans) Natl Bk Netwk.

Reay, Diane. Class Work: Mothers' Involvement in Their Children's Primary Schooling. LC 98-199174. (Women & Social Class Ser.). viii, 198 p. 1998. write for info. (1-85728-916-1) UCL Pr Ltd.

***Reay, Diane.** Class Work: Mothers' Involvement in Their Children's Primary Schooling. LC 98-199174. (Women & Social Class Ser.). 198p. 1998. 75.00 (1-85728-915-3, Pub. by UCL Pr Ltd) Taylor & Francis.

Reay, Barry. The Last Rising of the Agricultural Labourers: Rural Life & Protest in Nineteenth-Century England. (Illus.). 248p. 1990. 69.00 (0-19-820187-7) OUP.

Reay, Barry. Microhistories: Demography, Society & Culture in Rural England, 1800-1930. (Cambridge Studies in Population, Economy & Society in Past Time: No. 30). (Illus.). 313p. (C). 1996. text 59.95 (0-521-57028-X) Cambridge U Pr.

— Popular Culture in England 1550-1750. LC 98-16046. (Themes in British Social History Ser.). 288p. (C). 1998. pap. 24.60 (0-582-48954-7) Longman.

Reay, D. W., jt. ed. see Jenkins, J. D.

Reay, David A. Advance in Heat Pipe Technology. 1982. 75.00 (0-08-027286-X, Pergamon Pr) Elsevier.

— Advances in Heat Pipe Technology. 1981. pap. write for info. (0-08-027285-1, Pergamon Pr) Elsevier.

— History of Man-Powered Flight. 1977. 157.00 (0-08-021738-9, Pub. by Pergamon Repr) Franklin.

Reay, David A., ed. Energy Economics & Management in Industry: Proceedings of the European Congress Held Algarve, Portugal, 2-5 April 1984. 80p. 1985. pap. 22.00 (0-08-032548-3, Pergamon Pr) Elsevier.

— Innovation For Energy Efficiency. (Illus.). 400p. 1987. 97.00 (0-317-66351-8, Pergamon Pr) Elsevier.

Reay, David A. & Dunn, P. D. Heat Pipes. 4th ed. LC 93-41521. 358p. 1994. 107.50 (0-08-041903-8, Pergamon Pr) Elsevier.

Reay, David A. & MacMichael, D. B. Heat Pumps. 2nd ed. 347p. 1988. text 125.00 (0-08-033463-6, Pergamon Pr); pap. text 51.00 (0-08-033462-8, Pergamon Pr) Elsevier.

Reay, David A., et al. Energy & Environment: Proceedings of the International Conference on Energy & the Environment, 1995. LC 95-47802. 829p. 1995. 165.00 (1-56700-052-5) Begell Hse.

Reay, David A., jt. auth. see International Heat Pipe Conference Staff.

Reay, David G. Identifying Training Needs. 96p. 1994. pap. 25.00 (0-7494-1285-2, Kogan Pg Educ) Stylus Pub VA.

— Implementing Training. 96p. 1994. pap. 25.00 (0-7494-1287-9, Kogan Pg Educ) Stylus Pub VA.

***Reay, James.** Begin at Once to Live: Begin at Once to Live & Count Each Day as a New Life - Seneca. LC 00-190187. 2000. 25.00 (0-7388-1530-6); pap. 18.00 (0-7388-1531-4) Xlibris Corp.

Reay, John R. Generalizations of a Theorem of Caratheodory. LC 52-42839. (Memoirs Ser.: No. 1/54). 50p. 1965. pap. 16.00 (0-8218-1254-8, MEMO/1/54) Am Math.

Reazin, Ruth. Strong & Simple Messages for Children's Ministry: 59 Low-Prep, High Impact Ways to Teach Bible Truths. Brolsma, Jody, ed. LC 98-14421. (Illus.). 80p. 1998. per. 14.99 (0-7644-2051-8, Vital Ministry) Group Pub.

Reb, Sylvaine. L' Aufklarung Catholique a Salzbourg: L'Oeuvre Reformatrice (1772-1803) de Hieronymus von Colloredo, 2 vols. (Contacts Ser.: Vol. 33). (FRE.). xviii, 1044p. 1995. 103.95 (3-906754-19-7, Pub. by P Lang) P Lang Pubng.

Reba, Richard, et al. Diagnostic Imaging Medicine. 1983. text 282.00 (90-247-2798-7) Kluwer Academic.

Reba, Richard C., ed. see Diksic, Mirko.

Rebac, Zoran. Thai Boxing Dynamite: The Explosive Art of Muay Thai. (Illus.). 120p. 1987. reprint ed. pap. 16.00 (0-87364-426-3) Paladin Pr.

Rebach, H. M. & Bruhn, J. G. Handbook of Clinical Sociology. LC 90-7998. (Illus.). 434p. (C). 1991. pap. 37.50 (0-306-43579-9, Plenum Trade) Perseus Pubng.

Rebach, H. M. & Bruhn, J. G. Handbook of Clinical Sociology. LC 90-7998. (Illus.). 434p. (C). 1991. 70.00 (0-306-43559-4, Plenum Trade) Perseus Pubng.

Rebach, H. M., jt. auth. see Bruhn, J. G.

An Asterisk (*) at the beginning of an entry indicates that the title is appearing for the first time.

Rebach, Howard M., et al. Substance Abuse among Ethnic Minorities in America, Annotated Bibliography. LC 91-45032. (Library of Sociology: Vol. 20). 480p. 1992. text 25.00 (*0-8153-0066-2*, SS#737) Garland.

Rebagliato, I., et al. Metodologia de Investigacion en Epidemiologia. (SPA.). 223p. 1996. pap. 23.00 (*84-7978-265-X*, Pub. by Ediciones Diaz) IBD Ltd.

Reban, Milan J., jt. ed. see Klein, George.

***Rebane, Michael.** Where to Watch Birds in North & East Spain. 1999. pap. 21.95 (*0-7136-4700-0*) A & C Blk.

***Rebar, A. H., et al.** Hemogram Interpretation for Dogs & Cats. (Illus.). 108p. 1999. write for info. (*0-9678005-1-X*) Gloyd Grp Inc.

Rebarber, Theodor. State Policies for School Restructuring. 20p. 1992. pap. 10.00 (*1-55516-324-6*, 3114) Natl Conf State Legis.

Rebarber, Theodor, ed. see Finn, Chester E.

Rebaric, Joyce A. Apassionata. (Illus.). 200p. 1998. 20.00 (*0-9635084-3-1*) Nightshadow Prods.

— Crescendo. (Illus.). 200p. (Orig.). 1997. 20.00 (*0-9635084-1-5*) Nightshadow Prods.

— Nocturne. (Illus.). 130p. (Orig.). 1995. 17.00 (*0-9635084-2-3*) Nightshadow Prods.

— Variations. (Illus.). 250p. 1998. 20.00 (*0-9635084-4-X*) Nightshadow Prods.

Rebarto, Manuel. Spanish Cooking. 1289p. 1993. 12.98 (*1-55521-928-4*) Bk Sales Inc.

Rebay, Luciano. Alberto Moravia. LC 77-126544. (Columbia Essays on Modern Writers Ser.: No. 52). (Orig.). 1971. pap. text 12.00 (*0-231-02762-1*) Col U Pr.

— Introduction to Italian Poetry. 160p. 1991. pap. 5.95 (*0-486-26715-6*) Dover.

Rebbe Nachman of Breslov. The Empty Chair - Finding Hope & Joy: Timeless Wisdom from a Hasidic Master, Rebbe Nachman of Breslov. Mykoff, Moshe et al, eds. LC 94-6763. 128p. 1996. pap. text 9.95 (*1-879045-67-2*) Jewish Lights.

— The Gentle Weapon: Prayers for Everyday & Not-So-Everyday Moments. LC 98-47798. 144p. 1999. pap. text 9.95 (*1-58023-022-9*) Jewish Lights.

Rebbechi, B., et al. Dynamic Measurements of Gear Tooth Friction & Load. (Nineteen Ninety-One Fall Technical Meeting Ser.: Vol. 91FTM10). (Illus.). 11p. 1991. pap. text 30.00 (*1-55589-607-3*) AGMA.

***Rebbelmund, Romana.** Appropriation Art: Die Kopie Als Kunstform im 20. Jahrhundert. (Europaische Hochschulschriften Ser.: Vol. 28). (Illus.). 246p. 1999. 42.95 (*3-631-35343-X*) P Lang Pubng.

Rebber, Elizabeth. Seymour: A Pictorial History. (Indiana Pictorial History Ser.). (Illus.). 1990. write for info. (*0-943963-24-9*) G Bradley.

Rebbert, Richard L. Instructor's Manual to Accompany Experiments in Chemistry. 3rd ed. 104p. (C). 1989. pap. text 34.00 (*0-15-506464-9*) Harcourt Coll Pubs.

Rebbi, C., ed. Lattice Gauge Theories & Monte Carlo Simulations. 658p. 1983. text 89.00 (*9971-950-70-7*); pap. text 46.00 (*9971-950-71-5*) World Scientific Pub.

Rebbi, C. & Soliani, G., eds. Solitons & Particles. 836p. 1984. text 121.00 (*9971-966-42-5*); pap. text 52.00 (*9971-966-43-3*) World Scientific Pub.

Rebe, Bernd & Lang, Franz P., eds. Die Unvollendete Einheit: Bestandsaufnahme und Perspektiven fur die Wirtschaft. (Cloppenburger Wirtschaftsgesprache Ser.: Bd. 7). 446p. 1996. 45.00 (*3-487-10240-4*) G Olms Pubs.

Rebec, George, jt. auth. see Groves, Philip.

***Rebecca.** Housewives at Play. (Illus.). 64p. 1999. pap. 9.95 (*1-56097-353-6*, Eros Comics) Fantagraph Bks.

Rebecca. Rose of Rapture. 1984. mass mkt. 6.95 (*0-446-37613-2*, Pub. by Warner Bks) Little.

Rebeck, David P. Holy Words: Do They Mean? Key Words of Faith. LC 97-29585. 76p. 1997. pap. 9.25 (*0-7880-1186-3*) CSS OH.

Rebeck, Theresa. Sunday on the Rocks: A Comedy in Two Acts LC 97-215364. 112p. 1996. write for info. (*0-573-69553-9*) S French Trade.

— Theresa Rebeck: Complete Plays 1989-1998. LC 98-53027. 416p. 1999. 19.95 (*1-57525-172-8*) Smith & Kraus.

— View of the Dome. LC 98-213912. 83 p. 1998. write for info. (*0-573-62603-0*) S French Trade.

Rebecque, Constant De, see De Rebecque, Constant.

Rebedy, Lucy, jt. auth. see Clancy, Joe.

Rebeira, Perry De, see Saunders, D. & De Rebeira, Perry.

Rebeiz, Constantin A., jt. ed. see Duke, Stephen O.

Rebeiz, Gabriel M., jt. auth. see Eleftheriades, George V.

Rebeiz-Nielsen, Natalie. Caviar: A True Delicacy. (Illus.). 64p. 1995. 12.95 (*0-02-860375-3*) Macmillan.

Rebeiz-Nielsen, Natalie, jt. auth. see Boeckmann, Susie.

Rebeka, Jo, jt. auth. see Zimmerman, Kit.

Rebel, Gunther. Modern Jazz Ballett. (GER., Illus.). 144p. (C). 1990. 50.00 (*3-8170-4003-2*, Pub. by Knstvrlag Weingrtn) Intl Bk Import.

Rebel, Hermann. Peasant Classes: The Bureaucratization of Property & Family Relations under Early Habsburg Absolutism, 1511-1636. LC 82-47610. (Illus.). 373p. 1983. reprint ed. pap. 115.70 (*0-7837-9431-2*, 206017300004) Bks Demand.

Rebel Montgomery Temple Staff. Shadow of the Eagles. (Illus.). 157p. (Orig.). (J). 1982. pap. 3.75 (*0-89279-045-8*, TXU 90-499) S&S Trade.

Rebel, Thomas P. Sea Turtles & the Turtle Industry of the West Indies, Florida, & the Gulf of Mexico. LC 73-159293. 224p. 1990. pap. 19.95 (*0-87024-217-2*) U of Miami Pr.

Rebell, Gerbert & Taplin, David, eds. Dermatophytes: Their Recognition & Identification. 2nd rev. ed. LC 70-130448. (Illus.). 1974. pap. 22.95 (*0-87024-185-0*) U of Miami Pr.

Rebell, Michael A. & Block, Arthur R. Educational Policy-Making & the Courts: An Empirical Study of Judicial Activism. LC 81-16225. (Illus.). 336p. 1996. 36.00 (*0-226-70598-6*) U Ch Pr.

— Educational Policy Making & the Courts: An Empirical Study of Judicial Activism. LC 81-16225. 336p. reprint ed. pap. 104.20 (*0-608-09509-5*, 205431000005) Bks Demand.

— Equality & Education: Federal Civil Rights Enforcement in the New York City School System. LC 85-42700. 353p. 1985. reprint ed. pap. 109.50 (*0-7837-9301-4*, 206004000004) Bks Demand.

Rebellato, Dan. 1956 & All That: The Making of Modern British Drama. LC 98-29159. 1999. 65.00 (*0-415-18938-1*); pap. 21.99 (*0-415-18939-X*) Routledge.

***Rebello, Leonard.** Lizzie Borden: Past & Present. LC 99-94628. (Illus.). xxii, 642p. 1999. 49.95 (*0-9670739-0-1*) ALZach Pr.

Rebello, Stephen. Alfred Hitchcock & the Making of Psycho. LC 98-50245. 240p. 1998. pap. 14.95 (*0-312-20785-9*) St Martin.

— The Art of Hercules: The Chaos of Creation. LC 97-9058. 200p. 1997. 250.00 (*0-7868-6290-4*, Pub. by Hyprn Child) Time Warner.

— The Art of Pocahontas. (Illus.). 200p. (J). 1995. 50.00 (*0-7868-6158-4*, Pub. by Hyperion) Time Warner.

— The Art of the Hunchback of Notre Dame. LC 97-15617. (Disney Miniatures Ser.). (Illus.). 192p. (J). 1997. 10.95 (*0-7868-6334-X*, Pub. by Hyperion) Time Warner.

Rebello, Stephen & Allen, Richard. Reel Art: Great Posters from the Golden Age of the Silver Screen. (Illus.). 342p. 1992. 39.98 (*0-89660-033-5*, Artabras) Abbeville Pr.

— Reel Art: Great Posters from the Golden Age of the Silver Screen. (Tiny Folios Ser.). (Illus.). 271p. 1992. pap. 11.95 (*1-55859-403-5*) Abbeville Pr.

Rebello, Steven. The Art of Pocahontas. limited ed. (Illus.). 1995. 250.00 (*0-7868-6174-6*, Pub. by Disney Pr) Time Warner.

— The Art of the Hunchback of Notre Dame. limited ed. (Illus.). 200p. 1996. 250.00 (*0-7868-6214-9*, Pub. by Disney Pr) Time Warner.

Rebelsky, Samuel A., jt. ed. see Makedon, F.

Rebenich, Stefan. Theodor Mommsen und Adolf Harnack: Wissenschaft und Politik im Berlin des Ausgehenden 19. Jahrhunderts, Mit Einem Anhang: Edition und Kommentierung des Briefwechsels. (GER.). xxi, 1018p. (C). 1997. lib. bdg. 248.60 (*3-11-015079-4*) De Gruyter.

Reber, Arthur S. Implicit Learning & Tacit Knowledge: An Essay on the Cognitive Unconscious. (Oxford Psychology Ser.). (Illus.). 200p. 1996. pap. text 24.95 (*0-19-510658-X*) OUP.

— New Gambler's Bible: How to Beat the Casinos, the Track, Your Bookie & Your Buddies. LC 96-219807. 496p. 1996. pap. 18.00 (*0-517-88669-3*) Crown Pub Group.

***Reber, Deborah.** Blues Best Rainy Day. (Blue's Clues Ser.: No. 3). (Illus.). (J). (gr. k-3). 2000. pap. 3.50 (*0-689-83279-6*, Simon Spot) Litle Simon.

— Blue's Valentine's Day. (Blues Clues Ser.). 16p. (J). 2000. pap. 3.99 (*0-689-83062-9*) S&S Childrens.

— Magenta & Me: My First Preschool Ready to Read Pre-Level 1. LC 99-46900. Vol. 2. (Illus.). 24p. (J). (ps-3). 2000. pap. 3.99 (*0-689-83123-4*, Simon Spot) Litle Simon.

— Weather Games with Blue. (Blue's Clues Super Chubby Ser.: No. 3). 22p. (J). (gr. k-3). 1999. pap. 4.99 (*0-689-82949-3*) S&S Childrens.

Reber, Deborah, jt. auth. see Wilder, Alice.

Reber, Horst, jt. auth. see Meister, Peter W.

Reber, Howard, ed. Pancreatic Cancer: Pathogenesis, Diagnosis & Treatment. 360p. 1998. 125.00 (*0-89603-466-6*) Humana.

Reber, Howard A., ed. Atlas of Pancreatic Surgery. (Illus.). 300p. (C). (gr. 13). 2000. text 79.95 (*0-8151-7160-9*, 22453) Mosby Inc.

Reber, Jack. Eerie Canal: An Historical Adventure. 1990. pap. 9.99 (*0-88092-310-5*) Royal Fireworks.

Reber, Jan & Shaw, Paul. Executive Protection Manual. 1976. 29.95 (*0-916070-02-6*, MTI Film & Video); pap. 19.95 (*0-388-01062-2*, MTI Film & Video) Coronet.

Reber, Vera B. British Mercantile Houses in Buenos Aires, 1810-1880. LC 78-15743. (Studies in Business History: No. 29). (Illus.). 217p. 1979. 34.95 (*0-674-08245-1*) HUP.

Reberdy, Janet, jt. auth. see Benziger, Marieli.

Reberg, Evelyne. The Old Woman & the Ghost. (I Love to Read Collection). (Illus.). 46p. (J). (ps-3). 1992. lib. bdg. 12.79 (*0-89565-814-3*) Childs World.

Reberioux, Madeleine, jt. auth. see Mayeur, Jean-Marie.

Rebers, Paul A., jt. auth. see Landreth, Robert E.

Rebers, Paul A., jt. ed. see Cothern, C. Richard.

Rebert, Jo & O'Hara, Jean. Copper Enameling. (Ceramics Monthly Handbooks Ser.). (Illus.). 64p. 1956. pap. 7.95 (*0-934706-00-X*) Am Ceramic.

***Rebert, Paula.** La Gran Linea: Mapping the United States-Mexico Boundary, 1849-1857. LC 00-41771. 2001. write for info. (*0-292-77111-8*) U of Tex Pr.

Rebert, Sandi Z. Seventy Times Seven. 180p. (Orig.). 1982. pap. 4.95 (*0-89084-156-X*, 018176) Bob Jones Univ.

Rebeschi, Lisa & Brown, Mary. The Pediatric Nurse's Survival Guide. (Nurse's Survival Guide Ser.). 300p. (Orig.). (C). 1996. per. 29.95 (*1-56930-018-6*) Skidmore Roth Pub.

Rebeta-Burditt, Joyce. Buck Naked. LC 95-45699. 272p. 1996. 21.00 (*0-345-40136-0*) Ballantine Pub Grp.

Rebhan, Gail. Mother - Son Talk. (Artists' Books Ser.). (Illus.). 36p. (Orig.). 1996. pap. 18.00 (*0-89822-117-X*) Visual Studies.

Rebhlin, Joseph. Crisis of Morality & Reaction to the Holocaust. LC 98-65687. 157p. 1998. pap. 12.00 (*0-911707-51-4*) Univ of Verne Pr.

Rebholz. Pain Management. (Professional Reference - Nursing Ser.). 1998. student ed. 31.50 (*0-8273-7382-1*) Delmar.

***Rebholz, Joseph, ed.** Salsa for Sensitive Souls. rev. ed. 204p. 2000. pap. 15.00 (*0-910390-23-1*) Coda Publications.

Rebholz, R. A., ed. see Wyatt, Thomas.

Rebhorn, Wayne A. The Emperor of Men's Minds: Literature & the Renaissance Discourse of Rhetoric. LC 94-34553. (Rhetoric & Society Ser.). (Illus.). 304p. 1995. text 37.50 (*0-8014-2562-X*) Cornell U Pr.

— Foxes & Lions: Machiavelli's Confidence Men. LC 87-47824. 288p. 1988. text 37.50 (*0-8014-2095-4*) Cornell U Pr.

***Rebhorn, Wayne A.** Renaissance Debates on Rhetoric. LC 99-34446. 1999. pap. text 19.95 (*0-8014-8206-2*) Cornell U Pr.

Rebhun, Joseph. The Embers of Michael: An Historical Epic. 411p. 1993. per. 15.00 (*0-9614162-2-X*) OR Pub.

— God & Man in Two Worlds. 1985. lib. bdg. 16.95 (*0-9614162-1-1*) OR Pub.

***Rebhun, Joseph.** Leap to Life: Triumph over Nazi Evil. LC 00-29320. 2000. write for info. (*1-893357-05-8*) Ardor Scrib.

***Rebhun, Linda-Anne.** Heart Is Unknown Country: Love in The Changing Economy of Northeast Brazil. LC 99-28657. 1999. 45.00 (*0-8047-3601-4*) Stanford U Pr.

Rebhun, William C. Diseases of Dairy Cattle. LC 94-44191. (Illus.). 544p. 1995. 75.00 (*0-683-07193-9*) Lppncott W & W.

ReBibo, Kathy, ed. see Kannan, Narisimhan P.

Rebich, Edward R. & Garrett, Sally. Montana Cowboy: My Life Around the World. 498p. (Orig.). 1996. pap. 25.00 (*1-885916-01-9*) Unconvntl Pr.

***Rebick, Judy.** Imagine Democracy. 256p. 2000. 27.95 (*0-7737-3229-2*) Stoddart Publ.

Rebien, Claus C. Evaluating Development Assistance in Theory & in Practice. 218p. 1997. text 68.95 (*1-85972-408-6*, Pub. by Avebry) Ashgate Pub Co.

Rebind, jt. auth. see Weatherly.

Rebisz, Jacqueline, ed. see Metz, Mary S. & Helstrom, Jo.

Reble. Dejiny Pedagogiky. (SLO.). 296p. 1996. write for info. (*80-08-00487-8*, Pub. by Slov Pegagog Naklad) IBD Ltd.

Rebling, Kathinka. Carl Flesch. Die Hohe Schule des Fingersatzes. 1995. 85.95 (*3-631-46281-6*) P Lang Pubng.

Reblitz, Arthur A. Piano Servicing, Tuning, & Rebuilding: For the Professional, the Student, the Hobbyist. 2nd ed. LC 92-13175. (Illus.). 340p. 1993. 39.95 (*1-879511-02-9*, Vestal Pr); pap. 29.95 (*1-879511-03-7*, Vestal Pr) Madison Bks UPA.

— Player Piano Servicing & Rebuilding. LC 85-3140. (Illus.). 224p. 1985. pap. 24.95 (*0-911572-40-6*, Vestal Pr) Madison Bks UPA.

***Rebman, Rene C.** Runaway Teens. LC 00-9421. (Hot Issues Ser.). (Illus.). (J). 1999. write for info. (*0-7660-1640-4*) Enslow Pubs.

***Rebman, Renee C.** Life on Ellis Island. LC 99-30876. (Way People Live Ser.). (Illus.). 95p. (YA). (gr. 6-8). 2000. lib. bdg. 18.96 (*1-56006-533-8*) Lucent Bks.

— Prohibition. LC 98-34225. (World History Ser.). (J). (gr. 4-12). 1998. lib. bdg. 23.70 (*1-56006-444-7*) Lucent Bks.

— The Sistine Chapel. LC 99-46399. (Building History Ser.). (Illus.). 128p. (YA). (gr. 4-12). 2000. lib. bdg. 18.96 (*1-56006-640-7*) Lucent Bks.

Rebmann, Andrew & David, Edward. Cadaver Dog. 200p. 1999. 79.95 (*0-8493-1886-6*) CRC Pr.

Rebmann, Dieter, jt. auth. see Zierl, Oluf Fritz.

Rebmann, Gerhard. Dictionary of Garment Terminology. (ENG, FRE & GER.). 450p. 1984. 295.00 (*0-8288-0747-7*, M6966) Fr & Eur.

Rebne, Douglas. Determinants of Individual Productivity: A Study of Academic Researchers. (Monograph & Research Ser.: No. 53). 155p. 1990. pap. 12.50 (*0-89215-162-5*) U Cal LA Indus Rel.

Rebnord, Lisa, jt. auth. see Hendry, Linda.

Reboh, Linda, ed. see King, Randy E.

Reboiras, J. J. Basic Concepts of Medical Terminology: Conceptos Basicos de Terminologia Medica. (SPA.). 157p. 1982. 27.95 (*0-8288-1876-2*, S12385) Fr & Eur.

Rebold, Emmanuel, et al. A General History of Freemasonry in Europe Based upon the Ancient Documents Relating to, & the Monuments Erected by This Fraternity from Its Foundation in the Year 715 BC to the Present Time. 434p. 1997. reprint ed. pap. 35.00 (*0-7661-0023-5*) Kessinger Pub.

Rebolledo, Francisco. Rasero. 576p. 1996. pap. 12.95 (*0-14-026053-6*) Viking Penguin.

— Rasero: A Novel. Lane, Helen R., tr. from SPA. LC 95-22424. (Illus.). 552p. (C). 1995. 24.95 (*0-8071-2004-9*) La State U Pr.

***Rebolledo, R., ed.** Stochastic Analysis & Mathematical Physics: ANESTOC '98, Proceedings of the Third International Workshop. (Trends in Mathematics Ser.). 176p. 2000. 59.95 (*0-8176-4185-8*, Pub. by Birkhauser) Spr-Verlag.

Rebolledo, R., jt. ed. see Del Pino, G.

Rebolledo, Rolando, ed. Stochastic Analysis & Mathematical Physics (ANESTOC '96) Proceedings of the Second International Workshop Vina Del Mar, Chile, December 16-21, 1996. LC 98-14978. 250p. 1998. 58.00 (*981-02-3465-1*) World Scientific Pub.

Rebolledo, Rolando, jt. auth. see International Workshop on Stochastic Analysis & Mathematical Physics Staff.

Rebolledo, Tey D. Women Singing in the Snow: A Cultural Analysis of Chicana Literature. 250p. 1995. pap. 17.95 (*0-8165-1546-8*); lib. bdg. 36.00 (*0-8165-1520-4*) U of Ariz Pr.

***Rebolledo, Tey D. & Marquez, Maria T., eds.** La Diabla a Pie: Women's Cuentos from the New Mexico WPA. 224p. 2000. pap. 17.95 (*1-55885-312-X*) Arte Publico.

Rebolledo, Tey D. & Rivero, Eliana S., eds. Infinite Divisions: An Anthology of Chicana Literature. LC 92-45101. 387p. (Orig.). 1993. pap. 21.50 (*0-8165-1384-8*) U of Ariz Pr.

Rebollo Torio, Miguel A. Vocabulario Politico Republicano y Franquista: Republican & Franco-ite Political Vocabulary, 1931-1971. (SPA.). 184p. 1978. 24.95 (*0-8288-5277-4*, S50122) Fr & Eur.

Rebolo, R. & Zapatero-Osorio, M. R., eds. Very Low-Mass Stars & Brown Dwarfs. (Cambridge Astrophysics Ser.). (Illus.). 400p. 2000. 69.95 (*0-521-66335-0*) Cambridge U Pr.

Rebolo, Rafael, et al, eds. Brown Dwarfs & Extrasolar Planets. (ASP Conference Series Proceedings: Vol. 134). 563p. 1998. 34.00 (*1-886733-54-6*) Astron Soc Pacific.

Rebonato, Riccardo. Interest-Rate Option Models: Understanding, Analysing & Using Models for Exotic Interest-Rate Options. LC 97-43952. (Series in Financial Engineering). 546p. 1998. 95.00 (*0-471-97958-9*) Wiley.

***Rebonato, Riccardo.** Volatility & Correlation in the Pricing of Equity, FX & Interest-Rate Options. LC 99-35173. (Financial Engineering Ser.). 360p. 1999. 99.00 (*0-471-89998-4*) Wiley.

Rebora, Carrie & Staiti, Paul. John Singleton Copley in America. (Illus.). 368p. 1995. pap. 45.00 (*0-87099-745-9*) Metro Mus Art.

Rebora, Clemente. L' Imagine Tesa: Edizioni di Storia e Letteratura, Rome. enl. ed. 410p. 1974. reprint ed. pap. 30.00 (*0-614-10117-4*) Am Inst Ital Stud.

***Rebore, Ronald W.** Human Resources Administration in Education: A Management Approach. 6th ed. 360p. 2000. 75.00 (*0-205-32212-3*) Allyn.

Rebore, Ronald W. Personnel Administration in Education: A Management Approach. 2nd ed. (Illus.). 368p. (C). 1987. text 31.95 (*0-13-657719-9*) P-H.

— Personnel Administration in Education: A Management Approach. 5th ed. LC 97-16286. 360p. 1997. 75.00 (*0-205-26912-5*) Allyn.

Rebore, Ronald W., jt. auth. see Travers, Paul D.

Rebori, Stephen J. Disney & the Development of Vacation Destination Resorts. LC 95-36823. (CPL Bibliographies Ser.: Vol. 320). 39p. 1995. pap. 10.00 (*0-86602-320-8*, Sage Prdcls Pr) Sage.

— The Influence of Disney Entertainment Parks on Architecture & Development. LC 95-37535. (CPL Bibliographies Ser.: Vol. 321). 20p. 1995. pap. 10.00 (*0-86602-321-6*, Sage Prdcls Pr) Sage.

— Theme & Entertainment Parks: Planning, Design, Development & Management. LC 95-20913. (CPL Bibliographies Ser.: No. 319). 97p. 1995. 10.00 (*0-86602-319-4*, Sage Prdcls Pr) Sage.

Reboucas, Marcelo J., ed. see MacCallum, Malcolm A., et al.

Reboul, Antoine. Thou Shall Not Kill. Craig, Stephanie, tr. LC 77-77312. Orig. Title: Tu Ne Tueras Point. (J). (gr. 5-8). 1969. 26.95 (*0-87599-161-0*) S G Phillips.

Reboul, Pierre, jt. auth. see Wordingham, J. A.

Reboul, Pierre, ed. see De Chateaubriand, Rene.

Reboullet, et al. Methode Orange, Bk 1. (Methode Orange Ser.). (FRE., Illus.). (gr. 7-12). 1979. pap. text 5.25 (*0-88345-406-8*) Prentice ESL.

— Methode Orange-Workbook 1. (Methode Orange Ser.). (FRE., Illus.). (gr. 7-12). 1979. teacher ed. 6.75 (*0-88345-411-4*); pap. text 3.50 (*0-88345-408-4*); audio 85.00 (*0-686-60844-5*) Prentice ESL.

Rebourgeon, P., ed. Tennis Dictionary: Dictionnaire de Tennis. (FRE.). 160p. 1981. 89.95 (*0-8288-4442-9*, M9769) Fr & Eur.

Rebovich, Donald J. Dangerous Ground: The World of Hazardous Waste Crime. 168p. (C). 1992. text 39.95 (*1-56000-014-7*) Transaction Pubs.

Rebreanu, Liviu. Ion. 1965. 30.00 (*0-7206-4650-2*) Dufour.

— Ion. Aderman, Ralph M., ed. LC 67-25190. 1967. 13.50 (*0-8057-5695-7*) Irvington.

— The Uprising. Crandjean, P. & Hartauer, S., trs. from RUM. 384p. 1964. 30.00 (*0-7206-9382-9*, Pub. by P Owen Ltd) Dufour.

Rebrovich, Victor E. Star Menu: A Professional Menu & System Management Program for the IBM PC-XT-AT-PS2. rev. ed. Nugent, Kathy, ed. (Illus.). 80p. (C). 1990. 79.95 incl. disk (*0-9626641-0-3*) AstroSoft Data.

Rebryna, Debra. Canadian Heritage Bread Making. pap. 4.95 (*1-55105-016-1*) Lone Pine.

Rebsamen, Frederick. Beowulf: A Verse Translation. LC 91-55103. 144p. 1992. pap. 5.00 (*0-06-430212-1*, Perennial) HarperTrade.

Rebucci, G. G., et al, eds. Symposium on Lucunar Infarcts: Clinical Aspects & Diagnostic Examinations: Ravenna, April 1989. (Journal: European Neurology: Vol. 29, Suppl. 2, 1989). 50p. (C). 1989. pap. 54.50 (*3-8055-5124-X*) S Karger.

Rebuck, Linda & Fettke, Tom. To See a Miracle. 1983. 195.00 (*0-685-68650-7*, OR-9049) Lillenas.

— To See a Miracle. 40p. 1983. 5.99 (*0-8341-9350-7*, MB-522) Lillenas.

— To Tell the Truth. (J). 1985. 5.99 (*0-685-68203-X*, MB-546) Lillenas.

Rebuck, Linda, jt. auth. see Fettke, Tom.

Rebuffat, Gaston. Mont Blanc Massif: The 100 Finest Routes. 240p. 1996. 39.95 (*0-89886-477-1*) Mountaineers.

— Starlight & Storm: The Conquest of the Great North Faces

R

of the Alps. Krakauer, Jon, ed. LC 99-41400. (Modern Library Exploration Ser.). 160p. 1999. pap. 12.95 (*0-375-75506-3*) Modern Lib NY.

Rebus Planning Associates Staff, jt. auth. see Jablon, Judy R.

Rebuschi, Georges & Tuller, Laurice, eds. The Grammar of Focus. LC 99-22380. (Linguistik Aktuell/Linguistics Today Ser.: Vol. 24). vi, 366p. 1999. 99.00 (*1-55619-908-2*) J Benjamins Pubng Co.

Reca, Lucio G. & Echeverria, Ruben G. Agricultura, Medio Ambiente y Pobreza Rural en America Latina. (SPA.). 450p. 1998. pap. text 15.00 (*1-886938-32-6*) IADB.

***Recaman, Santos Bernardo.** Challenging Brainteasers. (Illus.). 2000. pap. 6.95 (*0-8069-2877-8*) Sterling.

Recamier, Jeanne F. Memoirs & Correspondence of Madame Recamier. LC 73-37715. (Illus.). reprint ed. 55.00 (*0-404-56808-4*) AMS Pr.

Recana, Mel R. & Parrott, Wanda S. How to Try Your Own Case in Court - & Win Bk. 1: Basic Instructions for the Non-Lawyer. LC 96-27216. 344p. (Orig.). 1997. pap. 24.95 (*1-880090-31-7*) Galde Pr.

Recanati, Francois. Direct Reference: From Thought to Language. LC 92-29857. 448p. 1997. pap. text 29.95 (*0-631-20634-5*) Blackwell Pubs.

***Recanati, Francois.** Oratio Obliqua, Oratio Recta: An Essay on Metarepresentation. (Representation & Mind Ser.). (Illus.). 450p. (C). 2000. pap. 24.95 (*0-262-68116-1*, Bradford Bks) MIT Pr.

Recardo, Ronald J. & Peluso, Luigi A. The People Dimension: Managing the Transition to World-Class Manufacturing. LC 92-11950. 224p. 1992. text 29.95 (*0-527-91666-8*, 916668) Productivity Inc.

Recardo, Ronald J., et al. Teams: Who Needs Them & Why? (Illus.). 224p. 1996. 39.95 (*0-88415-852-7*, 5852) Gulf Pub.

Recblin, jt. auth. see Jaiswal.

Reccenda, Ann B., ed. see Roede, Ann.

Recchia, Cheri, ed. see Bel'kovitch, V. M. & Sh'ekotov, M. N.

Recchio & Spellmen. Practical Theory in Composition. pap. text. write for info. (*0-312-07528-6*) St Martin.

Recco, Gregory, tr. see Nancy, Jean-Luc.

Recco, Gregory, tr. see Raffoul, Francois.

***Reccord, Bob.** Forged by Fire: How God Shapes Those He Loves. 224p. 2000. pap. 12.99 (*0-8054-2297-8*) Broadman.

Recent Advances in Optimization Techniques Symposium Staff. Recent Advances in Optimization Techniques: Proceedings of the Symposium, Carnegie Institute of Technology, 1965. Lavi, Abrahim & Vogl, Thomas P., eds. LC 66-4421. 670p. reprint ed. pap. 200.00 (*0-608-30915-X*, 200634900058) Bks Demand.

Recer, J. Dan. How to Disinherit Your Son-in-Law . . . & Stiff the IRS: Keep Your Money in Your Family. LC 97-74614. (Illus.). 260p. 1997. 29.95 (*0-9639846-2-4*) AFRI.

— Terms of Endowment: How Board Members Can Acquire the Big Gift. (Illus.). 150p. 1998. 23.95 (*0-9663432-0-4*) Eastrn Shore Pub MD.

Rech, Photina. Wine & Bread. LC 98-34597. (Illus.). 118p. 1998. pap. 15.00 (*1-56854-189-9*) Liturgy Tr Pubns.

Rech, R. H. & Gudelsky, G. A., eds. Five-HT Antagonists As Psychoactive Drugs. LC 88-61898. (Illus.). 308p. 1988. 50.00 (*0-916182-06-1*) NPP Bks.

Rechard, Noreen, ed. see Sedler, Michael D.

Rechcigi, M. Nutrient Elements & Toxicants. (Comparative Animal Nutrition Ser.: Vol. 2). (Illus.). 1977. 85.25 (*3-8055-2351-3*) S Karger.

***Rechcigl, Jack E.** Biological & Biotechnological Control of Insect Pests. LC 99-31226. 392p. 1999. boxed set 69.95 (*1-56670-479-0*) Lewis Pubs.

Rechcigl, Jack E., ed. Soil Amendments: Impacts on Biotic Systems. (Agriculture & Environment Ser.). 336p. 1994. lib. bdg. 95.00 (*0-87371-860-7*, L860) Lewis Pubs.

— Soil Amendments & Environmental Quality. 528p. 1995. lib. bdg. 110.00 (*0-87371-859-3*, L859) Lewis Pubs.

Rechcigl, Jack E. & MacKinnon, Herbert C., eds. Agricultural Uses of By-Products & Wastes, Vol. 668. LC 97-16403. (ACS Symposium Ser.: No. 668). (Illus.). 290p. 1997. text 105.00 (*0-8412-3514-7*, Pub. by Am Chemical) OUP.

***Rechcigl, Jack E. & Rechcigl, Nancy A.** Insect Pest Management: Techniques for Environmental Protection. LC 99-40543. 408p. 1999. boxed set 69.95 (*1-56670-478-2*) Lewis Pubs.

Rechcigl, Jack E., jt. auth. see Rechcigl, Nancy A.

Rechcigl, Miloslav. Diets, Culture, Media & Food Supplements: Culture Media for Cells, Organs & Embryos. LC 77-6287. (Handbook Series in Nutrition & Food: Vol. 4, Sec. G). 1978. 265.00 (*0-8493-2739-3*, CRC Reprint) Franklin.

— Diets, Culture, Media & Food Supplements: Diets for Mammals. LC 77-6287. (Handbook Series in Nutrition & Food: Vol. 1, Sec. G). 1977. 358.00 (*0-8493-2736-9*, CRC Reprint) Franklin.

— Diets, Culture, Media & Food Supplements: Food Habits, Diets, Invertibrate, Vertebrates, Zoo Diets. LC 77-6287. (Handbook Series in Nutrition & Food: Vol. 2, Sec. G). 1978. 261.00 (*0-8493-2737-7*, CRC Reprint) Franklin.

— Diets, Culture, Media, Food Supplement Section G, 3 vols., Set. LC 77-6287. 1977. 883.00 (*0-8493-2735-0*, CRC Reprint) Franklin.

Rechcigl, Miloslav, Jr. Handbook of Agricultural Productivity, Vol. I: Plant Productivity. 464p. 1982. 264.00 (*0-8493-3961-8*, S494, CRC Reprint) Franklin.

Rechcigl, Miloslav. Handbook Series in Nutrition & Food, 4 vols., Set. LC 77-6287. 1977. 1190.00 (*0-8493-2700-8*, CRC Reprint) Franklin.

— World Food Problem: Selective Bibliography of Reviews. LC 74-30748. 352p. 1975. 128.00 (*0-8493-5098-0*, CRC Reprint) Franklin.

Rechcigl, Miloslav, Jr., ed. Carbohydrates, Lipids & Accessory Growth Factors. (Comparative Animal Nutrition Ser.: Vol. 1). (Illus.). 1976. 85.25 (*3-8055-2268-1*) S Karger.

— CRC Handbook of Nutritive Value of Processed Food: Animal Foodstuffs, Vol. II. 520p. 1982. 155.00 (*0-8493-3953-7*, TX551, CRC Reprint) Franklin.

— Czechoslovak Contribution to World Culture. 1964. text 115.40 (*90-279-1032-4*) Mouton.

— Czechoslovakia Past & Present, Set. Incl. Vol. 1. Political, International, Social & Economic Aspects. 1968. Vol. 2. Essays on the Arts & Sciences. 1968. 1968. Set text 347.00 (*0-686-22479-5*) Mouton.

Rechcigl, Miloslav, ed. Food, Nutrition & Health. (World Review of Nutrition & Dietetics Ser.: Vol. 16). (Illus.). 350p. 1973. 156.75 (*3-8055-1398-4*) S Karger.

Rechcigl, Miloslav, Jr., ed. Handbook of Foodborne Diseases of Biological Origin. 535p. 1983. lib. bdg. 163.00 (*0-8493-3964-2*, RA1258, CRC Reprint) Franklin.

— Handbook of Naturally Occurring Food Toxicants. 360p. 1983. lib. bdg. 176.00 (*0-8493-3965-0*, TX531, CRC Reprint) Franklin.

— Handbook of Nutrition & Food. (Comparative & Qualitative Requirements Ser.). (Illus.). 576p. 1977. 99.00 (*0-8493-2721-0*, QH519, CRC Reprint) Franklin.

Rechcigl, Miloslav, ed. Handbook of Nutritional Requirements in a Functional Context, Vol. I. 560p. 1981. 304.00 (*0-8493-3956-1*, QP82, CRC Reprint) Franklin.

— Handbook of Nutritional Requirements in a Functional Context, Vol. II. 616p. 1981. 331.00 (*0-8493-3958-8*, QP82, CRC Reprint) Franklin.

Rechcigl, Miloslav, Jr., ed. Handbook of Nutritional Supplements, 2 Vols., Vol. I: Human Use. 576p. 1983. lib. bdg. 214.00 (*0-8493-3969-3*, TX553, CRC Reprint) Franklin.

— Handbook of Nutritional Supplements, 2 Vols., Vol. II: Agricultural Use. 424p. 1984. lib. bdg. 192.00 (*0-8493-3970-7*, CRC Reprint) Franklin.

— Handbook of Nutritive Value of Processed Food: Food for Human Use, Vol. I. 696p. 1982. 376.00 (*0-8493-3951-0*, TX551, CRC Reprint) Franklin.

— Nitrogen, Electrolytes Water & Metabolism. (Comparative Animal Nutrition Ser.: Vol. 3). (Illus.). 1979. 113.25 (*3-8055-2829-9*) S Karger.

— Physiology of Growth & Nutrition. (Comparative Animal Nutrition Ser.: Vol. 4). (Illus.). xii, 344p. 1981. pap. 216.75 (*3-8055-1199-X*) S Karger.

Rechcigl, Miroslav, ed. Nutrition & Food Deficiencies Animals. 1978. 307.00 (*0-8493-2797-0*, RC620, CRC Reprint) Franklin.

— Nutrition & Food Deficiencies Animals, Vol. III. 388p. 1978. 70.50 (*0-8493-2798-9*, CRC Reprint) Franklin.

Rechcigl, Nancy A. & Rechcigl, Jack E. Environmentally Safe Approaches to Crop Disease Control. LC 96-54596. (Agriculture & Environment Ser.). 400p. 1997. boxed set 89.95 (*0-8493-2627-3*) CRC Pr.

Rechcigl, Nancy A., jt. auth. see Rechcigl, Jack E.

Rechebei, Elizabeth D. History of Palau: Heritage of an Emerging Nation. LC 98-232763. xvii, 462p. 1997. write for info. (*0-9652776-3-1*) Hirano Design.

Rechel, Camille J., et al. UV/EB Curing Primer: Inks, Coatings & Adhesives. 5th ed. LC 97-70727. 90p. 1997. 35.00 (*1-878664-17-4*) RadTech Intl North Amer.

Rechelbacher, Horst. Aveda Rituals: A Daily Guide to Natural Beauty & Health. LC 98-32307. (Illus.). 288p. 1998. pap. 19.95 (*0-8050-5800-1*, Owl) H Holt & Co.

— Rejuvenation: A Wellness Guide for Women & Men. (Illus.). 224p. 1987. pap. 14.95 (*0-89281-248-6*) Inner Tradit.

Rechenauer, Georg. Thuykdides und die Hippokratische Medizin. (Spudasmata Ser.: Bd. XLVII). (GER.). xii, 396p. 1991. write for info. (*3-487-09226-3*) G Olms Pubs.

Rechenbach, Charles W. & Gesuga, Angelica W. Swahili-English Dictionary. LC 67-31438. 653p. reprint ed. pap. 200.00 (*0-608-16033-4*, 203313300084) Bks Demand.

Rechenberg, H., jt. auth. see Mehra, J.

Rechenberg, H., jt. auth. see Mehra, Jagdish.

Rechenberg, H. R., ed. Applications of the Mossbauer Effect: Proceedings of 1st Latin American Conference. 448p. (C). 1990. text 151.00 (*9971-5-0936-9*) World Scientific Pub.

Rechenberg, Helmut, jt. auth. see Brown, Laurie M.

Rechenberg, Helmut, jt. auth. see Mehra, Jagdish.

Rechenberg, I., jt. ed. see Donecker, J.

Recher & Lunney. Natural Legacy. 2nd ed. 1986. text 52.00 (*0-08-029864-8*, Pergamon Pr); pap. text 26.00 (*0-08-029863-X*, Pergamon Pr) Elsevier.

Rechin, Bill, jt. auth. see Boren, Jim.

Rechinger, K. H. Flora of Lowland Iraq. 1964. 95.00 (*3-7682-0217-8*) Lubrecht & Cramer.

Rechinger, Karl H. Flora Iranica. Flora des Iranischen Hochlandes und der Umrahmenden Gebirge. Persien, Afghanistan, Teile Von West-Pakistan, Nord-Iraq, Azerbaidjan, Turkmenistan, Fascicle 1-172. (GER., Illus.). 7500p. 1998. 5033.00 (*3-201-00728-5*, Pub. by Akademische Druck-und) Balogh.

Rechlin, Charles F. Securities Credit Regulation. LC 93-44704. (Securities Law Ser.). 1994. ring bd. 145.00 (*0-87632-984-9*) West Group.

Rechlin, Fred, jt. auth. see Rechlin, Harriet.

Rechlin, Harriet & Rechlin, Fred. Pioneer Jews: A New Life in the Far West. (Illus.). 256p. 1986. pap. 21.95 (*0-395-42639-1*) HM.

Rechs, Rober J. Building Gas Blimps. 3rd rev. ed. (Illus.). 200p. (C). 1997. pap. text 50.00 (*0-937568-28-7*) Recks Pubns.

Rechs, Robert J. Balloon Construction: Design Critera, Vol. 1. (Illus.). 176p. (Orig.). 1987. pap. 35.00 (*0-937568-15-5*, TL 638 R43 V1) Recks Pubns.

— Balloon Construction: Materials & Suppliers, Vol. 2. (Illus.). 176p. (Orig.). 1987. pap. text 35.00 (*0-937568-16-3*, TL 638 R43 V2) Recks Pubns.

— Balloon Construction: Plans & Construction, Vol. 3. (Illus.). 176p. (Orig.). 1987. pap. text 35.00 (*0-937568-17-1*, TL 638 R43 V3) Recks Pubns.

— Who's Who of Ballooning: 1783-1983. 362p. (Orig.). 1982. 35.00 (*0-937568-26-0*, TL 615 R43); pap. text 20.00 (*0-937568-27-9*) Recks Pubns.

Rechsteiner, M. Ubiquitin. LC 88-9809. (Illus.). 364p. 1988. 89.00 (*0-306-42850-4*, Kluwer Plenum) Kluwer Academic.

Recht, Christine. Herbs. (Mini Fact Finders Ser.). 64p. 1991. pap. 4.95 (*0-8120-4453-3*) Barron.

Recht, Christine & Wetterwald, Max. Bamboos. (Illus.). 128p. 1992. 32.95 (*0-88192-268-4*) Timber.

Recht, Marilyn. She Must Have Been a Giant. 41p. (Orig.). 1994. pap. write for info. (*1-877649-22-8*) Tesseract SD.

***Rechter, David.** The Jews of Vienna & the First World War. LC 00-34903. (Library of Jewish Civilization). 2000. write for info. (*1-874774-65-X*, Pub. by Littman Lib) Intl Spec Bk.

Rechtin, Eberhardt. Systems Architecting: Creating & Building Complex Systems. 352p. (C). 1990. 92.00 (*0-13-880345-5*) P-H.

— Systems Architecting of Organizations: Why Eagles Can't Swim. LC 99-26157. (Systems Engineering Ser.). 280p. 1999. boxed set 49.95 (*0-8493-8140-1*) CRC Pr.

Rechtin, Eberhardt, et al. The Art of Systems Architecting. LC 96-31918. (Systems Engineering Ser.). 288p. (C). 1996. boxed set 74.95 (*0-8493-7836-2*, 7836) CRC Pr.

Rechtin, Eberhardt, jt. auth. see Maier, Mark.

Rechtschaffen, Joseph S. & Carola, Robert. Dr. Rechtschaffen's Diet for Lifetime Weight Control & Better Health. 224p. 1995. pap. 10.00 (*1-56836-077-0*) Kodansha.

— Minding Your Body: 100 Ways to Eat Well & Live Positively, Includes Recipes. 256p. 1995. 18.00 (*1-56836-076-2*) Kodansha.

Rechtschaffen, Scott D., et al. Employee Handbook: How to Write One for Your Company. Kemp, Susan, ed. 175p. (Orig.). (C). 1999. pap. text 79.00 (*1-57997-015-X*) CA Chamber Commerce.

Rechtschaffen, Stephan. Timeshifting: Creating More Time to Enjoy Your Life. 256p. 1997. pap. 12.95 (*0-385-48390-2*, Main St Bks) Doubleday.

Rechtschaffen, Stephan & Cohen, Marc. Vitality & Wellness. LC 99-28317. (Omega Institute Mind, Body & Spirit Bks.). 272p. 1999. pap. 12.95 (*0-440-50868-1*) Dell.

Rechy, John. City of Night. LC 83-49451. 400p. 1988. pap. 13.00 (*0-8021-3083-6*, Grove) Grove-Atltic.

***Rechy, John.** Coming of the Night. 2000. pap. 12.00 (*0-8021-3742-3*, Grove) Grove-Atltic.

Rechy, John. The Coming of the Night. LC 99-22538. 256p. 1999. 23.00 (*0-8021-1650-7*, Grove) Grove-Atltic.

— The Fourth Angel. LC 83-10863. 160p. 1983. pap. 9.95 (*0-8021-5197-3*, Grove) Grove-Atltic.

— The Miraculous Day of Amalia Gomez. 256p. 1993. pap. 11.45 (*1-55970-203-6*, Pub. by Arcade Pub Inc) Time Warner.

— Numbers. LC 83-49450. 272p. 1990. pap. 13.00 (*0-8021-5198-1*, Grove) Grove-Atltic.

— Our Lady of Babylon: A Novel. 352p. 1996. 23.45 (*1-55970-335-0*, Pub. by Arcade Pub Inc) Time Warner.

— Rushes. 224p. 1997. reprint ed. pap. 12.00 (*0-8021-3497-1*, Grove) Grove-Atltic.

— The Sexual Outlaw: A Documentary. LC 83-49452. 304p. 1984. pap. 14.00 (*0-8021-3163-8*, Grove) Grove-Atltic.

Recinos, Adrian. Popol Vuh: Las Antiguas Historias Del Quiche (Indigenous Legends) (SPA.). 187p. 1960. pap. 9.99 (*968-16-0327-3*, Pub. by Fondo) Continental Bk.

Recinos, Adrian, tr. Popol Vuh: Las Antiguas Historias Del Quiche (Indigenous Legends) 268p. 1997. 9.95 (*84-8377-093-8*) Piedra Santa Editorial.

Recinos, Adrian, et al, trs. Popol Vuh: The Sacred Book of the Ancient Quiche Maya: Spanish Version of the Original Maya. LC 50-6643. (Civilization of the American Indian Ser.: No. 29). 288p. 1991. 29.95 (*0-8061-0205-5*) U of Okla Pr.

— Popol Vuh: The Sacred Book of the Ancient Quiche Maya: Spanish Version of the Original Maya. LC 50-6643. (Civilization of the American Indian Ser.: No. 29). 288p. 1991. reprint ed. pap. 13.95 (*0-8061-2266-8*) U of Okla Pr.

Recinos, Adrian & Goetz, Delia, trs. The Annals of the Cakchiquels. (Civilization of the American Indian Ser.: Vol. 37). 217p. 1974. pap. 9.95 (*0-8061-1152-6*) U of Okla Pr.

Recinos, Hal J. Jesus Weeps. 16.30 (*0-687-01385-2*) Abingdon.

— Jesus Weeps: Global Encounter on Our Doorstep. 112p. (Orig.). 1992. pap. 10.95 (*0-687-03185-0*) Abingdon.

Recinos, Harold J. Who Comes in the Name of the Lord? Jesus at the Margins. LC 97-39675. 160p. 1997. pap. 14.95 (*0-687-01002-0*) Abingdon.

Recio, L. M., ed. see Menendez Pidal, Ramon.

Recio, Roxana. Petrarca y Alvar Gomez: La Traduccion del "Triunfo de Amor" (Studies in the Humanities: Vol. 28). (SPA.). VIII, 213p. (C). 1997. text 45.95 (*0-8204-3309-8*) P Lang Pubng.

Recio, T., ed. see American Mathematical Society Special Session Staf.

Recio, T., jt. ed. see Dubois, D. W.

Recio, T., jt. ed. see Gonzalez-Vega, L.

Reciputi, Natalie S. Dante's Ratchet. 74p. (Orig.). 1993. pap. 7.00 (*0-944920-06-3*) Bellowing Ark Pr.

Reck, Andrew J. Introduction to William James: An Essay & Selected Texts. LC 67-25137. (Midland Bk.: No. MB105). 220p. reprint ed. pap. 68.20 (*0-608-10842-1*, 205521200011) Bks Demand.

Reck, Andrew J., ed. Knowledge & Value. (Tulane Studies in Philosophy: No. 21). 202p. 1972. pap. text 71.50 (*90-247-1321-8*, Pub. by M Nijhoff) Kluwer Academic.

Reck, Andrew J., ed. see Mead, George Herbert.

Reck, Carleen, ed. AIDS: A Catholic Educational Approach to HIV - Teacher's Manual. rev. ed. (Illus.). 176p. 1992. pap. 16.00 (*1-55833-111-5*); 5.00 (*1-55833-112-3*) Natl Cath Educ.

Reck, Carleen, jt. ed. see Hall, Suzanne E.

Reck, Carol, jt. auth. see Reck, David B.

Reck, David B. & Reck, Carol. Music of the Whole Earth. unabridged ed. LC 96-50895. (Illus.). 559p. 1997. pap. 27.50 (*0-306-80749-1*) Da Capo.

Reck, Gregory C. In the Shadow of Tlaloc: Life in a Mexican Village. (Illus.). 224p. (C). 1986. reprint ed. pap. text 11.95 (*0-88133-244-5*) Waveland Pr.

Reck, Hanne G. Aleman Para Estudiantes de Habla Espanola: Deutsch fur Studenten der Spanischer Sprache, Vol. II. 7.00 (*0-8477-3340-8*) U of PR Pr.

— Deutsch Fur Studenten Spicher Sprache-Aleman Para Estudiantes De Habla Espanola, Vol. 1. LC 78-18825. 193p. 1979. pap. text 6.00 (*0-8477-3321-1*) U of PR Pr.

Reck, JoAnn M., jt. auth. see Siskin, H. Jay.

Reck, Jurgen. Diccionario Riodeuro Matematica. 2nd ed. (SPA.). 224p. 1982. 35.00 (*0-7859-5069-9*) Fr & Eur.

— Herder-Lexikon Mathematik. (GER.). 238p. 1974. 39.95 (*0-8288-6050-5*, M7445) Fr & Eur.

Reck, Michael, tr. see Homer.

Reck, Philip Georg Friedrich Von, see Von Reck, Philip Georg Friedrich.

Reck, Rima D. Drieu la Rochelle & the Picture Gallery Novel: French Modernism in the Interwar Years. LC 89-48255. (Illus.). 247p. reprint ed. pap. 76.60 (*0-608-09817-5*, 206998500007) Bks Demand.

Reck, Ross R. The Win-Win Negotiator. 1989. per. 12.00 (*0-671-67698-9*) PB.

Reck, Ross R. & Long, Brian. Negotiating Techniques: How to Work Toward a Constructive Agreement. Guder, Robert F., ed. 1985. 14.95 (*0-910187-05-3*) Economics Pr.

Reck, Ruth A. & Hummel, John R., eds. Interpretation of Climate & Photochemical Models, Ozone & Temperature Measurements: AIP Conference Proceedings, No. 82, La Jolla Institute, March 9-11, 1981. LC 82-71345. 320p. 1982. 33.00 (*0-88318-181-9*) Am Inst Physics.

Reck, Sue, ed. see Baldry, Cherith.

Reck, Sue, ed. see Boyce, Kim & Abraham, Ken.

Reck, Sue, ed. see Erickson, Mary.

Reck, Sue, ed. see Kennedy, Pamela.

Reck, Sue, ed. see Levene, Nancy S.

Reck, Sue, ed. see Lord, Wendy.

Reck, Sue, ed. see McHenry, Janet H.

Reck, Sue, ed. see Sattgast, Linda J.

Reck, Vera T. Boris Pil'niak: A Soviet Writer in Conflict with the State. LC 76-356287. 255p. reprint ed. pap. 79.10 (*0-8357-7355-8*, 202385700034) Bks Demand.

Reck, Vera T., tr. see Pilnyak, Boris.

Reck, W. Emerson. A. Lincoln: His Last 24 Hours. LC 85-43587. (Illus.). 240p. 1987. lib. bdg. 32.50 (*0-89950-216-4*) McFarland & Co.

— A. Lincoln: His Last 24 Hours. LC 94-5648. (Illus.). 232p. (C). 1994. reprint ed. pap. 12.95 (*1-57003-008-1*) U of SC Pr.

Reck, William A. An Hour with Jesus, Vol. II. LC 94-65655. 65p. (Orig.). 1995. pap. 2.00 (*1-877678-35-X*) Queenship Pub.

— Just You & Jesus. LC 92-92086. 64p. (YA). (gr. 8-12). 1996. pap. 2.00 (*1-877678-43-0*) Queenship Pub.

— An Overview of the New Age Movement. LC 95-74802. 96p. 1995. pap. 4.50 (*1-877678-38-4*) Queenship Pub.

Recke, Walther-Albert M. Bucherkunde Zur Geschichte und Literatur des Konigreichs Polen. xi, 242p. reprint ed. write for info. (*0-318-71861-8*) G Olms Pubs.

Reckenwald, Gerald W. An Introduction to Numerical Methods with Matlab. (C). 2000. text. write for info. (*0-201-30860-6*) Addison-Wesley.

Recker, Jo A., jt. auth. see Siskin, H. Jay.

Recker, Jo Ann Marie. The "Appelle-Moi 'Pierrot'" Wit & Irony in "Lettres" of Madame de Sevigne. LC 86-20777. (Purdue University Monographs in Romance Languages: No. 21). ix, 128p. 1986. pap. 33.00 (*0-915027-70-4*) J Benjamins Pubng Co.

Recker, Kristie, jt. auth. see Darosky, Renee.

Recker, Robert R., ed. Bone Histomorphometry: Techniques & Interpretation. 312p. 1983. 179.00 (*0-8493-5373-4*, QM569, CRC Reprint) Franklin.

Recker, Wilfred W., jt. auth. see McNally, Michael G.

Recker, Wilfred W., jt. auth. see Paaswell, Robert E.

Reckers, Philip. Advances in Accounting, Vol. 16. 1999. 78.50 (*0-7623-0513-4*) Jai Pr.

Reckers, Philip M., ed. Advances in Accounting: In Preparation, Winter 1996, Vol. 14. 1996. 78.50 (*0-7623-0161-9*) Jai Pr.

Reckert, Stephen. Beyond Chrysanthemums: Perspectives on Poetry East & West. LC 92-26818. (Illus.). 286p. 1993. text 65.00 (*0-19-815165-9*, Clarendon Pr) OUP.

Reckford, Kenneth J. Aristophanes' Old-&-New Comedy Vol. 1: Six Essays in Perspective. LC 86-16188. xiv, 567p. (C). 1987. 59.95 (*0-8078-1720-1*) U of NC Pr.

Reckford, Kenneth J., ed. see Lembke, Janet.

Reckford, Kenneth J., tr. see Euripides.

Reckford, Laura, ed. & intro. see Lambert, Adam.

Reckford, Laura M. Frommer's Cape Cod, Nantucket, & Martha's Vineyard. (Frommer's Cape Cod, Martha's Vineyard & Nantucket Ser.). 310p. 1999. pap. 14.95 (*0-02-862762-8*, Pub. by Macmillan) S&S Trade.

***Reckford, Laura M.** Frommer's 98 Cape Cod, Nantucket & Martha's Vineyard: With the Best Beaches & Historic Inns. (Frommer's Travel Guides Ser.). (Illus.). 320p. 1998. pap. 14.95 (*0-02-862093-3*, Frommer) Macmillan Gen Ref.

Reckford, Thomas J., jt. auth. see Palmer, Ronald D.

Reckhow, David R., jt. auth. see Langlais, Bruno.

Reckhow, Kenneth H. & Chapra, Steven. Engineering Approaches for Lake Management, 2 vols., Vol. 1: Data Analysis & Empirical Modeling. LC 79-56115. 358p. 1983. 79.95 (*0-250-40344-7*) Buttrwrth-Heinemann.

Reckitt, Basil N. Diary of Anti-Aircraft Defence, 1938-1944. (C). 1990. 50.00 (*0-7223-2459-6*, Pub. by A H S Ltd) St Mut.

— William Reckitt. 1999. pap. 21.00 (*1-85072-057-6*, Pub. by W Sessions) St Mut.

Reckitt, Basil N., ed. Diary of Military Government in Germany, 1945. 78p. (C). 1989. 50.00 (*0-7223-2301-8*, Pub. by A H S Ltd) St Mut.

Reckitt, Helena, jt. ed. see Oppenheimer, Josh.

***Recklaw, Jesse.** Dreamtoons. LC 99-87278. 128p. 2000. pap. 10.95 (*1-57062-573-5*, Pub. by Shambhala Pubns) Random.

***Reckless.** Diabetes & Lipids: Pocketbook Edition. 2nd ed. 2000. 14.95 (*1-85317-614-1*, Pub. by Martin Dunitz) Blackwell Sci.

Reckless, Walter C. Vice in Chicago. LC 69-16243. (Criminology, Law Enforcement, & Social Problems Ser.: No. 84). 1969. reprint ed. 18.00 (*0-87585-084-7*) Patterson Smith.

***Reckling, Frederick W. & Reckling, JoAnn B.** A Brief History of the University of Wyoming Alumni Association, 1895-2000. (Illus.). (C). 2000. pap. write for info. (*0-9663851-0-1*) U Wyom Alumni Assn.

Reckling, JoAnn B., jt. auth. see Reckling, Frederick W.

Recknagel, A. B. Forest Management. 269p. (C). 1981. text 900.00 (*0-7855-6586-8*, Pub. by Intl Bk Distr) St Mut.

— Forest Management. 269p. 1985. 225.00 (*81-7089-034-9*, Pub. by Intl Bk Distr); pap. 250.00 (*0-614-09777-0*, Pub. by Intl Bk Distr) St Mut.

Recknagel, Carl. Just off the Ground: Memoirs of an Aviator. (Illus.). 176p. (Orig.). 1993. pap. 19.95 (*1-56474-067-6*) Fithian Pr.

Recknagel, E. & Soares, J. C., eds. Nuclear Physics Applications on Materials Science. (C). 1988. text 271.50 (*90-247-3703-6*) Kluwer Academic.

Recknagel, E., jt. ed. see Echt, O.

Recknagel, Friedrich. Meg's Wish. LC 99-17370. (Illus.). 32p. (J). (ps-2). 1999. lib. bdg. 15.88 (*0-7358-1117-2*, Pub. by North-South Bks NYC) Chronicle Bks.

***Recknagel, Friedrich.** Meg's Wish. LC 99-17370. (Illus.). 32p. (J). (ps-2). 1999. 15.95 (*0-7358-1116-4*, Pub. by North-South Bks NYC) Chronicle Bks.

Reckner, Jerald H. & Norton, Jeni F. The Power Within: Living with Your Full Potential. LC 87-71541. (Illus.). (Orig.). (C). 1987. pap. 8.95 (*0-943889-00-6*) Assoc Beta Cos.

Recknor, Ellen. Leaving Missouri. 368p. 1997. mass mkt. 5.99 (*0-425-15575-7*) Berkley Pub.

— Prophet Annie. LC 98-54331. 336p. 1999. pap. 12.00 (*0-380-79513-2*, Avon Bks) Morrow Avon.

***Recknor, Ellen.** Prophet Annie. 352p. 2000. mass mkt. 6.99 (*0-380-81122-7*, Avon Bks) Morrow Avon.

Recknor, Ellen. Prophet Annie, Vol. 1. LC 99-14979. 1999. 26.95 (*0-7862-1992-0*) Thorndike Pr.

Reckord, Barry. Does Fidel Eat More Than Your Father? Cuban Opinion. LC 72-180081. 191 p. 1971. write for info. (*0-233-96216-6*) Andre Deutsch.

Recks, Robert J. Muscle Powered Blimps: Ulta Light Gas Blimps. (Illus.). 225p. 1998. pap. text 30.00 (*0-937568-30-9*) Recks Pubns.

Recksiek, C. W., et al. Basic Fishery Science Programs: A Compendium of Microcomputer Programs & Manual Of Operation. (Developments in Aquaculture & Fisheries Science Ser.: No. 18). 230p. 1988. 119.75 (*0-444-43031-8*) Elsevier.

Recktenwald, Charles. Helping Children Succeed: How to Help Children Succeed in School & in Life. LC 88-80401. 138p. (Orig.). 1989. pap. 6.95 (*0-929089-00-6*) East Fork Pub Co.

Recktenwald, Diether & Radbruch, A. Cell Separation Methods & Applications. LC 97-33113. (Illus.). 352p. 1997. text 145.00 (*0-8247-9864-3*) Dekker.

***Recktenwald, Gerald W.** Numerical Methods with Matlab: Implementations & Applications. LC 00-42758. 2000. write for info. (*0-13-030802-1*) P-H.

Recktenwald, Horst C. Dictionary of Economics: Woerterbuch der Wirtschaft. 10th ed. (ENG & GER.). 706p. 1987. 59.95 (*0-8288-1279-9*, M6941) Fr & Eur.

Reclus, Elisee. Plant Physiognomies. 1973. 69.95 (*0-8490-0840-9*) Gordon Pr.

***Reclus, Elisee.** A Voyage to New Orleans: Anarchist Impressions of the Old South. Clark, John P. & Martin, Camille, eds.Tr. of Fragment d'an Voyage a la Nouvelle-Orleans. (Illus.). 85p. 1999. pap. 7.50 (*1-930180-03-9*, Pub. by Glad Day Bks VT) Enfield Pubs NH.

Recognition Systems Staff. Providing Recognition: A Handbook of Ideas. 1974. ring bd. 24.90 (*0-89401-103-0*) Didactic Syst.

***Record Commission of the City of Boston Staff.** Dorchester Births, Marriages & Deaths to the End of 1825. 396p. 2000. reprint ed. pap. write for info. (*0-7884-1516-6*, 1516) Heritage Bk.

***Record Commissioners of Boston, Massachusetts Staff.** A Volume of Records Relating to the Early History of Boston: Containing Boston Marriages from 1752-1809. 722p. 1999. pap. 45.50 (*0-7884-1341-4*, R116) Heritage Bk.

***Record Commissioners of Boston Staff.** Charlestown Land Records. 273p. 1999. reprint ed. pap. 23.50 (*0-7884-1204-3*, R115) Heritage Bk.

Record Commissioners of City of Boston Staff. Dorchester Town Records. 344p. 1999. pap. 26.50 (*0-7884-1138-1*, R111) Heritage Bk.

Record, Jeffrey. Force Reductions in Europe: Starting Over. LC 80-83753. (Special Reports). 92p. 1980. 11.95 (*0-89549-027-7*) Inst Foreign Policy Anal.

— Hollow Victory: A Contrary View of the Gulf War. LC 92-26885. 192p. 1993. 23.00 (*0-02-881046-5*, 4173M) Brasseys.

— NATO'S Theater Nuclear Force Modernization Program: The Real Issues. LC 81-84988. (Special Reports). 102p. 1981. 11.95 (*0-89549-038-2*) Inst Foreign Policy Anal.

— The Rapid Deployment Force & U. S. Military Intervention in the Persian Gulf. 2nd ed. LC 83-81086. (Special Reports). 83p. 1983. 11.95 (*0-89549-053-6*) Inst Foreign Policy Anal.

— Sizing up the Soviet Army. LC 75-26941. (Studies in Defense Policy). 61p. reprint ed. pap. 30.00 (*0-608-18048-3*, 202797100057) Bks Demand.

— Strategic Bombers: How Many Are Enough? LC 86-6. (National Security Papers: No. 3). 26p. 1986. 7.50 (*0-89549-069-2*) Inst Foreign Policy Anal.

— U. S. Nuclear Weapons in Europe: Issues & Alternatives. LC 74-23433. (Studies in Defense Policy). 70p. 1974. pap. 8.95 (*0-8157-7365-X*) Brookings.

— U. S. Strategic Airlift: Requirements & Capabilities. LC 85-23927. (National Security Papers: No. 2). 43p. 1986. 7.50 (*0-89549-068-4*) Inst Foreign Policy Anal.

— The Wrong War: Why We Lost in Vietnam. LC 97-47706. (Illus.). 212p. 1998. 27.95 (*1-55750-699-X*) Naval Inst Pr.

Record, Jeffrey, ed. The Future of the U. S. Military Commitment to Europe. 172p. (Orig.). (C). 1989. pap. text 10.95 (*0-685-37970-1*) Hudson Instit IN.

Record, Jeffrey & Hanks, Robert J. U. S. Strategy at the Crossroads: Two Views. LC 82-82774. (Foreign Policy Reports). 69p. 1982. 11.95 (*0-89549-044-7*) Inst Foreign Policy Anal.

Record, Jeffrey, et al. The INF Treaty: Pro & Con. 70p. (Orig.). (C). 1988. pap. 5.00 (*1-55813-032-2*) Hudson Instit IN.

— Salt II & American Security. 65p. 1980. 11.95 (*0-89549-024-2*) Inst Foreign Policy Anal.

Record, Jeffrey, jt. auth. see Binkin, Martin.

Record, Jeffrey, jt. auth. see Lawrence, Richard D.

***Record, Matthew.** Preparing a Winning Business Plan: How to Plan to Succeed & Secure Financial Banking. 3rd ed. (Business & Management Ser.). (Illus.). 160p. 2000. pap. 19.95 (*1-85703-542-9*, Pub. by How To Bks) Trans-Atl Phila.

Record, Melvyn. High Octane. 128p. 1995. 14.98 (*0-7858-0327-0*) Bk Sales Inc.

— Hot Rods & Dragsters. 128p. 10.99 (*1-57215-225-7*, JG2257) World Pubns.

— Hot Rods & Dragsters: The Definitive Guide To The Fastest-Accelerating Cars Ever Made. (Illus.). 128p. 1995. 14.95 (*0-7858-0342-4*) Bk Sales Inc.

Record, Richard, jt. auth. see Gastfield, Gail.

Record, Robert. The Castle of Knowledge. LC 74-28882. (English Experience Ser.: No. 760). 1975. reprint ed. 50.00 (*90-221-0760-4*) Walter J Johnson.

— The Grounde of Artes, Teachying the Worke & Practise of Arithmetike. LC 77-26032. (English Experience Ser.: No. 174). (Illus.). 1969. reprint ed. 35.00 (*90-221-0174-6*) Walter J Johnson.

— The Path-Way to Knowledge, Containing the First Principles of Geometrie. LC 74-80206. (English Experience Ser.: No. 687). 1974. reprint ed. 25.00 (*90-221-0687-X*) Walter J Johnson.

Record, Samuel J. & Hess, Robert W. Timbers of the New World. LC 73-140611. (Use & Abuse of America's Natural Resources Ser.). (Illus.). 718p. 1975. reprint ed. 63.95 (*0-405-02806-7*) Ayer.

Record, Samuel J., jt. auth. see Standley, Paul C.

Record, Sandra H., ed. see Atkinson, Chuck.

Records Committee of the Prince George's County Ge, compiled by. Gleanings from the Records of the Francis Gasch's Sons Funeral Home, Prince George's County, Maryland 1860-1940. 665p. 1996. 40.00 (*0-916805-09-3*) Prince Georges County Gen Soc.

Records, Laban S. Cherokee Outlet Cowboy: Recollections of Laban S. Records. Wheeler, Ellen J., ed. LC 94-37534. (Illus.). 370p. 1995. 24.95 (*0-8061-2694-9*) U of Okla Pr.

— Cherokee Outlet Cowboy: Recollections of Laban S. Records. Wheeler, Ellen J., ed. LC 94-37534. (Illus.). 392p. 1997. pap. 15.95 (*0-8061-2872-0*) U of Okla Pr.

Records, Maryla W. Domestic 007 - Eliminating Hidden Killers in Your Home: Ridding Your Home of Harmful Chemicals & Cancer-Causing Agents. Lane, Cynthia, ed. LC 96-38137. (Illus.). 102p. (Orig.). 1997. pap. 18.95 (*0-9655793-0-1*) Earth-Wise.

Records, Pam. Once upon a Rhyme: A Wizard's Wacky Story Time. (Shuffle-a-Book Ser.). (Illus.). 21p. (J). (ps). 1993. pap. 8.00 (*0-9639839-0-3*) MP Records.

Records, Shawn K. Poor Man's Notebook. Trusky, Tom, ed. (Illus.). (Orig.). 1994. pap. 6.95 (*0-916272-60-5*) Ahsahta Pr.

Recorvits, Helen. Goodbye, Walter Malinski. LC 97-35451. (Illus.). 96p. (J). (gr. 4-7). 1999. pap. text 15.00 (*0-374-32747-5*) FS&G.

***Recos, Gabriel F., Jr.** The Golden Round. 2000. pap. 14.95 (*1-893162-25-7*) Erica Hse.

Recouly, Raymond. Third Republic. Buckley, E. F., tr. LC 28-23849. (National History of France Ser.: No. 10). reprint ed. 45.00 (*0-404-50800-6*) AMS Pr.

Recourse Systems, Inc. Staff, jt. auth. see INFORM, Inc. Staff.

Recovery Alliance, Inc. Staff. The Impossible Diet Cookbook. LC 92-61954. 196p. 1992. pap. 12.95 (*0-9629391-0-2*) Recovery Alliance.

Recreation & Sport Dept. Staff. Heysen Trail Guide Book, Pt. 1. 128p. (C). 1989. pap. text 30.00 (*0-89771-020-7*, Pub. by Bob Mossel) St Mut.

— Heysen Trail Guide Book, Pt. 11: Parachilna to Hawker. (C). 1989. pap. text 30.00 (*0-89771-033-9*, Pub. by Bob Mossel) St Mut.

Recruiting New Teachers, Inc. Staff. The RNT Careers in Teaching Handbook. (Illus.). 104p. 1993. 12.95 (*1-884139-02-7*) Recruit New Tchrs.

— State Policies to Improve the Teacher Workforce: Shaping the Profession That Shapes America's Future. (Illus.). 48p. 1993. 6.95 (*1-884139-00-0*) Recruit New Tchrs.

— Take This Job & Love It! Making the Mid-Career Move to Teaching. LC 99-164245. 240p. 1998. 19.95 (*1-884139-04-3*) Recruit New Tchrs.

— Teaching's Next Generation. (Illus.). 160p. 1993. 9.95 (*1-884139-01-9*) Recruit New Tchrs.

Recski, A. Matroid Theory & Its Applications in Electric Network Theory & Statics. (Algorithms & Combinatorics Ser.: Vol. 6). 350p. 1989. 135.95 (*0-387-15285-7*) Spr-Verlag.

Rectanus, Cheryl. Area & Perimeter, Grades 5-6. (Math by All Means Ser.). (Illus.). 208p. 1997. pap. text 23.95 (*0-941355-18-7*) Math Solns Pubns.

— Geometry Grades 3-4. (Math by All Means Ser.). (Illus.). 160p. 1994. pap. text 23.95 (*0-941355-10-1*) Math Solns Pubns.

Rectanus, Mark W. & Hiller, Renate. Prisma: Dokumente, Literatur, Kommunikation. (GER.). 314p. (C). 1992. pap. text 31.96 (*0-669-20492-7*) HM Trade Div.

***Rector, Brent D. & McIntyre, Elizabeth M.** Occupational Health & Safety: Guide for Michigan Employers. 172p. 2000. pap. 99.00 (*1-893318-05-2*) Michigan Cham Com.

Rector, Brent E. & Newcomer, Joseph M. Developing Win 32 Applications for Windows 95. 1568p. (C). 1997. pap. text 57.95 (*0-201-63492-9*) Addison-Wesley.

Rector, Brent E. & Sells, Chris. ATL Internals. LC 99-11448. 656p. (C). 1999. pap. 54.95 (*0-201-69589-8*) Addison-Wesley.

Rector, C. H. The Story of Beautiful Puerto Rico: By Pen & Camera. 200p. 1974. lib. bdg. 250.00 (*0-8490-1128-0*) Gordon Pr.

Rector, Cherie, jt. auth. see Allender, Judith.

Rector, Floyd C., Jr., jt. auth. see Brenner, Barry M.

Rector, Gary, tr. see Man-Jo, Kim, et al.

Rector, Harry E. Guidelines for Monitoring Indoor Air Quality. (Illus.). 270p. (C). 1986. 68.95 (*0-89116-385-9*) Hemisp Pub.

Rector, Hartman, Jr Already to Harvest. 91p. 1985. pap. 9.95 (*0-934126-67-4*); pap. 5.95 (*0-934126-73-9*) CFI Dist.

Rector, Hartman, Jr Expect the Miracle of Conversion. pap. 9.98 (*1-55517-258-X*) CFI Dist.

Rector, Janice. How to Recognize & Overcome Depression: A Woman's Personal Experience. LC 93-85051. 112p. (Orig.). 1994. pap. 10.95 (*0-9637222-0-4*) Sunrise Internat.

Rector, Johnny. Encyclopedia of Guitar Chord Progressions. deluxe ed. 96p. 1997. pap. 19.95 incl. audio compact disk (*0-7866-3442-1*) Mel Bay.

— Encyclopedia of Jazz Guitar Runs, Fills, Licks, & Lines. deluxe ed. 84p. 1998. spiral bd. 19.95 (*0-7866-3446-4*) Mel Bay.

— Walking Bass. 96p. 1997. pap. 22.95 incl. audio compact disk (*0-7866-0828-5*, 95547BCD) Mel Bay.

Rector, Lallene J. & Santaniello, Weaver, eds. Psychological Perspectives & the Religious Quest: Essays in Honor of Orlo Strunk, Jr. LC 98-31582. 208p. 1998. 49.00 (*0-7618-1292-X*); pap. 26.50 (*0-7618-1293-8*) U Pr of Amer.

Rector, Lee T. Americana. Tibbetts, Laurene & Tibbetts, Kathleen I., eds. LC 81-90246. 168p. 1981. write for info. (*0-9606170-0-0*) Rector Pub.

— Melodies of the Wind & Other Poems. 89p. 1984. write for info. (*0-318-58392-5*) Rector Pub.

— Yesteryears. 117p. 1982. write for info. (*0-318-58391-7*) Rector Pub.

Rector, Liam. American Prodigals. LC 94-43891. 60p. 1994. 19.95 (*0-934257-21-3*); pap. 11.95 (*0-934257-22-1*) Story Line.

— The Sorrow of Architecture. LC 83-20685. 75p. 1984. 14.00 (*0-937872-16-4*); pap. 6.00 (*0-937872-17-2*) Dragon Gate.

Rector, Liam, ed. The Day I Was Older: Writings on the Poetry of Donald Hall. 289p. (Orig.). 1989. 24.95 (*0-934257-20-5*); pap. 15.95 (*0-934257-19-1*) Story Line.

Rector, Liam, ed. Frank Bidart: A Symposium on the Poetry. (Illus.). (C). text. write for info. (*0-472-10955-3*) U of Mich Pr.

Rector, Margaret, ed. Cowboy Life on the Texas Plains: The Photographs of Ray Rector. LC 82-5902. (Centennial Series of the Association of Former Students: Vol. 12). (Illus.). 124p. 1992. pap. 19.95 (*0-89096-529-3*) Tex A&M Univ Pr.

Rector, Margaret H. The Lady & the Commissioner of Airports: Playscript. LC 93-28279. 1993. pap. 5.00 (*0-88734-325-2*) Players Pr.

— The Lady & the Mortician: Playscript. LC 93-28300. 1993. pap. 5.00 (*0-88734-326-0*) Players Pr.

— The Wishfork Wedding. LC 95-10803. 16p. 1995. pap. 5.00 (*0-88734-327-9*) Players Pr.

Rector, Mark, jt. auth. see Talhoffer, Hans.

Rector-Page, Linda. Weight Loss & Cellulite Control: A Fighting Chance. 1998. pap. text 8.95 (*1-884334-66-0*) Hlthy Healing.

Rector-Page, Linda G. & Van, Douglas. Party Lights: Healthy Party Foods & Environmentally Conscious Decorations. (Illus.). (Orig.). 1994. pap. 19.95 (*1-884334-53-9*) Hlthy Healing.

Rector, Richard, jt. ed. see Haour-Knipe, Mary.

***Rector, Robert.** Impact of Welfare Reform. 2000. pap. 10.00 (*0-89195-080-X*) Heritage Found.

Rector, Robert & Lauber, William F. America's "Failed" $5.4 Trillion: War on Poverty. 120p. 1995. pap. 12.95 (*0-89195-062-1*) Heritage Found.

Rector, William F., ed. Leadership in Space - For Benefits on Earth, 28th Annual AAS Meeting, Oct. 26-29, 1981, San Diego, CA. LC 57-43769. (Advances in the Astronautical Sciences Ser.: Vol. 47). (Illus.). 310p. 1982. 45.00 (*0-87703-168-1*, Am Astronaut Soc) Univelt Inc.

Rector, William F., ed. Leadership in Space - For Benefits on Earth, 28th Annual AAS Meeting, Oct. 26-29, 1981, San Diego, CA. LC 57-43769. (Advances in the Astronautical Sciences Ser.: Vol. 47). (Illus.). 310p. 1982. pap. 35.00 (*0-87703-169-X*, Am Astronaut Soc) Univelt Inc.

Rector, William F. & Penzo, Paul A., eds. Space Shuttle: Dawn of an Era, 26th Annual AAS Meeting, Oct. 29-Nov. 1, 1979, Los Angeles, CA, Pt. 1. LC 57-43769. (Advances in the Astronautical Sciences Ser.: Vol. 41). 452p. 1980. 45.00 (*0-87703-111-8*, Am Astronaut Soc); pap. 35.00 (*0-87703-112-6*, Am Astronaut Soc) Univelt Inc.

— Space Shuttle: Dawn of an Era, 26th Annual AAS Meeting, Oct. 29-Nov. 1, 1979, Los Angeles, CA, Pt. 2. LC 57-43769. (Advances in the Astronautical Sciences Ser.: Vol. 41). 528p. 1980. 55.00 (*0-87703-113-4*, Am Astronaut Soc); pap. 40.00 (*0-87703-114-2*, Am Astronaut Soc) Univelt Inc.

Recuerda, Jose M. Carteles Rotos - Amadis de Gaula. Torres, Sixto E., ed. LC 94-62226. (Coleccion Teatro). (SPA.). 199p. (Orig.). 1995. pap. 19.00 (*0-89729-749-0*) Ediciones.

— Salvajes en Puente San Gil. (SPA.). 290p. 1978. 9.50 (*0-8288-7046-2*) Fr & Eur.

— The Theatre of Jose Martin Recuerda, Spanish Dramatist: Dramas of Franco & Post-Franco Spain. Torres, Sixto E., ed. LC 93-30131. (Hispanic Literature Ser.: Vol. 22). 408p. 1993. 109.95 (*0-7734-9356-5*) E Mellen.

Recuero, Pascal. Dicionario Basico Ladino - Espanol: Basic Ladino - Spanish Dictionary. (LAD, POR & SPA.). 153p. 1977. pap. 29.95 (*0-8288-9419-1*, S36126) Fr & Eur.

Recum, Andreas Von, see Von Recum, Andreas.

Recycling Consortium Staff. Coconut Uses: Uses for the Coconut. rev. ed. 1992. ring bd. 19.95 (*0-317-04791-4*) Prosperity & Profits.

— Corn Uses: Uses for Corn. rev. ed. 1992. ring bd. 19.95 (*0-317-04792-2*) Prosperity & Profits.

— Dandelion Uses: Uses for the Dandelion. rev. ed. 1992. ring bd. 19.95 (*0-317-04793-0*) Prosperity & Profits.

— Egg Uses: Uses for Eggs. rev. ed. 1992. ring bd. 19.95 (*0-317-04794-9*) Prosperity & Profits.

— Homes for the Moving: Recyclable Home Possibilities. rev. ed. 1992. ring bd. 26.95 (*0-317-04781-7*) Prosperity & Profits.

— Lemon Uses: Uses for the Lemon. rev. ed. 1992. ring bd. 19.95 (*0-317-04795-7*) Prosperity & Profits.

— Orange Uses: Uses for the Orange. rev. ed. 1992. ring bd. 19.95 (*0-317-04796-5*) Prosperity & Profits.

— Potato Uses: Uses for the Potato. rev. ed. 1992. ring bd. 19.95 (*0-317-04797-3*) Prosperity & Profits.

— Roses Uses: Uses for the Rose. rev. ed. 1992. ring bd. 19.95 (*0-317-04798-1*) Prosperity & Profits.

— Solicit, Remake & Resell: The Jeans & Denim Recycling Fundraising Project Workbook. 1991. ring bd., wbk. ed. 25.95 (*0-318-03755-6*) Prosperity & Profits.

— Solicit, Remake & Resell: The Panty Hose Recycling Fundraising Project Workbook. 1991. ring bd. 23.95 (*0-318-03754-8*) Prosperity & Profits.

— Watermelon Uses: Uses for the Watermelon. rev. ed. 1992. ring bd. 19.95 (*0-317-04799-X*) Prosperity & Profits.

Reczuch, Karen, jt. auth. see Munro, Margaret.

Reczynska, Anna. For Bread & a Better Future: Emigration from Poland to Canada, 1918-1939. LC 96-931418. (POL & ENG., Illus.). 300p. 1996. pap. 34.75 (*0-919045-70-7*) U of Toronto Pr.

Red. Pilgrim Hymnal. LC 58-1015. 1958. 12.95 (*0-8298-0107-3*) Pilgrim OH.

Red Deer College Pr. Staff. The Wine Journal: Wine Recording System. 228p. 1993. text 12.95 (*0-88995-107-1*, Pub. by Red Deer) Genl Dist Srvs.

Red Eagle, Philip H. Red Earth: A Vietnam Warrior's Journey. 160p. 1997. pap. text 12.95 (*0-930100-74-3*) Holy Cow.

Red Hat Press Staff. TCL - TK Unleashed. 1100p. 1999. 49.99 (*0-672-31143-7*) Sams.

Red Hawk, Richard. ABCs the American Indian Way. (Illus.). 55p. (Orig.). (J). (ps-8). 1988. pap. 6.95 (*0-940113-15-5*) Sierra Oaks Pub.

— Grandfather's Story of Navajo Monsters. (Illus.). 41p. (Orig.). (J). (ps-7). 1988. pap. 6.95 (*0-940113-11-2*) Sierra Oaks Pub.

Red Hawk, Richard. The Sioux Dog Dance. (CSU Poetry Ser.: No. XXXV). 60p. (Orig.). 1991. pap. 10.00 (*0-914946-90-0*) Cleveland St Univ Poetry Ctr.

Red Hawk, Richard. A Trip to a Pow Wow. (Illus.). 45p. (Orig.). (J). (gr. k-3). 1988. pap. 6.95 (*0-940113-14-7*) Sierra Oaks Pub.

Red Heart Yarn Staff. Red Heart Afghans & Crochet Classics. 144p. 1996. pap. text 14.95 (*0-8487-1513-6*) Oxmoor Hse.

R

Red, Henrietta. Rival Sisters. (Romance Ser.). 576p. 1983. pap. 3.95 (*0-373-20078-1*) Harlequin Bks.

Red Herring Poets Staff, et al. Matrix 22, Vol. 22. (Illus.). 58p. 1997. pap. 6.00 (*0-932884-78-4*) Red Herring.

Red Herring Staff. Matrix 21: Anthology of the Red Herring Poets. Olsen, Ray, ed. 48p. (Orig.). 1996. pap. 6.00 (*0-932884-77-6*) Red Herring.

Red Hot Chili Peppers. One Hot Minute. 80p. 1996. per. 18.95 (*0-7935-5825-5*); otabind 22.95 (*0-7935-5824-7*) H Leonard.

— One Hot Minute. 224p. 1997. per. 27.95 (*0-7935-6672-X*) H Leonard.

Red Iberoamericana de Tecnologia del Software Staff. String Processing & Information Retrieval: A South American Symposium, Santa Cruz de la Sierra, Bolivia, September 9-11, 1998. LC 98-86236. 111 p. 1998. write for info. (*0-8186-8664-2*) IEEE Comp Soc.

Red, James. The American Original Home Recipe Collection Series, 4 vols., Set. Lynn, Mary, ed. (Illus.). (Orig.). 1991. pap. 15.95 (*1-879490-04-8*) Timberline NM.

Red Lips, jt. auth. see Messer, Sam.

Red Point Publishing Staff. Meetings: How & Why. 1997. pap. text 3.95 (*0-9658795-2-6*) Red Pt Publ.

— Overcoming Objections. 1997. pap. text 3.95 (*0-9658795-3-4*) Red Pt Publ.

— Red Point System. 1997. pap. text 3.95 (*0-9658795-4-2*) Red Pt Publ.

Red Shirt, Delphine. Bead on an Anthill: A Lakota Childhood. LC 97-14418. 146p. 1998. text 30.00 (*0-8032-3908-4*) U of Nebr Pr.

— Bead on an Anthill: A Lakota Childhood. LC 97-14418. 146p. 1999. pap. 9.95 (*0-8032-8976-6*, Bison Books) U of Nebr Pr.

Red, William S. Texas Colonists & Religion, 1821-1836. 1993. reprint ed. lib. bdg. 75.00 (*0-7812-5947-9*) Rprt Serv.

Red Wing Business Systems Staff, jt. auth. see Armbruster, David B.

Reda, Jacques. The Ruins of Paris. Treharne, Mark, tr. from FRE. (Topographics Ser.). 144p. 1997. pap. 18.95 (*0-948462-93-0*, Pub. by Reaktion Bks) Consort Bk Sales.

Reda, Jacques, et al, prefs. Sempe - On Holiday. (Illus.). 88p. 1996. pap. 19.95 (*3-7913-1099-2*, Pub. by Prestel) te Neues.

Reda, Jacques, jt. auth. see Kamel Al Wajiz.

Reda, Mario, et al, eds. Systems & Processes: Collected Works in Sociology. (C). 1968. pap. 19.95 (*0-8084-0292-7*) NCUP.

Reda, Mario R. Toward A New Sociology: A Collection of Readings. 2nd ed. 332p. (C). 1997. pap. 30.40 (*0-536-59985-8*) S&S Trade.

Reda, Mario R. Toward a New Sociology: Collection of Readings. 288p. (C). 1995. text 37.80 (*0-536-58952-6*) Pearson Custom.

Reda, Youssef M. Al-Kamel Al-Kabir Plus. (FRE & ARA.). 1600p. 1996. 85.00 (*0-86685-689-7*) Intl Bk Ctr.

— Al Kamel Al Wajiz. (FRE & ARA.). 1084p. 1986. 18.00 (*0-86685-723-0*) Intl Bk Ctr.

Reda, Youssef M. Al Kamel Al Wajiz. (ARA & FRE.). 1084p. 1986. 16.00 (*0-86685-414-2*, LDL4630S, Pub. by Librairie du Liban) Intl Bk Ctr.

— Al-Kamel Al-Wasit: Al-Kamel al-Wasit. (ARA & FRE., Illus.). 2000p. 85.00 (*0-86685-463-0*, LDL4630, Pub. by Librairie du Liban) Intl Bk Ctr.

Reda, Youssef M., jt. auth. see Kamel De Poche.

Reday-Mulvey, Genevieve, jt. ed. see Delsen, Lei.

***Redbank, Tennant.** Rug Bug. LC 99-87424. (Between the Lions Ser.). (Illus.). (J). 2000. 7.99 (*0-307-16505-1*, Goldn Books) Gldn Bks Pub Co.

***Redbank, Tennant & DiFiori, Larry.** Rug Bug. LC 99-87424. (J). 2000. 10.99 (*0-307-36505-0*) Gldn Bks Pub Co.

Redbeard, Ragnar. Might Is Right. 1972. 250.00 (*0-87700-187-1*) Revisionist Pr.

Redbook Editors. Redbook Flavor Rules! More Than 250 Recipes Plus Hints, Tips & Tricks for Really Great Food. LC 98-32091. (Illus.). 192p. 1999. 24.95 (*0-688-16255-X*, Hearst) Hearst Commns.

Redbook Editors, ed. The Redbook Exercise Program for Pregnant Women. 1924. write for info. (*0-688-16374-2*, Hearst) Hearst Commns.

Redbook Florist Services Educational Advisory Comm. Advanced Floral Design. LC 92-80132. (Encycloflora Ser.). (Illus.). 326p. (Orig.). 1992. pap. text 34.95 (*1-56963-024-0*) Redbk Florist.

— Basic Floral Design. LC 91-61275. (Encycloflora Ser.). (Illus.). 286p. (Orig.). 1991. pap. text 34.95 (*1-56963-014-3*) Redbk Florist.

— Designing with Balloons & Flowers. LC 91-66385. (Encycloflora Ser.). (Illus.). 176p. (Orig.). 1991. pap. text 34.95 (*1-56963-020-8*) Redbk Florist.

— Encycloflora (TM) Series, 12 vols., Set. (Illus.). text 347.52 (*1-56963-000-3*) Redbk Florist.

— Floral Design for the Holidays. LC 91-73528. (Encycloflora Ser.). (Illus.). 566p. (Orig.). 1991. pap. text 39.95 (*1-56963-019-4*) Redbk Florist.

— Green & Blooming Plants. LC 92-60180. (Encycloflora Ser.). (Illus.). 296p. (Orig.). 1992. pap. text 34.95 (*1-56963-015-1*) Redbk Florist.

— Marketing & Promoting Floral Products. LC 92-85370. (Encycloflora Ser.). (Illus.). 468p. (Orig.). 1993. pap. text 39.95 (*1-56963-018-6*) Redbk Florist.

— Purchasing & Handling Fresh Flowers & Foliage. LC 91-66386. (Encycloflora Ser.). (Illus.). 332p. (Orig.). 1992. pap. text 34.95 (*1-56963-013-5*) Redbk Florist.

— Retail Flower Shop Operation. LC 91-73529. (Encycloflora Ser.). (Illus.). 478p. (Orig.). 1991. pap. text 39.95 (*1-56963-016-X*) Redbk Florist.

— Selling & Designing Party Flowers. LC 92-64275. (Encycloflora Ser.). (Illus.). 404p. (Orig.). 1992. pap. text 34.95 (*1-56963-021-6*) Redbk Florist.

— Selling & Designing Sympathy Flowers. LC 92-60503. (Encycloflora Ser.). (Illus.). 222p. (Orig.). 1992. pap. text 34.95 (*1-56963-023-2*) Redbk Florist.

— Selling & Designing Wedding Flowers. LC 91-60000. (Encycloflora Ser.). (Illus.). 304p. (Orig.). 1991. pap. text 34.95 (*1-56963-022-4*) Redbk Florist.

— Visual Merchandising for the Retail Florist. LC 91-67527. (Encycloflora Ser.). (Illus.). 246p. (Orig.). 1992. pap. text 34.95 (*1-56963-017-8*) Redbk Florist.

Redborg, Rita & Cohen, Judith L. You Can Be a Woman Cardiologist. LC 96-8865. (Illus.). 40p. (J). (gr. 3-6). 1996. pap. 6.00 (*1-880599-18-X*) Cascade Pass.

Redburn, David E. & McNamara, Robert P., eds. Social Gerontology. LC 97-22753. 288p. 1998. 59.95 (*0-86569-264-5*, Auburn Hse) Greenwood.

Redburn, F. Stevens & Buss, Terry. Public Policies for Communities in Economic Crisis. 1981. pap. 15.00 (*0-918592-54-2*) Pol Studies.

Redburn, F. Stevens & Buss, Terry F. Responding to America's Homeless: Public Policy Alternatives. LC 86-21186. 170p. 1986. 52.95 (*0-275-92231-6*, C2231, Praeger Pubs) Greenwood.

Redburn, F. Stevens, jt. auth. see Buss, Terry F.

Redburn, H. Ashley, jt. auth. see Langworth, Richard M.

Redburn, Ray, et al. Confessions of Empowering Organizations: Who's Doing It & How. LC 91-77165. (Illus.). 224p. (Orig.). 1992. pap. 19.95 (*0-9631461-0-6*) Assn Qual & Part.

***Redburn, Sandy.** Another 500 Heartwarming Expressions for Crafting, Painting, Stitching & Scrapbooking, Bk. 3. 3rd ed. (Illus.). 88p. 2000. pap. 9.95 (*0-9686648-0-6*, Pub. by CSP1) Leisure AR.

— 500 Heartwarming Expressions for Crafting, Painting, Stitching & Scrapbooking, Bk. 1. 3rd rev. ed. (Illus.). 88p. 2000. pap. 9.95 (*0-9699410-8-0*, Pub. by CSP1) Leisure AR.

— 500 More Heartwarming Expressions for Crafting, Painting, Stitching & Scrapbooking, Bk. 2. 3rd rev. ed. (Illus.). 88p. 2000. pap. 9.95 (*0-9699410-9-9*, Pub. by CSP1) Leisure AR.

Redburn, Tom, ed. see Bergstrand, Jeffrey H.

Redburn, Tom, ed. see Di Benedetto, Anthony & Kamins, Michael A.

Redburn, Tom, ed. see Skylar, S. Jay & Bongiovanni, Joseph N.

Redcay, Shirley. Friendship Fables: For Interactive Guidance Lessons for Classes or Small Groups. (Illus.). 64p. (J). (gr. k-6). 1998. pap. text 12.95 (*1-57543-059-2*) Mar Co Prods.

Redcay, T. J. Old Order Amish: In Plain Words & Pictures. (Illus.). 32p. 1996. pap. 4.00 (*1-890541-30-3*) Americana Souvenirs & Gifts.

Redcliffe Press, Ltd. Staff, ed. Dorset Essays. 168p. 1983. 45.00 (*0-905459-53-9*, Pub. by Redcliffe Pr Ltd) St Mut.

Redclift, M. R. Agrarian Reform & Peasant Organization on the Ecuadorian Coast. (Institute of Latin American Studies Monographs: No. 8). (Illus.). 186p. (C). 1978. text 44.50 (*0-485-17708-0*, Pub. by Athlone Pr) Humanities.

***Redclift, M. R.** Social Environmental Research in the European Union: Research Networks & New Agendas. LC 00-37610. 2000. write for info. (*1-84064-211-4*) E Elgar.

— Sustainability: Life Chances & Livelihoods. LC 99-29732. 208p. 1999. pap. 27.99 (*0-415-19618-3*) Routledge.

***Redclift, M. R. & Codd, Francis.** The Frontier Environment & Social Order: The Letters of Francis Codd from Upper Canada. LC 00-33169. 2000. write for info. (*1-84064-251-3*) E Elgar.

***Redclift, M. R., et al.** Agriculture & World Trade Liberalization: Socio-Environmental Perspectives on the Common Agricultural Policy. LC 98-29587. 288p. 1999. 75.00 (*0-85199-297-8*) OUP.

Redclift, Michael. Development & the Environment Crisis: Red or Green Alternatives. (Development & Underdevelopment Ser.). 176p. 1984. pap. 14.95 (*0-416-32140-2*, NO. 4020) Routledge.

— Sustainable Development: Exploring the Contradictions. 196p. (C). 1987. pap. 25.99 (*0-415-05085-5*) Routledge.

Redclift, Michael & Benton, Ted, eds. Social Theory & the Global Environment. LC 93-44072. (Global Environmental Change Ser.). 256p. (C). 1994. pap. 18.95 (*0-415-11170-6*, B3823) Routledge.

Redclift, Michael & Sage, Colin, eds. Strategies for Sustainable Development: Local Agendas for the Southern Hemisphere. LC 93-3272. 206p. 1994. 150.00 (*0-471-94278-2*) Wiley.

***Redclift, Michael & Woodgate, Graham, eds.** The International Handbook of Environmental Sociology. LC 97-22850. 512p. 2000. pap. 40.00 (*1-84064-243-2*) E Elgar.

Redclift, Michael & Woodgate, Graham, eds. The Sociology of the Environment, 3 vols., Set. (International Library of Critical Writings in Sociology Ser.: No. 1). 2004p. 1995. 630.00 (*1-85278-902-6*) E Elgar.

Redclift, Michael R. Development Policymaking in Mexico: The Sistema Alimentario Mexicano (SAM) (Research Reports: No. 24). 26p. (Orig.). (C). 1981. ring bd. 5.00 (*0-935391-23-1*, RR-24) UCSD Ctr US-Mex.

***Redclift, Michael R., ed.** Sustainability: Life Chances & Livelihoods. LC 99-29732. 208p. (C). 1999. text. write for info. (*0-415-19617-5*) Routledge.

Redclift, Michael R. & Woodgate, Graham, eds. The International Handbook of Environmental Sociology. LC 97-22850. 512p. (C). 1998. 160.00 (*1-85898-405-X*) E Elgar.

Redd. Revelations. 2nd ed. 336p. 1993. pap. text 35.20 (*0-536-58423-0*) Pearson Custom.

— Revelations: Expository Essays by & about Blacks. (C). 1991. pap. text 38.60 (*0-536-57971-7*) Pearson Custom.

Redd, Ann, jt. auth. see Redd, Robert O.

Redd, Fredrick, Jr. Estimating for Building Construction. 400p. (C). 2001. 53.33 (*0-13-757279-4*, Macmillan Coll) P-H.

Redd, James B., et al. Quality Control Manual for Citrus Processing Plants: Flavor, Vol. 111. unabridged ed. (Illus.). 338p. 1996. text 78.00 (*0-9631397-4-6*) AgScience.

— Quality Control Manual for Citrus Processing Plants: Processing & Operating Procedures, Blending Techniques, Formulating, Citrus Mathematics & Costs, Vol. 2. LC 91-42295. 290p. (C). 1992. text 68.00 (*0-9631397-0-3*) AgScience.

Redd, James E. & Hendrix, Charles M., eds. Quality Control Manual for Citrus Processing Plants, Vol. 1. 250p. 1986. 58.00 (*0-614-25176-1*) AgScience.

Redd, Jim. The Illinois & Michigan Canal: A Contemporary Perspective in Essays & Photographs. LC 91-2220. (Illus.). 144p. (C). 1993. 31.95 (*0-8093-1660-9*) S Ill U Pr.

Redd, Katie. Making Santas with Katie Redd. LC 97-61776. (Illus.). 92p. 1997. pap. 14.95 (*0-916809-94-3*) Scott Pubns MI.

Redd, Lorraine & Davis, Jack. Only in Mississippi: A Guide for the Adventurous Traveler. rev. ed. LC 93-32607. (Illus.). 112p. 1997. pap. 7.95 (*0-937552-54-2*) Quail Ridge.

Redd, Louise. Hangover Soup: A Novel. LC 99-18936. 272p. 1999. 23.00 (*0-316-47900-4*) Little.

***Redd, Louise.** Hangover Soup: A Novel. 288p. 2000. pap. 12.95 (*0-316-47997-7*, Back Bay) Little.

Redd, Louise. Playing the Bones. 1997. pap. 11.95 (*0-614-27265-3*, Plume) Dutton Plume.

Redd, Mary A. The World of Holly Prickle: For Women Who Have Worked for Men. LC 93-92632. 290p. (Orig.). 1993. pap. 10.00 (*0-9636548-0-2*) Shenandoah Bks.

Redd, Preston. From Horseback to Cadillac, I'm Still a Cowboy: True Tales of the Old West. Tegeler, Dorothy, ed. (Illus.). 355p. 1989. 27.50 (*0-9621360-2-6*) Tavas Cash Pr.

Redd, Rahn. The Final Challenge. LC 88-92273. 177p. (Orig.). 1988. pap. 10.95 (*0-922969-01-9*) Pebble Beach Pub.

Redd, Robert O. Achievers Never Quit - How to Create a Life Plan for the Years after Fifty: A Book for People Who Can't Quit. LC 89-50123. (Illus.). 150p. (Orig.). 1989. pap. 6.95 (*1-877756-00-8*) Thornapple Pub.

— 21 Humorous, New, Short Plays & Skits for Performing Grandparents: Easy to Stage, Performance Tested, No Royalty 1998 Mature Media Gold Award. large type ed. LC 97-62524. (Illus.). 155p. 1998. pap. 24.95 (*1-877756-07-5*) Thornapple Pub.

Redd, Robert O. & Redd, Ann. Whimsey, Wit & Wisdom: For the Wonderful Years after Fifty. LC 90-90119. 128p. 1990. pap. text 8.95 (*1-877756-03-2*) Thornapple Pub.

***Redd, Roberto.** 23 New, Humorous, Short Play Scripts for Performing Grand Parents: 17 Traditional Scripts, 6 Improv Scripts. (Illus.). 150p. 2000. spiral bd. 24.95 (*1-877756-08-3*) Thornapple Pub.

Redd, Teresa M., ed. Revelations: An Anthology of Expository Essays by & about Blacks. 3rd rev. ed. LC 99-180704. 354p. (C). 1997. pap. 28.20 (*0-536-00234-7*) Pearson Custom.

Redda, Kinfe K., et al, eds. Cocaine, Marijuana, Designer Drugs: Chemistry, Pharmacology, & Behavior. 248p. 1989. boxed set 208.95 (*0-8493-6853-7*, RM316) CRC Pr.

Reddan, Minnie & Clapham, Alfred W. The Church of St. Helen, Bishopsgate, Pt. 1. LC 74-6179. (London County Council. Survey of London Ser.: No. 9). reprint ed. 84.50 (*0-404-51659-9*, NA5470) AMS Pr.

Reddaway, Darlene & Pruul, Kajar, eds. Estonian Short Stories. Poom, Ritva, tr. from EST. (Writings from an Unbound Europe Ser.). 232p. (Orig.). 1995. text 39.95 (*0-8101-1240-X*) Northwestern U Pr.

— Estonian Short Stories. Poom, Ritva, tr. from EST. (Writings from an Unbound Europe Ser.). 232p. (Orig.). (C). 1995. pap. 14.95 (*0-8101-1241-8*) Northwestern U Pr.

Reddaway, Peter, ed. see Vassiliev, Dmitri Glinski.

Reddaway, T. F., et al. The Early History of the Goldsmiths' Company, 1327-1509. LC 76-367000. xxx, 378p. 1975. write for info. (*0-7131-5749-6*) OUP.

Reddaway, William F. Frederick the Great & the Rise of Prussia. LC 68-25262. (Studies in German Literature: No. 13). 1969. reprint ed. lib. bdg. 75.00 (*0-8383-0232-7*) M S G Haskell Hse.

— Frederick the Great & the Rise of Prussia. reprint ed. 13.00 (*0-403-00037-8*) Scholarly.

— Problems of the Baltic. LC 75-41224. reprint ed. 27.50 (*0-404-14588-4*) AMS Pr.

Reddel, Carl W., ed. Military History Symposium Series of the United States Air Force Academy. (Orig.). 1993. write for info. (*1-879176-14-9*) Imprint Pubns.

Reddell, Rayford Clayton. Cut-Flower Roses. LC 98-19182. (Illus.). 96p. 1999. 14.95 (*0-8118-2270-2*) Chronicle Bks.

— Heirloom Roses. LC 98-19183. (Illus.). 96p. 1999. 14.95 (*0-8118-2254-0*) Chronicle Bks.

— The Rose Bible. LC 98-6832. (Illus.). 252p. 1998. pap. 24.95 (*0-8118-2159-5*) Chronicle Bks.

Reddemann, Angela. Der Wille Gottes Als Handlungsregelndes Motiv in der Moraltheologie Kant-Mausbach-Vatikanum II: Der Beitrag J. Mausbachs Fur ein Personales Verstandnis der Antriebsstruktur Christlichen Handelns. (Europaische Hochschulschriften Ser.: Reihe 23, Bd. 483). (GER.). XIII, 281p. 1993. 49.95 (*3-631-45848-7*) P Lang Pubng.

Redden, jt. auth. see Schlueter.

Redden, Charlotte A. A Comparative Study of Colombian & Costa Rican Emigrants to the United States. Cortes, Carlos E., ed. LC 79-6218. (Hispanics in the United States Ser.). (Illus.). 1981. lib. bdg. 23.95 (*0-405-13166-6*) Ayer.

***Redden, Gabriele.** Oven-Baked Vegetarian Dishes. LC 99-86988. 2000. 14.95 (*0-7641-1279-1*) Barron.

Redden, J. C. The Best & the Rest of Redden's Rules of Thumb: Almost 200 Money-Saving, Money-Making Tips for the Cemetery/Mortuary Industry. 82p. 1993. 20.00 (*1-879111-24-1*) Lincoln-Bradley.

Redden, J. E. Twi Basic Course. (Hippocrene Basic Course Guides Ser.). 225p. 1995. pap. 16.95 (*0-7818-0394-2*) Hippocrene Bks.

Redden, J. E., ed. A Descriptive Grammar of Ewondo. (Occasional Papers on Linguistics: No. 4). 254p. 1979. reprint ed. pap. text 26.88 (*1-55567-491-7*) Coyote Press.

— Papers from the American Indian Languages Conferences Held at the University of California, Santa Cruz, July & August, 1991, Vol. 16. (Occasional Papers on Linguistics: No. 16). (Illus.). 240p. (C). 1991. reprint ed. pap. text 25.63 (*1-55567-481-X*) Coyote Press.

— Papers from the 1987 Hokan-Penutian Languages Workshop & Friends of Uto-Aztecan Workshop. (Occasional Papers on Linguistics: No. 14). (Illus.). 89p. (C). 1988. reprint ed. pap. text 10.00 (*1-55567-483-6*) Coyote Press.

— Papers from the 1983, 1984 & 1985 Hokan-Penutian Languages Conference. (Occasional Papers of Linguistics: No. 13). 116p. (C). 1986. reprint ed. pap. text 13.13 (*1-55567-484-4*) Coyote Press.

— Papers from the 1992 Hokan-Penutian Languages Conference & the J. P. Harrington Conference, Held at the University of California, Santa Barbara, & the Museum of Natural History, Santa Barbara, June 24-27, 1992, Vol. 17. (Occasional Papers on Linguistics: No. 17). (Illus.). (C). 1992. reprint ed. pap. text 16.25 (*1-55567-480-1*) Coyote Press.

— Proceedings of the 1st Yuman Languages Workshop. fac. ed. (Southern Illinois University, University Museum Ser.: No. 7). 159p. 1976. reprint ed. pap. text 17.50 (*1-55567-493-3*) Coyote Press.

— Proceedings of the 1980 Hokan Languages Workshop, Held at University of California, Berkeley. (Occasional Papers on Linguistics: No. 9). 135p. 1981. reprint ed. pap. text 15.00 (*1-55567-488-7*) Coyote Press.

— Proceedings of the 1981 Hokan Languages Workshop & Penutian Languages Conference. (Occasional Papers on Linguistics: No. 10). 87p. 1982. reprint ed. pap. text 10.00 (*1-55567-487-9*) Coyote Press.

— Proceedings of the 1978 Hokan Languages Workshop. (Occasional Papers on Linguistics: No. 5). 96p. 1979. reprint ed. pap. text 10.94 (*1-55567-490-9*) Coyote Press.

— Proceedings of the 1979 Hokan Languages Workshop, Held at University of California, Los Angeles. (Occasional Papers on Linguistics: No. 7). 83p. 1980. reprint ed. pap. text 9.38 (*1-55567-489-5*) Coyote Press.

— Proceedings of the 1977 Hokan-Yuman Languages Workshop, Held at University of Utah, Salt Lake City. (Occasional Papers on Linguistics: No. 2). 95p. 1978. reprint ed. pap. text 10.63 (*1-55567-492-5*) Coyote Press.

— Proceedings of the 1976 Hokan-Yuman Languages Workshop Held at University of California. (Occasional Papers on Linguistics: No. 11). 99p. 1977. reprint ed. pap. text 11.25 (*1-55567-494-1*) Coyote Press.

— Proceedings of the 1982 Conference on Far Western American Indian Languages, Held at University of California, Santa Cruz. (Occasional Papers on Linguistics: No. 11). (Illus.). 61p. (C). 1983. reprint ed. pap. text 7.19 (*1-55567-486-0*) Coyote Press.

Redden, J. E. & Owusu, N. TWI Intensive Cassette Course: Learn TWI Quickly. 226p. 1997. 184.00 incl. audio (*0-9631518-4-3*) Mltilingl Bks.

***Redden, Jim.** Snitch Culture: How Citizens Are Turned into the Eyes & Ears of the State. 2000. pap. 14.95 (*0-922915-63-6*) Feral Hse.

Redden, Kenneth & Schlueter, Linda. Punitive Damages, 1998 Cumulative Supplement, Vols. 1 & 2. 3rd ed. 340p. 1998. suppl. ed. write for info. (*0-327-00360-X*, 6647712) LEXIS Pub.

Redden, Kenneth R. Modern Legal Systems Cyclopedia Vols. 3 & 3A: Western Europe - E. E. C. Countries, 2 vols., Set. rev. ed. LC 83-82953. 1989. ring bd. 195.00 (*0-89941-303-X*, 306270) W S Hein.

Redden, Kenneth R., ed. Modern Legal Systems Cyclopedia Vols. 1 & 1A: North America, 2 vols., Set. rev. ed. LC 83-82953. 1988. ring bd. 195.00 (*0-89941-301-3*, 306250) W S Hein.

— Modern Legal Systems Cyclopedia Vols. 2 & 2A: Pacific Basin, 2 vols., Set. rev. ed. LC 83-82953. 1989. ring bd. 195.00 (*0-89941-302-1*, 306260) W S Hein.

— Modern Legal Systems Cyclopedia Vols. 4 & 4A: Western Europe Non - E. E. C. Countries, 2 vols., Set. rev. ed. LC 83-82953. 1989. ring bd. 195.00 (*0-89941-304-8*, 306280) W S Hein.

— Modern Legal Systems Cyclopedia Vols. 5 & 5A: Middle East, 2 vols., Set. rev. ed. LC 83-82953. 1990. ring bd. 195.00 (*0-89941-305-6*, 306290) W S Hein.

— Modern Legal Systems Cyclopedia Vols. 6 & 6A: Africa, 2 vols., Set. rev. ed. LC 83-82953. 1990. ring bd. 195.00 (*0-89941-306-4*, 306300) W S Hein.

— Modern Legal Systems Cyclopedia Vols. 7 & 7A: Central America & Caribbean, 2 vols., Set. rev. ed. LC 83-82953. 1989. ring bd. 195.00 (*0-89941-307-2*, 306310) W S Hein.

— Modern Legal Systems Cyclopedia Vols. 8 & 8A: Eastern Europe, 2 vols., Set. rev. ed. LC 83-82953. 1991. ring bd. 195.00 (*0-89941-308-0*, 306320) W S Hein.

— Modern Legal Systems Cyclopedia Vols. 9 & 9A: Asia, 2 vols., Set. rev. ed. LC 83-82953. 1991. ring bd. 195.00 (*0-89941-309-9*, 306330) W S Hein.

— Modern Legal Systems Cyclopedia Vols. 10 & 10A: South America. rev. ed. LC 83-82953. xlvii, 1021p. 1986. ring bd. 195.00 (*0-89941-310-2*, 306340) W S Hein.

— Modern Legal Systems Cyclopedia Indices. LC 83-82953. 1984. ring bd. 1995.00 (*0-89941-300-5*, 306670) W S Hein.

Redden, Kenneth R. & Beyer, Gerry W. Modern Dictionary for the Legal Profession, 1995: Supplement. LC 92-35678. xiii, 802p. 1993. pap., suppl. ed. 75.00 (*0-89941-829-5*, 307770) W S Hein.

— Modern Dictionary for the Legal Profession, 1995: Supplement. LC 92-35678. 78p. 1994. suppl. ed. 25.00 (*0-89941-865-1*, 308570) W S Hein.

Redden, Kenneth R., jt. auth. see Beyer, Gerry W.

Redden, Kenneth R., jt. auth. see Schlueter, Linda L.

Redden, Mary, jt. ed. see Stuart-Smith, Stephen.

Redden, Ric. Understanding Laminitis: Your Guide to Horse Health Care & Management. Duke, Jacqueline, ed. (Horse Health Care Library). (Illus.). 144p. 1998. pap. 14.95 (*0-939049-98-8*) Blood-Horse.

Redden, Steven. Good Grammar Matters, Pt. I. unabridged ed. 24p. 1992. pap. 39.50 incl. audio (*0-88432-527-X*, S04050) Audio-Forum.

Redden, Steven. Good Grammar Matters, Pt. II. unabridged ed. 24p. 1992. pap. 39.50 incl. audio (*0-88432-528-8*, S04060) Audio-Forum.

Redder, Howard. Paper, Mister? Downtown Dayton - 1935. 205p. (Orig.). 1995. pap. 14.95 (*0-9657401-0-2*) H J Redder.

Reddi, A. Harri, jt. auth. see Habal, Mutaz B.

Reddi, Agarala Easwara, see Easwara Reddi, Agarala, ed.

Reddi, Alluru S. Essentials of Renal Physiology. LC 98-74967. (Illus.). 350p. 1999. pap. text. write for info. (*0-9669823-0-4*) College Book.

Reddi, L. N. Soil Science Principles & Geoenvironmental Applications. (Books in Soils, Plants & the Environment). Date not set. write for info. (*0-8247-9438-9*) Dekker.

Reddi, L. N. & Inyang, H. Fundamentals of Geoenvironmental Engineering. (Books in Soils, Plants & the Environment). (Illus.). 311p. 2000. text. write for info. (*0-8247-0045-7*) Dekker.

Reddi, Lakshmi N., et al. Filtration & Drainage in Geotechnical Geoenvironmental Engineering. LC 98-40470. (Geotechnical Special Publication Ser.). 216p. 1998. 40.00 (*0-7844-0385-6*) Am Soc Civil Eng.

— Non-Aqueous Phase Liquids (NAPLS) in Subsurface Environment: Assessment & Remediation: Proceedings of the Specialty Conference Held in Conjunction with the ASCE National Convention, Washington, D. C., November 12-13, 1996. LC 96-44713. 864p. 1996. 84.00 (*0-7844-0203-5*) Am Soc Civil Eng.

Reddick. Internet Guide to Earth Science. LC 97-113861. (C). 1996. text 16.00 (*0-03-018842-3*, Pub. by Harcourt Coll Pubs) Harcourt.

— The Online Journalist. 3rd ed. (C). 1999. pap. text 37.50 (*0-15-506752-4*, Pub. by Harcourt Coll Pubs) Harcourt.

Reddick, jt. auth. see Cohen.

Reddick, Allen. The Making of Johnson's Dictionary, 1746-1773. 2nd ed. LC 96-151729. (Studies in Publishing & Printing History). (Illus.). 274p. (C). 1996. pap. text 19.95 (*0-521-56838-2*) Cambridge U Pr.

Reddick, DeWitt C. The Mass Media & the School Newspaper. 2nd ed. (Mass Communication). 1986. mass mkt. 24.75 (*0-534-03597-3*) West Pub.

Reddick, Don. Dawson City Seven. 272p. 1994. pap. write for info. (*0-86492-158-6*) Goose Ln Eds.

Reddick, Eddie J., et al, eds. An Atlas of Laparoscopic Surgery. LC 92-14363. 128p. 1993. sl. 236.50 (*0-88167-979-8*) Lppncott W & W.

— Atlas of Laparoscopic Surgery. LC 92-14363. (Illus.). 126p. 1993. reprint ed. pap. 39.10 (*0-608-07210-9*, 206743500009) Bks Demand.

Reddick, Ellen R. Back to Basics. 174p. (Orig.). 1997. pap. write for info. (*0-9656532-0-X*) University Pub.

*__Reddick, Henry W.__ Seventy-Seven Years in Dixie: The Boys in Gray of '61-'65. (Illus.). xx, 92p. 1999. pap. 9.00 (*0-9666805-2-9*) SWTAA.

Reddick, J. Rex, ed. F. W. Assmann & Sohne Sales Catalog. (Illus.). 108p. 1993. pap. 17.95 (*0-9624883-3-X*) Reddick Enterp.

Reddick, J. Rex, jt. auth. see Evans, C. Scott.

Reddick, J. Rex, ed. see Hicks, Kelly.

Reddick, J. Rex, ed. see Skotte, Anders.

Reddick, J. Rex, ed. see Wilson, Kit.

Reddick, John. Georg Buchner: The Shattered Whole. 406p. 1995. text 72.00 (*0-19-815812-2*) OUP.

Reddick, John, tr. & intro. see Buchner, Georg.

Reddick, Marshall E., jt. auth. see Cohen, William A.

Reddick, Norman C. The Keepers: The Tree. 198p. 1998. pap. 10.95 (*1-57502-965-0*, PO2675) Morris Pubng.

*__Reddick, Norman C.__ Murders Most Pleasant. 175p. 2000. pap. 10.95 (*0-9701192-0-8*) Carlisle TX.

Reddick, Randy. Saunders Internet Guide. (C). 1996. text 23.50 (*0-03-018858-X*) Harcourt.

Reddick, Randy & King, Elliot. The On-Line Journ@list: Using the Internet & Other Electronic Resources. 2nd ed. LC 96-80011. 288p. (C). 1997. pap. text 31.00 (*0-15-505222-5*, Pub. by Harcourt Coll Pubs) Harcourt.

— The On-Line Student: Making the Grade on the Internet. LC 95-81842. 337p. (C). 1995. pap. text 22.00 (*0-15-503189-9*, Pub. by Harcourt Coll Pubs) Harcourt.

— The Online Journalist: Using the Internet & Other Electronic Resources. (Illus.). 240p. (C). 1994. pap. text 27.00 (*0-15-502018-8*, Pub. by Harcourt Coll Pubs) Harcourt.

Reddicliffe, Sheila. The Cornish Mistress. 148p. (C). 1992. pap. 40.00 (*1-871330-04-1*, Pub. by Lightbody Pubns) St Mut.

Reddie, James. Inquiries Elementary & Historical in the Science of Law. LC 81-23554. viii, 216p. 1982. reprint ed. 32.95 (*0-8377-1034-0*, Rothman) W S Hein.

Reddiford, Gordon, jt. ed. see Beveridge, Michael.

Reddig, Jill S., jt. ed. see Eisel, Deborah D.

Reddig, William M. Tom's Town: Kansas City & the Pendergast Legend. LC 85-20888. 400p. (C). 1986. pap. 22.50 (*0-8262-0498-8*) U of Mo Pr.

Reddihough, Alison, jt. auth. see Lewis, Ian.

Reddin. Output Oriented Manager. 400p. 1989. 78.95 (*0-566-02711-9*) Ashgate Pub Co.

— Output Oriented Organization. 272p. 1989. 78.95 (*0-566-02710-0*) Ashgate Pub Co.

Reddin, Chitra P. Forms of Evil in the Gothic Novel. Varma, Devendra P., ed. LC 79-8472. (Gothic Studies & Dissertations). 1980. lib. bdg. 35.95 (*0-405-12669-7*) Ayer.

Reddin, Jane E. How to Avoid & Manage Sexual Harassment Claims. LC 96-16340. 56p. 1996. spiral bd. 47.00 (*0-925773-24-7*) M Lee Smith.

Reddin, Keith. Big Time & After School Special. 61p. (Orig.). 1987. pap. 5.95 (*0-88145-063-4*) Broadway Play.

— Black Snow. 1993. pap. 5.25 (*0-8222-1371-0*) Dramatists Play.

— Brutality of Fact. 1995. pap. 5.25 (*0-8222-1503-9*) Dramatists Play.

— Desperadoes, Throwing Smoke, Keyhole Lover. 1986. pap. 5.25 (*0-8222-0301-4*) Dramatists Play.

— The Innocents' Crusade. 1993. pap. 5.25 (*0-8222-1332-X*) Dramatists Play.

— Life & Limb. 1985. pap. 5.25 (*0-8222-0658-7*) Dramatists Play.

— Life During Wartime. 1991. pap. 5.25 (*0-8222-0659-5*) Dramatists Play.

— Rum & Coke. 1986. pap. 6.95 (*0-88145-042-1*) Broadway Play.

Reddin, Mike & Pilch, Michael. Can We Afford Our Future. (C). 1989. 40.00 (*0-86242-038-5*, Pub. by Age Concern Eng) St Mut.

Reddin, O. Enfrentamiento de Poderes.Tr. of Power Encounter. (SPA.). 272p. 1994. pap. 11.99 (*0-8297-0397-7*) Vida Pubs.

Reddin, William J. Using Tests to Improve Training: The Complete Guide to Selecting, Developing, & Using Training Instruments. LC 94-5600. 276p. (C). 1994. text 59.95 (*0-13-108556-5*) P-H.

Redding, Arthur. Raids on Human Consciousness: Writing, Anarchism & Violence. LC 97-45434. 275p. 1998. lib. bdg. 39.95 (*1-57003-230-0*) U of SC Pr.

Redding, Arthur F. Raids on Human Consciousness: Writing, Anarchism & Violence. LC 97-45434. (Cultural Frames, Framing Culture Ser.). 1998. pap. 18.95 (*1-57003-276-9*) U of SC Pr.

*__Redding, David A., ed.__ The Prayers I Love. 2nd rev. ed. (Illus.). 128p. 1999. pap. 15.95 (*0-9671701-0-9*, 1-A) Starborne Hse.

Redding, D'Eva, jt. auth. see Redding, Eric.

Redding, Eric & Redding, D'Eva. Great Big Beautiful Doll: The Anna Nicole Smith Story. LC 95-50720. (Illus.). 208p. 1996. 22.00 (*1-56980-079-0*) Barricade Bks.

Redding, Gene, ed. see Garrison, J. Gregory.

Redding, Gordon M. & Wallace, Benjamin. Adaptive Spatial Alignment. Link, Stephen W. & Townsend, James, eds. LC 96-41210. (Scientific Psychology Ser.). 216p. 1997. 49.95 (*0-8058-2395-6*) L Erlbaum Assocs.

Redding, J. Saunders. A Scholar's Conscience: Selected Writings of J. Saunders Redding. Berry, Faith, ed. 248p. 1992. 39.95 (*0-8131-1770-4*) U Pr of Ky.

— Stranger & Alone. (Northeastern Library of Black Literature). 320p. 1989. reprint ed. text 42.50 (*1-55553-055-9*); reprint ed. pap. text 16.95 (*1-55553-053-2*) NE U Pr.

— To Make a Poet Black. LC 86-47630. 184p. 1987. 32.50 (*0-8014-1982-4*); pap. text 11.95 (*0-8014-9438-9*) Cornell U Pr.

Redding, J. Saunders. Troubled in Mind: J. Saunders Redding's Early Years in Wilmington. LC 91-70169. (Illus.). 90p. (Orig.). 1991. pap. 4.00 (*0-924117-03-6*) Delaware HP.

Redding, J. Saunders & Joyce, Joyce A. The New Cavalcade I: African American Writing. Davis, Arthur P. et al, eds. 1991. pap. 32.95 (*0-88258-133-3*) Howard U Pr.

Redding, Jackie. Scotland the Green: The Alternative to Vegetarian & Vegan Hideaways in Scotland. (Illus.). 96p. (Orig.). 1997. pap. 9.95 (*1-899171-41-X*, Pub. by Findhorn Pr) Words Distrib.

Redding, Jackie & Weston, Tony. Rainbows & Wellies: The Taigh Na Mara Cookbook. (Illus.), 100p. 1995. 24.95 (*1-899171-70-3*, Pub. by Findhorn Pr) Words Distrib.

Redding, Jay S. To Make a Poet Black. 8.00 (*0-405-18495-6*) Ayer.

— To Make a Poet Black. (BCL1-PS American Literature Ser.). 142p. 1993. reprint ed. lib. bdg. 69.00 (*0-7812-6567-3*) Rprt Serv.

Redding, Joan & O'Conner, Diane V. Guide to Photographic Collections at the Smithsonian Institution Vol. IV: NASM. (Illus.). 328p. 1995. pap. text 60.00 (*1-56098-414-7*) Smithsonian.

*__Redding, John C.__ Radical Team Handbook: Harnessing the Power of Team Learning for Breakthrough Results. 2000. 34.95 (*0-7879-5161-7*) Jossey-Bass.

Redding, John C. & Catalanello, Ralph F. Strategic Readiness: The Making of a Learning Organization. LC 93-48673. (Business-Management Ser.). 200p. 1994. text 30.95 (*1-55542-633-6*) Jossey-Bass.

Redding, Judith M. & Brownworth, Victoria A. Film Fatales: Independent Women Directors. LC 97-29205. (Illus.). 286p. (Orig.). 1997. pap. 16.95 (*1-878067-97-4*) Seal Pr WA.

Redding, Judith M., jt. ed. see Brownworth, Victoria A.

Redding, M. W. Scarlet Book of Freemasonry: Containing, a Thrilling & Authentic Account of the Imprisonment, Torture, & Martyrdom of Freemasons & Knights Templars, for the Past Six Hundred Years; Also an Authentic Account of the Education, Remarkable Career & Tragic Death of the Renowned Philospher Pythagoras, Recent Remarkable Discovery of Masonic Emblems on an Ancient Obelisk in Egypt. 524p. 1992. reprint ed. pap. 29.95 (*1-56459-283-9*) Kessinger Pub.

Redding, M. Wolcott. Masonic Antiquities of the Orient Unveiled. 454p. 1997. reprint ed. pap. 35.00 (*0-7661-0016-2*) Kessinger Pub.

Redding, Mary L. Breaking & Mending: Divorce & God's Grace. LC 98-11786. 160p. 1998. pap. 12.00 (*0-8358-0855-6*, UR855) Upper Room Bks.

*__Redding, Michael.__ Great Themes: Understanding the Bible's Core Doctrines. (Bible 101 Ser.). 64p. 2000. pap. 4.99 (*0-8308-2067-1*) InterVarsity.

— Times & Places: Picturing the Events of the Bible. (Bible 101 Ser.). 64p. 2000. pap. 4.99 (*0-8308-2062-0*) InterVarsity.

Redding, Moses W. The Illustrated History of Freemasonry. 726p. 1997. reprint ed. pap. 50.00 (*0-7661-0033-2*) Kessinger Pub.

Redding, Noel & Appleby, Carol. Are You Experienced? The Inside Story of the Jimi Hendrix Experience. (Illus.). 258p. (Orig.). 1996. pap. 13.95 (*0-306-80681-9*) Da Capo.

Redding, Nora. Tied to a Chair. LC 98-84526. (Illus.). 116p. 1998. pap. 11.95 (*0-9663195-0-8*) Redding Pub.

Redding, Paul. Hegel's Hermeneutics. LC 95-25886. 288p. 1996. text 42.50 (*0-8014-3180-8*); pap. text 16.95 (*0-8014-8345-X*) Cornell U Pr.

— The Logic of Affect. LC 98-55361. 1999. 35.00 (*0-8014-3591-9*) Cornell U Pr.

— Wild West Shows. LC 98-58008. 368p. 1999. pap. 21.95 (*0-252-06787-8*) U of Ill Pr.

— Wild West Shows. LC 98-58008. 368p. 1999. 49.95 (*0-252-02464-8*) U of Ill Pr.

Redding, Phil. Tuning In: A Layman's Guide to Youth Ministry. 153p. 1990. pap. 5.95 (*1-882449-21-5*) Messenger Pub.

Redding, Richard W. & Knecht, Charles E. An Atlas of Electro-Encephalography in the Dog & Cat. LC 83-13693. (Illus.). 387p. 1984. 79.50 (*0-275-91448-8*, C1448, Praeger Pubs) Greenwood.

*__Redding, Richard W. & Papurt, M. L.__ Dogs Drugstore: A Dog Owner's Guide to Nonprescription Drugs & Their Safe Use in Veterinary Home Care. LC 00-27487. (Illus.). 300p. 2000. text 23.95 (*0-312-20888-X*) St Martin.

Redding, Robert & Yenne, Bill. Boeing: Planemaker to the World. LC 97-11330. (Illus.). 256p. 1997. 19.98 (*1-57145-045-9*, Thunder Bay) Advantage Pubs.

Redding, Robert H. Londagin. LC 97-93463. 192p. 1997. lib. bdg. 18.95 (*0-8034-9241-3*, Avalon Bks) Bouregy.

*__Redding, Robert H.__ McCall. LC 99-90986. 192p. 1999. 18.95 (*0-8034-9391-6*, Avalon Bks) Bouregy.

Redding, S. Gordon. International Cultural Differences. (International Library of Management). (Illus.). 544p. 1995. text 235.95 (*1-85521-422-9*, Pub. by Dartmth Pub) Ashgate Pub Co.

— The Spirit of Chinese Capitalism. (Studies in Organization: No. 22). xiv, 267p. (C). 1993. pap. text 24.95 (*3-11-013794-1*) De Gruyter.

Redding, S. Gordon, jt. ed. see Clegg, Stewart R.

Redding, Sandra, ed. Greensboro: A Portrait of Progress. LC 98-41683. (Illus.). 264p. 1998. 45.00 (*1-885352-84-0*) Community Comm.

Redding, Spencer W. & Montgomery, Michael T., eds. Dentistry in Systemic Disease: Diagnostic & Therapeutic Approach to Patient Management. LC 89-64175. (Illus.). 348p. 1990. pap. text 21.95 (*0-945892-00-4*) JBK Pub.

Redding, Stan, jt. auth. see Abagnale, Frank W., Jr.

Redding, Theresa, jt. auth. see Midlen, Alex.

Redding, Trilba N., ed. see Wilson, Charles A.

Reddingius, Joannes, jt. auth. see Den Boer, P. J.

Reddington, Linda. The Ants in Frants. LC 99-183585. 55 p. 1996. write for info. (*0-9660216-0-6*) Times-Beacon.

Reddington, Marge. Health, Happiness & Human Needs: An Introduction to Symbolization. LC 94-60127. 254p. 1994. pap. 19.95 (*0-9640594-0-1*) TDC Pubng.

Reddish, D. J., jt. auth. see Whittaker, Barry N.

Reddish, Mitchell G. An Introduction to the Gospels. LC 97-5098. 288p. 1997. pap. 19.95 (*0-687-00448-9*) Abingdon.

Reddish, Paul. Spirits of the Jaguar: The National History & Ancient Civilizations of the Caribbean & Central America. (Illus.). 224p. 1997. 32.95 (*0-563-38743-2*) BBC.

Redditt, Jo Ann T. The Chinese Shar-Pei: An Owner's Guide to a Happy Healthy Pet. (Owner's Guide to a Happy Healthy Pet Ser.). (Illus.). 160p. 1996. 12.95 (*0-87605-396-7*) Howell Bks.

Redditt, Jo Ann T., ed. see Steidel, Kitty.

*__Redditt, Paul L.__ Daniel. (New Century Bible Ser.). 211p. 1999. pap. 19.95 (*1-84127-009-1*, Pub. by Sheffield Acad) CUP Services.

Redditt, Paul L., jt. ed. see Penchansky, David.

Redditt, Paul Lewis. Haggai, Zechariah, Malachi. (New Century Bible Ser.). 196p. 1995. pap. 14.95 (*0-551-02832-7*, Pub. by Sheffield Acad) CUP Services.

Reddix, Valerie. Dragon Kite of the Autumn Moon. LC 91-1506. (Illus.). (J). (ps-3). 1992. lib. bdg. 13.93 (*0-688-11031-2*) Lothrop.

Reddock, Rhoda. Women, Labour & Politics in Trinidad & Tobago: A History. 304p. (C). 1994. text 27.50 (*1-85649-154-4*) Humanities.

— Women, Labour & Politics in Trinidad & Tobago: A History. 304p. (C). 1994. text 65.00 (*1-85649-153-6*, Pub. by Zed Books) St Martin.

Reddock, Rhoda, jt. ed. see Jain, Shobhita.

Reddrop, Bruce, jt. auth. see Reddrop, Mary.

Reddrop, Mary & Reddrop, Bruce. For Better, for Worse: A Guide to Contemporary Marriage Counselling. 256p. 1995. pap., teacher ed. 11.99 (*0-551-02825-4*) Zondervan.

R

Reddy & Medhat, eds. Concurrent Engineering: Simulation in. 100p. 1993. pap. 40.00 (*1-56555-054-4*, CE-1) Soc Computer Sim.

Reddy, jt. see Jacobs.

Reddy, Chris, jt. auth. see le Grange, Lesley.

Reddy, A. K., jt. auth. see Bockris, J. O.

Reddy, Allan C. A Macro Perspective on Technology Transfer. LC 95-51413. 160p. 1996. 57.95 (*0-89930-977-1*, Quorum Bks) Greenwood.

— Total Quality Marketing: The Key to Regaining Market Shares. LC 94-15885. 200p. 1994. 57.95 (*0-89930-893-7*, Quorum Bks) Greenwood.

Reddy, Allan C., ed. The Emerging High-Tech Consumer: A Market Profile & Marketing Strategy Implications. LC 96-46713. 176p. 1997. 59.95 (*1-56720-072-9*, Quorum Bks) Greenwood.

Reddy, Allan C. & Campbell, David P. Marketing's Role in Economic Development. LC 93-27715. 160p. 1993. 49.95 (*0-89930-766-3*, Quorum Bks) Greenwood.

Reddy, Amulya K., jt. auth. see Bockris, John O.

Reddy, Anne W. & Riffe, Andrew L., IV, eds. Richmond County, Virginia Marriage Books, 1797-1853. 158p. 1994. reprint ed. pap. 16.00 (*0-8328-4016-5*) Higginson Bk Co.

Reddy, B. D. Introductory Functional Analysis: With Applications to Boundary-Value Problems & Finite Elements, Vol. 127. Marsden, J. E. et al, eds. LC 97-24052. (Texts in Applied Mathematics Ser.: No. 27). (Illus.). 488p. 1997. 54.95 (*0-387-98307-4*) Spr-Verlag.

Reddy, B. D., jt. auth. see Ham, Weimin.

Reddy, Bandaru S. & Cohen, Leonard A., eds. Diet, Nutrition & Cancer: A Critical Evaluation. LC 85-15172. 184p. 1986. 109.00 (*0-8493-6332-2*, RC268, CRC Reprint); 112.00 (*0-8493-6333-0*) Franklin.

Reddy, Bayapa. Studies in Indian Writing in English. 128p. 1990. text 20.00 (*81-85218-26-9*, Pub. by Prestige) Advent Bks Div.

Reddy, C. A., ed. see International Symposium on Microbial Ecology (3rd:.

Reddy, D. P., ed. Seismic Design Technology for Breeder Reactor Structures: Special Topics in Earthquake Ground Motion, Vol. 1. LC 83-50358. 277p. 1983. pap. 36.50 (*0-87079-542-2*, DOE/SF/01011-T25, VOL. 1, DE84004808); fiche 9.00 (*0-87079-543-0*, DOE/SF/01011-T25, VOL. 1, DE84004808) DOE.

— Seismic Design Technology for Breeder Reactor Structures: Special Topics in Piping & Equipment, Vol. 4. 215p. 1983. pap. 36.50 (*0-87079-548-1*, DOE/SF/01011-T25, VOL. 4, DE84004811); fiche 9.00 (*0-87079-549-X*, DOE/SF/01011-T25, VOL. 4, DE84004811) DOE.

— Seismic Design Technology for Breeder Reactor Structures: Special Topics in Reactor Structures, Vol. 3. 167p. 1983. pap. 27.00 (*0-87079-546-5*, DOE/SF/01011-T25, VOL. 3, DE84004810); fiche 9.00 (*0-87079-547-3*, DOE/SF/01011-T25, VOL. 3, DE84004810) DOE.

— Seismic Design Technology for Breeder Reactor Structures: Special Topics in Soil Structure Interaction Analyses, Vol. 2. LC 83-50358. 134p. 1983. pap. 27.00 (*0-87079-544-9*, DOE/SF/01011-T25, VOL. 2, DE84004309); fiche 9.00 (*0-87079-545-7*, DOE/SF/01011-T25, VOL. 2, DE84004309) DOE.

Reddy, D. Subramanyam. Agrarian Relations & Peasant in Modern Andhra. 1990. 16.00 (*81-7035-073-5*, Pub. by Daya Pub Hse) S Asia.

Reddy, E. S., ed. Liberation of Southern Africa: Speeches of Olaf Palme. 1990. text 18.95 (*0-7069-5317-7*, Pub. by Vikas) Advent Bks Div.

— Socialism, Peace & Solidarity: Speeches of Olaf Palme. 1990. text 25.00 (*0-7069-5316-9*, Pub. by Vikas) S Asia.

Reddy, Francis. Discovery Atlas of Dinosaurs & Prehistoric Creatures. LC 93-43086. Orig. Title: Rand McNally Children's Atlas of Earth Through Time. (Illus.). 64p. (J). 1994. 4.95 (*0-528-83677-3*) Rand McNally.

Reddy, G. B., jt. ed. see Uzochukwu, G. A..

Reddy, G. Lokanadha. Education for Unorganised Sector. (C). 1992. 39.00 (*81-7024-490-0*, Pub. by Ashish Pub Hse) S Asia.

*__Reddy, G. N.__ When Maples Blush. 2000. pap. 18.00 (*0-7388-2214-0*) Xlibris Corp.

Reddy, G. Narayana & Ramana, Rao D. Women Organisation & Power Struggle. 1995. 18.00 (*81-85613-98-2*, Pub. by Chugh Pubns) S Asia.

Reddy, G. Ram. Higher Education in India. LC 95-901698. (C). 1995. write for info. (*81-207-1765-1*) Sterling Pubs.

— Patterns of Panchayati Raj in India. 1977. 9.50 (*0-8364-0046-1*) S Asia.

Reddy, G. Ram, ed. Government & Public Enterprise: Essays in Honour of Professor V. V. Ramanadham. 224p. 1985. 37.50 (*0-7146-3258-9*, Pub. by F Cass Pubs) Intl Spec Bk.

Reddy, Henry A. Nuclear War & Radioactive Fallout: Index of New Information with Authors, Subjects & References. 150p. 1997. 47.50 (*0-7883-1320-7*); pap. 44.50 (*0-7883-1321-5*) ABBE Pubs Assn.

Reddy, Indra K., ed. Ocular Therapeutics & Drug Delivery: A Multi-Disciplinary Approach. LC 94-60709. 525p. 1995. text 179.95 (*1-56676-213-8*) Technomic.

R

Reddy, Indra K., jt. auth. see Kahn, Mansoor A.

Reddy, Indra K., jt. auth. see Khan, Mansoor A.

Reddy, J. N. Applied Functional Analysis & Variational Methods in Engineering. 560p. (C). 1991. reprint ed. lib. bdg. 63.50 (*0-89464-585-4*) Krieger.

— Energy & Variational Methods in Applied Mechanics. LC 84-3605. 560p. 1984. 175.00 (*0-471-89673-X*) Wiley.

— An Introduction to the Finite Element Method. 2nd ed. LC 92-29532. (McGraw-Hill Series in Mechanical Engineering). 896p. (C). 1993. 95.94 (*0-07-051355-4*) McGraw.

— Mechanics of Laminated Composite Plates: Theory & Analysis. LC 96-38476. 800p. 1996. boxed set 104.95 (*0-8493-3101-3*, 3101) CRC Pr.

— Theory & Analysis of Elastic Plates. LC 98-48726. 1999. 99.95 (*1-56032-705-7*) Hemisp Pub.

Reddy, J. N., ed. Mechanics of Composite Materials: Selected Works of Nicholas J. Pagano. LC 94-30334. (Solid Mechanics & Its Applications Ser.). 1994. text 272.50 (*0-7923-3041-2*) Kluwer Academic.

Reddy, J. N. & Gartling, D. K. The Finite Element Method in Heat Transfer & Fluid Dynamics. LC 94-8277. 416p. 1994. boxed set 115.95 (*0-8493-9410-4*, 9410) CRC Pr.

Reddy, J. N. & Miravete, Antonio. Practical Analysis of Composite Laminates. LC 95-34343. 336p. 1995. boxed set 99.95 (*0-8493-9401-5*, 9401) CRC Pr.

Reddy, J. N. & Murty, A. V., eds. Composite Structures: Testing, Analysis & Design. (Illus.). 350p. 1993. 174.95 (*0-387-55879-9*) Spr-Verlag.

Reddy, J. N. & Reifsnyder, K. L., eds. Local Mechanics Concepts for Composite Material Systems: IUTAM Symposium, Blacksburg, VA, 1991. LC 92-17944. (International Union of Theoretical & Applied Mechanics Symposia Ser.). xi, 412p. 1992. 181.95 (*0-387-55547-1*) Spr-Verlag.

Reddy, J. N. & Scarpelli, Dante G. Experimental Pancreatic Carcinogenesis. LC 85-23391. 192p. 1986. 181.00 (*0-8493-5544-3*, CRC Reprint) Franklin.

Reddy, Janardan K. Peroxisomes: Biology & Role in Toxicology & Disease. LC 96-39418. (Annals of the New York Academy of Sciences Ser.). 801p. 1997. 150.00 (*0-89766-967-3*) NY Acad Sci.

Reddy, Jo, jt. auth. see Dobson, Paul.

Reddy, Joan C., jt. auth. see Roddy, Vernon.

Reddy, John, jt. photos by see Haney, Chuck.

Reddy, K. C. Sickness in Small Scale Industries. (C). 1988. 32.00 (*81-7024-212-6*, Pub. by Ashish Pub Hse) S Asia.

Reddy, K. J., ed. Practical Exercises for Bar Students. 300p. (C). 1991. 80.00 (*1-85352-893-5*, Pub. by HLT Pubns) St Mut.

Reddy, K. L. Psychological Immunity: Parent's First Line of Defense. LC 95-69778. 218p. (Orig.). (C). 1995. pap. 16.95 (*1-882792-11-4*) Proctor Pubns.

Reddy, K. N., jt. auth. see Kline, Daniel L.

***Reddy, K. R. & Hodges, H. F.** Climate Change & Global Crop Productivity. LC 99-57251. (CABI Publishing Ser.). 512p. 2000. text 140.00 (*0-85199-439-3*) C A B Intl.

Reddy, K. R. & Smith, W. H., eds. Aquatic Plants for Water Treatment & Resource Recovery. LC 87-61397. (Illus.). 1088p. 1987. 140.00 (*0-941463-00-1*) Magnolia FL.

Reddy, K. Ramesh. Phosphorus Biogeochemistry in Sub-Tropical Ecosystemst. LC 98-50246. 1998. 69.95 (*1-56670-331-X*) Lewis Pubs.

Reddy, K. Ramesh & Patrick, William H., Jr. Biogeochemistry of Wetlands. 1999. 55.00 (*1-56670-058-2*, L1058) Lewis Pubs.

Reddy, K. Venkata. Major Indian Novelists. 1991. text 22.50 (*81-85218-29-3*, Pub. by Prestige) Advent Bks Div.

***Reddy, Kumuda.** All Love Flows to the Self. 1999. pap. text. write for info. (*1-57582-057-9*) Samhita Enterprises.

— Ayurveda Baby Massage. (Illus.). 60p. 1999. pap. 4.95 (*1-929297-03-3*) Samhita Prodns.

Reddy, Kumuda. Eternal Story of Love. (Illus.). 235p. 1999. pap. text. write for info. (*1-57582-038-2*) Samhita Enterprises.

***Reddy, Kumuda.** The Eternal Story of Love. 235p. 1999. pap. 18.95 (*1-929297-04-1*) Samhita Prodns.

— Timeless Wisdom Stories: Magical & Enchanting "Timeless Stories", Vol. 1, Set. unabridged ed. (J). (gr. 1-6). 2000. 16.95 incl. audio (*1-929297-12-2*, Pub. by Samhita Prodns) ACCESS Pubs Network.

***Reddy, Kumuda & Egenes, Linda.** Conquering Chronic Disease: Through Maharishi Vedic Medicine. (Illus.). 350p. 2000. pap. 18.95 (*1-929297-00-9*, Pub. by Samhita Prodns) ACCESS Pubs Network.

***Reddy, Kumuda & Lane, Cynthia.** Living Life Free from Pain: Treating Arthritis, Joint Pain, Muscle Pain, & Fibromyalgia with Maharishi Vedic Medicine. (Illus.). 300p. 2000. pap. 18.95 (*1-929297-17-3*) Samhita Prodns.

Reddy, Kumuda & Pruitt, John. The Female Mouse. (Illus.). 31p. (J). (gr. 1-6). 1997. 13.67 (*1-929297-07-6*, Pub. by Samhita Prodns) ACCESS Pubs Network.

Reddy, Kumuda & Pruitt, John E. The Hares & the Elephants. (Illus.). 31p. (J). (gr. 1-6). 1997. 9.95 (*1-929297-10-6*, Pub. by Samhita Prodns) ACCESS Pubs Network.

— The Lion & the Hare. (Illus.). 31p. (J). (gr. 1-6). 1997. 13.67 (*1-929297-09-2*, Pub. by Samhita Prodns) ACCESS Pubs Network.

— The Money & the Crocodile. (Illus.). 31p. (J). (gr. 1-6). 1997. 13.67 (*1-929297-08-4*, Pub. by Samhita Prodns) ACCESS Pubs Network.

— The Wish That Came True. (Illus.). 31p. (J). (gr. 1-6). 2000. 9.95 (*1-929297-11-4*, Pub. by Samhita Prodns) ACCESS Pubs Network.

Reddy, Kumuda & Pruitt, Jon E. The Indigo Jackal. (Illus.). 31p. (J). (gr. 1-6). 1997. 9.95 (*1-929297-06-8*, Pub. by Samhita Prodns) ACCESS Pubs Network.

***Reddy, Kumuda & Willbanks, Sandra.** Golden Transition: Menopause Made Easy with Maharishi Vedic Medicine. (Illus.). 300p. 2000. pap. 18.95 (*1-929297-16-5*) Samhita Prodns.

***Reddy, Kumuda, et al.** All Love Flows to the Self: Eternal Stories from the Upanishads. (Illus.). 172p. 2000. pap. 24.95 (*1-929297-05-X*, Pub. by Samhita Prodns) ACCESS Pubs Network.

— All Love Flows to the Self Series: Eternal Stories from the Upanishads. Set. unabridged ed. 1999. 18.95 incl. audio (*1-929297-14-9*) Samhita Prodns.

— For a Blissful Baby: Healthy & Happy Pregnancy with Maharishi Vedic Medicine. (Illus.). 250p. 2000. pap. 16.95 (*1-929297-01-7*, Pub. by Samhita Prodns) ACCESS Pubs Network.

— For a Blissful Baby: Healthy & Happy Pregnancy with the Maharishi Vedic Approach to Health. (Illus.). 250p. 1999. pap. text 16.95 (*1-57582-020-X*) Samhita Enterprises.

Reddy, Kumuda, et al. Forever Healthy: Introduction to Maharishi Ayur-Veda Health Care. LC 98-142454. (Illus.). 198p. 1997. pap. 14.95 (*1-57582-021-8*, Pub. by Samhita Enterprises) ACCESS Pubs Network.

***Reddy, Kumuda, et al.** Playful & Awesome Timeless Stories, Vol. 2, set. unabridged ed. (Timeless Wisdom Stories Ser. : Vol. 2). (J). (gr. 1-6). 1999. 18.95 incl. audio (*1-929297-13-0*) Samhita Prodns.

Reddy, Linda A., jt. ed. see Pfeiffer, Steven I.

Reddy, M. Atchi. Lands & Tenants in South India: A Study of Nellore District, 1850-1990. LC 96-900191. 228p. (C). 1996. 19.95 (*0-19-563660-0*) OUP.

***Reddy, M. M. Krishna.** Marriage Population & Society: Demographic Perspectives of a Social Institution. LC 98-906907. 1998. 34.00 (*81-7391-255-6*, Pub. by Kaniska Pubs Dist) S Asia.

Reddy, M. Rami, jt. ed. see Parrill, Abby L.

Reddy, M. S. & Daniel, D. F., eds. Latest Advances in Power Generating Facilities Design, Operation & Maintenance & Environmental Improvements. (PWR Ser.: Vol. 22). 176p. 1993. 37.50 (*0-7918-0997-8*, H00829) ASME.

Reddy, M. Sankara. Reference Sources in Telugu: A Comprehensive Guide. (C). 1996. 22.00 (*81-7018-889-X*, Pub. by BR Pub) S Asia.

***Reddy, M. Venkata.** Command Area Development Programmes: Myths & Realities. LC 99-931778. 282p. 1998. pap. 120.00 (*81-7533-082-1*, Pub. by Print Hse) St Mut.

Reddy, M. Vikram. Management of Tropical Agroecosystems & the Beneficial Soil Biota. (Illus.). 350p. 1999. 90.00 (*1-57808-045-2*) Science Pubs.

Reddy, Manjulika S. Distance Education in India: A Model for Developing Countries. LC 99-939766. 1996. 30.00 (*81-259-0071-3*, Pub. by Vikas) S Asia.

Reddy, Marepally S. Fire in Passion. 32p. 1997. pap. 8.00 (*0-8059-4083-9*) Dorrance.

Reddy, Marisa E., jt. auth. see Hensler, Deborah R.

Reddy, Marlita A., ed. Statistical Record of Hispanic Americans. 2nd ed. 1141p. 1995. 115.00 (*0-8103-6422-0*, 102121) Gale.

— Statistical Record of Native North Americans. 2nd ed. 1272p. 1995. 109.00 (*0-8103-6421-2*, 102120) Gale.

Reddy, Marlita A. & Lazich, Robert S., eds. World Market Share Reporter 1: A Compilation of Reported World Market Share Data & Rankings on Companies Products & Services. 620p. 1994. 315.00 (*0-8103-9641-6*) Gale.

Reddy, Marlita A., jt. ed. see Darnay, Arsen J.

Reddy, Maureen. Creating Scientific Communities in the Elementary Classroom. LC 97-49090. 1997. pap. 27.00 (*0-325-00025-5*) Heinemann.

Reddy, Maureen T. Crossing the Color Line: Race, Parenting, & Culture. LC 94-535. 215p. 1996. pap. 16.95 (*0-8135-2374-5*) Rutgers U Pr.

— Crossing the Color Line: Race, Parenting, & Culture. LC 94-535. 215p. (C). 1996. 35.00 (*0-8135-2105-X*) Rutgers U Pr.

Reddy, Maureen T., ed. Everyday Acts Against Racism: Raising Children in a Multiracial World. 304p. (Orig.). 1996. pap. 15.95 (*1-878067-85-0*) Seal Pr WA.

Reddy, Maureen T., et al, eds. Mother Journeys: Feminists Write about Mothering. LC 94-18338. 300p. 1994. 29.95 (*1-883523-04-4*) Spinsters Ink.

Reddy, Maureen T., jt. ed. see Daly, Brenda O.

Reddy, Michael T. Securities Operations: A Guide to Operations & Information Systems in the Securities Industry. 512p. (C). 1989. text 75.00 (*0-13-799123-1*) NY Inst Finance.

— Securities Operations: A Guide to Operations & Information Systems in the Securities Industry. 2nd ed. (C). 1995. 80.00 (*0-13-161044-9*) P-H.

Reddy, Michelle, jt. auth. see Sweeney, Diane.

Reddy, N. Krishna. Intaglio Simultaneous Color Printmaking: Significance of Materials & Processes. LC 88-1516. (Illus.). 142p. (C). 1988. text 74.50 (*0-88706-739-5*); pap. text 24.95 (*0-88706-740-9*) State U NY Pr.

Reddy, N. R., ed. Phytates in Cereals & Legumes. 160p. 1989. lib. bdg. 153.00 (*0-8493-6108-7*, QP801) CRC Pr.

Reddy, N. R., et al. Legume-Based Fermented Foods. 272p. 1986. 151.00 (*0-8493-6286-5*, TX558, CRC Reprint) Franklin.

Reddy, N. Y. Values & Attitudes of Indian Youth. 244p. 1980. 24.95 (*0-940500-10-8*, Pub. by Light & Life Pubs) Asia Bk Corp.

Reddy, Nilufer M., tr. from TUR. Short Stories by Turkish Women Writers. 2nd ed. LC 94-76980. (Turkish Studies: Vol. 8). 172p. 1994. pap. text 16.95 (*1-878318-07-1*) IN Univ Turkish.

Reddy, P. Chenna. Guilds in Medieval Andhra Desa. (C). 1991. text 49.50 (*81-85067-70-8*, Pub. by Sundeep Prak) S Asia.

Reddy, P. Chinnappa. Physics of Sports: Basketball. (C). 1992. text 20.00 (*81-7024-511-7*, Pub. by Ashish Pub Hse) S Asia.

***Reddy, P. S.** Local Government Democratisation & Decentralisation: A Review of the Southern African Experience. 304p. 1999. pap. 27.95 (*0-7021-4979-9*, Pub. by Juta & Co) Intl Spec Bk.

Reddy, P. S. Readings in Local Government Management & Development: A Southern African Perspective. LC 97-129379. 333p. 1996. pap. 36.00 (*0-7021-3612-3*, Pub. by Juta & Co) Gaunt.

Reddy, P. S., et al, eds. Pericardial Disease. LC 81-23539. (Illus.). 391p. reprint ed. pap. 121.30 (*0-7837-7097-9*, 204692600004) Bks Demand.

***Reddy, Pingle J.** The Judiciary I Served. LC 99-933620. 291p. 1999. write for info. (*81-250-1617-1*, Pub. by Orient Longman Ltd) S Asia.

Reddy, R. G., et al, eds. Design Fundamentals of High Temperature Composites, Intermetallics, & Metal-Ceramics Systems: A Collection of Papers from the 1996 TMS Annual Meeting & Exhibition in Anaheim, California, February 4-8, 1996. (Illus.). 451p. 1996. 20.00 (*0-87339-305-8*, 3058) Minerals Metals.

Reddy, R. G. & Mishra, B., eds. Trace & Reactive Metals - Processing & Technology: Proceedings of the International Symposium on Extraction & Processing of Trace & Reactive Metals, Sponsored by the Extraction & Processing Et Al. LC 94-73543. 291p. 1995. 10.00 (*0-87339-280-9*, 2809) Minerals Metals.

Reddy, R. G., jt. auth. see Gokcen, N. A.

Reddy, R. G., ed. see Queneau, Paul E. International Symposium Staff.

Reddy, R. S., jt. auth. see Rao, V. K.

Reddy, Rajender, jt. auth. see Schiff, Eugene R.

Reddy, Rama N. & Ziegler, Carol. PL-1: Structured Programming & Problem Solving. (Illus.). 739p. (C). 1986. mass mkt. 63.00 (*0-314-93915-6*) West Pub.

Reddy, Ramana G., ed. see Metallurgical Society of AIME Staff.

Reddy, Ramana G., ed. see Minerals, Metals & Materials Society Staff.

Reddy, Robert. Beneficial Recipes: We Are What We Eat We Are What We Think. LC 96-83339. 200p. 1996. spiral bd. 9.95 (*0-9656200-4-2*, Future Library) Medical Library.

Reddy, Roma N. FORTRAN 77 with Applications. 2nd ed. Date not set. pap. text, teacher ed. write for info. (*0-314-03440-4*) West Pub.

Reddy, S. M. Microbial Biotechnology: Proceedings of National Symposium on Frontiers, UGC & CSIR November 1994, New Delhi. 1997. pap. 180.00 (*81-7233-153-3*, Pub. by Scientific Pubs) St Mut.

Reddy, Sanjeeva P. Different Sources of Irrigation: A Case Study of the Telangana Region. LC 97-905887. xx, 258p. 1997. 19.00 (*81-86562-31-1*, Pub. by Manak Pubns Pvt Ltd) Nataraj Bks.

***Reddy, Sharon L. Spinner.** Emperor Evolved. (Solastria Ser.: Vol. 1). 1999. disk 3.50 (*1-58338-017-5*) CrossrdsPub.

— Lone Ranger Legacy. 1998. disk 4.50 (*1-58338-019-1*) CrossrdsPub.

— Sapphire Wind. (Starvan Ser.: Vol. 2). 1998. disk 3.50 (*1-58338-022-1*) CrossrdsPub.

— Solastria Bks. I & II: Emperor Evolved & Task Worthy of Princes. 1999. disk 5.00 (*1-58338-045-0*) CrossrdsPub.

— Task Worthy of Princes. (Solastria Ser.: Vol. 2). 1998. disk 3.50 (*1-58338-018-3*) CrossrdsPub.

Reddy, Sigrid, ed. see Hodges, Maud.

Reddy, Suma N. Institutionalised Children. (C). 1989. 44.00 (*81-85076-57-X*, Pub. by Chugh Pubns) S Asia.

Reddy, T. Ramakrishna. India's Policy in the United Nations. LC 67-26816. 164p. 1975. 24.50 (*0-8386-6755-4*) Fairleigh Dickinson.

Reddy, Terrence R., jt. auth. see Long, Huey B.

Reddy, Torun, ed. see Tureen, Edward A.

Reddy, V. Madhusudan. Integral Yoga Psychology. 170p. (Orig.). 1990. pap. 7.95 (*0-941524-92-2*) Lotus Pr.

— The Vedic Epiphany No. 2: The Vedic Action. 572p. 1994. pap. text 39.50 (*81-85853-02-9*, Pub. by Inst Human Study) E-W Cultural Ctr.

— The Vedic Epiphany No. 3: The Vedic Fulfillment. 311p. 1996. pap. text 29.95 (*81-85853-04-5*, Pub. by Inst Human Study) E-W Cultural Ctr.

Reddy, V. Ramakrishan. Economic History of Hyderabad State: Warangal Suba (1911-1950) 834p. 1987. 40.00 (*81-212-0099-7*, Pub. by Gian Publng Hse) S Asia.

Reddy, V. Rami. Elements of Prehistory. (C). 1987. 20.00 (*81-7099-013-0*, Pub. by Mittal Pubs Dist) S Asia.

— Neolithic & Post-Neolithic Cultures. (C). 1991. text 15.00 (*81-7099-311-3*, Pub. by Mittal Pubs Dist) S Asia.

Reddy, Vishu, jt. ed. see Dawson, Sam.

Reddy, W. Brendan. Group-Level Team Assessment: A 10-Step Sequence to a Committed Team. LC 96-68139. (Illus.). 176p. 1996. ring bd. 99.95 (*0-88390-474-8*) Jossey-Bass.

— Intervention Skills: Process Consultation for Small Groups & Teams. LC 94-65468. 256p. 1994. 39.95 (*0-88390-434-9*, Pfffr & Co) Jossey-Bass.

Reddy, W. Brendan & Henderson, Clenard C., Jr., eds. Training Theory & Practice. LC 87-62132. 300p. (Orig.). 1987. pap. text 19.00 (*0-9610392-4-8*) NTL Inst.

Reddy, W. Brendan & Jamison, Kaleel, eds. Team Building: Blueprints for Productivity & Satisfaction. 225p. (Orig.). 1988. pap. text 19.95 (*0-9610392-5-6*) NTL Inst.

Reddy, William M. The Invisible Code: Honor & Sentiment in Postrevolutionary France, 1814-1848. LC 96-21675. (Illus.). 292p. 1997. 40.00 (*0-520-20536-7*, Pub. by U CA Pr) Cal Prin Full Svc.

Reddy, Y. Haragopal. Bonded Labour System in India: Causes, Practice, & Law. LC 95-901468. (C). 1995. 27.00 (*81-7100-703-1*, Pub. by Deep & Deep Pubns) S Asia.

Reddy, Y. Ramachandra. Grass-Root Democracy: Anantapur Area Under Madras Presidency. (C). 1993. 18.00 (*0-8364-2898-6*, Pub. by New Era Pub) S Asia.

Reddy, Y. Ramachandra & Sinha, Dharni P., eds. Business Scenarios for the Nineties: Strategic Perspectives. 168p. (C). 1992. 25.00 (*0-7069-5876-4*, Pub. by Vikas) S Asia.

Reddy, Y. Ranga. Guides to the Identification of Microinvertebrates of the Continental Waters of the World Vol. 5: Copepoda, Calanoida, Diaptomidae. Dumont, H. J., ed. (Illus.). viii, 221p. 1994. pap. 75.00 (*90-5103-089-4*, Pub. by SPB Acad Pub) Balogh.

Redecke, Sebashan, jt. ed. see Burg, Annegret.

Redecke, Sebastian & Stern, Ralph, eds. Foreign Affairs: New Embassy Buildings & the German Foreign Office in Berlin. (Illus.). 232p. 1997. 79.00 (*3-7643-5629-4*, Pub. by Birkhauser); pap. 65.00 (*3-7643-5618-9*, Pub. by Birkhauser) Princeton Arch.

Redecke, Sebastian, jt. ed. see Burg, Annegret.

Redeen, Kira S. I Never Say Goodbye. 2nd ed. 364p. 1988. pap. 8.00 (*0-9615501-0-4*) K Singh Pub.

— I Never Say Goodbye: Memories of a Visit with God. Redeen, Robert, ed. 300p. pap. 12.00 (*0-9615501-2-0*) K Singh Pub.

— Istina I Mirazh. (RUS.). 256p. (Orig.). 1992. pap. 14.00 (*0-934923-03-5*) Hermitage Pubs.

Redeen, Robert, ed. see Redeen, Kira S.

Redei, George P. Genetics: A Manual of Current Concepts & Terms. LC 98-198509. 1000p. 1998. lib. bdg. 78.00 (*981-02-2780-9*) World Scientific Pub.

Redei, Karoly. Zyrian Folklore Texts. (Bibliotheca Uralica: No. 3). 652p. (C). 1978. 171.00 (*963-05-1506-7*, Pub. by Akade Kiado) St Mut.

Redeker, Andrea. Abweichendes Verhalten und Moralischer Fortschritt: Zur Steuerungsfunktion der Normkritik in der Theologisch-Ethischen Reflexion. (Forum Interdisziplinare Ethik Ser.: Bd. 5). (GER.). IV, 426p. 1993. 61.80 (*3-631-46072-4*) P Lang Pubng.

Redeker, Hans. Bruno Bruni. Ayers, Helge, tr. from GER. (Bibliophilen Taschenbucher Ser.). (Illus.). 247p. (Orig.). 1981. pap. 15.00 (*3-921785-16-2*) J Szoke Edns.

Redeker, James R. Discipline, Policies & Procedure. LC 83-6053. 290p. reprint ed. pap. 89.90 (*0-7837-4609-1*, 204432800002) Bks Demand.

— Employee Discipline: Policies & Practices. LC 88-38546. 426p. 1989. trans. 36.00 (*0-87179-595-7*, 0595) BNA Books.

Redeker, Kit. Around the Fire. 24p. 1999. pap. 5.00 (*1-884226-06-X*) Dark River.

Redeker, Patty. The History & Development of the Saleen Mustang. LC 94-71001. (Illus.). 205p. (Orig.). 1994. pap. 12.95 (*0-9624908-8-1*) CA Mustang Sales.

***Redekop, Benjamin W.** Enlightenment & Community: Lessing, Abbt, Herder & the Quest for a German Public. 1999. 65.00 (*0-7735-1026-5*) McG-Queens Univ Pr.

Redekop, Benjamin W., jt. ed. see Redekop, Calvin W.

***Redekop, Calvin W.** Creation & the Environment: An Anabaptist Perspective on a Sustainable World. LC 00-8081. (Illus.). 296p. 2000. 45.00 (*0-8018-6422-4*) Johns Hopkins.

Redekop, Calvin W. Leaving Anabaptism: From Evangelical Mennonite Brethren to Fellowship of Evangelical Bible Churches. LC 98-28701. 268p. 1998. 19.99 (*0-9665021-0-8*) Pandora PA.

— Mennonite Society. LC 88-32013. 456p. (C). 1989. text 55.00 (*0-8018-3729-4*) Johns Hopkins.

— The Old Colony Mennonites: Dilemmas of Ethnic Minority Life. LC 69-13192. 322p. reprint ed. pap. 99.90 (*0-608-30354-2*, 202173700022) Bks Demand.

— Strangers Become Neighbors. LC 80-13887. (Studies in Anabaptist & Mennonite History: Vol. 22). (Illus.). 312p. 1980. 24.99 (*0-8361-1228-8*) Herald Pr.

Redekop, Calvin W., et al, eds. Anabaptist - Mennonite Faith & Economics. 444p. (Orig.). (C). 1994. pap. text 33.00 (*0-8191-9350-X*) U Pr of Amer.

Redekop, Calvin W. & Bender, Urie A. Who Am I? What Am I? A Christian View of Working. 352p. 1988. mass mkt. 14.95 (*0-310-35581-8*, 18090P) Zondervan.

Redekop, Calvin W. & Redekop, Benjamin W., eds. Entrepreneurs in the Faith Community: Profiles of Mennonites in Business. LC 95-52887. 272p. (Orig.). 1996. pap. 17.99 (*0-8361-9034-3*) Herald Pr.

Redekop, Calvin W., et al. Mennonite Entrepreneurs. LC 94-46177. (Illus.). 320p. 1995. text 34.95 (*0-8018-5003-7*) Johns Hopkins.

***Redekop, Calvin Wall.** Creation & the Environment: An Anabaptist Perspective on a Sustainable World. LC 00-8081. (Illus.). 296p. 2000. 19.95 (*0-8018-6423-2*) Johns Hopkins.

Redekop, Gloria N. The Work of Their Hands: Mennonite Women's Societies in Canada. xvi, 172p. 1996. pap. 24.95 (*0-88920-270-2*) W Laurier U Pr.

Redekop, John H. The Christian & Civil Disobedience. (Faith & Life Ser.). 42p. 1991. pap. text 2.50 (*0-921788-12-6*) Kindred Prods.

— A People Apart: Ethnicity & the Mennonite Brethren. 198p. 1987. pap. 2.95 (*0-919797-68-7*) Kindred Prods.

Redekop, John H. & Martens, Elmer A. On Capital Punishment. 32p. 1987. pap. 1.50 (*0-919797-69-5*) Kindred Prods.

Redekop, Vernon W. A Life for a Life? The Death Penalty on Trial. LC 89-26709. (Peace & Justice Ser.: Vol. 9). 104p. (Orig.). 1990. pap. 6.99 (*0-8361-3516-4*) Herald Pr.

***Redekopp, Dave, et al.** What You Can Do with a Science Degree: Opportunities for Canadians in a Global Economy. 133p. 1999. pap. 11.95 (*1-895579-96-1*, Pub. by Trifolium Inc) ACCESS Pubs Network.

An Asterisk (*) at the beginning of an entry indicates that the title is appearing for the first time.

Redekopp, Elsa. Two Worlds for Jash. 1991. pap. text 6.95 (*1-895308-04-6*) Windflower Comns.

Redekopp, Jean. A View from the Bucket: A Grand Lake & McNabs Island Memoir. LC 96-950133. 96p. 1996. pap. 11.25 (*0-921411-52-9*) Genl Dist Srvs.

Redel, D. Color Blood Flow Imaging of the Heart. (Illus.). 140p. 1988. 199.00 (*0-387-16521-5*) Spr-Verlag.

Redel, Matthew R. The Platoon Operations Order. (Illus.). 33p. 1998. pap. 8.95 (*1-884778-51-8*) Old Mountain.

Redel, Miklos. Quantum Logic in Algebraic Approach. LC 97-46597. (Fundamental Theories of Physics Ser.). 238p. 1998. 129.00 (*0-7923-4903-2*) Kluwer Academic.

Redel, Victoria. Already the World. LC 95-4151. (Wick Poetry First Bks.: No. 1). 72p. 1995. pap. 9.50 (*0-87338-531-4*); text 17.00 (*0-87338-530-6*) Kent St U Pr.

Redelinghuis, A., et al. Quantitative Methods for Managerial Decision Making. 2nd ed. 479p. 1989. pap. 49.95 (*0-409-10961-4*) Buttrwrth-Heinemann.

Redelmeier, T. E., jt. auth. see Schaefer, H.

Redemann, Hans. Innovations in Aircraft Construction: Thirty-Seven Influential Designs. Force, Edward, tr. from GER. LC 91-62736. (Illus.). 248p. 1991. 29.95 (*0-88740-338-7*) Schiffer.

Redemptorist Pastoral Communications Staff. Handbook for Today's Catholic: Fully Indexed to the Catechism of the Catholic Church. rev. ed. LC 94-75247. 112p. 1994. pap. 2.95 (*0-89243-671-9*) Liguori Pubns.

Redemptorist Pastoral Publication Staff. The Essential Catholic Handbook: A Summary of Beliefs, Practices & Prayers. rev. ed. LC 96-48426. (Redemptorist Pastoral Publication). 304p. (Orig.). 1997. pap. 9.95 (*0-89243-910-6*) Liguori Pubns.

— The Essential Mary Handbook: A Summary of Beliefs, Devotions & Prayers. Bauer, Judith A., ed. & compiled by by. LC 98-47844. 304p. 1999. pap. 13.00 (*0-7648-0383-2*) Liguori Pubns.

— Getting Confirmed: A Journey of Questions & Answers. 16p. (Orig.). 1996. pap. 2.95 (*0-7648-0048-5*) Liguori Pubns.

— Your Baby's Baptism: CSSR England. 16p. 1985. pap. 2.95 (*0-89243-445-7*) Liguori Pubns.

— Your Wedding: A Guide to Getting Married in the Catholic Church. 26p. 1995. pap. 3.95 (*0-89243-803-7*) Liguori Pubns.

Redemptorist Pastoral Publication Staff, jt. auth. see Liguori, Alphonsus.

Redemptorist Pastoral Pubns. Staff. El Bautismo De Su Bebe. (Redemptorist Pastoral Publicaitons). (ENG & SPA.). 16p. 1994. pap. 2.95 (*0-89243-627-1*) Liguori Pubns.

— Peace Be with You. rev. ed. (Illus.). 16p. 1987. pap. 2.95 (*0-89243-417-1*) Liguori Pubns.

— Your Child's First Communion. (Illus.). 16p. 1990. pap. 2.95 (*0-89243-328-0*) Liguori Pubns.

Redemptorist Pastoral Pubns. Staff & Liguori, Alfonso M. The Mission-Book of the Congregation of the Most Holy Redeemer. 1978. 42.95 (*0-405-10843-5*, 11848) Ayer.

Redemptorist Pastoral Staff. Faith for the Future: A New Illustrated Catechism. LC 97-76621. (Illus.). 200p. 1998. pap. 12.95 (*0-7648-0189-9*) Liguori Pubns.

Redemptoust Pastoral Publication Staff. Handbook for Today's Catholic Family-A Redemptorist Pastoral Publication. 64p. 1979. pap. 4.95 (*0-89243-112-1*) Liguori Pubns.

Reden, Gussi Von, see Niedner, Marie & Von Reden, Gussi.

Redenbach, Sandi. The Road Map to Consulting: An Educator's Guide. (Illus.). 157p. 1998. pap. 16.95 (*0-9632112-3-4*) Esteem Sem.

— Self-Esteem: The Necessary Ingredient for Success: A Student-Centered Approach to Restructuring Education. Cole, Carol S., ed. LC 91-90017. (Illus.). 135p. (Orig.). 1991. pap. 14.00 (*0-9632112-0-X*) Esteem Sem.

Redenbacher, Fritz. Platen-Bibliographie. viii, 186p. 1972. reprint ed. write for info. (*3-487-04095-6*) G Olms Pubs.

Redenbarger, Wayne J. Articulator Features & Portuguese Vowel Height. (Studies in Romance Languages: No. 37). (Illus.). 197p. (C). 1981. pap. 9.00 (*0-674-04815-6*) HUP.

Redenbaugh, Vicki J. Synseeds: Applications of Synthetic Seeds to Crop Improvement. 496p. 1992. lib. bdg. 239.00 (*0-8493-4906-0*) CRC Pr.

Reder, Alan & Baxter, John. Listen to This! Leading Musicians Recommend Their Favorite Artists & Recordings. LC 99-19504. 512p. 1999. pap. 16.95 (*0-7868-8260-3*, Pub. by Hyperion) Time Warner.

Reder, Alan, et al. The Whole Parenting Guide: Strategies, Resources, & Inspiring Stories for Holistic Parenting & Family Living. LC 98-37487. (Illus.). 448p. 1999. pap. 20.00 (*0-7679-0133-9*) Broadway BDD.

Reder, Anthony T., ed. Interferon Therapy of Multiple Sclerosis. LC 96-39953. (Illus.). 560p. 1997. text 195.00 (*0-8247-9764-7*) Dekker.

Reder, Lynne. Implicit Memory & Metacognition. Klahr, David, ed. LC 96-29383. (Carnegie Mellon Symposia on Cognition Ser.). 376p. 1996. 69.95 (*0-8058-1859-6*) L Erlbaum Assocs.

— Implicit Memory & Metacognition. Klahr, David, ed. LC 96-29383. (Carnegie Mellon Symposia on Cognition Ser.). 376p. 1996. pap. 36.00 (*0-8058-1860-X*) L Erlbaum Assocs.

Reder, Melvin W. Economics: The Culture of a Controversial Science. LC 98-8640. (Illus.). 376p. 1999. 35.00 (*0-226-70609-5*) U Ch Pr.

— Studies in the Theory of Welfare Economics. LC 68-54288. (Columbia University. Studies in the Social Sciences: No. 534). reprint ed. 20.00 (*0-404-51534-7*) AMS Pr.

Reder, Melvin W., jt. auth. see Hogarth, Robin M.

***Reder, Michael R., ed.** Conversations with Salman Rushdie. LC 99-57120. (Literary Conversations Ser.). 256p. 2000. pap. 18.00 (*1-57806-185-7*); text 45.00 (*1-57806-184-9*) U Pr of Miss.

Reder, Peter & Lucey, Clare, eds. Assessment of Parenting: Psychiatric & Psychological Contributions. LC 95-7618. 304p. (C). 1995. pap. 27.99 (*0-415-11454-3*) Routledge.

— Assessment of Parenting: Psychiatric & Psychological Contributions. LC 95-7618. 304p. (C). (gr. 13). 1995. 85.00 (*0-415-11453-5*) Routledge.

Reder, Peter, et al. Beyond Blame: Child Abuse Tragedies Revisited. (Illus.). 204p. (C). 1993. pap. 24.99 (*0-415-06679-4*, A7792) Routledge.

***Reder, Peter, et al.** Family Matters: Interfaces Between Child & Adult Mental Health. LC 00-23155. 2000. pap. write for info. (*0-415-22218-4*) Routledge.

***Reder, Stephen M.** State of Literacy in America: Estimates at the Local, State & National Levels. LC 98-132833. 635p. 1998. pap. 44.00 (*0-16-049404-4*) USGPO.

Reder, Stephen M., jt. ed. see Vogel, Susan A.

Reder, Timothy S. En el Principio... Meyer, Richard, ed. (Adult Sunday School Ser.). (SPA.). 88p. 1991. 4.40 (*1-879892-04-9*) Editorial Bautista.

Redes, Paula, ed. Irish Love Poems: Danta Gra. (IRI., Illus.). 146p. 1996. 17.50 (*0-7818-0396-9*) Hippocrene Bks.

REDEX Staff. Solar SNG: The Estimated Availability of Resources for Large-Scale Production of SNG by Anaerobic Digestion of Specially Grown Plant Material. 450p. 1979. pap. 15.00 (*0-318-12701-6*, M80779) Am Gas Assn.

Redey, George & Spatz, Eugene. A Comprehensive Diagnostic Test to Evaluate Motor & Cognitive Ability for the Ambulatory Severely Mentally Retarded. LC 76-23718. 100p. 1976. 5.00 (*0-935484-00-0*) Universe Pub Co.

Redfearn, D. H. Redfearn: History of the Redfearn Family. 2nd rev. ed. (Illus.). 377p. 1992. reprint ed. pap. 56.00 (*0-8328-2711-8*); reprint ed. lib. bdg. 66.00 (*0-8328-2710-X*) Higginson Bk Co.

Redfearn, David. Tolstoy: Principles for a New World Order. 196p. 1994. pap. text 18.95 (*0-85683-134-4*, Pub. by Shepheard-Walwyn Pubs) Paul & Co Pubs.

Redfearn, J. W. Parting, Clinging, Individulization. 1985. 20.00 (*0-7855-1943-2*) St Mut.

Redfearn, Joseph. The Exploding Self: The Creative & Destructive Nucleus of the Personality. LC 91-38084. 312p. (Orig.). 1992. pap. 16.95 (*0-933029-60-8*) Chiron Pubns.

Redfern, Angela, jt. auth. see Edwards, Viv.

Redfern, Christopher, ed. Retinoid Protocols. LC 97-44455. (Methods in Molecular Biology Ser.: Vol. 89). (Illus.). 456p. 1998. 99.50 (*0-89603-438-0*) Humana.

Redfern, Dareen, et al. Macsyma O. D. E. Lab Book. LC 97-34233. (Math Ser.). 192p. 1997. pap. 28.75 (*0-7637-0532-2*) Jones & Bartlett.

Redfern, Darren. The Maple Handbook. 400p. 1993. write for info. (*3-540-94054-5*) Spr-Verlag.

— The Maple Handbook. 2nd ed. LC 94-25796. 1995. 29.00 (*0-387-94331-5*) Spr-Verlag.

— The Maple Handbook. 4th ed. 495p. 1998. 31.95 (*0-387-98418-6*) Spr-Verlag.

— The Maple Handbook: Maple V Release 4. 3rd ed. 495p. 1996. 31.95 (*0-387-94538-5*) Spr-Verlag.

— Matlab Handbook. LC 96-10769. 520p. 1997. pap. 29.95 (*0-387-94200-9*) Spr-Verlag.

— The Practical Approach Utilities for Maple: Maple V, Release 4. 1996. pap. text 69.00 incl. disk (*0-387-14225-8*) Spr-Verlag.

Redfern, Darren & Chandler, E. Maple ODE Lab Book. LC 97-1341. 160p. 1996. pap. 29.95 (*0-387-94733-7*) Spr-Verlag.

Redfern, Darren & Doherty, D. The Practical Approach Utilities for Maple: Maple V, Release 3. (Illus.). 328p. 1995. 75.95 incl. disk (*0-387-14221-5*) Spr-Verlag.

Redfern, David. Unclosed Eye: The Music Photographs of David Redfern, 1. 1999. pap. text 30.00 (*1-86074-255-6*) Sanctuary Pr.

Redfern, E. J. Introduction to Pascal for Computational Mathematics. (Computer Science Ser.). (Illus.). 300p. (C). 1988. text 90.00 (*0-333-44430-2*); pap. text 35.00 (*0-333-44431-0*) Scholium Intl.

Redfern, H. B. Questions in Aesthetic Education. Snelders, Philip & Wringe, Colin, eds. 120p. 1986. pap. text 14.95 (*0-04-370163-9*) Routledge.

Redfern, James. A Lexical Study of Raeto-Romance & Contiguous Italian Dialect Areas. LC 70-159469. (Janua Linguarum, Ser. Practica: No. 120). (Illus.). 105p. (Orig.). 1971. pap. text 76.95 (*90-279-1908-9*) Mouton.

Redfern, John-Claude. Country Classic Recipes 'n Pastoral Prose. 87p. 1995. spiral bd. 5.00 (*0-9618238-1-X*) SBCAP.

— The New Wave & Human Rights of Constitutional Law Against the Dark Age in America: God's Truth Against the Secular Machine. LC 87-60754. 82p. (Orig.). (C). 1988. pap. 19.95 (*0-9618238-0-1*) SBCAP.

— The New Wave Millenium, Rural Economies, & Human Rights. (New Wave Ser.). (Illus.). 93p. 1999. per. 19.95 (*0-9618238-3-6*) SBCAP.

— The New Wave of the Future: The Sequel. LC 95-92767. 151p. (Orig.). 1996. spiral bd. 19.95 (*0-9618238-2-8*) SBCAP.

Redfern, Jon, jt. ed. see David, Jack.

Redfern, Liz, jt. auth. see Spouse, Jenny.

***Redfern, Martin.** Kingfisher Young Peoples Book of Planet Earth. LC 98-53276. 96p. (J). (gr. 4-8). 1999. 21.95 (*0-7534-5180-8*) LKC.

Redfern, Martin. The Kingfisher Young Peoples Book of Space. LC 97-51122. 96p. (J). (gr. 4-8). 1998. 19.95 (*0-7534-5136-0*) LKC.

***Redfern, Nicholas.** Cosmic Crashes. 336p. 2000. 24.50 (*0-684-87023-1*) S&S Trade.

— The FBI Files: The FBI's UFO Top Secrets Exposed. (Illus.). 368p. 2000. 24.50 (*0-684-86834-2*) S&S Trade.

Redfern, Paul. The Love Diseases. (Illus.). 150p. 1981. reprint ed. pap. 4.95 (*0-8065-0772-1*, Citadel Pr) Carol Pub Group.

Redfern, Paul, jt. ed. see Desai, Meghnad.

Redfern, Ray & Harmon, Barbara S. The Paintings of F. Grayson Sayre, 1879-1939. (Illus.). 76p. 1986. pap. 35.00 (*0-939370-06-9*) DeRus Fine Art.

Redfern, Sally J., ed. Nursing Elderly People. 2nd ed. (Illus.). 600p. (Orig.). 1991. pap. text 54.00 (*0-443-04138-5*) Church.

Redfern, Sally J., jt. auth. see Kogan, Maurice.

Redfern, W., ed. see Sartre, Jean-Paul.

Redfern, Walter. Feet First: Jules Valles. 240p. 1993. 60.00 (*0-85261-315-6*, Pub. by Univ of Glasgow) St Mut.

— Michel Tournier: Le Coq de Bruyere. LC 95-32323. 144p. (C). 1996. 27.50 (*0-8386-3627-6*) Fairleigh Dickinson.

***Redfern, Walter, ed.** Giono: Le Hussard Sur le Toit. 64p. 1999. pap. 35.00 (*0-85261-530-2*, Pub. by U of Glasgow) St Mut.

Redfern, Walter D. Private World of Jean Giono. LC 67-20396. 217p. reprint ed. 67.30 (*0-8357-9115-7*, 201792400010) Bks Demand.

Redfield, A. C., et al. Interaction of Sea & Atmosphere: A Group of Contributions. (Meteorological Monograph: Vol. 2, No. 10). (Illus.). 75p. (Orig.). 1957. pap. 17.00 (*0-933876-05-X*) Am Meteorological.

Redfield, Alden, ed. see Hulan, Richard & Lawrence, Stephen S.

Redfield, Bessie G., ed. Gods: A Dictionary of the Deities of All Lands Including Supernatural Beings, Mythical Heroes & Kings & Sacred Books of Religions. 1977. lib. bdg. 300.00 (*0-8490-1893-5*) Gordon Pr.

Redfield, Bryan. A Bartender's Guide on How to Pick-Up Women: With a Special Section for Women Only. (Illus.). 365p. (Orig.). 1990. pap. 19.95 (*0-9626455-0-8*) Bryan Redfield.

Redfield, Carol, jt. ed. see Bell, Benjamin.

Redfield, Dana. Ezekiel's Chariot. 2nd ed. 242p. 1997. reprint ed. pap. text 11.95 (*1-57174-081-3*) Hampton Roads Pub Co.

***Redfield, Dana.** Jonah. 400p. 2000. 22.95 (*1-57174-156-9*) Hampton Roads Pub Co.

Redfield, Dana. Lucy Blue & the Daughters of Light. LC 98-71588. 320p. 1998. pap. 13.95 (*1-57174-107-0*) Hampton Roads Pub Co.

— Summoned: Encounters with Alien Intelligence. LC 98-73905. 212p. 1999. pap. 13.95 (*1-57174-126-7*) Hampton Roads Pub Co.

Redfield, David & Bube, Richard H. Photo-Induced Defects in Semiconductors. (Studies in Semiconductor Physics & Microelectronic Engineering: No. 4). (Illus.). 229p. (C). 1996. text 59.95 (*0-521-46196-0*) Cambridge U Pr.

***Redfield, H. V.** Homicide North & South. (History of Crime & Criminal Justice Ser.). 240p. 2000. 40.00 (*0-8142-0851-7*); pap. 14.95 (*0-8142-5056-4*) Ohio St U Pr.

Redfield, Isaac F. A Practical Treatise upon the Law of Railways. 2nd ed. LC 70-37982. (American Law Ser.: The Formative Years). 850p. 1972. reprint ed. 53.95 (*0-405-04025-3*) Ayer.

Redfield, James. The Celestine Prophecy. 1997. mass mkt. 192.00 (*0-446-16578-6*) Warner Bks.

— The Celestine Prophecy. 256p. 1995. reprint ed. mass mkt. 13.95 (*0-446-67100-2*, Pub. by Warner Bks) Little.

— The Celestine Prophecy: A Pocket Guide to the Nine Insights. 72p. 1996. 6.95 (*0-446-91206-9*, Pub. by Warner Bks) Little.

— The Celestine Prophecy: An Adventure. 247p. 1994. 23.95 (*0-446-51862-X*, Pub. by Warner Bks) Little.

— The Celestine Prophecy: An Adventure. large type ed. LC 94-19119. 1994. pap. 26.95 (*1-56895-113-2*) Wheeler Pub.

— The Celestine Vision: Living the New Spiritual Awareness. LC 97-61468. 288p. 1997. 20.00 (*0-446-52274-0*, Pub. by Warner Bks) Little.

***Redfield, James.** The Celestine Vision: Living the New Spiritual Awareness. LC 97-61468. 288p. 1999. mass mkt. 13.99 (*0-446-67523-7*, Pub. by Warner Bks) Little.

Redfield, James. The Celestine Vision: Living the New Spiritual Awareness. large type ed. LC 98-22092. (Large Print Book Ser.). 1998. 26.95 (*1-56895-603-7*) Wheeler Pub.

— La Decima Revelacion: Sostener La Vision. Sardoy, Cristina, tr. LC 96-26520. (SPA.). 288p. 1996. mass mkt. 8.99 (*0-446-67301-3*, Pub. by Warner Bks) Little.

— La Profecia Celestina: Una Aventura. (SPA.). 320p. 1996. 16.95 (*0-446-52057-8*, Pub. by Warner Bks) Little.

— The Secret of Shambhala: In Search of the Eleventh Insight. 256p. 1999. 23.95 (*0-446-52308-9*, Pub. by Warner Bks) Little.

***Redfield, James.** The Secret of Shambhala: In Search of the Eleventh Insight. 256p. 1999. mass mkt. 16.00 (*0-446-67648-9*, Pub. by Warner Bks) Little.

— Secret of Shambhala: In Search of the Eleventh Insight. large type ed. (G. K. Hall Core Ser.). 2000. 30.95 (*0-7838-8953-4*, G K Hall Lrg Type) Mac Lib Ref.

Redfield, James. The Tenth Insight: Holding the Vision. LC 96-60026. 256p. 1996. 19.95 (*0-446-51908-1*, Pub. by Warner Bks) Little.

— The Tenth Insight: Holding the Vision. 1996. mass mkt. 8.99 (*0-446-67330-7*, Pub. by Warner Bks) Little.

— The Tenth Insight: Holding the Vision. large type ed. 1996. 26.95 (*0-7862-0817-1*, G K Hall Lrg Type) Mac Lib Ref.

— The Tenth Insight: Holding the Vision. 256p. 1998. reprint ed. mass mkt. 12.99 (*0-446-67457-5*, Pub. by Warner Bks) Little.

— The Tenth Insight: Holding the Vision - A Pocket Guide. LC 97-218067. 64p. 1997. 6.95 (*0-446-91213-1*, Pub. by Warner Bks) Little.

Redfield, James. The Tenth Insight: Holding the Vision: An Experiential Guide. LC 96-3245. 384p. (Orig.). 1996. mass mkt. 11.99 (*0-446-67299-8*, Pub. by Warner Bks) Little.

Redfield, James. The Tenth Insight: Holding the Vision: Further Adventures of the Celestine Prophecy. 236p. 1998. text 20.00 (*0-7881-5772-8*) DIANE Pub.

***Redfield, James.** La Vision Celestina; Para Experimentar el Nuevo Despertar Espiritual. 1999. pap. text. write for info. (*970-05-1041-7*) Grijalbo Edit.

Redfield, James & Adrienne, Carol. The Celestine Prophecy: An Experiential Guide. LC 94-35210. 304p. 1995. mass mkt. 12.95 (*0-446-67122-3*, Pub. by Warner Bks) Little.

Redfield, James & Lillegard, Dee. The Song of Celestine. LC 98-5874. (Illus.). 48p. (J). (gr. k-3). 1998. 14.95 (*0-316-73923-5*) Little.

Redfield, James, jt. auth. see Miller, Larry.

Redfield, James, tr. see Borgeaud, Philippe.

Redfield, James M. Nature & Culture in the "Iliad" The Tragedy of Hector. LC 93-32349. 336p. 1993. text 54.95 (*0-8223-1409-6*); pap. text 19.95 (*0-8223-1422-3*) Duke.

Redfield, Judy, jt. auth. see Rainwater, Dorothy T.

Redfield, Kent D. Cash Clout: Political Money in Illinois Legislative Elections. 2nd ed. LC 95-35616. (Illus.). 228p. 1995. pap. 10.00 (*0-938943-05-7*) U IL Spgfld Pub Affrs.

Redfield, Kent D., jt. auth. see Van Der Slik, Jack R.

Redfield, Linda. Adventures of Berington Bullsnake. (J). (gr. 3-7). 1998. pap. 10.95 (*0-533-12655-X*) Vantage.

Redfield, Marc. Phantom Formations: Aesthetic Ideology & the Bildungsroman. LC 96-17186. (Illus.). 256p. 1996. text 37.50 (*0-8014-3236-7*) Cornell U Pr.

Redfield, Margaret P., ed. see Redfield, Robert.

Redfield, Nayan L., tr. see D'Olivet, Fabre.

***Redfield, Peter.** Space in the Tropics: From Convicts to Rockets in French Guiana. LC 99-56834. (Illus.). 350p. 2000. 55.00 (*0-520-21984-8*, Pub. by U CA Pr); pap. 22.50 (*0-520-21985-6*, Pub. by U CA Pr) Cal Prin Full Svc.

Redfield, Robert. The Folk Culture of Yucatan. LC 41-15380. (University of Chicago Publications in Anthropology. Social Anthropology). 440p. reprint ed. pap. 136.40 (*0-608-16508-5*, 202674000051) Bks Demand.

— The Folk Society. (Reprint Series in Sociology). (C). 1993. reprint ed. pap. text 1.00 (*0-8290-2622-3*, S-229) Irvington.

— The Little Community. 266p. 1960. pap. text 5.00 (*0-226-70664-8*, P53) U Ch Pr.

— The Little Community. 1973. lib. bdg. 10.00 (*0-226-70649-4*) U Ch Pr.

— The Little Community & Peasant Society & Culture. 284p. 1989. pap. text 23.00 (*0-226-70670-2*, Midway Reprint) U Ch Pr.

— Papers of Robert Redfield, 2 vols., 2. Redfield, Margaret P., ed. LC 62-10995. (Illus.). 301p. reprint ed. pap. 93.40 (*0-8357-6250-5*, 205681800002) Bks Demand.

— Papers of Robert Redfield, 2 vols., Vol. 1: Human Nature & the Study of Society. Redfield, Margaret P., ed. LC 62-10995. (Illus.). 523p. reprint ed. pap. 162.20 (*0-8357-6249-1*, 205681800001) Bks Demand.

— The Primitive World & Its Transformations. 198p. 1957. pap. text 11.95 (*0-8014-9028-6*) Cornell U Pr.

— Tepoztlan, a Mexican Village: A Study of Folk Life. LC 30-15556. (Midway Reprint Ser.). 271p. reprint ed. pap. 84.10 (*0-608-16613-8*, 202678300052) Bks Demand.

Redfield, Robert & Villa, Rojas A. Chan Kom, a Maya Village. LC 62-2616. 246p. reprint ed. pap. 76.30 (*0-608-12116-9*, 202406200035) Bks Demand.

Redfield, Salle M. Meditations for Healing the Earth. 1997. write for info. (*0-446-52044-6*) Warner Bks.

***Redfield, Salle Merrill.** Creating a Life of Joy: A Meditative Guide. 1999. pap. text 24.98 incl. audio compact disk (*1-57042-804-2*) Time Wrner AudioBks.

— Creating a Life of Joy: A Meditative Guide. LC 99-17005. 160p. 1999. mass mkt. 9.99 (*0-446-67587-3*, Pub. by Warner Bks) Little.

Redfield, Salle Merrill. The Joy of Meditating: A Beginner's Guide to the Art of Meditation. LC 95-33297. 64p. 1995. reprint ed. mass mkt. 8.99 (*0-446-67234-3*, Pub. by Warner Bks) Little.

Redfield, Susan S. & Kupetsky, Lisa. Developing Subjective Test Items. (Illus.). 40p. (Orig.). 1987. pap. 16.50 (*0-87683-917-0*, A917-0) GP Courseware.

Redfield, W. C. Genealogical History of the Redfield Family in the United States, Being a Revision & Extension of the Genealogical Tables Compiled in 1839. (Illus.). 345p. 1989. reprint ed. pap. 55.00 (*0-8328-1011-8*); reprint ed. lib. bdg. 65.00 (*0-8328-1010-X*) Higginson Bk Co.

Redfieldx. The Celestine Insights: The Celestine Prophecy & The Tenth Insight. 1997. 25.00 (*0-446-52394-1*, Pub. by Warner Bks) Little.

Redford & Van Note. The Rise of the Church of the Nazarene. 104p. 1985. pap. 7.99 (*0-8341-0141-6*) Nazarene.

Redford, A. H., jt. auth. see Mills, B.

Redford, Arthur. The Economic History of England, 1760-1860: A Greenwood Archival Edition. LC 73-15244. 244p. 1974. reprint ed. lib. bdg. 69.50 (*0-8371-7166-0*, REEH, Greenwood Pr) Greenwood.

— Labour Migration in England, 1800-1850. 2nd ed. Chaloner, William H., ed. LC 68-6093. (Illus.). xx, 209p. 1968. lib. bdg. 37.50 (*0-678-06766-X*) Kelley.

— Manchester Merchants & Foreign Trade, 1794-1858. LC 73-1675. 251p. 1973. reprint ed. 37.50 (*0-678-00750-0*) Kelley.

R

Redford, Bruce. The Converse of the Pen: Acts of Intimacy in the Eighteenth Century Familiar Letter. LC 86-11237. (Illus.). 264p. 1987. lib. bdg. 34.00 (*0-226-70678-8*) U Ch Pr.

— The Converse of the Pen: Acts of Intimacy in the Eighteenth Century Familiar Letter. LC 86-11237. (Illus.). 264p. 1996. pap. text 14.95 (*0-226-70679-6*) U Ch Pr.

***Redford, Bruce.** James Boswell's Life of Johnson: An Edition of the Original Manuscript, 4 vols. 336p. 1999. 70.00 (*0-300-07969-9*) Yale U Pr.

Redford, Bruce. Venice & the Grand Tour. LC 96-26608. (Illus.). 160p. 1996. 35.00 (*0-300-06911-1*) Yale U Pr.

Redford, Bruce, ed. The Letters of Samuel Johnson, Vol. I: 1731-1772. LC 90-8806. (Illus.). 431p. 1992. text 47.50 (*0-691-06881-X*, Pub. by Princeton U Pr) Cal Prin Full Svc.

— The Letters of Samuel Johnson, Vol. II: 1773-1776. (Illus.). 389p. 1992. text 47.50 (*0-691-06928-X*, Pub. by Princeton U Pr) Cal Prin Full Svc.

— The Letters of Samuel Johnson, Vol. III: 1777-1781. (Illus.). 399p. 1992. text 47.50 (*0-691-06929-8*, Pub. by Princeton U Pr) Cal Prin Full Svc.

— The Letters of Samuel Johnson, Vol. IV: 1782-1784. (Illus.). 488p. 1993. text 47.50 (*0-691-06977-8*, Pub. by Princeton U Pr) Cal Prin Full Svc.

— The Letters of Samuel Johnson, Vol. V: Appendices & Comprehensive Index. (Illus.). 202p. 1993. text 47.50 (*0-691-06978-6*, Pub. by Princeton U Pr) Cal Prin Full Svc.

— The Letters of Samuel Johnson: Volume I: 1731-1772, Volume II: 1773-1776, Volume III: 1777-1781, 3 vols. (Illus.). 1909p. 1993. text 175.00 (*0-691-03389-7*, Pub. by Princeton U Pr) Cal Prin Full Svc.

Redford, D., ed. Standard Lesson Commentary King James Version 1999-2000. 456p. 1999. 17.99 (*0-7847-0959-9*, 74030) Standard Pub.

— The Standard Lesson Commentary, 1998-1999. 456p. 1998. 16.99 (*0-7847-0843-6*, 11-01999); pap. 12.99 (*0-7847-0842-8*, 11-74029) Standard Pub.

Redford, D., ed. see Standard Publishing Staff.

Redford, D. B. & Weavers, John W., eds. Studies on the Ancient Palestinian World: Presented to Professor F. V. Winnett on the Occasion of His Retirement, July 1971. LC 79-151397. (Toronto Semitic Texts & Studies: No. 2). (Illus.). 191p. reprint ed. pap. 59.30 (*0-608-18051-3*, 202647900049) Bks Demand.

Redford, D. B., jt. ed. see Wevers, John W.

Redford, Donald B. Akhenaten: The Heretic King. LC 83-22960. (Illus.). 281p. 1984. pap. 25.95 (*0-691-00217-7*, Pub. by Princeton U Pr) Cal Prin Full Svc.

— Egypt, Canaan, & Israel in Ancient Times. (Illus.). 505p. 1992. pap. text 19.95 (*0-691-00086-7*, Pub. by Princeton U Pr) Cal Prin Full Svc.

***Redford, Donald B.** The Oxford Encyclopedia of Ancient Egypt. LC 99-54801. 2000. write for info. (*0-19-513821-X*); write for info. (*0-19-513822-8*); write for info. (*0-19-513823-6*) OUP.

***Redford, Donald B., ed.** The Oxford Encyclopedia of Ancient Egypt, 3 vols. LC 99-54801. (Illus.). 1632p. 2000. text 450.00 (*0-19-510234-7*) OUP.

Redford, Donald B., et al. Aspects of Monotheism: How God is One : Symposium at the Smithsonian Institution, October 19, 1996, Sponsored by the Resident Associate Program. LC 97-34911. 1997. 21.95 (*1-880317-50-8*, 7H47) Biblical Arch Soc.

***Redford, Dorothy Spruill.** Somerset Homecoming: Recovering a Lost Heritage. LC 99-43644. (Chapel Hill Book Ser.). (Illus.). 240p. 2000. pap. 18.95 (*0-8078-4843-3*) U of NC Pr.

Redford, Doug. Stories for the Lord's Supper. LC 99-12644. (Communion & Offering Meditations Ser.). 112p. 1999. 6.99 (*0-7847-0945-9*) Standard Pub.

Redford, Doug, ed. KJV Standard Lesson Commentary, 1997-98. 456p. (Orig.). 1997. text 16.99 (*0-7847-0619-0*, 74028) Standard Pub.

Redford, Emmette S. Ideal & Practice in Public Administration. LC 57-14937. 168p. 1958. pap. 52.10 (*0-608-05147-0*, 206570800005) Bks Demand.

— The Never-Ending Search for the Public Interest. (Reprint Series in Social Sciences). (C). 1993. reprint ed. pap. text 5.00 (*0-8290-3667-9*, PS-236) Irvington.

— Water Resource Development & Management in the Edwards Aquifer Region. (Policy Research Project Report Ser.: No. 1). 63p. 1972. pap. 3.00 (*0-89940-600-9*) LBJ Sch Pub Aff.

Redford, Emmette S. & Blissett, Marlan. Organizing the Executive Branch: The Johnson Presidency. LC 81-1142. (Administrative History of the Johnson Presidency Ser.). (C). 1995. 30.00 (*0-226-70675-3*) U Ch Pr.

— Organizing the Executive Branch: The Johnson Presidency. LC 81-1142. (Administrative History of the Johnson Presidency Ser.). 287p. reprint ed. pap. 89.00 (*0-608-09510-9*, 205431100005) Bks Demand.

Redford, Emmette S. & McCulley, Richard T. White House Operations: The Johnson Presidency. LC 85-26437. (An Administrative History of the Johnson Presidency Ser.). 261p. reprint ed. pap. 81.00 (*0-608-20108-1*, 207138000011) Bks Demand.

Redford, Emmette S., ed. see Hammond, Paul Y.

Redford, Emmette S., ed. see Herring, George C.

Redford, Emmette S., ed. see Welborn, David M.

Redford, George, jt. auth. see Smith, T. Roger.

Redford, J. A. C. Wecome All Wonders: A Composer's Journey. LC 97-19487. 352p. (gr. 11). 1997. 18.99 (*0-8010-1120-5*) Baker Bks.

Redford, John. Play of Wit & Science. (Tudor Facsimile Texts. Old English Plays Ser.: No. 18). reprint ed. 59.50 (*0-404-53318-3*) AMS Pr.

***Redford, John.** What Is Catholicism? Hard Questions - Straight Answers. LC 99-70514. 304p. 1999. pap. 12.95 (*0-87973-587-2*) Our Sunday Visitor.

Redford, John, jt. ed. see Pasco, Rowanne.

Redford, John B., et al, eds. Orthotics: Clinical Practice & Rehabilitation Technology. LC 95-35492. 337p. 1995. pap. text 48.00 (*0-443-08992-2*) Church.

Redford, Kent H., et al, eds. Parks in Peril: People, Politics & Protected Areas. LC 98-23680. 400p. 1998. text 50.00 (*1-55963-607-6*); pap. text 30.00 (*1-55963-608-4*) Island Pr.

Redford, Kent H. & Eisenberg, John F. Mammals of the Neotropics Vol. 2: The Southern Cone: Chile, Argentina, Uruguay, & Paraguay. (Illus.). 460p. 1992. pap. text 48.00 (*0-226-70682-6*); lib. bdg. 110.00 (*0-226-70681-8*) U Ch Pr.

Redford, Kent H. & Mansour, Jane A., eds. Traditional Peoples & Biodiversity: Conservation in Large Tropical Landscapes. (Illus.). 278p. (Orig.). (C). 1996. pap. text 19.95 (*1-886765-02-2*, America Verde) Nature VA.

Redford, Kent H. & Padoch, Christine, eds. Conservation of Neotropical Forests: Working from Traditional Resource Use. (Biological Ser.). (Illus.). 432p. 1992. text 50.00 (*0-231-07602-9*) Col U Pr.

***Redford, Kent H. & Padoch, Christine, eds.** Conservation of Neotropical Forests: Working from Traditional Resource Use. (Biology & Resource Management Ser.). 475p. 1999. pap. 25.00 (*0-231-07603-7*) Col U Pr.

Redford, Kent H., jt. ed. see Robinson, John G.

Redford, M. H., et al, eds. The Condom: Increasing Utilization in the U. S. (Illus.). 1974. 15.00 (*0-911302-25-5*); pap. 15.00 (*0-317-58587-8*) San Francisco Pr.

***Redford, Pat.** The Gunslinger. large type ed. 224p. 1999. pap. 18.99 (*0-7089-5554-1*, Linford) Ulverscroft.

Redford, Robert, pref. The Legacy of Wildness: The Photographs of Robert Glenn Ketchum. 120p. 1993. 76.00 (*0-89381-498-9*) Aperture.

Redford, Scott. Archaeology of the Frontier in the Medieval Near East: Excavations at Gritille, Turkey. LC 98-40203. 1998. write for info. (*0-924171-65-0*) U Museum Pubns.

***Redgate, A. E.** The Armenians. (Peoples of America Ser.). 352p. 2000. pap. text 27.95 (*0-631-22037-2*, Pub. by Blackwell Publishers) Blackwell Pubs.

Redgate, A. E. The Armenians. LC 98-24617. (Peoples of America Ser.). (Illus.). 352p. 2000. text 59.95 (*0-631-14372-6*, Pub. by Blackwell Publishers) Blackwell Pubs.

***Redgate, Chris.** The Red Pencil #1. LC 00-190192. 263p. 1999. 25.00 (*0-7388-1542-X*); pap. 18.00 (*0-7388-1543-8*) Xlibris Corp.

Redgate, S., ed. see International Symposium on Brain-Pituitary-Adrenal.

Redgment, J. The Law Student's Companion: A Guide to the Study & Practice of Law. 2nd ed. 232p. 1988. pap. write for info. (*0-7021-2211-4*, Pub. by Juta & Co) Gaunt.

Redgrave, Corin. Michael Redgrave: My Father. (Illus.). 176p. 1996. 29.95 (*1-86066-000-2*, Pub. by R Cohen Bks) Trafalgar.

Redgrave, G. R., jt. ed. see Pollard, Alfred W.

Redgrave, Michael. The Actor's Ways & Means. 2nd ed. (Illus.). 144p. (C). (gr. 13). 1995. pap. 16.99 (*0-87830-059-7*, B7285, Thtre Arts Bks) Routledge.

Redgrave, Richard & Redgrave, Samuel. A Century of British Painters. Todd, Ruthven, ed. (Landmarks in Art History Ser.). (Illus.). 622p. 1981. pap. text 27.50 (*0-8014-9217-3*) Cornell U Pr.

Redgrave, Samuel, jt. auth. see Redgrave, Richard.

Redgrove, H. Stanley. Alchemy Ancient & Modern. 192p. 1992. reprint ed. pap. 17.95 (*1-56459-143-3*) Kessinger Pub.

— The Belief in Talismans. 1992. reprint ed. pap. 7.95 (*1-55818-200-4*, Sure Fire) Holmes Pub.

— Bygone Beliefs: An Excursion into the Occult & Alchemical Nature of Man. (Excursion into the Occult & Alchemical Nature of Man Ser.). 287p. 1981. pap. 20.00 (*0-89540-078-2*, SB-078) Sun Pub.

— Bygone Beliefs, Being a Series of Excursions in the Byways of Thought (1920) 225p. 1998. reprint ed. pap. 18.95 (*0-7661-0156-8*) Kessinger Pub.

— Magic & Mysticism: Studies in Bygone Beliefs. 1970. 7.95 (*0-8216-0111-3*) Carol Pub Group.

— Roger Bacon: Christian Mystic & Alchemist. 1994. pap. 6.95 (*1-55818-303-5*) Holmes Pub.

Redgrove, Peter. Abyssophone. 1995. write for info. (*1-873012-87-X*) SPD-Small Pr Dist.

— Assembling a Ghost. 64p. 1997. 15.95 (*0-224-04482-6*, Pub. by Jonathan Cape) Trafalgar.

— The Cyclopean Mistress: Selected Short Fiction 1960-1990. 156p. 1994. pap. 16.95 (*1-85224-207-8*, Pub. by Bloodaxe Bks) Dufour.

Redgwell, Catherine. Intergenerational Trusts & Environmental Protection. (Melland Schill Studies in International Law). 240p. 1998. text 79.95 (*0-7190-3489-2*, Pub. by Manchester Univ Pr) St Martin.

Redgwell, Catherine & Bowman, Michael, eds. International Law & the Conservation of Biological Diversity. LC 95-43223. (International Environmental Law & Policy Ser.). 1995. 105.00 (*90-411-0863-7*) Kluwer Law Intl.

***Redhawk, Jordan.** Tiopa Ki Lakota. 360p. 2000. pap. 18.99 (*1-930928-03-3*, 0014) Renaissance Alliance.

Redhawk, Randy. Grimadi Land of the Dragons. 210p. (YA). (gr. 6 up). 1998. reprint ed. pap. 18.95 (*0-9641861-6-0*) Redhawk Pubng.

— The Pow Wow Book: A Must for Every Pow Wow. 2nd rev. ed. LC 94-92187. (Illus.). 22p. (J). (gr. 3 up). 1994. pap. 5.00 (*0-9641861-0-1*) Redhawk Pubng.

Redhawk, Richard. Grandmother's Christmas Story: A True Tale of the Quechan Indians. (Illus.). 40p. (J). (ps-5). 1987. pap. 6.95 (*0-940113-08-2*) Sierra Oaks Pub.

Redhead. The Big Block of Chocolate. (J). (ps-2). 1989. 19.95 (*0-590-50157-7*) Scholastic Inc.

— Tropical Forestry. 1993. pap. text. write for info. (*0-582-77522-1*, Pub. by Addison-Wesley) Longman.

Redhead, Brian. Manchester: A Celebration. (Illus.). 170p. 1994. 45.00 (*0-233-98816-5*, Pub. by Andre Deutsch) Trafalgar.

— The North West of England. (Radio Times Around Britain Guides Ser.). (Illus.). 96p. 1994. 8.95 (*0-563-36953-1*, Pub. by BBC) Parkwest Pubns.

Redhead, Brian, ed. Political Thought from Plato to NATO. 288p. (C). 1988. pap. text 32.50 (*0-534-10801-6*) Harcourt.

Redhead, Brian, jt. auth. see Gumley, Frances.

Redhead, D. N. & Chalmers, N. Imaging. LC 94-11040. (Colour Guide Ser.). 1995. pap. text 16.95 (*0-443-05020-1*) Harcrt Hlth Sci Grp.

***Redhead, David.** Products of Our Time. LC 99-89524. (Illus.). 144p. 2000. pap. 38.00 (*3-7643-6234-0*, Pub. by Birkhauser) Princeton Arch.

Redhead, Janet S. Something Special for Miss Margery. LC 93-6632. (Voyages Ser.). (Illus.). (J). 1994. write for info. (*0-383-03673-9*) SRA McGraw.

Redhead, Janet S. & Dale, Christine. The Big Block of Chocolate. (Illus.). (J). pap. 4.95 (*0-908643-75-6*, Pub. by Ashton Scholastic) Scholastic Inc.

Redhead, Keith. Introduction to Financial Derivatives: An Introduction. LC 96-20800. 390p. 1996. pap. 40.00 (*0-13-241399-X*) P-H.

Redhead, Keith & Hughes, Steward. Financial Risk Management. 200p. 1988. text 72.95 (*0-566-02652-X*, Pub. by Gower) Ashgate Pub Co.

Redhead, Keith, jt. ed. see Stonham, Paul.

Redhead, Michael. From Physics to Metaphysics. (Illus.). 106p. (C). 1995. text 39.95 (*0-521-47405-1*) Cambridge U Pr.

— From Physics to Metaphysics. 150p. 1996. pap. text 18.95 (*0-521-58966-5*) Cambridge U Pr.

— Incompleteness, Nonlocality, & Realism: A Prolegomenon to the Philosophy of Quantum Mechanics. 200p. 1989. reprint ed. pap. text 24.95 (*0-19-824238-7*) OUP.

Redhead, P. A., et al. The Physical Basis of Ultrahigh Vacuum. LC 92-46643. (AVS Classics of Vacuum Science & Technology Ser.). 1993. write for info. (*1-56396-122-9*) Am Inst Physics.

***Redhead, Ray.** The International Party Guide: Where's the O#$! Beer!? LC 99-95066. (Illus.). 220p. 1999. pap. 16.95 (*0-9673586-0-4*) Exit Row.

Redhead, Steve. Post-Fandom & the Millennial Blues: The Transformation of Soccer Culture. LC 97-2916. 176p. (C). 1997. 75.00 (*0-415-11527-2*); pap. 22.99 (*0-415-11528-0*) Routledge.

— Subculture to Clubcultures: An Introduction to Popular Cultural Studies. LC 96-39887. (Illus.). (C). 1997. text 62.95 (*0-631-19788-5*) Blackwell Pubs.

— Subculture to Clubcultures: An Introduction to Popular Cultural Studies. LC 96-39887. (Illus.). (C). 1998. pap. text 23.95 (*0-631-19789-3*) Blackwell Pubs.

Redhead, Steve, ed. The Passion & the Fashion: Football Fandom in the New Europe. LC 93-3864. (Popular Cultural Studies). 224p. 1993. 59.95 (*1-85628-462-X*, Pub. by Avebry); pap. 24.95 (*1-85628-464-6*, Pub. by Avebry) Ashgate Pub Co.

— Rave Off: Politics & Deviance in Contemporary Youth Culture. (Popular Culture in the City Ser.). 202p. 1993. 59.95 (*1-85628-463-8*, Pub. by Avebry) Ashgate Pub Co.

Redheffer, Gordon. Introduction to Differential Equations. (Math Ser.). 480p. (C). 1992. 61.25 (*0-86720-289-0*) Jones & Bartlett.

Redheffer, Raymond M. Differential Equations. 800p. 1991. 63.75 (*0-86720-200-9*) Jones & Bartlett.

Redheffer, Raymond M., jt. auth. see Sokolnikoff, Ivan S.

Redhill, Michael. Asphodel. LC 97-148566. 112p. 1997. pap. text 10.95 (*0-7710-7354-2*) McCland & Stewart.

Redhill, Michael, ed. Blues & True Concussions: Six New Toronto Poets. LC 97-104842. 1996. pap. text 13.95 (*0-88784-581-9*) Stoddart Publ.

— Blues & True Confessions: Six New Toronto Poets. (Orig.). 1996. pap. 13.95 (*0-614-17721-9*, Pub. by Hse of Anansi Pr) Genl Dist Srvs.

Redhouse, James W. Redhouse English-Turkish Dictionary. 17th ed. (ENG & TUR.). 1152p. 1990. lib. bdg. 95.00 (*0-7859-0640-1*, M2050) Fr & Eur.

— Redhouse Turkish & English Lexicon. (ENG & TUR.). 2224p. 1994. 120.00 (*0-86685-127-5*, LDL1275, Pub. by Librairie du Liban) Intl Bk Ctr.

— Turkish-English Dictionary, 3 pts. (ENG & TUR.). 1977. reprint ed. 297.95 (*0-518-19005-6*) Ayer.

Redhouse, James W., tr. see Din, Shams U. & Ahmed, E.

Redhouse, James W., tr. see Shah, Nasir A.

Redi, C. A., jt. ed. see Olmo, E.

***Redi, Maurya, et al.** Hello Adirondacker. expanded rev. ed. (Adirondack Reidings Ser.: Vol. IV). xiv, 120p. 1998. pap. 8.95 (*1-890072-04-4*) Reid Pubns.

Redican, Kerry & Moore, Linda, des. AAHE Scholar Presentations, 1981-1995. (Illus.). 180p. 1997. pap. 21.95 (*0-88314-606-1*) AAHPERD.

Redican, Kerry J., et al. Organization of School Health Programs. 2nd ed. 496p. (C). 1992. text. write for info. (*0-697-13129-7*) Brown & Benchmark.

Redick, Donald D., ed. see Hefner, Hal.

Redick, Donald J., ed. see Compton, Scott.

Redick, Heather. Decorative Painting Zhostovo Style. LC 99-24605. (Illus.). 128p. 1999. pap. 24.99 (*0-89134-987-1*, 31458, North Lght Bks) F & W Pubns Inc.

Redick, Janet L. Bookkeeping Is Not a Four-Letter Word! A Guide to Basic Bookkeeping. (Illus.). 48p. 1998. spiral bd. 12.95 (*0-9668686-0-9*) J L Redick.

Redig, Ann, jt. auth. see Toal, James.

Redig, Clare, ed. see Yates, Lori L.

Redig, I. Wayan. Ganesa Images from India & Indonesia from Circa 7th to 15th Century AD. LC 96-900618. (C). 1996. 68.00 (*81-85067-96-1*, Pub. by Sundeep Prak) S Asia.

Redig, Patrick T., et al, eds. Raptor Biomedicine. 288p. (C). 1993. 49.95 (*0-8166-2219-1*) U of Minn Pr.

Rediger, G. Lloyd. Clergy Killers: Guidance for Pastors & Congregations under Attack. LC 96-79932. (Illus.). 208p. 1996. pap. 14.99 (*1-885361-03-3*) Logos Prods.

— Clergy Killers: Guidance for Pastors & Congregations under Attack. LC 97-723. 200p. 1997. pap. 15.00 (*0-664-25753-4*) Westminster John Knox.

— Fit to Be a Pastor: A Guide to Personal & Professional Fitness. LC 99-45357. 160p. 1999. pap. 14.95 (*0-664-25844-1*) Westminster John Knox.

***Rediger, Pat.** For the Love of Soccer. (For the Love of Sports Ser.). (Illus.). 24p. (J). (gr. k-3). 2000. write for info. (*1-930954-10-7*) Weigl Pubs.

Rediger, Pat. Great African Americans, 12 vols., Set. (Illus.). (YA). (gr. 4-10). 1995. pap. 107.40 (*0-86505-824-5*) Crabtree Pub Co.

Rediger, Pat. Great African Americans, 12 vols., Set. (Illus.). (YA). (gr. 4-10). 1995. lib. bdg. 255.36 (*0-86505-810-5*) Crabtree Pub Co.

— Great African Americans in Civil Rights. (Outstanding African Americans Ser.). (Illus.). (J). 1995. 14.40 (*0-606-18055-9*) Turtleback.

Rediker, Marcus. Between the Devil & the Deep Blue Sea: Merchant Seamen, Pirates & the Anglo-American Maritime World, 1700-1750. LC 87-6304. (Illus.). 352p. 1987. text 52.95 (*0-521-30342-7*) Cambridge U Pr.

— Between the Devil & the Deep Blue Sea: Merchant Seamen, Pirates, & the Anglo-American Maritime World, 1700-1750. (Canto Book Ser.). (Illus.). 340p. (C). 1993. pap. 11.95 (*0-521-45720-3*) Cambridge U Pr.

Rediker, Marcus, jt. auth. see Linebaugh, Peter.

Redin, Mats A. Word-Order in English Verse from Pope to Sassoon. 1977. lib. bdg. 59.95 (*0-8490-2842-6*) Gordon Pr.

Redinbaugh, Larry D. Retailing Management: A Planning Approach. (Illus.). 447p. (C). 1992. text 89.00 (*1-878907-68-9*) TechBooks.

Redinbaugh, Larry D. & Neu, Clyde W. Small Business Management: A Planning Approach. (Illus.). 475p. 1980. pap. text, teacher ed. write for info. (*0-314-52998-5*) West Pub.

Reding. CPR: MS Access 97 Basic. (Illustrated Ser.). (C). 1997. pap. 20.95 (*0-7600-5822-9*) Course Tech.

— Dynamic Html Four Point O Introductory. (C). 1998. pap. 21.95 (*0-7600-6079-7*) Thomson Learn.

— HTML Four Point O Illustrated Standard. (C). 1998. pap. text 21.95 (*0-7600-6078-9*) Thomson Learn.

Reding. Microsoft Publisher 98. (Illustrated Ser.). (C). 1998. mass mkt. 21.95 (*0-7600-6106-8*) Course Tech.

Reding. MS Publisher 97. (Illustrated Ser.). (Illus.). (C). 1997. pap. 21.95 (*0-7600-5591-2*) Course Tech.

***Reding & Beskeen.** Integrating Microsoft Office 2000. (C). 2000. pap. 21.95 (*0-7600-6552-7*) Course Tech.

***Reding & O'Keefe.** Crse Gde: Ill Ms Excel 2000 Basic. (C). 1999. pap. text 21.95 (*0-7600-6389-3*) Course Tech.

Reding, et al. Integrating Microsoft Office 97: Professional Edition. 10th ed. (Illustrated Ser.). (Illus.). 96p. (C). 1997. pap. 12.95 (*0-7600-4711-1*) Course Tech.

— Microsoft Office for Windows 95, Professional Edition: A First Course. (Illustrated Ser.). (Illus.). 512p. (C). 1996. pap., per. 38.00 (*0-7600-4797-9*) Course Tech.

— Microsoft Office 97 Professional Edition: A First Course. (Illustrated Ser.). (Illus.). 608p. (C). 1997. pap. 38.00 (*0-7600-4693-X*) Course Tech.

Reding, jt. auth. see Hurst.

Reding, jt. auth. see O'Keefe.

Reding, Andrew. Democracy & Human Rights in Guatemala. Schmuhl, Peter, ed. (World Policy Papers). 83p. 1997. pap. 10.00 (*0-911646-65-5*) World Policy.

— Democracy & Human Rights in Mexico. LC 95-61021. (World Policy Papers). 68p. (Orig.). 1995. pap. 7.50 (*0-911646-59-0*) World Policy.

Reding, Andrew, ed. see Borge, Tomas.

Reding, Andrew A., ed. Haiti: An Agenda for Democracy. (Papers). 1996. 5.00 (*0-911646-63-9*) World Policy.

Reding, Andrew A. & Whalen, Christopher. Fragile Stability: Reform & Repression in Mexico under Carlos Salinas. (North America Project Special Reports). 33p. 1992. pap. 5.00 (*0-911646-50-7*) World Policy.

Reding, Andrew A., ed. see Levinson, Jerome I.

Reding, Elizabeth E. Excel 97 Exam Prep. 10th ed. 432p. (C). 1997. pap. 29.99 (*1-57610-232-7*) Coriolis Grp.

Reding, Elizabeth E. Microsoft Access 7 for Windows 95: Illustrated Brief Edition, Incl. instr. resource kit, test mgr., Web pg. (Illustrated Ser.). (Illus.). 96p. 1996. pap. 11.95 (*0-7600-3812-0*) Course Tech.

— Microsoft Access 2000: Illustrated Complete Edition. 1999. pap. text 38.95 (*0-7600-6072-X*) Course Tech.

— Microsoft Excel 5 for Windows - Illustrated, Incl. instr. resource kit, test bank, transparency. (Illustrated Ser.). (Illus.). 192p. (C). 1996. pap. 20.95 (*1-56527-264-1*) Course Tech.

— Microsoft Excel 7 for Windows 95 - Illustrated Brief Edition, Incl. instr. resource kit, test mgr., Web pg. (Illustrated Ser.). (Illus.). 96p. 1995. text, mass mkt. 11.95 incl. 3.5 ld (*0-7600-3811-2*) Course Tech.

***Reding, Elizabeth E.** Microsoft Excel 2000: Illustrated Complete. (Illus.). 488p. 1999. pap. text 38.95 (*0-7600-6064-9*) Course Tech.

Reding, Elizabeth E. & Beskeen, David W. Integrating Microsoft Office for Windows 3.1: Illustrated Brief Edition. (Illustrated Ser.). (Illus.). 96p. (C). 1996. pap. 12.95 (*0-7600-4037-0*) Course Tech.

— Integrating Microsoft Office for Windows 95, Incl. instr.

An Asterisk (*) at the beginning of an entry indicates that the title is appearing for the first time.

R

resource kit, test mgr., Web pg. (Illustrated Ser.). (Illus.). 96p. 1996. text, mass mkt. 11.95 incl. 3.5 ld (*0-7600-4045-1*) Course Tech.

Reding, Elizabeth E. & Friedrichsen, Lisa. Microsoft Access 97: Illustrated Brief Edition. 10th ed. (Illustrated Ser.). (Illus.). 96p. (C). 1997. pap. 12.95 (*0-7600-4703-0*) Course Tech.

— Microsoft Access 97: Illustrated PLUS Edition. (Illustrated Ser.). (Illus.). 488p. (C). 1997. pap. 38.95 (*0-7600-5157-7*).Course Tech.

— Microsoft Access 97: Illustrated Standard Edition, a Second Course. 10th ed. (Illustrated Ser.). (Illus.). 192p. (C). 1997. pap. 21.95 (*0-7600-5154-2*) Course Tech.

— Microsoft Access 97 - Illustrated Standard Edition: A First Course. 10th ed. (Illus.). 192p. (C). 1997. pap. 21.95 (*0-7600-4697-2*) Course Tech.

Reding, Elizabeth E. & O'Keefe, Tara. Microsoft Excel 97: Illustrated Brief Edition. (Illus.). 96p. (C). 1997. pap., teacher ed. 40.00 (*0-7600-5310-3*) Course Tech.

— Microsoft Excel 97: Illustrated Brief Edition. 10th ed. (Illustrated Ser.). (Illus.). 96p. (C). 1997. pap. 12.95 (*0-7600-4701-4*) Course Tech.

— Microsoft Excel 97: Illustrated Plus Edition. (Illustrated Ser.). (Illus.). 488p. (C). 1997. pap. 38.95 (*0-7600-5149-6*) Course Tech.

— Microsoft Excel 97: Illustrated Standard Edition: A First Course. 10th ed. (Illustrated Ser.). (Illus.). 192p. (C). 1997. pap. 21.95 (*0-7600-4695-6*) Course Tech.

— Microsoft Excel 97: Illustrated Standard Edition: A Second Course. (Illustrated Ser.). (Illus.). 192p. (C). 1997. pap. 16.50 (*0-7600-5146-1*) Course Tech.

— Microsoft Excel 97 - Illustrated Standard Edition: A First Course. (Illus.). 192p. (C). 1997. teacher ed. 5.00 incl. 3.5 hd (*0-7600-5151-8*) Course Tech.

Reding, Elizabeth E., et al. Microsoft Office for Windows 95, Professional Edition: A First Course - Illustrated, Incl. instr. resource kit, test mgr., Web pg. (Illustrated Ser.). (Illus.). 512p. 1995. text, mass mkt. 50.95 incl. 3.5 ld (*0-7600-3531-8*) Course Tech.

Reding, Elizabeth E., et al. Microsoft Office for Windows 95 Professional Edition: A Second Course - Illustrated, Incl. instr. resource kit, test mgr., Web pg. (Illustrated Ser.). (Illus.). 600p. 1996. text 50.95 incl. 3.5 ld (*0-7600-3729-9*) Course Tech.

Reding, Elizabeth E., et al. Microsoft Office Professional for Windows 3.1 - Illustrated Enhanced Edition, Incl. instr. resource kit, test mgr., Web pg. (Illustrated Ser.). (Illus.). 576p. 1996. text, mass mkt. 50.95 incl. 3.5 ld (*0-7600-4034-6*) Course Tech.

Reding, Elizabeth E., jt. auth. see Shafer, Ann.

Reding, Elizabeth Eisner. Adobe Photoshop 5.5 - Illustrated Introductory. (Illus.). 240p. per. 21.95 (*0-7600-6337-0*, Pub. by Course Tech) Thomson Learn.

— HTML - Illustrated Brief. (Illus.). 120p. per. 12.95 (*0-7600-6077-0*, Pub. by Course Tech) Thomson Learn.

— HTML Four Point O Illustrated Complete. (C). 1998. text 38.95 (*0-7600-5842-3*) Thomson Learn.

— Microsoft Excel 2000 - Illustrated Brief. (Illus.). 112p. per. 12.95 (*0-7600-6061-4*, Pub. by Course Tech) Thomson Learn.

— Microsoft Publisher 2000 - Illustrated Introductory. (Illus.). 192p. per. 21.95 (*0-7600-6366-4*, Pub. by Course Tech) Thomson Learn.

Reding, Elizabeth Eisner & O'Keefe, Tara Lynn. Microsoft Excel 2000 - Illustrated Introductory. (Illus.). 208p. per. 21.95 (*0-7600-6062-2*) Course Tech.

— Microsoft Excel 2000 Certified: Course CBT. 26.95 (*0-619-00118-6*, Pub. by Course Tech) Thomson Learn.

— Mous Excel 2000 Exam Prep. LC 00-26971. 2000. write for info. (*1-57610-480-X*) Coriolis Grp.

Reding, Ginny, jt. auth. see Hurst, Beth.

Reding, Jaclyn. Stealing Heaven. 1996. mass mkt. 5.99 (*0-451-40649-4*, Onyx) NAL.

— White Heather. 1997. mass mkt. 5.99 (*0-451-40650-8*, Onyx) NAL.

— White Knight. 320p. 1999. mass mkt. 5.99 (*0-451-19852-2*, Sig) NAL.

— White Magic. 1998. mass mkt. 5.99 (*0-451-40855-1*, Topaz) NAL.

Reding, Liz. Easy PowerPoint for Windows 95. (Illus.). 250p. 1995. 19.99 (*0-7897-0627-X*) Que.

Reding, Malcolm E. Flood Insurance: The Insecurity Blanket. 1994. pap. 6.95 (*0-9638709-1-2*) Shade Tree Pr.

Reding, Malcolm E., ed. see Butcher, Clyde.

Reding, Malcolm E., ed. see Teger, Allan I.

Reding, Todd L., ed. Rockhurst Review, 1992: A Fine Arts Journal, Vol. V. 50p. 1992. pap. 5.00 (*1-886761-04-3*) Rockhurst Col.

Redinger, David H. Story of Big Creek. LC 98-42701. 1998. write for info. (*0-9628236-8-6*) Ironwood Press.

Redington & Burger. Redington Field Guides to Biological Interactions: Animals in Town. LC 98-67755. 710p. (C). 1998. per. 52.95 (*0-7872-5470-3*, 41547001) Kendall-Hunt.

Redington, Andrew, et al. Congenital Heart Disease in Adults: A Practical Guide. (Illus.). 270p. 1994. text 67.95 (*0-7020-1913-5*, Pub. by W B Saunders) Saunders.

Redington, James F., jt. auth. see Klimenko, Nicholas A.

Rediniotis, Othon K., et al, eds. ASME Fluids Engineering Division: Proceedings, ASME International Mechanical Engineering Congress & Exposition, 1996, Atlanta, Georgia. LC 96-78692. (FED Ser.: Vol. 242). 378p. 1996. pap. text 110.00 (*0-7918-1550-1*) ASME Pr.

Redisch, Edward F., jt. ed. see Risley, John S.

Redish, A. David. Beyond the Cognitive Map: From Place Cells to Episodic Memory. LC 98-41504. (Illus.). 636p. 1999. 45.00 (*0-262-18194-0*) MIT Pr.

***Redish, Angela.** Bimetallism: An Economic & Historical Analysis. LC 99-52882. (Studies in Macroeconomic History). (Illus.). 280p. (C). 2000. write for info. (*0-521-57091-3*) Cambridge U Pr.

Redish, Charles H. Pecos Pete. large type ed. Redish, Greg, ed. (Illus.). 32p. (J). (gr. k-8). 1996. 24.95 (*0-9643885-2-9*) Personal Profiles.

Redish, Edward F. & Rigden, John S., eds. The Changing Role of Physics Departments in Modern Universities: Proceedings of ICUPE, Pts. 1 & 2. (AIP Conference Proceedings Ser.: Vol. 399). (Illus.). 1096p. 1997. 165.00 (*1-56396-698-0*, 399, AIP Pr) Spr-Verlag.

Redish, Greg, ed. see Redish, Charles H.

Redish, Janice C., jt. auth. see Dumas, Joseph S.

Redish, Janice C., jt. auth. see Hackos, JoAnn T.

Redish, Martin H. The Constitution As Political Structure. LC 93-42364. 240p. 1995. text 52.00 (*0-19-507060-7*) OUP.

— The Federal Courts in the Political Order: Judicial Jurisdiction & American Political Theory. LC 90-85345. 200p. 1991. lib. bdg. 24.95 (*0-89089-411-6*) Carolina Acad Pr.

— Federal Jurisdiction. 2nd ed. (Black Letter Ser.). 234p. (C). 1990. pap., pap. text 24.50 incl. disk (*0-314-79273-2*) West Pub.

— Federal Jurisdiction. 3rd ed. (Black Letter Ser.). Date not set. pap. text. write for info. (*0-314-06771-X*) West Pub.

Redish, Martin H. & Nichol, Gene R. Comments & Questions on Federal Courts: Cases, Comments & Questions. 3rd ed. (American Casebook Ser.). 1000p. (C). 1994. text. write for info. (*0-314-03990-2*) West Pub.

Redish, Martin H. & Sherry, Suzanna. Federal Courts, Cases, Comments & Questions On. 4th ed. LC 97-52357. (American Casebook Ser.). 1000p. 1998. 62.50 (*0-314-23047-5*) West Pub.

Redish, Martin H., et al. Federal Courts Cases, Comments & Questions, 1996 Supplement to Redish & Nichol's. 3rd ed. (American Casebook Ser.). 75p. 1996. pap. text. write for info. (*0-314-20106-8*) West Pub.

Redivo, Zaglia M., jt. auth. see Brezinski, C.

Redkey, Edwin S., ed. A Grand Army of Black Men: Letters from African-American Soldiers in the Union Army, 1861-1865. LC 92-14632. (Cambridge Studies in American Literature & Culture: No. 63). 322p. (C). 1992. pap. 19.95 (*0-521-43998-1*) Cambridge U Pr.

— Respect Black: The Writings & Speeches of Henry McNeal Turner. LC 79-138695. 1971. 11.95 (*0-405-01984-X*) Ayer.

Redknap, Mark, jt. ed. see Gaimster, David.

Redl, E. & Oldal, E. Dictionary of Electronics, Telecommunications & Vacuum Technology, 2 vols., Set. (ENG, FRE, GER, HUN & RUS.). 1269p. 1983. 75.00 (*0-8288-0315-3*, M6649) Fr & Eur.

— Electronics, Telecommunications, Vacuum Technology Vols. 50-53, 2 vols. 1270p. 1983. 60.00 (*963-05-2674-3*, Pub. by Akade Kiado) St Mut.

Redl, E., et al. Electronics: Dictionary of Technical Information, 2 vols. 1270p. (C). 1983. 205.00 (*0-569-08782-1*, Pub. by Collets) St Mut.

Redl, Fritz & Wineman, David. Controls from Within: Techniques for the Treatment of the Aggressive Child. LC 52-8161. 1965. pap. 17.95 (*0-02-926040-X*) Free Pr.

Redl, H., jt. ed. see Schlag, Gunther O.

Redl, Heinz & Schlag, Gunther. Cytokines in Severe Sepsis & Septic Shock. LC 98-37008. (PIR/Progress in Inflammation Research Ser.). 1998. 179.00 (*0-8176-5877-7*); 179.00 (*3-7643-5877-7*) Birkhauser.

Redl, Heinz, jt. auth. see Schlag, Gunther.

Redl, Maureen, jt. auth. see Hayes, Jody.

Redl, Siegmund, et al. GSM & Personal Communications Handbook. LC 98-4710. 500p. 1998. 99.00 (*0-89006-957-3*) Artech Hse.

Redl, Siegmund H., et al. An Introduction to GSM. LC 94-23893. 379p. 1995. 99.00 (*0-89006-785-6*) Artech Hse.

Redl, William A., ed. Noise & Vibration Measurement: Proceedings of a Symposium Sponsored by the Environmental Engineering Division. 145p. 1985. 19.00 (*0-87262-445-5*) Am Soc Civil Eng.

Redlake, Kevin. The Sorrows below Apollyon, Vol. 1. Stohlmberg, Jacob, ed. (Illus.). 120p. 1995. pap. 5.00 (*0-9639186-0-5*) Stohlmberg Horror.

Redleaf, Angelica. Behind Closed Doors: Gender, Sexuality & Touch in the Doctor-Patient Relationship. LC 97-32947. 216p. 1998. 55.00 (*0-275-96146-X*, Praeger Pubs) Greenwood.

Redleaf Pr. Staff, ed. Calendar-Keeper Cookbook: 100 Keepsake Recipes. LC 96-41371. (Illus.). 120p. (Orig.). 1996. pap. 13.95 (*1-884834-23-X*, 1029) Redleaf Pr.

Redleaf, Rhoda. Busy Fingers, Growing Minds: Finger Plays, Verses & Activities for Whole Language Learning. LC 93-39636. (Illus.). 167p. (Orig.). (J). (ps). 1993. pap. 18.95 (*0-934140-79-0*, 4561) Redleaf Pr.

— Open the Door Let's Explore More! Field Trips of Discovery for Young Children. LC 96-14294. (Illus.). 368p. (Orig.). 1996. pap. 21.95 (*1-884834-13-2*, 4020) Redleaf Pr.

Redleaf, Rhoda & Robertson, Audrey. Learn & Play the Recycle Way: Homemade Toys That Teach. LC 99-29587. 1999. pap. text 18.95 (*1-884834-40-X*) Redleaf Pr.

***Redlich, Dieter.** Die Umkehrung der Hegelschen Dialektik. 322p. 1999. 47.95 (*3-906761-76-2*, Pub. by P Lang) P Lang Pubng.

Redlich, Frederick C., jt. auth. see Hollinghead, August B.

Redlich, Frederick C., jt. ed. see Brody, Eugene B.

Redlich, Fritz. Hitler: Diagnosis of a Destructive Prophet. LC 97-48888. (Illus.). 466p. 1998. 35.00 (*0-19-505782-1*) OUP.

***Redlich, Fritz.** Hitler: Diagnosis of a Destructive Prophet. (Illus.). 480p. 2000. pap. 17.95 (*0-19-513631-4*) OUP.

Redlich, Josef. Austrian War Government. (Economic & Social History of the World War Ser.). 1929. 100.00 (*0-685-69855-6*) Elliots Bks.

Redlich, Josef & Hirst, Francis W. The History of Local Government in England. 2nd ed. LC 71-110121. xvii, 284p. 1970. lib. bdg. 45.00 (*0-678-07005-9*) Kelley.

Redlich, Joseph. Osterreichische Regierung Und Verwaltung Im Weltkriege. (Wirtschafts-Und Sozialgeschichte des Weltkrieges (Osterreichische Und Ungarische Serie)). (GER.). 1925. 100.00 (*0-317-27532-1*) Elliots Bks.

— Procedure of the House of Commons, 3 vols. Steinthal, A. Ernest, tr. LC 77-77895. reprint ed. 165.00 (*0-404-05280-0*) AMS Pr.

Redlich, Marcellus D. Pedigrees of Some of the Emperor Charlemagne's Descendants, Vol. I. LC 71-39170. 320p. 1996. reprint ed. 25.00 (*0-8063-0494-4*) Genealog Pub.

Redlich, Norman. Constitutional Law. 3rd ed. 1996. text 50.36 (*0-256-22158-8*) McGraw.

— Professional Responsibility: A Problem Approach. 2nd ed. 288p. 1983. 23.00 (*0-316-73657-0*, Aspen Law & Bus) Aspen Pub.

— Standards of Professional Conduct for Lawyers & Judges. (C). 1984. pap. 16.00 (*0-316-73658-9*, Aspen Law & Bus) Aspen Pub.

Redlich, Norman, et al. Constitutional Law. 3rd ed. LC 96-27063. (Casebook Ser.). 1996. 56.00 (*0-8205-2701-7*) Bender.

***Redlich, Norman, et al.** Understanding Constitutional Law. 2nd ed. LC 99-17008. 1999. 30.00 (*0-8205-4057-9*) Bender.

Redlich, Norman, et al. Understanding Constitutional Law: 1995 Supplement. 32p. (C). 1996. pap. text 12.95 (*0-256-21910-9*, Irwn McGrw-H) McGrw-H Hghr Educ.

Redlich, Rosemarie, jt. auth. see Scherman, David E.

Redlich, Shimon. Propaganda & Nationalism in Wartime Russia: The Jewish Anti-Fascist Committee in the U. S. S. R., 1941-1948. (East European Monographs: No. 108). 236p. 1982. text 55.50 (*0-88033-001-5*, Pub. by East Eur Monographs) Col U Pr.

— War, Holocaust & Stalinism: A Documented History of the Jewish Anti-Fascist Committee in the USSR. (History of Russia Ser: Vol. 1). 510p. 1995. text 82.00 (*3-7186-5739-2*, Harwood Acad Pubs) Gordon & Breach.

Redlin, jt. auth. see Stewart.

Redlin, Lothar, jt. auth. see Stewart, James.

Redlin, Michael H. & Stipanuk, David M. Managing Hospitality Engineering Systems. LC 87-15712. (Illus.). 275p. (C). 1987. pap. text. write for info. (*0-86612-037-8*) Educ Inst Am Hotel.

Redlin, Scott C. & Carris, Lori M., eds. Endophytic Fungi in Grasses & Woody Plants: Systematics, Ecology, & Evolution. LC 96-83100. 231p. (Orig.). (C). 1996. pap. text 47.00 (*0-89054-213-9*) Am Phytopathol Soc.

Redman, Alvin, ed. see Wilde, Oscar.

Redman, B. R., tr. see Gobineau, Joseph A.

Redman, Barbara K. Measurement Tools in Patient Education. LC 97-29477. (Illus.). 408p. 1997. 59.95 (*0-8261-9860-0*) Springer Pub.

— Women's Health Needs in Patient Education. LC 99-27854. (Focus on Women Ser.). (Illus.). 160p. 1999. text 32.95 (*0-8261-1264-1*) Springer Pub.

Redman, Barbara K., et al, eds. Educating RNs for the Baccalaureate: Programs & Issues. LC 90-9533. (Teaching of Nursing Ser.: Vol. 12). 248p. 1990. 39.95 (*0-8261-7210-5*) Springer Pub.

Redman, Barbara K. & Klug, Barbara. The Practice of Patient Education. 8th ed. (Illus.). 304p. (C). (gr. 13). 1996. pap. text 34.00 (*0-8151-9357-2*, 29203) Mosby Inc.

Redman, Barbara K., ed. see American Association of Colleges of Nursing Staff.

Redman, Ben R. Edwin Arlington Robinson. LC 74-1444. (Studies in Poetry: No. 38). 1974. lib. bdg. 75.00 (*0-8383-2045-7*) M S G Haskell Hse.

Redman, Ben R., ed. see Voltaire.

Redman, Bridgette M. White Papers in Club Management. (Topical Reference Ser.: Vol. 2). (Illus.). (C). 1998. pap. write for info. (*0-86612-183-8*) Educ Inst Am Hotel.

— White Papers on Club Management. LC 97-25551. (Topical Reference Ser.). 240p. 1997. write for info. (*0-86612-164-1*) Educ Inst Am Hotel.

Redman, C. W., et al. The Human Placenta. (Illus.). 608p. 1992. 199.95 (*0-632-02721-5*) Blackwell Sci.

Redman, Charles L. Human Impact on Ancient Environments. LC 99-6237. (Illus.). 288p. 1999. pap. 22.95 (*0-8165-1963-3*) U of Ariz Pr.

***Redman, Charles L.** Human Impact on Ancient Environments. LC 99-6237. (Illus.). 288p. 1999. 45.00 (*0-8165-1962-5*) U of Ariz Pr.

Redman, Charles L. People of the Tonto Rim: Archaeological Discovery in Prehistoric Arizona. LC 92-25213. (Illus.). 224p. 1993. pap. text 17.95 (*1-56098-192-X*) Smithsonian.

Redman, Charles L., ed. Medieval Archeology. (Medieval & Renaissance Texts & Studies: Vol. 60). 320p. 1989. 24.00 (*0-86698-044-X*, MR60) MRTS.

Redman, Deborah A. A Reader's Guide to Rational Expectations: A Survey & Comprehensive Annotated Bibliography. 208p. 1992. text 95.00 (*1-85278-567-5*) E Elgar.

— The Rise of Political Economy As a Science: Methodology & the Classical Economists. LC 97-22275. (Illus.). 489p. 1997. 59.50 (*0-262-18179-7*) MIT Pr.

Redman, Deborah A., compiled by. Economic Methodology: A Bibliography with References to Works in the Philosophy of Science, 1860-1988, 9. LC 89-17195. (Bibliographies & Indexes in World History Ser.: No. 9). 301p. 1989. lib. bdg. 85.00 (*0-313-26859-2*, REG/, Greenwood Pr) Greenwood.

Redman, Eric. The Dance of Legislation. 320p. 1974. pap. 11.00 (*0-671-21746-1*, Touchstone) S&S Trade Pap.

***Redman, Eric.** Dance of Legislation. (Illus.). 320p. 2000. pap. 17.50 (*0-295-98023-0*) U of Wash Pr.

Redman, G. A. Mystic Hours of Spiritual Experiences. 388p. 1997. reprint ed. pap. 24.95 (*0-7661-0035-9*) Kessinger Pub.

Redman, George. A Casebook for Exploring Diversity in K-12 Classrooms. LC 98-2655. 164p. (C). 1998. pap. text 21.00 (*0-13-745878-9*, Merrill Coll) P-H.

— Teaching in Today's Classrooms. LC 98-18503. (C). 1998. pap. text 18.00 (*0-13-627167-7*, Scribners Ref) Mac Lib Ref.

***Redman, George.** Teaching in Today's Classrooms: Cases from Elementary School. LC 98-13900. 132p. (C). 1998. pap. text 21.00 (*0-13-627142-1*, Merrill Coll) P-H.

Redman, George L. Building Self-Esteem in Children: A Skill & Strategy Workbook for Parents. rev. ed. Gorham, Kerstin, ed. (Illus.). 95p. 1995. pap. 19.95 (*1-879276-02-X*) Parent Tching Pubns.

— Building Self-Esteem in Students: A Skill & Strategy Workbook for Teachers. Gorham, Kerstin, ed. (Illus.). 91p. 1992. pap. 19.95 (*1-879276-01-1*) Parent Tching Pubns.

Redman, Harry, Jr. Major French Milton Critics of the Nineteenth Century. LC 93-39661. (Duquesne Studies: Language & Literature Ser.: Vol. 14). 404p. (C). 1994. text 48.00 (*0-8207-0249-8*) Duquesne.

— The Roland Legend in Nineteenth-Century French Literature. LC 90-26581. 264p. 1991. text 34.95 (*0-8131-1732-1*) U Pr of Ky.

Redman, Helen C., et al. Emergency Radiology. (Illus.). 554p. 1992. text 120.00 (*0-7216-7491-7*, W B Saunders Co) Harcrt Hlth Sci Grp.

Redman, Helen C., jt. auth. see Weinreb, Jeffrey C.

Redman, Jim. Jim Redman - Six Times World Motorcycle Champion: The Autobiography. (Illus.). 288p. 1998. pap. 19.95 (*1-901295-35-4*) Vloce Pub.

Redman, John. Understanding State Economies Through Industry Studies. LC 94-5574. 1994. 15.95 (*0-934842-70-1*) CSPA.

Redman, John & Thomason, Michael E. John Redman's Essentials of the Golf Swing. (Illus.). 144p. 1994. pap. 13.95 (*0-452-27302-1*, Plume) Dutton Plume.

Redman, John E., jt. auth. see Ray, Ralph P.

Redman, Lenn. How to Draw Caricatures. (Illus.). 176p. (Orig.). 1984. pap. 18.95 (*0-8092-5685-1*, 568510, Contemporary Bks) NTC Contemp Pub Co.

Redman, Lipman, jt. auth. see Quiggle, James W.

Redman, Mark, et al. Agricultural Pollution: Problems & Practical Solutions. (Illus.). 256p. (C). (gr. 13). 1999. pap. 34.99 (*0-419-21390-2*, D5567, E & FN Spon) Routledge.

Redman, Michael, jt. auth. see Walker, D. J.

Redman, Michael E., et al. Traveling America: An Activity Book for the Whole Family. 56p. (Orig.). 1993. pap. write for info. (*0-9637442-0-8*) Mstr Designs.

Redman, Nina, jt. auth. see Whalen, Lucille.

***Redman, Nina E.** Food Safety: A Reference Handbook. 2000. lib. bdg. 39.50 (*1-57607-158-8*) ABC-CLIO.

***Redman, Rich.** Age of Apocalypse. (X-Men Ser.). 64p. 2000. pap. 9.95 (*0-7869-1664-8*) TSR Inc.

— Arms & Equipment Guide. (Alternity Ser.). 96p. 2000. pap. 18.95 (*0-7869-1616-8*) TSR Inc.

— Spider-Man, Mysterio's Ways. (Marvel Super Heroes Adventures Ser.). (Illus.). 32p. (J). 2000. pap. 4.95 (*0-7869-1669-9*) TSR Inc.

— X-Men, Resurrection of Cyclops. (Marvel Super Heroes Adventures Ser.). 2000. pap. 4.95 (*0-7869-1665-6*) TSR Inc.

Redman, Robert R., Jr. Reformulating Reformed Theology: Jesus Christ - The Theology of Hugh Ross MacKintosh. 304p. 1997. 40.00 (*0-7618-0515-X*) U Pr of Amer.

Redman, Stephanie. Taking the Leap into New Media. LC 99-17287. (Illus.). 144p. 1999. pap. 29.99 (*0-89134-953-7*, 31445, North Lght Bks) F & W Pubns Inc.

Redman, Stuart. English Vocabulary in Use: Pre-Intermediate & Intermediate Edition with Answers. 272p. (J). 1997. pap. text 15.95 (*0-521-55737-2*) Cambridge U Pr.

Redman, Stuart & Ellis, Robert. A Way with Words Level 1: Vocabulary Development Activities for Learners of English, Resource Pack Book. 1990. 29.95 (*0-521-47775-1*) Cambridge U Pr.

Redman, Stuart & Shaw, Ellen. Vocabulary in Use: Intermediate. (Illus.). 240p. (C). 1999. pap. text 18.95 (*0-521-63478-4*) Cambridge U Pr.

— Vocabulary in Use: Intermediate: Instructor's Manual. (Illus.). 304p. (C). 1999. pap. text, teacher ed. write for info. (*0-521-63477-6*) Cambridge U Pr.

Redman, Stuart, jt. auth. see Gairns, Ruth.

Redman, Thomas C. Data Quality for the Information Age. LC 96-37205. 303p. 1996. 75.00 (*0-89006-883-6*) Artech Hse.

Redman, Tim. Ezra Pound & Italian Fascism. (Cambridge Studies in American Literature & Culture: No. 47). 300p. (C). 1991. text 54.95 (*0-521-37305-0*) Cambridge U Pr.

***Redman, Tom.** Managing Human Resources. (C). 2000. pap. text. write for info. (*0-201-59613-X*) Addison-Wesley.

Redman, Warren. Portfolios for Development: A Guide for Trainers & Managers. 192p. (Orig.). 1994. pap. text 27.95 (*0-89397-394-7*) Nichols Pub.

— Portfolios for Development Guide for Trainers & Managers. 224p. (C). 1994. pap. 45.00 (*0-7494-1158-9*, Pub. by IPM Hse) St Mut.

R

Redmann, J. M. The Intersection of Law & Desire. 1997. mass mkt. 5.99 (*0-380-72819-2*, Avon Bks) Morrow Avon.
— Lost Daughters: A Micky Knight Mystery. LC 99-10422. 320p. 1999. text 24.95 (*0-393-04028-3*) Norton.
Redmann, R. E., jt. auth. see Ripley, E. A.
Redmayne, Ann. A Time to Forget. large type ed. (Linford Romance Library). 1989. pap. 16.99 (*0-7089-6791-4*) Ulverscroft.
— To Speak of Love. large type ed. (Linford Romance Library). 1991. pap. 16.99 (*0-7089-6988-7*) Ulverscroft.
***Redmayne, Ann.** To Walk in the Sun Again. large type ed. 208p. 2000. pap. 18.99 (*0-7089-5636-X*, Linford) Ulverscroft.
Redmayne, Barbara. Ambitious Angel. large type ed. (Romance Ser.). 336p. 1988. 27.99 (*0-7089-1855-7*) Ulverscroft.
— Lovely Day. large type ed. (Romance Ser.). 320p. 1988. 27.99 (*0-7089-1747-X*) Ulverscroft.
Redmayne, J. Equity Warrants. 170p. 1995. 170.00 (*1-85564-275-1*, Pub. by Euromoney) Am Educ Systs.
Redmayne, Julian. Equity Warrants. 2nd ed. 1998. pap. 215.00 (*1-85564-656-0*, Pub. by Euromoney) Am Educ Systs.
Redmayne, Julian, ed. Convertibles. 2nd ed. 1999. 170.00 (*1-85564-657-9*, Pub. by Euromoney) Am Educ Systs.
Redmayne, Robert A. British Coal-Mining Industry During the War: R. A. S. Redmayne. (Economic & Social History of the World War Ser.). 1923. 125.00 (*0-686-37864-4*) Elliots Bks.
Redmer, Pamela M., ed. see Bader, William C.
Redmill. System Safety. LC 98-55085. 258p. 1999. 99.95 (*0-471-98280-6*) Wiley.
Redmill, F. J. & Valdar, A. R. SPC Digital Telephone Exchanges. rev. ed. (Telecommunications Ser.: No. 21). 537p. 1994. pap. 45.00 (*0-86341-298-X*, TE021Z, Pub. by Peregrinus); boxed set 115.00 (*0-86341-301-3*, TE021, Pub. by Peregrinus) Dist Unknown.
Redmill, Felix. Software Projects: Evolutionary Versus Big Bang Theory. 274p. 1997. 80.00 (*0-471-93343-0*) Wiley.
Redmill, Felix & Anderson, Tom. Safer Systems: Proceedings of the Fifth Safety-Critical Systems Symposium, 4-6 February 1997, Brighton, U. K. LC 96-52064. 1997. pap. write for info. (*3-540-76134-9*) Spr-Verlag.
Redmill, Felix & Anderson, Tom, eds. Achievement & Assurance of Safety: Proceedings of the Third Safety-Critical Systems Symposium, Brighton, UK, 7-9 February, 1995. LC 94-46761. 1995. 69.00 (*3-540-19922-5*) Spr-Verlag.
— Directions in Safety-Critical Systems: Proceedings of the First Safety-Critical Systems Symposium, the Watershed Media Centre, Bristol, 9-11 February 1993. LC 92-43311. 1992. 69.00 (*0-387-19817-2*) Spr-Verlag.
— Industrial Perspectives of Safety-Critical Systems: Proceedings of the 6th Safety-Critical Systems Symposium, Birmingham, 1998. LC 97-53123. x, 238p. 1998. pap. 84.95 (*3-540-76189-6*) Spr-Verlag.
***Redmill, Felix & Anderson, Tom, eds.** Lessons in System Safety: Proceedings of the Eighth Safety-Critical Systems Symposium, Southampton, UK, 2000. LC 99-56289. x, 302p. 2000. pap. text 89.95 (*1-85233-249-2*) Spr-Verlag.
Redmill, Felix & Anderson, Tom, eds. Safety-Critical Systems: The Convergence of High Tech & Human Factors: Proceedings of the Fourth Safety-Critical Systems Symposium, Leeds, 6-8 February 1996. (Illus.). ix, 285p. 1996. pap. 75.00 (*3-540-76009-1*) Spr-Verlag.
— Technology & Assessment of Safety-Critical Systems: Proceedings of the Second Safety-Critical Systems Symposium, Birmingham, UK, 8-10 February 1994. LC 93-50853. 1994. 78.95 (*0-387-19859-8*) Spr-Verlag.
Redmill, Felix & Dale, Chris, eds. Life Cycle Management for Dependability. LC 96-27350. (Illus.). xviii, 235p. 1997. pap. 62.00 (*3-540-76073-3*) Spr-Verlag.
Redmill, Felix & Rajan, Jane. Human Factors in Safety: Critical Systems. LC 96-48632. (Illus.). 320p. 1997. text 80.00 (*0-7506-2715-8*) Buttrwrth-Heinemann.
Redmon, Curtis. Anointed Praise: The Ministry of Music in the Church Today. (Practical Church Ser.). 54p. 1992. pap. text 4.95 (*1-881685-00-4*) LUA Stand Minist.
— Chosen: The Pastor, the Preacher & His Wife. (Practical Church Ser.). (Orig.). 1993. pap. 6.95 (*1-881685-03-9*) LUA Stand Minist.
— Just Servants: The Ministry of the Deacon & the Usher. (Practical Church Ser.). (Orig.). 1993. pap. text 5.95 (*1-881685-02-0*) LUA Stand Minist.
— Ruling Well: Leadership in Our Church Today. (Practical Church Ser.). 129p. (Orig.). 1996. pap. text 7.95 (*1-881685-05-5*) LUA Stand Minist.
— What about the Children? The Ministry of the Sunday School. (Practical Church Ser.). (Orig.). 1993. pap. text 5.95 (*1-881685-01-2*) LUA Stand Minist.
***Redmon, George L.** Energy For Life: How to Manage Your Metabolic Potential. 240p. 2000. 15.95 (*1-890612-14-6*) Vital Health.
Redmon, George L. Managing & Preventing Arthritis: The Natural Alternatives. unabridged ed. LC 98-45831. 192p. 1999. pap. 12.95 (*0-934252-90-4*, Pub. by Hohm Pr) SCB Distributors.
***Redmon, George L.** Managing & Preventing Prostate Disorders: The Natural Alternatives. 185p. 2000. pap. 12.95 (*0-934252-97-1*, Pub. by Hohm Pr) SCB Distributors.
Redmon, George L. Minerals: What Your Body Really Needs & Why. LC 99-18141. 196p. 1998. pap. 10.95 (*0-89529-863-5*, Avery) Penguin Putnam.
Redmon, Hugo. Campamentos y Retiros Cristianos.Tr. of Christian Camps & Retreats. (SPA.). 128p. (Orig.). 1992. pap., teacher ed. 6.50 (*0-311-11051-7*) Casa Bautista.
Redmon, Jessie R. F. & Fauset, Jessie R. Comedy, American Style, Vol. 4. LC 94-24678. (African-American Women Writers,1910-1940, Ser.). 1995. 25.00 (*0-8161-1628-8*, G K Hall & Co) Mac Lib Ref.
Redmon, Laurel, ed. see Yi, Qiao & Stone, Al.
Redmon, Ronald. Panzergrenadiers in Action. (Combat Troops in Action Ser.). (Illus.). 1995. pap. 9.95 (*0-89747-096-6*, 3005) Squad Sig Pubns.
Redmon, Ronald & Cuccarese, James. Panzer Grenadier - Grossdeutschland. (Specials Ser.). (Illus.). 80p. 1993. pap. 14.95 (*0-89747-061-3*, 6009) Squad Sig Pubns.
Redmon, William K. & Dickinson, Alyce M. Promoting Excellence Through Performance Management. LC 90-4369. (Journal of Organizational Behavior Management: Vol. 11, No. 1). 289p. 1990. text 39.95 (*1-56024-015-6*) Haworth Pr.
Redmond. Balancing on the Wire. LC 98-71001. 1998. 35.07 (*0-395-93849-X*) HM.
***Redmond.** Citizen Ezra Pound. 1999. text 35.00 (*0-8050-6053-7*) St Martin.
— Come on You Reds. 2000. pap. 6.95 (*0-552-54558-9*, Pub. by Transworld Publishers Ltd) Trafalgar.
Redmond. Encyclopedia of Clinical Trial. text. write for info. (*0-471-82211-6*) Wiley.
***Redmond.** Penalty. 2000. pap. 6.95 (*0-552-54559-7*, Pub. by Transworld Publishers Ltd) Trafalgar.
Redmond, Anthony D., jt. auth. see Robertson, Colin E.
Redmond, Barbara, jt. auth. see Thomas, Eberle.
Redmond, C. F., jt. ed. see Lodge, Henry C.
Redmond, Chris. An Irregular Pictionary: Forty Words for Sherlockians. (Illus.). 40p. 1997. pap. 8.00 (*1-55246-000-2*) Battered Silicon.
Redmond, Christopher. In Bed with Sherlock Holmes: Sexual Elements in Arthur Conan Doyle's Stories of the Great Detective. 200p. 1993. 29.95 (*0-88924-142-2*, Pub. by SIM) Empire Pub Srvs.
Redmond, Christopher, compiled by. Quotations from Baker Street. 48p. (Orig.). 1994. pap. 8.00 (*1-896032-16-8*) Battered Silicon.
Redmond, Christopher, ed. Canadian Holmes: The First Twenty-Five Years. (Illus.). 305p. 1997. 36.50 (*1-899562-27-3*) Ash-Tree.
Redmond, David, jt. auth. see Johnson, Ron.
Redmond, Diane. The Odyssey. unabridged ed. (Curtain Up! Ser.: Vol. 8). (Illus.). 48p. (J). (gr. 2-6). 1998. pap. 16.95 (*0-7136-4628-4*, Pub. by A & C Blk) Midpt Trade.
Redmond, Don. Number Theory: An Introduction. (Monographs & Textbooks in Pure & Applied Mathematics: Vol. 201). (Illus.). 772p. 1996. text 175.00 (*0-8247-9696-9*) Dekker.
Redmond, Don, jt. auth. see Gregory, John.
Redmond, Donald A. Sherlock Holmes among the Pirates: Copywright & Conan Doyle in America 1890-1930, 36. LC 89-27280. (Contributions to the Study of World Literature Ser.: No. 36). 304p. 1990. 65.00 (*0-313-27230-1*, RSH/, Greenwood Pr) Greenwood.
Redmond, Elsa M. A Fuego y Sangre: Early Zapotec Imperialism in the Cuicatlan Canada, Oaxaca. Marcus, Joyce, ed. (Memoirs Series, Studies in Latin American Ethnohistory & Archaeology: No. 16, Vol. 1). (Illus.). 214p. 1983. pap. 15.00 (*0-932206-97-2*) U Mich Mus Anthro.
— Tribal & Chiefly Warfare in South America. Marcus, Joyce, ed. LC 94-18061. (Memoirs Ser., Prehistory & Human Ecology of the Valley of Oaxaca: No. 28, Vol. 5). 1994. 25.00 (*0-915703-35-1*) U Mich Mus Anthro.
Redmond, Elsa M., ed. Chiefdoms & Chieftaincy in the Americas. LC 98-8522. 416p. 1998. 55.00 (*0-8130-1620-7*) U Press Fla.
Redmond, Eugene B. The Eye in the Ceiling: Selected Poems. 156p. (Orig.). 1992. 22.00 (*0-86316-308-4*); pap. 12.00 (*0-86316-307-6*) Writers & Readers.
Redmond, Fiona. Farmyard Counting Book. (Board Counting Bks.). (Illus.). 20p. (J). (ps). 1996. bds. 5.98 (*1-85854-202-2*) Brimax Bks.
Redmond, Fiona. ABC. (Brimax Interactive Ser.). 12p. (J). (ps-k). 1996. bds. 6.98 (*1-85854-371-1*) Brimax Bks.
— One to Ten. (Board Counting Bks.). 20p. (J). (ps). 1996. bds. 5.98 (*1-85854-203-0*, 1 85854 203 0) Brimax Bks.
— 1 2 3. (Brimax Interactive Ser.). 12p. (J). (ps-k). 1996. bds. 6.98 (*1-85854-372-X*) Brimax Bks.
— Ten Little Kittens. 20p. (J). (ps). 1997. bds. 5.98 (*1-85854-589-7*) Brimax Bks.
— Turn & Learn. (Brimax Interactive Ser.). 12p. (J). (ps-k). 1996. bds. 6.98 (*1-85854-492-0*) Brimax Bks.
Redmond, Franke E., 3rd. DCOM: Microsoft Distributed Component Object Model. LC 97-73635. 384p. 1997. pap. 39.99 (*0-7645-8044-2*) IDG Bks.
Redmond, Geoffrey P. The Good News about Women's Hormones: Complete Information & Proven Solutions for the Most Common Hormonal Problems. 528p. 1995. mass mkt. 13.99 (*0-446-39454-8*, Pub. by Warner Bks) Little.
Redmond, Geoffrey P., ed. Androgenic Disorders. 356p. 1995. text 102.00 (*0-7817-0274-7*) Lppncott W & W.
— Lipids & Women's Health. (Illus.). 272p. 1990. 89.00 (*0-387-97318-4*) Spr-Verlag.
Redmond, Geoffrey P., jt. ed. see Soyka, Lester F.
Redmond, Gerald. The Sporting Scots of Nineteenth-Century Canada. LC 80-67124. (Illus.). 352p. 1982. 40.00 (*0-8386-3069-3*) Fairleigh Dickinson.
Redmond, Gerald, ed. see Olympic Scientific Congress (1984: Eugene, OR) Sta.
Redmond, Gerry. Wayne Gretzky: A Biography. (Illus.). 112p. (Orig.). 1993. pap. 9.95 (*1-55022-190-6*, Pub. by ECW) LPC InBook.
Redmond, Gerry, et al. The Arithmetic of Tax & Social Security Reform: A User's Guide to Microsimulation Methods & Analysis. LC 98-6160. (Department of Applied Economics Occasional Papers: No. 64). (Illus.). 300p. (C). 1998. 59.95 (*0-521-63224-2*) Cambridge U Pr.
Redmond, Gerry, jt. auth. see Hutton, Sandra.
Redmond, Gertrude T. & Ouellette, Frances. Concept & Case Studies Nursing: A Life Cycle Approach. 1983. pap. write for info. (*0-201-06207-0*, Health Sci) Addison-Wesley.
Redmond, Howard A. Christian Hedonism. LC 89-12344. (American University Studies: Theology & Religion: Ser. VII, Vol. 67). 156p. 1989. text 34.95 (*0-8204-1117-5*) P Lang Pubng.
— Our Hearts Are Restless: Meditations on Learning to Live. LC 96-53401. 96p. (Orig.). 1997. pap. 10.95 (*1-55612-859-2*, LL1859) Sheed & Ward WI.
***Redmond, Ian.** Elephant. (Eyewitness Books). (Illus.). (J). (gr. 4-7). 2000. 19.99 (*0-7894-6591-4*) DK Pub Inc.
— Elephant. (Eyewitness Books). (J). (gr. 4-7). 2000. 15.95 (*0-7894-5872-1*) DK Pub Inc.
— Gorilla. (Eyewitness Books). (Illus.). (J). (gr. 4-7). 2000. 19.99 (*0-7894-6613-9*) DK Pub Inc.
— Gorilla. (Illus.). 64p. (J). (gr. 5). 1995. lib. bdg. 20.99 (*0-679-97332-X*) Random.
***Redmond, Ian.** Gorilla, Monkey & Ape. (Eyewitness Books). (J). (gr. 4-7). 2000. 15.95 (*0-7894-6036-X*) DK Pub Inc.
Redmond, Ian. Gorilla, Monkey & Ape. (Illus.). 64p. (J). (gr. 5). 1995. 19.00 (*0-679-87332-5*) Random.
Redmond, J. A. Heat Treating Gears by Induction Heating. (Technical Papers: Vol. P129.08). (Illus.). 12p. 1950. pap. text 30.00 (*1-55589-330-9*) AGMA.
Redmond, James, ed. Drama, Dance & Music. (Themes in Drama Ser.: No. 3). (Illus.). 260p. 1981. write for info. (*0-521-22180-3*) Cambridge U Pr.
— Drama in Society. LC 77-54723. (Themes in Drama Ser.: No. 1). (Illus.). 1979. write for info. (*0-521-22076-9*) Cambridge U Pr.
— News from Nowhere. (Routledge English Texts Ser.). 236p. (C). 1972. pap. 20.99 (*0-415-07581-5*) Routledge.
Redmond, James, ed. see Morris, William.
Redmond, James, jt. ed. see Washington, Gregory.
Redmond, John. The Book of Irish Golf. LC 97-30639. (Illus.). 176p. 1997. 39.95 (*1-56554-327-0*) Pelican.
***Redmond, John.** Great Golf Courses of Ireland. (Illus.). 368p. 1999. 39.95 (*0-7171-2875-X*, Pub. by Gill & MacMill) Irish Bks Media.
Redmond, John. The Next Mediterranean Enlargement of the European Community: Turkey, Cyprus & Malta? 165p. 1993. 72.95 (*1-85521-281-1*, Pub. by Dartmth Pub) Ashgate Pub Co.
Redmond, John, ed. The External Relations of the European Community: The International Response to 1992. LC 92-4253. 200p. 1992. text 65.00 (*0-312-08051-4*) St Martin.
— The 1995 Enlargement of the European Union. LC 96-29590. 208p. 1997. 72.95 (*1-85521-823-2*, Pub. by Dartmth Pub) Ashgate Pub Co.
Redmond, John & Rosenthal, Glenda G., eds. The Expanding European Union: Past, Present, Future. LC 97-15802. 240p. 1997. 53.00 (*1-55587-623-4*) L Rienner.
Redmond, John, jt. auth. see Croft, Stuart.
Redmond, John, jt. ed. see Gower, Jackie.
Redmond, K. & Aapro, M. S., eds. Cancer in the Elderly: A Nursing & Medical Perspective. 110p. 1997. 95.00 (*0-444-82858-3*) Elsevier.
Redmond, Katherine G. Chartracker to the Intracoastal Waterway: Norfolk to Jacksonville. LC 98-30039. (Illus.). 184p. 1998. spiral bd. 39.95 (*1-892399-00-8*) Seaworthy WI.
Redmond, Kathy, jt. auth. see Hawthorn, Jan.
***Redmond, Kent C. & Smith, Thomas M.** From Whirlwind to MITRE: The R&D Story of the SAGE Air Defense Computer. LC 00-29228. (History of Computing Ser.). (Illus.). 566p. (C). 2000. 49.95 (*0-262-18201-7*) MIT Pr.
Redmond, LaGroon, ed. see Old Campbell County Historical Society Staff.
***Redmond, Laure.** Feel Good Naked: 10 No-Diet Secrets to a Fabulous Body. (Illus.). 2001. 22.95 (*1-86204-398-1*) Element MA.
Redmond, Layne. When Drummers Were Women: A Spiritual History of Rhythm. LC 97-186947. 1997. pap. 18.00 (*0-609-80128-7*) Random Hse Value.
Redmond, Liam. Death Is So Kind. 1959. 9.95 (*0-8159-5301-1*) Devin.
Redmond, Lula M. Surviving When Someone You Love Was Murdered: A Professional's Guide to Group Grief Therapy for Families & Friends of Murder Victims. 170p. (Orig.). (C). 1989. pap. 24.95 (*0-9624592-0-8*) Psychological Consult.
***Redmond, Marcia A.** The Trade - Pleasure for Money. 183p. 1998. pap. write for info. (*0-9684376-0-5*) Easly Reading.
Redmond, Marie, jt. ed. see Barrett, Edward.
Redmond, Marilyn. Henry Hamilton in Outer Space. LC 90-25176. (Illus.). 192p. (J). (gr. 4-7). 1991. 12.95 (*0-88289-820-5*) Pelican.
Redmond, Marilyn. Henry Hamilton in Outer Space. LC 90-25176. (Illus.). 192p. (J). (gr. 4-7). 1991. pap. 12.95 (*1-56554-532-X*) Pelican.
Redmond, Michael. Sixty Second Sells: Ninety-Nine Hot Radio Spots for Retail Businesses. LC 92-56684. 109p. 1993. lib. bdg. 23.50 (*0-89950-792-1*) McFarland & Co.
Redmond, P. W. & Shears, Peter. General Principles of English Law. 7th ed. 496p. 1993. pap. 54.50 (*0-7121-0858-0*, Pub. by Pitman Pub) Trans-Atl Phila.
Redmond, Pat H. History of Quincy & Its Men of Mark: Or Facts & Figures Exhibiting Its Advantages & Resources, Manufacturers & Commerce. (Illus.). 302p. 1997. reprint ed. lib. bdg. 37.50 (*0-8328-5787-4*) Higginson Bk Co.
Redmond, Patricia, jt. ed. see Baker, Houston A., Jr.
***Redmond, Patrick.** Something Dangerous. 2000. mass mkt. 7.50 (*0-7868-8957-8*) Hyprn Ppbks.
Redmond, Patrick. Something Dangerous: A Novel. 2000. mass mkt. write for info. (*0-7868-8972-1*, Pub. by Disney Pr) Little.
— Something Dangerous: A Novel. LC 98-56261. 320p. 1999. 23.95 (*0-7868-6552-0*, Pub. by Hyperion) Time Warner.
Redmond, Paul. Companies & Securities Law: Commentary & Materials. lxi, 912p. 1988. 120.00 (*0-455-20765-8*, Pub. by LawBk Co); pap. 79.00 (*0-455-20766-6*, Pub. by LawBk Co) Gaunt.
— Companies & Securities Law: Commentary & Materials, Incl. suppl. 2nd ed. 1221p. 1992. 171.00 (*0-455-21403-4*, Pub. by Cavendish Pubng); pap. 110.00 (*0-455-21397-6*, Pub. by Cavendish Pubng) Gaunt.
— Companies & Securities Law: Commentary & Materials, Suppl. 61p. 1996. pap. 20.00 (*0-455-21380-1*, Pub. by Cavendish Pubng) Gaunt.
Redmond, Paulinus. Seed & the Root. 272p. 1995. 39.95 (*1-899163-08-5*, Pub. by Quiller Pr) St Mut.
Redmond-Pyle, David, jt. auth. see Moore, Alan.
Redmond, R., ed. General Principles of English Law. 392p. (C). 1990. 130.00 (*0-7855-5675-3*, Pub. by Inst Pur & Supply) St Mut.
Redmond, R. & Lawson, L. An Introduction to Business Law. 320p. (C). 1990. 125.00 (*0-7855-6521-3*, Pub. by Inst Pur & Supply) St Mut.
Redmond, Sandra. Ready Steady Go. (J). (gr. k-6). 1995. pap. 6.00 (*0-87602-333-2*) Anchorage.
Redmond, Shirley-Raye. Grampa & the Ghost. 96p. (Orig.). (J). (gr. 3 up). 1994. pap. 3.50 (*0-380-77382-1*, Avon Bks) Morrow Avon.
Redmond, Stephen. The Fountain of Youth: Slowing the Aging Process. (Illus.). 308p. (Orig.). 1995. pap. 14.95 (*0-9643754-0-0*) Ridgeback Pr.
Redmond, Tim & Mason, John. Words of Promise for Leaders. 160p. 1997. pap. 6.99 (*1-56292-370-6*) Honor Bks OK.
Redmond, Tony. All-in-One: Managing & Programming in Version 3.0. LC 92-27295. (All-in-One Ser.). (Illus.). 552p. 1992. pap. text 62.95 (*1-55558-101-3*, EYM522EDP, Digital DEC) Buttrwrth-Heinemann.
— Microsoft Exchange Server. 1996. pap. 36.95 (*0-614-20270-1*, Digital DEC) Buttrwrth-Heinemann.
— Microsoft Exchange Server 5.5: Planning, Design & Implementation. LC 98-21457. 685p. 1998. pap. 54.95 (*1-55558-213-3*) DEC.
***Redmond, Tony.** Microsoft Exchange Server for Windows 2000: Planning, Design & Implementation. 656p. 2000. pap. 49.95 (*1-55558-224-9*, Digital DEC) Buttrwrth-Heinemann.
Redmond, Tony. Microsoft Exchange Server V5.0: Planning, Design & Implementation. LC 97-19416. 640p. 1997. pap. text 52.95 (*1-55558-189-7*, Digital DEC) Buttrwrth-Heinemann.
Redmond, W. B. A Bibliography of the Philosophy in the Iberian Colonies of America. (International Archives of the History of Ideas Ser.: No. 51). 188p. 1972. lib. bdg. 106.00 (*90-247-1190-8*) Kluwer Academic.
Redmond, William H. & Scott, A. Floyd. Atlas of Amphibians in Tennessee. LC 96-85311. (Illus.). 90p. (Orig.). 1996. pap. 7.50 (*1-880617-05-6*) APSU Ctr Fld Bio.
***Redmonds, George.** Stock Market Operators. (Investment Greats Ser.). 288p. 2000. 29.00 (*0-273-64311-8*) F T P H.
Redmont, Bernard S. Risks Worth Taking: The Odyssey of a Foreign Correspondent. 264p. (C). 1992. pap. text 29.50 (*0-8191-8852-2*); lib. bdg. 57.00 (*0-8191-8797-6*) U Pr of Amer.
***Redmont, Jane.** Believing Women: The Witness of Women in the Church. 280p. 2000. pap. 12.95 (*1-58051-079-5*) Sheed & Ward WI.
Redmont, Jane. Generous Lives: American Catholic Women Today. LC 93-15400. 384p. 1993. reprint ed. pap. text 14.95 (*0-89243-576-3*, Liguori Triumph) Liguori Pubns.
— When in Doubt, Sing: Experiencing Prayer in Everyday Life. LC 98-11849. 448p. 1999. 25.00 (*0-06-017439-0*) HarpC.
Redmont, P. W. Mercantile Law. 296p. (C). 1989. 80.00 (*0-7855-4633-2*, Pub. by Inst Pur & Supply) St Mut.
Redmore, G. B. Under the Southern Cross: South America, Australia, Africa. (Life & Livelihood Geographies Ser.: Bk. 2). (Illus.). pap. 8.95 (*0-685-20646-7*) Transatl Arts.
Redmount, R. S., et al. Grievance-Response Mechanisms in the Ghetto. LC 74-151046. (Symposia on Law & Society Ser.). 1971. reprint ed. lib. bdg. 19.50 (*0-306-70117-0*) Da Capo.
Redmount, Robert. The Red Sox Encyclopedia. (Illus.). 400p. 1998. 39.95 (*1-58261-012-6*) Sports Pub.
***Redmount, Robert.** The Red Sox Encyclopedia: Second Edition. 2nd ed. (Illus.). 320p. 2000. 39.95 (*1-58261-244-7*) Sports Pub.
Rednap, Mark. Artifacts from Wrecks. 1997. 68.00 (*1-900188-39-2*) Oxbow Bks.
Rednaur, Shar, ed. Virgin Territory. (Orig.). 1996. pap. 12.95 (*1-56333-457-7*, R Kasak Bks) Masquerade.
Redner, Harry. Malign Masters 20th Century. LC 96-37665. 240p. 1997. text 55.00 (*0-312-17324-5*) St Martin.
***Redner, Morton.** Getting Out. 1999. pap. 9.98 (*0-671-77507-3*, Pocket Books) PB.
***Redner, Shar.** The Femme's Guide to the Universe. 2000. pap. 14.95 (*1-55583-461-2*, Pub. by Alyson Pubns) Consort Bk Sales.

An Asterisk (*) at the beginning of an entry indicates that the title is appearing for the first time.

***Rednour, Shar, ed.** Starf*cker: A Twisted Collection of Superstar Fantasies. 304p. 2001. pap. 12.95 (*1-55583-516-3*, Pub. by Alyson Pubns) Consort Bk Sales.

Rednour, Shar, ed. Virgin Territory 2. (Orig.). 1997. pap. 12.95 (*1-56333-506-9*, R Kasak Bks) Masquerade.

Redo. Haikus to Fool With. 24p. 1998. pap. 4.95 (*1-893084-05-1*) Benway Inst.

Redo, jt. illus. see Cook, Joie.

***Redon, Odile.** Medieval Kitchen. (Illus.). 2000. pap. 18.00 (*0-226-70685-0*) U Ch Pr.

Redon, Odile, et al. The Medieval Kitchen: Recipes from France & Italy. Schneider, Edward, tr. from ENG. LC 97-31785. (Illus.). 348p. (ps). 1998. 32.50 (*0-226-70684-2*) U Ch Pr.

Redon, Odilon. To Myself: Notes on Life, Art, & Artists. Jacob, Mira & Wasserman, Jeanne L., trs. from FRE. 144p. 1996. pap. 14.95 (*0-8076-1146-8*) Braziller.

Redondi, Pietro, ed. Science: The Renaissance of a History: (Proceedings of the International Conference, Paris, June 1986), Vol. 4, No. 1-4. (History & Technology Ser.: Vol. 4, Nos. 1-4). iv, 582p. 1987. pap. text 237.00 (*3-7186-0441-8*) Gordon & Breach.

Redondi, Pietro & Fox, R., eds. French Institutions from the Revolution to the Restoration. (Special Issue of the Journal History & Technology Ser.: Vol. 5, Nos. 2-4). 230p. (C). 1988. pap. text 380.00 (*3-7186-4845-8*) Gordon & Breach.

Redondo, Jesus. Hereos & Villians Coloring Book, 1. 1999. pap. 2.99 (*0-375-80021-2*) Random.

***Redondo, Jesus.** Learning Word Sounds: Kindergarten. (Star Wars). 16p. (J). (ps-2). 1999. pap., wbk. ed. 4.99 (*0-375-80005-0*, Pub. by Random Bks Yng Read) Random.

— Writing Letters A to Z: Preschool - Kindergarten. (Star Wars). 16p. (J). (ps-2). 1999. pap., wbk. ed. 4.99 (*0-375-80006-9*, Pub. by Random Bks Yng Read) Random.

***Redondo, Jesuss.** Simple Adding & Subtracting. (Star Wars). 16p. (J). (ps-2). 1999. pap. 4.99 (*0-375-80003-4*, Pub. by Random Bks Yng Read) Random.

Redondo, Santiago, et al, eds. Advances in Psychology & Law: International Contributions. LC 97-22521. 542p. 1997. 132.00 (*3-11-015615-6*) De Gruyter.

Redondo, Susana. Vest Pocket Spanish. LC 89-15369. (ENG & SPA.). 1986. pap. 5.95 (*0-8489-5101-8*) Inst Lang Study.

Redonnet, Marie. Candy Story. Quinn, Alexandra, tr. LC 95-10304. (European Women Writers Ser.). v, 99p. 1995. pap. 10.00 (*0-8032-8958-8*) U of Nebr Pr.

— Forever Valley. Stump, Jordan, tr. LC 94-1315. (European Women Writers Ser.). v, 117p. 1994. pap. 10.00 (*0-8032-8951-0*, Bison Books) U of Nebr Pr.

— Hotel Splendid. Stump, Jordan, tr. LC 94-1314. (European Women Writers Ser.). ix, 117p. 1994. pap. 10.00 (*0-8032-8953-7*, Bison Books) U of Nebr Pr.

— Mobie-Diq. McGillicuddy, Dan, tr. from FRE. LC 95-71282. 96p. (Orig.). 1995. pap. 10.95 (*0-9648671-0-9*) DM Pubng.

— Nevermore. Stump, Jordon, tr. LC 96-1288. (European Women Writers Ser.). vi, 125p. 1996. pap. 12.00 (*0-8032-8959-6*, Bison Books) U of Nebr Pr.

— Nevermore. Stump, Jordan, tr. & intro. by. LC 96-1288. (European Women Writers Ser.). vi, 125p. 1996. text 40.00 (*0-8032-3912-2*) U of Nebr Pr.

— Rose Mellie Rose. Stump, Jordan, tr. LC 94-1313. (European Women Writers Ser.). vii, 123p. 1994. pap. 10.00 (*0-8032-8952-9*, Bison Books) U of Nebr Pr.

Redor, Dominique. Wage Inequalities in East & West. (Illus.). 230p. (C). 1993. text 59.95 (*0-521-39531-3*) Cambridge U Pr.

Redoseyev, P. Marxist Philosophy & Our Time. (Social Science Today Problems of the Contemporary World Ser.: No.109). 256p. 1983. pap. 30.00 (*0-7855-1231-4*, Pub. by Collets) St Mut.

Redoute, Pierre J. Les Roses. cd-rom 50.00 (*1-891788-28-0*, 28-0) Octavo Corp.

Redoute, Pierre-Joseph. Lilies & Related Flowers. LC 81-11021. (Illus.). 240p. 1982. 65.00 (*0-87951-135-4*, Pub. by Overlook Pr) Penguin Putnam.

***Redoute, Pierre-Joseph.** Redoute Lilies. (Illus.). 2000. 39.99 (*3-8228-6407-2*) Taschen Amer.

Redoute, Pierre-Joseph. Redoute Rose Prints. (Illus.). 1990. pap. 3.95 (*0-486-26270-7*) Dover.

***Redoute, Pierre-Joseph.** Redoute Rose Stained Glass Coloring Book. (Illus.). (J). 1999. pap. 4.95 (*0-486-40807-8*) Dover.

— Redoute Rose Stickers: 16 Pressure-Sensitive Designs. (Illus.). (J). 1992. pap. 1.00 (*0-486-27140-4*) Dover.

***Redoute, Pierre-Joseph.** Roses. 1999. 39.99 (*3-8228-6629-6*) Benedikt Taschen.

Redoute, Pierre-Joseph. Roses. Hinz, Petra-Andrea & Schulz, Barbara, eds. (Illus.). 256p. 1999. 39.99 (*3-8228-6528-1*) Taschen Amer.

Redpath, Alan. The Bible Speaks to Our Times: The Christian's Victory in Christ. (Alan Redpath Library). 128p. (gr. 11). 1993. reprint ed. pap. 9.99 (*0-8007-5492-1*) Revell.

— The Making of a Man of God: Studies in the Life of David. LC 62-10731. (Alan Redpath Library). 256p. (gr. 10). 1994. reprint ed. pap. 11.99 (*0-8007-5516-2*) Revell.

Redpath, Henry A., jt. auth. see Hatch, Edwin.

Redpath, James. Echoes of Harper's Ferry. LC 77-82215. (Anti-Slavery Crusade in America Ser.). 1970. reprint ed. 23.95 (*0-405-00654-3*) Ayer.

— Public Life of Captain John Brown. LC 79-126251. (Select Bibliographies Reprint Ser.). 1977. 34.95 (*0-8369-5478-5*) Ayer.

— The Roving Editor, Or, Talks with Slaves in the Southern States. McKivigan, John R., ed. LC 95-31729. 328p. 1996. 45.00 (*0-271-01532-2*) Pa St U Pr.

— The Roving Editor, Or, Talks with Slaves in the Southern States. McKivigan, John R., ed. LC 95-31729. (Illus.). 328p. 1996. pap. 16.95 (*0-271-01533-0*) Pa St U Pr.

Redpath, James, jt. auth. see Proctor, George R.

Redpath, Peter, ed. From Twilight to Dawn: The Cultural Vision of Jacques Maritain. LC 90-50611. 320p. (C). 1991. pap. text 17.50 (*0-268-00979-1*) U of Notre Dame Pr.

Redpath, Peter A. Help Me! My Child Is Missing! LC 84-71207. 106p. (Orig.). 1985. pap. 9.95 (*0-936049-00-6*) Child Savers.

— A Simplified Introduction to the Wisdom of St. Thomas. LC 80-5230. 180p. 1980. pap. text 21.00 (*0-8191-1059-0*) U Pr of Amer.

Redpath, Peter A., ed. see Crowley, Charles B.

Redpath, Philip. William Golding: A Structural Reading of His Fiction. LC 86-10710. 224p. 1986. 58.50 (*0-389-20647-4*, N8204) B&N Imports.

Redpath, S. M., et al, eds. Birds of Prey & Red Grouse. LC 98-122663. 148p. 1997. 45.00 (*0-11-702176-8*, Pub. by Statnry Office) Balogh.

Redshaw, Dai, jt. auth. see Dawber, Keith.

Redshaw, David. In a Mist. 186p. (Orig.). 1996. mass mkt. 7.95 (*1-56201-062-X*) Blue Moon Bks.

Redshaw, Mavis, jt. ed. see Orville-Thomas, W. J.

Redshaw, Peggy A., jt. ed. see Lincecum, Jerry B.

Redshaw, S. C., jt. auth. see Rushton, K. R.

Redshaw, Thomas D., jt. auth. see Montague, John.

Redshaw, Tom. Site Agent's Handbook: Construction under the Ice Conditions. 183p. 1990. text 58.50 (*0-7277-1540-2*, Pub. by T Telford) RCH.

Redsicker, David R. The Practical Methodology of Forensic Photography. 304p. 1992. boxed set 69.95 (*0-8493-9519-4*) CRC Pr.

Redsicker, David R. The Practical Methodology of Forensic Photography. 2nd ed. (Practical Aspects of Criminal & Forensic Investigation Ser.). 328p. ring bd. 79.95 (*0-8493-2004-6*) CRC Pr.

Redsicker, David R., ed. The Practical Methodology of Forensic Photography. (Illus.). 292p. 1991. 44.95 (*0-444-01597-3*, TR822) CRC Pr.

Redsicker, David R. & O'Connor, John J. Practical Fire & Arson Investigation. 2nd ed. LC 97-16777. (Practical Aspects of Criminal & Forensics Investigations Ser.). (Illus.). 432p. 1996. boxed set 74.95 (*0-8493-8155-X*, 8155) CRC Pr.

Redslob, Edwin. Schicksal und Dichtung: Goethe Aufsaetze Ed. by Wieland Schmidt. (GER.). 145p. 1985. 63.10 (*3-11-010472-5*) De Gruyter.

Redstone, Lilian J., ed. Parish of All Hallows Barking Pt. 1: The Parish Church. LC 74-138273. (London County Council. Survey of London Ser.: No. 12). reprint ed. 84.50 (*0-404-51662-9*, DA685) AMS Pr.

Redstone, Louis G. Louis G. Redstone: From Israeli Pioneer to American Architect. LC 89-11119. (Illus.). 206p. 1989. reprint ed. pap. 63.90 (*0-608-00142-2*, 206092300006) Bks Demand.

***Redstone, P. G.** When the Moon Comes over the Mountain. Ricotta, Kimberly, ed. Orig. Title: Federation. (Illus.). 244p. 2000. pap. 12.95 (*0-9673590-0-7*) Dansing Hrt.

Redverse-Mutton, Anthony. Plastics & Additives in Plastics in Europe. LC 98-120918. (Report Ser.: No. P-163). 163p. 1997. 3350.00 (*1-56965-274-0*, P-163) BCC.

Redway, A. R., jt. auth. see Brennan, Neil.

Redway, Jacques W. Making of the Empire State. 263p. 1993. reprint ed. lib. bdg. 79.00 (*0-7812-5196-6*) Rprt Serv.

Redway, Kathryn. Be a Rapid Reader. (Here's How Ser.). 112p. 1999. pap. 8.95 (*0-8442-2943-1*) NTC Contemp Pub Co.

— How to Be a Rapid Reader. LC 90-62788. (Illus.). 112p. 1995. pap. 7.95 (*0-8442-5174-7*, 51747, Natl Textbk Co) NTC Contemp Pub Co.

Redwine, Carole C. Basic Research Skills: A Review Handbook. 58p. (Orig.). (C). 1994. pap. text 6.00 (*0-87563-498-2*) Stipes.

Redwine, Cooper. Upgrading to FORTRAN 90. LC 95-12917. (Illus.). 416p. 1995. 44.95 (*0-387-97995-6*) Spr-Verlag.

Redwine, Mary F. Substitute Teacher's Handbook: Activities & Projects for Kindergarten Through Grade Six. 1970. pap. 6.99 (*0-8224-6600-7*) Fearon Teacher Aids.

Redwine, Robert P., jt. auth. see Enge, Harald A.

Redwood, Christopher. Delius Companion. 1991. pap. 11.95 (*0-7145-3826-4*) Riverrun NY.

Redwood, Daniel. Contemporary Chiropractic. LC 97-18583. 1997. text 43.00 (*0-443-07809-2*) Church.

— Edgar Cayce's Holistic Health Program. (Good Health Guides Ser.). 48p. 1996. pap. 3.95 (*0-87983-661-X*, 3661XK, Keats Publng) NTC Contemp Pub Co.

Redwood, John. The Death of Britain. LC 99-12709. 1999. text 65.00 (*0-312-22193-2*) St Martin.

Redwood, John. Our Currency, Our Country. LC 98-115526. 240p. pap. 15.95 (*0-14-026523-6*, Pub. by Pnguin Bks Ltd) Trafalgar.

Redwood, John, 3rd. World Bank Approaches to the Environment in Brazil. LC 93-14544. (Operations Evaluation Studies). 90p. 1993. pap. 22.00 (*0-8213-2511-6*, 12511) World Bank.

Redwood, John H. The Old Settler. 1998. pap. 5.25 (*0-8222-1642-6*) Dramatists Play.

Redwood, Ray. QTC: I Have a Message for You. Noe, Tom, ed. LC 88-90627. (Illus.). 376p. (Orig.). 1989. 15.00 (*0-945845-00-6*); pap. 9.95 (*0-945845-01-4*) Sequoia Pr TX.

Redwood, Rosaline. He Was There, Too: Reminiscences of a Christian Journalist. LC 98-90445. 1999. pap. 17.95 (*0-533-12810-2*) Vantage.

— On Copra Ships & Coral Isles. large type ed. 352p. 1992. 27.99 (*0-7089-2614-2*) Ulverscroft.

— Stranger from Shanghai. large type ed. (Linford Mystery Library). 384p. 1992. pap. 16.99 (*0-7089-7218-7*) Ulverscroft.

Redwood, Shawn. C' Est Facile! French Grammar Made Simple. 128p. 1999. pap. 14.00 (*0-8059-4501-6*) Dorrance.

***Redwood, Stephen, et al.** Action Management: Practical Strategies for Making Your Corporate Transformation a Success. LC 99-12823. 256p. 1999. 27.95 (*0-471-34547-4*) Wiley.

Ree. Lemon Twist: No Salt Added Cookbook. LC 87-92238. 204p. 1989. 19.45 (*0-929622-02-2*); pap. text 14.95 (*0-929622-00-6*) Nutrit Unltd Pubns.

Ree, jt. auth. see Meth-Cohn, K.

Ree, Erik Van, see Van Ree, Erik.

***Ree, Hans.** Human Comedy of Chess: Grandmaster's Chronicles. Tissot, Willem, tr. from DUT. LC 99-90790. Orig. Title: Schitterend Schaak. (Illus.). 334p. 2000. pap. 24.95 (*1-888690-06-2*) Russell Ent.

Ree, Harry. Educator Extraordinary: The Life & Achievement of Henry Morris, 1889-1961. 163p. 1985. pap. 19.95 (*0-7206-0700-0*, Pub. by P Owen Ltd) Dufour.

Ree, Jim. Cultural Renovation, the Start: The Book to Read. New Culture Club Staff, ed. (KOR., Illus.). 398p. (Orig.). 1997. pap. 15.00 (*0-9657434-1-1*) East West Inst.

Ree, Jonathan. Concise Encyclopedia of Western Philosophy & Philosophers. 3rd ed. Urmson, J. O., ed. 256p. (C). 1990. text 44.95 (*0-685-46018-5*); pap. text 16.95 (*0-685-46019-3*) Routledge.

***Ree, Jonathan.** I See a Voice: Deafness, Language & the Senses--A Philosophical History. (Illus.). 416p. 2000. pap. 16.00 (*0-8050-6255-6*) H Holt & Co.

— I See a Voice: Deafness, Language, & the Senses-A Philosophical History. LC 99-29061. (Illus.). 400p. 1999. 27.50 (*0-8050-6254-8*) H Holt & Co.

— Kierkegaard Biography. 2001. text 30.00 (*0-8050-6256-4*) St Martin.

Ree, Jonathan. Proletarian Philosophers: Problems in Socialist Culture in Britain, 1900-1940. (Illus.). 182p. (C). 1984. text 39.95 (*0-19-827261-8*) OUP.

***Ree, Jonathan.** Witcraft. 2000. text 25.00 (*0-8050-6257-2*) St Martin.

Ree, Jonathan & Chamberlain, Jane. Kierkegaard: A Critical Reader. LC 97-22299. (Critical Readers Ser.). 208p. (C). 1997. text 57.95 (*0-631-20198-X*); pap. text 26.95 (*0-631-20199-8*) Blackwell Pubs.

Ree, Jonathan, jt. ed. see Chamberlain, Jane.

Ree, Jonathan, ed. see Sartre, Jean-Paul.

Ree, Jonathan, jt. ed. see Urmson, J. O.

Ree, Jonathan, tr. see Hountondji, Paulin J.

Reeb, E. A., ed. & tr. see Lull, Ramon, pseud.

Reeb, Richard H. Taking Journalism Seriously: "Objectivity" As a Partisan Cause. LC 98-31011. 340p. 1999. 49.00 (*0-7618-1275-X*); pap. 27.50 (*0-7618-1276-8*) U Pr of Amer.

Reeb, William A. Start Consulting: How to Walk the Talk. Winters, Stephen L. & Winters, Stanley E., eds. LC 98-7431. (Illus.). 550p. 1998. pap. 44.00 (*0-87051-206-4*, 090439) Am Inst CPA.

Reebenacker, Noel. From the Blind Side. (Illus.). xii, 347p. 1998. 21.00 (*0-9664284-0-4*) Franklin Pubg.

Reeber, Heather. I Have a Story Just Like You. 1998. pap. 12.95 (*0-9656748-2-7*) Winter Again.

***Reece.** Reece Human Relations B. 4th ed. 1999. pap. text 25.77 (*0-395-96246-3*) HM.

***Reece, A. B. J. & Preston, T. W.** Finite Element Methods in Electrical Power Engineering. No. 46. (Illus.). 320p. 2000. text 95.00 (*0-19-856504-6*) OUP.

Reece, Albert E., et al. Handbook of Medicine of the Fetus & Mother. (Illus.). 512p. 1994. spiral bd. 52.00 (*0-397-51347-X*) Lppncott W & W.

Reece, Barry L. Effective Human Relations, 6 vols. (C). 1995. text, teacher ed., suppl. ed. 65.56 (*0-395-76570-6*) HM.

— Effective Human Relations, 6 vols. 6th ed. (C). 1995. pap. text, student ed. 19.96 (*0-395-74006-1*) HM.

— Human Relation B: Testbank, 3 vols. (C). 1996. pap., teacher ed. 11.96 (*0-395-79610-5*) HM.

— Human Relations, 2 vols. (C). 1994. pap., teacher ed. 3.96 (*0-395-68311-4*) HM.

— Human Relations, 3 vols. 3rd ed. (C). 1996. pap. text 27.96 (*0-395-79609-1*) HM.

Reece, Barry L. & Brandt, Rhonda. Effective Human Relations in Organizations, 4 vols. 4th ed. (C). 1989. student ed. 17.16 (*0-395-52991-3*) HM.

— Effective Human Relations in Organizations, 4 vols. 4th ed. (C). 1990. pap. text 3.96 (*0-395-52356-7*); 73.16 (*0-395-52993-X*) HM.

— Effective Human Relations in Organizations, 6 vols. 6th ed. 608p. (C). 1995. text 65.56 (*0-395-74005-3*) HM.

— Effective Human Relations in Organizations, 6 vols. 6th ed. (C). 1995. text, teacher ed. 11.96 (*0-395-74007-X*) HM.

***Reece, Barry L. & Brandt, Rhonda.** Effective Human Relations in Organizations. 7th ed. LC 98-72077. 533 p. 1999. text 55.77 (*0-395-90819-1*) HM.

Reece, Barry L. & Brandt, Rhonda. Human Relations: Principles & Practices, 2 vols. (C). 1993. pap. 27.96 (*0-395-52996-4*) HM.

Reece, Barry L., et al. Business, 2 vols. 2nd ed. (C). 1990. pap. text 5.16 (*0-395-52352-4*); 101.56 (*0-395-52952-2*) HM.

— Business, 2 vols. 2nd ed. (C). 1990. pap. text 5.56 (*0-395-52353-2*) HM.

Reece, Barry L., jt. auth. see Manning, Gerald L.

***Reece, Bob.** The Origins of Irish Convict Transportation to Australia. LC 00-27250. 308p. 2000. text 69.95 (*0-312-23211-X*) St Martin.

Reece, Byron H. Ballad of the Bones & Other Poems. LC 85-21338. 96p. 1985. reprint ed. 17.95 (*0-87797-100-5*) Cherokee.

— Better a Dinner of Herbs: A Novel by Byron Herbert Reece. LC 92-22952. (Brown Thrasher Bks.). 240p. 1992. reprint ed. pap. 16.00 (*0-8203-1489-7*) U of Ga Pr.

— Bow down in Jerico. LC 85-21335. 160p. 1985. reprint ed. 19.95 (*0-87797-102-1*) Cherokee.

— The Hawk & the Sun: A Novel. LC 85-2238. (Brown Thrasher Bks.). 200p. 1994. reprint ed. pap. 16.00 (*0-8203-1656-3*) U of Ga Pr.

— Season of Flesh. LC 85-21333. 96p. 1985. reprint ed. 17.95 (*0-87797-104-8*) Cherokee.

— Song of Joy & Other Poems. LC 85-22355. 128p. 1985. reprint ed. 18.95 (*0-87797-105-6*) Cherokee.

***Reece, Colleen.** Finding Your Way: Words of Wisdom for the Graduate. 40p. 2000. 1.99 (*1-57748-708-7*) Barbour Pub.

***Reece, Colleen L.** Come Home, Nurse Jenny. large type ed. LC 00-28681. 224p. 2000. 20.95 (*0-7862-2580-7*) Mac Lib Ref.

Reece, Colleen L. Everlasting Melody. large type ed. 192p. 1997. pap. 20.95 (*0-614-25139-7*, G K Hall Lrg Type) Mac Lib Ref.

— Everlasting Melody. large type ed. 1996. pap. 20.95 (*0-7862-0852-X*) Thorndike Pr.

***Reece, Colleen L.** Frontiers. 464p. 2000. pap. 4.97 (*1-57748-643-9*) Barbour Pub.

Reece, Colleen L. The Heritage of Nurse O'Hara. large type ed. LC 99-27127. 1999. pap. 18.95 (*0-7862-2033-3*) Mac Lib Ref.

***Reece, Colleen L.** In Search of Twilight LC 99-11205. 238 p. 1999. write for info. (*0-7540-3760-6*) Thorndike Pr.

Reece, Colleen L. In Search of Twilight. LC 99-11205. 1999. 19.95 (*0-7862-1872-X*) Mac Lib Ref.

— Mark of Our Moccasins. (Indian Culture Ser.). 45p. (J). (gr. 5-12). 1982. 5.95 (*0-89992-081-0*) Coun India Ed.

***Reece, Colleen L.** The Mayflower Adventure. (American Adventure Ser.: No. 1). (J). (gr. 3-6). 1998. 3.97 (*1-57748-059-7*) Barbour Pub.

Reece, Colleen L. The Mayflower Adventure. LC 98-7226. (American Adventure Ser.: No. 1). 144p. (J). (gr. 3-7). 1999. lib. bdg. 15.95 (*0-7910-5041-6*) Chelsea Hse.

— Mike. LC 96-119772. 96p. (J). (gr. 4-7). 1995. pap. 5.99 (*0-8280-0879-5*) Review & Herald.

— Mysterious Monday. (Juli Scott, Super Sleuth Ser.). 176p. (J). (gr. 4-10). 1997. pap. text 2.97 (*1-55748-983-1*) Barbour Pub.

***Reece, Colleen L.** Plymouth Pioneers. (American Adventure Ser.: No. 2). (J). (gr. 3-6). 1998. pap. 3.97 (*1-57748-060-0*) Barbour Pub.

Reece, Colleen L. Plymouth Pioneers. LC 98-7225. (American Adventure Ser.: No. 2). (Illus.). 142p. (J). (gr. 4-7). 1998. lib. bdg. 15.95 (*0-7910-5042-4*) Chelsea Hse.

— Saying Thank You. LC 82-21992. (Moods & Emotions Ser.). (Illus.). 32p. (J). (ps-2). 1982. lib. bdg. 21.36 (*0-89565-249-8*) Childs World.

***Reece, Colleen L.** Secrets of the Canyon. 1999. pap. write for info. (*0-8280-1389-6*) Review & Herald.

Reece, Colleen L. Thursday Trials. (Juli Scott, Super Sleuth Ser.: Bk. 4). 176p. (J). (gr. 4-10). 1998. pap. 2.97 (*1-57748-180-1*) Barbour Pub.

— Trouble on Tuesday. (Juli Scott, Super Sleuth Ser.). 176p. (J). (gr. 4-10). 1997. pap. text 2.97 (*1-55748-984-X*) Barbour Pub.

— Women of the Bible. unabridged ed. (Value Book Ser.: Vol. 4). 128p. 1996. mass mkt. 0.99 (*1-55748-817-7*) Barbour Pub.

— Writing Smarter, Not Harder: The Workbook Way. Lent, Penny, ed. (Illus.). 112p. (Orig.). 1995. pap. 13.95 (*1-885371-13-6*) Kldoscope Pr.

— Writing Smarter, Not Harder: The Workbook Way. Lent, Penny, ed. (Illus.). 80p. (J). (gr. 1-6). 1996. pap. 9.95 (*0-614-14790-5*) Kldoscope Pr.

***Reece, Colleen L.** Yellowstone Park Nurse. large type ed. LC 00-25937. (Paperback Ser.). 185p. 2000. pap. 23.95 (*0-7838-9024-9*, G K Hall Lrg Type) Mac Lib Ref.

Reece, Colleen L. & Donihue, Anita C. Apples for a Teacher: Lesson Plans for Life. LC 96-226201. 64p. 1996. 5.97 (*1-55748-780-4*) Barbour Pub.

— Joy to the World: A Treasury of Holiday Traditions, Stories, Prayers, Poetry, Recipes & More. (Illus.). 64p. 1996. 5.97 (*1-55748-849-5*) Barbour Pub.

***Reece, Colleen L. & Donihue, Anita C.** A Teacher's Heart: Thank You for Being My Teacher. LC 99-193267. 64p. (J). 1998. 5.97 (*1-57748-220-4*) Barbour Pub.

Reece, Colleen L. & Towns, Albert B. Crows' Nests & Mirrors. (Heartsong Ser.). 176p. 1994. pap. text 1.66 (*1-55748-466-X*) Barbour Pub.

Reece, Colleen L., et al. Inspirational Romance Reader Vol. 1: Historical Collection. unabridged ed. 500p. 1996. pap. 4.97 (*1-55748-796-0*) Barbour Pub.

— An Old-Fashioned Christmas. LC 98-101317. (Christmas Fiction Collection). 352p. 1997. pap. 4.97 (*1-57748-083-X*) Barbour Pub.

Reece, Connie. Holy Hatred: Militant Islam's War Against the West. 252p. 2000. pap. 10.99 (*0-7852-7499-5*) Nelson.

Reece, Connie, ed. see Hagee, John.

Reece, D. How to Do It. 3rd ed. 240p. 1995. pap. text 24.00 (*0-7279-0895-2*, Pub. by BMJ Pub) Login Brothers Bk Co.

Reece, D., ed. How to Do It. 3rd ed. 264p. 1995. pap. text 24.00 (*0-7279-0896-0*, Pub. by BMJ Pub) Login Brothers Bk Co.

— How to Do It, Vol. 1. 3rd ed. 272p. 1995. pap. text 24.00 (*0-7279-0848-0*, Pub. by BMJ Pub) Login Brothers Bk Co.

R

An Asterisk (*) at the beginning of an entry indicates that the title is appearing for the first time.

R

Reece, Debra. Make-Up Magic: A Complete Guide to a Beautiful New You. Settel, Trudy, ed. (Illus.). 64p. (Orig.). 1987. pap. 3.95 (*0-932523-01-3*) Briarcliff Pr.

Reece, E. Albert. Medicine of the Fetus & Mother. 1992. text 155.00 (*0-397-51339-9*) Lppncott W & W.

Reece, E. Albert & Coustan, Donald R., eds. Diabetes Mellitus in Pregnancy: Principles & Practice. (Illus.). 652p. 1988. text 105.00 (*0-443-08470-X*) Church.

— Diabetes Mellitus in Pregnancy: Principles & Practice. 2nd ed. LC 95-12415. 1995. text 96.00 (*0-443-08979-5*) Church.

Reece, E. Albert & Hobbins, John C. Medicine of the Fetus & Mother. 2nd ed. LC 98-29286. 1804p. 1998. text 149.00 (*0-397-51862-5*) Lppncott W & W.

Reece, E. Albert, et al. Fundamentals of Obstetric & Gynecologic Ultrasound. (Illus.). 272p. (C). 1994. pap. text 95.00 (*0-8385-9247-3*, A9247-6, Apple Lange Med) McGraw.

— Medicine of the Fetus & Mother. (Illus.). 1488p. 1992. text 145.00 (*0-397-51013-6*) Lppncott W & W.

— Review for Medicine of the Fetus & Mother. LC 92-25643. 210p. 1992. pap. text 19.95 (*0-397-51331-3*) Lppncott W & W.

Reece, Erik A. A Balance of Quinces: The Paintings & Drawings of Guy Davenport. LC 96-21805. (Illus.). 144p. (Orig.). 1996. pap. 25.00 (*0-8112-1336-6*, NDP813, Pub. by New Directions) Norton.

Reece, Gary T., jt. ed. see Schechter, Ellen M.

***Reece, Gary W.** Trauma, Loss & Bereavement: A Survivor's Handbook. 152p. 1999. pap. 17.00 (*1-57910-298-0*) Wipf & Stock.

Reece, Gerow, tr. see Kawai, Hayao.

Reece, Helen, jt. auth. see Freeman, Michael.

Reece, Ira T. Homicide - Index of Modern Authors & Subjects with Guide for Rapid Research. LC 90-56268. 200p. 1991. 47.50 (*1-55914-304-5*); pap. 44.50 (*1-55914-305-3*) ABBE Pubs Assn.

— Prisoners: Health & Medical Subject Analysis with Reference Bibliography. LC 85-48088. 150p. 1987. 47.50 (*0-88164-448-X*); pap. 44.50 (*0-88164-449-8*) ABBE Pubs Assn.

Reece, J. McGee, jt. auth. see Metzger, Walter P.

Reece, James S., et al. Accounting Principles. 6th ed. 440p. (C). 1992. text, wbk. ed. 29.37 (*0-256-13496-0*, Irwn McGrw-H) McGrw-H Hghr Educ.

Reece, Jane B., et al. The Soul Unbound: The Photographs of Jane Reece. LC 94-72369. 185p. 1997. write for info. (*0-937809-13-6*) Dayton Art.

Reece, June E. Jimmy & the Sun Drop. (Illus.). 24p. (Orig.). (J). (ps-3). 1992. pap. 3.50 (*0-9631934-0-6*) Sun Drop.

Reece, Katherine E., jt. auth. see Frascona, Oliver E.

Reece, Kim T. Kim Taylor Reece: Images of Hawaii's Ancient Hula. Chun, Kanoenani, ed. LC 98-206647. 176p. 1997. 49.95 (*0-9660395-9-9*) K T Reece.

Reece, Laurence H., III. Negotiating, Drafting & Enforcing Noncompetition Agreements: Includes Forms on Disk. Gill, Laurie S., ed. LC 97-70626. 112p. 1997. pap. text 59.00 incl. disk (*1-57589-063-1*, 97-04.40-QC) Mass CLE.

***Reece, Laurence H., III.** Protecting Trade Secrets. LC 97-76383. 138p. 1998. write for info. (*1-57589-080-1*) Mass CLE.

Reece, Linda W. Women of Oklahoma, 1890-1920. LC 97-7549. (Illus.). xviii, 366p. 1997. 28.95 (*0-8061-2955-7*) U of Okla Pr.

Reece, Louise. Thank You Lord. (Illus.). 164p. (Orig.). 1983. pap. 3.95 (*0-9614264-0-3*) Lovejoy Pr.

Reece, Marshall P. The Kansas Legislature: Structure & Process. 241p. 1992. spiral bd. 10.00 (*0-614-13969-4*) U of KS Cont Ed.

Reece, Nancy S., ed. see Mitchell, Richard L.

Reece-Podgorski, Ashley. Ultimate Performance System. LC 94-90309. 270p. 1993. 24.99 (*0-9644303-0-4*) Ultimate Perf.

— Ultimate Performance System II. LC 94-90308. 344p. (C). 1994. 44.95 (*0-9644303-1-2*) Ultimate Perf.

Reece, Ray. The Sun Betrayed: A Report on the Corporate Seizure of U. S. Solar Energy Development. LC 79-66992. 234p. 1979. 35.00 (*0-89608-072-2*); pap. 7.50 (*0-89608-071-4*) South End Pr.

— Sun Betrayed: A Study of the Corporate Seizure of Solar Energy Development. 234p. write for info. (*0-919618-08-1*); pap. write for info. (*0-919618-07-3*) Black Rose.

Reece, Regina, ed. see Chase, H. Peter.

Reece, Richard. Coinage in Roman Britain. (Illus.). 144p. 1987. lib. bdg. 45.00 (*0-900652-86-1*) S J Durst.

— Cotswold Studies Vol. II: Excavations, Survey & Records Around Cirencester. (Illus.). 128p. 1990. pap. 16.00 (*0-905853-26-1*) David Brown.

***Reece, Richard.** The Later Roman Empire. (Illus.). 208p. 1999. 32.50 (*0-7524-1449-6*, Pub. by Tempus Pubng) Arcadia Publng.

Reece, Richard. My Roman Britain. 164p. 1988. pap. 14.00 (*0-905853-21-0*) David Brown.

— Roman Coins from 140 Sites in Britain. (Illus.). 107p. 1991. pap. 18.00 (*1-873132-20-4*) David Brown.

Reece, Richard & James, Simon. Identifying Roman Coins. (Illus.). 48p. 1994. lib. bdg. 22.00 (*0-900652-79-9*) S J Durst.

Reece, Robert D. & Siegel, Harvey A. Studying People: A Primer in the Ethnics of Social Research. LC 86-18059. 272p. (Orig.). 1986. 29.95 (*0-86554-220-1*, H198); pap. 18.75 (*0-86554-221-X*, MUP/P028) Mercer Univ Pr.

Reece, Robert H. Night Bombing with the Bedouins. (Great War Ser.: No. 12). (Illus.). 120p. 1991. reprint ed. 29.95 (*0-89839-161-X*) Battery Pr.

Reece, Robert M. Child Abuse: Medical Diagnosis & Management. (Illus.). 466p. 1994. text 72.00 (*0-8121-1498-1*) Lppncott W & W.

***Reece, Robert M.** Treatment of Child Abuse: Common Ground for Mental Health, Medical & Legal Practitioners. LC 99-48750. 2000. 65.00 (*0-8018-6320-1*) Johns Hopkins.

Reece, Robert M., ed. Manual of Emergency Pediatrics. 4th ed. (Illus.). 586p. 1992. pap. text 69.00 (*0-7216-3289-0*, W B Saunders Co) Harcrt Hlth Sci Grp.

Reece, Robert M. & Ludwig, Stephen. Child Abuse: Medical Diagnosis & Management. 2nd ed. 500p. text 79.95 (*0-7817-2444-9*) Lppncott W & W.

***Reece, Rolland.** Pastoral Prayers for All Seasons. 2000. pap. 17.25 (*0-7880-1567-2*) CSS OH.

Reece, Sachiko, tr. see Kawai, Hayao.

Reece, Stephen. The Bear in the Air Scare. (Illus.). 12p. (J). (ps-3). 1998. pap. 2.95 (*1-892388-00-6*) Lttle Trucker.

— The Bedbugs Save Sidney. (Illus.). 16p. (J). (ps-3). 1998. pap. 3.65 (*1-892388-07-3*) Lttle Trucker.

— Bubblebath & the Christmas Truck. (Illus.). 12p. (J). (ps-3). 1998. pap. 3.65 (*1-892388-06-5*) Lttle Trucker.

— Little Trucker Books, Series One, 3 vols. (Illus.). 40p. (J). (ps-3). 1998. pap. 7.95 (*1-892388-03-0*) Lttle Trucker.

— Little Trucker Books, Series Two, 3 vols. (Illus.). 40p. (J). (ps-5). 1998. pap. 7.95 (*1-892388-04-9*) Lttle Trucker.

— The Little Trucker Counting Book. 16p. (J). (ps-3). 1998. pap. 3.65 (*1-892388-01-4*) Lttle Trucker.

— Mudflap & Logjam to the Rescue. (Illus.). 12p. (J). (ps-3). 1998. pap. 3.65 (*1-892388-05-7*) Lttle Trucker.

— My Dad Drives a Big Truck. (Illus.). 12p. (J). (ps-3). 1998. pap. 2.95 (*1-892388-02-2*) Lttle Trucker.

Reece, Steve. The Stranger's Welcome: Oral Theory & the Aesthetics of the Homeric Hospitality Scene. (Monographs in Classical Antiquity). 272p. (C). 1993. text 47.50 (*0-472-10386-5*, 10386) U of Mich Pr.

***Reece, Terence & Bird, David.** Bridge: The Modern Game. 192p. 1999. pap. 14.95 (*0-7090-6179-X*, Pub. by R Hale Ltd) Seven Hills Bk.

Reece, Trevor. Model Radio Control Yachts. (Illus.). 176p. 1989. pap. 24.50 (*0-85242-972-X*, Pub. by Nexus Special Interests) Trans-Atl Phila.

Reece, Trudy, jt. auth. see Pritikin, Enid.

Reece, William O. Physiology of Domestic Animals. LC 90-5543. (Illus.). 372p. 1990. pap. text 39.50 (*0-8121-1307-1*) Lppncott W & W.

— Physiology of Domestic Animals. 2nd ed. LC 96-18088. (Illus.). 464p. 1997. 44.95 (*0-683-07240-4*) Lppncott W & W.

Reece, William O., jt. ed. see Swenson, Melvin J.

Reecher, David, ed. see Sackheim, Maxwell.

Reeck, Karen Ann L., ed. see Rollins, Pamela L.

Reed. Cognition-Theory & Application. (Psychology). 1982. teacher ed. write for info. (*0-534-03430-6*) Wadsworth Pub.

— Cognitive Skills: Theory & Applications. 5th ed. LC 99-50364. 480p. 1999. 85.95 (*0-534-35641-9*) Thomson Learn.

— Equine Internal Medicine. LC 95-48272. 1997. text 135.00 (*0-7216-3524-5*, W B Saunders Co) Harcrt Hlth Sci Grp.

— Graceland Book Club. 2000. 45.00 (*0-00-255448-8*) HarperTrade.

— Hometown Rumble. Date not set. write for info. (*0-465-06891-X*) HarpC.

— Implementing Directory. 1999. 50.00 (*0-07-134409-8*) McGraw.

— In the Classroom. 3rd ed. LC 97-29578. 1997. boxed set (*0-697-29880-9*, WCB McGr Hill) McGrw-H Hghr Educ.

— In the Classroom. 3rd ed. LC 98-132064. 1997. (*0-697-29882-5*, WCB McGr Hill) McGrw-H Hghr Educ.

— Keeping the Faith: The Can-Do Spirit of Modern America. 1996. 25.00 (*0-02-874106-4*) Free Pr.

— Money & the Global Economy. 1998. ring bd. 99.95 (*0-8493-0552-7*) CRC Pr.

— Money & the Global Economy. 1998. boxed set 120.00 (*1-85573-411-7*, Pub. by Woodhead Pubng) Am Educ Systs.

— Nurse Education: A Practice-Reflective Based Approach. 216p. 1993. pap. 51.50 (*1-56593-212-9*, 0540) Singular Publishing.

— Nutrition. Date not set. pap. text, teacher ed. write for info. (*0-314-53518-7*) West Pub.

— Practical Skills in Biomolecular Sciences. 328p. (C). 1998. pap. text 64.00 (*0-582-29826-1*) Longman.

— Race in Post White America. 1999. write for info. (*0-201-62464-8*) Addison-Wesley.

— Schubert. 2nd ed. LC 96-34211. (Dent Master Musicians Ser.). (Illus.). 286p. (C). 1997. pap. text 16.95 (*0-19-816494-7*) OUP.

— William James: A Biography. pap. text. write for info. (*0-7167-2942-3*) W H Freeman.

Reed, ed. Multicultural Literature Anthology. (C). 1999. text. write for info. (*0-321-01055-8*) Addson-Wesley Educ.

Reed & Levine, eds. Locating the Transference: Actuality & Illusion in the Psychoanalytic Encounter. (Psychoanalytic Inquiry Ser.: Vol. 13, No. 4). 1993. 20.00 (*0-88163-941-9*) Analytic Pr.

Reed & Woerner. Software Radios. 1999. text 77.28 (*0-13-081158-0*) P-H.

Reed, jt. ed. see Levine.

Reed, A. Unmanned Aircraft. 110p. 1979. 35.95 (*0-08-027026-3*, Pergamon Pr) Elsevier.

Reed, A. D. & Reed, D. C. Devereux: Genealogy of Arthur Forrester Devereux & His Family. 146p. 1997. reprint ed. pap. 21.00 (*0-8328-8284-4*); reprint ed. lib. bdg. 31.00 (*0-8328-8283-6*) Higginson Bk Co.

— Devereux: Genealogy of Reuben Devereus of the 58th Generation of the Devereux Family. 149p. 1997. reprint ed. pap. 22.00 (*0-8328-8282-8*); reprint ed. lib. bdg. 32.00 (*0-8328-8281-X*) Higginson Bk Co.

***Reed, A. W.** Aboriginal Myths, Legends & Fables. LC 99-487900. 2000. pap. 16.95 (*1-876334-29-0*, Pub. by New Holland) BHB Intl.

— Aboriginal Stories. 2000. pap. 18.95 (*1-876334-34-7*, Pub. by New Holland) BHB Intl.

Reed, Abigail. Choices: A Novel. 1999. mass mkt. 6.99 (*0-8125-4528-1*, Pub. by Forge NYC) St Martin.

***Reed, Abigail.** Under Pressure. 2000. mass mkt. 6.99 (*0-8125-3928-1*) Forge NYC.

Reed, Adele. Old Mammoth: A First Hand Account. Smith, Genny, ed. LC 82-60130. (Illus.). 200p. 1994. reprint ed. pap. 17.95 (*0-931378-04-4*) Live Oak.

Reed, Adolph, Jr. Class Notes: Posing as Politics & Other Thoughts on the American Scene. 256p. 2000. 25.00 (*1-56584-482-3*, Pub. by New Press NY) Norton.

— Stirrings in the Jug: Black Politics in the Post-Segregation Era. LC 99-27301. 288p. 1999. pap. 18.95 (*0-8166-2681-2*, Pub. by U of Minn Pr); lib. bdg. 47.95 (*0-8166-2680-4*, Pub. by U of Minn Pr) Chicago Distribution Ctr.

Reed, Adolph, Jr., ed. Race, Politics & Culture: Critical Essays on the Radicalism of the 1960s, 95. LC 85-27162. (Contributions in Afro-American & African Studies: No. 95). 299p. 1986. 65.00 (*0-313-24480-4*, RRA/, Greenwood Pr) Greenwood.

— Without Justice for All: The New Liberalism & Our Retreat from Racial Equality. LC 98-49324. 480p. 1999. text 25.00 (*0-8133-2050-X*, Pub. by Westview) HarpC.

Reed, Adolph L., Jr. W. E. B. Du Bois & American Political Thought: Fabianism & the Color Line. LC 96-847. 296p. 1997. 45.00 (*0-19-505174-2*) OUP.

— W. E. B. Du Bois & American Political Thought: Fabianism & the Color Line. 296p. 1999. pap. 17.95 (*0-19-513098-7*) OUP.

Reed, Alan, ed. The Fact of Blackness: Frantz Fanon & Visual Representation. LC 96-11416. (Illus.). 212p. 1996. pap. 18.95 (*0-941920-43-7*) Bay Pr.

Reed, Alan, Sr., jt. auth. see Mayss, Abla.

Reed, Alan, Sr., jt. auth. see Mayss, Abla J.

Reed, Alan B. Collector's Encyclopedia of Pickard China. 216p. 1995. 29.95 (*0-89145-646-5*, 3964) Collector Bks.

Reed, Albert, tr. see Biorklund, Elis.

Reed, Alette E., ed. Drafting Wills & Trusts in Massachusetts, 1998 Supplement. LC 89-64081. 1998. ring bd. 59.95 (*1-57589-087-9*, 97-08.18-SP) Mass CLE.

Reed, Alette E., et al. Drafting Wills & Trusts in Massachusetts. LC 89-64081. 450p. 1990. ring bd. 95.00 (*0-944490-17-4*) Mass CLE.

— Drafting Wills & Trusts in Massachusetts, 1992. LC 89-64081. 1991. ring bd., suppl. ed. 24.50 (*0-944490-99-9*) Mass CLE.

— Drafting Wills & Trusts in Massachusetts, 1994. LC 94-78709. 1994. ring bd., suppl. ed. 34.50 incl. disk (*0-944490-70-0*) Mass CLE.

Reed, Alfred Z. Present-Day Law Schools in the United States & Canada. LC 75-22836. (America in Two Centuries Ser.). 1976. reprint ed. 51.95 (*0-405-07707-6*) Ayer.

— Present-Day Law Schools in the United States & Canada. LC 87-80146. (Historical Writings in Law & Jurisprudence Ser.: No. 12). xv, 508p. 1987. reprint ed. lib. bdg. 47.50 (*0-89941-546-6*, 305100) W S Hein.

— Territorial Basis of Government under the State Constitutions. LC 68-56685. (Columbia University. Studies in the Social Sciences: No. 106). reprint ed. 39.50 (*0-404-51106-6*) AMS Pr.

— Training for the Public Profession of the Law. LC 75-22837. (America in Two Centuries Ser.). 1976. reprint ed. 42.95 (*0-405-07708-4*) Ayer.

— Training for the Public Profession of the Law. Helmholz, R. H. & Reams, Bernard D., Jr., eds. LC 86-62932. (Historical Writings in Law & Jurisprudence Ser.: No. 2). xviii, 498p. 1986. reprint ed. lib. bdg. 47.50 (*0-89941-516-4*, 304520) W S Hein.

Reed, Allan P., ed. Clinical Cases in Anesthesia. 2nd ed. LC 94-23730. 1995. text 79.00 (*0-443-08899-3*) Church.

Reed, Allan P. & Kaplan, Joel A. Clinical Cases in Anesthesia. LC 89-17273. (Illus.). 350p. 1989. reprint ed. pap. 108.50 (*0-7837-9746-X*, 206047400005) Bks Demand.

Reed, Allen C. Grand Circle Adventure: The Story Behind the Scenery. Morales, Brigitte, tr. (GER., Illus.). 48p. (Orig.). 1994. pap. 8.95 (*0-88714-789-5*) KC Pubns.

— Grand Circle Adventure: The Story Behind the Scenery. LeBras, Yvon, tr. (FRE., Illus.). 48p. (Orig.). 1994. pap. 8.95 (*0-88714-790-9*) KC Pubns.

— Grand Circle Adventure: The Story Behind the Scenery. rev. ed. LC 94-75108. (Illus.). 48p. (Orig.). 1994. pap. 7.95 (*0-88714-082-3*) KC Pubns.

Reed, Alma. Jose Clemente Orozco. LC 76-6319. (Illus.). 272p. 1985. reprint ed. lib. bdg. 50.00 (*0-87817-204-1*) Hacker.

Reed, Alonzo & Kellogg, Brainerd. Higher Lessons in English. LC 87-4980. (American Linguistics, 1700-1900 Ser.). 336p. 1987. 50.00 (*0-8201-1422-7*) Schol Facsimiles.

Reed, Alvin, jt. ed. see Beougher, Timothy K.

Reed, Andrew & Herron, Jeffrey. Dan Screams. (Illus.). 64p. (Orig.). 1994. pap. 10.95 (*0-9633307-3-X*) Poets Farm Pr.

Reed, Ann, jt. auth. see Low, John.

***Reed, Archie.** Implementing Directory Services: Microsoft Active Directory Novell NDS, Netscape NDS, Cisco/Microsoft Directory-Enabled Networks. (Enterprise Computing Ser.). (Illus.). 752p. 2000. pap. 49.99 (*0-07-134408-X*) McGraw.

Reed, Arden, ed. Romanticism & Language. LC 84-45146. 327p. reprint ed. pap. 101.40 (*0-608-20939-2*, 207203800003) Bks Demand.

Reed, Arthea. Presenting Harry Mazer. large type ed. 1996. 28.00 (*0-8057-4512-2*, Twyne) Mac Lib Ref.

Reed, Arthea J. Comics to Classics: A Parent's Guide to Books for Teens & Preteens. LC 88-10171. 131p. 1988. reprint ed. pap. 40.70 (*0-608-00499-5*, 206131900008) Bks Demand.

— Reaching Adolescents: The Young Adult Book & the School. (Illus.). 502p. (Orig.). (C). 1993. text 45.80 (*0-02-398861-4*, Macmillan Coll) P-H.

Reed, Arthea J. & Bergemann, Verna E. Course Kit: In the Classroom: An Introduction to Education/Guide to Observation & Participation in the Classroom. 2nd ed. 627p. (C). 1995. text 43.50 (*0-697-29830-2*) Brown & Benchmark.

— A Guide to Participation & Observation in the Classroom. 2nd ed. (Illus.). 208p. (Orig.). (C). 1995. text 14.37 (*1-56134-320-X*, Dshkn McG-Hill) McGrw-H Hghr Educ.

— In the Classroom: An Introduction to Education. LC 91-77534. (Illus.). 624p. (C). 1992. text 36.95 (*0-87967-931-X*, Dshkn McG-Hill) McGrw-H Hghr Educ.

— In the Classroom: An Introduction to Education. 2nd ed. LC 94-69040. (C). 1995. text. write for info. (*1-56134-304-8*, Dshkn McG-Hill) McGrw-H Hghr Educ.

***Reed, Arthea J. S.** Norma Fox Mazer: A Writer's World / LC 00-38759. (Studies in Young Adult Literature). 2000. write for info. (*0-8108-3814-1*) Scarecrow.

Reed, B. J. & Swain, John W. Public Finance Administration. 2nd ed. LC 96-25311. 496p. 1996. 49.95 (*0-8039-7405-1*) Sage.

***Reed, Barbara.** High Notes Are Murder. LC 00-190436. 345p. 2000. pap. 11.95 (*0-9700024-0-8*) Rare Sound Pr.

Reed, Barbara. Nutritional Guidelines for Correcting Behavior. rev. ed. 1984. pap. 10.00 (*0-939956-07-1*) Natural Pr.

Reed, Barbara, et al. Food, Teens & Behavior. 307p. 1983. pap. 7.00 (*0-939956-04-7*) Natural Pr.

Reed, Barbara E. Culture & Customs of Taiwan. LC 97-43935. 280p. 1998. 45.00 (*0-313-30298-7*, Greenwood Pr) Greenwood.

Reed, Barbara F. Beyond the Great Darkness: Modern Missionary Pioneering in the Jungles of the Philippines. 1987. pap. 4.95 (*9971-972-55-7*) OMF Bks.

Reed, Barbara S., jt. ed. see Hutton, Frankie.

Reed, Barry. Choice. 1992. mass mkt. 5.99 (*0-312-92883-1*) St Martin.

— The Deception. 1997. 24.00 (*0-614-27935-6*) Crown Pub Group.

— The Deception. large type ed. (Niagara Large Print Ser.). 592p. 1997. 29.50 (*0-7089-5884-2*) Ulverscroft.

— The Deception: Courtroom Drama. 1998. mass mkt. 6.99 (*0-312-96494-3*) St Martin.

— Indictment. 1995. mass mkt. 6.99 (*0-312-95416-6*, Pub. by Tor Bks) St Martin.

— The Verdict. 1992. mass mkt. 5.99 (*0-312-92954-4*) St Martin.

Reed, Bella & Roth, Kevin. The Good Friends Song Book. 86p. 1985. pap. 9.95 (*0-931759-02-1*) Centerstream Pub.

Reed, Bernard. W-3: Way with Words. 32p. 1999. pap. 8.00 (*0-8059-4582-2*) Dorrance.

Reed, Beth G. & Garvin, Charles D., eds. Groupwork with Women - Groupwork with Men: An Overview of Gender Issues in Social Groupwork Practice. LC 83-12745. (Social Work with Groups Ser.: Vol. 6, Nos. 3-4). 195p. 1983. text 39.95 (*0-86656-258-3*); pap. text 17.95 (*0-86656-274-5*) Haworth Pr.

Reed, Betsy, ed. see Gluckman, Amy.

Reed, Betsy, jt. ed. see Gluckman, Amy.

Reed, Bika, tr. Rebel in the Soul: An Ancient Egyptian Dialogue Between a Man & His Destiny. LC 97-4969. (Illus.). 144p. 1997. pap. 19.95 (*0-89281-615-5*) Inner Tradit.

Reed, Bill. Business English Teacher's Resource Book. (Longman Resource Bks.). 1996. pap. 49.00 (*0-582-07843-1*) Longman.

— Hot from Harlem: Profiles in Classic African-American Entertainment. (Illus.). 292p. 1998. pap. 12.95 (*0-9661449-0-2*) Cellar Door.

— Tusk. 1998. pap. text 12.95 (*1-875657-86-X*, Pub. by Hyland Hse) Seven Hills Bk.

Reed, Billy, ed. The Final Four: Reliving America's Basketball Classic. (Illus.). 240p. 1987. 29.95 (*1-879688-06-9*) Host Comns Inc.

Reed, Billy, jt. auth. see Bolus, Jim.

***Reed, Bob.** Master Your Whole Life: Foundation for an Art, Science & Technology of Human Development. 124p. 2000. pap. 12.95 (*0-9686390-0-3*, Pub. by New Vision) Hushion Hse.

Reed, Bob. The Potluck Dinner That Went Astray: And Other Tales of Christian Life. 96p. 1996. pap. 11.00 (*1-57312-041-3*) Smyth & Helwys.

Reed, Bobbie. 501 Practical Ways to Teach Your Children Values. LC 97-37079. 1998. 12.99 (*0-570-04994-6*, 12-3343) Concordia.

— Learn to Risk. 1990. pap. 8.99 (*0-310-28711-1*) Zondervan.

— Life after Divorce: How to Grow Through a Divorce. 192p. (Orig.). 1993. pap. 10.99 (*0-570-04614-9*, 123199) Concordia.

— Listen to the Heart: Story Meditations on the Fruits of the Spirit. LC 97-29637. 1997. pap. text 11.99 (*0-8066-2827-8*, Augsburg) Augsburg Fortress.

— Singles' Ministry for Today. LC 95-23858. 1996. 12.99 (*0-570-04840-0*, 12-3277) Concordia.

— Surviving Your Child's Dating Years: 7 Vital Skills to Help Your Child Build Healthy Relationships. LC 95-7305. (How to Family Ser.). 160p. 1995. pap. 8.99 (*0-570-04826-5*, 12-3268) Concordia.

Reed, Bobbie, ed. Baker Handbook of Single-Parent Ministry. LC 98-3800. 304p. 1998. 24.99 (*0-8010-9052-0*) Baker Bks.

An Asterisk (*) at the beginning of an entry indicates that the title is appearing for the first time.

Reed, Bobbie & Westfall, John. Building Strong People: How to Lead Effectively. LC 96-52301. 224p. (gr. 11). 1996. pap. 13.99 (*0-8010-9028-8*) Baker Bks.

Reed, Bobbie, jt. auth. see Talley, Jim.

Reed, Boston. Corporate Training for Medical Assisting. 448p. (C). 1998. text 41.95 (*0-7668-0932-3*) Delmar.

***Reed, Bradly Ward.** Talons & Teeth. LC 99-41457. (Law, Society, & Culture in China Ser.). 2000. 55.00 (*0-8047-3758-4*) Stanford U Pr.

Reed, Brenda L. Easy-to-Make Decorative Paper Snowflakes. 64p. (Orig.). 1987. pap. 4.95 (*0-486-25408-9*) Dover.

Reed, C. P., ed. English Legal System. 324p. 1996. pap. 95.00 (*0-7510-0687-4*, Pub. by HLT Pubns) St Mut.

— English Legal System Cases. 222p. 1996. pap. 95.00 (*0-7510-0653-X*, Pub. by HLT Pubns) St Mut.

Reed, C. W. Mirror on the Wall. large type ed. (Dales Large Print Ser.). 365p. 1996. pap. 18.99 (*1-85389-685-3*, Dales) Ulverscroft.

Reed, Carla. Contents Under Pressure: 10 Team-Based Principles for Coping in an Ever-Changing World. 51p. 1998. pap. 4.95 (*0-9658659-6-7*) Tompkins Assocs.

Reed, Carlynn. And We Have Danced: The History of the Sacred Dance Guild, 1958-1978. Adams, Doug, ed. 1978. 5.95 (*0-941500-00-4*) Sharing Co.

Reed, Carol, jt. auth. see Reed, George A.

***Reed, Carol J.** Teaching with Power: Shared Decision-Making & Classroom Practice. LC 00-20500. (Series on School Reform). 2000. pap. write for info. (*0-8077-3940-5*) Tchrs Coll.

Reed, Carolyn. Maze Bright. 54p. 1986. pap. 6.00 (*0-912549-12-2*) Bread & Butter.

Reed, Carroll E. & Davison, Zeta C. English Archaisms in Pennsylvania German; A Word-List from The Appalachians & the Piedmont Area of North Carolina. (Publications of the American Dialect Society: No. 19). 19p. 1953. pap. 2.50 (*0-8173-0619-6*) U of Ala Pr.

Reed, Carroll E., et al. Washington Words; Wa'n't' The ADS Collections - Actuality & Possibility. (Publications of the American Dialect Society: No. 25). 31p. 1956. pap. 4.20 (*0-8173-0625-0*) U of Ala Pr.

Reed, Carson. Tie up the Strong Man. 50p. 1989. pap. 6.95 (*0-912549-14-9*) Bread & Butter.

Reed, Carson & Hawk, Doug. The Colorado Community College & Occupational Education System: A Silver Anniversary History. Van Lew, Carol & Fetter, Rosemary, eds. LC 95-622313. (Illus.). 163p. (C). 1994. pap. 15.00 (*0-9635787-0-7*) CO Comm Coll.

Reed, Cartwright, jt. auth. see Mark, Dave.

Reed, Cecil A. & Donovan, Priscilla. Fly in the Buttermilk: The Life Story of Cecil Reed. LC 93-18624. (Singular Lives: The Iowa Series in North American Autobiography). (Illus.). 208p. 1993. pap. 14.95 (*0-87745-416-7*); text 29.95 (*0-87745-415-9*) U of Iowa Pr.

Reed, Charles. Christ in the Now. 131p. 1998. pap. 7.95 (*1-888189-00-2*) Nance Pubng.

Reed, Charles A., ed. Origins of Agriculture. (World Anthropology Ser.). (Illus.). xvi, 1014p. 1977. 113.85 (*90-279-7919-7*) Mouton.

Reed, Charles A., jt. auth. see Schaffer, William M.

Reed, Charles B. The First, Great, Canadian: The Story of Pierre Le Moyne, Sieur d'Iberville. 1977. 27.95 (*0-8369-6987-1*, 7864) Ayer.

Reed, Charles E., jt. ed. see Dempsey, Jerome A.

Reed, Charles F., et al, eds. Psychopathology: A Source Book. LC 58-10405. (Illus.). 815p. 1958. 77.50 (*0-674-72200-0*) HUP.

***Reed, Charles Wellington & Campbell, Eric A.** A Grand Terrible Drama: From Gettysburg to Petersburg. LC 00-37587. (North's Civil War Ser.). 2000. pap. write for info. (*0-8232-1972-0*) Fordham.

Reed, Cheryl, jt. auth. see Formo, Dawn M.

Reed, Chip. Resource Track: Applying Biblical Principles to Personal Finances. (Illus.). 74p. (Orig.). 1989. pap., student ed. 10.00 (*0-9621353-1-3*) C Reed Assocs.

Reed, Chris. Computer Law. 2nd ed. 372p. 1993. pap. 40.00 (*1-85431-227-8*, Pub. by Blackstone Pr) Gaunt.

***Reed, Chris.** H-53 Sea Stallion in Action. (Aircraft in Action Ser.: Vol. 174). (Illus.). 50p. 2000. pap. 9.95 (*0-89747-417-1*, 1174) Squad Sig Pubns.

Reed, Chris. Lockheed C-130 Hercules & Its Variants. LC 98-87296. (Illus.). 136p. (Orig.). 1999. pap. 29.95 (*0-7643-0722-3*) Schiffer.

Reed, Chris, ed. Computer Law. 3rd ed. 396p. 1996. pap. 44.00 (*1-85431-448-3*, Pub. by Blackstone Pr) Gaunt.

Reed, Christine, jt. auth. see Reed, J. D.

Reed, Christine M., jt. auth. see Bruce, Willa M.

Reed, Christopher, ed. A Roger Fry Reader. 456p. 1996. lib. bdg. 50.00 (*0-226-26643-5*) U Ch Pr.

Reed, Christopher R. The Chicago NAACP & the Rise of Black Professional Leadership, 1910-1966. LC 97-9017. (Blacks in the Diaspora Ser.). 304p. 1997. 35.00 (*0-253-33313-X*) Ind U Pr.

***Reed, Christopher Robert.** All the World is Here! The Black Presence at White City. LC 99-29925. 1999. 39.95 (*0-253-33566-3*) Ind U Pr.

Reed, Cleota. Henry Chapman Mercer & the Moravian Pottery & Tile Works. (Illus.). 284p. (Orig.). 1996. reprint ed. pap. 36.50 (*0-8122-1601-6*) U of Pa Pr.

Reed, Cleota & Skoczen, Stan. Syracuse China. LC 97-14548. 272p. 1997. 60.00 (*0-8156-0474-2*) Syracuse U Pr.

Reed, Cleota, et al. The Genius Belt: The Story of the Arts in Bucks County, PA. Bush, George S., ed. (Illus.). 190p. (Orig.). 1996. pap. write for info. (*1-879636-07-7*) J A Michener.

Reed, Clyde G. Price Data & European Economic History: England, 1300-1600. Bruchey, Stuart, ed. LC 80-2826. (Dissertations in European Economic History Ser.: No. 2). (Illus.). 1981. lib. bdg. 17.95 (*0-405-14010-X*) Ayer.

Reed, Colin. Pastors, Partners & Paternalists: African Church Leaders & the Development of Missionary Paternalism in Kenya, 1850-1900. LC 96-48065. 168p. 1997. 78.00 (*90-04-10639-1*) Brill Academic Pubs.

Reed, Colin & Trent, Dennis R., eds. Promotion of Mental Health, 1995. (Mental Health Promotion Unit Ser.: No. 5). 429p. 1996. pap. 87.95 (*1-85972-284-9*, Pub. by Avebry) Ashgate Pub Co.

— Promotion of Mental Health, 1994, Vol. 4. (Mental Health Promotion Unit Ser.). 560p. 1995. 101.95 (*1-85972-065-X*, Pub. by Avebry) Ashgate Pub Co.

Reed, Colin, jt. auth. see Trent, Dennis R.

Reed, Colin A., jt. ed. see Trent, Denis R.

Reed, Colleen A., jt. ed. see Lewin, Jeanne E.

Reed Consulting Group, Inc. Staff. On the Brink of Competition: RCG's Guide to the Northeast Power Market. LC 98-138599. (Illus.). 202p. 1997. pap. write for info. (*0-9654813-0-1*) Reed Cnslting.

Reed Consumer Group Staff. Ocean World: A Duplo Carousel Playbook. (J). 1997. write for info. (*0-316-85336-4*) Little.

Reed, Cory A. The Novelist As Playwright: Cervantes & the Entremes Nuevo. LC 92-25216. (Studies on Cervantes & His Times: Vol. 4). 222p. (C). 1993. text 43.95 (*0-8204-1989-3*) P Lang Pubng.

Reed, Cynthia M. Phlebotomist Test Preparation. LC 94-45960. (Test Prep Ser.). 128p. 1995. pap. 29.60 (*0-8359-4945-1*, Arco) Macmillan Gen Ref.

Reed, Cynthia M. & Foley, David P. Using Arbitration in Commercial Disputes. Vol. L4. text 82.00 (*0-8205-2390-9*) Bender.

Reed, D. C., jt. auth. see Reed, A. D.

Reed, Dale, jt. compiled by see Palm, Charles G.

Reed, Damon, jt. auth. see Kenny, Herbert A.

Reed, Dan. Paid for the Privilege: Hearing the Voices of Autism. 163p. (Orig.). 1996. pap. 16.00 (*1-886928-06-1*) DRI Pr.

Reed-Danahay, Deborah. Education & Identity in Rural France: The Politics of Schooling. LC 96-135734. (Studies in Social & Cultural Anthropology: Vol. 98). (Illus.). 254p. (C). 1996. text 64.95 (*0-521-48312-3*) Cambridge U Pr.

Reed-Danahay, Deborah, ed. Auto-Ethnography: Rewriting the Self & the Social. LC 97-202405. 224p. 1997. 55.00 (*1-85973-970-9*, Pub. by Berg Pubs); pap. 19.50 (*1-85973-975-X*, Pub. by Berg Pubs) NYU Pr.

Reed, Daniel A. & Fujimoto, Richard M. Multicomputer Networks: Message-Based Parallel Processing. (Scientific Computation Ser.). 400p. 1987. 52.50 (*0-262-18129-0*) MIT Pr.

Reed, Daniel W. Emotion: The Treasure of Love. (Orig.). 1996. pap. write for info. (*1-57553-320-0*) Watermrk Pr.

***Reed, Daphne S.** The Secret World of Angels: Revelations from Another Dimension. 2nd ed. (Illus.). ix, 300p. 1999. spiral bd. 24.95 (*0-9655978-2-2*, 9544978-2) Owl Pubs.

Reed, Darren. Coco Ways: A Tribute to African American Women. 79p. 1999. per. 10.00 (*0-9670325-0-4*) Aya Pubg.

Reed, Dave. After Death - What? According to Jesus. (Illus.). 40p. 1997. 4.95 (*0-9637448-4-4*) Comments Friends.

— Web Tips: For Beginners & Professionals. (Illus.). 40p. (Orig.). 1997. write for info. (*0-9637448-3-6*) Comments Friends.

Reed, Dave, ed. see Kinsley, Michael J.

Reed, David. The Art & Craft of Stonescaping: Setting & Stacking Stone. LC 97-49856. 160p. 1998. 27.50 (*1-57990-018-6*, Pub. by Lark Books) Random.

— Education for Building a People's Movement. LC 81-51388. 208p. 1981. pap. 15.00 (*0-89608-121-4*) South End Pr.

***Reed, David.** Managing the Oracle Data Warehouse. 450p. 2000. pap. text 49.99 (*0-13-014923-3*) P-H.

Reed, David. Milwaukee's New Architecture: A Downtown Trail. (Publications in Architecture & Urban Planning: No. R86-2). (Illus.). 6p. 1986. 1.00 (*0-938744-48-8*) U of Wis Ctr Arch-Urban.

— The Rough Guide to Nepal. 4th ed. (Illus.). 496p. 1999. 18.95 (*1-85828-438-4*, Pub. by Rough Guides) Penguin Putnam.

Reed, David & Basualdo, Carlos. Two Bedrooms in San Francisco. Echavarren, Roberto, tr. (ENG & SPA., Illus.). 12p. (Orig.). 1992. pap. 5.00 (*0-930495-17-9*) San Fran Art Inst.

Reed, David, jt. ed. see Ryhn, Douglas.

Reed, David A. Answering Jehovah's Witnesses: Subject by Subject. LC 96-1102. 256p. (YA). (gr. 10). 1996. pap. 10.99 (*0-8010-5317-X*) Baker Bks.

— Behind the Watchtower Curtain. 160p. (Orig.). 1989. pap. write for info. (*0-925703-08-7*) Crown MA.

— Blood on the Altar: Confessions of a Jehovah's Witness Minister. LC 95-13435. 285p. 1996. 25.95 (*1-57392-059-2*) Prometheus Bks.

— Jehovah's Witnesses Answered Verse-by-Verse. 144p. (gr. 10). 1986. pap. 8.99 (*0-8010-7739-7*) Baker Bks.

— No Blood! 144p. (Orig.). 1995. pap. 7.95 (*0-9637448-2-8*) Comments Friends.

Reed, David A., ed. Index of Watchtower Errors: 1879 to 1989. 144p. (Orig.). (YA). (gr. 10). 1990. pap. 9.99 (*0-8010-7756-7*) Baker Bks.

Reed, David A. & Farkas, John R. Mormons Answered Verse by Verse. 160p. (Orig.). (gr. 11). 1992. pap. 9.99 (*0-8010-7761-3*) Baker Bks.

Reed, David A., jt. auth. see Farkas, John R.

Reed, David D. & Mroz, Glen. Resource Assessment in Forested Landscapes. LC 97-1735. 386p. 1997. 99.00 (*0-471-15582-9*) Wiley.

Reed, David M., jt. ed. see Whittington, Stephen L.

Reed, David P. Residential Fiber Optic Networks: An Engineering & Economic Analysis. LC 91-36112. (Artech House Telecommunications Library). (Illus.). 367p. 1992. reprint ed. pap. 113.80 (*0-7837-9698-6*, 206042800005) Bks Demand.

Reed, David W., ed. A Grower's Guide to Water, Media, & Nutrition for Greenhouse Crops. (Illus.). 322p. (C). 1996. pap. 56.95 (*1-883052-12-2*, B029) Ball Pub.

Reed, David W. & Bradley, F. W. Eastern Dialect Words in California; Supplementary List of South Carolina Words & Phrases. (Publications of the American Dialect Society: No. 21). 49p. 1954. pap. 4.90 (*0-8173-0621-8*) U of Ala Pr.

Reed, Deborah. California's Rising Income Inequality: Causes & Concerns. LC 98-55464. (Illus.). xxxv, 101p. 1999. pap. 12.00 (*1-58213-005-1*) Pub Policy Inst.

Reed, Deborah, et al. The Distribution of Income in California. LC 97-29809. (Illus.). xxix, 139p. 1996. pap. 12.00 (*0-9653184-0-0*) Pub Policy Inst.

Reed, Dee. Cahokia. LC 98-87145. (Images of America Ser.). (Illus.). 128p. 1998. pap. 16.99 (*0-7524-1286-8*) Arcadia Publng.

Reed, Dennis, jt. auth. see Wilson, Michael G.

Reed, Dick A. The Complete Investor's Guide to Silver Dollar Investing. 1982. 18.95 (*0-911349-00-6*) English Fact.

Reed, Dolores M. Fight City Hall & Win. 86p. (Orig.). 1985. pap. text. write for info. (*0-935543-00-7*) Inst Political Res.

— Kingmaker-Kingbreaker: A Political Campaign Primer. Polgar, Antoine, ed. (Inaugural Ser.). (Illus.). 128p. (Orig.). 1986. pap. text 12.85 (*0-935543-01-5*) Inst Political Res.

— No More Setasides: Women, Minorities, Business, & Politics. Polgar, Antoine, ed. (Inaugural Ser.). (Illus.). 19p. 1993. pap. text 5.90 (*0-318-20009-0*) Inst Political Res.

Reed, Don C. The Kraken. LC 93-74140. (Illus.). 217p. (YA). (gr. 5 up). 1997. pap. 7.95 (*1-56397-693-5*) Boyds Mills Pr.

Reed, Donald R. Following Kohlberg: Liberalism & the Practice of Democratic Community. LC 97-21491. (Revisions Ser.). 272p. 1998. 30.00 (*0-268-02851-6*) U of Notre Dame Pr.

***Reed, Donald Timothy, et al.** Actinide Speciation in High Ionic Strength Media: Experimental & Modeling Approaches to Predicting Actinide Speciation & Migration in the Subsurface LC 99-36676. 1999. write for info. (*0-306-46185-4*, Kluwer Plenum) Kluwer Academic.

***Reed, Donald Upham.** Donald's World: A Family History & Memoirs of a Journalist & Professor. LC 99-91122. 1999. 25.00 (*0-7388-0626-9*); pap. 18.00 (*0-7388-0627-7*) Xlibris Corp.

Reed, Donn & Reed, Jean. The Home School Source Book. 3rd ed. (Illus.). 352p. (Orig.). 2000. pap. 29.95 (*0-919761-28-3*) Brook Farm Bks.

HOME SCHOOL SOURCE BOOK, NEW-third edition of this much-loved classic. Jean & Donn Reed share 24 years of homeschooling experience. The Reeds speak honestly & with humor about homeschooling to help new & experienced homeschoolers. The new edition has more information to help readers create the best learning experience possible for their families with liberal arts resources from birth through adulthood. New "how to" essays & commentary - more resources for early learning, parenting, classic books, numerous new creative hands-on resources for math & science, educational games, maps, computers, support, college entrance, special needs & reference material. Everything reviewed; not listed. MILLLENNIUM WHOLE EARTH CATALOG says "A Whole Earth Catalog for homeschoolers." Bursting with ideas & resources for enriching the home schooling environment. Pat Faenga, publisher of GROWING WITHOUT SCHOOLING says "a wealth of information for beginning & experienced homeschoolers. HOME EDUCATION MAGAZINE says, "a veritable smorgasbord of articles, resources, essays, insights, honest & sometimes scathing, reviews, notes & commentary on home education." REAL GOOD NEWS says, "the only major home education resource guide that emphasizes comparative religions, cultural literacy, ecology, conservation & global awareness." A great collection of learning tools for families, resource centers & alternative schools. 0-919761-28-3, Brook Farm Books. Available from Brook Farm Books, PO Box 246, Bridgewater ME 04735. Standard trade discounts. STOP 40

. $3.50 shipping. Wholesalers: Baker, Taylor, Ingram

Publisher Paid Annotation.

Reed, Donna. Daddy's Little Girl: For Dad's & Little Girls of All Ages. (Illus.). 34p. (Orig.). 1994. pap. 8.00 (*0-9641434-1-0*) Westbury Pubng.

— Loving Me-Loving You: Loving Me Frees Me for Loving You. 151p. 1993. pap. 10.00 (*0-9641434-0-2*) Westbury Pubng.

Reed, Donna K. The Novel & the Nazi Past. LC 83-49004. (American University Studies: Germanic Languages & Literature: Ser. I, Vol. 28). X, 216p. (C). 1984. text 26.50 (*0-8204-0064-5*) P Lang Pubng.

Reed, Donna L. Spotlight on Conventions. LC 98-231705. (Spotlight Series of Leadership Handbooks). 16p. 1997. 3.00 (*1-884048-19-6*) Natl Assn Parliamentarians.

Reed, Donna L., et al, contrib. by. Spotlight on Meeting Planning. LC 99-170331. 16 p. 1997. 3.00 (*1-884048-21-8*) Natl Assn Parliamentarians.

R

Reed, Doris, see Robb, Dorian, pseud.

Reed, Douglas. Battle for Rhodesia. 1967. 9.95 (*0-8159-5102-7*) Devin.

Reed, Douglas. Behind the Scene. unabridged ed. 101p. 1951. reprint ed. pap. 8.00 (*0-945001-56-8*) GSG & Assocs.

Reed, Douglas. Behind the Scene, Pt. 2. 1976. pap. 6.95 (*0-911038-41-8*, 0007, Noontide Pr) Legion Survival.

Reed, Douglas. The Controversy of Zion. unabridged ed. 592p. 1978. reprint ed. pap. 30.00 (*0-945001-38-X*) GSG & Assocs.

Reed, Douglas. Far & Wide. 398p. 1951. pap. 10.00 (*0-913022-22-5*) CPA Bk Pub.

Reed, Douglas. Far & Wide: Part One: American Scene. Part Two: Behind the Scene, 2 vols. in 1. 2nd unabridged ed. 398p. 1951. reprint ed. pap. 15.00 (*0-945001-73-8*) GSG & Assocs.

— The Grand Design. unabridged ed. 45p. 1977. reprint ed. pap. 8.00 (*0-945001-57-6*) GSG & Assocs.

Reed, Douglas. Somewhere South of Suez. 9.95 (*0-8159-6816-7*) Devin.

Reed, Douglas, ed. see Givans, Ina.

Reed, Douglas, ed. see Martin, Jessy.

Reed, Douglas, ed. see Owens, Thomas & Owens, Derrick.

Reed, Douglas, ed. see Walker, Pat George.

Reed, Douglas S. Garden's Corner. 288p. (Orig.). 1997. pap. 15.00 (*0-9657272-4-6*) Kataza Bks.

Reed, Duffer. From Wishes to Wealth in Four Easy Steps: Plus the Idea Factory, Golf Lover's Edition. (Illus.). 52p. (Orig.). 1992. pap. 4.98 (*1-881878-04-X*) Gift Bks Am.

Reed, Duncan & Thomas, P. Essential HTML Fast. LC 97-29237. (Essential Ser.). x, 133p. 1998. pap. 24.95 (*3-540-76199-3*) Spr-Verlag.

Reed, Earl H. The Dune Country. (Illus.). 1979. reprint ed. 20.00 (*0-915056-09-7*) Hardscrabble Bks.

Reed, Ed. Requiem for a Kingfish. LC 86-71787. 250p. 1986. 24.95 (*0-9617384-0-5*) Award Pubns.

Reed, Edward. Masque: Photographs of Halloween. LC 80-54591. (Illus.). 60p. 1981. pap. 8.95 (*0-89822-012-2*) Visual Studies.

Reed, Edward, ed. see Center for the Study of Democratic Institutions St.

Reed, Edward A., jt. auth. see Eary, Donald F.

Reed, Edward B. English Lyrical Poetry. LC 67-30805. 1970. reprint ed. lib. bdg. 99.00 (*0-8383-0703-5*) M S G Haskell Hse.

— English Lyrical Poetry from Its Origins to the Present Time. (BCL1-PR English Literature Ser.). 616p. 1992. reprint ed. lib. bdg. 149.00 (*0-7812-7081-2*) Rprt Serv.

Reed, Edward S. Encountering the World: Toward an Ecological Psychology. LC 95-31908. (Illus.). 224p. 1996. text 35.00 (*0-19-507301-0*) OUP.

— From Soul to Mind: The Emergence of Psychology, from Erasmus Darwin to William James. LC 96-49051. 288p. 1997. 30.00 (*0-300-06967-7*); pap. 16.00 (*0-300-07581-2*) Yale U Pr.

— The Necessity of Experience. LC 96-5980. 200p. 1996. 30.00 (*0-300-06668-6*) Yale U Pr.

— Revolution in Perception: The Ecological Psychology of James J. Gibson. (C). 1988. 45.00 (*0-300-04289-2*) Yale U Pr.

Reed, Edward S., et al, eds. Values & Knowledge. (Jean Piaget Symposia Ser.). 192p. 1996. text 39.95 (*0-8058-1521-X*) L Erlbaum Assocs.

Reed, Edwin. Bacon & Shakespeare Parallelisms (1902) 450p. 1998. reprint ed. pap. 35.00 (*0-7661-0155-X*) Kessinger Pub.

— Francis Bacon Our Shake-speare. 250p. 1992. reprint ed. pap. 24.95 (*1-56459-136-0*) Kessinger Pub.

Reed, Eleanor C. Battle Invisible, & Other Stories. LC 71-125236. (Short Story Index Reprint Ser.). 1977. 19.95 (*0-8369-3603-5*) Ayer.

Reed, Eli. Black in America. LC 96-54490. 160p. 1997. 29.95 (*0-393-03995-1*) Norton.

Reed, Elizabeth, ed. see Evy & Chick Staff.

Reed, Ellen C. The Witches' Book of Names. (Illus.). 166p. (Orig.). Date not set. pap. 19.95 (*1-885569-10-6*) Solar Crown.

— The Witches Qabala: The Pagan Path & the Tree of Life. LC 97-9197. (Illus.). 232p. (Orig.). 1997. reprint ed. pap. 12.95 (*0-87728-880-1*) Weiser.

— The Witches Tarot Bk. II: The Witches Qabala. LC 88-45181. (Modern Witchcraft Ser.). (Illus.). 320p. (Orig.). 1989. pap. 12.95 (*0-87542-668-9*) Llewellyn Pubns.

— The Witches Tarot Kit. (Illus.). 320p. 1996. boxed set 34.95 (*1-56718-558-4*) Llewellyn Pubns.

***Reed, Ellen Cannon.** The Heart of Wicca: Wise Words from a Crone on the Path. 144p. 2000. pap. 12.95 (*1-57863-174-2*) Weiser.

Reed, Emily. Emily's Guides to the San Juan Islands - Washington, 3 bks. 5th ed. 75p. 1997. 14.50 (*1-882625-05-6*) Gus Pubns.

Reed, Emily F. The Penry Penalty: Capital Punishment & Offenders with Mental Retardation. LC 92-44124. 1993. 54.50 (*0-8191-9019-5*); pap. 29.50 (*0-8191-9020-9*) U Pr of Amer.

Reed, Emily L., jt. auth. see Dakin, A., Jr.

Reed, Erik K. Excavations in Mancos Canyon, Colorado. (Utah Anthropological Papers: No. 35). reprint ed. 40.00 (*0-404-60635-0*) AMS Pr.

An Asterisk (*) at the beginning of an entry indicates that the title is appearing for the first time.

R

Reed, Esther. Life of Esther De Berdt, Afterwards Esther Reed, of Pennsylvania. LC 72-140877. (Eyewitness Accounts of the American Revolution Ser.). 1971. reprint ed. 23.95 (*0-405-01208-X*) Ayer.

Reed, Esther D. A Theological Reading of Hegel's Phenomenology of Spirit, with Particular Reference to Its Themes of Identity, Alienation, & Community: Salvation in a Social Context. LC 95-20526. 240p. 1996. write for info. (*0-7734-8874-X*) E Mellen.

Reed, Evelyn. Is Biology Woman's Destiny? 2nd ed. 31p. 1985. reprint ed. pap. 3.00 (*0-87348-258-1*) Pathfinder NY.

— Problems of Women's Liberation: A Marxist Approach. LC 78-143808. 131p. (Orig.). 1970. reprint ed. pap. 12.95 (*0-87348-167-4*); reprint ed. lib. bdg. 30.00 (*0-87348-166-6*) Pathfinder NY.

— Sexism & Science. LC 77-92144. (Illus.). 1978. reprint ed. pap. 16.95 (*0-87348-541-6*); reprint ed. lib. bdg. 45.00 (*0-87348-540-8*) Pathfinder NY.

— Woman's Evolution: From Matriarchal Clan to Patriarchal Family. LC 74-26236. 491p. 1974. reprint ed. lib. bdg. 65.00 (*0-87348-421-5*) Pathfinder NY.

— Woman's Evolution: From Matriarchal Clan to Patriarchal Family. LC 74-26236. 491p. 1975. reprint ed. pap. 22.95 (*0-87348-422-3*) Pathfinder NY.

Reed, Evelyn D. Coyote Tales from the Indian Pueblos: Legends. LC 86-14544. (Illus.). 96p. (J). (gr. 4 up). 1988. pap. 8.95 (*0-86534-094-3*) Sunstone Pr.

Reed, F. Morton. Odd & Curious. (Illus.). 1979. pap. 10.00 (*0-915262-37-1*) S J Durst.

Reed, Frances. Experiencing Guidance: Inner Help in Life's Struggles. 240p. (Orig.). 1993. pap. 14.95 (*0-9627954-1-0*) LifeTime OR.

Reed, Frances K. Hilo Legends. (Illus.). 52p. 1987. pap. 5.95 (*0-912180-45-5*) Petroglyph.

Reed, Frances M., ed. see Wilde, Oscar.

Reed, Francis. The ABC of Stage Lighting. (Illus.). 144p. (C). 1992. pap. text 16.95 (*0-89676-119-3*, Drama Pubs) QSMG Ltd.

Reed, Frank C., jt. auth. see Firestone, David B.

*__Reed, Fred A.__ Anatolia Junction. 288p. 2000. pap. 16.95 (*0-88922-426-9*, Pub. by Talonbks) Genl Dist Srvs.

Reed, Fred A. Persian Postcards: Iran after Khomeini. 288p. 1994. pap. 16.95 (*0-88922-351-3*, Pub. by Talonbks) Genl Dist Srvs.

— Salonica Terminus: Travels into the Balkan Nightmare. 288p. 1996. pap. 16.95 (*0-88922-368-8*) Genl Dist Srvs.

*__Reed, G.__ Biotechnology: A Multi-Volume Comprehensive Treatise: Environmental Processes III, Vol. 11C, Environmental Processes III. 2nd ed. Rehm, H. J., ed. 518p. 2000. 340.00 (*3-527-28336-6*) Wiley.

Reed, G. B., et al, eds. Diseases of the Fetus & Newborn: Pathology, Imaging, Genetics & Management. 2nd ed. 1728p. 1994. text 225.00 (*0-412-39160-0*, Pub. by E A) OUP.

Reed, G. M., et al, eds. Topology & Category Theory in Computer Science. (Illus.). 402p. (C). 1991. text 79.00 (*0-19-853760-3*) OUP.

Reed, G. M., jt. ed. see Van Mill, Jan.

Reed, Gail, ed. see Frank, Marc.

Reed, Gail S. Transference Neurosis & Psychoanalytic Experience: Perspectives on Contemporary Clinical Practice. LC 94-1406. 240p. 1994. 35.00 (*0-300-05957-4*) Yale U Pr.

Reed, Gary. Pryor Rendering. 1996. write for info. (*0-614-09427-5*, Dutt) Dutton Plume.

— Raven Chronicles: Myths & Methods. (Illus.). 192p. 1997. pap. 16.95 (*0-941613-96-8*, Caliber Comics) Stabur Pr.

— RDF Accelerated Training Program. Marciniszyn, Alex & Cartier, Randi, eds. (Robotech RPG Adventures Ser.). (Illus.). 56p. (Orig.). (YA). (gr. 8 up). 1988. pap. 7.95 (*0-916211-32-0*, 555) Palladium Bks.

— RenField. (Illus.). 192p. (Orig.). 1995. pap. 8.95 (*0-941613-77-1*, Caliber Comics) Stabur Pr.

Reed, Gary & Davis, Guy. Baker Street: Honour among Punks. (Graphic Novel Ser.). (Illus.). 176p. 1993. 14.95 (*0-941613-42-9*) Stabur Pr.

Reed, Geoffrey, jt. auth. see Sodersten, Bo.

Reed, George. Dark Sky Legacy: Astronomy's Impact on the History of Culture. LC 89-10314. (Illus.). 199p. 1989. 31.95 (*0-87975-541-5*) Prometheus Bks.

*__Reed, George.__ Eyes on the Universe. (Story of Science Ser.). (Illus.). (J). 2000. 28.50 (*0-7614-1154-2*, Benchmark NY) Marshall Cavendish.

Reed, George. Murdered by Isaac Newton. 216p. 1984. 14.95 (*0-89697-146-5*) Intl Univ Pr.

*__Reed, George A. & Reed, Carol.__ Fort Ontario. LC 99-69479. (Images of America Ser.). (Illus.). 128p. 2000. pap. 18.99 (*0-7385-0284-7*) Arcadia Publng.

Reed, Gerald. C. S. Lewis & the Bright Shadow of Holiness. LC 99-13434. 192p. 1999. pap. text 14.99 (*0-8341-1752-5*) Beacon Hill.

Reed, Gerald & Nagodawithana, Tilak W., eds. Enzymes in Food Processing. 3rd ed. (Food Science & Technology Ser.). (Illus.). 480p. 1993. text 121.00 (*0-12-513630-7*) Acad Pr.

Reed, Gerald, jt. ed. see Nagodawithana, Tilak W.

Reed, Gerard A. The Liberating Law: 10 Steps to Freedom. 208p. (Orig.). 1996. pap. 13.99 (*0-8341-1617-0*) Beacon Hill.

Reed, Germaine M. Crusading for Chemistry: The Professional Career of Charles Holmes Herty. LC 94-25816. (Illus.). 496p. 1995. 45.00 (*0-8203-1671-7*) U of Ga Pr.

Reed, Gervais, jt. auth. see Moseley, Spencer.

Reed, Glenn & Gray, Roger. How to Do Business in Mexico: Your Essential & Up-to-Date Guide for Success. LC 96-22353. (Illus.). 200p. 1997. 30.00 (*0-292-77079-0*); pap. 12.95 (*0-292-77080-4*) U of Tex Pr.

Reed, Glenn, ed. see Simms, William Gilmore.

Reed, Gordon K. Living Life by God's Law. 124p. (Orig.). 1984. pap. 6.00 (*0-317-03221-6*) Word Ministries Inc.

Reed, Graham. The Psychology of Anomalous Experience. rev. ed. LC 88-61531. 209p. 1988. pap. 24.95 (*0-87975-435-4*) Prometheus Bks.

Reed, Graham, ed. Collected Works of Francis Bacon, 12 vols. 5216p. (C). 1996. 1400.00 (*0-415-14303-9*) Routledge.

Reed, Gregory J. Negotiation's Behind Closed Doors. 135p. text 22.00 (*1-882806-07-7*); pap. text 19.00 (*1-882806-08-5*) New Natl Pub.

— Progressive Cleric. 170p. 1992. text 35.00 (*1-882806-09-3*); pap. text 35.00 (*1-882806-10-7*) New Natl Pub.

— This Business of Boxing & Its Secrets. 300p. 1981. text 20.00 (*1-882806-03-4*); pap. text 20.00 (*1-882806-04-2*) New Natl Pub.

— This Business of Celebrity Estates. 1992. text 25.00 (*1-882806-06-9*); pap. text 19.50 (*1-882806-05-0*) New Natl Pub.

— This Business of Entertainment & Its Secrets. 295p. 1985. text 25.50 (*1-882806-01-8*); pap. text 19.50 (*1-882806-02-6*) New Natl Pub.

Reed, Gregory J., jt. auth. see Parks, Rosa.

Reed, Gretchen M. & Sheppard, Vincent F. Basic Structures of the Head & Neck: A Programmed Instruction in Clinical Anatomy for Dental Professionals. (Illus.). 716p. 1976. pap., teacher ed. write for info. (*0-7216-2035-3*, W B Saunders Co) Harcrt Hlth Sci Grp.

— Basic Structures of the Head & Neck: A Programmed Instruction in Clinical Anatomy for Dental Professionals. LC 75-298. (Illus.). 716p. 1976. pap. text 55.00 (*0-7216-7516-6*, W B Saunders Co) Harcrt Hlth Sci Grp.

Reed, Gwendolyn D. Thoughts from the Corners of My Mind. LC 97-61963. iii, 206p. 1997. pap. 15.00 (*0-9671798-0-7*) WOAM.

Reed, H. Clay & Miller, George J., eds. The Burlington Court Book: A Record of Quaker Jurisprudence in West New Jersey, 1680-1709. LC 98-70093. 427p. (J). 1998. reprint ed. 40.00 (*0-8063-1558-X*) Genealog Pub.

Reed, H. Owen. Basic Music: A Basic Theory Text with Correlated Ear Training & Keyboard Exercises. 2nd rev. ed. 157p. 1954. pap. text 15.00 (*0-7692-1678-1*, 90004) Wrner Bros.

Reed, Harold. Brains for Animals: How to Build Brains for Your Machine. LC 96-25951. (Illus.). 175p. 1996. 19.95 (*1-56072-320-3*) Nova Sci Pubs.

— Brains for Machines. (C). 1996. lib. bdg. 55.00 (*1-56072-370-X*) Nova Sci Pubs.

Reed, Harry. Platform for Change: The Foundations of the Northern Black Community, 1775-1865. LC 93-37526. 1994. 29.95 (*0-87013-341-1*) Mich St U Pr.

Reed, Harry A., jt. ed. see Henderson, John P.

Reed, Helen H. The Reader in the Picaresque Novel. (Monografias A Ser.: Vol. CXIV). 120p. (C). 1984. 41.00 (*0-7293-0204-0*, Pub. by Tamesis Bks Ltd) Boydell & Brewer.

Reed, Helen M. A Diet Pill, a Pretty Rock & a Live Snake for the Teacher. 100p. 1991. 8.95 (*0-9630217-0-2*) H M Reed.

Reed, Henrey H., jt. ed. see Cole, John.

Reed, Henry. Awakening Your Psychic Powers. 242p. 1996. mass mkt. 6.99 (*0-312-95868-4*) St Martin.

— Edgar Cayce on Channeling Your Higher Self. Cayce, Charles T., ed. 288p. 1989. reprint ed. mass mkt. 6.99 (*0-446-34980-1*, Pub. by Warner Bks) Little.

— Edgar Cayce on Mysteries of the Mind. 1989. mass mkt. 3.95 (*0-446-34976-3*, Pub. by Warner Bks) Little.

— Lectures on English History & Tragic Poetry. LC 72-174305. reprint ed. 36.50 (*0-404-05234-7*) AMS Pr.

— U. S. Capitol. Date not set. write for info. (*0-393-03831-9*) Norton.

— Your Mind: Unlocking Your Hidden Powers. LC 96-27778. Orig. Title: Edgar Cayce on Mysteries of the Mind. 258p. 1996. pap. 12.95 (*0-87604-365-1*, 480) ARE Pr.

Reed, Henry, ed. see Wordsworth, Christopher.

Reed, Henry H., jt. auth. see Farber, Joseph C.

Reed, Henry H., jt. auth. see Gillon, Edmund V.

Reed, Henry H., jt. ed. see Coles, William A.

Reed, Henry M. The A. B. Frost Book. (Illus.). 176p. 1993. 49.95 (*0-941711-13-7*) Wyrick & Co.

Reed-Hill, R. E., et al, eds. Deformation Twining: Proceedings, Gainesville, Florida, March 21-22, 1963. LC 64-8380. (Metallurgical Society Conference Ser.: Vol. 25). 476p. reprint ed. pap. 147.60 (*0-608-11228-3*, 200151300079) Bks Demand.

Reed-Hill, Robert E. & Abbaschian, Reza. Physical Metallurgy Principles. 3rd ed. (C). 1991. 82.00 (*0-534-92173-6*) PWS Pubs.

*__Reed, Holcomb.__ Wird Bird. LC 99-64438. (Illus.). 32p. (J). (ps-3). 2000. 16.50 (*0-9670198-1-8*); 18.00 (*0-9670198-0-X*); pap. 9.50 (*0-9670198-2-6*) T T Ink.

Reed, Holly, ed. see National Research Council Staff.

Reed, Horace B. & Loughran, Elizabeth L., eds. Beyond Schools: Education for Economic, Social & Personal Development. LC 84-70668. (Illus.). 253p. (C). 1984. pap. text 15.00 (*0-934210-10-1*) Devlp Commy.

— Beyond Schools: Education for Economic, Social & Personal Development. (Illus.). 266p. 1985. reprint ed. pap. text 27.00 (*0-8191-5174-2*) U Pr of Amer.

Reed, Howard. We the Angels: The Star-Born Story of Humanity's Celestial Origins. LC 97-77526. 200p. 1998. pap. 14.00 (*0-87516-711-X*) DeVorss.

Reed Information Services Staff, ed. KOMPASS Register of Business & Industry, 1996 Catalog Showcase. 32p. 1996. write for info. (*0-86268-352-1*, Kompass) Reed Info Srvcs.

— KOMPASS United States, 2 vols. Incl. Vol. 1. KOMPASS United States, 1997. 1997. (*0-86268-359-9*, Kompass); Vol. 2. KOMPASS United States, 1997. 1997. (*0-86268-360-2*, Kompass); write for info. (*0-86268-361-0*, Kompass) Reed Info Srvcs.

— KOMPASS United States, 1996: Register of Business & Industry of the United States, 2 vols. 3534p. 1996. 375.00 (*0-86268-351-3*, Kompass) Reed Info Srvcs.

— KOMPASS United States, 1996: Register of Business & Industry of the United States, Vol. 1. 1797p. 1996. write for info. (*0-86268-349-1*, Kompass) Reed Info Srvcs.

— KOMPASS United States, 1996: Register of Business & Industry of the United States, Vol. 2. 1737p. 1996. write for info. (*0-86268-350-5*, Kompass) Reed Info Srvcs.

Reed, Ione. Pioneering in Oregon's Coast Range: Surviving the Depression Years. (Illus.). 140p. (Orig.). 1983. pap. 7.95 (*0-934784-31-0*) Calapooia Pubns.

*__Reed, Irving S. & Chen, Xuemin.__ Error-Control Coding for Data Networks LC 99-24310. (Kluwer International Series in Engineering & Computer Science). 1999. write for info. (*0-7923-8528-4*) Kluwer Academic.

Reed, Ishmael. Flight to Canada. 180p. 1989. pap. 11.00 (*0-689-70733-9*, Pub. by Ctrl Bur voor Schimmel) Macmillan.

— Flight to Canada. 192p. 1998. per. 11.00 (*0-684-84750-7*) S&S Trade.

*__Reed, Ishmael.__ The Free-Lance Pallbearers. LC 99-35091. 192p. 1999. reprint ed. pap. 11.95 (*1-56478-225-5*, Pub. by Dalkey Arch) Chicago Distribution Ctr.

Reed, Ishmael. Japanese by Spring. 240p. 1996. pap. 11.95 (*0-14-025585-0*, Penguin Bks) Viking Penguin.

*__Reed, Ishmael.__ The Last Days of Louisiana Red. LC 00-20974. 179p. 2000. reprint ed. pap. 11.95 (*1-56478-236-0*, Pub. by Dalkey Arch) Chicago Distribution Ctr.

Reed, Ishmael. Mumbo Jumbo. 224p. 1996. per. 11.00 (*0-684-82477-9*) S&S Trade.

— New & Collected Poems. 256p. 1989. pap. 9.95 (*0-689-12004-4*) Atheneum Yung Read.

*__Reed, Ishmael.__ Reckless Eyeballing. 148p. 2000. pap. 11.50 (*1-56478-237-9*) Dalkey Arch.

Reed, Ishmael. The Reed Reader. 450p. 2000. 30.00 (*0-465-06893-6*) HarpC.

— A Secretary to the Spirits. (Poets Ser.). (Illus.). 42p. 1977. 11.95 (*0-88357-057-2*); pap. 4.95 (*0-88357-058-0*) NOK Pubs.

*__Reed, Ishmael.__ The Terrible Threes. LC 99-35666. 192p. 1999. reprint ed. pap. 11.95 (*1-56478-224-7*, Pub. by Dalkey Arch) Chicago Distribution Ctr.

Reed, Ishmael. The Terrible Twos. 192p. 1988. pap. 9.95 (*0-689-70727-4*, Pub. by Ctrl Bur voor Schimmel) Macmillan.

*__Reed, Ishmael.__ The Terrible Twos. LC 99-35665. 192p. 1999. reprint ed. pap. 11.95 (*1-56478-226-3*, Pub. by Dalkey Arch) Chicago Distribution Ctr.

Reed, Ishmael. Writing Is Fighting: Forty-Three Years of Boxing on Paper. 1998. pap. write for info. (*0-201-48399-8*) Addison-Wesley.

*__Reed, Ishmael.__ Yellow Back Radio Broke Down. LC 00-20976. 177p. 2000. reprint ed. pap. 11.95 (*1-56478-238-7*, Pub. by Dalkey Arch) Chicago Distribution Ctr.

Reed, Ishmael, ed. Multi-America: Essays on Cultural Wars & Cultural Peace. LC 96-9130. xxviii, 468p. 1998. pap. 14.95 (*0-14-025912-0*, Penguin Bks) Viking Penguin.

Reed, Ishmael, et al, eds. The Before Columbus Foundation Fiction Anthology: Selections from the American Book Awards 1980-1990. 400p. 1991. 22.95 (*0-393-03055-5*); pap. 14.95 (*0-393-30832-4*) Norton.

— The Before Columbus Foundation Poetry Anthology: Selections from the American Book Awards 1980-1990. 320p. 1991. 22.95 (*0-393-03056-3*); pap. 14.95 (*0-393-30833-2*) Norton.

Reed, Ishmael, ed. see Vizenor, Gerald R.

Reed, J. Moby Dick (Melville) (Barron's Book Notes Ser.). (C). 1984. pap. 2.50 (*0-8120-3428-7*) Barron.

Reed, J. & Proctor, S. Practitioner Research in Health Care: The Inside Story. (Illus.). 224p. 1994. pap. text 42.50 (*1-56593-189-0*, 0504) Singular Publishing.

Reed, J., jt. ed. see Black, M.

Reed, J., tr. see Nasrallah, Ibrahim.

Reed, J. C. Martin Luther King, Jr. A Big Biography. 16p. (J). (gr. 2-4). 1994. pap. 16.95 (*1-56784-350-6*) Newbridge Educ.

Reed, J. D., ed. Bion of Smyrna: The Fragments of the Adonis. LC 96-21684. (Cambridge Classical Texts & Commentaries Ser.: No. 33). 279p. (C). 1997. text 64.95 (*0-521-57316-5*) Cambridge U Pr.

Reed, J. D. & Reed, Christine. Exposure. LC 86-29772. 242p. 1987. 14.95 (*0-939149-00-1*) Soho Press.

Reed, J. E., jt. auth. see Herriott, W.

Reed, J. J., jt. auth. see Chamberlain, Nugent F.

Reed, J. L. The Reed Genealogy, Descendants of William Reade of Weymouth, Mass., from 1635-1902. (Illus.). 786p. 1989. reprint ed. pap. 109.00 (*0-8328-1015-0*); reprint ed. lib. bdg. 117.00 (*0-8328-1014-2*) Higginson Bk Co.

Reed, J. W. History of the Reed Family in Europe & America. (Illus.). 596p. 1989. reprint ed. pap. 89.00 (*0-8328-1013-4*); reprint ed. lib. bdg. 97.00 (*0-8328-1012-6*) Higginson Bk Co.

Reed, James. The Birth Control Movement & American Society: From Private Vice to Public Virtue, With a New Preface on the Relationship Between Historical Scholarship & Feminist Issues. LC 83-60459. 482p. reprint ed. pap. 149.50 (*0-7837-1420-3*, 204177500023) Bks Demand.

*__Reed, James.__ Bruised Reed. 285p. 1999. pap. 11.99 (*1-84030-054-X*) Ambassador Prodns Ltd.

— A Bruised Reed. 169p. 1999. pap. 11.99 (*1-889893-40-4*, Ambassador-Emerald) Emerald House Group Inc.

Reed, James. The Missionary Mind & American East Asia Policy, 1911-1915. (East Asian Monographs: No. 104). 300p. 1983. 30.00 (*0-674-57657-8*) HUP.

Reed, James, ed. Border Ballads: A Selection. pap. write for info. (*0-85635-906-8*, Pub. by Carcanet Pr) Paul & Co Pubs.

— Sir Walter Scott (1771-1832) Selected Poems. pap. write for info. (*0-85635-958-0*, Pub. by Carcanet Pr) Paul & Co Pubs.

Reed, James, jt. auth. see Williams, Walter E.

Reed, James B. State Legislation Relating to Native Americans, 1991. (State Legislative Reports: Vol. 16, No. 9). 19p. 1991. pap. text 5.00 (*1-55516-308-4*, 7302-1609) Natl Conf State Legis.

Reed, James B. & Calhoun, John A. The California Framework for Science. (State Legislative Reports: Vol. 17, No. 2). 7p. 1992. pap. text 15.00 (*1-55516-310-6*, 7302-1702) Natl Conf State Legis.

Reed, James B. & Furneaux, David. Hazardous Material Transport: Closing the Information Gap. (State Legislative Reports: Vol. 19, No. 2). 6p. 1994. 15.00 (*1-55516-096-4*, 7302-1902) Natl Conf State Legis.

Reed, James B. & Goehring, Janet. On the Road with NAFTA. 16p. 1995. 15.00 (*1-55516-399-8*, 7302-2014) Natl Conf State Legis.

Reed, James B. & Mahoney, Katherine A. Federal Training Assistance for the Transportation of Spent Fuel. (State Legislative Reports: Vol. 17, No. 10). 5p. 1992. pap. text 15.00 (*1-55516-282-7*, 7302-1710) Natl Conf State Legis.

Reed, James B. & Zelio, Judy A. States & Tribes: Building New Traditions. LC 96-106696. 79p. 1995. 25.00 (*1-55516-929-5*, 9354) Natl Conf State Legis.

Reed, James B., et al. State Tribal Legislation: 1992 & 1993 Legislations. LC 98-40273. 26p. 1994. 10.00 (*1-55516-926-0*, 9364) Natl Conf State Legis.

Reed, James C. Chest Radiology: Plain Film Patterns & Differential Diagnoses. 4th ed. (Illus.). 496p. (C). (gr. 13). 1996. text 95.00 (*0-8151-7122-6*, 27076) Mosby Inc.

*__Reed, James E.__ A History of Christian Education. 1998. pap. text 24.99 (*0-8054-1867-9*) Broadman.

Reed, James E. History of Erie County, Pennsylvania, 2 vols. (Illus.). 1288p. 1994. reprint ed. lib. bdg. 130.00 (*0-8328-4007-6*) Higginson Bk Co.

Reed, James N., et al. The Black Man's Guide to Good Health: Essential Advice for the Special Concerns of African-American Men. Shucker, Charlene & Shulman, Neil B., eds. LC 94-13443. 288p. (Orig.). 1994. pap. 12.00 (*0-399-52138-0*, Perigee Bks) Berkley Pub.

Reed, James S. Principles of Ceramics Processing. 2nd ed. 688p. 1995. 89.95 (*0-471-59721-X*) Wiley.

*__Reed, James W., et al.__ The Black Man's Guide to Good Health: Essential Advice for African American Men & Their Families. rev. ed. (Illus.). 256p. 2000. pap. 16.95 (*0-9675258-1-0*, Pub. by Hilton Pubg) IPG Chicago.

Reed, Jan & Ground, Ian. Nursing & Philosophy. LC 96-167803. 1997. write for info. (*0-340-61028-X*, Pub. by E A) Routldge.

— Philosophy for Nursing. (Illus.). 192p. (Orig.). 1996. pap. 45.00 (*1-56593-757-0*, 1472) Singular Publishing.

Reed, Jan & Procter, Sue, eds. Practitioner Research in Health Care. 208p. 1995. pap. 34.95 (*0-412-49810-3*) Chapman & Hall.

Reed, Jane L., jt. auth. see Grundberg, Andy.

Reed, Janet, ed. Early Learning Program, 3 bks., Set. (Illus.). 1994. pap. 44.85 (*1-56784-346-8*) Newbridge Educ.

Reed, Janet & Ellis, Linette, eds. 501 Teacher Timesavers. (Macmillan Instant Activities Program Ser.). (Illus.). 108p. 1995. ring bd. 24.95 (*1-56784-700-5*) Newbridge Educ.

— A Treasury of Critical & Creative Thinking Activities. (Macmillan Instant Activities Program Ser.). (Illus.). 408p. 1993. ring bd. 29.95 (*1-56784-701-3*) Newbridge Educ.

Reed, Janet, ed. see Berger, Melvin.

Reed, Janet, ed. see Gold, Kari J.

Reed, Janet, ed. see Nayer, Judy.

Reed, Janet, ed. see Rothman, Cynthia.

Reed, Janice, jt. auth. see MacDowell, Marsha.

*__Reed, Janna.__ Amphibians & Reptiles: Thematic Unit. Hale, Janet A., ed. (Illus.). 80p. (J). 1999. pap., teacher ed. 9.95 (*1-57690-378-6*, TCM2378) Tchr Create Mat.

Reed, Janna. Chocolate. (Thematic Unit Ser.). (Illus.). 80p. 1994. pap., teacher ed. 9.95 (*1-55734-239-3*) Tchr Create Mat.

Reed, Jay. Comprehensive Guide to Industrial Locomotives. 2nd ed. (Illus.). 416p. 1998. pap. 22.95 (*0-9647221-1-9*) Rio Hondo Pub.

Reed, Jean. Arco Resumes That Get Jobs. 8th ed. 1995. 9.95 (*0-02-860590-X*, Arco) Macmillan Gen Ref.

— Resumes That Get Jobs. 9th ed. 208p. 1997. 10.95 (*0-02-862206-5*, Arc) IDG Bks.

Reed, Jean & Potter, Ray. Resumes That Get Jobs: With Resume-Writing Software. 9th ed. 208p. 1997. pap. 24.95 incl. cd-rom (*0-02-862195-6*, Arc) IDG Bks.

Reed, Jean, jt. auth. see Reed, Donn.

Reed, Jeanne. Business English. 4th ed. 1986. text 61.64 (*0-07-051503-4*) McGraw.

Reed, Jeff. Becoming a Disciple: First Principles of the Faith. Reed, Nancy, ed. (First Principles Ser.). (Illus.). 64p. 1997. pap. 6.99 (*1-891441-00-0*) LearnCorp Res.

— Belonging to a Family of Families: First Principles of Community Life. Reed, Nancy, ed. (First Principles Ser.). (Illus.). 64p. 1997. pap. 6.99 (*1-891441-01-9*) LearnCorp Res.

— Building for Future Generations: First Principles of True Success. Reed, Nancy, ed. (First Principles Ser.: Series II). (Illus.). 64p. 1998. pap. 6.99 (*1-891441-07-8*) LearnCorp Res.

An Asterisk (*) at the beginning of an entry indicates that the title is appearing for the first time.

— Cultivating Habits of the Heart: First Principles of Disciplined Living. Reed, Nancy, ed. (First Principles Ser.). (Illus.). 64p. 1997. pap. 6.99 (*1-891441-03-5*) LearnCorp Res.
— Enjoying Your Relationship: First Principles of Marriage. Reed, Nancy, ed. (First Principles, Series II). (Illus.). 64p. 1998. pap. 6.99 (*1-891441-04-3*) LearnCorp Res.
— Envisioning Fruitful LifeWork: First Principles of Ministry. Reed, Nancy, ed. (First Principles Ser.: Series II). (Illus.). 64p. 1998. pap. 6.99 (*1-891441-06-X*) LearnCorp Res.
— Participating in the Mission of the Church: First Principles of Community Purpose. Reed, Nancy, ed. (First Principles Ser.). (Illus.). 64p. 1997. pap. 6.99 (*1-891441-02-7*) LearnCorp Res.
— Passing on Your Beliefs: First Principles of Family Life. Reed, Nancy, ed. (First Principles Ser.: Series II). (Illus.). 64p. 1998. pap. 6.99 (*1-891441-05-1*) LearnCorp Res.
Reed, Jeffery T., jt. ed. see Porter, Stanley E.
Reed, Jeffrey. Bent Nails & Chipped Bricks. 128p. (Orig.). 1996. pap. 9.99 (*1-56043-265-9*, Treasure Hse) Destiny Image.
— From the Cave to the Throne. LC 98-163775. 144p. 1997. pap. 9.99 (*1-56043-287-X*, Treasure Hse) Destiny Image.
Reed, Jeffrey G. & Baxter, Pam M. Library Use: A Handbook for Psychology. 2nd ed. 177p. (Orig.). (C). 1992. pap. text 19.95 (*1-55798-144-2*) Am Psychol.
Reed, Jeffrey H., et al, eds. Wireless Personal Communications: Advances in Coverage & Capacity. LC 96-43020. (Kluwer International Series in Engineering & Computer Science). 240p. (C). 1996. text 109.00 (*0-7923-9788-6*) Kluwer Academic.
Reed, Jeffrey T. A Discourse Analysis of Philippians: Method & Rhetoric in the Debate over Literary Integrity. (JSNTS Ser.: Vol. 136). 525p. 1997. 85.00 (*1-85075-638-4*, Pub. by Sheffield Acad) CUP Services.
Reed, Jeremy. Angels, Divas & Blacklisted Heroes. 112p. 1997. pap. 17.95 (*0-7206-1052-4*, Pub. by P Owen Ltd) Dufour.
— Another Tear Falls: An Appreciation of Scott Walker. (Illus.). 192p. 1998. pap. 17.95 (*1-871592-75-5*) Creation Books.
— Bitter Blue: Tranquillisers, Drugs, Dependency. 136p. 1996. 29.95 (*0-7206-0892-9*, Pub. by P Owen Ltd) Dufour.
— Black Sugar: Gay, Lesbian & Heterosexual Love Poems. (Illus.). write for info. (*0-614-20072-5*, Pub. by P Owen Ltd) Dufour.
— Black Sugar: Gay, Lesbian & Heterosexual Love Poems. 128p. 1993. pap. 21.00 (*0-7206-0871-6*, Pub. by P Owen Ltd) Dufour.
— Chasing Black Rainbows: A Novel about Antonin Artaud. 184p. 1996. pap. 18.95 (*0-7206-1008-7*, Pub. by P Owen Ltd) Dufour.
— Chasing Black Rainbows: A Novel Based on the Life of Artaud. LC 94-200611. 184p. 1995. 28.00 (*0-7206-0924-0*, Pub. by P Owen Ltd) Dufour.
— Delirium: An Interpretation of Arthur Rimbaud. 200p. 1994. pap. text 9.95 (*0-87286-296-8*) City Lights.
— Diamond Nebula. 200p. 1996. pap. 18.95 (*0-7206-0922-4*, Pub. by P Owen Ltd) Dufour.
— Diamond Nebula: A Novel. 200p. 1995. 28.00 (*0-7206-0891-0*, Pub. by P Owen Ltd) Dufour.
— Dicing for Pearls. 38p. (Orig.). 1990. 25.00 (*1-870612-85-X*, Pub. by Enitha Pr); pap. 10.95 (*1-870612-80-9*, Pub. by Enitha Pr) Dufour.
— Dorian: A Sequel to the Picture of Dorian Grey. LC 96-161435. 167p. 1998. 27.95 (*0-7206-1012-5*, Pub. by P Owen Ltd) Dufour.
— Inhabiting Shadows. 120p. 1990. 30.00 (*0-7206-0787-6*, Pub. by P Owen Ltd) Dufour.
— Isidore: A Novel about the Comte de Lautreamont. (Illus.). 150p. 1992. 29.00 (*0-7206-0831-7*, Pub. by P Owen Ltd) Dufour.
— Isidore: The Life of Comte de Lautreamont. 144p. (Orig.). 1996. pap. 12.95 (*1-871592-42-9*) Creation Books.
— Kicks. unabridged ed. LC 95-131374. 192p. 1996. pap. 13.95 (*1-871592-15-1*) Creation Books.
— The Last Decadent: A Study of Brian Jones. (Illus.). 192p. 1999. pap. 17.95 (*1-871592-71-2*, Pub. by Creation Books) Subterranean Co.
— The Last Star: A Study of Marc Almond. (Illus.). 192p. (Orig.). 1996. pap. 15.95 (*1-871592-61-5*) Creation Books.
— The Last Star: A Study of Marc Almond. 2nd rev. ed. (Illus.). 192p. (Orig.). 1999. pap. 17.95 (*1-84068-006-7*) Creation Books.
— Lipstick, Sex & Poetry: An Autobiography. 119p. 1991. 30.00 (*0-7206-0817-1*, Pub. by P Owen Ltd) Dufour.
— Madness: The Price of Poetry. LC 90-80803. 208p. 1990. 36.00 (*0-7206-0744-2*) Dufour.
***Reed, Jeremy.** Patron Saint of Eye-Liner. 160p. 2000. 19.95 (*1-84068-042-3*, Pub. by Creation Books) Subterranean Co.
— The Pleasure Chateau. 242p. (Orig.). 2000. pap. 14.95 (*1-84068-046-6*, Pub. by Creation Bks) Subterranean Co.
Reed, Jeremy. The Pleasure Chateau. (Velvet Ser.: Vol. 3). 192p. (Orig.). 1996. pap. 12.95 (*1-871592-52-6*) Creation Books.
— Red-Haired Android. 280p. (Orig.). 1993. pap. 12.95 (*0-87286-283-6*) City Lights.
— Red Hot Lipstick. 144p. 1996. 28.95 (*0-7206-0988-7*, Pub. by P Owen Ltd) Dufour.
— Red Hot Lipstick. 160p. 1997. pap. 19.95 (*0-7206-0943-7*, Pub. by P Owen Ltd) Dufour.
— Red Hot Lipstick. deluxe ed. 144p. 1996. boxed set. write for info. (*0-7206-0989-5*, Pub. by P Owen Ltd) Dufour.
— Sister Midnight. 160p. 1998. reprint ed. pap. 12.95 (*1-871592-80-1*, Velvet Pub) Creation Books.
— Sweet Sister Lyric. LC 96-183846. 80p. 1996. pap. 16.95 (*1-870612-62-0*, Pub. by Enitha Pr) Dufour.
— When the Whip Comes Down: A Novel about De Sade. 136p. 1993. 30.00 (*0-7206-0857-0*, Pub. by P Owen Ltd); pap. 18.95 (*0-7206-0858-9*, Pub. by P Owen Ltd) Dufour.
Reed, Jeremy, et al. Pop Stars. (Illus.). 94p. 1995. pap. 17.95 (*1-870612-29-9*, Pub. by Enitha Pr) Dufour.
Reed, Jeremy, jt. auth. see Montale, Eugenio.
Reed, Jeremy, ed. see Beckford, William.
Reed, Jeremy, ed. see Carroll, Lewis, pseud.
Reed, Jeremy, ed. see Wilde, Oscar.
Reed, Jeremy, tr. see Cocteau, Jean.
Reed, Jeremy, tr. see Friedrich von Hardenberg, Georg P.
Reed, Jim. Dad's Tweed Coat. LC 96-69013. 176p. 1999. 14.95 (*1-887654-30-5*) Premium Pr TN.
***Reed, Jim.** Everything Imus: All You Ever Wanted to Know about Don Imus. 224p. 1999. 18.95 (*1-55972-930-9*, Birch Ln Pr) Carol Pub Group.
Reed, Jim. Everything Imus: All You Ever Wanted to Know about Don Imus. LC 99-17691. (Illus.). 224p. 1999. 18.95 (*1-55972-504-4*, Birch Ln Pr) Carol Pub Group.
Reed, Jim, jt. ed. see Jemison, Marie S.
Reed, Jim, illus. see Byrne, Randy.
Reed, Jim H. The False Eunich. 179p. 1991. pap. 13.50 (*1-885411-04-9*) Columbia Lit.
— Golden Mountain. 158p. 1992. pap. 9.95 (*1-885411-03-0*) Columbia Lit.
— The Three Sons of Han. 390p. (Orig.). 1994. pap. 13.50 (*1-885411-00-6*) Columbia Lit.
Reed, John. The Collected Works of John Reed. 960p. 1995. 20.00 (*0-679-60144-9*) Modern Lib NY.
— Daughter of the Revolution, & Other Stories. LC 75-134975. (Short Story Index Reprint Ser.). 1977. 16.95 (*0-8369-3707-4*) Ayer.
— The Education of John Reed. Stuart, John, ed. 224p. 1972. reprint ed. pap. 2.75 (*0-7178-0354-6*) Intl Pubs Co.
— Insurgent Mexico. LC 69-14047. 325p. 1969. reprint ed. lib. bdg. 69.50 (*0-8371-0633-8*, REIM, Greenwood Pr) Greenwood.
— Insurgent Mexico. LC 69-17616. 292p. 1994. reprint ed. pap. 7.95 (*0-7178-0099-7*) Intl Pubs Co.
— Paul Weller: My Ever Changing Moods. (Illus.). 392p. 1996. 24.95 (*0-7119-5495-X*, OP 47810) Omnibus NY.
— Schubert. (Master Musicians Ser.). 1997. 35.00 (*0-02-864867-6*) S&S Trade.
***Reed, John.** A Still Small Voice. 288p. 2000. 23.95 (*0-385-33405-2*) Delacorte.
— The Story of Mod. (Illus.). 160p. 1999. write for info. (*0-7119-6813-6*) Omnibus NY.
Reed, John. Ten Days That Shook the World. LC 67-27252. (Illus.). 396p. (C). 1989. pap. 6.95 (*0-7178-0200-0*) Intl Pubs Co.
— Ten Days That Shook the World. LC 97-14782. (Illus.). 288p. 1997. text 35.00 (*0-312-17711-9*) St Martin.
— Ten Days That Shook the World. 1992. reprint ed. lib. bdg. 21.95 (*0-89968-271-5*, Lghtyr Pr) Buccaneer Bks.
— The Third Day. Miles, Kathy, ed. 117p. 1995. pap. 32.95 (*0-8464-4761-4*) Beekman Pubs.
— Whole Dog Catalog: More Than 800 Terrific Toys. LC 97-8077. 1997. pap. 19.95 (*0-609-80037-X*) Random Hse Value.
Reed, John, ed. see Vance, Rupert.
Reed, John, tr. see Oyono, Ferdinand.
Reed, John, tr. see Senghor, Leopold S.
Reed, John A., Jr. Germany & NATO. 265p. (Orig.). (C). 1995. pap. text 40.00 (*0-7881-2157-X*) DIANE Pub.
Reed, John C. Conduct of Lawsuits out of & in Court: Practically Teaching, & Copiously Illustrating, the Preparation & Forensic Management of Litigated Cases of All Kinds. LC 94-17732. xxvii, 434p. 1994. reprint ed. 52.50 (*0-8377-2576-3*, Rothman) W S Hein.
Reed, John C., Jr., et al, eds. Precambrian: Conterminous U. S. LC 92-30479. (DNAG, Geology of North America Ser.: Vol. C2). 1993. 49.25 (*0-8137-5218-3*) Geol Soc.
Reed, John C. & Love, J. D. Creation of Teton Landscape: The Geologic Story of Grand Teton National Park. Pecara, W. T. & U. S. Games Systems Staff, eds. (Illus.). 120p. 1995. reprint ed. pap. 12.95 (*0-931895-08-1*) Grand Teton NHA.
Reed, John E. History of Erie County, Pennsylvania, 2 vols., Set. (Illus.). 1288p. 1993. reprint ed. lib. bdg. 125.00 (*0-8328-3222-7*) Higginson Bk Co.
Reed, John F. Campaign to Valley Forge. 1980. reprint ed. 17.50 (*0-913150-42-8*) Pioneer Pr.
— Root & Shoot Growth of Shortleaf & Loblolly Pines in Relation to Certain Environmental Conditions. LC 40-13430. (Duke University, School of Forestry Bulletin Ser.: No. 4). 54p. reprint ed. pap. 30.00 (*0-7837-6052-3*, 204586500008) Bks Demand.
— Valley Forge, Crucible of Victory. LC 70-76769. (Revolutionary War Bicentennial Ser.). (Illus.). 1969. lib. bdg. 11.95 (*0-912480-04-1*) Freneau.
Reed, John H. The Application of Operations Research to Court Delay. LC 72-89647. (Special Studies in U. S. Economic, Social & Political Issues). 1973. 42.50 (*0-275-06690-8*) Irvington.
— Directory of Back Issue Treasure Magazine Buyers, Sellers, & Traders. 41p. (Orig.). 1987. pap. 5.95 (*0-940519-02-X*) Res Discover Pubns.
— Directory of Treasure Hunting, Prospecting & Related Organizations. LC 86-63262. 191p. 1987. pap. 9.95 (*0-940519-00-3*) Res Discover Pubns.
— Treasure Hunting Bibliography & Index to Periodical Articles. 425p. (Orig.). 1989. pap. 19.95 (*0-940519-04-6*) Res Discover Pubns.
Reed, John R. Decadent Style. LC 84-16545. (Illus.). 284p. (C). 1985. text 35.00 (*0-8214-0793-7*) Ohio U Pr.
— Dickens & Thackeray: Punishment & Forgiveness. LC 94-40416. 528p. 1997. pap. text 29.95 (*0-8214-1175-6*) Ohio U Pr.
— Great Lake & Other Poems. 73p. (Orig.). 1995. pap. 9.95 (*1-56439-044-6*) Ridgeway.
— Life Sentences. 86p. (Orig.). 1996. pap. 15.95 (*0-8143-2629-3*) Wayne St U Pr.
— The Natural History of H. G. Wells. LC 81-11261. 304p. 1982. lib. bdg. 30.00 (*0-8214-0628-0*) Ohio U Pr.
— Old School Ties: The Public School in British Literature. LC 64-23341. 344p. reprint ed. pap. 106.70 (*0-8357-3980-5*, 203667800005) Bks Demand.
— Victorian Conventions. LC 73-92908. 574p. 1975. pap. text 27.95 (*0-8214-0828-3*) Ohio U Pr.
— Victorian Conventions. LC 73-92908. 574p. 1975. 40.00 (*0-8214-0147-5*) Ohio U Pr.
— Victorian Will. LC 88-33695. 511p. 1989. lib. bdg. 39.95 (*0-8214-0928-X*) Ohio U Pr.
Reed, John S. The Enduring South: Subcultural Persistence in Mass Society. LC 86-40031. xxi, 150p. 1986. pap. 16.95 (*0-8078-4162-5*) U of NC Pr.
— Glorious Battle: The Cultural Politics of Victorian Anglo-Catholicism. LC 96-52009. (Illus.). 384p. 1996. 34.95 (*0-8265-1274-7*) Vanderbilt U Pr.
— Kicking Back: Further Dispatches from the South. 192p. (C). 1995. 22.50 (*0-8262-1004-X*) U of Mo Pr.
— My Tears Spoiled My Aim. 168p. 1994. pap. 8.95 (*0-15-600006-7*) Harcourt.
— My Tears Spoiled My Aim: And Other Reflections on Southern Culture. LC 92-37623. (Illus.). 168p. (C). 1993. 19.95 (*0-8262-0886-X*) U of Mo Pr.
— One South: An Ethnic Approach to Regional Culture. LC 81-19387. xxii, 218p. (C). 1982. pap. text 17.95 (*0-8071-1038-8*) La State U Pr.
— 1001 Things Everyone Should Know About the South. 272p. 1997. pap. 15.95 (*0-385-47442-3*) Doubleday.
— Southern Folk, Plain & Fancy: Native White Social Types. LC 86-1479. (Brown Thrasher Bks.). (Illus.). 136p. 1988. pap. 13.95 (*0-8203-1023-9*) U of Ga Pr.
— Surveying the South: Studies in Regional Sociology. LC 93-8561. 168p. (Orig.). (C). 1993. pap. 15.95 (*0-8262-0915-7*) U of Mo Pr.
— Surveying the South: Studies in Regional Sociology. LC 93-8561. 168p. (Orig.). (C). 1993. text 30.00 (*0-8262-0914-9*) U of Mo Pr.
— Whistling Dixie: Dispatches from the South. 264p. 1992. pap. 9.95 (*0-15-696174-1*, Harvest Bks) Harcourt.
— Whistling Dixie: Dispatches from the South. 200p. 1990. 29.95 (*0-8262-0758-8*) U of Mo Pr.
Reed, John S. & Watson, Harry L., eds. Sports in the South. (Southern Cultures Ser.: Vol. 3). 136p. 1997. 9.00 (*0-8078-5303-8*) U of NC Pr.
Reed, John S., jt. auth. see Black, Merle.
***Reed, John Sheldon.** Glorious Battle: The Cultural Politics of Victorian Anglo-Catholicism. 2000. reprint ed. pap. 21.95 (*0-8265-1380-8*) Vanderbilt U Pr.
Reed, John T. Aggressive Tax Avoidance for Real Estate Investors: How to Make Sure You Aren't Paying One More. 16th ed. 267p. 1998. pap. text 23.95 (*0-939224-41-0*) John T Reed.
— Coaching Youth Football. 2nd ed. LC 97-69472. (Illus.). 256p. 1997. pap. 21.95 (*0-939224-40-2*) John T Reed.
— Coaching Youth Football Defense. 2nd ed. LC 96-222147. (Illus.). 224p. 1996. pap. text 19.95 (*0-939224-36-4*) John T Reed.
— Football Clock Management. LC 97-91682. (Illus.). 240p. (Orig.). 1997. pap. 19.95 (*0-939224-39-9*) John T Reed.
— How to by Real Estate for at Least 20 Percent Below Market Value. 2nd ed. LC 96-92154. (Illus.). 280p. 1996. ring bd. 39.95 (*0-939224-37-2*) John T Reed.
— How to Increase the Value of Real Estate. 208p. 1986. ring bd. 39.95 (*0-939224-10-0*) John T Reed.
— How to Manage Residential Property for Maximum Cash Flow & Resale Value: How to Maximize Your Income & Minimize Your Expenses & Hassles. 5th rev. ed. LC 98-67085. (Illus.). 300p. 1998. pap. 23.95 (*0-939224-42-9*) John T Reed.
— How to Use Leverage to Maximize Your Real Estate Investment Return. 300p. 1991. ring bd. 39.95 (*0-939224-12-7*) John T Reed.
— Office Building Acquisition Handbook: Checklists for Making Sure You Don't Overlook Anything Important When You Buy an Office Building. LC 85-90317. 170p. 1985. ring bd. 39.95 (*0-939224-17-8*) John T Reed.
— Real Estate Investment Strategy: Selected Articles from the National Newsletter. 290p. 1991. ring bd. 39.95 (*0-939224-23-2*) John T Reed.
— Residential Property Acquisition Handbook: Checklists for Making Sure You Don't Overlook Anything Important When You Buy a House, Condo, Apartment Building. 250p. 1991. ring bd. 39.95 (*0-939224-22-4*) John T Reed.
***Reed, John T.** Youth Baseball Coaching. (Illus.). 256p. 2000. pap. 23.95 (*0-939224-38-0*, Pub. by John T Reed) Publishers Group.
***Reed-Johnson, Mary.** The World of Dreadlocks. (Illus.). vii, 65p. 2000. text 19.95 (*0-9679750-0-X*) Hair Is.
***Reed, Jonas.** History of Rutland, Worcester Co. MA, from Its Earliest Settlement: With a Biography of Its First Settlers. fac. ed. 168p. 2000. reprint ed. 27.00 (*0-8328-2499-2*) Higginson Bk Co.
Reed, Jonas. A History of Rutland, Worcester County, Massachusetts, from Its Earliest Settlement, with a Biography of Its First Settlers. 168p. 1992. reprint ed. lib. bdg. 24.50 (*0-8328-2522-0*) Higginson Bk Co.
***Reed, Jonathan.** Archaeology & the Galilean Jesus: A Reexamination of the Evidence. 256p. 2000. pap. 30.00 (*1-56338-324-1*) TPI PA.
Reed-Jones, Carol. Green Weddings That Don't Cost the Earth. LC 96-67124. (Illus.). 163p. (Orig.). 1996. pap. 10.95 (*0-9650833-0-6*) Paper Crane.
— The Tree in the Ancient Forest. (Illus.). 36p. (J). (ps-5). 1995. 16.95 (*1-883220-32-7*); pap. 7.95 (*1-883220-31-9*) Dawn CA.
Reed-Jones, Carol. The Tree in the Ancient Forest. 1995. 13.15 (*0-606-08891-1*, Pub. by Turtleback) Demco.
Reed, Joseph R., jt. auth. see Field, Homer H.
Reed, Joseph W., Jr. English Biography in the Early Nineteenth Century: 1801-1838. 1966. 59.50 (*0-685-45652-8*) Elliots Bks.
Reed, Joseph W., ed. see Reed, Kit.
Reed, Joseph W., Jr., ed. see Walpole, Horace.
***Reed, Joy.** Catherine's Wish. 2000. mass mkt. 5.50 (*0-8217-6645-7*, Zebra Kensgtn) Kensgtn Pub Corp.
Reed, Joy. The Duke & Miss Denny. 256p. 1998. pap. 4.99 (*0-8217-5931-0*) Kensgtn Pub Corp.
— Home for the Holidays. 256p. 1998. mass mkt. 4.99 (*0-8217-6071-8*) Kensgtn Pub Corp.
— An Inconvenient Engagement. 320p. 1997. mass mkt. 4.99 (*0-8217-5839-X*, Zebra Kensgtn) Kensgtn Pub Corp.
***Reed, Joy.** Lord Caldwell & the Cat, Vol. 1. (Zebra Regency Romance Ser.). 1999. mass mkt. 4.99 (*0-8217-6356-3*, Zebra Kensgtn) Kensgtn Pub Corp.
Reed, Joy. Lord Wyland Takes a Wife. 256p. 1997. mass mkt. 4.99 (*0-8217-5767-9*, Zebra Kensgtn) Kensgtn Pub Corp.
***Reed, Joy.** Miss Chambers Takes Charge. (Zebra Regency Romance Ser.). 2000. mass mkt. 4.99 (*0-8217-6581-7*, Zebra Kensgtn) Kensgtn Pub Corp.
Reed, Joy. The Seduction of Lady Carroll. 224p. 1996. mass mkt. 4.50 (*0-8217-5382-7*, Zebra Kensgtn) Kensgtn Pub Corp.
Reed, Joyce G. Take a Whistler's Walk. (Illus.). 77p. (J). (gr. 4-9). 1988. 12.95 (*0-943487-08-0*); pap. 4.95 (*0-943487-07-2*) Sevgo Pr.
Reed, Judith. Lauren Groveman's Kitchen: Nurturing Food for Family & Friends. LC 94-13263. 528p. 1994. 24.95 (*0-8118-0609-X*) Chronicle Bks.
***Reed, Karen.** The Complete Idiot's Guide to Woodworking. (Illus.). 400p. 2000. pap. 16.95 (*0-02-863237-0*) Macmillan Gen Ref.
Reed, Karen J. Music Is the Master Key. LC 97-40440. (Illus.). 160p. 1999. 18.95 (*0-944957-70-6*) Rivercross Pub.
Reed, Karen S. Betty Neuman: The Neuman Systems Model. (Notes on Nursing Theories Ser.: Vol. 11). (Illus.). 64p. (C). 1993. text 22.95 (*0-8039-4861-1*); pap. text 9.95 (*0-8039-4862-X*) Sage.
Reed, Katherine M., jt. ed. see Bartsch-Winkler, Susan.
***Reed, Kathlyn L.** Quick Reference to Occupational Therapy. 2nd ed. 1024p. 2000. pap. 49.00 (*0-8342-1631-0*) Aspen Pub.
Reed, Kathlyn L. & Cunningham, Sandra. Internet Guide for Rehabilitation Professionals. (Illus.). 224p. 1997. pap. text 32.00 (*0-397-55463-X*) Lppncott W & W.
Reed, Kathlyn L. & Nelson, Sharon R. Concepts of Occupational Therapy. 3rd ed. (Illus.). 410p. 1992. 36.00 (*0-683-07207-2*) Lppncott W & W.
Reed, Kathlyn L., jt. auth. see Pauls, Julie A.
Reed, Kathlyn L., jt. auth. see Pore, Sally G.
Reed, Kathryn L. Fetal Echocardiography: An Atlas. LC 88-686. (Illus.). 146p. 1988. 169.95 (*0-471-61733-4*) Wiley.
Reed, Kathryn L., jt. ed. see Copel, Joshua A.
Reed, Keith A., et al, eds. New York State Employment Laws & Regulations: How to Comply. 140p. 1995. pap. 75.00 (*0-923606-01-7*) Amer CC Pubs.
Reed, Keith A. & Mignin, Robert J., eds. Employment Discrimination: How to Comply. 174p. 1995. pap. 75.00 (*0-923606-04-1*) Amer CC Pubs.
— Federal Employment Laws & Regulations: How to Comply. 322p. 1995. pap. 75.00 (*0-685-67823-7*) Amer CC Pubs.
Reed, Keith A. & Mignini, Robert J., eds. Chicagoland Employment Law Manual. 456p. 1994. pap. 75.00 (*0-614-06735-9*) Amer CC Pubs.
Reed, Kelly, jt. ed. see Schunk, Carol.
Reed, Kelvin L. Rookie Year: Journey of a First-Year Teacher. LC 98-96642. 336p. 1999. 21.95 (*0-9667631-2-2*) Peralta Pub Co.
***Reed, Ken.** Introduction to Local Area Networks, NetPrep: Netprep WB26.0. rev. ed. Aust, Marilee, ed. 410p. (YA). 1999. write for info. (*1-58676-009-2*) WestNet Learn.
— Introduction to Local Area Networks, NetWorx: NetWorx, WB26.0. rev. ed. Aust, Marilee, ed. 410p. (YA). 1999. write for info. (*1-58676-010-6*) WestNet Learn.
— Introduction to Networking. rev. ed. (Tech Ser.: Vol. 3CS-111). (Illus.). 364p. (C). 1998. write for info. (*1-58676-034-3*) WestNet Learn.
— Introduction to Networking, NetWorx: NetWorx WB16.0. rev. ed. (Illus.). 364p. (C). 1998. write for info. (*1-58676-001-7*) WestNet Learn.
— Introduction to Wide Area Networks, NetPrep: NetPrep WB36.0. rev. ed. Aust, Marilee, ed. (Illus.). 415p. (C). 1999. write for info. (*1-58676-015-7*) WestNet Learn.
— Introduction to Wide Area Networks, NetWorx: NetWorx, WB36.0. rev. ed. Aust, Marilee, ed. (Illus.). 415p. (C). 1999. write for info. (*1-58676-016-5*) WestNet Learn.
— LAN Architectures. rev. ed. Aust, Marilee, ed. (Tech Ser.: Vol. 3CS-112). (Illus.). 410p. 1999. write for info. (*1-58676-035-1*) WestNet Learn.
Reed, Ken. Lectures in Psychiatry: The Functional Psychoses, Vol. 1. (Illus.). 304p. 1985. 37.50 (*0-87527-339-4*) Green.
Reed, Ken, photos by. Data Network Handbook: An Interactive Guide to Network Architecture & Operations. (Illus.). 391p. (Orig.). (C). 1996. text, teacher ed. 54.95 incl. cd-rom (*0-442-02299-9*) S-W Pub.
Reed, Ken C. & Graves, Jennifer A., eds. Mammalian Sex Chromosomes & Sex-Determining Genes. LC 92-1483. xviii, 410p. 1993. text 131.00 (*3-7186-5276-5*) Gordon & Breach.
Reed, Kenneth. Data Network Handbook. 1996. 49.95 (*0-614-20336-8*, VNR) Wiley.

An Asterisk (*) at the beginning of an entry indicates that the title is appearing for the first time.

R

Reed, Kenneth. Data Network Handbook: An Interactive Guide to Network Architecture & Operations. 400p. 1996. 75.00 (*0-471-28775-X*, VNR) Wiley.

— Introduction to Networking, NetPrep: NetPrep WBNP16.0. (Illus.). 364p. (C). 1998. write for info. (*1-58676-000-9*) WestNet Learn.

Reed, Kenny, tr. see Bogary, Hamza.

Reed, Kevin J. The Saratoga Yearling. Herold, Meri G., ed. (Illus.). 110p. (Orig.). (J). (gr. 5-9). 1985. pap. 3.95 (*0-9614546-0-1*) Chowder Pr.

— A Season for Dreams. LC 89-90670. (Illus.). 152p. (J). (gr. 5-7). 1989. pap. 5.95 (*0-9614546-3-6*) Chowder Pr.

Reed, Kevin J., jt. auth. see Warner, David C.

***Reed, Kit.** At Expectations. 256p. 2000. text 22.95 (*0-312-87486-3*) St Martin.

Reed, Kit. Fat. LC 73-22670. 1974. 7.95 (*0-672-51979-8*, Bobbs) Macmillan.

— Seven for the Apocalypse. LC 99-19334. 230p. 1999. pap. 16.95 (*0-8195-6382-X*, Wesleyan Univ Pr); text 40.00 (*0-8195-6381-1*, Wesleyan Univ Pr) U Pr of New Eng.

— Story First: The Writer As Insider. Reed, Joseph W., ed. 150p. 1982. 19.95 (*0-13-850487-3*) P-H.

— Thief of Lives. 192p. 1992. 24.95 (*0-8262-0850-9*) U of Mo Pr.

— Weird Women, Wired Women. LC 97-43287. 234p. 1998. pap. 17.95 (*0-8195-2255-4*, Wesleyan Univ Pr) U Pr of New Eng.

***Reed, Kjersti A.** Notes on a Broken Chandelier (Poems by Kjersti A. Reed) 33p. 2000. pap. 6.00 (*1-882983-45-9*) March Street Pr.

Reed, Lajou. Art M & A. 3rd ed. 1998. text 135.00 (*0-7863-1237-8*, Irwn Prfssnl) McGraw-Hill Prof.

Reed-Lajoux, Alexandra, jt. auth. see Reed, Stanley Foster.

Reed, Langford. Writer's Rhyming Dictionary. LC 61-16086. 1985. pap. 8.95 (*0-87116-143-5*) Writer.

Reed, Larry, ed. see Wirth, Steven & Farkas, May.

Reed, Larry, ed. see Wirth, Steven & Wirth, Sandra.

Reed, Larson. Divergent Realities. 1994. 22.95 (*0-02-918011-2*) S&S Trade.

Reed, Lawrence W. A Lesson from the Past: The Silver Panic of 1893. 93p. (Orig.). 1993. pap. 7.95 (*0-910614-90-3*) Foun Econ Ed.

Reed, Lawrence W., ed. Private Cures for Public Ills: The Promise of Privatization. LC 95-83090. 208p. (Orig.). 1996. pap. 10.95 (*1-57246-019-9*) Foun Econ Ed.

Reed, Lawrence W. & Haywood, Dale M. When We Are Free. 3rd ed. 403p. 17.50 (*0-87359-054-6*) Northwood Univ.

Reed, Lee O., jt. auth. see Corley, Robert N.

Reed, Lena F., jt. auth. see Brey, Catherine F.

Reed, Lena F., ed. see Tolhurst, William D.

Reed, Leslee, jt. auth. see Peyton, Joy K.

Reed, Lester. Old Time Cattlemen: And Other Pioneers of the Anza-Borrego Area. 3rd ed. 146p. 1986. reprint ed. pap. 7.95 (*0-910805-02-4*) Anza-Borrego.

Reed, Lewis. Specs: The Comprehensive Foodservice Purchasing & Specification Manual. 2nd ed. LC 92-12414. 712p. 1993. text 108.95 (*0-442-00705-1*, VNR) Wiley.

Reed, Lewis. Specs: The Comprehensive Foodservice Purchasing & Specification Manual. 2nd ed. 712p. 1993. 140.00 (*0-471-28424-6*, VNR) Wiley.

Reed, Lewis. Wenzel's Menu Maker. 3rd ed. 1997. text 166.95 (*0-442-01283-7*, VNR) Wiley.

Reed, Linda. Simple Decency & Common Sense: The Southern Conference Movement, 1938-1963. LC 91-7803. (Blacks in the Diaspora Ser.). (Illus.). 288p. 1991. text 31.50 (*0-253-34895-1*) Ind U Pr.

— Simple Decency & Common Sense: The Southern Conference Movement, 1938-1963. LC 91-7803. (Blacks in the Diaspora Ser.). 288p. 1994. pap. 11.95 (*0-253-20912-9*) Ind U Pr.

Reed, Linda, jt. auth. see Lane, Karen.

Reed, Lisa A. Toward Logical Form: An Exploration of the Role of Syntax in Semantics. Horn, Laurence, ed. LC 96-34690. (Outstanding Dissertations in Linguistics Ser.). 344p. 1996. text 75.00 (*0-8153-2555-X*) Garland.

Reed, Lorena. Blue Water Women. (Illus.). 320p. 1993. write for info. (*0-933858-12-4*) Kennebec River.

Reed, Lori S. & Reed, Paul F., eds. Cultural Diversity & Adaptation: The Archaic, Anasazi, & Navajo Occupation of the San Juan Basin. (Cultural Resources Ser.: No. 9). (Illus.). 182p. (Orig.). 1992. 8.00 (*1-878178-10-5*) Bureau of Land Mgmt NM.

Reed, Lou. Pass Thru Fire: The Collected Lyrics. LC 98-23415. (Illus.). 352p. 1999. 24.95 (*0-7868-6452-4*, Pub. by Hyperion) Time Warner.

Reed, Lynn R. Pedro, His Perro & the Alphabet Sombrero. large type ed. LC 94-28215. (Illus.). 32p. (J). (ps-3). 1995. 14.95 (*0-7868-0071-2*, Pub. by Hyprn Child) Little.

Reed, M. Landscape of Britain. (Illus.). 408p. (C). 1997. pap. 29.95 (*0-415-15745-5*, D4178) Routledge.

Reed, M. & Howard, V. Unbiased Stereology: A Practical Guide. LC 97-45235. (Microscopy Handbooks Ser.). (Illus.). 144p. 1997. pap. 32.95 (*0-387-91516-8*) Spr-Verlag.

Reed, M. Ann. Raven Brings to the People Another Gift: A Story Based on Native American Legend. (American Heritage Ser.: Vol. 5). (Illus.). 18p. (J). (gr. 3 up). 1997. 3.95 (*1-877976-19-9*) Tipi Pr.
True to tradition, this story begins with the storyteller in Raven mask (symbol of transformation) weaving a whole new story, one beginning where the legend of how Raven brings light to the people ends. In this new story, Raven is inspired by Crane & his brothers & sisters in China. He learns the pathway to wisdom by traveling it. He learns how each virtue plants its own seeds, seeds that bear their own stories. Author M. Ann Reed experienced the joy of receiving this story from the creative spirit in whom all new stories are born. She offers Young Authors' Creative Writing Workshops at Bamber Valley Elementary School in Rochester, Minnesota where she lives & writes poetry, drama & short stories. The Native American Sacred Circle & oral tradition is always part of her teaching of composition & communication. Illustrator Nakoma Volkman initiated Nakoma Art Traditions & is a traditional dancer & singer whose art & writings are devoted to sharing Native American values & spirituality. He has lectured, performed & presented educational programs for forty years, is enrolled with the National American Indian Enrollment Agency, & is a founding member & retired chairman of the Native American Center of Southeastern Minnesota. Order from Tipi Press, St. Joseph's Indian School, Chamberlain, SD 57326, 605-734-3300, 800-229-5684.
Publisher Paid Annotation.

Reed, Mabel, jt. auth. see Arnold, Mary E.

Reed, Marcelina. Seven Clans of the Cherokee Society. (Illus.). 32p. (YA). (gr. 5-12). 1993. pap. 4.00 (*0-935741-17-8*, Pub. by Cherokee Pubns) Book Pub Co.

***Reed, Marcia & Terminello, Verna.** Business Netiquette: Being a Good E-mmunity Netizen at Work. (Communicating Effectively & Responsibly Through E-Mail Ser.). 2000. write for info. (*1-930862-01-6*) E-mail E-mmun.

Reed, Marcia, jt. auth. see Terminello, Verna.

Reed, Marietta, jt. auth. see Timberlake, Lewis.

Reed, Mark. How to Find Your Gifts. (Illus.). 80p. (YA). (gr. 7-12). 1995. pap. 6.95 (*1-57515-080-8*) PPI Pubng.

Reed, Mark & Johnsen, Stale, eds. Produced Water 2: Environmental Issues & Mitigation Technologies. (Environmental Science Research Ser.: Vol. 52). (Illus.). 549p. (C). 1996. 167.00 (*0-306-45308-8*, Plenum Trade) Perseus Pubng.

Reed, Mark, jt. ed. see Spaulding, Malcolm L.

Reed, Mark A. & Kirk, Wiley P., eds. Nanostructure Physics & Fabrication. 544p. 1989. text 108.00 (*0-12-585000-X*) Acad Pr.

Reed, Mark A., jt. auth. see Melloch, Mike.

Reed, Mark L. Wordsworth: The Chronology of the Early Years, 1770-1799. LC 66-21344. 383p. 1967. reprint ed. pap. 118.80 (*0-7837-4182-0*, 205903100012) Bks Demand.

— Wordsworth: The Chronology of the Middle Years, 1800-1815. LC 74-77179. 768p. 1975. 54.50 (*0-674-95777-6*) HUP.

Reed, Mark L., ed. see Nichols, Gary.

Reed, Mark L., ed. see Wordsworth, William.

Reed, Martin H. Skeletal Radiology. (Illus.). 696p. 1991. 150.00 (*0-683-07212-9*) Lppncott W & W.

Reed, Martin H., jt. auth. see Webb, Randall.

Reed, Mary. Fruits & Nuts in Symbolism & Celebration. LC 92-23681. (Illus.). 248p. (Orig.). (C). 1992. pap. 21.95 (*0-89390-238-1*) Resource Pubns.

***Reed, Mary.** One for Sorrow. 288p. 2000. pap. 12.95 (*1-890208-42-6*) Poisoned Pen.

— Two for Joy. 2000. 23.95 (*1-890208-37-X*) Poisoned Pen.

***Reed, Mary, ed.** The ABC Art & Craft Event Directory: Year 2000 Edition. annot. ed. (Illus.). 320p. 1999. pap. 19.95 (*0-9667487-1-9*) ACD Dir.

***Reed, Mary & Mayer, Eric.** One for Sorrow. LC 99-61907. 302p. 1999. 23.95 (*1-890208-19-1*) Poisoned Pen.

Reed, Mary & Simon-Smolinski, Carole. Researching Local History. (Local History Technical Leaflets Ser.). (Illus.). 22p. (Orig.). 1985. pap. 1.50 (*0-931406-08-0*) Idaho State Soc.

Reed, Mary, jt. auth. see Ventura, John.

Reed, Mary E. Carol Ryrie Brink. LC 91-55034. (Western Writers Ser.: No. 100). (Illus.). 51p. 1991. 4.95 (*0-88430-099-4*) Boise St U W Writ Ser.

Reed, Mary E., jt. auth. see Petersen, Keith C.

Reed, Mary H. IEG Legal Guide to Sponsorship. 498p. 1989. 79.00 (*0-944807-01-1*) IEG.

***Reed, Mary Lou.** Grandparents Cry Twice: Help for Bereaved Grandparents. Morgan, John D., ed. LC 99-34925. (Death, Value & Meaning Ser.). 142p. 2000. pap. 23.95 (*0-89503-204-X*) Baywood Pub.

Reed, Mary M. An Investigation of Practices in First Grade Admission & Promotion. LC 70-177183. (Columbia University. Teachers College. Contributions to Education Ser.: No. 290). reprint ed. 37.50 (*0-404-55290-0*) AMS Pr.

Reed, Maxine, compiled by. And Baby Makes Three. 144p. 1995. 7.95 (*0-8092-3496-3*, 349630, Contemporary Bks) NTC Contemp Pub Co.

Reed, Maxine K. & Reed, Robert M. Career Opportunities in Television, Cable, Video & Multimedia: A Comprehensive Guide to More Than 100 Exciting Careers in Television, Video, & New Media. 4th ed. Phenner, Lee, ed. LC 98-51425. 288p. 1999. 35.00 (*0-8160-3940-2*, Checkmark); pap. 18.95 (*0-8160-3941-0*, Checkmark) Facts on File.

***Reed, Meredith, ed.** Into Teachers' Hands: Creating Classroom Success. 11th ed. (SDE Sourcebook Ser.). (Illus.). 336p. 1998. pap. 24.95 (*1-884548-22-9*, 5533, Crystal Spgs) Soc Dev Educ.

Reed, Merl E. Seedtime for the Modern Civil Rights Movement: The President's Committee on Fair Employment Practice, 1941-1946. LC 90-39656. 344p. 1991. pap. text 18.95 (*0-8071-1688-2*) La State U Pr.

Reed, Merl E., et al, eds. Southern Workers & Their Unions, Eighteen Eighty to Nineteen Seventy-Five: Selected Papers, the Second Southern Labor History Conference, 1978, 39. LC 80-24724. (Contributions in Economics & Economic History Ser.: No. 39). (Illus.). 249p. 1981. 65.00 (*0-313-22701-2*, RSW/) Greenwood.

Reed, Merl E., jt. ed. see Fink, Gary M.

Reed, Meryl L., et al. Guide to Troubled Businesses & Bankruptcies, 2 vols. 3rd ed. Incl. Vol. 2. 3rd rev. ed. 1995. ring bd. (*1-56433-819-3*); Vol. 1. 3rd rev. ed. 1995. ring bd. (*1-56433-820-7*); 140.00 (*1-56433-818-5*) Prctnrs Pub Co.

Reed, Michael. The Landscape of Britain: From the Beginnings to 1914. (Illus.). 368p. (C). 1990. text 83.00 (*0-389-20933-3*) B&N Imports.

Reed, Michael & Hughes, Michael. Rethinking Organization: New Directions in Organization Theory & Analysis. 320p. (C). 1992. text 62.00 (*0-8039-8287-9*); pap. text 22.00 (*0-8039-8288-7*) Sage.

Reed, Michael & Simon, Barry. Methods of Modern Mathematical Physics, 4 vols. Incl. Vol. 2. Fourier Analysis Self-Adjointness. 1975. text 71.00 (*0-12-585002-6*); Vol. 3. Scattering Theory. 1979. text 84.00 (*0-12-585003-4*); Vol. 4. 1978. text 71.00 (*0-12-585004-2*); write for info. (*0-318-50309-3*) Acad Pr.

Reed, Michael & Simon, Barry, eds. Methods of Modern Mathematical Physics: Functional Analysis, Vol. 1. 2nd enl. rev. ed. 1980. text 71.00 (*0-12-585050-6*) Acad Pr.

Reed, Michael, jt. auth. see Ray, Larry.

Reed, Michael, ed. see Lange, Ronald H.

Reed, Michael C. Fundamental Ideas of Analysis. LC 97-20683. 432p. 1997. text 95.95 (*0-471-15996-4*) Wiley.

— Practicing Anthropology in a Postmodern World: Lessons & Insights from Federal Contract Research. LC 97-6539. (NAPA Bulletin Ser.). 1997. write for info. (*0-913167-81-9*) Am Anthro Assn.

Reed, Michael C., jt. auth. see Barnes, James F.

Reed, Michael L. & Rohrer, Ronald A. Applied Introductory Circuit Analysis for Electrical & Computer Engineers. LC 98-40881. 499p. (C). 1998. 100.00 (*0-13-787631-9*, Macmillan Coll) P-H.

***Reed, Michael R.** International Trade in Agricultural Products. LC 00-20569. 256p. 2000. 85.00 (*0-13-084209-5*) P-H.

Reed, Michal. The Weight of the Body. (Artists' Books Ser.). (Illus.). 32p. (Orig.). 1995. pap. 12.00 (*0-89822-110-2*) Visual Studies.

Reed, Mick & Wells, Roger, eds. Class, Conflict & Protest in the English Countryside, 1700-1800. 236p. 1990. text 45.00 (*0-7146-3343-7*, Pub. by F Cass Pubs) Intl Spec Bk.

Reed, Millard & Forman, Jan R. It's Your Serve: A Practical Leadership for Pastors & Sunday School Superintendents. (Illus.). 152p. 1990. pap., student ed. 14.99 (*0-8341-1293-0*) Beacon Hill.

Reed, Mort. Coinology. 1985. 4.50 (*0-89637-005-4*) American Numismatic.

Reed, Murray K., ed. Commercial Applications of Ultrafast Lasers. LC 98-227302. (Proceedings of SPIE Ser.: Vol. 3269). 144p. 1998. 59.00 (*0-8194-2708-X*) SPIE.

***Reed, Murray K. & Neev, Joseph, eds.** Commercial & Biomedical Applications of Ultrafast Lasers. 186p. 1999. pap. text 72.00 (*0-8194-3086-2*) SPIE.

Reed, Myrtle. Flower of the Dusk. 1976. lib. bdg. 15.75 (*0-89968-109-3*, Lghtyr Pr) Buccaneer Bks.

— Lavender & Old Lace. 1976. lib. bdg. 13.50 (*0-89968-110-7*, Lghtyr Pr) Buccaneer Bks.

— A Spinner in the Sun. 1976. lib. bdg. 17.25 (*0-89968-111-5*, Lghtyr Pr) Buccaneer Bks.

Reed, Nancy, ed. see Reed, Jeff.

Reed, Nancy A. Cockatiels! Pets - Breeding - Showing. Erhart, Rainer R., ed. (Illus.). 256p. 1990. lib. bdg. 23.95 (*0-86622-640-0*, TS-140) TFH Pubns.

***Reed, Nancy B.** More Than Just a Game: The Military Nature of Greek Athletic Contests. (Illus.). 82p. 1999. pap. 15.00 (*0-89005-572-6*) Ares.

Reed, Naomi V. Breakfast at the Prince of Wales: A Bed & Breakfast Success Story. LC TX941.P75R44. 121p. (Orig.). 1997. pap. 13.95 (*0-9657541-9-7*) Bayberry Bks.

Reed, Nat. Danny, the Champion of the World: A Study Guide. Friedland, J. & Kessler, R., eds. (Novel-Ties Ser.). (J). (gr. 4-6). 1993. pap. text, student ed. 15.95 (*0-88122-897-4*) Lrn Links.

— Homer Price: A Study Guide. Friedland, J. & Kessler, R., eds. (Novel-Ties Ser.). (J). (gr. 5-7). 1994. pap. text, student ed. 15.95 (*1-56982-069-4*) Lrn Links.

— Thunderbird Gold. LC 96-45496. (Illus.). 154p. (J). 1997. pap. 6.49 (*0-89084-919-6*, 103325) Bob Jones Univ.

Reed, Nathanial. The Life of Texas Jack: Eight Years a Criminal - 41 Years Trusting in God. (American Biography Ser.). 66p. 1991. reprint ed. lib. bdg. 59.00 (*0-7812-8321-3*) Rprt Serv.

Reed, Nathaniel, ed. see Spratt, Robert.

Reed, Neil. Black Beauty. 96p. (J). (gr. 1-6). 1997. 9.98 (*1-85854-549-8*) Brimax Bks.

— Treasure Island. 96p. (J). (gr. 1-6). 1996. 9.98 (*1-85854-190-5*) Brimax Bks.

Reed, Nelson. The Caste War of Yucatan. (Illus.). xii, 308p. 1964. reprint ed. pap. 14.95 (*0-8047-0165-2*) Stanford U Pr.

Reed, Nelson A. Family Papers. (Illus.). 1990. 29.95 (*0-935284-78-8*) Patrice Pr.

Reed, Nicholas. Camille Pissaro at Crystal Palace. 1993. pap. 40.00 (*0-9515258-2-4*, Pub. by Lilburne Pr) St Mut.

— Pissarro in Essex. 1990. pap. 29.95 (*0-9515258-4-0*, Pub. by Lilburne Pr) St Mut.

— Pissarro in West London. 1990. pap. 29.95 (*0-7855-7038-1*, Pub. by Lilburne Pr) St Mut.

— Richmond & Kew Green: A Souvenir Guide. 1992. pap. 29.95 (*0-9515258-6-7*, Pub. by Lilburne Pr) St Mut.

— Sisley & the Thames. 1992. pap. 29.95 (*0-9515258-5-9*, Pub. by Lilburne Pr) St Mut.

Reed, Norman S. Ellie's Place. 477p. 1993. pap. write for info. (*0-932281-11-7*) Quill Pubns GA.

— A Place Fit Only for Refuse. (Illus.). 63p. 1985. pap. 12.95 (*0-317-53582-X*); pap. 7.95 (*0-317-53583-8*) Quill Pubns GA.

— A Place Fit Only for Refuse: Stories of Dump-Picking on Martha's Vineyard Island. 2nd ed. 1986. write for info. (*0-318-61140-6*) Quill Pubns GA.

— A Place Where the Eelgrass Flows. Vineyard Gazette Editors, ed. (Illus.). 81p. pap. 7.95 (*0-685-18165-0*) Quill Pubns GA.

Reed, Oscar F. 1 & 2 Corinthians. Greathouse, William M. & Taylor, Willard H., eds. (Bible Exposition Ser.: Vol. 7). 298p. 1976. 14.99 (*0-8341-0318-4*) Beacon Hill.

— Search the Scriptures, Old Testament Vol. 17: Hosea, Joel, Amos. 1967. pap. 1.99 (*0-8341-0044-4*) Beacon Hill.

Reed, Otis L. & Roland, George. The Camel Drivers: The 17th Aero Squadron in World War I. (Illus.). 160p. 1996. 45.00 (*0-7643-0071-7*) Schiffer.

Reed, P. B., jt. auth. see Brown, Robert H.

Reed, P. B., jt. auth. see Thomas, P. I.

Reed, P. I., et al, eds. New Trends in Gastric Cancer. (Developments in Oncology Ser.). (C). 1990. text 123.00 (*0-7923-8917-4*) Kluwer Academic.

Reed, Parker M. History of Bath, Maine. (Illus.). 526p. 1993. reprint ed. lib. bdg. 54.00 (*0-8328-3112-3*) Higginson Bk Co.

***Reed, Pat.** Container of Stars. 23p. 1999. pap. 10.00 (*0-9661505-2-X*, Pub. by Arcturus Edtns) SPD-Small Pr Dist.

Reed, Pat. Kismet. LC 90-60631. 96p. 1991. 8.00 (*1-882022-03-3*) O Bks.

***Reed, Pat.** Run Your Business Virtually Free: An Internet Guide to Free & Low Cost Business Tools, Services & Resources. 115p. 1999. ring bd. 59.00 incl. disk (*0-9672070-0-2*) J S Pubg.

Reed, Patrick. Happy Everything! (Illus.). 40p. (J). 1998. pap. 12.00 (*1-891989-01-4*) Fundbuilders USA.

— Theodore Elijah Bear Explores the United States. (Illus.). 40p. (J). 1998. pap. 12.00 (*1-891989-02-2*) Fundbuilders USA.

— Who Lives Here? (Illus.). 40p. (J). 1998. pap. 12.00 (*1-891989-00-6*) Fundbuilders USA.

Reed, Patrick C. The Role of Federal Courts in U. S. Customs & International Trade Law. LC 96-43143. 453p. 1997. 125.00 (*0-379-21375-3*) Oceana.

Reed, Patti. Reed's Guide to Farms & Barns in Eastern Pennsylvania, New Jersey, & Delaware. (Illus.). 112p. 1993. per. 10.95 (*0-9637181-0-X*) Horse Tales.

Reed, Paul. Back from the Brink: Reflections on Illness, Renewal, & Hope. 44p. 1996. 2.00 (*0-9641006-1-4*) Hse of Lillian.

— Combles Somme. 1999. pap. text 16.95 (*0-85052-674-4*) Leo Cooper.

***Reed, Paul.** Courcelette. 1998. pap. 16.95 (*0-85052-592-6*, Pub. by Leo Cooper) Trans-Atl Phila.

— Developing Applications with Visual Basic & UML. LC 99-42512. (Object Technology Ser.). (Illus.). 560p. 1999. pap. 39.95 (*0-201-61579-7*) Addison-Wesley.

Reed, Paul. Longing. LC 88-14994. 192p. 1990. pap. 7.95 (*0-89087-597-9*) Celestial Arts.

— Les Mains Sales, Satre: Critical Monographs in English. 64p. 1993. pap. 32.00 (*0-85261-247-8*, Pub. by Univ of Glasgow) St Mut.

— The Savage Garden: A Journal. 176p. 1994. 20.00 (*0-9641006-0-6*) Hse of Lillian.

***Reed, Paul.** Vertical Intercourse. 160p. (Orig.). 2001. pap. 16.00 (*1-892723-06-9*) Black Books.

— Walking the Salient. (Battleground Europe Ser.). 1998. pap. text 16.95 (*0-85052-617-5*, Pub. by Leo Cooper) Trans-Atl Phila.

Reed, Paul, ed. Fire-Emergency Services Sourcebook, 1990-91. 2nd ed. Orig. Title: Fire Service Directory of Training & Information Sources. 650p. 1990. text 79.95 (*0-940613-01-8*) Special Pubn Serv.

Reed, Paul & Schwarz, Ted. Kontum Diary: Captured Writings Bring Peace to a Vietnam Veteran. (Illus.). 312p. 1996. 22.95 (*1-56530-205-2*) Summit TX.

***Reed, Paul F.** Foundations of Anasazi Culture: The Basketmaker-Pueblo Transition. LC 99-50687. 2000. 60.00 (*0-87480-656-9*) U of Utah Pr.

Reed, Paul F., jt. ed. see Reed, Lori S.

Reed, Paula & Tate, Grover T. The Tenderfoot Bandits: Sam Bass & Joel Collins, Their Lives & Hard Times. (Great West & Indian Ser.: Vol. 51). (Illus.). 1987. 26.95 (*0-87026-066-9*) Westernlore.

Reed, Peter. Alvar Aalto: Between Humanism & Materialism. LC 97-76094. 320p. 1998. 55.00 (*0-87070-107-X*, 0-8109-6183-0, Pub. by Mus of Modern Art); pap. 29.95 (*0-87070-108-8*) Mus of Modern Art.

Reed, Peter, ed. Glasgow: The Forming of a City. (Illus.). 335p. 1993. text 110.00 (*0-7486-0246-1*, Pub. by Edinburgh U Pr) Col U Pr.

***Reed, Peter, ed.** Glasgow: The Forming of the City, New Edition. rev. ed. (Illus.). 254p. 1999. pap. 32.00 (*0-7486-1200-9*, Pub. by Edinburgh U Pr) Col U Pr.

Reed, Peter, ed. Alvar Aalto: Between Humanism & Materialism. (Museum of Modern Art Book Ser.). (Illus.). 320p. 1998. 55.00 (*0-8109-6183-0*, Pub. by Abrams) Time Warner.

Reed, Peter & Leeds, Marc, eds. The Vonnegut Chronicles: Interviews & Essays. 65. LC 95-4670. (Contributions to the Study of World Literature Ser.: Vol. 65). 288p. 1996. 59.95 (*0-313-29719-3*, Greenwood Pr) Greenwood.

Reed, Peter & Rothenberg, David, eds. Wisdom in the Open Air: The Norwegian Roots of Deep Ecology. (Illus.). 288p. (C). 1992. pap. 19.95 (*0-8166-2182-9*); text 49.95 (*0-8166-2150-0*) U of Minn Pr.

Reed, Peter, jt. auth. see Brown, Robert.

Reed, Peter, jt. ed. see Leeds, Marc J.

Reed, Peter J. The Short Fiction of Kurt Vonnegut. 1. LC 97-2236. (Contributions to the Study of American Literature: Vol. 1). 200p. 1997. 57.95 (*0-313-30235-9*, Greenwood Pr) Greenwood.

Reed, Peter S., et al. World War II & the American Dream: How Wartime Building Changed a Nation. Albrecht, Donald, ed. & intro. by. (Illus.). 328p. 1995. 55.00 (*0-262-01145-X*); pap. text 27.50 (*0-262-51083-9*) MIT Pr.

Reed, Philip. Bird Dog. LC 98-158137. 304p. 1997. 22.00 (*0-671-00163-9*, PB Hardcover) PB.

— Bird Dog. 1998. per. 6.50 (*0-671-00165-5*, Pocket Books) PB.

***Reed, Philip.** Churchill: The War Leader 1940-1945. 1999. 19.95 (*1-873162-68-5*) PRO Pubns.

Reed, Philip. Low Rider. large type ed. LC 98-50508. 1999. 26.95 (*0-7862-1758-8*) Mac Lib Ref.

— The Travel Diaries of Peter Pears: 1936-1978. (Aldeburgh Studies in Music Ser.: Vol. 2). (Illus.). 242p. 1999. pap. 29.95 (*0-85115-741-6*) Boydell & Brewer.

Reed, Philip, ed. On Mahler & Britten Vol. 3: Essays in Honour of Donald Mitchell on His Seventieth Birthday. (Aldeburgh Studies in Music). (Illus.). 374p. 1998. pap. 35.00 (*0-85115-614-2*, Boydell Pr) Boydell & Brewer.

Reed, Philip & Muggeridge, Richard. Boxe Francaise Savate. pap. 13.95 (*0-901764-74-4*, 93216, Pub. by P H Crompton) Midpt Trade.

Reed, Philip, jt. auth. see Amberry, Tom.

Reed, Philip, jt. ed. see Cooke, Mervyn.

Reed, Philip, jt. ed. see Mitchell, Donald.

Reed, Philip, ed. see Pears, Peter.

Reed, Philip C. Environmental Compliance Handbook, 3 vols., Set. rev. ed. 1993. ring bd. 279.95 (*1-55645-006-0*, 160005) Busn Legal Reports.

— Environmental Manager's Survival Guide. rev. ed. 1994. ring bd. 179.95 (*0-614-09101-2*, 170003) Busn Legal Reports.

Reed, Philippa, jt. auth. see Kinkade, Thomas.

Reed, Phillip. Low Rider. LC 98-15898. 336p. 1998. 23.00 (*0-671-00166-3*, Pocket Books) PB.

— Low Rider. 1999. mass mkt. 6.50 (*0-671-00167-1*) S&S Trade.

Reed, Porter B. National List of Plant Species That Occur in Wetlands: National Summary. 250p. 1988. pap. 15.00 (*0-16-003585-6*, S/N 024-010-00682-0) USGPO.

Reed, Presley. The Medical Disability Advisor: Workplace Guidelines for Disability Duration. LC 91-14155. 1994. 275.00 (*0-934753-52-0*) LRP Pubns.

— The Medical Disability Advisor: Workplace Guidelines for Disability Duration. 3rd rev. ed. (Illus.). 1935p. 1995. 345.00 (*1-889010-01-4*) Reed Grp Ltd.

— The Medical Speciality Selector: A Medical Speciality Referral Guide. 200p. (Orig.). 1996. pap. text 65.00 (*1-889010-00-6*) Reed Grp Ltd.

Reed Publishing Staff. American Express Amsterdam, Rotterdam & the Hague. 1994. pap. 13.00 (*0-671-88170-1*) S&S Trade.

— American Express Australia's Major Cities. 1994. pap. 13.00 (*0-671-88169-8*) S&S Trade.

— American Express Munich, Frankfurt. 1994. pap. 13.00 (*0-671-88171-X*) S&S Trade.

— American Express New York. 1994. pap. 13.00 (*0-671-88163-9*) S&S Trade.

— American Express Vienna, Budapest. 1994. pap. 13.00 (*0-671-88172-8*) S&S Trade.

— American Express Washington, D. C. 1994. pap. 13.00 (*0-671-88164-7*) S&S Trade.

Reed, R. Banker or Retailer? (C). 1989. 39.00 (*0-85297-245-8*, Pub. by Chartered Bank) St Mut.

Reed, R. & Rubin, U., eds. Connective Tissue Biology: Integration & Reductionism. (Wenner-Gren International Ser.: Vol. 71). 314p. (C). 1998. 127.50 (*1-85578-118-2*, Pub. by Portland Pr Ltd) Ashgate Pub Co.

Reed, R. A. Sustainable Sewerage: Guidelines for Community Schemes. 112p. (Orig.). 1995. pap. 17.50 (*1-85339-305-3*, Pub. by Intermed Tech) Stylus Pub VA.

Reed, R. Dale & Lister, Darlene. Wingless Flight: The Lifting Body Story. LC 97-40547. xxvi, 230 p. 1997. write for info. (*0-16-049390-0*) USGPO.

Reed, R. David, jt. auth. see Garter, Larry.

Reed, R. K., et al, eds. Interstitium, Connective Tissue & Lymphatics. (Portland Press Proceedings Ser.: Vol. 9). 350p. 1995. 127.50 (*1-85578-073-9*, Pub. by Portland Pr Ltd) Ashgate Pub Co.

Reed, R. P. & Fickett, F. R., eds. Advances in Cryogenic Engineering, Vol. 36. (Illus.). 1426p. 1990. 185.00 (*0-306-43598-5*, Plenum Trade) Perseus Pubng.

Reed, R. P., jt. ed. see Fickett, F. R.

Reed, R. P., jt. ed. see Read, D. T.

Reed, Ralph. Active Faith. 1998. pap. 14.00 (*0-684-83494-4*) S&S Trade.

— Active Faith: How Christians Are Changing the Face of American Politics. 304p. 1996. 25.00 (*0-684-00304-X*) Free Pr.

— Active Faith: How Christians Are Changing the Face of American Politics. 304p. 1996. 25.00 (*0-684-82758-1*) Free Pr.

Reed, Ralph D. Geology of California. 1992. reprint ed. lib. bdg. 75.00 (*0-7812-5076-5*) Rprt Serv.

Reed, Rebecca R., et al. A Veil of Fear: Nineteenth-Century Convent Tales by Rebecca Reed & Maria Monk. LC 98-55784. 1999. pap. 19.95 (*1-55753-134-X*) Purdue U Pr.

Reed, Rebecca T. Six Months in a Convent: The Narrative of Rebecca Theresa Reed & Supplement. LC 76-46097. (Anti-Movements in America Ser.). 1977. reprint ed. lib. bdg. 39.95 (*0-405-09970-3*) Ayer.

Reed, Rex. Metro Transportation Finance: Can Denver Avoid a Hollow Core? 24p. 1989. pap. text 8.00 (*1-57655-085-0*) Independ Inst.

— Rex Reed's Guide to Movies on TV & Video. 640p. (Orig.). 1992. mass mkt. 6.99 (*0-446-36206-9*, Pub. by Warner Bks) Little.

Reed, Rex & Holm, David W. The Monopoly Economics of Juvenile Custody: Could Private Competition Keep Costs Down? 10p. 1988. pap. text 8.00 (*1-57655-107-5*) Independ Inst.

Reed, Richard. Forest Dwellers, Forest Protectors: Indigenous Models for International Development. LC 97-151414. 135p. 1996. pap. text 20.00 (*0-205-19822-8*) Allyn.

— Practical Wisdom & Timely Advice. LC 98-93856. x, 342p. 1998. pap. 14.95 (*0-9666197-0-6*) Catawba Pr.

Reed, Richard C. Managing a Law Practice: The Human Side. LC 88-70279. 95p. 1988. pap. 34.95 (*0-89707-351-7*, 511-0248) Amer Bar Assn.

Reed, Richard C., ed. Applying Total Quality Management to the Law Office: An Investment in the Future of Your Practice. 175p. 1993. pap. 79.00 (*1-888286-01-6*) Altman Weil.

Reed, Richard J. North American Combustion Handbook Vol. I: Combustion, Fuels, Stoichiometry, Heat Transfer, Fluid Flow. 3rd ed. LC 86-11635. 332p. 1986. 55.00 (*0-9601596-2-2*) North Am Mfg Co.

Reed, Richard J., et al. A Guide to the Development of On-Site Sanitation. (ENG, FRE & SPA., Illus.). viii, 237p. 1992. pap. text 47.00 (*92-4-154443-0*, 1150380) World Health.

— North American Combustion Handbook Vol. II: A Basic Reference on the Art & Science of Industrial Heating. 3rd unabridged ed. (Illus.). 456p. 1997. 55.00 (*0-9601596-3-0*) North Am Mfg Co.

Reed, Richard J., jt. ed. see Gill, James H. & Quiel, John M.

Reed, Richard K. Prophets of Agroforestry: Guarani Communities & Commercial Gathering. LC 94-10634. (Illus.). 264p. (C). 1995. text 37.50 (*0-292-77067-7*) U of Tex Pr.

Reed, Richard P. & Clark, Alan F., eds. Materials at Low Temperature. LC 82-73607. (Illus.). 608p. reprint ed. pap. 188.50 (*0-7837-1873-X*, 204207400001) Bks Demand.

***Reed, Rick R.** A Face Without a Heart: A Modern-Day Version of Oscar Wilde's The Picture of Dorian Gray. 211p. 2000. pap. 15.95 (*1-891946-08-0*) Design Image.

Reed, Rip, et al. New Mexico Retirement & Relocation Guide. large type ed. (Retirement & Relocation Guides Ser.). (Illus.). 350p. Date not set. pap. 24.95 (*1-56559-108-9*) HGI-Over Fifty.

Reed, Rita. Growing up Gay: The Sorrows & Joys of Gay & Lesbian Adolescence. LC 96-47379. (Illus.). 128p. (C). 1997. 35.00 (*0-393-04092-5*); pap. 19.95 (*0-393-31659-9*) Norton.

Reed, Robert. Bears & Dolls in Advertising: Guide to Collectible Characters & Critters. LC 98-71065. (Illus.). 168p. 1998. pap. 24.95 (*0-930625-19-6*, Antique Trader) Krause Pubns.

— Beneath the Gated Sky. LC 97-15363. 384p. 1997. text 23.95 (*0-312-86269-5*) St Martin.

— Beneath the Gated Sky. 1998. pap. 16.95 (*0-312-86477-9*, Pub. by Tor Bks) St Martin.

— Beyond the Veil of Stars. 320p. 1995. 4.99 (*0-8125-2406-3*, Pub. by Tor Bks) St Martin.

— Crash! Travel Mishaps & Calamities. LC 98-89303. (Illus.). 176p. 1999. pap. 19.95 (*0-7643-0813-0*) Schiffer.

— The Dragons of Springplace. LC 98-37689. 320p. 1999. 23.95 (*0-9655901-6-X*) Golden Gryphon.

— An Exaltation of Larks. 1998. pap. 12.95 (*0-312-85887-6*) St Martin.

— The Leeshore. 272p. 1988. mass mkt. 3.50 (*0-445-20616-0*, Pub. by Warner Bks) Little.

***Reed, Robert.** Marrow. 384p. 2000. 25.95 (*0-312-86801-4*, Pub. by Tor Bks) St Martin.

Reed, Robert. Old Washington, D. C. in Early Photographs. LC 79-52841. (Illus.). 240p. (Orig.). 1980. pap. 12.95 (*0-486-23869-5*) Dover.

— Paper Advertising Collectibles: Treasures from Almanacs to Window Signs. (Illus.). 208p. 1998. pap. 24.95 (*0-930625-91-9*, Antique Trader) Krause Pubns.

— Six-Gun Salute: An Illustrated History of the Houston Colt .45s. LC 99-17649. 256p. 1999. 34.95 (*0-88415-283-9*, 5283) Gulf Pub.

Reed, Robert, jt. ed. see Reed, Tina.

Reed, Robert C. Smash-ups! LC 98-88801. (Illus.). 176p. (Orig.). 1999. pap. 19.95 (*0-7643-0766-5*) Schiffer.

— Train Wrecks: A Pictorial History of Accidents on the Main Line. LC 96-9539. 184p. (YA). (gr. 10). 1997. pap. 19.95 (*0-7643-0136-5*) Schiffer.

Reed, Robert D. Furnace Operations. 3rd ed. LC 80-26274. 240p. reprint ed. pap. 74.40 (*0-8357-2574-X*, 204026500015) Bks Demand.

Reed, Robert D. & Roy, R. R. Statistical Physics for Students of Science & Engineering. (Illus.). xi, 320p. 1995. pap. text 10.95 (*0-486-68568-3*) Dover.

Reed, Robert D., jt. auth. see Jacobs, Pamela D.

Reed, Robert F. The U. S. - Japan Alliance: Sharing the Burden of Defense. (Illus.). 68p. (C). 1998. pap. text 15.00 (*0-7881-4799-4*) DIANE Pub.

***Reed, Robert Lanier.** Shakespeare's Tragic Form: Spirit in the Wheel. LC 00-28623. 192p. 2000. 34.50 (*0-87413-725-X*) U Delaware Pr.

Reed, Robert M. Facts on File Dictionary of Television, Cable & Video. 234p. 1994. 27.95 (*0-8160-2947-4*) Facts on File.

Reed, Robert M., jt. auth. see Reed, Maxine K.

Reed, Robert R. Colonial Manila: The Context of Hispanic Urbanism & Process of Morphogenesis. LC 77-80476. (University of California Publications in Social Welfare: No. 22). 143p. reprint ed. pap. 44.40 (*0-608-18306-7*, 203157600075) Bks Demand.

— Crime & God's Judgment in Shakespeare. LC 83-19701. 231p. reprint ed. pap. 71.70 (*0-608-18507-8*, 203152400075) Bks Demand.

Reed, Robert R., ed. Patterns of Migration in Southeast Asia. unabridged ed. LC 90-86324. (Occasional Papers: Vol. 16). 302p. (Orig.). 1990. pap. text 19.50 (*0-944613-11-X*) UC Berkeley Ctrs SE Asia.

Reed, Robert W., jt. auth. see Brunelle, Richard L.

Reed, Roberta G., jt. auth. see Kotz, John C.

Reed, Robin R. Happiness Through Choice. Stern, Ellen Sue, ed. 91p. (Orig.). (YA). (gr. 9-12). 1995. pap. 18.95 (*0-9656420-0-3*) R R Reed.

Reed, Robyn. Arlington, VA. (Illus.). 150p. 2000. 38.95 (*1-890291-12-9*) Platinum Pubng.

Reed, Rod. The Cisco Kid. (U. S. Classics Ser.). (Illus.). 80p. (Orig.). 1983. pap. 5.95 (*0-912277-00-9*) K Pierce Bks.

Reed, Rodney J., jt. auth. see Guthrie, James W.

Reed, Roger & Hardwicke, Greer. Brookline. (Images of America Ser.). (Illus.). 128p. 1998. pap. 16.99 (*0-7524-1205-1*) Arcadia Publng.

Reed, Roland. The Miser. (J). (gr. 4-12). 1973. 6.00 (*0-87602-158-5*) Anchorage.

Reed, Ron. Historical Documents in Education. (C). 2000. pap. text. write for info. (*0-8013-3314-8*) Longman.

— Philosophical Documents in Education. (C). 1995. pap. text. write for info. (*0-8013-1725-8*) Addison-Wesley.

Reed, Ronald, ed. I Wish That I Could Live Outdoors: Mohican Outdoor School Student Poetry Contest Winners & Others. (Illus.). 100p. (Orig.). (J). (gr. 4-7). 1992. pap. 18.95 incl. audio (*0-685-53268-2*) Mohican Schl.

Reed, Ronald, jt. ed. see Pontelli, John P.

***Reed, Ronald F.** Philosophical Documents in Education. 2nd ed. LC 99-12144. 301p. (C). 1999. pap. text 33.53 (*0-8013-3316-4*) Longman.

Reed, Ronald F. Rebecca: A Novel for Children. (Illus.). 37p. (Orig.). (J). (ps-4). 1990. pap. 8.00 (*0-924303-00-X*) TX Wesleyan Coll.

— Talking with Children. LC 83-9990. 123p. (Orig.). 1983. 11.95 (*0-912869-00-3*); pap. 6.95 (*0-912869-01-1*) Arden Pr.

Reed, Ronald F. & Johnson, Tony W. Friendship & Moral Education: Twin Pillars of Philosophy for Children. LC 98-38610. (Rethinking Childhood Ser.: Vol. 7, No. 7). IX, 227p. (C). 1999. pap. text 29.95 (*0-8204-3776-X*) P Lang Pubng.

Reed, Ronald F., jt. ed. see Sharp, Ann M.

Reed, Rosalind & Lang, Thomas A. Health Behaviors. LC 85-26551. (Illus.). 602p. (C). 1986. pap. text, teacher ed. write for info. (*0-314-96653-6*) West Pub.

— Health Behaviors. 2nd ed. LC 85-26551. (Illus.). 602p. (C). 1986. mass mkt. 42.00 (*0-314-93409-X*) West Pub.

Reed, Rowena. Combined Operations in the Civil War. LC 92-37967. (Illus.). xxxvi, 468p. (C). 1993. pap. 17.95 (*0-8032-8943-X*, Bison Books) U of Nebr Pr.

Reed, Rowena, jt. auth. see Mullins, Michael A.

Reed, Rowland I., ed. see NATO Advanced Study Institute Staff.

Reed, Roy. Faubus: The Life & Times of an American Prodigal. LC 96-53868. 1997. pap. 22.00 (*1-55728-467-9*) U of Ark Pr.

— Looking for Hogeye. LC 85-28906. 142p. 1986. 16.00 (*0-938626-62-0*) U of Ark Pr.

Reed, Roy A., jt. auth. see Browning, Robert L.

Reed, Rubin, jt. auth. see Woods, Bunny R.

Reed, Russell D. & Marks, Robert J., II. Neural Smithing: Supervised Learning in Feedforward Artificial Neural Networks. LC 98-13416. (Illus.). 346p. 1999. 47.50 (*0-262-18190-8*, Bradford Bks) MIT Pr.

Reed, Ruth. The Illegitimate Family in New York City: Its Treatment by Social & Health Agencies. LC 78-169397. (Family in America Ser.). 408p. 1972. reprint ed. 19.95 (*0-405-03874-7*) Ayer.

— Negro Illegitimacy in New York City. LC 68-57577. (Columbia University. Studies in the Social Sciences: No. 277). reprint ed. 20.00 (*0-404-51277-1*) AMS Pr.

— Teaching Basic Skills Through Literature. (Professional's Guide Ser.). 80p. 1995. pap., teacher ed. 9.95 (*1-55734-839-1*) Tchr Create Mat.

Reed, Ruth A. Beyond the Egg Crate. 96p. 1993. pap. 5.95 (*1-880365-79-0*) Prof Pr NC.

Reed, S. B. Victorian Dwellings for Village & Country (1885) unabridged ed. LC 98-46320. (Illus.). 128p. 1999. pap. 8.95 (*0-486-40299-1*) Dover.

***Reed, S. B.** Village & Country Residences: And How to Build Them. LC 00-23083. (Illus.). 2000. write for info. (*1-58574-008-X*) Lyons Pr.

Reed, S. G. A History of the Texas Railroads & of Transportation Conditions under Spain & Mexico & the Republic & the State. Bruchey, Stuart, ed. LC 80-1339. (Railroads Ser.). (Illus.). 1981. reprint ed. lib. bdg. 106.86 (*0-405-13811-3*) Ayer.

Reed, S. J. Electron Microprobe Analysis. 2nd ed. 346p. 1997. pap. text 42.95 (*0-521-59944-X*) Cambridge U Pr.

— Electron Microprobe Analysis & Scanning Electron Microscopy in Geology. (Illus.). 213p. (C). 1996. text 80.00 (*0-521-48280-1*); pap. text 29.95 (*0-521-48350-6*) Cambridge U Pr.

Reed, Sabrina, ed. see Layton, Irving & Creeley, Robert.

Reed, Sally G. Library Volunteers - Worth the Effort! A Program Manager's Guide. LC 94-4568. 128p. 1994. pap. 27.50 (*0-7864-0004-8*) McFarland & Co.

— Saving Your Library: A Guide to Getting, Using & Keeping the Power You Need. LC 91-51207. 144p. 1992. pap. 29.95 (*0-89950-719-0*) McFarland & Co.

— Small Libraries: A Handbook for Successful Management. LC 90-50813. 156p. 1991. lib. bdg. 28.50 (*0-89950-596-1*) McFarland & Co.

Reed, Sally G., ed. Creating the Future: Essays on Librarianship in an Age of Great Change. LC 96-15089. 276p. 1996. lib. bdg. 39.95 (*0-7864-0236-9*) McFarland & Co.

Reed, Sally G., jt. auth. see Symons, Ann K.

Reed, Sampson. Observations on the Growth of the Mind Including GENIUS. 5th ed. LC 72-4971. (Romantic Tradition in American Literature Ser.). 110p. 1972. reprint ed. 20.95 (*0-405-04641-3*) Ayer.

— Observations on the Growth of the Mind with Remarks on Other Subjects. LC 78-100126. 200p. 1970. reprint ed. 50.00 (*0-8201-1070-1*) Schol Facsimiles.

— Sampson Reed: Primary Source Material for Emerson Studies. (Swedenborg Studies: No. 1). 53, xiip. 1992. pap. text 6.95 (*0-87785-180-8*) Swedenborg.

Reed, Scott. Miracle of Psycho Command Power: The New Way to Riches, Love & Happiness. 1972. 17.95 (*0-13-585679-5*, Reward) P-H.

Reed, Scott, ed. see B., Iris.

Reed-Scott, Jutta. Scholarship, Research Libraries, & Global Publishing: The Result of a Study Funded by the Andrew W. Mellon Foundation. (Illus.). 160p. 1996. pap. 30.00 (*0-918006-78-3*) Assn Res Lib.

***Reed-Scott, Jutta, ed.** Scholarship, Research Libraries & Global Publishing. LC 99-30030. (Journal of Library Administration: Vol. 27, Nos. 3 & 4). 155p. (C). 1999. 49.95 (*0-7890-0754-1*) Haworth Pr.

Reed-Scott, Jutta, jt. auth. see Oldham-Merrill, Jan.

Reed, Sharon. Sharon Shares from Where Eagles Soar. 95p. (Orig.). 1993. pap. text 12.95 (*0-9629735-1-3*) Sharon Reed.

Reed, Sharon R. The Bird Book. (Illus.). 24p. (J). (gr. k-6). 1999. spiral bd. 7.00 (*0-8059-4583-0*) Dorrance.

***Reed, Sherry.** Family & Friends: Address, Phone & Record Book. 76p. 1999. ring bd. 18.94 (*0-9675701-0-7*) S Reed.

Reed, Sherwood C. Guidance for Design & Construction of a Subsurface Flow Constructed Wetland. (Illus.). 22p. (C). 1997. reprint ed. pap. text 15.00 (*0-7881-3737-9*) DIANE Pub.

Reed, Smith, Shaw & McClay Staff. OSHA Compliance Handbook. 364p. 1992. pap. text 89.00 (*0-86587-290-2*) Gov Insts.

Reed, Stanley F. The Toxic Executive. 320p. 1994. reprint ed. pap. 13.50 (*0-88730-693-4*, HarpBusn) HarpInfo.

— The Toxic Executive: How to Report to, Work with, or Manage the S.O.B. down the Hall (& Maintain Some Sense of Dignity) LC 91-58509. 288p. 1993. 20.00 (*0-88730-562-8*, HarpBusn) HarpInfo.

Reed, Stanley F. & Lajoux, Alexandra R. The Art of M&A: A Merger Acquisition Buyout Guide. 3rd ed. LC 98-45524. (Illus.). 1000p. 1998. 179.95 (*0-07-052660-5*) McGraw-Hill Prof.

Reed, Stanley Foster & Reed-Lajoux, Alexandra. The Art of M & A: A Merger Acquisition Buyout Guide. 2nd ed. LC 94-10916. 1000p. 1994. text 125.00 (*1-55623-722-7*, Irwn Prfssnl) McGraw-Hill Prof.

Reed, Stephanie, ed. see Lonik, Larry.

Reed, Stephen K. Cognition: Theory & Applications. 2nd ed. LC 87-11785. (Experimental Psychology Ser.). 348p. (C). 1987. mass mkt. 40.50 (*0-534-08172-X*) Brooks-Cole.

— Cognition: Theory & Applications. 3rd ed. LC 91-14250. 400p. (C). 1992. text 41.80 (*0-534-14760-7*) Brooks-Cole.

— Cognition: Theory & Applications. 4th ed. LC 95-15683. 1995. mass mkt. 54.25 (*0-534-21954-3*) Brooks-Cole.

— Cognition: Theory & Applications. 4th ed. 1995. mass mkt., teacher ed. write for info. (*0-534-33888-7*) Brooks-Cole.

— Word Problems. (Studies in Mathematical Thinking & Learning Ser.). 256p. 1998. write for info. (*0-8058-2660-2*); pap. 27.50 (*0-8058-2661-0*) L Erlbaum Assocs.

Reed, Stephen W. The Making of Modern New Guinea. LC 75-30077. (Institute of Pacific Relations Ser.). (Illus.). 352p. 1982. reprint ed. 47.50 (*0-404-59554-5*) AMS Pr.

***Reed, Steve.** Pebbling the Walk: How to Survive Cancer Treatment When You're Not the Patient. 2000. pap. 13.95 (*0-936085-63-0*) Blue Heron OR.

Reed, Steven R. Japan Election Data: The House of Representatives, 1947-1990. LC 92-2509. xx, 602p. 1992. 67.50 (*0-939512-57-2*); pap. 34.95 (*0-939512-58-0*) U MI Japan.

— Making Common Sense of Japan. LC 93-12871. (Policy & Institutional Studies). 208p. (C). 1993. pap. 15.95 (*0-8229-5510-5*); text 49.95 (*0-8229-3757-3*) U of Pittsburgh Pr.

Reed, Sue W. French Prints from the Age of the Musketeers. LC 98-66928. (Illus.). 320p. 1998. pap. 35.00 (*0-87846-460-3*) Mus Fine Arts Boston.

Reed, Sue W. & Shapiro, Barbara S. Degas' Complete Graphic Work. (Painter As Printmaker Ser.). (Illus.). 344p. 1984. 125.00 (*1-55660-196-4*); pap. 75.00 (*0-915346-89-3*) A Wofsy Fine Arts.

Reed, Sue W. & Wallace, Richard. Italian Etchers of the Renaissance & Baroque. LC 88-62541. (Illus.). 352p. 1989. pap. text 29.95 (*0-87846-305-4*) Mus Fine Arts Boston.

***Reed, Sue W., et al.** Awash in Color: American Watercolors in the Museum of Fine Arts, Boston. (Illus.). 348p. 1999. pap. 40.00 (*0-8212-2619-3*, Pub. by Bulfinch Pr) Little.

Reed, Suzanne E. Presenting Ursula Le Guin. LC 96-38622. 1997. 28.00 (*0-8057-4609-9*, Twyne) Mac Lib Ref.

R

Reed, T. Occupational Stress Guide to Control. 1993. text 34.95 (0-442-00189-4, VNR) Wiley.

Reed, T. & Bryant, B. Densified Biomass: A New Form of Solid Fuel. 35p. 1978. spiral bd. 12.00 (1-890607-16-9) Biomass Energy.

Reed, T., jt. auth. see Gaur, S.

Reed, T. G., jt. auth. see Smith, David B.

Reed, T. J. The Classical Centre: Goethe & Weimar Seventeen Seventy-Five to Eighteen Thirty-Two. LC 79-54252. (Literary History of Germany Ser.: Vol. 5). 1980. text 44.00 (0-06-495825-6, N6651) B&N Imports.

— Classical Centre: Goethe & Weimar, 1775-1832. 270p. 1986. pap. text 18.95 (0-19-815842-4) OUP.

— Death in Venice: Making & Unmaking a Master. LC 94-4252. (Twayne's Masterwork Studies: No. 140). 125p. 1994. 29.00 (0-8057-8069-6, Twyne); pap. 13.95 (0-8057-8114-5, Twyne) Mac Lib Ref.

— Thomas Mann: The Uses of Tradition. 2nd ed. LC 96-7771. (Illus.). 484p. 1996. pap. text 32.00 (0-19-815915-3) OUP.

Reed, T. J. & Cram, David, eds. Heinrich Heine. LC 97-217476. (Everyman's Poetry Ser.). 1997. pap. 3.50 (0-460-87865-4, Everyman's Classic Lib) Tuttle Pubng.

***Reed, T. J. & Stillmark, Alexander, eds.** Heine und die Weltliteratur. (Legenda Ser.). 243p. (C). 2000. pap. 49.50 (1-900755-16-5, Pub. by E H R C) David Brown.

Reed, T. J., jt. auth. see Heine, Heinrich.

Reed, T. J., ed. see Goethe, J. W.

Reed, T. J., ed. see Goethe, Johann Wolfgang Von.

Reed, T. J., tr. see Heine, Heinrich.

Reed, T. V. Fifteen Jugglers, Five Believers: Literary Politics & the Poetics of American Social Movements. (New Historicism: Studies in Cultural Poetics: No. 22). (C). 1992. 40.00 (0-520-07521-8, Pub. by U CA Pr); pap. 17.95 (0-520-07522-6, Pub. by U CA Pr) Cal Prin Full Svc.

Reed, Ted. Syncopation for the Modern Drummer. 1996. pap. 7.00 (0-88284-795-3) Alfred Pub.

Reed, Teresa. The Big Bug Hunt Book No. 6. LC 96-68721. 24p. (ps-1). 1996. 3.25 (0-689-80822-4) S&S Childrens.

— Happy Birthday Daddy. LC 96-161759. (Gullah Gullah Island Ser.). 24p. (ps-1). 1996. 3.25 (0-689-80396-6) S&S Bks Yung.

— Keisha Leads the Way. (Magic Attic Club Ser.). (Illus.). 80p. (J). (gr. 2-6). 1996. 12.95 (1-57513-016-5); pap. 5.95 (1-57513-017-3) Magic Attic.

— Keisha the Fairy Snow Queen. (Magic Attic Club Ser.). (Illus.). 72p. (J). (gr. 2-6). 1995. 12.95 (1-57513-024-6); pap. 5.95 (1-57513-025-4) Magic Attic.

Reed, Teresa. Keisha the Fairy Snow Queen. (Magic Attic Club Ser.). (J). (gr. 2-6). 1995. 11.15 (0-606-08558-0, Pub. by Turtleback) Demco.

Reed, Teresa. Keisha to the Rescue. (Magic Attic Club Ser.). (Illus.). 80p. (J). (gr. 2-6). 1996. 12.95 (1-57513-069-6); pap. 5.95 (1-57513-070-X) Magic Attic.

— Rain, Rain Go Away. (Gullah Gullah Island Ser.). 24p. (ps-1). 1996. 3.25 (0-689-80395-8) S&S Bks Yung.

— Something's Fishy. 24p. (J). (ps-1). 1996. 3.25 (0-689-80821-6) S&S Childrens.

— Star Trek Movie Tie-in #1, No. 1. 32p. (J). (ps-2). 1996. 3.99 (0-689-80897-6) S&S Trade.

— Star Trek Movie Tie-in #2, No. 2. LC 96-41588. 32p. (J). (ps-2). 1996. pap. 3.99 (0-689-80898-4) S&S Trade.

— Three Cheers for Keisha. (Magic Attic Club Ser.). (Illus.). 72p. (J). (gr. 2-6). 1995. 12.95 (1-57513-008-4); pap. 5.95 (1-57513-009-2) Magic Attic.

Reed, Teresa. Three Cheers for Kiesha. (Magic Attic Club Ser.). (J). 1995. 11.15 (0-606-08644-7, Pub. by Turtleback) Demco.

Reed, Teresa. What's Up, Brother? (Moesha Ser.: Vol. 5). 176p. (YA). (gr. 8-12). 1998. mass mkt. 4.50 (0-671-02592-9) S&S Trade.

Reed, Terry & Cummings, John. Compromised: Clinton, Bush & the CIA. (Illus.). 682p. 1995. pap. 18.95 (1-883955-02-5) Penmarin Bks.

Reed, Thomas. An Illustrator Guide to Type Effects & Logo-Building. LC 98-100717. (Illus.). 391p. (Orig.). 1997. pap. 22.00 (0-9661154-0-6) Tumblereed Design.

***Reed, Thomas.** A Survey of Biomass Densification. 2000. (Illus.). 203p. 1999. spiral bd. 25.00 (1-890607-13-4) Biomass Energy.

Reed, Thomas B., ed. see Swedish Academy of Engineering Staff.

Reed, Thomas F. & Brandow, Karen. The Sky Never Changes: Testimonies from the Guatemalan Labor Movement. (ILR Press Book). (Illus.). 200p. 1996. 35.00 (0-87546-354-1); pap. 14.95 (0-87546-355-X) Cornell U Pr.

Reed, Thomas J. Tibbits' Boys: A History of the 21st New York Cavalry. LC 96-52016. 368p. 1997. 62.50 (0-7618-0688-1); pap. 42.50 (0-7618-0689-X) U Pr of Amer.

Reed, Thomas J. & Ross, Eunice L. Will Contests. LC 92-72560. 1992. ring bd. 135.00 (0-685-59866-7) West Group.

Reed, Thomas J., jt. ed. see Britton, Ann H.

Reed, Thomas L., Jr. Middle English Debate Poetry & the Aesthetics of Irresolution. 480p. 1990. text 43.00 (0-8262-0733-2) U of Mo Pr.

Reed, Thomas S. Directory of Music Notation Proposals. Johnston, Michael & Keislar, Douglas F., eds. LC 96-93025. (Illus.). 111p. 1997. spiral bd. 28.00 (0-9638849-2-1, Notation Res) Music Notation.

— A Profile of Brigadier General Alfred N. A. Duffie. 53p. 1982. pap. text 23.00 (0-89126-109-5) MA-AH Pub.

— 3rd MNMA Conference Proceedings 1994. LC 98-68688. (Illus.). 110p. 1999. pap. write for info. (0-9638849-3-X, Notation Res) Music Notation.

Reed, Thomas S., ed. Second MNMA Conference Proceedings, 1991: With Test Drive the New Notation Systems. LC 93-86922. 180p. (C). 1994. pap. 27.00 (0-9638849-0-5) Music Notation.

Reed, Thomas W. & Cameron, Bradley J. Above the Law: Covering Congress under Federal Employment Laws. LC 95-151371. 113p. 1994. 25.00 (0-916559-53-X, 2051-MO-4035) EPF.

Reed, Tina & Reed, Robert, eds. Speaking of Marriage: Irreverent Reflections on Matrimony. LC 94-39474. 1995. pap. 10.00 (0-399-51941-6, Perigee Bks) Berkley Pub.

Reed, Todd, ed. see Jerome, Gavin.

Reed, Tom. The Black Music History of Los Angeles - Its Roots: A Classical Pictorial History of Black Music in L. A. from 1920-1970. Graham, Julian, ed. (Illus.). 480p. (C). 1992. reprint ed. 65.00 (0-9632908-6-X) Black Accent.

— Teach Yourself Adobe Illustrator. (Illus.). 1995. pap. 21.95 (1-55828-435-4, MIS Pr) IDG Bks.

Reed, Toni. Demon-Lovers & Their Victims in British Fiction. LC 88-18126. 184p. 1988. 22.50 (0-8131-1663-5) U Pr of Ky.

Reed, Toni, jt. ed. see Button, Marilyn Demarest.

Reed, Tony. On the Wild Side. 200p. (Orig.). 1995. pap. write for info. (1-885591-67-5) Morris Pubng.

Reed, Uma. Developing Your Intuition with Magic Mirrors. LC 97-48963. (Illus.). 64p. 1998. 17.95 (1-56170-473-3, 863) Hay House.

Reed, V. B. & Williams, J. D. Case of Aaron Burr. 216p. Date not set. 20.95 (0-8488-2644-2) Amereon Ltd.

Reed, V. Delbert. Paul Bear Bryant: What Made Him a Winner. (Illus.). 209p. 1997. 29.95 (1-885219-01-6) Vision AL.

Reed, V. Steve. Litigation Support for Scientists & Engineers. (Geraghty & Miller Environmental Science & Engineering Ser.). Date not set. 59.95 (1-56670-210-0) Lewis Pubs.

Reed, Val, jt. auth. see Robinson, David.

Reed, Val, jt. auth. see Robinson, David K.

Reed, Verner Z. Southern Ute Indians of Early Colorado. Jones, William R., ed. (Illus.). 1980. reprint ed. pap. 2.95 (0-89646-067-3) Vistabooks.

Reed, Vernon. Presiding & Leading: How to Be a President. 113p. 1994. 23.95 (0-9641116-0-8) Woodflower Pr.

Reed, Veronica M., jt. auth. see Turner, Margery A.

Reed, Vicki A. An Introduction to Children with Language Disorders. 2nd ed. LC 93-2404. 544p. (C). 1993. 83.00 (0-02-399150-X, Macmillan Coll) P-H.

Reed-Victor, Evelyn, jt. auth. see Stronge, James H.

Reed, Vilia. Photographic Retouching. LC 87-81377. (Illus.). 116p. (Orig.). (C). 1998. pap. 24.95 (0-87985-474-X, E-97, Kodak) Saunders Photo.

Reed, Virginia. Not Half the Trubles: A Letter from Virginia Reed, May 16, 1847. Dodd, Charles H., ed. (Illus.). iii, 54p. (Orig.). 1996. pap. 9.95 (0-9653876-0-7) Ninetnth Cent Pub.

Reed, W. A., ed. Porcupine Literary Arts Magazine. (Illus.). 150p. 1998. pap. 8.95 (0-9663121-0-4) Porcupine Press.

Reed, W. F. The Descendants of Thomas Durfee, Vol. 2. (Illus.). 668p. 1989. reprint ed. pap. 97.00 (0-8328-0505-X); reprint ed. lib. bdg. 107.00 (0-8328-0504-1) Higginson Bk Co.

Reed, W. H. Reed. (Illus.). 529p. 1991. reprint ed. pap. 81.50 (0-8328-2052-0); reprint ed. lib. bdg. 91.50 (0-8328-2051-2) Higginson Bk Co.

Reed, W. L. National Anthems of the World. 9th ed. Bristow, M. J., ed. (Illus.). 608p. 1997. 95.00 (0-304-34925-9, Pub. by Cassell) Sterling.

Reed, W. L., jt. auth. see Winnett, Frederick V.

Reed, W. Michael & Burton, John K., eds. Educational Computing & Problem Solving. LC 87-2795. (Computers in the Schools Ser.: Vol. 4, Nos. 3-4). (Illus.). 217p. 1988. text 49.95 (0-86656-781-X) Haworth Pr.

Reed, Walt. Great American Illustrators. (Illus.). 160p. 1996. 19.95 (0-89659-075-5) Abbeville Pr.

— The Magic Pen of Joseph Clement Coll. 2nd ed. (Illus.). 176p. 1994. reprint ed. pap. 30.00 (0-9627642-0-5) Illustration Hse.

Reed, Walter L. Dialogues of the Word: The Bible As Literature According to Bakhtin. LC 92-36420. 248p. (C). 1993. text 52.00 (0-19-507997-3) OUP.

— An Exemplary History of the Novel: The Quixotic Versus the Picaresque. LC 80-17908. 336p. 1981. lib. bdg. 25.00 (0-226-70683-4) U Ch Pr.

— An Exemplary History of the Novel: The Quixotic Versus the Picaresque. LC 80-17908. 342p. reprint ed. pap. 106.10 (0-608-09511-7, 205431200005) Bks Demand.

— Meditations on the Hero: A Study of the Romantic Hero in Nineteenth-Century Fiction. LC 74-77068. 217p. reprint ed. 67.30 (0-8357-9384-2, 201676000005) Bks Demand.

Reed, Warren, jt. ed. see Little, Reg.

Reed, Warren A. Prophecies to America. 24p. 1996. pap. 7.00 (0-8059-4000-6) Dorrance.

Reed, William. Blood & Glory. (Soldiers of War Ser.: No. 1). 1991. per. 3.50 (0-373-63401-3) Harlequin Bks.

— Company of Heroes. (Soldiers of War Ser.: No. 02). 1991. per. 3.50 (0-373-63402-1) Harlequin Bks.

— Ki: A Practical Guide for Westerners. LC 85-81367. 224p. (Orig.). 1986. pap. 18.00 (0-87040-640-X) Japan Pubns USA.

— Ki: A Road That Anyone Can Walk. (Illus.). 272p. (Orig.). 1992. pap. 24.00 (0-87040-799-6) Japan Pubns USA.

— The Phantom of the Poles. 1996. reprint ed. spiral bd. 23.00 (0-7873-0711-4) Hlth Research.

— The Phantom of the Poles: Mysteries of the Polar Regions & the Interior of the Earth. 1991. lib. bdg. 79.95 (0-8490-4966-0) Gordon Pr.

— Shodo: The Art of Coordinating Mind, Body, & Brush. LC 88-81760. (Illus.). 212p. (Orig.). 1990. pap. 22.00 (0-87040-784-8) Japan Pubns USA.

— Study Skills: The Key to Student Success. 120p. (C). 1996. per. 25.95 (0-7872-2596-7, 41259601) Kendall-Hunt.

— Tide of Victory. (Soldiers of War Ser.: No. 03). 1991. per. 3.50 (0-373-63403-X) Harlequin Bks.

— The World of the Arts. LC 95-19642. (Child Horizons Ser.). (J). (gr. 4-6). 1996. 22.95 (0-87392-307-3) Ferguson.

Reed, William C. The Role of Traditional Rulers in Elective Politics in Nigeria. (Graduate Student Term Papers: No. 5). 1982. pap. text 2.00 (0-941934-41-1) Indiana Africa.

Reed, William F. The Descendants of Thomas Durfee of Portsmouth, R. I., Vol. 1. (Illus.). 593p. 1989. reprint ed. pap. 89.00 (0-8328-0503-3); reprint ed. lib. bdg. 99.00 (0-8328-0502-5) Higginson Bk Co.

Reed, William H. Elgar. 1988. reprint ed. lib. bdg. 59.00 (0-7812-0411-9) Rprt Serv.

— Elgar. LC 71-181234. 227p. 1949. reprint ed. 29.00 (0-403-01656-8) Scholarly.

***Reed, William S.** Bulletproof Asset Protection. 184p. 2000. 29.95 (1-886699-24-0) Five Corners.

Reed, Wilson Edward. The Politics of Community Policing: The Case of Seattle. Kappeler, Victor et al, eds. (Current Issues in Criminal Justice Ser.: Vol. 25). 168p. 1998. 44.00 (0-8153-3029-4, SS1179) Garland.

Reed, Wornie L., ed. Complete Series of Assessment of the Status of African-Americans. 700p. (Orig.). 1990. pap. 39.95 (1-878358-05-7) U MA W M Trotter Inst.

— Critiques of the NRC Study, a Common Destiny: Blacks & American Society. (Assessment of the Status of African-Americans Ser.). 56p. (Orig.). (C). 1990. pap. 3.95 (1-878358-06-5) U MA W M Trotter Inst.

— Health & Medical Care of African-Americans. LC 92-30000. 184p. 1993. 52.95 (0-86569-217-3, T217, Auburn Hse); pap. 18.95 (0-86569-218-1, R218, Auburn Hse) Greenwood.

— Health & Medical Care of African-Americans, Vol. V. (Assessment of the Status of African-Americans Ser.). 150p. (C). 1990. pap. 8.95 (1-878358-01-4) U MA W M Trotter Inst.

— Social, Political, & Economic Issues in Black America, Vol. IV. (Assessment of the Status of African-Americans Ser.). 150p. (Orig.). (C). 1990. pap. 8.95 (1-878358-03-0) U MA W M Trotter Inst.

— Summary of the Assessment of the Status of African-Americans, Vol. I. 100p. (Orig.). (C). 1990. pap. 5.95 (1-878358-04-9) U MA W M Trotter Inst.

Reed, Wornie L., et al, eds. African-Americans: Essential Perspectives. LC 92-31298. 184p. 1993. 49.95 (0-86569-221-1, T221, Auburn Hse); pap. 19.95 (0-86569-222-X, R222, Auburn Hse) Greenwood.

Reed, Wornie L. & Hill, Robert B., eds. Research on the African-American Family: A Holistic Perspective. LC 92-26624. 200p. 1993. 57.95 (0-86569-019-7, T019, Auburn Hse); pap. 18.95 (0-86569-021-9, R021, Auburn Hse) Greenwood.

Reed, Wornie L. & Simon, Mary E., eds. Cleveland's Children & Youth: A Status Report, 1993. 175p. 1993. pap. write for info. (0-9638675-0-4) CSU Urban Chld.

Reed-Wright, E. Reed-Read Lineage: Captain John Reed of Providence, Rhode Island, & Norwalk, Connecticut, & His Descendants Through His Sons, John & Thomas, 1660-1909. (Illus.). 796p. 1989. reprint ed. pap. 109.00 (0-8328-1017-7); reprint ed. lib. bdg. 117.00 (0-8328-1016-9) Higginson Bk Co.

Reeday, T. G. The Law Relating to Banking. 5th ed. 1985. pap. 46.00 (0-406-64769-0, U.K., MICHIE) LEXIS Pub.

Reeday, T. G. & Smart, P. E., eds. Legal Decisions Affecting Bankers 1879-1990. 1987. write for info. (0-406-99887-6, LDABVASET, MICHIE) LEXIS Pub.

Reede, Silver. Atlanta's Business & Employment Guide. (Illus.). 240p. (C). 1991. per. 29.95 (0-944449-08-5) Silver Reede Servs.

— Florida's Business & Employer's Directory for Orlando & the Space Coast: Orlando, Jacksonville, Titusville. (Illus.). 144p. (C). 1989. pap., per. 32.95 (0-944449-07-7) Silver Reede Servs.

— Florida's Gold Coast Business & Employer's Directory: Palm Beach, Ft. Lauderdale, Miami Metro Areas. rev. ed. (Illus.). 240p. (C). 1989. pap., per. 34.95 (0-944449-05-0) Silver Reede Servs.

— Florida's Gulf Coast Business & Employer's Directory: Tampa, Clearwater, St. Pete Metro Areas. rev. ed. (Illus.). 144p. (C). 1988. pap., per. 29.95 (0-944449-06-9) Silver Reede Servs.

Reeder Campion, Nardi. Casa Means Home. LC 79-98925. 134 p. (J). 1970. write for info. (0-03-084248-4) Holt R&W.

Reeder, Carolyn. Across the Lines. LC 96-31068. 224p. (J). (gr. 4-6). 1997. 16.00 (0-689-81133-0) Atheneum Yung Read.

***Reeder, Carolyn.** Across the Lines. 224p. (J). (gr. 4-7). 1998. mass mkt. 4.50 (0-380-73073-1, Avon Bks) Morrow Avon.

Reeder, Carolyn. Captain Kate. LC 98-24845. (Camelot Book Ser.). 224p. (J). (gr. 4-7). 1999. 15.00 (0-380-97628-5, Avon Bks) Morrow Avon.

***Reeder, Carolyn.** Captain Kate. LC 98-24845. 224p. (J). (gr. 3-7). 2000. mass mkt. 4.99 (0-380-79668-6) Morrow Avon.

— Captain Kate. (Illus.). (J). 1999. 10.34 (0-606-17963-1) Turtleback.

Reeder, Carolyn. Grandpa's Mountain. (J). 1991. 9.60 (0-606-05321-2, Pub. by Turtleback) Demco.

Reeder, Carolyn. Grandpa's Mountain. LC 90-27126. 176p. (J). 1993. reprint ed. mass mkt. 4.99 (0-380-71914-2, Avon Bks) Morrow Avon.

— Moonshiner's Son. 208p. (J). (gr. 4-7). 1995. mass mkt. 4.50 (0-380-72251-8, Avon Bks) Morrow Avon.

Reeder, Carolyn. Moonshiner's Son. LC 92-39570. 208p. (J). (gr. 3-7). 1993. lib. bdg. 14.95 (0-02-775805-2, Mac Bks Young Read) S&S Childrens.

— Moonshiner's Son. (J). 1995. 9.85 (0-606-07887-8) Turtleback.

— Shades of Gray. LC 89-31976. 160p. (J). (gr. 3-7). 1999. per. 4.50 (0-689-82696-6, 076714004993) Aladdin.

— Shades of Gray. LC 89-31976. 176p. (J). (gr. 3-7). 1989. lib. bdg. 15.00 (0-02-775810-9, Mac Bks Young Read) S&S Childrens.

— Shades of Gray. 1991. 9.60 (0-606-04873-1, Pub. by Turtleback) Demco.

Reeder, Carolyn & Reeder, Jack. Shenandoah Heritage: The Story of the People Before the Park. LC 78-61240. 88p. 1995. 7.00 (0-915746-10-7) Potomac Appalach.

— Shenandoah Secrets. 184p. 1991. pap. 12.95 (0-915746-41-7) Potomac Appalach.

— Shenandoah Vestiges: What the Mountain People Left Behind. LC 80-81761. 72p. 1993. pap. 5.00 (0-915746-14-X) Potomac Appalach.

Reeder, Clarence A., Jr. The History of Utah's Railroads, Eighteen Sixty-Nine to Eighteen Eighty-Three. Bruchey, Stuart, ed. LC 80-1288. (Railroads Ser.). (Illus.). 1981. lib. bdg. 49.95 (0-405-13759-1) Ayer.

Reeder, Curt. The In-Home VCR Mechanical Repair & Cleaning Guide. LC 96-67585. (Illus.). 222p. (Orig.). 1996. pap. 24.95 (0-7906-1076-0) Prompt Publns.

Reeder, Curt & Berquist, Carl. IC Projects. LC 97-65786. (Illus.). 212p. 1997. pap. 24.95 (0-7906-1116-3) Prompt Publns.

Reeder, D., jt. ed. see Diederiks, H. A.

Reeder, D., jt. ed. see Heller, K.

Reeder, Dan. Make Something Ugly... For a Change! The Definitive Guide to Papier & Cloth Mache. LC 99-17217. (Illus.). 80p. 1999. pap. 17.95 (0-87905-907-9) Gibbs Smith Pub.

— The Simple Screamer: A Guide to the Art of Papier & Cloth Mache. (Illus.). 96p. 1984. pap. 17.95 (0-87905-163-9) Gibbs Smith Pub.

Reeder, DeeAnn M., jt. ed. see Wilson, Don E.

Reeder, Dottie. From Blueberries to Wild Roses: A Northwoods Wild Foods Cookbook. LC 94-61838. (Illus.). 128p. (Orig.). 1995. pap., per. 9.95 (1-879432-15-3) Explorers Guide Pub.

Reeder, E. D., ed. Pandora: Women in Classical Greece. LC 95-60831. 400p. 1996. text 100.00 (0-691-01125-7, Pub. by Princeton U Pr) Cal Prin Full Svc.

Reeder, Edwin H. A Method of Directing Children's Study of Geography. LC 73-177184. (Columbia University. Teachers College. Contributions to Education Ser.: No. 193). reprint ed. 37.50 (0-404-55193-9) AMS Pr.

Reeder, Ellen D. Pandora: Women in Classical Greece. (Illus.). 434p. 1995. pap. 35.00 (0-911886-41-9) Walters Art.

Reeder, Ellen D., et al. Scythian Gold: Treasures from Ancient Ukraine. LC 99-14769. 352p. 1999. 60.00 (0-8109-4476-6, Pub. by Abrams) Time Warner.

Reeder, Glenn, jt. ed. see Pryor, John B.

Reeder, Harry P. The Work of Felix Kaufmann. (Current Continental Research Ser.: No. 220). 238p. (C). 1991. lib. bdg. 60.00 (0-8191-7728-8) U Pr of Amer.

Reeder, Jack, jt. auth. see Reeder, Carolyn.

Reeder, Jefferson, ed. see Bouchard, Ronald A.

Reeder, Jefferson, ed. see Dogherty, Jennifer D., et al.

Reeder, Jefferson, ed. see Gallot, Freddie, Jr., et al.

Reeder, Jefferson, ed. see National Association of College & University Busin.

Reeder, John. On Moral Sentiments: Contemporary Responses to Adam Smith. (Key Issues Ser.: No. 18). 256p. 1998. 72.00 (1-85506-549-5); pap. 22.00 (1-85506-550-9) Thoemmes Pr.

***Reeder, John.** Troubleshoot DC/AC Circuits Using Multisim 6.02. (Student Material TV Ser.). (C). 1999. pap. 34.95 (0-7668-1133-6) Delmar.

Reeder, John P., Jr. Killing & Saving: Abortion, Hunger, & War. LC 95-2510. 1996. 40.00 (0-271-01028-2); pap. 18.95 (0-271-01029-0) Pa St U Pr.

Reeder, John P., Jr., jt. ed. see Outka, Gene.

Reeder, Josh. Indexing Genealogy Publications. Earnest, Corinne P., ed. & pref. by. LC 94-241870. (Illus.). 48p. (Orig.). 1994. pap. 13.90 (1-879311-08-9) R D Earnest.

Reeder, Julie, jt. auth. see Weaver, Clarence M.

Reeder, Julie, ed. see Weaver, Clarence M.

Reeder, June K. Fundamental Microsoft Publisher 97. 1997. pap. text 29.99 (0-07-882347-1) Osborne-McGraw.

Reeder, Maurice M. Reeder & Felson's Gamuts in Bone, Joint, & Spine Radiology: Comprehensive Lists of Roentgen Differential Diagnosis. xx, 501p. 1993. 37.00 (0-387-94016-2) Spr-Verlag.

— Reeder & Felson's Gamuts in Cardiovascular Radiology: Comprehensive Lists of Radiographic & Angiographic Differential Diagnosis. LC 93-46633. 141p. 1994. 30.00 (0-387-94219-X) Spr-Verlag.

Reeder, Maurice M. & Bradley, William G., Jr. Reeder & Felson's Gamuts in Neuroradiology: Comprehensive Lists of Roentgen & MRI Differential Diagnosis. LC 93-10195. 357p. 1993. 36.00 (0-387-94034-0) Spr-Verlag.

Reeder, Maurice M. & Bradley, William G. Reeder & Felson's Gamuts in Radiology: Comprehensive Lists of Roentgen Differential Diagnosis. 1997. cd-rom 185.00 (0-387-14228-2) Spr-Verlag.

Reeder, Maurice M. & Bradley, William G., Jr. Reeder & Felson's Gamuts in Radiology: Comprehensive Lists of Roentgen Differential Diagnosis. 3rd ed. LC 92-49707. 640p. 1992. write for info. (3-540-97891-7) Spr-Verlag.

— Reeder & Felson's Gamuts in Radiology: Comprehensive Lists of Roentgen Differential Diagnosis. 3rd ed. LC 92-49707. 640p. 1993. 99.00 (0-387-97891-7) Spr-Verlag.

Reeder, Maurice M., jt. auth. see Palmer, Philip E.

An Asterisk (*) at the beginning of an entry indicates that the title is appearing for the first time.

Reeder, Maurice M., jt. auth. see Palmer, Philip E. S.

Reeder, P. L. De, see De Reeder, P. L., ed.

Reeder, Pat. Using PC Tools 6. Hanson, Kevin C., ed. (LogicNotes Ser.). (Illus.). (Orig.). 1990. pap. text 24.95 (*0-929978-30-7*) M-USA Busn Systs.

Reeder, R. J., ed. Carbonates: Mineralogy & Chemistry. (Reviews in Mineralogy Ser.: Vol. 11). 394p. 1983. 24.00 (*0-939950-15-4*) Mineralogical Soc.

Reeder, R. L., et al. Investigations in the Lower Perche-Hinkson Drainage. (Illus.). xvii, 258p. 1983. 10.00 (*0-917111-00-1*) Mus Anthro MO.

Reeder, Rachel. The Case Against Mercury: Rx for Pollution Prevention. (Illus.). 12p. (Orig.). 1995. pap. 4.95 (*1-880686-01-5*) Terrene Inst.

— Liturgy: Holy Places. (Quarterly Journal of The Liturgical Conference: Vol. 3, No. 4). (Illus.). 96p. (Orig.). 1983. pap. text 8.95 (*0-918208-32-7*) Liturgical Conf.

Reeder, Rachel, ed. The Art of Celebration. (Liturgy Ser.). 96p. (Orig.). 1990. pap. 8.95 (*0-918208-50-5*) Liturgical Conf.

— Glad Shouts. (Liturgy Ser.). 104p. (Orig.). 1990. pap. 8.95 (*0-918208-52-1*) Liturgical Conf.

— A Life to Share. (Liturgy Ser.). 92p. (Orig.). 1990. 10.95 (*0-918208-53-X*) Liturgical Conf.

— Liturgy: Celebrating Marriage, Vol. 4, No. 2. (Illus.). 80p. 1984. pap. text 8.95 (*0-918208-34-3*) Liturgical Conf.

— Liturgy: Central Symbols. (Quarterly Journal of The Liturgical Conference: Vol. 7, No. 1). (Illus.). 96p. (Orig.). 1988. pap. text 8.95 (*0-918208-45-9*) Liturgical Conf.

— Liturgy: Covenant with the World. (Quarterly Journal of The Liturgical Conference: Vol. 6, No. 4). 112p. 1987. pap. 8.95 (*0-918208-44-0*) Liturgical Conf.

— Liturgy: Diakonia. (Journals of The Liturgical Conference: Vol. 2, No. 4). (Illus.). 84p. (Orig.). 1982. pap. 8.95 (*0-918208-28-9*) Liturgical Conf.

— Liturgy: Ethics & Justice. (Quarterly Journal of The Liturgical Conference: Vol. 7, No. 4). (Illus.). 111p. (Orig.). 1989. pap. text 8.95 (*0-918208-48-3*) Liturgical Conf.

— Liturgy: Feasts & Fasting. (Quarterly Journal of The Liturgical Conference: Vol. 2, No. 1). (Illus.). 80p. (Orig.). 1981. pap. text 8.95 (*0-918208-25-4*) Liturgical Conf.

— Liturgy: In Spirit & Truth. (Quarterly Journal of The Liturgical Conference: Vol. 5, No. 3). (Illus.). 96p. (Orig.). 1986. pap. text 8.95 (*0-918208-39-4*) Liturgical Conf.

— Liturgy: Ministries to the Sick. (Quarterly Journal of The Liturgical Conference: Vol. 2, No 2 of Liturgy). (Illus.). 80p. 1982. 8.95 (*0-918208-26-2*) Liturgical Conf.

— Liturgy: One Church, Many Churches. (Quarterly Journal of The Liturgical Conference: Vol. 3, No. 2). (Illus.). 96p. (Orig.). 1983. pap. text 8.95 (*0-918208-30-0*) Liturgical Conf.

— Liturgy: Putting on Christ, Vol. 4, No. 1. (Illus.). 80p. 1983. pap. text 8.95 (*0-918208-33-5*) Liturgical Conf.

— Liturgy: Scripture & the Assembly. (Quarterly Journal of The Liturgical Conference: Vol. 2, No. 3 of Liturgy). (Illus.). 80p. 1982. 8.95 (*0-918208-27-0*) Liturgical Conf.

— Liturgy: Teaching Prayer. (Quarterly Journal of The Liturgical Conference: Vol. 5, No. 1). (Illus.). 96p. (Orig.). 1985. pap. text 8.95 (*0-918208-37-8*) Liturgical Conf.

— Liturgy: The Calendar. (Liturgy, the Quarterly Journal of the Liturgical Conference: Vol. 1, No. 2). (Illus.). 92p. 1980. pap. 8.95 (*0-918208-01-7*) Liturgical Conf.

— Liturgy: The Healing Word. (Quarterly Journal of The Liturgical Conference: Vol. 7, No. 2). (Illus.). 104p. (Orig.). 1988. pap. text 8.95 (*0-318-41831-2*) Liturgical Conf.

— Liturgy: The Holy Cross. (Liturgy, the Quarterly Journal of the Liturgical Conference: Vol. 1, No. 1). (Illus.). 76p. 1980. pap. 8.95 (*0-918208-00-9*) Liturgical Conf.

— Liturgy: The Power That Unites, Vol. 6, No. 2. (Illus.). 96p. (Orig.). 1986. pap. 8.95 (*0-918208-42-4*) Liturgical Conf.

— Liturgy: The Song of All Creation. (Quarterly Journal of The Liturgical Conference: Vol. 6 No. 3). (Illus.). 88p. (Orig.). 1987. pap. 8.95 (*0-918208-43-2*) Liturgical Conf.

— Liturgy: With All the Saints. (Quarterly Journal of The Liturgical Conference: Vol. 5, No. 2). (Illus.). 112p. (Orig.). 1985. pap. text 8.95 (*0-918208-38-6*) Liturgical Conf.

— Liturgy: With Lyre & Harp. (Quarterly Journal of The Liturgical Conference: Vol. 3, No. 3). (Illus.). 88p. (Orig.). 1983. pap. text 8.95 (*0-918208-31-9*) Liturgical Conf.

— Rhythms of Prayer. (Liturgy Ser.). 104p. (Orig.). 1990. pap. 8.95 (*0-918208-51-3*) Liturgical Conf.

— Riparian Road Guide: Managing Roads to Enhance Riparian Areas. (Illus.). 32p. (Orig.). 1994. pap. 9.95 (*1-880686-20-1*) Terrene Inst.

— A Watershed Approach to Urban Runoff: Handbook for Decisionmakers. (Illus.). 115p. (Orig.). 1996. pap. 16.95 (*1-880686-05-8*) Terrene Inst.

Reeder, Rachel, ed. see Alexander, Susan V.

Reeder, Rachel, ed. see McComas, Steve.

Reeder, Ray. Bach English-Title Index. LC 92-37177. (Reference Books in Music: No. 20). viii, 184p. 1993. 33.00 (*0-914913-23-9*, Fallen Lef Pr) Scarecrow.

Reeder, Robert H., jt. auth. see Fisher, Edward C.

Reeder, Roberta. Anna Akhmatova: Poet & Prophet. LC 95-21676. 640p. 1995. pap. 19.00 (*0-312-13429-0*, Picador USA) St Martin.

Reeder, Roberta, ed. see Akhmatova, Anna Andreevena.

Reeder, Roberta, tr. see Lezhnev, Abram.

Reeder, Rosalyn M. Divorcing the Corporation: One Woman's Fight to Save Her Family from Multinational Maneuvers. LC 98-94069. (Illus.). 283p. 1999. 22.00 (*0-9666586-0-4*) Hapi Haus.

Reeder, Rudolph R. How Two Hundred Children Live & Learn. LC 74-1701. (Children & Youth Ser.). 252p. 1974. reprint ed. 25.95 (*0-405-05978-7*) Ayer.

Reeder, S. Gail, ed. Succesful Machine Applique. LC 78-72878. (Illus.). 48p. 1978. pap. 6.00 (*0-932946-01-1*) Burdett CA.

Reeder, Sharon J., et al. Maternity Nursing: Family, Newborn & Women's Health Care. 18th ed. LC 96-15970. 1,312p. 1996. text 59.95 (*0-397-55166-5*) Lppncott W & W.

Reeder, T. Jefferson, ed. Financial Accounting & Reporting Manual for Higher Education. 1990. 545.00 (*0-915164-57-4*) NACUBO.

Reeder, T. Jefferson, ed. see Jenny, Hans H.

Reeder, Tony. The Black Lotus. 175p. (C). 1990. 39.00 (*0-947333-17-7*, Pub. by Pascoe Pub) St Mut.

Reeder, W. Fleming. The Long Journey Home: A Chronicle of Travel & Adventure. Williams, Don, ed. LC 98-60379. (Illus.). 280p. 1998. pap. 19.95 (*1-888338-10-5*) New Messenger Bks.

Reeders. Imaging in AIDS. (Illus.). 200p. 1998. text 140.00 (*0-7020-1904-6*) Bailliere Tindall.

Reeders, J., et al, eds. Imaging in Hepatobiliary & Pancreatic Disease: A Practical Clinical Guide. (Illus.). 305p. 1999. text 195.00 (*0-7020-1873-2*) W B Saunders.

Reeders, J. W., et al, eds. Diagnostic Imaging of AIDS. (Illus.). 147p. 1992. pap. 89.00 (*0-86577-416-1*) Thieme Med Pubs.

Reeders, Jacques W. & Rosenbusch, Gerd. Clinical Radiology & Endoscopy of the Colon. Winter, Peter, ed. Bergman, Clifford et al, trs. LC 93-30486. (Illus.). 1993. 199.00 (*0-86577-508-7*) Thieme Med Pubs.

Reeders, Jacques W., et al. Ischaemic Colitis. (Illus.). 200p. 1984. text 185.50 (*0-89838-645-4*) Kluwer Academic.

Reedijk, Jan & Bouwman, Elisabeth. Bioinorganic Catalysis. 2nd rev. expanded ed. LC 98-56651. (Illus.). 624p. 1999. text 225.00 (*0-8247-0241-7*) Dekker.

Reeds, Roger C. Biblical Graphics. 1977. 6.95 (*0-89265-058-3*) Randall Hse.

— Pupil Profiles. (Sunday School Workers Training Course Ser.: No. 3). (C). 1973. pap. 6.95 (*0-89265-010-9*) Randall Hse.

***Reeds, Roger C. & Montgomery, Susan J.** Phillips Academy, Andover: Campus Guide. (Illus.). 144p. 2000. pap. 24.95 (*1-56898-230-5*) Princeton Arch.

Reedstrom. Apache Wars. Date not set. write for info. (*0-8069-5828-6*) Sterling.

Reedstrom, E. L. Legendary Outlaws & Lawmen of the West. 1991. pap. 2.95 (*0-486-25995-1*) Dover.

Reedstrom, E. Lisle. Note Cards of Color-Bearers. 9.95 (*0-685-71943-X*, J M C & Co) Amereon Ltd.

— Story of Baseball Coloring Book. (Illus.). (J). (gr. k-3). 1991. pap. 2.95 (*0-486-26748-2*) Dover.

Reedstrom, Ernest L. Bugles, Banners, & War Bonnets. LC 77-165608. 384p. reprint ed. pap. 119.10 (*0-8357-7461-9*, 202306200031) Bks Demand.

Reedy. Electronic Marketing. (C). 1999. text 51.50 (*0-03-021107-7*, Pub. by Harcourt Coll Pubs) Harcourt.

Reedy, Chandra L. Himalayan Bronzes: Technology, Style, & Choices. LC 95-43231. (Illus.). 344p. (C). 1997. 95.00 (*0-87413-570-2*) U Delaware Pr.

Reedy, Chandra L., jt. auth. see Reedy, Terry F.

Reedy, Chandra L., jt. auth. see Reedy, Terry J.

Reedy, Daniel & Bustamante, Cecilia. Magda Portal's Truth & Hope: A XX Century Feminist of Latin America. (Seagreen Ser.). (Illus.). 200p. (C). 1989. pap. 12.95 (*0-685-30777-8*) Extramares Edit.

Reedy, Dennis, ed. School & Community History of Dickenson County, Virginia. (Illus.). 520p. 1994. 21.95 (*1-57072-010-X*) Overmountain Pr.

Reedy, G. V. Erotic Sculptures of Ancient India. (C). 1991. 42.00 (*81-210-0261-3*, Pub. by Inter-India Pubns) S Asia.

Reedy, Gerard. The Bible & Reason: Anglicans & Scripture in Late Seventeenth-Century England. LC 84-25608. 196p. reprint ed. pap. 60.80 (*0-608-03629-3*, 206445600009) Bks Demand.

— Robert South (1634-1716) An Introduction to His Life & Sermons. (Studies in Eighteenth-Century English Literature & Thought: No. 12). (Illus.). 185p. (C). 1992. text 57.95 (*0-521-40164-X*) Cambridge U Pr.

Reedy, Jeremiah, tr. from GRE. The Platonic Doctrines of Albinus. LC 91-25598. 81p. (Orig.). 1991. pap. 12.00 (*0-933999-15-1*) Phanes Pr.

Reedy, Jerry. Oklahoma. 2nd ed. LC 98-10772. (America the Beautiful Ser.). (J). 1998. lib. bdg. 32.00 (*0-516-20639-7*) Childrens.

Reedy, Jerry, jt. auth. see Hesburgh, Theodore M.

Reedy, Joel. Marketing to Consumers with Disabilities: How to Identify & Meet the Growing Market Needs of 43 Million Americans. 240p. 1993. text 32.50 (*1-55738-478-9*, Irwn Prfssnl) McGraw-Hill Prof.

Reedy, Lloyd. Allergic Skin Diseases of Dogs & Cats. 2nd ed. 1997. text 49.00 (*0-7020-1974-7*) Bailliere Tindall.

Reedy, Terry F. & Reedy, Chandra L. Principles of Experimental Design for Art Conservation Research. (Illus.). 114p. 1992. pap. 15.00 (*0-89236-243-X*, Getty Conservation Inst) J P Getty Trust.

Reedy, Terry J. & Reedy, Chandra L. Statistical Analysis in Art Conservation Research. LC 88-2994. (Research in Conservation Ser.). 108p. 1988. pap. 20.00 (*0-89236-097-6*, Pub. by J P Getty Trust) OUP.

Reef, Catherine. The African Diaspora. LC 98-11793. (Illus.). 160p. (J). 1998. 19.95 (*0-8160-3772-8*) Facts on File.

— Albert Einstein: Scientist of the 20th Century. LC 91-7560. (Taking Part Ser.). (Illus.). 64p. (J). (gr. 3 up). 1991. lib. bdg. 13.95 (*0-87518-462-6*, Dillon Silver Burdett) Silver Burdett Pr.

— Arlington National Cemetery. LC 91-17183. (Places in American History Ser.). (Illus.). 72p. (J). (gr. 4-6). 1991. text, lib. bdg. 14.95 (*0-87518-471-5*, Dillon Silver Burdett) Silver Burdett Pr.

— Baltimore. (Illus.). 60p. (J). (gr. 3 up). 1990. write for info. (*0-685-31388-3*, Mac Bks Young Read) S&S Childrens.

— Benjamin Davis, Jr. (African-American Soldiers Ser.). (Illus.). 80p. (J). (gr. 4-7). 1995. lib. bdg. 14.95 (*0-8050-2137-X*) TFC Bks NY.

— Black Explorers. LC 95-51552. (American Profiles Ser.). (J). 1996. lib. bdg. 19.95 (*0-8160-3315-3*) Facts on File.

— Black Fighting Men: A Proud History. (African-American Soldiers Ser.). (Illus.). 80p. (J). (gr. 4-7). 1995. lib. bdg. 17.90 (*0-8050-3106-5*) TFC Bks NY.

— Buffalo Soldiers: African-American Soldiers. (African-American Soldiers Ser.). (Illus.). 80p. (J). (gr. 4-7). 1995. lib. bdg. 22.90 (*0-8050-2372-0*) TFC Bks NY.

— Civil War Soldiers: African-American Soldiers. (African-American Soldiers Ser.). (Illus.). 80p. (J). (gr. 4-7). 1995. lib. bdg. 17.90 (*0-8050-2371-2*) TFC Bks NY.

— Colin Powell. (African-American Soldiers Ser.). (Illus.). 80p. (J). (gr. 4-7). 1995. lib. bdg. 17.90 (*0-8050-2136-1*) TFC Bks NY.

— Ellis Island. LC 91-18755. (Places in American History Ser.). (Illus.). 72p. (J). (gr. 4-6). 1991. text 14.95 (*0-87518-473-1*, Dillon Silver Burdett) Silver Burdett Pr.

— Ellis Island. (Places in American History Ser.). (Illus.). 72p. (J). (gr. 4). 1997. pap. 7.95 (*0-382-24772-8*, Dillon Silver Burdett) Silver Burdett Pr.

***Reef, Catherine.** George Gershwin: American Composer. LC 99-54031. (Masters of Music Ser.). (Illus.). 112p. (YA). (gr. 5 up). 2000. lib. bdg. 19.95 (*1-883846-58-7*) M Reynolds.

Reef, Catherine. Gettysburg. LC 91-43653. (Places in American History Ser.). (Illus.). 72p. (J). (gr. 4 up). 1992. lib. bdg. 14.95 (*0-87518-503-7*, Dillon Silver Burdett) Silver Burdett Pr.

— Henry David Thoreau: A Neighbor to Nature. (Earth Keepers Ser.). (Illus.). 72p. (J). (gr. 4-7). 1995. lib. bdg. 14.95 (*0-941477-39-8*) TFC Bks NY.

— John Steinbeck. LC 95-11500. (Illus.). 176p. (YA). (gr. 5 up). 1996. 17.95 (*0-395-71278-5*, Clarion Bks) HM.

— The Lincoln Memorial. LC 93-13708. (Places in American History Ser.). (Illus.). 72p. (J). (gr. 4 up). 1994. text 14.95 (*0-87518-624-6*, Dillon Silver Burdett) Silver Burdett Pr.

— Monticello. LC 91-15850. (Places in American History Ser.). (Illus.). 72p. (J). (gr. 4-6). 1991. lib. bdg. 14.95 (*0-87518-472-3*, Dillon Silver Burdett) Silver Burdett Pr.

— Mount Vernon. LC 91-33494. (Places in American History Ser.). (Illus.). 72p. (J). (gr. 4 up). 1992. lib. bdg. 14.95 (*0-87518-474-X*, Dillon Silver Burdett) Silver Burdett Pr.

***Reef, Catherine.** Paul Laurence Dunbar: Portrait of a Poet. LC 99-16456. (African-American Biographies Ser.). (Illus.). 128p. (gr. 6 up). 2000. lib. bdg. 20.95 (*0-7660-1350-2*) Enslow Pubs.

Reef, Catherine. Ralph David Abernathy. LC 94-28623. (People in Focus Ser.). (Illus.). (YA). (gr. 5 up). 1995. pap. 7.95 (*0-382-24965-8*, Dillon Silver Burdett) Silver Burdett Pr.

— Ralph David Abernathy. LC 94-28623. (People in Focus Ser.). (Illus.). (YA). (gr. 10 up). 1995. 13.95 (*0-87518-653-X*, Dillon Silver Burdett) Silver Burdett Pr.

— The Supreme Court. (Places in American History Ser.). (Illus.). 72p. (J). (gr. 4). 1997. pap. 7.95 (*0-382-24722-1*) Silver Burdett Pr.

— The United States Capitol. LC 98-51124. (Places in American History Ser.). 2000. write for info. (*0-382-42013-6*, Dillon Silver Burdett) Silver Burdett Pr.

— Walt Whitman. LC 94-7405. (Illus.). 148p. (J). (gr. 10 up). 1995. 16.95 (*0-395-68705-5*, Clarion Bks) HM.

— Washington, D. C. LC 89-12025. (Downtown America Ser.). (Illus.). 60p. (J). (gr. 3 up). 1990. lib. bdg. 13.95 (*0-87518-411-1*) Silver Burdett Pr.

— Washington, D. C. Downtown America. (Illus.). 64p. (J). (gr. 4-7). 1996. pap. text 7.95 (*0-382-24803-1*) Silver Burdett Pr.

***Reef, Catherine.** Working in America. LC 00-21058. (Illus.). 400p. 2000. lib. bdg. 50.00 (*0-8160-4022-2*) Facts on File.

Reef, Pat D. Bernard Langlais, Sculptor. LC 84-81337. (Illus.). 48p. (J). (gr. 3-7). 1985. pap. 9.95 (*0-933858-06-X*) Kennebec River.

— Dahlov Ipcar, Artist. (Maine Artists for Young Readers Ser.: No. 2). (Illus.). 48p. (J). (gr. 3-7). 1987. pap. 12.95 (*0-933858-20-5*) Kennebec River.

— William Thon, Painter. (Maine Artists for Young Readers Ser.: No. 3). (Illus.). 56p. (J). (gr. 4-7). 1991. pap. 12.95 (*0-933858-28-0*) Kennebec River.

Reef, Virginia B. Equine Diagnostic Ultrasound. Donley, Stephanie, ed. LC 97-48247. (Illus.). 400p. (C). 1998. text 125.00 (*0-7216-5023-6*, W B Saunders Co) Harcrt Hlth Sci Grp.

Reegen, Sidney L., jt. ed. see Frisch, Kurt C.

Reeh, Merrill J., et al. Ophthalmic Anatomy. (Illus.). 290p. 1981. 25.00 (*0-317-94082-1*) Am Acad Ophthal.

Reeher, Grant. Narratives of Justice: Legislators' Beliefs about Distributive Fairness. LC 96-532. 352p. (C). 1996. pap. text 22.95 (*0-472-06620-X*, 06620) U of Mich Pr.

— Narratives of Justice: Legislators' Beliefs about Distributive Fairness. LC 96-532. 352p. (C). 1996. text 52.50 (*0-472-09620-6*, 09620) U of Mich Pr.

Reeher, Grant & Cammarano, Joseph, eds. Education for Citizenship: Ideas & Innovations in Political Learning. LC 97-13580. 240p. 1997. pap. 20.95 (*0-8476-8366-4*); text 68.50 (*0-8476-8365-6*) Rowman.

Reehling, Robert S. & Stirba, Dave. The Dog Who Knew Too Much. (Illus.). 70p. (Orig.). 1995. pap. 9.95 (*0-9648080-0-5*) Mad Dog Bks.

Reehorst, Jane. Guided Meditations for Children: How to Teach Children to Pray Using Scripture. 1993. pap. text 11.00 (*0-697-02201-3*) Harcourt Religion.

Reejal, P. R. Monetary & Credit Policies of the Nepal Rastra Bank & Their Impact on the Nepalese Economy. 1986. 75.00 (*0-7855-0248-3*, Pub. by Ratna Pustak Bhandar) St Mut.

Reejal, P. R., ed. Monetary & Credit Policies of the Nepal Rastra Bank & Their Impact on the Nepalese Economy. 100p. (C). 1987. 220.00 (*0-89771-051-7*, Pub. by Ratna Pustak Bhandar) St Mut.

Reejhsinghani, Aroona. The Art of South Indian Cooking. 141p. 1990. 6.95 (*0-318-36302-X*) Asia Bk Corp.

— Cooking the Punjabi Way. 137p. 1990. 6.95 (*0-318-36283-X*) Asia Bk Corp.

— Delicious Bengali Dishes. 162p. 1980. 5.95 (*0-318-36285-6*) Asia Bk Corp.

— Delights from Goa. 135p. 1987. 5.95 (*0-318-36286-4*) Asia Bk Corp.

— Delights from Maharashtra. 162p. 1980. 5.95 (*0-318-36287-2*) Asia Bk Corp.

— Vegetarian Wonders from Gujarat. 140p. 1989. 5.95 (*0-318-36306-2*) Asia Bk Corp.

Reek, Kenneth. Pointers in C. LC 97-10744. 636p. (C). 1997. pap. text 51.00 (*0-673-99986-6*) Addison-Wesley.

Reeker, Hans-Dieter. Die Landschaft in der Aeneis. xii, 192p. 1971. write for info. (*0-318-71211-3*) G Olms Pubs.

Reekie, Duncan W. Managerial Economics. 4th ed. 576p. (C). 1995. pap. 88.00 (*0-13-100520-0*, Macmillan Coll) P-H.

Reekie, Duncan W. & Weber, Michael H. Profits, Politics & Drugs. LC 78-24496. 185p. 1979. 49.50 (*0-8419-0461-8*) Holmes & Meier.

Reekie, Gail. Measuring Immortality: Social Inquiry & the Problem of Illegitimacy. LC 98-26653. 284p. (C). 1998. 64.95 (*0-521-62034-1*); pap. 19.95 (*0-521-62974-8*) Cambridge U Pr.

Reekie, H. Martin, jt. auth. see Murray, Alan F.

Reekie, Robert. Llamados a Escribir.Tr. of Calle to Write. (SPA.). 115p. 1992. pap. 3.99 (*1-56063-108-2*, 498421) Editorial Unilit.

Reekie, Shirley H. Sailing Made Simple. LC 86-10393. (Illus.). 167p. (Orig.). reprint ed. pap. 51.80 (*0-608-07085-8*, 206731400009) Bks Demand.

Reekie, W. D. Industrial Economics: A Critical Introduction to Corporate Enterprise in Europe & America. 256p. 1989. pap. 20.00 (*1-85278-075-4*) E Elgar.

Reekie, W. Duncan. Government in Healthcare: Lessons from the U. K. (Illus.). 120p. (Orig.). 1995. pap. 6.95 (*1-883969-02-6*) CSU Smith Ctr.

— Medicine Prices & Innovations: An International Survey. (Choice in Welfare Ser.: No. 30). 65p. 1996. pap. 34.50 (*0-255-36369-9*, Pub. by Inst Economic Affairs) Coronet Bks.

— Prescribing the Price of Pharmaceuticals. (Choice in Welfare Ser.: No. 26). 120p. 1995. pap. 34.50 (*0-255-36363-X*, Pub. by Inst Economic Affairs) Coronet Bks.

Reekle, Gail. Temptations: Sex & Selling in the Department Store. (Illus.). 240p. 1993. pap. text 19.95 (*1-86373-342-6*, Pub. by Allen & Unwin Pty) Paul & Co Pubs.

Reeks, Lindsay S. Ancestors of Reeks & Rogers, Christchurch, Dorset. LC 88-83492. (Illus.). 235p. 1989. 27.00 (*0-9616950-1-3*) L S Reeks.

— Ontario Loyalist Ancestors. LC 92-73836. (Illus.). 235p. 1992. 30.00 (*0-9616950-2-1*) L S Reeks.

— Woodward-Woodard Ancestors of New England. LC 95-77604. (Illus.). 234p. 1995. 30.00 (*0-9616950-3-X*) L S Reeks.

***Reel, Guy.** Blood of Innocents. 2000. mass mkt. 6.50 (*0-7860-1363-X*) Kensgtn Pub Corp.

Reel, Guy. Unequal Justice: Wayne Dumond, Bill Clinton & the Politics of Rape in Arkansas. LC 93-28576. 263p. 1993. 26.95 (*0-87975-841-4*) Prometheus Bks.

Reel, Guy, et al. The Blood of Innocents. 432p. 1995. mass mkt. 4.99 (*0-7860-0177-1*, Pinncle Kensgtn) Kensgtn Pub Corp.

Reel, James. City Smart: Tucson. (City Smart Ser.). (Illus.). 224p. 1998. pap. 12.95 (*1-56261-368-5*, City Smart) Avalon Travel.

Reel, Jerome V., Jr. Index to Biographies of Englishmen, 1000-1485: Found in Dissertations & Theses. LC 74-19807. 689p. 1975. lib. bdg. 85.00 (*0-8371-7846-0*, RIB/, Greenwood Pr) Greenwood.

Reel, Joseph P. Use Both Brains. LC 80-82602. (Illus.). 104p. (Orig.). 1980. pap. 14.95 (*0-938024-00-0*) Human Dev Pr.

Reel, Judee, jt. auth. see Henninger-Chiang, Tracy.

Reel, Nancy. Macintosh Notebook: Chart. write for info. (*0-318-59656-3*) S&S Trade.

Reeling, Patricia & Varlejs, Jana, eds. Education for the Library - Information Profession: Strategies for the Mid-1990s. LC 92-51096. 96p. 1993. pap. 25.00 (*0-89950-892-8*) McFarland & Co.

Reeling, Viola C. Evanston Illinois: Its Land & Its People. (Illus.). 468p. 1997. reprint ed. lib. bdg. 45.00 (*0-8328-7075-7*) Higginson Bk Co.

***Reely, Trey.** Move over Mr. Holland: Insights, Humor & Philosophy on Music & Life. LC 99-93450. (Illus.). 198p. 2000. pap. 9.95 (*0-9673756-0-6*) T Reely.

R

An Asterisk (*) at the beginning of an entry indicates that the title is appearing for the first time.

R

Reeman, Douglas. The Destroyers. LC 74-196050. 317p. (J). 1974. write for info. (*0-09-119940-9*, Pub. by Hutchnson) Trafalgar.
Reeman, Douglas. Hostile Shore. 1973. 3.75 (*0-09-907880-5*) Arrow Bks.
— Killing Ground. 309p. 1991. pap. 15.95 (*0-330-31636-2*, Pub. by Pan) Trans-Atl Phila.
— Path of the Storm. large type ed. 1980. 12.00 (*0-7089-0486-6*) Ulverscroft.
— Prayer for the Ship. pap. 3.75 (*0-09-907890-2*) Arrow Bks.
— Send a Gunboat. 256p. 1986. reprint ed. lib. bdg. 19.95 (*0-89966-557-8*) Buccaneer Bks.
— Ship Must Die. pap. 3.75 (*0-09-922600-6*) Arrow Bks.
— Strike from the Sea. pap. 3.75 (*0-09-918780-9*) Arrow Bks.
— Surface with Daring. pap. 3.75 (*0-09-914540-5*) Arrow Bks.
— Torpedo Run. 1982. pap. 3.50 (*0-09-928380-8*) Arrow Bks.
— The White Guns. Date not set. mass mkt. 6.99 (*0-7493-2407-4*) Heinemann.
— Winged Escort. pap. 3.75 (*0-09-913380-6*) Arrow Bks.
— With Blood & Iron. 1976. pap. 3.75 (*0-09-906270-4*) Arrow Bks.
Reemes, Dana M. Directed by Jack Arnold. LC 87-46382. (Illus.). 255p. 1988. lib. bdg. 39.95 (*0-89950-331-4*) McFarland & Co.
Reems, Ernestine. In the Storm. 114p. (Orig.). 1996. pap. 8.99 (*1-56043-254-3*, Treasure Hse) Destiny Image.
Reemsnyder, H. S. & Throop, J. F., eds. Residual Stress Effects in Fatigue--STP 776. 241p. 1982. 26.50 (*0-8031-0711-0*, STP776) ASTM.
Reemtsa, Jan Philipp. More Than a Champion: The Style of Muhammad Ali. Woods, John E., tr. (Vintage Ser.). 192p. 1999. pap. 11.00 (*0-375-70005-6*) Vin Bks.
Reemtsen, R. & Uckmann, Jan J. R. Semi-Infinite Programming. LC 98-20075. 411p. 1998. write for info. (*0-7923-5054-5*) Kluwer Academic.
Reemtsma, Jan P. In the Cellar. Janeway, Carol B., tr. from GER. LC 98-35256. 223p. 1999. 24.00 (*0-375-40098-2*) Knopf.
— More Than a Champion: The Style of Muhammad Ali. Woods, John E., tr. from GER. LC 97-36675. 172p. 1998. 3.99 (*0-375-40030-3*) Knopf.
Reen, D. J., jt. ed. see Gosling, J. P.
Reenan, Antanas J. Van, see Van Reenan, Antanas J.
Reenberg, Annette & Markussen, Birgitte, eds. The Sahel Population: Integrated Rural Development Projects Research Components in Development Projects. LC 95-106314. (AAU Reports: No. 32). 182p. (C). 1994. pap. 12.95 (*87-87600-41-2*, Pub. by Aarhus Univ Pr) David Brown.
Reenen, Lani Van, see Van Reenen, Lani.
Reenen, Pieter Van, see Van Reenen, Pieter, ed.
Reenen-Stein, Karin Van, see Van Reenen, Pieter & Van Reenen-Stein, Karin, eds.
Reents-Budet, Dorie. Painting the Maya Universe: Royal Ceramics of the Classic Period. LC 93-29587. (Illus.). 402p. 1994. pap. text 42.95 (*0-8223-1438-X*) Duke.
Reents, Georg, jt. auth. see Kinzel, Wolfgang.
*__Reents, Stan.__ Sport & Exercise Pharmacology. (Illus.). 360p. 2000. 45.00 (*0-87322-937-1*) Human Kinetics.
Reents, Stan & Seymour, Jon. Clinical Pharmacology: An Electronic Drug Reference & Teaching Guide. 295.00 incl. cd-rom (*0-614-19731-7*, DSO46695WE) AMA.
*__Reep.__ Technical Writing: Principles, Strategies, & Readings. 4th ed. LC 99-25449. 572p. 1999. pap. text 58.00 (*0-205-29861-3*, Longwood Div) Allyn.
Reep, Diana C. The Rescue & Romances: Popular Novels Before World War 1. LC 82-61169. 144p. 1982. pap. 7.95 (*0-87972-212-6*) Bowling Green Univ Popular Press.
Reep, Diana C. & Sharp, Helen M. The Educator's Writing Handbook. LC 98-21618. 198p. (C). 1998. pap. 26.00 (*0-205-28519-8*) Allyn.
Reep, Diane C. The Rescue & Romances: Popular Novels Before World War 1. LC 82-61169. 144p. 1982. 13.95 (*0-87972-211-8*) Bowling Green Univ Popular Press.
Reep, Edward. A Combat Artist in World War II. LC 86-22380. 224p. 1987. reprint ed. pap. 69.50 (*0-608-02122-9*, 206277100004) Bks Demand.
Reep, James W. & Reep, Reynold F. Reep Family Bibliography. LC 81-85071. (Illus.). 196p. 1985. 14.00 (*0-9614602-0-2*) James Reep.
Reep, Marianna L. & Plass, Richard M. New York State Regents Biology Laboratory Manual. (Illus.). 138p. (YA). (gr. 8-11). 1989. 5.95 (*0-685-29317-3*) Amer Scholastic.
Reep, R., ed. Relationship Between Prefrontal & Limbic Cortex: A Comparative Anatomical Review. (Journal: Brains, Behavior & Evolution: Vol. 25, Nos. 1-2). (Illus.). 80p. 1985. pap. 48.00 (*3-8055-4033-7*) S Karger.
Reep, Reynold F., jt. auth. see Reep, James W.
Reep, Steve. Go to Hull. LC 97-162912. (Illus.). 270p. (Orig.). 1996. pap. 50.00 (*0-9639984-5-5*) Century Creations.
*__Reep, Thomas P.__ Abraham Lincoln 1831-1837: The Civil War President's Character-Building Years. LC 00-29140. (Illus.). 160p. 2000. 24.00 (*0-913337-36-6*) Southfarm Pr.
Reepen, Ronald. Lefty Meets Hefty. (Illus.). 40p. (J). (gr. 2-7). 1987. 6.95 (*0-930905-02-4*) Platypus Bks.
Rees. The Adventures of C P T Bonneville. 1990. 26.00 (*0-8057-3765-0*, Twyne) Mac Lib Ref.
— Biotechnology. (Illus.). 304p. (Orig.). 1999. write for info. (*0-412-63610-7*, Chap & Hall NY) Chapman & Hall.
— College Algebra. 10th ed. 1990. text, teacher ed. 26.87 (*0-07-051742-8*) McGraw.
— Environmental Quality. (Geoforum Ser.). 1984. pap. 51.00 (*0-08-031842-8*, Pergamon Pr) Elsevier.
*__Rees.__ Reforming the European Union. 304p. (C). 2000. pap. text 23.95 (*0-582-28986-6*) Addison-Wesley.
Rees. Skills of Management. 4th ed. (ITBP Textbooks Ser.). 1998. pap. 18.99 (*1-86152-482-X*) Thomson Learn.
*__Rees.__ Something Secret. (J). 2000. pap. 5.95 (*0-440-86339-2*, Pub. by Transworld Publishers Ltd) Trafalgar.
Rees & Davies. The Matter of Britain & the Matter of England. 28p. 1996. pap. text 8.95 (*0-19-951377-5*) OUP.
Rees, jt. auth. see Corre.
Rees, jt. auth. see Gravelle.
Rees, jt. auth. see Gravelle, Hugh.
Rees, jt. auth. see Willis.
Rees, A. L. A History of Experimental Film & Video. LC 99-495134. (Distributed for the British Film Institute Ser.). 256p. Date not set. pap. 23.50 (*0-85170-681-9*, Pub. by British Film Inst) Ind U Pr.
*__Rees, A. L.__ A History of Experimental Film & Video. LC 99-495134. (Distributed for the British Film Institute Ser.). 256p. Date not set. text 55.00 (*0-85170-684-3*, Pub. by British Film Inst) Ind U Pr.
Rees, A. L. & Borzello, Frances, eds. The New Art History. LC 87-2997. 176p. (C). 1988. reprint ed. pap. 17.50 (*0-391-03552-5*) Humanities.
Rees, A. R. Ornamental Bulbs, Corms & Tubers. (Crop Production Science in Horticulture Ser.: No. 1). (Illus.). 220p. 1992. pap. text 40.00 (*0-85198-656-0*) OUP.
Rees, A. R., ed. see Society for the Environmental Therapy, Inaugural C.
*__Rees, Alan M.__ Consumer Health Information Source Book. 6th ed. LC 99-52937. 304p. 2000. pap. 59.50 (*1-57356-123-1*) Oryx Pr.
Rees, Alan M. Consumer Health U. S. A. Essential Information from the Federal Health Network, Vol. 2. LC 94-37594. (Illus.). 608p. 1997. pap. text 65.00 (*1-57356-068-5*) Oryx Pr.
Rees, Alan M., ed. Consumer Health Information Service, 1985 Index. 58p. 1985. pap. 25.00 (*0-8357-0700-8*) Univ Microfilms.
— Consumer Health Information Service, 1985-1987 Index. 120p. 1987. pap. 25.00 (*0-8357-0721-0*) Univ Microfilms.
— Consumer Health Information Service, 1987-1989 Index. 143p. 1989. pap. 25.00 (*0-8357-0808-X*) Univ Microfilms.
— Consumer Health USA: Essential Information from the Federal Health Network. LC 94-37594. 552p. 1994. boxed set 55.00 (*0-89774-889-1*) Oryx Pr.
Rees, Albert E. The Economics of Trade Unions. LC 88-4848. x, 214p. 1989. pap. text 14.95 (*0-226-70710-5*) U Ch Pr.
— New Measures of Wage-Earner Compensation in Manufacturing, 1914-57. (Occasional Papers: No. 75). 38p. 1960. reprint ed. 20.00 (*0-87014-389-1*) Natl Bur Econ Res.
— Personal Health Reporter. 627p. 1992. 105.00 (*0-8103-8392-6*, 101230) Gale.
— Real Wages in Manufacturing, 1890-1914. LC 75-19735. (National Bureau of Economic Research Ser.). (Illus.). 1975. reprint ed. 20.95 (*0-405-07612-6*) Ayer.
— Real Wages in Manufacturing, 1890-1914. (General Ser.: No. 70). 179p. 1961. reprint ed. 46.60 (*0-87014-069-8*) Natl Bur Econ Res.
— Striking a Balance: Making National Economic Policy. LC 83-17881. (Illus.). x, 128p. 1984. 15.00 (*0-226-70707-5*) U Ch Pr.
— Striking a Balance: Making National Economic Policy. LC 83-17881. (Illus.). x, 128p. 1986. pap. text 8.50 (*0-226-70708-3*) U Ch Pr.
Rees, Albert E. & Hamermesh, Daniel S. The Economics of Work & Pay. 5th ed. LC 92-16939. (C). 1997. pap. 74.00 (*0-06-500448-5*) Addson-Wesley Educ.
Rees, Albert E. & Smith, Sharon P. Faculty Retirement in the Arts & Sciences. LC 91-10463. (Illus.). 119p. 1991. reprint ed. pap. 36.90 (*0-608-03198-4*, 206371000007) Bks Demand.
Rees, Albert E., ed. see Princeton University Conference on Discrimination.
Rees, Allan H., et al. Pediatric Cardiology Handbook. (Illus.). 194p. 1987. pap. 23.75 (*0-87527-348-3*) Green.
Rees, Alwyn D. Life in a Welsh Countryside. LC 97-102959. 200p. 1996. pap. 19.95 (*0-7083-1271-3*, Pub. by Univ Wales Pr) Paul & Co Pubs.
Rees, Alwyn D. & Rees, Brinley. Celtic Heritage: Ancient Tradition in Ireland & Wales. LC 78-63038. (Illus.). 1989. reprint ed. pap. 12.95 (*0-500-27039-2*, Pub. by Thames Hudson) Norton.
Rees, Ann M. Consumer Handbook. (Illus.). 160p. 1992. pap. 20.95 (*0-632-00692-7*) Blackwell Sci.
Rees, Anthony R., et al, eds. Protein Engineering: A Practical Approach. LC 92-49381. (Practical Approach Ser.). (Illus.). 424p. (C). 1993. 95.00 (*0-19-963139-5*); pap. 55.00 (*0-19-963138-7*) OUP.
Rees, B. R. Pelagius: Life & Letters. LC 98-28992. 552p. 1998. pap. 55.00 (*0-85115-714-9*, Boydell Pr) Boydell & Brewer.
*__Rees, Beth C.__ The Ideal Pentecostal Church. 88p. 1998. pap. 5.99 (*0-88019-378-6*) Schmul Pub Co.
Rees, Bill & Sheikh, Saleem. Pervasive Subjects. 250p. 1993. 34.00 (*1-85431-298-7*, Pub. by Blackstone Pr) Gaunt.
Rees, Bob & Sherwood, Marika. The Black Experience: In the U. S. A. & the Carribean. LC 94-38918. (Biographical History Ser.). (Illus.). 64p. (YA). (gr. 5 up). 1995. 17.95 (*0-87226-117-4*, 61174B, P Bedrick Books) NTC Contemp Pub Co.
*__Rees, Brian.__ Camille Saint-Saens: A Life. (Illus.). 485p. 2000. 45.00 (*1-85619-773-5*, Pub. by Chatto & Windus) Trafalgar.
Rees, Brian. Heal Your Self, Heal Your World: Turn Illness & Suffering into Health & Peace Through Scientifically Proven Methods. LC 96-8994. (Illus.). 350p. 1997. 27.50 (*0-9652319-3-3*) Manu Pub.
Rees, Brinley, jt. auth. see Rees, Alwyn D.
Rees, C. Ghost Chamber. (J). mass mkt. 8.95 (*0-340-68651-0*, Pub. by Hodder & Stought Ltd) Trafalgar.
— Soul Taker. (J). 1998. mass mkt. 8.95 (*0-340-68652-9*, Pub. by Hodder & Stought Ltd) Trafalgar.
Rees, C., et al, eds. Theory & Applications of Fourier Analysis. (Pure & Applied Mathematics Ser.: Vol. 59). (Illus.). 432p. 1981. text 175.00 (*0-8247-6903-1*) Dekker.
Rees, C. Roger, jt. auth. see Miracle, Andrew W., Jr.
Rees, C. W., jt. ed. see Capon, B.
Rees, C. W., jt. ed. see Katritzky, Alan R.
Rees, C. W., ed. see Matteson, D. S.
Rees, C. W., ed. see Simon, J. & Andre, J. J.
Rees, Carol. Hints for Upstairs, Downstairs. 134p. 1991. pap. text 7.95 (*0-941162-02-8*) D Gibson.
— Household Hints for Upstairs, Downstairs, & All Around the House. LC 87-28864. (Illus.). 1995. pap. 7.95 (*0-8050-0765-2*, Owl) H Holt & Co.
— Household Hints for Upstairs, Downstairs & All Around the House. 1993. 6.99 (*0-88365-815-1*) Galahad Bks.
*__Rees, Celia.__ Truth Out There. 240p. (J). (gr. 4-7). 2000. 16.95 (*0-7894-2668-4*) DK Pub Inc.
Rees, Charles S. Precalculus. LC 96-45922. (C). 1997. mass mkt. 88.95 (*0-314-06770-1*) West Pub.
Rees, Charles S., et al. Plane Trigonometry with Tables. 7th ed. (Illus.). 1977. text 23.95 (*0-685-03896-3*) P-H.
*__Rees, Chris.__ BMW M-Series: A Collector's Guide. (Illus.). 128p. 2000. pap. 19.95 (*1-899870-45-8*, 130083AE, Pub. by Motor Racing) Motorbooks Intl.
Rees, Chris. Caterham Sevens: The Official Story of a Unique British Sportscar. (Illus.). 208p. 1997. 59.95 (*0-947981-97-7*, Pub. by MRP Speedsport) Motorbooks Intl.
— Classic Car Buyer's Guide, 1998-99. 2nd ed. (Illus.). 244p. 1998. pap. 19.95 (*1-901432-07-6*, Bay View Bks) MBI Pubg.
— Classic Convertibles: An Invaluable Guide to Over 35 1st-Rate Models. 1999. 12.95 (*1-85967-889-0*, Lorenz Bks) Anness Pub.
— The Complete Mini. (Illus.). 160p. 1995. 34.95 (*0-947981-88-8*, Pub. by Motor Racing) Motorbooks Intl.
*__Rees, Chris.__ Concept Cars: An A-Z Guide to The World's Most Fabulous Futuristic Cars. 1999. 9.98 (*1-84038-402-6*) Hermes Hse.
— Dream Wheels. 256p. 2000. pap. 19.95 (*1-84215-149-5*) Anness Pub.
Rees, Chris. Encyclopedia of Dream Cars. 1998. 30.00 (*1-85967-699-5*) Anness Pub.
Rees, Chris. Essential Ford Capri: The Cars & Their Story, 1969-87. (Illus.). 80p. 1997. pap. 9.98 (*1-901432-01-7*) MBI Pubg.
Rees, Christine. The Judgement of Marvell. 224p. 1990. text 49.00 (*0-86187-805-1*) St Martin.
— The Judgement of Marvell. 260p. 1993. pap. 16.95 (*1-85567-165-4*) St Martin.
— Utopian Imagination & Eighteenth-Century Fiction. LC 95-13096. (Studies in Eighteenth & Nineteenth-Century Literature Ser.). 288p. (C). 1995. 73.00 (*0-582-06735-9*); pap. 36.93 (*0-582-06736-7*) Longman.
Rees, Claire, et al, eds. World Hotel Directory, 1999: An Essential Guide for Business Travellers, Including Conference Room Capacities. 24th ed. 890p. 1998. 249.50 (*0-273-63734-7*) F T P-H.
Rees, Compton, jt. auth. see Butler, Francelia.
Rees, D. Lectures on the Asymptotic Theory of Ideals. (London Mathematical Society Lecture Note Ser.: No. 113). 222p. 1989. pap. text 42.95 (*0-521-31127-6*) Cambridge U Pr.
Rees, D., ed. COSPAR International Reference Atmosphere, 1986 Pt. I: Thermosphere Models. (Advances in Space Research Ser.: Vol. 8). 476p. 1989. pap. 120.00 (*0-08-036888-3*, Pergamon Pr) Elsevier.
Rees, D., et al, eds. COSPAR International Reference Atmosphere, 1986 Pt. II: Middle Atmospher Models. (Advances in Space Research Ser.: Vol. 10). (Illus.). 528p. 1991. pap. 95.75 (*0-08-040789-7*, Pergamon Pr) Elsevier.
Rees, D., jt. ed. see Warwick, Kevin.
Rees, D. A., ed. & pref. see Farguharson, Arthur.
Rees, D. Ben. The Life & Work of Owen Thomas, 1812-1891: A Welsh Preacher. LC 91-4083. (Welsh Studies: Vol. 3). 336p. 1991. lib. bdg. 99.95 (*0-7734-9710-2*) E Mellen.
— The Welsh of Merseyside. LC 98-138958. (Illus.). 80p. 1997. pap. 14.95 (*0-901332-45-3*, Pub. by Modern Welsh) Intl Spec Bk.
Rees, D. Ben, ed. Local & Parliamentary Politics in Liverpool from 1800 to 1911. LC 99-26393. (Studies in British History: Vol. 55). 162p. 1999. text 79.95 (*0-7734-7990-2*) E Mellen.
Rees, D. G. Essential Statistics for Medical Practice: A Case-Study Approach. 224p. (gr. 13). 1994. ring bd. 31.95 (*0-412-59930-9*, Chap & Hall CRC) CRC Pr.
Rees, D. H., jt. auth. see Axford, J. S.
*__Rees, Dafydd & Crampton, Luke.__ Rock Stars Encyclopedia. 2nd ed. LC 99-24275. (Illus.). 1103p. (YA). (gr. 6-12). 1999. pap. 29.95 (*0-7894-4613-8*) DK Pub Inc.
Rees, Daniel, jt. auth. see English Benedictine Congregation Members Staff.
Rees, David. The Defeat of Japan. LC 97-3687. 232p. 1997. 59.95 (*0-275-95955-4*, Praeger Pubs) Greenwood.
— Jethro Tull: Minstrels in the Gallery. 1998. pap. 17.95 (*0-946719-22-5*, Pub. by Helter Skelter) Interlink Pub.
*__Rees, David.__ Korea: An Illustrated History. (Illustrated History Ser.). (Illus.). 150p. 2000. 14.95 (*0-7818-0785-9*) Hippocrene Bks.
Rees, David. The Marble in the Water: Essays on Contemporary Writers of Fiction for Children & Young Adults. LC 80-16623. 224p. 1980. pap. 9.95 (*0-87675-281-4*) Horn Bk.
— Packing It In. 160p. (Orig.). 1992. pap. 13.95 (*1-873741-07-3*, Pub. by Millvres Bks) LPC InBook.
— Painted Desert, Green Shade: Essays on Contemporary Writers for Children & Young Adults. LC 83-12996. 211p. 1984. pap. 13.95 (*0-87675-286-5*) Horn Bk.
— Sir Rhys Ap Thomas. 92p. 1992. pap. 30.00 (*0-86383-744-1*, Pub. by Gomer Pr) St Mut.
— Sir Rhys ap Thomas. 92p. 1992. pap. 12.95 (*0-8464-4672-3*) Beekman Pubs.
— Son of Prophecy: Henry Tudor's Road to Bosworth. (Illus.). 165p. 1997. pap. 10.95 (*1-871083-01-X*, Pub. by J Jones Pub) Intl Spec Bk.
— The Soviet Seizure of the Kuriles. LC 84-18373. 204p. 1985. 57.95 (*0-275-90154-8*, C0154, Praeger Pubs) Greenwood.
— What Do Draculas Do? Essays on Contemporary Writers of Fiction for Children & Young Adults. LC 90-8669. 260p. 1990. 31.00 (*0-8108-2320-9*) Scarecrow.
— Words & Music. 220p. 1994. pap. 14.95 (*1-873741-11-1*, Pub. by Millvres Bks) LPC InBook.
Rees, David, jt. ed. see Garrison, Terry.
Rees, David G. Essential Statistics. 256p. 1989. pap. 19.95 (*0-412-32030-4*, A3819) Chapman & Hall.
— Foundations on Statistics. 228p. (C). 1987. ring bd. 31.95 (*0-412-28560-6*, Chap & Hall CRC) CRC Pr.
*__Rees, David W.__ Mechanics of Solids & Structures. (Illus.). 2000. pap. 58.00 (*1-86094-218-0*) Imperial College.
Rees, David W. Satellite Communications: The First Quarter Century of Service. LC 88-33948. 329p. 1990. 123.00 (*0-471-62243-5*) Wiley.
Rees, Douglas. Lightning Time. LC 97-31028. (Illus.). 172p. (J). (gr. 5-9). 1997. 15.95 (*0-7894-2458-4*) DK Pub Inc.
— Lightning Time. LC 98-28615. 176p. (J). (gr. 5-9). 1999. pap. 4.99 (*0-14-130317-4*, PuffinBks) Peng Put Young Read.
Rees, E. A. Stalinism & Soviet Rail Transport, 1928-41. LC 94-30652. (Studies in Soviet History & Society Ser.). 307p. 1994. text 75.00 (*0-312-12381-7*) St Martin.
Rees, E. A., ed. Decision-Making in the Stalinist Command Economy, 1932-37. (Studies in Russian & East European History & Society). (Illus.). 304p. 1997. text 69.95 (*0-312-16564-1*) St Martin.
Rees, E. G. Notes in Geometry. (Universitext Ser.). (Illus.). 109p. 1993. 42.95 (*0-387-12053-X*) Spr-Verlag.
Rees, Eleanor. Hijacked Honeymoon. (Presents Ser.). 1994. per. 2.99 (*0-373-11645-4*, 1-11645-8) Harlequin Bks.
— Hijacked Honeymoon. large type ed. 1992. reprint ed. lib. bdg. 18.95 (*0-263-12900-4*) Thorndike Pr.
— Pirate's Hostage. (Presents Ser.: No. 452). 1992. per. 2.89 (*0-373-11452-4*, 1-11452-9) Harlequin Bks.
— The Seal Wife. large type ed. (Magna Large Print Ser.). 219p. 1997. 27.99 (*0-7505-1059-5*) Ulverscroft.
*__Rees, Elizabeth.__ Celtic Saints: Passionate Wanderers. LC 99-66195. (Illus.). 208p. 2000. 24.95 (*0-500-01989-4*, Pub. by Thames Hudson) Norton.
Rees, Elizabeth. Christian Symbols, Ancient Roots. 176p. 1996. pap. 22.95 (*1-85302-179-2*, Pub. by Jessica Kingsley) Taylor & Francis.
Rees, Elizabeth, jt. auth. see Jennings, Sue.
Rees, Elizabeth M. Body Lines, Bk. 2. LC 98-22315. (Heart Beats Ser.: Bk. 2). 192p. (J). (gr. 4-8). 1998. mass mkt. 3.99 (*0-689-81949-8*) S&S Childrens.
— Face the Music. LC 98-48981. (Heart Beats Ser.: Bk. 5). 224p. (J). (gr. 4-8). 1999. 3.99 (*0-689-81952-8*) S&S Childrens.
— In the Spotlight, Bk. 3. LC 98-30242. (Heart Beats Ser.: Bk. 3). 192p. (J). (gr. 5-8). 1998. mass mkt. 3.99 (*0-689-81950-1*) S&S Childrens.
*__Rees, Elizabeth M.__ Last Dance. LC 98-52338. (Heart Beats Ser.: Bk. 6). 224p. (J). (gr. 4-8). 1999. pap. text 3.99 (*0-689-81953-6*) S&S Childrens.
Rees, Elizabeth M. Latin Nights, Bk. 4. (Heart Beats Ser.: Bk. 4). 192p. (J). (gr. 4-8). 1998. mass mkt. 3.99 (*0-689-81951-X*) S&S Childrens.
— Moving as One. LC 98-17136. (Heart Beats Ser.: Bk. 1). 233p. (J). (gr. 4-8). 1998. mass mkt. 3.99 (*0-689-81948-X*) S&S Childrens.
— Plainsong for Caitlin. (American Dreams Ser.). 176p. (Orig.). (J). (gr. 7). 1996. mass mkt. 3.99 (*0-380-78216-2*, Avon Bks) Morrow Avon.
*__Rees, Elizabeth M., adapted by.__ Web Sight. (So Weird Ser.: No. 5). (Illus.). 144p. (J). (gr. 3-7). 2000. pap. 4.99 (*0-7868-4441-8*, Pub. by Disney Pr) Time Warner.
Rees, Emlyn. The Book of Dead Authors. 288p. 1998. pap. 11.95 (*0-7472-5721-3*, Pub. by Headline Bk Pub) Trafalgar.
Rees, Emlyn & Lloyd, Josie. Come Together. LC 98-31804. 304p. 1999. 21.95 (*0-375-50232-7*) Villard Books.
Rees, Ennis. Brer Rabbit & His Tricks. (J). (ps-3). 1990. pap. 5.95 (*0-929077-10-5*) WaterMark Inc.
— Brer Rabbit & His Tricks. LC 88-50415. (Illus.). 56p. (J). (gr. k-5). 1992. reprint ed. 12.95 (*1-56282-215-2*, Pub. by Hyprn Child) Time Warner.
— More Brer Rabbit & His Tricks. (J). 1990. pap. 5.95 (*0-929077-11-3*) WaterMark Inc.
— More of Brer Rabbit's Tricks. LC 93-32676. (Illus.). 48p. (J). (gr. k-5). 1994. reprint ed. pap. 5.95 (*1-56282-578-X*, Pub. by Hyprn Child) Little.
Rees, Ennis, et al. Lions & Lobsters & Foxes & Frogs: Fables from Aesop. LC 75-155912. 48p. (J). 1971. write for info. (*0-201-09246-8*) Peachpit Pr.
Rees, Ennis, tr. see Homer.

An Asterisk (*) at the beginning of an entry indicates that the title is appearing for the first time.

Rees, Erik. High Achievers: Glorifying God with Your Life! LC 99-173509. 176 p. 1998. write for info. (*1-892417-00-6*) High Achiev.

Rees, Fran. The Facilitator Excellence Handbook: Helping People Creatively & Productively Together, Profile. (Business Training Ser.). 16p. 1998. pap. 12.95 (*0-7879-3889-0*) Jossey-Bass.

— The Facilitator Excellence Handbook: Helping People Work Creatively & Productively Together. LC 98-25304. (Business Training Ser.). 256p. 1998. pap. 39.95 (*0-7879-3888-2*) Jossey-Bass.

— The Facilitator Excellence Handbook: Helping People Work Creatively & Productively Together, Instructor's Edition. (Business Training Ser.). 200p. 1998. teacher ed., ring bd. 99.95 (*0-7879-3887-4*) Jossey-Bass.

— How to Lead Work Teams: Facilitation Skills. LC 91-6561. 161p. 1991. pap. 24.95 (*0-88390-056-4*, Pfffr & Co) Jossey-Bass.

— Teamwork from Start to Finish: 10 Steps to Results. LC 97-4606. 176p. 1997. 24.95 (*0-7879-1061-9*, Pfffr & Co) Jossey-Bass.

Rees, Fran, intro. Twenty-Five Activities for Teams. LC 92-85291. 108p. (Orig.). 1993. pap. text 34.95 (*0-88390-362-8*) Jossey-Bass.

Rees, G. Wyn. Anglo-American Approaches to International Security, 1955-1960. 256p. 1996. text 69.95 (*0-312-12986-6*) St Martin.

Rees, G. Wyn, ed. International Politics in Europe: The New Agenda. LC 92-44820. 224p. (C). 1993. pap. 29.99 (*0-415-08283-8*, B2425) Routledge.

Rees, Gareth. The Remote Sensing Data Book. LC 98-30283. (Illus.). 262p. (C). 1999. text 39.95 (*0-521-48040-X*) Cambridge U Pr.

Rees, Gareth & Lambert, John. Cities in Crisis: The Political Economy of Urban Development in Post-War Britain. LC 86-128145. 200p. 1985. write for info. (*0-7131-6456-5*) St Martin.

Rees, Gareth, jt. auth. see Bartram, Jamie.

Rees, Gareth, jt. ed. see Bartram, Jamie.

Rees, Gareth J. Clinical Oncology. 368p. 1989. pap. 47.50 (*0-7194-0133-X*) OUP.

Rees, Garnet, ed. see Apollinaire, Guillaume.

Rees, Gary W. & Hoeber, Mary. A Catalogue of Sanborn Atlases at California State University, Northridge. LC 73-5773. (Occasional Papers: No. 1). (Illus.). 143p. (Orig.). 1973. pap. 4.00 (*0-939112-01-9*) Western Assn Map.

Rees, Geoffrey. Sex with Strangers. LC 93-1242. 245p. 1993. 20.00 (*0-374-26165-2*) FS&G.

Rees, Goronwy, tr. see Janouch, Gustav.

Rees, Graham, ed. see Bacon, Francis.

Rees, Graham L. Britain's Commodity Markets. 1972. 25.00 (*0-89979-002-X*) British Am Bks.

Rees, Gwendolen. Libraries for Children. (Library Science Ser.). 1980. lib. bdg. 55.00 (*0-8490-3131-1*) Gordon Pr.

Rees, Helen G. Guytons Galore: From French Huguenots to Oregon Pioneers. LC 85-73595. (Illus.). 294p. 1986. 19.95 (*0-8323-0448-4*) Binford Mort.

— Shaniko: From Wool Capital to Ghost Town. 2nd ed. LC 81-70285. (Illus.). 176p. 1990. reprint ed. pap. 10.00 (*0-8323-0399-2*) Binford Mort.

— Shaniko People. LC 82-73596. (Illus.). 256p. 1982. 10.95 (*0-8323-0414-X*); pap. 7.95 (*0-8323-0415-8*) Binford Mort.

Rees, Helen G., jt. auth. see Yung, Bell.

Rees, Herbert. Mold Engineering. LC 95-2590. 644p. 1995. 129.00 (*1-56990-131-7*) Hanser-Gardner.

— Understanding Injection Molding Technology. 140p. 1994. pap. 34.95 (*1-56990-130-9*) Hanser-Gardner.

— Understanding Product Design for Injection Molding. LC 96-32922. (Hanser Understanding Bks.). 116p. 1996. 34.95 (*1-56990-210-0*) Hanser-Gardner.

Rees, Humbert. The Best of Humbert Rees. 320p. (Orig.). 1995. pap. write for info. (*0-9649593-0-5*) Gran Farnum.

— The Rest of the Best of Humbert Rees. 352p. (Orig.). 1997. pap. write for info. (*0-9649593-2-1*) Gran Farnum.

Rees, Ievan, jt. auth. see Gullick, Michael.

Rees, Ioan B. Beyond National Parks. Stephens, Meic, ed. (Changing Wales Ser.). 50p. 1998. pap. 11.95 (*0-8464-4719-3*) Beekman Pubs.

Rees, Ioan B., ed. The Mountains of Wales: An Anthology in Verse & Prose. xvii, 299p. 1995. reprint ed. pap. write for info. (*0-7083-1163-6*, Pub. by Univ Wales Pr) Paul & Co Pubs.

Rees, J. G. Geology of the Country Around Stroke-on-Trent: Memoir for 1:50,000 Geological Sheet 123 (England & Wales) (Geological Survey of Great Britain - England & Wales - Memoirs; British Geological Survey - BGS Reports: No. 81023708). (Illus.). 152p. 1998. pap. 115.00 (*0-11-884537-3*, HM45373, Pub. by Statnry Office) Balogh.

Rees, James. Life of Edwin Forrest with Reminiscences & Personal Recollections. 524p. 1993. reprint ed. lib. bdg. 99.00 (*0-7812-5285-7*) Rprt Serv.

— Shakespeare & the Bible. LC 70-174307. reprint ed. 34.50 (*0-404-05235-5*) AMS Pr.

Rees, Jane & Rees, Mark. Christopher Gabriel & the Tool Trade in 18th Century London. (Illus.). 88p. 1997. pap. 16.95 (*1-879335-84-0*) Astragal Pr.

Rees, Jane, ed. see Goodman, W. L.

***Rees, Jenny.** Looking for Mr. Nobody: The Secret Life of Goronwy Rees. 2000. pap. 24.95 (*0-7658-0688-6*) Transaction Pubs.

Rees, Jenny. Looking for Mr. Nobody: The Secret Life of Goronwy Rees. (Illus.). 320p. 1995. 40.00 (*0-297-81430-3*, Pub. by Weidenfeld & Nicolson) Trafalgar.

Rees, Jim. Farewell to Famine. (Illus.). 165p. 1994. pap. 17.95 (*0-9519239-1-9*, Pub. by Dee-Jay) Irish Bks Media.

Rees, Jim, ed. The Trial of Billy Byrne of Ballymanus. 80p. (Orig.). 1996. pap. 11.95 (*0-9519239-4-3*, Pub. by Dee-Jay) Irish Bks Media.

Rees, Jim, intro. 2nd USENIX Symposium on Mobile & Location-Independent Computing Proceedings: Ann Arbor, MI. 132p. (Orig.). 1995. pap. text 24.00 (*1-880446-69-3*) USENIX Assn.

Rees, Joan. Shakespeare & the Story: Aspects of Creation. 239p. (C). 1978. pap. 18.95 (*0-485-12041-0*, Pub. by Athlone Pr) Humanities.

— Sir Philip Sidney & Arcadia. LC 89-46411. 1991. 32.50 (*0-8386-3406-0*) Fairleigh Dickinson.

— Writings on the Nile. (Illus.). 128p. 1995. pap. 19.95 (*0-948695-40-4*, Pub. by Rubicon Pr) David Brown.

Rees, John. Algebra of Revolution: The Dialectic & the Classical Marxist Tradition. LC 97-24653. (Revolutionary Studies). 304p. 1998. 55.00 (*0-391-04052-9*) Humanities.

— Algebra of Revolution: The Dialectic & the Classical Marxist Tradition. LC 97-24653. 1999. 75.00 (*0-415-19876-3*); pap. 24.99 (*0-415-19877-1*) Routledge.

Rees, John, ed. Technology, Regions, & Policy. 336p. (C). 1986. 59.50 (*0-8476-7409-6*, R7409) Rowman.

Rees, John, et al, eds. Industrial Locations & Regional Systems: Spatial Organization & the Economic Sector. LC 80-28399. (Illus.). 260p. (C). 1981. 39.95 (*0-89789-008-6*, Greenwood Pr) Greenwood.

Rees, John & Price, John. ABC of Asthma. 3rd ed. (Illus.). 49p. (C). 1997. pap. 19.00 (*0-7279-0882-0*, Pub. by BMJ Pub) Login Brothers Bk Co.

Rees, John, et al. Aids to Clinical Pharmacology & Therapeutics. 3rd ed. LC 92-49325. (Illus.). 350p. 1993. pap. text 29.00 (*0-443-04698-0*) Church.

Rees, John, jt. auth. see Clark, Tim.

Rees, John, jt. auth. see Weinstein, Bernard L.

Rees, John E. Idaho: Chronology, Nomenclature, Bibliography. fac. ed. (Shorey Historical Ser.). 135p. 1918. reprint ed. pap. 10.00 (*0-8466-0104-4*, S-104) Shoreys Bkstore.

***Rees-Jones, Deryn.** Carol Ann Duffy. (Writers & Their Works Ser.). 80p. 1999. pap. text 19.00 (*0-7463-0852-3*, Pub. by Northcote House) U Pr of Miss.

Rees-Jones, Deryn. Consorting with Angels: Modern Women Poets. 288p. 1997. 49.95 (*1-85224-391-0*, Pub. by Bloodaxe Bks); pap. 23.95 (*1-85224-392-9*, Pub. by Bloodaxe Bks) Dufour.

— The Memory Tray. 1995. 14.95 (*0-614-07442-8*, Pub. by Seren Bks) Dufour.

— Signs Round a Dead Body, Vol.1. 1999. pap. text 17.95 (*1-85411-241-4*) Poetry Wales Pr.

Rees-Jones, Deryn, et al. The Memory Tray. 64p. 1995. pap. 14.95 (*1-85411-116-7*) Dufour.

Rees-Jones, Deryn, jt. auth. see Mark, Alison.

***Rees-Jones, Trevor & Johnston, Moira.** The Bodyguard's Story: Diana, the Crash, & the Sole Survivor. 360p. 2000. 25.95 (*0-446-52775-0*) Warner Bks.

— The Bodyguard's Story: Diana, the Crash, & the Sole Survivor. 2000. reprint ed. mass mkt. 7.50 (*0-446-61004-6*) Warner Bks.

Rees, Joseph V. Hostages of Each Other: The Transformation of Nuclear Safety since Three Mile Island. LC 93-35819. 250p. 1994. 24.95 (*0-226-70687-7*) U Ch Pr.

— Hostages of Each Other: The Transformation of Nuclear Safety since Three Mile Island. (Illus.). 238p. (C). 1996. reprint ed. pap. text 15.95 (*0-226-70688-5*) U Ch Pr.

— Reforming the Workplace: A Study of Self-Regulation in Occupational Safety. LC 88-20822. (Law in Social Context Ser.). 320p. (C). 1988. text 44.95 (*0-8122-8132-2*) U of Pa Pr.

Rees, K. & Chapman, M. Limitation of Actions Handbook - Victoria. 372p. 1996. pap. write for info. (*0-409-31116-2*, MICHIE) LEXIS Pub.

***Rees, Katy & Jolly, Bonnie.** A Jolly Holiday. Worthingten, Kristina, ed. (Illus.). 40p. 1999. pap. 7.99 (*0-9674338-0-0*) Jolly Pubng.

Rees, L. V., ed. see International Conference on Zeolites Staff.

Rees, Laurence. The Nazis: A Warning from History. (Illus.). 256p. 1998. 25.00 (*1-56584-445-9*, Pub. by New Press NY); pap. 18.95 (*1-56584-551-X*, Pub. by New Press NY) Norton.

***Rees, Laurence.** War of the Century: When Hitler Fought Stalin. (Illus.). 255p. 2000. 27.95 (*1-56584-599-4*, Pub. by New Press NY) Norton.

Rees, Lesley, jt. ed. see Jolly, Brian.

Rees, Lesley H. & Van Wimersma Greidanus, T., eds. ACTH & LPH in Health & Disease. (Frontiers of Hormone Research Ser.: Vol. 8). (Illus.). x, 210p. 1981. 115.00 (*3-8055-1977-X*) S Karger.

Rees, Lesley H., jt. ed. see Bouloux, Pierre M.

Rees, Leslie. The Seagull Who Liked Cricket. LC 98-177067. (Illus.). 40p. (J). 1996. 18.95 (*1-875560-60-2*) Intl Spec Bk.

Rees, Linford, et al, eds. Textbook of Psychiatry. LC 97-206881. (Illus.). 250p. 1996. pap. text 28.95 (*0-340-57195-0*, Pub. by E A) OUP.

Rees, Lloyd. Lloyd Rees: An Artist Remembers. (Illus.). 160p. 1987. text 30.00 (*0-947131-08-6*) Gordon & Breach.

— The Show-Me State. 176p. 1995. pap. 16.95 (*1-85411-145-0*, Pub. by Seren Bks) Dufour.

Rees, Lucy. Keeping a Pony. (Illus.). 240p. 1995. pap. text 9.95 (*1-85310-585-X*, Pub. by Swan Hill Pr) Voyageur Pr.

***Rees, Lucy.** The Maze: A Desert Journey. 2000. 22.95 (*0-593-03858-4*, Pub. by Transworld Publishers Ltd) Trafalgar.

Rees, Lucy. The Maze: A Desert Journey. LC 97-26251. 189p. 1997. pap. 15.95 (*0-8165-1831-9*) U of Ariz Pr.

Rees, Mair. Drawing on Difference: Art Therapy with People Who Have Learning Difficulties. LC 97-38891. 264p. (C). 1998. pap. 25.99 (*0-415-15480-4*) Routledge.

— Drawing on Difference: Art Therapy with People Who Have Learning Difficulties. LC 97-38891. (Illus.). 280p. (C). 1998. 85.00 (*0-415-15479-0*) Routledge.

***Rees, Margaret.** Exploring Planet Earth: The Lab Manual. 188p. (C). 1999. 36.95 (*0-7872-6059-2*) Kendall-Hunt.

Rees, Margaret A. Alfred de Musset. LC 73-120495. (Twayne's World Authors Ser.). 1971. lib. bdg. 20.95 (*0-8057-2646-2*) Irvington.

Rees, Mark. Dear Sir or Madam? The Autobiography of a Female-to-Male Transsexual. LC 96-164119. (Sexual Politics Ser.). 288p. 1997. pap. 19.95 (*0-304-33394-8*) Continuum.

— Dear Sir or Madam? The Autobiography of a Female-to-Male Transsexual. LC 96-164119. (Sexual Politics Ser.). 288p. 1997. 69.95 (*0-304-33393-X*) Continuum.

Rees, Mark, intro. The Preston Catalogue. (Illus.). 224p. 1991. reprint ed. pap. 19.95 (*0-9618088-9-6*) Astragal Pr.

Rees, Mark, jt. auth. see Rees, Jane.

Rees, Mark, ed. see Goodman, W. L.

Rees, Martin. Just Six Numbers: The Deep Forces That Shape the Universe. (Illus.). 173p. 2000. 22.00 (*0-465-03672-4*, Pub. by Basic) HarpC.

— New Perspectives in Astrophysical Cosmology. 2nd ed. LC 99-21389. (Illus.). 168p. 2000. 24.95 (*0-521-64238-8*) Cambridge U Pr.

Rees, Martin, jt. auth. see Begelman, Mitchell.

Rees, Martin J. Before the Beginning: Our Universe & Others. LC 98-87223. 304p. 1998. pap. text 13.00 (*0-7382-0033-6*) Perseus Pubng.

— Perspectives in Astrophysical Cosmology. (Lezioni Lincee Lectures). (Illus.). 151p. (C). 1995. text 49.95 (*0-521-47530-9*); pap. text 21.95 (*0-521-47561-9*) Cambridge U Pr.

Rees, Martin J. & Stoneham, R. Supernovae: A Survey of Current Research. 1982. text 226.00 (*90-277-1442-8*) Kluwer Academic.

Rees, Matthew. From the Deck to the Sea: Blacks & the Republican Party. LC 91-34055. 300p. 1992. text 35.00 (*0-89341-684-3*, Longwood Academic) Hollowbrook.

Rees, Matthew, jt. auth. see Coe, Jeffery.

Rees, Matthew, jt. auth. see Coe, Jeffrey.

Rees, Mel. Principles to Live By. 96p. 1993. per. 4.95 (*0-945383-47-9*) Teach Servs.

Rees, Mike & Robson, David. Pract Compiling w/ Pascal. (Illus.). 256p. (C). 1988. pap. text 29.25 (*0-201-18487-7*) Addison-Wesley.

Rees-Miller, Janie, jt. ed. see Aronoff, Mark.

Rees-Mogg, Lord William, jt. auth. see Davidson, James D.

Rees, Naomi, jt. auth. see Watson, David.

Rees, Nigel. Brewer's Quotations. 448p. 1998. pap. 14.95 (*0-304-34832-5*, Pub. by Cassell) Sterling.

— Cassell Companion to Quotations. 1999. pap. 24.95 (*0-304-35192-X*) Continuum.

***Rees, Nigel.** Cassell Dictionary of Anecdotes. 384p. 2000. pap. text 19.95 (*0-304-35195-4*) Continuum.

Rees, Nigel. Cassell Dictionary of Cliches. 256p. 1996. 24.95 (*0-304-34698-5*, Pub. by Cassell) Sterling.

— Cassell Dictionary of Cliches. 1999. pap. text 14.95 (*0-304-34962-3*) Continuum.

— Cassell Dictionary of Humorous Quotations. LC 99-195310. 320p. 1999. 27.95 (*0-304-35095-8*) Continuum.

— The Cassell Pocket Dictionary. 1088p. 1998. pap. 14.95 (*0-304-35079-6*) Continuum.

***Rees, Nina.** School Choice. 2000. pap. 10.00 (*0-89195-076-1*) Heritage Found.

Rees, Nona. St. David of Dewisland. (Illus.). (C). 1993. pap. 21.00 (*0-86383-856-1*, Pub. by Gomer Pr) St Mut.

— St. David of Dewisland. 3rd ed. 37p. 1996. reprint ed. pap. 11.95 (*0-8464-4705-3*) Beekman Pubs.

Rees, Owen. Polyphony in Portugal, c. 1530-c. 1620: Sources from the Monastery of Santa Cruz, Coimbra. LC 95-16153. (Outstanding Dissertations in Music from British Universities Ser.). (Illus.). 482p. 1995. text 127.00 (*0-8153-2029-9*) Garland.

***Rees, Owen, ed.** Music by Pedro de Cristo (c. 1550-1618) (Illus.). 231p. 1998. text 60.00 (*90-5755-010-5*, Harwood Acad Pubs) Gordon & Breach.

Rees, P. John, jt. ed. see Williams, D. G.

Rees-Parnall. Face the Music. Date not set. pap. text, wbk. ed. write for info. (*0-582-02136-7*, Pub. by Addison-Wesley) Longman.

Rees, Pat. Positive Parenting: A Survival Guide. 1992. 50.00 (*1-85549-018-8*) St Mut.

Rees, Paul K., et al. College Algebra. 10th ed. 576p. (C). 1989. text, student ed. 20.50 (*0-07-051744-4*) McGraw.

Rees, Paul S. The Warrior Saint. 1987. pap. 7.99 (*0-88019-213-5*) Schmul Pub Co.

Rees, Peter, ed. see Briggs, Adrian.

Rees, Philip H. Margaret Atwood: A Critical Inquiry. LC 84-433. (Women Writers Ser.). 352p. (C). 1984. 50.00 (*0-389-20742-X*, 08034) B&N Imports.

— Residential Patterns in American Cities, 1960. LC 78-12169. (University of Chicago, Department of Geography, Research Paper Ser.: No. 189). 425p. 1979. reprint ed. pap. 131.80 (*0-608-02263-2*, 206290400004) Bks Demand.

Rees, Philip H., ed. Population Migration in the European Union. LC 95-24756. 410p. 1997. 140.00 (*0-471-94968-X*) Wiley.

Rees, Philip H., jt. ed. see Woods, Robert I.

Rees, R. A., jt. auth. see Styles, S. J.

Rees, R. C., ed. The Biology & Clinical Applications of Interleukin-2. (Illus.). 200p. 1991. 55.00 (*0-19-963137-9*) OUP.

***Rees, R. M., et al, eds.** The Sustainable Management of Soil Organic Matter. (CABI Publishing Ser.). (Illus.). 320p. 2000. text. write for info. (*0-85199-465-2*) OUP.

Rees, Richard. The Illuminati Conspiracy. large type ed. (Ulverscroft Large Print Ser.). 512p. 1997. 27.99 (*0-7089-3783-7*) Ulverscroft.

— The Shadow of the Mary Celeste. large type ed. (Ulverscroft Large Print Ser.). 672p. 1997. 27.99 (*0-7089-3726-8*) Ulverscroft.

Rees, Richard, tr. see Monnerot, Jules.

Rees, Richard, tr. see Permanyer, Lluis.

Rees, Robert A. & Harbert, Earl N., eds. Fifteen American Authors Before 1900: Bibliographic Essays on Research & Criticism. LC 77-157395. 456p. 1971. reprint ed. pap. 141.40 (*0-608-01971-2*, 206262600003) Bks Demand.

Rees, Robert A., jt. ed. see Harbert, Earl N.

Rees, Roberta. Beneath the Faceless Mountain. 240p. 1994. text 12.95 (*0-88995-106-3*, Pub. by Red Deer) Genl Dist Srvs.

— Eyes Like Pigeons. 120p. 1992. pap. 10.95 (*0-919626-61-0*, Pub. by Brick Bks) Genl Dist Srvs.

Rees, Roger, tr. see Turgenev, Ivan Sergeevich & Konovalov, S. M.

***Rees-Rohrbacher, Darhon.** Cantique de Noel (O Holy Night) 28p. 2000. pap. 12.50 (*1-882712-52-8*) Dragonflower.

Rees-Rohrbacher, Darhon. Come, Ye Sons of Art Processional Suite. 7p. 1998. pap. 7.00 (*1-882712-13-7*) Dragonflower.

***Rees-Rohrbacher, Darhon.** The Complete Ave Maria Book. 30p. 2000. pap. 15.00 (*1-882712-26-9*) Dragonflower.

Rees-Rohrbacher, Darhon. Festival Preludes & Postludes. rev. ed. 67p. 1999. pap. 20.00 (*1-882712-56-0*) Dragonflower.

— Micro Travelling: How to Travel the World with Only Carry-on Luggage. 75p. (Orig.). Date not set. pap. 8.00 (*1-882712-48-X*) Dragonflower.

— The Pocket Guide to Harp Composing. 2nd rev. ed. (Illus.). 80p. 1995. pap. text 9.00 (*1-882712-14-5*) Dragonflower.

Rees-Rohrbacher, Darhon, ed. Concerto in B Flat Major: Opus 4 Number 6. 15p. 1998. pap. 8.00 (*1-882712-50-1*) Dragonflower.

Rees, Rolf S., ed. Graphs, Matrices & Designs. LC 92-24370. (Lecture Notes in Pure & Applied Mathematics Ser.: Vol. 139). (Illus.). 344p. 1992. pap. text 165.00 (*0-8247-8790-0*) Dekker.

Rees, Ronald. Interior Landscapes: Gardens & the Domestic Environment. LC 92-536. (Illus.). 224p. 1993. 35.00 (*0-8018-4467-3*) Johns Hopkins.

***Rees, Ronald.** King Copper: South Wales & the Copper Trade, 1584-1895. 224p. 2000. 60.00 (*0-7083-1588-7*, Pub. by U Wales Pr); pap. 29.95 (*0-7083-1589-5*, Pub. by U Wales Pr) Paul & Co Pubs.

Rees, Ronald. St. Andrews & the Islands. LC 95-227519. (Illus.). 156p. 1998. pap. text 17.95 (*1-55109-115-1*) Nimbus Publ.

Rees, Rosemary. The Ancient Egyptians. LC 96-29763. (Understanding People in the Past Ser.). (J). 1997. pap. write for info. (*0-431-07803-3*) Buttrwrth-Heinemann.

— The Ancient Egyptians. LC 96-29763. (Understanding People in the Past Ser.). (Illus.). 64p. (J). 1998. 22.79 (*0-431-07789-4*) Buttrwrth-Heinemann.

— The Ancient Greeks. LC 96-53222. (Understanding People in the Past Ser.). (Illus.). 64p. (J). 1999. write for info. (*0-431-07790-8*) Heinemann Lib.

— The Aztecs. LC 98-43082. 1999. 22.79 (*1-57572-888-5*) Heinemann.

***Rees, Rosemary.** The Incas. LC 98-42722. (Understanding People in the Past Ser.). 1999. 22.79 (*1-57572-889-3*) Heinemann Lib.

Rees, Rosemary. The Romans. LC 98-43260. (Understanding People in the Past Ser.). 1999. 22.79 (*1-57572-890-7*) Heinemann Lib.

— The Western Front. LC 97-4476. (Heinemann History Depth Studies). (Illus.). 48p. (J). 1998. write for info. (*1-57572-217-8*) Heinemann Lib.

Rees, Roy. Manual of Soccer Coaching. 1988. pap. text 14.95 (*0-937347-19-1*) C & D Intl.

Rees, Roy & Van der Meer, Cor. Coaching Soccer Successfully. LC 96-15148. 240p. (Orig.). 1996. pap. 19.95 (*0-87322-444-2*, PREE0444) Human Kinetics.

***Rees, Russell E.** Ireland, 1905-25 No. 1: Text & Histiography. LC 98-230981. 360p. 1998. pap. 24.95 (*1-898392-19-6*, Pub. by Colourpoint) Irish Bks Media.

Rees, Saskiavan, et al. Women Giving Birth. (Illus.). 160p. (Orig.). 1995. pap. 18.95 (*0-89087-668-1*) Celestial Arts.

Rees, Seth C. The Holy War. 131p. 1995. pap. 9.99 (*0-88019-342-5*) Schmul Pub Co.

Rees, Shan & Graham, Roderick. Assertion Training: How to Be Who You Really Are. LC 90-36950. (Strategies for Mental Health Ser.). 160p. (C). 1991. pap. 22.99 (*0-415-01073-X*, A5409) Routledge.

Rees, Sian. A Guide to Ancient & Historic Wales: Dyfed. (Illus.). x, 241p. 1992. pap. 24.00 (*0-11-701220-3*, Pub. by Statnry Office) Seven Hills Bk.

***Rees, Sian.** Lighting Styles. (Illus.). 2000. pap. 17.95 (*0-600-60093-9*) P HM.

Rees, Sian. Natural Home Spa: Recreate the Luxurious Beauty Treatments of a Professional Spa in Your Own Home. LC 99-33940. 1999. 24.95 (*0-8069-6813-3*) Sterling.

Rees, Stuart. Social Work Face to Face: Clients & Social Workers' Perceptions of the Content & Outcome of Their Meetings. 1979. text 46.00 (*0-231-04764-9*) Col U Pr.

Rees, Stuart, ed. Achieving Power. 216p. 1991. pap. 17.95 (*0-04-442335-7*, Pub. by Allen & Unwin Pty) Paul & Co Pubs.

R

***Rees, Teresa.** Women & Work: 25 Years of Equality Legislation. 200p. 1999. pap. (*0-7083-1495-3*, Pub. by Univ Wales Pr) Paul & Co Pubs.

Rees, Teresa L. Mainstreaming Equality in the European Union. LC 97-17427. (Illus.). 280p. (C). 1998. 75.00 (*0-415-11533-7*); pap. 24.99 (*0-415-11534-5*) Routledge.

— Women & the Labour Market. LC 92-10512. 224p. 1993. pap. write for info. (*0-415-03802-2*) Routledge.

Rees, Thomas D. & LaTrenta, Gregory S. Aesthetic Plastic Surgery, 2 vols., Set. 2nd ed. (Illus.). 1384p. 1994. text. write for info. (*0-7216-3712-4*, W B Saunders Co) Harcrt Hlth Sci Grp.

Rees, Thomas R. The Technique of T. S. Eliot. LC 72-94500. (De Proprietatibus Litterarum, Ser. Practica: No. 39). (Illus.). 397p. (Orig.). 1974. pap. text 53.10 (*90-279-3190-9*) Mouton.

Rees, Tim & Thorpe, Andrew. International Communism & the Communist International, 1919-1943. LC 98-28361. 320p. 1999. 79.95 (*0-7190-5116-9*, Pub. by Manchester Univ Pr) St Martin.

***Rees, Tim & Thorpe, Andrew.** International Communism & the Communist International, 1919-1943. LC 98-28361. 1999. pap. 29.95 (*0-7190-5546-6*) Manchester Univ Pr.

Rees, Tim, jt. auth. see Donald, Moira.

Rees, Tim, jt. auth. see Grugel, Jean.

Rees, Tim, jt. auth. see Grugel, JEan.

Rees, Tina. Traditions. 230p. 1992. 13.95 (*0-929271-01-7*) D Gibson.

Rees, W. D. Advances in Peptic Ulcer Pathogenesis. 250p. 1988. text 155.00 (*0-7462-0062-5*) Kluwer Academic.

Rees, W. G. Physics by Example: Two Hundred Problems & Solutions. LC 93-34300. (Illus.). 388p. (C). 1994. pap. text 30.95 (*0-521-44975-8*) Cambridge U Pr.

***Rees, W. J., tr.** St. David of Wales (St. Dewi) From Lives of the Cambro British Saints. 1999. reprint ed. pap. 12.50 (*0-89979-118-2*) British Am Bks.

Rees, W. Michael, et al, eds. Multimedia & Megachange: New Roles for Educational Computing. (Computers in the Schools Ser.). (Illus.). 438p. 1995. lib. bdg. 59.95 (*1-56024-693-6*) Haworth Pr.

Rees, Wendy Van, see Van Rees, Wendy.

Rees, William. French Poetry. 1994. pap. 19.95 (*0-14-042385-0*, Viking) Viking Penguin.

Rees, William. A History of the Order of St. John of Jerusalem in Wales & on the Welsh Border: Including an Account of the Templars. LC 76-29839. (Illus.). reprint ed. 37.50 (*0-404-15427-1*) AMS Pr.

Rees, William & Wackernagel, Mathis. Our Ecological Footprint: Reducing Human Impact on the Earth. (Illus.). 176p. (Orig.). 1995. pap. 14.95 (*0-86571-312-X*) New Soc Pubs.

Rees, William, jt. ed. see Sheikh, Saleem.

Rees, William E. Sustainable Development & the Biosphere: Concepts & Principles. (Teilhard Studies: No. 23). 1990. pap. 3.50 (*0-89012-061-7*) Am Teilhard.

Rees, William S., Jr., ed. CVD of Nonmetals. (Illus.). 392p. 1996. 165.00 (*3-527-29295-0*, Wiley-VCH) Wiley.

Rees, Yvonne. Balconies & Roof Gardens. (Illus.). 144p. 1996. pap. 16.95 (*0-7063-7460-6*, Pub. by WrLock) Sterling.

— Essential English Country Style. (Illus.). 112p. 1997. pap. 12.95 (*0-7063-7637-4*, Pub. by WrLock) Sterling.

— Gilding & Antique Finishes: Practical Home Restoration. (Illus.). 96p. 1996. pap. 14.95 (*0-7063-7444-4*, Pub. by WrLock) Sterling.

— Practical Garden Design. (Illus.). 64p. pap. 8.95 (*1-85223-624-8*, Pub. by Cro1wood) Trafalgar.

— Practical Home Restoration: Stained Glass & Ceramics. (Illus.). 96p. 1996. pap. 14.95 (*0-7063-7468-1*, Pub. by WrLock) Sterling.

Rees, Yvonne & Palliser, David. Patio Gardening: Step by Step to Growing Success. (Crowood Gardening Guides Ser.). (Illus.). 128p. 1992. pap. 16.95 (*1-85223-507-1*, Pub. by Cro1wood) Trafalgar.

Rees, Yvonne, jt. auth. see Paul, Anthony.

Reese. Effective Human Relations, 5 vols. (C). 1993. pap., teacher ed. 3.96 (*0-395-63893-3*) HM.

— The Gillian Anderson Files. 1997. pap. 16.00 (*0-671-01492-7*, PB Trade Paper) PB.

— Master Deceptive Plays. pap. 3.95 (*0-575-04384-9*, Pub. by V Gollancz) Trafalgar.

— Muscle & Sensory Testing. LC 98-7961. (C). 1999. pap. 45.00 (*0-7216-5958-6*) Harcourt.

— Physics. 1999. mass mkt., student ed. 35.95 (*0-534-35234-0*) Brooks-Cole.

— Physics. LC 98-41666. (Physics Ser.). 1999. 74.00 (*0-534-24655-9*) Brooks-Cole.

Reese. Runners World 2000. write for info. (*1-57954-131-3*) Rodale Pr Inc.

Reese. University Physics. 1999. pap. text. write for info. (*0-534-36962-6*) Brooks-Cole.

***Reese.** University Physics. (Physics Ser.). (C). 2000. text 18.00 (*0-534-37727-0*) Brooks-Cole.

Reese. University Physics, Volume 1, Vol. 1. (Physics). 1999. 40.00 (*0-534-35658-3*) Brooks-Cole.

— University Physics Volume 2, Vol. 2. LC 98-41666. (Physics). (C). 1999. 40.00 (*0-534-35659-1*) Brooks-Cole.

Reese & Hoffman. Play It Again, Sam. 7.95 (*0-910791-21-X*, 0690) Devyn Pr.

Reese, Jean. Internet Books for Educators, Parents & Children. LC 99-26463. 200p. 1999. pap. 32.50 (*1-56308-697-2*) Libs Unl.

Reese, Randy, jt. auth. see Anderson, Keith R.

Reese, A. C. & Nair, C. N. Review Questions for Microbiology & Immunology. LC 98-35193. (Review Questions Ser.). (Illus.). 113p. 2000. pap. 20.95 (*1-85070-020-6*) Prthnon Pub.

Reese, Alexander. Industrial Energy Conservation: Where Do We Go from Here? LC 77-93745. 54p. reprint ed. pap. 30.00 (*0-7837-0331-7*, 204065000017) Bks Demand.

Reese, Andrew, jt. auth. see Barba, Rick.

Reese, Andrew J., jt. auth. see Debo, Thomas N.

Reese, Andrew J., jt. ed. see Pusey, Charles D.

Reese, Andy. Windows 95: Easy Installation Guide. 1995. pap. text 12.95 (*0-7615-0241-6*) Prima Pub.

Reese, Becky D., jt. auth. see Mayer, Susan M.

Reese, Bernie, et al. Tahquitz Exchange. Rietveld, Jeffrey, ed. 226p. (Orig.). (YA). (gr. 12). 1993. pap. 7.00 (*0-9628802-3-X*) DeChamp CA.

Reese, Bob. Abert & Kaibab: Big Book. (Grand Canyon Ser.). (Illus.). (J). (gr. k-6). 1987. 9.95 (*0-89868-226-6*); pap. 3.95 (*0-89868-227-4*) ARO Pub.

— Ape Escape. (Going Ape Ser.). (Illus.). (J). 1983. 9.95 (*0-89868-147-2*); pap. 3.95 (*0-89868-146-4*) ARO Pub.

— The Ape Team. (Going Ape Ser.). (Illus.). (J). 1983. 9.95 (*0-89868-145-6*); pap. 3.95 (*0-89868-144-8*) ARO Pub.

— Apricot Ape. (Going Ape Ser.). (Illus.). (J). 1983. 9.95 (*0-89868-141-3*); pap. 3.95 (*0-89868-140-5*) ARO Pub.

— Arbor Day. Jordan, Alton, ed. (Holiday Set). (Illus.). (J). (gr. k-3). 1984. 7.95 (*0-89868-031-X*, Read Res); pap. 3.95 (*0-89868-064-6*, Read Res) ARO Pub.

— Bubba Bear. (Yellowstone Ser.). (Illus.). (J). (gr. k-6). 1986. 9.95 (*0-89868-173-1*); pap. 3.95 (*0-89868-174-X*) ARO Pub.

— Bubba Bear: Big Big Book. (Yellowstone Ser.). (Illus.). (J). (gr. k-6). 1986. 22.00 (*0-614-24509-5*) ARO Pub.

— Buffa Buffalo. (Yellowstone Ser.). (Illus.). (J). (gr. k-6). 1986. 9.95 (*0-89868-175-8*); pap. 3.95 (*0-89868-176-6*) ARO Pub.

— Bugle Elk & Little Toot. (Yellowstone Ser.). (Illus.). (J). (gr. k-6). 1986. 9.95 (*0-89868-177-4*); pap. 3.95 (*0-89868-178-2*) ARO Pub.

— Camper Critters. (Yellowstone Ser.). (Illus.). (J). (gr. k-6). 1986. 9.95 (*0-89868-169-3*); pap. 3.95 (*0-89868-170-7*) ARO Pub.

— Can Do. (Ten Word Book Ser.). (Illus.). (J). (gr. k-3). 1994. pap. 3.95 (*0-89868-248-7*, Read Res); lib. bdg. 9.95 (*0-89868-247-9*, Read Res) ARO Pub.

— Cocos Berry Party. (Grand Canyon Ser.). (Illus.). (J). (gr. k-6). 1987. 9.95 (*0-89868-193-6*); pap. 3.95 (*0-89868-194-4*) ARO Pub.

— Crab Apple. Wasserman, Dan, ed. (Ten Word Book Ser.). (Illus.). (J). (gr. k-1). 1979. 9.95 (*0-89868-072-7*); pap. 3.95 (*0-89868-083-2*) ARO Pub.

— Easter. Jordan, Alton, ed. (Holiday Set). (Illus.). (J). (gr. k-3). 1984. 7.95 (*0-89868-032-8*, Read Res); pap. 3.95 (*0-89868-065-4*, Read Res) ARO Pub.

— For Keeps. (Ten Word Book Ser.). (Illus.). (J). (gr. k-3). 1994. pap. 3.95 (*0-89868-252-5*, Read Res); lib. bdg. 9.95 (*0-89868-251-7*, Read Res) ARO Pub.

— Forty Word Yellowstone Series, 6 bks., Set. (Illus.). (J). (gr. k-6). 1986. 59.70 (*0-89868-239-8*) ARO Pub.

— Going Bananas. (Going Ape Ser.). (Illus.). (J). 1983. 9.95 (*0-89868-143-X*); pap. 3.95 (*0-89868-142-1*) ARO Pub.

— El Gusano Curioso. Schaffer-Melendez, Gloria, tr. (Un Libro de Diaz Palabras Ser.). (SPA., Illus.). (J). (gr. k-3). 1994. pap. 3.95 (*0-89868-258-4*, Read Res); lib. bdg. 9.95 (*0-89868-257-6*, Read Res) ARO Pub.

— Honest Ape. (Going Ape Ser.). (Illus.). (J). 1983. 9.95 (*0-89868-149-9*); pap. 3.95 (*0-89868-148-0*) ARO Pub.

— The Jungle Train. (Going Ape Ser.). (Illus.). (J). 1983. 9.95 (*0-89868-151-0*); pap. 3.95 (*0-89868-150-2*) ARO Pub.

— The Jungle Train: Big Big Book. (Going Ape Ser.). (Illus.). (J). 1983. 22.00 (*0-614-24512-5*) ARO Pub.

— Little Dinosaur. Wasserman, Dan, ed. (Ten Word Book Ser.). (Illus.). (J). (gr. k-1). 1979. 9.95 (*0-89868-070-0*); pap. 3.95 (*0-89868-081-6*) ARO Pub.

— Mickey Moose. (Yellowstone Ser.). (Illus.). (J). (gr. k-6). 1986. 9.95 (*0-89868-171-5*); pap. 3.95 (*0-89868-172-3*) ARO Pub.

— Old Faithful. (Yellowstone Ser.). (Illus.). (J). (gr. k-6). 1986. 9.95 (*0-89868-167-7*); pap. 3.95 (*0-89868-168-5*) ARO Pub.

— Pamba & the Bink. (Illus.). (J). (gr. k-6). 1984. 9.95 (*0-89868-152-9*) ARO Pub.

— Para Siempre. Schaffer-Melendez, Gloria, tr. (Libro de Diaz Palabras Ser.). (SPA., Illus.). (J). (gr. k-3). 1994. pap. 3.95 (*0-89868-260-6*, Read Res); lib. bdg. 9.95 (*0-89868-259-2*, Read Res) ARO Pub.

— Podemos. Schaffer-Melendez, Gloria, tr. (Libro de Diaz Palabras Ser.). (SPA., Illus.). (J). (gr. k-3). 1994. pap. 3.95 (*0-89868-256-8*, Read Res); lib. bdg. 9.95 (*0-89868-255-X*, Read Res) ARO Pub.

— Raven's Roost. (Grand Canyon Ser.). (Illus.). (J). (gr. k-6). 1987. 9.95 (*0-89868-195-2*); pap. 3.95 (*0-89868-196-0*) ARO Pub.

— Sixty Word Grand Canyon Series, 6 bks., Set. (Illus.). (J). (gr. k-6). 1987. 59.70 (*0-89868-241-X*) ARO Pub.

— Slitherfoot Snake. (Grand Canyon Ser.). (Illus.). (J). (gr. k-6). 1987. 9.95 (*0-89868-191-X*); pap. 3.95 (*0-89868-192-8*) ARO Pub.

— St. Patrick's Day. Jordan, Alton, ed. (Holiday Set). (Illus.). (J). (gr. k-3). 1984. 7.95 (*0-89868-030-1*, Read Res); pap. 3.95 (*0-89868-063-8*, Read Res) ARO Pub.

— Sunshine. Wasserman, Dan, ed. (Ten Word Book Ser.). (Illus.). (J). (gr. k-1). 1979. 9.95 (*0-89868-073-5*); pap. 3.95 (*0-89868-084-0*) ARO Pub.

— Surefoot Mule. (Grand Canyon Ser.). (Illus.). (J). (gr. k-6). 1987. 9.95 (*0-89868-197-9*); pap. 9.95 (*0-89868-198-7*) ARO Pub.

— Who's a Silly Egg? Jordan, Alton, ed. (Buppet Bks.). (Illus.). (J). (gr. 1-4). 1980. 9.95 (*0-89868-092-1*, Read Res); pap. 3.95 (*0-89868-103-0*, Read Res) ARO Pub.

— Wild Turkey Run. (Grand Canyon Ser.). (Illus.). (J). (gr. k-6). 1987. 9.95 (*0-89868-199-5*); pap. 3.95 (*0-89868-225-8*) ARO Pub.

— Wonder Worm. (Ten Word Book Ser.). (Illus.). (J). (gr. k-3). 1994. pap. 3.95 (*0-89868-250-9*, Read Res); lib. bdg. 9.95 (*0-89868-249-5*, Read Res) ARO Pub.

— Zero Word Going Ape Series, 6 bks., Set. (Illus.). (J). 1983. 9.95 (*0-89868-139-1*); pap. 3.95 (*0-89868-138-3*) ARO Pub.

Reese, Bob & Preece-Sandoval, Pam. Libros de Diez Palabras Series, 4 bks., Set. Schaffer-Melendez, Gloria, tr. (SPA., Illus.). (J). (gr. k-3). 1994. pap. 15.80 (*0-89868-279-7*, Read Res); lib. bdg. 39.80 (*0-89868-278-9*, Read Res) ARO Pub.

— Ten Word Book Series, 4 bks., Set. (Illus.). (J). (gr. k-3). 1994. pap. 15.80 (*0-89868-274-6*, Read Res); lib. bdg. 99.50 (*0-89868-273-8*, Read Res) ARO Pub.

Reese, Bob & Reese, Nancy. Smiley Snake. Jordan, Alton, ed. (Illus.). (J). (gr. k-3). 1984. 7.95 (*0-89868-010-7*, Read Res); pap. 3.95 (*0-89868-043-3*, Read Res) ARO Pub.

Reese, Bob, et al. Big Big Book Series, 7 bks. (Illus.). (J). (gr. k-6). 1987. pap. 154.00 (*0-89868-244-4*) ARO Pub.

— I Can Read Underwater Series, 10 bks. Jordan, Alton, ed. (Illus.). (J). (gr. k-2). 1984. 79.50 (*0-89868-000-X*, Read Res); pap. 39.50 (*0-89868-033-6*, Read Res) ARO Pub.

— Ten Word Book Series, 10 bks., Set. (Illus.). (J). (gr. k-1). 1979. pap. 39.50 (*0-89868-077-8*, Read Res) ARO Pub.

Reese, Bob, jt. auth. see Preece-Sandoval, Pam.

Reese, Bob, jt. auth. see Reese, Nancy.

Reese, C. Roger & Miracle, Andrew W., eds. Sport & Social Theory. LC 85-19758. 352p. reprint ed. pap. 109.20 (*0-608-07066-1*, 206727200009) Bks Demand.

***Reese, Charles D.** Material Handling Systems: Designing for Safety & Health. LC 99-57159. 2000. write for info. (*1-56032-868-1*) Taylor & Francis.

Reese, Charles D. Palm Beach Roots & Recipes. (Illus.). 120p. (Orig.). 1991. reprint ed. pap. 12.95 (*0-9629266-0-4*) Palm Bch Roots.

***Reese, Charles D. & Edison, James V.** Annotated Dictionary of Construction Safety & Health. LC 99-42159. 264p. 1999. write for info. (*1-56670-514-2*) Lewis Pubs.

Reese, Charles Dennis & Eidson, James Vernon. Handbook of OSHA Construction Safety & Health. LC 98-51604. 1999. 89.95 (*1-56670-297-6*, L1297) Lewis Pubs.

Reese, Clyde M. NAEP 1996 Mathematics Report Card for the Nation & the States: Findings from the National Assessment of Educational Progress. LC 97-152431. 169p. 1997. pap. 13.00 (*0-16-049013-8*) USGPO.

Reese, Craig E. Deregulation & Environmental Quality: The Use of Tax Policy to Control Pollution in North America & Western Europe. LC 82-11266. (Illus.). 495p. 1983. 65.00 (*0-89930-018-9*, RDE/, Quorum Bks) Greenwood.

Reese, David. Prospects for North Korea's Survival, Vol. 323. LC 99-200844. (International Institute for Strategic Studies: 323). 96p. 1999. pap. text 26.95 (*0-19-922379-3*) OUP.

***Reese, David E.** Radio Production Worktext. 4th ed. 240p. 2001. pap. 39.95 (*0-240-80439-2*, Focal) Buttrwrth-Heinemann.

Reese, David E. & Gross, Lynne S. Radio Production Worktext: Studio & Equipment. 3rd ed. LC 97-23429. 224p. 1998. pap. 39.95 (*0-240-80283-7*, Focal) Buttrwrth-Heinemann.

***Reese, David E., et al.** Broadcast Announcing Worktext: Performing for Radio, Television & Cable. LC 99-42964. (Illus.). 200p. 2000. pap., wbk. ed. 36.95 incl. cd-rom (*0-240-80356-6*, Focal) Buttrwrth-Heinemann.

Reese, David M. Humbugs of New York. LC 77-37314. (Black Heritage Library Collection). 1977. reprint ed. 26.95 (*0-8369-8951-1*) Ayer.

Reese, Dawnell & Vondrak, Elizabeth, eds. Rockhurst Review, 1995: A Fine Arts Journal, Vol. VIII. 80p. 1995. pap. 6.00 (*1-886761-07-8*) Rockhurst Col.

Reese, Della. Angels along the Way. large type ed. LC 97-32530. (Americana Series). 1998. 27.95 (*0-7862-1309-4*) Thorndike Pr.

— God Inside of Me. 32p. (J). (ps-3). Date not set. pap. 15.99 (*0-7868-1311-3*, Pub. by Hyprn Child) Little.

— God Inside of Me. LC 98-45112. (Illus.). 32p. 1999. lib. bdg. 16.49 (*0-7868-2395-X*, Jump at the Sun) Hyprn Child.

— God Inside of Me. LC 98-45112. (Illus.). 32p. (J). (ps-2). 1999. 16.99 (*0-7868-0434-3*, Pub. by Hyprn Child) Time Warner.

Reese, Della, et al. Angels along the Way: My Life with Help from Above. (Illus.). 352p. 1998. reprint ed. mass mkt. 6.99 (*0-425-16573-6*) Blvd Books.

***Reese, Donald T., ed.** Classical Guitar Music in Print: 1998 Supplement. (Music in Print Ser.: Vol. 7s). 340p. 1998. lib. bdg. 95.00 (*0-88478-048-1*) Musicdata.

***Reese, Dresden.** Sailorboy: A Fleeting Glimpse. LC 00-190347. 319p. 2000. 25.00 (*0-7388-1736-8*); pap. 18.00 (*0-7388-1737-6*) Xlibris Corp.

Reese, Ed. Beyond Selling. LC 87-63208. 1988. 22.95 (*0-916990-19-2*) META Pubns.

Reese, Edward, compiled by. The Reese Chronological Bible. 1624p. 1980. reprint ed. text 39.99 (*0-87123-115-8*) Bethany Hse.

Reese, Elizabeth. Life: A Workback Schedule. 1997. mass mkt. 5.99 (*0-614-20508-5*) Harlequin Bks.

***Reese, Ellisa.** By Leads & Rebounds. 2000. mass mkt. 10.95 (*1-55279-023-1*) Picasso Publ.

Reese, Esther D., jt. auth. see Davis, Carol.

Reese, Francesca G., jt. auth. see Gardner, John W.

Reese, Gareth. New Testament History - Acts. 11th ed. (Bible Study Textbook Ser.). (Illus.). 1056p. 1976. 24.99 (*0-89900-055-X*) College Pr Pub.

Reese, George H. Database Programming with JDBC & Java. 240p. 1997. pap. write for info. (*1-56592-270-0*) Thomson Learn.

Reese, George H., ed. Journals & Papers of the Virginia State Convention of 1861, 3 vols., Set. LC 65-7459. 1966. text 49.95 (*0-88490-058-4*) Library of VA.

— Journals of the Council of the State of Virginia, 1786-1788, 5 vols., Vol. 4. LC 31-27557. x, 403p. 1967. 19.95 (*0-88490-024-X*) Library of VA.

— Proceedings in the Court of Vice-Admiralty of Virginia, 1698-1775. xiii, 121p. 1983. 12.50 (*0-88490-113-0*) Library of VA.

— Proceedings of the Virginia State Convention of 1861, 4 vols., Set. LC 65-7459. 1965. text 79.95 (*0-88490-057-6*) Library of VA.

Reese, George H. & Hickin, Patricia, eds. Journal of the Senate of Virginia, November Session, 1793. (Journals of the Senate of Virginia 1792-1803). vii, 110p. 1972. 10.00 (*0-88490-051-7*) Library of VA.

— Journal of the Senate of Virginia, Session of 1802-03. (Journals of the Senate of Virginia 1792-1803). vi, 131p. 1973. 10.00 (*0-88490-056-8*) Library of VA.

Reese, George H., jt. ed. see Van Horne, John C.

Reese, Gerd, tr. see Kirzner, Israel M.

Reese, Greg. Jazzkeepers: A Pictorial Tribute & Memoir. (Illus.). 200p. 1996. pap. 25.00 (*1-885066-14-7*) Four-G Pubs.

Reese, Gregory L. & Hawkins, Ernestine L. Stop Talking, Start Doing! LC 99-18329. 176p. 1999. 30.00 (*0-8389-0762-8*) ALA.

Reese, Gustave. Fourscore Classics of Music Literature. LC 78-87616. (Music Reprint Ser.). 1970. reprint ed. lib. bdg. 23.50 (*0-306-71620-8*) Da Capo.

— Music in the Middle Ages. (Illus.). (C). 1940. text 52.25 (*0-393-09750-1*) Norton.

— Music in the Renaissance. rev. ed. (Illus.). (C). 1959. text 50.75 (*0-393-09530-4*) Norton.

Reese, Gustave & Snow, Robert J., eds. Essays in Musicology: In Honor of Dragan Plamenac on His 70th Birthday. LC 77-4220. (Music Reprint Ser.). (Illus.). 1977. reprint ed. lib. bdg. 45.00 (*0-306-77408-9*) Da Capo.

Reese, Gustave, tr. see Einstein, Alfred, ed.

Reese, Harry. The Sandragraph: Between Printing & Painting. (Illus.). 20p. (C). 1987. 3000.00 (*0-923980-04-0*) Arundel Pr.

Reese, Harvey. The Adventures of Gentle Nellie, Incl. horse. (Illus.). 16p. (J). 1996. 25.00 (*1-890414-11-5*) Bow Tie.

— How to License Your Million Dollar Idea: Everything You Need to Know to Make Money from Your New Product Idea. LC 92-44310. 240p. 1993. pap. 19.95 (*0-471-58050-3*) Wiley.

Reese, Hayne W., ed. Advances in Child Development & Behavior, Vol. 24. (Illus.). 317p. (C). 1993. text 94.95 (*0-12-009724-9*) Acad Pr.

— Advances in Child Development & Behavior, Vol. 25. (Illus.). 385p. (C). 1994. text. write for info. (*0-12-009725-7*) Acad Pr.

— Advances in Child Development & Behavior, Vol. 26. (Illus.). 253p. (C). 1996. text 59.95 (*0-12-009726-5*) Acad Pr.

***Reese, Hayne W., ed.** Advances in Child Development & Behavior, Vol. 27. Vol. 27. (Illus.). 320p. 1999. 79.95 (*0-12-009727-3*) Acad Pr.

Reese, Hayne W. & Franzen, Michael D., eds. Biological & Neuropsychological Mechanisms: Life-Span Developmental Psychology. LC 96-17641. (West Virginia Conference on Life-Span Developmental Psychology Ser.). 264p. 1997. 59.95 (*0-8058-1152-4*) L Erlbaum Assocs.

Reese, Hayne W. & Parrott, Linda J., eds. Behavior Science: Philosophical, Methodological, & Empirical Advances. 272p. 1986. text 69.95 (*0-89859-766-8*) L Erlbaum Assocs.

Reese, Hayne W., jt. ed. see Puckett, James M.

Reese, Herbert H. Kellogg Arabians: Their Background & Influence. 1958. 25.00 (*0-87505-114-6*) Borden.

Reese, Ilinda. If I'm Looking for a Prince, Why Am I Still Kissing Frogs? (Illus.). 210p. 1998. pap. 24.95 (*0-942923-08-1*) NETWIC.

***Reese, J.** Worlds at War Minds at Peace. 1998. 21.95 (*0-9639103-4-5*) Intl Focus Pr.

Reese, J. Irving. Una Gui'a: Como Organizar y Conducir una Iglesia Bautista. (SPA.). 134p. 1997. pap. 6.95 (*1-879892-68-5*) Editorial Bautista.

Reese, James M. The Student's Guide to the Gospels. (Good News Studies: Vol. 24). 150p. (Orig.). 1992. pap. text 11.95 (*0-8146-5689-7*) Liturgical Pr.

***Reese, James T., Jr.** Sports Governance & Ethics. 208p. 2000. write for info. (*1-58692-016-2*) Copyright Mgmt.

Reese, Jeffrey G. Poems & Other Writings. (Illus.). (Orig.). 1994. pap. 20.00 (*0-9641717-0-8*) Am Vision Gallery.

***Reese, Jim.** This Ain't No Shoe Store! LC 99-96755. 2000. pap. 8.95 (*0-533-13341-6*) Vantage.

Reese, Joe. Katie Dee & Katie Haw: Letters from a Texas Farm Girl. (Illus.). 184p. (Orig.). (YA). (gr. 8-12). 1995. pap. 8.95 (*0-925854-13-1*) Defiant Pr.

Reese, John. Rich Man's Range. 1978. mass mkt. 1.75 (*0-451-08261-3*, E8261, Sig) NAL.

Reese, John H. Administrative Law: Principles & Practice. LC 94-49388. (American Casebook Ser.). 844p. (C). 1995. 57.50 (*0-314-04986-X*) West Pub.

— Administrative Law, Principles & Practice, Teacher's Manual to Accompany. (American Casebook Ser.). 65p. (C). 1995. pap. text. write for info. (*0-314-06261-0*) West Pub.

— Administrative Law, 1995 Statutory Supplement (Including Recent Cases) to Accompany. (American Casebook Ser.). 95p. 1995. pap. 16.50 (*0-314-07100-8*) West Pub.

Reese, John W. Flaming Feuds of Colorado County, Texas. (Illus.). 1962. 35.00 (*0-685-05000-9*) A Jones.

An Asterisk (*) at the beginning of an entry indicates that the title is appearing for the first time.

Reese, Judy S. Recasting Social Values in the Work of Virginia Woolf. LC 95-37374. 168p. 1996. 29.50 (*0-945636-83-0*) Susquehanna U Pr.

Reese, Karen J., ed. see North American Prairie Conference Staff.

Reese, Kenneth M., ed. A Century of Chemistry: The Role of Chemists & the American Chemical Society. LC 76-6126. 468p. (C). 1976. text 18.95 (*0-8412-0307-5*, Pub. by Am Chemical) OUP.

***Reese, Kimberly Ingalls.** Celebrate Jesus! At Christmas: Family Devotions for Advent Through Epiphany. LC 00-8510. 2000. write for info. (*0-570-07127-5*) Concordia.

***Reese, Laura.** Panic Snap. LC 99-56344. 352p. 2000. text 24.95 (*0-312-24229-8*) St Martin.

— Panic Snap. 2001. pap. write for info. (*0-312-27275-8*, St Martin Griffin) St Martin.

Reese, Laura. Topping from Below. LC 95-5798. 384p. 1996. pap. 12.95 (*0-312-14435-0*) St Martin.

Reese, Laura. Topping from Below. abr. ed. 1995. 16.95 incl. audio (*1-882071-58-1*) B&B Audio.

Reese, Laura A. & Lindenberg, Karen E. Implementing Sexual Harassment Policy: Challenges for the Public Sector Workplace. LC 98-19721. 214p. 1998. write for info. (*0-7619-1144-8*); pap. write for info. (*0-7619-1145-6*) Sage.

Reese, Laura A. & Urban Center Staff. Local Economic Development Policy: The United States & Canada. Bingham, Richard D., ed. LC 96-47040. (Contemporary Urban Affairs Ser.). (Illus.). 176p. 1997. text 37.00 (*0-8153-2383-2*, SS1109) Garland.

Reese, Laura A., jt. auth. see Blair, John P.

Reese, Linda. A guide to RCRA inspections. LC 98-38343. xi, 89 p. 1998. write for info. (*1-57073-606-5*) Amer Bar Assn.

Reese, Linda E. & Gasparis. Mental Health & Psychiatric Nursing. LC 91-5211. (Nursetest: A Review Ser.). 288p. 1991. pap. 21.95 (*0-87434-306-2*) Springhouse Corp.

Reese, Linda W. Women of Oklahoma, 1890-1920. LC 97-7549. (Illus.). 384p. 1997. pap. 18.95 (*0-8061-2999-9*) U of Okla Pr.

Reese, Lizette W. Selected Poems. (BCL1-PS American Literature Ser.). 187p. 1992. reprint ed. lib. bdg. 69.00 (*0-7812-6839-7*) Rprt Serv.

Reese, Luellen. Young Man's Journey with Aids: The Story of Nick Trevor. LC 97-21622. (Issues-Teen Ser.). (J). 1997. 24.00 (*0-531-11366-3*) Watts.

— A Young Man's Journey with AIDS: The Story of Nick Trevor. (YA). (gr. 9-12). 1998. pap. 9.95 (*0-531-15892-6*) Watts.

Reese, Lyn. The Bird of Destiny - Ancient Egypt: World History Unit for the Middle Grades. rev. ed. Dougherty, Mary A. & Wilkinson, Jean B., eds. (Illus.). 36p. (YA). (gr. 6-9). 1991. spiral bd. 10.00 (*0-9625880-8-3*) Wom Wrld Hist.

— The Eyes of the Empress: Women in Tang Dynasty China. Dougherty, Mary A. & Wilkinson, Jean, eds. (Illus.). 62p. (Orig.). (J). (gr. 6-10). 1996. pap., wbk. ed. 12.00 (*0-9625880-4-0*) Wom Wrld Hist.

— Fated to Be Friends - Coming of Age in Classical Athens: World History Unit for the Middle Grades. rev. ed. Dougherty, Mary A. & Wilkinson, Jean B., eds. (Illus.). 43p. (YA). (gr. 6-9). 1994. spiral bd. 10.00 (*1-890380-01-6*) Wom Wrld Hist.

— The Garnet-Eyed Brooch - Anglo-Saxon England: World History Unit for the Middle Grades. rev. ed. Dougherty, Mary A. & Wilkinson, Jean B., eds. (Illus.). 37p. (YA). (gr. 6-9). 1991. spiral bd. 10.00 (*0-9625880-9-1*) Wom Wrld Hist.

— Gifts for Queen Amina - African Songhay & Hausa Kingdoms: World History Unit for the Middle Grades. rev. ed. Dougherty, Mary A. & Wilkinson, Jean B., eds. (Illus.). 38p. (YA). (gr. 6-9). 1990. spiral bd. 10.00 (*0-9625880-7-5*) Wom Wrld Hist.

— I Will Not Bow My Head: Documenting Women's Political Resistance in World History. Wilkinson, Jean & Dougherty, Mary A., eds. (Illus.). 119p. (Orig.). (YA). (gr. 9-12). 1995. pap. text, student ed. 19.95 (*0-9625880-3-2*) Wom Wrld Hist.

— A Message for the Sultan - 16th Century Ottoman Turkey: World History Unit for the Middle Grades. rev. ed. Dougherty, Mary A. & Wilkinson, Jean B., eds. (Illus.). 45p. (YA). (gr. 6-9). 1994. spiral bd. 10.00 (*1-890380-03-2*) Wom Wrld Hist.

— The Needle & the Brush - Renaissance Florence: World History Unit for the Middle Grades. rev. ed. Dougherty, Mary A. & Wilkinson, Jean B., eds. (Illus.). 33p. (YA). (gr. 6-9). 1990. spiral bd. 10.00 (*0-9625880-6-7*) Wom Wrld Hist.

— Nothing Lasts Forever - Roman Pompeii: World History Unit for the Middle Grades. rev. ed. Dougherty, Mary A. & Wilkinson, Jean B., eds. (Illus.). 37p. (YA). (gr. 6-9). 1990. spiral bd. 10.00 (*0-9625880-5-9*) Wom Wrld Hist.

— Samurai Sisters - Early Feudal Japan: World History Unit for the Middle Grades. rev. ed. Dougherty, Mary A. & Wilkinson, Jean B., eds. (Illus.). 51p. (YA). (gr. 6-9). 1991. spiral bd. 10.00 (*1-890380-00-8*) Wom Wrld Hist.

— Spindle Stories: World History Units for the Middle Grades, Bk. 1. Dougherty, Mary A. & Wilkinson, Jean B., eds. (Illus.). 107p. (J). (gr. 5-9). 1991. pap. 16.95 (*0-9625880-0-8*) Wom Wrld Hist.

— Spindle Stories Bk. 3: Three Units on Women's World History. Wilkinson, Jean & Doughtery, Mary A., eds. (Spindle Stories Ser.). (Illus.). 138p. (Orig.). (YA). (gr. 6 up). 1994. pap. text 16.95 (*0-9625880-2-4*) Wom Wrld Hist.

— Spindle Stories Bk. Two: Three Units on Women's World History. Dougherty, Mary A. & Wilkinson, Jean B., eds. (Illus.). 123p. (J). (gr. 6-10). 1991. pap. text 16.95 (*0-9625880-1-6*) Wom Wrld Hist.

— Weaving the Heavens - Mayan Women in Precolumbian Guatemala: World History Unit for the Middle Grades. rev. ed. Dougherty, Mary A. & Wilkinson, Jean B., eds. (Illus.). 51p. (YA). (gr. 6-9). 1994. spiral bd. 10.00 (*1-890380-02-4*) Wom Wrld Hist.

— Women in the Muslim World: Personalities & Perspectives from the Past. rev. ed. Dougherty, Mary A. & Shabbas, Audrey, eds. (Illus.). 102p. (YA). (gr. 8 up). 1998. spiral bd. 19.95 (*1-890380-05-9*) Wom Wrld Hist.

Reese, Lyn, et al, eds. I'm on My Way Run. rev. ed. 304p. 2000. pap. 11.00 (*0-380-78050-X*, Avon Bks) Morrow Avon.

Reese, Lyn & Wilkinson, Jean. Women in the World: Annotated History Resources for the Secondary Student. LC 87-16436. (Illus.). 228p. 1987. 31.50 (*0-8108-2050-1*) Scarecrow.

Reese, Lyvita. A Teacher's Year-Timer: A Complete Organizer for Teachers. 1996. spiral bd. 19.95 (*1-889003-01-8*) LRW Publns.

Reese, M. E. Reese: Genealogy of the Reese Family in Wales & America from Their Arrival in America to the Present Time (1903) (Illus.). 322p. 1995. reprint ed. pap. 49.50 (*0-8328-4826-3*); reprint ed. lib. bdg. 59.50 (*0-8328-4825-5*) Higginson Bk Co.

Reese, M. R. Better Beer & How to Brew It. LC 81-7003. (Illus.). 128p. 1983. pap. 9.95 (*0-88266-257-0*, Garden Way Pub) Storey Bks.

Reese, Margaret C. Abstract of Augusta County, Virginia Death Registers, 1853-1896. 242p. 1983. pap. 14.95 (*0-935931-55-4*) Iberian Pub.

Reese, Mary A. Doing What Comes Naturally: Jobs, Career & Vocation, Vol. 3. Coffey, Kathy, ed. LC 98-159518. (Crossings). 80p. (YA). 1998. pap. 3.95 (*1-889108-27-8*) Liv Good News.

Reese, Maryann. How to Walk What You Talk: Your Personal NLP Development Manual. 160p. 1989. student ed. 39.95 (*0-9615502-3-6*) Southern Inst Pr.

Reese, Maryann & Yancar, Carol L. Practitioner Manual for Introductory Patterns of Neuro Linguistic Programming. 245p. 1986. 30.00 (*0-9615502-1-X*) Southern Inst Pr.

Reese, Merrill & Eckel, Mark. Merrill Reese: "It's Goooood!" (Illus.). 200p. 1998. 22.95 (*1-58261-000-2*) Sports Pub.

Reese, Michael, II. Autographs of the Confederacy. LC 81-68377. 225p. 1981. 54.95 (*0-940746-00-X*); 89.95 (*0-686-42866-8*) Cohasco.

— Luger Tips. rev. ed. 1992. reprint ed. 14.95 (*0-913150-36-3*) Pioneer Pr.

— Nineteen Hundred Luger-U. S. Test Trials. 2nd rev. ed. Pioneer Press Staff, ed. LC 71-117532. (Illus.). 1976. pap. 7.00 (*0-913150-35-5*) Pioneer Pr.

— A Travel Letter, 1871. 1988. write for info. (*0-318-65536-5*) Cloister Pr.

Reese, Mildred L. & Smith, Thelma D. Successful African-American Males - Teachers Make a Difference. McCann, Yvette, ed. & illus. by. 234p. (YA). (gr. 7-12). 1997. pap. 25.00 (*0-9657163-4-1*) Educ Resources.

Reese, Nancy. I Can Eat an Elephant. Jordan, Alton, ed. (I Can Eat an Elephant Ser.). (Illus.). (J). (gr. k-3). 1984. 7.95 (*0-89868-012-3*, Read Res); pap. 3.95 (*0-89868-045-X*, Read Res) ARO Pub.

— New Year's. Jordan, Alton, ed. (Holiday Set). (Illus.). (J). (gr. k-3). 1984. 7.95 (*0-89868-026-3*, Read Res); pap. 3.95 (*0-89868-059-X*, Read Res) ARO Pub.

— Silly Egg. Jordan, Alton, ed. (Illus.). (J). (gr. k-3). 1984. 7.95 (*0-89868-004-2*, Read Res); pap. 3.95 (*0-89868-037-9*, Read Res) ARO Pub.

— Valentine's Day. Jordan, Alton, ed. (Holiday Set). (Illus.). (J). (gr. k-3). 1984. 7.95 (*0-89868-029-8*, Read Res); pap. 3.95 (*0-89868-062-X*, Read Res) ARO Pub.

Reese, Nancy & Reese, Bob. The Bee. Jordan, Alton, ed. (Illus.). (J). (gr. k-3). 1984. 7.95 (*0-89868-005-0*, Read Res); pap. 3.95 (*0-89868-038-7*, Read Res) ARO Pub.

Reese, Nancy, et al. Elephant Set, 10 bks. Jordan, Alton, ed. (Illus.). (J). (gr. k-3). 1984. 79.50 (*0-89868-011-5*, Read Res); pap. 39.50 (*0-89868-044-1*, Read Res) ARO Pub.

Reese, Nancy, jt. auth. see Reese, Bob.

Reese, Pat, ed. In the Waters of My Mind. LC 95-75373. 350p. 1996. pap. text 23.50 (*0-9644993-1-2*) Joehenry.

Reese, Patricia D., ed. see Hill, Cora A.

Reese, Paul. Go East Old Man: Adventures of a Runner in His 70s Traveling 22 Western States. Henderson, Joe, ed. 288p. (Orig.). 1997. pap. 14.95 (*1-879628-15-5*) Keokee ID.

***Reese, Paul.** The Old Man & the Road: Reflections While Completing a Crossing of All 50 States on Foot at Age 80. Henderson, Joe, ed. 304p. (Orig.). 2000. pap. 14.95 (*1-879628-20-1*) Keokee ID.

Reese, Paul. Ten Million Steps. 226p. 1994. 12.95 (*0-915297-20-5*) Cedarwinds.

Reese, Pee Wee, intro. Gil Hodges: The Quiet Man. (Illus.). 256p. 1991. 19.95 (*0-8397-2957-X*) Eriksson.

***Reese, Peg.** Federal Power: Implications of Reduced Maintenance & Repairs of Federal Hydropower Plants. (Illus.). 71p. (C). 1999. pap. text 20.00 (*0-7881-8427-X*) DIANE Pub.

***Reese, Peter.** Bannockburn. 2000. pap. 16.95 (*0-86241-915-8*, Pub. by Canongate Books) Interlink Pub.

Reese, Peter. Journey: Signposts from the Healing Road. 1995. pap. 12.00 (*0-9629302-4-5*) Ramsey Found.

— The Scottish Commander: Scotland's Greatest Military Leaders from Wallace to World War II. 256p. 1999. pap. 16.00 (*0-86241-833-X*, Pub. by Canongate Books) Interlink Pub.

— Wallace: A Biography. (Illus.). 256p. 1996. pap. 11.95 (*0-86241-607-8*) Interlink Pub.

Reese, R. Thessalonians. 1989. pap. 21.00 (*0-86217-022-2*, Pub. by Veritas Pubns) St Mut.

Reese, R. Page. Don't Move. LC 94-75765. 325p. 1994. lib. bdg. 19.95 (*0-9609672-1-4*) Jeanies Classics.

Reese, Reuben A. True Doctrine of Ultra Vires in the Law of Corporations: Being a Concise Presentation of the Doctrine in Its Application to the Powers & Liabilities of Private & Municipal Corporations. lxxi, 338p. 1981. reprint ed. 52.50 (*0-8377-1031-6*, Rothman) W S Hein.

Reese, Richard E. & Betts, Robert F. Handbook of Antibiotics. 2nd ed. LC 92-48900. (Little, Brown Handbook Ser.). 672p. 1993. pap. text 38.00 (*0-316-73719-4*, Little Brwn Med Div) Lppncott W & W.

— Handbook of Antibiotics. 3rd ed. 352p. pap. text 34.95 (*0-7817-1611-X*) Lppncott W & W.

Reese, Richard E. & Betts, Robert F., eds. A Practical Approach to Infectious Diseases. 4th ed. 1200p. 1996. pap. text 74.95 (*0-316-73721-6*, Little Brwn Med Div) Lppncott W & W.

Reese, Richard G., Jr. & Reese, Suzanne L. Pilots Guide to Southwestern Airports. rev. ed. (Illus.). 550p. 1982. 34.95 (*0-9622494-0-8*) RGR Pubns.

Reese, Robert. Alaskan Gold. 1998. mass mkt. 5.99 (*0-425-16263-X*) Berkley Pub.

— Flying with One Wing. 176p. (Orig.). 1992. pap. 8.95 (*0-9633351-2-X*) Blue Pacific.

Reese, Robert T. & Kawahara, Wendell A. Handbook on Structural Testing. LC 93-9439. 141p. 1993. 68.00 (*0-88173-155-2*) Fairmont Pr.

Reese, Roger R. The Soviet Military Experience: A History of the Soviet Army, 1917-1991. LC 99-14259. (Warfare & History Ser.). 224p. 2000. pap. 21.99 (*0-415-21720-2*) Routledge.

***Reese, Roger R.** Soviet Military Experience: History of Soviet Army, 1917-1991. LC 99-14259. 224p. (C). 2000. text. write for info. (*0-415-21719-9*) Routledge.

Reese, Roger R. Stalin's Reluctant Soldiers: A Social History of the Red Army, 1925-1941. LC 96-4252. (Modern War Studies). (Illus.). 288p. 1996. 35.00 (*0-7006-0772-2*) U Pr of KS.

Reese, Ron. Crazy Cat. Jordan, Alton, ed. (Illus.). (J). (gr. k-3). 1984. 7.95 (*0-89868-002-6*, Read Res); pap. 3.95 (*0-89868-035-2*, Read Res) ARO Pub.

— Crazy Cat's Bad Day. Jordan, Alton, ed. (Buppet Bks.). (Illus.). (J). (gr. 1-4). 1980. 9.95 (*0-89868-090-5*, Read Res); pap. 3.95 (*0-89868-101-4*, Read Res) ARO Pub.

— Halloween. Jordan, Alton, ed. (Holiday Set). (Illus.). (J). (gr. k-3). 1984. 7.95 (*0-89868-023-9*, Read Res); pap. 3.95 (*0-89868-056-5*, Read Res) ARO Pub.

— Sammy Skunk. (Illus.). (J). (gr. k-3). 1984. 7.95 (*0-89868-009-3*, Read Res) ARO Pub.

— Sammy Skunk. Jordan, Alton, ed. (Illus.). (J). (gr. k-3). 1984. pap. 3.95 (*0-89868-042-5*, Read Res) ARO Pub.

— Toy Bear. Jordan, Alton, ed. (I Can Eat an Elephant Ser.). (Illus.). (J). (gr. k-3). 1984. 7.95 (*0-89868-016-6*, Read Res); pap. 3.95 (*0-89868-049-2*, Read Res) ARO Pub.

Reese, Ron, et al. Holiday Series, 10 bks. Jordan, Alton, ed. (Illus.). (J). (gr. k-3). 1984. 79.50 (*0-89868-022-0*, Read Res); pap. 39.50 (*0-89868-055-7*, Read Res) ARO Pub.

***Reese, Ronald L.** University Physics. LC 98-41666. 1267p. 2000. 99.95 (*0-534-36961-8*) Brooks-Cole.

— University Physics, Vol. 2. LC 98-41666. 561p. 2000. (*0-534-36965-0*) Brooks-Cole.

Reese, S. 3D Studio Max 2 Character. (CTI Coriolis Ser.). (C). 1998. mass mkt. 39.99 (*1-57610-218-1*) Coriolis Grp.

***Reese, Sara L.** Healthquest Diet. 2000. write for info. (*0-380-97561-0*, Wm Morrow) Morrow Avon.

***Reese, Sara L., et al, eds.** Healthquest: Staying Strong:Reclaiming The Wisdom Of African-American Healing. 352p. 1999. pap. 14.00 (*0-380-79402-0*, Avon Bks) Morrow Avon.

Reese, Stephen D., jt. auth. see Shoemaker, Pamela.

Reese, Stephen D., jt. auth. see Shoemaker, Pamela J.

Reese, Steven. Enough Light to Steer By. (Cleveland Poets Ser.: Vol. 50). 45p. (Orig.). 1997. pap. 8.00 (*1-880834-34-0*) Cleveland St Univ Poetry Ctr.

Reese, Suzanne L., jt. auth. see Reese, Richard G., Jr.

Reese, Taylor. Humor Is Where You Find It - Look No Further. LC 98-71020. (Illus.). xiii, 163p. 1998. pap. 12.95 (*0-9663666-0-3*) AAcorn Bks.

Reese, Taylor & Pyle, Jack R. You & the Man in the Moon: The Complete Guide to Using the Almanac. (Illus.). 123p. 1995. pap. 13.95 (*1-878086-44-8*, Pub. by Down Home NC) Blair.

Reese, Taylor, jt. auth. see Pyle, Jack R.

Reese, Terence. Bridge for Ambitious Players. 144p. 1988. pap. 15.95 (*0-575-04176-5*, Pub. by V Gollancz) Trafalgar.

— Bridge for Bright Beginners. 144p. 1973. reprint ed. pap. 5.95 (*0-486-22942-4*) Dover.

— C. C. Wei's Precision System. 98p. (Orig.). 1970. pap. 2.50 (*0-87643-033-7*) M Lisa Precision.

— Do You Really Want to Win at Bridge? 159p. 1989. pap. 15.95 (*0-575-04404-7*, Pub. by V Gollancz) Trafalgar.

— Learn Bridge in Five Days. LC 96-24650. 96p. 1996. pap. 7.95 (*0-8069-6166-X*) Sterling.

— Master Play in Contract Bridge. (Illus.). 144p. 1974. reprint ed. 5.95 (*0-486-20336-0*) Dover.

— Master Plays in a Single Suit. 8p. 1988. pap. 3.95 (*0-575-04132-3*, Pub. by V Gollancz) Trafalgar.

Reese, Terence & Bird, David. All You Need to Know about Bidding. (Illus.). 128p. 1993. 24.95 (*0-575-05378-X*, Pub. by V Gollancz) Trafalgar.

— All You Need to Know about Play. LC 94-45165. (Master Bridge Ser.). 120p. 1995. pap. 9.95 (*0-395-72861-4*) HM.

— All You Need to Know about Play. (Illus.). 128p. 1997. 24.95 (*0-575-05670-3*, Pub. by V Gollancz) Trafalgar.

— Cardinal Sins. 160p. 1996. pap. 15.95 (*0-575-06294-0*, Pub. by V Gollancz) Trafalgar.

— Divine Intervention. (Illus.). 128p. 1996. pap. 13.95 (*0-575-06112-X*, Pub. by V Gollancz) Trafalgar.

— Famous Bidding Decisions. 128p. 1996. pap. 13.95 (*0-575-06295-9*, Pub. by V Gollancz) Trafalgar.

— Famous Hands from Famous Matches. LC 91-4060. (Maxwell Macmillan Bridge Ser.). 156p. 1992. pap. 15.95 (*1-85744-501-5*, Pub. by CHES) Macmillan.

— Famous Play Decisions. 128p. 1997. pap. 13.95 (*0-575-06456-0*, Pub. by V Gollancz) Trafalgar.

— Miracles of Card Play. 160p. 1998. pap. 17.95 (*0-575-06594-X*, Pub. by V Gollancz) Trafalgar.

— Unholy Tricks: More Miraculous Card Play. 128p. 1995. pap. 13.95 (*0-575-05944-3*, Pub. by V Gollancz) Trafalgar.

Reese, Terence & Pottage, Julian. The Extra Edge in Play. 112p. 1994. pap. 13.95 (*0-575-05737-8*, Pub. by V Gollancz) Trafalgar.

Reese, Terence & Trezel, Roger. Blocking & Unblocking Plays in Bridge. (Master Bridge Ser.). (Illus.). 128p. 1991. pap. 9.95 (*0-575-02749-5*, Pub. by V Gollancz) Trafalgar.

— The Mistakes You Make at Bridge. (Master Bridge Ser.). 160p. 1984. pap. 13.95 (*0-575-05785-8*, Pub. by V Gollancz) Trafalgar.

— Safety Plays in Bridge. (Master Bridge Ser.). (Illus.). 64p. 1976. pap. 9.95 (*0-575-02748-7*, Pub. by V Gollancz) Trafalgar.

Reese, Terence & Watkins, A. T. How to Win at Poker. 1976. pap. 10.00 (*0-87980-070-4*) Wilshire.

Reese, Terence, jt. auth. see McNeil, Keith.

Reese, Terrence. Teach Yourself Bridge. 2nd ed. (Teach Yourself Ser.). 160p. 1999. pap. 11.95 (*0-8442-1338-1*, 13381, Teach Yrslf) NTC Contemp Pub Co.

Reese, Thomas J. Inside the Vatican: The Politics & Organization of the Catholic Church. (Illus.). 352p. 1996. 24.95 (*0-674-93260-9*) HUP.

— Inside the Vatican: The Politics & Organization of the Catholic Church. (Illus.). 336p. 1999. pap. text 15.95 (*0-674-93261-7*) HUP.

— The Politics of Taxation. LC 79-8413. (Illus.). 237p. 1980. 55.00 (*0-89930-003-0*, RPT/, Quorum Bks) Greenwood.

Reese, Thomas J. & Bernardin, Joseph Louis. A Flock of Shepherds: A Discussion on the National Conference of Catholic Bishops: Proceedings of a Symposium Sponsored by the Foundations & Donors Interested in Catholic Activities. LC 92-13530. 47p. (Orig.). 1992. pap. 19.95 (*1-55612-557-7*, LL1557) Sheed & Ward WI.

Reese, Timothy J. Sealed with Their Lives: The Battle for Crampton's Gap. (Illus.). 423p. 1998. 40.00 (*0-935523-67-7*) Butternut & Blue.

— Sykes' Regular Infantry Division, 1861-1864: A History of Regular United States Infantry Operations in the Civil War's Eastern Theater. LC 90-42746. (Illus.). 488p. 1990. lib. bdg. 57.50 (*0-89950-447-7*) McFarland & Co.

Reese, Will & Switzer, Phil. The Penny Tree. 2nd rev. ed. LC 94-910814. (Illus.). 30p. (J). 1994. pap. 7.95 (*1-55105-050-1*) Lone Pine.

Reese, William B., jt. auth. see Hoss, E. E.

Reese, William D. & Landry, Garrie. Acadiana Flora: Native & Naturalized Woody Plants of South-Central Louisiana. (Illus.). 126p. 1992. 15.00 (*0-940984-77-6*) Univ LA Lafayette.

Reese, William D., jt. auth. see Allen, Noris S.

Reese, William Dean. Mosses of the Gulf South: From the Rio Grande to the Apalachicola. LC 83-889. (Illus.). xvi, 252p. 1984. text 35.00 (*0-8071-1110-4*) La State U Pr.

Reese, William J. The Origins of the American High School. LC 94-24975. 352p. 1995. 35.00 (*0-300-06384-9*) Yale U Pr.

***Reese, William J.** The Origins of the American High School. (Illus.). 352p. 1999. 18.00 (*0-300-07943-5*) Yale U Pr.

Reese, William J. Power & Promise of School Reform: Grass Roots Movements During the Progressive Era. (Critical Social Thought Ser.). 320p. (C). 1986. text 39.95 (*0-7100-9952-5*, Routledge Thoemms); pap. text 14.95 (*0-7102-0767-0*, Routledge Thoemms) Routledge.

Reese, William J., ed. Hoosier Schools, Past & Present. LC 97-21565. (Midwestern History & Culture Ser.). (Illus.). 248p. 1998. 29.95 (*0-253-33362-8*); pap. 14.95 (*0-253-21154-9*) Ind U Pr.

Reese, William J., jt. ed. see McClellan, B. Edward.

Reese, William L. Dictionary of Philosophy & Religion. 1996. pap. 29.95 (*1-57392-621-3*) Prometheus Bks.

Reese, William L. Dictionary of Philosophy & Religion: Eastern & Western Thought. LC 98-50459. 1998. write for info. (*1-57392-426-1*, Humanity Bks) Prometheus Bks.

— Dictionary of Philosophy & Religion: Eastern & Western Thought. 2nd enl. ed. LC 78-12561. 768p. (C). 1996. 60.00 (*0-391-03864-8*); pap. 25.00 (*0-391-03865-6*) Humanities.

Reese, William L., ed. Freedom: A Study Guide with Readings. LC 99-46411. (Introduction to Philosophy Ser.). 245p. 2000. pap. 19.95 (*1-57392-736-8*, Humanity Bks) Prometheus Bks.

***Reese, William L., ed.** Values: A Study Guide with Readings. 250p. 2000. pap. 26.95 (*1-57392-870-4*) Prometheus Bks.

Reese, William L., jt. auth. see Hartshorne, Charles.

Reese, William L., jt. ed. see Hartshorne, Charles.

Reese, William S. The First Hundred Years of Printing in British North America: Printers & Collectors. 37p. 1990. reprint ed. pap. 5.00 (*0-944026-19-2*) Am Antiquarian.

— The Printers' First Fruits: An Exhibition of American Imprints, 1640-1742, from the Collections of the American Antiquarian Society. (Illus.). 52p. 1989. pap. 15.00 (*0-944026-15-X*) Am Antiquarian.

***Reese, William S.** Stamped with a National Character: Nineteenth Century American Color Plate Books: An Exhibition. 120p. 1999. 39.00 (*0-910672-27-X*, Pub. by Grolier Club) Wm Reece.

R

An Asterisk (*) at the beginning of an entry indicates that the title is appearing for the first time.

Reese, William S. & Saffron, Morris H. American Bibliographic Notes: Three Massachusetts Broadsides; Earliest Medical Broadsides. 25p. 1983. pap. 4.00 (*0-944026-79-6*) Am Antiquarian.
Reese, William S., jt. auth. see Field, Thomas W.
Reese, Willis L., et al. Conflict of Laws: Cases & Materials. 9th ed. (University Casebook Ser.). 1021p. 1990. text 43.50 (*0-88277-789-0*) Foundation Pr.
— Conflict of Laws: Cases & Materials. 9th ed. (University Casebook Ser.). 186p. 1990. pap. text, teacher ed. write for info. (*0-88277-851-X*) Foundation Pr.
Reeser, jt. auth. see Robison, Wade L.
Reeser, Jacki, ed. see Madewell, Terry.
Reeser, John, ed. Bicycling Magazine's Ultimate Ride Guide: Breakthrough Training Programs, Daily Logs, & Performance Secrets from the Pros. LC 98-45931. 1999. pap. 14.95 (*1-57954-056-2*) Rodale Pr Inc.
Reeser, Kelly, jt. auth. see Bumsted, Keith.
Reeser, Linda C. & Epstein, Irwin. Professionalization & Activism in Social Work. 196p. 1990. text 44.00 (*0-231-06788-7*) Col U Pr.
Reeser, M. P. Introduction to Public Utility Accounting. 407p. write for info. (*0-318-59899-X*) Am Gas Assn.
Reeser, Michael. Huan Ching & the Golden Fish. (Publish-a-Book Contest Ser.). (Illus.). 32p. (J). (gr. 1-6). 1988. lib. bdg. 22.83 incl. audio (*0-8172-2751-2*) Raintree Steck-V.
Reeser, Nellie W. Alt. Valentin Alt, His Children & His Grandchildren. (Illus.). 122p. 1997. reprint ed. pap. 21.00 (*0-8328-7253-9*); reprint ed. lib. bdg. 31.00 (*0-8328-7252-0*) Higginson Bk Co.
Reeser, Ralph. Manual of Indian Gaming Law. 1300p. 1995. ring bd. 329.00 (*1-882800-00-1*) Falmouth Inst.
Reeser, Renee, ed. see Wrath.
Reeser, Todd, jt. auth. see Heu, Helene.
Reesing, John. Milton's Poetic Art: A Mask, Lycidas, & Paradise Lost. LC 68-17632. 222p. reprint ed. 68.90 (*0-8357-9166-1*, 201701100006) Bks Demand.
Reesink, Carole J., ed. Teacher-Made Aids for Elementary School Mathematics Vol. 2: Readings from the Arithmetic Teacher. LC 73-21581. (Illus.). 185p. 1985. pap. 15.95 (*0-87353-225-2*) NCTM.
***Reesink, Carole J., ed.** Teacher-Made Aids for Elementary School Mathematics Vol. 3: Readings from the Arithmetic Teacher & Teaching Children Mathematics. (Illus.). 378p. 1998. pap. 23.50 (*0-87353-463-8*) NCTM.
Reesink, Ger P. Structures & Their Functions in Usan: A Papuan Language of Papua New Guinea. LC 86-17518. (Studies in Language Companion: Vol. 13). xviii, 369p. 1987. 97.00 (*90-272-3015-3*) J Benjamins Pubng Co.
Reesink, H. W., ed. Hepatitis C Virus. (Current Studies in Hematology & Blood Transfusion: No. 61). (Illus.). viii, 212p. 1994. 210.50 (*3-8055-5866-X*) S Karger.
— Hepatitis C Virus. 2nd rev. ed. LC 97-41314. (Current Studies in Hematology & Blood Transfusion: Vol. 62, 1997). (Illus.). x, 270p. 1998. 172.25 (*3-8055-6542-9*) S Karger.
Reesman. Jack London. LC 98-55670. 15p. 1999. 25.95 (*0-8057-1678-5*) S&S Trade.
Reesman, Ann E. The Americans with Disabilities Act: Medical Examinations & Inquiries. 18p. 1990. pap. 10.00 (*0-614-06164-4*, 2023B-PP-4040) EPF.
— The Americans with Disabilities Act: Qualified Individual with a Disability. 31p. 1990. pap. 10.00 (*0-614-06163-6*, 2023A-PP-4040) EPF.
— Should Federal Law Provide Monetary Damages for Harassment? 30p. 1991. pap. 10.00 (*0-614-06157-1*, 2028-PP-4040) EPF.
Reesman, Ann E., ed. Americans with Disabilities Act Desk Reference. 1160p. 1992. 90.00 (*0-916559-36-X*, 2002-MO-4035) EPF.
Reesman, Ann E., jt. auth. see Potter, Edward E.
Reesman, Ann E., jt. auth. see Yager, Daniel V.
Reesman, Jeanne C. American Designs: The Late Novels of James & Faulkner. LC 90-19272. 248p. (C). 1991. text 32.50 (*0-8122-8253-1*) U of Pa Pr.
— Speaking the Other Self: American Women Writers. LC 96-48850. 1997. 50.00 (*0-8203-1903-1*); pap. 24.95 (*0-8203-1909-0*) U of Ga Pr.
Reesman, Jeanne C., jt. auth. see Labor, Earl G.
Reesman, Jeanne C., jt. ed. see Cassuto, Leonard.
***Reesman, Jeanne Campbell.** Trickster Lives: Culture & Myth in American Fiction. LC 00-30228. 2001. pap. write for info. (*0-8203-2277-6*) U of Ga Pr.
***Reesoe, James B.** Three Mysteries Revealed: Three Books in One. LC 99-97535. 2000. pap. 8.95 (*0-533-13412-9*) Vantage.
***Reesom Haile Staff & Cantalupo, Charles.** We Have Our Voice: Selected Poems of Reesom Haile. LC 99-45185. 128p. 2000. 14.95 (*1-56902-133-3*) Red Sea Pr.
***Reet, Claudia G.** Fill It a Heart Full. 54p. 1999. pap. 5.00 (*0-9674775-1-4*) Coral Bell Pr.
Reetz, Dorothea. Clara Zetkin As a Socialist Speaker. LC 86-27178.Tr. of Clara Zetkin Als Sozialistische Rednerin. 76p. 1987. pap. 3.95 (*0-7178-0649-9*) Intl Pubs Co.
Reetz, Elaine. Come Back in Time, Vol. 2. (Illus.). 240p. 1982. pap. 9.95 (*0-939398-03-6*) Fox River.
Reetz, Elaine, et al. Come Back in Time: Communities, Vol. I. (Illus.). 184p. 1981. pap. 8.95 (*0-939398-00-1*) Fox River.
Reetz, Henry C. Electroplating. (Illus.). 99p. reprint ed. pap. 7.95 (*1-55918-008-0*) Lindsay Pubns.
Reetz, M. T. Organotitanium Reagents in Organic Synthesis. (Reactivity & Structure Ser.: Vol. 24). (Illus.). 240p. 1986. 149.95 (*0-387-15784-0*) Spr-Verlag.
Reeve. Henry James Short Fiction. 248p. 1997. text 49.95 (*0-312-16487-4*) St Martin.
***Reeve.** Readings & Issues in Cost Management. 2nd ed. LC 99-32107. (SWC-Accounting Ser.). 1999. pap. 37.95 (*0-324-02298-0*) Thomson Learn.
Reeve, ed. Ciceronis, M. Tulli. (LAT.). 1992. 39.50 (*3-8154-1179-3*, T1179, Pub. by B G Teubner) U of Mich Pr.
— Longi: Daphnis et Chloe. (GRE.). 1994. 29.95 (*3-8154-1932-8*, T1932, Pub. by B G Teubner) U of Mich Pr.
Reeve, jt. auth. see Hayward.
Reeve, jt. auth. see Warren.
Reeve, ed. see Cicero, Marcus Tullius.
Reeve, Agnesa & Reeve, Jack. Tex Mex New Mex: Southwestern Slim Cooking. (Illus.). 1997. pap. 15.95 (*0-9631401-7-5*) Cimarron CO.
Reeve, Agnesa L., compiled by. My Dear Mollie: Love Letters of a Texas Sheep Rancher. LC 90-41891. (Illus.). 192p. (J). (gr. 7 up). 1990. 8.95 (*0-937460-62-1*) Hendrick-Long.
Reeve, Agnesa L. & Reeve, Jack. Cooking with a Handful of Ingredients: Delicious Meals in the Palm of Your Hand. LC 91-77268. 272p. (Orig.). 1992. pap. 15.95 (*0-9631401-6-7*) Cimarron CO.
Reeve, Agnesa L., jt. auth. see Finney County Historical Society Staff.
Reeve, Alan, tr. see De Mul, Jos.
Reeve, Andrew, ed. Modern Theories of Exploitation. (Modern Politics Ser.: Vol. 14). 214p. (C). 1987. text 45.00 (*0-8039-8072-8*); pap. text 17.95 (*0-8039-8073-6*) Sage.
Reeve, Andrew, jt. auth. see Lively, Jack.
Reeve, Andru J. Turn Me on, Dead Man: The Complete Story of the Paul McCartney Death Hoax. (Rock & Roll Remembrances Ser.: No. 12). (Illus.). 224p. 1994. lib. bdg. 40.00 (*1-56075-035-9*) Popular Culture.
Reeve, Anne & Screech, M. A., eds. Erasmus' Annotations on the New Testament: Galatians to the Apocalypse, Facsimile of the Final Latin Text with All Earlier Variants. LC 93-29006. (Studies in the History of Christian Thought: No. 52). x, 29, 264p. 1993. 119.00 (*90-04-09906-9*) Brill Academic Pubs.
Reeve, Anne, ed. see Erasmus, Desiderius.
Reeve, Arthur B. Poisoned Pen. LC 70-150561. (Short Story Index Reprint Ser.). (Illus.). 1977. reprint ed. 23.95 (*0-8369-3858-5*) Ayer.
— The Silent Bullet: The Adventures of Craig Kennedy, Scientific Detective. LC 75-32795. (Literature of Mystery & Detection Ser.). (Illus.). 1976. reprint ed. 34.95 (*0-405-07896-X*) Ayer.
Reeve, C. D. Philosopher - Kings: The Argument of Plato's "Republic" (Illus.). 400p. 1989. reprint ed. pap. text 19.95 (*0-691-02094-9*, Pub. by Princeton U Pr) Cal Prin Full Svc.
— Practices of Reason: Aristotle's Nicomachean Ethics. 240p. 1995. pap. text 24.95 (*0-19-823565-8*) OUP.
— Socrates in the Apology: An Essay on Plato's Apology of Socrates. LC 89-33069. (Illus.). 224p. 1989. 37.95 (*0-87220-089-2*); pap. 14.95 (*0-87220-088-4*) Hackett Pub.
Reeve, C. D., tr. see Plato.
***Reeve, C. D. C.** Substantial Knowledge: Aristotle's Metaphysics. 320p. 2000. lib. bdg. 34.95 (*0-87220-515-0*) Hackett Pub.
Reeve, C. D. C., tr. & intro. see Aristotle.
Reeve, Catherine & Sward, Marilyn. The New Photography: A Guide to New Images, Processes, & Display Techniques for Photographers. (Quality Paperbacks Ser.). (Illus.). xiv, 242p. 1987. reprint ed. pap. 18.95 (*0-306-80295-3*) Da Capo.
Reeve, Charles & Watts, Jacqueline, eds. Groundwater, Drought, Pollution & Management: Proceedings of the International Conference, Brighton, 1994. (Illus.). 170p. (C). 1994. 123.00 (*90-5410-351-5*, Pub. by A A Balkema) Ashgate Pub Co.
Reeve, Christopher. Still Me. 324p. 1999. mass mkt. 7.99 (*0-345-43241-X*) Ballantine Pub Grp.
— Still Me: A Life. LC 98-10223. 299p. 1998. 25.00 (*0-679-45235-4*) Random.
— Still Me: A Life. large type ed. LC 97-31800. 1998. pap. 25.00 (*0-375-70234-2*) Random.
Reeve, Cintra, jt. auth. see Gray, Rebecca.
Reeve, D. A. C. I. I. Pension Scheme Design & Administration. No. 170-060. (C). 1984. 240.00 (*0-7855-4270-1*, Pub. by Witherby & Co) St Mut.
Reeve, Dana. Care Packages: Letters to Christopher Reeve from Strangers & Other Friends. LC 99-29304. 160p. 1999. 20.00 (*0-375-50076-6*) Random.
Reeve, David & McCarthy, James G. El Catolicismo: Una Fe en Crisis. 52p. (Orig.). 1994. pap. text 1.88 (*1-884833-01-2*) Lumen Prodns.
Reeve, Douglas W., jt. ed. see Dence, Carlton W.
Reeve, E. C. R., ed. Encyclopedia of Genetics. (Illus.). 900p. 1999. lib. bdg. 125.00 (*1-884964-34-6*) Fitzroy Dearborn.
Reeve, F. A. The Cambridge That Never Was. (Cambridge Town, Gown & County Ser.: Vol. 8). (Illus.). 1976. pap. 5.95 (*0-902675-72-9*) Oleander Pr.
Reeve, F. D. Concrete Music. LC 92-6099. 88p. 1992. 18.00 (*1-881119-56-4*); pap. 11.00 (*1-881119-72-6*) Pyncheon Hse.
— A Few Rounds of Old Maid & Other Stories. LC 94-79252. 144p. 1995. pap. text 12.95 (*1-885214-00-6*) Azul Edits.
***Reeve, F. D.** The Moon & Other Failures. (Illus.). 150p. 1999. pap. 17.95 (*0-87013-514-7*) Mich St U Pr.
Reeve, F. D. The White Monk: An Essay on Dostoevsky & Melville. LC 89-35562. 192p. 1990. 22.95 (*0-8265-1234-8*) Vanderbilt U Pr.
Reeve, F. D. & Meek, Jay, eds. After the Storm: Poems on the Persian Gulf War. LC 92-11673. 126p. 1992. pap. text 10.95 (*0-944624-16-2*) Maisonneuve Pr.
Reeve, Frank A. Cambridge College Walks. (Cambridge Town, Gown & County Ser.: Vol. 25). (Illus.). 1978. pap. 4.95 (*0-900891-42-4*) Oleander Pr.
— Cambridge College Walks French Edition. (Cambridge Town, Gown & County Ser.: Vol. 25). (FRE., Illus.). 1978. pap. 4.95 (*0-685-55599-2*) Oleander Pr.
— Cambridge College Walks German Edition. (Cambridge Town, Gown & County Ser.: Vol. 25). (GER., Illus.). 1978. pap. 4.95 (*0-685-55600-X*) Oleander Pr.
— The Cambridge Nobody Knows. (Cambridge Town, Gown & County Ser.: Vol. 14). (Illus.). 1977. pap. 5.95 (*0-900891-10-6*) Oleander Pr.
— Promenades a Cambridge. (Cambridge Town, Gown & County Ser.: Vol. 26). (FRE., Illus.). 1978. pap. 4.95 (*0-900891-43-2*) Oleander Pr.
— Spaziergange durch Cambridge. (Cambridge Town, Gown & County Ser.: Vol. 27). (GER., Illus.). 1978. pap. 4.95 (*0-900891-44-0*) Oleander Pr.
— Varsity Rags & Hoaxes. (Cambridge Town, Gown & County Ser.: Vol. 17). (Illus.). 1977. pap. 5.95 (*0-900891-16-5*) Oleander Pr.
Reeve, Frank D. Navajo Foreign Affairs, 1795-1846. 54p. 1983. pap. 4.00 (*0-912586-51-6*) Dine College Pr.
Reeve, Franklin D., ed. Contemporary Russian Drama. LC 68-20138. 1968. 39.00 (*0-672-53521-1*); pap. text 14.95 (*0-8290-2101-9*) Irvington.
Reeve, Helen, tr. see Zernova, Ruth.
Reeve, Helen H. Brown County, Indiana Obituaries, 1914-1984, 2 vols., I. 1708p. 1986. write for info. (*0-9616808-1-4*) Brown Cnty Hist Soc.
— Brown County, Indiana Obituaries, 1914-1984, 2 vols., II. 1708p. 1986. write for info. (*0-9616808-2-2*) Brown Cnty Hist Soc.
— Brown County, Indiana Obituaries, 1914-1984, 2 vols., Set. 1708p. 1986. 100.00 (*0-9616808-0-6*) Brown Cnty Hist Soc.
Reeve, Henry, tr. see De Tocqueville, Alexis.
Reeve, Hudson K., jt. ed. see Dugatkin, Lee A.
Reeve, Hudson Kern, jt. ed. see Dugatkin, Lee Alan.
Reeve, Jack, jt. auth. see Reeve, Agnesa.
Reeve, Jack, jt. auth. see Reeve, Agnesa L.
***Reeve, James.** Cocktails, Crises & Cockroaches: A Diplomatic Trail. 1999. 39.50 (*1-86064-445-7*, Pub. by I B T) St Martin.
Reeve, James H. Wolves in Sheeps' Clothing: How to Recognize False Prophets & Protect Your Family from Their Influence. (Orig.). 1994. pap. write for info. (*1-884781-00-4*) Quest For Excell.
Reeve, James K. The Art of Showing Art. rev. ed. LC 86-61319. (Illus.). 144p. (Orig.). 1995. pap. 14.95 (*0-933031-67-X*) Coun Oak Bks.
Reeve, James M. Managerial Accounting. 3rd ed. (AB - Accounting Principles Ser.). (C). 1994. mass mkt., student ed. 17.00 (*0-538-82186-8*) S-W Pub.
— Managerial Accounting - Working Papers. 3rd ed. (AB - Accounting Principles Ser.). (C). 1994. mass mkt., wbk. ed. 21.25 (*0-538-82187-6*) S-W Pub.
Reeve, James M., ed. Readings & Issues in Cost Management. LC 94-11412. (C). 1994. mass mkt. 26.95 (*0-538-84248-2*) S-W Pub.
Reeve, James M. & Warren, Carl S. Corporate Financial Accounting. 5th ed. (AM - Financial Accounting Ser.). 1996. pap. 53.95 (*0-538-85339-5*) S-W Pub.
— Corporate Financial Accounting. 6th ed. (AB - Accounting Principles Ser.). 1998. pap. 75.95 (*0-538-87356-6*) S-W Pub.
— Financial Accounting. 6th ed. (AB - Accounting Principles Ser.). 1998. pap., student ed. 18.00 (*0-538-87362-0*) S-W Pub.
— Financial/Managerial Accounting: Solutions Software Problem Booklet. 5th ed. (AB - Accounting Principles Ser.). 1999. pap. 12.95 (*0-538-86371-4*) S-W Pub.
— Managerial Accounting. 6th ed. (AB - Accounting Principles Ser.). 1998. pap. 75.95 (*0-538-87357-4*) S-W Pub.
— Managerial Accounting: Chapters 14-24. 6th ed. (AB - Accounting Principles Ser.). 1998. pap. 20.25 (*0-538-87363-9*) S-W Pub.
— Principles of Finance & Management Accounting. 5th ed. (AB - Accounting Principles Ser.). 1996. pap., student ed. 23.95 (*0-538-85310-7*) S-W Pub.
— Principles of Finance & Management Accounting. 5th ed. (Accounting Principles Ser.). 1996. pap., student ed. 22.95 (*0-538-85311-5*) S-W Pub.
— Working Papers - Managerial Accounting. 6th ed. (AB - Accounting Principles Ser.). 1998. pap. 22.25 (*0-538-87359-0*) S-W Pub.
Reeve, James M., jt. auth. see Warren, Carl S.
Reeve, Jeff, jt. auth. see Pritchard, David.
***Reeve, Jim.** God Never Wastes a Hurt. 224p. 2000. pap. 12.99 (*0-88419-738-7*) Creation House.
Reeve, John, et al. The Anglo-Saxons. (Illus.). (J). (gr. 2-6). pap. 5.95 (*0-7141-0537-6*, Pub. by British Mus Pr) Parkwest Pubns.
Reeve, John M. Motivating Others: A Teacher's Guide to Nurturing Innermotivational Resources. 256p. 1995. pap. text 46.00 (*0-205-16969-4*) Allyn.
— Understanding Motivation & Emotion. 2nd ed. 546p. (C). 1996. text 76.50 (*0-15-502654-2*, Pub. by Harcourt Coll Pubs) Harcourt.
Reeve, John T. Order Out of Chaos. 96p. (Orig.). 1996. pap. text 5.95 (*1-57087-205-8*) Prof Pr NC.
Reeve, Joseph R., Jr., ed. Cholecystokinin. LC 94-4554. (Annals Ser.: Vol. 713). 1994. pap. 130.00 (*0-89766-858-8*) NY Acad Sci.
Reeve, Kirk. Lolo & Red-Legs. LC 97-49969. 100p. (J). (gr. 5 up). 1998. lib. bdg. 12.95 (*0-87358-683-2*) Northland AZ.
— Lolo & Red Legs. LC 97-49969. (Illus.). 100p. (J). (gr. 3-6). 1998. pap. 6.95 (*0-87358-684-0*, Rising Moon Bks) Northland AZ.
Reeve, Lee. 27toUD Bk. 1: Malitajla. (27 to UD: 1). (Illus.). 1998. pap. write for info. (*0-9665458-4-2*) Virtual Ink.
Reeve, M. R., jt. ed. see Grice, G. D.
Reeve, Margaret, jt. auth. see Rotondi, Michael.
Reeve, Mike & Zenith, Steven E., eds. Parallel Processing & Artificial Intelligence. LC 89-16532. (Wiley Communicating Process Architecture Ser.). (Illus.). 307p. reprint ed. pap. 95.20 (*0-7837-6393-X*, 204610600010) Bks Demand.
Reeve, N. H. The Novels of Rex Warner: An Introduction. 190p. 1990. text 45.00 (*0-312-03703-1*) St Martin.
Reeve, N. H. & Kerridge, Richard. Nearly Too Much: The Poetry of J. H. Prynne. 244p. 1997. 34.95 (*0-85323-840-5*, Pub. by Liverpool Univ Pr); pap. 16.95 (*0-85323-850-2*, Pub. by Liverpool Univ Pr) Intl Spec Bk.
Reeve, Nigel. Hedgehogs. (Poyser Natural History Ser.). (Illus.). 350p. 1996. text 29.95 (*0-85661-081-X*) Acad Pr.
Reeve, Pamela. Parables by the Sea. LC 77-6209. (Illus.). 46p. 1976. pap. text 7.99 (*0-930014-11-1*) Multnomah Pubs.
— Parables of the Forest. Libby, Larry R., ed. LC 88-36472. (Illus.). 49p. (Orig.). 1989. pap. 7.99 (*0-88070-306-7*, Multnomah Bks) Multnomah Pubs.
— Relationships: What It Takes to Be a Friend. LC 96-44079. 96p. 1997. 10.99 (*1-57673-044-1*, Multnomah Bks) Multnomah Pubs.
Reeve, R., ed. Chlamydial Infections. (Illus.). 145p. 1987. 55.95 (*0-387-16552-5*) Spr-Verlag.
Reeve, Rachel, jt. ed. see Wintle, Michael.
Reeve, Richard, jt. ed. see Luzuriaga, Gerardo.
Reeve, Roger N. Environmental Analysis. Barnes, John D., ed. LC 95-115769. 284p. 1994. pap. 64.95 (*0-471-93833-5*) Wiley.
Reeve, Rowland B. Kaho'olawe. (Illus.). pap. 32.95 (*1-883528-02-X*) Ai Pohaku Pr.
Reeve, Simon. The New Jackals: Ramzi Yousef, Osama bin Laden, & the Future of Terrorism. LC 99-37245. (Illus.). 256p. 1999. 26.95 (*1-55553-407-4*) NE U Pr.
***Reeve, Simon.** One Day in September: The Story of the 1972 Munich Olympics Massacre. 2000. 25.95 (*1-55970-547-7*, Pub. by Arcade Pub Inc) Time Warner.
Reeve, Simon & McGhee, Colin. The Millennium Bomb: Countdown to a 400 Billion Pound Cata$trophe. (Illus.). 195p. 1999. pap. 15.95 (*1-883319-82-X*) Frog Ltd CA.
Reeve, Stuart A., et al. Myrtle Point: The Changing Land & People of a Lower Patuxent River Community. (Occasional Papers: No. 3). (Illus.). 209p. 1991. spiral bd. 18.00 (*1-878399-09-8*) Div Hist Cult Progs.
Reeve, T. G., jt. ed. see Proctor, R. W.
Reeve, T. M. & Woods, P. J. Revision of Dendrobium Section Oxyglossum (Orchidaceae) rev. ed. Gregory, N. M., ed. (Notes from the Royal Botanic Garden Edinburgh Ser.: Vol. 46, No. 2, 1989). 1989. pap. 44.00 (*0-11-493502-5*, HM5025, Pub. by Royal Botanic Edinburgh) Balogh.
Reeve, Tapping. The Law of Baron & Femme, of Parent & Child, of Guardian & Ward, of Master & Servant, & of the Powers of Court of Chancery. Helmholz, R H. & Reams, Bernard D., Jr., eds. LC 80-84865. (Historical Writings in Law & Jurisprudence Ser.: No. 11, Bk. 14). x, 502p. 1981. reprint ed. lib. bdg. 52.50 (*0-89941-066-9*, 301320) W S Hein.
— A Treatise on the Law of Descents, in the Several United States of America. Helmholz, R. H. & Reams, Bernard D., Jr., eds. LC 80-84864. (Historical Writings in Law & Jurisprudence Ser.: No. 12, Bk. 15). iv, 515p. 1981. reprint ed. lib. bdg. 55.00 (*0-89941-067-7*, 301330) W S Hein.
Reeve, Tapping, et al. The Law of Baron & Femme, of Parent & Child, Guardian & Ward, Master & Servant & of the Powers of the Courts of Chancery: With an Essay on the Terms Heir, Heirs, Heirs of the Body, 1862. 3rd ed. LC 98-36057. 1998. reprint ed. 75.00 (*1-886363-58-7*) Lawbk Exchange.
Reeve, W. Kannada-English Dictionary. rev. ed. (ENG & KAN.). 1040p. 1980. 75.00 (*0-8288-1144-X*, M 14009) Fr & Eur.
Reeve, W. D. Public Administration in Siam. LC 74-179236. reprint ed. 24.50 (*0-404-54863-6*) AMS Pr.
— The Republic of Korea: A Political & Economic Study. LC 79-9857. 197p. 1979. reprint ed. lib. bdg. 55.00 (*0-313-21265-1*, RERK, Greenwood Pr) Greenwood.
Reeve, W. D., ed. see NCTM Staff.
Reeve, Whitham D. Subscriber Loop Signaling & Transmission Handbook: Analog. LC 91-19685. (Telecommunications Handbook Ser.). (Illus.). 304p. (C). 1991. text 69.95 (*0-87942-274-2*, PC0268-3) Inst Electrical.
Reeve, Whitham D. Subscriber Loop Signaling & Transmission Handbook: Digital. (Telecommunications Handbook Ser.). 672p. 1995. 79.95 (*0-7803-0440-3*, PC3376) Inst Electrical.
Reeve, William. Hammer, Compass & Traverse-Wheel. 175p. (C). 1989. text 65.00 (*1-872795-33-1*, Pub. by Pentland Pr) St Mut.
Reeve, William C. The Federfuchser & Penpusher from Lessing to Grillparzer: A Study Focused on Grillparzer's Ein Bruderzwist in Habsburg. 184p. 1995. 65.00 (*0-7735-1298-5*, Pub. by McG-Queens Univ Pr) CUP Services.
***Reeve, William C.** Grillparzer's Libussa: The Tragedy of Separation. 1999. 65.00 (*0-7735-1831-2*) McG-Queens Univ Pr.
Reeve, William C. In Pursuit of Power: Heinrich von Kleist's Machiavellian Protagonists. 236p. 1987. text 35.00 (*0-8020-5702-0*) U of Toronto Pr.
— Kleist on Stage, 1804-1987. (Illus.). 256p. 1993. 65.00 (*0-7735-0941-0*, Pub. by McG-Queens Univ Pr) CUP Services.
— Kleist's Aristocratic Heritage & Das K[00e4]thchen von Heilbronn. 200p. 1991. 65.00 (*0-7735-0869-4*, Pub. by McG-Queens Univ Pr) CUP Services.
Reeven, John T., jt. auth. see Weir, E. Kenneth.

Reeves. Building Services. (Illus.). 304p. 1997. text. write for info. (*0-419-21640-5*, E & FN Spon) Routledge.
— Managing Human Resources. LC 94-164528. 1994. pap. text 12.75 (*0-314-03682-2*) West Pub.
— Medical Surgical Nursing. 1998. 37.00 (*0-07-134657-0*) McGraw.
***Reeves.** Network+ Exam Cram. (Networking Ser.). (C). 1999. pap. 15.60 (*0-619-01602-7*) Course Tech.
Reeves. The Suicide of American Churches. 1996. 25.00 (*0-02-925967-3*) Free Pr.
— The Technology of Fluid Power. (Mechanical Technology Ser.). 120p. 1997. pap. text, teacher ed. 14.00 (*0-8273-6665-5*) Delmar.
— The Technology of Fluid Power. (Mechanical Technology Ser.). 1995. lab manual ed. 15.95 (*0-8273-6666-3*, VNR) Wiley.
Reeves & Stevens. The Continuing Mission. LC 98-229110. (Star Trek Ser.). 1998. pap. 20.00 (*0-671-02559-7*) S&S Trade.
Reeves, jt. auth. see Hendrick.
Reeves, A. Compton, jt. ed. see Michalove, Sharon D.
Reeves, Adrienne E. Change of Heart. 288p. 1995. mass mkt. 4.99 (*0-8217-0103-7*, Zebra Kensgtn); mass mkt. 4.99 (*0-7860-0103-8*, Pinncle Kensgtn) Kensgtn Pub Corp.
— Love's Promise. 1998. 4.99 (*0-7860-0568-8*) Kensgtn Pub Corp.
Reeves, Adrienne Ellis. Destined. 1999. mass mkt. 4.99 (*1-58314-047-6*) BET Bks.
Reeves, Alexander G. Disorders of the Nervous System: A Primer. LC 80-24086. (Internal Medicine Ser.). 252p. reprint ed. pap. 78.20 (*0-608-15909-3*, 203085100071) Bks Demand.
Reeves, Alexander G., ed. Epilepsy & the Corpus Callosum. LC 85-3465. 520p. 1985. 135.00 (*0-306-41848-7*, Plenum Trade) Perseus Pubng.
Reeves, Alexander G. & Roberts, David W., eds. Epilepsy & the Corpus Callosum 2: Proceedings of the Second International Conference Held in Hanover, New Hampshire, August 14-18, 1991. (Advances in Behavioral Biology Ser.: Vol. 45). (Illus.). 322p. 1995. 110.00 (*0-306-45134-4*, Kluwer Plenum) Kluwer Academic.
Reeves, Alfred G. Treatise on the Law of Real Property, 2 vols. LC 97-47217. 1997. reprint ed. 225.00 (*0-8377-2585-2*, Rothman) W S Hein.
Reeves, Andree E. Congressional Committee Chairmen: Three Who Made an Evolution. LC 92-34812. (Illus.). 280p. 1993. text 39.00 (*0-8131-1816-6*) U Pr of Ky.
Reeves, Anne-Rose, jt. auth. see Barr, Randolph W.
Reeves, Arthur. The Golden Age of Crime. (Criminology Ser.). 1992. lib. bdg. 76.95 (*0-8490-5297-1*) Gordon Pr.
Reeves, Barbara. April Morning: A Study Guide. Friedland, J. & Kessler, R., eds. (Novel-Ties Ser.). (YA). (gr. 7-12). 1992. pap. text, student ed. 15.95 (*0-88122-714-5*) Lrn Links.
— Bunnicula: A Study Guide. Friedland, Joyce & Kessler, Rikki, eds. (Novel-Ties Ser.). (J). (gr. 2-5). 1991. pap. text, student ed. 15.95 (*0-88122-572-X*) Lrn Links.
— Cheaper by the Dozen: A Study Guide. Friedland, J. & Kessler, R., eds. (Novel-Ties Ser.). (YA). (gr. 7-12). 1994. pap. text, student ed. 15.95 (*1-56982-073-2*) Lrn Links.
— The Civil War: A Study Guide. (Historical Ties Ser.). (J). (gr. 5-8). 1991. pap. text 20.95 (*0-88122-688-2*) Lrn Links.
— The Dangerous Marquis. 240p. (Orig.). 1994. mass mkt. 3.99 (*0-380-77672-3*, Avon Bks) Morrow Avon.
— Farewell to Manzanar: A Study Guide. Friedland, Joyce & Kessler, Rikki, eds. (Novel-Ties Ser.). (J). (gr. 6-8). 1991. pap. text 15.95 (*0-88122-583-5*) Lrn Links.
— Georgina's Campaign. (Regency Novel Ser.). 192p. 1993. reprint ed. mass mkt. 3.99 (*0-380-71968-1*, Avon Bks) Morrow Avon.
— Hamlet: A Study Guide. Friedland, J. & Kessler, R., eds. (Novel-Ties Ser.). (YA). (gr. 9-12). 1995. pap. text, student ed. 15.95 (*1-56982-322-7*) Lrn Links.
— Lacy's Dilemma. 224p. (Orig.). 1995. mass mkt. 3.99 (*0-380-77673-1*, Avon Bks) Morrow Avon.
— A Lantern in Her Hand: A Study Guide. Friedland, J. & Kessler, R., eds. (Novel-Ties Ser.). (J). (gr. 6-8). 1992. pap. text, student ed. 15.95 (*0-88122-716-1*) Lrn Links.
— The Lilies of the Field: A Study Guide. Friedland, Joyce & Kessler, Rikki, eds. (Novel-Ties Ser.). (YA). (gr. 9-12). 1991. pap. text 15.95 (*0-88122-585-1*) Lrn Links.
— The Much Maligned Lord. 192p. (Orig.). 1993. mass mkt. 3.99 (*0-380-77332-5*, Avon Bks) Morrow Avon.
— Murder on the Orient Express: A Study Guide. Friedland, J. & Kessler, R., eds. (Novel-Ties Ser.). (YA). (gr. 9-12). 1992. pap. text, student ed. 15.95 (*0-88122-717-X*) Lrn Links.
— Number the Stars: A Study Guide. Friedland, Joyce & Kessler, Rikki, eds. (Novel-Ties Ser.). (J). (gr. 5-7). 1991. pap. text 15.95 (*0-88122-579-7*) Lrn Links.
— A Scandalous Courtship. 208p. 1994. mass mkt. 3.99 (*0-380-72151-1*, Avon Bks) Morrow Avon.
Reeves, Barbara. A Scandalous Courtship. 190p. 1993. 19.95 (*0-8027-1258-4*) Walker & Co.
Reeves, Barbara. Shabanu: A Study Guide. Friedland, J. & Kessler, R., eds. (Novel-Ties Ser.). (J). (gr. 6-8). 1996. pap. text 15.95 (*1-56982-672-2*) Lrn Links.
— The Slave Dancer: A Study Guide. Friedland, J. & Kessler, R., eds. (Novel-Ties Ser.). (J). (gr. 5-7). 1993. pap. text 15.95 (*0-88122-905-9*) Lrn Links.
— Thunder at Gettysburg: A Study Guide. Friedland, J. & Kessler, R., eds. (Novel-Ties Ser.). (J). (gr. 1-3). 1993. pap. text, student ed. 15.95 (*0-88122-881-8*) Lrn Links.
— A Treasury of Whole Language Literature Ideas. (Teacher Idea Bks.). 1998. teacher ed. 12.95 (*0-8167-2585-3*) Troll Communs.
— The War Between the Classes: A Study Guide. Friedland, Joyce & Kessler, Rikki, eds. (Novel-Ties Ser.). (YA). (gr. 9-12). 1991. pap. text 15.95 (*0-88122-586-X*) Lrn Links.
— When the Legends Die: A Study Guide. Friedland, J. & Kessler, R., eds. (Novel-Ties Ser.). (J). (gr. 6-8). 1993. pap. text, student ed. 15.95 (*0-88122-898-2*) Lrn Links.
Reeves, Barbara, ed. see Friedland, Joyce & Kessler, Rikki.
Reeves, Barbara M. The French Riviera Cote d'Azur: Self-Guided Tours. LC 94-93877. (Illus.). 183p. (Orig.). 1995. spiral bd. 17.95 (*0-9643520-0-1*) B Reeves.
Reeves, Betsy, ed. see Athology Reprints Staff.
Reeves, Bill. North Carolina Freedman's Savings & Trust Company Records. 598p. 1992. 25.00 (*0-936370-08-4*) N C Genealogical.
***Reeves, Bk.** My Buffalo Soldier. 2000. pap. 8.95 (*1-58571-013-X*, Pub. by Genesis Press) BookWorld.
Reeves, Byron & Nass, Clifford. The Media Equation: How People Treat Computers, Television, & New Media Like Real People & Places. 317p. (C). 1998. reprint ed. pap. 15.95 (*1-57586-053-8*) CSLI.
— The Media Equation: How People Treat Computers, Televisions, & New Media Like Real People & Places. (CSLI Lecture Notes Ser.). 350p. 1996. 28.95 (*1-57586-052-X*) CSLI.
Reeves, C., jt. auth. see Coblenz, R.
Reeves, C. C., Jr. Caliche-Origin Classification, Morphology & Uses. LC 76-2234. 1976. text 39.95 (*0-9652519-1-8*) Estacado Bks.
Reeves, C. C., Jr. & Reeves, Judy A. The Ogallala Aquifer (Of the Southern High Plains), Vol. 1. LC 96-84153. (Illus.). 360p. (Orig.). 1996. pap. 79.95 (*0-9652519-0-X*) Estacado Bks.
Reeves, C. N. After Tut 'Ankhamun: Research & Excavation in the Royal Necropolis at Thebes. LC 90-43443. 211p. 1992. 95.00 (*0-7103-0406-4*) Routledge.
Reeves, Carole. Egyptian Medicine. (Shire Egyptology Ser.). (Illus.). 72p. 1992. pap. 12.00 (*0-7478-0127-4*, Pub. by Shire Pubns) Lubrecht & Cramer.
Reeves, Carole, jt. auth. see Thornton, John L.
Reeves, Carolyn. My Daily Journey with My Utmost for His Highest: Personal Reflections That Draw Us Closer to God. LC 95-33978. 192p. 1995. pap., student ed. 12.99 (*1-57293-005-5*) Discovery Hse Pubs.
Reeves, Charlene, et al. Medical-Surgical Nursing. LC 98-20549. (Nursing Core Ser.). (Illus.). 750p. 1999. pap. text 37.00 (*0-07-105480-4*) McGraw-Hill HPD.
***Reeves, Charles B., Jr.** Carpe Diem: The Twentieth Century Pilgrimage of an Imparfit Knight. 380p. 1999. 27.95 (*0-9674253-0-1*, 1) C B Reeves.
Reeves, Charles E. An Analysis of Janitor Service in Elementary Schools. LC 77-177185. (Columbia University. Teachers College. Contributions to Education Ser.: No. 167). reprint ed. 37.50 (*0-404-55167-X*) AMS Pr.
Reeves, Charles H., tr. see Lenhart, John N.
Reeves, Clement. The Psychology of Rollo May: Reflections & Commentary by Rollo May. LC 76-50708. (Jossey-Bass Behavioral Science Ser.). 352p. reprint ed. pap. 109.20 (*0-8357-6885-6*, 203793700009) Bks Demand.
Reeves, Colin R. An Introduction to Logical Design of Digital Circuits. LC 77-182029. (Cambridge Computer Science Texts Ser.: No. 1). 198p. reprint ed. pap. 56.50 (*0-608-12171-1*, 2024532) Bks Demand.
Reeves, Colin R., jt. auth. see Banzhaf, Wolfgang.
Reeves, Compton. Pleasures & Pastimes in Medieval England. (Illus.). 248p. 1998. pap. 16.95 (*0-19-521423-4*) OUP.
***Reeves, Compton.** Pleasures & Pastimes in Medieval England. (Illus.). 228p. 1999. reprint ed. text 30.00 (*0-7881-6670-0*) DIANE Pub.
***Reeves, Crystal S. & Stanley, Kay.** IPA Management: Legal & Compliance Guidelines LC 99-35049. 1999. write for info. (*0-07-134297-4*) McGrw-H Intl.
Reeves, Dale, ed. Some Kind of Journey: On the Road with Audio Adrenaline. McCabe, Virginia & Burgen, Jim, trs. LC 97-229445. (Empowered Youth Products Ser.). (Illus.). 176p. (YA). 1997. pap. 12.99 incl. cd-rom (*0-7847-0744-8*, 03304) Standard Pub.
Reeves, Dale, ed. see Belknap, Bryan.
Reeves, Dale, ed. see Bundschuh, Rick.
Reeves, Dale, ed. see Burgen, Jim.
Reeves, Dale, ed. see Corey, Sheila.
Reeves, Dale, ed. see Cosper, John, Jr.
Reeves, Dale, ed. see Farah, Greg.
Reeves, Dale, ed. see Kast, Michael.
Reeves, Dale, ed. see Nappa, Mike.
Reeves, Dale, ed. see Senseman, Patricial Alderdice.
Reeves, Dale, ed. see St. Clair, Barry.
Reeves, Dale, ed. see St. Clair, Barry & Miller, Steve.
Reeves, Dale, ed. see Vogel, Jane.
Reeves, Dale, ed. see Warden, Michael.
Reeves, David E., ed. see Becker, H. Neil, et al.
Reeves, David S. & Ullmann, Uwe, eds. High Performance Liquid Chromatography in Medical Microbiology, Vol. 2. 272p. (Orig.). 1986. pap. text 65.00 (*0-89574-215-2*, Pub. by Gustav Fischer) Balogh.
Reeves, Dean. From the Kitchen Door: Recipes of Lyssa Gillespie. LC 97-75783. (Illus.). 80p. 1997. pap. 11.95 (*1-57736-074-5*, Hillsboro Pr) Providence Hse.
Reeves, Deborah L. A Rose of Thorns. 393p. (Orig.). 1996. pap. 6.99 (*0-9652862-0-7*) Weikel Publishing.
Reeves, Diana. Introduction to Drawing the Nude. 128p. 1993. 14.98 (*1-55521-901-2*) Bk Sales Inc.
Reeves, Diane L. Art. LC 97-32687. (Career Ideas for Kids Who Like Ser.). (Illus.). 240p. (YA). (gr. 5-9). 1998. 18.95 (*0-8160-3681-0*) Facts on File.
— Art. LC 97-32687. (Career Ideas for Kids Who Like Ser.). (Illus.). 176p. (YA). (gr. 5-9). 1998. pap. 12.95 (*0-8160-3687-X*) Facts on File.
— Career Ideas for Kids Who Like Science. LC 97-37048. (Career Ideas for Kids Ser.). (Illus.). 176p. (J). (gr. 4-8). 1998. 18.95 (*0-8160-3680-2*); pap. 12.95 (*0-8160-3686-1*) Facts on File.
— Career Ideas for Kids Who Like Sports. LC 98-15203. (Career Ideas for Kids Ser.). (Illus.). 176p. (J). (gr. 4-8). 1998. 18.95 (*0-8160-3684-5*) Facts on File.
— Career Ideas for Kids Who Like Talking. LC 97-50075. (Career Ideas for Kids Ser.). (Illus.). 176p. (YA). (gr. 5-9). 1998. 18.95 (*0-8160-3683-7*); pap. text 12.95 (*0-8160-3689-6*) Facts on File.
— Career Ideas for Kids Who Like Writing. LC 98-6229. (Career Ideas for Kids Ser.). (Illus.). 166p. (J). (gr. 4-8). 1998. pap. 12.95 (*0-8160-3691-8*) Facts on File.
— Child Care Crisis: A Reference Handbook. LC 92-38144. (Contemporary World Issues Ser.). 173p. 1992. lib. bdg. 39.50 (*0-87436-645-3*) ABC-CLIO.
***Reeves, Diane L., ed.** Career Ideas for Kids Who Like Writing. LC 98-6229. (Career Ideas for Kids Ser.). (Illus.). 166p. (J). (gr. 4-8). 1998. 18.95 (*0-8160-3685-3*) Facts on File.
Reeves, Diane L. & Bradbury. Majors Exploration: A Search & Find Guide for College & Career Direction. LC 98-47211. 234p. 1998. ring bd. 22.60 (*0-13-011379-4*) P-H.
Reeves, Diane L. & Heubeck, Nancy. Career Ideas for Kids Who Like Math. LC 99-30051. (Career Ideas for Kids Ser.). (Illus.). 192p. (J). (gr. 4-8). 2000. pap. 12.95 (*0-8160-4096-6*) Facts on File.
Reeves, Diane L. & Kent, Peter. Career Ideas for Kids Who Like Computers. LC 98-5199. (Career Ideas for Kids Ser.). (Illus.). 176p. (J). (gr. 4-8). 1998. 18.95 (*0-8160-3682-9*); pap. 12.95 (*0-8160-3688-8*) Facts on File.
— Career Ideas for Kids Who Like Sports. LC 98-15203. (Career Ideas for Kids Ser.). (Illus.). 176p. (J). (gr. 4-8). 1998. pap. 12.95 (*0-8160-3690-X*) Facts on File.
***Reeves, Diane Lindsey & Bryan, Gayle.** Career Ideas for Kids Who Like Money. (Career Ideas for Kids Ser.). (Illus.). 144p. (J). (gr. 4-8). 2001. pap. 12.95 (*0-8160-4320-5*, Checkmark); lib. bdg. 18.95 (*0-8160-4319-1*, Checkmark) Facts on File.
***Reeves, Diane Lindsey & Heubeck, Nancy.** Career Ideas for Kids Who Like Adventure. (Career Ideas for Kids Ser.). (Illus.). 176p. (J). (gr. 4-8). 2001. pap. 12.95 (*0-8160-4322-1*, Checkmark); lib. bdg. 18.95 (*0-8160-4321-3*, Checkmark) Facts on File.
— Career Ideas for Kids Who Like Animals & Nature. LC 99-37735. (Illus.). 192p. (J). (gr. 4-8). 2000. 18.95 (*0-8160-4097-4*, Checkmark); pap. 12.95 (*0-8160-4098-2*, Checkmark) Facts on File.
— Career Ideas for Kids Who Like Math. LC 99-30051. (Career Ideas for Kids Ser.). (Illus.). 192p. (J). (gr. 4-7). 2000. 18.95 (*0-8160-4095-8*) Facts on File.
Reeves, Don, jt. ed. see Cohen, Marc J.
Reeves, Donald. Down to Earth: A New Vision for the Church. 117p. 1997. reprint ed. pap. 14.95 (*0-264-67460-X*, BR115) A R Mowbray.
— Making Sense of Religion. (Illus.). 157p. 1992. pap. 7.95 (*0-563-20759-0*, BBC-Parkwest) Parkwest Pubns.
Reeves, Donna Rae Seamon, jt. auth. see Hermann, Fredrea Marlyn.
Reeves, Dorothea D. Resources for the Study of Economic History: A Preliminary Guide to Pre-Twentieth Century Printed Material in Collection. (Kress Library of Business & Economics Publication: No. 16). viiii, 62p. 1961. pap. 9.95 (*0-678-09917-0*) Kelley.
Reeves, Douglas B. Accountability in Action: A Blueprint for Learning Organizations. Barnes, Cynthia, ed. 325p. 1999. pap. 34.95 (*0-9644955-3-8*) Adv Learn.
— Making Standards Work: How to Implement Standards-Based Assessments in the Classroom, School & District. (Illus.). xviii, 226p. 1997. ring bd. 34.95 (*0-9644955-2-X*) Adv Learn.
Reeves, Douglas B. & Willis, Courtney. How to Prepare for the Colorado PLACE Exams. 3rd rev. ed. (Illus.). xv, 204p. (Orig.). 1996. pap. 19.95 (*0-9644955-1-1*) Adv Learn.
Reeves, E. Dios Te Ama.Tr. of God Loves You. (SPA.). (J). 1.89 (*0-7899-0477-2*, 498668) Editorial Unilit.
Reeves, E. Mi Primera Biblia Ilustrada. (Biblias para Ninos Ser.).Tr. of My First Picture Bible. (SPA., Illus.). (J). 1999. 9.99 (*0-7899-0456-X*, 496625) Editorial Unilit.
Reeves, E. Oraciones a la Hora de Dormir.Tr. of Prayer at Bedtime. (SPA.). (J). 1.89 (*0-7899-0478-0*, 498665) Editorial Unilit.
— El Padre Nuestro.Tr. of Lord's Prayer. (SPA.). (J). 1.89 (*0-7899-0480-2*, 498667) Editorial Unilit.
Reeves, E. Te Gustaria Conocer a Jesus?Tr. of Would You Like to Know Jesus?. (SPA.). (J). 0.99 (*1-56063-739-0*, 497740) Editorial Unilit.
Reeves, E. Yo Soy Valiente.Tr. of I Am Brave. (SPA.). (J). 1.89 (*0-7899-0479-9*, 498666) Editorial Unilit.
Reeves, E. A. Cable Management Systems. (Illus.). 336p. 1992. 89.95 (*0-632-02808-4*) Blackwell Sci.
— Newnes Electrical Pocket Book. 1988. 21.00 (*0-434-91716-8*) CRC Pr.
Reeves, E. A., ed. Newnes Electrical Pocket Book. 22nd ed. LC 95-20183. (Illus.). 544p. 1995. pap. text 29.95 (*0-7506-2566-X*) Buttrwrth-Heinemann.
Reeves, E. A., jt. auth. see Heathcote, Martin.
Reeves, E. A., ed. see Bush, K. G.
Reeves, Earl. Aviation's Place in Tomorrow's Business. (Airlines History Project Ser.). reprint ed. 35.00 (*0-404-19331-5*) AMS Pr.
Reeves, Earl, jt. ed. see Filipovitch, Anthony.
Reeves, Edward B. The Hidden Government: Ritual, Clientelism, & Legitimation in Northern Egypt. LC 90-52748. 240p. 1990. pap. 74.40 (*0-7837-8557-7*, 204937200011) Bks Demand.
***Reeves, Eileen.** Painting the Heavens. 320p. 1999. pap. 24.95 (*0-691-00976-7*, Pub. by Princeton U Pr) Cal Prin Full Svc.
Reeves, Eileen. Painting the Heavens: Art & Science in the Age of Galileo. LC 96-51631. 320p. 1997. text 45.00 (*0-691-04398-1*, Pub. by Princeton U Pr) Cal Prin Full Svc.
Reeves, Eira. La Historia de Jesus.Tr. of Story of Jesus. (SPA.). 64p. (J). 1992. 5.99 (*1-56063-350-6*, 494011) Editorial Unilit.
***Reeves, Eira.** The Little One's Bible with "Talkabouts" & Prayers. (Illus.). 384p. (J). (ps-1). 2000. 9.99 (*1-57748-846-6*, Promise Pr) Barbour Pub.
Reeves, Eira. My First Picture Bible. LC 98-206083. (Illus.). 128p. (J). 1998. 9.99 (*0-8024-6023-2*) Moody.
Reeves, Ellen G., jt. auth. see Stern, Lise.
Reeves, Ellen G., tr. see Beauvoir, Simone de.
Reeves-Ellington, Richard H. & Anderson, Adele. Business, Commerce, & Social Responsibility: Beyond Agenda. LC 97-37725. 288p. 1997. text 89.95 (*0-7734-8442-6*) E Mellen.
Reeves, Elton T. So You Want to Be an Executive. LC 73-138569. 254p. reprint ed. pap. 78.80 (*0-608-10882-0*, 205039800078) Bks Demand.
Reeves, Emma B. Minutes of the District Court of Nacogdoches County (Texas) (Minute Bk. A). 152p. (Orig.). 1981. pap. 12.50 (*0-911013-06-7*) E B Reeves.
— Three Centuries of Ballingers in America. LC 75-27993. (Illus.). 614p. 1977. lib. bdg. 20.00 (*0-911013-02-4*) E B Reeves.
Reeves, Faye C. The Birthday Wish Mystery. LC 94-18348. (Illus.). 64p. (J). (gr. 2-5). 1994. pap. 3.50 (*0-8167-3531-X*, Little Rainbow) Troll Communs.
— The Birthday Wish Mystery. LC 94-18348. (Illus.). 64p. (J). (gr. 2-5). 1997. lib. bdg. 14.00 (*0-8167-3530-1*, Little Rainbow) Troll Communs.
Reeves, Floyd W., et al, eds. Instructional Problems in the University. LC 71-168086. reprint ed. 34.50 (*0-404-05236-3*) AMS Pr.
Reeves, Frances, compiled by. Selected Passages from Sai Baba's Teachings. 1993. pap. 2.75 (*1-57836-047-1*, BW-175) Sathya Sai Bk Ctr.
Reeves, Francis. Business Ethics. 85p. (C). 1993. student ed. 19.74 (*1-56870-032-6*) RonJon Pub.
— Problems of Philosophy. 85p. (C). 1993. student ed. 16.11 (*1-56870-033-4*) RonJon Pub.
Reeves, Frank W. Race & Borough Politics. 318p. 1989. text 67.95 (*0-566-05573-2*, Pub. by Avebry) Ashgate Pub Co.
Reeves, Gary R., jt. ed. see Lawrence, Kenneth D.
Reeves, Geoffrey, jt. auth. see Hunt, Albert.
Reeves, Geoffrey D., ed. Workshop on the Earth's Trapped Particle Environment. (AIP Conference Proceedings Ser.: No. 383). (Illus.). 256p. 1996. 135.00 (*1-56396-540-2*, AIP Pr) Spr-Verlag.
Reeves, George. The New Idioms in Action. (J). 1975. pap. text 22.95 (*0-8384-2652-2*, Newbury) Heinle & Heinle.
Reeves, George E. Mining Lease Handbook. 300p. 1992. pap., student ed. 135.00 (*0-929047-32-X*, ML) Rocky Mtn Mineral Law Found.
***Reeves, Gordon & Todd, Ian.** Lecture Notes on Immunology. (Lecture Notes Ser.). (Illus.). 280p. (C). 2000. pap. 29.95 (*0-632-05636-3*) Blackwell Sci.
Reeves, Gordon, et al. Lecture Notes on Immunology. 3rd ed. LC 95-39681. (Lecture Notes Ser.). (Illus.). 226p. 1996. pap. 28.95 (*0-632-03812-8*) Blackwell Sci.
Reeves, Greg. Judy Ford: World Champion Cowgirl. (Illus.). 46p. (J). (gr. 4-8). 1992. pap. 5.95 (*0-938349-88-0*) State House Pr.
Reeves, Greg, jt. auth. see Reeves, Joel.
Reeves, H. Clyde, ed. Measuring Fiscal Capacity. LC 85-30979. (Lincoln Institute of Land Policy Bk.). 221p. reprint ed. pap. 68.60 (*0-7837-5754-9*, 204541600006) Bks Demand.
Reeves, H. Clyde & Ellsworth, Scott, eds. Funding Clean Water. LC 83-22202. (Lincoln Institute of Land Policy Bk.). 235p. reprint ed. pap. 72.90 (*0-7837-3271-6*, 204329000007) Bks Demand.
— The Role of the State in Property Taxation. LC 82-48536. (Lincoln Institute of Land Policy Bk.). 231p. reprint ed. pap. 71.70 (*0-7837-3272-4*, 204329100007) Bks Demand.
Reeves, Harriet R. Song & Dance Activities for Elementary Children. 1984. 17.95 (*0-13-260613-5*, Parker Publishing Co) P-H.
Reeves, Helen M. High Morals. 12p. 1999. pap. 7.00 (*0-8059-3809-5*) Dorrance.
— High Morals: Christian Living. 16p. 1999. spiral bd. 7.00 (*0-8059-4587-3*) Dorrance.
Reeves, Henry, jt. auth. see Shoaf, Mary J.
Reeves, Hershel C. Photo Guide for Appraising Surface Fuels in East Texas. (Illus.). 89p. (Orig.). 1988. 10.00 (*0-938361-04-X*) Austin Univ Forestry.
Reeves, Howard W. There Was An Old Witch. LC 98-6902. (Illus.). (J). (ps-3). 1998. 9.95 (*0-7868-0438-6*, Pub. by Hyperion) Time Warner.
Reeves, Howard W. There Was an Old Witch. LC 98-6902. (Illus.). 24p. (J). (ps-3). 1998. lib. bdg. 10.49 (*0-7868-2387-9*, Pub. by Hyperion) Little.
***Reeves, Howard W.** There Was an Old Witch. (Illus.). 32p. (J). (ps-3). 2000. pap. 5.99 (*0-7868-1492-6*) Hyprn Ppbks.
Reeves, Hubert. Evolution Stellaire et Nucleosynthese. (Cours & Documents de Mathematiques & de Physique Ser.). xiv, 100p. (Orig.). 1968. text 129.00 (*0-677-50150-1*) Gordon & Breach.
— Nuclear Reactions in Stellar Surfaces & Their Relations

R

with Stellar Evolution. (Illus.). xii, 88p. 1971. text 142.00 (0-677-02960-8); pap. text 101.00 (0-677-02965-9) Gordon & Breach.

Reeves, Hubert, et al. Origins: Cosmos, Earth & Mankind. LC 97-27830.Tr. of Plus Belle Historie du Monde. 192p. 1998. 22.45 (1-55970-408-X, Pub. by Arcade Pub Inc) Time Warner.

— Origins: Cosmos, Earth, & Mankind. 1999. pap. 12.95 (1-55970-458-6, Pub. by Arcade Pub Inc) Time Warner.

Reeves, I. S. The People, Art of Native Americans: Items from the Collection of Sara W. Reeves & I.S.K. Reeves V. (Illus.). 56p. (Orig.). 1992. pap. 15.00 (0-918548-03-9) Green APC.

Reeves, J. C., jt. auth. see Hutchins, J. D.

Reeves, J. Scott, jt. auth. see Dixon, Jerry.

Reeves, James. English Fables & Fairy Stories. 1993. 20.25 (0-8446-6660-2) Peter Smith.

Reeves, James. English Fables & Fairy Stories. (J). 1989. 18.05 (0-606-03265-7, Pub. by Turtleback) Demco.

— Fairy Tales from England. (Oxford Myths & Legends Ser.). (Illus.). 192p. 1999. pap. 12.95 (0-19-275014-3) OUP.

Reeves, James. Mr. Horrox & the Gratch. LC 91-13326. (Illus.). 32p. (J). (gr. 1-6). 1991. 13.95 (0-922984-08-5) Wellington IL.

Reeves, James, jt. ed. see Flower, Desmond.

*Reeves, James F., et al. Guide to Practical Estate Planning, 2 vols. 1999. ring bd. 180.00 (0-7646-0795-2) Prctnrs Pub Co.

Reeves, James F., et al. Guide to Practical Estate Planning, 2 vols. Incl. Vol. 1. 1997. ring bd. (0-7646-0253-5); Vol. 2. 1997. ring bd. (0-7646-0254-3); 168.00 (0-7646-0009-5); 170.00 (0-7646-0252-7) Prctnrs Pub Co.

— Guide to Practical Estate Planning, 2 vols., Set. 1995. ring bd. 168.00 (1-56433-711-1) Prctnrs Pub Co.

— Guide to Practical Estate Planning, Vol. 1. 1995. ring bd. write for info. (1-56433-712-X) Prctnrs Pub Co.

*Reeves, James F., et al. Guide to Practical Estate Planning, Vol. 1. 1999. ring bd. write for info. (0-7646-0796-0) Prctnrs Pub Co.

— Guide to Practical Estate Planning, Vol. 2. 1995. ring bd. write for info. (1-56433-713-8) Prctnrs Pub Co.

*Reeves, James F., et al. Guide to Practical Estate Planning, Vol. 2. 1999. ring bd. write for info. (0-7646-0797-9) Prctnrs Pub Co.

Reeves, Janet. The Apple a Day Cookbook. (Illus.). 256p. 1993. pap. 13.95 (0-921556-32-2, Pub. by Gynergy-Ragweed) U of Toronto Pr.

— One Potato, Two Potato: A Cookbook & More! 256p. 1994. pap. 13.95 (0-920304-70-2, Pub. by Gynergy-Ragweed) U of Toronto Pr.

Reeves, Jesse S. The International Beginnings of the Congo Free State. LC 78-63834. (Johns Hopkins University. Studies in the Social Sciences. Thirtieth Ser. 1912: 11-12). reprint ed. 34.50 (0-404-61094-3) AMS Pr.

— The Napoleonic Exiles in America: A Study in Diplomatic History, 1815-1819. LC 78-63910. (Johns Hopkins University. Studies in the Social Sciences. Thirtieth Ser. 1912: 9-10). reprint ed. 32.50 (0-404-61162-1) AMS Pr.

Reeves, Jim. The Songs of Jim Reeves. (Piano-Vocal-Guitar Personality Folio Ser.). (Illus.). 80p. 1985. per. 12.95 (0-88188-340-9, 00358033) H Leonard.

Reeves, Jimmie L. & Campbell, Richard. Cracked Coverage: Television News, the Anti-Cocaine Crusade, & the Reagan Legacy. LC 93-41411. 360p. 1994. text 59.95 (0-8223-1449-5); pap. text 19.95 (0-8223-1491-6) Duke.

*Reeves, Joel & Reeves, Greg. DoubleTake: Two by Two: A Touch of Frost & the Last Sighting of Melgor Lich. ed. 275p. 1999. 4.50 (1-928670-55-5) Awe Struck E Bks.

Reeves, John. History of the English Law, from the Time of the Saxons, to the End of the Reign of Philip & Mary, 4 vols. 2nd ed. 1969. reprint ed. 225.00 (0-8377-2526-7, Rothman) W S Hein.

— Reeves' History of the English Law from the Time of the Romans to the End of the Reign of Elizabeth, 5 vols. Finlason, W. F. et al, eds. LC 80-84861. (Historical Writings in Law & Jurisprudence Ser.: #24, Bks. 34-38). 2812p. 1981. reprint ed. lib. bdg. 260.00 (0-89941-240-8, 302480) W S Hein.

— The Rothschilds: Financial Rulers of Nations. 1975. 300.00 (0-87968-193-4) Gordon Pr.

*Reeves, John. The St. Matthew Passion: A Text for Voices. 2000. 14.00 (0-8028-3900-2) Eerdmans.

*Reeves, John & Finlason, W. F. Reeves' History of the English Law: From the Time of the Romans to the End of the Reign of Elizabeth : a New Edition in Three Volumes with Numerous Notes, & an Introductory Dissertation ... LC 99-73236. 2002p. 1999. 428.00 (1-56169-526-2) Gaunt.

Reeves, John, jt. auth. see Deardorff, William W.

Reeves, John A., jt. ed. see Simon, J. Malcolm.

Reeves, John C. Heralds of That Good Realm: Syro-Mesopotamian Gnosis & Jewish Traditions. LC 96-1795. (Nag Hammadi & Manichaean Studies). 1996. 98.00 (90-04-10459-3) Brill Academic Pubs.

— Jewish Lore in Manichaean Cosmogony: Studies in the "Book of Giants" Traditions. (Monographs of the Hebrew Union College: No. 14). 260p. 1992. 49.95 (0-87820-413-X) Hebrew Union Coll Pr.

Reeves, John C. & Kampen, John, eds. Pursuing the Text: Studies in Honor of Ben Zion Wacholder on the Occasion of His 70th Birthday. (JSOT Supplement Ser.: No. 184). 434p. 1994. 90.00 (1-85075-501-9, Pub. by Sheffield Acad) CUP Services.

Reeves, John R. & Maibach, Howard I. Clinical Dermatology Illustrated: A Regional Approach. 3rd ed. LC 97-13921. (Illus.). 510p. (C). 1997. spiral bd. 54.95 (0-8036-0279-0) Davis Co.

Reeves, John T. Literary Gems: A Reading List of Great Short Books. 2nd rev. ed. 46p. 1998. pap. 5.95 (1-882063-13-9) Cottage Pr MA.

Reeves, John T., ed. see Weir, Kenneth E.

*Reeves, Judy A. A Writer's Book of Days: A Spirited Companion & Lively Muse for the Writing Life. LC 99-31110. (Illus.). 240p. 1999. pap. 15.95 (1-57731-100-0, Pub. by New Wrld Lib) Publishers Group.

Reeves, Judy A., jt. auth. see Reeves, C. C., Jr.

Reeves, Kalinda, jt. auth. see Reeves, Scott.

Reeves, Kay, jt. auth. see Crawford, Barrie.

Reeves, Keith. Voting Hopes or Fears? White Voters, Black Candidates & Racial Politics in America. LC 96-36850. (Illus.). 200p. 1997. pap. 17.95 (0-19-510162-6) OUP.

Reeves, Keith H. The Resurrection Narrative in Matthew: A Literary-Critical Examination. LC 93-36660. (Biblical Press Ser.: Vol. 19). 124p. 1993. text 59.95 (0-7734-2384-2, Mellen Biblical Pr) E Mellen.

*Reeves, Kevin. The Composers: A History of Music. (Illus.). 160p. 1998. pap. 15.95 (0-920151-29-9, Pub. by Sound & Vision) Firefly Bks Ltd.

Reeves, Laura L., jt. auth. see Poe, Vidette.

Reeves, Linda. Get More Tail: A Guide to the Florida Lobster. rev. ed. (Illus.). (C). 1989. 3.95 (0-9622619-0-4) Sea Scripts.

— Get More Tail: A Guide to the Florida Lobster. 3rd ed. (Illus.). 48p. 1990. 3.95 (0-9622619-1-2) Sea Scripts.

Reeves, M. Why History? 1980. text. write for info. (0-582-36119-2, Pub. by Addison-Wesley) Longman.

Reeves, Margaret. A Strange Bird on the Lagoon. 224p. (C). 1990. pap. 39.00 (0-908175-95-7, Pub. by Boolarong Pubns) St Mut.

— Training Schools for Delinquent Girls. 1992. lib. bdg. 79.95 (0-8490-5298-X) Gordon Pr.

*Reeves, Margaret, et al. Fields of Poison: California Farmworkers & Pesticides. Reyes, Victor, tr. (ENG & SPA., Illus.). 103p. (C). 1999. pap. text 20.00 (0-7881-8418-0) DIANE Pub.

Reeves, Marjorie. Christian Thinking & Social Order: Conviction Politics from the 1930s to the Present Day. 192p. 1997. 75.00 (0-304-70247-1) Continuum.

— Christian Thinking & Social Order: Conviction Politics from the 1930s to the Present Day. LC 93-31913. 192p. (C). 1998. pap. 27.95 (0-304-70248-X) Continuum.

*Reeves, Marjorie. Favorite Hymns: 2000 Years of Magnificat. 2000. 28.95 (0-8264-4872-0) Continuum.

— Female Education & Non-Conformist Culture, 1700-1900. 2000. pap. text 24.95 (0-7185-0236-1) Leicester U Pr.

Reeves, Marjorie. The Influence of Prophecy in the Later Middle Ages: A Study in Joachimism. (C). 1994. reprint ed. pap. text 23.00 (0-268-01170-2) U of Notre Dame Pr.

— The Medieval Castle. (Then & There Ser.). 105p. (gr. 7-12). 1963. pap. text 8.60 (0-582-00381-4, 78062) Longman.

— The Medieval Monastery. (Then & There Ser.). (Illus.). 90p. (Orig.). (gr. 7-12). 1980. reprint ed. pap. text 8.60 (0-582-00380-6, 78064) Longman.

— The Medieval Town. (Then & There Ser.). (Illus.). 90p. (gr. 7-12). 1954. pap. text 8.60 (0-582-00385-7, 78065) Longman.

— The Medieval Village. 2nd ed. (Then & There Ser.). (Illus.). 90p. (Orig.). (gr. 7-12). 1954. pap. text 8.60 (0-582-00386-5, 78066) Longman.

— The Norman Conquest. (Then & There Ser.). (Illus.). 60p. (Orig.). (gr. 7-12). 1988. pap. text 8.60 (0-582-00384-9, 78110) Longman.

*Reeves, Marjorie. The Prophetic Sense of History in Medieval & Renaissance Europe: From Jerusalem to Cyprus. LC 99-31184. (Variorum Collected Studies). 1999. 97.95 (0-86078-805-9) Ashgate Pub Co.

Reeves, Marjorie. Pursuing the Muses: Female Education & Nonconformist Culture. LC 96-51474. 192p. 1997. 65.00 (0-7185-0105-5) Bks Intl VA.

— Why History? LC 81-111881. 159p. reprint ed. pap. 49.30 (0-7837-1597-8, 204188900024) Bks Demand.

Reeves, Marjorie & Gould, Warwick. Joachim of Fiore & the Myth of the Eternal Evangel in the Nineteenth Century. (Illus.). 264p. 1987. 85.00 (0-19-826672-3) OUP.

Reeves, Marjorie, jt. auth. see Rosenthal, Miriam.

Reeves, Marjorie, ed. see Beacroft, Bernard.

Reeves, Marjorie, ed. see Chamberlain, E. R.

Reeves, Marjorie, ed. see Mack, Donald W.

Reeves, Marjorie, ed. see Sylvester, David W.

Reeves, Marjorie, ed. see Turner, Derek.

Reeves, Marjorie, ed. see Williams, Ann.

Reeves-Marquardt, Dona B., jt. ed. see Lich, Glen E.

Reeves-Marquardt, Dona B., tr. see Beratz, Gottlieb.

Reeves, Martha & Bego, Mark. Dancing in the Street: Confessions of a Motown Diva. (Illus.). 304p. (J). 1994. 22.45 (0-7868-6024-3, Pub. by Hyperion) Time Warner.

— Dancing in the Street: Confessions of a Motown Diva. (Illus.). 304p. (J). 1995. pap. 14.45 (0-7868-8094-5, Pub. by Hyperion) Time Warner.

*Reeves, Martha E. Suppressed, Forced out & Fired: How Successful Women Lose Their Jobs. LC 99-56363. 256p. 2000. 59.95 (1-56720-356-6) Greenwood.

Reeves, Maud P. Round about a Pound a Week. large type ed. 256p. 1993. 22.95 (1-85695-030-1, Pub. by ISIS Lrg Prnt) Transaction Pubs.

Reeves, Mildred E. Old-Fashioned Love Story. 209p. 1974. 7.50 (0-318-04130-8) Prairie Pub.

— To Thee I Come. 220p. 1975. 7.50 (0-686-12109-0) Prairie Pub.

Reeves, Minou & Stewart, P. J. Muhammad in Europe: A Thousand Years of Western Myth-Making. LC 99-22794. 1999. text 34.50 (0-8147-7533-0) NYU Pr.

Reeves, Miriam G. Felicianas of Louisiana. 1967. 20.00 (0-87511-096-7) Claitors.

*Reeves, Miriam G. Governors of Louisiana. 5th ed. LC 98-234669. (Governors Ser.). (Illus.). 136p. 1998. 18.95 (1-56554-425-0) Pelican.

Reeves, Mona R. The Spooky Eerie Night Noise. LC 89-447. (Illus.). 32p. (J). (ps-2). 1989. lib. bdg. 13.95 (0-02-775732-3, Bradbury S&S) S&S Childrens.

Reeves, Mona Rabun. I Had a Cat. 1995. 10.15 (0-606-07682-4, Pub. by Turtleback) Demco.

Reeves, Nancy. Womankind: Beyond the Stereotypes. 2nd ed. LC 81-71348. 199p. 1982. pap. text 23.95 (0-202-30300-4); lib. bdg. 45.95 (0-202-30299-7) Aldine de Gruyter.

*Reeves, Nicholas. Ancient Egypt: The Great Discoveries. LC 99-69519. (Illus.). 256p. 2000. 40.00 (0-500-05105-4, Pub. by Thames Hudson) Norton.

Reeves, Nicholas. The Complete Tutankhamun: The King - The Tomb - The Royal Treasure. LC 90-70202. (Illus.). 224p. 1995. pap. 17.95 (0-500-27810-5, Pub. by Thames Hudson) Norton.

— Official British Film Propaganda During the First World War. 304p. 1986. 49.95 (0-7099-4225-7, Pub. by C Helm) Routldge.

— Power of Film Propaganda: Myth or Reality? LC 99-10122. 1999. 75.00 (0-304-33871-0); pap. 21.95 (0-304-33872-9) Continuum.

Reeves, Nicholas & Wilkinson, Richard H. The Complete Valley of the Kings: Tombs & Treasures of Ancient Egypt's Royal Burial Site. LC 96-60259. (Illus.). 224p. 1996. 29.95 (0-500-05080-5, Pub. by Thames Hudson) Norton.

Reeves, Nicholas, jt. auth. see Goring, Elizabeth.

Reeves, Nicholas, ed. see Maspero, Gaston C. & Brugsch, Emile.

Reeves, Nigel. Heinrich Heine: Poetry & Politics. 210p. 1994. pap. 24.95 (1-870352-57-2, Pub. by Libris) Paul & Co Pubs.

Reeves, Nigel & Kelly-Holmes, Helen, eds. The European Business Environment: Germany. 240p. 1996. pap. 69.95 (0-415-11702-X) Thomson Learn.

— The European Business Environment: Germany. LC 97-5337. 240p. 1997. pap. 18.99 (0-415-11703-8) Thomson Learn.

Reeves, Nigel & Wright, Colin. Linguistic Auditing: A Guide to Identifying Foreign Language Communication Needs in Corporations. LC 95-42195. (Topics in Translation Ser.: No. 9). 130p. 1996. 39.95 (1-85359-328-1, Pub. by Multilingual Matters); pap. 24.95 (1-85359-327-3, Pub. by Multilingual Matters) Taylor & Francis.

Reeves, Nigel, tr. see Von Kleist, Heinrich.

Reeves, P. Fusion of the Legal Profession: Are Two Legal Professions Necessary? (Legal & Social Policy Library). (Illus.). 128p. 1986. pap. 26.00 (0-08-039218-0, Pergamon Pr) Elsevier.

Reeves, Pamela. Ellis Island: Gateway to the American Dream. (Illus.). 144p. 1991. 16.99 (0-517-05905-3) Random Hse Value.

— Equatorial Guinea: 1996 Presidential Elections Observation Report. LC 96-3204. vi, 300p. 1996. pap. text 32.00 (1-879720-19-1) Intl Fndt Elect.

Reeves, Pamela & Klein, Keith. Republic in Transition: 1995 Elections in Tanzania & Zanzibar. iv, 348p. 1995. pap. text 37.00 (1-879720-29-9) Intl Fndt Elect.

Reeves, Paula. Women's Intuition: Unlocking the Wisdom of the Body. LC 99-22487. 288p. 1999. pap. 15.95 (1-57324-156-3) Conari Press.

Reeves, Peter. Landlords & Governments in Uttar Pradesh. (Illus.). 384p. 1992. 35.00 (0-19-562728-8) OUP.

Reeves, Philip N. & Coile, Russell C., Jr. Introduction to Health Planning. 4th ed. LC 89-81230. (Illus.). xvii, 321p. 1990. reprint ed. pap. 32.50 (0-87815-059-5) Info Resources.

Reeves, Phoebe. The Revenant. LC 98-88293. 5p. 1998. 25.00 (0-7388-0147-X); pap. 15.00 (0-7388-0148-8) Xlibris Corp.

*Reeves, Phoebe. Turning the Century: A Bits & Bytes Reader for Developing Writers. LC 99-12253. 365p. 1999. pap. text 32.40 (0-13-081305-2) P-H.

Reeves, Phoebe. What's the Big Idea? Writing Through Reading & Thinking. LC 97-53052. 327p. (C). 1998. pap. text 34.00 (0-13-629593-2) P-H.

*Reeves, Ralph & Dembeck, Len. An Improbable Machine Gunner. 157p. 1999. 8.00 (0-9675017-0-9) F Hancock.

Reeves, Randall R., et al. The Sierra Club Handbook of Seals & Sirenians. LC 92-946. (Illus.). 350p. (Orig.). 1992. pap. 18.00 (0-87156-656-7, Pub. by Sierra) Random.

Reeves, Randall R., jt. auth. see Leatherwood, Stephen.

Reeves, Randall R., jt. auth. see Leatherwood, Stephen P.

Reeves, Randall R., jt. auth. see Whitaker, John, Jr.

Reeves, Randall R., jt. ed. see Leatherwood, Stephen P.

Reeves, Randall R., jt. ed. see Twiss, John R.

Reeves, Ray. Signs of a Christian. 36p. 1995. pap. 3.95 (0-9647459-0-9) Kuppinger Pubng.

*Reeves, Rhonda. Tackling Tough Issues. Law, Jennifer, ed. (Illus.). 144p. 1999. pap. 8.99 (1-56309-299-9, N998108, New Hope) Womans Mission Union.

Reeves, Rhonda, Two Hundred Ways to Care for Preschoolers. (Illus.). 72p. (ps). 1997. pap. text 6.95 (1-56309-208-5, N978103, New Hope) Womans Mission Union.

Reeves, Rhonda, ed. see Law, Jennifer.

Reeves, Richard. President Kennedy. (Illus.). 480p. 1993. 30.00 (0-671-64879-9) S&S Trade.

— President Kennedy: Profile of Power. (Illus.). 800p. 1994. per. 15.00 (0-671-89289-4) S&S Trade Pap.

— Running in Place: How Bill Clinton Disappointed America. (Illus.). 128p. (Orig.). 1996. pap. 8.95 (0-8362-1091-3) Andrews & McMeel.

— What the People Know: Freedom & the Press. LC 98-22572. (Joanna Jackson Goldman Memorial Lecture on American Civilization & Government Ser.). 128p. 1998. 19.95 (0-674-61622-7) HUP.

— What the People Know: Freedom & the Press. 159p. 1999. pap. 12.95 (0-674-61623-5) HUP.

Reeves, Richard, jt. auth. see Iyengar, Shanto.

Reeves, Richard, jt. auth. see Pritchard, Elaine.

Reeves, Richard P., jt. ed. see DuBowy, Paul J.

Reeves, Richard S. Royal Blood: Fifty Years of Classic Thoroughbreds. 284p. 1994. text 75.00 (0-939049-63-5) Blood-Horse.

Reeves, Richard S., et al. Crown Jewels of Thoroughbred Racing: Original Paintings by Richard Stone Reeves. (Illus.). 192p. 1997. 75.00 (0-939049-90-2) Blood-Horse.

— Crown Jewels of Thoroughbred Racing: Original Paintings by Richard Stone Reeves. limited ed. (Illus.). 200p. 1997. 350.00 (0-939049-91-0) Blood-Horse.

Reeves, Robert. The Superpower Space Race: An Explosive Rivalry Through the Solar System. LC 94-28240. (Illus.). 452p. (C). 1994. 28.95 (0-306-44768-1, Plenum Trade) Perseus Pubng.

Reeves, Robert G. Flora of Central Texas. Orig. Title: Flora of South Central Texas. (C). 1977. reprint ed. pap. text 17.75 (0-934786-00-3) G Davis.

Reeves, Robert N. The Ridiculous to the Delightful: Comic Characters in Sidney's New Arcadia. LC 73-91641. (LeBaron Russell Briggs Prize Honors Essays in English Ser.). 64p. 1974. pap. 2.70 (0-674-76890-6) HUP.

Reeves, Rosser, jt. auth. see Martin, Ray.

Reeves, S., jt. ed. see Groves, L.

Reeves, Sally K., et al. Historic City Park: New Orleans. (Illus.). 256p. 1982. 24.95 (0-9610062-0-X) Friends City Park.

Reeves, Sally K., tr. see Lelievre, Jacques-Felix.

Reeves, Scott. NetWare 5 CNE. LC 98-88910. (Certification NetWare 5 Ser.). 448p. 1999. 39.99 (0-7821-2388-0) Sybex.

Reeves, Scott & Reeves, Kalinda. Network+ Exam Cram. LC 99-25789. (Exam Cram (Coriolis' Certification Insider Press) Ser.). (Illus.). 355p. 1999. pap. 29.99 (1-57610-405-2) Coriolis Grp.

Reeves, Scott D. Creative Beginnings. 310p. 1996. spiral bd. 33.33 (0-13-345463-0) P-H.

Reeves, Scott D. Creative Beginnings: An Introduction to Jazz Improvisation. 1997. 52.53 (0-13-760083-6) P-H.

— Creative Beginnings: Compact Disk. (C). 1996. text 21.80 (0-13-573098-8, Macmillan Coll) P-H.

Reeves, Scott D. Creative Jazz Improvisation. 2nd ed. LC 94-10657. 332p. 1994. pap. text 45.00 (0-13-303280-9) Prntice Hall Bks.

*Reeves, Scott D. Creative Jazz Improvisation. 3rd ed. LC 00-23670. (Illus.). 332p. 2000. spiral bd. 37.33 (0-13-088975-X) P-H.

Reeves-Smyth, Terence. Irish Gardens. (Appletree Pocket Guides Ser.). (Illus.). 96p. (Orig.). 1994. pap. 7.95 (0-86281-374-3, Pub. by Appletree Pr) Irish Bks Media.

Reeves, Stephen M. Wendover, Acme, & Virginia Point. LC 80-54382. 158p. 1981. 29.95 (0-938794-01-9) Red River Pub Co.

Reeves, Steve & Peterson, James A. Powerwalking. LC 81-18184. 1982. pap. write for info. (0-672-52713-8) Macmillan.

Reeves, Stevens G. Children of the Shroud. 1990. mass mkt. 4.95 (0-445-21014-1, Mysterious Paperbk) Warner Bks.

Reeves-Stevens, Garfield. Children of the Shroud. 1988. 19.95 (0-385-25139-4) Doubleday.

— Dark Matter. 1991. mass mkt. 5.99 (0-7704-2485-6) Bantam.

— Dreamland. 1991. mass mkt. 4.95 (0-446-36155-0) Warner Bks.

— The First Christmas Elf. (J). 2000. pap. 2.95 (0-689-71821-7); pap. 6.95 (0-689-71822-5) Aladdin.

Reeves-Stevens, Garfield & Reeves-Stevens, Judith. Icefire. (Illus.). 703p. 1999. reprint ed. per. 6.99 (0-671-01403-X, Pocket Books) PB.

— Star Trek. (Star Trek Ser.: No. 42). 1991. mass mkt. 5.50 (0-671-74359-7) PB.

Reeves-Stevens, Garfield, jt. auth. see Reeves-Stevens, Judith.

Reeves-Stevens, Judith. Federation. (Star Trek Ser.). 480p. 1995. per. 6.50 (0-671-89423-4) PB.

*Reeves-Stevens, Judith. Going to Mars: The Untold Story of Mars Pathfinder & NASA's Bold New Missions for the 21st Century. 288p. 1999. 40.00 (0-671-02796-4) PB.

— Prime Directive. 1999. pap. 12.98 (0-671-04465-6) PB.

Reeves-Stevens, Judith. Star Trek, Phase II. (Lost Ser.). 1997. pap. 128.00 (0-671-84007-X) PB.

Reeves-Stevens, Judith & Reeves-Stevens, Garfield. The Art of Star Trek. Ryan, Kevin, ed. 320p. 1995. 50.00 (0-671-89804-3, PB Hardcover) PB.

— The Art of Star Trek. 1997. per. 25.00 (0-671-01776-4) PB.

— The Continuing Mission. 10th anniversary ed. (Star Trek Ser.). 288p. 1997. 35.00 (0-671-87429-2) PB.

— The Day of Descent. Ryan, Kevin, ed. (Alien Nation Ser.: No. 1). 416p. (Orig.). 1993. mass mkt. 4.99 (0-671-73599-3, Pocket Star Bks) PB.

*Reeves-Stevens, Judith & Reeves-Stevens, Garfield. The Fall of Terok Nor. (Star Trek: Vol. 1). 464p. 2000. per. 6.50 (0-671-02401-9, Star Trek) PB.

Reeves-Stevens, Judith & Reeves-Stevens, Garfield. Icefire. 384p. 1998. 23.00 (0-671-01402-1, Pocket Books) PB.

*Reeves-Stevens, Judith & Reeves-Stevens, Garfield. Inferno. (Star Trek Ser.: Vol. 3). 448p. 2000. per. 6.50 (0-671-02403-5, Star Trek) PB.

Reeves-Stevens, Judith & Reeves-Stevens, Garfield. Prime Directive. Stern, Dave, ed. (Star Trek Ser.). 416p. 1991. reprint ed. mass mkt. 5.99 (0-671-74466-6) PB.

An Asterisk (*) at the beginning of an entry indicates that the title is appearing for the first time.

— Quick Silver. LC 00-503332. 496p. 1999. 23.00 (*0-671-02853-7*, PB Hardcover) PB.

— Quicksilver. 752p. 2000. reprint ed. per. 6.99 (*0-671-02854-5*, Pocket Books) PB.

— Star Trek Phase II: The Lost Series. LC 97-129139. (Illus.). 288p. 1997. pap. 16.00 (*0-671-56839-6*) S&S Trade.

***Reeves-Stevens, Judith & Reeves-Stevens, Garfield.** The War of the Prophets. (Star Trek: Vol. 2 2). 432p. 2000. per. 6.50 (*0-671-02402-7*, Star Trek) PB.

Reeves-Stevens, Judith, jt. auth. see Reeves-Stevens, Garfield.

Reeves, Sue. Country Rag Crafts: 50 Colorful Projects from Leftover Fabric. (Illus.). 128p. 1996. 24.95 (*0-7153-0290-6*, Pub. by D & C Pub) Sterling.

Reeves, T. Zane. The Politics of the Peace Corps & VISTA. LC 86-19194. (Illus.). 232p. 1988. text 34.95 (*0-8173-0323-5*) U of Ala Pr.

Reeves, T. Zane, ed. Cases in Public Human Resource Management. LC 98-67459. 200p. 1998. pap. text 27.50 (*0-87581-418-2*) F E Peacock Pubs.

Reeves, T. Zane, jt. auth. see Hays, Steven W.

Reeves, Thomas. A Question of Character: A Life of John F. Kennedy. 528p. 1997. per. 18.00 (*0-7615-1287-X*) Prima Pub.

Reeves, Thomas C. Empty Church: Does Organized Religion Matter Anymore? 288p. 1998. per. 12.00 (*0-684-83607-6*, Touchstone) S&S Trade Pap.

— The Empty Church: The Crisis of Liberal Christianity. 1996. 25.00 (*0-614-20416-X*) Free Pr.

— Gentleman Boss: The Life of Chester Alan Arthur. Speirs, Katherine E., ed. LC 91-71714. (Signature Ser.). (Illus.). 500p. 1991. reprint ed. 32.50 (*0-945707-03-7*) Amer Political.

— The Life & Times of Joe McCarthy. LC 79-3730. 1981. 19.95 (*0-8128-2337-0*, Scrbrough Hse) Madison Bks UPA.

— The Life & Times of Joe McCarthy: A Biography. LC 83-42968. (Illus.). 848p. 1983. pap. 14.95 (*0-8128-6200-7*, Scrbrough Hse) Madison Bks UPA.

— The Life & Times of Joe McCarthy: A Biography. LC 97-26679. (Illus.). 832p. 1997. reprint ed. pap. 19.95 (*1-56833-101-0*) Madison Bks UPA.

— A Question of Character: A Life of John F. Kennedy. (Illus.). 528p. 1992. pap. 13.95 (*1-55958-175-1*) Prima Pub.

— Twentieth-Century America: A Brief History. LC 98-50366. (Illus.). 320p. (YA). (gr. 9 up). 1999. 30.00 (*0-19-504483-5*) OUP.

***Reeves, Thomas C.** Twentieth-century America: A Brief History. LC 98-50366. 320p. 2000. 21.95 (*0-19-504484-3*) OUP.

Reeves, Thomas C., ed. John F. Kennedy: The Man, the Politician, the President. LC 89-33503. 178p. (C). 1990. pap. 11.50 (*0-89464-371-1*) Krieger.

— Mc Carthyism. 3rd ed. LC 88-13666. 154p. (C). 1989. pap. 11.50 (*0-89464-289-8*) Krieger.

Reeves, Thomas C., frwd. James Lloyd Breck: Apostle of the Wilderness. 194p. 1992. text 22.00 (*1-881648-00-1*); pap. text 12.95 (*1-881648-01-X*) Frontier Mission.

Reeves, Tom. Alchemy for Managers: Turning Your Experience into Achievement. LC 97-224301. 200p. 1997. pap. text 28.95 (*0-7506-3340-9*) Buttrwrth-Heinemann.

Reeves, Tracy, jt. auth. see Silvester, Steven.

Reeves, Trish. Returning the Question. LC 88-71364. (CSU Poetry Ser.: No. XXV). 62p. (Orig.). 1988. 12.00 (*0-914946-67-6*); pap. 6.00 (*0-914946-66-8*) Cleveland St Univ Poetry Ctr.

***Reeves, Walter & Glasener, Erica.** Month by Month Gardening in Georgia. (Illus.). 320p. 2000. pap. 18.95 (*1-888608-27-7*) Cool Springs Pr.

Reeves, Walter, jt. auth. see Glasener, Erica.

Reeves, Wayne W. Cognition & Complexity: The Cognitive Science of Managing Complexity. LC 95-49462. 192p. 1996. 30.00 (*0-8108-3101-5*) Scarecrow.

***Reeves, Wayne W.** Learner-Centered Design: A Cognitive View of Managing Complexity in Product Information & Environmental Design. LC 99-26072. 198p. 1999. 42.00 (*0-7619-0726-2*) Sage.

Reeves, William. The Bell of St. Patrick Called the Clog an Edachta. 1991. reprint ed. pap. 5.95 (*0-89979-055-0*) British Am Bks.

Reeves, William, ed. see Adamnan, Saint.

Reeves, William W. The Technology of Fluid Power. (Illus.). 320p. (C). 1987. text 45.00 (*0-8359-7525-8*) P-H.

Reeves, William W., ed. The Technology of Fluid Power. LC 96-11155. (Mechanical Technology Ser.). 480p. 1996. pap. 72.95 (*0-8273-6664-7*) Delmar.

Reevy, Anthony W. Ghost Train: American Railroad Ghost Legends. (Illus.). 160p. 1999. 14.95 (*1-883089-41-7*, Pub. by TLC VA) Motorbooks Intl.

Ref. Holman Giant Print Reference Bible: Imitation Leather. 1998. 19.97 (*1-55819-753-2*) Broadman.

***Refausse, Raymond.** Church of Ireland Records. (Maynooth Guides for Local History Research Ser.). (Illus.). 64p. 1999. pap. 14.50 (*0-7165-2701-4*, Pub. by Irish Acad Pr) Intl Spec Bk.

Refausse, Raymond, ed. The Register of Christ Church Cathedral, 1710-1900. LC 98-189239. 176p. 1998. boxed set 50.00 (*1-85182-344-1*, Pub. by Four Cts Pr) Intl Spec Bk.

Refausse, Raymond, ed. see Helferty, Seamus.

Refausse, Raymond, jt. ed. see Helferty, Seamus.

Refausse, Raymond, jt. ed. see McEnery, M. J.

Refenes, Apostolos-Paul, ed. Neural Networks in the Capital Markets. LC 94-37990. 392p. 1995. 105.00 (*0-471-94364-9*) Wiley.

Refenes, Apostolos-Paul, et al, eds. Neural Networks in Financial Engineering: Proceedings of the Third International Conference on Neural Networks in the Capital Markets, London, England October 1995. 300p. 1996. text 84.00 (*981-02-2480-X*, RuaKebMb-P2951) World Scientific Pub.

Refenes, Apostolos-Paul, jt. auth. see Zapranis, A. D.

***Referee Magazine Staff.** Successful Sports Officiating. Grunska, Jerry, ed. LC 99-30329. (Illus.). 184p. 1999. pap. 19.95 (*0-88011-748-6*, PREF0748) Human Kinetics.

Reference Division Staff, ed. see Cook, Claire K.

***Reference Press Staff.** Grantfinder: The Complete Guide to Postgraduate Funding. 2000. text 40.00 (*0-312-22893-7*) St Martin.

— GrantFinder: The Complete Guide to Postgraduate Funding; Science. 296p. 2000. text 40.00 (*0-312-22895-3*) St Martin.

— Who's Who 2000. 152nd ed. 2000p. 2000. text 255.00 (*0-312-22907-0*) St Martin.

Reference Service Press Staff. Scholarship Search Strategies. 1999. pap. text 4.50 (*0-918276-46-2*) Ref Serv Pr.

— Speaking the Language: Your Financial Aid Dictionary. 1999. pap. 5.50 (*0-918276-47-0*) Ref Serv Pr.

Refetoff, Samuel, jt. ed. see Braverman, Lewis E.

Reff, Daniel T., tr. see De Ribas, Andres Perez.

Reff, Theodore. Degas: The Artist's Mind. LC 87-11827. (Paperbacks in AA History Ser.). (Illus.). 352p. 1987. pap. 24.95 (*0-674-19543-4*) HUP.

— Manet & Modern Paris: One Hundred Paintings, Drawings, Prints, & Photographs by Manet & His Contemporaries. LC 82-18965. (Illus.). 280p. 1992. 39.95 (*0-226-70720-2*) U Ch Pr.

— The Notebooks of Edgar Degas: A Catalogue of the Thirty-Eight Note-Books in the Bibliotheque Nationale & Other Collections., 2 vols. 2nd rev. ed. LC 84-82426. (Illus.). 167p. 1985. reprint ed. lib. bdg. 195.00 (*0-87817-304-8*) Hacker.

Reff, Theodore & Shoemaker, Innis H. Paul Cezanne: 2 Sketchbooks. (Illus.). 244p. (Orig.). 1989. pap. 25.00 (*0-87633-080-4*) Phila Mus Art.

Reff, Theodore & Valdes-Forain, Florence. Jean-Louis Forain: The Impressionist Years: The Dixon Gallery & Gardens Collection. LC 95-6905. 1995. write for info. (*0-945064-00-4*) Dixon Gallery.

***Reffell, Massala, Sr.** The Black Mayflower. 2000. 21.95 (*0-533-13260-6*) Vantage.

Reffin-Smith, Brian. Soft Computing: Art & Design. 192p. (C). 1986. pap. text. write for info. (*0-318-61094-9*) Addison-Wesley.

Reffner, Corey, jt. ed. see McMillin, Challace J.

Reffo, G., jt. ed. see Gandini, A.

Refi, James J. Fiber Optic Cable: A LightGuide. (Specialized Ser.). (Illus.). 208p. 1991. pap. 39.95 (*1-56016-043-8*) ABC TeleTraining.

***Refinetti, Roberto.** Circadian Physiology. LC 99-51743. 1999. write for info. (*0-8493-2299-5*) CRC Pr.

Refinetti, Roberto, jt. ed. see Dank, Barry M.

Reflected Images Staff. The Perfect Wedding Workbook: A Bride's "Best Friend" 1996. 40.00 (*1-881263-22-3*) Reflect Images.

Refnes, Vera. Kinder Capers Songs: For Special Times & Special People. (Illus.). 23p. 1991. teacher ed. 10.00 (*0-9627108-1-4*) Refhouse Pubns.

Refnes, Vera & Milhous, Enid. Kinder Capers. (Illus.). 311p. 1990. teacher ed. 29.95 (*0-9627108-0-6*) Refhouse Pubns.

***Refoen, Raymond.** Micronesia's Never-Forgotten Island. (Illus.). 2000. pap. 17.49 (*0-9679288-0-X*) Virginia Pines.

Reformed Church in America Staff. Rejoice in the Lord: A Hymn Companion to the Scriptures. Routley, Erik, ed. 608p. 1985. 15.00 (*0-8028-9009-1*) Eerdmans.

Reformed Zion Union Apostolic Churches of America. History of the Reformed Zion Union Apostolic Churches of America. LC 97-39517. 1997. 39.95 (*1-55618-166-3*) Brunswick Pub.

Refregier, Philippe & Ahlers, Rolf-Juergen, eds. New Image Processing Techniques & Applications: Algorithms, Methods & Components II. LC 98-125171. (Europto Ser.: Vol. 3101). 352p. 1997. 69.00 (*0-8194-2521-4*) SPIE.

***Refregier, Philippe & Javidi, Bahram, eds.** Euro-American Workshop on Optoelectronic Information Processing: Proceedings of a Conference Held 31 May-2 June 1999, Colmar, France. LC 99-38973. (Critical Reviews of Optical Science & Technology Ser.: Vol. CR74). 309p. 1999. pap. 70.00 (*0-8194-3457-4*) SPIE.

Refregier, Philippe, ed. see Javidi, Bahram.

Refro, Nancy & Hunt, Tamara. Pocketful of Puppets: Mother Goose Rhymes. Schwalb, Ann W., ed. (Puppetry in Education Ser.). (Illus.). 80p. (Orig.). (J). (ps-2). 1982. spiral bd. 12.95 (*0-931044-06-5*) Renfro Studios.

Refsal, Harley. Woodcarving in the Scandinavian Style. LC 92-16979. (Illus.). 132p. 1992. pap. 14.95 (*0-8069-8633-6*) Sterling.

Refsgaard, J. C. & Karalis, E. A., eds. Operational Water Management: Proceedings of the International Conference, Copenhagen, 3-7 September 1997. (Illus.). 486p. (C). 1997. text 110.00 (*90-5410-897-5*, Pub. by A A Balkema) Ashgate Pub Co.

Refsgaard, Jens C., jt. ed. see Abbott, Michael B.

***Refsing, Kirsten, ed.** Early European Writings on Ainu Culture. (Ainu Library: Collection 3). 1999. text 695.00 (*0-7007-1155-4*, Pub. by Curzon Pr Ltd) UH Pr.

Refsing, Kirsten, ed. Early European Writings on the Ainu Language, 10 vols. (Ainu Library Collection). 4000p. (C). 1996. text 995.00 (*0-7007-0400-0*, Pub. by Curzon Pr Ltd) UH Pr.

— Origins of the Ainu Language: The Ainu Indo-European Controversy. (Ainu Library Collection: Vol. 2). 1998. lib. bdg. 695.00 (*0-7007-1034-5*, Pub. by Curzon Pr Ltd) UH Pr.

Reftery, Larry, ed. Worship His Majesty. 32p. 1981. pap. 0.75 (*0-88144-056-6*) Christian Pub.

Refugee Women in Development Staff. Understanding Family Violence within U. S. Refugee Communities: A Training Manual. Richie, Beth, ed. 1988. 8.00 (*0-9620653-0-7*) Ref Women Dev.

Rega, Alcides F. CA 2 Plus Pump of Plasma Membrane. Garrahan, Patricio J., ed. 184p. 1986. 108.00 (*0-8493-6253-9*, QH601, CRC Reprint) Franklin.

Rega Silva, J. J. Do, see Do Rega Silva, J. J.

Regal, David. Close-Up & Personal. (Illus.). 264p. 1999. 45.00 (*0-945296-25-8*) Hermetic Pr.

***Regal, David.** Jungle Mischief, Vol. 2. (Illus.). 24p. (ps-3). 2000. pap. 3.50 (*0-689-83228-1*, Simon Spot) Little Simon.

Regalado, Nancy F. Poetic Patterns in Rutebeuf: A Study in Noncourtly Poetic Modes of the Thirteenth Century. LC 70-104620. (Yale Romanitc Series, Second Ser.: No. 21). 384p. reprint ed. pap. 119.10 (*0-608-14258-1*, 202033300024) Bks Demand.

Regalado, Nancy F., ed. see Poirion, Daniel.

Regalado, Samuel O. Viva Baseball! Latin Major Leaguers & Their Special Hunger. LC 97-21066. (Sports & Society Ser.). 264p. 1998. text 39.95 (*0-252-02372-2*) U of Ill Pr.

Regalbuto, Robert J. A Guide to Monastic Guest Houses. 3rd ed. LC 97-38227. 280p. 1998. pap. 17.95 (*0-8192-1713-1*) Morehouse Pub.

***Regalbuto, Robert J.** A Guide to Monastic Guest Houses. 4th ed. 304p. 2000. pap. 19.95 (*0-8192-1848-0*, 6297) Morehouse Pub.

Regalia, Phillip. Adaptive IIR Filtering in Signal Processing & Control. LC 94-30294. (Electrical Engineering & Electronics Ser.: 90). (Illus.). 704p. 1994. text 185.00 (*0-8247-9289-0*) Dekker.

Regamey, Constantin, tr. from SAN. Three Chapters from the Samadhirajasutra. 112p. 1984. reprint ed. lib. bdg. 19.50 (*0-88181-003-7*) Canon Pubns.

Regamey, Konstanty. The Bhadramayakara-Vyakarana. 1990. reprint ed. 19.00 (*81-208-0761-8*, Pub. by Motilal Bnarsidass) S Asia.

Regamey, R. H., et al, eds. International Symposium on Brucellosis 2. (Developments in Biological Standardization Ser.: Vol. 31). (Illus.). 1976. 61.00 (*3-8055-2364-5*) S Karger.

— International Symposium on Vaccination of Man & Animals by the Non-Parenteral Route: Proceedings, Douglas 1975. (Developments in Biological Standardization Ser.: Vol. 33). (Illus.). 1976. 61.00 (*3-8055-2399-8*) S Karger.

— Joint OIE-IABS Symposium on Clostridial Products in Veterinary Medicine. (Developments in Biological Standardization Ser.: Vol. 32). 1976. 61.00 (*3-8055-2435-8*) S Karger.

Regamey, R. H. & Horodniceanu, F., eds. European Society of Animal Cell Technology, General Meeting. (Developments in Biological Standardization Ser.: Vol. 42). (Illus.). 1979. pap. 61.00 (*3-8055-2989-9*) S Karger.

Regamey, R. H., ed. see International Association of Biological Standardiz.

Regamey, R. H., jt. ed. see International Association of Biological Standardiz.

Regamey, R. H., ed. see International Congress of Microbiological Standard.

Regamey, R. H., ed. see International Symposium on BCG Vaccine Staff.

Regamey, R. H., ed. see International Symposium on Enterobacterial Vaccine.

Regamey, R. H., ed. see International Symposium on Smallpox Vaccine Staff.

Regamey, R. H., ed. see International Symposium on Standardization & Use of Vaccines in the Developing Countries Staff.

Regamey, R. H., ed. see Joint WHC-IABS Staff.

Regamey, R. H., ed. see Permanent Section of Microbiological Standardizati.

Regan. Troubleshooting the PC. LC 99-15344. (Illus.). 655p. 1999. pap. text 90.00 (*0-13-095796-8*) P-H.

Regan, Mariann. Immortality News. LC 98-74227. 290p. 1999. 24.50 (*0-88739-215-6*) Creat Arts Bk.

— Immortality News. LC 98-74227. 288p. 2000. pap. 16.50 (*0-88739-192-3*) Creat Arts Bk.

Regan, Brendan O. The Heart of Healing. (Illus.). 192p. 1999. reprint ed. text 25.00 (*0-7881-6430-9*) DIANE Pub.

Regan, Brian T. Which Business Structure Is Best for You? 40p. (Orig.). (C). 1995. pap. text 15.00 (*1-878630-69-5*) CA Chamber Commerce.

Regan, C. Summary of Technical Information & Agreements from Nuclear Management & Resources Council Industry Reports Addressing License Renewal. 186p. 1996. per. 18.00 (*0-16-062676-5*) USGPO.

Regan, Carol S. Flag of the United States. (Illus.). 51p. 1995. pap., wbk. ed. 8.95 (*0-9658144-0-8*) MCR.

Regan, Colm. People of the Islands. LC 98-10933. (Wide World Ser.). (J). 1998. 25.69 (*0-8172-5064-6*) Raintree Steck-V.

Regan, Colm & Cremin, Pedar. Africa. LC 96-30746. (Continents Ser.). 48p. (J). 1997. lib. bdg. 25.69 (*0-8172-4776-9*) Raintree Steck-V.

Regan, D., et al, eds. Systems Approach in Vision: Proceedings of a Workshop Held in Amsterdam, the Netherlands, 27-29 August 1984. (Illus.). 226p. 1986. 55.00 (*0-08-032033-3*, Pub. by PPL) Elsevier.

Regan, Dana. At My School: Paint Box Fun. 32p. (J). (ps-3). 1993. pap. 1.95 (*0-590-46291-1*) Scholastic Inc.

— I've Been Working on the Railroad. (Wheel Bks.). (Illus.). 10p. (J). (ps-k). 1996. 5.95 (*0-590-54317-2*, Cartwheel) Scholastic Inc.

***Regan, Dana.** Monkey See, Monkey Do. (All Aboard Reading Ser.). (Illus.). 32p. (J). (ps-3). 2000. pap. 3.99 (*0-448-42299-9*, Planet Dexter) Peng Put Young Read.

— Sing-Along Christmas. LC 98-65670. (Wee Sing Ser.). (Illus.). 12p. (J). (ps). 1998. pap. 9.99 (*0-8431-7836-1*) Putnam Pub Group.

Regan, Dana. Wee Sing Nursery Rhymes: With Cassette, 1. (Wee Sing Ser.). (Illus.). 12p. (J). (ps). 1999. pap. 9.99 (*0-8431-7508-7*, Price Stern) Peng Put Young Read.

— The Wheels on the Bus. (Wheel Bks.). 12p. (J). (ps-k). 1996. 5.95 (*0-590-54316-4*, Cartwheel) Scholastic Inc.

Regan, Dana. Baby Boo! 12p. (J). (ps-k). 1992. 6.99 (*0-679-81544-9*, Pub. by Random Bks Yng Read) Random.

— Busy, Busy Preschool. (Sticker Stories Ser.). 16p. (J). 1997. pap. text 4.95 (*0-448-41714-6*, G & D) Peng Put Young Read.

Regan, Dana, jt. auth. see Schoberle, Cecile.

Regan, Dana, jt. illus. see Packard, Mary.

Regan, David. Experience the Mystery: Pastoral Possibilities for Christian Mystagogy. 160p. (Orig.). 1994. pap. 11.95 (*0-8146-2328-X*, Liturg Pr Bks) Liturgical Pr.

***Regan, David.** Human Perception of Objects: Early Visual Processing of Spatial Form Defined by Luminance, Color, Texture, Motion & Binocular Disparity. LC 99-57028. 1999. pap. text 39.95 (*0-87893-753-6*) Sinauer Assocs.

Regan, David, ed. The New City Republics: Municipal Intervention in Defence. (C). 1990. 35.00 (*0-907967-87-6*, Pub. by Inst Euro Def & Strat) St Mut.

Regan, David J. Mourning Glory: The Making of a Marine. 1980. 9.95 (*0-8159-6218-5*) Devin.

***Regan, Dian C.** Monster of the Month Club, Class Set. unabridged ed. (J). (gr. 4). 1998. 89.70 incl. audio (*0-7887-2544-0*, 46714) Recorded Bks.

— Monster of the Month Club, Homework Set. unabridged ed. (J). 1998. 38.24 incl. audio (*0-7887-2239-5*, 40723) Recorded Bks.

Regan, Dian Curtis. The Class with the Summer Birthdays. (Illus.). 80p. (J). (gr. 2-4). 1995. 13.95 (*0-8050-1657-0*, Redfeather BYR) H Holt & Co.

— The Curse of the Trouble Dolls. LC 91-28572. (Illus.). 88p. (J). (gr. 2-4). 1995. 14.95 (*0-8050-1944-8*, Bks Young Read); pap. 4.95 (*0-8050-2952-4*, Bks Young Read) H Holt & Co.

— Daddies. LC 95-15938. (Illus.). 32p. (J). (ps-k). 1996. 5.95 (*0-590-47973-3*, Cartwheel) Scholastic Inc.

— Dear Dr. Sillybear. LC 96-44212. (Illus.). 40p. (J). 15.95 (*0-8050-5065-5*, Bks Young Read) H Holt & Co.

— Fangs-Giving. (J). (gr. 2-7). 1997. pap. 3.99 (*0-590-96821-1*) Scholastic Inc.

— The Friendship of Milly & Tug. LC 98-38100. (Illus.). (J). (gr. 1-3). 1999. 15.95 (*0-8050-5935-0*) H Holt & Co.

— Game of Survival. 144p. (Orig.). (J). 1989. pap. 2.75 (*0-380-75585-8*, Avon Bks) Morrow Avon.

— The Haunted Campground Mystery. (Ghost Twins Ser.: No. 06). 128p. (gr. 4-6). 1995. pap. 3.25 (*0-590-25242-9*) Scholastic Inc.

— The Haunted Campground Mystery. (Ghost Twins Ser.). 1995. 8.35 (*0-606-07630-1*, Pub. by Turtleback) Demco.

— The Initiation. 176p. (Orig.). (J). (gr. 5). 1993. pap. 3.50 (*0-380-76325-7*, Avon Bks) Morrow Avon.

— I've Got Your Number. 144p. 1986. pap. 2.50 (*0-380-75082-1*, Avon Bks) Morrow Avon.

— Jilly's Ghost. 144p. (Orig.). 1990. pap. 2.95 (*0-380-75831-8*, Avon Bks) Morrow Avon.

— Liver Cookies. 160p. (J). (gr. 4-6). 1991. pap. 2.75 (*0-590-44337-2*) Scholastic Inc.

— Monster of the Month. (J). 1997. mass mkt. 3.99 (*0-590-62391-5*) Scholastic Inc.

— Monster of the Month Club. 1997. 9.09 (*0-606-11635-4*, Pub. by Turtleback) Demco.

— Monsters & My One True Love. LC 97-50411. (Illus.). 198p. (J). (gr. 4-6). 1995. 15.95 (*0-8050-4676-3*) H Holt & Co.

— Monsters in Cyberspace. LC 96-37559. (J). 1995. 14.95 (*0-8050-4677-1*) H Holt & Co.

— Monsters in the Attic. LC 95-16174. (Illus.). 178p. (J). (gr. 4-7). 1995. 14.95 (*0-8050-3709-8*) H Holt & Co.

— Monsters in the Attic. (J). 1998. pap. 4.50 (*0-590-84473-3*) Scholastic Inc.

— Monsters in the Attic. 1998. 9.60 (*0-606-13620-7*, Pub. by Turtleback) Demco.

***Regan, Dian Curtis.** Monsters in the Attic. (Illus.). 178p. (J). (gr. 4-6). 1999. reprint ed. text 15.00 (*0-7881-6676-X*) DIANE Pub.

Regan, Dian Curtis. My Zombie Valentine. 112p. (J). (gr. 4-6). 1993. pap. 2.95 (*0-590-46038-2*) Scholastic Inc.

— The Mystery at Hanover School. (Ghost Twins Ser.: No. 7). 128p. (J). (gr. 4-6). 1995. pap. text 3.25 (*0-590-53884-5*) Scholastic Inc.

— The Mystery at Hanover School. (Ghost Twins Ser.). (J). 1995. 8.35 (*0-606-07914-9*, Pub. by Turtleback) Demco.

— Mystery at Kickingbird Lake. (Mystery at Kickingbird Lake Ser.: No. 01). 128p. (J). (gr. 4-6). 1994. pap. 3.25 (*0-590-48253-X*) Scholastic Inc.

— The Mystery of One Wish Pond. (Ghost Twins Ser.: No. 02). 128p. (J). (gr. 4-6). 1994. pap. 3.25 (*0-590-48254-8*) Scholastic Inc.

— The Mystery of the Disappearing Dogs. (Ghost Twins Ser.: No. 5). 128p. (J). (gr. 4-6). 1995. pap. 3.25 (*0-590-25241-0*) Scholastic Inc.

— The Mystery of the Disappearing Dogs. (Ghost Twins Ser.). (J). 1995. 8.35 (*0-606-07915-7*, Pub. by Turtleback) Demco.

— The Mystery of the Haunted Castle. (Ghost Twins Ser.: No. 8). (J). 1995. pap. 3.50 (*0-590-53885-3*) Scholastic Inc.

R

— Mystery of the Haunted Castle. (Ghost Twins Ser.). 1995. 8.60 (*0-606-08574-2*, Pub. by Turtleback) Demco.

— The Mystery on Walrus Mountain. (Ghost Twins Ser.: No. 03). 128p. (J). (gr. 4-6). 1995. pap. 3.25 (*0-590-48255-6*) Scholastic Inc.

— The Mystery on Walrus Mountain. (Ghost Twins Ser.). (J). 1995. 8.35 (*0-606-07917-3*, Pub. by Turtleback) Demco.

— The Perfect Age. 192p. 1987. pap. 2.50 (*0-380-75337-5*, Avon Bks) Morrow Avon.

— Princess Nevermore. LC 94-30020. 240p. (YA). (gr. 4-7). 1995. 14.95 (*0-590-45758-6*, Scholastic Hardcover) Scholastic Inc.

— Princess Nevermore. LC 94-30020. 240p. (J). (gr. 5-9). 1997. mass mkt. 4.50 (*0-590-45759-4*) Scholastic Inc.

Regan, Dian Curtis. Princess Nevermore. LC 94-30020. (Point Fantasy Ser.). 1995. 9.60 (*0-606-11765-2*, Pub. by Turtleback) Demco.

Regan, Dian Curtis. Vampire Who Came for Christmas. 112p. (J). (gr. 4-6). 1994. pap. 2.95 (*0-590-47862-1*) Scholastic Inc.

Regan, Donald H. Duties of Preservation. (Working Papers on the Preservation of Species). 1988. 2.50 (*0-318-33310-4*, PS1) IPPP.

Regan, Donald T. For the Record: From Wall Street to Washington. (Illus.). 352p. 1988. 21.95 (*0-15-163966-3*) Harcourt.

Regan, Edward V. Infrastructure Investment for Tomorrow: A Financing Plan to Eliminate the Deferred Maintenance on the Nation's Roads. (Public Policy Brief Ser.: No. 16). (Illus.). 64p. (Orig.). 1994. pap. write for info. (*0-941276-04-X*) J Levy.

***Regan, Edward V.** New Approach to Tax-Emempt Bonds: Infrastructure Financing with the AGIS Bond. (Public Policy Brief Ser.: No. 58). 40p. 1999. pap. write for info. (*0-941276-82-1*) J Levy.

— New Approach to Tax-Exempt Bonds. (Public Policy Brief Highlights Ser.: No. 58A). 6p. 1999. pap. write for info. (*0-941276-83-X*) J Levy.

***Regan, Elizabeth & O'Connor, Bridget.** End User Information Systems. 2nd ed. 608p. 2000. 65.33 (*0-13-018264-8*) P-H.

Regan, Elizabeth A. & O'Connor, Bridget N. End-User Information Systems: Perspectives for Managers & Information Systems Professionals. LC 93-20214. (Illus.). 604p. (C). 1993. text 52.35 (*0-02-399163-1*, Macmillan Coll) P-H.

Regan, F., jt. ed. see Vernon, J.

***Regan, Francis, et al, eds.** The Transformation of Legal Aid: Comparative & Historical Studies. LC 99-27431. 216p. 1999. text 75.00 (*0-19-826589-1*) OUP.

Regan, Frank, jt. auth. see Spencer, Gary.

Regan, Frank J. & Anandakrishnan, Satya M. Dynamics of Atmospheric Re-Entry. LC 92-33727. (Educ Ser.). 604p. 1993. 99.95 (*1-56347-048-9*, 48-9) AIAA.

Regan, Frauke, tr. see Mendelssohn, Moses.

Regan, G. & Shapiro, D. The Healer's Hand Book: A Step-by-Step Guide to Developing Your Latent Healing Abilities. 112p. 1993. pap. 11.95 (*1-85230-022-1*, Pub. by Element MA) Penguin Putnam.

Regan, Gary. The Bartender's Bible: One Thousand & One Mixed Drinks & Everything You Need to Know to Set up Your Bar. LC 91-55104. (Illus.). 352p. 1991. 18.00 (*0-06-016722-X*) HarperTrade.

— The Bartender's Bible: 1001 Mixed Drinks & Everything You Need to Know to Set up Your Own Bar. 400p. 1999. mass mkt. 6.99 (*0-06-109220-7*, Harp PBks) HarpC.

Regan, Gary & Regan, Mardee H. The Bourbon Companion: A Connoisseur's Guide. LC 97-76135. (Connoisseur Ser.). (Illus.). 192p. 1998. 19.95 (*0-7624-0013-7*) Running Pr.

— The Martini Companion: The Connoisseur's Guide. (Illus.). 192p. 1997. 19.95 (*0-7624-0061-7*) Running Pr.

— New Classic Cocktails. LC 96-40035. 144p. 1997. 21.00 (*0-02-861349-X*) Macmillan.

Regan, Geoffrey. Back Fire: The Tragic Story of Friendly Fire in Warfare from Ancient Times to the Gulf War. 253p. 1999. reprint ed. text 30.00 (*0-7881-6121-0*) DIANE Pub.

***Regan, Geoffrey.** Brassey's Book of Air Force Blunders. 2000. pap. 21.95 (*1-57488-254-6*) Brasseys.

Regan, Geoffrey. Brassey's Book of Military Blunders. (Illus.). 186p. 1998. pap. text 24.95 (*1-57488-189-2*) Brasseys.

***Regan, Geoffrey.** Brassey's Book of Military Blunders. 2000. pap. 19.95 (*1-57488-252-X*) Brasseys.

— Brassey's Book of More Military Blunders. 2000. pap. 21.95 (*1-57488-255-4*) Brasseys.

Regan, Geoffrey. Brassey's Book of Naval Blunders. (Illus.). 186p. 1998. pap. text 24.95 (*1-57488-188-4*) Brasseys.

***Regan, Geoffrey.** Brassey's Book of Naval Blunders. 2000. pap. 19.95 (*1-57488-253-8*) Brasseys.

— Great Military Blunders. 2000. 24.95 (*0-7522-1844-1*) Trans-Atl Phila.

Regan, Geoffrey. Guinness Book of Decisive Battles. 240p. 1992. 14.98 (*1-55859-431-0*) Abbeville Pr.

— Histrionics: A Treasury of Historical Anecdotes. (Illus.). 276p. 1997. pap. 12.95 (*1-86105-066-6*, Robson-Parkwest) Parkwest Pubns.

— Lionhearts: Richard I, Saladin & the Era of the Third Crusade. LC 98-53348. (Illus.). 288p. 1999. reprint ed. 25.00 (*0-8027-1354-8*) Walker & Co.

Regan, Geoffrey B. The Book of Military Blunders. 192p. 1991. lib. bdg. 45.00 (*0-87436-668-2*) ABC-CLIO.

— Fight or Flight. 320p. (Orig.). 1996. pap. 12.50 (*0-380-78019-4*, Avon Bks) Morrow Avon.

— Histrionics: A Treasury of Historical Anecdotes. 1996. 26.95 (*0-86051-928-7*, Robson-Parkwest) Parkwest Pubns.

— Saladin & the Fall of Jerusalem. 192p. 1988. lib. bdg. 55.00 (*0-7099-4208-7*, Pub. by C Helm) Routldge.

— Snafu: Great American Military Disasters. 296p. 1993. pap. 10.00 (*0-380-76755-4*, Avon Bks) Morrow Avon.

Regan, Helen B. & Brooks, Gwen H. Out of Women's Experience: Creating Relational Leadership. LC 95-12698. (Illus.). 136p. 1995. 45.95 (*0-8039-6233-9*) Corwin Pr.

Regan, Helen B., et al. Teacher: A New Definition & Model for Development. 118p. (Orig.). 1992. pap. 21.95 (*1-56602-048-4*) Research Better.

Regan, Hilary & Torrance, Alan J., eds. Christ & Context: The Confrontation Between Gospel & Culture. 288p. 1993. pap. text 29.95 (*0-567-29235-5*, Pub. by T & T Clark) Bks Intl VA.

Regan, Hilary, jt. ed. see Pfitzner, Victor.

Regan, James D., et al, eds. The Science of Photomedicine. LC 82-9072. (Photobiology Ser.). 680p. 1982. 125.00 (*0-306-40924-0*, Plenum Trade) Perseus Pubng.

Regan, Jane E. & Horan, Michael. Exploring the Catechism. 184p. (Orig.). 1995. pap. 12.95 (*0-8146-2152-X*) Liturgical Pr.

Regan, Jim. Winning at Slot Machines: A Guide to Making Money at the Most Popular of All Casino Games. 196p. 1995. pap. 5.95 (*0-8065-0973-2*, Citadel Pr) Carol Pub Group.

Regan, Joan M. Guide to Surviving Nursing School. 2nd ed. LC 95-9126. (Springhouse Notes Ser.). 144p. 1995. pap. 16.95 (*0-87434-816-1*) Springhouse Corp.

Regan, John. The Aged Client & the Law. 1990. text 44.00 (*0-231-06978-2*) Col U Pr.

***Regan, John.** The Irish Counter-Revolution: Treatyite Politics & Settlement in Independent Ireland, 1921-36. LC 99-22263. 1999. text 59.95 (*0-312-22727-2*) St Martin.

Regan, John, jt. auth. see Cronin, Mike.

Regan, John H. Memoirs, with Special Reference to Secession & the Civil War. (American Biography Ser.). 351p. 1991. reprint ed. lib. bdg. 79.00 (*0-7812-8322-1*) Rprt Serv.

Regan, John J. Tax, Estate & Financial Planning for the Elderly. 1985. ring bd. 230.00 (*0-8205-1289-3*) Bender.

Regan, John J., et al, eds. Atlas of Endoscopic Spine Surgery. (Illus.). 359p. 1995. 200.00 (*0-942219-73-2*) Quality Med Pub.

Regan, John J., et al. Atlas of Endoscopic Spine Surgery. (Illus.). 359p. 1995. 225.00 (*1-57626-046-1*, QMP) Quality Med Pub.

***Regan, Judith.** Quick & Delicious Meals in Minutes. 2000. pap. 22.00 (*0-06-095659-3*) HarpC.

Regan, Judith, ed. see Becker, Audrey.

Regan, Judith, ed. see Braiker, Harriet B.

Regan, Judith, ed. see Coupland, Douglas.

Regan, Judith, ed. see Kirn, Walter.

Regan, Judith, ed. see Limbaugh, Rush H., III.

Regan, Judith, ed. see Marcinko, Richard & Weisman, John.

Regan, Judith, ed. see Stumbo, Bella.

Regan, Judith, ed. see Walther, Anne.

Regan, Kevin. Twenty More Teen Prayer Services. LC 94-60339. 112p. (Orig.). 1994. pap. 9.95 (*0-89622-605-0*) Twenty-Third.

Regan, Leo. Public Enemies. (Illus.). 114p. 1994. pap. 19.95 (*0-233-98830-0*, Pub. by Andre Deutsch) Trafalgar.

Regan, M. Faithless. 36p. (Orig.). 1996. pap. 5.00 (*1-887289-19-4*) Rodent Pr.

Regan, M. Joanna & Keiss, Isabelle. Tender Courage: Reflections on the Life & Spirit of Catherine Mcauley. 158p. (Orig.). 1988. pap. 7.95 (*0-8199-0917-3*, Frncscn Herld) Franciscan Pr.

Regan, Madelyn, jt. auth. see Simpson, Richard L.

Regan, Mardee H., jt. auth. see Regan, Gary.

Regan, Mardee H., ed. see Wicks, Judy, et al.

***Regan, Margaret, compiled by.** Our Peaceable Kingdom: The Photographs of John Drysdale. (Illus.). 112p. 2000. 19.95 (*0-312-26588-3*) St Martin.

Regan, Maria Kassberg & Jonas, Steve. Help Your Man Get Healthy: An Essential Guide for Every Caring Woman. LC 99-25808. 288p. 1999. pap. 12.50 (*0-380-79769-0*, Avon Bks) Morrow Avon.

Regan, Mariann S. Love Words: The Self & the Text in Medieval & Renaissance Poetry. LC 81-15126. 288p. 1982. text 39.95 (*0-8014-1415-6*) Cornell U Pr.

Regan, Mary Beth, ed. see Race, Susan E.

Regan, Michael. American & European Furniture Price Guide. LC 94-79664. (Illus.). 256p. 1995. pap. 15.95 (*0-930625-46-3*) Krause Pubns.

***Regan, Michael.** How to Be a D. J. 2000. pap. 19.95 (*0-634-01136-7*) H Leonard.

Regan, Michael D. The Journey to Teams: A Practical Step-by-Step Implementation Plan. LC 98-93080. (Illus.). x, 198p. 1999. 19.95 (*0-9663549-5-8*) Holden Pr.

***Regan, Michael D.** The Kaizen Revolution: How to Use Kaizen Events to Implement Lean Manufacturing & Improve Quality, Cost & Delivery. (Illus.). 256p. 2000. 24.95 (*0-9663549-7-4*) Holden Pr.

Regan, Michael J., jt. auth. see Ajmera, Maya.

Regan, Milton C., Jr. Alone Together: Law & the Meanings of Marriage. LC 97-51283. 296p. 1999. text 45.00 (*0-19-511003-X*) OUP.

— Family Law & the Pursuit of Intimacy. LC 92-38948. 304p. (C). 1993. text 45.00 (*0-8147-7430-X*) NYU Pr.

— Family Law & the Pursuit of Intimacy. LC 92-38948. 304p. (C). 1995. pap. text 20.00 (*0-8147-7457-1*) NYU Pr.

Regan, Milton C., Jr., jt. auth. see Richardson, Elizabeth C.

Regan, Milton C., Jr., jt. ed. see Allen, Anita L.

Regan, Nancy. The Institute of Chartered Financial Analysts: A Twenty-Five Year History. (Orig.). (C). 1987. write for info. (*0-935015-00-0*); pap. write for info. (*0-935015-01-9*) Inst Charter Finan Analysts.

***Regan, Pamela C. & Berscheid, Ellen.** Lust: What We Know about Human Sexual Desire. LC 99-6175. 173p. 1999. 49.95 (*0-7619-1792-6*) Sage.

Regan, Pamela C. & Berscheid, Ellen. Lust: What We Know about Human Sexual Desire. LC 99-6175. (Series on Close Relationships). 1999. write for info. (*0-7619-1793-4*) Sage.

Regan, Pat. Watercolor: A Painting Study Guide. (Illus.). 68p. pap. 12.95 (*0-9615826-0-X*) P Regan.

Regan, Patrick. The Torch & the Spear. (Illus.). (Orig.). 1996. pap. 19.95 (*1-898307-72-5*, Pub. by Capall Bann Pubng) Holmes Pub.

Regan, Patrick, jt. auth. see Engelbreit, Mary.

***Regan, Patrick M.** Civil Wars & Foreign Powers: Outside Intervention in Intrastate Conflict. LC 99-59856. (Illus.). 224p. (C). 2000. text 39.50 (*0-472-11125-6*, 11125) U of Mich Pr.

Regan, Patrick M. Organizing Societies for War: The Process & Consequences of Societal Militarization. LC 93-8621. 208p. 1994. 55.00 (*0-275-94670-3*, C4670, Praeger Pubs) Greenwood.

Regan, Peter. Revenge of the Wizards. 156p. 1997. pap. 8.95 (*0-947962-61-1*) Dufour.

***Regan, Peter.** Riverside: Dynamo Rouge. 112p. 2000. pap. 7.95 (*1-901737-21-7*, Pub. by Anvil Books Ltd) Dufour.

Regan, Peter. Riverside: The London Trip. (Illus.). 112p. (YA). (gr. 3 up). 1999. pap. 7.95 (*1-901737-16-0*, Pub. by Anvil Books Ltd) Dufour.

***Regan, Peter.** Riverside Loot! 112p. 2000. pap. 7.95 (*1-901737-19-5*, Pub. by Anvil Books Ltd) Dufour.

Regan, Peter. The Street-League. LC 97-220207. (Riverside Ser.). 112p. 1996. pap. 6.95 (*0-947962-46-8*) Dufour.

— Teen Glory. 144p. 1993. pap. 8.95 (*0-947962-78-6*) Dufour.

— Urban Heroes. 176p. 1995. pap. 8.95 (*0-947962-62-X*) Dufour.

— Young Champions. 160p. 1995. pap. 8.95 (*0-947962-92-1*) Dufour.

Regan, Peter & Myler, Terry. The Croke Park Conspiracy. LC 98-228568. (Riverside Ser.). 112p. 1998. pap. 7.95 (*1-901737-04-7*) Dufour.

Regan, Peter F. & Schultze, Hans G. Education for the Health Professions: Policies for the 1980s. 93p. (Orig.). 1983. pap. text 28.00 (*91-22-00627-3*) Coronet Bks.

Regan, Peter J. & Neuner, Arthur J. Massachusetts Real Estate Principles & Practices. 4th ed. 301p. (C). 1995. 27.00 (*0-9627396-1-8*) Nrth Shr Pr.

Regan, Priscilla M. Legislating Privacy: Technology, Social Values, & Public Policy. LC 94-49544. 1995. 39.95 (*0-8078-2226-4*) U of NC Pr.

Regan, Rhonda, jt. auth. see Avila-Weil, Donna.

Regan, Richard J. Just War: Principles & Cases. LC 95-46533. 247p. 1996. pap. 19.95 (*0-8132-0856-4*) Cath U Pr.

— Just War: Principles & Cases. LC 95-46533. 247p. (C). 1996. text 39.95 (*0-8132-0855-6*) Cath U Pr.

Regan, Richard J., jt. auth. see Aquinas, Thomas, Saint.

Regan, Richard J., jt. auth. see Thomas.

Regan, Richard J., ed. see Aquinas, Thomas, Saint.

Regan, Richard J., tr. see Aquinas, Thomas, Saint.

Regan, Richard J., tr. & intro. see Aquinas, Thomas, Saint.

Regan, Robert D., jt. ed. see Watson, Ken.

Regan, Robert J. The Annual Meeting of Shareholders. 4th ed. (Corporate Practice Ser.: No. 12). 1998. 95.00 (*1-55871-368-9*) BNA.

Regan, S. Kevin. Teen Prayer Services: Twenty Themes for Reflection. LC 92-81797. 80p. (Orig.). 1992. pap. 9.95 (*0-89622-520-8*) Twenty-Third.

Regan, Sandy. Home for Sale by Owner: The FSBO Guide. (Illus.). 1989. pap. 8.95 (*0-317-89466-8*) R & R Pub.

***Regan, Star-Beth.** Sketches from the Attic of My Mind: A Collection of Short Stories. 2000. pap. 7.95 (*0-533-13351-3*) Vantage.

Regan, Stephen. Philip Larkin. LC 97-911. 240p. 1997. pap. 18.95 (*0-312-17349-0*); text 45.00 (*0-312-17348-2*) St Martin.

— The Year's Work in Critical & Cultural Theory, Vol. 1. 256p. 1996. 66.95 (*0-631-18858-4*) Blackwell Pubs.

Regan, Stephen, ed. The Politics of Pleasure. LC 92-19298. (Ideas & Production Ser.). 1992. pap. 34.95 (*0-335-09759-6*) OpUniv Pr.

Regan, Stephen & Treharne, Elaine, eds. The Year's Work in Critical & Cultural Theory, Vol.2. 368p. (C). 1996. 66.95 (*0-631-18859-2*) Blackwell Pubs.

Regan, Stephen D. In Bitter Tempest: The Biography of Admiral Frank Fletcher. LC 93-29772. (Illus.). 304p. 1994. text 44.95 (*0-8138-0778-6*) Iowa St U Pr.

Regan, Steven, ed. The Eagleton Reader. LC 97-16433. 400p. (C). 1997. 66.95 (*0-631-20248-X*); pap. 26.95 (*0-631-20249-8*) Blackwell Pubs.

Regan, Sylvia. Morning Star. pap. 5.95 (*0-8222-1729-5*) Dramatists Play.

Regan, Sylvia. Zelda: Manuscript Edition. 1969. pap. 13.00 (*0-8222-1292-7*) Dramatists Play.

Regan, Timothy E. Keyport. (Images of America Ser.). 1995. pap. 16.99 (*0-7524-0242-0*) Arcadia Publng.

— Keyport, Vol. II. (Images of America Ser.). 1997. pap. 16.99 (*0-7524-0537-3*) Arcadia Publng.

— Keyport in the 20th Century. LC 98-87870. (Images of America Ser.). 1998. write for info. (*0-7385-0016-X*) Arcadia Publng.

— New Brunswick. LC 96-208564. (Images of America Ser.). 1996. pap. 16.99 (*0-7524-0430-X*) Arcadia Publng.

Regan, Tom. Animal Sacrifices: Religious Perspectives on the Use of Animals in Science. LC 85-22093. (Ethics & Action Ser.). 288p. (C). 1987. pap. 18.95 (*0-87722-511-7*) Temple U Pr.

— The Case for Animal Rights. LC 83-1087. (C). 1983. pap. 16.95 (*0-520-05460-1*, CAL 741, Pub. by U CA Pr) Cal Prin Full Svc.

***Regan, Tom.** Defending Animal Rights. LC 00-8708. 2001. write for info. (*0-252-02611-X*) U of Ill Pr.

Regan, Tom. G. E. Moore: The Early Essays. LC 86-6007. 266p. 1986. 37.95 (*0-87722-442-0*) Temple U Pr.

— The Thee Generation: Reflections on the Coming Revolution. 176p. 1991. 27.95 (*0-87722-758-6*); pap. 19.95 (*0-87722-772-1*) Temple U Pr.

Regan, Tom, ed. Earthbound: Introductory Essays in Environmental Ethics. 392p. (C). 1990. reprint ed. pap. text 23.95 (*0-88133-568-1*) Waveland Pr.

— Matters of Life & Death. 3rd ed. LC 92-23158. 416p. (C). 1992. pap. 23.13 (*0-07-051330-9*) McGraw.

Regan, Tom & McCarthy, Colman. The Struggle for Animal Rights. 208p. (Orig.). 1987. pap. 5.95 (*0-9602632-1-7*) ISAR Inc.

Regan, Tom & Singer, Peter Albert David. Animal Rights & Human Obligations. 2nd ed. 288p. (C). 1989. pap. text 39.20 (*0-13-036864-4*) P-H.

Regan, Tom, jt. ed. see VanDeVeer, Donald.

Regan, Vera, ed. Contemporary Approaches to Second Language Acquisition in Social Context Crosslinguistic Perspectives: Crosslinguistic Perspectives. LC 98-173361. 208p. 1998. pap. 29.95 (*1-900621-14-2*) Dufour.

***Regan, William J.** The Maccordion Format: An Integrating Mosaic of American Society. (Illus.). 272p. 2000. write for info. (*0-9701015-0-3*) Pandemic.

Regani, Sarojini. Nizam-British Relations, 1724-1857. (C). 1989. 28.50 (*81-7022-195-1*, Pub. by Concept) S Asia.

Regard, Maurice, jt. auth. see Balzac, Honore de.

Regard, Maurice, ed. see Balzac, Honore de.

Regard, Maurice, ed. see Chateaubriand, Francois-Rene de.

Regardie, Israel. The Art of True Healing: The Unlimited Power of Prayer & Visualization. 2nd ed. Allen, Marc, ed. LC 96-43004. (Illus.). 112p. 1997. reprint ed. pap. 8.95 (*1-57731-012-8*) New Wrld Lib.

— The Complete Golden Dawn System of Magic. LC 83-81664. (Illus.). 1200p. 1991. reprint ed. 59.95 (*1-56184-037-8*) New Falcon Pubns.

— The Eye in the Triangle: An Interpretation of Aleister Crowley. rev. ed. LC 88-83355. 560p. 1993. reprint ed. pap. 18.95 (*1-56184-054-8*) New Falcon Pubns.

— Foundations of Practical Magic. (Illus.). 160p. (Orig.). 1986. pap. 9.95 (*0-85030-315-X*, Pub. by Aqn Pr) Harper SF.

— A Garden of Pomegranates. LC 74-18984. (High Magick Ser.). (Illus.). 160p. 1970. pap. 8.95 (*0-87542-690-5*) Llewellyn Pubns.

— A Garden of Pomegranates: Skrying on the Tree of Life. 3rd rev. ed. Cicero, Chic & Cicero, Sandra T., eds. LC 98-47612. (Illus.). 336p. 1999. 14.95 (*1-56718-141-4*) Llewellyn Pubns.

— The Golden Dawn. 6th rev. ed. LC 86-15247. (Golden Dawn Ser.). (Illus.). 848p. 1986. pap. 29.95 (*0-87542-663-8*) Llewellyn Pubns.

— Healing Energy, Prayer, & Relaxation. rev. ed. LC 82-83292. 80p. 1982. pap. 12.95 (*1-56184-055-6*) New Falcon Pubns.

— Middle Pillar: The Balance Between Mind & Magic. 3rd ed. LC 97-51493. (Illus.). 312p. 1998. pap. text 12.95 (*1-56718-140-6*) Llewellyn Pubns.

— The One Year Manual: Twelve Steps to Spiritual Enlightenment. rev. ed. LC 92-35344. 96p. 1981. reprint ed. pap. 9.95 (*0-87728-489-X*) Weiser.

— The Philosopher's Stone: A Modern Comparative Approach to Alchemy from the Psychological & Magical Points of View. 204p. 1993. reprint ed. pap. 17.95 (*1-56459-282-0*) Kessinger Pub.

— Roll Away the Stone: An Introduction to Aleister Crowleys Essays on the Psychology of Hashish. 249p. 1994. pap. 12.95 (*0-87877-194-8*) Newcastle Pub.

***Regardie, Israel.** The Tree of Life: An Illustrated Study in Magic. Cicero, Chic & Cicero, Sandra Tabatha, eds. (Illus.). 2000. pap. 19.95 (*1-56718-132-5*) Llewellyn Pubns.

Regardie, Israel. Tree of Life, a Study in Magic. LC 70-16403. (Illus.). 284p. 1972. reprint ed. pap. 14.95 (*0-87728-149-1*) Weiser.

— What You Should Know about the Golden Dawn. 6th rev. ed. LC 83-81663. (Illus.). 248p. 1993. pap. 12.95 (*1-56184-064-5*) New Falcon Pubns.

Regardie, Israel & Stephensen, P. R. The Legend of Aleister Crowley. LC 83-81836. 192p. 1983. pap. 14.95 (*1-56184-114-5*) New Falcon Pubns.

Regardie, William. Regardies 1997 Washington Desk Diary. (Illus.). 144p. 1996. 24.95 (*0-9655227-0-9*) Regardie & Regardie Pr.

Regardz, Beth, jt. auth. see Schultz, Joseph.

Regas, jt. auth. see Scavio.

Regas, James. Introductory Astronomy Laboratory Exercises. 3rd abr. ed. 216p. (C). 1997. spiral bd. 29.95 (*0-7872-3784-1*) Kendall-Hunt.

Regas, James L. Introduction to Astronomy Lab Exercises. 320p. (C). 1997. spiral bd. 46.95 (*0-7872-3304-8*) Kendall-Hunt.

Regazzi, John J. & Hines, Theodore C. A Guide to Indexed Periodicals in Religion. LC 75-22277. 328p. 1975. 26.50 (*0-8108-0868-4*) Scarecrow.

Regazzini, G. Italian-English - English-Italian Commercial Dictionary. (ENG & ITA.). 1167p. 1992. 125.00 (*0-7859-9596-X*) Fr & Eur.

Regazzoni, Carlo S., et al. Advanced Video-Based Surveillance Systems. LC 98-45582. (Series in Engineering & Computer Science). 227p. 1998. 115.00 (*0-7923-8392-3*) Kluwer Academic.

Regazzoni, P., jt. ed. see Aebi, M.

***Rege, Ron.** Skibber Bee Bye. (Illus.). 256p. 2000. pap. 18.95 (*0-9665363-8-X*) Highwater Bks.

An Asterisk (*) at the beginning of an entry indicates that the title is appearing for the first time.

R

An Asterisk (*) at the beginning of an entry indicates that the title is appearing for the first time.

R

— Heroes of God-Coloring Book. 1989. pap. text 9.90 (0-88271-186-5) Regina Pr.
— Holy Family. 1994. pap. 25.00 (0-88271-427-9) Regina Pr.
— Infant of Prague. 1993. pap. 25.00 (0-88271-344-2) Regina Pr.
— The Joy of Christmas. 1999. 9.95 (0-88271-675-1) Regina Pr.
— Keep His Passion in Mind. 1994. pap. 6.25 (0-88271-378-7) Regina Pr.
— Life of Jesus, 10 vols. 1998. pap. text 9.90 (0-88271-636-0) Regina Pr.
— Life of Mary, 10 Vols. 1998. pap. text 9.90 (0-88271-637-9) Regina Pr.
— Lord Look Kindly on the Child. 1994. pap. 6.25 (0-88271-348-5) Regina Pr.
— Mother Seton. 1994. pap. 25.00 (0-88271-448-1) Regina Pr.
— My First Book of Catholic Prayers. 1999. 5.95 (0-88271-753-7) Regina Pr.
— Noah & the Ark. 1999. 6.95 (0-88271-645-X) Regina Pr.
— Noah's Ark. 1999. 4.95 (0-88271-671-9); 5.95 (0-88271-712-X) Regina Pr.
— Old Testament for Children. (J). (ps-3). 1.95 (0-88271-044-3) Regina Pr.
— Our Lady Czestochowa. 1994. pap. 25.00 (0-88271-433-3) Regina Pr.
— Our Lady Lourdes. 1994. pap. 25.00 (0-88271-431-7) Regina Pr.
— Our Lady of Guadalupe. 1994. pap. text 25.00 (0-88271-435-X) Regina Pr.
— Our Lady of Mt. Carmel. 1994. pap. 25.00 (0-88271-425-2) Regina Pr.
— Our Lady of Mt. Carmel. 1995. pap. 25.00 (0-88271-434-1) Regina Pr.
— Our Lady of Perpetual Help. 1994. pap. 25.00 (0-88271-398-1) Regina Pr.
— Our Lady of Perpetual Help. 1994. pap. 25.00 (0-88271-444-9) Regina Pr.
— Our Lady of Vladamir. 1994. pap. 25.00 (0-88271-436-8) Regina Pr.
— Precious Moments: Book of Prayers. 1992. 15.95 (0-88271-276-4) Regina Pr.
— Precious Moments: My First Book of Prayers. (J). 1992. 6.95 (0-88271-277-2) Regina Pr.
— Precious Moments Catholic Ed. My First Book of Prayers. (Precious Moments Ser.). (J). 1991. 8.95 (0-88271-275-6) Regina Pr.
— El Rosario. 1993. pap. text 25.00 (0-88271-326-4) Regina Pr.
— Rosary, 10 vols. 1998. pap. text 9.90 (0-88271-633-6) Regina Pr.
— Sacred Heart. 1994. pap. 25.00 (0-88271-430-9) Regina Pr.
— St. Anthony. 1994. pap. 25.00 (0-88271-438-4) Regina Pr.
— St. Martin de Porres. 1994. pap. 25.00 (0-88271-446-5) Regina Pr.
— St. Therese. 1994. pap. 25.00 (0-88271-440-6) Regina Pr.
— Saints, 10 vols., Vol. 1. 1998. pap. text 9.90 (0-88271-634-4) Regina Pr.
— Saints, 10 vols., Vol. 2. 1998. pap. text 9.90 (0-88271-635-2) Regina Pr.
— The Story of Christmas, 10 vols. 1998. pap. text 9.90 (0-88271-640-9) Regina Pr.
— Teach Me Your Ways O Lord. 1994. pap. 6.25 (0-88271-379-5) Regina Pr.
— Thank You, God. 1999. 4.95 (0-88271-672-7) Regina Pr.
— Traditions of Advent for Children. 1999. pap. 2.50 (0-88271-683-2) Regina Pr.
— Way of the Cross, 10 vols. 1998. pap. text 9.90 (0-88271-643-3) Regina Pr.
— Who's Coming to Stay? 1999. 3.95 (0-88271-680-8) Regina Pr.

***Regina Press Staff, ed.** Catholic Bible. 2000. bds. 9.99 (0-88271-751-0) Regina Pr.

Regina Staff. Precious Moments My Guardian Angel. (J). (ps-3). 9.95 (0-88271-288-8) Regina Pr.
— Precious Moments Prayers for Boys & Girls. (J). (ps-3). bds. 3.95 (0-88271-291-8) Regina Pr.

Reginald, Charles, jt. auth. see Shrader, Ed.

Reginald, Jorge S. Smoking: Medical Subject Analysis & Research Guide with Bibliography. LC 84-45743. 150p. 1987. 47.50 (0-88164-270-3); pap. 44.50 (0-88164-271-1) ABBE Pubs Assn.

Reginald, R. Contemporary Science Fiction Authors. LC 74-16517. (Science Fiction Ser.). (Illus.). 358p. 1976. reprint ed. 26.95 (0-405-06332-6) Ayer.
— Science Fiction & Fantasy Literature Supplement, '87. 87th ed. 140.00 (0-8103-5511-6) Gale.

Reginald, R. & Elliot, Jeffrey M. If J. F. K. Had Lived: A Political Scenario. LC 81-19516. (Borgo Political Scenarios Ser.: Vol. 1). 64p. 1982. pap. 13.00 (0-89370-255-2) Millefleurs.
— Tempest in a Teapot: The Falkland Islands War. LC 83-8807. (Stokvis Studies in Historical Chronology & Thought: No. 3). (Illus.). 173p. 1983. pap. 21.00 (0-89370-267-6) Millefleurs.

Reginald, R. & Melville, Douglas, eds. Dreamers of Dreams: An Anthology of Fantasy. LC 77-84280. (Lost Race & Adult Fantasy Ser.). (Illus.). 1978. lib. bdg. 44.95 (0-405-11017-0) Ayer.
— Lost Race & Adult Fantasy Fiction Series, 69 bks., Set. (Illus.). 1978. lib. bdg. 2018.00 (0-405-10950-4) Ayer.
— They: Three Parodies of H. Rider Haggard's She. LC 77-84277. (Lost Race & Adult Fantasy Ser.). (Illus.). 242p. 1978. lib. bdg. 54.95 (0-405-11015-4) Ayer.
— Worlds of Never: An Original Anthology. LC 77-84278. (Lost Race & Adult Fantasy Ser.). (Illus.). 414 p. 1978. lib. bdg. 41.95 (0-405-11016-2) Ayer.

Reginald, R. & Menville, Douglas A., eds. Ancestral Voices: An Anthology of Early Science Fiction. LC 74-16508. (Science Fiction Ser.). 1977. reprint ed. 23.95 (0-405-06305-9) Ayer.
— Ancient Haunting: An Orginal Anthology. LC 75-46269. (Supernatural & Occult Fiction Ser.). (Illus.). 1976. lib. bdg. 39.95 (0-405-08163-4) Ayer.
— The Boyhood Days of Guy Fawkes: Or, the Conspirators of Old London. LC 75-46257. (Supernatural & Occult Fiction Ser.). (Illus.). (YA). (gr. 7 up). 1976. reprint ed. lib. bdg. 20.95 (0-405-08116-2) Ayer.
— King Solomon's Children: Some Parodies of H. Rider Haggard. LC 77-84281. (Lost Race & Adult Fantasy Ser.). (Illus.). 1978. lib. bdg. 54.95 (0-405-11018-9) Ayer.
— Phantasmagoria: An Original Anthology. LC 75-46292. (Supernatural & Occult Fiction Ser.). 1976. lib. bdg. 34.95 (0-405-08152-9) Ayer.
— R. I. P. Five Stories of the Supernatural. LC 75-1539. (Supernatural & Occult Fiction Ser.). (Illus.). 253p. 1976. lib. bdg. 26.95 (0-405-08425-0) Ayer.
— The Spectre Bridegroom & Other Horrors: Original Anthology. LC 75-46305. (Supernatural & Occult Fiction Ser.). (Illus.). 292 p. 1976. lib. bdg. 25.95 (0-405-08165-0) Ayer.
— Supernatural & Occult Fiction Series, 63 bks., Set. 1976. lib. bdg. 1516.50 (0-405-08107-3) Ayer.

Reginald, R., et al. Futurevisions: The New Golden Age of the Science Fiction Film. (Illus.). 192p. 1985. pap. 23.00 (0-89370-699-X) Millefleurs.

Reginald, R., jt. auth. see Menville, Douglas A.
Reginald, R., ed. see Ainsworth, William H.
Reginald, R., ed. see Ames, Joseph B.
Reginald, R., ed. see Anderson, Olof W.
Reginald, R., ed. see Arlen, Michael J.
Reginald, R., ed. see Arnold, Edwin L.
Reginald, R., ed. see Atkins, Frank.
Reginald, R., ed. see Balzac, Honore de.
Reginald, R., ed. see Bennet, Robert A.
Reginald, R., ed. see Bennett, Gertrude B.
Reginald, R., ed. see Benson, Edward F.
Reginald, R., ed. see Blackwood, Algernon.
Reginald, R., ed. see Boothby, Guy.
Reginald, R., ed. see Bramah, Ernest.
Reginald, R., ed. see Bruce, Muriel.
Reginald, R., ed. see Burrage, Alfred McLelland.
Reginald, R., ed. see Burton, Alice E.
Reginald, R., ed. see Campbell, Praed.
Reginald, R., ed. see Carew, Henry.
Reginald, R., ed. see Carnegie, James.
Reginald, R., ed. see Chambers, Robert W.
Reginald, R., ed. see Channing, Mark.
Reginald, R., ed. see Chester, George R.
Reginald, R., ed. see Clock, Herbert & Boetzel, Eric.
Reginald, R., ed. see Coblentz, Stanton A.
Reginald, R., ed. see Constantine, Murray.
Reginald, R., ed. see Cook, William W.
Reginald, R., ed. see Coppard, Alfred E.
Reginald, R., ed. see Cowan, Frank.
Reginald, R., ed. see Crawford, Francis M.
Reginald, R., ed. see Dalton.
Reginald, R., ed. see De Comeau, Alexander.
Reginald, R., ed. see De La Mare, Walter J.
Reginald, R., ed. see Doughty, Francis W.
Reginald, R., ed. see Dunn, Allan J.
Reginald, R., ed. see Eddison, Eric R.
Reginald, R., ed. see Erckmann, Emile & Erckmann, Alexandre.
Reginald, R., ed. see Ewers, Hanns H.
Reginald, R., ed. see Fielding, Henry.
Reginald, R., ed. see Fleckenstein, Alfred C.
Reginald, R., ed. see Fyne, Neal.
Reginald, R., ed. see Gautier, Theophile.
Reginald, R., ed. see Gillmore, Inez H.
Reginald, R., ed. see Gompertz, Martin L.
Reginald, R., ed. see Green, Fitzhugh.
Reginald, R., ed. see Gregory, Jackson.
Reginald, R., ed. see Griffith, George.
Reginald, R., ed. see Guthrie, Thomas A.
Reginald, R., ed. see Hadley, George.
Reginald, R., ed. see Haggard, H. Rider.
Reginald, R., ed. see Haldane, Charlotte.
Reginald, R., ed. see Harris, Burland.
Reginald, R., ed. see Hartmann, Franz.
Reginald, R., ed. see Harvey, William F.
Reginald, R., ed. see Hearn, Lafcadio.
Reginald, R., ed. see Hecht, Ben.
Reginald, R., ed. see Heron-Allen, Edward.
Reginald, R., ed. see Hodder, William R.
Reginald, R., ed. see Holmes, Oliver W.
Reginald, R., ed. see Housman, Clemence.
Reginald, R., ed. see Ingram, Elanor M.
Reginald, R., ed. see James, Montague R.
Reginald, R., ed. see Keller, David H.
Reginald, R., ed. see Kingsmill, Hugh, pseud.
Reginald, R., ed. see Knowles, Vernon.
Reginald, R., ed. see Kummer, Frederic A.
Reginald, R., ed. see Large, E. C.
Reginald, R., ed. see Le Queux, William T.
Reginald, R., ed. see Leroux, Gaston.
Reginald, R., ed. see Lindsay, David.
Reginald, R., ed. see Linklater, Eric.
Reginald, R., ed. see London, Jack.
Reginald, R., ed. see Machen, Arthur.
Reginald, R., ed. see MacKay, Mary.
Reginald, R., ed. see Marrat, Florence.
Reginald, R., ed. see Marshall, Sidney J.
Reginald, R., ed. see McHugh, Vincent.
Reginald, R., ed. see Merritt, Abraham.
Reginald, R., ed. see Moresby, Lily & Beck, Adams.
Reginald, R., ed. see Morris, Kenneth.
Reginald, R., ed. see Murray, G. G.
Reginald, R., ed. see Odell, Eric.
Reginald, R., ed. see O'Donnell, Elliot.
Reginald, R., ed. see Oliver, George.
Reginald, R., ed. see Owen, Frank F.
Reginald, R., ed. see Paget, Violet.
Reginald, R., ed. see Paine, Albert B.
Reginald, R., ed. see Phillpotts, Eden.
Reginald, R., ed. see Potter, Margaret H.
Reginald, R., ed. see Powys, John Cowper.
Reginald, R., ed. see Reynolds, George W.
Reginald, R., ed. see Rolfe, Frederick W., et al.
Reginald, R., ed. see Rosynyaine, J. H.
Reginald, R., ed. see Russell, William C.
Reginald, R., ed. see Savile, Frank.
Reginald, R., ed. see Scott, G. Firth.
Reginald, R., ed. see Sheldon-Williams, Miles.
Reginald, R., ed. see Sicard, Clara.
Reginald, R., ed. see Sinclair, Upton.
Reginald, R., ed. see Stewart, Mary L.
Reginald, R., ed. see Todd, Ruthven.
Reginald, R., ed. see Viereck, George S.
Reginald, R., ed. see Vivan, Charles E.
Reginald, R., ed. see Vivian, Charles E.
Reginald, R., ed. see Ward, Arthur Henry Sarsfield.
Reginald, R., ed. see Wells, H. G.
Reginald, R., ed. see Whiting, Sydney.

***Reginald, Robert.** Katydid & Other Critters. 256p. 2000. pap. 15.00 (0-8095-0004-3) Millefleurs.

Reginald, Robert. Xenograffiti: Essays on Fantastic Literature. LC 96-35246. (Evans Studies in the Philosophy & Criticism of Literature: No. 33). 224p. 1996. pap. 23.00 (0-8095-1900-3) Millefleurs.

Reginald, Robert, ed. Science Fiction & Fantasy Literature, 1975-1991, 2 vols. 86th ed. 1200p. 1992. 199.00 (0-8103-1825-3) Gale.

Reginald, Robert & Burgess, Mary A. Index Litteratus, 2 vols., Set. LC 96-3521. (Literary Guides Ser.: No. 11). Date not set. pap. write for info. (0-89370-903-4) Millefleurs.
— Index Litteratus, Vol. 1. LC 96-3521. (Literary Guides Ser.: No. 11). Date not set. pap. write for info. (0-89370-904-2) Millefleurs.
— Index Litteratus, Vol. 2. LC 96-3521. (Literary Guides Ser.: No. 11). Date not set. pap. write for info. (0-89370-905-0) Millefleurs.

Reginald, Robert & Burgess, Mary A., compiled by. BP 250: An Annotated Bibliography of the First 250 Publications of the Borgo Press, 1975-1996. LC 96-1744. (Borgo Literary Guides Ser.: No. 10). 192p. 1996. pap. 21.00 (0-8095-1206-8) Millefleurs.

Reginald, Robert & Slusser, George E., eds. Yesterday or Tomorrow? Questions of Vision in the Fiction of Robert A. Heinlein. (Starmont Studies in Literary Criticism: No. 5). 160p. Date not set. reprint ed. lib. bdg. 19.95 (0-89370-977-8) Millefleurs.

Reginald, Robert, jt. auth. see Elliot, Jeffrey M.
Reginald, Robert, jt. auth. see Kurtz, Katherine.
Reginald, Robert, jt. auth. see Mallett, Daryl F.
Reginato, Antonio J., jt. auth. see Schumacher, Ralph H.
Reginato, R. J., jt. auth. see Sposito, G.
Regine, Birute, jt. auth. see Lewin, Roger.

Reginer, Victor, et al. Best Practices in Assisted Living: Innovations in Design, Management & Financing. (Illus.). 166p. (C). 1991. 18.00 (1-881010-25-2) USC Andrus Geron.

Regini, Marino. The Future of Labour Movements. (International Sociology Ser.: Vol. 43). (Illus.). 272p. 1992. pap. text 26.95 (0-8039-7977-0) Sage.
— The Future of Labour Movements. (International Sociology Ser.: Vol. 43). (Illus.). 272p. (C). 1992. text 69.95 (0-8039-8761-7) Sage.
— Uncertain Boundaries: The Social & Political Construction of European Economies. (Cambridge Studies in Comparative Politics). (Illus.). 176p. (C). 1995. text 59.95 (0-521-47371-3) Cambridge U Pr.

Regini, Marino, et al, eds. From Tellers to Sellers: Changing Employment Relations in Banks. LC 99-25719. (Illus.). 432p. 1999. 39.95 (0-262-18193-2) MIT Pr.

Regini, Marino, jt. auth. see Esping-Andersen, Gsta.
Regini, Marino, jt. ed. see Esping-Andersen, Gosta.
Regini, Marino, jt. ed. see Lange, Peter.

***Regio, Jose.** The Flame-Coloured Dress. 352p. 2000. pap. 19.95 (1-85754-386-6, Pub. by Carcanet Pr) Paul & Co Pubs.

Regional Bureau for Europe & the CIS of the United. The Shrinking State: Governance & Human Development in Eastern Europe & the Commonwealth of Independent States. 125p. 1997. pap. 25.00 (92-1-126077-9, BF713) UN.

Regional Bureau for Europe & the CIS Staff. Human Development under Transition: Europe & CIS. 244p. 1997. pap. 35.00 (92-1-126076-0, BF713) UN.

Regional Bureau for Europe & the Commonwealth of I. Human Development in Europe & the CIS: Summaries of the 1995 National Human Development Reports for RBEC Programme Countries. (Development Programme Ser.). 165p. 1996. pap. 35.00 (92-1-126079-5, BF713) UN.

Regional Kidney Disease Program, Education Departm. The Patient's Guide to Understandng Hemodialysis. rev. ed. 150p. 1986. reprint ed. ring bd. 30.00 (1-56488-005-2) Dialyrn.

Regional Kidney Disease Program, Interstate Divisi. Home Hemodialysis Training. 194p. 1980. ring bd. 25.00 (1-56488-007-9) Dialyrn.

Regional Laboratory for Education Improvement Staf. What about Learning? 17p. 1993. pap. text. write for info. incl. VHS (1-878234-05-6) Reg Lab Educ IOT NE Isls.

Regional Plan Association Staff. A Framework for Transit Planning in the New York Region. (RPA Bulletin Ser.: No. 131). 130p. 1986. pap. 10.00 (0-318-21808-9) Regional Plan Assn.
— From Plan to Reality, 3 vols. LC 73-14026. (Metropolitan America Ser.). (Illus.). 330p. 1974. reprint ed. 33.95 (0-405-05437-8) Ayer.
— Jamaica Center, 1987: An Office Enterprise Zone. (RPA Bulletin Ser.: No. 132). 53p. 1986. 10.00 (0-318-16370-5) Regional Plan Assn.
— The Open Space Imperative I: Greenspaces & Greenways. (Illus.). 1987. pap. 5.00 (0-938085-00-X) Regional Plan Assn.
— The Open Space Imperative II: II: Where the Pavement Ends. 1987. 5.00 (0-938085-03-4) Regional Plan Assn.

Regional Plan Association Staff, jt. auth. see Citizens Crime Commission of New York City Staff.
Regional Plan Association Staff, jt. auth. see Citizens Crime Commission of New York Staff.

Regional Research Conference on Differential Games. Differential Games & Control Theory: Proceedings of a National Science Foundation-Conference Board of the Mathematical Sciences Regional Research Conference, Held at University of Rhode Island, Kingston, Rhode Island, June 4-8, 1973: the Invited Lectures & Contributed Papers. LC 74-21593. (Lecture Notes in Pure & Applied Mathematics Ser.: No. 10). 422p. reprint ed. pap. 130.90 (0-7837-4774-8, 204452900003) Bks Demand.

Regional Seminar on Distance Education Staff & Asian Development Bank Staff. Distance Education for Primary School Teachers: Papers & Proceedings of the Regional Seminar on Distance Education. LC 97-947321. ii, 416 p. 1997. write for info. (971-561-124-9) Asian Devel Bank.

Regional Workshop on Privatization & Financing of Municipalities in the Eastern Africa Sub-Region Staff, et al. Report of the Regional Workshop on Privatization & Financing of Municipalities in the Eastern Africa Sub-Region. LC 98-982861. iii, 57p. 1998. write for info. (92-1-131377-5) UN.

Regis, Atticus, jt. auth. see Fisher, Stephen.

Regis, Ed. The Biology of Doom: The History of America's Secret Germ Warfare Project. LC 99-15024. 244p. 1999. 25.00 (0-8050-5764-1) H Holt & Co.
— The Biology of Doom: The History of America's Secret Germ Warfare Project. 272p. 2000. pap. 15.00 (0-8050-5765-X, Owl) H Holt & Co.
— Great Mambo Chicken & the Transhuman Condition: Science Slightly Over the Edge. 1990. 18.22 (0-201-09258-1) Addison-Wesley.
— Great Mambo Chicken & the Transhuman Condition: Science Slightly Over the Edge. 288p. 1991. pap. 16.00 (0-201-56751-2) Addison-Wesley.
— Nano: The Emerging Science of Nanotechnology. 325p. (C). 1998. pap. text 15.00 (0-7881-5714-0) DIANE Pub.
— Nano: The Emerging Science of Nanotechnology. LC 94-35378. 1995. 23.95 (0-316-73858-1) Little.
— Nano: The Emerging Science of Nanotechnology. 1996. pap. 14.95 (0-614-97755-X) Little.

***Regis, Ed.** Virus Ground Zero. 256p. 1998. pap. 14.00 (0-671-02325-X, Pocket Books) PB.
— Virus Ground Zero: Stalking the Killer Viruses with the Center for Disease Control. 244p. 2000. reprint ed. text 23.00 (0-7881-6974-2) DIANE Pub.

Regis, Ed. Virus Ground Zero: Stalking the Killer Viruses with the Centers for Disease Control. 244p. 1996. 23.00 (0-671-55361-5, PB Hardcover) PB.

Regis, Edward. Who Got Einstein's Office? Eccentricity & Genius at the Institute for Advanced Study. LC 87-11568. (Illus.). 320p. 1988. pap. 15.00 (0-201-12278-2) Addison-Wesley.

Regis, Edward, Jr., ed. Gewirth's Ethical Rationalism: Critical Essays with a Reply by Alan Gewirth. LC 83-17965. 274p. (C). 1984. lib. bdg. 36.00 (0-226-70691-5) U Ch Pr.
— Gewirth's Ethical Rationalism: Critical Essays with a Reply by Alan Gewirth. LC 83-17965. 272p. (C). 1997. pap. text 15.00 (0-226-70692-3) U Ch Pr.

Regis, Emelina G. Dalawang Dula Ni Clarissa Sa Ecolohiya. (TAG.). 77p. (Orig.). 1993. pap. 6.50 (971-10-0504-2, Pub. by New Day Pub) Cellar.

Regis, Franki V., jt. auth. see Regis, Marc Y., 1st.
Regis, Iester M., ed. see Dillon, Helen M.
Regis, Iester M., ed. see Edwards, Randi & Edwards, Stevie.

Regis, Louis. The Political Calypso: True Opposition in Trinidad & Tabago, 1962-1987. LC 97-37804. 320p. 1998. 49.95 (0-8130-1580-4) U Press Fla.

Regis, Louis, jt. auth. see Roulston, Christine.

Regis, Louis-Marie. St. Thomas & Epistemology. (Aquinas Lectures). 1946. 15.00 (0-87462-110-0) Marquette.

Regis, Marc Y., 1st & Regis, Franki V. Deadly Road to Democracy. LC 98-65802. (Illus.). 192p. (gr. 7-12). 1998. 20.00 (0-9663952-0-4) JukeJoint Pub.

Regis, Margaret, jt. auth. see Kimmett, Larry.

Regis, Mark. Haiti Through My Eyes: The Poems of Marc Yves Regis. 72p. (Orig.). 1996. pap. 10.00 (1-57502-251-6) Morris Pubng.

***Regis, Pamela.** Describing Early America: Bartram, Jefferson, Crevecoeur, & the Influence of Natural History. LC 98-47416. 1999. pap. text 14.95 (0-8122-1686-5) U of Pa Pr.

Regis, Pamela. Describing Early America: Bartram, Jefferson, Crevecoeur, & the Rhetoric of Natural History. LC 91-28145. 189p. 1992. lib. bdg. 30.00 (0-87580-166-8) N Ill U Pr.

An Asterisk (*) at the beginning of an entry indicates that the title is appearing for the first time.

Register, L. B., tr. see Alvarez, A., et al.

Register, Alvaretta K., compiled by. Index to the 1830 Census of Georgia. LC 73-22267. 520p. 1999. reprint ed. pap. 38.50 (*0-8063-0609-2*) Clearfield Co.

Register, Charles A., et al. Canadian Economic Issues. 512p. (C). 1997. per. 52.95 (*0-256-20993-6*, Irwn McGrw-H) McGrw-H Hghr Educ.

— The Economics of Social Issues: Wall Street Journal Edition (With Study Guide) 12th ed. (C). 1996. text 56.50 (*0-256-23636-4*, Irwn McGrw-H) McGrw-H Hghr Educ.

Register, Cheri. Are Those Kids Yours? American Families with Children Adopted from Other Countries. 250p. 1990. 24.95 (*0-02-925750-6*) Free Pr.

— The Chronic Illness Experience: Embracing the Imperfect Life. LC 99-32734. 316p. 1999. pap. 15.00 (*1-56838-346-0*) Hazelden.

***Register, Cheri.** Packinghouse Daughter: A Memoir. LC 00-40214. 2000. pap. write for info. (*0-87351-392-4*) Minn Hist.

Register, Cheri, ed. see Rask, Mark.

Register, George & Gattis, L. S. Basic Coin Collecting for Pathfinders. (Illus.). 20p. (Orig.). 1987. pap., teacher ed. 9.95 (*0-936241-14-4*) Cheetah Pub.

— Basic Stamp Collecting. (Illus.). 20p. (Orig.). (YA). 1987. pap., teacher ed. 5.00 (*0-936241-13-6*) Cheetah Pub.

Register, James. Shadows of Old New Orleans. 1967. 12.50 (*0-87511-097-5*) Claitors.

Register, Jane. Blessed Assurance. 133p. (Orig.). 1993. pap. 12.95 (*1-880994-09-7*) Mt Olive Coll Pr.

— He's My Lord. 8p. 1993. 7.50 (*1-880994-27-5*) Mt Olive Coll Pr.

Register, Layton B. & Brunsken, E., eds. The Science of Legal Method. 1977. lib. bdg. 59.95 (*0-8490-2571-0*) Gordon Pr.

Register, Layton B., jt. tr. see Bruncken, Ernest.

Register, Layton B., tr. see Calisse, Carlo.

Register, Richard. Ecocity Berkeley: Building Cities for a Healthy Future. (Illus.). 140p. 1987. pap. 16.95 (*1-55643-009-4*) North Atlantic.

Regitz. Multiple Bonds & Low Coordination in Phosphorous Chemistry. 125.00 (*0-86577-380-7*) Thieme Med Pubs.

Reglar, Stephen, jt. auth. see Brugger, Bill.

Regler, David. Identifying Guide to Mushrooms. 80p. 1994. 6.98 (*0-7858-0048-4*) Bk Sales Inc.

Regler, Eva M. Postmoderne Textpraxis Im Heitigen Frankreich Am Beispiel von Denis Roche. 291p. 1997. 54.95 (*3-631-30728-4*) P Lang Pubng.

Regler, Margaret & Hoff, Rhoda. Uneasy Neighbors: Cuba & the United States. (International Affairs Ser.). 1997. lib. bdg. 24.00 (*0-531-11326-4*) Watts.

Regli, Brian. Wireless: Strategically Liberalizing the Telecommunications Market. LC 97-5611. (Telecommunications Ser.). viii, 287p. 1997. pap. 32.50 (*0-8058-2582-7*); text 69.95 (*0-8058-2581-9*) L Erlbaum Assocs.

Regli, Phil. Collector's Guide to Sports Illustrated & Sports Publications. 1999. pap. text 19.95 (*1-887432-72-8*) Beckett Pubns.

— The Collector's Guide to Sports Publications & Sports Illustrated. 1998. pap. text 19.95 (*1-887432-49-3*) Beckett Pubns.

Regli, Phil & Prothero, Steve. Collectors' Guide to Sports Illustrated. 152p. (Orig.). 1994. pap. 12.95 (*0-9655697-0-5*, PR-CGSP-001) P&R Pubns.

Regli, Philip. Collectors' Guide to Sports Illustrated & Sports Publications. 2nd rev. ed. LC 97-120743. 224p. 1996. pap. 19.95 (*0-9655697-1-3*, PR-CGSP-002) P&R Pubns.

Regli, Robert B., jt. auth. see Swami Rama.

Regli, Robert S. Kona Kai Farms Guide to the Kona Coast: A Coffee Lover's Guide to the Vacation Pleasures of the Kona Coast & the Big Island of Hawaii. 225p. (Orig.). 1995. pap. 8.95 (*0-9646128-0-1*) Kona Kai Farms.

Reglin, Gary L. Achievement for African-American Students: Strategies for the Diverse Classroom. LC 96-138479. 119p. (Orig.). 1995. pap. 21.95 (*1-879639-40-8*) Natl Educ Serv.

— At Risk "Parent & Family" School Involvement: Strategies for Low Income Families & African-American Families of Unmotivated & Underachieving Students. LC 93-19838. 128p. (C). 1993. 33.95 (*0-398-05877-6*) C C Thomas.

— At Risk "Parent & Family" School Involvement: Strategies for Low Income Families & African-American Families Unmotivated & Underachieving Students. 128p. 1993. pap. 20.95 (*0-398-06340-0*) C C Thomas.

— Motivating Low-Achieving Students: A Special Focus on Unmotivated & Underachieving African American Students. 190p. 1993. pap. 33.95 (*0-398-06341-9*); text 48.95 (*0-398-05852-0*) C C Thomas.

Regling, Gunter, ed. Wolff's Law & Connective Tissue Regulation: Modern Interdisciplinary Comments on Wolff's Law of Connective Tissue Regulation & Rational Understanding of Common Clinical Problems. LC 93-20493. 1993. 121.55 (*3-11-013909-X*) De Gruyter.

Regmi, G. P. Industrial Growth in Nepal: A Sectoral & Regional Analysis. 1994. pap. 53.00 (*0-7855-0454-0*, Pub. by Ratna Pustak Bhandar) St Mut.

Regmi, J. C. A Glossary of Himalayan Buddhism. 1994. pap. 60.00 (*0-7855-0445-1*, Pub. by Ratna Pustak Bhandar) St Mut.

Regmi, Jagdish C. A Glossary of Himalayan Buddhism. LC 94-902192. (Illus.). xvi, 212p. 1994. 20.00 (*81-85693-28-5*, Pub. by Nirala Pubns) Nataraj Bks.

***Regmi, M. C.** Landownership in Nepal. 1999. pap. 185.00 (*0-7855-7605-3*) St Mut.

— A Study in Neapli Economic History. 1999. 120.00 (*0-7855-7645-2*) St Mut.

Regmi, Mahesh C. Land Tenure & Taxation in Nepal. 1978. 150.00 (*0-7855-0247-5*, Pub. by Ratna Pustak Bhandar); 150.00 (*0-7855-0316-1*, Pub. by Ratna Pustak Bhandar) St Mut.

— Land Tenure & Taxation in Nepal: Mahesh Chandra Regmi, 4 vols. enl. rev. ed. 851p. (C). 1989. reprint ed. 350.00 (*0-89771-108-4*, Pub. by Ratna Pustak Bhandar) St Mut.

Regmi, Murari P., ed. The Himalayan Mind: A Nepalese Investigation. (Illus.). xiv, 240p. 1994. 20.00 (*81-85693-29-3*, Pub. by Nirala Pubns) Nataraj Bks.

Regmi, Rishikershab R. Kathmandu, Patan & Bhaktapur: An Archaeological Anthropology of the Royal Cities of the Kathmandu Valley. (C). 1993. 36.00 (*0-7855-0187-8*, Pub. by Ratna Pustak Bhandar) St Mut.

Regmi, Rishikeshab R. The Dhimals Miraculour Migrants of Himalyan Anthropological Study of a Nepalese Ethnic Group. (C). 1991. text 90.00 (*0-7855-0133-9*, Pub. by Ratna Pustak Bhandar) St Mut.

— Kathmandu, Patan & Bhaktapur: An Archaeological Anthropology of the Royal Cities of the Kathmandu Valley. 109p. 1993. 13.00 (*81-85693-30-7*, Pub. by Nirala Pubns) Nataraj Bks.

Regnard, C. & Hockley, J. M. Flow Diagrams in Advanced Cancer & Other Disease. 112p. 1996. pap. text 19.95 (*0-340-61389-0*, Pub. by E A) OUP.

Regnard, Claud G. & Tempest, Sue. Guide to Symptom Control in Advanced Disease. 4th ed. LC 98-155044. 80p. 1998. pap. text 17.50 (*1-898507-38-4*) Buttrwrth-Heinemann.

Regnart, Jacob, et al. Leise Settings of the Renaissance & Reformation Era. Riedel, Johannes, ed. (Recent Researches in Music of the Renaissance Ser.: Vol. RRR35). (Illus.). xxvi, 100p. 1980. pap. 40.00 (*0-89579-130-7*, RRR35) A-R Eds.

Regnauld, B. The Foot. Elson, Reginald A., tr. from FRE. (Illus.). 705p. 1986. 430.00 (*0-387-13222-8*) Spr-Verlag.

Regnault, Lucien. Day-to-Day Lives of the Desert Fathers in Fourth-Century Egypt. LC 98-45678. 1998. pap. 24.95 (*1-879007-34-7*) St Bedes Pubns.

Regnault, Paule & Daniel, Rollin K. Aesthetic Plastic Surgery: Principles & Techniques. 800p. 1984. 230.00 (*0-316-73851-4*, Little Brwn Med Div) Lppncott W & W.

Regner, Hermann, ed. Music for Children, 3 vols., 1. (Orff-Schulwerk Ser.). 1977. pap. 24.95 (*0-930448-12-X*, STAP012) Eur-Am Music.

— Music for Children, 3 vols., 2. (Orff-Schulwerk Ser.). 1977. pap. 39.95 (*0-930448-00-6*, STAP006) Eur-Am Music.

— Music for Children, 3 vols., 3. (Orff-Schulwerk Ser.). 1977. pap. 39.95 (*0-930448-08-1*, STAP008) Eur-Am Music.

Regnery, Henry. The Cliff Dwellers: A History of a Chicago Cultural Institution. (Illus.). 86p. 1990. text 20.00 (*0-924772-08-5*) CH Bookworks.

— Creative Chicago: From the Chap-Book to the University. LC 93-11130. 1993. 25.00 (*0-924772-24-7*) CH Bookworks.

— A Few Reasonable Words: Selected Writings. 348p. 1996. 19.95 (*1-882926-13-7*) ISI Books.

— Memoirs of a Dissident Publisher. LC 78-22269. 260p. 1979. pap. 9.95 (*0-89526-802-7*) Regnery Pub.

***Regnery, Henry.** Perfect Sowing: Reflections of a Bookman. Nelson, Jeffrey, ed. 406p. 1999. 24.95 (*1-882926-32-3*) ISI Books.

Regnery Publishing Staff. Cox Report: The Report of the Select Committee on U.S. National Security & Military/Commercial. 1999. pap. text 18.95 (*0-89526-262-2*) Regnery Pub.

Regnier, Adolphe. Lexique de la Langue de la Bruyere. lxxi, 380p. 1970. reprint ed. write for info. (*0-318-71399-3*) G Olms Pubs.

— Lexique de la Langue de Malherbe. lxxxvii, 680p. 1970. reprint ed. write for info. (*0-318-71400-0*) G Olms Pubs.

Regnier, Fred E., jt. ed. see Gooding.

Regnier, Gerard. Treasures of Musee Picasso: Mini Edition. 1998. pap. text 11.95 (*0-7892-0576-9*) Abbeville Pr.

— Treasures of the Musee Picasso. (Tiny Folios Ser.). (Illus.). 320p. 1996. pap. 11.95 (*1-55859-836-7*) Abbeville Pr.

Regnier, John, ed. see Budreck, Frank.

***Regnier, Katherine Frances & Regnier, Linda Black.** Best Easy Day Hikes: Santa Fe. LC 99-29378. (Illus.). 96p. 1999. pap. 6.95 (*1-56044-700-1*) Falcon Pub Inc.

Regnier, Linda Black, jt. auth. see Regnier, Katherine Frances.

Regnier, Paul, jt. auth. see Spillane, Robert R.

Regnier, Philippe. Singapore: City State in South-East Asia. 258p. (C). 1992. text 31.00 (*0-8248-1406-1*); pap. text 14.25 (*0-8248-1407-X*) UH Pr.

Regnier, Victor. Assisted Living Housing for the Elderly: Design Innovations from the United States & Europe. 212p. 1993. 54.95 (*0-471-28423-8*, VNR) Wiley.

— Assisted Living Housing for the Elderly: Innovations in Design & Planning. LC 92-43118. (Illus.). 208p. 1993. text 46.95 (*0-442-00702-7*, VNR) Wiley.

— Housing the Aged: Design Directives & Policy Considerations. Pynoos, Jon, ed. 517p. 1987. 65.00 (*0-444-01012-2*) P-H.

Regnier, Victor, et al. Assisted Living For the Aged & Frail: Innovations in Design, Management, & Financing. LC 93-38639. 271p. 1995. 39.00 (*0-231-08276-2*) Col U Pr.

Regniers, Beatrice S. De, see De Regniers, Beatrice S.

Regniers, Beatrice Schenk De, see Schenk De Regniers, Beatrice.

Regnon, Theodore De. Etudes De Theologie Positive Sur la Sainte Trinite: Theories Grecques Des Processions Divines. LC 80-2363. (Troisieme Ser., II). reprint ed. 67.00 (*0-404-18915-6*) AMS Pr.

Regnot, Franz, tr. see Nachman of Breslov.

Rego, Paul. Little Bits about . . . America Online3 for Macintosh. (Little Bits Ser.). (Illus.). 209p. 1996. spiral bd. 19.95 (*0-945876-11-4*) Insight Data.

— Little Bits about . . . How to Buy a Computer. Rego, Sylvia, ed. (Little Bits Ser.). (Illus.). 131p. 1996. spiral bd. 9.95 (*0-945876-09-2*) Insight Data.

— Little Bits about . . . Macintosh Resources. (Little Bits Ser.). 48p. 1996. spiral bd. 2.95 (*0-945876-10-6*) Insight Data.

Rego, Paula, jt. auth. see Morrison, Blake.

Rego, Richard J. The Gift Beyond Compare. 140p. 1996. pap. 7.95 (*1-885845-26-X*) Leaflet Missal.

Rego, Sylvia, ed. see Rego, Paul.

Regoeczi, Erwin. Iodine-Labeled Plasma Protein, Vol. IIA. (Illus.). 176p. 1987. 102.00 (*0-8493-6557-0*, CRC Reprint) Franklin.

— Iodine-Labeled Plasma Protein, Vol. IIB. (Illus.). 144p. 1987. 86.00 (*0-8493-6558-9*, CRC Reprint) Franklin.

Regoeczi, Erwin, ed. Iodine-Labeled Plasma Proteins, Vol. I. LC 96-7564. (Illus.). 240p. 1984. 135.00 (*0-8493-6556-2*, QP99, CRC Reprint) Franklin.

— Iodine-Labeled Plasma Proteins, Vol. 2. (Illus.). 1987. 322.00 (*0-8493-6555-4*, QP99, CRC Reprint) Franklin.

Regoli. Delinquency in Society. 4th ed. LC 99-18928. 512p. 1999. pap. 69.06 (*0-07-228603-2*) McGraw.

Regoli, Robert M. Criminal Justice. LC 95-16937. (Illus.). 813p. 1995. 58.00 (*0-02-399181-X*, Macmillan Coll) P-H.

Regoli, Robert M. & Hewitt, John D. Delinquency in Society. 3rd ed. LC 96-12713. (C). 1996. text 54.00 (*0-07-052203-0*) McGraw.

Regoli, Robert M., et al. Juvenile Delinquency & Juvenile Justice. 448p. (C). 1985. text 52.74 (*0-07-554409-1*) McGraw.

Regosin, Richard L. Montaigne's Unruly Brood: Textual Engendering & the Challenge to Paternal Authority. LC 95-6077. 255p. (C). 1996. 48.00 (*0-520-20194-9*, Pub. by U CA Pr) Cal Prin Full Svc.

Regt, L. J. De, see De Regt, L. J.

Regteren Altena, I. Van, see Van Regteren Altena, I.

Reguant, Montserrat. Etapas Reivindicativas de la Teoria Nacional Catalana: Verdaguer, Oller y Prat de la Riba. (Catalan Studies: Vol. 22). (SPA.). 152p. (C). 1997. text 41.95 (*0-8204-3053-6*) P Lang Pubng.

Regueiro & Riechenberger. Spanish Drama of the Golden Age, Vols. 1-2. 1984. 85.00 (*0-87535-137-9*) Hispanic Soc.

Regueiro, Jose R., et al. Human T-Lymphocyte Activation Deficiencies. LC 93-39483. (Medical Intelligence Unit Ser.). 208p. 1994. 99.00 (*1-57059-020-6*) Landes Bioscience.

Regueiro, M. Vocabulary of Iberian Languages: Vocabulario de las Lenguas Ibericas. (BAQ & SPA.). 169p. 1982. pap. 11.95 (*0-8288-1455-4*, S39893) Fr & Eur.

***Reguera, D., et al, eds.** Statistical Mechanics of Biocomplexity: Proceedings of the XV Sitges Conference, Held at Sitges, Barcelona, Spain, 8-12 June 1998. LC 99-50185. (Lecture Notes in Physics Ser.: Vol. 527). xi, 318p. 1999. 74.00 (*3-540-66245-6*) Spr-Verlag.

Reguera, D., jt. auth. see Sitges Conference on Statistical Mechanics Staff.

Regula, De Traci. Mysteries of Isis: Her Worship & Magick. LC 95-20520. (Llewellyn's World Religion & Magic Ser.). (Illus.). 320p. 1999. pap. 19.95 (*1-56718-560-6*) Llewellyn Pubns.

Regula, De Traci, jt. auth. see Harrington, David.

Regular Baptist Press Staff. Asi Que Eres Bautista! Meyer, Richard, ed. (Junior High Sunday School Ser.). (SPA.). 91p. 1995. 5.50 (*1-879892-50-2*) Editorial Bautista.

— La Betalla de las Edades (Battle of the Ages) Meyer, Richard, ed. (Junior High Sunday School Ser.). (SPA., Illus.). 89p. 1998. pap. 5.50 (*1-879892-69-3*, SI-889) Editorial Bautista.

— Contendiendo Por la Fe. Meyer, Richard, ed. (Adult Sunday School Ser.). (SPA.). 100p. 1993. 4.40 (*1-879892-02-2*) Editorial Bautista.

— Deja Que Dios Te Utilice (Let God Use You) Meyer, Richard, ed. (Junior High Sunday School Ser.). (SPA., Illus.). 79p. 1998. pap. 5.50 (*1-879892-70-7*) Editorial Bautista.

— Demuestra Tu Fe. Meyer, Richard, ed. (Adult Sunday School Ser.). (SPA.). 86p. 1993. 4.40 (*1-879892-38-3*) Editorial Bautista.

— Ellos Escucharon Su Voz (They Heard His Voice) Meyer, Richard, ed. (Junior High Sunday School Ser.). (SPA., Illus.). 79p. 1998. pap. 5.50 (*1-879892-71-5*, SI-891) Editorial Bautista.

— Fundamentos de la Verdad. Meyer, Richard, ed. (Junior High Sunday School Ser.). (SPA.). 90p. 1995. 5.50 (*1-879892-51-0*) Editorial Bautista.

— Jornadas en el Desierto. Meyer, Richard, ed. (Adult Sunday School Ser.). (SPA.). 100p. 1995. 4.40 (*1-879892-45-6*) Editorial Bautista.

— Respuestas A Tus Preguntas (Answers to Your Questions) Meyer, Richard, ed. (SPA., Illus.). 83p. 1998. pap. 5.50 (*1-879892-72-3*, SI892) Editorial Bautista.

— Una Salvacion Tan Grande: La Doctrina de la Salvacion. Meyer, Richard, ed. (Adult Sunday School Ser.). (SPA.). 88p. 1992. 4.40 (*1-879892-28-6*) Editorial Bautista.

— Yo Amo a la Iglesia. rev. ed. Meyer, Richard, ed. (Adult Sunday School Ser.). (SPA.). 103p. 1994. 4.40 (*1-879892-26-X*) Editorial Bautista.

Regulatory Compliance Associates, Inc. Staff. Community Reinvestment Act: Understanding & Implementing the New Requirements. LC 98-160060. 1995. write for info. (*1-55827-157-0*) Sheshunoff.

— Compliance Monitoring Program for State Member Banks LC 98-213549. (Compliance & Law Ser.). 1997. write for info. (*1-55827-230-5*) Sheshunoff.

— Data Management: PC/LAN Administration Manual. LC 98-214027. (Compliance & Law Ser.). 1998. write for info. (*1-55827-159-7*) Sheshunoff.

— Regulatory Compliance Desk Reference. 2nd ed. LC 96-10712. (Illus.). 224p. (C). 1996. text 75.00 (*0-7863-0967-9*, Irwn Prfssnl) McGraw-Hill Prof.

***Regulatory Compliance Associates, Inc. Staff.** Year 2000 Planning & Compliance Manual. LC 98-213921. (Compliance & Law Series). 1998. write for info. (*1-55827-250-X*) Sheshunoff.

Regulatory Compliance Associates, Inc. Staff, jt. auth. see Tipton, Elizabeth J.

Regulatory Impact Analysis Project, Inc. Staff. Choices in Risk Assessment: The Role of Science Policy in the Environmental Risk Management Process. 300p. (Orig.). 1994. pap. write for info. (*0-9643747-1-4*) Regulatory Impact.

— Toward Common Sense: Understanding & Including Science Policy in the Environmental Risk Management Debate. 300p. (Orig.). 1994. pap. write for info. (*0-9643747-0-6*) Regulatory Impact.

Regulatory Staff. Compliance Training Service. 1995. 295.00 (*0-7863-0720-X*, Irwn Prfssnl) McGraw-Hill Prof.

Regules, J. M. Aranda, see Aranda Regules, J. M.

Regulez, M., jt. auth. see Gardeazabal, J.

Regulski, Jerzy, et al, eds. Decentralization & Local Government: A Danish-Polish Comparative Study in Political Systems. 200p. 1989. pap. 39.95 (*0-88738-730-6*) Transaction Pubs.

***Regunathan, Sudhamahi.** Siku: Faith & Conversion: Donyipolo Movement in Arunachal Pradesh. 2000. 30.00 (*81-241-0099-3*, Pub. by Har-Anand Pubns) S Asia.

Regusa, Dan, ed. Nelson's Directory of Investment Managers, 1997, 2 vols. 5500p. 1997. pap., per. 495.00 (*0-922460-93-0*) Nelson Info.

Regush, Nicholas. The Breaking Point: Understanding Your Potential for Violence. 250p. 1998. pap. 24.95 (*1-55013-836-7*) Firefly Bks Ltd.

***Regush, Nicholas.** The Breaking Point: Understanding Your Potential for Violence. 194p. 1998. pap. 14.95 (*1-55013-988-6*) Firefly Bks Ltd.

— The Virus Within: A Coming Epidemic. LC 99-58326. 224p. 2000. 24.95 (*0-525-94534-2*, Dutt) Dutton Plume.

Regvald, R. Heidegger et la Probleme du Neant. (Phaenomenologica Ser.: Vol. 101). 212p. 1986. lib. bdg. 139.00 (*90-247-3388-X*, Pub. by M Nijhoff) Kluwer Academic.

Reh, Albert M., jt. ed. see Barner, Wilfried.

Reh, Jane G. Hands-on BASIC Workbook for Kids Commodore 64. (Illus.). 350p. 14.95 (*0-317-12841-8*) P-H.

Reh, Jane G. & Van Hoozer, Michael. Teach Yourself Microsoft Visual InterDev in 21 Days. LC 96-67211. 816p. 1997. 39.99 (*1-57521-093-2*) Sams.

Reh, Vincent. Railroad Radio: Hearing & Understanding Railroad Radio Communications & Systems. LC 96-96107. (Illus.). 208p. (Orig.). 1996. pap. 19.95 (*0-9651599-0-6*) Byron Hill.

Reh, Wouter, jt. auth. see Steenbergen, Clemens.

Rehab Choice Incorporated Staff. Establishing Dysphagia Programs: A Speech-Language Pathologist's Guide. (Illus.). 96p. (Orig.). (C). 1993. pap. text 43.95 (*0-937857-38-6*, 1521) Speech Bin.

Rehab Work Group Staff, jt. auth. see Enterprise Foundation Staff.

Rehabilitators of Wildlife Rescue of New Mexico St. Wildlife Rehabilitation: A Coloring & Activity Book. (Illus.). 32p. (Orig.). (J). (gr. 2-6). 1996. pap. 7.95 (*0-913945-55-2*) Horizon Comms.

***Rehad, Mitri.** Bethlehem 2000: Past & Present. 160p. 1999. 34.95 (*3-930378-21-3*, Pub. by Palmyra Pub Hse) Interlink Pub.

Rehage, H. & Peschel, G., eds. Structure, Dynamics & Properties of Dispersed Colloidal Systems. (Progress in Colloid & Polymer Science Ser.: Vol. 111). 203333p. 1998. 79.95 (*3-7985-1118-7*) Spr-Verlag.

Rehahn, Jens P. Dictionary of Telecommunication Terms: English, French, German. (ENG, FRE & GER.). 480p. 1992. 250.00 (*0-7859-9959-0*) Fr & Eur.

— Optical Communication Engineering Dictionary in Four Languages: English-German-French-Russian. (ENG, FRE, GER & RUS.). 156p. 1992. 49.00 (*0-7859-8912-9*) Fr & Eur.

— Technological Dictionary of Telecommunications: English - French - German. (ENG, FRE & GER.). 480p. 1992. lib. bdg. 275.00 (*0-7859-3657-2*, 3761170426) Fr & Eur.

Rehahn, Jens P. & Schafer, Natalja. Optical Communication Technology: Optische Kommunikationstechnik. (ENG, FRE, GER & RUS.). 176p. 1988. 95.00 (*0-8288-0874-0*, F18820) Fr & Eur.

Rehahn, Jens P., jt. auth. see Schafer, Natalja.

***Rehahn, Jens-Peter.** German Dictionary of Telecommunications/Fachworterbuch Telekommunikation: English-German/German-English. (Routledge Bilingual Specialist Dictionaries Ser.). 590p. (C). 1999. text 115.00 (*0-415-19372-9*) Routledge.

Rehak, Theo. Practical Typecasting. (Illus.). 240p. 1993. 64.95 (*0-938768-33-6*) Oak Knoll.

Rehart, Catherine M. The Heartland's Heritage: An Illustrated History of Fresno County. Parks, Lori, ed. LC 99-73080. (Illus.). 350p. 2000. 39.95 (*1-886483-32-9*, Pub. by Heritge Media) Sunbelt Pubns.

— The Valley's Legends & Legacies. LC 96-36997. (Illus.). 320p. 1996. pap. 18.95 (*1-884995-12-8*) Word Dancer.

— The Valley's Legends & Legacies II. (Illus.). 352p. 1997. pap. 18.95 (*1-884995-15-2*) Word Dancer.

***Rehart, Catherine M.** The Valley's Legends & Legacies III, Vol. 3. 352p. 1999. pap. 18.95 (*1-884995-18-7*) Word Dancer.

R

R

Rehart, Deborah. Introduction to Phonetics. (C). 1995. pap. text, wbk. ed. write for info. (*0-8013-0936-0*) Addison-Wesley.

Rehart, S. & Zichner, R., eds. Hand Surgery - A Current Concepts Review: Proceedings of the Frankfurt International Hand Surgery Conference, November, 1996. rev. ed. (Illus.). 100p. 1997. pap. 55.00 (*0-86577-723-3*) Thieme Med Pubs.

Rehbein, Ed. Remembering God's Word. (Orig.). 1991. pap. 5.99 (*0-89900-359-1*) College Pr Pub.

Rehbein, Edna A., jt. auth. see Rojas, Sonia R.

Rehbein, Jochen, jt. auth. see Ehlich, Konrad.

*__Rehberg, Andrea, ed.__ The Matter of Critique: Readings in Kant's Philosophy. 296p. 2000. pap. 29.95 (*1-903083-11-7*, Pub. by Clinamen Pr) Paul & Co Pubs.

Rehberg, Jeanne & Popa, Radu D., eds. Accidental Tourist on the New Frontier: An Introductory Guide to Global Legal Research. LC 97-32088. xv, 294p. 1998. 67.50 (*0-8377-1075-8*, Rothman) W S Hein.

Rehberg, Linda & Conway, Lois. The Bread Machine Magic. 160p. (Orig.). 1992. pap. 11.95 (*0-312-06914-6*, St Martin Griffin) St Martin.

— The Bread Machine Magic Book of Helpful Hints. rev. ed. (Illus.). 272p. 1995. pap. 11.95 (*0-312-13444-4*, St Martin Griffin) St Martin.

*__Rehberg, Linda & Conway, Lois.__ The Bread Machine Magic Book of Helpful Hints. 2nd ed. LC 99-36687. 256p. 1999. pap. 11.95 (*0-312-24123-2*, St Martin Griffin) St Martin.

Rehberg, Linda & Conway, Lois. The Bread Machine Magic Book of Helpful Hints: Dozens of Problem-Solving Hints & Troubleshooting Techniques for Getting the Most Out of Your Bread Machine. (Illus.). 224p. (Orig.). 1993. pap. 10.95 (*0-312-09759-X*) St Martin.

— More Bread Machine Magic. LC 97-20540. (Illus.). 224p. 1997. pap. 11.95 (*0-312-16935-3*, St Martin Griffin) St Martin.

Rehberger, Claudia. Humanisierung des Menschen und die Wiederversohnung Mit der Erde: Die Befreiungstheologie Rosemary Ruethers. (Internationale Theologie Ser.: Bd. 1). (GER.). 283p. 1996. 54.95 (*3-631-49993-0*) P Lang Pubng.

Rehbinder, Eckard. Integration Through Law: Environmental Protection Policy. Stewart, Richard, ed. (European University Institute, Series A (Law): No. 2). xxiv, 351p. 1985. 119.25 (*3-11-010200-5*) De Gruyter.

Rehbinder, Eckard & Stewart, Richard. Environmental Protection Policy. 351p. (C). 1988. pap. text 31.95 (*3-11-011490-9*) De Gruyter.

Rehbinder, Manfred. Einfuerung in die Rechtswissenschaft: Grundfragen, Grundlagen und Grundgedanken des Rechts. 254p. 1983. 24.60 (*3-11-009723-0*) De Gruyter.

Rehbinder, Manfred & Sonn, Ju-Chan, eds. Zur Rezeption des Deutschen Rechts in Korea. (GER.). 111p. 1990. pap. 27.00 (*3-7890-1968-2*, Pub. by Nomos Verlags) Intl Bk Import.

Rehbinder, Manfred, jt. ed. see Becker, Jurgen.

Rehbock, Helmut, jt. auth. see Henne, Helmut.

Rehbock, Philip F., ed. At Sea with the Scientifics: The Challenger Letters of Joseph Matkin. (Illus.). 424p. (C). 1993. text 39.00 (*0-8248-1424-X*) UH Pr.

Rehbock, Philip F., jt. ed. see MacLeod, Roy M.

Rehder, Alfred, jt. auth. see Wilson, Ernest.

Rehder, Denny & Fitch, Lucius W. The Shampoo King: F. W. Fitch & His Company. (Illus.). 160p. 1982. pap. 12.95 (*0-942240-05-7*) D Rehder.

Rehder, Ernest. Ibarguengoitia en Exelsior, 1968-1976: Una Bibliografia Anotada Con Introduccion Critica y Citas Memorables del Autor. LC 93-22214. (American University Studies, XXII: Latin American Literature: Vol. 23). (SPA.). 142p. (C). 1994. text 40.95 (*0-8204-2195-2*) P Lang Pubng.

Rehder, Harold A., contrib. by. Familiar Seashells of North America. (Illus.). 192p. 1988. pap. 9.00 (*0-394-75795-5*) Knopf.

Rehder, Harold A., jt. auth. see Audubon Society Staff.

*__Rehder, Henry, Jr.__ Creating a Beautiful Landscape: Henry Rehder's Daily Guide. (Illus.). 168p. 2000. 27.95 (*1-928556-10-8*) Coastal NC.

Rehder, Henry, Jr. Growing a Beautiful Garden: A Landscape Guide for the Coastal Carolinas. LC 96-84203. (Illus.). 240p. 1997. 34.95 (*0-9635967-9-9*) Banks Channel.

*__Rehder, John B.__ Delta Sugar: Louisiana's Vanishing Plantations Landscape. LC 99-20199. (Creating the North American Landscape Ser.). 352p. 1999. 45.00 (*0-8018-6131-4*) Johns Hopkins.

Rehder, Robert. The Compromises Will Be Different. LC 96-138879. 78p. (Orig.). 1996. pap. 14.95 (*1-85754-127-8*, Pub. by Sheep Meadow) U Pr of New Eng.

— Wordsworth & the Beginnings of Modern Poetry. 246p. 1981. 42.00 (*0-389-20209-6*, N6991) B&N Imports.

Rehder, Robert, ed. see Clarke, Charlotte.

Reher, David, jt. auth. see Colesworthy, Robert.

Reher, David, ed. see Navarro, Ramon Gil.

Reher, David S. Perspectives on the Family in Spain: Past & Present. (Illus.). 372p. 1997. text 85.00 (*0-19-823314-0*) OUP.

Reher, David S. & Schofield, Roger S., eds. Old & New Methods in Historical Demography. LC 93-6635. (Illus.). 440p. (C). 1994. text 75.00 (*0-19-828793-3*, Clarendon Pr) OUP.

Rehfeld, John E. Alchemy for a Lender: Combining Western & Japanese Management Skills to Transform Your Company. 251p. 1994. 22.95 (*0-471-00836-2*) Wiley.

Rehfeldt, Phillip. Getting the Most Out of Clarinets. 1985. 11.00 (*0-933251-06-8*) Mill Creek Pubns.

— Guide to Playing Woodwind Instruments. 1988. 29.00 (*0-933251-09-2*) Mill Creek Pubns.

— Making & Adjusting Single Reeds. 1991. 11.00 (*0-933251-02-5*) Mill Creek Pubns.

— New Directions for Clarinet. rev. ed. (New Instrumentation Ser.: Vol. 4). 1993. pap. 39.95 (*0-520-03379-5*, Pub. by U CA Pr) Cal Prin Full Svc.

— Playing Woodwind Instruments: A Guide for Teachers, Performers, & Composers. (Illus.). 211p. (C). 1998. pap. text 27.95 (*1-57766-028-5*) Waveland Pr.

— Research Materials in Music. (Music History Ser.). 98p. (C). 1990. pap. text 20.00 (*0-933251-11-4*) Mill Creek Pubns.

— Study Materials for Clarinet, 3 vols., 1. (Clarinet Ser.). 1985. 11.00 (*0-933251-05-X*) Mill Creek Pubns.

— Study Materials for Clarinet, 3 vols., 2. (Clarinet Ser.). 1985. 14.00 (*0-933251-18-1*) Mill Creek Pubns.

— Study Materials for Clarinet, 3 vols., 3. (Clarinet Ser.). 1985. 17.50 (*0-933251-19-X*) Mill Creek Pubns.

Rehfeldt, Phillip, ed. Handbook for Flute Doubling. 1985. 11.50 (*0-933251-04-1*) Mill Creek Pubns.

— White's Edition for Clarinet & Piano, 1027. (Editions for Clarinet Ser.). 1983. 16.50 (*0-933251-03-3*) Mill Creek Pubns.

Rehfuss, John. Rearranged Fairy Stories. 178p. 1998. pap. 6.95 (*0-9664940-0-8*) J Rehfuss.

Rehg, James A. Industrial Electronics. (C). 2001. 64.00 (*0-13-206418-9*, Macmillan Coll) P-H.

— Introduction to Robotics: A Systems Approach. (Illus.). 240p. (C). 1985. text 51.00 (*0-13-495581-1*) P-H.

— Introduction to Robotics in CIM Systems. 4th ed. LC 99-43721. 464p. 1999. text 91.00 (*0-13-901208-7*) S&S Trade.

*__Rehg, James A. & Kraebber, Henry W.__ Computer-integrated Manufacturing. 2nd ed. 512p. 2000. 76.00 (*0-13-087553-8*) P-H.

Rehg, Kenneth L. & Sohl, Damian G. Ponapean-English Dictionary. LC 79-19451. (PALI Language Texts, Micronesia Ser.). 278p. 1979. pap. text 17.00 (*0-8248-0562-3*) UH Pr.

— Ponapean Reference Grammar. LC 80-13276. (PALI Language Texts Micronesia Ser.). 420p. 1981. pap. text 19.00 (*0-8248-0718-9*) UH Pr.

Rehg, Virgil R., jt. auth. see Lloyd, Russell F.

Rehg, William. Insight & Solidarity: The Discourse Ethics of Jurgen Habermas. LC 93-23800. (Philosophy, Social Theory, & the Rule of Law Ser.: No. 1). 1994. 48.00 (*0-520-08204-4*, Pub. by U CA Pr) Cal Prin Full Svc.

— Insight & Solidarity: The Discourse Ethics of Jurgen Habermas. LC 93-23800. (Philosophy, Social Theory, & the Rule of Law Ser.: Vol. 1). 1997. pap. 18.95 (*0-520-20897-8*, Pub. by U CA Pr) Cal Prin Full Svc.

Rehg, William, jt. ed. see Bohman, James.

Rehg, William, tr. see Habermas, Jurgen.

Rehill, Anne C., jt. auth. see Wise, James E., Jr.

Rehill, Anne C., tr. see Chalon, Jean.

Rehkopf, Friedrich. Griechisch-Deutsches Woerterbuch Zum Neuen Testament. (GER & GRE.). 140p. 1992. 75.00 (*0-7859-8412-7*, 3525501188) Fr & Eur.

Rehl, Kathleen M., ed. Planning for the Times of Your Life: 45 Great Financial Planning Ideas, Practical Strategies to Help You to Take Charge of Your Finances. LC 99-60702. (Illus.). 76p. (C). 1999. pap. 19.95 (*0-9670673-0-8*) Cambridge Advisors LLC.

Rehm. Principles of Biology. 188p. 1998. pap. text 14.40 (*0-536-01432-9*) Pearson Custom.

Rehm, Diane. Finding My Voice. LC 99-18513. 256p. 1999. 24.00 (*0-375-40163-6*) Knopf.

Rehm, Donald S. The Myopia Myth: The Truth about Nearsightedness & How to Prevent It. LC 83-80453. (Illus.). 165p. 1983. reprint ed. pap. 15.00 (*0-9608476-0-X*) Intl Myopia.

Rehm, Ellen. Der Schmuck der Achameniden. (Altertumskunde des Vorderen Orients Ser.: Vol. 2). (GER., Illus.). xii, 468p. 1992. text 91.00 (*3-927120-11-1*, Pub. by UGARIT) Eisenbrauns.

Rehm, H. J., et al, eds. Biotechnology, 12 vols. 2nd rev. ed. 7215p. 1996. 5100.00 (*3-527-28310-2*) Wiley.

— Biotechnology Vol. 11B: Environmental Processes - Soil Decontamination, Off-Gas Treatment, Potable Water Preparation. Vol. 11B, Environmental Processes II. 2nd ed. 542p. 2000. 340.00 (*3-527-28323-4*) Wiley.

Rehm, H. J., ed. see Reed, G.

Rehm, Hans Jurgen, et al, eds. Biotechnology: A Multi-Volume Comprehensive Treatise, Vol. 8B, Biotransformations. 546p. 2000. 340.00 (*3-527-28324-2*) Wiley.

Rehm, Jurgen T. & Gadenne, V. Intuitive Predictions & Professional Forecasts: Cognitive Processes & Social Consequences. LC 90-31507. (International Series in Experimental Social Psychology: Vol. 20). (Illus.). 210p. 1990. 90.00 (*0-08-036763-1*, Pub. by Pergamon Repr) Franklin.

Rehm, Karl M. Left or Right? (J). 1991. 10.15 (*0-606-07778-2*) Turtleback.

Rehm, Margarete. Lexikon Buch, Bibliothek, Neue Medien. (GER.). 294p. 1991. 195.00 (*0-7859-8447-X*, 3598108893) Fr & Eur.

— Lexikon Buch, Bibliothek, Neue Medien. (GER.). 294p. 1991. pap. text 30.00 (*3-598-10851-6*) K G Saur Verlag.

Rehm, Mary T., jt. auth. see DePietro, Anne C.

Rehm, Pam. The Garment in Which No One Had Slept: Poems. (Poetry Ser.). 64p. 1993. pap. 8.00 (*0-930901-87-8*) Burning Deck.

— The Garment in Which No One Had Slept: Poems. limited ed. (Poetry Ser.). 64p. 1993. pap. 15.00 (*0-930901-88-6*) Burning Deck.

— Piecework. 1992. pap. 5.00 (*1-879645-06-8*) o-blek editions.

— To Give It Up. LC 95-15850. (New American Poetry Ser.: No. 16). 100p. 1995. pap. 9.95 (*1-55713-212-7*) Sun & Moon CA.

Rehm, Patrice K. Nuclear Medicine: Self-Study Program IV: Oncology. LC 97-41360. (Conventional Tumor Imaging Ser.: No. 2). (Illus.). 1997. pap. text 35.00 (*0-932004-53-9*) Soc Nuclear Med.

*__Rehm, Robert.__ People in Charge: Creating Self Managing Workplaces. (Illus.). 288p. 1999. pap. 29.95 (*1-869890-87-6*, Pub. by Hawthorn Press) Anthroposophic.

Rehm, Rush. Greek Tragic Theatre. (Theatre Production Ser.). (Illus.). 184p. (C). 1994. pap. 25.99 (*0-415-11894-8*, B4729) Routledge.

— Marriage to Death: The Conflation of Wedding & Funeral Rituals in Greek Tragedy. LC 93-39939. 264p. 1994. text 37.50 (*0-691-03369-2*, Pub. by Princeton U Pr); pap. text 16.95 (*0-691-02916-4*, Pub. by Princeton U Pr) Cal Prin Full Svc.

Rehm, S. Multilingual Dictionary of Agronomic Plants, English, French, German, Portugese & Spanish. (ENG, FRE, GER, POR & SPA.). 283p. 1994. 250.00 (*0-7859-9638-9*) Fr & Eur.

Rehm, S., ed. Multilingual Dictionary of Agronomic Plants. LC 94-19353. 1994. text 169.50 (*0-7923-2970-8*) Kluwer Academic.

*__Rehm, Sabine.__ Spiegel der Heilsgeschichte: Typologische Bildzyklen in der Glasmalerei Des 14. Bis 16. Jahrhunderts im Deutschsprachigen Raum. (Europaische Hochschulschriften, Reihe 28). (Illus.). xi, 758p. 1999. 90.95 (*3-631-35009-0*) P Lang Pubng.

Rehman, A. A., ed. see Taylor, Jeremy.

Rehman, Abdur. Encyclopedia of Remedy Relationships in Homeopathy. 362p. (C). 1997. text 79.00 (*3-7760-1545-4*, Pub. by K F Haug Pubs) Medicina Bio.

Rehman, Afzalur. Islamic Methodology in History. 1994. pap. 15.95 (*1-56744-102-5*) Kazi Pubns.

Rehman, Inamur. Public Opinion & Political Development in Pakistan, 1947-1958. 298p. (Orig.). 1983. pap. text 26.00 (*0-19-577268-7*) OUP.

*__Rehman, Javaid.__ The Weaknesses in the International Protection of Minority. 288p. 2000. 93.00 (*90-411-1350-9*) Kluwer Law Intl.

Rehman, Javaid, jt. auth. see Ali, Shaheen Sardar.

Rehman, M. M. Education, Work & Women: An Inquiry into Gender Bias. (C). 1993. 24.00 (*81-7169-251-6*, Commonwealth) S Asia.

*__Rehman, Rafeeq.__ HP-UX Certification: System & Network Administration. LC 00-24274. 750p. 2000. 59.99 (*0-13-018374-1*) P-H.

Rehman, Sajjad U. Management Theory & Library Education, 14. LC 86-22736. (New Directions in Information Management Ser.: No. 14). 158p. 1987. 49.95 (*0-313-25288-2*, RMN/, Greenwood Pr) Greenwood.

*__Rehman, Sajjad ur.__ Preparing the Information Professional: An Agenda for the Future, 93. LC 99-462056. (Contributions in Librarianship & Information Science Ser.: Vol. 93). 192p. 2000. 57.50 (*0-313-30673-7*, GM0673, Greenwood Pr) Greenwood.

Rehman, Scheherazade S. The Path to European Economic & Monetary Union. LC 97-17513. 1997. lib. bdg. 154.00 (*0-7923-9951-X*) Kluwer Academic.

Rehman, Scheherazade S., ed. Financial Crisis Management in Regional Blocs. LC 97-51644. 378p. 1998. 129.95 (*0-7923-8094-0*) Kluwer Academic.

Rehman, Sharaf N. You're Not Listening. 80p. (Orig.). (YA). pap. 7.95 (*1-883120-06-3*) Northern St U.

Rehman, T., jt. auth. see Romero, Carlos.

Rehman, Z. Payamber Vol. I, II, III: The Messenger. 1991. 12.50 (*0-933511-96-5*) Kazi Pubns.

Rehmann, Elsa, jt. auth. see Roberts, Edith A.

Rehmann, R. M., jt. ed. see Decker, K. M.

Rehmann, Ruth. The Man in the Pulpit (Questions for a Father) Lohmann, Christoph & Lohmann, Pamela, trs. from GER. LC 96-13097. (European Women Writers Ser.). xviii, 215p. 1997. pap. 15.00 (*0-8032-8960-X*, Bison Books); text 40.00 (*0-8032-3917-3*) U of Nebr Pr.

Rehmel, Judy. Complete Index to the Quilt Keys. LC 84-90562. 60p. (Orig.). 1984. pap. 2.00 (*0-913731-06-4*) J Rehmel.

— Key to 1000 Quilt Patterns. 3rd rev. ed. (Illus.). 240p. 1992. spiral bd. 15.00 (*0-913731-08-0*) J Rehmel.

— So, You Want to Write a Cookbook! (Illus.). 52p. 1982. pap. 8.95 (*0-913731-04-8*) J Rehmel.

Rehmel, Judy, jt. auth. see Schaffhausen, Suzanne.

Rehmus, Charles M. Professional Updating of Personnel-Industrial Relations Training. (Occasional Publications: No. 146). 11p. 1983. 1.00 (*0-318-04753-5*) U Hawaii.

Rehmus, Charles M., ed. Public Employment Labor Relations: An Overview of Eleven Nations. LC 74-22858. (Comparative Studies in Public Employment Labor Relations Ser.). 1974. 10.00 (*0-87736-025-1*); pap. 5.00 (*0-87736-026-X*) U of Mich Inst Labor.

Rehn, Detlef, jt. auth. see Simon, Denis F.

*__Rehn, Rudolf.__ Sprache und Dialektik in der Aristotelischen Philosophie. (Bochumer Studien zur Philosophie Ser.). (GER.). 375p. 2000. write for info. (*90-6032-358-0*, Pub. by B R Gruner) J Benjamins Pubng Co.

Rehn, Victor. ERATO & Japan's Dreams of Future Technology. 31p. (Orig.). (C). 1992. pap. text 25.00 (*1-56806-019-X*) DIANE Pub.

Rehnberg, Clas. The Organization of Public Health Care: An Economic Analysis of the Swedish Health Care System. (Linkoping Studies in Arts & Sciences: No. 58). 172p. (Orig.). 1991. pap. 55.00 (*91-7870-728-5*) Coronet Bks.

Rehnberg, Peter. Coast Adventures. (Illus.). 40p. 1992. pap. 6.95 (*1-878175-17-3*) F Amato Pubns.

— Skunked Again! (Illus.). 96p. 1996. pap. 7.95 (*0-9654253-0-4*, C-101) Osprey Isl.

*__Rehnberg, Peter, photos by.__ Critters & Kids: Clip Art for the Classroom. (Illus.). 96p. 2000. pap. 12.95 (*1-877673-41-2*) Cottonwood Pr.

Rehnborg, C. F. C. F. Rehnborg: A Collection of His Essays, Speeches, & Writings. Johnson, Lee, ed. (Illus.). 300p. (Orig.). 1985. pap. write for info. (*0-9606564-2-1*) C F Rehnborg.

Rehner, Jan. Infertility: Old Myths, New Meanings. 130p. 1994. pap. 14.95 (*0-929005-06-6*, Pub. by Sec Story Pr) LPC InBook.

— Practical Strategies for Critical Thinking: A Student's Handbook. (C). 1993. text, teacher ed. 2.36 (*0-395-67341-0*); pap. text 9.16 (*0-395-67340-2*) HM.

*__Rehnmark, Eva-Lena.__ Neither God nor Devil: Rethinking Our Perception of Wolves. (Illus.). 144p. 2000. 30.00 (*0-7649-1338-7*, A549) Pomegranate Calif.

Rehnquist, William H. All the Laws but One: Civil Liberties in Wartime. 288p. 2000. pap. 14.00 (*0-679-76732-0*) Knopf.

— All the Laws but One: Civil Liberties in Wartime. LC 98-12641. (Illus.). 256p. 1998. 26.00 (*0-679-44661-3*) McKay.

— Grand Inquests: The Historic Impeachments Of Justice Samuel Chase And President Andrew Johnson, 1. 304p. 1999. pap. 12.00 (*0-688-17171-0*, Wm Morrow) Morrow Avon.

*__Rehnstrom, Joel.__ Development Cooperation in Practice: The United Nations Volunteers in Nepal. 2000. pap. text 19.95 (*92-808-1037-5*) UN Univ Pr.

Rehof, Lars A. Guide to the Travaux Preparatories of the United Nations Convention on the Elimination of All Forms of Discrimination Against Women. LC 93-12629. (International Studies in Human Rights: Vol. 29). 408p. 1993. lib. bdg. 142.50 (*0-7923-2222-3*) Kluwer Academic.

Rehof, Lars A. & Gulmann, Claus, eds. Human Rights in Domestic Law & Development. (C). 1989. lib. bdg. 75.50 (*90-247-3743-5*) Kluwer Academic.

Rehon, Peter M. Obtaining a Writ of Attachment - Action Guide - Fall 1997. Tindel, Kay E., ed. 84p. 1997. ring bd. 58.00 (*0-7626-0155-8*, CP-11124) Cont Ed Bar-CA.

Rehon, Peter M. Obtaining a Writ of Possession Pts. 1 & 2: Summer, 1992, Action Guide. Lester, Ellen C. & Graber, Suzanne E., eds. 70p. 1992. pap. text 52.00 (*0-88124-554-2*, CP-11352) Cont Ed Bar-CA.

Rehor, John A. The Nickel Plate Story. (Illus.). 484p. 1966. 74.95 (*0-89024-012-4*) Kalmbach.

Rehr. A & L Quick Review: Physician. 4th ed. 1999. pap. text 29.95 (*0-8385-0394-2*) Appleton & Lange.

Rehr, Darryl. Antique Typewriters & Office Collectibles: Identification & Value Guide. LC 97-203014. (Illus.). 144p. 1997. pap. 19.95 (*0-89145-757-7*, 4845) Collector Bks.

Rehr, Helen, ed. Milestones in Social Work & Medicine. LC 82-18542. 1982. pap. 8.95 (*0-317-04157-6*, Prodist) Watson Pub Intl.

Rehr, Helen, et al, eds. Creative Social Work in Health Care: Challenges for the Profession. LC 97-52579. 208p. 1998. 39.95 (*0-8261-1199-8*) Springer Pub.

Rehr, Helen & Mailick, Mildred D., eds. In the Patient's Interest: Access to Hospital Care. LC 81-15781. 171p. 1982. text 17.50 (*0-88202-136-2*) Watson Pub Intl.

Rehr, Helen & Rosenberg, Gary, eds. The Changing Context of Social Health Care: Its Implications for Providers & Consumers. 143p. 1991. pap. 2.95 (*1-56024-144-6*) Haworth Pr.

— The Changing Context of Social Health Care: Its Implications for Providers & Consumers. 143p. 1991. 4.95 (*1-56024-143-8*) Haworth Pr.

Rehr, Helen, jt. ed. see Rosenberg, Gary.

Rehr, Stuart, jt. auth. see Lee, Kaiman.

Rehrig, William H. The Heritage Encyclopedia of Band Music: Composers & Their Music, 2 vols., Set. Bierley, Paul E., ed. LC 91-73637. 1087p. 1991. 110.00 (*0-918048-08-7*) Integrity.

— Supplement to the Heritage Encyclopedia of Band Music. Bierley, Paul E., ed. LC 96-77526. 1056p. 1996. 90.00 (*0-918048-12-5*) Integrity.

Rehuraldt, Cristine A. Cristine, May We Listen? Rehwaldt, Charles A., ed. & pref. by. (Illus.). 139p. 1998. pap. 9.00 (*0-9666527-0-3*) Charles A Renwaldt.

Rehva. International Dictionary of Heating, Ventilating & Air Conditioning. (DUT, ENG, FRE, GER & HUN.). 482p. 1982. 295.00 (*0-8288-0966-6*, M15644) Fr & Eur.

Rehwaldt, Charles A., ed. & pref. see Rehuraldt, Cristine A.

Rehwaldt, Susan S., jt. auth. see Higgerson, Mary L.

Rehwinkel, Alfred M. Flood. 2nd ed. (Orig.). (YA). (gr. 10-12). 1957. pap. 16.00 (*0-570-03183-4*, 12-2103) Concordia.

Rei, Shakura. The Spiritual Warrior. Charles, Rodney, ed. LC 97-65709. 250p. (Orig.). 1997. pap. 17.95 (*1-887472-28-2*) Sunstar Pubng.

Reia, Flora. Business Communications: Speaking & Writing Effectively. (Illus.). 250p. (C). 1987. pap. text 13.95 (*0-935920-47-1*, Ntl Pubs Blck) P-H.

Reib, John. The Making of Conair: And Some History of Auxiliary Equipment for Plastic Processors. LC 95-62105. 144p. 1996. text 34.95 (*1-56676-356-8*) Technomic.

Reib, Robert. Cruising Comfortably on a Budget. 2nd rev. ed. LC 98-91020. (Illus.). 185p. 1999. pap. 24.00 (*0-9662208-7-0*, CC) Skip Bob.

— Cruising the Rideau & Richelieu Canals. LC 98-92483. (Illus.). 50p. 1998. pap. 10.00 (*0-9662208-6-2*, RR) Skip Bob.

Reib, Robert D. Marinas along the Intracoastal Waterway. 3rd ed. LC 97-91147. 98p. 1999. pap. 14.00 (*0-9662208-0-3*, Marinas97) Skip Bob.

Reibaldi, A., et al, eds. Progress in Retinopathy of Prematurity. (Illus.). xii, 234p. (Orig.). 1997. pap. 71.50 (*90-6299-146-7*) Kugler Pubns.

An Asterisk (*) at the beginning of an entry indicates that the title is appearing for the first time.

Reibel, Daniel B. Registration Methods for the Small Museums. 3rd ed. LC 96-51217. (American Association for State & Local History Book Ser.). (Illus.). 192p. 1997. 59.00 (0-7619-8904-8); pap. 21.95 (0-7619-8905-6) AltaMira Pr.

Reibel, David, intro. Lindley Murray: The Educational Works. 5240p. (C). 1996. 1320.00 (0-415-12307-0) Routledge.

Reibel, David, jt. ed. see University of Tubingen.

Reibel, Paula. A Morning Moon. large type ed. 608p. 1987. 27.99 (0-7089-8399-5, Charnwood) Ulverscroft.

Reibenschuh, Gernot. Menschliches Denken: Eine Systematische Studie Am Boden der Kantischen Philosophie. (Kantstudien-Ergaenzungshefte Ser.: Vol. 129). (GER.). x, 306p. (C). 1997. lib. bdg. 102.10 (3-11-014270-8) De Gruyter.

Reiber, Beth. Frommer's Berlin, 1995-1996. 1995. pap. 13.00 (0-671-88478-6) S&S Trade.

— Frommer's Budget Travel Guide Berlin on $50 a Day, 1996-1997. 1995. pap. 12.00 (0-671-51873-9) S&S Trade.

— Frommer's Comprehensive Travel Guide to Hong Kong, 1996-1997. 1996. pap. 12.95 (0-671-51929-8, P-H Travel) Prntice Hall Bks.

— Frommer's Comprehensive Travel Guide Tokoyo, 1996-1997. 1996. per. 12.95 (0-671-51950-6) S&S Trade.

— Frommer's Tokyo. 320p. 1996. 14.95 (0-02-861124-1) Macmillan.

— Frommer's Tokyo. 5th ed. (Frommer's Travel Guides Ser.). 288p. 1998. pap. 14.95 (0-02-862061-5, Frommer) Macmillan Gen Ref.

— Tokyo, 1992-1993. (Frommer's Comprehensive Travel Guide Ser.). (Illus.). 288p. 1992. pap. 13.00 (0-13-333477-5, P-H Travel) Prntice Hall Bks.

Reiber, Beth & Spencer, Janie. Frommer's Japan. 608p. 1996. 19.95 (0-02-860927-1) Macmillan.

Reiber, Beth, jt. auth. see Spencer.

Reiber, Duke B., ed. The NASA Mars Conference. (Science & Technology Ser.: Vol. 71). (Illus.). 570p. 1988. 25.00 (0-87703-293-9, Am Astronaut Soc); pap. 15.00 (0-87703-294-7, Am Astronaut Soc) Univelt Inc.

Reiber, G. E. & King, H. Guidelines for the Development of a National Programme for Diabetes Mellitus. (ARA, ENG, FRE, RUS & SPA.). vii, 70p. 1991. pap. text 9.00 (0-614-08022-3, 1930055) World Health.

Reiber, J. H. & Vander Wall, E. What's New in Cardiovascular Imaging? LC 98-22461. (Developments in Cardiovascular Medicine Ser.). 441p. 1998. 159.00 (0-7923-5121-5) Kluwer Academic.

Reiber, Johan H., ed. Cardiovascular Imaging. LC 96-21220. (Developments in Cardiovascular Medicine Ser.). 600p. (C). 1996. text 239.50 (0-7923-4109-0) Kluwer Academic.

Reiber, Johan H., et al, eds. Advances in Imaging Techniques in Ischemic Heart Disease, Vol. 171. LC 95-23084. (Developments in Cardiovascular Medicine Ser.). 168p. (C). 1995. text 73.50 (0-7923-3620-8) Kluwer Academic.

Reiber, Johan H. & Serruys, Patrick W., eds. Advances in Quantitative Coronary Arteriography. LC 92-20819. (Developments in Cardiovascular Medicine Ser.: Vol. 137). 1993. text 414.50 (0-7923-1863-3) Kluwer Academic.

— New Developments in Quantitative Coronary Arteriography. (Developments in Cardiovascular Medicine Ser.). (C). 1988. text 226.50 (0-89838-377-3) Kluwer Academic.

— Progress in Quantitative Coronary Arteriography. LC 94-13374. (Developments in Cardiovascular Medicine Ser.: Vol. 155). 432p. (C). 1994. text 251.00 (0-7923-2814-0) Kluwer Academic.

— Quantitative Coronary Arteriography. (Developments in Cardiovascular Medicine Ser.). (C). 1991. text 272.50 (0-7923-0913-8) Kluwer Academic.

— State of the Art in Quantitative Coronary Arteriography. (Developments in Cardiovascular Medicine Ser.). 1986. text 251.50 (0-89838-804-X) Kluwer Academic.

Reiber, Johan H. & Van Der Wall, Ernst E., eds. Cardiovascular Nuclear Medicine & MRI. (Developments in Cardiovascular Medicine Ser.). 384p. (C). 1992. text 247.50 (0-7923-1467-0) Kluwer Academic.

Reiber, Johan H., jt. auth. see Simmons, M. L.

Reiber, John Ney. Books of Magic: Bindings. (Illus.). 112p. 1995. mass mkt. 12.95 (1-56389-187-5, Pub. by DC Comics) Time Warner.

***Reiber, John Ney.** Books of Magic: Girl in the Box. Moore, Stuart, ed. (Illus.). 192p. 1999. pap. text 14.95 (1-56389-539-0, Pub. by DC Comics) Time Warner.

Reiber, John Ney. Books of Magic: Reckonings. LC 99-232466. (Illus.). 192p. 1997. pap. 12.95 (1-56389-321-5, Pub. by DC Comics) Time Warner.

— Books of Magic: Summonings. (Illus.). 240p. 1996. mass mkt. 19.95 (1-56389-265-0, Pub. by DC Comics) Time Warner.

— Books of Magic: Transformations. LC 99-229773. (Illus.). 128p. 1998. pap. text 12.95 (1-56389-417-3, Pub. by DC Comics) Time Warner.

Reiber, John Ney, jt. auth. see Carlton, Bronwyn.

Reiber, Steve Harold & AWWA Research Foundation. A General Framework for Corrosion Control Based on Utility Experience. LC 98-121860. (Illus.). 1997. write for info. (0-89867-925-7) Am Water Wks Assn.

Reiber, Steven H. & Kukull, Walter A. Aluminum, Drinking Water, & Alzheimer's Disease. LC 97-107408. (Illus.). 93p. 1996. pap. 125.00 (0-89867-858-7, 90683) Am Water Wks Assn.

Reibetanz, John. The Lear World: A Study of King Lear in Its Dramatic Context. LC 76-54829. 154p. reprint ed. pap. 47.80 (0-8357-4028-5, 203672000005) Bks Demand.

— Midland Swimmer. LC 97-104852. 112p. 1996. pap. 12.95 (0-919626-86-6, Pub. by Brick Bks) Genl Dist Srvs.

Reible, Danny D. Fundamentals of Environmental Engineering. LC 98-22372. 544p. 1999. lib. bdg. 69.95 (1-56670-047-7) Lewis Pubs.

Reible, Danny D., jt. auth. see Choy, Bruce.

Reiblich, G. Kenneth. The Supreme Court of the United States, Summary of the October, 1980 Term. 1983. write for info. (0-318-58311-9) West Pub.

Reibman, James, et al. The Fredric Wertham Collection. (Illus.). 101p. 1990. pap. 14.95 (0-916724-75-1, 475-1) Harvard Art Mus.

Reibold, Fred. Alpha & Omega (1902) 110p. 1998. reprint ed. pap. 17.95 (0-7661-0329-3) Kessinger Pub.

***Reiboldt, J. Max.** IPA Management: Financial Guidelines. LC 99-53272. 1999. write for info. (0-07-134299-0) McGraw-Hill Sch.

Reiboldt, J. Max, jt. auth. see Stanley, Kay.

Reiboldt, Max. Physician Compensation Systems. Stanley, Kay, ed. 1998. 44.95 (0-89970-910-9) AMA.

Reiboldt, Max, jt. auth. see Mink, Lauretta.

Reibstein, Richard J., jt. auth. see Green, Ronald M.

Reich. Tests for United States History. 1988. pap. text, teacher ed. 10.00 (0-03-014812-X) Holt R&W.

— United States History. 1988. text 80.00 (0-03-014627-5); text 66.50 (0-03-014808-1); pap. text, teacher ed., wbk. ed. 18.75 (0-03-014807-3) Holt R&W.

***Reich.** WAN (Wide Area Network) Encyclopedia Bioethic. 2nd ed. 1998. 25000.00 (0-7838-0104-1, G K Hall & Co) Mac Lib Ref.

Reich. Workbook for United States History. 1988. pap. text, student ed. 15.50 (0-03-014809-X) Holt R&W.

— World History. 1990. text 67.25 (0-03-028898-3) Holt R&W.

— World History. 90th ed. 1990. pap. text, teacher ed. 45.00 (0-03-028899-1) Holt R&W.

— World History: Testmasters. 90th ed. 1990. pap. text, teacher ed. 11.00 (0-03-028908-4) Holt R&W.

Reich, A. R., et al, eds. Progress in HPLC Vol. 3: Flow Through Radioactivity Detection in HPLC. 214p. 1988. 115.00 (90-6764-114-6, Pub. by VSP) Coronet Bks.

Reich, Alice & Steele, Thomas J., eds. Fraser Haps & Mishaps: The Diary of Mary E. Cozens. LC 90-62379. (Illus.). 101p. (Orig.). 1990. pap. 5.95 (0-944340-03-2) Regis Coll.

Reich, Allen Z. Marketing Management for the Hospitality Industry: A Strategic Approach. LC 94-47535. 530p. 1997. 59.95 (0-471-31012-3) Wiley.

— Positioning of Tourist Destinations. (Advances in Tourism Applications Ser.: Vol. 4). (Illus.). 160p. 1999. pap. 16.95 (1-57167-261-3) Sagamore Pub.

Reich, Andreas. Friedrich Schleiermacher Als Pfarrer an der Berliner Dreifaltigkeitskirche 1809-1834. (Schleiermacher-Archiv Ser.: Bd. 12). (GER.). xiv, 568p. (C). 1992. lib. bdg. 190.80 (3-11-013636-8) De Gruyter.

Reich, Arie. International Public Procurement Law: The Evolution of International Regimes on Public Purchasing. LC 98-34014. (Studies in Transnational Economic Law: Vol. 12). 432p. 1999. 168.00 (90-411-9685-4) Kluwer Law Intl.

Reich, Asher. Long Distance. Barkan, Stanley H. & Alkaley-Gut, Karen, eds. (Review Israeli Writers Chapbook Ser.: No. 2). (ENG & HEB.). 48p. 1991. 15.00 (0-89304-381-8); 15.00 (0-89304-383-4); pap. 5.00 (0-89304-382-6); pap. 5.00 (0-89304-384-2) Cross-Cultrl NY.

Reich, Astrid, jt. ed. see Dittmar, Norbert.

Reich, Bernard. Arab-Israeli Conflict & Conciliation: A Documentary History. LC 95-36120. 304p. 1995. pap. 24.95 (0-275-95430-7, Praeger Pubs) Greenwood.

— Handbook of Political Research on the Middle East & North Africa. LC 97-37549. 400p. 1998. lib. bdg. 89.50 (0-313-27372-3, Greenwood Pr) Greenwood.

— Historical Dictionary of Israel. LC 92-5324. (Asian Historical Dictionaries Ser.: No. 8). (Illus.). 421p. 1992. 58.00 (0-8108-2535-X) Scarecrow.

— Quest for Peace: United States-Israel Relations & the Arab-Israeli Conflict. LC 76-45940. 495p. reprint ed. pap. 153.50 (0-608-13017-6, 202416000035) Bks Demand.

— Securing the Covenant: The United States - Israeli Relations after the Cold War. LC 94-37881. (Contibutions in Political Science Ser.: Vol. 351). 184p. 1995. pap. 16.95 (0-275-95121-9, Praeger Pubs) Greenwood.

— Securing the Covenant: United States - Israeli Relations after the Cold War, 351. LC 94-37881. (Contributions in Political Science Ser.: Vol. 351). 192p. 1995. 59.95 (0-313-29540-9, Greenwood Pr) Greenwood.

— The United States & Israel: Influence in the Special Relationship. LC 83-24795. (Studies of Influence in International Relations). 236p. 1984. 31.95 (0-275-91247-7, C1247, Praeger Pubs) Greenwood.

Reich, Bernard, ed. The Arab-Israeli Conflict & Conciliation: A Documentary History. LC 95-31620. 304p. 1995. lib. bdg. 85.00 (0-313-29856-4, Greenwood Pr) Greenwood.

— An Historical Encyclopedia of the Arab-Israeli Conflict. LC 95-6684. 672p. 1996. lib. bdg. 105.00 (0-313-27374-X, Greenwood Pr) Greenwood.

— Political Leaders of the Contemporary Middle East & North Africa: A Biographical Dictionary. LC 89-7498. 570p. 1990. lib. bdg. 99.50 (0-313-26213-6, RPC/, Greenwood Pr) Greenwood.

— The Powers & the Middle East: The Ultimate Strategic Arena. LC 86-21266. 361p. 1986. 49.95 (0-275-92304-5, C2304, Praeger Pubs) Greenwood.

Reich, Bernard & Dorr, Steven. Qatar. (Profiles of the Middle East Ser.). 1996. text 36.00 (0-8133-0344-3) Westview.

***Reich, Bernard & Goldberg, David H.** Political Dictionary of Israel. (Illus.). 528p. 2000. 75.00 (0-8108-3778-1) Scarecrow.

Reich, Bernard & Kieval, Gershon R., eds. Israel Faces the Future. LC 86-21278. (Illus.), 240p. 1986. 62.95 (0-275-92190-5, C2190, Praeger Pubs) Greenwood.

— Israeli National Security Policy: Political Actors & Perspectives, 210. LC 87-36099. (Contributions in Political Science Ser.: No. 210). 251p. 1988. 59.95 (0-313-26196-2, RHS/, Greenwood Pr) Greenwood.

— Israeli Politics in the 1990s: Key Domestic & Foreign Policy Factors, 285. LC 91-3956. (Contributions in Political Science Ser.: No. 285). 208p. 1991. 55.00 (0-313-27349-9, RIA, Greenwood Pr) Greenwood.

Reich, Bernard & Silverburg, Sanford R. U. S. Foreign Relations with the Middle East & North Africa: A Bibliography & Supplement. Woronoff, Jon, ed. & frwd. by. LC 99-11075. (Area Bibliographies Ser.: No. 19). 552p. 1999. 95.00 (0-8108-3615-7) Scarecrow.

Reich, Bernard, jt. auth. see Silverburg, Sanford R.

Reich, Bernard, jt. ed. see Long, David E.

Reich, Bernard, ed. see Silverburg, Sanford R.

Reich, Blaize H., jt. ed. see Cyr, Dianne H.

Reich, Carl M., jt. auth. see Barefoot, Robert R.

***Reich, Cary.** Financier: The Biography of Andre Meyer, a Story of Money, Power & the Reshaping of American. (Trailblazers Ser.). 400p. 1998. 29.95 (0-471-24741-3) Wiley.

Reich, Christopher. Numbered Account. 768p. 1998. mass mkt. 7.99 (0-440-22529-9) Dell.

— Numbered Account. large type ed. LC 98-19325. 1998. 28.95 (0-7862-1505-4) Thorndike Pr.

***Reich, Christopher.** The Runner. LC 99-89058. 448p. 2000. 26.95 (0-385-33366-8) Delacorte.

— The Runner. large type ed. LC 99-87234. 676p. 2000. 26.95 (0-375-40973-4) Random Hse Lrg Prnt.

Reich, David E. Designing High-Powered OS/23 Warp Applications: The Anatomy of Multithreaded Programs. 2nd ed. LC 95-12069. 368p. 1995. 34.95 (0-471-11586-X) Wiley.

Reich, David L., jt. auth. see Brooks, Jean S.

Reich, Deborah, jt. auth. see Gallup, Barbara.

Reich, Devorah. Turning Point: A Novel about Growth & Suspense in an English Seminary. 15.99 (0-89906-528-7, TURH); pap. 12.99 (0-89906-529-5, TURP) Mesorah Pubns.

Reich, Doris, ed. see Geier, Joan A.

Reich, Ellen J. Waiting: A Diary of Loss & Hope in Pregnancy. LC 91-8720. 132p. 1992. pap. 11.95 (0-918393-88-4) Haworth Pr.

— Waiting: A Diary of Loss & Hope in Pregnancy. LC 91-8720. 132p. 1992. lib. bdg. 3.95 (1-56024-087-3) Haworth Pr.

Reich, Emil. Hungarian Literature: Historical & Critical Survey. LC 72-80503. 1972. reprint ed. 20.95 (0-405-08876-0) Ayer.

Reich, Esther. The Ravine House Mystery. 1995. 14.95 (0-533-11086-6) Vantage.

Reich, H. J., jt. auth. see Uexkull, J. R.

Reich, Hans H., jt. ed. see Reid, Euan.

Reich, Hans J. & Rigby, James H. Handbook of Reagents for Organic Synthesis, Acidic & Basic Reagents. LC 98-53088. 508p. 1999. 115.00 (0-471-97925-2) Wiley.

***Reich, Hans J. & Rigby, James H.** Handbook of Reagents for Organic Synthesis Acidic & Basic Reagents. LC 98-53088. 564p. 1999. 115.00 (0-471-97926-0) Wiley.

Reich, Harry, jt. auth. see Garry, R.

Reich, Harry, jt. auth. see Hulka, Jaroslav F.

Reich, Herbert J. Principles of Electron Tubes: Understanding & Designing Simple Circuits. (Illus.). 379p. 1995. reprint ed. pap. text 34.95 (1-882580-07-9) Audio Amateur.

Reich, Hermann. Der Mimus. xii, 900p. 1974. reprint ed. write for info. (3-487-05109-5) G Olms Pubs.

Reich, Janet. Gus & the Green Thing. LC 92-33845. (J). 1993. 8.95 (0-8027-8252-3); lib. bdg. 9.85 (0-8027-8253-1) Walker & Co.

Reich, Jerome R. British Friends of the American Revolution. LC 97-14520. 196p. (C). (gr. 13). 1997. text 56.95 (0-7656-0073-0); pap. text 25.95 (0-7656-0074-9) M E Sharpe.

— Colonial America. 4th ed. LC 97-2114. 326p. 1997. pap. text 38.40 (0-13-749573-0) P-H.

***Reich, Jerome R.** Colonial America. 5th ed. 336p. 2000. pap. 32.00 (0-13-089565-2) P-H.

Reich, Jill N., et al, eds. Close up on Psychology: Supplemental Readings from the APA Monitor. LC 97-10904. 168p. 1997. pap. 9.95 (1-55798-427-1) Am Psychol.

Reich, Jon. Reich: The Nudes of Jon Reich. LC 90-91911. (Illus.). 130p. 1991. 59.95 (0-9627203-0-5) Predictable Pr.

Reich, Klaus. The Completeness of Kant's Table of Judgments. Kneller, Jane & Losonsky, Michael, trs. from GER. LC 91-38006. (Series in Philosophy). 160p. (C). 1992. 27.50 (0-8047-1934-9) Stanford U Pr.

Reich, Laurence R. New Jersey Corporation Law & Practice. (National Corporation Law Ser.). 1466p. 1992. ring bd. 155.00 (0-13-109257-X) Aspen Law.

Reich, Lee. The Joy of Pruning. LC 95-35875. 224p. 1996. 30.00 (0-02-860398-2) Macmillan Info.

— A Northeast Gardener's Year. 1992. 20.00 (0-201-55050-4) Addison-Wesley.

— A Northeast Gardener's Year. 1993. pap. 12.00 (0-201-62233-5) Addison-Wesley.

— The Pruning Book. LC 96-34301. (Illus.). 244p. 1997. 27.95 (1-56158-160-7, 070297) Taunton.

— The Pruning Book. (Illus.). 244p. 1999. pap. 19.95 (1-56158-316-2, 070440) Taunton.

— Uncommon Fruits Worthy of Attention: A Gardener's Guide. 1992. pap. 10.00 (0-201-60820-0) Addison-Wesley.

***Reich, Lee.** The Weedless Garden. (Illus.). 176p. 2001. pap. 9.95 (0-7611-1696-6) Workman Pub.

Reich, Lee, ed. Growing Fruits: Nature's Desserts. (Twenty-First Century Gardening Ser.: Vol. 147). (Illus.). 112p. 1996. pap. 9.95 (0-945352-93-X) Bklyn Botanic.

Reich, Leo & Schindler, A. Polymerization by Organometallic Compounds. LC 65-14732. (Polymer Rev. Ser.: Vol. 12). 750p. reprint ed. pap. 200.00 (0-608-30438-7, 201196500080) Bks Demand.

Reich, Leo & Stivala, Salvatore S. Autoxidation of Hydrocarbons & Polyolefins: Kinetics & Mechanisms. LC 68-17424. (Illus.). 541p. reprint ed. pap. 167.80 (0-7837-0775-4, 204108900019) Bks Demand.

Reich, Lilly J. The Viennese Pastry Cookbook. (Illus.). 336p. 1996. 9.98 (0-9643600-5-5) Biscuit Bks.

Reich, Liselotte B. Dreams Should Never Die. (Orig.). 1995. pap. write for info. (1-57553-020-1) Watermrk Pr.

Reich, Lou. Hume's Religious Naturalism. LC 97-38956. 128p. (C). 1997. text 44.00 (0-7618-0981-3) U Pr of Amer.

— Hume's Religious Naturalism. LC 97-38956. vii, 119p. (C). 1998. pap. text 24.50 (0-7618-0982-1) U Pr of Amer.

Reich, Mark & Youell, Judd. Estimating with Timberline Precision Version 5.2. 762p. 1994. mass mkt. 52.00 (0-8273-6002-9) Delmar.

Reich, Mary W., jt. auth. see Shah, Dayna K.

Reich, Max I. Sweet Singer of Israel: Unfinished Poems & Devotional Thoughts. LC 70-38312. (Biography Index Reprint Ser.). 1977. reprint ed. 17.95 (0-8369-8127-8) Ayer.

Reich, Menachem M. Amukah - The Hidden Valley. 150p. 1992. write for info. (1-56062-129-X) CIS Comm.

Reich, Michael. Racial Inequality: A Political-Economic Analysis. LC 80-8573. (Illus.). 358p. 1981. reprint ed. pap. 111.00 (0-7837-8181-4, 204788600008) Bks Demand.

Reich, Michael R. Toxic Politics: Responsing to Chemical Disasters. LC 91-55054. 392p. 1991. text 49.95 (0-8014-2434-8); pap. text 19.95 (0-8014-9986-0) Cornell U Pr.

***Reich, Michael R., ed.** An Assessment of U. S. Pharmaceutical Donations: Players, Processes & Products. 280p. 1999. pap. 15.00 (0-9673960-0-X) Harvard Pub Hlth.

Reich, Michael R. & Marui, Eiji, eds. International Cooperation for Health: Problems, Prospects & Priorities. LC 88-35321. 416p. 1989. 65.00 (0-86569-189-4, Auburn Hse) Greenwood.

Reich, Michael R. & Okubo, Toshiteru, eds. Protecting Workers' Health in the Third World: National & International Strategies. LC 92-6991. 328p. 1992. 59.95 (0-86569-026-X, T026, Auburn Hse) Greenwood.

Reich, Michael R., jt. auth. see Bell, David E.

Reich, Michelle. Gold Ring of Betrayal. large type ed. (Harlequin Romance Ser.). 1997. 20.95 (0-263-15046-1) Mac Lib Ref.

Reich, Mira, tr. see Sed-Rajna, Gabrielle.

Reich, Nancy B. Clara Schumann: The Artist & the Woman. LC 84-45798. (Illus.). 352p. 1987. pap. 16.95 (0-8014-9388-9) Cornell U Pr.

— Clara Schumann: The Artist & the Woman. 2000. pap. text 18.95 (0-8014-8637-8) Cornell U Pr.

Reich, Nathaniel E. The Facts of Life. LC 98-90306. 1999. pap. 10.95 (0-533-12766-1) Vantage.

Reich, Neil. American Passages: An Anthology of Readings on Our Immigrant Experience. (Illus.). 300p. (C). pap. text 21.95 (0-472-08757-6) U of Mich Pr.

Reich, Neil. Now & Then. 196p. 1996. pap. text 29.95 (0-312-14783-X) St Martin.

— Now & Then: Reading & Writing about the American Immigrant Experience. 240p. (C). 1996. pap. text 18.95 (0-521-65756-3) Cambridge U Pr.

— Now & Then: Reading & Writing about the American Immigrant Experience: Instructor's Manual. 32p. (C). 1996. pap., teacher ed. 6.00 (0-521-65755-5) Cambridge U Pr.

Reich, Norbert, jt. auth. see Micklitz, Hans W.

Reich, Paul R. Hematology: Physiopathologic Basis for Clinical Practice. 2nd ed. 528p. 1984. 31.00 (0-316-73863-8, Little Brwn Med Div) Lppncott W & W.

Reich, Peter, tr. see Konrad, George.

Reich, Peter A. Language Development. 400p. 1986. 45.00 (0-13-523069-1) P-H.

Reich, Peter L. Mexico's Hidden Revolution: The Catholic Church in Law & Politics since 1929. LC 95-16516. (From the Helen Kellogg Institute for International Ser.). (C). 1996. text 28.95 (0-268-01418-3) U of Notre Dame Pr.

— Statistical Abstract of the United States-Mexico Borderlands. (Statistical Abstract of Latin America Supplement Ser.: Vol. 9). 204p. 1984. 45.00 (0-87903-243-X) UCLA Lat Am Ctr.

Reich, Philipp E. Aus dem Leben des Buchhandlers. reprint ed. write for info. (0-318-71732-8) G Olms Pubs.

Reich, Richard. House Without Windows: Manuscript Edition. 1952. pap. 13.00 (0-8222-0538-6) Dramatists Play.

Reich, Robert B. American Competitiveness & American Brains. (Philip Morris Lectures on Business & Society Ser.). 20p. 1993. pap. write for info. (1-884663-03-6) Baruch Coll Cty U.

***Reich, Robert B.** The Future of Success. LC 00-40552. 2001. write for info. (0-375-41112-7) Knopf.

— Good for Business: Making Full Use of the Nation's

Human Capital, the Environmental Scan, a Fact- Finding Report of the Federal Glass Ceiling Commission. 251p. 1995. pap. text 18.00 (*0-16-045547-2*) USGPO.

Reich, Robert B. Locked in the Cabinet. 338p. 1997. 3.99 (*0-375-40064-8*) Knopf.

— Locked in the Cabinet. LC 97-35525. 1998. pap. 13.00 (*0-375-70061-7*) Vin Bks.

— Locked in the Cabinet. large type ed. LC 97-27595. (Americana Series). 668p. 1997. pap. 25.95 (*0-7862-1216-0*) Thorndike Pr.

— The Resurgent Liberal. LC 90-50146. 320p. 1991. pap. 15.00 (*0-679-73152-0*) Vin Bks.

— Tales of a New America: The Anxious Liberal's Guide to the Future. LC 87-45915. 304p. 1988. reprint ed. pap. 14.00 (*0-394-75706-8*) Vin Bks.

— The Work of Nations: Preparing Ourselves for 21st Century Capitalism. 1992. pap. 13.00 (*0-679-73615-8*) Vin Bks.

Reich, Robert B., ed. The Power of Public Ideas. 272p. 1990. pap. 15.95 (*0-674-69590-9*) HUP.

— The Power of Public Ideas. LC 87-1371. 264p. 1987. 24.95 (*0-88730-128-2*, HarpBusn) HarpInfo.

Reich, Ron. Cerf-Volant Precision: Votre Guide Complet Pour le Pilotage de Cerfs-Volants Acrobatiques. Fosset, Raoul, tr. from ENG. & intro. by. (FRE., Illus.). 184p. (Orig.). 1994. pap. 14.95 (*0-9639010-3-6*) Tutor Text.

— Kite Precision: Your Comprehensive Guide for Flying Controllable Kites. LC 93-61552. (Illus.). 180p. (Orig.). 1994. pap. 14.95 (*0-9639010-2-8*) Tutor Text.

Reich, S., jt. auth. see Goebel, K.

Reich, S., jt. ed. see Deuflhard, P.

Reich, Sheldon. Andrew Dasburg: His Life & Art. LC 85-48158. (Illus.). 144p. 1989. 45.00 (*0-8387-5098-2*) Bucknell U Pr.

— John Marin Drawings, 1886-1951: A Retrospective Exhibition Honoring John Marin's Centennial, Organized by the University of Utah Museum of Fine Arts. LC 79-83660. (Illus.). 120p. reprint ed. pap. 37.20 (*0-8357-4381-0*, 203721200007) Bks Demand.

Reich, Simeon, jt. auth. see Censor, Yair Al.

Reich, Simon. The Fruits of Fascism: Postwar Prosperity in Historical Perspective. LC 90-55136. (Cornell Studies in Political Economy). 384p. 1990. text 52.50 (*0-8014-2440-2*); pap. text 18.95 (*0-8014-9729-9*) Cornell U Pr.

— The Reagan Administration, the Auto Producers, & the 1981 Agreement with Japan. (Pew Case Studies in International Affairs). 50p. (C). 1992. pap. text 3.50 (*1-56927-119-4*) Geo U Inst Dplmcy.

— Restraining Trade to Invoke Investment: MITI & the Japanese Auto Producers. (Pew Case Studies in International Affairs). 50p. (C). 1992. pap. text 3.50 (*1-56927-150-X*) Geo U Inst Dplmcy.

Reich, Simon & Markovits, Andrei S. The German Predicament: Memory & Power in the New Europe. LC 96-42943. 1997. pap. write for info. (*0-8014-8074-4*) Cornell U Pr.

Reich, Simon, jt. auth. see Markovits, Andrei S.

***Reich, Susanna.** Clara Schumann: Piano Virtuoso. LC 98-24510. (Illus.). 128p. (YA). (gr. 3-12). 1999. 18.00 (*0-395-89119-1*, Clarion Bks) HM.

Reich, T. E., jt. auth. see Shoup, C. S.

Reich, Tova. The Jewish War: A Novel. 272p. 1995. 22.00 (*0-679-43987-0*) Pantheon.

— The Jewish War: A Novel. LC 96-43640. (Library of Modern Jewish Literature). 288p. 1997. pap. 17.95 (*0-8156-0452-1*) Syracuse U Pr.

***Reich, Tova.** Mara: A Novel. LC 00-35396. (Library of Modern Jewish Literature). 2000. write for info. (*0-8156-0659-1*) Syracuse U Pr.

— Master of the Return. LC 99-34313. 256p. 1999. pap. text 17.95 (*0-8156-0620-6*) Syracuse U Pr.

Reich, Vivianna. My Soul Is Free LC 92-236428. iv, 108p. 1992. write for info. (*1-56043-506-2*) Destiny Image.

Reich, Walter. Orgins of Terrorism: Psychologies, Ideologies, Theologies, States of Mind. LC 98-24652. 302p. 1998. pap. text 18.95 (*0-943875-89-7*) W Wilson Ctr Pr.

Reich, Walter, ed. Origins of Terrorism: Psychologies, Ideologies, Theologies, States of Mind. (Woodrow Wilson Center Ser.). 300p. (C). 1990. pap. text 21.95 (*0-521-38589-X*) Cambridge U Pr.

Reich, Warren T. Encyclopedia of Bioethics, Vol. 1. 2nd ed. 1995. 100.00 (*0-02-897353-4*) Macmillan.

— Encyclopedia of Bioethics, Vol. 2. 2nd ed. 1995. 100.00 (*0-02-897354-2*) Macmillan.

— Encyclopedia of Bioethics, Vol. 3. 2nd ed. 1995. 100.00 (*0-02-897356-9*) Macmillan.

— Encyclopedia of Bioethics, Vol. 4. 2nd ed. 1995. 100.00 (*0-02-897357-7*) Macmillan.

— Encyclopedia of Bioethics, Vol. 5. 2nd ed. 1995. 100.00 (*0-02-897352-6*) Macmillan.

Reich, Warren T., ed. Encyclopedia of Bioethics, Vol. 2. 1982. 100.00 (*0-02-925940-1*) Mac Lib Ref.

***Reich, Wilhelm.** American Odyssey: Letters & Journals, 1940-1947. Higgins, Mary Boyd, ed. Jordan, Derek et al, trs. from GER. LC 98-48372. (Illus.). 320p. 1999. text 27.00 (*0-374-10436-0*) FS&G.

Reich, Wilhelm. Beyond Psychology: Letters & Journals, 1934-1939. Higgins, Mary B., ed. & intro. by. LC 94-14721. 320p. 1994. text 25.00 (*0-374-11247-9*) FS&G.

— Character Analysis. 3rd rev. ed. Carfagno, Vincent R., tr. from GER. 576p. 1980. pap. 20.00 (*0-374-50980-8*) FS&G.

— The Function of the Orgasm: Discovery of the Orgone, Vol. 1. rev. ed. 400p. 1986. pap. 20.00 (*0-374-50204-8*) FS&G.

— Funksiyon-e Orgazm: Kashf-e Energi-ye Orgon: The Function of the Orgasm: The Discovery of the Orgone. Simonian, Stephan, tr. & intro. by. LC 94-75384. (PER., Illus.). 448p. (Orig.). 1994. pap. 18.00 (*0-936347-38-4*) IBEX.

— Listen, Little Man! Manheim, Ralph, tr. from GER. Vol. 271. (Illus.). 144p. 1974. pap. 11.00 (*0-374-50401-6*) FS&G.

— The Mass Psychology of Fascism. 3rd ed. Carfagno, Vincent R., tr. from GER. 126p. 1980. pap. 18.00 (*0-374-50884-4*) FS&G.

— Passion of Youth: An Autobiography, 1897-1922. Higgins, Mary B. & Raphael, Chester M., eds. Schmitz, Philip & Tompkins, Jerri, trs. 240p. 1988. 17.95 (*0-374-22995-3*) FS&G.

— Passion of Youth: An Autobiography, 1897-1922. (Illus.). 178p. 1994. pap. 10.95 (*1-56924-929-6*) Marlowe & Co.

Reich, Wilhelm, et al. On Wilhelm Reich & Orgonomy. DeMeo, James, ed. (Illus.). 176p. (Orig.). (C). 1994. pap. text 20.00 (*0-9621855-3-1*) Natural Energy.

Reich, Willi, ed. see Webern, Anton.

Reich, William. Studies in Psychology. 2nd ed. (C). 1991. pap. text 24.80 (*0-536-58075-8*) Pearson Custom.

***Reicha, Anton & Landey, Peter M.** Treatise on Melody: Considered Apart from Its Relationship with Harmony, Followed by a Supplement on the Art of Accompanying Melody with Harmony, Where the Former Is Dominant, All Demonstrated by the Best Melodic Models. LC 00-34018. 2000. write for info. (*1-57647-031-8*) Pendragon NY.

Reichard. Hubert Humphrey. 1996. 26.95 (*0-8057-7777-6*, Twyne) Mac Lib Ref.

— UNIX in Plain English. 3rd ed. LC QA76.76.O63R4448. 400p. 1999. 24.99 (*0-7645-7011-0*) IDG Bks.

Reichard & Yakal. Teach Yourself . . . Microsoft Internet Explorer 4. 1997. 24.95 (*0-8052-8572-5*, M&T Bks) IDG Bks.

Reichard, Birge D. & Siewers, Christiane M. The Small Group Trainer's Survival Guide. Rodenhauser, Paul, ed. 168p. (C). 1992. text 42.00 (*0-8039-4740-2*); pap. text 19.50 (*0-8039-4757-7*) Sage.

Reichard, Dan & Gilbert, Larry A. Team Evangelism for Youth. Spear, Cindy G., ed. (Illus.). 26p. 1995. ring bd. 65.95 incl. audio (*1-57052-046-1*) Chrch Grwth VA.

— Team Ministry for Youth: A Guide to Gift Discovery & Involvement in Ministry. Spear, Cindy G., ed. (Illus.). 27p. 1996. ring bd., wbk. ed. 65.95 incl. audio (*1-57052-054-2*) Chrch Grwth VA.

Reichard, David C. Version Three Supplement to Exploring CADKEY. 176p. 1988. pap. text 8.40 (*0-13-296120-2*) P-H.

***Reichard de Cancio, Haydee E.** Tales from la Isla del Encanto. LC 99-93792. 1999. pap. 8.50 (*0-533-13144-8*) Vantage.

Reichard, Gary W. Politics as Usual: The Age of Truman & Eisenhower. Eisenstadt, A. S. & Franklin, John H., eds. LC 87-20726. 222p. (C). 1988. pap. text 11.95 (*0-88295-856-9*) Harlan Davidson.

— The Reaffirmation of Republicanism: Eisenhower & the 83rd Congress. LC 75-1017. (Twentieth-Century America Ser.). 330p. reprint ed. pap. 102.30 (*0-8357-8607-2*, 203500400091) Bks Demand.

Reichard, Gary W., jt. ed. see Bremner, Robert H.

Reichard, Gladys A. Analysis of Coeur d'Alene Indian Myths. LC 48-2411. (AFS Memoirs Ser.). 1972. reprint ed. 30.00 (*0-527-01093-6*) Periodicals Srv.

— Melanesian Design: A Study of Style in Wood & Tortoiseshell Carving. LC 70-82256. (Illus.). reprint ed. 95.00 (*0-404-50568-6*) AMS Pr.

— Navaho Grammar. LC 73-15404. (American Ethnological Society Publications: No. 21). reprint ed. 57.50 (*0-404-58171-4*) AMS Pr.

— Navaho Religion: A Study of Symbolism. LC 63-14455. (Bollingen Ser.: Vol. 18). 863p. reprint ed. 200.00 (*0-8357-9504-7*, 201488000093) Bks Demand.

— Navajo Medicine Man Sand Paintings. (Illus.). 132p. 1977. reprint ed. pap. 12.95 (*0-486-23329-4*) Dover.

— Navajo Shepherd & Weaver. LC 68-25390. (Beautiful Rio Grande Classics Ser.). (Illus.). 280p. 1984. pap. 12.00 (*0-87380-143-1*) Popular E Commerce.

— Prayer: The Compulsive Word. LC 84-45512. (American Ethnological Society Monographs: No. 7). 1988. reprint ed. 29.50 (*0-404-62907-5*) AMS Pr.

— Social Life of the Navajo Indians. LC 76-82350. (Columbia Univ. Contributions to Anthropology Ser.: Vol. 7). reprint ed. 31.00 (*0-404-50557-0*) AMS Pr.

— Spider Woman: A Story of Navajo Weavers & Chanters. (Illus.). 344p. 1987. pap. 12.00 (*0-87380-160-1*) Popular E Commerce.

— Spider Woman: A Story of Navajo Weavers & Chanters. LC 96-43353. 292p. 1997. pap. 16.95 (*0-8263-1793-6*) U of NM Pr.

— Weaving a Navajo Blanket. LC 73-86437. (Illus.). 222p. 1974. reprint ed. 6.95 (*0-486-22992-0*) Dover.

— Wiyot Grammer & Texts. fac. ed. (University of California Publications in American Archaeology & Ethnology: Vol. 22: 1). 215p. (C). 1925. reprint ed. pap. text 23.13 (*1-55567-255-8*) Coyote Press.

Reichard, Gladys A. & La Farge, Oliver. Navaho Religion: A Study of Symbolism. (Bollingen Ser.: No. XVIII). 872p. (C). 1950. pap. text 24.95 (*0-691-01906-1*, Pub. by Princeton U Pr) Cal Prin Full Svc.

Reichard, Gladys A., jt. auth. see Newcomb, Franc J.

Reichard, John, ed. 1997 Comparative Performance Data Sourcebook. (Illus.). 558p. 1996. pap. text 195.00 (*1-881393-84-4*) Faulkner & Gray.

— The 1997 Healthcare Alliance & Network Sourcebook. 700p. 1996. pap. 265.00 (*1-881393-22-4*) Faulkner & Gray.

Reichard, Kevin. Power Programming Motif. 2nd ed. 1995. pap. 59.95 incl. disk (*1-55828-322-6*, MIS Pr) IDG Bks.

— Teach Yourself . . . Netscape Navigator 2. LC 96-15534. 89p. 1996. pap. 21.95 (*1-55828-471-0*, MIS Pr) IDG Bks.

***Reichard, Kevin.** Teach Yourself Linux. 408p. 2000. 24.99 (*1-55828-598-9*, MIS Pr) IDG Bks.

Reichard, Kevin. UNIX for DOS & Windows Users. 1994. pap. 19.95 (*1-55828-361-7*, MIS Pr) IDG Bks.

— UNIX Shareware & Freeware. 1994. pap. 24.95 incl. cd-rom (*1-55828-382-X*, MIS Pr) IDG Bks.

Reichard, Kevin & Foster-Johnson, Eric. Teach Yourself UNIX. 4th ed. LC 97-45826. (Teach Yourself Ser.). 416p. 1999. pap. 19.99 (*1-55828-588-1*, MIS Pr) IDG Bks.

— UNIX in Plain English. 2nd ed. 1997. pap. write for info. (*0-614-28502-X*, MIS Pr) IDG Bks.

Reichard, Kevin & Johnson, Eric. Advanced X Windows Applications Programming. 2nd ed. LC 94-34030. 89p. 1994. pap. 44.95 incl. cd-rom (*1-55828-344-7*, M&T Bks) IDG Bks.

Reichard, Kevin & Johnson, Eric F. UNIX Systems Administrators Guide to X Windows with CD ROM. LC 94-13565. 89p. 1994. pap. 44.95 (*1-55828-347-1*, MIS Pr) IDG Bks.

— Using X: Troubleshooting X Windows, Mofit, Open Systems. 89p. 1995. pap. 29.95 (*1-55828-212-2*, MIS Pr) IDG Bks.

Reichard, Max. The Human Journey. 2nd ed. 372p. (C). 1992. pap. text 43.00 (*0-536-58129-0*) Pearson Custom.

Reichard, Richard W. From the Petition to the Strike: A History of Strikes in Germany, 1869-1914. LC 90-46469. (American University Studies: History: Ser. IX, Vol. 67). (Illus.). VII, 337p. (C). 1991. text 55.95 (*0-8204-0905-7*) P Lang Pubng.

Reichard, Sherwood M. & Filkens, James P., eds. The Reticuloendothelial System: A Comprehensive Treatise, Vol. 7A: Physiology. LC 79-25933. 436p. 1984. 105.00 (*0-306-41422-8*, Plenum Trade) Perseus Pubng.

Reichard, Sherwood M. & Filkins, James P., eds. The Reticuloendothelial System Vol. 7B: A Comprehensive Treatise: Physiology. LC 79-25933. 558p. 1984. 115.00 (*0-306-41423-6*, Plenum Trade) Perseus Pubng.

Reichard, Suzanne, et al. Aging & Personality: A Study of Eighty-Seven Older Men. Stein, Leon, ed. LC 79-8680. (Growing Old Ser.). (Illus.). 1980. reprint ed. lib. bdg. 25.95 (*0-405-12797-9*) Ayer.

Reichard, William. Alchemy in the Bones: Poems. LC 97-69843. (Minnesota Voices Project Ser.: Vol. 90). 88p. 1999. pap. 13.95 (*0-89823-194-9*, Pub. by New Rivers Pr) Consort Bk Sales.

Reichardi, Veronica, jt. auth. see Wolffe, Mary.

Reichardt, Anna Katharina & Kubli, Eric. Menschenbilder. 24.95 (*3-906762-49-1*, Pub. by P Lang) P Lang Pubng.

Reichardt, Charles S. & Rallis, Sharon F., eds. The Qualitative-Quantitative Debate: New Perspectives. LC 85-644749. (New Directions for Evaluation Ser.: No. PE 61). 98p. (Orig.). 1994. pap. 20.00 (*0-7879-9967-9*) Jossey-Bass.

Reichardt, Charles S., ed. see Cook, Thomas D.

Reichardt, Charles S., ed. see Evaluation Studies Review Annual Staff.

Reichardt, Christian. Solvents & Solvent Effects in Organic Chemistry, 2.rE. 2nd enl. rev. ed. (Illus.). 534p. 1988. 185.00 (*3-527-26805-7*, Wiley-VCH) Wiley.

Reichardt, E. Noel. The Significance of Ancient Religions in Relation to Human Evolution & Brain Development (1912) 450p. 1998. reprint ed. pap. 29.95 (*0-7661-0164-9*) Kessinger Pub.

Reichardt, Erwin. Die Diatomeen der Altmuehl. (Bibliotheca Diatomologica Ser.: Vol. 6). (GER., Illus.). 170p. 1985. lib. bdg. 39.00 (*3-7682-1411-7*) Lubrecht & Cramer.

Reichardt, Erwin, jt. auth. see Lange-Bertalot, Horst.

Reichardt, Hans-Jurgen. Sachstand & Probleme Umweltorientierter Unternehmensfuhrung in der Mittelstandischen Industrie: Ergebnisse & Losungsansatze aus Einer Empirischen Untersuchung. (GER., Illus.). 251p. 1996. 51.95 (*3-631-30734-9*) P Lang Pubng.

Reichardt, Helmut. Gentle Exercises for Better Backs. LC 98-3366. (Illus.). 80p. 1998. 10.95 (*0-8069-9451-7*) Sterling.

Reichardt, Johann F., jt. ed. see Kunzen, Friedrich L.

Reichardt, Louise. Songs. LC 80-22799. (Women Composers Ser.). 1980. 27.50 (*0-306-79552-3*) Da Capo.

Reichardt, Mary R. A Web of Relationship: Women in the Short Fiction of Mary Wilkins Freeman. LC 91-32352. 208p. 1992. text 32.50 (*0-87805-555-X*) U Pr of Miss.

Reichardt, Mary R. & Freeman, Mary E. Wilkins. Mary E. Wilkins Freeman: A Study of the Short Fiction. LC 97-18464. 1997. 29.00 (*0-8057-4626-9*, Twyne) Mac Lib Ref.

Reichardt, Mary R., ed. see Freeman, Mary E. Wilkins.

Reichardt, Mary R., ed. & intro. see Freeman, Mary E. Wilkins.

Reichardt, Peg. Conceptbuilding: Developing Meaning Through Narratives & Discussion. LC 91-43896. 144p. 1992. pap. 29.00 (*0-930599-71-3*) Thinking Pubns.

Reichardt, Robert H. & Muskens, George, eds. Post-Communism, the Market & the Arts: First Sociological Assessments. LC 92-36724. 205p. 1992. 40.00 (*3-631-45313-2*) P Lang Pubng.

Reichardt, Rolf, jt. auth. see Lusebrink, Hans-Jurgen.

Reichardt, W. Acoustics Dictionary. 1983. text 134.50 (*90-247-2707-3*) Kluwer Academic.

Reichardt, Walter L., jt. ed. see Hunter, Paul R.

Reichart, Elisabeth. February Shadows. Hoffmeister, Donna L., tr. from GER. & comment by. (Studies in Austrian Literature, Culture & Thought). (Orig.). 1989. pap. 13.95 (*0-929497-02-3*) Ariadne CA.

***Reichart, Elisabeth.** "La Valse" & "Foreign" Demeritt, Linda C., tr. 2000. pap. 15.95 (*0-7914-4774-X*) State U NY Pr.

— La Valse & Foreign. Demeritt, Linda C., tr. (C). 2000. text 47.50 (*0-7914-4773-1*) State U NY Pr.

Reichart, John F. & Sturm, Steven R., eds. American Defense Policy. 5th ed. LC 81-48186. 874p. reprint ed. pap. 200.00 (*0-8357-6906-2*, 203796400009) Bks Demand.

***Reichart, Matthias.** Umweltschutz Durch Volkerrechtliches Strafrecht. XX, 650p. 1999. 85.95 (*3-631-33822-8*) P Lang Pubng.

***Reichart, Peter A. & Philipsen, Hans Peter.** Color Atlas of Oral Pathology. (Illus.). 304p. 2000. 199.00 (*0-86577-932-5*) Thieme Med Pubs.

Reichart-Wallrabenstein, Maike, jt. auth. see Decke-Cornill, Helene.

Reichart, Walter A., ed. see Irving, Washington.

Reichblum, Charles. Knowledge in a Nutshell. 2nd ed. (Knowledge in a Nutshell Ser.). 248p. (YA). (gr. 2-12). 1997. reprint ed. mass mkt. 7.50 (*0-9660991-8-4*) arpr inc.

KNOWLEDGE IN A NUTSHELL is a paperback the whole family will love. The ultimate "share toy." Want to be surprised by the truth? Discover how you've been misled for years? Get a kick out of crazy coincidences? Children of all ages...from 8 to over 80 love this book. Wild, wacky, absolutely true facts, real-life, bizarre accounts. You'll have heaps of fun with this endlessly entertaining book. Crack open KNOWLEDGE IN A NUTSHELL & find out the U.S. State that no longer exists. The only man who was present when THREE U.S. Presidents were assassinated. What animal has one name in winter & another name in summer. Over 500 amazing, astounding, fun facts - a treasure chest for trivia buffs. Radio hosts say: "The king of trivia books." "...the best trivia book I have--& I collect them--(because) these aren't just facts, but wonderful stories." "Knowledge in a Nutshell is the best gift you can give to yourself or anyone else." "This is a fun book. I couldn't put it down." Every fact fully explained with a fascinating story. Eighteen chapters, 248 pages, written in a style everyone understands. Available direct from publisher 1-800-633-3082, IPG, Ingram, Baker & Taylor. When bookstores stock, we promote location during media interviews.
Publisher Paid Annotation.

***Reichblum, Charles. Knowledge in a Nutshell on Popular Products: Heinz Edition. (Knowledge in a Nutshell Ser.). 224p. 2000. mass mkt. 9.50 (*0-9660991-1-7*) arpr inc.**

Knowledge in a Nutshell on Popular Products Heinz Edition looks inside one of the world's most famous companies with surprising facts & stories. How did ketchup get its name?...Why is it sometimes spelled "catsup"?...How did Henry Heinz, founder, H.J. Heinz, literally "sink" his competition?...Why did he choose the famous slogan "57 Varieties" when he was already producing more than 60?...What unique things do Britons do with baked beans?...What popular food was first used as a medicine in 400 B.C.?...How can vinegar help you with hundreds of household chores?...Why do we call accountants "bean counters"?...and much more, including international recipes. This 224-page paperback book is the first in the KNOWLEDGE IN A NUTSHELL series on POPULAR PRODUCTS & joins KNOWLEDGE IN A NUTSHELL (general information) & KNOWLEDGE IN A NUTSHELL ON SPORTS, each with over 500 amazing, astounding fun facts. A treasure chest for trivia buffs of all ages. ***Publisher Paid Annotation.***

–Knowledge in a Nutshell on Sports. 2nd rev. ed. LC 99-483505. (Knowledge in a Nutshell Ser.). 192p. (YA). (gr. 2-12). 1998. pap. 9.50 (*0-9660991-6-8*) arpr inc.

KNOWLEDGE IN A NUTSHELL ON SPORTS is another in the KNOWLEDGE IN A NUTSHELL series. Sports lovers, young or old, will love the sports facts & anecdotes. The ultimate "share toy." Over 500 amazing, astounding fun facts - a treasure chest for trivia buffs. Crack open KNOWLEDGE IN A NUTSHELL ON SPORTS & find out about the 6-inch home run. Why golf courses have 18 holes. The major leaguer who caught his own home run. The great football team that never existed. The invisible field goal in an NFL game. Radio hosts say: "This will keep you talking sports all night."... "This

is not just for American sports fans, it's for us Canadians, too."... "Best sports trivia book I've seen."... "We thought we knew a lot about sports, but this book has stuff we never knew." Every fact fully explained with a fascinating story. Seven chapters, 192 pages, written in a style everyone understands. Available direct from publisher 1-800-NUTSHELL (688-7435), Ingram, Baker & Taylor. When bookstores stock, we promote location during media interviews. Just let us know. *Publisher Paid Annotation.*

Reiche, Andrzej, jt. ed. see Hausleiter, Arnulf.

***Reiche, Danyel T. & Krebs, Carsten.** Der Einstieg in die Okologische Steuerreform: Aufstieg, Restriktionen und Durchsetzung eines Umweltpolitischen Themas. 337p. 1999. 37.95 (*3-631-35561-0*) P Lang Pubng.

Reiche, Hans. Maintenance Minimization for Competitive Advantage: A Life-Cycle Approach for Product Manufacturers & End-Users. LC 92-46257. 208p. 1994. text 68.00 (*2-88124-589-7*) Gordon & Breach.

Reiche, Rainer. Ein Rheinisches Schulbuch Aus Dem 11: Jahrhundert. (Munchener Beitrage zur Mediavistik und Renaissance-Forschung Ser.: Bd. 24). (GER.). xvi, 487p. 1976. 55.00 (*3-615-00157-5*) G Olms Pubs.

***Reichek, Elaine.** When This You See... (Illus.). 2000. 30.00 (*0-8076-1460-2*) Braziller.

Reichel, Alicia D., jt. auth. see Reichel-Dolmatoff, Gerardo.

Reichel, Cara. A Stone Promise. Thatch, Nancy R., ed. LC 91-15059. (Books for Students by Students). (Illus.). 26p. (YA). (gr. 5 up). 1991. lib. bdg. 15.95 (*0-933849-35-4*) Landmark Edns.

Reichel-Dolmatoff, Gerardo. Amazonian Cosmos: The Sexual & Religious Symbolism of the Tukano Indians. LC 73-133491. xxiv, 290p. 1992. reprint ed. pap. text 7.95 (*0-226-70732-6*, P574) U Ch Pr.

— The Sacred Mountain of Colombia's Kogi Indians. LC 90-2138. (Iconography of Religions Ser.: Vol. IX, Pt. 2). (Illus.). ix, 38p. 1990. pap. 48.00 (*90-04-09274-9*) Brill Academic Pubs.

— Yurupari: Studies of an Amazonian Foundation Myth. LC 95-41259. (Religions of the World Ser.). 348p. 1996. 24.95 (*0-945454-08-2*) Harvard U Wrld Relig.

Reichel-Dolmatoff, Gerardo & Reichel, Alicia D. People of Aritama. LC 60-14234. (Illus.). 495p. 1962. lib. bdg. 36.00 (*0-226-70791-1*) U Ch Pr.

Reichel, Elias & Puliafito, Carmen A. Atlas of Indocyanine Green Angiography. LC 96-6149. (Illus.). 120p. 1996. 98.50 (*0-89640-310-6*) Igaku-Shoin.

Reichel, Horst. Initial Computability, Algebraic Specifications, & Partial Algebras. (International Series of Monographs on Computer Science: No. 2). (Illus.). 224p. 1987. 65.00 (*0-19-853806-5*) OUP.

— Structural Induction on Partial Algebras. 206p. (C). 1984. 85.00 (*0-7855-4973-0*, Pub. by Collets) St Mut.

Reichel, Horst, et al, eds. Fundamentals of Computation Theory: 10th International Conference, FCT '95, Dresden, Germany, August 22-25, 1995, Proceedings, Vol. IX. LC 95-37622. (Lecture Notes in Computer Science Ser.: Vol. 965). 433p. 1995. 68.00 (*3-540-60249-6*) Spr-Verlag.

Reichel, Horst, ed. see Symposium on Theoretical Aspects of Computer Science.

Reichel, Jurgen, jt. ed. see Totten, George E.

Reichel, Lothar, et al, eds. Numerical Linear Algebra: Proceedings of the Conference in Numerical Linear Algebra & Scientific Computation, Kent (Ohio), March 13-14, 1992. LC 93-8437. ix, 199p. 1993. lib. bdg. 95.95 (*3-11-013784-4*) De Gruyter.

Reichel, Norbert. Politik und Praxis der Umwelterziehung. 170p. 1995. 27.95 (*3-631-49925-6*) P Lang Pubng.

Reichel, Philip, ed. Criminal Justice. (Perspectives Ser.). (YA). (gr. 9-12). 1998. pap. 13.70 (*1-56510-900-7*); lib. bdg. 22.45 (*1-56510-901-5*) Greenhaven.

Reichel, Philip L. Comparative Criminal Justice Systems. 2nd ed. LC 98-8606. 403p. 1998. pap. 55.00 (*0-13-080908-X*) P-H.

— Corrections. LC 96-3256. 675p. 1996. 65.00 (*0-314-09980-8*) West Pub.

Reichel, William, et al, eds. Care of the Elderly: Clinical Aspects of Aging. 4th ed. LC 94-26125. (Illus.). 672p. 1995. 65.00 (*0-683-07209-9*) Lppncott W & W.

Reichelt, Karl L. Truth & Tradition in Chinese Buddhism. 1972. 59.95 (*0-8490-1234-1*) Gordon Pr.

— Truth & Tradition in Chinese Buddhism. (Illus.). 415p. 1990. reprint ed. pap. 30.00 (*957-9482-17-9*) Oriental Bk Store.

Reichelt, Marie H. Yes, There Is Life after Aerospace: Career Transition from Military Defense - Aerospace to Commercial Civilian Life. Franklin, Reece & Fischer, Joanne, eds. LC 94-71162. (Illus.). 132p. (Orig.). 1994. pap. 14.95 (*0-9639036-5-9*) ABP Assocs.

Reichelt, Marie W. History of Deerfield. (Illus.). 215p. 1997. reprint ed. pap. 24.50 (*0-8328-5734-3*); reprint ed. lib. bdg. 32.50 (*0-8328-5733-5*) Higginson Bk Co.

Reichelt, Richard. Heartland Blacksmiths: Conversations at the Forge. LC 88-4482. (Shawnee Bks.). (Illus.). 192p. (C). 1988. pap. 21.95 (*0-8093-1476-2*) S Ill U Pr.

***Reichen, Frederick.** The Lost Legends of New Jersey: A Novel. LC 99-57774. 320p. 2000. 24.00 (*0-15-100507-9*) Harcourt.

Reichen, J. & Poupon, R. E., eds. Surrogate Markers to Assess Efficacy of Treatment in Chronic Liver Diseases: Proceedings of the International Falk Workshop Held in Basel, Switzerland, October 23-24, 1995. LC 96-17380. 1996. text 110.50 (*0-7923-8705-8*) Kluwer Academic.

Reichen, J., ed. see Falk Symposium Staff.

Reichenbach, B. A., tr. from GER. The Meaning of This Life. LC 98-67456. 63p. 1998. pap. 12.00 (*0-915034-06-9*) Kober Pr.

Reichenbach, B. A., tr. see Bo Yin Ra.

Reichenbach, Bodo A., tr. see Bo Yin Ra.

Reichenbach, Bruce. Evil & a Good God. LC 82-71120. xv, 198p. 1982. reprint ed. 30.00 (*0-8232-1080-4*); reprint ed. pap. 18.00 (*0-8232-1081-2*) Fordham.

***Reichenbach, Bruce R.** Introduction to Critical Thinking. LC 00-21488. 2000. write for info. (*0-07-366027-2*) McGraw.

Reichenbach, Bruce R. & Anderson, V. Elving. On Behalf of God: A Christian Ethic for Biology. (Studies in a Christian World View). 368p. (Orig.). 1995. pap. 23.00 (*0-8028-0727-5*) Eerdmans.

Reichenbach, Charles Von, see Von Reichenbach, Charles.

Reichenbach, Frank, ed. Greenberg's Guide to Ives Trains Vol. I: Wide Gauges & Accessories, 1901-1932. (Illus.). 176p. 1991. 39.95 (*0-89778-108-2*, 10-6785, Greenberg Books) Kalmbach.

— Greenberg's Guide to Ives Trains Vol. II: O Gauge. (Illus.). 176p. 1992. 39.95 (*0-89778-124-4*, 10-7185, Greenberg Books) Kalmbach.

Reichenbach, H. Selected Writings, 1909-1953, Vol. I. Reichenbach, Maria & Cohen, Robert S., eds. Schneewind, Elizabeth H., tr. (Vienna Circle Collection: No. 4a). 518p. 1978. lib. bdg. 187.00 (*90-277-0291-8*) Kluwer Academic.

— Selected Writings, 1909-1953, Vol. II. Reichenbach, Maria & Cohen, Robert S., eds. Schneewind, Elizabeth H., tr. (Vienna Circle Collection: No. 4b). 446p. 1978. lib. bdg. 171.00 (*90-277-0909-2*) Kluwer Academic.

Reichenbach, Hans. Direction of Time. LC 99-49141. 292p. 2000. pap. text 10.95 (*0-486-40926-0*) Dover.

— Experience & Prediction: An Analysis of the Foundations & the Structure of Knowledge. LC BD0163.R4. (Midway Reprint Ser.). 421p. reprint ed. pap. 130.60 (*0-608-12117-7*, 202406300035) Bks Demand.

— From Copernicus to Einstein. Winn, Ralph B., tr. (Illus.). 123p. 1998. reprint ed. 5.95 (*0-486-23940-3*) Dover.

— Philosophic Foundations of Quantum Mechanics. unabridged ed. LC 98-40052. 192p. 1998. pap. 8.95 (*0-486-40459-5*) Dover.

— Philosophy of Space & Time. Reichenbach, Maria, tr. 295p. 1998. pap. text 8.95 (*0-486-60443-8*) Dover.

— The Rise of Scientific Philosophy. 1951. pap. 17.95 (*0-520-01055-8*, Pub. by U CA Pr) Cal Prin Full Svc.

Reichenbach, Heinrich G. Die Vollstandigste Naturgeschicte der Affen. LC 78-72725. reprint ed. 72.50 (*0-404-18298-4*) AMS Pr.

Reichenbach, Maria, ed. see Reichenbach, H.

Reichenbach, Maria, tr. see Reichenbach, Hans.

Reichenbach, Sandra, ed. see Swears, Linda.

Reichenbach, Wendy A. Studying Density Using Salad Oil & Vinegar. Neidig, H. Anthony, ed. (Modular Laboratory Program in Chemistry Ser.). 7p. (C). 1993. pap. text 1.50 (*0-87540-393-X*, PROP 393-0) Chem Educ Res.

Reichenberg, Monte. Cheating Chet. (Illus.). 32p. (Orig.). (J). (ps-4). 1992. pap. 3.95 (*0-9640260-1-5*) MM & I Ink.

— It'll Feel Better When It Quits Hurtin' rev. ed. (Illus.). 52p. 1998. pap. 7.95 (*0-9640260-3-1*) MM & I Ink.

— It'll Feel Better When It Quits Hurtin' 2nd ed. 44p. 1993. pap. 5.95 (*0-9640260-0-7*) MM & I Ink.

— Sam, Old Kate & I. (Illus.). 32p. (Orig.). (J). (ps-4). 1994. pap. 3.95 (*0-9640260-2-3*) MM & I Ink.

Reichenberg, Neil. Family & Medical Leave Act Regulations. (Monographs). 1995. pap. 10.00 (*0-914945-09-2*) Intl Personnel Mgmt.

— FLSA Exemptions: An Update. (Monographs). 1992. pap. 10.00 (*0-914945-08-4*) Intl Personnel Mgmt.

— The FLSA Salary Basis Test. (Monographs). 1996. pap. 10.00 (*0-614-23984-2*) Intl Personnel Mgmt.

Reichenberg, Norman & Raphael, Alan J. Advanced Psychodiagnostic Interpretation of the Bender Gestalt Test: Adults & Children. LC 91-37456. 176p. 1992. 47.95 (*0-275-94163-9*, C4163, Praeger Pubs) Greenwood.

Reichenberg, Shaul. Procedure for Setting Aside T'rumot & Ma'asrot. 1991. pap. 4.95 (*1-58330-141-0*) Feldheim.

***Reichenberg-Ullman, Judith.** Whole Woman Homeopathy: The Comprehensive Guide to Treating PMS, Menopause, Cystitis & Other Problems. (Illus.). 384p. 2000. pap. 18.00 (*0-7615-2411-8*) Prima Pub.

***Reichenberg-Ullman, Judyth.** Rage-Free Kids: The Homeopathic Answer for Angry, Aggressive & Defiant Children. LC 99-16191. 1999. pap. 15.00 (*0-7615-2027-9*) Prima Pub.

Reichenberg-Ullman, Judyth & Ullman, Robert. Ritalin-Free Kids: Safe & Effective Homeopathic Medicine for ADD & Other Behavioral & Learning Problems. 320p. 1996. pap. 15.00 (*0-7615-0719-1*) Prima Pub.

Reichenberg-Ullman, Judyth, jt. auth. see Ullman, Robert W.

Reichenberger, Arnold G., ed. see de Vega, Lope.

Reichenburg, Louisette. Contribution a l'histoire de la "querelle des Bouffons" LC 76-43938. (Music & Theatre in France in the 17th & 18th Centuries Ser.). reprint ed. 32.50 (*0-404-60188-X*) AMS Pr.

Reichenfeld, Robert. Windsurfing: Step by Step to Success. (Illus.). 176p. 1993. pap. 24.95 (*1-85223-746-5*, Pub. by Crolwood) Trafalgar.

Reichenfeld, Robert & Bruechert, Anna M. Skiing: Step by Step to Success with Alpine Skiing, Snowboarding & Telemarking. (Illus.). 160p. 1993. pap. 24.95 (*1-85223-707-4*, Pub. by Crolwood) Trafalgar.

— Snowboarding. LC 94-28366. (Outdoor Pursuits Ser.). (Illus.). 144p. (Orig.). 1994. pap. 13.95 (*0-87322-677-1*, PREI0677) Human Kinetics.

Reichenstein, Hermann W., ed. see Dedad, John A.

Reichenstein, William & Dorsett, Dovalee. Time Diversification Revisited. 82p. (Orig.). 1995. pap. text 30.00 (*0-943205-30-1*) RFICFA.

Reicher, Murray A. & Kellerhouse, Leland E. MRI of the Wrist & Hand. LC 90-8561. 219p. 1990. reprint ed. pap. 67.90 (*0-608-03440-1*, 206414100008) Bks Demand.

Reicher, Stephen, jt. auth. see Emler, Nicholas.

Reichersberg, Gerhoch. Letter to Pope Hadrian about the Novelties of the Day. Haring, Nikolaus M., ed. (LAT.). 125p. 16.57 (*0-88844-024-3*) Brill Academic Pubs.

Reichert, Amy. Bustop the Cat & Mrs. Lin. (Illus.). 48p. (Orig.). (J). (gr. 1-4). 1994. pap. 9.95 (*1-880812-12-6*) S Ink WA.

— A Home for Ernie. (Illus.). 48p. (Orig.). (J). (gr. 2-6). 1994. pap. 9.95 (*1-880812-11-8*) S Ink WA.

Reichert-Facilides, Fritz, et al, eds. International Insurance Contract Law: Proceedings of a Comparative Law Conference Held at the European University Institute, Florence, May 23-24, 1991. LC 92-40852. 1993. 76.50 (*90-6544-676-1*) Kluwer Law Intl.

***Reichert, Gwen.** Signposts Language Arts Activities for Grade 2 Teacher's Manual. Barbe, Walter B., ed. (Illus.). 80p. 2000. 16.95 (*1-56762-123-6*) Modern Learn Pr.

Reichert, Heinrich. Introduction to Neurobiology. (Illus.). 272p. (C). 1993. reprint ed. pap. text 42.95 (*0-19-521010-7*) OUP.

Reichert, Herbert W. Basic Concepts in the Philosophy of Gottfried Keller. LC 49-11614. (North Carolina. University. Studies in the Germanic Languages & Literatures: No. 1). reprint ed. 27.00 (*0-404-50901-0*) AMS Pr.

Reichert, Herbert W. & Salinger, Herman, eds. Studies in Arthur Schnitzler. LC 63-62703. (North Carolina. University. Studies in the Germanic Languages & Literatures: No. 42). reprint ed. 31.50 (*0-404-50942-8*) AMS Pr.

Reichert, J., jt. ed. see Meyer, W. E.

Reichert, Jake. Special Edition Using Java Network Applications. 600p. 1997. 44.99 (*0-7897-1465-5*) Que.

— Using Java Network: Special Edition. 1997. pap. text 44.99 incl. cd-rom (*1-56276-569-8*, Ziff-Davis Pr) Que.

Reichert, John. Making Sense of Literature. LC 77-24455. 234p. 1978. lib. bdg. 10.00 (*0-226-70769-5*) U Ch Pr.

— Milton's Wisdom: Nature & Scripture in Paradise Lost. LC 92-20087. 312p. (C). 1992. text 47.50 (*0-472-10324-5*, 10324) U of Mich Pr.

Reichert, Kathryn J. Nutrition for Recovery: A Patient's Guide. 1993. 36.95 (*0-8493-8652-7*, RC552) CRC Pr.

— Nutrition for Recovery: Eating Disorders. 144p. 1993. 65.00 (*0-8493-8651-9*, RC552) CRC Pr.

Reichert, Marcus. Verdon Angster. 247p. (Orig.). 1995. pap. 12.95 (*0-9645655-0-1*) BurnhillWolf.

Reichert, Marimargaret & Young, Jack H. Sterilization Technology for the Health Care Facility. LC 93-18193. 320p. 1993. 145.00 (*0-8342-0373-1*, 20373) Aspen Pub.

Reichert, Marimargaret & Young, Jack H., eds. Sterilization Technology for the Health Care Facility. 2nd ed. LC 97-8366. 400p. 1997. ring bd. 89.00 (*0-8342-0838-5*, 20838) Aspen Pub.

Reichert, Michael, jt. auth. see Bloom, Sandra L.

Reichert, Mickey Z. Beyond Ragnarok. (Renshai Chronicles Ser.: Vol. 1). 688p. 1995. 21.95 (*0-88677-658-9*, Pub. by DAW Bks) Penguin Putnam.

— Beyond Ragnarok. (Renshai Chronicles Ser.: Vol. 1). 744p. 1996. mass mkt. 5.99 (*0-88677-701-1*, Pub. by DAW Bks) Penguin Putnam.

***Reichert, Mickey Z.** Bifrost Guardians, Bks. 1-3. 2000. mass mkt. 7.50 (*0-88677-919-7*, Pub. by DAW Bks) Penguin Putnam.

Reichert, Mickey Z. By Chaos Cursed. (Bifrost Guardians Ser.: No. 5). 304p. (Orig.). 1991. mass mkt. 4.50 (*0-88677-474-8*, Pub. by DAW Bks) Penguin Putnam.

— Child of Thunder. (Last of the Renshai Ser.: Bk. 3). 592p. (Orig.). 1993. mass mkt. 6.99 (*0-88677-549-3*, Pub. by DAW Bks) Penguin Putnam.

— The Children of Wrath. (Renshai Chronicles Ser.). 688p. 1998. 24.95 (*0-88677-785-2*, Pub. by DAW Bks) Penguin Putnam.

— The Children of Wrath. (Last of the Renshai Ser.). 640p. 1999. mass mkt. 6.99 (*0-88677-860-3*, Pub. by DAW Bks) Penguin Putnam.

— Dragonrank Master. (Bifrost Guardians Ser.: No. 3). 304p. 1989. reprint ed. mass mkt. 4.99 (*0-88677-366-0*, Pub. by DAW Bks) Penguin Putnam.

— Godslayer. (Bifrost Guardians Ser.: No. 1). 224p. 1987. reprint ed. mass mkt. 3.99 (*0-88677-372-5*, Pub. by DAW Bks) Penguin Putnam.

— The Last of the Renshai. 640p. (Orig.). 1992. mass mkt. 5.99 (*0-88677-503-5*, Pub. by DAW Bks) Penguin Putnam.

— The Legend of Nightfall. 496p. (Orig.). 1993. mass mkt. 6.99 (*0-88677-587-6*, Pub. by DAW Bks) Penguin Putnam.

— Prince of Demons. LC 96-228053. (Renshai Chronicles Ser.: Vol. 2). 688p. 1996. pap. 22.95 (*0-88677-715-1*, Pub. by DAW Bks) Penguin Putnam.

— Prince of Demons Vol. 2: The Renshai Chronicles, Vol. 2. 704p. 1997. mass mkt. 6.99 (*0-88677-759-3*, Pub. by DAW Bks) Penguin Putnam.

— Shadow Climber. (Bifrost Guardians Ser.: No. 2). 304p. (Orig.). 1988. reprint ed. mass mkt. 4.99 (*0-88677-284-2*, Pub. by DAW Bks) Penguin Putnam.

— Shadow's Realm. (Bifrost Guardians Ser.: No. 4). 304p. 1990. mass mkt. 4.99 (*0-88677-419-5*, Pub. by DAW Bks) Penguin Putnam.

— The Unknown Soldier. 320p. (Orig.). 1994. mass mkt. 4.99 (*0-88677-600-7*, Pub. by DAW Bks) Penguin Putnam.

— The Western Wizard. (Renshai Chronicles Ser.: Bk. 2). (Illus.). 640p. (Orig.). 1992. mass mkt. 6.99 (*0-88677-520-5*, Pub. by DAW Bks) Penguin Putnam.

Reichert, Mickey Z. & Wingert, Jennifer. Spirit Fox. LC 99-165899. 368p. 1998. 23.95 (*0-88677-806-9*, Pub. by DAW Bks) Penguin Putnam.

— Spirit Fox. 464p. 1999. mass mkt. 6.99 (*0-88677-807-7*, Pub. by DAW Bks) Penguin Putnam.

***Reichert, Mickey Zucker.** Bifrost Guardians 2. 2000. mass mkt. 7.50 (*0-88677-934-0*, Pub. by DAW Bks) Penguin Putnam.

Reichert, Richard J. Simulation Games for Religious Education. LC 75-142. 112p. 1975. pap. 5.95 (*0-88489-060-0*) St Marys.

Reichert, Ronald G. Kava Kava. LC 97-27617. (Good Herb Guides Ser.). 96p. 1997. pap. 4.95 (*0-87983-870-1*, 38701K, Keats Publng) NTC Contemp Pub Co.

Reichert, U. The Pharmacology of Topical Retinoids. Schaefer, H. et al, eds. (Journal: Skin Pharmacology: Vol. 6, Suppl. 1, 1993). (Illus.). vi, 84p. 1994. pap. 38.50 (*3-8055-5922-4*) S Karger.

Reichert, U. & Shroot, B., eds. Pharmacology of Retinoids in the Skin: 8th CIRD Symposium on Advances in Skin Pharmacology, Cannes, September 1988. (Pharmacology & the Skin Ser.: Vol. 3). (Illus.). x, 282p. 1989. 207.00 (*3-8055-4909-1*) S Karger.

Reichert, William O. & Ludd, Steven O., eds. Outlook on Ohio. (Orig.). 1983. pap. 13.50 (*0-940390-04-3*) Comwealth Bks NJ.

Reicherts, Michael, jt. auth. see Perrez, Meinrad.

Reichertz, Ronald. The Making of the Alice Books: Lewis Carroll's Uses of Earlier Children's Literature. LC 98-219961. 264p. 1997. text 55.00 (*0-7735-1625-5*, Pub. by McG-Queens Univ Pr) CUP Services.

***Reichertz, Ronald.** The Making of the Alice Books: Lewis Carroll's Uses of Earlier Children's Literature. 256p. 2000. pap. 22.95 (*0-7735-2081-3*, Pub. by McG-Queens Univ Pr) CUP Services.

Reichheld, Frederick F., ed. The Quest for Loyalty: Creating Value Through Partnership. 252p. 1996. 29.95 (*0-87584-745-5*) Harvard Busn.

Reichheld, Frederick F. & Teal, Thomas. The Loyalty Effect: The Hidden Force Behind Growth, Profits, & Lasting Value. (Illus.). 323p. (C). 1996. 24.95 (*0-87584-448-0*) Harvard Busn.

***Reichhold, Jane.** Geography Lens. LC 99-64271. 1999. 12.00 (*0-944676-44-8*, Pub. by AHA Bks) Amazon Com.

Reichhold, Jane. Wave of Mouth Stories. 184p. (Orig.). 1993. pap. 9.00 (*0-944676-09-X*) AHA Bks.

Reichhold, Jane & Higginson, William J., eds. Narrow Road to Renga: A Collection of Renga. 270p. (Orig.). 1989. pap. 12.95 (*0-944676-19-7*) AHA Bks.

Reichhold, Jane & Reichhold, Werner. In the Presence: Tanka. 128p. 1997. pap. 10.00 (*0-944676-22-7*) AHA Bks.

Reichhold, Jane & Reichhold, Werner, eds. Wind Five-Folded. 230p. 1994. 15.00 (*0-944676-21-9*) AHA Bks.

Reichhold, Jane, jt. auth. see Walker, Bambi.

Reichhold, Jane, ed. see Eulert, Don.

Reichhold, Jane, jt. ed. see Swede, George.

Reichhold, Jane, tr. see Baha, Akiko.

Reichhold, Jane, tr. see Saito, Fumi.

Reichhold, Werner. Bridge of Voices. (ENG, FRE, GER & ITA., Illus.). 190p. (Orig.). 1990. pap. 11.00 (*0-944676-13-8*) AHA Bks.

— Handshake: In the Spirit of Exchange. (Illus.). 125p. (Orig.). 1989. pap. 10.00 (*0-944676-11-1*) AHA Bks.

— Sensescapes. (Illus.). 65p. (Orig.). 1991. pap. 8.00 (*0-944676-14-6*) AHA Bks.

— Tidal Wave. (Illus.). 170p. (Orig.). 1989. pap. 14.00 (*0-944676-12-X*) AHA Bks.

Reichhold, Werner, jt. auth. see Reichhold, Jane.

Reichhold, Werner, jt. ed. see Reichhold, Jane.

***Reichholf-Riehm, Helgard.** Birds of America. 1999. pap. 9.99 (*3-8228-7032-3*) Random.

Reichholf-Riehm, Helgard. Field Guide to Butterflies & Moths of Britain & Europe. (Illus.). 287p. 1992. pap. 22.95 (*1-85223-593-4*, Pub. by Crolwood) Trafalgar.

Reichl, Alexander J. Reconstructing Times Square: Politics & Culture in Urban Development. LC 98-55259. (Studies in Government & Public Policy). (Illus.). 264p. 1999. 39.95 (*0-7006-0949-0*); pap. 19.95 (*0-7006-0950-4*) U Pr of KS.

Reichl, Christopher A., tr. & pref. see Takayasu, Rokuro.

Reichl, H., ed. Micro Systems Technologies 90: First International Conference on Micro, Electro, Mechanic Systems & Components, Berlin, 10-13 September 1990. (Illus.). xv, 858p. 1990. 238.95 (*0-387-53025-8*) Spr-Verlag.

***Reichl, Karl.** Singing the Past: Turkic & Medieval Heroic Poetry. (Myth & Poetics Ser.). 2000. 39.95 (*0-8014-3736-9*) Cornell U Pr.

Reichl, Karl. Turkic Oral Epic Poetry: Tradition, Forms, Poetic Structure. LC 92-16726. (Albert Bates Lord Studies in Oral Tradition: Vol. 7). 408p. 1992. text 10.00 (*0-8240-7210-3*, H01247) Garland.

Reichl, Karl & Sauer, Walter. A Concordance to Six Middle English Tail-Rhyme Romances. LC 92-39411. (Illus.). X, 932p. 1993. 124.00 (*3-631-43026-4*) P Lang Pubng.

Reichl, Karl, jt. ed. see Harris, Joseph.

Reichl, L. E. The Transition to Chaos: In Conservative Classical Systems: Quantum Manifestations. (Institute for Nonlinear Science Ser.). (Illus.). xv, 551p. 1994. 54.95 (*0-387-97753-8*) Spr-Verlag.

Reichl, L. E., jt. ed. see Horton, C. W., Jr.

Reichl, Linda. A Modern Course in Statistical Physics. 2nd ed. LC 97-13550. 832p. 1998. 99.95 (*0-471-59520-9*) Wiley.

Reichl, Ruth. Tender at the Bone: Growing up at the Table. LC 97-14720. 282p. 1998. 23.00 (*0-679-44987-6*) Random.

An Asterisk (*) at the beginning of an entry indicates that the title is appearing for the first time.

— Tender at the Bone: Growing up at the Table. large type ed. LC 98-36821. 392p. 1998. 26.95 (*0-7838-0365-6*, G K Hall Lrg Type) Mac Lib Ref.

— Tender at the Bone: Growing up at the Table. LC 98-46550. 304p. 1999. reprint ed. pap. 13.00 (*0-7679-0338-2*) Broadway BDD.

Reichl, Ruth, et al. New York Times Guide to Restaurants in New York City, 2000. 400p. 1999. pap. 14.95 (*0-9668659-2-8*, Pub. by NY Times) Publishers Group.

Reichle, D. E. Dynamic Properties of Forest Ecosystems. (C). 1991. text 910.00 (*0-89771-648-5*, Pub. by Intl Bk Distr) St Mut.

Reichle, D. E., jt. ed. see Trabalka, J. R.

Reichle, Joe & Wacker, David, eds. Communicative Alternatives to Challenging Behavior: Integrating Functional Assessment & Intervention Strategies. LC 93-14787. 496p. 1993. boxed set 45.00 (*1-55766-082-4*) P H Brookes.

Reichlen, H., et al. The Scientific Expedition of Leon De Cessac to California, 1877-1879 & a Bibliography of the Chumash & Their Predecessors. fac. ed. (Reports of the University of California Archaeological Survey: No. 61). (Illus.). 74p. 1964. reprint ed. pap. 8.75 (*1-55567-376-7*) Coyote Press.

***Reichler, Gayle.** Active Wellness: A Personalized 10 Step Plan for Health Empowerment. LC 98-25072. (Illus.). 319p. (gr. 11). 1999. 24.95 (*0-7370-0006-6*) Time-Life.

Reichler, Joseph L. Baseball Trade Register. 1984. 19.95 (*0-02-603110-8*) Macmillan.

— Baseball's Great Moments, 1990 Edition. 1990. 7.98 (*0-88365-754-6*) Galahad Bks.

— Great All Time Baseball Record. 1981. 19.95 (*0-02-603100-0*) Macmillan.

Reichley, A. James. Conservatives in an Age of Change: The Nixon & Ford Administrations. LC 81-1672. 482p. 1981. 39.95 (*0-8157-7380-3*); pap. 18.95 (*0-8157-7379-X*) Brookings.

***Reichley, A. James.** The Life of the Parties: A History of American Political Parties. 512p. 2000. pap. 29.95 (*0-7425-0888-9*) Rowman.

Reichley, A. James. Religion in American Public Life. LC 85-21312. 402p. 1985. 42.95 (*0-8157-7378-1*); pap. 18.95 (*0-8157-7377-3*) Brookings.

Reichley, A. James, ed. Elections American Style. LC 87-34156. 292p. 1987. 38.95 (*0-8157-7382-X*); pap. 16.95 (*0-8157-7381-1*) Brookings.

Reichley, David. Jasper & Sam. (Illus.). (J). (gr. 4-6). 1992. 14.95 (*1-879260-04-2*) Evanston Pub.

Reichley, James. The Art of Government. (Reprint Series in Sociology). (Illus.). 1972. reprint ed. pap. 12.95 (*0-89197-664-7*); reprint ed. lib. bdg. 29.50 (*0-697-00222-5*) Irvington.

Reichlin, Seymour, ed. The Neurohypophysis: Psychological & Clinical Aspects. LC 84-4861. 240p. 1984. 65.00 (*0-306-41642-5*, Kluwer Plenum) Kluwer Academic.

— Somatostatin: Basic & Clinical Status. (Serono Symposia U. S. A. Ser.). (Illus.). 364p. 1987. 85.00 (*0-306-42573-4*, Plenum Trade) Perseus Pubng.

Reichlin, Seymour, et al, eds. The Hypothalamus. fac. ed. LC 77-83691. (Association for Research in Nervous & Mental Disease Research Publications: No. 56). (Illus.). 502p. pap. 155.70 (*0-7837-7350-1*, 204715900005) Bks Demand.

Reichlin, Seymour, jt. ed. see Bigazzi, Pierluigi E.

Reichman. Time Bomb. write for info. (*0-07-135244-9*) McGraw.

***Reichman.** Timebomb. 320p. 2000. pap. 24.95 (*0-07-135924-9*) McGraw.

Reichman, Barry. The Pre-Calculus & Calculus Workbook & Videotape. (Pre-Calculus Ser.). 100p. (J). (gr. 6-12). 1990. 225.00 (*0-685-38398-9*) Video Tutorial Serv.

Reichman, Dick. Tanker on the Rocks. 1997. pap. text 5.95 (*1-877900-02-8*) Prince W Sound.

Reichman, Harold. Reshimos Shiurim: Succah. Kuntz, Y., ed. (Notes on Jewish Talmud Ser.). 300p. (C). 1989. text 15.00 (*0-685-29013-1*) Torah Study.

Reichman, Helmut. Cross Country Soaring. rev. ed. 172p. 1993. text 39.50 (*1-883813-01-8*) Soaring Soc.

— Flying Sailplanes. 128p. 1980. text 25.00 (*1-883813-00-X*) Soaring Soc.

Reichman, Henry F. Censorship & Selection: Issues & Answers for Schools. LC 88-16815. 151p. reprint ed. pap. 46.90 (*0-7837-6155-4*, 204587700009) Bks Demand.

— Censorship & Selection: Issues & Answers for Schools. rev. ed. LC 93-19711. 160p. 1993. pap. text 20.00 (*0-8389-0620-6*) ALA.

Reichman, James B. Philosophy of the Human Person. 346p. 1985. 12.95 (*0-8294-0504-6*) Loyola Pr.

Reichman, Judith. I'm Not in the Mood: What Every Woman Should Know about Improving Her Libido. LC 98-28544. 160p. 1998. 21.95 (*0-688-16515-X*, Wm Morrow) Morrow Avon.

***Reichman, Judith.** I'm Not in the Mood: What Every Woman Should Know about Improving Her Libido. 208p. 1999. reprint ed. pap. 12.00 (*0-688-17225-3*, Wm Morrow) Morrow Avon.

Reichman, Judith. I'm Too Young to Get Old: Health Care for Women after Forty. LC 94-34614. 400p. 1996. 25.00 (*0-8129-2417-7*, Times Bks) Crown Pub Group.

— I'm Too Young to Get Old: Health Care for Women after Forty. LC 95-34614. 512p. 1997. pap. 16.00 (*0-8129-2425-8*, Times Bks) Crown Pub Group.

***Reichman, Judith.** Relax, This Won't Hurt: Painless Answers to Women's Most Pressing Health Questions. LC 99-53257. (Illus.). 384p. 2000. 25.00 (*0-688-16301-7*, Wm Morrow) Morrow Avon.

Reichman, Lee & Hershfield, Earl, eds. Tuberculosis: A Comprehensive International Approach. LC 93-20307. (Lung Biology in Health & Disease Ser.: Vol. 66). (Illus.). 784p. 1993. text 240.00 (*0-8247-8852-4*) Dekker.

***Reichman, Lee B. & Hershfield, Earl S.** Tuberculosis: A Comprehensive International Approach. 2nd rev. expanded ed. LC 00-22917. (Lung Biology in Health & Disease Ser.). (Illus.). 2000. write for info. (*0-8247-8121-X*) Dekker.

***Reichman, Louis & Borzellino, Joe.** Documents of American Democracy & Citizenship Literacy. 174p. 1998. pap. text 17.95 (*1-56226-423-0*) CAT Pub.

Reichman, Louis & Borzellino, Joe. Documents of American Democracy & Citizenship Literacy Test Bank. 22p. 1998. pap. text. write for info. (*1-56226-399-4*) CAT Pub.

— Documents of American Democracy & Citizenship Literacy Vocabulary Workbook. 76p. 1998. pap. text, wbk. ed. 10.95 (*1-56226-395-1*) CAT Pub.

Reichman, O. J. Konza Prairie: A Tallgrass Natural History. LC 87-18903. (Illus.). xii, 228p. (C). 1988. pap. 12.95 (*0-7006-0450-2*) U Pr of KS.

Reichman, Rachel. Getting Computers to Talk Like You & Me: Discourse, Context, Focus & Semantics; an ATN Model. (Comput'l Models Ser.). (Illus.). 144p. 1985. 31.50 (*0-262-18118-5*, Bradford Bks) MIT Pr.

Reichman, Steven, jt. ed. see Tien, John K.

Reichman, Sylvia. Transitions: Recent Midwifery in the U.S. Stewart, David & Stewart, Lee, eds. LC 87-63157. (Illus.). 160p. 1987. pap. 9.95 (*0-934426-15-5*) NAPSAC Reprods.

Reichman, William E. & Katz, Paul R., eds. Psychiatric Care in the Nursing Home. (Illus.). 328p. 1996. text 49.95 (*0-19-508515-9*) OUP.

Reichmanis, Elsa, et al, eds. Irradiation of Polymeric Materials: Processes, Mechanisms, & Applications. LC 93-22431. (ACS Symposium Ser.: No. 527). (Illus.). 388p. 1993. text 98.00 (*0-8412-2662-8*, Pub. by Am Chemical) OUP.

— Microelectronics Technology: Polymers in Advanced Imaging & Packaging Developed from a Symposium Sponsored by the ACS Division of Polymeric Materials: Science & Engineering, Inc., & the Polymers for Microelectronics Division of the Society of Polymer Science, Japan, at the 209th National Meeting of the American Chemical Society, Anaheim, California, April 2-6, 1995. LC 95-44669. (Symposium Ser.: Vol. 614). 590p. 1995. text 145.00 (*0-8412-3332-2*, Pub. by Am Chemical) OUP.

Reichmanis, Elsa & O'Donnell, James H., eds. The Effects of Radiation on High-Technology Polymers. LC 88-39298. (ACS Symposium Ser.: Vol. 381). 280p. 1989. reprint ed. pap. 86.80 (*0-608-03287-5*, 206380500007) Bks Demand.

Reichmanis, Elsa, jt. auth. see O'Donnell, James J.

Reichmann & Co. Staff. Die Mittelatterlichen Munzen. (ENG & GER., Illus.). 151p. 1977. 15.00 (*0-915018-32-2*) Attic Bks.

Reichmann, Eberhard, ed. Hoosier German Tales: Small & Tall. (Illus.). xx, 258p. 1991. pap. 8.00 (*1-880788-00-4*) MKGAC & IGHS.

Reichmann, Eberhard, et al, eds. Emigration & Settlement Patterns of German Communities in North America. (Illus.). 414p. (Orig.). 1995. pap. 28.00 (*1-880788-04-7*) MKGAC & IGHS.

Reichmann, Eberhard, jt. auth. see Probst, George T.

Reichmann, Eberhard, ed. & tr. see Adams, Willi P.

Reichmann, Eberhardt, ed. see Asala, Joanne.

Reichmann, Felix. The Sources of Western Literacy: The Middle Eastern Civilizations, 29. LC 79-8292. (Contributions in Librarianship & Information Science Ser.: No. 29). 274p. 1980. 59.95 (*0-313-20948-0*, RWL/, Greenwood Pr) Greenwood.

***Reichmann, James B.** Evolution, Animal 'Rights' & The Environment. LC 98-47146. 1999. 49.95 (*0-8132-0931-5*) Cath U Pr.

— Evolution, Animal 'Rights' & the Environment. LC 98-47146. 400p. (C). 2000. pap. 29.95 (*0-8132-0954-4*) Cath U Pr.

Reichmann, Rebecca L. Brazil. text 65.00 (*1-85973-263-1*); pap. text 19.50 (*1-85973-268-2*) Berg Pubs.

— Race in Contemporary Brazil: From Indifference to Inequality. LC 98-37292. 1999. 55.00 (*0-271-01905-0*); pap. text 19.95 (*0-271-01906-9*) Pa St U Pr.

Reichmann, Rebecca L., jt. auth. see Correa, Sonia.

Reichmann, Thomas. Controlling: Concepts of Management Control, Controllership, & Ratios. LC 97-15309. (Illus.). xiv, 338p. 1997. 89.00 (*3-540-62722-7*) Spr-Verlag.

Reichmeider, Philip. The Equivalence of Some Combinatorial Matching Theorems. LC 84-11746. (Illus.). 127p. 1985. 15.50 (*0-936428-09-0*) Polygonal Pub.

Reichmuth, Stefan. Der Arabische Dialekt der Sukriyya Im Ostsudan. (Studien Zur Sprachwissenschaft Ser.: Vol. 2). 325p. 1983. write for info. (*3-487-07457-5*) G Olms Pubs.

***Reichold, Klaus & Graf, Bernhard.** Buildings That Changed the World. LC 99-65365. (Illus.). 192p. 1999. 29.95 (*3-7913-2150-1*, Pub. by Prestel) te Neues.

Reichold, Klaus & Graf, Bernhard. Paintings That Changed the World: From Lascaux to Picasso. LC 98-231241. (Illus.). 192p. 1998. 29.95 (*3-7913-1983-3*) te Neues.

Reichow, Alan W., jt. auth. see Stoner, Michael W.

Reichs, Kathleen J., ed. Forensic Osteology: Advances in the Identification of Human Remains. 2nd ed. LC 97-24812. (Illus.). 584p. 1997. text 94.95 (*0-398-06804-6*) C C Thomas.

***Reichs, Kathy.** Deadly Decisions. large type ed. 464p. 2000. 25.00 (*0-7432-0429-8*) S&S Trade.

— Deadly Decisions: A Novel. LC 00-22220. 416p. 2000. 25.00 (*0-684-85971-8*) Scribner.

— Death du Jour. 1999. mass mkt. 7.99 (*0-671-03472-3*) PB.

Reichs, Kathy. Death du Jour. LC 98-48763. 384p. 1999. 25.00 (*0-684-84118-5*) Scribner.

***Reichs, Kathy.** Death du Jour. LC 99-26441. (Basic Ser.). (FRE.). 1999. pap. 27.95 (*0-7862-1997-1*) Thorndike Pr.

— Death du Jour. large type ed. LC 99-26441. 688p. 1999. 29.95 (*0-7862-1996-3*) Thorndike Pr.

— Death du Jour. 480p. 2000. reprint ed. mass mkt. 7.99 (*0-671-01137-5*, Pocket Star Bks) PB.

Reichs, Kathy. Deja Dead. 532p. 1998. per. 6.99 (*0-671-01136-7*) PB.

— Deja Dead. LC 97-2990. 416p. 1997. 24.00 (*0-684-84117-7*) Scribner.

Reichs, Kathy. Deja Dead. 1997. 282.00 (*0-684-00611-1*) Scribner.

— Deja Dead. (J). 1998. write for info. (*0-434-00427-8*, Pub. by W Heinemann) Random Bks Yng Read.

Reichs, Kathy. Deja Dead. large type ed. LC 97-38401. 697p. 1997. 28.95 (*0-7862-1265-9*) Thorndike Pr.

Reichsman, F., ed. Epidemiologic Studies in Psychosomatic Medicine. (Advances in Psychosomatic Medicine Ser.: Vol. 9). (Illus.). 1977. 49.75 (*3-8055-2654-7*) S Karger.

Reichstein, Andreas V. Rise of the Lone Star: The Making of Texas. Willson, Jeanne R., tr. LC 89-30386. (Illus.). 328p. 1989. 36.95 (*0-89096-318-5*) Tex A&M Univ Pr.

Reichstein, Gail. Wood Becomes Water: An Introduction to Chinese Medicine & the Five Element Cycle. LC 97-31947. 240p. 1998. 20.00 (*1-56836-209-9*) Kodansha.

Reichter, Eric. Chemical Processing with a Basic Computer. (Illus.). 120p. 1982. pap. text 14.95 (*0-917410-05-X*) Basic Sci Pr.

Reichwage, Randall J., ed. see McGrew, J. R., et al.

Reichwaye, Randall J., ed. see Moorhead, et al.

Reichwein, A. China & Europe. 1972. 59.95 (*0-87968-853-X*) Gordon Pr.

Reichwein, Jeffrey. Emergence of Native American Nationalism in the Columbia Plateau. LC 90-21298. (Evolution of North American Indians Ser.: Vol. 17). 416p. 1991. reprint ed. text 10.00 (*0-8240-2512-1*) Garland.

Reick, Franklin G. Flying the Stock Market: Pilot Your Dollars to Success. LC 96-75841. (Illus.). 310p. 1997. 24.95 (*0-944435-41-6*) Glenbridge Pub.

Reicke, Bo I. The Disobedient Spirits & Christian Baptism: Study of First Peter, III-19 & Its Context. LC 79-8117. 288p. 1984. reprint ed. 41.50 (*0-404-18430-8*) AMS Pr.

— The New Testament Era: The World of the Bible from 500 B. C. to A.D. 100. LC 68-15864. 352p. 1974. pap. 20.00 (*0-8006-1080-6*, 1-1080, Fortress Pr) Augsburg Fortress.

Reid. America, New Mexico. LC 97-21238. 264p. 1998. 40.00 (*0-8165-1851-3*); pap. 16.95 (*0-8165-1876-9*) U of Ariz Pr.

— Atlas of Colposcopy. 1996. text. write for info. (*0-7216-3555-5*, W B Saunders Co) Harcrt Hlth Sci Grp.

— Bed & Breakfast: Caribbean. 1995. pap. 16.00 (*0-671-89928-7*) S&S Trade.

— Bed & Breakfast: Hawaii. 1994. pap. 16.00 (*0-671-89929-5*) Howell Bks.

***Reid.** Borderland. (Illus.). 258p. 2000. pap. 16.00 (*0-8133-3792-5*, Pub. by Westview) HarpC.

Reid. Chemical Thermodynamics. 1990. text, student ed. 35.31 (*0-07-051770-3*) McGraw.

— Corrections. 2nd ed. (C). 1997. text. write for info. (*0-15-501313-0*) Harcourt Coll Pubs.

— Crime & Criminology. 7th ed. 1994. teacher ed. 12.81 (*0-697-27464-0*, WCB McGr Hill) McGrw-H Hghr Educ.

— Crime & Criminology. 9th ed. LC 99-22329. 496p. 1999. 52.50 (*0-07-228604-0*) McGraw.

— Criminal Justice. 4th ed. 1996. pap. 40.63 (*1-56134-454-0*, Dshkn McG-Hill) McGrw-H Hghr Educ.

— Criminal Law. 5th ed. 480p. 2000. 64.06 (*0-07-232153-9*) McGraw.

— DSM-IV Training Guide. 1995. pap. 195.00 (*0-87630-774-8*); sl. 195.00 (*0-87630-773-X*) Brunner-Mazel.

— DSM-IV Training Program Complete, Set. 1995. text 425.00 incl. VHS, sl. (*0-87630-771-3*); text 425.00 incl. trans., VHS (*0-87630-772-1*) Brunner-Mazel.

— Dyslexia In Adults. pap. text. write for info. (*0-471-85205-8*) Wiley.

Reid. Hospitality Marketing Management. 1988. pap. text 22.95 (*0-471-28978-7*) Wiley.

Reid. Hospitality Marketing Management. 3rd ed. 400p. 1998. text 46.95 (*0-442-01754-5*, VNR) Wiley.

— Integrator - Criminal Justice: Test Item File. 4th ed. 1996. teacher ed. 11.25 (*0-697-35632-9*, WCB McGr Hill) McGrw-H Hghr Educ.

— The Last Stand of Asian Autonomies, 1750-1900. LC 96-46165. (Illus.). 344p. 1997. text 75.00 (*0-312-17249-4*) St Martin.

— Lehi Jones, a Man of Grace. 7.95 (*1-56684-249-2*) Evans Bk Dist.

— Linear System Fundamentals. 1983. text, student ed. 28.75 (*0-07-051809-2*) McGraw.

Reid. Peru. pap. text 10.00 (*0-85345-698-4*) Monthly Rev.

Reid. Presenting Young Adult Science Fiction. LC 98-35178. 1998. 28.00 (*0-8057-1653-X*, Twyne) Mac Lib Ref.

— Sales Manual. Date not set. pap. text, teacher ed. write for info. (*0-314-88426-2*) West Pub.

— Sorcerers & Healing Spirits. (Australian National University Press Ser.). 1983. pap. text 32.00 (*0-08-032902-0*, Pergamon Pr) Elsevier.

— Understanding Buildings. (C). 1984. pap. text. write for info. (*0-582-00971-5*, Pub. by Addison-Wesley) Longman.

— Verb & Noun Number in English. Date not set. text. write for info. (*0-582-08616-7*, Pub. by Addison-Wesley) Longman.

Reid, ed. Critical Think Skill Philosophy. 5th ed. 1999. pap. text 6.00 (*0-13-086183-9*) S&S Trade.

***Reid & Barrington.** Training Interventions: Promoting Learning Opportunities. 512p. 2000. pap. 59.95 (*0-8464-5151-4*) Beekman Pubs.

Reid & Mercer. Administrative Law & Practice. 3rd ed. 704p. 137.00 (*0-409-80933-0*, MICHIE) LEXIS Pub.

Reid, et al. Cell Signalling: Experimental Strategies, No. 92. 1991. 187.00 (*0-85186-436-8*) CRC Pr.

Reid, jt. auth. see Brownlow.

Reid, jt. auth. see Connerton.

Reid, jt. auth. see Connerton, Patrice.

Reid, jt. auth. see Kondo.

Reid & Priest Staff. Electric Power Purchasing Handbook. 2nd ed. 316p. 1994. pap. 110.00 (*0-471-11268-2*) Wiley.

Reid, A. Reminiscences of the Revolution. 32p. 1995. reprint ed. pap. 6.50 (*0-910746-44-3*) Hope Farm.

Reid, A. & Tripatra Engineers Staff. Project Management: Getting It Right. 200p. 1999. boxed set 63.00 (*1-85573-420-6*) Am Educ Systs.

Reid, A. H. Reid's Branson Instruction to Juries, 7 vols. 3rd ed. 1966. suppl. ed. 275.00 (*0-672-84048-0*, 66580-10, MICHIE) LEXIS Pub.

Reid, Ace. Ace Reid & the Cowpoke Cartoons. LC 98-25330. (Southwestern Writers Collection Ser.). 176p. 1999. pap. 19.95 (*0-292-77097-9*) U of Tex Pr.

— Ace Reid's Cowpokes Cartoons Recollections Exaggerations. (Illus.). 64p. (Orig.). 1995. pap. 6.00 (*1-879894-11-4*) Cowpokes.

— Cowpokes Comin' Yore Way. 5th ed. (Illus.). 64p. 1966. reprint ed. pap. 6.00 (*0-917207-05-X*) Cowpokes.

— Cowpokes Cookbook & Cartoons. 12th ed. (Illus.). 64p. 1969. reprint ed. pap. 6.00 (*0-917207-06-8*) Cowpokes.

— Cowpokes Cow Country Cartoons. 14th ed. (Illus.). 56p. 1958. reprint ed. pap. 6.00 (*0-917207-00-9*) Cowpokes.

— Cowpokes Home Remedies. 7th ed. (Illus.). 56p. 1971. reprint ed. pap. 6.00 (*0-917207-07-6*) Cowpokes.

— Cowpokes Ole Jake. (Illus.). 64p. 1987. pap. 6.00 (*0-917207-11-4*) Cowpokes.

— Cowpokes Rarin' to Go. 2nd ed. (Illus.). 74p. 1978. reprint ed. pap. 6.00 (*0-917207-09-2*) Cowpokes.

— Cowpokes Ride Again. 4th ed. (Illus.). 64p. 1974. reprint ed. pap. 6.00 (*0-917207-08-4*) Cowpokes.

— Cowpokes Tales & Cartoons. 2nd ed. (Illus.). 64p. 1981. reprint ed. pap. 6.00 (*0-917207-10-6*) Cowpokes.

— Cowpokes Wanted. 12th ed. (Illus.). 62p. 1964. reprint ed. pap. 6.00 (*0-917207-02-5*) Cowpokes.

— Draggin' S Ranch Cowpokes. 14th ed. (Illus.). 65p. 1966. reprint ed. pap. 6.00 (*0-917207-04-1*) Cowpokes.

— More Cowpokes. 14th ed. (Illus.). 60p. 1960. reprint ed. pap. 6.00 (*0-917207-01-7*) Cowpokes.

— On the Hunt. (Illus.). 64p. (Orig.). 1992. pap. 6.00 (*1-879894-02-5*) Saratoga Pub.

Reid, Agnes J. Letters of Long Ago. 4th rev. ed. Just, Rick et al, eds. (Illus.). 132p. 1997. pap. 13.95 (*0-9653539-4-X*) Cedar Creek ID.

Reid, Aileen. I. M. Pei. (Illus.). 112p. 1998. pap. 19.95 (*1-57715-055-4*) Knckerbocker.

Reid, Alan. Castles of Wales. (Illus.). 140p. 1998. pap. 24.95 (*0-8464-4862-9*) Beekman Pubs.

Reid, Alan. The Castles of Wales. (Illus.). 140p. pap. 13.95 (*1-871083-41-9*, Pub. by J Jones Pub) Dufour.

Reid, Alan & Osborne, Brian. Discovering Scottish Writers. LC 98-131188. 96p. 1990. pap. 24.00 (*1-898218-84-6*) St Mut.

Reid, Alastair. An Alastair Reid Reader: Selected Prose & Poetry. LC 94-20521. (Bread Loaf Series of Contemporary Writers). 255p. 1994. 19.95 (*0-87451-692-7*) U Pr of New Eng.

— Oases: Poems & Prose LC 98-145218. 328 p. 1997. write for info. (*0-86241-717-1*) Canongate Books.

— Weathering: Poems & Translations. LC 87-30048. 144p. 1988. pap. 14.95 (*0-8203-0990-7*) U of Ga Pr.

— Whereabouts: Notes on Being a Foreigner. 206p. 1990. reprint ed. pap. 10.00 (*1-877727-10-5*) White Pine.

Reid, Alastair, jt. auth. see Neruda, Pablo.

Reid, Alastair, tr. see Neruda, Pablo.

Reid, Alastair, tr. see Padilla, Heberto.

Reid, Alastair J. Social Classes & Social Relations in Britain, 1850-1914. (New Studies in Economic & Social History: No. 19). 82p. (C). 1995. text 34.95 (*0-521-55278-8*); pap. text 10.95 (*0-521-55775-5*) Cambridge U Pr.

Reid, Alexandra. Glitter's Slumber Party. (Sky Dancers Ser.). (Illus.). 24p. (J). (ps). 1997. 2.50 (*0-694-01013-8*, HarpFestival) HarpC Child Bks.

Reid, Alistair J., jt. auth. see Pelling, Henry.

Reid, Alvin L. Introduction to Evangelism. LC 98-13631. (Illus.). 384p. 1998. pap. text 14.99 (*0-8054-1143-7*) Broadman.

Reid, Alvin L., jt. auth. see McDow, Malcolm.

Reid, Andrew & Morris, Karen. Daniel: Our Faithful God. (Faith Walk Bible Studies). 80p. 1999. pap. 4.99 (*1-58134-095-8*) Crossway Bks.

— Isaiah: The Road to God. (Faith Walk Bible Studies). (Illus.). 80p. 1999. pap. 4.99 (*1-58134-094-X*) Crossway Bks.

Reid, Andy, jt. auth. see Sexton, Mike.

Reid, Angus. Shakedown: How the New Economy Is Changing Our Lives. 368p. 1997. mass mkt. 9.99 (*0-7704-2761-8*) Bantam.

***Reid, Anita.** Allergen-Free Living: How to Create a Healthy, Allergen-Free Home & Lifestyle. 2000. 24.95 (*1-84000-233-6*) Mitchell Beazley.

Reid, Ann C., ed. Population Change, Natural Resources & Regionalism. (Breaking New Ground Ser.: No. 1). 104p. 1986. pap. 15.00 (*0-938549-00-6*) Grey Towers Pr.

Reid, Anna. Borderland: A Journey Through the History of Ukraine. LC 99-25541. (Illus.). 272p. 1999. 25.00 (*0-8133-3674-0*, Pub. by Westview) HarpC.

An Asterisk (*) at the beginning of an entry indicates that the title is appearing for the first time.

Reid, Annette. The Toll of Victory. LC 79-144169. (Short Story Index Reprint Ser.). 1977. reprint ed. 19.95 (*0-8369-3784-8*) Ayer.

***Reid, Anthony.** Charting the Shape of Early Modern Southeast Asia. 296p. 2000. pap. 17.50 (*974-7551-06-3*, Pub. by Silk Worm Bks) U of Wash Pr.

— The Indonesian National Revolution 1945-1950. LC 86-22768. (Studies in Contemporary Southeast Asia). (Illus.). 205p. 1986. reprint ed. lib. bdg. 59.75 (*0-313-25376-5*, REIN, Greenwood Pr) Greenwood.

Reid, Anthony. Southeast Asia in the Age of Commerce, 1450-1680 Vol. 1: The Lands Below the Winds. 291p. (C). 1990. reprint ed. pap. 18.00 (*0-300-04750-9*) Yale U Pr.

— Southeast Asia in the Age of Commerce, 1450-1680 Vol. 2: Expansion & Crisis. (C). 1995. pap. 18.00 (*0-300-06516-7*) Yale U Pr.

Reid, Anthony, ed. Sojourners & Settlers: Histories of Southeast Asia & the Chinese. (Illus.). 232p. 1996. pap. 24.95 (*1-86373-990-4*, Pub. by Allen & Unwin Pty) Paul & Co Pubs.

— Southeast Asia in the Early Modern Era: Trade, Power, & Belief. LC 92-54969. (Asia East by South Ser.). (Illus.). 286p. 1993. text 47.50 (*0-8014-2848-3*); pap. text 16.95 (*0-8014-8093-0*) Cornell U Pr.

Reid, Anthony & Akira, Oki, eds. The Japanese Experience in Indonesia: Selected Memoirs of 1942-1945. LC 82-90736. (Monographs in International Studies, Southeast Asia Ser.: No. 72). (Illus.). 424p. 1986. pap. text 20.00 (*0-89680-132-2*) Ohio U Pr.

Reid, Anthony, jt. ed. see Chirot, Daniel.

Reid, Anthony, jt. ed. see Kelly, David.

Reid, Arch & Kaiser, C. H. Creekside to Gourmet Cooking: Ozark Hills to Texas Society. (Illus.). (Orig.). 1986. pap. 8.95 (*0-9616178-0-2*) K & R Pub.

***Reid, Arnold P.** Project Management: Getting It Right. LC 99-38743. 1999. write for info. (*0-8493-0645-0*) CRC Pr.

Reid, Art. Fishing Southern Illinois. LC 86-3717. (Shawnee Bks.). (Illus.). 160p. (Orig.). 1986. 16.95 (*0-8093-1294-8*); pap. 16.95 (*0-8093-1295-6*) S Ill U Pr.

Reid, Asa E. Ace Reid & the Cowpoke Cartoons. LC 98-25330. (Southwestern Writers Collection Ser.). 176p. 1999. 40.00 (*0-292-77096-0*) U of Tex Pr.

Reid, Augusta T. Poems & Verses. 50p. (Orig.). 1997. pap. 20.00 (*0-9634518-2-0*) Longinus Pr.

Reid, B. A., ed. see Robinson, Linton H., et al.

Reid, B. C. A Casebook on Patents. (Waterlow Practitioner's Library). (Illus.). 388p. 1988. pap. 60.00 (*0-08-033087-8*, Pergamon Pr) Elsevier.

— Confidentiality & the Law. (Waterlow Practitioner's Library). 224p. 1986. 49.00 (*0-08-039236-9*, Pergamon Pr) Elsevier.

Reid, B. L. Necessary Lives: Biographical Reflections. 176p. 1990. 24.95 (*0-8262-0736-7*) U of Mo Pr.

***Reid, Barbara.** Acorn to Oak Tree. (Illus.). 14p. (J). 2000. 6.95 (*0-00-224006-8*) HarpC Child Bks.

— Caterpillar to Butterfly. (Illus.). 14p. (J). 2000. 6.95 (*0-00-224007-6*) HarpC Child Bks.

Reid, Barbara. Fun with Modeling Clay. (Illus.). 40p. (J). (gr. 3 up). 1998. pap. 5.95 (*1-55074-510-7*, Pub. by Kids Can Pr) Genl Dist Srvs.

— The Party. LC 98-29778. (Illus.). 32p. (J). (ps-2). 1999. 15.95 (*0-590-97801-2*) Scholastic Inc.

— Two by Two. 1996. pap. text 4.95 (*0-590-64942-6*) Scholastic Inc.

Reid, Barbara, jt. auth. see Bogart, Jo E.

Reid, Barbara E. Choosing the Better Part? Women in the Gospel of Luke. 248p. (Orig.). 1996. pap. 17.95 (*0-8146-5494-0*, M Glazier) Liturgical Pr.

— Parables for Preachers: The Gospel of Mark - Year B. LC 99-28090. 1999. pap. text 11.95 (*0-8146-2551-7*) Liturgical Pr.

***Reid, Barbara E.** Parables for Preachers Year C: The Gospel of Luke. 144p. 2000. pap. 11.95 (*0-8146-2552-5*) Liturgical Pr.

— A Retreat with Luke: Stepping Out on the Word. (Retreat with Ser.). 2000. pap. 9.95 (*0-86716-332-1*) St Anthony Mess Pr.

Reid, Barbara V., jt. ed. see Whitehead, Tony L.

Reid, Bernice D., ed. Tapestry Vol. I: A Multicultural Volume. 200p. 1992. pap. 12.00 (*0-9636974-0-4*) Lamar HS.

Reid, Bernice D., et al, eds. Tapestry Vol. II: A Multicultural Volume. 2nd ed. (Illus.). 253p. 1993. pap. 15.00 (*0-9636974-1-2*) Lamar HS.

Reid, Beryl, intro. V & A Cats. (Illus.). 96p. 1998. reprint ed. 19.95 (*1-85177-056-9*, Pub. by V&A Ent) Antique Collect.

Reid, Bethany. The Coyotes & My Mom. 48p. (Orig.). 1989. pap. 4.00 (*0-944920-03-9*) Bellowing Ark Pr.

Reid, Betsy, et al. Organizing a Conference on National Security. 1986. spiral bd. 7.50 (*0-937115-00-2*) Comm Natl Security.

Reid, Bill. The Raven Steals the Light. 2nd ed. LC 95-48942. 109p. (C). (ps up). 1996. reprint ed. pap. 14.95 (*0-295-97524-5*) U of Wash Pr.

Reid, Bill & Bringhurst, Robert. The Raven Steals the Light. limited ed. LC 84-47978. (Illus.). 94p. 1984. 200.00 (*0-295-96194-5*) U of Wash Pr.

Reid, Bill G. Five for the Land & Its People. (Illus.). 154p. 1989. 12.00 (*0-911042-37-7*) NDSU Inst Reg.

Reid, Brian H. The Origins of the American Civil War. (Origins of Modern Wars Ser.). 416p. (C). 1996. pap. 34.60 (*0-582-49178-9*) Longman.

Reid, Brian H. The Origins of the American Civil War. (Origins of Modern Wars Ser.). 416p. (C). 1996. 83.00 (*0-582-49177-0*) Longman.

Reid, Brian H., contrib. by. Studies in British Military Thought: Debates with Fuller & Liddell Hart. LC 97-30296. xix, 287p. 1998. text 50.00 (*0-8032-3927-0*) U of Nebr Pr.

Reid, Brian H., ed. Military Power: Land Warfare in Theory & Practice. LC 96-54594. 272p. (C). 1997. 42.50 (*0-7146-4768-3*, Pub. by Irish Acad Pr); pap. 22.00 (*0-7146-4325-4*, Pub. by Irish Acad Pr) Intl Spec Bk.

Reid, Brian H. & White, John, eds. Americana: Essays in Honour of Marcus Cunliffe. 350p. 1998. pap. 29.95 (*0-85958-670-7*, Pub. by Univ of Hull Pr) Paul & Co Pubs.

Reid, Brian Holden. The American Civil War & the Wars of the Industrial Revolution. LC 99-495002. (Illus.). 224p. 1999. 29.95 (*0-304-35230-6*, Pub. by Cassell) Sterling.

Reid, Brian Holden, jt. auth. see Grant, Susan-Mary.

***Reid, Bruce J. & Foster, William, eds.** Achieving Cultural Change in Networked Libraries. 288p. 2000. 96.95 (*0-566-08200-4*, Pub. by Gower) Ashgate Pub Co.

Reid, C. Courant: In Goettingen & New York. LC 76-17062. (Illus.). 1976. 59.95 (*0-387-90194-9*) Spr-Verlag.

— Hilbert-Courant. (Illus.). 610p. 1986. 39.95 (*0-387-96256-5*) Spr-Verlag.

— Neyman. (Illus.). 308p. 1997. pap. 34.95 (*0-387-98357-0*) Spr-Verlag.

Reid, C. & Dyer, R. Allen. A Review of the Southern African Species of Cyrtanthus. Beauchamp, R. Mitchel, ed. (Illus.). 68p. (Orig.). 1984. pap. 12.00 (*0-930653-00-9*) Intl Bulb Soc.

Reid, C. E. Chemical Thermodynamics. 332p. (C). 1990. 95.31 (*0-07-051769-X*) McGraw.

Reid, Calvin, jt. intro. see Lee, Spike.

Reid, Carlos. Out of the Hood: And into God's Purpose. LC 99-231698. 154p. 1997. pap. 8.99 (*1-884369-68-5*, EBED Pubns) McDougal Pubng.

Reid, Carol. Catastrophic Cooking: Eating Right When All Is Wrong. Harrington, David, tr. & photos by by. (Illus.). 222p. 1998. pap. 19.95 (*0-9669800-4-2*) Catastrophic.

Reid, Charles. The Natural Way to Paint: Rendering the Figure in Watercolor Simply & Beautifully. LC 94-28590. (Illus.). 144p. 1994. 29.95 (*0-8230-3158-6*) Watsn-Guptill.

***Reid, Charles.** Natural Way to Paint: Rendering the Figure in Watercolor Simply & Beautifully. (Illus.). 144p. 2000. pap. 19.95 (*0-8230-3173-X*) Watsn-Guptill.

Reid, Charles. Painting What You Want to See. (Illus.). 144p. 1987. pap. 18.95 (*0-8230-3879-3*) Watsn-Guptill.

Reid, Charles F. Education in the Territories & Outlying Possessions of the United States. LC 70-177186. (Columbia University. Teachers College. Contributions to Education Ser.: No. 825). reprint ed. 37.50 (*0-404-55825-9*) AMS Pr.

Reid, Charles F., III. Guide to Residential Financing. 3rd ed. Mascari, Claude J. et al, eds. LC 84-61252. 286p. 1984. 34.95 (*0-9603790-3-7*) PaineWebber Mortgage.

***Reid, Charles R.** Education & Evolution: School Instruction & the Human Future. LC 99-56969. 270p. 2000. 44.50 (*0-7618-1595-3*) U Pr of Amer.

Reid, Charles R. Environment & Learning: The Prior Issues. LC 75-36526. 1977. 33.50 (*0-8386-1711-5*) Fairleigh Dickinson.

Reid, Charlotte B. Tiki: Spirit Unbroken. LC 94-90588. (Illus.). 144p. (Orig.). 1995. pap. 11.95 (*0-9643061-3-1*) Egret Press.

Reid, Chisholm, jt. auth. see Reid, Stuart.

Reid, Christina. Plays, No. 1. LC 97-223101. (Contemporary Dramatists Ser.). 1997. pap. 14.95 (*0-413-71220-6*) Methn.

Reid, Christine. How to Use Microsoft Word for Windows Version 2.X. unabridged ed. Hargrave, Sally, ed. 98p. 1992. pap. text 175.00 incl. audio, disk (*1-56562-011-9*, 440) OneOnOne Comp Trng.

Reid, Christopher. Expanded Universes. 96p. (Orig.). 1996. pap. 11.95 (*0-571-17924-X*) Faber & Faber.

Reid, Christopher, jt. ed. see Mullan, John.

Reid, Christopher E., et al. Signal Processing in C. 352p. 1991. pap. 59.99 (*0-471-52713-0*) Wiley.

Reid, Clara, et al. Seven Tutuila Writers. (Illus.). 82p. 1989. pap. 5.00 (*0-930773-15-2*) Black Heron Pr.

Reid, Clarice D., et al, eds. Management & Therapy of Sickle Cell Disease. 3rd rev. ed. (Illus.). 114p. 1997. pap. text 40.00 (*0-7881-3853-7*) DIANE Pub.

Reid, Colin W. Open Secret. LC 86-63639. (Illus.). 92p. 1987. pap. 12.95 (*0-86140-240-5*, Pub. by Smyth) Dufour.

Reid, Constance. Courant. LC 96-33749. (Copernicus Bks.). (Illus.). 318p. 1996. reprint ed. 15.00 (*0-387-94670-5*) Spr-Verlag.

— From Zero to Infinity. 4th ed. LC 92-60161. 200p. 1992. pap. 19.00 (*0-88385-505-4*, ZTI) Math Assn.

— Hilbert. LC 96-33753. (Illus.). 228p. 1996. reprint ed. 15.00 (*0-387-94674-8*) Spr-Verlag.

— Jerzy Neyman-From Life. (Illus.). 320p. 1982. 65.95 (*0-387-90747-5*) Spr-Verlag.

— Julia: A Life in Mathematics. LC 96-77366. (Spectrum Ser.). (Illus.). 136p. (YA). (gr. 9 up). 1996. 31.95 (*0-88385-520-8*, JULIA) Math Assn.

— The Search for E. T. Bell: Also Known As John Taine. LC 93-78369. (MAA Spectrum Ser.). (Illus.). 384p. 1993. 30.95 (*0-88385-508-9*, BELL) Math Assn.

Reid, Cornelius L. Bel Canto: Principles & Practices. LC 76-368704. 1999. reprint ed. pap. 14.95 (*0-915282-01-1*) J Patelson Mus.

— A Dictionary of Vocal Terminology. (Illus.). 480p. 1994. reprint ed. text 40.00 (*0-9663862-0-5*, 560) Recital Pubns.

— Essays on the Nature of Singing. 280p. 1992. text 32.50 (*0-9663862-1-3*, 426) Recital Pubns.

— The Free Voice: A Guide to Natural Singing. LC 65-18533. 1999. reprint ed. pap. 14.95 (*0-915282-02-X*) J Patelson Mus.

— Voice: Psyche & Soma. LC 74-30987. (Orig.). 1975. pap. 6.95 (*0-915282-00-3*) J Patelson Mus.

Reid, D. C. Sports Injury Assessment & Rehabilitation. 2nd ed. 1998. write for info. (*0-443-08996-5*) Church.

Reid, D. Kim, et al. Cognitive Approaches to Learning Disabilities. 3rd ed. LC 90-19787. 686p. 1996. text 43.00 (*0-89079-685-8*, 7820) PRO-ED.

Reid, D. Kim, jt. auth. see Fahey, Kathleen R.

Reid, D. M., jt. ed. see Pharis, R. P.

Reid, Daniel. The Complete Book of Chinese Health & Healing: Guarding the Three Treasures. LC 93-26702. 496p. 1994. pap. 22.95 (*1-57062-071-7*, Pub. by Shambhala Pubns) Random.

***Reid, Daniel.** A Complete Guide to Chi-Gung. 336p. 2000. pap. 19.95 (*1-57062-543-3*, Pub. by Shambhala Pubns) Random.

Reid, Daniel. A Handbook of Chinese Healing Herbs. 336p. 1995. pap. 15.95 (*1-57062-093-8*, Pub. by Shambhala Pubns) Random.

— Harnessing the Power of the Universe: A Complete Guide to the Principles & Practice of Chi-gung. LC 98-5002. 304p. 1998. 25.00 (*1-57062-337-6*, Pub. by Shambhala Pubns) Random.

— Koh Samui & Environs: Koh Sammi. 2nd ed. LC 94-69773. (Illus.). 172p. (Orig.). 1995. pap. 15.95 (*0-8442-9921-9*, 99219, Passprt Bks) NTC Contemp Pub Co.

— Korea, the Land of Morning Calm. (Asian Guides Ser.). (Illus.). 206p. 1993. pap. 9.95 (*0-8442-9715-1*, Passprt Bks) NTC Contemp Pub Co.

— The Shambhala Guide to Traditional Chinese Medicine. LC 95-23897. (Illus.). 224p. (Orig.). 1996. pap. 12.00 (*1-57062-141-1*, Pub. by Shambhala Pubns) Random.

Reid, Daniel, jt. auth. see Passmore, Jacki.

Reid, Daniel G., et al, eds. Concise Dictionary of Christianity in America. abr. ed. LC 95-40444. 350p. (Orig.). 1995. pap. 16.99 (*0-8308-1446-9*, 1446) InterVarsity.

— Dictionary of Christianity in America: A Comprehensive Resource on the Religious Impulse That Shaped a Continent. LC 89-29953. 1306p. 1990. 44.99 (*0-8308-1776-X*, 1776) InterVarsity.

Reid, Daniel P. Chinese Herbal Medicine. LC 86-17814. (Illus.). 180p. 1987. reprint ed. pap. 25.00 (*0-87773-398-8*, Pub. by Shambhala Pubns) Random.

— The Tao of Health, Sex & Longevity: A Modern Practical Guide to the Ancient Way. 416p. 1989. pap. 15.00 (*0-671-64811-X*, Fireside) S&S Trade Pap.

Reid, David. Ever Hearing & Ever Seeing: A Book Reflecting on Science Through the Ears & Eyes of a Scientist, Vol. 1. LC 99-93083. (Illus.). 120p. 1999. pap. 11.95 (*0-9669041-0-9*) Plumbline Pub.

— The Humanism of Milton's Paradise Lost. 224p. (C). 1993. text 50.00 (*0-7486-0401-4*, Pub. by Edinburgh U Pr) Col U Pr.

***Reid, David.** The Metaphysical Poets. LC 99-86025. (Medieval & Renaissance Library). 272p. 2000. pap. 27.00 (*0-582-29835-0*) Longman.

— The Metaphysical Poets. LC 99-86025. 272p. 2001. 69.95 (*0-582-29834-2*) Longman.

Reid, David. New Wine: The Cultural Shaping of Japanese Christianity. LC 91-7732. (Nanzan Studies in Asian Religions: Vol. 2). (Illus.). 250p. (C). 1991. pap. text 20.00 (*0-89581-932-5*) Asian Humanities.

— Sustainable Development Introduction Guide. 1995. 26.00 (*1-85383-241-3*, Pub. by Escan Pubns) Island Pr.

Reid, David, ed. Sex, Death, & God in L. A. LC 93-38872. 1994. pap. 15.95 (*0-520-08640-6*, Pub. by U CA Pr) Cal Prin Full Svc.

Reid, David & Jerald, John. Pure Silver: The Second Best of Everything. 1987. 14.95 (*0-15-179950-4*, Harvest Bks); pap. 6.95 (*0-685-19152-4*, Harvest Bks) Harcourt.

Reid, David & Jerald, Jonathan. Pure Silver: The Second Best of Everything. 320p. 1988. pap. 10.95 (*0-15-679960-X*) Harcourt.

Reid, David, jt. ed. see Tamaru, Noriyoshi.

Reid, David A. The Sales Presentation Manual: Role Playing for Sales Effectiveness. Burvikovs, ed. 231p. (C). 1992. pap. text 27.25 (*0-314-92681-X*) West Pub.

Reid, David A., jt. auth. see Weverka, Peter.

Reid, David C. Sports Injury Assessment & Rehabilitation. (Illus.). 1269p. 1991. text 165.00 (*0-443-08662-1*) Church.

Reid, David G., ed. Protein NMR Techniques. LC 97-17906. (Methods in Molecular Biology Ser.: Vol. 60). (Illus.). 429p. 1997. 79.50 (*0-89603-309-0*) Humana.

Reid, David P. What Are They Saying about the Prophets? LC 80-80869. (What Are They Saying about...Ser.). 112p. (Orig.). 1980. pap. 3.95 (*0-8091-2304-5*) Paulist Pr.

Reid, David T., ed. see Jacobs, Paul F.

Reid, Dee, jt. auth. see Sansome, Rosemary.

Reid, Dennis. A Concise History of Canadian Painting. 2nd ed. (Illus.). 432p. 1989. pap. text 19.95 (*0-19-540663-X*) OUP.

***Reid, Dennis, ed.** Krieghoff: Images of Canada. (Illus.). 360p. 1999. 85.00 (*1-55054-725-9*, Pub. by DGL) Orca Bk Pubs.

Reid, Dennis H. Soccer Made Simple for Parents & Spectators: A Quick Guide for Understanding Terminology & Rules. 100p. 1996. write for info. (*0-9645562-1-9*) Habilit Mgt Consult.

Reid, Dennis H., ed. Organizational Behavior Management & Developmental Disabilities Services: Accomplishments & Future Directions. LC 98-39134. 258p. 1998. 49.95 (*0-7890-0662-6*) Haworth Pr.

Reid, Dennis H. & Parsons, Marsha B. Motivating Human Service Staff: Supervisory Strategies for Maximizing Work Effort & Work Enjoyment. LC 95-79661. 218p. 1995. pap. 27.00 (*0-9645562-0-0*, Pub. by Habilit Mgt Consult) Quality Bks IL.

Reid, Dennis H., et al. Staff Management in Human Services: Behavioral Research & Application. (Illus.). 248p. 1989. pap. 41.95 (*0-398-06343-5*) C C Thomas.

— Staff Management in Human Services: Behavioral Research & Application. (Illus.). 248p. (C). 1989. text 62.95 (*0-398-05547-5*) C C Thomas.

Reid, Dennis H., jt. auth. see Everson, Jane M.

Reid, Derek A. A Monograph of the Stipitate Steroid Fungi. (Illus.). 1965. pap. 145.00 (*3-7682-5418-6*) Lubrecht & Cramer.

Reid, Desmond A. Dana Meets the Cow Who Lost Its Moo. 32p. 1985. 5.95 (*0-912444-29-0*) DARE Bks.

Reid, Don. Rock Climbing Yosemite's Select. 2nd rev. ed. LC 98-17872. (Illus.). 144p. 1998. pap. 15.00 (*1-57540-115-0*) Falcon Pub Inc.

— Yosemite Climbs: Free Climbs. (Illus.). 424p. (Orig.). 1994. pap. 25.00 (*0-934641-59-5*) Falcon Pub Inc.

— Yosemite Climbs Big Walls. rev. ed. (Illus.). 216p. 1996. pap. 20.00 (*0-934641-54-4*) Falcon Pub Inc.

— Yosemite Select. rev. ed. (Illus.). 130p. 1993. pap. 15.00 (*0-934641-41-2*) Falcon Pub Inc.

Reid, Don & Falkenstein, Chris. Rock Climbs of Tuolumne Meadows. 3rd ed. (Illus.). 184p. (Orig.). 1992. pap. 20.00 (*0-934641-47-1*) Falcon Pub Inc.

Reid, Donald. The Miners of Decazeville: A Genealogy of Deindustrialization. (Illus.). 336p. 1985. 38.50 (*0-674-57634-9*) HUP.

— Paris Sewers & Sewermen: Realities & Representations. LC 90-40617. (Illus.). 248p. 1991. 45.00 (*0-674-65462-5*, REIPAR) HUP.

— Paris Sewers & Sewermen: Realities & Representations. (Illus.). 248p. (C). 1993. pap. 18.00 (*0-674-65463-3*) HUP.

— Travel Diary. (Illus.). 80p. 1998. pap. 9.95 (*1-85368-434-1*) Globe Pequot.

Reid, Donald M. Cairo University & the Making of Modern Egypt. (Cambridge Middle East Library: No. 23). (Illus.). 314p. (C). 1990. text 69.95 (*0-521-36641-0*) Cambridge U Pr.

— Lawyers & Politics in the Arab World, 1880-1960. LC 80-71053. (Studies in Middle Eastern History: No. 5). 435p. (C). 1981. 40.00 (*0-88297-028-3*) Bibliotheca.

— The Odyssey of Farah Antun: A Syrian Christian's Quest for Secularism. LC 74-80598. (Studies in Middle Eastern History: No. 2). 1975. 25.00 (*0-88297-009-7*) Bibliotheca.

***Reid, Donna.** Thinking & Writing about Art. 2nd ed. 43p. (C). 1999. pap. text 11.80 (*0-13-022358-1*) P-H.

Reid, Dorothy E. Coach into Pumpkin. LC 71-144727. (Yale Series of Younger Poets: No. 20). reprint ed. 18.00 (*0-404-53820-7*) AMS Pr.

***Reid, Duke.** Ultimate Guide to Assembling a Home Freeze Drying Machine. (Illus.). 136p. 1999. pap. 24.95 (*0-9654309-3-6*) Surety Pr.

— Ultimate Guide to VLT - "Very Long Term" Food Storage. unabridged ed. (Illus.). 182p. 1999. pap. 24.95 (*0-9654309-2-8*) Surety Pr.

Reid, Duncan. Energies of the Spirit: Trinitarian Models in Eastern Orthodox & Western Theology. LC 97-5574. (American Academy of Religion Academy Ser.). 149p. 1997. pap. 19.95 (*0-7885-0345-6*, 010196) OUP.

— Energies of the Spirit: Trinitarian Models in Eastern Orthodox & Western Theology. LC 97-5574. 149p. 1997. 49.95 (*0-7885-0344-8*, 010196) OUP.

Reid, E., et al, eds. Bioanalysis of Drugs & Metabolites: Especially Anti-Inflammatory & Cardiovascular. LC 88-22412. (Methodological Surveys in Biochemistry & Analysis Ser.: Vol. 18). (Illus.). 430p. 1988. 110.00 (*0-306-42996-9*, Plenum Trade) Perseus Pubng.

— Cells, Membranes & Disease: Including Renal. LC 87-22060. (Methodological Surveys in Biochemistry & Analysis Ser.: Vol. 17). (Illus.). 506p. (C). 1987. text 174.00 (*0-306-42678-1*, Kluwer Plenum) Kluwer Academic.

Reid, E. & Hill, H. M., eds. Drug Development Assay Approaches: Including Molecular Imprinting & Biomarkers. 300p. 1999. 225.00 (*0-85404-748-4*) Royal Soc Chem.

Reid, E., et al. Complete Set of Readers & Workbooks: Short Vowels, Long Vowels, & Digraphs, 30 vols., Set. (Start Reading Ser.: Sets A,B,C). 440p. (J). (ps-3). 1986. pap. text 69.95 (*1-56422-045-1*) Start Reading.

— Digraph Readers, 5 vols., Set. (Start Reading Ser.: Set C). 40p. (J). (ps-3). 1986. pap. text 14.95 (*1-56422-038-9*) Start Reading.

— Digraph Readers & Workbooks, 10 vols., Set. (Start Reading Ser.: Set C). 144p. (J). (ps-3). 1986. pap. text 28.95 (*1-56422-044-3*); pap. text 369.95 (*1-56422-048-6*) Start Reading.

— Digraph Workbooks, 5 vols., Set. (Start Reading Ser.: Set C). 104p. (J). (ps-3). 1986. pap. text 14.95 (*1-56422-041-9*) Start Reading.

— Long Vowel Readers, 5 vols., Set. (Start Reading Ser.: Set B). 40p. (J). (ps-3). 1986. pap. text 14.95 (*1-56422-037-0*) Start Reading.

— Long Vowel Readers & Workbooks, 10 vols., Set. (Start Reading Ser.: Set B). 164p. (J). (ps-3). 1986. pap. text 28.95 (*1-56422-043-5*); pap. text 369.95 (*1-56422-047-8*) Start Reading.

— Long Vowel Workbooks, 5 vols., Set. (Start Reading Ser.: Set B). 124p. (J). (ps-3). 1986. pap. text 14.95 (*1-56422-040-0*) Start Reading.

— Mastery Workbook for Ann: Short "a" Sound. (Start Reading Ser.: No. A1). 12p. (J). (ps-3). 1986. pap., student ed. 2.99 (*1-56422-015-X*) Start Reading.

— Mastery Workbook for Get Set: Short "e" Sound. (Start Reading Ser.: No. A5). 16p. (J). (ps-3). 1986. pap., student ed. 2.99 (*1-56422-019-2*) Start Reading.

— Mastery Workbook for the Blue Boat: Long "o" Sound. (Start Reading Ser.: No. B2). 28p. (J). (ps-3). 1986. pap., student ed. 2.99 (*1-56422-023-0*) Start Reading.

R

— Mastery Workbook for the Brown Mule: Long "u" Sound. (Start Reading Ser.: No. B5). 16p. (J). (ps-3). 1986. pap., student ed. 2.99 (*1-56422-024-9*) Start Reading.
— Mastery Workbook for the Chimp: "Ch" Sound. (Start Reading Ser.: No. C3). 20p. (J). (ps-3). 1986. pap., student ed. 2.99 (*1-56422-027-3*) Start Reading.
— Mastery Workbook for the Green Jeep: Long "e" Sound. (Start Reading Ser.: No. B3). 28p. (J). (ps-3). 1986. pap., student ed. 2.99 (*1-56422-021-4*) Start Reading.
— Mastery Workbook for the Queen: "Qu" Sound. (Start Reading Ser.: No. C4). 20p. (J). (ps-3). 1986. pap., student ed. 2.99 (*1-56422-028-1*) Start Reading.
— Mastery Workbook for the Red Plane: Long "a" Sound. (Start Reading Ser.: No. B1). 32p. (J). (ps-3). 1986. pap., student ed. 2.99 (*1-56422-020-6*) Start Reading.
— Mastery Workbook for the Shark: "Sh" Sound. (Start Reading Ser.: No. C2). 20p. (J). (ps-3). 1986. pap., student ed. 2.99 (*1-56422-026-5*) Start Reading.
— Mastery Workbook for the Thing: "Th" Sound. (Start Reading Ser.: No. C5). 20p. (J). (ps-3). 1986. pap., student ed. 2.99 (*1-56422-029-X*) Start Reading.
— Mastery Workbook for the Whale: "Wh" Sound. (Start Reading Ser.: No. C1). 24p. (J). (ps-3). 1986. pap., student ed. 2.99 (*1-56422-025-7*) Start Reading.
— Mastery Workbook for the White Bike: Long "i" Sound. (Start Reading Ser.: No. B4). 20p. (J). (ps-3). 1986. pap., student ed. 2.99 (*1-56422-022-2*) Start Reading.
— Mastery Workbook for Tip: Short "i" Sound. (Start Reading Ser.: No. A2). 20p. 1986. pap., student ed. 2.99 (*1-56422-017-6*) Start Reading.
— Mastery Workbook for Top Dog: Short "o" Sound. (Start Reading Ser.: No. A3). 24p. (J). (ps-3). 1986. pap., student ed. 2.99 (*1-56422-016-8*) Start Reading.
— Mastery Workbook for up & Up: Short "u" Sound. (Start Reading Ser.: No. A4). 20p. (J). (ps-3). 1986. pap., student ed. 2.99 (*1-56422-018-4*) Start Reading.
— Mastery Worksheets. (Start Reading Ser.: Set A). 72p. (J). (ps-3). 1989. 44.95 (*1-56422-032-X*) Start Reading.
— Mastery Worksheets. (Start Reading Ser.: Set B). 86p. (J). (ps-3). 1989. 44.95 (*1-56422-033-8*) Start Reading.
— Mastery Worksheets. (Start Reading Ser.: Set C). 73p. (J). (ps-3). 1989. 44.95 (*1-56422-034-6*) Start Reading.
— Short Vowel, Long Vowel, Digraph Readers & Workbooks, 450 vols., Set. (Start Reading Ser.: Sets A,B,C). 6600p. (J). (ps-3). 1986. pap. text 949.95 (*1-56422-049-4*) Start Reading.
— Short Vowel Readers, 5 vols., Set. (Start Reading Ser.: Set A). 40p. (J). (ps-3). 1986. pap. text 14.95 (*1-56422-036-2*) Start Reading.
— Short Vowel Readers & Workbooks, 10 vols., Set. (Start Reading Ser.: Set A). 132p. (J). (ps-3). 1986. pap. text 28.95 (*1-56422-042-7*); pap. text 369.95 (*1-56422-046-X*) Start Reading.
— Short Vowel Workbooks, 5 vols., Set. (Start Reading Ser.: Set A). 92p. (J). (ps-3). 1986. pap. text 14.95 (*1-56422-039-7*) Start Reading.
— The Start Reading Series: Instructor's Manual. 36p. 1986. teacher ed. 12.95 (*1-56422-030-3*) Start Reading.
— Start Reading with Get Set: Short "e" Sound. (Start Reading Ser.: No. A5). 8p. (J). (ps-3). 1986. pap. text 2.99 (*1-56422-004-4*) Start Reading.
— Start Reading with Red Plane: Long "a" Sound. (Start Reading Ser.: No. B1). 8p. (J). (ps-3). 1986. pap. text 2.99 (*1-56422-005-2*) Start Reading.
— Start Reading with the Blue Boat: Long "o" Sound. (Start Reading Ser.: No. B2). 8p. (J). (ps-3). 1986. pap. text 2.99 (*1-56422-006-0*) Start Reading.
— Start Reading with the Brown Mule: Long "u" Sound. (Start Reading Ser.: No. B5). 8p. (J). (ps-3). 1986. pap. text 2.99 (*1-56422-009-5*) Start Reading.
— Start Reading with the Chimp: Ch Sound. (Start Reading Ser.: No. C3). 8p. (J). (ps-3). 1986. pap. text 2.99 (*1-56422-012-5*) Start Reading.
— Start Reading with the Green Jeep: Long "e" Sound. (Start Reading Ser.: No. B3). 8p. (J). (ps-3). 1986. pap. text 2.99 (*1-56422-007-9*) Start Reading.
— Start Reading with the Queen: Qu Sound. (Start Reading Ser.: No. C4). 8p. (J). (ps-3). 1986. pap. text 2.99 (*1-56422-013-3*) Start Reading.
— Start Reading with the Shark: Sh Sound. (Start Reading Ser.: No. C2). 8p. 1986. pap. text 2.99 (*1-56422-011-7*) Start Reading.
— Start Reading with the Thing: Th Sound. (Start Reading Ser.: No. C5). 8p. (J). (ps-3). 1986. pap. text 2.99 (*1-56422-010-9*) Start Reading.
— Start Reading with the Whale: Wh Sound. (Start Reading Ser.: No. C1). 8p. (J). (ps-3). 1986. pap. text 2.99 (*1-56422-014-1*) Start Reading.
— Start Reading with the White Bike: Long "i" Sound. (Start Reading Ser.: No. B4). 8p. (J). (ps-3). 1986. pap. text 2.99 (*1-56422-008-7*) Start Reading.
— Start Reading with Tip: Short "i" Sound. (Start Reading Ser.: No. A2). 8p. (J). (ps-3). 1986. pap. text 2.99 (*1-56422-001-X*) Start Reading.
— Start Reading with Top Dog: Short "o" Sound. (Start Reading Ser.: No. A3). 8p. (J). (ps-3). 1986. pap. text 2.99 (*1-56422-002-8*) Start Reading.
— Start Reading with up & Up: Short "u" Sound. (Start Reading Ser.: No. A4). 8p. (J). (ps-3). 1986. pap. text 2.99 (*1-56422-003-6*) Start Reading.
Reid, E. Lee. Marketing Made Easy! Basics for Home Builders. LC 94-46812. (Illus.). (Orig.). 1995. pap. 24.75 (*0-86718-403-5*) Home Builder.
Reid, E. R. The Proverbs 31 Woman. 112p. 1993. pap. 8.99 (*1-56043-612-3*, Treasure Hse) Destiny Image.
Reid, Ebenezer E. Chemistry Through the Language Barrier: How to Scan Chemical Articles in Foreign Languages with Emphasis on Russian & Japanese. LC 75-112360. 150p. 1970. reprint ed. pap. 46.50 (*0-608-08142-6*, 200389300037) Bks Demand.
Reid, Ed. The Green Felt Jungle. 23.95 (*0-8488-1457-6*) Amereon Ltd.
Reid, Ed & Demaris, Ovid. The Green Felt Jungle. 256p. 1991. reprint ed. lib. bdg. 35.95 (*0-89966-783-X*) Buccaneer Bks.
Reid, Edward. Ready or Not, Here He Comes. 256p. (Orig.). 1997. pap. 14.99 (*1-878951-37-8*) Review & Herald.
Reid, Edward, jt. ed. see Hitti, Angela.
Reid, Edwin A. Camps & Critters Vol. 6: Adirondack Reidings. unabridged ed. (Illus.). 120p. 1996. pap. 8.95 (*1-890072-06-0*) Reid Pubns.
***Reid, Edwin A.** Where the Pavement Ends. (Adirondack Reidings Ser.: Vol. VII). (Illus.). 1999. per. 10.95 (*1-890072-07-9*) Reid Pubns.
Reid, Elizabeth. Moms & Dads Bilingual Coloring Book: Mamis y Papis Libro Bilingue para Iluminar. 2nd ed. (ENG & SPA., Illus.). 32p. (J). (gr. k-3). 1996. pap. 1.95 (*0-9627080-5-4*) In One EAR.
— Native Speaker: Teach English & See the World. 96p. 1996. per. 5.00 (*1-881791-06-8*) In One EAR.
— Spanish Crossword Puzzles for Beginners: Crucigramas Para Principiantes. (SPA., Illus.). 32p. (Orig.). 1995. student ed. 1.95 (*1-881791-04-1*) In One EAR.
— Spanish Lingo for the Savvy Gringo: A Do-It-Yourself Guide to the Language, Culture & Slang. expanded rev. ed. (Illus.). 216p. 2000. reprint ed. pap. 14.95 (*1-881791-08-4*) In One EAR.
***Reid, Elizabeth.** Spanish Lingo for the Savvy Gringo: A Do-It-Yourself Guide to the Language, Culture & Slang. (Illus.). 216p. 2000. reprint ed. 10.00 (*1-881791-20-3*) In One EAR.
Reid, Elizabeth, ed. HIV & AIDS: The Global Inter-Connection. LC 94-43316. (Kumarian Press Books for a World That Works). 240p. (Orig.). (C). 1995. pap. 14.95 (*1-56549-041-X*) Kumarian Pr.
Reid, Elizabeth, ed. Bilingual Cooking: La Cocina Bilingue. (ENG & SPA., Illus.). 224p. 1992. pap. 5.00 (*0-9627080-3-8*) In One EAR.
Reid, Elmer T. Practical Guide for Royal Arch Chapter Officers & Companions. rev. ed. (Illus.). x, 92p. 1980. reprint ed. pap. 6.95 (*0-88053-015-4*, M-063) Macoy Pub.
Reid, Elwood. If I Don't Six. LC 97-40416. 272p. 1998. 22.95 (*0-385-49119-0*) Doubleday.
— If I Don't Six: A Novel. 272p. 1999. pap. 12.95 (*0-385-49120-4*) Doubleday.
***Reid, Elwood.** Midnight Sun. LC 00-22719. 288p. 2000. 23.95 (*0-385-49736-9*) Doubleday.
Reid, Elwood. What Salmon Know: Stories. LC 98-55516. 240p. 1999. 21.95 (*0-385-49121-2*) Doubleday.
***Reid, Elwood.** What Salmon Know: Stories. 256p. 2000. reprint ed. pap. 12.00 (*0-385-49122-0*, Anchor NY) Doubleday.
Reid, Eric, et al, eds. Bioactive Analytes, Including CNS Drugs, Peptides, & Enantiomers. LC 86-21204. (Methodological Surveys in Biochemistry & Analysis Ser.: Vol. 16). 436p. 1986. 105.00 (*0-306-42400-2*, Plenum Trade) Perseus Pubng.
— Biofluid & Tissue Analysis for Drugs, Including Hypolipidaemics. 434p. 1994. 189.00 (*0-85186-644-1*, R6644) CRC Pr.
Reid, Eric & Wilson, Ian D. Analysis/Drugs & Metabolites, Including Anti-Infective Agent. 1990. 175.00 (*0-85186-956-4*) CRC Pr.
Reid, Eric, et al. Biochemical Approaches to Cellular Calcium. 1989. 176.00 (*0-85186-926-2*) CRC Pr.
Reid, Escott. Hungary & Suez, 1956: A View from Delhi. 160p. 1994. 24.95 (*0-88962-297-3*); pap. 14.95 (*0-88962-296-5*) Mosaic.
— On Duty: A Canadian at the Making of the United Nations, 1945 to 1946. LC 83-12021. 203p. reprint ed. pap. 63.00 (*0-7837-1342-8*, 204149000020) Bks Demand.
— Radical Mandarin: The Memoirs of Escott Reid. 1989. text 35.00 (*0-8020-5811-6*) U of Toronto Pr.
— Radical Mandarin: The Memoirs of Escott Reid. 432p. 1992. pap. text 19.95 (*0-8020-7365-4*) U of Toronto Pr.
Reid, Esmond. Understanding Buildings: A Multidisciplinary Approach. (Illus.). 225p. 1988. pap. text 19.50 (*0-262-68054-8*) MIT Pr.
Reid, Euan & Reich, Hans H., eds. Breaking the Boundaries: A Comparative Evaluation of the Pilot Projects Supported by the EC from 1986-89 on the Education of Children of Migrant Workers. 270p. 1992. 84.95 (*1-85359-134-3*, Pub. by Multilingual Matters); pap. 34.95 (*1-85359-133-5*, Pub. by Multilingual Matters) Taylor & Francis.
Reid, F. H. & Goldie, W., eds. Gold Plating Technology. 630p. 1974. 133.00 (*0-318-12538-2*) Am Electro Surface.
Reid, F. Lee. Marketing Made Easy. Tennyson, Dorris, ed. 96p. 1994. write for info. (*0-86718-428-0*) Home Builder.
Reid, Fiona A. A Field Guide to the Mammals of Central America & Southeast Mexico. (Illus.). 456p. 1998. pap. 29.95 (*0-19-506401-1*); text 60.00 (*0-19-506400-3*) OUP.
Reid, Forrest. Apostate. 240p. 1998. reprint ed. lib. bdg. 24.00 (*1-58287-009-8*) North Bks.
— Pender among the Residents. 1988. reprint ed. lib. bdg. 59.00 (*0-7812-0344-9*) Rprt Serv.
— Pender among the Residents. LC 70-131812. 1971. reprint ed. 39.00 (*0-403-00699-6*) Scholarly.
— Pirates of the Spring. LC 76-145255. 1971. reprint ed. 24.00 (*0-403-01170-1*) Scholarly.
— Private Road. LC 75-41225. reprint ed. 37.50 (*0-404-14587-6*) AMS Pr.
— W. B. Yeats: A Critical Study. LC 72-1317. (Studies in Irish Literature: No. 16). 1972. reprint ed. lib. bdg. 75.00 (*0-8383-1434-1*) M S G Haskell Hse.
— Walter De La Mare: A Critical Study. LC 73-131813. 1970. reprint ed. 39.00 (*0-403-00700-3*) Scholarly.
— Young Tom & the Retreat. large type ed. 525p. 1995. lib. bdg. 24.00 (*0-939495-85-6*) North Bks.
Reid, Frances, jt. auth. see Connerton, Patrice.
Reid, Francis. ABC of Stage Technology. (Illus.). 136p. 1995. pap. 14.95 (*0-435-08684-7*, 08684) Heinemann.
— Designing for the Theatre. 2nd ed. (Illus.). 112p. (C). 1996. pap. 19.99 (*0-87830-062-7*, Thtre Arts Bks) Routledge.
— Discovering Stage Lighting. LC 92-43267. (Illus.). 144p. 1993. pap. text 39.95 (*0-240-51345-2*, Focal) Buttrwrth-Heinemann.
— Discovering Stage Lighting. 2nd ed. LC 98-30048. (Illus.). 144p. 2000. pap. text 37.95 (*0-240-51545-5*, Focal) Buttrwrth-Heinemann.
— Sing A Song Of Mother Goose. large type ed. 40p. (J). (gr. 1-4). 1993. text 19.95 (*0-590-71380-9*) Scholastic Inc.
— Stage Lighting Handbook. LC 76-8319. (Illus.). 1976. pap. 13.95 (*0-87830-988-8*, Thtre Arts Bks) Routledge.
— Stage Lighting Handbook. 1987. pap. 10.45 (*0-87830-156-9*) Routledge.
— Stages for Tomorrow. LC 98-6416. 128p. 1998. pap. text 28.95 (*0-240-51515-3*, Focal) Buttrwrth-Heinemann.
— The Staging Handbook. 1996. pap. 16.95 (*0-435-08682-0*, 08682) Heinemann.
— The Staging Handbook. (Illus.). 1978. 14.95 (*0-87830-160-7*, Thtre Arts Bks) Routledge.
Reid, Frank, III. Nehemiah Plan, No. 1. LC 94-200437. Vol. 1. 140p. (Orig.). 1993. pap. 9.99 (*1-56043-766-9*, Treasure Hse) Destiny Image.
***Reid, Frank, III.** Restoring the House of God. 160p. 2000. pap. 11.99 (*1-56043-349-3*) Destiny Image.
Reid, Frank M., 3rd, et al. When Black Men Stand up for God: Reflections on the Million Man March. LC 96-217842. (Illus.). 226p. (Orig.). 1996. pap. text 12.95 (*0-913543-48-9*) African Am Imag.
Reid, Freda M., ed. Torrey Pines State Reserve: A Scientific Reserve of the Department of Parks & Recreation, State of California. 3rd rev. ed. LC 91-65594. (Illus.). 108p. 1991. pap., student ed. 4.00 (*0-9629917-0-8*) Torrey Pines.
Reid, Frederick H. Best of the West: Telephone Pioneers of America, Chap. 8. LC 91-37816. 1994. per. 8.00 (*0-87197-321-9*) Favorite Recipes.
Reid, G. Edward. It's Your Money, Isn't It? LC 93-12429. 1993. pap. 8.99 (*0-8280-0726-8*) Review & Herald.
Reid, G. S. & Oliver, M. R. The Premiers of Western Australia, 1890-1982. (Illus.). viii, 122p. 1983. 16.95 (*0-85564-214-9*, Pub. by Univ of West Aust Pr) Intl Spec Bk.
Reid, G. T., jt. ed. see Robinson, D. W.
Reid, Garnett. Defeating Doubt. 1982. pap. 1.95 (*0-89265-076-1*) Randall Hse.
— How to Grow in Grace. 1982. pap. 1.95 (*0-89265-077-X*) Randall Hse.
— How to Know God's Will. 1982. pap. 1.95 (*0-89265-078-8*) Randall Hse.
— How to Know You're Saved. 1982. pap. 1.95 (*0-89265-075-3*) Randall Hse.
Reid, Gary. Linear System Fundamentals: Continuous, Discrete & Modern. (McGraw-Hill Series in Electrical Engineering). (Illus.). 512p. (C). 1983. 99.38 (*0-07-051808-4*) McGraw.
Reid, Gavin. Dyslexia: A Practitioner's Handbook. 2nd ed. LC 97-17407. 264p. 1998. pap. 48.50 (*0-471-97391-2*) Wiley.
— Value Distribution & Capital: Essays in Honour of Pierangelo Garengnani. 2nd ed. LC 98-29696. 288p. (C). 1995. 75.00 (*0-415-14277-6*) Routledge.
Reid, Gavin C. Small Business Enterprise: Economic Analysis. 352p. (C). 1996. pap. 29.99 (*0-415-13207-X*) Routledge.
— Venture Capital Investment: An Agency Analysis of Practice. 352p. (C). (gr. 13). 1998. 85.00 (*0-415-17968-8*, D6366) Routledge.
— Venture Capital Investment: An Agency Analysis of Practice. LC 98-6504. 11p. 1999. write for info. (*0-415-17969-6*) Routledge.
Reid, Gavin C. & Jacobsen, Lowell R. The Small Entrepreneurial Firm. (David Hume Papers). 100p. 1988. pap. text 19.95 (*0-08-036577-9*, Pub. by Aberdeen U Pr) Macmillan.
Reid, George A. Pitman Shorterhand Dictionary. Angus, Marion, ed. LC 96-36410. 1930. 15.00 (*0-273-04229-7*) F T P-H.
Reid, George H. Marine Salvage: A Guide for Boaters & Divers. LC 96-16995. (Illus.). 176p. 1996. 23.50 (*0-924486-99-6*) Sheridan.
Reid, George H. Primer of Towing. 2nd rev. ed. LC 92-13816. (Illus.). 256p. 1992. pap. text 17.00 (*0-87033-430-1*) Cornell Maritime.
Reid, George H. The Quick & Easy Guide to Compass Correction. LC 97-24701. (Illus.). 64p. 1997. pap. 9.95 (*1-57409-023-2*) Sheridan.
— Shiphandling with Tugs. LC 86-47712. (Illus.). 279p. 1986. text 18.00 (*0-87033-354-2*) Cornell Maritime.
Reid, George K. Guide to Pond Life. (Golden Guide Ser.). 1990. 11.05 (*0-606-11759-8*, Pub. by Turtleback) Demco.
Reid, Gerard, ed. Great Irish Voices: Over 400 Years of Irish Oratory. LC 98-43173. (Illus.). 416p. 1999. 34.50 (*0-7165-2674-3*, Pub. by Irish Acad Pr) Intl Spec Bk.
Reid, Gerry. ASK for Success! 21 Ways to Enhance Your Image & Maximize Your Potential. 304p. (Orig.). 1994. pap. 16.95 (*0-9643260-0-0*) E Thomas & Sons.
Reid, Glenn C. PostScript Language Program Design. Adobe Systems Inc. Staff, ed. (Adobe Postscript Ser.: Bk. 3). 240p. (C). 1988. pap. text 26.95 (*0-201-14396-8*) Addison-Wesley.
Reid, Gordon. The Dinosaur Provincial Park: Land of Vanished Dinosaurs. rev. ed. (Illus.). 64p. 1994. pap. 12.95 (*0-88962-556-5*) Mosaic.
— A Nest of Hornets. (Illus.). 1983. 39.95 (*0-19-554358-0*) OUP.
— The Wind from the Stars: Through the Year with George MacDonald. 380p. 1992. pap. 17.95 (*0-00-599320-2*, Pub. by T & T Clark) Bks Intl VA.
Reid, Gordon, ed. Poor Bloody Murder: Personal Memoirs of the First World War. 260p. 1992. 19.95 (*0-88962-123-3*); pap. 12.95 (*0-88962-122-5*) Mosaic.
Reid, Graeme A., jt. ed. see Chapman, Steven K.
Reid, Grant. From Concept to Form in Landscape Design. 162p. 1993. pap. 39.95 (*0-471-28509-9*, VNR) Wiley.
Reid, Grant W. From Concept to Form in Landscape Design. LC 92-22661. (Illus.). 176p. 1993. pap. 39.95 (*0-442-01247-0*, VNR) Wiley.
— Landscape Graphics. (Illus.). 216p. 1987. pap. 19.95 (*0-8230-7331-9*, Whitney Lib) Watsn-Guptill.
Reid-Green, Marcia, ed. see Matrau, Henry.
Reid-Green, Marcia M., ed. see Matrau, Henry.
Reid, Greg. Nobodys Angel: A Book of Satanic Abuse. LC 97-93064. 96p. 1998. pap. 14.95 (*0-9657066-9-9*) Magic Press.
— Teen Satanism: Redeeming the Devil's Children. 32p. (Orig.). 1990. pap. 10.00 (*1-877858-04-8*, TS-RDC) Amer Focus Pub.
— Treasures from the Master's Heart. 107p. (Orig.). 1991. pap. 10.00 (*1-877858-39-0*, TFTMH) Amer Focus Pub.
Reid, H. Extra South. (Illus.). 144p. 1986. pap. 21.95 (*0-911868-53-4*, C53) Carstens Pubns.
Reid, H. A. Advanced Engineering Studies: Business, Society & the Environment. 176p. (Orig.). 1996. pap. 29.50 (*0-7487-2595-4*, Pub. by S Thornes Pubs) Trans-Atl Phila.
Reid, H. Bruce, jt. auth. see Virkar, Raghunat.
Reid, H. W., ed. The Management & Health of Farmed Deer. (Current Topics in Veterinary Medicine & Animal Science Ser.). (C). 1988. text 137.50 (*0-89838-408-7*) Kluwer Academic.
Reid, Harry. Searchlight: The Camp That Didn't Fail. LC 97-18226. 288p. 1998. 19.95 (*0-87417-310-8*) U of Nev Pr.
Reid, Harvey. Long: Biographical Sketch of Enoch Long, an Illinois Pioneer (with Genealogy) (Illus.). 134p. 1996. reprint ed. pap. 19.00 (*0-8328-5615-0*); reprint ed. lib. bdg. 29.00 (*0-8328-5614-2*) Higginson Bk Co.
Reid, Harvey, jt. auth. see Kuhn, Terry.
Reid, Heather. Preparing Music for Celebration. LC 96-6577. (Preparing for Liturgy Ser.). 1997. pap. 3.95 (*0-8146-2480-4*) Liturgical Pr.
Reid, Henrietta. New Boss at Birchfields. large type ed. 1991. 27.99 (*0-7089-2524-3*) Ulverscroft.
Reid, Howard & Croucher, Michael. The Way of the Warrior: The Paradox of the Martial Arts. (Illus.). 240p. 1991. 35.00 (*0-87951-433-7*, Pub. by Overlook Pr) Penguin Books.
— The Way of the Warrior: The Paradox of the Martial Arts. (Illus.). 240p. 1995. pap. 23.95 (*0-87951-626-7*, Pub. by Overlook Pr) Penguin Putnam.
Reid, Howard, et al. The Book of Soft Martial Arts: Finding Personal Harmony with Chi Kung, Hsing I, Pa Kua & T'ai Chi. LC 98-17561. (Illus.). 192p. 1998. pap. 17.95 (*0-8348-0460-3*) Weatherhill.
Reid, Hugh B. Sheet Metal Layout Simplified, 3 vols., Vol. 1. 1981. 19.50 (*0-685-77694-8*) H B Reid.
— Sheet Metal Layout Simplified, 3 vols., Vol. 2. 1981. 19.50 (*0-685-41577-5*) H B Reid.
— Sheet Metal Layout Simplified, 3 vols., Vol. 3. 1981. 19.50 (*0-685-41578-3*) H B Reid.
Reid, Ian. Higher Education or Education for Hire? LC 97-172439. v, 171p. 1996. pap. 19.95 (*1-875998-13-6*, Pub. by Central Queensland) Accents Pubns.
— Narrative Exchanges. 240p. (C). (gr. 13 up). 1992. text 52.95 (*0-415-07234-4*) Routledge.
— Rhumbs. Kaplan, Peter, ed. LC 75-10586. 1975. 1.50 (*0-915176-07-6*) Pourboire.
Reid, Ian, ed. The Place of Genre in Learning: Current Debates. 124p. (C). 1987. 50.00 (*0-7300-0247-0*, Pub. by Deakin Univ) St Mut.
Reid, Ian W., jt. ed. see Berthof, Robert J.
Reid, Inez S. Together Black Women. 2nd ed. LC 73-83156. 348p. 1974. reprint ed. 29.95 (*0-89388-114-7*); reprint ed. pap. 19.95 (*0-89388-115-5*) Okpaku Communications.
Reid, Ira D. In a Minor Key Negro Yoyth. LC 73-160450. (Illus.). 134p. 1971. reprint ed. lib. bdg. 65.00 (*0-8371-3346-7*, RENY, Greenwood Pr) Greenwood.
— Negro Immigrant: His Background, Characteristics & Social Adjustment, 1899-1937. LC 68-58615. (Columbia University. Studies in the Social Sciences: No. 449). reprint ed. 20.00 (*0-404-51449-9*) AMS Pr.
— Negro Immigrant: His Background, Characteristics & Social Adjustment, 1899-1937. LC 69-18771. (American Immigration Collectio. Series 1). 1975. reprint ed. 19.95 (*0-405-00537-7*) Ayer.
Reid, Isaiah. Grace & Spiritual Growth. 1989. pap. 5.99 (*0-88019-253-4*) Schmul Pub Co.
Reid, Ivan. Class in Britain. LC 98-29549. 288p. 1998. 59.95 (*0-7456-1891-X*); pap. 26.95 (*0-7456-1892-8*) Blackwell Pubs.
— The Sociology of School & Education. 320p. 1986. pap. 23.00 (*1-85396-183-3*, Pub. by P Chapman) Taylor & Francis.
Reid, Ivan & Stratta, Drica, eds. Sex Differences in Britain. 2nd ed. (Illus.). 1989. text 64.95 (*0-566-05595-3*, Pub. by Gower); pap. text 33.95 (*0-566-05804-9*, Pub. by Gower) Ashgate Pub Co.
Reid, J. Arch of Ancient Arizona. LC 96-25188. (Illus.). 310p. 1996. 40.00 (*0-8165-1380-5*); pap. 17.95 (*0-8165-1709-6*) U of Ariz Pr.

An Asterisk (*) at the beginning of an entry indicates that the title is appearing for the first time.

R

Reid, J., jt. auth. see Katz, L.
Reid, J. B. A Complete Word & Phrase Concordance to the Poems & Songs of Robert Burns, Incorporating a Glossary of Scotch Words. (BCL1-PR English Literature Ser.). 568p. 1992. reprint ed. lib. bdg. 99.00 (*0-7812-7468-0*) Rprt Serv.
Reid, J. D. & Yang, K. H., eds. Crashworthiness & Occupant Protection in Transportation Systems. LC 89-46297. 319p. 1993. pap. 70.00 (*0-7918-1022-4*) ASME.
Reid, J. Gavin, jt. auth. see Hay, James G.
Reid, J. H. The Origins of the British Labour Party. LC 55-11709. 272p. reprint ed. pap. 84.40 (*0-608-14618-8*, 205589900039) Bks Demand.
— Writing Without Taboos: The New East German Literature. 268p. 1990. 19.50 (*0-85496-020-1*) Berg Pubs.
Reid, J. Jefferson, ed. Cholla Project Archaeology: Ceramic Studies. (Archaeological Ser.: No. 161). (Illus.). 438p. 1981. pap. 16.95 (*1-889747-34-3*) Ariz St Mus.
Reid, J. Jefferson, jt. ed. see Fish, Paul.
Reid, J. Jefferson, ed. see Haury, Emil W.
Reid, J. K., tr. see Calvin, John.
Reid, J. L. Total Geostrophic South Pacific: Flow Patterns, Tracers & Transports. 1985. pap. 50.00 (*0-08-034011-3*, Pub. by PPL) Elsevier.
Reid, J. M., et al. Fluid Gasification of Oil. (Research Bulletin Ser.: No. 16). iv, 48p. 1953. pap. 25.00 (*1-58222-021-2*) Inst Gas Tech.
— Natural Gas Supplements by Cyclic-Regenerative Hydrogasification of Oils. (Research Bulletin Ser.: No. 28). iv, 78p. 1960. pap. 25.00 (*1-58222-031-X*) Inst Gas Tech.
Reid, J. Norman & Dubin, Elliott. Federal Funds to Rural Areas: Fair Share? Right Mix? (New Alliances for Rural America Ser.). (Orig.). 1988. pap. text 6.00 (*1-55877-019-4*) Natl Governor.
Reid, J. Norman, jt. ed. see Sears, David W.
Reid, J. R., et al, eds. Crashworthiness & Occupant Protection in Transportation Systems - 1995. LC 97-138987. (1995 ASME International Mechanical Engineering Congress & Exposition Ser.: AMD-Vol. 210/BED-Vol. 30). 568p. 1995. 150.00 (*0-7918-1721-0*, H01003) ASME.
Reid, J. S. The Municipalities of the Roman Empire. Date not set. 35.00 (*0-89005-551-3*) Ares.
Reid, J. S., et al. Rubber Dam in Clinical Practice. (Illus.). 108p. 1991. pap. text 34.00 (*1-85097-011-4*) Quint Pub Co.
Reid, J. S., ed. see Cicero, Marcus Tullius.
Reid, Jack. Watercolor Basics: Let's Get Started. LC 98-4285. (Watercolor Basics Ser.). (Illus.). 128p. 1998. pap. 18.99 (*0-89134-867-0*, North Lght Bks) F & W Pubns Inc.
***Reid, Jack.** Watercolor Basics: Painting Snow & Water. LC 99-54495. (Watercolor Basics Ser.). (Illus.). 128p. 2000. pap. 18.99 (*0-89134-918-9*, North Lght Bks) F & W Pubns Inc.
Reid, James. Edward Seago: The Landscape Art. 264p. 1992. 90.00 (*0-85667-402-8*) Sothebys Pubns.
***Reid, James.** Marvelous Reality: The Fascination of South America. (Illus.). 1999. write for info. (*0-9675934-0-9*) Alexandr Glob.
Reid, James & Apesteguia, Raul. The Textile Art of Peru. De Lavalle, Jose A. & Gonzalez, Jose A., eds. Hare, Isabel, tr. (Illus.). 373p. (Orig.). 1993. 65.00 (*0-9647468-0-8*) Industrial Textil.
***Reid, James & Reisner, M. E.** The Diary of a County Clergyman, 1848-1851. (Illus.). 472p. 2000. 65.00 (*0-7735-2000-7*, Pub. by McG-Queens Univ Pr) CUP Services.
Reid, James D. The Telegraph in America: Its Founders, Promoters & Noted Men. LC 74-7493. (Telecommunications Ser.). (Illus.). 926p. 1974. reprint ed. 69.95 (*0-405-06056-4*) Ayer.
Reid, James D., jt. ed. see Willis, Sherry.
Reid, James H. Heinrich Boll: A German for His Time. LC 87-15783. 245p. 1988. 19.50 (*0-85496-533-5*) Berg Pubs.
— Narration & Description in the French Realist Novel: The Temporality of Lying & Forgetting. LC 92-39126. (Cambridge Studies in French: No. 44). 238p. (C). 1993. text 69.95 (*0-521-42092-X*) Cambridge U Pr.
***Reid, James J.** Studies in Safavid Mind, Society & Culture. LC 99-87121. (Illus.). 460p. 2000. text 45.00 (*1-56859-089-X*) Mazda Pubs.
Reid, James J., ed. Tribalism & Society in Islamic Iran 1500-1629. (Studies in Near Eastern Culture & Society Ser.: Vol. 4). xiv, 220p. 1983. pap. 24.00 (*0-89003-124-X*) Undena Pubns.
Reid, James M. Better Business Letters John Deere Special Edition. 4th ed. pap. 14.49 (*0-201-56337-1*) Addison-Wesley.
Reid, James M. & Silleck, Anne. Better Business Letters: A Programmed Book to Develop Skill in Writing. 3rd ed. LC 84-24457. 208p. 1985. pap. text 16.95 (*0-201-06350-6*) Addison-Wesley.
Reid, Jamie. Easy Money. 1987. 17.95 (*0-8027-0999-0*) Walker & Co.
Reid, Jamie. Home on the Range. 319p. 1995. 24.95 (*1-85158-563-X*, Pub. by Mainstream Pubng) Trafalgar.
— Home on the Range. 256p. 1996. pap. 15.95 (*1-85158-794-2*, Pub. by Mainstream Pubng) Trafalgar.
— Prez: Homage to Lester Young. 1993. pap. text 9.95 (*0-88982-129-1*, Pub. by Oolichan Bks) Genl Dist Srvs.
***Reid, Jan.** Close Calls: Jan Reid's Texas. LC 00-30242. 304p. 2000. 29.95 (*0-89096-965-5*) Tex A&M Univ Pr.
Reid, Jan. The Improbable Rise of Redneck Rock. LC 76-30434. (Quality Paperbacks Ser.). (Illus.). 1977. pap. 6.95 (*0-306-80065-9*) Da Capo.
Reid, Jan, ed. see Sansom, Andrew.
Reid, Jane D. A Guide to Classical Subjects in the Arts, Vol. 2. LC 92-35374. 1344p. 1993. text 275.00 (*0-19-504998-5*) OUP.
Reid, Jean B., jt. ed. see Fields, Margaret U.
***Reid, Jefferson.** Grasshopper Pueblo: A Story of Archeology & Ancient Life. LC 99-6572. (Illus.). 192p. 1999. 29.95 (*0-8165-1913-7*); pap. 15.95 (*0-8165-1914-5*) U of Ariz Pr.
Reid, Jeffrey. How to Build Ponds & Waterfalls & Much More. Klein, Mary, ed. (Illus.). 81p. 1997. 24.95 (*0-9656905-0-4*) Tranquility Ponds.
— How to Build Ponds & Waterfalls & Much More... The Complete Guide. 1998. pap. text 14.95 (*1-56465-195-9*) Tetra Pr.
Reid, Jeffrey, jt. tr. see Braud, Philippe.
Reid, Jennings B. Jesus: God's Emptiness, God's Fullness: The Christology of St. Paul. LC 90-36837. 160p. 1990. pap. 7.95 (*0-8091-3165-X*) Paulist Pr.
Reid, Jenny. Secret of the Silver Sea. LC 97-178304. (J). 1996. pap. 6.95 (*1-85594-182-1*, Pub. by Attic Press) Intl Spec Bk.
Reid, Jill, jt. auth. see Brown, Cynthia.
Reid, Jim. A Telemedicine Primer: Understanding the Issues. LC 96-94441. xi, 294p. 1996. spiral bd. 75.00 (*0-9653045-0-7*) Innvtve Med.
Reid, Joan A., jt. auth. see Rocky Mountain Mineral Law Staff.
Reid, Joanie. Life Line: A Journal for Parents Grieving a Miscarriage, Stillbirth or Other Early Infant Death. LC 93-86825. 100p. 1994. 15.95 (*1-878526-30-8*) Pineapple MI.
Reid, JoAnne, et al. Small Group Learning in the Classroom. LC 90-35956. 95p. (C). 1990. pap. text 16.50 (*0-435-08542-5*, 08542) Heinemann.
Reid, John. The Best Little Boy in the World. 256p. 1993. pap. 11.00 (*0-345-38176-9*) Ballantine Pub Grp.
— The Best Little Boy in the World: 1998 Edition. LC 98-15284. 1998. 15.95 (*0-679-60314-X*) Modern Lib NY.
— Living with Teenagers: A Survival Manual for Adults. LC 81-70265. 268p. (Orig.). 1983. pap. 7.95 (*0-9607234-0-4*) Ampersand Pub.
— The Magnificent Society & the Democracy Amendments: How to Free Your Congressmen from the Control of the Special Interests. LC 80-85474. 220p. 1981. 11.95 (*0-939428-00-8*); pap. 8.95 (*0-939428-01-6*) Pony X Pr.
Reid, John & Eaton, John. The Life of Andrew Jackson. Owsley, Frank L., Jr., ed. LC 74-2567. (Southern Historical Publications: No. 19). 536p. reprint ed. 166.20 (*0-8357-9619-1*, 201321500083) Bks Demand.
Reid, John C. The Best Is Yet to Be: A Christian Interpretation of Life Beyond Death. 4th ed. 36p. 1994. pap. 2.95 (*0-914733-00-1*) Desert Min.
— God's Promises & My Needs. 80p. 1993. pap. 3.95 (*0-914733-06-0*) Desert Min.
— My Commitment. 68p. 1993. pap. 3.95 (*0-914733-14-1*) Desert Min.
Reid, John C., jt. auth. see Wilkes, G. A.
Reid, John C., jt. ed. see Buckner, Phillip A.
Reid, John G. Mount Allison University: A History, to 1963, Vol. 1. LC 84-175462. (Illus.). 441p. 1984. reprint ed. pap. 136.80 (*0-8357-3663-6*, 203639000001) Bks Demand.
— Mount Allison University: A History, to 1963, Vol. 2: 1914-1963. LC 84-175462. (Illus.). 544p. 1984. reprint ed. pap. 168.70 (*0-8357-3664-4*, 203639000002) Bks Demand.
Reid, John G., jt. ed. see Axelrod, Paul.
Reid, John K. The Authority of Scripture: A Study of the Reformation & Post-Reformation Understanding of the Bible. LC 79-8716. 286p. 1981. reprint ed. lib. bdg. 65.00 (*0-313-22191-X*, REAS, Greenwood Pr) Greenwood.
Reid, John K., jt. auth. see Metcalf, Michael.
Reid, John L., et al. Lecture Notes on Clinical Pharmacology. 5th ed. LC 96-859. 1996. pap. 29.95 (*0-08-654665-1*) Blackwell Sci.
Reid, John M. Homeward Journey. (Classics Ser.). 192p. 1992. pap. 9.95 (*0-86241-178-5*, Pub. by Canongate Books) Interlink Pub.
Reid, John M., jt. auth. see Spencer, Merrill P.
Reid, John P. Chief Justice: The Judicial World of Charles Doe. LC 67-12102. (Illus.). 499p. 1967. 40.00 (*0-674-11400-0*) HUP.
— The Concept of Liberty in the Age of the American Revolution. LC 87-14971. viii, 232p. 1988. 31.50 (*0-226-70896-9*) U Ch Pr.
— The Concept of Representation in the Age of the American Revolution. LC 89-32139. 260p. 1989. 38.50 (*0-226-70898-5*) U Ch Pr.
— Constitutional History of the American Revolution. LC 94-39045. 176p. 1995. text 29.95 (*0-299-14660-X*) U of Wis Pr.
— Constitutional History of the American Revolution. abr. ed. LC 94-39045. 176p. 1995. pap. text 14.95 (*0-299-14664-2*) U of Wis Pr.
— Constitutional History of the American Revolution Vol. 1: The Authority of Rights. LC 86-40058. 1987. text 35.00 (*0-299-10870-8*) U of Wis Pr.
— Constitutional History of the American Revolution Vol. 2: The Authority to Tax. LC 87-8256. 384p. (C). 1987. text 35.00 (*0-299-11290-X*) U of Wis Pr.
— Constitutional History of the American Revolution Vol. 3: The Authority to Legislate. LC 91-50326. 508p. (C). 1991. 35.00 (*0-299-13070-3*) U of Wis Pr.
— Constitutional History of the American Revolution Vol. 4: The Authority of Law. LC 86-40058. 288p. (C). 1993. 35.00 (*0-299-13980-8*) U of Wis Pr.
— In a Defiant Stance: The Conditions of Law in Massachusetts Bay, the Irish Comparison, & the Coming of the American Revolution. LC 76-42453. 1977. 30.00 (*0-271-01240-4*) Pa St U Pr.
— In Defiance of the Law: The Standing-Army Controversy, the Two Constitutions, & the Coming of the American Revolution. LC 80-14002. (Studies in Legal History). 295p. reprint ed. pap. 91.50 (*0-7837-5236-9*, 204497000005) Bks Demand.
— Law for the Elephant: Property & Social Behavior on the Overland Trail. LC 79-26989. 447p. reprint ed. pap. 138.60 (*0-7837-5287-3*, 204504100005) Bks Demand.
— Law for the Elephant: Property & Social Behavior on the Overland Trail. LC 97-131833. 446p. 1997. reprint ed. pap. 15.00 (*0-87328-164-0*) Huntington Lib.
***Reid, John P.** Patterns of Vengeance. LC 99-52258. 1999. write for info. (*0-9635086-1-X*) Ninth Judicial CHS.
Reid, John P. Policing the Elephant: Crime, Punishment, & Social Behavior on the Overland Trail. LC 96-30677. (Illus.). (Orig.). 1996. pap. 15.00 (*0-87328-159-4*) Huntington Lib.
***Reid, John P., et al.** Law as Culture & Culture as Law: Essays in Honor of John Phillip Reid. LC 00-26743. 2000. write for info. (*0-945612-99-0*) Madison Hse.
Reid, John T. & Hunter, J. R. History of Humbold County, Nevada. 48p. 1986. reprint ed. 10.00 (*0-8466-9174-5*, S-174, Shorey Pubns) Shoreys Bkstore.
Reid, John Z. Born to Win: A Poetic Biography of African-Americans. LC 95-68267. (Illus.). 64p. (YA). (gr. 6-12). 1995. 17.95 (*1-887214-01-1*); pap. 12.95 (*1-887214-02-X*) Caribbean TX.
Reid, Joseph L. Northwest Pacific Ocean Waters in Winter. LC 72-12351. (Johns Hopkins Oceanographic Studies: No. 5). (Illus.). 96p. 1973. reprint ed. pap. 30.00 (*0-608-04008-8*, 206474400011) Bks Demand.
Reid, Joseph L., ed. Antarctic Oceanology One. LC 78-151300. (Antarctic Research Ser.: Vol. 15). (Illus.). 343p. 1971. 28.50 (*0-87590-115-8*) Am Geophysical.
Reid, Joseph L., jt. ed. see Capurro, Luis R.
Reid, Joy M. Basic Writing. 2nd ed. (Illus.). 256p. (C). 1996. pap. text 30.47 (*0-13-353657-2*) P-H.
— Learning Styles in the ESL/EFL. 240p. (J). 1995. mass mkt. 33.95 (*0-8384-6158-1*) Heinle & Heinle.
— The Process of Composition. (Illus.). 224p. (C). 1982. pap. text 11.95 (*0-13-723015-X*) P-H.
— The Process of Composition. 2nd ed. (Illus.). 256p. (C). 1988. pap. text 33.27 (*0-13-723065-6*) P-H.
***Reid, Joy M.** The Process of Composition. 3rd ed. LC 99-38017. 368p. 1999. pap. text 33.27 (*0-13-021317-9*) P-H.
Reid, Joy M. Process of Paragraph Writing. 2nd ed. 272p. (C). 1994. pap. text 33.27 (*0-13-101205-3*) P-H.
— Teaching ESL Writing. 368p. (C). 1993. pap. 31.20 (*0-13-888215-0*) P-H.
— Understanding Learning Styles in the Second Language Classroom. LC 97-25281. 224p. (C). 1998. pap. text 26.33 (*0-13-281636-9*) P-H.
Reid, Joyce M., ed. Classic Scottish Short Stories. 352p. 1990. pap. 13.95 (*0-19-282686-7*) OUP.
***Reid, Judith P.** Family Ties in England, Scotland, Wales & Ireland: Sources for Genealogical Research. LC 96-42143. 108p. 1998. pap. 25.01 (*0-8444-0911-1*, Library of Cong); per. 5.50 (*0-16-061816-9*, Library of Cong) USGPO.
Reid, Judith P., ed. Family Ties in England, Scotland, Wales & Ireland: Sources for Genealogical Research. (Illus.). 108p. (C). 1999. pap. text 25.00 (*0-7881-7791-5*) DIANE Pub.
***Reid, Judith Prowse & Fowler, Simon.** Genealogical Research in England's Public Record Office: A Guide for North Americans. 2nd ed. (Illus.). 164p. 2000. 22.50 (*0-8063-1632-2*) Genealog Pub.
Reid, K. A Guide to the Use of Otoliths in the Study of Predators at South Georgia. 40p. 1996. pap. 25.00 (*0-86556-184-2*, Pub. by Brit Antarctic Surv) Balogh.
Reid, K. B., jt. auth. see Law, S. K.
Reid, K. F. Properties & Reactions of Bonds in Organic Molecules. LC 79-365421. 570p. reprint ed. pap. 176.70 (*0-608-10832-4*, 200455100043) Bks Demand.
***Reid, Kathryn G.** Children Together: Teaching Girls & Boys to Value Themselves & Each Other. 2000. pap. 14.95 (*0-8298-1380-2*) Pilgrim OH.
Reid, Kathryn G. Preventing Child Sexual Abuse: A Curriculum for Children Ages Five Through Eight. LC 94-3395. (Illus.). 160p. (Orig.). 1994. pap. 11.95 (*0-8298-1016-1*) Pilgrim OH.
Reid, Kathryn G. & Fortune, Marie M. Preventing Child Sexual Abuse: A Curriculum for Children Ages Nine Through Twelve. LC 89-33084. (Illus.). 128p. (Orig.). (YA). 1989. pap. 9.95 (*0-8298-0810-8*) Pilgrim OH.
Reid, Kathryn Goering & Reid, Stephen Breck. Uncovering Racism. LC 99-23619. (Covenant Bible Studies Ser.). 120p. 1999. pap. 5.95 (*0-87178-016-X*, FaithQuest) Brethren.
Reid, Kaye, ed. Maxine Sommers Presents Savory Soups: A Celebration of Exquisite Flavors! (Illus.). 6p. (Orig.). 1993. pap. 3.00 (*0-943991-29-3*) Pound Sterling Pub.
***Reid, Keith.** Penguin. (Natural World Ser.). (Illus.). (J). 2000. 9.95 (*0-7398-3128-3*); 27.12 (*0-7398-2767-7*) Raintree Steck-V.
Reid, Ken. Disaffection from School. 230p. 1988. pap. text 15.95 (*0-423-51550-0*) Routledge.
***Reid, Ken.** Tackling Truancy in Schools: A Practical Manual for Primary & Secondary Schools. LC 99-32847. 265p. 2000. pap. write for info. (*0-415-20508-5*) Routledge.
Reid, Ken. Truancy in Schools. LC 99-27648. 256p. 1999. pap. write for info. (*0-415-20509-3*) Routledge.
Reid, Kenneth E. From Character Building to Social Treatment: The History of the Use of Groups in Social Work. LC 79-6567. 249p. 1981. 45.00 (*0-313-22016-6*, RCB/, Greenwood Pr) Greenwood.
— Social Work Practice with Groups: A Clinical Perspective. 2nd ed. LC 96-31830. (Miscellaneous/Catalogs Ser.). 306p. (C). 1996. mass mkt. 53.95 (*0-534-34548-4*) Brooks-Cole.
Reid, Kenneth G. & Gretton, George L. An Introduction to the Scottish Law of Property. 1995. pap. text. write for info. (*0-406-10517-0*, UK, MICHIE) LEXIS Pub.
Reid, Kenneth G., et al. Reid: The Law of Property in Scotland. 1996. write for info. (*0-406-99917-1*, RSPL, MICHIE) LEXIS Pub.
Reid, Kenneth R. Social Work Practice with Groups: A Clinical Perspective. 311p. (C). 1996. pap. 49.75 (*0-534-14820-4*) Brooks-Cole.
Reid, Kenneth S., tr. see Marias Aquilera, Julian.
Reid, L. D., ed. Opioids, Bulimia, & Alcohol Abuse & Alcoholism. xi, 393p. 1990. 89.95 (*0-387-97242-0*) Spr-Verlag.
Reid, Laura. Adventures in Creating Earrings. Smith, Monte, ed. LC 90-82647. (Illus.). 96p. 1990. per. 9.95 (*0-943604-28-1*, BOO/14) Eagles View.
— New Adventures in Beading Earrings. Smith, Monte, ed. (Illus.). 64p. (Orig.). 1989. pap., per. 9.95 (*0-943604-18-4*, BOO/07) Eagles View.
Reid, Laurie, jt. auth. see Guest, Barbara.
Reid, Lawrence A. An Ivatan Syntax. LC 68-64243. (Oceanic Linguistics Special Publication Ser.: No. 2). 168p. (Orig.). reprint ed. pap. 52.10 (*0-8357-8679-X*, 205683600092) Bks Demand.
Reid, Legh W. The Elements of the Theory of Algebraic Numbers. LC 10-23524. 474p. reprint ed. pap. 147.00 (*0-608-10039-0*, 202074300018) Bks Demand.
Reid, Leonard N., ed. Proceedings of the Conference of the American Academy of Advertising, 1992. 1992. pap. 25.00 (*0-931030-15-3*) Am Acad Advert.
Reid, Leslie M. Research & Cumulative Watershed Effects. (Illus.). 118p. (Orig.). (C). 1995. pap. text 35.00 (*0-7881-1894-3*) DIANE Pub.
Reid, Linda. Crossing the Threshold: The Astrology of Dreaming. Sullivan, Erin, ed. LC 98-129586. (Arkana Contemporary Astrology Ser.). (Illus.). xvi, 185p. 1998. pap. 12.95 (*0-14-019528-9*) Viking Penguin.
Reid, Lisa. Raising Kids with Just a Little Cash. LC 96-96469. (Illus.). 1740p. (Orig.). 1996. pap. 12.95 (*0-9651651-0-8*) Ferguson-Carol Pubs.
Reid, Lloyd D., jt. auth. see Etkin, Bernard.
Reid, Lola M., jt. ed. see Zern, Mark A.
Reid, Loren. Finally It's Friday: School & Work in Mid-America, 1921-1933. LC 80-27453. (Illus.). 304p. 1981. 32.50 (*0-8262-0330-2*) U of Mo Pr.
— Hurry Home Wednesday: Growing Up in a Small Missouri Town, 1905-1921. LC 77-25401. (Illus.). 304p. 1978. text 32.50 (*0-8262-0247-0*) U of Mo Pr.
— Professor on the Loose. LC 92-96967. (Illus.). vi, 334p. (Orig.). 1992. pap. 13.95 (*0-9634518-0-4*) Longinus Pr.
— Speech Teacher: A Random Narrative. LC 90-63139. (Illus.). 109p. (C). 1990. pap. 7.00 (*0-944811-05-1*) Natl Comm Assn.
Reid, Lorene. Thinking Skills Resource Book. 70p. 1990. pap. 14.95 (*0-936386-58-4*) Creative Learning.
Reid, Loretta G. Control & Communication in Programs. Stone, Harold, ed. LC 82-6893. (Computer Science: Systems Programming Ser.: No. 13). 175p. 1982. reprint ed. pap. 54.30 (*0-8357-1349-0*, 207004600063) Bks Demand.
Reid, Lori. The Art of Hand Reading. 120p. 1996. 24.95 (*0-7894-1060-5*) DK Pub Inc.
— Astrology. (Pocket Prophecy Ser.). (Illus.). 64p. 2000. text 7.95 (*1-86204-483-X*, Pub. by Element MA) Penguin Putnam.
Reid, Lori. Chinese Horoscopes. rev. ed. (Illus.). 96p. 1994. pap. 6.95 (*0-7063-7222-0*, Pub. by WrLock) Sterling.
Reid, Lori. Chinese Horoscopes for Lovers: Dog. (Chinese Horoscopes Ser.). 1996. 8.95 (*1-85230-771-4*, Pub. by Element MA) Penguin Putnam.
— Chinese Horoscopes for Lovers: Dragon. (Chinese Horoscopes Ser.). 1996. 8.95 (*1-85230-765-X*, Pub. by Element MA) Penguin Putnam.
— Chinese Horoscopes for Lovers: Horse. (Chinese Horoscopes Ser.). 1996. 8.95 (*1-85230-767-6*, Pub. by Element MA) Penguin Putnam.
— Chinese Horoscopes for Lovers: Monkey. (Chinese Horoscopes Ser.). 1996. 8.95 (*1-85230-769-2*, Pub. by Element MA) Penguin Putnam.
— Chinese Horoscopes for Lovers: Ox. LC 95-46830. (Chinese Horoscopes Ser.). (Illus.). 48p. 1996. 8.95 (*1-85230-762-5*, Pub. by Element MA) Penguin Putnam.
— Chinese Horoscopes for Lovers: Pig. (Chinese Horoscopes Ser.). 1996. 8.95 (*1-85230-772-2*, Pub. by Element MA) Penguin Putnam.
— Chinese Horoscopes for Lovers: Rabbit. (Chinese Horoscopes Ser.). 1996. 8.95 (*1-85230-764-1*, Pub. by Element MA) Penguin Putnam.
— Chinese Horoscopes for Lovers: Rat. (Chinese Horoscopes Ser.). 48p. 1996. 8.95 (*1-85230-759-5*, Pub. by Element MA) Penguin Putnam.
— Chinese Horoscopes for Lovers: Rooster. (Chinese Horoscopes Ser.). 48p. (Orig.). 1996. 8.95 (*1-85230-770-6*, Pub. by Element MA) Penguin Putnam.
— Chinese Horoscopes for Lovers: Sheep. (Chinese Horoscopes Ser.). 1996. 8.95 (*1-85230-768-4*, Pub. by Element MA) Penguin Putnam.
— Chinese Horoscopes for Lovers: Snake. (Chinese Horoscopes Ser.). 1996. 8.95 (*1-85230-766-8*, Pub. by Element MA) Penguin Putnam.
— Chinese Horoscopes for Lovers: Tiger. (Chinese Horoscopes Ser.). 1996. 8.95 (*1-85230-763-3*, Pub. by Element MA) Penguin Putnam.
— Color Crazy: A Guide to Understanding the Colors in Your Life. LC 98-29525. (Illus.). 96p. (YA). (gr. 5 up). 1998. 19.95 (*1-901881-61-X*, Pub. by Element MA) Penguin Putnam.

An Asterisk (*) at the beginning of an entry indicates that the title is appearing for the first time.

— The Complete Book of Chinese Horoscopes. LC 98-189082. 136p. 1997. write for info. (1-86204-063-X) Element MA.

— The Complete Book of Chinese Horoscopes. 112p. 1997. pap. 19.95 (1-85230-941-5, Pub. by Element MA) Penguin Putnam.

***Reid, Lori.** The Complete Illustrated Guide to Chinese Astrology. (Illus.). 2001. pap. 19.95 (1-86204-386-8) Element MA.

Reid, Lori. Dream Catcher: Unravel the Mysteries of Your Sleeping Mind. 1997. 29.95 (1-86204-268-3, Pub. by Element MA) Penguin Putnam.

***Reid, Lori.** The Dream Catcher: Unravel the Mysteries of Your Sleeping Mind. 2000. pap. 18.95 (1-86204-551-8) Element MA.

Reid, Lori. East West Astrology: Combining the Chinese & Western Traditions to Chart Your Destiny. LC 98-46638. (Illus.). 224p. 1999. pap. 24.95 (1-86204-462-7, Pub. by Element MA) Penguin Putnam.

— Elements of Handreading. (Elements of...Ser.). 1997. pap. 9.95 (1-86204-075-3, Pub. by Element MA) Penguin Putnam.

— Health in Your Hands: How to Gain a Detailed Picture of Your State of Health from Your Hands. 256p. 1993. 13.00 (1-85538-182-6, Pub. by Aqrn Pr) Harper SF.

— Mix & Match Astrology. 128p. 1997. 24.95 (0-7641-5054-5) Barron.

***Reid, Lori.** Moon Blessings Pack: Let the Creative Energies of the Moon Enhance Your Life & Illuminate Your Soul with Book & Cards & Other. 2000. pap. 24.95 (1-85868-857-4, Pub. by Carlton Bks Ltd) Natl Bk Netwk.

Reid, Lori. Sweet Dreamer: A Guide for Young Dreamers Including Feathers, Beads, String, Plastic Circle to Make a Dream Catcher & Dream Journal. (Cosmic Kits Ser.). (Illus.). 96p. (YA). (gr. 5 up). 1998. pap. 19.95 (1-901881-55-5, Pub. by Element MA) Penguin Putnam.

— The Sweet Dreamer: A Guide to Understanding Your Dreams. 96p. 1999. pap. 5.95 (1-901881-75-X, Pub. by Element MA) Penguin Putnam.

— Tea Leaves, Herbs & Flowers: Fortune Telling the Gypsy Way! (Elements of the Extraordinary Ser.). (Illus.). 125p. (J). (gr. 4-7). 1998. pap. text 5.95 (1-901881-82-2, Pub. by Element Child) Penguin Putnam.

Reid, Louann & Golub, Jeffrey N., eds. Reflective Activities: Helping Students Connect with Texts. (Classroom Practices in Teaching English Ser.: Vol. 30). 220p. 1998. pap. 22.95 (0-8141-1755-4) NCTE.

***Reid, Louann & Neufeld, Jamie, eds.** Rationales for Teaching Young Adult Literature. LC 99-32781. 224p. 1999. pap. text 22.50 (1-893056-04-X, 05604-X) Calendar Islands.

Reid, Louis A. A Study in Aesthetics. LC 70-114546. 415p. 1973. reprint ed. lib. bdg. 75.00 (0-8371-4794-8, RESA, Greenwood Pr) Greenwood.

— Ways of Knowledge & Experience. 287p. 1961. 69.50 (0-614-00166-8) Elliots Bks.

Reid, Lydia J., jt. ed. see Backstrom, T. E.

Reid, Lynne M., jt. auth. see Legg, Merle A.

Reid, M. Undergraduate Algebraic Geometry. (London Mathematical Society Student Texts Ser.: No. 12). (Illus.). 144p. 1989. pap. text 21.95 (0-521-35662-8) Cambridge U Pr.

Reid, M., et al, eds. Mathematical Papers in Honor of Yuri Ivanovich Manin. 650p. (C). 1987. text 143.00 (0-8223-0798-7) Duke.

Reid, M. J. & Moran, J. M., eds. The Impact of VLBI on Astrophysics & Geophysics. (C). 1988. lib. bdg. 208.00 (90-277-2704-X) Kluwer Academic.

***Reid, Macgregor S. & Flury, Walter, eds.** Space Safety & Rescue, 1998: Including Space Activities Impact on Environment. 398p. 2000. 55.00 (0-87703-464-8, Am Astronaut Soc) Univelt Inc.

Reid, Malcolm. Prehistoric Houses in Britain. (Archaeology Ser.: No. 70). (Illus.). 72p. 1989. pap. 10.50 (0-7478-0218-1, Pub. by Shire Pubns) Parkwest Pubns.

— The Shouting Signpainters: A Literary & Political Account of Quebec Revolutionary Nationalism. LC 75-158922. 320p. 1972. pap. 10.00 (0-85345-283-0, Pub. by Monthly Rev) NYU Pr.

Reid, Margaret, et al. Training Interventions. 3rd ed. 456p. (C). 1992. pap. text 95.00 (0-85292-480-1, Pub. by IPM Hse) St Mut.

Reid, Margaret, jt. auth. see Kenney, John.

Reid, Margaret A. The Polemics of Poetry: The Harlem Renaissance & Sixties in Retrospect. LC 94-11768. (Studies in African & African-American Culture: Vol. 8). 1994. write for info. (0-8204-2482-X) P Lang Pubng.

Reid, Margaret A. & Barrington, Harry. Training Interventions: Managing Employee Development. 456p. (C). 1994. pap. 60.00 (0-85292-566-2, Pub. by IPM Hse) St Mut.

Reid, Margaret G. Consumers & the Market. 3rd ed. LC 75-39270. (Getting & Spending: The Consumer's Dilemma Ser.). (Illus.). 1976. reprint ed. 51.95 (0-405-08042-5) Ayer.

— Food for People. LC 75-26312. (World Food Supply Ser.). (Illus.). 1976. reprint ed. 54.95 (0-405-07790-4) Ayer.

Reid, Margarette S. The Button Box. LC 89-38566. (Illus.). 24p. (J). (ps-2). 1990. 14.99 (0-525-44590-0, Dutton Child) Peng Put Young Read.

— The Button Box. (Illus.). 24p. (J). (ps-2). 1995. pap. 5.99 (0-14-055495-5, PuffinBks) Peng Put Young Read.

— Button Box. 1995. 11.19 (0-606-07328-0, Pub. by Turtleback) Demco.

— La Caja de los Botones.Tr. of Button Box. (J). 1995. 10.19 (0-606-07767-7) Turtleback.

— A String of Beads. LC 97-10686. (Illus.). 32p. (J). (ps-4). 1997. 14.99 (0-525-45721-6) NAL.

Reid, Margo, ed. Law & Accounting: Nineteenth-Century American Legal Cases. (Foundations in Accounting Ser.: No. 15). 295p. 1989. reprint ed. text 10.00 (0-8240-6130-6) Garland.

***Reid, Marie E. & Hammersley, Richard.** Communicating Successfully in Groups: A Practical Introduction for the Workplace. LC 99-57361. 2000. pap. write for info. (0-415-20103-9) Routledge.

Reid, Marion. A Plea for Woman. LC 88-61923. 98p. 1988. reprint ed. pap. 12.95 (0-948275-56-1) Dufour.

Reid, Marion E. & Lomas-Francis, Christine, eds. The Blood Group Antigen Factsbook. LC 96-36684. (Factsbooks Ser.). (Illus.). 384p. 1996. pap. text 42.00 (0-12-585965-1) Morgan Kaufmann.

Reid, Marion E. & Nance, Sandra J., eds. Red Cell Transfusion: A Practical Guide. LC 97-39691. (Contemporary Hematology Ser.). (Illus.). 240p. 1997. 99.50 (0-89603-412-7) Humana.

***Reid, Mark.** Parochial. 2000. pap. 16.95 (1-86368-277-5, Pub. by Fremantle Arts) Intl Spec Bk.

Reid, Mark A. PostNegritude Visual & Literary Culture. LC 96-20292. (SUNY Series, Cultural Studies in Cinema/Video). 192p. (C). 1997. text 54.50 (0-7914-3301-3); pap. text 17.95 (0-7914-3302-1) State U NY Pr.

— Redefining Black Film. 1993. pap. 17.95 (0-520-07902-7, Pub. by U CA Pr) Cal Prin Full Svc.

Reid, Mark A., ed. Spike Lee's "Do the Right Thing" (Cambridge Film Handbooks Ser.). (Illus.). 174p. (C). 1997. text 49.95 (0-521-55076-9); pap. text 13.95 (0-521-55954-5) Cambridge U Pr.

***Reid-Maroney, Nina.** Philadelphia's Enlightenment, 1740-1800: Kingdom of Christ, Empire of Reason, Vol. 81. (Contributions to the Study of World History Ser.: Vol. 81). 2000. write for info. (0-313-31472-1, Greenwood Pr) Greenwood.

Reid, Martine. Indians of the Northwest. (J). (gr. 1-9). 1992. pap. 4.95 (0-88388-112-8) Bellerophon Bks.

Reid, Martine, ed. Yale French Studies, 84: Boundaries: Writing & Drawing. 1993. pap. 18.00 (0-300-05836-5) Yale U Pr.

Reid, Marty L. Augustinian & Pauline Rhetoric in Romans Five: A Study of Early Christian Rehetoric. LC 96-891. (Mellen Biblical Press Ser.: No. 30). 216p. 1996. 89.95 (0-7734-2367-2, Mellen Biblical Pr) E Mellen.

Reid, Mary. How Have I Grown? LC 93-44811. (Illus.). (J). 1993. 19.95 (0-590-72911-X) Scholastic Inc.

— Karaleen. (Serenade Serenata Ser.: No. 32). 1986. pap. 1.49 (0-310-47362-4) Zondervan.

Reid, Mary & Chessen, Betsey. Bugs, Bugs, Bugs! LC 97-29202. (Science Emergent Readers Ser.). (Illus.). (J). 1997. pap. 2.50 (0-590-39792-3) Scholastic Inc.

Reid, Mary, jt. auth. see Canizares, Susan.

Reid, Mary C. Big Island Search. (Backpack Mysteries Ser.: No. 2). (Illus.). 8p. (J). (gr. 2-5). 1996. pap. 3.99 (1-55661-716-X) Bethany Hse.

— Phantom Gardener, Vol. 3. (Backpack Mystery Ser.). 8p. (J). (gr. 2-5). 1997. pap. 3.99 (1-55661-717-8) Bethany Hse.

— Rock Patrol, 6. LC 97-21039. (Backpack Mystery Ser.). 8p. (J). 1997. pap. 3.99 (1-55661-720-8) Bethany Hse.

— Secret in the Swamp, 5. LC 97-21038. (Backpack Mystery Ser.). 8p. (J). 1997. pap. 3.99 (1-55661-719-4) Bethany Hse.

— Too Many Treasures. (Backpack Mysteries Ser.: No. 1). (Illus.). 8p. (J). (gr. 2-5). 1996. pap. 3.99 (1-55661-715-1) Bethany Hse.

— Twin Trouble, Vol. 4. LC 97-4650. (Backpack Mysteries Ser.). 8p. (J). (gr. 2-5). 1997. pap. 3.99 (1-55661-718-6) Bethany Hse.

Reid, Mary Carpenter. Backpack Mysteries, Vols. 1-6. (Backpack Mystery Ser.). (J). 1997. boxed set 23.99 (0-7642-8193-3, 258193) Bethany Hse.

Reid, Mary E. Bicycles. (Let's Find Out Library Ser.). (Illus.). 24p. (J). (ps-2). 1997. pap. text 4.95 (0-590-73802-X) Scholastic Inc.

— Let's Find Out about Ice Cream. (Let's Find Out Library Ser.). 24p. (J). (ps-2). 1997. pap. text 4.95 (0-590-73800-3) Scholastic Inc.

***Reid, Mary E. & World Book, Inc. Staff.** Howlers & Other New World Monkeys. LC 00-21639. (Animals of the World Ser.). (Illus.). 64p. (J). (gr. 1-4). 2000. write for info. (0-7166-1209-7) World Bk.

— Owls & Other Birds of Prey. LC 00-21634. (Animals of the World Ser.). (Illus.). 64p. (J). (gr. 1-4). 2000. write for info. (0-7166-1203-8) World Bk.

— Wolves & Other Wild Dogs. LC 00-21636. (Animals of the World Ser.). (Illus.). 64p. (J). (gr. 1-4). 2000. write for info. (0-7166-1206-2) World Bk.

Reid, Mary F. The Camera-Shy Cupid. LC 97-97214. (Cupid Romance Ser.: Vol. 13K1). 192p. 1998. 18.95 (0-8034-9284-7, Avalon Bks) Bouregy.

— The Electric Cupid. LC 98-96332. 192p. 1998. lib. bdg. 18.95 (0-8034-9312-6, Avalon Bks) Bouregy.

— The Gourmet Cupid. LC 98-96224. (Cupid Romance Ser.: Bk. 2). 192p. 1998. 18.95 (0-8034-9302-9, Avalon Bks) Bouregy.

***Reid, Maureen Murphy.** I Remember Fannie. 204p. 2000. 23.95 (0-7541-1290-X, Pub. by Minerva Pr) Unity Dist.

***Reid, Maurya M., et al.** Make Them Hunters. expanded rev. ed. (Adirondack Reidings Ser.: Vol. I). x, 137p. 1998. pap. 9.95 (1-890072-01-X) Reid Pubns.

Reid, Mehry M. Gourmet Cooking Persian Style. LC 89-91992. (Illus.). 192p. 1989. 30.00 (0-9623790-1-8) Ceresville Pub Co.

— Persian Calligraphic Designs. (International Design Library). (Illus.). 48p. (Orig.). 1995. pap. 5.95 (0-88045-130-0) Stemmer Hse.

— Persian Carpet Designs. (International Design Library). (Illus.). 48p. 1982. pap. 5.95 (0-88045-005-3) Stemmer Hse.

— Persian Ceramic Designs. (International Design Library). (Illus.). 48p. (Orig.). 1983. pap. 5.95 (0-88045-024-X) Stemmer Hse.

— Persian Etching Designs. (International Design Library). (Illus.). 48p. 1985. pap. 5.95 (0-88045-061-4) Stemmer Hse.

— Persian Textile Designs. (International Design Library). (Illus.). 48p. (Orig.). 1984. pap. 5.95 (0-88045-027-4) Stemmer Hse.

Reid, Melissa E. Charlottesville for Families: A Guide to Activities for Families & Children. 288p. 1998. pap. 14.95 (0-9641731-3-1) Featherstne Inc.

Reid-Merritt, Patricia. Sister Power: How Phenomenal Black Women Are Rising to the Top. LC 96-4208. 214p. 1996. 22.95 (0-471-10461-2) Wiley.

— Sister Power: How Phenomenal Black Women Are Rising to the Top. 214p. 1997. pap. 14.95 (0-471-19355-0) Wiley.

Reid, Michael, tr. see Wright, Machaelle S.

Reid, Michaela. Ask Sir James. large type ed. (Illus.). 524p. 1989. 27.99 (0-7089-1966-9) Ulverscroft.

Reid, Michelle. Coercion to Love. (Presents Ser.). 1993. mass mkt. 2.99 (0-373-11597-0, 1-11597-1) Harlequin Bks.

— Corazon Rendido. 1999. per. 3.50 (0-373-33516-4, 1335165) Harlequin Bks.

— The Dark Side of Desire. (Presents Ser.). 1993. pap. 2.89 (0-373-11533-4, 1-11533-6) Harlequin Bks.

— Esclavos del Amor. (Bianca Ser.). (SPA.). 1996. per. 3.50 (0-373-33373-0, 1-33373-1) Harlequin Bks.

— Fruto de la Traicion: Gold Ring of Betrayal. (Bianca Ser.: Vol. 125). (SPA.). 1998. per. 3.50 (0-373-33475-3, 1-33475-4) Harlequin Bks.

— Gold Ring of Betrayal. 1997. per. 3.50 (0-373-11917-8, 1-11917-1) Harlequin Bks.

— House of Glass Presents Plus. (Presents Ser.). 1994. per. 2.99 (0-373-11615-2, 1-11615-1) Harlequin Bks.

***Reid, Michelle.** The Italian's Revenge. (Presents Ser.). 2000. mass mkt. 3.99 (0-373-12121-0, 1-12121-9) Harlequin Bks.

Reid, Michelle. Lost in Love. (Presents Ser.). 1994. per. 2.99 (0-373-11665-9, 1-11665-6) Harlequin Bks.

— Marriage on the Rebound. (Presents Ser.: Vol. 1973). 1998. per. 3.75 (0-373-11973-9, 1-11973-4) Harlequin Bks.

— Marriage on the Rebound. large type ed. (Mills & Boon Large Print Ser.). 288p. 1998. 24.99 (0-263-15564-1, Pub. by Mills & Boon) Ulverscroft.

— The Marriage Surrender. (Presents Ser.: No. 2014). 1999. per. 3.75 (0-373-12014-1, 1-12014-6) Harlequin Bks.

— The Mistress Bride: Society Weddings. (Presents Ser.: No. 2056). 1999. per. 3.75 (0-373-12056-7, 1-12056-7) Harlequin Bks.

***Reid, Michelle.** The Mistress Bride: Society Weddings. large type ed. (Romance Ser.). 1999. 21.95 (0-263-16247-8) Mills & Boon.

Reid, Michelle. The Morning After. 1997. per. 3.50 (0-373-11859-7, 1-11859-5) Silhouette.

— The Morning After. large type ed. (Harlequin Ser.). 1996. 20.95 (0-263-14752-5) Thorndike Pr.

— No Way to Begin. large type ed. 285p. 1991. reprint ed. lib. bdg. 18.95 (0-263-12697-8) Mac Lib Ref.

— Passion Becomes You. LC 95-13569. (Presents Ser.). 187p. 1995. per. 3.25 (0-373-11752-3, 1-11752-2) Harlequin Bks.

— Passionate Scandal. 1994. per. 2.99 (0-373-11695-0, 1-11695-3) Harlequin Bks.

— The Price of a Bride. (Presents Ser.: No. 2033). 1999. per. 3.75 (0-373-12033-8, 1-12033-6, Harlequin) Harlequin Bks.

— Slave to Love. LC 96-503. 186p. 1995. per. 3.25 (0-373-11776-0) Harlequin Bks.

— Slave to Love. large type ed. (Harlequin Romance Ser.). 1995. 19.95 (0-263-14288-4) Mac Lib Ref.

***Reid, Michelle.** The Spanish Husband. (Presents Ser.). 2000. mass mkt. 3.99 (0-373-12145-8, 1121458) Harlequin Bks.

— Tycoon's Bride. (Presents Ser.: Vol. 2106). 185p. 2000. per. 3.99 (0-373-12106-7) Harlequin Bks.

Reid, Michelle. The Ultimate Betrayal (Wedlocked!) LC 96-703. 188p. 1996. per. 3.50 (0-373-11799-X, 1-11799-3) Harlequin Bks.

Reid, Mick. A Treasury of Stories for Eight Year Olds. LC 94-30241. 160p. (J). (ps-4). 1995. pap. 6.95 (1-85697-545-2) LKC.

Reid, Miles. Undergraduate Commutative Algebra. (London Mathematical Society Student Texts Ser.: No. 29). (Illus.). 167p. (C). 1996. text 59.95 (0-521-45255-4) Cambridge U Pr.

— Undergraduate Commutative Algebra. (London Mathematical Society Student Texts Ser.: No. 29). (Illus.). 167p. (C). 1996. pap. text 21.95 (0-521-45889-7) Cambridge U Pr.

Reid, Miles, tr. see Shafarevich, Igor R.

Reid, Mitchell. Civil War Soldiers. 288p. 1997. pap. 12.95 (0-14-026333-0) Viking Penguin.

Reid, Monty. Crawlspace: New & Selected Poems. 122p. (Orig.). 1993. pap. 14.95 (0-88784-539-8, Pub. by Hse of Anansi Pr) Genl Dist Srvs.

— Flat Side: Poems. LC 99-170151. 1998. pap. 9.95 (0-88995-188-8, Pub. by Red Deer) Genl Dist Srvs.

Reid, Muriel F. Speak the Thought: How to Read & Speak in Public, with Bible-Lesson Applications. 2nd exp. ed. 64p. 1984. 7.00 (0-915878-05-4) Joseph Pub Co.

Reid, N., jt. auth. see Cox, D. R.

Reid, Nancy, jt. auth. see Liermann, Sheila.

Reid, Nancy G., ed. see Duncan, Mike.

***Reid, Neill & Hawley, Suzanne L.** New Light on Dark Stars: Red Dwarfs, Low-Mass Stars, Brown Dwarfs. LC 99-49519. (Praxis Bks.). 415p. 2000. pap. 146.00 (1-85233-100-3) Spr-Verlag.

Reid, Nicholas, jt. ed. see Harvey, Mark.

Reid, Norma. Health Care Research by Degrees. LC 92-28523. (Illus.). 224p. 1993. pap. 29.95 (0-632-03466-1) Blackwell Sci.

Reid, Norman, jt. ed. see Sears, David.

Reid, P. C., et al, eds. Protozoa & Their Role in Marine Processes. (NATO ASI Series G: Ecological Sciences: Vol. 25). x, 506p. 1991. 272.95 (0-387-18565-8) Spr-Verlag.

Reid, P. Carey. Swimming in the Starry River. 384p. (J). 1994. 19.45 (0-7868-6005-7, Pub. by Hyperion) Time Warner.

Reid, P. Nelson, jt. ed. see Lowe, Gary R.

Reid, Pamela J. Excel-Erated Learning: Explaining in Clear English How Dogs Learn & How Best to Teach Them. (Illus.). 172p. 1996. pap. 16.95 (1-888047-07-0) J & K Pubs.

Reid, Pamela J., ed. see McHugh, Joy Jackson.

***Reid, Panthea, ed.** Conversations with Ellen Douglas. (Literary Conversations Ser.). 256p. 2000. pap. 18.00 (1-57806-280-2); lib. bdg. 45.00 (1-57806-279-9) U Pr of Miss.

Reid, Patricia. The New GED Tests Overview Viewer's Guide. (GED Staff Development Videotape Ser.). teacher ed. 9.50 (0-8092-4932-4) NTC Contemp Pub Co.

Reid, Patrick, ed. Readings in Western Religious Thought: The Ancient World. 304p. (Orig.). 1987. pap. 22.95 (0-8091-2850-0) Paulist Pr.

Reid, Patrick V., ed. Readings in Western Religious Thought II: The Middle Ages Through the Reformation. 400p. (Orig.). (C). 1995. pap. 24.95 (0-8091-3533-7) Paulist Pr.

Reid, Paul C. Swimming in the Starry River. LC 95-41213. 384p. (J). 1995. pap. 11.95 (0-312-14136-X) St Martin.

Reid, Peggy A. Litigation Support: For the Proactive Corporate Information Manager. (Illus.). 149p. (Orig.). 1990. student ed. 129.95 (0-9625994-0-9, TX2 817 405) Independent.

Reid, Peter L. Tenth-Century Latinity: Rather of Verona. LC 80-54672. (Humana Civilitas Ser.: Vol. 6). 139p. 1981. pap. 23.00 (0-89003-070-7) Undena Pubns.

Reid-Pharr, Robert F. Conjugal Union: The Body, the House, & the Black American. LC 98-35936. (Race & American Culture Ser.). (Illus.). 192p. 1999. 35.00 (0-19-510402-1) OUP.

Reid-Pharr, Robert F. Gay Black Man. write for info. (0-8147-7502-0) NYU Pr.

Reid, Philip D., et al, eds. Tissue Printing: Tools for the Study of Anatomy, Histochemistry, & Gene Expression. (Illus.). 188p. 1992. student ed., spiral bd. 32.00 (0-12-585970-8) Acad Pr.

Reid, Proctor P., ed. see National Academy of Engineering Staff.

Reid, Proctor R., ed. see National Academy of Engineering, Committee on Engi.

Reid, R. A., ed. see Demosthenes.

Reid, R. A., jt. ed. see Oberst, B. B.

Reid, R. Dan & Riegel, Carl D. Purchasing Practices of Large Foodservice Firms. Ketchum, Carol L., ed. LC 89-60232. 76p. (Orig.). (C). 1989. pap. text 20.00 (0-945968-02-7) Ctr Advanced Purchasing.

***Reid, R. L.** Owners of Nuclear Power Plants. 82p. 2000. pap. 8.00 (0-16-059183-X) USGPO.

Reid, R. M., Jr. Romie & Rudolph: An Intimate History Told in Letters of Friendship, Family, Courtship & Marriage. 226p. 1995. pap. 20.00 (0-9648967-0-2) M Reid Pubns.

***Reid Rambo, Teresa J. & Pflaum, Leanne J.** Legal Writing by Design: A Guide to Great Briefs & Memos. 2000. pap. text. write for info. (0-89089-910-X) Carolina Acad Pr.

Reid, Randall. Fiction of Nathanael West: No Redeemer, No Promised Land. LC 67-30949. 1992. pap. text 2.25 (0-226-70925-6, P434) U Ch Pr.

Reid, Randy, jt. auth. see Kaysing, Bill.

Reid, Rebecca L. & Flagg, William R. Oregon: A Statistical Overview, 1996. 140p. 1996. pap. 30.00 (0-9653878-0-1) Sthrn Oregon Reg.

Reid, Richard. The Georgian House & Its Details. 1989. 29.95 (0-900873-93-0, Pub. by Bishopsgte Pr) Intl Spec Bk.

Reid, Richard, ed. see Sophocles.

Reid, Richard J. The Army That Buell Built. LC 94-92107. 78p. (Orig.). 1994. pap. write for info. (1-877713-05-8) R J Reid.

— The Battle of Tippecanoe. LC 89-155804. (Illus.). 66p. 1997. reprint ed. pap. write for info. (1-877713-00-7) R J Reid.

— Death Rides the Zollie Trail. LC 96-92352. (Illus.). 120p. (Orig.). 1996. pap. write for info. (1-877713-08-2) R J Reid.

— The Fight for Middle Creek. LC 91-93267. (Illus.). 52p. (Orig.). 1992. pap. write for info. (1-877713-03-1) R J Reid.

— Fourth Indiana Cavalry Regiment: A History. LC 94-69868. (Illus.). 244p. 1994. pap. 14.95 (1-877713-06-6) R J Reid.

— Morgan's Coming Again: Civil War Books. (Morgan's Comin' Agin! Ser.). (Illus.). 160p. 1999. 10.00 (1-877713-09-0) R J Reid.

— Stones River Ran Red. LC 89-189682. (Illus.). 83p. (Orig.). 1998. reprint ed. pap. write for info. (1-877713-02-3) R J Reid.

— They Met at Perryville. 2nd rev. ed. LC 95-94782. (Illus.). 94p. (Orig.). 1995. reprint ed. pap. 7.95 (1-877713-07-4) R J Reid.

Reid, Richard S., ed. see Dreiss, Joseph G.

Reid, Rob. Children's Jukebox: A Subject Guide to Musical Recordings & Programming Ideas for Songsters Ages One to Twelve. LC 95-6163. 270p. (Orig.). 1995. pap. 25.00 (0-8389-0650-8, 0650-8-2045) ALA.

An Asterisk (*) at the beginning of an entry indicates that the title is appearing for the first time.

*Reid, Rob. Family Storytime. LC 98-40765. 176p. 1999. 28.00 (0-8389-0751-2) ALA.
Reid, Rob. Wave Goodbye. LC 95-21733. (Illus.). 24p. (J). (ps-1). 1996. 14.95 (1-880000-30-X) Lee & Low Bks.
Reid, Robert. Architects of the Web: 1,000 Days That Build the Future of Business. LC 97-1826. 416p. 1997. 27.95 (0-471-17187-5) Wiley.
— Architects of the Web: 1,000 Days That Built the Future of Business. 1997. 27.95 (0-614-28019-2) Wiley.
— Architects of the Web: 1,000 Days That Built the Future of Business. 416p. 1999. pap. 16.95 (0-471-32573-2) Wiley.
— Bed & Breakfast: Rockies. 1995. pap. 16.00 (0-671-89927-9) S&S Trade.
— Frommer's Bed & Breakfast Guides: Rockies. (Illus.). 128p. 1995. 16.00 (0-02-860455-5) Macmillan.
— Hospitality Marketing Management. 2nd ed. (Illus.). 384p. (C). 1989. 22.95 (0-442-31915-0, VNR) Wiley.
— Introduction to Hospital Management. (Hospitality, Travel & Tourism Ser.). 1997. text 34.95 (0-442-00856-2, VNR) Wiley.
— Mikhail Lermontov: From Russia to the Caucasus. Date not set. write for info. (1-57181-995-9) Berghahn Bks.
— Venus & Mars: The Signs of Love & Passion. 304p. 1998. pap. 14.95 (0-7225-3703-4) Thorsons PA.
— Year One: An Intimate Look Inside Harvard Business School. 336p. 1995. reprint ed. pap. 11.00 (0-380-72559-2, Avon Bks) Morrow Avon.
*Reid, Robert & Fairmont, Press. The Roofing & Cladding Systems Handbook: A Guide for Facility Managers. 288p. 1999. 82.00 (0-13-026357-5) P-H.
Reid, Robert, jt. auth. see Berger, Terry.
Reid, Robert Associates Staff. Bed & Breakfasts: Caribbean. (Frommer's Travel Guide Ser.). (Illus.). 128p. 1995. 16.00 (0-02-860063-0) Macmillan.
Reid, Robert C., et al. The Properties of Gases & Liquids. 4th ed. (Illus.). 741p. 1987. 110.00 (0-07-051799-1) McGraw.
Reid, Robert D. Hospitality Marketing Management. 2nd ed. 416p. 1988. 59.95 (0-471-28952-3, VNR) Wiley.
— Hospitality Marketing Management. 2nd ed. (Illus.). 399p. (C). 1988. text 52.95 (0-442-27848-9, VNR) Wiley.
Reid, Robert F., III. And Then There Was Now. LC 80-82920. (Illus.). (Orig.). 1980. pap. 4.25 (0-9603490-5-7) Noble Hse.
Reid, Robert G. Evolutionary Theory: The Unfinished Synthesis. 416p. (C). 1985. text 45.00 (0-8014-1831-3) Cornell U Pr.
Reid, Robert H. & Guerrero, Eileen. Corazon Aquino & the Brushfire Revolution. LC 95-30684. (Illus.). 248p. (C). 1995. 29.95 (0-8071-1980-6) La State U Pr.
Reid, Robert L. Mountains of the Great Blue Dream. LC 97-37793. 208p. 1998. reprint ed. pap. 16.95 (0-8263-1923-8) U of NM Pr.
— Picturing Texas: The FSA-OWI Photographers in the Lone Star State, 1935-1943. LC 94-21684. (Illus.). 224p. 1995. 49.95 (0-87611-140-1) Tex St Hist Assn.
Reid, Robert L., ed. Always a River: The Ohio River & the American Experience. LC 90-25293. (Illus.). 269p. 1991. reprint ed. pap. 83.40 (0-608-01073-1, 205938100001) Bks Demand.
— Back Home Again: Indiana in the Farm Security Administration Photographs, 1935-1943. LC 86-46377. (Illus.). 158p. 1987. 28.95 (0-253-31133-0) Ind U Pr.
— Picturing Minnesota, 1936-1943: Photographs from the Farm Security Administration. LC 89-13104. (Illus.). viii, 200p. (Orig.). 1989. pap. 19.95 (0-87351-248-0) Minn Hist.
Reid, Robert L. & Fuller, Dan H. Pilgrims on the Ohio: The River Journey & Photographs of Reuben Gold Thwaites, 1894. LC 97-24067. (Illus.). vii, 105p. 1997. pap. 29.95 (0-87195-118-5) Ind Hist Soc.
Reid, Robert L. & Rogers, Thomas E. A Good Neighbor: The First Fifty Years at Crane 1941-1991. (Illus.). 118p. (Orig.). 1991. pap. write for info. (0-9640288-1-6) Univ So IN.
*Reid, Robert L. & Viskochil, Larry A., eds. Chicago & Downstate: Illinois As Seen by the Farm Security Administration Photographers, 1936-1943. (Illus.). 194p. 2000. pap. 25.00 (0-7881-9430-5) DIANE Pub.
Reid, Robert L. & Viskochil, Larry A., eds. Chicago & Downstate: Illinois As Seen by the Farm Security Administration Photographers, 1936-1943. LC 88-27873. (Visions of Illinois Ser.). (Illus.). 216p. 1989. text 29.95 (0-252-01635-1); pap. text 19.95 (0-252-06078-4) U of Ill Pr.
Reid, Robert L., ed. see Conference on Systems Simulation, Economic Analysi.
Reid, Robert L., ed. see Haley, Margaret A.
*Reid, Robert N. Roofing & Cladding Systems Handbook: A Guide for Facility Managers. LC 99-43145. 265p. 2000. 82.00 (0-88173-330-X) Fairmont Pr.
Reid, Robert S. Preaching Mark. LC 99-37930. 1999. pap. 19.99 (0-8272-2958-5) Chalice Pr.
Reid, Robert W. Science Experiments for the Primary Grades. 1962. pap. 3.99 (0-8224-6300-8) Fearon Teacher Aids.
Reid, Robin A. Arthur C. Clarke. LC 96-37046. (Critical Companions to Popular Contemporary Writers Ser.). 224p. 1997. 29.95 (0-313-29529-8, Greenwood Pr) Greenwood.
*Reid, Robin Anne. Ray Bradbury: A Critical Companion. LC 00-22332. (Critical Companions to Popular Contemporary Writers Ser.). 170p. 2000. 30.00 (0-313-30901-9, GR0901) Greenwood.
Reid, Roddey. Families in Jeopardy: Regulating the Social Body in France, 1750-1910. LC 93-16664. 384p. (C). 1993. 42.50 (0-8047-2224-2) Stanford U Pr.
*Reid, Roddey & Traweek, Sharon. Doing Science + Culture. LC 99-56916. 400p. 2000. pap. 24.99 (0-415-92112-0) Routledge.
*Reid, Roddey & Traweek, Sharon, eds. Doing Science & Culture. LC 99-56916. 400p. (C). 2000. text 80.00 (0-415-92111-2) Routledge.
Reid, Rolland R. & McMannis, William J. Precambrian Geology of North Snowy Block, Beartooth Mountains, Montana. LC 74-28529. (Geological Society of America, Special Paper: No. 157). 188p. reprint ed. pap. 58.30 (0-608-13544-5, 202547000044) Bks Demand.
Reid, Ronald F. American Rhetorical Discourse. 2nd rev. ed. xx, 841 p. (C). 1995. pap. text 29.95 (0-88133-839-7) Waveland Pr.
— Edward Everett: Unionist Orator, 7. LC 89-27281. (Critical Studies, Speeches & Sources: No. 7). 304p. 1990. lib. bdg. 59.95 (0-313-26164-4, REE/, Greenwood Pr) Greenwood.
Reid, Russell. Sakakawea: The Bird Woman. 4th ed. (Illus.). 27p. 1986. reprint ed. pap. 2.50 (1-891419-11-0) State Hist ND.
Reid, Russell, ed. Lewis & Clark in North Dakota. 2nd ed. (Illus.). 347p. 1988. reprint ed. pap. 15.95 (1-891419-08-0) State Hist ND.
*Reid, Russell & Gannon, Clell. Birds & Mammals Observed by Lewis & Clark in North Dakota. (Illus.). 14p. 1999. reprint ed. pap. 3.95 (1-891419-18-8) State Hist ND.
*Reid, S. Criminal Justice. (C). 1998. pap. text 19.47 (0-395-96600-0) HM.
Reid, S. Invention & Discovery. (Illustrated Dictionaries Ser.). (Illus.). 128p. (J). (gr. 7-11). 1987. pap. 12.95 (0-86020-956-3) EDC.
— Invention & Discovery. (Illustrated Dictionaries Ser.). (Illus.). 128p. (J). (gr. 7-11). 1999. lib. bdg. 20.95 (0-88110-231-8) EDC.
— Inventors. (Famous Lives Ser.). (Illus.). 48p. (J). (gr. 5-9). 1994. pap. 7.95 (0-7460-0705-1, Usborne) EDC.
— Inventors. (Famous Lives Ser.). (Illus.). 48p. (YA). (gr. 5 up). 1999. lib. bdg. 15.95 (0-88110-698-4, Usborne) EDC.
— Memory Skills. (Superskills Ser.). (Illus.). 48p. (YA). (gr. 6-10). 1988. pap. 5.95 (0-7460-0162-2); lib. bdg. 13.95 (0-88110-305-5) EDC.
— Space Facts. (Facts & Lists Ser.). (Illus.). 48p. (J). (gr. 3-7). 1987. pap. text 5.95 (0-7460-0024-3) EDC.
Reid, S. & Fara, P. Scientists. (Famous Lives Ser.). (Illus.). 48p. (J). (gr. 5 up). 1993. pap. 7.95 (0-7460-1009-5) EDC.
— Scientists. (Famous Lives Ser.). (Illus.). 48p. (J). (gr. 5 up). 1999. lib. bdg. 15.95 (0-88110-587-2) EDC.
Reid, S., jt. auth. see Everett, Felicity.
Reid, S. R., ed. Metal Forming & Impact Mechanics. (Illus.). 360p. 1985. 163.00 (0-08-031679-4, Pub. by PPL) Franklin.
Reid, S. R. & Zhou, G., eds. Impact Behaviour of Fibre-Reinforced Composite Materials & Structures. 280p. 2000. boxed set 170.00 (1-85573-423-0) Am Educ Systs.
Reid, S. W., ed. see Brown, Charles Brockden.
Reid, S. W., ed. see Conrad, Joseph.
Reid, Sally H. Close Call. 320p. 1994. mass mkt. 4.50 (0-8217-4627-8, Zebra Kensgtn) Kensgtn Pub Corp.
— Undertow. 320p. 1992. mass mkt. 4.50 (0-8217-3962-X, Zebra Kensgtn) Kensgtn Pub Corp.
Reid, Sally L. Mommakitty's Surprise: Skyler. large type ed. (Illus.). 36p. (J). (gr. k-3). 1997. 12.00 (0-614-30156-4) Surge Pub.
Reid, Samuel C., Jr. Scouting Expeditions of McCulloch's Texas Rangers: Or, the Summer & Fall Campaign of the Army of the United States in Mexico 1846. LC 72-126252. (Select Bibliographies Reprint Ser.). 1977. 20.95 (0-8369-5479-3) Ayer.
Reid, Sarah, ed. see Hopkins, Jeanne.
Reid, Saralou L. Mommakitty's Surprise: "Skyler" LC 88-60613. (Illus.). (J). (gr. k-3). 1997. 12.00 (0-9620420-0-5); ring bd. 18.00 (0-9620420-1-3) Surge Pub.
— Mommakitty's Surprise: "Skyler" LC 88-60613. (Illus.). (J). (gr. k-3). 1997. lib. bdg. 35.00 (0-9620420-3-X) Surge Pub.
Reid, Scott. Canada Remapped. 1994. per. 14.95 (0-88978-249-0, Pub. by Arsenal Pulp) LPC InBook.
Reid, Scott, ed. see Fortescue, Adrian.
Reid, Scott M. General Sacramental Absolution: An Historical, Canonical & Pastoral Perspective. 40p. 1998. pap. 4.50 (1-901157-65-2) St Augustines Pr.
Reid, Scott M., ed. see Waugh, Evelyn & Hennan, John C.
Reid, Sheila. Art Without Rejection. (Illus.). 242p. (Orig.). 1993. 39.00 (0-9646268-1-0); pap. 18.00 (0-9646268-0-2) Rush Eds.
Reid, Shell. Eddy Hulbert: Montana Silversmith. Morris, Chandra, ed. (Illus.). 95p. 1998. 24.95 (0-9658264-0-6) Bar B Diamond.
Reid, Shirley W. Roots & Blossoms: An Anthology of 13 African American Plays African & Caribbean Plays with a Critical Introduction & Bibliographies. 620p. (Orig.). (C). 1991. pap. 21.00 (0-911557-03-2) Bedford Publishers.
Reid, Stanley D., jt. ed. see Rosson, Philip J.
Reid, Stephanie M. Food for the Soul: Inspirational Poems. (Illus.). ix, 45p. (Orig.). 1997. pap. 6.50 (0-9657711-0-5) S M R Inspirations.
Reid, Stephen. The Prentice Hall Guide for College Writers. LC 88-25341. Date not set. write for info. (0-13-150160-7) P-H.
— The Prentice Hall Guide for College Writers. 5th ed. LC 99-24814. 736p. 1999. write for info. (0-13-022547-9) P-H.
— Prentice Hall Guide for College Writers: Full Edition with Handbook. 5th ed. 701p. 1999. pap. 47.00 (0-13-021028-5) P-H.
Reid, Stephen, ed. Purpose & Process. 3rd ed. 572p. 1996. pap. text 39.60 (0-13-237389-0) P-H.
— Purpose & Process: A Reader for Writers. 4th ed. 592p. (C). 2000. pap. 30.00 (0-13-021026-9) P-H.
Reid, Stephen A., jt. ed. see Kuespert, Jonathon G.
Reid, Stephen B. Enoch & Daniel: A Form Critical & Sociological Study of Historical Apocalypses. Endres, John & Christensen, Duane L., eds. LC 88-72056. (Bibal Monograph Ser.: No. 2). 147p. 1989. pap. 12.95 (0-941037-07-X, BIBAL Press) D & F Scott.
— Experience & Tradition: A Primer in Black Biblical Hermeneutics. LC 90-43485. 1991. pap. 11.95 (0-687-12400-X) Abingdon.
— Listening In: A Multicultural Readings of the Psalms. LC 97-42691. 176p. 1997. pap. 19.95 (0-687-01194-9) Abingdon.
Reid, Stephen B., ed. Prophets & Paradigms: Essays in Honor of Gene M. Tucker. (JSOTS Ser.: No. 229). 248p. 1996. 70.00 (1-85075-630-9, Pub. by Sheffield Acad) CUP Services.
Reid, Stephen Breck, jt. auth. see Reid, Kathyrn Goering.
*Reid, Stephen J. Ozone & Climate Change: A Beginner's Guide. 220p. 2000. text 45.00 (90-5699-232-5, G & B Science); pap. text 23.00 (90-5699-233-3, G & B Science) Gordon & Breach.
Reid, Steven, jt. auth. see Schaefer, Charles E.
Reid, Steven E., jt. ed. see Schaefer, Charles.
*Reid, Straun. Castle Life. (Age of Castles Ser.). (Illus.). 48p. (J). (gr. 4-8). 1998. pap. 7.95 (0-8172-8120-7) Raintree Steck-V.
*Reid, Struan. Alexander Graham Bell. LC 00-24355. (Groundbreakers Ser.). (Illus.). (YA). 2000. lib. bdg. write for info. (1-57572-366-2) Heinemann Lib.
Reid, Struan. Castle Life. LC 97-51140. (Age of Castles Ser.). (J). (gr. 4-8). 1998. 25.69 (0-8172-5119-7) Raintree Steck-V.
— Castle Life. LC 97-51140. (Age of Castles Ser.). (J). (gr. 4-8). 1998. write for info. (0-7502-2145-3) Raintree Steck-V.
— Castle under Seige. LC 97-51140. (Age of Castles Ser.). 48 p. (J). (gr. 4-8). 1998. write for info. (0-8172-5120-0) Raintree Steck-V.
— The Children's Atlas of Lost Treasures. LC 96-42453. 96p. (J). (gr. 2-6). 1997. lib. bdg. 27.40 (0-7613-0219-0) Millbrook Pr.
— The Children's Atlas of Lost Treasures. LC 96-42453. (Illus.). 96p. (J). (gr. 2-6). 1997. pap. 14.95 (0-7613-0240-9) Millbrook Pr.
— Cultures & Civilizations. (Silk & Spice Routes Ser.). (Illus.). 48p. (YA). (gr. 6 up). 1994. lib. bdg. 15.95 (0-02-726315-0) Silver Burdett Pr.
Reid, Struan. Exploration by Sea. (Silk & Spice Routes Ser.). (Illus.). 48p. (J). 1993. pap. 14.95 (0-88780-236-2, Pub. by Formac Publ Co) Formac Dist Ltd.
Reid, Struan. Exploration by Sea. LC 93-14693. (Silk & Spice Routes Ser.). (Illus.). 48p. (YA). (gr. 6 up). 1994. lib. bdg. 15.95 (0-02-775801-X) Silver Burdett Pr.
Reid, Struan. Inventions & Trade. (Silk & Spice Routes Ser.). (Illus.). 48p. (J). 1994. pap. 14.95 (0-921921-30-6, Pub. by Formac Publ Co) Formac Dist Ltd.
Reid, Struan. Inventions & Trade. (Silk & Spice Routes Ser.). (Illus.). 48p. (YA). (gr. 6 up). 1994. lib. bdg. 15.95 (0-02-726316-9, New Dscvry Bks) Silver Burdett Pr.
*Reid, Struan. John Logie Baird. LC 00-35012. (Groundbreakers Ser.). (Illus.). (J). 2000. lib. bdg. write for info. (1-57572-372-7) Heinemann Lib.
Reid, Struan, ed. Dictionary of Horses & Ponies. (Illus.). 128p. (YA). (gr. 4-7). 1999. pap. 14.95 (0-7460-2492-4, Usborne) EDC.
— Dictionary of Horses & Ponies. (Illus.). 128p. (YA). (gr. 6 up). 1999. lib. bdg. 22.95 (1-58086-117-2, Usborne) EDC.
*Reid, Struan & Einstein, Albert. Albert Einstein. LC 00-29591. (Groundbreakers Ser.). 2000. lib. bdg. write for info. (1-57572-365-4) Heinemann Lib.
Reid, Struan, jt. ed. see Miles, Lisa.
Reid, Stuart. All the King's Armies: A Military History of the English Civil War, 1642-1651. (Illus.). 296p. 1997. 34.95 (1-86227-028-7, Pub. by Spellmnt Pubs) St Mut.
— British Redcoat Vol. 2: 1793-1815. (Warrior Ser.: Vol. 20). (Illus.). 64p. 1997. pap. 12.95 (1-85532-556-X, Pub. by Ospry) Stackpole.
— British Redcoat, 1740-1793. (Warrior Ser.: No. 19). 1997. pap. 12.95 (1-85532-554-3, Pub. by Ospry) Stackpole.
— The Campaigns of Montrose. 208p. 1989. 64.00 (0-901824-92-5, Pub. by Mercat Pr Bks) St Mut.
— Eighteenth Century Highlanders. (Men-at-Arms Ser.). (Illus.). 48p. 1993. pap. 12.95 (1-85532-316-8, 9232, Pub. by Ospry) Stackpole.
— Highland Clansman 1689-1746. (Men-at-Arms Ser.: Vol. 21). (Illus.). 64p. 1997. 12.95 (1-85532-660-4, Pub. by Ospry) Stackpole.
*Reid, Stuart. Highlander: Fearless Celtic Warriors. (Illus.). 2000. 34.95 (1-903040-03-5) Military Illustrated.
— Hot Stuff: James Wolfe & King George's Army. 256p. 1997. 80.00 (1-86227-084-8, Pub. by Spellmnt Pubs) St Mut.
Reid, Stuart. King George's Army, 1740-93, Vol. 2. (Men-at-Arms Ser.). (Illus.). 48p. 1995. pap. 12.95 (1-85532-564-0, Pub. by Ospry) Stackpole.
— King George's Army, 1740-93, Vol. 3. (Illus.). 48p. 1996. pap. 12.95 (1-85532-565-9, Pub. by Ospry) Stackpole.
— Scots Armies of the English Civil Wars, 331. 1999. pap. text 12.95 (1-85532-836-4) Ospry.
— 1745: A Military History of the Last Jacobite Rising. (Illus.). 264p. 1996. 24.95 (1-885119-28-3) Sarpedon.
Reid, Stuart. 1745: A Military History of the Last Jacobite Rising. 256p. 1997. 80.00 (1-873376-59-6, Pub. by Spellmnt Pubs) St Mut.
Reid, Stuart. Wellington's Highlanders. (Men-at-Arms Ser.: No. 253). (Illus.). 48p. pap. 11.95 (1-85532-256-0, 9224, Pub. by Ospry) Stackpole.
— Who Built the Pyramids? (Starting Point History Ser.). (Illus.). 32p. (J). (gr. 1 up). 1996. lib. bdg. 12.95 (0-88110-796-4, Usborne) EDC.
*Reid, Stuart. Wolfe: The Career of General James Wolfe, from Culloden & Quebec. 2000. 32.95 (1-885119-73-9) Sarpedon.
Reid, Stuart & Reid, Chisholm. Who Built the Pyramids? (Starting Point History Ser.). (Illus.). (J). (gr. 1 up). 1996. pap. 4.95 (0-7460-2036-8, Usborne) EDC.
Reid, Stuart & Wingate, Philippa. Who Were the First North Americans. (Starting Point History Ser.). (Illus.). 32p. (J). (gr. k up). 1996. lib. bdg. 12.95 (0-88110-786-7, Usborne) EDC.
— Who Were the First North Americans. (Starting Point History Ser.). (Illus.). (J). (gr. 1 up). 1996. pap. 4.95 (0-7460-2040-6, Usborne) EDC.
Reid, Stuart J. A Sketch of the Life & Times of Sydney Smith. 1972. 59.95 (0-8490-1060-8) Gordon Pr.
Reid, Stuart J., ed. see Blount, Edward.
Reid, Sue, ed. see Woolf, Virginia.
Reid, Sue T. Crime & Criminology. 7th ed. (C). 1994. text. write for info. (0-697-27463-2) Brown & Benchmark.
— Crime & Criminology. 8th ed. LC 96-85636. 720p. (C). 1996. text, boxed set. write for info. (0-697-35299-4); text. write for info. (0-697-28921-4) Brown & Benchmark.
— Criminal Law. 4th ed. LC 97-20451. 567p. 1997. 64.06 (0-07-065349-6) McGraw.
Reid, Sue Titus. Criminal Justice. 5th ed. 1998. pap. text 33.00 (0-697-35612-4) McGraw.
Reid, Susan. Understanding Your 2 Year Old. Osborne, Elsie, ed. (Understanding Your Child Ser.: Vol. 3). 96p. 1997. pap. 8.95 (1-894020-02-2) Warwick Publ.
Reid, Susan & Tavistock Clinic Staff. Developments in Infant Observation: The Tavistock Model. LC 96-43621. 248p. (C). 1997. 80.00 (0-415-14940-1); pap. 27.99 (0-415-14941-X) Routledge.
*Reid, Susan E. & Crowley, David, eds. Style & Socialism: Modernity & Material Culture in Post-War Eastern Europe. (Illus.). 256p. 2000. 65.00 (1-85973-234-8, Pub. by Berg Pubs); pap. 19.50 (1-85973-239-9, Pub. by Berg Pubs) NYU Pr.
Reid, Suzan. Follow That Bus. (Illus.). 32p. (Orig.). (J). (gr. 1-4). 1993. pap. 4.95 (0-920501-88-5) Orca Bk Pubs.
— The Meat Eaters Arrive. (Illus.). 32p. (J). (ps-3). 1996. pap. 4.95 (1-55209-004-3) Firefly Bks Ltd.
Reid, Suzan & Hendry, Linda. The Meat Eaters Arrive. (Tell Me a Story Ser.). (Illus.). 32p. (J). pap. 12.99 incl. audio (0-590-24540-6) Scholastic Inc.
Reid, Suzanne. Presenting Cynthia Voigt. (Young Adult Authors Ser.). 1995. 28.00 (0-8057-8219-2, Twyne) Mac Lib Ref.
Reid, T. J. Fashion, Fun & Feelings: A Lady Looks at Life. Porter, Carolyn, ed. LC 83-93566. (Illus.). 196p. (Orig.). 1994. pap. 14.95 (1-880522-48-9) Retail Res.
— 52 Promotions: A Year's Worth of Profit! (Illus.). 128p. (Orig.). 1996. pap. 24.95 (1-880522-46-2) Retail Res.
— More Retail Details Mother Forgot to Mention. (Illus.). 128p. 1999. pap. 34.95 (1-880522-25-X) Retail Res.
— What Mother Never Told Ya about Retail: A Small Store Survival Guide. 2nd rev. ed. Porter, Carolyn, ed. (Illus.). 119p. (C). 1994. pap. 29.95 (1-880522-24-1) Retail Res.
Reid, T. R. Confucius Lives Next Door: What Living in the East Teaches Us about Living in the West. LC 98-36438. 288p. 1999. 24.95 (0-679-45624-4) Random.
— Confucius Lives Next Door: What Living in the East Teaches Us about Living in the West. 1999. pap. 13.00 (0-679-77760-1) Vin Bks.
— Ski Japan! Calogeras, Meagan, ed. (Illus.). 240p. 1994. pap. 20.00 (4-7700-1680-8) Kodansha.
Reid, T. R., tr. see Inamori, Kazuo.
Reid, T. W. Charlotte Bronte. LC 75-130243. (English Biography Ser.: No. 31). 1970. reprint ed. lib. bdg. 75.00 (0-8383-1133-4) M S G Haskell Hse.
Reid, Tamaya. Incomplete Package. Edit Ink Staff, ed. 1999. pap. write for info. (0-9672064-0-5) T Reid.
*Reid, Thomas. Baldur's Gate II: D & D Guidebook. (Illus.). 224p. 2000. pap. 18.95 (0-7869-1674-5) TSR Inc.
Reid, Thomas. Essays on the Active Powers of Man. 1986. reprint ed. pap. 32.95 (0-935005-64-1); reprint ed. lib. bdg. 48.95 (0-935005-63-3) Lincoln-Rembrandt.
— Essays on the Intellectual Powers of Man. Woozley, A. D., ed. 1986. reprint ed. pap. 44.95 (0-935005-14-5); reprint ed. lib. bdg. 61.95 (0-935005-15-3) Lincoln-Rembrandt.
— Eye of Doom. 1996. 7.95 (0-7869-0427-5, Pub. by TSR Inc) Random.
— Inquiry & Essays. Beanblossom, Ronald E. & Lehrer, Keith, eds. LC 83-22864. (HPC Classics Ser.). lxii, 430p. (C). 1983. reprint ed. pap. text 12.95 (0-915145-85-5); reprint ed. lib. bdg. 34.95 (0-915145-86-3) Hackett Pub.
— An Inquiry into the Human Mind. Duggan, Timothy, ed. LC 74-108880. 331p. reprint ed. pap. 102.70 (0-608-11849-4, 201697400006) Bks Demand.
— Inquiry into the Human Mind on the Principle of Common Sense. 3rd ed. 1986. reprint ed. pap. 27.95 (0-935005-32-3); reprint ed. lib. bdg. 43.95 (0-935005-30-7) Lincoln-Rembrandt.
— An Inquiry into the Human Mind, on the Principles of Common Sense: 1785 Edition. 510p. 1996. reprint ed. 75.00 (1-85506-081-7) Bks Intl VA.
— Philosophical Works: With Notes & Supplementary Dissertations by Sir William Hamilton, 2 vols., Set. 8th ed. 1983. reprint ed. 154.70 (3-487-01617-6) G Olms Pubs.
— Practical Ethics. Haakonssen, Knud, ed. (Illus.). 544p. 1990. text 79.50 (0-691-07350-3, Pub. by Princeton U Pr) Cal Prin Full Svc.
— The Tale of the Comet. 1997. 30.00 (0-7869-0653-7, Pub. by TSR Inc) Random.

R

An Asterisk (*) at the beginning of an entry indicates that the title is appearing for the first time.

R

— The Works of Thomas Reid, 2 vols. Hamiliton, Sir William, ed. 1986. reprint ed. lib. bdg. 126.95 (*0-935005-68-4*) Lincoln-Rembrandt.

Reid, Thomas & Brookes, Derek R. Thomas Reid, an Inquiry into the Human Mind: On the Principles of Common Sense. LC 97-16293. 1997. 55.00 (*0-271-01741-4*) Pa St U Pr.

Reid, Thomas M. The Boy Hunters. LC 68-23725. (Americans in Fiction Ser.). reprint ed. pap. text 13.95 (*0-89197-685-X*); reprint ed. lib. bdg. 20.00 (*0-8398-1750-9*) Irvington.

***Reid, Thomas M.** Gridrunner. (Star Drive Bks.). (Illus.). 320p. 2000. mass mkt. 6.99 (*0-7869-1573-0*) Wizards Coast.

Reid, Thomas M. The Quadroon: Or, Adventures in the Far West. LC 67-29278. (Americans in Fiction Ser.). (Illus.). 447p. reprint ed. pap. text 6.95 (*0-89197-912-3*); reprint ed. lib. bdg. 39.00 (*0-8398-1751-7*) Irvington.

— The White Chief: A Legend of North Mexico. LC 68-23726. (Americans in Fiction Ser.). (Illus.). 401p. reprint ed. pap. text 5.95 (*0-89197-975-1*); reprint ed. lib. bdg. 32.50 (*0-8398-1752-5*) Irvington.

Reid, Tom, jt. auth. see Bowen, Barbara C.

Reid, Tommy. Kingdom Now but Not Yet. 128p. 1988. pap. 6.95 (*0-917595-18-1*) Kingdom Pubs.

***Reid, Tristan.** Server-Side Scripting & Security: A4, Version 4.07. McKenna, Jill, ed. (CIW Application Developer Track A4 Ser.). (Illus.). 1999. pap. write for info. (*1-58143-075-2*) Prosoft I-net.

— Server-Side Scripting & Security: Version 4.07. McKenna, Jill, ed. (CIW Application Developer Track Ser.). (Illus.). 1999. pap. write for info. (*1-58143-039-6*) Prosoft I-net.

Reid Turner, Freda. Greene County, Georgia, Wills 1786-1877. LC 98-60998. 397p. 1998. 25.00 (*1-883793-30-0*) Wolfe Pubng.

Reid, V. S. The Leopard. (Caribbean Writers Ser.). 110p. (C). 1980. pap. 7.95 (*0-435-98660-0*, 98660) Heinemann.

— The Leopard. 159p. 1972. reprint ed. 15.00 (*0-911860-08-8*) Chatham Bkseller.

Reid, Van. Cordelia Underwood: or The Marvelous Beginnings of the Moosepath League. 416p. 1999. pap. 12.95 (*0-14-028010-3*) Viking Penguin.

— Cordelia Underwood: or The Marvelous Beginnings of the Moosepath League. LC 99-19130. 1999. write for info. (*1-56895-649-5*) Wheeler Pub.

Reid, Van. Mollie Peer: Or the Underground Adventures of the Moosepath League. LC 99-17375. 336p. 1999. 24.95 (*0-670-88633-5*, Viking) Viking Penguin.

***Reid, Van.** Mollie Peer: Or the Underground Adventures of the Moosepath League. 368p. 2000. pap. 12.95 (*0-14-029185-7*) Viking Penguin.

Reid, W. H., jt. auth. see Drazin, P. G.

Reid, W. Max. Mohawk Valley. 455p. 1993. reprint ed. lib. bdg. 99.00 (*0-7812-5133-8*) Rprt Serv.

— The Mohawk Valley - Its Legends & Its History. (Illus.). 455p. 1993. reprint ed. lib. bdg. 47.50 (*0-8328-3188-3*) Higginson Bk Co.

— Story of Old Fort Johnson. 455p. 1993. reprint ed. lib. bdg. 99.00 (*0-7812-5132-X*) Rprt Serv.

Reid, Walter & Myddelton, David R. The Meaning of Company Accounts. 6th ed. 360p. 1996. 43.95 (*0-566-07821-X*, Pub. by Gower) Ashgate Pub Co.

***Reid, Walter & Myddelton, David R.** The Meaning of Company Accounts. 7th ed. LC 00-42972. 368p. 2000. pap. 54.95 (*0-566-08378-7*, Pub. by Ashgate Pub) Ashgate Pub Co.

Reid, Walter, jt. ed. see Goldemberg, Jose.

Reid, Walter V. & Miller, Kenton R. Keeping Options Alive: The Scientific Basis for Conserving Biodiversity. 128p. 1989. pap. 15.00 (*0-915825-41-4*) World Resources Inst.

Reid, Walter V. & Trexler, Mark C. Drowning the National Heritage: Climate Change & Coastal Biodiversity in the United States. 48p. 1991. pap. 10.00 (*0-915825-62-7*, REDNP) World Resources Inst.

Reid, Walter V., et al. Bankrolling Successes Vol. 1: A Portfolio of Sustainable Development Projects. (Illus.). 48p. (Orig.). 1988. pap. 25.00 (*0-945051-05-0*) Friends of Earth.

Reid, Whitelaw. American & English Studies, 2 Vols. LC 68-29240. (Essay Index Reprint Ser.). 1977. reprint ed. 41.95 (*0-8369-0815-5*) Ayer.

***Reid, William.** Echoes of Flight 67: The Rest of the Story. (Illus.). 100p. 2000. mass mkt. 15.00 (*0-9677911-0-3*) High Flight Pubns.

Reid, William, ed. Authentic Records of Revival, Now in Progress in the United Kingdom. (Revival Library). viii, 478p. 1980. reprint ed. lib. bdg. 17.50 (*0-940033-17-8*) R O Roberts.

Reid, William, jt. auth. see Fortune, Anne.

Reid, William, jt. auth. see Ross, Graham.

Reid, William A. Curriculum As Institution & Practice: Essays in the Deliberative Tradition. LC 98-39832. (Studies in Curriculum Theory Ser.). 232p. 1998. 49.95 (*0-8058-2981-4*) L Erlbaum Assocs.

— The Pursuit of Curriculum: Schooling & the Public Interest. LC 93-46339. 198p. 1994. pap. 39.50 (*1-56750-051-X*); text 73.25 (*0-89391-980-2*) Ablx Pub.

Reid, William D. Death Notices of Ontario (1810-1849) 417p. 1997. reprint ed. pap. 35.00 (*0-8063-4682-5*) Clearfield Co.

Reid, William D. The Loyalists in Ontario: The Sons & Daughters of the American Loyalists of Upper Canada. (Illus.). 418p. 1994. reprint ed. 27.00 (*0-8063-1440-0*, 4865) Clearfield Co.

***Reid, William D.** Marriage Notices of Ontario, 1813-1854. 550p. 2000. reprint ed. pap. 38.50 (*0-8063-4983-2*, Pub. by Clearfield Co) ACCESS Pubs Network.

Reid, William H. A Clinician's Guide to Legal Issues in Therapy Practice: Or Proceed with Caution. LC 99-19558. 200p. 1999. pap. 22.95 (*1-891944-08-8*) Zeig Tucker.

— The Treatment of Psychiatric Disorders: Revised for the DSM-III-R. 2nd enl. rev. ed. LC 88-19468. 438p. 1989. text 43.95 (*0-87630-536-2*) Brunner-Mazel.

Reid, William H., ed. Mathematical Problems in the Geophysical Sciences I: Geophysical Fluid Dynamics. LC 62-21481. (Lectures in Applied Mathematics). 383p. 1972. text 66.00 (*0-8218-1113-4*, LAM/13) Am Math.

— Mathematical Problems in the Geophysical Sciences, No. 2: Inverse Problems, Dynamo Theory & Tides. LC 62-21481. (Lectures in Applied Mathematics: Vol. 14). 370p. 1972. text 62.00 (*0-8218-1114-2*, LAM/14) Am Math.

Reid, William H., et al, eds. Unmasking the Psychopath: Antisocial Personality & Related Syndromes. (Professional Bks.). 1986. 34.95 (*0-393-70025-9*) Norton.

Reid, William H. & Wise, Michael G. DSM-IV Training Guide. 384p. 1995. 50.00 (*0-87630-768-3*) Brunner-Mazel.

— DSM-IV Training Guide. LC 95-9947. 384p. 1995. pap. text 26.95 (*0-87630-763-2*, 7632) Brunner-Mazel.

Reid, William H., et al. The Treatment of Psychiatric Disorders: Revised for DSM-4. 3rd rev. ed. LC 96-7478. 514p. 1997. 69.95 (*0-87630-765-9*) Brunner-Mazel.

Reid, William H., ed. see Lebovitz, Norman, et al.

Reid, William H., ed. see Summer Seminar on Applied Mathematics, 6th, 1970,.

Reid, William J. Family Problem Solving. 360p. 1985. text 46.00 (*0-231-06056-4*) Col U Pr.

— Task Strategies: An Empirical Approach to Clinical Social Work. (Illus.). 320p. 1992. text 44.00 (*0-231-07550-2*) Col U Pr.

Reid, William J. & Epstein, Laura. Task-Centered Casework. LC 72-4931. 350p. (C). 1972. text 44.00 (*0-231-03466-0*) Col U Pr.

— Task-Centered Practice. LC 76-28177. 1977. text 44.00 (*0-231-04072-5*) Col U Pr.

Reid, William J. & Shyne, Ann W. Brief & Extended Casework. LC 70-79192. 1969. text 46.00 (*0-231-03219-6*) Col U Pr.

Reid, William J. & Smith, Audrey D. Research in Social Work. 2nd ed. 360p. 1989. text 43.50 (*0-231-06420-9*) Col U Pr.

Reid, William J., jt. auth. see Smith, Audrey D.

Reid, William J., jt. ed. see Sherman, Edmund.

Reid, William J., jt. ed. see Videka-Sherman, Lynn.

***Reid, William James.** The Task Planner: An Intervention Resource for Human Service Professionals. LC 99-38236. 2000. text 49.50 incl. cd-rom (*0-231-10646-7*) Col U Pr.

Reid, William T. Sturmian Theory for Ordinary Differential Equations. (Applied Mathematical Sciences Ser.: Vol. 31). 559p. 1981. pap. 69.00 (*0-387-90542-1*) Spr-Verlag.

Reida, Clara M. & Brothers, David, eds. Stephanie: A Love Story. LC 96-84148. (Illus.). 353p. (Orig.). 1996. pap. 12.95 (*1-881872-18-1*) Acclaim Pub.

Reida, Clara M., ed. see Haga, Michael W.

***Reidar, Dale.** Organisations & Development: Strategies, Structures & Processes. LC 00-33278. 2000. pap. write for info. (*0-7619-9430-0*) Sage.

Reidel, Arthur, ed. Fundamental Rock Climbing. 1973. pap. 2.00 (*0-9601698-0-6*) MIT Outing.

Reidel-Geubtner, Virginia, jt. auth. see Boushahla, Jo J.

Reidel, James, ed. see Kees, Weldon.

Reidel, Johannes, jt. auth. see Schafer, William J.

Reidel, S. P. & Hooper, P. R., eds. Volcanism & Tectonism in the Columbia River Flood-Basalt Province. (Special Papers: No. 239). 400p. 1990. 26.00 (*0-8137-2239-X*) Geol Soc.

Reidel, Susan. PSpice. (C). 1996. pap. text. write for info. (*0-201-51055-3*) Addison-Wesley.

Reidelbach. Visual Reference for Word 97. (Visual Reference Basics Ser.). spiral bd. 17.00 (*1-56243-458-6*, G-20HC) DDC Pub.

— Visual Reference Word 97. LC 97-174139. pap., spiral bd. 15.00 (*1-56243-435-7*, G-20) DDC Pub.

Reidelbach, Maria. Completely Mad: A History of the Comic Book & Magazine. (Illus.). 208p. 1998. text 50.00 (*0-7881-5587-3*) DIANE Pub.

— Completely Mad: A Hisrtory of the Comic Book & Magazine. (Illus.). 216p. 1992. pap. 24.95 (*0-316-73891-3*) Little.

— Microsoft Access. 1993. pap. 12.00 (*1-56243-115-3*, MA-18) DDC Pub.

— Quick Reference Guide Access 7 Windows 95. 1996. 12.00 (*1-56243-296-6*, AX95) DDC Pub.

— Quick Reference Guide for Access 7 Windows 95. 1996. 13.00 (*1-56243-309-1*, AX95HC) DDC Pub.

— Quick Reference Guide for Access 2.O for Windows. LC 94-224257. 1994. spiral bd. 12.00 (*1-56243-193-5*, OAX2) DDC Pub.

— Quick Reference Guide for Works 4 for Windows 95. 1996. 15.00 (*1-56243-314-8*, WKW4HC); pap. 12.00 (*1-56243-293-1*, WKW4) DDC Pub.

Reidelbach, Maria, jt. auth. see Garfinkel, Nina.

Reidelbach, Maria, jt. auth. see McDougall.

Reidelbach-Schwartz, Rain. Visual Reference Office 97. LC 97-174148. (Visual Reference Basics Ser.). 1997. spiral bd. 15.00 (*1-56243-434-9*, G-19) DDC Pub.

Reidelberger, Penelope L., jt. auth. see Hermanson, Susan.

Reidemeister, Kurt. Knot Theory. Boron, Leo F. et al, trs. from GER. LC 83-72870. Orig. Title: Knotentheorie. (Illus.). 143p. (C). 1983. pap. text 20.00 (*0-914351-00-1*) BCS Assocs.

— Kombinatorische Topologie. 14.95 (*0-8284-0076-8*) Chelsea Pub.

Reidenbach, Eric, jt. auth. see Goeke, Reg.

Reidenbach, R. Eric & McClung, Gordon W. The Wizardry of Customer Value: An Action Guide to Measuring & Managing Loyalty. LC 99-190480. (Illus.). 150p. 1998. pap. 29.95 (*1-893066-00-2*) Rhumb Line.

Reidenbach, R. Eric, jt. auth. see Grubbs, M. Ray.

***Reidenbaugh, Lowell.** Cooperstown Baseball's Hall of Famers. LC 99-20480. 1999. 19.99 (*0-517-19464-3*) Gramrcy Bks.

Reidenbaugh, Lowell. Jackson's Valley Campaign - The Battle of Kernstown. (Virginia Civil War Battles & Leaders Ser.). (Illus.). 174p. 1996. 19.95 (*1-56190-094-X*) H E Howard.

— Thirty-Third Virginia Infantry. (Virginia Regimental Histories Ser.). (Illus.). 151p. 1987. 19.95 (*0-930919-37-8*) H E Howard.

— Twenty-Seventh Virginia Infantry. (Virginia Regimental Histories Ser.). (Illus.). 191p. 1993. 19.95 (*1-56190-044-3*) H E Howard.

Reidenberg, Joel R., jt. auth. see Schwartz, Paul.

Reidenberg, Joel R., jt. auth. see Schwartz, Paul M.

Reidenberg, Marcus S. & Erill, Sergio, eds. Drug-Protein Binding: Esteve Foundation Symposium I. LC 85-12479. (Clinical Pharmacology & Therapeutics Ser.: Vol. 6). 380p. 1985. 49.95 (*0-275-90010-X*, C0010, Praeger Pubs) Greenwood.

Reider, Andrea, ed. see Corkin, Bud & Averill, Mary.

Reider, Andrea, ed. see Corrado, Frank.

Reider, Andrea, ed. see Magid, Renee Y. & Codkind, Melissa.

Reider, Andrea, ed. see Pinsker, Richard.

Reider, Barbara E. A Hooray Kind of Kid: A Child's Self-Esteem & How to Build It. MacLain, M., ed. (Illus.). 133p. (Orig.). 1988. pap. 8.95 (*0-9621156-0-6*) Sierra Hse Pub.

— Notes in the Lunchbox: How to Help Your Child Succeed at School. Reimer, Kathleen & Ritter, Mary, eds. (Illus.). 144p. (Orig.). 1993. pap. 9.95 (*0-9621156-1-4*) Sierra Hse Pub.

Reider, Barbara E., jt. auth. see Charbonneau, Manon P.

Reider, Bruce. The Orthopaedic Physical Examination. Lampert, Richard, ed. LC 98-38025. (Illus.). 525p. 1999. text. write for info. (*0-7216-7437-2*, W B Saunders Co) Harcrt Hlth Sci Grp.

Reider, Freda. The Hallah Book: Recipes, History & Traditions. 1987. 19.95 (*0-88125-111-9*) Ktav.

***Reider, H. Robert.** Operational Review: Maximum Results at Efficient Costs. 2nd ed. LC 98-23563. 552p. 1998. 135.00 (*0-471-25204-2*) Wiley.

Reider, Ines, tr. see Bierman, Pieke.

Reider, Katja. Snail Started It! Lanning, Rosemary, tr. LC 96-44944. (Illus.). 32p. (J). (gr. k-3). 1997. 15.95 (*1-55858-706-3*, Pub. by North-South Bks NYC); lib. bdg. 15.88 (*1-55858-707-1*, Pub. by North-South Bks NYC) Chronicle Bks.

***Reider, Katja.** Snail Started It! LC 96-44944. (Illus.). 32p. (J). (gr. k-3). 1999. pap. 6.95 (*0-7358-1142-3*, Pub. by North-South Bks NYC) Chronicle Bks.

— Todo Empezo Con Caracol. Lasconi, Diego, tr. LC 99-12678.Tr. of Snail Started It!. (SPA., Illus.). 32p. (J). (gr. k-3). 1999. 15.95 (*0-7358-1143-1*, Pub. by North-South Bks NYC); pap. 6.95 (*0-7358-1144-X*, Pub. by North-South Bks NYC) Chronicle Bks.

Reider, Marge D., jt. auth. see Mundahl, Steve.

Reider, Rob. Benchmarking Strategies: A Tool for Profit Improvement. LC 99-16341. 288p. 1999. text 75.00 (*0-471-34464-8*) Wiley.

***Reider, Rob.** Operational Review: Maximum Results at Efficient Costs. 78p. 1999. pap. 60.00 (*0-471-36134-8*) Wiley.

Reidesel, C. Alan & Clements, Douglas H. Coping with Computers in the Elementary & Middle Schools. (Illus.). 384p. (C). 1985. pap. text 35.00 (*0-13-172420-7*) P-H.

Reidhead, C. Ty. The Phunny Pharm. LC 96-29285. (Illus.). 225p. (Orig.). 1996. pap. text 21.00 (*1-56053-114-2*) Hanley & Belfus.

***Reidhead, S. J.** Dust Devil. LC 99-94388. 288p. 1999. pap. 9.95 (*1-892508-08-7*) Jingle Bob Pr.

Reidinger, Edward A. Turned-On Advising: Computer & Video Resources for Educational Advising. 96p. 1995. pap. text 18.00 (*0-912207-73-6*) NAFSA Washington.

***Reidinger, Paul.** The City Kid. 2001. 14.95 (*1-56023-168-8*); pap. 39.95 (*1-56023-169-6*) Haworth Pr.

Reidinger, Richard B., jt. auth. see Miller, Barbara A.

Reidinger, Rudolf. Der Codex Vindobonensis 418: Seine Vorlage und Seine Schreiber. (C). 1989. pap. text 106.00 (*0-7923-0350-4*) Kluwer Academic.

Reidl, John O. A Catalogue of Renaissance Philosophers. 192p. 1982. 10.00 (*0-87462-433-9*) Marquette.

Reidle, James, jt. auth. see Spielman, Patrick.

Reidt, Wilford H. John G. Lake: A Man Without Compromise. 188p. (Orig.). 1989. pap. 7.99 (*0-89274-316-6*, HH-316) Harrison Hse.

Reidy, Carolyn, ed. see Davis, Burke.

Reidy, David & Wallace. The Solar System: A Practical Guide. pap. 19.95 (*0-04-442260-1*, Pub. by Allen & Unwin Pty) Paul & Co Pubs.

Reidy, David & Wallace, Ken. The Solar System: Practical Guide. 1991. 29.95 (*0-04-442288-1*, Pub. by Allen & Unwin Pty) Paul & Co Pubs.

Reidy, David, jt. auth. see Wallace.

Reidy, Denis, ed. The Italian Book, 1465-1800. (British Library Studies in the History of the Book). (Illus.). 424p. 1993. 120.00 (*0-7123-0295-6*, Pub. by B23tish Library) U of Toronto Pr.

Reidy, Hannah. What Do You Like to Wear? LC 98-44724. 1999. 7.95 (*1-84089-152-1*) LKC.

***Reidy, Hannah.** What Noises Can You Hear? LC 98-44725. 1999. 7.95 (*1-84089-153-X*) LKC.

Reidy, John, ed. see Norton, Thomas.

Reidy, Joseph P. From Slavery to Agrarian Capitalism in the Cotton Plantation South: Central Georgia, 1800-1880. LC 92-53620. (Fred W. Morrison Series in Southern Studies). xvi, 360p. (C). 1992. 55.00 (*0-8078-2061-X*) U of NC Pr.

— From Slavery to Agrarian Capitalism in the Cotton Plantation South: Central Georgia, 1800-1880. LC 92-53620. (Fred W. Morrison Series in Southern Studies). (Illus.). 376p. (C). 1995. pap. text 19.95 (*0-8078-4552-3*) U of NC Pr.

Reidy, Mary Denis. Maudlin Scourge. 228p. mass mkt. 4.99 (*1-896329-43-8*) Picasso Publ.

Reidy, R. Municipal Solid Waste Recycling in Western Europe to 1996. 246p. 1992. pap. 1110.00 (*1-85617-138-8*, Pub. by Elsvr Adv Tech) Elsevier.

Reidy, Robert W., jt. auth. see Jones, William L.

Reidy, Roisin, compiled by. Profile of the International Pump Industry: Market Prospects to 1988. 2nd ed. LC 95-117280. 280p. 1994. pap. 855.00 (*1-85617-225-2*, Pergamon Pr) Elsevier.

Reidy, Roisin, ed. Profile of the International Fluid Sealing Industry: Market Prospects to 1999. LC 95-215107. 204p. 1995. spiral bd. 855.00 (*1-85617-227-9*) Elsevier.

***Reidy, Sue.** The Visitation. 2000. pap. 10.95 (*0-552-99696-3*, Pub. by Transworld Publishers Ltd) Trafalgar.

***Reier, Sharon.** The Bridges of New York. 2000. pap. 12.95 (*0-486-41230-X*) Dover.

Reiersen, Johan R. Pathfinder for Norwegian Emigrants. LC 81-132209. (Norwegian-American Historical Association. Travel & Description Ser.: No. 9). 253p. reprint ed. pap. 78.50 (*0-608-15446-6*, 202929300059) Bks Demand.

Reiersen, Olav, jt. auth. see Ansteinsson, J.

Reierson, Art. Allen Family: Descendants of Ralph Allen (b. 1540, England) Through His Son George of Weymouth, England & Massachusetts. (Illus.). 213p. 1998. reprint ed. pap. 34.00 (*0-8328-7231-8*); reprint ed. lib. bdg. 44.00 (*0-8328-7230-X*) Higginson Bk Co.

— Cooper Family of Buckinghamshire, England, & Long Island. (Illus.). 187p. 1998. reprint ed. pap. 27.00 (*0-8328-8040-X*); reprint ed. lib. bdg. 37.00 (*0-8328-8039-6*) Higginson Bk Co.

— Cornell Family: Descendants of George Cornell (b. 1550, Essex, England) in England & New York. (Illus.). 339p. 1998. pap. 51.00 (*0-8328-8060-4*); lib. bdg. 61.00 (*0-8328-8059-0*) Higginson Bk Co.

— Corwin. William Corwin Family (Descendants of William Corwin of New Jersey & Pennsylvania) 86p. 1998. pap. 17.00 (*0-8328-8066-3*); lib. bdg. 27.00 (*0-8328-8065-5*) Higginson Bk Co.

— Egolf Genealogy: Descendants of Michael, 1670, of Germany. 88p. 1998. pap. 16.00 (*0-8328-9561-X*); lib. bdg. 26.00 (*0-8328-9560-1*) Higginson Bk Co.

— Fones Family: (New York & New England) Descendants of William Fones of Saxby, England. (Illus.). 250p. 1998. pap. 38.00 (*0-8328-8592-4*); lib. bdg. 48.00 (*0-8328-8591-6*) Higginson Bk Co.

— Hallett Family: Descendants of Richard Hallett of Dorset, England & Long Island, New York. (Illus.). 96p. 1998. reprint ed. pap. 18.00 (*0-8328-8912-1*); reprint ed. lib. bdg. 28.00 (*0-8328-8911-3*) Higginson Bk Co.

— Johnson Family: Descendants of Elkanah Johnson of Wales & Rhode Island. (Illus.). 131p. 1998. pap. 23.00 (*0-8328-9341-2*); lib. bdg. 33.00 (*0-8328-9340-4*) Higginson Bk Co.

— Johnson. Genealogy: Descendants of William, 1625, of Portsmouth, England (Through Elkanah of Rhode Island) 89p. 1998. pap. 17.50 (*0-8328-9565-2*); lib. bdg. 27.50 (*0-8328-9564-4*) Higginson Bk Co.

— Maltby Family of Massachusetts. (Illus.). 374p. 1998. pap. 58.00 (*0-8328-9467-2*); lib. bdg. 68.00 (*0-8328-9466-4*) Higginson Bk Co.

— Winthrop Genealogy: Descendants of William Wynethorpe, 1400, Wynethorpe, England. 233p. 1998. pap. 36.00 (*0-8328-9563-6*); lib. bdg. 46.00 (*0-8328-9562-8*) Higginson Bk Co.

— Woody Family: Descendants of Richard Wooddy of England & Massachusetts. (Illus.). 329p. 1998. pap. 49.50 (*0-8328-9553-9*); lib. bdg. 59.50 (*0-8328-9552-0*) Higginson Bk Co.

— Woolsey Genealogy: Descendants of Cardinal Robert Wulcy, 1440, Ipswich, England. 171p. 1998. pap. 25.00 (*0-8328-9559-8*); lib. bdg. 35.00 (*0-8328-9558-X*) Higginson Bk Co.

— Zullman - Zollmann - Zolman Families: U. S. Descendants of Johannes Zullman of Mensfelden, Germany. (Illus.). 562p. 1998. pap. 84.00 (*0-8328-9555-5*); lib. bdg. 94.00 (*0-8328-9554-7*) Higginson Bk Co.

— Zumbrun Family of Switzerland & Montgomery County, Maryland. (Illus.). 422p. 1998. pap. 65.00 (*0-8328-9557-1*); lib. bdg. 75.00 (*0-8328-9556-3*) Higginson Bk Co.

Reierson, Gary B. The Art in Preaching: The Intersection of Theology, Worship, & Preaching with the Arts. LC 87-34943. 176p. (Orig.). (C). 1988. pap. 19.50 (*0-8191-6883-1*); lib. bdg. 43.50 (*0-8191-6882-3*) U Pr of Amer.

Reierson, Vickie. Start Your Business: A Beginner's Guide. 3rd ed. LC 98-48610. 178p. 1999. 10.95 (*1-55571-485-4*) PSI Resch.

Reierson, Vickie, ed. see DeThomas, Arthur R.

Reierson, Vickie, ed. see Keup, Erwin J.

Reiese, U. Erich. Sea Anemones As a Hobby. (Illus.). 320p. 1993. 47.95 (*0-86622-539-0*, TT027) TFH Pubns.

Reiesen, DeLoss & Reiesen, Ruby. Counseling & Marriage. (Resources for Christian Counseling Ser.: Vol. 19). 246p. 18.99 (*0-8499-0501-X*) Word Pub.

Reiesen, Ruby, jt. auth. see Reiesen, DeLoss.

Reif. International Ombudsman Anthology. LC 98-43827. 1997. lib. bdg. 159.00 (*90-411-0490-9*) Kluwer Law Intl.

An Asterisk (*) at the beginning of an entry indicates that the title is appearing for the first time.

Reif, Arnold E., ed. Immunity & Cancer in Man: An Introduction. LC 75-145. (Immunology Ser.: No. 3). (Illus.). 187p. reprint ed. pap. 58.00 (*0-7837-0652-9*, 204099100019) Bks Demand.

***Reif, Charles Braddock.** Toxamok, a Troll at Summer Camp. (Illus.). 75p. (J). (gr. 4-6). 1999. write for info. (*0-9666156-1-1*) Keepsake Chron.

Reif, Daniel K. Home Office - Small Office Quick Planner: Reusable, Peel & Stick Furniture & Architectural Symbols. (Illus.). 11p. 1995. pap. 18.95 (*1-880301-05-9*) Gardeners.

— Home Quick Planner: Reusable, Peel & Stick Furniture & Architectural Symbols. (Illus.). 12p. 1993. pap., student ed. 18.95 (*1-880301-03-2*) Gardeners.

Reif, Emil & Moeller, Therald B. Pocket Atlas of Radiographic Positioning. LC 97-110619. (Illus.). 290p. 1996. pap. text 19.90 (*0-86577-640-7*) Thieme Med Pubs.

***Reif, Emil & Moeller, Toreten B.** Pocket Atlas of Radiographic Anatomy. 2nd ed. LC 99-40802. (Illus.). 391p. 1999. pap. 34.00 (*0-86577-874-4*) Thieme Med Pubs.

Reif, Emil, et al. Pocket Atlas of Cross-Sectional Anatomy: Computer Tomography & Magnetic Resonance Imaging, Head, Neck, Spine & Joints, Vol. 1. Bergman, Clifford, tr. LC 93-43883. 1993. pap. 28.50 (*0-86577-510-9*) Thieme Med Pubs.

Reif, Emil, jt. auth. see Moeller, Torsten B.

Reif, Emil, jt. auth. see Moller, Torsten B.

Reif, Emil, ed. see Moeller, Torsten B., et al.

Reif, Frederick. Fundamentals of Statistical & Thermal Physics. (Fundamentals of Physics Ser.). 651p. (C). 1965. 100.31 (*0-07-051800-9*) McGraw.

— Understanding Basic Mechanics. LC 94-44982. 272p. 1995. pap. 20.95 (*0-471-11623-8*); pap., student ed. 37.95 (*0-471-11624-6*); pap. text 32.00 (*0-471-10337-3*) Wiley.

Reif, J. A., jt. auth. see Tirkel, Eliezer.

Reif, J. A., ed. see Tirkel, Eliezer.

Reif, J. H., ed. VLSI Algorithms & Architectures. (Lecture Notes in Computer Science Ser.: Vol. 319). x, 476p. 1988. 79.95 (*0-387-96818-0*) Spr-Verlag.

Reif, Jennifer. Mysteries of Demeter: Rebirth of the Pagan Way. LC 99-29771. (Illus.). 344p. 1999. 35.00 (*1-57863-133-5*) Weiser.

***Reif, Jennifer.** Mysteries of Demeter: Rebirth of the Pagan Way. LC 99-29771. (Illus.). 320p. 2000. pap. 19.95 (*1-57863-141-6*) Weiser.

Reif, Joe & Shahmanesh, Nargess. The Global Road Warrior: 100 - Country Handbook for the International Business Traveler. Kosaka, Minoru & Rabello, Camilla, eds. LC 98-21032. (Illus.). 666p. 1997. pap. 24.95 (*1-885073-49-6*) Wrld Trade Pr.

Reif, Joe, et al. Services--The Export of the 21st Century: A Guidebook for U. S. Service Exporters. LC 96-33514. 1996. write for info. (*1-885073-41-0*) Wrld Trade Pr.

Reif, John H., ed. Synthesis of Parallel Algorithms. 1993. text 63.95 (*1-55860-135-X*) Morgan Kaufmann.

***Reif, Joseph.** Hebrew Basic Course with 35 Cassettes. (Multilingual Books Intensive Cassette Foreign Language Ser.). 620p. 1999. pap. text 250.00 (*1-58214-032-4*) Mltilingl Bks.

Reif, Joseph A. & Levinson, Hanna. Spoken Modern Hebrew. (Spoken Language Ser.). 590p. 1980. pap. 30.00 (*0-87950-683-0*); pap. 220.00 incl. audio (*0-87950-685-7*); audio 190.00 (*0-87950-684-9*) Spoken Lang Serv.

Reif, Karlheinz, ed. Ten European Elections: Campaigns & Results of the 1979-81 First Direct Elections to the European Parliament. LC 84-18874. 232p. 1985. text 79.95 (*0-566-00694-4*) Ashgate Pub Co.

Reif, Karlheinz & Melich, Anna. Euro-Barometer Thirty: Immigrants & Out-Groups in Western Europe, October-November 1988. LC 91-70507. 836p. 1991. write for info. (*0-89138-868-0*) ICPSR.

— Euro-Barometer Twenty-Nine: Environmental Problems & Cancer, March-April 1988. LC 90-85881. 472p. 1990. write for info. (*0-89138-869-9*) ICPSR.

— Euro-Barometer 31: European Elections, 1989; Pre-Election Survey, March-April, 1989. 536p. 1991. write for info. (*0-89138-866-4*) ICPSR.

— Euro-Barometer, 31A: European Elections, 1989: Post-Election Survey, June-July 1989. LC 93-78540. 864p. 1993. write for info. (*0-89138-862-1*) ICPSR.

— Euro-Barometer 38.0: European Court of Justice, Passive Smoking, & Consumer Issues, September-October 1992. 2nd ed. LC 92-70498. 976p. 1995. pap. write for info. (*0-89138-864-8*) ICPSR.

Reif, Laura & Martin, Karen S. Nurses & Consumers: Partners in Assuring Quality Care in the Home. 60p. 1995. pap. text 20.95 (*1-55810-120-9*, CH-49) Am Nurses Pub.

Reif, Laura & Trager, Brahna, eds. International Perspectives on Long-Term Care. LC 85-8442. (Home Health Care Services Quarterly Ser.: Vol. 5, Nos. 3 & 4). 341p. 1985. text 79.95 (*0-86656-400-4*); pap. text 24.95 (*0-86656-445-4*) Haworth Pr.

Reif-Lehrer, Liane. Grant Application Writers Handbook. 3rd ed. 496p. (C). 1995. pap. text 40.00 (*0-86720-874-0*) Jones & Bartlett.

— Writing a Successful Grant Application. 2nd rev. ed. 304p. 1989. pap. 25.00 (*0-86720-104-5*) Jones & Bartlett.

***Reif, Linda C.** The International Ombudsman Yearbook, 1999, Vol. 3. 316p. 2000. 61.00 (*90-411-1352-5*) Kluwer Law Intl.

Reif, Linda C., ed. The International Ombudsman Yearbook, Vol. 1. 224p. 1997. 62.00 (*90-411-0498-4*) Kluwer Academic.

Reif, Linda C., jt. ed. see International Ombudsman Institute Staff.

Reif, R., et al, eds. Environmental, Safety, & Health Issues in IC Production. LC 97-11466. (Materials Research Society Symposium Proceedings Ser.: No. 447). 154p. 1997. text 75.00 (*1-55899-351-7*) Materials Res.

Reif, R., jt. auth. see Munchow, L.

Reif, Rafael, ed. see Symposium on Reduced Temperature Processing for VL.

Reif, Stefan C. Hebrew Manuscripts at Cambridge University Library: A Description & Introduction. LC 96-46043. (University of Cambridge Oriental Publications: No. 52). (Illus.). 646p. (C). 1997. text 125.00 (*0-521-58339-X*) Cambridge U Pr.

Reif, Stefan C., jt. ed. see Blau, Joshua.

Reif, W. E., et al, eds. Studies in Paleoecology: Report 1979-1981. (Neues Jahrgb. f. Geologie und Palaeontologie Ser.: Vol. 164 1/2). (ENG & GER., Illus.). 1982. pap. text 110.00 (*0-945345-33-X*) Lubrecht & Cramer.

Reif, Wolf-Ernst, ed. see Schindewolf, Otto H.

Reife, Abraham & Freeman, Harold S., eds. Environmental Chemistry of Dyes & Pigments. LC 95-6113. 352p. 1995. 115.00 (*0-471-58927-6*, Wiley-Interscience) Wiley.

Reifel, Michael, jt. ed. see McClelland, Bramlette.

Reifel, Stuart. Advances in Early Education & Day Care: Foundations Adult Dynamics, Teacher Education & Play, Vol. 10. 1999. 78.50 (*0-7623-0425-1*) Jai Pr.

***Reifel, Stuart.** Play & Culture Studies, Vol. 2. 1999. 73.25 (*1-56750-422-1*); pap. 39.50 (*1-56750-423-X*) Ablx Pub.

— Theory in Context & Out. 2000. lib. bdg. write for info. (*1-56750-487-6*) Greenwood.

— Theory in Context & Out. Vol. V.3. 2000. write for info. (*1-56750-486-8*) Greenwood.

Reifel, Stuart, ed. Advances in Early Education & Day Care, Vol. 2. 264p. 1982. 78.50 (*0-89232-149-0*) Jai Pr.

— Advances in Early Education & Day Care, Vol. 3. 200p. 1984. 78.50 (*0-89232-206-3*) Jai Pr.

— Advances in Early Education & Day Care, Vol. 4. 224p. 1985. 78.50 (*0-89232-454-6*) Jai Pr.

— Advances in Early Education & Day Care, Vol. 6. 304p. 1995. 78.50 (*1-55938-767-X*) Jai Pr.

— Advances in Early Education & Day Care, Vol. 8. 328p. 1996. 78.50 (*0-7623-0092-2*) Jai Pr.

— Advances in Early Education & Day Care: Perspectives on Developmentally Appropriate Practice, Vol. 5. 244p. 1993. 78.50 (*0-89232-811-8*) Jai Pr.

— Advances in Early Education & Day Care: Social Contexts of Early Development & Education, Vol. 7. 352p. 1995. 78.50 (*1-55938-952-4*) Jai Pr.

Reifel, Stuart & Kilmer, Sally, eds. Advances in Early Education & Day Care, Vol. 1. 240p. 1980. 78.50 (*0-89232-127-X*) Jai Pr.

Reifel, Toni & Woodward, Bette. Mama Cooks a Day Ahead. (Illus.). 260p. 1990. write for info. (*0-9628049-0-8*) Mama Cooks.

— Mama Cooks a Day Ahead. (Illus.). 260p. 1991. reprint ed. write for info. (*0-9628049-1-6*) Mama Cooks.

— Mama Cooks a Day Ahead. (Illus.). 260p. 1993. reprint ed. write for info. (*0-9628049-4-0*) Mama Cooks.

— Mama Cooks for Christmas. (Illus.). 190p. 1991. 7.95 (*0-9628049-2-4*) Mama Cooks.

— Mama Cooks with Kids in the Kitchen. Jamieson, Suzanne, ed. & illus. by. 108p. 1992. write for info. (*0-9628049-3-2*) Mama Cooks.

Reifen, David. The Juvenile Court in a Changing Society: Young Offenders in Israel. LC 73-178000. 280p. 1973. 28.95 (*0-8122-7649-3*) U of Pa Pr.

Reifen, R., et al, eds. Pediatric Nutrition, No. 8. LC 98-12387. (Pediatric & Adolescent Medicine Ser.: Vol. 8 (1998)). (Illus.). viii, 262p. 1998. 275.00 (*3-8055-6652-2*) S Karger.

Reifenberg, A. Ancient Jewish Coins from the Persian Time to the 2nd Revolt. 6th ed. (Illus.). 84p. 1974. 21.00 (*965-09-0004-7*, 73890, Pub. by R Mass Ltd) Lambda Pubs.

Reifer, Donald J. Managing Software Reuse. LC 97-1743. 374p. 1997. 59.99 (*0-471-57853-3*) Wiley.

— Software Management. 5th ed. LC 97-20501. 550p. 1997. 70.00 (*0-8186-8001-6*) IEEE Comp Soc.

Reifer, Donald J. & IEEE Computer Society Members. Tutorial, Software Management. 3rd ed. LC 86-80073. vii, 518 p. 1986. write for info. (*0-8186-4678-0*) IEEE Comp Soc.

Reifer, Donald J., jt. auth. see Marciniak, John J.

Reifers, Kate & Dorning, Stacee. What's for Lunch? Experience the Multi-Cultural Cuisine of the Golden Triangle. 150p. 1998. pap. 8.95 (*0-9666265-0-8*) San Diego Tech.

Reiff. Communication Skills, Achievement Tests. 2nd ed. (EC - HS Communication/English Ser.). 1985. 4.95 (*0-538-23663-9*) S-W Pub.

— Communication Skills for the Processing of Words. 2nd ed. (EC - HS Communication/English Ser.). 1985. mass mkt. 16.95 (*0-538-23660-4*) S-W Pub.

— Communication Skills for the Processing of Words. 3rd ed. (EC - HS Communication/English Ser.). (C). 1990. mass mkt. 23.95 (*0-538-60684-3*) S-W Pub.

— Communication Skills for the Processing of Words. 4th ed. (EC - HS Communication/English Ser.). 1996. mass mkt. 5.95 (*0-538-65135-0*) S-W Pub.

— Integrated Keyboarding/Communication Skills. 2nd ed. (TA - Typing/Keyboarding Ser.). 1989. pap. 9.50 (*0-538-60105-1*) S-W Pub.

— Introduction to Corporate Travel. (Hospitality, Travel & Tourism Ser.). (C). 1993. pap., wbk. ed. 25.25 (*0-538-70966-9*) S-W Pub.

Reiff & Ament. Steps in Home Living. 3rd ed. (gr. 7-9). 1984. text 26.99 (*0-02-665750-3*) Glencoe.

Reiff, Annette. Introduction to Corporate Travel. 285p. 1994. pap., teacher ed. write for info. (*0-538-70967-7*) S-W Pub.

Reiff, D. D., ed. see Pressure Vessels & Piping Conference Staff.

Reiff, Dan W. & Reiff, Kathleen K. Eating Disorders: Nutrition Therapy in the Recovery Process. (Illus.). 554p. 1997. pap. 85.00 (*0-9668941-0-3*) Life Ent.

Reiff, Daniel. Small Georgian Houses in England & Virginia: Origins & Development Through the 1750s. LC 83-40521. (Illus.). 352p. 1986. 85.00 (*0-87413-254-1*) U Delaware Pr.

***Reiff, Daniel D.** Houses from Books. LC 99-46642. 2001. write for info. (*0-271-01943-3*) Pa St U Pr.

Reiff, Dora. The Beauty of His Presence. 9p. 1980. 0.20 (*0-89814-048-X*) Grace Publns.

Reiff, Henry B., et al. Exceeding Expectations: Successful Adults with Learning Disabilities. LC 96-34106. 234p. 1997. pap. text 27.00 (*0-89079-705-6*, 7474) PRO-ED.

Reiff, Henry B., jt. ed. see Gerber, Paul J.

Reiff, Janice L. Digitizing the Past: The Use of Computers & Communication Technologies in History. (Illus.). 160p. 2000. pap. 10.00 (*0-87229-104-9*) Am Hist Assn.

Reiff, Judith. Learning Styles. (What Research Says to the Teacher Ser.). 40p. 1992. pap. 3.95 (*0-8106-1092-2*) NEA.

Reiff, Judith, jt. auth. see Fortson, Laura R.

Reiff, Kathleen K., jt. auth. see Reiff, Dan W.

Reiff, Richard F. Living & Learning for International Interchange: A Sourcebook for Housing Personnel. 28p. 1986. pap. text 12.00 (*0-912207-13-2*) NAFSA Washington.

Reiff, Robert & Scheerer, Martin. Memory & Hypnotic Age Regression: Developmental Aspects of Cognitive Function Explored Through Hypnosis. LC 59-13120. 253p. 1970. 40.00 (*0-8236-3340-3*) Intl Univs Pr.

Reiff, Robert S. Drunk Driving & Related Offenses: 1998 Supplement. LC 97-70981. 1998. suppl. ed. 35.00 (*0-327-00212-3*, 61241-10) LEXIS Pub.

— Drunk Driving & Related Vehicular Offenses. LC 97-70981. 505p. 1997. text 100.00 (*1-55834-482-9*, 61240-10, MICHIE) LEXIS Pub.

***Reiff, Robert S.** Drunk Driving & Related Vehicular Offenses: The Complete Lawyer's Guidebook to Drunk Driving. 2nd ed. LC 99-67363. 600p. 1999. 110.00 (*0-327-04973-1*, 6124011) LEXIS Pub.

Reiff, Roseanne. Communication Skills for Processing of Words. 4th ed. (EC - HS Communication/English Ser.). 240p. 1996. mass mkt. 27.95 (*0-538-65134-2*) S-W Pub.

Reiff, Sandra. Jacques Cousteau Finds the Lost Syntax. (By-Invitation-Only Ser.). 11p. 1992. pap. 6.00 (*1-882448-01-4*, Machiavellian) Mac-Kinations.

Reiff, Tana. Beauty & the Business. LC 94-76141. (Working for Myself Ser.). 80p. 1994. pap. 4.95 (*0-7854-1106-2*, 40831) Am Guidance.

— Caring. LC 94-79122. (That's Life Ser.: Bk. 6). 95p. 1994. pap. 4.95 (*0-7854-1091-0*, 40706); audio 10.95 (*0-7854-1100-3*, 40716) Am Guidance.

— Clean As a Whistle. LC 94-76147. (Working for Myself Ser.). 80p. 1994. pap. 4.95 (*0-7854-1107-0*, 40837) Am Guidance.

— Crafting a Business. LC 94-76142. (Working for Myself Ser.). 80p. 1994. pap. 4.95 (*0-7854-1109-7*, 40832) Am Guidance.

— Deals on Wheels. LC 94-79121. (That's Life Ser.: Bk. 5). 1994. pap. 4.95 (*0-7854-1090-2*, 40705); audio 10.95 (*0-7854-1099-6*, 40715) Am Guidance.

— Emergency. LC 94-79117. (That's Life Ser.: Bk. 1). 96p. 1994. pap. 4.95 (*0-7854-1086-4*, 40701) Am Guidance.

— Fables: Reading Level 2-3. (Timeless Tales Ser.). 1993. 4.95 (*0-88336-270-8*) New Readers.

— The Flower Man. (Working for Myself Ser.). 80p. 1994. pap. 4.95 (*0-7854-1110-0*, 40838) Am Guidance.

— Folktales: Reading Level 2-3. (Timeless Tales Ser.). 1993. 4.95 (*0-88336-271-6*) New Readers.

— The Green Team. LC 94-76144. (Working for Myself Ser.). 80p. 1994. pap. 4.95 (*0-7854-1111-9*, 40834) Am Guidance.

— Handy All Around. LC 94-76145. (Working for Myself Ser.). 80p. 1994. pap. 4.95 (*0-7854-1112-7*, 40835) Am Guidance.

— In a Family Way. LC 94-79120. (That's Life Ser.: Bk. 4). 96p. 1994. pap. 4.95 (*0-7854-1089-9*, 40704) Am Guidance.

— Layoff. (That's Life Ser.: Bk. 3). 96p. 1994. pap. 4.95 (*0-7854-1088-0*, 40703); audio 10.95 (*0-7854-1097-X*, 40713) Am Guidance.

— Legends: Reading Level 2-3. (Timeless Tales Ser.). 1993. 4.95 (*0-88336-273-2*) New Readers.

— Mr. & Ms. LC 94-79116. (That's Life Ser.: Bk. 8). 96p. (YA). (gr. 6-12). 1994. pap. 4.95 (*0-7854-1093-7*, 40708) Am Guidance.

— One More for the Road. LC 94-79118. (That's Life Ser.: Bk. 2). 96p. (YA). (gr. 6-12). 1994. pap. 4.95 (*0-7854-1087-2*, 40702); audio 10.95 (*0-7854-1096-1*, 40712) Am Guidance.

— Other People's Pets. LC 94-76143. (Working for Myself Ser.). 80p. 1994. pap. 4.95 (*0-7854-1113-5*, 40833) Am Guidance.

— Tax Time. LC 94-79115. (That's Life Ser.: Bk. 7). 96p. 1994. pap. 4.95 (*0-7854-1092-9*, 40707); audio 10.95 (*0-7854-1101-1*, 40717) Am Guidance.

— That's Life Basic Set, 8 bks. 1994. pap. 49.95 (*0-7854-1084-8*, 40700) Am Guidance.

— That's Life Classroom Library, 24 bks. 1994. pap., teacher ed. 99.95 (*0-7854-1083-X*, 40710) Am Guidance.

— That's Life Curriculum Guide. 272p. 1994. pap. 29.95 (*0-7854-1094-5*, 40709) Am Guidance.

Reiff, Tana. Timeless Tales Fables. (Timeless Tales Ser.). (J). 1993. audio 10.00 (*0-88336-266-X*) New Readers.

Reiff, Tana. Working for Myself Basic Set, 10 bks. 1994. pap. 44.95 (*0-7854-1104-6*, 40828) Am Guidance.

— Working for Myself Classroom Library, 30 bks. 1994. pap. 129.95 (*0-7854-1103-8*, 40840) Am Guidance.

— Working for Myself Curriculum Guide. 96p. 1994. pap. 19.50 (*0-7854-1105-4*, 40839) Am Guidance.

— You Call, We Haul. LC 94-76140. (Working for Myself Ser.). 80p. 1994. pap. 4.95 (*0-7854-1114-3*, 40830) Am Guidance.

— Your Kids & Mind. LC 94-76139. (Working for Myself Ser.). 80p. 1994. pap. 4.95 (*0-7854-1115-1*, 40829) Am Guidance.

Reiff, Tana & Clews, Vince. That's Life DramaTapes Cassette Program, 8 bks. 1994. pap., teacher ed. 99.95 incl. audio (*0-7854-1085-6*, 40720) Am Guidance.

Reiff, Tara. Myths: Reading Level 2-3, Reading Level 2-3. (Timeless Tales Ser.). 1993. 4.95 (*0-88336-272-4*) New Readers.

Reiffel, James, et al, eds. Psychosocial Aspects of Cardiovascular Disease. LC 79-27765. 365p. 1980. 12.50 (*0-930194-32-2*) Ctr Thanatology.

Reiffen, Hannelotte, ed. see Barth, Karl.

Reiffenstuhl, Gunther, et al. Vaginal Operations: Surgical Anatomy & Technique. 2nd ed. Imig, John R., ed. Bond, Julika, tr. LC 95-39425. (Illus.). 320p. 1996. 150.00 (*0-683-07285-4*) Lppncott W & W.

Reifferscheid, Augustus, ed. Bibliotheca Patrum Latinorum Italica, 2 vols. in 1. 1033p. 1976. reprint ed. write for info. (*3-487-05966-5*) G Olms Pubs.

Reifferscheid, Augustus, ed. see Suetonius, C.

Reifler, David M., ed. The American Society of Ophthalmic Plastic & Reconstructive Surgery (ASOPRS) History of Ophthalmic Plastic Surgery, 2500 BC-1995 AD: The First Twenty-Five Years 1969-1994. LC 94-7908. (Illus.). 493p. 1994. 75.00 (*0-930405-64-1*) Norman SF.

Reifler, Sam. I Ching. 288p. 1991. pap. 12.95 (*0-553-35424-8*) Bantam.

Reifman, Noah. Certification Review for Pharmacy Technicians. 1996. pap. text 32.95 (*0-914373-34-X*) Wieser & Wieser.

Reifner, Udo & Ford, Janet, eds. Banking for People: I. Social Banking & New Poverty, II. Consumer Debts & Unemployment in Europe, National Reports. xxxii, 673p. (C). 1992. lib. bdg. 169.25 (*3-11-012675-3*) De Gruyter.

Reifsnider, K. L. Fatigue of Composite Materials. (Composite Materials Ser.: Vol. 4). 520p. 1991. 262.50 (*0-444-70507-4*, CCS 4) Elsevier.

Reifsnider, K. L., ed. Damage in Composite Materials - STP 775. 282p. 1982. 33.50 (*0-8031-0696-3*, STP775) ASTM.

— Progress in Durability Analysis of Composite Systems: Proceedings of the 2nd International Conference, Blacksburg, Virginia, 14-17 September 1997. 500p. 1998. 101.00 (*90-5410-960-2*, Pub. by A A Balkema) Ashgate Pub Co.

Reifsnider, K. L. & Hyer, M. W., eds. Proceedings of the Sixth Japan-U. S. Conference on Composite Materials. LC 92-85213. 875p. 1993. text 219.95 (*1-56676-021-6*) Technomic.

Reifsnider, K. L. & Lauritis, K. N., eds. Fatigue of Filamentary Composite Materials- STP 636. 282p. 1970. 26.00 (*0-8031-0347-6*, STP636) ASTM.

Reifsnider, K. L., jt. ed. see Noor, A. K.

Reifsnyder, Constance A., jt. auth. see Bartolomei, Sonja.

Reifsnyder, K. L., jt. ed. see Reddy, J. N.

Reifsnyder, William E. High Huts of the White Mountains. 2nd ed. (Illus.). 256p. 1993. pap. 12.95 (*1-878239-20-1*) AMC Books.

Reifsynder, William E. & Lull, Howard W. Radiant Energy in Relation to Forests. LC 77-10239. (U. S. Department of Agriculture. Technical Bulletin Ser.: 1344). reprint ed. 39.50 (*0-404-16217-7*) AMS Pr.

Reig, Daniel. Arabic-French, French-Arabic Dictionary: Dictionnaire Arabe-Francais-Arabe. (ARA & FRE.). 1448p. 1983. 95.00 (*0-8288-0442-7*, F290) Fr & Eur.

— Dictionnaire Arabe-Francais. (ARA & FRE.). 1991. write for info. (*0-7859-8607-3*, 203451209X) Fr & Eur.

Reig, Teddy & Berger, Edward. Reminiscing in Tempo: The Life & Times of a Jazz Hustler. LC 90-36355. (Studies in Jazz: No. 10). (Illus.). 238p. 1990. 32.00 (*0-8108-2326-8*) Scarecrow.

Reigart, John F. The Lancasterian System of Instruction in the Schools of New York City. LC 72-89220. (American Education: Its Men, Institutions, & Ideas. Series 1: Its Men, Institutions & Ideas, Ser. 1). 1975. reprint ed. 13.95 (*0-405-01459-7*) Ayer.

Reigate, Emily. An Illustrated Guide to Lace. (Illus.). 264p. 1986. 49.50 (*1-85149-003-5*) Antique Collect.

Reigber, Christoph. Solid Earth Geophysics, ser. vol. 6. (Advances in Space Research Ser.). 1988. pap. 56.00 (*0-08-036644-9*, Pergamon Pr) Elsevier.

Reigber, Christoph, jt. ed. see Montag, Horst.

Reigel, Donald H., jt. ed. see Rowley-Kelly, Fern L.

Reigelman, Milton M. The Midland: A Venture in Literary Regionalism. LC 75-28219. 154p. (Orig.). 1975. pap. text 9.95 (*0-87745-054-4*) U of Iowa Pr.

Reigeluth, Charles, ed. Instructional Design Theories & Models: A New Paradigm of Instructional Theory, Vol. II. 728p. 1999. 45.00 (*0-8058-2859-1*) L Erlbaum Assocs.

Reigeluth, Charles M. Instructional Design Theories & Models: An Overview of Their Current Status. 512p. 1983. text 45.00 (*0-89859-275-5*) L Erlbaum Assocs.

Reigeluth, Charles M., ed. Instructional Theories in Action: Lessons Illustrating Selected Theories & Models. 360p. (C). 1987. 39.95 (*0-89859-825-7*) L Erlbaum Assocs.

Reigeluth, Charles M., et al, eds. Comprehensive Systems Design: A New Educational Technology. (NATO ASI Series F: Computer & Systems Sciences, Special Programme AET: Vol. 95). ix, 437p. 1993. write for info. (*3-540-56677-5*) Spr-Verlag.

An Asterisk (*) at the beginning of an entry indicates that the title is appearing for the first time.

R

— Comprehensive Systems Design: A New Educational Technology. LC 93-11329. (NATO ASI Series F: Computer & Systems Science: Vol. 95). 1993. 119.95 (0-387-56677-5) Spr-Verlag.

Reigeluth, Charles M. & Garfinkle, Robert J., eds. Systemic Change in Education. LC 93-36654. 184p. 1994. 34.95 (0-87778-271-7) Educ Tech Pubns.

Reigeluth, George, jt. auth. see Wolman, Harold.

***Reiger, George.** The Complete Book of North American Waterfowling: A Handbook of Techniques & Strategies. 3rd ed. LC 00-32710. 2000. pap. 24.95 (1-58574-125-6) Lyons Pr.

Reiger, George. Heron Hill Chronicle. LC 94-22675. 192p. 1994. 19.95 (1-55821-296-5) Lyons Pr.

***Reiger, George.** Profiles in Saltwater Angling: A History of the Sport - Its People & Places, Tackle & Techniques. 2nd rev. ed. LC 99-35356. 470p. 1999. 24.95 (0-89272-449-8) Down East.

Reiger, George. The Striped Bass Chronicles. LC 97-1925. (Illus.). 192p. 1997. 22.95 (1-55821-478-X) Lyons Pr.

Reiger, George, compiled by. The Best of Zane Grey, Outdoorsman: Hunting & Fishing Tales. LC 91-35932. (Classics of American Sport Ser.). (Illus.). 368p. 1992. pap. 16.95 (0-8117-2599-5) Stackpole.

Reiger, George W. The Birder's Journal: And Illustrated Lifelist. Baughman, Mel M., ed. (Illus.). 1989. 30.00 (0-9623149-0-0) Baughman Co.

***Reiger, John F.** American Sportsmen & the Origins of Conservation. 3rd ed. (Illus.). 352p. 2000. pap. 24.95 (0-87071-487-2) Oreg St U Pr.

Reiger, John F. "Gifford Pinchot with Rod & Reel" - "Trading Places: From Historian to Environmental Activist" Two Essays in Conservation History. (Pinchot Lecture Series). 63p. 1994. pap. 8.95 (0-685-75416-2) Grey Towers Pr.

Reiger, Kerreen. The Disenchantment of the Home: Modernizing the Australian Family, 1880-1940. (Illus.). 1985. text 29.95 (0-19-554594-X) OUP.

Reiger, Kurt E., jt. auth. see Shenkman, Richard.

Reighard, Dwight. Treasures from the Dark: A Book for Every Person Who Has Lost a Loved One. rev. ed. 298p. 1998. pap. 17.99 (1-888237-16-3) Baxter Pr.

Reighard, Dwight & Springle, Pat. Discovering Your North Star: Charting Your Course for Success & Significance. (Illus.). 368p. 1998. 25.00 (1-888237-17-1) Baxter Pr.

— The North Star Journal. 312p. 1998. 35.00 (1-888237-19-8) Baxter Pr.

Reighard, Frank H., & Assistants Staff, ed. Standard History of Fulton County: Authentic Narrative of the Past, with an Extended Survey of Modern Developments in the Progress of Town & County. With Modern Every-Name Index Compiled by the Fulton County Chapter, Ohio Genealogical Society, 2 vols. (Illus.). 1205p. 1997. reprint ed. lib. bdg. 121.00 (0-8328-6317-3) Higginson Bk Co.

Reighard, John, compiled by see Camara, Joaquim M.

Reighley, Kurt. Marilyn Manson: God of Fuck. LC 97-46172. 192p. 1998. pap. 10.95 (0-312-18133-7) St Martin.

Reighley, Kurt B. Looking for the Perfect Beat: The Art & Culture of the DJ. 244p. 2000. per. 12.95 (0-671-03869-9, MTV Bks) PB.

Reigle, David. The Books of Kiu-Te in the Tibetan Buddhist Tantras. LC 83-60416. (Secret Doctrine Reference Ser.). (Illus.). 80p. (Orig.). 1983. pap. 6.00 (0-913510-49-1) Wizards.

— Kalacakra Sadhana & Social Responsibility. (Illus.). 48p. (Orig.). 1996. pap. 12.95 (0-9651315-1-3) Spirit of the Sun.

***Reigle, David & Reigle, Nancy.** Blavatsky's Secret Books: 20 Years Research into the Tibetan Books of Kiu-Te. LC 99-73808. 208p. 1999. 15.00 (0-913510-76-9) Wizards.

Reigle, James E., jt. auth. see Riegel, Carl R.

Reigle, Nancy, jt. auth. see Reigle, David.

Reigler, Timothy J. Of Other Worlds. 128p. 1992. pap. 4.95 (0-9633459-0-7) Top Shelf Pr.

Reigns, Miranda. CyberWebs, 192p. 1999. mass mkt. 7.95 (1-56201-115-4) Blue Moon Bks.

***Reigns, Miranda.** Cyberwebs No. II: Sweet Revenge. 192p. 1999. mass mkt. 7.95 (1-56201-147-2) Blue Moon Bks.

Reigot, Betty P. A Book about Planets & Stars. (Illus.). 48p. (J). (gr. 2-5). 1988. pap. 4.99 (0-590-40593-4) Scholastic Inc.

— Questions & Answers about Bees. (Illus.). (J). 1996. pap. 4.95 (0-590-52839-4) Scholastic Inc.

Reigot, Betty P. & Spina, Rita K. Beyond the Traditional Family: Voices of Diversity. 288p. 1996. 36.95 (0-8261-9030-8) Springer Pub.

Reigstad, Paul. Rolvaag: His Life & Art. LC 70-175804. 182p. 1972. reprint ed. pap. 56.50 (0-608-02041-9, 206269400003) Bks Demand.

Reihan, Mireille De, see De Reihan, Mireille.

Reihe, D. Erdgas: Reserven - Exploration - Produktion. rev. ed. (Geologische Jahrbuch Ser.: Heft 109). (ENG & GER., Illus.). 86p. 1998. pap. 25.00 (3-510-95817-9, Pub. by E Schweizerbartsche) Balogh.

Reihe, G. Hydrogeologische Kartieranleitung. (Geologische Jahrbuch Ser.: Heft 2). 1998. write for info. (3-510-95818-7, Pub. by E Schweizerbartsche) Balogh.

Reiher, Ruth, ed. Sprache Im Konflikt: Zur Rolle der Sprache in Sozialen, Politischen und Militaerischen Auseinandersetzung. (Sprache, Politik, Oeffentlichkeit Ser.: No. 5). (GER.). 480p. (C). 1994. lib. bdg. 204.65 (3-11-013958-8) De Gruyter.

Reiher, Ruth, et al, eds. Sprache Als Mittel Von Identifikation und Distanzierung. (Leipziger Arbeiten zur Sprach- und Kommunikationsgeschichte Ser.: Band 5). (GER.). 321p. 1998. pap. 51.95 (3-631-31638-0) P Lang Pubng.

***Reihman.** Biological Sciences, No. 5. 140p. (C). 1998. pap. text, lab manual ed. 19.60 (0-536-01584-8) Pearson Custom.

Reihne, G. UaG-Hintergrundwerte der Ad-Hoc - AG Geochemie. (Geologische Jahrbuch Ser.: Heft 6). 1998. write for info. (3-510-95819-5, Pub. by E Schweizerbartsche) Balogh.

Reijen, Willem Van, see Bolz, Norbert & Van Reijen, Willem.

Reijen, Willem Van, see Maas, Utz & Van Reijen, Willem, eds.

Reijinders, Jan, ed. Economics & Evolution. LC 97-30494. (Belgian-Dutch Association for Post-Keynesian Studies). 224p. 1997. 80.00 (1-85898-555-2) E Elgar.

Reijinders, Peter J., ed. Seals, Fur Seals, Sea Lions & Walruses: An Action Plan for Their Conservation. 88p. (C). 1993. pap. text 27.00 (2-8317-0141-4, Pub. by IUCN) Island Pr.

Reijinders, Peter J., jt. ed. see Wolff, W. J.

Reijnders, Jan. Long Waves in Economic Development: Kondratieff, Schumpter & the Enigma of Long Waves. (Illus.). 320p. 1990. text 95.00 (1-85278-339-7) E Elgar.

Reijnders, Jan, jt. ed. see Louca, Francisco.

Reijnen, Gijsbertha C. & De Graaff, W. Pollution of Outer Space: Scientific, Policy & Legal Aspects. (C). 1989. lib. bdg. 94.50 (90-247-3750-8) Kluwer Academic.

Reijns, G. L. & Luo, J., eds. Transputing for Numerical & Neural Network Applications. LC 92-73167. (Transputer & Occam Engineering Ser.: Vol. 30). 264p. (gr. 12). 1992. pap. 79.00 (90-5199-100-2) IOS Press.

Reik, L. Lyme Disease & the Nervous System. (Illus.). 192p. 1991. text 59.00 (0-86577-394-7) Thieme Med Pubs.

Reik, Theodor. Compulsions to Confess: On the Psycho Analysis of Crime & Punishment. LC 72-1146. (Essay Index Reprint Ser.). 1977. reprint ed. 36.95 (0-8369-2856-3) Ayer.

— Dogma & Compulsion. LC 72-9369. 332p. 1973. reprint ed. lib. bdg. 69.50 (0-8371-6577-6, REDC, Greenwood Pr) Greenwood.

— Psychology of Sex Relations. LC 74-28525. 243p. 1975. reprint ed. lib. bdg. 65.00 (0-8371-7916-5, RESR, Greenwood Pr) Greenwood.

— Ritual. 1976. pap. 24.95 (0-8236-8269-2, 025840) Intl Univs Pr.

— The Unknown Murderer. 1978. pap. 24.95 (0-8236-8320-6, 26700) Intl Univs Pr.

Reik, Wolf & Surani, Azim, eds. Genomic Imprinting: Frontiers in Molecular Biology. LC 97-6804. (Frontiers in Molecular Biology Ser.: No. 18). (Illus.). 268p. 1997. text 125.00 (0-19-963626-5); pap. text 55.00 (0-19-963625-7) OUP.

Reiken, Frederick. The Odd Sea. 224p. 1999. pap. 9.95 (0-385-33338-2, Delta Trade) Dell.

— The Odd Sea. LC 97-40675. 224p. 1998. 22.00 (0-15-100360-2) Harcourt.

Reikes, Ursula. Quilts for Baby: Easy as ABC. (Illus.). 80p. 2000. pap. 19.95 (1-56477-282-9, B403, That Patchwrk Pl) Martingale & Co.

Reikes, Ursula, jt. auth. see Doak, Carol.

Reikes, Ursula, ed. see Bonsib, Sandy.

Reikes, Ursula, ed. see Dietrich, Mimi.

Reikes, Ursula, ed. see Doak, Carol.

Reikes, Ursula, ed. see Lehman, Libby.

Reikes, Ursula, ed. see Martin, Nancy J.

Reikes, Ursula, ed. see Noble, Maurine & Hendricks, Elizabeth.

Reikes, Ursula, ed. see Thomas, Donna L.

Reikes, Ursula, ed. see Torrence, Lorraine.

Reikes, Ursula G. Quilts for Baby: Easy as ABC. LC 93-28647. 1993. pap. 9.95 (1-56477-041-9, B168) Martingale & Co.

Reikes, Ursula G., ed. see Barnes, Christine.

Reikes, Ursula G., ed. see Berg, Alice, et al.

Reikes, Ursula G., ed. see Doak, Carol.

Reikes, Ursula G., ed. see Greenberg, Lesly-Claire.

Reikes, Ursula G., ed. see Hammond, Suzanne Tessier.

Reikes, Ursula G., ed. see Hickey, Mary & Hanson, Joan.

Reikes, Ursula G., ed. see Kime, Janet.

Reikes, Ursula G., ed. see McConnell, Donna.

Reikes, Ursula G., ed. see Noble, Maurine.

Reikes, Ursula G., ed. see Rolfe, Margaret.

Reikes, Ursula G., ed. see Schneider, Sally.

Reikes, Ursula G., ed. see Tesene, Connie & Tendall, Mary.

Reikichi, Ueda. Netsuke Handbook of Ueda Reikichi. Bushell, Raymond, tr. LC 61-8139. (Illus.). 325p. 1961. 45.00 (0-8048-0424-9) Tuttle Pubng.

Reil, A. Dictionary Film & Video: German/English/German. 2nd ed. (ENG & GER.). 265p. 1992. 59.95 (0-320-00601-8) Fr & Eur.

Reil, Theodor. Beitrage zur Kenntnis des Gewerbes im Hellenistischen Agypten. Finley, Moses, ed. LC 79-5001. (Ancient Economic History Ser.). (GER.). 1979. reprint ed. lib. bdg. 21.95 (0-405-12390-6) Ayer.

Reiland, Dan. From a Father's Heart: Letters of Encouragement to Children & Grandchildren. LC 98-48625. 168p. 1999. 14.99 (0-7852-7043-4) Nelson.

— Shoulder to Shoulder: Strengthening Your Church by Supporting Your Pastor. LC 96-39916. 192p. 1997. pap. 10.99 (0-7852-7248-8) Nelson.

— Small Business Anthology. 1999. pap. 18.13 (0-07-234774-0) McGraw.

Reiley, Eldon H. Guidebook to Security Interests in Personal Property. 2nd ed. LC 85-16673. 1986. ring bd. 130.00 (0-87632-481-2) West Group.

Reiley, H. Edward. Introductory Horticulture. 5th ed. LC 95-15151. 560p. (Orig.). (C). 1995. mass mkt. 68.95 (0-8273-6766-X) Delmar.

— Introductory Horticulture. 5th ed. (Agriculture Ser.). 32p. (Orig.). 1996. lab manual ed. 12.75 (0-8273-6916-6) Delmar.

— Introductory Horticulture. 5th ed. (Agriculture Ser.). 368p. (Orig.). 1996. 89.95 (0-8273-6768-6, VNR); teacher ed. 12.75 (0-8273-6767-8, VNR) Wiley.

— Introductory Horticulture. 5th rev. ed. (Agriculture Ser.). (Orig.). 1996. 100.00 (0-8273-7489-5) Delmar.

***Reiley, H. Edward.** Introductory Horticulture. 6th ed. (Orig.). (C). 2000. pap. 45.00 (0-7668-1567-6) Delmar.

Reiley, H. Edward. Introductory Horticulture: Lab Manual. 5th ed. (Agriculture Ser.). 240p. 1996. mass mkt., lab manual ed. 17.00 (0-8273-6915-8) Delmar.

Reiley, H. Edward & Shry, Carroll L., Jr. Introductory Horticulture. 4th ed. 576p. (Orig.). 1991. pap. 42.95 (0-8273-4512-7); text, teacher ed. 12.00 (0-8273-4513-5) Delmar.

Reiley, Mark A. Guidelines for Prescribing Foot Orthotics. LC 95-17726. (Illus.). 1995. pap. 35.00 (1-55642-280-6) SLACK Inc.

***Reiley, Mary C.** Re-Evaluation of the State-of-the-Science for Water Quality Criteria Development. (Illus.). 2000. write for info. (1-880611-30-9, SETAC Pr) SETAC.

Reiley, Roxanne. Deadbeat Dad Buster: How to Collect Child Support When He Won't Pay, the Support Agency Can't Find Him, & You Can't Afford a Lawyer. Johnson, Jennifer, ed. 64p. 1998. 7.95 (1-892871-00-9) Blackmarket Pr.

Reiling, J. & Swellengrebel, J. L. A Handbook on the Gospel of Luke. LC 92-40061. (UBS Handbook Ser.). Orig. Title: Translator's Handbook on the Gospel of Mark. xv, 798p. 1971. pap. 27.99 (0-8267-0157-4, 102675) Untd Bible Soc.

Reill, Peter H. & Wilson, Ellen J. Encyclopedia of the Enlightenment. LC 95-11962. 496p. 1996. 50.00 (0-8160-2989-X) Facts on File.

Reill, Peter H., jt. ed. see Miller, David P.

Reilley, C. N. & Sawyer, Donald T. Experiments for Instrumental Methods. LC 78-24543. 420p. 1979. reprint ed. pap. text 30.50 (0-88275-816-0) Krieger.

Reilley, Robert R., jt. auth. see Dillard, John M.

Reilley, Timothy A., ed. Raising Money Through an Institutionally Related Foundation. 83p. 1985. 10.00 (0-89964-225-X, 23501) Coun Adv & Supp Ed.

Reillo, Michelle. AIDS under Pressure: Hyperbaric Medicine in the Management of HIV Disease. LC 97-12032. 1997. 39.50 (0-88937-153-9) Hogrefe & Huber Pubs.

Reilly. Communication in the Hospitality & Travel Industries. (Hospitality, Travel & Tourism Ser.). 1990. pap., teacher ed. 11.00 (0-8273-3126-6) Delmar.

— Constitutional Amendments. 1998. 8.00 (0-07-233003-1) McGraw.

— A Guide To U.s. History. 1998. pap. 8.50 (0-07-233004-X) McGraw.

— Investment Analysis. 5th ed. (C). 1996. pap. text, student ed. 26.50 (0-03-019138-6, Pub. by Harcourt Coll Pubs) Harcourt.

Reilly. Investment Analysis. 5th ed. 1997. teacher ed. 15.25 (0-03-020454-2, Pub. by Harcourt Coll Pubs) Harcourt.

Reilly. Investment Analysis & Portfoilo Management. 5th ed. 1996. pap. text 8.75 (0-03-020923-4) Harcourt Coll Pubs.

— Investment Analysis & Portfolio Management. 5th ed. (C). 1996. pap. text 6.50 (0-03-021139-5) Harcourt Coll Pubs.

***Reilly.** Investment Analysis & Portfolio Management. 6th ed. 1120p. 1999. 97.50 (0-03-025809-X) Harcourt.

— Investment Analysis & Practice Management. 6th ed. (C). 1999. pap. text, student ed. 7.50 (0-03-025806-5, Pub. by Harcourt Coll Pubs) Harcourt.

Reilly. Investments. 5th ed. LC 98-85990. (C). 1999. text 92.50 (0-03-022343-1, Pub. by Harcourt Coll Pubs) Harcourt.

— Landscaping with Annuals. (Country Wisdom Bulletins Ser.: Vol. A-108). 1988. pap. 2.95 (0-88266-539-1) Storey Bks.

— Landscaping with Bulbs. (Country Wisdom Bulletins Ser.: Vol. A-99). 1988. pap. 2.95 (0-88266-498-0) Storey Bks.

— Pascalgorithms. (C). 1988. pap. text, teacher ed. 2.76 (0-395-45300-3) HM.

— Start Keyboarding & Information Processing. 1995. pap. text. write for info. (0-582-80693-3, Pub. by Addison-Wesley) Longman.

— Starting Seeds Indoors. 1988. pap. 2.95 (0-88266-519-7) Storey Bks.

— Travel & Tourism Marketing Techniques. 2nd ed. (Hospitality, Travel & Tourism Ser.). 1988. pap., teacher ed. 11.50 (0-8273-3301-3) Delmar.

— Worlds of History, Vol. 1. Vol. 1. 1999. pap. text 32.95 (0-312-15789-4) St Martin.

— Worlds of History, Vol. 2. 1999. pap. text 32.95 (0-312-15788-6) St Martin.

Reilly, jt. auth. see Love.

Reilly, jt. auth. see Ralston.

Reilly, A., jt. ed. see Karunasagar, I.

Reilly, Abigail P., ed. The Communication Game: Perspectives on the Development of Speech, Language & Non-Verbal Communication Skills. (Pediatric Round Table Ser.: No. 4). 98p. 1980. 10.00 (0-931562-05-8) J & J Consumer Prods.

Reilly, Ann. Enjoying Roses. LC 94-67705. (Illus.). 352p. 1995. pap. 24.95 (0-89721-271-1, UPC05607) Meredith Bks.

— Gardening Naturally: A Guide to Growing Chemical-Free Flowers, Vegetables & Herbs. LC 96-36401. 1997. write for info. (1-56799-224-2, Friedman-Fairfax) M Friedman Pub Grp Inc.

— Ortho's Guide to Enjoying Roses. LC 92-70585. (Illus.). 352p. 1996. 29.95 (0-89721-293-2, Ortho Bks) Meredith Bks.

— Taylor's Pocket Guide to Herbs & Edible Flowers. Hughes, Amy, ed. LC 89-85027. (Taylor's Guides to Gardening Ser.: Vol. 8). (Illus.). 1990. pap. 5.95 (0-395-52246-3) HM.

Reilly, Ann, jt. auth. see Oster, Maggie.

Reilly, Ann, ed. see Doty, Walter L.

Reilly, Ann T., jt. ed. see LoPucki, Lynn M.

Reilly, Barbara A., jt. auth. see Reilly, Robert R.

Reilly, Becky. Oh No! Not Another Christmas Play! 24p. (Orig.). 1997. pap. 5.25 (0-7880-1037-9) CSS OH.

Reilly, Ben, et al. Electoral Systems & Conflict in Divided Societies. 72p. 1999. pap. 18.00 (0-309-06446-5) Natl Acad Pr.

***Reilly, Bernard.** Journey to Compostela. 2000. 24.95 (1-58097-042-7) Combined Pub.

Reilly, Bernard. The Secret of Santiago: A Novel of Medieval Spain. LC 96-32516. 256p. 1996. 24.95 (0-938289-60-8, 289608) Combined Pub.

Reilly, Bernard F. The Contest of Christian & Muslim Spain: 1031-1157. (History of Spain Ser.). (Illus.). 284p. 1995. pap. 28.95 (0-631-19964-0) Blackwell Pubs.

— The Kingdom of Leon-Castilla under King Alfonso VI, 1065-1109. LC 87-3502. (Illus.). 427p. 1988. reprint ed. pap. 132.40 (0-608-01601-2, AU0047300002) Bks Demand.

— Kingdom of Leon-Castilla under King Alfonso VII, 1126-1157. LC 98-6677. (Middle Ages Ser.). 416p. 1998. 65.00 (0-8122-3452-9) U of Pa Pr.

— The Kingdom of Leon-Castilla under Queen Urraca, 1109-1126. LC 81-47949. (Illus.). 431p. 1982. reprint ed. pap. 133.70 (0-608-01602-0, AU0047400002) Bks Demand.

— The Medieval Spains. LC 92-23379. (Cambridge Medieval Textbooks Ser.). 240p. (C). 1993. text 59.95 (0-521-39436-8); pap. text 19.95 (0-521-39741-3) Cambridge U Pr.

Reilly, Bernard F., Jr. Prints & Photographs: An Illustrated Guide. 80p. 1995. pap. text 8.00 (0-16-045377-1, Library of Cong) USGPO.

Reilly, Brendan M. Practical Strategies in Outpatient Medicine. 2nd ed. (Illus.). 1328p. 1990. text 155.00 (0-7216-2821-4, W B Saunders Co) Harcrt Hlth Sci Grp.

Reilly, Brian. Create PowerPoint Presentations in a Weekend. LC 97-69600. (Computer Bks.). 360p. 1997. per. 19.99 (0-7615-1294-2) Prima Pub.

Reilly, Carol, jt. ed. see Taylor, Tom.

Reilly, Catherine, compiled by. Winged Words: Poetry & Verse. LC 95-167615. 174p. 1995. pap. 19.95 (1-870612-24-8) Dufour.

Reilly, Catherine W. Late Victorian Poetry, 1880-1899: A Biobibliography. 416p. 1995. 140.00 (0-7201-2001-2) Continuum.

***Reilly, Catherine W.** Mid-Victorian Poetry, 1860-1879. LC 99-26552. 2000. 140.00 (0-7201-2318-6) Continuum.

Reilly, Charles. Shenanigan. Ingham, Donna, ed. LC 98-61084. 288p. 1998. pap. 14.95 (1-881636-31-3) Windsor Hse Pub Grp.

— Shenanigan. LC 98-61084. 300p. 2000. reprint ed. 18.95 (1-881636-65-8) Windsor Hse Pub Grp.

Reilly, Charles A., ed. New Paths to Democratic Development in Latin America: The Rise of NGO-Municipal Collaboration. LC 94-31381. 376p. 1995. pap. text 29.95 (1-55587-557-2) L Rienner.

Reilly, Charles H. McKim, Mead & White. LC 71-180028. (Illus.). 1972. reprint ed. 17.95 (0-405-08877-9) Ayer.

— Representative British Architects of the Present Day. LC 67-26774. (Essay Index Reprint Ser.). 1977. reprint ed. 15.95 (0-8369-0818-X) Ayer.

Reilly, Charlie. Ballads & Ballast: Traditional Ballads, Myths & Negro Spirituals - Textbook Edition. 3rd rev. ed. (Illus.). 181p. (C). 1998. pap. 23.00 (0-9638132-3-4) Clydewater Pubs.

Reilly, Charlie, ed. Conversations with Amiri Baraka. LC 93-43532. (Literary Conversations Ser.). 288p. 1994. pap. 15.95 (0-87805-687-4); text 39.50 (0-87805-686-6) U Pr of Miss.

***Reilly, Colleen.** Yabagouchy. unabridged ed. 1999. mass mkt. 3.95 (1-891371-12-6) Angel Ministries.

***Reilly, Cyril & Reilly, Renee.** An Irish Blessing: A Photographic Interpretation. LC 99-61902. (Illus.). 64p. 1999. pap. 13.95 (1-893732-01-0) SORIN BKS.

Reilly, Cyril A. Song of Creation. 64p. 1983. 9.95 (0-86683-710-8) Harper SF.

Reilly, Daniel F. School Controversy, 1891-1893. LC 76-89221. (American Education: Its Men, Institutions, & Ideas. Series 1). 1975. reprint ed. 26.95 (0-405-01460-0) Ayer.

Reilly, Darryl & Jenks, Bill. U. S. Glass: The States Patterns. LC 99-474295. (Illus.). 100p. 1998. 19.95 (0-9648111-2-X) Author Author Bks.

Reilly, Darryl, jt. auth. see Jenks, Bill.

Reilly, David H. Education: The Captive Profession: Theory, Practice, & Prospects for Achieving Improvements in Educational Outcomes. LC 96-84889. 424p. 1996. text 77.95 (1-85972-376-4, Pub. by Avebry) Ashgate Pub Co.

— How to Have Successful Schools: What Parents & Teachers Need to Know to Improve Children's Learning. 252p. (Orig.). (C). 1995. pap. text 24.50 (0-7618-0019-0); lib. bdg. 53.00 (0-7618-0018-2) U Pr of Amer.

Reilly, David P., jt. auth. see Wei, William.

Reilly, Dawn, jt. auth. see Reilly, Michael.

***Reilly, Dee Dee.** Teaching Agnes to Dance. large type ed. LC 99-63761. (Illus.). 40p. (J). (ps-3). 1999. 14.95 (0-9669497-0-6) Reilly Ent.

Reilly, Dorothy E. & Oermann, Marilyn H. Behavioral Objectives: Evaluation in Nursing. 3rd ed. 278p. 1990. 22.95 (0-88737-500-6) Natl League Nurse.

— Clinical Teaching in Nursing Education. 2nd ed. 528p. (C). 1992. pap. text 26.95 (0-88737-549-9) Natl League Nurse.

***Reilly, Dorothy E. & Oermann, Marilyn H.** Clinical Teaching in Nursing Education 2nd ed. LC 99-203157. xiv, 507p. 1999. write for info. (0-7637-0943-3) Jones & Bartlett.

An Asterisk (*) at the beginning of an entry indicates that the title is appearing for the first time.

Reilly, Douglas J. Inside Server-Based Applications. LC 99-46394. 448p. (C). (gr. 8). 1999. pap. 49.99 (1-57231-817-1) Little.

Reilly, Douglas J. Win32 Client/Server Developer's Guide. 480p. 1996. pap. 39.95 incl. disk (0-201-40762-0) Addison-Wesley.

Reilly, Ed & McMannus, Maggie. Monkees - A Manufactured Image: The Ultimate Reference Guide to Monkee Memories & Memorabilia. Schultheiss, Thomas, ed. (Rock & Roll Reference Ser.). (Illus.). 324p. 1993. reprint ed. 39.50 (1-56075-032-4) Popular Culture.

Reilly, Edward C. Jim Harrison. 1996. 32.00 (0-8057-3978-5) Macmillan.

— William Kennedy. (Twayne's United States Authors Ser.: No. 570). 152p. 1990. 24.95 (0-8057-7611-7) Macmillan.

Reilly, Edward J. Anniversary Haiku. 28p. 1997. pap. 5.00 (0-913719-80-3, High Coo Pr) Brooks Books.

***Reilly, Edward J.** Baseball: A Dictionary of Popular Culture. 2000. 65.00 (1-57607-103-0) ABC-CLIO.

Reilly, Edward R. Quantz & His Versuch: Three Studies. (Studies & Documents: Vol. 5). 180p. 1971. pap. 10.00 (1-878528-07-6) Am Musicological.

Reilly, Edwin D. & Federighi, Francis D. Pascalgorithms. 700p. (C). 1987. text. write for info. (0-318-62601-2) HM.

Reilly, Edwin D., Jr., jt. auth. see Ralston, Anthony.

Reilly, Edwin D., Jr., jt. ed. see Ralston, Anthony.

Reilly, Francis E. Charles Peirce's Theory of Scientific Method. LC 79-105527. (Orestes Brownson Series on Contemporary Thought & Affairs: No. 7). 208p. reprint ed. pap. 64.50 (0-7837-0465-8, 204078800018) Bks Demand.

Reilly, Frank K. Study Guide-Investments. 4th ed. (C). 1995. pap. text, student ed. 26.00 (0-03-001023-3) Harcourt Coll Pubs.

Reilly, Frank K., ed. High-Yield Bonds: Analysis & Risk Assessment. (Orig.). 1990. pap. text 30.00 (1-879087-02-2) Assn I M&R.

Reilly, Frank K. & Brown, Keith C. Investment Analysis & Portfolio Management. 5th ed. LC 96-83161. 1122p. (C). 1996. text 107.50 (0-03-018683-8) Dryden Pr.

Reilly, Frank K. & Norton, Edgar A. Investments. 4th ed. 656p. (C). 1994. text 92.50 (0-03-000907-3) Dryden Pr.

Reilly, George. Beginning ATL COM Programming with Visual C. (Illus.). 400p. 1998. pap. 39.95 (1-86100-011-1) Wrox Pr Inc.

Reilly Giff, Patricia. Next Stop, New York City! The Polk Street Kids on Tour. (Polk Street Special Ser.: No. 9). (Illus.). 128p. 1997. pap. 3.99 (0-440-41362-1) Dell.

— Oh Boy, Boston! (Polk Street Special Ser.: No. 10). (Illus.). 128p. (Orig.). (J). (gr. 1-4). 1997. pap. 3.99 (0-440-41365-6) BDD Bks Young Read.

Reilly, Gladys B., jt. auth. see Bogue, Merwyn.

Reilly, H. Edward. Success with Rhododendrons & Azaleas. (Illus.). 314p. 1995. pap. 22.95 (0-88192-331-1) Timber.

Reilly, H. Pat. From the Balloon to the Moon Vol. 2: New Jersey's Amazing Aviation History. 2nd rev. ed. Suplee, Carol, ed. (Illus.). 136p. 1997. 29.95 (0-9632295-2-4) H V Pubs.

Reilly, H. V. The Balloon to the Moon: Chronology of New Jersey's Distinguished Aviation History. Suplee, Carol, ed. (Illus.). 340p. (Orig.). 1992. pap. 29.95 (0-9632295-0-8) H V Pubs.

Reilly, Harold J. Edgar Cayce Handbook for Health Through Drugless Therapy. 348p. 1988. pap. 14.95 (0-87604-215-9, 2073) ARE Pr.

Reilly, Helen. McKee of Centre Street. 299p. 1980. reprint ed. lib. bdg. 14.25 (0-89968-214-6, Lghtyr Pr) Buccaneer Bks.

Reilly, Hugh J. & Hyland, Terry L. Letters from the Front: Boys Town on the Battlefield from Pearl Harbor to the Persian Gulf. Lonnborg, Barbara A. & Manley, David, eds. (Illus.). 272p. (Orig.). 1995. pap. 10.99 (0-938510-51-7, 19-007) Boys Town Pr.

Reilly, I., tr. see Marussi, A.

Reilly, J. Patrick. Applied Bioelectricity: From Electrical Stimulation to Electropathology. LC 97-48860. (Illus.). 632p. 1998. 89.95 (0-387-98407-0) Spr-Verlag.

— Electrical Stimulation & Electropathology. (Illus.). 522p. (C). 1992. text 95.00 (0-521-41791-0) Cambridge U Pr.

Reilly, J. S., ed. Euthanasia of Animals Used for Scientific Purposes. 71p. 1993. pap. 50.00 (0-646-11803-X, Pub. by Univs Fed Animal Welfare) St Mut.

Reilly, James. The Albumen & Salted Paper Book. LC 80-14340. (Extended Photo Media Ser.: No. 2). (Illus.). 1980. pap. text 8.95 (0-87992-014-9) Light Impressions.

Reilly, James M. Care & Identification of Nineteenth Century Photographic Prints. LC 85-81727. (Illus.). 116p. (Orig.). (C). 1998. pap. 29.95 (0-87985-365-4, G-25, Kodak) Saunders Photo.

Reilly, James M., et al. New Tools for Preservation: Assessing Long-Term Environmental Effects on Library & Archive Collections. LC 96-126478. 35p. 1995. pap. 10.00 (1-887334-46-7) Coun Lib & Info.

***Reilly, James R.** Richard Griffith & His Valuation of Ireland: With an Inventory of the Books of the General Valuation of Rateable Property in Ireland. 108p. 2000. pap. 21.95 (0-8063-4954-9, Pub. by Clearfield Co) ACCESS Pubs Network.

Reilly, James R., jt. auth. see Murphy, Helen M.

Reilly, Jane A. Public Librarian As Adult Learners' Advisor: An Innovation in Human Services, 38. LC 80-27307. (Contributions in Librarianship & Information Science Ser.: No. 38). (Illus.). 152p. 1981. 45.00 (0-313-22134-0, REP/) Greenwood.

Reilly, Jill M. Mentorship: The Essential Guide for Schools & Business. LC 91-42116. (Illus.). 274p. 1992. pap. 20.00 (0-910707-18-9) Gifted Psych Pr.

Reilly, Jill M., jt. auth. see Featherstone, Bonnie D.

Reilly, Jim. Eliot. (Life & Works Ser.: Set II). (Illus.). 112p. (YA). (gr. 7 up). 1990. lib. bdg. 18.95 (0-86593-022-8); lib. bdg. 14.95 (0-685-36353-8) Rourke Corp.

— Joseph Conrad. (Life & Works Ser.: Set II). (Illus.). 112p. (YA). (gr. 7 up). 1990. lib. bdg. 18.95 (0-86593-021-X) Rourke Corp.

— Shadowtime: History & Representation in Hardy, Conrad & George Eliot. LC 92-16199. 192p. (C). 1994. pap. 27.99 (0-415-11893-X, B4788) Routledge.

Reilly, Jim, et al. Life & Works, 6 bks., Set. (Illus.). 672p. (YA). (gr. 7 up). 1990. lib. bdg. 119.64 (0-86593-015-5) Rourke Corp.

Reilly, Jo, et al, eds. Belsen in History & Memory. LC 97-198223. (Illus.). 248p. (C). 1997. 49.95 (0-7146-4767-5, Pub. by F Cass Pubs); pap. 24.95 (0-7146-4323-8, Pub. by F Cass Pubs) Intl Spec Bk.

Reilly, Joanne. Belsen: British Responses. LC 97-20026. 256p. (C). 1998. 80.00 (0-415-13827-2) Routledge.

Reilly, John E. The Image of Poe in American Poetry. 1976. pap. 2.50 (0-910556-05-9) Enoch Pratt.

Reilly, John E., ed. John Henry Ingram's Poe Collection at the University of Virginia. 2nd ed. (C). 1994. pap. text 30.00 (0-8139-1552-X) U Pr of Va.

Reilly, John H. Arthur Adamov. LC 74-2162. (Twayne's World Authors Ser.). 177p. (C). 1974. lib. bdg. 20.95 (0-8057-2005-7) Irvington.

Reilly, John H., ed. see Giraudoux, Jean.

Reilly, John J. Spengler's Future. 198p. 1993. pap. 14.95 (0-9639606-0-1) Millennium.

Reilly, John J., ed. see Riepe, Jack.

***Reilly, John M.** Larry Mcmurtry: A Critical Companion. LC 99-49695. (Critical Companions to Popular Contemporary Writers Ser.). 216p. 2000. 29.95 (0-313-30300-2) Greenwood.

Reilly, John M. Tony Hillerman: A Critical Companion. LC 95-50459. (Critical Companions to Popular Contemporary Writers Ser.). 240p. 1996. 29.95 (0-313-29416-X, Greenwood Pr) Greenwood.

Reilly, John W. Agency Relationships in Real Estate. 2nd rev. ed. LC 94-8705. 235p. (C). 1994. pap. text 54.95 (0-7931-0787-3, 1560-0802, Real Estate Ed) Dearborn.

— The Language of Real Estate. 4th ed. LC 93-8367. 455p. 1993. pap. 32.95 (0-7931-0583-8, 19610104, Real Estate Ed) Dearborn.

***Reilly, John W.** The Language of Real Estate. 5th ed. LC 00-44556. 2000. write for info. (0-7931-3193-6, Real Estate Ed) Dearborn.

Reilly, John W. & Vitousek, Paige B. Questions & Answers to Help You Pass the Real Estate Exam. 5th ed. LC 96-8013. 1996. pap. 27.95 (0-7931-1505-1, 1970-0405, Real Estate Ed) Dearborn.

***Reilly, John W. & Vitousek, Paige Bovee.** Questions & Answers to Help You Pass the Real Estate Exam. 6th ed. LC 00-27969. 2000. pap. 27.95 (0-7931-3582-6) Dearborn.

Reilly, John W. & Williams, Martha R. Agency Relationships in California Real Estate. 2nd ed. LC 87-4762. 1995. 7.95 (0-7931-1449-7, 1560-1002, Real Estate Ed) Dearborn.

Reilly, John W., et al. Texas Real Estate Agency. 3rd ed. LC 98-4097. 1998. pap. 34.95 (0-7931-2717-3, 15600503, G&C Learning) Dearborn.

Reilly, Joseph J. Dear Prue's Husband, & Other People. LC 68-8487. (Essay Index Reprint Ser.). 1977. 21.95 (0-8369-0816-3) Ayer.

— Of Books & Men. LC 68-57336. (Essay Index Reprint Ser.). 1977. 23.95 (0-8369-0817-1) Ayer.

Reilly, Joseph P. Human Fulfillment. LC 83-71415. 421p. (C). 1983. 16.00 (0-912987-00-6); pap. 12.00 (0-912987-01-4) Bionomic.

Reilly, Judith S., jt. ed. see Thal, Donna J.

Reilly, Judy S., jt. ed. see Emmorey, Karen.

Reilly, Julie A. Are You Prepared? A Guide to Emergency Planning LC 97-75451. ii, 68p. 1997. write for info. (0-933307-13-6) Nebraska Hist.

Reilly, Katie. Nobody's Daughter: A Woman's Poetic Journal. Wolf, Barbara, ed. LC 96-71980. 100p. 1997. 13.95 (0-9656367-0-4) Slow Please Pr.

Reilly, Kevan, jt. auth. see Dempsey, Paul.

Reilly, Kevin. The West & the World Vol. I: A History of Civilization from the Ancient World to 1700. LC 96-37674. 368p. (C). 1999. pap. text 19.95 (1-55876-152-7) Wiener Pubs Inc.

— The West & the World Vol. II: A History of Civilization from 1500 to Modern Times. 444p. (C). 2000. pap. text 19.95 (1-55876-153-5) Wiener Pubs Inc.

Reilly, Kevin, et al, eds. World History: Selected Course Outlines from Leading American Colleges & Universities. 4th ed. LC 98-28365. (Orig.). 1998. pap. text 16.95 (1-55876-136-5) Wiener Pubs Inc.

Reilly, Kevin, jt. auth. see Shaffer, Lynda N.

Reilly, Kevin, jt. ed. see Jolly, Karen L.

Reilly, Kevin, tr. see Stavrianos, L. S.

Reilly, Kevin V. The Beach Bank: Your Treasure Teller. 64p. (Orig.). 1996. pap. 9.95 (1-881777-04-9) Pirate Express.

Reilly, Kurt, jt. illus. see Parsons, Bob.

Reilly, Lambert. Because There Is Jesus: A Call to Be New-Made in Christ. LC 97-75019. 1998. pap. 14.95 (0-87029-305-2) Abbey.

***Reilly, Lee.** Teaching Maggie: Letters on Life, Writing & the Virtues of Solid Food. 223p. 2000. 23.00 (1-886913-36-6, Pub. by Ruminator Bks) Consort Bk Sales.

Reilly, Leo. How to Outnegotiate Anyone (Even a Car Dealer!) LC 93-34576. 144p. (Orig.). 1993. pap. 7.95 (1-55850-283-1) Adams Media.

Reilly, Lisa A. An Architectural History of Peterborough Cathedral. LC 96-47067. (Clarendon Studies in the History of Art: Vol. 17). (Illus.). 164p. (C). 1997. text 110.00 (0-19-817520-5, Clarendon Pr) OUP.

Reilly, Lucille. The Hammered Dulcimer: A-Chording to Lucille Reilly. LC 90-39604. (Illus.). 170p. 1990. pap. 27.95 (0-9613356-3-7, SP-05) Shadrach.

— Striking Out & Winning! A Music-Maker's Guide for the Hammered Dulcimer. 2nd ed. LC 84-199357. (Illus.). 170p. 1984. pap. 35.00 (0-9613356-4-5) Shadrach.

Reilly, Margaret A. Pharmacology. LC 97-3055. (Rypins' Intensive Reviews Ser.). (Illus.). 200p. 1997. pap. text 19.95 (0-397-51550-2) Lppncott W & W.

Reilly, Maria. Now That I Am Old: Meditations on the Meaning of Life. LC 92-63179. 128p. (Orig.). 1994. pap. 7.95 (0-89622-559-3) Twenty-Third.

Reilly, Mary, ed. Play As Exploratory Learning: Studies of Curiosity Behavior. LC 72-98044. 317p. 1974. reprint ed. pap. 98.30 (0-608-01448-6, 205949200001) Bks Demand.

Reilly, Mary A. Achieving Reading & Writing Competence: An EWT Companion. 198p. (YA). (gr. 7-10). 1996. wbk. ed. 19.95 (1-886292-13-2) CEO Sftware.

— Achieving Reading & Writing Competence Bk. 1: Narrative Text. 224p. (YA). (gr. 9-12). 1994. text 19.95 (1-886292-07-8) CEO Sftware.

— Achieving Reading & Writing Competence Bk. 2: Informational Text. 248p. (YA). (gr. 9-12). 1994. text 19.95 (1-886292-06-X) CEO Sftware.

— Achieving Reading & Writing Competence Bk. 3: Persuasive-Argumentative Text. 242p. (YA). (gr. 9-12). 1994. text 19.95 (1-886292-05-1) CEO Sftware.

— Achieving Reading & Writing Competence Bk. 4: Workplace Text. 306p. (YA). (gr. 9-12). 1994. text 19.95 (1-886292-04-3) CEO Sftware.

— Achieving Reading & Writing Competence: An EWT Companion: Answer Key. 22p. 1996. teacher ed. 19.95 (1-886292-09-4) CEO Sftware.

— ESPA Companion: Achieving Language Art Literacy. (Illus.). 184p. (J). 1998. pap. text 39.95 (1-886292-25-6) CEO Sftware.

— ESPA Companion Answer Key. 19p. 1998. 19.95 (1-886292-26-4) CEO Sftware.

— GEPA Companion: Achieving Language Arts Literacy. (Illus.). 208p. (J). (gr. 7-8). 1999. 39.95 (1-886292-33-7) CEO Sftware.

— Strategic Reading & Writing for HSPT Competency, Vol. 1. CEO Solutions Staff, ed. 200p. (Orig.). (YA). (gr. 8-12). 1997. pap. text, wbk. ed. 19.95 (1-886292-22-1) CEO Sftware.

Reilly, Mary A., jt. ed. see Lott, Bernice.

Reilly, Mary E., jt. auth. see Luebke, Barbara.

Reilly, Mary L. & Olson, Lynn F. It's Time for Music: Songs & Lesson Outlines for Early Childhood Music. 80p. 1985. pap., teacher ed. 16.95 (0-88284-339-7, 2456) Alfred Pub.

Reilly, Mary Louise & Olson, Lynn Freeman. It's Time for Music, Teacher's Handbook: Songs & Lesson Outlines for Early Childhood Music. 36p. 1985. pap., teacher ed. 12.95 (0-7390-0529-4, 2458) Alfred Pub.

***Reilly, Matthew J.** Ice Station. 528p. 1999. mass mkt. 6.99 (0-312-97123-0) St Martin.

Reilly, Matthew J. Ice Station. 2nd ed. LC 99-23845. 390p. 1999. 24.95 (0-312-20551-1, Thomas Dunne) St Martin.

***Reilly, Maureen.** California Couture. (Illus.). 208p. 1999. 49.95 (0-7643-0940-4) Schiffer.

Reilly, Maureen. Hot Shoes: One Hundred Years. (Illus.). 224p. 1998. 49.95 (0-7643-0435-6) Schiffer.

Reilly, Maureen, et al. Women's Hats of the 20th Century for Designers & Collectors. LC 96-38119. (Illus.). 240p. 1997. 49.95 (0-7643-0204-3) Schiffer.

***Reilly, Maureen E.** Swing Style: Fashions of the 1930's-1950's. (Illus.). 159p. 2000. 29.95 (0-7643-1009-7) Schiffer.

Reilly, Maureen E., jt. auth. see Fleishman, Edwin A.

Reilly, Michael. Reilly of the White House. (American Autobiography Ser.). 248p. 1995. reprint ed. lib. bdg. 79.00 (0-7812-8623-9) Rprt Serv.

Reilly, Michael, ed. When the Waves Rolled upon Us: Essays in Nineteenth Century Maori History. LC 99-236510. (Illus.). 1998. pap. 39.95 (1-877133-20-5, Pub. by Univ Otago Pr) Intl Spec Bk.

Reilly, Michael & Reilly, Dawn. The Bumper Sticker Book: Plus Games on the Go. (Illus.). 96p. (Orig.). 1992. pap. 5.95 (0-930753-10-0) Spect Ln Pr.

Reilly, Michael, jt. auth. see Pompa, Delia.

Reilly, Michael, jt. auth. see Poolet, Michelle.

Reilly, Michael E., jt. auth. see Law, Gordon T., Jr.

Reilly, Michael K. Gravity & Electronics: The Gates to Paradise. LC 98-92214. 1997. write for info. (0-09-579127-2) Trafalgar.

Reilly, Micheal, jt. auth. see Boyd & Fraser Staff.

Reilly, Niamh, jt. auth. see Bunch, Charlotte.

***Reilly, Norman B.** Team Based Product Development Guidebook. LC 99-24687. (Illus.). 256p. 1999. 38.50 (0-87389-451-0) ASQ Qual Pr.

Reilly, Norman R., jt. auth. see Petrich, Mario.

Reilly, P. T., et al. Lee's Ferry: From Mormon Crossing to National Park. Webb, Robert H., ed. LC 98-58050. (Illus.). 480p. 1998. 39.95 (0-87421-261-8) Utah St U Pr.

— Lee's Ferry: From Mormon Crossing to National Park. Webb, Robert H., ed. LC 98-58050. (Illus.). 542p. 1999. pap. 21.95 (0-87421-260-X) Utah St U Pr.

Reilly, Paddy. The Paddy Reilly Songbook. (Illus.). 64p. 1989. pap. 14.95 (0-7119-1825-2, AM74733) Music Sales.

Reilly, Pat. Paperweights: The Collector's Guide to Selecting & Enjoying New & Antique Paperweights. 1999. pap. text 12.95 (1-57715-075-9) Knckerbocker.

Reilly, Patricia. Today Was a Terrible Day. (Story Tapes Ser.). (J). (ps-6). 1988. pap. 6.95 incl. audio Peng Put Young Read.

Reilly, Patricia G. Next Year I'll Be Special. (Illus.). 32p. (J). (gr. k-3). 1996. pap. 4.99 (0-440-41031-2) Dell.

Reilly, Patricia L. Be Full of Yourself. 1997. write for info. (0-517-70675-X) Harmony Bks.

— Be Full of Yourself! The Journey from Self-Criticism to Self-Celebration. 320p. (Orig.). 1998. pap. 15.00 (0-9661642-0-2) Open Wind Creat.

— A God Who Looks Like Me: Discovering a Woman-Affirming Spirituality. 368p. 1996. pap. 12.00 (0-345-40233-2) Ballantine Pub Grp.

***Reilly, Patricia Lynn.** I Promise Myself: Making a Commitment to Yourself & Your Dreams. 256p. 2000. pap. 14.95 (1-57324-178-4) Conari Press.

Reilly, Patricia Lynn. Imagine a Woman in Love with Herself: Embracing Your Wisdom & Wholeness. LC 99-16071. 192p. 1999. pap. 12.95 (1-57324-169-5) Conari Press.

Reilly, Patrick. Jonathan Swift: The Brave Desponder. LC 81-85639. 295p. 1982. 26.95 (0-8093-1075-9) S Ill U Pr.

— Lord of the Flies: Fathers & Sons. (Masterwork Studies). 170p. 1992. 23.95 (0-8057-7999-X, Twyne); pap. 18.00 (0-8057-8049-1, Twyne) Mac Lib Ref.

— 1984: Past, Present & Future. (Masterwork Studies). 160p. 1989. 25.95 (0-8057-8065-3, Twyne); pap. 13.95 (0-8057-8110-2, Twyne) Mac Lib Ref.

— Tom Jones: Adventure & Providence. (Twayne's Masterworks Ser.: No. 72). 192p. 1991. 23.95 (0-8057-9422-0); pap. 13.95 (0-8057-8143-9) Macmillan.

***Reilly, Patrick.** Treasured Friends. 2000. 4.99 (1-56245-399-8) Great Quotations.

Reilly, Paul A. Making Your Way: A Practical Guide to Life. 97p. (Orig.). 1996. pap. 12.00 (0-9655159-0-7) Expanding Awareness.

Reilly, Pauline. Bilby. (Picture Roo Bks.). 1997. pap. text 6.95 (0-86417-785-2) Intl Spec Bk.

— Bilby Picture Roo. (Picture Roo Bks.). (Illus.). 32p. (Orig.). (J). (gr. 2-7). 1997. pap. 6.95 (0-86417-737-2, Pub. by Kangaroo Pr) Seven Hills Bk.

— Echidna. (Picture Roo Bks.). (Illus.). 32p. (Orig.). (J). 1993. pap. 6.95 (0-86417-285-0, Pub. by Kangaroo Pr) Seven Hills Bk.

— Emu That Walks Toward Rain. 2nd ed. (Picture Roo Bks.). (Illus.). 32p. (J). (gr. 2-6). 1994. pap. 6.95 (0-86417-571-X, Pub. by Kangaroo Pr) Seven Hills Bk.

— Frillneck: An Australian Dragon. (Picture Roo Bks.). (Illus.). 32p. (Orig.). (J). 1993. pap. 6.95 (0-86417-414-4, Pub. by Kangaroo Pr) Seven Hills Bk.

— Galah. (Picture Roo Bks.). (Illus.). 32p. (Orig.). (J). 1993. pap. 6.95 (0-86417-346-6, Pub. by Kangaroo Pr) Seven Hills Bk.

— Kiwi. (Picture Roo Bks.). (Illus.). 32p. (Orig.). (J). 1993. pap. 6.95 (0-86417-488-8, Pub. by Kangaroo Pr) Seven Hills Bk.

— Koala. (Picture Roo Bks.). (Illus.). 32p. (Orig.). (J). 1993. pap. 6.95 (0-86417-243-5, Pub. by Kangaroo Pr) Seven Hills Bk.

— Kookaburra. 2nd ed. (Picture Roo Bks.). (Illus.). 32p. (J). (gr. 2-6). 1994. pap. 6.95 (0-86417-528-0, Pub. by Kangaroo Pr) Seven Hills Bk.

— The Lyrebird: A Natural History. (Illus.). 102p. 1988. pap. 24.95 (0-86840-083-1, Pub. by New South Wales Univ Pr) Intl Spec Bk.

— Lyrebird That Is Too Busy to Dance. (Picture Roo Bks.). (Illus.). 32p. (Orig.). (J). 1993. pap. 6.95 (0-86417-086-6, Pub. by Kangaroo Pr) Seven Hills Bk.

— Pelican Picture Roo. (Picture Roo Bks.). (Illus.). 32p. (J). 1997. pap. 6.95 (0-86417-830-1, Pub. by Kangaroo Pr) Seven Hills Bk.

— Penguin Picture Roo. (Picture Roo Bks.). (Illus.). 32p. (Orig.). (J). (ps-3). 1997. pap. 6.95 (0-86417-826-3, Pub. by Kangaroo Pr) Seven Hills Bk.

— The Penguin That Walks at Night. (Picture Roo Bks.). (Illus.). 32p. (Orig.). (J). 1993. pap. 6.95 (0-86417-034-3, Pub. by Kangaroo Pr) Seven Hills Bk.

— Penguins of the World. (Illus.). 176p. 1994. pap. 17.95 (0-19-553547-2) OUP.

— Platypus. (Picture Roo Bks.). (Illus.). 32p. (Orig.). (J). (ps-3). 1994. pap. 6.95 (0-86417-391-1, Pub. by Kangaroo Pr) Seven Hills Bk.

— Pobblebonk the Frog Picture Roo. (Picture Roo Bks.). (Illus.). 32p. (Orig.). (J). (gr. 2-7). 1997. pap. 6.95 (0-86417-802-6, Pub. by Kangaroo Pr) Seven Hills Bk.

— Python: Picture Roo Book. (Illus.). 32p. (Orig.). (J). (gr. 3-7). 1995. pap. 6.95 (0-86417-698-8, Pub. by Kangaroo Pr) Seven Hills Bk.

— Roobook the Owl. (Picture Roo Bks.). 32p. 1998. pap. 6.95 (0-86417-966-9, Pub. by Kangaroo Pr) Seven Hills Bk.

— Sugar Glider. (Picture Roo Bks.). (Illus.). 32p. (J). (gr. 2-6). 1994. pap. 6.95 (0-86417-590-6, Pub. by Kangaroo Pr) Seven Hills Bk.

— Tasmanian Devil. (Picture Roo Bks.). (Illus.). 32p. (Orig.). (J). 1993. pap. 6.95 (0-86417-207-9, Pub. by Kangaroo Pr) Seven Hills Bk.

— Wombat. (Picture Roo Bks.). (Illus.). 32p. (Orig.). (J). 1993. pap. 6.95 (0-86417-148-X, Pub. by Kangaroo Pr) Seven Hills Bk.

Reilly, Pauline, jt. auth. see Massam, Katherine.

***Reilly, Peter.** Flexibility at Work: Balancing the Interests of Employer & Employee. 224p. 2000. 79.95 (0-566-08259-4, Pub. by Ashgate Pub) Ashgate Pub Co.

Reilly, Peter & Bullock, Ross, eds. Head Injury: Pathophysiology & Management of Severe Closed Injury. LC 97-66517. (Illus.). 478p. 1997. text 135.00 (0-412-58540-5, Pub. by E A) OUP.

Reilly, Peter J. & Francis, Paul. Really Bad Swing Thoughts. LC 97-33471. 1998. 8.95 (0-8362-5190-3) Andrews & McMeel.

***Reilly, Philip.** Abraham Lincoln's DNA: Adventures in Genetics. LC 00-29467. 2000. write for info. (0-87969-580-3) Cold Spring Harbor.

R

An Asterisk (*) at the beginning of an entry indicates that the title is appearing for the first time.

Reilly, Philip R. Genes & Your Fate: Understanding Your Genetic Heritage. 1994. text 24.95 (0-02-926045-0) Free Pr.

— The Surgical Solution: A History of Involuntary Sterilization in the United States. LC 90-5090. 208p. 1991. 29.95 (0-8018-4096-1) Johns Hopkins.

— To Do No Harm: A Journey Through Medical School. LC 86-26576. 309p. 1987. 49.95 (0-86569-162-2, Auburn Hse); pap. 16.95 (0-86569-163-0, Auburn Hse) Greenwood.

Reilly, R. Wedgwood, 2 vols. LC 89-21609. 1989. 250.00 (0-935859-85-3) Groves Dictionaries.

Reilly, Raymond E. Human Performance in the Undersea Environment: An Annotated Bibliography. LC 76-135084. 90p. 1970. 15.00 (0-403-04530-4) Scholarly.

Reilly, Renee, jt. auth. see Reilly, Cyril.

***Reilly, Rick.** The Life of Reilly: Three Decades Under the Blimp: The Best of Sports Illustrated's Rick Reilly. 224p. 2000. 22.95 (1-892129-88-4) Total Sprts.

Reilly, Rick. Missing Links. 288p. 1997. pap. 12.95 (0-385-48886-6, Main St Bks) Doubleday.

— Sir Charles: The Wit & Wisdom of Charles Barkley, an Exclusive Interview. abr. ed. 1994. audio 10.00 (1-57042-121-8, 4-521218, Pub. by Warner Bks) Little.

***Reilly, Rick.** Slo Mo! 304p. 2000. reprint ed. pap. 14.00 (0-7679-0551-2) Broadway BDD.

— Slo Mo! My Untrue Story. LC 99-33240. 304p. 1999. 23.95 (0-385-48884-X) Doubleday.

Reilly, Rob, ed. see Rhody, Kurt.

Reilly, Robert. Drug Comparison Handbook. 3rd rev. ed. LC 98-232107. 550p. (C). 1998. per. 42.95 (1-56930-075-5) Skidmore Roth Pub.

Reilly, Robert, ed. The Transcendent Adventure: Studies of Religion in Science Fiction-Fantasy, 12. LC 84-542. (Contributions to the Study of Science Fiction & Fantasy Ser.: No. 12). 266p. 1985. 65.00 (0-313-23062-5, RET/, Greenwood Pr) Greenwood.

Reilly, Robert, et al. The Pharmacy Tech: Basic Pharmacology & Calculations. (Illus.). 140p. (C). 1994. per. 29.95 (1-56930-005-4) Skidmore Roth Pub.

Reilly, Robert F. Handbook of Advanced Business Valuation. LC 99-21968. 512p. 1999. 95.00 (0-07-134769-0) McGraw.

Reilly, Robert F. & Schweihs, Robert P. Value Accounting Practices. LC 96-34963. 304p. 1997. 105.00 (0-471-17224-3) Wiley.

— Valuing Intangible Assets. LC 98-13959. (Irwin Library of Investment & Finance). 600p. 1998. 95.00 (0-7863-1065-0) McGraw-Hill Prof.

Reilly, Robert M. American Socket Bayonets & Scabbards. LC 90-81582. (Illus.). 208p. 1998. reprint ed. 45.00 (0-917218-45-0) A Mowbray.

— United States Martial Flintlocks. LC 86-60684. (Illus.). 263p. 1997. reprint ed. 40.00 (0-917218-21-3) A Mowbray.

— United States Military Small Arms, 1816-1865. 1983. 39.95 (0-88227-019-2) Gun Room.

Reilly, Robert R. & Reilly, Barbara A. MMPI-2 Tutorial Workbook. 212p. 1991. pap. text 22.00 (0-89079-267-4, 1510) PRO-ED.

Reilly, Robert T. Communication in the Travel & Hospitality Industry. (Hospitality, Travel & Tourism Ser.). 1990. pap. 31.50 (0-8273-3125-8) Delmar.

— Handbook of Professional Tour Management: Instructor's Guide. 2nd ed. 1991. pap., teacher ed. 11.50 (0-8273-3526-1) Delmar.

— Public Relations in Action. 1981. 34.00 (0-13-738526-9) P-H.

— Rebels in the Shadows. LC 78-66069. 192p. (YA). (gr. 3-7). 2000. pap. 12.95 (0-8229-5304-8) U of Pittsburgh Pr.

— Red Hugh, Prince of Donegal. LC 97-73495. (Living History Library). (Illus.). 155p. (YA). (gr. 5 up). 1997. pap. 11.95 (1-883937-22-1, 22-1) Bethlehem ND.

Reilly, Robin. Wedgwood, 2 Vols. 1600p. 1989. 250.00 (0-935859-83-7) Groves Dictionaries.

Reilly, Robin. Wedgwood: The New Illustrated Dicitonary. LC 96-134170. (Illus.). 516p. 1995. 89.50 (1-85149-209-7) Antique Collect.

— Wedgwood Jasper. LC 94-60284. (Illus.). 408p. 1994. 60.00 (0-500-01624-0, Pub. by Thames Hudson) Norton.

Reilly, Robin L. Complete Shotokan Karate: History, Philosophy, & Practice. (Illus.). 238p. 1998. pap. 19.95 (0-8048-2108-9) Tuttle Pubng.

— Japan's Complete Fighting System: Shin Kage Ryu. LC 88-50069. (Illus.). 320p. 1989. 35.00 (0-8048-1536-4) Tuttle Pubng.

Reilly, Rosemary M., ed. see American Institute of Certified Public Accountants.

Reilly, Sarah C. Public Pension Plans: The State Regulatory Framework. 115p. write for info. (0-318-60967-3) Natl Coun Teach.

Reilly, Saskia & Kalisky, Lorin. Living, Studying & Working in France: Everything You Need to Know to Fulfill Your Dreams of Living Abroad. LC 99-11623. 272p. 1999. pap. 16.00 (0-8050-5947-4, Owl) H Holt & Co.

Reilly, Shauna. Freedom in My Soul. LC 98-8849. 416p. 1998. 22.50 (0-87081-503-2) Univ Pr Colo.

***Reilly, Sheena.** Schedule for Oral Motor Assessment. 1999. pap. text 140.00 (1-86156-134-2) Whurr Pub.

Reilly, Stephen M., jt. ed. see Wainwright, Peter C.

Reilly, Susan S., et al. The Quality System Compendium: GMP Requirements & Industry Practice. (Orig.). 1996. pap. 295.00 (1-57020-076-9, GMPS-209) Assn Adv Med Instrn.

Reilly, Susan S., jt. auth. see Goodall, Hillary.

Reilly, T. Science & Soccer. (Illus.). 408p. (C). 1995. pap. 39.99 (0-419-18880-0, E & FN Spon) Routledge.

— Sports Technology. 1995. pap. text. write for info. (0-419-12130-7, E & FN Spon) Routledge.

Reilly, T., et al, eds. Biomechanics & Medicine in Swimming. (Illus.). 420p. (C). 1992. 125.00 (0-419-15600-3, A6115, E & FN Spon) Routledge.

— Physiology of Sports. (Illus.). 320p. 1990. 63.00 (0-419-13580-4, A4403, E & FN Spon) Routledge.

— Physiology of Sports. (Illus.). 512p. (C). 1990. pap. 45.00 (0-419-13590-1, A4407, E & FN Spon) Routledge.

— Science & Football. 500p. 1988. text 57.50 (0-419-14360-2, E & FN Spon) Routledge.

— Science & Football, No. 2. 2nd ed. 768p. (gr. 13). 1992. mass mkt. 160.95 (0-419-17850-3, A9478) Chapman & Hall.

Reilly, T., et al. Biological Rhythms & Exercise. (Illus.). 172p. 1996. text 76.50 (0-19-262525-X) OUP.

— Biological Rhythms & Exercise. (Illus.). 172p. 1996. pap. text 49.95 (0-19-262524-1) OUP.

Reilly, T., jt. auth. see Eston, R. G.

Reilly, T., jt. ed. see Atkinson.

Reilly, Terence, jt. auth. see Clemen, Robert T.

Reilly, Teresa M. Five Seasons of Wall Quilts: Original Quilt Designs Following the Seasons. (Illus.). 71p. 1994. pap. 17.95 (1-881588-10-6, 882670162) EZ Quilting.

Reilly, Thomas. Jannus, an American Flier. LC 97-23419. 248p. 1997. 29.95 (0-8130-1544-8) U Press Fla.

— Jannus, an American Flier. (Illus.). 240p. 1997. 29.95 (0-614-29834-2) U Press Fla.

Reilly, Thomas, jt. auth. see Homan, Lynn.

Reilly, Thomas, jt. auth. see Homan, Lynn M.

Reilly, Thomas P. Simple Psychology: Simple Living in a Complicated World. LC 96-94359. 171p. 1996. 19.95 (0-944448-11-9) Motivation Pr.

— Tom Reilly's Guide to Better Probing: "How to Ask Better Questions & Listen to Your Customer" (Thinker Ser.). 22p. 1998. pap. text 5.00 (0-944448-12-7) Motivation Pr.

— Tom Reilly's Guide to Better Sales Letters: "How to Use Letters in the Value Added Sales Process" (Thinker Ser.). 43p. 1998. pap. text 5.00 (0-944448-13-5) Motivation Pr.

— Value Added Sales Management: A Manager's Guide to Creating the Value Added Sales Culture. LC 92-63228. 176p. (C). 1993. 24.95 (0-944448-08-9) Motivation Pr.

— Value Added Selling Techniques. LC 87-90744. 1987. 19.95 (0-944448-07-0) Motivation Pr.

***Reilly, Tom.** Crush Price Objections: Hold the Line on Prices! 159p. 1999. pap. 19.95 (0-944448-14-3) Motivation Pr.

Reilly, Tom. Value-Added Customer Service. 224p. 1996. pap. 11.95 (0-8092-3190-5, 319050, Contemporary Bks) NTC Contemp Pub Co.

— Value Added Customer Service: Every Employee's Guide for Creating Satisfied Customers. LC 94-79761. (Illus.). 70p. (Orig.). (C). 1995. pap. 5.00 (0-944448-10-0) Motivation Pr.

— Value-Added Sales Management. LC 92-43380. 160p. 1993. pap. 12.95 (0-8092-3787-3, 378730, Contemporary Bks) NTC Contemp Pub Co.

— What You Need to Know Before You Win the Lottery. Glenn-Reilly, Rosa, ed. De Tagle, Lillian, tr. 50p. (Orig.). 1996. pap. 10.00 (0-9651636-0-1) OdysseyPtrns.

Reilly, Vanessa & Ward, Sheila. Very Young Learners. (Illus.). 208p. 1997. pap. text 18.95 (0-19-437209-X) OUP.

Reilly, Wayne E., ed. Sarah Jane Foster, Teacher of the Freedmen: A Diary & Letters. 240p. 1990. pap. text 16.50 (0-8139-1305-5) U Pr of Va.

Reilly, William J. Marketing Investigations. Assael, Henry, ed. LC 78-251. (Century of Marketing Ser.). 1979. reprint ed. lib. bdg. 23.95 (0-405-11176-2) Ayer.

Reilly, William K., jt. auth. see Skinner, Samuel K.

Reilman, Beverly. When the Family Gathers: An International Cookbook & Calendar for Special Times. LC 96-76506. (Illus.). 176p. 1996. pap. 16.95 (1-56352-288-8) Longstreet.

Reily, John R. Read That Back, Please: Memoirs of a Court Reporter. LC 98-33821. (Illus.). 288p. 1999. pap. 14.95 (1-56474-284-9) Fithian Pr.

Reily, Nancy. I Am at an Age. 1991. 18.95 (1-878096-02-8) Best E TX Pubs.

Reily, Nancy H. Joseph A. Imhof: Artist of the Pueblos. LC 97-27712. (Illus.). 320p. 1998. 60.00 (0-86534-259-8) Sunstone Pr.

***Reily, Nancy Hopkins.** Classic Outdoor Color Portraits: A Guide for Photographers: It's Your Turn to Make a Portrait. (Illus.). 256p. 2000. pap. 22.95 (0-86534-302-0) Sunstone Pr.

***Reily, Philip K.** The Rocket Scientists: Achievement in Science, Technology & Industry at Atlantic Research Corporation. LC 98-90132. 1999. 35.00 (0-533-12710-6) Vantage.

Reiman, Alan. Mentoring & Supervision for Teacher Development. LC 97-21568. (Illus.). 384p. (C). 1997. pap. text 70.00 (0-8013-1539-5) Addison-Wesley.

Reiman, Donald H. Intervals of Inspiration: The Skeptical Tradition & the Psychology of Romanticism. 437p. 1988. write for info. (0-913283-23-1) Penkevill.

— Percy Bysshe Shelley. (Twayne's English Authors Ser.: No. 81). 200p. 1989. 28.95 (0-8057-6981-1, Twyne) Mac Lib Ref.

— Romantic Texts & Contexts. 408p. 1988. text 39.95 (0-8262-0649-2) U of Mo Pr.

Reiman, Donald H. The Study of Modern Manuscripts: Public, Confidential & Private. LC 92-43641. 224p. (C). 1993. text 29.95 (0-8018-4590-4) Johns Hopkins.

Reiman, Donald H., contrib. by. Shelley's Last Notebook: Bodleian MSS Shelley Adds, Nos. e.15 & e.20. 9003rd ed. (Bodleian Shelley Manuscripts Ser.: Vol. VII). 665p. 1990. text 95.00 (0-8240-6983-8) Garland.

Reiman, Donald H., jt. auth. see Shelley, Percy Bysshe.

Reiman, Donald H., ed. see Darwin, Erasmus.

Reiman, Donald H., ed. see Hayley, William.

Reiman, Donald H., ed. see Shelley, Percy Bysshe.

Reiman, Donald H., ed. see Wiffen, Jeremiah H.

Reiman, Donald H., ed. & intro. see Shelley, Percy Bysshe.

Reiman, Jeffrey. Abortion & the Ways We Value Life. LC 98-39537. 144p. 1998. pap. 18.95 (0-8476-9208-6) Rowman.

***Reiman, Jeffrey.** Abortion & the Ways We Value Life. LC 98-39537. 144p. 1998. 55.00 (0-8476-9207-8) Rowman.

Reiman, Jeffrey & Pojman, Louis. The Death Penalty: For & Against. LC 97-27795. (Point/Counterpoint Ser.: No. 94). 188p. 1997. 55.50 (0-8476-8632-9); pap. 17.95 (0-8476-8633-7) Rowman.

Reiman, Jeffrey H. Critical Moral Liberalism: Theory & Practice. (Studies in Social, Political, & Legal Philosophy: Vol. 70). 294p. 1996. 66.00 (0-8476-8313-3); pap. 24.95 (0-8476-8314-1) Rowman.

Reiman, Jeffrey H. The Rich Get Richer & the Poor Get Prison: Ideology, Class & Criminal Justice. 5th ed. LC 97-16285. 226p. 1997. pap. text 27.00 (0-205-26487-5) Allyn.

— The Rich Get Richer & the Poor Get Prison: Ideology, Class & Criminal Justice. 6th ed. LC 00-23784. 256p. 2000. pap. text 24.00 (0-205-30557-1) Allyn.

Reiman, Joey. Best Year of Your Life. 1996. pap. text 5.95 (1-56352-349-3) Longstreet.

— Success - The Original Hand Book: Life's Five Greatest Secrets Are Right in Your Hand. LC 92-71789. 128p. 1992. 14.95 (1-56352-044-3) Longstreet.

— Thinking for a Living: Creating Ideas That Revitalize Your Business & Career. LC 97-76265. 208p. 1998. 20.00 (1-56352-469-4) Longstreet.

Reiman, Michael, jt. auth. see Kaaz, Carsten.

Reiman Publication Staff. Taste of Home Recipe Book. 1997. 12.95 (0-89821-213-8) Reiman Pubns.

Reiman Publications Staff. At Ease. Beno, Mike, ed. LC 95-70942. 160p. 1996. 16.95 (0-89821-152-2, 20291) Reiman Pubns.

— Best of Country Cooking. 1996. 24.95 (0-89821-179-4, 24122) Reiman Pubns.

— Best of Country Cooking. 2nd ed. 1996. 24.95 (0-89821-187-5, 24123) Reiman Pubns.

— The Best of Country Cooking, 1998. Schnittka, Julie, ed. 188p. 1998. 19.95 (0-89821-235-9) Reiman Pubns.

— Bountiful Harvest. 1996. 12.95 (0-89821-189-1, 24158) Reiman Pubns.

— Cookin' up Country Breakfasts. 1996. 12.95 (0-89821-190-5, 24159) Reiman Pubns.

— Country Chicken. 1996. 12.95 (0-89821-196-4, 24227) Reiman Pubns.

— Country Ground Beef. 1996. 12.95 (0-89821-188-3, 24157) Reiman Pubns.

— Dining During the Depression. Thibodeau, Karen, ed. LC 95-72660. 208p. 1996. 14.95 (0-89821-156-5, 20288) Reiman Pubns.

— Grandmas Great Desserts. 100p. 1996. 12.95 (0-89821-197-2, 24226) Reiman Pubns.

— Iron Will. LC 96-71402. 164p. 1997. 19.95 (0-89821-193-X, 24230) Reiman Pubns.

— Motorin' Along. Martin, Mike, ed. LC 97-76274. 164p. 1998. 16.95 (0-89821-232-4) Reiman Pubns.

— 1998 Taste of Home Annual Recipes. Schnittke, Julie, ed. 324p. 1997. 24.95 (0-89821-216-2, 24510) Reiman Pubns.

— 1,112 Down to Earth Garden Secrets. LC 98-65083. 180p. 1998. 16.95 (0-89821-233-2) Reiman Pubns.

— 601 Sayings to Make You Smile. LC 97-65776. 228p. 1997. 11.95 (0-89821-212-X, 24497) Reiman Pubns.

— 1628 Country Shortcuts from 1628 Country People. 1996. pap. text 12.95 (0-89821-172-7, 20371) Reiman Pubns.

— The Taste of Home Recipe Book. 116p. 1996. 12.95 (0-89821-178-6, 24124) Reiman Pubns.

— Taste of Home 30-Minute Cookbook. Schnittka, Julie, ed. LC 97-68129. 210p. 1997. 24.95 (0-89821-215-4, 24727) Reiman Pubns.

— Taste of Home's Down-Home Diabetic Cookbook. Schnittka, Julie, ed. LC 95-71713. 320p. 1996. 17.95 (0-89821-153-0, 20287) Reiman Pubns.

— Taste of the Country. 100p. 1994. 12.95 (0-89821-180-8) Reiman Pubns.

— Taste of the Country. 2nd ed. 100p. 1994. 12.95 (0-89821-181-6) Reiman Pubns.

— Taste of the Country. 4th ed. 100p. 1994. 12.95 (0-89821-183-2) Reiman Pubns.

— Taste of the Country. 5th ed. 100p. 1995. 12.95 (0-89821-184-0) Reiman Pubns.

— Taste of the Country. 6th ed. 100p. 1995. 12.95 (0-89821-185-9) Reiman Pubns.

— Taste of the Country. 7th ed. 100p. 1996. 12.95 (0-89821-186-7) Reiman Pubns.

— Taste of the Country. 8th ed. 100p. 1996. 12.95 (0-89821-191-3, 24133) Reiman Pubns.

— We Made Our Own Fun! Miller, Bettina, ed. LC 95-72529. 164p. 1996. 14.95 (0-89821-155-7, 20290) Reiman Pubns.

Reiman, Robert, jt. auth. see Lovingood, Paul.

Reiman, Roy, ed. 1,628 Country Shortcuts...from 1,628 Country People. LC 95-68774. 196p. 1995. 16.95 (0-89821-148-4, 20102) Reiman Pubns.

Reimanis, Ivar E., et al, eds. Ceramic Joining. (Ceramic Transactions Ser.: Vol. 77). 197p. 1997. 95.00 (1-57498-022-X, CT077) Am Ceramic.

Reimann, Andreas, jt. auth. see Francis, Mark.

Reimann, Bernard C. Managing for Value: A Guide to Value-Based Strategic Management. 256p. 1987. 33.00 (0-912841-26-5) Planning Forum.

Reimann, Clemens & De Caritat, Patrice. Chemical Elements in the Environment: Factsheets for the Geochemist & Environmental Scientist. LC 97-39319. 410p. 1998. 110.00 (3-540-63670-6) Spr-Verlag.

Reimann, Harry. The Semi-Simple Zeta Function of Quaternionic Shimura Varieties. LC 97-6505. (Lecture Notes in Mathematics Ser.: Vol. 165). 1997. pap. write for info. (3-540-62645-X) Spr-Verlag.

Reimann, Hobart A. The Pneumonias. LC 78-166458. (Illus.). 224p. 1971. 12.50 (0-87527-119-7) Green.

Reimann, James, ed. see Chambers, Oswald.

Reimann, James, jt. ed. see Chambers, Oswald.

Reimann, James, ed. see Cowman, Lettie B.

Reimann, James, ed. see Sheldon, Charles M.

Reimann, Katya. A Tremor in the Bitter Earth. 1999. mass mkt. 6.99 (0-8125-4934-1, Pub. by Tor Bks) St Martin.

— A Tremor in the Bitter Earth, No. 2. LC 98-11423. (Tielmaran Chronicles Ser.). 384p. 1998. text 24.95 (0-312-86008-0) St Martin.

— Wind from a Foreign Sky. (Tielmaran Chronicles Ser.). 1997. mass mkt. 6.99 (0-8125-4933-3, Pub. by Tor Bks) St Martin.

Reimann, Klaus U. Geology of Bangladesh. (Beitraege Zur Regionalen Geologie der Erde. Ser.: Vol. 20). (GER., Illus.). viii, 160p. 1993. 73.00 (3-443-11020-7, Pub. by Gebruder Borntraeger) Balogh.

Reimann, Mathias. Conflict of Laws in Western Europe: A Guide Through the Jungle. LC 95-21942. 1995. text 85.00 (1-57105-005-1) Transnatl Pubs.

Reimann, Peter & Spada, Hans, eds. Learning in Humans & Machines. LC 95-25493. (Illus.). 324p. 1995. 74.75 (0-08-042569-0, Pergamon Pr) Elsevier.

Reimbert, A., jt. auth. see Reimbert, M.

Reimbert, M. & Reimbert, A. Silos: Theory & Practice. (Bulk Materials Handling Ser.: Vol. 1, No. 3). (Illus.). 251p. (C). 1976. text 35.00 (0-87849-014-0, Pub. by Trans T Pub) Enfield Pubs NH.

— Study of Passive Resistance in Foundation Structures Vol. 2: (Retaining Walls) LC 74-77789. (Rock & Soil Mechanics Ser.).Tr. of Murs De Soutenement Tome Ii. (Illus.). 200p. (C). 1976. text 54.00 (0-87849-013-2, Pub. by Trans T Pub) Enfield Pubs NH.

Reimel, J. Christopher. Image Processing & Optical Character Recognition: How They Work & How to Implement Them. LC 93-32942. 1993. 16.00 (0-87051-142-4) Am Inst CPA.

Reimensnyder, Barbara L. Powwowing in Union County: A Study of Pennsylvania German Folk Medicine in Context. LC 88-35082. (Immigrant Communities & Ethnic Minorities in the U. S. & Canada Ser.: No. 31). 1989. 55.00 (0-404-19441-9) AMS Pr.

Reimer. Atlas of Equine Ultrasonography. LC 97-27369. (Illus.). 328p. (C). (gr. 13). 1997. text 84.95 (0-8151-2146-6, 30756) Mosby Inc.

Reimer & Safarik. Quotations on the Jays. 96p. 1994. per. 4.95 (0-88978-273-3, Pub. by Arsenal Pulp) LPC InBook.

Reimer, et al. The Clinical Rotation Handbook: The Practicum Guide for Nurses. 240p. (C). 1998. text 26.95 (0-7668-0540-9) Delmar.

Reimer, jt. auth. see Safarik, Allan.

Reimer, A. James. Paul Tillich & Emanuel Hirsch Debate: A Study in the Political Ramifications of Theology. LC 89-13568. (Toronto Studies in Theology: Vol. 42). 384p. 1989. lib. bdg. 109.95 (0-88946-991-1) E Mellen.

Reimer, A. James, ed. The Influence of the Frankfurt School on Contemporary Theology: Critical Theory & the Future of Religion: Dubrovnik Papers in Honour of Rudolf J. Siebert. LC 92-36327. (Toronto Studies in Theology: Vol. 64). 364p. 1992. text 99.95 (0-7734-9169-4) E Mellen.

***Reimer, Bennett.** Performing with Understanding: The Challenge of the National Standards for Music Education. 216p. (Orig.). 2000. pap. 26.00 (1-56545-118-X, 1672) MENC.

Reimer, Bennett. Philosophy of Music Education. 2nd ed. 240p. 1988. text 45.00 (0-13-663881-3) P-H.

Reimer, Bennett & Evans, Edward. The Experience of Music. (Illus.). 384p. (C). 1973. lp 302.40 (0-13-294892-3); lp 129.95 (0-686-76953-8) P-H.

Reimer, Bennett & Smith, Ralph A., eds. The Arts, Education, & Aesthetic Knowing. (National Society for the Study of Education Publication Ser.). 288p. 1992. 27.50 (0-226-60158-7) U Ch Pr.

Reimer, Bennett & Wright, Jeffrey E., eds. On the Nature of Musical Experience. 327p. (C). 1992. text 39.95 (0-87081-248-3) Univ Pr Colo.

Reimer-Bohner, Ute, tr. see Buchanan, Brian.

Reimer, Carol J., jt. auth. see Reimer, Robert C.

Reimer, Catherine Swan. Counseling the Inupiat Eskimo, 36. LC 98-51220. (Contributions in Psychology Ser.: Vol. 36). 192p. 1999. 59.95 (0-313-30934-5) Greenwood.

Reimer, Charles W., jt. auth. see Patrick, Ruth.

Reimer, David, jt. ed. see Barton, John.

Reimer, David J. The Oracles Against Babylon in Jeremiah 50-51: A Horror among the Nations. LC 92-29514. 340p. 1992. text 99.95 (0-7734-9821-4) E Mellen.

Reimer, Doug. Older Than Ravens. 1997. pap. 10.95 (0-88801-137-7, Pub. by Turnstone Pr) Genl Dist Srvs.

Reimer, Earl. Cell 66. 1995. pap. write for info. (1-57514-181-7) Encore Perform Pub.

— The Rehearsal. (Christian Theatre Ser.). 23p. 1994. pap. 3.00 (1-57514-138-8, 1104) Encore Perform Pub.

— She Was Only a Garbageman's Daughter: But She Was Nothing to Be Sniffed At. 63p. (Orig.). 1995. pap. 4.50 (1-57514-229-5, 0091) Encore Perform Pub.

— Worship & Dramatize. 72p. 1998. pap. 5.00 (0-87440-070-8) Bakers Plays.

Reimer, Elaine, ed. see Reimer, Wilbert.

Reimer, Everett. Futuros Alternativos. LC 76-14982. (Planning Ser.: No. S-4: Graduate Program in Planning). 110p. (Orig.). 1976. pap. text 2.80 (0-8477-2434-4) U of PR Pr.

Reimer, G. C., tr. see Freytag, Gustav.

Reimer, Gail T. & Kates, Judith A., eds. Beginning Anew. LC 97-24410. 384p. 1997. per. 14.00 (*0-684-82687-9*, Touchstone) S&S Trade Pap.

Reimer, Gail T., jt. ed. see Kates, Judith A.

Reimer, Ivoni R. Women in the Acts of the Apostles: A Feminist Liberation Perspective. Maloney, Linda M., tr. LC 95-23363. 288p. 1995. pap. 29.00 (*0-8006-2840-3*, 1-2840) Augsburg Fortress.

Reimer, James A. Emanuel Hirsch und Paul Tillich: Theologie und Politik in Einer Zeit der Krise. (GER.). xxi, 489p. (C). 1995. lib. bdg. 152.30 (*3-11-012933-7*) De Gruyter.

Reimer, Jeffrey A., jt. auth. see Duncan, T. Michael.

***Reimer, Johannes.** Liberty in Confinement: A Story of Faith in the Red Army.Tr. of Verweigerer. 164p. 2000. mass mkt. 3.95 (*0-921788-59-2*, Pub. by Kindred Prods) Spring Arbor Dist.

Reimer, Joseph. Succeeding at Jewish Education: How One Synagogue Made It Work. LC 97-19889. 201p. 1997. pap. 12.95 (*0-8276-0623-0*) JPS Phila.

Reimer, Joseph, et al. Promoting Moral Growth: From Piaget to Kohlberg. 2nd ed. 285p. (C). 1990. reprint ed. pap. text 19.95 (*0-88133-570-3*) Waveland Pr.

Reimer, Kathleen, ed. see Reider, Barbara E.

Reimer, Keith A., jt. auth. see Hackel, Donald B.

Reimer, L. Scanning Electron Microscopy: Physics of Image Formation & Microanalysis. 2nd rev. ed. MacAdam, D. L. et al, eds. LC 98-26178. (Springer Series in Optical Sciences: Vol. 45). (Illus.). 510p. 1998. 89.95 (*3-540-63976-4*) Spr-Verlag.

Reimer, Lawrence & Wagner, James. The Hospital Handbook: A Practical Guide to Hospital Visitation. LC 84-61207. 176p. 1984. pap. 13.95 (*0-8192-1470-1*) Morehouse Pub.

Reimer, Ludwig. Image Formation in Low-Voltage Scanning Electron Microscopy. LC 92-43451. (Tutorial Texts in Optical Engineering Ser.: Vol. TT 12). 1993. pap. 20.00 (*0-8194-1206-6*) SPIE.

— Scanning Electron Microscopy. (Optical Sciences Ser.: Vol. 45). (Illus.). 480p. 1985. 106.95 (*0-387-13530-8*) Spr-Verlag.

— Transmission Electron Microscopy: Physics of Image Formation & Microanalysis. 3rd ed. LC 93-27996. (Optical Sciences Ser.: Vol. 36). 1993. 69.00 (*0-387-56849-2*) Spr-Verlag.

— Transmission Electron Microscopy: Physics of Image Formation & Microanalysis. 4th ed. LC 97-6983. (Series in Optical Sciences). 608p. 1997. 69.95 (*3-540-62568-2*) Spr-Verlag.

Reimer, Ludwig, ed. Energy-Filtering Transmission Electron Microscopy. LC 94-43581. (Series in Optical Sciences: Vol. 71). 1995. 75.95 (*3-540-58479-X*) Spr-Verlag.

Reimer, Luetta & Reimer, Wilbert. Mathematicians Are People, Too: Stories from the Lives of Great Mathematicians, Vol. 1. (Illus.). 143p. (Orig.). (J). (gr. 3-10). 12.95 (*0-86651-509-7*, 2001) Seymour Pubns.

— Mathematicians Are People, Too: Stories from the Lives of Great Mathematicians, Vol. 2. (Illus.). 150p. (Orig.). (J). (gr. 3 up). 11.95 (*0-86651-823-1*, 2004) Seymour Pubns.

Reimer, Luetta, jt. auth. see Reimer, Wilbert.

Reimer, Mavis, ed. Such a Simple Little Tale: Critical Responses to L. M. Montgomery's Anne of Green Gables. LC 92-7392. (Children's Literature Association Ser.). 210p. 1992. 26.50 (*0-8108-2560-0*) Scarecrow.

Reimer, Michael J. Colonial Bridgehead: Government & Society in Alexandria, 1807-1882. LC 97-960788. xiii, 2p. 1997. write for info. (*977-424-418-4*) Am Univ Cairo Pr.

— Colonial Bridgehead: Government & Society in Alexandria, 1807-1882. LC 97-25933. (State, Culture & Society in Arab North Africa Ser.). (C). 1997. text 75.00 (*0-8133-2777-6*, Pub. by Westview) HarpC.

Reimer, Naomi. The Taken. LC 97-73587. vii, 72p. 1997. pap. 10.00 (*0-9659933-0-2*) Birch Bay.

Reimer, Neal. The Future of the Democratic Revolution: Toward a More Prophetic Politics. LC 84-8254. 305p. 1984. 69.50 (*0-275-91250-7*, C1250, Praeger Pubs) Greenwood.

Reimer, P., et al, eds. Clinical MR-Imaging: A Practical Approach. LC 98-53094. (Illus.). 550p. 1999. pap. 129.00 (*3-540-64098-3*) Spr-Verlag.

Reimer, Pierce. Greenhouse Gas Mitigation: Technologies for Activities Implemented Jointly: Proceedings of Technologies for Activities Implemented Jointly 26th-29th, May 1997, the Westin Bayshire Hotel, Vancouver, Canada. LC 97-48253. 1998. 217.00 (*0-08-043325-1*) Elsevier.

Reimer, Pierce & Mills, Steven. Custom Fords. (Illus.). 152p. 1987. 29.95 (*0-85429-581-X*, F581, Pub. by GT Foulis) Haynes Manuals.

Reimer, Ramon. The $1.89 Christmas Tree. LC 96-54012. (Illus.). (J). 1997. write for info. (*1-56763-318-8*); pap. write for info. (*1-56763-319-6*) Ozark Pub.

***Reimer, Robert, ed.** Cultural History Through a National Socialist Lens: Essays on the Cinema of Nazi Germany. LC 99-89973. (Studies in German Literature, Linguistics & Culture). (Illus.). 240p. 2000. 49.50 (*1-57113-164-7*, Pub. by Camden Hse) Boydell & Brewer.

Reimer, Robert C. & Reimer, Carol J. Nazi-Retro Film: How German Narrative Cinema Remembers the Past. LC 92-18054. (Twayne's Filmmakers Ser.). 200p. 1992. pap. 15.95 (*0-8057-9316-X*, Twyne) Mac Lib Ref.

Reimer, Susan. Motherhood Is a Contact Sport. LC 98-70956. 212p. (Orig.). 1998. pap. 11.95 (*0-9649819-6-3*) Baltimore Sun.

Reimer, T. O., tr. see Mainquet, M.

Reimer, Thomas, tr. see Devillers, Charles & Chaline, Jean.

Reimer, Thomas, tr. see Dvillers, C. & Chaline, Jean.

Reimer, Thomas, tr. see Enay, R.

Reimer, Wilbert. What's Next? Vol. 1: A Pattern Discovery Approach to Problem Solving. Reimer, Elaine, ed. (What's Next Ser.: Vol. 1). (Illus.). 60p. (Orig.). 1995. teacher ed., wbk. ed. 16.95 (*1-881431-54-1*, 1660) AIMS Educ Fnd.

— What's Next? Vol. 2: A Pattern Discovery Approach to Problem Solving. Reimer, Elaine, ed. (What's Next Ser.: No. 2). (Illus.). 60p. (Orig.). 1996. teacher ed., wbk. ed. 16.95 (*1-881431-55-X*, 1665) AIMS Educ Fnd.

— What's Next? Vol. 3: A Pattern Discovery Approach to Problem Solving, 3 vols. Reimer, Elaine, ed. (What's Next Ser.: No. 3). (Illus.). 60p. (Orig.). 1996. teacher ed., wbk. ed. 16.95 (*1-881431-56-8*, 1670) AIMS Educ Fnd.

Reimer, Wilbert & Reimer, Luetta. Historical Connections in Mathematics: Resources for Using History of Mathematics in the Classroom, Vol. I. (Illus.). 103p. (Orig.). (J). (gr. 4-10). 1992. 16.95 (*1-881431-35-5*, 2002) AIMS Educ Fnd.

— Historical Connections in Mathematics: Resources for Using History of Mathematics in the Classroom, Vol. II. (Illus.). 120p. (Orig.). (J). (gr. 4-10). 1993. 16.95 (*1-881431-38-X*, 2003) AIMS Educ Fnd.

— Historical Connections in Mathematics: Resources for Using History of Mathematics in the Classroom, Vol. III. (Illus.). 120p. (Orig.). (J). (gr. 4-10). 1995. 16.95 (*1-881431-49-5*, 2005) AIMS Educ Fnd.

Reimer, Wilbert, jt. auth. see Reimer, Luetta.

***REIMERS, CATHY L & Brungers, Bruce A.** ADHD in the Young Child: Driven to Redirection; A Guide for Parents & Teachers of Young Children with ADHD. LC 99-388861. (Illus.). 202p. 1999. pap. 18.95 (*1-886941-32-7*, Pub. by Spec Pr FL) Partners Pubs Grp.

Reimers, Cathy L., jt. auth. see Brunger, Bruce A.

Reimers, David M. A Land of Immigrants. Stotsky, Sandra, ed. LC 95-13820. (Immigrant Experience Ser.). (Illus.). 120p. (YA). (gr. 5 up). 1995. lib. bdg. 19.95 (*0-7910-3361-9*) Chelsea Hse.

— Still the Golden Door: The Third World Comes to America. LC 84-29273. 320p. 1987. pap. text 22.50 (*0-231-05771-7*) Col U Pr.

— Still the Golden Door: The Third World Comes to America. 350p. 1992. pap. text 20.00 (*0-231-07681-9*) Col U Pr.

— Teaching Immigration of People of Color to the United States. Painter, Nell I. & Bustamante, Antonio R., eds. LC 99-30891. (Teaching Diversity Ser.). 52 p. 1999. pap. 8.00 (*0-87229-110-3*) Am Hist Assn.

— Unwelcome Strangers: American Identity & the Turn Against Immigration. LC 97-52683. 218p. 1998. 27.50 (*0-231-10956-3*) Col U Pr.

— Unwelcome Strangers: American Identity & the Turn Against Immigration. LC 97-52683. 199p. 1999. pap. 17.50 (*0-231-10957-1*) Col U Pr.

Reimers, David M. & Binder, Frederick M. All the Nations Under Heaven: An Ethnic & Racial History of New York City. 353p. 1996. pap. 17.50 (*0-231-07879-X*) Col U Pr.

Reimers, David M., jt. auth. see Binder, Frederick M.

Reimers, David M., jt. ed. see Binder, Frederick M.

***Reimers, Fernando.** Unequal Schools, Unequal Chances: The Challenges to Equal Opportunity in the Americas. 410p. 2000. pap. 24.95 (*0-674-00375-6*) HUP.

Reimers, Fernando & McGinn, Noel F. Informed Dialogue: Using Research to Shape Education Policy Around the World. LC 96-50323. 224p. 1997. 62.95 (*0-275-95442-0*, Praeger Pubs); pap. 20.95 (*0-275-95443-9*, Praeger Pubs) Greenwood.

Reimers, Fernando, jt. auth. see Warwick, Donald P.

Reimers, Henry L. The Abrams Story. 60p. 1977. 7.50 (*0-87770-181-4*) Ye Galleon.

— Fight & Fright on the Oregon Trail. 16p. pap. 2.95 (*0-614-16727-2*) Ye Galleon.

— The Secret Saga of Five-Sack. 25p. 1975. pap. 4.95 (*0-87770-145-8*) Ye Galleon.

Reimers, Sigurd & Treacher, Andrew. Introducing User-Friendly Family Therapy. LC 94-10723. 240p. (C). 1994. 80.00 (*0-415-07430-4*, B4450); pap. 27.99 (*0-415-07431-2*, B4454) Routledge.

Reimers, Ulrich. Digital Video Broadcasting: The International Standard for Digital HDTV. 300p. 2000. 89.95 (*3-540-60946-6*) Spr-Verlag.

Reimers, W., jt. auth. see Hauk, V.

Reimherr, Otto, ed. Quest for Faith, Quest for Freedom: Aspects of Pennsylvania's Religious Experience. LC 86-61790. (Illus.). 208p. 1987. 36.50 (*0-941664-26-0*) Susquehanna U Pr.

Reimlinger, Hans. Organisch-Chemische Nomenklatur. (GER.). 620p. (C). 1997. lib. bdg. 87.40 (*3-11-014863-3*) De Gruyter.

Reimold, Cheryl. How to Write What People Like to Read. 24p. (Orig.). 1994. pap. 15.00 (*0-89852-280-3*, 0101R235) TAPPI.

— The Language of Business. 168p. (Orig.). 1992. pap. 58.00 (*0-614-10341-X*, 0101R200) TAPPI.

— The Language of Business: A TAPPI Press Anthology of Published Papers 1980-1991. LC 92-3287. 175p. reprint ed. pap. 54.30 (*0-7837-1978-7*, 204225200002) Bks Demand.

Reimold, Cheryl & Reimold, Peter. How to Prepare & Deliver Outstanding Presentations: A Practical Guide. 120p. 1999. pap. 19.95 (*0-7803-3415-9*, PC5686-QOE) Inst Electrical.

Reimold, Peter, jt. auth. see Reimold, Cheryl.

Reimold, Robert J., ed. Watershed Management: Practice, Policies, & Coordination. LC 98-25965. (Illus.). 608p. 1998. 79.95 (*0-07-052299-5*) McGraw-Hill Prof.

Reimonenq, Alden. Hoodoo Headrag. 100p. 2000. pap. 10.00 (*1-883573-14-9*) Pride & Imprints.

Reimonenq, Alden, et al. Milking Black Bull: 12 Gay Black Poets. LC 95-725. 168p. 1995. pap. 12.00 (*1-880729-11-3*) Vega Pr.

Reimpell, Jornsen & Stoll, Helmutt. The Automotive Chassis: Engineering Principles. 368p. 1995. text 49.00 (*1-56091-736-9*, R-165) Soc Auto Engineers.

Reimschneider, Burkhard, jt. ed. see Grosenick, Uta.

Rein. Language of Advertising & Merchandising in English. 1987. pap. 20.40 (*0-13-523291-0*) P-H.

Rein, David. Grammar Exercises Part Two: Intermediate ESL. Clark, Raymond C., ed. (Interplay ESL Ser.). (Illus.). 224p. (Orig.). (gr. 8 up). 1986. pap. text 14.00 (*0-86647-014-X*) Pro Lingua.

— Vardis Fisher: Challenge to Evasion. 1992. lib. bdg. 79.95 (*0-8490-5475-3*) Gordon Pr.

Rein, David P., jt. auth. see Graves, Kathleen.

Rein, Gustav A. Sir John Robert Seeley: A Study of the Historian. LC 82-18662. 155p. 1987. text 25.00 (*0-89341-550-2*, Longwood Academic) Hollowbrook.

Rein-Hagen, Mark, jt. auth. see Tweet, Jonathan.

Rein, Harald. Allgemeine Einfuhrung: Die Anglikanisch-Altkatholischen Beziehungen. (Europaische Hochschulschriften Ser.: Reihe 23, Bd. 477). (GER.). 482p. 1993. 60.80 (*3-906750-72-8*, Pub. by P Lang) P Lang Pubng.

Rein, Harold. Die Anglikanisch-Orthodoxen Beziehungen - Die Orthodox-Altkatholischen Beziehungen - Das Ekklesiologische Selbstverstandnis und die Beziehungen Dieser Drei Zu Anderen Kirchen. (Europaische Hochschulschriften Ser.: Reihe 23, Bd. 511). (GER.). 572p. 1994. 62.95 (*3-906752-32-1*, Pub. by P Lang) P Lang Pubng.

Rein, Harry. The Primer on Medical Malpractice. 400p. 1988. student ed. 100.00 (*1-55917-569-9*, 132B) Natl Prac Inst.

— The Primer on Soft Tissue Injuries. 272p. 1988. student ed. 25.00 (*1-55917-566-4*, 131B) Natl Prac Inst.

— The Primer on Thermography. 275p. 1988. 85.00 (*1-55917-563-X*, 133B) Natl Prac Inst.

Rein, Horst, jt. ed. see Ruckpaul, Klaus.

Rein, Irving, et al. High Visibility: The Making & Marketing of Celebrities. LC 97-17534. (Illus.). 176p. 1997. 24.95 (*0-8442-3448-6*, NTC Business Bks) NTC Contemp Pub Co.

Rein, J. J. The Industries of Japan: Together with an Account of Its Agriculture, Forestry, Arts & Commerce. fac. ed. (Illus.). 580p. (C). 1996. text 395.00 (*0-7007-0351-9*, Pub. by Curzon Pr Ltd) UH Pr.

— Japan: Travel & Researches. (Illus.). 550p. 1998. text 375.00 (*0-7007-1016-7*, Pub. by Curzon Pr Ltd) UH Pr.

Rein, Kurt, jt. ed. see Keel, William.

Rein, Martin. Social Policy: Issues of Choice & Change. abr. ed. LC 82-19676. 384p. 1983. reprint ed. pap. 119.10 (*0-7837-9981-0*, 206070800006) Bks Demand.

Rein, Martin, et al, eds. Enterprise & Social Benefits after Communism. (Illus.). 344p. (C). 1997. text 74.95 (*0-521-58403-5*) Cambridge U Pr.

Rein, martin & Rainwater, Lee, eds. Public - Private Interplay in Social Protection. LC 86-11911. (Comparative Public Policy Analysis Ser.). 256p. (gr. 13). 1986. pap. text 42.95 (*0-87332-498-6*) M E Sharpe.

Rein, Martin & Rainwater, Lee, eds. Public & Private Interplay in Social Protection. LC 86-11911. (Comparative Public Policy Analysis Ser.). 256p. (gr. 13). 1986. text 85.95 (*0-87332-383-1*) M E Sharpe.

Rein, Martin & Wadensjo, Eskil. Enterprise & the Welfare State. LC 97-24228. 416p. 1998. pap. 40.00 (*1-85898-664-8*) E Elgar.

Rein, Martin & Wadensjo, Eskil, eds. Enterprise & the Welfare State. LC 97-24228. 416p. 1997. 100.00 (*1-85898-379-7*) E Elgar.

Rein, Martin, et al. Income Packaging in the Welfare State. (Illus.). 296p. 1987. 65.00 (*0-19-828482-9*) OUP.

Rein, Martin, jt. auth. see Marris, Peter.

Rein, Martin, jt. auth. see Peattie, Lisa.

Rein, Martin, jt. auth. see Schon, Donald A.

Rein, Martin, jt. ed. see Epsing-Andersen, Gosta.

***Rein, Mei L., et al, eds.** The American Family: Reflected a Changing Nation. (Reference Ser.). (Illus.). 160p. 1999. pap. text 25.95 (*1-57302-090-7*) Info Plus TX.

***Rein, Mei Ling, ed.** Immigration & Illegal Aliens: Burden or Blessing? rev. ed. (Information Plus Reference Ser.). (Illus.). 160p. 1999. pap. text 25.95 (*1-57302-100-8*) Info Plus TX.

— Nutrition: A Key to Good Health. rev. ed. (Information Plus Reference Ser.). (Illus.). 1999. pap. text 25.95 (*1-57302-101-6*) Info Plus TX.

***Rein, Mei Ling, et al, eds.** Child Abuse: Betraying a Trust. 10th ed. (Reference Ser.). (Illus.). 136p. 1999. pap. text 25.95 (*1-57302-091-5*) Info Plus TX.

Rein, Mei Ling, et al, eds. Death & Dying: Who Decides. rev. ed. (Reference Ser.). 180p. 1998. pap. text 26.95 (*1-57302-027-3*) Info Plus TX.

Rein, Michael F., jt. ed. see Mandell, Gerald L.

Rein, Mildred. Dilemmas of Welfare Policy: Why Work Strategies Haven't Worked. LC 82-3726. 179p. 1982. 52.95 (*0-275-90883-6*, C0883, Praeger Pubs) Greenwood.

Rein, Monica. Politics & Education in Argentina, 1946-1962. Grenzeback, Martha, tr. LC 97-29381. (Latin American Realities Ser.). (Illus.). 240p. (C). (gr. 13). 1998. text 65.95 (*0-7656-0209-1*); pap. text 29.95 (*0-7656-0210-5*) M E Sharpe.

Rein, Raanan. In the Shadow of the Holocaust & the Inquisition: Israel's Relations with Francoist Spain. Grenzeback, Martha, tr. from HEB. LC 96-53973. 288p. 1997. 54.50 (*0-7146-4796-9*, Pub. by F Cass Pubs); pap. 26.50 (*0-7146-4351-3*, Pub. by F Cass Pubs) Intl Spec Bk.

***Rein, Raanan, ed.** Spain & the Mediterranean since 1898. LC 98-45229. 256p. 1999. 49.50 (*0-7146-4945-7*, Pub. by F Cass Pubs); pap. 24.50 (*0-7146-8004-4*, Pub. by F Cass Pubs) Intl Spec Bk.

Rein, Rachel, jt. auth. see Rein, Raelynne P.

Rein, Raelynne P. & Rein, Rachel. How to Develop Your Child's Gifts & Talents During the Elementary Years. 2nd rev. ed. LC 99-201972. 160p. 1999. pap. 13.95 (*0-7373-0088-4*, 00884W) NTC Contemp Pub Co.

***Rein, Richard K., ed.** U. S. 1 Business Directory 2000 Vol. 13: Business to Business Resource Guide for Central New Jersey. 296p. 2000. pap. 12.95 (*1-889000-04-3*) U S One Pub.

Reina, Dennis S. & Reina, Michelle L. Trust & Betrayal in the Workplace: Building Effective Relationships in Your Organization. LC 99-41538. 173p. 1999. 27.95 (*1-57675-070-1*) Berrett-Koehler.

Reina, Jacqueline, ed. see Juusola, Detta.

Reina, Michelle L., jt. auth. see Reina, Dennis S.

Reina, Richard & Muller, William A. Partyboat Fishing with the Experts. (With the Experts Ser.). (Illus.). 269p. 1987. text 14.95 (*0-9625187-1-9*) Wavecrest Comns.

— Surf Fishing with the Experts. (With the Experts Ser.). (Illus.). 242p. 1984. text 14.95 (*0-9625187-0-0*) Wavecrest Comns.

Reina, Richard, jt. auth. see Muller, William A.

Reina, Ruben E. Parana: Social Boundaries in an Argentine City. LC 72-8265. (Latin American Monographs: No. 31). 446p. reprint ed. pap. 127.20 (*0-8357-7758-8*, 2036116) Bks Demand.

— Shadows: A Mayan Way of Knowing. 1984. 13.95 (*0-88282-008-7*) New Horizon NJ.

Reina, Ruben E., jt. ed. see Kensinger, Kenneth.

Reinach, Adolf. Samtliche Werke: Textcritical Edition in Two Volumes, Set. Schuhmann, Karl & Smith, Barry, eds. (Philosophia Resources Library). (GER.). xviii, 848p. 1989. 199.00 (*3-88405-015-X*) Philosophia Pr.

Reinach, Adolf, et al. Epistemology. Seifert, Josef, ed. & tr. by. Crosby, John, ed. LC 81-6249. (Aletheia-an International Journal of Philosophy: Vol. 2). 272p. (Orig.). (C). 1982. pap. 25.00 (*0-86663-780-X*) Ide Hse.

Reinach, Adolph J. Rapport sur les Fouilles de Koptos (Janvier-Fevrier, 1910) (FRE., Illus.). 58p. 1988. reprint ed. pap. 30.00 (*0-933175-21-3*) Van Siclen Bks.

Reinach, Salomon. Orpheus: A History of Religions. Simmonds, Florence, tr. 497p. 1996. reprint ed. pap. 39.00 (*1-56459-568-4*) Kessinger Pub.

— Repertoire de Peintures du Moyen Age et de la Renaissance (1280-1580), 6 Vols. 1974. pap. 560.00 (*0-8115-0047-0*) Periodicals Srv.

— Repertoire des Vases Peints Grecs et Etrusques, 2 Vols. 1974. 130.00 (*0-8115-4856-2*) Periodicals Srv.

Reinach, T. Jewish Coins. (Illus.). 1966. lib. bdg. 15.00 (*0-932106-36-6*) S J Durst.

Reinach, Theodore. Mithradates Eupator, Koenig von Pontos: Mit Berichtigung und Nachtraegen Ins Deutsche Uebersetzt. Goetz, A., tr. (GER.). 488p. 1975. reprint ed. lib. bdg. 125.00 (*3-487-05585-6*) G Olms Pubs.

— Textes d'Auteurs Grecs et Romains Relatifs au Judaisme. xx, 376p. 1983. reprint ed. write for info. (*3-487-00346-5*) G Olms Pubs.

Reinacher, Eduard. Eine Bibliographie Seiner Werke. (Bibliographien Zur Deutschen Literature Ser.: Vol. 4). lii, 272p. 1984. write for info. (*3-487-07598-9*) G Olms Pubs.

***Reinagel, Wayne A.** Secrets of Evening Primrose Oil. 224p. 2000. mass mkt. 5.99 (*0-312-97298-9*) St Martin.

Reinagel, Wayne A., see Warlock, Adam, pseud.

Reinagle, Alexander. Alexander Reinagle: The Philadelphia Sonatas. Hopkins, Robert, ed. (Recent Researches in American Music Ser.: No. RRAM5). (Illus.). 84, xxivp. 1978. pap. 35.00 (*0-89579-107-2*) A-R Eds.

— Four Sonatas: Andante, Theme & Variation & Adagio for Piano. (Music Reprint Ser.). 100p. 1987. reprint ed. lib. bdg. 24.50 (*0-306-76254-4*) Da Capo.

Reinagle, Damon J. Draw! Medieval Fantasies. LC 95-31190. 1995. 14.15 (*0-606-09213-7*, Pub. by Turtleback) Demco.

— Draw Alien Fantasies. LC 96-9894. (Draw! Bks.). (Illus.). 64p. (Orig.). (J). (gr. 2-8). 1996. pap. 8.95 (*0-939217-31-7*) Peel Prod.

— Draw Medieval Fantasies. LC 95-31190. (Draw Bks.). (Illus.). 64p. (J). (gr. 4-7). 1995. pap. 8.95 (*0-939217-30-9*) Peel Prod.

— Draw Sports Figures. LC 97-25457. (Draw! Bks.). (Illus.). 64p. (J). (gr. 3-9). 1997. pap. 8.95 (*0-939217-32-5*) Peel Prod.

Reinalter, Helmut. Aufklarung - Vormarz - Revolution: Jahrbuch der Internationalen Forschungsstelle Demokratische Bewegungen in Mitteleuropa Von 1770-1850 an der Universitat Innsbruck Bd. 13/14/15 (1993/95) (GER.). 358p. 1997. 57.95 (*3-631-48395-3*) P Lang Pubng.

Reinalter, Helmut, ed. Der Illuminatenorden (1776-1785/87) Ein Politischer Geheimbund der Aufklaerungszeit. (Schriftenreihe der Internationalen Forschungsstelle "Demokratische Bewegungen in Mitteleuropa, 1770-1850" Ser.: Band 24). (GER.). 418p. 1998. pap. 56.95 (*3-631-32227-5*) P Lang Pubng.

***Reinalter, Helmut & Pelinka, Anton.** Die Anfange der Demokratischen Bewegung in Osterreich von der Spataufklarung Bis Zur Revolution, 1848-1849: Eine Kommentierte Quellenauswahl. (Demokratische Bewegungen in Mitteleuropa, 1770-1850 Ser.). 588p. 1999. 74.95 (*3-631-49257-X*) P Lang Pubng.

Reinalter, Helmut & Pelinka, Anton, eds. Die Demokratische Bewegung in Deutschland von der Spaetaufklaerung bis zur Revolution 1848-49: Eine Kommentierte Quellenauswahl. (Schriftenreihe der Internationalen Forschungsstelle "Demokratische

An Asterisk (*) at the beginning of an entry indicates that the title is appearing for the first time.

Bewegungen in Mitteleuropa, 1770-1850" Ser.: Band 25). (GER., Illus.). 403p. 1998. pap. 56.95 (*3-631-32240-2*) P Lang Pubng.

Reinard. Introduction to Comparative Research. 2nd ed. 1999. write for info. (*0-07-236864-0*) McGraw.

— An Introduction to Communications. 1994. teacher ed. 26.87 (*0-697-06459-X*) McGraw.

Reinard, John C. Foundations of Argument: Effective Communication for Critical Thinking. 512p. (C). 1990. text. write for info. (*0-697-05338-5*) Brown & Benchmark.

— Introduction to Communication Research. 384p. (C). 1994. text. write for info. (*0-697-06458-1*) Brown & Benchmark.

— Introduction to Communication Research. 2nd ed. LC 97-21501. 416p. (C). 1997. text. write for info. (*0-697-32730-2*, WCB McGr Hill) McGrw-H Hghr Educ.

Reinard, Ken. The Colonial Angler's Manual of Flyfishing & Flytying. 106p. 1995. 29.95 (*1-56523-070-1*) Fox Chapel Pub.

— The Colonial Angler's Manual of Flyfishing & Flytying Manual. (Illus.). 106p. 1995. pap. 19.95 (*1-56523-039-6*) Fox Chapel Pub.

Reinard, Patsy, jt. auth. see Wolberg, Donald.

Reinard, R. Douglas & LaRusch, Cynthia. Sermons from the Mystery Box: Object Lessons for Children. 1991. pap. 8.95 (*0-687-37534-7*) Abingdon.

Reinardt Schuhmann International Symposium on Inno, et al. The Reinhardt Schuhmann International Symposium on Innovative Technology & Reactor Design in Extraction Metallurgy: 1986: Colorado Springs, CO. Gaskell, D. R. et al, eds. LC 86-23469. (Illus.). 1080p. reprint ed. pap. 200.00 (*0-8357-5545-2*, 203516000093) Bks Demand.

Reinares, Fernando, ed. European Democracies Against Terrorism: Governmental Policies & Intergovernmental Cooperation. LC 99-15645. (Onati International Series in Law & Society). 250p. 1999. text 87.95 (*0-7546-2015-8*, Pub. by Ashgate Pub) Ashgate Pub Co.

***Reinares-Nestares, Fernando.** European Democracies Against Terrorism: Governmental Policies & Intergovernmental Cooperation LC 99-15645. (Odnati International in Law & Society Ser.). 1999. 43.95 (*0-7546-2019-0*, Pub. by Ashgate Pub) Ashgate Pub Co.

Reinarman, Craig. American States of Mind: Political Beliefs & Behavior among Private & Public Workers. LC 86-26752. 272p. reprint ed. pap. 84.40 (*0-7837-4550-8*, 208034100005) Bks Demand.

Reinarman, Craig & Levine, Harry G. Crack in America: Demon Drugs & Social Justice. LC 96-47765. 359p. 1997. 48.00 (*0-520-20241-4*, Pub. by U CA Pr); pap. 18.95 (*0-520-20242-2*, Pub. by U CA Pr) Cal Prin Full Svc.

Reinartz, Dirk. Richard Serra: La Mormaire. LC 98-152349. (Illus.). 120p. 1996. 70.00 (*3-928762-54-0*, 620792, Pub. by Richter Verlag) Dist Art Pubs.

Reinartz, Dirk, jt. auth. see Serra, Richard.

Reinartz, Kay F. Tukwila - Community at the Crossroads. (Illus.). 264p. (Orig.). 1991. 35.00 (*0-9629652-0-0*); pap. 18.00 (*0-9629652-1-9*) City Tukwila.

***Reinartz, Thomas.** Focusing Solutions for Data Mining: Analytical Studies & Experimental Results in Real-World Domains. Carbonell, J. G. & Siekmann, J., eds. LC 99-44746. (Lecture Notes in Computer Science Ser.: Vol. 1623). xv, 309p. 1999. pap. 56.00 (*3-540-66429-7*) Spr-Verlag.

Reinarz, Robert C. Property & Liability Reinsurance Management: A Recognized Text on P. & L. Reinsurance. LC 68-59174. (C). 1969. 15.95 (*0-916910-01-6*) Mission Pub.

Reinaud, M., tr. see Abu al-Fida.

Reinbach, Salomon. Traite d'Epigraphie Grecque. xliv, 560p. reprint ed. write for info. (*0-318-71401-9*); reprint ed. write for info. (*0-318-72106-6*) G Olms Pubs.

Reinberg, Alain. Clinical Chronopharmacology. 260p. 1990. 109.00 (*0-89116-943-1*) Hemisp Pub.

Reinberg, Alain, et al, eds. Annual Review of Chronopharmacology, Vol. 2. (Illus.). 334p. 1986. 108.00 (*0-08-034135-7*, Pub. by PPL) Elsevier.

— Night & Shift Work - Biological & Social Aspects: Proceedings of the 5th International Symposium on Night & Shift Work-Scientific Committee on Shift Work of the Permanent Commission & International Association on Occupational Health (PCIAIH, Rouen, 12-16 May 1980. (Illus.). 509p. 1981. 100.00 (*0-08-025516-7*, Pergamon Pr) Elsevier.

— Recent Advances of the Chronobiology of Allergy & Immunology: Symposium on Chronobiology in Allergy & Immunology, Israel, 1979. LC 80-41028. (Illus.). 358p. 1980. 76.00 (*0-08-025891-3*, Pergamon Pr) Elsevier.

Reinberg, Alain, ed. see International Congress of Pharmacology Staff.

Reinberg, Linda. In the Field: The Language of the Vietnam War. fac. ed. LC 90-41550. 283p. 1991. reprint ed. pap. 87.80 (*0-7837-8127-X*, 204793400008) Bks Demand.

Reinberg, Steven. Persona. LC 97-11848. (Illus.). 160p. 1997. pap. 35.00 (*0-8478-2046-7*, Pub. by Rizzoli Intl) St Martin.

Reinberg, Steven E. First Aid & Safety for Day Care Provider's Instructor's Guide. (Illus.). 50p. (C). 1994. ring bd. 110.00 incl. sl., fiche (*1-884225-04-7*) Communs Skills.

Reinberg, Steven E., ed. see Paturas, James L. & Werdmann, Michael J.

Reinbold, Paul J., jt. auth. see Burgess, David R.

Reinbold, Wolfgang. Der Aelteste Bericht Ueber den Tod Jesu: Literarische Analyse & Historische Kritik der Passionsdarstellungen der Evangelien. (Beihefte zur Zeitschrift fuer die Neutestamentliche Wissenschaft Ser.: Band 69). (GER.). xii, 357p. (C). 1993. lib. bdg. 112.00 (*3-11-014198-1*) Mouton.

***Reinbold, Wolfgang.** Mythenbildungen Und Nationalismus. 319p. 1999. 47.95 (*3-906762-04-1*) P Lang Pubng.

Reinbolt, Jacob C. Meeting Statutory Deadlines: Business Entities' Filing Requirements & Deadlines, Winter 1993, Action Guide, Pt. 7. Lester, Ellen C., ed. (Meeting Statutory Deadlines Ser.). 90p. 1993. pap. text 47.00 (*0-88124-603-4*, BU-11422) Cont Ed Bar-CA.

Reinbolt, William, III. Moses Rose. Danbury, Richard S., ed. 220p. (Orig.). 1996. pap. text 10.95 (*0-89754-125-1*, 12077354-0998) Dan River Pr.

Reinburg, Claire E., jt. auth. see Holmes, Ann.

Reinburg, Claire E., ed. see Harmon, Daniel E.

Reinburg, Claire E., ed. see Holmes, Ann E.

Reinburg, Claire E., jt. ed. see Nadelson, Carol C.

Reinburg, J. Hunter. Aerial Combat Escapades. Ebersole, Michael J., ed. 280p. 1988. pap. 14.95 (*0-9613218-2-2*) GCBA.

Reinburg, Peggy K. Arp Schnitger, Organ Builder: Catalyst for the Centuries. LC 81-47829. 188p. reprint ed. pap. 58.30 (*0-7837-3725-4*, 205790300009) Bks Demand.

Reinburg, Virginia, ed. see Boston College Museum of Art Staff.

Reinburg, Virginia, jt. ed. see Netzer, Nancy.

Reinckens, Sunnhild. Making Dolls. Maclean, Donald, tr. (GER., Illus.). 56p. (J). (ps-3). 1989. reprint ed. pap. 10.95 (*0-86315-093-4*, Pub. by Floris Bks) Gryphon Hse.

Reindeau, Roger, jt. auth. see Rogozinski, Jan.

Reinders. Borrowed Gods & Foreign Bodies. 2000. 59.00 (*0-8133-6715-8*) Westview.

***Reinders, Hans S.** The Future of the Disabled in Liberal Society: An Ethical Analysis. (Revisions Ser.). 344p. 2000. 35.00 (*0-268-02856-7*, Pub. by U of Notre Dame Pr); pap. 17.00 (*0-268-02857-5*, Pub. by U of Notre Dame Pr) Chicago Distribution Ctr.

Reinders, Judy A. & Ross, Steven C. Understanding & Using Supercalc 4. 212p. (C). 1988. pap. text 28.75 (*0-314-34291-5*) West Pub.

Reinders, Judy A., jt. auth. see Ross, Steven C.

Reinders, L. J., tr. see Berezinskii, V. S., et al.

Reinders, Lucas, ed. Environmentally Improved Production Processes & Products: An Introduction. (Environment & Management Ser.: Vol. 6). 112p. (C). 1996. text 73.00 (*0-7923-3786-7*) Kluwer Academic.

Reinders, M. J. Model Adaptations for Image Coding. (Illus.). x, 148p. (Orig.). 1995. pap. 59.50 (*90-407-1203-4*, Pub. by Delft U Pr) Coronet Bks.

Reinders, Reinder & Paul, Kees, eds. Carvel Construction Technique. (Oxbow Monographs in Archaeology: No. 12). (Illus.). 189p. 1991. pap. 42.00 (*0-946897-34-4*, Pub. by Oxbow Bks) David Brown.

Reine, W. F. Prud'homme van, see Prud'homme van Reine, W. F.

Reineccius, Gary. Source Book of Flavors. 2nd ed. 928p. 1993. 209.00 (*0-8342-1307-9*) Aspen Pub.

Reineccius, Gary A., jt. ed. see Risch, Sara J.

Reineck & Reineck Staff. Karte & Fuhrer Zum Yosemite Valley.Tr. of Map & Guide to Yosemite Valley. (GER.). 1992. pap. 2.50 (*0-939666-61-8*) Yosemite Assn.

Reineck & Reineck Staff, tr. see Medley, Steven P.

Reineck & Reineck Staff, tr. see Shenk, Dean.

Reineck, H. E. & Singh, I. B. Depositional Sedimentary Environments-with Reference to Terrigenous Classics. (Illus.). 439p. 1992. 98.95 (*0-387-10189-6*) Spr-Verlag.

Reinecke, C. Sonata, Opus 167: Undine for No Flute & Piano Great Performer's Edition. 32p. 1986. otabind 10.95 (*0-7935-1562-9*, 50336260) H Leonard.

Reinecke, Elisabeth, tr. see Rudin, Josef.

Reinecke, Hans P. Cents Frequency Period: Umrechnungstabellen fuer musikalische Akustik und Musikethnologie. (ENG & GER.). (C). 1970. 36.95 (*3-11-006397-2*) De Gruyter.

Reinecke, Herb. Whittling Simplified: Everything You Need to Know. LC 85-11136. (Illus.). 162p. 1999. pap. 12.95 (*0-930256-14-X*, Vestal Pr) Madison Bks UPA.

Reinecke, John A., et al. Introduction to Business. 6th ed. 750p. 1989. boxed set 46.00 (*0-205-11832-1*, H18328) Allyn.

— Introduction to Business. 6th ed. 750p. 1989. 6.67 (*0-685-44204-7*, H20043); teacher ed. write for info. (*0-318-63844-4*, H18351); teacher ed. write for info. incl. trans. (*0-318-63845-2*, H18377); student ed. 18.00 (*0-685-44205-5*, H25299); write for info. (*0-685-21996-8*, H18369); write for info. (*0-318-63846-0*, H18393); write for info. (*0-685-21997-6*); trans. write for info. (*0-318-63847-9*, H18401) P-H.

Reinecke, John E. The Filipino Piecemeal Sugar Strike of 1924-1925. Beechert, Edward D. & Beechert, Alice, eds. LC 96-35183. 192p. 1996. pap. text 23.00 (*0-8248-1896-2*) UH Pr.

— A Man Must Stand Up: The Autobiography of a Gentle Activist. Beechert, Alice M. & Beechert, Edward D., eds. (Biography Monograph/Pacific & Asian Personal Papers). 96p. (Orig.). 1993. pap. text 12.00 (*0-8248-1517-3*) UH Pr.

Reinecke, Jost, jt. ed. see Engel, Uwe.

Reinecke, Louise. Prayer - Songs for the Very Young & Their Families. LC 98-93396. (Illus.). vi, 22p. (J). (ps-6). 1998. pap. write for info. (*0-9665302-0-9*) Garm Co.

Reinecke, M. F. General Principles of Insurance. (Lawsa Student Text Ser.). 323p. 1989. pap. text 64.00 (*0-409-05046-6*, SA, MICHIE) LEXIS Pub.

Reinecke, Mark A., et al, eds. Cognitive Therapy with Children & Adolescents: A Casebook for Clinical Practice. LC 95-36991. 416p. 1995. lib. bdg. 46.00 (*1-57230-022-1*, 0022) Guilford Pubns.

Reinecke, Mark A., jt. auth. see Freeman, Arthur.

***Reinecke, Martin.** The Sled & Other Stories. 124p. 1999. pap. write for info. (*1-57579-174-9*, Pub. by Pine Hill Pr) Penmarch Pub.

Reinecke, Robert D. & Farrell, Thomas A. Fundamentals of Ophthalmology: A Programmed Text. 1989. 12.50 (*0-317-94087-2*) Am Acad Ophthal.

Reinecke, Robert D. & Herm, Robert. Refraction: A Programmed Text. 3rd ed. (Illus.). 373p. (C). 1983. pap. text 39.95 (*0-8385-8300-8*, A8300-4) Appleton & Lange.

Reinecke, Robert D., ed. see Ophthalmology Annual Staff.

***Reinecke, Thomas C.** Hildegard Jone, 1891-1963: Untersuchungen Zu Leben, Werk und Veroffentlichungskontexten Zugleich eine Studie Zu Einigen Figuren im Denken Anton Weberns und Den von Ihm Vertonten Texten. (Europaische Hochschulschriften: Reihe 1, Deutsche Sprache und Literatur Ser.). 434p. 1999. 52.95 (*3-631-34773-1*) P Lang Pubng.

Reinecke, Thomas C. To Know, Love & Serve God. (Illus.). 200p. (Orig.). 1994. pap. write for info. (*0-9643291-0-7*) Faith Hope & Love.

***Reinecke, William G., ed.** 18th International Symposium on Ballistics, Vols. 1 & 2. LC 99-67717. 1455p. 1999. text 259.95 (*1-56676-901-9*) Technomic.

Reinecker, Herbert. Falle fur den Kommissar: C Level. text 8.95 (*0-88436-920-X*) EMC-Paradigm.

— Der Kommissar Lasst Bitten: Level B. text 8.95 (*0-88436-291-4*) EMC-Paradigm.

Reinefeld, A., jt. ed. see Hellwagner, H.

Reinehr, Frances G. Bloody Mary: Gentle Woman. LC 89-84199. (Illus.). 104p. 1989. pap. 6.95 (*0-934988-16-1*) Foun Bks.

Reinehr, Robert C., jt. auth. see Swartz, Jon D.

Reineke, Martha J. Sacrificed Lives: Kristeva on Women & Violence. LC 96-53642. 1997. 35.00 (*0-253-33299-0*); lib. bdg. 18.95 (*0-253-21128-X*) Ind U Pr.

Reineke, R. K. Veterinary Helminthology. (Illus.). 1983. 52.95 (*0-409-11262-3*) Buttrwrth-Heinemann.

Reineke, Robert A. Challenging the Mind, Touching the Heart: Best Assessment Practices. LC 97-21152. (Illus.). 152p. 1997. 65.95 (*0-8039-6629-6*); pap. 29.95 (*0-8039-6630-X*) Corwin Pr.

Reineker, P., jt. auth. see Kenkre, V. M.

Reineking, James. Logical Space. LC 74-82737. (Illus.). 90p. 1975. 25.00 (*0-8150-0703-5*) Oolp Pr.

Reinelda, Bob & Verbeek, Bertjan. Autonomous Policy-Making by International Organizations. LC 98-7428. 232p. (C). 1998. 85.00 (*0-415-16486-9*) Routledge.

Reinelt, Gerhard. The Traveling Salesman, Vol. 840. LC 94-31562. 1994. 39.95 (*0-387-58334-3*) Spr-Verlag.

Reinelt, Janelle, jt. ed. see Aston, Elaine.

Reinelt, Janelle, jt. ed. see Case, Sue-Ellen.

Reinelt, Janelle G. After Brecht: British Epic Theater. 248p. (Orig.). 1996. pap. text 18.95 (*0-472-08408-9*, 08408) U of Mich Pr.

Reinelt, Janelle G., ed. Crucibles of Crisis: Performing Social Change. LC 96-4110. 256p. (C). 1996. pap. text 19.95 (*0-472-06618-8*, 06618) U of Mich Pr.

— Crucibles of Crisis: Performing Social Change. LC 96-4110. 256p. (C). 1996. text 49.50 (*0-472-09618-4*, 09618) U of Mich Pr.

Reinelt, Janelle G. & Roach, Joseph R., eds. Critical Theory & Performance. (Theater: Theory - Text - Performance Ser.). (Illus.). 464p. (C). 1992. text 55.00 (*0-472-09458-0*, 09458); pap. text 22.95 (*0-472-06458-4*, 06458) U of Mich Pr.

Reinelt, Sabine. Magic of Character Doll. LC 95-146721. (Illus.). 96p. 1999. 29.95 (*0-87588-414-8*) Hobby Hse.

— Zauber der Charakterpuppen: Ebenbilder der Kinder. (GER., Illus.). 96p. (C). 1993. 34.00 (*3-8170-1013-3*, Pub. by Knstvrlag Weingrtn) Intl Bk Import.

— Zauber der Puppenwelt. (GER., Illus.). 128p. (C). 1992. 67.00 (*3-8170-1010-9*, Pub. by Knstvrlag Weingrtn) Intl Bk Import.

Reinen, David P. Guitar Tools: Guitar Study Course. 128p. 1992. student ed. 19.95 (*0-9631942-0-8*) Driftwood Pubns.

Reinen, Judy. Dog Record Book. (Animal Antics Ser.). 1997. 19.95 (*1-57977-004-5*) Havoc Pub.

Reiner, Angela, ed. see Cook, Catherine Holloran & Pfeifer, Janet McGivney.

Reiner, Angela, ed. see Ledbetter, Darriel & Graham, Leland.

Reiner, Annie. The Naked I. 90p. (Orig.). 1994. pap. text 9.95 (*1-881168-22-0*) Red Danceflr.

— The Potty Chronicles: A Story to Help Children Adjust to Toilet Training. LC 91-86. (Illus.). 32p. (J). (ps-1). 1991. pap. 8.95 (*0-945354-35-5*) Am Psychol.

— Visit to the Art Galaxy. LC 91-16989. (Illus.). (J). (gr. 1 up). 1991. 15.95 (*0-671-74957-9*, Green Tiger S&S) S&S Childrens.

Reiner, Anton, jt. ed. see Smeets, Wilhelmus J.

Reiner, Beatrice S. & Kaufman, Irving. Character Disorders in Parents of Delinquents. LC 59-15631. 183p. reprint ed. pap. 56.80 (*0-608-30557-X*, 201994500015) Bks Demand.

Reiner, Carl. All Kinds of Love. LC 92-35890. 1993. 18.95 (*1-55972-163-4*, Birch Ln Pr) Carol Pub Group.

— Continue Laughing: A Novel. LC 94-44308. 288p. 1995. 19.95 (*1-55972-273-8*, Birch Ln Pr) Carol Pub Group.

— How Paul Robeson Saved My Life & Other Mostly Happy Stories. LC 99-31107. 176p. 1999. 20.00 (*0-06-019451-0*, Cliff Street) HarperTrade.

***Reiner, Carl.** How Paul Robeson Saved My Life & Other Stories. 176p. 2000. pap. 10.00 (*0-06-093251-1*, Cliff Street) HarperTrade.

Reiner, Carl, jt. auth. see Brooks, Mel.

Reiner, Christopher. Ogling Anchor. 68p. 1998. pap. 10.00 (*1-880713-14-4*, Pub. by AVEC Bks) SPD-Small Pr Dist.

Reiner, David. Deluxe Anthology of Fiddle Styles. 1979. pap., spiral bd. 18.95 incl. audio (*0-87166-499-2*, 93647P) Mel Bay.

— Deluxe Anthology of Fiddle Styles. 88p. 1979. spiral bd. 9.95 (*0-87166-497-6*, 93647) Mel Bay.

— Deluxe Anthology of Fiddle Styles. 1979. audio 9.98 (*0-87166-498-4*, 93647C) Mel Bay.

Reiner, David & Anick, Peter. Old-Time Fiddling Across America. 184p. 1989. pap. 17.95 (*0-87166-766-5*, 94205); audio 9.98 (*1-56222-641-X*, 94205C) Mel Bay.

— Old-Time Fiddling Across America. 1993. pap., spiral bd. 23.95 incl. audio (*0-7866-0975-3*, 94205P) Mel Bay.

— You Can Teach Yourself Recorder. 1996. VHS 29.95 (*0-7866-2057-9*, 94337VX) Mel Bay.

***Reiner-Drehwald, M. Elena.** Bryophytorum Bibliotheca. (Dissertationes Botanicae Ser.: Bank 54). (Illus.). 102p. 1999. 39.00 (*3-443-62026-4*, Pub. by Gebruder Borntraeger) Balogh.

Reiner, Elsa, et al, eds. Enzymes Hydrolising Organophosphorus Compounds. 1989. text 59.95 (*0-470-21447-3*) P-H.

Reiner, Eric L. Series Sixty-Two Exam Preparations. 184p. (Orig.). 1989. pap. text 69.95 (*0-932889-10-7*) Examco Inc.

Reiner, Erica. Astral Magic in Babylonia. LC 95-76539. (Transactions Ser.: Vol. 85, Pt. 4). (Illus.). 150p. (C). 1995. pap. 15.00 (*0-87169-854-4*, T854-ree) Am Philos.

— Your Thwarts in Pieces, Your Mooring Rope Cut: Poetry from Babylonia & Assyria. Matejka, Ladislav, ed. (Michigan Studies in the Humanities: No. 5). (C). 1985. 10.00 (*0-936534-04-4*) Mich Studies Human.

Reiner, Erica, et al, eds. The Assyrian Dictionary of the Oriental Institute of the University of Chicago, Vol. 11, N, Pts. 1 & 2. LC 56-58292. 1980. lib. bdg. 130.00 (*0-918986-17-6*) Orient Inst.

— The Assyrian Dictionary of the Oriental Institute of the University of Chicago, Vol. 13, Q. LC 56-58292. xxiv, 332p. 1982. text 70.00 (*0-918986-24-9*) Orient Inst.

— The Assyrian Dictionary of the Oriental Institute of the University of Chicago, Vol. 17, S, Pt. 1. LC 56-58292. xxviii, 492p. 1989. 100.00 (*0-918986-55-9*) Orient Inst.

— The Assyrian Dictionary of the Oriental Institute of the University of Chicago, Vol. 17, S, Pt. 2. LC 56-58292. xxiii, 453p. 1992. lib. bdg. 120.00 (*0-918986-78-8*) Orient Inst.

Reiner, Erica & Pingree, D. Babylonian Planetary Omens Pt. 2: Enumu Anu Enlil, Tablet 50-51. LC 79-67168. (Bibliotheca Mesopotamica Ser.: Vol. 2, Pt. 2). 100p. 1981. pap. 20.00 (*0-89003-049-9*) Undena Pubns.

Reiner, Erica, jt. auth. see Pingree, D.

Reiner, Erica, jt. ed. see Oppenheim, A. Leo.

Reiner, Hans. Duty & Inclination: The Fundamentals of Morality. 320p. 1983. lib. bdg. 176.50 (*90-247-2818-5*, Pub. by M Nijhoff) Kluwer Academic.

Reiner, Irving. Class Groups & Picard Groups of Group Rings & Orders. LC 76-10337. (CBMS Regional Conference Series in Mathematics: Vol. 26). 44p. 1986. reprint ed. pap. 21.00 (*0-8218-1676-4*, CBMS/26C) Am Math.

Reiner, Irving, ed. Representation Theory of Finite Groups & Related Topics: Proceedings of the Symposia in Pure Mathematics-Madison, Wis.-1970. LC 79-165201. (Proceedings of Symposia in Pure Mathematics Ser.: Vol. 21). 178p. 1971. text 41.00 (*0-8218-1421-4*, PSPUM/21) Am Math.

Reiner, Irving & Roggenkamp, Klaus W., eds. Orders & Their Applications. (Lecture Notes in Mathematics Ser.: Vol. 1142). x, 306p. 1985. 46.95 (*0-387-15674-7*) Spr-Verlag.

Reiner, Irving, jt. auth. see Curtis, Charles W.

Reiner, Larry. Minute of Silence. LC 90-34659. 268p. 1990. lib. bdg. 18.95 (*0-9626148-0-7*) Integra Pr.

— The Other Shore. unabridged ed. LC 97-50517. 288p. 1998. lib. bdg. 24.75 (*0-9626148-4-X*) Integra Pr.

Reiner, Laurence E. Methods & Materials of Residential Construction. (Illus.). 336p. 1981. text 48.00 (*0-13-578864-1*) P-H.

Reiner, M. Dialogue & Instruction. Beun, Robert-Jan & Baker, M., eds. (NATO ASI Ser.: Vol. 142). 368p. 1995. 90.00 (*3-540-58834-5*) Spr-Verlag.

Reiner, M. Leon, et al. Palestine--Divided or United? The Case for a Bi-National Palestine Before the United Nations. LC 80-39531. 104p. 1983. reprint ed. lib. bdg. 59.75 (*0-8371-2617-7*, MAPA, Greenwood Pr) Greenwood.

***Reiner, Marian, compiled by.** Month-By-Month Poetry: December, January & February. 1999. pap. text 9.95 (*0-590-37900-3*) Scholastic Inc.

Reiner, Martha, ed. see Kleinberg, Howard.

Reiner, Michael B. The Whole Psychology Catalog. 5th ed. 366p. (C). 1996. pap. text 32.25 (*0-15-504153-3*) Harcourt Coll Pubs.

Reiner, Robert. The Blue-Coated Worker: A Sociological Study of Police Unionism. LC 77-85695. (Cambridge Studies in Sociology: No. 10). 307p. reprint ed. pap. 87.50 (*0-8357-7329-9*, 2030616) Bks Demand.

— Policing, 2 vols., Vols. I & II. (International Library of Criminology, Criminal Justice & Penology). (Illus.). 1000p. 1996. text 349.95 (*1-85521-390-7*, Pub. by Dartmth Pub) Ashgate Pub Co.

— The Politics of the Police. 280p. 2000. text 55.00 (*0-19-876544-4*) OUP.

— The Politics of the Police. 2nd ed. 334p. 1993. text 60.00 (0-8020-2942-6); pap. text 19.95 (0-8020-7769-2) U of Toronto Pr.

***Reiner, Thomas.** Semiotics of Musical Time. LC 99-29427. (Berkeley Insights in Linguistics & Semiotics Ser.: Vol. 43). 264p. (C). 2000. text 56.95 (0-8204-4525-8) P Lang Pubng.

Reiner, Thomas A. Trucking Terminal Impact & Community Response: Case Studies in the Philadelphia Region. (Discussion Papers: No. 86). 1975. pap. 10.00 (1-55869-127-8) Regional Sci Res Inst.

Reiner, Traudl & Reiner, Walter. Fitness for Cats: Fight Feline Flab. (Illus.). 82p. 1998. 10.00 (0-7881-5419-2) DIANE Pub.

Reiner, V. Quotients of Coexter Complexes & P-Partitions. LC 91-36297. (Memoirs Ser.: No. 460). 134p. 1992. pap. 27.00 (0-8218-2525-9, MEMO/95/460) Am Math.

Reiner, Walter, jt. auth. see Reiner, Traudl.

Reinerman, Alan J. Austria & the Papacy in the Age of Metternich: Between Conflict & Cooperation, 1809-1830, Vol. 1. LC 79-774. 264p. 1979. reprint ed. pap. 81.90 (0-7837-9188-7, 204988800001) Bks Demand.

— Austria & the Papacy in the Age of Metternich II Vol. 2: Revolution & Reaction 1830-1838. LC 79-774. 429p. 1989. 49.95 (0-8132-0669-3) Cath U Pr.

Reiners, Kenneth G. Addicted to the Addict: From Codependency to Recovery. LC 87-50843. 64p. (Orig.). (YA). (gr. 9-12). 1987. pap. 5.95 (0-934104-06-9) Woodland.

— There's More to Life Than Pumpkins, Drugs & Other False Gods. LC 80-50424. 64p. (Orig.). 1980. pap. 5.95 (0-934104-03-4) Woodland.

Reiners, Kimberly. Life's Winding Roads. 1998. pap. write for info. (1-57553-753-2) Watermrk Pr.

Reinersdorff-Paczensky, Uta Von, see Von Reinersdorff-Paczensky, Uta.

Reinersmann, Elisabeth E., tr. see Heuler, Oliver.

Reinerstsen, H., et al. Fish Farming Technology: Proceeding of the First International Conference, Trondheim, Norway, August 1993. (Illus.). 496p. (C). 1993. text 149.00 (90-5410-326-4, Pub. by A A Balkema) Ashgate Pub Co.

Reinert & Huang, Allen. Children in Conflict: Educational Strategies for the Emotionally Disturbed & Behaviorally Disordered. 3rd ed. 320p. (C). 1990. pap. text 50.20 (0-675-20740-1, Merrill Coll) P-H.

Reinert, Andy & Burke, Bink. I'll Walk Again: Faith, Love, Laughter. LC 86-72724. (Illus.). 240p. (Orig.). 1986. pap. text 14.50 (0-86516-183-6) Bolchazy-Carducci.

Reinert, Benedikt. Haqani als Dichter: Poetische Logik und Phantasie. (Studien zur Sprache, Geschichte und Kultur des Islamischen Orients: Vol. 4). (GER.). viii, 120p. (C). 1972. 46.95 (3-11-002481-0) De Gruyter.

Reinert, Dale R. Sexual Abuse & Incest. LC 97-6704. (Teen Issues Ser.). 104p. (YA). (gr. 6 up). 1997. lib. bdg. 20.95 (0-89490-916-9) Enslow Pubs.

Reinert, Duane F. Love God . . . Clean House . . . Help Others. 72p. 1996. pap. 4.95 (0-8091-3643-0, 3643-0) Paulist Pr.

Reinert, Eric A. Grant's Tomb. (Illus.). 24p. 1997. pap. 3.95 (1-888213-11-6) Eastern National.

Reinert, Gerard H. Death Certificates of the Rich & Famous. (Illus.). 160p. (Orig.). 1996. pap. 19.95 (0-9652340-5-3) Perpetual Pub.

Reinert, J., ed. Chloroplasts. (Results & Problems in Cell Differentiation Ser.: Vol. 10). (Illus.). 280p. 1980. 64.95 (0-387-10082-2) Spr-Verlag.

Reinert, J. & Bajaj, Y. P. S., eds. Applied & Fundamental Aspects of Plant Cell, Tissue, & Organ Culture. (Illus.). xviii, 803p. 1989. reprint ed. 165.95 (0-387-07677-8) Spr-Verlag.

Reinert, J. & Binding, H., eds. Differentiation of Protoplasts & of Transformed Plant Cells. (Results & Problems in Cell Differentiation Ser.: Vol. 12). (Illus.). 180p. 1986. 71.95 (0-387-16539-8) Spr-Verlag.

Reinert, Kenneth A., jt. ed. see Francois, Joseph F.

Reinert, Kevin H., ed. see SETAC Staff.

Reinert, Otto & Arnott, Peter D. Twenty-Three Plays: An Introductory Anthology. (C). 1978. pap. text 32.00 (0-673-39234-1) Addson-Wesley Educ.

Reinert, Paul C. & Shore, Paul. Seasons of Change: Reflections of a Half Century at St. Louis University. LC 96-28829. 186p. 1997. 29.95 (0-9652929-0-8) St Louis Univ.

— Seasons of Change: Reflections on a Half Century at Saint Louis University. xi, 188p. 1996. 29.95 (0-9525929-0-8) St Louis Univ.

Reinert, Rita C. Boots: Trailing the Appalachians. 80p. 1995. pap. 9.95 (0-9645648-0-7) Atir Pr.

— Welcome in the House You Were Born In. Scott, Whitney, ed. 206p. 1999. pap. 14.95 (0-9645648-1-5) Atir Pr.

Reinert, Thomas. Regulating Confusion: Samuel Johnson & the Crowd. LC 95-32412. 208p. 1996. text 49.95 (0-8223-1707-9); pap. text 16.95 (0-8223-1717-6) Duke.

Reinertsen, Donald. Managing the Design Factory: A Toolkit for Product Developers. LC 97-20343. (Illus.). 256p. 1997. 29.50 (0-684-83991-1) Free Pr.

Reinertsen, Donald G., jt. auth. see Smith, Preston G.

Reinertsen, Helge & Haaland, Herborg, eds. Sustainable Fish Farming: Proceedings of the First International Symposium of Sustainable Fish Farming, Oslo, Norway, August 1984. (Illus.). 350p. (C). 1996. text 128.00 (90-5410-567-4, Pub. by A A Balkema) Ashgate Pub Co.

Reinertsen, Lauren D. Clipart Book of Promotional & Program Artwork. 2nd ed. LC 74-84398. (Illus.). 64p. 1974. pap. 11.95 (0-87874-013-9) Galloway.

Reinertsen, Maureen C., tr. see Detaille, Edouard.

Reinertsen, Maureen Carlson, tr. see Detaille, Edouard.

Reinertsen, R. E., jt. ed. see Bech, C.

***Reinertson, Debbie.** Whose Nose? Whose Toes? (Illus.). 16p. (J). (ps). 1999. 7.00 (0-570-05490-7, 56-1953GJ) Concordia.

Reinertson, Raymond N., jt. auth. see Adams, Richard M., II.

Reines, Alvin J. Polydoxy: Explorations in a Philosophy of Liberal Religion. LC 87-2259. 219p. 1987. 32.95 (0-87975-399-4) Prometheus Bks.

Reines, Alvin J., jt. auth. see Abravanel, Isaac.

Reines, Frederick, ed. Cosmology, Fusion & Other Matters: George Gamow Memorial Volume. LC 77-159018. (Illus.). 334p. reprint ed. pap. 103.60 (0-8357-5503-7, 203511800093) Bks Demand.

Reines, Kathryn. The Kiss. 304p. (Orig.). 1996. mass mkt. 5.99 (0-380-78347-9, Avon Bks) Morrow Avon.

Reines, Lew, ed. see Rockwood, Charles A., Jr. & Matsen, III, Frederick A., 3rd.

Reines, Lew, ed. see Roizen, Michael F. & Fleisher, Lee A.

Reinfeld. Chess in a Nutshell. 1990. mass mkt. 5.99 (0-671-73513-6) PB.

Reinfeld, Barbara K. Karel Havlicek. (East European Monographs: No. 98). 135p. 1982. text 52.50 (0-914710-92-3, Pub. by East Eur Monographs) Col U Pr.

Reinfeld, Eric & London, Sherry. Real World after Effects. LC 98-161690. 458p. (C). 1997. write for info. incl. cd-rom (0-201-69619-3) Seymour Pubns.

Reinfeld, Eric, jt. auth. see London, Sherry.

Reinfeld, Fred. Beginner's Guide to Winning Chess. 1980. pap. 10.00 (0-87980-215-4) Wilshire.

— Beginner's Guide to Winning Chess. 2nd rev. ed. 224p. 1996. pap. 13.95 (0-572-02022-8, Pub. by W Foulsham) Trans-Atl Phila.

— Chess for Children, with Moves & Positions Pictured in Photo & Diagram. rev. ed. LC 80-128763. 1980. pap. 9.99 (0-8069-4905-8) Sterling.

— Chess Problems for Beginners. 1979. pap. 7.00 (0-87980-017-8) Wilshire.

— Complete Chess Course. LC 59-13043. 704p. 1959. 26.95 (0-385-00464-8) Doubleday.

— The Complete Chess Player. 300p. 1992. per. 10.00 (0-671-76895-6) S&S Trade.

— Great Brilliancy Prize Games of the Chess Masters. (Illus.). xv, 222p. 1995. pap. text 7.95 (0-486-28614-2) Dover.

— Great Short Games of the Chess Masters. unabridged ed. LC 96-22567. 224p. 1996. reprint ed. pap. text 7.95 (0-486-29266-5) Dover.

— How to Be A Winner at Chess. 1996. pap. 10.00 (0-449-91206-X) Fawcett.

— How to Force Checkmate. (Illus.). 112p. 1947. pap. 3.95 (0-486-20439-1) Dover.

— How to Win at Checkers. 1977. pap. 7.00 (0-87980-068-2) Wilshire.

— Hypermodern Chess. 221p. 1948. pap. 6.95 (0-486-20448-0) Dover.

— Immortal Gamea of Capablanca. 239p. 1990. pap. 7.95 (0-486-26333-9) Dover.

— One Thousand One Brilliant Ways to Checkmate. (Illus.). 1969. reprint ed. pap. 10.00 (0-87980-110-7) Wilshire.

— One Thousand One Winning Chess Sacrifices & Combinations. 1969. reprint ed. pap. 10.00 (0-87980-111-5) Wilshire.

— Pony Express. LC 64-21330. (Illus.). 135p. 1973. pap. 7.00 (0-8032-5786-4, Bison Books) U of Nebr Pr.

— Win at Chess. 120p. 1945. pap. 3.95 (0-486-20438-3) Dover.

Reinfeld, Fred, ed. Chess Tactics for Beginners. 1975. pap. 10.00 (0-87980-019-4) Wilshire.

Reinfeld, Fred, jt. auth. see Hobson, Burton H.

Reinfeld, Fred, ed. see Mason, James.

Reinfeld, Fred, ed. see Spielmann, Rudolf.

Reinfeld, Fred, ed. see Znosko-Borovsky, Eugene.

Reinfeld, Linda. Language Poetry: Writing As Rescue. LC 91-24848. (Horizons in Theory & American Culture Ser.). 192p. 1992. text 27.50 (0-8071-1698-X) La State U Pr.

Reinfeld, Nyles V. Open Heart Surgery: A Second Chance. 192p. 1983. 22.00 (0-13-637520-0); pap. 14.95 (0-13-637512-X) P-H.

Reinfeld, W. Vel. Index of Outreach Programs in Israel. 98p. 1989. pap. write for info. (0-9623723-0-7) AVI CHAI.

Reinfelder, Monika, ed. Amazon to Zami: Towards a Global Lesbian Feminism. LC 96-222750. (Sexual Politics Ser.). 224p. 1997. pap. 21.95 (0-304-33203-8) Continuum.

— Amazon to Zami: Towards a Global Lesbian Feminism. LC 96-222750. (Sexual Politics Ser.). 224p. 1997. 89.50 (0-304-33193-7) Continuum.

Reinforced Concrete Research Council Staff. Long Reinforced Concrete Columns. (Bulletin Ser.: No. 21). 250p. 1986. 5.00 (0-87262-537-0) Am Soc Civil Eng.

Reinganum, Marc R. & Institute of Chartered Financial Analysts Staff. Selecting Superior Securities LC 99-207583. xv, 85 p. 1988. write for info. (0-943205-01-8) RFICFA.

***Reingold, Beth.** Representing Women: Sex, Gender & Legislative Behavior in Arizona & California. LC 99-53084. (Illus.). 368p. 2000. pap. 19.95 (0-8078-4850-6); lib. bdg. 55.00 (0-8078-2538-7) U of NC Pr.

Reingold, Carmel B. The 7 Most Effective Ways to Jumpstart Your Diet. LC 99-191147. 1999. mass mkt. 5.99 (0-440-22587-6) Dell.

Reingold, Carmel B. & Kaufman, William I. The Gourmet Fondue Cookbook. LC 76-15136. 112 p. 1970. write for info. (0-88365-156-4) Galahad Bks.

Reingold, Carmel B., jt. auth. see Burke, David.

Reingold, Edward M., jt. auth. see Dershowitz, Nachum.

Reingold, Edward M., jt. auth. see Kamin, Philip.

Reingold, Ida H., jt. ed. see Reingold, Nathan.

Reingold, Jacquelyn. Girl Gone. LC 97-208568. 1995. pap. 5.25 (0-8222-1471-7) Dramatists Play.

Reingold, Nathan. Science, American Style. LC 90-9068. 414p. (C). 1991. text 42.00 (0-8135-1660-9); pap. text 18.00 (0-8135-1661-7) Rutgers U Pr.

Reingold, Nathan, ed. The Papers of Joseph Vol. 1: The Albany Years, December 1797-October 1832. 496p. 1972. text 80.00 (0-87474-123-8, REP1) Smithsonian.

— The Papers of Joseph Henry Vol. 2: The Princeton Years, November 1832-December 1835. 564p. 1976. text 80.00 (0-87474-164-5, REP2) Smithsonian.

— The Papers of Joseph Henry Vol. 3: The Princeton Years, January 1836-December 1837. LC 72-2005. (Illus.). 585p. 1979. text 80.00 (0-87474-174-2, REP3) Smithsonian.

— The Papers of Joseph Henry Vol. 5: The Princeton Years, January 1841-December 1843. LC 72-2005. (Joseph Henry Papers). (Illus.). 500p. 1985. text 80.00 (0-87474-793-7, REP5) Smithsonian.

— Science in Nineteenth-Century America: A Documentary History. LC 85-1021. xii, 352p. 1997. pap. text 15.00 (0-226-70947-7) U Ch Pr.

Reingold, Nathan & Reingold, Ida H., eds. Science in America: A Documentary History, 1900-1939. LC 81-2584. 504p. 1981. 45.00 (0-226-70946-9) U Ch Pr.

Reingold, Nathan & Rothenberg, Marc, eds. Scientific Colonialism: A Cross-Cultural Comparison - Papers at a Conference at Melbourne, May 25-30, 1981. LC 85-43238. 264p. (Orig.). (C). 1986. pap. text 19.95 (0-87474-785-6) Smithsonian.

Reingold, Ted. Management Strategies That Make U. S. Firms Competitive in the Global Economy. rev. ed. LC 98-9415. (Studies on Industrial Productivity). (Illus.). 250p. 1998. text 50.00 (0-8153-3091-X) Garland.

Reingruber, Michael C. The Data Modeling Hancbook: A Best Practice Approach to Building Quality Data Models. 384p. 1994. 64.99 (0-471-05290-6) Wiley.

***Reinhard, B. J.** Sanji's Seed. (Backyard Ser.). (Illus.). (J). 2000. 12.99 (0-7642-2210-4) Bethany Hse.

***Reinhard, Barbara.** Glow-in-the-Dark Fish: And 59 More Ways to See God Through His Creation. LC 00-8272. (Illus.). 160p. (J). (gr. 1-7). 2000. 12.99 (0-7642-2262-7) Bethany Hse.

Reinhard, D. & Asmussen, J. Diamond Thin Films Handbook. (Illus.). Date not set. text. write for info. (0-8247-9577-6) Dekker.

Reinhard, Dale W. Simply Celebrating Children: Parties As Unique & Special As a Child. 132p. (J). 1991. 12.95 (0-9628888-0-X) Pressed Duck.

Reinhard, David W. The Republican Right since 1945. LC 82-40460. 304p. 1983. 32.50 (0-8131-1484-5) U Pr of Ky.

Reinhard, Donald K. Introduction to Integrated Circuit Engineering. LC 86-80842. 480p. (C). 1987. teacher ed. 6.36 (0-395-37069-8) Lppncott W & W.

Reinhard, Gaup Von, see Von Reinhard, Gaup.

Reinhard, Henry J., jt. auth. see Lambert, James F.

Reinhard, Johan. Discovering the Inca Ice Maiden: My Adventures on Ampato. (My Adventures Ser.). (Illus.). 48p. (YA). (gr. 5 up). 1998. per. 17.45 (0-7922-7142-4, Pub. by Natl Geog) Publishers Group.

Reinhard, John. Burning the Prairie. Vol. 31. 86p. 1988. pap. 5.00 (0-89823-104-3) New Rivers Pr.

— On the Road with Patsy Cline: Poems. Minczeski, John, ed. LC 96-67818. (Minnesota Voices Project Ser.: No. 77). 88p. 1996. pap. 11.95 (0-89823-171-X) New Rivers Pr.

Reinhard, John R., tr. Medieval Pageant. LC 75-129969. (Studies in European Literature: No. 56). 1970. reprint ed. lib. bdg. 75.00 (0-8383-1166-0) M S G Haskell Hse.

Reinhard, Kenneth, jt. auth. see Lupton, Julia R.

Reinhard, Lisa A. The Nutmeg Adventure. (Illus.). 40p. (J). (ps-2). 1994. 9.95 (0-87935-099-7) Colonial Williamsburg.

Reinhard, Margaret. Smart Fast Food Meals. LC 99-220273. 176p. 1999. pap. 8.95 (0-471-34798-1) Wiley.

Reinhard, Margaret, jt. auth. see Forester, Anne.

***Reinhard, Martin & Drefahl, Axel.** Toolkit for Estimating Physicochemical Properties of Organic Compounds. 4p. 1999. cd-rom 295.00 (0-471-19492-1) Wiley.

Reinhard, Martin, jt. auth. see Drefahl, Axel.

Reinhard, Mary B. Acting the Part: An Approach to Moral Education Through Drama. (J). (gr. 5-7). 1982. 24.50 (1-881678-26-1) CSEE.

Reinhard, Michael & Drefahl, Axel. Handbook for Estimating Physiochemical Properties of Organic Compounds. LC 98-15969. (Illus.). 228p. 1998. 69.95 (0-471-17264-2, Wiley-Interscience) Wiley.

***Reinhard, Michael & Drefahl, Axel.** Handbook for Estimating Physiochemical Properties of Organic Compounds. 224p. 1999. 325.00 incl. cd-rom (0-471-17263-4) Wiley.

Reinhard, P. G., jt. auth. see Goeke, K.

Reinhard, Tonia. The Vitamin Sourcebook. LC 98-34410. 320p. 1998. pap. 17.00 (1-56565-878-7, 08787W, Pub. by Lowell Hse) NTC Contemp Pub Co.

Reinhard, Wolfgang, ed. Power Elites & State Building. (The Origins of the Modern State in Europe Ser.). (Illus.). 332p. (C). 1996. text 85.00 (0-19-820547-3) OUP.

Reinhardstoettner, Karl Von, see Von Reinhardstoettner, Karl.

***Reinhardt.** Flash 4 Bible. LC 99-47389. (Bible Ser.). (Illus.). 648p. 2000. 39.99 (0-7645-3356-8) IDG Bks.

Reinhardt, Al S. Jewish Communities of Russian Carpathia: From Early Settlement to WWI. LC 89-85091. (HEB.). 192p. 1989. pap. 12.50 (0-911437-75-4) Labyrinthos.

Reinhardt, C. A., ed. Alternatives to Animal Testing: New Ways in the Biomedical Sciences, Trends & Progress. LC 93-44359. 182p. 1994. pap. 165.00 (3-527-30043-0) Wiley.

Reinhardt, Carl, et al. The Prudent Investor's Guide to Beating the Market. 1996. text 22.35 (0-7863-1160-6, Irwn Prfssnl) McGraw-Hill Prof.

Reinhardt, Christoph A., ed. Alternatives to Animal Testing: New Ways in the Biomedical Sciences, Trends, & Progress. LC 93-44359. 1994. pap. 90.00 (1-56081-831-X, Wiley-VCH) Wiley.

Reinhardt, Curt. Brainwashed. 232p. 1993. pap. write for info. (0-9631949-2-5) Graphic Pub Williamsbrg.

Reinhardt, David P., jt. auth. see Kimbaall, Russell D.

Reinhardt, Dietrich & Schmidt, Eberhard, eds. Food Allergy. LC 88-42557. (Nestle Nutrition Workshop Ser.: Vol. 17). 319p. 1988. reprint ed. pap. 98.90 (0-608-00332-8, 206104900007) Bks Demand.

Reinhardt, Ed & Rogers, Hal. How to Make Your Own Picture Frames. 3rd ed. (Illus.). 144p. 1989. pap. 14.95 (0-8230-2452-0) Watsn-Guptill.

***Reinhardt, Forest L.** Down to Earth. LC 99-30610. 1999. 29.95 (1-57851-192-5, Pub. by Harvard Busn) Random.

Reinhardt, Forest L. & Vietor, Richard H. Business Management & the Natural Environment: Cases & Text. LC 95-30969. (C). 1995. pap. 97.95 (0-538-84328-4) S-W Pub.

Reinhardt, H. J. Analysis of Approximation Methods for Differential & Integral Equations. (Applied Mathematical Sciences Ser.: Vol. 57). (Illus.). xi, 398p. 1985. 89.95 (0-387-96214-X) Spr-Verlag.

Reinhardt, H. W. Penetration & Permeability of Concrete: Barriers to Organic & Contaminating Liquids: State-of-the-Art Report Prepared by Members of the RILEM Technical Committee 146-TCF. LC 98-107870. (Rilem Report Ser.). x, 331p. 1997. write for info. (0-419-22560-9, E & FN Spon) Routledge.

Reinhardt, H. W., ed. Testing During Concrete Construction: Proceedings of RILEM Colloquium, Darmstadt, 1990. (Illus.). 420p. 1991. 85.95 (0-442-31389-6) Chapman & Hall.

Reinhardt, H. W., jt. ed. see Naaman, A. E.

Reinhardt, Hazel, et al. The Changing Reader: Understanding the Forces Changing Newspapers. 128p. 1997. pap. 17.50 (0-9656018-1-1) NMC.

Reinhardt, Hugo, jt. auth. see Alkofer, Reinhard.

Reinhardt, J., jt. auth. see Greiner, W.

Reinhardt, J., jt. auth. see Greiner, Walter.

Reinhardt, J., jt. auth. see Muller, B.

Reinhardt, Jennifer B. The Giant's Toybox. (Illus.). 32p. (J). 1995. 13.95 (0-941711-20-X) Wyrick & Co.

Reinhardt, Jerry. Carving Miniature Carousel Animals: Country Fair Style. (Illus.). 72p. 1996. pap. 12.95 (1-879511-22-3, Vestal Pr) Madison Bks UPA.

Reinhardt, Joachim, jt. auth. see Greiner, Walter.

Reinhardt, Jon M. Foreign Policy & National Integration: The Case of Indonesia. LC 70-175548. (Monographs: No. 17). vi, 230p. 1971. 8.50 (0-938692-12-7) Yale U SE Asia.

Reinhardt, Juergen & Sigleo, Wayne R., eds. Paleosols & Weathering Through Geologic Time: Principles & Applications. LC 87-35459. (Geological Society of America Ser.: Vol. 216). (Illus.). 193p. 1988. reprint ed. pap. 59.90 (0-608-07742-9, 206783000010) Bks Demand.

Reinhardt, K. & Eyrich, K., eds. Sepsis. (Illus.). 410p. 1989. 122.95 (0-387-17763-9) Spr-Verlag.

Reinhardt, Karen & Pranis, Eve. GrowLab Workshop Planning Packet. LC 98-87227. (Growing Science Inquiry Ser.). 144p. (J). 1998. ring bd. 18.00 (0-915873-40-0, 310) Natl Gardening Assn.

Reinhardt, Karen, et al. GrowLab Consultants' Toolkit. LC 98-87227. (Growing Science Inquiry Ser.). 258p. 1998. ring bd. 60.00 (0-915873-39-7, 315) Natl Gardening Assn.

Reinhardt, Karl. Poseidonios, 2 vols. viii, 895p. 1976. write for info. (3-487-06106-6); write for info. (0-318-71005-6); write for info. (0-318-71006-4) G Olms Pubs.

Reinhardt, Klaus. Moscow: The Turning Point? 495p. 1992. 47.50 (0-85496-695-1) Berg Pubs.

Reinhardt, Kurt F. Germany: Two Thousand Years, 2 vols., Vol. 1. rev. ed. LC 60-53139. 1981. pap. 19.95 (0-8044-6692-0) F Ungar Bks.

— Germany: Two Thousand Years, Vol. 2. rev. ed. LC 60-53139. 1981. pap. 19.95 (0-8044-6693-9) F Ungar Bks.

— Germany: Two Thousand Years, 2 vols., Vol. 2. rev. ed. LC 60-53139. 350p. 1992. pap. text 19.95 (0-8044-1784-9) F Ungar Bks.

Reinhardt, Laurel A. The Girl Who Kept Her Magic. (Illus.). 90p. (Orig.). (YA). (gr. 3 up). 1995. pap. 12.00 (0-9648168-0-6) Weaver Dream.

— Seasonal Magic. (Girl Who Kept Her Magic Ser.). 32p. (J). (gr. 4-9). 1997. text, wbk. ed. 3.00 (0-9648168-3-0) Weaver Dream.

***Reinhardt, Lisa, ed.** Davenport's Art Reference & Price Guide, 2000-2001. 2000. 195.00 (0-931036-84-4) Gordon s Art.

— Gordon's Photography Price Annual International, 2000. 2000. 125.00 (0-931036-56-9) Gordon s Art.

— Gordon's Print Price Annual, 2000. 2000. 245.00 (0-931036-19-4) Gordon s Art.

— Lawrence's Dealer Print Prices, 2000. 2000. 145.00 (0-931036-78-X) Gordon s Art.

Reinhardt, Lloyd, jt. ed. see Freadman, Richard.

Reinhardt, Madge. The Unclean Bird. LC 85-72901. 135p. 1986. pap. 8.00 (0-917162-10-2) Back Row Pr.

— The Voice of the Stranger. LC 81-65402. (Illus.). 477p. 1982. pap. 11.00 (0-917162-06-4) Back Row Pr.

R

— The Year of the Silence. LC 78-59573. 177p. 1978. pap. 6.50 (0-917162-08-0) Back Row Pr.

— You've Got to Ride the Subway. LC 76-4760. 278p. 1977. pap. 7.00 (0-917162-02-1) Back Row Pr.

Reinhardt, Mark. The Art of Being Free: Taking Liberties with Tocqueville, Marx, & Arendt. LC 96-46294. (Contestations Ser.). 256p. 1996. text 39.95 (0-8014-3137-9); pap. text 16.95 (0-8014-8424-3) Cornell U Pr.

Reinhardt, Mark W. The Perfectly Contented Meat-Eater's Guide to Vegetarianism: A Book for Those Who Really Don't Want to Be Hassled about Their Diet. LC 97-41023. (Illus.). 252p. 1998. pap. 17.95 (0-8264-1082-0) Continuum.

Reinhardt, Mona. Programmer's Desk Reference for Your Commodore 64. write for info. (0-318-58214-7) P-H.

Reinhardt, Peter A., et al, eds. Pollution Prevention & Waste Minimization in Laboratories. 512p. 1995. lib. bdg. 85.00 (0-87371-975-1, L975) Lewis Pubs.

Reinhardt, Peter A. & Gordon, Judith G. Infectious & Medical Waste Management. (Illus.). 296p. 1990. boxed set 99.95 (0-87371-158-0, L158) Lewis Pubs.

*Reinhardt, Sophie. Tizian In England: Zur Kunstrezeption Am Hof Karls I. (GER.). 379p. 1999. 57.00 (3-631-34592-5) P Lang Pubng.

Reinhardt, Stefan. Die Darstellung der Revolution Von 1848/49 In Den Lebenserinnerungen Von Carl Schurz und Otto Von Corvin. 101p. 1999. 26.95 (3-631-34340-X) P Lang Pubng.

Reinhardt, Steven G. Justice in the Sarladais, 1770-1790. LC 90-28831. (Illus.). 336p. 1991. text 47.50 (0-8071-1587-8); pap. text 19.95 (0-8071-1658-0) La State U Pr.

Reinhardt, Steven G., ed. The Sun King: Louis XIV & the New World. (Studies in Louisiana Culture: Vol. III). (Illus.). 344p. (Orig.). 1984. write for info. (0-916137-00-7); pap. write for info. (0-916137-01-5) L A Mus Foun.

Reinhardt, Steven G. & Cawthon, Elisabeth A., eds. Essays on the French Revolution: Paris & the Provinces. LC 91-22146. (Walter Prescott Webb Memorial Lectures: No. 25). 144p. 1992. 25.95 (0-89096-498-X) Tex A&M Univ Pr.

Reinhardt, Steven G., jt. ed. see Buisseret, David.

Reinhardt, Steven G., jt. ed. see Morris, Christopher.

Reinhardt, Thomas A., et al. Ornamental Grasses: Design Ideas, Uses, & Varieties. LC 95-13522. Orig. Title: Ornamental Grass Gardening. (Illus.). 128p. 1995. pap. 14.95 (1-56799-219-6, Friedman-Fairfax) M Friedman Pub Grp Inc.

Reinhardt, Timothy E. & Ottmar, Roger D. Smoke Exposure among Wildland Firefighters: A Review & Discussion of Current Literature. 72p. 1997. reprint ed. 14.20 (0-89904-678-9, Ecosytems Resrch); reprint ed. pap. 8.20 (0-89904-679-7, Ecosytems Resrch) Crumb Elbow Pub.

Reinhardt, Uwe E., jt. ed. see Altman, Stuart H.

Reinhardt, Uwe E., jt. ed. see Shortell, Stephen M.

Reinhardt, W. P., jt. auth. see Blumel, R.

Reinhardt Werba Bowen Advisory Services Staff. The Prudent Investor's Guide to Beating the Market. 192p. 1996. pap. 30.00 (0-7863-0365-4, Irwn Prfssnl) McGraw-Hill Prof.

Reinhardt, Werner, et al. Deutsche Fachsprache der Technik. (Studien Zu Sprache und Technik Ser.: Bd. 3). (GER.). xi, 174p. 1992. write for info. (3-487-09608-0) G Olms Pubs.

*Reinhart. Everyday Math Made E-Z. 224p. 2000. pap. 17.95 (1-56382-448-5) E-Z Legal.

Reinhart. Rainmakers Off Wall Street. 2000. 24.95 (0-07-135606-1) McGraw.

Reinhart, A. Kevin. Before Revelation: The Boundaries of Muslim Moral Thought. 225p. 1996. pap. 19.95 (0-614-21213-8, 1417) Kazi Pubns.

— Before Revelation: The Boundaries of Muslim Moral Thought. LC 94-13372. (SUNY Series in Middle Eastern Studies). 267p. (C). 1995. text 59.50 (0-7914-2289-5); pap. text 19.95 (0-7914-2290-9) State U NY Pr.

Reinhart, B. L. Differential Geometry of Folitations: The Fundamental Integrability Problem, Set. (Ergebnisse der Mathematik Ser.: Folge 2, Vol. 99). 195p. 1983. 111.95 (0-387-12269-9) Spr-Verlag.

Reinhart, C., et al, eds. Irritation Testing of Skin & Mucous Membranes: Proceedings of a Workshop Held at the Karthhaus-Ittingen, near Frauenfeld, Switzerland, April 1984. (Illus.). 180p. 1985. pap. 41.00 (0-08-032004-X, Pub. by PPL) Elsevier.

*Reinhart, Carlene. The Pad Process Guide; The Pad Process Toolbox; Performance, Analysis & Development, 2 vols., Set. (Illus.). 106p. 1999. pap. 125.00 (0-9672850-1-1) Manta Press.

Reinhart, Carlene, jt. auth. see Chalofsky, Neal E.

*Reinhart, Carmen M., ed. Accounting for Saving: Financial Liberalization, Capital Flows & Growth in Latin America & Europe. 469p. 1999. 24.95 (1-886938-58-X) IADB.

Reinhart, Carmen M., et al. Dealing with Capital Inflows: Are There Any Lessons? LC 97-188482. (Research for Action Ser.). ix, 46p. 1996. write for info. (952-9520-42-5) UN.

Reinhart, Carmen M., jt. ed. see Khan, Mohsin S.

Reinhart, Cornell, ed. & intro. see Johnson, Isaac.

Reinhart, Debra, ed. see American Society of Civil Engineers Staff.

Reinhart, Debra R. & Townsend, Timothy G. Landfill Bioreactor Design & Operation. LC 97-22220. 208p. 1997. boxed set 69.95 (1-56670-259-3) Lewis Pubs.

Reinhart, Dietrich, jt. auth. see Kwatera, Michael.

Reinhart, G. D., jt. ed. see Jameson, D. M.

Reinhart, Gregory A. & Carey, Daniel P., eds. Recent Advances in Canine & Feline Nutrition Vol. II: 1998 Iams Nutrition Symposium Proceedings. LC 99-158843. 564p. 1998. text 11.00 (1-882203-21-6) Orange Frazer.

Reinhart, Gunther, jt. ed. see Ahlers, Rolf-Juergen.

Reinhart, H. W. & Naaman, A. E., eds. High Performance Fiber-Reinforced Cement Composites: Proceedings of the International Rilem-ACI Workshop. (Rilem Proceedings Ser.). (Illus.). 584p. 1992. mass mkt. 156.50 (0-419-17630-6, E & FN Spon) Routledge.

Reinhart, J. R. The Power of Knowing Who I Am in Christ. LC 82-73254. 220p. 1983. pap. 8.95 (0-918060-04-4) Burn Hart.

Reinhart, Jo A., jt. auth. see Morgan, Sharon R.

Reinhart, Johanna M., ed. Small Boat Design. (Illus.). 79p. 1983. pap. text 12.00 (0-89955-393-1, Pub. by ICLARM) Intl Spec Bk.

Reinhart, K., et al, eds. Sepsis: Current Perspectives in Pathophysiology & Therapy. LC 94-373. (Update in Intensive Care & Emergency Medicine Ser.: Vol. 18). 1994. 98.00 (0-387-57349-6) Spr-Verlag.

Reinhart, K. & Eyrich, K., eds. Clinical Aspects of O2-Transport & Tissue Oxygenation. (Illus.). xiii, 511p. 1989. 146.00 (0-387-51470-8, 3312) Spr-Verlag.

Reinhart, Kimberly K. Successfully Prepare Your Child for Life: Straight-to-the-Point Parenting Tips, Guidelines, Activities & Resources Guaranteed to Prepare Your Child for Kindergarten & Beyong. (Children's Activities; Resources; Tips for Parenting Success Ser.). (Illus.). 85p. (Orig.). 1997. pap. 15.99 (0-9659126-0-4) Principles Pub.

Reinhart, L. P., jt. auth. see Streeter, M. K.

*Reinhart, Mark S. Abraham Lincoln on Screen: A Filmography of Dramas & Documentaries Including Television, 1903-1997. LC 99-33316. (Illus.). 304p. 1999. lib. bdg. 49.95 (0-7864-0602-X) McFarland & Co.

*Reinhart, Max. Imperiled Heritage: Tradition, History & Utopia in Early Modern German Literature. LC 00-25370. (Studies in European Cultural Transition). 2000. 82.95 (0-7546-0059-9, Pub. by Ashgate Pub) Ashgate Pub Co.

Reinhart, Max. Infinite Boundaries: Order, Disorder, & Reorder in Early Modern German Culture. LC 97-32755. (Sixteenth Century Essays & Studies: Vol. 40). 408p. 1998. 45.00 (0-940474-43-3, SCJP) Truman St Univ.

— Johann Hellwig: A Descriptive Bibliography. LC 92-42474. (GERM Ser.). x, 160p. 1993. 65.00 (1-879751-46-1) Camden Hse.

Reinhart, Max, jt. auth. see Hellwig, Johann.

Reinhart, Melani. Chiron & the Healing Journey. LC 99-220283. 1999. pap. 14.95 (0-14-019573-4, PuffinBks) Peng Put Young Read.

*Reinhart, Peter. Bread upon the Waters: A Pilgrimage Toward Self-Discovery & Spiritual Truth. 192p. 2000. 22.00 (0-7382-0183-9) Perseus Pubng.

Reinhart, Peter. Brother Juniper's Bread Book: Slow Rise as Method & Metaphor. (Illus.). 224p. 1993. pap. 12.00 (0-201-62467-2) Addison-Wesley.

— Crust & Crumb: Bread Revolution. LC 98-18538. (Illus.). 352p. 1998. 29.95 (1-58008-003-0) Ten Speed Pr.

— The Recovery of Sacred Psychology. 1998. write for info. (0-201-48396-3) Addison-Wesley.

— Sacramental Magic in a Smalltown Cafe. 240p. 1994. 20.00 (0-201-62259-9) Addison-Wesley.

Reinhart, Richard B. FAA Medical Certification: Guidelines for Pilots. 3rd ed. LC 97-18886. 264p. 1997. pap. 24.95 (0-8138-2769-8) Iowa St U Pr.

Reinhart, Richard O. Basic Flight Physiology. 248p. 1992. 34.95 (0-8306-3890-3, 4141) McGraw-Hill Prof.

— Basic Flight Physiology. 2nd ed. 285p. 1996. pap. 59.95 (0-07-052223-5) McGraw.

— FAA Medical Certification: The New Rules. 2nd ed. LC 91-31005. (Illus.). 272p. 1996. pap. text 24.95 (0-07-052251-0) McGraw.

— Fit for Flight: Flight Physiology & Human Factors for Aircrew. 2nd ed. LC 99-27343. (Illus.). 266p. 1999. pap. 27.95 (0-8138-1567-3) Iowa St U Pr.

— Fit to Fly: A Pilot's Guide to Health & Safety. 1992. 24.95 (0-07-051822-X) McGraw.

— Fit to Fly: A Pilot's Guide to Health & Safety. (Illus.). 208p. 1992. 24.95 (0-8306-2070-2, 3682); pap. 15.95 (0-8306-2059-1, 3682) McGraw-Hill Prof.

Reinhart, Robert. Telling Moments: 15 Gay Monologues. LC 93-45366. (Acting Ser.). 96p. 1994. pap. 8.95 (1-55783-163-7) Applause Theatre Bk Pubs.

Reinhart, Rodney E. Splinters on the Wind. (Illus.). 1985. 3.00 (0-931081-01-7) Operation DOME.

Reinhart, Shirley Rogers. The Blue Scarab. LC 98-83258. 336p. 2000. pap. 16.50 (0-88739-250-4) Creat Arts Bk.

Reinhart, Susan M. Testing Your Grammar. 160p. 1985. pap. text 13.95 (0-472-08054-7, 08054) U of Mich Pr.

*Reinhart, Susan M. & Fisher, Ira. Speaking & Social Interaction: Activities for Intermediate to Advanced Esl Students. 2nd ed. (Illus.). 128p. (C). 2000. pap. text 16.95 (0-472-08650-2, 08650) U of Mich Pr.

Reinhart, Susan M., jt. auth. see Madden, Carolyn G.

Reinhart, T. S., ed. see International SAMPE Technical Conference Staff.

Reinhart, Tamany. Last Night While I Lay Dreaming. 1998. pap. write for info. (1-58235-024-8) Watermrk Pr.

Reinhart, Tanya. Anaphora & Semantic Interpretation. LC 84-16267. 208p. 1985. reprint ed. pap. text 10.95 (0-226-70955-8) U Ch Pr.

Reinhart, Theodore R., ed. The Archaeology of 18th Century Virginia, No. 35. (Illus.). 365p. (C). 1996. pap. 28.00 (1-884626-28-9) Archeolog Soc.

— The Archaeology of Shirley Plantation. fac. ed. LC 84-15245. (Illus.). 238p. 1984. reprint ed. pap. 73.80 (0-7837-7983-6, 204773900008) Bks Demand.

— A Cumulative Index to the Quarterly Bulletin of the Archeological Society of Virginia 1940-1990, No. 24. 179p. 1991. pap. 28.00 (1-884626-10-6) Archeolog Soc.

Reinhart, Theodore R. & Hodges, Mary E., eds. Early & Middle Archaic Research in Virginia, a Synthesis, Vol. 22. 173p. 1990. pap. 28.00 (1-884626-08-4) Archeolog Soc.

— Late Archaic & Early Woodland Research in Virginia, a Synthesis, Vol. 23. 275p. 1991. pap. 28.00 (1-884626-09-2) Archeolog Soc.

— Middle & Late Woodland Research in Virginia, a Synthesis, Vol. 29. 311p. 1992. pap. 28.00 (1-884626-12-2) Archeolog Soc.

Reinhart, Theodore R. & Pogue, Dennis J., eds. The Archaeology of 17th Century Virginia, a Synthesis, Vol. 30. 402p. 1993. pap. 28.00 (1-884626-13-0) Archeolog Soc.

Reinhart, Theodore R., jt. ed. see Sprinkle, John H., Jr.

Reinhartsen & Riherd. Language Through Literature. 256p. (C). 1997. per. 48.95 (0-7872-3737-X, 41373701) Kendall-Hunt.

Reinhartz, jt. auth. see Beach.

Reinhartz, Adele. "Why Ask My Name?" Anonymity & Identity in Biblical Narrative. LC 97-44216. 240p. 1998. text 39.95 (0-19-509970-2) OUP.

Reinhartz, Dennis. The Cartographer & the Literati Herman Moll & His Intellectual Circle. LC 97-10515. (Illus.). 256p. 1997. text 89.95 (0-7734-8604-6) E Mellen.

— Milovan Djilas: A Revolutionary As a Writer. (East European Monographs: No. 89). 112p. 1981. text 58.00 (0-914710-83-4, Pub. by East Eur Monographs) Col U Pr.

Reinhartz, Dennis & Colley, Charles C., eds. The Mapping of the American Southwest. LC 86-22992. (Special Collections Publication of the University of Texas at Arlington Ser.: No. 1). (Illus.). 112p. 1987. reprint ed. 29.95 (0-89096-237-5) Tex A&M Univ Pr.

Reinhartz, Dennis & Maizlish, Stephen E., eds. Essays on Walter Prescott Webb & the Teaching of History. LC 85-40047. (Walter Prescott Webb Memorial Lectures: No. 19). 116p. 1985. 18.95 (0-89096-234-0) Tex A&M Univ Pr.

Reinhartz, Dennis & Reinhartz, Judy. Geography Across the Curriculum. 96p. 1990. pap. 10.95 (0-8106-3070-2) NEA.

*Reinhartz, Dennis & Saxon, Gerald D., eds. The Mapping of the Entradas into the Greater Southwest. annot. ed. (Illus.). 256p. 1998. 37.50 (0-8061-3047-4) U of Okla Pr.

Reinhartz, Dennis, jt. ed. see Palmer, Stanley.

Reinhartz, Jehuda & Mosse, George L. The Impact of Western Nationalisms. (Illus.). 336p. (C). 1992. 69.95 (0-8039-8766-8) Sage.

Reinhartz, Judy, ed. Teacher Induction. 128p. 1989. pap. 14.95 (0-8106-3003-6) NEA.

Reinhartz, Judy & Beach, Don M. Teaching & Learning in the Elementary School: Focus on Curriculum. LC 96-33011. 1996. text 60.00 (0-02-399285-9, Merrill Pub Co) Macmillan.

Reinhartz, Judy & Van Cleef, Daniel. Teach - Practice - Apply: The TPA Instructional Model, K-8. 112p. 1986. pap. 10.95 (0-8106-1830-3) NEA.

Reinhartz, Judy, jt. auth. see Reinhartz, Dennis.

Reinharz, Jehuda & Mendes-Flohr, Paul R., eds. The Jew in the Modern World: A Documentary History. 2nd ed. (Illus.). 766p. (C). 1995. pap. text 36.95 (0-19-507453-X) OUP.

Reinharz, Jehuda & Shapira, Anita, eds. Essential Papers on Zionism. (Essential Papers on Jewish Studies). 750p. (C). 1995. text 75.00 (0-8147-7448-2); pap. text 27.50 (0-8147-7449-0) NYU Pr.

Reinharz, Jehuda, jt. auth. see Halpern, Ben.

Reinharz, Peter. Killer Kids, Bad Law: Tales of the Juvenile Court System. LC 95-51179. 336p. 1996. 24.95 (1-56980-070-7) Barricade Bks.

Reinharz, Shulamit. On Becoming a Social Scientist. 466p. (C). 1991. pap. 24.95 (0-87855-968-X) Transaction Pubs.

— On Becoming a Social Scientist. LC 79-83577. (Jossey-Bass Social & Behavioral Science Ser.). 442p. reprint ed. pap. 137.10 (0-8357-6886-4, 203793800009) Bks Demand.

— Social Research Methods, Feminist Perspectives. (Athene Ser.). 1993. text 50.01 (0-08-032794-X, Pub. by PPI); pap. text 21.01 (0-08-032793-1, Pub. by PPI) Elsevier.

Reinharz, Shulamit & Davidman, Lynn. Feminist Methods in Social Research. 424p. 1992. pap. text 29.95 (0-19-507386-X, 3474) OUP.

Reinharz, Shulamit & Rowles, Graham D., eds. Qualitative Gerontology. 336p. (C). 1987. 36.95 (0-8261-5230-9) Springer Pub.

Reinharz, Shulamit, jt. ed. see Conrad, Peter.

Reinheimer, Brent A. USMLE Step 1 Recall: Buzzwords for the Boards. 18p. 28.00 (0-683-30639-1) Lppncott W & W.

— USMLE Step 1 Recall: Buzzwords for the Boards. LC 98-55690. (Recall Ser.). 1999. 15.95 (0-683-30713-4) Lppncott W & W.

Reinherz, E. L., et al, eds. Leukocyte Typing II: Human B Lymphocytes, Vol. 2. (Illus.). 530p. 1985. 215.00 (0-387-96176-3) Spr-Verlag.

— Leukocyte Typing II: Human Myeloid & Hematopoietic Cells, Vol. 3. (Illus.). xvi, 366p. 1985. 174.00 (0-387-96177-1) Spr-Verlag.

— Leukocyte Typing II: Human T Lymphocytes, Vol. 1. (Illus.). 575p. 1985. 215.00 (0-387-96175-5) Spr-Verlag.

Reinhold. Golden Age of August. 1978. 39.95 (0-88866-585-7); 19.95 (0-88866-586-5) Edgar Kent.

— Past & Present. 1972. 29.95 (0-88866-508-3); 39.95 (0-88866-509-1) Edgar Kent.

*Reinhold, Ludwig. RF Circuit Design: Theory & Applications. 3rd ed. 642p. 2000. pap. 100.00 (0-13-095323-7, Prentice Hall) P-H.

Reinhold, Amy J., jt. auth. see Colletta, Nat J.

Reinhold, Barbara B. Toxic Work. 288p. 1997. pap. 12.95 (0-452-27275-0, Plume) Dutton Plume.

Reinhold, Gerd. Soziologie-Lexikon. 2nd ed. (GER.). 677p. 1992. 85.00 (0-614-00539-6, 3486223402) Fr & Eur.

*Reinhold, Janet E. How to Bury a Stainless Steel Time Capsule: If You Really Want to Do That. 4th rev. ed. (Illus.). 52p. 1999. pap. 15.00 (1-891406-27-2, FPP L003) Future Pubg.

Reinhold, Janet E. How to Bury Our Stainless Steel Time Capsule. 3rd rev. ed. (Illus.). iv, 18p. (YA). 1997. reprint ed. 9.00 (1-891406-06-X, FPP 003); reprint ed. 9.00 (1-891406-08-6, FPP 003); reprint ed. ring bd. 9.00 (1-891406-07-8, FPP 003) Future Pubg.

*Reinhold, Janet E. A Sampling of Time Capsule Contents. 4th rev. ed. (Illus.). 126p. 2000. pap. 25.00 (1-891406-30-2, FPP L001) Future Pubg.

— Time Capsule Preservation. (Illus.). 22p. 1999. pap. 15.00 (1-891406-25-6, FPP L100) Future Pubg.

Reinhold, Janet E. Your Time Capsule: Brainstorming Container & Ceremony. 3rd rev. ed. (Illus.). 25p. (YA). 1997. reprint ed. 15.00 (1-891406-03-5, FPP 006); reprint ed. 15.00 (1-891406-05-1, FPP 006); reprint ed. ring bd. 15.00 (1-891406-04-3, FPP 006) Future Pubg.

*Reinhold, Janet E. Your Time Capsule: Brainstorming Container & Ceremony. 4th rev. ed. (Illus.). 50p. 1999. pap. 15.00 (1-891406-23-X, FPP L006) Future Pubg.

Reinhold, Janet E., ed. see Kunkle, James E.

Reinhold, Janet H. A Sampling of Time Capsule Contents. 2nd rev. ed. (Illus.). ii, 50p. (YA). 1997. reprint ed. 15.00 (1-891406-00-0, FPP 001); reprint ed. 15.00 (1-891406-02-7, FPP 001); reprint ed. ring bd. 15.00 (1-891406-01-9, FPP 001) Future Pubg.

*Reinhold, Janet R. Our Expectations for Preservation. large type ed. (Illus.). 8p. 1999. 5.00 (1-891406-26-4) Future Pubg.

Reinhold, Kathy, et al, eds. Favorite Hymns: And High Contrast Photographs. large type ed. (Harvard Ranch Ser.: No. 3). (Illus.). 60p. 1999. 24.95 (1-893630-27-7) Harvard Ranch.

— Verses from the Bible: Illuminated by Stained Glass Windows. large type ed. (Harvard Ranch Ser.: No. 1). (Illus.). 60p. 1999. 24.95 (1-893630-26-9) Harvard Ranch.

— A Walk in the Garden: An Illustrated Journey with Verse. large type ed. (Harvard Ranch Ser.: No. 2). (Illus.). 48p. 1999. 24.95 (1-893630-25-0) Harvard Ranch.

Reinhold, L., et al, eds. Progress in Phytochemistry, 2 vols., 5. LC 68-24347. 1978. 105.00 (0-08-022645-0, Pub. by Pergamon Repr) Franklin.

Reinhold, L. & Liwschitz, Y., eds. Progress in Phytochemistry, 1. LC 68-24347. 731p. 1968. reprint ed. pap. 200.00 (0-608-08324-0, 201617700001) Bks Demand.

— Progress in Phytochemistry, 2. LC 68-24347. 523p. 1970. reprint ed. pap. 162.20 (0-608-08325-9, 201617700002) Bks Demand.

Reinhold, Margaret. How to Survive in Spite of Your Parents. Date not set. pap. 5.99 (0-7493-2198-9) Heinemann.

Reinhold, Meyer. From Republic to Principate: An Historical Commentary on Cassius Dio's; Roman History; Books 49-52. LC 87-9498. (American Philological Association Philological Monographs). 261p. 1988. pap. 27.00 (1-55540-246-1, 40 00 34) OUP.

Reinhold, Meyer, jt. ed. see Lewis, Naphtali.

Reinhold, Meyer, jt. ed. see Feldman, Louis H.

Reinhold, Meyer, jt. ed. see Haase, Wolfgang.

Reinhold, Michael. Why Rush Limbaugh Is Wrong: A Look at the Man & the Issues Surrounding Him. LC 95-77891. 275p. (Orig.). 1996. pap. write for info. (0-9647470-1-4) Mighty Pen.

Reinhold, Michael, jt. auth. see Rahman, Michael.

Reinhold, Ronald W. & Astle, Richard M. The Commonsense MBA! Lessons & Encouragement for the Entrepreneur. LC 93-90237. 248p. (Orig.). pap. 16.95 (0-9636366-5-0) Entrep Grp.

Reinhold, Ruth M. Sky Pioneering: Arizona in Aviation History. LC 81-11514. (Illus.). 232p. 1982. pap. 16.95 (0-8165-0757-0) U of Ariz Pr.

Reinhold, Timothy A., ed. see International Workshop on Wind Tunnel Modeling Criteria & Techniques in Civil Engineering Application Staff.

Reinhold, Walter. Culture 3.0 Workbook. 3rd rev. ed. 188p. 1997. pap. text 29.00 (0-9624372-6-3) Cultural Rescs.

Reinhold, Walter W. Culture 2.0 Workbook: Interdisciplinary Lessons. rev. ed. 310p. 1992. pap. 45.00 (0-9624372-4-7) Cultural Rescs.

*Reinholdsson, Peter. Making Music Together: An Interactionist Perspective on Small-Group Performance in Jazz. LC 98-215452. (Studia Musicologica Upsaliensia Nova Ser.: Vol. 14). 440 p. 1998. pap. 97.50 (91-554-4243-9, Pub. by Almqvist Wiksell) Coronet Bks.

Reinholdt, Bill, jt. auth. see Andersen, Honey.

Reinholdt, Bill, jt. auth. see Anderson, Honey.

Reinholtz, Charles F., jt. auth. see Mabie, Hamilton H.

Reinhorn, Marc. Dictionnaire Laotien-Francais, 2 vols., Set.Tr. of Laotian-French Dictionary. (FRE & LAO.). 2000p. 1970. 175.00 (0-8288-6527-2, M-6481) Fr & Eur.

Reinhoudt, D. N. Structure & Activity of Anti-Tumour Agents. 1982. text 155.50 (90-247-2783-9) Kluwer Academic.

— Supramolecular Materials & Technologies. LC 99-18991. 320p. 1999. 185.00 (0-471-97367-X) Wiley.

An Asterisk (*) at the beginning of an entry indicates that the title is appearing for the first time.

Reinicke, Wolfgang H. Banking, Politics & Global Finance: American Commercial Banks & Regulatory Change, 1980-1990. (Studies in International Political Economy). 256p. 1995. 90.00 (*1-85898-176-X*) E Elgar.

— Building a New Europe: The Challenge of System Transformation & Systemic Reform. 216p. (C). 1993. pap. 14.95 (*0-8157-7391-9*) Brookings.

— Deepening the Atlantic: Toward a New Transatlantic Marketplace? 96p. 1996. pap. 12.00 (*3-89204-802-9*) Brookings.

— Global Public Policy: Governing Without Government? LC 98-8941. 308p. 1998. 42.95 (*0-8157-7390-0*) Brookings.

Reinicke, Wolfgang H., jt. auth. see Heilemann, Ullrich.

Reinier, Jacqueline S. American Childhood 1775 to 1865. LC 96-25091. 1996. 33.00 (*0-8057-4102-X*, Twyne) Mac Lib Ref.

Reinier, Jacqueline S., jt. auth. see Clement, Priscilla F.

Reinig, Christa. Idleness Is the Root of All Love. Mueller, Ilze, tr. from GER. LC 91-11708. 114p. 1991. 18.95 (*0-934971-22-6*); pap. 10.00 (*0-934971-21-8*) Calyx Bks.

Reiniger, Anne, et al. NYSPCC Professionals' Handbook Identifying & Reporting Child Abuse & Neglect. 7th rev. ed. Charnizon, Marlene, ed. (Illus.). 80p. 1997. pap. text 12.95 (*0-9628247-0-4*) NYSPCC.

***Reiniger, Anne, et al.** NYSPCC Professionals' Handbook on Providing Supervised Visitation. 158p. 2000. pap. 15.00 (*0-9628247-1-2*) NYSPCC.

Reinikka, Merle A. A History of the Orchid. rev. ed. (Illus.). 340p. 1995. 29.95 (*0-88192-325-7*) Timber.

Reining, Conrad C. The Zande Scheme: An Anthropological Case Study of Development in Africa. LC 65-24665. (Northwestern University African Studies Ser.: No. 17). 285p. reprint ed. pap. 88.40 (*0-608-14324-3*, 201672100004) Bks Demand.

Reining, Priscilla & Tinker, Irene, eds. Population: Dynamics, Ethics & Policy. LC 75-4498. (AAAS Miscellaneous Publications: No. 75-5). 192p. reprint ed. pap. 59.60 (*0-7837-0062-8*, 204030900016) Bks Demand.

Reininger, Gustave, ed. Centering Prayer in Daily Life & Ministry. LC 97-33168. 144p. 1997. pap. 11.95 (*0-8264-1041-3*) Continuum.

Reininges, Gustave, ed. The Diversity of Centering Prayer. LC 99-18005. 128p. 1998. pap. 11.95 (*0-8264-1115-0*) Continuum.

***Reinink, Adriaan W. & Stumpel, Jeroen.** Memory & Oblivion. LC 99-51941. 1999. write for info. (*0-7923-4213-5*) Kluwer Academic.

***Reinink, G. J. & Klugkist, A. C.** After Bardaisan: Studies on Continuity & Change in Syriac Christianity in Honour of Professor Han. J. W. Drijvers. xvi, 366p. 1999. 103.00 (*90-429-0735-5*, Pub. by Peeters Pub) Bks Intl VA.

Reinis, J. G. The Portrait Medallions of David D'Angers: An Illustrated Catalogue of David's Contemporary & Retrospective Portraits. (Illus.). 528p. 1999. text 285.00 (*0-937370-01-0*) Polymath Pr.

Reinis, Stanislav & Goldman, Jerome M. The Chemistry of Behavior: A Molecular Approach to Neuronal Plasticity. LC 82-13294. 622p. 1982. 110.00 (*0-306-41161-X*, Plenum Trade) Perseus Pubng.

***Reinisch, August.** International Organizations Before National Courts. LC 99-11072. (Cambridge Studies in International & Comparative Law: Vol. 10). 448p. (C). 2000. 85.00 (*0-521-65326-6*) Cambridge U Pr.

Reinisch, June M. The Kinsey Institute New Report on Sex. 1994. pap. 7.99 (*0-312-95184-1*) St Martin.

Reinisch, June M. & Beasley, Ruth. The Kinsey Institute New Report on Sex. 560p. 1991. pap. 17.95 (*0-312-06386-5*) St Martin.

Reinisch, K. & Thoma, M., eds. Large Scale Systems: Theory & Applications, 1989. (IFAC Proceedings Ser.: No. 9009). 580p. 1990. 255.75 (*0-08-035731-8*, Pergamon Pr) Elsevier.

Reinisch, Leonhard, ed. Theologians of Our Time. LC 64-17067. 1964. pap. 10.50 (*0-268-00378-5*) U of Notre Dame Pr.

Reinisch, R., jt. ed. see Kajzar, F.

Reinisch, Raymond, jt. ed. see Ostrowsky, Daniel B.

Reinitz, Neale, ed. see Wilson, Edmund.

Reinitz, R. Tensions in American Puritanism. LC 70-100325. (Problems in American History Ser.). 208p. reprint ed. pap. 64.50 (*0-8357-9991-3*, 201929200011) Bks Demand.

Reinitz, Richard. Irony & Consciousness: American Historiography & Reinhold Niebuhr's Vision. LC 77-92574. 232p. 1978. 34.50 (*0-8387-2062-5*) Bucknell U Pr.

Reinitz, Yehonason David, ed. see Schneersohn, Shmuel.

Reinitzer, Heimo & Bibel-Archiv, Deutches, eds. Naturalis Historia Bibliae. Schriften Zur Biblischen Naturkunde Des 16.-18. Jahrhunderts Vol. 1: Hermann Heinrich Frey - Therobiblia. Biblische Thierbuch - Vogelbuch - Fischbuch. fac. ed. (GER., Illus.). 1390p. 1978. reprint ed. 87.00 (*3-201-01042-1*, Pub. by Akademische Druck-und) Balogh.

Reinitzer, Heimo & Bibel-Archiv, Deutsches, eds. Naturalis Historia Bibliae. Schriften Zur Biblischen Naturkunde Des 16.-18. Jahrhunderts Vol. 2: Joachim Camerarius - Symbola et Emblemata, 4 vols. fac. ed. (GER., Illus.). 704p. 1986. reprint ed. 115.00 (*3-201-01309-9*, Pub. by Akademische Druck-und) Balogh.

Reinke, Betty, compiled by. The War Years & the People of Antelope County, Nebraska. 168p. 1995. 35.00 (*0-88107-249-4*) Curtis Media.

Reinke, Bodo. Synergiemanagement im Handel: Grundzuge Einer Handelsbetrieblichen Synergiekonzeption unter Berucksichtigung Empirischer Untersuchungen im Deutschen Konsumguterhandel. (GER., Illus.). XXIV, 262p. 1996. 54.95 (*3-631-30464-1*) P Lang Pubng.

Reinke, Christen J. How to Avoid the 10 Biggest Mistakes When Owner Financing Real Estate: Insider Tips for Your Protection & Peace of Mind. (Illus.). 134p. 1998. pap. Price not set. (*1-57833-037-8*) Todd Commns.

Reinke, Danny C. & Swartz, Lucy. The NEPA Reference Guide. LC 99-21501. 1999. pap. 45.00 (*1-57477-068-3*) Battelle.

Reinke, Edgar C., tr. & anno. see Briggs, Ward W. & Kopff, E. Christian, eds.

Reinke, Janet. Juvenile Law. (Contemporary Legal Issues Ser.). 1996. lib. bdg. 39.50 (*0-87436-798-0*) ABC-CLIO.

Reinke, K., jt. auth. see Hirschfeld, U.

Reinke, Michael. The Kite Flyer: Poems by Michael Reinke. Baker, R. D., ed. (Poetry Chapbook Ser.). (Illus.). 28p. (Orig.). 1995. pap. 4.00 (*1-887641-05-X*) Argonne Hotel Pr.

Reinke, Wilhelm W. Quotations in Nudes. (Illus.). 96p. 1996. 65.00 (*3-908162-46-7*, Pub. by Edit Stemmle) Dist Art Pubs.

Reinke, William A., ed. Health Planning for Effective Management. (Illus.). 304p. 1988. text 35.00 (*0-19-505337-0*) OUP.

Reinke, William A. & Williams, Kathleen N., eds. Health Planning: Qualitative Aspects & Quantitative Techniques. LC 79-189139. (Illus.). 360p. 1972. 12.00 (*0-912888-00-8*) Dept Intl Health.

Reinken, Gunter. Deer Farming: A Practical Guide to German Techniques. Meadowcroft, P., tr. (Illus.). 300p. 1990. 39.95 (*0-85236-206-4*, Pub. by Farming Pr) Diamond Farm Bk.

Reinken, Patrick. Judgment Day. 448p. 1996. 23.00 (*0-684-80762-9*) S&S Trade.

Reinking. Teaching Composition. 5th ed. (C). 1998. write for info. (*0-13-095510-8*, Macmillan Coll) P-H.

— Writing for College & Career. 1998. 26.74 (*0-07-229196-6*) McGraw.

Reinking, David, ed. Reading & Computers: Issues for Theory & Practice. LC 87-10053. (Computers & Education Ser.). 219p. 1987. reprint ed. pap. 67.90 (*0-608-02759-6*, 206382200007) Bks Demand.

Reinking, David, et al, eds. Handbook of Literacy & Technology: Transformations in a Post-Typographic World. LC 97-42351. 400p. 1998. 99.95 (*0-8058-2642-4*) L Erlbaum Assocs.

***Reinking, Donna.** Lincoln in Bloomington - Normal: A Historical Tour of Lincoln Sites in Bloomington & Normal Illinois. (Illus.). 24p. 1998. pap. 3.50 (*0-943788-18-8*) McLean County.

Reinking, James A. Strategies for Successful Writing: A Rhetoric, Research Guide & Reader. 5th ed. LC 98-28680. 607p. 1998. pap. text 41.00 (*0-13-956392-X*) P-H.

— Strategies for Successful Writing: A Rhetoric, Research Guide, Reader & Handbook. 5th ed. LC 98-28780. 735p. 1998. pap. text 47.00 (*0-13-956400-4*) P-H.

Reinman, Fred M. Archeological Investigations at Whale Rock Reservoir, Cayucos, California. (Publications of the Department of Parks & Recreation: No. 2). (Illus.). 56p. (C). 1961. reprint ed. pap. text 6.88 (*1-55567-454-2*) Coyote Press.

Reinman, Jacob J. The Book of Esther. LC 94-70048. 124p. (C). 1993. 11.95 (*1-56062-247-4*); pap. 8.95 (*1-56062-248-2*) CIS Comm.

— The Passover Haggadah. Marmorstein, Arnohom, tr. LC 94-70476. (Illus.). 130p. 1994. 12.95 (*1-56062-251-2*); pap. 8.95 (*1-56062-252-0*) CIS Comm.

Reinman, Y. Y., ed. see Gold, Avner.

Reinman, Y. Y., ed. see Teichman, Avigail.

Reinman, Yaakov Yosef. Destiny Vol. 1: The Story of the Jewish People & the Western World. 1995. pap. 12.95 (*0-9626226-5-6*) Feldheim.

Reinmiller, Elinor C., jt. auth. see Chapman, Carl B.

Reinmuller, Berit, jt. auth. see Ljungqvist, Bengt.

Reinmuth. Regulation of Reciprocal Insurance Exchanges. (C). 1967. 10.50 (*0-256-00676-8*, Irwn McGrw-H) McGrw-H Hghr Educ.

Reinmuth, Dean. Tension Free Golf: Unleashing Your Greatest Shots More Often. (Illus.). 256p. 1997. reprint ed. pap. 19.95 (*1-57243-039-7*) Triumph Bks.

Reinmuth, Dieter. Yukon Travel Adventure Guide. LC 98-105433. 1997. 24.95 (*1-895907-94-2*) ITMP Pub.

Reinmuth, Howard S., Jr., ed. Early Stuart Studies: Essays in Honor of David Harris Wilson. LC 71-139962. 283p. reprint ed. pap. 87.80 (*0-608-15085-1*, 205590000039) Bks Demand.

Reinmuth, James E., jt. auth. see Mendenhall, William.

Reino, Joseph. Stephen King: The First Decade, Carrie to Pet Sematary. (United States Authors Ser.: No. 531). 176p. 1988. 32.00 (*0-8057-7512-9*) Macmillan.

Reinoehl, Richard & Hanna, Thomas, eds. Computer Literacy in Human Services. LC 89-71738. (Computers in Human Services Ser.: Vol. 6, Nos. 1-4). 337p. 1990. text 69.95 (*0-86656-866-2*) Haworth Pr.

Reinoehl, Richard & Mueller, B. Jeanne. Computer Literacy in Human Services Education. LC 90-34943. (Computers in Human Services Ser.: Vol. 7, Nos. 1-4). 381p. 1990. text 12.95 (*0-86656-980-4*) Haworth Pr.

Reinold, E. Ultrasonics in Early Pregnancy: Diagnostic Scanning & Fetal Motor Activity. Keller, P. J., ed. (Contributions to Gynecology & Obstetrics Ser.: Vol. 1). 1976. 51.50 (*3-8055-2332-7*) S Karger.

Reinold, E., ed. Fortbildungstagung und Jahrestagung der Oesterreichischen Gesellschaft Fuer Gynaekologie und Geburtshilfe, Gmunden, Juni 1992. (Gynaekologische Rundschau Journal: Vol. 32, Suppl. 1). (Illus.). iv, 160p. 1992. pap. 48.75 (*3-8055-5725-6*) S Karger.

— Gitsch, E., Festschrift. (Journal: Gynaekologische Rundschau: Vol. 30, No. 4, 1990). (Illus.). xiv, 64p. 1991. pap. 32.25 (*3-8055-5393-5*) S Karger.

— Jahrestagung der Oesterreichischen Gesellschaft Fuer Gyaekologie und Geburtshilfe, Krems, June 1980. (Gynaekologische Rundschau Journal: Vol. 20, Suppl. 2, 1981). (Illus.). xviii, 294p. 1981. pap. 57.50 (*3-8055-2191-X*) S Karger.

— Oesterreichische Gesellschaft fuer Gynaekologie & Geburtshilfe, Bayerische Gesellschaft fuer Geburtshilfe & Frauenheilkunde, Jahrestagung, Salzburg, June 1993. (Journal: Gynaekologisch Geburtshilfliche Rundschau: Vol. 33, Suppl. 1, 1993). (Illus.). x, 354p. 1993. pap. 158.50 (*3-8055-5916-X*) S Karger.

— Oesterreichische Gesellschaft fuer Gynaekologie und Geburtshilfe, Jahrestagung, Bregenz, June 1994: Journal: Gynaekologisch-geburtshilfliche Rundschau, 1994, Vol. 34, Supp. 1. (Illus.). viii, 214p. 1994. pap. 96.75 (*3-8055-6108-3*) S Karger.

Reinold, E., jt. auth. see Gitsch, Eduard.

Reinold, E., jt. ed. see Gitsch, Eduard.

Reinold, E., jt. ed. see Winter, R.

Reinoso-Suarez, Fernando & Ajmone-Marsan, Cosimo, eds. Cortical Integration: Basic, Archicortical, & Cortical Association Levels of Neural Integration. LC 84-17798. (International Brain Research Organization Monograph Ser.: No. 11). (Illus.). 454p. 1984. reprint ed. pap. 140.80 (*0-7837-9555-6*, 206030400005) Bks Demand.

Reinsch, Paul S. American Legislatures & Legislative Methods. LC 91-55447. (American State Ser.). x, 337p. 1991. reprint ed. 85.00 (*0-912004-97-5*) Gaunt.

— Colonial Government, an Introduction to the Study of Colonial Institutions. LC 72-107829. (Select Bibliographies Reprint Ser.). 1977. 29.95 (*0-8369-5221-9*) Ayer.

— English Common Law in the Early American Colonies. 1976. lib. bdg. 200.00 (*0-8490-1373-9*) Gordon Pr.

— English Common Law in the Early American Colonies. LC 75-110969. (American Constitutional & Legal History Ser). 1970. reprint ed. lib. bdg. 16.95 (*0-306-71910-X*) Da Capo.

— Intellectual & Political Currents in the Far East. LC 79-165804. (Select Bibliographies Reprint Ser.). 1977. reprint ed. 26.95 (*0-8369-5960-4*) Ayer.

Reinsch, Roger W., jt. auth. see Maxwell, Kimera K.

Reinschke, K. J. Multivariable Control - A Graph-Theoretic Approach. (Lecture Notes in Control & Information Sciences: Vol. 108). 275p. 1988. 51.95 (*0-387-18899-1*) Spr-Verlag.

Reinsel, G. C. Elements of Multivariate Time Series Analysis. 2nd ed. LC 96-49573. (Springer Series in Statistics). (Illus.). 376p. 1997. 59.95 (*0-387-94918-6*) Spr-Verlag.

Reinsel, G. C. & Velu, R. P. Multivariate Reduced-Rank Regression. Bickel, P. et al, eds. LC 98-29393. (Lecture Notes in Statistics Ser.: Vol. 136). 272p. 1998. pap. 39.95 (*0-387-98601-4*) Spr-Verlag.

Reinsel, Gregory C. Elements of Multivariate Time Series Analysis. (Series in Statistics). (Illus.). 250p. 1993. write for info. (*3-540-94063-4*) Spr-Verlag.

— Elements of Multivariate Time Series Analysis. 2nd rev. ed. LC 93-13954. (Series in Statistics). (Illus.). 263p. 1995. 54.95 (*0-387-94063-4*) Spr-Verlag.

Reinshagen, Hans G. Paris - 1961. (FRE & GER., Illus.). 96p. (C). 1996. 41.00 (*3-8170-2514-9*, Pub. by Knstvrlag Weingrtn) Intl Bk Import.

Reinsma, Carol. Credo Canyon Kids: Stories for Life. LC 98-5894. (Devotional Stories for Life Ser.). 255p. (J). 1998. pap. 14.95 (*1-56212-342-4*, 1701-0100) CRC Pubns.

***Reinsma, Carol.** Rooftop Kids: Stories for Life. LC 99-30245. 254p. 1999. pap. 14.95 (*1-56212-407-2*, 1701-0125) CRC Pubns.

Reinsma, Carol. Wanna Trade? LC 95-17545. (J). 1995. pap. 7.95 (*1-56212-111-1*) CRC Pubns.

— With a Cherry on Top: Daily Devotions for Kids. LC 96-30007. 87p. (J). 1997. pap. 7.95 (*1-56212-236-3*, 1701-0403) CRC Pubns.

Reinsma, Carol, jt. auth. see Bruno, Bonnie.

Reinsma, Luke M. Aelfric: An Annotated Bibliography. LC 85-45125. (Reference Library of the Humanities). 328p. 1987. text 10.00 (*0-8240-8665-1*) Garland.

Reinsmith, William A. Archetypal Forms in Teaching: A Continuum, 56. LC 91-44433. (Contributions to the Study of Education Ser.: No. 56). 232p. 1992. 52.95 (*0-313-28405-9*, RTG/, Greenwood Pr) Greenwood.

Reinstatler, Laura & Smith, Kerry, eds. Fine Art Quilts: Works by Artists of the Contemporary QuiltArt Association. LC 97-16857. (Illus.). 112p. (Orig.). 1997. pap. 29.95 (*1-56477-193-8*, B307, Fiber Studio Pr) Martingale & Co.

Reinstatler, Laura, ed. see Holmberg, Nannette.

Reinstatler, Laura, ed. see Wilder, Donna.

Reinstatler, Laura M., ed. see Edie, Marge.

Reinstatler, Laura M., ed. see Halferty, Suzette & Porter, Carol C.

Reinstatler, Laura M., ed. see Hopkins, Judy D.

Reinstatler, Laura M., ed. see Kime, Janet.

Reinstatler, Laura M., ed. see Rozmyn, Mia.

Reinstatler, Laura M., ed. see Swain, Gabrielle.

Reinstedt, Randall A. Ghost Notes: Haunted Happenings on California's Historic Monterey Peninsula. LC 88-82533. (Illus.). 190p. 1991. pap. 9.95 (*0-933818-09-2*) Ghost Town.

— Ghostly Tales & Mysterious Happenings of Old Monterey. LC 79-110356. (Illus.). 64p. 1977. pap. 5.95 (*0-933818-04-1*) Ghost Town.

— Ghosts, Bandits & Legends of Old Monterey. expanded rev. ed. Bergez, John, ed. LC 74-189524. (Illus.). 88p. 1995. pap. 6.95 (*0-933818-00-9*) Ghost Town.

— Incredible Ghosts of Old Monterey's Hotel Del Monte. LC 80-131190. (Illus.). 48p. 1980. pap. 4.95 (*0-933818-07-6*) Ghost Town.

— Incredible Ghosts of the Big Sur Coast. LC 82-164106. (Illus.). 56p. 1981. pap. 5.95 (*0-933818-08-4*) Ghost Town.

— Lean John, California's Horseback Hero. Bergez, John, ed. (History & Happenings of California Ser.). (Illus.). 62p. (J). (gr. 3-6). 1996. 13.95 (*0-933818-26-2*); pap. 9.95 (*0-933818-81-5*) Ghost Town.

— Monterey's Mother Lode. LC 79-110351. Orig. Title: Gold in the Santa Lucias. (Illus.). 104p. 1977. pap. 7.95 (*0-933818-01-7*) Ghost Town.

— Mysterious Sea Monsters of California's Central Coast. Bergez, John, ed. LC 80-114610. (Illus.). 74p. 1993. pap. 6.95 (*0-933818-06-8*) Ghost Town.

— One-Eyed Charley: The California Whip. Bergez, John, ed. LC 90-81382. (History & Happenings of California Ser.). (Illus.). 84p. (J). (gr. 3-6). 1990. 13.95 (*0-933818-23-8*); pap. 9.95 (*0-933818-77-7*) Ghost Town.

— Otters, Octopuses & Odd Creatures of the Deep: A Tale of History, Science, & Mystery. Bergez, John, ed. LC 87-82106. (History & Happenings of California Ser.). (Illus.). 64p. (J). (gr. 3-6). 1987. 13.95 (*0-933818-21-1*); pap. 9.95 (*0-933818-76-9*) Ghost Town.

— Shipwrecks & Sea Monsters of California's Central Coast. LC 76-350548. (Illus.). 168p. 1975. pap. 8.95 (*0-933818-02-5*) Ghost Town.

— Stagecoach Santa. Bergez, John, ed. LC 86-81735. (History & Happenings of California Ser.). (Illus.). 46p. (J). (gr. 3-6). 1986. 12.95 (*0-933818-20-3*); pap. 8.95 (*0-933818-75-0*) Ghost Town.

— The Strange Case of the Ghosts of the Robert Louis Stevenson House. Bergez, John, ed. LC 88-81933. (History & Happenings of California Ser.). (Illus.). 70p. (J). (gr. 3-6). 1988. 13.95 (*0-933818-22-X*); pap. 9.95 (*0-933818-78-5*) Ghost Town.

— Tales & Treasures of California's Missions. LC 92-73253. (History & Happenings of California Ser.). (Illus.). 120p. (J). (gr. 3-6). 1992. pap. 10.95 (*0-933818-79-3*) Ghost Town.

— Tales & Treasures of California's Missions. Bergez, John, ed. LC 92-73253. (History & Happenings of California Ser.). (Illus.). 120p. (J). (gr. 3-6). 1992. 14.95 (*0-933818-24-6*) Ghost Town.

— Tales & Treasures of California's Ranchos. Bergez, John, ed. (History & Happenings of California Ser.). (Illus.). 128p. (J). (gr. 3-6). 1998. 14.95 (*0-933818-29-7*); pap. 10.95 (*0-933818-82-3*) Ghost Town.

— Tales & Treasures of the California Gold Rush. Bergez, John, ed. (History & Happenings of California Ser.). (Illus.). 112p. (J). (gr. 3-6). 1994. 14.95 (*0-933818-28-9*); pap. 10.95 (*0-933818-80-7*) Ghost Town.

— Tales, Treasures, & Pirates of Old Monterey. LC 79-110354. (Illus.). 72p. 1976. pap. 5.95 (*0-933818-03-3*) Ghost Town.

— Where Have All the Sardines Gone? A Pictorial History of Steinbeck's Cannery Row & Old Monterey's Fisherman's Wharf & Sardine Industry. LC 79-101716. (Illus.). 168p. 1978. pap. 8.95 (*0-933818-05-X*) Ghost Town.

Reinstein, Alan, jt. auth. see Weinrich, Thomas R.

Reinstein, Mike, jt. auth. see Reinstein, Reina J.

***Reinstein, Norbert, ed.** Promoting Health Promotion: Anatomy of a Hospital-Based Approach. 2nd ed. (Illus.). 180p. 2000. pap. 15.95 (*1-888822-09-0*) Singlish Pub.

Reinstein, Reina J. & Reinstein, Mike. Don't Blame Me, I'm a Gemini! Astrology for Teenagers. LC 95-19890. (Illus.). 162p. (J). (gr. 8 up). 1996. pap. 5.95 (*0-8120-9524-3*) Barron.

***Reinstein, Robert.** Practical Windows 2000 Server. 700p. 2000. pap. text 29.99 (*0-7897-2141-4*) Que.

Reinstein, Robert, et al. Windows NT Troubleshooting & Configuration. LC 96-68962. 1032p. 1997. 59.99 (*0-672-30941-6*) Sams.

Reinstra, Marchiene V. The Swallow's Nest: A Feminine Reading of the Psalms. 1992. pap. 18.95 (*0-377-00248-8*) Friendship Pr.

Reinsvold, Robert. Diversity of Plants, Fungi & Microbes: A Lab Manual. 2nd ed. 192p. (C). 1998. pap. text, lab manual ed. 30.95 (*0-7872-5433-9*, 41543301) Kendall-Hunt.

Reintgen, D., jt. auth. see Whitman, Eric.

Reintgen, Douglas & Clark, Robert A., eds. Cancer Screening. LC 95-33562. (Illus.). 304p. (C). (gr. 13). 1996. text 74.00 (*0-8151-7142-0*, 24303) Mosby Inc.

Reinthaler, Joan. Mathematics & Music: Some Intersections. 1990. 2.50 (*0-940790-08-4*) Mu Alpha Theta.

Reintjes, Afton E. How to Research "A Little Bit of Indian" 109p. 1989. pap. 25.50 (*0-940764-39-3*) Genealog Inst.

— Scotch-Irish Sources of Research. 50p. 1986. pap. 16.50 (*0-940764-46-6*) Genealog Inst.

— Tennessee Research. 50p. 1986. pap. 19.50 (*0-940764-45-8*) Genealog Inst.

Reintjes, Anna G., jt. auth. see Branciforte, Suzanne.

Reintjes, Frank. Strategische Koordination von Beschaffung und Absatz Vol. XXI: Entwicklung Einer Konzeption zur Analyse und Gestaltung eines Koordinationssystems zur Abstimmung Beschaffungs- und Absatzwirtschaftlicher Ziel-, Strategie- und Marktorientierter Instrumentenentscheidungen. (Marktorientierte Unternehmensfuhrung Ser.: Bd. 20). (GER., Illus.). 345p. 1995. pap. 55.95 (*3-631-48728-2*) P Lang Pubng.

Reintjes, J. F., jt. ed. see Fisher, R. A.

Reintjes, J. Francis. Numerical Control: Making a New Technology. (Oxford Series on Advanced Manufacturing: No. 9). (Illus.). 240p. (C). 1991. text 57.00 (*0-19-506772-X*) OUP.

Reintjes, Liz, ed. Influence & Originality: Ivon Hitchens, Frances Hodgkins, Winifred Nicholson Landscape c. 1920-50. (Illus.). 64p. 1996. pap. 24.95 (*0-85331-687-2*, Pub. by Lund Humphries) Antique Collect.

Reintzell, John F. The Police Officer's Guide to Survival, Health & Fitness. 152p. 1990. pap. 24.95 (0-398-06344-3) C C Thomas.

Reintzell, John F. The Police Officer's Guide to Survival, Health & Fitness. 152p. 1990. 36.95 (0-398-05711-7) C C Thomas.

Reinuehl, Charles M. & Eckhart, George B. Eckardt: History of an Eckhar(d)t Family, Whose Three Sons (John, Henry, George) Came to America Before 1850, Including Records of a Pullman Family. 78p. 1997. reprint ed. pap. 15.50 (0-8328-8432-4); reprint ed. lib. bdg. 25.50 (0-8328-8431-6) Higginson Bk Co.

Reinvang, Ivar. Aphasia & Brain Organization. LC 85-9545. (Applied Psycholinguistics & Communication Disorders Ser.). 208p. 1985. 59.50 (0-306-41975-0, Plenum Trade) Perseus Pubng.

Reipurth, Bo & Bertout, C. Herbig-Haro Flows & the Birth of Low Mass Stars. LC 97-23407. xx, 596p. 1997. lib. bdg. 210.00 (0-7923-4660-2) Kluwer Academic.

Reiquam, Steve W., ed. Solidarity & Poland: Impacts East & West. LC 87-29537. (Illus.). 72p. (Orig.). (C). 1988. pap. text 9.00 (0-943875-02-1); lib. bdg. 20.25 (0-943875-05-6) W Wilson Ctr Pr.

Reis, ed. Ciceronis, M. Tulli Fascicule 5: Orator. (LAT.). 1993. reprint ed. pap. 19.95 (3-519-01173-5, T1173, Pub. by B G Teubner) U of Mich Pr.

Reis, A., ed. Economics & Management of Energy in Industry: Proceedings of the European Congress, Algarve, Portugal, 2-5 April 1984, 2 vols. 700p. 1985. 160.00 (0-08-030558-X, 310884, Pub. by Pergamon Repr) Franklin.

Reis, Augie. Painting Flowers with Augie. 48p. 1984. pap. text 6.50 (1-56770-152-3) S Scheewe Pubns.

Reis, Bernard J. False Security: The Betrayal of the American Investor. LC 75-2663. (Wall Street & the Security Market Ser.). 1975. 33.95 (0-405-06987-1) Ayer.

Reis, Brian. Australian Film: A Bibliography. LC 96-28623. 480p. 1997. 125.00 (0-7201-2315-1) Continuum.

Reis, Carlos A. Towards a Semiotics of Ideology. LC 92-21173. (Approaches to Semiotics Ser.: No. 109). vii, 163p. (C). 1993. lib. bdg. 90.80 (3-11-011829-7) Mouton.

Reis, Claire R. Composers in America. LC 77-4158. (Music Reprint Ser.: 1977). 1977. reprint ed. lib. bdg. 42.50 (0-306-70893-0) Da Capo.

Reis, Donald J., et al, eds. The Imidazoline Receptor: Pharmacology, Functions, Ligands, & Relevance to Biology & Medicine. (Annals of the New York Academy of Sciences Ser.: Vol. 763). 707p. 1995. 190.00 (0-89766-935-5) NY Acad Sci.

— The Imidazoline Receptor: Pharmacology, Functions, Ligands, & Relevance to Biology & Medicine. LC 95-316. (Annals of the New York Academy of Sciences Ser.: Vol. 763). 707p. 1995. pap. 190.00 (0-89766-936-3) NY Acad Sci.

Reis, Donald J. & Posner, Jerome B., eds. Frontiers of Neurology. LC 97-32679. (Annals of the New York Academy of Sciences Ser.: No. 835). 421p. 1998. 90.00 (1-57331-096-4) NY Acad Sci.

— Frontiers of Neurology: A Symposium in Honor of Fred Plum. LC 97-32679. (Annals of the New York Academy of Sciences Ser.: No. 835). 421p. 1998. pap. 90.00 (1-57331-097-2) NY Acad Sci.

Reis, Elisa P., jt. ed. see Asmerom, H. K.

Reis, Elizabeth. Damned Women: Sinners & Witches in Puritan New England. LC 96-53411. (Illus.). 248p. 1996. text 32.50 (0-8014-2834-3) Cornell U Pr.

— Damned Women: Sinners & Witches in Puritan New England. 1999. pap. text 16.95 (0-8014-8611-4) Cornell U Pr.

***Reis, Elizabeth, ed.** Sexual Histories. 2000. 64.95 (0-631-22080-1); pap. 27.95 (0-631-22081-X) Blackwell Pubs.

Reis, Elizabeth, ed. Spellbound: Women & Witchcraft in America. LC 97-49092. (Worlds of Women Ser.: Vol. 4). (Illus.). 184p. 1998. 55.00 (0-8420-2576-6); pap. 18.95 (0-8420-2577-4) Scholarly Res Inc.

***Reis, Harry T. & Judd, Charles M., eds.** Handbook of Research Methods in Social & Personality Psychology. LC 99-16937. (Illus.). 576p. (C). 2000. 69.95 (0-521-55128-5); pap. 34.95 (0-521-55903-0) Cambridge U Pr.

Reis, Henrique L. Dos, see Dos Reis, Henrique L., ed.

Reis, Henrique L. Dos, see Djordjeuc, B. Boro & Dos Reis, Henrique L., eds.

Reis, Jaime, ed. International Monetary Systems in Historical Perspective. LC 95-4171. 288p. 1995. text 79.95 (0-312-12540-2) St Martin.

***Reis, James F., ed.** 1999-2000 Colorado International Trade Directory. 164p. 1999. pap. 50.00 (0-9643267-3-6) Wrld Trade Ctr.

Reis, Jim. Pieces of the Past. (Illus.). 200p. (Orig.). 1988. pap. 9.95 (0-9621043-0-2) KY Post.

— Pieces of the Past, Pt. II. (Illus.). 190p. (Orig.). 1991. pap. 9.95 (0-9624673-3-2) Picture This Bks.

Reis, Joao J. Slave Rebellion in Brazil: The Muslim Uprising of 1835 in Bahia. Brakel, Arthur, tr. from POR. (Studies in Atlantic History & Culture). (Illus.). 320p. 1995. reprint ed. pap. text 16.95 (0-8018-5250-1) Johns Hopkins.

— Slave Rebellion in Brazil: The Muslim Uprising of 1853 in Bahia. Brakel, Arthur, tr. from POR. LC 92-27067. (Studies in Atlantic History & Culture). (Illus.). 320p. 1993. text 48.00 (0-8018-4462-2) Johns Hopkins.

Reis, John C. Environmental Control in Petroleum Engineering. (Illus.). 288p. 1996. 65.00 (0-88415-273-1, No. 5273) Gulf Pub.

Reis, Joyce G., jt. auth. see Good, Julia P.

Reis, Leo Van Der, see Van Der Reis, Leo, ed.

Reis, Leo Van Der, see Williams, Erin & Van Der Reis, Leo.

Reis, M. D., jt. ed. see Pinkerton, P. H.

Reis, Marion J., jt. tr. see Lemon, Lee T.

Reis, Patricia. Daughters of Saturn: From Father's Daughter to Creative Woman. 288p. 1996. pap. 15.95 (0-8264-0893-1) Continuum.

***Reis, Pedro Cabrita.** About Light & Space. (Illus.). 2000. pap. 35.00 (88-8158-254-6) Charta.

Reis, Richard H. George MacDonald's Fiction: A Twentieth Century View. 1989. pap. 8.95 (0-940652-32-3) Sunrise Bks.

Reis, Rick. Tomorrow's Professor: Preparing for Academic Careers in Science & Engineering. LC 96-37355. 416p. 1997. pap. 39.95 (0-7803-1136-1, PP5602) Inst Electrical.

Reis, Roberto. The Pearl Necklace: Toward an Archaeology of the Brazilian Transition Discourse. (Illus.). 192p. (C). 1992. 49.95 (0-8130-1105-1) U Press Fla.

Reis, Roberto, ed. Toward Socio-Criticism: Selected Proceedings of the Conference "Luso-Brazilian Literatures, a Socio-Critical Approach" LC 91-563. 236p. (Orig.). 1991. text 25.00 (0-87918-074-9) ASU Lat Am St.

Reis, Roberto, jt. ed. see Foster, David W.

Reis, Ronald A. Digital Electronics. 1991. pap. text, lab manual ed. 46.00 (0-675-21254-5, Merrill Coll) P-H.

— Digital Electronics Through Project Analysis. 541p. (C). 1990. pap. text 35.20 (0-675-21141-7, Merrill Coll) P-H.

— Electronic Project Design & Fabrication. 4th ed. LC 97-32740. 525p. (C). 1998. pap. text 89.00 (0-13-776055-8) P-H.

— Understanding Electronic & Computer Technology. 3rd ed. (Illus.). 384p. (Orig.). 1996. pap. text 25.00 (0-911908-23-4) Tech Ed Pr.

Reis, Ronald A., jt. auth. see Webb, John W.

Reis, S., jt. ed. see Friedrich, R.

***Reis, Sally M.** Work Left Undone: Choices & Compromises of Talented Women. 442p. 1998. pap. 19.95 (0-936386-76-2) Creative Learning.

Reis, Sally M. & Renzulli, Joseph S. The Secondary Triad Model: A Practical Plan for Implementing Gifted Programs at the Junior & Senior High School Levels. 1985. pap. 16.95 (0-936386-33-9) Creative Learning.

Reis, Sally M. & Ruezulli, Joseph S. Secondary Action Information Message. 1987. pap. 24.95 (0-936386-48-7) Creative Learning.

Reis, Sally M., et al. Curriculum Compacting: The Complete Guide to Modifying the Regular Curriculum for High Ability Students. 1992. pap. 24.95 (0-936386-63-0) Creative Learning.

Reis, Sally M., jt. auth. see Renzulli, Joseph S.

Reis, Sally M., jt. auth. see Rezulli, Joseph S.

Reis, Sally M., jt. ed. see Renzulli, Joseph S.

Reis, Sherry. Basic Quiltmaking Techniques for Divided Circles. LC 98-24783. (Your First Quilt Book Ser.). (Illus.). 79p. 1998. pap. 14.95 (1-56477-238-1, B347, Pub. by Martingale & Co) F & W Pubns Inc.

— Basic Quiltmaking Techniques for Eight-Pointed Stars. LC 98-46527. (Basic Quiltmaking Techniques Ser.). (Illus.). 80p. 1999. pap. 14.95 (1-56477-249-7, B370, That Patchwrk Pl) Martingale & Co.

Reis, Siri V. Von, see Von Reis, Siri V.

Reis, Stuart. King George's Army, 1740-93 Vol. 1: Infantry. (Men-at-Arms Ser.). (Illus.). 48p. 1995. pap. 12.95 (1-85532-515-2, Pub. by Ospry) Stackpole.

Reisberg, jt. auth. see Gleitman.

Reisberg, Barry. Alzheimer's Disease: The Clinical Syndrome. 1994. 19.18 (0-02-926050-7) S&S Trade.

— Alzheimer's Disease: The Reference Text. 1994. 67.50 (0-02-926235-6) S&S Trade.

— A Guide to Alzheimer's Disease: For Families, Spouses & Friends. LC 80-69717. 216p. (C). 1984. pap. 13.95 (0-02-926370-0) Free Pr.

Reisberg, Daniel. Cognition cHAPTERS 4-7. (C). pap. text (0-393-10317-X, Norton Paperbks) Norton.

— Cognitive Psychology: Exploring the Science of the Mind. (C). 1996. 76.50 (0-393-96925-8) Norton.

Reisberg, Daniel, ed. Auditory Imagery. 288p. 1992. text 65.00 (0-8058-0556-7) L Erlbaum Assocs.

Reisberg, Daniel, jt. auth. see Schwartz, Barry.

Reisberg, Liz A. Argentina: A Study of the Educational System & a Guide to the Placement of Students in Educational Institutions in the United States. (World Education Ser.). (Illus.). 150p. 1993. pap. text 45.00 (0-929851-17-X) Am Assn Coll Registrars.

Reisberg, Mira. Baby Rattlesnake. LC 89-9892. 32p. (YA). (ps-3). 1989. 14.95 (0-89239-049-2) Childrens Book Pr.

Reisberg, Veg. Elinda Who Danced in the Sky: An Estonia Folktale. LC 99-2247. 32p. (YA). (gr. 4-7). 1990. 14.95 (0-89239-066-2) Childrens Book Pr.

Reisbick, Anna M., jt. ed. see Olson, Marie M.

Reisbig. Thermodynamics for the Engineering Sciences. (C). 1999. pap. text, teacher ed. write for info. (0-673-97794-3) Addison-Wesley.

***Reisbig.** Thermodynamics for the Engineering Sciences. (C). 1999. text. write for info. (0-673-98409-5) Addison-Wesley.

Reisburg, Mira. Baby Rattlesnake. LC 88-9892. 32p. (YA). (ps-3). 1993. pap. 7.95 (0-89239-111-1) Childrens Book Pr.

Reisch, Joan S., jt. auth. see Parker, Harry J.

Reisch, Michael & Gambrill, Eileen. Social Work in the 21st Century. LC 96-45367. 1997. pap. 29.95 (0-8039-9091-X) Pine Forge.

Reisch, Michael, jt. auth. see Wenocur, Stanley.

Reischaue, jt. auth. see Fairbank.

Reischauer, August K. Studies in Japanese Buddhism. LC 73-107769. reprint ed. 37.50 (0-404-05237-1) AMS Pr.

Reischauer, Edwin O. Ennin's Travels in T'ang China. LC 55-6273. 357p. reprint ed. pap. 110.70 (0-608-11810-9, 201236700081) Bks Demand.

— Japan: The Story of a Nation. LC 79-565893. 384p. reprint ed. pap. 119.10 (0-608-14950-0, 202611500048) Bks Demand.

— Japan: The Story of a Nation. 4th ed. 448p. (C). 1989. pap. 34.06 (0-07-557074-2) McGraw.

— The Japanese Today: Change & Continuity. LC 87-14904. (Illus.). 436p. 1988. 39.95 (0-674-47181-4) Belknap Pr.

— The Japanese Today: Change & Continuity. LC 87-14904. (Illus.). 436p. 1989. pap. text 12.95 (0-674-47182-2) HUP.

Reischauer, Edwin O., tr. Ennin's Diary: The Record of a Pilgrimage to China in Search of the Law. LC 55-5553. (Illus.). 478p. reprint ed. pap. 148.20 (0-8357-9521-7, 201236600081) Bks Demand.

Reischauer, Edwin O. & Craig, Albert M. Japan: Tradition & Transformation, 2 vols. 2nd ed. LC 77-77979. (Illus.). (C). 1989. pap. text 38.36 (0-395-49696-9) HM.

Reischauer, Edwin O. & Jansen, Marius B. The Japanese Today: Change & Continuity. enl. ed. LC 94-31346. 471p. 1995. text 16.95 (0-674-47184-9) Belknap Pr.

Reischauer, Haru M. Samurai & Silk: A Japanese & American Heritage. (Illus.). 400p. 1986. 35.00 (0-674-78800-1) Belknap Pr.

— Samurai & Silk: A Japanese & American Heritage. 400p. 1988. reprint ed. pap. text 18.95 (0-674-78801-X) Belknap Pr.

Reischauer, Robert D. Reforming School Finance. LC 73-1080. (Brookings Institution Studies in Social Experimentation). 199p. reprint ed. pap. 61.70 (0-608-12469-9, 202540100043) Bks Demand.

Reischauer, Robert D., ed. Setting National Priorities: Budget Choices for the Next Century. LC 96-45888. 316p. 1996. 42.95 (0-8157-7398-6); pap. 18.95 (0-8157-7397-8) Brookings.

Reischauer, Robert D., et al, eds. Medicare: Preparing for the Challenges of the 21st Century. LC 97-33931. 329p. 1998. pap. 19.95 (0-8157-7399-4) Brookings.

Reischauer, Robert D. & Aaron, Henry J., eds. Setting National Priorities, 1999. 350p. 1998. 44.95 (0-8157-7402-8); pap. 18.95 (0-8157-7401-X) Brookings.

Reischauer, Robert D., jt. auth. see Aaron, Henry J.

Reischauer, Robert K. Japan, Government-Politics. LC 75-41226. reprint ed. 20.00 (0-404-14589-2) AMS Pr.

Reische, Diana. Electing a U. S. President. LC 91-32339. (Democracy in Action Ser.). (Illus.). 128p. (YA). (gr. 7-12). 1992. lib. bdg. 24.00 (0-531-11043-5) Watts.

Reischl, Dennis & Miller, Claire S. Customer Service in Government: A Pratical Guide for Managers & Employees. abr. ed. (Illus.). 65p. 1996. pap. text 14.95 (0-936295-71-6) FPMI Comns.

Reischl, Dennis K., jt. auth. see Smith, Ralph R.

Reischl, Udo, ed. Molecular Diagnosis of Infectious Diseases. LC 97-29087. (Methods in Molecular Medicine Ser.: Vol. 13). 648p. 1997. 125.00 (0-89603-485-2) Humana.

— Molecular Diagnostics of Infectious Diseases. (Methods in Molecular Medicine Ser.: Vol. 13). (Illus.). 648p. 1997. spiral bd. 89.50 (0-89603-398-8) Humana.

Reischl, Udo, jt. auth. see Kochanowski, Bernd.

Reischl, W. C., ed. see Hierosolymitanus, Cyrillus.

Reischuk, R. Udiger & Morvan, Michel. STACS, '97 Vol. 120: 14th Annual Symposium on Theoretical Aspects of Computer Science, Lubeck, Germany, February-March 1997: Proceedings. LC 97-7674. (Lecture Notes in Computer Science Ser.). 1997. 91.00 (3-540-62616-6) Spr-Verlag.

Reischuk, Rudiger, jt. ed. see Puech, Claude.

Reisdorf, Phyllis. Water, Water, Everywhere, So Many Drops to Drink. (Illus.). 52p. (Orig.). 1988. pap. 4.95 (0-317-93900-9) P Reisdorf.

Reisdorff, Earl, et al. Emergency Radiology. Schwartz, David T., ed. LC 98-36343. (Illus.). 608p. 1999. text 89.00 (0-07-050827-5) McGraw-Hill HPD.

Reisdorff, Earl J., et al. Pediatric Emergency Medicine. (Illus.). 1190p. 1992. text 164.00 (0-7216-3281-5, W B Saunders Co) Harcrt Hlth Sci Grp.

Reisdorff, James J., ed. see Barak, Anthony J.

Reisdorff, James J., ed. see Stensvad, Arthur E.

Reisdorph, Kent. Borland C++ Builder 4 Unleashed. LC 98-87917. (Sams Unleashed Series). (Illus.). 1223p. (Orig.). 1999. pap. 59.99 (0-672-31510-6) Sams.

— Borland C++Builder 4. 1999. pap. text 49.99 (0-672-31627-7) Sams.

— Sams Teach Yourself Borland C++ Builder 3 in 21 Days. (Teach Yourself Ser.). 832p. 1998. pap. text 39.99 (0-672-31266-2) Sams.

***Reisdorph, Kent.** Teach Yourself Borland C++ Builder 4 in 24 Hours. LC 98-83060. (Teach Yourself . . . Ser.). (Illus.). 451p. 1999. pap. 24.99 (0-672-31626-9) Sams.

Reisdorph, Kent & Henderson, Ken. Teach Yourself Borland C++ Builder in 21 Days. LC 97-65225. 840p. 1997. 39.99 (0-672-31020-1) Sams.

Reise, K. Tidal Flat Ecology. (Ecological Studies: Vol. 54). (Illus.). 210p. 1985. 93.95 (0-387-15447-7) Spr-Verlag.

Reise, Steve, jt. auth. see Embretson, Susan E.

Reisel, Esther & Reisel, Rudi. Modern Jewish Identity: A Rationalistic Approach to Judaism. LC 98-12251. 1998. 24.95 (965-229-163-3) Gefen Bks.

Reisel, Jerome, jt. auth. see Weschler, Irving R.

Reisel, Robert R. Elementary Theory of Metric Spaces: A Course in Constructing Mathematical Proofs. (Universitext Ser.). 120p. 1982. 59.95 (0-387-90706-8) Spr-Verlag.

Reisel, Rudi, jt. auth. see Reisel, Esther.

***Reisem, Richard O.** Erie Canal Legacy. LC 00-90736. (Illus.). 200p. 2000. 39.95 (0-9641706-6-3) Landmark Soc.

Reisem, Richard O. Field Guide to Forest Lawn Cemetery, Buffalo, New York. (Illus.). 64p. 1998. pap. 10.00 (0-9652756-1-2) Forest Lawn.

— Mt. Hope: America's First Municipal Victorian Cemetery. (Illus.). 128p. 1995. 39.95 (0-9641706-3-9) Landmark Soc.

— 200 Years of Rochester Architecture & Gardens. (Illus.). 144p. 1994. 39.95 (0-9641706-1-2) Landmark Soc.

***Reisem, Richard O. & Michaels, Albert L.** Classic Buffalo: A Heritage of Distinguished Architecture. LC 99-74516. (Illus.). 160p. 1999. 39.95 (0-9671480-0-6) Canisius Coll Pr.

Reisem, Richard O., et al. Forest Lawn Cemetery: Buffalo History Preserved. 160p. 1996. 39.95 (0-9652756-0-4) Forest Lawn.

Reisen, Helmut. Debts, Deficits & Exchange Rates. 256p. 1994. 90.00 (1-85278-930-1) E Elgar.

***Reisen, Helmut.** Pensions, Savings & Capital Flows: From Ageing to Emerging Markets. LC 99-49040. (Organisation for Economic Co-Operation & Development Ser.). 288p. 2000. 90.00 (1-84064-308-0) E Elgar.

Reisen, Helmut. Public Debt, External Competitiveness, & Fiscal Discipline in Developing Countries. LC 89-24746. (Studies in International Finance: No. 66). 30p. 1989. pap. text 13.50 (0-88165-238-5) Princeton U Int Finan Econ.

Reisen, Helmut, jt. auth. see Fischer, Bernhard.

Reisen, Helmut, jt. ed. see Hausmann, Ricardo.

Reisen, Mirjam Van, see Van Reisen, Mirjam.

Reisenauer, Cindy. How to Draw Creepy Creatures. (How to Draw Ser.). 32p. (J). 1991. 3.98 (1-56156-019-7); pap. 2.95 (1-56156-064-2) Kidsbks.

Reisenberger, John R., jt. auth. see Moran, Robert T.

Reisenfeld, Robin. The German Print Portfolio 1890-1930: Serial for Private Sphere. (Illus.). 160p. 1992. 80.00 (0-85667-147-9, Pub. by P Wilson) Scala Books.

— The German Print Portfolio 1890-1930: Serials for a Private Sphere. LC 92-80372. (Illus.). 159p. 1992. pap. 29.95 (0-85667-417-6) D & A Smart Museum.

Reiser, Bob, jt. auth. see Francis, Panama.

Reiser, Carl, jt. auth. see Kaplan, Daniel I.

Reiser, Christa. Reflections on Anger: Women & Men in a Changing Society. LC 98-33626. 168p. 1999. 55.00 (0-275-95777-2, Praeger Pubs) Greenwood.

***Reiser, David R., et al.** J. K. Lasser Pro Wealth Building: Investment Strategies for Retirement & Estate Planning. (J. K. Lasser Pro Ser.). 224p. 2000. 49.95 (0-471-38807-6) Wiley.

Reiser, Dee & Dormer, Teresa. Best of Friends. LC 85-90457. (Illus.). 168p. (Orig.). 1985. pap. 9.95 (0-9615950-5-1) Best Friends.

Reiser, Dee, jt. auth. see Dormer, Teresa.

Reiser, Gwendolyn M. & Schaefer, G. Bradley. Cancer Genetics: A Guide for Counseling Families. (Illus.). 63p. 1996. ring bd. 45.00 (1-889843-00-8) Munroe-Meyer Inst.

Reiser, Howard. Barry Sanders: Lion with a Quiet Roar. LC 93-19780. (Sports Stars Ser.). (Illus.). 48p. (J). (gr. 2-8). 1993. pap. 4.50 (0-516-44377-1); lib. bdg. 19.00 (0-516-04377-3) Childrens.

— The Georgetown Hoyas Men's Basketball Team. LC 98-19229. (Great Sports Teams Ser.). 48p. (J). (gr. 4-10). 1999. lib. bdg. 18.95 (0-7660-1160-7) Enslow Pubs.

— Muggsy Bogues: Tall on Talent. LC 95-33637. (Sports Stars Ser.). (Illus.). 48p. (J). (gr. 2-8). 1996. lib. bdg. 19.00 (0-516-04396-X) Childrens.

— Nolan Ryan: Strikeout King. LC 92-35741. (Sports Stars Ser.). (Illus.). 48p. (J). (gr. 3-4). 1993. lib. bdg. 19.00 (0-516-04365-X) Childrens.

— Patrick Ewing: Center of Attention. LC 94-14399. (Sports Stars Ser.). (Illus.). 48p. (J). (gr. 2-8). 1994. lib. bdg. 19.00 (0-516-04388-9) Childrens.

— Scottie Pippen: Prince of the Court. LC 92-42023. (Sports Stars Ser.). (Illus.). 48p. (J). (gr. 2-8). 1993. pap. 5.95 (0-516-44366-6) Childrens.

— Scottie Pippen: Prince of the Court. LC 92-42023. (Sports Stars Ser.). (Illus.). 48p. (J). (gr. 3-4). 1993. lib. bdg. 19.00 (0-516-04366-8) Childrens.

Reiser, J., jt. ed. see Fiechter, A.

Reiser, Jean-Marc. Les Copines. (FRE.). 135p. 1985. pap. 16.95 (0-7859-4219-X, 2070376362) Fr & Eur.

— Fous d'Amour. (FRE.). 107p. 1989. pap. 13.95 (0-7859-4320-X, 2070381552) Fr & Eur.

— Gros Degueulasse. (FRE.). 1985. pap. 11.95 (0-7859-4235-1) Fr & Eur.

— Mon Papa. (FRE.). 1976. pap. 10.95 (0-7859-4067-7) Fr & Eur.

— On Vit une Epoque Formidable. (FRE.). 1978. pap. 10.95 (0-7859-4092-8) Fr & Eur.

Reiser, Joseph C., jt. auth. see Beck, Jill.

Reiser, Lynn. Any Kind of Dog. (Illus.). (J). (ps-2). 1996. 24.95 incl. audio (0-87499-380-6) Live Oak Media.

— Any Kind of Dog. (Illus.). (J). (ps-4). 1996. pap. 15.95 incl. audio (0-87499-379-2) Live Oak Media.

— Any Kind of Dog. LC 91-12771. 1994. 10.15 (0-606-06180-0, Pub. by Turtleback) Demco.

— Any Kind of Dog, 4 bks., Set. (Illus.). (J). (ps-2). 1996. pap. 31.95 incl. audio (0-87499-381-4) Live Oak Media.

— Earthdance. LC 98-41378. (Illus.). 32p. (J). (gr. k-3). 1999. 16.00 (0-688-16326-2, Grenwillow Bks) HarpC Child Bks.

***Reiser, Lynn.** Earthdance. LC 98-41378. (Illus.). 32p. (J). (gr. k-3). 1999. 15.89 (0-688-16327-0, Grenwillow Bks) HarpC Child Bks.

Reiser, Lynn. Little Clam. LC 97-34511. (Illus.). 24p. (J). (ps-3). 1998. 15.00 (0-688-15908-7, Grenwillow Bks) HarpC Child Bks.

***Reiser, Lynn.** Little Clam. LC 97-34511. (Illus.). 24p. (J). (ps-3). 1998. 14.89 (0-688-15909-5, Grenwillow Bks) HarpC Child Bks.

Reiser, Lynn. Margaret & Margarita, Margarita y Margaret. LC 92-29012. 1996. 10.15 (0-606-10482-8, Pub. by Turtleback) Demco.

— The Surprise Family. LC 93-16249. (Illus.). 32p. (J). 1997. pap. 4.95 (*0-688-15476-X*, Wm Morrow) Morrow Avon.
— The Surprise Family. (J). 1997. 10.15 (*0-606-11947-7*, Pub. by Turtleback) Demco.
Reiser, Lynn W. Any Kind of Dog. LC 91-12771. 24p. (J). (ps-3). 1992. 14.00 (*0-688-10914-4*, Grenwillow Bks) HarpC Child Bks.
Reiser, Lynn W. Any Kind of Dog. Cohn, Amy, ed. LC 91-12771. (Illus.). 24p. (J). (ps up). 1994. reprint ed. mass mkt. 4.95 (*0-688-13572-2*, Wm Morrow) Morrow Avon.
— Beach Feet. LC 95-12208. (Illus.). 32p. (J). (ps-3). 1996. 15.00 (*0-688-14400-4*, Grenwillow Bks) HarpC Child Bks.
Reiser, Lynn W. Beach Feet. LC 95-12208. (Illus.). 32p. (J). (ps-3). 1996. lib. bdg. 14.93 (*0-688-14401-2*, Grenwillow Bks) HarpC Child Bks.
Reiser, Lynn W. Best Friends Think Alike. LC 96-25924. (Illus.). 32p. (J). (ps up). 1997. 16.00 (*0-688-15199-X*, Grenwillow Bks) HarpC Child Bks.
— Cherry Pies & Lullabies. LC 95-2259. (Illus.). 40p. (J). (ps-3). 1998. 16.00 (*0-688-13391-6*, Grenwillow Bks) HarpC Child Bks.
*__Reiser, Lynn W.__ Cherry Pies & Lullabies. LC 95-2259. (Illus.). 40p. (J). (ps-3). 1998. 15.89 (*0-688-13392-4*, Grenwillow Bks) HarpC Child Bks.
Reiser, Lynn W. Margaret & Margarita, Margarita y Margaret. LC 92-29012. (SPA., Illus.). 32p. (J). (ps-3). 1993. 15.95 (*0-688-12239-6*, Grenwillow Bks) HarpC Child Bks.
— Margaret & Margarita, Margarita y Margaret. LC 92-29012. (SPA & ENG., Illus.). 32p. (J). (ps up). 1993. lib. bdg. 15.93 (*0-688-12240-X*, Grenwillow Bks) HarpC Child Bks.
*__Reiser, Lynn W.__ My Cat Tuna. LC 98-50518. (J). 2001. 9.95 (*0-688-16874-4*, Grenwillow Bks) HarpC Child Bks.
Reiser, Lynn W. My Dog Truffle. LC 98-50913. (J). 2001. 9.95 (*0-688-16875-2*, Grenwillow Bks) HarpC Child Bks.
— Night Thunder & the Queen of the Wild Horses. LC 93-25734. (Illus.). 32p. (J). (ps-3). 1995. 15.00 (*0-688-11791-0*, Grenwillow Bks) HarpC Child Bks.
— The Surprise Family. LC 93-16249. (Illus.). 32p. (J). (ps-3). 1994. 16.00 (*0-688-11671-X*, Grenwillow Bks) HarpC Child Bks.
— The Surprise Family. LC 93-16249. (Illus.). 32p. (J). (ps up). 1994. lib. bdg. 15.93 (*0-688-11672-8*, Grenwillow Bks) HarpC Child Bks.
— Tomorrow on Rocky Pond. LC 91-45801. (Illus.). 32p. (J). (ps up). 1993. lib. bdg. 13.93 (*0-688-10673-0*, Grenwillow Bks) HarpC Child Bks.
*__Reiser, Lynn W.__ Tortillas & Lullabies, Tortillas y cancioncitas. LC 97-7096. (SPA & ENG., Illus.). 40p. (J). (ps-3). 1998. 16.00 (*0-688-14628-7*, Grenwillow Bks); 15.93 (*0-688-14629-5*, Grenwillow Bks) HarpC Child Bks.
Reiser, Lynn W. Two Mice in Three Fables. LC 93-35935. (Illus.). 32p. (J). (ps up). 1995. lib. bdg. 14.93 (*0-688-13390-8*, Grenwillow Bks) HarpC Child Bks.
Reiser, M. & Rostoker, N., eds. Collective Methods of Acceleration. (Accelerators & Storage Rings Ser.: Vol. 2). xxviii, 724p. 1979. text 274.00 (*3-7186-0005-6*) Gordon & Breach.
Reiser, M., jt. ed. see Heuck, Andreas.
Reiser, Marius. Jesus & Judgment: The Eschatological Proclamation in Its Jewish Context. Maloney, Linda M., tr. LC 97-13241. 352p. 1997. pap. 29.00 (*0-8006-2623-0*, Fortress Pr) Augsburg Fortress.
Reiser, Martin. Handbook of Investigative Hypnosis. LC 79-53215. 1980. 24.95 (*0-934486-00-X*) Martin Reiser.
— Police Psychology: Collected Papers. LC 81-82247. 1982. 24.95 (*0-934486-01-8*) Martin Reiser.
— Theory & Design of Charged Particle Beams. 632p. 1994. 125.00 (*0-471-30616-9*) Wiley.
Reiser, Martin, et al, eds. Heavy Ion Inertial Fusion: AIP Conference Proceedings, No. 152. LC 86-73185. 638p. 1987. lib. bdg. 80.00 (*0-88318-352-8*) Am Inst Physics.
Reiser, Morton F. Memory in Mind & Brain: What Dream Imagery Reveals. 232p. 1994. pap. 17.00 (*0-300-06032-7*) Yale U Pr.
Reiser, Morton F., jt. auth. see Leigh, Hoyle.
Reiser, Oliver L. The Alchemy of Light & Color. 78p. 1996. reprint ed. pap. 12.95 (*1-56459-630-3*) Kessinger Pub.
— Cosmic Humanism & World Unity. LC 73-86468. (World Institute Creative Findings Ser.). (Illus.). xii, 274p. 1975. pap. text 68.00 (*0-677-03875-5*) Gordon & Breach.
Reiser, Paul. Babyhood. LC 97-29894. 224p. 1997. 22.00 (*0-688-14979-0*, Wm Morrow) Morrow Avon.
— Babyhood. large type ed. 288p. 1998. mass mkt. 6.99 (*0-380-72872-9*, Avon Bks) Morrow Avon.
— Couplehood. 224p. 1995. reprint ed. mass mkt. 6.50 (*0-553-57313-6*) Bantam.
Reiser, Ramon F., ed. see Hart, Scott A.
Reiser, Robert A., jt. auth. see Dick, Walter.
Reiser, Robert S., jt. auth. see Seeger, Pete.
Reiser, Ronald J. Florida Passport. (Illus.). 36p. (Orig.). 1989. 3.95 (*0-9625515-0-3*) VJR Passports.
— Illinois Passport. (Illus.). 36p. (Orig.). 1990. 3.95 (*0-9625515-1-1*) VJR Passports.
— Indiana Passport. (Illus.). 36p. (Orig.). (YA). (gr. 9-12). 1991. 3.95 (*0-9625515-5-4*) VJR Passports.
— Kentucky Passport. (Illus.). 36p. (Orig.). (YA). (gr. 9-12). 1991. 3.95 (*0-9625515-9-7*) VJR Passports.
— Michigan Passport. (Illus.). 36p. (Orig.). (YA). (gr. 9-12). 1991. 3.95 (*0-9625515-7-0*) VJR Passports.
— North Carolina Passport. (Illus.). 36p. (Orig.). (YA). (gr. 9-12). 1991. 3.95 (*0-9625515-8-9*) VJR Passports.
— Ohio Passport. (Illus.). 36p. (Orig.). (YA). (gr. 9-12). 1991. 3.95 (*0-9625515-6-2*) VJR Passports.
Reiser, Sheldon. Metabolic Effects of Utilizable Dietary Carbohydrates. LC 82-10079. (Illus.). 358p. reprint ed. pap. 111.00 (*0-7837-0669-3*, 204100400019) Bks Demand.
Reiser, Sheldon & Hallfrisch, Judith, eds. Metabolic Effects of Dietary Fructose. LC 86-31687. 176p. 1987. 105.00 (*0-8493-6457-4*, QP702, CRC Reprint) Franklin.
Reiser, Stanley J. Medicine & the Reign of Technology. LC 77-87389. (Illus.). 328p. (Orig.). 1981. pap. text 24.95 (*0-521-28223-3*) Cambridge U Pr.
Reiser, Stanley J., et al, eds. Divided Staffs, Divided Selves: A Case Approach to Mental Health Ethics. LC 86-28416. (Illus.). 164p. 1987. pap. text 15.95 (*0-521-31890-4*) Cambridge U Pr.
Reiser, Stanley J. & Anbar, Michael, eds. The Machine at the Bedside: Strategies for Using Technology in Patient Care. (Illus.). 384p. 1984. pap. text 28.95 (*0-521-31832-7*) Cambridge U Pr.
Reiser, Stanley J., jt. auth. see Rosen, David H.
Reiser, Stanley J., jt. ed. see Bulger, Ruth E.
Reiser, Stewart. The Israeli Arms Industry: Foreign Policy, Arms Transfers, & Military Doctrine of a Small State. LC 89-2205. 250p. 1989. 55.00 (*0-8419-1028-6*) Holmes & Meier.
— Israeli's Defense Industry. (C). 1996. pap. text 19.50 (*0-8133-7010-8*) Westview.
Reiser, Virginia S., ed. Best Loved Poems in Large Print. large type ed. (General Ser.). 1983. 23.95 (*0-8161-3575-4*, G K Hall Lrg Type) Mac Lib Ref.
— Favorite Poems in Large Print. large type ed. (General Ser.). 1981. lib. bdg. 21.95 (*0-8161-3160-0*, G K Hall Lrg Type) Mac Lib Ref.
*__Reiser, William.__ Jesus in Solidarity with His People: A Theologian Looks at Mark. 2000. pap. text. write for info. (*0-8146-2717-X*) Liturgical Pr.
Reiser, William E. Forever Faithful: The Unfolding of God's Promise to Creation. 104p. (Orig.). 1993. pap. 7.95 (*0-8146-5849-0*, M Glazier) Liturgical Pr.
— To Hear Gods Word Listed to the World. LC 96-29367. 144p. (Orig.). 1997. pap. 17.95 (*0-8091-3696-1*) Paulist Pr.
— What Are They Saying about Dogma? LC 78-58955. (What Are They Saying about...Ser.). 1978. pap. 3.95 (*0-8091-2127-1*) Paulist Pr.
Reiser, William E., ed. Love of Learning: Desire for Justice: Undergraduate Education & the Option for the Poor. LC 94-60876. 138p. 1995. 22.00 (*0-940866-41-2*) U Scranton Pr.
Reisfeld, Eric. Consumer Karate: A Guide to Economic Survival. 5.95 (*0-686-18908-6*) Meridian Ed.
Reisfeld, R., jt. ed. see Jorgensen, C. K.
Reisfeld, Ralph A. & Ferrone, Soldano, eds. Current Trends in Histocompatability, 2 vols. Incl. Vol. 1. Immunogenetic & Molecular Profiles. LC 80-18211. 570p. 1981. 110.00 (*0-306-40480-X*, Kluwer Plenum); Vol. 2. Biological & Clinical Concepts. LC 80-18211. 326p. 1981. 85.00 (*0-306-40481-8*, Kluwer Plenum); LC 80-18211. 1981. write for info. (*0-318-55317-1*, Plenum Trade) Perseus Pubng.
— Melanoma Antigens & Antibodies. LC 82-5288. 462p. 1982. 95.00 (*0-306-40852-X*, Plenum Trade) Perseus Pubng.
Reisfeld, Ralph A., jt. ed. see Sell, Stewart.
Reisfeld, Randi. All You Need Is a Love Spell. (Sabrina, the Teenage Witch Ser.: No. 7). (YA). (gr. 7-12). 1998. per. 4.50 (*0-671-01695-4*, Archway) PB.
— An American Betty in Paris. (Clueless Ser.: No. 3). (YA). (gr. 7 up). 1996. mass mkt. 4.99 (*0-671-56869-8*, PB Trade Paper) PB.
— American Gladiators: The Official Book. 1995. pap. 12.00 (*0-671-51966-2*) PB.
— The Bar - Bat Mitzvah Survival Guide. (Illus.). 144p. 1992. pap. 9.95 (*0-8065-1295-4*, Citadel Pr) Carol Pub Group.
— The Bar/Bat Mitzvah Survival Guide. 196p. 1999. reprint ed. lib. bdg. 26.95 (*0-7351-0106-X*) Replica Bks.
— The Boy Who Would Be King: A Biography of Prince William. (YA). (gr. 7 up). 1997. pap. 3.99 (*0-614-28881-9*, Archway) PB.
— Cher Goes Enviro-Mental. (Clueless Ser.: No. 7). (YA). (gr. 6 up). 1997. pap. 3.99 (*0-614-28884-3*, Archway) PB.
— Cher Goes Enviro-Mental, No. 6. (Clueless Ser.: No. 7). 160p. (YA). (gr. 8 up). 1997. per. 4.99 (*0-671-00324-0*) PB.
— Cher's Furiously Fit Workout, No. 4. (Clueless Ser.: No. 5). (YA). (gr. 6 up). 1996. per. 4.99 (*0-671-00322-4*) PB.
— Chronically Crushed. (Clueless Ser.: No. 14). (YA). (gr. 6 up). 1998. per. 4.99 (*0-671-01904-X*) PB.
— Dude with a 'Tude. (Clueless Ser.: No. 16). (YA). (gr. 8-12). 1998. mass mkt. 4.99 (*0-671-02090-0*) PB.
— Extreme Sisterhood. (Clueless Ser.: No. 18). 160p. (YA). (gr. 6-12). 1998. mass mkt. 4.99 (*0-671-02092-7*) PB.
*__Reisfeld, Randi.__ Got Issues Much? Celebrities Share Their Traumas & Triumphs. 1999. pap. text 47.92 (*0-439-04359-X*) Scholastic Inc.
Reisfeld, Randi. Got Issues Much? Celebrities Share Their Traumas & Triumphs. LC 99-231500. (Illus.). 144p. (gr. 3-9). 1999. pap. 5.99 (*0-590-63274-4*) Scholastic Inc.
— He's Not What You Think. (Love Stories Ser.). 192p. (YA). (gr. 7-12). 1997. mass mkt. 3.99 (*0-553-57077-3*) Bantam.
*__Reisfeld, Randi.__ How to Draw Digimon: The Official Guide. (Digimon Ser.). (Illus.). 48p. (J). (ps-3). 2000. pap. 4.99 (*0-439-21058-5*) Scholastic Inc.
Reisfeld, Randi. Meet the Stars of Animorphs. (Animorphs Ser.). (J). (gr. 3-7). 1999. pap. text 59.88 (*0-439-07272-7*); mass mkt. 4.99 (*0-439-06165-2*) Scholastic Inc.
— Melrose Place: Meet the Stars of Today's Hottest New Show. Clancey, Lisa, ed. 192p. (YA). (gr. 5 up). 1992. mass mkt. 4.50 (*0-671-79781-6*) PB.
— The Parent's Bar/Bas Mitzvah Guide: Everything You Need to Know about Planning Your Child's Special Day. rev. ed. (Illus.). 208p. 1997. 18.95 (*1-55972-417-X*, Birch Ln Pr) Carol Pub Group.
— Prince William: The Boy Who Will Be King. LC 99-195322. (Illus.). (YA). (gr. 5 up). 1997. per. 4.99 (*0-671-88785-8*, Archway) PB.
— Prince William: The Boy Who Will Be King. rev. ed. (J). 1998. pap. 4.99 (*0-671-02358-6*, Archway) PB.
Reisfeld, Randi. Prince William, the Boy Who Will Be King: An Unauthorized Biography. LC 49-252540. (J). 1997. 10.09 (*0-606-11763-6*, Pub. by Turtleback) Demco.
Reisfeld, Randi. Sarah Michelle Gellar: She is the Slayer. (J). 1998. pap. text 3.99 (*0-590-64308-8*) Scholastic Inc.
— This Is the Sound: The Best of Alternative Rock. (Illus.). 128p. (YA). (gr. 7 up). 1996. mass mkt. 7.99 (*0-689-80670-1*) Aladdin.
— Too Hottie to Handle. (Clueless Ser.: No. 9). 160p. (YA). (gr. 6 up). 1997. per. 3.99 (*0-671-01160-X*, Archway) PB.
— True Blue Hawaii. (Clueless Ser.: No. 11). 176p. (YA). (gr. 6 up). 1997. per. 3.99 (*0-671-01162-6*) PB.
— Young Stars. Clancy, Lisa, ed. 144p. (Orig.). (J). 1992. per. 3.50 (*0-671-76987-1*) PB.
*__Reisfeld, Randi, ed.__ Digimon: The Official Picture Scrapbook. 48p. (ps-3). 2000. pap. 5.99 (*0-439-21057-7*) Scholastic Inc.
Reisfeld, Randi & Fields, Danny. Who's Your Fave Rave? Who's Your Fave Rave? 256p. (YA). 1997. pap. 14.00 (*1-57297-253-X*) Blvd Books.
Reisfeld, Randi & Gilmour, H. B. Cher Goes Enviro-Mental; Cher's Furiously Fit Workout; Friend or Faux; Baldwin from Another Planet. (Clueless Ser.: Nos. 5-8). (YA). (gr. 4-7). 1997. pap. 15.96 (*0-671-87834-4*) PB.
Reisfeld, Randi, jt. auth. see Preston-Gomez, Cheryl.
Reisgies, Teresa, jt. auth. see Salzman, Marian.
Reish, Donald J. Marine Life of Southern California. 240p. (C). 1995. pap. text 21.00 (*0-7872-1045-5*) Kendall-Hunt.
Reishus, Nancy B. Gone to the Dogs. (Illus.). (Orig.). 1981. lib. bdg. 6.95 (*0-938571-00-1*) Glorycliff Pub.
*__Reisig, Michael.__ Brothers of the Sword - Children of Time, 2 bks. in 1. 400p. 2000. 7.99 (*0-9651240-3-7*) Clear Creek Pr.
— The Fledgling Author's Handbook. 100p. (C). 2000. pap. 9.95 (*0-9651240-5-3*) Clear Creek Pr.
— The Hawks of Kamalon. 436p. 1999. mass mkt. 7.99 (*1-885173-60-1*) Write Way.
Reisig, Michael. The Intrepid Arkansas Traveler, Vol. 1. (Illus.). 240p. (Orig.). 1996. pap. 8.95 (*0-9651240-0-2*) Clear Creek Pr.
— The New Madrid Run. 312p. 1998. mass mkt. 5.95 (*0-9651240-1-0*) Clear Creek Pr.
*__Reisig, Michael.__ The Old Man's Letters. 110p. 1999. pap. 5.99 (*0-9651240-4-5*) Clear Creek Pr.
Reisig, W. Elements of Distributed Algorithms: The Petri Net Approach. LC 98-22854. 300p. 1997. 39.95 (*3-540-62752-9*) Spr-Verlag.
— A Primer in Petri Net Design. Muchnick, S. S. & Schnupp, Peter, eds. (Compass International Ser.). (Illus.). xiv, 120p. 1992. 51.95 (*0-387-52044-9*) Spr-Verlag.
Reisig, W., jt. ed. see Girault, C.
Reisiger, Hans. Johann Gottfried Herder: Sein Leben in Selbstzeugnissen, Briefen und Berichten. 352p. 1970. reprint ed. write for info. (*0-318-71943-6*) G Olms Pubs.
Reisigl, Martin. Sekundare Interjektionen: Eine Diskursanalytische Annaherung. (Illus.). 259p. 1998. 45.95 (*3-631-32973-3*) P Lang Pubng.
*__Reisigl, Martin & Wodak, Ruth.__ Discourse & Discrimination: Rhetorics of Racism & Antisemitism. LC 00-38259. 2000. pap. write for info. (*0-415-23150-7*) Routledge.
Reising, Chris. Noedgelines. (Illus.). (Orig.). 1986. pap. 7.00 (*0-937061-00-X*) Earhart Pr.
Reising, Peggy. Word for Windows Essentials, IM, Level 2. 1996. teacher ed., ring bd. 49.99 (*1-57576-277-3*) Que Educ & Trng.
— Word for Windows 95 Essentials, Level 2. 1996. pap. text 22.99 (*1-57576-276-5*) Que Educ & Trng.
*__Reising, Peggy, et al.__ Word for Windows 95 Essentials, Level Ii. 2nd ed. 174p. (C). 1998. pap. text 18.67 (*1-58076-153-4*) Que Educ & Trng.
Reising, Russell J. Loose Ends: Closure & Crisis in the American Social Text. LC 96-24672. (New Americanists Ser.). (Illus.). 392p. 1997. pap. text 18.95 (*0-8223-1891-1*); lib. bdg. 54.95 (*0-8223-1887-3*) Duke.
— The Unusable Past: Theory & the Study of American Literature. 224p. 1986. text 35.00 (*0-416-01311-2*, 9811) Routledge.
Reisinger, A., tr. see Duran, Jacques.
Reisinger, Anette. Radiocaesium in Pilzen. (Bibliotheca Mycologica: Vol. 155). (GER., Illus.). x, 342p. 1994. 89.00 (*3-443-59057-8*, Pub. by Gebruder Borntraeger) Balogh.
Reisinger, Axel, tr. see Klein, Etienne & Lachieze-Rey, Marc.
Reisinger, Axel, tr. see Thuan, Trin Xuan.
Reisinger, Axel R., tr. see Pullman, Bernard.
Reisinger, Ernest C. The Carnal Christian: What Should We Think of the Carnal Christian? 75p. 1992. reprint ed. 2.00 (*0-85151-389-1*) Banner of Truth.
— The Law & the Gospel. LC 97-197. 232p. (Orig.). 1997. pap. 9.99 (*0-87552-387-0*) P & R Pubng.
— Lord & Christ: The Implications of Lordship for Faith & Life. LC 94-33274. 198p. (Orig.). 1994. pap. 8.99 (*0-87552-388-9*) P & R Pubng.
— Today's Evangelism: It's Message & Methods. 1982. pap. 8.99 (*0-87552-417-6*) P & R Pubng.
*__Reisinger, Ernest C.__ Whatever Happened to the Ten Commandments. (Illus.). 109p. 1999. pap. 6.99 (*0-85151-763-3*) Banner of Truth.
Reisinger, Heribert. Goodness-of-Fit-Mabe in Linearen Regressions- und Logit-Modellen: Theorie und Anwendung in der Empirischen Marktforschung. (Europaische Hochschulschriften: Reihe 5: Bd. 2007). (GER., Illus.). 222p. 1996. pap. 42.95 (*3-631-30777-2*) P Lang Pubng.

R

Reisinger, Hester A. A Soul's Quest: Soliloquies. 165p. 1997. pap. 9.00 (*0-9644370-7-4*) Dryden Publ.
Reisinger, John. An Appointment You Will Keep. pap. 0.06 (*0-87377-125-7*) GAM Pubns.
*__Reisinger, John.__ Nassau. 284p. 2000. pap. 14.95 (*0-595-00093-2*, Writers Club Pr) iUniversecom.
*__Reisinger, John G.__ Abraham's Four Seeds: A Biblical Examination of the Presuppositions of Covenant Theology. 151p. 1998. pap. 10.95 (*0-9660845-4-3*) New Convenant.
Reisinger, John G. But "I" Say unto You. 112p. (Orig.). 1989. pap. write for info. (*0-925703-04-4*) Crown MA.
*__Reisinger, John G.__ Chosen in Eternity. 39p. 2000. pap. 5.50 (*1-928965-04-0*) New Convenant.
— Christ - Lord & Lawgiver over the Church. 20p. 1998. pap. 2.50 (*0-9660845-2-7*) New Convenant.
— Grace. 57p. 1999. pap. write for info. (*0-9660845-6-X*) New Convenant.
Reisinger, John G. The Law - Grace Controversy. 1989. pap. 1.49 (*0-87377-092-7*) GAM Pubns.
— The Sovereignty of God in Providence. 40p. (Orig.). 1989. reprint ed. pap. write for info. (*0-925703-06-0*) Crown MA.
— Tablets of Stone. 120p. (Orig.). 1989. pap. write for info. (*0-925703-05-2*) Crown MA.
*__Reisinger, John G.__ What Is the Christian Faith? A Biblical Study of 1 Corinthians 15:1-4. 14p. 1998. pap. 2.50 (*0-9660845-1-9*) New Convenant.
Reisinger, John G. When Should a Christian Leave a Church?: or An Open Letter to Pastors & Elders. 1994. pap. 1.49 (*0-87377-079-X*) GAM Pubns.
Reisinger, Steven M. Valuation of Privately-Owned Businesses. 155p. 1981. pap. 24.95 (*0-940694-00-X*) Acquisition Plan.
Reisinger, William M. Energy & the Soviet Bloc: Alliance Politics after Stalin. LC 91-55530. 200p. reprint ed. pap. 62.00 (*0-608-20940-6*, 207203900003) Bks Demand.
Reisinger, Wolfgang. Ancient Myth & Philosophy in Peter Russell's "Agamemnon in Hades" LC 97-525. 264p. 1996. text 89.95 (*0-7734-4197-2*) E Mellen.
— Ancient Myth & Philosophy in Peter Russell's Agamemnon in Hades. 263p. 1997. pap. 29.95 (*3-7052-0080-1*, Pub. by Poetry Salzburg) Intl Spec Bk.
Reiskin, Allan B. Advances in Oral Radiology. LC 79-21095. (Postgraduate Dental Handbook Ser.: No. 12). (Illus.). 328p. reprint ed. pap. 101.70 (*0-8357-7600-X*, 205692200096) Bks Demand.
Reisler, Jim. Babe Ruth Slept Here: The Baseball Landmarks of New York City. LC 98-30819. 1998. pap. 18.95 (*1-888698-15-2*) Diamond Communications.
— Black Writers - Black Baseball: An Anthology of Articles from Black Sportswriters Who Covered the Negro Leagues. LC 94-6936. (Illus.). 183p. 1994. lib. bdg. 24.95 (*0-7864-0002-1*) McFarland & Co.
Reisler, Mark. By the Sweat of Their Brow: Mexican Immigrant Labor in the United States, 1900-1940. LC 76-5329. 298p. (Orig.). 1976. 65.00 (*0-8371-8894-6*, RPE/, Greenwood Pr) Greenwood.
Reisman, A. & Kiley, M. Health Care Delivery Planning, Vol. 2. (Studies in Operations Research). x, 374p. 1973. text 171.00 (*0-677-04570-0*) Gordon & Breach.
Reisman, Albert F. Business Loan Workouts, 1988. (Commercial Law & Practice Course Handbook Ser.). 1073p. 1988. 17.50 (*0-685-69387-2*) PLI.
Reisman, Arnold. Management Science Knowledge: Its Creation, Generalization, & Consolidation. LC 91-44705. 324p. 1992. 62.95 (*0-89930-739-6*, RMK/, Quorum Bks) Greenwood.
Reisman, Arnold & Reisman, Ellen, eds. Welcome Tomorrow. LC 82-91107. (Illus.). 1982. pap. 6.95 (*0-686-39632-4*); 4.17 (*0-912269-00-6*) North Coast Pubs.
Reisman, Bernard & Rosen, Gladys. Single-Parent Families at Camp: The Essence of an Experience. LC 84-70480. 54p. 1984. pap. 2.50 (*0-87495-061-9*) Am Jewish Comm.
Reisman, Daniel & Durst, Sanford J. Buying & Selling Country Land. (Illus.). 1981. lib. bdg. 25.00 (*0-915262-40-1*) S J Durst.
Reisman, David. Anthony Crosland: The Mixed Economy. LC 96-1509. 175p. 1996. text 75.00 (*0-312-15950-1*) St Martin.
— Croslands Future: Opportunity & Outcome. LC 96-1989. 300p. 1996. text 75.00 (*0-312-16089-5*) St Martin.
— Market & Health. LC 93-17299. 254p. 1993. text 45.00 (*0-312-09981-9*) St Martin.
Reisman, David, ed. Democratic Socialism in Britain: Classic Texts in Economic & Political Thought, 1825-1952, 10 vols. LC 96-26896. 3700p. 1997. 950.00 (*1-85196-285-9*, Pub. by Pickering & Chatto) Ashgate Pub Co.
— Economic Thought & Political Theory. LC 93-42898. (Recent Economic Thought Ser.). 256p. (C). 1994. lib. bdg. 127.00 (*0-7923-9433-X*) Kluwer Academic.
— The Political Economy of James Buchanan. LC 89-4435. (Economics Ser.: No. 10). 216p. 1990. 39.50 (*0-89096-430-0*) Tex A&M Univ Pr.
— Theories of the Mixed Economy, 10 vols. 1995. 950.00 (*1-85196-213-1*, Pub. by Pickering & Chatto) Ashgate Pub Co.

An Asterisk (*) at the beginning of an entry indicates that the title is appearing for the first time.

Reisman, Ellen, jt. ed. see Reisman, Arnold.

Reisman, George. Capitalism: A Complete & Integrated Understanding of the Nature & Value of Human Economic Life. LC 96-78105. 1096p. 1997. 95.00 (0-915463-73-3) Jameson Bks.

— The Government Against the Economy. LC 79-83689. 225p. 1985. reprint ed. pap. 16.95 (0-915463-23-7) Jameson Bks.

Reisman, H. B., ed. Economic Analysis of Fermentation Processes. (Biotechnologists & Microbiologists Ser.). 272p. 1988. 219.00 (0-8493-6886-3, TP156) CRC Pr.

Reisman, Howard M. Fishes You Can Color! Atlantic Coast Coloring Book & Guide. (Illus.). 40p. (J). (ps-6). 1996. spiral bd. 4.95 (0-9628492-4-3) Waterline Bks.

Reisman, Jane, jt. auth. see Kohl, Jeanne.

Reisman, Jane, jt. auth. see Zeigler, Harmon.

Reisman, Jane, jt. ed. see Borman, Kathryn M.

Reisman, John, ed. Behavioral Disorders in Infants, Children, & Adolescents. 416p. 1986. text 36.00 (0-89859-887-7) L Erlbaum Assocs.

Reisman, John M. Anatomy of Friendship. LC 79-12857. 1979. 22.95 (0-89197-646-9) Irvington.

— A History of Clinical Psychology. 2nd ed. 424p. 1991. 99.95 (1-56032-041-9); pap. 36.95 (1-56032-188-1) Hemisp Pub.

— A History of Clinical Psychology: Enlarged Edition of the Development of Clinical Psychology. LC 75-40102. 430p. 1983. reprint ed. pap. text 19.95 (0-8290-0873-X) Irvington.

— Toward the Integration of Psychotherapy. LC 77-147236. (Wiley Series on Psychological Disorders). 169p. reprint ed. pap. 52.40 (0-608-30407-7, 201188400080) Bks Demand.

Reisman, Judith A. Kinsey: Crimes & Consequences: The Red Queen & the Grand Scheme. Ray, Eunice V., ed. (Illus.). 340p. 1999. pap. 24.95 (0-9666624-0-7) Inst Media Educ.

Reisman, Kimberly D., jt. auth. see Dunnam, Maxie.

***Reisman, Kimberly Dunnam.** The Christ-Centered Woman: Finding Balance in World of Extremes. Halverson, Holly, ed. 96p. 2000. pap. 12.00 (0-8358-0913-7) Upper Room Bks.

Reisman, Kimberly Dunnam, jt. auth. see Dunnam, Maxie.

Reisman, L., et al. The New Orleans Voter: A Handbook of Political Description, Vol. 2. LC 56-3785. 1955. 11.00 (0-930598-01-6) Tulane Stud Pol.

***Reisman, Michael, ed.** Jurisdiction in International Law. LC 98-43824. (Library of Essays in International Law). 620p. 1999. text 222.95 (1-84014-093-3, Pub. by Ashgate Pub) Ashgate Pub Co.

Reisman, Nancy. House Fires. LC 99-29218. (Iowa Short Fiction Award Ser.). 224p. 1999. pap. 18.95 (0-87745-692-5) U of Iowa Pr.

***Reisman, Paul Joseph.** Forming the Future through Knowledge of the Past: Two Thousand Years of Christian History. 2000. pap. 16.00 (0-8059-4947-X) Dorrance.

Reisman, Robert E., jt. ed. see Slavin, Raymond G.

Reisman, Rose. Light Vegetarian Cooking. (Illus.). 192p. 1998. pap. text 17.95 (1-896503-66-7) R Rose Inc.

— Rose Reisman Brings Home Light Pasta. (Illus.). 242p. 1995. 27.95 (1-896503-06-3, Pub. by R Rose Inc); pap. 16.95 (1-896503-04-7, Pub. by R Rose Inc) Firefly Bks Ltd.

— Rose Reisman's Enlighted Home Cooking. (Illus.). 256p. (Orig.). 1996. pap. 18.95 (1-896503-16-0, Pub. by R Rose Inc) Firefly Bks Ltd.

Reisman, Rosemary M. & Canfield, Christopher J. Contemporary Southern Women Fiction Writers. 237p. 1994. 36.00 (0-8108-2832-4) Scarecrow.

Reisman, Sorel, ed. Multimedia Computing: Preparing for the Twenty-First Century. 600p. (C). 1996. text 59.95 (1-878289-22-5) Idea Group Pub.

Reisman, Stanley, jt. auth. see Ritter, Arthur B.

Reisman, W. Michael. The Art of the Possible: Diplomatic Alternatives in the Middle East. LC 70-136196. 169p. reprint ed. pap. 52.40 (0-8357-8806-7, 203338300085) Bks Demand.

— Law in Brief Encounters. LC 99-13730. 240p. 1999. 27.50 (0-300-07569-3) Yale U Pr.

— Systems of Control in International Adjudication & Arbitration: Breakdown & Repair. LC 91-33033. 188p. 1992. text 37.95 (0-8223-1202-6) Duke.

Reisman, W. Michael & Baker, James. Regulating Covert Action: Practices, Contexts, & Policies of Covert Coercion Abroad in International & American Law. 256p. (C). 1992. 37.50 (0-300-05059-3) Yale U Pr.

Reisman, W. Michael & Schreiber, Aaron M. Jurisprudence: Understanding & Shaping Law. LC 87-11243. (Illus.). 640p. (C). 1987. text 42.95 (0-913275-00-X) New Haven Pr.

Reisman, W. Michael & Westerman, Gayl L. Straight Baselines in International Maritime Boundary Delimitation. 210p. 1992. text 59.95 (0-312-06034-3) St Martin.

Reisman, W. Michael & Willard, Andrew R., eds. International Incidents: The Law That Counts in World Politics. LC 87-25846. 291p. 1988. reprint ed. pap. 90.30 (0-608-07161-7, 206738600009) Bks Demand.

Reisman, W. Michael, et al. International Commercial Arbitration, Cases, Materials & Notes on the Resolution of International Business Disputes. LC 97-223333. (University Casebook Ser.). 1346p. 1997. text. write for info. (1-56662-554-8) Foundation Pr.

— International Commercial Arbitration, Cases, Materials & Notes on the Resolution of International Business Disputes, Documentary Supplement To. (University Casebook Ser.). 804p. 1997. pap. text. write for info. (1-56662-555-6) Foundation Pr.

Reisman, W. Michael, jt. auth. see McDougal, Myres S.

Reisman, Yisroel. The Laws of Ribbis. 23.99 (0-89906-126-5, LORH); pap. 19.99 (0-89906-127-3, LORP) Mesorah Pubns.

Reismann, Herbert & Pawlik, Peter S. Elasticity: Theory & Applications. 446p. (C). 1991. reprint ed. lib. bdg. 68.50 (0-89464-532-3) Krieger.

Reismann, John M. Anatomy of Friendship. 1987. pap. text 6.95 (0-8290-2116-7) Irvington.

***Reisner, Frank.** Posting the Mail. 224p. 1999. pap. 16.00 (0-8059-4629-2) Dorrance.

Reisner, G. A. Excavations at Kerma, Pts. I-III. Hooton, E. A. & Bates, Natica I., eds. (Harvard African Studies: Vol. 5). 1972. lib. bdg. 160.00 (0-527-01028-6) Periodicals Srv.

— Excavations at Kerma, Pts. IV-V. Hooton, E. A. & Bates, Natica I., eds. (Harvard African Studies: Vol. 5). 1972. lib. bdg. 140.00 (0-527-01029-4) Periodicals Srv.

Reisner, George A. The Egyptian Conception of Immortality. ix, 85p. (Orig.). 1989. reprint ed. pap. 15.00 (0-933175-22-1) Van Siclen Bks.

— Egyptian Conception of Immortality: The Ingersoll Lecture of 1911. 96p. 1998. reprint ed. pap. 11.95 (0-7661-0446-X) Kessinger Pub.

— A History of the Giza Necropolis. (Illus.). 600p. 1998. reprint ed. 150.00 (1-57898-146-8) Martino Pubng.

— Mycerinus: The Temples of the Third Pyramid at Giza. (Illus.). 400p. 1998. reprint ed. 125.00 (1-57898-145-X) Martino Pubng.

Reisner, M. E., jt. auth. see Reid, James.

Reisner, Marc P. Cadillac Desert. 608p. 1999. pap. write for info. (0-14-026510-4) Viking Penguin.

— Cadillac Desert: The American West & Its Disappearing Water. rev. ed. (Illus.). 582p. 1993. pap. 15.95 (0-14-017824-4, Penguin Bks) Viking Penguin.

Reisner, Marc P. & Bates, Sarah F. Overtapped Oasis: Reform or Revolution for Western Water. LC 89-24459. (Illus.). 197p. (C). 1990. pap. 19.95 (0-933280-75-0); text 38.00 (0-933280-76-9) Island Pr.

Reisner, Ralph, et al, eds. Administracion de la Deuda de los Paises Latinoamericanos: Aspectos Juridicos y Reglamentarios. 332p. 1992. 14.50 (0-940602-50-4) IADB.

— Latin American Sovereign Debt Management: Legal & Regulatory Aspects. (Illus.). 273p. 1992. pap. text 14.50 (0-940602-33-4) IADB.

Reisner, Ralph & Gruson, Michael. Regulation of Foreign Banks: United States & International. 900p. 1993. suppl. ed. 35.00 (0-685-74147-8, MICHIE) LEXIS Pub.

— Regulation of Foreign Banks: United States & International, 2 vols. 2nd ed. 750p. 1993. 160.00 (0-88063-287-9, MICHIE) LEXIS Pub.

Reisner, Ralph & Slobogin, Christopher. Law & the Mental Health System: Civil & Criminal Aspects. 2nd ed. (American Casebook Ser.). 1117p. (C). 1990. text 54.50 (0-314-73302-7) West Pub.

— Law & the Mental Health System: Civil & Criminal Aspects, Teacher's Manual to Accompany. 2nd ed. (American Casebook Ser.). 68p. (C). 1992. pap. text. write for info. (0-314-01378-4) West Pub.

— Law & the Mental Health System: Civil & Criminal Aspects, 1992. 2nd ed. (American Casebook Ser.). 73p. (C). 1992. pap. text, suppl. ed. 8.00 (0-314-01301-6) West Pub.

Reisner, Ralph, jt. auth. see Gruson, Michael.

Reisner, Ralph, jt. auth. see Slobogin, Christopher.

Reisner, Robert G., ed. Bird: The Legend of Charlie Parker. LC 74-30084. (Roots of Jazz Ser.). (Illus.). 256p. 1975. reprint ed. pap. 13.95 (0-306-80069-1); reprint ed. lib. bdg. 29.50 (0-306-70677-6) Da Capo.

Reisner, Trudi. Easy AMI PRO 3.1 for Windows. LC 94-67604. (Illus.). 256p. (Orig.). 1994. 19.99 (1-56529-996-5) Que.

— Easy Microsoft Office 97. LC 96-71447. 320p. 1996. 24.99 (0-7897-1078-1) Que.

— Easy Windows 3.1. 246p. 1994. 19.99 (1-56529-832-2) Que.

— Easy Word for Windows 95. (Illus.). 251p. (Orig.). 1995. 19.99 (0-7897-0081-6) Que.

— EasyWord Perfect for Windows 95. (Illus.). 256p. (Orig.). 1996. 19.99 (0-7897-0145-6) Que.

— Microsoft Excel 2000 Exam Cram. 1999. pap. text 26.99 (1-57610-512-1) Coriolis Grp.

— Microsoft Excel 97. 10th ed. LC 98-11496. (Exam Cram Ser.). xxiv, 384 p. (C). 1999. mass mkt. 26.99 (1-57610-221-1) Coriolis Grp.

***Reisner, Trudi.** Microsoft Word 2000. LC 99-15717. (One Step at a Time Ser.). 360p. 1999. pap. 29.99 (0-7645-3295-2) IDG Bks.

Reisner, Trudi. Office Max - Easy Microsoft Office. 1994. 24.99 (0-7897-0697-0) Que.

— Outlook, '97 One Step at a Time. LC 97-76682. (New Tutorial Ser.). 350p. 1997. pap. 29.99 (0-7645-3128-X) IDG Bks.

— 10 Minute Guide to Windows 95. (Illus.). 180p. (Orig.). 1995. 12.99 (1-56761-515-5, Alpha Ref) Macmillan Gen Ref.

— Word 97 One Step at a Time. LC 97-76686. (New Tutorial Ser.). 352p. 1997. pap. 29.99 (0-7645-3129-8) IDG Bks.

— WordPerfect Solutions. 608p. 1993. pap. 24.95 (0-471-58935-7) Wiley.

Reisner, Trudi & Acklen, Laura. Windows 3.11 QuickStart Supplemental Version. LC 94-67368. (Illus.). 246p. 1994. 21.99 (1-56529-865-9) Que.

Reisner, Trudi, jt. auth. see Darnell, Rick.

Reisner, Trudi, jt. auth. see Kasser, Barbara.

Reison, Dennis S., ed. Physician's Reference Guide to Cardiology. 935p. 1992. write for info. (1-878212-00-1) Prof & Tech Pub.

Reiss. Family Systems in America. 4th ed. (C). 1988. pap. text, teacher ed. 42.00 (0-03-020578-6) Harcourt Coll Pubs.

— Flamingo. 1990. pap. write for info. (0-312-92368-6) Tor Bks.

— Marx: A Clear Guide. LC 96-28836. 1996. 44.95 (0-7453-1015-X, Pub. by Pluto GBR) Stylus Pub VA.

Reiss, jt. auth. see Hall.

Reiss, Albert J., Jr. & Tonry, Michael H., eds. Communities & Crime. LC 80-642217. (Studies in Crime & Justice: Vol. 8). viii, 430p. (C). 1986. lib. bdg. 33.00 (0-226-80802-5) U Ch Pr.

— Communities & Crime. LC 80-642217. (Studies in Crime & Justice: Vol. 8). viii, 429p. (C). 1987. pap. text 19.95 (0-226-80798-3) U Ch Pr.

Reiss, Albert J., Jr., et al. Occupations & Social Status. Stein, Leon, ed. LC 77-70525. (Illus.). 1977. reprint ed. lib. bdg. 33.95 (0-405-10193-7) Ayer.

Reiss, Albert J., Jr., ed. see National Research Council, Panel on the Understand.

Reiss, Albert J., Jr., ed. see National Research Council Staff.

Reiss, Albert J., Jr., jt. ed. see Tonry, Michael H.

Reiss, Albert J., Jr., ed. see Wirth, Louis.

Reiss, Alvin H. Arts Management: A Guide to Finding Funds & Winning Audiences. 267p. 1992. 45.00 (0-930807-32-4, 600321) Fund Raising.

— Arts Management Reader. (Illus.). 704p. 1979. text 75.00 (0-8247-6850-7) Dekker.

— Cash In! Funding & Promoting the Arts. LC 86-23040. (Illus.). 240p. 1986. 24.95 (0-930452-62-3) Theatre Comm.

***Reiss, Alvin H.** CPR for Nonprofits: Creating Strategies for Successful Fundraising, Marketing, Communications & Management. (Illus.). 2000. pap. 26.95 (0-7879-5241-9) Jossey-Bass.

Reiss, Alvin H. Don't Just Applaud, Send Money! The Most Successful Strategies for Funding & Marketing the Arts. (Illus.). 200p. (Orig.). 1995. pap. 15.95 (1-55936-105-0) Theatre Comm.

Reiss, Barry S. Pharmacological Aspects of Nursing Care. 5th ed. (Nursing Education Ser.). 112p. 1996. teacher ed. 10.50 (0-8273-7669-3) Delmar.

Reiss, Barry S. & Evans, Mary E. Pharmacological Aspects of Nursing Care. 4th ed. LC 92-49601. 766p. 1993. pap. 44.95 (0-8273-4846-0) Delmar.

— Pharmacological Aspects of Nursing Care. 5th ed. (Nursing Education Ser.). 816p. (C). 1995. mass mkt. 63.95 (0-8273-6662-0) Delmar.

— Pharmacological Aspects of Nursing Care: Computerized Testmaker & Testbank for DOS Compatible Computers. 4th ed. 1993. 49.95 (0-685-70404-1) Delmar.

— Pharmacological Aspects of Nursing Care: Instructor's Guide. 4th ed. 139p. 1993. pap. 16.95 (0-8273-5447-9) Delmar.

Reiss, Bob. The Last Spy. large type ed. LC 93-22359. 563p. 1993. lib. bdg. 21.95 (1-56054-696-4) Thorndike Pr.

— Purgatory Road. large type ed. LC 96-35542. 1996. pap. 22.95 (1-56895-384-4, Compass) Wheeler Pub.

***Reiss, Bob & Cruikshank, Jeffrey L.** Low Risk, High Reward: Starting & Growing a Business with Minimal Risk. 352p. 2000. 27.50 (0-684-84962-3) Free Pr.

***Reiss, C., et al, eds.** Advances in Molecular Toxicology. 568p. 1998. 225.00 (90-6764-278-9, Pub. by VSP) Coronet Bks.

Reiss, Carol A. Experiments in Plant Physiology. LC 93-2239. (Illus.). 292p. (C). 1997. pap. text 51.00 (0-13-701285-3, Pub. by P-H) S&S Trade.

Reiss, David. The Family's Construction of Reality. (Illus.). 440p. 1981. pap. 20.50 (0-674-29416-5) HUP.

— Relationship Code: Deciphering Genetic & Social Influences on Adolescent Development. LC 99-38680. 532p. 2000. 55.00 (0-674-00054-4) HUP.

— 3 Outta 4. unabridged ed. LC 99-90004. 288p. 1999. pap. 14.95 (1-884778-61-5) Old Mountain.

Reiss, David, ed. Psychosocial Treatments. 104p. 1994. pap. text 14.95 (0-89862-298-0, 2298) Guilford Pubns.

Reiss, David, jt. ed. see Cole, Robert.

Reiss, David S. M*A*S*H: The Exclusive Inside Story of the TV's Most Popular Show. rev. ed. LC 89-19743. 168p. 1983. pap. 9.95 (0-672-52762-6, Bobbs) Macmillan.

Reiss, Dolan. Wordperfect Function Key Template. 1989. 1.00 (0-538-80946-9) Thomson Learn.

Reiss, Donna, et al, eds. Electronic Communication Across the Curriculum. LC 97-47688. (Illus.). 327p. 1998. pap. 26.95 (0-8141-1308-7) NCTE.

Reiss, Donna, jt. auth. see Hickey, Dona J.

Reiss, Donna, ed. see Bogger, Tommy L. & Wiggins, William B.

Reiss, Edward. Marx. 192p. 1997. pap. 15.95 (0-7453-1014-1, Pub. by Pluto GBR) Stylus Pub VA.

— The Strategic Defense Initiative. (Studies in International Relations: No. 23). (Illus.). 263p. (C). 1992. text 64.95 (0-521-41097-5) Cambridge U Pr.

Reiss, Ellen, ed. see Siegel, Eli.

Reiss, Eric L. The Compleat Talking Machine: A Collector's Guide to Antique Phonographs. 3rd rev. ed. LC 98-228311. (Illus.). 272p. 1998. pap. 29.95 (1-886606-12-9) Sonoran Pub.

Reiss-Evans. Pharmacological Aspect of Nursing Care. 6th ed. (Nursing Education Ser.). (C). 2001. pap. text 35.95 (0-7668-0502-6) Delmar.

Reiss, Fern. The Infertility Diet: Get Pregnant & Prevent Miscarriage. LC 98-48227. (Illus.). 288p. 1999. pap. 24.95 (1-893290-39-5) Peanut Butt & Jelly.

— The Infertility Diet: Get Pregnant & Prevent Miscarriage. LC 98-48227. (Illus.). 288p. 2000. 39.95 (1-893290-38-7) Peanut Butt & Jelly.

— Taking Time off in Israel. LC 85-1225. (Illus.). 149p. 1985. pap. 9.95 (0-915361-15-9) Lambda Pubs.

Reiss, Frederick, ed. The Standard Guide to the Jewish & Civil Calendars: A Parallel Jewish & Civil Calender from 1899-2050. 160p. 1986. pap. text 19.95 (0-87441-428-8) Behrman.

***Reiss, Gary.** Changing Ourselves, Changing the World. LC 99-61060. 224p. 2000. pap. 14.95 (1-56184-143-9) New Falcon Pubns.

Reiss, Geoff. Programme Management Demystified: Managing Multiple Projects Successfully. LC 95-72359. (Illus.). 272p. (Orig.). 1996. pap. 34.99 (0-419-21350-3, E & FN Spon) Routledge.

— Project Management Demystified. 1992. pap. text 30.95 (0-419-16920-2, E & FN Spon) Routledge.

— Project Management Demystified: Today's Tools & Techniques. 2nd ed. (Illus.). 240p. 1995. pap. 29.99 (0-419-20750-3, E & FN Spon) Routledge.

Reiss, H. Radiative Transfer in Nontransparent, Dispersed Media. (Tracts in Modern Physics Ser.: Vol. 113). (Illus.). ix, 205 p. 1988. 80.95 (0-387-18608-5) Spr-Verlag.

Reiss, H., et al, eds. Progress in Solid State Chemistry, Vol. 5. 1971. 98.00 (0-08-015846-3, Pub. by Pergamon Repr) Franklin.

— Progress in Solid State Chemistry, Vol. 6. 1971. 98.00 (0-08-016723-3, Pub. by Pergamon Repr) Franklin.

— Progress in Solid State Chemistry, Vol. 7. 1972. 98.00 (0-08-016916-3, Pub. by Pergamon Repr) Franklin.

***Reiss, H. D.** Poems for Lovers. LC 99-93893. 1999. pap. 7.95 (0-533-13178-2) Vantage.

Reiss, H. S., ed. see Kant, Immanuel.

Reiss, Harriet M., jt. auth. see Reiss, Ira L.

Reiss, Herbert. Reproductive Medicine: From A to Z. LC 97-35789. (Illus.). 162p. 1998. pap. text 49.95 (0-19-262901-8) OUP.

Reiss, Howard R. Methods of Thermodynamics. unabridged ed. LC 96-35379. (Illus.). 238p. 1997. reprint ed. pap. text 8.95 (0-486-69445-3) Dover.

Reiss, Ira L. & Reiss, Harriet M. Solving America's Sexual Crisis. LC 97-37334. 287p. 1997. pap. text 18.95 (1-57392-172-6) Prometheus Bks.

Reiss, James. The Parable of Fire. LC 94-68938. (Poetry Ser.). 58p. (C). 1996. 20.95 (0-88748-238-4); pap. 11.95 (0-88748-239-2) Carnegie-Mellon.

Reiss, Jill, ed. see Templeton, Michael.

Reiss, Johanna. The Journey Back. LC 76-12615. (Trophy Keypoint Bk.). 224p. (YA). (gr. 7 up). 1987. pap. 4.95 (0-06-447042-3, HarpTrophy) HarpC Child Bks.

— Journey Back. LC 76-12615. 1987. 10.05 (0-606-03518-4, Pub. by Turtleback) Demco.

— The Upstairs Room. (J). 1984. mass mkt. 2.50 (0-553-24784-0) Bantam.

— The Upstairs Room. LC 77-187940. 208p. (YA). (gr. 7 up). 1972. 15.95 (0-690-85127-8) HarpC Child Bks.

— The Upstairs Room. LC 77-187940. 208p. (J). (gr. 7 up). 1990. pap. 5.95 (0-06-440370-X, HarpTrophy) HarpC Child Bks.

***Reiss, Johanna.** The Upstairs Room. (J). 1999. 9.95 (1-56137-657-4) Novel Units.

Reiss, Johanna. The Upstairs Room. (J). 1972. 10.05 (0-606-04132-X, Pub. by Turtleback) Demco.

— Upstairs Room, The (rack) LC 77-187940. (Trophy Keypoint Bk.). 192p. (J). (gr. 7 up). 1987. reprint ed. mass mkt. 4.95 (0-06-447043-1, HarpTrophy) HarpC Child Bks.

***Reiss, Julie H.** From Margin to Center: The Spaces of Installation Art. LC 99-41769. (Illus.). 208p. 2000. 32.95 (0-262-18196-7) MIT Pr.

Reiss, Kathryn. Dollhouse of the Dead. (Ghost in the Dollhouse Ser.). (J). (gr. 4-7). 1997. pap. 3.99 (0-614-29026-0, Apple Classics) Scholastic Inc.

Reiss, Kathryn. Dollhouse of the Dead. (Ghost in the Dollhouse Ser.). 1997. 9.09 (0-606-11370-3, Pub. by Turtleback) Demco.

Reiss, Kathryn. Dreadful Sorry. LC 92-38780. (gr. 7 up). 1996. mass mkt. 4.99 (0-590-48406-0) Scholastic Inc.

— Dreadful Sorry. LC 92-38780. 1996. 10.09 (0-606-09216-1, Pub. by Turtleback) Demco.

— Ghost Dollhouse. (J). 1997. mass mkt. 3.99 (0-590-60360-4) Scholastic Inc.

— The Glass House People. LC 91-26850. 288p. (YA). (gr. 7 up). 1992. 16.95 (0-15-231040-1, Harcourt Child Bks) Harcourt.

— The Glass House People. LC 91-26850. 288p. (YA). (gr. 7 up). 1996. pap. 6.00 (0-15-201293-1) Harcourt.

— Glass House People. (YA). (gr. 7 up). 1992. pap. 6.95 (0-15-231041-X, Harcourt Child Bks) Harcourt.

— Headless Bride. (Ghost in the Dollhouse Ser.). 1997. 9.09 (0-606-11371-1, Pub. by Turtleback) Demco.

— Headless Bride, Vol. 2. (Ghost in the Dollhouse Ser.). 1997. pap. 3.99 (0-590-60361-2, Apple Paperbacks) Scholastic Inc.

— Pale Phoenix. LC 93-32299. (J). (gr. 5 up). 1994. pap. 3.95 (0-15-200031-3) Harcourt.

— Pale Phoenix. LC 93-32299. 256p. (YA). (gr. 7 up). 1994. 10.95 (0-15-200030-5) Harcourt.

— Pale Phoenix. (J). 1997. pap. 4.99 (0-590-48405-2, Point) Scholastic Inc.

— Pale Phoenix. 1997. 10.09 (0-606-13012-8, Pub. by Turtleback) Demco.

— Paperquake: A Puzzle. LC 97-33217. 264p. (J). (gr. 5-9). 1998. 17.00 (0-15-201183-8) Harcourt.

— Rest in Peace. (Ghost in the Dollhouse Ser.). 1997. 9.09 (0-606-11372-X, Pub. by Turtleback) Demco.

— Rest in Peace, Vol. 3. (Ghost in the Dollhouse Ser.). (J). 1997. pap. text 3.99 (0-590-60362-0, Apple Paperbacks) Scholastic Inc.

— Time Windows. LC 90-22018. 272p. (J). (gr. 4-7). 1991. 17.00 (0-15-288205-7, Harcourt Child Bks) Harcourt.

***Reiss, Kathryn.** Time Windows. 192p. (J). (gr. 4-7). 2000. pap. 6.00 (0-15-202399-2, Harcourt Child Bks) Harcourt.

An Asterisk (*) at the beginning of an entry indicates that the title is appearing for the first time.

R

Reiss, Leonard, jt. auth. see Weber, Christopher.

Reiss, Levi. The Eudora User's Guide. (Illus.). 296p. 1996. pap. text 19.95 (*0-12-586355-1*) Acad Pr.

— UNIX System Administration Guide. 672p. 1993. pap. 34.95 (*0-07-881951-2*) McGraw.

— Using Paradox for Windows. (C). 1993. text 21.50 (*0-07-052018-6*) McGraw.

Reiss, Louis H. Reservoir Engineering Aspects of Fractured Formation. (Illus.). 120p. (C). 1980. 220.00 (*2-7108-0374-7*, Pub. by Edits Technip) Enfield Pubs NH.

Reiss, Michael & Straughan, Roger. Improving Nature? The Science & Ethics of Genetic Engineering. (Illus.). 304p. (C). 1998. reprint ed. pap. 15.95 (*0-521-63754-6*) Cambridge U Pr.

Reiss, Michael J. The Allometry of Growth & Reproduction. (Illus.). 200p. (C). 1989. text 64.95 (*0-521-36091-9*) Cambridge U Pr.

— The Allometry of Growth & Reproduction. (Illus.). 198p. (C). 1991. pap. text 24.95 (*0-521-42358-9*) Cambridge U Pr.

— Science Education for a Pluralist Society. LC 92-47138. (Developing Science & Technology Education Ser.). 1993. pap. 31.95 (*0-335-15760-2*) OpUniv Pr.

Reiss, Michael J. & Straughan, Roger. Improving Nature? The Science & Ethics of Genetic Engineering. (Illus.). 298p. (C). 1996. text 29.95 (*0-521-45441-7*) Cambridge U Pr.

Reiss, Michael J., jt. ed. see King, Anna S.

***Reiss, Mike.** How Murray Saved Christmas. (Illus.). 32p. (J). (ps up). 2000. 10.99 (*0-8431-7610-5*, Price Stern) Peng Put Young Read.

Reiss, Mitchell. Bridled Ambition: Why Countries Constrain Their Nuclear Capabilities. LC 95-2646. (Special Studies). 360p. 1995. pap. 16.95 (*0-943875-71-4*); text 45.00 (*0-943875-72-2*) W Wilson Ctr Pr.

Reiss, Mitchell & Litwak, Robert S., eds. Nuclear Proliferation after the Cold War. (Woodrow Wilson Center Press Ser.). 320p. (C). 1994. text 45.00 (*0-943875-64-1*); pap. text 16.95 (*0-943875-57-9*) Johns Hopkins.

Reiss, Nira. Speech Acts Taxonomy As a Tool for Ethnographic Description: An Analysis Based on Videotapes of Continuous Behavior in Two New York Households. LC 86-8207. (Pragmatics & Beyond Ser.: No. VI:7). x, 153p. 1985. pap. 53.00 (*0-915027-93-3*) J Benjamins Pubng Co.

Reiss, Oscar. Blacks in Colonial America. LC 97-10009. 301p. 1997. lib. bdg. 45.00 (*0-7864-0339-X*) McFarland & Co.

— Medicine & the American Revolution: How Diseases & Their Treatments Affected the Colonial Army. LC 98-20088. 286p. 1998. lib. bdg. 48.50 (*0-7864-0338-1*) McFarland & Co.

***Reiss, Oscar.** Medicine in Colonial America. 536p. 2000. 64.50 (*0-7618-1576-7*) U Pr of Amer.

***Reiss, Paul J.** Dad: A Son's Perspective on the Life & Legacy of Julian J. Reiss. (Illus.). xvi, 168p. 2000. 25.00 (*0-9643452-1-8*) Graphics North.

Reiss, Philip. That's a Good One! LC 97-90579. 1998. 8.95 (*0-533-12429-8*) Vantage.

Reiss, R. D. Approximate Distributions of Order Statistics. (Series in Statistics). (Illus.). xii, 355p. 1989. 84.95 (*0-387-96851-2*) Spr-Verlag.

***Reiss, R. D.** Children Learning Science. LC 99-44088. (Illus.). 2000. pap. write for info. (*0-335-19769-8*) Open Univ TX.

— Understanding Science Lessons. LC 99-44088. (Illus.). (J). 2000. write for info. (*0-335-19770-1*, Pub. by OpUniv Pr) Taylor & Francis.

Reiss, R. D. & Thomas, M. Statistical Analysis of Extreme Values. LC 97-23442. 1997. write for info. (*0-8176-5768-1*) Birkhauser.

— Statistical Analysis of Extreme Values. LC 97-23442. 336p. 1997. text 64.50 (*3-7643-5768-1*) Spr-Verlag.

Reiss, R. D., et al. A Course on Point Processes. Fienberg, Stephen E. et al, eds. LC 92-29587. (Series in Statistics). (Illus.). 264p. 1992. 72.95 (*0-387-97924-7*) Spr-Verlag.

Reiss, R. D., jt. ed. see Husler, J.

Reiss, Ray. Red Wing Art Pottery 2: Including Poterry Made for RumRill. (Illus.). 1999. 39.00 (*0-9642087-2-5*) Property IL.

— Red Wing Dinnerware: Price & Identification Guide. LC 97-195131. (Illus.). 40p. 1997. pap. 12.95 (*0-9642087-1-7*) Property IL.

Reiss, Ronald & Schipper, Merle, contrib. by. Roland Reiss: A Seventeen-Year Survey. LC 91-73980. (Illus.). 96p. 1991. pap. 24.00 (*0-911291-19-9*, Pub. by Fellows Cont Art) RAM Publications.

Reiss, Stephen. The Child Art of Peggy Somerville. (Illus.). 96p. 1992. 25.00 (*1-871569-17-6*, NAB) I R Dee.

— Peggy Somerville: An English Impressionist. (Illus.). 200p. 1997. 49.50 (*1-85149-260-7*) Antique Collect.

***Reiss, Stephen.** Thomas Churchyard,1798-1865. 72p. 1999. pap. text 35.00 (*1-85149-312-3*) Antique Collect.

Reiss, Steven. Handbook of Challenging Behavior: Mental Health Aspects of Mental Retardation. LC 94-77561. 301p. (C). 1994. text 29.95 (*0-9642598-1-8*) IDS Pubng.

***Reiss, Steven.** Who Am I? The 16 Basic Desires That Motivate Our Actions & Define Our Personalities. LC 00-27268. (Illus.). 288p. 2000. 24.95 (*1-58542-045-X*, Tarcher Putnam) Putnam Pub Group.

Reiss, Steven & Aman, Michael G., eds. Psychotropic Medications & Developmental Disabilities Vol. 1: The International Consensus Handbook. 300p. 1998. text 80.00 (*0-9658966-0-9*) OSU Nisonger.

***Reiss, Steven & Feineman, Neil.** Thirty Frames per Second: The Visionary Art of the Music Video. LC 00-26629. (Illus.). 272p. 2000. 39.95 (*0-8109-4357-3*, Pub. by Abrams) Time Warner.

Reiss, Steven P. The Field Programming Environment: A Friendly Integrated Environment for Learning & Development. (International Series in Engineering & Computer Science, Natural Language Processing & Machine Translation). 312p. (C). 1994. text 127.00 (*0-7923-9537-9*) Kluwer Academic.

— Object-Oriented Software Design with C++ LC 98-38753. (Worldwide Series in Computer Science). 544p. 1998. pap. 67.95 (*0-471-24213-6*) Wiley.

Reiss, Thomas H. Recognizing Planar Objects Using Invariant Image Features. LC 93-19397. 1993. 35.00 (*0-387-56713-5*) Spr-Verlag.

Reiss, Timothy J. Knowledge, Discovery & Imagination in Early Modern Europe: The Rise of Aesthetic Rationalism. (Cambridge Studies in Renaissance Literature & Culture: No. 15). 256p. (C). 1997. text 59.95 (*0-521-58221-0*); pap. text 21.95 (*0-521-58795-6*) Cambridge U Pr.

— The Meaning of Literature. LC 91-23344. 408p. 1992. pap. text 17.95 (*0-8014-9947-X*) Cornell U Pr.

— Tragedy & Truth: Studies in the Development of a Renaissance & Neoclassical Discourse. LC 80-10413. 344p. reprint ed. pap. 106.70 (*0-7837-4549-4*, 208033800005) Bks Demand.

— The Uncertainty of Analysis: Problems in Truth, Meaning, & Culture. LC 88-47741. 312p. 1988. 39.95 (*0-8014-2162-4*) Cornell U Pr.

— The Uncertainty of Analysis: Problems in Truth, Meaning & Culture. LC 88-47741. 315p. reprint ed. pap. 97.70 (*0-608-20941-4*, 207204000003) Bks Demand.

***Reiss, Tom.** Man From the East. 2000. 25.00 (*0-06-019765-X*) HarpC.

— Man from the East. 2000. pap. 14.00 (*0-06-095704-2*) HarpC.

***Reiss, Uzzi & Zucker, Martin.** Natural Hormone Balance for Women. 2001. 24.95 (*0-7434-0665-6*, PB Hardcover) PB.

Reiss, Winold. Blackfoot Indian Portraits. (Illus.). 1992. pap. 3.95 (*0-486-27088-2*) Dover.

Reissenberger, Karl, jt. auth. see Deutschen Akademie der Wissenschaften Staff.

Reisser, Anne N., jt. auth. see McCue, Noelle B.

Reisser, Craig, tr. see Lichtenberger, Elisabeth.

Reisser, Linda, jt. auth. see Chickering, Arthur W.

Reisser, Lynn. Margaret & Margarita, Margarita y Margaret. LC 92-29012. (Illus.). 32p. (J). 1996. mass mkt. 5.95 (*0-688-14734-8*, Wm Morrow) Morrow Avon.

Reisser, Paul C. Complete Book of Baby & Child Care. 1999. pap. 19.99 (*0-8423-3512-9*) Focus Family.

Reisser, Paul C. & Focus on the Family Physicians Resource Council St. The Focus on the Family Complete Book of Baby & Child Care. LC 97-23617. 928p. 1997. 34.99 (*0-8423-0889-X*) Tyndale Hse.

Reisser, Teri K. Help for the Post-Abortion Woman. 96p. 1989. mass mkt. 6.99 (*0-310-34332-1*) Zondervan.

— Solitary Sorrow: Finding Healing & Wholeness after Abortion. LC 99-36846. 150p. 1999. pap. 11.99 (*0-87788-774-8*, H Shaw Pubs) Waterbrook Pr.

Reisser, W. Algae & Symbioses: Plants, Animals, Fungi, Viruses, Interactions Explored. (Illus.). 750p. 1992. 130.00 (*0-948737-15-8*, Pub. by Biopress) Balogh.

Reissiger, Friedrich A., jt. auth. see Kortsen, Bjarne.

Reissigl, H., et al, eds. Infusionstherapie bei Volumenmangel und bei rheologischen Indikationen. (Beitraege zur Infusionstherapie und Klinische Ernaehrung Ser.: Band 2). 1979. pap. 15.00 (*3-8055-3014-5*) S Karger.

Reissigl, H. & Schoenitzer, D. Transfusionsmedizin und Schock. (Handbuch der Infusionstherapie und Klinischen Ernaehrung Ser.: Band 3). xii, 256p. 1986. 108.75 (*3-8055-3744-1*) S Karger.

Reissigl, H., et al. Wasser und Elektrolythaushalt: Physiologie und Pathophysiologie. (Handbuch der Infusionstherapie und Klinischen Ernaehrung Ser.: Band 1). viii, 160p. 1984. 68.75 (*3-8055-3745-X*) S Karger.

Reissman, Rose. The Evolving Multicultural Classroom. LC 94-25103. 1994. pap. 16.95 (*0-87120-233-6*) ASCD.

Reissner, Eric. Selected Works in Applied Mechanics & Mathematics. (Math Ser.). 624p. 1995. 81.25 (*0-86720-968-2*) Jones & Bartlett.

Reissner, Eric, ed. see Applied Mathematics Symposium Staff, et al.

Reissner, Will, jt. auth. see Frankel, Dave.

Reist, A., et al, eds. Diabetes und Graviditaet. (Fortschritte der Geburtshilfe & Gynaekologie Ser.: Vol. 54). (GER., Illus.). 1975. pap. 16.75 (*3-8055-2144-8*) S Karger.

Reist, A., ed. see Held, E., et al.

Reist, Linnaeus L. The Colorful Landis Brothers: Founders of the Landis Valley Museum. Severs, Susan B., ed. & illus. by. LC 87-90447. 100p. (Orig.). (YA). (gr. 11-12). 1987. pap. write for info. (*0-9618501-0-8*) S R Severs.

Reist, Parker C. Aerosol Science & Technology. 2nd ed. 379p. 1993. 74.95 (*0-07-051882-3*) McGraw.

— Applied Mathematics for Environmental Engineers & Scientists. LC 98-28082. 239p. 1998. 69.95 (*0-07-052543-9*) McGraw.

Reiswig, Gary. Water Boy. 304p. 1993. 20.00 (*0-671-79506-6*) S&S Trade.

Reisz, Karel. Technique of Film Editing. 2nd ed. 426p. 1995. pap. text 44.95 (*0-240-51437-8*, Focal) Buttrwrth-Heinemann.

Reisz, Robert R. A Diapsid Reptile from the Pennsylvanian of Kansas. (Special Publications: No. 7). 74p. (Orig.). 1981. pap. 5.00 (*0-89338-011-3*) U KS Nat Hist Mus.

Reisz, Thomas, jt. auth. see Meyer-Ortmanns, Hildegard.

Reit, Seymour. Behind Rebel Lines: The Incredible Story of Emma Edmonds, Civil War Spy. 1988. 11.10 (*0-606-04874-X*, Pub. by Turtleback) Demco.

Reit, Seymour. Guns for General Washington: A Story of the American Revolution. (Great Episodes Ser.). 1990. 11.10 (*0-606-01034-3*, Pub. by Turtleback) Demco.

Reit, Seymour V. Behind Rebel Lines: The Incredible Story of Emma Edmonds, Civil War Spy. LC 87-28079. 144p. (J). (gr. 3-7). 1988. 12.95 (*0-15-200416-5*, Gulliver Bks) Harcourt.

— Behind Rebel Lines: The Incredible Story of Emma Edmonds, Civil War Spy. LC 90-45524. (Odyssey Ser.). 144p. (J). (gr. 3-7). 1991. pap. 6.00 (*0-15-200424-6*, Gulliver Bks) Harcourt.

— Guns for General Washington. LC 90-4871. (Great Episodes Ser.). (Illus.). 144p. (J). (gr. 3-7). 1992. pap. 6.00 (*0-15-232695-2*, Gulliver Bks) Harcourt.

Reitan, Daniel K. Reflections on Interstellar Space Travel. (Illus.). iii, 80p. 1999. per. 10.00 (*0-9670757-0-X*) Diamond Bay.

— The Visual Perception of Relativistically Moving Objects. (Illus.). vii, 188p. 1999. per. 10.00 (*0-9670757-1-8*) Diamond Bay.

Reitan, Earl A. Crossing the Bridge: Growing up Norwegian-American in Depression & War. LC 98-89808. (Illus.). 160p. 1999. pap. 12.95 (*1-883477-28-X*) Lone Oak MN.

— Politics, War & Empire: The Rise of Britain to a World Power, 1688-1792. Eubank, Keith, ed. (European History Ser.). 200p. (C). 1994. pap. text 11.95 (*0-88295-899-2*) Harlan Davidson.

— Tory Radicalism: Margaret Thatcher, John Major, & the Transformation of Modern Britain, 1979-1997. LC 97-18649. 234p. 1997. 66.50 (*0-8476-8524-1*); pap. 25.95 (*0-8476-8525-X*) Rowman.

Reitan, Earl A., ed. The Best of the Gentleman's Magazine, 1731-1754. LC 87-1709. (Studies in British History: Vol. 4). (Illus.). 432p. 1987. lib. bdg. 109.95 (*0-88946-457-X*) E Mellen.

Reitan, Eric, jt. auth. see Garver, Newton.

Reitan, Ralph M. Aphasia & Sensory-Perceptual Deficits in Children. 208p. (Orig.). 1985. pap. text 32.00 (*0-934515-01-8*) Neuropsych Pr.

Reitan, Ralph M. & Wolfson, Deborah. The Halstead-Reitan Neuropsychological Test Battery: Theory & Clinical Interpretation. LC 85-71561. 486p. 1985. teacher ed. write for info. (*0-934515-04-2*); text 39.95 (*0-934515-02-6*) Neuropsych Pr.

— Neuroanatomy & Neuropathology: A Clinical Guide for Neuropsychologists. LC 85-61660. (Illus.). 353p. 1985. teacher ed. write for info. (*0-934515-05-0*); text 39.95 (*0-934515-03-4*) Neuropsych Pr.

— Traumatic Brain Injury: Pathophysiology & Neuropsychological Evaluation, Vol. 1. LC 86-60951. (Illus.). 425p. 1986. text 59.95 (*0-934515-06-9*) Neuropsych Pr.

— Traumatic Brain Injury: Recovery & Rehabilitation, Vol. 2. LC 86-60952. (Illus.). 400p. 1987. text 59.95 (*0-934515-07-7*) Neuropsych Pr.

Reitan, Ruth. The Rise & Decline of an Alliance: Cuba & African-American Leaders in the 1960s. LC 98-39714. xvi, 155 p. 1999. 22.95 (*0-87013-498-1*) Mich St U Pr.

Reitano, Joanne. The Tariff Question: Confronting Industrialism in the Gilded Age. LC 93-5313. 190p. 1994. 35.00 (*0-271-01035-5*) Pa St U Pr.

Reitano, John. What If the Zebra Lost Their Stripes? LC 98-14643. (Illus.). 30p. (J). (ps up). 1998. 16.95 (*0-8091-6649-6*, 6649-6) Paulist Pr.

Reitano, Michael V. Sexual Health: Questions You Have... Answers You Need. LC 98-44625. 1999. pap. 12.95 (*1-882606-43-4*) Peoples Med Soc.

Reitano, Michael V., ed. see Stern, Jerry O., et al.

Reite, Martin. Concise Guide to Evaluation & Management of Sleep Disorders. LC 89-17711. (American Psychiatric Press Ser.). (Illus.). 199p. 1990. reprint ed. pap. 61.70 (*0-608-06655-9*, 206685200009) Bks Demand.

Reite, Martin L., et al. Concise Guide to Evaluation & Management of Sleep Disorders. 2nd ed. (Concise Guides/American Psychiatric Press Ser.). 304p. 1997. pap. text 22.95 (*0-88048-906-5*, 8906) Am Psychiatric.

Reiten, Brent. Transient Sex. 60p. (Orig.). 1989. pap. 8.00 (*0-317-94038-4*) Scalding Pr.

Reiten, I. & Van Den Bergh, M. Two-Dimensional Tame & Maximal Orders of Finite Representation Type. LC 89-15024. (Memoirs Ser.: Vol. 80/408). 72p. 1989. pap. 18.00 (*0-8218-2469-4*, MEMO/80/408) Am Math.

Reiten, Idun, et al, eds. Algebras & Modules I: Workshop on Representations of Algebras & Related Topics, July 29-August 3, 1996, Trondheim, Norway. LC 98-3695. (Conference Proceedings, Canadian Mathematical Society Ser.: Vol. 23). 198p. 1998. pap. 39.00 (*0-8218-0850-8*, CMSAMS/23) Am Math.

— Algebras & Modules II. LC 98-6550. (Conference Proceedings, Canadian Mathematical Society Ser.). 569p. 1998. pap. 99.00 (*0-8218-1076-6*, CMSAMS/24) Am Math.

Reiten, Idun, ed. see Auslander, Maurice.

Reiter. Islamic Institutions in Jerusalem, Vol. AILS 15. 1997. write for info. (*90-411-0383-X*) Kluwer Law Intl.

Reiter & Russel. Melatonin. 1996. mass mkt. 8.99 (*0-553-85114-4*) Bantam.

***Reiter, Andrea Ilse Maria.** Narrating the Holocaust. LC 00-22678. (Illus.). 2000. pap. write for info. (*0-8264-4737-6*) Continuum.

***Reiter, Barry J. & Shishler, Melanie A.** Joint Ventures: Legal & Business Perspectives. xxvi, 404p. 1999. pap. 44.95 (*1-55221-036-7*, Pub. by Irwin Law) Gaunt.

Reiter, Bernhard F. Walter Hasenclevers Mystische Periode: Die Dramen der Jahre, 1917-1925. (Europaische Hochschulschriften Ser.: Reihe 1, Bd. 1632). (GER., Illus.). 305p. 1997. 57.95 (*3-631-31297-0*) P Lang Pubng.

Reiter, Beth L. Coastal Georgia. (Illus.). 1985. 19.95 (*0-932958-02-8*); pap. 9.95 (*0-932958-03-6*) Golden Coast.

Reiter-Brandwein, Donna, ed. see Frishberg, Nancy.

Reiter, Clifford A. & Jones, William R. APL with a Mathematical Accent. 205p. (C). (gr. 13). 1990. text, mass mkt., boxed set 68.95 (*0-534-12864-5*, Chap & Hall CRC) CRC Pr.

Reiter, Dan. Crucible of Beliefs: Learning, Alliances, & World Wars. LC 95-42350. (Studies in Security Affairs). (Illus.). 264p. 1996. text 37.50 (*0-8014-3188-3*) Cornell U Pr.

Reiter, David P. The Snow in Us. (Illus.). 64p. (C). 1989. 39.00 (*0-9587972-3-4*, Pub. by Five Isl Pr) St Mut.

***Reiter, Ehud & Dale, Robert.** Building Natural Language Generation Systems. LC 99-14937. (Studies in Natural Language Processing). (Illus.). 288p. 2000. 59.95 (*0-521-62036-8*) Cambridge U Pr.

Reiter, Elmar R. Atmospheric Transport Processes, Pt. 1: Energy Transfers & Transformations. LC 76-603262. (DOE Critical Review Ser.). 253p. 1969. pap. 14.25 (*0-87079-396-9*, TID-24868); fiche 9.00 (*0-87079-397-7*) DOE.

— Atmospheric Transport Processes, Pt. 2: Chemical Tracers. LC 76-603262. (DOE Critical Review Ser.). 382p. 1971. pap. 17.50 (*0-87079-140-0*, TID-25314); fiche 9.00 (*0-87079-141-9*, TID-25314) DOE.

— Atmospheric Transport Processes, Pt. 3: Hydrodynamic Tracers. LC 76-603262. (DOE Critical Review Ser.). 216p. 1972. pap. 36.50 (*0-87079-142-7*, TID-25731); fiche 9.00 (*0-87079-143-5*, TID-25731) DOE.

— Atmospheric Transport Processes, Pt. 4: Radioactive Tracers. LC 76-603262. (DOE Critical Review Ser.). 615p. 1978. 23.50 (*0-87079-114-1*, TID-27114); fiche 9.00 (*0-87079-145-1*, TID-27114) DOE.

— Jet-Stream Meteorology. LC 63-13074. 529p. reprint ed. pap. 164.00 (*0-608-30635-5*, 202015300016) Bks Demand.

— Jet Streams: How Do They Affect Our Weather? LC 78-25793. (Illus.). 189p. 1979. reprint ed. lib. bdg. 35.00 (*0-313-20782-8*, REJS, Greenwood Pr) Greenwood.

Reiter, Ester. Making Fast Food: From the Frying Pan into the Fryer. 224p. (C). 1991. 65.00 (*0-7735-0843-0*) McG-Queens Univ Pr.

— Making Fast Food: From the Frying Pan into the Fryer, 224p. 1992. pap. 9.95 (*0-7735-0947-X*, Pub. by McG-Queens Univ Pr) CUP Services.

— Making Fast Food: From the Frying Pan into the Fryer. 2nd ed. (Illus.). 224p. (C). 1995. pap. 19.95 (*0-7735-1387-6*, Pub. by McG-Queens Univ Pr) CUP Services.

Reiter, Frederick J. They Built Utopia: The Jesuit Missions in Paraguay: 1610-1768. (Illus.). x, 401p. 1995. 75.00 (*1-882528-11-5*) Scripta.

Reiter, G., et al, eds. Dynamics of Magnetic Fluctuations in High-Temperature Superconductors. (NATO ASI Ser.: Vol. 246). (Illus.). 368p. (C). 1991. text 144.00 (*0-306-43810-0*, Kluwer Plenum) Kluwer Academic.

Reiter, H. Metaplectic Groups & Segal Algebra. (Lecture Notes in Mathematics Ser.: Vol. 1382). xi, 128p. 1989. 29.95 (*0-387-51417-1*) Spr-Verlag.

***Reiter, Hans & Stegeman, Jan D.** Classical Harmonic Analysis & Locally Compact Groups. (London Mathematical Society Monographs: Vol. 22). 320p. 2000. text 100.00 (*0-19-851189-2*) OUP.

Reiter, Henry H. Compendium of Abnormal Psychology. 2nd ed. 110p. 1980. pap. text 5.00 (*0-9606044-0-5*) Psychometric.

Reiter, Herbert, jt. auth. see Della Porta, Donatella.

Reiter, Irene, ed. see Baker, Katherine.

***Reiter, Jerry.** Live from the Gates of Hell: An Insider's Look at the Anti-Abortion Underground. 280p. 2000. 26.00 (*1-57392-840-2*) Prometheus Bks.

Reiter, Joel, jt. auth. see Richard, Adrienne.

Reiter, Karin. Die Metalle im Alten Orient: Unter Besonderer Berucksichtigung Altbabylonischer Quellen. (Alter Orient und Altes Testament Ser.). (GER.). xlvii, 471p. 1997. text 84.00 (*3-927120-49-9*, 249, Pub. by Ugarit-Verlag) Eisenbrauns.

Reiter, Kurt. Von Helden und Schelmen: Tall Tales & Legends for Intermediate Students of German. (GER.). 88p. (C). 1998. pap. 9.95 (*0-8442-2259-3*, X2259-3) NTC Contemp Pub Co.

Reiter, Leon. Earthquake Hazard Analysis. 1991. text 83.00 (*0-231-06534-5*) Col U Pr.

Reiter, M., ed. Dynamics of Business Cycles: Contributions to Economics. 215p. 1995. 54.00 (*3-7908-0823-7*) Spr-Verlag.

***Reiter, Margaret E.** Senior Moments: Life in Barefoot Bay. LC 99-97594. 2000. pap. 7.95 (*0-533-13441-2*) Vantage.

***Reiter, Martin.** Die Identifikation von Tektonischen Storungen: Eine Semiotische Analyse Geologischer Arbeitsweisen. vii, 240p. 1999. 37.95 (*3-631-35356-1*) P Lang Pubng.

Reiter, Mary J. Weaving a Life: The Story of Mary Meigs Atwater. Patterson, Veronica, ed. 208p. (Orig.). 1992. pap. 14.95 (*0-934026-77-7*) Interweave.

Reiter, Pauline, jt. auth. see Jacobs, Linda.

Reiter, Prosper, Jr. Profits, Dividends & the Law: Profits Available for Dividends from Standpoint of Law & Best Accounting Practice. LC 75-18481. (History of Accounting Ser.). (Illus.). 1979. reprint ed. 23.95 (*0-405-07563-4*) Ayer.

Reiter, Russel J. & Robinson, Jo. Melatonin: Your Body's Natural Wonder Drug. 416p. 1996. mass mkt. 6.99 (*0-553-57484-1*) Bantam.

Reiter, Russell J. Fields, Currents & Aerosols in the Lower Troposphere. Kothekar, V. S., tr. from GER. (ENG.). 736p. (C). 1986. text 168.00 (*90-6191-469-8*, Pub. by A A Balkema) Ashgate Pub Co.

— Phenomena in Atmospheric & Environmental Electricity. LC 92-5574. (Developments in Atmospheric Science Ser.: Vol. 20). 542p. 1992. 219.75 (*0-444-89286-9*) Elsevier.

— Pineal Gland Series, 3 vols. 465.00 (*0-8493-5713-6*, CRC Reprint) Franklin.

R

Reiter, Russell J., ed. The Pineal & Reproduction. (Progress in Reproductive Biology & Medicine Ser.: Vol. 4). (Illus.). 1978. 103.50 (*3-8055-2815-9*) S Karger.

— The Pineal Gland. LC 84-4762. (Comprehensive Endocrinology Ser.). (Illus.). 394p. 1984. reprint ed. pap. 122.20 (*0-7837-9579-3*, 206032800005) Bks Demand.

— The Pineal Gland, Vol. I. 1981. 186.00 (*0-8493-5714-4*, QP188, CRC Reprint) Franklin.

— The Pineal Gland: Reproductive Effects, Vol. II. 240p. 1981. 137.00 (*0-8493-5716-0*, QP188, CRC Reprint) Franklin.

Reiter, Russell J., et al, eds. Electromagnetic Fields & Circadian Rhythmicity. (Circadian Factors in Human Health & Performance Ser.). vii, 210p. 1993. 60.00 (*0-8176-3552-1*) Birkhauser.

— Melatonin: A Universal Photoperiodic Signal with Diverse Actions: International Symposium, Hong Kong, September 1995. LC 96-44662. (Frontiers of Hormone Research Ser.: Vol. 21, 1996). (Illus.). viii, 208p. 1996. 198.25 (*3-8055-6344-2*) S Karger.

— The Pineal Gland & Its Hormones: Fundamentals & Clinical Perspectives: Proceedings of NATO ASI Held in Erice, Italy, June 7-13, 1994. LC 95-33471. (NATO ASI Ser.: Series A, Vol. 277). (Illus.). 244p. (C). 1995. text 95.00 (*0-306-45105-0*) Plenum.

— Therapeutic Potential of Melatonin: 2nd Locarno Meeting on Neuroendocrinoimmunology, Locarno, May 1996. LC 97-5492. (Frontiers of Hormone Research Ser.: Vol. 23, 1997). (Illus.). 178p. 1997. 172.25 (*3-8055-6439-2*) S Karger.

Reiter, Russell J. & Webb, Susan M., eds. The Pineal Gland: Update 1996: From Molecular Mechanisms to Clinical Implications. LC 97-50031. 1996. 69.95 (*0-915340-19-4*) PJD Pubns.

Reiter, Russell J., jt. ed. see Follett, B. K.

Reiter, Seymour. A Study of Shelley's Poetry. LC 67-22735. 1967. 20.00 (*0-8263-0085-5*) Lib Soc Sci.

Reiter, Seymour, jt. auth. see Henry, O.

Reiter, Sheila, ed. see Fajors, Nique.

Reiter, Sheila, ed. see Pearce, Robert.

Reiter, Shunit, jt. ed. see Retish, Paul.

Reiter, Stephen E., jt. auth. see Poirier, Charles C.

Reiter, Thomas. Crossovers. LC 95-2450. 62p. 1995. pap. 12.50 (*0-910055-20-3*) East Wash Univ.

— Crossovers: Poems. LC 95-2450. 62p. 1995. 23.00 (*0-910055-19-X*) East Wash Univ.

*__Reiter, Thomas.__ Pearly Everlasting. LC 99-55820. 80p. 2000. 22.50 (*0-8071-2542-3*); pap. 14.95 (*0-8071-2543-1*) La State U Pr.

Reiter, Thomas. Time in the Air. Ellis, Ron, ed. 36p. (Orig.). 1990. pap. write for info. (*0-9624746-1-4*) Woodhenge.

Reiter, Tom. Basketball Inbound Attack. (Illus.). 128p. (Orig.). 1993. pap. 12.95 (*0-940279-60-6*, 79606H, Mstrs Pr) NTC Contemp Pub Co.

— Basketball's Offensive Sets. 128p. 1995. pap. 12.95 (*1-57028-040-1*, 80401H, Mstrs Pr) NTC Contemp Pub Co.

*__Reiter, Tom.__ First Strike: Basketball's Secondary Break Offense. (Illus.). 130p. 2000. pap. 16.95 (*1-58382-032-9*) Coaches Choice.

Reiter, Wellington. Vessels & Fields. LC 98-44893. (Illus.). 192p. 1999. pap. 24.95 (*1-56898-187-2*) Princeton Arch.

Reiter, William A. Aemilius Paullus, Conqueror of Greece. 160p. 1988. lib. bdg. 55.00 (*0-7099-4285-0*, Pub. by C Helm) Routldge.

Reiter, Yitzhak. Islamic Endowments in Jerusalem under British Mandate. LC 96-15450. 272p. (Orig.). (C). 1997. 52.50 (*0-7146-4670-9*, Pub. by F Cass Pubs); pap. 25.00 (*0-7146-4342-4*, Pub. by F Cass Pubs) Intl Spec Bk.

Reiter, Ytizhak. Islamic Institutions in Jerusalem: Palestinian Muslim Organization under Jordanian & Israeli Rule. LC 97-2854. (Arab & Islamic Laws Ser.: No. 15). 120p. 1997. 62.00 (*90-411-0382-1*) Kluwer Academic.

Reiterer, Friedrich V., ed. Freundschaft bei Ben Sira: Beitraege des Symposions zu Ben Sira - Salzburg 1995. (GER.). viii, 265p. (C). 1996. lib. bdg. 117.05 (*3-11-015261-4*) De Gruyter.

*__Reith.__ Who Am I? 1999. 8.95 (*0-7459-4066-8*, Pub. by Lion Pubng) Trafalgar.

Reith, A., jt. auth. see Feger, O.

Reith, Adrian, jt. auth. see Wroe, Martin.

Reith, Alastair D. Protein Kinase Protocols. (Methods in Molecular Biology Ser.: Vol. 124). (Illus.). 400p. 2000. 89.50 (*0-89603-700-2*) Humana.

Reith, Albrecht & Mayhew, Terry M., eds. Stereology & Morphometry in Election Microscopy: Some Problems & Their Solutions. (Ultrastructural Pathology Publication). 215p. 1988. 104.00 (*0-89116-623-8*) Hemisp Pub.

Reith, Charles. The Blind Eye of History: A Study of the Origins of the Present Police Era (With Intro. Added) LC 74-26636. (Criminology, Law Enforcement, & Social Problems Ser.: No. 203). (C). 1975. reprint ed. 25.00 (*0-87585-203-3*) Patterson Smith.

— Police Principles & the Problem of War. 1992. lib. bdg. 88.75 (*0-8490-5299-8*) Gordon Pr.

Reith, Charles, jt. auth. see Caldwell, Jack A.

Reith, Charles C. & Thomson, Bruce M., eds. Deserts As Dumps? The Disposal of Hazardous Materials in Arid Ecosystems. LC 92-16983. 330p. 1993. pap. 15.95 (*0-8263-1298-5*) U of NM Pr.

Reith, Gerda. The Age of Chance: Gambling in Western Culture. LC 99-24303. 232p. 1999. 90.00 (*0-415-17997-1*) Routledge.

Reith, Gerry, ed. Neutron Gun. 2nd ed. (Illus.). 72p. 1987. pap. 4.95 (*0-911627-12-X*) Neither-Nor Pr.

Reith, H. B. Sonographie des Knochens: Experimentelle und Klinische Ergebnisse Zur Verlaufskontrolle Nach Frakturen und Spongiosatransplantationen. (Illus.). vi, 58p. 1994. pap. 28.00 (*3-8055-5965-8*) S Karger.

Reith, H. B., jt. ed. see Kozuschek, W. A.

*__Reith, Maarten E. A., ed.__ Cerebral Signal Transduction: From First to Fourth Messengers. LC 99-38476. (Contemporary Neuroscience Ser.). 428p. 2000. 125.00 (*0-89603-608-1*) Humana.

Reith, Maarten E. A., ed. Neurotransmitter Transporters: Structure, Function & Regulation. LC 96-36600. (Contemporary Neuroscience Ser.). (Illus.). 416p. 1996. 150.00 (*0-89603-372-4*) Humana.

Reith, Mary K., ed. see Zobel, Herbert L.

Reither, Joseph. The Development of Tactical Doctrines at AAFSAT & AAFTAC. (USAF Historical Studies: No. 13). 121p. 1944. pap. text 27.95 (*0-89126-036-6*) MA-AH Pub.

— World History: A Brief Introduction. LC 65-17275. Orig. Title: World History at a Glance. (Illus.). 512p. (C). 1973. reprint ed. pap. text 12.95 (*0-07-051875-0*) McGraw.

Reither, Joseph, jt. auth. see England, J. Merton.

Reithmaier. Standard Aircraft Handbook. 6th ed. LC 99-29590. 292p. 1999. pap. 24.95 (*0-07-134836-0*) McGraw.

Reithmaier, Larry W. Mach One & Beyond: The Illustrated Guide to High-Speed Flight. LC 94-1421. (Illus.). 273p. 1994. pap. text 24.95 (*0-07-052021-6*) McGraw-Hill Prof.

— Standard Aircraft Handbook. 5th ed. (Illus.). 224p. 1991. pap. 12.95 (*0-07-157642-8*) McGraw.

— Standard Aircraft Handbook. 5th ed. (Illus.). 256p. 1991. vinyl bd. 12.95 (*0-8306-8634-7*, 3634, TAB-Aero) TAB Bks.

Reitlinger, Gerald. The Economics of Taste, 3 Vols. LC 82-80311. (Illus.). 1959p. 1982. reprint ed. 100.00 (*0-87817-288-2*) Hacker.

— The S. S. Alibi of a Nation, 1922-1945. (Quality Paperbacks Ser.). (Illus.). 534p. 1989. reprint ed. pap. 16.95 (*0-306-80351-8*) Da Capo.

Reitlinger, Joanna, jt. auth. see Bulgakov, Sergius.

Reitman, Alan, ed. Price of Liberty: Perspectives on Civil Liberties by Member of the A.C.L.U. (C). 1969. pap. 2.00 (*0-393-00505-4*) Norton.

Reitman, E. Edward. Hungry for Love: Psychological Tidbits to Nourish an Empty Heart. LC 98-74309. 240p. 1998. pap. 14.95 (*1-58151-014-4*) BookPartners.

Reitman, Jeffrey B. & Weisblatt, Harold. Checks, Drafts & Notes. 1983. ring bd. 240.00 (*0-8205-1074-2*) Bender.

Reitman, Jerry I. Beyond 2000: The Future of Direct Marketing. (Illus.). 296p. 1996. pap. 27.95 (*0-8442-3447-8*, NTC Business Bks) NTC Contemp Pub Co.

Reitman, Jerry I., compiled by. Beyond Two Thousand: The Future of Direct Marketing: 28 of the World's Leading Experts Predict the Changes Which Will Impact You, Your Job, & Your Company. LC 93-42158. (Illus.). 296p. 1994. 34.95 (*0-8442-3450-8*, NTC Business Bks) NTC Contemp Pub Co.

Reitman, Judith. Bad Blood: Crisis in the American Red Cross. LC 96-76491. (Illus.). 304p. 1996. 24.95 (*1-57566-115-2*, Knsington) Kensgtn Pub Corp.

— Blood Legacy. 1999. pap. 19.95 (*0-525-93962-8*) NAL.

Reitman, Judith, ed. American Proverbs. LC 99-52234. (Illus.). 100p. 1999. 14.95 (*0-7818-0753-0*) Hippocrene Bks.

Reitman, Robert, ed. see Jenenko, Patricia.

Reitman, Sanford W. The Educational Messiah Complex: American Faith in the Culturally Redemptive Power of Schooling. 224p. 1992. pap. text 19.95 (*1-880192-00-4*) Caddo Gap Pr.

Reitmeister, Lewis A. If Tomorrow Comes: A Tale of Two Worlds. LC 74-154458. (Utopian Literature Ser.). (Illus.). 1976. reprint ed. 28.95 (*0-405-03540-3*) Ayer.

Reitner, J. & Keupp, H., eds. Fossil & Recent Sponges. (Illus.). 608p. 1991. 238.95 (*0-387-52509-2*) Spr-Verlag.

Reitner, R. J., jt. auth. see Fraschini, F.

Reitsch, Arthur G., jt. auth. see Hanke, John E.

Reitsch, Hanna. The Sky My Kingdom. LC 97-5033. 1997. pap. 17.95 (*1-85367-262-9*) Greenhill Bks.

Reitsma, Pieter & Verhoeven, Ludo T., eds. Acquisition of Reading in Dutch: A State of the Art. (Studies on Language Acquisition). 160p. (Orig.). (C). 1989. pap. 46.15 (*90-6765-490-6*) Mouton.

Reitter, Mary S., ed. National Directory of Brain Injury Rehabilitation Services, 1997. Orig. Title: National Directory of Head Injury Rehabilitation Services. 1997. pap. text 50.00 (*0-614-30066-5*) Brain Injury Assoc.

Reittinger, Janice. Iowa's Complete Guide to Antique Shops & Malls. 5th ed. 206p. 1998. pap. text 4.95 (*0-9640314-4-2*) DJs Pubng.

— Iowa's Complete Guide to Antique Shops & Malls. 6th ed. 225p. 1999. pap. 4.95 (*0-9640314-5-0*) DJs Pubng.

*__Reittinger, Janice.__ Iowa's Complete Guide to Antique Shops & Malls. 7th ed. 230p. 2000. pap. text 4.95 (*0-9640314-6-9*) DJs Pubng.

Reitz. Congenital Cardiac Surgery. (C). 2000. 195.00 (*0-8385-1542-8*) Appleton & Lange.

Reitz, jt. auth. see Baumgartner, Fritz.

Reitz, Allen, jt. auth. see Maryanoff, Bruce E.

Reitz, Allen B., ed. Inositol Phosphates & Derivatives: Synthesis, Biochemistry, & Therapeutic Potential. LC 91-17716. (Symposium Ser.: No. 463). (Illus.). 235p. 1991. text 65.00 (*0-8412-2086-7*, Pub. by Am Chemical) OUP.

*__Reitz, Andrea & Schommartz, Heike, eds.__ Take off in German: A Complete Language Learning Pack. 256p. 2000. audio compact disk 32.50 (*0-19-860294-4*) OUP.

— Take Off In German Book: A Complete Language Learning Pack. 256p. 2000. 24.95 incl. audio (*0-19-860275-8*) OUP.

Reitz, Charles. Art, Alienation, & the Humanities: A Critical Engagement with Herbert Marcuse. LC 99-38495. (C). 2000. pap. text 17.95 (*0-7914-4462-7*) State U NY Pr.

Reitz, Charles R. Art, Alienation, & the Humanities: A Critical Engagement with Herbert Marcuse. LC 99-38495. (C). 2000. text 54.50 (*0-7914-4461-9*) State U NY Pr.

Reitz, Charles R., ed. see Farnsworth, Edward Allan, et al.

Reitz, Christiane. Zur Gleichnistechnik des Apollonios von Rhodos. (Studien Zur Klassischen Philologie Ser.: Bd. 99). (GER.). VII, 170p. 1996. 42.95 (*3-631-30751-9*) P Lang Pubng.

Reitz, Curtis R. Consumer Product Warranties under Federal & State Laws. 2nd ed. 286p. 1987. text 16.00 (*0-8318-0484-X*, B484) Am Law Inst.

Reitz, Curtis R., jt. auth. see Honnold, John O.

Reitz, Del. Little Lieu: And Other Waifs. LC 97-166101. 20p. 1997. 8.95 (*0-917835-02-6*) Newsletter Inago.

Reitz, Deneys. Boer Commando: An Afrikaner Journal of the Boer War. 288p. 1993. reprint ed. pap. 12.95 (*0-9627613-3-8*) Sarpedon.

— Trilogy of Deneys Reitz, Commando - Trekking On - No Outspan: A Boer Journal of the Boer War. 971p. 1994. 45.00 (*1-879356-39-2*) Wolfe Pub Co.

Reitz, Donald J. Moral Crisis in the Schools: What Parents & Teachers Need to Know. LC 98-23768. 174p. 1998. pap. 18.00 (*1-885938-09-8*) Cathdrl Fndtn Pr.

Reitz, E. J., et al. Case Studies in Environmental Archaeology. (Interdisciplinary Contributions to Archaeology Ser.: Interdisciplinary Contribution to Archaeology Ser.). (Illus.). 376p. (C). 1996. pap. 41.00 (*0-306-45253-7*, Plenum Trade) Perseus Pubng.

Reitz, Elizabeth J., et al, eds. Case Studies in Environmental Archaeology. (Interdisciplinary Contributions to Archaeology Ser.). (Illus.). 376p. (C). 1996. 83.00 (*0-306-45252-9*, Plenum Trade) Perseus Pubng.

Reitz, Elizabeth J. & Wing, Elizabeth S. Zooarchaeology. LC 98-7989. (Manuals in Archaeology Ser.). (Illus.). 500p. (C). 1999. 80.00 (*0-521-48069-8*); pap. 34.95 (*0-521-48529-0*) Cambridge U Pr.

Reitz, J. J. Reitz: Family History & Record Book of the Descendants of Johan Friedrich Reitz, the Pioneer, Who Landed at Philadelphia, Sept. 7, 1748. (Illus.). 289p. 1994. reprint ed. pap. 44.50 (*0-8328-4054-8*); reprint ed. lib. bdg. 54.50 (*0-8328-4053-X*) Higginson Bk Co.

Reitz, Jeffery G., jt. auth. see Lazardfeld, Paul.

*__Reitz, Jeffrey G.__ Warmth of the Welcome. 312p. 1999. pap. 25.00 (*0-8133-6802-2*) Westview.

Reitz, Jeffrey G., jt. auth. see Lazarsfeld, Paul F.

Reitz, John R., et al. Foundations of Electromagnetic Theory. 3rd ed. LC 78-18649. (Physics Ser.). (Illus.). 1979. text 54.95 (*0-201-06332-8*) Addison-Wesley.

— Foundations of Electromagnetic Theory. 4th ed. LC 91-36491. 630p. (C). 1992. 109.00 (*0-201-52624-7*) Addison-Wesley.

Reitz, M. Die Alge im System der Pflanzen: Nanochlorum Eucaryotum - Eine Alge mit Minimalen Eukaryotischen Kriterien. (GER., Illus.). 273p. 1986. lib. bdg. 70.00 (*3-437-30523-9*) Lubrecht & Cramer.

Reitz, Mercedes M. & Reitz, Russell T. The Black Wolves of Yellow Mountain. (Yellow Mountain Ser.). (Illus.). 198p. (Orig.). (J). (gr. 4 up). 1994. pap. 11.95 (*0-9625344-5-5*) Creative Multi-Media.

— The Dreadful Monsters of Yellow Mountain. (Yellow Mountain Ser.). (Illus.). 216p. (Orig.). (J). (gr. 4 up). 1991. pap. 9.95 (*0-9625344-3-9*); text 19.95 (*0-9625344-2-0*) Creative Multi-Media.

Reitz, Mercedes M., et al. Trouble Double on Yellow Mountain. (Yellow Mountain Ser.). (Illus.). 184p. (Orig.). (J). (gr. 3 up). 1990. pap. 9.95 (*0-9625344-1-2*) Creative Multi-Media.

Reitz, Miriam & Watson, Kenneth W. Adoption & the Family System: Strategies for Treatment. LC 91-44266. 340p. 1992. lib. bdg. 40.00 (*0-89862-797-4*) Guilford Pubns.

*__Reitz, Mullenix Elizabeth.__ Wearing the Breeches: Gender On The Antebellum Stage. LC 99-59917. 1999. text 45.00 (*0-312-22349-8*) St Martin.

Reitz, Raymond L. Photography in Life Sciences: Index of Modern Authors & Subjects with Guide for Rapid Research. LC 90-56305. 160p. 1991. 47.50 (*1-55914-396-7*); pap. 44.50 (*1-55914-397-5*) ABBE Pubs Assn.

Reitz, Ric. The Journey of Sir Douglas Fir. Bell, Suzanne, ed. (Illus.). 48p. (J). (gr. 2-6). 1999. 27.95 incl. audio compact disk (*0-9670160-0-2*, Sir Fir Bks) Sir Fir Ent.

Reitz, Robert, ed. see Ask, Robert W.

Reitz, Russell T., jt. auth. see Reitz, Mercedes M.

Reitze, Arnold W., Jr. Air Pollution Law. LC 95-77498. 1257p. 1995. 105.00 (*1-55834-234-6*, 66621-10, MICHIE) LEXIS Pub.

Reitzel, J. David, et al. Contemporary Business Law & the Legal Environment: Principles & Cases. 5th rev. ed. LC 93-37330. Orig. Title: Contemporary Business Law. (C). 1994. text 72.74 (*0-07-051912-9*) McGraw.

Reitzel, Rick W. From the Flower to the Vein. Hilvosky, Judy, ed. LC 89-30725. 1991. pap. 13.95 (*0-87949-287-2*) Ashley Bks.

Reitzel, Robert. Adventures of a Greenhorn: An Autobiographical Novel. Erhardt, Jacob, tr. from GER. LC 91-28511. (New German-American Studies - Neue Deutsch-Amerikanische Studien: Vol. 3). XVII, 94p. (C). 1992. text 35.95 (*0-8204-1330-5*) P Lang Pubng.

Reitzenstein, Richard. Epigramm und Skolion. 296p. 1970. reprint ed. write for info. (*0-318-70820-5*) G Olms Pubs.

— The Hellenistic Mystery-Religions. Steely, John E., tr. from GER. LC 77-12980. (Pittsburgh Theological Monographs: No. 15). Orig. Title: Die Hellenistischen Mysterienreligionen Nach Ihren Arundgedanken und Wirkungen. 1978. pap. text 20.00 (*0-915138-20-4*) Pickwick.

Reitzer, Stefan, jt. ed. see Korn, Matthias.

Reitzes, Frelta, et al. Wonderplay: Interactive & Developmental Games, Crafts, & Creative Activities for Infants, Toddlers, & Preschoolers. LC 94-67769. (Illus.). 120p. 1995. pap. 12.95 (*1-56138-575-1*) Running Pr.

Reitzes, Lisa B., jt. auth. see Wright, Patricia.

Reitzug, Ulrich C., jt. auth. see Kowalski, Theodore J.

Reiver, Jules. The United States Early Silver Dollars, 1794 to 1803. rev. ed. (Illus.). 120p. 1998. 37.95 (*0-87341-602-3*, ESD) Krause Pubns.

Reizbaum, Marilyn. James Joyce's Judaic Other. LC 98-36896. (Contraversions Ser.). 1999. write for info. (*0-8047-3255-8*); pap. 16.95 (*0-8047-3473-9*) Stanford U Pr.

Reizbaum, Marilyn, jt. ed. see Devlin, Kimberly J.

Reizenstein, Milton. The Economic History of the Baltimore & Ohio Railroad. 1827-1853. LC 78-63858. (Johns Hopkins University. Studies in the Social Sciences. Thirtieth Ser. 1912: 7-8). reprint ed. 32.50 (*0-404-61114-1*) AMS Pr.

Reizenstein, P., jt. ed. see Mathe, G.

Reizenstein, Peter. Hematologic Stress Syndrome: The Biological Response to Disease. LC 83-4023. 190p. 1983. 57.95 (*0-275-91408-9*, C1408, Praeger Pubs) Greenwood.

Reizer, Jonathan & Peterkofsky, Alan. Sugar Transport & Metabolism in Gram-Positive Bacteria. (Topics in Enzyme & Fermentation Biotechnology Ser.). 560p. 1987. text 126.95 (*0-470-20818-X*) P-H.

Reizes, Haim. The Mechanics of Vehicle Collisions. (Illus.). 152p. 1973. 35.95 (*0-398-02639-4*); pap. 23.95 (*0-398-06345-1*) C C Thomas.

Reizner, Jayne. Pursuing the Permanent: Meeting the Part of You That Lives Forever. LC 96-61106. 184p. 1997. pap. 9.99 (*1-56384-126-6*, Vital Issue Pr) Huntington Hse.

Rejab, F. I. The Crocodile & the Elephant. (Illus.). 40p. (J). 1995. 9.95 (*983-9808-25-7*, Pub. by Delta Edits) Weatherhill.

— The Fiery Cave. (Illus.). 40p. (J). 1995. 9.95 (*983-9808-29-X*, Pub. by Delta Edits) Weatherhill.

— The Hero of Indera Kayangan. (Illus.). 40p. 1995. 9.95 (*983-9808-27-3*, Pub. by Delta Edits) Weatherhill.

— The Magic Frog. (Illus.). 40p. (J). 1995. 9.95 (*983-9808-14-1*, Pub. by Delta Edits) Weatherhill.

— Mahsuri: The Legend of Langkawi. (Illus.). 40p. (J). 1995. 9.95 (*983-9808-24-9*, Pub. by Delta Edits) Weatherhill.

— The Merchant's Two Daughters. (Illus.). 40p. (J). 1995. 9.95 (*983-9808-23-0*, Pub. by Delta Edits) Weatherhill.

— The Mousedeer & the Tiger Cubs. (Illus.). 24p. (J). 1994. 9.95 (*983-9808-15-X*, Pub. by Delta Edits) Weatherhill.

— The Prince of Mount Kinabalu. (Illus.). 40p. (J). 1995. 9.95 (*983-9808-26-5*, Pub. by Delta Edits) Weatherhill.

— The Young Heroes. (Illus.). 40p. (J). 1995. 9.95 (*983-9808-28-1*, Pub. by Delta Edits) Weatherhill.

*__Rejai, M. & Phillips, Kay.__ The Young George Washington in Psychobiographical Perspective. LC 00-38679. 132p. 2000. 69.95 (*0-7734-7694-6*) E Mellen.

Rejai, Mostafa. Political Ideologies: A Comparative Approach. 216p. 1991. pap. text 34.95 (*0-87332-807-8*) M E Sharpe.

Rejai, Mostafa. Political Ideologies: A Comparative Approach. LC 90-26349. 216p. (C). (gr. 13). 1991. text 69.95 (*0-87332-806-X*) M E Sharpe.

Rejai, Mostafa. Political Ideologies: A Comparative Approach. 2nd ed. LC 94-29696. 256p. (YA). (gr. 13). 1994. pap. text 32.95 (*1-56324-142-0*) M E Sharpe.

Rejai, Mostafa & Phillips, Kay. Demythologizing an Elite: American Presidents in Empirical, Comparative, & Historical Perspective. LC 92-31840. 172p. 1993. 49.95 (*0-275-94331-3*, C4331, Praeger Pubs) Greenwood.

— Leaders & Leadership: An Appraisal of Theory & Research. LC 96-53942. 144p. 1997. 49.95 (*0-275-95880-9*, Praeger Pubs) Greenwood.

— World Military Leaders: A Collective & Comparative Analysis. LC 95-22011. 192p. 1996. 57.95 (*0-275-95386-6*, Praeger Pubs) Greenwood.

Rejai, Mostafa, jt. auth. see Phillips, Kay.

Rejali, Roxanna, ed. Llewellyn's 1998 Pocket Planner. (Illus.). 208p. (Orig.). 1997. otabind 7.95 (*1-56718-936-9*) Llewellyn Pubns.

— Llewellyn's 1999 Astrological Pocket Planner: Daily Ephemeris & Aspectarian, 1999-2000. 176p. 1999. 7.95 (*1-56718-944-X*) Llewellyn Pubns.

Rejali, Roxanna, ed. see Star, Gloria.

Rejaner, Jeanne. 100 Best Careers in Fashion & Modeling. 304p. 1999. pap. 15.95 (*0-02-862177-8*) Macmillan.

Rejda. Personal Financial Planning. (C). 1998. pap. text. write for info. (*0-321-02102-9*) Addison-Wesley.

— Principles of Risk Management & Insurance. 6th ed. 336p. (C). 1997. text, student ed. 30.00 (*0-321-00026-9*) Addison-Wesley.

— Social Insurance & Economy Security. 6th ed. 399p. 1998. pap. text 92.00 (*0-13-020441-2*) P-H.

Rejda, ed. Personal Financial Planning. (C). 1997. text. write for info. (*0-673-99878-9*) Addison-Wesley.

Rejda, George E. Personal Financial Planning. 2nd ed. (C). 2000. text (*0-321-04307-3*) Addson-Wesley Educ.

— Principles of Risk Management & Insurance. 4th ed. (C). 1992. 25.00 (*0-673-46542-X*) Addson-Wesley Educ.

— Principles of Risk Management & Insurance. 5th ed. LC 94-17221. (C). 1997. 97.00 (*0-673-99027-3*) Addson-Wesley Educ.

— Principles of Risk Management & Insurance. 6th ed. (C). 1997. text. write for info. (*0-321-00677-1*) Addson-Wesley Educ.

*__Rejda, George E.__ Principles of Risk Management & Insurance. 7th ed. LC 00-41633. 2000. write for info. (*0-321-05065-7*) Addson-Wesley Educ.

Rejda, George E. Social Insurance & Economic Security. 2nd ed. (Illus.). 512p. (C). 1984. 33.00 (*0-13-815845-2*) P-H.

An Asterisk (*) at the beginning of an entry indicates that the title is appearing for the first time.

Rejda, George E., ed. Principles of Risk Management & Insurance. 6th ed. LC 97-28269. 566p. (C). 1997. 98.00 (*0-321-01451-0*) Addson-Wesley Educ.

Rejda, George E., et al. Personal Insurance. 3rd ed. LC 97-73241. 382p. (C). 1997. pap. text 31.00 (*0-89462-117-3*, 2202) IIA.

Rejebian, Gary P. Think Green! A Retailer's Environmental Idea Book. (Illus.). 50p. (Orig.). 1992. pap. 25.00 (*1-885337-00-0*) IL Retail Merchants.

Rejeski, W. Jack & Kenney, Elizabeth A. Fitness Motivation: Preventing Participant Dropout. LC 88-4584. (Illus.). 168p. 1988. pap. text 18.00 (*0-87322-928-2*, BREJ0928) Human Kinetics.

Rejhon, Annalee C. C'An Rolant: The Medieval Welsh Version of the Song of Roland. LC 82-20031. (University of California Publications in Entomology: No. 113). (ENG & WEL.). 276p. 1984. pap. 85.60 (*0-7837-8422-8*, 204922400010) Bks Demand.

Rejnis, Carolyn J. Complete Idiot's Guide to Retiring in Comfort. 1998. 16.99 (*0-02-861374-0*, Pub. by Macmillan) S&S Trade.

Rejnis, Ruth. Careers with Creatures Great & Small. 192p. 1999. 14.95 (*0-87605-027-5*) Howell Bks.

— The Everything Homebuying Book. LC 98-17889. (Illus.). 352p. 1998. pap. 12.95 (*1-58062-074-4*) Adams Media.

***Rejnis, Ruth.** The Everything Homeselling Book. LC 99-55560. (Illus.). 304p. 2000. pap. 12.95 (*1-58062-304-2*) Adams Media.

— The Everything Saints Book: Discover the Lives of the Saints & the Saints in Your Life. (Everything Ser.). (Illus.). 304p. 2000. pap. 12.95 (*1-58062-399-9*) Adams Media.

Rejnis, Ruth & Walter, Claire. Buying Your Vacation Home: For Fun & Profit. 224p. (Orig.). 1996. pap. 19.95 (*0-7931-1583-3*, 1913-3601, Real Estate Ed) Dearborn.

Rejnis, Ruth, jt. auth. see Century 21 Editors.

Rejnis, Ruth, jt. auth. see Janik, Carol.

Rejnis, Ruth, jt. auth. see Janik, Carolyn.

Rejnis, Ruth, jt. auth. see Johnson, Ann M.

Rejouis, Joel, tr. see Dongala, Emmanuel.

Rejouis, Rose-Myriam, tr. see Chamoiseau, Patrick.

Rejwan, Nissim. Arabs Face the Modern World: Religious, Cultural, & Political Responses to the West. LC 97-39680. 256p. 1998. 39.95 (*0-8130-1559-6*) U Press Fla.

***Rejwan, Nissim.** Israel in Search of Identity: Reading The Formative Years. LC 98-53889. 1999. 59.95 (*0-8130-1664-9*) U Press Fla.

Rejwan, Nissim. Israel's Place in the Middle East: A Pluralist Perspective. LC 98-6104. 224p. 1998. 49.95 (*0-8130-1601-0*) U Press Fla.

— Israel's Place in The Middle East: A Pluralist Perspective. 1999. pap. text 19.95 (*0-8130-1723-8*) U Press Fla.

***Rejwan, Nissim.** The Many Faces of Islam. LC 00-32587. 2000. write for info. (*0-8130-1807-2*) U Press Fla.

Rejwan, Nissim. Nasserist Ideology: Its Exponents & Critics. 271p. 1974. boxed set 39.95 (*0-87855-162-X*) Transaction Pubs.

— Nasserist Ideology: Its Exponents & Critics. LC 74-2116. (Shiloah Center for Middle Eastern & African Studies. The Monograph Ser.). 282p. reprint ed. pap. 87.50 (*0-8357-8962-4*, 203358300086) Bks Demand.

Rekany, Ilonia M. Dental Practice & Research: Index of Modern Information. LC 88-47950. 150p. 1990. 47.50 (*1-55914-132-8*); pap. 44.50 (*1-55914-133-6*) ABBE Pubs Assn.

Rekate, Harold L., ed. Comprehensive Management of Spina Bifida. 264p. 1990. lib. bdg. 129.00 (*0-8493-0151-3*, RJ496) CRC Pr.

Rekdal, Jan E., jt. ed. see Corrain, Ailbhe O.

***Rekdal, Paisley.** A Crash of Rhinos: Poems by Paisley Rekdal. 80p. 2000. pap. 15.95 (*0-8203-2273-3*) U of Ga Pr.

— The Night My Mother Met Bruce Lee: Observations on Not Fitting In. 224p. 2000. 22.00 (*0-375-40937-8*) Pantheon.

***Rekela, George R.** Brett Favre: Star Quarterback. LC 99-49659. (Sports Reports Ser.). (Illus.). 104p. (J). (gr. 4-10). 2000. lib. bdg. 20.95 (*0-7660-1332-4*) Enslow Pubs.

Rekela, George R. Hakeem Olajuwon: Tower of Power. LC 92-38905. (Achievers Ser.). (J). (gr. 4-9). 1993. lib. bdg. 18.60 (*0-8225-0518-5*, Lerner Publctns) Lerner Pub.

— Karl Malone: Star Forward. LC 97-25560. (Sports Reports Ser.). (Illus.). 104p. (J). (gr. 4-10). 1998. lib. bdg. 20.95 (*0-89490-931-2*) Enslow Pubs.

— Sports Great Anfernee Hardaway. LC 95-20298. (Sports Great Bks.). 64p. (J). (gr. 4-10). 1996. lib. bdg. 17.95 (*0-89490-758-1*) Enslow Pubs.

— Sports Great Muggsy Bogues. LC 96-14170. (Sports Great Bks.). (Illus.). 64p. (J). (gr. 4-10). 1997. lib. bdg. 17.95 (*0-89490-876-6*) Enslow Pubs.

— State Champions: The Story of the Buhl Bulldogs' Rise to Glory in 1941 & 1942. (Orig.). 1991. pap. 5.95 (*0-9619505-0-1*) Milkees Pr.

Reken, Randal S. Van, see Van Reken, Randal S.

Reken, Ruth E. Van, see Knuckles, Barbara.

Rekenthaler, Doug, Jr., ed. see DiGregorio, Ron.

***Reker, Gary T. & Chamberlain, Kerry.** Optimizing Human Development: Existential Meaning Across the Life Span. LC 99-6281. 1999. write for info. (*0-7619-0994-X*) Sage.

***Reker, Gary T. & Chamberlain, Kerry, eds.** Exploring Existential Meaning: Optimizing Human Development Across the Life Span. LC 99-6281. 221p. 2000. 64.95 (*0-7619-0993-1*) Sage.

Reker, Les, jt. auth. see Butler, Tom.

Rekers, George A. Counseling Families. (Resources for Christian Counseling Ser.: Vol. 14). 211p. 18.99 (*0-8499-0595-8*) Word Pub.

— Handbook of Child & Adolescent Sexual Problems. LC 94-40653. (Series in Scientific Foundations of Clinical & Counseling Psychology). 500p. 1995. 45.00 (*0-02-926317-4*) Jossey-Bass.

— Susan Smith: Victim or Murderer. LC 95-79296. 230p. 1995. 21.95 (*0-944435-38-6*) Glenbridge Pub.

Rekha Chowdhury. Ideology & Politics of Ruling Parties in India. 1991. 19.00 (*81-7100-301-X*, Pub. by Deep & Deep Pubns) S Asia.

Rekhter, Yakov, jt. auth. see Davie, Bruce S.

Reklaitis, G. V. Introduction to Material & Energy Balances. LC 82-23800. 704p. (C). 1983. text 99.95 (*0-471-04131-9*) Wiley.

Reklaitis, G. V., ed. Large Scale Optimization: Annual Meeting of the American Institute of Chemical Engineers, 1982. 100p. 1983. write for info. (*0-08-030270-X*, Pergamon Pr) Elsevier.

Reklaitis, G. V., et al. Engineering Optimization: Methods & Applications. LC 83-3545. 704p. 1983. 150.00 (*0-471-05579-4*) Wiley.

Reklaitis, G. V., jt. ed. see Squires, Robert G.

Rekon, Peter, jt. compiled by see Appleby, Amy.

Rekowski, Mary, et al. Mind-Altering Drugs Desk Reference: A Guide to the History, Uses & Effects of Psychoactive Drugs. 2nd rev. ed. Bankston, Karen & Holzhecht, Terri, eds. 346p. 1998. ring bd. 25.95 (*1-882145-04-6*) U WI Clearinghse.

Reksten, Harald & Boyer, Reba. Index to McMinn County, Tennessee, Tax Lists, 1829-1832 & 1836, & Detail from 1836 Tax List. LC 96-218218. 127p. (Orig.). 1996. pap. 16.00 (*0-7884-0490-3*, R147) Heritage Bk.

***Reksten, Linda E.** Using Technology to Increase Student Learning. LC 99-50607. (One-Off Ser.). 176p. 2000. pap. 34.95 (*0-8039-6814-0*); lib. bdg. 74.95 (*0-8039-6813-2*) Corwin Pr.

Reksten, Terry. More English Than the English. (Illus.). 192p. 1986. pap. 12.95 (*0-920501-03-6*) Orca Bk Pubs.

Rektorys, Karel. The Method of Discretization in Time. 1982. text 251.00 (*90-277-1342-1*) Kluwer Academic.

— Solving Ordinary & Partial Boundary Value Problems in Science & Engineering. LC 98-25766. (Computational Mechanics & Applied Analysis Ser.). 224p. 1998. boxed set 74.95 (*0-8493-2552-8*, 2552) CRC Pr.

— Survey of Applicable Mathematics, 2 vols. 2nd rev. ed. (Mathematics & Its Applications Ser.). 1769p. 1994. lib. bdg. 595.00 (*0-7923-0679-1*) Kluwer Academic.

— Variational Methods in Mathematics, Science & Engineering. Basch, Michael, tr. from CZE. 572p. 1980. text 122.00 (*90-277-1060-0*) Kluwer Academic.

Rektorys, Karel, jt. auth. see Maia.

Rekus, John F. Complete Confined Spaces Handbook. 400p. 1994. lib. bdg. 85.00 (*0-87371-487-3*, L487) Lewis Pubs.

Rekus, Jurgen. Schulfach und Ethik. 141p. 1991. write for info. (*3-487-09409-6*) G Olms Pubs.

Rela, Walter, compiled by. A Bibliographical Guide to Spanish American Literature: Twentieth-Century Sources, 13. LC 88-15443. (Bibliographies & Indexes in World Literature Ser.: No. 13). 400p. 1988. lib. bdg. 65.00 (*0-313-25861-9*, RBG/, Greenwood Pr) Greenwood.

Rela, Walter, ed. Uruguayan Literature: A Selective Bibliography. LC 86-15989. (Special Studies: No. 26). 86p. 1987. pap. 12.95 (*0-87918-060-9*) ASU Lat Am St.

Rela, Walter, jt. auth. see Foster, David W.

Relais et Chateaux Staff, ed. Relais et Chateaux, 1997. 1997. pap. 19.95 (*0-7859-9396-7*) Fr & Eur.

Relais Routiers Staff. Guide des Relais Routiers 1998. (FRE.). 1998. 49.95 (*0-7859-9714-8*) Fr & Eur.

Relander, Click. Drummers & Dreamers. (Illus.). 345p. (Orig.). 1986. reprint ed. pap. text 9.95 (*0-914019-09-0*) NW Interpretive.

Relation, Sylvia. Knotted Stems. 88p. 1999. 42.70 (*0-89002-347-6*); pap. 13.95 (*0-89002-345-X*) Northwoods Pr.

Relative Value Studies, Inc. Staff. The McGraw-Hill Complete RBRVS: The Resource Based Relative Value Scale. 1996. pap. 189.95 incl. disk (*0-07-810222-7*) McGraw.

— The McGraw-Hill Complete RBRVS: The Resource Based Relative Value Scale. 1996. 89.95 (*0-07-600823-1*) McGraw.

— Relative Values for Physicians, 1996-1997. 1996. 249.00 (*0-07-600822-3*) McGraw.

Rele, J. R. Fertility Analysis Through Extension of Stable Population Concepts & Stochastic Model of Human Reproduction, Vol. 2. LC 76-5439. (Population Monograph: No. 11). 1976. reprint ed. lib. bdg. 55.00 (*0-8371-8826-1*, REFA, Greenwood Pr) Greenwood.

Rele, J. R. & Kanitkar, Tara. Fertility & Family Planning in Greater Bombay. 217p. 1980. 22.95 (*0-940500-87-6*, Pub. by Popular Prakashan) Asia Bk Corp.

Rele, Vasant G. The Mysterious Kundalini. 92p. (Orig.). 1985. reprint ed. spiral bd. 13.00 (*0-7873-1032-8*) Hlth Research.

Relei. Bird Designs Stained Glass Pattern Book. (Illus.). 64p. pap. 5.95 (*0-486-25947-1*) Dover.

— Decorative Doorways Stained Glass Pattern Book. (Illus.). 64p. pap. 5.95 (*0-486-26494-7*) Dover.

Relei, Carolyn. Marine Animals Stained Glass Pattern Book. (Illus.). 64p. 1992. pap. 6.95 (*0-486-27016-5*) Dover.

— Traditional Doorways Stained Glass Pattern Book. LC 97-5735. (Illus.). 64p. 1997. pap. 6.95 (*0-486-29692-X*) Dover.

Relei, Carolyn. Tropical Flowers Stained Glass. (Illus.). (J). 1997. pap. 4.50 (*0-486-29780-2*) Dover.

Relei, Carolyn. William Morris Stained Glass Pattern Book. LC 98-27758. (Illus.). 64p. 1998. pap. 6.95 (*0-486-40288-6*) Dover.

Re'lem, Dyob, see Melger, Boyd A., pseud.

Re'lem, Dyob, pseud. High Bloodpressures, Heart Attack, Diagrams. rev. ed. LC 89-92415. (Illus.). 90p. 1989. pap. write for info. (*0-9622463-2-8*) B Melger.

— Hoge Bloeddruk, Hart Infarct, Grafieken. rev. ed. (DUT., Illus.). 90p. 1989. pap. write for info. (*0-9622463-3-6*) B Melger.

Re'lem, Dyob, pseud & Melger, Boyd A. Hoge Bloeddruk, Myocardiale Infarct, Grafieken. (DUT., Illus.). 69p. (Orig.). 1989. pap. write for info. (*0-9622463-1-X*) B Melger.

Relethford, John H. Fundamentals of Biological Anthropology. 2nd rev. ed. (Illus.). xiv, 386p. (C). 1996. pap. text 49.95 (*1-55934-667-1*, 1667) Mayfield Pub.

— Fundmentals of Biological Anthropology: Instructor's Manual. 2nd rev. ed. 113p. (C). 1996. pap. text, teacher ed. write for info. (*1-55934-668-X*, 1668) Mayfield Pub.

— The Human Species: An Introduction to Biological Anthropology. 4th ed. LC 99-22904. xvii,499p. 1999. pap. text 56.95 (*0-7674-1171-4*, 1171-4) Mayfield Pub.

***Relf, Pat.** A Dinosaur Named Sue: The Story of the Colossal Fossil: The World's Most Complete T. Rex. (Illus.). 64p. (J). (gr. 1-5). 2000. 15.95 (*0-439-09985-4*) Scholastic Inc.

Relf, Patricia. El Autobus Magico Planta Una Semilla: Un Libro Sobre Como Crecen Los Seres Vivos. (J). 1995. 8.19 (*0-606-07471-6*, Pub. by Turtleback) Demco.

— El Autobus Magico Salta Hasta Llegar A Casa: Un Libro Sobre Los Habitats De Los Animales. (J). 1995. 7.70 (*0-606-07472-4*, Pub. by Turtleback) Demco.

***Relf, Patricia.** The Magic School Bus Gets Eaten: A Book about Food Chains. (Magic School Bus Ser.). (Illus.). (J). (gr. k-2). 1999. pap. 10.55 (*0-7857-7530-7*) Econo-Clad Bks.

Relf, Patricia. The Magic School Bus Gets Eaten: A Book about Food Chains. Duchesne, Lucie, tr. (Magic School Bus Ser.). (FRE., Illus.). 32p. (J). (gr. k-2). 1996. pap. 5.99 (*0-590-16038-9*) Scholastic Inc.

— The Magic School Bus Gets Eaten: A Book about Food Chains. LC 96-181116. (Magic School Bus Ser.). (Illus.). (J). (ps-3). 1996. pap. 2.99 (*0-590-48414-1*) Scholastic Inc.

— The Magic School Bus Gets Eaten: A Book about Food Chains. (Magic School Bus Ser.). (Illus.). (J). (gr. k-2). 1996. 8.19 (*0-606-09587-X*, Pub. by Turtleback) Demco.

— The Magic School Bus Hops Home: A Book about Animal Habitats. LC 94-25969. (Magic School Bus Ser.). (Illus.). 32p. (J). (ps-3). 1995. pap. 2.50 (*0-590-48413-3*) Scholastic Inc.

— The Magic School Bus Hops Home: A Book about Animal Habitats. (Magic School Bus Ser.). (Illus.). (J). (gr. k-2). 1995. 8.19 (*0-606-07821-5*, Pub. by Turtleback) Demco.

***Relf, Patricia.** The Magic School Bus Plants Seeds: A Book about How Living Things Grow. (Magic School Bus Ser.). (Illus.). (J). (ps-3). 1999. pap. 10.55 (*0-7857-5621-3*) Econo-Clad Bks.

Relf, Patricia. The Magic School Bus Plants Seeds: A Book about How Living Things Grow. LC 94-38345. (Magic School Bus Ser.). (Illus.). 32p. (J). (ps-3). 1995. pap. 2.99 (*0-590-22296-1*) Scholastic Inc.

— The Magic School Bus Plants Seeds: A Book about How Living Things Grow. (Magic School Bus Ser.). (Illus.). (J). (gr. k-2). 1995. 8.19 (*0-606-07826-6*, Pub. by Turtleback) Demco.

— The Magic School Bus Wet All Over: A Book about the Water Cycle. (Magic School Bus Ser.). (Illus.). (J). (ps-3). 1996. pap. 2.99 (*0-590-50833-4*) Scholastic Inc.

Relf, Patricia. The Magic School Bus Wet All Over: A Book about the Water Cycle. (Magic School Bus Ser.). (Illus.). (J). (gr. k-2). 1996. 8.19 (*0-606-09589-6*, Pub. by Turtleback) Demco.

— Tonka: Look Inside Trucks. (Tonka Trucks Storybook Ser.). (Illus.). 5p. (J). (ps-1). 1999. bds. 9.95 (*0-439-05020-0*, Pub. by Scholastic Inc) Penguin Putnam.

Relf, Patricia. Tonka Big Book of Trucks. LC 95-47928. (Illus.). 32p. (J). (ps-3). 1996. 11.95 (*0-590-84572-1*, Cartwheel) Scholastic Inc.

***Relf, Patricia.** Tonka Trucks Night & Day. LC 99-43602. (Illus.). 40p. (J). (ps-3). 2000. 12.95 (*0-439-12196-5*, Cartwheel) Scholastic Inc.

— What's Happening? A Book of Explanations. (Illus.). 32p. (J). (gr. 3-7). 2000. 15.95 (*1-57255-841-5*) Mondo Pubng.

Relf, Patricia & Cole, Joanna. Se Salpica Todo (Wet All Over) (Autobus Magico Ser.). (ENG & SPA.). (J). (gr. 1-4). 1996. pap. text 2.99 (*0-590-85951-X*) Scholastic Inc.

Relfe, Mary S. Civilization Ambushed--Banks Fail... Dollars Die... The Y2K Apocalypse: New Offering. 306p. 1999. pap. 12.00 (*0-9607986-5-X*) League Prayer.

— Cure of All Ills: Revival Cycles of the Past 250 Years. 175p. 1988. pap. 7.00 (*0-9607986-2-5*) League Prayer.

— The Day Banks Close & Other Unthinkables. 64p. 1998. pap. 6.00 (*0-9607986-4-1*) League Prayer.

— The New Money System. 272p. 1982. pap. 7.00 (*0-9607986-1-7*) League Prayer.

— When Your Money Fails. 234p. (Orig.). 1981. pap. text 6.00 (*0-9607986-0-9*) League Prayer.

***Relfe, Mary S., contrib. by.** Y2K & End-Time Updates. 164p. 1999. pap. 8.00 (*0-9607986-6-8*) League Prayer.

Relfe, Mary S., ed. see Bunyan, John.

Relgis, Eugene. Max Nettlau, Rudolf Rocker, Han Ryner, Rodolfo Gonzalez Pacheco, Joseph Ishill & Other Essays in Anarchism, Humanism, Libertarianism & Freedom. (History of Anarchism Ser.). 1984. lib. bdg. 250.00 (*0-8490-3234-2*) Gordon Pr.

— Muted Voices. 1972. reprint ed. lib. bdg. 250.00 (*0-87968-001-6*) Gordon Pr.

Reliance Medical Information, Inc. Staff, et al, eds. The CareWise Guide: Self-Care from Head to Toe. 2nd rev. ed. LC 96-83132. (Illus.). 448p. 1996. pap. 19.95 (*1-886444-01-3*) CareWise.

Relier, J. P., ed. XIXes Journees Nationales de Neonatologie, 1989. (Progres en Neonatologie Ser.: Vol. 9). (Illus.). 268p. 1989. pap. 115.75 (*3-8055-5060-X*) S Karger.

— XVIIes Journees Nationales de Neonatologie, 1987. (Paris, Mai Ser.: Vol. 7). vi, 382p. 1987. pap. 139.25 (*3-8055-4652-1*) S Karger.

— XXVes Journees Nationales de Neonatologie, 1995. (Progres en Neonatologie Ser.: Vol. 15). (Illus.). vi, 332p. 1995. pap. 170.50 (*3-8055-6208-X*) S Karger.

— XXIes Journees Nationales de Neonatologie, 1990. (Progres en Neonatologie Ser.: Vol. 10). (Illus.). vi, 312p. 1990. pap. 137.50 (*3-8055-5249-1*) S Karger.

— Twenty-First Journees Nationales de Neonatologie, 1991. (Progres en Neonatologie Ser.: Vol. 11). (Illus.). vi, 370p. 1991. pap. 161.00 (*3-8055-5446-X*) S Karger.

— XXIVemes Journees Nationales de Neonatologies, 1994, No. 14. (Progres en Neonatologie Ser.: Vol. 14). (Illus.). iv, 256p. 1994. pap. 170.50 (*3-8055-6015-X*) S Karger.

— XXIIes Journees Nationales De Neonatologie Paris, May 1992. (Progres en Neonatologie Ser.: Vol. 12). (Illus.). vi, 326p. 1992. pap. 169.75 (*3-8055-5636-5*) S Karger.

Reliford, Joe L., Sr. From Batboy to the Hall of Fame. (Illus.). 80p. 1997. pap. 10.00 (*0-9660934-0-2*) Relifords Pub.

Religious Education Committee. Quakers on the Move: A Storybook of Quaker History. (Illus.). 128p. (J). (gr. 2-5). 1996. pap. 9.00 (*1-888305-03-7*) Friends Genl Conf.

Religious Research Writers Group Staff. Death with Understanding. LC 87-61427. 284p. (Orig.). 1987. pap. 12.95 (*0-915151-10-3*) Religious Res Pr.

Relihan, Constance C. Fashioning Authority: The Development of Elizabethan Novelistic Discourse. LC 93-32278. (Illus.). 192p. 1994. lib. bdg. 24.00 (*0-87338-495-4*) Kent St U Pr.

Relihan, Constance C., ed. Framing Elizabethan Fictions: Contemporary Approaches to Early Modern Narrative Prose. LC 96-7331. (Illus.). 284p. (C). 1997. text 35.00 (*0-87338-551-9*) Kent St U Pr.

Relihan, Joel C. Ancient Menippean Satire. LC 92-36271. 344p. (C). 1993. text 49.95 (*0-8018-4524-6*) Johns Hopkins.

Relihan, Joel C., tr. see Tischler, Hans, ed.

Relihan, Taun, jt. auth. see Deasy, Victoria.

Relis, Nurie & Strauss, Gail. Sewing for Fashion Design. 2nd ed. LC 96-26800. 196p. 1996. spiral bd. 58.00 (*0-13-496753-4*) P-H.

Relis, Nurie, jt. auth. see Jaffe, Hilde.

Reljic, L. & Radovanovic, D. Folk Embroidery in Yugoslavia. (Illus.). 176p. (C). 1988. text 225.00 (*0-7855-5879-9*, Pub. by Collets) St Mut.

Relkin, Donald B., jt. auth. see Miller, Donald E.

Relkin, Norman R., et al, eds. Apolipoprotein E Genotyping in Alzheimer's Disease: Proceedings of a Conference Sponsored by the National Institute on Aging & the Alzheimer's Association, October 21-22, 1995, Vol. 802. 1996. 80.00 (*1-57331-048-4*) NY Acad Sci.

Relkin, Norman R., et al. Apolipoprotein E Genotyping in Alzheimer's Disease. LC 96-45654. (Annals Of The New York Academy Of Sciences,). 225p. 1997. pap. 80.00 (*1-57331-049-2*) NY Acad Sci.

Rella, Franco. The Myth of the Other: Lacan, Foucault, Deleuze, Bataille. Moe, Nelson, tr. from ITA. & intro. by. (Post Modern Positions Ser.: Vol. 7). 120p. (C). 1994. pap. text 11.95 (*0-944624-21-9*); lib. bdg. 29.95 (*0-944624-20-0*) Maisonneuve Pr.

Reller, John E., ed. The Diaries & Writing of Ann Morrison Reed, 1849-1921. 1978. 10.00 (*0-910312-48-6*) Calif Hist.

Reller, L. Barth, et al. Clinical Internal Medicine. 1979. 28.50 (*0-316-73970-7*, Little Brwn Med Div) Lppncott W & W.

Reller, Theodore L., jt. ed. see Erickson, Donald A.

Relles, Daniel A., jt. auth. see Brelsford, William M.

Rellich, F. Perturbation Theory of Eigenvalue Problems. x, 128p. 1969. text 195.00 (*0-677-00680-2*) Gordon & Breach.

Rellimeo. Within the Holy of Holies: Attitudes of Attainment. rev. ed. 1996. reprint ed. spiral bd. 10.00 (*0-7873-0712-2*) Hlth Research.

***Relling, William, Jr.** Deadly Vintage. No. 330. 1999. mass mkt. 4.99 (*0-373-26330-9*, Wrldwide Lib) Harlequin Bks.

Relling, William, Jr. The Infinite Man. (Illus.). 1988. lib. bdg. 25.00 (*0-910489-25-4*) Scream Pr.

***Relling, William, Jr.** Sweet Poison. (Mystery Ser.: No. 336). 2000. mass mkt. 4.99 (*0-373-26336-8*, 1-26336-8, Wrldwide Lib) Harlequin Bks.

Relman, Arnold S. When More Is Less: The Paradox of American Health Care & How to Resolve It. 224p. 1993. 19.95 (*0-393-03579-4*) Norton.

Relman, Arnold S., ed. see Curran, William J.

Relman, Arnold S., ed. see Lister, John.

Relman, John P. Housing Discrimination Practice Manual. LC 91-37449. (Civil Rights Ser.). 1992. ring bd. 130.00 (*0-87632-828-1*) West Group.

***Relova, Lia.** How to Self-Publish Your Own Book. (Illus.). 50p. 1999. pap. 10.00 (*0-9676252-4-6*) Pumpkin.

— The Job Hunter's Survival Kit. 80p. 1999. pap. 25.00 (*0-9676252-2-X*) Pumpkin.

— Sacred Places. (Illus.). 90p. 1998. pap. 10.00 (*0-9676252-0-3*) Pumpkin.

— The Self-Publisher's Writing Journal: The Writings & Artwork of Lia Price Relova. (Illus.). 80p. 1999. pap. 25.00 (*0-9676252-1-1*) Pumpkin.

Relova, Lia, ed. & illus. see Davies, Susan G.

Relph, Edward. The Modern Urban Landscape: 1880 to the Present. LC 87-3809. 288p. (Orig.). 1987. pap. text 16.95 (*0-8018-3560-7*) Johns Hopkins.

R

R

— Rational Landscapes & Humanistic Geography. LC 81-10782. 232p. 1981. 58.50 (*0-389-20237-1*, N7033) B&N Imports.

Relton, Frederic, jt. auth. see Overton, John H.

Relton, J., jt. auth. see Hohenadel, P.

Relton, V., jt. auth. see Hohenadel, P.

Rely, Len. Mono: A Collection of Dark Fiction. unabridged ed. 198p. 1998. pap. 14.95 (*1-892896-22-2*) Buy Books.

Relyea, Douglas B. Practical Application of SPC in the Flexible Packaging Industry. 176p. 1992. pap. text 21.50 (*0-527-91645-5*, 916455) Productivity Inc.

— Practical Application of SPC in the Wire & Cable Industry. (Illus.). 176p. 1990. pap. 21.50 (*0-527-91643-9*, 916439) Productivity Inc.

Relyea, Harold C. Evolution & Organization of Intelligence Activities in the United States. 321p. 1988. pap. 34.80 (*0-89412-156-1*); lib. bdg. 44.30 (*0-89412-157-X*) Aegean Park Pr.

— Silencing Science: National Security Controls & Scientific Communication. LC 93-50697. (Information Management, Policies & Services Ser.). 272p. 1994. pap. 39.50 (*1-56750-097-8*); text 73.25 (*1-56750-096-X*) Ablx Pub.

Relyea, Harold C., ed. The Executive Office of the President: A Historical, Biographical, & Bibliographical Guide. LC 96-5790. (Encyclopedia of the Federal Government Ser.). 696p. 1997. lib. bdg. 99.50 (*0-313-26476-7*, Greenwood Pr) Greenwood.

Relyea, Harold C., et al. The Presidency & Information Policy. 216p. (Orig.). 1981. 10.00 (*0-938204-03-3*); pap. 8.00 (*0-938204-04-1*) Ctr Study Presidency.

Remafedi, Gary, ed. Death by Denial: Studies of Suicide in Gay & Lesbian Teenagers. LC 95-120623. 205p. 1993. pap. 9.95 (*1-55583-260-1*) Alyson Pubns.

Remagen, jt. auth. see Greenspan, Adam.

Remak, Henry H. Structural Elements of the German Novella from Goethe to Thomas Mann. (North American Studies in Nineteenth-Century German Literature: Vol. 14). XIX, 322p. (C). 1996. text 54.95 (*0-8204-3451-5*) P Lang Pubng.

Remak, Jeannette. XB-70 Valkyrie: The Ride to Valhalla. LC 98-37887. (Illus.). 128p. 1998. pap. 19.95 (*0-7603-0555-2*) MBI Pubg.

Remak, Joachim. The Gentle Critic: Theodor Fontane & German Politics, 1848-1898. LC 64-16920. 116p. reprint ed. pap. 36.00 (*0-608-15208-0*, 202740200055) Bks Demand.

— The Nazi Years: A Documentary History. 178p. (C). 1990. reprint ed. pap. text 10.95 (*0-88133-527-4*) Waveland Pr.

— The Origins for World War I, 1871-1914. 2nd ed. LC 94-77240. (Illus.). 170p. (C). 1994. pap. text 29.50 (*0-15-501438-2*, Pub. by Harcourt Coll Pubs) Harcourt.

Remak, Joachim, ed. The Nazi Years: A Documentary History. LC 69-11359. 1969. pap. text 5.95 (*0-13-610535-1*, S195, Spectrum IN) Macmillan Gen Ref.

— War, Revolution & Peace: Essays in Honor of Charles B. Burdick. (Illus.). 298p. (C). 1987. lib. bdg. 50.00 (*0-8191-6342-2*) U Pr of Amer.

Remakel, John, jt. auth. see Moore, Chris.

Remakus, Bernard L. Keystone. Costa, Gwen, ed. LC 89-17582. 441p. (Orig.). 1992. 22.95 (*0-87949-294-5*) Ashley Bks.

— The Malpractice Epidemic: A Layman's Guide to Medical Malpractice. O'Donnell, Cara, ed. LC 89-17582. 1990. 22.95 (*0-87949-295-3*) Ashley Bks.

Remaley, Alan, et al. Clinical Pathology. 1997. write for info. (*0-89189-315-6*) Am Soc Clinical.

Reman, Edward. The Norse Discoveries & Explorations in America. LC 76-1871. (Illus.). 201p. 1976. reprint ed. lib. bdg. 38.50 (*0-8371-8745-1*, REND, Greenwood Pr) Greenwood.

Remand, B., jt. auth. see Ohta, M.

Remane, Adolf & Schlieper, Carl. Biology of Brackish Water. 2nd ed. (Binnengewasser Ser.: Vol. 25). (Illus.). x, 372p. 1971. 42.00 (*3-510-40034-8*, Pub. by E Schweizerbartsche) Balogh.

Remane, Katja, ed. see United Nations Food & Agriculture Organization Staff.

Remanufacturing Symposium, et al. 1998 APICS Remanufacturing Symposium Proceedings, May 18-19, 1998, San Diego, California: New Oportunities in Remanufacturing, Strategies & Tactics for Improving Your Business. LC 98-170466. 1998. write for info. (*1-55822-141-7*) Am Prod & Inventory.

Remar, Robert B. & Hubert, Richard N. Georgia. LC 96-19783. (Law & Mental Health Professionals Ser.). 510p. (C). 1996. text 59.95 (*1-55798-364-X*, 431-5090) Am Psychol.

Remark, Robert. Anatomical & Microscopic Observations on the Structure of the Nervous System. fac. ed. (Fascimiles of Classical Medical-Science Theses Ser.). (ENG & LAT., Illus.). 50p. (C). 1994. pap. text 19.50 (*0-930329-66-X*) Kabel Pubs.

Remarque, Erich-Maria. All Quiet on the Western Front. (Classics Illustrated Study Guides Ser.). (Illus.). 1998. mass mkt. 4.99 (*1-57840-056-2*, Pub. by Acclaim Bks) Penguin Putnam.

— All Quiet on the Western Front. 20.95 (*0-8488-1459-2*) Amereon Ltd.

— All Quiet on the Western Front. (Barron's Book Notes Ser.). (C). 1984. pap. 3.95 (*0-8120-3401-5*) Barron.

— All Quiet on the Western Front. 304p. 1987. mass mkt. 5.99 (*0-449-21394-3*, Crest) Fawcett.

— All Quiet on the Western Front. LC 96-96745. 295p. 1996. pap. 12.00 (*0-449-91149-7*) Fawcett.

— All Quiet on the Western Front. 248p. (gr. 8). 1929. 24.95 (*0-316-73992-8*) Little.

Remarque, Erich-Maria. All Quiet on the Western Front. 1984. 11.09 (*0-606-00101-8*, Pub. by Turtleback) Demco.

Remarque, Erich-Maria. All Quiet on the Western Front. large type ed. Wheen, A. W., tr. from ENG. LC 97-24791. (Perennial Ser.). 260p. 1997. lib. bdg. 24.95 (*0-7838-8259-9*, G K Hall Lrg Type) Mac Lib Ref.

— All Quiet on the Western Front. 391p. 1981. reprint ed. lib. bdg. 21.95 (*0-89966-292-7*) Buccaneer Bks.

— All Quiet on the Western Front: The Illustrated Edition. Wheen, A. W., tr. from GER. (Illus.). 208p. 1996. 29.95 (*0-8212-2312-7*) Little.

— Arch of Triumph. LC 97-90644. 464p. 1998. pap. 13.95 (*0-449-91245-0*) Fawcett.

— The Black Obelisk. LC 98-96090. 1998. pap. 13.95 (*0-449-91244-2*) Fawcett.

— The Black Obelisk. Lindley, Denver, tr. LC 57-8840. 440p. 1957. 19.95 (*0-15-113181-3*) Harcourt.

— Les Camarades, 2 vols. 1976. pap. 11.95 (*0-7859-4070-7*); pap. 11.95 (*0-7859-4071-5*) Fr & Eur.

— Drei Kameraden. (C). 1957. pap. 18.00 (*0-442-22070-7*) Heinle & Heinle.

— Heaven Has No Favorites. LC 98-96091. 1998. pap. 13.95 (*0-449-91249-3*) Fawcett.

— The Night in Lisbon. LC 98-96092. 1998. pap. 13.95 (*0-449-91243-4*) Fawcett.

— Shadows in Paradise. LC 98-96093. 1998. pap. 0.13 (*0-449-91248-5*) Fawcett.

— A Time to Love & a Time to Die. 1998. pap. 13.95 (*0-449-91250-7*) Fawcett.

Remarque, Erich-Maria, jt. auth. see Center for Learning Network Staff.

Remas, William A. What's Stopping You? Attitude Adjustment for the About-to-Be Entrepreneur. (Know How Now Ser.). 55p. 1995. pap. 5.00 (*0-9639557-0-5*, Know How Now) A R K Co.

Remaud, B., et al. Topics in Atomic & Nuclear Collisions. (NATO ASI Ser.: Vol. 321). (Illus.). 478p. (C). 1994. text 139.50 (*0-306-44662-6*, Kluwer Plenum) Kluwer Academic.

Rembaum, Alan & Selegny, Eric, eds. Charged & Reactive Polymers: Polyelectrolytes & Their Applications, Vol. 2. LC 74-34151. 350p. 1975. text 184.00 (*90-277-0561-5*) Kluwer Academic.

Rembaum, Alan & Tokes, Zoltan A., eds. Microspheres Medical & Biological Applications. LC 88-7343. 272p. 1988. 140.00 (*0-8493-6571-6*, RS201, CRC Reprint) Franklin.

Rembaum, Alan, ed. see Symposium on Biomedical Polymers Staff.

Rember, John. Cheerleaders from Gomorrah: Tales from the Lycra Archipelago. LC 93-71409. 125p. 1994. 15.00 (*1-881090-03-5*); pap. 12.00 (*1-881090-06-X*) Confluence Pr.

— Coyote in the Mountains: And Other Stories. (Illus.). 102p. (Orig.). 1989. pap. 12.00 (*0-931659-05-1*) Limberlost Pr.

***Rembert, Ron.** From Roaring Boys to Dreaming Spires: Essays in Honor of John Wilson. LC 99-36802. 152p. 1999. 37.00 (*0-7618-1482-5*) U Pr of Amer.

Rembielinski, Jakub, ed. Particle, Fields & Gravitation. LC 98-88573. 586p. 1998. 145.00 (*1-56396-837-1*) Am Inst Physics.

Rembold, et al. Computeranwendungen in der Produktion. (GER.). (C). 1991. text. write for info. (*0-201-55961-7*) Addison-Wesley.

Rembold, Kristen S. Coming into This World. 38p. (Orig.). 1992. pap. 3.00 (*1-880575-13-2*) Hot Pepper.

— Felicity. LC 94-13615. (First Novel Ser.). 192p. (Orig.). 1994. pap. 12.00 (*0-922811-19-9*) Mid-List.

Rembold, Ulrich, ed. Robot Technology & Applications. (Manufacturing Engineering & Materials Processing Ser.: Vol. 34). (Illus.). 696p. 1990. text 230.00 (*0-8247-8206-2*) Dekker.

Rembold, Ulrich & Dillman, R., eds. Computer-Aided Design & Manufacturing. 2nd rev. ed. (Symbolic Computation Ser.). (Illus.). 510p. 1986. 140.95 (*0-387-16321-2*) Spr-Verlag.

Rembold, Ulrich & Horman, K., eds. Languages for Sensor-Based Control in Robotics. (NATO ASI Series H: Vol. 29). x, 625p. 1987. 127.95 (*0-387-17665-9*) Spr-Verlag.

Rembold, Ulrich, et al. Computer-Integrated Manufacturing Technology & Systems. LC 85-16052. (Manufacturing Engineering & Materials Processing Ser.: No. 16). (Illus.). 804p. reprint ed. pap. 200.00 (*0-608-09647-4*, 206976300006) Bks Demand.

— Computers in Manufacturing. LC 76-11945. (Manufacturing Engineering & Materials Processing Ser.: Vol. 1). (Illus.). 590p. reprint ed. pap. 182.90 (*0-608-08978-8*, 206961300005) Bks Demand.

— Interface Technology for Computer Controlled Manufacturing Processes. (Manufacturing Engineering & Materials Processing Ser.: Vol. 9). (Illus.). 376p. 1983. text 150.00 (*0-8247-1836-4*) Dekker.

Rembold, Ulrich, jt. auth. see Fatikow, S.

Rembold, Ulrich, jt. ed. see Dillman, R.

Remboldt, Carole. Chemical Dependence: Yes, You Can Do Something. 20p. 1987. pap. 2.95 (*0-935908-35-8*, 3222, HazeldenJohnson Inst) Hazelden.

— Chemical Dependence & Recovery: A Family Affair. 32p. 1980. pap. 2.75 (*0-935908-00-5*, 8105, HazeldenJohnson Inst) Hazelden.

— The Family Enablers. rev. ed. 16p. 1982. pap. 2.75 (*0-935908-09-9*, 3221, HazeldenJohnson Inst) Hazelden.

— Getting Off the Hook: Solving Alcohol & Other Drug Problems at Work. 1992. pap., wbk. ed. 5.50 (*1-56246-073-0*, 3283, HazeldenJohnson Inst) Hazelden.

— Good Intentions, Bad Results: Preventing Teenage Peer Enabling & Chemical Use: a Guide for Educators. LC 93-21083. 106p. 1993. pap. 9.95 (*1-56246-076-5*, 3116, HazeldenJohnson Inst) Hazelden.

— Good Intentions, Bad Results: Preventing Teenage Peer Enabling & Chemical Use: a Guide for Educators, Am I An Enabler? 32p. 1993. pap., student ed. 6.50 (*1-56246-077-3*, 3118, HazeldenJohnson Inst) Hazelden.

— Good Intentions, Bad Results: Preventing Teenage Peer Enabling & Chemical Use: a Guide for Educators, How Chemical Use Becomes Chemical Dependence. 40p. 1993. pap., student ed. 5.50 (*1-56246-081-1*, 3117, HazeldenJohnson Inst) Hazelden.

— Helping Kids Handle Anger Without Violence. LC 96-38969. (Johnson Institute Resources for Parenting Ser.). 1997. 2.25 (*1-56246-138-9*, 3193, HazeldenJohnson Inst) Hazelden.

— Helping Kids Resolve Conflicts Without Violence. LC 96-38951. (Resources for Parenting Ser.). 1997. 2.25 (*1-56246-139-7*, 3192, HazeldenJohnson Inst) Hazelden.

— How to Teach Kids to Handle Anger Without Violence. LC 97-3374. (Johnson Institute Resources for Parenting Ser.). 1997. 2.25 (*1-56246-125-7*, 3140, HazeldenJohnson Inst) Hazelden.

— How to Teach Kids to Resolve Conflicts Without Violence. LC 97-3376. (Johnsons Institute Resources for Parenting Ser.). 1997. 2.25 (*1-56246-126-5*, 3146, HazeldenJohnson Inst) Hazelden.

Remboldt, Carole. Making Choices: How to Prevent Alcohol & Other Drug Problems at Work. 1994. wbk. ed. 27.50 (*1-56246-097-8*, 328810, HazeldenJohnson Inst) Hazelden.

Remboldt, Carole. Recovery Is a Family Affair. 48p. 1993. pap., wbk. ed. 9.95 (*1-56246-113-3*, 3258, HazeldenJohnson Inst) Hazelden.

— Solving Violence Problems in Your School: Why a Systematic Approach Is Necessary. 52p. 1994. pap. 3.25 (*1-56246-095-1*, 3036, HazeldenJohnson Inst) Hazelden.

— Violence in Schools: The Enabling Factor. 48p. 1994. pap. 3.25 (*1-56246-096-X*, 3035, HazeldenJohnson Inst) Hazelden.

— What to Say or Do If Your Child... A Parent's Quick Reference for Handling Common Behavior Problems. LC 98-12281. 110p. 1998. pap. 16.95 (*1-56246-147-8*, P724, HazeldenJohnson Inst) Hazelden.

Remboldt, Carole & Zimman, Richard. Respect & Protect: A Practical Step-by-Step Violence Prevention & Intervention Program for Schools & Communities. LC 95-44082. 424p. (Orig.). 1995. pap. 109.95 (*1-56246-098-6*, 3034, HazeldenJohnson Inst) Hazelden.

Remboldt, Carole, ed. see Wilmens, David J.

Rembrandt. Drawings of Rembrandt, 2 vols., Vol. 1. Slive, Seymour, ed. (Illus.). 630p. 1965. pap. 17.95 (*0-486-21485-0*) Dover.

— Drawings of Rembrandt, 2 vols., Vol. 2. Slive, Seymour, ed. (Illus.). 1965. pap. 17.95 (*0-486-21486-9*) Dover.

Rembrandt Harmenszoon van Rijn Staff & Montgomery Museum of Fine Arts Staff. Rembrandt, Beyond the Brush: Master Prints from the Weil Collection. LC 99-19970. 1999. 22.00 (*0-89280-037-2*) Montgomery Mus.

Rembrandt Harmenszoon van Rijn Staff, jt. auth. see Maan, Tony.

Rembrandt Research Project Staff. A Corpus of Rembrandt Paintings Vol. III: 1635-1642. (C). 1990. lib. bdg. 783.50 (*90-247-3781-8*) Kluwer Academic.

Rembry, J. Control of Feral Cat Populations by Long Term Administration of Magestrol Acetate. 1978. 16.00 (*0-7855-1105-9*) St Mut.

***Remec, I.** H. B. Robinson-2 Pressure Vessel Benchmark. 62p. 1998. pap. 5.00 (*0-16-062891-1*) USGPO.

— Neutron Exposure Parameters for Capsule 10. 05 in the Heavy Section Steel Irradiation Program Tenth Irradiation Series. 49p. 1998. pap. 4.25 (*0-16-062958-6*) USGPO.

— Neutron Exposure Parameters for the Dosimetry Capsule in the Heavy Section Steel Irradiation Program Tenth Irradiation Series. 47p. 1998. pap. 4.25 (*0-16-062959-4*) USGPO.

— Pool Critical Assembly Pressure Vessel Facility Benchmark. 50p. 1997. pap. 4.50 (*0-16-054689-3*) USGPO.

Remedio, E. M. Export Processing Zone in the Philippines: A Review of Employment, Working Conditions & Labour Relations. (Multinational Enterprises Programme Working Papers: No. 77). vii, 44p. 1996. 13.50 (*92-2-110056-1*) Intl Labour Office.

Remeika, Paul & Lindsay, Lowell. Geology of Anza-Borrego: Edge of Creation. LC 92-33102. (Natural History Bks.). (Illus.). 208p. (Orig.). 1993. pap. 12.95 (*0-932653-17-0*) Sunbelt Pubns.

Remeis, Mot & Siemer, Thomas K. Cruise Missiles: A Drama about Nuclear First Strike Planning. 142p. (Orig.). (C). 1989. pap. 14.95 (*0-685-30774-3*) Abbeyhills O C.

Remele, Larry, ed. The North Dakota State Capitol: Architecture & History. (Illus.). 63p. 1989. pap. 6.50 (*1-891419-09-9*) State Hist ND.

Remele, Patricia. Money Freedom: Finding Your Inner Source of Wealth. Skidmore, Kenneth M., ed. 242p. 1995. pap. 14.95 (*0-87604-333-3*, 422) ARE Pr.

Remen, Rachel N. Kitchen Table Wisdom: Stories That Heal. 368p. 1997. pap. 12.95 (*1-57322-610-6*, Riverhd Trade) Berkley Pub.

***Remen, Rachel N.** My Grandfather's Blessings: Stories of Strength, Refuge & Belonging. LC 99-58061. 368p. 2000. 24.95 (*1-57322-150-3*, Riverhead Books) Putnam Pub Group.

***Remender, Rick & Jaten, Harper.** Captain Dingleberry: Unplugged. (Illus.). 144p. 1999. pap. 19.95 (*0-943151-17-1*) Slave Labor Bks.

Remensnyder, Amy G. Remembering Kings Past: Monastic Foundation Legends in Medieval Southern France. (Illus.). 376p. 1996. text 52.50 (*0-8014-2954-4*) Cornell U Pr.

Remeny, K. Combustion Stability. 176p. 1980. 89.75 (*0-569-08640-X*) St Mut.

***Remenyi & Brown, Ann.** IT Management Critical Business Issues for Ensuring Success. 256p. 2000. 75.95 (*0-7506-5034-6*) Buttrwrth-Heinemann.

Remenyi, D., et al. Achieving Maximum Value from Information Systems: An Active Benefit Realisation Approach. LC 97-9287. (Wiley Series in Information Systems). 278p. 1997. 82.95 (*0-471-97500-1*) Wiley.

Remenyi, D. S., jt. ed. see Berghout, E. W.

***Remenyi, Dan.** Stop IT Project Failures Through Risk Management. 227p. 1999. 44.95 (*0-7506-4503-2*) Buttrwrth-Heinemann.

Remenyi, Dan & Sherwood-Smith, Michael. IT Investment: Making a Business Case. 160p. 1999. pap. text 49.95 (*0-7506-4504-0*) Buttrwrth-Heinemann.

***Remenyi, Dan, et al.** Doing Research in Business & Management: An Introduction to Process & Method. 336p. 1998. 74.50 (*0-7619-5949-1*); pap. 26.50 (*0-7619-5950-5*) Sage.

Remenyi, J. V. Agricultural Research Systems. 190p. (Orig.). 1985. pap. 87.00 (*0-949511-18-8*) St Mut.

***Remenyi, Joe & Quidnones, B.** Microfinance & Poverty Alleviation: Case Studies from Asia & the Pacific. LC 99-44978. (Global Development & the Environment Ser.). 2000. pap. 82.95 (*1-85567-643-5*) P P Pubs.

Remenyi, Joe, et al. Aid Trade & Development: An Interpretive Essay. 1993. pap. 35.00 (*0-7300-1601-3*, SSS338, Pub. by Deakin Univ) St Mut.

Remenyi, Joseph. World Literatures. 315p. 1977. 19.95 (*0-8369-1010-9*) Ayer.

Remenyi, K. Combustion Stability. 174p. 1980. 45.00 (*963-05-2023-0*, Pub. by Akade Kiado) St Mut.

— Industrial Firing. 496p. 1987. 162.00 (*963-05-4165-3*, Pub. by Akade Kiado) St Mut.

— Industrial Firing. 498p. (C). 1987. 400.00 (*0-569-09004-0*, Pub. by Collets) St Mut.

— The Theory of Grindability & the Comminution of Binary Mixtures. 144p. (C). 1974. 40.00 (*963-05-0231-3*, Pub. by Akade Kiado) St Mut.

Remer, Abby. Discovering Native American Art. LC 95-83877. (Illus.). 64p. (YA). (gr. 9-12). 1996. pap. 15.55 (*0-87192-305-X*) Davis Mass.

— Pioneering Spirits: The Life & Times of Remarkable Women Artists in Western History. LC 96-85574. (Illus.). 160p. (YA). (gr. 9-12). 1997. 27.00 (*0-87192-317-3*) Davis Mass.

Remer, Charles F. Foreign Investments in China. LC 67-24594. (C). 1968. 55.00 (*0-86527-067-8*) Fertig.

— A Study of Chinese Boycotts, with Special References to Their Economic Effectiveness. 1979. 28.95 (*0-405-10620-3*) Ayer.

Remer, Charles F. & Kawai, Saburo. Japanese Economics: A Guide to Japanese Reference & Research Materials, No. 5--5. LC 78-5534. (University of Michigan Center for Japanese Studies Bibliographical Ser.: No. 5). 91p. 1978. reprint ed. lib. bdg. 57.50 (*0-313-20435-7*, REJE) Greenwood.

Remer, Daniel & Dunaway, Robert. Legal Care for Your Software. rev. ed. 368p. 1993. pap. 39.95 (*0-9636256-0-8*) RDS Pub.

Remer, Gary. Humanism & the Rhetoric of Toleration. LC 95-9739. 302p. 1996. 48.50 (*0-271-01480-6*) Pa St U Pr.

Remer, Jane. Beyond Enrichment: Building Effective Arts Partnerships with Schools & Your Communities. LC 96-5119. 557p. 1996. pap. 24.95 (*1-879903-24-5*) Am for the Arts.

— Changing Schools Through the Arts: How to Build on the Power of an Idea. LC 90-1293. 284p. 1990. pap. 17.95 (*0-915400-86-3*, ACA Bks) Am for the Arts.

Remer, John H., Jr. The New Bull Terrier. (Illus.). 288p. 1989. 25.95 (*0-87605-096-8*) Howell Bks.

Remer, Nicolaus. Laws of Life in Agriculture. Castelliz, K. et al, trs. from GER. (Illus.). 158p. 1995. pap. 12.95 (*0-938250-40-X*) Bio-Dynamic Farm.

Remer, Pam, jt. auth. see Worell, Judith.

Remer, Rosalind. Printers & Men of Capital: Philadelphia Book Publishers in the New Republic. (Early American Studies). (Illus.). 224p. 1996. text 34.95 (*0-8122-3337-9*) U of Pa Pr.

Remers, William A. The Chemistry of Antitumor Antibiotics, Vol. 1. LC 78-12436. 299p. reprint ed. pap. 92.70 (*0-608-08116-7*, 201740100007) Bks Demand.

— The Chemistry of Antitumor Antibiotics, Vol. 2. 290p. 1988. 180.00 (*0-471-08180-9*) Wiley.

***Remers, William A.** Chemists at War: Accounts of Chemical Research in the United States in World War II. viii, 216p. 2000. pap. 14.95 (*0-9677940-0-5*) Clarice Pubns.

Remers, William A., jt. auth. see Delgado, Jaime N.

Remesh, T., jt. auth. see Razkova, S.

Remfert, Matt H. How to Survive Auto Repairs. 95p. (Orig.). 1995. pap. 6.95 (*0-614-11215-X*) Pygmalion Press.

Remfrew, Colin, jt. ed. see Cunliffe, Barry.

Remfry, J., jt. auth. see Neville, Peter.

Remgen, J. V., ed. Studies in Ornithology Honoring Ted Parker. (Ornithological Monographs: Vol. 48). (Illus.). 918p. 1997. 49.95 (*0-935868-93-3*) Am Ornithologists.

Remiasz, Stella V. Designing Bridal Veils, Headpieces & Hats. (Illus.). 136p. (Orig.). (C). 1992. pap. text 15.95 (*0-9617414-1-4*) Hat Tree Studio.

— Hats, Design & Construction. 2nd ed. LC 86-82042. (Illus.). 160p. 1990. pap. text 15.95 (*0-9617414-0-6*) Hat Tree Studio.

Remich, Daniel. History of Kennebunk, from Its Earliest Settlement to 1890, Including Biographical Sketches. (Illus.). 580p. 1992. reprint ed. lib. bdg. 55.00 (*0-8328-2526-3*) Higginson Bk Co.

Remick, jt. auth. see Mitchell.

Remick, jt. compiled by see Mitchell.

An Asterisk (*) at the beginning of an entry indicates that the title is appearing for the first time.

Remick, Daniel G. & Friedland, Jan S., eds. Cytokines in Health & Disease. 2nd ed. LC 97-12544. (Illus.). 704p. 1997. text 195.00 (*0-8247-9823-6*) Dekker.

Remick, Helen. Comparable Worth & Wages: Economic Equity for Women. (Occasional Publications: No. 149). 14p. 1984. 1.00 (*0-318-04754-3*) U Hawaii.

Remick, Helen, ed. Comparable Worth & Wage Discrimination: Technical Possibilities & Political Realities. (Women in the Political Economy Ser.). 320p. 1985. pap. 24.95 (*0-87722-385-8*) Temple U Pr.

Remick, Jack. The Stolen House. LC 79-91912. (Fiction Ser.). 168p. (Orig.). 1980. pap. 5.95 (*0-917530-13-6*) Pig Iron Pr.

— Terminal Weird. 160p. (Orig.). 1994. pap. 10.95 (*0-930773-34-9*); lib. bdg. 20.95 (*0-930773-33-0*) Black Heron Pr.

Remick, Jack, jt. auth. see Robert, Robert J.

Remick, Mary K. Searching for Blanche. LC 99-209843. 310p. 1998. 19.95 (*0-9667128-0-3*) Pen Oak Pr.

***Remick, Mary Kay.** Sweet & Sour. 290p. 2000. 21.95 (*0-9667128-1-1*) Pen Oak Pr.

***Remick, Norman T.** Mr. Jefferson's Academy: The Real Story Behind West Point. LC 98-91578. (Illus.). 440p. 1999. 25.00 (*0-9674879-0-0*) N T Remick.

Remick, Oliver P. A Record of the Services of the Commissioned Officers & Enlisted Men of Kittery & Eliot, Maine, in the American Revolution. LC 86-60507. (Illus.). 235p. 1986. reprint ed. 25.00 (*0-89725-062-1*, 1217) Picton Pr.

— A Record of the Services of the Commissioned Officers & Enlisted Men of Kittery & Eliot, Who Served Their Country...in the Revolution, 1775-1783. (Illus.). 223p. 1997. reprint ed. pap. 25.00 (*0-8328-5864-1*) Higginson Bk Co.

Remick, Sue & Bay Area Consumer's Checklist Editors Staff. Guide to Bay Area Restaurants. rev. ed. 128p. 1998. pap. 7.95 (*1-888124-05-9*) Ctr Study Serv.

Remick, Sue, jt. auth. see Consumers' Checkbook Magazine Editors.

Remie, Cornelius H. & Lacroix, Jean-Michel, eds. Canada on the Threshold of the 21st Century: European Reflections upon the Future of Canada. Selected Papers of the First All-European Studies Conference, The Hague, The Netherlands, Oct 24-27, 1990. LC 91-20633. xx, 565p. 1991. 50.00 (*1-55619-124-3*) J Benjamins Pubng Co.

Remie, R., jt. auth. see Van Dongen, J. J.

Remillard, Francois. New York City: Ulysses Travel Guide. Ulysses Travel Guide Staff, ed. (Ulysses Travel Guide Ser.). (Illus.). 432p. 1998. pap. 14.95 (*2-89464-088-9*) Ulysses Travel.

***Remillard, Francois.** New York City 2000-2001. 2nd ed. (Illus.). 2000. pap. 14.95 (*2-89464-236-9*, Pub. by Ulysses Travel) Globe Pequot.

Remillard, Francois. Quebec: Ulysses Travel Guide. Ulysses Travel Guide Staff, ed. (Ulysses Travel Guide Ser.). (Illus.). 1999. 21.95 (*2-89464-202-4*) Ulysses Travel.

***Remillard, Francois & Marceau, Stephane G.** Quebec City. 2000. pap. 12.95 (*2-89464-277-6*, Pub. by Ulysses Travel) Globe Pequot.

Remillard, Francois, et al. Montreal. Ulysses Travel Guide Staff, ed. (Ulysses Travel Guide Ser.). (Illus.). 416p. 1999. pap. 14.95 (*2-89464-190-7*) Ulysses Travel.

***Remillard, Francois, et al.** Ulysses Travel Guide - Montreal, 2000-2001. (Illus.). 2000. pap. 14.95 (*2-89464-260-1*, Pub. by Ulysses Travel) Globe Pequot.

Remillieux, J., et al, eds. Shim 89: Proceedings of the First International Symposium on Swift Heavy Ions in Matter, Caen, France, May 18-19, 1989: A Special Issue of the Journal Radiation Effects & Defects in Solids. x, 228p. 1989. pap. text 500.00 (*0-677-25960-3*) Gordon & Breach.

ReMine, Walter J. The Biotic Message: Evolution Versus Message Theory. LC 93-92637. 538p. (C). 1993. text 44.95 (*0-9637999-0-8*) St Paul Sci.

ReMine, William H., et al. Manual of Upper Gastrointestinal Surgery. (Comprehensive Manuals of Surgical Specialties Ser.). (Illus.). xiv, 124p. 1985. 162.00 (*0-387-96148-8*) Spr-Verlag.

Remington, ed. Politics in Russia. (C). 1999. text. write for info. (*0-673-99358-2*) Addison-Wesley.

Remington, Bob, ed. The Challenge of Severe Mental Handicap: A Behavior Analytic Approach. LC 90-13162. (Clinical Psychology Ser.: No. 1837). 416p. 1991. 375.00 (*0-471-92503-9*) Wiley.

Remington, Dennis W. & Higa, Barbara W. Back to Health: A Comprehensive Medical & Nutritional YEAST Control Program. (Illus.). 256p. 1986. pap. 10.95 (*0-912547-03-0*, 801-224-9214) Vitality Hse Int Inc.

Remington, Dennis W., et al. How to Lower Your Fat Thermostat: The No-Diet Reprogramming Plan for Lifelong Weight Control. LC 83-80794. (Illus.). 256p. 1983. pap. 9.95 (*0-912547-01-4*) Vitality Hse Int Inc.

Remington, Douglas. The Answer to the Secret of Life. LC 87-206430. 125p. (Orig.). 1989. pap. 5.00 (*0-614-13956-2*) Two Fortyeight.

— The Answer to the Secret of Life, I. 125p. (Orig.). 1989. write for info. (*0-318-65917-4*) Two Fortyeight.

— The Answer to the Secret of Life, II. LC 87-206430. 125p. (Orig.). 1989. write for info. (*0-614-13957-0*) Two Fortyeight.

Remington, F. Remington's Old West Postcards. 1989. pap. 4.95 (*0-486-25889-0*) Dover.

Remington, Frank J., jt. ed. see Ohlin, Lloyd E.

Remington, Frederic. Collective Writings Frederic Remington. 12.98 (*1-55521-115-1*) Bk Sales Inc.

Remington, Frederic. Crooked Trails. LC 74-101820. (Short Story Index Reprint Ser.). 1998. 3.95 (*0-8369-3208-0*) Ayer.

— Crooked Trails. (Illus.). 226p. 1992. reprint ed. pap. 18.00 (*1-55613-566-1*) Heritage Bk.

— Crooked Trails. LC 72-104547. (Illus.). 1979. reprint ed. lib. bdg. 20.00 (*0-8398-1753-3*) Irvington.

— Frederic Remington: One Hundred Seventy-Three Drawings & Illustrations. Pitz, Henry C., ed. & intro. by. LC 78-158963. (Illus.). 140p. 1972. pap. 9.95 (*0-486-20714-5*) Dover.

— Frederic Remington: One Hundred Seventy-Three Drawings & Illustrations. 1990. 23.25 (*0-8446-4601-6*) Peter Smith.

— Frederic Remington's Own West. 256p. 1994. 9.98 (*0-88394-005-1*) Promntory Pr.

— Frederick Remington: Selected Writings. 484p. 1992. 7.98 (*0-89009-441-1*) Bk Sales Inc.

— John Ermine of the Yellowstone. LC 68-20020. (Americans in Fiction Ser.). (Illus.). reprint ed. pap. text 8.95 (*0-89197-810-0*); reprint ed. lib. bdg. 22.50 (*0-8398-1754-1*) Irvington.

— Pony Tracks. 22.95 (*0-89190-780-7*) Amereon Ltd.

— Pony Tracks. (Western Frontier Library: No. 19). (Illus.). 1975. reprint ed. 12.95 (*0-8061-1248-4*) U of Okla Pr.

— Stories of Peace & War. LC 75-125237. (Short Story Index Reprint Ser.). 1977. 15.95 (*0-8369-3604-3*) Ayer.

— The Way of an Indian. LC 76-50438. 1976. 25.00 (*0-89436-000-0*) Memento.

Remington, Frederic, jt. auth. see Bourke, John G.

Remington, Frederic, jt. auth. see Neff, Emily B.

Remington, Gary, jt. ed. see Baskys, Andrius.

***Remington, Gwen.** The Cheyenne. LC 00-8653. 2000. write for info. (*1-56006-750-0*) Lucent Bks.

— The Sioux (North America) LC 99-32703. (Indigenous Peoples Ser.). (Illus.). 144p. (YA). (gr. 6-9). 2000. lib. bdg. 23.70 (*1-56006-615-6*) Lucent Bks.

Remington, Jack S. Current Clinical Topics in Infectious Diseases 13, Vol. 13. (Illus.). 392p. 1993. 79.95 (*0-86542-278-8*) Blackwell Sci.

***Remington, Jack S. & Klein, Jerome O.** Infectious Diseases of the Fetus & Newborn Infant. 5th ed. (Illus.). 1375p. 2000. text. write for info. (*0-7216-7976-5*, W B Saunders Co) Harcrt Hlth Sci Grp.

Remington, Jack S. & Klein, Jerome O., eds. Infectious Diseases of the Fetus & Newborn Infant. 4th ed. LC 94-23372. (Illus.). 1373p. 1994. text 210.00 (*0-7216-6782-1*, W B Saunders Co) Harcrt Hlth Sci Grp.

Remington, Jack S. & Swartz, M. N., eds. Current Clinical Topics in Infectious Diseases 14, Vol. 14. (Illus.). 320p. 1994. 79.95 (*0-86542-359-8*) Blackwell Sci.

Remington, Jack S. & Swartz, Morton, eds. Current Clinical Topics in Infectious Disease, Vol.16. (Illus.). 304p. 1996. 79.95 (*0-86542-477-2*) Blackwell Sci.

Remington, Jack S. & Swartz, Morton N. Current Clinical Topics in Infectious Disease, Vol. 17. (Illus.). 336p. 1997. 79.95 (*0-86542-575-2*) Blackwell Sci.

***Remington, Jack S. & Swartz, Morton N.** Current Clinical Topics in Infectious Disease, Vol. 19. (Illus.). 1999. 79.95 (*0-632-04402-0*) Blackwell Sci.

— Current Clinical Topics in Infectious Diseases, Vol. 20. (Illus.). 384p. 2000. 79.95 (*0-632-04427-6*) Blackwell Sci.

Remington, Jack S. & Swartz, Morton N., eds. Current Clinical Topics in Infectious Diseases, 15. (Illus.). 300p. 1995. 79.95 (*0-86542-397-0*) Blackwell Sci.

— Current Clinical Topics in Infectious Diseases, Vol. 18. LC 80-643590. (Illus.). 315p. 1998. 79.95 (*0-632-04398-9*) Blackwell Sci.

— Current Clinical Topics in Infectious Diseases 12, Vol. 12. (Illus.). 352p. (C). 1992. 79.95 (*0-86542-207-9*) Blackwell Sci.

Remington, Jack S., jt. auth. see Peterson, Phillip K.

Remington, Jim & Remington, Leona. Avioanxiety Becomes Controlled: Now, Fly Without Fear. (Illus.). 160p. (Orig.). 1992. 9.95 (*1-879855-01-1*) Inner Marker.

Remington, Kathleen. Ten Secrets of Highly Successful Women. White, Tim, ed. & illus. by. 220p. 1994. pap. 59.95 (*1-887126-92-9*) Natl Bus Bur.

Remington, Lee A. Clinical Anatomy of the Visual System. LC 97-16054. 272p. 1997. text 68.00 (*0-7506-9558-7*) Buttrwrth-Heinemann.

Remington, Leona, jt. auth. see Remington, Jim.

Remington, R. Roger. Lester Beall: Trailblazer of American Graphic Design. (Illus.). 320p. 1996. 60.00 (*0-393-73002-6*) Norton.

Remington, Richard D., jt. auth. see Schork, M. Anthony.

Remington, Thomas F. Building Socialism in Bolshevik Russia: Ideology & Industrial Organization, 1917-1921. LC 84-3603. (Series in Russian & East European Studies: No. 6). 232p. 1984. pap. 72.00 (*0-7837-8543-7*, 204935800011) Bks Demand.

— Politics in Russia. LC 98-4968. 368p. (C). 1998. pap. 41.40 (*0-321-00493-0*) Addison-Wesley Educ.

Remington, Vanessa, jt. auth. see Lloyd, Christopher.

Remini, Robert O., jt. auth. see Clark, James I.

Remini, Robert V. Andrew Jackson Vol. 1: The Course of American Empire, 1767-1821. LC 97-75802. (Illus.). 544p. reprint ed. pap. 17.95 (*0-8018-5911-5*) Johns Hopkins.

— Andrew Jackson Vol. 2: The Course of American Freedom, 1822-1832. LC 97-75802. (Illus.). 504p. pap. 17.95 (*0-8018-5912-3*) Johns Hopkins.

— Andrew Jackson & the Bank War. (Essays in American History Ser.). (C). 1967. pap. text 11.25 (*0-393-09757-9*) Norton.

— Andrew Jackson & the Course of American Democracy, 1833-1845, Vol. 3. LC 97-75802. (Illus.). 672p. 1998. pap. 17.95 (*0-8018-5913-1*) Johns Hopkins.

— The Battle of New Orleans: Andrew Jackson & America's First Military Victory. LC 99-19837. 199p. 1999. 24.95 (*0-670-88551-7*, Viking) Viking Penguin.

— Daniel Webster: The Man & His Time. LC 97-24371. 850p. 1997. 39.95 (*0-393-04552-8*) Norton.

— The Era of Good Feelings & the Age of Jackson, 1816-1841. LC 79-84211. (Goldentree Bibliographies Series in American History). (C). 1979. pap. text 19.95 (*0-88295-579-9*) Harlan Davidson.

***Remini, Robert V.** Gathering History: Marian S. Carson Collection of Americana. 134p. 1999. pap. 21.00 (*0-16-061819-3*, Library of Cong) USGPO.

Remini, Robert V. Henry Clay: Statesman for the Union. 880p. 1993. pap. 19.95 (*0-393-31088-4*) Norton.

— The Jacksonian Era. 2nd ed. Eisenstadt, A. S. & Franklin, John H., eds. LC 96-41307. (American History Ser.). (Illus.). 150p. (C). 1997. pap. text 11.95 (*0-88295-931-X*) Harlan Davidson.

— The Legacy of Andrew Jackson: Essays on Democracy, Indian Removal, & Slavery. LC 87-24137. (Walter Lynwood Fleming Lectures in Southern History). 117p. 1988. pap. text 12.95 (*0-8071-1642-4*) La State U Pr.

— The Life of Andrew Jackson. (Illus.). 416p. 1990. pap. 14.95 (*0-14-013267-8*, Penguin Bks) Viking Penguin.

Remini, Robert V. & Rupp, Robert O. Andrew Jackson: A Bibliography, 7. LC 90-41976. (Bibliographies of the Presidents of the United States Ser.: No. 7). 352p. 1990. lib. bdg. 79.50 (*0-313-28165-3*, AP07, Greenwood Pr) Greenwood.

***Remini, Robert Vincent.** Andrew Jackson. 272p. 1999. reprint ed. mass mkt. 14.00 (*0-06-080132-8*, P132, Perennial) HarperTrade.

Remini, Susan, ed. The Rainbow Book of Adventures. (Illus.). 114p. (Orig.). 1983. pap. 7.95 (*0-932471-01-3*) Falsoft.

Remini, William C., ed. Evaluation of Current Developments in Municipal Waste Treatment: Proceedings. LC 77-10538. (ERDA Symposium Ser.). 130p. 1977. pap. 11.25 (*0-87079-201-6*, CONF-770108); fiche 9.00 (*0-87079-205-9*, CONF-770108) DOE.

***Reminick, Gerald.** Patriots & Heroes: True Stories of the U. S. Merchant Marine in World War II. unabridged ed. LC 00-26432. (Illus.). xii, 298p. 2000. pap. 21.95 (*1-889901-14-8*) Glencannon Pr.

Reminick, Joan. Exploring Long Island with Newsday: 20 Historical Long Island Day Trips. (Illus.). 204p. 1998. pap. 11.95 (*1-885134-13-4*) Newsday.

Remis, Rafael. Remis: An Autobiography. (Illus.). 55p. 1998. pap. 9.00 (*0-8059-4401-X*) Dorrance.

Remizov, Aleksei. Iveren. Raevsky-Hughes, Olga, ed. (Modern Russian Literature & Culture, Studies & Texts: Vol. 7). (RUS.). 400p. (Orig.). 1986. pap. 19.00 (*0-933884-35-4*) Berkeley Slavic.

— Rossiia V Pis'menakh: Tom 1. LC 79-91965. (RUS., Illus.). 232p. 1982. reprint ed. pap. 7.95 (*0-89830-013-4*) Russica Pubs.

— Tsar Maksimilian. (RUS.). 128p. 1988. reprint ed. pap. 8.00 (*0-933884-55-9*) Berkeley Slavic.

Remkiewicz, Frank, jt. auth. see Kline, Suzy.

Remkus, Susan, ed. see Dennison, Susan.

Remkus, Susan, ed. see Drew, Naomi.

Remkus, Susan, ed. see Kovelman, Joyce A.

Remkus, Susan, ed. see Sunbeck, Deborah.

Remkus, Susan, ed. see Whitaker-Duncklee, Deborah.

Remland Nonverbal Communication Everyday Staff. Remland Nonverbal Comm Everday. Date not set. pap. text 33.27 (*0-395-88856-5*) HM.

Remler, Mary H. & Hamilton County Chapter of the Ohio Genealogical S. Hamilton County, Ohio Burial Records Vol. 10: Green Township. 204p. 1998. pap. 30.50 (*0-7884-0856-9*, H157) Heritage Bk.

Remler, Mary H., ed. see Hamilton County Chapter of the Ohio Genealogical Society Staff.

Remler, P. Ascomyceten auf Ericaceen in den Ostalpen. (Bibliotheca Mycologica Ser.: No. 68). (GER., Illus.). 1980. lib. bdg. 64.00 (*3-7682-1248-3*) Lubrecht & Cramer.

***Remler, Pat.** Egyptian Mythology A to Z: A Young Reader's Companion. LC 99-58590. (Mythology A to Z Ser.). (Illus.). 144p. (YA). 2000. 19.95 (*0-8160-3984-4*) Facts on File.

Remley, David. Adios Nuevo Mexico: The Santa Fe Journal of John Watts in 1859. LC 98-61628. 1999. 24.95 (*1-881325-30-X*) Yucca Tree Pr.

***Remley, David.** History of the Bell Ranch: Cattle Ranching in the Southwest, 1824-1947. 2000. pap. 19.00 (*1-881325-42-3*) Yucca Tree Pr.

Remley, David A. Bell Ranch: Cattle Ranching in the Southwest, 1824-1947. LC 92-23474. (Illus.). 409p. 1993. reprint ed. pap. 126.80 (*0-608-07274-5*, 206750200009) Bks Demand.

Remley, Frederick M., frwd. Tomorrow's Television. (Illus.). 256p. 1982. pap. text 30.00 (*0-940690-06-3*) Soc Motion Pic & TV Engrs.

Remley, Mary L. Women in Sport: An Annotated Bibliography. 178p. 1991. 40.00 (*0-8161-8977-3*, Hall Reference) Macmillan.

Remley, Paul G. Old English Biblical Verse: Studies in Genesis, Exodus & Daniel. LC 96-176696. (Studies in Anglo-Saxon England: No. 16). 493p. (C). 1996. text 80.00 (*0-521-47454-X*) Cambridge U Pr.

Remley, Theodore P., Jr. ACA Legal Series Vol. 1: Preparing for Court Appearances. 66p. (C). 1991. pap. text 18.95 (*1-55620-077-3*, 72020) Am Coun Assn.

Remley, Theodore P., Jr., ed. see Bullis, Ronald K.

Remley, Theodore P., jt. ed. see Huey, Wayne C.

Remley, Theodore P., Jr., ed. see Mitchell, Robert W.

Remley, Theodore P., Jr., ed. see Salo, Mark M. & Shumate, Stephen G.

Remley, Theodore P., Jr., ed. see Weikel, William J. & Hughes, Paula R.

Remling, John. Brakes. 2nd ed. (Wiley Auto Ser.). (C). 1989. pap. text 49.60 (*0-13-093196-9*) P-H.

— Steering & Suspension. 2nd ed. 1989. pap. text 51.80 (*0-13-859398-1*) P-H.

Remling, John, jt. auth. see Patten, Donald W.

Remlinger-Trounstine, Connie. The Worst Christmas Ever. LC 94-14326. (Illus.). 128p. (J). (gr. 3-6). 1996. pap. 3.95 (*0-8167-3516-6*, Rainbow NJ) Troll Communs.

Remme, Camille. Birds & Bees & Butterflies Too. (Illus.). 80p. (Orig.). pap. 17.95 (*0-929950-10-0*) ME Pubns.

— Braid & Chevron Updated. (Illus.). 72p. (Orig.). pap. 17.95 (*0-929950-09-7*) ME Pubns.

— Celtic Geometric Quilts. LC 96-44789. (Illus.). 96p. 1997. spiral bd. 16.95 (*0-89145-870-0*, 4626, Am Quilters Soc) Collector Bks.

— Frogs & Flowers: Impressions of Ponds & Gardens Made into Quilts. Shimp, Mimi, ed. & illus. by. Shimp, John, illus. 96p. (Orig.). 1991. pap. 17.95 (*1-879844-03-6*) Boyd Pub.

— Modular Magic. Shimp, John, ed. & illus. by. 80p. (Orig.). 1992. pap. 18.00 (*0-929950-07-0*) ME Pubns.

— Starburst Mosaic. (Illus.). (Orig.). pap. 14.95 (*0-929950-12-7*) ME Pubns.

Remme, W. I., jt. ed. see Hjalmarson, A.

Remmel, Jeffrey B., jt. auth. see Clote, Peter.

Remmel, Jeffrey B., jt. ed. see Clote, Peter.

Remmen, J. Fundamentals of Data Bases. (Illus.). 208p. (C). 1985. text 37.50 (*0-13-336090-3*) P-H.

Remmer, Karen L. Military Rule in Latin America. 208p. 1989. 39.95 (*0-04-445479-1*) Routledge.

Remmerden, H. Van, see Van Remmerden, H.

Remmers, Hermann H. Anti-Democratic Attitudes in American Schools. LC 63-11565. 356p. reprint ed. 110.40 (*0-8357-9447-4*, 201542800001) Bks Demand.

— Introduction to Opinion & Attitude Measurement. LC 74-138127. 437p. 1972. reprint ed. lib. bdg. 75.00 (*0-8371-4166-4*, REOA, Greenwood Pr) Greenwood.

Remmert, Erhard. Jugendstilfenster in Deutschland. (GER., Illus.). 144p. (C). 1996. 67.00 (*3-8170-2028-7*, Pub. by Knstvrlag Weingrtn) Intl Bk Import.

— Jugendstilfenster in Norddeutschland. (GER., Illus.). 144p. (C). 1993. 118.00 (*3-8170-2022-8*, Pub. by Knstvrlag Weingrtn) Intl Bk Import.

— Jugendstilfenster in Ostdeutschland. (GER., Illus.). 152p. (C). 1994. 118.00 (*3-8170-2023-6*, Pub. by Knstvrlag Weingrtn) Intl Bk Import.

— Jugendstilfenster in Suddeutschland. (GER., Illus.). 144p. (C). 1992. 118.00 (*3-8170-2021-X*, Pub. by Knstvrlag Weingrtn) Intl Bk Import.

— Originale Fensterentwurfe Des Jugendstils: Art Nouveau Stained-Glass Window Designs. Hattery-Beyer, Lynn, tr. (ENG & GER., Illus.). 272p. (C). 1991. 228.00 (*3-8170-2020-1*, Pub. by Knstvrlag Weingrtn) Intl Bk Import.

Remmert, Hermann. Arctic Animal Ecology. (Illus.). 250p. 1980. 59.95 (*0-387-10169-1*) Spr-Verlag.

— Ecology: A Textbook. (Illus.). 300p. 1980. 53.95 (*0-387-10059-8*) Spr-Verlag.

Remmert, Hermann, ed. Minimum Animal Populations. LC 93-34010. 1995. 96.95 (*0-387-56684-8*) Spr-Verlag.

Remmert, Hermann, et al, eds. Ecological Heterogeneity. (Ecological Studies: Vol. 86). (Illus.). 400p. 1991. 105.95 (*0-387-97418-0*) Spr-Verlag.

— Ecology & Decline of Red Spruce in the Eastern United States. (Ecological Studies: Vol. 96). (Illus.). 417p. 1992. 120.00 (*0-387-97786-4*) Spr-Verlag.

— The Ecology of Aquatic Hyphomycetes. (Ecological Studies: Vol. 94). (Illus.). 214p. 1992. 158.95 (*0-387-54400-3*) Spr-Verlag.

— Fire in South African Mountain Fynbos: Ecosystem, Community & Species Response at Swartboskloof. (Ecological Studies: Vol. 93). (Illus.). 272p. 1992. 158.95 (*0-387-53301-X*) Spr-Verlag.

— Fire in the Tropical Biota: Ecosystem Processes & Global Challenges. (Ecological Studies: Vol. 84). (Illus.). 528p. 1990. 216.95 (*0-387-52115-1*) Spr-Verlag.

— The Mosaic-Cycle Concept of Ecosystems. (Ecological Studies: Vol. 85). (Illus.). 200p. 1991. 136.95 (*0-387-52502-5*) Spr-Verlag.

— Plantago: A Multidisciplinary Study. (Ecological Studies: Vol. 89). (Illus.). 400p. 1992. 199.95 (*0-387-53632-9*) Spr-Verlag.

— Quantitative Methods in Landscape Ecology: The Analysis & Interpretation of Landscape Heterogeneity. (Ecological Studies: Vol. 82). (Illus.). 520p. 1992. 130.95 (*0-387-97326-5*) Spr-Verlag.

— The Rivers of Florida. (Ecological Studies: Vol. 83). (Illus.). 240p. 1990. 105.00 (*0-387-97363-X*) Spr-Verlag.

Remmert, Hermann & Kranz, Jacqueline L. Epidemics of Plant Diseases: Mathematical Analysis & Modeling. 2nd rev. ed. (Ecological Studies: Vol. 13). (Illus.). 304p. 1990. 142.95 (*0-387-52116-X*) Spr-Verlag.

Remmert, Hermann, ed. see Tamm, C. O.

Remmert, Hermann, ed. see Trillmich, F. & Ono, K. A.

Remmert, Reinhold. Classical Topics in Complex Function Theory, Vol. 172. Kay, Leslie, tr. from GER. LC 97-10091. (Graduate Texts in Mathematics Ser.). 343p. 1997. 49.95 (*0-387-98221-3*) Spr-Verlag.

— Theory of Complex Functions. Burckel, Robert B., tr. from GER. (Graduate Texts in Mathematics Ser.: Vol. 122). (Illus.). xix, 453p. 1995. 64.95 (*0-387-97195-5*) Spr-Verlag.

Remmert, Reinhold & Kozlov, Valery V. Symmetries, Topology, & Resonances in Hamiltonian Mechanics. LC 95-1802. (Ergebnisse der Mathematik und ihrer Grenzgebiete: Vol. 31). (Illus.). 402p. 1995. 154.95 (*0-387-57039-X*) Spr-Verlag.

Remmert, Reinhold, et al. Non-Archimedean Analysis. (Grundlehren der Mathematischen Wissenschaften Ser.: Vol. 261). 450p. 1984. 182.95 (*0-387-12546-9*) Spr-Verlag.

Remmert, Reinhold, jt. auth. see Grauert, H.

Remmey, G. Bickley, Jr. Firing Ceramics. LC 94-21247. 220p. 1994. text 67.00 (*981-02-1678-5*); pap. text 41.00 (*981-02-1679-3*) World Scientific Pub.

R

R

*Remmey, G. Bickley, Jr. Planning & Cruising Guide to the Great Circle Cruise: Around the Eastern U. S. A. (Illus.). 1999. pap. 34.95 (0-9669987-0-7) G B Remmey.

Remmler, Karen. Waking the Dead: Correspondences Between Walter Benjamin's Concept of Remembrance & Ingeborg Bachmann's Ways of Dying. (Studies in Austrian Literature, Culture, & Thought). 174p. 1996. 26.95 (1-57241-028-0) Ariadne CA.

Remmler, Karen, jt. ed. see Gilman, Sander L.

Remmling, Gunter W. South American Sociologists, a Directory. LC HM0022.L29. (Guides & Bibliographies Ser.). 57p. reprint ed. pap. 30.00 (0-608-16480-1, 202732600055) Bks Demand.

Remmling, Gunter W. & Campbell, Robert B. Basic Sociology. (Quality Paperback Ser.: No. 229). 384p. 1976. reprint ed. pap. 7.95 (0-8226-0229-6) Littlefield.

Remnant, G. L. A Catalogue of Misericords in Great Britain. LC 98-219813. (Illus.). 244p. (C). 1998. text 125.00 (0-19-817164-1) OUP.

Remnant, Mary. Early English Bowed Instruments. (Oxford Monographs on Music). (Illus.). 206p. 1987. text 110.00 (0-19-816134-4) OUP.

Remnant, Mary, ed. Plays by Women, Vol. 5. (Methuen New Theatrescripts Ser.). 181p. (C). 1988. pap. write for info. (0-413-41570-8, A0221, Methuen Drama) Methn.

Remnant, Mary, intro. Plays by Women, Vol. 6. (Methuen New Theatrescripts Ser.). 126p. (C). 1988. pap. write for info. (0-413-14080-6, A0222, Methuen Drama) Methn.

Remnant, Peter, ed. see Leibniz, Gottfried Wilhelm.

Remnant Publications Staff. The Heavenly Music Hymnal. 1998. 14.95 (1-883012-64-3, RP-5510) Remnant Pubns.

Remnick, David. The Devil Problem. 432p. 1997. pap. 14.00 (0-679-77752-0) Vin Bks.

*Remnick, David. The Gilded Age. 2000. 25.95 (0-375-50541-5) Random.

— King of the World. (Illus.). 1999. pap. 13.00 (0-375-70229-6) Knopf.

Remnick, David. King of the World: Muhammad Ali & the Rise of an American Hero. LC 98-24539. 336p. 1998. 25.00 (0-375-50065-0) Random.

— Lenin's Tomb: The Last Days of the Soviet Empire. 1994. pap. 14.00 (0-679-75125-4) Vin Bks.

— Resurrection: The Struggle for a New Russia. LC 98-218520. 416p. 1998. pap. 15.00 (0-375-75023-1) Vin Bks.

*Remnick, David. Wonderful Town: New York City Stories from the New Yorker. LC 99-48838. 480p. 2000. 26.95 (0-375-50356-0) Random.

*Remnick, David & Choi, Susan M., eds. Life Stories: Profiles from the New Yorker. LC 99-53712. 480p. 2000. 26.95 (0-375-50355-2) Random Hse Value.

Remnyi, Dan. Measuring & Managing IT Costs & Benefits. LC 96-115805. 350p. 1995. pap. 51.95 (0-7506-2432-9) Buttrwrth-Heinemann.

Remo, John L., ed. Near-Earth Objects: The United Nations International Conference, Vol. 822. LC 97-20561. 1997. 140.00 (1-57331-040-9) NY Acad Sci.

Remocker. Action Speaks Louder. 6th ed. LC 98-40030. (C). 1998. pap. text 39.95 (0-443-05865-2) Church.

Remocker, A. Jane & Storch, Elizabeth T. Action Speaks Louder: A Handbook of Structured Group Techniques. 5th ed. (Illus.). 190p. (Orig.). 1992. pap. text 50.00 (0-443-04364-7) Church.

Remoff, Heather Trexler. February Light: A Love Letter to the Seasons During a Year of Cancer & Recovery. LC 97-16245. 176p. 1997. text 20.95 (0-312-16839-X) St Martin.

Remoissenet, M. Waves Called Solitons: Concepts & Experiments. LC 93-36462. 1994. 49.00 (0-387-57000-4) Spr-Verlag.

— Waves Called Solitons: Concepts & Experiments. 2nd ed. (Illus.). 255p. 1996. pap. 49.95 (3-540-60502-9) Spr-Verlag.

*Remoissenet, M. Waves Called Solitons: Concepts & Experiments. 3rd enl. rev. ed. LC 99-23783. (Illus.). xxii, 325p. 1999. pap. 59.95 (3-540-65919-6) Spr-Verlag.

Remoissenet, M. & Peyrard, M., eds. Nonlinear Coherent Structures in Physics & Biology: Proceedings of the 7th Interdisciplinary Workshop Held at Dijon, France, 4-6 June 1991. (Lecture Notes in Physics Ser.: Vol. 393). xii, 398p. 1991. 79.95 (0-387-54890-4) Spr-Verlag.

Remole, Mary J. Food Fun & Laughter. 1997. 15.95 (0-9620670-0-8) Mary Janes Cookbook.

Remond, G., et al. Luminescence Vol. 9: Scanning Microscopy Supplement. (Illus.). 288p. 1998. pap. 66.00 (0-931288-48-7) Scanning Microscopy.

Remond, Gabriel. Royer-Collard. Mayer, J. P., ed. LC 78-67377. (European Political Thought Ser.). (FRE.). 1980. reprint ed. lib. bdg. 17.95 (0-405-11727-2) Ayer.

Remondino, Peter C. History of Circumcision, from the Earliest Times to the Present. LC 72-9675. (Physicians' & Students' Ready Reference Ser.). reprint ed. 47.50 (0-404-57492-0) AMS Pr.

Remp, Richard, jt. auth. see Etzioni, Amitai.

Rempe, Gary L. The Los-Fat, Great-Tasting, Good-For-You Supermarket cookbook: More Than 150 Quick & Easy Recipes Using Today's Reduced-Fat Foods. 176p. 1998. pap. 14.95 (0-8092-2972-2) NTC Contemp Pub Co.

— 1001 Simple Ways to Lose Weight. LC 96-47054. 336p. 1997. pap. 14.95 (0-8092-3080-1, 308010, Contemporary Bks) NTC Contemp Pub Co.

Rempe, Jennifer & Santucci, Louis, eds. CTFA List of Japanese Cosmetic Ingredients. 3rd rev. ed. LC 96-72067. 165p. 1997. pap. 225.00 (1-882621-19-0, 8050) Cosmetic T&FA.

Rempe, Jennifer M., ed. see CTFA Staff.

Rempel, Gerhard. Hitler's Children: The Hitler Youth & the SS. LC 88-28036. (Illus.). xiv, 354p. (C). 1991. reprint ed. pap. 21.95 (0-8078-4299-0) U of NC Pr.

Rempel, Henry & Hourse, William J. The Kenyan Employment Problem. 1978. 24.95 (0-19-572453-4) OUP.

Rempel, John, ed. Minister's Manual. 242p. 1998. pap. 24.95 (0-87303-320-5); pap. 32.95 incl. disk (0-87303-327-2) Faith & Life.

Rempel, John D. The Lord's Supper in Anabaptism: A Study in the Christology of Balthasar Hubmaier, Pilgram Marpeck, & Dirk Philips. LC 93-78630. (Studies in Anabaptist & Mennonite History: Vol. 33). 272p. 1993. 29.99 (0-8361-3112-6) Herald Pr.

Rempel, John I. Building with Wood & Other Aspects of Nineteenth Century Building in Central Canada. rev. ed. LC 81-116855. 470p. reprint ed. pap. 145.70 (0-8357-7473-2, 202638700049) Bks Demand.

Rempel, Michael. Citizen Politics in Post-Industrial Cities: Interest Groups Transformed. Clark, Terry N., ed. LC 97-15839. (Urban Policy Challenges Ser.). (C). 1997. text 69.00 (0-8133-8987-9, Pub. by Westview) HarpC.

*Rempel, Richard A., ed. The Collected Papers of Bertrand Russell: Uncertain Roads to Freedom. 608p. 1999. 195.00 (0-415-09411-9) Routledge.

Rempel, Richard A., et al, eds. Prophesy & Dissent, 1914-16. (The Collected Papers of Bertrand Russell: Vol. 13). 774p. 1988. 140.00 (0-415-10463-7, A9421) Routledge.

Rempel, Roy. Counterweights: The Failure of Canada's German & European Policy, 1955-1995. LC 97-187301. (Illus.). 288p. 1996. 49.95 (0-7735-1507-0, Pub. by McG-Queens Univ Pr) CUP Services.

Rempel, Siegfried. The Care of Photographs. (Illus.). 160p. (Orig.). 1987. pap. 16.95 (0-941130-48-7) Lyons Pr.

Rempel, Siegfried & Rempel, Wolfgang. Health Hazards for Photographers. (Illus.). 224p. 1992. pap. 16.95 (1-55821-181-0) Lyons Pr.

Rempel, Wolfgang, jt. auth. see Rempel, Siegfried.

*Rempp, P. Polymer Synthesis. 1998. 54.95 (3-527-29721-9) Wiley.

Rempt, Raymond D. & Broz, Alfred L., eds. Nondestructive Evaluation of Aging Aircraft, Airports & Aerospace Hardware, Vol. 2945. 462p. 1996. 94.00 (0-8194-2349-1) SPIE.

Remsberg, Charles. The Tactical Edge: Surviving High-Risk Patrol. LC 85-73162. (Illus.). 544p. (C). 1986. text 39.95 (0-935878-05-X) Calibre Pr.

— Tactics for Criminal Patrol: Vehicle Stops, Drug Discovery & Officer Survival. LC 95-67002. (Illus.). 520p. 1995. text 39.95 (0-935878-12-2) Calibre Pr.

Remsberg, Charles, jt. auth. see Gallagher, Richard.

*Remsberg, Rich. Riders for God: The Story of a Christian Motorcycle Gang. LC 99-50473. (Illus.). 240p. 2000. 55.00 (0-252-02521-0); pap. 34.95 (0-252-06943-9) U of Ill Pr.

Remsburg, George J., jt. auth. see Remsburg, John E.

Remsburg, John E. The Christ: A Critical Review & Analysis of the Evidence of His Existence. LC 94-32833. 437p. (C). 1994. 32.95 (0-87975-924-0) Prometheus Bks.

Remsburg, John E. & Remsburg, George J. Charley Reynolds: Soldier, Hunter, Scout & Guide. Carroll, John M., ed. 1985. 17.95 (0-8488-0249-7, J M C & Co) Amereon Ltd.

Remschmidt, H., ed. Child & Adolescent Psychiatry in Europe. 350p. 1999. 56.95 (3-7985-1170-5, Pub. by D Steinkopff) Spr-Verlag.

Remschmidt, H. & Schmidt, M. H., eds. Anorexia Nervosa. LC 90-4848. (Child & Youth Psychiatry: European Perspectives Ser.: Vol. 1). (Illus.). 200p. 1990. text 64.00 (0-88937-041-9) Hogrefe & Huber Pubs.

— Developmental Psychopathology. LC 90-4957. (Child & Youth Psychiatry: European Perspectives Ser.: Vol. 2). (Illus.). 200p. 1992. text 64.00 (0-88937-051-6) Hogrefe & Huber Pubs.

*Remschmidt, Helmut, ed. Schizophrenia in Children & Adolescents. (Cambridge Child & Adolescent Psychiatry Ser.). (Illus.). 288p. 2000. pap. write for info. (0-521-79428-5) Cambridge U Pr.

Remsem, Jim. Intermarriage Handbook: A Guide for Christians & Jews. 1988. 22.95 (0-88795-976-8) Willms Wallce.

*Remsen, Glenn C., et al. Voice of the New Reformation, Vol. 2, Issue 2. unabridged ed. (Illus.). 36p. 1999. lib. bdg. 6.50 (1-929479-05-0, Grace Baptist) Remnant Bks.

Remsen, J. V., Jr. Community Ecology of Neotropical Kingfishers. LC 90-46525. (Publications in Zoology: Vol. 124). (Illus.). 128p. 1991. pap. 13.00 (0-520-09673-8, Pub. by U CA Pr) Cal Prin Full Svc.

Remsen, J. V., Jr. & Traylor, Melvin A., Jr. Annotated List of the Birds of Bolivia. LC 89-61415. (Illus.). 1989. 15.00 (0-931130-16-6) Harrell Bks.

Remsen, Jim, jt. auth. see Petsonk, Judy.

Remski, Matthew. Dying for Veronica. LC 97-156656. 224p. 1997. pap. 14.99 (1-895837-40-5) Insomniac.

— Silver. LC 99-166851. 528p. 1998. pap. text 15.99 (1-895837-23-5) Insomniac.

Remson, Al. Where Did Christmas Come From? LC 96-7821. 96p. 1996. pap. 8.00 (0-399-52247-6) Berkley Pub.

*Remson, Al, ed. A Christmas Celebration in Song & Story. LC 99-39290. 208p. 1999. pap. 12.95 (0-399-52552-1, Perigee Bks) Berkley Pub.

*Remstein, Henna. William Sherman. (Famous Figures of the Civil War Era Ser.). (Illus.). 2000. pap. 8.95 (0-7910-6143-4) Chelsea Hse.

— William Sherman. (Famous Figures of the Civil War Era Ser.). (Illus.). (J). 2000. 18.95 (0-7910-6005-5) Chelsea Hse.

Remub, Angela. Einfuhrung Quattro Pro. (GER.). (C). 1991. text. write for info. (0-201-55947-1) Addison-Wesley.

Remus, Harold. Jesus As Healer. LC 96-36260. (Understanding Jesus Today Ser.: No. 7). 159p. (C). 1997. text 39.95 (0-521-58469-8); pap. text 12.95 (0-521-58574-0) Cambridge U Pr.

— Pagan - Christian Conflict over Miracle in the Second Century. LC 83-6729. (Patristic Monograph: No. 10). xiii, 371p. 1983. pap. 11.00 (0-915646-09-9) N Amer Patristic Soc.

Remus, Martin. Menschenbildvorstellungen Im Ijob-Buch: Ein Beitrag zur Alttestamentlichen Anthropologie. (Beitrage zur Erforschung des Alten Testaments & Antiken Judentums Ser.: Bd. 21). (GER.). 132p. 1993. 28.80 (3-631-42465-5) P Lang Pubng.

*Remus, Tim. How to Build Hot Rod Chassis. (Illus.). 160p. 2000. pap. 19.95 (0-7603-0836-5, 129795AP, Pub. by MBI Pubg) Motorbooks Intl.

— How to Build the Ultimate America. 1998. pap. 19.95 (0-9641358-8-4) Wolfgang Pubns.

Remus, Tim. How to Customize Your Harley Davidson in Color. LC 97-43422. (Illus.). 160p. 1998. pap. 24.95 (0-7603-0359-2) MBI Pubg.

*Remus, Tim. Motorcycle Cruiser Performance & Customizing Guide. (Illus.). 144p. 2000. pap. 24.95 (1-929133-02-2, 130731AE, Pub. by Wolfgang Pubns) Motorbooks Intl.

— Triumph Bonneville & TR6: Motorcycle Color History. (Motorcycle Color History Ser.). (Illus.). 128p. 2000. pap. 21.95 (0-7603-0665-6, 129789AP, Pub. by MBI Pubg) Motorbooks Intl.

Remus, Tim. Triumph Twins & Triples. (Enthusiast Color Ser.). (Illus.). 96p. 1997. pap. 13.95 (0-7603-0312-6) MBI Pubg.

*Remus, Tim. The Ultimate Hot Rod Hardware Book: Nuts, Bolts, Hoses & Clamps. (Illus.). 128p. 2000. pap. 19.95 (1-929133-01-4, 129891AE) Wolfgang Pubns.

Remus, Timothy. Ultimate Sheet Metal Fabrication Book. (Illus.). 144p. 1999. pap. 19.95 (0-9641358-9-2) Wolfgang Pubns.

Remus, Timothy, jt. auth. see Overholser, Dennis.

Remus, Timothy S. America's Best Harley-Davidson Customs. LC 92-29760. 160p. 1993. pap. 5.98 (0-87938-702-5) MBI Pubg.

— Boyd Coddington's How to Build Hot Rod Bodywork. (Power Pro Ser.). (Illus.). 160p. 1993. pap. 19.95 (0-87938-798-X) MBI Pubg.

— Boyd Coddington's How to Paint Your Hot Rod. LC 94-23273. (Boyd Coddington How-to Ser.). (Illus.). 152p. 1994. pap. 19.95 (0-87938-942-7) MBI Pubg.

— Harley-Davidson: The Customs of Arlen Ness. (Illus.). 128p. 1994. pap. text 19.95 (0-9641358-0-9) Wolfgang Pubns.

— Harley-Davidson Customs. (Enthusiast Color Ser.). (Illus.). 96p. 1995. pap. 13.95 (0-87938-989-3) MBI Pubg.

— How to Build the Ultimate American V-Twin Motorcycle: Build a Bike That Is Really Your Own. (Illus.). 144p. 1995. pap. text 19.95 (0-9641358-2-5) Wolfgang Pubns.

— Ultimate U-Twin Motorcycle Chassis: Forks, Shocks, Brakes, Wheels & Tires. (Illus.). 144p. 1998. pap. 19.95 (0-9641358-7-6) Wolfgang Pubns.

Remus, Timothy S. & Chisenhall, Jack. How to Air Condition Your Car. LC 93-1775. (Illus.). 144p. 1993. 19.95 (0-87938-765-3) MBI Pubg.

Remusat, Charles F. Histoire de la Philosophie en Angleterre depuis Bacon Jusqu'a Locke, 2 vols. viii, 836p. reprint ed. write for info. (0-318-71402-7) G Olms Pubs.

Remusat, Charles F. De, see De Remusat, Charles F.

Remusat, M. M. Pilgrimage of Fa Hian. (C). 1990. reprint ed. text 31.50 (0-685-50087-X, Pub. by Mittal Pubs Dist) S Asia.

Remuzzi, Giuseppe, ed. Renal Protective Effect of ACE Inhibition & Angiotensin II Blockade. (Journal Ser.: Vol. 4, Supplement 1, 1996). (Illus.). iv, 62p. 1996. pap. 28.75 (3-8055-6442-2) S Karger.

— Renal Transplant Tolerance: Molecular Mechanisms of T Cell Regulation. (Journal: Experimental Nephrology: Vol. 1, No. 2, 1993). (Illus.). 76p. 1992. pap. 40.00 (3-8055-5699-3) S Karger.

Remy, Arthur. The Influence of India & Persia on the Poetry of Germany. 1976. lib. bdg. 59.95 (0-8490-2059-X) Gordon Pr.

Remy, Carole. Fantasy Impromptu. (Orig.). 1997. mass mkt. 6.50 (1-56333-513-1) Masquerade.

Remy, Dorothy, jt. auth. see Sacks, Karen B.

Remy, H., jt. auth. see Remy-Jardin, M.

Remy, J. L., jt. ed. see Rusinowitch, Michael.

Remy-Jardin, M. & Remy, H. Spiral CT of the Chest: Medical Radiology, Diagnostic Imaging & Radiation Oncology. (Illus.). 352p. 1996. 198.00 (3-540-59185-0) Spr-Verlag.

Remy, Jean-Pierre. La Vie d'Adrian Putney, Poete. (FRE.). 1979. pap. 10.95 (0-7859-4119-3) Fr & Eur.

Remy, M. Jules. Contributions of a Venerable Native to the Ancient History of the Hawaiian Islands. Alexander, W. D. & Brigham, William T., trs. (Illus.). 1979. pap. 2.00 (0-89646-056-8) Vistabooks.

Remy, Mark N. A New Teacher's Survival Guide: Everything They Forget to Tell You During Credentialing. LC 97-92217. (Illus.). 134p. 1997. pap. 15.95 (0-9659349-1-8, 001) Siena Pub.

Remy, Michael H., et al. Guide to the California Environmental Quality Act. 10th rev. ed. 750p. 1999. pap. 70.00 (0-923956-56-5) Solano Pr.

Remy, Michel. Surrealism in Britain. LC 98-50874. (Illus.). 1999. text 87.95 (1-85928-282-2, Pub. by Ashgate Pub) Ashgate Pub Co.

Remy, Patrick. Strip. 1998. 19.99 (3-88243-548-8) Steidl.

Remy, Patrick & Ricard-Konig, Susanne, eds. Paradise. (Illus.). 224p. 1999. pap. 19.95 (3-88243-640-9, Pub. by Steidl) Dist Art Pubs.

Remy, Patrick, jt. ed. see Lovatt-Smith, Lisa.

*Remy, Richard C. United States Government: Democracy in Action. LC 98-232596. 1999. teacher ed. write for info. (0-02-822081-1) Glencoe.

Remy, Richard C. United States Government: Democracy in Action 104th ed. LC 96-101854. 938p. 1996. write for info. (0-02-822948-7) Glencoe.

Remy, Richard C., jt. auth. see Patrick, John J.

Remy, Richard C., jt. ed. see Merryfield, Merry M.

Remy, Tristan. Clown Scenes. Sahlins, Bernard, tr. from FRE. & frwd. by. LC 96-38289. 256p. 1997. 25.00 (1-56663-144-0, Pub. by I R Dee) Natl Bk Netwk.

Ren, D. L. Topics in Integral Geometry. 256p. 1994. text 55.00 (981-02-1101-5); pap. text 32.00 (981-02-1107-4) World Scientific Pub.

Ren, F., et al, eds. Compound Semiconductor Power Transistors & State-of-the-Art Program on Compound Semiconductors (SOTAPOCS XXIX) LC 99-161350. (Proceedings Ser.: Vol. 98-12). (Illus.). 320p. 1998. 57.00 (1-56677-222-2) Electrochem Soc.

— High Speed III-V Electronics for Wireless Applications: State-of-the-Art Program on Compound Semiconductors XXV. LC 95-83757. (Proceedings Ser.: Vol. 96-15). (Illus.). 346p. 1996. 63.00 (1-56677-165-X) Electrochem Soc.

— State-of-the-Art Program on Compound Semiconductors XXIV. LC 95-83749. (Proceedings Ser.: Vol. 96-2). (Illus.). 278p. 1996. 53.00 (1-56677-152-8) Electrochem Soc.

— Wide Bandgap Semiconductors & Devices: State-of-the-Art Program on Compound Semiconductors XXIII. LC 95-61594. (Proceedings Ser.: Vol. 95-21). (Illus.). 510p. 1995. 53.00 (1-56677-116-1) Electrochem Soc.

Ren, F., et al. State-of-the-Art Program on Compound Semiconductors XXI. (Proceedings Ser.: Vol. 94-34). 312p. 1995. pap. 40.00 (1-56677-093-9) Electrochem Soc.

Ren Gan, tr. see Shipei Liu.

Ren, Hai-cang, jt. ed. see Feng, Sun-qi.

Ren, Marah, ed. see Alexander, Skye.

Ren, Marah, ed. see Ford, Norman.

Ren, Marah, ed. see Konraad, Sandor.

Ren, Marah, ed. see Steiger, Brad.

Ren, Marah, ed. see Van Pelt, Tamise.

Ren, Xin. Tradition of the Law & Law of the Tradition: Law, State & Social Control in China, 50. LC 96-20676. (Contributions in Criminology & Penology Ser.: No. 50). 200p. 1997. 59.95 (0-313-29096-2, Greenwood Pr) Greenwood.

Ren, Z. D., jt. auth. see Rao, M. M.

Renahan, Doug. Goldilocks & Little Bear's Birthday. 1988. pap. 4.15 (0-89137-072-2) Quality Pubns.

Renahan, Doug. Little Bear & His Teddy Bear. 1989. 6.95 (0-89137-060-9) Quality Pubns.

— Little Bear Visits His Grandparents. (J). 1994. 6.95 (0-89137-066-8) Quality Pubns.

Renaissance Symposium Staff. The Renaissance: A Reconsideration of the Theories & Interpretations of the Age, Proceedings of the Symposium, University of Wisconsin, 1959. Helton, Tinsley, ed. LC 80-21869. 160p. 1980. reprint ed. lib. bdg. 49.75 (0-313-22797-7, SYRE) Greenwood.

Renaissance Vinoy Staff, jt. auth. see Vinoy, Prudy T.

*Renaker, John. Dr. Strangelove & the Hideous Epoch: Deterrence in the Nuclear Age. LC 00-34153. 2000. write for info. (0-941690-99-7) Red Sea Pr.

Renal Resource Center Staff. Healthy Eating on a Renal Diet: A Cookbook for People with Kidney Disease. 183p. 1991. pap. 33.00 (0-8036-9887-9) Davis Co.

Renal Stone Research Symposium Staff. Urinary Calculi: Recent Advances in Aetiology, Stone Structure & Treatment, Proceedings of the Renal Stone Research Symposium, Madrid, Sept. 1972. Cifuentes Delatte, L. et al, eds. (Illus.). 1974. 113.25 (3-8055-1618-5) S Karger.

Renaldi, Joseph T. The Wailing Wind: A Tale of Love & Obsession. Kroitzsh, H. Donald, ed. 392p. 1999. pap. 13.95 (1-886699-17-8) Five Corners.

Renaldi, Thomas W. The Two Versions of Mariano Azuela's "Los De Abajo" A Comparative Study. 1978. lib. bdg. 250.00 (0-8490-1396-8) Gordon Pr.

Renaldo, Debbie. Astral Stalker. LC 98-83102. 365p. 1999. 25.00 (0-7388-0331-6); pap. 15.00 (0-7388-0332-4) Xlibris Corp.

Renan, Ari. Le Costume en France, 1890. (Illus.). 274p. pap. 25.00 (0-87556-185-3) Saifer.

Renan, Ary. Le Costume in France: 1890. (Illus.). 274p. 1984. reprint ed. pap. 25.00 (0-87556-689-8) Saifer.

Renan, Ernest. Averroes et l'Averroisme. xvi, 486p. 1987. reprint ed. write for info. (3-487-07816-3) G Olms Pubs.

— Caliban. Vickery, Eleanor G., tr. LC 70-169928. (Shakespeare Society of New York. Publications: No. 9a). reprint ed. 27.50 (0-404-54209-3) AMS Pr.

— Histoire et Paroles: Oeuvres Diverses. (FRE.). 1984. pap. 36.95 (0-7859-3404-9) Fr & Eur.

— Histoires des Origines du Christianisme: Marc Aurele et la Fin du Monde. (FRE.). 1984. pap. 16.95 (0-7859-3416-2) Fr & Eur.

— Lectures on the Influence of the Institutions, Thought & Culture of Rome, on Christianity & the Development of the Catholic Church. Beard, Charles Austin, tr. LC 77-27170. (Hibbert Lectures: 1880). reprint ed. 32.00 (0-404-60402-1) AMS Pr.

— The Life of Jesus. LC 91-61904. (Great Minds Ser.). 235p. (Orig.). 1991. pap. 11.95 (0-87975-704-3) Prometheus Bks.

— Oeuvres Completes, 10 tomes, Set. Psichari, Henriette, ed. 175.00 (0-685-34960-8) Fr & Eur.

— La Reforme Intellectuelle et Morale de la France. (FRE.). 1990. pap. 24.95 (0-7859-3333-6, 2870273614) Fr & Eur.

An Asterisk (*) at the beginning of an entry indicates that the title is appearing for the first time.

— Souvenirs D'Enfance et de Jeunesse. (FRE.). 1992. pap. 8.95 (*0-7859-3173-2*, 2253061751) Fr & Eur.

— Vie de Jesus. (FRE.). 1974. pap. 11.95 (*0-7859-4034-0*) Fr & Eur.

— Vie de Jesus. (Folio Ser.: No. 618). (FRE.). 1974. pap. 9.95 (*2-07-036618-9*) Schoenhof.

Renan, Sheldon. Treasure. (Illus.). 80p. (Orig.). 1984. mass mkt. 12.95 (*0-446-38160-8*, Pub. by Warner Bks) Little.

Renard, C., ed. Crop Residues in Sustainable Mixed Crop/Livestock Farming Systems. LC 97-13553. (CAB International Publications). 336p. 1997. text 95.00 (*0-85199-177-7*) OUP.

Renard, Georges. Guilds in the Middle Ages. Terry, Dorothy, tr. LC 68-55330. (Reprints of Economic Classics Ser.). xxv, 139p. 1986. reprint ed. 29.50 (*0-678-00438-2*) Kelley.

Renard, John. All the King's Falcons: Rumi on Prophets & Revelation. 220p. 1996. 57.50 (*0-614-21250-2*, 1419); pap. 18.95 (*0-614-21249-9*, 1419) Kazi Pubns.

— All the King's Falcons: Rumi on Prophets & Revelation. LC 94-2307. 216p. (C). 1994. text 21.50 (*0-7914-2221-6*) State U NY Pr.

— In the Footsteps of Muhammad: Understanding the Islamic Experience. 176p. 1996. pap. 9.95 (*0-614-21710-5*, 494) Kazi Pubns.

— In the Footsteps of Muhammad: Understanding the Islamic Experience. LC 92-11396. 184p. 1992. pap. 9.95 (*0-8091-3316-4*) Paulist Pr.

— Islam & the Heroic Image: Themes in Literature & the Visual Arts. 368p. 1999. pap. 24.95 (*0-86554-640-1*) Mercer Univ Pr.

— Responses to 101 Questions on Hinduism. LC 98-49026. 176p. 1999. pap. 8.95 (*0-8091-3845-X*) Paulist Pr.

— Responses to 101 Questions on Islam. LC 98-4301. (Responses to 101 Questions Ser.). 192p. 1998. pap. 12.95 (*0-8091-3803-4*) Paulist Pr.

***Renard, John.** Responses to 101 Questions on Buddhism. LC 99-27867. 208p. 1999. pap. 12.95 (*0-8091-3878-6*) Paulist Pr.

— Seven Doors to Islam: Spirituality & Religious Life of Muslims. (Illus.). 349p. 1998. 39.50 (*81-215-0852-5*, Pub. by M Manoharial) Coronet Bks.

Renard, John. Seven Doors to Islam: Spirituality & the Religious Life of Muslims. 317p. 1996. pap. 16.95 (*0-614-21343-6*, 1452) Kazi Pubns.

— Seven Doors to Islam: Spirituality & the Religious Life of Muslims. LC 95-45130. 317p. 1996. pap. 17.95 (*0-520-20417-4*, Pub. by U CA Pr) Cal Prin Full Svc.

— Seven Doors to Islam: Spirituality & the Religious Life of Muslims. LC 95-45130. (Illus.). 317p. (C). 1996. 48.00 (*0-520-20095-0*, Pub. by U CA Pr) Cal Prin Full Svc.

***Renard, John.** Windows on the Hosue of Islam: Muslim Sources on Spirituality & Religious Life. (Illus.). 66p. 1999. 42.50 (*81-215-0883-5*, Pub. by M Manoharial) Coronet Bks.

Renard, John. Windows on the House of Islam: Muslim Sources on Spirituality & Religious Life. LC 97-9853. 450p. 1998. 50.00 (*0-520-20976-1*, Pub. by U CA Pr); pap. 22.00 (*0-520-21086-7*, Pub. by U CA Pr) Cal Prin Full Svc.

Renard, John & Schimmel, Annemarie, trs. Ibn 'Abbad of Ronda: Letters on the Sufi Path. (Classics of Western Spirituality Ser.: No. 49). 256p. 1986. pap. 19.95 (*0-8091-2730-X*) Paulist Pr.

— IBN Abbad of Ronda, Letters on the Sufi Path. (Classics of Western Spirituality Ser.: No. 49). 256p. 1986. 12.95 (*0-8091-0365-6*) Paulist Pr.

Renard, John, tr. see Abbad, Ibn.

Renard, Jules. L' Ecornifleur. (FRE.). 1980. pap. 10.95 (*0-7859-4128-2*) Fr & Eur.

— Histoires Naturelles. unabridged ed. (FRE.). pap. 5.95 (*2-87714-216-7*, Pub. by Bookking Intl) Distribks Inc.

— Histoires Naturelles, Nos Freres Farouches, Ragotte. (FRE.). 1984. pap. 15.95 (*0-7859-4207-6*) Fr & Eur.

— Journal, 1887-1910. Guichard, Henri, ed. (FRE.). 1504p. 1960. lib. bdg. 125.00 (*0-7859-3783-8*, 2070104737) Fr & Eur.

— Journal, 1887-1910. (FRE.). 1990. pap. 48.95 (*0-7859-3031-0*) Fr & Eur.

— Journal, 1887-1910, 4 vols., Set. Guichard, Leon & Sigaux, Gilbert, eds. (Bibliotheque de la Pleiade Ser.). pap. 34.95 (*0-685-34964-0*) Fr & Eur.

— Journal, 1887-1910, 4 vols., Vol. 1: 1887-1895. Guichard, Leon & Sigaux, Gilbert, eds. (Bibliotheque de la Pleiade Ser.). pap. 18.95 (*0-7859-3185-6*, 2264006102) Fr & Eur.

— Journal, 1887-1910, 4 vols., Vol. 2: 1897-1901. Guichard, Leon & Sigaux, Gilbert, eds. (Bibliotheque de la Pleiade Ser.). pap. 16.95 (*0-7859-3186-4*, 2264006110) Fr & Eur.

— Journal, 1887-1910, 4 vols., Vol. 3: 1902-1905. Guichard, Leon & Sigaux, Gilbert, eds. (Bibliotheque de la Pleiade Ser.). pap. 16.95 (*0-685-67477-0*) Fr & Eur.

— Journal, 1887-1910, 4 vols., Vol. 4: 1906-1910. Guichard, Leon & Sigaux, Gilbert, eds. (Bibliotheque de la Pleiade Ser.). pap. 16.95 (*0-7859-3187-2*, 2264006358) Fr & Eur.

— Journal, 1902-1905, Vol. 3. (FRE.). 1984. pap. 16.95 (*0-7859-3448-0*) Fr & Eur.

— Oeuvres, Tome II. Guichard, ed. (Pleiade Ser.). (FRE.). 61.95 (*2-07-010634-9*) Schoenhof.

— Oeuvres, Vol. 1. Guichard, Leon, ed. (FRE.). 1120p. 1970. lib. bdg. 105.00 (*0-7859-3784-6*, 2070104745) Fr & Eur.

— Oeuvres, Vol. 2. Guichard, Leon, ed. (FRE.). 1971. 100.00 (*0-7859-3809-5*) Fr & Eur.

— Poil de Carotte. (FRE.). 1957. pap. 6.95 (*0-8288-6913-8*) Fr & Eur.

— Poil de Carotte. 90p. 1965. 6.95 (*0-685-61098-5*) Fr & Eur.

— Poil de Carotte. unabridged ed. (FRE.). pap. 5.95 (*2-87714-171-3*, Pub. by Bookking Intl) Distribks Inc.

Renard, Jules. Poil de Carotte: Level A. text 7.95 (*0-8219-1450-2*) EMC-Paradigm.

Renard, Jules. Poil de Carotte la Bigote. (Folio Ser.: No. 1090). (FRE.). pap. 9.95 (*2-07-037090-9*) Schoenhof.

— Poil de Carotte Suivi de la Bigote. (FRE.). 1979. pap. 11.95 (*0-7859-4114-2*) Fr & Eur.

Renard, K. G. Predicting Soil Erosion by Water: A Guide to Conservation Planning with the Revised Universal Soil Loss Equation (rusle) 404p. 1997. boxed set 47.00 (*0-16-060813-9*, Agriculture Dept) USGPO.

Renard, Kenneth G., jt. ed. see Replogle, John A.

Renard, Lisa, ed. see Rogers, Spence.

Renard, Louis. Fishes, Crayfishes, & Crabs: Louis Renard's Natural History of the Rarest Curiosities of the Seas of the Indies, Vol. 2. Pietsch, Theodore W., ed. LC 93-49411. (Foundations of Natural History Ser.). (Illus.). 480p. 1995. text 95.00 (*0-8018-4790-7*) Johns Hopkins.

***Renard, Muriel.** Medium Rare: Reminiscences of a Clairvoyant. 1998. pap. 22.95 (*1-86163-027-1*, Pub. by Capall Bann Pubng) Holmes Pub.

Renard, P., et al. Sales & Distribution Guide to Thailand. (Southeast Asian Business Guides Ser.: No. 2). 144p. 1988. text 59.00 (*0-08-035838-1*, Pub. by Pergamon Repr) Franklin.

Renard, Pierre. The Solar Revolution & the Prophet. (Testimonials Ser.). (Illus.). 193p. (Orig.). 1980. pap. 13.95 (*2-85566-135-8*, Pub. by Prosveta) Prosveta USA.

Renard, Ronald D. The Burmese Connection: Illegal Drugs & the Making of the Golden Triangle. LC 95-21261. 170p. 1996. lib. bdg. 38.00 (*1-55587-618-8*) L Rienner.

Renard, Rosamunde. Handbook for Caribbean Early Childhood Education Caregivers. 90p. 1998. pap. 12.95 (*1-85856-102-7*, Trentham Bks) Stylus Pub VA.

***Renardy, Michael.** Mathematical Analysis of Viscoelastic Flows. (CBMS-NSF Regional Conference Ser.: Vol. 73). 2000. pap. 35.00 (*0-89871-457-5*) Soc Indus-Appl Math.

Renardy, Michael & Rogers, Robert C. A First Graduate Course in Partial Differential Equations. LC 92-37449. (Texts in Applied Mathematics Ser.: Vol. 13). (Illus.). 428p. 1996. 49.95 (*0-387-97952-2*) Spr-Verlag.

Renardy, Yuriko Y., et al, eds. Advances in Multi-Fluid Flows. LC 96-69427. (Proceedings in Applied Mathematics Ser.: No. 86). xvi, 432p. 1996. pap. 79.50 (*0-89871-377-3*, PR86) Soc Indus-Appl Math.

Renardy, Yuriko Y., jt. auth. see Joseph, Daniel D.

Renart, Jean. The Romance of the Rose; Or Guillaume de Dole: The Late Medieval Resistance to the Renaissance. Terry, Patricia & Durling, Nancy V., eds. & trs. by. from FRE. LC 93-16414. (Middle Ages Ser.). 136p. (Orig.). (C). 1993. text 27.50 (*0-8122-3111-2*) U of Pa Pr.

Renata, Kathryn. Poems for Living. 39p. 1998. pap. 5.00 (*1-892019-01-9*) G D Frummox.

Renate, jt. auth. see Klein.

Renatus, Flavius V. Epitoma Rei Militaris. Stelten, Leo F., ed. & tr. by. from LAT. LC 90-40049. (American University Studies: Classical Languages & Literature: Ser. XVII, Vol. 11). (Illus.). XXX, 334p. (C). 1991. text 49.00 (*0-8204-1403-4*) P Lang Pubng.

Renatus, Flavius Vegetius, see Vegetius Renatus, Flavius.

Renau, Lynn S. Freebee the Story of a Good-for-Nothing Horse. (Illus.). 125p. (J). (gr. 4-12). 1997. pap. 7.95 (*0-9646111-2-0*) Herr Hse.

— Jockeys, Belles & Bluegrass Kings. (Illus.). 170p. (Orig.). 1996. pap. 9.95 (*0-9646111-3-9*) Herr Hse.

— Racing Around Kentucky. limited ed. (Illus.). 218p. (Orig.). 1995. pap. 16.95 (*0-9646111-0-4*) Herr Hse.

Renaud, Ary. Book of Poems, Vol. I. (Illus.). 140p. 1996. pap. 19.95 (*0-9645708-9-0*) Sea of Fanta Pubns.

— Dimensional Shift: Dream Journal, Vol. II. Date not set. write for info. (*0-9645708-8-2*) Sea of Fanta Pubns.

— The First 48: An Autobiography - Ary Renaud. (Illus.). 170p. 1996. 29.95 (*0-9645708-6-6*) Sea of Fanta Pubns.

— God Is a White Man: And Other Stupid Notions. Date not set. lib. bdg. write for info. (*0-9645708-5-8*) Sea of Fanta Pubns.

— Gods of the Firewind: First Journessy. 2000. lib. bdg. write for info. (*0-9645708-3-1*) Sea of Fanta Pubns.

— In Search of the Lost Sword: Journessy III-Color. (Illus.). 382p. 1995. lib. bdg. 49.95 (*0-9645708-4-X*) Sea of Fanta Pubns.

— In Search of the Lost Sword Vol. III, B: Journessy-B&W. (Illus.). 382p. 1995. lib. bdg. 39.95 (*0-9645708-1-5*) Sea of Fanta Pubns.

— Invasion, 2279: Journessy IV. (Illus.). 270p. 1999. lib. bdg. 29.95 (*0-9645708-2-3*) Sea of Fanta Pubns.

— Journey to the Far Side of the Earth: Journessy II, No. 2. (Illus.). 222p. 1994. lib. bdg. 22.79 (*0-9645708-0-7*) Sea of Fanta Pubns.

— Squirrel Wars: Adventures in Bird Feeding. (Illus.). 120p. 1996. pap. 14.95 (*0-9645708-7-4*) Sea of Fanta Pubns.

Renaud, Bertrand, et al, eds. Markets at Work: Dynamics of the Residential Real Estate Market in Hong Kong. LC 98-170590. (Illus.). 128p. 1997. pap. 32.50 (*962-209-438-4*, Pub. by HK Univ Pr) Coronet Bks.

Renaud, Bertrand, jt. auth. see Bertaud, Alain.

Renaud, Bertrand, jt. ed. see Mera, Koichi.

Renaud, Beth, jt. auth. see Renaud, Rick.

Renaud, Frank. The Future of the Steel Industry. 188p. 1995. 2750.00 (*1-56965-228-7*, GB-183) BCC.

— Insulation Materials Markets: Competition, Applications, Trends. LC 96-120798. 164p. 1995. 2650.00 (*1-56965-159-0*, E-057) BCC.

Renaud, Frank, contrib. by. Future of Electric Utilities: Impact of New Technologies. 222p. 1996. 2850.00 (*1-56965-161-2*, E-075) BCC.

Renaud, Georges & Kahn, Victor. Art of the Checkmate. 208p. 1953. pap. 5.95 (*0-486-20106-6*) Dover.

Renaud, Jacqueline. Train Your Brain for a Track Career. 288p. 1997. pap. text 17.95 (*0-572-02290-5*, Pub. by W Foulsham) Trans-Atl Phila.

Renaud, Jeanne. Still No Sign of Them. LC 98-84055. 96p. 1998. pap. 10.95 (*1-888996-08-0*, Red Hen Press) Valentine CA.

Renaud, Jessica, ed. see Moser, Barry.

Renaud, Michelle & Kresse, Elizabeth. Profiles of Activities to Reduce Perinatal Transmission of HIV: Assessing the Response. (Illus.). 115p. (C). 1998. pap. text 25.00 (*0-7881-7379-0*) DIANE Pub.

Renaud, Michelle L. Women at the Crossroads: A Prostitute Community's Response to AIDS in Urban Senegal. 192p. 1997. text 39.00 (*90-5699-530-8*); pap. text 14.00 (*90-5699-531-6*) Gordon & Breach.

Renaud, P., jt. ed. see Adey, R. A.

Renaud, P. S. Applied Political Economic Modeling. (Studies in Contemporary Economics). (Illus.). xii, 246p. 1989. pap. 47.00 (*0-387-51597-6*, 3424) Spr-Verlag.

Renaud, Paul E. Introduction to Client - Server Systems: A Practical Guide for Systems Professionals. 2nd ed. LC 96-1875. 596p. 1996. pap. 49.99 (*0-471-13333-7*) Wiley.

Renaud, Rick & Renaud, Beth. The Best 50 Brown Bag Lunches. (Illus.). 168p. 1999. per. 4.95 (*1-55867-234-6*) Bristol Pub Ent CA.

Renaud, S., ed. see Inserm-International Symposium Staff.

Renaudo, Andre. Peynet Collections. (ENG & FRE., Illus.). 108p. 55.00 (*0-903685-60-4*, Pub. by R Dennis) Antique Collect.

Renauer, Albin. Personal Recordkeeper: Version 5. LC 98-16995. 1998. 59.95 (*0-87337-483-5*) Nolo com.

Renauld, Christiane. Journey in a Shell. (Child's World Library). (Illus.). 32p. (J). (gr. k-5). 1992. lib. bdg. 18.50 (*0-89565-752-X*) Childs World.

— The Magic Shoes. (Child's World Library). (Illus.). 32p. (J). (gr. k-5). 1992. lib. bdg. 18.50 (*0-89565-753-8*) Childs World.

— A Pal for Martin. (Child's World Library). (Illus.). 32p. (J). (gr. k-5). 1992. lib. bdg. 18.50 (*0-89565-756-2*) Childs World.

— Tomorrow Will Be a Nice Day. (Child's World Library). (Illus.). 32p. (J). (gr. k-5). 1992. lib. bdg. 18.50 (*0-89565-763-5*) Childs World.

Renault, Francois. Cardinal Lavigerie: Churchman & Missionary 1825-1892. O'Donohue, John, tr. from FRE. LC 94-2304. 360p. (C). 1994. text 60.00 (*0-485-11453-4*, Pub. by Athlone Pr) Humanities.

Renault, Mable. Avenue of Ghosts. 120p. (Orig.). 1988. pap. text 10.00 (*0-685-28898-6*) Rivendell Hse Ltd.

— Queen Esther. 60p. (Orig.). 1988. pap. text 6.00 (*0-685-28899-4*) Rivendell Hse Ltd.

***Renault, Mary.** The Bull from the Sea. LC 00-23405. 340p. 2000. 32.95 (*0-7658-0783-1*) Transaction Pubs.

Renault, Mary. The Bull from the Sea. 352p. 1975. pap. 10.00 (*0-394-71504-7*) Vin Bks.

— Bull from the Sea. 351p. Date not set. 25.95 (*0-8488-2380-X*) Amereon Ltd.

— Charioteer. 348p. 1994. pap. 10.95 (*0-15-616768-9*) Harcourt.

— Fire from Heaven. 384p. 1977. pap. 12.00 (*0-394-72291-4*) Vin Bks.

— Kind Are Her Answers. 287p. reprint ed. lib. bdg. 23.95 (*0-89244-078-3*, Queens House) Amereon Ltd.

— The King Must Die. 1984. mass mkt. 4.95 (*0-553-26065-0*) Bantam.

— The King Must Die. LC 86-46178. 406p. 1988. pap. 12.00 (*0-394-75104-3*) Random.

— The Last of the Wine. 480p. 1975. pap. 10.00 (*0-394-71653-1*) Vin Bks.

— The Mask of Apollo. LC 86-46177. 400p. 1988. pap. 13.00 (*0-394-75105-1*) Vin Bks.

— Middle Mist. 23.95 (*0-89244-080-5*, Queens House) Amereon Ltd.

— The Nature of Alexander. LC 74-15152. 288p. 1979. pap. 11.00 (*0-394-73825-X*) Pantheon.

— North Face. 286p. 1976. reprint ed. lib. bdg. 23.95 (*0-88411-072-9*, Queens House) Amereon Ltd.

— The Persian Boy. LC 86-46179. 432p. 1988. pap. 13.00 (*0-394-75101-9*) Vin Bks.

— Promise of Love. 382p. reprint ed. lib. bdg. 26.95 (*0-89244-079-1*) Amereon Ltd.

— Return to Night. 23.95 (*0-88411-073-7*) Amereon Ltd.

***Renaut, Alain.** The Era of the Individual. (New French Thought Ser.). 290p. (C). 1999. pap. text 17.95 (*0-691-02938-5*, Pub. by Princeton U Pr) Cal Prin Full Svc.

Renaut, Alain. The Era of the Individual: A Contribution to a History of Subjectivity. DeBevoise, M. B. & Philip, Franklin, trs. from FRE. LC 96-45263. (New French Thought Ser.). 290p. 1997. text 29.95 (*0-691-00637-7*, Pub. by Princeton U Pr) Cal Prin Full Svc.

Renaut, Alain, jt. auth. see Ferry, Luc.

Renaut, Alain, ed. see Ferry, Luc.

Renaut, R. W. & Last, W. M., eds. Sedimentology & Geochemistry of Modern & Ancient Saline Lakes. LC 95-107859. (SEPM Special Publications: No. 50). (Illus.). 348p. 1994. text 97.00 (*1-56576-014-X*) SEPM.

Renaux, Sigrid. The Turn of the Screw: A Semiotic Reading. LC 92-26035. (American University Studies: American Literature: Ser. XXIV, Vol. 46). (Illus.). XII, 290p. 1994. 46.95 (*0-8204-2017-4*) P Lang Pubng.

Renay. They Drivem Pickup Trucks, They Shootem Shotguns. LC 96-183041. (Illus.). 40p. (Orig.). 1996. pap. 3.00 (*1-888431-06-7*) ASGP.

Renberg, Dalia H. The Complete Family Guide to Jewish Holidays. LC 84-11008. (Illus.). (J). (gr. 4 up). 1985. pap. 22.95 (*0-915361-09-4*) Lambda Pubs.

Renberg, Werner. Getting Organized. 2nd ed. 192p. 2000. pap. 10.95 (*0-02-863613-9*) Macmillan.

— 10 Minute Guide to Mutual Funds. LC 96-68540. (Best-Selling Ser.). 144p. 1996. pap. 10.95 (*0-02-861284-1*, Pub. by Macmillan) S&S Trade.

Renborg, B. A. International Drug Control: A Study of International Administration by & Through the League of Nations. (Studies in the Administration of International Law & Organization). 1941. reprint ed. 25.00 (*0-527-00885-0*) Periodicals Srv.

Renbourn, John. Complete Anthology of Medieval & Renaissance Music. 176p. 1995. pap. 17.95 (*0-7866-0365-8*, 95394); pap. 23.95 incl. audio (*0-7866-1312-2*, 95394P) Mel Bay.

— Complete Anthology of Medieval & Renaissance Music for Guitar. 176p. 2000. spiral bd. write for info. incl. audio compact disk (*0-7866-5476-7*, 95394BCD) Mel Bay.

— John Renbourn Fingerstyle Guitar. 120p. 2000. spiral bd. write for info. incl. audio compact disk (*0-7866-5024-9*, 98511BCD) Mel Bay.

Renbourn, John, jt. auth. see Grossman, Stefan.

Renc, Bill, jt. auth. see Bansemer, Roger.

Rench, Janice E. Family Violence: How to Recognize & Survive It. (Coping with Modern Issues Ser.). 64p. (J). (gr. 4 up). 1991. lib. bdg. 19.93 (*0-8225-0047-7*, Lerner Publctns) Lerner Pub.

Rencher, Alvin C. Linear Model in Statistics. LC 99-30176. 578p. 1999. 84.95 (*0-471-31564-8*) Wiley.

Rencher, Alvin C. Methods of Multivariate Analysis: Basic Applications, Vol. 1. (Series in Probability & Mathematics). 648p. 1995. 99.95 incl. disk (*0-471-57152-0*) Wiley.

Rencher, Alvin C. Multivariate Statistical Inference & Application, Vol. 2. LC 97-5255. (Series in Probability & Statistics). 592p. 1997. 89.95 incl. disk (*0-471-57151-2*) Wiley.

Rencher, William F. Vaginal Microbicide Formulations Workshop. 132p. text 69.00 (*0-7817-1932-1*) Lppncott W & W.

Rencis, J. J. & Brebbia, Carlos A., eds. Boundary Elements XV, 2 vols. LC 93-71026. (BEM Ser.: Vol. 15). 1356p. 1993. 459.00 (*1-56252-161-6*, 2378) Computational Mech MA.

— Boundary Elements XV Vol. 1: Fluid Flow & Computational Aspects. LC 93-71026. (BEM Ser.: Vol. 15). 706p. 1993. 242.00 (*1-56252-197-7*, 2734) Computational Mech MA.

— Boundary Elements XV Vol. 2: Stress Analysis. LC 93-71026. (BEM Ser.: Vol. 15). 650p. 1993. 224.00 (*1-56252-198-5*, 2742) Computational Mech MA.

Rencis, J. J., jt. ed. see Brebbia, C. A.

Rencis, Joseph J. & Mullens, Robert L., eds. Structural Engineering & Microcomputers. 80p. 1987. 3.00 (*0-87262-585-0*) Am Soc Civil Eng.

***Rencken, Robert H.** Brief & Extended Interventions in Sexual Abuse. 2nd ed. LC 99-57771. 240p. 2000. pap. text 33.95 (*1-55620-178-8*, 72691) Am Coun Assn.

Rencken, Robert H. Intervention Strategies for Sexual Abuse. 186p. 1989. pap. text 28.95 (*1-55620-057-9*, 72002) Am Coun Assn.

Renckens, Han. A Bible of Your Own: Growing with the Scriptures. Forest-Flier, Nancy, tr. LC 94-45525. 159p. reprint ed. pap. 49.30 (*0-608-20240-1*, 207149900012) Bks Demand.

Renckens, Hans. A Bible of Your Own: Growing with the Scriptures. Forest-Flier, Nancy, tr. from DUT. LC 94-45525. 125p. (Orig.). 1995. pap. 13.00 (*1-57075-007-6*) Orbis Bks.

Renckly, Richard G. Human Resources. LC 96-37522. (Barron's Business Library). 224p. 1997. pap. 18.95 (*0-7641-0061-0*) Barron.

Rencz, Andrew N., ed. Remote Sensing for the Earth Sciences, Vol. 3. 3rd ed. 728p. 1999. 198.00 (*0-471-29405-5*) Wiley.

Renda, Lex. Running on the Record: Civil War-Era Politics in New Hampshire. LC 96-37995. 1997. 32.50 (*0-8139-1722-0*) U Pr of Va.

Renda, Sandy, jt. auth. see Cinderella, Joe.

Rendahl, J. Stanley. Working with Older Adults. LC 84-80708. (Equipping Ser.). (Illus.). 130p. (Orig.). 1984. pap. 5.95 (*0-935797-08-4*) Harvest IL.

Rendal, Justine. The Girl Who Listened to Sinks. (J). (ps-6). 1993. pap. 14.00 (*0-671-77745-9*) S&S Bks Yung.

— A Very Personal Computer. LC 95-2252. (Joanna Cotler Bks.). 224p. (J). (gr. 4-7). 1995. 15.95 (*0-06-025404-1*) HarpC Child Bks.

Rendall, Carol W., jt. auth. see Kohl, Wilfred L.

Rendall, G. H., tr. Apology. (Loeb Classical Library: No. 250). (Illus.). 15.50 (*0-674-99276-8*) HUP.

Rendall, Gerald H. Shakespeare: Handwriting & Spelling. LC 76-169107. (Studies in Shakespeare: No. 24). 1971. reprint ed. lib. bdg. 75.00 (*0-8383-1335-3*) M S G Haskell Hse.

Rendall, Ivan. Checkered Flag: Hundred Years of Auto Racing. 1993. 34.98 (*1-55521-961-6*) Bk Sales Inc.

***Rendall, Ivan.** Power Game: The History of Formula 1 & the World Championship. 2000. 29.95 (*0-304-35399-X*) Continuum.

— Rolling Thunder: Jet Combat from World War II to the Gulf War. 400p. 2000. mass mkt. 6.50 (*0-440-23639-8*) Dell.

— Rolling Thunder: The Story of Jet Combat from World War II to the Gulf War. LC 98-55505. (Illus.). 352p. 1999. 24.50 (*0-684-85780-4*) Free Pr.

Rendall, Jane, jt. auth. see Mendus, Susan.

Rendall, Jaydine. Sacramento Family Resorce Guide. 1998. pap. text 12.95 (*0-9633777-9-5*) Im Expecting.

Rendall, Jonathan. This Bloody Mary Is The Last Thing I Own. LC 97-30884. 208p. 1999. 23.95 (*0-88001-601-9*) HarpC.

***Rendall, Jonathan.** This Bloody Mary Is The Last Thing I Own. LC 97-30884. 187p. 1999. pap. 15.00 (*0-88001-685-X*) HarpC.

Rendall, Norline. Just a Taste of Honey. (Quiet Time Books for Women). (J). pap. 4.99 (*0-8024-4494-6*, 411) Moody.

R

Rendall, Stephen, tr. see Le Goff, Jacques.

Rendall, Steve, et al. The Way Things Aren't: Rush Limbaugh's Reign of Error. LC 94-46494. 128p. 1995. 6.95 (*1-56584-260-X*, Pub. by New Press NY) Norton.

Rendall, Steven. Distinguo: Reading Montaigne Differently. 148p. 1992. text 45.00 (*0-19-815180-2*) OUP.

Rendall, Steven, ed. Honore d'Urfe, Astrea. LC 94-32421. (Medieval & Renaissance Texts & Studies: 134). 416p. 1997. reprint ed. 30.00 (*0-86698-142-X*, MR134) MRTS.

Rendall, Steven, tr. see Benabou, Marcel.

Rendall, Steven, tr. see De Crenne, Helisenne.

Rendall, Steven, tr. see Habermas, Jurgen.

Rendall, Steven, tr. see Hosle, Nora K. & Hosle, Vittorio.

Rendall, Steven, tr. see Rojtman, Betty.

Rendall, Steven, tr. see Steinert, Marlis.

Rendall, Steven, tr. see Zoller, Michael.

Rendall, Steven F., tr. see De Certeau, Michel.

Rende, Michael L. Lonergan on Conversion: The Development of a Notion. 238p. (C). 1990. lib. bdg. 41.00 (*0-8191-7525-0*) U Pr of Amer.

Rende, Victoria D. Weathering the Storm. LC 97-90250. 1998. 13.95 (*0-533-12740-8*) Vantage.

Rendeird, Elisabeth, et al. Decisions about Drug Use. 254p. 1994. ring bd. 30.00 (*1-878848-35-6*, 167) Natl Res Ctr.

Rendel, Peter. Understanding the Chakras: Discovering & Using the Energy of Your 7 Vital Force Centers. 1991. pap. 10.00 (*1-85538-009-9*, Thorsons PA) HarpCollins.

Rendell-Baker, Leslie, jt. auth. see Mushin, William W.

Rendell, Catherine. Wills, Probate & Administration. (London Guildhall-Cavendish Legal Practice Course Companion Ser.). 360p. 1994. pap. 26.00 (*1-874241-99-6*, Pub. by Cavendish Pubng) Gaunt.

Rendell, D. A., jt. auth. see Hill, Roger.

Rendell, Jane, et al. Gender Space Architecture: Interdisciplinary Introduction. LC 99-12322. (Architext Ser.). 1999. pap. 29.99 (*0-415-17253-5*, E & FN Spon) Routledge.

***Rendell, Jane, et al.** Gender Space Architecture: Interdisciplinary Introduction. 1999. text. write for info. (*0-415-17252-7*, E & FN Spon) Routledge.

Rendell, Kenneth W. Forging History: The Detection of Fake Letters & Documents. LC 94-2098. (Illus.). 184p. 1994. 24.95 (*0-8061-2636-1*) U of Okla Pr.

— History Comes to Life: Collecting Historical Letters & Documents. LC 95-1984. (Illus.). 288p. 1995. 29.95 (*0-8061-2764-3*) U of Okla Pr.

Rendell, Ruth. The Best Man to Die. 208p. 1994. mass mkt. 5.99 (*0-345-34530-4*) Ballantine Pub Grp.

— The Best Man to Die. reprint ed. lib. bdg. 20.95 (*0-89190-887-0*, Am Repr) Amereon Ltd.

— Blood Lines. 320p. 1996. 26.95 (*0-385-25550-0*) Doubleday.

— Bloodlines. 224p. 1997. mass mkt. 7.99 (*0-7704-2735-9*) Bantam.

— Bloodlines. large type ed. LC 97-715. (Large Print Book Ser.). 256p. 1997. 24.95 (*1-56895-417-4*) Wheeler Pub.

— The Bridesmaid. 272p. 1990. mass mkt. 7.99 (*0-7704-2383-3*) Bantam.

— The Bridesmaid. 272p. 1989. 22.95 (*0-385-25223-4*) Doubleday.

— The Bridesmaid. 259p. 1989. 17.95 (*0-89296-388-3*, Pub. by Mysterious Pr) Little.

— The Bridesmaid. large type ed. 462p. 1990. reprint ed. lib. bdg. 11.95 (*0-89621-948-8*) Thorndike Pr.

— The Copper Peacock & Other Stories. 192p. 1992. mass mkt. 5.99 (*0-7704-2516-X*) Bantam.

— The Crocodile Bird. 368p. 1994. mass mkt. 7.99 (*0-7704-2598-4*) Bantam.

— The Crocodile Bird. 384p. 1994. mass mkt. 6.50 (*0-440-21865-9*) Dell.

— The Crocodile Bird. large type ed. LC 93-37403. 507p. 1994. lib. bdg. 21.95 (*0-7862-0091-X*) Thorndike Pr.

— The Crocodile Bird. large type ed. LC 93-37403. 526p. 1994. pap. 15.95 (*0-7862-0092-8*) Thorndike Pr.

— Death Notes. (Chief Inspector Wexford Ser.). 224p. 1986. mass mkt. 5.99 (*0-345-34198-8*) Ballantine Pub Grp.

— A Demon in My View. lib. bdg. 19.95 (*0-8488-2015-0*) Amereon Ltd.

— A Demon in My View. LC 99-22589. 208p. 2000. pap. 11.00 (*0-375-70491-4*) Vin Bks.

— Face of Trespass. lib. bdg. 21.95 (*0-8488-0617-4*) Amereon Ltd.

— The Fallen Curtain. lib. bdg. 19.95 (*0-8488-2017-7*) Amereon Ltd.

***Rendell, Ruth.** The Fallen Curtain. 2000. pap. write for info. (*0-375-70492-2*) Vin Bks.

Rendell, Ruth. The Fever Tree & Other Stories of Suspense. lib. bdg. 19.95 (*0-8488-2109-2*) Amereon Ltd.

— From Doon with Death. (Chief Inspector Wexford Ser.). 160p. 1988. mass mkt. 5.99 (*0-345-34817-6*) Ballantine Pub Grp.

— Going Wrong. 272p. 1991. mass mkt. 6.99 (*0-7704-2435-X*) Bantam.

— Going Wrong. 1991. mass mkt. 4.99 (*0-446-40028-9*, Pub. by Warner Bks) Little.

— A Guilty Thing Surprised. 174p. Date not set. 19.95 (*0-8488-2381-8*) Amereon Ltd.

— A Guilty Thing Surprised. (Chief Inspector Wexford Ser.). 176p. 1987. mass mkt. 5.99 (*0-345-34811-7*) Ballantine Pub Grp.

***Rendell, Ruth.** Harm Done. LC 99-20432. 336p. 1999. 24.00 (*0-609-60547-X*, Crown) Crown Pub Group.

— Harm Done. 2000. pap. 12.00 (*0-375-72484-2*) Knopf.

Rendell, Ruth. Heartstones. lib. bdg. 16.95 (*0-8488-2110-6*) Amereon Ltd.

***Rendell, Ruth.** A Judgement in Stone. 1998. 21.95 (*0-89190-888-9*) Amereon Ltd.

Rendell, Ruth. A Judgement in Stone. LC 99-22573. 208p. 2000. pap. 11.00 (*0-375-70496-5*) Vin Bks.

— Judgment in Stone. 1978. pap. 4.50 (*0-09-917140-6*) Arrow Bks.

— The Keys to the Street. 1997. mass mkt. 8.99 (*0-7704-2760-X*) Bantam.

— The Keys to the Street. 384p. 1997. mass mkt. 6.50 (*0-440-22392-X*) Dell.

— The Keys to the Street. 352p. 1996. 27.95 (*0-385-25598-5*) Doubleday.

— Kissing the Gunner's Daughter. 368p. 1993. mass mkt. 6.99 (*0-7704-2515-1*) Bantam.

— Kissing the Gunner's Daughter. 384p. 1993. mass mkt. 6.99 (*0-446-40334-2*, Pub. by Warner Bks) Little.

***Rendell, Ruth.** Kissing the Gunner's Daughter. large type ed. LC 00-31645. 543p. 2000. 27.95 (*1-58547-050-3*) Ctr Point Pubg.

Rendell, Ruth. Live Flesh. 1987. mass mkt. 5.99 (*0-345-34485-5*) Ballantine Pub Grp.

— Make Death Love Me. lib. bdg. 19.95 (*0-8488-2018-5*) Amereon Ltd.

— Make Death Love Me. 1998. lib. bdg. 23.95 (*1-56723-150-0*, 159) Yestermorrow.

— Master of the Moor. 256p. 1986. mass mkt. 5.95 (*0-345-34147-3*) Ballantine Pub Grp.

— Murder Being Once Done. 1998. 21.95 (*0-89190-372-0*) Amereon Ltd.

— Murder Being Once Done. LC 98-52890. (Vintage Crime/Black Lizard Series). 201p. 1999. pap. text 11.00 (*0-375-70488-4*) Vin Bks.

***Rendell, Ruth.** Murder Being Once Done: An Inspector Wexford Mystery. 224p. 1999. pap. 11.00 (*0-679-70488-4*) Vin Bks.

Rendell, Ruth. No More Dying Then. 21.95 (*0-89190-373-9*) Amereon Ltd.

***Rendell, Ruth.** No More Dying Then. LC 98-52546. (Vintage Crime/Black Lizard Series). 203p. 1999. pap. text 11.00 (*0-375-70489-2*) Vin Bks.

— No More Dying Then: An Inspector Wexford Mystery. 224p. 1999. pap. 11.00 (*0-679-70489-2*) Vin Bks.

Rendell, Ruth. One Across, Two Down. 1999. lib. bdg. 21.95 (*1-56723-149-7*, 158) Yestermorrow.

— Put on by Cunning. 1982. pap. 3.75 (*0-09-927730-1*) Arrow Bks.

— Road Rage: A Chief Inspector Wexford Mystery. (Inspector Wexford Mysteries Ser.). 400p. 1998. mass mkt. 6.50 (*0-440-22602-3*) Dell.

— Road Rage: A Chief Inspector Wexford Mystery. LC 98-104916. (Illus.). 320p. 1997. 29.95 (*0-385-25682-5*) Doubleday.

— Road Rage: International Edition. 400p. 1998. mass mkt. 5.99 (*0-440-29558-0*) Dell.

— The Secret House of Death. reprint ed. lib. bdg. 21.95 (*0-88411-144-X*) Amereon Ltd.

***Rendell, Ruth.** Shake Hands Forever. LC 99-87711. (Crime - Black Lizard Ser.). 192p. 2000. pap. 11.00 (*0-375-70495-7*) Vin Bks.

Rendell, Ruth. A Sight for Sore Eyes. LC 98-27654. 336p. 1999. 24.00 (*0-609-60417-1*) Crown Pub Group.

— A Sight for Sore Eyes. large type ed. LC 98-51568. 352p. 1999. pap. 24.00 (*0-375-70573-2*) Random.

***Rendell, Ruth.** A Sight for Sore Eyes. 400p. 2000. reprint ed. mass mkt. 6.50 (*0-440-23544-8*) Dell.

— A Sight For Sore Eyes Signed Edition. 1999. 24.00 (*0-609-50208-5*) Crown Pub Group.

Rendell, Ruth. Simisola. 336p. 1996. mass mkt. 6.50 (*0-7704-2714-6*) Bantam.

— Simisola. 384p. 1996. mass mkt. 6.50 (*0-440-22202-8*) Dell.

— Simisola. 336p. 1995. 27.95 (*0-385-25498-9*) Doubleday.

— Sins of the Fathers. (Chief Inspector Wexford Ser.). 1986. mass mkt. 5.99 (*0-345-34253-4*) Ballantine Pub Grp.

— Sins of the Fathers. 1994. reprint ed. lib. bdg. 29.95 (*1-56849-322-3*) Buccaneer Bks.

— A Sleeping Life. lib. bdg. 19.95 (*0-8488-2019-3*) Amereon Ltd.

— A Sleeping Life. (Inspector Wexford Mystery Ser.). 1998. audio 29.95 (*0-7540-7523-0*) Chivers N Amer.

***Rendell, Ruth.** A Sleeping Life. LC 99-87718. (Crime - Black Lizard Ser.). 192p. 2000. pap. 11.00 (*0-375-70493-0*) Vin Bks.

Rendell, Ruth. Some Lie & Some Die. lib. bdg. 20.95 (*0-8488-2020-7*) Amereon Ltd.

— Some Lie & Some Die. LC 98-52888. (Vintage Crime - Black Lizard Ser.). 181p. 1999. pap. text 11.00 (*0-375-70490-6*) Vin Bks.

— Speaker of Mandarin. lib. bdg. 21.95 (*0-8488-2016-9*) Amereon Ltd.

***Rendell, Ruth.** Thornapple. 2000. pap. 3.95 (*1-86092-032-2*, Pub. by Travelman Pub) IPG Chicago.

Rendell, Ruth. To Fear a Painted Devil. 208p. 1987. mass mkt. 5.99 (*0-345-34951-2*) Ballantine Pub Grp.

— The Tree of Hands. LC 85-8148. 320p. 1986. mass mkt. 5.99 (*0-345-31200-7*) Ballantine Pub Grp.

— An Unkindness of Ravens. 352p. 1986. mass mkt. 5.99 (*0-345-32746-2*) Ballantine Pub Grp.

— Vanity Dies Hard. 20.95 (*0-89190-374-7*) Amereon Ltd.

— The Veiled One. 320p. 1989. mass mkt. 5.99 (*0-345-35994-1*) Ballantine Pub Grp.

— Wexford: An Omnibus. 1992. pap. 10.00 (*0-09-956640-0*) Random.

— Wolf to the Slaughter. 224p. 1987. mass mkt. 5.99 (*0-345-34520-7*) Ballantine Pub Grp.

Rendell, Ruth, see Vine, Barbara, pseud.

Rendell, Sharon. Living with Big Cats: The Story of Jungle Larry, Safari Jane, & David Tetzlaff. LC 94-31632. (Illus.). 222p. 1995. pap. 11.95 (*0-9642604-0-9*) Intl Zool Soc.

Rendell-Smock, Sharon, ed. Getting Hooked: Fiction's Opening Sentences 1950s-1990s. 104p. (Orig.). 1996. pap. 7.95 (*0-9654981-0-7*) S Rendell-Smock.

Rendell, Stephen, tr. see Passelecq, Georges & Suchecky, Bernard.

Render, jt. auth. see Heizer.

Render, Barry. Quantitative Analysis for Management. 7th ed. LC 99-21605. 766p. 1999. text 97.33 incl. audio compact disk (*0-13-021538-4*) P-H.

Render, Barry, et al. Cases & Readings in Management Science. 2nd ed. 350p. 1990. teacher ed. write for info. (*0-318-66342-2*, H23039) P-H.

— Microcomputer Software for Management Science & Operations Management. 2nd ed. 1989. 3.5 hd 26.67 (*0-205-11969-7*) Allyn.

— Microcomputer Software for Management Science & Operations Management. 2nd ed. 1989. pap. 24.00 (*0-685-44218-7*) P-H.

Render, Barry, jt. auth. see Heizer, Jay.

Render, Edwin R., et al, eds. Eighth Annual Labor & Employment Law Institute: Prevailing Issues in Labor & Employment Law (University of Louisville School of Law, June 20-21, 1991) LC 97-30344. viii, 290p. 1998. 72.50 (*0-8377-1049-9*, Rothman) W S Hein.

— Tenth Annual Labor & Employment Law Institute: Labor & Employment Law: Strategies for the 1990s (University of Louisville School of Law, May 20-21, 1993) LC 98-13675. viii, 304p. 1998. 72.50 (*0-8377-1076-6*, Rothman) W S Hein.

Render, Lorne E. The Mountains & the Sky. LC 75-27295. (Illus.). 224p. 1976. 35.00 (*0-295-95462-0*) U of Wash Pr.

Render, Shirley. No Place for a Lady: The Story of Canadian Women Pilots, 1928-1992. (Illus.). 389p. 1992. 39.95 (*0-9694264-2-9*) Peguis Pubs Ltd.

Render, Sylvia L., ed. The Short Fiction of Charles W. Chesnutt. LC 81-6314. 428p. (C). 1981. pap. 12.95 (*0-88258-092-2*) Howard U Pr.

Rendero, Thomasine, ed. see Albano, Charles.

Renders, Eileen. Food Additives, Nutrients, Supplements A-Z: A Shoppers Guide. LC 98-11905. 288p. 1999. pap. 14.95 (*1-57416-008-7*) Clear Light.

Rendig, Victor V., jt. ed. see Grunes, D. L.

Rendina, Claudio & Listor, Massimo. Palaces of Rome. (Art & Architecture Ser.). (Illus.). 400p. 1999. 39.95 (*3-8290-1348-5*, 520774) Konemann.

Rendina, Dave. Eastern Treasure Hunter. 1978. pap. 10.00 (*0-686-14204-7*) D Rendina.

Rendle, Alfred B. The Classification of Flowering Plants, Vol. 1: Gymnosperms & Monocotyledons. 2nd ed. 428p. reprint ed. pap. 122.00 (*0-608-12500-8*, 2024529) Bks Demand.

— The Classification of Flowering Plants, Vol. 2: Dicotyledons. 2nd ed. 660p. reprint ed. pap. 180.00 (*0-608-16149-7*, 2024529) Bks Demand.

Rendle, Ellen. The Ghosts of Market Street: Merchants of Yesteryear. (Illus.). xii, 80p. 1998. 24.95 (*1-892142-03-1*, 111) Cedar Tree Bks.

— Judy Johnson Vol. 1: Delaware's Invisible Hero. (Illus.). xi, 82p. (Orig.). 1994. 24.95 (*0-9657328-5-1*, 105) Cedar Tree Bks.

— P. S. We Love You, Vol. 1. (Illus.). xi, 75p. 1993. 24.95 (*0-9657328-4-3*, 104) Cedar Tree Bks.

Rendle, Gilbert R. Behavioral Covenants in Congregations: A Handbook for Honoring Differences. 1998. pap. 12.25 (*1-56699-209-5*, AL199) Alban Inst.

— Leading Change in the Congregation: Spiritual & Organizational Tools for Leaders. LC 97-73984. 1997. pap. 15.75 (*1-56699-187-0*) Alban Inst.

— Transforming Congregations for the Future: The Once & Future Church. 64p. 1995. pap., student ed. 11.95 (*1-56699-159-5*, AL129sg) Alban Inst.

Rendle-Short, John. Green Eye of the Storm. 285p. 1998. pap. 19.99 (*0-85151-727-7*) Banner of Truth.

— Reasonable Christianity. 1991. pap. 8.99 (*0-85234-289-6*, Pub. by Evangelical Pr) P & R Pubng.

Rendle, Steve & Coombs, Mark. Holden Barina Automotive Repair Manual. LC 97-81216. (Automotive Repair Manual Ser.). 1997. write for info. (*1-56392-307-6*) Haynes Manuals.

Rendle, Steve & Warren, Larry. Holden Camira Automotive Repair Manual. LC 97-81291. (Haynes Automotive Repair Manual Ser.). 1997. write for info. (*1-56392-308-4*) Haynes Manuals.

Rendleman, Danny. Asylum. 1977. per. 3.00 (*0-88031-040-5*) Invisible-Red Hill.

— The Middle West. 78p. (Orig.). 1995. pap. 10.00 (*1-56439-049-7*) Ridgeway.

— Victrola. 28p. (Orig.). 1994. pap. text 6.00 (*1-56439-033-0*) Ridgeway.

Rendleman, Danny L. Signals to the Blind. LC 72-19183. 50p. 1972. 2.95 (*0-87886-015-0*, Greenfld Rev Pr) Greenfld Rev Lit.

— The Winter Rooms. LC 75-315873. 65p. 1975. 3.50 (*0-87886-061-4*, Greenfld Rev Pr) Greenfld Rev Lit.

Rendleman, Doug. Enforcement of Judgements & Leins in Virginia 1999 Cumulative Supplement. 2nd ed. 75p. 1998. write for info. (*0-327-00835-0*, 6661315) LEXIS Pub.

— Enforcement of Judgments & Liens in Virginia. LC 94-76709. 590p. 1994. 75.00 (*1-55834-158-7*, 66610-11, MICHIE) LEXIS Pub.

Rendleman, Doug, jt. auth. see Fiss, Owen M.

Rendleman, Douglas. Cases & Materials on Remedies. 6th ed. LC 98-30864. (American Casebook Ser.). 900p. 1998. 57.50 (*0-314-22338-X*) West Pub.

Rendleman, Edith B. All Anybody Ever Wanted of Me Was to Work: The Memoirs of Edith Bradley Rendleman. Adams, Jane, ed. & intro. by. LC 94-37252. (Shawnee Bks.). (Illus.). 232p. (C). 1996. 39.95 (*0-8093-1931-4*) S Ill U Pr.

***Rendleman, Richard.** Option Pricing. 350p. 2000. 74.95 (*0-631-21589-1*); pap. 34.95 (*0-631-21590-5*) Blackwell Pubs.

Rendleman, Ron. A Line in the Sand. LC 97-66514. 200p. 1997. pap. 11.95 (*0-9650884-1-3*) Sterling Prodns.

— Red Sky. vi, 160p. (Orig.). 1996. pap. 9.95 (*0-9650884-0-5*) Sterling Prodns.

Rendler, Elaine. In the Midst of the Assembly. Colombari, Bari, ed. 192p. (Orig.). 1994. pap. 9.95 (*0-915531-37-2*) OR Catholic.

— This Is the Day. Colombari, Bari, ed. 255p. 1995. pap. text 11.95 (*0-915531-42-9*) OR Catholic.

Rendler, Elaine, jt. auth. see Hansen, James.

Rendoff, Patty. An Exceptional Resource Guide for the Gifted: For Home Schooling & Or Supplementing Education. 75p. 1994. 14.95 (*0-9644479-1-6*) Diggies Do It All.

— Special Needs Resource Guide: For Home Schooling & Supplementing. 100p. 1994. 20.95 (*0-9644479-0-8*) Diggies Do It All.

Rendon, A. Perez, jt. auth. see Garcia, P. L.

Rendon, Al, photos by. San Antonio. LC 94-43910. (Texas Sights & Scenes Ser.). (Illus.). 64p. 1995. pap. 7.95 (*0-87719-261-8*, 9261) Gulf Pub.

Rendon, Laura I. & Hope, Richard O. Educating a New Majority: Transforming America's Educational System for Diversity. (Higher & Adult Education Ser.). 528p. 1995. text 36.95 (*0-7879-0130-X*) Jossey-Bass.

Rendon, Marcie R. Powwow Summer: A Family Celebrates the Circle of Life. (Illus.). (J). (gr. k-3). 1996. pap. 7.95 (*1-57505-011-0*, Carolrhoda) Lerner Pub.

— Powwow Summer: A Family Celebrates the Circle of Life. LC 95-36777. (Illus.). 1996. lib. bdg. 16.95 (*0-87614-986-7*, Carolrhoda) Lerner Pub.

***Rendon, Marcie R. & Bellville, Cheryl Walsh.** Farmer's Market: Families Working Together. LC 00-9481. 2001. lib. bdg. write for info. (*1-57505-462-0*, Carolrhoda) Lerner Pub.

Rendon, Marion B. & Kranz, Rachel. Straight Talk about Money. (Straight Talk Ser.). 128p. (YA). (gr. 6-12). 1992. lib. bdg. 19.95 (*0-8160-2612-2*) Facts on File.

Rendon, Ricardo. Breve Historia de Tlaxcala (Concise History of Tlaxcala) (Breves Historias de los Estados de Mexico Ser.). (SPA.). 1996. pap. 13.99 (*968-16-4542-1*, Pub. by Fondo) Continental Bk.

Rendsberg, Gary A., jt. ed. see Gordon, Cyrus H.

Rendsburg, Gary. The Bible & the Ancient Near East. rev. ed. 384p. 1998. pap. 14.95 (*0-393-31689-0*) Norton.

Rendsburg, Gary A. Diglossia in Ancient Hebrew. (American Oriental Ser.: Vol. 72). xxi, 233p. 1990. text 26.00 (*0-940490-72-2*) Am Orient Soc.

Rendsburg, Gary A., et al. The Bible World: Essays in Honor of Cyrus H. Gordon. 1981. 49.50 (*0-87068-758-1*) Ktav.

Rendsburg, Gary A., jt. ed. see Gordon, Cyrus H.

Rendtorff, Rolf. Canon & Theology: Overtures to an Old Testament Theology. Kohl, Margaret, ed. Kohl, Margeret, tr. from GER. LC 93-22408. (Overtures to Biblical Theology Ser.).Tr. of Kanon & Theologie. 248p. 1993. pap. 23.00 (*0-8006-2665-6*, 1-2665, Fortress Pr) Augsburg Fortress.

Rendtorff, Rolf. Covenant Formula: An Exegetical & Theological Investigation. 128p. 37.95 (*0-567-08605-4*) T&T Clark Pubs.

Rendtorff, Rolf. The Old Testament: An Introduction. Bowden, John, tr. LC 85-47728. (GER.). 320p. 1991. pap. 21.00 (*0-8006-2544-7*, 1-2544, Fortress Pr) Augsburg Fortress.

— The Problem of the Process of Transmission in the Pentateuch. (Journal for the Study of the Old Testament Supplement Ser.: Vol. 89). 214p. 1990. 43.75 (*1-85075-229-X*, Pub. by Sheffield Acad) CUP Services.

Rendtorff, Rolf, et al. Canonical Criticism. 300p. 1997. 74.25 (*90-04-10467-4*) Brill Academic Pubs.

Rene, E. Hands & How to Read Them. 1996. reprint ed. spiral bd. 12.00 (*0-7873-0713-0*) Hlth Research.

Rene, Gabriel, jt. auth. see De la Lance, Mennessier.

Rene-Jacques. Mont Saint-Michel. (Panorama Bks.). (FRE.). 62p. 3.95 (*0-685-23348-0*) Fr & Eur.

Rene, Remond. Religion & Society in Modern Europe. LC 99-19777. (Making of Europe Ser.).Tr. of Religion et Societe en Europe. 240p. 1999. text 62.95 (*0-631-20817-8*); pap. text 27.95 (*0-631-20818-6*) Blackwell Pubs.

Rene, Wendy, ed. see Rochester, David, Jr.

Reneau, Don, tr. see Asendorf, Christoph.

Reneau, Don, tr. see Gebauer, Gunter & Wulf, Christopher.

Reneau, Don, tr. see Godeau, Abigail S., et al.

Reneau, Don, tr. see Riesebrodt, Martin.

Reneau, Don, tr. see Sachs, Wolfgang.

Reneau, Fred. Long Term Care. 1996. 10.74 (*0-07-011925-2*) McGraw.

Reneau, Jack & Reneau, Susan C., eds. Records of North American Big Game, 1993. 10th ed. LC 93-72098. (Illus.). 632p. 1993. 49.95 (*0-940864-20-7*) Boone & Crockett.

— Records of North American Caribou & Moose. LC 97-74095. (Illus.). 384p. 1997. 24.95 (*0-940864-29-0*) Boone & Crockett.

— Records of North American Elk & Mule Deer, (1996) 2nd ed. LC 96-84237. (Illus.). 368p. 1996. 24.95 (*0-940864-27-4*) Boone & Crockett.

— Records of North American Sheep, Goats & Pronghorn. LC 96-84238. (Illus.). 400p. 1996. 24.95 (*0-940864-28-2*); per. 18.95 (*0-940864-26-6*) Boone & Crockett.

— Records of North American Whitetail Deer, 1995. 3rd ed. LC 95-79533. (Illus.). 458p. 1995. pap. 19.95 (*0-940864-24-X*) Boone & Crockett.

Reneau, Jack, jt. ed. see Byers, C. Randall.

Reneau, Jack, jt. ed. see Nesbitt, W. H.

Reneau, Jack, ed. see Nesbitt, William H. & Wright, Philip L.

Reneau, Jack, jt. ed. see Nesbitt, William H.

Reneau, Jack, ed. see Scwarzkopf, H. Norman, et al.

*__Reneau, Mike & Clark, Brian.__ Biblical Evangelism. 70p. 1999. 5.00 (*1-888220-11-2*) Reality Living.

Reneau, Susan C. The Adventures of Moccasin Joe: The True Life Story of Sgt. George S. Howard. LC 91-73719. (Illus.). 224p. (Orig.). 1994. pap. 19.95 (*0-9611376-1-4*) Colo Big Game.

— The Adventures of Moccasin Joe: The True Life Story of Sgt. George S. Howard. limited ed. LC 91-73719. (Illus.). 224p. (Orig.). 1996. 29.95 (*0-9611376-3-0*) Colo Big Game.

— Cpsi Assessment Learner Performnce. 1996. 14.50 (*0-07-011926-0*) McGraw.

Reneau, Susan C., ed. see Gray, Prentiss N.

Reneau, Susan C., jt. ed. see Reneau, Jack.

Reneaux, J. J. Cajun Folktales. 176p. (J). (gr. 5 up). 1992. 19.95 (*0-87483-283-7*); pap. 11.95 (*0-87483-282-9*) August Hse.

— Haunted Bayou, & Other Cajun Ghost Stories. LC 94-27774. (Illus.). 176p. (J). 1994. pap. 9.95 (*0-87483-385-X*) August Hse.

— How Animals Saved the People. LC 99-52379. (J). 2000. 17.95 (*0-688-16253-3*, Wm Morrow) Morrow Avon.

— How Animals Saved the People. LC 99-52379. (J). 2001. lib. bdg. 17.89 (*0-688-16254-1*, Wm Morrow) Morrow Avon.

— Why Alligator Hates Dog: A Cajun Folktale. LC 94-46965. (Illus.). (J). (ps-2). 1995. 15.95 (*0-87483-412-0*) August Hse.

Renebome, Joyce, jt. auth. see Ristau, Debra A.

*__Renee, Antonette.__ Essence of Passion. 184p. 1999. mass mkt. 9.99 (*1-55279-009-6*) Picasso Publ.

*__Renee, Janina.__ Tarot: Your Everyday Guide. 312p. 2000. pap. 12.95 (*1-56718-565-7*) Llewellyn Pubns.

Renee, Janina. Tarot Spells. LC 89-77199. (New Age Tarot Ser.). (Illus.). 288p. (Orig.). 1990. pap. 12.95 (*0-87542-670-0*) Llewellyn Pubns.

Renee, 1929-. The Snowball Waltz. LC 98-147510. 1997. write for info. (*0-14-026885-5*) Penguin Books.

Renegar, James, et al, eds. The Mathematics of Numerical Analysis: 1995 Summer Seminar on Mathematics of Numerical Analysis, July 17-August 11, 1995, Park City, Utah, Vol. 32. LC 96-14611. (Lectures in Applied Mathemathics). 929p. 1996. pap. 125.00 (*0-8218-0530-4*, LAM/32) Am Math.

Renehan, Edward J., Jr. Great American Websites: An Online Discovery of Hidden America. LC 97-185330. 640p. 1997. pap. text 24.99 (*0-07-882304-8*) Osborne-McGraw.

— John Burroughs: An American Naturalist. LC 92-19579. (Illus.). 368p. reprint ed. pap. 114.10 (*0-608-08575-8*, 206909800002) Bks Demand.

— John Burroughs: An American Naturalist. 2nd ed. LC 98-15903. (Illus.). 372p. 1998. reprint ed. pap. 19.95 (*1-883789-16-8*) Blk Dome Pr.

— The Lion's Pride: Theodore Roosevelt & His Family in Peace & War. LC 98-23998. (Illus.). 320p. 1998. 27.50 (*0-19-512719-6*) OUP.

Renehan, Edward J. The Lion's Pride: Theodore Roosevelt & His Family in Peace & War. (Illus.). 320p. 1999. pap. 16.95 (*0-19-513424-9*) OUP.

Renehan, Edward J., Jr. Net Worth: Creating & Maximizing Wealth with the Internet. LC 97-155554. 560p. 1996. pap. 49.95 incl. cd-rom (*1-884133-28-2*, Jamsa Press) Gulf Pub.

— 1001 Programming Resources. LC 97-171645. 528p. 1996. pap. 49.95 incl. cd-rom (*1-884133-50-9*, Jamsa Press) Gulf Pub.

— 1001 Really Cool Web Sites. LC 96-142662. 548p. 1995. pap. 39.95 incl. cd-rom (*1-884133-22-3*, Jamsa Press) Gulf Pub.

— The Secret Six: The True Tale of the Men Who Conspired with John Brown. LC 96-47366. (Illus.). 318p. 1997. reprint ed. pap. 16.95 (*1-57003-181-9*) U of SC Pr.

Renehan, Robert. Greek Textual Criticism: A Reader. LC 72-82297. (Loeb Classical Monographs). 164p. reprint ed. pap. 50.90 (*0-7837-2319-9*, 205740700004) Bks Demand.

Renella, R. R. Microsurgery of the Temporo-Medical Region. (Illus.). 220p. 1989. 126.00 (*0-387-82144-9*) Spr-Verlag.

Reneman, R. S. & Bollinger, A., eds. Serotonin & Microcirculation. (Mikrozirkulation in Forschung und Klinik; Progress in Applied Microcirculation Ser.: Vol. 10). (Illus.). x, 92p. 1986. pap. 57.50 (*3-8055-4163-5*) S Karger.

Reneman, Robert S. & Hoeks, Arnold P., eds. Doppler Ultrasound in the Diagnosis of Cerebrovascular Disease. LC 81-19854. (Ultrasound in Biomedicine Ser.: No. 5). (Illus.). 312p. reprint ed. pap. 96.80 (*0-8357-6097-9*, 203423500089) Bks Demand.

Reneman, Robert S. & Strackee, Jan, eds. Data in Medicine. (Instrumentation & Techniques in Clinical Medicine Ser.: No. 1). 1979. text 162.50 (*90-247-2150-4*) Kluwer Academic.

Rener, ed. Raymundi de Rocosello. (LAT.). 1980. 32.50 (*3-519-01951-5*, T1951, Pub. by B G Teubner) U of Mich Pr.

Renert, Ian L. The Disguised Eurodollar Loan Syndication. 192p. 1993. pap. 150.00 (*0-9659948-2-1*) Hawthorne-Sterling.

— Easy Money: Profiting from Restricted Securities. 159p. 1997. pap. 150.00 (*0-9659948-1-3*) Hawthorne-Sterling.

— Standby Letters of Credit: The Private Primary Market. 4th rev. ed. LC TX3601173. 157p. 1992. pap. 150.00 (*0-9659948-0-5*) Hawthorne-Sterling.

Renes, Robert M. & Ollila, Dale G. Independent Contracting: A Primer. (Going Independent Ser.). (Illus.). 270p. 1993. pap. 24.95 (*1-883487-24-2*); ring bd. 29.95 (*1-883487-23-4*) Eagle Pr Ltd.

Renesch, John. Setting Goals. 3rd ed. 170p. 1983. pap. 15.00 (*0-932654-08-8*) Context Pubns.

Renesch, John, ed. New Traditions in Business: Spirit & Leadership in the 21st Century. LC 92-52970. (Illus.). 270p. 1992. pap. 17.95 (*1-881052-03-6*) Berrett-Koehler.

— New Traditions in Business: Spirit & Leadership in the 21st Century. 256p. 1991. 24.75 (*0-9630390-0-8*) New Leaders.

Renesch, John, et al. The New Bottom Line: Bringing Heart & Soul to Business. LC 96-69103. 350p. 1996. 33.95 (*0-9630390-9-1*) New Leaders.

— The New Bottom Line: Bringing Heart & Soul to Business. LC 96-69103. 350p. 1998. reprint ed. pap. 21.95 (*1-886710-04-X*, Pub. by New Leaders) Natl Bk Netwk.

Renesch, John, jt. ed. see Chawla, Sarita.

Renesch, John, ed. see Youngblood, Mark D.

Renesch, John E. Conscious Organization: Multiple Perspectives on Organizational Transformation, 1. 2000. pap. text 16.95 (*1-886710-06-5*) New Leaders.

— Elegant Solutions: The Power of Systems Thinking. 2000. pap. text 18.95 (*1-886710-07-4*) New Leaders.

Renesse, Robert V., jt. auth. see Birman, Kenneth P.

Renesse, Rudolf L. Van, see Van Renesse, Rudolf L., ed.

Renetzky, Alvin. Listening to Myself. LC 78-50943. 1978. pap. 3.95 (*0-930946-02-2*) Newaves Pub.

Reneville, J. D. De, see De Reneville, J. D.

*__Renew Staff.__ Arrested in the Kingdom. 1999. pap. 5.99 (*1-85240-249-0*) SOV5.

— Cuba for Christ. 1999. pap. 5.99 (*1-85240-250-4*) SOV5.

— Great Bible Women of China. 1999. pap. text. write for info. (*1-85240-252-0*) SOV5.

— Travellers on the Narrow Road. 1999. pap. 5.99 (*1-85240-251-2*) SOV5.

Renewal in Education, Inc. Associates Staff. City of Magnificent Intentions: A History of the District of Columbia. rev. ed. (Illus.). 615p. 1993. text 26.50 (*0-685-61095-0*) Intac.

Reney, Caren & Lagasse, E. Lee. The Complete E/M Documentation Compliance Manual. LC 96-94733. (Illus.). 180p. 1998. spiral bd. 122.50 (*0-9653884-1-7*) Hlthcare Quality.

Renfer, Linda H., ed. Daily Readings from Quaker Writings Ancient & Modern, Vol. II. 384p. 1995. 31.95 (*0-9620869-1-6*) Serenity Pr.

Renfer, Linda H., ed. Daily Readings from Quaker Writings Ancient & Modern. 400p. 1988. 31.95 (*0-9620869-0-8*) Serenity Pr.

— Daily Readings from Quaker Writings Ancient & Modern, 2 vols., Set. 784p. 1995. 63.90 (*0-9620869-2-4*) Serenity Pr.

Renford, Raymond K. The Non-Official British in India to 1920. (Illus.). 400p. 1987. text 34.00 (*0-19-561388-0*) OUP.

Renforth, William & Raveed, Sion. A Comparative Study of Multinational Corporation Joint International Business Ventures with Family Firm or Non-Family Firm Partners. Bruchey, Stuart, ed. LC 80-782. (Multinational Corporations Ser.). 1981. lib. bdg. 23.95 (*0-405-13395-2*) Ayer.

Renfree, Marilyn, jt. auth. see Tyndale-Biscoe, C. Hugh.

*__Renfrew.__ Atlas of Spine Imaging. 2002. text. write for info. (*0-7216-9071-8*, W B Saunders Co) Harcrt Hlth Sci Grp.

Renfrew & McCormick. Midwifery Research Database Miriad Supplement, No. 1. 60p. 1997. pap. text, suppl. ed. 42.00 (*1-898507-46-5*) Buttrwrth-Heinemann.

*__Renfrew, A. Colin, ed.__ America Past, America Present: Genes & Language in the Americas & Beyond. (Papers in the Prehistory of Languages). (Illus.). 175p. (C). 2000. pap. 54.95 (*1-902937-01-5*, Pub. by McDonald Inst) David Brown.

*__Renfrew, A. Colin & Nettle, Daniel, eds.__ Nostratic: Examining a Linguistic Macrofamily. (Papers in the Prehistory of Languages). 999p. 1999. pap. 54.00 (*1-902937-00-7*, Pub. by McDonald Inst) David Brown.

Renfrew, Alasdair, jt. auth. see Hindmarsh, John.

Renfrew, Charles. Rambling Through Life. (C). 1988. 39.00 (*0-85439-236-X*, Pub. by St Paul Pubns) St Mut.

Renfrew, Colin. Approaches to Social Archaeology. (Illus.). 440p. 1984. 44.50 (*0-674-04165-8*) HUP.

— Archaeology. 2nd ed. LC 95-70511. (C). 1996. pap. 34.95 (*0-500-27867-9*) Norton.

— Archaeology & Language: The Puzzle of Indo-European Origins. (Illus.). 368p. (C). 1990. pap. text 22.95 (*0-521-38675-6*) Cambridge U Pr.

— Before Civilization: The Radiocarbon Revolution & Prehistoric Europe. LC 73-173730. 292 p. 1973. write for info. (*0-224-00790-4*) Jonathan Cape.

— British Prehistory: A New Outline. LC 75-315089. xiv, 348 p. 1974. 6.95 (*0-7156-0670-0*) G Duckworth.

— Cycladic Spirit: Masterpieces from the Nicholas P. Goulandris Collection. (Illus.). 207p. 1991. 49.50 (*0-8109-3169-9*, Pub. by Abrams) Time Warner.

— Investigations in Orkney. LC 80-510107. (Reports of the Research Committee of the Society of Antiquaries of London). (Illus.). 328p. reprint ed. pap. 101.70 (*0-7837-6402-2*, 204611800010) Bks Demand.

*__Renfrew, Colin.__ The Salisbury Hoard. (Illus.). 176p. 1998. 29.99 (*0-7524-1404-6*, Tempus Publng) Arcadia Publng.

*__Renfrew, Colin & Bahn, Paul.__ Archaeology: Theories, Methods, & Practice. LC 99-70861. (Illus.). 624p. 2000. pap. 44.50 (*0-500-28147-5*) Thames Hudson.

*__Renfrew, Colin & Boyle, Katie, eds.__ Molecular Genetics in Early Europe: Papers in Population Prehistory. 350p. (C). 2000. 80.00 (*1-902937-08-2*, Pub. by McDonald Inst) David Brown.

Renfrew, Colin & Scarre, Chris, eds. Cognition & Material Culture: The Archaeology of Symbolic Storage. (Monographs Ser.). (Illus.). 188p. 1998. 70.00 (*0-9519420-6-9*, Pub. by McDonald Inst) David Brown.

Renfrew, Colin & Zubrow, Ezra B., eds. The Ancient Mind: Elements of Cognitive Archaeology. (New Directions in Archaeology Ser.). (Illus.). 209p. (C). 1994. pap. text 23.95 (*0-521-45620-7*) Cambridge U Pr.

Renfrew, Colin, et al. Excavations at Sitagroi No. 1: A Prehistoric Village in Northeast Greece, Vol. 1. LC 85-11928. (Monumenta Archaeologica Ser.: No. 13). (Illus.). 515p. 1986. 48.00 (*0-917956-51-6*) UCLA Arch.

Renfrew, Colin, jt. auth. see Research Seminar in Archaeology & Related Subjects Staff.

Renfrew, Colin, jt. ed. see Hardy, D. A.

Renfrew, Jane, ed. New Light on Early Farming. 1991. text 95.00 (*0-7486-0131-7*, Pub. by Edinburgh U Pr) Col U Pr.

Renfrew, John W. Aggression & Its Causes: A Biopsychosocial Approach. LC 95-31920. (Illus.). 288p. (C). 1996. text 61.95 (*0-19-508229-X*); pap. text 23.95 (*0-19-508230-3*) OUP.

Renfrew, Malcolm M. & Ashbrook, Peter C., eds. Safe Laboratories: Principle - Practices - Design - Remodeling. (Illus.). 184p. 1991. lib. bdg. 95.00 (*0-87371-200-5*, L200) Lewis Pubs.

Renfrew, Mary, et al. Bestfeeding: Getting Breastfeeding Right for You. rev. ed. LC 89-920. 240p. 2000. pap. 14.95 (*0-89087-571-5*) Celestial Arts.

*__Renfrew, Mary, et al.__ Breastfeeding. rev. ed. (Illus.). 272p. 2000. pap. 14.95 (*0-89087-955-9*) Celestial Arts.

Renfrew, Mary, jt. ed. see Marsh, Geoffrey.

Renfrew, Tom. Orienteering. LC 96-10885. (Outdoor Pursuits Ser.). (Illus.). 136p. (Orig.). 1996. pap. 14.95 (*0-87322-885-5*, PREN0885) Human Kinetics.

Renfro, Anthony C. A Guide for a Single Man in Relationship to Women. 147p. 1984. pap. 9.99 (*0-9621521-2-9*) Renfro Pub.

— A Guide for a Single Woman in Relationship to Men. 151p. (Orig.). 1988. pap. 9.99 (*0-9621521-0-2*) Renfro Pub.

Renfro, Elizabeth. The Shasta Indians of California & Their Neighbors. Brown, Keven, ed. (Illus.). 126p. 1992. pap. 8.95 (*0-87961-221-5*) Naturegraph.

Renfro, Mike. Under the X in Texas: Little Stories from the Big Country. LC 95-32155. (C). 1995. 21.95 (*0-89672-355-0*) Tex Tech Univ Pr.

Renfro, Nancy. Bags Are Big: A Paper Bag Craft Book. Cromack, Celeste, ed. (Illus.). 78p. (J). (gr. 1-6). 1983. pap. 16.95 (*0-931044-10-3*) Renfro Studios.

— Puppet Shows Made Easy! Cromack, Celeste, ed. (Puppetry in Education Ser.). (Illus.). 96p. (Orig.). (J). (gr. 2-12). 1995. spiral bd. 16.95 (*0-931044-13-8*) Renfro Studios.

— Puppetry Language & the Special Child: Discovering Alternate Languages. Cromack, Celeste, ed. (Puppetry in Education Ser.). (Illus.). 160p. (Orig.). (J). (ps-6). 1984. spiral bd. 17.95 (*0-931044-12-X*) Renfro Studios.

Renfro, Nancy & Frazier, Nancy. Imagination: At Play with Puppets & Creative Drama. Schwalb, Ann W., ed. (Puppetry in Education Ser.). (Illus.). 96p. (J). (gr. 1-6). 1987. pap. 18.95 (*0-931044-16-2*) Renfro Studios.

Renfro, Nancy & Sullivan, Debbie. Puppets U. S. A. - Texas: Exploring Folklore, Music & Crafts with Puppets. Schwalb, Ann W. & Marion, Craig A., eds. (Puppetry in Education Ser.). (Illus.). 96p. (Orig.). (J). (gr. 1-6). 1985. pap., spiral bd. 17.95 (*0-931044-11-1*) Renfro Studios.

Renfro, Nancy, jt. auth. see Hunt, Tamara.

Renfro, Nancy, jt. auth. see Sullivan, Debbie.

Renfro, Sheila T., jt. ed. see Mooney, J. M.

Renfro, William L. Issues Management in Strategic Planning. LC 93-18244. 200p. 1993. 49.95 (*0-89930-785-X*, RIC/, Quorum Bks) Greenwood.

Renfroe, Earl W. Edgewise. LC 74-671. 512p. reprint ed. pap. 158.80 (*0-608-12686-1*, 205600600043) Bks Demand.

Renfroe, Fred. Arabic-Ugaritic Lexical Studies. (Abhandlungen Zur Literatur Alt-Syrien-Palastinas Ser.: Vol. 5). xii, 198p. 1992. text 55.00 (*3-927120-09-X*, Pub. by UGARIT) Eisenbrauns.

Renfroe, Walter J., Jr., tr. see Delbruck, Hans.

*__Renfron, Kenon D.__ A Ragtime Christmas. 16p. 1998. pap. 5.50 (*0-7390-0577-4*, 18755) Alfred Pub.

— A Sacred Collectional, Bk. 1. 24p. 1994. pap. 5.95 (*0-7390-0567-7*, 11736) Alfred Pub.

Renfrow, Cindy. A Sip Through Time: A Collection of Old Brewing Recipes, in a Single Illustrated Volume, Containing Hundreds of Old Recipes for Ale, Beer, Mead, Metheglin, Cider, Perry, Brandy, Liqueurs, Distilled Waters, Hypocras, Wines, etc., Dating from 1800 B. C. to Modern Times. (Illus.). 335p. (Orig.). 1995. pap. 18.00 (*0-9628598-3-4*) C Renfrow.

— Take a Thousand Eggs or More: A Translation of Medieval Recipes from Harleian MS.279, Harleian MS.4016, & Extracts of Ashmole MS.1439, Laud MS.553, & Douce MS.55, with over 100 Recipes Adapted to Modern Cookery, 2 vols. 2nd ed. LC 98-153998. (Illus.). 670p. (Orig.). 1998. pap., spiral bd. 27.00 (*0-9628598-4-2*) C Renfrow.

Renfrow, Jan. Cryptoverse! 16p. (Orig.). 1994. pap. 4.95 (*0-9613072-8-5*) Jan Renfrow.

— For the Feeling Heart. (Illus.). 24p. (Orig.). 1989. pap. 8.95 (*0-9613072-3-4*) Jan Renfrow.

— Songs of Love. (Illus.). 32p. (Orig.). 1987. pap. 10.00 (*0-9613072-2-6*) Jan Renfrow.

— Stranger in the Wind. 28p. (Orig.). 1983. pap. 6.00 (*0-9613072-0-X*) Jan Renfrow.

— What Compassionate Men Need to Know about Women. 1991. pap. 7.00 (*0-9613072-5-0*) Jan Renfrow.

— Within & Beyond. (Illus.). 34p. (Orig.). 1993. pap. 10.00 (*0-9613072-7-7*) Jan Renfrow.

Renfrow, Kenon D. Christmas Collection, Bk. 1. 24p. 1991. pap. 5.95 (*0-7390-0881-1*, 6047) Alfred Pub.

— Christmas Collection, Bk. 2. 24p. 1992. pap. 5.95 (*0-7390-0755-6*, 6549) Alfred Pub.

— A Merry Little Christmas, Bk. 1. 16p. 1996. pap. 5.50 (*0-7390-0851-X*, 16883) Alfred Pub.

Renfrow, Kenon D., jt. auth. see Lancaster, E. L.

Renfrow, Kenon D., jt. ed. see Lancaster, E. L.

Rengachary, Setti S., et al, eds. Techniques in Spinal Fusion & Stabilization. (Illus.). 408p. 1994. 135.00 (*0-86577-523-0*) Thieme Med Pubs.

Rengachary, Setti S. & Benzel, Edward C., eds. Calvarial & Dural Reconstruction. 198p. 95.00 (*1-879284-63-4*) Am Assn Neuro.

Rengachary, Setti S. & Wilkins, Robert H., eds. Neurosurgical Operative Atlas, Vol. 4. (Illus.). 257p. 1995. ring bd. 165.00 (*1-879284-39-1*) Am Assn Neuro.

— Neurosurgical Operative Atlas, Vol. 5. (Illus.). 250p. 1996. ring bd. 165.00 (*1-879284-41-3*) Am Assn Neuro.

— Neurosurgical Operative Atlas, Vol. 6. 277p. 1997. 165.00 (*1-879284-50-2*) Am Assn Neuro.

Rengachary, Setti S. & Wilkins, Robert H., eds. Neurosurgical Operative Atlas, Vol. 7. 267p. 165.00 (*1-879284-56-1*) Am Assn Neuro.

— Neurosurgical Operative Atlas, Vol. 8. 276p. 165.00 (*1-879284-67-7*) Am Assn Neuro.

Rengachary, Setti S. & Wilkins, Robert H., eds. Principles of Neurosurgery. LC 93-10153. (gr. 13). 1994. 210.00 (*1-56375-022-8*) Mosby Inc.

Rengachary, Setti S., jt. ed. see Doty, James R.

Rengachary, Setti S., jt. ed. see Wilkins, Robert H.

*__Rengarajan, T.__ Glossary of Hinduism. 628p. 1999. mass mkt. 17.95 (*81-204-1348-2*, Pub. by Oxford & IBH Pubng) Enfield Pubs NH.

Rengel, Marian. Encyclopedia of Birth Control. (Illus.). 312p. 2000. boxed set 55.00 (*1-57356-255-6*) Oryx Pr.

Rengel, Zdenko, ed. Mineral Nutrition of Crops: Fundamental Mechanisms & Implications. LC 98-48697. (Illus.). 399p. (C). 1999. lib. bdg. 149.95 (*1-56022-880-6*, Food Products) Haworth Pr.

*__Rengel, Zdenko, ed.__ Nutrient Use in Crop Production. LC 98-39020. 267p. 1998. 79.95 (*1-56022-061-9*, Food Products) Haworth Pr.

— Nutrient Use in Crop Production. 267p. 2000. pap. 39.95 (*1-56022-076-7*, Food Products) Haworth Pr.

Rengen, Wilfried Van, see Van Rengen, Wilfried.

Renger-Patzsch, Albert. Albert Renger-Patzsch: The Late Work. 1996. pap. text 55.00 (*3-89322-879-9*, Pub. by Edition Cantz) Dist Art Pubs.

— World of Plants. 1998. 50.00 (*3-89322-946-9*, Pub. by Edition Cantz) Dist Art Pubs.

Rengers, Christopher. Mary of the Americas: Our Lady of Guadalupe. LC 88-8155. 154p. (Orig.). 1988. pap. 8.95 (*0-8189-0543-3*) Alba.

— The Youngest Prophet: The Life of Jacinta Marto, Fatima Visionary. LC 85-30789. 144p. (Orig.). 1986. pap. 5.95 (*0-8189-0496-8*) Alba.

Rengers, Niek, ed. Engineering Geology of Quaternary Sediments: Proceedings of the Twenty-Year Jubilee Symposium of the INGEOKRING, Delft, Netherlands, June 1994. (Illus.). 146p. (C). 1994. text 65.00 (*90-5410-398-1*, Pub. by A A Balkema) Ashgate Pub Co.

Rengert, George. Geography of Illegal Drugs. 160p. (C). 1998. pap. text 22.00 (*0-8133-6650-X*, Pub. by Westview) HarpC.

*__Rengert, George F. & Wasilchick, John V.__ A Suburban Burglary: A Tale of Two Suburbs. 2nd ed. LC 00-37713. 2000. pap. write for info. (*0-398-07085-7*) C C Thomas.

Rengert, George F. & Wasilchick, John V. Suburban Burglary: A Time & a Place for Everything. (Illus.). 136p. 1985. pap. text 20.95 (*0-398-06648-5*) C C Thomas.

— Suburban Burglary: A Time & a Place for Everything. (Illus.). 136p. (C). 1985. text 31.95 (*0-398-05142-9*) C C Thomas.

Rengger, A. Bericht Uber die Armen-Erziehungsanstalt: 1815/1820 Editions. Stern, Jeffrey, ed. & intro. by. (Classics in Education Ser.). 322p. 1996. reprint ed. 95.00 (*1-85506-308-5*) Bks Intl VA.

Rengger, N. J. International Relations Political Theory & Problem of Order: Beyond International Relations Theory? LC 99-32333. (New International Relations Ser.). 288p. 1999. pap. 29.99 (*0-415-09584-0*) Routledge.

*__Rengger, N. J.__ International Relations Political Theory & Problem of Order: Beyond International Relations Theory? LC 99-32333. 288p. (C). 1999. text. write for info. (*0-415-09583-2*) Routledge.

Rengger, N. J. Political Theory, Modernity & Postmodernity. 200p. (C). 1995. pap. 24.95 (*0-631-19159-3*) Blackwell Pubs.

— Political Theory, Modernity & Postmodernity. 200p. (C). 1995. 61.95 (*0-631-19158-5*) Blackwell Pubs.

Rengger, N. J., jt. ed. see Baylis, John.

Rengger, Nicholas. Treaties & Alliances of the World. 5th ed. 1991. 120.00 (*0-582-05733-7*) Longman.

Rengger, Nick. Retreat from the Modern. 128p. 1995. pap. 14.95 (*0-906097-29-0*) LPC InBook.

Renggli, Bernard J. & Blankenship, G. Wesley. The Development of a CNC Spur Gear Generating System. (Nineteen Eighty-Eight Fall Technical Meeting Ser.: Vol. 88FTMS2). (Illus.). 19p. 1988. pap. text 30.00 (*1-55589-522-0*) AGMA.

Rengier, John & Blankman, Howard. By Hex. 1956. pap. 5.25 (*0-8222-0170-4*) Dramatists Play.

*__Rengifo, Carolina.__ Actividades Biblicas para Ninos, Tomo 1. (SPA., Illus.). 48p. 2000. pap. 5.00 (*0-311-46200-6*, Edit Mundo) Casa Bautista.

Rengo, F., jt. ed. see Vigorito, C.

R

An Asterisk (*) at the beginning of an entry indicates that the title is appearing for the first time.

R

Rengstorf, Karl, et al, eds. Die Mischna: Text, Ubersetzung und Ausfuhrliche Erklarung mit Eingehenden Gesschichtlichten und Sprachelichen Einleitungen und Textkritischen Anhangen. (GER.). x, 188p. (Orig.). (C). 1991. pap. text 104.65 (3-11-012464-5, 147-91) De Gruyter.

Reniak, Anthony L. We the People: To Save America. LC 97-224109. 32p. 1997. pap. 7.00 (0-8059-4066-9) Dorrance.

Renich, Fred C. When the Chisel Hits the Rock: The Sculpting of a Leader. 2nd ed. 132p. 1998. reprint ed. pap. write for info. (0-942381-13-0) Sammamish Pr.

Renich, Jill. So You're a Teenage Girl. (Orig.). (J). (gr. 8 up). 1966. pap. 3.95 (0-310-31802-5, 10706S) Zondervan.

Renich, T. Elizabeth. Matter of Trust. (Shadowcreek Chronicles Ser.: Bk. 2). 1995. pap. 8.99 (1-883002-14-1) Emerald WA.

— Not Without Courage. (Shadowcreek Chronicles Ser.: Bk. 3). 340p. 1996. pap. 8.99 (1-883002-32-X) Emerald WA.

— Word of Honor. LC 95-41622. (Shadowcreek Chronicles Ser.: Bk. 1). 300p. 1994. pap. 8.99 (1-883002-10-9) Emerald WA.

Renick, Barbara. Internet for Genealogists. 4th ed. 1998. pap. 16.99 (0-938717-41-3) Shumway Family Hist.

— The Internet for Genealogists: A Beginner's Guide. LC 98-169174. 197p. 1997. write for info. (0-938717-32-4) Shumway Family Hist.

Renick, Butera, jt. auth. see Caluori.

Renick, Clay, jt. auth. see Kruppenbach, Jack.

Renick, Robert M. From Red Hot to Monkey's Eyebrow: Unusual Kentucky Place Names. LC 97-30247. (Illus.). 96p. 1997. pap. 11.50 (0-8131-0931-0) U Pr of Ky.

Renick, Saundra. Affirmative but No Action: The First Minority Law Books, Vol. 1. large type ed. Kaye, Saundra, ed. ix, 250p. 1996. text 90.00 (0-9654618-1-5) ABNA Publns.

— Affirmative but No Action: The First Minority Law Books, Vol. 2. large type ed. Kaye, Saundra, ed. ix, 250p. 1996. text 90.00 (0-9654618-2-3) ABNA Publns.

Renie, William A. Goldberg's Genetic & Metabolic Eye Disease. 2nd ed. 608p. 1986. 142.00 (0-316-74016-0, Little Brwn Med Div) Lppncott W & W.

Renier, Fernand G. Beginner's Dutch. (Hippocrene Beginner's Language Ser.). (DUT & ENG.). 200p. 1999. pap. 14.95 (0-7818-0735-2) Hippocrene Bks.

— Colloquial Dutch. 1986. pap. 13.95 (0-7100-0785-X, Routledge Thoemms) Routledge.

— Dutch-English-English-Dutch Dictionary. 590p. 1982. pap. 21.99 (0-415-04610-6) Routledge.

— Dutch-English-English-Dutch Dictionary. (DUT & ENG.). 40.95 (0-87557-014-3) Saphrograph.

Renier, Fernand G., ed. Dutch-English & English-Dutch Dictionary. (DUT & ENG.). 1949. pap. 13.95 (0-7100-9352-7, Routledge Thoemms) Routledge.

Renier, Fernand G., tr. see Ciliga, Ante.

Renier, G. J., tr. see Blok, Petrus J.

Renieri, A., jt. auth. see Dattoli, G.

Reniewicz, Frank. For God, Country & Polonia: One Hundred Years of the Orchard Lake Schools. LC 85-72080. (Illus.). 177p. 1985. 9.95 (0-9615564-0-4) Ctr Polish.

Renik. Interpretation & Its Consequences. (Psychoanalytic Inquiry Ser.: Vol. 12, No. 2). 1992. 20.00 (0-88163-947-8) Analytic Pr.

Renik, Owen, ed. Knowledge & Authority in the Psychoanalytic Relationship. LC 97-29287. 280p. 1998. pap. 40.00 (0-7657-0139-1) Aronson.

Reniker, S., jt. ed. see Maruyama, M.

Reniker, Sherry, ed. World's Edge: An Anthology. 1991. pap. 12.00 (0-87924-077-6) Membrane Pr.

Reninger, T. Douceur. Mrazovich, Christine, ed. (Illus.). 36p. 1999. 5.99 (0-9665521-4-8) Dead End St.

Renino, Christopher. Way Home Is Longer. LC 96-40464. 1997. text 23.95 (0-312-15686-3) St Martin.

Renino, Marjorie C., compiled by. The Guide to Genealogical Research for Westchester County. rev. ed. LC 88-151242. (Illus.). xviii, 228p. (Orig.). 1987. reprint ed. per. 35.00 (0-9615866-0-5) M Renino.

Renique, Gerardo, jt. auth. see Poole, Deborah.

Renirkens, Clement. Love with Your Eyes Open. Lucas, Marc & Lucas, Claudia, trs. from FRE. LC 85-28669. 145p. (Orig.). 1986. pap. 7.95 (0-8189-0491-7) Alba.

Renish, Peggy. Home Educator's Guide for Washington State. LC 86-90511. 136p. 1986. pap. 5.50 (0-9617607-0-2) R & R Publish.

Renjifo, Juan M. Ranas y Sapos de Colombia. deluxe ed. (SPA., Illus.). 1998. 100.00 (958-638-214-1) Editorial Colina.

Renjilian-Burgy, Joy. Justina: Homenaje a Justina Ruiz de Conde en Su Ochenta Cumpleanos. Gascon-Vera, Elena, ed. (Homenajes De ALDEEU Ser.). (ENG & SPA., Illus.). 224p. (C). 1992. pap. 25.00 (0-9626630-1-8) Spanish Profs Amer.

Renjun, Zou. Fundamentals of Pyrolysis in Petrochemical Technology. 1993. 116.00 (0-8493-7760-9) CRC Pr.

Renk, jt. auth. see Atlas, Ronald M.

Renk, Kathleen. Caribbean Shadows & Victorian Ghosts: Women's Writing & Decolonization. LC 98-35057. 208p. 1999. pap. text 16.50 (0-8139-1836-7) U Pr of Va.

Renk, Ernst. Spiegelungen. (GER.). 291p. 1985. text 29.50 (0-930329-40-6) Kabel Pubs.

Renk, Kathleen J. Caribbean Shadows & Victorian Ghosts: Women's Writing & Decolonization. LC 98-35057. 208p. 1999. text 49.50 (0-8139-1835-9) U Pr of Va.

Renke, Adria. Easy Home Tutoring: A Parent's Guide. O'Brien, Greg, ed. 84p. (Orig.). 1995. pap. text 7.95 (1-887086-00-5) Stony Brook Pr.

Renke, Kurt, ed. Enzyklopadie des Marchens: Handwortenbuch zur Historischen und Vergleichenden Erzahlforschung. 1422p. 1996. 104.00 (3-11-014338-0) De Gruyter.

Renkema, Barb. Fabric Foto Framers: Picture & Greeting Card Mats in Counted Cross-Stitch. 20p. 1986. 5.98 (0-88290-314-4) Horizon Utah.

Renkema, Guillermo. Credos y Confesiones I-bL-Alumno. (SPA.). 1989. pap. 1.75 (1-55955-014-7) CRC Wrld Lit.

— Credos y Confesiones I-C-Alumno. (SPA.). 1992. pap. 1.75 (1-55955-142-9) CRC Wrld Lit.

— Credos y Confesiones I-C-Maestro. (SPA.). 1992. pap. 1.50 (1-55955-143-7) CRC Wrld Lit.

— Credos y Confesiones I-Db-Alumno. (SPA.). 1989. pap. 1.75 (1-55955-012-0) CRC Wrld Lit.

— Credos y Confesiones I-Db-Maestro. (SPA.). 1989. pap. 1.50 (1-55955-013-9) CRC Wrld Lit.

— Credos y Confesiones II: C-Alumno. (SPA.). 1993. pap. 1.75 (1-55955-165-8) CRC Wrld Lit.

— Credos y Confesiones II: C-Maestro. (SPA.). 1993. pap. 2.00 (1-55955-166-6) CRC Wrld Lit.

— Credos y Confesiones II-bL-Alumno. (SPA.). 1993. pap. 1.75 (1-55955-158-5) CRC Wrld Lit.

— Credos y Confesiones II-bL-Maestro. (SPA.). 1993. pap. 2.00 (1-55955-159-3) CRC Wrld Lit.

— Credos y Confesiones II-Db-Alumno. (SPA.). 1993. pap. 1.75 (1-55955-156-9) CRC Wrld Lit.

— Credos y Confesiones II-Db-Maestro. (SPA.). 1993. pap. 2.00 (1-55955-157-7) CRC Wrld Lit.

— Credos y Confesiones I-bL-Maestro. (SPA.). 1989. pap. 1.50 (1-55955-015-5) CRC Wrld Lit.

Renkema, Jan. Discourse Studies: An Introductory Textbook. LC 93-1453. x, 224p. 1993. 53.00 (1-55619-492-7); pap. 22.95 (1-55619-493-5) J Benjamins Pubng Co.

***Renkema, Theo J. W.** Managing the IT Value Quest: How to Capture the Business Value of IT-Based Infrastructure. LC 99-50119. (Series in Information Systems). (Illus.). 278p. 2000. 55.00 (0-471-98817-0) Wiley.

Renken, Anthony L., jt. auth. see Karony, Stephenie.

***Renken, Laura.** My Lord Pirate. (Seduction Romance Ser.). 2000. mass mkt. 5.99 (0-515-12984-4, Jove) Berkley Pub.

Renken, Maxine. Bibliography of Henry Miller. LC 72-4735. (American Literature Ser.: No. 49). 1972. reprint ed. lib. bdg. 75.00 (0-8383-1592-5) M S G Haskell Hse.

Renkens, Jack H. Recruiting Realities Vol. I: Educating High School Counselors, Coaches, Parents & Student-Athletes in the Recruiting Process. 3rd rev. ed. (Illus.). 110p. (Orig.). (YA). (gr. 9-12). 1998. pap., mass mkt. 19.95 (0-9647041-9-6) Brookes & John.

Renker, Elizabeth. Strike Through the Mask: Herman Melville & the Scene of Writing. LC 95-31870. (Illus.). 200p. (C). 1996. text 35.00 (0-8018-5230-7) Johns Hopkins.

— Strike Through the Mask: Herman Melville & the Scene of Writing. LC 95-31870. (Illus.). 216p. 1998. reprint ed. pap. text 15.95 (0-8018-5875-5) Johns Hopkins.

Renker, Skip. Sifting the Visible. 36p. 1998. pap. 6.50 (0-932412-13-0) Mayapple Pr.

Renkes, Ashley. Stories, Poems & Other Things. LC 97-75371. (Illus.). 32p. (Orig.). (J). (gr. k-7). 1999. 14.95 (1-882792-40-8) Proctor Pubns.

Renkes, Jim. The Quad-Cities & the People. LC 94-24648. (Illus.). 112p. (Orig.). 1994. pap. 9.95 (1-56037-067-X) Am Wrld Geog.

Renkes, Robert N., ed. see Upton, Howard.

Renkewitz, Heinz. Hochmann von Hochenau, 1670-1721. Willoughby, William G., tr. (Monographs: No. 4). 148p. (C). 1993. 30.00 (0-936693-24-X) Brethren Encyclopedia.

Renkiewicz, Frank & Bjorkquist Ng, Anne, compiled by. Guide to Polish-American Newspapers & Periodicals in Microform. 60p. 1988. pap. 5.00 (0-932833-06-3, G-4) Immig His Res.

Renkikoff, Charles. Selected Letters of Charles Reznikoff 1917-1976. Hindus, Milton, ed. LC 97-25367. 350p. 1997. 27.50 (1-57423-035-2); pap. 17.50 (1-57423-034-4) Black Sparrow.

— Selected Letters of Charles Reznikoff 1917-1976. deluxe ed. Hindus, Milton, ed. LC 97-25367. 350p. 1997. 35.00 (1-57423-036-0) Black Sparrow.

Renkin, Eugene M. & Michel, C. Charles, eds. Handbook of Physiology: Section 2, The Cardiovascular System, Vol. IV, Pts. 1 & 2: Microcirculation. (American Physiological Society Book). (Illus.). 1124p. 1988. text 275.00 (0-19-520666-5) OUP.

Renkl, Margaret. The Marigold Poems. 28p. (Orig.). 1992. pap. 5.00 (1-877801-25-9) Still Waters.

Renn, Derek, ed. Life, Death, & Money: Actuaries & the Development of Social & Financial Markets. LC 97-38759. 339p. 1998. 78.95 (0-631-20906-9) Blackwell Pubs.

Renn, Dorothy L. Emotional Abuse of the Child. LC 87-92179. 1988. 16.95 (0-87212-216-6) Libra.

Renn, Jurgen, et al. Einstein in Context. (Science in Context Ser.: Vol. 6). (Illus.). 360p. (C). 1993. pap. text 39.95 (0-521-44834-4) Cambridge U Pr.

Renn, Leslie, jt. auth. see Lewis, Jerre G.

Renn, Leslie D. & Lewis, Jerre G. How to Start & Manage a Bicycle Shop Business: Step by Step Guide to Business Success. (Illus.). 125p. 1999. pap. 18.95 (1-57916-004-2) Lewis Renn.

Renn, Leslie D., jt. auth. see Lewis, Jerre G.

Renn, Ludwig. Warfare: The Relation of War to Society. Fitzgerald, Edward, tr. LC 79-160989. (Select Bibliographies Reprint Ser.). 1977. reprint ed. 23.95 (0-8369-5857-8) Ayer.

Renn, Ortwin, et al, eds. Fairness & Competence in Citizen Participation: Evaluating Models for Environmental Discourse. (Technology, Risk & Society Ser.). 400p. (C). 1995. pap. text 59.00 (0-7923-3518-X, Pub. by Kluwer Academic) Kluwer Academic.

— Fairness & Competence in Citizen Participation: Evaluating Models for Environmental Discourse. LC 95-12720. (Technology, Risk & Society Ser.: Vol. 10). 400p. (C). 1995. lib. bdg. 99.50 (0-7923-3517-1, Pub. by Kluwer Academic) Kluwer Academic.

***Renn, Ortwin & Rohrmann, Bernd.** Cross-Cultural Risk Perception: A Survey of Empirical Studies. LC 99-89699. (Technology, Risk & Society Ser.). 2000. write for info. (0-7923-7747-8) Kluwer Academic.

Renn, Ortwin, jt. ed. see Pinkau, Klaus.

Renn, Walter, et al. The Treatment of the Holocaust in Textbooks: The Federal Republic of Germany, Israel, the United States. (Holocaust Studies). 333p. 1987. text 58.50 (0-88033-955-1, Pub. by East Eur Monographs) Col U Pr.

Renna, Giani, jt. auth. see Shore, Donna.

***Rennack, Diane E.** Legislation on Foreign Relations Through 1998, March 1999, Current Legislation & Related Executive Orders. 881p. 1999. per. 41.00 (0-16-058495-7) USGPO.

***Rennack, Dianne E.** Legislation on Foreign Relations Through 1997, March 1998, Current Legislation & Related Executive Orders. 820p. 1998. per. 37.00 (0-16-056344-5) USGPO.

— Legislation on Foreign Relations Through 1999: Current Legislation & Related Executive Orders, March 2000, Vol. 1a. 937p. 2000. per. 47.00 (0-16-060502-4) USGPO.

***Renne.** Animals up Close, 6 bks. Incl. Animal Males & Females. (Illus.). 38p. (J). (gr. 3 up). 2000. lib. bdg. 21.27 (0-8368-2712-0); Animal Trail & Tracks. (Illus.). 38p. (J). (gr. 3 up). 2000. lib. bdg. 21.27 (0-8368-2713-9); Animals & Their Eggs. (Illus.). 38p. (J). (gr. 3 up). 2000. lib. bdg. 21.27 (0-8368-2714-7); Animals That Live in Water. (Illus.). 38p. (J). (gr. 3 up). 2000. lib. bdg. 21.27 (0-8368-2715-5); Why Animals Have Tails. (Illus.). 38p. (J). (gr. 3 up). 2000. lib. bdg. 21.27 (0-8368-2716-3); Young Animals & Their Parents. (Illus.). 38p. (J). (gr. 3 up). 2000. lib. bdg. 21.27 (0-8368-2717-1); (Illus.). (J). (gr. 3 up). 2000. Set lib. bdg. 127.62 (0-8368-2711-2) Gareth Stevens Inc.

Renne, Elisha P. Cloth That Does Not Die: The Meaning of Cloth in Bunu Social Life. LC 94-12014. (McLellan Bks.). (Illus.). 216p. (C). 1995. 40.00 (0-295-97392-7) U of Wash Pr.

Renneberg, Monkia & Walker, Mark. Science, Technology & National Socialism. LC 92-41633. (Illus.). 442p. (C). 1993. text 74.95 (0-521-40374-X) Cambridge U Pr.

Renneberg, Prue, ed. see Ronneberg, Rod L.

Renneberg, Robert C. The Winchester Model 94. LC 90-63918. (Illus.). 208p. 1991. 34.95 (0-87341-161-7, WN01) Krause Pubns.

Renneisen, Robert. How to Be Treated Like a High Roller: Even Though You're Not One. 128p. 1992. pap. 7.95 (0-8184-0556-2, L Stuart) Carol Pub Group.

— How to Be Treated Like a High Roller Even Though You're Not One. 124p. 1996. pap. 8.95 (0-8184-0580-5, L Stuart) Carol Pub Group.

Renneker, Mark. Sick Surfers Ask the Surf Docs & Dr. Geoff. 389p. 1993. pap. 12.95 (0-923521-26-7) Bull Pub.

— Understanding Cancer. 3rd ed. 1991. pap. 39.95 (0-923521-29-1) Bull Pub.

Rennell, Diane S., ed. Appendix Materials. rev. ed. (Service Technology Ser.). 52p. 1989. write for info. (0-924635-02-9); text 90.00 (0-924635-01-0) Natl Spa Pool.

— Basic Pool & Spa Technology. rev. ed. (Service Technology Ser.). (Illus.). 390p. 1989. pap. text 140.00 (0-924635-00-2); pap. text 90.00 (0-685-25190-X) Natl Spa Pool.

Rennell, Francis J. British Military Administration of Occupied Territories in Africa During the Years of 1941-1947. 1970. reprint ed. lib. bdg. 85.00 (0-8371-4319-5, REBM, Greenwood Pr) Greenwood.

Rennell, James, jt. auth. see Park, Mungo.

Rennels, K. E. & Zecher, J. E. What Every Engineer Should Know about CAD/CAM. 2nd ed. (What Every Engineer Should Know Ser.). Date not set. write for info. (0-8247-9619-5) Dekker.

Rennels, Max R. The Art of Appreciation: A Cultural Awareness Perspective. 160p. 1995. per. 32.95 (0-8403-7078-4) Kendall-Hunt.

Rennenberg, H., et al, eds. Sulfur Nutrition & Sulfur Assimilation in Higher Plants: Fundamental Environmental & Agricultural Aspects. (Illus.). 276p. 1990. 89.00 (90-5103-038-X, Pub. by SPB Acad Pub) Balogh.

Rennenberg, Heinz. Trees - Contributions to Modern Tree Physiology. Eschrich, Walter & Ziegler, Hubert, eds. (Illus.). 565p. 1997. 130.50 (90-73348-67-6) Balogh.

Renner. Basic Hotel Front Office Prrocedures. 3rd ed. 1994. text. write for info. (0-471-28579-X) Wiley.

Renner. Diccionario de Modismos y Lenguaje Coloquial: Espanol - Aleman. (GER & SPA.). 1991. write for info. (0-7859-3704-8, 8428318506) Fr & Eur.

Renner, Shirley. Inflation & the Enforcement of Contracts. LC 98-33207. (New Horizons in Environmental Economics Ser.). 192p. 1999. 75.00 (1-84064-062-6) E Elgar.

Renner, Adrienne G., jt. auth. see Layman, Katie.

Renner, Brian, jt. auth. see Weatherford, William H., Sr.

Renner, Bruce. The Language of Light Ambits. 53p. per. 8.00 (0-934332-48-7) LEpervier Pr.

— Song Made Out of a Pale Smoke. LC 81-15617. 51p. text 9.95 (0-934332-37-1); pap. text 4.95 (0-934332-36-3) LEpervier Pr.

— Wakefulness. LC 78-71828. 78p. (Orig.). 1978. pap. 3.75 (0-934332-10-X) LEpervier Pr.

Renner, Don. Hands-On Water/Wastewater Equipment Maintenance, Vol. 1. LC 98-85950. 225p. 1998. 104.95 (1-56676-428-9) Technomic.

***Renner, Don.** Hands-On Water/Wastewater Equipment Maintenance, Vol. 2. LC 98-85950. 256p. 2000. pap. text 110.95 (1-56676-817-9) Technomic.

Renner, Eric. The International Pinhole Photography Exhibition. Center for Contemporary Arts Staff, ed. (Illus.). 64p. (Orig.). 1989. pap. text 18.00 (0-929762-01-0) CCA Santa Fe.

— Pinhole Photography: Rediscovering a Historic Technique. (Illus.). 192p. 1994. pap. text 29.95 (0-240-80231-4, Focal) Buttrwrth-Heinemann.

***Renner, Eric.** Pinhole Photography: Rediscovering a Historic Technique. 2nd ed. LC 99-25672. 228p. 1999. pap. text 32.95 (0-240-80350-7, Focal) Buttrwrth-Heinemann.

Renner, Franz C. & Seemann, Max. Viennese Stained Glass Designs in Full Color. (Illus.). 32p. 1988. reprint ed. pap. 6.95 (0-486-25590-5) Dover.

Renner, Frederic G., jt. auth. see Yost, Karl.

Renner, Gail K. In Pursuit of Excellence: Missouri Southern State College, 1937-1992. LC 93-29631. 1993. write for info. (0-89865-876-4) Donning Co.

Renner, Ginger K. Charles M. Russell: The Frederic G. Renner Collection. 80p. (Orig.). 1981. pap. 10.00 (0-910407-09-6) Phoenix Art.

Renner, Gregory J., jt. auth. see Zitsch, Robert P., III.

Renner, Gregory J., jt. auth. see Zitsch, Robert P., 3rd.

Renner, James, ed. see Lebrun, Rico.

Renner, Jeff. Northwest Marine Weather: From the Columbia River to Cape Scott, Including Puget Sound, the San Juan & Gulf Islands, & the Straits of Juan de Fuca, Georgia, Johnstone, & Queen Charlotte. 144p. 1993. 10.95 (0-89886-376-7) Mountaineers.

— Northwest Mountain Weather: Understanding & Forecasting for the Backcountry User. LC 91-46559. (Illus.). 96p. (Orig.). 1992. pap. 10.95 (0-89886-297-3) Mountaineers.

Renner, John H. Healthsmarts: How to Spot the Quacks, Avoid the Nonsense & Get the Facts that Affect Your Health. Vaughn, Lewis, ed. 160p. (Orig.). 1990. pap. 12.95 (0-9626145-0-5) Health Facts Pub.

Renner, John H., ed. A Self-Administered Patient Education Audit for Family Practices. 19p. 1990. 10.00 (0-9626145-1-3) Health Facts Pub.

Renner, K. Edward. The New Agenda for Higher Education: Choices Universities Can Make to Ensure a Brighter Future. (Illus.). 160p. (Orig.). 1995. pap. text. write for info. (1-55059-113-4) Detselig Ents.

Renner, Karl. Wandlungen der Modernen Gesellschaft: Transformations of Modern Society. LC 74-25776. (European Sociology Ser.). 227p. 1975. reprint ed. 24.95 (0-405-06530-2) Ayer.

Renner, Louis L. Father Tom of the Arctic. LC 85-71951. (Illus.). 176p. (Orig.). 1985. 24.95 (0-8323-0445-X); pap. 10.95 (0-8323-0443-3) Binford Mort.

Renner, M. J. & Rosenzweig, Mark R. Enriched & Impoverished Environments. (Recent Research in Psychology Ser.). (Illus.). 150p. 1987. 59.95 (0-387-96523-8) Spr-Verlag.

Renner, Michael. Budgeting for Disarmament: The Costs of War & Peace. 70p. (Orig.). 1994. pap. 5.00 (1-878071-23-8) Worldwatch Inst.

— Critical Juncture: The Future of Peacekeeping. 70p. (Orig.). 1993. pap. 5.00 (1-878071-15-7) Worldwatch Inst.

— Economic Adjustments after the Cold War: Strategies for Conversion. 1992. 66.95 (1-85521-259-5, Pub. by Dartmth Pub) Ashgate Pub Co.

— Ending Violent Conflict, Vol. 146. Peterson, Jane A., ed. 80p. 1999. pap. 5.00 (1-878071-48-3) Worldwatch Inst.

— Fighting for Survival: Environmental Decline, Social Conflict, & the New Age of Insecurity. LC 96-232410. 224p. 1996. 19.95 (0-393-03996-X); pap. 11.00 (0-393-31568-1) Norton.

— Jobs in a Sustainable Economy. 70p. (Orig.). 1991. pap. 5.00 (1-878071-05-X) Worldwatch Inst.

— National Security: The Economic & Environmental Dimension. 1989. pap. write for info. (0-916468-90-9) Worldwatch Inst.

— Psychology Smartbox: Introduction to Psychology. 9th ed. (Prentice Hall College Titles Ser.). (C). 1996. text 81.00 (0-13-443250-9, Macmillan Coll) P-H.

— Rethinking the Role of the Automobile. (Papers). 72p. (Orig.). (C). 1988. pap. 5.00 (0-916468-85-2) Worldwatch Inst.

— Small Arms, Big Impact: The Next Challenge of Disarmament. (Illus.). 77p. (C). 1998. pap. text 25.00 (0-7881-7188-7) DIANE Pub.

— Swords into Plowshares: Converting to a Peace Economy. 70p. (Orig.). 1990. pap. 5.00 (0-916468-97-6) Worldwatch Inst.

Renner, Michael & Worldwatch Institute Staff. Small Arms, Big Impact: The Next Challenge of Disarmament. Schwartz, Daniel, ed. LC 97-61351. (Worldwatch Papers). 77 p. 1997. 5.00 (1-878071-39-4) Worldwatch Inst.

Renner, Michelle. The Girl Who Swam with the Fish. LC 94-13763. (Illus.). 32p. (J). (gr. 2 up). 1995. 15.95 (0-88240-442-3, Alaska NW Bks) Gr Arts Ctr Pub.

***Renner, Michelle.** Girl Who Swam with the Fish: An Athabascan Legend. (Illus.). (J). 1999. 14.40 (0-606-17948-8) Turtleback.

Renner, Michelle. The Girl Who Swam with the Fish: An Athabascan Legend. (Illus.). (J). (gr. 2-4). 1999. 8.95 (0-88240-523-3, Alaska NW Bks) Gr Arts Ctr Pub.

An Asterisk (*) at the beginning of an entry indicates that the title is appearing for the first time.

Renner, Peter F. Basic Hotel Front Office Procedures. 3rd ed. 224p. 1993. pap. 54.95 (*0-471-29064-5*, VNR) Wiley.
— Basic Hotel Front Office Procedures. 3rd ed. 1994. text. write for info. (*0-442-01612-3*, VNR) Wiley.
Renner, Peter F. & Quinlivan-Hall, David. In Search of Solutions: Sixty Ways to Guide Your Problem-Solving Group. LC 96-153763. 176p. 1993. pap. 12.95 (*0-89384-236-2*, Pfffr & Co) Jossey-Bass.
Renner, R. G. Hopper. 1994. pap. 9.99 (*3-8228-0543-2*) Taschen Amer.
Renner, Richard R., ed. see Latin American Conference Staff.
Renner, Rick. Dream Thieves: Don't Be Robbed of Your Divine Destiny. 160p. 1996. pap. 8.99 (*1-880089-09-2*, Pub. by Albury Pub) Appalach Bk Dist.
— Dressed to Kill: You Don't Have to Take It Anymore, Because You Are... 320p. 1996. pap. 10.99 (*1-880089-06-8*, Pub. by Albury Pub) Appalach Bk Dist.
— The Dynamic Duo: The Holy Spirit & You. 1994. pap. 10.99 (*0-88419-362-4*) Creation House.
***Renner, Rick.** If You Were God, Would You Choose You? 330p. 2000. pap. 12.00 (*0-9621436-6-9*) R Renner Minst.
Renner, Rick. Living in the Combat Zone. 256p. 1996. pap. 10.99 (*1-880089-02-5*, Pub. by Albury Pub) Appalach Bk Dist.
— Merchandising the Anointing: Developing Discernment for These Last Days. 272p. 1997. pap. 10.99 (*1-880089-08-4*, AP-908, Pub. by Albury Pub) Appalach Bk Dist.
— The Point of No Return: Tackling Your Next New Assignment with Courage & Common Sense. 176p. 1996. pap. 9.99 (*1-880089-20-3*, Pub. by Albury Pub) Appalach Bk Dist.
— Seducing Spirits & Doctrines of Demons. MacKall, Phyllis, ed. (Orig.). 1988. 6.95 (*0-9621436-0-X*) R Renner Minst.
— Seducing Spirits & Doctrines of Demons: Last-Day Supernatural Confrontation. 176p. (Orig.). 1997. pap. 9.99 (*1-880089-07-6*, Pub. by Albury Pub) Appalach Bk Dist.
— Spiritual Weapons to Defeat the Enemy: Overcoming the Wiles, Devices & Deceptions of the Devil. 64p. 1996. pap. 5.99 (*1-880089-11-4*, Pub. by Albury Pub) Appalach Bk Dist.
***Renner, Rick.** Who Is Ready for a Spiritual Promotion? 246p. 2000. pap. 12.00 (*0-9621436-7-7*) R Renner Minst.
Renner, Robert, ed. QDT. 1993. (Illus.). 188p. (Orig.). 1993. pap. text 54.00 (*0-86715-186-2*) Quint Pub Co.
Renner, Robert C., et al. Self-Assessment Guide for Surface Water Treatment Plant Optimization. LC 97-27310. 1997. pap. write for info. (*0-89867-928-1*, 90730) Am Water Wks Assn.
Renner, Robert P. & Boucher, Louis J. Removable Partial Dentures. (Illus.). 416p. 1987. text 62.00 (*0-86715-189-7*, 1897) Quint Pub Co.
Renner, Rolf G. Hopper, 11 vols. (Thunder Bay Artists Ser.). (Illus.). 96p. 1997. pap. text 4.99 (*1-57145-099-8*, Thunder Bay) Advantage Pubs.
— Hopper. (SPA.). 1996. pap. 9.99 (*3-8228-0228-X*) Taschen Amer.
Renner, Ron. Secrets to Decorating & Moving to Florida. LC 91-91378. (Orig.). 1991. pap. 14.95 (*0-9631435-0-6*) Renner FL.
Renner, Rudiger. Economic Terminology English-German, German-English. 4th ed. (ENG & GER.). 543p. 1992. 125.00 (*0-7859-6872-5*) Fr & Eur.
Renner, Rudiger & Tooth, Jeffery. Legal Terminology English & German. (ENG & GER.). 76.00 (*3-19-006201-3*) Adlers Foreign Bks.
Renner, Rudiger & Tooth, Jeffrey. English & German Legal Terminology. (ENG & GER.). 526p. 1971. 95.00 (*0-8288-6466-7*) Fr & Eur.
Renner, Rudiger, jt. auth. see Haensch, G.
Renner, Susanne S. A History of Botanical Exploration in Amazonian Ecuador, 1739-1988. LC 92-5840. (Smithsonian Contributions to Botany Ser.: No. 82). 43p. reprint ed. pap. 30.00 (*0-7837-5166-4*, 204489500004) Bks Demand.
— Systematic Studies in the Melastomataceae: Bellucia, Loreya & Macairea. LC 88-39155. (Memoirs Ser.: No. 50). (Illus.). 111p. 1989. pap. 24.00 (*0-89327-335-X*) NY Botanical.
Renner, Susanne S., jt. auth. see Kubitzki, Klaus.
Renner, Tari. Statistics Unraveled: A Practical Guide to Using Data in Decision Making. 198p. (Orig.). 1988. pap. text 28.00 (*0-87326-934-9*) Intl City-Cnty Mgt.
Renner, Thomas C., jt. auth. see Giancana, Antoinette.
Renner, Thomas L., ed. see Michigan Intercollegiate Athletic Association Staf.
Renner, William, Jr. Kicking the Football. LC 97-12108. (Illus.). 184p. (Orig.). 1997. pap. 16.95 (*0-88011-685-4*, PREN0685) Human Kinetics.
Renner, Zainabu. Ethics in African Dress. 52p. (J). (gr. 3-4). 1996. pap. write for info. (*1-57579-038-6*) Pine Hill Pr.
— My Grandma & I. 16p. 1998. pap. write for info. (*1-57579-107-2*) Pine Hill Pr.
Rennert, Amy, ed. Helen Mirren: Prime Suspect. LC 95-24944. (Illus.). 144p. (Orig.). 1995. pap. 16.95 (*0-912333-69-3*) BB&T Inc.
Rennert, Hal H. Eduard Moerike's Reading & the Reconstruction of His Extant Library. LC 83-49184. (American University Studies: Comparative Literature: Ser. III, Vol. 8). 230p. (C). 1985. 26.00 (*0-8204-0080-7*) P Lang Pubng.
Rennert, Hugo A. Life of Lope de Vega. LC 67-13337. 1972. reprint ed. 30.95 (*0-405-08878-7*) Ayer.
— Spanish Pastoral Romances. LC 67-29552. 1968. reprint ed. 30.00 (*0-8196-0214-0*) Biblo.
Rennert, Jack. Elegant Posters, Vol. 10. (Illus.). 1990. 40.00 (*1-929530-08-0*) Pstr Auctns Intl.
Rennert, Jack. 100 Posters of Paul Colin. (Illus.). 112p. Date not set. 30.00 (*0-9664202-2-5*) Posters Please.
— One Hundred Years of Bicycle Posters. (Illus.). 1977. pap. 30.00 (*0-601-35336-6*) Darien Hse.
Rennert, Jack. Positively Posters, Vol. XXII. 1996. 40.00 (*0-9664201-7-9*) Pstr Auctns Intl.
— Poster Allure Vol. XXX: PAI XXX. (Illus.). 192p. 2000. 50.00 (*1-929530-15-3*) Pstr Auctns Intl.
— Poster Classics, Vol. 17. (Illus.). 1993. 40.00 (*1-929530-02-1*) Pstr Auctns Intl.
— Poster Delights, Vol. XXIII. (Illus.). 1996. 40.00 (*0-9664201-6-0*) Pstr Auctns Intl.
— Poster Jubilee, Vol. 13. (Illus.). 1991. 40.00 (*1-929530-05-6*) Pstr Auctns Intl.
— Poster Palette, Vol. 9. (Illus.). 1989. 40.00 (*1-929530-09-9*) Pstr Auctns Intl.
— Poster Panache, Vol. 12. (Illus.). 1991. 40.00 (*1-929530-06-4*) Pstr Auctns Intl.
— Poster Panorama, Vol. XX. 1995. 40.00 (*0-9664201-9-5*) Pstr Auctns Intl.
— Poster Parade, Vol. 16. (Illus.). 1993. 40.00 (*1-929530-03-X*) Pstr Auctns Intl.
— Poster Passion, Vol. 11. (Illus.). 1990. 40.00 (*1-929530-07-2*) Pstr Auctns Intl.
— Poster Pizzazz, Vol. 5. (Illus.). 1987. 40.00 (*1-929530-11-0*) Pstr Auctns Intl.
— Poster Pleasures, Vol. XXIV. (Illus.). 1997. 40.00 (*0-9664201-5-2*) Pstr Auctns Intl.
— Poster Treasures, Vol. 8. (Illus.). 1989. 40.00 (*1-929530-10-2*) Pstr Auctns Intl.
Rennert, Jack. Poster Vogue, Vol. XXVIII. (Illus.). 176p. Date not set. 40.00 (*0-9664201-2-8*) Pstr Auctns Intl.
— Postermania, No. XXVI. (Illus.). 160p. 1998. 50.00 (*0-9664201-0-1*) Pstr Auctns Intl.
***Rennert, Jack.** Posters for the Millennium, Vol. XXIX. (Illus.). 378p. 1999. 50.00 (*1-929530-13-7*) Pstr Auctns Intl.
Rennert, Jack. Posters of the Belle Epoque: The Wine Spectator Collection. (Illus.). 256p. Date not set. 75.00 (*0-9664202-1-7*) Posters Please.
Rennert, Jack. Prestige Posters, Vol. 4. (Illus.). 1987. 40.00 (*1-929530-12-9*) Pstr Auctns Intl.
— Prima Posters, Vol. 19. (Illus.). 1994. 40.00 (*1-929530-00-5*) Pstr Auctns Intl.
— Rarest Posters, Vol. 15. (Illus.). 1992. 40.00 (*1-929530-04-8*) Pstr Auctns Intl.
— Sterling Posters, Vol. XXV. (Illus.). 1997. 40.00 (*0-9664201-4-4*) Pstr Auctns Intl.
— Timeless Posters, Vol. XXI. 1995. 40.00 (*0-9664201-8-7*) Pstr Auctns Intl.
— Winning Posters, Vol. 18. (Illus.). 1994. 40.00 (*1-929530-01-3*) Pstr Auctns Intl.
Rennert, Jack & Terry, Walter. One Hundred Years of Dance Posters. (Illus.). 1977. pap. 30.00 (*0-88201-010-7*) Darien Hse.
Rennert, Kate A., jt. auth. see Alderson, Jo B.
Rennert, Maggie. I Love You. (Illus.). (J). (ps up). 1987. 9.95 (*0-915361-71-X*) Lambda Pubs.
Rennert, Owen M. & Chan, Wayiee, eds. Metabolism of Trace Metals in Man, Vol. I. 192p. 1984. 110.00 (*0-8493-5798-5*, QP534, CRC Reprint) Franklin.
— Metabolism of Trace Metals in Man, Vol. II. 168p. 1984. 99.00 (*0-8493-5799-3*, QP534, CRC Reprint) Franklin.
Rennert, Ricahrd S., ed. Book of Firsts: Sports Heroes. LC 93-18437. (Profiles of Great Black Americans Ser.). (Illus.). 64p. (J). (gr. 3 up). 1993. lib. bdg. 15.95 (*0-7910-2055-X*, Chelsea Juniors) Chelsea Hse.
Rennert, Richard. Performing Artists. (Profiles of Great Black Americans Ser.). (J). 1994. 12.15 (*0-606-08004-X*) Turtleback.
Rennert, Richard S. African American Answer Book. (Illus.). 64p. (gr. 5). 1994. 89.70 (*0-7910-3200-0*) Chelsea Hse.
Rennert, Richard S. African American Answer Book: Arts & Entertainment. LC 94-29999. (Illus.). 64p. (YA). (gr. 5 up). 1995. pap. 4.95 (*0-7910-3202-7*); lib. bdg. 12.95 (*0-7910-3201-9*) Chelsea Hse.
— African American Answer Book: Biography. LC 94-30201. (Illus.). 64p. (YA). (gr. 5 up). 1995. pap. 3.95 (*0-7910-3204-3*) Chelsea Hse.
— African American Answer Book: Biography. LC 94-30201. (Illus.). 64p. (YA). (gr. 7 up). 1995. lib. bdg. 12.95 (*0-7910-3203-5*) Chelsea Hse.
— African American Answer Book: Facts & Trivia. LC 94-30203. (Illus.). 6p. (YA). (gr. 5 up). 1995. pap. 4.95 (*0-7910-3212-4*) Chelsea Hse.
— African American Answer Book: History. LC 94-30202. 64p. (YA). (gr. 5 up). 1995. pap. 3.95 (*0-7910-3210-8*) Chelsea Hse.
— African American Answer Book: Sports. (Illus.). 64p. (YA). (gr. 5 up). 1995. pap. 3.95 (*0-7910-3206-X*); lib. bdg. 12.95 (*0-7910-3205-1*) Chelsea Hse.
Rennert, Richard S. African American Answer Book: Science & Discovery. (Illus.). 64p. (YA). (gr. 5 up). 1995. pap. 3.95 (*0-7910-3208-6*) Chelsea Hse.
Rennert, Richard S. Henry Aaron: Baseball Great. (Black American Ser.). (Illus.). 192p. (YA). 1993. mass mkt. 3.95 (*0-87067-780-2*, Melrose Sq) Holloway.
— Jesse Owens: Champion Athlete. (Junior Black Americans of Achievement Ser.). (Illus.). 76p. (J). (gr. 3-6). 1991. lib. bdg. 16.95 (*0-7910-1570-X*) Chelsea Hse.
— Jesse Owens: Champion Athlete. (Junior Black Americans of Achievement Ser.). (Illus.). 76p. (J). (gr. 3-6). 1992. pap. 4.95 (*0-7910-1955-1*) Chelsea Hse.
— Julius Erving: Basketball Great. Huggins, Nathan I., ed. LC 94-13206. (Black Americans of Achievement Ser.). (Illus.). 124p. (YA). (gr. 5 up). 1992. lib. bdg. 19.95 (*0-7910-1125-9*) Chelsea Hse.
— Male Writers. (Profiles of Great Black Americans Ser.). (Illus.). 64p. (J). (gr. 3 up). 1994. pap. 5.95 (*0-7910-2062-2*) Chelsea Hse.
— Pioneers of Discovery. (Profiles of Great Black Americans Ser.). (Illus.). 64p. (J). (gr. 3 up). 1994. pap. 5.95 (*0-7910-2068-1*) Chelsea Hse.
Rennert, Richard S., ed. African American Answer Book: Facts & Trivia. LC 94-30203. (Illus.). 64p. (YA). (gr. 5 up). 1995. lib. bdg. 12.95 (*0-7910-3211-6*) Chelsea Hse.
— Book of Firsts: Leaders of America. LC 93-25878. (Profiles of Great Black Americans Ser.). (Illus.). 64p. (YA). (gr. 3 up). 1993. pap. 5.95 (*0-7910-2065-5*) Chelsea Hse.
— Book of Firsts: Sports Heroes. LC 93-18437. (Profiles of Great Black Americans Ser.). (Illus.). 64p. (J). (gr. 3 up). 1993. pap. 5.95 (*0-7910-2056-8*) Chelsea Hse.
— Civil Rights Leaders. LC 92-37655. (Profiles of Great Black Americans Ser.). (Illus.). 64p. (J). (gr. 3 up). 1993. lib. bdg. 15.95 (*0-7910-2051-7*) Chelsea Hse.
— Female Leaders. (Profiles of Great Black Americans Ser.). (Illus.). 64p. (J). (gr. 3 up). 1993. lib. bdg. 15.95 (*0-7910-2057-6*) Chelsea Hse.
— Female Leaders. (Profiles of Great Black Americans Ser.). (Illus.). 64p. (J). (gr. 3 up). 1994. pap. 5.95 (*0-7910-2058-4*) Chelsea Hse.
— Female Writers. LC 93-21673. (Profiles of Great Black Americans Ser.). (Illus.). 64p. (J). (gr. 3 up). 1993. pap. 5.95 (*0-7910-2064-9*) Chelsea Hse.
— Jazz Stars. (Profiles of Great Black Americans Ser.). (Illus.). 64p. (YA). (gr. 5-8). 1993. lib. bdg. 16.95 (*0-7910-2059-2*) Chelsea Hse.
— Male Writers. (Profiles of Great Black Americans Ser.). (Illus.). 64p. (J). (gr. 3 up). 1993. lib. bdg. 14.95 (*0-7910-2061-4*) Chelsea Hse.
— Performing Artists. (Profiles of Great Black Americans Ser.). (Illus.). 64p. (J). (gr. 3 up). 1993. lib. bdg. 15.95 (*0-7910-2069-X*, Chelsea Juniors) Chelsea Hse.
— Performing Artists. (Profiles of Great Black Americans Ser.). (Illus.). 64p. (J). (gr. 3 up). 1994. pap. 5.95 (*0-7910-2070-3*) Chelsea Hse.
— Pioneers of Discovery. (Profiles of Great Black Americans Ser.). (Illus.). 64p. (J). (gr. 3 up). 1993. lib. bdg. 15.95 (*0-7910-2067-3*) Chelsea Hse.
— Profiles of Great Black Americans, 10 vols., Set. (Illus.). (J). (gr. 3 up). 1993. lib. bdg. 149.50 (*0-7910-2050-9*) Chelsea Hse.
— Shapers of America. LC 92-39962. (Profiles of Great Black Americans Ser.). (Illus.). 64p. (YA). (gr. 3 up). 1993. lib. bdg. 15.95 (*0-7910-2053-3*) Chelsea Hse.
— Shapers of America. LC 92-39962. (Profiles of Great Black Americans Ser.). 64p. (YA). (gr. 3 up). 1994. pap. 5.95 (*0-7910-2054-1*) Chelsea Hse.
Rennert, Richard Scott. Book of Firsts: Leaders of America. (Profiles of Great Black Americans Ser.). 1994. 11.15 (*0-606-07312-4*, Pub. by Turtleback) Demco.
— Civil Rights Leaders. (Profiles of Great Black Americans Ser.). 1993. 11.15 (*0-606-07374-4*, Pub. by Turtleback) Demco.
— Female Leaders. (Profiles of Great Black Americans Ser.). (J). 1994. 12.40 (*0-606-07507-0*) Turtleback.
— Female Writers. (Profiles of Great Black Americans Ser.). (J). 1994. 11.15 (*0-606-07508-9*) Turtleback.
— Jesse Owens. (Junior World Biographies). 1992. 10.15 (*0-606-07739-1*, Pub. by Turtleback) Demco.
— Male Writers. (Profiles of Great Black Americans Ser.). (J). 1994. 12.40 (*0-606-07833-9*) Turtleback.
— Pioneers of Discovery. (Profiles of Great Black Americans Ser.). (J). 1994. 11.15 (*0-606-08016-3*) Turtleback.
Rennert, Rick. Shapers of America. (Profiles of Great Black Americans Ser.). (J). 1993. 12.40 (*0-606-08152-6*) Turtleback.
Rennes, Jacob J. Van, see Van Rennes, Jacob J.
Renneville, ed. see Rimbaud, Arthur.
***Renney, Sandra, ed.** Golf - The Game for Life: The 2000 Official Guide to Junior Golf. 3rd ed. (Illus.). 200p. 2000. pap. 6.95 (*1-891965-03-4*) Belmont Intl.
— Semper - Fi: Celebrating 225 Years of the U. S. Marine Corps. (Illus.). 200p. 1999. pap. 6.95 (*1-891965-02-6*) Belmont Intl.
***Rennick, Penny.** Russian America, Vol. 26, No. 4. Alaska Geographic Staff, ed. LC 72-92087. (Illus.). 112p. 1999. pap. 21.95 (*1-56661-047-8*) Alaska Geog Soc.
— Seals, Sea Lions & Sea Otters. 2000. pap. 21.95 (*1-56661-052-4*) Alaska Geog Soc.
Rennick, Penny, ed. Alaska's Southern Panhandle. (Alaska Geographic Ser.: Vol. 24, No. 1). (Illus.). (Orig.). 1997. pap. 19.95 (*1-56661-035-4*) Alaska Geog Soc.
***Rennick, Penny, ed.** The Bering Sea. LC 72-92087. (Illus.). 112p. 1999. pap. 21.95 (*1-56661-048-6*) Alaska Geog Soc.
Rennick, Penny, ed. Commercial Fishing in Alaska. (Alaska Geographic Ser.: Vol. 24, No. 3). (Illus.). (Orig.). 1997. pap. 19.95 (*1-56661-038-9*) Alaska Geog Soc.
— Kuskokwim River. (Alaska Geographic Ser.: Vol. 15, No. 4). (Illus.). 96p. 1989. pap. 19.95 (*0-88240-187-4*) Alaska Geog Soc.
— Mammals of Alaska. (Alaska Geographic Guides Ser.). (Illus.). 176p. (Orig.). 1996. pap. 17.95 (*1-56661-034-6*) Alaska Geog Soc.
Rennick, Penny & Campbell, L. J. Alaska: The Great Land. LC 72-92087. (Alaska Geographic Ser.: Vol. 19, No. 2). (Illus.). 112p. 1992. pap. 9.95 (*1-56661-002-8*) Alaska Geog Soc.
— Sitka (Travel Guide) LC 95-40004. (Alaska Geographic Guides Ser.). (Illus.). 144p. 1995. pap. 9.95 (*1-56661-029-X*) Alaska Geog Soc.
— World War II in Alaska. (Alaska Geographic Ser.: Vol. 22, No. 4). (Illus.). 96p. (Orig.). 1996. pap. 19.95 (*1-56661-028-1*) Alaska Geog Soc.
Rennick, Penny, jt. auth. see Campbell, L. J.
Rennick, Penny, ed. see Alaska Geographic Editors.
Rennick, Penny, ed. see Alaska Geographic Society Staff.
Rennick, Penny, ed. see Alaska Geographic Society Staff & Doogan, Mike.
Rennick, Penny, ed. see Campbell, L. J.
Rennick, Penny, ed. see Campbell, L. J., & Staff & Alaska Geographic Society Staff.
Rennick, Penny, ed. see Campbell Staff, L. J.
Rennick, Penny, ed. see Campbell Staff, L. J. & Alaska Geographic Society Staff.
Rennick, Penny, ed. see Emanuel, Richard P.
Rennick, Penny, ed. see Emanuel, Richard P., et al.
Rennick, Penny, ed. see Matzkanin, George A.
Rennick, Penny, ed. see McDonald, Lucile.
Rennick, Penny, ed. see Piper, Ernest.
Rennick, Penny, ed. see Simpson, Sherry & Alaska Geographic Society Staff.
Rennick, Robert M. Kentucky Place Names. LC 87-31617. 400p. 1988. pap. 22.00 (*0-8131-0179-4*) U Pr of Ky.
Rennicke, Jeff. Colorado Wildlife. 2nd ed. (Illus.). 66p. 1996. reprint ed. pap. 19.95 (*1-56044-515-7*) Falcon Pub Inc.
— Isle Royale: Moods, Magic & Mystique. (Illus.). 40p. (Orig.). 1989. pap. 11.95 (*0-935289-01-1*) Isle Royale Hist.
— The Smoky Mountain Black Bear: Spirit of the Hills. Kemp, Steve, ed. (Illus.). 60p. (Orig.). 1991. pap. 7.95 (*0-937207-04-7*) GSMNH.
Rennie. Textbook of Neonatology. 3rd ed. LC 98-48318. (C). 1998. text. write for info. (*0-443-05541-6*) Church.
Rennie, A. R., jt. ed. see Ottewill, Ronald H.
Rennie, Andrew, jt. auth. see Baxter, Martin.
Rennie, Bryan S. Reconstructing Eliade: Making Sense of Religion. LC 95-12358. 293p. (C). 1996. text 59.50 (*0-7914-2763-3*); pap. text 19.95 (*0-7914-2764-1*) State U NY Pr.
***Rennie, Bryan S., ed.** Changing Religious Worlds: The Meaning & End of Mircea Eliade. LC 00-22911. (C). 2000. pap. text 24.95 (*0-7914-4730-8*) State U NY Pr.
— Changing Religious Worlds: The Meaning & End of Mircea Eliade. LC 00-22911. (C). 2000. text 73.50 (*0-7914-4729-4*) State U NY Pr.
Rennie, C. Goal Behind the Curtain. Date not set. 4.99 (*1-871676-47-9*, Pub. by Christian Focus) Spring Arbor Dist.
— Offside in Ecuatina. Date not set. 4.99 (*1-871676-69-X*, Pub. by Christian Focus) Spring Arbor Dist.
— True Gold. 1995. 4.99 (*1-871676-90-8*, Pub. by Christian Focus) Spring Arbor Dist.
Rennie, Caroline & MacLean, Alair. Salvaging the Future: Waste-Based Production. LC 89-11209. (Illus.). 160p. 1989. pap. text 20.00 (*0-917582-37-3*) Inst Local Self Re.
Rennie, David L. Person-Centred Counselling: An Experimental Approach LC 97-62420. vi, 153p. 1998. write for info. (*0-7619-5345-0*) Sage.
Rennie, David L., jt. auth. see Toukmanian, Shake G.
Rennie, Dorothy A., jt. ed. see Isaacson, Martin J.
Rennie, E. Cowal. Date not set. pap. 11.95 (*1-874744-08-4*, Pub. by Birlinn Ltd) Dufour.
Rennie, Frank, jt. ed. see Bruce, George.
Rennie, Gordon. Starship Troopers. (Illus.). 1998. pap. text 16.95 (*1-56971-314-6*) Dark Horse Comics.
Rennie, James. The Operators: Inside 14 Intelligence Company. (Illus.). 256p. 1996. 35.00 (*0-7126-7730-5*, Pub. by CEN3) Trafalgar.
Rennie, Janet M. Neonatal Cerebral Ultrasound. LC 96-13980. (Illus.). 254p. (C). 1997. text 95.00 (*0-521-45079-9*) Cambridge U Pr.
Rennie, Jeanne, jt. ed. see Holt, Daniel D.
Rennie, John A., jt. ed. see Lafferty, Kevin.
Rennie, John C. Exportise: An International Trade Sourcebook for the Smaller Company Executive. 3rd ed. (Illus.). 260p. 1990. pap. text 49.50 (*0-912501-02-2*) Small Bus Amer.
Rennie, John C., ed. Exportise: An International Trade Source Book for Smaller Company Executives. rev. ed. (Illus.). 237p. 1987. reprint ed. pap. 29.50 (*0-912501-01-4*) Small Bus Amer.
Rennie, Leonie J., et al, eds. Gender, Science & Mathematics: Shortening the Shadow. LC 95-30191. (Science & Technology Education Libary: Vol. 2). 1996. lib. bdg. 120.00 (*0-7923-3535-X*) Kluwer Academic.
Rennie, M. J. Permission/The Perfect Wife. 1998. mass mkt. 6.95 (*1-56333-695-2*) Masquerade.
Rennie, Neil. Far-Fetched Facts: The Literature of Travel & the Idea of the South Seas. (Illus.). 338p. 1999. reprint ed. pap. text 26.00 (*0-19-818627-4*) OUP.
Rennie, Robert. Rennie: Solicitors' Negligence. 1997. write for info. (*0-406-99610-5*, RSN, MICHIE) LEXIS Pub.
Rennie, Robert & Cusine, Douglas J. Rennie & Cusine: The Requirements of Writing. 1995. write for info. (*0-406-06331-1*, RCRW1, MICHIE) LEXIS Pub.
Rennie, Robert, jt. auth. see Cusine, Douglas J.
Rennie, William R., jt. ed. see Cruess, Richard L.
Rennie, Ysabel F. The Argentine Republic. LC 74-12767. (Illus.). 431p. 1975. reprint ed. lib. bdg. 38.50 (*0-8371-7739-1*, REAR, Greenwood Pr) Greenwood.
Rennilson, Jay J. & Hale, W. N., Jr., eds. Review & Evaluation of Appearance: Method & Techniques, STP 914. LC 86-7999. (Special Technical Publication Ser.). (Illus.). 112p. 1986. text 24.00 (*0-8031-0480-4*, STP914) ASTM.
Renning, Adair N. The Utimate Treasure Hunt: Offering Hope to Children with Autism. (Illus.). 281p. 1995. pap. 19.95 (*0-9648773-0-9*) A Renning.
Renning, Adair N., jt. auth. see Bolander, Anne M.
***Renning, Anne Holden, et al.** Graduate Prospects in a Changing Society. LC 98-228088. (Education on the Move Ser.). 397 p. 1998. (*92-3-103497-9*) Bernan Associates.

An Asterisk (*) at the beginning of an entry indicates that the title is appearing for the first time.

R

Renninger, Dana, jt. auth. see Renninger, Jodi.

***Renninger, Gwen.** The Perfect Hand. (Illus.). ii, 35p. 2000. spiral bd. 6.99 (*0-9679838-0-0*) G G Renninger.

Renninger, Jodi & Renninger, Dana. Helping Youth Make Difficult Decisions: A Classroom Program to Help Students Develop Decision-Making Skills Grades 4-8. 68p. 1989. pap. text 9.95 (*1-57543-052-5*) Mar Co Prods.

Renninger, John P., ed. The Future Role of the United Nations in an Interdependent World. (C). 1990. lib. bdg. 110.00 (*0-7923-0532-9*) Kluwer Academic.

Renninger, K. Ann, et al, eds. The Role of Interest in Learning & Development. 368p. 1992. text 79.95 (*0-8058-0718-7*) L Erlbaum Assocs.

Renninger, K. Ann, jt. ed. see Amsel, Eric.

Renninger, K. Ann, jt. ed. see Cocking, Rodney R.

***Rennings, K., et al, eds.** Social Costs & Sustainable Mobility. (ZEW Economic Studies: Vol. 7). (Illus.). vi, 212p. 2000. pap. 63.00 (*3-7908-1260-9*) Spr-Verlag.

Renninson, Keith E. The Pain & Joy of Love. 100p. 1995. pap. 15.00 (*0-9648551-4-3*) Namaste Pub.

Rennison, John R. Koromfe. LC 96-7548. 560p. (C). 1997. 190.00 (*0-415-15257-7*) Routledge.

Rennison, Louise. Angus, Thongs & Full-Frontal Snogging: Confessions of Georgia Nicolson. LC 99-40591. 256p. (J). (gr. 7 up). mass mkt. 4.95 (*0-06-447227-2*) HarpC.

— Angus, Thongs & Full-Frontal Snogging: Confessions of Georgia Nicolson. LC 99-40591. (Illus.). 256p. (YA). (gr. 7-12). 2000. lib. bdg. 15.89 (*0-06-028871-X*) HarpC Child Bks.

— Anugs, Thongs & Full-Frontal Snogging. LC 99-40591. 256p. (YA). (gr. 7-12). 2000. 15.95 (*0-06-028814-0*) HarpC Child Bks.

— Georgia Sequel. 192p. (gr. 7 up). 15.95 (*0-06-028813-2*) HarpC.

— Georgia Sequel. 192p. (J). (gr. 12 up). 15.89 (*0-06-028872-8*) HarpC Child Bks.

Rennison, N. & Schmidt, M., eds. Poets on Poets: An Anthology. LC 98-146544. 420p. 1998. pap. 18.95 (*1-85754-339-4*, Pub. by Carcanet Pr) Paul & Co Pubs.

Rennison, Robert Nicholas. London Blue Plaque Guide. 2000. pap. text 16.95 (*0-7509-2091-2*) Sutton Pub Ltd.

Rennison, Roderick, jt. auth. see Chapman, Robert E.

Rennke, Helmut G., jt. auth. see Rose, Burton D.

Renny, Arnold J. Consumers' Data Book of Activities, Investigations, Satisfactions & Organizations: Index of New Information. 150p. 1994. 47.50 (*0-7883-0130-6*); pap. 44.50 (*0-7883-0131-4*) ABBE Pubs Assn.

Renny, Gerard. The Men of the Pacific Street Social Club Cook Italian: Home-Style Recipes And Unforgettable Stories. LC 98-31047. (Illus.). 160p. 1999. 23.00 (*0-688-15617-7*, Wm Morrow) Morrow Avon.

Reno, Bill. Sundance. large type ed. LC 92-28127. (Nightingale Ser.). 336p. 1993. pap. 14.95 (*0-8161-5630-1*, G K Hall Lrg Type) Mac Lib Ref.

Reno, Carolyn. Almost... but Lost. pap. 0.59 (*1-56632-013-5*) Revival Lit.

***Reno, Carolyn.** Almost... But Lost.Tr. of Casi... Pero Perdida. (SPA.). 25p. 1999. pap. 0.59 (*1-56632-105-0*) Revival Lit.

Reno, Dawn E. Advertising: Identification & Price Guide. 572p. (Orig.). 1993. pap. 15.00 (*0-380-76884-4*, Avon Bks) Morrow Avon.

— The Candace: Warrior Queens of the Kingdom of Kush. LC 99-72736. (Illus.). 120p. 1999. pap. text 8.95 (*1-58521-009-9*) Bks Black Chldn.

— Contemporary Native American Artists. 1995. pap. 18.00 (*0-9641509-6-4*) Allian Pubng.

— The Encyclopedia of Black Collectibles: A Value & Identification Guide. LC 95-11637. (Illus.). 320p. 1996. pap. 19.95 (*0-87069-703-X*, Wllce-Homestd) Krause Pubns.

— Native American Collectibles: Identification & Price Guide. 538p. (Orig.). 1994. pap. 17.00 (*0-380-77069-5*, Avon Bks) Morrow Avon.

Reno, Dawn E. & Tiegs, Jacque. Collecting Romance Novels. LC 96-197005. (Instant Expert Ser.). 120p. 1995. pap. 12.00 (*0-9641509-5-6*) Allian Pubng.

Reno, Deb, ed. 1998 OR Product Directory. 458p. 1998. pap. 25.00 (*1-888460-01-6*) Assn Oper Rm Nurses.

Reno, Frank D. Historic Figures of the Arthurian Era: Authenticating the Enemies & Allies of Britain's Post-Roman King. LC 99-55343. (Illus.). 358p. 2000. lib. bdg. 39.95 (*0-7864-0648-8*) McFarland & Co.

— The Historic King Arthur: Authenticating the Celtic Hero of Post-Roman Britian. LC 96-22231. (Illus.). 458p. 1996. lib. bdg. 42.50 (*0-7864-0266-0*) McFarland & Co.

Reno, Fred, jt. ed. see Burton, Richard D.

Reno, Harley W., et al. Pocket Guide to Lure Fishing for Trout in a Stream. (Illus.). 28p. 1995. spiral bd. 12.95 (*1-886127-06-9*) Greycliff Pub.

— Pocket Guide to Target - Field Archery. (Illus.). 28p. 1994. spiral bd. 12.95 (*1-886127-01-8*) Greycliff Pub.

***Reno, J. Paul.** Daniel Nash: Prevailing Prince of Prayer.Tr. of Poderoso Principe De la Oracion. (SPA.). 27p. 1999. pap. 1.99 (*1-56632-104-2*) Revival Lit.

Reno, J. Paul. Daniel Nash - Prevailing Prince of Prayer. 1989. pap. 1.99 (*1-56632-089-5*) Revival Lit.

— To Fight or Not to Fight. 1984. pap. 2.49 (*1-56632-012-7*) Revival Lit.

Reno, Janet. Ishmael Alone Survived. LC 89-45971. 176p. 1991. 32.50 (*0-8387-5171-7*) Bucknell U Pr.

Reno, John L., ed. Narrow Gap Semiconductors, 1995: Proceedings of the Seventh International Conference on Narrow Gap Semiconductors, Santa Fe, New Mexico, 8-12 January 1995. LC 95-42877. (Institute of Physics Conference Ser.: Vol. 144). 388p. 1995. 200.00 (*0-7503-0341-7*) IOP Pub.

Reno, Kelly. Good Gifts from the Home: Oils, Lotions & Other Luxuries: Make Beautiful Gifts to Give (or Keep) LC 95-44916. (Gifts from the Home Ser.). (Illus.). 96p. 1996. text 12.00 (*0-7615-0334-X*) Prima Pub.

— Good Gifts from the Home: Soaps, Shampoos & Other Suds. LC 95-44917. (Good Gifts from the Home Ser.). (Illus.). 96p. 1997. 14.00 (*0-7615-0335-8*) Prima Pub.

***Reno, Kelly.** Good Gifts from the Home - Candles, Bubble Baths & Other Romantic Indulgences: Make Beautiful Gifts to Give (or Keep) (Good Gifts from the Home Ser.). 2000. 14.95 (*0-7615-2342-1*) Prima Pub.

— Good Gifts from the Home - Oils, Lotions & Other Luxuries: Make Beautiful Gifts to Give (or Keep) (Good Gifts from the Home Ser.). 2000. 14.95 (*0-7615-2544-0*) Prima Pub.

— Good Gifts from the Home - Perfumes, Scented Gifts & Other Fragrances: Make Beautiful Gifts to Give (or Keep) LC 00-28543. (Good Gifts from the Home Ser.). (Illus.). 96p. 2000. 14.95 (*0-7615-2341-3*) Prima Pub.

— Good Gifts from the Home - Soaps, Shampoos & Other Suds: Make Beautiful Gifts to Give (or Keep) (Good Gifts from the Home Ser.). 2000. 14.95 (*0-7615-2543-2*) Prima Pub.

Reno, Kelly. 100 Great Freelance Careers. 256p. 1997. 14.95 (*0-02-861938-2*) Macmillan.

***Reno, Kelly.** The 101 Best Freelance Careers. LC 99-217722. 224p. (Orig.). 1999. pap. 12.00 (*0-425-16865-4*) Berkley Pub.

Reno, Kelly. Perfumes, Potions & Fanciful Formulas. Smith, Sally, ed. 112p. Date not set. 14.95 (*1-891437-00-3*, V900) Victorian Essence.

— 77 No Talent, No Experience, & (Almost) No Cost Businesses You Can Start Today! 192p. 1995. pap. 12.95 (*0-7615-0246-7*) Prima Pub.

Reno, Liz & Devrais, Joanna. Allergy-Free Eating. LC 95-21878. 490p. 1995. pap. 16.95 (*0-89087-745-9*) Celestial Arts.

Reno, Margarida F., et al. Spoken Portuguese, Bk. I. (ENG & POR.). 1978. pap. 90.00 incl. audio (*0-87950-186-3*) Spoken Lang Serv.

Reno, Margarida F., et al. Spoken Portuguese, Bk. I. (ENG & POR.). 1978. audio 75.00 (*0-87950-185-5*) Spoken Lang Serv.

Reno, Margarida F., et al. Spoken Portuguese, Bk. I, Units 1-12. (ENG & POR.). 218p. 1978. 15.00 (*0-87950-180-4*) Spoken Lang Serv.

— Spoken Portuguese, Bk. II, Units 13-30. (ENG & POR.). 307p. 1978. 15.00 (*0-87950-181-2*) Spoken Lang Serv.

Reno, Ottie W. Reno & Apsaalooka Survive Custer. LC 96-23800. (Illus.). 336p. 1997. 29.95 (*0-8453-4862-0*, Cornwall Bks) Assoc Univ Prs.

— State of Ohio vs. Isaac Milton Smith, Murder. LC 90-55329. (Illus.). 376p. 1991. 24.95 (*0-8453-4832-9*, Cornwall Bks) Assoc Univ Prs.

***Reno, R. R. & Hook, Brian S.** Heroism & the Christian Life. LC 99-86534. 256p. 2000. pap. 23.95 (*0-664-25812-3*, Pub. by Westminster John Knox) Presbyterian Pub.

Reno, Robert C. Radiation in Medicine. 2nd ed. LC 94-73544. (Illus.). 104p. (C). 1994. pap. text 27.95 (*0-916615-05-7*) Bks of Sci.

Reno, Robert P. The Gothic Visions of Ann Radcliffe & Matthew G. Lewis. Varma, Devendra P., ed. LC 79-8473. (Gothic Studies & Dissertations). 1980. lib. bdg. 31.95 (*0-405-12648-4*) Ayer.

Reno, Russell R., Jr. & Simmons, Wilbur E. Maryland Real Estate Forms, 2 vols., Set. 900p. 1986. spiral bd. 229.00 incl. disk (*0-87189-281-2*, MICHIE) LEXIS Pub.

Reno, Russell R., Jr., et al. Maryland Real Estate Forms, No. 13. Kosmas, Michael S., ed. LC 84-149438. 100p. 1998. ring bd. write for info. (*0-327-00318-9*, 81605-13) LEXIS Pub.

***Reno, Russell R., Jr., et al.** Maryland Real Estate Forms, No. 14. 120p. 1999. ring bd. write for info. (*0-327-01585-3*, 8160514) LEXIS Pub.

Reno, Virginia P., et al, eds. Disability: Challenges for Social Insurance, Health Care Financing, & Labor Market Policy. LC 96-45847. 202p. 1997. pap. 19.95 (*0-8157-7405-2*) Brookings.

Reno, Virginia P., jt. ed. see Mashaw, Jerry L.

Reno, William. Corruption & State Politics in Sierra Leone. (African Studies: 83). (Illus.). 242p. (C). 1995. text 64.95 (*0-521-47179-6*) Cambridge U Pr.

Reno, William. Warlord Politics & African States. LC 97-32752. 257p. 1998. lib. bdg. 53.50 (*1-55587-673-0*) L Rienner.

***Reno, William.** Warlord Politics & African States. 260p. 1999. pap. 19.95 (*1-55587-883-0*) L Rienner.

Renoir, Alain. A Key to Old Poems: Oral-Formulaic Rhetorical Context & the Interpretation of Traditional West-Germanic Poetry. LC 86-43040. 260p. 1988. 35.00 (*0-271-00482-7*) Pa St U Pr.

Renoir, Alain & Hernandez, Ann, eds. Approaches to Beowulfian Scansion: Four Essays by John Miles Foley, Winfred P. Lehmann, Robert Creed, & Dolores Warwick Frese. (Old English Colloquium Ser.: No. 1). 64p. 1985. reprint ed. pap. text 15.00 (*0-8191-4518-1*) U Pr of Amer.

Renoir, Auguste, jt. auth. see Crepaldi, Gabriele.

Renoir, Jean. An Interview: Jean Renoir. (Green Integer Ser.: No. 6). 96p. 1998. pap. 9.95 (*1-55713-330-1*) Green Integer.

— My Life & My Films. Denny, Norman, tr. from FRE. (Quality Paperbacks Ser.). (Illus.). 287p. 1991. reprint ed. pap. 14.95 (*0-306-80457-3*, Pub. by Da Capo) HarpC.

— Pierre-Auguste Renoir, Mon Pere. (FRE.). 1981. pap. 13.95 (*0-7859-4151-7*) Fr & Eur.

***Renoir, Pierre-Auguste.** Renoir: 16 Art Stickers. (Illus.). (J). 1999. pap. 1.00 (*0-486-40605-9*) Dover.

— Renoir Paintings Cards. (Illus.). (J). 1997. pap. 1.00 (*0-486-29592-3*) Dover.

Renoir, Pierri Auguste. Renoir Lithographs: Thirty Two Works. LC 93-32998. (Illus.). 32p. 1993. pap. 3.95 (*0-486-27884-0*) Dover.

Renou, Louis. Civilization in Ancient India. Spratt, Philop, tr. (C). 1997. 29.50 (*81-215-0744-8*, Pub. by M Manoharial) Coronet Bks.

— Religions of Ancient India. 1972. 16.00 (*0-8364-2614-2*, Pub. by M Manoharial) S Asia.

Renou, M., jt. ed. see Van Mens-Verhulst, Janneke.

Renou, Philippe. Dictionnaire du Diabetique. (FRE.). 320p. 1991. 79.95 (*0-8288-9478-7*) Fr & Eur.

Renouard, A. A. Annales de L'Imprimerie des Estienne, 2 vols. (FRE.). 586p. 1998. reprint ed. 75.00 (*1-57898-112-3*) Martino Pubng.

Renouard, Frank & Rangert, Bo. Risk Factors & Implant Treatment: Clinical Assessment & Rationale. LC 99-19894. 1999. write for info. (*0-86715-355-5*) Quint Pub Co.

Renouard, H. Dictionary of Information Services & Technology, German-English/English-German. 2nd enl. rev. ed. (ENG & GER.). 400p. 1993. 175.00 (*0-7859-3719-6*, F140270) Fr & Eur.

— Imprimeurs et Libraires Parisiens Du XVIe Siecle. Incl. Tome I. Abada Avril. 135.00 Tome II. Baaleu Banville. 165.00 write for info. (*0-318-52031-1*) Fr & Eur.

— Repertoire Des Imprimeurs Parisiens, Libraires, Foundeurs De Caracteres et Correcteurs De l'Imprimerie Depius l'Introduction De l'Imprimerie (1470) Jusqu'a la Fin Du Xvie Siecle. 61.95 (*0-685-35952-2*) Fr & Eur.

Renouard, H. E. Dictionary of Electronic Media & Services. (GER.). 382p. 1997. 182.00 (*3-540-61766-3*, Pub. by Spr-Verlag) IBD Ltd.

Renouard, Horst. Dictionary of Electronic Media & Services, German/English-English/German. (ENG & GER.). 497p. 1997. 295.00 (*0-7859-9518-8*) Fr & Eur.

— Dictionary of Information Services & Technology, German-English/English-German. 3rd ed. (ENG & GER.). 400p. 1996. 195.00 (*0-7859-9531-5*) Fr & Eur.

***Renouard, Phillippe.** Bibliographie des Editions de Simon de Colines. fac. ed. 519p. 2000. 75.00 (*1-57898-200-6*) Martino Pubng.

Renouf, Antoinette, ed. Explorations in Corpus Linguistics. LC 98-222136. (Language & Computers Ser.: No. 23). 292p. 1998. 83.00 (*90-420-0751-6*) Editions Rodopi.

Renouf, Kathy, jt. auth. see Renouf, Norman.

Renouf, Nicholas. Jean-Philippe Rameau, 1683-1764: A Tercentenary Tribute: An Exhibition of Instruments by French Makers, Contemporary Graphics, Printed Music & Books. 10p. (Orig.). 1983. pap. 1.50 (*0-929530-03-9*) Yale U Coll Musical Instruments.

— Musical Instruments in the Viennese Tradition, 1750-1850: An Exhibition of Instruments by Austrian Makers with Supplementary Exhibits of Contemporary Graphics, Printed Music & Books. (Illus.). 32p. (Orig.). 1981. pap. 4.00 (*0-929530-02-0*) Yale U Coll Musical Instruments.

— A Yankee Lyre: Musical Instruments by American Makers: An Exhibition of Instruments by 19th-Century American Makers with Supplementary Exhibits of Graphics, Books & Furniture. (Illus.). 62p. (Orig.). 1985. pap. 5.00 (*0-929530-04-7*) Yale U Coll Musical Instruments.

Renouf, Nicholas & Rephann, Richard T. The Robyna Neilson Ketchum Collection of Bells. (Illus.). 28p. (Orig.). 1975. pap. 3.00 (*0-929530-00-4*) Yale U Coll Musical Instruments.

Renouf, Norman & Renouf, Kathy. Georgia & the Carolinas. (Adventure Guides Ser.). (Illus.). 256p. 1999. pap. 15.95 (*1-55650-854-9*) Hunter NJ.

Renouf, Norman, jt. auth. see Howard, Blair.

Renouf, Norman P. Daytrips Spain & Portugal: 50 One-Day Adventures by Car, Rail or Ferry. LC 96-79109. (Illus.). 300p. 1997. pap. text 14.95 (*0-8038-9389-2*) Hastings.

— Daytrips Switzerland: 45 One-Day Adventures by Rail, Bus & Car. (Illus.). 304p. 1999. pap. text 16.95 (*0-8038-9414-7*, Pub. by Hastings) Midpt Trade.

— Spain & Portugal by Rail. (Bradt Rail Guides Ser.). (Illus.). 326p. 1994. pap. 15.95 (*1-56440-553-2*, Pub. by Bradt Pubns) Globe Pequot.

***Renouf, Norman P. T.** Daytrips Spain & Portugal: 58 One Day Adventures by Rail, Bus or Car. 2nd ed. (Illus.). 368p. 2001. pap. 16.95 (*0-8038-2012-7*, Pub. by Hastings) Midpt Trade.

Renouf, Peter L. Lectures on the Origin & Growth of Religion As Illustrated by the Religion of Ancient Egypt. 2nd ed. LC 77-27171. (Hibbert Lectures: 1879). reprint ed. 39.00 (*0-404-60401-3*) AMS Pr.

Renouil, Yves & Traversay, Yves de. Dictionnaire du Vin.Tr. of Dictionary of Wine. (FRE.). 1962. 95.00 (*0-8288-6809-3*, M-6482) Fr & Eur.

Renouprez, A. J. & Jobic, H., eds. Catalysis by Metals: Course Held in Les Houches, 19-29 March 1996. LC 98-102266. xv, 214p. 1997. pap. 79.95 (*3-540-63708-7*) Spr-Verlag.

Renouvin, Pierre. Forms of War Government in France. (Economic & Social History of the World War Ser.). 1927. 100.00 (*0-685-69856-4*) Elliots Bks.

Renoux, Andre. Remembering Paris. (Illus.). 144p. 1999. 29.95 (*2-08-013659-3*) Abbeville Pr.

Renov, Michael. Hollywood's Wartime Woman: Representation & Ideology. LC 87-25546. (Studies in Cinema: No. 42). 285p. reprint ed. pap. 88.40 (*0-8357-1813-1*, 207063600011) Bks Demand.

Renov, Michael, ed. Theorizing Documentary. (AFI Film Readers Ser.). (Illus.). 256p. (C). 1993. pap. 21.99 (*0-415-90382-3*, A5181) Routledge.

Renov, Michael & Suderberg, Erika, eds. Resolutions: Contemporary Video Practices. 512p. 1995. pap. 21.95 (*0-8166-2330-9*); text 59.95 (*0-8166-2327-9*) U of Minn Pr.

Renov, Michael, jt. auth. see Gaines, J.

Renove, Norman. Romantic Weekends in Virginia, Washington DC & Maryland. 2nd ed. (Romantic Weekends Ser.). (Illus.). 408p. 1998. pap. 16.95 (*1-55650-835-2*) Hunter NJ.

***Renowden, Gareth.** The Olive Book. (Illus.). 114p. (Orig.). 1999. pap. 39.95 (*0-908812-80-9*, Pub. by Canterbury Univ) Accents Pubns.

Renpenning, Kathie M., jt. auth. see Allison, Sarah E.

***Renquist, Thomas A.** Topsy-Turvy Living in the Biblical World: Gospel Sermons for Sundays after Pentecost (Middle Third), Cycle C. LC 00-35801. 84p. 2000. pap. 8.95 (*0-7880-1737-3*); disk 8.95 (*0-7880-1738-1*) CSS OH.

Renquist, Thomas A. What Grace They Received: Worship Commemorations for 12 Ancient & Modern Saints. 1992. pap. 9.95 (*1-55673-567-7*, 9314) CSS OH.

***Renreng, Abdullah.** Introduction to Theoretical Physics. (Pure & Applied Physics Ser.). 2000. 89.95 (*0-8493-0816-X*) CRC Pr.

***Rens, Jean-Guy.** The Invisible Empire: A History of the Telecommunications Industry in Canada, 1846-1956. 320p. 2000. 49.95 (*0-7735-2052-X*, Pub. by McG-Queens Univ Pr) CUP Services.

Rens, Kevin L., ed. Forensic Engineering: Proceedings of the 1st Congress, Minneapolis, MN, October 5-8, 1997. LC 97-30968. (Illus.). 352p. 1997. pap. text 34.00 (*0-7844-0277-9*, 40277-9) Am Soc Civil Eng.

***Rens, Kevin L., et al.** Forensic Engineering: Proceedings of the Second Congress, May 21-23, 2000, San Juan, Puerto Rico. LC 00-26652. 2000. write for info. (*0-7844-0482-8*) Am Soc Civil Eng.

Rensalier, Dolores Van, see Alaya, Flavia & Van Rensalier, Dolores.

Rensbaw, Janet, jt. auth. see Lister, Ted.

Rensbergen, Johan Van, see D'Ydewalle, Gery & van Rensbergen, Johan, eds.

Rensberger, Boyce. Instant Biology: From Single Cells to Human Beings, & Beyond. (Illus.). 256p. 1996. pap. 10.00 (*0-449-90701-5*) Fawcett.

— Life Itself: Exploring the Realm of the Living Cell. LC 96-33679. (Illus.). 304p. 1997. 30.00 (*0-19-510874-4*) OUP.

— Life Itself: Exploring the Realm of the Living Cell. (Illus.). 304p. 1998. reprint ed. pap. 15.95 (*0-19-512500-2*) OUP.

Rensberger, David. Johannine Faith & Liberating Community. LC 88-10052. 168p. 1988. pap. 22.95 (*0-664-25041-6*) Westminster John Knox.

Rensberger, David K. 1 John, 2 John, 3 John. LC 97-14992. (Abingdon New Testament Commentaries Ser.). 176p. 1997. pap. 19.95 (*0-687-05722-1*) Abingdon.

Rensberger, John M. Successions of Meniscomyine & Allomyine Rodents (Aplodontidae) in the Oligo-Miocene John Day Formation, Oregon. LC 83-1403. (Publications in Geological Sciences: Vol. 124). 176p. (C). 1983. pap. 27.50 (*0-520-09668-1*, Pub. by U CA Pr) Cal Prin Full Svc.

Rensburg, B. G. Van, see Van Rensburg, B. G.

Rensburg, Chris Van, see Robertson, Thomas Dolby & Van Rensburg, Chris.

Rensburg, Ronel S. & Bredenkamp, Christian. Aspects of Business Communication. (Communicamus Ser.: Vol. 9). 125p. (C). 1994. reprint ed. text 29.00 (*0-7021-2488-5*, Pub. by Juta & Co) Intl Spec Bk.

Rensburg, Sally Van, see Van Rensburg, Sally.

Rensch, Bernhard. Biophilosophy. Sym, Cecilia, tr. from GER. LC 72-132692. 1971. 61.00 (*0-231-03299-4*) Col U Pr.

Rensch, Hero E. Historic Spots in California, 2 vols., Set. 1992. reprint ed. lib. bdg. 180.00 (*0-7812-5077-3*) Rprt Serv.

Rensch, Joseph R., ed. Papers of the Eighth International Conference on Liquefied Natural Gas: Los Angeles, U. S. A., June 15-19, 1986, 2 vols., Set. 768p. 1986. pap. 85.00 (*0-910091-59-5*) Inst Gas Tech.

Rensch, Roslyn. Harps & Harpists. LC 88-37609. (Illus.). 344p. 1998. pap. 29.95 (*0-253-21209-X*) Ind U Pr.

Rensel, Jan & Rodman, Margaret, eds. Home in the Islands: Housing & Social Change in the Pacific. LC 97-789. 1997. pap. text 24.95 (*0-8248-1934-9*) UH Pr.

— Home in the Islands: Housing & Social Change in the Pacific. LC 97-789. (Illus.). 288p. 1997. text 39.00 (*0-8248-1682-X*, Kolowalu Bk) UH Pr.

Rensenbrink, John. Against All Odds: The Green Transformation of American Politics. LC 99-19472. 256p. 1999. pap. 19.95 (*0-9660629-1-4*) Leopold Pr.

— Poland Challenges a Divided World. LC 88-1393. 256p. 1988. text 35.00 (*0-8071-1446-4*) La State U Pr.

Renshall, Michael. Mametz Wood: Somme. (Battleground Europe Ser.). 1999. pap. text 16.95 (*0-85052-664-7*) Leo Cooper.

Renshall, Michael & Walmsley, Keith, eds. Butterworths Company Law Guide. 2nd ed. 560p. 1990. pap. 49.00 (*0-406-19702-4*, UK, MICHIE) LEXIS Pub.

Renshaw, Betty, jt. auth. see Hacker, Diana.

Renshaw, Betty B., et al. Values & Voices: A College Reader. 3rd ed. 372p. (C). 1986. pap. text 20.75 (*0-03-071039-1*) Harcourt Coll Pubs.

***Renshaw, Camille.** Best of Pif Magazine: Off-Line. 150p. 1999. pap. write for info. (*1-928704-75-1*) Authorlink.

Renshaw, Clarence. Hayes, Seay, Mattern & Mattern - Fifty Years of Form & Function. (Illus.). 96p. 1998. pap. 19.95 (*0-9666185-0-5*) HSMM Inc.

Renshaw, Corinne. The Hand of Aquila Possett. 2nd ed. 143p. (J). (gr. 4). 1996. reprint ed. pap. 13.95 (*0-8464-4816-5*) Beekman Pubs.

— The Sunhouse & Other Stories. 103p. 1996. pap. 17.95 (*0-8464-4624-3*) Beekman Pubs.

Renshaw, Domeena. Seven Weeks to Better Sex. 1995. write for info. (*0-614-32212-X*) Random.

An Asterisk (*) at the beginning of an entry indicates that the title is appearing for the first time.

Renshaw, Domeena C. Incest: Understanding & Treatment. 1982. 38.95 (*0-316-74031-4*, Little Brwn Med Div) Lppncott W & W.

Renshaw, Eric, ed. Modelling Biological Populations in Space & Time. (Cambridge Studies in Mathematical Biology: No. 11). 421p. (C). 1993. pap. text 35.95 (*0-521-44855-7*) Cambridge U Pr.

Renshaw, Geoffrey T. Adjustment & Economic Performance in Industrialized Countries: A Synthesis. (Employment, Adjustment & Industrialisation Ser.: No. 8). xiii, 110p. (Orig.). 1986. 36.00 (*92-2-105509-4*); pap. 27.00 (*92-2-105510-8*) Intl Labour Office.

Renshaw, Geoffrey T., ed. Employment, Trade & North-South Co-Operation: (A WEP Study) xiv, 263p. (Orig.). 1981. pap. 24.75 (*92-2-102531-4*) Intl Labour Office.

— Market Liberalisation, Equity & Development. xiv, 181p. 1989. pap. 22.50 (*92-2-106397-6*) Intl Labour Office.

Renshaw, J., et al. Care in the Community: The First Steps. 201p. 1988. text 64.95 (*0-566-05737-9*, Pub. by Avebry) Ashgate Pub Co.

Renshaw, Janet, jt. auth. see Lister, Ted.

Renshaw, Jean R. Kimono in the Boardroom: The Invisible Evolution of Japanese Women Managers. LC 98-3075. (Illus.). 304p. 1999. 35.00 (*0-19-511765-4*) OUP.

Renshaw, Jeffrey H. The American Wind Symphony Commissioning Project: A Descriptive Catalog of Published Editions 1957-1991, 34. LC 91-30220. (Music Reference Collection: No. 34). 408p. 1991. lib. bdg. 75.00 (*0-313-28146-7*, RWY/, Greenwood Pr) Greenwood.

Renshaw, Joyce. Teaching Children to Read Art. Renshaw, Ken, ed. LC 94-21286. (Illus.). 115p. (Orig.). 1992. pap. 16.50 (*0-9616620-8-5*) Constellation Pr.

Renshaw, Joyce & Renshaw, Ken. Easy K-5 DBAE Art Lesson Plans for Teachers & Parents-Docents. (Illus.). 128p. 1999. pap. 22.00 (*0-9616620-6-9*) Constellation Pr.

Renshaw, Joyce, jt. auth. see Renshaw, Ken.

Renshaw, Ken & Renshaw, Joyce. Teaching Children the Love of Art: Step-by-Step DBAE Lessons. (Illus.). 102p. 1998. pap. 20.00 (*0-9616620-7-7*) Constellation Pr.

Renshaw, Ken, jt. auth. see Renshaw, Joyce.

Renshaw, Ken, ed. see Renshaw, Joyce.

Renshaw, Martin, jt. auth. see Barnes, Alan.

Renshaw, Patrick. American Labor & Consensus Capitalism, 1935-1990. LC 91-13034. 258p. 1992. text 38.50 (*0-87805-536-3*); pap. text 16.95 (*0-87805-537-1*) U Pr of Miss.

— The Longman Companion to America: From Wilson to Roosevelt, 1910-45. Cook, Chris & Stevenson, John, eds. LC 95-23386. (Longman Companions to History Ser.). 256p. (C). 1995. text 55.00 (*0-582-09116-0*, Pub. by Addison-Wesley) Longman.

— The Wobblies: The Story of the IWW & Syndicalism in the United States. LC 99-32039. 264p. 1999. pap. 14.95 (*1-56663-273-0*, Pub. by I R Dee) Natl Bk Netwk.

Renshaw, Polly & Levens, Ann. Teacher's Guide for Uncle Noel's Fun Fables. (Illus.). 52p. 1991. student ed. 5.95 (*0-9630734-1-9*) Aesop Systs.

Renshaw, Samuel, et al. Children's Sleep: A Series of Studies on the Influence of Motion Pictures. LC 76-124031. (Literature of Cinema Ser.). 1970. reprint ed. 21.95 (*0-405-01631-X*) Ayer.

Renshaw, Vernon, et al. Nebraska Population Projections: State, County, Region & Town, 1975-2020. 232p. (Orig.). 1973. pap. 14.00 (*1-55719-111-5*) U NE CPAR.

Renshon, Stanley A. High Hopes: The Clinton Presidency & the Politics of Ambition. 402p. (C). 1996. text 45.00 (*0-8147-7463-6*) NYU Pr.

— High Hopes: The Clinton Presidency & the Politics of Ambition. 416p. 1998. reprint ed. pap. 17.99 (*0-415-92147-3*) Routledge.

— The Political Psychology of the Gulf War: Leaders, Publics, & the Process of Conflict. LC 92-34182. (Series in Policy & Institutional Studies). 408p. (C). 1993. pap. 22.95 (*0-8229-5495-8*); text 49.95 (*0-8229-3744-1*) U of Pittsburgh Pr.

— The Psychological Assessment of Presidential Candidates. 496p. (C). 1996. text 45.00 (*0-8147-7469-5*) NYU Pr.

— The Psychological Assessment of Presidential Candidates. LC 98-11839. 528p. (C). 1998. reprint ed. pap. 24.99 (*0-415-92146-5*) Routledge.

Renshon, Stanley A. & Duckitt, J. H. Political Psychology: Cultural & Cross-Cultural Foundations. LC 99-26248. 2000. pap. text 22.50 (*0-8147-7537-3*) NYU Pr.

***Renshon, Stanley A. & Duckitt, John, eds.** Political Psychology: Cultural & Cross-Cultural Foundations. LC 99-26248. 400p. 2000. text 65.00 (*0-8147-7536-5*) NYU Pr.

Renshow, Linda, ed. see Jerman, Patricia L.

Rensi, Ray C. & Williams, H. David. Gold Fever: America's First Gold Rush. (Georgia Humanities Council Publications). (Illus.). 54p. 1991. pap. 9.95 (*0-8203-1314-9*) U of Ga Pr.

Rensick, Lauren B., jt. ed. see Wirt, John G.

Rensin, David, jt. auth. see Brillstein, Bernie.

Rensin, David K., et al. SQL Server 7 Secrets. LC 99-30646. 744p. 1999. 49.99 (*0-7645-3245-6*) IDG Bks.

Rensing, L. & Jaeger, N. I., eds. Temporal Order. (Synergetics Ser.: Vol. 29). (Illus.). ix, 325p. 1985. 80.95 (*0-387-15274-1*) Spr-Verlag.

Rensing, L. & Mackey, M. C., eds. Temporal Disorder in Human Oscillatory Systems. (Synergetics Ser.: Vol. 36). (Illus.). 270p. 1987. 79.95 (*0-387-17765-5*) Spr-Verlag.

Rensselaer, Alexander Van, see Van Rensselaer, Alexander.

Rensselaer Dey, Frederic Van, see Van Rensselaer Dey, Frederic.

Rensselaer, John K. Van, see Van Rensselaer, John K.

Rensselaer, Mariana Van, see Van Rensselaer, Mariana.

Renstrom, Mary. Legislative Television Programming in the States. (State Legislative Reports: Vol. 17, No. 13). 16p. 1992. pap. text 15.00 (*1-55516-284-3*, 7302-1713) Natl Conf State Legis.

— Public Information & Media Relations in State Legislatures. (State Legislative Reports: Vol. 17, No. 22). 29p. 1992. pap. text 15.00 (*1-55516-295-9*, 7302-1722) Natl Conf State Legis.

Renstrom, Peter G. The American Law Dictionary. LC 90-24114. (Clio Dictionaries in Political Science Ser.). 308p. 1990. lib. bdg. 52.00 (*0-87436-226-1*) ABC-CLIO.

— Constitutional Law & Young Adults. 2nd ed. LC 96-28831. 497p. 1996. 55.00 (*0-87436-850-2*) ABC-CLIO.

— Constitutional Law for Young Adults: A Handbook on the Bill of Rights & the Fourteenth Amendment. LC 91-47990. 413p. 1992. lib. bdg. 35.00 (*0-87436-483-3*) ABC-CLIO.

— Constitutional Rights Sourcebook. LC 99-13197. 770p. (YA). (gr. 10 up). 1999. lib. bdg. 75.00 (*1-57607-061-1*) ABC-CLIO.

***Renstrom, Peter G.** The Stone Court: Justices, Rulings, & Legacy. 2001. lib. bdg. 60.00 (*1-57607-153-7*) ABC-CLIO.

Renstrom, Peter G. & Rogers, Chester B. Electoral Politics Dictionary. LC 88-34440. 350p. 1989. pap. text 20.50 (*0-87436-518-X*) ABC-CLIO.

— Electoral Politics Dictionary. LC 88-34440. 350p. 1989. lib. bdg. 49.00 (*0-87436-517-1*) ABC-CLIO.

Renstrom, Richard. Motorcycle Milestones, Vol. 1. LC 80-66669. (Illus.). 112p. 1980. 20.00 (*0-936660-00-7*) Classics Unltd.

Rensvold, Sandy. A Ride on the Historical Virginia V. (J). (gr. 2-3). 1995. pap. text 7.95 (*0-9647088-0-9*) Keeper Bks.

Rentel, Victor, et al. Psychophysiological Aspects of Reading & Learning. (Monographs in Psychobiology). xx, 352p. 1985. text 174.00 (*2-88124-000-3*); pap. text 83.00 (*2-88124-025-9*) Gordon & Breach.

***Rentel, Victor M. & Dittmer, Allan, eds.** Themes & Issues in Faculty Development: Case Studies in Innovative Practice in Teacher Education. LC 99-40356. 240p. 1999. 57.00 (*0-7618-1514-7*); pap. 34.50 (*0-7618-1513-9*) U Pr of Amer.

Renteln, Alison D. International Human Rights: Universalism vs. Relativism. (Frontiers of Anthropology Ser.: Vol. 6). 208p. (C). 1990. text 52.00 (*0-8039-3505-6*); pap. text 25.00 (*0-8039-3506-4*) Sage.

Renteln, Alison D. & Dundes, Alan, eds. Folk Law: Essays in the Theory & Practice of Lex Non Scripta. LC 93-29340. (Folklore Casebks.: Vol. 7). 1072p. 1994. text 176.00 (*0-8153-1314-4*, H1715) Garland.

— Folk Law: Essays in the Theory & Practice of Lex Non Scripta. LC 94-812. 1994. pap. 39.95 (*0-299-14344-9*) U of Wis Pr.

Renter, Bertha. The Courage to Rise Again: A Journey from Tears to Testimony. 233p. 1999. pap. 15.95 (*0-7414-0052-9*) Buy Books.

Renterghem, Omer Van, see Roos, Wilma & Van Renterghem, Omer.

Renteria, Tamis H. Chicano Professionals: Culture, Conflict, & Identity. LC 97-35336. (Latino Communities Ser.). 200p. 1998. 50.00 (*0-8153-3093-6*) Garland.

Renteros, Exora. Pensar Es un Pecado. LC 93-74793. (Coleccion Caniqui). 198p. 1994. pap. 16.00 (*0-89729-720-2*) Ediciones.

***Rentfro, Anne R. & McCampbell, Linda.** Nursing Care of Infants & Children. 6th ed. 352p. (C). 1998. text, student ed. write for info. (*0-323-00104-1*) Mosby Inc.

Rentfrow, David J. Yo! Dudes! Dudettes! You Got a Call! 130p. (Orig.). 1995. pap. write for info. (*1-57502-069-6*) Morris Pubng.

Rentfrow, Stephen M. Stevie Ray's Medium-Sized Book of Comedy: What We Laugh at... & Why. v, 287p. 1999. pap. 12.95 (*0-9671786-0-6*) Punchline Pubns.

Rentiis, Dina De, see Zimmermann, Margarete & De Rentiis, Dina, eds.

Rentmeister, Jean. Marriage & Death Notices Extracted from the Genius of Liberty & Fayette Advertiser of Uniontown, Pa., 1805-1854. 52p. 1981. per. 8.50 (*0-933227-41-8*, 244) Closson Pr.

Renton, Andrew. Technique Anglaise: Current Trends in British Art. LC 91-65285. (Illus.). 224p. (Orig.). 1991. pap. 19.95 (*0-500-97396-2*, Pub. by Thames Hudson) Norton.

Renton, B. Andrew. Psyched on Bikes: The Bicycle Owner's Handbook. 184p. 1992. pap. 14.95 (*0-8306-1987-9*, 3668) McGraw-Hill Prof.

Renton, Dave. Fascism: Theory & Practice. LC 98-53606. 160p. 1999. 59.95 (*0-7453-1475-9*, Pub. by Pluto GBR) Stylus Pub VA.

***Renton, Dave.** Fascism: Theory & Practice. LC 98-53606. 160p. 1999. pap. 16.95 (*0-7453-1470-8*, Pub. by Pluto GBR) Stylus Pub VA.

— Fascism, Anti-fascism & Britain in the 1940s. LC 99-15878. 1999. text 65.00 (*0-312-22501-6*) St Martin.

Renton, J. D. Applied Elasticity: Matrix & Tensor Analysis of Elastic Continua. (Mechanical Engineering Ser.). 1987. text 67.95 (*0-470-20878-3*) P-H.

Renton, Jeanne L., jt. auth. see Eble, Mary M.

Renton, John. Physical Geology. Date not set. pap. text, teacher ed. write for info. (*0-314-03403-X*) West Pub.

— Physical Geology: Testbank. Date not set. pap. text, suppl. ed. write for info. (*0-314-03228-2*) West Pub.

Renton, N. E. Guide for Meetings. 5th ed. xxiii, 225p. 1990. pap. 19.50 (*0-455-21004-7*, Pub. by LawBk Co) Gaunt.

— Guide for Voluntary Associations. 5th ed. xix, 237p. 1991. pap. 19.50 (*0-455-21001-2*, Pub. by LawBk Co) Gaunt.

— Metaphorically Speaking: A Dictionary of 3,800 Picturesque Idiomatic Expressions. 1992. reprint ed. mass mkt. 11.99 (*0-446-39353-3*, Pub. by Warner Bks) Little.

Renton, R., jt. auth. see MacDonald, J.

Renton, R. W. & MacDonald, J. A. Scottish Gaelic-English - English-Scottish Gaelic Dictionary. 162p. (Orig.). 1994. pap. 8.95 (*0-7818-0316-0*) Hippocrene Bks.

***Rentsch, Walt.** The Angler Poet. 158p. 1999. pap. 14.95 (*0-7392-0413-0*) Morris Pubng.

***Rentschiler, William H.** Goldwater: Conservative Icon of Integrity. (Illus.). 224p. 2000. 18.95 (*0-8092-9556-3*, Contemporary Bks) NTC Contemp Pub Co.

Rentschler, Bill. Live Each New Day. 1991. pap. 8.95 (*0-913617-14-8*) Highlander Pr.

Rentschler, Bill, jt. auth. see Hale, Jon M.

Rentschler, Eric. The Ministry of Illusion: Nazi Cinema & Its Afterlife. LC 96-11731. (Illus.). 480p. 1996. 62.50 (*0-674-57639-X*); pap. 26.00 (*0-674-57640-3*) HUP.

Rentschler, Eric, ed. The Films of G. W. Pabst. (Films in Print Ser.). (Illus.). 350p. (C). 1990. pap. 17.95 (*0-8135-1534-3*) Rutgers U Pr.

— German Film & Literature: Adaptations & Transformations. (Illus.). 384p. 1986. lib. bdg. 45.00 (*0-416-60331-9*, 9885) Routledge.

— German Film & Literature: Adaptations & Transformations. (Illus.). 384p. (C). 1986. pap. 24.99 (*0-416-60341-6*, 9866) Routledge.

— West German Filmmakers on Film: Visions & Voices. LC 87-14856. (Modern German Voices Ser.). 300p. 1988. 49.00 (*0-8419-0984-9*); pap. 22.50 (*0-8419-0985-7*) Holmes & Meier.

Rentschler, Evan, et al. The Compleat Baseball Advocate, 1995. 325p. 1995. pap. 15.95 (*0-9635768-2-8*) CBPS Pub.

Rentschler, I. & Epstein, D. Beauty & the Brain. 250p. 1988. 79.00 (*0-8176-1924-0*) Birkhauser.

Rentschler, L. A. Jitters: A Novel about Pre-Marital Stress. 288p. 1995. pap. 12.95 (*0-9640583-0-8*) White Willow.

— Jitters-Display. 1997. 64.75 (*0-9640583-1-6*) White Willow.

Rentschler, Ray. A Guide to Personal Defense. 96p. 1997. pap. 9.95 (*1-57502-624-4*, PO1780) Morris Pubng.

***Rentschler, Ruth, ed.** Innovative Arts Marketing. (Illus.). 2000. pap. 35.00 (*1-86448-993-6*, Pub. by Allen & Unwin Pty) Paul & Co Pubs.

Renty, Ivan de. Lexique Quadrilingue des Affaires (ENG, FRE, GER & SPA.). 702p. 1977. 59.95 (*0-8288-5497-1*, M6483) Fr & Eur.

Renty, Ivan De, see De Renty, Ivan.

Rentz, Audrey L. Student Affairs Practice in Higher Education. 2nd ed. Orig. Title: Student Affairs Functions in Higher Education. (Illus.). 426p. 1996. pap. 57.95 (*0-398-06675-2*) C C Thomas.

Rentz, Audrey L., ed. Student Affairs: A Profession's Heritage. 2nd ed. LC 94-19521. 782p. (C). 1995. pap. text 44.50 (*1-883485-06-1*) Am Coll Personnel.

— Student Affairs: A Profession's Heritage. 28th ed. LC 94-19521. 782p. (C). 1994. lib. bdg. 75.00 (*1-883485-05-3*) Am Coll Personnel.

— Student Affairs Practice in Higher Education. 2nd rev. ed. LC 96-12918. Orig. Title: Student Affairs Functions in Higher Education. (Illus.). 426p. 1996. 73.95 (*0-398-06658-2*) C C Thomas.

Rentz, Bill. Geronimo! U. S. Airborne Uniforms, Insignia & Equipment in World War II. LC 98-86443. (Illus.). 1999. 59.95 (*0-7643-0677-4*) Schiffer.

Rentz, D. C. A Monograph of the Tettigoniidae of Australia Vol. 1: The Tettigoniinae, with an Appendix by D. H. Colles. (Illus.). 384p. 1985. lib. bdg. 70.00 (*0-685-25035-0*) Lubrecht & Cramer.

— The Tettigoniidae, Vol. 1. 384p. 1985. text 80.00 (*0-643-03839-6*, Pub. by CSIRO) Accents Pubns.

— Tettigoniidae of Australia Vol. 2: The Austrosaginae, Zaprochilinae & Phasmodinae. (Illus.). 386p. 1993. text 80.00 (*0-643-05424-3*, Pub. by CSIRO) Accents Pubns.

Rentz, David C. & Weissman, David B. Faunal Affinities, Systematics, & Bionomics of the Orthoptera of the California Channel Islands. LC 80-26399. (University of California Publications in Social Welfare: No. 94). (Illus.). 254p. reprint ed. pap. 78.80 (*0-608-18313-X*, 203158500075) Bks Demand.

Rentz, John N. Bougainville & the Northern Solomons. (Elite Unit Ser.: No. 22). (Illus.). 166p. reprint ed. 39.95 (*0-89839-137-7*) Battery Pr.

— Marines in the Central Solomons. (Elite Unit Ser.: No. 24). (Illus.). 216p. 1989. reprint ed. 39.95 (*0-89839-143-1*) Battery Pr.

Rentz, Lisa T., jt. auth. see Mullen, Denise.

Rentz, Mark D. The Reader's Journal: Authentic Reading for Writers. 272p. (C). 1992. pap. text 28.60 (*0-13-755273-4*) P-H.

Rentz, Otto, et al. Joint Implementation in Deutschland: Stand & Perspektiven aus Sicht von Politik, Industrie & Forschung. (GER., Illus.). 162p. 1996. 32.95 (*3-631-30872-8*) P Lang Pubng.

Rentzch, H. German & English Electric Motor Handbook. (ENG & GER.). 861p. 1992. 85.00 (*0-7859-8899-8*) Fr & Eur.

Rentzel, Lori, jt. auth. see Davies, Bob.

Rentzepis, P. M., jt. auth. see Helliwell, John R.

Rentzepis, Peter M. & Capellos, Christos, eds. Advances in Chemical Reaction Dynamics. 1986. text 261.50 (*90-277-2312-5*) Kluwer Academic.

Rentzsch, H. German & English Electric Motor Handbook. 861p. 1992. 116.00 (*3-590-80853-5*, Pub. by Cornelsen) IBD Ltd.

Rentzsch, S. B. Electronics Terms: German & English. (GER.). 861p. 1992. 49.95 (*0-8288-1377-9*, M15121) Fr & Eur.

Renu, Ma, ed. see Baba Hari Dass.

Renu, Ma, ed. & frwd. see Baba Hari Dass.

Renu, Phanishwar N. The Third Vow & Other Stories. Hansen, Kathryn, tr. 1986. 18.50 (*81-7001-013-6*, Pub. by Chanakya) S Asia.

— The Third Vow & Other Stories. (C). 1996. pap. 11.00 (*81-7001-105-1*, Pub. by Chanakya) S Asia.

Renugopalakrishnan. Proteins. 423p. 1991. text 245.00 (*90-72199-09-X*) Kluwer Academic.

Renversez, F. Dictionnaire Encyclopedique Economique. (FRE.). 1998. 39.95 (*0-320-00357-4*) Fr & Eur.

Renvoize, Jean. Incest: A Family Pattern. 224p. 1985. pap. 11.95 (*0-7102-0681-X*, Routledge Thoemms) Routledge.

— Innocence Destroyed: A Study of Child Sexual Abuse. LC 92-49994. 196p. (C). 1993. pap. 24.99 (*0-415-06284-5*, B0232) Routledge.

Renvoize, S. A. Gramineas de Bolivia. (SPA., Illus.). 642p. 1998. pap. 96.00 (*1-900347-38-5*, Pub. by Royal Botnic Grdns) Balogh.

— The Grasses of Bahia. 301p. 1984. pap. 22.00 (*0-947643-00-1*, Pub. by Royal Botnic Grdns) Balogh.

— Hatschbach's Parana Grasses. 76p. 1988. pap. 17.00 (*0-947643-06-0*, Pub. by Royal Botnic Grdns) Balogh.

Renwick. Americas Identity. LC 99-11252. 2000. text 69.95 (*0-312-22322-6*) St Martin.

Renwick, jt. auth. see Bergman.

Renwick, Andrew, jt. auth. see Waller, Derek.

Renwick, David. One Foot in the Grave: The Basis of a British Comedy. large type ed. 21.95 (*1-85695-361-0*, Pub. by ISIS Lrg Prnt) Transaction Pubs.

Renwick, E. S. Thermostatic Incubator: Raising Chickens by Hand. 98p. pap. 15.00 (*0-87556-360-0*) Saifer.

Renwick, E. S. Thermostatic Incubator: Raising Chickens by Hand. 98p. 1996. pap. 25.00 (*0-87556-756-8*) Saifer.

Renwick, George W. A Fair Go for All: Australian & American Interactions. LC 91-9628. (InterAct Ser.). 96p. (Orig.). 1991. pap. text 11.95 (*0-933662-96-3*) Intercult Pr.

Renwick, James. Life of David Rittenhouse. 1993. reprint ed. lib. bdg. 89.00 (*0-7812-5822-7*) Rprt Serv.

Renwick, John. Language Rhetoric: Rhetoric & the Revolution. 160p. 1990. 60.00 (*0-7486-0122-8*, Pub. by Edinburgh U Pr) Col U Pr.

— Three Guns for Guadla. large type ed. (Dales Large Print Ser.). 195p. 1997. pap. 18.99 (*1-85389-687-X*) Ulverscroft.

Renwick, Neil. Japan's Alliance Politics & Defense Production. LC 95-577. 256p. 1995. text 55.00 (*0-312-12675-1*) St Martin.

Renwick, Neil, jt. auth. see Krause, Jill.

Renwick, Rebecca, et al. Quality of Life in Health Promotion & Rehabilitation: Conceptual Approaches, Issues, & Applications. LC 95-41770. (Illus.). 320p. 1996. 58.00 (*0-8039-5913-3*); pap. 26.95 (*0-8039-5914-1*) Sage.

Renwick, Robin. Unconventional Diplomacy. LC 96-32086. 176p. 1997. text 45.00 (*0-312-16533-1*) St Martin.

Renwick, Trudi J. Poverty & Single Parent Families. rev. ed. LC 98-8511. (Children of Poverty Ser.). (Illus.). 156p. 1998. 40.00 (*0-8153-3172-X*) Garland.

Renwick, W. M. The Accounting Equation. 1991. pap. 21.00 (*0-409-49283-3*, Austral, MICHIE) LEXIS Pub.

Renwick, Whitney, jt. ed. see Heyen, Chris.

Renwick, William. Analyzing Fugue: A Schenkerian Approach. LC 94-47622. (Harmonologia Ser.: No. 8). 1995. 58.00 (*0-945193-52-1*) Pendragon NY.

***Renwick, William.** The Langloz Manuscript: Fugal Improvisation Through Figured Bass. (Early Music Ser.). (Illus.). 208p. 2001. text 72.00 (*0-19-816729-6*) OUP.

Renwick, William, jt. auth. see Cutter, Susan L.

Renwick, William L. The Beginnings of English Literature to Skelton, Fifteen Nine. 1988. reprint ed. lib. bdg. 69.00 (*0-7812-0190-X*) Rprt Serv.

— Burns As Others Saw Him. 52p. 1982. 30.00 (*0-7855-7318-6*, 085411015, Pub. by Saltire Soc) St Mut.

— Edmund Spenser: An Essay on Renaissance Poetry. (BCL1-PR English Literature Ser.). 198p. 1992. reprint ed. lib. bdg. 69.00 (*0-7812-7228-9*) Rprt Serv.

Renwick, William L., ed. see Spenser, Edmund.

Reny, Philip J., jt. auth. see Jehle, Geoffrey Alexander.

Renyi, Alfred. Foundations of Probability. LC 72-105221. 366p. 1970. 44.00 (*0-8162-7114-3*) Holden-Day.

Renyi, Judith. Going Public: Schooling for a Diverse Democracy. LC 92-56918. 304p. 1994. 25.00 (*1-56584-083-6*, Pub. by New Press NY) Norton.

Renyi, Pierre & Amrouni, Dominique. English - French Dictionary of Electronics & Electrical Engineering: Dictionnaire Anglais-Francais De l'Electronique et De l'Electrotechnique. (ENG & FRE.). 1122p. 1986. 125.00 (*0-8288-0282-3*, F12765) Fr & Eur.

Renyi, Pierre & Langenscheidt Staff. Langenscheidt Picture Dictionary. (ENG & GER., Illus.). 190p. (J). (gr. 4-7). 1993. 19.95 (*0-88729-852-4*); pap. 14.95 (*0-88729-858-3*) Langenscheidt.

Renyi-Vamos, F. & Balogh, F. Pyelonephritis. 190p. (C). 1979. 55.00 (*963-05-1724-8*, Pub. by Akade Kiado) St Mut.

Renyl, Pierre & Amroundi, Dominique. Dictionary of Electronics & Electrical Engineering: English-French. (ENG & FRE., Illus.). 1130p. 1986. 715.00 (*0-921137-01-X*, Pub. by Edits Technip) Enfield Pubs NH.

Renyolds, Adrian, jt. illus. see Grindley, Sally.

Renz, Mark. Fossiling in Florida: A Guide for Diggers & Divers. LC 99-17917. (Illus.). 1999. pap. 19.95 (*0-8130-1677-0*) U Press Fla.

Renz, C. J., ed. Ruah, 1995, Vol. 5. 28p. 1995. 5.00 (*1-883734-06-1*) Power of Poetry.

Renz, C. J., et al, eds. Ruah Vol. IX: A Journal of Spiritual Poetry. (Illus.). 70p. 1999. 10.00 (*1-883734-09-6*) Power of Poetry.

Renz, C. J. & Thielen, Gregory, eds. Ruah: A Journal of Spiritual Poetry. (Illus.). 70p. 1998. 10.00 (*1-883734-08-8*) Power of Poetry.

An Asterisk (*) at the beginning of an entry indicates that the title is appearing for the first time.

— Ruah. 1997. (Ruah: Vol. VII). (Orig.). 1997. pap. 5.00 (*1-883734-07-X*) Power of Poetry.

Renz, Chris, ed. Ruah, 1993, Vol. 3. 44p. 1993. pap. 5.00 (*1-883734-04-5*) Power of Poetry.

Renz, Loren & Massarsky, Cynthia W. Program-Related Investments: A Guide to Funders & Trends. 189p. 1995. 45.00 (*0-87954-558-5*, PRI) Foundation Ctr.

Renz, Loren, ed. see Foundation Center Staff.

Renz, Loren, ed. see Greenberg, Barbara R., et al.

Renz, Loren, ed. see Jacobs, Nancy F. & Sommers, Ira B.

Renz, Mary Ann & Greg, John B. Effective Small Group Communication in Theory & Practice. LC 99-26149. 342p. (C). 1999. pap. text 45.33 (*0-205-28201-6*, Macmillan Coll) P-H.

Renz, Michael E. Practical Groundwater Hydrology. 1995. 49.95 (*0-87371-643-4*, L643) Lewis Pubs.

Renza, Louis A. A "White Heron" & the Question of Minor Literature. LC 84-40157. (Wisconsin Project on American Writers Ser.: No. 1). 256p. 1984. text 25.00 (*0-299-09960-1*) U of Wis Pr.

— White Heron & the Question of Minor Literature. LC 84-40157. (Wisconsin Project on American Writers Ser.: No. 1). 256p. 1985. pap. text 12.95 (*0-299-09964-4*) U of Wis Pr.

Renza, Louis A., ed. see Jewett, Sarah Orne.

Renzelli, Gastone. 3 Layer Architecture for Business. text. write for info. (*0-471-48930-1*) Wiley.

Renzenbrink, Udo. Diet & Cancer. pap. 11.95 (*0-85440-766-9*, 415, Pub. by R Steiner Pr) Anthroposophic.

Renzetti. Living Sociology & Study Guide, 2 bks. 1998. text, student ed. 77.00 (*0-205-28841-3*) Allyn.

***Renzetti.** Living Sociology with Interactive Companion Cd-rom. 2nd ed. 1999. pap., suppl. ed. 19.00 (*0-205-31765-0*) Allyn.

Renzetti & Curran. Telecourse: Living Sociology. 1998. pap. text, student ed. write for info. (*0-205-29655-6*) Allyn.

— Women Men & Society. 4th ed. 450p. 1998. pap. text 44.00 (*0-205-26562-6*, Longwood Div) Allyn.

Renzetti, jt. auth. see Curran.

Renzetti & Curran. Living Sociology. 2nd ed. LC 99-45958. 645p. 1999. 70.00 incl. cd-rom (*0-205-30910-0*) Allyn.

Renzetti, Claire M. Violent Betrayal: Partner Abuse in Lesbian Relationships. 168p. (C). 1992. text 58.00 (*0-8039-3888-8*); pap. text 24.50 (*0-8039-3889-6*) Sage.

Renzetti, Claire M. & Curran, Daniel J. Living Sociology. LC 97-44354. 736p. 1997. 70.00 (*0-205-15144-2*) P-H.

— Women, Men, & Society: The Sociology of Gender. 400p. 1989. pap. text. write for info. (*0-205-11898-4*, H18989) Allyn.

Renzetti, Claire M. & Lee, Raymond M. Researching Sensitive Topics. (Focus Editions Ser.: Vol. 152). (Illus.). 312p. (C). 1992. 59.95 (*0-8039-4844-1*); pap. 26.00 (*0-8039-4845-X*) Sage.

Renzetti, Claire M. & Miley, Charles H., eds. Violence in Gay & Lesbian Domestic Partnerships. LC 95-52579. (Journal of Gay & Lesbian Social Services: Vol. 4, No. 1). 144p. 1996. 29.95 (*1-56024-753-3*); pap. 12.95 (*1-56023-074-6*, Harrington Park) Haworth Pr.

Renzetti, Claire M., jt. auth. see Curran, Daniel J.

Renzetti, Claire M., jt. ed. see Hamberger, L. Kevin.

Renzey, Fred. Blackjack Bluebook: The Right Stuff for the Serious Player. 2nd ed. 184p. 1997. pap. 14.00 (*1-886094-69-1*) Chicago Spectrum.

Renzglia, Karen S. Comparative Developmental Investigation of the Gametophyte Generation in the Metzgeriales (Hepatophyta) (Bryophytorum Bibliotheca Ser.: Vol. 24). (Illus.). 253p. (Orig.). 1982. text 84.00 (*3-7682-1336-6*) Lubrecht & Cramer.

Renzi, Thomas C. Jules Verne on Film: A Filmography of the Cinematic Adaptations of His Works, 1902-1997. LC 97-48528. (Illus.). 244p. 1998. lib. bdg. 55.00 (*0-7864-0450-7*) McFarland & Co.

— The Rhetorical Function of the Book of Ezekiel LC 99-19921. 1999. write for info. (*90-04-11362-2*) Brill Academic Pubs.

Renzi, William A. & Roehrs, Mark D. Never Look Back: A History of World War II in the Pacific. LC 90-25884. 240p. (gr. 13). 1991. 47.95 (*0-87332-808-6*) M E Sharpe.

Renzini, Alvio. Physical Processes in Red Giants. Iben, Icko, Jr., ed. xviii, 488p. 1981. text 176.50 (*90-277-1284-0*) Kluwer Academic.

Renzini, Alvio, jt. ed. see Chiosi, Cesare.

Renzini, Alvio, jt. ed. see Da Costa, Nicolaci.

Renzini, Alvio, jt. ed. see Kron, Richard G.

Renzini, Alvio, jt. ed. see Maeder, Andre.

Renzini, Alvio, jt. ed. see Rood, R. T.

Renzler, Carol A. The Healing Power of Soy: The Enlightened Person's Guide to Nature's Wonder Food. LC 98-33576. 240p. 2000. pap. 15.00 (*0-7615-1471-6*) Prima Pub.

Renzo, Anthony Di, see Di Renzo, Anthony.

Renzo, D. J., ed. Ceramic Raw Materials. LC 87-22002. (Illus.). 890p. 1988. 144.00 (*0-8155-1143-4*) Noyes.

Renzo, G. C. Di, see Cosmi, E. V., ed.

Renzo, G. C. Di, see Cosmi, E. V. & Di Renzo, G. C., eds.

Renzo, G. C. Di, see Di Renzo, G. C.

Renzo, G. C. Di, see Cosmi, E. V., ed.

Renzo, G. C. Di, see Cosmi, E. V. & Di Renzo, G. C., eds.

Renzo, Olivia di, see Houle, Paul & di Renzo, Olivia.

Renzoni, Aristeo, ed. Contaminants in the Environment: A Multidisciplinary Assessment of Risks to Man & Other Organisms. 304p. 1994. lib. bdg. 104.95 (*0-87371-853-4*, L853) Lewis Pubs.

Renzoni, Tommy. Baccarat: Everything You Want to Know About Playing & Winning. abr. ed. 1977. reprint ed. pap. 4.95 (*0-8065-0603-2*, Citadel Pr) Carol Pub Group.

***Renzotti, Claire M. & Goodstein, Lynne, eds.** Women, Crime & Criminal Justice: Contemporary Perspectives (Original Essays) (Illus.). 350p. 2000. pap. text. write for info. (*1-891487-39-6*) Roxbury Pub Co.

Renzulli, Joseph S. Building a Bridge Between Gifted Education & Total School Improvement. 38p. (C). 1996. reprint ed. pap. text 15.00 (*0-7881-3712-3*) DIANE Pub.

— The Enrichment Triad Model: A Guide for Developing Defensible Programs for the Gifted & Talented. (Illus.). 88p. 1977. pap. 9.95 (*0-936386-01-0*) Creative Learning.

— The Interest-A-Lyzer. 1977. pap. 29.95 (*0-936386-28-2*) Creative Learning.

Renzulli, Joseph S. Interest-a-Lyzer Family of Instruments: A Manual for Teachers. 80p. 1997. pap., teacher ed. 15.95 (*0-936386-69-X*) Creative Learning.

— New Directions in Creativity: Mark 1. 2000. pap. 25.95 (*0-936386-81-9*) Creative Learning.

— New Directions in Creativity: Mark 2. 2000. pap. 25.95 (*0-936386-82-7*) Creative Learning.

— Schools for Talent Development: A Practical Plan for Total School Improvement. 1994. pap. 39.95 (*0-936386-65-7*) Creative Learning.

Renzulli, Joseph S., ed. Systems & Models for Developing Programs for the Gifted & Talented. 1986. pap. text 38.95 (*0-936386-44-4*) Creative Learning.

***Renzulli, Joseph S. & Callahan, C. M.** New Directions in Creativity: Mark 3. 2000. pap. 25.95 (*0-936386-83-5*) Creative Learning.

Renzulli, Joseph S. & Reis, Sally M. Action Information Message, Set. 1981. pap. 24.95 (*0-936386-27-4*) Creative Learning.

— The Complete Triad Trainer's Inservice Manual: Including General Guidelines for Conducting Successful Inservice Programs. 140p. 1991. pap. 22.95 (*0-936386-57-6*) Creative Learning.

Renzulli, Joseph S. & Reis, Sally M., eds. The Triad Reader. 218p. 1986. pap. 22.95 (*0-936386-35-5*) Creative Learning.

Renzulli, Joseph S. & Smith, Linda H. The Compactor Set: Individual Programming Guide. 1978. pap. 22.95 (*0-936386-25-8*) Creative Learning.

— A Guidebook for Developing Individualized Educational Programs for Gifted & Talented Students. 56p. 1979. pap. 12.95 (*0-936386-13-4*) Creative Learning.

— Learning Styles Inventory: A Measure of Student Preference for Instructional Techniques. 40p. 1978. pap. 8.95 (*0-936386-14-2*) Creative Learning.

— The Strength-a-Lyzer: Individual Programming Guide. 1978. pap. 22.95 (*0-936386-24-X*) Creative Learning.

Renzulli, Joseph S., et al. Scales for Rating Behavioral Characteristics of Superior Students. 1997. pap. 8.95 (*0-936386-00-2*) Creative Learning.

Renzulli, Joseph S., jt. auth. see Purcell, Jeanne H.

Renzulli, Joseph S., jt. auth. see Reis, Sally M.

Renzulli, Joseph S., jt. ed. see Barbe, Walter B.

Renzulli, L. Marx. Maryland: The Federalist Years. LC 70-149405. 354p. 1975. 39.50 (*0-8386-7903-X*) Fairleigh Dickinson.

***Renzulli, M. J., et al.** New Directions in Creativity: Mark A. 2000. pap. 25.95 (*0-936386-79-7*) Creative Learning.

Renzulli, Maria L. Zen Runes Kit. 130p. 1998. 27.95 (*1-86204-316-7*, Pub. by Element MA) Penguin Putnam.

Renzulli, William F. William F. Renzulli Celebrates Wilmington. (Illus.). 120p. (Orig.). 1985. 35.00 (*0-9615598-1-0*); pap. 19.95 (*0-9615598-0-2*) Studio Pr PA.

Renzulli, William F. & Margaral, Brian. A Century of Serving. LC 98-66872. 225p. 1998. 19.95 (*0-9666357-0-1*) Jr Brd Christiana Care.

Reo, Vincent M. Finding Hot Horses: How to Pick Horses That Can Win for You. 135p. 1993. pap. 12.00 (*0-929387-96-1*) Bonus Books.

— Workouts & Maidens. 165p. 1994. pap. 11.95 (*1-56625-000-5*) Bonus Books.

Reohr, Janet R. Friendship: An Exploration of Structure & Processes. LC 91-19930. 152p. 1991. text 10.00 (*0-8240-7242-1*, SS431) Garland.

Reorganized Church of Jesus Christ of Latter Day S. Couples Who Care: An Essay to Use Resource to Create a Premarital Discussion Process for Engaged Couples in Your Congregation. Young, Leonard M., ed. LC 94-45060. 68p. (Orig.). 1995. pap. text 10.00 (*0-8309-0699-1*) Herald Pub Hse.

Reorganized Church of Jesus Christ of Latter Day S, jt. auth. see Young, Leonard M.

Reouven, Rene. Diccionario de los Asesinos. (SPA.). 386p. 1976. pap. 24.95 (*0-8288-5595-1*, S50083) Fr & Eur.

— Dictionnaire des Assassins. rev. ed. (FRE.). 429p. 1986. 85.00 (*0-7859-4844-9*) Fr & Eur.

Rep. Home Staff. Built Ins. 1980. 10.95 (*0-8094-2432-0*) Time-Life.

Repa, Barbara K. Avoid Employee Lawsuits: Auntie Nolo's Guide to Minding Your Business. LC 99-42369. 300p. 1999. pap. 24.95 (*0-87337-463-0*) Nolo com.

— Firing Without Fear. (Orig.). 1998. pap. 29.95 (*0-87337-435-5*) Nolo com.

— Your Rights in the Workplace. 4th ed. LC 98-18642. 528p. 1999. 21.95 (*0-87337-472-X*) Nolo com.

Repa, Barbara K., et al. Willmaker 7. LC 98-16977. 1998. 69.95 (*0-87337-482-7*) Nolo com.

— Willmaker 6.0 Windows. 6th ed. 1997. pap. 49.95 incl. cd-rom (*0-87337-314-6*) Nolo com.

Repa, Barbara K., jt. auth. see Petrocelli, William.

Repa, Barbara K., ed. see Randolph, Mary.

***Repa, Barbara Kate.** Your Rights in the Workplace. 5th ed. LC 00-37215. 2000. pap. 29.95 (*0-87337-597-1*) Nolo com.

Repacholi, M. H., et al, eds. Ultrasound: Medical Applications, Biological Effects, & Hazard Potential. 386p. 1987. 89.50 (*0-306-42411-8*, Plenum Trade) Perseus Pubng.

Repacholi, Michael H. & Benwell, Deirdre A., eds. Essentials of Medical Ultrasound: A Practical Introduction to the Principles, Techniques &... LC 80-85522. (Medical Methods Ser.). (Illus.). 330p. 1982. 120.00 (*0-89603-028-8*) Humana.

Repak, Terry A. Waiting on Washington: Central American Workers in the Nation's Capital. (Illus.). 240p. (Orig.). (C). 1995. pap. text 19.95 (*1-56639-302-7*); lib. bdg. 69.95 (*1-56639-301-9*) Temple U Pr.

***Repanshek, Kurt.** Hidden Utah. (Hidden Travel Ser.). (Illus.). 312p. 2000. pap. 14.95 (*1-56975-125-0*, Pub. by Ulysses Pr) Publishers Group.

Repar, John. Morsels. 150p. 1998. pap. 5.00 (*0-9661910-1-3*) J Repar.

— Plethora. unabridged ed. 150p. 1995. pap. 5.00 (*0-9661910-0-5*) J Repar.

Repas, Bob. Contract Administration: A Guide for Stewards & Local Officers. LC 84-9857. 264p. reprint ed. pap. 81.90 (*0-608-04263-3*, 206501800012) Bks Demand.

Repath, Austin. The Waterbearer. LC 94-152662. 200p. (Orig.). 1994. pap. 12.95 (*0-9697399-0-7*) Reed Pr.

Repato, Al. Children First: Reengineering California Education. 300p. (C). 1996. pap. 9.95 (*0-9621101-9-1*) Light Pub Hse.

Repchuk, Caroline. The Easter Chicks: A Lift-the-Flap Storybook. Vol. 1. LC 94-72889. (Illus.). 16p. (J). (gr. k-3). 1996. 7.95 (*0-316-83679-6*) Little.

— The Forgotten Garden. LC 96-42692. (Illus.). 32p. (J). (gr. k-4). 1997. 14.95 (*0-7613-0141-0*) Millbrook Pr.

— My Little Supermarket. LC 96-42691. (Illus.). 1996. 12.95 (*0-7613-0145-3*) Millbrook Pr.

— The Snow Tree. LC 97-214686. (Illus.). 32p. (J). 1997. 15.99 (*0-525-45903-0*, Dutton Child) Peng Put Young Read.

Repchuk, Caroline, jt. auth. see Lee, Kate.

Repede, John, et al. Microsoft Visual Basic 4: Introductory Concepts & Techniques. LC 96-32235. 304p. 1996. pap. 38.95 (*0-7895-0728-5*) Course Tech.

Reperant, Dominique, photos by. The Most Beautiful Villages of France. LC 90-70389. (Illus.). 220p. 1990. 45.00 (*0-500-54162-0*, Pub. by Thames Hudson) Norton.

Repertory Theatre of St. Louis, Backers Volunteer. Opening Night Entertaining, 2 vols., Set, Vols. 1-2. (Illus.). (Orig.). 1993. pap. 16.95 (*0-9605504-1-0*) Repertory Theatre SL.

— Opening Night Entertaining, 2 vols., Vols. 1-2. (Illus.). 72p. (Orig.). 1993. write for info. (*0-318-72146-5*); write for info. (*0-318-72147-3*) Repertory Theatre SL.

Repetitive Manufacturing S. I. G. Staff & Elster, Bernard J. Flattened Bill of Material (BOM) Training Aid. LC 96-84044. 56p. (Orig.). 1996. pap. 35.00 (*1-55822-125-5*) Am Prod & Inventory.

Repetitive Manufacturing S. I. G. Staff, jt. auth. see Boeder, Steven M.

Repetto-Alaia, Margherita, jt. ed. see Coppa, Frank J.

Repetto, Nadia, jt. auth. see Wurtz, Maruizio.

Repetto, Robert & Austin, Duncan. The Costs of Climate Protection: A Guide for the Perplexed. LC 97-60932. 60p. 1997. pap. 20.00 (*1-56973-222-1*) World Resources Inst.

— Pure Profit: The Financial Implications of Environmental Performance. 80p. 2000. pap. 20.00 (*1-56973-442-9*) World Resources Inst.

Repetto, Robert, et al. Has Environmental Protection Really Reduced Productivity Growth? We Need Unbiased Measures. 56p. 1996. pap. 20.00 (*1-56973-101-2*) World Resources Inst.

Repetto, Robert C. Economic Equality & Fertility in Developing Countries. LC 78-20533. (Resources for the Future Ser.). 204p. 1979. text 16.50 (*0-8018-2212-2*) Johns Hopkins.

— Economic Equality & Fertility in Developing Countries. LC 78-20533. 208p. reprint ed. pap. 64.50 (*0-608-18096-3*, 203216200078) Bks Demand.

— Jobs, Competitiveness & Environmental Regulation: What Are the Real Issues? LC 95-1197. 1995. 20.00 (*1-56973-030-X*) World Resources Inst.

— Paying the Price: Pesticide Subsidies in Developing Countries. 40p. 1985. pap. text 10.00 (*0-915825-12-0*) World Resources Inst.

— Promoting Environmentally Sound Economic Progress: What the North Can Do. 20p. 1990. pap. 15.00 (*0-915825-57-0*, REPEP) World Resources Inst.

— The Second India Revisited: Population, Poverty, & Environmental Stress over Two Decades. 95p. 1994. pap. 20.00 (*0-915825-96-1*, RESIP) World Resources Inst.

— Time in India's Development Programmes. LC 71-143230. (Economic Studies: No. 137). (Illus.). 249p. 1971. 16.50 (*0-674-89180-5*) HUP.

Repetto, Robert C. & Baliga, Sanjay S. Pesticides & the Immune System: The Public Health Risks. LC 96-12739. 100p. (Orig.). 1996. pap. 20.00 (*1-56973-087-3*) World Resources Inst.

Repetto, Robert C. & Cruz, Wilfrido. The Environmental Effects of Stabilization & Structural Adjustment Programs: The Philippines Case. large type ed. 90p. 1992. pap. 20.00 (*0-915825-81-3*, CRSAP) World Resources Inst.

Repetto, Robert C. & Gillis, Malcolm, eds. Public Policy & the Misuse of Forest Resources. 448p. 1988. pap. text 42.95 (*0-521-33574-4*) Cambridge U Pr.

Repetto, Robert C., et al. Green Fees: How a Tax Shift Can Work for the Environment & the Economy. 100p. 1992. pap. 20.00 (*0-915825-76-7*, REKCP) World Resources Inst.

— Population Growth, Poverty, & Environmental Stress: Frontier Migration in the Philippines & Costa Rica. enl. ed. 90p. 1992. pap. 20.00 (*0-915825-86-4*, MEPPP) World Resources Inst.

Repetto, Robert C., jt. auth. see Heaton, George R.

Repetto, Vittoria. Head for the Van Wyck. 23p. 1994. 6.00 (*0-9666378-0-1*) Monkey Cat.

***Repetzki, Michael M.** John Evelyn's Translation of Titus Lucretius Carus De Rerum Natura: An Old-Spelling Critical Edition. (Munster Monographs on English Literature: Vol. 22). cxiii, 275p. 2000. pap. 52.95 (*0-8204-4388-3*) P Lang Pubng.

Rephann, Richard & Germann, Sheridan. Historical Harpsichord, No. 4. (Historical Harpsichord Ser.). 2000. 54.00 (*0-945193-75-0*) Pendragon NY.

Rephann, Richard T. A Catalogue of the Pedro Traversari Collection of Musical Instruments. Odiaga, Lola, tr. (ENG & SPA., Illus.). 146p. (Orig.). 1978. pap. 10.00 (*0-929530-01-2*) Yale U Coll Musical Instruments.

— The Schambach-Kaston Collection of Musical Instruments. (Illus.). 88p. (Orig.). 1988. pap. 15.00 (*0-929530-05-5*) Yale U Coll Musical Instruments.

Rephann, Richard T., jt. auth. see Renouf, Nicholas.

Repic, Ed. Managing Engineers. (Illus.). (Orig.). 1981. pap. 25.00 (*0-939740-00-1*) Effect Mgmt.

Repic, Oljan. Principles of Process Research & Chemical Development in the Pharmaceutical Industry. LC 97-13904. 240p. 1997. 84.95 (*0-471-16516-6*) Wiley.

***Repicci, Albert J.** Nantucket Musings. (Illus.). 60p. 2000. 15.99 (*1-930348-00-2*) KHP Museum.

Repici, Anthony. Cathexis: An Energy Source for Life. (Illus.). 96p. 1997. pap. 10.00 (*0-8059-4165-7*) Dorrance.

— Love-Life Poems, Vol. 2. (Orig.). 1997. pap. write for info. (*1-57553-490-8*) Watermrk Pr.

Repin, I. E. Distant, Yet Familiar. 1982. 46.00 (*0-7855-1535-6*) St Mut.

Repine, J. E., jt. ed. see Cheronis, J. C.

Repine, Jim. Pacific Rim Fly Fishing: The Unrepentant Predator. (Illus.). 64p. 1995. pap. 9.95 (*1-57188-025-9*) F Amato Pubns.

Repington, Charles A. The First World War, 2 vols., Set. (Modern Revivals in Military History Ser.). 638p. 1992. 123.95 (*0-7512-0038-7*, Pub. by Gregg Revivals) Ashgate Pub Co.

Repinski, Cynthia A. The Univex Story. LC 91-71477. (Illus.). 272p. 1991. 34.95 (*0-931838-17-7*) Centennial Photo Serv.

Repinski, Karyn. Complete Idiot's Guide to Successful Dressing. (Complete Idiot's Guide Ser.). 352p. 1998. pap. 16.95 (*0-02-862729-6*) Macmillan Gen Ref.

Repishti, Sami, jt. ed. see Pippa, Arshi.

Repka, Joseph. Calculus with Analytic Geometry. (Illus.). 1344p. (C). 1993. text 18.75 (*0-697-16777-1*, WCB McGr Hill); text 18.75 (*0-697-16778-X*, WCB McGr Hill); text 18.75 (*0-697-21296-3*, WCB McGr Hill) McGrw-H Hghr Educ.

— Calculus with Analytic Geometry. (Illus.). 1344p. (C). 1994. text 21.25 (*0-697-12197-6*, WCB McGr Hill); text 22.50 (*0-697-11365-5*, WCB McGr Hill) McGrw-H Hghr Educ.

Repka, Kathleen M., jt. auth. see Repka, William.

Repka, William & Repka, Kathleen M. Dangerous Patriots: Canada's Unknown Prisoners of War. 250p. 1982. pap. 12.95 (*0-919573-07-X*, Pub. by New Star Bks) Genl Dist Srvs.

Repke, John T., ed. Intrapartum Obstetrics. LC 95-32785. 575p. 1995. text 130.00 (*0-443-08949-3*) Church.

Replansky, Dennis. Truth-in-Lending & Regulation Z. LC 84-71018. (Illus.). xvi, 297p. 1984. 9.50 (*0-8318-0242-1*, B242) Am Law Inst.

Replansky, Naomi. Twenty-One Poems: Old & New. (Orig.). 1988. pap. 5.95 (*0-9619869-0-5*) Gingko Pr.

Replinger, Peter J., jt. auth. see Labbe, John T.

Replogle, Elaine M. Head Start As a Family Support Program: Renewing a Community Ethic. 96p. 1995. pap. text 8.00 (*0-9630627-4-3*) Harvard Fam.

Replogle, Emma A. Earnest Genealogy: Indian Eve & Her Descendants, an Indian Story of Bedford Co. (Illus.). 128p. 1997. reprint ed. pap. 21.00 (*0-8328-8408-1*); reprint ed. lib. bdg. 31.00 (*0-8328-8407-3*) Higginson Bk Co.

Replogle, John A. & Renard, Kenneth G., eds. Water Today & Tomorrow: Proceedings of a Specialty Conference Sponsored by the Irrigation & Drainage Division. 740p. 1984. 8.00 (*0-87262-408-0*) Am Soc Civil Eng.

Replogle, Justin. Ancesters on the Frontier: Cripe, Metzger, Miller, Replogle, Shively, Ulrich. unabridged ed. (Illus.). 400p. 1998. pap. 19.95 (*0-9664693-0-5*) Kaehlers Mill Pr.

Replogle, Ron. Recovering the Social Contract. LC 87-33024. 256p. (C). 1989. 56.50 (*0-8476-7591-2*) Rowman.

Repo, Satu. What's a Friend. (Where We Live Ser.). (Illus.). 73p. (J). 1985. bds. 12.95 (*0-88862-188-4*, Pub. by J Lorimer) Formac Dist Ltd.

— What's a Friend? (Where We Live Ser.). (Illus.). 73p. (J). 1985. pap. 5.95 (*0-88862-178-7*, Pub. by J Lorimer) Formac Dist Ltd.

Repo, Satu, et al. Marco & Michela. (Where We Live Ser.). (Illus.). 79p. (J). 1985. pap. 5.95 (*0-88862-172-8*, Pub. by J Lorimer); bds. 12.95 (*0-88862-181-7*, Pub. by J Lorimer) Formac Dist Ltd.

REPOhistory Staff. Choice Histories: Framing Abortion: An Artists' Book by REPOhistory. 44p. 1992. 8.00 (*0-9636132-0-0*) REPOhistory.

Repond, Jose & Krakauer, Daniel, eds. Deep Inelastic Scattering & QCD: 5th International Workshop. LC 97-74677. (Conference Proceedings Ser.: Vol. 407). (Illus.). 1058p. 1997. 220.00 (*1-56396-716-2*) Am Inst Physics.

Report of a Study Group Staff. Toward Arab-Israeli Peace: Guidelines for American Policy. LC 88-70490. 49p. 1988. pap. 6.95 (*0-8157-7291-2*) Brookings.

An Asterisk (*) at the beginning of an entry indicates that the title is appearing for the first time.

Report of a Working Party Staff. Materials Technology Foresight on Aerospace Structural Materials. (Materials Strategy Commission Ser.: Bk. 624). 37p. 1995. pap. 40.00 (*0-901716-88-X*, Pub. by Inst Materials) Ashgate Pub Co.

Report of the National Performance Review Staff & Gore, Al, Jr. Creating a Government That Works Better & Costs Less. 1994. pap. write for info. (*0-929306-20-1*) Silicon Pr.

Report of the Price Statistics Review Committee. The Price Statistics of the Federal Government. (General Ser.: No. 73). 518p. 1961. reprint ed. 134.70 (*0-87014-072-8*) Natl Bur Econ Res.

Reporter. Reporter Reader. Ascoli, Max, ed. LC 74-93373. (Essay Index Reprint Ser.). 1977. 28.95 (*0-8369-1428-7*) Ayer.

Reporter on Economic Products to the Government of, ed. Races of Rice in India. 594p. 1996. pap. 300.00 (*81-85880-91-3*, Pub. by Print Hse) St Mut.

Reporters of the New York Times Staff, jt. auth. see Brody, Jane E.

Reposa, Carol C. The Facts of Life: Carol Coffee Reposa Poems. (American Regional Book Ser.: Vol. 8). 128p. (Orig.). 1999. pap. 12.95 (*0-9651359-7-7*, 1308, Pub. by Browder Springs) Herveys Bklink.

***Reposa, Carol Coffee.** The Green Room. 34p. 1998. pap. 7.00 (*1-877603-59-7*) Pecan Grove.

Repov, Du San & Semenov, Pavel. Continuous Selections of Multivalued Mappings. LC 98-36873. (Mathematics & Its Applications Ser.). 1998. write for info. (*0-7923-5277-7*) Kluwer Academic.

Repp. Functional Analysis of Problem Behavior. LC 98-44913. (Special Education Ser.). 1999. pap. 70.95 (*0-534-34850-5*) Brooks-Cole.

— Radium Pool. 5.00 (*0-686-00478-7*); pap. 2.00 (*0-686-00479-5*) Fantasy Pub Co.

— Stellar Missiles. 5.00 (*0-686-00483-3*); pap. 2.00 (*0-686-00484-1*) Fantasy Pub Co.

Repp & McCarthy. Machine Tool Technology. 1999. teacher ed. 19.03 (*0-02-671600-3*) Glencoe.

— Machine Tool Technology: Study Guide 1. 5th ed. (Illus.). 70p. (gr. 6-12). 1999. student ed. 11.61 (*0-02-671580-5*) Glencoe.

— Machine Tool Technology: Study Guide 2. 5th ed. (Illus.). 137p. (gr. 6-12). 1999. student ed. 11.61 (*0-02-671590-2*) Glencoe.

Repp, Alan C. & Singh, Nirbhay N., eds. Current Perspectives in the Use of Nonaversive & Aversive Interventions for Persons with Developmental Disabilities. (Illus.). 300p. (C). 1990. write for info. (*0-318-66893-9*) Sycamore Pub.

— Perspectives on the Use of Nonaversive & Aversive Interventions for Persons with Developmental Disabilities. 533p. 1993. 60.25 (*0-534-21672-2*) Brooks-Cole.

Repp, Alan C., jt. auth. see Coutinho, Martha J.

Repp, Alan C., ed. see O'Neill, Robert, et al.

Repp, Arthur C., Sr. Luther's Catechism Comes to America: Theological Effects on the Issues of the Small Catechism Prepared in or for America Prior to 1850. LC 82-5453. (American Theological Library Association Monograph: No. 18). 329p. 1982. text 34.50 (*0-8108-1546-X*) Scarecrow.

***Repp, Debbie.** My Confirmation Journal. (Illus.). 48p. 1998. pap. 1.95 (*0-7648-0257-7*) Liguori Pubns.

Repp, Gloria. Mik-Shrok. LC 98-8838. 133p. (J). 1998. pap. 6.49 (*1-57924-069-0*) Bob Jones Univ.

— Night Flight. (Light Line Ser.). 164p. (YA). 1991. pap. 6.49 (*0-89084-563-8*, 052191) Bob Jones Univ.

— Noodle Soup. LC 93-42417. (Illus.). 32p. (J). 1994. pap. 5.49 (*0-89084-582-4*, 055681) Bob Jones Univ.

— Nothing Daunted: The Story of Isobel Kuhn. Cooper, Manda, ed. LC 94-15531. (Light Line Ser.). 168p. 1994. pap. 6.49 (*0-89084-753-3*, 080481) Bob Jones Univ.

— A Question of Yams. (Light Line Ser.). (Illus.). 67p. (J). 1992. pap. 6.49 (*0-89084-614-6*, 057885) Bob Jones Univ.

— Secret of the Golden Cowrie. (Illus.). 192p. (J). (gr. 4-6). 1988. pap. 6.49 (*0-89084-459-3*, 042887) Bob Jones Univ.

— The Stolen Years. 152p. (YA). (gr. 7-12). 1989. pap. 6.49 (*0-89084-481-X*, 044412) Bob Jones Univ.

— Trouble at Silver Pines Inn. LC 97-48271. 149p. (J). 1998. pap. 6.49 (*1-57924-000-3*) Bob Jones Univ.

Repp, John. Thirst Like This: Poems. 64p. 1990. 18.95 (*0-8262-0762-6*); pap. 10.95 (*0-8262-0765-0*) U of Mo Pr.

Repp, Philip C. Words & Images: Land Within the Maumee. (Illus.). 83p. (Orig.). 1990. pap. write for info. (*0-9623291-1-8*) Minnetrista.

Repp, Stan. Super Chief: Train of the Stars. 3rd ed. LC 80-18725. (Illus.). 258p. 1980. reprint ed. 17.00 (*0-87095-081-9*) Gldn West Bks.

Repp, Thomas A. Route 66: The Empires of Amusement. LC 98-96936. (Illus.). 192p. 1999. 34.95 (*0-9669148-0-5*) Mock Turtle Pr.

Repp, Victor E. Metalwork: Technology & Practice. 9th ed. 1999. teacher ed. 11.29 (*0-02-676485-7*) Glencoe.

— Metalwork: Technology & Practice. 9th ed. (Illus.). 192p. (YA). (gr. 6-12). 1999. pap., student ed., wbk. ed. 7.60 (*0-02-676486-5*) Glencoe.

Repp, Victor E. & McCarthy, Williard J. Metalwork: Technology & Practice. 9th ed. (Illus.). 702p. (YA). (gr. 6-12). 1994. text, student ed. 40.20 (*0-02-676484-9*) Glencoe.

Repp, William. Complete Handbook of Business English. 1982. 29.50 (*0-13-160960-2*, Busn) P-H.

Reppen, Erik. Independence War: Prima's Official Strategy Guide. LC 98-67774. 244p. 1998. per. 19.99 (*0-7615-1817-7*) Prima Pub.

Reppen, Joseph. Becoming a Psychotherapist. LC 98-4116. 1998. 50.00 (*0-7657-0170-7*) Aronson.

— More Analysts at Work. LC 96-13800. 268p. 1997. pap. 50.00 (*1-56821-857-5*) Aronson.

Reppen, Joseph, ed. Analysts at Work: Practice, Principles, & Techniques. LC 94-36490. 268p. 1995. pap. text 50.00 (*1-56821-423-5*) Aronson.

Reppen, Joseph & Charney, Maurice, eds. The Psychoanalytic Study of Literature. LC 84-16791. 296p. reprint ed. pap. 91.80 (*0-8357-2737-8*, 203984600013) Bks Demand.

Reppen, Joseph, jt. ed. see Charney, Maurice.

Reppen, Joseph, jt. ed. see Ellman, Carolyn S.

Repper, J., jt. auth. see Perkins, R.

Reppert. Growing & Using Rosemary. LC 96-43192. (Storey Publishing Bulletin Ser.: Vol. A-161). 1996. pap. 2.95 (*0-88266-607-X*) Storey Bks.

Reppert, Bertha. The Bride's Herbal. 182p. 1989. pap. 12.00 (*0-9617210-3-0*) Remembrance.

— Growing Your Herb Business. Balmuth, Deborah, ed. LC 93-36518. (Illus.). 144p. 1994. pap. 12.95 (*0-88266-612-6*, Storey Pub) Storey Bks.

— Herbs of the Zodiac. 68p. 1984. pap. 6.00 (*0-9617210-7-3*) Remembrance.

— Herbs with Confidence. LC 86-90486. (Illus.). 268p. (Orig.). 1986. pap. 12.00 (*0-9617210-0-6*) Remembrance.

— A Heritage of Herbs: History, Early Gardening & Old Recipes. 192p. 1976. pap. 9.00 (*0-9617210-6-5*) Remembrance.

— Mrs. Reppert's Twelve Month Herbal: A Day-by-Day Journal in the Herb Garden. (Illus.). 375p. (Orig.). 1996. pap. 17.50 (*0-9617210-8-1*) Remembrance.

— Wreaths of All Sorts. 40p. 1987. pap. 6.50 (*0-9617210-1-4*) Remembrance.

Reppert, Bertha & Humphries, Pat. Potpourri: Recipes & Crafts. 40p. 1973. pap. 5.00 (*0-9617210-2-2*) Remembrance.

Reppert, Joan D. The Spirit of Jubilee. 1.25 (*0-687-02678-4*) Abingdon.

Reppert, Marjorie L. Guidance for Choosing a Career in the Visual Arts. 66p. 1992. pap. 7.95 (*0-9617210-4-9*) Remembrance.

Reppert, Marjorie L., ed. see Hydro, Vince.

Reppert, Pat. Mad about Garlic. (Illus.). 157p. 1997. spiral bd. 9.95 (*1-57166-106-9*) Hearts N Tummies.

Reppert, S., jt. auth. see Moore, R.

Reppert, Steven M., ed. Development of Circadian Rhythmicity & Photoperiodism in Mammals. LC 89-23095. (Research in Perinatal Medicine Ser.: No. IX). (Illus.). 1989. 102.50 (*0-916859-42-8*) Perinatology.

***Reppetto, Thomas A. & Lardner, James.** NYPD: The Inside Story of New York's Legendary Police Department. (Illus.). 384p. 2000. 27.50 (*0-8050-5578-9*, J Macrae Bks) H Holt & Co.

Repplier, Agnes. Americans & Others. LC 70-121503. (Essay Index Reprint Ser.). 1977. 23.95 (*0-8369-2025-2*) Ayer.

— Book of Famous Verse. LC 71-86802. (Granger Index Reprint Ser.). 1977. 18.95 (*0-8369-6086-6*) Ayer.

— Compromises. LC 78-98626. reprint ed. 27.50 (*0-404-05259-2*) AMS Pr.

— Compromises. (BCL1-PS American Literature Ser.). 277p. 1992. reprint ed. lib. bdg. 79.00 (*0-7812-6840-0*) Rprt Serv.

— Compromises. 1971. reprint ed. 8.00 (*0-403-00701-1*) Scholarly.

— Counter-Currents. LC 73-121504. (Essay Index Reprint Ser.). 1977. 23.95 (*0-8369-2026-0*) Ayer.

— Essays in Idleness. LC 70-121290. 1970. reprint ed. 27.50 (*0-404-05278-9*) AMS Pr.

— Essays in Idleness. (BCL1-PS American Literature Ser.). 224p. 1992. reprint ed. lib. bdg. 79.00 (*0-7812-6841-9*) Rprt Serv.

— Essays in Idleness. LC 70-131815. 1970. reprint ed. 8.00 (*0-403-00702-X*) Scholarly.

— Essays in Miniature. LC 70-112790. reprint ed. 27.50 (*0-404-05279-7*) AMS Pr.

— Essays in Miniature. (BCL1-PS American Literature Ser.). 217p. 1992. reprint ed. lib. bdg. 79.00 (*0-7812-6842-7*) Rprt Serv.

— Essays in Miniature. LC 74-131816. 1970. reprint ed. 8.00 (*0-403-00703-8*) Scholarly.

— A Happy Half-Century: And Other Essays. (BCL1-PS American Literature Ser.). 249p. 1992. reprint ed. lib. bdg. 79.00 (*0-7812-6843-5*) Rprt Serv.

— In Our Convent Days. (BCL1-PS American Literature Ser.). 256p. 1992. reprint ed. lib. bdg. 79.00 (*0-7812-6917-2*) Rprt Serv.

— In Our Convent Days. 1971. reprint ed. 8.00 (*0-403-00704-6*) Scholarly.

— Philadelphia, the Place & Its People. 1993. reprint ed. lib. bdg. 89.00 (*0-7812-5823-5*) Rprt Serv.

— Points of Friction. LC 77-121505. (Essay Index Reprint Ser.). 1977. 23.95 (*0-8369-2027-9*) Ayer.

— Times & Tendencies. LC 71-128297. (Essay Index Reprint Ser.). 1977. 21.95 (*0-8369-2028-7*) Ayer.

— Under Dispute. LC 75-167406. (Essay Index Reprint Ser.). 1977. reprint ed. 23.95 (*0-8369-2668-4*) Ayer.

Reppucci, N. Dickon. Preventing Child Abuse & Neglect Through Parent Education. LC 97-9036. 1997. pap. text 25.95 (*1-55766-289-4*) P H Brookes.

Reppucci, N. Dickon, et al, eds. Children, Mental Health, & the Law. LC 83-21116. (Sage Annual Reviews of Community Mental Health Ser.: No. 4). 312p. reprint ed. pap. 96.80 (*0-8357-4847-2*, 203777800009) Bks Demand.

Reppucci, N. Dickon, jt. auth. see Haugaard, Jeffrey J.

Reppy. Gilbert Community Property. 16th ed. 1994. pap. text 18.95 (*0-15-900235-4*) Harcourt Legal.

Reppy, A., jt. auth. see Field, David Dudley.

Reppy, Dean A. Introduction to Civil Procedure: Actions & Pleading at Common Law. LC 53-12996. xiv, 860p. 1954. 38.50 (*0-89941-619-5*, 501990) W S Hein.

Reppy, Jessie M. & Shaffer-Koros, Carole M. Explorations in World Literature: Readings to Enhance Academic Skills: Instructor's Manual. 60p. (C). 1994. pap., teacher ed. 6.00 (*0-521-65803-9*) Cambridge U Pr.

Reppy, Jessie M., jt. auth. see Shaffer-Koros, Carole M.

***Reppy, John H.** Concurrent Programming in ML. LC 99-20465. (Illus.). 336p. 1999. 44.95 (*0-521-48089-2*) Cambridge U Pr.

Reppy, John H., jt. ed. see Gansner, Emden R.

Reppy, Judith. Conversion of Military R & D. LC 98-8308. 304p. 1998. text 69.95 (*0-312-21802-8*) St Martin.

Reppy, Judith, jt. ed. see Hampson, Fen O.

Reppy, Judith, jt. ed. see Katzenstein, Mary F.

Reppy, William & Samuel, Cynthia. Community Property in the United States, 1997. 460p. 1997. ring bd. 66.00 (*1-879581-71-X*) Lupus Pubns.

Reppy, William A., Jr., jt. auth. see McKnight, Joseph W.

Reprogle, Rod, et al. The Mother of All Car Books: How to Get More Fun & Profit Buying, Showing & Selling Vintage & Classic Cars. LC 91-58795. 270p. 1995. pap. 14.95 (*0-911663-78-9*) Dunclifffs Intl.

Reps, jt. auth. see Crumbley.

Reps, John William. Bird's Eye Views: Historic Lithographs of North American Cities. LC 98-25784. (Illus.). 116p. 1998. 65.00 (*1-56898-146-5*) Princeton Arch.

Reps, David. Son of Prophecy: Henry Tudor's Road to Bosworth. 172p. 1998. pap. 19.95 (*0-8464-4859-9*) Beekman Pubs.

Reps, David N. Managerial Finance for Business Planning. 2nd ed. (Illus.). 220p. (Orig.). (C). 1996. pap. text 23.95 (*0-943025-68-0*) Cummngs & Hath.

— Managerial Finance for Business Planning. 3rd rev. ed. (Illus.). 248p. (Orig.). (C). 1996. pap. text 24.95 (*0-943025-88-5*) Cummngs & Hath.

Reps, John W. Cities of the Mississippi: Nineteenth-Century Images of Urban Development. LC 93-44630. (Illus.). 352p. (C). 1994. pap. 59.95 (*0-8262-0939-4*) U of Mo Pr.

— The Forgotten Frontier: Urban Planning in the American West Before 1890. LC 81-10322. 184p. 1981. pap. 14.95 (*0-8262-0352-3*); text 27.00 (*0-8262-0351-5*) U of Mo Pr.

— The Making of Urban America: A History of City Planning in the United States. (Illus.). 590p. 1965. pap. text 45.00 (*0-691-00618-0*, Pub. by Princeton U Pr) Cal Prin Full Svc.

— Panoramas of Promise: Pacific Northwest Cities & Towns on Nineteenth-Century Lithographs. LC 84-13164. (Illus.). 93p. 1984. 18.75 (*0-87422-016-5*); pap. 10.95 (*0-87422-017-3*) Wash St U Pr.

— St. Louis Illustrated: Nineteenth-Century Engravings & Lithographs of a Mississippi River Metropolis. LC 88-20914. (Illus.). 208p. (C). 1989. 44.95 (*0-8262-0698-0*) U of Mo Pr.

— Town Planning in Frontier America. LC 68-20877. 336p. 1981. reprint ed. pap. 16.95 (*0-8262-0316-7*) U of Mo Pr.

— Views & Viewmakers of Urban America: Lithographs of Towns & Cities in the United States & Canada, Notes on the Artists & Publishers, & a Union Catalog of Their Work, 1825-1925. LC 83-6495. (Illus.). 588p. 1984. text 89.50 (*0-8262-0416-3*) U of Mo Pr.

— Washington on View: The Nation's Capital since 1790. LC 90-46782. (Illus.). 308p. reprint ed. pap. 95.50 (*0-608-10414-0*, 205442500010) Bks Demand.

Reps, Paul. Let Good Fortune Jump on You. (Illus.). 75p. 1990. reprint ed. pap. 7.95 (*0-9620812-7-2*) Good Karma.

— Zen Telegrams. (Illus.). 92p. (Orig.). 1995. pap. 11.95 (*0-8048-2023-6*) Tuttle Pubng.

Reps, Paul, ed. Zen Flesh, Zen Bones: A Collection of Zen & Pre-Zen Writings. 192p. 1960. pap. 9.95 (*0-385-08130-8*, A233, Anchor NY) Doubleday.

Reps, Paul & Senzaki, Nyogen, compiled by. Zen Flesh, Zen Bones: A Collection of Zen & Pre-Zen Writings. (Illus.). 212p. 1998. pap. 12.95 (*0-8048-3186-6*) Tuttle Pubng.

Reps, Paul, jt. tr. see Senzaki, Nyogen.

Reps, T. W. & Teitelbaum, T. The Synthesizer Generator. (Texts & Monographs in Computer Science). (Illus.). xiii, 310p. 1988. 78.95 (*0-387-96857-1*) Spr-Verlag.

— The Synthesizer Generator: Reference Manual. 3rd ed. (Texts & Monographs in Computer Science). (Illus.). viii, 165p. 1990. 40.95 (*0-387-96910-1*) Spr-Verlag.

— The Synthesizer Generator: The Synthesizer Reference Manual, 2 vols., Set. (Texts & Monographs in Computer Science). (Illus.). 1989. 55.00 (*0-387-97100-9*) Spr-Verlag.

Repsher, Brian. The Rite of Church Dedication in the Early Medieval Era. LC 97-51516. 208p. 1998. text 89.95 (*0-7734-2231-5*) E Mellen.

Repstad, Pal, ed. Religion & Modernity: Modes of Coexistence. 240p. 1996. 43.00 (*82-00-22656-5*) Scandnvan Univ Pr.

Repton, Humphry. The Art of Landscape Gardening. LC 76-51839. (Illus.). 1976. reprint ed. 25.00 (*0-913728-20-9*) Theophrastus.

Republic of China Staff. Laws, Ordinances, Regulations, & Rules Relating to the Judicial Administration of the Republic of China. LC 76-11420. (Studies in Chinese Government & Law). 364p. 1976. reprint ed. lib. bdg. 75.00 (*0-313-26957-2*, U6957) Greenwood.

Republic of Texas Press Staff, ed. see Adare, Sierra.

Repyev, Alexander, tr. see Frolov, K. V.

Repyev, Alexander, tr. see Logunov, A. A.

Requa-Clark, Barbara S. Applied Pharmacology for the Dental Hygienist. 3rd ed. LC 95-106202. (Illus.). 416p. (C). (gr. 13). 1994. pap. text 44.00 (*0-8151-7233-8*, 23812) Mosby Inc.

— Applied Pharmacology for the Dental Hygienist. 4th ed. LC 99-16182. (Illus.). 512p. (C). (gr. 13). 1999. pap. text 39.95 (*0-8151-3630-7*, 28851) Mosby Inc.

Requa, Richard S. Inside Lights on the Building of San Diego's Exposition, 1935. (Illus.). 168p. 1997. reprint ed. pap. 15.00 (*0-9661224-0-2*) P H Jackson.

Requena, Luis, et al. Ackerman's Histopathologic Diagnosis of Adnexal Neoplasms. (Illus.). 800p. 1998. text 179.00 (*0-397-58793-7*) Lppncott W & W.

Requena, Yves. Character & Health. Felt, Robert L., ed. Bell, Carol, tr. from FRE. (Illus.). 224p. (Orig.). 1995. pap. text 25.00 (*0-912111-23-2*) Paradigm Publns.

— Chi Kung: The Chinese Art of Mastering Energy. (Illus.). 160p. 1996. pap. 16.95 (*0-89281-639-2*, Heal Arts VT) Inner Tradit.

— Terrains & Pathology in Acupuncture, Vol. 2. 2nd ed. Felt, Robert L., ed. Ducharne, Allan, tr. (FRE., Illus.). 448p. 1996. text 30.00 (*0-912111-49-6*) Paradigm Publns.

Requena, Yves, jt. auth. see Kenner, Dan.

***Requier-Desjardins, Denis, et al.** Environmental Policy & Societal Aims. LC 99-53175. (Studies in Ecological Economics). 1999. write for info. (*0-7923-6040-0*) Kluwer Academic.

Requin, Jean & Stelmach, G. E. Tutorials in Motor Behavior II. (Advances in Psychology Ser.: Vol. 87). 960p. 1992. 203.25 (*0-444-88801-2*, North Holland) Elsevier.

Requin, Jean & Stelmach, George E. Tutorials in Motor Neuroscience: Proceedings of the NATO Advanced Study Institute. 696p. (C). 1991. text 326.00 (*0-7923-1385-2*) Kluwer Academic.

Requin, Jean, jt. auth. see Stelmach, George E.

Requin, Jean, ed. see International Symposium on Attention & Performance.

Requin, Jean, jt. ed. see Kornblum, Sylvan.

Rerdeen, Lars. Robinson Island. 1999. 44.95 (*3-932657-04-7*) Taoran Pr.

Reres, Mary E. Managed Care: Managing the Process. 238p. 1996. pap. text 30.00 (*0-9660741-0-6*) Natl Prof Educ.

Rericha, Robert & Franke, Christopher. Killing Time: Vis-a-Vis Redivivus. 48p. 1990. pap. 5.00 (*0-9601640-2-2*) Deciduous.

Rerick, Rowland H. State Centennial History of Ohio, Covering the Periods of Indian, French & British Dominion, the Territory Northwest, & the Hundred Years of Statehood. 425p. 1995. reprint ed. lib. bdg. 45.00 (*0-8328-4616-3*) Higginson Bk Co.

Rerreault, Heidi R., ed. Classroom Strategies - The Methodology of Business Education: 1996 NBEA Yearbook. (Yearbook Ser.). 203p. 1996. pap. 15.00 (*0-933964-47-1*) Natl Busn Ed Assoc.

Resano, Francisco, jt. auth. see Ibanez, Aniceto.

***Resbstock, Michael & Hildebrand, Knut.** SAP R-3 Management. LC 99-24998. (Illus.). 210p. 1999. pap. 39.99 (*1-57610-454-0*) Coriolis Grp.

Rescar, Jennifer G. Pneumocystic Carinii: Index of New Information. 1998. 47.50 (*0-7883-1814-4*); pap. 47.50 (*0-7883-1815-2*) ABBE Pubs Assn.

Resch, Chico, jt. auth. see Fischler, Stan.

Resch, Elyse, jt. auth. see Tribole, Evelyn.

Resch, Gerhard, jt. auth. see Gutmann, Viktor.

Resch, H. & Beck, E. Arthroscopy of the Shoulder: Diagnosis & Therapy. Antoft, M. L. & Marschall, B., trs. from GER. (Illus.). 190p. 1992. 158.00 (*0-387-82339-5*) Spr-Verlag.

Resch, John P. Suffering Soldiers: Revolutionary War Veterans, Moral Sentiment & Political Culture in the Early Republic. LC 99-33065. 328p. 2000. text 40.00 (*1-55849-232-1*) U of Mass Pr.

Resch, Kathleen & Robin, Marcy. Dark Shadows in the Afternoon. (Illus.). 112p. (Orig.). 1991. pap. 12.95 (*0-685-50337-2*) Retro Vision.

Resch, Kenneth E. & Schicker, Vicki D. Using Film in the High School Curriculum: A Practical Guide for Teachers & Librarians. LC 92-50316. (Illus.). 176p. 1992. pap. 32.50 (*0-89950-750-6*) McFarland & Co.

Resch, Kurt M. A World of Bus: Toys & Models. LC 99-60097. (Illus.). 160p. 1999. pap. 29.95 (*0-7643-0814-9*) Schiffer.

Resch, Margit. Understanding Christa Wolf: Returning Home from a Foreign Land. LC 96-51242. (Understanding Modern European Literature Ser.). 190p. 1997. text 29.95 (*1-57003-148-7*) U of SC Pr.

Resch, Margit, ed. Seltene Augenblicke: Interpretations of Poems by Hugo von Hofmannsthal. LC 88-62942. (Studies in German Literature, Linguistics & Culture: Vol. 40). (Illus.). 224p. 1989. 39.95 (*0-938100-63-7*) Camden Hse.

Resch, Michael L. Stone Walls & Deep Waters. 32p. (Orig.). 1996. pap. 5.00 (*1-886405-51-4*) White Crow Pr.

Resch, Peter, jt. ed. see Balon, Brett.

Resch, Robert P. Althusser & the Renewal of Marxist Social Theory. LC 91-3014. (C). 1992. 50.00 (*0-520-06082-2*, Pub. by U CA Pr) Cal Prin Full Svc.

Resch, Tyler. Bill Tague's Berkshires. (Images of America Ser.). 128p. 1996. pap. 16.99 (*0-7524-0401-6*) Arcadia Publng.

— Bill Tague's Berkshires, Vol. II. (Images of America Ser.). (Illus.). 128p. 1998. pap. 16.99 (*0-7524-0975-1*) Arcadia Publng.

— Dorset: In the Shadow of the Marble Mountain. LC 89-25511. (Illus.). 416p. 1989. 30.00 (*0-914659-44-8*) Phoenix Pub.

— The Rutland Herald History: Bicentennial Chronicle. 1995. write for info. (*0-9643308-2-2*); lib. bdg. write for info. (*0-9643308-3-0*) Herald Assn.

R

R

Resch, Tyler, ed. The Bob Mitchell Years: An Anthology of Editorials by the Publisher of the Rutland Herald. 528p. 1994. write for info. (0-9643308-0-6); pap. write for info. (0-9643308-1-4) Herald Assn.

Rescher, Nicholas. American Philosophy Today & Other Philosophical Studies. LC 94-16451. 188p. 1994. reprint ed. lib. bdg. 52.50 (0-8476-7935-7) Rowman.
— Baffling Phenomena: And Other Studies in the Philosophy of Knowledge & Valuation. 188p. (C). 1990. lib. bdg. 49.50 (0-8476-7638-2) Rowman.
— Cognitive Economy: The Economic Dimension of the Theory of Knowledge. LC 89-5425. 179p. 1989. pap. 55.50 (0-608-05085-7, 206563900005) Bks Demand.
— Communicative Pragmatism: And Other Philosophical Essays on Language. LC 98-22530. 224p. 1998. 65.00 (0-8476-9090-3); pap. 23.95 (0-8476-9091-1) Rowman.
— Complexity: A Philosophical Overview. LC 98-28312. 162p. 1998. text 32.95 (1-56000-377-4) Transaction Pubs.
— The Development of Arabic Logic. LC 64-13361. 262p. reprint ed. pap. 81.30 (0-608-30659-2, 201557100094) Bks Demand.
— Dialectics: A Controversy-Oriented Approach to the Theory of Knowledge. LC 77-9542. 128p. (C). 1977. text 19.50 (0-87395-372-X) State U NY Pr.
— Essays in the History of Philosophy. LC 95-76330. 373p. 1995. 87.95 (1-85628-970-2, Pub. by Avebry) Ashgate Pub Co.
— Ethical Idealism: An Inquiry into the Nature & Function of Ideals. 1987. pap. 14.95 (0-520-07888-8, Pub. by U CA Pr) Cal Prin Full Svc.
— Forbidden Knowledge. 170p. (C). 1987. text 122.00 (90-277-2410-5, D Reidel) Kluwer Academic.
— G. W. Leibniz's Monadology: An Edition for Students. LC 90-24820. 480p. (C). 1991. pap. 22.50 (0-8229-5449-4); text 49.95 (0-8229-3670-4) U of Pittsburgh Pr.
— Human Interests: Reflections on Philosophical Anthropology. LC 90-30349. (Series in Philosophy). 212p. 1990. 35.00 (0-8047-1811-3) Stanford U Pr.
— Induktion: Zur Rechtfertigung Induktiven Schliessens. Schaffner, Gerhard, tr. from ENG. (Introductiones Ser.).Tr. of Induction: An Essay on the Justification of Inductive Reasoning. (GER.). 246p. 1987. 46.00 (3-88405-051-6); pap. 36.00 (3-88405-078-8) Philosophia Pr.

*Rescher, Nicholas. Inquiry Dynamics. 110p. 2000. 29.95 (0-7658-0007-1) Transaction Pubs.

Rescher, Nicholas. Instructive Journey: An Essay in Autobiography. LC 96-44938. (Illus.). 320p. 1996. 57.50 (0-7618-0585-0); pap. 32.50 (0-7618-0586-9) U Pr of Amer.

*Rescher, Nicholas. Kant & the Reach of Reason: Studies in Kant's Theory of Rational Systematization. LC 99-25919. 196p. (C). 1999. 54.95 (0-521-66100-5); pap. 19.95 (0-521-66791-7) Cambridge U Pr.

Rescher, Nicholas. Leibniz: An Introduction to His Philosophy. (Modern Revivals in Philosophy Ser.). 176p. 1994. 51.95 (0-7512-0275-4, Pub. by Gregg Revivals) Ashgate Pub Co.
— Leibniz's Metaphysics of Nature: A Group of Essays. (University of Western Ontario Series in Phylosophy of Science: No. 18). 140p. 1981. pap. text 59.00 (90-277-1253-0); lib. bdg. 70.50 (90-277-1252-2) Kluwer Academic.
— The Limits of Science. LC 99-6562. 280p. 1999. pap. 19.95 (0-8229-5713-2) U of Pittsburgh Pr.
— The Logic of Decision & Action. LC 67-18272. 236p. reprint ed. pap. 73.20 (0-608-30824-2, 201049500068) Bks Demand.
— Luck: The Brilliant Randomness of Everyday Life. LC 95-17421. 237p. 1995. 19.00 (0-374-19428-9) FS&G.
— Many-Valued Logic. (Modern Revivals in Philosophy Ser.). 376p. 1993. 67.95 (0-7512-0274-6, Pub. by Gregg Revivals) Ashgate Pub Co.
— Metaphilosophical Inquiries. LC 93-5179. (System of Pragmatic Idealism Ser.: Vol. 3). 288p. 1994. text 55.00 (0-691-07394-5, Pub. by Princeton U Pr) Cal Prin Full Svc.
— Mid-Journey: An Unfinished Autobiography. LC 82-45083. (Illus.). 204p. (Orig.). 1983. pap. 18.75 (0-8191-2523-7); lib. bdg. 50.50 (0-8191-2522-9) U Pr of Amer.
— Moral Absolute: An Essay on the Nature & Rationale of Morality. (Studies in Moral Philosophy: Vol. 2). X, 115p. (C). 1989. text 29.00 (0-8204-0797-6) P Lang Pubng.
— Objectivity: The Obligations of Impersonal Reason. LC 96-26431. 264p. (C). 1997. text 35.00 (0-268-03701-9); pap. text 16.00 (0-268-03703-5) U of Notre Dame Pr.
— Philosophical Standardism: An Empiricist Approach to Philosophical Methodology. 224p. (C). 1994. text 49.95 (0-8229-3790-5) U of Pittsburgh Pr.

*Rescher, Nicholas. Philosophical Standardism: An Empiricist Approach to Philosophical Methodology. (Philosophy Ser.). 224p. 2000. pap. 19.95 (0-8229-5739-6) U of Pittsburgh Pr.

Rescher, Nicholas. Pluralism: Against the Demand for Consensus. (Clarendon Library of Logic & Philosophy). (Illus.). 216p. 1995. reprint ed. pap. text 19.95 (0-19-823601-8) OUP.
— Predicting the Future: An Introduction to the Theory of Forecasting. LC 97-1986. 315p. (C). 1997. text 65.50 (0-7914-3553-9); pap. text 21.95 (0-7914-3554-7) State U NY Pr.
— Priceless Knowledge? Natural Science in Economic Perspective. LC 96-18508. 198p. 1996. 55.50 (0-8476-8244-7); pap. 23.95 (0-8476-8245-5) Rowman.
— Process Metaphysics: An Introduction to Process Philosophy. LC 95-8784. (SUNY Series in Philosophy). 213p. (C). 1996. text 36.50 (0-7914-2817-6); pap. text 17.95 (0-7914-2818-4) State U NY Pr.

*Rescher, Nicholas. Process Philosophy: A Survey of Basic Issues. 120p. 2000. 27.50 (0-8229-4142-2) U of Pittsburgh Pr.

Rescher, Nicholas. Profitable Speculations: Essays on Current Philosophical Themes. LC 97-17812. 300p. 1997. 71.50 (0-8476-8677-9); pap. 26.95 (0-8476-8678-7) Rowman.
— Public Concerns: Philosophical Studies of Social Science. 208p. (Orig.). (C). 1995. pap. text 21.95 (0-8476-8126-2); lib. bdg. 52.50 (0-8476-8125-4) Rowman.
— Realistic Pragmatism: An Introduction to Pragmatic Philosophy. LC 99-15030. (SUNY Series in Philosophy). 288p. (C). 1999. text 65.50 (0-7914-4407-4); pap. text 21.95 (0-7914-4408-2) State U NY Pr.
— Reason & Rationality in Natural Science: A Group of Essays. 228p. (Orig.). 1985. lib. bdg. 49.50 (0-8191-4763-X) U Pr of Amer.
— Risk: A Philosophical Introduction to the Theory of Risk Evaluation & Management. LC 82-21970. (Nicholas Rescher Ser.). 218p. (Orig.). 1983. pap. text 23.00 (0-8191-2270-X) U Pr of Amer.
— Satisfying Reason: Studies in the Theory of Knowledge. LC 94-33491. (Episteme Ser.: Vol. 21). 256p. (C). 1995. lib. bdg. 114.50 (0-7923-3148-6, Pub. by Kluwer Academic) Kluwer Academic.
— Scientific Realism: A Critical Reappraisal. (University of Western Ontario Series in Phylosophy of Science: No. 40). 182p. 1987. pap. text 62.50 (90-277-2528-4); lib. bdg. 110.00 (90-277-2442-3) Kluwer Academic.
— The Strife of Systems: An Essay on the Grounds & Implications of Philosophical Diversity. LC 84-21958. 295p. 1985. reprint ed. pap. 91.50 (0-608-02053-2, 206270600003) Bks Demand.
— Studies in the History of Arabic Logic. LC 63-17521. 108p. reprint ed. pap. 33.50 (0-608-30822-6, 201049900068) Bks Demand.
— A System of Pragmatic Idealism Vol. 2: The Validity of Values - A Normative Theory of Evaluative Rationality. 296p. 1993. text 55.00 (0-691-07393-7, Pub. by Princeton U Pr) Cal Prin Full Svc.
— Temporal Modalities in Arabic Logic. (Foundations of Language Supplementary Ser.: No. 2). 50p. 1966. text 57.00 (90-277-0083-4) Kluwer Academic.
— Topics in Philosophical Logic. (Synthese Library: No. 17). 347p. 1968. text 171.00 (90-277-0084-2, D Reidel) Kluwer Academic.
— Unpopular Essays on Technological Progress. LC 79-21648. (Illus.). 132p. 1980. text 49.95 (0-8229-3411-6) U of Pittsburgh Pr.
— Unselfishness: The Role of the Vicarious Affects in Moral Philosophy & Social Theory. LC 75-9123. 138p. 1975. text 49.95 (0-8229-3308-X) U of Pittsburgh Pr.
— A Useful Inheritance: Evolutionary Aspects of the Theory of Knowledge. LC 89-27509. 148p. (C). 1990. lib. bdg. 46.50 (0-8476-7615-3) Rowman.
— Welfare: The Social Issues in Philosophical Perspective. LC 70-158184. 198p. reprint ed. pap. 61.40 (0-608-12656-X, 202544400043) Bks Demand.

Rescher, Nicholas, ed. Aesthetic Factors in Natural Science. LC 89-35898. 110p. (C). 1990. lib. bdg. 37.50 (0-8191-7576-5) U Pr of Amer.
— Evolution, Cognition, & Realism: Studies in Evolutionary Epistemology. (CPS Publications in Philosophy of Science). 144p. (C). 1990. pap. text 19.00 (0-8191-7755-5); lib. bdg. 39.00 (0-8191-7754-7) U Pr of Amer.
— Heritage of Logical Positivism. (CPS Publications in Philosophy of Science). 186p. (Orig.). 1985. pap. text 23.00 (0-8191-4471-1) U Pr of Amer.
— Leibnizian Inquiries: A Group of Essays. LC 88-37059. (CPS Publications in Philosophy of Science). 196p. (Orig.). (C). 1989. pap. text 19.50 (0-8191-7359-2); lib. bdg. 37.00 (0-8191-7358-4) U Pr of Amer.
— Scientific Inquiry in Philosophical Perspective. (CPS Publications in Philosophy of Science). (Illus.). 308p. (Orig.). 1987. pap. text 26.00 (0-8191-5799-6) U Pr of Amer.

Rescher, Nicholas, et al, eds. Essays in Honor of Carl G. Hempel: A Tribute on the Occasion of His Sixty-Fifth Birthday. (Synthese Library: No.24). 279p. 1969. text 153.00 (90-277-0085-0, D Reidel) Kluwer Academic.

Rescher, Nicholas, tr. see Al-Farabi.

Reschke, Angelika, et al. Voila: Glanzstucke Historischer Moden 1750-1960 (Masterpieces of Fashion 1750-1960) Hornsbostel, Wilhelm, ed. (GER., Illus.). 192p. 1991. 80.25 (3-7913-1117-4, Pub. by Prestel) te Neues.

Reschke, Claus. Life As a Man: Contemporary Male-Female Relationships in the Novels of Max Frisch. LC 89-39785. (Studies in Modern German Literature: Vol. 34). 409p. (C). 1990. text 72.95 (0-8204-1163-9) P Lang Pubng.

Reschke, H. & Schelle, H., eds. Dimensions of Project Management: Fundamentals, Techniques, Organization, Applications. (Illus.). xvii, 336p. 1990. pap. 77.00 (0-387-53157-2) Spr-Verlag.

*Reschly, Daniel J., et al, eds. Special Education in Transition: Functional Assessment & Noncategorical Programming. 1999. pap. 27.50 (1-57035-227-5, 131 NONCAAT) Sopris.

*Reschly, Steven D. Amish on the Iowa Prairie, 1840 to 1910. (Illus.). 256p. 2000. 42.50 (0-8018-6388-0) Johns Hopkins.

Rescigno, A. & Boicelli, A., eds. Cerebral Blood Flow: Mathematical Models, Instrumentation, & Imaging Techniques. LC 88-25519. (NATO ASI Series A, Life Sciences: Vol. 153). (Illus.). 272p. 1988. 95.00 (0-306-43019-3, Plenum Trade) Perseus Pubng.

Rescigno, A. & Thakur, A. K., eds. New Trends in Pharmacokinetics. (NATO ASI Ser.: Vol. 221). (Illus.). 456p. (C). 1992. text 168.00 (0-306-44089-X, Kluwer Plenum) Kluwer Academic.

Rescigno, A., jt. ed. see Pecile, A.

Rescigno, Dolores. Behavior Modification in Business & Industry: A Selected Bibliography. (CPL Bibliographies Ser.: No. 140). 58p. 1984. 10.00 (0-86602-140-X, Sage Prdcls Pr) Sage.

Rescigno, Federico, jt. auth. see Connell, Stanley W.

*Rescorla, Eric. SSL & TLS: Building & Designing Secure Systems. 2000. pap. 34.95 (0-201-61598-3) Addison-Wesley.

Rescorla, Leslie, et al, eds. Academic Instruction in Early Childhood: Challenge or Pressure? LC 85-644581. (New Directions for Child Development Ser.: No. CD 53). 1991. pap. 25.00 (1-55542-769-3) Jossey-Bass.

Rescue American Red Cross Staff. American Red Cross CPR for the Professional Rescue. 160p. (gr. 13). 1993. pap. text 11.90 (0-8016-7067-5) Mosby Inc.

Rescue Training Associates, Ltd. Staff, et al. Vehicle Rescue. (Illus.). 1975. teacher ed. 7.95 (0-87618-611-8); pap. text 24.95 (0-89303-118-6) P-H.

Rescue Training Association Staff. Action Guide for Emergency Service Personnel. 656p. 1985. pap. text 39.00 (0-89303-301-4) P-H.

Research & Education Association Staff. Act. 1998. pap. text 29.95 incl. cd-rom (0-87891-213-4) Res & Educ.
— ACT-American College Testing. 1000p. 2000. pap. text 17.95 (0-87891-967-8) Res & Educ.
— Act with Testware: Book Plus Software. 2000. pap. text 29.95 (0-87891-794-2) Res & Educ.
— Advanced Calculus Problem Solver. rev. ed. LC 81-52799. (Illus.). 1056p. 1999. pap. text 29.95 (0-87891-533-8) Res & Educ.
— Advanced Placement Examination in Biology. rev. ed. LC 88-90702. (Illus.). 592p. 2000. pap. text 17.95 (0-87891-652-0) Res & Educ.
— Advanced Placement Examination in Calculus BC. rev. ed. (Illus.). 368p. 2000. pap. text 17.95 (0-87891-647-4) Res & Educ.
— Advanced Placement Examination in Physics. rev. ed. (Illus.). 1998. pap. text 17.95 (0-87891-881-7) Res & Educ.
— Advanced Placement Examination in Psychology. rev. ed. (Illus.). 336p. 2000. pap. text 19.95 (0-87891-883-3) Res & Educ.
— Algebra & Trigonometry Problem Solver. rev. ed. LC 76-334. (Illus.). 924p. (C). 1999. pap. text 23.95 (0-87891-508-7) Res & Educ.
— AP Examination in English Literature & Composition. rev. ed. LC 97-68615. (Illus.). 368p. 2000. pap. text 17.95 (0-87891-843-4) Res & Educ.
— AP Statistics. LC 97-65092. 1998. pap. text 20.95 (0-87891-082-4) Res & Educ.
— Authoritative Guide to the Top 100 Careers to Year 2005. LC 96-67991. 368p. 1997. pap. 19.95 (0-87891-062-X) Res & Educ.
— Automatic Control Systems-Robotic Problem Solver. rev. ed. LC 82-61485. (Illus.). 1088p. 1999. pap. text 29.95 (0-87891-542-7) Res & Educ.
— Best Test Preparation for CLEP General Examinations. LC 95-68426. 1108p. 1998. pap. text 19.95 (0-87891-901-5) Res & Educ.
— The Best Test Preparation for the Advanced Placement Examination in European History. rev. ed. (Rea Test Preps Ser.). (Illus.). 592p. 1999. pap. 20.95 (0-87891-863-9) Res & Educ.
— The Best Test Preparation for the Advanced Placement Examination in United States History. rev. ed. (Illus.). 622p. 2000. pap. 20.95 (0-87891-844-2) Res & Educ.
— The Best Test Preparation for the ASVAB, Armed Services Vocational Aptitude Battery. 600p. 1998. pap. 19.95 (0-87891-895-7) Res & Educ.
— Best Test Preparation for the Place: Program for Licensing Assessments for Colorado Educators. LC 97-69317. 900p. 1998. pap. 29.95 (0-87891-093-X) Res & Educ.
— Biology Builder for Standardized Tests. 512p. 1998. pap. text 15.95 (0-87891-940-6) Res & Educ.
— Biology of Mental Disorders. 192p. 1995. pap. text 15.95 (0-87891-960-0) Res & Educ.
— Biology Problem Solver. rev. ed. LC 78-63610. (Illus.). 1088p. 1999. pap. text 23.95 (0-87891-514-1) Res & Educ.
— Business, Accounting & Finance Problem Solver. rev. ed. LC 78-64582. (Illus.). 862p. 1999. pap. text 24.95 (0-87891-516-8) Res & Educ.
— Calculus Problem Solver. rev. ed. Weisbecker, Henry, ed. LC 74-17899. (Illus.). 1088p. (C). 1999. pap. text 23.95 (0-87891-505-2) Res & Educ.
— Chemical Engineering Handbook. LC 98-73108. 1500p. 1999. pap. text 38.95 (0-87891-982-1) Res & Educ.
— Chemistry Builder for Standardized Tests. 544p. 1998. pap. text 15.95 (0-87891-939-2) Res & Educ.
— Chemistry Problem Solver. rev. ed. LC 77-70335. (Illus.). 1056p. 1999. pap. text 23.95 (0-87891-509-5) Res & Educ.
— CLEP - Analysis & Interpretation of Literature. LC 97-68344. (CLEP Ser.). 368p. 1998. pap. text 26.95 (0-87891-897-3) Res & Educ.
— CLEP - College Algebra. LC 95-68212. (CLEP Ser.). 368p. 2000. pap. text 26.95 (0-87891-898-1) Res & Educ.
— CLEP - Freshman College Composition. (CLEP Ser.). 312p. 1998. pap. text 25.95 (0-87891-899-X) Res & Educ.
— CLEP - General Examinations Review Book. LC 96-68950. (CLEP Ser.). 1008p. 1998. pap. text 24.95 (0-87891-900-7) Res & Educ.
— CLEP - History of U. S. I, No. 1. LC 97-68613. (CLEP Ser.). 400p. 1999. pap. text 26.95 (0-87891-896-5) Res & Educ.
— CLEP - Human Growth & Development. LC 95-69957. (CLEP Ser.). 400p. 2000. pap. text 26.95 (0-87891-902-3) Res & Educ.
— CLEP - Introductory Sociology. (CLEP Ser.). 320p. 1998. pap. text 25.95 (0-87891-903-1) Res & Educ.
— CLEP - Principles of Marketing. (CLEP Ser.). 312p. 1999. pap. text 25.95 (0-87891-904-X) Res & Educ.
— Differential Equations Problem Solver. rev. ed. LC 78-63609. (Illus.). 1408p. 2000. pap. text 29.95 (0-87891-513-3) Res & Educ.
— Economics Problem Solver. rev. ed. LC 80-53175. (Illus.). 1088p. (Orig.). (C). 1998. pap. text 23.95 (0-87891-524-9) Res & Educ.
— Electric Circuits Problem Solver. rev. ed. LC 79-92401. (Illus.). 1176p. 1998. pap. text 29.95 (0-87891-517-6) Res & Educ.
— Electrical Engineering Handbook. 1500p. 1996. pap. text 38.95 (0-87891-981-3) Res & Educ.
— Electrical Machines Problem Solver. rev. ed. LC 83-62280. (Illus.). 800p. 1994. pap. text 29.95 (0-87891-551-6) Res & Educ.
— Electromagnetics Problem Solver. rev. ed. LC 83-62279. (Illus.). 1008p. 2000. pap. 29.95 (0-87891-550-8) Res & Educ.
— Electronic Communications Problem Solver. rev. ed. LC 84-61814. (Illus.). 960p. 1994. pap. text 29.95 (0-87891-558-3) Res & Educ.
— Electronics Problem Solver. rev. ed. LC 82-61484. (Illus.). 1310p. 2000. pap. text 29.95 (0-87891-543-5) Res & Educ.
— ELM - CA State University Entry Level Mathematics Test. LC 97-65003. 1997. pap. 16.95 (0-87891-909-0) Res & Educ.
— English Handbook of Grammar, Style, & Composition. rev. ed. LC 83-62275. (Illus.). 320p. 1998. pap. text 20.95 (0-87891-552-4) Res & Educ.
— Essential of Canadian History, Prehistory to 1867. 104p. 2000. pap. 6.95 (0-87891-916-3) Res & Educ.
— Essentials of Accounting I. rev. ed. (Illus.). 96p. 2000. pap. text 6.95 (0-87891-667-9) Res & Educ.
— Essentials of Advanced Accounting I. rev. ed. LC 96-67812. (Illus.). 96p. 2000. pap. text 6.95 (0-87891-692-X) Res & Educ.
— Essentials of Advanced Accounting II. rev. ed. (Illus.). 128p. 2000. pap. text 5.95 (0-87891-905-8) Res & Educ.
— Essentials of Advanced Calculus I. rev. ed. (Illus.). 80p. 1994. pap. text 5.95 (0-87891-567-2) Res & Educ.
— Essentials of Advanced Calculus II. rev. ed. (Illus.). 64p. 1994. pap. text 5.95 (0-87891-568-0) Res & Educ.
— Essentials of Algebra & Trigonometry I. rev. ed. (Illus.). 96p. 1999. pap. text 6.95 (0-87891-569-9) Res & Educ.
— Essentials of Algebra & Trigonometry II. rev. ed. (Illus.). 80p. 1999. pap. text 5.95 (0-87891-570-2) Res & Educ.
— Essentials of Anatomy & Physiology. 96p. 1999. pap. text 6.95 (0-87891-922-8) Res & Educ.
— Essentials of Ancient History 4,500 BC-500 AD. rev. ed. (Illus.). 96p. 2000. pap. text 5.95 (0-87891-704-7) Res & Educ.
— Essentials of Anthropology. rev. ed. LC 98-68564. (Illus.). 128p. 1999. pap. text 6.95 (0-87891-722-5) Res & Educ.
— Essentials of Art History. (Essentials Ser.). 96p. 1999. 6.95 (0-87891-792-6) Res & Educ.
— Essentials of Astronomy. LC 94-67852. 100p. 1998. pap. text 5.95 (0-87891-965-1) Res & Educ.
— Essentials of Automatic Control Systems - Robotics II. rev. ed. (Illus.). 96p. 1994. pap. 5.95 (0-87891-572-9) Res & Educ.
— Essentials of BASIC. rev. ed. (Illus.). 128p. 2000. pap. text 6.95 (0-87891-684-9) Res & Educ.
— Essentials of Biology I. rev. ed. (Illus.). 64p. 2000. pap. text 6.95 (0-87891-573-7) Res & Educ.
— Essentials of Biology II. rev. ed. (Illus.). 64p. 1998. pap. text 5.95 (0-87891-574-5) Res & Educ.
— Essentials of Boolean Algebra. rev. ed. (Illus.). 112p. 1994. pap. text 5.95 (0-87891-698-9) Res & Educ.
— Essentials of Business Law II. rev. ed. (Illus.). 128p. 1999. pap. text 5.95 (0-87891-729-2) Res & Educ.
— Essentials of Business Law I. rev. ed. (Illus.). 128p. 1998. pap. text 6.95 (0-87891-690-3) Res & Educ.
— Essentials of Business Statistics I. rev. ed. LC 96-67266. (Illus.). 112p. 1998. pap. text 5.95 (0-87891-841-8) Res & Educ.
— Essentials of Business Statistics II. rev. ed. (Illus.). 128p. 1995. pap. text 5.95 (0-87891-842-6) Res & Educ.
— Essentials of C Programming Language. rev. ed. (Illus.). 128p. 1998. pap. text 5.95 (0-87891-696-2) Res & Educ.
— Essentials of Calculus I. rev. ed. (Illus.). 80p. 1999. pap. text 6.95 (0-87891-577-X) Res & Educ.
— Essentials of Calculus III. rev. ed. (Illus.). 80p. 1999. pap. text 6.95 (0-87891-579-6) Res & Educ.
— Essentials of Calculus II. rev. ed. (Illus.). 64p. 1999. pap. text 6.95 (0-87891-578-8) Res & Educ.
— Essentials of Canadian History since 1867. 112p. 1998. pap. 5.95 (0-87891-917-1) Res & Educ.
— Essentials of Chemistry. rev. ed. (Illus.). 96p. 1998. pap. text 6.95 (0-87891-580-X) Res & Educ.
— Essentials of COBOL II. rev. ed. (Illus.). 112p. 1994. pap. text 5.95 (0-87891-680-6) Res & Educ.
— Essentials of College & University Writing. 100p. 1999. pap. text 6.95 (0-87891-964-3) Res & Educ.
— Essentials of Complex Variables I. rev. ed. (Illus.). 112p. 1994. pap. text 5.95 (0-87891-661-X) Res & Educ.
— Essentials of Complex Variables II. rev. ed. (Illus.). 112p. 1994. pap. text 5.95 (0-87891-662-8) Res & Educ.
— Essentials of Computer Science I. LC 96-67993. (Essentials Ser.). 96p. 2000. 6.95 (0-87891-670-9) Res & Educ.
— Essentials of Computer Science II. LC 96-67992. (Essentials Ser.). 96p. 1998. 5.95 (0-87891-671-7) Res & Educ.
— Essentials of Cost & Managerial Accounting I. rev. ed. LC 97-75935. (Illus.). 96p. 1998. pap. text 5.95 (0-87891-664-4) Res & Educ.

An Asterisk (*) at the beginning of an entry indicates that the title is appearing for the first time.

— Essentials of Cost & Managerial Accounting II. rev. ed. LC 96-71058. (Illus.). 96p. 1997. pap. text 5.95 (*0-87891-668-7*) Res & Educ.
— Essentials of Data Structures I. rev. ed. LC 96-68367. (Illus.). 112p. 1996. pap. text 5.95 (*0-87891-728-4*) Res & Educ.
— Essentials of Data Structures II. rev. ed. (Illus.). 112p. 2000. pap. text 6.95 (*0-87891-837-X*) Res & Educ.
— Essentials of Differential Equations I. rev. ed. (Illus.). 96p. 1998. pap. text 5.95 (*0-87891-581-8*) Res & Educ.
— Essentials of Differential Equations II. rev. ed. (Illus.). 96p. 1994. pap. text 5.95 (*0-87891-582-6*) Res & Educ.
— Essentials of Discrete Structures. rev. ed. (Illus.). 96p. 1994. pap. text 5.95 (*0-87891-723-3*) Res & Educ.
— Essentials of Electric Circuits I. rev. ed. (Illus.). 64p. 1994. pap. text 5.95 (*0-87891-585-0*) Res & Educ.
— Essentials of Electromagnetics I. rev. ed. (Illus.). 80p. 1994. pap. text 5.95 (*0-87891-587-7*) Res & Educ.
— Essentials of Electromagnetics II. rev. ed. (Illus.). 64p. 1994. pap. text 5.95 (*0-87891-588-5*) Res & Educ.
— Essentials of Electronic Communications I. rev. ed. (Illus.). 80p. 1994. pap. text 5.95 (*0-87891-589-3*) Res & Educ.
— Essentials of Electronic Communications II. rev. ed. (Illus.). 112p. 1994. pap. text 5.95 (*0-87891-590-7*) Res & Educ.
— Essentials of Electronics I. rev. ed. LC 97-67031. (Illus.). 112p. 1998. pap. text 5.95 (*0-87891-591-5*) Res & Educ.
— Essentials of Electronics II. rev. ed. (Illus.). 112p. 1994. pap. text 5.95 (*0-87891-592-3*) Res & Educ.
— Essentials of English Language. (Essentials Ser.). 138p. 2000. 6.95 (*0-87891-789-6*) Res & Educ.
— Essentials of European History, 1848-1914. rev. ed. (Illus.). 96p. 1997. pap. text 5.95 (*0-87891-709-8*) Res & Educ.
— Essentials of European History, 1450-1648. rev. ed. (Illus.). 96p. 1999. pap. text 5.95 (*0-87891-706-3*) Res & Educ.
— Essentials of European History, 1914-1935. rev. ed. (Illus.). 128p. 1997. pap. text 5.95 (*0-87891-710-1*) Res & Educ.
— Essentials of European History, 1789-1848. rev. ed. (Illus.). 96p. 1999. pap. text 6.95 (*0-87891-708-X*) Res & Educ.
— Essentials of European History since 1935. rev. ed. (Illus.). 128p. 1997. pap. text 5.95 (*0-87891-711-X*) Res & Educ.
— Essentials of Financial Management. rev. ed. (Illus.). 128p. 1998. pap. text 5.95 (*0-87891-724-1*) Res & Educ.
— Essentials of Fluid Mechanics - Dynamics I. rev. ed. (Illus.). 80p. 1994. pap. text 5.95 (*0-87891-594-X*) Res & Educ.
— Essentials of Fortran. rev. ed. (Illus.). 128p. 1994. pap. text 5.95 (*0-87891-663-6*) Res & Educ.
— Essentials of Fourier Analysis. rev. ed. (Illus.). 80p. 1994. pap. text 5.95 (*0-87891-697-0*) Res & Educ.
— Essentials of French. LC 98-66570. (FRE.). 96p. 1999. pap. text 5.95 (*0-87891-926-0*) Res & Educ.
— Essentials of Geometry I. rev. ed. LC 98-65414. (Illus.). 80p. 2000. pap. text 6.95 (*0-87891-606-7*) Res & Educ.
— Essentials of Geometry II. rev. ed. (Illus.). 96p. 1998. pap. text 5.95 (*0-87891-607-5*) Res & Educ.
— Essentials of German. (GER.). 96p. 1998. pap. text 5.95 (*0-87891-927-9*) Res & Educ.
— Essentials of Group Theory I. rev. ed. (Illus.). 112p. 1994. pap. text 5.95 (*0-87891-686-5*) Res & Educ.
— Essentials of Group-Theory II. rev. ed. (Illus.). 96p. 1994. pap. text 5.95 (*0-87891-687-3*) Res & Educ.
— Essentials of Heat Transfer II. rev. ed. (Illus.). 80p. 1994. pap. text 5.95 (*0-87891-609-1*) Res & Educ.
— Essentials of HIV-AIDS. 100p. 1995. pap. text 5.95 (*0-87891-984-8*) Res & Educ.
— Essentials of Intermediate Accounting I. rev. ed. (Illus.). 112p. 1999. pap. text 5.95 (*0-87891-682-2*) Res & Educ.
— Essentials of Intermediate Accounting II. rev. ed. LC 98-67285. (Illus.). 128p. 1999. pap. text 6.95 (*0-87891-683-0*) Res & Educ.
— Essentials of Italian. (ITA.). 96p. 1995. pap. text 5.95 (*0-87891-929-5*) Res & Educ.
— Essentials of La Place Transforms. rev. ed. (Illus.). 128p. 1994. pap. text 5.95 (*0-87891-726-8*) Res & Educ.
— Essentials of Linear Algebra. rev. ed. (Illus.). 96p. 1998. pap. text 5.95 (*0-87891-610-5*) Res & Educ.
— Essentials of Macroeconomics II. rev. ed. (Illus.). 96p. 1998. pap. text 5.95 (*0-87891-719-5*) Res & Educ.
— Essentials of Macroeconomics I. rev. ed. (Illus.). 96p. 1998. pap. text 6.95 (*0-87891-700-4*) Res & Educ.
— Essentials of Marketing Principles. rev. ed. (Illus.). 128p. 1996. pap. text 5.95 (*0-87891-693-8*) Res & Educ.
— Essentials of Math for Computer Applications. LC 98-67990. 70p. 1999. pap. 6.95 (*0-87891-314-9*) Res & Educ.
— Essentials of Mathematics for Engineers II. rev. ed. (Illus.). 128p. 1994. pap. text 5.95 (*0-87891-891-4*) Res & Educ.
— Essentials of Mechanics I. rev. ed. (Illus.). 96p. 1994. pap. text 5.95 (*0-87891-611-3*) Res & Educ.
— Essentials of Mechanics III. rev. ed. (Illus.). 96p. 1994. pap. text 5.95 (*0-87891-613-X*) Res & Educ.
— Essentials of Mechanics II. rev. ed. (Illus.). 96p. 1994. pap. text 5.95 (*0-87891-612-1*) Res & Educ.
— Essentials of Medieval History, 500-1450 AD. rev. ed. (Illus.). 96p. 1998. pap. text 5.95 (*0-87891-705-5*) Res & Educ.
— Essentials of Microbiology. 96p. 1999. pap. text 6.95 (*0-87891-924-4*) Res & Educ.
— Essentials of Microeconomics. rev. ed. (Illus.). 128p. 1999. pap. text 6.95 (*0-87891-660-1*) Res & Educ.
— Essentials of Modern Algebra. rev. ed. (Illus.). 80p. 1999. pap. text 6.95 (*0-87891-681-4*) Res & Educ.
— Essentials of Molecular Structures of Life. 128p. 1995. pap. text 5.95 (*0-87891-983-X*) Res & Educ.
— Essentials of Money & Banking I. rev. ed. (Illus.). 112p. 1995. pap. text 5.95 (*0-87891-691-1*) Res & Educ.
— Essentials of Money & Banking II. rev. ed. (Illus.). 128p. 1994. pap. text 5.95 (*0-87891-720-9*) Res & Educ.
— Essentials of Numerical Analysis, II. rev. ed. (Illus.). 96p. 1994. pap. text 5.95 (*0-87891-615-6*) Res & Educ.
— Essentials of Numerical Analysis I. rev. ed. (Illus.). 96p. 1994. pap. text 5.95 (*0-87891-614-8*) Res & Educ.
— Essentials of Organic Chemistry I. rev. ed. (Illus.). 128p. 1999. pap. text 6.95 (*0-87891-616-4*) Res & Educ.
— Essentials of Organic Chemistry II. rev. ed. (Illus.). 128p. 1998. pap. text 5.95 (*0-87891-617-2*) Res & Educ.
— Essentials of PASCAL I. rev. ed. (Illus.). 80p. 1994. pap. text 5.95 (*0-87891-694-6*) Res & Educ.
— Essentials of PASCAL II. rev. ed. (Illus.). 96p. 1994. pap. text 5.95 (*0-87891-718-7*) Res & Educ.
— Essentials of Physical Chemistry, II. rev. ed. (Illus.). 128p. 1994. pap. text 5.95 (*0-87891-621-0*) Res & Educ.
— Essentials of Physical Chemistry I. rev. ed. LC 96-72632. (Illus.). 128p. 1994. pap. text 5.95 (*0-87891-620-2*) Res & Educ.
— Essentials of Physics I. rev. ed. (Illus.). 96p. 2000. pap. 6.95 (*0-87891-618-0*) Res & Educ.
— Essentials of Physics II. rev. ed. LC 97-68108. (Illus.). 80p. 1998. pap. 5.95 (*0-87891-619-9*) Res & Educ.
— Essentials of PL-1 Programming. rev. ed. (Illus.). 112p. 1994. pap. text 5.95 (*0-87891-695-4*) Res & Educ.
— Essentials of Political Science. LC 95-71343. (Essentials Ser.). 96p. 1996. 5.95 (*0-87891-791-8*) Res & Educ.
— Essentials of Pre-Calculus. rev. ed. (Illus.). 128p. 1998. pap. text 6.95 (*0-87891-877-9*) Res & Educ.
— Essentials of Probability. rev. ed. (Illus.). 128p. 1997. pap. text 5.95 (*0-87891-840-X*) Res & Educ.
— Essentials of Psychology I. 96p. 1996. pap. text 6.95 (*0-87891-930-9*) Res & Educ.
— Essentials of Psychology II. 96p. 1995. pap. text 6.95 (*0-87891-931-7*) Res & Educ.
— Essentials of Real Variables. (Illus.). 96p. 1994. pap. text 5.95 (*0-87891-921-X*) Res & Educ.
— Essentials of Set Theory. rev. ed. (Illus.). 80p. 1994. pap. text 5.95 (*0-87891-657-1*) Res & Educ.
— Essentials of Sociology. LC 97-68610. 100p. 1999. pap. text 5.95 (*0-87891-966-X*) Res & Educ.
— Essentials of Spanish. LC 94-65503. (SPA.). 96p. 1996. pap. text 6.95 (*0-87891-928-7*) Res & Educ.
— Essentials of Statistics I. rev. ed. LC 95-68121. (Illus.). 112p. 1999. pap. text 6.95 (*0-87891-658-X*) Res & Educ.
— Essentials of Statistics II. rev. ed. (Illus.). 128p. 1998. pap. text 5.95 (*0-87891-659-8*) Res & Educ.
— Essentials of Strength of Materials I. rev. ed. (Illus.). 128p. 1994. pap. text 5.95 (*0-87891-624-5*) Res & Educ.
— Essentials of Strength of Materials II. rev. ed. (Illus.). 128p. 1994. pap. text 5.95 (*0-87891-625-3*) Res & Educ.
— Essentials of Thermodynamics I. rev. ed. (Illus.). 64p. 1998. pap. text 5.95 (*0-87891-626-1*) Res & Educ.
— Essentials of Thermodynamics II. rev. ed. (Illus.). 64p. 1994. pap. text 5.95 (*0-87891-627-X*) Res & Educ.
— Essentials of Topology. rev. ed. (Illus.). 112p. 1994. pap. text 5.95 (*0-87891-685-7*) Res & Educ.
— Essentials of Transport Phenomena I. rev. ed. (Illus.). 96p. 1994. pap. text 5.95 (*0-87891-628-8*) Res & Educ.
— Essentials of Transport Phenomena II. rev. ed. (Illus.). 112p. 1994. pap. text 5.95 (*0-87891-629-6*) Res & Educ.
— Essentials of U. S. History, 1841-1877. rev. ed. (Illus.). 96p. 2000. pap. text 6.95 (*0-87891-714-4*) Res & Educ.
— Essentials of U. S. History, 1877-1912. rev. ed. LC 97-68340. (Illus.). 96p. 1995. pap. text 5.95 (*0-87891-715-2*) Res & Educ.
— Essentials of U. S. History, 1500-1789. rev. ed. LC 96-67268. (Illus.). 96p. 2000. pap. text 6.95 (*0-87891-712-8*) Res & Educ.
— Essentials of U. S. History, 1789-1841. rev. ed. (Illus.). 112p. 2000. pap. text 6.95 (*0-87891-713-6*) Res & Educ.
— Essentials of Vector Analysis. rev. ed. (Illus.). 128p. 1994. pap. text 5.95 (*0-87891-630-X*) Res & Educ.
— European History Builder for Admission & Standardized Tests. 544p. 1995. pap. text 14.95 (*0-87891-782-9*) Res & Educ.
— ExCET: Texas Education Certification. (Illus.). 336p. 2000. pap. text 25.95 (*0-87891-971-6*) Res & Educ.
— Finite & Discrete Math Problem Solver. rev. ed. LC 84-61815. (Illus.). 1032p. 1999. pap. text 24.95 (*0-87891-559-1*) Res & Educ.
— Fluid Mechanics-Dynamics Problem Solver. rev. ed. LC 83-62278. (Illus.). 960p. 1999. pap. text 29.95 (*0-87891-547-8*) Res & Educ.
— GED - General Educational Development Test, Canadian Edition. (Illus.). 1024p. 1994. pap. text 15.95 (*0-87891-918-X*) Res & Educ.
— GED - H. S. Equivalency Diploma Test. rev. ed. LC 98-68563. (Illus.). 912p. 2000. pap. text 17.95 (*0-87891-869-8*) Res & Educ.

***Research & Education Association Staff.** Genetics Problem Solver. rev. ed. LC 85-62730. (Illus.). 640p. 1999. pap. text 23.95 (*0-87891-560-5*) Res & Educ.

Research & Education Association Staff. Geometry Problem Solvers: Plane, Solid, & Analytic. rev. ed. LC 77-70336. (Illus.). 1080p. 1998. pap. text 23.95 (*0-87891-510-9*) Res & Educ.
— GRE Biology Test Preparation. rev. ed. (Illus.). 736p. 1999. pap. text 23.95 (*0-87891-602-4*) Res & Educ.
— GRE Chemistry Test Preparation. rev. ed. (Illus.). 480p. 2000. pap. text 26.95 (*0-87891-600-8*) Res & Educ.
— GRE Computer Science Test Preparation. rev. ed. (Illus.). 272p. 2000. pap. text 23.95 (*0-87891-847-7*) Res & Educ.
— GRE Economics Test Preparation. rev. ed. LC 88-90711. (Illus.). 672p. 1999. pap. text 27.95 (*0-87891-632-6*) Res & Educ.
— GRE Engineering Test Preparation. rev. ed. LC 98-68562. (Illus.). 640p. 1999. pap. text 28.95 (*0-87891-601-6*) Res & Educ.
— GRE Literature in English Test Preparation. rev. ed. (Illus.). 786p. 1999. pap. text 27.95 (*0-87891-634-2*) Res & Educ.
— GRE Mathematics Test Preparation. rev. ed. LC 98-68360. (Illus.). 352p. 1999. pap. text 28.95 (*0-87891-637-7*) Res & Educ.
— GRE Physics Test Preparation. rev. ed. (Illus.). 416p. 1999. pap. text 27.95 (*0-87891-848-5*) Res & Educ.
— GRE Psychology Test Preparation. rev. ed. LC 86-60827. (Illus.). 592p. 1999. pap. text 23.95 (*0-87891-599-0*) Res & Educ.
— GRE Sociology. 400p. 1999. pap. text 25.95 (*0-87891-999-6*) Res & Educ.
— H. S. P. T.-High School Proficiency Test. (Orig.). 1999. 19.95 (*0-87891-788-8*) Res & Educ.
— Handbook & Guide for Comparing & Selecting Computer Languages. LC 84-61817. (Illus.). 128p. 1989. pap. 8.95 (*0-87891-561-3*) Res & Educ.
— Handbook of Mathematical, Scientific, & Engineering Formulas, Tables, Functions, Graphs, Transforms. rev. ed. LC 80-52490. (Illus.). 1248p. (Orig.). (C). 1997. 34.95 (*0-87891-521-4*) Res & Educ.
— Heat Transfer Problem Solver. rev. ed. LC 84-61813. (Illus.). 840p. 1999. pap. text 29.95 (*0-87891-557-5*) Res & Educ.
— High School Algebra Tutor. rev. ed. LC 85-62004. (Illus.). 320p. 2000. pap. text 16.95 (*0-87891-564-8*) Res & Educ.
— High School Biology Tutor. 352p. 2000. pap. 15.95 (*0-87891-907-4*) Res & Educ.
— High School Chemistry Tutor. 2nd rev. ed. LC 86-63873. (Illus.). 360p. 1999. pap. text 16.95 (*0-87891-596-6*) Res & Educ.
— High School Earth Science Tutor. LC 95-67786. 496p. 1995. pap. text 13.95 (*0-87891-975-9*) Res & Educ.
— High School Geometry Tutor. rev. ed. LC 85-62003. (Illus.). 352p. 2000. pap. text 16.95 (*0-87891-565-6*) Res & Educ.
— High School Physics Tutor. rev. ed. (Illus.). 288p. 1999. pap. text 16.95 (*0-87891-597-4*) Res & Educ.
— High School Pre-Algebra Tutor. 324p. 1997. pap. text 16.95 (*0-87891-483-8*) Res & Educ.
— High School Pre-Calculus Tutor. 360p. (YA). (gr. 9-12). 1999. pap. 16.95 (*0-87891-910-4*) Res & Educ.
— High School Probability Tutor. 300p. 1996. pap. text 14.95 (*0-87891-958-9*) Res & Educ.
— High School Trigonometry Tutor. rev. ed. LC 85-62002. (Illus.). 352p. 1997. pap. text 15.95 (*0-87891-566-4*) Res & Educ.
— How to Create Catalogs That Sell. 208p. Date not set. pap. text 29.95 (*0-87891-976-7*) Res & Educ.
— How to Create Great Advertising by the Most Creative People in the Field. 208p. Date not set. pap. text 29.95 (*0-87891-977-5*) Res & Educ.
— Linear Algebra Problem Solver. rev. ed. LC 79-92402. (Illus.). 1022p. 1999. pap. text 29.95 (*0-87891-518-4*) Res & Educ.
— LSAT - Law School Admission Test. rev. ed. LC 97-68607. (Illus.). 688p. 1998. pap. text 20.95 (*0-87891-854-X*) Res & Educ.
— LSAT with Testware. 510p. 1999. pap. text 34.95 incl. disk (*0-87891-471-4*) Res & Educ.
— Machine Design Problem Solver. rev. ed. (Illus.). 928p. 1994. pap. text 29.95 (*0-87891-605-9*) Res & Educ.
— MAT - The Miller Analogies Test. 256p. 2000. pap. text 15.95 (*0-87891-864-7*) Res & Educ.
— Math Builder for Standardized Tests. rev. ed. LC 97-69309. (Illus.). 1998. pap. 15.95 (*0-87891-876-0*) Res & Educ.
— Mathematics for Engineers Problem Solver. rev. ed. (Illus.). 816p. 1996. pap. text 29.95 (*0-87891-838-8*) Res & Educ.
— Max Notes - A Raisin in the Sun. (Illus.). 96p. 1994. pap. text 3.95 (*0-87891-945-7*) Res & Educ.
— Max Notes - A Tale of Two Cities. LC 94-65957. (Illus.). 128p. 1994. pap. text 3.95 (*0-87891-949-X*) Res & Educ.
— Max Notes - Gone with the Wind. (Illus.). 128p. 1994. pap. text 3.95 (*0-87891-955-4*) Res & Educ.
— Max Notes - Hamlet. LC 94-65964. (Illus.). 128p. 2000. pap. text 3.95 (*0-87891-952-X*) Res & Educ.
— Max Notes - Huckleberry Finn. (Illus.). 128p. 1994. pap. text 3.95 (*0-87891-953-8*) Res & Educ.
— Max Notes - I Know Why the Caged Bird Sings. (Illus.). 128p. 1994. pap. text 3.95 (*0-87891-956-2*) Res & Educ.
— Max Notes - Julius Caesar. 1500p. 1994. pap. text 3.95 (*0-87891-948-1*) Res & Educ.
— Max Notes - Les Miserables. (Illus.). 128p. 1994. pap. text 3.95 (*0-87891-951-1*) Res & Educ.
— Max Notes - Macbeth. (Illus.). 128p. 1994. pap. text 3.95 (*0-87891-944-9*) Res & Educ.
— Max Notes - The Grapes of Wrath. (Illus.). 128p. 1994. pap. text 3.95 (*0-87891-947-3*) Res & Educ.
— Max Notes - The Great Gatsby. (Illus.). 128p. 1994. pap. text 3.95 (*0-87891-942-2*) Res & Educ.
— Max Notes - The Odyssey. (Illus.). 100p. 2000. pap. text 3.95 (*0-87891-943-0*) Res & Educ.
— Max Notes - To Kill a Mockingbird. (Illus.). 128p. 1994. pap. text 3.95 (*0-87891-946-5*) Res & Educ.
— MaxNotes - Great Expectations. 128p. 1994. pap. text 3.95 (*0-87891-954-6*) Res & Educ.
— MaxNotes - Plato's Republic. LC 98-66192. (MaxNotes Ser.). (Illus.). 128p. 1999. pap. text 3.95 (*0-87891-987-2*) Res & Educ.
— MaxNotes a Midsummer Night's Dream. (MaxNotes Ser.). (Illus.). 128p. (Orig.). 1996. pap. 3.95 (*0-87891-030-1*) Res & Educ.
— MaxNotes a Passage to India. (MaxNotes Ser.). (Illus.). 128p. (Orig.). 1996. pap. 3.95 (*0-87891-039-5*) Res & Educ.
— MaxNotes a Portrait of the Artist. (MaxNotes Ser.). (Illus.). 128p. (Orig.). 1996. pap. 3.95 (*0-87891-041-7*) Res & Educ.
— MaxNotes Absalom, Absalom. (MaxNotes Ser.). (Illus.). 128p. (Orig.). 1996. pap. 3.95 (*0-87891-000-X*) Res & Educ.
— MaxNotes Antony & Cleopatra. LC 96-67443. (MaxNotes Ser.). (Illus.). 128p. (Orig.). 1996. pap. 3.95 (*0-87891-002-6*) Res & Educ.
— MaxNotes As I Lay Dying. LC 96-67417. (MaxNotes Ser.). (Illus.). 128p. (Orig.). 1996. pap. 3.95 (*0-87891-059-X*) Res & Educ.
— MaxNotes As You Like It. LC 96-67405. (MaxNotes Ser.). (Illus.). 128p. (Orig.). 1996. pap. 3.95 (*0-87891-003-4*) Res & Educ.
— MaxNotes Beloved. LC 95-71345. (MaxNotes Ser.). (Illus.). 128p. 1999. pap. 3.95 (*0-87891-006-9*) Res & Educ.
— MaxNotes Billy Budd. (MaxNotes Ser.). (Illus.). 128p. (Orig.). 1996. pap. 3.95 (*0-87891-007-7*) Res & Educ.
— MaxNotes Death in Venice. LC 96-67419. (MaxNotes Ser.). (Illus.). 128p. (Orig.). 1996. pap. 3.95 (*0-87891-010-7*) Res & Educ.
— MaxNotes Divine Comedy Vol. I: Inferno. (MaxNotes Ser.). (Illus.). 128p. (Orig.). 1996. pap. 3.95 (*0-87891-991-0*) Res & Educ.
— MaxNotes Dubliners. (MaxNotes Ser.). (Illus.). 128p. (Orig.). 1996. pap. 3.95 (*0-87891-011-5*) Res & Educ.
— MaxNotes Emma. (MaxNotes Ser.). (Illus.). 128p. (Orig.). 1996. pap. 3.95 (*0-87891-012-3*) Res & Educ.
— MaxNotes Frankenstein. (MaxNotes Ser.). (Illus.). 128p. (Orig.). 1996. pap. 3.95 (*0-87891-014-X*) Res & Educ.
— MaxNotes Gulliver's Travels. LC 96-67403. (MaxNotes Ser.). (Illus.). 128p. (Orig.). 1996. pap. 3.95 (*0-87891-015-8*) Res & Educ.
— MaxNotes Hard Times. (MaxNotes Ser.). (Illus.). 128p. (Orig.). 1996. pap. 3.95 (*0-87891-016-6*) Res & Educ.
— MaxNotes Heart of Darkness. (MaxNotes Ser.). (Illus.). 128p. (Orig.). 1996. pap. 3.95 (*0-87891-017-4*) Res & Educ.
— MaxNotes Henry V. LC 96-67445. (MaxNotes Ser.). (Illus.). 128p. 1996. pap. 3.95 (*0-87891-019-0*) Res & Educ.
— MaxNotes Henry IV, Pt. I. (MaxNotes Ser.). (Illus.). 128p. (Orig.). 1996. pap. 3.95 (*0-87891-018-2*) Res & Educ.
— MaxNotes Invisible Man. LC 96-67424. (MaxNotes Ser.). (Illus.). 128p. (Orig.). 1996. pap. 3.95 (*0-87891-021-2*) Res & Educ.
— MaxNotes Jane Eyre. (MaxNotes Ser.). (Illus.). 128p. (Orig.). 1996. pap. 3.95 (*0-87891-022-0*) Res & Educ.
— MaxNotes Jazz. (MaxNotes Ser.). (Illus.). 128p. (Orig.). 1996. pap. 3.95 (*0-87891-023-9*) Res & Educ.
— MaxNotes Metamorphosis. LC 96-67406. (MaxNotes Ser.). (Illus.). 128p. (Orig.). 1996. pap. 3.95 (*0-87891-028-X*) Res & Educ.
— MaxNotes Middlemarch. LC 96-67451. (MaxNotes Ser.). (Illus.). 128p. (Orig.). 1996. pap. 3.95 (*0-87891-029-8*) Res & Educ.
— MaxNotes Moll Flanders. (MaxNotes Ser.). (Illus.). 128p. (Orig.). 1996. pap. 3.95 (*0-87891-031-X*) Res & Educ.
— MaxNotes Mrs. Dalloway. (MaxNotes Ser.). (Illus.). 128p. (Orig.). 1996. pap. 3.95 (*0-87891-032-8*) Res & Educ.
— MaxNotes Much Ado about Nothing. (MaxNotes Ser.). (Illus.). 128p. (Orig.). 1996. pap. 3.95 (*0-87891-033-6*) Res & Educ.
— MaxNotes My Antonia. (MaxNotes Ser.). (Illus.). 128p. (Orig.). 1996. pap. 3.95 (*0-87891-034-4*) Res & Educ.
— MaxNotes Native Son. LC 96-67428. (MaxNotes Ser.). (Illus.). 128p. (Orig.). 1996. pap. 3.95 (*0-87891-035-2*) Res & Educ.
— MaxNotes Oedipus Trilogy. (MaxNotes Ser.). (Illus.). 128p. (Orig.). 1996. pap. 3.95 (*0-87891-036-0*) Res & Educ.
— MaxNotes on the Road. (MaxNotes Ser.). (Illus.). 128p. (Orig.). 1996. pap. 3.95 (*0-87891-037-9*) Res & Educ.
— MaxNotes Othello. (MaxNotes Ser.). (Illus.). 128p. 2000. pap. 3.95 (*0-87891-038-7*) Res & Educ.
— MaxNotes Pride & Prejudice. (MaxNotes Ser.). (Illus.). 128p. (Orig.). 1996. pap. 3.95 (*0-87891-042-5*) Res & Educ.
— MaxNotes Richard II. LC 96-67421. (MaxNotes Ser.). (Illus.). 128p. (Orig.). 1996. pap. 3.95 (*0-87891-043-3*) Res & Educ.
— MaxNotes Sir Gawain & the Green Knight. (MaxNotes Ser.). (Illus.). 128p. (Orig.). 1996. pap. 3.95 (*0-87891-044-1*) Res & Educ.
— MaxNotes Slaughterhouse-Five. LC 96-67404. (MaxNotes Ser.). (Illus.). 128p. (Orig.). 1996. pap. 3.95 (*0-87891-045-X*) Res & Educ.
— MaxNotes Song of Solomon. LC 96-67449. (MaxNotes Ser.). (Illus.). 128p. (Orig.). 1996. pap. 3.95 (*0-87891-046-8*) Res & Educ.
— MaxNotes the Aeneid of Virgil. (MaxNotes Ser.). (Illus.). 128p. (Orig.). 1996. pap. 3.95 (*0-87891-001-8*) Res & Educ.
— MaxNotes the Awakening. (MaxNotes Ser.). (Illus.). 128p. (Orig.). 1996. pap. 3.95 (*0-87891-005-0*) Res & Educ.
— MaxNotes the Bluest Eye: A Novel. LC 96-67418. (MaxNotes Ser.). (Illus.). 128p. (Orig.). 1996. pap. 3.95 (*0-87891-008-5*) Res & Educ.
— MaxNotes the Color Purple. (MaxNotes Ser.). (Illus.). 128p. (Orig.). 1996. pap. 3.95 (*0-87891-009-3*) Res & Educ.

R

An Asterisk (*) at the beginning of an entry indicates that the title is appearing for the first time.

— MaxNotes the House on Mango Street. (MaxNotes Ser.). (Illus.). 128p. (Orig.). 1996. pap. 3.95 (0-87891-020-4) Res & Educ.

— MaxNotes the Joy Luck Club. (MaxNotes Ser.). (Illus.). 128p. (Orig.). 1996. pap. 3.95 (0-87891-024-7) Res & Educ.

— MaxNotes the Merchant of Venice. (MaxNotes Ser.). (Illus.). 128p. (Orig.). 1996. pap. 3.95 (0-87891-026-3) Res & Educ.

— MaxNotes the Metamorphoses of Ovid. LC 96-67410. (MaxNotes Ser.). (Illus.). 128p. (Orig.). 1996. pap. 3.95 (0-87891-027-1) Res & Educ.

— MaxNotes the Portrait of a Lady. LC 96-67450. (MaxNotes Ser.). (Illus.). 128p. (Orig.). 1996. pap. 3.95 (0-87891-040-9) Res & Educ.

— MaxNotes the Scarlet Letter. (Illus.). 128p. 1994. pap. text 3.95 (0-87891-950-3) Res & Educ.

— MaxNotes the Sound & the Fury. (MaxNotes Ser.). (Illus.). 128p. (Orig.). 1996. pap. 3.95 (0-87891-047-6) Res & Educ.

— MaxNotes the Stranger. (MaxNotes Ser.). (Illus.). 128p. (Orig.). 1996. pap. 3.95 (0-87891-048-4) Res & Educ.

— MaxNotes the Taming of the Shrew. LC 96-67412. (MaxNotes Ser.). (Illus.). 128p. (Orig.). 1996. pap. 3.95 (0-87891-050-6) Res & Educ.

— MaxNotes the Tempest. (MaxNotes Ser.). (Illus.). 128p. (Orig.). 1996. pap. 3.95 (0-87891-052-2) Res & Educ.

— MaxNotes Their Eyes Were Watching God. (MaxNotes Ser.). (Illus.). 128p. (Orig.). 1996. pap. 3.95 (0-87891-053-0) Res & Educ.

— MaxNotes to the Lighthouse. LC 96-67414. (MaxNotes Ser.). (Illus.). 128p. (Orig.). 1996. pap. 3.95 (0-87891-054-9) Res & Educ.

— MaxNotes Twelfth Night. (MaxNotes Ser.). (Illus.). 128p. (Orig.). 1996. pap. 3.95 (0-87891-055-7) Res & Educ.

— MaxNotes Uncle Tom's Cabin. (MaxNotes Ser.). (Illus.). 128p. (Orig.). 1996. pap. 3.95 (0-87891-056-5) Res & Educ.

— MaxNotes Waiting for Godot. LC 96-67420. (MaxNotes Ser.). (Illus.). 128p. (Orig.). 1996. pap. 3.95 (0-87891-057-3) Res & Educ.

— MaxNotes Wuthering Heights. (MaxNotes Ser.). (Illus.). 128p. (Orig.). 1996. pap. 3.95 (0-87891-058-1) Res & Educ.

— MCAT Medical College Admission Test. rev. ed. LC 98-67276. (Illus.). 1008p. 2000. pap. 44.95 (0-87891-872-8) Res & Educ.

— Mechanical Engineering Handbook. 1536p. 1999. pap. text 38.95 (0-87891-980-5) Res & Educ.

— Mechanics Problem Solver. rev. ed. LC 79-92403. (Illus.). 1088p. 1997. pap. text 29.95 (0-87891-519-2) Res & Educ.

— Modern Microelectronics: Circuit Design, IC Applications, Fabrication Technology, 2 vols., Set. 2nd ed. LC 81-50168. (Illus.). 1408p. 1986. 36.75 (0-87891-520-6) Res & Educ.

— MSAT - Multiple Subject Assessment for Teachers. 400p. 1998. pap. text 25.95 (0-87891-749-7) Res & Educ.

— NCLEX-RN. 600p. Date not set. pap. text 24.95 (0-87891-865-5) Res & Educ.

— NTE - Core Battery with Cassettes. rev. ed. LC 97-68606. (Illus.). 768p. 2000. pap. text 23.95 incl. audio (0-87891-851-5) Res & Educ.

— Numerical Analysis Problem Solver. rev. ed. LC 83-62277. (Illus.). 896p. 1994. pap. text 29.95 (0-87891-549-4) Res & Educ.

— NYSTCE - The New York State Teacher Certification Exam. LC 97-65091. 592p. 1999. pap. text 30.95 (0-87891-866-3) Res & Educ.

— Operations Research Problem Solver. rev. ed. LC 83-62276. (Illus.). 1068p. 1996. pap. text 29.95 (0-87891-548-6) Res & Educ.

— Optics Problem Solver. rev. ed. LC 81-50899. 832p. 1994. pap. 29.95 (0-87891-526-5) Res & Educ.

— Organic Chemistry Problem Solver. rev. ed. LC 77-19370. 1408p. 1998. pap. text 29.95 (0-87891-512-5) Res & Educ.

— Physical Chemistry Problem Solver. rev. ed. LC 81-522778. (Illus.). 800p. 1997. pap. text 29.95 (0-87891-532-X) Res & Educ.

— Physics Builder for Standardized Tests. 544p. 1995. pap. text 12.95 (0-87891-941-4) Res & Educ.

— Physics Problem Solver. rev. ed. LC 76-332. (Illus.). 1200p. (C). 2000. pap. text 23.95 (0-87891-507-9) Res & Educ.

— PPST - Pre-Professional Skills Test. 350p. 2000. pap. text 21.95 (0-87891-867-1) Res & Educ.

— Pre-Calculus Problem Solver: A Complete Solution Guide to Any Textbook. rev. ed. LC 84-61812. (Illus.). 960p. 2000. pap. text 23.95 (0-87891-556-7) Res & Educ.

— Proven Successful Brochures & Methods for Direct Marketing. 208p. Date not set. pap. text 29.95 (0-87891-979-1) Res & Educ.

— Psychology Problem Solver. rev. ed. LC 80-53174. (Illus.). 1056p. (C). 1999. pap. text 23.95 (0-87891-523-0) Res & Educ.

— Reading Comprehension Builder. LC 96-67458. 608p. 1998. pap. 16.95 (0-87891-793-4) Res & Educ.

— REA's Authoritative Guide to Law Schools. LC 97-66116. 432p. 1997. pap. 21.95 (0-87891-478-1) Res & Educ.

— REA's Authoritative Guide to Medical/Dental School. 1997. pap. 21.95 (0-87891-479-X) Res & Educ.

— SAT I Math Tutor. 325p. 1999. pap. text 16.95 (0-87891-962-7) Res & Educ.

— SAT I Verbal Tutor. LC 94-67718. 256p. 1999. pap. text 16.95 (0-87891-963-5) Res & Educ.

— SAT II American History & Social Studies. rev. ed. LC 96-67269. (Illus.). 508p. 2000. pap. text 16.95 (0-87891-845-0) Res & Educ.

— SAT II Chemistry. rev. ed. LC 91-139417. (Illus.). 368p. 2000. pap. text 17.95 (0-87891-603-2) Res & Educ.

— SAT II French. (FRE.). 288p. 1998. pap. 14.95 (0-87891-969-4) Res & Educ.

— SAT II German. LC 97-69998. (GER.). 288p. 1998. pap. 15.95 (0-87891-970-8) Res & Educ.

— SAT II Literature. rev. ed. (Illus.). 288p. 2000. pap. text 16.95 (0-87891-846-9) Res & Educ.

— SAT II Physics. rev. ed. LC 96-71059. (Illus.). 288p. 1999. pap. text 15.95 (0-87891-870-1) Res & Educ.

— SAT with Testware. 1000p. 1999. pap. text 29.95 incl. disk (0-87891-468-4) Res & Educ.

— Statistics Problem Solver. rev. ed. LC 78-64581. (Illus.). 1056p. 1999. pap. text 23.95 (0-87891-515-X) Res & Educ.

— Strength of Materials & Mechanics of Solids Problem Solver. rev. ed. LC 80-83305. (Illus.). 1152p. (Orig.). (C). 1996. pap. text 29.95 (0-87891-522-2) Res & Educ.

— Superstar Entrepreneurs. LC 97-76349. 208p. 1998. pap. text 19.95 (0-87891-978-3) Res & Educ.

— TASP - Texas Academic Skills Program. rev. ed. LC 97-68648. 528p. 1999. pap. text 19.95 (0-87891-893-0) Res & Educ.

— Thermodynamics Problem Solver. rev. ed. LC 84-61810. (Illus.). 892p. 1995. pap. text 29.95 (0-87891-555-9) Res & Educ.

— Top 100 Business Schools Directory. 352p. 1996. pap. text 19.95 (0-87891-747-0) Res & Educ.

— Topology Problem Solver. (Illus.). 1008p. 1998. pap. text 29.95 (0-87891-925-2) Res & Educ.

— Transport Phenomena Problem Solver. rev. ed. LC 84-61816. (Illus.). 864p. 1994. pap. text 29.95 (0-87891-562-1) Res & Educ.

— U. S. History Builder. LC 97-68605. 640p. 2000. pap. text 16.95 (0-87891-961-9) Res & Educ.

— Vector Analysis Problem Solver. rev. ed. LC 84-61811. (Illus.). 1296p. 1994. pap. text 29.95 (0-87891-554-0) Res & Educ.

— Verbal Builder for Standardized Tests. rev. ed. (Illus.). 368p. 2000. pap. 15.95 (0-87891-875-2) Res & Educ.

— Writing Your A+ Scientific Technical Paper. 112p. 1997. pap. 9.95 (0-87891-913-9) Res & Educ.

— Writing Your A+ Term Paper. 1996. pap. text 7.95 (0-87891-785-3) Res & Educ.

— Writing Your A+ Research Paper. LC 97-68341. 1998. pap. text 8.95 (0-87891-786-1) Res & Educ.

— Writing Your A+ Thesis. 2000. pap. text 9.95 (0-87891-787-X) Res & Educ.

***Research & Education Association Staff, ed.** GRE General Cat Testbuster. 2000. pap. 34.95 (0-87891-292-4) Res & Educ.

Research & Education Association Staff, ed. Technical Design Graphics Problem Solver. rev. ed. LC 81-86648. (Illus.). 960p. (Orig.). 1994. pap. 23.95 (0-87891-534-6) Res & Educ.

Research & Education Association Staff & Berger, Vance. Probability Problem Solver. LC 98-68175. 1000p. 1999. 24.95 (0-87891-839-6) Res & Educ.

Research & Education Association Staff & Burnside, William H. Essentials of European History, 1648-1789. rev. ed. (Illus.). 128p. 1996. pap. text 5.95 (0-87891-707-1) Res & Educ.

Research & Education Association Staff & Cezzar, Ruknet. Essentials of COBOL I. rev. ed. (Illus.). 128p. 1994. pap. text 5.95 (0-87891-679-2) Res & Educ.

Research & Education Association Staff & Conner, E. SAT II Writing Test. 362p. 2000. pap. 16.95 (0-87891-935-X) Res & Educ.

***Research & Education Association Staff & Goldman, L.** Best Test Preparation for the CLEP College-Level Examination Program Spanish. LC 98-66856. 480p. 1999. pap. 34.95 incl. audio (0-87891-221-5) Res & Educ.

Research & Education Association Staff & Grimes, Charles. Thomas Hardy's Tess of the D'Urbervilles. (MaxNotes Ser.). (Illus.). 128p. (Orig.). 1996. pap. 3.95 (0-87891-051-4) Res & Educ.

Research & Education Association Staff & Jones, Cynthia. Thomas Hardy's Jude the Obscure. (MaxNotes Ser.). (Illus.). 128p. (Orig.). 1996. pap. 3.95 (0-87891-025-5) Res & Educ.

Research & Education Association Staff & Milano, Duane R. Essentials of Accounting II. rev. ed. (Illus.). 80p. 2000. pap. text 6.95 (0-87891-672-5) Res & Educ.

Research & Education Association Staff & Turner, William. Essentials of U. S. History, 1912-1941. rev. ed. (Illus.). 128p. 2000. pap. text 6.95 (0-87891-716-0) Res & Educ.

Research & Education Association Staff & Underiner, Tamara L. MaxNotes Euripedes' Electra & Medea. LC 95-72125. (MaxNotes Ser.). (Illus.). 128p. (Orig.). 1996. pap. 3.95 (0-87891-013-1) Res & Educ.

Research & Education Association Staff, et al. MaxNotes the Autobiography of Malcolm X. (MaxNotes Ser.). (Illus.). 128p. 1996. pap. 3.95 (0-87891-004-2) Res & Educ.

Research & Education Association Staff, jt. auth. see Fogiel, M.

Research & Education Association Staff, jt. auth. see Giove, Frank C.

Research & Education Association Staff, jt. auth. see Segal, Mark A.

Research & Education Associaton Staff. Mcat with Testware: Book Plus Software. 1997. pap. text 52.95 (0-87891-807-8) Res & Educ.

***Research & Education Associaton Staff, ed.** The Best Test Preparation for the Advanced Placement Examination: European History. (Illus.). 2000. pap. 29.95 incl. cd-rom (0-87891-330-0) Res & Educ.

— Biology. (Illus.). 1999. pap. 8.95 (0-87891-153-7) Res & Educ.

Research & Education Staff, contrib. by. Commercial Driver License Exam. LC 98-66384. 1998. pap. text 16.95 (0-87891-109-X) Res & Educ.

— MaxNotes "Tar Baby" LC 98-66563. (MaxNotes Ser.). 1999. pap. text 3.95 (0-87891-230-4) Res & Educ.

— MaxNotes "The Sun Also Rises" (MaxNotes Ser.). (Illus.). 128p. 1996. pap. text 3.95 (0-87891-049-2) Res & Educ.

Research & Policy Committee of the Committee for E. American Workers & Economic Change. LC 96-11810. (CED Statement on National Policy Ser.). 1996. 18.00 (0-87186-122-4) Comm Econ Dev.

— Connecting Students to a Changing World: A Technology Strategy for Improving Mathematics & Science Education: A Statement. 1995. 15.00 (0-87186-121-6) Comm Econ Dev.

— Rebuilding Inner City Communities: An Emerging National Strategy Against Urban Decay. LC 95-1695. 1995. 18.00 (0-87186-120-8) Comm Econ Dev.

— U. S. Trade Policy Beyond the Uraguay Round: A Statement. LC 94-14783. 1994. 10.00 (0-87186-098-8) Comm Econ Dev.

— The United States in the New Global Economy: A Rallier of Nations. LC 92-34022. 90p. 1992. pap. 17.50 (0-87186-094-5) Comm Econ Dev.

Research & Policy Committee of the Economic Develo, ed. Who Will Pay for Your Retirement? The Looming Crisis. LC 95-3345. 1995. 20.00 (0-87186-119-4) Comm Econ Dev.

Research & Reference Division Staff. Mass Media in India, 1981 to 83. 269p. 1984. 21.95 (0-318-37285-1) Asia Bk Corp.

Research & Technology Coordinating Committee (U. S & National Research Council (U. S.) Staff. The Future Highway Transportation System & Society: Suggested Research on Impacts & Interaction. LC 97-48811. 183p. 1997. 18.00 (0-309-06218-7, FUTURE) Natl Acad Pr.

Research & Technology Coordinating Committee (U. S, jt. auth. see National Research Council (U. S.) Transportation Research Board Staff.

Research (Princeton-Williamsburg) Conference on Cerebrovascular Diseases Staff. Cerebrovascular Diseases: Fourteenth Research (Princeton-Williamsburg) Conference. Plum, Fred & Pulsinelli, William A., eds. LC 75-25125. (Illus.). 281p. 1985. reprint ed. pap. 87.20 (0-7837-9527-0, 206027600005) Bks Demand.

Research Associates Company Staff. Food for Sex: How to Improve Sex Through the Foods You Eat. LC 88-63835. 63p. (Orig.). 1989. reprint ed. pap. 9.95 (0-317-93479-1) Res Assocs Co.

Research Committee of the Muskoka Pioneer Village. Huntsville: Pictures from the Past. LC 97-154685. (Illus.). 160p. 1997. pap. 15.95 (0-919783-23-6, Pub. by Boston Mills) Genl Dist Srvs.

Research Communications Ltd. Staff, ed. see Crane, Valerie, et al.

Research Conference on Geriatric Blindness & Severe Visual Impairment Staff. Proceedings of the Research Conference on Geriatric Blindness & Severe Visual Impairment, September, 7-8, 1967, Washington, D. C. Clark, Leslie L., ed. LC RE0091.R4. 91p. reprint ed. pap. 30.00 (0-7837-0134-9, 204042300016) Bks Demand.

Research Conference on Structure & Property of Engineering Materials Staff. Materials Science Research: Proceedings of the Research Conference on Structure & Property of Engineering Materials, North Carolina State University, Raleigh, Nov. 16-18, 1964. Palmour, Hayne & Kriegel, W. Wurth, eds. LC 63-17645. (Illus.). 645p. reprint ed. pap. 200.00 (0-608-30329-1, 201940900003) Bks Demand.

Research Conference on Subjective Probability, Uti, et al. Contributions to Decision Making: Subjective Probability, Utility & Decision Making (SPUDM) Caverni, Jean-Paul, ed. LC 95-2215. 372p. 1995. 155.00 (0-444-82181-3) Elsevier.

Research Division Staff. Financial Derivatives: New Instruments & Their Uses. 242p. 1993. per. 15.00 (0-9624159-1-X) FRB Atlanta.

Research Education Association Staff. Math Applied to Space Science: Interesting Problems & Their Solutions. LC 97-69458. 1998. pap. text 14.95 (0-87891-217-7) Res & Educ.

Research Grant Guides Staff. Directory of Operating Grants. 1998. pap. 59.50 (0-945078-20-X) Rsch Grant Guides.

Research Group on Living & Surviving Staff. Inhabiting the Earth as a Finite World. 1979. lib. bdg. 71.50 (0-89838-018-9) Kluwer Academic.

Research Igos Staff. Advanced Magick Quest Course, Bk. 4: Milanthros. 107p. 1994. 35.00 (1-57179-037-3) Intern Guild ASRS.

Research in Marketing, Incorporated Staff, jt. auth. see American Nurses Association Staff.

Research Institute of Acupuncture & Moxibustion, China. Chinese Therapeutical Methods of Acupuncture & Moxibustion. 18p. 1994. reprint ed. spiral bd. 8.00 (0-7873-1023-9) Hlth Research.

Research Institute of America Staff. The Complete Internal Revenue Code, January 1999. annuals rev. ed. 2848p. 1999. pap. text 54.95 (0-7811-0207-3) Res Inst Am.

— January 1, 1999 Stock Market Values. annuals rev. ed. 372p. 1999. pap. text 21.00 (0-7811-0212-X) Res Inst Am.

***Research Institute of America Staff.** 1998 Corporation & Partnership Tax Return Guide. rev. ed. 140p. 1999. pap. text 15.75 (0-7811-0214-6) Res Inst Am.

— 1998 Fiduciary Tax Return Guide. rev. ed. 160p. 1999. pap. text 15.75 (0-7811-0215-4) Res Inst Am.

— 1998 Individual Tax Return Guide. rev. ed. 160p. 1999. pap. text 15.75 (0-7811-0213-8) Res Inst Am.

— 1999 Guide to Sales & Use Taxes. annuals rev. ed. 992p. 1999. pap. text 59.95 (0-7811-0206-5) Res Inst Am.

Research Inst. of America Staff. RIA Federal Tax Regulations, July 1996, Vols. 1-4. rev. ed. 8080p. 1996. pap. text 56.95 (0-7811-0142-5) Res Inst Am.

Research Institute for Peace & Security Staff. Asian Security 1987-1988: Asia 3. (Asia Ser.: No. 3). 212p. 1987. 28.75 (0-317-66310-0, Pergamon Pr) Elsevier.

— Asian Security 1995-96. 224p. 1995. 37.50 (1-85753-114-0, Pub. by Brasseys) Brasseys.

Research Institute for Peace & Security Staff, ed. Asian Security, 1985. 226p. 1985. 38.50 (0-08-031208-X, Pergamon Pr); pap. 19.95 (0-08-031209-8, Pergamon Pr) Elsevier.

— Asian Security, 1986. (Asia Ser.: No. 2). 212p. 1986. 38.50 (0-08-033610-8, Pergamon Pr); pap. 19.95 (0-08-033611-6, Pergamon Pr) Elsevier.

Research Institute for Peace Staff. Asian Security 1996-1997. 244p. 1997. 40.00 (1-85753-206-6, Pub. by Brasseys) Brasseys.

— Asian Security 1997-98. 256p. 1997. 39.95 (1-85753-248-1, Pub. by Brasseys) Brasseys.

Research Institute for the Study of Man Staff. Testament: Life & Work of M. G. Smith, 1921-1993. (InterAmericas Ser.: No. 3). 47p. (Orig.). 1994. 7.00 (0-9633741-3-3) RI Study of Man.

Research Institute of America, Inc. Staff. Stock Market Values & Yields, 1993. rev. ed. 192p. 1993. pap. text 19.50 (0-7811-0065-8) Res Inst Am.

***Research Institute of America Staff.** All States Tax Handbook, 1999. annuals 384p. 1999. pap. text 35.75 (0-7811-0200-6) Res Inst Am.

Research Institute of America Staff. All States Tax Handbook 1994. rev. ed. 410p. 1993. pap. text 30.00 (0-7811-0079-8) Res Inst Am.

***Research Institute of America Staff.** The Complete Internal Revenue Code, January 2000. rev. ed. 2856p. 2000. pap. 59.95 (0-7811-0227-8) Res Inst Am.

Research Institute of America Staff. The Complete Internal Revenue Code, July 1998. rev. ed. 2842p. 1998. pap. text 48.00 (0-7811-0188-3) Res Inst Am.

— Federal Tax Regulations, January 1999, 5 vols. rev. ed. 8584p. 1999. pap. text 78.00 (0-7811-0204-9) Res Inst Am.

***Research Institute of America Staff.** Federal Tax Regulations, January 2000, 5 vols. rev. ed. 8898p. 2000. pap. 94.00 (0-7811-0224-3) Res Inst Am.

— RIA Federal Tax Handbook Vol. I: 1999 Edition. rev. ed. 888p. 1998. pap. text 41.95 (0-7811-0203-0) Res Inst Am.

— RIA Federal Tax Handbook 2000. (Illus.). 1999. pap. 45.00 (0-7811-0223-5) Res Inst Am.

Research Institute of America Staff. Stock Market Values, January 1, 1994. rev. ed. 195p. 1994. pap. text 19.50 (0-7811-0083-6) Res Inst Am.

Research Institute on the Social Welfare Consequen. Migration & Social Welfare: Report. LC 72-144344. 256p. reprint ed. pap. 79.40 (0-608-15426-1, 202927500059) Bks Demand.

Research International Staff, ed. Freelancers of North America. 2nd ed. pap. 37.95 (0-911085-05-X) Author Aid.

Research Libraries Group, Inc. Staff. International Conference on Research Library Cooperation. (Collection Management: Vol. 9, Nos. 2-3). 162p. 1988. 49.95 (0-86656-596-5) Haworth Pr.

Research Libraries of the New York Public Library. Bibliographic Guide to Government Publications - Foreign: 1990, 2 vols., Set. (Bibliographic Guides Ser.). 1600p. 1991. 550.00 (0-8161-7139-4, G K Hall & Co) Mac Lib Ref.

— Bibliographic Guide to Soviet & East European Studies: 1990, 3 vols., Set. (Bibliographic Guides Ser.). 2980p. 1991. 610.00 (0-8161-7148-3, G K Hall & Co) Mac Lib Ref.

Research Libraries of the New York Public Library & Library of Congress Staff. Bibliographic Guide to Psychology, 1991. (Bibliographic Guides Ser.). 154p. 1992. 205.00 (0-8161-7168-8, G K Hall & Co) Mac Lib Ref.

Research Libraries of the New York Public Library, jt. auth. see Library of Congress Staff.

Research Publications, Inc. Staff. American Medical Periodicals. LC 98-176074. 750p. 1986. 150.00 (0-89235-150-0, Resch Pubns) Primary Srce Media.

Research Publications, Inc. Staff. Goldsmiths' Kress Library of Economic Literature: A Consolidated Guide to the Microfilm Collection, 1976-1983, 7 vols. 1976. 2100.00 (0-89235-077-6) Primary Srce Media.

— Goldsmiths' Kress Library of Economic Literature: A Consolidated Guide to the Microfilm Collection, 1976-1983, Vol. 1. 481p. 1976. 250.00 (0-89235-004-0) Primary Srce Media.

— Goldsmiths' Kress Library of Economic Literature: A Consolidated Guide to the Microfilm Collection, 1976-1983, Vol. 2. 509p. 1977. 300.00 (0-89235-143-8) Primary Srce Media.

— Goldsmiths' Kress Library of Economic Literature: A Consolidated Guide to the Microfilm Collection, 1976-1983, Vol. 3. 457p. 1978. 300.00 (0-89235-142-X) Primary Srce Media.

— Goldsmiths' Kress Library of Economic Literature: A Consolidated Guide to the Microfilm Collection, 1976-1983, Vol. 4. 582p. 1982. 250.00 (0-89235-036-9) Primary Srce Media.

— Goldsmiths' Kress Library of Economic Literature: A Consolidated Guide to the Microfilm Collection, 1976-1983, Vol. 5. 629p. 1983. 250.00 (0-89235-079-2) Primary Srce Media.

— Goldsmiths' Kress Library of Economic Literature: A Consolidated Guide to the Microfilm Collection, 1976-1983, Vol. 6. 1146p. 1986. 250.00 (0-89235-102-0) Primary Srce Media.

— Goldsmiths' Kress Library of Economic Literature: A

An Asterisk (*) at the beginning of an entry indicates that the title is appearing for the first time.

R

Consolidated Guide to the Microfilm Collection, 1976-1983, Vol. 7. 225p. 1987. suppl. ed. 275.00 (*0-89235-144-6*) Primary Srce Media.

Research Publications, Inc. Staff, ed. American Fiction: Cumulative Author Index to the Microfilm Collection, 1901-1910. 217p. 1984. lib. bdg. 150.00 (*0-89235-082-2*) Primary Srce Media.

— American Poetry 1609-1870: A Guide to the Microfilm Collection. LC 82-7641. 592p. 1982. 300.00 (*0-89235-039-3*) Primary Srce Media.

— City Directories of the United States, Pre-1860 to 1901. 487p. 1984. 300.00 (*0-89235-081-4*) Primary Srce Media.

— Early British Fiction - Pre-1750: A Guide to the Microfilm Collection. LC 82-3864. 50p. 1982. 65.00 (*0-89235-034-2*) Primary Srce Media.

— The Eighteenth Century: Guide to the Microfilm Collection, Units 26-40. 850p. 1986. lib. bdg. 300.00 (*0-89235-105-5*) Primary Srce Media.

— The Eighteenth Century: Guide to the Microfilm Collection, Units 1-10, Set. 435p. 1984. lib. bdg. 250.00 (*0-89235-083-0*) Primary Srce Media.

— The Eighteenth Century: Guide to the Microfilm Collection, Units 11-25. 1200p. 1985. lib. bdg. 400.00 (*0-89235-101-2*) Primary Srce Media.

— History of Photography: Bibliography & Reel Guide to the Microfilm Collection. LC 82-15002. 91p. 1982. text 100.00 (*0-89235-058-X*) Primary Srce Media.

— Nineteenth-Century Legal Treatises: A Guide to the Microfiche Collections, Units 7-12. 268p. 1987. lib. bdg. 250.00 (*0-89235-123-3*) Primary Srce Media.

— Nineteenth-Century Legal Treatises: A Guide to the Microfilm Collections, Units 1-6. 363p. 1987. lib. bdg. 250.00 (*0-89235-118-7*) Primary Srce Media.

— Sex Research-Early Literature from Statistics to Erotica: Guide to the Microfilm Collection. 130p. 1983. 110.00 (*0-89235-075-X*) Primary Srce Media.

Research Publications, Inc. Staff & Budeit, Janice L., eds. Papers of William H. Seward: Guide & Index to the Microfilm Collection. 402p. 1983. 325.00 (*0-89235-073-3*) Primary Srce Media.

Research Publications, Inc. Staff & Del Cervo, Diane M., eds. The Faber Birren Collection of Books on Color. 65p. 1983. 80.00 (*0-89235-080-6*) Primary Srce Media.

Research Publications International Staff. Incunabula, the Printing Revolution in Europe, 1455-1500: A Guide to the [Number of] Units of the Microfiche Collection. LC 95-194229. 1995. write for info. (*0-86257-167-7*) Primary Srce.

Research Seminar in Archaeology & Related Subjects Staff & Renfrew, Colin. The Explanation of Culture Change: Models in Prehistory: Proceedings of a Meeting of the Research Seminar in Archaeology & Related Subjects Held at the University of Sheffield. LC 73-179549. xv, 788 p. 1973. write for info. (*0-7156-0673-5*) G Duckworth.

Research Society of Sun Tzu Staff, tr. see Michaelson, Gerald A.

Research Systems Staff. IDL: The Interactive Data Language. 1998. 99.50 (*1-891044-00-1*) Res Sys Inc.

— Learning IDL. 1997. pap. write for info. (*1-891044-01-X*) Res Sys Inc.

Resehtnyak, Y. G. Geometry IV: Nonregular Riemannian Geometry. Primrose, E., tr. from RUS. (Encyclopedia of Mathematical Sciences Ser.: Vol. 70). (Illus.). 270p. 1993. write for info. (*3-540-54701-0*) Spr-Verlag.

Reseigh Long, Donna, see Long, Donna Reseigh.

Resek, Carl. Lewis Henry Morgan, American Scholar. LC 60-5468. (Midway Reprint Ser.). (Illus.). 196p. reprint ed. pap. 60.80 (*0-608-09512-5*, 205431300005) Bks Demand.

— Lewis Henry Morgan, American Scholar. (Midway Reprint Ser.). (Illus.). 1974. reprint ed. pap. text 8.00 (*0-226-71012-2*) U Ch Pr.

Resek, Carl, ed. The Progressives. (Orig.). (C). 1967. pap. write for info. (*0-672-60084-6*, AHSJ4, Bobbs) Macmillan.

Resek, Carl, ed. see Bourne, Randolph S.

Resek, Elizabeth A., jt. auth. see Barbash, Jack E.

Reselbach, Jennifer & Hathorn, Clay. The Pacific Rim, Vol. 1. Haupt, Jennifer, ed. WA Academy of Languages Staff, tr. from ENG. LC 93-61377. (JPN., Illus.). 160p. 1994. text 49.95 (*0-9634100-1-6*) Wyndham Pubns.

— The Pacific Rim, Vol. 2. Haupt, Jennifer, ed. WA Academy of Languages Staff, tr. LC 93-61377. (Illus.). 160p. 1994. text 49.95 (*0-9634100-2-4*) Wyndham Pubns.

Reseliep, Raymond. The Earth We Swing On. (Illus.). 64p. (Orig.). 1984. 9.95 (*0-86683-711-6*, 8327) Harper SF.

Reselman, Bob. Practical Visual Basic 6. 850p. 1999. pap. 29.99 (*0-7897-2145-7*) Que.

— Using Visual Basic 5. LC 97-69810. 436p. 1997. pap. text 24.99 incl. cd-rom (*0-7897-1453-1*) Que.

— Using Visual Basic X. LC 98-84137. 838p. 1998. pap. text 29.99 (*0-7897-1633-X*) Que.

Resende, Andre L., contrib. by. Policies for Growth: The Latin American Experience: Proceedings of a Conference Held in Mangaratiba, Rio de Janeiro, Brazil, March 16-19, 1994. 1995. 24.00 (*1-55775-517-5*) Intl Monetary.

Resendez, Carlos C. Trade Liberalization in Mexico & the North American Free Trade Agreement. (U. S. - Mexican Occasional Papers: No. 3). 36p. 1993. pap. 7.00 (*0-614-01235-X*) LBJ Sch Pub Aff.

Resendez, Carlos Cabeza. Trade Liberalization in Mexico & the North American Free Trade Agreement. (U. S. - Mexican Occasional Papers: Vol. 3). 36p. 1993. pap. 7.00 (*0-89940-585-1*) LBJ Sch Pub Aff.

Resendiz, Daniel & Romo, Miguel P., eds. Soft-Ground Tunnelling: Failures & Displacements. 110p. (C). 1981. text 91.00 (*90-6191-201-6*, Pub. by A A Balkema) Ashgate Pub Co.

Resenikoff, H. L. The Illusion of Reality. (Illus.). 385p. 1988. 89.95 (*0-387-96398-7*) Spr-Verlag.

Reser, David W., compiled by. Toward a New Beginning in Cooperative Cataloging: The History, Progress, & Future of the Cooperative Cataloging Council. LC 94-42740. 1994. write for info. (*0-8444-0867-0*) Lib Congress.

Reser, Harry. Picture Chords for Guitar. 2nd ed. Stang, Aaron, ed. 60p. (Orig.). (C). 1981. pap. text 7.95 (*0-7692-1345-6*, GF0195) Wrner Bros.

Reserve Assets Study Group Staff. Towards a Less Unstable International Monetary System. (Report Ser.). 19p. 1980. pap. 10.00 (*1-56708-052-9*) Grp of Thirty.

Resetar, Robert J. & Schulte, Mary K. Princess Nada & the City of Ice. LC 97-37475. (New Tales of the Arabian Nights Ser.: Vol. 1). (Illus.). 32p. (J). (gr. k-5). 1997. 16.95 (*1-880090-55-4*) Galde Pr.

Resetar, S. A., et al. Environmental Management in Design: Lessons from Volvo & Hewlitt-Packard for the Department of Defense. (Illus.). 170p. 1998. pap. text 15.00 (*0-8330-2660-7*, MR1009-OSD) Rand Corp.

Resetar, Susan. Technology Forces at Work: Profiles of Environmental Research & Development at Dupont, Intel, Monsanto & Xerox. LC 99-20456. (Illus.). 175p. 1999. pap. 15.00 (*0-8330-2728-X*, MR-1068-OSTP) Rand Corp.

Resetar, Susan, et al. Technology Forces at Work: Profiles of Environmental Research & Development at DuPont, Intel, Monsanto, & Xerox. 24p. (Orig.). 1999. pap. 15.00 (*0-8330-2739-5*, MR-1068/1-OSTP) Rand Corp.

Resetarits, Paul J. Using CADKEY. (CAD/CAM Ser.). 1987. teacher ed. 16.00 (*0-8273-2967-9*) Delmar.

— Using CADKEY 4.0: Instructor's Guide. 3rd ed. 1991. pap. 15.00 (*0-8273-4946-7*) Delmar.

— Using CADKEY Light. (CAD/CAM Ser.). 1991. pap., teacher ed. 16.00 (*0-8273-4736-7*) Delmar.

Resetarits, Paul J. & Bertoline, Gary R. Using CADKEY. 2nd ed. 400p. 1991. pap. 42.95 (*0-8273-3632-2*) Delmar.

— Using CADKEY & Its Applications, Vols. 5-6. 36p. 1993. teacher ed. 16.00 (*0-8273-5718-4*) Delmar.

— Using CADKEY & Its Applications Versions 5 & 6. 4th ed. LC 92-21484. 652p. 1994. pap. 43.95 (*0-8273-5607-2*) Delmar.

— Using CADKEY Light. 301p. 1992. mass mkt. 42.50 (*0-8273-4735-9*) Delmar.

— Using CADKEY Version 7. (Illus.). 832p. (C). 1995. pap., mass mkt. 73.95 incl. disk (*0-8273-7009-1*) Delmar.

Resetarits, William J. Experimental Ecology: Issues & Perspectives. Bernardo, Joseph, ed. (Illus.). 488p. 1998. text 85.00 (*0-19-510241-X*) OUP.

Resh, Howard M. Hydroponic Food Production: A Definitive Guidebook for the Advanced Home Gardener & the Commercial Hydroponic Grower. 5th rev. ed. LC 95-22823. (Illus.). 528p. 1995. 49.50 (*0-88007-212-1*) Woodbridge Pr.

— Hydroponic Home Food Gardens: Abundant Production with Automated Care. LC 90-12143. (Illus.). 196p. 1990. pap. 12.95 (*0-88007-178-8*) Woodbridge Pr.

— Hydroponic Tomatoes for the Home Gardener. LC 93-18128. (Illus.). 142p. (Orig.). 1993. pap. 9.95 (*0-88007-199-0*) Woodbridge Pr.

— Hydroponics: Questions & Answers for Successful Growing: Problem-Solving Conversations with Howard M. Resh. LC 98-6582. (Illus.). 208p. 1998. pap. 13.95 (*0-88007-220-2*) Woodbridge Pr.

Resh, Nura, jt. auth. see Dar, Yehezkel.

***Resh, Vincent H.** Distribution, Ecology & Potential Impacts of the Chinese Mitten Crab (Eriocheir sinesis) in San Francisco Bay. (Illus.). 2000. pap. text. write for info. (*1-887192-12-3*) U Cal CWWR.

Resh, Vincent H. & Rosenberg, David M., eds. Ecology of Aquatic Insects. LC 83-21199. 625p. 1984. 65.00 (*0-275-91248-5*, C1248, Praeger Pubs) Greenwood.

Reshetar, John S., Jr. The Ukrainian Revolution, 1917-1920: A Study in Nationalism. LC 72-4292. (World Affairs Ser.: National & International Viewpoints). 376p. 1980. reprint ed. 31.95 (*0-405-04584-0*) Ayer.

Reshetar, John S., Jr., ed. see Meissner, Boris.

Reshetnyak. Geometry IV: Non-Regular Riemannian Geometry. LC 93-13858. (Encyclopedia of Mathematical Sciences Ser.: Vol. 70).Tr. of Geometriia IV. 1993. 118.95 (*0-387-54701-0*) Spr-Verlag.

— Stability Theorems in Geometry & Analysis, 304. LC 94-33303. (Mathematics & Its Applications Ser.).Tr. of Theoremy Ustoichivosti v Geometrii i Analize. 1994. text 225.00 (*0-7923-3118-4*) Kluwer Academic.

Reshetnyak, jt. auth. see Alexandrov, A. D.

Reshetnyak, jt. auth. see Gol'dshtein, V. M.

Reshetnyak, jt. auth. see Makarets, M. V.

Reshetnyak, ed. see Alexandrov, A. D.

Reshetov, D. N. & Portman, V. T., eds. Accuracy of Machine Tools. 304p. 1988. 68.00 (*0-7918-0004-0*, 800040) ASME Pr.

Reshetylo-Rothe, Daria A. Rilke & Russia: A Re-Evaluation. (Studies in Modern German Literature: Vol. 18). XIV, 357p. (C). 1990. text 62.50 (*0-8204-0560-4*) P Lang Pubng.

Reshevsky, Samuel. Art of Positional Play. 1980. pap. 15.00 (*0-679-14101-4*) McKay.

Reshtenyak, Y. Space Mappings with Bounded Distortion. McFaden, H. H., tr. LC 89-72. (Translations of Mathematical Monographs: Vol. 73). 362p. 1989. text 150.00 (*0-8218-4526-8*, MMONO/73) Am Math.

Resibois, Pierre & DeLeener, M. Classical Kinetic Theory of Fluids. LC 76-58852. 430p. reprint ed. pap. 133.30 (*0-608-15370-2*, 205635000060) Bks Demand.

Resick, Patricia A. & Schnicke, Monica K. Cognitive Processing Therapy for Rape Victims: A Treatment Manual. (Interpersonal Violence: the Practice Ser.: Vol. 4). (Illus.). 174p. (C). 1993. text 48.00 (*0-8039-4901-4*); pap. text 21.50 (*0-8039-4902-2*) Sage.

Resident Members of the University of Oxford. Essays Introductory to the Study of English Constitutional History. Wakeman, Henry O. & Hassall, Arthur, eds. vii, 349p. 1998. reprint ed. 105.00 (*1-56169-369-5*) Gaunt.

***Residents of Central Iowa Staff, et al.** The Continuing History of Marshall County Iowa, 1997. (Illus.). 1000p. 1999. 67.50 (*0-9670650-0-3*) History Comm Marshall.

Residents of Stockbridge Staff. The Stockbridge Story: Seventeen Thirty-Nine to Nineteen Eighty-Nine. (Illus.). 1989. 25.00 (*0-685-27189-7*) Town Stockbridge.

Residuals & Biosolids Management Conference Staff, et al. 10th Annual Residuals & Biosolids Management Conference: 10 Years of Progress & a Look Toward the Future, August 18-21, 1996, Denver Marriott Tech Center, Denver, Colorado. LC 98-228848. 1996. pap. write for info. (*1-57278-031-2*) Water Environ.

Resing, Henry A., jt. ed. see Fraissard, Jacques P.

Resinger. Evangelizacion de Hoy - Today's Evangelism: Su Mensaje y Sus Metodos. (SPA.). write for info. (*1-56063-564-9*) Editorial Unilit.

Resinger, H. & Gomez Gutierrez, J. M. Elsevier's Dictionary of Terrestrial Plant Ecology. 680p. 1992. 178.50 (*0-444-88977-9*) Elsevier.

Resinger, H. & Gutierrez, J. M. Elsevier's Dictionary of Terrestrial Plant Ecology: English - Spanish, Spanish - English. (ENG & SPA.). 664p. 1992. 250.00 (*0-8288-9216-4*) Fr & Eur.

Resintatler, Laura M., ed. see Eddy, Ellen A.

Resis, Albert, ed. see Molotov, V. M.

Reske, Charles F. Mac-V-SOG Command History Annex B, 1971-1972: The Last Secret of the Vietnam War, 2 vols., Set. (Illus.). 350p. (Orig.). 1990. pap. 49.95 (*0-939427-63-X*, 09053) Alpha Pubns OH.

— Mac-V-SOG Command History Annex B, 1971-1972: The Last Secret of the Vietnam War, 2 vols., Vol. 1. (Illus.). 350p. (Orig.). 1990. pap. 26.95 (*0-939427-60-5*) Alpha Pubns OH.

— Mac-V-SOG Command History Annex B, 1971-1972: The Last Secret of the Vietnam War, 2 vols., Vol. 2. (Illus.). 350p. (Orig.). 1990. pap. 26.95 (*0-939427-61-3*) Alpha Pubns OH.

— MACV-SOG Command Histories (Annexes A, N & M), 1964-1966: First Secrets of the Vietnam War. LC 92-82789. (Illus.). 178p. (Orig.). 1992. pap. 19.95 (*0-939427-62-1*) Alpha Pubns OH.

Reskiewicz, A. Polish-English, English-Polish Dictionaries. (ENG & POL.). 1992. write for info. (*0-8288-7279-1*) Fr & Eur.

Reskin, Barbara F. Sex Differences in the Professional Life Changes of Chemists. Zuckerman, Harriet & Merton, Robert K., eds. LC 79-9041. (Dissertations on Sociology Ser.). 1980. lib. bdg. 44.95 (*0-405-12987-4*) Ayer.

Reskin, Barbara F., ed. Sex Segregation in the Workplace: Trends, Explanations, Remedies. LC 84-8342. 323p. reprint ed. pap. 100.20 (*0-7837-5357-8*, 204511900005) Bks Demand.

Reskin, Barbara F. & Padavic, Irene. Women & Men at Work. 240p. 1994. pap. 18.95 (*0-8039-9022-7*) Pine Forge.

Reskin, Barbara F. & Roos, Patricia A. Job Queues, Gender Queues: Explaining Women's Inroads into Male Occupations. (Women in the Political Economy Ser.). 368p. 1990. 39.95 (*0-87722-743-8*); pap. 24.95 (*0-87722-744-6*) Temple U Pr.

Reskin, Melvin A., jt. auth. see Rohan, Patrick J.

Resko, John. Reprieve: The Testament of John Resko. LC 75-17464. 285p. 1975. reprint ed. lib. bdg. 65.00 (*0-8371-8311-1*, RERE, Greenwood Pr) Greenwood.

Resla, W. J. The Best of People & the Other Animals. abr. rev. ed. 200p. 1988. reprint ed. 14.00 (*0-318-35260-5*) Grant Dahlstrom.

— The Best of People & the Other Animals. Marshall, Elva, ed. 200p. 1988. reprint ed. 14.00 (*0-9620682-0-9*) W J Resla.

— The Rest of People & Other Stories. rev. ed. Kroll, William, ed. (Illus.). 160p. 1997. 11.00 (*0-9658101-0-0*) W J Resla.

Resler, Michael, tr. see Stricker, Der.

Resler, Michael, tr. & comment see Von Hartmann, Aue.

Resler, Nancy D., jt. auth. see De Paoli, Geri.

Resler, Nancy D., ed. see Nixon, Bruce & Hopps, Walter.

Reslin-Williams, Anne. The Border Terrier Today. 160p. 1996. 25.95 (*0-87605-054-2*) Howell Bks.

Resling, Darlene E. Old Testament VALUable Bible Plays. (VALUable Bible Plays Ser.: Bk. 1). 48p. 1998. 6.95 (*1-878669-78-8*) Crea Tea Assocs.

Resling, Darlene E. & Lindel, Albert. Benjamin Franklin. (Our Changing Lives Ser.). (Illus.). 80p. (YA). (gr. 4-12). 1997. pap. text 7.95 (*1-55596-170-3*, LW2030) Learning Well.

— Booker T. Washington. (Our Changing Lives Ser.). (Illus.). 64p. (YA). (gr. 4-12). 1997. pap. text 7.95 (*1-55596-174-6*, LW2060) Learning Well.

— Gandhi. (Our Changing Lives Ser.). (Illus.). 64p. (YA). (gr. 4-12). 1997. pap. text 7.95 (*1-55596-168-1*, LW2010) Learning Well.

— Golda Meir. (Our Changing Lives Ser.). (Illus.). 64p. (YA). (gr. 4-12). 1997. pap. text 7.95 (*1-55596-172-X*, LW2040) Learning Well.

— Lee Iacocca. (Our Changing Lives Ser.). (Illus.). 64p. (YA). (gr. 4-12). 1997. pap. text 7.95 (*1-55596-169-X*, LW2020) Learning Well.

— Phillis Wheatley. (Our Changing Lives Ser.). (Illus.). 64p. (YA). (gr. 4-12). 1997. pap. text 7.95 (*1-55596-171-1*, LW2070) Learning Well.

— Sitting Bull. (Our Changing Lives Ser.). (Illus.). 64p. (YA). (gr. 4-12). 1997. pap. text 7.95 (*1-55596-173-8*, LW2050) Learning Well.

— Susan B. Anthony. (Our Changing Lives Ser.). (Illus.). 64p. (YA). (gr. 4-12). 1997. pap. text 7.95 (*1-55596-167-3*, LW2000) Learning Well.

Resmer, Mark, et al. Computers for All Students: A Strategy for Universal Access to Information Resources. 1995. 15.00 (*1-881543-07-2*) SHEEO.

Resmini. Rhode Island Practice: Tort & Personal Injury, 1998 Cumulative Supplement. 350p. 1998. write for info. (*0-327-00630-7*, 8235813) LEXIS Pub.

Resmini, Ronald. Rhode Island Civil Practice & Procedure: 1996 Edition, 2 vols. LC 96-78036. 1997. text 150.00 (*1-55834-405-5*, 66675-10, MICHIE) LEXIS Pub.

Resmini, Ronald J. Rhode Island Civil Practice & Procedure 1999 Cumulative Supplement, 2 vols. Incl. Vol. 1. 1999. (*0-327-01506-3*); Vol. 2. 1999. (*0-327-01507-1*); 171p. 1999. suppl. ed. write for info. (*0-327-01505-5*, 6668111) LEXIS Pub.

***Resmini, Ronald J.** Rhode Island Practice: Tort & Personal Injury, 2 vols., Set. 2nd ed. 1999. 180.00 (*0-327-01662-0*, 8235511) LEXIS Pub.

— Rhode Island Practice: Tort & Personal Injury, Vol. 1. 2nd ed. 1500p. 1999. write for info. (*0-327-01663-9*, 8235611) LEXIS Pub.

— Rhode Island Practice: Tort & Personal Injury, Vol. 2. 2nd ed. 1500p. 1999. write for info. (*0-327-01664-7*, 8235711) LEXIS Pub.

Resmini, Ronald J. Rhode Island Practice: Tort Law & Personal Injury Practice, 2 vols. 1300p. 1990. boxed set 165.00 (*0-88063-408-1*, 82535-10, MICHIE) LEXIS Pub.

— Rhode Island Practice: Tort Law & Personal Injury Practice, 2 vols. 1300p. 1993. suppl. ed. 37.00 (*0-685-74298-9*, MICHIE) LEXIS Pub.

— Rhode Island Practice: Tort Law & Personal Injury Practice. 1300p. 1994. boxed set 165.00 (*0-614-05962-3*, MICHIE) LEXIS Pub.

Resmini, Ronald J., jt. auth. see Pope, Daniel C.

Resnekov, Orna & Von Gabain, A., eds. Post-Transcriptional Control of Gene Expression: Proceedings of the NATO Advanced Study Institute, Held on the Island of Spetsai, Greece, August 1992. LC 96-14087. (NATO ASI - Cell Biology Ser.: Vol. 97). 288p. 1996. 139.00 (*0-387-56847-6*) Spr-Verlag.

Resnekov, Orna, ed. see Von Gabain, Alexander.

Resner, Andre, Jr. Preacher & Cross: Person & Message in Theology & Rhetoric. LC 98-53604. 205p. 1999. pap. 18.00 (*0-8028-4640-8*) Eerdmans.

***Resnick.** Hunger in Soul. 1999. mass mkt. write for info. (*0-8125-2347-4*) Tor Bks.

Resnick. Marketing & Selling the Travel Product. (Hospitality, Travel & Tourism Ser.). (C). 1990. mass mkt. 36.50 (*0-538-70277-X*) S-W Pub.

— Surgery of the Prostate. 1997. text 110.00 (*0-443-07533-6*, W B Saunders Co) Harcrt Hlth Sci Grp.

Resnick. Whole Language Reading. (C). 1999. teacher ed. write for info. (*0-321-40644-3*) Addison-Wesley.

***Resnick.** Whole Language Reading. 1999. pap. 26.00 (*0-321-04578-5*) Longman.

Resnick, A., et al. Every Day's a Holiday. 1991. 22.99 (*0-8224-6372-5*) Fearon Teacher Aids.

***Resnick, Abraham.** Due to the Weather: Ways the Elements Affect Our Lives. LC 99-88484. 180p. 2000. 45.00 (*0-313-31344-X*, GR1344, Greenwood Pr) Greenwood.

Resnick, Abraham. Money. (Lucent Overview Ser.). (Illus.). (YA). (gr. 5-8). 1995. lib. bdg. 22.45 (*1-56006-165-0*) Lucent Bks.

Resnick, Alan N., et al. Bankruptcy Practice & Strategy. 1987. 210.00 (*0-88712-652-9*) Warren Gorham & Lamont.

Resnick, Alan N., jt. auth. see Weintraub, Benjamin.

Resnick, Alan N., jt. ed. see Wypyski, Eugene M.

Resnick, Barry, jt. auth. see Burke, James.

Resnick, Barry, jt. auth. see Capwell, Gerald.

Resnick, Barry P., jt. auth. see Capwell, Gerald K.

Resnick, Bruce & Eun, Cheol. International Financial Management. LC 97-5124. 672p. (C). 1997. text 45.60 (*0-256-16046-5*, Irwn McGrw-H) McGrw-H Hghr Educ.

Resnick, Daniel P. The White Terror & the Political Reaction after Waterloo. LC 66-18254. (Historical Studies: No. 77). 161p. 1966. 15.00 (*0-674-95190-5*) HUP.

Resnick, David M. Professional Ethics for Audiologists & Speech-Language Pathologists. LC 92-34723. (Illus.). 196p. (Orig.). (C). 1993. pap. text 39.95 (*1-56593-087-8*, 0392) Thomson Learn.

Resnick, David M., jt. auth. see Margolis, Michael.

Resnick, Donald. Bone & Joint Imaging. 2nd ed. Bralow, Lisette, ed. LC 95-37882. (Illus.). 944p. 1996. text 195.00 (*0-7216-6043-6*, W B Saunders Co) Harcrt Hlth Sci Grp.

— Diagnosis of Bone & Joint Disorders, 6 vols., Set. 3rd ed. LC 93-48321. (Illus.). 1994. text 725.00 (*0-7216-5066-X*, W B Saunders Co) Harcrt Hlth Sci Grp.

— Internal Derangements of Joints. LC 96-20546. (C). 1997. text 255.00 (*0-7216-6760-0*) Harcourt.

Resnick, Donald & Pak, Charles Y. Urolithiasis. (Illus.). 352p. 1990. text 115.00 (*0-7216-2439-1*, W B Saunders Co) Harcrt Hlth Sci Grp.

Resnick, Donald, et al. Disease (Fourth Series) Test & Syllabus. (Professional Self-Evaluation & Continuing Education Program Ser.: Vol. 25). (Illus.). 900p. (C). 1989. 165.00 (*1-55903-025-9*) Am Coll Radiology.

Resnick, Donald, jt. auth. see Kang.

Resnick, Donald, jt. auth. see Taylor, John.

Resnick, Elizabeth, jt. auth. see Kubasiewicz, Jan.

Resnick, Estelle P., jt. auth. see Bystydzienski, Jill M.

Resnick-Gallo, Laurie, ed. see Alperin-Hochman, Marlene.

Resnick, Greg, ed. Natural for DB2 Developers Handbook. 560p. 1991. pap. 65.00 (*1-878960-06-7*) WH&O Intl.

Resnick, Hy, ed. Electronic Tools for Social Work Practice & Education. (Computers in Human Services Ser.). (Illus.). 434p. 1994. lib. bdg. 59.95 (*1-56024-658-8*) Haworth Pr.

Resnick, Idrian N. Controlling Consulting: A Manual for Native American Governments & Organizations. 75p. 1990. reprint ed. pap. 10.00 (*0-9626861-1-5*) Frst Nations Dev.
— The Long Transition: Building Socialism in Tanzania. LC 80-8089. 416p. 1982. 28.00 (*0-85345-554-6*, Pub. by Monthly Rev); pap. 12.00 (*0-85345-555-4*, Pub. by Monthly Rev) NYU Pr.
Resnick, Irven M. Divine Power & Possibility in St. Peter Damian's De Divina Omnipotencia. LC 91-43923. (Studien und Texte zur Geistesgeschichte des Mittelalters Ser.: No. 31). viii, 130p. 1992. 60.00 (*90-04-09572-1*) Brill Academic Pubs.
Resnick, Irven M., intro. On Original Sin & A Disputation with the Jew, Leo, Concerning the Advent of Christ, the Son of God: Two Theological Treatises. LC 94-16217. (Middle Ages Ser.). 168p. (Orig.). (C). 1994. pap. text 13.95 (*0-8122-1540-0*) U of Pa Pr.
Resnick, Irven M., jt. ed. see Kitchell, Kenneth F., Jr.
Resnick, Irven M., tr. see Odo of Tournai.
Resnick, Jane. Loving Tea. LC 98-127241. 1997. mass mkt. 6.50 (*0-425-16119-6*) Berkley Pub.
Resnick, Jane P. All about Seals, Sea Lions & Walruses. LC 94-60734. (Sea World All about Library). (Illus.). 32p. (J). (gr. 1-8). 1994. pap. 3.95 (*1-884506-13-5*) Third Story.
— All about Sharks. LC 93-61829. (Sea World All about Library). (Illus.). 32p. (Orig.). (J). (gr. 1-8). 1994. pap. 3.95 (*1-884506-10-0*) Third Story.
— All about Training Shamu. LC 93-61830. (Sea World All about Library). (Illus.). 32p. (Orig.). (J). (gr. 1-8). 1994. pap. 3.95 (*1-884506-11-9*) Third Story.
— The Everything Bartender's Book. LC 95-34446. (Everything Ser.). (Illus.). 288p. 1995. pap. 9.95 (*1-55850-536-9*) Adams Media.
— Everything Pasta Book. LC 97-477. (Illus.). 304p. 1997. pap. text 12.95 (*1-55850-719-1*) Adams Media.
— Eyes on Nature: Fish. (Illus.). 32p. (J). 1992. pap. 4.95 (*1-56156-150-9*) Kidsbks.
— The Fox & the Crow. (Aesop's Fables Ser.). (Illus.). (J). 1992. bds. 3.25 (*0-8378-2525-3*) Gibson.
Resnick, Jane P. A Friend Makes All the Difference. (Illus.). 32p. 1984. 6.95 (*0-8378-2037-5*) Gibson.
Resnick, Jane P. The International Connoisseur's Guide to Cigars. (Illus.). 192p. 1996. 10.98 (*1-884822-88-6*) Blck Dog & Leventhal.
— Shamu's Secrets of the Sea. LC 93-61822. (Shamu's Little Library). (Illus.). 12p. (J). (ps). 1994. 6.95 (*1-884506-03-8*) Third Story.
— The Tortoise & the Hare. (Aesop's Fables Ser.). (Illus.). (J). 1992. bds. 3.25 (*0-8378-2524-5*) Gibson.
Resnick, Jane P., ed. The Classic Treasury of Silly Poetry. LC 94-73894. (Illus.). 56p. (J). (ps up). 1996. 9.98 (*1-56138-486-0*, Courage) Running Pr.
Resnick, Jane P., ed. The Little Golf Treasury. 400p. 1966. 8.98 (*1-884822-50-9*) Blck Dog & Leventhal.
Resnick, Jane P. & Aesop. The Ant & the Dove. (Aesop's Fables Ser.). (Illus.). (J). 1992. bds. 3.25 (*0-8378-2523-7*) Gibson.
— The Lion & the Mouse. (Aesop's Fables Ser.). (Illus.). (J). 1992. bds. 3.25 (*0-8378-2526-1*) Gibson.
Resnick, Jane P. & Tallarico, Tony. The Kids' Fun-Filled Question & Answer Book, 2 Vols. LC 98-229073. (J). 1996. write for info. (*1-56156-576-8*) Kidsbks.
Resnick, Jennifer, ed. see Brault, Jim.
Resnick, Judy. I've Been Rich. I've Been Poor. Rich Is Better. 216p. 1999. pap. 13.00 (*1-58238-023-6*, Whitman Coin) St Martin.
— On Our Own. unabridged ed. LC 97-25527. 224p. 1998. text 22.00 (*0-307-44005-2*, Whitman Coin) St Martin.
— The Rich Is Better Workbook. (Illus.). 176p. 1998. pap., wbk. ed. 14.95 (*1-58238-020-1*, Whitman Coin) St Martin.
Resnick, Kathleen. Kermit Learns Windows. (Muppet Computer Bks.). (Illus.). 48p. (J). (gr. 5 up). 1993. 9.95 (*1-55958-366-5*) Prima Pub.
Resnick, Laibel. A Time to Weep. LC 93-72409. 200p. 1993. pap. 11.95 (*1-56062-212-1*) CIS Comm.
Resnick, Laura. Blonde in Africa: Resnick's Library of African Adventure. LC 96-23455. 1997. pap. text 16.95 (*1-57090-030-2*) Alexander Dist.
Resnick, Laura. In Legend Born. LC 98-14529. 464p. 1998. text 25.95 (*0-312-89055-9*) St Martin.
***Resnick, Laura.** In Legend Born. 2000. mass mkt. 6.99 (*0-8125-5547-3*) Tor Bks.
Resnick, Laura & Klopfer, Leopold, eds. Toward the Thinking Curriculum: Current Cognitive Research. (Yearbook, 1989 Ser.). (Illus.). 221p. (Orig.). 1989. pap. 18.95 (*0-87120-156-9*, 610-89012) ASCD.
Resnick, Lauren B. Education & Learning to Think. LC 87-43107. 72p. 1987. reprint ed. pap. 30.00 (*0-608-02330-2*, 206297100004) Bks Demand.
Resnick, Lauren B., ed. Knowing, Learning & Instructions: Essays in Honor of Robert Glaser. 528p. (C). 1989. pap. 49.95 (*0-8058-0460-9*) L Erlbaum Assocs.
— The Nature of Intelligence. 364p. 1976. text 69.95 (*0-89859-137-6*) L Erlbaum Assocs.
Resnick, Lauren B., et al, eds. Discourse, Tools, & Reasoning: Essays on Situated Cognition. LC 97-35966. (NATO ASI Series F: Vol. 160). xii, 474p. 1998. 109.00 (*3-540-63511-4*) Spr-Verlag.
— Perspectives on Socially Shared Cognition. 429p. 1991. pap. 19.95 (*1-55798-376-3*) Am Psychol.
Resnick, Lauren B. & Ford, Wendy W. The Psychology of Mathematics for Instruction. LC 80-29106. 288p. 1981. text 59.95 (*0-89859-029-9*) L Erlbaum Assocs.
Resnick, Lauren B. & Weaver, Phyllis A. Theory & Practice of Early Reading, Vol. 2. LC 79-23784. 368p. 1980. text 79.95 (*0-89859-010-8*) L Erlbaum Assocs.
Resnick, Lauren B. & Weaver, Phyllis A., eds. Theory & Practice of Early Reading, Vol. 1. LC 79-22322. 416p. 1980. text 79.95 (*0-89859-003-5*) L Erlbaum Assocs.
— Theory & Practice of Early Reading, Vol. 3. 400p. 1980. text 79.95 (*0-89859-011-6*) L Erlbaum Assocs.
Resnick, Martin I. Manual Complete Urology Asia. 1989. 10.95 (*0-316-74052-7*, Little Brwn Med Div) Lppncott W & W.
— Manual Complete Urology ISE. 1989. 15.95 (*0-316-74053-5*, Little Brwn Med Div) Lppncott W & W.
— Manual of Clinical Problems in Urology. 298p. 1989. spiral bd. 36.00 (*0-316-74054-3*, Little Brwn Med Div) Lppncott W & W.
Resnick, Martin I. & Novick, Andrew, eds. Urology Secrets. 2nd ed. LC 99-24451. (Secrets Ser.). (Illus.). 300p. 1999. pap. text 38.00 (*1-56053-320-X*) Hanley & Belfus.
Resnick, Martin I. & Older, Robert A. Diagnosis of Genitourinary Disease. 2nd ed. (Illus.). 688p. 1997. text 149.00 (*0-86577-573-7*) Thieme Med Pubs.
Resnick, Martin I. & Schaeffer, Anthony, eds. Urology Pearls. LC 99-32134. (Pearls Ser.). (Illus.). 225p. 1999. pap. text 39.00 (*1-56053-351-X*) Hanley & Belfus.
Resnick, Martin I. & Spirnak, J. Patrick, eds. Topics in Urology: New Diagnostic Tests. LC 95-32007. (Topics in Clinical Urology Ser.). (Illus.). 216p. 1995. 69.50 (*0-89640-290-8*) Igaku-Shoin.
***Resnick, Martin I. & Thompson, Ian M.** Advanced Therapy of Prostatic Disease. 672p. 1999. boxed set 129.00 incl. cd-rom (*1-55009-102-6*) DEKR.
Resnick, Martin I. & Thompson, Ian M. Surgery of the Prostate. LC 97-23368. 1997. write for info. (*0-04-435576-9*) Church.
Resnick, Melvyn C. Introduccion a la Historia de la Lengua Espanola. LC 81-7209. 196p. (Orig.). (C). 1981. reprint ed. pap. text 13.50 (*0-87840-083-4*) Georgetown U Pr.
— Phonological Variants & Dialect Identification in Latin American Spanish. LC 73-80498. (Janua Linguarum, Series Practica: No. 201). (Illus.). 484p. 1975. pap. text 84.65 (*90-279-3227-1*) Mouton.
Resnick, Meredith G. Adjusting to Your New Community. (Spotlight on Military Issues Ser.). (Illus.). 8p. 1997. pap. 1.25 (*1-56688-390-3*) Bur For At-Risk.
— After the Move: Adjustments & Opportunities. (Spotlight on Military Issues Ser.). (Illus.). 8p. 1998. pap. 1.25 (*1-56688-435-7*) Bur For At-Risk.
— Building Emotional Health & Resiliency. (Spotlight on Military Issues Ser.). (Illus.). 8p. 1997. pap. 1.25 (*1-56688-391-1*) Bur For At-Risk.
— The Complete Relocation Checklist. (Spotlight on Military Issues Ser.). (Illus.). 8p. 1998. pap. 1.25 (*1-56688-431-4*) Bur For At-Risk.
— Day to Day Money Management. (Spotlight on Military Issues Ser.). (Illus.). 8p. 1997. pap. 1.25 (*1-56688-387-3*) Bur For At-Risk.
— Getting the Interview: Getting the Job. (Spotlight on Military Issues Ser.). (Illus.). 8p. 1997. pap. 1.25 (*1-56688-385-7*) Bur For At-Risk.
— Job Search Tools. (Spotlight on Military Issues Ser.). (Illus.). 8p. 1997. pap. 1.25 (*1-56688-386-5*) Bur For At-Risk.
— Networking for Success. (Spotlight on Military Issues Ser.). (Illus.). 8p. 1997. pap. 1.25 (*1-56688-384-9*) Bur For At-Risk.
— Planning for Your Financial Future. (Spotlight on Military Issues Ser.). (Illus.). 8p. 1997. pap. 1.25 (*1-56688-388-1*) Bur For At-Risk.
— Relocating Overseas: Your Adventure Abroad. (Spotlight on Military Issues Ser.). (Illus.). 8p. 1998. pap. 1.25 (*1-56688-434-9*) Bur For At-Risk.
— Relocation: Family Feelings & Fears. (Spotlight on Military Issues Ser.). (Illus.). 8p. 1998. pap. 1.25 (*1-56688-433-0*) Bur For At-Risk.
— Relocation Basics: Answers to Key Family Questions. (Spotlight on Military Issues Ser.). (Illus.). 8p. 1998. pap. 1.25 (*1-56688-432-2*) Bur For At-Risk.
— Smart Credit Management for a Debt-Free Life. (Spotlight on Military Issues Ser.). (Illus.). 8p. 1997. pap. 1.25 (*1-56688-389-X*) Bur For At-Risk.
— Transferring to a New School: Tips for Parents & Kids. (Spotlight on Military Issues Ser.). (Illus.). 8p. 1998. pap. 1.25 (*1-56688-436-5*) Bur For At-Risk.
— Transition: How the Military Can Help. (Spotlight on Military Issues Ser.). (Illus.). 8p. 1997. pap. 1.25 (*1-56688-383-0*) Bur For At-Risk.
— When You're a Bicultural Family. (Spotlight on Military Issues Ser.). (Illus.). 8p. 1997. pap. 1.25 (*1-56688-392-X*) Bur For At-Risk.
Resnick, Michael A., jt. auth. see Bracey, Gerald W.
***Resnick, Michael D.** In Space No One Can Hear You Laugh. LC 00-29384. 2000. write for info. (*1-57090-106-6*, Farthest Star) Alexander Dist.
Resnick, Michael D. Tales of the Galactic Midway, 4 vols. in 1. LC 98-42573. 448p. 2000. pap. 18.95 (*1-57090-086-8*, Pub. by Alexander Dist) Midpt Trade.
Resnick, Mike. Birthright: The Book of Man. LC 96-36683. 148p. 1997. reprint ed. pap. 14.99 (*1-57090-044-2*, Farthest Star) Alexander Dist.
— Bwana - Bully. 1991. mass mkt. 3.99 (*0-8125-1246-4*, Pub. by Tor Bks) St Martin.
— Eros at Zenith. 1984. 17.00 (*0-932096-32-8*) Phantasia Pr.
***Resnick, Mike.** A Hunger in the Soul. LC 98-50739. 1999. 24.95 (*0-7838-8511-3*) Macmillan Gen Ref.
Resnick, Mike. A Hunger in the Soul. LC 98-5552. 224p. 1998. text 21.95 (*0-312-85438-2*) St Martin.
— A Hunger in the Soul. 1999. pap. 11.95 (*0-312-86918-5*, Pub. by Tor Bks) St Martin.
— Inferno. 304p. 1995. 4.99 (*0-8125-2345-8*, Pub. by Tor Bks) St Martin.
— Ivory. 1989. mass mkt. 4.95 (*0-8125-0042-3*) Tor Bks.
— Kirinyaga: A Fable of Utopia. LC 97-44476. 293p. 1998. 25.00 (*0-345-41701-1*, Del Rey) Ballantine Pub Grp.
— Kirinyaga: A Fable of Utopia. 293p. 1999. pap. 12.95 (*0-345-41702-X*, Del Rey) Ballantine Pub Grp.
— A Miracle of Rare Design. 256p. 1996. pap. write for info. (*0-614-05523-7*); mass mkt. 5.99 (*0-8125-2424-1*, Pub. by Tor Bks) St Martin.
— Oracle. 256p. (Orig.). 1992. mass mkt. 4.99 (*0-441-58694-5*) Ace Bks.
— Paradise. 1990. mass mkt. 4.99 (*0-8125-0716-9*) Tor Bks.
— Purgatory. 320p. 1994. mass mkt. 4.99 (*0-8125-3535-9*) Tor Bks.
— Return of the Dinosaurs. 320p. 1997. mass mkt. 5.99 (*0-88677-753-4*, Pub. by DAW Bks) Penguin Putnam.
— Second Contact. 1990. pap. 3.95 (*0-8125-1113-1*, Pub. by Tor Bks) St Martin.
— Solo Flights Through Shard Worlds by Mike Resnick. (Illus.). 172p. pap. 8.99 (*1-888993-01-4*) Dark Regions.
— Solo Flights Through Shard Worlds by Mike Resnick. limited ed. (Illus.). 172p. 19.95 (*1-888993-00-6*) Dark Regions.
— Stalking the Unicorn. 320p. (Orig.). 1990. mass mkt. 3.95 (*0-8125-0985-4*) Tor Bks.
— Stalking the Wild Resnick. limited ed. (Boskone Bks.). (Illus.). viii, 216p. 1991. 15.00 (*0-915368-45-5*) New Eng SF Assoc.
— Through Darkest Resnick with Gun & Camera. 200p. 1990. 35.00 (*0-9621725-1-0*) Washington Sci Fiction.
— The Widowmaker in Spring. (Widowmaker Trilogy: Bk. 1). 304p. 1996. mass mkt. 5.99 (*0-553-57160-5*) Bantam.
— The Widowmaker Reborn. (Widowmaker Trilogy: Bk. 2). 304p. 1997. mass mkt. 5.99 (*0-553-57161-3*, Spectra) Bantam.
— The Widowmaker Unleashed. 240p. 1998. mass mkt. 5.99 (*0-553-57162-1*) Bantam.
— Will the Last Person to Leave the Planet . . . 368p. 1994. pap. 12.95 (*0-312-89010-9*) Orb NYC.
Resnick, Mike, ed. Alternate Kennedys. 416p. 1992. mass mkt. 4.99 (*0-8125-1955-8*) Tor Bks.
— Alternate Outlaws. 544p. (Orig.). (C). 1994. mass mkt. 4.99 (*0-8125-3344-5*, Pub. by Tor Bks) St Martin.
— Alternate Presidents. 1992. mass mkt. 4.99 (*0-8125-1192-1*, Pub. by Tor Bks) St Martin.
— Alternate Tyrants. LC 97-204867. 544p. (Orig.). 1996. mass mkt. 6.99 (*0-8125-4835-3*, Pub. by Tor Bks) St Martin.
— Alternate Warriors. 448p. (Orig.). 1993. mass mkt. 4.99 (*0-8125-2346-6*) Tor Bks.
Resnick, Mike & Greenberg, Martin H., eds. Sherlock Holmes in Orbit. 320p. (Orig.). 1995. pap. 5.50 (*0-88677-636-8*, Pub. by DAW Bks) Penguin Putnam.
Resnick, Mike, et al. Girls for the Slime God. (Illus.). 224p. 1997. pap. 15.00 (*0-9659569-0-3*, Obscura Pr) Wunzen Pub Co.
Resnick, Mike, jt. ed. see Greenberg, Martin H.
Resnick, Mike, ed. see Lake, Alexander.
Resnick, Mike, ed. see Malzberg, Barry N.
Resnick, Mitchel. Turtles, Termites, & Traffic Jams: Explorations in Massively Parallel Microworlds. (Illus.). 184p. 1997. reprint ed. pap. text 13.50 (*0-262-68093-9*, Bradford Bks) MIT Pr.
Resnick, Mitchel, jt. ed. see Kafai, Yasmin B.
***Resnick, Paul.** Everything You Need to Know to Manage a Small Business. LC 98-29613. 230p. 1998. pap. 12.95 (*0-471-32117-6*) Wiley.
Resnick, Paul. The Small Business Bible: The Make-or-Break Factors for Survival & Success. LC 88-17207. 240p. 1988. pap. 22.95 (*0-471-62985-5*) Wiley.
Resnick, Philip. The Masks of Proteus: Canadian Reflections on the State. 352p. (C). 1990. 65.00 (*0-7735-0731-0*, Pub. by McG-Queens Univ Pr) CUP Services.
— The Masks of Proteus: Canadian Reflections on the State. 352p. 1997. pap. text 24.95 (*0-7735-1694-8*, Pub. by McG-Queens Univ Pr) CUP Services.
— Toward a Canada-Quebec Union. 136p. (C). 1991. pap. text 24.95 (*0-7735-0865-1*, Pub. by McG-Queens Univ Pr) CUP Services.
— Twenty-First Century Democracy. 192p. 1997. pap. 19.95 (*0-7735-1659-X*, Pub. by McG-Queens Univ Pr); text 60.00 (*0-7735-1658-1*, Pub. by McG-Queens Univ Pr) CUP Services.
Resnick, Philip & Latouche, Daniel. Letters to a Qu[00e9]b[00e9]cois Friend. 136p. (C). 1990. pap. 17.95 (*0-7735-0777-9*, Pub. by McG-Queens Univ Pr) CUP Services.
— Letters to a Quibicois Friend. 136p. (C). 1990. 55.00 (*0-7735-0772-8*, Pub. by McG-Queens Univ Pr) CUP Services.
Resnick, Rachel. Go West Young F*cked-Up Chick: A Novel of Separation. LC 98-40599. 256p. 1999. text 22.95 (*0-312-19889-2*) St Martin.
***Resnick, Rachel.** Go West Young F*cked-Up Chick: A Novel of Separation. 2000. pap. 12.95 (*0-312-26329-5*) St Martin.
Resnick, Robert, jt. auth. see Creasy, Robert K.
Resnick, Robert, jt. auth. see Porfiri, Lynne.
Resnick, Robert E. Introduction to Special Relativity. 248p. 1968. pap. 70.95 (*0-471-71725-8*) Wiley.
Resnick, Robert E. & Halliday, David. Basic Concepts in Relativity & Early Quantum Theory. 2nd ed. (Illus.). 352p. (C). 1991. pap. 28.60 (*0-02-399340-5*, Macmillan Coll) P-H.
— Fundamentals of Physics. 3rd ed. LC 87-31703. 1988. write for info. (*0-318-63029-X*) Wiley.
Resnick, Robert E. & Wilson, Jack. Conference on the Introductory Physics Course on the Occasion of the Retirement of Robert Resnick. LC 96-1948. 347p. 1996. text 49.95 (*0-471-15557-8*) Wiley.
Resnick, Robert E., et al. Fundamentals of Physics. expanded ed. LC 97-159472. 1080p. 1996. text 125.95 (*0-471-10559-7*) Wiley.
— Fundamentals of Physics. 5th ed. 384p. 1996. pap. 34.95 (*0-471-14561-0*) Wiley.
— Fundamentals of Physics. 5th ed. LC 96-203538. 1080p. 1996. text 120.95 (*0-471-10558-9*) Wiley.
— Fundamentals of Physics, Vol. 1. 5th ed. 624p. 1996. text 74.95 (*0-471-15662-0*) Wiley.
— Fundamentals of Physics, Vol. 1 & 2. 1996. text 89.00 (*0-471-16666-9*) Wiley.
— Fundamentals of Physics, Vol. 2. 5th ed. 688p. 1996. text 77.95 (*0-471-15663-9*) Wiley.
— Physics, 2 vols., Vol. 2. 4th ed. 1136p. (C). 1992. text 59.50 (*0-471-56898-8*) Wiley.
— Physics: Extended Version, 2 vols., Vol. 2. 4th ed. 1344p. (C). 1992. text 61.00 (*0-471-56897-X*) Wiley.
— Physics: Extended Version, 2 vols., Vol. 2 Extended. 4th ed. LC 92-24917. 688p. (C). 1992. text 81.95 (*0-471-54804-9*) Wiley.
— Physics: With Tanner Interactive Learningware, MAC, Pt. 2. 4th expanded ed. 688p. 1994. text 41.00 incl. disk (*0-471-11107-4*) Wiley.
— Physics: With Tanner Interactive Learningware, Vol. 1. 4th ed. 656p. 1994. text 41.00 incl. disk (*0-471-11108-2*) Wiley.
— Physics: With Tanner Interactive Learningware-IBM, Part 2. 4th expanded ed. 688p. 1994. text 41.00 incl. disk (*0-471-11109-0*) Wiley.
Resnick, Robert E., jt. auth. see Eisberg, Robert M.
Resnick, Robert J. & McEvoy, Kathleen, eds. Attention-Deficit/Hyperactivity Disorder: Abstracts of the Psychological & Behavioral Literature, 1971-1994. (Bibliographies in Psychology Ser.: No. 14). 204p. 1994. pap. 19.95 (*1-55798-274-0*) Am Psychol.
Resnick, Robert J. & Rozensky, Ronald H., eds. Health Psychology Through the Life Span: Practice & Research Opportunities. LC 96-41438. 464p. 1996. boxed set 39.95 (*1-55798-378-X*, 431-7780); pap. 34.95 (*1-55798-391-7*) Am Psychol.
Resnick, Robert J., jt. ed. see Lowman, Rodney L.
Resnick, Rosalind & Taylor, Dave. The Internet Business Guide. 2nd ed. (Illus.). 496p. (Orig.). 1995. pap. 25.00 (*1-57521-004-5*) Sams.
Resnick, Rose. Dare to Dream: The Rose Resnick Story. LC 88-4944. (Illus.). 236p. (Orig.). 1988. pap. 9.95 (*0-89407-089-4*) Strawberry Hill.
Resnick, S. Adventures in Stochastic Processes. xii, 626p. 1994. 64.50 (*0-8176-3591-2*) Birkhauser.
— Extreme Values, Regular Variation & Point Processes. (Applied Probability Ser.). 345p. 1987. 96.95 (*0-387-96481-9*) Spr-Verlag.
— A Probability Path. LC 98-21749. xii, 453 p. 1999. 64.50 (*0-8176-4055-X*) Birkhauser.
Resnick, Seymour. En Breve: A Concise Review of Spanish Grammar. 3rd ed. LC 93-77580. (C). 1994. pap. text 49.50 (*0-15-500748-3*) Harcourt.
— Essential French Grammar. 159p. (Orig.). 1963. pap. 4.95 (*0-486-20419-7*) Dover.
— Essential Spanish Grammar. 115p. (Orig.). 1963. pap. 4.95 (*0-486-20780-3*) Dover.
***Resnick, Seymour.** 1001 Most Useful English Words for Spanish-Speaking People. 2000. pap. 1.50 (*0-486-41128-1*) Dover.
Resnick, Seymour. 1001 Most Useful Spanish Words. (ENG & SPA.). 64p. (Orig.). 1996. pap. text 1.50 (*0-486-29113-8*) Dover.
— Spanish-American Poetry: A Dual-Language Anthology. rev. ed. LC 96-7769. 64p. 1996. reprint ed. pap. text 4.95 (*0-486-29380-7*) Dover.
— Teach Yourself French: Essential Grammar. (Teach Yourself Ser.). 1992. 14.95 (*0-8288-8326-2*) Fr & Eur.
— Teach Yourself Spanish: Essential Grammar. (Teach Yourself Ser.). 1992. 12.95 (*0-8288-8397-1*) Fr & Eur.
Resnick, Seymour & Giuliano, William. En Breve: A Concise Review of Spanish Grammar. 4th ed. LC 97-70693. (SPA.). 352p. (C). 1997. pap. text 44.50 (*0-03-024569-9*) Holt R&W.
Resnick, Seymour & Pasmantier, Jeanne. Nueve Siglos de Literatura Espanola: Nine Centuries of Spanish Literature: A Dual-Language Anthology. unabridged ed. LC 94-19769. 480p. 1994. pap. text 9.95 (*0-486-28271-6*) Dover.
Resnick, Sol D., jt. ed. see Issar, Arie S.
Resnick, Stella. The Pleasure Zone: Why We Resist Good Feelings & How to Let Go & Be Happy. LC 97-15651. 320p. 1997. 21.95 (*1-57324-071-0*) Conari Press.
— Pleasure Zone: Why We Resist Good Feelings & How to Let Go & be Happy. 320p. 1998. pap. text 14.95 (*1-57324-150-4*) Conari Press.
Resnick, Stephen A. & Wolff, Richard D. Knowledge & Class: A Marxian Critique of Political Economy. LC 86-32631. viii, 360p. 1989. pap. text 22.00 (*0-226-71023-8*) U Ch Pr.
— Knowledge & Class: A Marxian Critique of Political Economy. LC 86-32631. viii, 352p. 1994. 32.50 (*0-226-71021-1*) U Ch Pr.
Resnick, Steven, jt. ed. see Wolff, Richard.
Resnick, Susan, tr. see Schwaller De Lubicz, Isha.
***Resnick, Susan Kushner.** Sleepless Days: One Woman's Journey Through Postpartum Depression. LC 99-89675. 208p. 2000. text 22.95 (*0-312-25336-2*) St Martin.
Resnicoff, Stanley. The Seal of Approval. LC 98-42172. (J). 1999. pap. 3.25 (*0-679-89466-7*, Pub. by Random Bks Yng Read) Random.
Resnicoff, Steven H., jt. auth. see Lewis, Wayne K.
Resnicow, Herbert. The Dead Room. 224p. 1989. reprint ed. spiral bd. 3.50 (*0-373-26020-2*) Harlequin Bks.
***Resnik, David, et al.** Human Germ-Line Therapy: Scientific, Moral & Political Issues. LC 98-43505. 189p. 1999. 99.00 (*1-57059-586-0*) Landes Bioscience.

An Asterisk (*) at the beginning of an entry indicates that the title is appearing for the first time.

Resnik, David B. The Ethics of Science: An Introduction. LC 97-40514. 232p. (C). 1998. 75.00 (*0-415-16697-7*); pap. 24.99 (*0-415-16698-5*) Routledge.

Resnik, Gail & Trost, Scott. All You Need to Know about the Movie & TV Business. 336p. 1996. per. 12.00 (*0-684-80064-0*) S&S Trade.

Resnik, H. L., ed. Suicidal Behaviors: Diagnosis & Management. LC 94-32435. 568p. 1995. pap. text 50.00 (*1-56821-263-1*) Aronson.

Resnik, H. L., jt. auth. see Mitchell, Jeffrey.

Resnik, H. L., jt. auth. see Mitchell, Jeffrey T.

Resnik, Hank, ed. Skills For Adolescence. (Illus.). 436p. 1985. student ed. 4.85 (*0-933419-09-0*) Quest Intl.

— Youth & Drugs: Society's Mixed Messages. 174p. (Orig.). (C). 1994. pap. text 30.00 (*0-7881-0296-6*) DIANE Pub.

Resnik, Hank, jt. auth. see Schimmels, Cliff.

Resnik, Hank, ed. see Barr, Linda & Gerber, Carole.

Resnik, Judith, jt. auth. see Fiss, Owen M.

***Resnik, Linda & Brock, Dee.** Food FAQs: Substitutions, Yields & Equivalents. LC 98-93812. 224p. 2000. pap. 12.95 (*0-9667179-0-2*) FAQs Pr.

Resnik, Michael D. Choices: An Introduction to Decision Theory. LC 86-11307. 234p. 1987. pap. 17.95 (*0-8166-1440-7*) U of Minn Pr.

— Frege & the Philosophy of Mathematics. 240p. 1980. text 37.50 (*0-8014-1293-5*) Cornell U Pr.

— Mathematics As a Science of Patterns. LC 96-51610. (Illus.). 298p. 1997. text 45.00 (*0-19-823608-5*) OUP.

— Mathematics As a Science of Patterns. (Illus.). 304p. 2000. pap. text 19.95 (*0-19-825014-2*) OUP.

Resnik, Michael D., ed. Mathematical Objects & Mathematical Knowledge. LC 95-5672. (International Research Library of Philosophy). (Illus.). 672p. 1995. text 235.95 (*1-85521-638-8*, Pub. by Dartmth Pub) Ashgate Pub Co.

Resnik, Muriel. Any Wednesday. 1966. pap. 5.25 (*0-8222-0059-7*) Dramatists Play.

Resnik, Philip, jt. ed. see Klavans, Judith L.

Resnik, Philip, jt. ed. see Klavans, Judith.

Resnik, Robert, jt. ed. see Creasy, Robert K.

Resnik, Salomon. Mental Space. 144p. 1995. pap. text 28.00 (*1-85575-058-9*, Pub. by H Karnac Bks Ltd) Other Pr LLC.

— The Theatre of the Dream. LC 87-6538. 260p. (C). 1987. lib. bdg. 45.00 (*0-422-61040-2*, Pub. by Tavistock) Routldge.

— The Theatre of the Dream. LC 87-6538. 260p. (C). 1995. pap. text 22.99 (*0-422-61830-6*, Pub. by Tavistock) Routldge.

Resnik, Susan. Blood Saga: The Social History of the U. S. Hemophilia Community, 1948-1998. LC 98-14150. 1999. 29.95 (*0-520-21195-2*, Pub. by U CA Pr) Cal Prin Full Svc.

Resnikoff, H. L. & Wells, R. O. Mathematics in Civilization. LC 72-83805. (Illus.). reprint ed. 29.50 (*0-03-085035-5*) Irvington.

Resnikoff, H. L. & Wells, R. O., Jr. Mathematics in Civilization. (Popular Science Ser.). (Illus.). 448p. 1999. reprint ed. pap. 11.95 (*0-486-24674-4*) Dover.

— Wavelet Analysis: The Scalable Structure of Information. LC 97-44442. (Illus.). 536p. 1998. text 59.00 (*0-387-98383-X*) Spr-Verlag.

Resnikoff, Irene & Motzkin, Linda. Tall Tales Told in Biblical Hebrew. (Illus.). 144p. (Orig.). 1994. pap. 16.95 (*0-939144-20-4*) EKS Pub Co.

Resnikoff, Irene, et al. OG Returns: OG's Further Adventures in Prayerbook Hebrew. Goldstien, Jessica, ed. (OG the Terrible Ser.: Vol. 2). (HEB., Illus.). 24p. (J). (gr. 1-6). 1998. pap. 3.95 (*0-939144-27-1*) EKS Pub Co.

Resnikoff, Irene, jt. auth. see Simon, Ethelyn.

Resnikoff, Marvin. The Next Nuclear Gamble: Transportation & Storage of Nuclear Waste. 378p. 1985. 39.95 (*0-88738-095-6*) Transaction Pubs.

Resolution Business Press Staff. Northwest High Tech. 6th ed. 1997. 34.95 (*0-945264-21-6*) Resolution Busn Pr.

Resolve Staff, jt. auth. see Aronson, Diane.

Resor, Stanley R., Jr. & Kutt, Henn, eds. The Medical Treatment of Epilepsy. (Neurological Disease & Therapy Ser.: Vol. 10). (Illus.). 760p. 1991. text 255.00 (*0-8247-8549-5*) Dekker.

Resource Center, United Way of San Diego County St. Directions 1997: Directory of Health & Human Care Services in San Diego County. unabridged ed. 256p. (Orig.). 1996. 38.00 (*0-9629793-5-X*) United Way SD.

Resource Center, United Way of San Diego County Staff. Directions 1996: Directory of Health & Human Care Services in San Diego County. 700p. 1995. 38.00 (*0-9629793-4-1*) United Way SD.

Resource Engineering, Inc. Staff. FMEA Investigator Workbook: The Official Companion Guide to the FMEA Investigator Personal Trainer Series. 64p. 1998. pap. 7.95 (*1-882307-24-0*) Res Engineering.

— SPC Workout Workbook: The Official Companion Guide to the SPC Workout. (Illus.). 58p. (C). 1996. 7.95 (*1-882307-23-2*) Res Engineering.

Resource Pathway's Editors. Going Solo: The Best Resources for Entrepreneurs & Freelancers. Mason, Stanley, ed. 288p. 1999. pap. 24.95 (*1-892148-12-9*, Pub. by Res Pathways) Natl Bk Netwk.

***Resource Pathways Staff, ed.** Stepparenting: The Best Resources to Help Blend Your Family. LC 99-65820. (Parenting Ser.). 288p. 2000. pap. 24.95 (*1-892148-13-7*) Res Pathways.

Resource Staff. Pocket Dictionary-Flag Blue, Blue. 326p. 1994. pap. text 7.95 (*0-15-900257-5*) Harcourt Legal.

— Pocket Dictionary-Hunter Green, Green. 326p. 1994. pap. text 7.95 (*0-15-900258-3*) Harcourt Legal.

— Pocket Dictionary-Maroon, Burgundy. 326p. 1994. pap. text 7.95 (*0-15-900256-7*) Harcourt Legal.

Resource World Staff, compiled by. The Art of Architectural Illustration. 220p. 1994. 49.99 (*1-56496-074-9*) Rockport Pubs.

— The Art of Architectural Illustration. (Illus.). 226p. 1996. pap. text 34.99 (*1-56496-201-6*) Rockport Pubs.

***Resources for Global Sustainability Staff. Environmental Grant Making Foundations 2000. 8th ed. Thiele, Corinne Szymko, ed. 1061p. (Orig.). 2000. pap. 105.00 (*0-9631943-7-2*) Res Global Sus.**
The best selling comprehensive guide to 889 independent, community & corporate foundations that give environmental grants. Together these foundations give over $600 million annually for environmental purposes. Foundation profiles include: contact information, history & philosophy, financial data, funding analysis, sample grants & application process. Multiple indexes allow easy cross-referencing. Also available in CD-ROM format. To order, contact RGS by phone (800-724-1857), fax (919-363-9841) e-mail (rgs@environmentalgrants.com) or by mail: RGS: PO B ox 3665, Cary, NC 27519-3665. Visit www.environmentalgrants.com for detailed information. *Publisher Paid Annotation.*

Resources for Rehabilitation Organization. A Woman's Guide to Coping with Disability. 2nd ed. LC 96-51596. 1997. pap. 42.95 (*0-929718-19-4*) Resc Rehab.

***Resources for Rehabilitation Organization Staff.** Meeting the Needs of Employees with Disabilities. 3rd ed. LC 99-33733. 1999. pap. 44.95 (*0-929718-25-9*) Resc Rehab.

Resources for Rehabilitation Staff. Living with Low Vision: A Resource Guide for People with Sight Loss. 5th large type ed. 1998. pap. 44.95 (*0-929718-20-8*) Resc Rehab.

— Making Wise Medical Decisions: How to Get the Information You Need. LC 98-23960. 219p. 1998. pap. 39.95 (*0-929718-21-6*) Resc Rehab.

— A Man's Guide to Coping with Disability. 2nd ed. LC 98-55559. 1999. pap. 44.95 (*0-929718-23-2*) Resc Rehab.

— Resources for Elders with Disabilities. 4th large type ed. LC 99-17664. (Orig.). 1999. pap. 49.95 (*0-929718-24-0*) Resc Rehab.

— Resources for People with Disabilities & Chronic Conditions. 4th ed. LC 98-41349. 1999. pap. 54.95 (*0-929718-22-4*) Resc Rehab.

Resources for the Future, Inc. Staff. Agricultural Development in the Mekong Basin: Goals, Priorities, & Strategies: A Staff Study. LC 70-158820. 116p. reprint ed. pap. 36.00 (*0-8357-5269-0*, 202381000034) Bks Demand.

— Design for a World Wide Study of Regional Development: Report to the United Nations on a Proposed Research-Training Program. LC 66-19959. 92p. reprint ed. pap. 30.00 (*0-608-12544-X*, 202381100034) Bks Demand.

— Forest Credit in the United States: A Survey of Needs & Facilities; Report of a Committee Appointed by Resources for the Future, Inc. LC 58-8252. 176p. reprint ed. pap. 54.60 (*0-608-13098-2*, 205210500034) Bks Demand.

— Publications of Resources for the Future, Inc., 12 vols., Set. reprint ed. write for info. (*0-404-60325-4*) AMS Pr.

— A Report on Planning, Policy Making & Research Activities. LC 61-14884. 46p. reprint ed. pap. 30.00 (*0-608-13095-8*, 205210600034) Bks Demand.

— United States Energy Policies: An Agenda for Research. LC 68-28767. 166p. reprint ed. pap. 51.50 (*0-608-12545-8*, 202381200034) Bks Demand.

Resources for the Future, Inc. Staff & Farm Foundation Staff. Land Economics Research: Papers Presented at a Symposium Held at Lincoln, Nebraska, June 16-23, 1961. Clawson, Marion et al, eds. LC 77-86388. (Resources for the Future, Inc. Publications). 296p. reprint ed. 55.00 (*0-404-60327-0*) AMS Pr.

Respess, Kathryn. The Children of Israel: A Workbook Introduction to Ancient Israel. 124p. (YA). (gr. 9-12). 1984. student ed. 25.50 (*1-881678-08-3*) CSEE.

— The Children of Israel: A Workbook Introduction to Ancient Israel. (Illus.). (YA). (gr. 9-12). 1984. pap. 9.00 (*1-881678-09-1*) CSEE.

Respighi, Ottorino. Fountains of Rome in Full Score. 1999. pap. 9.95 (*0-486-40630-X*) Dover.

Respighi, Elsa. Fifty Years of a Life in Music, 1905-1955: Cinquant Anni De Vita Nella Musica. Fontecchio, Giovanni & Johnson, Roger, trs. from ITA. LC 93-27440. (Studies in the History & Interpretation of Music: Vol. 42). 348p. 1993. 99.95 (*0-7734-9364-6*) E Mellen.

Respiratory Nursing Society Staff, jt. auth. see American Nurses Association Staff.

Respondek, W., jt. auth. see Jakubczyk, Bronisaw.

Respress, Linda. Hairstylists, Barbers, & All That Jazz. 1999. pap. 8.95 (*0-533-12931-1*) Vantage.

Ress, David. The Burundi Ethnic Massacres, 1988. LC 91-45122. 136p. 1992. lib. bdg. 69.95 (*0-7734-9878-8*) E Mellen.

Ress, Georg, ed. Entwicklung des Europaischen Urheberrechts: Intellectual Property Rights & EC Law. (GER.). 135p. 1989. pap. 44.00 (*3-7890-1817-1*, Pub. by Nomos Verlags) Intl Bk Import.

Ress, Pat. Armageddon: Headress, Uniforms & Equipment. 98p. 1998. 20.00 (*1-57179-075-6*) Intern Guild ASRS.

Resseguie, Jacqueline, jt. auth. see Thompson, Stephen.

Resseguie, James L. Revelation Unsealed: A Narrative Critical Approach to John's Apocalypse. LC 97-47635. (Biblical Interpretation Ser.). xii, 234p. 1998. 89.00 (*90-04-11129-8*) Brill Academic Pubs.

Resseguier, Gertrude. The First Love: About Joy in the Priesthood. Stephens, Charlotte E., tr. from GER. LC 98-10387. 128p. 1998. pap. 9.95 (*1-879007-27-4*, FIRS) St Bedes Pubns.

Ressi, Michele. Dictionnaire des Citations de l'Histoire de France. (FRE.). 800p. 1992. pap. 155.00 (*0-7859-7880-1*, 2268010171) Fr & Eur.

Ressich, John. Voices in the Wilderness. LC 79-152954. (Short Story Index Reprint Ser.). 1977. reprint ed. 19.95 (*0-8369-3869-0*) Ayer.

Ressis, Jim. The Art of Cooking for Singles. 106p. 1996. 9.95 (*0-9650456-0-9*) J Ressis.

Ressler, D. Michael & United States Staff. Historical Perspective on the President's Own, U.S. Marine Band. LC 98-177659. 36p. 1998. write for info. (*0-16-049644-6*) USGPO.

Ressler, Lawrence, jt. ed. see Schrock-Shenk, Carolyn.

Ressler, Lawrence E., ed. Hearts Strangely Warmed: Reflections of Biblical Passages Relevant to Social Work. 48p. 1994. pap. 8.00 (*0-9623634-3-X*) N American Assn.

Ressler, Martin E., et al. Lancaster County Churches in the Revolutionary War Era. Harrison, Matthew W., Jr., ed. LC 76-21210. (Illus.). 96p. 1976. pap. 5.00 (*0-915010-11-9*) Sutter House.

Ressler, Pauline. God's Detour. (Illus.). 240p. (YA). (gr. 7-10). 1993. 9.10 (*0-7399-0125-7*, 2247) Rod & Staff.

— Poems for Praise & Power. (Illus.). 157p. 1978. pap. 5.90 (*0-7399-0167-2*, 2350) Rod & Staff.

Ressler, Ralph. A World of Choice: Careers & You - Student Workbook. LC 77-4182. (Illus.). (YA). (gr. 9-12). 1978. pap., teacher ed. 19.95 (*0-88280-051-5*); pap., student ed. 14.95 (*0-88280-050-7*) ETC Pubns.

Ressler, Robert K. I Have Lived with the Monster: True Crime Special Release. (True Crime Library). 1998. mass mkt. 6.50 (*0-312-96429-3*) St Martin.

— Justice Is Served. 1996. mass mkt. 5.99 (*0-312-95615-0*, Pub. by Tor Bks) St Martin.

Ressler, Robert K., et al, eds. Sexual Homicide: Patterns, Motives & Procedures for Investigation. 256p. 1988. 39.95 (*0-669-16559-X*) Free Pr.

Ressler, Robert K. & Schachtman, Thomas. Whoever Fights Monsters: A Brilliant FBI Detective's Career-Long War Against Serial Killers. 1993. mass mkt. 5.99 (*0-312-95044-6*) St Martin.

Ressler, Robert K., jt. auth. see Burgess, Ann W.

Rest, D., jt. auth. see Varshavsky, T.

Rest, Friedrich O. Our Christian Symbols. LC 53-9923. (Illus.). 96p. 1954. pap. 5.95 (*0-8298-0099-9*) Pilgrim OH.

Rest, Gregory, jt. auth. see Salant, Stephen W.

Rest, Hillard C. How to Profit from Your Investment Personality: What You Need to Know to Identify Your Investment Personality & Increase Your Profits. Martin, Alice, ed. & illus. by. LC 90-84885. 224p. 1992. pap. 16.95 (*1-879250-00-4*) Hilmar Pub.

Rest, James, et al. Postconventional Moral Thinking: A Neo-Kohlbergian Approach. LC 98-43690. 240p. 1999. 49.95 (*0-8058-3285-8*) L Erlbaum Assocs.

Rest, James R. Development in Judging Moral Issues. LC 79-22755. 327p. reprint ed. pap. 101.40 (*0-608-15977-8*, 203328500084) Bks Demand.

— Moral Development: Advances in Research & Theory. LC 86-21708. 241p. 1986. 55.00 (*0-275-92254-5*, C2254, Praeger Pubs) Greenwood.

Rest, James R. & Narvaez, Darcia F., eds. Moral Development in the Professions: Psychology & Applied Ethics. 248p. 1994. pap. 27.50 (*0-8058-1539-2*); text 39.95 (*0-8058-1538-4*) L Erlbaum Assocs.

Rest, Kathleen, ed. Proceedings of the Association of Occupational & Environmental Clinics (AOEC) Workshop on Multiple Chemical Sensitivity - Advancing the Understanding of Multiple Chemical Sensitivity. LC 92-64374. (Toxicology & Industrial Health Ser.: Vol. 8, No. 4). (Illus.). 1992. pap. text 65.00 (*0-911131-74-4*) Specialist Journals.

Rest, Stanley M., jt. auth. see Casciani, Joseph M.

Resta. Educational Technology. (MML Ser.: Vol. 4, Nos. 2-3). 1994. 40.00 (*0-8058-9962-6*) L Erlbaum Assocs.

Resta, Bart. Health & Wholeness. (Lifesearch Ser.). 64p. (Orig.). 1994. pap. 4.95 (*0-687-77869-7*) Abingdon.

Resta, Stefano. Fish Bird Stone Star. 1996. 10.00 (*0-9650738-7-4*) Wooden Fish.

Restack, Richard. Older & Wiser. LC 97-14232. 304p. 1997. 23.50 (*0-684-82976-2*) S&S Trade.

Restad, Penne L. Christmas in America: A History. (Illus.). 240p. 1996. reprint ed. pap. 12.95 (*0-19-510980-5*) OUP.

Restagno, Enzo, jt. auth. see Carter, Elliott.

Restaino, Joyce & Keenan, Judy. New Jersey Property Tax Assessments: A Homeowner's Guided Tour to Understanding Assessments, Appeals, Revluations, & Reassessments. 2nd rev. ed. (Illus.). 50p. 1995. 12.95 (*0-9628989-1-0*) Milford Pr.

Restaino-Kelly, Rudolph. Building Literacy Through Child Development: A Source for the Field. 166p. (C). 1997. per. 23.95 (*0-7872-4458-9*, 41445801) Kendall-Hunt.

***Restaino, Sergio, et al, eds.** Catching the Perfect Wave: Adaptive Optics & Interferometry in the 21st Century. LC 99-64822. (Conference Series Proceedings: Vol. 174). 256p. 1999. text 52.00 (*1-886733-96-1*) Astron Soc Pacific.

***Restak, Richard.** Mysteries of the Mind. 2000. 35.00 (*0-7922-7941-7*) Natl Geog.

Restak, Richard, jt. auth. see Mahoney, David.

Restak, Richard M. Brainscapes: An Introduction to What Neuroscience Has Learned about the Structure, Function & Abilities of the Brain. LC 95-14774. (Illus.). 160p. (J). 1995. 19.45 (*0-7868-6113-4*, Pub. by Hyperion) Time Warner.

— Brainscapes: An Introduction to What Neuroscience Has Learned about the Structure, Function & Abilities of the Brain. (Illus.). 160p. (J). 1996. pap. 10.45 (*0-7868-8190-9*, Pub. by Hyperion) Time Warner.

— The Modular Brain. 256p. 1994. 22.00 (*0-684-19544-5*, Scribners Ref) Mac Lib Ref.

— The Modular Brain: How New Discoveries in Neuroscience Are Answering Age-Old Questions about Memory, Free Will, Consciousness, & Personal Identity. 1995. pap. 14.00 (*0-684-80126-4*, Touchstone) S&S Trade Pap.

***Restak, Richard M.** Mysteries of the Mind. LC 00-27668. 2000. write for info. (*0-7922-7640-X*) Natl Geog.

— Older & Wiser: How to Maintain Peak Mental Ability for As Long As You Live. 272p. 1999. reprint ed. pap. 12.95 (*0-425-16586-8*) Berkley Pub.

Restall, Eric, jt. auth. see Bark, Conrad V.

***Restall, Greg.** An Introduction to Substructural Logics LC 99-15946. 1999. pap. text. write for info. (*0-415-21534-X*) Routledge.

— Introduction to Substructural Logics. LC 99-15946. 400p. (C). 2000. text. write for info. (*0-415-21533-1*) Routledge.

Restall, John & Hebbs, Donald. How to Make Wines with a Sparkle. (Illus.). 132p. (Orig.). 1993. reprint ed. pap. 10.95 (*0-9619072-6-6*) G W Kent.

— Making Sparkling Wines. 2nd ed. (Illus.). 144p. (Orig.). 1995. pap. 14.95 (*1-85486-119-0*, Pub. by Nexus Special Interests) Trans-Atl Phila.

Restall, Matthew. Life & Death in a Maya Community: The Ixil Testaments of the 1760s. LC 94-77123. (Illus.). 200p. (Orig.). 1995. pap. 20.00 (*0-911437-31-2*) Labyrinthos.

— Maya Conquistador. LC 98-15751. (Illus.). 272p. 1998. 25.00 (*0-8070-5506-9*) Beacon Pr.

— Maya Conquistador. LC 98-15751. (Illus.). 272p. 1999. pap. 18.00 (*0-8070-5507-7*) Beacon Pr.

— The Maya World: Yucatec Culture & Society, 1550-1850. LC 96-26167. 1997. 66.00 (*0-8047-2745-7*) Stanford U Pr.

— Maya World: Yucatec Culture & Society, 1550-1950. 1999. pap. text 24.95 (*0-8047-3658-8*) Stanford U Pr.

Restall, Matthew, jt. ed. see Kellogg, Susan.

Restall, Robin. Munias & Mannikins. LC 96-61495. (Illus.). 340p. 1997. 60.00 (*0-300-07109-4*) Yale U Pr.

Restany, Pierre. G. H. Rothe Master of the Mezzotint. Newell, Cam, ed. LC 83-81130. (Illus.). 271p. 1983. 60.00 (*0-9611570-0-3*); 60.00 (*0-9611570-1-1*) Hammer Gal.

— Hundertwasser: Power of Art: The Painter-King with the 5 Skins. 1998. pap. text 9.99 (*3-8228-7641-0*) Taschen Amer.

— Yves Klein: Fire at the Heart of the Void. Ottmann, Klaus, ed. Loselle, Andrea, tr. from FRE. (Journal of Contemporary Art Editions Ser.). (Illus.). 160p. (Orig.). (C). 1993. pap. 20.00 (*0-9634713-0-9*) Jrnl Contemp.

Restany, Pierre & Brauer, Erich. Brauer: Oils, Gouaches, Watercolours & Etchings. (Illus.). 102p. 1975. 40.00 (*1-55660-279-0*) A Wofsy Fine Arts.

Restany, Pierre & De Vree, Freddy. Cremer: Grafiek - Prints 1956-1998. (Illus.). 252p. pap. (*90-6868-210-5*, Pub. by U Thoth) Bks Nippan.

Restany, Pierre, et al. Dani Karavan. (Illus.). 159p. 1992. 70.00 (*3-7913-1237-5*, Pub. by Prestel) te Neues.

— Niki de Saint Phalle: The Tarot Garden. LC 99-178176. (Illus.). 120p. 1998. pap. 25.00 (*88-8158-167-1*, Pub. by Charta) Dist Art Pubs.

Restany, Pierre, jt. auth. see Greene, Alison D.

Restaurant Business Inc. Staff. Menu Planning & Foods Merchandising. LC 73-163322. 1971. teacher ed. 6.67 (*0-672-96094-X*, Bobbs); student ed. 7.50 (*0-672-96093-1*, Bobbs) Macmillan.

***Restayn, Jean.** Tiger I in the East. 1999. 37.95 (*2-908182-82-3*, 182815) Histoire.

— Tiger I on the Eastern Front. 1999. 37.95 (*2-908182-81-5*) Histoire.

— Tiger I on the Western Front. (Illus.). 2000. 37.95 (*2-913903-13-4*, Pub. by Histoire) Combined Pub.

Restelli, Giambattista, ed. Dimethylsulphide - Oceans, Atmosphere & Climate: Proceedings of the International Symposium Held in Belgirate, Italy, 13-15 October 1992. LC 93-30136. 412p. (C). 1993. text 214.50 (*0-7923-2490-0*) Kluwer Academic.

Restelli, Giambattista, jt. ed. see Angeletti, G.

Rester, A. C., Jr. & Trombka, J. I., eds. High-Energy Radiation Background in Space. LC 89-83833. (AIP Conference Proceedings Ser.: No. 186). 520p. 1989. lib. bdg. 80.00 (*0-88318-386-2*) Am Inst Physics.

Rester-Zodrow, Gina, jt. auth. see Chancer, Joni.

Restif De La Bretonne, Nicholas E. Monsieur Nicholas, Vol. 2. Testud, Jean-Yves, ed. (FRE.). 1989. lib. bdg. 170.00 (*0-7859-3888-5*) Fr & Eur.

Restif de la Bretonne, Nicholas E. Nuits de Paris. (Folio Ser.: No. 1739). (FRE.). 1986. pap. 14.95 (*2-07-037739-3*) Schoenhof.

— La Vie de Mon Pere, 2 vols. in 1. iv, 291p. 1979. reprint ed. write for info. (*3-487-06844-3*) G Olms Pubs.

Restifo, Robert A. Illustrated Key to the Mosquitoes of Ohio: Biological Notes, No. 17. (Illus.). 56p. 1982. pap. text 7.00 (*0-86727-092-6*) Ohio Bio Survey.

Restine, L. Nan. Women in Administration: Facilitators for Change. Herman, Jerry J. & Herman, Janice L., eds. LC 93-16917. (Road Maps to Success Ser.). 64p. 1993. pap. 14.95 (*0-8039-6059-X*) Corwin Pr.

Restivo, Sal, jt. ed. see Croissant, Jennifer.

R

An Asterisk (*) at the beginning of an entry indicates that the title is appearing for the first time.

R

Restivo, Sal P. Mathematics in Society & History: Sociological Inquiries. LC 92-13695. 208p. (C). 1992. lib. bdg. 127.50 (*0-7923-1765-3*, Pub. by Kluwer Academic) Kluwer Academic.

— Science, Society, & Values: Toward a Sociology of Objectivity. LC 92-85310. 1994. 39.50 (*0-934223-21-1*) Lehigh Univ Pr.

— The Social Relations of Physics, Mysticism & Mathematics. 318p. 1983. lib. bdg. 133.00 (*90-277-1536-X*, D Reidel) Kluwer Academic.

— The Social Relations of Physics, Mysticism & Mathematics. (Pallas Paperbacks Ser.). 308p. 1985. pap. text 61.50 (*90-277-2084-3*, D Reidel) Kluwer Academic.

Restivo, Sal P., et al, eds. Math Worlds: Philosophical & Social Studies of Mathematics & Mathematics Education. LC 92-4252. (SUNY Series in Science, Technology, & Society). 292p. (C). 1993. text 22.50 (*0-7914-1329-2*) State U NY Pr.

***Restle, Barbara.** Shadow over Fiji: A Memoir. LC 99-93570. 1999. pap. 13.95 (*0-533-13069-7*) Vantage.

Restle, Frank & Castellan, N. J., Jr., eds. Cognitive Theory, Vol. 3. 336p. 1978. 69.95 (*0-89859-438-3*) L Erlbaum Assocs.

***Restle, Nicole.** Vokales und instrumentales Komponieren in Johann Hermann Scheins Opella Nova Ander Theil. 2000. 42.95 (*3-631-35776-1*) P Lang Pubng.

Reston, James. Artillery of the Press. LC 67-11330. 128p. reprint ed. 39.70 (*0-8357-9150-5*, 200215900012) Bks Demand.

Reston, James, Jr. Collision at Home Plate: The Lives of Pete Rose & Bart Giamatti. LC 96-46316. (Illus.). ix, 344p. 1997. pap. 16.00 (*0-8032-8964-2*, Bison Books) U of Nebr Pr.

Reston, James. The Last Apocalypse. (Illus.). 336p. 1999. pap. 14.95 (*0-385-48336-8*) Doubleday.

— Shermans March & Vietnam. 1985. 14.95 (*0-02-602300-8*) Macmillan.

Reston, James, jt. ed. see Childs, Marquis W.

***Restorick, Rita.** Death of a Soldier: A Mother's Search for Peace in Northern Ireland. 2000. pap. 19.95 (*0-85640-670-8*, Pub. by Blackstaff Pr) Dufour.

***Restoring Southern Gardens & Landscape Conference Staff.** Breaking Ground: Examining the Vision & Practice of Historic Landscape Restoration. LC 99-12458. 1999. write for info. (*1-879704-06-4*) Old Salem NC.

Restout, Denise, tr. see Chambonnieres, Jacques C.

Restrepo. Sweet Intimacy Spa. (SPA.). 208p. 1999. pap. 10.00 (*0-06-092822-0*) HarpC.

Restrepo, Jaime. Internet para Todos. LC 98-48788. 1999. pap. 14.95 (*0-375-70350-0*) Random Ref & Info.

Restrepo, Jaime A. De Dos a Windows. 1996. pap. 12.95 (*0-679-77378-9*) McKay.

***Restrepo, Jaime A.** Internet Para Todos. (Illus.). (J). 1999. 20.30 (*0-606-18498-8*) Turtleback.

Restrepo, Jamie. Windows 95-98 Para Todos. rev. ed. LC 99-70178. (SPA., Illus.). 224p. (YA). (gr. 9 up). 1999. pap. 13.95 (*0-375-70361-6*) Random Ref & Info.

***Restrepo, Laura.** The Angel of Galilea: A Novel. 1999. pap. 12.00 (*0-375-70649-6*) Vin Bks.

— The Leopard in the Sun. (International Ser.). 256p. 2000. pap. 12.00 (*0-375-70508-2*) Vin Bks.

— Leopard in the Sun. LC 99-13509. 256p. 1999. 22.00 (*0-609-60386-8*, Crown) Crown Pub Group.

Restrepo, Maria C. Llano, see Llano Restrepo, Maria C.

Restrepo, Tanya E., jt. auth. see Alley, Alyson B.

***Restuccia, Frances L.** Melancholics in Love: Representing Women's Depression & Domestic Abuse. LC 99-45718. 160p. 2000. pap. 22.95 (*0-8476-9829-7*); text 65.00 (*0-8476-9828-9*) Rowman.

Restuccia, Nancy. Hold It! How to Sew Bags, Totes, Duffels, Pouches & More! LC 93-48333. (Illus.). 144p. 1994. pap. 17.95 (*0-8019-8494-7*) Krause Pubns.

Restyn & Buffeteaut. Tanks of World War II. (Jane's Gem Ser.). (Illus.). 256p. (Orig.). 1995. pap. 8.00 (*0-00-470847-4*, Perennial) HarperTrade.

Resumil De Sanfilippo, Olga E. Criminologia General. 309p. 1995. 22.95 (*0-8477-3033-6*) U of PR Pr.

Resumil de Sanfilippo, Olga E. Derecho Procesal Penal, 2 Tomos. (SPA.). 400p. 1994. boxed set 120.00 (*0-88063-691-2*, 82895-10, MICHIE) LEXIS Pub.

Resumil de Sanfilippo, Olga E., see Resumil de Sanfilippo, Olga E.

Resurreccion, Anna V. Consumer Sensory Testing for Product Development. LC 97-48866. 304p. 1998. 75.00 (*0-8342-1209-9*) Aspen Pub.

Reswick, Irmtraud. Traditional Textiles of Tunisia & Related North African Weaving. (Illus.). 272p. 1985. pap. 24.95 (*0-295-96281-X*) U of Wash Pr.

Reswick, James B., jt. ed. see Hambrecht, F. Terry.

Resye, Robert T., ed. In Tune with Tradition: Wisconsin Folk Musical Instruments. (Illus.). 72p. (Orig.). 1990. pap. 10.00 (*0-9625597-0-9*) Cedarburg Cultural Ctr.

Resz, E. English-Hungarian & Hungarian-English Tourists Dictionary. 315p. (C). 1988. 350.00 (*0-569-19611-6*, Pub. by Collets) St Mut.

Reszat, Beate. The Japanese Foreign Exchange Market. LC 97-12497. (Illus.). 248p. (C). 1997. 90.00 (*0-415-14232-6*) Routledge.

Reszat, Beate, jt. auth. see Menkhoff, Lukas.

Reszegh, Carol A., ed. 1997 Annual Potato Statistical Yearbook. (Illus.). 72p. 1997. 25.00 (*0-318-19543-7*) Natl Potato Coun.

Retail Advertising & Marketing Association Staff, ed. Excellence in Advertising: The Thirty-Ninth RAC Awards. (Illus.). 224p. 1992. 49.95 (*0-934590-43-5*) Visual Refer.

Retail Entertainment Data Publishing Staff. Gramophone Annual Guide to Classical Recordings, 1996. (C). 1995. 90.00 (*0-02-864514-6*, Schirmer Books) Mac Lib Ref.

— MusicMasters & Gramophone Annuals, 1996, 3 vols., Set. (C). 1996. 175.00 (*0-02-864521-9*, Schirmer Books) Mac Lib Ref.

— MusicMasters & Gramophone Annuals, 1996, 3 vols., Set. (C). 1996. text 350.00 incl. cd-rom (*0-02-864523-5*, Schirmer Books) Mac Lib Ref.

— MusicMasters Annual Guide to Popular Recordings, 1996, 2 vols., Set. 1996. 115.00 (*0-02-864576-6*, Hall Reference) Macmillan.

Retail Partners, Inc., Staff. Eight Steps to Business Success: A Handbook for Independent Merchants. 105p. 1991. 14.95 (*0-9629238-0-X*) URA Pittsburgh.

Retail Reporting Staff. Cafes & Coffee Shops. 1995. 55.00 (*0-688-14322-9*, Wm Morrow) Morrow Avon.

— Corporate Interiors 3. 1999. 55.00 (*0-688-17256-3*, Wm Morrow) Morrow Avon.

— Corporate Interiors 2. 1998. 55.00 (*0-688-16057-3*, Wm Morrow) Morrow Avon.

***Retail Reporting Staff.** 11 Stores of the Year. 1998. 55.00 (*0-688-16522-2*, Wm Morrow) Morrow Avon.

— Entertainment Places. 1999. 45.00 (*0-688-17257-1*, Wm Morrow) Morrow Avon.

Retail Reporting Staff. 5 Winning Shopping Center Designs. 1998. 29.95 (*0-688-16521-4*, Wm Morrow) Morrow Avon.

— Hospitality Environments. 1999. 49.95 (*0-688-15070-5*, Wm Morrow) Morrow Avon.

— Point of Purchase. 6th ed. 1999. 39.95 (*0-688-16475-7*, Wm Morrow) Morrow Avon.

— Point Purchase: Merchandizing. 1998. 39.95 (*0-688-16473-0*, Wm Morrow) Morrow Avon.

— Retail Entertainment. 1998. 42.50 (*0-688-15720-3*, Wm Morrow) Morrow Avon.

— Specialty Food Store Design. 1999. 42.50 (*0-688-16523-0*, Wm Morrow) Morrow Avon.

— Store Windows. 9th ed. 1997. 55.00 (*0-688-14970-7*, Wm Morrow) Morrow Avon.

— Streetscapes. 1998. 42.50 (*0-688-16045-X*, Wm Morrow) Morrow Avon.

— 3 Points of Purchase. 1995. 55.00 (*0-688-14259-1*, Wm Morrow) Morrow Avon.

— 12 Stores of the Year. 1999. 47.50 (*0-688-17260-1*, Wm Morrow) Morrow Avon.

— Urban Spaces. 1999. 55.00 (*0-688-16715-2*, Wm Morrow) Morrow Avon.

Retakh, V., jt. ed. see Gelfand, I. M.

Retallack, Alexa, jt. auth. see Hodges, Terry.

***Retallack, Greg J., et al.** Eocene & Oligocene Paleosols of Central Oregon. LC 99-52006. (Special Papers). 1999. write for info. (*0-8137-2344-2*) Geol Soc.

Retallack, Gregory J. Colour Guide to Paleosols: A Handbook. LC 96-37349. 188p. 1997. 100.00 (*0-471-96711-4*) Wiley.

— Late Eocene & Oligocene Paleosols from Badlands National Park, South Dakota. LC 83-5675. (Geological Society of America, Special Paper: No. 193). 90p. reprint ed. pap. 30.00 (*0-7837-2685-6*, 204306200006) Bks Demand.

— Soils of the Past: An Introduction to Paleopedology. 300p. 1990. pap. 134.50 (*0-04-551128-4*) Thomson Learn.

Retallack, James. Germany in the Age of Kaiser Wilhelm II. (Studies in European History). 152p. 1996. pap. 11.95 (*0-312-16031-3*) St Martin.

Retallack, James, ed. Saxony in German History: Culture, Society, & Politics, 1830-1933. (Social History, Popular Culture, & Politics in Germany). (Illus.). 376p. (C). text 59.50 (*0-472-11104-3*, 11104) U of Mich Pr.

Retallack, James, jt. ed. see Jones, Larry E.

Retallack, James N. Notables of the Right: The Conservative Party & Political Mobilization in Germany, 1876-1918. 224p. (C). 1988. text 55.00 (*0-04-900038-1*) Routledge.

Retallack, James N., jt. ed. see Jones, Larry E.

Retallack, Joan. Afterimages. LC 94-48727. (Wesleyan Poetry Ser.). 115p. 1995. pap. 13.95 (*0-8195-1223-0*, Wesleyan Univ Pr) U Pr of New Eng.

— Afterrimages. LC 94-48727. (Wesleyan Poetry Ser.). 115p. 1995. text 27.50 (*0-8195-2219-8*, Wesleyan Univ Pr) U Pr of New Eng.

— Circumstantial Evidence: Poems 1976-1983. LC 84-51705. 87p. (Orig.). 1985. pap. 6.00 (*0-911809-01-5*) Moon Lake Bks.

— Errata Suite. 63p. (Orig.). 1994. pap. 8.00 (*0-9619097-5-7*) Edge Bks.

— How to Do Things with Words. (Sun & Moon Classics Ser.: No. 168). 96p. 1998. pap. 10.95 (*1-55713-213-5*) Sun & Moon CA.

— Mongrelisme. (Isthmus Project Ser.). 48p. 1999. pap. 5.00 (*0-945926-54-5*) Paradigm RI.

Retallic, Ken. Flyfisher's Guide to Wyoming. LC 98-5197. (Illus.). 320p. 1998. pap. 26.95 (*1-885106-37-8*) Wild Adven Pr.

— Greater Yellowstone Fly Fisher's Stream Guide. unabridged ed. (Illus.). 80p. (Orig.). 1996. pap. 14.95 (*0-9652775-0-X*) GBHink.

Retallic, Ken & Barker, Rocky. Fly Fisher's Guide to Idaho. rev. ed. LC 95-62176. (Illus.). 350p. (Orig.). 1997. pap. 26.95 (*1-885106-30-0*) Wild Adven Pr.

— Wingshooter's Guide to Idaho: Upland Birds & Waterfowl. LC 97-60642. (Illus.). 320p. 1997. pap. 26.95 (*1-885106-27-0*) Wild Adven Pr.

Retallick, John, et al. Learning Communities in Education. LC 98-36953. 1999. write for info. (*0-415-19760-0*) Routledge.

Retamal, Gonzala. Education as a Humanitarian Response. 1997. 75.00 (*0-304-70193-9*) Continuum.

Retamar, Roberto F. Caliban & Other Essays. Baker, Edward, tr. from SPA. 168p. (Orig.). 1989. pap. 14.95 (*0-8166-1743-0*) U of Minn Pr.

Retan, Walter. Armies of Ants. LC 93-29782. (Hello Reader! Ser.: Level 4). (Illus.). 48p. (J). (gr. 2-3). 1994. pap. 3.99 (*0-590-47616-5*, Cartwheel) Scholastic Inc.

***Retan, Walter.** Armies of Ants, 1 vol. (Hello Reader! Level 4 Ser.). (SPA., Illus.). 48p. (gr. 2-3). 1999. pap. text 3.99 (*0-439-08742-2*) Scholastic Inc.

Retan, Walter. Bunnies, Bunnies, Bunnies. (J). 1998. pap. 7.95 (*0-671-88247-3*) S&S Bks Yung.

Retan, Walter. Easy-to-Read Little Engine That Could. (All Aboard Bks.). (J). 1986. 8.15 (*0-606-03774-8*, Pub. by Turtleback) Demco.

Retan, Walter. One Hundred & One Facts about Snakes & Reptiles. 96p. (J). (gr. 4-6). 1992. pap. 1.95 (*0-590-44891-9*) Scholastic Inc.

— 101 Wacky Facts about Snakes & Reptiles. (J). 1991. 7.05 (*0-606-01771-2*, Pub. by Turtleback) Demco.

— Piggies Piggies Piggies. (J). (gr. 3 up). 1993. pap. 15.00 (*0-671-75244-8*) S&S Bks Yung.

Retan, Walter, ed. Bunnies, Bunnies, Bunnies. LC 90-41486. (Illus.). 96p. (J). (ps-2). 1991. pap. 14.95 (*0-671-73221-8*) S&S Bks Yung.

Retan, Walter & Risom, Ole. The Busy, Busy World of Richard Scarry. LC 97-1756. (Illus.). 160p. 1997. 39.95 (*0-8109-4000-0*, Pub. by Abrams) Time Warner.

***Retana, Alvaro.** EIGRP for IP: Basic Operation & Configuration. (Networking Basics Ser.). 168p. 2000. pap. text 19.95 (*0-201-65773-2*) Addison-Wesley.

Retana, Alvaro, et al. CCIE Professional Development: Advanced IP Network Design. (Illus.). 343p. 1999. 55.00 (*1-57870-097-3*) Cisco Press.

Retana, Guillermo, tr. see Retana, Maria L.

Retana, Maria L. Born into the Pack/Nacer en la Manada. Retana, Guillermo, tr. (SPA., Illus.). 32p. (Orig.). (J). (gr. k-3). 1997. pap. 6.95 (*0-9652920-4-5*) Hgh Desert Prods.

— The Pig That Is Not a Pig: El Cerdo Que No es Cerdo. (SPA., Illus.). 32p. (Orig.). (J). (gr. k-2). 1997. pap. 6.95 (*0-9652920-8-8*) Hgh Desert Prods.

— Tall Tails from a Mountain Slope. Retana, Guillermo, tr.Tr. of Rabos Altos de la Ladera. (SPA., Illus.). 32p. (Orig.). (J). (gr. k-3). 1999. pap. 6.95 (*0-9652920-0-2*, Pub. by Hgh Desert Prods) Treas Chest Bks.

Retana, Maria Luisa, tr. see Fisher, Norma Grusy.

Retat, Pierre. Le Dictionnaire de Bayle et la Lute Philosophique au 18e Siecle. (FRE.). 556p. 1972. pap. 45.00 (*0-7859-0731-9*, FA-410) Fr & Eur.

Retecki, Richard. Rainbow Dance Studio. Mycue, Edward, ed. (Took Modern Poetry in English Ser.: No. 8). (Illus.). 28p. (Orig.). 1993. pap. 3.00 (*1-879457-02-4*) Norton Coker Pr.

***Retegan, Mihai.** In the Shadow of the Prague Spring: Romanian Foreign Policy & the Crisis in Czechoslovakia 1968. 300p. 1999. 49.00 (*973-98392-9-0*) Intl Spec Bk.

Reteguiz, Jo-Ann & Cornel-Avendano, Beverly. Mastering the Objective Structured Clinical Examination & Clinical Skills Assessment. LC 98-55698. (Illus.). 300p. 1999. pap. 39.95 (*0-07-135012-8*) McGraw-Hill HPD.

Reth & Earl, Peter E. Psychological Economics. 1987. lib. bdg. 110.50 (*0-89838-234-3*) Kluwer Academic.

Rethati, L., jt. auth. see Kezdi, A.

Rethati, L., jt. ed. see Kezdi, A.

Retherford, J. R. Hilbert Space: Compact Operators & the Trace Theorem. (London Mathematical Society Student Texts Ser.: No. 27). 143p. (C). 1993. text 69.95 (*0-521-41884-4*); pap. text 25.95 (*0-521-42933-1*) Cambridge U Pr.

Retherford, Kristine S. Guide Applied: Production Characteristics of Language Impaired Children. LC 92-23583. 1992. pap., ring bd. 39.00 incl. audio (*0-930599-78-0*) Thinking Pubns.

— Guide to Analysis of Language Transcripts. 2nd rev. ed. LC 93-19445. 296p. (C). 1993. spiral bd. 39.00 (*0-930599-87-X*) Thinking Pubns.

***Retherford, Kristine S.** Guide to Analysis of Language Transcripts. 3rd ed. LC 00-21945. (Illus.). 2000. pap. write for info. (*1-888222-41-7*) Thinking Pubns.

Retherford, Ralph. When Chicken Soup Is Not Enough: Finding the Key to Health, Wellness & Beyond Through the Mind-Body Connection. (Illus.). 192p. 1998. pap. text 14.95 (*1-888820-06-3*, Millennium) Millennium Calif.

— When Chicken Soup Is Not Enough: Revolutionary Healing Through the Mind-Body Connection. 192p. 1999. pap. 14.95 (*0-8119-1005-9*) F Fell Pubs Inc.

***Retherford, Ralph.** When Chicken Soup Is Not Enough: Revolutionary Healing Through the Mind-Body Connection. 1999. pap. 14.95 (*0-88391-003-9*) F Fell Pubs Inc.

Retherford, Robert D. The Changing Sex Differential in Mortality, 1. LC 74-19808. (Studies in Demography & Urban Population). (Illus.). 139p. 1975. 47.95 (*0-8371-7848-7*, RSX/, Greenwood Pr) Greenwood.

Retherford, Robert D. & Choe, Minja K. Statistical Models for Causal Analysis. 272p. 1993. 84.95 (*0-471-55802-8*) Wiley.

***Rethmann, Petra.** Intimate Relations: History & Gender in the Russian Far East. LC 00-27429. (Post-Communist Cultural Studies Ser.). 2000. write for info. (*0-271-02058-X*) Pa St U Pr.

Rethorst, John. Teach Yourself WordPerfect 3.0 for Macintosh. LC 94-186645. 400p. 1994. pap. 21.95 (*1-55828-307-2*, M&T Bks) IDG Bks.

Rethwisch, David G., jt. ed. see Lewis, Kenrich M.

Reti, Ingrid. Echoes of Silence. 64p. (Orig.). 1989. pap. 6.95 (*0-939821-49-4*) HerBooks.

Reti, Irene, ed. Childless by Choice: An Anthology. 96p. 1992. pap. 9.95 (*0-939821-03-6*) HerBooks.

— Unleashing Feminism: A Critique of Lesbian Sadomasochism in the Gay Nineties. 160p. 1993. pap. 8.95 (*0-939821-04-4*) HerBooks.

Reti, Irene & Chase, Valerie J., eds. Garden Variety Dykes: Lesbian Traditions in Gardening. 128p. 1994. 10.00 (*0-939821-05-2*) HerBooks.

— A Transported Life: Memories of Kindertransport: The Oral History of Thea Eden. (Illus.). 96p. (Orig.). 1995. pap. text 9.00 (*0-939821-07-9*) HerBooks.

Reti, Richard. Modern Ideas in Chess. 183p. 1960. pap. 8.95 (*0-486-20638-6*) Dover.

Reti, Rudolph. Thematic Patterns in Sonatas of Beethoven. (Music Reprint Ser.). 1992. 27.50 (*0-306-79714-3*) Da Capo.

Reti, Rudolph R. The Thematic Process in Music. LC 77-13622. 362p. 1978. reprint ed. lib. bdg. 69.75 (*0-8371-9875-5*, RETH, Greenwood Pr) Greenwood.

— Tonality, Atonality, Pantonality: A Study of Some Trends in Twentieth Century Music. LC 78-6162. (Illus.). 166p. 1978. reprint ed. lib. bdg. 38.50 (*0-313-20478-0*, RETO, Greenwood Pr) Greenwood.

Reti, Steven P. Silver & Gold: The Political Economy of International Monetary Conferences, 1867-1892, 194. LC 97-31991. (Contributions in Economics & Economic History Ser.: Vol. 194). 224p. 1998. 59.95 (*0-313-30409-2*, Greenwood Pr) Greenwood.

Retian, Ralph M. Aphasia & Sensory-Perceptual Deficits in Adults. 173p. (Orig.). 1984. pap. text 34.00 (*0-934515-00-X*) Neuropsych Pr.

***Retich, Kayla.** How-To Easy Crafts Handbook. (Illus.). 2000. spiral bd. 8.95 (*0-9679325-0-5*) K Retich.

Retief, E., et al. Plants of the Northern Provinces of South Africa: Keys & Diagnostic Characters. (Strelitzia Ser.: Vol. VI). (Illus.). 1977. 15.00 (*1-874907-30-7*, Pub. by Natl Botanical Inst) Balogh.

***Retief, Frank.** Divorce. 2000. pap. text 9.99 (*1-85792-421-5*) Christian Focus.

Retif de la Bretonne, A. Monsieur Nicolas, Vol. 1. (FRE.). 1989. lib. bdg. 150.00 (*0-8288-3531-4*, F26670) Fr & Eur.

Retik, A., jt. ed. see Kumar, B.

Retinger, J. H. Conrad & His Contemporaries. LC 81-65546. (Illus.). 182p. 1981. 14.50 (*1-881284-08-5*) Am Inst Polish.

Retinger, Joseph. Conrad & His Contemporaries. LC 72-6504. (Studies in Conrad: No. 8). 156p. 1972. reprint ed. lib. bdg. 59.00 (*0-8383-1621-2*) M S G Haskell Hse.

***Retirement Workshop Staff.** Taxation of Federal Retirement Benefits for Tax Year 1999. LC 98-210015. 30p. 2000. 12.95 (*0-910582-50-5*) Fed Employees.

Retish, Paul. Exceptional Person. (Special Education Ser.). 1994. teacher ed. 12.00 (*0-8273-4697-2*) Delmar.

Retish, Paul & Reiter, Shunit, eds. Adults with Disabilities: An International Perspective. LC 98-35593. 368p. 1999. 79.95 (*0-8058-2424-3*) L Erlbaum Assocs.

Retnakaran, Arthur, jt. ed. see Wright, James E.

Retore, Christian, ed. Logical Aspects of Computational Linguistics: Selected Papers, 1st International Conference, LACL '96, Nancy, France, April 23-25, 1996. LC 97-43015. (Lecture Notes in Artificial Intelligence Ser.: Vol. 1328). viii, 435p. 1997. pap. 67.00 (*3-540-63700-1*) Spr-Verlag.

Retowski, O. F. The Genoese-Tatar Coinage. Zander, R., tr. from RUS. (Illus.). 62p. (Orig.). 1983. pap. 12.00 (*0-912671-05-X*) Russian Numis.

Retsinis, Joan M. It's OK Mom: The Nursing Home From a Sociological Perspective. LC 86-50614. 192p. (Orig.). 1986. 10.95 (*0-913292-14-1*) Tiresias Pr.

Retske, Gene. The International Callback Book: An Insider's View: How to Save 65on Your International Telephone Calls, How to Set up an International Callback Company. (Illus.). 340p. 1995. 34.95 (*0-936648-65-1*) Telecom Bks.

Retskin, Bill. The Matchcover Collector's Price Guide. 2nd rev. ed. LC 97-72680. (Illus.). 304p. 1998. pap. 21.95 (*0-930625-77-3*) Krause Pubns.

Retso, Jan. Diathesis in the Semitic Languages: A Comparative Morphological Study. LC 89-39786. (Studies in Semitic Languages & Linguistics: Vol. XIV). xvii, 254p. 1989. 77.00 (*90-04-08818-0*) Brill Academic Pubs.

Rettaliata, Janis, et al, photos by. Welcome Home: The Enterprise Foundation & Homeownership, Pt. 4. (Illus.). 20p. 1997. pap. 20.00 (*0-942901-06-1*) Enterprise Fnd.

Rettelbusch. Handbook of Historic Ornament from Ancient Times to Biedermeier. LC 96-22173. (Illus.). 272p. pap. 15.95 (*0-486-29240-1*) Dover.

***Rettenmaier, Andrew J. & Saving, Thomas R.** The Economics of Medicare Reform. (C). 2000. write for info. (*0-88099-212-3*); pap. write for info. (*0-88099-211-5*) W E Upjohn.

***Rettenmaier, Andrew J. & Saving, Thomas R., eds.** Medicare Reform: Issues & Answers. LC 99-23001. (Volume in the Bush School Series in the Economics of Public Policy). 176p. 1999. 25.00 (*0-226-71013-0*) U Ch Pr.

Rettenmayr, M., jt. ed. see Roosz, A.

Rettenmund, Matthew. Blind Items. LC 98-34222. 288p. 1998. text 22.95 (*0-312-19242-8*) St Martin.

***Rettenmund, Matthew.** Blind Items. 288p. 2000. pap. 13.95 (*0-312-26295-7*) St Martin.

Rettenmund, Matthew. Boy Culture. 192p. 1996. pap. 10.95 (*0-312-14553-5*) St Martin.

— Madonnica: The Woman & the Icon from A to Z. LC 94-48309. 1995. pap. 16.95 (*0-312-11782-5*) St Martin.

— The Totally Awesome 80's: A Lexicon of the Music, Videos, Movies, TV Shows, Stars & Trends of That Awesome Decade. (Illus.). 224p. 1996. pap. 15.95 (*0-312-14436-9*) St Martin.

Retter, G. J. Matrix & Space - Phasor Theory of Electrical Machines. 412p. (C). 1987. 335.00 (*0-569-09003-2*, Pub. by Collets) St Mut.

Retterstol, Nils. Suicide: A European Perspective. (Illus.). 273p. (C). 1993. text 64.95 (*0-521-42099-7*) Cambridge U Pr.

An Asterisk (*) at the beginning of an entry indicates that the title is appearing for the first time.

Retterstol, Nils, et al, eds. The Delusional Misidentification Syndromes. (Journal: Psychopathology: Vol. 27, No. 3-5, 1994). (Illus.). 156p. 1994. pap. 126.25 (*3-8055-6082-6*) S Karger.
Retterstol, Nils & Dahl, A., eds. Functional Psychoses: Classification & Prognosis. (Journal: Psychopathology: Vpl. 29, No. 1-2, 1986). (Illus.). 92p. 1986. pap. 68.00 (*3-8055-4317-4*) S Karger.
Retterstol, Nils, et al. Functional Psychoses: Recent Follow-up Studies, 1991 - Psychopathology Journal, Vol. 24, No. 5. (Illus.). 92p. 1991. pap. 38.50 (*3-8055-5534-2*) S Karger.
Rettger, J. F. The Development of Ablaut in the Strong Verbs of the East Midland Dialects of Middle English. (LD Ser.: No. 18). 1972. reprint ed. 25.00 (*0-527-00764-1*) Periodicals Srv.
Rettich. Pennsylvania Dutch Designs. 1998. pap. 3.95 (*0-486-24496-2*) Dover.
Rettie, Dwight F. Our National Park System: Caring for America's Greatest Natural & Historic Treasures. LC 94-22632. 320p. 1995. 34.95 (*0-252-02148-7*) U of Ill Pr.
— Our National Park System: Caring for America's Greatest Natural & Historic Treasures. (Illus.). 320p. 1996. 21.95 (*0-252-06558-1*) U of Ill Pr.
Rettig, jt. auth. see Johnson.
Rettig, jt. auth. see Strickland.
Rettig, John W., tr. see Augustine, Saint.
Rettig, Marc. Recreating the Web Site. 400p. 1997. pap. text 39.99 (*1-56830-332-7*) Hayden.
Rettig, Michael D., jt. auth. see Canady, Robert L.
Rettig, Michael D., jt. ed. see Canady, Robert L.
Rettig, Perry R. & Khodavandi, Mehraban. Recruiting Minority Teachers: The UTOP Program. (Fastback Ser.: No. 436). 46p. 1998. pap. write for info. (*0-87367-636-X*, FB436) Phi Delta Kappa.
Rettig, Perry R., jt. auth. see Henson, Kenneth T.
Rettig, R., et al, eds. Salt & Hypertension. 385p. 1989. 118.00 (*0-387-50063-4*) Spr-Verlag.
Rettig, Rainer, tr. see Vanderlip, Sharon L.
Rettig, Richard A. Health Care in Transition: Technology Assessment in the Private Sector. LC 96-41468. (Illus.). 156p. 1997. pap. 15.00 (*0-8330-2444-2*, MR-754-DHHS/ASP) Rand Corp.
— Military Use of Drugs Not Yet Approved by the FDA for CW/BW Defense: Lessons from the Gulf War. LC 98-31679. (Illus.). 120p. 1999. pap. 15.00 (*0-8330-2683-6*, MR-1018/9-OSD) Rand Corp.
Rettig, Richard A., ed. see Committee to Study the Use of Advisory Committees.
Rettig, Richard A., ed. see Institute of Medicine, Committee for the Study of.
Rettig, Richard A., jt. ed. see Yarmolinsky, Adam.
Rettig, Richard P. Manny: A Criminal-Addict's Story. 202p. (C). 1999. pap. 11.95 (*1-57766-058-7*) Waveland Pr.
Rettig, Rudi. Das Investitions und Finanzierungsverhalten Deutscher Grossunternehmen 1880-1911. Bruchey, Stuart, ed. LC 80-2827. (Dissertations in European Economic History Ser.).Tr. of Investment & Financial Behavior of German Large Scale Enterprises. (Illus.). 1981. lib. bdg. 35.95 (*0-405-14019-3*) Ayer.
Rettig, S. The Discursive Social Psychology of Evidence: Symbolic Construction of Reality. LC 90-7911. (Illus.). 232p. (C). 1990. 54.50 (*0-306-43701-5*, Plenum Trade) Perseus Pubng.
Rettig, Sam & French, Drucie. Sam's WIT: Water Interval Training for Fabulous People of Every Kind. large type ed. (Illus.). 118p. 1993. pap. 20.00 (*0-9637470-2-9*) DFC Seminars.
Rettig, Terrence W. & Hahn, Joseph, eds. Completing the Inventory of the Solar System. Vol. 107. (ASP Conference Series Proceedings). 512p. 1996. 34.00 (*1-886733-27-9*) Astron Soc Pacific.
Rettig, Tom & Moody, Debby. Expert Advisor: dBASE III Plus. (Illus.). 400p. 1988. pap. 22.95 (*0-201-17197-X*) Addison-Wesley.
***Rettig, W. & Seifert, H. J., eds.** Applied Fluorescence in Chemistry, Biology & Medicine. LC 98-40878. (Illus.). 500p. 1998. 169.00 (*3-540-64451-2*) Spr-Verlag.
Rettinger, Michael. Handbook of Architecture & Noise Control: A Manual For Architects & Engineers. (Illus.). 272p. 1988. 32.95 (*0-8306-2686-7*, 2686) McGraw-Hill Prof.
Rettke, Mari. Practical Data Communications. 256p. (C). 1990. text 32.50 (*0-07-067667-4*) McGraw.
Rettner, Raphael. Vegetarian Cooking for People with Allergies: Delicious Recipes for Vibrant Health. LC 97-30405. 192p. 1997. pap. 12.95 (*1-57067-045-5*) Book Pub Co.
Retton, Mary L. The Olympic Ideal of Vision Vol. 2: Personal Leadership Through the Olympic Ideals. Moore, Nancy, ed. (U. S. Olympic Committee's Curriculum Guide Ser.). (Illus.). 16p. (YA). 1997. pap., wbk. ed. 3.95 (*1-58000-001-0*) Griffin CA.
***Retton, Mary Lou.** Mary Lou Retton's Gateways to Happiness: 7 Ways to a More Peaceful, More Accomplished, More Satisfying Life. LC 99-86417. (Illus.). 288p. 2000. 22.95 (*0-7679-0439-7*) Broadway BDD.
— Mary Lou Retton's Gateways to Happiness: 7 Ways to a More Peaceful, More Prosperous, More Satisfying Life with Others, 8 vols. 2000. 183.60 (*0-7679-9899-5*) Broadway BDD.
***Retton, Mary Lou & Bender, David.** Mary Lou Retton's Gateways to Happiness: 8 Ways to a More Peaceful, More Prosperous, More Satisfying Life with Others. 2000. 22.95 (*1-57856-347-X*) Waterbrook Pr.
Rettori, A. & Pescia, D. Fundamental Aspects of Thin Film Magnetism. 280p. 1997. text 71.00 (*981-02-2309-9*) World Scientific Pub.
Retz, Jean-Francois De, see De Retz, Jean-Francois.
Retzer, Fernon & Speegle, Mike. You Can Understand the Bible. rev. ed. (Illus.). 32p. 1996. pap. 5.95 (*1-57847-001-3*) MAGCOS-DA.
Retzer, Henry, tr. see Barth, R. Carl, ed.
Retzer, Michael E., et al. Fishes of the Lower Green River Drainage, Kentucky. unabridged ed. (Kentucky Nature Preserves Commission Scientific & Technical Ser.: Vol. 3). (Illus.). 48p. 1983. pap. 3.89 (*0-9673646-2-0*) KY State Nature.
Retzii, A. J. Observationes Botanicae: Six Fascicmles, 1779-1791. 1987. 160.00 (*0-7855-2032-5*, Pub. by Scientific) St Mut.
Retzinger, Suzanne M. Violent Emotions: Shame & Rage in Marital Quarrels. 256p. (C). 1991. 58.00 (*0-8039-4183-8*) Sage.
Retzlaff, Ewald. Dictionary of Code Symbols for Cables & Insulated Cords According to UDE, CENELEC & IEC: German-English. 4th ed. (ENG & GER.). 152p. 1993. 49.95 (*0-7859-8693-6*, 380071860x) Fr & Eur.
Retzlaff, John A., et al. Lens Implant Power Calculation: A Manual for Ophthalmologists & Biometrists. 3rd ed. LC 90-53345. 58p. 1990. pap. 25.00 (*1-55642-186-9*) SLACK Inc.
Retzlaff, Kay. Irish Myths & Legends. LC 97-36156. 1998. write for info. (*1-56799-564-0*, Friedman-Fairfax) M Friedman Pub Grp Inc.
***Retzlaff, Kay.** Women of Mythology. LC 99-26787. 1999. 24.98 (*1-56799-757-0*, MetroBooks) M Friedman Pub Grp Inc.
Retzlaff, Michael. Back to Basics. (Illus.). 65p. (Orig.). 1995. pap. 10.00 (*1-887560-02-5*) M Poll Pub.
Retzlaff, Nancy. Gods in the Making or How to Have Fun in the Galaxy. Roerden, Chris, ed. 78p. (Orig.). 1993. pap. 14.95 (*0-9635188-1-X*) Gemini Moon.
Retzlaff, Paul D., ed. Psychotherapy of the Personality Disorders: A MOMI-III-Based Approach. 288p. (C). 1995. 49.00 (*0-205-15932-X*, Longwood Div) Allyn.
Reu, Johann M. The Augsburg Confession. LC 83-45650. reprint ed. 76.50 (*0-404-19859-7*) AMS Pr.
— Luther's German Bible. LC 83-45651. reprint ed. 75.00 (*0-404-19860-0*) AMS Pr.
— Thirty-Five Years of Luther Research. LC 79-13505. (Illus.). reprint ed. 36.50 (*0-404-05284-3*) AMS Pr.
Reubart, Dale. Anxiety & Musical Performance. LC 84-21422. (Music Ser.). 250p. 1985. 35.00 (*0-306-76253-6*) Da Capo.
Reuben. The Chess Organiser's Handbook. 1997. pap. text 14.95 (*1-85744-199-0*) S&S Trade.
Reuben, jt. auth. see Hirsch.
Reuben, Bryan G., jt. auth. see Wittcoff, Harold A.
Reuben, Bunny. Raj Kapoor: Fabulous Showman: An Intimate Biography. (C). 1995. pap. 21.00 (*81-7223-196-2*, Pub. by Indus Pub) S Asia.
Reuben, Carolyn. Antioxidants: Your Complete Guide. LC 93-49709. (Illus.). 240p. 1994. pap. 12.95 (*1-55958-522-6*) Prima Pub.
— Antioxidants for Life. LC 98-18105. 1998. pap. 14.00 (*0-7615-1446-5*) Prima Pub.
— Cleansing the Body, Mind, & Spirit. LC 99-176658. 1998. mass mkt. 6.99 (*0-425-16191-9*) Berkley Pub.
***Reuben, David.** Dr. David Reuben's Quick Weight-Gain Program. 271p. 2000. reprint ed. text 23.00 (*0-7881-6898-3*) DIANE Pub.
— Everything You Always Wanted. 2000. pap. 13.00 (*0-06-095496-5*) HarpC.
— Everything You Always Wanted to Know about Sex (but Were Afraid. 400p. 2000. reprint ed. mass mkt. 7.99 (*0-312-97656-9*) St Martin.
— Everything You Always Wanted to Know About Sex But Were Afraid to Ask: Reuben&MD, David. 1999. audio 18.00 (*0-694-52109-4*) HarperAudio.
Reuben, David B., et al, eds. Geriatrics Review Syllabus: A Core Curriculum in Geriatric Medicine. 3rd ed. 690p. 1996. pap. 350.00 (*0-7872-1992-4*) Kendall-Hunt.
Reuben, David R. Everything You Always Wanted to Know about Nutrition. 1979. mass mkt. 4.50 (*0-380-44370-8*, Avon Bks) Morrow Avon.
— Everything You Always Wanted to Know About Sex: * But. 30th anniversary ed. LC 98-43025. 384p. 1999. 25.00 (*0-06-019267-4*) HarpC.
Reuben, Davis. Recollections of Mississippi & Mississippians. (American Biography Ser.). 456p. 1991. reprint ed. lib. bdg. 89.00 (*0-7812-8100-8*) Rprt Serv.
Reuben, Elaine & Hoffmann, Leonore, eds. Unladylike & Unprofessional: Academic Women & Academic Unions. fac. ed. LC LB2842.2.U58. 63p. 1975. reprint ed. pap. 30.00 (*0-7837-8033-8*, 20477890008) Bks Demand.
Reuben, Gabriel. Electricity Experiments for Children. (Illus.). 88p. (J). (gr. 5-9). 1968. pap. 3.95 (*0-486-22030-3*) Dover.
Reuben, J., jt. auth. see Berliner, L. J.
Reuben, Jacques, jt. ed. see Berliner, Lawrence J.
Reuben, Julie A. The Making of the Modern University: Intellectual Transformation & the Marginalization of Morality. 376p. 1996. pap. text 18.95 (*0-226-71020-3*) U Ch Pr.
— The Making of the Modern University: Intellectual Transformation & the Marginalization of Morality. 376p. 1996. lib. bdg. 55.00 (*0-226-71018-1*) U Ch Pr.
Reuben, Robert. Materials in Marine Technology. LC 93-15462. 1994. 315.95 (*0-387-19789-3*) Spr-Verlag.
Reuben, Ruth, tr see Sheldon, Charles M.
Reuben, S., jt. auth. see Hartston, William R.
***Reuben, Shelly.** Come Home, Love, Dad. 200p. 2000. pap. 14.95 (*0-9662868-1-2*) Bernard St Bks.
Reuben, Shelly. Origin & Cause: A Crime Novel. 352p. 1994. 20.00 (*0-684-19702-2*, Scribners Ref) Mac Lib Ref.
— Spent Matches. 240p. 1996. 20.50 (*0-684-80107-8*) S&S Trade.
Reuben, Steven C. Making Interfaith Marriage Work: A Nonjudgmental Guide to Coping with the Spiritual, Emotional, & Psychological Issues. LC 93-48111. 256p. 1994. pap. 12.95 (*1-55958-506-4*) Prima Pub.
— Raising Jewish Children in a Contemporary World: The Modern Parent's Guide to Creating a Jewish Home. (Illus.). 244p. 1991. 18.95 (*1-55958-150-6*) Prima Pub.
— Raising Jewish Children in a Contemporary World: The Modern Parent's Guide to Creating a Jewish Home. 240p. 1993. pap. 12.95 (*1-55958-319-3*) Prima Pub.
Reuben, Stewart. Chess Opening, Your Choice. 1994. pap. 17.95 (*1-85744-070-6*) S&S Trade.
— Chess Openings: Your Choice. (Chess Ser.). (Illus.). 150p. 1985. 23.95 (*0-08-026895-1*, Pub. by PPL); pap. 17.90 (*0-08-026894-3*, Pub. by PPL) Elsevier.
— Chess Openings: Your Choice! 240p. 1993. pap. 15.95 (*1-85744-024-2*, Pub. by Cadgn Bks) Macmillan.
Reuben, Stewart, jt. auth. see Ciaffone, Bob.
Reubens, Beatrice G., ed. Youth at Work: An International Survey. LC 83-8631. (Conservation of Human Resources Ser.: No. 22). 366p. (C). 1983. text 76.50 (*0-86598-101-9*) Rowman.
Reubens, Edwin P., ed. The Challenge of the New International Economic Order. (Special Studies in International Business & Economics). 220p. 1981. text 52.00 (*0-89158-762-4*) Westview.
Reubens, Peggy. Vocational Education for Immigrant & Minority Youth. 42p. 1983. 4.25 (*0-318-22240-X*, IN257) Ctr Educ Trng Employ.
Reubenstein, Howard. Knowledge-Based Software Engineering. Setliff, Dorothy E., ed. LC 96-36330. 116p. (C). 1996. text 105.00 (*0-7923-9789-4*) Kluwer Academic.
Reuber, Grant L., jt. auth. see Caves, Richard E.
***Reubsamen, Helga.** The Song & the Truth. LC 00-23274. 384p. 2000. 26.00 (*0-375-40261-6*) Knopf.
Reuchlin, Johann. Briefwechsel. (GER.). 372p. 1973. reprint ed. write for info. (*0-318-70505-2*) G Olms Pubs.
— De Arte Cabalistica. Goodman, Martin & Goodman, Sarah, trs. LC 77-86231. (Janus Ser.).Tr. of Art of the Kabbalah. 384p. 1983. lib. bdg. 35.00 (*0-913870-56-0*) Abaris Bks.
— On the Art of the Kabbalah. Goodman, Martin & Goodman, Sarah, trs. LC 93-13872. (ENG & LAT.). xxix, 376p. 1993. pap. 15.00 (*0-8032-8946-4*, Bison Books) U of Nebr Pr.
Reuchlin, Johannes. Briefwechsel. (Bibliothek des Literarischen Vereins in Stuttgart Ser.: No. 126). (GER.). 372p. 1973. reprint ed. write for info. (*3-487-05034-X*) G Olms Pubs.
***Reuchlin, Johannes.** Recommendation Whether to Confiscate, Destroy & Burn All Jewish Books. Wortsman, Peter, ed. & tr. by. 88p. 2000. pap. 9.95 (*0-8091-3972-3*) Paulist Pr.
Reuck, K. M. De, see Wagner, W. & De Reuck, K. M.
Reucroff, Stephen, jt. ed. see Nath, Pran.
Reucroft, Stephen, jt. ed. see Nath, Pran.
Reudelhuber, Timothy L. & Deschepper, Christian. Molecular Biology in Medicine: A Practical Guide for the Health Care Physician. Date not set. write for info. (*0-8247-9411-7*) Dekker.
Reuder, Bruce. Sports Medicine: The School Age Athlete. 2nd ed. Lampert, Richard, ed. LC 95-36916. (Saunders Text & Review Ser.). (Illus.). 704p. 1996. text 149.00 (*0-7216-5673-0*, W B Saunders Co) Harcrt Hlth Sci Grp.
Reudor. The Doodle Family Passover Haggadah. (Reudor's the Doodle Family Ser.). (Illus.). 80p. (Orig.). (J). 1997. pap. 7.95 (*1-886611-13-0*) Atara Publ.
— The Doodled Family Haggadah. 2nd ed. LC 96-83601. (ENG & HEB., Illus.). 80p. (J). (gr. 1 up). 1995. 24.95 (*1-886611-22-X*) Atara Publ.
— The Gang of Four: Kung-Fooey to the Rescue. 1999. 16.95 (*0-943706-07-6*) Pitspopany.
— Hebrew Letters Tell Their Story. 1999. pap. write for info. (*0-943706-03-3*) Pitspopany.
***Reudor.** Hebrew Letters Tell Their Story. (Illus.). 48p. 1999. 16.95 (*0-943706-24-6*) Pitspopany.
— Hebrew Letters Tell Their Story. (Illus.). 48p. 1999. pap. text 9.95 (*0-943706-23-8*) Pitspopany.
Reudor. Oodles of Doodles for Hanukkah: A Color, Activity, Sticker Book. (Illus.). 35p. (Orig.). (J). (ps up). 1996. pap. 4.95 (*1-886611-08-4*) Atara Publ.
— Oodles of Doodles for Passover: A Color, Activity, Sticker Book. (Reudor's the Doodle Family Ser.). (Illus.). 34p. (J). (ps-6). 1997. pap. 4.95 (*1-886611-06-8*) Atara Publ.
— The Young Maccabees. (Reudor's the Doodle Family Ser.). (Illus.). 22p. (J). (gr. 3-12). 1998. 8.95 (*1-886611-07-6*) Atara Publ.
Reudor Staff. Are Pigeons Kosher? (Reudor's the Doodle Family Ser.). (Illus.). 96p. (J). (gr. 3-12). 1998. pap. 5.95 (*1-886611-05-X*) Atara Publ.
— My Bubbe's Arms: Reudor's the Doodle Family. (Rhyme Time Doodles Ser.). (Illus.). 24p. (J). (gr. 1-12). 1998. 7.95 (*1-886611-00-9*) Atara Publ.
— My Dog Is Jewish: Reudor's the Doodle Family. (Rhyme Time Doodles Ser.). (Illus.). 24p. (J). (gr. 1-12). 1998. 7.95 (*1-886611-03-3*) Atara Publ.
Reue, Karen, jt. auth. see Doolittle, Mark.
Reuen, Christiane. Vergangenheitsbezuge in der Kindersprache: Eine Untersuchung Zum Gebrauch der Tempora und des Temporalen Lexikons Bei Kindern. (Europaische Hochschulschriften Ser.: Reihe 1, Band 1672). (GER., Illus.). 204p. 1998. 37.95 (*3-631-33304-8*) P Lang Pubng.
***Reuer, Barbara L., ed.** Best Practice in Music Therapy: Utilizing Group Percussion Strategies for Promoting Volunteerism in Well Older Adults. 2nd ed. 1999. write for info. (*1-884914-02-0*) Amer Music Therapy.
Reuer, Barbara L., jt. auth. see Crowe, Barbara.
Reufenacht, Peter, jt. auth. see Bauer, Fred.
Reuhl, K. R., jt. auth. see Lowndes, H. E.
Reuijl, Jan C. On the Determination of Advertising Effectiveness: An Empirical Study of the German Cigarette Market. 1982. lib. bdg. 126.00 (*0-89838-125-8*) Kluwer Academic.
Reul, David G. Getting Started with Middle Level Band. (Getting Started Ser.). 72p. 1994. pap. 12.25 (*1-56545-049-3*, 1631) MENC.
Reul, I. H., ed. see International Conference on Mechanics in Medicine.
***Reuland, Eric, ed.** Arguments & Case: Explaining Burzio's Generalization. LC 99-462297. (Linguistik Aktuell/Linguistics Today Ser.: Vol. 34). xii, 239p. 2000. 65.00 (*1-55619-918-X*) J Benjamins Pubng Co.
Reuland, Eric, jt. ed. see Koster, Jan.
Reuland, Eric J. & Ter Meulen, Alice G. The Representation of InDefiniteness. (Current Studies in Linguistics: Vol. 14). 370p. 1987. 44.00 (*0-262-18126-6*) MIT Pr.
Reuland, Melissa, ed. Information Management & Crime Analysis: Practitioners' Recipe for Success. LC 96-71911. 152p. (Orig.). 1997. pap. text 21.00 (*1-878734-48-2*) Police Exec Res.
Reuland, R., jt. ed. see Cassee, E.
Reuland, Walter P. Cartridges for the Springfield Trap-Door Rifles & Carbines 1865-1898. 3rd ed. 60p. 1996. pap. 8.00 (*0-9646463-1-5*) Heritage Concepts.
***Reule, Bruno & Estes, James F.** Bruno: A Young Boy's Survival in War-Torn Europe. rev. ed. Wagner, Barbara Christy, ed. Orig. Title: Bruno: The Story of a Young Boy. (Illus.). 200p. 2000. pap. 20.00 (*0-615-11788-0*) Ger Russ Pub.
Reule, Tracy D. The Church in American History. LC 95-36457. 94p. (Orig.). (C). 1995. pap. text 18.50 (*0-7618-0090-5*) U Pr of Amer.
Reulen, H. J., et al, eds. Brain Edema, No. VIII. (Acta Neurochirugica - Supplementum Ser.: No. 51). (Illus.). xiii, 416p. 1991. 230.00 (*0-387-82240-2*) Spr-Verlag.
— Training in Neurosurgery. (Acta Neurochirurgica Ser.: Suppl. 69). (Illus.). 220p. 1997. 73.00 (*3-211-83002-2*) Spr-Verlag.
***Reum, Debby.** Author Studies on the Computer: Grade 4-6+ Evans, Marilyn, ed. (Teaching & Learning on the Computer Ser.). (Illus.). 80p. 2000. pap., teacher ed. 16.95 (*1-55799-763-2*, 072) Evan-Moor Edu Pubs.
— Intermediate Math Activities on the Computer: Grade 4-6+ Evans, Marilyn, ed. (Teaching & Learning on the Computer Ser.). (Illus.). 80p. 2000. pap., teacher ed. 16.95 (*1-55799-761-6*, 069) Evan-Moor Edu Pubs.
— Language Arts Activities Using the World Wide Web: Grade 4-6+ Evans, Marilyn, ed. (Teaching & Learning with the Computer Ser.: Vol. 1). 80p. 1999. pap., teacher ed. 16.95 (*1-55799-747-0*, 068) Evan-Moor Edu Pubs.
— Social Studies Activities Using the World Wide Web: Grade 4-6+ Evans, Marilyn, ed. (Teaching & Learning with the Computer Ser.: Vol. 3). 80p. 1999. pap., teacher ed. 16.95 (*1-55799-729-2*, 071) Evan-Moor Edu Pubs.
Reum, Earl. The Spirit of Student Council. Bros, C., ed. (J). (gr. 7-9). 1981. pap. 7.00 (*0-88210-117-X*) Natl Assn Principals.
Reuman, Robert E. Walls: Physical & Psychological. LC 66-24444. (Orig.). 1966. pap. 4.00 (*0-87574-147-9*) Pendle Hill.
Reumann, John H. Stewardship & the Economy of God. fac. ed. LC 92-24696. (Library of Christian Stewardship). 171p. 1992. reprint ed. pap. 53.10 (*0-7837-7971-2*, 204772700008) Bks Demand.
— Variety & Unity in New Testament Thought. (Oxford Bible Ser.). (Illus.). 344p. 1991. pap. text 24.95 (*0-19-826204-3*) OUP.
Reumann, John H., jt. ed. see Taylor, Walter F., Jr.
Reumaux, Patrick, jt. auth. see Moenne-Loccoz, Pierre.
Reunert, Theodore. Diamonds & Gold in South Africa. LC 72-3916. (Black Heritage Library Collection). 1977. reprint ed. 32.95 (*0-8369-9106-0*) Ayer.
Reunhold, Niebuhr. The Nature & Destiny of Man Vol. I: Human Nature. 305p. (C). 1980. pap. text 17.80 (*0-02-387510-0*, Macmillan Coll) P-H.
Reuning, Winifred. Antarctic Journal of the United States, Review 1995 No. 5, Vol. 30. 411p. 1997. per. 37.00 (*0-16-061862-2*) USGPO.
— Antarctic Journal of the United States, Review 1996 No. 2, Vol. 31. 290p. 1998. per. 23.00 (*0-16-061864-9*) USGPO.
Reupke, Dietrich. Buhnenschiedsgerichte in der Bewahrung. (Europaische Hochschulschriften: Reihe 2: Bd. 2050). (GER.). 252p. 1997. 51.95 (*3-631-31144-3*) P Lang Pubng.
Reupke, P. & Duff, A. Review of the Activated Carbon Industry & Scope for Oil Palm Kernel Shell As a Raw Material. 1993. pap. 25.00 (*0-85954-326-9*, Pub. by Nat Res Inst) St Mut.
Reupke, P. & Tariq, A. S. Biomass-Fuelled Indirect Air Heater for Agro-Processing Industries: Design Approach. 1994. pap. 40.00 (*0-85954-370-6*, Pub. by Nat Res Inst) St Mut.
Reurs, Catherine. Splendid Needlepoint: 40 Beautiful & Distinctive Designs. Morgenthal, Deborah, ed. (Illus.). 128p. 1997. 27.95 (*1-887374-22-1*, Pub. by Lark Books) Random.
Reus-Smit, Christian. The Moral Purpose of the State: Culture, Social Identity & Institutional Rationality in International Relations. LC 98-33162. (Princeton Studies in International History & Politics). 208p. 1999. 35.00 (*0-691-02735-8*, Pub. by Princeton U Pr) Cal Prin Full Svc.
Reusch, B., et al, eds. Computational Intelligence: Theory & Applications. LC 99-30076. (Lecture Notes in Computer Science Ser.: Vol. 1625). xiv, 710p. 1999. pap. 102.00 (*3-540-66050-X*) Spr-Verlag.
— Computational Intelligence Theory & Applications: Proceedings International Conference, 5th Fuzzy Days,

An Asterisk (*) at the beginning of an entry indicates that the title is appearing for the first time.

R

Dortmund, Germany, April 28-30, 1997. LC 97-13048. (Lecture Notes in Computer Science Ser.: No. 1226). xiii, 609p. 1997. pap. 91.00 (*3-540-62868-1*) Spr-Verlag.

Reusch, Gary M., jt. auth. see Hartwig, Eric P.

Reusch, Johann P. Systema Logicum Antiquiorum Atque Recentiorum Item Propria Praecepta Exhibens. (Materialien und Dokumente Ser.: Bd. 26). (GER.). 1016p. 1990. reprint ed. write for info. (*3-487-09349-9*) G Olms Pubs.

— Systema Metaphysicum Antiquiorum Atque Recentiorum Item Propria Dogmata et Hypotheses Exhibens. (Materialien und Dokumente Ser.: Bd. 27, No. 2). (GER.). 1218p. 1980. reprint ed. write for info. (*3-487-09330-8*) G Olms Pubs.

Reusch, William. An Introduction to Organic Chemistry. LC 76-50855. 1977. text 37.95 (*0-8162-7161-5*) Holden-Day.

Reuschemeyer, Marilyn, et al. Soviet Emigre Artists. LC 84-23558. 184p. (C). (gr. 13). 1985. text 69.95 (*0-87332-296-7*) M E Sharpe.

Reuscher, John A. A Concordance to the 'Critique of Pure Reason' LC 92-36438. (American University Studies Series V: Vol. 148). XIII, 409p. (C). 1996. text 59.95 (*0-8204-2108-1*) P Lang Pubng.

— Essays on the Metaphysical Foundation of Personal Identity. LC 80-6067. 111p. (C). 1981. lib. bdg. 44.00 (*0-8191-1471-5*) U Pr of Amer.

Reuschlein, Harold G. Jurisprudence: Its American Prophets; a Survey of Taught Jurisprudence. LC 70-158741. 527p. 1971. reprint ed. lib. bdg. 79.50 (*0-8371-6180-0*, REJU, Greenwood Pr) Greenwood.

Reuschlein, Harold G. & Gregory, William A. The Law of Agency & Partnership: Student Edition. 2nd ed. (Hornbook Ser.). 683p. (C). 1990. 38.50 (*0-314-56279-6*) West Pub.

Reuse, Ruth B., jt. auth. see O'Donnell, Joe.

Reuse, Willem J. De, see Chelliah, Shobhana L. & De Reuse, Willem J., eds.

Reusink, J. H., jt. ed. see Wardenier, J.

Reusner, Nicolas. Emblemata Partim Ethica, et Physica: Partim Vero Historica et Hieroglyphica. (GER.). xxvi, 374p. 1990. reprint ed. write for info. (*3-487-09407-X*) G Olms Pubs.

Reuss, Carol & Silvis, Donn. Inside Organizational Communication. 2nd ed. (Series in Public Communication). 384p. (C). 1989. pap. text 20.76 (*0-582-28538-0*) Addison-Wesley.

Reuss, Carol, jt. auth. see Hiebert, Ray E.

Reuss, Frederick. Henry of Atlantic City. LC 99-26946. 1999. 22.00 (*1-878448-89-7*) MacMurray & Beck.

— Horace Afoot. LC 97-21601. 278p. 1997. 25.00 (*1-878448-79-X*) MacMurray & Beck.

— Horace Afoot. LC 98-18167. 288p. 1999. pap. 13.00 (*0-375-70378-0*) Vin Bks.

Reuss, Frederick G. Fiscal Policy for Growth Without Inflation: The German Experiment. LC 63-17669. (Goucher College Ser.). 334p. reprint ed. pap. 103.60 (*0-608-13742-1*, 202073400018) Bks Demand.

Reuss, Henry S. When Government Was Good: Memories of a Life in Politics. LC 98-48747. (Illus.). 192p. 1999. 22.95 (*0-299-16190-0*) U of Wis Pr.

Reuss, Henry S. & Reuss, Margaret M. The Unknown South of France: A History Buff's Guide. LC 90-47384. (Illus.). (Orig.). 1991. pap. 12.95 (*1-55832-030-X*) Harvard Common Pr.

Reuss-Ianni, Elizabeth. Two Cultures of Policing: Street Cops & Management Cops. 145p. (C). 1993. pap. text 21.95 (*1-56000-654-4*) Transaction Pubs.

Reuss, J. O. & Johnson, D. W. Acid Deposition & Acidification of Soils & Waters. (Ecological Studies: Vol. 59). (Illus.). viii, 119p. 1986. 89.95 (*0-387-96290-5*) Spr-Verlag.

Reuss, JoAnne C., jt. auth. see Reuss, Richard A.

Reuss, M., jt. ed. see Heinzle, E.

Reuss, Margaret M., jt. auth. see Reuss, Henry S.

***Reuss, Martin.** Designing the Bayous: Control of Water in the Atchafalaya Basin, 1800-1995. 490p. 1998. per. 29.00 (*0-16-061270-5*) USGPO.

Reuss, Martin, ed. Water Resources Administration in the United States: Policy, Practice, & Emerging Issues. LC 93-7668. 300p. (C). 1993. 40.00 (*0-87013-333-0*) Mich St U Pr.

Reuss, Martin, ed. see National Forum on Water Management Policy Staff.

Reuss, Monica, tr. see Misgeld, Dieter & Nicholson, Graeme, eds.

Reuss, Richard A. Songs of American Labor, Industrialization & the Urban Work Experience: A Discography. Lockwood, Yvonne, ed. (Program on Workers Culture Ser.). (Illus.). 109p. 1983. pap. 4.75 (*0-87736-344-7*) U of Mich Inst Labor.

***Reuss, Richard A. & Reuss, JoAnne C.** American Folk Music & Left-Wing Politics, 1927-1957. Smith, Ralph Lee & Cohen, Ronald C., eds. (American Folk Music & Musicians Ser.: No. 4). (Illus.). 328p. 2000. 55.00 (*0-8108-3684-X*) Scarecrow.

Reuss, Suzanne, jt. auth. see Burkhart, Patrick J.

Reusse, Patrick, jt. auth. see Hartman, Sid.

Reust, Hans R. & Cooper, Dennis. Raymond Pettibon. 352p. Date not set. pap. 50.00 (*3-85780-106-9*) Dist Art Pubs.

Reuten, Geert & Williams, Mike. Value Form & the State: The Tendencies of Accumulation & the Determination of Economic Policy in Capitalist Society. 320p. 1989. 75.00 (*0-415-00088-2*, A3585); pap. 21.95 (*0-415-03893-6*, A3589) Routledge.

Reuten, Geert, jt. ed. see Arthur, Christopher J.

Reutenauer, C., jt. auth. see Berstel, J.

Reutenauer, Christophe. Free Lie Algebras. LC 92-27318. (London Mathematical Society Monographs: New Series 7). (Illus.). 286p. 1993. text 110.00 (*0-19-853679-8*, Clarendon Pr) OUP.

Reuter. End of the Rainbow. 1999. pap. 15.99 (*0-525-45166-8*) NAL.

— Pathology of the Testes. 1997. text. write for info. (*0-7216-4977-7*) Harcourt.

— Thieme LexiMed Pocket, English-German - German-English. (ENG & GER.). 1024p. 1998. pap. 35.00 (*0-86577-788-8*) Thieme Med Pubs.

Reuter, et al, eds. Fracture Mechanics. 834p. 1995. 99.00 (*0-8031-1996-8*, STP1256) ASTM.

Reuter, Andreas, jt. auth. see Gray, Jim.

Reuter, Anna H., jt. auth. see Trahey, Jane.

Reuter, Bjarne. Boys from St. Petri. 1996. 10.09 (*0-606-08704-4*, Pub. by Turtleback) Demco.

Reuter, C., jt. auth. see Reuter, P.

Reuter, Cathie. Healing in His Hands: A Collection of Poems Bringing Comfort to the Broken-Hearted. unabridged ed. LC 97-119514. 80p. (Orig.). 1996. pap. 9.95 (*0-9654939-3-8*) Anderine Pub.

Reuter, Christian. Doing Business in the United States. (GER.). 64p. 1995. 30.00 (*0-86640-052-4*) German Am Chamber.

— Schelmuffsky. Wonderley, Wayne, tr. LC 62-62959. (North Carolina. University. Studies in the Germanic Languages & Literatures: No. 33). reprint ed. 27.00 (*0-404-50933-9*) AMS Pr.

Reuter, Christoph. Die Auditive Diskrimination von Orchesterinstrumenten: Verschmelzung und Heraushorbarkeit von Instrumentalklangfarben im Ensemblespiel. (Europaische Hochschulschriften, Reihe 36: Bd. 162). (GER., Illus.). 339p. 1996. 57.95 (*3-631-30886-8*) P Lang Pubng.

***Reuter, Claus.** Brunswick Troops in North America, 1776-1783. 114p. 1999. pap. 21.00 (*0-7884-1348-1*, R187) Heritage Bk.

Reuter, D. J. & Robinson, J. B., eds. Plant Analysis: An Interpretation Manual. 2nd rev. ed. (Illus.). 572p. 1997. 89.95 (*0-643-05938-5*, Pub. by CSIRO) Accents Pubns.

Reuter, D. J., jt. auth. see Walker, J.

Reuter, Donald F. Heartthrob: 100 Years of Beautiful Men. (Illus.). 160p. 1998. 29.95 (*0-7893-0224-1*, Pub. by Universe) St Martin.

— Heavenly: A Hundred Years of Unforgettable Women. (Illus.). 160p. 1999. 29.95 (*0-7893-0377-9*, Pub. by Universe) St Martin.

***Reuter, Donald F.** Shirtless! The Hollywood Male Physique. (Illus.). 2000. 29.95 (*0-7893-0508-9*) Universe.

Reuter, Edward B. The Mulatto in the United States. LC 70-100495. (Studies in Black History & Culture: No. 54). 1970. lib. bdg. 75.00 (*0-8383-1216-0*) M S G Haskell Hse.

— The Mulatto in the United States. LC 69-16569. 417p. 1969. reprint ed. lib. bdg. 52.50 (*0-8371-0938-8*, REM&) Greenwood.

Reuter, Elisabeth. Best Friends. Orig. Title: Judith & Lisa. 26p. (J). (gr. 1-4). 1993. 12.95 (*0-943706-18-1*) Pitspopany.

— Best Friends. Orig. Title: Judith & Lisa. 26p. (J). (gr. 2-5). 1993. 12.95 (*0-614-18955-1*) Pitspopany.

Reuter, Frank, jt. auth. see Orman, Mort.

Reuter, Frank, ed. see Greenberg, Michael A.

Reuter, Frank, ed. see Lucier, Thomas J.

Reuter, Frank, ed. see Schwartz, Bob & Schwartz, Leah.

Reuter, Frank, ed. see Van Buskirk, Kathleen, et al.

Reuter, Frank T., jt. auth. see Tucker, Spencer C.

Reuter, Frederick A. Moments Divine - Before the Blessed Sacrament. 290p. 1995. pap. 8.50 (*0-89555-533-6*) TAN Bks Pubs.

Reuter, Fritz. When the French Were Here. Bayerschmidt, Carl F., tr. 200p. 1984. 28.50 (*0-8386-3230-0*) Fairleigh Dickinson.

Reuter, Gabriele. From a Good Family. LC 98-55669. 1999. 49.50 (*1-57113-149-3*) Camden Hse.

Reuter, Helmut. Aseptic Packaging of Food. LC 89-50658. 284p. 1989. pap. 49.95 (*0-87762-694-4*) Technomic.

Reuter, Helmut, ed. Aseptic Processing of Foods. (Illus.). 313p. 1993. pap. 104.95 (*1-56676-058-5*, 760585) Technomic.

***Reuter, Jeff.** Let's Cut the Small Talk: The Adult Party Game for the 21st Century. 304p. 2000. 6.95 (*0-9663303-0-7*) Corporate Designs.

Reuter, Joe, tr. see Steiner, Rudolf.

Reuter, Klaus. Lebensgeschichte und Religiose Sozialisation: Aspekte der Subjektivitat in Arbeiterautobiographien Aus der Zeit der Industrialisierung Bis 1914. (Erfahrung und Theologie Ser.: Bd. 19). (GER.). 230p. 1991. 46.80 (*3-631-43475-8*) P Lang Pubng.

Reuter, Laurel, ed. see Camrud, Madelyn.

Reuter, Laurel J. Georgie Papageorge. (Illus.). 108p. (Orig.). 1995. pap. 29.95 (*0-943107-05-9*) ND Mus Art.

— JudyLand: The Art of Judy Onofrio. (Illus.). 66p. (Orig.). 1993. pap. 18.00 (*0-943107-03-2*) ND Mus Art.

Reuter, Laurel J., jt. auth. see Constantine, Mildred.

Reuter, Laurel J., jt. auth. see Ratcliff, Carter.

Reuter, M., jt. auth. see Dittrich, W.

Reuter, Marianne. Text und Bild Im Codex 132 der Bibliothek von Montecassino "Liber Rabani de Originibus Rerum" (Munchener Beitrage zur Mediavistik und Renaissance-Forschung Ser.: Bd. 34). (GER.). x, 228p. 1984. 65.00 (*3-615-00165-6*) G Olms Pubs.

Reuter, P. Leximed Compact: Dictionary of Clinical Medicine: Deutsch-Englisch. 1997. 49.00 (*0-86577-735-7*) Thieme Med Pubs.

— Leximed Compact: Dictionary of Clinical Medicine: English-German. 1997. 49.00 (*0-86577-734-9*) Thieme Med Pubs.

— Thieme Compact Medical Dictionary Vol. 1: German to English. (ENG & GER.). 738p. 1997. 125.00 (*0-320-00424-4*) Fr & Eur.

— Thieme Compact Medical Dictionary Vol. 2: English to German. (ENG & GER.). 804p. 1997. 125.00 (*0-320-00425-2*) Fr & Eur.

Reuter, P. & Reuter, C. Thieme Leximed: Dictionary, Vol. 1. (ENG & GER.). 400p. 1995. 140.00 (*3-13-100471-1*, Pub. by G Thieme) Thieme Med Pubs.

— Thieme Leximed: Dictionary, Vol. 2. (ENG & GER.). 841p. 1996. 140.00 (*3-13-100491-6*, Pub. by G Thieme) Thieme Med Pubs.

Reuter, Paul. Introduction to the Law of Treaties. Mico, Jose & Haggenmacher, Peter, trs. LC 94-44908. (Publication of the Graduate Institute of International Studies, Geneva).Tr. of Introduction au Droit des Traites. (ENG & FRE.). 1994. write for info. (*0-7103-0502-8*) Routledge.

— Introduction to the Law of Treaties.Tr. of Introduction au Droit des Traites. 250p. 1989. text 57.50 (*0-86187-954-6*) St Martin.

— Introduction to the Law of Treaties.Tr. of Introduction au Droit des Traites. 252p. 1992. pap. text 29.50 (*0-7185-1440-8*) St Martin.

***Reuter, Peter.** Birkhauser Dictionary of Human Biology (Birkhauser Whorterbuch der Humanbiologie) English-German - German-English. LC 00-22420. (GER & ENG., Illus.). 750p. 2000. 120.00 (*3-7643-6198-0*) Birkhauser.

Reuter, Peter. English/German Medical Dictionary. (ENG & GER.). 1994. 295.00 (*0-7859-9984-1*) Fr & Eur.

— German/English Medical Dictionary. (ENG & GER.). 837p. 1995. 295.00 (*0-7859-9983-3*) Fr & Eur.

Reuter, Peter, et al. Comparing Western European & North American Drug Policies: An International Conference Report. LC 93-28666. 1993. pap. text 15.00 (*0-8330-1431-5*, MR-237-GMF/SF) Rand Corp.

Reuter, Peter, ed. see National Research Council Staff.

Reuter, Rainer. Synopse Zu Den Breifen des Neuen Testaments Teil II: Die Pastoralbriefe, Vol. 2. (Arbeiten zur Religion und Geschichte des Urchristentums Ser.: Bd. 6).Tr. of Synopsis of the New Testament Letters: The Pastoral Epistles. (ENG & GER.). 592p. 1998. 79.95 (*3-631-31457-4*) P Lang Pubng.

***Reuter, Reiner.** Synopse zu den Breifen des Neuen Testame (Synopsis of the New Testament Letters) Teil II: Die Pastoralbriefe (Vol. II: The Pastoral Epistles) (Arbeiten zur Religion und Geschichte des Urchristentums: Vol. 6). 592p. 1998. 79.95 (*0-8204-3593-7*) P Lang Pubng.

Reuter, Theodore. The Minnesota House of Representatives & the Professionalization of Politics. LC 94-982. 244p. (Orig.). 1994. pap. 28.50 (*0-8191-9452-2*); lib. bdg. 54.00 (*0-8191-9451-4*) U Pr of Amer.

Reuter, Timothy. Germany in the Early Middle Ages, C. 800-1056. LC 00-46393. text. write for info. (*0-582-08156-4*) Longman.

Reuter, Timothy, ed. The New Cambridge Medieval History Vol. 3: c. 900 - c. 1024. (New Cambridge Medieval History Ser.). (Illus.). 890p. (C). 2000. 110.00 (*0-521-36447-7*) Cambridge U Pr.

— Warriors & Churchmen in the High Middle Ages: Essays Presented to Karl Leyser. LC 92-22268. 304p. 1992. 55.00 (*1-85285-063-9*) Hambledon Press.

Reuter, Timothy, ed. see Leyser, Karl J.

Reuter, Timothy, tr. see Fuhrmann, Horst.

Reuter, Timothy, tr. see Tellenbach, Gerd.

Reuter, Walter G. Surface Crack Growth: Models, Experiments, & Structures. Underwood, John H. & Newman, James C., Jr., eds. LC 89-49360. (Special Technical Publication (STP) Ser.: No. 1060). (Illus.). 425p. 1990. text 88.00 (*0-8031-1284-X*, STP1060) ASTM.

Reuter, Walter G., ed. Nondestructive Evaluation of Utilities & Pipelines II, Vol. 3398. LC 98-209972. 224p. 1998. 59.00 (*0-8194-2847-7*) SPIE.

***Reuter, Walter G., ed.** Nondestructive Evaluation of Utilities & Pipelines III. 106p. 1999. pap. text 50.00 (*0-8194-3058-7*) SPIE.

Reuter, William. Winning with Reverse Chess Strategy. 1999. pap. text 19.95 (*0-938650-95-5*) Thinkers Pr.

Reuter, Yves, ed. Les Interactions Lecture-Ecriture: Actes du Colloque Organise par l'Equipe Theodile-Crel (Universite Charles-de-Gaulle - Lille III, 22-24 Novembre 1993) 2nd ed. (Exploration Ser.). (FRE., Illus.). xii, 404p. 1997. 51.95 (*3-906759-36-9*, Pub. by P Lang) P Lang Pubng.

Reuterdahl, Arvid. Scientific Theism. 1926. 25.00 (*0-8159-6805-1*) Devin.

Reutern, Gerhard-Michael Von, see Von Reutern, Gerhard-Michael.

Reuters. EMU Explained: A Guide to Markets & Monetary Union. 1997. pap. text 24.95 (*0-7494-2377-3*) Kogan Page Ltd.

— Introduction to Equities. LC 99-30667. 350p. 1999. 69.95 (*0-471-83171-9*) Wiley.

***Reuters.** Risk Management. (C). 1999. text 46.00 (*0-471-83175-1*) Wiley.

Reuters America Staff. Six Drown Saving Chicken: And Other Stories from Reuters's "Oddly Enough File" Basler, Robert, ed. (Illus.). 160p. 1996. pap. 8.95 (*0-7867-0369-5*) Carroll & Graf.

Reuters, Anna H. Friendship & Love in the Middle English Metrical Romances. (European University Studies: Anglo-Saxon Language & Literature: Ser. 14, Vol. 226). 249p. 1991. pap. 47.00 (*3-631-43499-5*) P Lang Pubng.

***Reuters Limited Staff.** Debt Markets. LC 99-37481. 300p. 2000. 49.95 (*0-471-83174-3*) Wiley.

— Introduction to Derivatives. LC HG6024.A3I59 1998. 216p. 1999. 59.95 (*0-471-83176-X*) Wiley.

— Money Markets & Foreign Exchange. LC 99-17730. 352p. 1999. 69.95 (*0-471-83128-X*) Wiley.

— Technical Analysis. 192p. 1999. 59.95 (*0-471-83127-1*) Wiley.

***Reuters Limited Staff, ed.** Commodities, Energy & Shipping. 250p. 2000. text 49.95 (*0-471-83150-6*) Wiley.

Reuters Staff. The Reuters Glossary: A Dictionary of International Economic & Financial Terms. 1989. pap. 12.95 (*0-582-04286-0*) Longman.

Reuth, Ralf G. Goebbels. Winston, Krishna, tr. from GER. LC 93-15900. (ENG.). 1993. 27.95 (*0-15-136076-6*) Harcourt.

— Goebbels. (Illus.). 480p. 1994. pap. 16.95 (*0-15-600139-X*) Harcourt.

Reuther, David & Thorn, John, eds. The Armchair Mountaineer: The Triumphs & Tragedies of Ascent, from Fact & Fiction. (Illus.). 342p. 1989. reprint ed. pap. 15.95 (*0-89732-092-1*) Menasha Ridge.

Reuther, Kathy. Kathy's Secret Garden. 2nd ed. (Illus.). 38p. 1997. 9.95 (*1-57377-018-3*) Easl Pubns.

Reuther, R. Geochemical Approaches to Environmental Engineering of Metals, Vol. 323. LC 96-2747. (Environmental Science Ser.). 1996. write for info. (*0-387-58848-5*) Spr-Verlag.

Reuther, R., ed. Geochemical Approaches for Environmental Engineering of Metals. 224p. 1996. 74.95 (*3-540-58848-5*) Spr-Verlag.

***Reuther, Ruth E.** For Children of All Ages. (Illus.). 34p. 2000. pap. write for info. (*0-9622632-2-2*) Wee-Chee-Taw.

Reuther, Ruth E. Meet at the Falls: The Story of the Pioneers. McCall, Jody, ed. (Series 2). (Illus.). (J). 1989. pap. text. write for info. (*0-9622632-1-4*) Wee-Chee-Taw.

Reuther, Ruth E. & Richardson, A. G. Meet Me at the Falls: Activities Book. (Series 1). (Illus.). (Orig.). 1989. pap. text 5.98 (*0-9622632-0-6*) Wee-Chee-Taw.

Reuther, Walter, et al, eds. The Citrus Industry Vol. 4. Crop Protection. LC 67-63041. 362p. 1978. 30.00 (*0-931876-24-9*, 4088) ANR Pubns CA.

— The Citrus Industry, Vol. V: Crop Protection, Postharvest Technology, & Early History of Citrus Research in California. LC 67-63041. (Illus.). 388p. 1989. 42.00 (*0-931876-87-7*, 3326) ANR Pubns CA.

Reuther, Walter P. Education & the Public Good. Incl. Challenge to Education in a Changing World. LC 64-25934. 1964. LC 64-25934. 67p. 1964. 6.50 (*0-674-23875-3*) HUP.

Reutiman, Sherry, ed. see Engelmann, Barbara A. & Engelmann, Michael A.

Reutlinge. Wills, Trusts, & Estates. 288p. 1993. 23.95 (*0-316-74112-4*, Aspen Law & Bus) Aspen Pub.

Reutlinger, Mark. Evidence: Essential Terms & Concepts. 336p. 1997. pap. text 24.95 (*1-56706-494-9*, 64949) Panel Pubs.

— Wills, Trusts, & Estates: Essential Terms & Concepts. 2nd ed. LC 97-50050. (Essentials for Law Students Ser.). 300p. 1998. pap. text. write for info. (*1-56706-767-0*) Panel Pubs.

Reutlinger, Shlomo. Techniques for Project Appraisal under Uncertainty. LC 74-94827. (World Bank Staff Occasional Papers: No. 10). (Illus.). 109p. (Orig.). reprint ed. pap. 33.80 (*0-7837-5385-3*, 204514900005) Bks Demand.

Reutlinger, Shlomo & Selowsky, Marcelo. Malnutrition & Poverty: Magnitude & Policy Options. LC 76-17240. (World Bank Staff Occasional Papers: No. 23). 96p. reprint ed. pap. 30.00 (*0-7837-5384-5*, 204514800005) Bks Demand.

Reutner, Richard. Lexikalische Studien Zum Dialekt Im Wiener Volksstuck Vor Nestroy: Mit Einer Edition von Baeuerles "Die Fremden in Wien" (1814) Wiesinger, Peter, ed. (Schriften zur Deutschen Sprache in Osterreich Ser.: Band 25). (GER.). 454p. 1998. pap. 67.95 (*3-631-32534-7*) P Lang Pubng.

Reutov, O. A. Theoretical Principles of Organic Chemistry. Mir Publishers Staff, tr. 500p. (C). 1975. text 35.00 (*0-8464-0919-4*) Beekman Pubs.

Reutov, Oleg A., et al. Ambident Anions. Michael, J. P., ed. & tr. by. from RUS. LC 83-10137. (Illus.). 352p. 1983. reprint ed. pap. 109.20 (*0-608-05421-6*, 206589000006) Bks Demand.

Reutter, E. Edmund, Jr The Law of Public Education. 4th ed. 1015p. 1994. text 48.00 (*1-56662-154-2*) Foundation Pr.

Reutter, E. Edmund. Schools & the Law. 5th ed. LC 81-80361. 126p. reprint ed. pap. 39.10 (*0-608-18141-2*, 203279700081) Bks Demand.

Reutter, Jeffrey M., jt. auth. see Kershner, Kelly.

Reutter, Klaus-Joachim, et al, eds. Tectonics of the Southern Central Andes: Structure & Evolution of an Active Continental Margin. LC 93-15961. 1994. 238.95 (*0-387-55232-4*) Spr-Verlag.

Reutter, M. On the Wings of the Zephyr. 352p. 2000. 27.50 (*0-06-018233-4*) HarperTrade.

Reutter, Rainer. Synopse Zu Den Briefen des Neuen Testaments (Synopsis of the New Testament Letters) Teil I (Vol. I) Kolosser-, Epheser-, II. Thessalonicherbrief (Colossians, Ephesians II. Thessalonians) (Arbeiten zur Religion und Geschichte des Urchristentums Ser.: No. 5). (ENG & GER.). 774p. 1997. 114.95 (*3-631-31456-6*) P Lang Pubng.

Reutter, Werner, ed. Orotic Acid. 1981. text 84.00 (*0-85200-294-7*) Kluwer Academic.

Reutter, Werner, et al, eds. Modulation of Liver Cell Expression. (Falk Ser.: No. 43). 1987. text 268.50 (*0-85200-677-2*) Kluwer Academic.

— Structural Carbohydrates in the Liver: Falk Symposium, No 34. 600p. 1983. text 272.50 (*0-85200-711-6*) Kluwer Academic.

Reutter, Werner, jt. ed. see Wieland, F.

Reutzel. Teaching Children to Read. 2nd ed. 1999. pap. text 43.75 (*0-13-022524-X*) S&S Trade.

An Asterisk (*) at the beginning of an entry indicates that the title is appearing for the first time.

Reutzel & Cooter, Robert. Teaching Children to Read: Putting the Pieces Together. 3rd ed. LC 99-17100. (Illus.). 654p. 1999. 71.00 (*0-13-099835-4*) P-H.

Reutzel, D. Ray, jt. auth. see Cooter, Robert B.

Reuven, Yisrael B. Male & Female He Created Them: A Guide to Classical Torah Commentary on the Roles & Natures of Men & Women. 222p. 1996. 17.95 (*1-56871-096-8*) Targum Pr.

Reuveni, Amnon. In the Name of the "New World Order" Manifestations of Decadent Powers in World Politics. Nunhofer, Nicholas & Boardman, Terry, trs. (Illus.). 152p. 1996. pap. 16.95 (*0-904693-81-3*, Pub. by Temple Lodge) Anthroposophic.

Reuveni, Reuven. Novel Approaches to Integrated Pest Management. 384p. 1995. boxed set 94.95 (*0-87371-881-X*, L881) Lewis Pubs.

Reuver, H. A., jt. auth. see Hanken, A. F.

Reuver, Marc. Requiem for Constantine: A Vision of the Future of Church & State in the West. LC 96-208828. 262 p. 1996. write for info. (*90-242-6354-9*) KOK Pharos.

Reuvid, Johathan. Doing Business with China. 2nd ed. 1997. pap. text 140.00 (*0-7494-1741-2*) Kogan Page Ltd.

Reuvid, Jonathan, jt. auth. see Millar, Roderick.

Reuzeau, Jean-Yves, ed. French Poets of Today. 2nd rev. ed. LC 97-78147. (Essential Poets Ser.: Vol. 21). (FRE & ENG.). 195p. 1999. reprint ed. pap. 13.00 (*0-920717-82-9*) Guernica Editions.

Revankar, Ratna G. The Indian Constitution: A Case Study of Backward Classes. LC 76-120067. 361p. 1975. 49.50 (*0-8386-7670-7*) Fairleigh Dickinson.

***Revankar, S. T.** Single-Phase & Two-Phase Natural Circulation Tests in the Puma Facility. 288p. 1998. per. 23.00 (*0-16-062950-0*) USGPO.

Revans, Reginald. The ABC of Action Learning. (Orig.). 1998. pap. text 17.95 (*1-898001-42-1*) Lemos & Crane.

Revard. Family Matters, Tribal Affairs. LC 97-21139. (Sun Tracks Ser.). 219p. 1998. 40.00 (*0-8165-1842-4*) U of Ariz Pr.

***Revard.** Family Matters, Tribal Affairs. LC 97-21139. (Sun Tracks Ser.). xx, 202p. 1998. pap. 16.95 (*0-8165-1843-2*) U of Ariz Pr.

Revard, Carter C. An Eagle Nation. LC 93-12720. (Sun Tracks Ser.: Vol. 24). 123p. 1993. pap. 14.95 (*0-8165-1403-8*); lib. bdg. 36.00 (*0-8165-1355-4*) U of Ariz Pr.

Revard, James M. The Progressive Cavity Pump Handbook. LC 95-10764. 1995. 79.95 (*0-87814-445-5*) PennWell Bks.

Revard, Stella P. Milton & the Tangles of Neaera's Hair: The Making of the 1645 Poems. LC 97-360. 304p. 1997. spiral bd. 44.95 (*0-8262-1100-3*) U of Mo Pr.

Revard, Stella P., et al, eds. Acta Conventus Neo-Latini Guelpherbytani: Proceedings of Sixth International Congress, 1985, at Wolfenbuttel. LC 88-11889. (Medieval & Renaissance Texts & Studies: Vol. 53). (Illus.). 720p. 1988. 60.00 (*0-86698-037-7*, MR53) MRTS.

Revauger, Jean-Paul, jt. auth. see Edwards, John.

Revauger, Jean-Paul, jt. ed. see Edwards, John.

Revault, Jacques. Designs & Patterns from North African Carpets & Textiles. Applebaum, Stanley, tr. from FRE. (Illus.). 128p. (Orig.). 1973. pap. 9.95 (*0-486-22850-9*) Dover.

Reveal, Betsy, jt. auth. see Chase, Gordon.

Reveal, James L., jt. contrib. by see Harper, K. T.

Revealed Book Staff. The Holy Qur'an: Text, Translation & Commentary. Ali, S. V., tr. LC 87-51715. 1928p. (C). 1995. reprint ed. 29.95 (*0-940368-84-6*, 135); reprint ed. pap. 39.95 (*0-940368-85-4*, 135A) Tahrike Tarsile Quran.

Reveaux, Tony. Cool Mac Clip Art Plus, Incl. disk. 1993. 24.95 incl. disk (*0-672-48551-6*) Hayden.

Reveill, Ken, jt. auth. see Walters, Dennis A.

Revel, Alain & Riboud, Christophe. American Green Power. LC 86-2706.Tr. of Les/Etats-Unis et la Strategie Alimentaire Mondiale. (Illus.). 240p. reprint ed. pap. 74.40 (*0-608-06113-1*, 206644600008) Bks Demand.

Revel Guest, jt. auth. see St. George, Andrew.

Revel, J., et al, eds. Oeuvres de Pierre Curie. 624p. 1984. pap. text 73.00 (*2-903928-07-X*) Gordon & Breach.

Revel, J. P., et al, eds. The Science of Biological Specimen Preparation for Microscopy & Microanalysis. (Proceedings of the Pfefferkorn Conference Ser.: No. 2). (Illus.). x, 246p. 1984. text 40.00 (*0-931288-32-0*) Scanning Microscopy.

Revel, Jacques. Histories: French Constructions of the Past Postwar French Thought, Vol. I. 1998. pap. 19.95 (*1-56584-435-1*, Pub. by New Press NY) Norton.

Revel, Jean-Francois. Culture & Cuisine: A Journey Through the History of Food. Lane, Helen R., tr. from FRE. (Quality Paperbacks Ser.). (Illus.). 300p. 1984. reprint ed. pap. 12.95 (*0-306-80222-8*) Da Capo.

— Democracy Against Itself: The Future of the Democratic Impulse. 300p. 1993. text 27.95 (*0-02-926387-5*) Free Pr.

***Revel, Jean-Francois & Ricard, Matthieu.** The Monk & the Philosopher: A Father & Son Discuss the Meaning of Life. Canti, John, tr. from FRE. 2000. pap. 14.00 (*0-8052-1103-9*) Schocken.

Revelas, Joanna M., ed. see Lint, Gregg L.

***Revelation Lugia Staff.** Art of Pokemon: The Movie: Revelation Lugia 2000. (Illus.). (J). 2000. pap. 9.95 (*1-56931-502-7*) Viz Commns Inc.

Revelation Technologies Staff. Continuing Development in Advanced Revelation Training Manual. 200p. 1988. 50.00 (*0-923387-20-X*) Revelation Sftware.

— Introduction to Development in Advanced Revelation Training Manual. 200p. 1988. 50.00 (*0-923387-18-8*) Revelation Sftware.

— Introduction to Development in Advanced Revelation Training Manual (Instructor Manual) 150p. 1989. 100.00 (*0-923387-19-6*) Revelation Sftware.

— Programming in Advanced Revelation Training Manual. 150p. 1990. 50.00 (*0-923387-22-6*) Revelation Sftware.

— Programming in Advanced Revelation Training Manual (Instructor Manual) 75p. 1990. 100.00 (*0-923387-23-4*) Revelation Sftware.

— SQL-I Training Manual. 90p. 1990. 50.00 (*0-923387-39-0*) Revelation Sftware.

— Using Advanced Revelation Applications I Training Manual. 100p. 1989. 30.00 (*0-923387-26-9*) Revelation Sftware.

— Using Advanced Revelation Applications I Training Manual (Instructor Manual) 75p. 1989. 60.00 (*0-923387-27-7*) Revelation Sftware.

Reveles, Daniel. Enchiladas, Rice, & Beans. 256p. (Orig.). 1994. pap. 10.00 (*0-345-38426-1*) One Wrld.

Reveley, Edith. A Pause for Breath. LC 82-22293. 210p. 1983. 15.95 (*0-87951-165-6*, Pub. by Overlook Pr) Penguin Putnam.

***Reveley, Michael A. & Deakin, J. F. William, eds.** The Psychopharmacology of Schizophrenia. (An Arnold Publication). 2000. 55.00 (*0-340-75912-7*, Pub. by E A) OUP.

***Reveley, Shirley, et al.** Nurse Practitioners: Developing the Role in the Hospital Setting. 256p. 2000. pap. 40.00 (*0-7506-4761-2*) Buttrwrth-Heinemann.

Revelis, B. G. Greek-English Letterwriting. (ENG & GRE.). 10.00 (*0-685-09036-1*) Divry.

Revelis, B. O. Greek-English Guide to Letterwriting. (ENG & GRE.). 224p. 1960. pap. 19.95 (*0-8288-6838-7*, M-9440) Fr & Eur.

Revell, Alex. Victoria Cross: WWI Airmen & Their Aircraft. LC 98-162565. (Illus.). 96p. 1997. pap. 29.95 (*1-891268-00-7*) Flying Machines.

Revell, Alex & Davis, Mick. High in the Empty Blue: History of 56 Squadron RFC/RAF 1916-1919. (Illus.). 456p. 1995. 49.95 (*0-963710-3-2*) Flying Machines.

Revell, Don. The Broken Juke. Wilcox, Patricia, ed. LC 75-21920. (Iris Poets Ser.: Vol. 1). 55p. 1975. pap. 5.00 (*0-916078-00-0*) Iris Pr.

Revell, Don, jt. auth. see Gillham, Skip.

Revell, Donald. Beautiful Shirt. LC 94-20492. (Wesleyan Poetry Ser.). 67p. 1994. pap. 12.95 (*0-8195-1219-2*, Wesleyan Univ Pr); text 25.00 (*0-8195-2216-3*, Wesleyan Univ Pr) U Pr of New Eng.

— Erasures. LC 92-12429. (Wesleyan Poetry Ser.). 58p. 1992. pap. 12.95 (*0-8195-1206-0*, Wesleyan Univ Pr); text 25.00 (*0-8195-2203-1*, Wesleyan Univ Pr) U Pr of New Eng.

— The Gaza of Winter. LC 87-12523. (Contemporary Poetry Ser.). 80p. 1988. pap. 14.95 (*0-8203-0989-3*) U of Ga Pr.

— New Dark Ages. LC 89-49759. (Wesleyan Poetry Ser.). 72p. 1990. pap. 12.95 (*0-8195-1186-2*, Wesleyan Univ Pr) U Pr of New Eng.

— There Are Three: Poems. LC 98-16359. (Wesleyan Poetry Ser.). 59p. 1998. pap. 12.95 (*0-8195-2247-3*, Wesleyan Univ Pr); text 25.00 (*0-8195-2246-5*, Wesleyan Univ Pr) U Pr of New Eng.

Revell, Donald, tr. see Apollinaire, Guillaume.

Revell, Dorothy T. Food Tips for a Healthy Life Style. 232p. 1999. 19.95 (*1-58244-017-4*) Rutledge Bks.

Revell, E. J. Hebrew Text with Palestinian Vocalization. LC 76-18746. (Near & Middle East Ser.: No. 7). 242p. reprint ed. pap. 75.10 (*0-608-11032-9*, 205121500093) Bks Demand.

Revell, Elizabeth, ed. The Later Letters of Peter of Blois. (Auctores Britannici Medii Aevi British Academy Ser.: No. XIII). 424p. 1993. text 125.00 (*0-19-726108-6*) OUP.

Revell, Glenda. Glenda's Story. LC 95-107597. 122p. 1994. pap. 7.99 (*0-8474-1154-0*) Back to Bible.

— With Love from a Mother's Heart. 1999. pap. text 12.99 (*0-8474-1103-6*) Back to Bible.

Revell, Jack, ed. Europe Inc. LC 99-35169. 206p. 1999. 45.00 (*0-471-62388-1*) Wiley.

***Revell, N.** House of the Spirit Levels. 1998. pap. text 17.95 (*0-7472-7638-2*, Pub. by Headline Bk Pub) Trafalgar.

Revell, Norman, et al, eds. Database & Expert Systems Applications: 6th International Conference, DEXA '95, London, United Kingdom, September 4-8, 1995, Proceedings, Vol. XV. LC 95-37100. (Lecture Notes in Computer Science Ser.: Vol. 978). 654p. 1995. 100.00 (*3-540-60303-4*) Spr-Verlag.

***Revell, Oliver.** G-Man's Journal: A Legendary Career Inside the FBI; From the Kennedy Assassination to the Oklahoma City Bombing. (Illus.). 1999. per. 7.99 (*0-671-56800-0*) PB.

Revell, Oliver & Williams, Dwight. A G-Man's Journal: From the Kennedy Assassination to the Oklahoma City Bombing. LC 99-168120. (Illus.). 528p. 1998. 23.00 (*0-671-56801-9*, PB Hardcover) PB.

Revell, P. A. Pathology of Bone. (Illus.). 320p. 1985. 204.00 (*0-387-15418-3*) Spr-Verlag.

Revell, Peter. Quest in Modern American Poetry. (Critical Studies). 246p. 1981. 44.00 (*0-389-20238-X*, 07028) B&N Imports.

***Revell, Phil.** Kayaking. LC 99-27663. (Radical Sports Ser.). 1999. lib. bdg. write for info. (*1-57572-943-1*) Heinemann Lib.

Revell, Richard A. & Slyn, Alan T. Kentucky Divorce: Practice Systems Library Manual. LC 79-91145. 1992. suppl. ed. 120.00 (*0-318-11937-4*) West Group.

— Kentucky Divorce: Practice Systems Library Manual. 1993. suppl. ed. 75.00 (*0-317-03267-4*) West Group.

Revell, Rod. Highly Recommended. (Illus.). 112p. 1989. pap. text, teacher ed. 14.95 (*0-19-437648-6*) OUP.

Revell, Rod & Scott, Chris. Highly Recommended. 68p. 1995. pap. text, teacher ed. 14.95 (*0-19-437666-4*) OUP.

— Highly Recommended. 2nd ed. (Illus.). 112p. 1995. pap. text, student ed. 13.95 (*0-19-437665-6*) OUP.

— Highly Recommended: English for the Hotel & Catering Industry. (Illus.). 64p. 1993. pap. text, wbk. ed. 6.95 (*0-19-437664-8*) OUP.

Revell, Rod & Sweeney, Simon. In Print: Reading Business English. 128p. (C). 1993. pap. text 15.95 (*0-521-38303-X*) Cambridge U Pr.

Revell, Stephen. Capital Markets Forum Yearbook Vol. 2: 1994/95. 680p. 1997. 163.00 (*90-411-0659-6*) Kluwer Law Intl.

Revell, Stephen, ed. Capital Markets Forum Yearbook Vol. 1: 1993. (International Bar Association Ser.). 370p. (C). 1994. lib. bdg. 113.00 (*1-85966-066-5*, Pub. by Graham & Trotman) Kluwer Academic.

Revell, William J., jt. auth. see Brookes, Murray.

Revelle. Environment:issues & Choices. 1981. pap. text 20.50 (*0-87150-758-7*) PWS Pubs.

ReVelle, Charles. Optimizing Reservoir Resources: A New Model for Reservoir Reliability. LC 98-38927. 200p. 1999. 69.95 (*0-471-18877-8*) Wiley.

Revelle, Charles S. The Global Environment: Securing a Sustainable Future. (Life Science Ser.). 496p. (C). 1992. 55.00 (*0-86720-321-8*) Jones & Bartlett.

ReVelle, Charles S. & McGarity, Arthur, eds. Civil & Environmental Engineering Systems: An Advanced Applications Text. LC 97-52. 752p. 1997. 110.00 (*0-471-12816-3*) Wiley.

ReVelle, Charles S., et al. Civil & Environmental Engineering Systems. LC 96-220. 507p. (C). 1996. 105.00 (*0-13-138678-6*) P-H.

ReVelle, Jack B., et al. The QFD Handbook. LC 97-6508. 432p. 1998. text 99.00 incl. disk (*0-471-17381-9*) Wiley.

Revelle, Penelope L., jt. auth. see Johnson.

Revelle, Roger, et al. Science with a Human Face: In Honor of Roger Randall Revelle. LC 97-20687. 1997. pap. 14.95 (*0-674-79483-4*) HUP.

Revelli, Clare. Color & You: A Guide to Determining Your Best Colors. rev. ed. (Illus.). 96p. 1994. reprint ed. pap. 7.99 (*0-9608092-3-6*) Revelli.

— Design & You: Your Guide to Decorating with Style. rev. ed. (Illus.). 96p. 1994. pap. 7.99 (*0-9608092-1-X*) Revelli.

— Style & You: Every Woman's Guide to Total Style. (Illus.). 96p. 1993. reprint ed. pap. 7.99 (*0-9608092-2-8*) Revelli.

Revelo, H., jt. auth. see Pennington, T. D.

***Revels, DeBorah Anne.** Reflections of the Soul, Pts. 1-7. (Illus.). 96p. 2000. pap. 20.00 (*0-9675909-0-6*) Rockettes.

***Revels, James C.** The Deepest of Red Wines: Poems from a Spiritual Journey. LC 00-130559. 100p. 2000. pap. 9.95 (*0-9676460-0-6*) White Swan FL.

Revelstroke, Simon & Corben, Richard. The Bodyssey. (Illus.). 64p. 1993. reprint ed. pap. 12.95 (*0-9623841-8-6*) Fantagor Pr.

Revelt, Janet G. Opening Doors: A Job Search Guide for Graduates. 1996. pap. 27.50 (*0-938609-04-1*) Graduate Group.

Revely, Edith. In Good Faith. LC 84-22677. 272p. 1985. 22.95 (*0-87951-992-4*, Pub. by Overlook Pr) Penguin Putnam.

Revenga, Ana, jt. ed. see Coricelli, Fabrizio.

Revenga, Carmen, et al. Watersheds of the World: Ecological Value & Vulnerability. 200p. 1998. pap. 30.00 (*1-56973-254-X*) World Resources Inst.

Revenga, Luis & Lopez-Vidriero, M. L., eds. Tesoros de Espana, Ten Centuries of Spanish Books. (ENG & SPA., Illus.). 440p. 1985. pap. 19.95 (*84-398-4960-5*) NY Pub Lib.

***Revenscroft, Helena.** Black Lace Stand & Deliver. (Black Lace Ser.). 1999. pap. 9.99 (*0-352-33340-5*) Virgin Bks.

Revenson, Tracey A., jt. auth. see Singer, Dorothy G.

Revenstein, E. G., ed. Journal of the First Voyage of Vasco De Gama. (C). 1995. 44.00 (*81-206-1136-5*, Pub. by Asian Educ Servs) S Asia.

Reventlow, Henning G., ed. Eschatology in the Bible & in Jewish & Christian Tradition. (JSOTS Ser.: Vol. 243). 272p. 1997. 75.00 (*1-85075-664-3*, Pub. by Sheffield Acad) CUP Services.

Reventlow, Henning G. & Farmer, William, eds. Biblical Studies & the Shifting of Paradigms, 1850-1914. (JSOT Supplement Ser.: Vol. 192). 297p. 1995. 85.00 (*1-85075-532-9*, Pub. by Sheffield Acad) CUP Services.

Reventlow, Henning G., jt. ed. see Uffenheimer, Benjamin.

Revenue Canada Staff, ed. NAFTA Customs Procedures Manual. 2nd ed. LC 95-705441. 1995. ring bd. 69.95 (*0-660-16268-7*, Pub. by Canadian Govt Pub) Accents Pubns.

Reverand, Cedric D., II. Dryden's Final Poetic Mode: The Fables. LC 88-10768. 254p. (C). 1988. text 37.50 (*0-8122-8121-7*) U of Pa Pr.

Reverby, Susan M. Ordered to Care: The Dilemma of American Nursing, 1850-1945. (Cambridge History of Medicine Ser.). (Illus.). 320p. 1987. pap. text 19.95 (*0-521-33565-5*) Cambridge U Pr.

***Reverby, Susan M., ed.** Tuskegee's Truths: Rethinking the Tuskegee Syphilis Study. LC 99-56379. (Studies in Social Medicine). (Illus.). 608p. 2000. pap. 27.50 (*0-8078-4852-2*); lib. bdg. 69.95 (*0-8078-2539-5*) U of NC Pr.

Reverby, Susan M., jt. ed. see Helly, Dorothy O.

Reverchon, Alain & Ducamp, Marc. Mathematical Software Tools in C++ LC 93-13741. 520p. 1993. pap. 90.00 (*0-471-93792-4*) Wiley.

Reverdot, Jean-Philipe, photos by. The Proof: Photographs by Jean-Philipe Reverdot. (Illus.). 60p. 1998. 45.00 (*1-899235-50-7*, 811032, Pub. by Dewi Lewis) Dist Art Pubs.

Reverdy, Pierre. Cette Emotion Appelee Poesie: Ecrits sur la Poesie. (FRE.). 288p. 1989. pap. 29.95 (*0-7859-1599-0*, 208060659X) Fr & Eur.

— Ferraille & Plein Verre, le Chant des Morts, Bois Verts, Pierres Blanches. (FRE.). 1981. pap. 10.95 (*0-8288-3869-0*, F105190) Fr & Eur.

— Ferraille & Plein Verre, le Chant, des Morts, Buis Verts, Pierres Blanches. (Poesie Ser.). (FRE.). 256p. 1981. pap. 9.95 (*2-07-032207-6*) Schoenhof.

— Flacques de Verre. (FRE.). 1984. pap. 10.95 (*0-7859-2984-3*) Fr & Eur.

— Lettres a Jean Rousselot (1949-1954) Avec: Rousselot, Jean. Pierre Reverdy Romancier, ou quand le Poete Se Dedouble. Rousselot, Jean, ed. 87p. 1973. 9.95 (*0-686-54722-5*) Fr & Eur.

— Le Livre de Mon Bord, Notes (1930-1936) (FRE.). 272p. 1989. pap. 18.95 (*0-686-54724-1*, 271521572X) Fr & Eur.

— Main-d'oeuvre: Poemes, 1913-1949. (FRE.). 548p. 1989. pap. 49.95 (*0-7859-1542-7*, 2715215819) Fr & Eur.

— Note Eternelle du Present: Ecrits sur l'Art (1923-1960) 288p. 16.95 (*0-686-54726-8*) Fr & Eur.

— La Plupart du Temps, Vol. 1. (FRE.). 1970. pap. 10.95 (*0-8288-3870-4*, F121000) Fr & Eur.

— La Plupart du Temps, Vol. 2. (FRE.). 1989. pap. 10.95 (*0-8288-3871-2*, F121001) Fr & Eur.

— Plupart du Temps, 1915-1922. (Poesie Ser.). pap. 18.95 (*2-07-032532-6*) Schoenhof.

— Selected Poems. Bent, Timothy, ed. Ashbery, John et al, trs. from FRE. LC 90-72092. (French Poetry in Translation Ser.). 179p. 1991. 18.95 (*0-916390-47-0*) Wake Forest.

— Selected Poems. Bree, Germaine, ed. Ashbery, John et al, trs. from FRE. LC 90-72092. (French Poetry in Translation Ser.). 179p. 1991. pap. 12.95 (*0-916390-46-2*) Wake Forest.

— Selected Poems. limited rev. ed. 25.00 (*0-8112-0512-6*, Pub. by New Directions) Norton.

— Sources du Vent: Avec: La Balle au Bond. (FRE.). 256p. 1971. pap. 10.95 (*0-7859-1355-6*, 2070317919) Fr & Eur.

— Sources du Vent - Balle au Bond. (FRE.). 1971. pap. 10.95 (*0-8288-3872-0*, F121020) Fr & Eur.

— Sources du Vent - La Balle au Bond. (Poesie Ser.). (FRE.). 256p. 1971. pap. 9.95 (*2-07-031791-9*) Schoenhof.

— Le Voleur de Talan. 181p. 1967. 8.95 (*0-686-54733-0*) Fr & Eur.

***Revere, Alan.** Art of Jewelry Making: Classic & Original Designs. LC 99-35806. 144p. 1999. 24.95 (*0-8069-2070-X*) Sterling.

Revere, Alan. Professional Goldsmithing: A Contemporary Guide to Traditional Jewelry Techniques. LC 90-35140. 1991. text 62.95 (*0-442-23898-3*) Chapman & Hall.

— Professional Goldsmithing: A Contemporary Guide to Traditional Jewelry Techniques. 4th ed. (Illus.). 240p. Date not set. reprint ed. 69.95 (*0-9651049-0-7*, Revere Acad) RAJA.

— Ring Repair, 6 vols. (Professional Jewelry Repair Ser.). (Illus.). 124p. 1999. pap. 44.95 (*0-9651049-1-5*, Revere Acad) RAJA.

Revere, Elizabeth. Cricket Moon: New & Selected Poems. LC 92-5472. (Illus.). 80p. 1992. pap. 7.95 (*0-918606-09-8*) Heidelberg Graph.

— Windows of Snow: Collected Poems by Elizabeth Revere. LC 85-8722. 78p. 1985. pap. 5.95 (*0-918606-08-X*) Heidelberg Graph.

Revere, Glenn. All about Carpets: A Consumer Guide. (Illus.). 160p. 1988. 15.95 (*0-8306-0646-7*, 2646); pap. 9.95 (*0-8306-0446-4*, 2646) McGraw-Hill Prof.

Revere, John, tr. see Magendie, Francois.

Revere, Lawrence. Playing Blackjack As a Business. (Illus.). 192p. 1995. pap. 15.95 (*0-8184-0064-1*, Citadel Pr) Carol Pub Group.

— Playing Blackjack As a Business. 192p. 1999. reprint ed. 27.95 (*0-7351-0090-X*) Replica Bks.

Revere, Michael R. Fire & Rain: Poems. LC 97-42306. 96p. 1997. pap. 12.50 (*1-887905-08-1*) Pkway Pubs.

Revere, Paul Memorial Association Staff. Paul Revere, Artisan, Businessman, & Patriot: The Man Behind the Myth. (Artisans & the Arts Ser.). (Illus.). 192p. 1988. pap. text 6.00 (*0-9619999-1-8*); lib. bdg. 25.00 (*0-9619999-0-X*) Paul Revere Mem Assn.

Reverman, Ardys. All about the Whole You: The Riddle of Me at the Heart-Wood Tree, Vol. 4. (Friendly Universe Collection). (Illus.). 196p. 1998. pap. 9.95 incl. audio (*0-9625385-5-8*) Friendly Univ Pr.

— All about You Vol. 1: In the Creative Circle. large type ed. LC 92-90748. (Friendly Universe Collection). (Illus.). 150p. (J). (gr. 6). 1993. pap. 14.95 incl. VHS (*0-9625385-3-1*, 5000) Friendly Univ Pr.

— All about You Vol. 2: Teamwork Is Child's Play. large type ed. LC 92-91277. (Friendly Universe Collection). (Illus.). 1995. 14.95 incl. VHS (*0-9625385-2-3*) Friendly Univ Pr.

— Team Smart SQ: Redefining What It Means to Be Smart. LC 98-60225. (Friendly Universe Collection: No. 3). (Illus.). 196p. 2001. pap. 14.95 (*0-9625385-1-5*) Friendly Univ Pr.

Reverte, Arturo P. La Table de Flandes (The Chess Master) 424p. 1995. pap. 16.95 (*0-679-76090-3*) Vin Bks.

Reves, Cynthia, et al, eds. Linguistics & Language Teaching: Proceedings of the 6th Joint LSH-HATESL Conference. (Technical Report Ser.: No. 10). 368p. 1996. pap. text 20.00 (*0-8248-1851-2*) Sec Lang Tching.

Reves, J. G. Cardiothoracic Anesthesia, Vol. 8. LC 98-35854. (Atlas of Anesthesia Ser.). 1998. text 135.00 (*0-443-07974-9*) Church.

Revest, P. & Longstaff, A. Molecular Neuroscience. LC 98-17627. (Illus.). 240p. 1997. pap. 34.95 (*0-387-91519-2*) Spr-Verlag.

Revest, Patricia, jt. ed. see Longstaff, Alan.

R

Revesz, Akos G., jt. ed. see Walrafen, George E.

Revesz, Gabor, jt. auth. see Ehrlich, Eva.

Revesz, Geza. Introduction to the Psychology of Music. De Courcy, G., tr. from GER. LC 54-5937. (Illus.). 288p. reprint ed. pap. 89.30 (*0-608-18561-2*, 201099900073) Bks Demand.

— Psychology of a Musical Prodigy. LC 70-114890. (Select Bibliographies Reprint Ser.). 1977. 19.95 (*0-8369-5294-4*) Ayer.

— Psychology of a Musical Prodigy. LC 78-100832. 180p. 1970. reprint ed. lib. bdg. 49.75 (*0-8371-4004-8*, REMP, Greenwood Pr) Greenwood.

— The Psychology of a Musical Prodigy. LC 77-173178. (Illus.). 1972. reprint ed. 20.95 (*0-405-08879-5*) Ayer.

— The Psychology of a Musical Prodigy. 180p. 1990. reprint ed. lib. bdg. 59.00 (*0-7812-9002-3*) Rprt Serv.

Revesz, Gyorgy E. Introduction to Formal Languages. 199p. 1991. pap. 7.95 (*0-486-66697-2*) Dover.

Revesz, P. Random Walk in Random & Non-Random Environments. 348p. (C). 1990. text 48.00 (*981-02-0237-7*) World Scientific Pub.

Revesz, P., et al, eds. First Pannonian Symposium on Mathematical Statistics: Proceedings. (Lecture Notes in Statistics Ser.: Vol. 8). 308p. 1981. 72.95 (*0-387-90583-9*) Spr-Verlag.

Revesz, Pal. Random Walks of Infinitely Many Particles. 220p. 1994. text 58.00 (*981-02-1784-6*) World Scientific Pub.

Revesz, Peter. Constraint Databases. 1999. 49.95 (*0-387-98729-0*) Spr-Verlag.

Revesz, Richard L. Foundations of Environmental Law & Policy. (Interdisciplinary Readers in Law Ser.). (Illus.). 352p. (C). 1996. text 57.00 (*0-19-509151-5*); pap. text 26.95 (*0-19-509152-3*) OUP.

***Revesz, Richard L., et al, eds.** Environmental Law, the Economy & Substainable Development: The United States, the European Union & the International Community. LC 99-47718. 336p. (C). 2000. text. write for info. (*0-521-64270-1*) Cambridge U Pr.

Revesz, Richard L. & Stewart, Richard B., eds. Analyzing Superfund: Economics, Science, & Law. 263p. 1995. text 50.00 (*0-915707-75-6*) Resources Future.

Revesz, Tamas. New York. 14.95 (*0-393-05023-8*) Norton.

Revett, Nicholas, jt. auth. see Stuart, James.

Revette, Debbie, jt. auth. see Mansfield, Richard.

Reveyoso, Jean-Paul, jt. auth. see Hutton, John P.

Revhaug, A. Acute Catabolic State. 320p. 1996. 134.00 (*3-540-58445-5*) Spr-Verlag.

Revhaug, A., ed. Acute Catabolic State. LC 95-10442. (Update Intensive Care & Emergency Medicine Ser.: Vol. 21). 1995. write for info. (*0-387-58445-5*) Spr-Verlag.

***Revi, Albert C.** American Cut & Engraved Glass. LC 00-8505. (Illus.). 2000. write for info. (*0-7643-1005-4*) Schiffer.

Revi, Aromar. Shelter in India. 1990. text 27.95 (*0-7069-4937-4*, Pub. by Vikas) S Asia.

Revich, S. J. The Camel Boy. (Tales from the East Ser.). (Illus.). 158p. (J). (gr. 5-8). 1987. 11.95 (*0-935063-44-7*); pap. 9.95 (*0-935063-45-5*) CIS Comm.

— Ezra the Physician. (Tales from the East Ser.). (Illus.). 126p. (J). (gr. 5-7). 1988. 12.95 (*0-935063-63-3*); pap. 9.95 (*0-935063-64-1*) CIS Comm.

— Ibrahim the Magician. (Tales from the East Ser.). (Illus.). 126p. (J). (gr. 4-7). 1987. 12.95 (*0-935063-33-1*); pap. 9.95 (*0-935063-34-X*) CIS Comm.

— The Lion Tamer. 140p. (J). (ps-8). 1990. 12.95 (*1-56062-038-2*); pap. 9.95 (*1-56062-054-4*) CIS Comm.

— The Poet & the Thief. (Tales from the East Ser.). (Illus.). 158p. (J). (gr. 5-7). 1989. 13.95 (*0-935063-71-4*); pap. 10.95 (*0-935063-72-2*) CIS Comm.

— The Prince & the Scholar. LC 92-70596. 128p. 1992. 12.95 (*1-56062-111-7*); pap. 9.95 (*1-56062-112-5*) CIS Comm.

Reviczky, Adam. Wars Lost Battles Won: Lost Wars. 384p. 1993. text 59.50 (*0-88033-246-8*, 349, Pub. by East Eur Monographs) Col U Pr.

Reviczky, Bela. It's a Long Way to Tipperary. 64p. 1999. pap. 21.00 (*963-13-3582-8*, Pub. by Corvina Bks) St Mut.

Revie. Uhlig's Corrosion Handbook. 2nd ed. LC 99-30123. 1302p. 2000. 195.00 (*0-471-15777-5*) Wiley.

Revie, R. W., et al, eds. Materials Performance Maintenance: Proceedings of the International Symposium on Materials Performance Maintenance, Ottawa, Ontario, Canada, August 18-21, 1991. (Proceedings of Metallurgical Society of the Canadian Institute of Mining & Metallurgy Ser.: No. 25). (Illus.). 360p. 1991. 137.25 (*0-08-041441-9*, Pergamon Pr) Elsevier.

Revie, R. Winston, jt. auth. see Uhlig, Herbert H.

Revien, Leon. When Every Moment Counts, Count on Provision. 16p. 1987. pap. text 4.95 (*0-940429-02-0*) M B Glass Assocs.

Reviere, Rebecca, et al, eds. Needs Assessment: A Creative & Practical Guide for Social Scientists. LC 96-21821. 233p. 1996. 59.95 (*1-56032-375-2*); pap. 29.95 (*1-56032-376-0*) Taylor & Francis.

Reviere, Susan L. Memory of Childhood Trauma: A Clinician's Guide to the Literature. LC 96-10813. 178p. 1996. pap. text 21.00 (*1-57230-110-4*, 0104); lib. bdg. 36.95 (*1-57230-109-0*) Guilford Pubns.

Review & Herald Publishing Editors. He Is Our Song. 1988. 9.99 (*0-8280-0440-4*) Review & Herald.

— My Prayer Notebook. 1995. ring bd. 17.99 (*0-8280-0776-4*) Review & Herald.

— Sing for Joy. 1998. pap. 9.99 (*0-8280-0471-4*) Review & Herald.

Review for Religious Staff, ed. Index: Topical & Author. 320p. (Orig.). (C). 1995. pap. text 20.00 (*0-924768-04-5*) Review Relig.

***Review Noire Magazine Staff.** African Cities. (Revue Noire Magazine Ser.). 1999. 22.00 (*2-909571-42-4*) Revue Noire.

Review of Personality & Social Psychology Staff. Review of Personality & Social Psychology, 5 vols., 2. Wheeler, Ladd, ed. LC 80-649712. 295p. pap. 91.50 (*0-8357-8404-5*, 203467700002) Bks Demand.

— Review of Personality & Social Psychology, 5 vols., 3. Wheeler, Ladd, ed. LC 80-649712. 287p. pap. 89.00 (*0-8357-8405-3*, 203467700003) Bks Demand.

— Review of Personality & Social Psychology, 5 vols., 4. Wheeler, Ladd, ed. LC 80-649712. 328p. pap. 101.70 (*0-8357-8406-1*, 203467700004) Bks Demand.

— Review of Personality & Social Psychology, 5 vols., 5. Wheeler, Ladd, ed. LC 80-649712. 312p. pap. 96.80 (*0-8357-8407-X*, 203467700005) Bks Demand.

— Review of Personality & Social Psychology, 5 vols., Vol. 1. Wheeler, Ladd, ed. LC 80-649712. 352p. pap. 109.20 (*0-8357-8403-7*, 203467700001) Bks Demand.

Review of Politics Staff. Image of Man. Fitzsimons, M. A. et al, eds. LC 72-156710. (Essay Index Reprint Ser.). 1977. reprint ed. 30.95 (*0-8369-2369-3*) Ayer.

Review of Research in Education Staff. Review of Research in Education, Vol. 3. Kerlinger, Fred N., ed. LC 72-89719. (Illus.). 311p. reprint ed. pap. 96.50 (*0-608-06232-4*, 206656100003) Bks Demand.

— Review of Research in Education, Vol. 5. Shulman, Lee S. & Mowry, Susan, eds. LC 72-89719. (Illus.). 407p. reprint ed. pap. 126.20 (*0-608-06233-2*, 206656200005) Bks Demand.

— Review of Research in Education, Vol. 6. Shulman, Lee S., ed. LC 72-89719. (Illus.). 411p. reprint ed. pap. 127.50 (*0-608-06234-0*, 206656300006) Bks Demand.

— Review of Research in Education, Vol. 7. Berliner, David C., ed. LC 72-89719. 461p. reprint ed. pap. 143.00 (*0-608-06235-9*, 206656400007) Bks Demand.

— Review of Research in Education, Vol. 9. Berliner, David C., ed. LC 72-89719. 455p. reprint ed. pap. 141.10 (*0-608-06236-7*, 206656500009) Bks Demand.

— Review of Research in Education, Vol. 10. Gordon, Edmund W., ed. LC 72-89719. 428p. reprint ed. pap. 132.70 (*0-608-06237-5*, 206656600010) Bks Demand.

— Review of Research in Education, Vol. 13. Rothkopf, Ernst Z., ed. LC 72-89719. 410p. reprint ed. pap. 127.10 (*0-608-06238-3*, 206656700013) Bks Demand.

— Review of Research in Education, Vol. 15. Rothkopf, Ernst Z., ed. LC 72-89719. 487p. reprint ed. pap. 151.00 (*0-608-06239-1*, 206656800015) Bks Demand.

— Review of Research in Education, Vol. 16. Cazden, Courtney B., ed. LC 72-89719. 431p. reprint ed. pap. 133.70 (*0-608-06240-5*, 206656900016) Bks Demand.

— Review of Research in Education, Vol. 17. Grant, Gerald, ed. LC 72-89719. 498p. reprint ed. pap. 154.40 (*0-608-06241-3*, 206657000017) Bks Demand.

Review Publications, Inc. Staff. Virginia Review Directory of State & Local Government Officials. annuals 13th ed. Taylor-White, Alyson, ed. (Illus.). 400p. 1998. ring bd. 39.95 (*1-883263-08-5*) Review Pubns.

Review Pubns., Inc. Staff. Virginia Review Directory of State & Local Government Officials. annuals Taylor-White, Alyson L., ed. (Illus.). 400p. 1997. ring bd. write for info. (*1-883263-06-9*) Review Pubns.

Revilio, Bill. Namibia. Globetrotter Staff, ed. (Globe Trotter Travel Guides Ser.). (Illus.). 128p. 1996. pap. 30.00 (*1-85368-364-7*, Pub. by New5 Holland) Globe Pequot.

Revill, David. The Roaring Silence: A Biography of John Cage. (Illus.). 272p. 1992. 27.45 (*1-55970-166-8*, Pub. by Arcade Pub Inc) Time Warner.

— The Roaring Silence: John Cage: A Life. 384p. 1993. pap. 14.45 (*1-55970-220-6*, Pub. by Arcade Pub Inc) Time Warner.

Revill, Janie. A Compilation of the Original Lists of Protestant Immigrants to South Carolina, 1763-1773. LC 68-25937. 161p. 1999. reprint ed. pap. 17.50 (*0-8063-0599-1*, 4870, Pub. by Clearfield Co) ACCESS Pubs Network.

— Edgefield County, South Carolina, Records. 246p. 1984. 30.00 (*0-89308-531-6*) Southern Hist Pr.

— Some South Carolina Genealogical Records. 456p. 1985. 35.00 (*0-89308-539-1*) Southern Hist Pr.

Revilla, jt. auth. see Paya.

Revilla, Federico. Diccionario de Iconografia. (SPA.). 408p. 1990. pap. 32.95 (*0-7859-6001-5*, 8437609291) Fr & Eur.

Revilla, Linda A., et al, eds. Bearing Dreams, Shaping Visions: Asian Pacific American Perspectives. LC 93-1862. (Association for Asian American Studies). 298p. 1993. pap. 30.00 (*0-87422-099-8*) Wash St U Pr.

Revillard, J. P., jt. ed. see Brown, F.

Reville, Albert D. Lectures on the Origin & Growth of Religion As Illustrated by the Native Religions of Mexico & Peru. LC 77-27167. (Hibbert Lectures: 1884). 45.00 (*0-614-07017-1*) AMS Pr.

— Lectures on the Origin & Growth of Religion As Illustrated by the Native Religions of Mexico & Peru. 1977. lib. bdg. 59.95 (*0-8490-2140-5*) Gordon Pr.

Reville, Albert D. & Wicksteed, Philip H. The Native Religions of Mexico & Peru: Hibbert Lectures. LC 77-27167. 224p. (C). 1983. reprint ed. 45.00 (*0-404-60405-6*) AMS Pr.

Reville, John C., jt. auth. see St. Francis De Sales.

Reville, Julie D. The Many Voices of Paws: A Workbook for Young Stutterers. (Illus.). 64p. (J). (ps-3). 1989. 18.95 (*0-937857-11-4*, 1568) Speech Bin.

Reville, Nicholas. Broadcasting: The New Law. 1991. pap. 33.00 (*0-406-00137-5*, UK, MICHIE) LEXIS Pub.

Revillout, Eugene & Eisenlohr. Corpus Papyrorum Aegypti, 3 vols. in 1. xii, 67p. 1978. reprint ed. write for info. incl. 3.5 hd (*3-487-06440-5*) G Olms Pubs.

Revis, Johan. Encounters with M. 210p. (Orig.). 1992. pap. 9.95 (*0-9629956-0-6*) Destel-Bergen.

Revitch, Eugene & Schlesinger, Louis B. Sex Murder & Sex Aggression: Phenomenology, Psychopathology, Psychodynamics & Prognosis. (Illus.). 152p. 1989. pap. 28.95 (*0-398-06346-X*) C C Thomas.

— Sex Murder & Sex Aggression: Phenomenology, Psychopathology, Psychodynamics & Prognosis. (Illus.). 152p. (C). 1989. text 41.95 (*0-398-05556-4*) C C Thomas.

Revitch, Eugene, jt. ed. see Schlesinger, Louis B.

Reviv, Hanoch. The Elders in Ancient Israel: A Study of a Biblical Institution. 222p. 1989. text 18.00 (*965-223-901-1*, Pub. by Magnes Pr) Eisenbrauns.

Revkin, Andrew C. Death in the Rain Forest. 1990. write for info. (*0-318-65605-1*) HM.

— Global Warming: Understanding the Forecast. (Illus.). 180p. 1992. 9.98 (*1-55859-310-1*) Abbeville Pr.

Revland, Catherine, jt. auth. see Garey, Carol C.

Revna, S. P. & Downs, R. E., eds. Deadly Developments: Capitalism, States & War. 292p. 1999. text 32.00 (*90-5699-589-8*); pap. text 25.00 (*90-5699-590-1*) Gordon & Breach.

Revoir, Trudie W. & Pipe, John H. Legends & Traditions of Christmas: Devotional Ideas for Family & Group Use During Advent & Christmas. LC 98-36794. (Illus.). 96p. 1998. pap. 12.00 (*0-8170-1286-9*) Judson.

Revoir, William H. Respiratory Protection Handbook. LC 96-47080. 464p. 1997. lib. bdg. 75.00 (*0-87371-281-1*, L281) Lewis Pubs.

Revolutionary Communist Party, U. S. A. Staff. The Chicano Struggle & the Struggle for Socialism. 2nd ed. (Illus.). 1979. pap. 1.50 (*0-89851-003-1*) RCP Pubns.

— Cuba: The Evaporation of a Myth, from Anti-Imperialist Revolution to a Pawn of Social-Imperialism. 2nd ed. 1983. pap. 1.50 (*0-89851-008-2*) RCP Pubns.

Revolutionary Communist Party, U S A. Staff. New Programme & New Constitution of the Revolutionary Communist Party, U. S. A. 128p. (Orig.). (C). 1981. pap. 3.00 (*0-89851-037-6*) RCP Pubns.

Revolutionary Communist Party, U. S. A. Staff. Revolution & Counter-Revolution: The Revisionist Coup in China & the Struggle in the Revolutionary Communist Party, U. S. A. 1978. pap. 4.95 (*0-89851-016-3*) RCP Pubns.

Revonsuo, Antti & Kamppinen, Matti, eds. Consciousness in Philosophy & Cognitive Neuroscience. 312p. 1994. text 59.95 (*0-8058-1509-0*) L Erlbaum Assocs.

Revonsuo, Antti, jt. ed. see Rossetti, Yves.

Revoyr, Jack. The New Complete "How to" Guide to Collegiate Licensing. 139p. (Orig.). 1990. pap. 34.95 (*0-9627106-0-1*) Kent Communs.

— A Primer on Licensing. 2nd ed. 264p. 1996. 37.95 (*0-9627106-4-4*); pap. 15.95 (*0-9627106-5-2*) Kent Communs.

Revoyr, Nina. The Necessary Hunger. LC 96-32999. 368p. (YA). 1997. 22.50 (*0-684-83234-8*) S&S Trade.

— The Necessary Hunger. LC 97-50577. 1998. pap. 13.95 (*0-312-18142-6*) St Martin.

Revsbech, N. P. & Sorensen, J. Denitrification in Soil & Sediment. LC 91-7400. (FEMS Symposium Ser.: No. 56). (Illus.). 358p. (C). 1990. text 110.00 (*0-306-43721-X*, Kluwer Plenum) Kluwer Academic.

***Revsin, Leslie.** Fast & Fabulous: Food You Can Make in an Hour That Tastes Like It Took All Day. LC 00-37946. (Illus.). 2001. pap. write for info. (*0-7679-0608-X*) Broadway BDD.

Revsin, Leslie. Great Fish, Quick: Delicious Dinners from Fillets & Shellfish. LC 97-3067. (Illus.). 320p. 1997. 27.50 (*0-385-48538-7*) Doubleday.

Revsine. Financial Reporting & Analysis. 1998. pap. text, student ed. 21.60 (*0-13-921941-2*) P-H.

Revsine, Lawrence, et al. Financial Reporting & Analysis. LC 97-39357. 998p. (C). 1998. 105.00 (*0-13-768623-4*) P-H.

Revters, contrib. by. EMU Explained: A Guide to Markets & Monetary Union. 2nd ed. LC 98-201570. 242p. 1998. pap. 30.00 (*0-7494-2654-3*) Kogan Page Ltd.

Revue Fiduciaire Staff. Dictionnaire Fiduciaire Paye 1998. (FRE.). 1998. 125.00 (*0-320-00243-8*) Fr & Eur.

— Dictionnaire Social, 1992. (FRE.). 1992. 85.00 (*0-7859-8141-1*, 2-86521-191-6) Fr & Eur.

Revue Musicale Staff. Wagner et la France. LC 77-4006. (Music Reprint Ser.: 1977). (Illus.). 1977. reprint ed. lib. bdg. 32.50 (*0-306-70889-2*) Da Capo.

***Revue Noire Editions Staff.** Anthology of African Photography. (Illus.). 432p. 1999. 85.00 (*2-909571-30-0*, Pub. by Revue Noire) Dist Art Pubs.

Revue Noire Editions Staff. Namibia: Photographies. (Illus.). 1996. pap. text 19.95 (*2-909571-12-2*, Pub. by Revue Noire) Dist Art Pubs.

***Revue Noire Editors, ed.** Suites Marocaines: La Jeune Creation au Maroc. (SPA.). 2000. pap. 18.00 (*2-909571-50-5*) Revue Noire.

***Revue Noire Magazine Editors.** Nigeria. (Revue Noire Magazine Ser.: 30). (Illus.). 1999. pap. 22.00 (*2-909571-41-6*) Revue Noire.

***Revue Noire Magazine Staff.** Revue Noire Magazine: Sensualite & Spiritualite, Vol. 35. (Illus.). 96p. (Orig.). 2000. pap. 22.00 (*2-909571-47-5*) Dist Art Pubs.

Revuelta, Gutierrez, tr. see Brown, Steven F., ed.

Revutsky, Valerian & Zinkewych, Osyp, eds. Les Kurbas: Collection of Works on Theatre, Essays by His Contemporaries, Documents (in Ukrainian) LC 89-62916. 1040p. 1989. 45.50 (*0-914834-59-2*) Smoloskyp.

***Revuz, D. & Yor, M.** Continuous Martingales & Brownian Motion. 3rd ed. LC 98-53189. (Grundlehren der Mathematischen Wissenschaften Ser.: Vol. 293). xiii, 602 p. 1999. 119.00 (*3-540-64325-7*) Spr-Verlag.

Revuz, Daniel. Markov Chains. rev. ed. (Mathematical Library: Vol. 11). 374p. 1984. 149.50 (*0-444-86400-8*, I-548-83, North Holland) Elsevier.

Revuz, Daniel & Yor, M. Continuous Martingales & Brownian Motion. (Grundlehren der Mathematischen Wissenschaften Ser.). (Illus.). 576p. 1990. 98.00 (*0-387-52167-4*) Spr-Verlag.

Revuz, Daniel & Yor, Marc. Continuous Martingales & Brownian Motion. LC 94-15097. (Grundlehren der Mathematischen Wissenschaften Ser.: Vol. 293). 1995. 141.95 (*0-387-57622-3*) Spr-Verlag.

Revzan, David A. Wholesaling in Marketing Organization. Assael, Henry, ed. LC 78-256. (Century of Marketing Ser.). 1979. reprint ed. lib. bdg. 58.95 (*0-405-11181-9*) Ayer.

Revzen, M., jt. ed. see Mann, A.

Revzin, Arnold, ed. Biology of Non-Specific DNA Protein Interaction. 272p. 1990. lib. bdg. 195.00 (*0-8493-6177-X*, QP624) CRC Pr.

— Footprinting of Nucleic Acid-Protein Complexes. (Separation, Detection, & Characterization of Biological Macromolecules Ser.). (Illus.). 193p. 1993. pap. 45.00 (*0-12-586500-7*) Acad Pr.

Rew, Alan, jt. auth. see Campbell, John R.

Rew, Lois J. God's Green Liniment. LC 81-84183. (Illus.). 204p. (Orig.). (J). (gr. 3-8). 1981. pap. 8.99 (*0-938462-02-4*) Green Leaf CA.

— Introduction to Technical Writing. 2nd ed. 1993. pap. text, teacher ed. 5.00 (*0-312-08069-7*) St Martin.

— Introduction to Technical Writing: Process & Practice. 2nd ed. LC 92-50047. (Illus.). 631p. (Orig.). (C). 1993. pap. text 60.95 (*0-312-06781-X*) St Martin.

— Trends & Issues in Professional Nursing. (Nursing Education Ser.). (C). 1998. 31.95 (*0-8273-7879-3*) Delmar.

Rew, Lynn. Awareness in Healing. (Nurse as Healer Ser.). 216p. 1995. pap. 31.95 (*0-8273-6397-4*) Delmar.

Rew, Robert S., jt. ed. see Campbell, William C.

***Rew, Terry.** Feng Shui Today. (Illus.). 176p. 2000. pap. write for info. (*0-8230-6638-X*) Watsn-Guptill.

***Rewa.** Molly May on the High Seas. LC 99-50916. (Illus.). 96p. (J). (gr. 2-5). 2000. pap. 9.95 (*1-56474-340-3*) Fithian Pr.

Rewald, Enrique. Immune Crossover: The Two Faces of Immunity: An Approach to the Dangers of Plague. (Illus.). 134p. 1998. 25.00 (*1-85070-018-4*) Prthnon Pub.

Rewald, John. Aristide Maillol: 1861-1944. LC 75-42576. (Illus.). 140p. 1975. pap. 9.95 (*0-89207-000-5*) S R Guggenheim.

— Cezanne: A Biography. (Illus.). 288p. 1996. 75.00 (*0-8109-0775-5*, Pub. by Abrams) Time Warner.

— Cezanne & America: Dealers, Collectors, Artists & Critics, 1891-1921. LC 88-22578. (Bollingen Ser.: Vol. 28). (Illus.). 352p. reprint ed. pap. 109.20 (*0-608-09110-3*, 206974200005) Bks Demand.

— Cezanne (Paul) the Watercolors: A Catalogue Raisonne. (Illus.). 486p. 1984. boxed set 200.00 (*1-55660-167-0*) A Wofsy Fine Arts.

— Degas's Complete Sculpture: A Catalogue Raisonne. rev. ed. (Illus.). 216p. 1990. 125.00 (*1-55660-045-3*) A Wofsy Fine Arts.

— Pissarro. (Masters of Art Ser.). (Illus.). 128p. 1989. 24.95 (*0-8109-1499-9*, Pub. by Abrams) Time Warner.

— Seurat: A Biography. (Illus.). 240p. 1990. 75.00 (*0-8109-3814-6*) Abrams.

— Seurat: A Biography. (Illus.). 240p. 1992. pap. 34.98 (*0-8109-8124-6*, Pub. by Abrams) Time Warner.

— Studies in Impressionism. Gordon, Irene & Weitzenhoffer, Frances, eds. (Illus.). 232p. 1986. 39.95 (*0-8109-1617-7*, Pub. by Abrams) Time Warner.

— Studies in Post-Impressionism. (Illus.). 296p. 1986. 39.95 (*0-8109-1632-0*, Pub. by Abrams) Time Warner.

Rewald, John, ed. Cezanne Letters. 5th rev. ed. LC 81-81716. (Illus.). 400p. 1985. lib. bdg. 50.00 (*0-87817-276-9*) Hacker.

Rewald, John & Near, Pinkney L. French Paintings: The Collection of Mr. & Mrs Paul Mellon in the Virginia Museum of Fine Arts. Cruger, George A., ed. LC 85-21707. (Illus.). 156p. 1985. 29.95 (*0-917046-20-X*); pap. 19.95 (*0-917046-19-6*) Va Mus Arts.

Rewald, John, et al. The Paintings of Paul Cezanne: A Catalogue Raisonne, 2 vols. LC 96-10853. (Illus.). 880p. 1996. boxed set 400.00 (*0-8109-4044-2*, Pub. by Abrams) Time Warner.

Rewald, John, ed. see Cezanne, Paul.

Rewald, John, ed. see Pissarro, Camille.

Rewald, Sabine. Paul Klee: The Berggruen Klee Collection in the Metropolitan Museum of Art. (Illus.). 320p. 1988. pap. 45.00 (*0-87099-513-8*, 0-8109-2447-1) Abrams.

Rewald, Sabine, jt. auth. see Lieberman, William S.

***Rewers, Ewa.** Language & Space: The Poststructuralist Turn in the Philosophy of Culture. (Literary & Cultural Theory Ser.). 169p. 1999. pap. 35.95 (*3-631-34444-9*) P Lang Pubng.

— Language & Space: The Poststructuralist Turn in the Philosophy of Culture. LC 99-46407. (Literary & Cultural Theory Ser.). 169p. (C). 1999. pap. 35.95 (*0-8204-4304-2*) P Lang Pubng.

Rewes, Ralph. El Diario de un Cubanito. LC 87-82650. (Coleccion Caniqui). (SPA.). 180p. (Orig.). 1988. pap. 9.95 (*0-89729-464-5*) Ediciones.

Rewolinski, Leah. Space Fido Frontier, Vol. 1. (Star Wreck Ser.: No. 07). 1994. mass mkt. 4.50 (*0-312-95362-3*) St Martin.

— Star Wreck the Generation Gap. 1992. mass mkt. 3.99 (*0-312-92802-5*) St Martin.

Rewt, Pauline, jt. ed. see Edwards, Paul.

Rex. Society of Ethnic Conflict. Date not set. text. write for info. (*1-85043-906-0*) I B T.

***Rex, Andrew F.** Integrated Physics & Calculus. LC 99-35366. 592p. (C). 1999. pap. text 45.00 (*0-201-47396-8*) Addison-Wesley.

An Asterisk (*) at the beginning of an entry indicates that the title is appearing for the first time.

Rex, Andrew F. & Jackson, Martin. Integrated Physics & Calculus, Vol. 2. 955p. (C). 2000. pap. 45.00 (*0-201-47397-6*) Benjamin-Cummings.

Rex, Andrew F., jt. auth. see Thornton, Stephen T.

Rex, David & Roberts, Thomas, eds. Recording the Performance of U. S. Undergraduates at British Institutions: Guidelines Toward Standardized Reporting for Study Abroad. 9p. 1988. 12.00 (*0-912207-22-1*) NAFSA Washington.

Rex, Douglas K. & Lewis, Blair S. Flexible Sigmoidoscopy. LC 95-22330. 200p. 1995. pap. 46.95 (*0-86542-369-5*) Blackwell Sci.

Rex, Evelyn, et al, eds. Foundations of Braille Literacy. 160p. 1995. pap. 37.95 (*0-89128-934-8*) Am Foun Blind.

Rex, Evelyn J., et al. Foundations of Braille Literacy. braille ed. 153p. 1995. pap. 37.95 (*0-89128-935-6*) Am Foun Blind.

Rex, Janet & Appelman, Bernard R., eds. The Economics of Protective Coatings: Proceedings of SSPC 7th Annual Symposium Held November 13-17, 1988, Baltimore, MD. 108p. 1988. pap. text 50.00 (*0-938477-36-6*) SSPC.

Rex, Janet & Appleman, Bernard R., eds. Lead Paint Removal from Industrial Structures: Proceedings of the SSPC Lead Paint Removal Conference, Feb. 27-Mar. 1, 1989. 114p. 1989. pap. text 40.00 (*0-938477-45-5*, SSPC 89-02) SSPC.

— Protective Coatings for Industrial Structures: Proceedings of the 1989 SSPC National Conference Seminars. (Illus.). 140p. 1989. pap. text 45.00 (*0-938477-44-7*, SSPC 89-14) SSPC.

— Protective Coatings for Pulp & Paper Mills. 83p. 1988. pap. text 30.00 (*0-938477-37-4*) SSPC.

— Protective Coatings for Pulp & Paper Mills: Proceedings of the Second Annual SSPC Pulp & Paper Industry Seminar (1989) 69p. 1990. pap. text 30.00 (*0-938477-49-8*, SSPC 89-15) SSPC.

Rex, Janet & Drisko, R., eds. Improving the Field Reliability of Protective Coatings: Proceedings of the 6th SSPC Symposium (Nov. 2-5, 1987, Orlando) 1987. pap. text 50.00 (*0-938477-33-1*, 87-07) SSPC.

Rex, John. Ethnic Minorities in the Modern Nation State: Working Papers in the Theory of Multiculturalism & Political Integration. LC 95-35009. (Migration, Minorities, & Citizenship Ser.). 256p. 1996. text 65.00 (*0-312-12923-8*) St Martin.

— The Ghetto & the Underclass: Essays on Race & Social Policy. 235p. 1988. text 72.95 (*0-566-05651-8*, Pub. by Avebry) Ashgate Pub Co.

— Immigrant Association in Europe. (Studies in European Migration (EFS): Vol. 1). 1987. text 67.95 (*0-566-05474-4*, Pub. by Avebry) Ashgate Pub Co.

— Race & Ethnicity. LC 86-5197. (Concepts in Social Sciences Ser.). 160p. 1986. pap. 22.95 (*0-335-15385-2*) OpUniv Pr.

Rex, John & Drury, Beatrice, eds. Ethnic Mobilisation in a Multi-Cultural Europe. (Research in Ethnic Relations Ser.). 192p. 1994. 72.95 (*1-85628-573-1*, Pub. by Avebry) Ashgate Pub Co.

Rex, John, jt. auth. see Binstock, Andrew.

Rex, John, jt. ed. see Guibernau, Montserrat.

Rex-Johnson, Braiden. Inside the Pike Place Market: Exploring America's Most Beloved Farmer's Market. LC 99-20535. (Illus.). 128p. 1999. pap. 19.95 (*1-57061-176-9*) Sasquatch Bks.

— The Pike Place Market Cookbook: Recipes, Anecdotes, & Personalities from Seattle's Renowned Public Market. (Illus.). 272p. (Orig.). 1992. pap. 15.95 (*0-912365-52-8*) Sasquatch Bks.

— Pike Place Public Market Seafood Cookbook. LC 97-3447. (Illus.). 341p. 1997. pap. 24.95 (*0-89815-872-9*) Ten Speed Pr.

Rex-Johnson, Braiden & Wasson, David. That's Fresh! Seasonal Recipes for Young Cooks. (Illus.). 96p. (Orig.). (J). (gr. 2 up). 1995. pap. 14.95 (*1-57061-017-7*) Sasquatch Bks.

Rex, Leda F., et al. George Rex Genealogy: Ancestry & Descendants of George Rex, First of England to Pennsylvania in 1771. 2nd ed. LC 99-208006. xi, 270 p. 1998. 30.00 (*0-7884-1006-7*) Heritage Bk.

***Rex, Michael.** Brooms Are for Flying. LC 99-44493. (Illus.). 32p. (J). (ps-2). 2000. 16.00 (*0-8050-6410-9*) H Holt & Co.

— My Fire Engine. LC 98-6611. (Illus.). (J). (ps-k). 1999. 15.95 (*0-8050-5391-3*) H Holt & Co.

— My Race Car. LC 99-31773. 32p. 2000. 15.95 (*0-8050-6101-0*) H Holt & Co.

Rex, Michael. The Painting Gorilla. LC 96-44209. (Illus.). 32p. (J). 1997. 15.95 (*0-8050-5020-5*, Bks Young Read) H Holt & Co.

***Rex, Michael.** The Pie is Cherry. 2001. text (*0-8050-6308-0*) H Holt & Co.

Rex, Michael. Who Builds? LC 99-212491. 16p. (ps-k). 1999. 6.95 (*0-694-01249-1*) HarpC Child Bks.

— Who Digs? LC 99-212490. 16p. (J). (ps-k). 1999. 6.95 (*0-694-01254-8*) HarpC Child Bks.

Rex, Michael, jt. auth. see London, Jonathan.

Rex, Patricia. Bear Essentials. 1988. pap. 8.99 (*0-8224-0697-7*) Fearon Teacher Aids.

— Best of the West Activity/Resource Book. LC 96-48204. 64p. (Orig.). (J). (gr. k-3). 1997. pap. 12.95 (*1-885777-15-9*) Hendrick-Long.

Rex, Percy F. The Prolific Pencil. Burrows, Fredrika A. & Sullwold, Stephen W., eds. LC 80-51482. (Illus.). 312p. 1980. 15.00 (*0-88492-037-2*) W S Sullwold.

Rex, Richard. Henry VIII & the English Reformation. (British History in Perspective Ser.). 1993. pap. text 16.95 (*0-333-56749-8*, Pub. by Macmillan) Humanities.

— The Sins of Madame Eglentyne: And Other Essays on Chaucer. LC 94-48358. 208p. 1995. 35.00 (*0-87413-567-2*) U Delaware Pr.

— The Theology of John Fisher: A Study in the Intellectual Origins of the Counter-Reformation. 305p. (C). 1991. text 75.00 (*0-521-39177-6*) Cambridge U Pr.

Rex, Richard, tr. see Berce, Yves-Marie.

Rex, Stella H. Practical Hooked Rugs. (Illus.). 1975. 20.00 (*0-89166-004-6*); pap. 15.00 (*0-89166-003-8*) Cobblesmith.

Rex, W. Essays on Pierre Bayle & Religious Controversy. (International Archives of the History of Ideas Ser.: No. 8). 286p. 1965. lib. bdg. 81.00 (*90-247-0184-8*) Kluwer Academic.

Rexach, Nilda L. The Hispanic-American Cookbook. 224p. 1985. 12.00 (*0-8184-0363-2*) Carol Pub Group.

— The Hispanic Cookbook: Traditional & Modern Recipes in English & Spanish. (SPA & ENG.). 190p. 1995. pap. 9.95 (*0-8065-1601-1*, Citadel Pr) Carol Pub Group.

Rexach, Rosario. Dos Figuras Cubanas Y Una Sola Actitud: Felix Varela 1788-1853 - Jorge Manach 1898-1961. LC 90-86072. 258p. 1991. pap. 19.00 (*0-89729-592-7*) Ediciones.

— Rumbo al Punto Cierto. 1979. pap. 7.50 (*84-499-2644-0*) Edit Mensaje.

Rexed, B., et al. Guidelines for the Control of Narcotic & Psychotropic Substances in the Context of the International Treaties. (FRE, RUS & SPA.). 141p. 1984. pap. text 17.00 (*92-4-154172-5*, 1150215) World Health.

Rexer, Lyle. Self-Taught Outsider Art Brut: Masterpieces from the Robert M. Greenberg Collection. (Illus.). 96p. 1998. pap. 25.00 (*0-9669498-0-3*) R Maresca Gal.

Rexford, Eveoleen N., ed. A Developmental Approach to Problems of Acting Out. rev. ed. LC 77-17666. 223p. 1978. 35.00 (*0-8236-1221-X*) Intl Univs Pr.

Rexford, Eveoleen N., et al, eds. Infant Psychiatry: A New Synthesis. LC 75-2774. (Monographs of the Journal of the American Academy of Child Psychiatry: No. 2). (Illus.). 370p. reprint ed. pap. 114.70 (*0-8357-8183-6*, 203386600087) Bks Demand.

Rexford, John. What Handwriting Indicates: An Analytical Graphology. 1991. lib. bdg. 79.95 (*0-8490-4528-2*) Gordon Pr.

— What Handwriting Indicates: An Analytical Graphology. 142p. 1996. reprint ed. spiral bd. 14.00 (*0-7873-1082-4*) Hlth Research.

Rexford, Kenneth. Electrical Control for Machines. (Electrical Trades Ser.). 1987. lab manual ed. 17.50 (*0-8273-2794-3*) Delmar.

— Electrical Controls for Machines. 5th ed. 152p. 1996. teacher ed. 15.00 (*0-8273-8163-8*); mass mkt., lab manual ed. 19.00 (*0-8273-8162-X*) Delmar.

Rexford, Kenneth B. Electrical Control for Machines. 4th ed. 1992. text 39.95 (*0-8273-4868-1*) Delmar.

— Electrical Control for Machines. 4th ed. 416p. 1993. pap., student ed. 18.95 (*0-8273-4880-0*) Delmar.

— Electrical Control for Machines: Instructor's Guide. 4th ed. 105p. 1992. pap. 15.95 (*0-8273-4870-3*) Delmar.

— Electrical Control for Machines: Student Manual. 4th ed. 120p. 1993. student ed. 14.95 (*0-685-66866-5*) Delmar.

— Electrical Controls for Machines. 5th ed. LC 96-44175. (Electrical Trades Ser.). 544p. 1996. mass mkt. 68.95 (*0-8273-7644-8*) Delmar.

***Rexford, Nancy E.** Women's Shoes in America, 1795-1930. LC 99-55197. (Illus.). 2000. 60.00 (*0-87338-656-6*) Kent St U Pr.

Rexin, Cecelia. Testament to Courage: The Concentration Camp Diary (1940-1945) of a Courageous German Woman Who Risked Her Life to Save Others. Shaw, Mark, ed. Evans, Nancy R., tr. (Illus.). 250p. 1998. 24.95 (*1-57860-056-1*) Guild Pr IN.

Rexine, John E. Constantine Cavarnos' Works Surveyed Vol. II: A Continuation of the Volume an Explorer of Realms of Art, Life, & Thought. LC 97-61106. (Illus.). 142p. 1997. 15.00 (*1-884729-27-4*) Inst Byzantine.

— Constantine Cavarnos' Works Surveyed Vol. II: A Continuation of the Volume "An Explorer of Realms of Art, Life, & Thought" LC 97-61106. (Illus.). 142p. 1997. pap. 7.50 (*1-884729-28-2*) Inst Byzantine.

— An Explorer of Realms of Art, Life & Thought: A Survey of the Works of Philosopher & Theologian Constantine Cavarnos. LC 85-81278. (Illus.). 184p. 1985. 15.00 (*0-914744-69-0*); pap. 7.50 (*0-914744-70-4*) Inst Byzantine.

— Religion in Plato & Cicero. LC 68-28581. 72p. 1968. reprint ed. lib. bdg. 49.50 (*0-8371-0198-0*, RERP, Greenwood Pr) Greenwood.

Rexroad, Eileen. Teaching Elementary School Music. 320p. (C). 1992. pap. text 39.80 (*0-13-039983-3*) P-H.

Rexroad, Michael L. Angels Don't Lie. 90p. (Orig.). 1996. pap. 8.95 (*1-879559-08-0*) Galaxy OH.

Rexroad, Zoe. 'Miz Liz Do You Dye Your Hair? 140p. (Orig.). (J). (gr. 5-6). 1997. pap. 6.95 (*1-57502-490-X*, P01457) Morris Pubng.

Rexroat, Kelsey. Zangy, the Watchdog. LC 96-27278. (Illus.). (J). 1997. write for info. (*1-56763-233-5*); pap. write for info. (*1-56763-234-3*) Ozark Pub.

Rexroat, Stephen V. For Our Good: The Ten Commandments from a Positive Perspective. 106p. (Orig.). 1990. pap. 7.95 (*0-942381-05-X*) Sammamish Pr.

Rexroth, Kenneth. An Autobiographical Novel. rev. ed. Hamalian, Linda, ed. LC 91-4785. (New Directions Classics Ser.). 528p. 1991. pap. 14.95 (*0-8112-1179-7*, NDP725, Pub. by New Directions) Norton.

— Beyond the Mountains. LC 51-9631. 192p. 1974. pap. 3.25 (*0-8112-0552-5*, NDP384, Pub. by New Directions) Norton.

— A Bird in the Bush. LC 75-111860. (Essay Index Reprint Ser.). 1977. 21.95 (*0-8369-1623-9*) Ayer.

— Classics Revisited. LC 85-31088. (New Directions Classics Ser.). 256p. 1986. reprint ed. pap. 10.95 (*0-8112-0988-1*, NDP621, Pub. by New Directions) Norton.

— Classics Revisited. LC 85-31088. (New Directions Classics Ser.). 256p. 1986. reprint ed. 23.95 (*0-8112-0987-3*, Pub. by New Directions) Norton.

— The Collected Longer Poems. LC 68-25549. 1970. reprint ed. pap. 12.95 (*0-8112-0177-5*, NDP309, Pub. by New Directions) Norton.

— Collected Shorter Poems. LC 66-17818. 1966. pap. 14.95 (*0-8112-0178-3*, NDP243, Pub. by New Directions) Norton.

— More Classics Revisited. Morrow, Bradford, ed. LC 88-22789. (Revived Modern Classics Ser.). 160p. 1989. pap. 10.95 (*0-8112-1083-9*, NDP668, Pub. by New Directions) Norton.

— One Hundred More Poems from the Chinese: Love & the Turning Year. LC 71-114845. 1970. 12.00 (*0-8112-0369-7*, Pub. by New Directions); pap. 9.95 (*0-8112-0179-1*, NDP308, Pub. by New Directions) Norton.

— Poems from the Greek Anthology. expanded ed. LC 99-32302. (Ann Arbor Paperbacks Ser.). 152p. 1999. pap. text 15.95 (*0-472-08608-1*, 08608) U of Mich Pr.

— Quarterly Review of Literature: The 1950s, Homestead Called Damascus, Vol. IX, No. 2. 1950. pap. 10.00 (*1-888545-23-2*) Quarterly Rev.

— Sacramental Acts: The Love Poems of Kenneth Rexroth. Hamill, Sam & Kleiner, Elaine Laura, eds. 130p. 1997. pap. 15.00 (*1-55659-080-6*) Copper Canyon.

— Selected Poems. Morrow, Bradford, ed. LC 84-9972. (Illus.). 160p. 1984. pap. 9.95 (*0-8112-0917-2*, NDP581, Pub. by New Directions) Norton.

— Sky, Sea, Birds, Trees, Earth, House, Beast. 2nd ed. LC 76-134750. (Illus.). 30p. 1973. 17.50 (*0-87775-044-0*); pap. 10.00 (*0-87775-048-3*) Unicorn Pr.

***Rexroth, Kenneth.** Swords That Shall Not Strike: Poems of Protest & Rebellion. Gardner, Geoffrey, ed. 2000. 14.00 (*1-930180-02-0*, 3) Glad Day Bks VT.

Rexroth, Kenneth. Women Poets of China. LC 72-6791. Vol. 528. Orig. Title: The Orchid Boat. 160p. 1982. reprint ed. pap. 9.95 (*0-8112-0821-4*, NDP528, Pub. by New Directions) Norton.

— World Outside the Window: The Selected Essays of Kenneth Rexroth. Morrow, Bradford, ed. LC 86-28610. 352p. 1987. 24.95 (*0-8112-1024-3*, Pub. by New Directions); pap. 12.95 (*0-8112-1025-1*, NDP639, Pub. by New Directions) Norton.

Rexroth, Kenneth, tr. from JPN. One Hundred More Poems from the Japanese. LC 76-7486. (Illus.). 120p. 1976. pap. 9.95 (*0-8112-0619-X*, NDP420, Pub. by New Directions) Norton.

— One Hundred Poems from the Chinese. LC 56-13351. 1965. pap. 9.95 (*0-8112-0180-5*, NDP192, Pub. by New Directions) Norton.

— One Hundred Poems from the Japanese. LC 56-2557. (ENG & JPN.). 140p. 1964. pap. 9.95 (*0-8112-0181-3*, NDP147, Pub. by New Directions) Norton.

Rexroth, Kenneth & Atsumi, Ikuko, trs. from JPN. Women Poets of Japan. LC 77-1833. 192p. 1982. reprint ed. pap. 9.95 (*0-8112-0820-6*, NDP527, Pub. by New Directions) Norton.

Rexroth, Kenneth, ed. see Li-Ching-Chao.

Rexroth, Kenneth, ed. see Shiraishi, Kazuko.

Rexroth, Kenneth, tr. see De L. Milosz, O. V.

Rexroth, Kenneth, tr. see Hamill, Sam, ed.

Rexxxxx, Don J. Modem Love: Step-by-Step Guide to Sex on the Information Highway. 1995. pap. 12.00 (*0-8217-4921-8*, Zebra Kensgtn) Kensgtn Pub Corp.

Rey, A. Robert Dictionary Historique Langue Francaise, 2 vols. (FRE.). 2391p. 1995. 395.00 (*0-320-00532-1*) Fr & Eur.

— Robert Dictionnaire des Expressions et Locutions. (FRE.). 888p. 1997. 69.95 (*0-320-00494-5*); 34.95 (*0-320-00433-3*) Fr & Eur.

— Robert Micro (Med) (FRE.). 1506p. 1998. 59.95 (*0-320-00414-7*) Fr & Eur.

— Robert Micro Poche Vol. 1: Langue Francaise. (FRE.). 1506p. 1998. pap. 34.95 (*0-320-00416-3*) Fr & Eur.

— Robert Micro Poche Vol. 2: Noms Propres. (FRE.). 1120p. 1994. pap. 34.95 (*0-320-00584-4*) Fr & Eur.

Rey, Agapito, jt. ed. see Hammond, George P.

Rey, Alain. Dictionnaire des Expressions et Locutions: Les Tresors des Manieres de Dire Anciennes et Nouvelles. (FRE.). 1322p. 1989. 34.95 (*0-7859-9213-8*) Fr & Eur.

— Dictionnaire des Expressions et Locutions Figurees. (FRE.). 1036p. 1990. 125.00 (*0-7859-9222-7*) Fr & Eur.

— Dictionnaire Historique de la Langue Francaise: Mille Ans de Langue Francaise. (FRE.). 2391p. 1992. 395.00 (*0-7859-9208-1*) Fr & Eur.

— Essays on Terminology. Sager, Juan C., ed. & tr. by. from FRE. LC 94-45807. (Benjamins Translation Library: No. 9). xiv, 223p. 1995. pap. 24.95 (*1-55619-689-X*); lib. bdg. 69.00 (*1-55619-688-1*) J Benjamins Pubng Co.

— Petit Robert des Noms Propres Dictionnaire: Universel Illustre en Couleurs Alphabetique Analogique. (FRE.). 2259p. 1995. 175.00 (*0-7859-9195-6*) Fr & Eur.

— Le Robert Micro. (FRE.). 1995. 49.95 (*0-7859-9309-6*) Fr & Eur.

— Le Robert Micro: Dictionnaire du Bon Usage & des Difficultes (Nouvelle Edition) (FRE.). 1472p. 1992. 59.95 (*0-7859-9187-5*) Fr & Eur.

— Robert Micro Poche Langue Francaise. (FRE.). 1510p. 1993. 34.95 (*0-7859-9189-1*) Fr & Eur.

— Robert Micro Poche Noms Propres. (FRE.). 1120p. 1994. 34.95 (*0-7859-9200-6*) Fr & Eur.

Rey, Alfonso, ed. see De Quevedo, Francisco.

Rey, Anthony M. & Wieland, Ferdinand. Managing Service in Food & Beverage Operations. LC 85-12962. (Illus.). 395p. 1985. text. write for info. (*0-86612-023-8*) Educ Inst Am Hotel.

Rey, Antonio B. Concierto de Primavera. (Romance Real Ser.). 180p. 1981. pap. 1.50 (*0-88025-001-1*) Roca Pub.

***Rey, Bret.** Bullets in Buzzards Creek. large type ed. 240p. 1999. pap. 18.99 (*0-7089-5498-7*, Linford) Ulverscroft.

Rey, Bret. The Devil Rode a Pinto. large type ed. (Linford Western Large Print Ser.). 240p. 1997. pap. 16.99 (*0-7089-5042-6*) Ulverscroft.

— Gunsmoke in a Colorado Canyon. large type ed. (Linford Western Library). 240p. 1993. pap. 16.99 (*0-7089-7440-6*) Ulverscroft.

— Kill Conway. large type ed. (Linford Western Large Print Ser.). 224p. 1998. pap. 17.99 (*0-7089-5273-9*, Linford) Ulverscroft.

— A Killing in Horseshoe Bend. large type ed. (Dales Large Print Ser.). 224p. 1998. pap. 19.99 (*1-85389-786-8*, Dales) Ulverscroft.

— Marshal Without a Badge. large type ed. (Linford Western Library). 272p. 1993. pap. 16.99 (*0-7089-7362-0*, Linford) Ulverscroft.

— Outlaw's Woman. large type ed. (Linford Western Library Ser.). 208p. 1997. pap. 16.99 (*0-7089-5152-X*) Ulverscroft.

— Runaway. large type ed. (Linford Western Library). 256p. 1992. pap. 16.99 (*0-7089-7151-2*) Ulverscroft.

— Texas Pilgrim. large type ed. (Linford Western Library). 1995. pap. 16.99 (*0-7089-7767-7*, Linford) Ulverscroft.

— Trouble Valley. large type ed. (Linford Western Library). 1991. pap. 16.99 (*0-7089-7010-9*) Ulverscroft.

***Rey, Bret.** West of the Brazos. large type ed. 208p. 2000. 20.99 (*1-84137-018-5*, Pub. by Mgna Lrg Print) Ulverscroft.

Rey, C., jt. ed. see Sedel, L.

Rey, Caroline. The Mammoth Book of Love & Sensuality. LC 96-40924. (Mammoth Book Ser.). (Illus.). 512p. 1997. pap. 11.95 (*0-7867-0374-1*) Carroll & Graf.

Rey, Charles. Monarch of All I Survey: Bechuanaland Diaries, 1929-1937. Parsons, Neil & Crowder, Michael, eds. LC 87-12570. (Illus.). 282p. 1988. text 39.50 (*0-936508-22-1*) Barber Pr.

Rey-Debove, G. Dictionnaire des Anglicismes.Tr. of Dictionary of Anglicisms. (FRE.). 1150p. 1990. 75.00 (*0-7859-4769-8*, M3259) Fr & Eur.

Rey-Debove, Josette. Dictionaire de Citations Francaises de Chateaubriand a Simenon, Vol. 2. (FRE.). 980p. 1990. 34.95 (*0-7859-9209-X*) Fr & Eur.

— Dictionnaire des Anglicismes. (FRE.). 1150p. 1990. 79.95 (*0-7859-9217-0*) Fr & Eur.

— Le Metalanguage. 326p. 1978. 49.95 (*0-7859-9207-3*) Fr & Eur.

— Nouveau Petit Robert: Dictionnaire Alphabetique & Analogique de la Langue Francaise. (FRE.). 2551p. 1995. 150.00 (*0-7859-9206-5*) Fr & Eur.

— Le Petit Robert des Enfants: Dictionnaire de la Langue Francaise. (FRE.). 1187p. 1990. 95.00 (*0-7859-9225-1*) Fr & Eur.

— Le Robert des Jeunes. (FRE.). 1292p. 1991. 95.00 (*0-7859-9223-5*) Fr & Eur.

— Robert Dictionnaire des Anglicismes. (FRE.). 1150p. 1988. 69.95 (*0-7859-7121-1*, 2850360279) Fr & Eur.

— Le Robert Methodique. (FRE.). 1617p. 1982. 95.00 (*0-7859-9212-X*) Fr & Eur.

Rey-Debove, Josette, ed. Recherches sur les Systemes Significants: Symposium de Varsovie, 1968. (Approaches to Semiotics Ser.: No. 18). (Illus.). 1973. 140.00 (*90-279-2379-5*) Mouton.

Rey, Donna, ed. see Figueroa-Faxton, Carlita.

Rey, E. De La, see De La Rey, E.

Rey, Eibe-Rudolf & Bailer, Josef. Prognose und Verlauf Ersthospitalisierter Schizophrener: Unter Mitarbeit von Wolfgang Brauer, Dagmar Laubenstein, Michael Handel & Martin Volz. (Illus.). 199p. 1997. 38.95 (*3-631-30074-3*) P Lang Pubng.

Rey, Emmanuel. Colonies Franques De Syrie Aux Dix-Septieme & Dix-Huitieme Siecles. LC 75-168087. reprint ed. 55.00 (*0-404-05285-1*) AMS Pr.

Rey, F., jt. auth. see Estep, K. W.

Rey, Georges. Contemporary Philosophy of Mind: A Contentiously Clasical Approach. LC 96-21571. (Contemporary Philosophy Ser.). 384p. (C). 1996. text 60.95 (*0-631-19069-4*) Blackwell Pubs.

— Contemporary Philosophy of Mind: A Eontentiously Classical Approach. LC 96-21571. (Contemporary Philosophy Ser.). 384p. (C). 1996. pap. text 28.95 (*0-631-19071-6*) Blackwell Pubs.

Rey, Greta. For Caregivers, with Love. LC 95-42627. 160p. (YA). (gr. 10). 1996. pap. 9.99 (*0-8010-5705-1*) Baker Bks.

Rey, H. A. Anybody at Home? rev. ed. 22p. (J). 1998. pap. 4.95 (*0-395-90692-X*) HM.

An Asterisk (*) at the beginning of an entry indicates that the title is appearing for the first time.

— Cecily G. & the Nine Monkeys, 001. (Illus.). 32p. (J). (gr. 1-3). 1974. 16.00 (*0-395-18430-4*) HM.

— Cecily G. & the Nine Monkeys. LC 88-37188. (Illus.). 32p. (J). (ps-3). 1989. pap. 5.95 (*0-395-50651-4*, Sandpiper) HM.

Rey, H. A. Cecily G. & the 9 Monkeys. 1989. 11.15 (*0-606-10771-1*, Pub. by Turtleback) Demco.

Rey, H. A. Curious George. LC 73-162780. (Curious George Ser.). (Illus.). 56p. (J). (ps-3). 1973. 14.95 (*0-395-15993-8*) HM.

— Curious George. (Curious George Ser.). (J). (ps-3). 1993. pap. 9.95 incl. audio (*0-395-66490-X*, 494351) HM.

— Curious George. LC 93-40088. (Curious George Ser.). (Illus.). 56p. (J). (ps-3). 1994. pap. 19.95 (*0-395-69803-0*) HM.

— Curious George. (Curious George Ser.). (J). (ps-2). 1973. 11.15 (*0-606-02923-0*, Pub. by Turtleback) Demco.

— Curious George. (Curious George Ser.). (J). (ps-2). 1995. reprint ed. lib. bdg. 27.95 (*1-56849-658-3*) Buccaneer Bks.

— Curious George, 001. LC 73-162780. (Curious George Ser.). (Illus.). 48p. (J). (ps-3). 1973. reprint ed. pap. 5.95 (*0-395-15023-X*, Sandpiper) HM.

— Curious George Comes Home, Vol. 2. (J). 1997. 10.30 (*0-395-85435-0*) HM.

— Curious George Gets a Medal. LC 57-7206. (Curious George Ser.). (Illus.). 48p. (J). (ps-3). 1957. 14.95 (*0-395-16973-9*) HM.

— Curious George Gets a Medal. (Curious George Ser.). (J). (ps-2). 1957. 11.15 (*0-606-02909-5*, Pub. by Turtleback) Demco.

— Curious George Gets a Medal. LC 57-7206. (Curious George Ser.). (Illus.). 48p. (J). (ps-3). 1974. reprint ed. pap. 5.95 (*0-395-18559-9*, Sandpiper) HM.

— Curious George Gets a Medal. unabridged ed. (Curious George Ser.). (J). (ps-3). 1998. pap. 9.95 incl. audio (*0-395-89115-9*, 494862, Clarion Bks) HM.

— Curious George Learns the Alphabet. LC 62-12261. (Curious George Ser.). (Illus.). 72p. (J). (ps-1). 1963. 14.95 (*0-395-16031-6*) HM.

— Curious George Learns the Alphabet. LC 62-12261. (Curious George Ser.). (Illus.). 72p. (J). (ps-3). 1973. pap. 5.95 (*0-395-13718-7*, Sandpiper) HM.

— Curious George Learns the Alphabet. (Curious George Ser.). (J). (ps-2). 1963. 11.15 (*0-606-00511-0*, Pub. by Turtleback) Demco.

— Curious George Learns the Alphabet. unabridged ed. (Curious George Ser.). (Illus.). (J). (ps-3). 1998. pap. 9.95 incl. audio (*0-395-89113-2*, 482595, Clarion Bks) HM.

— Curious George Paper Doll. (J). 1982. pap. 4.95 (*0-486-24386-9*) Dover.

— Curious George Rides a Bike. LC 73-180856. (Curious George Ser.). (Illus.). 48p. (J). (ps-3). 1952. 14.95 (*0-395-16964-X*) HM.

— Curious George Rides a Bike. LC 52-8728. (Curious George Ser.). (Illus.). 48p. (J). (ps-3). 1997. pap. 9.95 incl. audio (*0-395-85760-0*) HM.

— Curious George Rides a Bike. (Curious George Ser.). (J). (ps-2). 1973. 11.15 (*0-606-02924-9*, Pub. by Turtleback) Demco.

— Curious George Rides a Bike. (Curious George Ser.). (Illus.). 48p. (J). (ps-2). 1973. reprint ed. pap. 5.95 (*0-395-17444-9*, Sandpiper) HM.

— Curious George Takes a Job. (Curious George Ser.). (Illus.). 48p. (J). (ps-3). 1973. 14.95 (*0-395-15086-8*) HM.

— Curious George Takes a Job. (Curious George Ser.). (Illus.). 48p. (J). (ps-3). 1974. pap. 5.95 (*0-395-18649-8*, Sandpiper) HM.

— Curious George Takes a Job. (Curious George Ser.). (J). (ps-2). 1975. 11.15 (*0-606-02925-7*, Pub. by Turtleback) Demco.

— Curious George Takes a Job. unabridged ed. (Curious George Ser.). (J). (ps-2). 1998. pap. 9.95 incl. audio (*0-395-89114-0*, 494388, Clarion Bks) HM.

— Edward's John Alden, 4 vols. Date not set. pap. 9.68 (*0-395-52221-8*) HM.

***Rey, H. A.** Elizabite: Adventures of a Carnivorous Plant. (Illus.). 32p. (J). (gr. k-3). 1999. 15.00 (*0-395-97702-9*) HM.

— Elizabite: Adventures of a Carnivorous Plant. LC 90-4834. (Illus.). 32p. (J). (gr. k-4). 1999. pap. 5.95 (*0-395-97704-5*) HM.

— Elizabite: Adventures of a Carnivorous Plant. (Illus.). (J). 2000. pap. 9.95 (*0-618-08125-9*) HM.

Rey, H. A. Feed the Animals. rev. ed. 22p. (J). 1998. pap. 4.95 (*0-395-90693-8*) HM.

— Find the Constellations, 001. rev. ed. LC 54-9051. (Illus.). 72p. (J). (gr. 4-7). 1976. pap. 9.95 (*0-395-24418-8*, Sandpiper) HM.

— Find the Constellations, 001. rev. ed. (Illus.). 80p. (J). (gr. 3-7). 1976. 20.00 (*0-395-24509-5*) HM.

***Rey, H. A.** How Do You Get There? 22p. 1998. pap. 4.95 (*0-395-90694-6*) HM.

Rey, H. A. Jorge el Curioso, 001. (SPA., Illus.). 64p. (J). (gr. k-3). 1961. 14.95 (*0-395-17075-3*) HM.

— Jorge el Curioso, 001. LC 61-12429. (SPA., Illus.). 64p. (J). (ps-3). 1976. pap. 5.95 (*0-395-24909-0*, Sandpiper) HM.

— Jorge El Curioso. 1990. 11.15 (*0-606-09494-6*, Pub. by Turtleback) Demco.

— Our George. (J). 1974. pap. 1.95 (*0-590-02043-9*) Scholastic Inc.

— See the Circus. rev. ed. 22p. (J). 1998. pap. 4.95 (*0-395-90695-4*) HM.

— The Stars: A New Way to See Them, 001. 160p. (J). (gr. 4 up). 1976. pap. 11.95 (*0-395-24830-2*) HM.

— The Stars: A New Way to See Them, 001. 3rd ed. (Illus.). 160p. (J). (gr. 8 up). 1973. 25.00 (*0-395-08121-1*) HM.

— Where's My Baby? rev. ed. 22p. 1998. pap. 4.95 (*0-395-90696-2*) HM.

***Rey, H. A.** Whiteblack the Penguin. LC 00-23196. (Illus.). (J). 2000. write for info. (*0-618-07390-6*) HM.

— Whiteblack the Penguin Sees the World. (Illus.). (J). 2000. 15.00 (*0-618-07389-2*) HM.

Rey, H. A. & Rey, Margret. Curious George: A Pop-up Book. (Curious George Ser.). (Illus.). 12p. (J). (ps-3). 1987. 15.95 (*0-395-45347-X*) HM.

***Rey, H. A. & Rey, Margret.** Curious George & the Dump Truck. LC 99-31533. (Curious George Ser.). (Illus.). 32p. (J). (ps-3). 1999. pap. 3.95 (*0-395-97836-X*); bds. 7.95 (*0-395-97844-0*) HM.

— Curious George Goes to the Beach. LC 99-31534. (Curious George Ser.). (Illus.). 32p. (J). (ps-3). 1999. pap. 3.95 (*0-395-97838-6*); bds. 7.95 (*0-395-97846-7*) HM.

— Curious George's Pop-Up Storybook House. (Curious George Ser.). (Illus.). 43p. (J). (ps-2). 1999. 20.00 (*0-395-97908-0*) HM.

Rey, H. A. & Rey, Margret. The Original Curious George: Collector's Edition. LC 98-71472. (Curious George Ser.). (Illus.). 64p. (J). (ps-2). 1998. 25.00 (*0-395-92272-0*) HM.

Rey, H. A., jt. auth. see Rey, Margret.

Rey, Henri. Universals of Psychoanalysis: In the Treatment of Psychotic & Borderline States. Magagna, Jeanne, ed. 319p. (C). 1994. pap. 37.00 (*1-85343-370-5*, Pub. by Free Assoc Bks) NYU Pr.

Rey, Iran O., ed. Julio Larraz: Paintings - Pinturas. Yobst, Julia, tr. (ENG & SPA., Illus.). 80p. 1997. 36.00 (*0-9650650-3-0*) Palette Pubns.

— Peter von Artens: Paintings Portraits - Pinturas Retratos. Yobst, Julia, tr. (ENG & SPA., Illus.). 80p. 1996. 36.00 (*0-9650650-1-4*) Palette Pubns.

Rey, J. French Dictionary of the Difficulties of the English Version. 287p. pap. 29.50 (*2-7080-0066-7*) IBD Ltd.

Rey, J. J. Robust Statistical Methods. (Lecture Notes in Mathematics Ser.: Vol. 690). 1978. 18.95 (*0-387-09091-6*) Spr-Verlag.

Rey, Jean. Dictionnaire Selectif et Commente des Difficultes de la Vers. (FRE.). 1973. write for info. (*0-7859-7927-1*, 2-7080-0066-7) Fr & Eur.

Rey, Jean, jt. ed. see Ballabriga, Angel.

Rey, Jean N. Video France - Optiques: La Vie Quotidienne. 80p. 1995. reprint ed. pap. 149.95 (*0-8442-1468-X*, Passprt Bks) NTC Contemp Pub Co.

— Video France - Panorama de la France. (Illus.). 80p. 1995. reprint ed. pap. 149.95 (*0-8442-1485-X*, Natl Textbk Co) NTC Contemp Pub Co.

— Video France - Profiles des Francaise. 80p. 1995. reprint ed. pap. 149.95 (*0-8442-1471-X*, Natl Textbk Co) NTC Contemp Pub Co.

Rey, Jorge R. & Kain, Tim. A Guide to the Salt Marsh Impoundments of Florida. (Illus.). 1990. pap. write for info. (*0-9615224-3-7*) Fla Med Entom.

***Rey, Joseph.** Is My Teenager in Trouble? A Parent's Guide to Serious Adolescent Problems. 200p. 2000. per. 12.00 (*0-684-87204-8*) S&S Trade.

Rey, Louis, ed. Arctic Underwater Operations. 360p. 1985. lib. bdg. 163.00 (*0-86010-631-4*) G & T Inc.

Rey, Louis, et al, eds. Unveiling the Arctic. (Illus.). 292p. 1985. 55.00 (*0-919034-09-8*) U of Alaska Pr.

Rey, Louis & May, Joan C. Freeze-Drying/Lyophilization of Pharmaceutical & Biological Products. LC 99-26168. (Drugs & the Pharmaceutical Sciences Ser.). (Illus.). 496p. 1999. text 195.00 (*0-8247-1983-2*) Dekker.

Rey, Marc L., jt. auth. see NATO Advanced Study Institute on Theoretical & Observational Cosmology Staff.

Rey, Marcos. Memoirs of a Gigolo. 224p. 1987. pap. 7.95 (*0-380-75000-7*, Avon Bks) Morrow Avon.

Rey, Margret. Curious George Pop-Up Book. (Illus.). (J). (ps-3). 1997. 15.95 (*0-614-28827-4*) HM.

— Pretzel. LC 96-9669. (Illus.). 32p. (J). 1997. pap. 4.95 (*0-395-83733-2*) HM.

— Pretzel. LC 96-9669. (Illus.). 32p. (J). 1997. 15.00 (*0-395-83737-5*) HM.

— Pretzel. LC 44-9584. (Trophy Picture Bk.). (Illus.). 32p. (J). (ps-3). 1984. pap. 5.95 (*0-06-443051-0*, HarpTrophy) HarpC Child Bks.

— Spotty. LC 96-26818. (Illus.). 32p. 1997. 14.95 (*0-395-83736-7*) HM.

— Spotty. LC 96-26818. (Illus.). 32p. (ps-3). 1997. pap. 5.95 (*0-395-83732-4*) HM.

Rey, Margret. Spotty. LC 96-26818. 1997. 11.15 (*0-606-11880-2*, Pub. by Turtleback) Demco.

Rey, Margret & Rey, H. A. The Complete Adventures of Curious George, 3 bks., Set. LC 96-112596. (Curious George Ser.). (Illus.). 405p. (J). (ps-3). 1995. 29.95 (*0-395-75410-0*) HM.

— Curious George & the Bunny. LC 97-74215. (Curious George Ser.). 12p. (J). (ps-2). 1998. bds. 5.95 (*0-395-89922-2*) HM.

— Curious George & the Dinosaur. LC 89-32366. (Curious George Ser.). 32p. (J). (ps-3). 1989. 12.00 (*0-395-51942-X*) HM.

— Curious George & the Dinosaur. LC 89-32366. (Curious George Ser.). (Illus.). 30p. (J). (ps-3). 1989. pap. 3.95 (*0-395-51936-5*) HM.

— Curious George & the Dinosaur. (Curious George Ser.). (Illus.). 1p. (J). (ps-3). 1990. pap. 9.95 incl. audio (*0-395-56484-0*, 494303, Clarion Bks) HM.

— Curious George & the Hot Air Balloon. LC 98-21326. (Curious George Ser.). (Illus.). (J). (ps-3). 1998. pap. 3.95 (*0-395-91909-6*) HM.

— Curious George & the Hot Air Balloon. LC 98-21326. (Curious George Ser.). (Illus.). 24p. (J). (ps-3). 1998. 12.00 (*0-395-91918-5*); bds. 7.95 (*0-395-92338-7*) HM.

— Curious George & the Pizza. LC 85-2434. (Curious George Ser.). 32p. (J). (ps-3). 1985. 12.00 (*0-395-39039-7*); pap. 3.95 (*0-395-39033-8*) HM.

— Curious George & the Pizza. (Curious George Ser.). 1p. (J). (ps-2). 1988. pap. 9.95 incl. audio (*0-395-48874-5*, 494294) HM.

— Curious George & the Pizza. (Curious George Ser.). (J). (ps-2). 1985. 9.15 (*0-606-12232-X*, Pub. by Turtleback) Demco.

— Curious George & the Puppies. LC 97-50444. (Curious George Ser.). (J). (ps-3). 1998. 12.00 (*0-395-91217-2*) HM.

— Curious George & the Puppies. LC 97-50444. (Curious George Ser.). (Illus.). 24p. (J). (ps-3). 1998. pap. 3.95 (*0-395-91215-6*); bds. 7.95 (*0-395-92334-4*) HM.

— Curious George at the Fire Station. LC 85-2471. (Curious George Ser.). (Illus.). 32p. (J). (ps-3). 1985. 12.00 (*0-395-39037-0*); pap. 3.95 (*0-395-39031-1*) HM.

— Curious George at the Fire Station. (Curious George Ser.). 1p. (J). (ps-2). 1988. pap. 9.95 incl. audio (*0-395-48875-3*, 494295) HM.

— Curious George at the Parade. LC 99-21454. (Curious George Ser.). (Illus.). 32p. (J). (ps-3). 1999. 12.00 (*0-395-97833-5*); pap. 3.95 (*0-395-97837-8*) HM.

***Rey, Margret & Rey, H. A.** Curious George at the Parade. (Curious George Ser.). (Illus.). 32p. (J). (ps-3). 1999. bds. 7.95 (*0-395-97845-9*) HM.

Rey, Margret & Rey, H. A. Curious George Feeds the Animals. LC 98-21327. (Curious George Ser.). (Illus.). 24p. (J). (ps-3). 1998. pap. 3.95 (*0-395-91910-X*); bds. 7.95 (*0-395-92340-9*) HM.

— Curious George Flies a Kite. (Curious George Ser.). (Illus.). 80p. (J). (ps-2). 1973. 15.00 (*0-395-16965-8*) HM.

— Curious George Flies a Kite. LC 58-8163. (Curious George Ser.). (Illus.). 80p. (J). (ps-3). 1977. pap. 5.95 (*0-395-25937-1*) HM.

— Curious George Flies a Kite. LC 58-8163. (Curious George Ser.). (Illus.). 89p. (J). (ps-2). 1997. pap. 9.95 incl. audio (*0-395-85759-7*) HM.

— Curious George Flies a Kite. (Curious George Ser.). (J). (ps-2). 1986. 11.15 (*0-606-01093-9*, Pub. by Turtleback) Demco.

***Rey, Margret & Rey, H. A.** Curious George Goes Camping. LC 99-21453. (Curious George Ser.). (Illus.). 32p. (J). (ps-3). 1999. pap. 3.95 (*0-395-97835-1*); bds. 7.95 (*0-395-97843-2*) HM.

— Curious George Goes Camping. LC 99-21453. (Curious George Ser.). (Illus.). 32p. (J). (ps-3). 1999. 12.00 (*0-395-97831-9*) HM.

Rey, Margret & Rey, H. A. Curious George Goes to a Chocolate Factory. LC 97-50446. (Curious George Ser.). (Illus.). 24p. (J). (ps-3). 1998. 12.00 (*0-395-91216-4*) HM.

— Curious George Goes to a Chocolate Factory. LC 97-50446. (Curious George Ser.). (Illus.). 24p. (J). (ps-3). 1998. pap. 3.95 (*0-395-91214-8*); pap. 7.95 (*0-395-92331-X*) HM.

— Curious George Goes to a Movie. LC 98-12370. (Curious George Ser.). (Illus.). 24p. (J). (ps-3). 1998. 12.00 (*0-395-91901-0*); pap. 3.95 (*0-395-91906-1*); bds. 7.95 (*0-395-92335-2*) HM.

— Curious George Goes to an Ice Cream Shop. (Curious George Ser.). (Illus.). 32p. (J). (ps-2). 1989. pap. 3.95 (*0-395-51937-3*) HM.

— Curious George Goes to School. (Curious George Ser.). (Illus.). 32p. (J). (ps-2). 1989. 12.00 (*0-395-51944-6*) HM.

— Curious George Goes to School. LC 89-32362. (Curious George Ser.). (Illus.). 30p. (J). (ps-3). 1989. pap. 3.95 (*0-395-51939-X*) HM.

— Curious George Goes to School. (Curious George Ser.). (Illus.). 1p. (J). (ps-3). 1990. pap. 9.95 incl. audio (*0-395-56483-2*, 494302) HM.

— Curious George Goes to the Aquarium. LC 84-16828. (Curious George Ser.). (Illus.). 32p. (J). (ps-3). 1984. 12.00 (*0-395-36634-8*); pap. 3.95 (*0-395-36628-3*) HM.

— Curious George Goes to the Dentist. (Curious George Ser.). (Illus.). 32p. (J). (ps-2). 1989. 9.95 (*0-685-26499-8*) HM.

— Curious George Goes to the Hospital. LC 65-19301. (Curious George Ser.). (Illus.). 48p. (J). (ps-3). 1966. pap. 5.95 (*0-395-07062-7*) HM.

— Curious George Goes to the Hospital. LC 65-19301. (Curious George Ser.). (Illus.). 48p. (J). (ps-3). 1973. 14.95 (*0-395-18158-5*) HM.

— Curious George Goes to the Hospital. (Curious George Ser.). (Illus.). 48p. (J). (ps-3). 1995. pap. 9.95 incl. audio (*0-395-72026-5*, 494395) HM.

— Curious George Goes to the Hospital. (Curious George Ser.). (J). (ps-2). 1966. 11.15 (*0-606-00836-5*, Pub. by Turtleback) Demco.

— Curious George in the Snow. LC 98-14162. (Curious George Ser.). (J). (ps-2). 1998. 12.00 (*0-395-91902-9*); bds. 7.95 (*0-395-92336-0*) HM.

***Rey, Margret & Rey, H. A.** Curious George in the Snow. LC 98-14162. (Curious George Ser.). (Illus.). 24p. (J). (ps-3). 1998. pap. 3.95 (*0-395-91907-X*) HM.

Rey, Margret & Rey, H. A. Curious George Learns Phonics & Spelling. (Curious George Ser.). (J). (ps-2). 1998. 24.72 (*0-395-85431-8*) HM.

— Curious George Makes Pancakes. LC 98-12350. (Curious George Ser.). (Illus.). 24p. (J). (ps-3). 1998. 12.00 (*0-395-91903-7*); pap. 3.95 (*0-395-91908-8*); bds. 7.95 (*0-395-92337-9*) HM.

— Curious George Plays Baseball. LC 86-10609. (Curious George Ser.). (Illus.). 32p. (J). (ps-2). 1986. 12.00 (*0-395-39041-9*) HM.

— Curious George Plays Baseball. LC 86-10609. (Curious George Ser.). 32p. (J). (ps-3). 1986. pap. 3.95 (*0-395-39035-4*) HM.

— Curious George Visits the Zoo. LC 85-2415. (Curious George Ser.). 32p. (J). (ps-3). 1985. 12.00 (*0-395-39036-2*) HM.

Rey, Margret & Rey, H. A. Curious George Visits the Zoo. LC 85-2415. (Curious George Ser.). (Illus.). 30p. (J). (ps-2). 1985. pap. 3.95 (*0-395-39030-3*) HM.

Rey, Margret & Rey, H. A. Curious George Visits the Zoo. (Curious George Ser.). (J). (ps-6). 1988. pap. 9.95 incl. audio (*0-395-48876-1*, 494296) HM.

— Curious George Visits the Zoo. (Curious George Ser.). (J). (ps-2). 1985. 9.15 (*0-606-12233-8*, Pub. by Turtleback) Demco.

— Curious George's ABCs. LC 97-74216. (Curious George Ser.). (Illus.). 12p. (J). (ps-2). 1998. bds. 5.95 (*0-395-89925-7*) HM.

— Curious George's Are you Curious? LC 97-74214. (Curious George Ser.). (Illus.). 8p. (J). (ps-2). 1998. bds. 5.95 (*0-395-89924-9*) HM.

— Curious George's Dream. (Curious George Ser.). (J). (ps-2). 1998. pap. 7.95 (*0-395-92342-5*) HM.

— Curious George's Dream. LC 98-14163. (Curious George Ser.). (Illus.). 24p. (J). (ps-3). 1998. 12.00 (*0-395-91905-3*); pap. 3.95 (*0-395-91911-8*) HM.

— Curious George's Opposites. LC 97-74212. (Curious George Ser.). (Illus.). (J). (ps-2). 1998. bds. 5.95 (*0-395-89923-0*) HM.

***Rey, Margret & Rey, H. A.** Margret & H. A. Rey's Curious George Goes to an Ice Cream Shop. Vipah Interactive Staff, ed. LC 00-21117. (Illus.). (J). 2000. bds. write for info. (*0-618-06575-X*) HM.

***Rey, Margret, et al.** Margret & H. A. Rey's Curious George Goes to a Costume Party. LC 00-21804. (J). 2000. pap. write for info. (*0-618-06569-5*) HM.

Rey, Margret, jt. auth. see Rey, H. A.

Rey, Maria Del. Obsession. 1999. mass mkt. 6.95 (*0-352-33375-8*) Nexus.

Rey-Meret, Theodule. Moral Choices Series 1: The Moral Theology of Saint Alphonsus. Laverdure, Paul, tr. from FRE. LC 98-12012. 208p. 1998. reprint ed. pap. 14.95 (*0-7648-0233-X*) Liguori Pubns.

Rey, Michael, jt. auth. see Meisler, Andy.

Rey, Patrick, jt. auth. see Farr, Amanda.

Rey, R. Poussin: Paintings. (Rhythm & Color One Ser.). 1970. 9.95 (*0-8288-9504-X*) Fr & Eur.

Rey, Rosa R. El Agua Quieta. (SPA.). 108p. (Orig.). (C). 1991. pap. 7.00 (*0-9626221-2-5*) Vista Pubns FL.

— El Cuchillo del Mendigo. (SPA.). 80p. (Orig.). (C). 1987. pap. 6.00 (*0-9626221-0-9*) Vista Pubns FL.

— El Salvador de Buques. (SPA.). 98p. (Orig.). (C). 1993. pap. 7.00 (*0-9626221-3-3*) Vista Pubns FL.

***Rey, Rosa R.** Ningun Lugar Sagrado. (Biblioteca Breve Ser.). (SPA.). 1999. 14.95 (*84-322-0762-4*) E Seix Barral.

Rey-Rosa, Rodrigo. The Beggar's Knife. Bowles, Paul, tr. from SPA. 112p. (Orig.). 1985. pap. 5.95 (*0-87286-164-3*) City Lights.

— Dust on Her Tongue. 124p. (Orig.). 1992. pap. 7.95 (*0-87286-272-0*) City Lights.

Rey, Roselyne. The History of Pain. Wallace, Louise E. et al, trs. from FRE. LC 94-31948.Tr. of Histoire de la Douleur. 1995. text 44.00 (*0-674-39967-6*, REYHIS) HUP.

— History of Pain. 400p. 1998. pap. text 18.95 (*0-674-39968-4*) HUP.

Rey, S. J., jt. auth. see Krauss, Lawrence M.

Rey, Terry. Our Lady of Class Struggle: The Cult of the Virgin Mary in Haiti. LC 98-31306. 400p. 1998. 79.95 (*0-86543-694-0*); pap. 21.95 (*0-86543-695-9*) Africa World.

Rey, W. J. Introduction to Robust & Quasi-Robust Statistical Methods. (Universitext Ser.). (Illus.). 250p. 1983. 51.95 (*0-387-12866-2*) Spr-Verlag.

Rey, William H. Essays Zur Deutschen Literatur. Hertling, Gunter & Behler, Ernst, eds. LC 97-40835. (GER.). 420p. 1997. 109.95 (*0-7734-8458-2*) E Mellen.

Reybaud, Louis. Etudes Sur les Reformateurs Ou Socialistes Modernes, 2 vols. Mayer, J. P., ed. LC 78-67379. (European Political Thought Ser.). (FRE.). 1980. reprint ed. lib. bdg. 68.95 (*0-405-11729-9*) Ayer.

Reybold, L. Earle, ed. Revolutions for Freedom: The Mass Media in Eastern & Central Europe. LC 91-19063. 250p. (Orig.). (C). 1993. reprint ed. pap. 17.95 (*0-943089-02-6*) U GA CFIMCTR.

Reybold, Laura. Everything You Need to Know about the Dangers of Tattooing & Body Piercing, 8 vols. LC 95-20227. (Need to Know Library). (Illus.). 64p. (YA). (gr. 5-7). 1996. lib. bdg. 17.95 (*0-8239-2151-4*) Rosen Group.

Reybold, Laura, jt. auth. see Rosen Group Staff.

Reybold, W. U. & Petersen, G. W. Soil Survey Techniques. (Special Publications: No. 20). 112p. 1987. 10.00 (*0-89118-783-9*) Soil Sci Soc Am.

Reyburn, Philip J. & Wilson, Terry L., eds. "Jottings from Dixie" The Civil War Dispatches of Sergeant Major Stephen F. Fleharty, U. S. A. LC 98-51114. (Illus.). 232p. 1999. 29.95 (*0-8071-2347-1*) La State U Pr.

Reyburn, Hugh Y. John Calvin: His Life, Letters & Work. LC 83-45630. reprint ed. 45.00 (*0-404-19847-3*) AMS Pr.

Reyburn, Scott. Art of the Impressionists. (Illus.). 128p. 10.99 (*1-57215-248-6*, JG2486) World Pubns.

Reyburn, Stanley. Sherlock Holmes in the Case of the Phantom Brigade. LC 98-28406. (Radio Plays Ser.). 1998. pap. 6.00 (*0-88734-732-0*) Players Pr.

***Reyburn, Stanley.** Sherlock Holmes in the Kiannan Blueprint. unabridged ed. LC 99-46896. 16p. 1999. pap. 6.00 (*0-88734-731-2*) Players Pr.

Reyburn, Stanley, jt. auth. see Doyle, Arthur Conan.

Reyburn, Stanley S. Alphabetically Eclectic: An A-to-Z Poetry Anthology. Carangelo, Lori, ed. 150p. 1999. pap. 9.95 (*0-942605-08-X*) Access Pr CA.

An Asterisk (*) at the beginning of an entry indicates that the title is appearing for the first time.

R

— Holmes Hiatus - The Parisian Affair. unabridged ed. Landes, William-Alan, ed. LC 98-28684. 55p. 1998. pap. 6.00 (*0-88734-739-8*) Players Pr.

*__Reyburn, Stanley S.__ JOBS2000: Starting, Buying & Selling Businesses. 200p. 2000. pap. 29.95 (*0-942605-09-8*) Access Pr CA.

Reyburn, Stanley S. Real Estate Finance. 582p. (C). 1994. pap. text 29.95 (*1-884811-00-0*) Felde Pubng.

— Sherlock Holmes in the Case of the Crafty Cracksman. unabridged ed. Landes, William-Alan, ed. LC 99-26435. (Radio Plays Ser.). 15p. 1999. pap. 6.00 (*0-88734-744-4*) Players Pr.

— Sherlock Holmes in the Case of the Derailed Shipment. Landes, William-Alan, ed. LC 97-49024. 55p. 1998. pap. 6.00 (*0-88734-734-7*) Players Pr.

— Sherlock Holmes in the Case of the Fatal Poppy. Landes, William-Alan, ed. LC 97-51919. 55p. 1998. pap. 6.00 (*0-88734-741-X*) Players Pr.

— Sherlock Holmes in the Case of the Nervous Nanny. Landes, William-Alan, ed. LC 97-49035. 55p. 1998. pap. 6.00 (*0-88734-737-1*) Players Pr.

— Sherlock Holmes in the Case of the Perilous Pawn. unabridged ed. Landes, William-Alan, ed. LC 98-28687. (Radio Plays Ser.). 55p. 1998. pap. 6.00 (*0-88734-733-9*) Players Pr.

— Sherlock Holmes in the Manitoba Marauder. unabridged ed. Landes, William-Alan, ed. LC 98-28686. (Radio Plays Ser.). 55p. 1998. pap. 6.00 (*0-88734-730-4*) Players Pr.

— Sherlock Holmes in the Meiji Experience. Landes, William-Alan, ed. LC 97-46910. 55p. 1998. pap. 6.00 (*0-88734-743-6*) Players Pr.

— Sherlock Holmes in the Murray River Mystery. unabridged ed. Landes, William-Alan, ed. LC 98-28407. (Radio Plays Ser.). 55p. 1998. pap. 6.00 (*0-88734-738-X*) Players Pr.

*__Reyburn, Stanley S.__ Sherlock Holmes in The Scarab of Abu-Simbel. unabridged ed. LC 99-51855. (Orig.). 1999. pap. 6.00 (*0-88734-735-5*) Players Pr.

— Sherlock Holmes in The Soong Conspiracy. unabridged ed. LC 99-47944. 16p. (Orig.). 1999. pap. 6.00 (*0-88734-736-3*) Players Pr.

Reyburn, Stanley S. Sherlock Holmes in the Voyage of Sven Sigerson. unabridged ed. Landes, William-Alan, ed. LC 99-26064. (Radio Plays Ser.). 15p. 1999. pap. 6.00 (*0-88734-740-1*) Players Pr.

— What a Wonderful World This Could Be. (Illus.). 28p. (Orig.). 1990. pap. 7.50 (*0-910147-87-6*) World Poetry Pr.

Reyburn, Wallace. Flushed with Pride: The Story of Thomas Crapper. (Illus.). 128p. 1998. pap. 9.95 (*1-85702-860-0*, Pub. by Fourth Estate) Trafalgar.

Reyburn, William D. A Handbook on Lamentations. LC 92-22755. (UBS Handbook Ser.). ix, 166p. 1992. pap. 11.99 (*0-8267-0124-8*, 104975) Untd Bible Soc.

— A Handbook on the Book of Job. LC 92-12735. (UBS Handbook Ser.). (Illus.). ix, 806p. 1992. pap. 19.99 (*0-8267-0117-5*, 104880) Untd Bible Soc.

Reyburn, William D. & Fry, Euan M. A Handbook on Genesis. LC 97-43855. (UBS Handbook Ser.). x, 1149p. 1998. write for info. (*0-8267-0100-0*) Untd Bible Soc.

*__Reyburn, William D. & Fry, Euan M.__ A Handbook on the Book of Proverbs. LC 99-87069. (Helps for Translators Ser.). 800p. 2000. 19.99 (*0-8267-0120-5*, 109186, Pub. by Untd Bible Soc) Am Bible.

Reyburn, William D., jt. auth. see Bratcher, Robert G.

*__Reychler, Luc.__ Democratic Peace-Building & Conflict Prevention: The Devil Is in the Transition. (Illus.). 176p. 1999. pap. 45.00 (*90-6186-985-4*, Pub. by Leuven Univ) Coronet Bks.

*__Reychler, Luc & Paffenholz, Thania, eds.__ Peacebuilding: A Field Guide. 600p. 2001. 65.00 (*1-55587-912-8*); pap. 29.95 (*1-55587-937-3*) L Rienner.

Reychler, Luc, jt. ed. see Rudney, Robert.

Reychman, J. Hungarian-Polish Comprehensive Dictionary. 2nd rev. ed. (HUN & POL.). 1059p. 1985. 75.00 (*0-8288-1064-8*, M 8566) Fr & Eur.

Reychman, Jan & Zajaczkowski, Ananiasz. Handbook of Ottoman-Turkish Diplomatics. rev. ed. Ehrenkreutz, Andrew S., tr. (Publications in Near & Middle East Studies: Ser. A, No. 7). (Illus.). 1968. 69.25 (*90-279-0513-4*) Mouton.

Reydams-Schils, Gretchen. An Anthology of Snakebites: On Women, Love, & Philosophy. LC 99-48236. 152p. (C). 1999. pap. text 19.95 (*1-889119-13-X*) Seven Bridges.

Reyden, Susan Van Der, see Ochs, Linnea L. & Van Der Reyden, Susan, eds.

Reyder, Rimma. Jewish Ceremonial Designs. (International Design Library). (Illus.). 48p. 1987. pap. 5.95 (*0-88045-087-8*) Stemmer Hse.

Reyer, Carolyn, ed. see Monroe, Mark.

Reyer, Philip, et al, eds. The Heritage of Limestone County, Alabama. (Heritage of Alabama Ser.). (Illus.). 316p. 1998. 55.00 (*1-891647-17-2*) Herit Pub Consult.

Reyerson, Donald M. The American Commercial Nuclear Power Industry Programs, Business Processes, & Organizational Evolutions - A Global Assessment & Prognosis. (ICONE 4 - Technical Papers). 1996. write for info. (*0-614-16715-9*, 96-NE-3) ASME.

Reyerson, Kathryn, jt. auth. see Chiat, Marilyn Segal.

Reyerson, Kathryn L. Business, Banking & Finance in Medieval Montpellier. xvi, 184p. pap. text 25.14 (*0-88844-075-8*) Brill Academic Pubs.

— Society, Law & Trade in Medieval Montpellier. (Collected Studies Ser.: No. CS475). 330p. 1995. 109.95 (*0-86078-460-6*, Pub. by Variorum) Ashgate Pub Co.

Reyerson, Kathryn L. & Drendel, J., eds. Urban & Rural Communities in Medieval France: Provence & Languedoc, 1000-1500. LC 98-35745. (Medieval Mediterranean Ser.: Vol. 18). (Illus.). xxiv, 336p. 1998. 122.50 (*90-04-10850-5*) Brill Academic Pubs.

Reyerson, Kathryn L., jt. ed. see Hanawalt, Barbara A.

Reyes, A. T. Archaic Cyprus: A Study of the Textual & Archaeological Evidence. LC 93-26237. (Oxford Monographs on Classical Archaeology). (Illus.). 224p. (C). 1994. text 90.00 (*0-19-813227-1*, Clarendon Pr) OUP.

Reyes, Adelaida. Songs of the Caged, Songs of the Free: Music & the Vietnamese Refugee Experience. LC 98-54778. (Illus.). 248p. 1999. 59.50 (*1-56639-685-9*); pap. 19.95 (*1-56639-686-7*) Temple U Pr.

Reyes, Alfonso. La Experiencia Literaria. (SPA.). pap. 7.99 (*968-16-1258-2*, Pub. by Fondo) Continental Bk.

— Mexico en una Nuez. (Fondo 2000 Ser.). (SPA.). pap. 2.99 (*968-16-5056-5*, Pub. by Fondo) Continental Bk.

— Position of America & Other Essays. De Onis, Harriet, tr. LC 77-142690. (Essay Index Reprint Ser.). 1977. 19.95 (*0-8369-2067-8*) Ayer.

— La Trayectoria de Goethe. (Breviarios Ser.). (SPA.). pap. 6.99 (*968-16-3118-8*, Pub. by Fondo) Continental Bk.

Reyes, Alina. Behind Closed Doors. Watson, David, tr. from FRE. 352p. 1997. pap. 14.00 (*0-8021-3505-6*, Grove) Grove-Atltic.

— The Butcher: And Other Erotica. Watson, David, tr. from FRE. LC 95-1761. 208p. 1996. reprint ed. pap. 11.00 (*0-8021-3450-5*, Grove) Grove-Atltic.

— The Fatal Bodice. 99p. 1995. pap. 5.99 (*0-7493-2178-4*) Buttrwrth-Heinemann.

Reyes, Belinda I. Dynamics of Immigration: Return Migration to Western Mexico. LC 97-29806. (Illus.). xxi, 99 p. 1997. pap. 10.00 (*0-9653184-2-7*) Pub Policy Inst.

Reyes, Benito F. Conscious Dying: Psychology of Death & Guidebook to Liberation. LC 86-51403. (Illus.). 212p. (Orig.). (C). 1986. pap. 15.00 (*0-939375-15-X*) World Univ Amer.

— Dialogues with God: Sonnet Psalms on the Significance of Being Human. LC 78-244706. 139p. 1969. reprint ed. pap. 10.00 (*0-939375-37-0*) World Univ Amer.

— Education for World Peace. 112p. 1971. pap. 10.00 (*0-939375-12-5*) World Univ Amer.

— The Essence of All Religions: In Search of Meaning. 38p. (C). 1983. pap. 5.00 (*0-939375-14-1*) World Univ Amer.

— The Essence of All Religions: In Search of Meaning. 38p. (C). 1995. pap. text 5.00 (*0-939375-40-0*) World Univ Amer.

— The Eternal Christ: Sonnet Prayer for the Second Coming. 18p. 1977. pap. 5.50 (*0-939375-00-1*) World Univ Amer.

— Inspired Meditations in Upper Ojai. 177p. (Orig.). 1990. pap. 7.50 (*0-939375-17-6*) World Univ Amer.

— Inspired Meditations in Upper Opai: A Treasured String of Pearls. 177p. 1990. pap. 6.75 (*0-939375-18-4*) World Univ Amer.

— Meditation: Cybernetics of Consciousness. Volz, Fred J., ed. 152p. 1978. pap. 10.00 (*0-939375-04-4*) World Univ Amer.

— Moments Without Self. 4th ed. LC 61-21760. 198p. 1970. reprint ed. 10.00 (*0-939375-36-2*) World Univ Amer.

— On World Peace. 24p. 1977. pap. text 1.50 (*0-939375-10-9*) World Univ Amer.

— Our Father: Sonnet Symphony. 28p. (Orig.). 1994. pap. 3.00 (*0-939375-39-7*) World Univ Amer.

— The Practice of Conscious Dying: Off-Ramp to Liberation & Freeway to Conscious Immortality. 134p. (Orig.). 1990. pap. 6.75 (*0-939375-16-8*) World Univ Amer.

— The Process of Moral Choice. (Ethics 101 Ser.). 142p. 1967. pap. 10.00 (*0-939375-28-1*) World Univ Amer.

— Sonnet Adoration of the Avatar: The Splendor of the Sathya Sai. (Illus.). 300p. 1985. reprint ed. pap. 20.00 (*0-939375-06-0*) World Univ Amer.

Reyes, Bernardo. Retrato de Familia: Neruda 1904-1920. (Illus.). 1996. pap. 14.95 (*0-8477-0296-0*) U of PR Pr.

Reyes, Carlos. Nightmarks. LC 88-26747. 1990. 15.95 (*0-89924-060-7*); pap. 8.00 (*0-89924-059-3*) Lynx Hse.

— A Suitcase Full of Crows: Poems. LC 95-10394. 1995. pap. 10.00 (*1-878325-12-4*) Bluestem Press.

Reyes, Carlos, tr. from SPA. Open Doors. LC 98-54781.Tr. of Puertas Abiertas. 32p. 1999. pap. 7.00 (*0-932264-25-5*) Trask Hse Bks.

Reyes, Carlos, tr. see de la Torre, Josefina.

Reyes, Carlos, tr. see de la Torre, Josephina.

Reyes, Carlos, tr. see Millares, Selena.

Reyes, Carmen S. Redaccion Comercial. 381p. 1992. pap. text 12.95 (*0-8477-3679-2*) U of PR Pr.

Reyes, Chris, et al. The Table Rocks of Jackson County: Islands in the Sky. LC 93-91595. (Illus.). 142p. (Orig.). (C). 1994. pap. 14.00 (*0-9637486-0-2*) Last Minute.

Reyes, Christiane, tr. see Cooper, Helen.

Reyes, David & Waldman, Tom. Land of a Thousand Dances: Chicano Rock 'n' Roll from Southern California. LC 97-50573. 178p. 1998. 50.00 (*0-8263-1929-7*) U of NM Pr.

— Land of a Thousand Dances: Chicano Rock 'n' Roll from Southern California. LC 97-50573. (Illus.). 178p. 1998. pap. 18.95 (*0-8263-1883-5*) U of NM Pr.

Reyes, Dominga L. Meditations: 365 Days with Shai Sathya Baba. 1987. 6.00 (*0-939375-01-X*) World Univ Amer.

— The Story of Two Souls. 80p. 1984. pap. 5.50 (*0-939375-02-8*) World Univ Amer.

Reyes, E. Manual de Procedimientos.Tr. of Operations Manual. (SPA.). 224p. 1994. pap. 9.99 (*0-8297-2040-5*) Vida Pubs.

Reyes, Felix O. Peregrinos de la Libertad. (Caribbean Collection). 245p. 1992. 29.95 (*0-8477-0898-5*) U of PR Pr.

Reyes, Felix O., ed. La Manigua en Paris: Correspondencia Diplomatica De Betances. (SPA.). 156p. (Orig.). 1984. pap. 6.00 (*1-878483-09-9*) Hunter Coll CEP.

Reyes, Felix Ojeda, see Ojeda Reyes, Felix.

Reyes, G. E. & Moerdijk, Izak. Models for Smooth Infinitesimal Analysis. (Illus.). x, 399p. 1990. 95.95 (*0-387-97489-X*) Spr-Verlag.

Reyes-Garcia, Ismael. Actualidad del Quijote y Otros Ensayos. LC 83-21679. (UPREX, Ensayo Ser.: No. 66). (SPA.). 121p. (Orig.). 1984. pap. 3.00 (*0-8477-0066-6*) U of PR Pr.

*__Reyes, Ginny.__ Addie's Knight, 1 vol. (Time Passages Ser.). 1999. mass mkt. 5.99 (*0-515-12506-7*, Jove) Berkley Pub.

Reyes, Ginny. Faerie Tale. (Magical Love Ser.). 1998. mass mkt. 5.99 (*0-515-12338-2*, Jove) Berkley Pub.

Reyes, Gracianus R. Death in the Cordilleras. 77p. (Orig.). (C). 1989. pap. 7.50 (*971-10-0371-6*, Pub. by New Day Pub) Cellar.

— The Moon & Bai Insiang & Other Stories. 108p. (Orig.). (C). 1990. pap. 10.75 (*971-10-0276-0*, Pub. by New Day Pub) Cellar.

— The Uncommitted. 90p. (Orig.). 1986. pap. 6.50 (*971-10-0249-3*, Pub. by New Day Pub) Cellar.

Reyes, Gracianus R. & Allego, Antonio M. Double Jeopardy: Fourteen Stories. 96p. (Orig.). (C). 1992. pap. 7.50 (*971-10-0459-3*, Pub. by New Day Pub) Cellar.

*__Reyes, Guillermo.__ Men on the Verge of a His-Panic Breakdown. 49p. (C). 1998. pap. 5.60 (*0-87129-899-6*, MB5) Dramatic Pub.

*__Reyes, Gullermo, et al.__ Rowing to America: The Immigrant Project. 94p. (YA). (gr. 10 up). 1999. pap. 5.60 (*0-87129-902-X*, R51) Dramatic Pub.

Reyes, Gustavo, jt. auth. see Pumarino, Jose Maria.

Reyes, H. B., et al, eds. Pregnancy, Sex Hormones, & the Liver: Proceedings of the 89th Falk Symposium, Held in Santiago, Chile, 10-11 November 1995. LC 96-17382. 1996. text 147.00 (*0-7923-8704-X*) Kluwer Academic.

Reyes, Isabelo De Los, see De Los Reyes, Isabelo.

*__Reyes, Jericho.__ Ero Gami. (Illus.). 48p. 2000. pap. 9.95 (*1-56167-613-6*) Am Literary Pr.

*__Reyes, Jesse Marinoff.__ Next: The New Generation in Graphic Design. LC 00-29201. (Illus.). 160p. 2000. write for info. (*0-89134-999-5*) North Lght.

*__Reyes, Jesus.__ Guide to Selecting & Applying to Master of Social Work Programs. 4th rev. ed. LC 99-68549. 252p. (C). 2000. pap. 19.95 (*1-929109-01-6*) White Hat.

Reyes, Jesus. Guide to Selecting & Applying to Master of Social Work Programs, 1999. 1999th ed. 220p. 1999. pap. 19.95 (*0-9653653-3-6*) White Hat.

Reyes, Jorge, jt. auth. see Walton, Harold F.

Reyes, Jose A. Epistola a los Filipenses.Tr. of Epistle to the Phillipians. (SPA.). 1991. pap., student ed. 2.99 (*0-945792-50-6*, 498511) Editorial Unilit.

— Epistola a los Romanos. (Estudiante Serie Encuentros - Student Bible Studies).Tr. of Epistle to the Romas. (SPA.). 60p. 1989. pap. 2.99 (*0-945792-30-1*, 498510) Editorial Unilit.

Reyes, Jose S. Legislative History of America's Economic Policy Toward the Philippines. LC 23-11140. (Columbia University. Studies in the Social Sciences: No. 240). reprint ed. 20.00 (*0-404-51240-2*) AMS Pr.

Reyes, Jun C. Utos Ng Hari at Iba Pang Kuwento. (TAG., Illus.). 130p. 1981. pap. 10.75 (*971-10-0221-3*, Pub. by New Day Pub) Cellar.

Reyes, Karen W., et al. Lambda Gray: A Practical, Emotional & Spiritual Guide for Gays & Lesbians Who Are Growing Older. Farrell, Lorena F., ed. 160p. (Orig.). 1993. pap. 12.95 (*0-87877-179-4*) Newcastle Pub.

Reyes, Ken, Jr. Handbook to Higher Consciousness: The Workbook. 228p. (Orig.). 1989. pap. 8.95 (*0-915972-16-6*) Love Line Bks.

Reyes Lagunes, I. & Poortinga, Ype H., eds. From a Different Perspective. vi, 390p. 1985. pap. 58.25 (*90-265-0672-4*) Swets.

*__Reyes, Luis.__ Hispanics in Hollywood: A Celebration of 100 Years in Film & Television. (Illus.). 550p. 2000. pap. text 21.95 (*1-58065-025-2*) Lone Eagle Pub.

Reyes, Luis & Rubie, Peter, eds. Hispanics in Hollywood: An Encyclopedia of Film & Television. LC 93-40607. (Illus.). 592p. 1994. text 100.00 (*0-8153-0827-2*, H1761) Garland.

Reyes, Luis E. Modelo Antiguo: A Novel of Mexico City. Franco, Sharon & Hayes, Joe, trs. LC 97-28170.Tr. of Modelo Antiguo. 160p. (Orig.). 1997. pap. 11.95 (*0-938317-32-6*) Cinco Puntos.

Reyes, Luis I. Made in Paradise: Hollywood's Films of Hawai'i & the South Seas. (Illus.). 320p. (Orig.). 1995. 45.00 (*1-56647-089-7*) Mutual Pub HI.

Reyes, Lynda A. The Textiles of the Southern Philippines. 170p. (C). 1992. text 28.00 (*971-542-005-2*, Pub. by U of Philippines Pr); pap. text 17.95 (*971-542-006-0*, Pub. by U of Philippines Pr) UH Pr.

Reyes, Marily A. Rincon Bohemio/Bohemian Corner: Gala del Ricon Escrita/Writers Gala. 104p. 1998. pap. 9.00 (*0-88100-104-X*) Natl Writ Pr.

Reyes, Mario. Le Meridien Dallas Cookbook. (Illus.). 106p. (Orig.). 1995. pap., spiral bd. 14.95 (*0-9651298-8-8*) Le Meridien Dallas.

Reyes, Narciso G. Lupang Tinubuan & Selected Works in English. 118p. (Orig.). (C). 1991. pap. 10.75 (*971-10-0407-0*, Pub. by New Day Pub) Cellar.

Reyes, Nestor, jt. auth. see Hales, John.

Reyes, Norman. Child of Two Worlds: The Autobiography of a Filipino-American...or Vice-Versa. (Illus.). 289p. 1995. 35.00 (*0-89410-777-1*, Three Contnts); pap. 16.95 (*0-89410-778-X*, Three Contnts) L Rienner.

Reyes, Oscar, tr. see Smith, Karen S. & Ciangio, Donna L.

Reyes, Oscar, tr. see Smith, Karen S. & Ciangion, Donna L.

Reyes, Oscar, tr. see Smith, Karen S., et al.

Reyes, Oscar, tr. see Subcommittee for the Third Millennium/Jubilee Year.

Reyes, Pedro, ed. Teachers & Their Workplace: Commitment, Performance, & Productivity. (Focus Editions Ser.: Vol. 122). (Illus.). 320p. (C). 1990. pap. 29.95 (*0-8039-3689-3*) Corwin Pr.

Reyes, Pedro, et al. Lessons from High-Performing Hispanic Schools: Creating Learning Communities. LC 98-51496. (Critical Issues in Educational Leadership Ser.). 240p. 1999. pap. text 23.95 (*0-8077-3830-1*) Tchrs Coll.

— Lessons from High-Performing Hispanic Schools: Creating Learning Communities, Vol. #5. Scribner, Alicia Paredes, ed. LC 98-51496. 5. 240p. 1999. 52.00 (*0-8077-3831-X*) Tchrs Coll.

Reyes, Ray. The Ten Commandments for Teaching: A Teacher's View. 48p. 1991. pap. 8.95 (*0-8106-1539-8*) NEA.

Reyes, Rebecca. Fajita Fiesta. (Illus.). 60p. 1985. pap. 3.57 (*0-9622394-0-2*) Fajita Fiesta.

Reyes, Reynaldo & Wilson, J. K. Rafaga: The Life Story of a Nicaraguan Miskito Comandante. Sloan, Tod S., ed. LC 92-54141. (Illus.). 232p. 1992. 27.95 (*0-8061-2453-9*) U of Okla Pr.

Reyes, Rose. New Life for the Elderly: God's Vision to a Home Care Provider. LC 96-119674. 112p. (Orig.). 1994. pap. 8.00 (*0-9636577-1-2*) Trego-Hill.

Reyes, RoseMarie A. Treasure & Other Poems. (Illus.). 28p. (Orig.). 1996. pap. 6.95 (*0-9654775-0-9*) R M A R Publns.

Reyes, Sandra, ed. Oblivion & Stone: A Selection of Contemporary Bolivian Poetry & Fiction. DuVal, John et al, trs. from SPA. LC 97-51161. 256p. 1998. 38.00 (*1-55728-511-X*); pap. 22.00 (*1-55728-512-8*) U of Ark Pr.

Reyes, Sandra, tr. see Parra, Nicanor.

Reyes, Simone. Astrology for Dogs. Caton, Patrick, ed. LC 98-71849. 168p. 1998. pap. 5.95 (*1-56245-344-0*) Great Quotations.

Reyes, Simone & Compton, Ken. Astrology for Cats. Caton, Patrick, ed. LC 97-77656. (Illus.). 168p. 1998. pap. 5.95 (*1-56245-340-8*) Great Quotations.

Reyes, Spindola. Una Carta Para Ti de Angel de la Guarda. 1997. pap. text 10.98 (*968-890-163-6*) Edit Diana.

Reyes, Teresa, ed. see Shelley, Mary Wollstonecraft.

Reyes, Victor, tr. see Laufer, Peter.

Reyes, Victor, tr. see Reeves, Margaret, et al.

Reyes, Vinicio H. Bicultural-Bilingual Education for Latino Students. Cordasco, Francesco, ed. LC 77-90553. (Bilingual-Bicultural Education in the U. S. Ser.). 1978. lib. bdg. 36.95 (*0-405-11092-8*) Ayer.

Reyes, Z., jt. auth. see Cotts, D.

*__Reyfman, Irina.__ Ritualized Violence Russian Style: The Duel in Russian Culture & Literature. LC 99-21520. 1999. 49.50 (*0-8047-3412-7*) Stanford U Pr.

Reyfman, Irina. Vasilii Trediakovsky: The Fool of the "New" Russian Literature. LC 90-9682. (Illus.). 336p. 1991. 42.50 (*0-8047-1824-5*) Stanford U Pr.

Reyher, Becky. My Mother Is the Most Beautiful Woman in the World. (Illus.). 40p. (J). (gr. k-3). 1944. lib. bdg. 16.93 (*0-688-51251-8*) Lothrop.

Reyher, Ken. Antoine Robidoux & Fort Uncompahgre: The Story of a Western Colorado Fur Trader. LC 98-87114. (Illus.). 88p. 1998. pap. 9.95 (*1-890437-13-1*) Western Reflections.

Reyher, Paul. Les Masques Anglais. LC 64-14712. 1972. 36.95 (*0-405-08880-9*, Pub. by Blom Pubns) Ayer.

Reyher, Rebecca H. Zulu Woman: The Life Story of Christina Sibiya. LC 98-41326. (Women Writing Africa Ser.). 256p. 1998. 45.00 (*1-55861-202-5*, Pub. by Feminist Pr) Consort Bk Sales.

*__Reyher, Rebecca Hourwich.__ Zulu Woman: The Life of Christina Sibiya. 252p. 1999. pap. 21.95 (*0-86980-964-4*, Pub. by Univ Natal Pr) Intl Spec Bk.

Reyher, Rebecca Hourwich. Zulu Woman: The Life Story of Christina Sibiya. LC 98-41326. 256p. 1998. pap. 15.95 (*1-55861-203-3*, Pub. by Feminist Pr) Consort Bk Sales.

Reyhner, Jon, ed. Teaching American Indian Students. LC 92-54136. (Illus.). 344p. 1994. pap. 15.95 (*0-8061-2674-4*) U of Okla Pr.

Reyhner, Jon & Eder, Jeanne. A History of Indian Education. 150p. 1989. pap. 8.95 (*0-89992-515-4*) Coun India Ed.

Reyhner, Jon, ed. see Holland, Royce Q., et al.

Reyhons, Kenneth. Recruiting Sales Associates. 2nd ed. LC 86-63281. 153p. 1990. 22.00 (*0-913652-62-8*) Realtors Natl.

— Strategic Planning for the Real Estate Manager. 2nd rev. ed. Bettin, Christopher, ed. (Illus.). 125p. 1989. reprint ed. pap. 22.00 (*0-913652-68-7*) Realtors Natl.

— Strategic Planning for the Real Estate Manager. 3rd ed. Bettin, Christopher, ed. LC 93-4861. 1993. 22.00 (*0-913652-78-4*) Realtors Natl.

Reyhons, Kenneth, jt. auth. see Godi, Art.

Reyle, Uwe & Rohrer, C., eds. Natural Language Parsing & Linguistic Theories. 1988. lib. bdg. 143.50 (*1-55608-055-7*) Kluwer Academic.

Reyle, Uwe, jt. auth. see Kamp, Hans.

Reyles, Carlos. Castanets. Le Clerq, Jacques, tr. 1977. lib. bdg. 59.95 (*0-8490-1583-9*) Gordon Pr.

Reyman, A., tr. see Arnol'd, V. I. & Novikov, S. P., eds.

Reyman, Jonathan E. The Gran Chichimeca: Essays on the Archaeology & Ethnohistory of North Meso America. (Worldwide Archaeology Series 12). 260p. 1995. 87.95 (*1-85628-711-4*, Pub. by Avebry) Ashgate Pub Co.

Reyman, Randall G. The Jazz Sax Primer. (Building Excellence Ser.). 1991. pap. 6.95 (*1-56222-090-X*, 94530) Mel Bay.

— Jazz Trombone Primer. 36p. 1992. pap. 5.95 (*1-56222-398-4*, 94652) Mel Bay.

— Jazz Trumpet Primer. 96p. 1992. pap. 5.95 (*1-56222-388-7*, 94651) Mel Bay.

*__Reyment, R. A. & Savazzi, E.__ Aspects of Multivariate Statistical Analysis in Geology. 292p. 1999. pap. 76.00 (*0-444-50412-5*) Elsevier.

*__Reyment, R. A. & Savazzi, Enrico.__ Aspects of Multivariate Statistical Analysis in Geology. LC 99-44753. 292p. 1999. write for info. (*0-444-82568-1*) Elsevier.

R

Reyment, Richard A. Multidimensional Palaeobiology. 426p. 1991. 173.00 (*0-08-037231-7*, Pergamon Pr); pap. 60.00 (*0-08-041001-4*, Pergamon Pr) Elsevier.

Reyment, Richard A. & Joreskog, K. G. Applied Factor Analysis in the Natural Sciences. 2nd ed. 383p. 1996. pap. text 39.95 (*0-521-57556-7*) Cambridge U Pr.

Reyment, Richard A., jt. ed. see Cubitt, J. M.

Reymer & Gersin Associates Staff. Building Bridges with Cable: A Survey of Local Cable System Operators & MSO Executives. 130p. (Orig.). 1990. pap. 40.00 (*0-89324-087-7*) Natl Assn Broadcasters.

Reymert, Martin L., ed. Feelings & Emotions: The Wittenberg Symposium. LC 73-2986. (Classics in Psychology Ser.). 1974. reprint ed. 28.95 (*0-405-05158-1*) Ayer.

Reymes, Ellen. Christmas Party. LC 99-188029. (You're Invited to Mary-Kate & Ashley's Ser.). 48p. (J). (gr. 2-4). 1997. 12.95 (*0-590-76958-8*) Scholastic Inc.

Reymes, William, tr. see Secchi, Nicolo.

Reymond, Arnold. History of the Sciences in Greco-Roman Antiquity. Bray, Ruth G. De, tr. LC 63-18046. 1963. 30.00 (*0-8196-0128-4*) Biblo.

Reymond, E. A. & Barns, J. W., eds. Four Martyrdoms from the Pierpont Morgan Coptic Codices. 278p. 1974. 24.95 (*0-19-815448-8*) OUP.

Reymond, Henri & Mailick, Sidney. International Personnel Policies & Practices. 256p. 1985. 62.95 (*0-275-90155-6*, C0155, Praeger Pubs) Greenwood.

Reymond, Jean-Pierre. Metals: Born of Earth & Fire. LC 87-34596. (Illus.). 38p. (J). (gr. k-5). 1988. 5.95 (*0-944589-19-7*, 197) Young Discovery Lib.

Reymond, Lizelle. The Dedicated: A Biography of Nivedita. 380p. 1985. 10.95 (*0-910261-16-4*, Arcana Pubng) Lotus Pr.

— To Live Within: A Woman's Spiritual Pilgrimmage in a Himalayan Hermitage. 326p. (Orig.). 1995. pap. 14.95 (*0-915801-54-X*) Rudra Pr.

***Reymond, M. A., et al.** Port-Site & Wound Recurrences in Cancer Surgery: Incidence - Pathogenesis - Prevention. Jack, A., tr. from GER. (Illus.). 210p. 2000. 104.00 (*3-540-66929-9*) Spr-Verlag.

Reymond, P. Dictionary of Biblical Hebrew & Aramean. (FRE & HEB.). 1104p. 1991. 125.00 (*0-8288-6920-0*, 2204044636) Fr & Eur.

Reymond, Robert L. Jesus, Divine Messiah: The Old Testament Witness. 13.50 (*0-906731-94-1*, Pub. by Christian Focus) Spring Arbor Dist.

— Systematic Theology of the Christian Faith. LC 97-12939. 1998. 39.99 (*0-8499-1317-9*) Word Pub.

Reymond, Robert L., intro. see Hodge, Charles.

Reymond, Sama. Embalmers' Archives from Hawara Vol. 1: Catalogue of Demotic Papyri in the Ashmolean Museum. (Illus.). 187p. 1973. 85.00 (*0-900416-08-4*, Pub. by Aris & Phillips) David Brown.

Reyna, Bessy. She Remembers. 1997. pap. 7.00 (*0-916897-28-1*) Andrew Mtn Pr.

Reyna, Jimmie V. Passport to North American Trade: Rules of Origin & Customs Procedures under NAFTA. LC 95-22565. (NAFTA Ser.). 1995. pap. write for info. (*0-07-172582-2*) Shepards.

Reyna, Jose L., et al. Understanding Mexico: Historical Perspective & Future Potential. Blachman, Morris M. et al, eds. LC 85-62047. (Papers on International Issues: No. 7). 63p. (Orig.). 1985. pap. 5.00 (*0-935082-09-3*) Southern Ctr Intl Stud.

Reyna, Rene. El Sol Tiene Manchas. LC 92-71445. (Coleccion Caniqui). (SPA.). 177p. (Orig.). 1992. pap. 19.95 (*0-89729-643-5*) Ediciones.

Reyna, Ruth, ed. Dictionary of Oriental Philosophy. 419p. 1993. 57.50 (*81-215-0118-0*, Pub. by M Manoharial) Coronet Bks.

Reyna, Sergio, ed. see Gonzalez de Mireles, Jovita.

Reyna, Stephen P., jt. ed. see Downs, R. E.

***Reynaert, Ingrid.** Study of the Cystic Fibrosis Transmembrane Conductance Regulator (CFTR) Protein in Human & Mouse VAS Deferens. (Acta Biomedica Lovaniensia Ser.: Vol. 189). (Illus.). 140p. 1998. pap. 47.50 (*90-6186-940-4*, Pub. by Leuven Univ) Coronet Bks.

Reynal, F. Pedagogie, Dictionnaire Concepts Cles. (FRE.). 1998. 110.00 (*0-320-00190-3*) Fr & Eur.

Reynal, G. Dictionnaire des Theologiens, Theologie Chretienne. (FRE.). 1998. 105.00 (*0-320-00362-0*) Fr & Eur.

Reynal, Vicente. Civilizaciones de Occidente: Cuadecno de Trabajo - Introduccion a la Humanidades. (SPA., Illus.). 320p. (Orig.). (C). 1995. wbk. ed. 15.95 (*1-56328-043-4*) Edit Plaza Mayor.

— Civilizaciones de Occidente: Cuadecno de Trabajo - Introduccion a la Humanidades. 8th ed. (Textbook Ser.). (SPA., Illus.). 470p. (Orig.). 1991. reprint ed. pap. text 17.95 (*1-56328-006-X*) Edit Plaza Mayor.

— Introduccion a las Humanidades. LC 90-43241. (SPA.). 85p. 1990. pap. 4.75 (*0-8477-2833-1*) U of PR Pr.

Reynal, Vicente, ed. & tr. see Seneca, Lucius Annaeus.

Reynaldo, Andres. La Sombra del Arquero. (SPA.). Date not set. pap. write for info. (*0-89729-821-7*) Ediciones.

Reynard, Alan M., jt. auth. see Smith, Cedric M.

Reynard, K. W., jt. ed. see Barry, T.

Reynard, Michael. Money Secrets of the Rich & Famous. LC 99-28130. 256p. 1999. 24.95 (*1-58115-032-6*) Allworth Pr.

Reynard, Robert. Secret Code Breaker: A Crtptanalysis Handbook. (Illus.). 96p. 1996. pap. 12.95 incl. disk (*1-889668-00-1*) S & D.

***Reynard, Robert.** Secret Code Breaker III. 124p. 1999. pap. text 12.95 (*1-889668-13-3*) S & D.

***Reynard, Sue & Weiss, David.** Streetwise Sales Letters: 2,500 Professionally Written Sales & Marketing Letters - With CD-ROM for Windows. (Streetwise Ser.). (Illus.). 400p. 2000. pap. 24.95 incl. cd-rom (*1-58062-440-5*) Adams Media.

Reynard, Sue, jt. auth. see Joiner Assocs., Inc. Staff.

Reynard, Sue, ed. see Joiner Associates Inc. Staff.

Reynard, Sue, ed. see Joiner Associates Inc. Staff & GOAL/QPC Staff.

Reynard, Sue, ed. see Joiner Assocs., Inc. Staff.

Reynard, Sue, ed. see Joiner Assocs., Inc. Staff & Goal/QPC Staff.

Reynard, Sue, ed. see Joiner, Brian L.

Reynard, Susan, ed. see Conzemius, Anne & O'Neill, Jan.

Reynarowych, Z., tr. see Sachs, L.

***Reynaud, Emmanuel.** Social Dialogue & Pension Reform: U. K., U. S., Germany, Japan, Swede, Italy, Spain. 112p. 2000. pap. text 14.95 (*92-2-110835-X*, Pub. by ILO) ILO Pubns Ctr.

Reynaud, Emmanuel, et al, eds. International Perspectives on Supplementary Pensions: Actors & Issues. LC 95-38753. 272p. 1996. 77.50 (*0-89930-967-4*, Quorum Bks) Greenwood.

Reynaud, Joyce. Samoyeds. (Illus.). 224p. 1994. 9.95 (*0-7938-1053-1*, KW-072) TFH Pubns.

Reynaud, Patricia. Fiction et Faillite: Economie et Metaphores dans Madame Bovary. (American University Studies, Series II, Romance Languages & Literature: Vol. 202). (FRE.). 233p. (C). 1994. text 42.95 (*0-8204-2047-6*) P Lang Pubng.

Reynaud, S., ed. see Zinn-Justin, Jean.

Reyneau, Betsy G., jt. illus. see Waring, Laura W.

Reyneke, Johan P., et al. Introduction to Orthognathic Surgery: A Color Atlas. Hacke, Gregory, ed. (Illus.). 125p. 1991. text 55.00 (*0-912791-84-5*, Ishiyaku EuroAmerica) Med Dent Media.

Reynel, C. & Pennington, T. D. El Genero Inga en el Peru: Morfologia, Distribucion y Usos. (Illus.). viii, 236p. 1997. pap. 54.00 (*1-900347-19-9*, Pub. by Royal Botnic Grdns) Balogh.

Reyner, David B., ed. see Martin, Gary.

Reyner, David B., ed. see Massey, James P.

Reyner, J. H. Gurdjieff in Action. 117p. 1982. 24.95 (*0-04-294117-2*) Routledge.

Reyner, Mark, ed. see Barron, Kirk W.

Reyner, Mark, ed. see Koury, Jen.

Reynhout, Robert. God's Wisdom for Handling Money. Simons, Cheryl, ed. 192p. (Orig.). 1995. pap. write for info. (*0-9646412-0-8*) R A Reynhout & Assocs.

Reyniak, J. Victor & Lauersen, Niels H., eds. Principles of Microsurgical Techniques in Infertility. LC 81-3045. 310p. 1982. 65.00 (*0-306-40781-7*, Kluwer Plenum) Kluwer Academic.

Reynierse, James H., ed. Current Issues in Animal Learning: A Colloquium. LC 78-98389. (Illus.). 402p. reprint ed. pap. 124.70 (*0-8357-2944-3*, 203920000011) Bks Demand.

Reynnells, M. Louise. Hazardous & Toxic Waste Management: Bibliography January 1989-May 1993. 56p. (Orig.). (C). 1995. pap. text 25.00 (*0-7881-2198-7*) DIANE Pub.

Reynnells, M. Louise, ed. Federal Funding Sources for Rural Areas: Fiscal Year 1998. rev. ed. 128p. (C). 1999. pap. text 25.00 (*0-7881-4383-2*) DIANE Pub.

— Federal Funding Sources for Rural Areas (1995) 117p. 1996. reprint ed. pap. text 35.00 (*0-7881-3354-3*) DIANE Pub.

Reynold. Little Journeys into Storyland. 235p. 1992. pap. 6.95 (*1-881545-06-7*) Angelas Bkshelf.

Reynold, jt. auth. see Matthews.

Reynold, Charles B. Old Saint Augustine, a Story of Three Centuries. (Illus.). 144p. 1997. reprint ed. pap. 21.00 (*0-8328-6616-4*) Higginson Bk Co.

Reynold, Ralph, ed. see Purcell, Wayne.

Reynold, Valda. A Practical Guide to Child Development, 2 vols., Vol. 2. 134p. (C). 1987. pap. 27.50 (*0-85950-240-6*, Pub. by S Thornes Pubs) Trans-Atl Phila.

Reynolds. Across the Alamedas. 24.11 (*0-673-20724-2*, GoodYrBooks) Addson-Wesley Educ.

Reynolds. AIDS Clinical Chemistry. 1986. pap. text 22.00 (*0-443-03145-2*, W B Saunders Co) Harcrt Hlth Sci Grp.

— As Long As I'm Laughing. LC 99-88439. (Illus.). 240p. 2000. text 24.95 (*1-57826-036-1*) Norton.

— Assessment & Protocols for Older Adults. (C). 2000. pap. text. write for info. (*0-7216-6548-9*, W B Saunders Co) Harcrt Hlth Sci Grp.

***Reynolds.** Autobiography of a Thief. 2000. 27.95 (*0-593-03779-0*, Pub. by Transworld Publishers Ltd); pap. 10.95 (*0-552-14275-1*, Pub. by Transworld Publishers Ltd) Trafalgar.

Reynolds. Down Under: Vanishing Cultures. 1992. pap. 4.25 (*0-15-200142-5*) Harcourt.

— Educational Psychology. (C). Date not set. pap. text, teacher ed. write for info. (*0-15-507965-4*) Harcourt Coll Pubs.

— Educational Psychology. (C). 2000. pap. text. write for info. (*0-15-503523-1*) Harcourt Coll Pubs.

***Reynolds.** Encyclopedia of Special Education: A Reference for the Education of the Handicapped & Other Exceptional Children & Adults, Vol. 1. 2nd ed. LC 99-15333. 641p. 1999. 125.00 (*0-471-25323-5*) Wiley.

Reynolds. Engineering Thermodynamics. 2nd ed. 1977. text 34.68 (*0-07-052047-X*) McGraw.

— Far North: Vanishing Cultures. 1992. pap. 2.50 (*0-15-200146-8*) Harcourt.

***Reynolds.** Handbook of Psychology 3rd ed. 1999. text 107.00 (*0-471-38132-2*) Wiley.

Reynolds. Hemingway :The Homecoming. 288p. 1999. pap. 13.95 (*0-393-31981-4*) Norton.

***Reynolds.** Introduction to College Writing. 544p. 2000. pap. 33.33 (*0-13-080328-6*) P-H.

Reynolds. Political Sociology: An Australian Perspective. Date not set. pap. text. write for info. (*0-582-66397-0*, Pub. by Addison-Wesley) Longman.

— Portfolio Keeping. 1999. pap. text, student ed. 6.95 (*0-312-19151-0*) St Martin.

***Reynolds.** Portfolio Keeping: A Guide For Teachers. 2000. pap. text, teacher ed. 13.95 (*0-312-19809-4*) St Martin.

Reynolds. Portfolio Programs Guide. 2000. pap. text. write for info. (*0-312-19811-6*) St Martin.

— Reading Connections. (Developmental Study/Study Skill Ser.). 1994. mass mkt., teacher ed. 19.25 (*0-534-24457-2*) Wadsworth Pub.

— Sentence Power. (C). 1991. pap. text, teacher ed. 34.00 (*0-03-026334-4*) Harcourt Coll Pubs.

Reynolds. Snow Country II, Document Processing. 4th ed. 1992. pap. 17.25 (*0-538-61178-2*) Sth-Wstrn College.

— Twentieth-Century American Women's Fiction. LC 99-15611. 272p. 1999. pap. 18.95 (*0-312-22637-3*) St Martin.

Reynolds. Vocabulary Connections. 112p. 1997. pap. 13.44 (*0-07-052628-1*); pap. 13.44 (*0-07-052629-X*) McGraw.

— Vocabulary Connections Books. 1997. pap. 20.00 (*0-07-289786-4*) McGraw.

Reynolds & Corwin. General Chemistry, Vol. 1. 116p. 1996. pap. text, lab manual ed. 18.00 (*0-536-59393-0*) Pearson Custom.

Reynolds, jt. auth. see Moreland.

Reynolds, jt. auth. see Ryan.

Reynolds, jt. auth. see Stair.

Reynolds, A. Managing Mental Health Service. LC 98-30735. (Health Services Management Ser.). 1999. pap. 29.95 (*0-335-19833-3*); pap. 95.00 (*0-335-19834-1*) OpUniv Pr.

Reynolds, Nicholas E. Just Cause: Marine Operations in Panama, 1988-1990. LC 96-215996. vii, 50 p. 1996. write for info. (*0-16-048729-3*) USGPO.

Reynolds, A. G. Bilingualism, Multiculturalism, & Second Language Learning: The McGill Conference in Honour of Wallace E. Lambert. 288p. (C). 1991. text 59.95 (*0-8058-0694-6*) L Erlbaum Assocs.

Reynolds, A. J. Advanced FORTH. 150p. 1987. pap. text 27.95 (*0-470-20759-0*) P-H.

— The Finances Engineering Companies. (Business Communication Ser.). 1993. pap. 24.50 (*0-340-56828-3*, VNR) Wiley.

— Turbulent Flows in Engineering. LC 73-8464. (Illus.). 478p. reprint ed. pap. 148.20 (*0-608-11704-8*, 205161700001) Bks Demand.

***Reynolds, Adrian.** Pete & Polo's Big School Adventure. LC 99-51523. (Illus.). 32p. (J). 2000. 15.95 (*0-531-30275-X*) Orchard Bks Watts.

Reynolds, Adrian. Mystery Stories. LC 96-1435. (Story Library). 260p. (J). (gr. 1 up). 1996. pap. 7.95 (*0-7534-5025-9*) LKC.

Reynolds, Adrian, jt. auth. see Whybrow, Ian.

Reynolds, Albert B. Bluebells & Nuclear Energy. LC 96-84323. (Illus.). 302p. (Orig.). 1996. pap. text 22.95 (*0-944838-63-4*) Med Physics Pub.

Reynolds, Alfred. Jesus vs. Christianity. 314p. (C). 1988. pap. 60.00 (*0-946101-02-7*) St Mut.

Reynolds, Althea C. & Brunetti, Argentina. Teatro, Prosa, Poesia. (Illus.). 160p. 1982. pap. text 29.50 (*0-915838-12-5*) Anma Libri.

Reynolds, Amy & McCombs, Maxwell, eds. The Poll with a Human Face: The National Issues Convention Experiment in Political Communication. LC 98-42667. (LEA's Communication Ser.). 272p. 1999. 49.95 (*0-8058-2974-1*) L Erlbaum Assocs.

***Reynolds, Andrew.** Election '99 South Africa: From Mandela to Mbeki. LC 99-41117. 1999. 49.95 (*0-312-22870-8*) St Martin.

— Election '99 South Africa: From Mandela to Mbeki. LC 99-41117. 2000. pap. 24.95 (*0-312-22871-6*) St Martin.

Reynolds, Andrew. Election 1994 South Africa: The Campaigns, Results & Future Prospects. 237p. 1995. pap. 18.95 (*0-312-12763-4*) St Martin.

— Electoral Systems & Democratization in Southern Africa. LC 98-30682. (Illus.). 356p. 1999. text 80.00 (*0-19-829510-3*) OUP.

***Reynolds, Andrew.** Later Anglo-Saxon England. (Illus.). 208p. 1999. 32.50 (*0-7524-1432-1*, Pub. by Tempus Pubng) Arcadia Publng.

Reynolds, Andrew, jt. auth. see Sisk, Timothy D.

Reynolds, Angus. Multimedia Training: Developing Technology-Based Systems. LC 95-32922. 1996. pap. text 50.00 incl. disk (*0-07-912012-1*) McGraw.

Reynolds, Angus, jt. auth. see Marguardt, Michael.

Reynolds, Ann B. Strength for the Journey. LC 96-85495. 96p. (Orig.). 1996. pap. 9.95 (*1-888257-02-4*, 257) Cameron Press.

Reynolds, Anne & Waddington, Raymond, eds. Renaissance Humanism at the Court of Clement VII: Francesco Berni's Dialogue Against Poets in Context. LC 96-41561. (Garland Studies in the Renaissance: Vol. 7). (Illus.). 400p. 1997. text 110.00 (*0-8153-2020-5*) Garland.

Reynolds, Annette. Always & Forever: A Wedding Treasury. 1992. 7.98 (*0-88486-060-4*) Arrowood Pr.

— Remember the Time. 432p. 1997. mass mkt. 5.50 (*0-553-57652-6*) Bantam.

Reynolds, Annie & Gordon, Albert. Stage to Yosemite: Recollections of Wawona's Albert Gordon. Vocelka, Mary & Bentle, Jane, eds. LC 94-220519. (Illus.). 180p. (Orig.). 1994. pap. 19.95 (*0-9639148-0-4*) A L Reynolds.

***Reynolds, Annie & Phillips, Thomas Bruce.** Yosemite's Forgotten Pioneers: The Bruces of Wawona. Bentle, Jane, ed. (Illus.). 128p. 1999. pap. 17.95 (*0-9668150-0-9*) Chilnualna Bks.

Reynolds, Anthony, jt. auth. see Mills, Arlen C.

Reynolds, Arianna. Myth & Magic of Cats. (Illus.). 64p. 1998. 12.95 (*0-7938-0240-7*, WW074) TFH Pubns.

Reynolds, Arlene, ed. The Civil War Memories of Elizabeth Bacon Custer: Reconstructed from Her Notes & Diaries. LC 94-1759. 1994. 24.95 (*0-292-71168-9*) U of Tex Pr.

Reynolds, Arthur J. Success in Early Intervention: The Chicago Child-Parent Centers. LC 99-45985. (Child, Youth, & Family Serivces Ser.). (Illus.). 272p. 2000. text 50.00 (*0-8032-3936-X*) U of Nebr Pr.

Reynolds, Arthur J. & Walberg, Herbert J., eds. Evaluation Methods for Educational Productivity. (Advances in Educational Productivity Ser.: Vol. 7). 1998. 78.50 (*0-7623-0253-4*) Jai Pr.

Reynolds, Arthur J., et al. Promoting Positive Outcomes in Children. LC 99-25170. 402p. 1999. pap. 39.95 (*0-87868-759-9*, CWLA Pr) Child Welfare.

Reynolds, Arthur J., jt. ed. see Walberg, Herbert J.

Reynolds, Audree. Critical & High Acuity in Nursing Care. (Outline Ser.). (Illus.). 300p. (C). 1994. per. 23.95 (*1-56930-028-3*) Skidmore Roth Pub.

— Critical & High Acuity Nursing Care. 2nd rev. ed. (Outline Ser.). 250p. (C). 1998. per. 23.95 (*1-56930-094-1*) Skidmore Roth Pub.

— Medical-Surgical Nursing. 2nd rev. ed. (Outline Ser.). 275p. (C). 1998. per. 23.95 (*1-56930-068-2*) Skidmore Roth Pub.

Reynolds, Audrey L. Exploring Written English: A Guide for Basic Writers. (C). 1983. 20.60 (*0-673-39290-2*, Scott Frsmn) Addson-Wesley Educ.

Reynolds-Ball, E. A. Paris in Splendor, 2 vols., Set. 1976. lib. bdg. 200.00 (*0-8490-2412-9*) Gordon Pr.

Reynolds, Barbara. And Still We Rise. 1988. 14.95 (*0-944347-02-9*) USA Today Bks.

— The Concise Cambridge Italian Dictionary. (ITA.). 792p. 1975. pap. 15.95 (*0-14-051064-8*, Penguin Bks) Viking Penguin.

— Dorothy L. Sayers. 1997. pap. 16.95 (*0-312-15353-8*) St Martin.

— The Passionate Intellect: Dorothy L. Sayers' Encounter with Dante. LC 88-13930. (Illus.). 286p. 1989. reprint ed. pap. 88.70 (*0-608-07360-1*, 206758800009) Bks Demand.

Reynolds, Barbara, ed. see Sayers, Dorothy L.

Reynolds, Barbara, tr. & intro. see Ariosto, Ludovico.

Reynolds, Barbara, tr. & intro. see Dante Alighieri.

Reynolds, Barbara A. No, I Won't Shut Up: Thirty Years of Telling It Like It Is. LC 98-67027. 332p. (C). 1998. pap. 17.95 (*0-9665073-0-4*) Reynolds News.

Reynolds, Barbara E., jt. auth. see Hastings, Nancy B.

Reynolds, Barbara E., jt. auth. see Hastings, Nancy Baxter.

Reynolds, Barrie & Stott, Margaret A. Material Anthropology: Contemporary Approaches to Material Culture. (Illus.). 242p. (Orig.). 1987. lib. bdg. 47.50 (*0-8191-6543-3*) U Pr of Amer.

Reynolds, Barry & Berryman, John. Pike on the Fly: The Flyfishing Guide to Northerns, Tigers, & Muskies. LC 93-38057. (Illus.). 160p. (Orig.). 1993. pap. 16.95 (*1-55566-113-0*, Sprng Creek Pr) Johnson Bks.

Reynolds, Barry, et al. Carp on the Fly: A Flyfishing Guide. LC 97-18257. (Illus.). 176p. 1997. 26.00 (*1-55566-207-2*, Sprng Creek Pr); pap. 17.50 (*1-55566-186-6*, Sprng Creek Pr) Johnson Bks.

Reynolds, Beatrice. Proponents of Limited Monarchy in Sixteenth Century France. LC 68-58616. (Columbia University. Studies in the Social Sciences: No. 334). reprint ed. 22.50 (*0-404-51334-4*) AMS Pr.

Reynolds, Becky. Graveyard Cleaning-Off Day. 41p. 1990. pap. 3.50 (*0-87129-001-4*, G54) Dramatic Pub.

Reynolds, Ben, et al. Writing Instruction for Verbally Talented Youth: The Johns Hopkins Model. rev. ed. 204p. (YA). 1994. pap. text, teacher ed. 27.00 (*1-881622-14-2*) JHU IAAY.

Reynolds, Ben, tr. see Le Roy-Ladurie, Emmanuel.

Reynolds, Benn P., jt. auth. see DeGeer, Maria E.

Reynolds, Bertha C. Social Work & Social Living: Explorations in Philosophy & Practice. LC 75-29534. (NASW Classics Ser.). 176p. 1975. reprint ed. pap. 8.95 (*0-87101-071-2*) Natl Assn Soc Wkrs.

— An Uncharted Journey: Fifty Years in Social Work by One of Its Great Teachers. LC 90-28265. 352p. 1991. reprint ed. 21.95 (*0-87101-193-X*) Natl Assn Soc Wkrs.

Reynolds, Beth. Sisters of Courage: Survivors of Breast & Cervical Cancer. Date not set. mass mkt. 20.00 (*0-9673284-0-3*) Photo-document.

Reynolds, Bethany S. Magic Stack-n-Whack Quilts. LC 97-46322. 1998. pap. text 19.95 (*1-57432-704-6*, 4995, Am Quilters Soc) Collector Bks.

***Reynolds, Bethany S.** Stars a la Carte. Smith, Barbara, ed. (Illus.). 128p. 2000. pap. 21.95 (*1-57432-739-9*, Am Quilters Soc) Collector Bks.

Reynolds, Betty. Clueless in Tokyo: An Explorer's Sketchbook of Weird & Wonderful Things in Japan. LC 96-48871. (Illus.). 48p. 1997. pap. 14.95 (*0-8348-0386-0*) Weatherhill.

***Reynolds, Betty.** Squeamish about Sushi: And Other Food Adventures in Japan. 2000. 16.95 (*0-8048-3301-X*, Periplus Eds) Tuttle Pubng.

— Squeamish about Sushi & Other Food Adventures in Japan. LC 00-29907. (Illus.). 2000. pap. write for info. (*0-8048-3300-1*) Tuttle Pubng.

Reynolds, Betty. Tokyo Friends. (Illus.). 64p. 1999. 12.95 (*0-8048-2123-2*) Tuttle Pubng.

Reynolds, Bill. Bodybuilding for Beginners. (Illus.). 144p. (Orig.). 1983. pap. 12.95 (*0-8092-5499-9*, 549990, Contemporary Bks) NTC Contemp Pub Co.

— The Complete Weight Training Book. LC 75-32443. (Illus.). 222p. 1979. pap. 4.95 (*0-89037-149-0*) Anderson World.

An Asterisk (*) at the beginning of an entry indicates that the title is appearing for the first time.

— Fall River Dreams: A Team's Quest for Glory, a Town's Search for It's Soul. (Illus.). 368p. 1995. pap. 13.95 (*0-312-13491-6*) St Martin.
— 50 Years of Classic Sports Cars. (Illus.). 288p. 1998. pap. 15.98 (*1-85833-603-1*) Quadrillion Pubng.
— Glory Days: On Sports, Men, Memory, & Dreams That Don't Die. LC 97-40489. 246p. 1998. text 22.95 (*0-312-18105-1*) St Martin.
— Lost Summer: The '67 Red Sox & the Impossible Dream. 328p. 1993. mass mkt. 5.50 (*0-446-36427-4*, Pub. by Warner Bks) Little.
— Weight Training for Beginners. (Illus.). 96p. 1982. pap. 8.95 (*0-8092-5728-9*, 572890, Contemporary Bks) NTC Contemp Pub Co.
Reynolds, Bill & Jayde, Negrita. Sliced. (Illus.). 320p. (Orig.). 1991. pap. 16.95 (*0-8092-4116-1*, 411610, Contemporary Bks) NTC Contemp Pub Co.
Reynolds, Bill & Vedral, Joyce L. Supercut. (Illus.). 288p. (Orig.). 1985. pap. 14.95 (*0-8092-5387-9*, 538790, Contemporary Bks) NTC Contemp Pub Co.
Reynolds, Bill, et al. Complete Training & Nutrition Encyclopedia. (Gold's Gym Ser.). (Illus.). 288p. 1992. pap. 17.95 (*0-8092-3947-7*, 394770, Contemporary Bks) NTC Contemp Pub Co.
— Gold's Gym Nutrition Bible. 224p. (Orig.). 1986. pap. 16.95 (*0-8092-5188-4*, 518840, Contemporary Bks) NTC Contemp Pub Co.
— Imagineering: A "Yes, We Can!" Sourcebook for Early Technology Experiences. (Illus.). (J). (gr. k-3). 1999. pap., teacher ed. 24.95 (*1-895579-19-8*) Trifolium Inc.
Reynolds, Bill, jt. auth. see Langer, Anja.
Reynolds, Bill, jt. auth. see McLish, Rachel.
Reynolds, Bill, jt. auth. see Napoli, Dede.
Reynolds, Bill, jt. auth. see Pirie, Lynne.
Reynolds, Bill, jt. auth. see Pitino, Rick.
Reynolds, Bill, jt. auth. see Sprague, Ken.
Reynolds, Bill, jt. auth. see Weider, Joe.
Reynolds, Billie I. Planning Is the Key. 1983. 10.00 (*0-915807-00-9*) Hidden Valley Bks.
Reynolds, Blair. The Relationship of Calvin to Process Theology As Seen Through His Sermons. LC 93-32120. (Texts & Studies in Religion: Vol. 61). 112p. 1993. text 59.95 (*0-7734-9355-7*) E Mellen.
— Toward a Process Pneumatology. LC 88-43326. 216p. 1990. 34.50 (*0-941664-97-X*) Susquehanna U Pr.
***Reynolds, Blair & Heinicke, Patricia.** The Naked Being of God: Making Sense of Love Mysticism. LC 00-36445. 160p. 2000. pap. 27.50 (*0-7618-1704-2*) U Pr of Amer.
***Reynolds, Blair & Heinicke, Patricia, Jr.** The Naked Being of God: Making Sense of Love Mysticism. 160p. 2000. 49.00 (*0-7618-1703-4*) U Pr of Amer.
Reynolds, Blair, tr. see Benz, Ernest.
Reynolds, Blair, tr. see Calvin, Jean.
Reynolds, Blair, tr. see Descartes, Rene.
Reynolds, Blair, tr. see Heyer, Henri.
Reynolds, Bob. Understanding Derivatives: What You Really Need to Know about the Wild-Card of Finance. LC 96-145357. (Illus.). 256p. 1995. 30.00 (*0-273-61378-2*) F T P-H.
Reynolds, Bonnie H. Space, Time & Crisis: The Theatre of Rene Marques. LC 87-61514. 118p. 1988. 20.00 (*0-938972-13-8*) Spanish Lit Pubns.
Reynolds, Bonnie J., jt. auth. see Choudhury, Bikram.
Reynolds, Brad. Cruel Sanctuary No. 3: A Father Mark Townsend Mystery. (A Father Mark Townsend Mystery Ser.: No. 3). 352p. 1999. mass mkt. 5.99 (*0-380-79843-3*, Avon Bks) Morrow Avon.
***Reynolds, Brad.** Deadly Harvest, Vol. 1. (Father Mark Townsend Mystery Ser.). 304p. 1999. mass mkt. 5.99 (*0-380-79844-1*, Avon Bks) Morrow Avon.
Reynolds, Brad. Pull & Be Damned. (Orig.). 1997. mass mkt. 5.50 (*0-614-27710-8*, Avon Bks) Morrow Avon.
— A Ritual Death: A Father Mark Townsend Mystery. (A Father Mark Townsend Mystery Ser.). 256p. (Orig.). 1997. mass mkt. 5.50 (*0-380-78401-7*, Avon Bks) Morrow Avon.
— The Story Knife: A Father Mark Townsend Mystery. 256p. 1996. mass mkt. 5.99 (*0-380-78400-9*, Avon Bks) Morrow Avon.
Reynolds, Brian. A Chance to Serve: Peer Ministers' Handbook. 84p. 1983. pap. 5.95 (*0-88489-154-2*); pap., teacher ed. 10.95 (*0-88489-153-4*) St Marys.
***Reynolds-Brittain, Melissa & Slemp, Chris, eds.** Conducting Effective Research Using the Internet. (Illus.). 126p. (C). 1998. pap. write for info. (*0-7423-0009-9*) ComputerPREP.
Reynolds, Bronwyn. Literacy in the Pre-School. 72p. 1997. pap. 11.95 (*1-85856-075-6*, Trentham Bks) Stylus Pub VA.
Reynolds, Bruce L., ed. Reform in China: Challenges & Choices. LC 87-23537. 240p. (C). (gr. 13). 1987. pap. text 42.95 (*0-87332-459-5*, East Gate Bk) M E Sharpe.
Reynolds, Bruce L., jt. ed. see Kim, Ilpyong J.
Reynolds, Bruford S. Becoming Self Sufficient with Dollars & Sense. 1977. pap. 3.95 (*0-89036-070-7*) Liahona Pub Trust.
— How to Survive with Sprouting. 112p. 1970. pap. 4.95 (*0-89036-028-6*) Liahona Pub Trust.
Reynolds, Burt. My Life. (Illus.). 352p. (J). 1994. 22.45 (*0-7868-6130-4*, Pub. by Hyperion) Time Warner.
Reynolds, C. E. Letters Plus: Communications on the Job. 136p. 1987. pap. text 7.56 (*0-07-052057-7*) McGraw.
Reynolds, C. E. & Steedman, James C. Examples of the Design of Reinforced Concrete Buildings to BS8110. 4th ed. (Illus.). 336p. 1992. pap. 69.95 (*0-442-31417-5*) Chapman & Hall.
— Examples of the Design of Reinforced Concrete Buildings to BS8110. 4th ed. (Illus.). 320p. 1991. 79.95 (*0-419-16990-3*, E & FN Spon) Routledge.
— Reinforced Concrete Designer's Handbook. (Illus.). 500p. 1988. text 95.00 (*0-419-14530-3*, E & FN Spon) Routledge.
Reynolds, C. R. Cognitive Assessment: A Multidisciplinary Perspective. (Perspectives on Individual Differences Ser.). (Illus.). 284p. (C). 1994. 49.50 (*0-306-44434-8*, Plenum Trade) Perseus Pubng.
Reynolds, C. S., et al, eds. Intermediate Disturbance Hypothesis in Phytoplankton Ecology: Proceedings of the 8th Workshop of the International Association of Phytoplankton Taxonomy & Ecology Held in Baja (Hungary), 5-15 July 1992. LC 92-41133. (Developments in Hydrobiology Ser.: Vol. 81). 208p. (C). 1993. text 178.50 (*0-7923-2097-2*) Kluwer Academic.
Reynolds, C. W. & Wiltrout, R. H. Functions of the Natural Immune System. LC 88-22488. (Illus.). 506p. (C). 1989. text 145.00 (*0-306-42951-9*, Kluwer Plenum) Kluwer Academic.
Reynolds, Calvin. Compensating Globally Mobile Employees: Approaches to Developing Expatriate Pay Strategies for the Evolving International Corporation. (Building Blocks Ser.: Vol. 26). (Illus.). 24p. (Orig.). 1995. pap. 24.95 (*1-57963-028-6*, A046) Am Compensation.
— Compensation Basics for North American Expatriates: Developing an Effective Program for Employees Working Abroad. (Building Blocks Ser.: Vol. 15). (Illus.). 24p. (Orig.). 1994. pap. 24.95 (*1-57963-018-9*, A0035) Am Compensation.
Reynolds, Caroline. Dimensions in Professional Development. 3rd ed. (C). 1987. mass mkt. 35.50 (*0-538-11651-X*, K65) S-W Pub.
— Dimensions in Professional Development. 4th ed. LC 92-18247. (C). 1993. mass mkt. 43.95 (*0-538-61416-1*) S-W Pub.
Reynolds, Carolyn. The Book of Lovers: Men Who Excite Women, Women Who Excite Men. LC 91-46568. (Popular Astrology Ser.). 464p. 1999. pap. 14.95 (*0-87542-289-6*) Llewellyn Pubns.
***Reynolds, Carolyn.** The Book of Lovers: Men Who Excite Women, Women Who Excite Men. LC 99-46529. 1999. 10.99 (*0-517-20949-7*) Random Hse Value.
Reynolds, Carolyn. El Libro Para Amantes: Los Hombres Que Excitan a las Mujeres, las Mujeres Que Excitan a los Hombres. LC 95-35995.Tr. of Book of Lovers: Men Who Excite Women Women Who Excite Men. (SPA.). 480p. 1999. pap. 20.00 (*1-56718-569-X*) Llewellyn Pubns.
Reynolds, Carter E. Eventually They'll Grow Up: A Work of Condensed-Prose. 54p. 1998. pap. 3.95 (*0-9662412-1-5*) Full Circle Creat.
Reynolds, Catherine. The Highwayman. (Regency Romance Ser.). 1993. per. 2.99 (*0-373-31209-1*, 1-31209-9) Harlequin Bks.
— The Highwayman. 1999. per. 3.75 (*0-373-31231-8*) Harlequin Bks.
***Reynolds, Cecil R.** Encyclopedia of Special Education: A Reference for the Education of the Handicapped & Other Exceptional Children & Adults, Vol. 2. 2nd ed. LC 99-15333. 670p. 1999. 125.00 (*0-471-25324-3*) Wiley.
Reynolds, Cecil R., ed. Detection of Malingering During Head Injury Litigation. LC 97-34812. (Critical Issues in Neuropsychology Ser.). 304p. (C). 1997. 45.00 (*0-306-45655-9*, Plenum Trade) Perseus Pubng.
Reynolds, Cecil R. & Brown, Robert T., eds. Perspectives on Bias in Mental Testing. (Perspectives on Individual Differences Ser.). 594p. 1984. 85.00 (*0-306-41529-1*, Plenum Trade) Perseus Pubng.
Reynolds, Cecil R. & Fletcher-Janzen, Elaine. Concise Encyclopedia of Special Education. LC 90-12684. 1215p. 1990. 250.00 (*0-471-51527-2*) Wiley.
***Reynolds, Cecil R. & Fletcher-Janzen, Elaine.** Encyclopedia of Special Education, Vol. 3. 2nd ed. LC 99-15333. 687p. 1999. write for info. (*0-471-25325-1*) Wiley.
Reynolds, Cecil R. & Fletcher-Janzen, Elaine, eds. Encyclopedia of Special Education, 3 vols. 2nd ed. LC 99-15333. 2016p. 2000. 375.00 (*0-471-25309-X*) Wiley.
— Handbook of Clinical Child Neuropsychology. LC 88-39536. (Critical Issues in Neuropsychology Ser.). (Illus.). 612p. 1989. 85.00 (*0-306-42879-2*, Plenum Trade) Perseus Pubng.
— Handbook of Clinical Child Neuropsychology. 2nd ed. LC 96-52991. (Critical Issues in Neuropsychology Ser.). 762p. (C). 1997. 95.00 (*0-306-45257-X*, Kluwer Plenum) Kluwer Academic.
***Reynolds, Cecil R. & Gutkin, Terry B., eds.** The Handbook of School Psychology. 3rd ed. LC 98-17618. 1216p. 1998. text 112.95 (*0-471-12205-X*) Wiley.
Reynolds, Cecil R. & Kamphaus, Randy W., eds. Handbook of Psychological & Educational Assessment of Children: Intelligence & Achievement. LC 89-38018. 814p. 1990. lib. bdg. 85.00 (*0-89862-391-X*) Guilford Pubns.
— Handbook of Psychological & Educational Assessment of Children: Personality, Behavior & Context. LC 89-38018. 618p. 1990. lib. bdg. 75.00 (*0-89862-392-8*) Guilford Pubns.
Reynolds, Cecil R. & Mann, Lester. Encyclopedia of Special Education: A Reference for the Education of the Handicapped & Other Exceptional Children & Adults, Vol. 1. 1987. text 215.00 (*0-471-63004-7*) Wiley.
— Encyclopedia of Special Education: A Reference for the Education of the Handicapped & Other Exceptional Children & Adults, Vol. 2. 1987. text 215.00 (*0-471-63005-5*) Wiley.
— Encyclopedia of Special Education: A Reference for the Education of the Handicapped & Other Exceptional Children & Adults, Vol. 3. 1987. text 215.00 (*0-471-63006-3*) Wiley.
Reynolds, Cecil R. & Mann, Lester, eds. Encyclopedia of Special Education: Reference for the Education of the Handicapped & Other Exceptional Children & Adults 3 vols., Vol. 3. LC 86-33975. 1824p. 1987. text 645.00 (*0-471-82858-0*) Wiley.
Reynolds, Cecil R. & Willson, Victor L., eds. Methodological & Statistical Advances in the Study of Individual Differences. LC 85-17042. (Perspectives on Individual Differences Ser.). (Illus.). 492p. (C). 1985. 114.00 (*0-306-41962-9*, Plenum Trade) Perseus Pubng.
Reynolds, Cecil R., jt. auth. see Gutkin, Terry B.
Reynolds, Cecil R., jt. auth. see Kamphaus, Randy W.
Reynolds, Cecil R., jt. ed. see Goldstein, Sam.
Reynolds, Cecilia & Young, Beth, eds. Women & Leadership on Canadian Education. 253p. (Orig.). 1995. pap. text. write for info. (*1-55059-116-9*) Detselig Ents.
Reynolds, Charles. Card Magic. LC 98-130889. (Blackstone Family Magic Shoppe Ser.). (Illus.). 48p. (J). (gr. 1 up). 1997. pap. 6.95 (*1-57102-300-3*, Ideals Child) Hambleton-Hill.
— The World of States: An Introduction to Explanation & Theory. 256p. 1992. 90.00 (*1-85278-133-5*); pap. 30.00 (*1-85278-134-3*) E Elgar.
Reynolds, Charles H., et al, eds. Computer-Aided Molecular Design: Applications in Agrochemicals, Materials, & Pharmaceuticals. LC 95-2511. (ACS Symposium Ser.: No. 589). (Illus.). 428p. 1995. text 120.00 (*0-8412-3160-5*, Pub. by Am Chemical) OUP.
Reynolds, Cheryl L. & Leininger, Madeleine. Madeleine Leininger: Cultural Care Diversity & Universality Theory. (Notes on Nursing Theories Ser.: Vol. 8). (Illus.). 64p. (C). 1993. text 22.95 (*0-8039-5097-7*); pap. text 9.95 (*0-8039-5098-5*) Sage.
Reynolds, Christopher. Public Health Law in Australia. 290p. 1995. pap. 39.00 (*1-86287-158-2*, Pub. by Federation Pr) Gaunt.
Reynolds, Christopher, ed. An Anthology of Sinhalese Literature of the Twentieth Century. 344p. (C). 1996. pap. text 25.00 (*0-904404-53-6*, Pub. by Curzon Pr Ltd) UH Pr.
Reynolds, Christopher, et al, eds. Beethoven Forum, No. 1. (Illus.). xiv, 250p. 1992. text 65.00 (*0-8032-3906-8*) U of Nebr Pr.
— Beethoven Forum, No. 2. ix, 236p. 1993. text 65.00 (*0-8032-3909-2*) U of Nebr Pr.
— Beethoven Forum, No. 3. xi, 189p. 1995. text 65.00 (*0-8032-4246-8*) U of Nebr Pr.
— Beethoven Forum, No. 4. (Illus.). xi, 204p. 1995. text 65.00 (*0-8032-3916-5*) U of Nebr Pr.
Reynolds, Christopher A. Papal Patronage & the Music of St. Peter's, 1380-1513. LC 94-5292. (Illus.). 410p. 1995. 65.00 (*0-520-08212-5*, Pub. by U CA Pr) Cal Prin Full Svc.
Reynolds, Clark G. Admiral John H. Towers: The Struggle for Naval Air Supremacy. LC 91-14694. (Illus.). 576p. 1991. 45.00 (*0-87021-031-9*) Naval Inst Pr.
— Civil War. (Illus.). 128p. 1997. 24.95 (*1-85833-703-8*, Pub. by CLib Bks) Whitecap Bks.
— Command of the Sea: The History & Strategy of Maritime Empires - Maps, 2 vols. LC 83-6129. 358p. 1983. reprint ed. text 8.00 (*0-89874-630-2*) Krieger.
— The Fast Carriers: The Forging of an Air Navy. LC 91-39437. (Illus.). 576p. 1992. reprint ed. 35.00 (*1-55750-701-5*) Naval Inst Pr.
— The Fighting Lady: New Yorktown in the Pacific War. LC 86-61530. (Illus.). 360p. 1986. pap. 19.95 (*0-933126-78-6*) Pictorial Hist.
— Navies in History. LC 98-6112. 267p. 1998. pap. 22.95 (*1-55750-715-5*) Naval Inst Pr.
— Navies in History. LC 98-6112. (Illus.). 304p. 1998. 29.95 (*1-55750-716-3*) Naval Inst Pr.
Reynolds, Clark W., et al, eds. The Dynamics of North American Trade & Investment: Canada, Mexico, & the United States. LC 90-41907. 300p. 1991. 47.50 (*0-8047-1864-4*) Stanford U Pr.
***Reynolds, Clay.** Cheating Old Age. (Illus.). 156p. 2000. pap. 15.95 (*0-9700019-0-8*) DTZ Inc.
Reynolds, Clay. A Hundred Years of Heroes: A History of the Southwestern Exposition & Livestock Show. 1995. pap. 16.95 (*0-87565-149-6*) Tex Christian.
***Reynolds, Clay.** Monuments. LC 99-89489. 400p. 2000. 29.95 (*0-89672-433-6*) Tex Tech Univ Pr.
Reynolds, Clay. The Players. LC 97-4265. 432p. 1997. 24.00 (*0-7867-0407-1*) Carroll & Graf.
— Players. 448p. 1998. mass mkt. 5.99 (*0-7860-0598-X*, Pinnacle Kensgtn) Kensgtn Pub Corp.
— Twenty Questions: Answers for the Inquiring Writer. 115p. (Orig.). 1997. pap. 12.95 (*0-9651359-2-6*) Browder Springs.
Reynolds, Clay, ed. Taking Stock: A Larry McMurtry Casebook. LC 88-43316. (Southwest Life & Letters Ser.). 448p. 1989. 26.95 (*0-87074-291-4*); pap. 15.95 (*0-87074-261-2*) SMU Press.
Reynolds, Clay & Schein, Marie. A Hundred Years of Heroes: A History of the Southwestern Exposition & Livestock Show. LC 95-15428. (Illus.). 352p. 1995. 29.95 (*0-87565-145-3*) Tex Christian.
Reynolds, Colin S. & Watanabe, Yasunori, eds. Vertical Structure in Aquatic Environments & Its Impact on Trophic Linkages & Nutrient Fluxes. (Advances in Limnology Ser.: Vol. 35). (GER., Illus.). vi, 159p. 1992. pap. 52.00 (*3-510-47036-2*, Pub. by E Schweizerbartsche) Balogh.
***Reynolds, Colin S., et al.** The Trophic Spectrum Revisited. 164p. 2000. 103.00 (*0-7923-6385-X*) Kluwer Academic.
Reynolds-Cornell, Regine, tr. see Marguerite of Angouleme.
Reynolds, Cort. The Final Problems - Sherlock Holmes Mystery Trivia Vol. 1. (Illus.). 80p. (Orig.). 1997. pap. 10.00 (*0-9648665-2-8*) Corts Ct.
— Home Run Derby Trivia. 80p. 1999. pap. 10.00 (*0-9648665-3-6*) Corts Ct.
Reynolds, Cort D. The Ultimate Basketball Trivia Challenge: It's a Basketball Game & Trivia Game in One! 84p. (Orig.). 1995. pap. 10.00 (*0-9648665-1-X*) Corts Ct.
— The Ultimate Hoosier Hoops Trivia Challenge: It's a Basketball Game & Trivia Game in One! 68p. (Orig.). 1995. pap. 9.00 (*0-9648665-0-1*) Corts Ct.
Reynolds, Cory, ed. see Halley, Peter.
Reynolds, Craig J. Thai Radical Discourse: The Real Face of Thai Feudalism Today. (Studies on Southeast Asia: No. 3). (Illus.). 186p. (Orig.). (C). 1994. pap. text 16.00 (*0-87727-702-8*) Cornell SE Asia.
— Thai Radical Discourse: The Real Face of Thai Feudalism Today. LC DS0568.R49. (Studies on Southeast Asia). (Illus.). 192p. (Orig.). reprint ed. pap. 59.60 (*0-8357-3117-0*, 203937500012) Bks Demand.
Reynolds, Craig J., ed. see Cushman, Jennifer.
Reynolds, Cuyler. Albany Chronicles: History of the City Arranged Chronologically, from the Earliest Settlement to the Present Time (1906) (Illus.). 808p. 1997. reprint ed. lib. bdg. 82.00 (*0-8328-6098-0*) Higginson Bk Co.
***Reynolds, Cuyler.** The Banquet Book. LC 99-28920. 1999. lib. bdg. 40.00 (*0-7808-0301-9*) Omnigraphics Inc.
— Genealogical & Family History of Southern New York & the Hudson: A Record of the Achievements of Her People in the Making of a Commonwealth & the Building of a Nation, 3 vols. 1482p. 1997. reprint ed. pap. 150.00 (*0-8063-4675-2*) Clearfield Co.
— Hudson-Mohawk Genealogical & Family Memoirs: A Record of Achievements of the People of the Hudson & Mohawk Valleys in New York State. xxxii, 1848p. 1999. pap. 180.00 (*0-8063-4914-X*) Clearfield Co.
Reynolds, Cuyler. Hudson-Mohwawk Genealogical & Family Memoirs, 4 vols. (Illus.). 1847p. 1994. reprint ed. lib. bdg. 195.00 (*0-8328-3991-4*) Higginson Bk Co.
Reynolds, D. R. & Riley, J. R. Flight Behaviour & Migration of Insect Pests: Radar Studies in Developing Countries. 114p. 1997. pap. 60.00 (*0-85954-470-2*, Pub. by Nat Res Inst) St Mut.
Reynolds, D. R. & Taylor, J. W., eds. The Fungal Holomorph: Mitotic, Meiotic & Pleomorphic Speciation in Fungal Systematics. (Illus.). 350p. 1993. text 80.00 (*0-85198-865-2*) OUP.
Reynolds, D. W. The Truth, the Whole Truth & Nothing But . . . A Police Officer's Guide to Testifying in Court. 90p. (C). 1990. text 25.95 (*0-398-05656-0*) C C Thomas.
Reynolds, D. William. Powerbuilder 5.0, Set. LC 94-37381. 448p. 1995. 39.95 incl. disk (*0-201-40886-4*) Addison-Wesley.
Reynolds, Dale, ed. see Fountain, Thomas E.
Reynolds, Dan. The Toilet Zone. Carle, Cliff, ed. (Illus.). 88p. 1999. pap. 6.95 (*1-57644-094-X*) CCC Pubns.
Reynolds, Dana. Be an Angel. (Illus.). 128p. 1994. 16.45 (*0-671-89694-6*) S&S Trade.
Reynolds, Daniel, tr. see Gogal, Nikolai.
Reynolds, David. Britannia Overruled. (Studies in Modern History). (Illus.). 360p. (C). 1995. pap. 49.00 (*0-582-55276-1*, 78925) Addison-Wesley.
— Britannia Overruled. (Studies in Modern History). (Illus.). 360p. (C). 1991. text 70.95 (*0-582-08427-X*, 78924) Longman.
***Reynolds, David.** Britannia Overruled: British Policy & World Power in the Twentieth Century. 2nd ed. 416p. 2000. pap. 24.00 (*0-582-38249-1*) Longman.
— Britannia Overruled: British Policy & World Power in the Twentieth Century. 2nd ed. 416p. 2000. 75.00 (*0-582-43725-3*) Longman.
Reynolds, David. The Creation of the Anglo-American Alliance, 1937-1941: A Study in Competitive Cooperation. LC 81-16503. 411p. reprint ed. pap. 127.50 (*0-7837-6864-8*, 204669300003) Bks Demand.
— Democracy Unbound: Progressive Challenges to the Two Party System. LC 96-46276. 369p. 1997. 40.00 (*0-89608-564-3*); pap. 22.00 (*0-89608-563-5*) South End Pr.
— Handle with Care: Balanced Guidelines for Raising Today's Children. 298p. (Orig.). pap. 9.95 (*1-877917-11-7*) Alpha Bible Pubns.
— Making History. 1998. write for info. (*0-679-45743-7*) Random.
— New Mexico Creditor - Debtor Law, 1989-1992, Issue 8. rev. ed. 326p. 1997. ring bd. 60.00 (*0-409-25140-2*, 82135-12, MICHIE) LEXIS Pub.
— New Mexico Creditor/Debtor Law. rev. ed. Date not set. ring bd. 120.00 (*0-327-00951-9*, 82134, MICHIE) LEXIS Pub.
— New Mexico Creditor/Debtor Law: 1989 Edition. 1995. ring bd. 120.00 (*0-409-25395-2*, 82134-10, MICHIE) LEXIS Pub.
— One World Divisible: A Global History Since 1945. LC 99-33903. 860p. 2000. text 35.00 (*0-393-04821-7*) Norton.
***Reynolds, David.** One World Divisible: A Global History Since 1945. (Illus.). 920p. 2000. pap. 18.95 (*0-393-32108-8*) Norton.
Reynolds, David. Paras: The Illustrated History of Britain's Airborne Forces. LC 99-188000. (Illus.). 288p. 1998. 49.95 (*0-7509-1723-7*, Pub. by Sutton Pub Ltd) Intl Pubs Mktg.
Reynolds, David, ed. The Origins of the Cold War in Europe: International Perspectives. LC 93-61583. 352p. 1994. 35.00 (*0-300-05892-6*) Yale U Pr.
Reynolds, David, et al. Advances in School Effectiveness Research & Practice. LC 94-15705. 200p. 1994. text 74.75 (*0-08-042392-2*, Pergamon Pr) Elsevier.
Reynolds, David, jt. auth. see Elferdink, Jim.
Reynolds, David, ed. see Dalin, Per.
Reynolds, David, ed. see Ribbins, Peter & Whale, Elizabeth.

An Asterisk (*) at the beginning of an entry indicates that the title is appearing for the first time.

R

Reynolds, David, ed. see Scheerens, Jaap.

Reynolds, David, jt. ed. see Teddlie, Charles.

Reynolds, David, ed. see Wallace, Mike & McMahon, Agnes.

Reynolds, David K. Constructive Living. 128p. 1984. pap. 9.95 (*0-8248-0871-1*) UH Pr.

— A Handbook for Constructive Living. 320p. 1997. reprint ed. pap. 12.00 (*0-688-15130-2*, Quil) HarperTrade.

— Naikan Psychotherapy: Meditation for Self-Development. LC 82-21862. 184p. 1983. 17.50 (*0-226-71029-7*) U Ch Pr.

— Playing Ball on Running Water: Living Morita Psychotherapy - The Japanese Way to Building a Better Life. LC 84-8399. 160p. 1984. pap. 8.95 (*0-688-03913-8*, Quil) HarperTrade.

— The Quiet Therapies: Japanese Pathways to Personal Growth. LC 80-17611. 144p. 1982. reprint ed. pap. 9.95 (*0-8248-0801-0*) UH Pr.

Reynolds, David K., ed. Plunging Through the Clouds: Constructive Living Currents. LC 91-45686. 199p. (C). 1993. text 19.50 (*0-7914-1313-6*) State U NY Pr.

Reynolds, David K. & Farberow, Norman L. Suicide: Inside & Out. LC 75-22661. 1976. pap. 14.95 (*0-520-03506-2*, CAL 370, Pub. by U CA Pr) Cal Prin Full Svc.

Reynolds, David K., jt. auth. see Kalish, Richard A.

Reynolds, David K., tr. see Kora, Takehisa.

Reynolds, David R. There Goes the Neighborhood: Rural School Consolidation at the Grass Roots in Early Twentieth-Century Iowa. LC 99-29743. (Illus.). 318p. 1999. text 39.95 (*0-87745-693-3*) U of Iowa Pr.

Reynolds, David S. Beneath the American Renaissance: The Subversive Imagination in the Age of Emerson & Melville. LC 89-31146. (Illus.). 656p. 1989. pap. 22.50 (*0-674-06565-4*) HUP.

— Faith in Fiction: The Emergence of Religious Literature in America. LC 80-20885. 280p. (C). 1981. 57.00 (*0-674-29172-7*) HUP.

— Walt Whitman's America: A Cultural Biography. (Illus.). 704p. 1996. pap. 19.00 (*0-679-76709-6*) Vin Bks.

***Reynolds, David S., ed.** A Historical Guide to Walt Whitman. LC 99-12608. (Illus.). 288p. 2000. pap. 15.95 (*0-19-512082-5*); text 35.00 (*0-19-512081-7*) OUP.

Reynolds, David S. & Rosenthal, Debra J., eds. The Serpent in the Cup: Temperance in American Literature. 240p. 1997. pap. 18.95 (*1-55849-082-5*); text 55.00 (*1-55849-081-7*) U of Mass Pr.

Reynolds, David S., ed. & intro. see Lippard, George.

Reynolds, David West. Star Wars: Incredible Cross-Sections. (Star Wars Ser.). (Illus.). 32p. 1998. 399.00 (*0-7894-3865-8*) DK Pub Inc.

— Star Wars: Incredible Cross-Sections. LC 98-22878. (Star Wars Ser.). (Illus.). 32p. (J). 1998. 19.95 (*0-7894-3480-6*) DK Pub Inc.

— Star Wars: The Visual Dictionary. LC 98-22877. (Star Wars Ser.). (Illus.). 64p. (J). 1998. 19.95 (*0-7894-3481-4*) DK Pub Inc.

— Star Wars: Episode I: The Visual Dictionary. (Star Wars Ser.). (Illus.). 64p. 1998. 399.00 (*0-7894-3866-6*) DK Pub Inc.

— Star Wars: Episode I: The Visual Dictionary. LC 99-18082. (Star Wars Ser.). (Illus.). 64p. 1999. 19.95 (*0-7894-4701-0*) DK Pub Inc.

Reynolds, David West & D K Publishing Staff. Star Wars: Episode I: Incredible Cross Sections. LC 99-10178. (Star Wars Ser.). (Illus.). 32p. (J). (gr. 4-8). 1999. 19.95 (*0-7894-3962-X*) DK Pub Inc.

***Reynolds, Deanna.** Treasury of Year-Round Preschool Activities: Early Childhood. (Illus.). 304p. 2000. pap., teacher ed. 24.95 (*1-57690-594-2*, TCM 2594) Tchr Create Mat.

Reynolds, Debbie. Debbie: My Life. 1991. mass mkt. 5.95 (*0-671-74248-5*) PB.

Reynolds, Dee. Symbolist Aesthetics & Early Abstract Art: Sites of Imaginary Space. (Cambridge Studies in French: No. 51). (Illus.). 308p. (C). 1995. text 69.95 (*0-521-42102-0*) Cambridge U Pr.

***Reynolds, Denise A. & Reynolds, Douglas.** Quixtar.com Click-by-Click. LC 00-190292. (Illus.). 177p. 2000. pap. 19.95 (*0-9679347-0-2*) click-by-click.

Reynolds, Dennis J., ed. Citizen Rights & Access to Electronic Information: The 1991 LITA President's Program Presentations & Background Papers. LC 92-19782. 201p. 1992. pap. 11.00 (*0-8389-7601-8*) ALA.

Reynolds, Diana H., ed. Florida Senior Managers Handbook. 5th ed. 750p. 1993. ring bd. 69.95 (*0-932143-01-6*) FL Ctr Public.

Reynolds, Dinah. Worcester Porcelain: Marshall Collection. (Illus.). 80p. 1995. 19.95 (*1-85444-040-3*, 75X) A Schwartz & Co.

— Worcester Porcelain: Marshall Collection. (Illus.). 80p. 1996. pap. 12.95 (*0-907849-75-X*, 75XP, Pub. by Ashmolean Mus) A Schwartz & Co.

Reynolds, Dona & Older, Ricki. So Now You Own a Food Processor. (Illus.). 285p. 1984. pap. text 10.95 (*0-931955-00-9*) East-West Pub.

Reynolds, Donald E. Editors Make War: Southern Newspapers in the Secession Crisis. LC 71-129050. 315p. reprint ed. pap. 97.70 (*0-8357-3263-0*, 203948400013) Bks Demand.

— Professor Mayo's College: A History of East Texas State University. (Illus.). 212p. 1993. 24.95 (*0-9637092-0-8*) E TX Mayo Pr.

Reynolds, Donald E. & Means, R. S., Co. Engineering Staff, eds. Residential & Light Commercial Construction Standards. (Illus.). 600p. 1998. pap. 59.95 (*0-87629-499-9*, 67322) R S Means.

Reynolds, Donald M. The Architecture of New York City: Histories & Views of Important Structures, Sites & Symbols. 2nd rev. ed. 408p. 1994. pap. 34.95 (*0-471-01439-7*) Wiley.

— Masters of American Sculpture: The Figurative Tradition. (Illus.). 276p. 1993. 67.50 (*1-55859-276-8*) Abbeville Pr.

— Monuments & Masterpieces: Histories & Views of Public Sculpture in New York City. LC 96-61457. (Illus.). 496p. 1997. pap. 19.95 (*0-500-01774-3*, Pub. by Thames Hudson) Norton.

Reynolds, Donald M., ed. Remove Not the Ancient Landmark: Public Monuments & Moral Values. (Documenting the Image Ser.: Vol. III). 237p. 1996. text 39.00 (*2-88124-602-8*, ECU38, Harwood Acad Pubs); pap. text 14.00 (*2-88449-204-6*, ECU18, Harwood Acad Pubs) Gordon & Breach.

Reynolds, Donald M., ed. see Wittkower, Rudolf.

Reynolds, Doreen. Straight from the Heart. LC 96-61378. 80p. 1997. pap. 9.95 (*1-887798-05-6*) WriteMore Pubns.

***Reynolds, Doris.** Remembering the Language of God by Angela Passidomo Trafford: The Forgotten Path. (Illus.). 300p. 1998. pap. 19.95 (*0-9628173-1-7*) Enterprse Pubg.

Reynolds, Douglas, jt. auth. see Reynolds, Denise A.

Reynolds, Douglas R. China, Eighteen Ninety-Eight to Nineteen Twelve: The Xinzheng Revolution & Japan. (East Asian Monographs: No. 160). (Illus.). 200p. (C). 1993. text 32.00 (*0-674-11660-7*) HUP.

Reynolds, Douglas R., ed. China, 1895-1912 State Sponsored Reforms & China's Late-Qing Revolution: Selected Essays from Zhongguo Jindai Shi (Modern Chinese History, 1840-1919) (Special Studies in Chinese History). 191p. (C). 1996. pap. text 93.95 (*1-56324-749-6*) M E Sharpe.

Reynolds, Dwight F. Heroic Poets, Poetic Heroes: The Ethnography of Performance in an Arabic Oral Epic Tradition. (Myth & Poetics Ser.). (Illus.). 304p. 1995. text 45.00 (*0-8014-3174-3*) Cornell U Pr.

Reynolds, E. Bruce. Thailand & Japan's Southern Advance, 1940-1945. LC 93-26125. 1994. text 55.00 (*0-312-10402-2*) St Martin.

Reynolds, E. E. Life of St. Francis of Assisi. 128p. 1994. reprint ed. mass mkt. 6.95 (*0-940147-28-9*) Source Bks CA.

Reynolds, E. L. Distribution of Subcutaneous Fat in Childhood & Adolescence. (SRCD Ser.: Vol. 15, No. 2). 1950. 25.00 (*0-527-01551-2*) Periodicals Srv.

Reynolds, Earle L. The Forbidden Voyage. LC 74-27390. (Illus.). 281p. 1975. reprint ed. lib. bdg. 69.50 (*0-8371-7906-8*, REFV, Greenwood Pr) Greenwood.

Reynolds, Ed. Confidence in Writing. 3rd ed. (C). 1995. text 37.00 (*0-15-501552-4*, Pub. by Harcourt Coll Pubs); pap. text, teacher ed. 28.00 (*0-15-503241-0*) Harcourt Coll Pubs.

Reynolds, Ed & Mixdorf, Marcia. Confidence in Writing: A Basic Text. 2nd ed. 350p. (C). 1990. pap. text 36.00 (*0-15-512987-2*, Pub. by Harcourt Coll Pubs) Harcourt.

Reynolds, Edward. A Commentary on Ecclesiastes: Volume 4 of Works, Vol. 4. LC 99-208656. (Works of Edward Reynolds: Vol. 4). 479p. 1998. 29.95 (*1-57358-076-7*) Soli Deo Gloria.

— Evolution of the Human Pelvis in Relation to the Mechanics of the Erect Posture. (HU PMP Ser.: Vol. 11, No. 5). 1931. pap. 25.00 (*0-527-01222-X*) Periodicals Srv.

— The Exaltation of Christ: Volume 2 of the Works. (Works of Edward Reynolds Ser.: Vol. 2). 466p. 1993. reprint ed. 29.95 (*1-877611-62-X*) Soli Deo Gloria.

***Reynolds, Edward.** Meditations on the Holy Sacrament of the Lord's Last Supper: Volume 3 of the Works. 2000. 29.95 (*1-57358-100-3*) Soli Deo Gloria.

Reynolds, Edward. Sinfulness of Sin: Volume 1 of the Works. (Works of Edward Reynolds Ser.: Vol. 1). 549p. 1991. reprint ed. 29.95 (*1-877611-44-1*) Soli Deo Gloria.

— Stand the Storm: A History of the Atlantic Slave Trade. 1989. pap. 6.95 (*0-85031-586-7*) Allison & Busby.

— Stand the Storm: A History of the Atlantic Slave Trade. 192p. 1993. reprint ed. pap. text 8.95 (*1-56663-020-7*, Elephant Paperbacks) I R Dee.

— Treatise of the Passions & Faculties of the Soule of Man. LC 79-161935. (History of Psychology Ser.). 536p. 1971. 75.00 (*0-8201-1095-7*) Schol Facsimiles.

— A Treatise on the Soul: Volume 6 of the Works. (Works of Edward Reynolds: Vol. 6). 392p. 1996. reprint ed. 29.95 (*1-57358-048-1*) Soli Deo Gloria.

Reynolds, Edward N., jt. auth. see Harris, Scott O.

Reynolds, Elaine, jt. auth. see Frazier, Kathy.

Reynolds, Elaine A. Before the Bobbies: The Night Watch & Police Reform in Metropolitan London, 1720-1830. LC 97-62111. (Illus.). 256p. 1998. 49.50 (*0-8047-3369-4*) Stanford U Pr.

Reynolds, Eleanor. Guiding Young Children: A Child-Centered Approach. 2nd ed. LC 95-9019. (Illus.). viii, 408p. (C). 1995. pap. text 35.95 (*1-55934-446-6*, 1446) Mayfield Pub.

***Reynolds, Eleanor.** Guiding Young Children: A Problem-Solving Approach. 3rd ed. LC 00-26305. 2000. write for info. (*0-7674-1796-8*) Mayfield Pub.

Reynolds, Eleanor D. LetterFun ABC Book. (Illus.). 32p. (J). 1999. pap. 5.95 (*0-9660157-1-1*) FunStuff Prodns.

Reynolds, Elisabeth B., ed. Income Security in Canada: Changing Needs, Changing Means. LC 95-198876. (Illus.). 230p. 1993. pap. 15.95 (*0-88645-149-3*, Pub. by Inst Res Pub) Ashgate Pub Co.

Reynolds, Elsdon & Reynolds, Stewart. A Town in Action Vol. 4: Voluntary Networks in Retford (Adult Learning in Voluntary Organisation) 1994. pap. 20.00 (*1-85041-047-X*, Pub. by Univ Nottingham) St Mut.

Reynolds, Eric. Dirty Stories. pap. 12.95 (*1-56097-246-7*, Pub. by Fantagraph Bks) Seven Hills Bk.

Reynolds, Eric. The Glass of John Walsh, 1850-1951. 148p. 1999. pap. 40.00 (*0-903685-69-8*, Pub. by R Dennis) Antique Collect.

Reynolds, Ernest. Early Victorian Drama: 1830-1870. LC 65-16248. 170p. 1972. 21.95 (*0-405-08881-7*, Pub. by Blom Pubns) Ayer.

Reynolds, Ernest E. Thomas More & Erasmus. LC 65-26739. (Illus.). 278p. reprint ed. pap. 86.20 (*0-7837-5582-1*, 204537000005) Bks Demand.

Reynolds-Feighn, A. J. The Effects of Deregulation on U. S. Air Networks. Batten, David F., ed. (Advances in Spatial & Network Economics Ser.). (Illus.). xiv, 131p. 1992. 71.95 (*0-387-54758-4*) Spr-Verlag.

Reynolds, Felicity, ed. Effects on the Baby of Maternal Analgesia & Anaesthesia. (Illus.). 292p. 1993. text 60.00 (*0-7020-1574-1*, Pub. by W B Saunders) Saunders.

Reynolds, Fiona. War in the Far East. 80p. (Orig.). (C). 1995. pap. text 6.50 (*0-435-31882-9*) Heinemann.

Reynolds, Fleur. Bonded. (Orig.). 1997. mass mkt. 5.95 (*0-352-33192-5*, Pub. by BLA4) London Brdge.

— Conquered. (Black Lace Ser.). 1995. mass mkt. 5.95 (*0-352-33025-2*, Pub. by Virgin Bks) London Brdge.

— The House in New Orleans. (Black Lace Ser.). 1995. mass mkt. 5.95 (*0-352-32951-3*, Pub. by Virgin Bks) London Brdge.

— Odalisque. (Black Lace Ser.). 1995. mass mkt. 5.95 (*0-352-32887-8*, Pub. by Virgin Bks) London Brdge.

Reynolds, Flora E. Guide to the Book Artifacts Collection. (Illus.). 62p. 1999. pap. 7.50 (*1-893663-04-3*) Bancroftd Lib.

Reynolds, Flora E., jt. auth. see Lyon, Margaret.

Reynolds, Francis E. The Complete Resort Golfer's Handbook: Did You See That? (Illus.). 72p. 1996. 9.95 (*0-9618116-2-5*) Sarge Pubns.

Reynolds, Francis F. Griffith: Smoke on the Waters. (Illus.). 308p. 1996. pap. 16.95 (*0-9618116-3-3*) Sarge Pubns.

— Pewabic: Deadly Waters. LC 99-188045. 170p. 1998. pap. 11.95 (*0-9618116-4-1*) Sarge Pubns.

Reynolds, Frank E. & Capps, Donald, eds. The Biographical Process: Studies in the History & Psychology of Religion. (Religion & Reason, Method & Theory in the Study & Interpretation of Religion Ser.: No. 11). 1976. text 75.40 (*90-279-7522-1*) Mouton.

***Reynolds, Frank E. & Carbine, Jason A., eds.** The Life of Buddhism. (Life of Religion Ser.). (Illus.). 247p. 2000. pap. 17.95 (*0-520-22337-3*) U CA Pr.

— The Life of Buddhism. LC 00-30260. (Life of Religion Ser.: Vol. 1). (Illus.). 247p. 2000. 45.00 (*0-520-21105-7*) U CA Pr.

Reynolds, Frank E. & Reynolds, Mani B., eds. Three Worlds According to King Ruang: A Thai Buddhist Cosmology. (Berkeley Buddhist Studies). (Illus.). 383p. 1982. 30.00 (*0-87725-314-5*) U of Cal IAS.

Reynolds, Frank E. & Tracy, David, eds. Discourse & Practice. LC 91-18680. (SUNY Series, Toward a Comparative Philosophy of Religions). 316p. (C). 1992. pap. text 21.95 (*0-7914-1024-2*) State U NY Pr.

— Myth & Philosophy. LC 89-48910. (SUNY Series, Toward a Comparative Philosophy of Religions). 382p. (C). 1990. pap. text 21.95 (*0-7914-0418-8*) State U NY Pr.

— Myth & Philosophy. LC 89-48910. (SUNY Series, Toward a Comparative Philosophy of Religions). 382p. (C). 1990. text 64.50 (*0-7914-0417-X*) State U NY Pr.

— Religion & Practical Reason: New Essays in the Comparative Philosophy of Religions. LC 94-7298. (SUNY Series, Toward a Comparative Philosophy of Religions). 444p. (C). 1994. text 64.50 (*0-7914-2217-8*); pap. text 21.95 (*0-7914-2218-6*) State U NY Pr.

Reynolds, Frank E., jt. ed. see Lovin, Robin W.

***Reynolds, Frank H.** I Looked at My Feet. (Illus.). 44p. 1999. pap. 14.95 (*0-7392-0402-5*, PO3635) Morris Pubng.

Reynolds, Frank J. Capture the Flag, 2 vols. 1994. pap. write for info. (*1-886457-01-8*) Intl Projects.

— Capture the Flag, Vol. I. 108p. 1994. pap. 45.00 (*1-886457-02-6*) Intl Projects.

— Capture the Flag, Vol. I. abr. ed. 108p. 1995. pap. 35.00 (*1-886457-04-2*) Intl Projects.

— Capture the Flag, Vol. II. 170p. 1994. pap. 45.00 (*1-886457-03-4*) Intl Projects.

— Capture the Flag, Vol. II. abr. ed. 170p. 1995. pap. 35.00 (*1-886457-05-0*) Intl Projects.

— Incoterms for Americans. 124p. 1993. pap. 39.00 (*1-886457-00-X*) Intl Projects.

***Reynolds, Frank J.** Incoterms for Americans, 2000. 2nd rev. ed. (Illus.). 150p. 1999. pap. 43.00 (*1-886457-06-9*) Intl Projects.

Reynolds, Fred D. & Barksdale, Hiram C., eds. Marketing & the Quality of Life. LC 78-17765. (American Marketing Association, Proceedings Ser.). 88p. reprint ed. pap. 30.00 (*0-608-11941-5*, 202336200032) Bks Demand.

Reynolds, Frederick. The Life & Times of Frederick Reynolds, 2 Vols., 1 bk. 2nd ed. LC 74-88489. 840p. 1972. 49.95 (*0-405-08882-5*, Pub. by Blom Pubns) Ayer.

Reynolds, G., tr. see Birkmayer, W. & Riederer, P.

Reynolds, G. F. Some Principles of Elizabethan Staging. LC 78-130233. reprint ed. 22.50 (*0-404-05286-X*) AMS Pr.

Reynolds, G. W., III. Jetty Man. 462p. 1999. pap. 22.95 (*1-58244-027-1*) Rutledge Bks.

***Reynolds, G. W., III.** Mullet Run. LC 99-69399. 510p. 1999. pap. 22.95 (*1-58244-078-6*) Rutledge Bks.

Reynolds, Gail, jt. auth. see MacAdam, Don.

Reynolds, Gaius, ed. see Neiman, Tummy & Reynolds, Sue.

Reynolds, Gary A. American Bronze Sculpture: 1850 to the Present. Sweeney, Mary S., ed. LC 84-22616. (Illus.). 72p. (Orig.). 1984. pap. 12.95 (*0-932828-20-5*) Newark Mus.

Reynolds, Gary A. & Wright, Beryl J. Against the Odds: African-American Artists & the Harmon Foundation. LC 89-27552. 298p. 1990. 40.00 (*0-932828-21-3*); pap. 20.00 (*0-932828-22-1*) Newark Mus.

Reynolds, George & Sjodahl, Janne M. Commentary on the Book of Mormon, 7 vols, Vol. 4. 451p. 9.95 (*0-87747-042-1*) Deseret Bk.

***Reynolds, George A.** M'aidez. LC 99-74761. 192p. 2000. pap. 13.95 (*1-57197-196-3*, Pub. by Pentland Pr) Assoc Pubs Grp.

Reynolds, George G. The Distribution of Power to Regulate Interstate Carriers Between the Nation & the States. LC 68-57578. (Columbia University. Studies in the Social Sciences: No. 295). reprint ed. 34.50 (*0-404-51295-X*) AMS Pr.

***Reynolds, George G.** The Distribution of Power to Regulate Interstate Carriers Between the Nation & the States. (Studies in History, Economics & Public Law: No. 295). 434p. 1999. reprint ed. 108.50 (*1-56169-570-X*, 18411) Gaunt.

Reynolds, George P. & Wigginton, Eliot. Foxfire Ten: Railroad Lore, Boarding Houses, Depression-Era Appalachia, Chairmaking, Whirligigs, Snakes Canes, & Gourd Art. Walker, Susan et al, eds. LC 92-24634. 512p. 1993. pap. 15.95 (*0-385-42276-8*, Anchor NY) Doubleday.

Reynolds, George W. The Mysteries of London, 4 vols., 2 bks., Set. LC 79-8192. reprint ed. 84.50 (*0-404-62106-6*) AMS Pr.

— The Necromancer: A Romance. Reginald, R. & Menville, Douglas A., eds. LC 75-46304. (Supernatural & Occult Fiction Ser.). (Illus.). 1976. reprint ed. lib. bdg. 23.95 (*0-405-08164-2*) Ayer.

Reynolds, George W., jt. auth. see Stair, Ralph M.

Reynolds, Gerald G. History of the Santa Clarita Valley. Worden, Leon, ed. (Illus.). 200p. 1997. text 29.95 (*0-9660253-0-X*) Old Town Newhall.

Reynolds, Gil. The Fused Glass Handbook. 3rd ed. LC 87-25114. (Illus.). 102p. 1994. pap. 24.95 (*0-915807-02-5*) Hidden Valley Bks.

Reynolds, Glenn H. Outer Space: Problems of Law & Policy. 2nd ed. 464p. 1998. pap. 40.00 (*0-8133-6680-1*, Pub. by Westview) HarpC.

Reynolds, Glenn H., jt. auth. see Morgan, Peter W.

Reynolds, Graham. British Portrait Miniatures. (Fitzwilliam Museum Handbooks Ser.). (Illus.). 146p. (C). 1998. text 59.95 (*0-521-59202-X*); pap. text 19.95 (*0-521-59781-1*) Cambridge U Pr.

— Constable: The Natural Painter. (Illus.). 144p. 1977. reprint ed. pap. 5.95 (*0-586-04401-9*) Academy Chi Pubs.

— The Early Paintings & Drawings of John Constable. (Studies in British Art). (C). 1996. 185.00 (*0-300-06337-7*) Yale U Pr.

— English Portrait Miniatures. rev. ed. (Illus.). 211p. (C). 1992. pap. text 38.95 (*0-521-33920-0*) Cambridge U Pr.

— English Watercolors. (Illus.). 160p. (C). 1988. 35.00 (*0-941533-43-3*, NAB) I R Dee.

— The Later Paintings & Drawings of John Constable, 2 vols., Set. LC 84-40186. (Studies in British Art). (Illus.). 880p. 1984. 300.00 (*0-300-03151-3*) Yale U Pr.

— Sixteenth & Seventeenth Century Miniatures in the Collection of Her Majesty the Queen. LC 99-70870. (Royal Collection). (Illus.). 320p. 1999. 220.00 (*0-500-97482-9*, Pub. by Thames Hudson) Norton.

— Turner. (World of Art Ser.). (Illus.). 216p. 1985. pap. 14.95 (*0-500-20083-1*, Pub. by Thames Hudson) Norton.

— The Wallace Collection Catalogue of Miniatures. (Illus.). 366p. 1980. pap. 19.95 (*0-900785-21-7*, Pub. by Wallace Collect) Antique Collect.

— Watercolors: A Concise History. (World of Art Ser.). (Illus.). 1986. pap. 14.95 (*0-500-20109-9*, Pub. by Thames Hudson) Norton.

Reynolds, Graham, et al, texts. John Constable R. A. (Illus.). 201p. 1988. pap. 50.00 (*1-58821-008-1*) Salander OReilly.

Reynolds, Graham & Baetjer, Katharine. European Miniatures: In the Metropolitan Museum of Art. LC 96-22153. (Illus.). 224p. 1996. 65.00 (*0-8109-6503-8*, Pub. by Abrams) Time Warner.

Reynolds, Gretchen. Heiress & the Horse Killers. 1996. write for info. (*0-8092-3253-7*) NTC Contemp Pub Co.

Reynolds, Gretchen & Jones, Elizabeth. Master Players. (Early Childhood Education Ser.: Vol. 60). 144p. (C). 1996. text 36.00 (*0-8077-3582-5*); pap. text 16.95 (*0-8077-3581-7*) Tchrs Coll.

Reynolds, Gretchen, jt. auth. see Jones, Elizabeth.

Reynolds, Guy. Twentieth-Century American Women's Fiction: A Critical Introduction. LC 99-15611. 253p. 1999. text 59.95 (*0-312-22636-5*) St Martin.

Reynolds, H. T. Analysis of Nominal Data. 2nd ed. (Quantitative Applications in the Social Sciences Ser.: Vol. 7). 82p. 1984. 10.95 (*0-8039-0653-6*) Sage.

Reynolds, H. W. Dutch Houses in the Hudson Valley Before 1776. 467p. 1993. reprint ed. lib. bdg. 99.00 (*0-7812-5303-9*) Rprt Serv.

— Dutchess County Doorways, 1730-1830. 280p. 1993. reprint ed. lib. bdg. 79.00 (*0-7812-5304-7*) Rprt Serv.

Reynolds, Hanson, jt. ed. see Warner, Joseph.

Reynolds, Harold R. Fifty Ways to Get a Date Without Bars, Singles Clubs or Computers. Riddle, Florence K., ed. LC 84-62106. 64p. (Orig.). 1992. pap. 7.00 (*0-9613987-2-8*) Reliant Pub.

Reynolds, Harry W., Jr., ed. Ethics in American Public Service. LC 94-66220. (Annals of the American Academy of Political & Social Science Ser.: Vol. 537). 1995. 28.00 (*0-8039-5882-X*); pap. 18.00 (*0-8039-5883-8*) Am Acad Pol Soc Sci.

Reynolds, Harry W., jt. auth. see American Academy of Political & Social Science Sta.

Reynolds, Helen. The Economics of Prostitution. 218p. 1985. pap. text 29.95 (*0-398-07036-9*) C C Thomas.

Reynolds, Helen. The Economics of Prostitution. (Illus.). 218p. (C). 1985. 40.95 (*0-398-05161-5*) C C Thomas.

Reynolds, Helen, jt. auth. see Reynolds, Ivan G.

An Asterisk (*) at the beginning of an entry indicates that the title is appearing for the first time.

Reynolds, Henry. Aboriginal Sovereignty: Reflections on Race, State & Nation. LC 96-192248. 240p. 1997. pap. text 17.95 (*1-86373-969-6*, Pub. by Allen & Unwin Pty) Paul & Co Pubs.
— Dispossession. xiv, 226 p. 1996. write for info. (*1-86448-141-2*, Pub. by Allen & Unwin Pty) Paul & Co Pubs.
— Dispossession: Black Australians & White Invaders. (Illus.). 226p. (C). 1990. pap. text 17.95 (*0-04-370182-5*) Routledge.
— Frontier. 248p. 1997. pap. 17.95 (*1-86448-191-9*, Pub. by Allen & Unwin Pty) Paul & Co Pubs.
— This Whispering in Our Hearts. LC 98-205517. 320p. 1998. pap. 17.95 (*1-86448-581-7*, Pub. by Allen & Unwin Pty) Paul & Co Pubs.
Reynolds, Henry, ed. 1995-96 HomeTech Housebuilders Cost Estimator. (Illus.). (Orig.). 1995. pap. 69.50 (*1-882379-17-9*) HomeTech Info Systs.
— 1996 HomeTech Remodeling & Renovation Cost Estimator, Field Manual. rev. ed. 278p. 1995. pap. 34.50 (*1-882379-18-7*) HomeTech Info Systs.
— 1996 HomeTech Remodeling & Renovation Cost Estimator, Manager's Manual. rev. ed. 278p. 1995. pap. 69.50 (*1-882379-19-5*) HomeTech Info Systs.
Reynolds, Hugh, ed. The Executive Branch of the U. S. Government: A Bibliography, 11. LC 88-24704. (Bibliographies & Indexes in Law & Political Science Ser.: No. 11). 389p. 1988. lib. bdg. 69.50 (*0-313-26568-2*, GEX/, Greenwood Pr) Greenwood.
Reynolds, Ignatius A., jt. auth. see England, John.
Reynolds, Ivan G. & Reynolds, Helen. Treasure of Charter Oak: Growing up in the Masonic Home for Children, 1928-1938. LC 89-34633. (Illus.). 80p. (Orig.). 1989. pap. 7.95 (*0-931832-34-9*) Fithian Pr.
Reynolds, J. Down Under. LC 91-9791. (Illus.). 32p. (J). (gr. 2 up). 1992. 16.95 (*0-15-224182-5*, Harcourt Child Bks) Harcourt.
— Material & Energy Balances: A Self Instructional Problem Workbook. 240p. (C). 1992. pap. text 60.00 (*1-882767-07-1*) ETS.
Reynolds, J. & Theodore, Louis. Thermodynamics: A Self Instructional Problem Workbook. 248p. (C). 1992. pap. text 60.00 (*1-882767-04-7*) ETS.
Reynolds, J., jt. auth. see Dupont, R.
Reynolds, J. B., ed. Fish Ecology in Arctic North America. LC 97-70116. (AFS Symposium Ser.: Vol. 19). 345p. 1997. pap. 103.00 (*0-913235-96-2*, 540.19P) Am Fisheries Soc.
Reynolds, J. B., jt. auth. see MacGougan, Denny.
Reynolds, J. Frederick, ed. Rhetorical Memory & Delivery: Classical Concepts for Contemporary Composition. (Communications, Rhetoric & Public Address Ser.). 192p. 1993. pap. 22.50 (*0-8058-1293-8*); text 45.00 (*0-8058-1292-X*) L Erlbaum Assocs.
Reynolds, J. R., et al, eds. Electrical, Optical, & Magnetic Properties of Organic Solid-State Materials IV Vol. 488: Materials Research Society Symposium Proceedings. LC 98-15398. 954p. 1998. text 76.00 (*1-55899-393-2*) Materials Res.
Reynolds, Jack. Assessing Community Health Needs & Coverage Module 2: User's Guide. (Primary Health Care Management Advancement Programme (PHC MAP) Modules Ser.). 227p. 1993. pap. text. write for info. (*1-882839-01-3*) Aga Khan Fnd.
— Assessing Information Needs Module 1: User's Guide. (Primary Health Care Management Advancement Programme (PHC MAP) Modules Ser.). 54p. 1993. pap. text. write for info. (*1-882839-00-5*) Aga Khan Fnd.
— Cost Analysis Module 8: User's Guide. (Primary Health Care Management Advancement Programme (PHC MAP) Modules Ser.). 97p. 1993. pap. text. write for info. (*1-882839-06-4*) Aga Khan Fnd.
Reynolds, Jack & Stinson, Wayne. Sustainability Analysis Module 9: User's Guide. (Primary Health Care Management Advancement Programme (PHC MAP) Modules Ser.). 105p. 1993. pap. text. write for info. (*1-882839-07-2*) Aga Khan Fnd.
Reynolds, Jack, et al. Better Management - 100 Tips: Manager's Guide. (Primary Health Care Management Advancement Programme (PHC MAP) Modules Ser.). 64p. 1993. pap. text. write for info. (*1-882839-17-X*) Aga Khan Fnd.
Reynolds, Jackie. Out of Jackie's Smoke House. (Illus.). 110p. (Orig.). 1996. pap. 19.95 (*0-9657632-1-8*, 76653-46873) Out Back Ranch.
Reynolds, Jaime, jt. auth. see Coutouvidis, John.
Reynolds, James, ed. Martindale Extra Pharmacopoeia. 31st ed. 2739p. 1996. text 299.00 (*0-85369-342-0*, Pub. by Pharmaceutical Pr) Rittenhouse.
Reynolds, James. Traildust: Cowboys, Cattle & Country: The Art of James Reynolds. LC 97-15123. 156p. 1997. 39.95 (*0-86713-035-0*) Greenwich Wrkshop.
Reynolds, James A. Applied Transformed Circuit Theory for Technology. LC 84-7525. 335p. 1985. text 49.95 (*0-471-09819-1*) P-H.
— Catholic Emancipation Crisis in Ireland, 1823-1829. LC 74-95134. 204p. 1970. reprint ed. lib. bdg. 55.00 (*0-8371-3141-3*, RECE, Greenwood Pr) Greenwood.
Reynolds, James A. & Grenon, Brian J., eds. 17th Annual BACUS Symposium on Photomask Technology & Management. LC 98-184513. 564p. 1997. 107.00 (*0-8194-2669-5*) SPIE.
Reynolds, James A., jt. ed. see Sheldon, Gilbert V.
Reynolds, James F. & Tenhunen, John D., eds. Landscape Function & Disturbance in Arctic Tundra. (Ecological Studies: Vol. 120). (Illus.). 429p. 1996. 139.00 (*3-540-59263-6*) Spr-Verlag.
Reynolds, James F., jt. auth. see Ludwig, John A.
Reynolds, James H. Computing in Psychology: An Introduction to Programming Methods & Concepts. (Illus.). 320p. 1987. pap. text 36.40 (*0-13-165812-3*) P-H.
Reynolds, James J., ed. Modern Poetry for Children, Bk. 8. LC 30-10164. (Granger Poetry Library). (J). (gr. 4). 1979. reprint ed. 20.00 (*0-89609-167-8*) Roth Pub Inc.
Reynolds, James J., jt. auth. see Harshbarger, Ronald J.
Reynolds, Jan. Amazon Basin. LC 92-21089. (Vanishing Cultures Ser.). (Illus.). 32p. (J). (gr. 2 up). 1993. pap. 10.00 (*0-15-202832-3*, Harcourt Child Bks) Harcourt.
— Frozen Land. LC 92-30324. (Illus.). 32p. (J). (gr. 2 up). 1993. 16.95 (*0-15-238787-0*); pap. 8.95 (*0-15-238788-9*) Harcourt.
— Himalaya. LC 90-36197. (Illus.). 32p. (J). (gr. 2 up). 1991. 17.00 (*0-15-234465-9*) Harcourt.
— Mongolia. LC 93-1351. (Vanishing Cultures Ser.). (Illus.). 32p. (J). (gr. 3-7). 1994. 16.95 (*0-15-255312-6*); pap. 8.95 (*0-15-255313-4*) Harcourt.
— Mother & Child: Visions of Parenting from Indigenous Cultures. LC 96-32597. (Illus.). 112p. 1996. pap. 19.95 (*0-89281-637-6*, Inner Trad) Inner Tradit.
— Sahara. LC 90-37653. (Illus.). 32p. (J). (gr. 2 up). 1991. pap. 10.00 (*0-15-269958-9*) Harcourt.
Reynolds, Jane L. Sing to the Earth. 16p. (J). (gr. k-4). 1978. write for info. (*0-932320-01-5*); write for info. (*0-932320-02-3*); write for info. (*0-932320-03-1*); write for info. (*0-932320-04-X*); pap. write for info. (*0-932320-00-7*) Solar Studio.
— Skits for Seniors Only. 20p. 1980. write for info. (*0-932320-06-6*); write for info. (*0-932320-07-4*); write for info. (*0-932320-05-8*) Solar Studio.
Reynolds, Janet, jt. auth. see Rob, Caroline.
Reynolds, Jean. Pygmalion's Wordplay: The Postmodern Shaw. LC 99-10186. 1999. 49.95 (*0-8130-1681-9*) U Press Fla.
— Sentence Power. (C). 1991. pap. text 36.00 (*0-03-026333-6*, Pub. by Harcourt Coll Pubs) Harcourt.
Reynolds, Jean A. Succeeding in College. 400p. 1996. pap. text 27.00 (*0-205-16041-7*) P-H.
Reynolds, Jean E. & Cross, Carol. Kisses from Hanna: From Holland to America: WWII Memoirs. LC 98-145262. (Illus.). 293p. 1997. pap. 14.95 (*0-9657160-0-7*) Cross & Reynolds.
Reynolds, Jeanette & McCann, Annes, eds. Cased-Hole Logging. (Oil & Gas Production Ser.). (Illus.). 75p. (Orig.). (C). 1981. pap. text 15.00 (*0-88698-107-7*, 3.30510) PETEX.
— Open-Hole Logging. (Oil & Gas Production Ser.). (Illus.). 87p. (Orig.). (C). 1981. pap. text 15.00 (*0-88698-108-5*, 3.30410) PETEX.
Reynolds, Jeanie, ed. see Stanton, Bette L.
Reynolds, Jerry D. What You Need to Know about Improving Basic English Skills. 288p. 1994. pap. 12.95 (*0-8442-5285-9*, Natl Textbk Co) NTC Contemp Pub Co.
— What You Need to Know about Improving Basic English Skills. 2nd ed. 1997. pap. 12.95 (*0-8442-5969-1*) NTC Contemp Pub Co.
Reynolds, Jerry D. & Steet, Marion L. What You Need to Know about Improving Basic English Skills. 2nd ed. LC 97-12336. (NTC's Skill Builders Ser.). 256p. (J). 1997. student ed. write for info. (*0-8442-5967-5*) NTC Contemp Pub Co.
Reynolds, Jerry D., et al. What You Need to Know about Improving Basic English Skills: Intermediate Through Advanced. 256p. (YA). 1994. pap. text 15.95 (*0-8442-5283-2*, Natl Textbk Co) NTC Contemp Pub Co.
— What You Need to Know about Improving Basic English Skills: Intermediate Through Advanced. annot. ed. 256p. (YA). 1994. teacher ed. 19.95 (*0-8442-5284-0*, Natl Textbk Co) NTC Contemp Pub Co.
Reynolds, Jerry D., jt. auth. see Mueller, Lavonne.
Reynolds, Jill & MIT List Visual Arts Center Staff. Jill Reynolds: The Shape of Breath. LC 97-36762. 1997. pap. 7.00 (*0-938437-55-0*) MIT List Visual Arts.
Reynolds, Jim. Norton: The Legend Continues. 96p. 1995. 12.98 (*0-7858-0310-6*) Bk Sales Inc.
— The Outer Path: Finding My Way in Tibet. Hallam, Kathleen, ed. LC 91-21086. (Illus.). 184p. (Orig.). 1992. pap. 10.95 (*0-933271-06-9*) Fair Oaks CA.
Reynolds, Joanne, ed. see Reynolds, Yvonne.
Reynolds, Jock. American Abstraction at the Addison. LC 91-71558. (Illus.). 96p. (Orig.). 1991. pap. 15.00 (*1-879886-30-8*) Addison Gallery.
Reynolds, Jock, ed. George B. Luks - Bronx Park, May 8, 1904. (Illus.). 96p. (Orig.). 1990. pap. 8.00 (*1-879886-28-6*) Addison Gallery.
Reynolds, Jock & Walker, Rebecca. House & Home: Spirits of the South. LC 94-70777. (Illus.). 100p. 1994. pap. 24.95 (*1-879886-35-9*) Addison Gallery.
Reynolds, Jock, jt. auth. see Keller, Andrea M.
Reynolds, Jock, jt. auth. see Powell, Richard.
Reynolds, Jock, jt. auth. see Powell, Richard J.
Reynolds, Joe. Out Front Leadership: Discovering, Developing, & Delivering Your Potential. 1993. 19.95 (*0-9636391-0-2*) Mott & Carlisle.
Reynolds, John. Andre Citroen. LC 96-31935. (Illus.). 256p. 1997. text 35.00 (*0-312-16505-6*) St Martin.
— Case Method in Management Development: Guide for Effective Use. (Management Development Ser.: No. 17). vi, 264p. 1992. reprint ed. 27.00 (*92-2-102363-X*) Intl Labour Office.
— Designing Transportation Fuels for a Cleaner Environment. LC 98-46897. 1999. 95.00 (*1-56032-813-4*) Hemisp Pub.
— Engines & Enterprises The Life & Work of Harry Ricardo. LC 99-492088. 1999. 36.00 (*0-7509-1712-1*) Bks Intl VA.
— Going South: An Antarctic Experience. 1987. pap. 5.95 (*0-310-55342-3*, 19036P) Zondervan.
— The Halo Effect: How Volunteering Can Lead to a More Fulfilling Life & a Better Career. unabridged ed. LC 98-7098. 224p. 1998. text 21.95 (*0-307-44071-0*, Whitman Coin) St Martin.
— Perfect Directions for All English Gold, Now Currant in This Kingdome. LC 77-7426. (English Experience Ser.: No. 886). 1977. reprint ed. lib. bdg. 20.00 (*90-221-0886-4*) Walter J Johnson.
— Self Liberation Through Seeing Everything in Its Nakedness. 1989. 29.95 (*0-88268-058-7*) Station Hill Pr.
— The Triumphs of God's Revenge Against the Crying & Execrable Sinne of Murther (1639), Bks. I-II, Vol. 1. Walmsley, Joan M., ed. LC 94-38864. 332p. 1995. text 99.95 (*0-7734-8992-4*) E Mellen.
Reynolds, John & DeLange, Jan. Original Critoen DS: The Restorer's Guide to All DS & ID Models 1955-75. (Illus.). 144p. 1996. 36.95 (*1-870979-71-0*, Bay View Bks) MBI Pubg.
Reynolds, John, jt. auth. see Stein, Benjamin.
Reynolds, John C. Theories of Programming Languages. LC 98-20462. 400p. (C). 1998. 49.95 (*0-521-59414-6*) Cambridge U Pr.
Reynolds, John C., jt. ed. see Wootton, Lutian R.
Reynolds, John D. Fexible Benefits Handbook. LC 92-82081. 111.00 (*0-7913-1515-0*) Warren Gorham & Lamont.
— Flexible Benefits Handbook. 1993. text 111.00 (*0-685-69670-7*, FLEX) Warren Gorham & Lamont.
Reynolds, John D. & Bischoff, Robin N. Health Insurance Answer Book. 3rd ed. Haffeman, JoAnne S., ed. 454p. 1990. 96.00 (*1-878375-18-0*) Panel Pubs.
Reynolds, John D., et al. Health Insurance Answer Book: 1992 Supplement. 200p. 1991. pap. text 49.00 (*1-878375-56-3*) Panel Pubs.
Reynolds, John E. Readings in Natural Resource Economics. 199p. (C). 1974. text 32.00 (*0-685-50581-2*) Irvington.
— Thames Ship Towage, 1933-1992. (C). 1989. text 75.00 (*1-85821-028-3*, Pub. by Pentland Pr) St Mut.
Reynolds, John E., III & Odell, Daniel K. Manatees & Dugongs. (Illus.). 192p. 1991. 24.95 (*0-8160-2436-7*) Facts on File.
Reynolds, John E., III & Rommel, Sentiel A., eds. Biology of Marine Mammals. LC 98-27808. (Illus.). 896p. 1999. 75.00 (*1-56098-375-2*) Smithsonian.
***Reynolds, John Earle.** In French Creek Valley. (Illus.). 430p. 1999. pap. 31.50 (*0-7884-1322-8*, R196) Heritage Bk.
***Reynolds, John Elliott, et al.** The Bottlenose Dolphin: Biology & Conservation. LC 00-29899. 2000. 34.95 (*0-8130-1775-0*) U Press Fla.
Reynolds, John F. Testing Democracy: Electoral Behavior & Progressive Reform in New Jersey, 1880-1920. LC 87-31947. (Illus.). 263p. 1988. pap. 81.60 (*0-608-05222-1*, 206575900001) Bks Demand.
Reynolds, John F., ed. Christian Fuerchtegott Gellert Briefwechsel: Kritische Gesamtausgabe, Vol. IV: 1764-1766. (GER.). ix, 308p. (C). 1996. lib. bdg. 130.40 (*3-11-014609-6*) De Gruyter.
— Gellert, Christian Furchtegott Briefwechsel: Kritische Gesamtausgabe, 5 vols., Bd. III. (GER.). xii, 560p. (C). 1991. lib. bdg. 172.35 (*3-11-009886-5*) De Gruyter.
— Rhetoric, Cultural Studies, & Literacy: Selected Papers from the 1994 Conference of the Rhetoric Society of America. 200p. 1995. 45.00 (*0-8058-1608-9*) L Erlbaum Assocs.
— Rhetoric, Cultural Studies, & Literacy: Selected Papers from the 1994 Conference of the Rhetoric Society of America. 200p. 1995. pap. 22.50 (*0-8058-1609-7*) L Erlbaum Assocs.
Reynolds, John F., et al. Writing & Reading Mental Health Records: Issues & Analysis. (Illus.). 144p. 1992. 34.00 (*0-8039-4097-1*); pap. 15.95 (*0-8039-4098-X*) Sage.
— Writing & Reading Mental Health Records: Issues & Analysis in Professional Writing & Scientific Rhetoric. 2nd ed. 120p. 1995. pap. 17.50 (*0-8058-2002-7*); text 29.95 (*0-8058-2001-9*) L Erlbaum Assocs.
Reynolds, John F., ed. see Gellart, Christian.
Reynolds, John H. The Letters of John Hamilton Reynolds. Jones, Leonidas M., ed. LC 72-90342. 122p. reprint ed. pap. 37.90 (*0-8357-3811-6*, 203653800003) Bks Demand.
— Selected Prose. Jones, Leonidas M., ed. LC 66-15653. (Illus.). 502p. 1966. 51.95 (*0-674-79935-6*) HUP.
Reynolds, John J. & Szmuk, Szilvia E. Spanish Golden Age Drama: An Annotated Bibliography of United States Doctoral Dissertations, 1899-1992. LC 98-10630. 600p. 1998. lib. bdg. 35.00 (*0-87352-570-1*, D360C) Modern Lang.
Reynolds, John J., jt. auth. see Dominicis, Maria C.
Reynolds, John L. Ballroom Dancing: The Romance, Rhythm & Style. LC 98-17096. (Illus.). 192p. 1998. 29.95 (*1-57145-621-X*, Laurel Glen Pub) Advantage Pubs.
Reynolds, John M. An Introduction to Applied & Environmental Geophysics. LC 96-14061. 806p. 1997. pap. 59.95 (*0-471-95555-8*) Wiley.
Reynolds, John M., tr. from TIB. The Golden Letters: The Three Statements of Garab Dorje, the First Teacher of Dzogchen, Together with a Commentary by Dza Patrw Rinpoche Entitled "The Special Teaching of the Wise & Glorious King" 392p. 1996. pap. 18.95 (*1-55939-050-6*) Snow Lion Pubns.
Reynolds, John M., tr. see Padmasambhava.
***Reynolds, John Myrdhin, tr.** Self-Liberation: Seeing with Naked Awareness. 172p. 2000. pap. 14.95 (*1-55939-144-8*) Snow Lion Pubns.
Reynolds, John T. From Scotland to America: The Descendants of William & Joanna Burns (1718-1987) LC 89-50772. 187p. 1989. pap. 25.00 (*0-9623150-1-X*); lib. bdg. 30.00 (*0-9623150-0-1*) W Burns Assn.
***Reynolds, John W.** The Corn Invaders: A Hunter's Tale. LC 99-93588. 1999. pap. 10.95 (*0-533-13072-7*) Vantage.
Reynolds, John W. The Earthworms, Lumbricidae & Sparganophilidae of Ontario. (Illus.). 152p. 22.86 (*0-88854-191-0*) Brill Academic Pubs.
***Reynolds, John W.** Lingering Memories: A Scrapbook of Southern Rural Life. (Illus.). 96p. 1999. pap. 9.95 (*1-886699-23-2*) Five Corners.
Reynolds, Jonathan. Rubbers & Yanks Three Detroit Zero Top of the Seventh: Two Plays. 1976. pap. 5.25 (*0-8222-0974-8*) Dramatists Play.
Reynolds, Jonathan & Smith, Heather. Kayaking Georgian Bay. 1999. pap. 13.95 (*1-55046-280-6*, Pub. by Boston Mills) Genl Dist Srvs.
***Reynolds, Jonathan M.** Maekawa Kunio & the Emergence of the Japanese Modernist Architecture. LC 00-37406. 2001. write for info. (*0-520-21495-1*) U CA Pr.
Reynolds, Jonathan T. The Time of Politics (Zamanin Siyasa) Islam & the Politics of Legitimacy in Northern Nigeria 1950-1966. 320p. 1998. 74.95 (*1-57309-272-X*) Intl Scholars.
Reynolds, Joseph P. Introduction to PRO/II: A Process Flowsheet Simulator: A Self-Instructional Problem Workbook. (Illus.). 288p. (Orig.). 1995. pap. text, wbk. ed. 60.00 (*1-882767-15-2*) ETS.
— Materials Science & Engineering: A Self-Instructional Problem Workbook. 224p. 1994. pap. text 60.00 (*1-882767-11-X*) ETS.
Reynolds, Joseph P. & Farag, Ihab H. Heat Transfer: A Self-Instructional Problem Workbook. (Illus.). 580p. (Orig.). (C). 1996. pap. text 60.00 (*1-882767-21-7*) ETS.
Reynolds, Joseph P., et al. Hazardous Waste Incineration Calculations: Problems & Software. LC 91-11047. 249p. 1991. 105.00 (*0-471-50782-2*) Wiley.
— Health, Safety & Accident Prevention: Industrial Applications: A Self-Instructional Problem Workbook. (Illus.). 314p. (Orig.). (C). 1996. pap. text, wbk. ed. 60.00 (*1-882767-18-7*) ETS.
Reynolds, Joseph P., jt. auth. see Theodore, Louis.
***Reynolds, Josh, photos by.** The Port of Gloucester: Photographs by Josh Reynolds. (New England Landmarks Ser.). (Illus.). 64p. 2000. 16.95 (*1-889833-17-7*, Commonwealth Eds) Memoirs Unltd.
Reynolds, Joshua. Discourses on Art. LC 97-80423. (Illus.). 388p. 1997. pap. text 17.00 (*0-300-07327-5*) Yale U Pr.
— Discourses on Art. Wark, Robert R., ed. (Illus.). 388p. 1997. 40.00 (*0-300-07345-3*) Yale U Pr.
— A Journey to Flanders & Holland. Mount, Harry, ed. LC 95-13807. (Art, Patrons & Public Ser.). (Illus.). 348p. (C). 1997. text 85.00 (*0-521-45129-9*) Cambridge U Pr.
Reynolds, Joshua & Malone, Edmond. The Works: To Which Is Prefixed an Account of the Life & Writings of the Author, 2 vols., Set. (Anglistica & Americana Ser.: No. 129). 1971. reprint ed. 180.70 (*0-685-66509-7*, 05103014) G Olms Pubs.
Reynolds, Joyce K., jt. auth. see Fitzpatrick, Robert L.
Reynolds, Joyce K., ed. see Stoll, Charles S. & White, Ronald C.
Reynolds, Judith. Historic Properties: Preservation & the Valuation Process. 115p. 1982. 17.00 (*0-911780-56-4*) Appraisal Inst.
— Historic Properties: Preservation & the Valuation Process. 2nd ed. LC 96-37188. 1996. 25.00 (*0-922154-34-1*) Appraisal Inst.
Reynolds, Judy, ed. Reference Services in the Humanities. LC 94-26131. (Reference Librarian Ser.: No. 47). 161p. 1994. lib. bdg. 49.95 (*1-56024-692-8*) Haworth Pr.
Reynolds, K. D. Aristocratic Women & Political Society in Victorian Britain. LC 97-47538. 272p. 1998. text 65.00 (*0-19-820727-1*) OUP.
Reynolds Kaelin, Celinda. Journey Song: A Spiritual Legacy of the American Indian. LC 98-92949. (Illus.). 250p. 1998. pap. 14.95 (*0-9645173-8-8*) Four Dir Pub.
Reynolds, Karen E. & Barba, Roberta R. Technology Teaching & Learning Science. 304p. 1996. pap. text 33.00 (*0-205-16287-8*) Allyn.
Reynolds, Katherine. Abstracts of Wills of Cumberland Country, Virginia Will Book 1 & 2, 1749-1782. 104p. 1984. 17.50 (*0-89308-430-1*) Southern Hist Pr.
Reynolds, Katherine & Wiebvsch, John. Park City. (Illus.). 72p. 1984. 23.00 (*0-916873-50-1*) Weller Inst.
Reynolds, Katherine C. Visions & Vanities: John Andrew Rice of Black Mountain College. LC 97-51834. (Southern Biography Ser.). (Illus.). 288p. 1998. text 35.00 (*0-8071-2203-3*) La State U Pr.
Reynolds, Kay. Groundbreakers: The Key 100 Growth Companies in the UK. LC 97-21293. 438p. 1997. pap. 89.95 (*0-471-96453-0*) Wiley.
Reynolds, Keith. Tennis. (Successful Sports Ser.). (J). 1996. write for info. (*1-57572-070-1*) Heinemann Lib.
— Tennis. LC 96-52604. (Successful Sports Ser.). (J). 1998. (*1-57572-200-3*) Heinemann Lib.
Reynolds, Kerry E. Healing a Broken Heart: How to "Grow on" When the Relationship Is Really Over. LC 97-94024. 104p. (Orig.). 1997. pap. 12.00 (*0-9652906-4-6*) Blazin Bks.
Reynolds, Kev. Walking in the Alps. LC 99-39739. 496p. 2000. pap. 22.95 (*1-56656-343-7*) Interlink Pub.
Reynolds, Kimberley. Children's Literature. (Writers & Their Work Ser.). 95p. 1996. pap. text 15.00 (*0-7463-0728-4*, Pub. by Northcote House) U Pr of Miss.
— Girls Only: Gender & Popular Children's Fiction in Britian 1880-1910. (Illus.). 160p. 1990. 27.95 (*0-87722-737-3*) Temple U Pr.
Reynolds, Kimberley & Humble, Nicola. Victorian Heroines: Representations of Feminity in Nineteenth-Century Literature & Art. LC 93-27468. (C). 1993. text 45.00 (*0-8147-7361-3*); pap. text 18.50 (*0-8147-7362-1*) NYU Pr.

R

Reynolds, Kimberley & Tucker, Nicholas. Children's Book Publishing in Britain since 1945. LC 97-19546. (Illus.). 250p. 1997. text 69.95 (*1-85928-236-9*, Pub. by Scolar Pr) Ashgate Pub Co.

*__Reynolds, Kirk & Oroszi, Dave.__ Baltimore & Ohio Railroad: Railroad Color History. LC 99-52185. (Railroad Color History Ser.). (Illus.). 128p. 2000. pap. 21.95 (*0-7603-0746-6*, Pub. by MBI Pubg) Motorbooks Intl.

Reynolds, Kristian S. Finger Lakes Panoramas. LC 99-20187. (Illus.). 128p. 1999. 39.95 (*0-935526-55-2*) McBooks Pr.

Reynolds, L. D., ed. see Cicero, Marcus Tullius.

Reynolds, L. D., ed. see Sallust.

Reynolds, Larry. The Trust Effect: Creating the High Trust, High Performance Organization. LC 97-33455. (People Skills for Professionals Ser.). (Illus.). 224p. 1997. pap. 17.95 (*1-85788-186-9*) Nicholas Brealey.

Reynolds, Larry, et al. Autorobics. (Illus.). 52p. (Orig.). 1989. pap. 6.95 (*0-685-26250-2*) Autorobics.

Reynolds, Larry, jt. ed. see Cox, Jeffrey.

Reynolds, Larry A. The Mudsock Scrapbook: A Pictorial Perspective of Fishers, Indiana the Early Years. LC 93-80648. 200p. 1993. 49.95 (*0-9639445-0-9*) Hoosier Cider.

Reynolds, Larry A. & La Belle, Tim. The Bear in the Basement: Includes the Story "The Foggy Frog of SoggySwamp" Anderson, Beth, ed. (Illus.). 48p. (J). 1998. pap. 10.00 (*0-9639445-1-7*) Hoosier Cider.

Reynolds, Larry J. European Revolutions & the American Literary Renaissance. LC 88-3784. 207p. (C). 1988. 32.50 (*0-300-04242-6*) Yale U Pr.

— Successful Site-Based Management: A Practical Guide. rev. ed. LC 96-51301. (Illus.). 200p. 1997. pap., wbk. ed. 32.95 (*0-8039-6560-5*, 80758) Corwin Pr.

— Successful Site-Based Management: A Practical Guide. rev. ed. LC 96-51301. (Illus.). 200p. 1997. wbk. ed. 69.95 (*0-8039-6559-1*, 80757) Corwin Pr.

Reynolds, Larry J., jt. auth. see Fuller, Margaret.

Reynolds, Larry T. Interactionism: Exposition & Critique. 3rd ed. LC 92-73398. 320p. 1993. pap. text 24.95 (*0-685-60899-9*); lib. bdg. 38.95 (*0-685-60898-0*) Gen Hall.

*__Reynolds, Larry T.__ Reflexive Sociology: Working Papers in Self-critical Analysis. 230p. (C). 1999. pap. 29.95 (*1-929416-28-8*) Magner Pubg.

— Self-Analytical Sociology: Essays & Explorations in the Reflexive Mode. 728p. 2000. 49.95 (*1-929416-27-X*) Magner Pubg.

— Self-Analytical Sociology: Essays & Explorations in the Reflexive Mode. 728p. (C). 2000. pap. 39.95 (*1-929416-26-1*) Magner Pubg.

Reynolds, Larry T. & Lieberman, Leonard, eds. Race & Other Misadventures: Essays in Honor of Ashley Montagu in His Ninetieth Year. LC 95-82132. (Illus.). 432p. 1996. text 65.95 (*1-882289-35-8*) Gen Hall.

Reynolds, Larry T., jt. ed. see Herman, Nancy J.

Reynolds, Larry T., ed. see Leggett, John C. & Malm, Suzanne.

Reynolds, Laura, ed. see Weindorf, Grace O.

Reynolds, Leah J. My Soliloquy. (Illus.). 43p. (Orig.). 1992. pap. 5.95 (*1-56411-022-2*) Untd Bros & Sis.

Reynolds, Leamon T. Love Em . . . And Leave Em. 184p. (Orig.). (C). 1989. pap. 6.95 (*1-877917-06-0*) Alpha Bible Pubns.

Reynolds, Leighton D., ed. Text & Transmission: Survey of Latin Classics. (Illus.). 556p. 1984. text 125.00 (*0-19-814456-3*) OUP.

Reynolds, Leighton D. & Wilson, N. G. Scribes & Scholars: A Guide to the Transmission of Greek & Latin Literature. 3rd ed. (Illus.). 330p. 1991. pap. text 39.95 (*0-19-872146-3*) OUP.

Reynolds, Leighton D., ed. see Seneca, Lucius Annaeus.

*__Reynolds, Leonard C.__ Dog Boats at War: Royal Navy D Class MTBs & MGBs, 1939-1945. (Illus.). 288p. 2000. pap. 21.95 (*0-7509-2454-3*) Sutton Publng.

Reynolds, Leonard C. Dog Boats at War: Royal Navy MGBs & MTBs in Action, 1939-45. LC 99-188193. (Illus.). 288p. 2000. 45.00 (*0-7509-1817-9*, Pub. by Sutton Publng) Intl Pubs Mktg.

Reynolds, Lesley, jt. auth. see Leatherbarrow, Liesbeth.

Reynolds, Lily, jt. auth. see Jones, Mary G.

Reynolds, Linda & Barrett, Stephen. Signs & Guiding for Libraries. LC 80-140234. 158p. 1981. reprint ed. pap. 49.00 (*0-608-02471-6*, 206311500004) Bks Demand.

Reynolds, Linda & Simmonds, Doig. Presentation of Data in Science. 223p. 1981. lib. bdg. 104.50 (*90-247-2398-1*) Kluwer Academic.

— Presentation of Data in Science. 223p. 1982. pap. text 73.00 (*90-247-3054-6*) Kluwer Academic.

Reynolds, Linda, jt. auth. see Simmonds, Doig.

Reynolds, Lisette, jt. auth. see Hallman, Tim.

Reynolds, Lloyd. Italic Calligraphy & Handwriting: Exercises & Text. (Illus.). pap. 5.95 (*0-8008-4284-7*) Taplinger.

— My Dear Runemeister: A Voyage Through the Alphabet. LC 89-16400. (Illus.). 80p. (Orig.). 1990. reprint ed. pap. 9.95 (*0-87595-219-4*) Oregon Hist.

Reynolds, Lloyd G. Image & Reality in Economic Development. LC 77-76312. 497p. 1977. 60.00 (*0-300-02088-0*) Yale U Pr.

— Macroeconomics: Analysis & Policy. 3rd ed. (C). 1979. 14.95 (*0-256-02173-2*, Irwn McGrw-H) McGrw-H Hghr Educ.

— The Three Worlds of Economics. LC 71-151588. (Studies in Comparative Economics: No. 12). 358p. reprint ed. pap. 111.00 (*0-8357-8352-9*, 203387000087) Bks Demand.

Reynolds, Lloyd G., ed. Agriculture in Development Theory. LC 74-20085. (Economic Growth Center, Yale University Publication Ser.). 522p. reprint ed. pap. 161.90 (*0-8357-8013-9*, 203386700087) Bks Demand.

Reynolds, Lloyd G. & Michas, Nicholas. Principles of Economics, Macro: Personal Learning Aid. 4th ed. (Plaid Ser.). 1983. pap. 13.00 (*0-87094-430-4*, Irwn Prfssnl) McGraw-Hill Prof.

Reynolds, Lloyd G. & Shister, Joseph. Job Horizons: Study of Job Satisfaction & Labor Mobility. Stein, Leon, ed. LC 77-70526. (Work Ser.). (Illus.). 1977. reprint ed. lib. bdg. 19.95 (*0-405-10194-5*) Ayer.

Reynolds, Lloyd G. & Torruellas, Luz M. Wages, Productivity, & Industrialization in Puerto Rico. LC 65-12407. (Yale University, Economic Growth Center, Publications). 373p. reprint ed. pap. 115.70 (*0-608-14256-5*, 202203400024) Bks Demand.

Reynolds, Lloyd G., et al. Labor Economics & Labor Relations. 11th ed. LC 97-10346. 581p. 1997. 96.00 (*0-13-263310-8*) P-H.

Reynolds, Lloyd J. Straight Impressions. LC 78-60187. (Illus.). 1979. 12.50 (*0-931474-06-X*) TBW Bks.

— Straight Impressions. LC 78-60187. (Illus.). 1984. pap. 5.95 (*0-931474-07-8*) TBW Bks.

Reynolds, Lois A., ed. see Pharmacists in Ophthalmic Practice, Inc. Staff.

Reynolds, Lorna. Kate O'Brien: A Literary Portrait. LC 85-30612. 150p. 1986. 41.00 (*0-389-20613-X*, N8168) B&N Imports.

Reynolds, Loys, jt. auth. see Rafferty, Bob.

Reynolds, Lura Schield, jt. auth. see Naylor, Phyllis Reynolds.

*__Reynolds, M.__ Wrong Kind of Shirts. 1998. pap. 8.95 (*1-85702-873-2*, Pub. by Fourth Estate) Trafalgar.

Reynolds, M. C., ed. Knowledge Base for the Beginning Teacher. 317p. 1989. text 129.25 (*0-08-036767-4*, Pergamon Pr) Elsevier.

Reynolds, M. H. The History & Descendants of John & Sarah Reynolds (1630?- 1923), of Watertown, Mass., & Wethersfield, Stamford, & Greenwich, Connecticut. (Illus.). 509p. 1993. reprint ed. pap. 79.50 (*0-8328-3054-2*); reprint ed. lib. bdg. 89.50 (*0-8328-3053-4*) Higginson Bk Co.

— Reynolds: History & One Line of Descendants of Robert & Mary Reynolds (1630? - 1928) of Boston, with the Hyatt Family of Princeton, New Jersey. (Illus.). 92p. 1993. reprint ed. pap. 18.00 (*0-8328-3391-6*); reprint ed. lib. bdg. 28.00 (*0-8328-3390-8*) Higginson Bk Co.

Reynolds, M. H., compiled by. Reynolds: History & Some of the Descendants of Robert & Mary Reynolds (1630? - 1931) of Boston, Massachusetts. (Illus.). 236p. 1993. reprint ed. pap. 37.50 (*0-8328-3393-2*); reprint ed. lib. bdg. 47.50 (*0-8328-3392-4*) Higginson Bk Co.

Reynolds, Mack. Compounded Interests. LC 82-62697. (Boskone Bks.). (Illus.). xii, 161p. 1983. 13.00 (*0-915368-20-X*) New Eng SF Assoc.

— Star Trek: Mission to Horatius. (Star Trek Ser.). (Illus.). 208p. 1999. 16.00 (*0-671-02812-X*, PB Hardcover) PB.

Reynolds, Majorie, ed. see Bolduc, Henry L.

Reynolds, Malvina. Magic Penny Big Book: Black & White Nellie Edge I Can Read & Sing Big Book. (Illus.). (J). (ps-2). 1988. pap. text 21.00 (*0-922053-19-7*) N Edge Res.

— Malvina Reynolds Songbook. 4th enl. ed. LC 74-20175. (Illus.). 112p. 1984. pap. 7.00 (*0-915620-07-3*) Schroder Music.

— Morningtown Ride. (Illus.). 32p. (J). (ps-12). 1996. 14.95 (*0-89594-763-3*) Crossing Pr.

— Morningtown Ride. (Illus.). 20p. (J). (ps-4). 1984. pap. 4.95 (*0-931793-00-9*) Turn-the-Page.

— Not in Ourselves, nor in Our Stars Either. 40p. 1975. pap. 1.00 (*0-915620-03-0*) Schroder Music.

— Tweedles & Foodles for Young Noodles. LC 73-80670. (Illus.). 42p. (J). (gr. k-4). 1961. pap. 5.75 (*0-915620-08-1*) Schroder Music.

Reynolds, Mani B., jt. ed. see Reynolds, Frank E.

Reynolds, Marcia. Being in the Zone. (Smart Tapes Ser.). 28p. 1997. pap. 19.95 incl. audio (*1-55678-064-8*, 3280) Learn Inc.

*__Reynolds, Marcia.__ Capture the Rapture: How to Step Out of Your Head & Leap into Life. 240p. 2000. pap. write for info. (*0-9655250-0-7*) Covision.

Reynolds, Marcia. Golf in the Zone. (Smart Tapes Ser.). 28p. (YA). (gr. 10 up). 1997. pap. text 19.95 incl. audio (*1-55678-065-6*, 3285) Learn Inc.

Reynolds, Margaret, ed. The Penguin Book of Lesbian Short Stories. LC 93-34061. 1999. text. write for info. (*0-670-84321-0*, Viking) Viking Penguin.

— The Penguin Book of Lesbian Short Stories. 464p. 1994. reprint ed. pap. 15.95 (*0-14-024018-7*, Penguin Bks) Viking Penguin.

Reynolds, Margaret, ed. see Browning, Elizabeth Barrett.

Reynolds, Margaret, jt. ed. see Leighton, Angela.

Reynolds, Marianne C. Reading Connections. LC 94-31933. 222p. (C). 1994. 28.25 (*0-534-24456-4*) Wadsworth Pub.

— Reading for Understanding. 451p. (C). 1992. pap. 25.95 (*0-534-17064-1*) Wadsworth Pub.

— Reading for Understanding. 2nd ed. LC 94-31932. 466p. (C). 1994. 32.50 (*0-534-23274-4*) Wadsworth Pub.

*__Reynolds, Marie.__ Browns Mills: New Jersey. LC 00-102561. (Images of America Ser.). (Illus.). 128p. 2000. pap. 18.99 (*0-7385-0451-3*) Arcadia Publng.

Reynolds, Marilyn. Baby Help. LC 97-40246. (True-to-Life Series from Hamilton High: Vol. 6). 192p. (Orig.). (YA). (gr. 7 up). 1997. 15.95 (*1-885356-26-9*); pap. 8.95 (*1-885356-27-7*) Morning Glory.

— Baby Help Teacher's Guide. 1998. pap., teacher ed. 2.50 (*1-885356-28-5*) Morning Glory.

— Beyond Dreams. LC 95-17802. (True-to-Life Series from Hamilton High). (Illus.). 192p. (Orig.). (YA). (gr. 7-12). 1996. pap. 8.95 (*1-885356-00-5*) Morning Glory.

— Beyond Dreams. LC 95-12802. (True-to-Life Series from Hamilton High). 192p. (Orig.). (YA). (gr. 7-13). 1996. 15.95 (*1-885356-01-3*) Morning Glory.

Reynolds, Marilyn. Beyond Dreams: True to Life Series from Hamilton High. 1995. 14.05 (*0-606-10995-1*, Pub. by Turtleback) Demco.

Reynolds, Marilyn. But What about Me? LC 96-23108. 192p. (YA). (gr. 7 up). 1996. pap. 8.95 (*1-885356-10-2*, 56102) Morning Glory.

— Detour for Emmy. 256p. 1993. pap. 8.95 (*0-930934-76-8*) Morning Glory.

— Detour for Emmy. 1993. 14.05 (*0-606-07159-8*, Pub. by Turtleback) Demco.

— If You Loved Me. LC 99-29522. 223p. (gr. 7-10). 1999. 15.95 (*1-885356-54-4*, Pub. by Morning Glory) IPG Chicago.

— If You Loved Me. 223p. (J). (gr. 7-10). 1999. pap. 8.95 (*1-885356-55-2*, Pub. by Morning Glory) IPG Chicago.

*__Reynolds, Marilyn.__ If You Loved Me Teacher's Guide. 1999. pap., teacher ed. 2.50 (*1-885356-59-5*) Morning Glory.

Reynolds, Marilyn. Telling. 186p. 1989. pap. 6.95 (*0-929848-01-2*) Peace Ventures Pr.

— Telling. rev. ed. LC 95-39149. 160p. (YA). (gr. 7-12). 1996. reprint ed. pap. 8.95 (*1-885356-03-X*) Morning Glory.

— Too Soon for Jeff. 224p. (Orig.). (YA). (gr. 7 up). 1994. 15.95 (*0-930934-90-3*); pap. 8.95 (*0-930934-91-1*) Morning Glory.

Reynolds, Marilyn & Doty, David. True-to-Life Series from Hamilton High Teaching Guide. Lindsay, Jeanne W., ed. 1996. pap., teacher ed. 21.95 (*1-885356-07-2*) Morning Glory.

Reynolds, Marilyn M. Regional Transit Guide: San Francisco Bay Area. Kahn, Brenda, ed. (Illus.). 128p. (Orig.). 1989. pap. 3.95 (*0-9624272-0-9*) Metro Trans Comm.

— Regional Transit Guide, 1991: San Francisco Bay Area. Kahn, Brenda, ed. (Illus.). 128p. 1990. pap. 3.95 (*0-9624272-1-7*) Metro Trans Comm.

Reynolds, Marilynn. Belle's Journey. (Illus.). 32p. (J). (gr. 1-4). 1994. pap. 6.95 (*1-55143-021-5*) Orca Bk Pubs.

— A Dog for a Friend. (Illus.). 32p. (J). (ps-3). 1994. reprint ed. pap. 6.95 (*1-55143-020-7*) Orca Bk Pubs.

— The New Land: A First Year on the Prairie. LC 96-72452. (Illus.). 32p. (J). (ps-3). 1997. pap. 6.95 (*1-55143-071-1*) Orca Bk Pubs.

*__Reynolds, Marilynn.__ The Prairie Fire. LC 98-89928. (Illus.). 32p. (J). (ps-3). 1999. 14.95 (*1-55143-137-8*) Orca Bk Pubs.

*__Reynolds, Marjorie.__ The Civil Wars of Jonah Moran: A Novel. LC 99-34222. 336p. 1999. 24.00 (*0-688-15975-3*, Wm Morrow) Morrow Avon.

Reynolds, Marjorie. Horse Called Mystery. LC 64-11830. (I Can Read Bks.). (Illus.). (J). (ps-3). 1972. pap. 2.95 (*0-06-440018-2*, HarpTrophy) HarpC Child Bks.

— The Starlite Drive-In. 304p. 1998. pap. 6.99 (*0-425-16572-8*) Berkley Pub.

*__Reynolds, Marjorie.__ Starlite Drive-in. 1999. pap. 13.95 (*0-425-17264-3*) Berkley Pub.

Reynolds, Marjorie. The Starlite Drive-In: A Novel. LC 97-728. 224p. 1997. 23.00 (*0-688-15389-5*, Wm Morrow) Morrow Avon.

Reynolds, Marjorie, ed. Your Creative Voice: Reaching & Teaching from Your Experience. (Illus.). 212p. 1996. pap., per. 14.95 (*0-9601302-0-9*) Adventures Time.

Reynolds, Mark. Haynes BSA A50 & A65 Twins Owners Workshop Manual, No. 155: '62-'73. (Illus.). 1979. 23.95 (*0-85696-155-8*) Haynes Manuals.

Reynolds, Mark, compiled by. The Wrong Kind of Shirts: Outrageous Football Excuses, Whinges & Verbal Own Goals. (Illus.). 112p. 1997. pap. 8.95 (*1-85702-602-0*, Pub. by Fourth Estate) Trafalgar.

— The Wrong Kind of Shirts Vol. 2: More Curious Quips & Accusations from the Soccer World. 2nd ed. 128p. 1997. pap. 8.95 (*1-85702-760-4*) Trafalgar.

Reynolds, Mark & Rota, Gian-Carlo, eds. Science, Computers, & People: From the Tree of Mathematics, Stanislaw Ulam. (Illus.). 1986. 48.00 (*0-8176-3276-X*) Birkhauser.

Reynolds, Mark, jt. auth. see Gabbay, Dov M.

Reynolds, Mark C. Object-Oriented Programming in Java. (Illus.). 336p. 1997. pap., pap. text 39.95 incl. cd-rom (*0-07-913250-2*) McGraw.

Reynolds, Mark C. & Wooldridge, Andrew. Special Edition Using JavaScript. 2nd ed. LC 97-65024. 856p. 1997. 49.99 (*0-7897-1138-9*) Que.

Reynolds, Martha, jt. auth. see Reynolds, Rick.

*__Reynolds, Mary D., ed.__ Educating, Respecting, Protecting: 1998 IWRC Conference Proceedings. 185p. 1999. pap. 20.00 (*1-884196-10-1*) IWRC.

Reynolds, Mary D., ed. From Science to Reality - A Bridge to the 21st Century: 1997 IWRC Conference Proceedings. 240p. 1998. pap. 20.00 (*1-884196-09-8*) IWRC.

— Uncommon Care for Common Animals: 1995 IWRC Conference Proceedings. (Illus.). 223p. (Orig.). 1996. pap. 18.00 (*1-884196-05-5*) IWRC.

Reynolds, Mary D., ed. Wild Today, Wild Tomorrow: 1996 IWRC Conference Proceedings. (Illus.). 190p. 1997. pap. 20.00 (*1-884196-06-3*) IWRC.

Reynolds, Mary T. Interdepartmental Committees in the National Administration, 1932-1936. LC 68-58618. (Columbia University. Studies in the Social Sciences: No. 450). reprint ed. 20.00 (*0-404-51450-2*) AMS Pr.

— Joyce & Dante: The Shaping Imagination. LC 80-7550. 396p. 1981. reprint ed. pap. 122.80 (*0-608-02913-0*, 206397700008) Bks Demand.

Reynolds, Mary T., ed. James Joyce: A Collection of Critical Essays. LC 92-16520. (New Century Views Ser.). 238p. 1992. pap. text 9.80 (*0-13-512211-2*) P-H.

Reynolds, Marylee. From Gangs to Gangsters: How American Sociology Organized Crime 1918-1994. LC 95-34255. 178p. (C). 1995. 48.50 (*0-911577-30-0*, HM22, Criminal Justice) Willow Tree NY.

*__Reynolds, Matthew.__ Beginning E-Commerce: With VB, ASP, ADO & MTS. 1000p. 2000. pap. 39.99 (*1-86100-398-6*) Wrox Pr Inc.

Reynolds, Matthew T. Test & Evaluation of Complex Systems. LC 96-28134. 186p. 1997. 110.00 (*0-471-96719-X*) Wiley.

Reynolds, Maynard C. Categories & Variables in Special Education. (Augustana College Library Occasional Papers, Wallin Lecture: No. 9). 16p. 1968. pap. 1.00 (*0-910182-39-6*) Augustana Coll.

Reynolds, Maynard C., jt. ed. see Wang, Margaret C.

Reynolds, Merrill J., jt. auth. see Dott, Robert Henry.

Reynolds Metzger, Anne. The Phoenix. 1998. pap. write for info. (*1-57553-909-8*) Watermrk Pr.

Reynolds, Michael. A Coming of Wizards. (Illus.). 234p. (Orig.). 1989. pap. 12.95 (*0-9614010-3-6*) High Mesa Pr.

*__Reynolds, Michael.__ Construction Litigation Practice. 280p. 1999. (*1-85811-214-1*, Pub. by CLT Prof) Gaunt.

Reynolds, Michael. Dead Ends. (Illus.). 304p. (Orig.). 1992. mass mkt. 4.99 (*0-446-36282-4*, Pub. by Warner Bks) Little.

— The Devil's Adjutant: Jochen Peiper, Panzer Leader. (Illus.). 320p. 1995. 27.50 (*1-885119-15-1*) Sarpedon.

Reynolds, Michael. The Devil's Adjutant: Jochen Peiper, Panzer Leader. 336p. 1997. 80.00 (*1-873376-41-3*, Pub. by Spellmnt Pubs) St Mut.

Reynolds, Michael. Earthship, Vol. III: Evolution Beyond Economics. 250p. 1993. 24.95 (*0-9626767-2-1*) Solar Survival.

*__Reynolds, Michael.__ Ernest Hemingway. (Literary Masters Ser.: Vol. 2). (Illus.). 61p. 2000. 49.95 (*0-7876-3961-3*) Gale.

Reynolds, Michael. Group Work in Education & Training. Bell, Chris, ed. 144p. 1994. pap. 24.95 (*0-7494-1027-2*, Kogan Pg Educ) Stylus Pub VA.

*__Reynolds, Michael.__ Hemingway: The Final Years. 416p. 2000. pap. 15.95 (*0-393-32047-2*) Norton.

— Men of Steel: SS Panzer Corps in the Ardennes & on the Eastern Front, 1944-45. (Illus.). 336p. 1999. write for info. (*1-885119-66-6*) Sarpedon.

Reynolds, Michael. Steel Inferno: The 1st S. S. Panzer Corps in Normandy. (Illus.). 320p. 1997. 27.50 (*1-885119-44-5*) Sarpedon.

Reynolds, Michael. Steel Inferno: 1st SS Panzer Corps in Normandy. 432p. 1998. mass mkt. 6.50 (*0-440-22596-5*) Doubleday.

Reynolds, Michael. Steel Inferno: 1st SS Panzer Corps in Normandy. 336p. 1997. 80.00 (*1-873376-90-1*, Pub. by Spellmnt Pubs) St Mut.

*__Reynolds, Michael, ed.__ Men of Steel: 1st Panzer Corps 1944-45: The Ardennes & Eastern Front. 336p. 1999. 80.00 (*1-86227-051-1*, Pub. by Spellmnt Pubs) St Mut.

Reynolds, Michael, jt. ed. see Burgoyne, John.

Reynolds, Michael D. & Sweetsir, Richard A. Observe Eclipses. pap. write for info. (*1-886336-10-5*) Chabot Observ.

Reynolds, Michael D., jt. auth. see Huebner, Jay S.

Reynolds, Michael E. Earthship: How to Build Your Own, Vol. 1. (Illus.). 240p. 1990. 24.95 (*0-9626767-0-5*) Solar Survival.

— Earthship: Systems & Components, Vol. II. (Illus.). 230p. 1991. 24.95 (*0-9626767-1-3*) Solar Survival.

Reynolds, Michael M., ed. Reader in the Academic Library. LC 71-112300. 378p. 1983. lib. bdg. 69.50 (*0-313-24034-5*, ZRB/, Greenwood Pr) Greenwood.

Reynolds, Michael P. Arbitration. 188p. 1993. 60.00 (*1-85044-550-8*) LLP.

Reynolds, Michael P. & King, Philip S. The Expert Witness & His Evidence. 2nd ed. LC 92-11007. (Illus.). 288p. 1992. 69.95 (*0-632-03389-4*) Blackwell Sci.

Reynolds, Michael S. Hemingway: An Annotated Chronology. (Omni Chronology Ser.). 155p. 1991. lib. bdg. 54.00 (*1-55888-427-0*) Omnigraphics Inc.

— Hemingway: The Final Years. LC 99-17141. (Illus.). 352p. 1999. text 30.00 (*0-393-04748-2*) Norton.

— Hemingway: The Paris Years. 402p. 1999. pap. 15.95 (*0-393-31879-6*) Norton.

— Hemingway: The 1930s. LC 96-43113. (Illus.). 384p. 1997. 30.00 (*0-393-04093-3*) Norton.

— Hemingway: The 1930s. (Illus.). 288p. 1998. pap. 14.95 (*0-393-31778-1*) Norton.

— The Sun Also Rises: A Novel of the Twenties. (Masterwork Studies: No. 16). 118p. 1988. 29.00 (*0-8057-7962-0*); pap. 18.00 (*0-8057-8015-7*) Macmillan.

— The Young Hemingway. (Illus.). 304p. 1998. pap. 13.95 (*0-393-31776-5*) Norton.

Reynolds, Michael S., jt. auth. see Voss, Frederick S.

Reynolds, Michelle. Carousel. 1997. mass mkt. 3.99 (*1-85487-934-0*) London Brdge.

Reynolds, Mike, ed. Camouflage & Markings: Luftwaffe 1939-1945. (Illus.). 48p. (Orig.). 1992. pap. 13.95 (*1-85486-066-6*) Nexus Special Interests.

— Camouflage & Markings: Royal Air Force 1939-1945. (Illus.). 48p. (Orig.). 1992. pap. 13.95 (*1-85486-065-8*) Nexus Special Interests.

Reynolds, Mike, et al. Three Strikes & You're Out! . . . A Promise to Kimber: The Chronicle of America's Toughest Anti-Crime Law. (Illus.). 272p. 1996. 24.95 (*1-884956-12-2*) Quill Driver.

*__Reynolds, Milena.__ Italian in Three Months. LC 97-47223. (ITA.). 1998. pap. 29.95 incl. audio (*0-7894-3232-3*) DK Pub Inc.

Reynolds, Moira D. Coping with An Immigrant Parent. Rosen, Ruth C., ed. (Coping Ser.). (YA). (gr. 7-12). 1992. lib. bdg. 17.95 (*0-8239-1462-3*) Rosen Group.

An Asterisk (*) at the beginning of an entry indicates that the title is appearing for the first time.

Reynolds, Moira D. & Strazzabosco, Gina. The Telephone: Uses & Abuses. LC 93-25717. (Lifeskills Library). (Illus.). 48p. (YA). (gr. 7-12). 1994. lib. bdg. 14.95 (0-8239-1608-1) Rosen Group.

***Reynolds, Moira Davison.** American Women Scientists: 23 Inspiring Biographies, 1900-2000. LC 99-14603. (Illus.). 159p. 1999. 33.50 (0-7864-0649-6) McFarland & Co.

Reynolds, Monica. Multiply Your Success with Real Estate Assistants: How to Hire, Train & Manage Your Assistant: Featuring 93 Ready-to-Use Forms. LC 93-32671. 247p. (Orig.). 1994. pap. 24.95 (0-7931-0776-8, 56088801, Real Estate Ed) Dearborn.

Reynolds, Monica & Rosen, Linda. The Professional Assistant: A Guide to Success for Real Estate Assistants. LC 95-50124. 1996. pap. 34.95 (0-7931-1774-7, 1550-0101, Real Estate Ed) Dearborn.

Reynolds, Morgan O. Crime & Punishment in America. 27p. 1995. pap. 10.00 (1-56808-058-1, 193) Natl Ctr Pol.

— Crime & Punishment in Texas: Update. 34p. 1996. pap. 10.00 (1-56808-068-9, 202) Natl Ctr Pol.

— Crime & Punishment in Texas a 1993 Update. rev. ed. (Illus.). 28p. 1993. pap. 10.00 (0-943802-79-2, 175) Natl Ctr Pol.

— Crime in Texas. 1991. pap. 10.00 (0-943802-61-X, 158) Natl Ctr Pol.

— Crime Pays, but So Does Imprisonment. 1990. pap. 10.00 (0-943802-52-0, 149) Natl Ctr Pol.

— Factories Behind Bars. 1996. write for info. (1-56808-074-3, 206) Natl Ctr Pol.

— The History & Economics of Labor Unions. Pejovich, Steve & Dethloff, Henry, eds. (Series on Public Issues: No. 16). 18p. 1985. pap. 2.00 (0-86599-052-2) PERC.

— How Much Government Does Texas Need? An Analysis of the Texas State Budget. 1989. pap. 10.00 (0-943802-41-5, 138) Natl Ctr Pol.

— Using the Private Sector to Deter Crime. 42p. (Orig.). 1994. pap. text 10.00 (1-56808-015-8, 181) Natl Ctr Pol.

— Why Does Crime Pay? 1991. pap. 5.00 (0-943802-89-X, BG110) Natl Ctr Pol.

— Why Does Crime Pay? rev. ed. (Illus.). 15p. 1992. pap. 5.00 (1-56808-006-9, BG 123) Natl Ctr Pol.

Reynolds, Morgan O. & Caruth, W. W., III. Myths about Gun Control. 1992. pap. 10.00 (0-943802-99-7, 176) Natl Ctr Pol.

Reynolds, Moria D. Immigrant American Women Role Models: Fifteen Inspiring Biographies, 1850-1950. LC 97-34100. 176p. 1997. lib. bdg. 32.50 (0-7864-0409-4) McFarland & Co.

Reynolds, Myra. The Learned Lady in England, 1650-1760. 1976. lib. bdg. 59.95 (0-8490-2136-7) Gordon Pr.

— The Learned Lady in England, 1650-1760. 1990. 16.50 (0-8446-1382-7) Peter Smith.

— The Treatment of Nature in English Poetry Between Pope & Wordsworth. LC 66-29468. 388p. 1966. reprint ed. 50.00 (0-87752-091-7) Gordian.

Reynolds, Myra, ed. & intro. see Finch, Anne K.

Reynolds, N. Dance History. 1999. pap. write for info. (0-14-009485-7, Viking) Viking Penguin.

Reynolds, N. J., jt. auth. see Dalton, H. R.

Reynolds, Nancy H. Older Volunteer Leaders in the Rural Community. LC 91-32211. (Studies on the Elderly in America). 152p. 1992. text 25.00 (0-8153-0528-1) Garland.

Reynolds, Nancy T. Adopting Your Child: Options, Answers, & Actions. (Reference Ser.). 288p. 1993. pap. 12.95 (0-88908-295-2) Self-Counsel Pr.

Reynolds, Neil B. & Manning, Ellis L., eds. Excursions in Science. LC 72-1237. (Essay Index Reprint Ser.). 1977. reprint ed. 22.95 (0-8369-2857-1) Ayer.

Reynolds, Noel B. Book of Mormon Authorship Revisited: The Evidence for Ancient Origins. LC 97-19147. 1997. write for info. (0-934893-25-X, F A R M S) Brigham.

Reynolds, Noel B. & Saxonhouse, Arlene W., eds. Thomas Hobbes: Three Discourses: A Critical Modern Edition of Newly Identified Work of the Young Hobbes. LC 95-12724. 192p. 1995. 27.50 (0-226-34545-9) U Ch Pr.

Reynolds, Nood. Minnesota, Land of Lakes & Innovation: Entering the 21st Century. LC 98-71769. (Illus.). 416p. 1998. 49.95 (1-882933-21-4) Cherbo Pub Grp.

Reynolds, Oliver. Almost. LC 99-488486. 64p. 1999. pap. 11.00 (0-571-19747-7) Faber & Faber.

Reynolds, Ora E. The Social & Economic Status of College Students. LC 71-177189. (Columbia University. Teachers College. Contributions to Education Ser.: No. 272). reprint ed. 37.50 (0-404-55272-2) AMS Pr.

Reynolds, Osborne M. Hornbook on Local Government Law. LC 82-8573. (Hornbook Ser.). 860p. (C). reprint ed. 37.50 (0-314-65452-6) West Pub.

Reynolds, Osborne M., Jr. Local Government Law, 1996: Pocket Part. (Handbook Edition). 190p. 1996. write for info. (0-314-09763-5) West Pub.

— Local Government Law, 1993: Pocket Part. (Hornbook Ser.). 200p. 1993. pap. text 12.50 (0-314-02256-2) West Pub.

Reynolds, Osborne M., Jr., jt. auth. see Kutner, Peter B.

Reynolds, P. A. Introduction To International Relations. 3rd ed. LC 93-2567. (C). 1995. pap. 38.00 (0-582-21318-5, 76670) Addison-Wesley.

***Reynolds, P. H.** Inducible Gene Expression in Plants. LC 98-25843. 256p. 1999. text 85.00 (0-85199-259-5) OUP.

Reynolds, P. K. The Banana: Its History & Cultivation. 1977. lib. bdg. 250.00 (0-8490-1474-3) Gordon Pr.

— The Vigiles of Imperial Rome. LC 96-163443. 133 p. 1996. pap. 15.00 (0-89005-552-1) Ares.

Reynolds, P. O., jt. ed. see Schandelmeier, H.

Reynolds, P. Preston. Watts Hospital of Durham, North Carolina, 1895-1976: Keeping the Doors Open. LC 91-77158. (Illus.). 133p. 1992. pap. 15.95 (0-9631387-0-7) Fund Adv Sci.

Reynolds, Pamela. Childhood in Crossroads: Cognition & Society in South Africa. LC HQ0792.S6R49. (Illus.). 276p. (Orig.). reprint ed. pap. 85.60 (0-7837-5560-0, 204533500005) Bks Demand.

— Dance, Civet Cat: Tonga Children & Labour in the Zambezi Valley. LC 89-22860. 208p. 1990. text 24.95 (0-8214-0946-8) Ohio U Pr.

— Dance, Civet Cat: Tonga Children & Labour in the Zambezi Valley. LC 89-22860. xxxi, 176 p. 1991. per. write for info. (0-86232-933-7) St Martin.

***Reynolds, Pamela.** Silly Soup. Wise, Noreen, ed. (Book-a-Day Collection). (Illus.). 32p. (YA). (ps up). 2000. pap. 5.95 (1-58584-434-9) Huckleberry CT.

Reynolds, Pamela. Traditional Healers & Childhood in Zimbabwe. LC 94-47391. (Illus.). 208p. (C). 1995. text 39.95 (0-8214-1121-7); pap. text 17.95 (0-8214-1122-5) Ohio U Pr.

Reynolds, Pat. Tom's Friend. LC 93-170. (J). 1994. write for info. (0-383-03797-2) SRA McGraw.

***Reynolds, Patrice.** Family 101. Bridges, Catina, ed. 200p. (Orig.). 1999. pap. 8.95 (0-9676114-9-0) Affirmative Pubg.

Reynolds, Patricia A. I Can Add. (Step Ahead Workbooks Ser.). (Illus.). 32p. (J). (ps-3). 1986. 2.09 (0-307-03590-5, 03590, Goldn Books) Gldn Bks Pub Co.

Reynolds, Patrick & Shachtman, Tom. The Gilded Leaf: Triumph, Tragedy & Tobacco: Three Generations of the R. J. Reynolds Family & Fortune. (Illus.). 384p. 1989. 19.95 (0-316-74121-3) Little.

Reynolds, Patrick M. Big Apple Almanac. Vol. 1. (Illus.). 112p. (Orig.). 1989. pap. 14.95 (0-932514-19-7) Red Rose Studio.

— Big Apple Almanac, No. 2. Vol. 2. (Illus.). 112p. (Orig.). 1991. pap. 14.95 (0-932514-24-3) Red Rose Studio.

— Big Apple Almanac, No. 3. Vol. 3. (Illus.). 112p. (Orig.). 1994. pap. 14.95 (0-932514-29-4) Red Rose Studio.

— The Book of Silly Lists. LC 92-38660. (J). 1993. pap. 1.25 (0-89375-354-8) Troll Communs.

***Reynolds, Patrick M.** A Cartoon History of Texas. (Illus.). 200p. 2000. pap. 17.95 (1-55622-780-9, Rep of TX Pr) Wordware Pub.

Reynolds, Patrick M. A Cartoon History of the District of Columbia. LC 96-170033. (Flashbacks Ser.: Vol. 1). (Illus.). 106p. (Orig.). 1995. pap. 14.95 (0-932514-31-6) Red Rose Studio.

— Colorful Characters of Pennsylvania: Pennsylvania Profiles, Vol. 12. Vol. 12. (Illus.). 56p. (Orig.). 1987. pap. 3.95 (0-932514-17-0) Red Rose Studio.

— District of Columbia Neighborhoods: A Cartoon History by Patrick M. Reynolds. (Flashbacks Ser.: Vol. 2). (Illus.). 112p. (Orig.). (YA). (gr. 6-12). 1997. pap. 14.95 (0-932514-33-2) Red Rose Studio.

— It Started in Pennsylvania. (Pennsylvania Profiles Ser.: Vol. 14). (Illus.). 56p. (Orig.). 1990. pap. 3.95 (0-932514-22-7) Red Rose Studio.

— The Johnstown Flood & Other Stories about Pennsylvania. (Pennsylvania Profiles Ser.: Vol. 13). (Illus.). 56p. (Orig.). 1989. pap. 3.95 (0-932514-20-0) Red Rose Studio.

— Keystone Chronicles. (Pennsylvania Profiles Ser.: Vol. 15). (Illus.). 56p. (Orig.). 1991. pap. 3.95 (0-932514-25-1) Red Rose Studio.

— Lone Star Legacies. (Texas Lore Ser.: Vol. 8). (Illus.). 56p. (Orig.). 1990. pap. 3.75 (0-932514-23-5) Red Rose Studio.

— Pennsylvania Firsts: The Famous, Infamous, & Quirky of the Keystone State. LC 98-49234. (Illus.). 192p. 1999. pap. 9.95 (0-940159-46-5) Camino Bks.

— Pennsylvania Profiles, Vol. 11. (Illus.). 56p. 1987. pap. 3.95 (0-932514-16-2) Red Rose Studio.

— Pennsylvania Profiles Series, Vol. 9. (Pennsylvania Profiles Ser.). (Illus.). 56p. (Orig.). 1985. pap. 3.95 (0-932514-12-X) Red Rose Studio.

— Pennsylvania's Hectic Heritage. (Pennsylvania Profiles Ser.: Vol. VI). (Illus.). 56p. (YA). (gr. 7-12). 1982. pap. 3.95 (0-932514-06-5) Red Rose Studio.

Reynolds, Patrick M. Scraping up Pennsylvania's Past. (Pennsylvania Profiles Ser.: Vol. 8). (Illus.). 56p. (Orig.). 1984. pap. 3.95 (0-932514-10-3) Red Rose Studio.

Reynolds, Patrick M. Texas' Action History. (Texas Lore Ser.: Vol. 7). (Illus.). 56p. (Orig.). 1990. pap. 3.75 (0-932514-21-9) Red Rose Studio.

— Texas Lore, Vol. 5. Vol. 5. (Illus.). 56p. (Orig.). 1987. pap. 3.75 (0-932514-15-4) Red Rose Studio.

— Texas Lore, Vol. 9. Vol. 9. (Illus.). 56p. (Orig.). 1991. pap. 3.75 (0-932514-26-X) Red Rose Studio.

— Texas Lore, Vols. 1, 2, 3, & 4. (Illus.). 228p. (Orig.). (YA). (gr. 7-12). 1992. pap. 12.95 (0-932514-27-8) Red Rose Studio.

— Texas Lore: The Era of the Missions, Vols. 11 & 12. Vol. 11. (Illus.). 104p. (Orig.). 1995. pap. 6.95 (0-932514-30-8) Red Rose Studio.

— Texas Lore 10. (Texas Lore Ser.: Vol. 10). (Illus.). 56p. (Orig.). 1992. pap. 3.75 (0-932514-28-6) Red Rose Studio.

— Unusual Stories from Texas' History. (Texas Lore Ser.: Vol. 6). (Illus.). 56p. (Orig.). 1988. pap. 3.75 (0-932514-18-9) Red Rose Studio.

Reynolds, Patti, jt. ed. see Bottoni, Lois.

Reynolds, Patti, jt. ed. see Fisher, Jean.

Reynolds, Patti, ed. see Jordens, Carol.

Reynolds, Paul, jt. auth. see Cowling, Mark.

Reynolds, Paul, jt. auth. see Lancaster, Geoff.

Reynolds, Paul, Jr., jt. ed. see Abrams, Marc.

Reynolds, Paul D. Ethical Dilemmas & Social Science Research. LC 79-88110. (Jossey-Bass Social & Behavioral Science Ser.). 527p. reprint ed. pap. 163.40 (0-8357-6887-2, 203793900009) Bks Demand.

— Primer in Theory Construction. 194p. (Orig.). (C). 1971. pap. text 34.00 (0-02-399600-5, Macmillan Coll) P-H.

***Reynolds, Paul D., et al, eds.** Frontiers of Entrepreneurship 1999: Proceedings of the 19th Annual Entrepreneurship Research Conference. 19th unabridged ed. (Illus.). 750p. 1999. pap. 65.00 (0-910897-20-4) Babson College.

Reynolds, Paul D., et al, eds. Frontiers of Entrepreneurship Research, 1996: Proceedings of the 16th Annual Entrepreneurship Research Conference. (Frontiers of Entrepreneurship Research Ser.: Vol. 16). 683p. (Orig.). 1996. pap. text 65.00 (0-910897-17-4) Babson College.

— Frontiers of Entrepreneurship Research, 1997: Proceedings of the 17th Annual Entrepreneurship Research Conference. unabridged ed. (Illus.). 750p. 1997. pap. 65.00 (0-910897-18-2) Babson College.

— Frontiers of Entrepreneurship Research, 1998 Vol. 18: Proceedings of the 18th Annual Entrepreneurship Research Conference. annuals 18th unabridged ed. (Illus.). 765p. 1998. pap. 65.00 (0-910897-19-0) Babson College.

Reynolds, Paul D. & White, Sammis B. The Entrepreneurial Process: Economic Growth, Men, Women & Minorities. LC 97-19229. 256p. 1997. 59.95 (1-56720-012-5, Quorum Bks) Greenwood.

Reynolds, Paula B. & Andrus, Jenny G. Bay Area Baby: The Essential Guide to Local Resources for Pregnancy, Childbirth & Parenthood. LC 87-28445. (Illus.). 324p. (Orig.). 1991. pap. 14.95 (0-944296-05-X) Spirit Pr.

Reynolds, Peter. Dealing with Crime & Aggression at Work: A Handbook for Organizational Action. LC 94-34351. 1994. 18.95 (0-07-707932-9) McGraw.

— How to Live & Work in Greece: Essential Advice for Visitors & New Residents. 168p. 1996. pap. 22.50 (1-85703-191-1, Pub. by How To Bks) Trans-Atl Phila.

— Practical Approaches to Teaching Shakespeare. Gill, Roma, ed. (Oxford School Shakespeare Ser.). 128p. (YA). (gr. 6 up). 1992. pap. text 12.95 (0-19-831954-1) OUP.

Reynolds, Peter & Bailey, Marcella. How to Design & Deliver Retirement Training. (Practical Trainer Ser.). 142p. 1993. pap. 25.00 (0-7494-0947-9, Kogan Pg Educ) Stylus Pub VA.

Reynolds, Peter & Phelan, Peter D. Argument & Evidence: Critical Analysis for the Social Sciences. LC 95-15784. 247p. (C). 1995. pap. 18.99 (0-415-11373-3) Routledge.

Reynolds, Peter, jt. auth. see Hahlo, Richard.

Reynolds, Peter, jt. auth. see Phelan, Peter.

Reynolds, Peter C. Stealing Fire: The Atomic Bomb as Symbolic Body. (Illus.). 304p. 1991. 24.00 (0-9629261-0-8) Iconic Anthro.

Reynolds, Peter H. The North Star. LC 97-94615. (Illus.). 108p. 1997. 22.00 (1-891405-01-2) FableVision.

Reynolds, Peter J., ed. On Clusters & Clustering: From Atoms to Fractals. LC 93-9513. (Random Materials & Processes Ser.). 422p. 1993. pap. 93.25 (0-444-89022-X, North Holland) Elsevier.

Reynolds, Philip L. Marriage in the Western Church: The Christianization of Marriage During the Patristic Medieval Periods. LC 94-570. (Supplements to Vigiliae Christianae Ser.: Vol. 24). 1994. 134.50 (90-04-10022-9) Brill Academic Pubs.

***Reynolds, Philip Lyndon.** Food & the Body: Some Peculiar Questions in High Medieval Theology. LC 99-42619. (Studien Und Texte Zur Geistesgeschichte des Mittelalters Ser.: 69). 448p. 1999. text 230.00 (90-04-11532-3) Brill Academic Pubs.

Reynolds, Phyllis C. & Dimon, Elizabeth F. Trees of Greater Portland. LC 92-19585. (Illus.). 216p. 1993. pap. 19.95 (0-88192-263-3) Timber.

Reynolds, Quentin. Amazing Mr. Doolittle: A Biography of Lieutenant General James H. Doolittle. LC 71-169434. (Literature & History of Aviation Ser.). 1976. reprint ed. 25.95 (0-405-03778-3) Ayer.

— Courtroom. LC 77-119943. (Select Bibliographies Reprint Ser.). 1977. 30.95 (0-8369-5386-X) Ayer.

— I, Willie Sutton. (Illus.). 283p. 1993. reprint ed. pap. 13.95 (0-306-80510-3) Da Capo.

— Quentin Reynolds. 26.95 (0-8488-1126-7) Amereon Ltd.

— The Wright Brothers. LC 50-11766. (Landmark Ser.). (Illus.). 160p. (J). (gr. 5-9). 1981. pap. 5.99 (0-394-84700-8, Pub. by Random Bks Yng Read) Random.

— Wright Brothers, Pioneers of American Aviation. (Landmark Bks.). (J). 1981. 11.09 (0-606-12118-8, Pub. by Turtleback) Demco.

Reynolds, R. A. Computing for Architects. 2nd ed. LC 93-3314. 224p. 1993. pap. text 59.95 (0-7506-1516-8, Butterwrth Archit) Buttrwrth-Heinemann.

— Computing for Architects. 2nd ed. LC 93-3314. (Illus.). 226p. reprint ed. pap. 70.10 (0-608-04419-9, 206520000001) Bks Demand.

— Introduction to International Relations. 200p. 1971. pap. 11.95 (0-582-48818-4) Schenkman Bks Inc.

Reynolds, R. C. Stage Left: The Development of the American Social Drama in the Thirties. LC 85-52030. xxx, 175p. 1986. 45.00 (0-87875-311-7) Whitston Pub.

Reynolds, R. C., Jr., jt. ed. see Walker, J. R.

Reynolds, R. D. Ascomycete Systematics: The Luttrellian Concept. (Microbiology Ser.). (Illus.). 272p. 1981. 159.00 (0-387-90488-3) Spr-Verlag.

Reynolds, R. J., jt. intro. see Moore, Bob.

Reynolds, Ralph. Growing up Cowboy: Confessions of a Luna Kid. LC 91-71366. 192p. (Orig.). 1991. pap. 12.95 (1-55591-086-6) Fulcrum Pub.

— Making Full Proof of Our Ministry. 5th ed. 152p. (C). 1989. pap. 5.95 (1-877917-07-9) Alpha Bible Pubns.

Reynolds, Ralph, jt. auth. see Walsh, Bill.

Reynolds, Ralph, ed. see Bowers, Wendell.

Reynolds, Ralph, ed. see Grozinger, Jim & Thompson, Brian.

Reynolds, Ralph, ed. see Peterson, Chester, Jr.

Reynolds, Ralph D. John Hobbs, 16??-1731: A Genealogy of the Hobbs Family of Ohio. 2nd ed. LC 96-114769. (Illus.). 400p. 1994. 29.00 (0-925861-01-4) Quaint Pub Co.

Reynolds, Ralph V. Alpha Bible Course, 6 vols. 2nd ed. 1728p. (C). 1987. pap. text 124.95 (0-685-27256-7) Alpha Bible Pubns.

— Can a Believer Be Lost? 2nd ed. 118p. (C). 1986. pap. 5.50 (1-877917-00-1) Alpha Bible Pubns.

— The Cry of the Unborn. (Orig.). (C). 1989. pap. 5.95 (0-685-27250-8) Alpha Bible Pubns.

— The Cry of the Unborn: Understanding the Spiritual Birth Process. 125p. (Orig.). (YA). pap. 5.95 (1-877917-09-5) Alpha Bible Pubns.

— Dear Pastor: If the Sheep Could Speak. 144p. (Orig.). (C). 1988. pap. 5.95 (1-877917-01-X) Alpha Bible Pubns.

— Dividing the Word of Truth. 193p. (YA). (gr. 9). pap. 14.95 (1-877917-08-7) Alpha Bible Pubns.

— Dividing the Word of Truth. 9th ed. 193p. (C). 1987. pap. 14.95 (0-685-27252-4) Alpha Bible Pubns.

— If the Sheep Could Speak. 144p. (Orig.). (C). 1988. pap. 5.95 (0-685-27255-9) Alpha Bible Pubns.

— Living the Crucified Life. 118p. (Orig.). (C). 1987. pap. 5.50 (1-877917-02-8) Alpha Bible Pubns.

— Portraits of the Bride. 142p. (Orig.). (C). 1985. pap. 5.95 (0-685-27254-0) Alpha Bible Pubns.

— Truth Shall Triumph. 9th ed. 111p. 1983. pap. 6.99 (0-912315-07-5) Word Aflame.

— Unbroken Vows. 132p. (Orig.). (C). 1986. pap. 6.95 (0-685-27253-2) Alpha Bible Pubns.

— Usando Bien la Palabra De Verdad. Geissler, Darry & Geissler, Kimberly, eds. Crossley, Darry, tr. (SPA.). 220p. (Orig.). (YA). pap. 14.95 (1-877917-12-5) Alpha Bible Pubns.

— Usando Bien la Palabra De Verdad. Geissler, Darry & Geissler, Kimberly, eds. Crossley, Darry, tr. from ENG. (Dividing the World of Truth Ser.). (SPA.). 220p. (Orig.). (C). 1988. pap. 14.95 (0-685-27251-6) Alpha Bible Pubns.

Reynolds, Ray. California the Curious. (Illus.). 200p. (Orig.). 1989. pap. 12.95 (0-939919-25-7) Bear Flag Bks.

— Catspaw Utopia: Alfred K. Owen, the Adventurer of Topolobampo Bay, & the Last Grand Utopian Scheme. enl. rev. ed. Quarton, Barbara A., ed. LC 93-12180. (West Coast Studies: No. 4). (Illus.). 160p. 1997. pap. 21.00 (0-8095-3803-2) Millefleurs.

Reynolds, Ray, jt. auth. see Barlow, Ronald S.

Reynolds, Rebecca A. Bring Me the Ocean: Nature As Teacher, Messenger & Intermediary. LC 94-61765. (Illus.). 120p. 1995. 21.95 (0-9641089-2-5) VanderWyk & Burnham.

Reynolds, Reginald. John Woolman & the Twentieth Century. (C). 1958. pap. 4.00 (0-87574-096-0) Pendle Hill.

Reynolds, Renny. The Art of the Party: Design Ideas for Successful Entertaining. (Illus.). 288p. 1992. 55.00 (0-670-83054-2, Pub. by Studio Bks) Penguin Books.

Reynolds, Rex, jt. auth. see Friedl, Francis P.

Reynolds, Richard. The Foundation of Rhetoric. LC 45-7205. 160p. 1977. reprint ed. 50.00 (0-8201-1210-0) Schol Facsimiles.

— On Doctoring: Stories, Poems, Essays. rev. expanded ed. 448p. 1995. 29.50 (0-684-80255-4) S&S Trade.

— Super Heroes: A Modern Mythology. (Illus.). 134p. 1998. pap. text 14.00 (0-7881-5642-X) DIANE Pub.

— Super Heroes: A Modern Mythology. LC 93-48411. (Studies in Popular Culture). (Illus.). 134p. 1994. reprint ed. text 35.00 (0-87805-693-9) U Pr of Miss.

Reynolds, Richard, photos by. Texas Hill Country. (Littlebook Ser.). (Illus.). 64p. 1996. 14.95 (1-56579-145-2) Westcliffe Pubs.

— Texas Reflections. (Littlebook Ser.). (Illus.). 64p. 1996. 14.95 (1-56579-144-4) Westcliffe Pubs.

— Texas Wildflowers. (Littlebook Ser.). (Illus.). 64p. 1996. 14.95 (1-56579-143-6) Westcliffe Pubs.

Reynolds, Richard, ed. see Ireland, Patrick J.

Reynolds, Richard C., et al. The Health of a Rural County: Perspectives & Problems. LC 75-35753. 203p. reprint ed. pap. 63.00 (0-7837-4946-5, 204461200004) Bks Demand.

Reynolds, Richard D. The Ancient Art of Colima, Mexico. LC 88-92600. (Illus.). 96p. (Orig.). 1993. 18.95 (0-9618577-1-4) Squibob Pr.

— Cry for War: The Story of Suzan & Michael Carson. 368p. (Orig.). 1987. pap. 7.95 (0-9618577-2-2) Squibob Pr.

Reynolds, Richard D., ed. Squibob: An Early California Humorist. LC 89-61831. (Illus.). 256p. 1989. 15.95 (0-9618577-5-7); pap. 10.95 (0-9618577-6-5) Squibob Pr.

Reynolds, Richard T. Heart of the Storm: The Genesis of the Air Campaign Against Iraq. LC 94-16836. (Illus.). 169p. 1995. pap. 11.00 (1-58566-052-3) Air Univ.

Reynolds, Rick & Reynolds, Martha. Cat Nips! 96p. (Orig.). 1992. pap. 8.95 (0-425-13512-8) Berkley Pub.

***Reynolds, Rita.** Blessing the Bridge: What Animals Teach Us about Death & Dying. (Illus.). 168p. 2000. pap. text 12.95 (0-939165-38-4) New Riders Pub.

Reynolds, Rob. George Washington, Jesus Christ & Uncle Fred. LC 94-65020. 112p. (Orig.). 1994. pap. 11.95 (1-880222-18-3) Red Apple Pub.

Reynolds, Robert. Are You Chicken? A Coward's Guide to Roller Coasters. (Illus.). 64p. (Orig.). 1997. pap. 9.95 (0-9657353-3-8) Nrthn Lights FL.

— Roller Coasters, Flumes & Flying Saucers: The Story of Ed Morgan & Karl Bacon, Ride Inventors of the Modern Amusement Parks. LC 98-96860. (Illus.). 192p. 1999. 19.95 (0-9657353-5-4) Nrthn Lights FL.

— Thomas Wolfe: Memoir of a Friendship. LC 65-23163. 173p. reprint ed. pap. 53.70 (0-8357-7717-0, 203607400002) Bks Demand.

R

Reynolds, Robert & Muench, David, photos by. New Mexico, Rio Grande & Other Essays. (Illus.). 96p. 1992. 27.50 (*1-55868-093-4*) Gr Arts Ctr Pub.

Reynolds, Robert C., Jr., jt. auth. see Moore, Duane M.

Reynolds, Robert G., jt. ed. see McDonnell, John R.

Reynolds, Robert L. Europe Emerges: Transition Toward an Industrial World-Wide Society, 600-1750. LC 61-6175. (Illus.). 543p. reprint ed. pap. 168.40 (*0-608-20469-2*, 207172100002) Bks Demand.

***Reynolds, Robert M., photos by.** Washington Wine Country. LC 99-57154. 2000. pap. 24.95 (*1-55868-528-6*) Gr Arts Ctr Pub.

Reynolds, Robert W., photos by. Oregon's National Forests. LC 89-81617. (Illus.). 84p. 1990. 26.50 (*1-55868-016-0*) Gr Arts Ctr Pub.

***Reynolds, Roger E.** Clerical Orders in the Early Middle Ages: Duties & Ordination. (Variorum Collected Studies Ser.: Vol. CS670). 368p. 2000. text 106.95 (*0-86078-809-1*, Pub. by Ashgate Pub) Ashgate Pub Co.

— Clerics in the Early Middle Ages: Heirarchy & Image. (Variorum Collected Studies Ser.: Vol. CS669). (Illus.). 352p. 2000. text 110.95 (*0-86078-808-3*, Pub. by Ashgate Pub) Ashgate Pub Co.

Reynolds, Roger E. Law & Liturgy in the Latin Church, 5th-12th Centuries. LC 94-4774. (Collected Studies: No. CS457). 1994. 109.95 (*0-86078-405-3*, Pub. by Variorum) Ashgate Pub Co.

— The Ordinals of Christ from Their Origins to the Twelfth Century. (C). 1978. 110.00 (*3-11-007058-8*) De Gruyter.

Reynolds, Ron, jt. auth. see O'Morrow, Gerald.

Reynolds, Ronald P. & O'Morrow, Gerald S. Problems, Issues & Concepts in Therapeutic Recreation. 304p. (C). 1985. text 39.00 (*0-13-717430-6*) P-H.

Reynolds, Ronald P., jt. auth. see O'Morrow, Gerald S.

***Reynolds, Ross.** The Cambridge Guide to the Weather. (Illus.). 192p. (C). 2000. pap. 14.95 (*0-521-77489-6*) Cambridge U Pr.

Reynolds-Rush, Jacquie, jt. auth. see Blitzer, Roy J.

Reynolds, Ruth. Riva: If Ya Wanna Look Good, Honey, Your Feet Gotta Hurt. LC 98-5140. (Illus.). 64p. 1998. pap. text 16.95 (*1-57120-048-7*, 10172) C & T Pub.

Reynolds, Ruth M. Campus in Bondage: A Nineteen Forty-Eight Microcosm of Puerto Rico in Bondage. Erazo, Blanca V., ed. (Illus.). 334p. (Orig.). 1989. pap. 12.00 (*1-878483-00-5*) Hunter Coll CEP.

Reynolds, Sarah. 50 Best Mashed Potatoes. LC 97-40476. (Illus.). 96p. (Orig.). 1997. pap. 10.00 (*0-7679-0043-X*) Broadway BDD.

— 365 All American Favorites. LC 96-28422. 272p. 1997. 16.95 (*0-06-017294-0*) HarpC.

Reynolds, Scott-Childress, ed. see Childress, Rennie.

Reynolds, Sean. Against the Giants: The Liberation of Geoff, Silver Anniversary ed. (AD&D Accessory Ser.). 1999. 17.95 (*0-7869-1413-0*, Pub. by TSR Inc) Random.

***Reynolds, Sean & Miller, Steve.** Into the Dragon's Lair. 96p. 2000. pap. 17.95 (*0-7869-1634-6*) Wizards Coast.

***Reynolds, Sean K.** Beyond Science: A Guide to FX. (Alternity Ser.). 96p. 2000. pap. 18.95 (*0-7869-1619-2*) TSR Inc.

— Beyond Science: Guide to Fx. 1999. text 18.95 (*0-7869-1432-7*) TSR Inc.

Reynolds, Sean K. Crypt of Lyzandred the Mad. 1998. 11.95 (*0-7869-1251-0*, Pub. by TSR Inc) Random.

***Reynolds, Sean K.** Slavers. (Advanced Dungeons & Dragons Gamebook Ser.). (Illus.). 128p. 2000. pap. 18.95 (*0-7869-1621-4*) TSR Inc.

Reynolds, Sean K. The Star Cairns. 1998. 11.95 (*0-7869-1250-2*, Pub. by TSR Inc) Random.

Reynolds, Sharon E., ed. see Brown, Drollene P.

Reynolds, Sheri. Bitterroot Landing. 288p. 1995. mass mkt. 6.99 (*0-425-15044-5*) Berkley Pub.

— Bitterroot Landing. 1997. pap. 12.00 (*0-425-16246-X*) Berkley Pub.

— A Gracious Plenty. 208p. 1999. pap. 12.00 (*0-609-80387-5*) Crown Pub Group.

— A Gracious Plenty. large type ed. LC 98-41991. Date not set. 30.00 (*0-7862-1683-2*) Thorndike Pr.

— The Rapture of Canaan. 320p. 1997. pap. 12.00 (*0-425-16244-3*) Berkley Pub.

— The Rapture of Canaan. large type ed. LC 97-25364. (Core Ser.). 364p. 1997. lib. bdg. 28.95 (*0-7838-8270-X*, G K Hall Lrg Type) Mac Lib Ref.

***Reynolds, Sheri.** The Rapture of Canaan. 320p. 1999. reprint ed. pap. text 12.00 (*0-7881-6169-5*) DIANE Pub.

Reynolds, Sherri T., jt. auth. see Goldsmith, Malcolm.

***Reynolds, Sherrie.** Learning Is a Verb: The Psychology of Teaching & Learning. LC 99-59722. 160p. (C). 1999. pap. 18.95 (*1-890871-24-9*) Holcomb Hath.

Reynolds, Sian. Brittanica's Typesetters: Women Compositors in Edwardian Edinburgh. (Edinburgh Education & Society Ser.). (Illus.). 160p. 1990. pap. 25.00 (*0-85224-652-8*, Pub. by Edinburgh U Pr) Col U Pr.

— France Between the Wars: Gender & Politics. 296p. (C). 1996. 85.00 (*0-415-12736-X*); pap. 29.99 (*0-415-12737-8*) Routledge.

Reynolds, Sian, ed. Women, State, & Revolution: Essays on Power & Gender in Europe Since 1789. LC 86-16074. (Illus.). 208p. 1986. lib. bdg. 27.50 (*0-87023-552-4*) U of Mass Pr.

***Reynolds, Sian & Kidd, William, eds.** Contemporary French Cultural Studies. 288p. 2000. pap. 19.95 (*0-340-74050-7*, Pub. by E A); text 65.00 (*0-340-74049-3*, Pub. by E A) OUP.

Reynolds, Sian, tr. see Bramly, Serge.

Reynolds, Sian, tr. see Braudel, Fernand.

Reynolds, Sian, tr. see Lambrichs, Louise.

Reynolds, Sian, tr. see Le Roy-Ladurie, Emmanuel.

Reynolds, Simon. Generation Ecstasy. LC 99-22695. 1999. pap. 17.99 (*0-415-92373-5*) Routledge.

— Generation Ecstasy: Into the World of Techno & Rave Culture. LC 98-14754. (Illus.). 464p. (gr. 8). 1998. 25.00 (*0-316-74111-6*) Little.

— The Vision of Simeon Solomon. 183p. 1984. write for info. (*0-904995-07-0*, Pub. by Catalpa Pr Ltd) Penguin Books.

Reynolds, Simon & Albert, Bill. Blissed Out: The Apocalypse of Rock. LC 90-60291. 256p. (Orig.). 1990. pap. 15.95 (*1-85242-199-1*) Serpents Tail.

Reynolds, Simon & Press, Joy. The Sex Revolts: Gender, Rebellion, & Rock 'n' Roll. LC 94-30683. 432p. 1995. text 24.95 (*0-674-80272-1*, REYSER) HUP.

— The Sex Revolts: Gender, Rebellion, & Rock 'n' Roll. 432p. 1996. pap. 15.95 (*0-674-80273-X*) HUP.

Reynolds, Simon, jt. auth. see Buffett, Warren.

Reynolds, Siri. House of Rooms. 200p. (Orig.). 1997. pap. 15.95 (*0-7486-6230-8*, Pub. by Polygon) Subterranean Co.

Reynolds, Stephen. Beyond the Killing Tree: A Journey of Discovery. (Illus.). 192p. 1995. 19.95 (*0-945397-42-9*) Epicenter Pr.

— Voyage of the New Hazard to the Northwest Coast, Hawaii & China, 1810-1813. 1970. 24.95 (*0-87770-076-1*) Ye Galleon.

Reynolds, Steven & Lomax, Ian. Enforcement in the Magistrates' Courts. 240p. 1996. pap. 59.50 (*1-85811-095-5*, Pub. by CLT Prof) Gaunt.

Reynolds, Steven, jt. auth. see Davis, George H.

Reynolds, Steven, jt. auth. see Lomax, Ian S.

Reynolds, Steven, jt. auth. see Stewart, Chris.

Reynolds, Stewart, jt. auth. see Reynolds, Elsdon.

Reynolds-Strauss, Karen & Gligor, Adrian. Romanian Fairy Tales. (Illus.). 85p. (Orig.). (J). (ps-6). 1992. pap. text 11.95 (*0-9634797-0-9*) K Strauss & A Gligor.

Reynolds, Stuart. Construction Site Equipment, Vol. I-4. (Single Market Review Ser.). 1998. 70.00 (*0-7494-2308-0*) Kogan Page Ltd.

— Technical Barriers to Trade, Vol. III-1. (Single Market Review Ser.). 1998. 80.00 (*0-7494-2324-2*) Kogan Page Ltd.

Reynolds, Sue. New Horizons the Complete Guide to Horse Careers. Host, Bobette, ed. LC 98-65621. 1998. per. 29.95 (*0-9663559-0-3*) New Horizons CO.

Reynolds, Sue, jt. auth. see Neiman, Tummy.

Reynolds, Susan. Fiefs & Vassals: The Medieval Evidence Reinterpreted. 556p. 1996. reprint ed. pap. text 19.95 (*0-19-820648-8*) OUP.

— Ideas & Solidarities of the Medieval Laity: England & Western Europe. LC 95-1530. (Collected Studies: Vol. 495). 264p. 1995. 97.95 (*0-86078-485-1*, Pub. by Variorum) Ashgate Pub Co.

— Kingdoms & Communities in Western Europe, 900-1300. 2nd ed. LC 97-222648. 462p. 1997. text 85.00 (*0-19-873148-5*); pap. text 26.00 (*0-19-873147-7*) OUP.

Reynolds, Suzanne. Medieval Reading: Grammar, Rhetoric & the Classical Text. (Studies in Medieval Literature: No. 27). (Illus.). 251p. (C). 1996. text 59.95 (*0-521-47257-1*) Cambridge U Pr.

Reynolds, Suzanne & Craig, Kenneth. North Carolina Family Law, 1998 Cumulative Supplement, Vol. 1. (Illus.). 1998. write for info. (*0-327-00648-X*, 64281-15) LEXIS Pub.

— North Carolina Family Law, 1998 Cumulative Supplement, Vol. 2. (Illus.). 1998. write for info. (*0-327-00650-1*, 64282-15) LEXIS Pub.

— North Carolina Family Law, 1998 Cumulative Supplement, Vol. 3. 4th ed. (Illus.). 1998. write for info. (*0-327-00651-X*, 64283-15) LEXIS Pub.

— North Carolina Family Law, 1998 Cumulative Supplement, Vol. 4. 4th ed. (Illus.). 1998. write for info. (*0-327-00652-8*, 64284-15) LEXIS Pub.

Reynolds, T. Cyberlane Commuter. 2nd ed. 1999. pap. 14.95 (*1-881116-97-2*) Black Forest Pr.

Reynolds, T., jt. ed. see Harley, R. M.

Reynolds, T. J. The Complete Book of Blackjack: A Comprehensive Guide to Winning Strategies. LC 97-44737. (Illus.). 224p. 1998. pap. 14.95 (*0-8184-0602-X*, L Stuart) Carol Pub Group.

Reynolds, T. James, jt. auth. see Goldstein, Robert H.

Reynolds, Terrence. The Coherence of Life Without God Before God: The Problem of Earthly Desires in the Later Theology of Dietrich Bonhoeffer. 190p. (C). 1989. lib. bdg. 39.00 (*0-8191-7237-5*) U Pr of Amer.

Reynolds, Terry. The Echocardiographer's Pocket Reference. 180p. 34.95 (*0-9635767-0-4*) AZ Heart Inst.

***Reynolds, Terry.** The Pediatric Echocardiographers Pocket Reference. Pan, Yeng & Dubovec, Patricia, eds. (Illus.). 250p. 1999. 64.95 (*0-9635767-7-1*) AZ Heart Inst.

Reynolds, Terry S. Stronger Than a Hundred Men: A History of the Vertical Water Wheel. LC 82-15346. (Johns Hopkins Studies in the History of Technology; New Ser.: Vol. 7). 472p. 1983. reprint ed. pap. 146.40 (*0-608-03744-3*, 206456900009) Bks Demand.

Reynolds, Terry S., ed. The Engineer in America: A Historical Anthology from Technology & Culture. 440p. 1991. pap. text 19.95 (*0-226-71032-7*); lib. bdg. 52.00 (*0-226-71031-9*) U Ch Pr.

Reynolds, Terry S. & Cutcliffe, Stephen H. Technology & the West: A Historical Anthology from Technology & Culture. LC 97-5926. 448p. 1997. pap. text 18.95 (*0-226-71034-3*); lib. bdg. 37.50 (*0-226-71033-5*) U Ch Pr.

Reynolds, Terry S., jt. auth. see Cutcliffe, Stephen H.

Reynolds, Thomas H. & Flores, Arturo A. Foreign Law: Current Sources of Codes & Basic Legislation in Jurisdictions of the World, 3 vols. in 6 bks. Incl. Vol. 1. Western Hemisphere. 1989. ring bd. 375.00 (*0-8377-0134-1*, Rothman); Vol. 2. Western & Eastern Europe & the European Communities. LC 89-10223. 1160p. ring bd. 375.00 (*0-8377-0138-4*, Rothman); Vol. 3. Africa, Asia & Australasia. LC 89-10223. x, 1366p. Date not set. ring bd. 375.00 (*0-8377-0139-2*, Rothman); (AALL Publications: No. 33). 1989. Set ring bd. 2100.00 (*0-8377-0140-6*, Rothman) W S Hein.

Reynolds, Thomas J. & Olson, Jerry C., eds. Consumer Decision Making: A Means End Approach to Marketing & Advertising Strategy. LC 99-47703. 350p. 2000. write for info. (*0-8058-1730-1*) L Erlbaum Assocs.

***Reynolds, Thomas J. & Olson, Jerry C., eds.** Consumer Decision Making: A Means End Approach to Marketing & Advertising Strategy. 350p. 2000. pap. write for info. (*0-8058-1731-X*) L Erlbaum Assocs.

Reynolds, Thomas P., III. Belle of the Brawl. (Illus.). 266p. 1996. 24.95 (*1-56311-308-2*) Turner Pub KY.

Reynolds, Tim. Dawn Chorus. LC 80-24377. 42p. 1980. 4.00 (*0-87886-111-4*, Greenfld Rev Pr) Greenfld Rev Lit.

— Que. LC 76-155304. 1971. 25.00 (*0-912604-06-9*); pap. 3.50 (*0-912604-05-0*) Halty Ferguson.

Reynolds, Timothy D., jt. auth. see Butler, Bret W.

***Reynolds, Tom.** Wild Ride: How Outlaw Motorcycle Myth Conquered America. (Illus.). 400p. 2000. 27.95 (*1-57500-145-4*, Pub. by TV Bks) HarpC.

Reynolds, Tom D. Unit Operations & Processes in Environmental Engineering. 1982. mass mkt. 63.50 (*0-8185-0493-5*) PWS Pubs.

— Unit Operations & Processes in Environmental Engineering. 2nd ed. (C). 1995. mass mkt. 109.95 (*0-534-94884-7*) Wadsworth Pub.

***Reynolds, Tom D. & Richards.** Unit Operations & Processes in Environmental Engineering 3e. 3rd ed. (C). 2002. pap. 75.50 (*0-534-37810-2*) Thomson Learn.

Reynolds, Tonga & Cousins, Colleen C. Lwaano Lwanyika: Tonga Book of the Earth. (Illus.). 250p. 1994. pap. 19.95 (*1-870670-30-2*) Paul & Co Pubs.

Reynolds, Tony. Cities in Crisis, Set II. (World Issues Ser.). (Illus.). 48p. (J). (gr. 5 up). 1990. lib. bdg. 25.27 (*0-86592-118-0*) Rourke Enter.

Reynolds, Tony, et al. World Issues, 2 bks. (Illus.). 336p. (YA). (gr. 5 up). 1990. lib. bdg. 94.50 (*0-685-36375-9*) Rourke Corp.

Reynolds, Tulsi. The Little Cat Who Had No Name. LC 90-62915. (Illus.). 32p. 1990. pap. 9.25 (*1-877675-04-0*) Midmarch Arts.

Reynolds, V. Forty Eight Etudes for French Horn. 56p. 1986. pap. 11.95 (*0-7935-5275-3*, 50329860) H Leonard.

Reynolds, V. & Boyce, A. J., eds. Human Populations: Diversity & Adaptation. (Illus.). 294p. 1995. text 135.00 (*0-19-852294-0*) OUP.

***Reynolds, V. Raye & Wilson, Marjorie P.** The Cat's Pajamas! A Personal Journal & Record Book. (Illus.). 60p. 2000. pap. 29.95 (*1-930335-00-8*) Rayeson Enterp.

Reynolds, Valda. A Practical Guide to Child Development. (Teacher's Books ser.). 48p. (C). 1988. pap., teacher ed. 27.50 (*0-85950-525-1*, Pub. by S Thornes Pubs) Trans-Atl Phila.

— A Practical Guide to Child Development, 2 vols., Vol. 1. 302p. (C). 1987. pap. 29.50 (*0-85950-221-X*, Pub. by S Thornes Pubs) Trans-Atl Phila.

***Reynolds, Valrae.** From the Sacred Realm: Treasures of Tibetan Art from the Neward Museum. (Illus.). 240p. 1999. 65.00 (*3-7913-2148-X*, Pub. by Prestel) te Neues.

Reynolds, Valrae. The Newark Museum Tibetan Buddhist Altar. VanDecker, Lori & Price, Mary S., eds. (Illus.). 32p. (Orig.). 1991. pap. 8.00 (*0-932828-25-6*) Newark Mus.

Reynolds, Valrae, et al. The Newark Museum Tibetan Collection: Sculpture & Painting, Vol. III. 2nd rev. ed. (Illus.). 208p. 1987. pap. 20.00 (*0-932828-15-9*) Newark Mus.

Reynolds, Valrae, jt. auth. see Pal, Pratapaditya.

Reynolds, Verne. The Horn Handbook. LC 96-13672. 250p. 1997. 33.95 (*1-57467-016-6*, Amadeus Pr) Timber.

Reynolds, Vernon, ed. The Sociobiology of Ethnocentrism: Evolutionary Dimensions of Xenophobia, Discrimination, Racism & Nationalism. (Illus.). 336p. 1986. 45.00 (*0-7099-4222-2*, Pub. by C Helm) Routldge.

Reynolds, Vernon & Kellett, John, eds. Mating & Marriage. (Biosocial Society Ser.: No. 3). (Illus.). 176p. 1991. 57.00 (*0-19-858406-7*) OUP.

Reynolds, Vernon & Tanner, Ralph. The Social Ecology of Religion. (Illus.). 336p. (C). 1995. text 49.95 (*0-19-506973-0*); pap. text 23.95 (*0-19-506974-9*) OUP.

Reynolds, Vernon, jt. auth. see Quiatt, Duane.

Reynolds, Vernon, jt. ed. see Landers, John.

***Reynolds, Virginia.** 101 Reasons Why You're the Greatest Mom. (Charming Petites Ser.). (Illus.). 80p. 2000. 4.95 (*0-88088-514-9*) Peter Pauper.

— The Spirit of Christmas: A History of Our Best-Loved Carols. (BookNotes with CDs Ser.). (Illus.). 64p. 2000. 13.99 incl. cd-rom (*0-88088-414-2*) Peter Pauper.

— You're My Cup of Tea: Special Moments, Special Friends. (Charming Petites Ser.). (Illus.). 80p. 2000. 4.95 (*0-88088-396-0*) Peter Pauper.

Reynolds, W. M. & Johnston, H. F., eds. Handbook of Depression in Children & Adolescents. (Issues in Clinical Child Psychology Ser.). (Illus.). 632p. (C). 1994. text 95.00 (*0-306-44742-8*, Kluwer Plenum) Kluwer Academic.

Reynolds, Walter F. Dry Strength Additives. LC 79-67261. (Press Reports). 188p. 1980. 28.00 (*0-89852-044-4*, 0102B044) TAPPI.

Reynolds, Walter F., ed. The Sizing of Paper. 2nd ed. 156p. 1989. 73.00 (*0-89852-051-7*, 0102B051) TAPPI.

Reynolds, Walter F., ed. see Technical Association of the Pulp & Paper Industry.

Reynolds, Wednesday. B/W: Minor Verse Faux Haiku False Koans Translations Apocrypha New Grass. (Monkey in Winter Ser.). (Illus.). 33p. 1999. pap. 8.00 (*0-9665390-1-X*) Emerick Bell.

Reynolds, William. The Lonely Years: Don't Look Like I'll Be an Old Man. (Illus.). 86p. (Orig.). 1996. pap. 7.50 (*1-57502-270-2*, P0956) Morris Pubng.

— The Mysteries of London. Thomas, Trefor, ed. (Illus.). 384p. 1998. 50.00 (*1-85331-111-1*, Pub. by Edinburgh U Pr) Col U Pr.

— Theory of the Law of Evidence: As Established in the United States & of the Conduct of the Examination of Witnesses. 3rd ed. xix, 206p. 1983. reprint ed. 36.00 (*0-8377-1039-1*, Rothman) W S Hein.

Reynolds, William & Pinar, William F., eds. Understanding Curriculum as Phenomenological & Deconstructed Text. (Critical Issues in Curriculum Ser.: No. 2). 272p. (C). 1991. text 46.00 (*0-8077-3114-5*); pap. text 21.95 (*0-8077-3113-7*) Tchrs Coll.

Reynolds, William & Rand, Ritch. The Cowboy Hat Book. LC 94-33734. (Illus.). 96p. 1995. pap. 19.95 (*0-87905-659-2*) Gibbs Smith Pub.

Reynolds, William & Trembley, Elizabeth, eds. It's a Print! Detective Fiction from Page to Screen. LC 94-70906. 235p. (C). 1994. 46.95 (*0-87972-661-X*); pap. 18.95 (*0-87972-662-8*) Bowling Green Univ Popular Press.

Reynolds, William, jt. auth. see Mackay, Roderick.

Reynolds, William, jt. auth. see MacKay, Roderick.

Reynolds, William, ed. see Splaver, Bernard R.

Reynolds, William B., jt. auth. see Wasserstrom, Richard A.

Reynolds, William C. & Perkins, Henry C. Engineering Thermodynamics. 2nd ed. 544p. (C). 1977. 105.31 (*0-07-052046-1*) McGraw.

Reynolds, William D. The Call That Changed My Life: A Man's Journey Toward Love. 72p. (Orig.). 1995. pap. 6.00 (*1-881568-08-3*) Healing Spirit.

Reynolds, William J. Drive-By: A Nebraska Mystery. Emmel, Gayle, ed. LC 95-1513. 329p. 1995. pap. 5.95 (*0-944287-14-X*) Ex Machina.

***Reynolds, William J.** South Dakota: The Face of the Future. 188p. 1999. write for info. (*1-882933-28-1*) Cherbo Pub Grp.

Reynolds, William J. & Price, Milburn. A Survey of Christian Hymnody. rev. ed. LC 87-81996. (Illus.). 300p. 1987. pap. text 27.95 (*0-916642-32-1*, 904) Hope Pub.

Reynolds, William L. Judicial Process in a Nutshell. 2nd ed. (Nutshell Ser.). 308p. (C). 1991. pap. 21.00 (*0-314-88430-0*) West Pub.

Reynolds, William L., jt. auth. see Richman, William M.

Reynolds, William M. Reading Curriculum Theory: The Development of a New Hermeneutic. (American University Studies: Language: Ser. XIV, Vol. 19). XIII, 238p. (C). 1989. text 30.95 (*0-8204-1001-2*) P Lang Pubng.

Reynolds, William M., ed. Internalizing Disorders in Children & Adolescents. LC 91-40212. (Series on Personality Processes: No. 1341). 352p. 1992. 150.00 (*0-471-50648-6*) Wiley.

Reynolds, William M., jt. auth. see Martusewicz, Rebecca A.

Reynolds, William N., ed. see Splaver, Bernard.

Reynolds, Woodson. And I Remember. LC 87-90716. (Illus.). 59p. 1987. pap. text 12.50 (*0-9619147-0-X*) Midnight Pubns.

— In Those Days. (Illus.). 55p. 1982. pap. text 12.50 (*0-614-30047-9*) Midnight Pubns.

Reynolds, Yvonne. An Ox Tale. LC 98-96220. (Illus.). 24p. (J). (gr. 2-5). 1998. pap. write for info. (*0-9650824-1-5*) Lolot Pr.

— Talent - Worth Its Weight in Gold. Reynolds, Joanne, ed. LC 95-95297. (Illus.). 176p. (Orig.). 1996. pap. 12.95 (*0-9650824-0-7*) Lolot Pr.

Reynoldson, Fiona. Conflict & Change, 1650-1800. LC 92-20460. (Illustrated History of the World Ser.). (Illus.). 80p. (J). (gr. 4-9). 1993. 19.95 (*0-8160-2790-0*) Facts on File.

Reynoldson, Floria. Women & War. LC 93-4889. (World War Two Ser.). (Illus.). 48p. (J). (gr. 5-9). 1993. lib. bdg. 24.26 (*1-56847-082-7*) Raintree Steck-V.

Reynoldson, George. Let's Reach for the Sun: Thirty Original Solar & Earth Sheltered Home Designs. rev. ed. (Illus.). 144p. 1981. pap. 12.95 (*0-9603570-1-7*) Space-Time WA.

Reynoldson, Ray W. Heat Treatment in Fluidized Bed Furnaces. LC 93-35827. 250p. 1993. 69.00 (*0-87170-485-4*, 6330) ASM.

Reynoldson, T. B. A Key to the British Species of Freshwater Triclads. 2nd ed. 1978. 60.00 (*0-900386-34-7*) St Mut.

Reynoldson, T. B. & Coates, K. A., eds. Aquatic Oligochaete Biology V: Proceedings of the 5th Symposium, Held in Tallinn, Estonia, 1991. LC 93-47117. (Developments in Hydrobiology Ser.). 328p. (C). 1994. text 276.00 (*0-7923-2686-5*) Kluwer Academic.

Reynosa, Larry, jt. auth. see Billingiere, Joseph.

Reynosa, Mark A. The M-1 Helmet: A History of the U. S. M-1 Helmet in World War II. (Illus.). 112p. 1996. 39.95 (*0-7643-0074-1*) Schiffer.

***Reynosa, Mark A.** Personnel Armor System Ground Troops Helmet: Illust.Study of Us Military Current Issue Helmet. (Illus.). 80p. 2000. pap. 19.95 (*0-7643-1034-8*) Schiffer.

— Post-World War II M-1 Helmets, An Illustrated Study. (Illus.). 136p. 2000. 39.95 (*0-7643-1033-X*) Schiffer.

Reynosa, Mark A. U. S. Combat Helmets of the 20th Century: Mass Production Helmets. LC 97-67427. 160p. 1997. 39.95 (*0-7643-0357-0*) Schiffer.

Reynoso, Anthony, jt. auth. see Chacon, Jeff.

Reynoso, Gerardo S., jt. auth. see Acosta, Virginia G.

Reynoso-Sydenham, Silvia, tr. see Fay, Jim & Cline, Foster W.

An Asterisk (*) at the beginning of an entry indicates that the title is appearing for the first time.

Reyntiens, Patrick. Stained Glass Christmas. LC 98-20944. (Illus.). 24p. 1998. 19.95 (*1-55670-846-7*) Stewart Tabori & Chang.

Reyntjens, Filip. Burundi - Landet Med Kuppen Utan Slut. (Afrikafakta Ser.: Nr. 3). 36p. 1996. write for info. (*91-7106-382-X*, Pub. by Nordic Africa) Transaction Pubs.

Reyoung. Unbabbling. LC 97-23672. 256p. 1997. pap. 13.95 (*1-56478-164-X*) Dalkey Arch.

Reyre, Dominique & Mohafez, Siawosh. First Contribution to the NIOC-ERAP Agreements to the Knowledge of Iranian Geology (A) 1972. 145.00 (*2-7108-0178-7*, Pub. by Edits Technip) Enfield Pubs NH.

Reys, Barbara J., et al. Developing Number Sense in the Middle Grades. Curcio, Frances, ed. LC 91-12623. (Curriculum & Evaluation Standards for School Mathematics Addenda Ser.). (Illus.). 56p. 1991. pap. 14.95 (*0-87353-322-4*) NCTM.

— Number Sense: Simple Effective Number Sense Experiences. Gideon, Joan & Anderson, Catherine, eds. (Illus.). 238p. (Orig.). (J). (gr. 4-6). 1996. pap. text, teacher ed. 18.95 (*1-57232-263-2*, 21802) Seymour Pubns.

— Number Sense: Simple Effective Number Sense Experiences. Gideon, Joan, ed. (Number Sense Ser.). (Illus.). 214p. (Orig.). (J). (gr. 3-4). 1996. pap. text 18.95 (*1-57232-262-4*, 21801) Seymour Pubns.

— Number Sense: Simple Effective Number Sense Experiences. Gideon, Joan, ed. (Illus.). 182p. (Orig.). 1997. pap. text, teacher ed. 18.95 (*1-57232-261-6*, 21800) Seymour Pubns.

— Simple, Effective Number Sense. Gideon, Joan, ed. (Number Sense Ser.). (Illus.). 213p. (Orig.). (J). (gr. 6-8). 1996. pap. text 18.95 (*1-57232-264-0*, 21803) Seymour Pubns.

Reys, Georges, jt. ed. see Loewer, Barry.

Reys, Robert E. Helping Children Learn Math. 1995. pap. text 54.00 (*0-205-16471-4*) Allyn.

***Reys, Robert E.** Helping Children Learn Mathematics. 5th ed. (Illus.). 400p. 1998. pap., teacher ed. 56.95 (*0-471-36536-X*) Wiley.

— Helping Children Learn Mathematics: Activity Cards. 5th ed. 158p. 1998. pap. 25.95 (*0-471-36525-4*) Wiley.

Reys, Robert E. & Nohda, Nobuhiko, eds. Computational Alternatives for the 21st Century: Cross-Cultural Perspectives from Japan & the United States. LC 93-48037. (Illus.). 211p. 1994. pap. 15.50 (*0-87353-368-2*) NCTM.

***Reys, Robert E., et al.** Helping Children Learn Mathematics. 6th ed. 400p. 2001. pap. write for info. (*0-471-36785-0*) Wiley.

Reys, Robert E., et al. Helping Children Learn Mathematics: Instructor's Manual with Test Questions. 5th ed. 1998. pap. text, teacher ed. write for info. (*0-205-27193-6*, T7193-0) Allyn.

Reyssat, Eric. Surfaces de Riemann. (Progress in Mathematics Ser.: No. 77). 256p. 1989. 60.50 (*0-8176-3441-X*) Birkhauser.

Reza, jt. auth. see Fadaei.

Reza, Fazlollah M. An Introduction to Information Theory. unabridged ed. LC 94-27222. (Illus.). 496p. 1994. pap. text 12.95 (*0-486-68210-2*) Dover.

Reza-Vaez-Zadeh, jt. ed. see Downes, Patrick.

Reza, Yasmina. Art. (Orig.). 1999. pap. 5.25 (*0-8222-1658-2*) Dramatists Play.

— Art. Hampton, Christopher, tr. from FRE. 96p. (Orig.). 1997. pap. 12.95 (*0-571-19014-6*) Faber & Faber.

***Reza, Yasmina.** Hammerklavier. Cosman, Carol, tr. from FRE. LC 99-56688. 128p. 2000. 20.00 (*0-8076-1451-3*, Pub. by Braziller) Norton.

Reza, Yasmina. Unexpected Man. Hampton, Christopher, tr. 80p. 1998. pap. 11.95 (*0-571-19604-7*) Faber & Faber.

Rezabek-Turner, Ellie. A Bouquet of Night Flowers: Journey of a Soul Through Loss, Grief & Healing. (Illus.). 80p. (Orig.). 1995. pap. 12.00 (*0-9646595-3-0*) LinkaAges.

Rezaian, S. Mahmoud. Modern Management of Spinal Injury. (Illus.). 152p. 1996. pap. 50.00 (*0-8059-3966-0*) Dorrance.

Rezak, Richard & Henry, Vernon J., eds. Contributions on the Geological & Geophysical Oceanography of the Gulf of Mexico. LC 72-170029. (Texas A & M University Oceanographic Studies: No. 3). (Illus.). 319p. reprint ed. pap. 98.90 (*0-608-18174-9*, 203289000081) Bks Demand.

Rezak, Richard & Lavoie, D. L., eds. Carbonate Microfabrics. LC 93-3272. (Frontiers in Sedimentary Geology Ser.). 1993. 116.00 (*0-387-94035-9*) Spr-Verlag.

Rezak, Richard, et al. Geology of Calcareous Algae: Notes for a Short Course. (Sedimenta Ser.: Vol. I). (Illus.). 70p. (Orig.). 1972. 9.00 (*0-932981-01-1*) Univ Miami CSL.

Rezakovic, D. & Alpert, J. S., eds. Nitrate Therapy & Nitrate Tolerance: Current Concepts & Controversies. LC 92-49386. (Illus.). x, 548p. 1993. 252.25 (*3-8055-5669-1*) S Karger.

Rezanov, I. A. Catastrophes in the Earth's History. 168p. 1984. pap. 40.00 (*0-7855-2040-6*) St Mut.

Rezanov, Nikolai P. The Rezanov Voyage to Nueva California in 1806. limited ed. 1988. 29.95 (*0-87770-448-1*) Ye Galleon.

Rezatto, Helen. Tales of the Black Hills. 8th ed. LC 89-84829. (Illus.). 288p. 1996. pap. text. write for info. (*0-913062-07-3*) Fenwyn Pr.

Rezau, Pierre. Dictionnaire du Francais Parle. rev. ed. (FRE.). 382p. 1991. pap. 17.95 (*0-7859-7627-2*, 2020128683) Fr & Eur.

***Rezazadeh, Fred.** Collectible Silver Jewelry: Identification & Value Guide. (Illus.). 256p. 2000. 24.95 (*1-57432-188-9*) Collector Bks.

Rezazadeh, Fred. Costume Jewelry - a Practical Handbook & Value Guide. (Illus.). 224p. 1997. 24.95 (*1-57432-013-0*, 4940) Collector Bks.

Rezazadeh, Reza. Iraq & Democracy: A Futuristic Perspective. LC 93-72961. 220p. 1994. 24.00 (*0-9629032-1-3*) Etarnalist.

— Technodemocratic Economic Theory: From Capitalism & Socialism to Democracy. LC 91-70823. 359p. (C). 1992. lib. bdg. 20.00 (*0-9629032-0-5*) Etarnalist.

Rezba, Richard. Learning Science Process Skills. 3rd ed. 288p. 1996. pap., per. 24.95 (*0-8403-8430-0*) Kendall-Hunt.

— Readings for Teaching Science in Elementary & Middle Schools Pak. 538p. (C). 1996. pap. text 57.95 (*0-7872-2654-8*, 41265401) Kendall-Hunt.

Rezeau, Pierre. Dictionnaire du Francais Regional de Poitou-Charentes et de Vendee. (FRE.). 159p. 1990. 50.00 (*0-8288-9480-9*, 2862530972) Fr & Eur.

Rezen, Susan V. & Hausman, Carl. Coping with Hearing Loss: A Guide for Adults & Their Families. rev. ed. LC 92-36728. 224p. 1993. 17.95 (*0-942637-83-6*) Barricade Bks.

Rezende, Ricardo. Rio Maria: Song of the Earth. Adriance, Madeleine, ed. & tr. by. LC 93-49654. 168p. reprint ed. pap. 52.10 (*0-608-20265-7*, 207152400012) Bks Demand.

Rezende, Sergio M., jt. ed. see Coutinho-Filho, Mauricio D.

***Rezendes, Paul.** Tracking & the Art of Seeing: How to Read Animal Tracks & Sign. 2nd ed. LC 98-45867. 336p. 1999. pap. 25.00 (*0-06-273524-1*) HarpC.

Rezendes, Paul. The Wild Within: Adventures in Nature & Animal Teachings. LC 98-11725. (Illus.). 240p. (J). 1998. 24.95 (*0-87477-931-6*, Tarcher Putnam) Putnam Pub Group.

***Rezendes, Paul & McKibben, Bill.** The Wild Within: Adventures in Nature & Animal Teachings. 1999. reprint ed. pap. 12.00 (*0-425-17157-4*) Berkley Pub.

Rezendes, Paul & Roy, Paulette M. Wetlands: The Web of Life. LC 96-14942. (Illus.). 160p. 1996. pap. 25.00 (*0-87156-878-0*, Pub. by Sierra) Random.

Rezendes, Victor S. Alternative-Fueled Vehicles: Progress Made in Accelerating Federal Purchases, but Benefits & Costs Remain Uncertain. (Illus.). 120p. (Orig.). (C). 1994. pap. text 45.00 (*0-7881-1370-4*) DIANE Pub.

— Electromagnetic Fields: Federal Efforts to Determine Health Effects Are Behind Schedule. (Illus.). 54p. (Orig.). (C). 1994. pap. text 25.00 (*0-7881-1394-1*) DIANE Pub.

— Geothermal Energy: Barriers to the Use of Geothermal Heat Pumps. (Illus.). 80p. (Orig.). (C). 1994. pap. text 25.00 (*0-7881-1308-9*) DIANE Pub.

***Rezendes, Victor S.** Nuclear Nonproliferation: Concerns with DOE[0012]s Efforts to Reduce the Risks Posed by Russia[0012]s Unemployed Weapons Scientists. (Illus.). 105p. (C). 2000. pap. text 25.00 (*0-7567-0014-0*) DIANE Pub.

Rezendes, Victor S., ed. Best Practices: Elements Critical to Successfully Reducing Unneeded RDT&E Infrastructure. (Illus.). 93p. (C). 1998. pap. text 20.00 (*0-7881-7345-6*) DIANE Pub.

— Department of Energy: Proposed Budget in Support of the President's Climate Change Technology Initiative. (Illus.). 58p. (C). 1999. pap. text 20.00 (*0-7881-7790-7*) DIANE Pub.

***Rezendes, Victor S., ed.** Federal Power: Options for Selected Power Marketing Administrations' Role in a Changing Electricity Industry. 164p. (C). 1999. reprint ed. pap. text 25.00 (*0-7881-8263-3*) DIANE Pub.

Rezits, David. Culinary Harmony: Favorite Recipes of the World's Finest Classical Musicians. Deatsman, Gerald, ed. LC 97-91706. (Illus.). 486p. 1997. pap. 24.95 (*0-9658851-0-0*) DIR Pubs.

Rezits, Joseph. Guitar Music in Print. LC 80-84548. 500p. (Orig.). 1983. pap. 95.00 (*0-8497-7802-6*, PM9) Kjos.

Rezmer, Martin G., jt. auth. see Porter, Alan G.

***Rezmerski, John C.** What Do I Know? New & Selected Poems. LC 99-88118. 134p. 2000. 13.95 (*0-930100-95-6*) Holy Cow.

Rezmerski, John C., ed. & intro. see Manfred, Frederick, pseud.

Rezmovic, Evi L. Abortion Clinics: Information on the Effectiveness of the Freedom of Access to Clinic Entrances Act. (Illus.). 108p. (C). 1999. text 25.00 (*0-7881-7740-0*) DIANE Pub.

***Rezmovic, Evi L.** Illegal Aliens: Significant Obstacles to Reducing Unauthorized Alien Employment Exist. (Illus.). 48p. (C). 1999. pap. text 20.00 (*0-7881-8424-5*) DIANE Pub.

Rezmovic, Evi L., et al. Illegal Immigration: Southwest Border Strategy Results Inconclusive; More Evaluation Needed. (Illus.). 104p. (C). 1998. pap. text 25.00 (*0-7881-7451-7*) DIANE Pub.

— INS Management: Follow-Up on Selected Problems. (Illus.). 126p. (C). 1998. pap. text 25.00 (*0-7881-7551-3*) DIANE Pub.

Rezneck, Samuel. Business Depressions & Financial Panics: Collected Essays in American Business & Economic History, 5. LC 68-28644. 201p. 1969. 49.95 (*0-8371-1501-9*, REB/, Greenwood Pr) Greenwood.

Reznek, Lawrie. Evil or Ill? Justifying the Insanity Defence. LC 97-11034. 344p. (C). 1997. 80.00 (*0-415-16699-3*); pap. 24.99 (*0-415-16700-0*) Routledge.

Reznicek, E. K. Hendrick Goltzius. Drawings Rediscovered 1962-1992: Supplement to "Die Zeichnungen von Hendrick Goltzius" Haverkamp-Begemann, Egbert & Allen, Elizabeth, eds. Gordenker, Emilie E., tr. from DUT. LC 93-80160. (Illus.). 92p. 1993. reprint ed. pap. text 75.00 (*0-9613754-1-8*) Mstr Draw Assn.

Reznicek, Rados, ed. Flow Visualization V: Proceedings of the Fifth International Symposium. 1064p. 1990. 198.00 (*0-89116-887-7*) Hemisp Pub.

Reznick, A. Z. Oxidative Stress in Skeletal Muscle. LC 98-6332. (Molecular & Cell Biology Updates Ser.). 1998. 140.00 (*0-8176-5820-3*) Birkhauser.

Reznick, A. Z., et al, eds. Oxidative Stress in Skeletal Muscle. LC 98-6332. (Molecular & Cell Biology Updates Ser.). 500p. 1998. 140.00 (*3-7643-5820-3*) Birkhauser.

Reznick, B. Sum of Even Powers of Real Linear Forms. LC 91-44877. (Memoirs Ser.). 155p. 1992. pap. 29.00 (*0-8218-2523-2*, MEMO/96/463) Am Math.

Reznick, J. Steven. Longitudinal Study on Intelligence in the Second Year. 1997. pap. text 15.00 (*0-226-71041-6*) U Ch Pr.

Reznick, J. Steven, ed. Perspectives on Behavioral Inhibition. LC 89-32463. (John D. & Catherine T. MacArthur Foundation Series on Mental Health & Development). (Illus.). 326p. 1989. 39.95 (*0-226-71040-8*) U Ch Pr.

Reznick, Leibel. The Holy Temple Revisited. LC 89-27465. (Illus.). 256p. 1990. 25.00 (*0-87668-843-1*) Aronson.

Reznick-Schuller, Hildegard M. Compare Ultrastructural Path: Selected Tumors in Man & Animals. 208p. 1989. boxed set 179.00 (*0-8493-5662-8*, RC269) CRC Pr.

Reznicki, Jack. Studio & Commercial Photography. LC 98-8493. (Kodak Pro Workshop Ser.). (Illus.). 160p. 1998. pap. 29.95 (*0-87985-783-8*, PW-2, Kodak) Saunders Photo.

Reznik, Bob, jt. auth. see Garrett, John.

Reznik, Bob, jt. auth. see Hochschuler, Stephen.

Reznik, Gerd K., jt. ed. see Stinson, Sherman F.

Reznik, John W., et al. Racquetball for Men & Women. (Illus.). 1984. pap. 7.40 (*0-87563-246-7*) Stipes.

Reznik, Leon. Fuzzy Controllers: How to Design Them, How They Work. LC 97-222053. 240p. 1997. pap. text 52.95 (*0-7506-3429-4*, Newnes) Buttrwrth-Heinemann.

Reznik-Schuller, Hildegard M. Comparative Respiratory Tract Carcinogenesis, 2 Vols. 272p. 1983. 148.00 (*0-8493-5421-8*, RC280, CRC Reprint); 128.00 (*0-8493-5422-6*, RC280, CRC Reprint) Franklin.

Reznik, Semyon. The Nazification of Russia: Antisemitism in the Post-Soviet Era. Martin, Maureen, ed. LC 96-83319. (Illus.). 276p. 1996. 24.95 (*0-9651350-9-4*); pap. 15.95 (*0-9651360-8-6*) Challenge VA.

Reznikoff, Charles. By the Waters of Manhattan. LC 86-50262. (Masterworks of Modern Jewish Writings). (Illus.). 264p. (C). 1986. reprint ed. pap. 9.95 (*0-910129-55-X*) Wiener Pubs Inc.

— Family Chronicle. LC 87-40102. (Masterworks of Modern Jewish Writings). 320p. 1988. reprint ed. pap. 9.95 (*0-910129-74-6*) Wiener Pubs Inc.

— Poems, 1918-1975: The Complete Poems of Charles Reznikoff. LC 89-17816. 450p. (C). 1995. reprint ed. pap. 17.50 (*0-87685-790-X*) Black Sparrow.

— Testimony: The United States, 1885-1915, Vol. 1. Cooney, Seamus, ed. LC 78-7618. 280p. 1978. 25.00 (*0-87685-322-X*) Black Sparrow.

— Testimony: The United States, 1885-1915, Vol. 2. Cooney, Seamus, ed. LC 78-7618. 250p. 1979. 25.00 (*0-87685-333-5*) Black Sparrow.

— Testimony: The United States, 1885-1915, Vol. 2. Cooney, Seamus, ed. LC 78-7618. Vol. 2. 250p. 1979. pap. 13.00 (*0-87685-332-7*) Black Sparrow.

— Testimony, the United States 1885-1890, Recitative. LC 65-15675. 1965. 10.00 (*0-685-79043-6*); 5.00 (*0-685-79044-4*) SPD-Small Pr Dist.

Reznikoff, Charles, tr. see Benjamin, Israel B.

Reznikoff, Natalie. Ognennaia Pamiat' Vospominaniia o Aleksee Remizove. (Modern Russian Literature & Culture, Studies & Texts: Vol. 4). (RUS., Illus.). 147p. 1980. pap. 8.50 (*0-933884-14-1*) Berkeley Slavic.

Reznikoff, S. C. Interior Graphic & Design Standards. (Illus.). 624p. 1986. 95.00 (*0-8230-7298-3*, Whitney Lib) Watsn-Guptill.

— Specifications for Commercial Interiors. rev. ed. (Illus.). 352p. 1989. 49.95 (*0-8230-4893-4*, Whitney Lib) Watsn-Guptill.

Reznikoff, William S., jt. ed. see Miller, Jeffrey H.

Reznikov, A. & Schappacher, N. Regulators in Analysis, Geometry & Number Theory. LC 99-44333. (Progress in Mathematics Ser.: Vol. 171). 400p. 1999. 69.95 (*0-8176-4115-7*, Pub. by Birkhauser) Spr-Verlag.

***Reznikov, Alexander & Schappacher, Norbert.** Regulators in Analysis, Geometry & Number Theory. LC 99-44333. (Progress in Mathematics Ser.). 1999. write for info. (*3-7643-4115-7*) Birkhauser.

Reznikov, K. Y. Cell Proliferation & Cytogenesis in the Mouse Hippocampus. Beck, F. et al, eds. (Advances in Anatomy, Embryology & Cell Biology Ser.: Vol. 122). (Illus.). 96p. 1991. pap. 72.00 (*0-387-53689-2*) Spr-Verlag.

Reznikov, L. M., et al, eds. Fuzzy Systems Design: Social & Engineering Applications. LC 98-26737. (Studies in Fuzziness & Soft Computing: Vol. 17). (Illus.). xvi, 334p. 1998. 90.00 (*3-7908-1118-1*) Spr-Verlag.

Reznikov, L. M., jt. auth. see Korenev, Boris G.

Rezulli, Joseph S. & Reis, Sally M. The Schoolwide Enrichment Model: A How-To Guide for Educational Excellence. 2nd rev. ed. 424p. 1997. pap. text 42.95 (*0-936386-70-3*) Creative Learning.

Rezun, Miron. Europe & War in the Balkans: Toward a New Yugoslav Identity. LC 95-4289. 256p. 1995. 62.95 (*0-275-95238-X*, Praeger Pubs) Greenwood.

***Rezun, Miron.** Europe's Nightmare: The Struggle for Kosovo. LC 00-32378. 2001. write for info. (*0-275-97072-8*, Praeger Pubs) Greenwood.

Rezun, Miron. Intrigue & War in Southwest Asia: The Struggle for Supremacy from Central Asia to Iraq. LC 91-16688. 168p. 1991. 52.95 (*0-275-94105-1*, C4105, Praeger Pubs) Greenwood.

— Saddam Hussein's Gulf Wars: Ambivalent Stakes in the Middle East. LC 92-4197. 164p. 1992. 47.95 (*0-275-94324-0*, C4324, Praeger Pubs) Greenwood.

— Science, Technology, & Ecopolitics in the U. S. S. R. LC 95-22010. 240p. 1996. 59.95 (*0-275-95383-1*, Praeger Pubs) Greenwood.

Rezun, Miron, ed. The Impact of Nationalism in the U. S. S. R. The Collapse of an Empire? LC 92-4219. 208p. 1992. 55.00 (*0-275-94320-8*, C4320, Praeger Pubs) Greenwood.

Rezvan, Jerena B., ed. see Laskey, Carolyn T.

Rezvan, Jerina B., ed. see Clark, Carolyn C.

Rezvani. Enigma. Donougher, Christine, tr. from FRE. (Europe 1998 Ser.). 210p. 1998. pap. 13.99 (*1-873982-28-3*, Pub. by Dedalus) Subterranean Co.

Rezvani, Kate A. Story Spinner: The Easy Way to Write a Story Outline. Lane, Jay, ed. LC 94-96237. (Illus.). 64p. 1995. per. 19.95 (*0-9641318-4-6*) Lrning Circle.

RGA Publishing Group Staff. Baby's ABCs. LC 90-193562. (Illus.). 24p. (J). (ps). 1997. 4.99 (*0-689-81271-X*) S&S Childrens.

— Baby's Clothes. (Illus.). 24p. (J). (ps up). 1997. 4.99 (*0-689-81264-7*) S&S Childrens.

— Baby's Friends. (Illus.). 24p. (J). (ps up). 1997. 4.99 (*0-689-81268-X*) S&S Childrens.

— Baby's Home. (Illus.). 12p. (J). (ps up). 1997. 4.99 (*0-689-81269-8*) S&S Childrens.

— Daddy & Me. (Illus.). 12p. (J). (ps up). 1997. 4.99 (*0-689-81266-3*) S&S Childrens.

— Grandma & Me. (Illus.). 12p. (J). (ps). 1998. 4.99 (*0-689-81270-1*) S&S Childrens.

— Mommy & Me. (Illus.). 12p. (J). (ps up). 1997. 4.99 (*0-689-81267-1*) S&S Childrens.

RGA Publishing Staff. Baby Colors. (Super Chubby Board Bks.). (Illus.). 12p. (J). (ps-k). 1996. 4.99 (*0-689-81239-6*) S&S Childrens.

Rgya-mTsho, Nag-dBan B. A History of Tibet by the Fifth Dalai Lama of Tibet. Ahmad, Zahiruddin, tr. from TIB. LC 94-65581. (Oriental Ser.: Vol. VII). 328p. 1995. 45.00 (*0-933070-32-2*) Ind U Res Inst.

RH Value Publishing Staff. The Bible on Faith, Hope & Love. 112p. 1997. 4.99 (*0-517-18387-0*) Random Hse Value.

— Harvest of Hope. 1997. 18.00 (*0-517-20023-6*) Random Hse Value.

— Random House Crossword Puzzle Dictionary. LC 98-15217. 1094p. 1996. 12.99 (*0-517-15008-5*) Random Hse Value.

— Webster's Encyclopedia Unabridged Dictionary. rev. deluxe ed. (Illus.). 2272p. 1996. 20.00 (*0-517-15026-3*) Random Hse Value.

Rha, Chokyun, ed. Theory, Determination & Control of Physical Properties of Food Materials. LC 74-76481. (Food Material Science Ser: No. 1). xi, 315p. 1975. text 220.00 (*90-277-0468-6*) Kluwer Academic.

***Rhaishanen, Heikki.** Reading the Bible in the Global Village: Helsinki. LC 00-37534. 2000. pap. write for info. (*0-88414-019-9*) Soc Biblical Lit.

Rham, G. De, see De Rham, G.

Rhamot, Anna. Language Development Through Content: America, after Independence. 112p. 1987. pap. text 13.40 (*0-201-12930-2*) Addison-Wesley.

Rhea. Herriot Country, Vol. 1. 1999. text 27.95 (*0-312-18509-X*) St Martin.

Rhea, jt. ed. see Dean, Jr.

Rhea, A., ed. see Riley, R.

Rhea, Alice. Good Cats, Bad Habits: The Complete A-to-Z Guide for When Your Cat Misbehaves. LC 95-32200. (Illus.). 256p. 1995. pap. 12.00 (*0-684-81113-8*, Fireside) S&S Trade Pap.

Rhea, Buford, ed. The Future of the Sociological Classics. 224p. (C). 1982. text 21.95 (*0-04-301136-5*) Routledge.

Rhea, D. L. How the Colt Navy .36 Revolver Was Gunsmithed & Fired in the Field During the Civil War: Techniques Learned from Civil War Veterans & Old-Time Gunsmiths. deluxe limited ed. 76p. 1985. 20.00 (*0-9627171-1-8*) Hera Pub.

Rhea, Dan. The Marvelous Garments of Brother Diego: And Other Short Stories. deluxe limited unabridged ed. 52p. 1994. pap. 15.00 (*0-9627171-2-6*) Hera Pub.

Rhea, Gordon C. Battle of the Wilderness, May 5-6, 1864. LC 93-42110. (Illus.). 536p. 1994. 34.95 (*0-8071-1873-7*) La State U Pr.

— Battles for Spotsyvania Court House & the Road to Yellow Tavern. LC 96-49575. (Illus.). 512p. 1997. 34.95 (*0-8071-2136-3*) La State U Pr.

***Rhea, Gordon C.** To the North Anna River: Grant & Lee, May 13-25, 1864. LC 99-50637. (Illus.). 475p. 2000. 34.95 (*0-8071-2535-0*) La State U Pr.

Rhea, Gordon C. Wilderness & Spotsylvania. (Civil War Ser.). (Illus.). 56p. 1995. pap. 4.95 (*0-915992-88-4*) Eastern National.

Rhea, Homer G. A New Creation. LC 83-62003. 183p. (Orig.). 1997. reprint ed. pap. 9.99 (*0-87148-630-X*) Pathway Pr.

Rhea, Homer G., compiled by. The Holy Spirit in Action: The Person & Work of the Holy Spirit. 189p. 1996. pap. 10.99 (*0-87148-419-6*) Pathway Pr.

Rhea, Homer G., ed. Sermon Resource Manual, Vol. 4. Vol. 4. (Illus.). 1992. 13.99 (*0-87148-960-0*) Pathway Pr.

Rhea, J. Michelle. From the Kitchen Table & Beyond: (If-I-Can-Do-It-You-Can-Do-It) Guide to Creating a Home Based Medical Transcription Business. Hughes, Peggy, ed. (Illus.). 100p. 1999. pap. 14.95 (*0-9670859-0-X*, Souled Out Bks) Souled Out.

Rhea, James T. & Vansonnenberg, Eric. Emergency Radiology. 256p. 1988. 72.95 (*0-316-74200-7*, Little Brwn Med Div) Lppncott W & W.

Rhea, Joseph T. Race Pride & the American Identity. LC 97-22046. 224p. 1997. 26.00 (*0-674-56681-5*) HUP.

Rhea, Kathlyn. Mind Sense: Fine Tuning Your Intellect & Intuition--A Practical Workbook. 214p. 1988. pap. 12.95 (*0-89087-529-4*) Celestial Arts.

R

An Asterisk (*) at the beginning of an entry indicates that the title is appearing for the first time.

Rhea, Nicholas. Constable about the Parish. large type ed. (Magna Large Print Ser.). 313p. 1997. 27.99 (*0-7505-1149-4*, Pub. by Mgna Lrg Print) Ulverscroft.

***Rhea, Nicholas.** Constable at the Gate. large type ed. 352p. 1998. 35.40 (*0-7505-1273-3*) Ulverscroft.

Rhea, Nicholas. Constable on Call. large type ed. (Magna Large Print Ser.). 1994. 26.95 (*0-7505-0693-8*, Pub. by Mgna Lrg Print) Ulverscroft.

***Rhea, Nicholas.** Constable over the Stile. large type ed. 352p. 1999. 31.99 (*0-7505-1363-2*, Pub. by Mgna Lrg Print) Ulverscroft.

— Constable under the Gooseberry Bush. large type ed. 352p. 2000. write for info. (*0-7505-1501-5*, Pub. by Mgna Lrg Print) Ulverscroft.

Rhea, Nicholas. Constable vs. Greengrass. large type ed. (Magna Large Print Ser.). 297p. 1996. 27.99 (*0-7505-1044-7*, Pub. by Mgna Lrg Print) Ulverscroft.

— Major Incident. large type ed. (Dales Large Print Ser.). 288p. 1998. pap. 19.99 (*1-85389-785-X*, Dales) Ulverscroft.

— Murder after the Holiday. large type ed. (Dales Large Print Ser.). 272p. 1998. pap. 19.99 (*1-85389-784-1*, Dales) Ulverscroft.

— Murder Beneath the Trees. large type ed. (Dales Large Print Ser.). 297p. 1996. pap. 18.99 (*1-85389-624-1*, Dales) Ulverscroft.

— Murder by the Lake. large type ed. (Dales Large Print Ser.). 304p. 1996. pap. 18.99 (*1-85389-622-5*, Dales) Ulverscroft.

— Omens of Death. large type ed. (Magna Large Print Ser.). 416p. 1998. 29.99 (*0-7505-1219-9*, Pub. by Mgna Lrg Print) Ulverscroft.

— Superstitious Death. 224p. 1998. 27.00 (*0-09-478620-8*, Pub. by Constable & Co) Trafalgar.

— Suspect. large type ed. (Dales Large Print Ser.). 340p. 1997. pap. 18.99 (*1-85389-722-1*) Ulverscroft.

— Target Criminal. large type ed. (Dales Large Print Ser.). 306p. 1997. pap. 18.99 (*1-85389-783-3*, Dales) Ulverscroft.

Rhea, Randall W. HF Filter Design & Computer Simulation. (Illus.). 448p. 1994. 59.00 (*1-884932-25-8*) Noble Pubng.

— Oscillator Design & Computer Simulation. 2nd ed. (Illus.). 320p. 1996. 65.00 (*0-07-052415-7*) McGraw.

— Oscillator Design & Computer Simulation. 2nd ed. (Illus.). 320p. 1995. 64.00 (*1-884932-30-4*) Noble Pubng.

Rhea, Randall W., ed. see Smith, Phillip H. & Parker, Glenn A.

Rhea, Robert A. The Dow Theory. LC 93-72199. 252p. (C). 1993. reprint ed. pap. 17.00 (*0-87034-110-3*) Fraser Pub Co.

Rhea, Robert A., et al. Harnessing AutoCAD. 1472p. 1992. pap. 41.95 (*0-8273-4685-9*) Delmar.

Rhea, Robert A., jt. auth. see Parisher, Roy A.

Rhea, Russell J. Provisional Patents: The Laymans Guide to Invention Security & Product Surety. (Illus.). 150p. (Orig.). 1996. pap. 29.95 (*0-9654309-0-1*) Surety Pr.

***Rhead, Louis.** Speckled Brook Trout. (Illus.). 200p. 2000. pap. 16.95 (*1-56833-157-6*) Madison Bks UPA.

Rheams, Samson. Tests of Bapak. 1997. pap. 8.00 (*1-890549-01-0*) Alpha Pub Grp.

Rheatown United Methodist Women Staff. Rheatown, Tennessee. (Illus.). 113p. 1997. pap. 9.95 (*1-57072-069-X*) Overmountain Pr.

Rheaume, Manon. Manon: Alone in Front of the Net. 1993. pap. write for info. (*0-00-638029-8*) HarpC.

Rheaume, Manon & Gilbert, Chantal. Manon: Alone in Front of the Net. Daley, Mark, tr. LC 95-5213. (Illus.). ix, 179p. 1998. mass mkt. 5.50 (*0-00-638031-X*) HarpC.

Rhee, C. H. van, jt. auth. see Jolowicz, J. A.

***Rhee, Chi S.** Letters to Hyun A: Bridging Two Cultures. 1999. pap. 8.95 (*1-57087-480-8*) Prof Pr NC.

— Love of Choon Hyang. 2000. pap. 7.95 (*1-57087-518-9*) Prof Pr NC.

Rhee, Douglas J. Wills Eye Manual: Office & Emergency Room Diagnosis & Treatment of Eye Disease. 3rd ed. LC 98-31758. 1999. write for info. (*0-7817-1602-0*) Lppncott W & W.

Rhee, Douglas J., et al. The Wills Eye Drug Guide: Diagnostic & Therapeutic Medications. LC 98-9871. 128p. 1998. pap. text. write for info. (*0-7817-1705-1*) Lppncott W & W.

Rhee, Hyun-Ku, et al. First-Order Partial Differential Equations: Theory & Application of Single Equations. (Illus.). 480p. 1986. text 56.33 (*0-685-11828-2*) P-H.

Rhee, Jhoon. Chon-Ji of Tae Kwon Do Hyung. Alvarez, Roberto, tr. LC 74-120124. (Korean Arts Ser.). (ENG & SPA., Illus.). 1970. pap. text 13.95 (*0-89750-000-8*, 102) Ohara Pubns.

— Chung-Gun & Toi Gye of Tae Kwon Do Hyung. LC 76-163381. (Series 108). (Illus.). 1971. pap. text 14.95 (*0-89750-003-2*) Ohara Pubns.

— Hwa-Rang & Chung-Mu of Tae Kwon Do Hyung. LC 77-163382. (Korean Arts Ser.). (Illus.). 1971. pap. text 15.95 (*0-89750-004-0*, 109) Ohara Pubns.

— Tan-Gun & To-San of Tae Kwon Do Hyung. LC 71-150320. (Korean Arts Ser.). (Illus.). 1971. pap. text 16.95 (*0-89750-001-6*, 106) Ohara Pubns.

— Won-Hyo & Yul-Kok of Tae Kwon Do Hyung. LC 70-157046. (Korean Arts Ser.). (Illus.). 1971. pap. text 14.95 (*0-89750-002-4*, 107) Ohara Pubns.

Rhee, K. C., jt. ed. see Koseoglu, S. Sefa.

Rhee, M. J. The Doomed Empire: Japan in Colonial Korea. LC 97-73530. (Illus.). 192p. 1997. text 73.95 (*1-85972-469-8*, Pub. by Ashgate Pub) Ashgate Pub Co.

Rhee, Man Y. CDMA Cellular Mobile Communications. LC 97-26391. 544p. (C). 1997. 88.00 (*0-13-598418-1*) P-H.

— Cryptography & Secure Communications. 400p. 1993. 55.00 (*0-07-112502-7*) McGraw.

Rhee, Nami. Magic Spring. (Whitebird Bks.). (Illus.). 32p. (J). (ps-3). 1993. lib. bdg. 15.95 (*0-399-22420-3*, G P Putnam) Peng Put Young Read.

Rhee, Nami. Woodcutter & Tiger Brother. LC 98-87686. 32p. (J). (ps-1). 1999. 14.95 (*1-56591-093-1*) Hollym Intl.

Rhee, Nari, et al, eds. Guide to Uncovering the Right on Campus. 2nd ed. (Illus.). 128p. 1997. pap. 8.00 (*0-945210-07-8*) Public Search.

Rhee, Robin. Korea Through Myths & Legends. LC 96-80108. (Illus.). 182p. 1997. lib. bdg. 24.50 (*1-56591-109-1*) Hollym Intl.

Rhee, S. C. & Chang, R. P. Pacific Basin Capital Markets Research. 592p. 1990. 127.50 (*0-444-88459-9*) Elsevier.

Rhee, S. G. & Chang, R. P. Pacific-Basin Capital Markets Research, Vol. III. 506p. 1992. 127.50 (*0-444-89288-5*, North Holland) Elsevier.

Rhee, S. K., ed. see International Conference on Wear of Materials Staf.

Rhee, Song N., jt. ed. see Aikens, C. Melvin.

***Rhee, Syngman & Kim, Han-Kyo.** The Spirit of Independence: A Primer for Korean Modernization & Democratic Reform. LC 00-33779. (Illus.). 2001. write for info. (*0-8248-2349-4*) UH Pr.

Rhee, Wolfgang, tr. see Sylvanus, Erwin.

Rhee, Yung W., et al. Korea's Competitive Edge: Managing Entry into World Markets. LC 84-47956. 173p. reprint ed. pap. 53.70 (*0-7837-4249-5*, 204393900012) Bks Demand.

Rheede, R. Hortus Malabaricus, Set, Vols. 1-12. (C). 1988. 4000.00 (*0-7855-3308-7*) St Mut.

Rheede-Van Oudtshoorn, Karen Van, see Van Rheede-Van Oudtshoorn, Karen.

***Rheeders, Kate.** The Qabalah: A Beginner's Guide. (Headway Guides for Beginners Ser.). (Illus.). 96p. 2000. pap. 11.95 (*0-340-74262-3*, Pub. by Headway) Trafalgar.

Rheeders, Kate. The Qabalah: A Beginner's Guide. (Beginners Ser.). (Illus.). 96p. 1996. pap. 11.95 (*0-340-67339-7*, Pub. by Hodder & Stought Ltd) Trafalgar.

— Some Traditional African Beliefs: A Beginner's Guide. (Illus.). 96p. 1997. pap. 11.95 (*0-340-70471-3*, Pub. by Headway) Trafalgar.

Rheenen, Gailyn Van, see Van Rheenen, Gailyn.

Rhees, David J., jt. auth. see Heitmann, John A.

Rhees, R. Ward, jt. auth. see Van De Graaff, Kent.

***Rhees, Rush.** Discussions of Simone Weil. LC 99-45377. (C). 2000. pap. text 18.95 (*0-7914-4428-7*) State U NY Pr.

Rhees, Rush. Discussions of Wittgenstein. (Wittgenstein Studies). 169p. 1996. pap. 16.00 (*1-85506-492-8*) Bks Intl VA.

***Rhees, Rush.** Moral Questions by Rush Rhees. LC 99-17493. 1999. text 65.00 (*0-312-22355-2*) St Martin.

Rhees, Rush. Rush Rhees on Religion & Philosophy. Phillips, D. Z., ed. 411p. (C). 1997. text 69.95 (*0-521-56410-7*) Cambridge U Pr.

Rhees, Rush, ed. Ludwig Wittgenstein: Personal Recollections. LC 79-28474. 246p. 1981. 53.50 (*0-8476-6253-5*) Rowman.

***Rhees, Rush, et al, eds.** Discussions of Simone Weil. LC 99-45377. 200p. (C). 2000. text. write for info. (*0-7914-4427-9*) State U NY Pr.

Rhees, Rush, ed. see Wittgenstein, Ludwig Josef Johann.

Rhees, William J. An Account of the Smithsonian Institution: Its Founder, Building, Operations, Etc. Cohen, I. Bernard, ed. LC 79-8404. (Three Centuries of Science in America Ser.). (Illus.). 1980. reprint ed. lib. bdg. 15.95 (*0-405-12582-8*) Ayer.

— The Smithsonian Institution: Documents Relative to Its History, 2 Vols. Cohen, I. Bernard, ed. LC 79-8405. (Three Centuries of Science in America Ser.). (Illus.). 1980. lib. bdg. 86.00 (*0-686-65997-X*) Ayer.

— The Smithsonian Institution: Documents Relative to Its History, 2 vols., Set. Cohen, I. Bernard, ed. LC 79-8405. (Three Centuries of Science in America Ser.). (Illus.). 1980. lib. bdg. 189.95 (*0-405-12583-6*) Ayer.

— The Smithsonian Institution: Documents Relative to Its History, 2 vols., Vol. 1. Cohen, I. Bernard, ed. LC 79-8405. (Three Centuries of Science in America Ser.). (Illus.). 1980. 94.95 (*0-405-12597-6*) Ayer.

— The Smithsonian Institution: Documents Relative to Its History, 2 vols., Vol. 2. Cohen, I. Bernard, ed. LC 79-8405. (Three Centuries of Science in America Ser.). (Illus.). 1980. lib. bdg. 94.95 (*0-405-12599-2*) Ayer.

— William J. Rhees on James Smithson: An Original Anthology, 2 vols. Cohen, I. Bernard, ed. LC 79-7996. (Three Centuries of Science in America Ser.). (Illus.). 1980. lib. bdg. 25.95 (*0-405-12581-X*) Ayer.

Rhees, William J., jt. auth. see Gonzalez, Fernando.

Rheidt, Klaus. Altertumer von Pergamon, Die Stadtgrabung, Band XV-2 Teil 2: Die Byzantinische Wohnstadt. (GER., Illus.). xviii, 253p. (C). 1991. lib. bdg. 229.25 (*3-11-012621-4*) De Gruyter.

Rheiffen, H. V. Die Dame zu Pferde. (Illus.). xii, 324p. 1907. write for info. (*3-487-08330-2*) G Olms Pubs.

Rheil, Mary, jt. ed. see Suchoff, David.

Rheims, Bettina. Bettina Rheims. 1999. pap. 19.95 (*3-570-19202-4*) Gruner & Jahr AG &.

— Bettina Rheims. (JPN., Illus.). 120p. 1998. pap. 29.95 (*3-929078-60-0*, Kehayoff) te Neues.

— Bettina Rheims: Animal. (Illus.). 120p. 1998. 45.00 (*3-929078-19-8*) te Neues.

***Rheims, Bettina.** Chambre Close. (Illus.). 144p. 1999. 19.95 (*3-929078-86-4*, Kehayoff) te Neues.

Rheims, Bettina & Harlow, Kim. Kim. (Illus.). 64p. 1998. 19.95 (*3-929078-21-X*, Kehayoff) te Neues.

Rheims, Bettina, jt. auth. see Bramly, Serge.

Rheims, Maurice. L' Art ou le Style Jules Verne, 1900. (FRE., Illus.). 424p. 1965. lib. bdg. 125.00 (*0-8288-3997-2*) Fr & Eur.

— Buffet's Complete Engravings, 1948-1980. (Illus.). 244p. 1983. 250.00 (*1-55660-046-1*) A Wofsy Fine Arts.

— Le Saint Office. (FRE.). 1985. pap. 17.95 (*0-7859-4230-0*) Fr & Eur.

Rhein, Betsy & Drummond, Sandy. Smart Snacks: Groups Size Snacks for Kids of All Ages. 121p. (Orig.). 1995. pap. 9.95 (*0-9647228-0-1*) TBM Pubns.

Rhein, Bob, jt. auth. see Baer-Brown, Leslie.

Rhein, Donna E. The Handprinted Books of Leonard & Virginia Woolf at the Hogarth Press, 1917-1932. LC 85-14144. (Studies in Modern Literature: No. 52). 182p. reprint ed. pap. 56.50 (*0-8357-1694-5*, 207051900097) Bks Demand.

Rhein, Elaine, ed. see Inge, Lori R.

***Rhein, Elaine M.** Do You Noah Your ABC's? (Illus.). 28p. (J). (ps-3). 1999. pap. 8.98 (*0-9676333-0-3*) Jubilation Creat.

Rhein, Ernestus, jt. ed. see Mann, Friedhelm.

Rhein, John Von, see Porter, Andrew & Von Rhein, John, eds.

Rhein, Linda D. & Rieger, Martin M., eds. Surfactants in Cosmetics. 2nd ed. LC 97-57. (Surfactant Science Ser.). (Illus.). 656p. 1997. text 225.00 (*0-8247-9805-8*) Dekker.

Rhein, Michael J., jt. auth. see Crompton, Samuel Willard.

Rhein, Phillip H. Albert Camus. rev. ed. (World Authors Ser.: No. 69). 152p. 1989. 32.00 (*0-8057-8253-2*, Twyne) Mac Lib Ref.

— The Verbal & Visual Art of Alfred Kubin. (Studies in Austrian Literature, Culture, & Thought). (Illus.). 188p. 1989. 24.95 (*0-929497-01-5*) Ariadne CA.

Rhein, Robert. German Grammar Flipper, No. 2. (GER.). 49p. (YA). (gr. 8 up). 1992. 6.95 (*1-878383-23-X*) C Lee Pubns.

Rhein, T. Black Heart Shining. (Illus.). 60p. 1998. pap. 12.95 (*0-9663037-0-9*) Luna Daeolin.

Rheinberger, Hans-Jorg. Toward a History of Epistemic Things: Synthesizing Proteins in the Test Tube. LC 96-47145. (Writing Science Ser.). 1997. write for info. (*0-8047-2785-6*); pap. 19.95 (*0-8047-2786-4*) Stanford U Pr.

Rheinboldt, W. C., jt. auth. see Ortega, James M.

Rheinboldt, Werner C. Methods for Solving Systems of Nonlinear Equations. 2nd rev. ed. LC 98-27321. (CBMS-NSF Regional Conference Series in Applied Mathematics: No. CB70). (Illus.). ix, 148p. 1998. pap. 34.00 (*0-89871-415-X*, BKCB0070) Soc Indus-Appl Math.

— Numerical Analysis of Parameterized Nonlinear Equations. LC 84-21974. (Lecture Notes in the Mathematical Sciences Ser.). 299p. 1986. pap. 150.00 (*0-471-88814-1*) Wiley.

Rheinboldt, Werner C., jt. auth. see Rabier, Patrick J.

Rheinfelder, Hans. Kultsprache und Profansprache in Den Romanischen Landern. (Bibliotheca Dell' "Archivum Romanicum", Ser.: No. 2-18). v, 481p. 1982. reprint ed. write for info. (*3-487-07236-X*) G Olms Pubs.

Rheingold, Andy & Sonneborn, Scott. MTV's Beavis & Butt-Head Chicken Soup for the Butt: A Guide to Finding your Inner Butt. (Bea). 96p. 1998. pap. 14.00 (*0-671-02598-8*, MTV Bks) PB.

Rheingold, Harriet L. The Psychologist's Guide to an Academic Career. LC 94-532. 203p. 1994. pap. text 19.95 (*1-55798-227-9*) Am Psychol.

Rheingold, Howard. Livin' on the Net, Vol. 1. 1996. 9.99 (*0-941188-55-8*) M Wiese.

— Livin' on the Net, Vol. 2. 1996. 9.95 (*0-941188-56-6*) M Wiese.

— They Have a Word for It: A Lighthearted Lexicon of Untranslatable Words & Phrases. 224p. 2000. reprint ed. pap. 16.95 (*1-889330-46-9*, Pub. by Sarabande Bks) Consort Bk Sales.

— Tools for Thought: The History & Future of Mind-Expanding Technology. LC 99-87051. (Illus.). 336p. 2000. pap. 17.95 (*0-262-68115-3*) MIT Pr.

— The Virtual Community: Homesteading on the Electronic Frontier. 360p. (C). 2000. reprint ed. pap. 18.95 (*0-262-68121-8*) MIT Pr.

Rheingold, Howard. Virtual Reality: The Revolutionary Technology of Computer-Generated Artificial Worlds - & How It Promises to Transform Society. 416p. 1992. pap. 12.00 (*0-671-77897-8*, Touchstone) S&S Trade Pap.

Rheingold, Howard, jt. auth. see Laberge, Stephen.

Rheingold, Hugh, ed. see Rheingold, Todd.

Rheingold, Paul D. New York Law of Product Liability. 250p. 1990. ring bd. 65.00 (*0-929179-49-8*) Juris Pubng.

Rheingold, Todd. Dispelling the Myths: An Analysis of American Attitudes & Prejudices. LC 93-90296. 174p. 1993. 22.95 (*0-912526-75-0*) Believe Dream.

— Dispelling the Myths: An Analysis of American Attitudes & Prejudices. Rheingold, Hugh, ed. LC 93-90296. (Illus.). 178p. 1993. 22.95 (*0-9662197-0-8*) Believe Dream.

Rheingrover, Jean S. Veronica's First Year. (Illus.). 24p. (J). (ps-4). 1996. lib. bdg. 13.95 (*0-8075-8474-6*) A Whitman.

Rheinhardt, Emil A. The Life of Eleanora Duse. LC 73-82841. 292p. 1972. 24.95 (*0-405-08883-3*, Pub. by Blom Pubns) Ayer.

Rheinhardt, Harrison-Simms. No China Doll: Enemy-in-Waiting. (Illus.). 308p. (Orig.). 1990. 25.00 (*0-9626181-1-X*); lib. bdg. 14.95 (*0-9626181-0-1*) Simms Pub.

Rheinstein, Max. Marriage Stability, Divorce, & the Law. LC 79-169582. 496p. 1995. lib. bdg. 42.00 (*0-226-71773-9*) U Ch Pr.

Rheinstrom, Carroll. Psyching the Ads: The Case Book of Advertising; the Methods & Results of 180 Advertisements. LC 75-39271. (Getting & Spending:The Consumer's Dilemma Ser.). (Illus.). 1976. reprint ed. 31.95 (*0-405-08043-3*) Ayer.

Rheker, Uwe. Integration Through Games & Sports. 1998. pap. text. write for info. (*3-89124-467-3*) Meyer & Meyer.

***Rheker, Uwe.** Integration Through Games & Sports. 2000. pap. 17.95 (*1-84126-012-6*) Meyer & Meyer.

Rhema Ministerial Association International Staff, ed. Missionary Strategies. 120p. 1995. pap. 14.95 (*0-89276-957-2*) Faith Lib Pubns.

— Pioneering Strategies. 72p. 1994. pap. 9.95 (*0-89276-956-4*) Faith Lib Pubns.

Rhemann, Maureen. Strategic Marketing in Telecommunications: How to Win Customers, Eliminate Churn & Increase Profits in the Telecom Marketplace. LC 99-87521. 280p. 2000. pap. 39.95 (*1-890154-17-2*) Aegis Pub Grp.

Rhemick, John R. A New People of God: A Study in Salvationism. 261p. (C). 1993. write for info. (*1-883719-00-3*) Salvat Army Supp.

Rhemtulla, Akbar, jt. auth. see Mura, Roberta.

Rhenanus, Beatus. Briefwechsel. (GER.). xxiv, 700p. 1966. reprint ed. write for info. (*0-318-70506-0*) G Olms Pubs.

— Briefwechsel. Horawitz, A. & Hartfelder, K., eds. xxiv, 700p. 1966. reprint ed. write for info. (*0-318-71276-8*) G Olms Pubs.

***Rhenisch, Harold.** The Blue Mouth of Morning. LC 99-200920. 104p. 1998. pap. 14.95 (*0-88982-173-9*, Pub. by Oolichan Bks) Genl Dist Srvs.

— Tom Thomson's Shack. 256p. 2000. pap. 16.00 (*0-921586-75-2*, Pub. by New Star Bks) Genl Dist Srvs.

Rhenman, Eric. Organization Theory for Long-Range Planning. LC 72-5724. 222p. reprint ed. pap. 68.90 (*0-8357-6246-7*, 203423600089) Bks Demand.

Rhett, Blanche S. Two Hundred Years of Charleston Cooking. 3rd ed. Gay, Lettie, ed. LC 70-120919. 311p. 1982. reprint ed. pap. 14.95 (*0-87249-348-2*) U of SC Pr.

Rhett, Kathryn. Near Breathing: A Memoir of a Difficult Birth. LC 96-51228. (Emerging Writers in Creative Nonfiction Ser.). 215p. 1997. 24.95 (*0-8207-0277-3*); pap. text 16.95 (*0-8207-0278-1*) Duquesne.

— Survival Stories: Memoirs of Crisis. 416p. 1998. pap. 14.00 (*0-385-48450-X*) Doubleday.

Rhett, Robert, jt. auth. see Steele, John.

Rhetts, Paul, jt. auth. see Awalt, Barbe.

Rhetts, Paul, ed. see Steele, Thomas J.

Rheuban, Joyce. Harry Langdon: The Comedian as Metteur-en-Scene. LC 81-65868. (Illus.). 248p. 1983. 35.00 (*0-8386-3111-8*) Fairleigh Dickinson.

***Rheubottom, David.** Age, Marriage, & Politics in Fifteenth-century Ragusa. LC 99-50136. 360p. 2000. 72.00 (*0-19-823412-0*) OUP.

Rhiannon, Thea, ed. see Chaney, Casey.

Rhiannon, Thea, ed. see Parkel, Paula.

Rhie, Gene S. & Jones, B. J. Mini Dictionary of English - Korean, Korean - English: Romanized. (ENG & KOR.). 780p. 1995. pap. 16.50 (*1-56591-011-7*) Hollym Intl.

— Standard English-Korean Dictionary for Foreigners. LC 81-84204. (ENG & KOR., Illus.). 386p. 1998. 14.95 (*0-930878-21-3*) Hollym Intl.

— Standard Korean-English Dictionary for Foreigners: Romanized. LC 85-80494. 394p. 1988. 14.95 (*0-930878-49-3*) Hollym Intl.

Rhie, Gene S., jt. auth. see Jones, B. J.

Rhie, Gene S., jt. ed. see Jones, B. J.

Rhie, Marylin M. Early Buddhist Art of China & Central Asia. LC 98-31898. (Handbuch der Orientalistik Ser.). 1998. 259.00 (*90-04-11201-4*) Brill Academic Pubs.

Rhie, Marylin M. & Thurman, Robert A. Wisdom & Compassion: The Sacred Art of Tibet. expanded ed. LC 95-39484. (Illus.). 488p. 1996. 75.00 (*0-8109-3985-1*, Pub. by Abrams) Time Warner.

— Worlds of Transformation: Tibetan Art of Wisdom & Compassion. (Illus.). 480p. 1999. 95.00 (*0-8109-6387-6*, Pub. by Abrams) Time Warner.

***Rhie, Marylin M. & Thurman, Robert A. F.** Wisdom & Compassion: The Sacred Art of Tibet. expanded ed. (Illus.). 488p. 2000. 34.98 (*0-8109-8204-8*, Pub. by Abrams) Time Warner.

Rhie, Schi-Zhin. Soon-Hee in America. LC 77-81780. (Illus.). 36p. (J). (gr. k-3). 1977. 8.50 (*0-930878-00-0*) Hollym Intl.

Rhiel, Mary. The Discursive Construction of Authorial Subjectivity in West Re-Viewing Kleist: Kleist German Films. LC 90-22998. (Studies in Modern German Literature: Vol. 44). 163p. (C). 1991. text 37.95 (*0-8204-1526-X*) P Lang Pubng.

Rhijn, Patricia Van, see Van Rhijn, Patricia.

Rhim, Johng S. & Dritschilo, Anatoly, eds. Neoplastic Transformation in Human Cell Culture: Mechanisms of Carcinogenesis. LC 91-35328. (Experimental Biology & Medicine Ser.: Vol. 25). (Illus.). 408p. 1991. 115.00 (*0-89603-227-2*) Humana.

Rhind, David. Framework for the World. LC 97-218852. 310p. 1997. 90.00 (*0-470-24440-2*) Wiley.

Rhind, David W. & Taylor, D. R., eds. Cartography Past, Present, & Future - a Festschrift for F. J. Ormeling: Published on Behalf of the International Cartographic Association. 194p. 1989. 97.75 (*1-85166-336-3*) Elsevier.

Rhind, Graham R. Building & Maintaining a European Direct Marketing Database. LC 94-174. 318p. 1994. 127.95 (*0-566-07471-0*, Pub. by Gower) Ashgate Pub Co.

An Asterisk (*) at the beginning of an entry indicates that the title is appearing for the first time.

— Global Sourcebook of Address Data Management: A Guide to Address Formats & Data in 193 Countries. LC 98-28991. 400p. 1998. 331.95 (*0-566-08109-1*, Pub. by Gower) Ashgate Pub Co.
Rhind, Nancy, jt. ed. see Chan, Cecilia L.
Rhind, Susan, jt. auth. see Andrew, David.
Rhind, Susan, jt. auth. see Hunter, Luke.
Rhine, C. D., jt. ed. see Roberts, F. X.
Rhine, Edward E., ed. Best Practices: Excellence in Corrections. LC 98-26064. 608p. 1998. pap. 24.95 (*1-56991-077-4*, 232) Am Correctional.
Rhine, Edward E., ed. see American Correctional Association Staff.
Rhine, Edward E., jt. ed. see Hartjen, Clayton A.
Rhine, J. B. Extra-Sensory Perception. 1997. pap. 15.95 (*0-8283-1464-0*) Branden Bks.
Rhine, J. B., et al. Parapsychology from Duke to FRNM. LC 65-28963. 121p. 1965. pap. 2.75 (*0-911106-00-6*) Parapsych Pr.
Rhine, Joseph B. New Frontiers of the Mind: The Story of the Duke Experiments. LC 71-178080. (Illus.). 275p. 1972. reprint ed. lib. bdg. 49.75 (*0-8371-6279-3*, RHNF, Greenwood Pr) Greenwood.
Rhine, Louisa E. Manual for Introductory Experiments in Parapsychology. 2nd ed. LC 68-70901. 24p. 1977. 2.00 (*0-911106-01-4*) Parapsych Pr.
Rhine, Mordechai. The Magic of Shabbos: An Introductory Guide. Goldman, Bonnie, ed. 224p. 1998. 13.95 (*1-880582-25-2*); pap. 9.95 (*1-880582-26-0*) Judaica Pr.
Rhine, Paul E. Locomotive Engineering Guide to Fuel Conservation: If Trains Are So Efficient, Why Does It Take So Much Fuel to Run Them? LC 96-69154. (Illus.). 76p. 1996. pap. 19.95 (*0-911382-17-8*) Simmons-Boardman.
Rhine, Robert S. My Brain Escapes Me. LC 99-19398. 352p. 1999. pap. 16.95 (*0-941543-18-8*) Sun Dog Pr.
— My Brain Escapes Me: Signed Paper. LC 99-19398. 352p. 1999. pap. 21.95 (*0-941543-19-6*) Sun Dog Pr.
Rhine, Stanley. Bone Voyage: A Journey in Forensic Anthropology. LC 98-23459. (Illus.). 268p. 1998. 49.95 (*0-8263-1967-X*); pap. 16.95 (*0-8263-1968-8*) U of NM Pr.
Rhine, W. E., et al, eds. Synthesis & Processing of Ceramics: Scientific Issues. (Symposium Proceedings Ser.: Vol. 249). 581p. 1992. text 17.50 (*1-55899-143-3*) Materials Res.
Rhinefort, Andrew. Air-Conditioning & Refrigeration Control. (C). 1995. pap. text 30.34 (*1-56870-213-2*) RonJon Pub.
— Commercial Refrigeration. 206p. (C). 1994. 60.49 (*1-56870-156-X*) RonJon Pub.
***Rhinehart & Friedman.** Infection Control in Home Care. LC 98-32394. 250p. 1999. spiral bd. 55.00 (*0-8342-1143-2*, 11432) Aspen Pub.
***Rhinehart, Kandy.** Sunset Dreams. 1999. pap. write for info. (*1-58235-093-0*) Watermrk Pr.
Rhinehart, Luke. The Dice Man. LC 98-10743. 328p. 1998. pap. 15.95 (*0-87951-864-2*, Pub. by Overlook Pr) Penguin Putnam.
— Long Voyage Back. 1996. pap. text 14.95 (*0-07-052507-2*) McGraw.
— Long Voyage Back: A Novel. LC 82-23586. (Bluejacket Paperback Ser.). 408p. 1995. pap. 15.95 (*1-55750-130-0*) Naval Inst Pr.
Rhinehart, Marilyn D. A Way of Work & a Way of Life: Coal Mining in Thurber, Texas, 1888-1926. LC 91-35907. (Southwestern Studies: No. 9). (Illus.). 192p. 1992. 39.50 (*0-89096-499-8*) Tex A&M Univ Pr.
Rhinehart, Mary R. The Door. 352p. 1986. mass mkt. 3.50 (*0-8217-1895-9*, Zebra Kensgtn) Kensgtn Pub Corp.
***Rhinehart, Raymond.** Princeton University: The Campus Guide. LC 99-29961. (Illus.). 188p. 2000. pap. 21.95 (*1-56898-209-7*) Princeton Arch.
Rhinehart, Ric, jt. auth. see Rasmussen, Wendy.
***Rhinehart, Richard J.** Colorado Caves. (Illus.). 2000. 24.95 (*1-56579-381-1*) Westcliffe Pubs.
— Without Rival: The Story of the Wonderful Cave of the Winds. (Illus.). 64p. 2000. per. 9.95 (*1-57864-113-6*, Pub. by Donning Co) Cave of the Winds.
Rhinehart, Russell, jt. auth. see Bethea, Robert M.
Rhinelander, Anthony L. Prince Michael Vorontsov: Viceroy to the Tsar. 304p. (C). 1990. text 65.00 (*0-7735-0747-7*, Pub. by McG-Queens Univ Pr) CUP Services.
Rhinelander, John B. & Scheinman, Adam M., eds. At the Nuclear Crossroads: Choices about Nuclear Weapons & Extension of the Non-Proliferation Treaty. LC 95-3155. (Illus.). 120p. (Orig.). (C). 1995. pap. text 21.50 (*0-8191-9818-8*); lib. bdg. 42.00 (*0-8191-9817-X*) U Pr of Amer.
Rhines, Frederick N., jt. auth. see DeHoff, Robert T.
Rhines, Jesse A. Black Film, White Money. LC 95-33932. (Illus.). 200p. (C). 1996. pap. 17.95 (*0-8135-2267-6*); text 48.00 (*0-8135-2266-8*) Rutgers U Pr.
Rhinesmith, Stephen H. Bring Home the World: A Management Guide for Community Leaders of International Exchange Programs. 223p. 1986. pap. 9.95 (*0-8027-7289-7*) Walker & Co.
— A Manager's Guide to Globalization: Six Keys to Success in a Changing World. LC 92-19470. (Illus.). 240p. 1992. 30.00 (*1-55623-904-1*, Irwn Prfssnl) McGraw-Hill Prof.
— A Manager's Guide to Globalization: Six Skills for Success in a Changing World. 2nd rev. ed. LC 95-45171. (Illus.). 256p. 1996. text 29.95 (*0-7863-0545-2*, Irwn Prfssnl) McGraw-Hill Prof.
— Manger's Guide Globalization 3/e. 2000. 29.95 (*0-07-135480-8*) McGraw.
Rhino Records Staff. Bar-B-Que Soul-a-Bration! Party Pack. 24.98 incl. audio (*1-56826-937-4*) Rhino Enter.
— Taz in a Scary Tale from Down Under. (Illus.). 24p. (J). (ps-3). 1998. pap. 7.99 incl. audio (*1-56826-821-1*, KR9) Rhino Enter.
***Rhinosoft Corporation Staff.** James Earl Jones Mulmed Bible. 1998. sl. 14.95 (*5-559-26998-0*) Rhinosoft Interactive.
Rhipidon Society Staff, ed. see Outland, Breck, et al.
Rho, Mannaque & Brown, G. E. APCTP Workshop on Astro-Hadron Physics: Properties of Hadrons in Matter: In Honor of Prof. Mannque Rho's 60th Birthday. LC 98-51622. 650p. 1999. 86.00 (*981-02-3768-5*) World Scientific Pub.
Rhoades. Body Art - Human Physiology. 3rd ed. (C). 1995. pap. text, teacher ed. 30.00 (*0-03-015862-1*) Harcourt Coll Pubs.
— Garden Crafts for Kids: 50 Reasons to Get Your Hands Dirty. (Illus.). 144p. (J). (gr. 3-7). 1998. pap. 14.95 (*0-8069-0999-4*) Sterling.
— Human Physiology. 3rd ed. (C). 1995. pap. text, student ed. 28.00 (*0-03-015863-X*) Harcourt.
— Oht's T/a Human Physiology 3/e Rv. 3rd ed. (C). 1996. pap. text 246.00 (*0-03-019774-0*) Harcourt Coll Pubs.
Rhoades, C. V. Strike Like Lightning: Meditations on Nature for Martial Artists. (Illus.). 112p. 1999. pap. 9.95 (*1-880336-28-6*) Turtle CT.
Rhoades-Baum, Patrice, et al, eds. Help Desk & Customer Support Practices Report 1995: May 1995 Survey Results. (Illus.). 56p. (Orig.). pap. write for info. (*1-57125-051-4*) Help Desk Inst.
— The 1995 Help Desk Salary Survey. (Illus.). 52p. (Orig.). pap. write for info. (*1-57125-024-7*) Help Desk Inst.
— 1995-1996 Help Desk Buyers Guide. (Illus.). 128p. (Orig.). pap. write for info. (*1-57125-052-2*) Help Desk Inst.
Rhoades-Baum, Patrice, jt. auth. see Case, Gary.
Rhoades-Baum, Patrice, ed. see Bultema, Patrick.
Rhoades-Baum, Patrice, ed. see Rainwater, Holly.
Rhoades-Baum, Patrice, ed. see Svendsen, Eric & Svendsen, Virginia.
Rhoades, Carol, tr. see Pagoldh, Susanne.
Rhoades, Chuck, jt. auth. see Cooperman, Carolyn.
Rhoades, Deb, jt. ed. see Weldon, Jay-Louise.
Rhoades, Dennis K. Legacy of Vietnam Veterans & Their Families: Survivors of War, Catalysts for Change, Papers from the 1994 National Symposium. 518p. 1995. per. 36.00 (*0-16-048205-4*) USGPO.
Rhoades, Dennis K., et al, eds. The Legacy of Vietnam Veterans & Their Families: Survivors of War: Catalysts for Change. LC 95-7814. 520p. (Orig.). 1995. write for info. (*0-9647667-0-1*); pap. 34.00 (*0-9647667-1-X*) Agent Orange.
— The Legacy of Vietnam Veterans & Their Families: Survivors of War: Catalysts for Change. (Illus.). 520p. (Orig.). (C). 1996. pap. text 40.00 (*0-7881-3255-5*) DIANE Pub.
Rhoades, Diane. Garden Crafts for Kids: 50 Great Reasons to Get Your Hands Dirty. LC 94-37108. (Illus.). 144p. (J). (gr. 3-7). 1995. 21.95 (*0-8069-0998-6*) Sterling.
Rhoades, Duane, compiled by. The Independent Monologue in Latin American Theater: A Primary Bibliography with Selective Secondary Sources, 5. LC 85-21947. (Bibliographies & Indexes in World Literature Ser.: No. 5). 242p. 1985. lib. bdg. 65.00 (*0-313-25080-4*, RIN/) Greenwood.
Rhoades, Gary. Managed Professionals: Unionized Faculty & Restructuring Academic Labor. LC 97-22368. (SUNY Series, Frontiers in Education). 320p. (C). 1998. text 73.50 (*0-7914-3715-9*); pap. text 24.95 (*0-7914-3716-7*) State U NY Pr.
***Rhoades, Jacqueline.** Rhoades to Reading: Teaching Reading to Secondary & Adult Students, Level I. 286p. (C). 1999. 82.00 (*1-930006-00-4*) Rhoades.
— Rhoades to Reading: Teaching Reading to Secondary & Adult Students, Level II. 226p. (C). 1999. pap. 90.00 (*1-930006-01-2*) Rhoades.
— Rhoades to Reading: Teaching Reading to Secondary & Adult Students, Level III. 264p. (C). 1999. 90.00 (*1-930006-02-0*) Rhoades.
— Rhoades to Reading: Teaching Reading to Secondary & Adult Students, Level IV. 305p. (C). 1999. 90.00 (*1-930006-03-9*) Rhoades.
— Rhoades to Reading: Teaching Reading to Secondary & Adult Students, Level V. 112p. (C). 1999. 81.00 (*1-930006-04-7*) Rhoades.
— Rhoades to Reading: Teaching Reading to Secondary & Adult Students, Blackline Masters, Level I. 140p. 1999. 40.00 (*1-930006-06-3*) Rhoades.
— Rhoades to Reading: Teaching Reading to Secondary & Adult Students, Blackline Masters, Level II. 104p. 1999. 40.00 (*1-930006-07-1*) Rhoades.
— Rhoades to Reading: Teaching Reading to Secondary & Adult Students, Blackline Masters, Level III. 149p. 1999. 40.00 (*1-930006-08-X*) Rhoades.
— Rhoades to Reading: Teaching Reading to Secondary & Adult Students, Blackline Masters, Level IV. 166p. 1999. 40.00 (*1-930006-09-8*) Rhoades.
— Rhoades to Reading: Teaching Reading to Secondary & Adult Students, Blackline Masters, Level V. 79p. 1999. 40.00 (*1-930006-10-1*) Rhoades.
— Rhoades to Reading: Teaching Reading to Secondary & Adult Students Teacher Handbook. 80p. 1999. teacher ed. 81.00 (*1-930006-05-5*) Rhoades.
— Rhoades to Reading: Teaching Reading to Secondary & Adult Students Teacher Handbook, Blackline Masters. 27p. 1999. 40.00 (*1-930006-11-X*) Rhoades.
Rhoades, Jacqueline & McCabe, Margaret E. The Cooperative Classroom: Social & Academic Activities. LC 98-160792. 151p. (Orig.). 1992. pap. 19.95 (*1-879639-16-5*) Natl Educ Serv.
— How to Stop Fighting with Your Kids. 39p. (Orig.). 1986. pap. 3.95 (*0-933935-02-1*) ITA Pubns.
Rhoades, Jacqueline, et al. Simple Cooperation in the Classroom. (Illus.). 165p. (Orig.). (J). (ps up). 1985. pap. 15.95 (*0-933935-07-2*) ITA Pubns.
Rhoades, Jacqueline, jt. auth. see McCabe, Margaret E.
***Rhoades, Jason.** Snowball. 1999. 45.00 (*3-89322-969-8*) Dr Cantz sche Druckerei GmbH.
Rhoades, Jeffrey A. The Nursing Home Market: Supply & Demand for the Elderly. LC 98-29802. (Studies on the Elderly in America). (Illus.). 160p. 1998. 42.00 (*0-8153-3201-7*) Garland.
***Rhoades, Jeffrey A., et al.** Health Insurance Status of the Civilian Noninstitutionalized Population, 1998. (MEPS Research Findings Ser.: Vol. 11). 2000. pap. write for info. (*1-58763-003-6*) Agency Healthcare.
***Rhoades, Joy.** The Compliance Handbook: Managing Compliance in Asian Emerging Markets. 1999. 150.00 (*962-936-051-9*, Pub. by Asia Law & Practice) Am Educ Systs.
Rhoades, Lawrence J. A History of the American Sociological Association: 1905-1980. 90p. 5.00 (*0-317-36340-9*) Am Sociological.
Rhoades, Lawrence J., ed. Cost Guide for Automatic Finishing Processes. LC 80-52614. 219p. reprint ed. pap. 67.90 (*0-608-14868-7*, 202615900048) Bks Demand.
Rhoades, Nancy L. Croquet: An Annotated Bibliography from the Rendell Rhoades Croquet Collection. LC 92-12217. (Illus.). 244p. 1992. 31.00 (*0-8108-2571-6*) Scarecrow.
Rhoades, Randy. How to Solve Calculus Problems. rev. ed. (Illus.). 180p. (C). 1988. pap. text 14.95 (*0-944492-00-2*) SW Res Grp Pubns.
— How to Solve Calculus Problems. 3rd rev. ed. (Illus.). 214p. (C). 1992. pap. text 14.95 (*0-944492-02-9*) SW Res Grp Pubns.
— How to Solve Word Problems. (Illus.). 64p. (Orig.). (C). 1988. pap. text 5.95 (*0-944492-01-0*) SW Res Grp Pubns.
Rhoades, Raphael H., ed. Therapy Through Hypnosis. 1976. pap. 5.00 (*0-87980-162-X*) Wilshire.
Rhoades, Robert E., ed. see Moock, Joyce L.
Rhoades, Robert E., jt. ed. see Moock, Joyce L.
Rhoades, Rodney. Human Physiology. 3rd ed. LC 95-74829. (C). 1995. text 97.00 (*0-03-005159-2*, Pub. by Harcourt Coll Pubs) Harcourt.
Rhoades, Rodney A. & Tanner, George A., eds. Medical Physiology. LC 94-24639. (Illus.). 839p. 1995. text 59.95 (*0-316-74228-7*, Little Brwn Med Div) Lppncott W & W.
Rhoades, Roxanne. Destination: Paraguay - Study Guide. (Illus.). 74p. 1997. reprint ed. pap. text 25.00 (*0-7881-4272-0*) DIANE Pub.
Rhoades, Ruby, jt. frwd. see Brubaker, Pamela K.
Rhoades, Rufus V. & Langer, Marshall J. U. S. International Taxation & Tax Treaties. 337p. 1996. 1230.00 (*0-8205-2778-5*) Bender.
Rhoades, Snowy. Diary of a Coastwatcher in the Solomons. 1984. pap. 5.00 (*0-934841-00-4*) Adm Nimitz Foun.
Rhoades, Weldon E. Flying MacArthur to Victory. LC 86-26105. (Military History Ser.: No. 1). (Illus.). 584p. 1987. 29.95 (*0-89096-266-9*) Tex A&M Univ Pr.
***Rhoads, Ann F. & Block, Timothy A.** The Plants of Pennsylvania: An Illustrated Manual. LC 99-89946. (Illus.). 1040p. 2000. 65.00 (*0-8122-3535-5*) U of Pa Pr.
Rhoads, Ann F. & Klein, William M. The Vascular Flora of Pennsylvania: Annotated Checklist & Atlas. LC 92-85316. (Memoirs Ser.: Vol. 207). (Illus.). 600p. (C). 1993. 25.00 (*0-87169-207-4*, M207-RHA) Am Philos.
Rhoads, B. Eric. Blast from the Past. (Illus.). 472p. 1996. 39.99 (*1-886745-06-4*) Streamline Pr.
Rhoads, David. Challenge of Diversity: The Witness of Paul & the Gospels. 144p. 1996. pap. 15.00 (*0-8006-2982-5*, 1-2982, Fortress Pr) Augsburg Fortress.
***Rhoads, David & Syreeni, Kari, eds.** Characterization in the Gospels. (JSNT Supplement Ser.: No. 184). 350p. 1999. 85.00 (*1-84127-004-0*, Pub. by Sheffield Acad) CUP Services.
Rhoads, David, et al. Mark as Story: An Introduction to the Narrative of a Gospel. 2nd ed. LC 99-12061. 192p. 1999. pap. 18.00 (*0-8006-3160-9*, 1-3160, Fortress Pr) Augsburg Fortress.
Rhoads, Diana A. Shakespeare's Defense of Poetry: A Midsummer Night's Dream & the Tempest. 264p. (Orig.). 1986. pap. text 26.00 (*0-8191-4980-2*); lib. bdg. 58.50 (*0-8191-4979-9*) U Pr of Amer.
Rhoads, Donald C. & Lutz, Richard A., eds. Skeletal Growth of Aquatic Organisms: Biological Records of Environmental Change. LC 79-25825. (Topics in Geobiology Ser.: Vol. 1). (Illus.). 762p. 1980. 140.00 (*0-306-40259-9*, Plenum Trade) Perseus Pubng.
Rhoads, Dorothy. The Corn Grows Ripe. LC 92-24888. (Illus.). (YA). (gr. 8-12). 1993. pap. 4.99 (*0-14-036313-0*, PuffinBks) Peng Put Young Read.
— The Corn Grows Ripe. (J). 1994. 18.75 (*0-8446-6756-0*) Peter Smith.
— The Corn Grows Ripe. (J). 1993. 10.19 (*0-606-05215-1*, Pub. by Turtleback) Demco.
Rhoads, Edward J. China's Republican Revolution: The Case of Kwangtung, 1895-1913. LC 74-84090. (East Asian Monographs: No. 81). 392p. 1975. 25.00 (*0-674-11980-0*) HUP.
Rhoads, Edward J., et al. Chinese Red Army, Nineteen Twenty-Seven to Nineteen Sixty-Three: An Annotated Bibliography. LC 65-1422. (East Asian Monographs: No. 16). 202p. 1964. pap. 20.00 (*0-674-12500-2*) HUP.
***Rhoads, Edward J. M.** Manchus & Han: Ethnic Relations & Political Power in Late Qing & Early Republican China, 1861-1928. LC 00-8470. (Illus.). 384p. 2000. 55.00 (*0-295-97938-0*) U of Wash Pr.
Rhoads, Ella, see Higginson, Ella, pseud.
Rhoads, F. D. & Edwards, J. Law Office Guide to Small Computers. (General Publications). (Illus.). 431p. 1984. text 95.00 (*0-07-052091-7*) Shepards.
Rhoads, Gwen, ed. see Mitchell, Robert B., et al.
Rhoads, John K. Critical Issues in Social Theory. 352p. 1991. 45.00 (*0-271-00709-5*); pap. 19.95 (*0-271-00753-2*) Pa St U Pr.
Rhoads, Loren & Jones, Mason, eds. Lend the Eye a Terrible Aspect: A Collection of Essays & Fiction. LC 93-72388. (Illus.). 165p. (Orig.). 1994. pap. 9.99 (*0-9636794-0-6*) Automatism Pr.
Rhoads, Mary, ed. Andrews' Deskbook: Aids. 50p. 1998. pap. 85.00 (*1-890155-06-3*) Andrews Pubns.
— Andrews' Deskbook: Pollution Exclusion. 51p. 1998. pap. 85.00 (*1-890155-04-7*) Andrews Pubns.
— Andrews' Deskbook: Tobacco. 55p. 1998. pap. 85.00 (*1-890155-05-5*) Andrews Pubns.
Rhoads, Rick, jt. auth. see Isenberg, Marc.
Rhoads, Robert A. Coming Out in College: The Struggle for a Queer Identity. LC 94-16454. 208p. 1994. 57.95 (*0-89789-378-6*); pap. 17.95 (*0-89789-421-9*, Bergin & Garvey) Greenwood.
— Community Service & Higher Learning: Explorations of the Caring Self. LC 96-49881. 254p. (C). 1997. pap. text 19.95 (*0-7914-3522-9*) State U NY Pr.
Rhoads, Robert A. Freedom's Web: Student Activism in an Age of Cultural Diversity. LC 98-5004. 288p. 1998. 38.00 (*0-8018-5887-9*) Johns Hopkins.
***Rhoads, Robert A.** Freedom's Web: Student Activism in an Age of Cultural Diversity. 288p. 2000. pap. 16.95 (*0-8018-6411-9*) Johns Hopkins.
Rhoads, Robert A. & Valadez, James R. Democracy, Multiculturalism, & the Community College: A Critical Perspective. LC 95-48972. (Critical Education Practice Ser.: Vol. 05). 256p. 1996. text 44.00 (*0-8153-2197-X*, SS1081) Garland.
— Democracy, Multiculturalism, & the Community College: A Critical Perspective. LC 95-48972. (Critical Education Practice Ser.: Vol. 5). 256p. 1996. pap. text 22.95 (*0-8153-2324-7*, SS1081) Garland.
Rhoads, Robert A., jt. auth. see Tierney, William G.
Rhoads, Samuel E. The Sky Tonight: A Guided Tour of the Stars over Hawaii. (Illus.). 202p. 1996. spiral bd. 29.95 (*0-930897-93-5*) Bishop Mus.
Rhoads, Samuel E. & Gearen, Michael V. Data Structures Using PASCAL. 400p. (C). 1991. text 56.75 (*0-697-11173-3*, Irwn McGrw-H) McGrw-H Hghr Educ.
Rhoads, Steven E. The Economist's View of the World: Government, Markets, & Public Policy. 336p. 1985. pap. text 21.95 (*0-521-31764-9*) Cambridge U Pr.
— Incomparable Worth: Pay Equity Meets the Market. (Illus.). 335p. (C). 1994. pap. text 20.95 (*0-521-47828-6*) Cambridge U Pr.
— Valuing Life: Public Policy Dilemmas. (Special Studies in Public Policy & Public Systems Management). 1982. text 44.50 (*0-89158-650-4*) Westview.
Rhoads, Steven F. Incomparable Worth: Pay Equity Meets the Market. LC 92-39227. 335p. (C). 1993. text 37.95 (*0-521-44187-0*) Cambridge U Pr.
Rhoda, Janice T. The ABC's of Violin for the Advanced, Vol. ABC5. (Illus.). 40p. 1998. 8.95 (*0-9663731-3-8*) ABCs MA.
— The ABC's of Violin TM Easy Piano Accompaniment for Book 2, Vol. ABC4. 35p. 1998. 8.95 (*0-9663731-4-6*) ABCs MA.
Rhode, Bill. Down to Paradise. 80p. 1997. 9.00 (*0-8059-4251-3*) Dorrance.
Rhode, David, jt. ed. see Madsen, David.
Rhode, Deborah. Professional Responsibility: Ethics by the Pervasive Method. 1994. teacher ed. 40.00 (*0-316-66508-8*, 65088) Aspen Law.
— Professional Responsibility: Ethics by the Pervasive Method. LC 93-80778. 912p. 1994. pap. 35.00 (*0-316-74232-5*, 42325) Aspen Law.
***Rhode, Deborah L.** Ethics in Practice. LC 99-58064. 352p. 2000. 35.00 (*0-19-512961-X*) OUP.
— In the Interests of Justice: Reforming the Legal Profession. 272p. 2000. 27.50 (*0-19-512188-0*) OUP.
Rhode, Deborah L. Justice & Gender. LC 89-30854. 440p. 1989. 47.50 (*0-674-49100-9*) HUP.
— Justice & Gender. 440p. (C). 1991. pap. 20.50 (*0-674-49101-7*) HUP.
— Professional Responsibility: Ethics by the Pervasive Method. 2nd ed. LC 97-51275. 1998. pap. text 40.00 (*1-56706-542-2*) Aspen Law.
— Speaking of Sex: The Denial of Gender Equality. LC 94-49905. 341p. 1999. pap. 17.95 (*0-674-83178-0*) HUP.
— Speaking of Sex: The Denial of Gender Inequality. LC 96-49905. (Illus.). 352p. 1997. 29.95 (*0-674-83177-2*) HUP.
— Teacher's Manual for Legal Ethics. (University Casebook Ser.). 118p. 1995. pap. text, teacher ed. write for info. (*1-56662-283-2*) Foundation Pr.
Rhode, Deborah L. & Luban, David J. Legal Ethics Teacher's Manual. (University Casebook Ser.). 177p. 1991. pap. text. write for info. (*0-88277-979-6*) Foundation Pr.
Rhode, Deborah L., jt. auth. see Luban, David.
Rhode, Deborah L., jt. auth. see Luban, David J.
Rhode, Deborah L., ed. see Hazard, Geoffrey C., Jr.
Rhode, Deborah L., jt. ed. see Lawson, Annette.
Rhode, Dennis L. Pizza: A Slice of the New West. LC 97-17037. (Illus.). 144p. 1997. pap. 9.95 (*0-87358-677-8*) Northland AZ.
Rhode, Eric. A History of the Cinema: From Its Origins to 1970. (Quality Paperbacks Ser.). (Illus.). 684p. 1985. reprint ed. pap. 13.95 (*0-306-80233-3*) Da Capo.
— On Hallucination, Intuition, & the Becoming of "O" (Illus.). 230p. 1998. pap. text 29.95 (*1-883881-26-9*, 26-9) S Freud RT&PF.
— Psychotic Metaphysics. 344p. 1994. pap. text 25.00 (*1-85575-074-0*, Pub. by H Karnac Bks Ltd) Other Pr LLC.

R

An Asterisk (*) at the beginning of an entry indicates that the title is appearing for the first time.

R

*Rhode, Franklin W. & Hahn, Robert W. Pike's Peek at the World of Sherlock Holmes. (Illus.). 68p. 1998. pap. 10.00 (1-55246-108-4) Battered Silicon.
Rhode, Ginger, et al. The Tough Kid Book: Practical Classroom Management Strategies. (Tough Kid Ser.). (Illus.). 120p. 1992. pap. text, teacher ed. 19.50 (0-944584-54-3, 40TK) Sopris.
Rhode, Grant F. & Whitlock, Reid E. Treaties of the People's Republic of China, 1949-1978: An Annotated Compilation. (Special Studies on China & East Asia). (Illus.). 208p. 1980. text 42.00 (0-89158-761-6) Westview.
Rhode, Harold & Sack, Sallyann A. Jewish Vital Records, Revision Lists & Other Holdings in the Lithuanian Archives. 154p. 1996. pap. 35.00 (1-886223-02-5) Avotaynu.
Rhode Island. Dept. of the Attorney General, jt. auth. see Rhode Island. Insurance Dept.
Rhode Island Historical Society Staff. Rhode Island Land Evidences Vol. 1: 1648-1696, Abstracts (All Published) LC 79-77882. (Illus.). 271p. 1998. reprint ed. pap. 26.50 (0-8063-0391-3) Clearfield Co.
Rhode Island Historical Society Staff, ed. The Early Records of the Town of Warwick (R. I.) 362p. 1993. lib. bdg. 39.50 (0-8328-3535-8) Higginson Bk Co.
*Rhode Island. Insurance Dept & Rhode Island. Dept. of the Attorney General. Rhode Island Regulations: Containing Regulations of the Insurance Department & Selected Attorney General's Opinions. LC 98-67599. (Illus.). 1998. write for info. (0-89246-384-8) NILS Pub.
Rhode, John. Death at the Inn. large type ed. 416p. 1998. pap. 17.99 (0-7089-5392-1, Linford) Ulverscroft.
Rhode, P. T., jt. auth. see Elsasser, Albert B.
*Rhode, Robert. The Harvest Story. 2000. 27.95 (1-55753-208-7) Purdue U Pr.
Rhode, Robert B. Booms & Busts on Bitter Creek: A History of Rock Springs, Wyoming. 2nd rev. ed. (Illus.). 256p. 1999. 28.00 (0-87108-051-6) F Pruett.
Rhode, Robert D. Setting in the American Short Story of Local Color, 1865-1900. (Studies in English Literature: No. 30). 190p. (Orig.). 1975. pap. text 55.40 (90-279-3281-6) Mouton.
Rhode, R.W. & Swearengen, eds. Mechanical Testing for Deformation Model Development - STP 765. 478p. 1982. 51.50 (0-8031-0737-4, SPT765) ASTM.
Rhode, Stephen J. & Ginsberg, Stephen P., eds. Ophthalmic Technology: A Guide for the Eye Care Assistant. (Illus.). 508p. 1987. pap. text 50.00 (0-88167-276-9) Lppncott W & W.
*Rhode, Steve & Kidwell, Mike. Get Out of Debt: Smart Solutions to Your Money Problems. (Illus.). 232p. 1999. pap. 19.95 (0-9670255-0-8, Pub. by Debt Counsel Am) BookMasters.
Rhode, William. Chewing Gum, Baling Wire & Guts: Story of the Gates Flying Circus. (Illus.). 194p. 1994. reprint ed. pap. write for info. (0-9632295-1-6) H V Pubs.
Rhodehamel, John. The Great Experiment: George Washington & the American Republic. LC 98-60559. (Illus.). 160p. 1998. 27.50 (0-300-07614-2) Yale U Pr.
Rhodehamel, John & Schwartz, Thomas F. The Last Best Hope on Earth: Abraham Lincoln & the Promise of America. (Illus.). 80p. 1993. pap. 9.00 (0-87328-142-X, 142X, Pub. by Huntington Lib) A Schwartz & Co.
Rhodehamel, John, ed. see Washington, George.
*Rhodehamel, John H., et al. The Great Experiment: George Washington & the American Republic. LC 98-60559. xxi, 176 p. 1998. pap. 18.95 (0-87328-174-8) Huntington Lib.
*Rhoden, Clare & Gordon, Christine Turskey. Studying Engineering at University. (Illus.). 208p. 2000. pap. 14.95 (1-86508-203-1, Pub. by Allen & Unwin Pty) Paul & Co Pubs.
Rhoden, Clare, jt. auth. see Chesterman, Simon.
Rhoden, David & Grabowski, John. Awesome Almanacs - New York. 208p. (J). (gr. 4-12). 1995. pap. 14.95 (1-880190-26-5) B&B Pub.
Rhoden, J. Lyn, jt. auth. see Robinson, Bryan E.
Rhoden, Maureen, jt. auth. see Balchin, Paul N.
*Rhoden, Nancy L. The Human Tradition in the American Revolution. LC 99-29787. (Human Tradition in America Ser.). 430p. 1999. 50.00 (0-8420-2747-5) Scholarly Res Inc.
Rhoden, Nancy L. The Human Tradition in the American Revolution. Steele, Ian K., ed. LC 99-29787. (Human Tradition in America Ser.). 430p. 1999. pap. 18.95 (0-8420-2748-3) Scholarly Res Inc.
— Revolutionary Anglicanism: The Colonial Church of England During the American Revolution. LC 98-31403. 224p. 1999. text 40.00 (0-8147-7519-5) NYU Pr.
Rhoden, Nancy L., jt. ed. see Steele, Ian K.
Rhoder, Carol, jt. auth. see French, Joyce N.
Rhoderick, E. H. Metal-Semiconductor Contacts. (Monographs in Electrical & Electronic Engineering). (Illus.). 1978. text 22.00 (0-19-859323-6) OUP.
Rhoderick, E. H., jt. auth. see Rose-Innes, A. C.
Rhoderick, Elin & Elin, Rhoderick. Smoking, Stop: Quit for Good! 31p. 1990. pap. 39.50 incl. audio (0-88432-287-4, S01670) Audio-Forum.
Rhoderick, George C., Jr. The Early History of Middletown, Maryland. LC 89-51152. (Illus.). 412p. 1989. 35.00 (0-9623594-9-1) Mddltwn Val Hist Soc.
*Rhodes. Cara's Land. 2000. pap. 10.95 (0-552-13636-0, Pub. by Transworld Publishers Ltd) Trafalgar.
Rhodes. Cases in International Relations. (C). 1999. text 22.00 (0-15-503517-7, Pub. by Harcourt Coll Pubs) Harcourt.
— European Social Policy. (C). 1999. pap. 19.00 (0-582-30490-3) Addison-Wesley.
— Future European Welfare: A New Social Contract? LC 97-38223. 304p. 1998. text 69.95 (0-312-21195-3) St Martin.
— How to Identify Musical Instruments from Ancient to Modern Times. (Getting Started Ser.). 1990. 7.95 (0-685-32032-4, 85-44) Hansen Ed Mus.
— Implementing New Technologies. 1994. 50.95 (0-631-17805-8) Blackwell Pubs.
*Rhodes. Madeleine. (J). 2000. pap. 10.95 (0-552-13309-4, Pub. by Transworld Publishers Ltd) Trafalgar.
Rhodes. Nucleic Acid-Binding Protein FactsBook. 192p. 1997. write for info. (0-12-587078-7) Acad Pr.
— Picture Tests in Surgery. 1996. pap. text 16.95 (0-443-05187-9, W B Saunders Co) Harcrt Hlth Sci Grp.
*Rhodes. Rainbow Through Rain. (J). 2000. pap. 10.95 (0-552-13870-3, Pub. by Transworld Publishers Ltd) Trafalgar.
Rhodes. Technical Mathematics. 370p. (C). 1998. pap. text 15.75 (0-536-01193-1) S&S Trade.
Rhodes & Biers. Essential Element Bk. 1: Oboe. 32p. 1992. pap. 10.00 (0-7935-0451-1, 08721629) H Leonard.
— Essential Elements: Alto Clarinet, Bk. 2. 32p. 1992. pap. 10.00 (0-7935-0472-4, 08721649) H Leonard.
— Essential Elements: Alto Sax, Bk. 2. 32p. 1991. pap. 10.00 (0-7935-0474-0, 08721651) H Leonard.
— Essential Elements: B Flat Bass Clarinet, Bk. 1. 32p. 1991. pap. 5.50 (0-7935-1255-7, 00863506) H Leonard.
— Essential Elements: B Flat Bass Clarinet, Bk. 2. 32p. 1991. pap. 5.50 (0-7935-1273-5, 00863524) H Leonard.
— Essential Elements: B Flat Clarinet, Bk. 1. 32p. 1991. pap. 5.50 (0-7935-1253-0, 00863504) H Leonard.
— Essential Elements: B Flat Clarinet, Bk. 2. 32p. 1991. pap. 5.50 (0-7935-1271-9, 00863522) H Leonard.
— Essential Elements: B Flat Tenor Saxophone, Bk. 1. 32p. 1991. pap. 5.50 (0-7935-1257-3, 00863508) H Leonard.
— Essential Elements: B Flat Tenor Saxophone, Bk. 2. 32p. 1991. pap. 5.50 (0-7935-1275-1, 00863526) H Leonard.
— Essential Elements: B Flat Trumpet. 32p. 1991. pap. 5.50 (0-7935-1277-8, 00863528) H Leonard.
— Essential Elements: B Flat Trumpet, Bk. 1. 32p. 1991. pap. 5.50 (0-7935-1259-X, 00863510) H Leonard.
— Essential Elements: B Flat Tuba T. C., Bk. 1. 32p. 1992. pap. 5.50 (0-7935-1731-1, 00863544) H Leonard.
— Essential Elements: Baritone BC. 32p. 1991. pap. 5.50 (0-7935-1280-8, 00863531) H Leonard.
— Essential Elements: Baritone BC, Bk. 1. 32p. 1991. pap. 5.50 (0-7935-1262-X, 00863513) H Leonard.
— Essential Elements: Baritone BC, Bk. 1. 32p. 1992. pap. 10.00 (0-7935-0462-7, 08721640) H Leonard.
— Essential Elements: Baritone BC, Bk. 2. 32p. 1992. pap. 10.00 (0-7935-0480-5, 08721657) H Leonard.
— Essential Elements: Baritone Sax, Bk. 1. 32p. 1992. pap. 10.00 (0-7935-0458-9, 08721636) H Leonard.
— Essential Elements: Baritone Sax, Bk. 2. 32p. 1992. pap. 10.00 (0-7935-0476-7, 08721653) H Leonard.
— Essential Elements: Baritone TC. 32p. 1991. pap. 5.50 (0-7935-1281-6, 00863532) H Leonard.
— Essential Elements: Baritone TC, Bk. 1. 32p. 1991. pap. 5.50 (0-7935-1263-8, 00863514) H Leonard.
— Essential Elements: Baritone TC, Bk. 1. 32p. 1992. pap. 10.00 (0-7935-0463-5, 08721641) H Leonard.
— Essential Elements: Baritone TC, Bk. 2. 32p. 1992. pap. 10.00 (0-7935-0481-3, 08721658) H Leonard.
— Essential Elements: Bass Clarinet, Bk. 2. 32p. 1992. pap. 10.00 (0-7935-0473-2, 08721650) H Leonard.
— Essential Elements: Bassoon, Bk. 1. 32p. 1991. pap. 5.50 (0-7935-1252-2, 00863503) H Leonard.
— Essential Elements: Bassoon, Bk. 1. 32p. 1992. pap. 10.00 (0-7935-0452-X, 08721630) H Leonard.
— Essential Elements: Bassoon, Bk. 2. 32p. 1991. pap. 5.50 (0-7935-1270-0, 00863521) H Leonard.
— Essential Elements: Bassoon, Bk. 2. 32p. 1992. pap. 10.00 (0-7935-0470-8, 08721647) H Leonard.
— Essential Elements: Clarinet, Bk. 2. 32p. 1991. pap. 10.00 (0-7935-0471-6, 08721648) H Leonard.
— Essential Elements: Conductor. 336p. 1991. pap. 19.95 (0-7935-1285-9) H Leonard.
— Essential Elements: Conductor, Bk. 1. 320p. 1991. spiral bd. 19.95 (0-7935-1267-0, 00863518); spiral bd. write for info. (0-7935-0467-8, 08721644) H Leonard.
— Essential Elements: Conductor, Bk. 2. 336p. 1991. spiral bd. write for info. (0-7935-0485-6, 08721661) H Leonard.
— Essential Elements: E Flat Alto Clarinet, Bk. 1. 32p. 1991. pap. 5.50 (0-7935-1254-9, 00863505) H Leonard.
— Essential Elements: E Flat Alto Clarinet, Bk. 2. 32p. 1991. pap. 5.50 (0-7935-1272-7, 00863523) H Leonard.
— Essential Elements: E Flat Alto Saxophone, Bk. 1. 32p. 1991. pap. 5.50 (0-7935-1256-5, 00863507) H Leonard.
— Essential Elements: E Flat Alto Saxophone, Bk. 2. 32p. 1991. pap. 5.50 (0-7935-1274-3, 00863525) H Leonard.
— Essential Elements: E Flat Baritone Saxophone, Bk. 1. 32p. 1991. pap. 5.50 (0-7935-1258-1, 00863509) H Leonard.
— Essential Elements: E Flat Baritone Saxophone, Bk. 2. 32p. 1991. pap. 5.50 (0-7935-1276-X, 00863527) H Leonard.
— Essential Elements: E Flat Tuba T. C., Bk. 2. 32p. 1992. pap. 5.50 (0-7935-1726-5, 00863539) H Leonard.
— Essential Elements: Flute, Bk. 1. 32p. 1991. pap. 5.50 (0-7935-1250-6, 00863501); pap. 10.00 (0-7935-0450-3, 08721628) H Leonard.
— Essential Elements: Flute, Bk. 2. 32p. 1991. pap. 10.00 (0-7935-0468-6, 08721645) H Leonard.
— Essential Elements: Flute, Bk. 2. 32p. 1992. pap. 5.50 (0-7935-1268-9, 00863519) H Leonard.
— Essential Elements: French Horn. 32p. 1991. pap. 5.50 (0-7935-1278-6, 00863529) H Leonard.
— Essential Elements: French Horn, Bk. 1. 48p. 1991. pap. 5.50 (0-7935-1260-3, 00863511); pap. 10.00 (0-7935-0460-0, 08721638) H Leonard.
— Essential Elements: French Horn, Bk. 2. 32p. 1991. pap. 10.00 (0-7935-0478-3, 08721655) H Leonard.
— Essential Elements: Keyboard Percussion, Bk. 1. 32p. 1991. pap. 5.50 (0-7935-1266-2, 00863517) H Leonard.
— Essential Elements: Keyboard Percussion, Bk. 2. 32p. 1991. pap. 5.50 (0-7935-1284-0, 00863535) H Leonard.
— Essential Elements: Oboe, Bk. 1. 32p. 1991. pap. 5.50 (0-7935-1251-4, 0863502) H Leonard.
— Essential Elements: Oboe, Bk. 2. 32p. 1991. pap. 5.50 (0-7935-1269-7, 00863520) H Leonard.
— Essential Elements: Oboe, Bk. 2. 32p. 1992. pap. 10.00 (0-7935-0469-4, 08721646) H Leonard.
— Essential Elements: Tenor Sax, Bk. 2. 32p. 1992. pap. 10.00 (0-7935-0475-9, 08721652) H Leonard.
— Essential Elements: Trombone. 32p. 1991. pap. 5.50 (0-7935-1279-4, 00863530) H Leonard.
— Essential Elements: Trombone, Bk. 1. 32p. 1991. pap. 5.50 (0-7935-1261-1, 00863512); pap. 10.00 (0-7935-0461-9, 08721639) H Leonard.
— Essential Elements: Trombone, Bk. 2. 32p. 1991. pap. 10.00 (0-7935-0479-1, 08721656) H Leonard.
— Essential Elements: Trumpet, Bk. 2. 32p. 1991. pap. 10.00 (0-7935-0477-5, 08721654) H Leonard.
— Essential Elements: Tuba. 32p. 1991. pap. 5.50 (0-7935-1282-4, 00863533) H Leonard.
— Essential Elements: Tuba, Bk. 1. 32p. 1991. pap. 5.50 (0-7935-1264-6, 00863515) H Leonard.
— Essential Elements: Tuba, Bk. 1. 32p. 1992. pap. 10.00 (0-7935-0464-3, 08721642) H Leonard.
— Essential Elements: Tuba, Bk. 2. 32p. 1992. pap. 10.00 (0-7935-0482-1, 08721659) H Leonard.
— Essential Elements Bk. 1: Alto Clarinet. 32p. 1992. pap. 10.00 (0-7935-0454-6, 08721632) H Leonard.
— Essential Elements Bk. 1: Alto Sax. 32p. 1992. pap. 10.00 (0-7935-0456-2, 08721634) H Leonard.
— Essential Elements Bk. 1: Bass Clarinet. 32p. 1992. pap. 10.00 incl. 5.25 hd (0-7935-0455-4, 08721633) H Leonard.
— Essential Elements Bk. 1: Clarinet. 32p. 1992. pap. 10.00 (0-7935-0453-8, 08721631) H Leonard.
— Essential Elements Bk. 1: E Flat Tuba T. C., Bk. 2. 32p. 1992. pap. 5.50 (0-7935-1730-3, 00863543) H Leonard.
— Essential Elements Bk. 1: Keyboard. 32p. 1992. pap. 10.00 (0-7935-0466-X, 08721695) H Leonard.
— Essential Elements Bk. 1: Tenor Sax. 32p. 1992. pap. 10.00 (0-7935-0457-0, 08721635) H Leonard.
— Essential Elements Bk. 1: Trumpet. 32p. 1992. pap. 10.00 (0-7935-0459-7, 08721637) H Leonard.
— Essential Elements Bk. 2: B Flat Trombone T. C. 32p. 1992. pap. 5.50 (0-7935-1725-7, 00863538); pap. 5.50 (0-7935-1729-X, 00863542) H Leonard.
— Essential Elements Bk. 2: B Flat Tuba T. C. 32p. 1992. pap. 5.50 (0-7935-1727-3, 00863540) H Leonard.
— Essential Elements Bk. 2: E Flat Alto Horn. 32p. 1992. pap. 5.50 (0-7935-1728-1, 00863541) H Leonard.
— Essential Elements Bk. 2: E Flat Alto Horn, Bk. 1. 32p. 1992. pap. 5.50 (0-7935-1724-9, 00863537) H Leonard.
— Essential Elements Bk. 2: Percussion. 32p. 1991. pap. 5.50 (0-7935-1283-2, 00863534) H Leonard.
— Essential Elements Bk. 2: Percussion, Bk. 1. 64p. 1991. pap. 5.50 (0-7935-1265-4, 00863516); pap. 10.00 (0-7935-0465-1, 08721643) H Leonard.
— Essential Elements Bk. 2: Percussion, Bk. 2. 64p. 1991. pap. 10.00 (0-7935-0483-X, 08721660) H Leonard.
— Essential Elements Bk. 2: Percussion, Bk. 2. 32p. 1992. pap. 10.00 (0-7935-0484-8, 08721696) H Leonard.
— Essential Technique B Flat Bass Clarinet: Intermediate to Advanced Studies. 48p. 1993. pap. 5.95 (0-7935-1805-9, 00863550) H Leonard.
— Essential Technique B Flat Tenor Saxophone: Intermediate to Advanced Studies. 48p. 1993. pap. 5.95 (0-7935-1807-5, 00863552) H Leonard.
— Essential Technique B Flat Trumpet: Intermediate to Advanced Studies. 48p. 1993. pap. 5.95 (0-7935-1809-1, 00863554) H Leonard.
— Essential Technique B Flat Tuba T. C. Intermediate to Advanced Studies. 48p. 1993. pap. 5.95 (0-7935-1821-0, 00863566) H Leonard.
— Essential Technique Baritone B. C. Intermediate to Advanced Studies. 48p. 1993. pap. 5.95 (0-7935-1812-1, 00863557) H Leonard.
— Essential Technique Baritone T. C. Intermediate to Advanced Studies. 48p. 1993. pap. 5.95 (0-7935-1813-X, 00863558) H Leonard.
— Essential Technique Bassoon: Intermediate to Advanced Studies. 48p. 1993. pap. 5.95 (0-7935-1802-4, 00863547) H Leonard.
— Essential Technique Conductor: Intermediate to Advanced Studies. 296p. 1993. spiral bd. 24.95 (0-7935-1817-2, 00863562) H Leonard.
— Essential Technique E Flat Alto Clarinet: Intermediate to Advanced Studies. 48p. 1993. pap. 5.95 (0-7935-1804-0, 00863549) H Leonard.
— Essential Technique E Flat Alto Horn: Intermediate to Advanced STudies. 48p. 1993. pap. 5.95 (0-7935-1818-0, 00863563) H Leonard.
— Essential Technique E Flat Alto Saxophone: Intermediate to Advanced Studies. 48p. 1993. pap. 5.95 (0-7935-1806-7, 00863551) H Leonard.
— Essential Technique E Flat Tuba T. C. Intermediate to Advanced Studies. 48p. 1993. pap. 5.95 (0-7935-1820-2, 00863565) H Leonard.
— Essential Technique Flute: Intermediate to Advanced Studies. 48p. 1993. pap. 5.95 (0-7935-1800-8, 00863545) H Leonard.
— Essential Technique French Horn: Intermediate to Advanced Studies. 48p. 1993. pap. 5.95 (0-7935-1810-5, 00863555) H Leonard.
— Essential Technique Keyboard Percussion: Intermediate to Advanced Studies. 48p. 1993. pap. 5.95 (0-7935-1816-4, 00863561) H Leonard.
— Essential Technique Oboe: Intermediate to Advanced Studies. 48p. 1993. pap. 5.95 (0-7935-1801-6, 00863546) H Leonard.
— Essential Technique Percussion: Intermediate to Advanced Studies. 88p. 1993. pap. 5.95 (0-7935-1815-6, 00863560) H Leonard.
— Essential Technique Trombone: Intermediate to Advanced Studies. 48p. 1993. pap. 5.95 (0-7935-1811-3, 00863556) H Leonard.
— Essential Technique Tuba: Intermediate to Advanced STudies. 48p. 1993. pap. 5.95 (0-7935-1814-8, 00863559) H Leonard.
— Essential Technqiue E Flat Baritone Saxophone: Intermediate to Advanced Studies. 48p. 1993. pap. 5.95 (0-7935-1808-3, 00863553) H Leonard.
— Instant Success Primer. 200p. 1993. teacher ed., spiral bd. 12.95 (0-7935-2483-0, 00862536) H Leonard.
— Instant Success Primer: B Flat Bass Clarinet. 16p. 1993. pap. 3.50 (0-7935-2472-5, 00862525) H Leonard.
— Instant Success Primer: B Flat Clarinet. 16p. 1993. pap. 3.50 (0-7935-2470-9, 00862523) H Leonard.
— Instant Success Primer: B Flat Tenor Saxophone. 16p. 1993. pap. 3.50 (0-7935-2474-1, 00862527) H Leonard.
— Instant Success Primer: B Flat Trumpet. 16p. 1993. pap. 3.50 (0-7935-2476-8, 00862529) H Leonard.
— Instant Success Primer: Baritone B C. 16p. 1993. pap. 3.50 (0-7935-2479-2, 00862532) H Leonard.
— Instant Success Primer: Baritone T C. 16p. 1993. pap. 3.50 (0-7935-2480-6, 00862533) H Leonard.
— Instant Success Primer: Bassoon. 16p. 1993. pap. 3.50 (0-7935-2469-5, 00862522) H Leonard.
— Instant Success Primer: Complete Percussion. 24p. 1993. pap. 3.50 (0-7935-2482-2, 00862535) H Leonard.
— Instant Success Primer: E Flat Alto Saxophone. 16p. 1993. pap. 3.50 (0-7935-2473-3, 00862526) H Leonard.
— Instant Success Primer: E Flat Baritone Saxophone. 16p. 1993. pap. 3.50 (0-7935-2475-X, 00862528) H Leonard.
— Instant Success Primer: Flute. 16p. 1993. pap. 3.50 (0-7935-2467-9, 00862520) H Leonard.
— Instant Success Primer: French Horn. 16p. 1993. pap. 3.50 (0-7935-2477-6, 00862530) H Leonard.
— Instant Success Primer: Oboe. 24p. 1993. pap. 3.50 (0-7935-2468-7, 00862521) H Leonard.
— Instant Success Primer: Trombone. 16p. 1993. pap. 3.50 (0-7935-2478-4, 00862531) H Leonard.
— Instant Success Primer: Tuba. 16p. 1993. pap. 3.50 (0-7935-2481-4, 00862534) H Leonard.
Rhodes & Cook. Basic Engineer Drawings. 2nd ed. 1991. pap. text. write for info. (0-582-06594-1, Pub. by Addison-Wesley) Longman.
Rhodes & Monkhouse, eds. Drug Products for Clinical Trials: An International Guide to Formulation-Production-Quality Control. LC 97-31539. (Drugs & the Pharmaceutical Sciences Ser.: Vol. 87). (Illus.). 408p. 1997. text 175.00 (0-8247-9852-X) Dekker.
Rhodes & Stone. The Language of the Earth. 350p. 1981. pap. 42.00 (0-08-025980-4, Pergamon Pr) Elsevier.
Rhodes, jt. auth. see Bowen.
Rhodes, jt. ed. see Wilsey.
Rhodes, A. Widowhood. Date not set. pap. 16.95 (1-879041-20-0) Sigo Pr.
Rhodes, Alexandra, jt. auth. see Papi, Stefano.
Rhodes, Ann. Take Care: A Practical Guide for Helping Elders. 199p. 1998. pap. text 15.00 (0-7881-5979-8) DIANE Pub.
Rhodes, Anthony. D'Annunzio: The Poet As Superman. 1960. 18.95 (0-8392-1022-1) Astor-Honor.
Rhodes, Anthony R. The Vatican in the Age of the Dictators, 1922-1945. LC 72-91593. 383p. 1974. write for info. (0-03-007736-2) Holt R&W.
Rhodes, Arnold B. Mighty Acts of God. 1964. pap., student ed. 22.95 (0-8042-9010-5) Westminster John Knox.
*Rhodes, Arnold B. & March, W. Eugene. Mighty Acts of God. rev. ed. 320p. 2000. pap. write for info. (0-664-50076-5, Pub. by Geneva Press) Presbyterian Pub.
Rhodes, Barbara J., jt. auth. see Streeter, William.
Rhodes, Benjamin D. The Anglo-American Winter War with Russia, 1918-1919: A Diplomatic & Military Tragicomedy, 71. LC 87-23645. (Contributions in Military Studies Ser.: No. 71). 168p. 1988. 42.95 (0-313-26132-6, RHF/, Greenwood Pr) Greenwood.
— James P. Goodrich, Indiana's "Governor Strangelove" A Republican's Infatuation with Soviet Russia. LC 95-25533. 192p. 1996. 32.50 (0-945636-82-2) Susquehanna U Pr.
Rhodes, Bennie. Christopher Columbus: Adventurer of Faith & Courage. LC 76-5788. (Sower Ser.). (Illus.). 146p. (YA). (gr. 5-9). 1977. reprint ed. pap. 7.99 (0-915134-26-8) Mott Media.
Rhodes, C. J. The Rabbit, the Skunk & the Cuckoo. Spears-Stewart, Reta, ed. (Illus.). 36p. (J). 1998. pap. 12.00 (0-9638648-5-8) Barnabs Pub.
Rhodes, C. K., et al, eds. Excimer Lasers, Nineteen Eighty-Three: OSA, Lake Tahoe, Nevada. LC 83-71437. (AIP Conference Proceedings Ser., Subseries: Particle & Fields: No. 100, 3). 354p. 1983. lib. bdg. 36.50 (0-88318-199-1) Am Inst Physics.
Rhodes, C. N., jt. auth. see Clark, J. H.
Rhodes, Carl C., jt. auth. see Garrick, John.
Rhodes, Carol. Friend of the Court, Enemy of the Family: Surviving the Child Support Enforcement System & Divorce Racket. LC 98-94782. 200p. 1998. pap. 14.95 (0-9668161-0-2) C Rhodes.
Rhodes, Carolyn. Reciprocity, U. S. Trade Policy, & the GATT Regime. 256p. 1993. text 37.50 (0-8014-2864-5) Cornell U Pr.
Rhodes, Carolyn, ed. The European Union in the World Community. 265p. 1998. lib. bdg. 52.00 (1-55587-780-X) L Rienner.

An Asterisk (*) at the beginning of an entry indicates that the title is appearing for the first time.

Rhodes, Carolyn & Mazey, Sonia, eds. The State of the European Union Vol. 3: Building a European Polity? LC 95-9034. 520p. 1995. 55.00 (*1-55587-605-6*) L Rienner.

Rhodes, Carolyn H., ed. American Notes & Queries Supplement, First Person Female American, Vol. II. LC 77-93778. xlx, 404p. 1980. 48.50 (*0-87875-140-8*) Whitston Pub.

Rhodes, Cheryl, jt. auth. see Bove, Anthony.

Rhodes, Cheryl, jt. auth. see Bove, Tony.

Rhodes, Chip. Structures of the Jazz Age. LC 98-30213. (Haymarket Ser.). 288p. 2000. 60.00 (*1-85984-833-8*); pap. 19.00 (*1-85984-200-3*) Routledge.

Rhodes, Christine P. The Encyclopedia of Beer. 502p. 1997. pap. text 18.95 (*0-8050-5554-1*) H Holt & Co.

Rhodes, Christine P., et al, eds. The Encyclopedia of Beer: The Beer Lover's Bible. LC 95-24963. (Henry Holt Reference Bks.). (Illus.). 509p. 1995. 35.00 (*0-8050-3799-3*) H Holt & Co.

Rhodes, Christopher, jt. ed. see Lund, Anders.

***Rhodes, Christopher J.** Toxicology of the Human Environment: The Critical Role of Free Radicals. LC 99-31651. 2000. 144.95 (*0-7484-0916-5*) Tay Francis Ltd.

Rhodes, Christopher T., jt. ed. see Banker, Gilbert S.

Rhodes, Clifford, ed. Authority in a Changing Society. LC 70-398288. 231p. reprint ed. pap. 71.70 (*0-8357-5901-6*, 205127700093) Bks Demand.

Rhodes, Colbert. An Introduction to Gerontology: Aging in American Society. (Illus.). 240p. 1998. pap. text 28.95 (*0-398-06649-3*) C C Thomas.

— An Introduction to Gerontology: Aging in American Society. (Illus.). 240p. (C). 1998. text 43.95 (*0-398-05376-6*) C C Thomas.

***Rhodes, Colin.** Outsider Art: Spontaneous Alternatives. LC 99-65579. (World of Art Ser.). (Illus.). 224p. 2000. pap. 14.95 (*0-500-20334-2*, Pub. by Thames Hudson) Norton.

Rhodes, Colin. Primitivism & Modern Art. LC 94-60286. (World of Art Ser.). (Illus.). 216p. (Orig.). 1995. pap. 14.95 (*0-500-20276-1*, Pub. by Thames Hudson) Norton.

***Rhodes, Crystal.** Sin. 2000. pap. 8.95 (*1-58571-017-2*, 909-096, Pub. by Genesis Press) BookWorld.

***Rhodes, Dan.** Anthropology. 240p. 2000. 18.95 (*0-375-50421-4*) Villard Books.

Rhodes, Dan, jt. auth. see Paulk, Earl.

***Rhodes, Daniel.** Clay & Glazes for the Potter. 3rd expanded rev. ed. (Illus.). 352p. 2000. pap. 39.95 (*0-87341-863-8*, CGFP3) Krause Pubns.

Rhodes, Daniel. Vampires: Emotional Predators Who Want to Suck the Life Out of You. LC 97-39228. 197p. 1998. 23.95 (*1-57392-191-2*) Prometheus Bks.

Rhodes, Darrel. Probing the Proverbs. 276p. (Orig.). 1996. pap. write for info. (*1-57502-350-4*, PO1133) Morris Pubng.

***Rhodes, Darrel A.** Preaching the Cross. 1998. pap. 9.45 (*0-9678509-1-6*) D A Rhodes.

Rhodes, Darrel A. Preaching the Cross. Studor, Douglas A., ed. 230p. 1999. pap. 9.45 (*0-7392-0182-4*, PO3149) Morris Pubng.

***Rhodes, Darrel A.** Probing the Proverbs. 1998. pap. 10.95 (*0-9678509-0-8*) D A Rhodes.

Rhodes, Darrell R. Medical Graduates of Foreign Nations: Index of New Information Including Social & Professional Discrimination, Selection, Performance & Problems. 135p. 1997. 47.50 (*0-7883-1636-2*); pap. 44.50 (*0-7883-1637-0*) ABBE Pubs Assn.

Rhodes, David. The Advent Adventure. 128p. 1998. pap. text 9.95 (*0-281-05159-3*) Intl Pubs Mktg.

Rhodes, David, jt. auth. see Wright, Mike.

Rhodes, David L., jt. ed. see Wilsey, Phil E.

Rhodes, Dennis E. Silent Printers: Anonymous Printing at Venice in the Sixteenth Century. LC 95-214505. (British Library Studies in the History of the Book). (Illus.). 306p. 1995. 120.00 (*0-7123-0385-5*) U of Toronto Pr.

— Studies in Early Italian Printing LC 81-190246. 343 p. 1982. write for info. (*0-907132-02-2*) Pindar.

Rhodes, Dennis E., ed. Bookbindings & Other Bibliophily. LC 95-154324. (Illus.). 368p. 1994. 125.00 (*88-85033-26-1*) Oak Knoll.

— A Catalogue of Incunabula in All the Libraries of Oxford Outside the Bodleian. 486p. 1982. text 145.00 (*0-19-818175-2*) OUP.

Rhodes, Dent M & Riegle, Rod. Language & Logic of Educational Policy. 2nd ed. 124p. (C). 1990. pap. 30.60 (*0-536-57695-5*) Pearson Custom.

Rhodes, Diane B., jt. auth. see Bell, George H.

Rhodes, Donald R. Introduction to Monopulse. LC 80-65818. (Illus.). 129p. reprint ed. pap. 40.00 (*0-608-17722-9*, 203013000067) Bks Demand.

***Rhodes, Donna McKee.** Even More Little Stories for Little Children: A Worship Resource, 3 vols. (Illus.). 128p. (J). 2000. pap. 7.99 (*0-8361-9129-3*) Herald Pr.

Rhodes, Donna McKee. Little Stories for Little Children: A Worship Resource. LC 94-38280. 128p. (J). (ps-6). 1995. pap. 7.99 (*0-8361-9000-9*) Herald Pr.

— More Little Stories for Little Children: A Worship Resource, 2 vols. LC 96-32340. 128p. (J). 1997. pap. 7.99 (*0-8361-9059-9*) Herald Pr.

Rhodes, Dorothy. Angel with Broken Wings. LC 95-81759. 88p. 1996. 18.95 (*1-878208-78-0*) Guild Pr IN.

Rhodes, E. G. & Moslow, T. F. Marine Clastic Reservoirs: Examples & Analogues. Bouma, A. H., ed. (Frontiers in Sedimentary Geology Ser.). (Illus.). 360p. 1992. 161.00 (*0-387-97788-0*) Spr-Verlag.

Rhodes, E. W. Defensor's Liber Scintillarum. (EETS, OS Ser.: No. 93). 1972. reprint ed. 54.00 (*0-527-00092-2*) Periodicals Srv.

Rhodes, Edward. International Relations: Introductory Readings. 296p. (C). 1995. per. 39.95 (*0-8403-8093-3*) Kendall-Hunt.

***Rhodes, Edward.** International RelationsI: Introductory Readings. 364p. (C). 1998. per. 45.95 (*0-7872-4688-3*) Kendall-Hunt.

Rhodes, Edward, ed. see Trubowitz, Peter.

Rhodes, Elizabeth. The Unrecognized Precursors of Montemayor's Diana. 280p. (C). 1992. text 32.50 (*0-8262-0818-5*) U of Mo Pr.

***Rhodes, Elvi.** The Bright One. 2000. pap. 8.95 (*0-552-14057-0*, Pub. by Transworld Publishers Ltd) Trafalgar.

— Doctor Rose. (J). 2000. pap. 8.95 (*0-552-12607-1*, Pub. by Transworld Publishers Ltd) Trafalgar.

— The House of Bonneau. (J). 2000. pap. 9.95 (*0-552-13481-3*, Pub. by Transworld Publishers Ltd) Trafalgar.

Rhodes, Elvi. The Merry Month of May. 224p. 1997. 24.00 (*0-7278-5163-2*) Severn Hse.

***Rhodes, Elvi.** The Mountain. 2000. 27.95 (*0-593-03932-7*, Pub. by Transworld Publishers Ltd); pap. 10.95 (*0-552-14400-2*, Pub. by Transworld Publishers Ltd) Trafalgar.

— Opal. 2000. pap. 8.95 (*0-552-12367-6*, Pub. by Transworld Publishers Ltd) Trafalgar.

— Portrait of Chloe. 2000. 27.95 (*0-593-04216-6*, Pub. by Transworld Publishers Ltd) Trafalgar.

— Spring Music. large type unabridged ed. 1999. 26.95 (*0-7531-5999-6*, 159996, Pub. by ISIS Lrg Prnt) ISIS Pub.

Rhodes, Ernest L. Henslowe's Rose: The Stage & Staging. LC 73-80466. 348p. reprint ed. pap. 107.90 (*0-7837-5778-6*, 204544400006) Bks Demand.

Rhodes, Erroll F., tr. see Lapide, Phinn E.

Rhodes, F. M., ed. Power up for the Recovery: Industrial Power Conference, 1983. 104p. 1983. pap. text 25.00 (*0-317-02641-0*, I00159) ASME.

Rhodes, Frank H. Fossils. (Golden Guide Ser.). Date not set. 11.05 (*0-606-11346-0*, Pub. by Turtleback) Demco.

— A Neglected Challenge: Minority Participation in Higher Education, No. 17. 13p. 1987. pap. 2.00 (*0-685-66149-0*) Acad Educ Dev.

Rhodes, Frank H., ed. Successful Fund Raising for Higher Education: The Advancement of Learning. LC 97-22597. (American Council on Education/Oryx Press Series on Higher Education). 232p. (C). 1997. boxed set 34.95 (*1-57356-072-3*) Oryx Pr.

Rhodes, Frank H., et al. Cornell Collects: A Celebration of American Art from the Collections of Alumni & Friends. LC 90-82601. (Illus.). 196p. (Orig.). (C). 1993. pap. 32.50 (*0-8122-1507-9*) U of Pa Pr.

Rhodes, Frank H. T., ed. & intro. see Nyiri, Alan.

Rhodes, Frank H.T. Guide to Geology. (Golden Guide Ser.). 1991. 11.05 (*0-606-11363-0*, Pub. by Turtleback) Demco.

Rhodes, Frederick L. Beginnings of Telephony. LC 07-4694. (Telecommunications Ser.). (Illus.). 286p. 1974. reprint ed. 28.95 (*0-405-06057-2*) Ayer.

***Rhodes, G.** Sweet Dreams. 1998. text 40.00 (*0-340-71239-2*, Pub. by Hodder & Stought Ltd) Trafalgar.

Rhodes, Gale. Crystallography Made Crystal Clear. 2nd ed. 256p. 1999. 42.00 (*0-12-587072-8*) Acad Pr.

— Crystallography Made Crystal Clear: A Guide for Users of Macromolecular Models. (Illus.). 202p. 1993. pap. text 42.00 (*0-12-587075-2*) Acad Pr.

***Rhodes, Gary.** Gary Rhodes Fabulous Food. 2000. 24.95 (*0-7894-6809-3*) DK Pub Inc.

— More Roads Around Britain. 2000. 26.95 (*1-884656-15-3*) W One Hund Seventy Five.

Rhodes, Gary. Rhodes Around Britain. LC 98-34995. (Great Food Ser.). (Illus.). 256p. 1998. pap. 19.95 (*1-884656-07-2*) W One Hund Seventy Five.

***Rhodes, Gary & Van der Meer, Ron.** The Cook Pack: Twenty No-Fail Three Course Meals for Two. 2000. 29.95 (*1-902413-41-5*, Pub. by Van der Meer) Abbeville Pr.

Rhodes, Gary D. Lugosi: His Life in Film, on Stage, & in the Hearts of Horror Lovers. LC 96-46131. (Illus.). 430p. 1997. boxed set 55.00 (*0-7864-0257-1*) McFarland & Co.

Rhodes, George F., Jr., et al, eds. Advances in Econometrics, Vol. 1. 310p. 1982. 78.50 (*0-89232-138-5*) Jai Pr.

— Advances in Econometrics, Vol. 9. 265p. 1991. 78.50 (*1-55938-341-0*) Jai Pr.

— Advances in Econometrics: Co-Integration, Spurious Regressions, & Unit Roots, Vol. 8. 342p. (Orig.). 1990. 78.50 (*1-55938-038-1*) Jai Pr.

— Advances in Econometrics: Computation & Simulation, Vol. 6. 261p. 1987. 78.50 (*0-89232-795-2*) Jai Pr.

— Advances in Econometrics: Exact Distribution Analysis in Linear Simultaneous Equation Models, Vol. 2. 231p. 1983. 78.50 (*0-89232-183-0*) Jai Pr.

— Advances in Econometrics: Innovations in Quantitative Economics: Essays in Honor of Robert L. Basmann. (Advances in Econometrics Ser.: Vol. 5). 368p. 1987. 78.50 (*0-89232-686-7*) Jai Pr.

— Advances in Econometrics: Nonparametric & Robust Inference, Vol. 7. 328p. (Orig.). 1989. 78.50 (*0-89232-911-4*) Jai Pr.

— Advances in Econometrics: Simulating & Analyzing Industrial Structure, Vol. 10. 170p. (Orig.). 1994. 78.50 (*1-55938-461-1*) Jai Pr.

— Advances in Econometrics Suppl. 1: International Evidence on Consumption Patterns. 212p. (Orig.). 1989. suppl. ed. 78.50 (*1-55938-046-2*) Jai Pr.

— Survey Methods & Measurements. (Advances in Econometrics Ser.: Vol. 4). 243p. 1985. 78.50 (*0-89232-580-1*) Jai Pr.

Rhodes, George F., Jr., ed. see Basmann, R. L.

Rhodes, George S. Numbers-a-Minute Timing Copy for Ten-Key Adding & Calculating Machines. 36p. (Orig.). (C). 1980. pap. text 6.95 (*0-89420-219-7*, 126000); audio 19.25 (*0-89420-226-X*, 126004) Natl Book.

— Three-Minute Timings for Typing. 2nd ed. Calhoun, Calfrey C., ed. 81p. 1983. pap. text 6.95 (*0-89420-228-6*, 296951) Natl Book.

Rhodes, Ginger, jt. auth. see Rhodes, Richard.

Rhodes, Greg & Erardi, John. Big Red Dynasty: How Bob Howsam & Sparky Anderson Built the Big Red Machine. (Illus.). 298p. 1998. pap. 19.95 (*0-9641402-3-3*) Road West.

Rhodes, Greg & Stang, Mark. Reds in Black & White: 100 Years of Cincinnati Reds Images. (Illus.). 200p. 1999. 29.95 (*0-9641402-4-1*, Pub. by Road West) Partners Pubs Grp.

Rhodes, Gregory L. & Erardi, John. Big Red Dynasty: How Bob Howsam & Sparky Anderson Built the Big Red Machine. (Illus.). 320p. 1997. 35.00 (*0-9641402-2-5*) Road West.

— Crosley Field: The Illustrated History of a Classic Ballpark. (Illus.). 1995. pap. 24.95 (*0-9641402-1-7*) Road West.

Rhodes, Gregory L., jt. ed. see Regina, Karen.

Rhodes, Gwen R. The History of the South Carolina Army National Guard, 1670-1987. (Illus.). 400p. (C). 1988. 30.00 (*0-9619911-0-0*) SC Army Natl Guard.

***Rhodes, Heidi Andrea.** Venus Rising. (Poetry Chapbks.: No. 3). 40p. 2000. pap. 8.00 (*1-930259-02-6*) Anabasis.

Rhodes, Helen. Psychoma (Soul-Sleep) 1908. 150p. 1998. reprint ed. pap. 19.95 (*0-7661-0411-7*) Kessinger Pub.

Rhodes, Herbert. How to Identify Musical Instruments. LC 85-44. (Self Improvement Ser.). (Illus.). 96p. (Orig.). 1985. pap. text 7.95 (*0-8494-1721-X*) Hansen Ed Mus.

Rhodes, Howard J. Rhodes Family in America: A Genealogy & History, from 1497 to the Present Day. (Illus.). 525p. 1992. reprint ed. pap. 79.00 (*0-8328-2391-0*); reprint ed. lib. bdg. 89.00 (*0-8328-2390-2*) Higginson Bk Co.

Rhodes, J., ed. Monoids & Semigroups Theory with Applications. 548p. (C). 1991. text 113.00 (*981-02-0117-6*) World Scientific Pub.

Rhodes, J., et al, eds. Social History in Museums: Handbook for Professionals. 344p. 1992. 80.00 (*0-11-290529-3*, HM05293, Pub. by Statnry Office) Bernan Associates.

Rhodes, J. & Walker, A. C., eds. Developments in Thin-Walled Structures, Vol. 3. 3rd ed. 290p. 1987. mass mkt. 132.95 (*1-85166-076-3*) Elsevier.

Rhodes, J. Michael & Lockwood, John P., eds. Mauna Loa Revealed: Its Structure, Composition, History, & Hazards. (Geophysical Monographs: Vol. 92). 348p. 1995. 70.00 (*0-87590-049-6*) Am Geophysical.

***Rhodes, J. Philip.** Wicca Unveiled: The Complete Rituals of Modern Witchcraft. 210p. 2000. pap. 14.99 (*0-9536745-0-9*, Pub. by Speaking Tree Bks) SCB Distributors.

Rhodes, Jack. Intercity Bus Lines of the Southwest: A Photographic History. LC 88-2207. (Centennial Series of the Association of Former Students: No. 29). (Illus.). 176p. 1988. 24.95 (*0-89096-374-6*) Tex A&M Univ Pr.

Rhodes, Jack W. Keats's Major Odes: An Annotated Bibliography of the Criticism. LC 83-16634. 224p. 1984. lib. bdg. 45.00 (*0-313-23809-X*, RHK/, Greenwood Pr) Greenwood.

Rhodes, Jack W., jt. ed. see Evert, Walter H.

Rhodes, James. Boothby. 1999. pap. write for info. (*0-14-012334-2*, Viking) Viking Penguin.

Rhodes, James F. History of the United States from the Compromise of 1850. abr. ed. Nevins, Allan, ed. LC 66-23695. (Orig.). 1992. pap. text 3.95 (*0-226-71056-4*, P238) U Ch Pr.

— History of the United States from the Compromise of 1850 to the End of the Roosevelt Administration, 6 vols., Set. rev. ed. (BCL1 - U. S. History Ser.). 1991. reprint ed. lib. bdg. 540.00 (*0-7812-6039-6*) Rprt Serv.

— Lectures on the American Civil War. LC 73-160990. (Select Bibliographies Reprint Ser.). 1977. reprint ed. 21.95 (*0-8369-5858-6*) Ayer.

Rhodes, James Ford. History of the Civil War, 1861-1865. LC 99-40604. 544p. 1999. pap. text 14.95 (*0-486-40900-7*) Dover.

Rhodes, James R. James R. Rhodes' Poems. LC 82-20374. (Lewiston Poetry Ser.). 112p. 1982. lib. bdg. 24.95 (*0-88946-999-7*) E Mellen.

— Little Vine. (Lewiston Poetry Ser.: Vol. 12). (Illus.). 84p. 1986. lib. bdg. 24.95 (*0-88946-049-3*) E Mellen.

Rhodes, Jamie. Prey, Messiah. 150p. 1998. pap. 9.95 (*0-9661752-0-4*) Twnty-Fifth Dynasty.

Rhodes, Jane. Mary Ann Shadd Cary: The Black Press & Protest in the Nineteenth Century. LC 98-19997. (Illus.). 304p. 1998. lib. bdg. 39.95 (*0-253-33446-2*) Ind U Pr.

***Rhodes, Jane.** Mary Ann Shadd Cary: The Black Press & Protest in the Nineteenth Century. (Illus.). 304p. 2000. pap. 18.95 (*0-253-21350-9*) Ind U Pr.

***Rhodes, Janice.** Information on Standards: A Guide to Sources. 130p. 1998. pap. 59.00 (*0-7123-0832-6*) L Erlbaum Assocs.

Rhodes, Janis, jt. auth. see McClure, Nancee.

Rhodes, Jeanne. Fat to Fit Without Dieting. (Illus.). 288p. 1990. pap. 14.95 (*0-8092-4158-7*, 415870, Contemporary Bks) NTC Contemp Pub Co.

Rhodes, Jennifer D. The Fitness Solution with Jennifer Rhodes: The Ultimate Exercise & Injury Prevention Program. (Illus.). 225p. 1999. pap. 19.95 (*0-9666732-4-7*) Tomchie Pub.

***Rhodes, Jennifer D.** Peak Performance Fitness: Maximizing Your Fitness Potential Without Injury or Strain. (Illus.). 2000. 24.95 (*0-89793-297-8*); pap. 14.95 (*0-89793-296-X*) Hunter Hse.

Rhodes, Jewell P. Magic City: A Novel. 288p. 1998. pap. 13.00 (*0-06-092907-3*) HarpC.

— Voodoo Dreams: A Novel of Marie Laveau. 4th ed. LC 94-45088. 1995. pap. 14.00 (*0-312-11931-3*) St Martin.

Rhodes, Jewell Parker. Free Within Ourselves: Fiction Lessons for Black Authors. LC 99-21963. 352p. 1999. pap. 12.95 (*0-385-49175-1*) Doubleday.

Rhodes, Joan L., jt. auth. see Kutie, Rita C.

Rhodes, John. Branch Lines to Ramsey. 76p. (C). 1985. 39.00 (*0-85361-323-0*) St Mut.

— Kettering-Huntingdon Line. (C). 1985. 65.00 (*0-85361-301-X*) St Mut.

— Rejoice or Cry - Diary of a Recon Marine - Vietnam, 1967-68. (Illus.). 219p. (Orig.). 1996. pap. 7.95 (*0-9655655-0-5*) J Rhodes.

***Rhodes, John.** Videoconferencing for the Real World. (Illus.). 272p. 2000. pap. 34.95 (*0-240-80416-3*, Focal) Buttrwrth-Heinemann.

Rhodes, John D. Theory of Electrical Filters. LC 75-30767. 234p. reprint ed. pap. 72.60 (*0-608-10195-8*, 202210300024) Bks Demand.

Rhodes, John H. The History of Battery B, First Regiment Rhode Island Light Artillery. (Army of the Potomac Ser.). (Illus.). 406p. (C). 1997. reprint ed. 40.00 (*0-935523-64-2*) Butternut & Blue.

Rhodes, Johnathan M. Clinical Problems in Gastroenterology. 280p. (C). (gr. 13). 1995. pap. text 47.95 (*0-8151-7334-2*, 23042) Mosby Inc.

Rhodes, Jonathan M. & Milton, Jeremy D., eds. Lectin Methods & Protocols. LC 97-28305. (Methods in Molecular Medicine Ser.: Vol. 9). 650p. 1997. 99.50 (*0-89603-396-1*) Humana.

Rhodes, Judy C. The Hunter's Heart. LC 92-47025. 192p. (J). (gr. 5 up). 1993. lib. bdg. 14.95 (*0-02-773935-X*, Bradbury S&S) S&S Childrens.

Rhodes, Karen. Booking "Hawaii Five-O" An Episode Guide & Critical History of the 1968-1980 Television Detective Series. LC 96-39668. (Illus.). 341p. 1997. lib. bdg. 48.50 (*0-7864-0171-0*) McFarland & Co.

— Shining Tide. 320p. 1992. mass mkt. 3.99 (*0-8217-3839-9*, Zebra Kensgtn) Kensgtn Pub Corp.

— Strings of Fortune. (Lucky in Love Ser.: No. 25). 320p. 1993. mass mkt. 3.50 (*0-8217-4111-X*, Zebra Kensgtn) Kensgtn Pub Corp.

Rhodes, Kathleen F. Kathleen's Secrets for an Adequate Lifesytle: A Guide for Living the Good Enough Life. LC 98-96839. 100p. 1999. pap. 9.95 (*0-9667934-0-4*) Adequate Enters.

Rhodes, Katy. Emperor's New Clothes: Fairy Tale Fun. LC 96-83207. Orig. Title: kejserens nye klaeder. (Illus.). 14p. (J). 1996. 4.95 (*0-8120-6613-8*) Barron.

— Old MacDonald's Pop-Up Farm. (Illus.). 12p. (J). 1997. 13.95 (*0-7641-5055-3*) Barron.

— Sleeping Beauty: Fairy Tale Fun. LC 96-83213. (Illus.). 14p. 1996. 4.95 (*0-8120-6610-3*) Barron.

Rhodes, Katy. Bedtime Rhymes. (Carousel Ser.). (J). (ps-1). 1994. boxed set 7.95 (*1-884628-10-9*, Flyng Frog) Allied Pub MD.

— Nursery Rhymes. (Carousel Ser.). (J). (ps-1). 1994. boxed set 7.95 (*1-884628-09-5*, Flyng Frog) Allied Pub MD.

***Rhodes, Keith A.** Year 2000 Computing Crisis: Readiness of the Electric Power Industry & Status of the Water. (Illus.). 86p. (C). 1999. pap. text 20.00 (*0-7881-8416-4*) DIANE Pub.

Rhodes, L. & Rhodes, T. G. Lovell. Biographical Genealogy of the Lovell Family in England & America. 219p. 1998. reprint ed. pap. 33.50 (*0-8328-9677-2*); reprint ed. lib. bdg. 43.50 (*0-8328-9676-4*) Higginson Bk Co.

Rhodes, Lelia G. Jackson State University: The First Hundred Years, 1877-1977. LC 77-18107. (Illus.). 436p. reprint ed. pap. 135.20 (*0-8357-4348-9*, 203715100007) Bks Demand.

Rhodes, Leon. Tunnel to Eternity: Beyond Near-Death. LC 97-24863. xvii, 107p. (Orig.). 1997. pap. 12.95 (*0-87785-378-9*, Chrysalis Books) Swedenborg.

Rhodes, Linda A., jt. auth. see Taylor, Wiley R.

Rhodes, Lisa. Coretta Scott King: Humanitarian. LC 97-36364. (Black Americans of Achievement Ser.). (Illus.). 144p. (YA). (gr. 5 up). 1999. 19.95 (*0-7910-4690-7*); pap. 8.95 (*0-7910-4691-5*) Chelsea Hse.

Rhodes, Lisa R. Barbara Jordan: Voice of Democracy. LC 98-24134. (Book Report Biography Ser.). (J). 1998. 22.00 (*0-531-11450-3*) Watts.

Rhodes, Lodis. Funds, Force, Friction: Intergovernmental Relations in Programs for Children & Youth in Texas, No. 48. (Policy Research Project Report Ser.). 96p. 1982. pap. 7.50 (*0-89940-651-3*) LBJ Sch Pub Aff.

— Housing Low-Income Austinites: New Roles for the Austin Housing Authority. (Policy Research Project Report Ser.: No. 87). 122p. 1989. pap. 10.00 (*0-89940-694-7*) LBJ Sch Pub Aff.

— Runaways in Texas: A Statistical Estimate, 1985. (Special Project Reports). 33p. 1985. pap. 5.00 (*0-89940-852-4*) LBJ Sch Pub Aff.

— Teacher Retirement System of Texas: Survey of Annuitants & State Teacher Retirement Systems. (Policy Research Project Report Ser.: No. 79). 75p. 1986. pap. 8.00 (*0-89940-683-1*) LBJ Sch Pub Aff.

— Welfare Reform, No. 28. Incl. Vol. II. Income Maintenance Policy: An Analysis of Historical & Legislative Precedents. 145p. 1978. pap. 3.00 (*0-89940-622-X*); Vol. III. Analyses of Contemporary Welfare Reform Issues. 98p. 1978. pap. 3.00 (*0-89940-623-8*); Vol. IV. Family Independence Project: An Alternative Welfare Reform Approach. 130p. 1978. pap. 3.00 (*0-89940-624-6*); (Policy Research Project Report Ser.). 1978. 12.00 (*0-89940-503-7*) LBJ Sch Pub Aff.

Rhodes, Lodis, contrib. by. Welfare Reform, Vol. 28. (Policy Research Project Report Ser.). 1978. 12.00 (*0-89940-620-3*) LBJ Sch Pub Aff.

Rhodes, Lodis & Hadden, Susan G. Evolution of Universal Service Policy. (Policy Research Project Report: No. 116). 90p. 1995. pap. 15.00 (0-89940-724-2) LBJ Sch Pub Aff.

Rhodes, Lorna. Book of Children's Foods. (Illus.). 120p. 1992. pap. 12.00 (1-55788-047-6, HP Books) Berkley Pub.

— The Book of Salads. (Book of...Ser.). (Illus.). 120p. (Orig.). 1989. pap. 12.00 (0-89586-791-5, HP Books) Berkley Pub.

— Book of Soups. (Illus.). 120p. (Orig.). 1989. pap. 12.00 (0-89586-818-0, Price Stern) Peng Put Young Read.

Rhodes, Lorna A. Emptying Beds: The Work of an Emergency Psychiatric Unit. LC 90-11161. (Comparative Studies of Health Systems & Medical Care: Vol. 27). (Illus.). 199p. 1991. 40.00 (0-520-07054-2, Pub. by U CA Pr) Cal Prin Full Svc.

— Emptying Beds: The Work of an Emergency Psychiatric Unit. (Comparative Studies of Health Systems & Medical Care: Vol. 27). (Illus.). 199p. 1995. pap. 14.95 (0-520-20351-8, Pub. by U CA Pr) Cal Prin Full Svc.

Rhodes, Lorne. Book of Fondues. Staub, Susan, ed. LC 87-15052. (Book of...Ser.). (Illus.). 120p. (Orig.). 1989. pap. 12.00 (0-89586-667-6, HP Books) Berkley Pub.

Rhodes, Lucien, jt. auth. see Little, Jeffrey B.

Rhodes, Lucy, et al. Walking Tours of Wisconsin's Historic Towns. Roerden, Chris, ed. LC 98-75060. (Illus.). 128p. 1998. pap. 14.95 (0-915024-67-5) Trails Media.

Rhodes, Lynette I. American Folk Art: From the Traditional to the Naive. LC 79-104017. (Themes in Art Ser.). (Illus.). 116p. reprint ed. pap. 36.00 (0-8357-5368-9, 202266100029) Bks Demand.

— The Roycroft Shops, 1894-1915. (Illus.). 20p. 1975. pap. 8.95 (0-9616623-8-7) Erie Art Mus.

— Science Within Art. LC 79-93193. (Illus.). 72p. reprint ed. pap. 30.00 (0-608-18575-2, 202266000029) Bks Demand.

Rhodes, Lynn K., ed. Literacy Assessment: A Handbook of Instruments. LC 92-1619. 181p. (C). 1992. pap. text 28.00 (0-435-08759-2, 08759) Heinemann.

Rhodes, Lynn K. & Dudley-Marling, Curt. Readers & Writers with a Difference: A Holistic Approach to Teaching Learning Disabled & Remedial Students. LC 87-23819. 344p. (Orig.). (C). 1988. pap. text 28.00 (0-435-08453-4, 08453) Heinemann.

— Readers & Writers with a Difference: A Holistic Approach to Teaching Struggling Readers & Writers. 2nd ed. LC 96-5894. 1996. pap. text 32.50 (0-435-07215-3) Heinemann.

Rhodes, Lynn K. & Shanklin, Nancy. Windows into Literacy: Assessing Learners K-Eight. LC 92-25297. 456p. (J). (gr. k). 1993. pap. text 35.00 (0-435-08757-6, 08757) Heinemann.

Rhodes, Lynn N. Co-Creating: A Feminist Vision of Ministry. LC 87-10518. 132p. (C). 1987. pap. 14.95 (0-664-24032-1) Westminster John Knox.

***Rhodes, M. J.** Introduction to Particle Technology. LC 98-7737. 336p. 1998. pap. 74.95 (0-471-98483-3) Wiley.

Rhodes, M. J., ed. Principles of Powder Technology. LC 89-70570. 452p. 1990. 250.00 (0-471-92422-9) Wiley.

Rhodes, M. J., jt. ed. see Charlwood, Barry V.

Rhodes, M. J., jt. ed. see Robins, R. J.

Rhodes, Margaret L. Ethical Dilemmas in Social Work Practice. LC 91-17352. 216p. 1991. pap. 18.95 (0-87304-255-7) Manticore Pubs.

— Ethical Dilemmas in Social Work Practice. 192p. 1986. pap. text 12.95 (0-415-90157-X, Routledge Thoemms) Routledge.

***Rhodes, Marion B.** Selected Papers on Optical Microscopy. LC 00-34437. (Milestone Ser.). 2000. write for info. (0-8194-3802-2) SPIE.

Rhodes, Mark, ed. New York Actions & Remedies Vols. 1-5, 5 vols., Set. Incl. Set. New York Actions & Remedies Vols. 3 & 4: Corporate & Commercial Law., 2 vols. 1300p. 1991. ring bd. 170.00 (0-88063-445-6, MICHIE); Vol. 5. New York Actions & Remedies Vol. 5: Family Law, Wills & Trusts. 500p. 1991. ring bd. 85.00 (1-56257-165-6, MICHIE); Vols. 1 & 2. New York Actions & Remedies Vols. 1 & 2: Tort Law. 1000p. 1991. ring bd. 170.00 (1-56257-164-8, MICHIE); 1991. Set ring bd. 400.00 (1-56257-661-5, MICHIE) LEXIS Pub.

Rhodes, Mark S. The Handbook of Insurance Agency Law. Standard Publishing Corporation Staff, ed. 480p. 1994. text 119.00 (0-923240-10-1) Stndrd Publishing.

— The Law of Commercial Insurance. 1992. 138.00 (0-923240-00-4) Stndrd Publishing.

— Orfield's Criminal Procedure under the Federal Rules, 7 vols., Set. 2nd ed. LC 85-50534. 1985. 710.00 (0-685-59839-X) West Group.

— Tort & Insurance Litigation Reference, 5 vols., Set. LC 92-71126. 1992. ring bd. 420.00 (0-685-59871-3) West Group.

Rhodes, Mark S. & Ohlsson, Gordon L. Workers' Compensation Answer Book, 1. annuals 834p. 1997. boxed set 125.00 (1-56706-401-9, 64019) Panel Pubs.

Rhodes, Martha. At the Gate, Vol. IV. Busa, Christopher, ed. LC 94-73949. (Provincetown Poets Ser.: IV). (Illus.). 72p. (Orig.). 1995. 35.00 (0-944854-19-2); pap. text 10.00 (0-944854-18-4) Provincetown Arts.

***Rhodes, Martha.** Perfect Disappearance. 51p. 1999. 22.00 (0-932826-98-9); pap. 12.00 (0-932826-99-7) WMU Poetry & Prose.

Rhodes, Martha E. Food Protection Technology, Vol. 2. (Illus.). 416p. 1990. boxed set 95.00 (0-87371-377-X, L377) Lewis Pubs.

Rhodes, Martha E., ed. see Nagy, et al.

Rhodes, Martin. Southern European Welfare States: Between Crisis & Reform. LC 97-10305. 296p. 1997. 45.00 (0-7146-4788-8, Pub. by F Cass Pubs); pap. 19.50 (0-7146-4344-0, Pub. by F Cass Pubs) Intl Spec Bk.

Rhodes, Martin, ed. The Regions & the New Europe: Patterns in Core & Periphery Development. LC 95-4963. (European Policy Research Unit Studies: No. 1). 320p. 1996. text 79.95 (0-7190-4251-8, Pub. by Manchester Univ Pr) St Martin.

Rhodes, Martin & Bull, Martin J. Crisis & Transition in Italian Politics. LC 97-2653. (Illus.). 253p. (C). 1997. 37.50 (0-7146-4816-7, Pub. by Irish Acad Pr); pap. 19.50 (0-7146-4366-1, Pub. by Irish Acad Pr) Intl Spec Bk.

Rhodes, Martin, et al. Developments in West European Politics. LC 96-52116. 1997. pap. 19.95 (0-312-17340-7); text 55.00 (0-312-17339-3) St Martin.

Rhodes, Martin, jt. auth. see Bardi, Luciano.

Rhodes, Martin, jt. ed. see Fererra, Maurizio.

Rhodes, Michael. The Secret Enemy. 1999. pap. 11.95 (0-7414-0039-1) Buy Books.

Rhodes, N. G. & Gabrisch, K. The Coinage of Nepal: From Earliest Times to 1911. (Illus.). 201p. 1989. lib. bdg. 110.00 (1-886720-04-5) S J Durst.

Rhodes, Nancy C. & Branaman, Lucinda E. Foreign Language Instruction in the United States: A National Survey of Elementary & Secondary Schools. LC 98-55507. (Language in Education Ser.). 1999. write for info. (1-887744-43-6) Delta Systems.

Rhodes, Naomi. Twenty One Voices: The Art of Presenting the Performing Arts. Robins, Melinda, ed. (Illus.). 324p. (Orig.). 1990. pap. 27.00 (0-926517-09-0) Assn Perf Arts Presenters.

Rhodes, Neil. Breaking Loose: Taking Your Marriage to a Higher Level of Fulfillment. LC 98-150647. 182p. (Orig.). 1997. pap. 8.99 (1-884369-57-X, EBED Pubns) McDougal Pubng.

— The Power of Eloquence & English Renaissance Literature. LC 92-14672. 1992. text 49.95 (0-312-08421-8) St Martin.

***Rhodes, Neil.** Renaissance Computer: Knowledge Technology in the First Age of Print. LC 99-87623. 2000. 85.00 (0-415-22063-7) Routledge.

Rhodes, Neil, ed. English Renaissance Prose: History, Language & Politics. LC 97-15525. (Medieval & Renaissance Texts & Studies: No. 164). 320p. 1997. 24.00 (0-86698-205-1, MR164) MRTS.

***Rhodes, Neil & McKeehan, Julie.** Palm Programming: The Developers Guide. Stone, Mark, ed. (Illus.). 457p. 1998. pap. 32.95 incl. cd-rom (1-56592-525-4) OReilly & Assocs.

Rhodes, Neil & Rhodes, Noline. Refilling the Jars: Finding Hope after Adultery. 182p. 1996. pap. 9.99 (1-884369-31-6, EBED Pubns) McDougal Pubng.

***Rhodes, Neil & Sawday, Jonathan.** The Renaissance Computer: Knowledge Technology in the First Age of Print. LC 99-87623. 2000. pap. 25.99 (0-415-22064-5) Routledge.

Rhodes, Nick, ed. see Cowper, William.

Rhodes, Noline, jt. auth. see Rhodes, Neil.

Rhodes, Norman. Ibsen & the Greeks: Selected Works of Henrik Ibsen as Mediated by German & Scandinavian Culture. LC 94-24280. 208p. 1995. 36.50 (0-8387-5298-5) Bucknell U Pr.

Rhodes, Olin E., Jr., et al, eds. Population Dynamics in Ecological Space & Time. (Illus.). 336p. 1996. lib. bdg. 50.00 (0-226-71057-2) U Ch Pr.

Rhodes, Olin E., et al, eds. Population Dynamics in Ecological Space & Time. (Illus.). 336p. 1996. pap. text 18.00 (0-226-71058-0) U Ch Pr.

Rhodes, Oliver. Overcoming Addiction Without a Twelve Step Conviction. Tradas, Nick, ed. LC 98-96213. (Illus.). 330p. (Orig.). 1997. pap., mass mkt. 19.95 (0-9658665-0-5, 001) Corp Hlth.

Rhodes, P., ed. see International Conference on the Physics of Transit.

Rhodes, P. H. Organic Chemists Desk Reference. 6th ed. 174p. (gr. 13). 1995. lib. bdg. 40.00 (0-412-54100-9) Chapman & Hall.

Rhodes, P. J. A Commentary on the Aristotelian Athenaion Politeia. (Illus.). 822p. 1993. reprint ed. pap. text 49.95 (0-19-814942-5) OUP.

— The Decrees of the Greek States. 654p. 1998. text 165.00 (0-19-814973-5) OUP.

— The Greek City States: A Source Book. LC 86-3375. 286p. 1986. 39.95 (0-8061-2010-X) U of Okla Pr.

Rhodes, P. J., ed. Thucydides Vol. IV.1-V.24: History. (Classical Texts Ser.). 360p. 1998. 59.95 (0-85668-701-4); pap. 32.00 (0-85668-702-2) David Brown.

Rhodes, P. J., jt. auth. see Mitchell, Lynette G.

Rhodes, P. J., ed. see Lewis, David M.

Rhodes, P. J., ed. see Thucydides.

Rhodes, P. J., tr. & intro. see Aristotle.

Rhodes, P. Malcolm & Stanbury, Peter F., eds. Applied Microbial Physiology: A Practical Approach, Vol. 183. LC 97-7854. (The Practical Approach Ser.: No. 183). (Illus.). 290p. 1997. text 115.00 (0-19-963578-1); pap. text 55.00 (0-19-963577-3) OUP.

***Rhodes, Pam.** Trespassers. large type ed. 464p. 2000. write for info. (0-7505-1479-5, Pub. by Mgna Lrg Print) Ulverscroft.

Rhodes, Pam. With Hearts & Hymns & Voices. LC 98-22570. 1998. pap. text 11.99 (0-7459-3854-X) Lion USA.

Rhodes, Penny J. Racial Matching in Fostering: The Challenge to Social Work Practice. 225p. 1992. 72.95 (1-85628-264-3, Pub. by Avebry) Ashgate Pub Co.

Rhodes, Peter, jt. auth. see Fincham, Robin.

Rhodes, Peter, jt. ed. see Rowland, Fytton.

Rhodes, Peter D. Building a Network: How to Specify, Design, Procure & Install a Corporate LAN. LC 95-21559. (Illus.). 222p. 1995. 40.00 (0-07-052134-4) McGraw.

Rhodes, Peter S. The Aim Workbook: A Spiritual Growth Method Developed from Swedenborg & Gurdjieff. 176p. pap. (0-9626795-4-2) J Appleseed & Co.

Rhodes, Peter S., jt. auth. see Fincham, Robin.

Rhodes, Phyllis. A Big Backyard: Nature's Musical Verse for Children. LC 97-94593. (Illus.). iv, 76p. (J). (ps-1). 1998. 30.00 incl. audio (0-9661359-0-3) Curio Pr.

Rhodes, R. El Falso Cristo de la Nueva Era.Tr. of Counterfeit Christ of New Age Movement. (SPA.). 100. pap. 9.99 (1-56063-665-3, 590278) Editorial Unilit.

— Understanding Governance: Policy Networks, Governance, Reflexivity & Accountability. LC 96-49949. (Public Policy & Management Ser.). 192p. 1997. 98.95 (0-335-19728-0); pap. 33.95 (0-335-19727-2) OpUniv Pr.

***Rhodes, R. A.** Control & Power in Central-Local Government Relations. 2nd ed. LC 99-15646. 220p. 1999. text 78.95 (1-84014-778-4, Pub. by Ashgate Pub) Ashgate Pub Co.

Rhodes, R. A., ed. United Kingdom, Vols. I & II. LC 99-63447. (International Library of Politics & Comparative Government). 460p. 1999. text 148.95 (1-84014-045-3, Pub. by Ashgate Pub) Ashgate Pub Co.

Rhodes, R. A. & Dunleavy, Patrick, eds. Prime Minister, Cabinet, & Core Executive. LC 94-49141. 1995. text 65.00 (0-312-12616-6) St Martin.

Rhodes, R. A. & Wright, V., eds. Tensions in the Territorial Politics of Western Europe. (Illus.). 176p. 1988. text 37.50 (0-7146-3329-1, Pub. by F Cass Pubs) Intl Spec Bk.

Rhodes, R. A., jt. ed. see Marsh, David.

***Rhodes, R. A. W.** Transforming British Government. LC 00-39063. 2000. pap. write for info. (0-312-23584-4) St Martin.

Rhodes, R. J., ed. see Thucydides.

Rhodes, R. Sanders, II. Paleoecology & Regional Paleoclimatic Implications of the Farmdalian Craigmile & Woodfordian Waubonsie Mammalian Local Faunas, Southwestern Iowa. (Reports of Investigations: No. 40). (Illus.). viii, 51p. (Orig.). 1984. pap. 5.00 (0-89792-103-8) Ill St Museum.

Rhodes, Raphael. Hypnosis - Theory, Practice & Application. LC 97-75631. 192p. 1998. reprint ed. 6.98 (1-56731-244-6, MJF Bks) Fine Comms.

Rhodes, Richard. Dark Sun: The Making of the Hydrogen Bomb. (Illus.). 731p. 1998. text 33.00 (0-7881-5658-6) DIANE Pub.

— Dark Sun: The Making of the Hydrogen Bomb. 1999. pap. 12.98 (0-671-04452-4) PB.

— Dark Sun: The Making of the Hydrogen Bomb. (Illus.). 736p. 1995. 32.95 (0-684-80400-X) S&S Trade.

— Dark Sun: The Making of the Hydrogen Bomb. (Illus.). 736p. 1996. per. 16.00 (0-684-82414-0, Touchstone) S&S Trade Pap.

— Deadly Feasts: The "Prion" Controversy & the Public's Health. (Illus.). 272p. 1998. per. 12.00 (0-684-84425-7, Touchstone) S&S Trade Pap.

— Deadly Feasts: Tracking the Secrets of a Terrifying New Plague. LC 97-320. 259p. 1997. 24.00 (0-684-82360-8) S&S Trade.

— Farm: A Year in the Life of an American Farmer. LC 97-17687. (Illus.). 333p. 1997. pap. 16.95 (0-8032-8965-0, Bison Books) U of Nebr Pr.

***Rhodes, Richard.** Hole in the World: An American Boyhood. 10th anniversary ed. 2000. pap. text 16.95 (0-7006-1038-3) U Pr of KS.

Rhodes, Richard. How to Write: Advice & Reflections. 240p. 1996. pap. 12.00 (0-688-14948-0, Quil); pap. 12.00 (0-614-20467-4, Quil) HarperTrade.

— The Inland Ground: An Evocation of the American Middle West. rev. ed. LC 91-26020. (Illus.). xvi, 328p. 1991. reprint ed. pap. 15.95 (0-7006-0499-5) U Pr of KS.

— The Inland Ground: An Evocation of the American Middle West. rev. ed. LC 91-26020. (Illus.). xvi, 328p. 1991. reprint ed. 25.00 (0-7006-0498-7) U Pr of KS.

— The Making of the Atomic Bomb. 928p. 1995. per. 17.00 (0-684-81378-5, Touchstone) S&S Trade Pap.

— Nuclear Renewal. 1999. pap. 10.95 (0-14-024134-5) Viking Penguin.

Rhodes, Richard. Why They Kill: The Discoveries of a Maverick Criminologist. LC 99-18920. 352p. 1999. 26.95 (0-375-40249-7) Knopf.

***Rhodes, Richard.** Why They Kill: The Discoveries of a Maverick Criminologist. 2000. pap. 14.00 (0-375-70248-2) Vin Bks.

Rhodes, Richard, ed. Visions of Technology. LC 98-37209. (Sloan Technology Ser.). (Illus.). 400p. 1999. 30.00 (0-684-83903-2) S&S Trade.

Rhodes, Richard & Rhodes, Ginger. Trying to Get Some Dignity: Stories of Triumph over Childhood Abuse. LC 96-22608. 320p. 1996. 25.00 (0-688-14096-3, Wm Morrow) Morrow Avon.

***Rhodes, Richard & Rhodes, Ginger.** Trying to Get Some Dignity: Stories of Triumph over Childhood Abuse. 368p. 1998. reprint ed. pap. 14.00 (0-688-16109-X, Quil) HarperTrade.

Rhodes, Richard, ed. & intro. see Serber, Robert.

Rhodes, Richard A. Eastern Ojibwa-Chippewa-Ottawa Dictionary. (Trends in Linguistics, Documentation Ser.: No. 3). liv, 626p. 1985. 144.65 (0-89925-114-5) Mouton.

— Eastern Ojibwa-Chippewa-Ottawa Dictionary. LC 92-37126. 1993. pap. 39.95 (3-11-013749-6) Mouton.

Rhodes, Richard A., ed. see Societas Linguistica Europaea Staff.

Rhodes, Rick. Honduras & Its Bay Islands: A Mariner's Guide, 1. LC 99-188646. 1999. pap. text 17.95 (0-9665866-1-1) Rick Rhodes.

Rhodes, Rita M. Women & the Family in Post-Famine Ireland: Status & Opportunity in a Patriarchal Society. LC 92-836. (Modern European History Ser.). 384p. 1992. text 30.00 (0-8153-0673-3) Garland.

Rhodes, Robert. Nonstop Neurotic Cabaret. 192p. 1998. pap. 14.95 (0-85449-278-X) Gay Mens Pr.

Rhodes, Robert, tr. see Numata Center for Buddhist Translation & Research.

Rhodes, Robert B., ed. Low Temperature Lubricant Rheology Measurement & Relevance to Engine Operation. LC 92-39198. (Special Technical Publication Ser.: No. 1143). (Illus.). 90p. 1993. 47.00 (0-8031-1438-9, STP1143) ASTM.

Rhodes, Robert E., jt. ed. see Casey, Daniel J.

Rhodes, Robert H. All for the Union: The Civil War Diary & Letters of Elisha Hunt Rhodes. 272p. 1992. pap. 13.00 (0-679-73828-2) Vin Bks.

— General A. P. Hill. 1992. pap. 15.00 (0-679-73888-6) Vin Bks.

Rhodes, Robert I. Imperialism & Underdevelopment: A Reader. LC 70-122736. (Illus.). 432p. reprint ed. pap. 134.00 (0-7837-6991-1, 204680300004) Bks Demand.

Rhodes, Robert P. Health Care Politics, Policy, & Distributive Justice: The Ironic Triumph. LC 90-10364. (SUNY Series in Health Care Politics & Policy). 339p. (C). 1991. pap. text 21.95 (0-7914-0778-0) State U NY Pr.

— Health Care Politics, Policy, & Distributive Justice: The Ironic Triumph. LC 90-10364. (SUNY Series in Health Care Politics & Policy). 339p. (C). 1992. text 64.50 (0-7914-0777-2) State U NY Pr.

Rhodes, Robin F. Architecture & Meaning on the Athenian Acropolis. (Illus.). 236p. (C). 1995. pap. text 17.95 (0-521-46981-3) Cambridge U Pr.

Rhodes, Robson. Personal Financial Planning Manual, 1996-1997. 12th ed. 368p. 1996. pap. 51.00 (0-406-99089-1, MICHIE) LEXIS Pub.

— Tolley's Estate Planning 1998-99. 1998. pap. write for info. (1-86012-839-4, Pub. by Tolley Pubng) St Mut.

Rhodes, Ron. Angels: What You Need to Know: Quick Reference Guide. (Quick Reference Guide Ser.). 10p. (Orig.). 1997. pap. 1.99 (1-56507-576-5) Harvest Hse.

— Angels Among Us. LC 94-22294. (Orig.). 1994. pap. 9.99 (1-56507-271-5) Harvest Hse.

***Rhodes, Ron.** Believing in Jesus: What You Need to Know. (Quick Reference Guide Ser.). 16p. 2000. pap. 1.99 (0-7369-0269-4) Harvest Hse.

— Bible Translations: What You Need to Know. (Quick Reference Guide Ser.). 16p. 2000. pap. 1.99 (0-7369-0261-9) Harvest Hse.

Rhodes, Ron. The Complete Book of Bible Answers: Answers to the Tough Questions. LC 97-8440. 350p. (Orig.). 1997. pap. 11.99 (1-56507-721-0) Harvest Hse.

***Rhodes, Ron.** Find It Fast in the Bible: Your Complete Topical Reference. LC 99-57243. 350p. 2000. pap. 10.99 (0-7369-0210-4) Harvest Hse.

— Islam: What You Need to Know. (Quick Reference Guide Ser.). 16p. 2000. pap. 1.99 (0-7369-0209-0) Harvest Hse.

Rhodes, Ron. Jehovah's Witnesses: What You Need to Know: Quick Reference Guide. (Quick Reference Guide Ser.). 10p. (Orig.). 1997. pap. 1.99 (1-56507-510-2) Harvest Hse.

***Rhodes, Ron.** Miracles Around Us: How to Recognize God at Work Today. 250p. 2000. pap. 9.99 (0-7369-0211-2) Harvest Hse.

— Reasoning from the Scriptures with Catholics. LC 99-43335. 400p. 2000. pap. 12.99 (0-7369-0208-2) Harvest Hse.

Rhodes, Ron. Reasoning from the Scriptures with the Jehovah's Witnesses. LC 93-3488. 1993. pap. 12.99 (1-56507-106-9) Harvest Hse.

— What Did Jesus Mean? Making Sense of the Difficult Sayings of Jesus. LC 98-42006. 300p. 1999. pap. 10.99 (0-7369-0049-7) Harvest Hse.

Rhodes, Ron & Bodine, Marian M. Reasoning from the Scriptures with the Mormons. 1995. pap. 12.99 (1-56507-328-2) Harvest Hse.

Rhodes, Ron & Gomes, Alan W. New Age Movement. (Guide to Cults & Religious Movements Ser.). 64p. 1995. pap. 5.99 (0-310-70431-6) Zondervan.

Rhodes, Ron, jt. auth. see Geisler, Norman L.

Rhodes, Ron D. & Decker. The Masonic Lodge: What You Need to Know: Quick Reference Guide. (Quick Reference Guide Ser.). 10p. 1997. pap. 1.99 (1-56507-566-8) Harvest Hse.

— Mormonism: What You Need to Know: Quick Reference Guide. (Quick Reference Guide Ser.). 10p. (Orig.). 1997. pap. 1.99 (1-56507-511-0) Harvest Hse.

Rhodes, Royal W., jt. auth. see McCarthy, George E.

Rhodes, Sammie J. The Best of Old Times Not Forgotten. LC 91-90544. 210p. 1991. pap. 11.95 (0-9630257-0-8) Cty Rhodes.

Rhodes, Samuel, ed. Contemporary Etudes & Solos for the Viola. (Contemporary Etudes Project Ser.). 40.00 (0-614-25499-X, 1902S) Am String Tchrs.

Rhodes, Sara B., ed. see Klein, Eric.

Rhodes, Sara B., ed. see Martin, Randy W.

Rhodes, Schuyler. Words to the Silence. 112p. 1994. pap. 12.95 (1-877871-74-5, 3536) Ed Ministries.

***Rhodes, Stephen.** The Velocity of Money. 512p. 1999. mass mkt. 6.99 (0-380-73284-X, Avon Bks) Morrow Avon.

Rhodes, Stephen. The Velocity of Money: A Novel of Wall Street. LC 97-20626. 352p. 1997. 24.00 (0-688-15538-3, Wm Morrow) Morrow Avon.

Rhodes, Stephen A. Where the Nations Meet: The Church in a Multicultural World. LC 98-17881. 240p. 1998. pap. 14.99 (0-8308-1936-3, 1936) InterVarsity.

Rhodes, Susan L., jt. ed. see Schwenk, Charles R.

Rhodes, T. & Hartnoll, R., eds. AIDS Drugs & Prevention: Perspectives on Individual & Community Action. (Illus.). 256p. (C). 1996. 85.00 (0-415-10203-0, C0221) Routledge.

Rhodes, T., jt. auth. see Czernecki, Stefan.

An Asterisk (*) at the beginning of an entry indicates that the title is appearing for the first time.

Rhodes, T. G., jt. auth. see Rhodes, L.

***Rhodes, Terrel L.** Republicans in the South: Voting for the State House, Voting for the White House. LC 99-55880. 160p. 2000. 49.95 (*0-275-96817-0*, Praeger Pubs) Greenwood.

Rhodes, Tim & Hartnoll, Richard, eds. AIDS Drugs & Prevention: Perspectives on Individual & Community Action. (Illus.). 256p. (C). 1996. pap. 27.99 (*0-415-10204-9*) Routledge.

Rhodes, Timothy, jt. auth. see Czernecki, Stefan.

Rhodes, Tom. Stress Without Tears. (Illus.). 130p. (Orig.). 1990. 22.50 (*0-9615234-1-7*) Jacobs Pub.

Rhodes, Tony, ed. Syndicated Lending. 2nd ed. 520p. 1996. pap. 170.00 (*1-85564-518-1*, Pub. by Euromoney) Am Educ Systs.

Rhodes, Tricia M. Contemplating the Cross: Pilgrimage of Prayer. LC 97-33855. 192p. 1998. pap. 10.99 (*0-7642-2049-7*) Bethany Hse.

***Rhodes, Tricia M.** Taking up Your Cross: The Incredible Gain of the Crucified Life. LC 99-50880. 207p. 1999. pap. 10.99 (*0-7642-2206-6*) Bethany Hse.

RHODES, TRICIA MCCARY. The Soul at Rest. 224p. 1999. pap. text 9.99 (*0-7642-2227-9*) Bethany Hse.

Rhodes, V. James & Dauve, Jan L. The Agriculture Marketing System. 5th ed. LC 97-7421. 500p. 1997. pap. text 53.95 (*1-890871-01-X*) Holcomb Hath.

Rhodes, Vicki. Pumpkin Decorating. LC 97-1936. (Illus.). 96p. 1997. 10.95 (*0-8069-9574-2*) Sterling.

Rhodes, Warren A. & Brown, Waln K., eds. Why Some Children Succeed Despite the Odds. LC 90-49203. 208p. 1991. 52.95 (*0-275-93705-4*, C3705, Praeger Pubs) Greenwood.

Rhodes, Warren A. & Hoey, Kim. Overcoming Childhood Misfortune: Children Who Beat the Odds. LC 93-19611. 168p. 1993. 52.95 (*0-275-94081-0*, Praeger Pubs) Greenwood.

***Rhodes, Willard.** Songs of the Apache. 14p. 1999. reprint ed. pap. 14.95 incl. audio (*1-57970-041-1*, 511157) J Norton Pubs.

— Songs of the Kiowa. 21p. 1999. reprint ed. pap. 14.95 incl. audio (*1-57970-045-4*, S511154) J Norton Pubs.

— Songs of the Navajo. 18p. 1999. reprint ed. pap. 14.95 incl. audio (*1-57970-042-X*, 511153) J Norton Pubs.

***Rhodes, Willard & Densmore, Frances.** Songs of the Sioux, Set. 30p. 1999. reprint ed. pap. 29.50 incl. audio (*1-57970-044-6*, S11158) J Norton Pubs.

Rhodes, William. What America's Users Spend on Illegal Drugs, 1988-1995. (Illus.). 108p. (C). 1999. pap. text 25.00 (*0-7881-7797-4*) DIANE Pub.

***Rhodes, William.** What America's Users Spend on Illegal Drugs, 1988-1995. LC 98-136342. 110p. 1998. pap. text 9.00 (*0-16-049509-1*) USGPO.

Rhodes, Xantha. A Volcanic Affair. (Orig.). 1997. mass mkt. 5.95 (*0-352-33184-4*, Pub. by BLA4) London Brdge.

Rhodier, Vicki. Reading Points-in-Time Coloring Book. (Illus.). 32p. (J). 1994. pap. text 5.00 (*1-887762-03-5*) His Soc Brks Cnty.

Rhodin, Anders G., ed. see Pritchard, Peter C.

Rhodin, Thor N., ed. Physical Metallurgy of Stress Corrosion Fracture. LC 59-14890. (Metallurgical Society Conference Ser.: Vol. 4). 409p. reprint ed. pap. 126.80 (*0-608-11559-2*, 200066700038) Bks Demand.

Rhodios, Apollonius. The Argonautika. Green, Peter, tr. LC 96-24772. (Hellenistic Culture & Society Ser.). 1997. 60.00 (*0-520-07686-9*, Pub. by U CA Pr) Cal Prin Full Svc.

— The Argonautika: The Story of Jason & the Quest for the Golden Fleece. Green, Peter, tr. LC 96-24773. 1997. pap. 14.95 (*0-520-07687-7*, Pub. by U CA Pr) Cal Prin Full Svc.

Rhodius, Apollonius. The Argonautica, Bk. III. (GER.). xlviii, 160p. 1989. reprint ed. 31.20 (*3-487-04590-7*) G Olms Pubs.

— Argonautica Book III. Hunter, R. L., ed. (Cambridge Greek & Latin Classics Ser.). 288p. (C). 1989. text 65.00 (*0-521-32031-3*); pap. text 22.95 (*0-521-31236-1*) Cambridge U Pr.

— Scholia in Apollonium Rhodium Vetera. Wendel, Karl, ed. (GER.). xxviii, 402p. 1974. write for info. (*3-296-15400-0*) G Olms Pubs.

Rhodus, Dennis. Headfirst. (Read-along Radio Dramas Ser.). (J). (gr. 6-10). 1987. ring bd. 38.00 (*1-878298-07-0*) Balance Pub.

Rhody, Alan & Ross, Franz. Holography MarketPlace: The Industry Reference Text & Sourcebook. 7th ed. 224p. 1998. pap. 19.95 (*0-89496-025-3*) Ross Bks.

Rhody, Alan & Ross, Franz, eds. Holography MarketPlace: The Industry Reference Text & Sourcebook. 8th ed. (Illus.). 224p. 1999. pap. 22.95 (*0-89496-110-1*) Ross Bks.

Rhody, Alan, jt. ed. see Ross, Franz.

Rhody, Kurt. Rendezvous: Reliving the Fur Trading Era of 1825 to 1840. Reilly, Rob, ed. (Illus.). 80p. (Orig.). 1996. pap. 17.95 (*0-939365-49-9*) Panorama Intl.

Rhody, Ron. The CEO's Playbook: Handling the Outside Forces That Shape Success. 128p. 1999. pap. 19.95 (*0-9670679-0-1*) Academy Pub.

Rhody, Sean. Powerbuilder Classwizard: How to Build Class Libraries?: PowerBuilder Developer's Journal. (PowerBuilder Training Ser.). (Illus.). 384p. (Orig.). 1996. pap. 37.75 (*1-886141-04-5*) SYS-Con Pubns.

Rholes, W. Steven, jt. ed. see Simpson, Jeffry A.

***Rhomberg, Lorenz.** Strategies to Protect the Health of Deployed U. S. Forces: Analytical Framework for Assessing Risks. 130p. 2000. 29.75 (*0-309-06895-9*) Natl Acad Pr.

Rhomberg, Valerie, jt. auth. see Hall, Nadia S.

Rhomer, Kay, jt. auth. see Puder, Arno.

Rhonda, Janice T. The ABC's of Violin Easy Piano Accompaniment for Book 1. (ABC's of Violin Ser.: Vol. PA-1). 34p. 1998. 8.95 (*0-9663731-2-X*, ABC's-PA-1) ABCs MA.

— The ABC's of Violin for the Absolute Beginner. (ABC's of Violin Ser.: Bk. 1). (Illus.). 41p. 1998. reprint ed. 8.95 (*0-9663731-0-3*, ABC's-1) ABCs MA.

— The ABC's of Violin for the Intermediate. (ABC's of Violin Ser.: Bk. 2). 32p. 1998. 8.95 (*0-9663731-1-1*, ABC's-2) ABCs MA.

Rhondda, Margaret H. Notes on the Way. LC 68-8488. (Essay Index Reprint Ser.). 1977. 19.95 (*0-8369-0822-8*) Ayer.

Rhone, Christine, jt. auth. see Michell, John.

Rhone, Christine, tr. see Faivre, Antoine.

Rhone, Christine, tr. see Richer, Jean.

Rhone, L. C. Total Auto Body Repair. LC 75-2551. (Illus.). 1976. 23.95 (*0-672-97659-5*, Bobbs) Macmillan.

— Total Auto Body Repair. LC 75-2551. 1978. teacher ed. write for info. (*0-672-97137-2*, 2319); student ed. write for info. (*0-672-97200-X*) Macmillan.

— Total Auto Body Repair. 3rd ed. 44p. 1999. teacher ed. 11.86 (*0-02-682163-X*) Glencoe.

— Total Auto Body Repair. 3rd ed. (Illus.). 118p. (gr. 6-12). 1999. student ed., wbk. ed. 12.66 (*0-02-682162-1*) Glencoe.

— Total Auto Body Repair. 21st ed. 1983. pap. 12.64 (*0-02-682130-3*) Macmillan.

— Total Auto Body Repair, No. 3. 3rd ed. 1990. 48.14 (*0-02-682161-3*) Macmillan.

Rhone, L. C. & Yates, H. David. Total Auto Body Repair. 2nd ed. 464p. (C). 1982. teacher ed., student ed. write for info. (*0-672-97969-1*); student ed. write for info. (*0-672-97968-3*); text. write for info. (*0-672-97967-5*) Macmillan.

Rhone, Rudolph F. The Principles of the Sanctuary Services. LC 99-176304. 222 p. 1997. write for info. (*1-55630-826-4*) Brentwood Comm.

Rhonheimer, Martin. Natural Law & Practical Reason: A Thomist View of Moral Autonomy. Malsbary, Gerald, tr. LC 99-89242. (Moral Philosophy & Theology Ser.: Vol. 1). 540p. 1999. 45.00 (*0-8232-1978-X*, Pub. by Fordham) BookMasters.

— Natural Law & Practical Reason: A Thomist View of Moral Autonomy. Malsbary, Gerald, tr. LC 99-89242. (Moral Philosophy & Theology Ser.: Vol. 1). 540p. 2000. pap. 19.95 (*0-8232-1979-8*, Pub. by Fordham) BookMasters.

Rhoodie, Eschel M. Discrimination Against Women: A Global Survey of the Economic, Educational, Social & Political Status of Women. LC 89-42748. 630p. 1989. lib. bdg. 65.00 (*0-89950-448-5*) McFarland & Co.

Rhorer, Norm, ed. see Anderson, David.

Rhorer, Richard L., ed. Proceedings from ASPE, 1991 Annual Conference. 233p. 1991. pap. write for info. (*1-887706-06-2*) Am Soc Prec Engr.

Rhorer, Richard L., et al, eds. Proceedings from ASPE Spring Topical Meeting on Principles of Cutting Mechanics. 99p. 1993. pap. write for info. (*1-887706-09-7*) Am Soc Prec Engr.

***Rhose, David, et al, eds.** Dimensions Volume Fourteen: Discipline. (Illus.). 208p. (C). 2000. Price not set. (*1-891197-12-6*) U Mich Arch.

Rhoton, Albert L., Jr. & Natori, Yoshihiro. The Orbit & Sellar Region: Microsurgical Anatomy & Operative Approaches. (Illus.). 380p. 1996. text 189.00 (*0-86577-531-1*) Thieme Med Pubs.

Rhoton, Dale. How Much for the Man - Chinese Edition. Chiu, Peter, tr. (CHI.). 47p. 1988. pap. 1.50 (*1-56582-070-3*) Christ Renew Min.

***Rhoton, Daphne.** The Coloring Tree. (J). 2001. pap. 9.99 (*1-57532-231-5*) Press-Tige Pub.

— The Coloring Tree. (Illus.). 32p. (YA). 2001. pap. 14.95 (*1-57532-228-5*) Press-Tige Pub.

Rhoton, Elaine. Un Barco Llamado Logos.Tr. of Logos Story. (SPA.). 160p. 1989. pap. 4.99 (*0-945792-49-2*, 498454) Editorial Unilit.

— Logos Story. rev. ed. (Illus.). 192p. 1992. reprint ed. pap. text 5.99 (*0-9630908-4-4*) O M Lit.

Rhoton, Jack & Bowers, Patricia, eds. Issues in Science Education. (Illus.). 240p. 1996. pap. 24.95 (*0-87355-137-0*, PB127X) Natl Sci Tchrs.

Rhoton, Jared, tr. see Rinpoche, Deshung K.

Rhoton, Jessian L. The Magic Treble Tree. Vol. I. (Illus.). 48p. (J). 1989. lib. bdg. write for info. (*0-318-65826-7*) Happy Music Pub.

— The Magic Treble Tree. (All about the Magic of Music Ser.). (Illus.). 48p. (J). 1990. write for info. (*0-9624162-9-0*) Happy Music Pub.

Rhoton, John. Programmer's Guide to Internet Mail: SMTP, POP, IMAP & LDAP. LC 99-36739. 291p. 1999. pap. 39.95 (*1-55558-212-5*, Digital DEC) Buttrwrth-Heinemann.

— SMTP, X.500, X.400: An Introduction. LC 97-14875. 207p. 1997. pap. text 34.95 (*1-55558-165-X*) Buttrwrth-Heinemann.

***Rhowbotham, Kevin.** Field Event:Field Space: Architecture & Urbanism 2. (Illus.). 64p. 1999. pap. 15.95 (*1-901033-40-6*, Pub. by Black Dog Pubg) RAM Publications.

RHR Collective Staff. Radical History Review Vol. 69: Culture & Poverty. (Radical History Review Ser.: No. 69). 200p. (C). 1998. pap. 19.95 (*0-521-63762-7*) Cambridge U Pr.

— Radical History Review Vol. 70: Women & Power. (Radical History Review Ser.: No. 70). 200p. (C). 1998. pap. 19.95 (*0-521-63761-9*) Cambridge U Pr.

— Radical History Review Vol. LXXII: New Models for Labor & Community Education. 226p. (C). 1999. pap. 21.95 (*0-521-64472-0*) Cambridge U Pr.

RHR Collective Staff, ed. Radical History Review: The Praxis of Anthropology & History, Vol. 65. (Illus.). 180p. (C). 1996. pap. 19.95 (*0-521-57690-3*) Cambridge U Pr.

— Radical History Review Vol. 68: Ethnicity, Identity, & Representation in the Academy & Museums. (Illus.). 206p. (C). 1998. pap. text 19.95 (*0-521-59906-7*) Cambridge U Pr.

Rhschendorf, Ludger, jt. auth. see Rachev, S. T.

Rhu, Lawrence F. The Genesis of Tasso's Narrative Theory: English Translations of the Early Poetics & a Comparative Study of Their Significance. LC 92-45872. 192p. 1993. pap. 19.95 (*0-8143-2119-4*); text 29.95 (*0-8143-2118-6*) Wayne St U Pr.

Rhuda, Charles A., ed. see American Institute of Certified Public Accountants.

Rhudy, Elizabeth, ed. see King, Claudia.

Rhue, Judith W., et al, eds. Handbook of Clinical Hypnosis. 765p. 1993. pap. 49.95 (*1-55798-440-9*) Am Psychol.

Rhue, Judith W., jt. ed. see Lynn, Steven Jay.

Rhue, Judith W., jt. ed. see Lynn, Steven J.

Rhue, Morton. The Wave. 144p. (YA). (gr. 7 up). 1981. mass mkt. 5.50 (*0-440-99371-7*, LLL BDD) BDD Bks Young Read.

Rhum, Michael R. The Ancestral Lords: Gender, Descent, & Spirits in a Northern Thai Village. (Special Reports: No. 29). (Illus.). 202p. 1994. pap. text 18.95 (*1-877979-79-1*) SE Asia.

Rhyden, Mari. Writing on the Backs of Blacks. LC 96-184962. 185p. 1996. 25.95 (*0-7022-2890-7*, Pub. by Univ Queensland Pr) Intl Spec Bk.

Rhyder, Robert F. Manufacturing Process Design & Optimization. LC 97-5719. (Manufacturing Engineering & Materials Processing Ser.: Vol. 50). (Illus.). 351p. 1997. text 137.50 (*0-8247-9909-7*) Dekker.

Rhymer, Eve. Legendary, Lexical, Loquacious Love. Alatalo, Sally, ed. 343p. 1996. pap. 16.00 (*1-888636-09-2*) Sara Ranchouse.

Rhymer, Joseph. The End of Time. 160p. (C). 1991. 39.00 (*0-85439-404-4*, Pub. by St Paul Pubns) St Mut.

— Illustrated Atlas of the Bible. 1995. 6.98 (*0-7858-0339-4*) Bk Sales Inc.

— The Miracles of Jesus. 152p. (C). 1996. pap. 39.95 (*0-85439-387-0*, Pub. by St Paul Pubns) St Mut.

Rhymer, Joseph, tr. The Psalms. 448p. 1996. pap. 39.95 (*0-85439-474-5*, Pub. by St Paul Pubns) St Mut.

— 365 Days with the Psalms. 382p. 1996. pap. 39.95 (*0-85439-514-8*, Pub. by St Paul Pubns) St Mut.

Rhyn, Heinz, jt. auth. see Oelkers, Jurgen.

Rhynard-Geil, Bonnie, ed. see Rhynard, Marie E.

Rhynard, Marie E. How to Set the Table & Use Utensils: For Every Day or Entertaining with Basic Tips on Good Manners. Rhynard-Geil, Bonnie & Staver, Frederick L., eds. (Illus.). 94p. 1997. pap. text. write for info. (*0-9659090-0-X*) BRG Design & Prod.

Rhyne, Charles S. Expanding the Circle: The Art of Guud San Glans, Robert Davidson. LC 99-234503. (Illus.). 76p. 1999. pap. 24.95 (*0-295-97776-0*) U of Wash Pr.

Rhyne, Elisabeth H. Small Business, Banks, & SBA Loan Guarantees: Subsidizing the Weak or Bridging a Credit Gap? LC 87-36098. 188p. 1988. 57.95 (*0-89930-256-4*, RSB/, Quorum Bks) Greenwood.

Rhyne, Elisabeth H., jt. ed. see Otero, Maria.

Rhyne, J. J., ed. see American Institute of Physics.

Rhyne, Janie. Gestalt Art Experience: Patterns that Connect. 2nd ed. LC 94-72915. (Illus.). 230p. (C). 1995. pap. text 26.95 (*0-9613309-6-1*) Magnolia St Pub.

Rhyne, Jennings J. Some Southern Cotton Mill Workers & Their Villages. Stein, Leon, ed. LC 77-70527. (Illus.). 1977. reprint ed. lib. bdg. 23.95 (*0-405-10195-3*) Ayer.

Rhyne, Nancy. Alice Flagg: The Ghost of the Hermitage. LC 89-28782. 256p. 1990. 19.95 (*0-88289-760-8*) Pelican.

— Carolina Seashells. LC 81-17342. (Illus.). 1989. pap. 6.95 (*0-87844-077-1*) Sandlapper Pub Co.

— Chronicles of the South Carolina Sea Islands. LC 97-40069. 1998. pap. 9.95 (*0-89587-208-0*) Blair.

— Coastal Ghosts: Haunted Places from Wilmington, North Carolina to Savannah, Georgia. rev. ed. LC 88-36234. (Illus.). 188p. (YA). (gr. 7 up). 1989. reprint ed. pap. 9.95 (*0-87844-049-6*) Sandlapper Pub Co.

— The Jack O'Lantern Ghost. (Illus.). 144p. (YA). (gr. 9-12). 1995. pap. 10.95 (*1-56554-132-4*) Pelican.

— John Henry Rutledge: The Ghost of Hampton Plantation. Stone, Barbara, ed. LC 96-42355. (Illus.). 160p. (Orig.). (YA). (gr. 7-12). 1996. pap. 9.95 (*0-87844-131-X*) Sandlapper Pub Co.

— More Tales of the South Carolina Low Country. LC 84-21710. 121p. 1984. pap. 6.95 (*0-89587-042-8*) Blair.

— Murder in the Carolinas. 176p. (Orig.). 1998. reprint ed. pap. 12.95 (*1-888105-32-1*) Avisson Pr.

— Once upon a Time on a Plantation. LC 88-9896. (Illus.). 160p. 1988. 13.95 (*0-88289-702-0*) Pelican.

— Plantation Tales. LC 88-37029. (YA). (gr. 7 up). 1989. pap. 12.95 (*0-87844-093-3*) Sandlapper Pub Co.

— The South Carolina Lizard Man. LC 92-17289. (Illus.). 144p. (J). (gr. 5-9). 1992. pap. 8.95 (*0-88289-907-4*) Pelican.

— Southern Recipes & Legends. Stone, Barbara, ed. 350p. (Orig.). 1996. 19.95 (*0-87844-133-6*); pap. 14.95 (*0-87844-134-4*) Sandlapper Pub Co.

— Tales of the South Carolina Low Country. LC 82-9710. 112p. 1982. pap. 6.95 (*0-89587-027-4*) Blair.

— Touring the Coastal Georgia Backroads. LC 93-47130. (Touring the Backroads Ser.). (Illus.). 188p. (Orig.). 1994. pap. 14.95 (*0-89587-111-4*) Blair.

— Touring the Coastal South Carolina Backroads. LC 91-41378. (Touring the Backroads Ser.). (Illus.). 276p. (Orig.). 1992. pap. 14.95 (*0-89587-090-8*) Blair.

***Rhyne, Nancy.** Voices of Carolina Slave Children. LC 99-28396. 1999. pap. 9.95 (*0-87844-150-6*) Sandlapper Pub Co.

Rhyne, Patricia J., jt. auth. see Ritter, Beverly L.

Rhyne, Patricia J., ed. see Nash, Jacqueline A. & Kinkaid, Joann.

Rhyne, Patricia J., ed. see Ritter, Beverly L.

Rhyne, William R. Hazardous Materials Transportation Risk Analysis: Quantitative Approaches for Truck & Train. LC 93-38050. 272p. 1994. text 65.95 (*0-442-01413-9*, VNR) Wiley.

Rhyne, William R. Hazardous Materials Transportation Risk Analysis: Quantitative Approaches for Truck & Train. (Industrial Health & Safety Ser.). 254p. 1994. 74.95 (*0-471-28554-4*, VNR) Wiley.

RhyneRhyne, Robert, et al, eds. Community-Oriented Primary Care: Health Care for the 21st Century. LC 98-74064. 228p. 1998. pap. 39.00 (*0-87553-236-5*) Am Pub Health.

Rhys, Bloomfield, ed. Wales, 1937-1940. 310p. 1969. 55.00 (*0-7146-2217-6*, Pub. by F Cass Pubs) Intl Spec Bk.

Rhys-Davids, Caroline A. Buddhist Manual of Psychological Ethics. 1975. reprint ed. 24.00 (*0-8364-2573-1*, Pub. by M Manoharial) S Asia.

— Buddhist Manual of Psychological Ethics. (C). 1996. reprint ed. 32.00 (*81-215-0717-0*, Pub. by M Manoharial) Coronet Bks.

— Stories of the Buddha. 288p. 1989. pap. 7.95 (*0-486-26149-2*) Dover.

Rhys-Davids, Caroline A., jt. auth. see Stede, William.

Rhys-Davids, T. W. Cosmic Law in Ancient Thought. 1998. pap. 3.95 (*1-55818-386-8*, Sure Fire) Holmes Pub.

Rhys, Ernest. Browning & His Poetry. LC 73-120992. (Poetry & Life Ser.). reprint ed. 27.50 (*0-404-52529-6*) AMS Pr.

— Lyric Poetry. LC 70-174315. (Channels of English Literature Ser.: No. 6). reprint ed. 43.50 (*0-404-07816-8*) AMS Pr.

— Modern English Essays, 5 vols. LC 73-174316. reprint ed. 60.00 (*0-404-08070-7*) AMS Pr.

— Rabindranath Tagore. LC 78-133286. (Studies in Asiatic Literature: No. 57). 1970. reprint ed. lib. bdg. 75.00 (*0-8383-1185-7*) M S G Haskell Hse.

Rhys, Ernest, compiled by. A Book of Nonsense. LC 83-45786. reprint ed. 37.50 (*0-404-20215-2*, PN6110) AMS Pr.

Rhys, Ernest, ed. Fairy Gold: A Book of Classic English Fairy Tales. LC 98-27816. (Library of Folklore). (Illus.). 236p. (J). (gr. 3-4). 1999. 14.95 (*0-7818-0700-X*) Hippocrene Bks.

— Fairy Gold: A Book of Old English Fairy Tales. LC 77-114912. (Select Bibliographies Reprint Ser.). 1977. 41.95 (*0-8369-5317-7*) Ayer.

Rhys, Ernest, ed. see Shelley, Percy Bysshe.

Rhys, Grace. Quest of the Ideal (1913) 62p. 1998. reprint ed. pap. 7.95 (*0-7661-0568-7*) Kessinger Pub.

Rhys-Gruffydd, Karol, jt. auth. see MacBay, Shannon.

Rhys, Horton. A Theatrical Trip for a Wager. LC 73-81217. 1972. 24.95 (*0-405-08884-1*, Pub. by Blom Pubns) Ayer.

Rhys, Jean. After Leaving Mr. MacKenzie. 192p. 1997. pap. 11.00 (*0-393-31547-9*) Norton.

— Collected Short Stories. lib. bdg. 27.95 (*0-614-30399-0*) Amereon Ltd.

— The Collected Short Stories. 1992. pap. 12.95 (*0-393-30625-9*) Norton.

— Good Morning, Midnight. (Shoreline Bks.). 192p. 1999. pap. 12.00 (*0-393-30394-2*) Norton.

— The Left Bank & Other Stories. LC 79-134976. (Short Story Index Reprint Ser.). 1977. 26.95 (*0-8369-3698-1*) Ayer.

— La Prisonniere de Sargasses. (FRE.). 1977. pap. 10.95 (*0-7859-4083-9*) Fr & Eur.

— Quai des Grand-Augustins. (FRE.). 1981. pap. 10.95 (*0-7859-4156-8*) Fr & Eur.

— Quartet. 192p. 1997. pap. 11.00 (*0-393-31546-0*) Norton.

— Quatuor. (FRE.). 1982. pap. 10.95 (*0-7859-4166-5*) Fr & Eur.

— Tigers Are Better-Looking. lib. bdg. 21.95 (*0-8488-1885-7*) Amereon Ltd.

— Voyage dans les Tenebres. (FRE.). 1978. pap. 10.95 (*0-7859-4108-8*) Fr & Eur.

— Voyage in the Dark. 1994. pap. 11.00 (*0-393-31146-5*) Norton.

— Wide Sargasso Sea. 190p. 1992. pap. 12.00 (*0-393-30880-4*) Norton.

***Rhys, Jean.** Wide Sargasso Sea. 192p. 1999. reprint ed. 29.95 (*1-56849-729-6*) Buccaneer Bks.

Rhys, Jean & Bronte, Charlotte. Wide Sargasso Sea. Raiskin, Judith L., ed. LC 98-14266. (Critical Editions Ser.). (C). 1998. pap. 11.25 (*0-393-96012-9*) Norton.

— Wide Sargasso Sea. large type ed. LC 93-35502. 209p. 1994. lib. bdg. 21.95 (*0-7862-0073-1*) Thorndike Pr.

Rhys, John. Celtic Folklore, 2 vols., Set. 1973. lib. bdg. 500.00 (*0-87968-099-7*) Gordon Pr.

— Lectures on the Origin & Growth of Religion As Illustrated by Celtic Heathendom. LC 77-27165. (Hibbert Lectures: 1886). reprint ed. 67.50 (*0-404-60407-2*) AMS Pr.

Rhys, John & Evans, John G., eds. Series of Old Welsh Texts, 11 vols., bk.14, Set. reprint ed. 600.00 (*0-404-60580-X*) AMS Pr.

Rhys, John & Evans, John G., eds. The Text of the Bruts from the Red Book of Hergest. LC 78-72662. (Series of Old Welsh Texts: Vol. 2). reprint ed. 62.50 (*0-404-60582-6*) AMS Pr.

— The Text of the Mabinogion from the Red Book of Hergest. LC 78-72663. (Series of Old Welsh Texts: Vol. 1). reprint ed. 52.50 (*0-404-60581-8*) AMS Pr.

Rhys, John & Jones, David B. Welsh People. LC 68-25263. (British History Ser.: No. 30). 1969. reprint ed. lib. bdg. 75.00 (*0-8383-0233-5*) M S G Haskell Hse.

Rhys, John & Morris Jones, John, eds. Eleucidarium. (Anecdota Oxoniensia Ser.: No. 6). 1988. reprint ed. 82.50 (*0-404-63956-9*) AMS Pr.

An Asterisk (*) at the beginning of an entry indicates that the title is appearing for the first time.

R

Rhys, John, jt. ed. see Evans, John G.

Rhys, John L. Celtic Folklore: Welsh & Manx, 2 vols., 1 bk. LC 72-80504. 762p. 1980. reprint ed. 53.95 (*0-405-08885-X*, Pub. by Blom Pubns) Ayer.

— England Is My Village. LC 72-152955. (Short Story Index Reprint Ser.). 1977. reprint ed. 18.95 (*0-8369-3870-4*) Ayer.

***Rhys-Jones, Graham.** The Loss of the Bismarck: An Avoidable Disaster. (Illus.). 256p. 2000. 32.95 (*1-55750-533-0*) Naval Inst Pr.

Rhys, Jones T. Teach Yourself Welsh. (Teach Yourself Ser.). 1992. 15.95 (*0-8288-8411-0*, 828884110); 45.00 incl. audio (*0-8288-8413-7*) Fr & Eur.

— Teach Yourself Welsh: A Complete Course for Beginners. (ENG & WEL.). 334p. 1995. pap. 14.95 (*0-8442-3841-4*, Teach Yrslf) NTC Contemp Pub Co.

— Teach Yourself Welsh Complete Course. (WEL.). 334p. 1995. pap. 25.95 incl. audio (*0-8442-3874-0*, Teach Yrslf) NTC Contemp Pub Co.

Rhys-Jones, T. N., ed. see Rhythm & News Staff.

Rhys, Natalie. Call Me Mistress: Memoirs of a Phone Sex Performer. LC 93-79544. 128p. (Orig.). 1993. pap. 10.00 (*0-9637672-0-8*) Miwok Pr.

Rhys, Terry Van, see Star, Brenda, ed.

Rhythm & News Staff. Surface Stability. Rhys-Jones, T. N., ed. (Characterisation of High-Temperature Materials Ser.: No. 6). (Illus.). 296p. 1989. pap. text 52.50 (*0-901462-61-6*, Pub. by Inst Materials) Ashgate Pub Co.

RIA In-House Professional Staff. All States Tax Handbook. rev. ed. 400p. 1992. pap. text 25.00 (*0-7811-0062-3*) Res Inst Am.

— All States Tax Handbook 1995. rev. ed. 410p. 1994. pap. text 29.95 (*0-7811-0092-5*) Res Inst Am.

— California Income Tax Laws: 1993 Edition. rev. ed. 1000p. 1992. pap. text 64.50 (*0-7811-0064-X*) Res Inst Am.

— Collection Field Function Allowable Expenses. 34p. 1995. pap. text 21.95 (*0-7811-0107-7*) Res Inst Am.

— The Complete Internal Revenue Code: January 1993 Edition. rev. ed. 2400p. 1993. pap. text 32.00 (*0-7811-0074-7*) Res Inst Am.

— The Complete Internal Revenue Code: January 1993 Edition. rev. ed. 2500p. 1994. pap. text 33.50 (*0-7811-0084-4*) Res Inst Am.

— The Complete Internal Revenue Code: January 1993 Edition. rev. ed. 2576p. 1996. pap. text 35.50 (*0-7811-0124-7*) Res Inst Am.

— The Complete Internal Revenue Code: January 1995 Edition. rev. ed. 2500p. 1995. pap. text 34.50 (*0-7811-0098-4*) Res Inst Am.

— The Complete Internal Revenue Code: July 1995 Edition. rev. ed. 2576p. 1995. pap. text 35.50 (*0-7811-0108-5*) Res Inst Am.

— The Complete Internal Revenue Code: Summer 1993 Edition. rev. ed. 2700p. 1993. pap. text 32.00 (*0-7811-0075-5*) Res Inst Am.

— Corporation & Partnership Tax Return Guide, 1992. rev. ed. (Illus.). 134p. 1993. pap. text 10.00 (*0-7811-0072-0*) Res Inst Am.

— Federal Estate & Gift Taxes - Internal Revenue Code & Regulations. 2016p. (Orig.). Date not set. pap. text 42.95 (*0-7811-0112-3*) Res Inst Am.

— Fiduciary Tax Return Guide, 1992. rev. ed. (Illus.). 140p. 1993. pap. text 10.00 (*0-7811-0073-9*) Res Inst Am.

— Individual Tax Return Guide, 1992. rev. ed. (Illus.). 158p. 1993. pap. text 10.00 (*0-7811-0071-2*) Res Inst Am.

— January 1, 1995 Stock Market Values. rev. ed. 200p. 1995. pap. text 14.95 (*0-7811-0100-X*) Res Inst Am.

— January 1, 1996 Stock Market Values. rev. ed. 290p. 1996. pap. text 15.95 (*0-7811-0129-8*) Res Inst Am.

— 1995 Corporation & Partnership Tax Return Guide. rev. ed. 142p. 1996. pap. text 11.50 (*0-7811-0131-X*) Res Inst Am.

— 1995 Fiduciary Tax Return Guide. rev. ed. 142p. 1996. pap. text 11.50 (*0-7811-0132-8*) Res Inst Am.

— 1995 Individual Tax Return Guide. rev. ed. 160p. 1996. pap. text 11.50 (*0-7811-0130-1*) Res Inst Am.

— Pension & Benefits Law, 1995. rev. ed. 1456p. 1995. pap. text 55.00 (*0-7811-0102-6*) Res Inst Am.

— Pension & Benefits Law, 1996. rev. ed. LC 97-117134. 1744p. 1996. pap. text 55.00 (*0-7811-0133-6*) Res Inst Am.

— Pension & Benefits Law, 1993. rev. ed. 2200p. 1993. pap. text 55.00 (*0-7811-0068-2*) Res Inst Am.

— Pension & Benefits Law, 1994. rev. ed. 1712p. 1994. pap. text 55.00 (*0-7811-0087-9*) Res Inst Am.

— Pension & Benefits Regulations, 1994. 2880p. 1994. pap. text 75.00 (*0-7811-0086-0*) Res Inst Am.

— Pension & Benefits Regulations, 1995. rev. ed. 2912p. 1995. pap. text 75.00 (*0-7811-0103-4*) Res Inst Am.

— Pension & Benefits Regulations, 1996. rev. ed. 2192p. 1996. pap. text 75.00 (*0-7811-0134-4*) Res Inst Am.

— Pension & Benefits Regulations, 1993. rev. ed. 2700p. 1993. pap. text 75.00 (*0-7811-0069-0*) Res Inst Am.

— Preambles to Pension & Benefits Regulations, 1993. rev. ed. 1400p. 1993. pap. text 49.00 (*0-7811-0070-4*) Res Inst Am.

— Preambles to Pension & Benefits Regulations, 1994 Edution. rev. ed. 1504p. 1994. pap. 49.00 (*0-7811-0088-7*) Res Inst Am.

— Preambles to Pension & Benefits Regulations, 1995. 1570p. 1995. pap. text 49.00 (*0-7811-0104-2*) Res Inst Am.

— Preambles to Pension & Benefits Regulations, 1996. rev. ed. 1728p. 1996. pap. 49.00 (*0-7811-0135-2*) Res Inst Am.

— The RIA Complete Analysis of the Revenue Reconciliation Act of 1993. rev. ed. 800p. 1993. pap. text 34.95 (*0-7811-0078-X*) Res Inst Am.

— RIA Federal Tax Handbook, 1994 Edition. rev. ed. 760p. 1993. pap. text 24.00 (*0-7811-0077-1*) Res Inst Am.

— RIA Federal Tax Handbook, 1995 Edition. rev. ed. 765p. 1994. pap. text 25.95 (*0-7811-0091-7*) Res Inst Am.

— RIA Federal Tax Regulations, Vols. I-IV. rev. ed. 1996. pap. text 55.95 (*0-7811-0125-5*) Res Inst Am.

— RIA Federal Tax Regulations, January 1995 Edition, 4 vols., Set. rev. ed. 8000p. 1995. pap. text 55.95 (*0-7811-0101-8*) Res Inst Am.

— RIA Federal Tax Regulations, January 1994, Vols. I-IV. 1994. pap. text 54.00 (*0-7811-0085-2*) Res Inst Am.

— RIA Federal Tax Regulations, July 1993 Edition, 4 vols., Set. rev. ed. 1993. pap. 54.00 (*0-7811-0076-3*) Res Inst Am.

— RIA Federal Tax Regulations, July 1995 Edition, Set, Vols. I-IV. rev. ed. 1995. pap. text 55.95 (*0-7811-0111-5*) Res Inst Am.

— RIA Federal Tax Regulations, 1993, 4 vols. Incl. Vol. I. RIA Federal Tax Regulations, 1993. rev. ed. 2300p. 1993. pap. Vol. II. RIA Federal Tax Regulations, 1993., 4 vols. rev. ed. 1850p. 1993. pap. Vol. III. RIA Federal Tax Regulations, 1993., 4 vols. rev. ed. 2000p. 1993. pap. Vol. IV. RIA Federal Tax Regulations, 1993., 4 vols. rev. ed. 2300p. 1993. pap. 1993. 52.00 (*0-7811-0067-4*) Res Inst Am.

— Tax Guide Controller's Edition: (1996) 2008p. (Orig.). 1995. pap. text 195.00 (*0-7811-0119-0*) Res Inst Am.

Riach, Alan. First & Last Songs. LC 95-164961. 64p. 1995. pap. 12.95 (*1-86940-125-5*, Pub. by Auckland Univ) Paul & Co Pubs.

— Hugh MacDiarmid's Epic Poetry. 1991. text 25.00 (*0-7486-0257-7*, Pub. by Edinburgh U Pr) Col U Pr.

Riach, Alan, ed. Hugh MacDiarmid: Albyn: Shorter Books & Monographs. LC 97-168222. 320p. 1997. text 45.00 (*1-85754-233-9*, Pub. by Carcanet Pr) Paul & Co Pubs.

Riach, Alan, ed. see MacDiarmid, Hugh.

Riach, P. A., jt. ed. see Harcourt, G. C.

Riad, Eva, jt. ed. see Kronholm, Tryggve.

Riad, S. & Baars, D. L., eds. Proceedings of the Fifth International Conference on Basement Tectonics. (Illus.). 350p. 1986. 37.50 (*0-317-43039-4*) Intl Basement.

Riahi-Belkaoui, Ahmed. Accounting, a Multiparadigmatic Science. LC 96-2215. 208p. 1996. 65.00 (*1-56720-048-6*, Quorum Bks) Greenwood.

***Riahi-Belkaoui, Ahmed.** Accounting & the Investment Opportunity Set. LC 99-56362. 216p. 2000. 69.50 (*1-56720-367-1*, Q367, Quorum Bks) Greenwood.

Riahi-Belkaoui, Ahmed. Accounting in the Developing Countries. LC 93-50070. 232p. 1994. 65.00 (*0-89930-821-X*, Quorum Bks) Greenwood.

***Riahi-Belkaoui, Ahmed.** Accounting Theory. 4th ed. (ITBP Textbooks Ser.). 2000. 28.99 (*1-86152-520-6*) Thomson Learn.

— Advanced Management Accounting. LC 00-37268. 2000. write for info. (*1-56720-343-4*) Greenwood.

Riahi-Belkaoui, Ahmed. Capital Structure: Determination, Evaluation & Accounting. LC 98-24565. 224p. 1999. 65.00 (*1-56720-234-9*, Quorum Bks) Greenwood.

— Corporate Social Awareness & Financial Outcomes. LC 98-34291. 208p. 1999. 65.00 (*1-56720-243-8*, Quorum Bks) Greenwood.

— Critical Financial Accounting Problems: Issues & Solutions. LC 97-22748. 200p. 1998. 59.95 (*1-56720-116-4*, Quorum Bks) Greenwood.

— The Cultural Shaping of Accounting. LC 94-45274. 176p. 1995. 55.00 (*0-89930-953-4*, Quorum Bks) Greenwood.

— Earnings Measurement, Determination, Management, & Usefulness: An Empirical Approach. LC 99-27826. 200p. 1999. 65.00 (*1-56720-330-2*, Quorum Bks) Greenwood.

***Riahi-Belkaoui, Ahmed.** Evaluating Capital Projects. 2001. write for info. (*1-56720-357-4*) Greenwood.

Riahi-Belkaoui, Ahmed. Financial Analysis & the Predictability of Important Economic Events. LC 97-32991. 240p. 1998. 69.50 (*1-56720-164-4*, Quorum Bks) Greenwood.

— The Linguistic Shaping of Accounting. LC 95-19470. 192p. 1995. 59.95 (*0-89930-992-5*, Quorum Bks) Greenwood.

— Long-Term Leasing: Accounting, Evaluation, Consequences. LC 97-22749. 160p. 1998. 59.95 (*1-56720-147-4*, Quorum Bks) Greenwood.

— Morality in Accounting. LC 92-7485. 224p. 1992. 57.95 (*0-89930-729-9*, BUN, Quorum Bks) Greenwood.

— Multinationality & Firm Performance. LC 96-15510. 152p. 1996. 59.95 (*1-56720-077-X*, Quorum Bks) Greenwood.

— The Nature & Consequences of the Multidivisional Structure. LC 94-32084. 208p. 1995. 65.00 (*0-89930-904-6*, Quorum Bks) Greenwood.

— The Nature & Determinants of Disclosure Adequacy: An International Perspective. LC 96-26868. 240p. 1997. 69.50 (*1-56720-086-9*, Quorum Bks) Greenwood.

— Performance Results in Value Added Reporting. LC 95-46276. 192p. 1996. 59.95 (*1-56720-024-9*, Quorum Bks) Greenwood.

— Performance Results of Multinationality. LC 98-44554. 200p. 1999. 65.00 (*1-56720-277-2*, Quorum Bks) Greenwood.

— Quality & Control: An Accounting Perspective. LC 92-34942. 240p. 1993. 67.95 (*0-89930-767-1*, BQC, Quorum Bks) Greenwood.

— Research Perspectives in Accounting. LC 97-1697. 176p. 1997. 59.95 (*1-56720-100-8*, Quorum Bks) Greenwood.

***Riahi-Belkaoui, Ahmed.** The Role of Corporate Reputation for Multinational Firms: Accounting, Organizational & Market Considerations. LC 00-32816. 2000. write for info. (*1-56720-408-2*, Quorum Bks) Greenwood.

Riahi-Belkaoui, Ahmed. Significant Current Issues in International Taxation. LC 98-4977. 200p. 1998. 59.95 (*1-56720-185-7*, Quorum Bks) Greenwood.

— Value Added Reporting & Research: State of the Art. LC 99-14847. 200p. 1999. 65.00 (*1-56720-301-9*, Quorum Bks) Greenwood.

Riahi-Belkaoui, Ahmed & Monti-Belkaoui, Janice. Human Resource Valuation: A Guide to Strategies & Techniques. LC 94-39658. 192p. 1995. 59.95 (*0-89930-931-3*, Quorum Bks) Greenwood.

Riahi-Belkaoui, Ahmed & Pavlik, Ellen L. Accounting for Corporate Reputation. LC 92-8401. 272p. 1992. 65.00 (*0-89930-717-5*, BKK, Quorum Bks) Greenwood.

Riahi-Belkaoui, Ahmed, jt. auth. see Monti-Belkaoui, Janice.

Riahi-Blekaoui, Ahmed. Organizational & Budgetary Slack. LC 93-30990. 144p. 1994. 55.00 (*0-89930-884-8*, Quorum Bks) Greenwood.

***Riahi, D. N.** Flow Transition, Vol. II. 280p. 2000. 145.00 (*1-85312-785-X*) Computational Mech MA.

Riahi, D. N. Mathematical Modeling & Simulation in Hydrodynamic Stability. 350p. 1996. text 86.00 (*981-02-2308-0*) World Scientific Pub.

Riahi, D. N., jt. ed. see Debnath, L.

***Riahi, Dan N.** Flow Instability. 256p. 2000. pap. text 145.00 (*1-85312-701-9*, 7019) Computational Mech MA.

Riahi, Daniel N., jt. ed. see Debnath, Lokenath.

Riahi, Hasana. Study of the Critical Points at Infinity Arising from the Failure of the Palais-Smale Condition for N-body Type Problems. LC 98-53119. (Memoirs of the American Mathematical Society Ser.). 1999. write for info. (*0-8218-0873-7*) Am Math.

***Riain, Flann.** Townlands of Leinster & the People Who Lived There. 192p. 2000. pap. 19.95 (*1-85182-465-0*, Pub. by Four Cts Pr) Intl Spec Bk.

Riain, Noirin Ni. Gregorian Chant Experience: Sing & Meditate With Noirin Ni Riain. 176p. 1997. pap. 17.95 (*0-86278-465-4*) Irish Amer Bk.

— Gregorian Chant Experience: Sing & Meditate With Noirin Ni Riain. 176p. 1997. audio compact disk 29.95 (*0-86278-474-3*, Pub. by OBrien Pr) Irish Amer Bk.

Riain, Sean O. Irish Is Fun-Tastic! (IRI.). 1990. pap. 6.95 (*0-86243-207-3*) Intl Spec Bk.

Rial, Dickson, jt. auth. see Glass, Bill.

Rial, Horacio V. Frontera Sur (Southern Border) 468p. 1995. pap. 16.95 (*0-679-76339-2*) Vin Bks.

Riale, Frank N. Sinless, Sickless, Deathless Life (1913) 264p. 1998. reprint ed. pap. 18.95 (*0-7661-0649-7*) Kessinger Pub.

Riall, Lucy. The Italian Risorgimento: State, Society & National Unification. LC 93-33882. (Historical Connections Ser.). (Illus.). 112p. (C). 1994. pap. 16.99 (*0-415-05775-2*, B2251) Routledge.

— Sicily & the Unification of Italy: Liberal Policy & Local Power 1859-1866. LC 97-18125. (Illus.). 264p. 1998. text 65.00 (*0-19-820680-1*) OUP.

***Riall, Lucy & Laven, David, eds.** Napoleon's Legacy: Problems of Government in Restoration Europe. (Illus.). 256p. 2000. 65.00 (*1-85973-244-5*, Pub. by Berg Pubs); pap. 19.50 (*1-85973-249-6*, Pub. by Berg Pubs) NYU Pr.

Riall, Nicholas. Boer War Diaries: The Diaries & Photographs of Malcolm Riall. (Illus.). 1998. 29.95 (*1-85753-266-X*, Pub. by Brasseys) Brasseys.

Rialp, Rosa Ma, see Suris Jorda, Jordi & Ma Rialp, Rosa.

Rialp Staff. Diccionario de Cine. (SPA.). 912p. 1991. write for info. (*0-7859-5902-5*, 8432128252) Fr & Eur.

— Enciclopedia Sistematica Acta, 2000, 9 vols., Set. 11th ed. (SPA.). 4500p. 1978. 295.00 (*0-8288-5229-4*, S50492) Fr & Eur.

— Gran Enciclopedia Rialp, 24 vols., Set. (SPA.). 21500p. 1976. 2995.00 (*0-8288-5673-7*, S50493) Fr & Eur.

Rialp, Victoria. Children & Hazardous Work in the Philippines. (ILO Child Labour Collection). x, 72p. 1993. pap. 13.50 (*92-2-106474-3*) Intl Labour Office.

Rian, Edwin H. The Presbyterian Conflict. 242p. 1992. reprint ed. pap. 11.95 (*0-934688-67-2*) Comm Hist Orthodox.

***Riande, Evaristo.** Polymer Viscoelasticity: Stress & Strain in Practice. LC 99-40874. (Plastics Engineering Ser.). (Illus.). 904p. 1999. text 235.00 (*0-8247-7904-5*) Dekker.

Riani, M., jt. auth. see Atkinson, A.

Riano, J. F. Critical & Biographical Notes on Early Spanish Music. LC 79-158958. (Music Ser.). 1971. reprint ed. lib. bdg. 29.50 (*0-306-70193-6*) Da Capo.

Riano, Pilar, ed. Women in Grassroots Communication: Effecting Global Social Change. (Communication & Human Values Ser.: Vol. 15). 332p. (C). 1994. text 52.00 (*0-8039-4905-7*); pap. text 24.95 (*0-8039-4906-5*) Sage.

RIAS Staff. Central Glasgow. 208p. (C). 1989. pap. 59.00 (*1-85158-200-2*, Pub. by Royal Inc Architects) St Mut.

— Fife. 208p. (C). 1990. pap. 80.00 (*1-85158-258-4*, Pub. by Royal Inc Architects) St Mut.

— Orkney. 104p. (C). 1991. pap. 75.00 (*1-873190-02-6*, Pub. by Royal Inc Architects) St Mut.

Riasanovsky, A. V. & Zubarev, Vera. Slovo O Polku Igoreve/Prince Igor in Search of Glory: Kniaz' Igor' V Poiskakh Slavy. Patton, Fred, tr. LC 96-10583. (ENG & RUS.). 110p. (Orig.). 1996. pap. 12.00 (*1-55779-088-4*) Hermitage Pubs.

Riasanovsky, Nicholas V. Collected Writings: 1947-1994. (Illus.). viii, 312p. (C). 1993. 39.95 (*1-884445-00-4*) C Schlacks Pub.

— The Emergence of Romanticism. 128p. 1995. pap. text 22.00 (*0-19-509646-0*) OUP.

— A History of Russia. 6th ed. LC 98-56640. (Illus.). 776p. (C). 1999. text 55.00 (*0-19-512179-1*) OUP.

— The Image of Peter the Great in Russian History & Thought. (Illus.). 352p. 1992. pap. text 24.95 (*0-19-507480-7*) OUP.

— Nicholas I & Official Nationality in Russia, 1825-1855. LC 59-11316. (Russian & East European Studies). 308p. reprint ed. pap. 95.50 (*0-7837-4750-0*, 204449700003) Bks Demand.

Riasanovsky, Nicholas V., et al, eds. California Slavic Studies, Vols. 5, 7-10. Incl. Vol. I. 1960. pap. 27.50 (*0-520-09037-3*); Vol. II. 1963. pap. 27.50 (*0-520-09038-1*); Vol. V. 1970. pap. 27.50 (*0-520-09043-8*); Vol. VII. 1974. pap. 27.50 (*0-520-09485-9*); Vol. 8. 1975. pap. 30.00 (*0-520-09519-7*); Vol. 9. 1976. pap. 27.50 (*0-520-09541-3*); Vol. 10. 1977. pap. 27.50 (*0-520-09564-2*); Vol. 11. 1980. pap. 34.00 (*0-520-03584-4*); pap. write for info. (*0-318-55999-4*) U CA Pr.

Riasanovsky, Nicholas V., jt. auth. see Watson, William.

Riasanovsky, Valentin A. Chinese Civil Law. LC 76-20214. (Studies in Chinese Government & Law). 310p. 1976. reprint ed. lib. bdg. 65.00 (*0-313-26965-3*, U6965, Greenwood Pr) Greenwood.

— Fundamental Principles of Mongol Law. LC 65-63020. (Uralic & Altaic Ser.: Vol. 43). 343p. 1965. write for info. (*0-87750-063-0*) Mongolia.

Riase, Gwendolyn. How to Have the Wedding of Your Dreams on a Nightmare Budget: 150 Money-Saving Strategies to Slash Your Wedding Costs. (Illus.). 74p. 1992. pap. 16.95 (*0-9632446-4-7*) Applesauce.

Riaskoff. Diabetic Retinopathy. 1976. pap. 144.00 (*90-6193-554-7*, Pub. by Kluwer Academic) Kluwer Academic.

Riaz, Fahmida A. Pakistan Literature & Society. 1986. 14.00 (*81-7050-021-4*, Pub. by Abhinav) S Asia.

***Riaz, Mian N., ed.** Extruders in Food Applications. LC 99-68515. 232p. 2000. text 99.95 (*1-56676-779-2*) Technomic.

Riazanov, David. Karl Marx & Friedrich Engels: An Introduction to Their Lives. Kunitz, Joshua, tr. LC 73-8055. 237p. reprint ed. pap. 73.50 (*0-7837-6992-X*, 204680400004) Bks Demand.

Riaziat, M. L. Introduction to High-Speed Electronics & Optoelectronics. LC 95-10083. 312p. 1995. 93.50 (*0-471-01582-2*) Wiley.

Riazuddin, Fayyazuddin. A Modern Introduction to Particle Physics. 676p. 1994. text 78.00 (*981-02-1072-8*); pap. text 44.00 (*981-02-1073-6*) World Scientific Pub.

— Modern Introduction to Particle Physics. 2nd ed. (High Energy Physics Ser.). 700p. 1999. 86.00 (*981-02-3876-2*); pap. text 54.00 (*981-02-3877-0*) World Scientific Pub.

— Quantum Mechanics. 504p. (C). 1990. text 61.00 (*9971-5-0752-8*) World Scientific Pub.

Riba, Carles. Diccionari de Robotica. 2nd ed. (CAT.). 92p. 1991. 35.00 (*0-7859-6251-4*, 8476531443) Fr & Eur.

Riba, J. Illustrated Encyclopedia of Cacti & Other Succulents. 1993. 12.98 (*1-55521-878-4*) Bk Sales Inc.

Riba, Michelle B. & Balon, Richard, eds. Psychopharmacology & Psychotherapy: A Collaborative Approach. 1999. 36.45 (*0-88048-913-8*, 8913) Am Psychiatric.

Riba, Michelle B., jt. ed. see Oldham, John M.

Riba, Michelle B., jt. ed. see Tasman, Allan.

Riback, Billy. The Home Improvement Guide to Household Repair: Complete Plans for Fixing Your Marriage, Your Children & Other Major Appliances. (Illus.). 96p. 1993. pap. 7.70 (*1-56282-755-3*, Pub. by Hyperion) Little.

Riback, Christopher, jt. auth. see Goddard, Taegan D.

***Riback, Estelle.** Henry Ward Ranger: Modulator of Harmonious Color. 72p. 2000. pap. 21.95 (*1-882897-48-X*) Lost Coast.

Ribak, Charles E., ed. Inhibition in the Brain. LC 82-642121. 173p. 1987. pap. 24.00 (*0-930195-04-3*) Inst Mind Behavior.

Ribak, Charles E., et al, eds. The Dentate Gyrus & Its Role in Seizures. LC 92-18288. (Epilepsy Research Ser.: No. 7). 318p. 1992. 314.25 (*0-444-81447-7*) Elsevier.

Ribakov, R. B. & Senkevich, A. N., eds. Indian Traditions Through the Ages. 1990. 22.50 (*81-202-0288-0*, Pub. by Ajanta) S Asia.

Ribal, Lizzy. Lizzy Gets a New Liver. unabridged ed. Basham, Beth, ed. LC 97-17815. (Illus.). 40p. (Orig.). (J). (gr. 6 up). 1997. pap. 14.95 (*1-57895-019-8*, Bridge Res) Curriculm Presbytrn KY.

Riband, Herbert F., jt. auth. see Minguela, Santiago C.

Ribar, John. Byte's Windows Programmer's Cookbook. 256p. 1994. pap., pap. text 34.95 incl. cd-rom (*0-07-882037-5*) Osborne-McGraw.

— FORTRAN Programming for Windows. 1992. pap. 29.95 (*0-07-881908-3*) Osborne-McGraw.

— Powerbuilder Construction Kit. 512p. 1994. pap. text 24.95 (*0-07-882079-0*) Osborne-McGraw.

— Programming Primer a Guide to Programming Fundamentals. 1994. pap. text 16.95 (*0-07-881999-7*) McGraw.

***Ribar, Sandy.** Operation - Rescue in the Redwoods: Readalong - Singalong Pack. unabridged ed. (Kids on Assignment - The Adventures of Rex & Ruby Ser.: Vol. 1). (J). (ps-5). 1999. pap. 11.49 incl. audio (*1-893401-08-1*, KOA000RR) Pure & Simple.

— Operation-Rescue in the Redwoods: Mini-Musical Production Guide. (Kids on Assignment - The Adventures of Rex & Ruby Ser.: Vol. 1). (Illus.). 40p. (J). (gr. k-5). 1999. pap. 7.95 (*1-893401-00-6*, KOA010) Pure & Simple.

— Operation-Rescue in the Redwoods: Mini-Musical Production Pack. (Kids on Assignment - The Adventures of Rex & Ruby Ser.). (Illus.). 40p. (J). (ps-4). 1999. pap. 98.00 (*1-893401-07-3*, KOA00RR) Pure & Simple.

— Operation-Rescue in the Redwoods: Storybook. (Kids on Assignment - The Adventures of Rex & Ruby Ser.: Vol. 8). (Illus.). 40p. (J). 1999. pap. 3.99 (*1-893401-06-5*, KOA081RR) Pure & Simple.

— Operation-Rescue in the Redwoods: Teacher's Resources.

An Asterisk (*) at the beginning of an entry indicates that the title is appearing for the first time.

Johnson, Henley B., ed. (Kids on Assignment - The Adventures of Rex & Ruby Ser.: Vol. 7). (Illus.). 1999. pap., teacher ed. 7.95 (*1-893401-05-7*, KOA0061RR) Pure & Simple.

Ribaric, M. & Sustersic, L. Conservation Laws & Open Questions of Classical Electrodynamics. 348p. (C). 1990. text 48.00 (*981-02-0151-6*) World Scientific Pub.

Ribarich, Cindy, jt. auth. see Delzio, Suzanne.

Ribas, Andres Perez De, see De Ribas, Andres Perez.

Ribas, Armando P. Cuba Entre la Independencia y la Libertad. LC 94-71842. (Coleccion Cuba y sus Jueces). (SPA.). 91p. (Orig.). 1994. pap. 12.00 (*0-89729-745-8*) Ediciones.

Ribas, Oscar B. Uanga--Fetico: Romance Folclorico Angolano. 2nd ed. (B. E. Ser.: No. 69). (POR.). 1969. 30.00 (*0-8115-3019-1*) Periodicals Srv.

Ribaudo, Linda & Walker, Darlyne. Coming to America. LC 94-5511. (Today's World Ser.). (Illus.). 1994. 3.33 (*1-56420-055-8*) New Readers.

— Teacher's Guide: Family Issues, Community Issues, Work Issues. LC 94-5516. (Today's World Ser.). 1994. 10.95 (*1-56420-067-1*) New Readers.

— Working Parents. LC 94-5504. (Today's World Ser.). 1994. 3.33 (*1-56420-058-2*) New Readers.

Ribaupierre, Anik De, see De Ribaupierre, Anik, ed.

Ribbans, Geoffrey. Conflicts & Conciliations: The Evolution of Galdos's "Fortunata y Jacinta" LC 97-12450. (Purdue Studies in Romance Literatures: No. 14). (Illus.). 344p. 1997. 44.95 (*1-55753-108-0*) Purdue U Pr.

Ribbans, Geoffrey. Cruelty to Animals & Interpersonal Violence Readings in Research & Application: The Evolution of Galdos' "Fortunata y Jacinta" LC 97-12450. (Studies in Romance Literatures). 1997. pap. text 29.95 (*1-55753-106-4*) Purdue U Pr.

Ribbe, Paul H., ed. see Kerrick, Derrill M.

Ribbe, Paul H., jt. ed. see Veblen, D. R.

Ribbe, Wolfgang, jt. ed. see Hansen, Reimer.

Ribbeck, Otto. Die Romische Tragodie Im Zeitalter der Republik. viii, 692p. 1968. reprint ed. write for info. (*0-318-71213-X*) G Olms Pubs.

Ribbeck, Otto, ed. Scaenicae Romanorum Poesis Fragmenta, Bd. I: Tragicorum Fragmenta. ccxiv, 876p. 1978. reprint ed. write for info. (*0-318-71215-6*) G Olms Pubs.

— Scaenicae Romanorum Poesis Fragmenta, Bd. II: Comicorum Fragmenta. ccxiv, 876p. 1978. reprint ed. write for info. (*0-318-71216-4*) G Olms Pubs.

— Scaenicae Romanorum Poesis Fragmenta, 2 vols., Set. ccxiv, 876p. 1978. reprint ed. write for info. (*0-318-71214-8*) G Olms Pubs.

Ribbeck, Otto, ed. see Virgil.

Ribbel, Arthur. Yesterday in San Diego. LC 90-61926. (Illus.). (Orig.). 1990. pap. 8.95 (*0-9627384-0-9*) Rancho Pr CA.

***Ribbens, Jack A.** Simultaneous Engineering for New Product: Development: Manufacturing Applications. LC 99-46112. 344p. 2000. 80.00 (*0-471-25265-4*) Wiley.

Ribbens, Jane. Mothers & Their Children: A Feminist Sociology of Childrearing. 240p. 1995. 69.95 (*0-8039-8834-6*); pap. 22.95 (*0-8039-8835-4*) Sage.

Ribbens, Katherine A. & Carlson, D. S., eds. Craniofacial Growth During Adolescence. (Craniofacial Growth Ser.: Vol. 20). (Illus.). 226p. 1987. 49.00 (*0-929921-16-X*) UM CHGD.

Ribbens, Katherine A. & Vig, Peter S., eds. Science & Clinical Judgment in Orthodontics. (Craniofacial Growth Ser.: Vol. 19). (Illus.). 251p. 1986. 49.00 (*0-929921-15-1*) UM CHGD.

Ribbens, Katherine A., jt. ed. see McNamara, James A., Jr.

Ribbens, Peter, jt. auth. see Pascal, Christine.

Ribbens, William B. Understanding Automotive Electronics. 5th ed. LC 98-154017. 392p. 1998. pap. text 29.95 (*0-7506-7008-8*, Newnes) Buttrwrth-Heinemann.

— Understanding Automotive Electronics: Illustrated How-To Guide for Understanding Automotive Electronics. 4th ed. LC 97-223930. (Illus.). 392p. 1998. pap. text 24.95 (*0-7506-7068-1*, Newnes) Buttrwrth-Heinemann.

Ribbins, Peter, ed. Leaders & Leadership in the School, College & University. LC 97-224026. (Management & Leadership in Education Ser.). (Illus.). 240p. 1997. 89.95 (*0-304-33887-7*); pap. 35.00 (*0-304-33888-5*) Continuum.

Ribbins, Peter & Raynor, Steve. Headteachers & Leadership in Special Education. 240p. 1999. 75.00 (*0-304-33971-7*); 27.95 (*0-304-33972-5*) Continuum.

Ribbins, Peter & Sherratt, Brian. Radical Educational Policies & Conservative Secretaries of State. LC 97-179491. (Management & Leadership in Education Ser.). 230p. 1997. 85.00 (*0-304-33906-7*, LC93, Pub. by Cassell) LPC InBook.

Ribbins, Peter & Whale, Elizabeth. Improving Education: Promoting Quality in Schools. Reynolds, David & Hopkins, David, eds. (School Development Ser.). (Illus.). 176p. 1993. 75.00 (*0-304-32743-3*); pap. 35.00 (*0-304-32735-2*) Weidner & Sons.

Ribble, Anne G., jt. auth. see Ribble, Frederick G.

Ribble, Frederick G. & Ribble, Anne G. Fielding's Library: An Annotated Catalogue. LC 97-148571. 1997. 30.00 (*1-883631-04-1*) Biblgraph Soc.

Ribble, Ronald G. Apples, Weeds, & Doggie Poo. (Illus.). 56p. (Orig.). 1995. pap. text 7.95 (*1-883331-08-0*) Anderie Poetry.

***Ribble, Ronald G.** For Heaven's Sake, Don't Eat the Snake: The Garden of Fools. 1999. pap. text 7.50 (*0-9671703-0-3*) Towers & Rushing.

Ribblett, David L. Nelly Custis: Child of Mount Vernon. LC 93-12419. 1993. pap. 7.95 (*0-931917-23-9*) Mt Vernon Ladies.

Ribblett, David L., jt. auth. see Samford, Patricia.

Ribbon Art Publishing Company Staff. Old-Fashioned Ribbon Art: Ideas & Designs for Accessories & Decorations. (Illus.). 32p. 1986. pap. 2.95 (*0-486-25174-8*) Dover.

Ribbons, D. W., jt. ed. see Norris, John R.

Ribbons, William B. Understanding Automotive Electronics. 5th ed. 400p. 1998. 30.00 (*0-7680-0211-7*) Soc Auto Engineers.

Ribe, Tom. Los Alamos, New Mexico: A Visitors & Newcomers Guide to the Area. (Illus.). 104p. 1997. pap. 8.95 (*0-9645703-4-3*) Otowi Crossing Pr.

Ribeiro. The Lizard's Smile. 320p. 1994. text 21.00 (*0-689-12125-3*) Atheneum Yung Read.

Ribeiro, Aileen. The Art of Dress: Fashion in England & France 1750 to 1820. LC 94-35347. 257p. 1995. 65.00 (*0-300-06287-7*) Yale U Pr.

— Dress & Morality. LC 86-14839. 170p. 1986. 47.95 (*0-8419-1091-X*) Holmes & Meier.

— Fashion in the French Revolution. LC 88-21242. (Costume & Civilization Ser.). (Illus.). 144p. 1988. 49.95 (*0-8419-1197-5*) Holmes & Meier.

***Ribeiro, Aileen.** The Gallery of Fashion. (Illus.). 240p. 2000. 60.00 (*0-691-05092-9*) Princeton U Pr.

— Ingres in Fashion: Representations of Dress & Appearance in Ingres's Images of Women. LC 98-47308. (Illus.). 268p. 1999. 55.00 (*0-300-07927-3*) Yale U Pr.

Ribeiro, Aileen & Cumming, Valerie. The Visual History of Costume: Seven Centuries of Costume History in One Volume. (Illus.). 240p. 1997. reprint ed. pap. 35.00 (*0-89676-221-1*, Costume & Fashion Pr) QSMG Ltd.

Ribeiro, Alex. Quien de Veras Gano la Copa? (Who Won the World Cup?) (SPA.). 1997. 6.99 (*0-88113-495-3*, B112-4953) Caribe Betania.

Ribeiro, Alex Dias. Quien Gano la Copa Mundial. 1998. pap. 14.99 (*0-88113-523-2*) Caribe Betania.

Ribeiro, Alvaro & Basker, James G. Tradition in Transition: Women Writers, Marginal Texts, & the Eighteenth-Century Canon. (Illus.). 368p. 1996. text 75.00 (*0-19-818288-0*) OUP.

Ribeiro, Branca T. Coherence in Psychotic Discourse. LC 92-49156. (Oxford Studies in Sociolinguistics). (Illus.). 336p. 1994. text 75.00 (*0-19-506597-2*) OUP.

***Ribeiro, Darcy & Rabassa, Gregory.** The Brazilian People: The Formation & Meaning of Brazil. LC 99-86541. 2000. write for info. (*0-8130-1777-7*) U Press Fla.

Ribeiro, E. Sousa, jt. ed. see Grossman, N. F.

Ribeiro, Edgard T. I Would Have Loved Him If I Had Not Killed Him: A Novel. 208p. 1996. pap. 9.95 (*0-312-14360-5*) St Martin.

Ribeiro, F. Ramoa, jt. auth. see NATO Advanced Study Institute Staff.

Ribeiro, Gustavo L. Transnational Capitalism & Hydropolitics in Argentina: The Yacyreta High Dam. LC 93-33426. (Center for Latin American Studies, University of Florida). (Illus.). 216p. (C). 1994. 49.95 (*0-8130-1280-5*) U Press Fla.

Ribeiro, Jodao & Pieris, P. E. The Historic Tragedy of the Island of Ceilead 4th ed. LC 99-932486. xvi, 266 p. 1999. write for info. (*81-206-1334-1*, Pub. by Asian Educ Servs) S Asia.

Ribeiro, Julio. Bullet for Bullet: My Life as a Police Officer. LC 99-932062. 397 p. 1998. 30.00 (*0-670-87871-5*, Viking) Viking Penguin.

Ribeiro, Lair. Adelgazar Comiendo. 1997. pap. text 15.98 (*84-7953-117-7*) Urano.

Ribeiro, Leonidio. Brazilian Medical Contributions. 1976. lib. bdg. 69.95 (*0-8490-1548-0*) Gordon Pr.

Ribeiro, O. K. A Source Book of the Genus Phytophtora. (Illus.). 1978. lib. bdg. 45.00 (*3-7682-1200-9*) Lubrecht & Cramer.

Ribeiro, O. K., jt. auth. see Erwin, D. C.

Ribeiro, Paulo F. Modeling & Simulation of Power System Harmonics. 1999. audio compact disk 138.00 (*0-7803-4597-5*) IEEE Standards.

Ribeiro, Rita A. Soft Computing in Financial Engineering. LC 98-52534. 1999. write for info. (*3-7908-1173-4*) Spr-Verlag.

Ribeiro, Robert. Engineering Contracts. LC 97-202559. (Illus.). 320p. 1997. 69.95 (*0-7506-2498-1*) Buttrwrth-Heinemann.

Ribeiro, Stella C. Sambaqui: A Novel of Prehistory. Van der Heuvel, Claudia, tr. (POR.). 144p. 1987. pap. 3.95 (*0-380-89624-9*, Avon Bks) Morrow Avon.

Ribeiro, Susan, ed. Arts from the Scholar's Studio Selected Oriental Masterpieces in Painting Lacquer, Glass, Ceramic, Wood, Metal & Stone. (Illus.). 287p. 1988. lib. bdg. 150.00 (*0-7103-0321-1*) Routledge.

Ribelin, William E. & Migaki, George, eds. Pathology of Fishes. LC 73-15261. (Illus.). 1016p. 1975. 75.00 (*0-299-06520-0*, 652) U of Wis Pr.

Ribelli, Piero. Jah Pickney: Children of Jamaica. (Illus.). 128p. 1996. 29.95 (*976-8100-71-0*, Pub. by Ian Randle); pap. 16.95 (*976-8100-72-9*, Pub. by Ian Randle) Paul & Co Pubs.

Riben, M. Shedding Light On . . . The Dark Side of Adoption. 1988. pap. 12.95 (*0-9662060-0-2*) Mirage.

Ribenboim, P. Fermat's Last Theorem for Amateurs. LC 98-41246. 362p. 1999. 39.95 (*0-387-98508-5*) Spr-Verlag.

Ribenboim, Paulo. The Book of Prime Number Records. 385p. 1988. 49.80 (*0-387-96573-4*) Spr-Verlag.

— The Book of Prime Number Records. 2nd ed. xxiii, 479p. 1989. 49.80 (*0-387-97042-8*, 3007) Spr-Verlag.

***Ribenboim, Paulo.** Classical Theory of Algebraic Numbers. 2nd ed. LC 00-40044. (Universitext Ser.). (Illus.). 2000. write for info. (*0-387-95070-2*) Spr-Verlag.

— Collected Papers of Paulo Ribenboim. LC 98-231739. (Illus.). 1997. write for info. (*0-88911-735-7*); write for info. (*0-88911-783-7*); write for info. (*0-88911-785-3*); write for info. (*0-88911-787-X*); write for info. (*0-88911-789-6*); write for info. (*0-88911-791-8*); write for info. (*0-88911-793-4*); write for info. (*0-88911-795-0*) Queens U Inst Intergov.

Ribenboim, Paulo. The Little Book of Big Primes. 304p. 1993. 32.95 (*0-387-97508-X*) Spr-Verlag.

***Ribenboim, Paulo.** My Numbers, My Friends. LC 99-42458. 450p. 2000. pap. 39.95 (*0-387-98911-0*) Spr-Verlag.

Ribenboim, Paulo. The New Book of Prime Number Records. 3rd rev. ed. LC 95-5441. 541p. 1996. 59.95 (*0-387-94457-5*) Spr-Verlag.

— Thirteen Lectures on Fermant's Last Theorem. 1995. 59.95 (*0-387-90432-8*) Spr-Verlag.

***Ribenboim, Paulo, ed.** Wolfgang Krull: Gesammelte Abhandlungen Collected Papers, 2 vols. 1730p. 1999. 248.95 (*3-11-012771-7*) De Gruyter.

Ribenboim, Paulo, jt. auth. see Alling, Norman L.

Ribenhoim, Paulo. The Theory of Classical Valuations. LC 98-4349. (Monographs in Mathematics). 328p. 1998. 69.95 (*0-387-98525-5*) Spr-Verlag.

Riber, Lorenzo, ed. see Fuenmayor, Antonio de.

Riber, Louise. Neria Production Notes. (Illus.). 15p. (Orig.). (C). 1992. pap. text write for info. (*0-936731-26-5*) Devel Self Rel.

Ribera, Chevremont E. Canto de Mi Tierra. 97p. (C). 1971. 2.00 (*0-8477-3213-4*) U of PR Pr.

— Obra Poetica, 2 vols., Set. LC 76-41873. (SPA., Illus.). cii, 1665p. (Orig.). 1976. 30.00 (*0-8477-3218-5*); pap. 25.00 (*0-8477-3233-9*) U of PR Pr.

Ribera Chevremont, Evaristo. Obra Poetica. (SPA.). xix, 568p. 1980. 15.00 (*0-8477-3227-4*); 15.00 (*0-8477-3228-2*); pap. 12.50 (*0-8477-3231-2*) U of PR Pr.

Ribera, Feliciano, jt. auth. see Meier, Matt S.

Ribera, Gilbert J. Calculating for Business. 336p. (C). 1993. pap. text, per. 37.95 (*0-8403-8624-9*) Kendall-Hunt.

— Machine Calculation for Business & Personal Use. 200p. (C). 1994. pap. text, spiral bd. 27.01 (*0-8403-9483-7*) Kendall-Hunt.

— Machine Calculation for Business & Personal Use. 2nd ed. LC 79-83523. 1979. pap. text 18.95 (*0-8162-7180-1*); teacher ed. 5.00 (*0-8162-7181-X*) Holden-Day.

Ribera, Julian. Music in Ancient Arabia & Spain: Being la Musica de las Cantigas. LC 70-87614. (Music Ser.). 1970. reprint ed. lib. bdg. 45.00 (*0-306-71622-4*) Da Capo.

Ribera y Tarrago, Julian. Historia de la Musica Arabe Medieval y Su Influencia en la Espanola. LC 78-178587. reprint ed. 47.50 (*0-404-56664-2*) AMS Pr.

Ribera Y Tarrago, Julian. La Musica Andaluza Medieval en las Canciones de Trovadores, Troveros, 3 vols. in 1. LC 71-178588. reprint ed. 57.50 (*0-404-56665-0*) AMS Pr.

***Riberio, E., et al.** Flora de Reserva Ducke (Flora of the Rucke Reserve) Guia de Identificaca das Plantas Vasculares de Uma Floresta de Terra-Firme na Amazonia (Field Guide to the Fascular Plants of a Terra Firma Forest in Central Amazonia) (POR., Illus.). xvi, 800p. 1999. pap. 50.00 (*85-211-0011-6*, Pub. by Royal Botnic Grdns) Balogh.

Ribes, Emilio, jt. ed. see Bijou, Sidney W.

Ribes-Inesta, Emilio, jt. ed. see Bandura, Albert.

***Ribes, L. & Zalesskii, P.** Profinite Groups. (Ergebnisse der Mathematik und Ihrer Grenzgebiete Ser.: Vol. 40). 450p. 2000. 109.00 (*3-540-66986-8*) Spr-Verlag.

Ribes, Peter. More Parables & Fables. 144p. 1996. pap. 39.95 (*0-85439-431-1*, Pub. by St Paul Pubns) St Mut.

— Parables & Fables for Modern Man. 184p. (C). 1990. text 60.00 (*0-85439-325-0*, Pub. by St Paul Pubns) St Mut.

Ribesky, Mary, ed. see Godeau, Abigail S., et al.

Ribet, K. Current Trends in Arithmetical Algebraic Geometry. LC 87-11506. (CONM Ser.: Vol. 67). 293p. 1987. reprint ed. pap. 38.00 (*0-8218-5074-1*, CONM-67) Am Math.

Ribeyre, Francis, jt. ed. see Boudou, Alain.

Ribeyro, Julio R. Marginal Voices: Selected Stories. Douglas, Dianne, tr. from SPA. LC 92-30359. (Texas Pan American Ser.). 153p. (Orig.). (C). 1993. pap. 11.95 (*0-292-77058-8*); text 27.50 (*0-292-77057-X*) U of Tex Pr.

***Ribeyro, Julio Ramon.** Cuentos Completos, Ribeyro. LC 94-199644. (SPA.). 1998. pap. 25.95 (*84-204-8142-4*) Santillana.

***Ribi, Alfred.** Die Suche Nach Den Eigenen Wurzeln: Die Bedeutung Von Gnosis, Hermetik und Alchemie Fur C. G. Jung und Marie-Louise Von Franz und Deren Einfluss Auf das Moderne Verstandnis Dieser Disziplin. 290p. 1999. 45.95 (*3-906761-60-6*, Pub. by P Lang) P Lang Pubng.

***Ribiat, Dovid.** 39 Melochos, 4 vols. 1999. 89.95 (*1-58330-368-5*) Feldheim.

Ribil, Soltan & Kallai, Gabor. Winning with the English. (Batsford Chess Library). 192p. 1993. pap. 20.95 (*0-8050-2642-8*, Owl) H Holt & Co.

Ribman, Ronald. The Ceremony of Innocence. 1968. pap. 5.25 (*0-8222-0195-X*) Dramatists Play.

— Passing Through from Exotic Places. 1970. pap. 5.25 (*0-8222-0876-8*) Dramatists Play.

— The Rug Merchants of Chaos & Other Plays. LC 92-2568. 240p. 1992. 24.95 (*1-55936-050-X*); pap. 12.95 (*1-55936-049-6*) Theatre Comm.

Ribner, David, jt. auth. see Schindler, Ruben.

Ribner, Irving & Huffman, Clifford C. Tudor & Stuart Drama. 2nd ed. LC 76-5215. (Goldentree Bibliographies Series in Language & Literature). (C). 1978. text 24.95 (*0-88295-572-1*); pap. text 14.95 (*0-88295-554-3*) Harlan Davidson.

Ribner, Jonathan P. Broken Tablets: The Cult of the Law in French Art from David to Delacroix. LC 92-23046. 1993. 58.00 (*0-520-07749-0*, Pub. by U CA Pr) Cal Prin Full Svc.

Ribner, Melinda. Jewish Way of Meditation: A Practical Guide to Tranquillity & Personal Growth. LC 98-14413. 192p. 1998. pap. 12.95 (*0-8065-1980-0*, Citadel Pr) Carol Pub Group.

***Ribner, Melinda.** New Age Judaism: Ancient Wisdom for the Modern World. 200p. 2000. pap. 9.95 (*1-55874-789-3*, Simcha Press) Health Comm.

Ribner, Melinda. New Age Judaism: Unlocking the Modern Secrets of Ancient Wisdoms. LC 98-53969. 192p. 1999. 19.95 (*1-55972-511-7*, Birch Ln Pr) Carol Pub Group.

Ribner, Mindy G. Fresh from the Kitchen: Kosher Cooking for Beginners to Gourmets. (Illus.). 450p. 1995. 29.95 (*1-56871-079-8*) Targum Pr.

***Ribner, Neil.** The First Session with Teenagers: A Step-by-Step Guide. LC 99-6908. 256p. 2000. 36.95 (*0-7879-4982-5*, Pfffr & Co) Jossey-Bass.

Ribner, Richard. Living Without Fatigue. 160p. (Orig.). pap. 9.95 (*0-8159-6117-0*) Devin.

Ribner, Susan & Chin, Richard. The Martial Arts. LC 76-58713. (Trophy Bk.). (Illus.). 160p. (J). (gr. 5 up). 1984. pap. 4.95 (*0-06-440139-1*, HarpTrophy) HarpC Child Bks.

Ribo, Duran L. Diccionario de Derecho. (SPA.). 916p. 1995. 595.00 incl. cd-rom (*0-7859-9768-7*) Fr & Eur.

Riboldi, Silvia. Goya. (Masters of Art Ser.). 64p. (J). 1999. lib. bdg. 22.50 (*0-87226-529-3*, 65293B, P Bedrick Books) NTC Contemp Pub Co.

Riboli, E. & Delendi, M., eds. Autopsy in Epidemiology & Medical Research. (IARC Scientific Publications: No. 112). (Illus.). 298p. 1991. pap. text 57.50 (*92-832-2112-5*) OUP.

Riboli, E. & Saracci, R. Diet, Hormones & Cancer: Methodological Issues for Prospective Studies. (IARC Technical Report Ser.: No. 4). 159p. 1988. text 30.00 (*92-832-1415-3*) World Health.

Ribolini, Gabriele, jt. auth. see Leonardi, Leonardo.

Riboni, Josiane. Dea Mandarins aux Samourais: La Fin d'un Mythe. (Currents in Comparative Romance Languages & Literatures Ser.: Vol. 50). (FRE.). X, 155p. (C). 1997. text 39.95 (*0-8204-3339-X*) P Lang Pubng.

Riboni, M. Dora. The Snake in Gambling.Tr. of Vibora en Arriesgar. (Illus.). 112p. 1996. 19.95 (*1-880470-38-1*) Creative Des.

Ribot, Jesse C., et al, eds. Climate Variability, Climate Change & Social Vulnerability in the Semi-Arid Tropics. (Internationsl Hydrology Ser.). (Illus.). 188p. (C). 1996. text 89.95 (*0-521-48074-4*) Cambridge U Pr.

Ribot, Theodule A. Diseases of Memory, 1. Smith, W. H. & Snell, M. M., trs. LC 77-72191. (Contributions to the History of Psychology Ser.: Vol. 1, Pt. C, Medical Psychology). 134p. 1977. reprint ed. lib. bdg. 75.00 (*0-313-26940-8*, U6940, Greenwood Pr) Greenwood.

— Essay on the Creative Imagination. LC 73-2987. (Classics in Psychology Ser.). 1978. reprint ed. 26.95 (*0-405-05159-X*) Ayer.

Ribot, Theodule A. German Psychology of To-Day. 333p. 90.00 (*1-85506-667-X*) Thoemmes Pr.

Ribot, Theodule A. Heredity: A Psychological Study of Its Phenomena, Laws, Causes, & Consequences. LC 78-72821. (Brainedness, Handedness, & Mental Abilities Ser.). reprint ed. 40.00 (*0-404-60890-6*) AMS Pr.

Riboud, Christophe, jt. auth. see Revel, Alain.

Riboud, Michelle. Ivory Coast, 1960-1986. 28p. 1987. pap. 9.95 (*0-917616-99-5*) ICS Pr.

Ribowsky, Mark. A Complete History of the Negro Leagues, 1884-1955. (Illus.). 400p. 1995. 24.95 (*1-55972-283-5*, Birch Ln Pr) Carol Pub Group.

***Ribowsky, Mark.** Don't Look Back: Satchel Paige in the Shadow of Baseball. (Illus.). 368p. 2000. pap. text 16.00 (*0-306-80963-X*, Pub. by Da Capo) HarpC.

— He's a Rebel: Phil Spector - Rock & Roll's Legendary Producer. (Illus.). 2000. pap. 18.95 (*0-8154-1044-1*, Pub. by Cooper Sq) Natl Bk Netwk.

Ribowsky, Mark. The Power & the Darkness: The Life of Josh Gibson in the Shadows of the Game. 322p. 1999. reprint ed. lib. bdg. 29.95 (*0-7351-0058-6*) Replica Bks.

— Twice Golden: The Story of Michael Johnson & His Triumphs in Atlanta. LC 97-22321. (Illus.). 240p. 1997. 19.95 (*1-55972-425-0*, Birch Ln Pr) Carol Pub Group.

Ribowsky, Mark & Feinberg, Bill. The Beach Boys. (Illus.). 240p. 1986. 17.45 (*0-671-53013-5*); pap. 7.95 (*0-671-54135-8*) S&S Trade.

Ribstein, Larry E. Business Associations. 2nd ed. 1990. teacher ed. write for info. (*0-8205-0276-6*); write for info. (*0-8205-0275-8*) Bender.

Ribstein, Larry E. Business Associations 1996. 3rd ed. 1996. text 57.00 (*0-8205-2719-X*) Bender.

Ribstein, Larry E. Unincorporated Business Entities. LC 96-21369. 518p. 1996. pap. 37.95 (*0-87084-766-X*) Anderson Pub Co.

Ribstein, Larry E., jt. auth. see Bromberg, Alan R.

Ribstein, Larry E., jt. auth. see Butler, Henry N.

Ribstein, Larry E., jt. auth. see Butler, Henry W.

Ribuffo, Leo P. Right Center Left: Essays in American History. LC 91-5030. 325p. (C). 1992. text 45.00 (*0-8135-1775-3*); pap. text 19.00 (*0-8135-1776-1*) Rutgers U Pr.

Ribush, Nicholas, ed. & compiled by see Yeshe, Lama Thubten.

RIC Staff. Engineering Services Forms of Cost Analysis. 156p. (C). 1985. 60.00 (*0-85406-292-0*, Pub. by Surveyors Pubns) St Mut.

RIC Staff, jt. auth. see Charness, Ann L.

Rica, Amoros, jt. auth. see Merlin-Walch, Olivier.

Rica, Narciso Amoros, see Merlin-Walch, Olivier & Amoros Rica, Narciso.

Ricalton, James. James Ricalton's Photographs of China During the Boxer Rebellion: His Illustrated Travelogue of 1900. Lucas, Christopher, ed. LC 89-13574. (Studies in the Photographic Arts: Vol. 1). (Illus.). 344p. 1990. lib. bdg. 99.95 (*0-88946-508-8*) E Mellen.

Rican, Rudolf. History of the Unity of Brethren: A Protestant Hussite Church in Bohemia & Moravia. Crews, C. Daniel, tr. from CZE. LC 92-62999. 446p. (Orig.). 1993. pap. 22.00 (*1-878422-05-7*) Moravian Ch in Amer.

Ricapito, J. V., ed. A Tri-Linear Edition of Lazarillo de Tormes of 1554, Burgos, Alcala de Henares, Amberes. xviii, 82p. 1987. 12.50 (*0-942260-91-0*) Hispanic Seminary.

Ricapito, Joseph V. Florentine Streets & Other Poems. LC 96-40474. (VIA Folios Ser.: Vol. 9). 60p. 1997. pap. 9.00 (*1-884419-08-9*) Bordighera.

— Formalistic Aspects of Cervante's Novelas Ejemplares. LC 97-26219. (Studies in Renaissance Literature: No. 16). 151p. 1997. text 79.95 (*0-7734-8556-2*) E Mellen.

Ricapito, Joseph V., ed. Hispanic Studies in Honor of Joseph H. Silverman: Special Memorial Edition. (Homenajes Ser.: Vol. 5). 382p. 1988. pap. 17.50 (*0-936388-46-3*) Juan de la Cuesta.

Ricapito, Joseph V., tr. see De Valdes, Alfonso.

***Ricard, Kelly, reader.** The Ugly Duckling. (Pocketaudio Ser.). (Illus.). (J). (ps-2). 2000. boxed set 9.95 incl. audio (*2-921997-86-X*, Pub. by Coffragants) Penton Overseas.

***Ricard, Jacques.** Biological Complexity & the Dynamics of Life Processes. LC 99-57247. (New Comprehensive Biochemistry Ser.). 2000. write for info. (*0-444-50081-2*) Elsevier.

Ricard, Jimmy L. The Statutory Affair. LC 98-169313. 154p. 1998. pap. 12.00 (*1-881524-22-1*) Milligan Bks.

Ricard-Konig, Susanne, jt. ed. see Remy, Patrick.

Ricard, Laura, jt. auth. see Long, Patrick D.

Ricard, Matthieu. Journey to Enlightenment: The Life & World of Khyentse Rinpoche, Spiritual Teacher from Tibet. LC 96-83980. (Illus.). 152p. 1996. 68.00 (*0-89381-679-5*) Aperture.

— The Mystery of Animal Migration. LC 72-172577. 235p. reprint ed. pap. 72.90 (*0-608-13596-8*, 205128200093) Bks Demand.

***Ricard, Matthieu.** Spirit of Tibet: The Life & World of Khyentse Rinpoche Spiritual Teacher. (Illus.). 144p. 2000. pap. 29.95 (*0-89381-903-4*) Aperture.

Ricard, Matthieu, jt. auth. see Revel, Jean-Francois.

Ricard, Michel, ed. Ouvrage Didie a la Memoire Du Professor Henry Germain (1903-1989) Avec la Collaboration de Michel Coste. (Illus.). 265p. 1990. 150.00 (*3-87429-322-X*, Pub. by Koeltz Sci Bks) Lubrecht & Cramer.

Ricard, Raymond, ed. see Racine, Jean.

Ricard, Rene. God with Revolver. 120p. (Orig.). 1989. 20.00 (*0-937815-31-4*); pap. 12.00 (*0-937815-30-6*) Hanuman Bks.

— Love Poems. (Illus.). 37p. 1999. pap. 5.95 (*0-9666328-6-9*) CUZ Ed.

***Ricard, Rene.** Philip Taaffe: Recent Paintings. Foye, Raymond, ed. (Illus.). 20p. 1999. pap. 40.00 (*1-880154-31-5*) Gagosian Gallery.

Ricard, Rene. Trusty Sarcophagus Co. Igliori, Paola & Zalopany, Michele, eds. 98p. (Orig.). 1990. pap. 25.00 (*0-9625119-1-9*) Inanout Pr.

— Trusty Sarcophagus Co. Igliori, Paola & Zalopany, Michele, eds. Lhardy, Patricia, tr. 100p. (Orig.). 1990. pap. 25.00 (*0-9625119-2-7*) Inanout Pr.

— Trusty Sarcophagus Co. Igliori, Paola & Zalopany, Michele, eds. Ramaseder, Josef, tr. 100p. (Orig.). 1990. pap. 25.00 (*0-9625119-3-5*) Inanout Pr.

— Trusty Sarcophagus Co. Igliori, Paola & Zalopany, Michele, eds. Diacono, Mario, tr. 100p. (Orig.). 1990. pap. 25.00 (*0-9625119-4-3*) Inanout Pr.

— Trusty Sarcophagus Co. (Illus.). 100p. (Orig.). 1990. pap. 25.00 (*0-685-64744-7*) Petersburg Pr.

Ricard, Virginia B. Developing Intercultural Communication Skills. LC 92-11171. (Professional Practices in Adult Education & Human Resource Development Ser.). 198p. (Orig.). (C). 1993. lib. bdg. 23.00 (*0-89464-663-X*) Krieger.

Ricardez, Rafael E., tr. see Cano, Robin B.

Ricardo-Campbell, Rita. The Economics & Politics of Health. LC 81-13377. 397p. pap. 123.10 (*0-608-05221-3*, 20657580001) Bks Demand.

— Food Safety Regulation: A Study of the Use & Limitations of Cost-Benefit Analysis. LC 74-14148. (AEI-Hoover Policy Studies: No. 12). 66p. reprint ed. pap. 30.00 (*0-608-13991-2*, 202224800025) Bks Demand.

— Resisting Hostile Takeovers: The Case of Gillette. LC 97-12811. 272p. 1997. 67.95 (*0-275-95830-2*, Praeger Pubs) Greenwood.

— Social Security: Promise & Reality. LC 77-83830. (Publication Ser.: No. 179). 351p. 1977. 6.38 (*0-8179-6791-5*) Hoover Inst Pr.

Ricardo-Campbell, Rita & Lazear, Edward P., eds. Issues in Contemporary Retirement. (Publication Ser.: No. 370). 427p. 1988. text 14.38 (*0-8179-8701-0*) Hoover Inst Pr.

Ricardo-Campbell, Rita, et al. Health Care in the United States: What We Should Keep & What We Should Change. LC 94-10295. (Essays in Public Policy Ser.: No. 50). 1994. pap. 5.00 (*0-8179-5552-6*) Hoover Inst Pr.

Ricardo, Catherine. Mastering Computer Applications. 2nd ed. 166p. (C). 1993. text 32.00 (*0-536-58447-8*) Pearson Custom.

Ricardo, Catherine & Bailie, Frances. Mastering Computer Applications. 3rd ed. 166p. (C). 1994. text 32.00 (*0-536-58661-6*) Pearson Custom.

Ricardo, David. Minor Papers on the Currency Question, 1809-1823. 1979. 21.95 (*0-405-10624-6*) Ayer.

— Notes on Malthus's Measure of Value. Porta, Pier L., ed. 84p. (C). 1992. text 39.95 (*0-521-40298-0*) Cambridge U Pr.

— On the Principles of Political Economy & Taxation. 597p. 1977. reprint ed. 96.20 (*3-487-06311-5*) G Olms Pubs.

— The Principles of Political Economy & Taxation. LC 96-28486. (Great Minds Ser.). 305p. 1996. pap. 10.95 (*1-57392-109-2*) Prometheus Bks.

— Works & Correspondence: Index, Vol. 11. Sraffa, P. & Dobb, Maurice H., eds. 146p. 1973. text 69.95 (*0-521-20039-3*) Cambridge U Pr.

— Works & Correspondence: Principles of Political Economy, Vo. 1. Sraffa, P., ed. 447p. 1981. pap. text 29.95 (*0-521-28505-4*) Cambridge U Pr.

***Ricardo, David & McCulloch, J. R.** The Works of David Ricardo, Esq., M. P. With a Notice of the Life & Writings of the Author. LC 99-39612. 2000. 90.00 (*1-58477-028-7*) Lawbk Exchange.

Ricardo-Gil, Jose, ed. see Saloom, Barbara B.

Ricardo, Gloria. Amistad e Intimidad. (Serie Realidades - Realities Ser.).Tr. of Friendship & Intimacy. (SPA.). 25p. 1988. pap. 1.99 (*0-945792-70-0*, 498108) Editorial Unilit.

— Amistad E Intimidad. 28p. 1992. pap. 1.15 (*1-885630-17-4*) HLM Producciones.

— Cuando la Mujer Ora. (Estudio Biblico para Mujeres Ser.). 72p. (Orig.). 1992. pap. 4.00 (*1-885630-29-8*) HLM Producciones.

— Cuando Una Mujer Ora Por Sus Hijos. (SPA.). 34p. (Orig.). 1996. pap. 1.15 (*1-885630-37-9*) HLM Producciones.

— Curso la Mujer de Excelencia: Estudio Biblico Individual O En Grupo. (SPA.). 68p. 1997. pap. 3.00 (*1-885630-42-5*) HLM Producciones.

— De Mujer A Mujer. 18p. 1992. pap. 1.15 (*1-885630-15-8*) HLM Producciones.

— Diez Mujeres Biblicas y Lecciones Actuales, No. 1. (Estudio Biblico para Mujeres Ser.). (SPA.). 50p. 1992. pap. 4.00 (*1-885630-21-2*) HLM Producciones.

— Diez Mujeres Biblicas y Lecciones Actuales, No. 2. (Estudio Biblico para Mujeres Ser.). (SPA.). 50p. 1992. pap. 4.00 (*1-885630-22-0*) HLM Producciones.

— La Excelencia en la Mujer. (Serie Realidades - Realities Ser.).Tr. of Excellence in the Woman. (SPA.). 37p. 1989. pap. 1.99 (*0-945792-69-7*, 498107) Editorial Unilit.

— Mas Que Vencedores: Secretos para Conquistar Actitudes Negativas. (SPA.). 56p. (Orig.). 1994. pap. 4.00 (*0-614-11599-X*) HLM Producciones.

— La Mujer De Excelencia. 36p. 1992. pap. 1.15 (*1-885630-10-7*) HLM Producciones.

— La Mujer y Sus Emociones. (Estudio Biblico Para Mujeres Ser.). 76p. 1992. pap. 4.00 (*1-885630-23-9*) HLM Producciones.

— El Perfil de una Mujer de Dios. 75p. 1994. pap. 3.00 (*1-885630-30-1*) HLM Producciones.

— Proverbios y la Mujer Moderna. (Estudio Biblico Para Mujeres Ser.). 76p. 1992. pap. 4.00 (*1-885630-26-3*) HLM Producciones.

— Quien Puede Entender a los Hombres? Transforma Tu Matrimonio y Tus Relaciones Con Otros Hombres en Tu Vida! (SPA.). 1998. pap. 3.00 (*1-885630-46-8*) HLM Producciones.

— Sus Hijos, Barro en Sus Manos. 26p. 1992. pap. 1.15 (*1-885630-12-3*) HLM Producciones.

— La Verdadera Liberacion Femenina. 26p. 1993. pap. 1.15 (*1-885630-04-2*) HLM Producciones.

Ricardo, Gloria, jt. auth. see Ricardo, Victor.

Ricardo, Jack. The Night G. A. A. Died. (Stonewall Inn Mysteries Ser.). 208p. 1993. 8.95 (*0-312-09353-5*) St Martin.

Ricardo, Jack, ed. Leathermen Speak Out: An Anthology on Leathersex, Vol. 1. 192p. (Orig.). 1991. pap. 14.95 (*0-943595-33-9*) Leyland Pubns.

— Leathermen Speak Out: An Anthology on Leathersex, Vol. 2. 192p. (Orig.). 1993. pap. 14.95 (*0-943595-40-1*) Leyland Pubns.

***Ricardo-Livingstone, Rod.** Campesino Fingerprints. 2nd ed. (Chapbook Ser.: Vol. 1). (Illus.). 32p. 2000. 5.00 (*0-9660773-2-6*) Calaca Pr.

Ricardo, Maryann. The Risk Management Handbook: Protecting You & Your Practice from Legal Action. 250p. 1995. reprint ed. ring bd. 49.95 (*1-57066-033-6*, ME057) Practice Mgmt Info.

Ricardo, Roger. Guantanamo: The Bay of Discord. LC 94-166621. (Illus.). 50p. 1995. pap. 7.95 (*1-875284-56-7*) Ocean Pr NJ.

Ricardo, Victor. Catorce Reglas para el Conflicto Matrimonial. 1992. pap. 1.15 (*1-885630-14-X*) HLM Producciones.

— Catorce Reglas para Manejar Conflictos/Matrimonio. (Serie Realidades - Realities Ser.).Tr. of Fourteen Rules to Handle Conflicts in Your Marriage. (SPA.). 28p. 1989. pap. 1.99 (*0-945792-68-9*, 498106) Editorial Unilit.

— Como Romper la Maldicion De la Pobreza. 30p. 1992. pap. 1.15 (*1-885630-16-6*) HLM Producciones.

— El Dominio Del Creyente. 28p. 1992. pap. 1.15 (*1-885630-13-1*) HLM Producciones.

— 11 Mitos Mortales vs. la Verdad. (SPA., Illus.). 24p. (Orig.). 1996. pap. 1.15 (*1-885630-40-9*) HLM Producciones.

— El Joven y Su Sexualidad. 32p. 1992. pap. 1.15 (*1-885630-19-0*) HLM Producciones.

— Ni Macho . . . Ni Raton . . . Sino Verdadero Varon! (SPA.). 36p. (Orig.). 1996. pap. 1.15 (*1-885630-39-5*) HLM Producciones.

— La Oracion Que da Resultados. (Serie Realidades - Realities Ser.).Tr. of Prayer That Produces Results. (SPA.). 36p. 1989. pap. 1.99 (*0-945792-67-0*, 498105) Editorial Unilit.

— Orando Para Lograr Resultados. 32p. 1992. pap. 1.15 (*1-885630-20-4*) HLM Producciones.

— La Persona Que Dios Usa. 32p. 1993. pap. 1.15 (*1-885630-05-0*) HLM Producciones.

— Poder en Tu Boca. 26p. 1992. pap. 1.15 (*1-885630-02-6*) HLM Producciones.

— Respuestas Biblicas a 10 Preguntas Actuales. (Estudio Biblico Para Mujeres Ser.). 57p. 1992. pap. 4.00 (*1-885630-27-1*) HLM Producciones.

— Rompiendo Ataduras. 28p. 1992. pap. 1.15 (*1-885630-01-8*) HLM Producciones.

— El Secreto para Cambiar Su Familia y Su Mundo. 26p. 1992. pap. text 1.00 (*1-885630-09-3*) HLM Producciones.

— Siete Cosas Que James Aceptare: El Secreto Para Vivir En Perdon, Paz, Confianza, Fuerza, Victoria Abundancia y Salud. 30p. 1992. pap. 1.15 (*1-885630-00-X*) HLM Producciones.

— Usted Puede Ganar en la Vida. 26p. 1992. pap. 1.15 (*1-885630-11-5*) HLM Producciones.

Ricardo, Victor & Ricardo, Gloria. Como Experimentar la Presencia De Dios. 35p. 1993. pap. 2.00 (*1-885630-08-5*) HLM Producciones.

— Conociendo a Dios: Dios Se Revela a Traves de Sus Nombres. 64p. 1994. pap. text 4.00 (*1-885630-31-X*) HLM Producciones.

— Cuando los Hijos Se Rebelan. 32p. 1993. pap. 1.15 (*1-885630-03-4*) HLM Producciones.

— Curso De Matrimonios: Una Aventura Amorosa Les Puede Suceder A Ustedes y A Su Conyuge. 66p. 1992. pap. 4.00 (*1-885630-24-7*) HLM Producciones.

— La Familia Feliz. 28p. 1992. pap. 1.15 (*1-885630-18-2*) HLM Producciones.

— Gocese en el Senor: Como el Poder del Gozo Puede Cambiar Su Mundo. 34p. 1995. pap. text 1.15 (*1-885630-36-0*) HLM Producciones.

— Matrimonio Al Maximo: Como Complementarse y No Fastidiarse. 36p. 1993. pap. 1.15 (*1-885630-06-9*) HLM Producciones.

— El Plan de Dios para la Familia. (Estudio Biblico Para Mujeres Ser.). 98p. 1992. pap. 4.00 (*1-885630-25-5*) HLM Producciones.

— Verdades Que Transforman. (Estudio Biblico Para Mujeres Ser.). 66p. 1992. pap. 4.00 (*1-885630-28-X*) HLM Producciones.

Ricardou, J. Le Nouveau Roman, les Raison de l'Ensemble. (FRE.). 1990. pap. 16.95 (*0-7859-2718-2*) Fr & Eur.

***Ricart, Alberto.** Active Server Pages 3 Developer's Guide. (Illus.). 600p. 2000. pap. text 39.99 (*0-7645-4715-1*) IDG Bks.

***Ricart, Manuel A.** E-Speak: The Definitive Guide for Developers. 400p. 2000. pap. 49.99 (*0-13-087071-4*) P-H.

Ricart, Manuel Alberto. Complete Idiot's Guide to Linux. LC 98-87629. 320p. 1998. 16.99 (*0-7897-1826-X*) Que.

Ricart, Matas J. Diccionario Biografico de la Musica. 2nd ed. (SPA.). 1144p. 1986. 150.00 (*0-7859-5124-5*) Fr & Eur.

Ricatto, Paul A. Basket-Ball - Unbelievable Discoveries - Only True American Sport. (Illus.). 100p. (Orig.). 1996. pap. 9.00 (*0-9655949-0-4*) P A Ricatto.

Ricaud, Lulu C. Crosland: Family of Edward & Ann Snead Crosland, 1740-1957. (Illus.). 546p. 1994. reprint ed. pap. 83.00 (*0-8328-4206-0*); reprint ed. lib. bdg. 93.00 (*0-8328-4205-2*) Higginson Bk Co.

— The Family of Edward & Ann Snead Crosland, 1740-1957. LC 87-4274. (Illus.). 561p. 1988. reprint ed. 30.00 (*0-87152-422-8*) Reprint.

Ricca, Franco & Lo Bue, Erberto. The Great Stupa of Gyantse: A Complete Tibetan Pantheon of the Fifteenth Century. (Illus.). 320p. 1994. 90.00 (*0-906026-30-X*, Pub. by Serindia) Weatherhill.

Ricca, Sergio. International Migration in Africa: Legal & Administrative Aspects. xii, 190p. (Orig.). 1989. 33.75 (*92-2-106502-2*); pap. 24.75 (*92-2-106501-4*) Intl Labour Office.

Riccardi, A. C. The Cretaceous System of Southern South America. LC 87-32081. (Geological Society of America Ser.: Vol. 168). (Illus.). 175p. reprint ed. pap. 54.30 (*0-608-07717-8*, 206780500010) Bks Demand.

Riccardi, A. C., ed. Advances in Jurassic Research, 2 vols., Set. (GeoResearch Forum Ser.: Vols. 1 & 2). (Illus.). 508p. 1996. text 128.00 (*0-87849-717-X*, Pub. by Trans T Pub) Enfield Pubs NH.

Riccardi, C., jt. ed. see Santoni, A.

Riccardi, Gregory. Databases, Java & the Internet. 464p. (C). 2000. 70.00 (*0-201-61247-X*) Addison-Wesley.

Riccardi, Margaret B., ed. see Bruno, Michael.

Riccardi, Margaret B., ed. see Coats, Warren L., Jr., et al.

Riccardi, Margaret B., ed. see Giovannini, Alberto.

Riccardi, Margaret B., ed. see Larrain, Felipe & Velasco, Andres.

Riccardi, Margaret B., ed. see Mussa, Michael L.

Riccardi, Margaret B., ed. see Padoa-Schioppa, Tommaso.

Riccardi, Margaret B., ed. see Tavlas, George S.

Riccardi, Pietro. Saggio di una Bibliografia Euclidea, 4 pts. in 1. 260p. 1974. reprint ed. write for info. (*3-487-05407-8*) G Olms Pubs.

Riccardi, Theodore, ed. A Nepali Version of the Vetalapancavimsati. (American Oriental Ser.: Vol. 54). ix, 206p. 1971. pap. 17.50 (*0-940490-54-4*) Am Orient Soc.

Riccardi, Theodore, Jr., ed. see Lewis, Todd T.

Riccardi, V. M., ed. Optic Pathway Gliomas. (Journal: Neurofibromatosis: Vol. 1, No. 4). (Illus.). 60p. 1989. pap. 33.25 (*3-8055-4945-8*) S Karger.

Riccardi, Vincent M. Neurofibromatosis: Phenotype, Natural History, & Pathogenesis. 2nd rev. ed. (Illus.). 520p. 1992. text 95.00 (*0-8018-4348-0*) Johns Hopkins.

Riccardo, Edward. Perspectives. 238p. 1993. pap. 14.00 (*0-911541-26-8*) Gregory Pub.

— The Wisdom of Love. (Illus.). 255p. (Orig.). 1995. pap. 14.00 (*0-911541-06-3*) Gregory Pub.

Riccardo, Martin V. Liquid Dreams of Vampires. LC 96-9053. (Illus.). 264p. (Orig.). 1999. pap. 14.95 (*1-56718-571-1*) Llewellyn Pubns.

Riccardo, Renee, jt. auth. see Laster, Paul.

Riccardo, Thomas. Wedding Warnings: What Every Bride & Groom Must Know but Were Never Told until Now! Becka, Brenda, ed. 120p. (Orig.). pap. text. write for info. (*0-9633972-0-6*) Club Wed Pubns.

Riccards, Michael P. The Ferocious Engine of Democracy, Vol. 1. 420p. 1997. pap. text 19.95 (*1-56833-102-9*) Madison Bks UPA.

— The Ferocious Engine of Democracy, Vol. 2. 480p. 1997. pap. text 19.95 (*1-56833-103-7*) Madison Bks UPA.

— The Ferocious Engine of Democracy: A History of the American Presidency, 2 vols., Set. 1995. 69.95 (*1-56833-052-9*) Madison Bks UPA.

— The Ferocious Engine of Democracy Vol. 1: The American Presidency from 1789 to 1989: From the Origins Through McKinley, Vol. 1. 420p. (C). 1997. lib. bdg. 34.95 (*1-56833-041-3*) Rowman.

— The Ferocious Engine of Democracy Vol. 2: The American Presidency from 1789 to 1989: From Theodore Roosevelt Through George Bush, Vol. 2. 480p. 1997. lib. bdg. 34.95 (*1-56833-042-1*) Rowman.

***Riccards, Michael P.** The Presidency & the Middle Kingdom: China, the United States & Executive Leadership. 256p. 2000. 60.00 (*0-7391-0129-3*) Lxngtn Bks.

Riccards, Michael P. A Republic, If You Can Keep It: The Foundation of the American Presidency, 1700-1800, 167. LC 86-29595. (Contributions in Political Science Ser.: No. 167). 242p. 1987. 59.95 (*0-313-25462-1*, RRE/, Greenwood Pr) Greenwood.

— Vicars of Christ: Popes, Power, & Politics in the Modern World. LC 97-33160. 300p. 1998. 29.95 (*0-8245-1694-X*) Crossroad NY.

Riccella, Christopher J. Muhammad Ali: World Heavyweight Boxing Champion. (Black American Ser.). (Illus.). 192p. (YA). 1991. mass mkt. 3.95 (*0-87067-574-5*, Melrose Sq) Holloway.

Ricceri, Biagio & Simons, S. Minimax Theory & Applications. LC 98-6569. (Nonconvex Optimization & Its Applications Ser.). 1998. 119.00 (*0-7923-5064-2*) Kluwer Academic.

Riccero, Delores & Bingham, Joan. More Haunted Houses. Peters, Sally, ed. 336p. (Orig.). 1991. pap. 9.00 (*0-671-69585-1*) PB.

Ricchiardi, Sherry & Young, Virginia. Women on Deadline: A Collection of America's Best. LC 90-41648. 224p. 1991. reprint ed. pap. 69.50 (*0-608-06870-5*, 206707700009) Bks Demand.

Ricchio, Daniel E. A Complete Guide to Planning, Building, Buying, Maintaining Inground Swimming Pools. (Illus.). 160p. 1996. pap. text 9.95 (*0-9651293-1-4*) DR Pool.

Ricchio, Paul P., jt. auth. see Buttram, Harold E.

Ricchiute. Auditing: Study Guide. 3rd ed. (SWC-Accounting). Date not set. pap., student ed. write for info. (*0-538-81693-7*) Thomson Learn.

— Auditing & Assurance Systems. 6th ed. 2000. pap. 87.95 (*0-324-02402-9*) Thomson Learn.

Ricchiute, David N. Auditing. 5th ed. LC 97-12700. (Miscellaneous/Catalogs Ser.). (C). 1997. mass mkt. 63.95 (*0-538-86952-6*); mass mkt., student ed. 19.95 (*0-538-86953-4*) S-W Pub.

— Auditing: Concepts & Standards. 4th ed. (SWC-Accounting). (C). 1994. mass mkt., student ed. 20.75 (*0-538-83885-X*) S-W Pub.

Ricchiute, David N., jt. auth. see Campbell.

Ricchiuti, Paul B. Ellen: Trial & Triumph on the American Frontier. LC 76-44051. 160p. (YA). (gr. 6 up). 1988. reprint ed. pap. 7.95 (*0-945460-03-1*) Upward Way.

***Ricchiuti, Paul B.** Ellen White Friend of Angels: Stories from Her Amazing Adventures, Travels & Relationships. Holt, B. Russell, ed. LC 98-47469. 124p. 1999. pap. 8.99 (*0-8163-1707-0*) Pacific Pr Pub Assn.

Ricchiuti, Paul B. Where's Moo Cow? Tig's Tale. LC 94-23758. (J). (ps-2). 1994. pap. 6.99 (*0-8280-0890-6*) Review & Herald.

Ricchiuto, Jack. Collaborative Creativity: Unleashing the Power of Shared Thinking. LC 96-43757. 130p. 1996. pap. 12.95 (*1-886939-12-8*, Pub. by OakHill Pr VA) ACCESS Pubs Network.

Ricchiuto, Steven R. & De Zoete Wedd, Barclays. The Rate Reference Guide to the U. S. Treasury Market. 2nd ed. 400p. 1996. text 55.00 (*1-55738-790-7*, Irwn Prfssnl) McGraw-Hill Prof.

Ricci & Rowe. Health & Environmental Risk Assessment. 1985. 60.00 (*0-08-031579-8*, Pergamon Pr) Elsevier.

Ricci, ed. see Berlinger, Eli & Zirkel, Gene.

Ricci, ed. see Hirsch, Lewis R. & Goodman, Arthur.

Ricci, ed. see Smith, Terry M.

Ricci, Benjamin. Experiments in the Physiology of Human Performance. LC 76-102701. 218p. reprint ed. pap. 67.60 (*0-608-15598-5*, 205657400074) Bks Demand.

Ricci, Carla. Mary Magdalene & Many Others: Women Who Followed Jesus. 240p. 1994. pap. 20.00 (*0-8006-2718-0*, Fortress Pr) Augsburg Fortress.

— Mary Magdalene & Many Others: Women Who Followed Jesus. 240p. 1994. pap. 40.00 (*0-86012-208-5*, Pub. by Srch Pr) St Mut.

Ricci, David. The Tragedy of Political Science. LC 84-3510. 352p. 1987. pap. 18.00 (*0-300-03760-0*, Y-631) Yale U Pr.

Ricci, David M. The Tragedy of Political Science: Politics, Scholarship, & Democracy. LC 84-3510. 352p. 1984. 47.50 (*0-300-03088-6*) Yale U Pr.

— The Transformation of American Politics: The New Washington & the Rise of Think Tanks. 320p. 1994. pap. 18.00 (*0-300-06123-4*) Yale U Pr.

An Asterisk (*) at the beginning of an entry indicates that the title is appearing for the first time.

— The Transformation of American Politics: The New Washington & the Rise of Washington Think Tanks. LC 92-36419. 280p. (C). 1993. 37.50 (*0-300-05340-1*) Yale U Pr.

Ricci, Doris R., tr. see Melzer, John T.

Ricci, Elisa. Italian Lace Designs: 243 Classic Examples. LC 93-16990. (Pictorial Archive Ser.). 96p. 1993. pap. 7.95 (*0-486-27588-4*) Dover.

Ricci, Franco. Difficult Games: A Reading of "I Racconti" by Italo Calvino. 200p. (C). 1990. text 29.95 (*0-88920-990-1*) W Laurier U Pr.

Ricci, Fred J. & Schutzer, Daniel. U. S. Military Communications: The Force Multiplier. LC 84-23783. 300p. (C). 1986. text 46.40 (*0-7167-8036-4*, Computer Sci Pr) W H Freeman.

Ricci, Frederick. Personal Communications Systems Applications. LC 96-42322. (Feher/Prentice Hall Digital & Wireless Communciation Ser.). 304p. 1996. 77.00 (*0-13-255878-5*) P-H.

Ricci, G., ed. Decision Processes in Economics: Proceedings of the VI Italian Conference on Game Theory Held in Modena, Italy, October 9-10, 1989. (Lecture Notes in Economics & Mathematical Systems Ser.: Vol. 353). (Illus.). iii, 209p. 1991. 38.95 (*0-387-53592-6*) Spr-Verlag.

Ricci, Gabriel R. & Gottfried, Paul, eds. Culture & Consumption Vol. 31: Religion & Public Life. 116p. 1999. pap. 19.95 (*0-7658-0629-0*) Transaction Pubs.

Ricci, Giorgio, et al, eds. Therapeutic Selectivity & Risk-Benefit Assessment of Hypolipidemic Drugs. LC 81-40550. (Illus.). 351p. 1982. reprint ed. pap. 108.90 (*0-7837-9541-6*, 206029000005) Bks Demand.

Ricci, Isolina. Mom's House, Dad's House: A Complete Guide for Parents Who Are Separated, Divorced, or Living Apart. 2nd ed. LC 97-29867. (Illus.). 381p. 1997. per. 13.00 (*0-684-83078-7*, Fireside) S&S Trade Pap.

Ricci, J. Elsevier's Banking Dictionary. 3rd enl. rev. ed. (DUT, ENG, FRE, GER & ITA.). 360p. 1990. 250.00 (*0-8288-9259-8*, M7911) Fr & Eur.

Ricci, J., ed. Elsevier's Banking Dictionary. 3rd rev. ed. (DUT, ENG, FRE, GER & ITA.). 370p. 1990. 188.50 (*0-444-88067-4*) Elsevier.

Ricci, James. Development of Gynaecological Surgery & Instruments. (Illus.). 594p. 1990. reprint ed. 165.00 (*0-930405-28-5*) Norman SF.

***Ricci, James.** One Hundred Years of Gynaecology. 651p. 2000. reprint ed. 85.00 (*1-57898-218-9*) Martino Pubng.

Ricci, Julio. Falling Through the Cracks. Zlotchew, Clark M., tr. 81p. 1989. pap. 8.00 (*0-934834-25-3*) White Pine.

Ricci, Laura. The Magic of Winning Proposals, Vol. 1. Wilkerson, George, ed. LC 98-93370. 100p. 1998. ring bd. 250.00 (*0-9657399-1-0*) RThree.

Ricci, Laura & Wilkerson, George. 12 Views: From Women's Eyes: Managing the New Majority. LC 97-91622. (Illus.). 144p. (Orig.). 1997. pap. 14.95 (*0-9657399-0-2*) RThree.

Ricci, Luigi. Un Avventura di Scaramuccia. LC 86-755124. (Italian Opera Ser., 1810-1840: Vol. 44). 312p. 1987. text 30.00 (*0-8240-6593-X*) Garland.

Ricci, Luigi, tr. see Machiavelli, Niccolo, et al.

Ricci, M., jt. ed. see Marone, Gianni.

Ricci, Mark, jt. auth. see Conway, Michael.

Ricci, Mark, jt. auth. see Vermilye, Jerry.

Ricci, Matteo. The True Meaning of the Lord of Heaven. Malatesta, Edward J., ed. LC 84-80944. (Jesuit Primary Sources in English Translation Ser.: No. 6). (CHI & ENG., Illus.). xiv, 485p. 1985. 39.00 (*0-912422-78-5*); 34.00 (*0-912422-77-7*) Inst Jesuit.

Ricci, Michael A. & Szabo, Joseph G. Was It Worth It? A Collection of International Cartoons about Columbus & His Trip to America. 112p. 1992. pap. 12.95 (*0-9631600-0-1*) WittyWrld ICM.

Ricci, Nino. In a Glass House. 288p. 1998. pap. 13.00 (*0-312-18691-6*) St Martin.

— In a Glass House: A Novel. LC 95-21020. 275p. 1995. text 22.00 (*0-312-13520-3*, Picador USA) St Martin.

— Journey Prize Anthology: The Best of Canada's New Writers. 168p. 1998. pap. text 15.95 (*0-7710-4425-9*) McCland & Stewart.

— Lives of the Saints: A Novel. LC 95-21022. 1995. pap. 11.00 (*0-312-13441-X*, Picador USA) St Martin.

— Where She Has Gone. LC 98-22709. 336p. 1998. text 25.00 (*0-312-18700-9*) St Martin.

— Where She Has Gone. 336p. 1999. pap. 13.00 (*0-312-20681-X*) St Martin.

Ricci, Paolo F., et al. Technological Risk Assessment. 1984. text 160.50 (*90-247-2961-0*) Kluwer Academic.

Ricci, Paolo F., ed. see Cox, L. A.

Ricci, Paul. Fundamentals of Critical Thinking. 2nd ed. (C). 1991. text 56.00 (*0-536-57941-5*) Pearson Custom.

Ricci, Phillip & Spruill, Wanda G. Accounting Principles, Printer Recharge, Inc. A Corporate Practice Set. 4th ed. (C). 1993. pap. text 26.88 (*0-07-059206-3*) McGraw.

Ricci, Phillip, jt. auth. see Spruill, Wanda G.

Ricci, Ralph V. Multiple Choice Questions in Preparation for the AP Biology Examination. 2nd ed. 115p. 1991. student ed. 15.95 (*1-878621-12-2*) D & S Mktg Syst.

— Multiple Choice Questions in Preparation for the AP Biology Examination. 2nd ed. 71p. (YA). (gr. 11-12). 1991. teacher ed. write for info. (*1-878621-13-0*) D & S Mktg Syst.

Ricci, Seymour De, see Cohen, Henry & De Ricci, Seymour.

Ricci, Seymour De, see De Ricci, Seymour.

Ricci, Stefano, et al. Ambulatory Phlebectomy: A Practical Guide for Treating Varicose Veins. (Illus.). 256p. (C). (gr. 13). 1995. text 138.00 (*0-8151-7045-9*, 24829) Mosby Inc.

Ricci, Stephen, jt. ed. see Nowell-Smith, Geoffry.

Ricci, Susan C., jt. auth. see Stebbins, Theodore R., Jr.

Ricci, Vincent L., jt. auth. see Duffy, James P.

Riccia, G. Della, et al, eds. Learning, Networks & Statistics. (CISM International Centre for Mechanical Sciences Ser.: No. 382). (Illus.). viii, 230p. 1997. pap. 64.00 (*3-211-82910-5*) Spr-Verlag.

Ricciardi, Antonio. St. Maximilian Kolbe. Daughters of St. Paul Staff, tr. from ITA. LC 82-18316. (Illus.). 314p. 1982. pap. 7.95 (*0-8198-6837-X*) Pauline Bks.

Ricciardi-Castagnoli, Paola, ed. Dendritic Cells in Fundamental & Clinical Immunology: Proceedings of the 4th International Symposium Held in Venice, Italy, October 5-10, 1996, Vol. 3. LC 97-8041. (Advances in Experimental Medicine & Biology Ser.: Vol. 417). 610p. (C). 1997. text 149.50 (*0-306-45592-7*, Kluwer Plenum) Kluwer Academic.

Ricciardi, Cynthia B., ed. see Griffith, Elizabeth, et al.

Ricciardi, John, jt. auth. see Meston, Zach.

Ricciardi, Luigi M. Diffusion Processes & Related Topics in Biology. LC 77-7464. (Lecture Notes in Biomathematics Ser.: Vol. 14). 1977. 32.00 (*0-387-08146-1*) Spr-Verlag.

Ricciardi, Luigi M., ed. Biomathematics & Related Computational Problems. (C). 1988. text 321.00 (*90-277-2726-0*) Kluwer Academic.

Ricciardi, Sherry. Bosnia: The Struggle for Peace. (Headliners Ser.). (Illus.). 64p. (J). (gr. 5-8). 1996. lib. bdg. 23.40 (*0-7613-0031-7*) Millbrook Pr.

Ricciardi, Stephen & Gobuzas, Thomas. Quest for Power: Darkness in the Light. Schonenberg, Douglas & Samuels, Steven, eds. (Quest for Power Ser.). (Illus.). 1996. boxed set 29.95 (*0-9653496-0-8*, DL1001) Infinite Imag.

Ricciardone, Sal, jt. auth. see Young, William G.

Riccio, Anthony V. Portrait of an Italian American Neighborhoo: The North End of Boston. LC 97-35581. (Illus.). 204p. 1998. 39.95 (*1-57703-006-0*) CMS.

Riccio, Barry D. Walter Lippmann: Odyssey of a Liberal. LC 92-37471. 376p. (C). 1993. text 39.95 (*1-56000-096-1*) Transaction Pubs.

— Walter Lippmann - Odyssey of a Liberal. 260p. (Orig.). (C). 1995. pap. text 24.95 (*1-56000-859-8*) Transaction Pubs.

Riccio, Dolores. Antioxidant Power: 366 Delicious Recipies for Great Health & Long Life. LC 98-38178. 401p. 1999. pap. 17.95 (*0-452-27728-0*, Plume) Dutton Plume.

— Superfoods for Life: 250 Anti-Aging Recipes for Foods That Keep You Feeling Fit & Fabulous. LC 97-15698. 368p. 1998. pap. 14.00 (*1-55788-280-0*, HP Books) Berkley Pub.

— 366 Delicious Ways to Cook Pasta with Vegetables. LC 97-17697. 1997. pap. 16.95 (*0-452-27727-2*, Plume) Dutton Plume.

Riccio, James & Brooks, Lisa. Nuclear Lemons. 5th ed. 75p. 1996. pap. 15.00 (*0-937188-58-1*) Pub Citizen.

Riccio, Nina. Five Kids & a Monkey Banish the Stinkies: A Learning Adventure about Keeping Clean & Healthy. LC 96-86336. (Five Kids & a Monkey Ser.: No. 3). (Illus.). 32p. (Orig.). (J). (gr. 2-6). 1997. pap. 7.95 (*0-9653955-2-9*) Creative Attic.

— Five Kids & a Monkey Banish the Stinkies Vol. 3: Complete with Unit Study & Poster! (Five Kids & a Monkey Ser.). (Illus.). 32p. (J). (gr. 2-6). 1997. pap. 12.95 (*0-9653955-9-6*) Creative Attic.

— Five Kids & a Monkey Investigate a Vicious Virus: A Learning Adventure about Germs & the Immune System. LC 96-86331. (Five Kids & a Monkey Ser.: No. 1). (Illus.). 32p. (J). (gr. 2-6). 1997. pap. 7.95 (*0-9653955-0-2*) Creative Attic.

— Five Kids & a Monkey Investigate a Vicious Virus Vol. 1: Complete with Unit Study & Poster! (Five Kids & a Monkey Ser.). (Illus.). 32p. (J). (gr. 2-6). 1997. pap. 12.95 (*0-9653955-7-X*) Creative Attic.

— Five Kids & a Monkey Manage Magenta Mayhem: A Learning Adventure about Making Decisions. (Five Kids & a Monkey Ser.: No. II). (Illus.). 32p. (Orig.). (J). (gr. 2-6). 1998. pap. 7.95 (*0-9653955-6-1*) Creative Attic.

— Five Kids & a Monkey Solve the Great Cupcake Caper: A Learning Adventure about Healthy Eating & Exercise. LC 96-86398. (Five Kids & a Monkey Ser.: No. 2). (Illus.). 32p. (Orig.). (J). (gr. 2-6). 1997. pap. 7.95 (*0-9653955-1-0*) Creative Attic.

— Five Kids & a Monkey Solve the Great Cupcake Caper Vol. 2: Complete with Unit Study & Poster!, 3 vols. (Five Kids & a Monkey Ser.). (Illus.). 32p. (J). (gr. 2-6). 1997. pap. 12.95 (*0-9653955-8-8*) Creative Attic.

Riccio, Nina M. Five Kids & a Monkey Dump the Grump: A Learning Adventure about Handling Disagreements. (Five Kids & a Monkey Ser.: No. II). (Illus.). 32p. (Orig.). (J). (gr. 2-6). 1998. pap. 7.95 (*0-9653955-4-5*) Creative Attic.

— Five Kids & a Monkey Series, 3 vols., Set. (Illus.). (J). (gr. 2-6). 23.85 (*0-9653955-3-7*) Creative Attic.

— Five Kids & a Monkey Unscramble Violet: A Learning Adventure about Handling Emotions. (Five Kids & a Monkey Ser.: No. II). (Illus.). 32p. (Orig.). (J). (gr. 2-6). 1998. pap. 7.95 (*0-9653955-5-3*) Creative Attic.

Riccio, Ottone, ed. see Thayer, Virginia.

Riccio, Peter. Italian Authors of Today. LC 75-128298. (Essay Index Reprint Ser.). 1977. 18.95 (*0-8369-1842-8*) Ayer.

***Ricciotti, Abbot G.** The Age of Martyrs: Christianity from Diocletian (284) to Constantine (337) Bull, Anthony, tr. from ITA. LC 98-61402. 305p. 1999. reprint ed. pap. 16.50 (*0-89555-631-6*, 1582) TAN Bks Pubs.

— Julian the Apostate: Roman Emperor 361-363. Costelloe, M. Joseph, tr. from ITA. (Illus.). 275p. 1999. reprint ed. pap. 16.50 (*0-89555-632-4*, 1583) TAN Bks Pubs.

Ricciotti, Hope & Connelly, Vincent. The Menopause Cookbook: How to Eat Now & for the Rest of Your Life. LC 99-34029. 256p. 2000. pap. 15.95 (*0-393-31983-0*, Norton Paperbks) Norton.

— The Pregnancy Cookbook. LC 95-6383. (Illus.). 336p. 1996. pap. 15.95 (*0-393-31386-7*) Norton.

Riccitelli, James M. Sing a New Song: When Music Divides the Church. LC 98-177661. 176p. 1997. pap. write for info. (*0-9658900-0-7*) H & E Berk.

Ricciuti, Edward. Natural History of North America. (Illus.). 224p. 1997. 17.99 (*1-85833-757-7*, Pub. by CLib Bks) Whitecap Bks.

***Ricciuti, Edward.** Natural History of North America. (Illus.). 224p. 2000. reprint ed. 30.00 (*0-7881-9357-0*) DIANE Pub.

Ricciuti, Edward R. America's Top 10 Bridges. LC 96-52998. (America's Top 10 Ser.). (Illus.). 24p. (J). (gr. 3-5). 1997. lib. bdg. 15.95 (*1-56711-197-1*) Blackbirch.

— America's Top 10 Natural Wonders. LC 97-3639. (America's Top 10 Ser.). (Illus.). 24p. (J). (gr. 3-5). 1997. lib. bdg. 15.95 (*1-56711-192-0*) Blackbirch.

— America's Top 10 Skyscrapers. LC 97-3637. (America's Top 10 Ser.). (Illus.). 24p. (J). (gr. 3-5). 1997. lib. bdg. 15.95 (*1-56711-193-9*) Blackbirch.

— Amphibians. LC 93-20658. (Our Living World Ser.). (Illus.). 64p. (J). (gr. 4-8). 1993. lib. bdg. 19.45 (*1-56711-045-2*) Blackbirch.

— Birds. LC 92-44037. (Our Living World Ser.). (Illus.). 64p. (J). (gr. 4-8). 1993. lib. bdg. 19.45 (*1-56711-038-X*) Blackbirch.

— Crustaceans. LC 93-44545. (Our Living World Ser.). (Illus.). 64p. (J). (gr. 4-8). 1994. lib. bdg. 19.45 (*1-56711-046-0*) Blackbirch.

— Fish. LC 92-44038. (Our Living World Ser.). (Illus.). 64p. (J). (gr. 4-8). 1993. lib. bdg. 19.45 (*1-56711-041-X*) Blackbirch.

— Fish of the Atlantic. (Illus.). 96p. 1982. pap. 7.95 (*0-88839-155-2*) Hancock House.

— The Menominee. LC 97-560. (Native American People Ser.: Set V). 32p. (J). (gr. 5-8). 1997. lib. bdg. 22.60 (*0-86625-603-2*) Rourke Pubns.

— Older Than the Dinosaurs: The Origin & Rise of the Mammals. LC 77-26606. (Illus.). 96p. (J). (gr. 5-12). 1980. 8.20 (*0-690-01328-0*); lib. bdg. 12.89 (*0-690-03879-8*) HarpC Child Bks.

— Secrets of Potfishing. (Illus.). 74p. pap. 3.50 (*0-88839-085-8*) Hancock House.

— Secrets of Shellfishing. (Illus.). 70p. pap. 3.50 (*0-88839-140-4*) Hancock House.

***Ricciuti, Edward R.** Snake Almanac. 2000. 29.95 (*1-58574-178-7*) Lyons Pr.

Ricciuti, Edward R. What on Earth Is a Capybara? Glassman, Bruce, ed. LC 94-36827. (What on Earth Is...? Ser.). 32p. (J). (gr. 2-5). 1995. lib. bdg. 16.95 (*1-56711-097-5*) Blackbirch.

— What on Earth Is a Chuckwalla? Glassman, Bruce, ed. LC 94-28248. (What on Earth Is . . . ? Ser.). 32p. (J). (gr. 2-5). 1994. lib. bdg. 16.95 (*1-56711-089-4*) Blackbirch.

— What on Earth Is a Galago? Glassman, Bruce, ed. LC 94-40356. (Illus.). 32p. (J). (gr. 2-5). 1995. lib. bdg. 16.95 (*1-56711-101-7*) Blackbirch.

— What on Earth Is a Hyrax? Glassman, Bruce, ed. LC 94-36411. (What on Earth Is . . . ? Ser.). (Illus.). 32p. (J). (gr. 2-5). 1996. lib. bdg. 16.95 (*1-56711-100-9*) Blackbirch.

— What on Earth Is a Pangolin? Glassman, Bruce, ed. LC 94-22517. (What on Earth Is . . . ? Ser.). (Illus.). 32p. (J). (gr. 2-5). 1994. lib. bdg. 16.95 (*1-56711-090-8*) Blackbirch.

— What on Earth Is a Pout? Glassman, Bruce S., ed. LC 95-43326. (What on Earth Is...? Ser.). (Illus.). 32p. (J). (gr. 2-5). 1996. lib. bdg. 16.95 (*1-56711-103-3*) Blackbirch.

— What on Earth Is a Skink. Glassman, Bruce S., ed. LC 94-28249. (What on Earth Is . . . ? Ser.). (Illus.). 32p. (J). (gr. 2-5). 1994. lib. bdg. 16.95 (*1-56711-096-7*) Blackbirch.

— Wildlife Special Agent: Protecting Endangered Species. Glassman, Bruce S., ed. & photos by. Carpenteri, Steve, photos by. LC 95-48143. (Risky Business Ser.). (Illus.). 32p. (J). (gr. 2-5). 1996. lib. bdg. 16.95 (*1-56711-160-2*) Blackbirch.

— The Yakama. LC 97-5899. (Native American People Ser.: Set V). (Illus.). 32p. (J). (gr. 5-8). 1997. lib. bdg. 22.60 (*0-86625-604-0*) Rourke Pubns.

Ricciuti, Edward R., compiled by. The Cats of Our Lives: Heartwarming Reminiscences of Feline Companions. (Illus.). 190p. 1997. 19.95 (*1-55972-414-5*, Birch Ln Pr) Carol Pub Group.

Ricciuti, Edward R. & National Audubon Society Staff. National Audubon Society First Field Guide: Rocks & Minerals. LC 97-17991. (Illus.). 160p. (J). (gr. 3-7). 1998. vinyl bd. 10.95 (*0-590-05484-8*) Scholastic Inc.

— National Audubon Society First Field Guide: Rocks & Minerals. LC 97-17991. (Illus.). 160p. (YA). (gr. 3-7). 1998. 17.95 (*0-590-05463-5*) Scholastic Inc.

Ricciuti, Edward R., jt. auth. see Albano, Lou.

Ricciuti, Henry N., jt. auth. see Caldwell, Bettye M.

Ricco, A. J., et al, eds. Chemical & Biological Sensors & Analytical Electrochemical Methods. LC 97-197229. (Proceedings Ser.: Vol. 97-19). 1110p. 1997. 98.00 (*1-56677-147-1*) Electrochem Soc.

***Riceo, Cia.** Living As If Your Life Depended on It! Twelve Gateways to a Life That Works. LC 00-190093. 184p. 2000. pap. 19.95 (*0-9678849-1-8*) Life Cre.

Riccobene, Samuel P. & Senior Adult Council Staff. Are Your Affairs in Order? A Planning Guide & Resource Book. (Older Adult Issues Ser.). 50p. 1999. pap. 4.95 (*0-664-50085-4*) Geneva Press.

***Riccoboni, Bartolomea.** Life & Death in a Venetian Convent: The Chronicle & Necrology of Corpus Domini, 1395-1436. Bornstein, Daniel Ethan, ed. & tr. by. from ITA. LC 99-37584. (Other Voice in Early Modern Europe Ser.). (Illus.). 109p. 2000. pap. text 12.00 (*0-226-71789-5*); lib. bdg. 35.00 (*0-226-71788-7*) U Ch Pr.

Riccoboni, Luigi. A General History of the Stage from Its Origin....with Two Essays: On the Art of Speaking in Public & a Comparison Between the Ancient & Modern Drama. LC 76-43937. (Music & Theatre in France in the 17th & 18th Centuries Ser.). reprint ed. 57.50 (*0-404-60187-1*) AMS Pr.

Riccoboni, Marie. Histoire D'Ernestine. Stewart, Joan H. & Stewart, Philip, eds. (MLA Texts & Translations Ser.: No. 5a). (FRE.). 100p. 1998. pap. 7.95 (*0-87352-785-2*, P006P) Modern Lang.

— The Story of Ernestine. Stewart, Joan H. & Stewart, Philip, trs. from FRE. LC 98-38996. (MLA Texts & Translations Ser.: No. 6b). 100p. 1998. pap. 7.95 (*0-87352-786-0*, Q006P) Modern Lang.

Riccomini, Donald R. & Rosenzweig, Philip M. Unexpected Japan: Why American Business Should Return to Its Own Traditional Values--& Not Imitate the Japanese. 144p. 1985. 12.95 (*0-8027-0858-7*) Walker & Co.

Riccucci, Norma M. Unsung Heroes: Federal Execucrats Making a Difference. LC 95-7073. 266p. 1995. 45.00 (*0-87840-592-5*); pap. 17.95 (*0-87840-595-X*) Georgetown U Pr.

— Women, Minorities & Unions in the Public Sector, 28. LC 89-7481. (Contributions in Labor Studies: No. 28). 201p. 1990. 52.95 (*0-313-26043-5*, RWM, Quorum Bks) Greenwood.

Riccucci, Norma M., jt. auth. see Ban, Carolyn.

Rice. Apple Surprise. (Easy Theme Reader Ser.). (Illus.). 16p. (J). (ps-1). 1996. pap. 2.49 (*1-55734-928-2*) Tchr Create Mat.

Rice. Calculus & Analytic Geometry Instructor. (Physics Ser.). 1990. pap., teacher ed. 30.00 (*0-8273-3871-6*) Delmar.

— Calculus & Analytical Geometry for Engineering Technology. (Physics). (C). 1986. pap. 72.75 (*0-8273-3868-6*) Thomson Learn.

— Cases in Child & Adolecent Development. 1996. pap. text, student ed. 25.20 (*0-13-573825-3*) P-H.

— Cases in Human Development. 3rd ed. 1998. pap. text, student ed. 17.10 (*0-13-888314-9*) P-H.

— College Algebra. (Mathematics Ser.). 1977. 14.00 (*0-87150-226-7*) PWS Pubs.

***Rice.** Glencoe Computer Applications & Keyboarding: Teacher's Wraparound Edition. 1998. teacher ed. 52.50 (*0-02-803397-3*) Glencoe.

— Handbook of Home Health Nursing Procedures. 2nd ed. (C). 1999. text 31.95 (*0-323-00911-5*) Mosby Inc.

Rice. Health Psychology with InfoTrac. (Psychology Ser.). 1998. 48.50 incl. cd-rom (*0-534-36359-8*) Brooks-Cole.

***Rice.** A History of Psychology. 1999. pap. text. write for info. (*0-582-30375-3*) Addison-Wesley.

— Home Care Nursing Practice. 3rd ed. 2000. pap. text. write for info. (*0-323-01107-1*) Mosby Inc.

Rice. Home Health Handbook of Pediatric Procedures. (Illus.). 462p. (C). (gr. 13). 1998. text 28.95 (*0-8151-3819-9*, 31842) Mosby Inc.

***Rice.** Human Development. 4th ed. 2001. pap., student ed. 22.67 (*0-13-018569-8*) P-H.

Rice. Idea Tasting. 4th ed. 112p. (C). 1998. pap. text 24.95 (*0-536-58914-3*) Pearson Custom.

— Introduction to Taxation: A Decision-Making Approach - 1999 Edition. 1998. 76.95 (*0-87393-763-5*) Dame Pubns.

— Irtro to Taxation: A Decision Making Approach. (SWC-Taxation). 1999. 80.95 (*0-87393-839-9*) Dame Pubns.

***Rice.** Marketing Manager's Troubleshooter. (C). 2000. 59.95 (*0-13-923574-4*, Macmillan Coll) P-H.

— May Monthly Activities. (J). (ps). 1996. pap. text, wbk. ed. 9.95 (*1-55734-868-5*) Tchr Create Mat.

Rice. Medications & Math for Allied Health Professions. (ALLIED HEALTH). (C). 2000. pap. 26.50 (*0-7668-1090-9*) Delmar.

— Medications & Math for the Nurse - IML. 8th ed. 96p. 1998. teacher ed. 15.95 (*0-8273-8329-0*) Delmar.

— Movies & Meaning: An Introduction to Film. 2nd ed. 432p. (C). 2000. pap. 36.75 (*0-205-31415-5*) Allyn.

Rice. November Monthly Activities. (Illus.). 80p. (J). (ps-1). 1996. pap., wbk. ed. 9.95 (*1-55734-862-6*) Tchr Create Mat.

— October Monthly Activities. (Monthly Activities Ser.). (Illus.). 80p. (J). (ps-1). 1996. pap., wbk. ed. 9.95 (*1-55734-861-8*) Tchr Create Mat.

Rice. Porosity of Ceramics. LC 97-52813. (Illus.). 560p. 1998. text 195.00 (*0-8247-0151-8*) Dekker.

***Rice.** Practical Horticulture. 4th ed. LC 99-23130. (Illus.). 455p. (C). 1999. 89.00 (*0-13-020610-5*) P-H.

Rice. Principles of Pharmacology for Medical Assistants. (Medical Assisting Ser.). 1989. pap., teacher ed. 14.00 (*0-8273-3093-6*) Delmar.

— Principles of Pharmacology for Medical Assisting - IML. 3rd ed. 112p. 1998. teacher ed. 19.95 (*0-7668-0326-0*) Delmar.

Rice. September Monthly Activities. (Monthly Activities Ser.). 80p. (J). (ps-1). 1996. pap. 9.95 (*1-55734-860-X*) Tchr Create Mat.

Rice. Stress & Health. (Psychology Ser.). 1987. text, teacher ed. write for info. (*0-534-07609-2*) Brooks-Cole.

— Stress & Health. 3rd ed. LC 98-7726. (Psychology Ser.). 1998. pap. 46.95 (*0-534-26502-2*) Brooks-Cole.

— Terminology of Health & Medicine: Instructor's Manual. 112p. (C). 1997. pap. text, teacher ed. 25.00 (*0-8385-8858-1*, A-8858-1) Appleton & Lange.

— Travel Perspectives: A Guide to Becoming a Travel Agent. 2nd ed. (Hospitality, Travel & Tourism Ser.). 64p. 1996. teacher ed. 19.00 (*0-8273-6534-9*) Delmar.

Rice & Cerbus. Grandparents. (Thematic Units Ser.). 80p. (J). (gr. 1-3). 1997. pap. 9.95 (*1-57690-112-2*) Tchr Create Mat.

R

An Asterisk (*) at the beginning of an entry indicates that the title is appearing for the first time.

Rice & Cerbus, Deborah P. Changing Seasons. (Easy Theme Reader Ser.). (Illus.). 16p. (J). (ps-1). 1996. pap. 2.49 (1-55734-899-5) Tchr Create Mat.
— My Senses Work for Me. (Easy Theme Reader Ser.). (Illus.). 16p. (J). (ps-1). 1996. pap. 2.49 (1-55734-929-0) Tchr Create Mat.
— Rocks Are Everywhere. (Easy Theme Reader Ser.). (Illus.). 16p. (J). (ps-1). 1996. pap. 2.49 (1-55734-927-4) Tchr Create Mat.
— What Kind of Weather? (Easy Theme Reader Ser.). (Illus.). 16p. (J). (ps-1). 1996. pap. 2.49 (1-55734-898-7) Tchr Create Mat.
Rice & Strange. College Algebra with Applications: Student Manual. 4th ed. (Mathematics Ser.). 1989. pap., student ed. 21.95 (0-534-10208-5) Brooks-Cole.
— College Algebra with Applications: Study Guide. 4th ed. (Mathematics Ser.). 1989. student ed. 18.95 (0-534-10207-7) Brooks-Cole.
— Finite Math for College Students. (Mathematics Ser.). 1992. pap. 25.95 (0-534-17174-5) Brooks-Cole.
— Ordinary Differential Equations with Applications. 2nd ed. (Mathematics Ser.). 1988. student ed. 20.00 (0-534-09907-6) Brooks-Cole.
— To Accompany Plane Trigonometry: Partial Solutions Manual. 4th ed. (C). 1986. mass mkt., student ed. 13.50 (0-87150-914-8, 33L4044) PWS Pubs.
Rice & Todd. Travel Perspectives PCDI Edition. (Hospitality, Travel & Tourism Ser.). (C). 1991. pap. 17.00 (0-8273-4884-3) Delmar.
Rice, jt. auth. see Berg.
Rice, jt. auth. see Bragger.
Rice, jt. auth. see Prigogine.
Rice, A. H. A Genealogical History of the Rice Family & Descendants of Deacon Edward Rice, Who Came from Berkhamstead, England, & Settled at Sudbury, Mass., in 1638. 387p. 1989. reprint ed. pap. 41.00 (0-8328-1019-3); reprint ed. lib. bdg. 51.00 (0-8328-1018-5) Higginson Bk Co.
***Rice, A .K.** Learning for Leadership: Interpersonal & Intergroup. 212p. 1999. pap. 38.00 (1-85575-233-6, Pub. by H Karnac Bks Ltd) Other Pr LLC.
***Rice, A. L.** Decommissioning the Brent Spar. LC 98-46095. 1999. write for info. (0-419-24080-2, E & FN Spon); pap. write for info. (0-419-24090-X, E & FN Spon) Routledge.
Rice, Alan, jt. ed. see Lockley, M. G.
Rice, Alan J. & Crawford, Martin, eds. Liberating Sojourn: Frederick Douglass & Transatlantic Reform. LC 99-23997. (Illus.). 217p. 1999. 45.00 (0-8203-2102-8); pap. 20.00 (0-8203-2129-X) U of Ga Pr.
Rice, Albert R. The Baroque Clarinet. (Early Music Ser.: No. 13). (Illus.). 218p. 1992. text 95.00 (0-19-816188-3) OUP.
Rice, Alice C. Happiness Road. LC 68-58810. (Essay Index Reprint Ser.). 1977. 17.95 (0-8369-0123-1) Ayer.
Rice, Alice H. Lovey Mary. 211p. 20.95 (0-8488-1133-X) Amereon Ltd.
— Mr. Opp. 336p. 25.95 (0-8488-1132-1) Amereon Ltd.
— Mrs. Wiggs of the Cabbage Patch. 19.95 (0-89190-859-5) Amereon Ltd.
— Mrs. Wiggs of the Cabbage Patch. (J). 1992. reprint ed. lib. bdg. 19.95 (0-89968-273-1, Lghtyr Pr) Buccaneer Bks.
— My Pillow Book. 17.95 (0-8488-1134-8) Amereon Ltd.
— The Peninsula. 23.95 (0-89190-728-9) Amereon Ltd.
— Quin. 402p. 27.95 (0-8488-1135-6) Amereon Ltd.
— Romance of Billy-Goat Hill. 27.95 (0-8488-1136-4) Amereon Ltd.
— Sandy. 326p. 24.95 (0-8488-1137-2) Amereon Ltd.
Rice, Alison. Explorations. (J). 1991. mass mkt. 22.95 (0-8384-3355-3) Heinle & Heinle.
Rice, Alison M. Teaching with Video: Techniques & Activities with Family Album, U. S. A. LC 92-5414. (C). 1992. pap. text 22.20 (0-02-881250-6) Macmillan.
Rice, Alison M., jt. auth. see Graves, Kathleen.
Rice, Allan L. Gothic Prepositional Compounds in Their Relation to the Greek Originals. (LD Ser.: No. 11). 1932. 25.00 (0-527-00757-9) Periodicals Srv.
— Swedish, a Practical Grammar. rev. ed. LC 58-13379. 110p. reprint ed. pap. 34.10 (0-608-16839-4, 202695000053) Bks Demand.
Rice, Allan L., tr. see Cavalli-Bjorkman, Gorel & Lindwall, Bo, eds.
Rice, Allan L., tr. see Langewiesche, Karl R.
Rice, Allen. The Road to New Beginning: A History of Tyro United Methodist Church Lexington, North Carolina. (Illus.). 112p. 1997. write for info. (1-57736-054-0) Providence Hse.
Rice, Allen T., ed. Reminiscences of Abraham Lincoln. LC 72-13766. (Concordance Ser.: No. 37). 1971. reprint ed. lib. bdg. 75.00 (0-8383-1227-6) M S G Haskell Hse.
***Rice, Andrew.** Frommer's Great Outdoor Guide to Northern California. (Illus.). 284p. 1999. pap. 15.95 (0-02-863308-3, Frommer) Macmillan Gen Ref.
— Frommer's Great Outdoor Guide to Southern California & Baja. (Outside Magazine's Adventure Guides Ser.). (Illus.). 352p. 1999. pap. 16.95 (0-02-861832-7, Frommer) Macmillan Gen Ref.
Rice, Andrew. Great Outdoors: Northern California. 384p. 1996. 15.95 (0-02-860623-X) Macmillan.
Rice, Ann S. Family Life Management. (C). 1986. teacher ed. write for info. (0-318-60353-5) Macmillan.
Rice, Anne. Cry to Heaven. 544p. 1991. pap. 14.00 (0-345-37370-7) Ballantine Pub Grp.
— Cry to Heaven. 1995. mass mkt. 6.99 (0-345-39693-6) Ballantine Pub Grp.
— Cry to Heaven. LC 81-19368. 1982. 29.95 (0-394-52351-2) Knopf.
— The Feast of All Saints. 640p. 1986. mass mkt. 7.99 (0-345-33453-1) Ballantine Pub Grp.
— The Feast of All Saints. 576p. 1992. pap. 14.00 (0-345-37604-8) Ballantine Pub Grp.
— Interview with the Vampire. (Vampire Chronicles: Bk. 1). 352p. 1986. mass mkt. 6.99 (0-345-33766-2) Ballantine Pub Grp.
— Interview with the Vampire. (Vampire Chronicles: Bk. 1). 1997. pap. 14.00 (0-345-40964-7) Ballantine Pub Grp.
— Interview with the Vampire. LC 96-232882. (Vampire Chronicles: Bk. 1). 1976. 27.50 (0-394-49821-6) Knopf.
— Interview with the Vampire. (Vampire Chronicles: Bk. 1). 320p. 1991. reprint ed. lib. bdg. 35.95 (0-89966-781-3) Buccaneer Bks.
Rice, Anne. El Ladron de Cuerpos. 1996. pap. text 13.95 (950-08-1433-1, Pub. by Atlantida) Libros Fronteras.
Rice, Anne. Lasher. 628p. 1995. mass mkt. 7.99 (0-345-39781-9) Ballantine Pub Grp.
— Lasher. LC 93-12246. 1993. 30.00 (0-679-41295-6) Knopf.
— Lasher. LC 93-12246. 592p. 1994. pap. 14.00 (0-345-37764-8) Knopf.
— Memnoch the Devil. (Vampire Chronicles: Bk. 5). 480p. 1996. pap. 14.00 (0-345-38940-9) Ballantine Pub Grp.
— Memnoch the Devil. (Vampire Chronicles: Bk. 5). 368p. 1995. 25.00 (0-679-44101-8) Knopf.
— Memnoch the Devil. limited ed. (Vampire Chronicles: Bk. 5). 354p. 1995. boxed set 150.00 (0-9631925-4-X) B E Trice.
— Merrick. LC 99-88556. 320p. 2000. 26.95 (0-679-45448-9) Knopf.
***Rice, Anne.** Merrick. large type ed. 2000. 26.95 (0-375-43077-6) Random.
Rice, Anne. The Mummy, or Ramses the Damned. 1989. pap. 14.00 (0-345-36000-1) Ballantine Pub Grp.
— The Mummy, or Ramses the Damned. 416p. 1991. mass mkt. 6.99 (0-345-36994-7) Ballantine Pub Grp.
— Pandora. (New Tales of the Vampires Ser.: Bk. 1). 1999. mass mkt. 6.99 (0-345-42238-4) Ballantine Pub Grp.
— Pandora. LC 97-49457. (New Tales of the Vampires Ser.: Bk. 1). 288p. 1998. 19.95 (0-375-40159-8) Random.
— Pandora. large type ed. LC 97-40717. (New Tales of the Vampires Ser.: Bk. 1). 288p. 1998. pap. 19.95 (0-375-70218-0) Random.
— Pandora. limited ed. (New Tales of the Vampires Ser.: Bk. 1). 356p. 1998. 150.00 (1-890885-02-9) B E Trice.
— The Queen of the Damned. LC 88-45311. (Vampire Chronicles: Bk. 3). 432p. 1988. 25.00 (0-394-55823-5) Ballantine Pub Grp.
— The Queen of the Damned. (Vampire Chronicles: Bk. 3). 491p. 1989. mass mkt. 6.99 (0-345-35152-5) Ballantine Pub Grp.
— The Queen of the Damned. (Vampire Chronicles: Bk. 3). 1997. pap. 14.00 (0-345-41962-6) Ballantine Pub Grp.
— Servant of the Bones. 1997. 7.50 (0-345-41231-1, Del Rey); pap. 14.00 (0-345-40966-3) Ballantine Pub Grp.
— Servant of the Bones. 1998. mass mkt. 7.99 (0-345-38941-7) Ballantine Pub Grp.
— Servant of the Bones. LC 95-49357. 387p. 1996. 26.00 (0-679-42832-1) Knopf.
— Servant of the Bones. 400p. 1996. 26.00 (0-679-43301-5) Random.
— Servant of the Bones. large type ed. (Large Print Ser.). 1996. pap. 26.00 (0-679-75904-2) Random.
— Servant of the Bones. limited ed. 387p. 1996. boxed set 150.00 (0-9631925-6-6) B E Trice.
— The Tale of the Body Thief. (Vampire Chronicles: Bk. 4). 448p. 1993. mass mkt. 6.99 (0-345-38475-X) Ballantine Pub Grp.
— The Tale of the Body Thief. 1997. pap. 14.00 (0-345-41963-4) Ballantine Pub Grp.
— The Tale of the Body Thief. LC 92-53085. (Vampire Chronicles). 428p. 1992. text 23.50 (0-394-22317-9) Knopf.
— The Tale of the Body Thief. LC 92-5308. (Vampire Chronicles: Bk. 4). 1992. 27.95 (0-679-40528-3) Knopf.
Rice, Anne. The Tale of the Body Thief, Set. abr. ed. (Vampire Chronicles Ser.: No. 4). 1992. pap. 18.00 incl. audio (0-679-41162-3) Random AudioBks.
Rice, Anne. Taltos. 480p. 1995. pap. 14.00 (0-345-39471-2) Ballantine Pub Grp.
— Taltos. 563p. 1996. mass mkt. 6.99 (0-345-40431-9) Ballantine Pub Grp.
— Taltos. 1994. 25.00 (0-679-42573-X) Knopf.
— Taltos. limited ed. 467p. 1994. boxed set 150.00 (0-9631925-1-5) B E Trice.
— The Vampire Armand. (New Tales of the Vampires Ser.: Bk. 2). 1999. pap. 14.95 (0-345-40927-2) Ballantine Pub Grp.
***Rice, Anne.** The Vampire Armand. 2000. mass mkt. 7.99 (0-345-43480-3) Ballantine Pub Grp.
Rice, Anne. The Vampire Armand. LC 98-14579. (New Tales of the Vampires Ser.: Bk. 2). 384p. 1998. 26.95 (0-679-45447-0) Knopf.
— The Vampire Armand. large type ed. LC 98-26240. (New Tales of the Vampires Ser.: Bk. 2). 565p. 1998. pap. 26.95 (0-375-70415-9) Random Hse Lrg Prnt.
— The Vampire Armand. limited ed. (Vampire Chronicles: Bk. 6). 1998. boxed set 150.00 (1-890885-06-1) B E Trice.
— The Vampire Chronicles, 4 vols. (Vampire Chronicles). 1993. pap., boxed set 27.96 (0-345-38540-3) Ballantine Pub Grp.
— The Vampire Chronicles, 3 vols. (Vampire Chronicles). 1990. 99.50 (0-394-58186-5) Random.
— The Vampire Chronicles, 4 vols., Set. (Vampire Chronicles). 1989. boxed set 20.97 (0-345-36422-8) Ballantine Pub Grp.
— The Vampire Lestat. (Vampire Chronicles: Bk. 2). 560p. 1986. mass mkt. 7.99 (0-345-31386-0) Ballantine Pub Grp.
— The Vampire Lestat. (Vampire Chronicles: Bk. 2). 1997. pap. 14.00 (0-345-41964-2) Ballantine Pub Grp.
— The Vampire Lestat. (Vampire Chronicles: Bk. 2). 384p. 1991. 39.95 (1-56521-002-6) Innovative.
— The Vampire Lestat. LC 85-40123. (Vampire Chronicles: Bk. 2). 512p. 1985. 27.50 (0-394-53443-3) Knopf.
— Violin. 1998. 7.50 (0-345-42446-8, Del Rey) Ballantine Pub Grp.
— Violin. 289p. 1998. pap. 14.00 (0-345-38942-5) Ballantine Pub Grp.
— Violin. 372p. 1999. mass mkt. 7.99 (0-345-42530-8) Ballantine Pub Grp.
— Violin. LC 96-38581. 1997. 25.95 (0-679-43302-3) Knopf.
— Violin. deluxe limited ed. 304p. 1997. boxed set 150.00 (1-890885-00-2) B E Trice.
— Violin. large type ed. LC 97-11708. (Large Print Ser.). 1997. pap. 25.95 (0-679-77444-0) Random.
— Violin: A Novel, unabridged ed. 1997. 39.95 incl. audio (0-679-46066-7, 105975, Pub. by Random AudioBks) Lndmrk Audiobks.
— Vittorio the Vampire. LC 98-14209. (New Tales of the Vampires Ser.: Bk. 3). 304p. 1999. 19.95 (0-375-40160-1) Knopf.
— Vittorio the Vampire. large type ed. LC 98-52777. (New Tales of the Vampires Ser.: Bk. 3). 304p. 1999. pap. 19.95 (0-375-70572-4) Random.
***Rice, Anne.** Vittorio the Vampire, 2. limited ed. (New Tales of the Vampires Ser.: Bk. 3). 292p. 1999. boxed set 150.00 (1-890885-07-X) B E Trice.
Rice, Anne. The Witching Hour. 976p. 1991. pap. 14.00 (0-345-36789-8) Ballantine Pub Grp.
Rice, Anne. The Witching Hour. 1056p. 1993. mass mkt. 6.99 (0-345-38446-6) Ballantine Pub Grp.
— The Witching Hour. 1990. 29.95 (0-394-58786-3) Knopf.
Rice, Anne, et al. Getting It On: A Condom Reader. Roberson, Mitch & Dubner, Julia, eds. 256p. 1999. 24.00 (1-56947-145-2) Soho Press.
— Getting It On: A Condom Reader. Roberson, Mitch & Dubner, Julia, eds. LC 98-3722. 240p. 1999. pap. 15.00 (1-56947-125-8) Soho Press.
Rice, Anne, see Rampling, Anne, pseud.
Rice, Anne, see Roquelaure, Ann N., pseud.
Rice, Anne, jt. auth. see Riley, Michael H.
***Rice, Anne-Christine.** Cinema for French Conversation: A New Way to Spoken French. (FRE., Illus.). (C). 1999. pap. text. write for info. (0-941051-84-6) Focus Pub-R Pullins.
— Cinema for French Conversation. Cahier du Professeur. (FRE., Illus.). 100p. 1999. pap. text, teacher ed. write for info. (0-941051-85-4) Focus Pub-R Pullins.
Rice, Anthony. Voyages of Discovery: Three Centuries of Natural History Exploration. LC 99-32989. 336p. 1999. 60.00 (0-609-60536-4) Crown Pub Group.
Rice, Arnold M., et al. United States History from 1865. 20th ed. LC 90-56006. (HarperCollins College Outline Ser.). (Illus.). 496p. (Orig.). 1991. pap. 17.00 (0-06-467100-3, Harper Ref) HarpC.
— United States History to 1877. 8th ed. LC 90-56006. (College Outline Ser.). (Illus.). 320p. (Orig.). 1991. pap. 16.00 (0-06-467111-9, Harper Ref) HarpC.
Rice, Arnold S. The Ku Klux Klan in American Politics. LC 72-1152. (Southern Literature & History Ser.: No. 65). 1972. reprint ed. lib. bdg. 75.00 (0-8383-1427-9) M S G Haskell Hse.
***Rice, Arthur.** Born of the Spirit, Child of a King. 1999. pap. write for info. (1-58235-243-7) Watermrk Pr.
— So Be It. 2000. write for info. (1-58235-595-9) Watermrk Pr.
Rice, B. Lewis. Mysore & Coorg from the Inscriptions. (Illus.). 256p. 1986. reprint ed. write for info. (0-8364-1700-3, Pub. by Manohar) S Asia.
Rice, Barbara, ed. see Institute of Medicine, Committee to Increase Minor.
Rice, Bebe Faas. The Jungle. (Doomsday Mall Ser.). (J). (gr. 3-7). 1996. pap. 3.99 (0-614-15550-9, Skylark BDD) BDD Bks Young Read.
***Rice, Ben.** Pobby & Dingan. (Illus.). 80p. 2000. 16.00 (0-375-41127-5) Knopf.
Rice, Bernard J. Plane Trigonometry. (Mathematics Ser.). 1995. text 12.75 (0-534-93464-1) Brooks-Cole.
— Plane Trigonometry. (Mathematics Ser.). Date not set. mass mkt. 12.00 (0-87150-540-1) PWS Pubs.
— Plane Trigonometry. 2nd ed. (Mathematics Ser.). 1978. 15.00 (0-87150-250-X) PWS Pubs.
Rice, Bernard J. & Strange. Plane Trigonometry. 6th ed. (Mathematics Ser.). 1992. pap., student ed. 17.50 (0-534-93121-9) PWS Pubs.
Rice, Bernard J. & Strange, Jerry. Ordinary Differential Equations W/apps. 2nd ed. LC 88-21725. (Math). (Illus.). 465p. (C). 1988. mass mkt. 58.50 (0-534-09906-8) Brooks-Cole.
Rice, Bernard J. & Strange, Jerry D. Algebra & Trigonometry Class Test. 3rd ed. LC 84-14917. (Math). (Illus.). 560p. (C). 1985. mass mkt. 37.75 (0-534-03600-7) Brooks-Cole.
— Ordinary Differential Equations W/apps. LC 85-29901. (Math). 325p. (C). 1986. mass mkt. 40.00 (0-534-06366-7) Brooks-Cole.
— Plane Trigonometry. 3rd ed. LC 80-26108. 322p. (C). 1981. mass mkt. 27.75 (0-87150-297-6, 2381) PWS Pubs.
— Plane Trigonometry. 4th ed. (C). 1986. mass mkt. 33.50 (0-87150-913-X, 33L4040) PWS Pubs.
— Plane Trigonometry. 5th ed. (Math). 384p. (C). 1989. mass mkt. 39.25 (0-534-91562-0) PWS Pubs.
— Plane Trigonometry. 6th ed. 400p. 1992. text 50.00 (0-534-92894-3) PWS Pubs.
— Plane Trigonometry. 7th ed. (Mathematics Ser.). 1995. mass mkt. 49.00 (0-534-94824-3) PWS Pubs.
Rice, Bernard J., et al. Finite Mathematics for College Students. 500p. (C). 1992. text 75.95 (0-534-17172-9) Brooks-Cole.
Rice, Bernard J., et al. Plane Trigonometry. 7th ed. (Math Ser.). 1995. pap., student ed. 21.25 (0-534-94825-1) Brooks-Cole.
Rice, Betty, et al. We, the Arcturian's. LC 90-82682. (Illus.). 336p. (Orig.). 1990. pap. 14.95 (0-9627417-0-1) Athena NM.
Rice, Bob. Nursery & Landscape Weed Control Manual. 264p. 1992. pap. 29.95 (0-913702-42-0) Thomson Pubns.
Rice, Bradley R. Progressive Cities: The Commission Government Movement in America, 1901-1920. LC 77-8458. 180p. reprint ed. pap. 55.80 (0-7837-1013-5, 204132400020) Bks Demand.
Rice, Bradley R., jt. auth. see Jackson, Harvey, III.
Rice, Bradley R., jt. auth. see Jackson, Harvey H.
Rice, Bradley R., ed. see McCarley, J. Britt, et al.
Rice, Brian. Astronomy: It's Out of This World. (Four-H Ser.). (Illus.). 36p. (J). (gr. 3-7). 1995. pap. 9.50 (1-57753-212-0, 132LM1) Corn Coop Ext.
Rice, Bruce. Descent into Lima. 88p. 1996. pap. 8.95 (1-55050-097-X, Pub. by Coteau) Genl Dist Srvs.
Rice, C. 50 Questions on Natural Law. 1993. pap. text 14.95 (0-89870-551-7) Ignatius Pr.
Rice, C. & Rice, M. Essential Budapest. (Essential Travel Guides Ser.). (Illus.). 128p. (Orig.). 1995. pap. 7.95 (0-8442-8902-7, Passprt Bks) NTC Contemp Pub Co.
— Essential Prague. (Essential Travel Guides Ser.). (Illus.). 128p. (Orig.). 1995. pap. 7.95 (0-8442-8948-5, Passprt Bks) NTC Contemp Pub Co.
Rice, C. Colliver. Persian Women & Their Ways. 1976. lib. bdg. 59.95 (0-8490-2424-2) Gordon Pr.
Rice, C. David, jt. auth. see Foley, William E.
Rice, C. David, jt. ed. see McClure, Arthur F.
Rice, C. M., jt. ed. see Hagedorn, C. H.
Rice, C. S. Gear Shaper Cutters. (Technical Papers: Vol. P129.22). (Illus.). 42p. 1977. pap. text 30.00 (1-55589-166-7) AGMA.
— Rice. "We Sought the Wilderness" (Memoirs of Some Descendants of Dea. Edmund Rice) 257p. 1991. reprint ed. pap. 39.50 (0-8328-1976-X); reprint ed. lib. bdg. 49.50 (0-8328-1975-1) Higginson Bk Co.
Rice, Cale Y. Selected Plays & Poems. LC 27-16490. xviii, 786p. 1972. reprint ed. 79.00 (0-403-01174-4) Scholarly.
***Rice, Candy K.** The Coach's Computer Resource: Basic Documents & Internet-Email Tasks. (No Sweat Learning Tools Ser.). (Illus.). 50p. 1999. 20.00 (0-9673896-1-5); spiral bd. 10.00 (0-9673896-0-7); spiral bd. 20.00 (0-9673896-2-3); spiral bd. 100.00 (0-9673896-3-1) C K Rice.
Rice, Cathy. Sign Language for Everyone: A Basic Course in Communication with the Deaf. LC 77-14592. 1978. 19.99 (0-8407-9002-3) Nelson.
Rice, Cecil A. Inpatient Group Psychotherapy. 1987. 26.95 (0-07-105351-4) McGraw.
— The Letters & Friendships of Sir Cecil Spring Rice, 2 vols, Set. Gwynn, Stephen L., ed. LC 73-110868. (Illus.). 1971. reprint ed. lib. bdg. 85.00 (0-8371-4545-7, SPLE) Greenwood.
— The Letters & Friendships of Sir Cecil Spring Rice, 2 vols, Vol. 1. Gwynn, Stephen L., ed. LC 73-110868. (Illus.). 1971. reprint ed. lib. bdg. 45.00 (0-8371-4546-5, SPLF) Greenwood.
— The Letters & Friendships of Sir Cecil Spring Rice, 2 vols, Vol. 2. Gwynn, Stephen L., ed. LC 73-110868. (Illus.). 1971. reprint ed. lib. bdg. 45.00 (0-8371-4547-3, SPLG) Greenwood.
— The Letters & Friendships of Sir Cecil Spring Rice: A Record, 2 Vols., Set. Gwynn, Stephen L., ed. LC 79-37912. (Select Bibliographies Reprint Ser.). 1977. reprint ed. 58.95 (0-8369-6750-X) Ayer.
Rice, Charles D. The Rise & Fall of Black Slavery. LC 72-9149. (Illus.). 443p. reprint ed. pap. 137.40 (0-608-09824-8, 206999200007) Bks Demand.
— The Scots Abolitionists, 1833-1861. fac. ed. LC 81-3789. 235p. 1981. reprint ed. pap. 72.90 (0-7837-7818-X, 204757400007) Bks Demand.
Rice, Charles E. Hole. History of the Hole Family in England & America. 134p. 1997. reprint ed. pap. 21.00 (0-8328-9178-9); reprint ed. lib. bdg. 31.00 (0-8328-9177-0) Higginson Bk Co.
— The Supreme Court & Public Prayer: The Need for Restraint. LC 64-18392. 216p. reprint ed. pap. 67.00 (0-7837-0466-6, 204078900018) Bks Demand.
***Rice, Charles E.** The Winning Side: Questions on Living the Culture of Life. 365p. 1999. pap. 24.95 (0-9674691-0-4) E M R Pubng.
Rice, Charles L., ed. Elements of Pennsylvanian Stratigraphy, Central Appalachian Basin. LC 94-32979. (Special Papers-Geological Society of America Ser.: Vol. 294). 1994. pap. 30.00 (0-8137-2294-2) Geol Soc.
Rice, Charles L., jt. ed. see Lyons, Paul C.
Rice, Cheryl F., et al. Early Childhood Units for Predictable Books. (Whole Language Units Ser.). 1995. pap. text 12.95 (1-55734-206-7) Tchr Create Mat.
— The U. S. Economy in the Light of Justice, Solidarity, & Complementarity: An Interdisciplinary Perspective. LC 96-186750. (Studies in Social Science). 212p. (Orig.). 1994. per. write for info. (1-883199-04-2) St U W Georgia.
Rice, Cheryl F., jt. auth. see Cerbus, Deborah P.
Rice, Cheryl Feichtenbiner, jt. auth. see Cerbus, Deborah P.
***Rice, Chris.** Essential Austria. (AAA Essential Guides Ser.). (Illus.). 128p. 2000. pap. 8.95 (0-658-00373-9, 003739, Passprt Bks) NTC Contemp Pub Co.

An Asterisk (*) at the beginning of an entry indicates that the title is appearing for the first time.

Rice, Chris & Perkins, Spencer. More Than Equals: Racial Healing for the Sake of the Gospel. LC 93-7442. (Illus.). 244p. (Orig.). 1993. pap. 12.99 (*0-8308-1318-7*, 1318) InterVarsity.

***Rice, Chris & Rice, Melanie.** Crusades: The Battle for Jerusalem. LC 00-24161. 2000. write for info. (*0-7894-6503-5*) DK Pub Inc.

Rice, Chris & Rice, Melanie. How Children Lived. LC 94-33412. (Illus.). 48p. (J). (gr. 2 up). 1995. 14.95 (*1-56458-876-9*) DK Pub Inc.

Rice, Chris, jt. auth. see Perkins, Spencer.

Rice, Chris, jt. auth. see Rice, Melanie.

***Rice, Christopher.** A Density of Souls. LC 00-35072. 304p. (YA). (gr. 8-12). 2000. 23.95 (*0-7868-6646-2*, Pub. by Hyperion) Time Warner.

Rice, Christopher. My First Body Book. (Illus.). (J). 22.99 (*0-590-24611-9*) Scholastic Inc.

***Rice, Christopher & Rice, Melanie.** Signpost Guides: Brittany & Normandy. LC 99-88340. (Thomas Cook Signpost Guides Ser.). (Illus.). 1999. pap. 22.95 (*0-7627-0680-5*) Globe Pequot.

Rice, Christopher & Rice, Melanie, contrib. by. Moscow. LC 98-7232. 256p. 1998. 22.95 (*0-7894-3529-2*) DK Pub Inc.

Rice, Christopher J., jt. auth. see Rice, Melanie.

Rice, Cindi, ed. see Conners, William W.

***Rice, Clarence.** The Fig Tree & the Trumpets. 146p. 1999. pap. 5.00 (*0-7392-0464-5*, PO3776) Morris Pubng.

Rice, Clarence. My Simple Life & Revelation Plus. 140p. (Orig.). 1996. pap. write for info. (*1-57502-230-3*) Morris Pubng.

— Simplicity: And Spiritual Mysteries. 152p. 1998. pap. 6.00 (*1-57502-838-7*, PO2302) Morris Pubng.

Rice, Clyde. A Heaven in the Eye. LC 84-6238. (Illus.). 1990. reprint ed. pap. 10.95 (*0-932576-84-2*) Breitenbush Bks.

— Night Freight. LC 87-808. 144p. 1987. 17.95 (*0-932576-50-8*); pap. 7.95 (*0-932576-57-5*) Breitenbush Bks.

— Nordi's Gift. LC 90-1948. 460p. 1990. 21.95 (*0-932576-77-X*) Breitenbush Bks.

Rice, Condoleezza. The Soviet Union & the Czechoslovak Army, 1948-1983: Uncertain Allegiance. LC 84-42566. 318p. 1984. reprint ed. pap. 98.60 (*0-7837-9432-0*, 206017400004) Bks Demand.

Rice, Condoleezza, jt. auth. see Zelikow, Philip D.

***Rice, Connie P.** Our Monongalia: A History of African Americans in Monongalia County, WV. (Illus.). 272p. 1998. 29.95 (*0-929915-26-7*) Headline Bks.

Rice, Craig. The Big Midget Murders. 365p. 1992. pap. 6.95 (*1-55882-112-0*) Intl Polygonics.

— The Corpse Steps Out. LC 89-85720. 304p. 1989. reprint ed. pap. 7.95 (*1-55882-022-1*, Lib Crime Classics) Intl Polygonics.

— Eight Faces at Three. 256p. 1989. reprint ed. pap. 5.95 (*1-55882-007-8*, Lib Crime Classics) Intl Polygonics.

— Home Sweet Homicide. 107p. 1947. pap. 5.50 (*0-87129-838-4*, H25) Dramatic Pub.

— The $100,000 Resume. LC 98-23199. 256p. 1998. pap. 16.95 (*0-07-052586-2*, BusinessWeek Bks) McGraw.

— Trial by Fury. LC 91-70598. 255p. 1991. pap. 5.95 (*1-55882-091-4*, Lib Crime Classics) Intl Polygonics.

— The Wrong Murder. LC 90-80762. 312p. 1990. reprint ed. pap. 7.95 (*1-55882-067-1*) Intl Polygonics.

Rice, Craig M. Auditing ESD & Cleanroom Processes: A Step-By-Step Workbook for Understanding & Assessing Effective Process Controls. (Illus.). 98p. 1996. wbk. ed. 24.95 (*0-9647684-1-0*) Integrat Mgmt.

— Calibration System Workbook: An Auditor's Guide for ISO Standards Compliance. 86p. 1994. 24.95 (*0-9647684-0-2*) Integrat Mgmt.

***Rice, Craig S.** Dodging Downsizing: Proven Strategies for Job Security in Tough Times. LC 98-10855. (Illus.). 240p. 1998. pap. 14.95 (*0-8442-6133-5*, 61335, VGM Career) NTC Contemp Pub Co.

Rice, Craig S. How to Market Your Book & Get Published: Just the Nuts & Bolts. LC 95-26138. 137p. 1996. 34.00 (*1-56072-287-8*); pap. 19.50 (*1-56072-277-0*, Nova Kroshka Bks) Nova Sci Pubs.

— Marketing Without a Marketing Budget. (Illus.). 320p. 1989. pap. 10.95 (*1-55850-986-0*) Adams Media.

— 101 Answers to Dilbert People Problems. LC 97-41229. 169p. 2000. pap. 18.95 (*1-56072-460-9*, Nova Kroshka Bks) Nova Sci Pubs.

— Strategic Planning for the Small Business: Situations, Weapons, Objectives & Tactics. 300p. 1990. pap. 10.95 (*1-55850-858-9*) Adams Media.

Rice, Cy, jt. auth. see Wander, Chester.

Rice, D. D. & Gluskoter, H. J. Economic Geology: U. S. Taylor, R. B. et al, eds. (DNAG, Geology of North America Ser.: Vol. P2). (Illus.). 630p. 1991. 40.00 (*0-8137-5214-0*) Geol Soc.

Rice, D. S. The Wade Cup in the Cleveland Museum of Art. (Islamic Art Reprint Ser.: No. 2). (Illus.). 64p. (C). 1988. reprint ed. lib. bdg. 15.00 (*0-939214-57-1*) Mazda Pubs.

Rice, Dale. Salivary Glands: Radiology, Surgery, Pathology, 2. Hanafee & Ward, eds. LC 94-30197. (Clinical Correlations in the Head & Neck Ser.: Vol. 2). (Illus.). 59p. 1994. 59.00 (*0-86577-364-5*) Thieme Med Pubs.

Rice, Dale H. & Schaefer, Steven D. Endoscopic Paranasal Sinus Surgery. 2nd ed. LC 92-17094. (Illus.). 272p. 1992. text 132.00 (*0-88167-946-1*) Lppncott W & W.

Rice, Dale H., jt. auth. see Batsakis, John G.

Rice, Dale W. & Wolman, Alan A. The Life History & Ecology of the Gray Whale (Eschrichteus Robustus) (ASM Special Publications: No 3). (Illus.). viii, 142p. 1971. pap. 6.00 (*0-943612-02-0*) Am Soc Mammalogists.

Rice, Dan. Akitas. LC 97-1064. (Complete Pet Owner's Manual Ser.). (Illus.). 120p. 1997. pap. 6.95 (*0-7641-0075-0*) Barron.

— Bengal Cats: Everything about Purchase, Care, Nutrition, Breeding, Diseases, & Behavior. (Complete Pet Owner's Manual Ser.). (Illus.). 1995. pap. 6.95 (*0-8120-9243-0*) Barron.

— Brittanys. LC 98-13204. (Complete Pet Owner's Manual Ser.). (Illus.). 1998. pap. 6.95 (*0-7641-0448-9*, 835908Q) Barron.

— Chesapeake Bay Retrievers: Everything about Purchase, Care, Nutrition, Behavior & Training. LC 98-29267. (Complete Pet Owner's Manual Ser.). (Illus.). 104p. 1999. pap. 6.95 (*0-7641-0657-0*) Barron.

— The Complete Book of Cat Breeding. LC 96-21778. (Illus.). 168p. (Orig.). 1996. pap. 9.95 (*0-8120-9764-5*) Barron.

— The Complete Book of Dog Breeding. 184p. 1996. pap. 9.95 (*0-8120-9604-5*) Barron.

***Rice, Dan.** The Dog Handbook. LC 99-23129. 173p. 1999. pap. text 9.95 (*0-7641-1152-3*) Barron.

Rice, Dan. Dogs from A to Z: A Dictionary of Canine Terms. LC 97-22432. (Illus.). 430p. 1998. pap. 14.95 (*0-7641-0158-7*) Barron.

***Rice, Dan.** German Shepherd. LC 99-12149. (Training Your Pet Ser.). (Illus.). 176p. 1999. pap. 11.95 (*0-7641-0852-2*) Barron.

Rice, Dan. The Well-Mannered Cat. LC 97-40167. (Illus.). 96p. 1998. pap. 9.95 (*0-7641-0222-2*) Barron.

Rice, Dan, jt. auth. see Ludwig, Gerd.

Rice, Daniel F. Reinhold Niebuhr & John Dewey: An American Odyssey. LC 92-4270. (Illus.). 358p. (C). 1993. text 22.50 (*0-7914-1345-4*) State U NY Pr.

Rice, Daniel M., ed. see Taylor, Phyllis.

Rice, Daniel R. The Clifford Years: The University of North Dakota, 1971-1992. LC 92-621838. (Illus.). 224p. 1992. pap. 10.00 (*0-9608700-9-1*) U NDak Pres.

Rice, Darcy. Yearbook - Musical. 113p. (YA). (gr. 9-12). 1996. pap. 5.95 (*0-87129-658-6*, Y03) Dramatic Pub.

Rice, Daryl H. A Guide to Plato's Republic. LC 96-43917. 160p. 1997. pap. 14.95 (*0-19-511284-9*); text 29.95 (*0-19-511283-0*) OUP.

Rice, David. Because Brian Hugged His Mother. LC 98-46381. (Sharing Nature with Children Book Ser.). (Illus.). 32p. (J). (ps-7). 1999. 16.95 (*1-883220-90-4*) Dawn CA.

— Because Brian Hugged His Mother. LC 98-46381. (Sharing Nature with Children Book Ser.). (Illus.). 32p. (YA). (ps up). 1999. pap. 7.95 (*1-883220-89-0*) Dawn CA.

— Blood Guilt. 247p. 1995. pap. 12.95 (*0-85640-531-0*) Dufour.

Rice, David. Give the Pig a Chance & Other Stories. LC 95-31048. 179p. (Orig.). (YA). (gr. 9 up). 1996. pap. 12.00 (*0-927534-54-1*) Biling Rev-Pr.

Rice, David. Shattered Vows: Priests Who Leave. LC 91-29569. 288p. 1992. pap. 9.95 (*0-89243-507-0*, Liguori Triumph) Liguori Pubns.

— Slavery Inconsistent with Justice & Good Policy. LC 70-82216. (Anti-Slavery Crusade in America Ser.). 1970. reprint ed. 11.95 (*0-405-00655-1*) Ayer.

Rice, David, jt. auth. see Nelson, Charles.

Rice, David G. Preliminary Report: Marmes Rockshelter Archaeological Site, Southern Columbia Plateau. fac. ed. (Washington Archaeological Laboratory of Anthropology Ser.). (Illus.). 205p. (C). 1969. reprint ed. pap. text 21.88 (*1-55567-506-9*) Coyote Press.

— The Windust Phase in Lower Snake River Region Prehistory. (Washington State University, Laboratory of Archaeology & History Ser.: No. 50). (Illus.). 241p. (C). 1972. reprint ed. pap. text 25.63 (*1-55567-595-6*) Coyote Press.

Rice, David G., jt. auth. see Rice, Joy K.

Rice, David L. Lifetimes. Hovemann, Glenn J., ed. (Illus.). 36p. (YA). (gr. k up). 1997. 16.95 (*1-883220-58-0*) Dawn CA.

— Lifetimes. Hovemann, Glenn J., ed. (Illus.). 32p. (YA). (ps up). 1997. pap. 7.95 (*1-883220-59-9*) Dawn CA.

— Lock This Man Up. LC 77-91707. 67p. 1978. per. 5.00 (*0-916418-14-6*) Lotus.

***Rice, David L. & Calvert, Trudy L.** Do Animals Have Feelings Too? LC 99-32162. (Sharing Nature with Children Book Ser.). 36p. (YA). (gr. 4 up). 2000. 16.95 (*1-58469-003-8*) Dawn CA.

— Do Animals Have Feelings Too? LC 99-32162. (Sharing Nature with Children Book Ser.). (Illus.). 32p. (YA). (gr. 4 up). 2000. pap. 7.95 (*1-58469-004-6*) Dawn CA.

Rice, David T. Art of the Byzantine Era. (World of Art Ser.). (Illus.). 288p. 1985. pap. 14.95 (*0-500-20004-1*, Pub. by Thames Hudson) Norton.

— Islamic Painting. 185p. 1979. 42.50 (*0-85224-112-7*, Pub. by Edinburgh U Pr) Col U Pr.

***Rice, Dean.** Snapshots of Enlightenment: Observations Made from the Business Side of High-Tech. (Illus.). 110p. 1999. spiral bd. 9.95 (*0-9675112-0-8*) byRice.

Rice, Denis T. & Ortmeyer, Charles P. Securities Regulation Forms, 3 vols., Set. LC 88-17561. 1988. ring bd. 395.00 (*0-87632-606-8*) West Group.

— Securities Regulation Forms, 3 vols., Set with forms on disk. (Securities Law Ser.). 1988. 495.00 incl. disk (*0-614-07308-1*) West Group.

Rice, Dennis G. English Porcelain Animals of the Nineteenth Century. (Illus.). 282p. 1989. 49.50 (*1-85149-085-X*) Antique Collect.

Rice, Dolores, et al. 100 of the World's Tallest Buildings. (Illus.). 220p. 1998. 59.95 (*3-927258-60-1*) Gingko Press.

Rice, Dolores B., jt. ed. see Beedle, Lynn S.

Rice, Dolores B., ed. see Council on Tall Buildings & Urban Habitats Staff.

Rice, Don, ed. Famous Nineteenth Century Faces. LC 91-70263. 128p. 1991. text 14.50 (*0-88108-082-9*) Art Dir.

— The New Testament: A Pictorial Archive from Nineteenth-Century Sources. (Pictorial Archive Ser.). (Illus.). 192p. (Orig.). 1986. pap. 9.95 (*0-486-25073-3*) Dover.

***Rice, Don, et al.** Collapse, Transition & Transformation: New Views of the End of the Classic Period in the Maya Lowlands. 480p. 1999. 75.00 (*0-8133-3601-5*) Westview.

Rice, Don A. Challenges Facing Distributors. 180p. 1994. pap. 31.00 (*1-881154-11-4*) Darco Pr.

— Financial Transactions of the Wholesale Distributor. 146p. (C). 1994. reprint ed. pap. 24.00 (*1-881154-04-1*) Darco Pr.

— The Guidebook to Service Quality. 264p. 1993. pap. 25.00 (*1-881154-25-4*) Darco Pr.

— Planning & Managing for Greater Profit. 65p. 1989. pap., teacher ed. 14.00 (*1-881154-08-4*); pap., student ed. 14.00 (*1-881154-09-2*) Darco Pr.

— Planning & Managing for Greater Profit, 2 cass., No. 1 & 2. 1989. pap. 300.00 incl. VHS (*1-881154-07-6*) Darco Pr.

— The Wholesale Distributor: Purpose & Function. 246p. 1990. pap. 24.00 (*1-881154-01-7*) Darco Pr.

Rice, Don A. & Rice, Sara V. Financial Freedom: How to Attain It. 166p. 1991. pap. 12.00 (*1-881154-15-7*) Darco Pr.

Rice, Don S., ed. Latin American Horizons: A Symposium at Dumbarton Oaks, 11th & 12th October, 1986. LC 92-14833. (Illus.). 382p. 1993. 30.00 (*0-88402-207-2*, RIHO, Dumbarton Rsch Lib) Dumbarton Oaks.

Rice, Don S., jt. ed. see Hanks, William F.

Rice, Dona & La Bounty, Blanca A. Theme of the Month. (J). (gr. 1-3). 1995. pap. text 14.95 (*1-55734-509-0*) Tchr Create Mat.

Rice, Dona H. Addition Practice Double Digits: Basic Skills. 32p. (J). (gr. 2-3). 1997. pap. 2.95 (*1-57690-252-8*) Tchr Create Mat.

— Addition Practice Facts to 20: Basic Skills. 32p. (J). (gr. 1-2). 1997. pap. 2.95 (*1-57690-251-X*) Tchr Create Mat.

— Alphabet: Beginning Skills. 32p. (J). (gr. k-1). 1997. pap. 2.95 (*1-57690-237-4*) Tchr Create Mat.

— April Monthly Activities. (Illus.). 80p. 1996. pap., teacher ed. 9.95 (*1-55734-877-4*, TCM877); pap., teacher ed. 9.95 (*1-55734-867-7*,) Tchr Create Mat.

— Consonant Blends & Diagraphs. 16p. (J). (gr. 1-2). 1997. pap. 2.95 (*1-57690-242-0*) Tchr Create Mat.

— Consonant Sounds B-J. 16p. (J). (gr. k-1). 1997. pap. 2.95 (*1-57690-240-4*) Tchr Create Mat.

— Consonant Sounds K-R. 16p. (J). (gr. k-1). 1997. pap. 2.95 (*1-57690-241-2*) Tchr Create Mat.

— Consonant Sounds S-Z. 16p. (J). (gr. k-1). 1997. pap. 2.95 (*1-57690-264-1*) Tchr Create Mat.

— Crossword Puzzles & Word Searches 1. 16p. 1997. pap. 2.95 (*1-57690-261-7*) Tchr Create Mat.

— Crossword Puzzles & Word Searches 3. 16p. 1997. pap. 2.95 (*1-57690-263-3*) Tchr Create Mat.

— Crossword Puzzles & Word Searches 2. 16p. 1997. pap. 2.95 (*1-57690-262-5*) Tchr Create Mat.

— December Monthly Activities. (Illus.). 80p. 1996. pap., teacher ed. 9.95 (*1-55734-873-1*, TCM873) Tchr Create Mat.

— December Monthly Activities. (Monthly Activities Ser.). 80p. 1997. pap. 9.95 (*1-55734-863-4*) Tchr Create Mat.

— February Monthly Activities-Early Childhood. 1997. pap. text 9.95 (*1-55734-865-0*) Tchr Create Mat.

— February Monthly Activities-Intermediate. 1997. pap. text 9.95 (*1-55734-875-8*) Tchr Create Mat.

— Handwriting. (Basic Skills Practice Bks.). (Illus.). 32p. (J). 1997. pap., teacher ed. 2.95 (*1-57690-244-7*, TCM2244) Tchr Create Mat.

— Harriet the Spy. (Literature Unit Ser.). (Illus.). 48p. pap., teacher ed. 7.95 (*1-57690-133-5*, TCM2133) Tchr Create Mat.

— How to Manage Learning Centers in the Classroom. LC 97-146413. 1997. pap. text 24.95 (*1-57690-037-1*) Tchr Create Mat.

— Ice Cream. (Thematic Units Ser.). 80p. (J). (gr. 1-3). 1997. pap. 9.95 (*1-57690-117-3*) Tchr Create Mat.

— January Monthly Activities. (J). (gr. 3-5). 1997. pap. text 9.95 (*1-55734-874-X*) Tchr Create Mat.

— January Monthly Activities. (J). (ps-2). 1997. pap. text 9.95 (*1-55734-864-2*) Tchr Create Mat.

— Ladybugs. (Thematic Units Ser.). 80p. (J). (gr. 1-3). 1997. pap. 9.95 (*1-57690-370-2*) Tchr Create Mat.

— Laura Ingalls Wilder. (Favorite Authors Ser.). 112p. (J). (gr. 3-5). 1997. pap. 11.95 (*1-55734-452-3*) Tchr Create Mat.

— Long Vowel A. (Vowel Workbks.). 32p. (J). (gr. k-2). 1997. pap. 2.95 (*1-57690-231-5*) Tchr Create Mat.

— Long Vowel E. (Vowel Workbks.). 32p. (J). (gr. k-2). 1997. pap. 2.95 (*1-57690-232-3*) Tchr Create Mat.

— Long Vowel I. (Vowel Workbks.). (J). (gr. k-2). 1997. pap. 2.95 (*1-57690-233-1*) Tchr Create Mat.

— Long Vowel O. (Vowel Workbks.). 32p. (J). (gr. k-2). 1997. pap. 2.95 (*1-57690-234-X*) Tchr Create Mat.

— Long Vowel Review. (Vowel Workbks.). 32p. (J). (gr. k-2). 1997. pap. 2.95 (*1-57690-236-6*) Tchr Create Mat.

— Long Vowel U. (Vowel Workbks.). 32p. (J). (gr. k-2). 1997. pap. 2.95 (*1-57690-235-8*) Tchr Create Mat.

— March Monthly Activities. (Illus.). 80p. 1996. pap., teacher ed. 9.95 (*1-55734-876-6*, TCM876) Tchr Create Mat.

— March Monthly Activities. (Monthly Activities Ser.). 80p. (J). (ps-k). 1997. pap. 9.95 (*1-55734-866-9*) Tchr Create Mat.

— May Monthly Activities. (Illus.). 80p. 1996. pap., teacher ed. 9.95 (*1-55734-878-2*, TCM878) Tchr Create Mat.

— November Monthy Activities. (Illus.). 80p. 1996. pap., teacher ed. 9.95 (*1-55734-872-3*, TCM872) Tchr Create Mat.

— Numbers: Beginning Skills. (Basic Skills Ser.). 32p. (J). (gr. k-1). 1997. pap. 2.95 (*1-57690-238-2*) Tchr Create Mat.

— October Monthly Activities. (Illus.). 80p. 1996. pap., teacher ed. 9.95 (*1-55734-871-5*, TCM871) Tchr Create Mat.

— Printing Practice. 32p. (J). (gr. k-2). 1997. pap. 2.95 (*1-57690-243-9*) Tchr Create Mat.

— Puzzles & Games to Reinforce Basic Skills. (Illus.). 334p. (J). 1998. pap., teacher ed. 24.95 (*1-57690-208-0*, TCM2208) Tchr Create Mat.

— Reading Comprehension. 32p. (J). (gr. 1 up). 1997. pap. 2.95 (*1-57690-248-X*) Tchr Create Mat.

— Reading Comprehension. 32p. (J). (gr. 2 up). 1997. pap. 2.95 (*1-57690-249-8*) Tchr Create Mat.

— Reading Comprehension, Grade 3. (Basic Skills Practice Bks.). (Illus.). 32p. (J). (gr. 3). 1997. pap. 2.95 (*1-57690-250-1*, TCM2250) Tchr Create Mat.

— Second Grade Brain Teasers. (Illus.). 80p. (J). (gr. 2). 1995. pap. 9.95 (*1-55734-487-6*) Tchr Create Mat.

— September Monthly Activities. (Illus.). 80p. 1996. pap., teacher ed. 9.95 (*1-55734-870-7*, TCM870) Tchr Create Mat.

— Shapes & Colors. 32p. (J). (gr. k-1). 1997. pap. 2.95 (*1-57690-239-0*) Tchr Create Mat.

— Short Vowel A. (Vowel Workbks.). 32p. (J). (gr. k-2). 1997. pap. 2.95 (*1-57690-225-0*) Tchr Create Mat.

— Short Vowel E. (Vowel Workbks.). 32p. (J). (gr. k-2). 1997. pap. 2.95 (*1-57690-226-9*) Tchr Create Mat.

— Short Vowel I. (Vowel Workbks.). 32p. (J). (gr. k-2). 1997. pap. 2.95 (*1-57690-227-7*) Tchr Create Mat.

— Short Vowel O. (Vowel Workbks.). 32p. (J). (gr. k-2). 1997. pap. 2.95 (*1-57690-228-5*) Tchr Create Mat.

— Short Vowel U. (Basic Skills Practice Bks.). (Illus.). 32p. (J). (gr. k-2). 1997. pap., teacher ed. 2.95 (*1-57690-229-3*, TCM2229) Tchr Create Mat.

— Subtraction Practice. (Basic Skills Ser.). 32p. (J). (gr. 2-3). 1997. pap. 2.95 (*1-57690-254-4*) Tchr Create Mat.

— Subtraction Practice Facts to 20. (Basic Skills Ser.). 32p. (J). (gr. 1-2). 1997. pap. 2.95 (*1-57690-253-6*) Tchr Create Mat.

— Writing Skill & Grammar, Grade 3. (Basic Skills Practice Bks.). (Illus.). 32p. (J). (gr. 3). 1997. pap., teacher ed. 2.95 (*1-57690-247-1*, TCM2247) Tchr Create Mat.

— Writing Skills & Grammar. (Illus.). 32p. (J). (gr. 2 up). 1997. pap., teacher ed. 2.95 (*1-57690-246-3*, TCM2246) Tchr Create Mat.

— Writing Skills & Grammar, Grade 1. (Basic Skills Practice Bks.). (Illus.). 32p. (J). (gr. 1). 1997. pap., teacher ed. 2.95 (*1-57690-245-5*, TCM2245) Tchr Create Mat.

Rice, Dona H., jt. auth. see Sterling, Mary E.

***Rice, Dona Herweck.** Practice & Learn. (Illus.). 304p. (J). (gr. 3). 1999. pap., teacher ed. 14.95 (*1-57690-713-9*, TCM2713) Tchr Create Mat.

— Practice & Learn: What Every 4th Grader Needs to Know. (Illus.). 304p. (J). (gr. 4). 1999. pap., teacher ed. 14.95 (*1-57690-714-7*, TCM2714) Tchr Create Mat.

— 20th Century 1910-1919. (Illus.). 96p. (J). 1999. pap., teacher ed. 11.95 (*1-57690-023-1*, TCM2023) Tchr Create Mat.

— 20th Century the Eighties. (Twentieth Century Ser.). (Illus.). 96p. (J). 1999. pap., teacher ed. 11.95 (*1-57690-030-4*, TCM2030) Tchr Create Mat.

Rice, Dona Herweck, ed. see Teacher Created Materials Staff & Robbins, Mari Lu.

Rice, Donald. Asset Financial Set. 1990. 145.00 (*0-316-74311-9*, Aspen Law & Bus) Aspen Pub.

— Countdown! (J). 1991. mass mkt. 22.95 (*0-8384-3379-0*) Heinle & Heinle.

Rice, Donald & Bragger. Allons Voir. (C). 1992. mass mkt. 39.95 (*0-8384-2136-9*) Heinle & Heinle.

— Allons Voir. (C). 1992. student ed. 41.95 (*0-8384-3913-6*) Heinle & Heinle.

— Allons Voir. (C). 1992. VHS 119.95 (*0-8384-2137-7*) Heinle & Heinle.

— Allons-Y! Le Francais par Etapes. 3rd ed. (C). 1992. pap., student ed. 27.50 (*0-8384-2427-9*) Heinle & Heinle.

— Du Tac Au Tac: Managing Conversations in French. (C). 1987. pap. write for info. (*0-8384-1511-3*) Heinle & Heinle.

— On y Va, Level 1. 1989. VHS. write for info. (*0-685-30549-X*) Heinle & Heinle.

— On y Va, Level 2. (YA). (gr. 7-12). 1989. pap. 44.95 (*0-8384-1682-9*) Heinle & Heinle.

— On y Va, Level 3. (YA). (gr. 7-12). 1990. mass mkt. 48.95 (*0-8384-1925-9*); mass mkt. 49.95 (*0-8384-1926-7*) Heinle & Heinle.

— On Y Va! Level 1, Level 1. 2nd ed. (Secondary French Ser.). 1994. pap., suppl. ed. 17.95 (*0-8384-4152-1*) Heinle & Heinle.

— On Y Va! Level 1 Text, Level 1. (Secondary French). 1989. pap. 31.75 (*0-8384-1614-4*) Heinle & Heinle.

— On Y Va! Level 2, Level 2. 2nd ed. (Secondary French Ser.). 1993. mass mkt., suppl. ed. 182.95 (*0-8384-4183-1*) Heinle & Heinle.

— On Y Va! Level 2, Level 2. 2nd ed. (Secondary French Ser.). 1994. mass mkt., suppl. ed. 13.95 (*0-8384-4169-6*) Heinle & Heinle.

— On Y Va! Level 3 Laboratory Tape Program, Level 3. (Secondary French). (YA). (gr. 7-12). 1990. 347.95 (*0-8384-1928-3*) Heinle & Heinle.

Rice, Donald & Schofer. Autour de la Litterature. 2nd ed. (C). 1991. pap. 38.95 (*0-8384-1980-1*) Heinle & Heinle.

— Autour de la Litterature. 2nd ed. (C). 1991. 14.95 (*0-8384-2114-8*) Heinle & Heinle.

— Autour de la Litterature. 2nd ed. (C). 1991. pap. 16.50 (*0-8384-2202-0*) Heinle & Heinle.

Rice, Donald & Schofer, Peter. Rhetorical Poetics: Theory & Practice of Figural & Symbolic Reading in Modern French Literature. LC 83-47768. 256p. 1983. text 22.50 (*0-299-09440-5*) U of Wis Pr.

R

— Rhetorical Poetics: Theory & Practice of Figural & Symbolic Reading in Modern French Literature. LC 83-47768. 267p. reprint ed. pap. 82.80 (*0-608-20470-6*, 207172200002) Bks Demand.

Rice, Donald, et al. On Y Va! Level 3, Level 3. 2nd ed. (Secondary French Ser.). 1993. mass mkt., suppl. ed. 182.95 (*0-8384-4176-9*) Heinle & Heinle.

Rice, Donald, jt. auth. see Balas, Robert S.

Rice, Donald, jt. auth. see Bragger, J.

Rice, Donald, jt. auth. see Bragger, Jeanette D.

Rice, Donald, jt. auth. see Bragger, Jeannette.

Rice, Donald, jt. auth. see Bragger, Jeannette D.

Rice, Donald, jt. auth. see Schofer, Peter.

Rice, Donald E. The Rhetorical Uses of the Authorizing Figure: Fidel Castro & Jose Marti. LC 91-35027. 192p. 1992. 49.95 (*0-275-94214-7*, C4214, Praeger Pubs) Greenwood.

Rice, Donald E. & Fisher, Joseph. Selected Experiments in College Chemistry: Some Basic Concepts & Techniques. 288p. 1994. spiral bd. 20.95 (*0-8403-7907-2*) Kendall-Hunt.

Rice, Donald L., ed. The Agitator: A Collection of Diverse Opinions from America's Not So Popular Press. LC 74-178271. (Schism Anthology Ser.). 462p. reprint ed. pap. 143.30 (*0-8357-5261-5*, 202418800035) Bks Demand.

Rice, Donna H. Short Vowel Review. (Vowel Workbks.). 32p. (J). (gr. k-2). 1997. pap. 2.95 (*1-57690-230-7*) Tchr Create Mat.

***Rice, Donna Herweck.** 20th Century 1900-1909. (Illus.). 96p. (J). 1999. pap., teacher ed. 11.95 (*1-57690-022-3*, TCM2022) Tchr Create Mat.

Rice, Donna Herweck, ed. see Young, Ruth M.

Rice, Dorothy. Beverly Hills with Love: Paintings & Text. LC 97-34564. (Illus.). 176p. 1998. 60.00 (*0-918269-03-2*) Glen Hse.

— Los Angeles with Love. (Illus.). 100p. (Orig.). 1984. pap. text 17.95 (*0-918269-00-8*) Glen Hse.

Rice, Dorothy. Israel with Love. LC 92-10106. 144p. 1992. 45.00 (*0-918269-01-6*) Glen Hse.

Rice, Dorothy M. & Payne, Lucille M. The Seventeenth Child. LC 98-28614. (Illus.). 101p. (YA). (gr. 7 up). 1998. lib. bdg. 18.50 (*0-208-02414-X*, Linnet Bks) Shoe String.

Rice, Dorothy M., jt. auth. see Branch, Muriel M.

Rice, Dorothy P., ed. see Institute of Medicine Staff.

Rice, Doug. Blood of Mugwump. 150p. (Orig.). 1996. pap. 8.95 (*1-57366-018-3*) Fiction Coll.

— A Good Cunt Boy is Hard to Find. (Illus.). 76p. 1998. pap. 5.00 (*1-886988-08-0*) Jasmine Sail.

Rice, Dudley D., ed. Oil & Gas Assessment: Methods & Applications. LC 86-14158. (AAPG Studies in Geology: No. 21). (Illus.). 275p. reprint ed. pap. 85.30 (*0-7837-2598-1*, 204276200006) Bks Demand.

Rice, Dudley D. & Gautier, Donald L. Patterns of Sedimentation, Diagenesis, & Hydrocarbon Accumulation in Cretaceous Rocks of the Rock Mountains. LC QE0571.R53. (SEPM Short Course Ser.: No. 11). (Illus.). 343p. 1983. pap. 106.40 (*0-608-05574-3*, 206603400006) Bks Demand.

Rice, Dudley D., jt. ed. see Law, Ben E.

Rice, Durwin. New Decoupage. LC 97-45787. (Illus.). 144p. 1998. 25.00 (*0-517-70560-5*) Random.

Rice, E. B. Paddy Irrigation & Water Management in Southeast Asia. (Operations & Evaluation Studies). 84p. 1997. pap. 22.00 (*0-8213-3914-1*, 13914) World Bank.

Rice, E. E. Cleopatra. 1999. pap. text 9.95 (*0-7509-2057-2*) Sutton Pub Ltd.

Rice, E. E., ed. The Sea & History. LC 97-150451. (Illus.). 224p. 1996. 63.00 (*0-7509-1096-8*, Pub. by Sutton Pub Ltd) Intl Pubs Mktg.

Rice, E. P. A History of Kannada Literature. (Illus.). 128p. 1986. reprint ed. 14.00 (*0-8364-1701-1*, Pub. by Manohar) S Asia.

Rice, Earle, Jr. The Attack on Pearl Harbor. (Great Battles Ser.). (Illus.). 112p. (J). (gr. 5-12). 1996. lib. bdg. 26.20 (*1-56006-421-8*) Lucent Bks.

— The Battle of Belleau Wood: Battles of World War I. LC 95-31680. (Battle Ser.). (Illus.). 112p. (J). (gr. 5-12). 1996. lib. bdg. 26.20 (*1-56006-424-2*) Lucent Bks.

— The Battle of Britain: Battles of World War II. LC 95-16224. (Battle Ser.). (Illus.). 112p. (YA). (gr. 5-12). 1996. lib. bdg. 26.20 (*1-56006-414-5*) Lucent Bks.

— The Battle of the Little Bighorn. LC 97-9870. (World History Ser.). (Illus.). (YA). (gr. 4-12). 1997. lib. bdg. 22.45 (*1-56006-453-6*) Lucent Bks.

***Rice, Earle, Jr.** The Cold War: Collapse of Communism. LC 00-8311. (History's Great Defeats Ser.). 133p. 2000. 18.96 (*1-56006-634-2*) Lucent Bks.

Rice, Earle. The Final Solution. LC 97-10847. (Holocaust Library). (J). 1997. lib. bdg. 22.45 (*1-56006-095-6*) Lucent Bks.

Rice, Earle, Jr. The Inchon Invasion: Battles of the Twentieth Century. LC 95-11698. (Battle Ser.). (Illus.). 112p. (J). (gr. 5-12). 1996. lib. bdg. 26.20 (*1-56006-418-8*) Lucent Bks.

***Rice, Earle, Jr.** Kamikazes (WWII) LC 99-23543. (American War Library). (Illus.). 128p. (YA). (gr. 7 up). 2000. lib. bdg. 23.70 (*1-56006-373-4*) Lucent Bks.

Rice, Earle, Jr. Life among the Great Plains Indians. LC 97-27149. (Way People Live Ser.). (Illus.). 112p. (J). (gr. 6-9). 1997. lib. bdg. 22.45 (*1-56006-347-5*) Lucent Bks.

— Life During the Crusades. LC 97-27994. (Way People Live Ser.). (Illus.). 96p. (YA). (gr. 4-12). 1997. lib. bdg. 22.45 (*1-56006-379-3*) Lucent Bks.

Rice, Earle. Life During the Middle Ages. LC 97-48275. (Way People Live Ser.). (Illus.). 96p. (YA). (gr. 7 up). 1998. lib. bdg. 22.45 (*1-56006-386-6*) Lucent Bks.

Rice, Earle, Jr. Nazi War Criminals. LC 97-9811. (Holocaust Library). (Illus.). (YA). (gr. 6 up). 1997. lib. bdg. 22.45 (*1-56006-097-2*) Lucent Bks.

Rice, Earle, Jr. The Nuremberg Trials. (Famous Trials Ser.). (Illus.). 112p. (J). (gr. 6). 1996. lib. bdg. 22.45 (*1-56006-269-X*) Lucent Bks.

— The O. J. Simpson Trial. (Famous Trials Ser.). (Illus.). (YA). 1996. lib. bdg. 22.45 (*1-56006-271-1*) Lucent Bks.

***Rice, Earle.** Pearl Harbor. LC 99-50970. (World History Ser.). (Illus.). 2000. write for info. (*1-56006-652-0*) Lucent Bks.

Rice, Earle, Jr. The Salem Witch Trials. (Famous Trials Ser.). (Illus.). 1996. lib. bdg. 22.45 (*1-56006-272-X*) Lucent Bks.

***Rice, Earle, Jr.** Strategic Battles in Europe (WWII) LC 99-31358. (American War Library). (Illus.). 144p. (YA). (gr. 6-9). 2000. lib. bdg. 23.70 (*1-56006-536-2*) Lucent Bks.

— Strategic Battles in the Pacific (WWII) LC 99-45479. (American War Library). (Illus.). 144p. (YA). (gr. 6-9). 2000. lib. bdg. 23.70 (*1-56006-537-0*) Lucent Bks.

Rice, Earle, Jr. The Tet Offensive. LC 96-14227. (Great Battles Ser.). (Illus.). 112p. (J). (gr. 5-12). 1996. lib. bdg. 26.20 (*1-56006-422-6*) Lucent Bks.

***Rice, Earle, Jr.** The Third Reich. (History's Great Defeats Ser.). 133p. (YA). (gr. 4-12). 2000. 18.96 (*1-56006-630-X*) Lucent Bks.

Rice, Earle. Tiger, Lion, Hawk: A Story of Flying Tigers. (Pacemaker Bks.). 1977. 16.60 (*0-606-02441-7*, Pub. by Turtleback) Demco.

***Rice, Earle.** Weapons of War. LC 00-9557. (Illus.). 2001. write for info. (*1-56006-719-5*) Lucent Bks.

***Rice, Ed.** Corps Apocalypse: Worldbook for Corps. Porter, Greg, ed. (Illus.). 128p. 1999. pap. text 17.00 (*0-943891-36-1*, BTRC 7104, Pub. by Blacksburg Tactical) Alliance Bk Co.

Rice, Edward. The Man in the Sycamore Tree: The Good Life & Hard Times of Thomas Merton. LC 84-22490. (Illus.). 192p. 1985. pap. 6.95 (*0-15-656960-4*, Harvest Bks) Harcourt.

Rice, Edward E. Wars of the Third Kind: Conflict in Underdeveloped Countries. 186p. 1988. pap. 15.95 (*0-520-07195-6*, Pub. by U CA Pr) Cal Prin Full Svc.

Rice, Edwin W. Sunday-School Movement, 1780-1917 & the American Sunday-School Union, 1817-1917. LC 70-165728. (American Education Ser.: No. 2). (Illus.). 1977. reprint ed. 39.95 (*0-405-03717-1*) Ayer.

Rice, Elaine. Julia. 224p. 1996. mass mkt. 7.95 (*1-56201-102-2*) Blue Moon Bks.

Rice, Elaine, jt. auth. see Abbott, James.

Rice, Elaine M., jt. auth. see Abbott, James A.

Rice, Elizabeth T., ed. see Rice, Tamara T.

Rice, Ellen. Alexander the Great. LC DF234.R53 1997. (Get a Life...Pocket Biographies Ser.). (Illus.). 128p. 1997. pap. 9.95 (*0-7509-1528-5*, Pub. by Sutton Pub Ltd) Intl Pubs Mktg.

Rice, Elmer. Court of Last Resort. (Lost Play Ser.). 1985. pap. 3.95 (*0-912262-87-7*) Proscenium.

— Dream Girl. 1950. pap. 5.25 (*0-8222-0332-4*) Dramatists Play.

— The Grand Tour: Manuscript Edition. 1952. pap. 13.00 (*0-8222-0474-6*) Dramatists Play.

— The Winner. 1954. pap. 5.25 (*0-8222-1263-3*) Dramatists Play.

Rice, Elroy L. Allelopathy: (Monograph) 2nd ed. LC 83-11782. (Physiological Ecology Ser.). 1983. text 153.00 (*0-12-587055-8*) Acad Pr.

— Biological Control of Weeds & Plant Diseases: Advances in Applied Allelopathy. LC 94-23242. (Illus.). 439p. 1995. 55.00 (*0-8061-2698-1*) U of Okla Pr.

Rice, Emanuel. Freud & Moses: The Long Journey Home. LC 89-77695. 266p. (C). 1990. text 21.50 (*0-7914-0453-6*) State U NY Pr.

Rice, Eric W. The Martinsville Seven: Race, Rape & Capital Punishment. (Constitutionalism & Democracy Ser.). 226p. 1998. reprint ed. pap. 14.50 (*0-8139-1830-8*) U Pr of Va.

Rice, Eugene F., Jr. The Prefatory Epistles of Jacques Lefevre d'Etaples & Related Texts. LC 71-123577. 480p. (C). 1972. text 90.50 (*0-231-03163-7*) Col U Pr.

— The Renaissance Idea of Wisdom. LC 72-12117. (Illus.). 220p. 1973. reprint ed. lib. bdg. 35.00 (*0-8371-6712-4*, RIRI, Greenwood Pr) Greenwood.

Rice, Eugene F., Jr. & Grafton, Anthony. The Foundation of Early Modern Europe, 1460-1559. 2nd ed. LC 93-11535. (C). 1994. pap. text 18.75 (*0-393-96304-7*) Norton.

Rice, Eugene F., Jr., jt. auth. see Mommsen, Theodor.

Rice-Evans, Catherine A. Free Radicals & Oxidative Stress: Environment, Drugs & Food Additives. (Biochemical Society Symposium Ser.: Vol. 61). (Illus.). 288p. (C). 1995. text 110.50 (*1-85578-069-0*, Pub. by Portland Pr Ltd) Ashgate Pub Co.

Rice-Evans, Catherine A. & Burdon, Roy H., eds. Free Radical Damage & Its Control. LC 93-40154. 408p. 1994. 201.25 (*0-444-89716-X*) Elsevier.

Rice-Evans, Catherine A., jt. ed. see Bruckdorfer, K. R.

Rice-Evans, Catherine T. & Packer, Lester, eds. Flavonoids in Health & Disease. LC 97-29218. (Antioxidants in Health & Disease Ser.: Vol. 7). (Illus.). 536p. 1997. text 195.00 (*0-8247-0096-1*) Dekker.

Rice, Eve. Benny Bakes a Cake. LC 80-17313. 32p. (J). (ps-3). 1993. 14.00 (*0-688-11579-9*, Grenwillow Bks) HarpC Child Bks.

Rice, Eve. Once in a Wood: Ten Tales from Aesop. 1993. 10.15 (*0-606-05522-3*, Pub. by Turtleback) Demco.

— Sam Who Never Forget. LC 76-30370. (Illus.). 40p. (J). (ps up). 1987. mass mkt. 5.95 (*0-688-07335-2*, Wm Morrow) Morrow Avon.

Rice, Eve. Swim! LC 95-25081. (Illus.). 24p. (J). (ps up). 1996. 15.00 (*0-688-14274-5*, Grenwillow Bks); lib. bdg. 14.93 (*0-688-14275-3*, Grenwillow Bks) HarpC Child Bks.

Rice, F. Philip. The Adolescent: Development, Relationships & Culture. 6th ed. 650p. 1989. text 45.00 (*0-205-12310-4*, H23104) Allyn.

— The Adolescent: Development, Relationships, & Culture. 9th ed. LC 98-5164. 517p. 1998. 82.00 (*0-205-27617-2*) Allyn.

— Child & Adolescent Development. LC 96-12716. 588p. (C). 1996. 80.00 (*0-13-566019-X*) P-H.

— Human Development: A Life Span Approach. (Illus.). 608p. (C). 1992. write for info. (*0-318-69919-2*) Macmillan.

— Human Development: A Life-Span Approach. 3rd ed. LC 97-17210. 759p. 1997. 79.00 (*0-13-805276-X*) P-H.

— Intimate Relationships, Marriages, & Families. 4th ed. LC 98-3327. xxiii, 680p. 1998. pap. text 43.95 (*0-7674-0211-1*, 0211-1) Mayfield Pub.

Rice, F. Philip & Kohl, Jeanne. Intimate Relationships, Marriages & Families: Study Guide. 4th rev. ed. vii, 231p. (C). 1998. pap. text 19.95 (*0-7674-0502-1*, 0502-1) Mayfield Pub.

***Rice, F. Philip.** Human Development. 4th ed. 736p. 2000. write for info. (*0-13-018565-5*) P-H.

Rice, Ferill J. & McMichael, LaVeria, eds. Caught in the Butterfly Net. 140p. 1992. pap. 19.95 (*0-9632974-0-6*) Fenton Art Glass.

Rice, Frances, jt. auth. see Rice, Wallace.

Rice, Frank A. Mines of Ouray (Colorado) County. rev. ed. Benham, Jack L., ed. (Illus.). 56p. (Orig.). 1980. reprint ed. pap. 3.95 (*0-941026-05-1*) Bear Creek Pub.

Rice, Frank A. & Sa'id, Majed F. Eastern Arabic. LC 79-22782. 400p. 1979. pap. 16.95 (*0-87840-021-4*) Georgetown U Pr.

— Eastern Arabic. unabridged ed. (ARA.). 400p. 185.00 incl. audio (*0-88432-201-7*, AFA450) Audio-Forum.

Rice, Frank A. & Saiid, Majed F. Eastern Arabic-English, English-Eastern Arabic Dictionary & Phrasebook. rev. ed. (ARA & ENG.). 220p. 1998. pap. 11.95 (*0-7818-0685-2*) Hippocrene Bks.

Rice, G. Wesley. Pecans - A Grower's Perspective: Popular Varieties, Propagation, Culture, & More. LC TX-3-864-43. (Illus.). xiii, 198p. 1994. pap. 39.50 (*0-9656644-0-6*) Pecan Creek.

— When a Man's Fancy Turns to Cooking. (Illus.). 144p. 1996. spiral bd. 13.95 (*0-9656644-1-4*) Pecan Creek.

— When a Man's Fancy Turns to Cooking. (Illus.). 136p. 1996. pap. 13.95 (*0-89745-988-1*) Sunflower U Pr.

***Rice, Geoffrey W.** Christchurch Changing: An Illustrated History. (Illus.). 240p. (Orig.). 1999. pap. 29.95 (*0-908812-53-1*, Pub. by Canterbury Univ) Accents Pubns.

Rice, Geoffrey W., ed. The Oxford History of New Zealand. 2nd ed. (Illus.). 774p. 1993. pap. text 45.00 (*0-19-558257-8*) OUP.

Rice, George. My Adventures with Your Money. (Illus.). 332p. 1986. 25.00 (*0-913814-75-X*) Nevada Pubns.

Rice, George A., compiled by. Vital Records of Pepperell, Massachusetts, to the Year 1850. LC 84-16660. 323p. 1985. 10.00 (*0-88082-008-X*) New Eng Hist.

Rice, George G. My Adventures with Your Money. 1975. 10.00 (*0-685-54481-8*) Bookfinger.

Rice, George H., Jr. The Governing of Organizations. unabridged ed. 308p. (C). 1998. pap. text 42.00 (*0-9627034-2-7*) Wheelock Pr.

Rice, George W. Audrey J. Williamson: Woman of the Word. 56p. 1992. pap. 2.99 (*0-8341-1434-8*) Beacon Hill.

— Facing the Dawn. 1970. pap. 1.00 (*0-8341-1010-5*) Nazarene.

— Hymns from a Woman's Heart. 55p. (Orig.). 1993. pap. 2.99 (*0-8341-1461-5*, 55707) Beacon Hill.

— Mary: A Mother Highly Favored. 56p. 1994. pap. 2.99 (*0-8341-1524-7*) Beacon Hill.

Rice, George W. Monica: A Prodigal's Praying Mother. 48p. 1989. pap. 2.99 (*0-8341-1286-8*) Beacon Hill.

Rice, George W. A Preacher Named Emma. 70p. 1995. pap. 2.49 (*0-8341-1564-6*) Beacon Hill.

— Shipping Days of Old Boothbay (Maine) LC 84-61955. (Illus.). 463p. 1984. reprint ed. 45.00 (*0-89725-054-0*, 1203) Picton Pr.

Rice, Glen E. A Synthesis of Tonto Basin Prehistory: The Roosevelt Archaeology Studies, 1989 to 1998. LC 98-53066. (Anthropological Field Studies). 1998. write for info. (*1-886067-12-0*) ASU Office Cultural Res.

Rice, Graham. The Complete Book of Perennials. LC 95-13645. (Illus.). 240p. 1996. 30.00 (*0-89577-825-4*, Pub. by RD Assn) Penguin Putnam.

— Discovering Annuals. LC 99-11612. (Illus.). 192p. 1999. 34.95 (*0-88192-465-2*) Timber.

— Hardy Perennials. (Illus.). 209p. 1995. 27.95 (*0-88192-338-9*) Timber.

— Hardy Perennials. LC 96-51644. (Illus.). 209p. 1997. reprint ed. pap. 17.95 (*0-88192-401-6*) Timber.

Rice, Graham & Strangman, Elizabeth. The Gardener's Guide to Growing Hellebores. (Gardener's Guide Ser.). (Illus.). 160p. 1993. 29.95 (*0-88192-266-8*) Timber.

Rice, Graham, jt. auth. see Lloyd, Christopher.

Rice, Grantland S. The Duffer's Handbook of Golf. rev. ed. (Illus.). 165p. 1989. reprint ed. text 28.00 (*0-940889-20-X*) Classics Golf.

— The Transformation of Authorship in America. LC 96-43890. 1997. pap. text 17.95 (*0-226-71124-2*); lib. bdg. 42.00 (*0-226-71123-4*) U Ch Pr.

Rice, Gregory E. & Brennecke, Shaun P., eds. Molecular Aspects of Placental & Fetal Autacoids. LC 92-48814. 480p. 1993. lib. bdg. 232.00 (*0-8493-6239-3*, QP281) CRC Pr.

Rice, H. & Dutton. Structural Glass. (Illus.). 144p. 1995. pap. 59.95 (*0-419-19940-3*, E & FN Spon) Routledge.

Rice, H. & Moore, S. Winning Football with the Air Option Passing Game. LC 85-3593. 178p. (C). 1985. text 27.95 (*0-13-961038-3*) P-H.

Rice, Harvey. How Do You Pronounce Artaxerxes: A Comprehensive Guide to Pronouncing Bible Names & Places. 256p. (Orig.). 1997. pap. write for info. (*1-57502-429-2*, PO1311) Morris Pubng.

Rice, Harvey L. The Book of Revelation . . . Plus. 211p. 1998. pap. 12.00 (*1-57502-955-3*, PO2624) Morris Pubng.

— It Happened in Church & a Few Other Places. 157p. 1998. pap. 7.00 (*1-57502-956-1*, PO2625) Morris Pubng.

— The Truth about Romans. 242p. 1998. pap. 12.00 (*1-57502-954-5*, PO2623) Morris Pubng.

Rice, Helen Steiner. Always a Springtime: Poems of Hope & Renewal. LC 87-12675. (Illus.). 96p. (gr. 10). 1987. 13.99 (*0-8007-1556-X*) Revell.

— Blossoms of Friendship. LC 91-41049. (Illus.). 96p. (gr. 10). 1992. 13.99 (*0-8007-1664-7*) Revell.

— A Book of Blessings. (Illus.). 96p. 1995. 13.99 (*0-8007-1714-7*) Revell.

— A Book of Courage. LC 97-102051. (Illus.). 96p. (YA). (gr. 10). 1996. 13.99 (*0-8007-1731-7*) Revell.

— A Book of Hope. (Illus.). 96p. (YA). (gr. 10). 1996. 13.99 (*0-8007-1722-8*) Revell.

— A Book of Prayer. (Illus.). 96p. (YA). (gr. 10). 1995. 13.99 (*0-8007-1707-4*) Revell.

— A Book of Thanks. LC 93-3967. (Illus.). 104p. (YA). (gr. 10). 1993. 13.99 (*0-8007-1695-7*) Revell.

— Bouquet of Joy. (Thumbprint Bks.). (Illus.). 92p. (gr. 10). 1999. 4.99 (*0-8007-7147-8*) Revell.

— Christmas Blessings. (Illus.). 80p. 2000. 9.99 (*0-517-20871-7*) Random Hse Value.

— Christmas Blessings. 2nd ed. LC 96-8450. (Illus.). 80p. (YA). (gr. 10). 1996. 19.99 (*0-8007-1729-5*) Revell.

— A Collection of Love Gifts. 64p. 1995. 5.97 (*1-55748-747-2*) Barbour Pub.

— Daily Bouquets. (Illus.). 96p. (gr. 10). 1989. 13.99 (*0-8007-1637-X*) Revell.

— Daily Pathways. (Illus.). 96p. 1989. 13.99 (*0-8007-1625-6*) Revell.

— Daily Reflections. (Illus.). 96p. (gr. 10). 1990. 13.99 (*0-8007-1642-6*) Revell.

— Daily Stepping Stones. LC 89-32210. (Illus.). 96p. (gr. 10). 1988. 13.99 (*0-8007-1616-7*) Revell.

— Especially for Mothers. LC 97-105694. 64p. 1996. 5.97 (*1-55748-834-7*) Barbour Pub.

— Everyone Needs Someone. LC 78-11999. 96p. (gr. 11). 1987. 13.99 (*0-8007-1555-1*) Revell.

— Eyes of Tenderness. LC 96-37889. (Illus.). 96p. 1997. 19.99 (*0-8007-1737-6*) Revell.

— For Each New Day. (Thumbprint Bks.). (Illus.). 92p. (gr. 10). 1995. 4.99 (*0-8007-7143-5*) Revell.

— Friend to Friend. (Thumbprint Bks.). 92p. (gr. 10). 1999. 4.99 (*0-8007-7146-X*) Revell.

Rice, Helen Steiner. From the Heart: A Daily Inspirational Calendar. (Perpetual Calendars Ser.). 384p. (gr. 11 up). 1992. spiral bd. 11.99 (*0-8007-7500-7*) Revell.

Rice, Helen Steiner. Gems of Inspiration. (Illus.). 160p. (gr. 10). 1996. 11.99 (*0-8007-7152-4*) Revell.

— Gifts of Love. LC 92-23413. (Illus.). 96p. (YA). (gr. 10). 1993. 13.99 (*0-8007-1677-9*) Revell.

— God's Promises from A to Z. LC 98-30449. (Illus.). 96p. (C). (gr. 13). 1999. 14.99 (*0-8007-1762-7*) Revell.

— Heart Gifts. 3rd ed. LC 99-22032. (Illus.). 96p. 1999. reprint ed. 13.99 (*0-8007-1767-8*) Revell.

— Inspiration for Living. (Thumbprint Bks.). (Illus.). 92p. (gr. 10). 1995. 4.99 (*0-8007-7142-7*) Revell.

— Joy for the Heart. LC 92-12413. 96p. (YA). (gr. 10). 1992. 13.99 (*0-8007-1674-4*) Revell.

— Loving Promises. (Illus.). 128p. (gr. 10). 1988. 16.99 (*0-8007-1600-0*) Revell.

— Lovingly: Poems for All Seasons. LC 77-123061. 96p. (gr. 11). 1987. 13.99 (*0-8007-1521-7*) Revell.

***Rice, Helen Steiner.** Mother, I Love You. 2001. 8.99 (*0-517-16284-9*) Crown Pub Group.

Rice, Helen Steiner. A New Beginning. (Thumbprint Bks.). (Illus.). 92p. (gr. 10). 1999. 4.99 (*0-8007-7141-9*) Revell.

— Poems of Faith. 1984. 14.95 (*0-89952-086-3*) Littlebrook.

— Precious Moments Caring Angels. LC 94-17006. (Illus.). 64p. (gr. 11). 1994. 11.99 (*0-8007-7139-7*) Revell.

— Precious Moments Christmas Angels. LC 94-17018. (Illus.). 64p. (gr. 11). 1994. 11.99 (*0-8007-7140-0*) Revell.

— Precious Moments of Celebration. LC 93-6575. (Illus.). 64p. (gr. 11). 1993. 11.99 (*0-8007-1691-4*) Revell.

— The Priceless Gift of Christmas. 1990. 14.95 (*0-89952-060-X*) Littlebrook.

— Showers of Blessings. 96p. (gr. 10). 1987. 13.99 (*0-8007-1567-5*) Revell.

— Somebody Loves You. 2nd adapted ed. LC 97-12527. (Illus.). 80p. 1998. 19.99 (*0-8007-1747-3*) Revell.

— Someone Cares. 2nd abr. ed. LC 98-12885. (Illus.). 80p. (C). 1998. 14.99 (*0-8007-1748-1*) Revell.

— Sunshine of Joy. (Illus.). 96p. (gr. 10). 1988. 13.99 (*0-8007-1568-3*) Revell.

— Time for Reflection. abr. ed. (Thumbprint Bks.). 92p. (gr. 10). 1999. 4.99 (*0-8007-7144-3*) Revell.

— To Mother with Love. 96p. (YA). (gr. 10). 1992. 13.99 (*0-8007-1649-3*) Revell.

— To Mother with Love. large type ed. 96p. 1995. pap. 12.95 (*0-8027-2690-9*) Walker & Co.

— Wings of Encouragement. LC 94-46001. (Illus.). 96p. (gr. 10). 1995. 19.99 (*0-8007-1704-X*) Revell.

Rice, Helen Steiner & Ruehlmann, Virginia J. Celebrating the Golden Years. large type ed. LC 98-4920. 96p. 1998. 19.99 (*0-8007-1749-X*) Revell.

***Rice, Helen Steiner & Ruehlmann, Virginia J.** Gifts of Love. 2nd rev. ed. LC 99-42717. 96p. (gr. 13). 2000. 19.99 (*0-8007-1770-8*) Revell.

An Asterisk (*) at the beginning of an entry indicates that the title is appearing for the first time.

Rice, Helen Steiner & Ruehlmann, Virginia J. Mother, I Love You. LC 98-41203. (Illus.). 80p. 1999. 14.99 (*0-8007-1764-3*) Revell.
— An Old-Time Christmas. LC 97-15594. (Illus.). 96p. 1997. 19.99 (*0-8007-1744-9*) Revell.
Rice, Helen Steiner, jt. auth. see Allen, Charles L.
Rice, Herbert W. Toni Morrison & the American Tradition: A Rhetorical Reading, Vol. 60. 2nd ed. (American University Studies: No. XXIV). 155p. (C). 1998. reprint ed. pap. text 24.95 (*0-8204-4117-1*) P Lang Pubng.
Rice, Hilary. Stars of Dawson's Creek. LC 98-208130. 1998. mass mkt. 4.95 (*1-58260-006-6*) Infnty Plus One.
***Rice, Homer.** Lessons for Leaders. LC 00-105059. 208p. 2000. 22.00 (*1-56352-632-8*) Longstreet.
Rice, Horace R. The Buffalo Ridge Cherokee: A Remnant of a Great Nation Divided. (Illus.). 256p. (Orig.). 1995. pap. 24.00 (*0-7884-0296-X*) Heritage Bk.
Rice, Howard. The Pastor As Spiritual Guide. Collett, Rita, ed. LC 97-23359. 208p. 1998. pap. 17.00 (*0-8358-0846-7*, UR846) Upper Room Bks.
Rice, Howard C., Jr. New Jersey Road Maps of the Eighteenth Century. (Illus.). 42p. 1981. pap. 5.00 (*0-87811-024-0*) Princeton Lib.
Rice, Howard C. Rudyard Kipling in New England. LC 72-6747. (English Biography Ser.: No. 31). 39p. 1972. reprint ed. lib. bdg. 75.00 (*0-8383-1635-2*) M S G Haskell Hse.
Rice, Howard C., Jr. Thomas Jefferson's Paris. (Illus.). 156p. (C). 1998. pap. text 20.00 (*0-7881-5525-3*) DIANE Pub.
Rice, Howard C. Thomas Jefferson's Paris. LC 75-30203. (Illus.). 168p. reprint ed. pap. 52.10 (*0-8357-3569-9*, 203464900090) Bks Demand.
Rice, Howard L. Reformed Spirituality: An Introduction for Believers. 192p. (Orig.). 1991. pap. 22.95 (*0-664-25230-3*) Westminster John Knox.
Rice, Howard L. & Williamson, Lamar, Jr., eds. A Book of Reformed Prayers. LC 97-28818. 1997. pap. 15.00 (*0-664-25701-1*) Westminster John Knox.
***Rice, Hugh A.** God & Goodness. 156p. 2000. 29.95 (*0-19-825028-2*) OUP.
***Rice, Iain.** Small, Smart & Practical Track Plans. (Model Railroader Ser.). (Illus.). 2000. pap. 18.95 (*0-89024-416-2*) Kalmbach.
Rice, J. Before the Great Spirit: The Many Faces of Sioux Spirituality. LC 97-37094. 175p. 1998. 45.00 (*0-8263-1868-1*) U of NM Pr.
— False Doctrines. 1994. pap. 9.95 (*0-87398-282-7*) Sword of Lord.
— Golden Path Success Soul Winning. 1988. pap. 5.95 (*0-87398-306-8*) Sword of Lord.
— Lodges Examined by the Bible. 1988. pap. 1.95 (*0-87398-510-9*) Sword of Lord.
Rice, J. & Boisvert, R. F. Solving Elliptic Problems Using ELLPACK. (Computational Mathematics Ser.: Vol. 2). (Illus.). 350p. 1985. 79.95 (*0-387-90910-9*) Spr-Verlag.
Rice, J. & DeMillo, R. A. Studies in Computer Science: In Honor of Samuel D. Conte. (Software Science & Engineering Ser.). (Illus.). 254p. (C). 1994. 75.00 (*0-306-44697-9*, Kluwer Plenum) Kluwer Academic.
Rice, J. M. Public School System of the United States. LC 77-89224. (American Education: Its Men, Institutions, & Ideas. Series 1). 1975. reprint ed. 26.95 (*0-405-01461-9*) Ayer.
— Scientific Management in Education. LC 70-89225. (American Education). 1975. reprint ed. 23.95 (*0-405-01462-7*) Ayer.
Rice, J. R., ed. Mathematical Aspects of Scientific Software. (IMA Volumes in Mathematics & Its Applications Ser.: Vol. 14). (Illus.). xi, 208p. 1988. 45.95 (*0-387-96706-0*) Spr-Verlag.
***Rice, James.** Cajun Christmas Cards. (Illus.). 1999. 7.95 (*1-56554-693-8*) Pelican.
— Cajun Night before Christmas Coloring Book. (Illus.). 32p. (J). (ps-3). 1976. reprint ed. text 2.75 (*0-88289-138-3*) Pelican.
Rice, James. Christmas at the J-O. LC 95-13568. (Illus.). 32p. (J). (ps-3). 1995. 14.95 (*1-56554-087-5*) Pelican.
— Cowboy Alphabet. 1982. pap. 10.95 (*0-08-829427-7*, Pergamon Pr) Elsevier.
— Cowboy Alphabet. 2nd ed. LC 88-33087. (Illus.). 40p. (gr. k-3). 1990. 14.95 (*0-88289-726-8*) Pelican.
— Cowboy Night Before Christmas. 2nd ed. LC 90-7280. Orig. Title: Praire Night Before Christmas. (Illus.). 32p. (J). (ps-3). 1986. reprint ed. 14.95 (*0-88289-811-6*) Pelican.
— Cowboy Night Before Christmas Coloring Book. (Illus.). 32p. (Orig.). (J). (ps-3). 1994. pap. 2.95 (*1-56554-093-X*) Pelican.
— Cowboy Rodeo. LC 91-34924. (Illus.). 32p. (J). (gr. 2 up). 1992. 14.95 (*0-88289-903-1*) Pelican.
***Rice, James.** Gaston Goes to Mardi Gras. (Illus.). 32p. (J). (ps-3). 2000. pap. 3.25 (*1-56554-773-X*) Pelican.
Rice, James. Gaston Goes to Mardi Gras. 2nd ed. LC 97-3561. (Illus.). 40p. (J). (ps-3). 1999. 14.95 (*1-56554-286-X*) Pelican.
— Gaston Goes to Texas. LC 78-12490. (Illus.). 32p. (J). (ps-3). 1978. 14.95 (*0-88289-204-5*) Pelican.
— Gaston Goes to the Kentucky Derby. LC 94-2196. (Illus.). 32p. (J). (ps-3). 1994. 14.95 (*1-56554-065-4*) Pelican.
— Gaston the Green-Nosed Alligator. LC 75-310918. (Illus.). 40p. (J). (ps-3). 1974. reprint ed. 14.95 (*0-88289-049-2*) Pelican.
— Gaston, the Green-Nosed Alligator. 2nd ed. LC 99-31229. (Illus.). 40p. (J). (gr. k-3). 1998. 14.95 (*1-56554-285-1*) Pelican.
— The Ghost of Pont Diable. LC 96-24041. (Illus.). 176p. (J). (gr. 5-8). 1996. 14.95 (*1-57168-109-4*, Eakin Pr); pap. 8.95 (*1-57168-130-2*, Eakin Pr) Sunbelt Media.
— La Nochebuena South of the Border. Smith, Ana, tr. LC 93-13002. (ENG & SPA., Illus.). 32p. (J). (gr. 4-7). 1993. reprint ed. 14.95 (*0-88289-966-X*) Pelican.
Rice, James, Jr. Teaching Library Use: A Guide for Library Instruction, 37. LC 80-21337. (Contributions in Librarianship & Information Science Ser.: No. 37). (Illus.). 169p. 1981. 49.95 (*0-313-21485-9*, RTL/, Greenwood Pr) Greenwood.
Rice, James. Texas Alphabet. LC 87-31159. (Illus.). 40p. (J). (ps-3). 1988. 14.95 (*0-88289-692-X*) Pelican.
— Texas Night Before Christmas. LC 86-9445. (Illus.). 32p. (J). (ps-3). 1986. reprint ed. 14.95 (*0-88289-603-2*) Pelican.
— Trail Drive. LC 96-23057. (Illus.). 32p. (J). (gr. 1-4). 1996. 14.95 (*1-56554-163-4*) Pelican.
— Vaqueros. LC 97-37428. (SPA., Illus.). 32p. (ps-3). 1998. 14.95 (*1-56554-309-2*) Pelican.
Rice, James. An Irish Night Before Christmas. LC 94-42911. 32p. (J). (ps-3). 1995. reprint ed. 14.95 (*1-56554-086-7*) Pelican.
***Rice, James & Besant, Walter.** The Chaplain of the Fleet. 252p. 2000. pap. 9.95 (*0-594-00429-2*) Eightn Hundrd.
Rice, James, jt. auth. see Besant, Walter.
Rice, James B., jt. ed. see Slater, Courtenay.
Rice, James L. Freud's Russia: National Identity in the Evolution of Psychoanalysis. LC 92-31244. 210p. (C). 1993. text 39.95 (*1-56000-091-0*) Transaction Pubs.
— Modern Cabins: A Memoir of the Sixties. LC 96-79976. 240p. (Orig.). 1997. pap. 10.95 (*0-9656250-3-6*) Mohawk Pr.
Rice, James M. Peoria City & County: Record of Settlement, Organization, Progress & Achievement, 2 vols. (Illus.). 905p. 1997. reprint ed. lib. bdg. 97.00 (*0-8328-5781-5*) Higginson Bk Co.
Rice, Jane. Instructor's Guide & Testbank for Medical Terminology with Human Anatomy. 3rd ed. (C). 1994. pap. text, teacher ed. 29.95 (*0-8385-6272-8*, A6272-7) Appleton & Lange.
— The Key to Medical Terminology. (Illus.). 384p. 1986. pap. text 21.95 (*0-13-515032-9*) P-H.
— Medical Terminology with Human Anatomy. 3rd ed. (Illus.). 574p. (C). 1994. pap. text 32.95 (*0-8385-6268-X*, A6268-5) Appleton & Lange.
— Medical Terminology with Human Anatomy: Instructor's Guide. 4th ed. 1998. pap., teacher ed. 25.00 (*0-8385-6291-4*, Medical Exam) Appleton & Lange.
— Medications & Math for the Nurse. 6th ed. (LPN/LVN Nursing Ser.). 1988. pap. 33.95 (*0-8273-2841-9*) Delmar.
— Medications & Mathematics for the Nurse. 8th ed. LC 97-13780. 652p. (C). 1997. mass mkt. 45.95 (*0-8273-8328-2*) Delmar.
— Meidcal Terminology with Human Anatomy & Student Disk. 4th ed. LC 98-15836. 574p. 1998. pap. 39.95 incl. audio (*0-8385-6274-4*, Medical Exam) Appleton & Lange.
— Principles of Pharmacology for Medical Assisting. 2nd ed. LC 93-26739. 548p. (C). 1994. pap. 32.00 (*0-8273-5744-3*) Delmar.
— Principles of Pharmacology for Medical Assisting. 3rd ed. LC 98-21887. 560p. (C). 1998. text 45.95 (*0-7668-0325-2*) Delmar.
— Principles of Pharmacology for Medical Assisting: Instructor's Guide. 2nd ed. 89p. 1994. 16.00 (*0-8273-6353-2*) Delmar.
— Spellright: A Medical Word Book. 772p. (C). 1990. pap. text 22.95 (*0-8385-6290-6*, A6290-9) Appleton & Lange.
Rice, Jane & Skelley, Esther G. Medications & Mathematics for Nursing. 7th ed. LC 92-18283. 620p. 1993. text 33.95 (*0-8273-5119-4*) Delmar.
— Medications & Mathematics for the Nurse: Instructor's Guide. 7th ed. 87p. 1993. pap. 12.95 (*0-8273-5120-8*) Delmar.
Rice, Janett, jt. auth. see Brown, Patty.
Rice, Jayne. Bonnet House: The Life & Gift. (Illus.). 48p. (Orig.). 1990. pap. text 6.00 (*0-9624757-1-8*) Bonnet Hse.
— Reflections of a Legacy: The Bonnet House Story. Robinson, Jayme, ed. (Illus.). 152p. 1989. 35.00 (*0-9624757-0-X*) Bonnet Hse.
Rice, Jean & Henke, James. Friendly BASIC: Apple Version. (Illus.). 125p. 14.95 (*0-317-13086-2*) P-H.
Rice, Jeffrey B. The Love of the Father. LC 98-60603. (Illus.). 32p. (J). (gr. 3-6). 1998. 14.95 (*1-890394-24-6*); pap. 9.95 (*1-890394-23-8*) Rhodes & Easton.
Rice, Jeffrey C. & Salisbury, Irving, III. Advanced Java Programming. LC 97-24537. (Illus.). 476p. 1997. pap., pap. text 39.95 incl. cd-rom (*0-07-913089-5*) McGraw.
Rice, Jeffrey C. & Salisbury, Irving. Advanced Java 1.1 Programming. LC 97-24537. (Java Masters Ser.). 1997. write for info. (*0-07-052426-2*); write for info. incl. cd-rom (*0-07-852998-0*) McGraw.
Rice, Jenny & Sullivan, Tim. Groupwork. 180p. 1996. ring bd. 199.00 (*0-7494-1868-0*, Kogan Pg Educ) Stylus Pub VA.
Rice, Jim & Hayhoe, Mike. Writing from Canada. LC 93-11687. (Figures in a Landscape Ser.). 1996. pap. 9.95 (*0-521-42305-8*) Cambridge U Pr.
Rice, Jim, jt. auth. see Onword Press Development Team Staff.
Rice, Joe, contrib. by. Metalworking: The Best of Projects in Metal 1990-1991, Bk. 2. (Illus.). 240p. (C). 1994. text 32.00 (*0-941653-17-X*) Village Pr Pubns.
Rice, Joe, ed. Projects 6. LC 95-74799. (Illus.). 250p. 1995. 35.00 (*0-941653-19-6*) Village Pr Pubns.
Rice, Joe, jt. auth. see Allen, JoCindee.
Rice, Joe D., ed. The Best of Live Steam: Nineteen Sixty-Six to Nineteen Seventy-One, Vol. 1. LC 85-51037. (Illus.). 176p. 1985. 26.95 (*0-914104-08-X*) Wildwood Pubns MI.
Rice, Joe D., ed. Projects 2. 200p. 1988. 24.95 (*0-941653-03-X*) Village Pr Pubns.
Rice, John. Better Food for Patients: New Menus, Cooking, & Ward Service for Hospital Patients, 3 vols. (King Edward's Hospital Fund Ser.). 1975. pap. 25.00 (*0-8464-0191-6*) Beekman Pubs.
— Chess Wizardry: The New ABC of Chess Problems. LC 96-77759. (New American Batsford Chess Library). 352p. 1996. pap. 26.95 (*1-879479-33-8*) ICE WA.
— The Dreams of Night Fishers: Scottish Islands in Poems & Photographs. 80p. 1994. pap. 24.00 (*1-84017-025-5*) St Mut.
***Rice, John.** DTV Production Demystified. (Demystified Ser.). (Illus.). 400p. 2000. pap. text 49.95 (*0-07-135966-4*) McGraw-Hill Prof.
Rice, John, jt. auth. see Murray, Michael K.
Rice, John A. Antonio Salieri & Viennese Opera. LC 97-32585. 1998. pap. write for info. (*0-226-71126-9*) U Ch Pr.
— Antonio Salieri & Viennese Opera. LC 97-32585. (Illus.). 578p. 1999. 95.00 (*0-226-71125-0*) U Ch Pr.
— Mathematical Statistics & Data Analysis. (Statistics). 595p. (C). 1987. pap. 56.00 (*0-534-08247-5*) Wadsworth Pub.
— Mathematical Statistics & Data Analysis. 2nd ed. 602p. 1994. pap. 106.95 (*0-534-20934-3*) Wadsworth Pub.
***Rice, John R.** Great Women of the Bible. 22p. 1999. pap. write for info. (*0-87398-341-6*) Sword of the Lord.
Rice, John R. Numerical Methods, Software, & Analysis. 2nd ed. (Illus.). 720p. 1992. text 71.00 (*0-12-587755-2*) Acad Pr.
Rice, John S. A Disease of One's Own: Psychotherapy, Addiction, & the Emergence of Co-Dependency. 264p. (C). 1996. text 39.95 (*1-56000-241-7*) Transaction Pubs.
— A Disease of One's Own: Psychotherapy, Addiction, & the Emergence of Co-Dependency. 253p. 1998. pap. 24.95 (*0-7658-0454-9*) Transaction Pubs.
Rice-Johnson. Tactical Management: The Paradox. LC 99-231261. (ITBP Textbooks Ser.). 1999. pap. 19.99 (*1-86152-376-9*) Thomson Learn.
Rice, Jonathan. Curiosities of Cricket. pap. text 11.95 (*1-85793-270-6*, Pub. by Pavilion Bks Ltd) Trafalgar.
Rice, Jonathan. Curiosities of Golf. (Illus.). 160p. 1996. reprint ed. pap. 9.95 (*1-85793-671-X*, Pub. by Pavilion Bks Ltd) Trafalgar.
Rice, Jonathan & Clarke, Roy. Hyacinth Bucket's Hectic Social Calendar. LC 97-74407. (Illus.). 160p. 1997. 20.95 (*0-563-37186-2*, BBC-Parkwest) Parkwest Pubns.
Rice, Jonathan, jt. auth. see Clarke, Roy.
Rice, Jonathon. Start of Play: The Curious Origins of Our Favorite Sports. LC 99-224305. (Illus.). 256p. 1998. 32.95 (*1-85375-281-9*) Prion.
Rice, Joseph. Irving: A Texas Odyssey-An Illustrated History. 144p. 1989. 29.95 (*0-89781-300-6*, 5312) Am Historical Pr.
Rice, Josette, jt. auth. see Knox, Dahk.
Rice, Josette, ed. see Elrick, Harold.
Rice, Josette, ed. see Hansen, Burdette.
Rice, Joy. Grandad Doesn't Live Here Anymore. (Contemporary Literature for Children Ser.: No. 2). (Illus.). 28p. (Orig.). (J). (ps-5). 1986. pap. 5.95 (*0-317-57377-2*, 104) Order of Legion.
Rice, Joy K. & Rice, David G. Living Through Divorce: A Developmental Approach to Divorce Therapy. LC 85-27173. (Family Therapy Ser.). 303p. 1985. lib. bdg. 42.00 (*0-89862-061-9*) Guilford Pubns.
Rice, Joyce. Making & Painting Victorian Birdhouses. LC 98-40475. (Illus.). 128p. 1999. pap. 24.99 (*0-89134-881-6*, 31359, North Lght Bks) F & W Pubns Inc.
Rice, Judith. Those Itsy-Bitsy Teeny-Tiny Not-So-Nice Head Lice. LC 98-12626. (SPA & ENG., Illus.). (J). (ps-1). 1998. 12.95 (*1-884834-54-X*) Redleaf Pr.
— Those Mean Nasty Dirty Downright Disgusting but... Invisible Germs. LC 97-9060. (Illus.). (J). 1997. pap. 12.95 (*1-884834-31-0*) Redleaf Pr.
Rice, Judith A. The Kindness Curriculum: Introducing Young Children to Loving Values. LC 95-7275. (Illus.). 122p. (Orig.). 1995. pap. 14.95 (*1-884834-02-7*, 3022) Redleaf Pr.
— Let's Party! How to Plan Special Events & Raise Money in Early Childhood Programs. LC 97-34166. (Illus.). (Orig.). 1997. pap. 13.95 (*1-884834-41-8*, 5320) Redleaf Pr.
Rice, Judith Anne. Those Icky Sticky Smelly Cavity-Causing but--Invisible Germs. LC 97-9059. (Illus.). (J). 1997. pap. 12.95 (*1-884834-30-2*) Redleaf Pr.
***Rice, Judith Anne.** Those Ooey Gooey Winky Blinky but... Invisible Pinkeye Germs: Esos Pringosos Viscosos Pestaneantes Parpadeantes Pero... Invisibles Germenes Que Causan Conjuntivitis. De la Vega, Eida, tr. (Children's Health Ser.: Vol. 4). (Illus.). (J). (ps-3). 2000. pap. 12.95 (*1-884834-89-2*, 181801, Pub. by Redleaf Pr) Gryphon Hse.
Rice, Judith R. Learning Workplace Writing. LC 93-15880. 336p. 1994. pap. text 52.00 (*0-13-337437-8*) P-H.
Rice, Julian. Before the Great Spirit: The Many Faces of Sioux Spirituality. LC 97-37094. (Illus.). 175p. 1998. pap. 22.50 (*0-8263-1898-3*) U of NM Pr.
— Black Elk's Story: Distinguishing Its Lakota Purpose. 165p. 1994. pap. 16.95 (*0-8263-1497-X*) U of NM Pr.
Rice, Kathleen F., jt. auth. see Brooks, Carolyn S.
***Rice, Kathleen L.** SL200 Introduction to Service in Multicultural Communities & WRSI361s: Foundations of Wellness: Service Learning. 126p. 1999. pap. write for info. (*1-58692-002-2*) Copyright Mgmt.
Rice, Keren. A Grammar of Slave. xliv, 1370p. (C). 1989. lib. bdg. 236.70 (*0-89925-140-4*) Mouton.
***Rice, Keren.** Morpheme Order & Semantic Scope: Word Formation in the Athapaskan Verb. LC 99-20442. (Cambridge Studies in Linguistics: No. 90). 288p. (C). 2000. 64.95 (*0-521-58354-3*) Cambridge U Pr.
Rice, Keren, jt. ed. see Cook, Eung D.
Rice, Keren D., jt. ed. see Murray, Laura J.
Rice, Kym S. Early American Taverns: For the Entertainment of Friends & Strangers. (Illus.). 168p. (Orig.). 1983. pap. text 15.00 (*0-9616415-1-7*) Fraunces Tavern.
Rice, Kym S., jt. auth. see Bernstein, Richard B.
Rice, Kym S., jt. ed. see Campbell, Edward D., Jr.
Rice, L., jt. ed. see Cope, L.
Rice, L. S., jt. auth. see Keyes, M. A.
Rice, Larry. Baja to Patagonia: Latin American Adventures. (Illus.). 234p. (Orig.). 1993. pap. 15.95 (*1-55591-113-7*) Fulcrum Pub.
Rice, Larry & American Bar Association Staff. The Complete Guide to Divorce Practice: Forms & Procedures for the Lawyer. 2nd ed. LC 98-27812. xxx, 732p. 1998. 74.95 (*1-57073-614-6*, ABA Genl Prac) Amer Bar Assn.
***Rice, Laura.** Maryland History in Prints, 1752-1900. (Illus.). 320p. 2000. 65.00 (*0-938420-71-2*, Pub. by MD Hist) A C Hood.
Rice, Laura, ed. & tr. see Eberhardt, Isabelle.
Rice, Lee M. & Vernam, Glenn R. They Saddled the West. LC 75-5734. (Illus.). 202p. reprint ed. pap. 62.70 (*0-8357-4431-0*, 203726200008) Bks Demand.
Rice, Leland D., intro. New Portfolios. (Illus.). 24p. 1976. 2.00 (*0-915478-35-8*) Montgomery Gallery.
Rice, Leonard & White, Michael D. Engineering Aspects of Water Law. 216p. (C). 1991. reprint ed. lib. bdg. 44.50 (*0-89464-548-X*) Krieger.
Rice, Lesley Ogilvie. Introduction to Open VMS. 5th ed. 2000. pap. 39.95 (*1-55558-194-3*) DEC.
Rice, Leslie, jt. auth. see Goodman, Nancy.
Rice, Lewis, ed. Naga Varmma's Karnataka Bhasha-Bhushana. (C). 1985. reprint ed. 12.00 (*0-8364-2407-7*, Pub. by Asian Educ Servs) S Asia.
Rice-Licare, Jennifer & Delaney-McLoughlin, Katharine. Cocaine Solutions: Help for Cocaine Abusers & Their Families. LC 90-4843. (Addiction Treatment Ser.). 150p. 1990. pap. text 14.95 (*0-918393-82-5*) Haworth Pr.
— Cocaine Solutions: Help for Cocaine Abusers & Their Families. LC 90-4843. (Addiction Treatment Ser.). 150p. 1990. 39.95 (*1-56024-035-0*) Haworth Pr.
Rice, Linda J., jt. auth. see Ashburn, Michael A.
Rice, Louise. The Altars & Altarpieces of New St. Peter's: Outfitting the Basilica, 1621-1666. LC 96-36272. (Monuments of Papal Rome Ser.). (Illus.). 494p. (C). 1998. text 95.00 (*0-521-55470-5*) Cambridge U Pr.
— Character Reading from Handwriting. (Illus.). 320p. 1996. pap. 14.95 (*0-87877-232-4*) Newcastle Pub.
Rice, Luanne. Blue Moon. 352p. 1994. mass mkt. 6.50 (*0-553-56818-3*) Bantam.
— Blue Moon. large type ed. LC 93-44120. 547p. 1994. lib. bdg. 22.95 (*0-7862-0148-7*) Thorndike Pr.
— Cloud Nine. 1999. 21.95 (*0-553-09729-6*) Bantam.
***Rice, Luanne.** Cloud Nine. 400p. 2000. mass mkt. 6.50 (*0-553-58099-X*) Bantam.
Rice, Luanne. Cloud Nine. LC 99-13818. 1999. write for info. (*1-56895-708-4*) Wheeler Pub.
***Rice, Luanne.** Follow the Stars Home. LC 99-40593. 368p. 2000. 19.95 (*0-553-11073-X*) Bantam.
— Follow the Stars Home. large type ed. LC 00-26015. (Large Print Book Ser.). 2000. 25.95 (*1-56895-864-1*) Wheeler Pub.
Rice, Luanne. Home Fires. 368p. 1996. mass mkt. 5.99 (*0-553-57322-5*) Bantam.
— Home Fires. 1996. pap. 5.99 (*0-614-98036-4*) Bantam.
— Home Fires. large type ed. LC 96-1845. 1996. 24.95 (*1-56895-299-6*) Wheeler Pub.
Rice, Lyn P., jt. contrib. by see Kaufman, Lois L.
Rice, Lynn, ed. see Jambro, Donald J.
Rice, Lynn, ed. see Siebold, Bert A.
Rice, M. Handbook of Airfoil Sections for Light Aircraft. (Illus.). 134p. 1974. pap. 10.25 (*0-87994-015-8*) Aviat Pub.
Rice, M., jt. auth. see Rice, C.
Rice, M. A. & Sammes, A. J. Command & Control Support Systems in the Gulf War. 1994. 43.01 (*1-85753-010-1*) Macmillan.
— Command & Control Support Systems in the Gulf War: Land Warfare: Brassey's Battlefield Weapons Systems & Technology. LC 95-171209. (Land Warfare: Brassey's New Battlefield Weapons & Technology Ser.: Vol. 13). 1994. 25.00 (*1-85753-015-2*, Pub. by Brasseys) Brasseys.
— Communications & Information Systems for Battlefield Command & Control. Lee, R. G. & Hartley, Frank, eds. (Land Warfare: Brassey's New Battlefield Weapons & Technology Ser.: Vol. 5). 276p. 1989. 40.00 (*0-08-036266-4*, Pub. by Brasseys); 25.00 (*0-08-036267-2*, Pub. by Brasseys) Brasseys.
Rice, M. S., ed. see Curtiss Aeroplane & Motor Corp.
Rice, Mabel L., ed. Toward a Genetics of Language. 432p. 1996. text 89.95 (*0-8058-1677-1*) L Erlbaum Assocs.
— Toward a Genetics of Language. 432p. 1996. pap. 49.95 (*0-8058-1678-X*) L Erlbaum Assocs.
Rice, Mabel L. & Wilcox, Kim A. Building a Language-Focused Curriculum for the Preschool Classroom Vol. I: A Foundation for Lifelong Communication, vol. 1. LC 94-49085. 248p. 1995. pap. 35.00 (*1-55766-177-4*) P H Brookes.
Rice, Marian L. Sexology Encyclopedia Vol. 16: Herpes Genitalis: Index & Reference Books of New Information. Bartone, John C., ed. (Illus.). 145p. 1996. 49.95 (*0-7883-0880-7*); pap. 39.95 (*0-7883-0881-5*) ABBE Pubs Assn.
Rice, Marion, jt. auth. see De Vorsey, Louis, Jr.
Rice, Mark P. & Mathews, Jana B. Growing New Ventures - Creating New Jobs: Principles & Practices of Successful Business Incubation. LC 95-34541. (Entrepreneurship: Principles & Practices Ser.). 176p. 1995. 39.95 (*1-56720-033-8*, Quorum Bks) Greenwood.

An Asterisk (*) at the beginning of an entry indicates that the title is appearing for the first time.

R

Rice, Martha & Burns, Jane. Thinking-Writing: An Introduction to the Writing Process for Students of ESL. (Illus.). 200p. (C). 1985. pap. text 29.60 (*0-13-918244-6*) P-H.

Rice, Martin P., tr. see Cizevskij, Dmitry.

Rice, Mary E., jt. ed. see Harrison, Frederick W.

Rice, Mary K. Sintesis de Distancia e Immersion en Cuatro Obras de Antonio Buero Vallejo. LC 91-3802. (American University Studies: Romance Languages & Literature: Ser. II, Vol. 169). 112p. (C). 1992. text 35.95 (*0-8204-1555-3*) P Lang Pubng.

Rice, Matthew. Traditional Houses of Rural Britain. (Illus.). 160p. 1992. 29.95 (*1-55859-338-1*, Cross Riv Pr) Abbeville Pr.

— The Village Buildings of Britain. 1991. write for info. (*0-316-88866-4*) Little.

Rice-Maximin, Edward. Accommodation & Resistance: The French Left, Indochina & the Cold War, 1944-1954, 2. LC 86-4624. (Contributions to the Study of World History Ser.: No. 2). 186p. 1986. 49.95 (*0-313-25355-2*, RMX/, Greenwood Pr) Greenwood.

Rice-Maximin, Edward, jt. auth. see Buhle, Paul.

Rice-Maximin, Micheline. Karukera: Presence Litteraire de la Guadeloupe. (Francophone Cultures & Literatures Ser.: Vol. 9). (FRE., Illus.). VIII, 197p. (C). 1998. pap. text 29.95 (*0-8204-2696-2*) P Lang Pubng.

***Rice, Mel.** Fire on the Hillside. (Lone Star Heroines Ser.). (Illus.). 128p. (YA). (gr. 4-7). 2000. pap. 8.95 (*1-55622-789-2*, Rep of TX Pr) Wordware Pub.

— Messenger on the Battlefield. (Lone Star Heroines Ser.). (Illus.). 128p. (YA). 2000. pap. 8.95 (*1-55622-788-4*, Rep of TX Pr) Wordware Pub.

— Secrets in the Sky. (Illus.). 120p. (YA). 2000. pap. 8.95 (*1-55622-787-6*, Rep of TX Pr) Wordware Pub.

Rice, Melanie. The Complete Book of Children's Activities. LC 92-30859. (J). 1993. pap. 9.95 (*1-85697-907-5*, Kingfisher) LKC.

***Rice, Melanie.** Play Together, Learn Together. (Illus.). 160p. (YA). 2000. pap. 12.95 (*0-7534-5294-4*, Kingfisher) LKC.

***Rice, Melanie & Rice, Chris.** Independent Traveler's Guide: New Zealand 2000. 2000. pap. 19.95 (*0-7627-0675-9*) Globe Pequot.

Rice, Melanie & Rice, Christopher J. My First Body Book. LC 94-40835. (Illus.). 48p. (J). (gr. k-3). 1995. 16.95 (*1-56458-893-9*, 5-70553) DK Pub Inc.

Rice, Melanie, jt. auth. see Rice, Chris.

Rice, Melanie, jt. auth. see Rice, Christopher.

Rice, Melanie, jt. contrib. by see Rice, Christopher.

Rice, Michael. The Archaeology of the Arabian Gulf. LC 93-7006. (Illus.). 392p. (C). (gr. 13). 1994. 90.00 (*0-415-03268-7*) Routledge.

— Egypt's Legacy: The Archetypes of Western Civilization 3000-30 B. C. LC 96-36661. (Illus.). 256p. (C). 1997. 60.00 (*0-415-15779-X*) Routledge.

— Egypt's Making: The Origins of Ancient Egypt 5000-2000 BC. (Illus.). 352p. (C). 1991. pap. 27.99 (*0-415-06454-6*, A5838) Routledge.

— False Inheritance: Israel in Palestine & the Search for a Solution. LC 93-28499. 232p. 1994. 34.00 (*0-7103-0473-0*) Routledge.

— The Golden Age of Ancient Egypt. 192p. (C). 1988. lib. bdg. 65.00 (*0-7103-0296-7*) Routledge.

— The Power of the Bull. LC 97-11049. (Illus.). 336p. (C). 1998. 60.00 (*0-415-09032-6*) Routledge.

— Who's Who in Ancient Egypt. 1999. 29.99 (*0-415-15448-0*) Routledge.

Rice, Michael, jt. ed. see Al-Khalifa, Shaikh A.

Rice, Michael A. The Northern Quahog: The Biology of Mercenaria Mercenaria. Jaworski, Carole & Schwartz, Malia, eds. (Illus.). (Orig.). 1992. pap. text 5.00 (*0-938412-33-7*) Sea Grant Pubns.

Rice, Michael D. Asset Financing. 770p. 1989. 145.00 (*0-316-74313-5*, Aspen Law & Bus) Aspen Pub.

Rice, Michael S., ed. see Dzik, Stanley J.

Rice, Miriam C. How to Use Mushrooms for Color. rev. ed. (Illus.). 145p. 1980. pap. text 18.50 (*0-916422-19-4*) Mad River.

Rice, Mitchell F. Diversity & Public Organizations: Theory, Issues & Perspectives. 256p. (C). 1996. pap. text, per. 36.95 (*0-7872-2739-0*) Kendall-Hunt.

Rice, Mitchell F. & Jones, Woodrow, Jr. Public Policy & the Black Hospital: From Slavery to Segregation to Integration, 165. LC 93-4851. (Contributions in Afro-American & African Studies: No. 165). 176p. 1994. 55.00 (*0-313-26309-4*, RBP/, Greenwood Pr) Greenwood.

Rice, Mitchell F. & Jones, Woodrow, Jr., compiled by. Black American Health: An Annotated Bibliography, 17. LC 86-25745. (Bibliographies & Indexes in Afro-American & African Studies: No. 17). 133p. 1987. lib. bdg. 55.00 (*0-313-24887-7*, RBH/, Greenwood Pr) Greenwood.

— Health of Black Americans from Post-Reconstruction to Integration, 1871-1960: An Annotated Bibliography of Contemporary Sources, 26. LC 89-78161. (Bibliographies & Indexes in Afro-American & African Studies: No. 26). 256p. 1990. lib. bdg. 65.00 (*0-313-26314-0*, RHB/, Greenwood Pr) Greenwood.

Rice, Mitchell F. & Jones, Woodrow, Jr., eds. Contemporary Public Policy Perspectives & Black Americans: Issues in an Era of Retrenchment Politics, 77. LC 84-717. (Contributions in Afro-American & African Studies: No. 77). (Illus.). 213p. 1984. 57.95 (*0-313-23711-5*, RIP/) Greenwood.

Rice, Mitchell F., jt. ed. see Jones, Woodrow, Jr.

Rice, Molly. Chance Encounter. (Superromance Ser.: No. 490). 1992. mass mkt. 3.39 (*0-373-70490-9*, 1-70490-7) Harlequin Bks.

— Krystal's Bodyguard. 1997. per. 3.75 (*0-373-22432-X*, 1-22432-8) Harlequin Bks.

***Rice, Molly.** Protecting His Own. 2000. per. 4.25 (*0-373-22562-8*) Harlequin Bks.

Rice, Molly. Silent Masquerade. LC 95-7078. (Intrigue Ser.). 250p. 1995. per. 3.50 (*0-373-22315-3*, 1-22315-5) Harlequin Bks.

— Unforgettable. LC 95-22380. 248p. 1995. per. 3.50 (*0-373-22348-X*) Harlequin Bks.

Rice, N. L. God Sovereign & Man Free. 1993. 16.99 (*0-87377-919-3*) GAM Pubns.

Rice, N. L., jt. auth. see Blanchard, Jonathan.

Rice, Nicky. Coming up to Midnight. 68p. 1994. pap. 14.95 (*1-870612-48-5*, Pub. by Enitha Pr) Dufour.

Rice, Otis K. Frontier Kentucky. LC 93-7821. 160p. 1993. 19.95 (*0-8131-1840-9*) U Pr of Ky.

— The Hatfields & the McCoys. LC 82-1916. (Illus.). 168p. 1979. reprint ed. 22.00 (*0-8131-1459-4*) U Pr of Ky.

— Lewisburg United Methodist Church: A Bicentennial History. 111p. 1988. pap. text. write for info. (*0-9620189-0-2*) Lewisburg United.

Rice, Otis K. & Brown, Stephen W. The Mountain State: An Introduction to West Virginia. Rowley, James W., ed. LC 97-60861. (Illus.). (J). (gr. 8). 1997. 30.00 (*0-914498-14-2*) WV Hist Ed Found.

— West Virginia: A History. 2nd ed. LC 93-17819. (Illus.). 376p. 1993. 32.00 (*0-8131-1854-9*) U Pr of Ky.

Rice, Patricia. Change & Conflict: Britain, Ireland & Europe from the Late 16th to the Early 18th Centuries. (Irish History in Perspective Ser.). (Illus.). 80p. 1994. pap. 13.95 (*0-521-46603-2*) Cambridge U Pr.

— Change & Conflict: Teachers Resource Book: Britain, Ireland & Europe from the Late 16th to the Early 18th Centuries. (Irish History in Perspective Ser.). (Illus.). 30p. 1995. pap. text, teacher ed. 19.95 (*0-521-46604-0*) Cambridge U Pr.

— Clouds. 375p. 1998. mass mkt. 5.99 (*0-449-15063-1*, GM) Fawcett.

— Denim & Lace. 1996. mass mkt. 6.99 (*0-451-40688-5*, Topaz) NAL.

— Garden of Dreams. 1998. mass mkt. 5.99 (*0-449-15062-3*, GM) Fawcett.

***Rice, Patricia.** Impossible Dreams. LC 99-91678. 344p. 2000. mass mkt. 6.50 (*0-449-00601-8*) Ballantine Pub Grp.

— Merely Magic. 2000. mass mkt. 6.99 (*0-451-20049-7*, Sig) NAL.

Rice, Patricia. Moonlight Mistress. 1999. mass mkt. 5.99 (*0-8217-6175-7*, Zebra Kensgtn) Kensgtn Pub Corp.

***Rice, Patricia.** Nobody's Angel. 2001. mass mkt. 6.99 (*0-449-00602-6*) Ballantine Pub Grp.

Rice, Patricia. Paper Moon. 382p. 1996. mass mkt. 5.99 (*0-451-40652-4*, Topaz) NAL.

— Surrender. 512p. 1998. mass mkt. 5.99 (*0-8217-6000-9*, Zebra Kensgtn) Kensgtn Pub Corp.

— Volcano. 1999. mass mkt. 5.99 (*0-449-15064-X*, GM) Fawcett.

***Rice, Patricia.** Volcano, 1. 1999. mass mkt. 5.99 (*0-449-00609-3*) Fawcett.

Rice, Patricia. Wayward Angel. 1997. mass mkt. 5.99 (*0-451-40724-5*) NAL.

— A Wedding Bouquet. 352p. 1996. mass mkt. 5.99 (*0-451-18785-7*, Sig) NAL.

Rice, Patricia C. Doing Archaeology: A Hands-On Laboratory Manual. LC 97-27978. xiv, 214p. 1997. pap. text 27.95 (*1-55934-845-3*, 1845) Mayfield Pub.

***Rice, Patricia C.** Strategies for Teaching Anthropology. (Illus.). 181p. 1999. pap. 25.20 (*0-13-025683-8*) P-H.

Rice, Patricia O. & Ogburn, Joyce L., eds. The Serials Partnership: Teamwork, Technology, & Trends. LC 89-28050. (Serials Librarian Ser.: Vol. 17, Nos. 3-4). (Illus.). xii, 215p. 1990. text 6.95 (*0-86656-991-X*) Haworth Pr.

Rice, Patricia O. & Robillard, Jane A., eds. The Future of Serials: Proceedings of the North American Serials Interest Group, Inc. (Serials Librarian Ser.: Vol. 19, Nos. 3-4). (Illus.). 260p. 1991. text 49.95 (*1-56024-081-4*) Haworth Pr.

***Rice, Patrick.** Infrared Wedding Photography: Techniques & Images in Black & White. (Illus.). 128p. 2000. pap. 29.95 (*1-58428-020-4*) Amherst Media.

Rice, Patty. Baby Talk: Quotations & Quips for New Mothers. LC 98-121362. (Illus.). 128p. 1997. pap. text 6.95 (*0-8362-3620-3*) Andrews & McMeel.

— Manmade Heartbreak. 48p. 1998. 5.00 (*1-889289-33-7*) Ye Olde Font Shoppe.

***Rice, Patty.** Somethin' Extra: A Novel. LC 99-54747. 368p. 2000. 22.50 (*0-684-85340-X*) S&S Trade.

Rice, Patty C. Amber: The Golden Gem of the Ages. 3rd ed. LC 97-42904. (Illus.). 336p. 2000. 75.00 (*0-945005-29-6*); pap. 40.00 (*0-945005-28-8*) Geoscience Pr.

Rice, Paul & Rice, Valeta. Potential: The Name Analysis Book. 192p. (Orig.). 1987. pap. 8.95 (*0-87728-632-9*) Weiser.

Rice, Paul F. Negotiating Your Contracts. 8p. (Orig.). 1988. 3.95 (*0-9620188-5-6*) Lifestyle Group.

— Selecting Your Accountant. 8p. (Orig.). 1988. 3.95 (*0-9620188-2-1*) Lifestyle Group.

— Selecting Your Financial Advisors: Keys to Choosing a Good Accountant, Lawyer, Securities Broker, Financial Planner & Other Sources of Financial Advice. 52p. (Orig.). 1988. pap. 7.95 (*0-318-23895-0*) Lifestyle Group.

— Selecting Your Lawyer. 8p. (Orig.). 1988. 3.95 (*0-9620188-1-3*) Lifestyle Group.

— Selecting Your Securities Broker & Financial Planner. 8p. (Orig.). 1988. 3.95 (*0-9620188-3-X*) Lifestyle Group.

Rice, Paul F., ed. An Edited Collection of the Theatre Music of John Abraham Fisher: The Druids, & Witches Scenes from Macbeth. (Studies in the History & Interpretation of Music: Vol. 48). 232p. 1996. text 89.95 (*0-7734-8865-0*) E Mellen.

Rice, Paul F. & Hoffman, Edward S. Structural Design Guide to AISC Specifications for Buildings. LC 75-40491. (Illus.). 368p. reprint ed. pap. 114.10 (*0-608-11680-7*, 200787700067) Bks Demand.

Rice, Paul R. Attorney-Client Privileges in the U. S. LC 92-73901. 1993. ring bd. 125.00 (*0-317-05382-5*) West Group.

— Evidence: Common Law & Federal Rules of Evidence. 3rd ed. (C). 1996. text 47.95 (*0-8205-2498-0*, 606) Bender.

***Rice, Paul W.** The Artistry of Paul W. Rice. (Illus.). 116p. 1999. pap. 14.95 (*1-929733-10-0*) MicroPress.

— God's Not So Odd Couple. (Illus.). 1999. pap. 9.95 (*1-929733-13-5*) MicroPress.

— The Remnants of Divorce. 76p. 1999. pap. 12.95 (*1-929733-12-7*) MicroPress.

— Voyage Through Innocence. 172p. 1999. pap. 19.95 (*1-929733-11-9*) MicroPress.

Rice, Peter. Peter Rice: An Engineer Imagines. 1998. pap. 29.00 (*1-899858-11-3*) Watsn-Guptill.

Rice, Peter, et al. Columbia Documents of Architecture & Theory Vol. 1: D. (Illus.). 150p. (Orig.). 1992. pap. 20.00 (*0-9623829-5-7*) CUGSA.

Rice, Peter L. Battletech #31: Highfligh. 1999. pap. 5.50 (*0-451-45587-8*, ROC) NAL.

Rice, Phil. Phil Rice's Correct Method for the Banjo. Ayers, Joseph W., ed. (Illus.). 64p. 1997. pap. 18.00 (*0-9633593-3-9*) Tuckahoe Music.

Rice, Philip. Modern Literary Theory: A Reader. 3rd ed. LC 96-17312. 400p. 1996. pap. text 19.95 (*0-340-64585-7*, Pub. by E A) OUP.

Rice, Philip & Waugh, Patricia. Modern Literary Theory: A Reader. 200p. 1989. 49.50 (*0-7131-6596-0*, Pub. by E A); pap. 15.95 (*0-7131-6541-3*, Pub. by E A) Routldge.

Rice, Philip & Waugh, Patricia, eds. Modern Literary Theory: A Reader. 2nd ed. LC 92-19707. 368p. 1995. text 16.95 (*0-340-57599-9*, Pub. by E A) St Martin.

Rice, Philip A., jt. auth. see Dellock, Jean.

Rice, Philip L. Health Psychology. LC 97-11794. (Psychology Ser.). 1997. pap. 45.75 (*0-534-33915-8*) Wadsworth Pub.

Rice, Phillip A. Church Records of the Bethany Evangelical Congregational Church (Formerly Bethany United Evangelical Church) 197p. 1994. per. 22.95 (*1-55856-179-X*) Closson Pr.

— German Protestant Cemetery of Mahanoy City Located in Mahonoy Township, Schuylkill County, Pennsylvania. 152p. 1995. per. 16.95 (*1-55856-180-3*, 047) Closson Pr.

— Index to the Obituaries As Found in the Pottsville Republican & Citizen Standard for the Year 1992. LC 95-118526. 82p. 1994. pap. text 9.75 (*1-55856-200-1*, 083) Closson Pr.

Rice, Phillip A., tr. from GER. St. John's Lutheran Church Near Berrysburg, Mifflin Township, Dauphin County, Pennsylvania. LC 96-85598. 139p. 1996. per. 15.00 (*1-55856-239-7*, 270) Closson Pr.

Rice, Phillip A. & Dellock, Jean. Church Records of St. David's Lutheran & Reformed Church at Hebe, Jordan Township, Northumberland County, Pennsylvania. 74p. 1995. per. 9.95 (*1-55856-181-1*, 082) Closson Pr.

Rice, Phillip A. & Dellock, Jean A. Collected Church Records of Berks County, Pennsylvania. 587p. 1995. per. 49.95 (*1-55856-184-6*, 095) Closson Pr.

— Dauphin County, Pennsylvania Archives, Vol. 2. LC 96-8557. 380p. 1996. per. 35.00 (*1-55856-237-0*, 014) Closson Pr.

— Early Lutheran Records from Dauphin County, Pennsylvania. LC 96-71481. 1997. per. 29.95 (*1-55856-251-6*, 269) Closson Pr.

— St. Paul's (White Church) Cemetery & Reformed Congregation Records (1874-1913) with Collected Cemeteries of Union Township & North Union Township, Schuylkill County, Pennsylvania. LC 94-214132. 260p. 1994. pap. text 24.95 (*1-55856-161-7*, 401) Closson Pr.

— Trinity Lutheran Church of Reading, (Baptisms 1751-1790), Pt. 1. 122p. 1990. per. 14.00 (*1-55856-054-8*, 392) Closson Pr.

Rice, Phillip A. & Dellock, Jean A., compiled by. Early Methodism in Ashland & Girardville, Schuylkill County, Pennsylvania: Records of the Methodist Episcopal Church at Ashland & Methodist Episcopal Church at Girardville. LC 96-85597. 222p. 1997. per. 24.95 (*1-55856-238-9*, 403) Closson Pr.

Rice, Phillip A. & Dellock, Jean A., eds. Circuit & Circuit Riders, Set, Vols. I & II. LC 96-216277. 638p. 1996. per. 49.95 (*1-55856-216-8*, 087) Closson Pr.

Rice, Phillip A., jt. auth. see Dellock, Jean.

Rice, Phillip A., jt. auth. see Dellock, Jean A.

Rice, Phillip A., jt. auth. see Schuylkill Roots Staff.

Rice, Phillip A., jt. compiled by see Dellock, Jean A.

Rice, Phillip L. Stress & Health. 2nd ed. 1992. pap., teacher ed. write for info. (*0-534-17281-4*) Brooks-Cole.

— Stress & Health. 2nd ed. LC 91-36428. 436p. (C). 1996. pap. 29.50 (*0-534-17280-6*) Brooks-Cole.

— Stress & Health: Principles & Practice for Coping & Wellness. LC 86-26875. (Psychology Ser.). 380p. (C). 1987. mass mkt. 21.25 (*0-534-07608-4*) Brooks-Cole.

***Rice, Pierce.** Man as Hero: The Human Figure in Western Art. (Illus.). 160p. 2000. pap. text 15.95 (*0-393-73056-5*) Norton.

Rice, Pranee L. & Manderson, Lenore. Maternity & Reproductive Health in Asian Societies. 320p. 1996. text 39.00 (*90-5702-021-1*, Harwood Acad Pubs) Gordon & Breach.

***Rice, Pranee Liamputtong.** Hmong Women & Reproduction. LC 99-55890. 2000. write for info. (*0-89789-679-3*, Bergin & Garvey) Greenwood.

***Rice, Pranee Liamputtong & Ezzy, Douglas.** Qualitative Reaseach Methods: A Health Focus. 240p. 2000. pap. text 29.95 (*0-19-550610-3*) OUP.

Rice, Prudence M. Macanche Island, el Peten, Guatemala: Excavations, Pottery, & Artifacts. LC 87-2040. (Illus.). 280p. (C). 1987. 49.95 (*0-8130-0838-7*) U Press Fla.

— Pottery Analysis: A Sourcebook. LC 86-24958. (Illus.). xxiv, 584p. (C). 1987. 65.00 (*0-226-71118-8*) U Ch Pr.

Rice, Prudence M., ed. The Prehistory & History of Ceramic Kilns. (Ceramics & Civilization Ser.: Vol. VII). 262p. 1997. 95.00 (*1-57498-026-2*, CC07) Am Ceramic.

Rice, R. Talking Turkey. (C). 1989. text 29.95 (*0-948032-38-3*, Pub. by Rosters Ltd) St Mut.

Rice, R. C., ed. see Tritsch, D.

Rice, R. Hugh. Dragonflies. (Books for Young Learners). (Illus.). 12p. (J). (gr. k-2). 1996. pap. text 5.00 (*1-57274-019-1*, A2445) R Owen Pubs.

— Flip Flop. (Books for Young Learners).Tr. of Flip Flop. (Illus.). 12p. (J). (gr. k-2). 1998. pap. text 5.00 (*1-57274-115-5*, A2455) R Owen Pubs.

— Libelulas. Torres, Raquel, tr. (Books for Young Learners).Tr. of Dragonflies. (SPA., Illus.). 12p. (J). (gr. k-2). 1996. pap. text 5.00 (*1-57274-032-9*, A2875) R Owen Pubs.

***Rice, R. Hugh.** Log Garfish. (Books for Young Learners). (Illus.). 16p. (J). (gr. k-2). 1999. pap. text 5.00 (*1-57274-267-4*, A2754) R Owen Pubs.

— Mother Octopus. (Books for Young Learners). (Illus.). 12p. (J). (gr. k-2). 1999. pap. text 5.00 (*1-57274-272-0*, A2472) R Owen Pubs.

Rice, R. Hugh & Romo, Alberto. Flip Flop. (Books for Young Learners).Tr. of Flip Flop. (SPA., Illus.). 12p. (J). (gr. k-2). 1999. pap. text 5.00 (*1-57274-289-5*) R Owen Pubs.

Rice, R. J. Fundamentals of Geomorphology. 2nd ed. 1996. pap. 31.00 (*0-582-30151-3*, Pub. by Addison-Wesley) Longman.

Rice, R. P., et al. Fruit & Vegetable Production in Warm Climates. (Illus.). 496p. (Orig.). 1990. pap. text 35.00 (*0-333-46850-3*) Scholium Intl.

***Rice, R. W.** Mechanical Properties of Ceramics & Composites: Grain & Particle Effects. LC 00-28151. (Materials Engineering Ser.). (Illus.). 2000. write for info. (*0-8247-8874-5*) Dekker.

***Rice, Railton, ed.** Enviromental Activity K 8. 1999. pap. text 27.95 (*0-205-28552-X*) A&B Bks.

Rice, Ralph S. & Rice, Terence R. California Family Tax Planning, 2 vols. 2nd ed. 1963. ring bd. 465.00 (*0-8205-1184-6*, 184) Bender.

Rice, Randall W., jt. auth. see Perry, William E.

Rice, Richard. The Reign of God: An Introduction to Christian Theology from a Seventh-Day Adventist Perspective. 2nd rev. ed. 464p. (C). 1997. text 34.95 (*1-883925-16-9*) Andrews Univ Pr.

Rice, Richard, jt. auth. see Sizer, Nigel.

Rice, Richard A., jt. ed. see Campbell, Oscar J.

Rice, Richard B., et al. The Elusive Eden: A New History of California. 2nd ed. LC 95-82034. (C). 1996. text 62.81 (*0-07-553403-7*) McGraw.

Rice, Richard C. & Society of Automotive Engineers Staff. SAE Fatigue Design Handbook. 3rd ed. LC 96-39685. 1997. 89.00 (*1-56091-917-5*, AE-22) Soc Auto Engineers.

Rice, Richard G. & Do, Duong D. Applied Mathematics & Modeling for Chemical Engineers. 720p. 1994. text 99.95 (*0-471-30377-1*) Wiley.

Rice, Richard L., Jr., jt. auth. see Jaffe, Richard S.

Rice, Rip G., ed. First International Symposium on Ozone for Water & Wastewater Treatment. LC 74-28539. (Illus.). 1974. text 15.00 (*0-918650-03-8*); text 20.00 (*0-918650-04-6*) Pan Am Intl Ozone.

— Safe Drinking Water: The Impact of Chemicals on a Limited Resource. LC 84-25105. (Illus.). 280p. 1984. 162.00 (*0-9614032-0-9*, CRC Reprint) Franklin.

— Safe Drinking Water: The Impact of Chemicals on a Limited Resource. 275p. 1985. 34.95 (*0-317-01439-0*); 29.95 (*0-318-17815-X*) Intl Bottled Water.

Rice, Rip G., et al, eds. International Symposium on Ozone Technology. 2nd. LC 76-28267. (Illus.). 1976. text 18.00 (*0-918650-07-0*); text 23.00 (*0-918650-08-9*) Pan Am Intl Ozone.

Rice, Rip G. & Browning, Myron E., eds. Ozone: Analytical Aspects & Odor Control. LC 76-17611. (Illus.). 1976. text 25.00 (*0-918650-09-7*) Pan Am Intl Ozone.

Rice, Rip G. & Cotruvo, Joseph A., eds. Ozone Chlorine-Dioxide Oxidation Products of Organic Materials. LC 78-53924. (Illus.). 1978. text 50.00 (*0-918650-02-X*) Pan Am Intl Ozone.

***Rice, Robert.** Agent of Judgement. LC 80-27974. (Illus.). 320p. 2000. text 23.95 (*0-312-87050-7*) St Martin.

Rice, Robert. The Last Pendragon. 340p. 1992. 19.95 (*0-8027-1180-4*) Walker & Co.

— The Last Pendragon. large type ed. 368p. 1992. reprint ed. 17.95 (*1-56054-432-5*) Thorndike Pr.

Rice, Robert F., et al, eds. A Book for All Nations! (Illus.). 64p. 1991. 1.00 (*1-877596-20-5*) Literacy & Evangelism.

— Firm Foundations: The First English Language Adult Literacy Series in the 20th Century with Bible-Content Lessons - Projected for the 21st Century, Bk. 1. rev. ed. LC 89-80387. (Illus.). 64p. 1989. 3.00 (*1-877596-14-0*) Literacy & Evangelism.

— Firm Foundations: The First English Language Adult Literacy Series in the 20th Century with Bible-Content Lessons - Projected for the 21st Century, Bk. 2. rev. ed. LC 89-80387. (Illus.). 56p. 1989. 3.00 (*1-877596-16-7*) Literacy & Evangelism.

— Firm Foundations: The First English Language Adult Literacy Series in the 20th Century with Bible-Content Lessons - Projected for the 21st Century, Bk. 3. rev. ed. LC 89-80387. (Illus.). 56p. 1989. 3.00 (*1-877596-18-3*) Literacy & Evangelism.

— Firm Foundations: The First English Language Adult

An Asterisk (*) at the beginning of an entry indicates that the title is appearing for the first time.

Literacy Series in the 20th Century with Bible-Content Lessons - Projected for the 21st Century, Pre-Reader. rev. ed. LC 89-80387. (Illus.). 32p. 1989. 3.00 (*1-877596-13-2*) Literacy & Evangelism.

— Firm Foundations: The First English Language Adult Literacy Series in the 20th Century with Bible-Content Lessons - Projected for the 21st Century, Vol. ESL. LC 89-80387. (Illus.). 80p. 1989. teacher ed. 3.00 (*1-877596-12-4*) Literacy & Evangelism.

— Firm Foundations: The First English Language Adult Literacy Series in the 20th Century with Bible-Content Lessons - Projected for the 21st Century, Wkbk. 1. LC 89-80387. (Illus.). 56p. 1989. student ed. 3.00 (*1-877596-15-9*) Literacy & Evangelism.

— Firm Foundations: The First English Language Adult Literacy Series in the 20th Century with Bible-Content Lessons - Projected for the 21st Century, Wkbk. 2. LC 89-80387. (Illus.). 56p. 1989. student ed. 3.00 (*1-877596-17-5*) Literacy & Evangelism.

— Firm Foundations: The First English Language Adult Literacy Series in the 20th Century with Bible-Content Lessons - Projected for the 21st Century, Wkbk. 3. LC 89-80387. (Illus.). 56p. 1989. student ed. 3.00 (*1-877596-19-1*) Literacy & Evangelism.

— Firm Foundations in Learning English: The First English Language Adult Literacy Series in the 20th Century with Bible-Content Lessons - Projected for the 21st Century, 7 bks., Set. rev. ed. LC 89-80387. (Illus.). 456p. 1989. pap. 20.00 (*1-877596-11-6*) Literacy & Evangelism.

Rice, Robert P., Jr. Thomson's English-Spanish - Spanish-English Illustrated Agricultural Dictionary. 160p. 1993. pap. 27.95 (*0-913702-56-0*) Thomson Pubns.

Rice, Robyn. Handbook of Home Health Nursing Procedures. (Illus.). 512p. (C). (gr. 13). 1994. spiral bd. 31.95 (*0-8016-6946-4*, 06946) Mosby Inc.

— Home Health Nursing Practice: Concepts & Application. 2nd rev. ed. (Illus.). 512p. (C). (gr. 13). 1995. pap. text 36.95 (*0-8151-7240-0*, 26255) Mosby Inc.

— Manual of Home Health Nursing Procedures. (Illus.). 400p. (C). (gr. 13). 1994. text 115.00 (*0-8016-6945-6*, 06945) Mosby Inc.

***Rice, Robyn.** Manual of Home Health Nursing Procedures. 2nd ed. LC 99-26972. 1999. text 55.00 (*0-323-00912-3*) Harcourt.

— Manual of Home Health Nursing Procedures: Update. (Illus.). 400p. 1998. write for info. (*1-55664-414-0*) Mosby Inc.

***Rice, Rochelle & Silberger, Nancy.** Real Fitness for Real Women: A Unique Workout Program for Plus-Size Women. 2001. pap. write for info. (*0-446-67621-7*) Warner Bks.

Rice, Rodney R. One Hundred One Weapons for Women: Implement Weaponry. Jones, Lynn, ed. (Illus.). 128p. 1992. pap. 10.95 (*0-9632402-1-8*) RiJo Prods.

Rice, Ron. Reflections of the Heart. (Illus.). 28p. (Orig.). 1995. pap. 6.95 (*0-9646093-0-4*) Kerley Pub Servs.

Rice, Ronald E. & Atkin, Charles K., eds. Public Communication Campaigns. 2nd ed. 416p. (C). 1989. text 58.00 (*0-8039-3262-6*); pap. text 24.50 (*0-8039-3263-4*) Sage.

Rice, Ronald E. & Paisley, William J., eds. Public Communication Campaigns. LC 81-2706. 328p. reprint ed. pap. 101.70 (*0-8357-4848-0*, 203777900009) Bks Demand.

Rice, Ronald E., et al. The New Media: Communication, Research, & Technology. LC 84-3287. (Illus.). 352p. reprint ed. pap. 109.20 (*0-7837-4560-5*, 204408800003) Bks Demand.

Rice, Ross R. Carl Hayden: Builder of the American West. LC 93-43763. 372p. (C). lib. bdg. 57.50 (*0-8191-9399-2*) U Pr of Amer.

Rice, Russ. Joe B. Hall: My Own Kentucky Home. LC 81-52628. (College Sports Bks.). 1981. 12.95 (*0-87397-196-5*, Strode Pubs) Circle Bk Service.

Rice, Russell. Adolph Rupp: Kentucky's Basketball Baron. LC 94-68641. (Illus.). 250p. 1994. 19.95 (*0-915611-98-8*) Sports Pub.

Rice, Ruth. English Teacher's Book of Instant Word Games. 288p. 1992. pap. text 28.95 (*0-87628-303-2*) Ctr Appl Res.

Rice, Sally, jt. ed. see Brett, Jane.

Rice, Samuel O., ed. Fundamentals of Investment. LC 75-2664. (Wall Street & the Security Market Ser.). 1975. reprint ed. 34.95 (*0-405-06988-X*) Ayer.

Rice, Sandra R. To Run the Race with Joy. LC 96-51817. (Orig.). 1997. pap. 14.75 (*0-7880-1064-6*) CSS OH.

Rice, Sara S., compiled by. Holiday Selections: For Readings & Recitations; Specially Adapted to Christmas, New Year... LC 72-39402. (Granger Index Reprint Ser.). 1977. reprint ed. 18.95 (*0-8369-6348-2*) Ayer.

Rice, Sara V., jt. auth. see Rice, Don A.

Rice, Sarah. He Included Me: The Autobiography of Sarah Rice. Westling, Louise, ed. LC 88-38690. (Illus.). 200p. 1989. 14.95 (*0-8203-1141-3*) U of Ga Pr.

Rice, Scott. From Reading to Revision. 336p. 1996. 24.25 (*0-534-21996-9*) Wadsworth Pub.

Rice, Sean M. Did Ya See the Masked Man? Playscript. LC 91-51083. (Orig.). 1985. pap. 5.00 (*0-88734-304-X*) Players Pr.

Rice, Sederick C. Must Be the Music Vol. I: Memoirs of a Musical Dynasty. (Illus.). 220p. 1999. pap. 15.95 (*0-7392-0245-6*, PO3250) Morris Pubng.

Rice, Shelley. Parisian Views. LC 97-7986. 1997. 35.00 (*0-262-18184-3*) MIT Pr.

— Parisian Views. (Illus.). 288p. 1999. pap. 18.00 (*0-262-68107-2*) MIT Pr.

Rice, Shelley, ed. Inverted Odysseys: Claude Cahun, Maya Deren, Cindy Sherman. LC 99-26888. (Illus.). 256p. 1999. pap. 35.00 (*0-262-68106-4*) MIT Pr.

Rice-Spearman, Lori & Larsen, Hal S. The Rotation Manual for Clinical Laboratory Science. LC 94-38433. 1994. write for info. (*0-683-04821-X*) Lppncott W & W.

— The Rotation Manual for Clinical Laboratory Science. 224p. 1995. pap. 35.00 (*0-683-07259-5*) Lppncott W & W.

Rice, Stan. Fear Itself. 112p. 1997. pap. 14.00 (*0-679-76600-6*) Knopf.

— Fear Itself. LC 95-42770. 679p. 1995. 20.00 (*0-679-44441-6*) Random.

— New & Selected Poems. LC 91-43573. 226p. 1992. 24.00 (*0-679-41145-3*) McKay.

— Paintings. LC 97-73826. 1997. 35.00 (*0-375-40026-5*) Knopf.

***Rice, Stan.** The Radiance of Pigs. LC 98-43232. 96p. 1999. 22.00 (*0-375-40485-6*) Knopf.

— The Radiance of Pigs: Poems. 96p. 2001. pap. 15.00 (*0-375-70434-5*) Knopf.

Rice, Stan. Singing Yet: New & Selected Poems. 1993. pap. 14.00 (*0-679-74733-8*) Knopf.

— Whiteboy. 1975. pap. 3.00 (*0-685-52155-9*) Mudra.

Rice, Stan & More, Alan S., eds. Collecting Assessments: An Operational Guide. 3rd ed. (GAP Reports: No. 10). 20p. (C). 1994. reprint ed. pap. 17.50 (*0-944715-29-X*) CAI.

Rice, Stanley. Book Design: Systematic Aspects. LC 77-28186. (Illus.). 274p. 1978. 34.95 (*0-8352-1044-8*) Bowker.

— Book Design: Text Format Models. LC 77-26908. 215p. 1978. 34.95 (*0-8352-1045-6*) Bowker.

***Rice, Stanley.** Botany Laboratory Manual & Study Sheets. 1999. pap. text 20.68 (*1-56870-352-X*) RonJon Pub.

Rice, Stanley D., et al, eds. Proceedings of the Exxon Valdez Oil Spill Symposium. LC 96-85358. (American Fisheries Society Symposium Ser.: No. 18). (Illus.). 931p. 1996. text 35.00 (*0-913235-95-4*, 540.18) Am Fisheries Soc.

Rice, Steve. Travel Adventures & Trivia Map: California. 1986. 2.95 (*0-912831-04-9*) Map Ink.

Rice, Steven J. An Introduction to Taxation. 4th ed. LC 95-11381. 1995. pap. 71.95 (*0-538-85528-2*) S-W Pub.

***Rice, Steven V., et al.** Optical Character Recognition: An Illustrated Guide to the Frontier. LC 99-20879. (Kluwer International Series in Engineering & Computer Science). 1999. write for info. (*0-7923-8492-X*) Kluwer Academic.

Rice, Stuart A. Farmers & Workers in American Politics. LC 78-82242. (Columbia University. Studies in the Social Sciences: No. 253). reprint ed. 31.50 (*0-404-51253-4*) AMS Pr.

***Rice, Stuart A.** Fragile X. 500p. 1999. mass mkt. write for info. (*1-890939-04-8*) Century Creations.

Rice, Stuart A. & Freed, Karl F., eds. Statistical Mechanics: New Concepts, New Problems, New Applications. LC 72-85434. 434p. reprint ed. pap. 134.60 (*0-608-30620-7*, 201996500015) Bks Demand.

***Rice, Stuart A. & Zhao, Meishan.** Optical Control of Molecular Dynamics. LC 99-49631. 420p. 2000. text 89.95 (*0-471-35423-6*, Wiley-Interscience) Wiley.

Rice, Stuart A., jt. auth. see Prigogine, I.

Rice, Stuart A., jt. ed. see Prigogine, Ilya.

Rice, Stuart A., jt. ed. see Prigogine, I.

Rice, Susan. A Compound of Excelsior. (Illus.). 93p. (Orig.). 1991. pap. 10.95 (*0-938501-14-3*) Wessex.

— Milwaukee for Free (or the Next Thing to It!) LC 97-12640. 144p. 1997. pap. 8.95 (*1-879483-37-8*) Prairie Oak Pr.

Rice, Susan & Todd, Ginger. Travel Perspectives: A Guide to Becoming a Travel Agent. 300p. 1991. pap. 47.95 (*0-8273-4570-4*) Delmar.

— Travel Perspectives: A Guide to Becoming a Travel Agent. 300p. 1992. pap., teacher ed. 12.95 (*0-8273-4571-2*) Delmar.

— Travel Perspectives Update One. 1992. pap. 8.00 (*0-8273-4569-0*) Delmar.

Rice, Susan, jt. auth. see Todd, Ginger.

Rice, Tamara T. Tamara: Memoirs of St. Petersburg, Paris, Oxford & Byzantium. Rice, Elizabeth T., ed. (Illus.). 272p. 1996. 40.00 (*0-7195-5721-6*, Pub. by John Murray) Trafalgar.

Rice, Tanya. Mother Teresa. LC 97-26030. (Life & Times of...Ser.). (Illus.). 48p. (YA). (gr. 5 up). 1999. lib. bdg. 15.95 (*0-7910-4637-0*) Chelsea Hse.

Rice, Ted, jt. auth. see Turner, Karla.

Rice, Terence R. Evidence: Common Law & Federal Rules of Evidence. 2nd ed. 1990. teacher ed. write for info. (*0-8205-0345-2*) Bender.

Rice, Terence R., jt. auth. see Rice, Ralph S.

Rice, Thomas. The Economics of Health Reconsidered. 251p. 1998. pap. text 40.00 (*1-56793-077-8*, EHRS-1019) Health Admin Pr.

Rice, Thomas A., jt. auth. see Wilkinson, Charles P.

Rice, Thomas J. Joyce, Chaos, & Complexity. LC 96-9969. (Illus.). 224p. 1997. text 34.95 (*0-252-02279-3*); pap. text 14.95 (*0-252-06583-2*) U of Ill Pr.

Rice, Thomas R. And the Sea Rolls on Forever. (Illus.). viii, 720p. 1997. 34.00 (*1-889074-04-7*) Elkhorn Pr.

— Thunder on the Western Front. (Illus.). vi, 102p. 1998. 15.95 (*1-889074-06-3*) Elkhorn Pr.

Rice, Tim & John, Elton. Circle of Life. (Illus.). 48p. (J). 1994. 9.70 (*0-7868-6148-7*, Pub. by Hyperion) Time Warner.

Rice, Timothy. Deep Run Mennonite Church East: A 250 Year Pilgrimage, 1746-1996 LC 96-76792. 144p. 1996. write for info. (*1-883294-39-8*) Masthof Pr.

— May It Fill Your Soul: Experiencing Bulgarian Music. LC 93-34083. (Chicago Studies in Ethnomusicology). 386p. (C). 1994. pap. text 27.50 (*0-226-71122-6*); lib. bdg. 65.00 (*0-226-71121-8*) U Ch Pr.

Rice, Timothy. Mosby's Rounds: Interactive Case Studies in Internal Medicine, Windows. 32p. 1995. write for info. incl. disk (*0-8151-6478-5*) Mosby Inc.

Rice, Timothy, et al, eds. Europe. (Encyclopedia of World Music Ser.: Vol. 8). (Illus.). 1000p. 1999. 195.00 incl. cd-rom (*0-8240-6034-2*, H1169) Garland.

***Rice, Tony.** Deep Ocean. LC 00-28537. (Illus.). 2000. pap. 14.95 (*1-56098-867-3*) Smithsonian.

— New Acoustic Guitar. 24p. 1996. pap. 19.95 (*0-7935-6048-9*) H Leonard.

Rice, Tony, jt. auth. see Grisman, David.

Rice University Staff. Prehistoric Man in the New World. Jennings, Jesse D. & Norbeck, Edward, eds. LC 63-18852. (Rice University Semicentennial Publications). (Illus.). 643p. reprint ed. pap. 199.40 (*0-608-09418-8*, 205421800004) Bks Demand.

Rice, Valeta, jt. auth. see Rice, Paul.

Rice, Wallace & Rice, Frances. The Humbler Poets: Second Series; a Collection of Newspaper & Periodical Verse, 1885-1910. LC 70-39395. (Granger Index Reprint Ser.). 1977. reprint ed. 23.95 (*0-8369-6349-0*) Ayer.

***Rice, Wayne.** Cleared for Takeoff. LC 00-36484. 160p. 2000. pap. 12.99 (*0-8499-4201-2*) Word Pub.

Rice, Wayne. Enjoy Your Middle Schooler. 144p. 1994. 10.99 (*0-310-40581-5*) Zondervan.

— Junior High Ministry: A Guide to Early Adolescence for Youth Workers. LC 97-32389. 1998. pap. 15.99 (*0-310-22442-X*) Zondervan.

— Junior High Ministry: A Guidebook for the Leading & Teaching of Early Adolescents. 1978. pap. 6.95 (*0-310-34971-0*, 10825P) Zondervan.

— More Hot Illustrations for Youth Talks: 100 More Attention-Getting Stories, Parables, & Anecdotes. LC 95-35691. 112p. 1996. pap. 14.99 (*0-310-20768-1*) Zondervan.

***Rice, Wayne.** Reality 101: What the Bible Says to Teens about Real-Life Questions. LC 98-43532. (Illus.). 221p. 1999. pap. 9.99 (*0-8423-3575-7*) Tyndale Hse.

Rice, Wayne. Still More Hot Illustrations for Youth Talks No. 3: 100 More Attention-Getting Stories, Parables, & Anecdotes. LC 98-51646. (Illus.). 208p. 1999. pap. 14.99 (*0-310-22464-0*) Zondervan.

— Understanding Your Teen. (YA). 1992. pap., wbk. ed. 49.99 incl. VHS (*0-310-54528-5*) Zondervan.

***Rice, Wayne.** Understanding Your Teenager. LC 99-30289. 208p. 1999. pap. 14.99 (*0-8499-3750-7*) Word Pub.

Rice, Wayne, compiled by. Hot Illustrations for Youth Talks: 100 Attention-Getting Stories, Parables, & Anecdotes. LC 93-30815. 240p. 1994. pap. 12.99 (*0-310-40261-1*) Zondervan.

Rice, Wayne & Yaconelli, Mike. Creative Activities for Small Youth Groups. (Creative Resources for Youth Ministry Ser.). (Illus.). 104p. (YA). (gr. 7-12). 1991. pap. 12.95 (*0-88489-264-6*) St Marys.

— Creative Communication & Discussion Activities. (Creative Resources for Youth Ministry Ser.). (Illus.). 96p. (YA). (gr. 7-12). 1991. pap. 12.95 (*0-88489-266-2*) St Marys.

— Creative Crowd-Breakers, Mixers & Games. LC 92-122163. (Creative Resources for Youth Ministry Ser.). (Illus.). 96p. 1991. pap. 12.95 (*0-88489-265-4*) St Marys.

— The Greatest Skits on Earth, 2 vols., Vol. 1. 237p. (Orig.). (J). (gr. 3-7). 1986. pap. 12.99 (*0-310-35141-3*, 10775P) Zondervan.

— Juegos para Cada Ocasion. Lazo, Julia A., tr. from ENG.Tr. of Play It!. (SPA.). 192p. (Orig.). 1988. pap., teacher ed. 9.99 (*0-311-11047-9*) Casa Bautista.

— Play It: Great Games for Groups. 285p. 1986. pap. 12.99 (*0-310-35191-X*, 10799P) Zondervan.

Rice, Wayne & Yaconelli, Mike, eds. Play It Again! More Great Games for Groups. 240p. 1993. pap. 12.99 (*0-310-37291-7*) Zondervan.

Rice, Wayne, et al. New Directions for Youth Ministry: Practical Strategies to Reach Teenagers. Simpson, Amy, ed. LC 98-7059. 128p. 1998. per. 16.99 (*0-7644-2103-4*, Vital Ministry) Group Pub.

Rice, Wayne, jt. auth. see McPherson, Miles.

Rice, William. Steak Lover's Cookbook. LC 96-38749. (Illus.). 256p. 1996. 23.95 (*0-7611-0631-6*, 10631); pap. 13.95 (*0-7611-0080-6*, 10080) Workman Pub.

Rice, William C., jt. auth. see Lovelace, Austin C.

Rice, William G. The Carillon in Literature. 1977. lib. bdg. 59.95 (*0-8490-1576-6*) Gordon Pr.

— Carillon Music & Singing Towers of the Old World & the New. 1977. lib. bdg. 59.95 (*0-8490-1577-4*) Gordon Pr.

— Carillons of Belgium & Holland. 1977. lib. bdg. 59.95 (*0-8490-1578-2*) Gordon Pr.

— Tale of Two Courts: Judicial Settlement of Controversies Between the States of the Swiss & American Federations. LC 67-20758. 149p. reprint ed. pap. 46.20 (*0-608-14615-3*, 202371800033) Bks Demand.

***Rice, William H.** An Index of the Estate Records: In the Basement. 40p. 2000. pap. 9.50 (*0-87012-607-5*) McClain.

Rice, William T. Pearl Harbor Story. pap. 4.95 (*1-884485-01-4*) Tongg Pub.

Ricekit, T. R. Pennsylvania Pete. LC 98-119936. (Illus.). 171p. (Orig.). (YA). (gr. 7 up). 1995. pap. 9.99 (*0-88092-250-8*, 2508) Royal Fireworks.

***Ricento, Thomas K.** Ideology, Politics & Language Policies: Focus on English. LC 00-39818. (Impact Ser.). 2000. write for info. (*1-55619-670-9*) J Benjamins Pubng Co.

Ricento, Thomas K. & Burnaby, Barbara, eds. Language & Politics in the United States & Canada: Myths & Realities. LC 97-38464. 256p. 1998. 79.95 (*0-8058-2838-9*); pap. 39.95 (*0-8058-2839-7*) L Erlbaum Assocs.

Rich. Asia's Modern Century. 1986. pap. text. write for info. (*0-582-68246-0*, Pub. by Addison-Wesley) Longman.

— Clinician's Guide to the Healing Journey. LC 99-167145. (Healing Journey Ser.). 41p. 1998. pap. 14.95 (*0-471-29745-3*) Wiley.

— Clinician's Guide to the Healing Journey for Couples. (Healing Journey Ser.). 50p. 1998. pap. 14.95 (*0-471-29744-5*) Wiley.

***Rich.** Clinician's Guide to the Healing Journey Through Divorce. LC 99-174038. (Healing Journey Ser.). 32p. 1998. pap. 12.95 (*0-471-29951-0*) Wiley.

— Clinician's Guide to the Healing Journey Through Grief. LC 99-174032. (Healing Journey Ser.). 21p. 1998. pap. 12.95 (*0-471-29950-2*) Wiley.

— Healing Journey: Your Journey of Self-Discovery & Clinician's Guide to the Healing Journey. pap. 29.95 (*0-471-34858-9*) Wiley.

— Healing Journey for Couples: Your Journal of Mutual Discovery & Clinician's Guide to the Healing Journey for Couples. pap. 29.95 (*0-471-34857-0*) Wiley.

— Healing Journey Through Divorce: Your Journey of Understanding & Renewal & Clinical's Guide to the Healing Journey Through Divorce. pap. 29.95 (*0-471-34859-7*) Wiley.

— Healing Journey Through Grief: Your Journey for Reflection & Recovery & Clinician's Guide to the Healing Journey Through Grief. pap. 29.95 (*0-471-34860-0*) Wiley.

Rich. Housing & Community Development Policy. (C). 1999. text. write for info. (*0-321-00547-3*) Addison-Wesley Educ.

— News Writing. (Mass Communication). 1995. pap., teacher ed. 54.25 (*0-534-19073-1*) Wadsworth Pub.

— News Writing Student Telecourse. 2nd ed. (Mass Communication Ser.). 1996. pap. 21.00 (*0-534-52254-8*) Wadsworth Pub.

— Telecourse for Writing & Reporting News. 3rd ed. (Mass Communication). 1999. pap., student ed. 21.00 (*0-534-55983-2*) Wadsworth Pub.

— Vascular Trauma. 2nd ed. (C). 2000. text. write for info. (*0-7216-4071-0*, W B Saunders Co) Harcrt Hlth Sci Grp.

— Velvet. 1998. per. 6.50 (*0-671-00046-2*, Pocket Books) PB.

— Writing & Reporting News. (Mass Communication Ser.). 1993. mass mkt., wbk. ed. 16.50 (*0-534-19076-6*) Wadsworth Pub.

— Writing & Reporting News. 2nd ed. (Mass Communication Ser.). 1996. wbk. ed. 19.50 (*0-534-50880-4*) Wadsworth Pub.

Rich, ed. Housing & Com Dev Policy. (C). 1997. text 18.25 (*0-06-501396-4*) Addison-Wesley.

— Housing & Community Development Policy. (C). 1999. text. write for info. (*0-673-98564-4*) Addison-Wesley.

Rich & Berkow. News Writing: Student Telecourse. (Mass Communication Ser.). 1995. pap., student ed. 17.50 (*0-534-19079-0*) Wadsworth Pub.

Rich, A., ed. see Moore, G. R. & Pettigrew, G. W.

Rich, Adrienne. Adrienne Rich's Poetry & Prose. 2nd ed. Gelpi, Barbara C. & Gelpi, Albert, eds. LC 92-28640. (Critical Editions Ser.). 434p. (C). 1993. pap. text 12.50 (*0-393-96147-8*) Norton.

— An Atlas of the Difficult World: Poems 1988-1991. 64p. 1991. pap. 10.00 (*0-393-30831-6*) Norton.

— Blood, Bread & Poetry. 1994. pap. 11.95 (*0-393-31162-7*) Norton.

— Collected Early Poems: 1950-1970. 464p. 1995. pap. 15.00 (*0-393-31385-9*) Norton.

— Dark Fields of the Republic: Poems, 1991-1995. 80p. 1995. pap. 10.00 incl. audio (*0-393-31398-0*, Norton Paperbks) Norton.

— Dark Fields of the Republic: Poems, 1991-1995. LC 95-2272. 80p. 1995. 25.00 (*0-393-03868-8*) Norton.

— The Dream of a Common Language: Poems 1974-1977. 88p. 1993. pap. 10.95 (*0-393-31033-7*) Norton.

— Driving into the Wreck: Poems, 1971-1972. 1994. pap. 10.00 (*0-393-31163-5*) Norton.

— The Facts of a Doorframe: Poems Selected & New: 1950-1984. 360p. 1994. pap. 13.95 (*0-393-31075-2*) Norton.

— French in Thirty-Two Lessons. (Gimmick Ser.). 1979. pap. 10.95 (*0-393-04531-5*) Norton.

***Rich, Adrienne.** Midnight Salvage: Poems 1995-1998. LC 98-19293. 96p. 1999. pap. 22.00 (*0-393-04682-6*) Norton.

Rich, Adrienne. Midnight Salvage: Poems 1995-1998. 96p. 1999. pap. 11.00 (*0-393-31984-9*, Norton Paperbks) Norton.

— Of Woman Born: Motherhood As Experience & Institution. 352p. 1995. pap. 14.95 (*0-393-31284-4*, Norton Paperbks) Norton.

— On Lies, Secrets & Silence: Selected Prose, 1966-1978. 320p. 1995. pap. 13.95 (*0-393-31285-2*, Norton Paperbks) Norton.

— Sources. deluxe ed. LC 83-81462. (Illus.). 48p. (Orig.). 1983. 225.00 (*0-940592-15-0*); pap. 19.00 (*0-940592-16-9*) Heyeck Pr.

— Time's Power: Poems 1985-1988. 1989. pap. 9.95 (*0-393-30575-9*) Norton.

— What Is Found There? Notebooks on Poetry & Politics. LC 93-9912. 1993. 20.00 (*0-393-03565-4*) Norton.

— What Is Found There? Notebooks on Poetry & Politics. 320p. 1994. pap. 11.00 (*0-393-31246-1*) Norton.

— A Wild Patience Has Taken Me This Far: Poems 1978-1981. 1981. 12.95 (*0-393-01494-0*) Norton.

— A Wild Patience Has Taken Me This Far: Poems 1978-1981. 72p. 1993. pap. 10.00 (*0-393-31037-X*) Norton.

— Your Native Land, Your Life. 128p. 1993. reprint ed. pap. 10.00 (*0-393-31082-5*) Norton.

Rich, Adrienne, ed. see Lehman, David.

Rich, Adrienne, tr. see Alarcon, Francisco X.

R

R

Rich, Adrienne C. Change of World. LC 72-144754. (Yale Series of Younger Poets: No. 48). reprint ed. 18.00 (*0-404-53848-7*) AMS Pr.

Rich, Alan. American Pioneers: Ives to Cage & Beyond. (20th Century Composers Ser.). (Illus.). 240p. (Orig.). (C). 1995. pap. 19.95 (*0-7148-3173-5*, Pub. by Phaidon Press) Phaidon Pr.

— George Frideric Handel: Play by Play; The Complete Water Music. LC 96-15448. 160p. 1996. 25.00 incl. cd-rom (*0-06-263558-1*) Harper SF.

— Romantics - Play by Play: Symphonie Fantastique, Opus 14, Orchestre Revolutionnaire Et... LC 96-15447. 160p. 1996. 25.00 (*0-06-263559-X*) Harper SF.

Rich, Alan, text. George Frideric Handel: The Complete Water Music. (Play by Play Ser.). 1996. 25.00 (*0-614-96871-2*) Harper SF.

— The Romantics: Symphonie Fantastique. (Play by Play Ser.). 1996. 25.00 (*0-614-96872-0*) Harper SF.

Rich, Andrea & Hitt, Katherine. The Woodcuts of Andrea Rich. deluxe limited ed. (Illus.). 96p. 1998. 300.00 (*0-9652575-2-5*, Pub. by Many Names) Bookpeople.

Rich, Anne J. Instructor's Manual to Accompany Maher - Stickney - Weil, Managerial Accounting, 5th Ed. 5th ed. 199p. (C). 1994. pap. text 36.75 (*0-03-098474-2*) Dryden Pr.

***Rich, Annette.** Botanical Embroidery. (Craft Ser.). (Illus.). 2000. 24.95 (*1-86351-242-X*) Sally Milner.

Rich, Annette. Wildflower Embroidery. (Illus.). 104p. 1995. pap. 14.95 (*1-86351-141-5*, Pub. by Sally Milner) Sterling.

Rich, Anthony. Dictionnaire des Antiquites Romaines et Gracques. (FRE.). 740p. 1987. pap. 79.95 (*0-7859-8067-9*, 2851994255) Fr & Eur.

Rich, Antoinette. The Buddha's Secret. 130p. mass mkt. 4.95 (*1-896329-45-4*) Picasso Publ.

Rich, B. Ruby. Chick Flicks: Theories & Memories of the Feminist Film Movement. LC 98-12052. 448p. 1998. pap. 18.95 (*0-8223-2121-1*) Duke.

Rich, Barnabe. Faultes, Faults & Nothing Else but Faultes. LC 65-10396. 264p. 1978. reprint ed. 50.00 (*0-8201-1266-6*) Schol Facsimiles.

Rich, Barnaby. Newes from Virginia, the Lost Flocke Triumphant. LC 70-25514. (English Experience Ser.: No. 269). 16p. 1970. reprint ed. 15.00 (*90-221-0269-6*) Walter J Johnson.

— A Path-Way to Military Practice. LC 75-25920. (English Experience Ser.: No. 177). 88p. 1969. reprint ed. 20.00 (*90-221-0177-0*) Walter J Johnson.

Rich, Barnett. Review of Elementary Mathematics. (Schaum's Outline Ser.). (Orig.). 1977. pap. text 11.95 (*0-07-052260-X*) McGraw.

— Schaum's Outline of Geometry. 2nd ed. (Outline Ser.). 322p. (C). 1989. pap. 14.95 (*0-07-052246-4*) McGraw.

— Schaum's Outline of Review of Elementary Mathematics. 2nd ed. LC 97-8029. (Illus.). 288p. (C). 1997. pap. 15.95 (*0-07-052279-0*) McGraw.

— Schaum's Outline of Theory & Problems of Elementary Algebra. 2nd rev. ed. LC 92-18533. 389p. (C). 1993. pap. 15.95 (*0-07-052262-6*) McGraw.

— Schaum's Outline of Theory & Problems of Geometry. 3rd rev. ed. 322p. 1999. pap. 15.95 (*0-07-052766-0*, Schaums Outlne) McGraw-Hill Prof.

Rich, Beatrice. ABCDEFGHIJKLMNOPQRSTUVWXYZ in English & French. LC 81-20838. (Illus.). 64p. (J). (gr. k-2). 1983. lib. bdg. 15.95 (*0-87460-353-6*) Lion Bks.

Rich, Ben R. & Janos, Leo. Skunk Works. (Illus.). 400p. 1996. pap. 13.95 (*0-316-74300-3*) Little.

Rich, Bennett M. The Presidents & Civil Disorder, 42. LC 79-26839. (Institute for Government Research of the Brookings Institution, Studies in Administration Ser.: No. 42). 235p. 1980. reprint ed. lib. bdg. 65.00 (*0-313-22299-1*, RIPD) Greenwood.

Rich, Bill & Nielsen, Rick. Guitars of the Stars: Rick Nielsen, Vol. 1. (Illus.). 180p. 1993. 39.95 (*0-9635279-0-8*) GOTS Pub.

Rich, Bruce. Mortgaging the Earth: The World Bank, Environmental Impoverishment, & the Crisis of Development. LC 93-3848. 384p. 1995. pap. 16.00 (*0-8070-4707-4*) Beacon Pr.

Rich, Buddy. Buddy Rich - Jazz Legend, 1917-1987: Transcriptions & Analysis of the World's Greatest Drummer. (Illus.). 1997. pap. text 16.95 (*0-7692-1690-0*) Wrner Bros.

Rich, Buddy & Adler, Henry. Buddy Rich's Modern Interpretation of Snare Drum Rudiments. (Illus.). 100p. 1942. pap. 12.95 (*0-8256-1003-6*, AM36419) Music Sales.

Rich C & Crawford,R.D.L, C. & Crawford, R.D.L. Food Lover's Guide to Canning: Contemporary Recipes & Techniques. 1999. pap. 18.95 (*1-57990-118-2*) Lark Books.

Rich, C. B. Life, Times & Poetry of C. B. Rich. (Orig.). 1992. pap. 7.95 (*0-9633062-0-0*) Double Arrow.

— Memories from the Mountains. 200p. (Orig.). 1992. pap. 7.95 (*0-9633062-1-9*) Double Arrow.

Rich, Carol. Writing & Reporting the News: A Coaching Method. 2nd ed. (Mass Communication Ser.). (Illus.). 624p. (C). 1996. pap. 40.25 (*0-534-50879-0*) Wadsworth Pub.

Rich, Carole. Creating Online Media: A Guide to Research, Writing & Design on the Internet. LC 98-2963. 1998. 34.50 (*0-07-303415-0*) McGraw.

— Writing & Reporting News: A Coaching Method. 3rd ed. (Mass Communication). 1999. pap., wbk. ed. 21.75 (*0-534-55982-4*) Wadsworth Pub.

— Writing & Reporting News: A Coaching Method. 3rd ed. LC 99-12602. (Mass Communication Ser.). 640p. 1999. mass mkt. 63.95 (*0-534-55980-8*) Wadsworth Pub.

— Writing & Reporting the News: A Coaching Method. 590p. (C). 1993. mass mkt. 33.75 (*0-534-19074-X*) Wadsworth Pub.

Rich, Charles. Charles Rich: Autobiography. LC 90-52664. 143p. (Orig.). 1991. pap. 9.95 (*0-932506-80-1*) St Bedes Pubns.

— How to Become Really Rich: The Facsimile of His Original & Annotated Notes on the Song of Songs. LC 96-53167. 1997. 7.95 (*1-879007-23-1*) St Bedes Pubns.

— Reflections. LC 86-17732. 131p. 1986. pap. 10.95 (*0-932506-49-6*) St Bedes Pubns.

Rich, Charles & Waters, Richard C., eds. Readings in Artificial Intelligence & Software Engineering. LC 86-18627. (Illus.). 624p. (Orig.). 1986. pap. text 34.95 (*0-934613-12-5*) Morgan Kaufmann.

Rich, Chris. The Book of Paper Cutting: A Complete Guide to All the Techniques with More than 100 Project Ideas. LC 92-21536. (Illus.). 128p. 1994. pap. 14.95 (*0-8069-0286-8*) Sterling.

— Stained Glass Basics: Techniques, Tools, Projects. (Illus.). 128p. 1997. pap. text 14.95 (*0-8069-4877-9*) Sterling.

Rich, Chris & Crawford, Lucy C. The Food Lover's Guide to Canning: Contemporary Recipes & Techniques. LC 97-14631. (Illus.). 128p. 1997. 24.95 (*1-887374-46-9*) Lark Books.

Rich, Chris, jt. auth. see Morgenthal, Deborah.

Rich, Chris, ed. see Clayton, Peirce.

Rich, Chris, ed. see Cushing, Val M.

Rich, Chris, ed. see Eberle, Bettina.

Rich, Chris, ed. see Mallow, Judy M.

Rich, Chris, ed. see Murashima, Kumiko.

Rich, Chris, ed. see Owens-Celli, Morgyn G.

Rich, Chris, ed. see Rosenstein, Mark.

Rich, Clayton, et al, eds. From Pragmatism to Vision: Leadership & Values in Academic Health Centers. 150p. (Orig.). 1991. pap. 14.95 (*1-879694-02-6*) AAH Ctrs.

Rich, Curt. Drive to Survive. (Illus.). 128p. 1998. pap. 14.95 (*0-7603-0525-0*) MBI Pubg.

Rich, Cynthia. Desert Years: Undreaming the American Dream. LC 89-35667. 120p. (Orig.). 1989. pap. 7.95 (*0-933216-67-X*) Spinsters Ink.

Rich, Cynthia, jt. auth. see Macdonald, Barbara.

***Rich, D.** Denver Hiking Guide. (Illus.). 1999. pap. 12.95 (*1-889593-58-3*) ThreeD Pr.

Rich, Daniel, jt. ed. see Byren, John.

Rich, Daniel, jt. ed. see Byrne, John.

Rich, Daniel C. Degas. (Masters of Art Ser.). (Illus.). 128p. (Orig.). 1985. 24.95 (*0-8109-0829-8*, Pub. by Abrams) Time Warner.

— Henri Rousseau. LC 75-86436. (Museum of Modern Art Publications in Reprint). (Illus.). 1969. reprint ed. 17.95 (*0-405-01543-7*) Ayer.

Rich, Dave. Boulderides: The Mountain Biking Guide to Boulder, Colorado. 2nd ed. (Fat Tire Guides Ser.). (Orig.). 1995. pap. 12.95 (*0-9634607-1-4*) ThreeD Pr.

— The Denver Hiking Guide: 40 Trails Within 45 Minutes. 96p. (Orig.). 1996. pap. write for info. (*0-9634607-7-3*) ThreeD Pr.

— Denverides: The Mountain Bike Guide to Denver. 2nd ed. (Fat Tire Guides Ser.). 62p. 1995. pap. 12.95 (*0-9634607-2-2*) ThreeD Pr.

— Tellurides: A Mountain Biking Guide to Telluride, Colorado. 1994. pap. 11.95 (*0-943727-18-9*) Wayfinder Pr.

Rich, Dave & Swenson, Pete. Pedro's Simple Trailside Repair. 2nd ed. 1995. pap. 6.95 (*0-9634607-4-9*) ThreeD Pr.

Rich, Dave, ed. see Daniel, Alice.

Rich, Dave, ed. see Judd, Janis.

Rich, Dave, ed. see St. John, Bill.

Rich, David. Breckenridge Mountain Biking & Hiking Guide Map. Date not set. pap. 8.95 (*0-9634607-3-0*) ThreeD Pr.

— The Kinemage Supplement & Introduction to Protein Structure: For Windows 3.1, 3.5 Disk. 930910p. Date not set. write for info. (*0-8153-1602-X*) Garland.

***Rich, David A., Jr.** Zu True: An Urban Adventure. 1999. pap. 12.95 (*0-9672664-0-8*, 2/101) LazerBks.

Rich, David C. The Industrial Geography of Australia. Thompson, Ian, ed. (Croom Helm Industrial Geography Ser.). 350p. 1987. 75.00 (*0-7099-2214-0*, Pub. by C Helm) Routldge.

Rich, David Z. Contemporary Economics: A Unifying Approach. LC 85-16762. 208p. 1985. 57.95 (*0-275-92033-X*, C2033, Praeger Pubs) Greenwood.

— The Dynamics of Knowledge: A Contemporary View, 36. LC 87-36100. (Contributions in Philosophy Ser.: No. 36). 240p. 1988. 55.00 (*0-313-26102-4*, RDY/, Greenwood Pr) Greenwood.

— The Economic Theory of Growth & Development. LC 93-23474. 272p. 1994. 59.95 (*0-275-94687-8*, Praeger Pubs) Greenwood.

— The Economics of International Trade: An Independent View. LC 91-33600. 216p. 1992. 59.95 (*0-89930-753-1*, RIT, Quorum Bks) Greenwood.

— The Economics of Welfare: A Contemporary Analysis. LC 89-30899. 212p. 1989. 62.95 (*0-275-93309-1*, C3309, Praeger Pubs) Greenwood.

***Rich, David Z.** Order & Disorder. 288p. 2001. 64.00 (*0-275-96787-5*, Praeger Pubs) Greenwood.

Rich, David Z., compiled by. Crisis Theory. LC 96-53945. 248p. 1997. 62.95 (*0-275-95722-5*, Praeger Pubs) Greenwood.

Rich, Deike, jt. auth. see Begg, Ean.

Rich, Diana, ed. see Jarvis, Frederick D.

Rich, Diane. In the Beginning - My ABC Book. Koger, Dorothy P. & Battle, Jacqueline M., eds. (Illus.). 50p. write for info. (*1-882821-24-6*) DPK Pubns.

Rich, Doris. The Magnificent Moisants: Champions of Early Flight. LC 98-6876. 264p. 1998. 24.95 (*1-56098-860-6*) Smithsonian.

Rich, Doris L. Amelia Earhart: A Biography. (Illus.). 322p. 1996. pap. 16.95 (*1-56098-725-1*) Smithsonian.

— Queen Bess: Daredevil Aviator. (Illus.). 172p. 1995. pap. 14.95 (*1-56098-618-2*) Smithsonian.

Rich, Dorothy. Helping Your Child Succeed in School: With Activities for Children Aged 5 Through 11. Martin, Margery, ed. (Illus.). 50p. (Orig.). (C). 1993. pap. text 15.00 (*1-56806-385-7*) DIANE Pub.

— Learning & Working: Basics for Children. 96p. (Orig.). 1996. pap. 15.95 (*0-8106-2002-2*, 2002-2) NEA.

— MegaSkills. expanded rev. ed. LC 97-44833. 384p. 1998. pap. 14.00 (*0-395-87757-1*, Mariner Bks) HM.

— Megaskills Moments for Teachers: How-To's for Building Personal & Professional Effectiveness For The Classroom & Beyond. LC 98-24154. 1998. pap. 11.95 (*0-8106-2006-5*) NEA.

— Schools & Families: Issues & Actions. 128p. 1987. pap. 11.95 (*0-8106-0276-8*) NEA.

— What Do We Say? What Do We Do? LC 97-7858. 240p. (J). 11.95 (*0-312-85433-1*, Pub. by Tor Bks) St Martin.

Rich, E. E., ed. Copy-Book of Letters Outward Etc. Begins 29 May, 1680, Ends 5 July, 1687. (Hudson's Bay Record Society Publications: Vol. 11). 1972. reprint ed. pap. 65.00 (*0-8115-3185-6*) Periodicals Srv.

— The Letters of John McLoughlin in from Fort Vancouver to the Governor & Committee: First Series, 1825-1838. (Hudson's Bay Record Society Publications: Vol. 4). 1969. reprint ed. pap. 65.00 (*0-8115-3178-3*) Periodicals Srv.

— The Letters of John McLoughlin in from Fort Vancouver to the Governor & Committee: Second Series, 1839-1844. (Hudson's Bay Record Society Publications: Vol. 6). 1969. reprint ed. pap. 65.00 (*0-8115-3180-5*) Periodicals Srv.

— The Letters of John McLoughlin in from Fort Vancouver to the Governor & Committee: Third Series, 1844-1846. (Hudson's Bay Record Society Publications: Vol. 7). 1969. reprint ed. pap. 65.00 (*0-8115-3181-3*) Periodicals Srv.

— Minutes of the Hudson's Bay Company, 1671-1674. (Hudson's Bay Record Society Publications: Vol. 5). 1974. reprint ed. pap. 65.00 (*0-8115-3179-1*) Periodicals Srv.

— Minutes of the Hudson's Bay Company, 1679-1684, Pt. 1. (Hudson's Bay Record Society Publications: Vol. 8). 1974. reprint ed. pap. 65.00 (*0-8115-3182-1*) Periodicals Srv.

— Part of Dispatch from George Simpson, Esquire, Governor of Ruperts Land, to the Governor & Committee of the Hudson's Bay Company, London, March 1, 1829: Continued & Completed March 24 & June 5, 1829. (Hudson's Bay Record Society Publications: Vol. 10). 1974. reprint ed. pap. 65.00 (*0-8115-3184-8*) Periodicals Srv.

Rich, Elaine, ed. Machine Translation in Japan. (JTEC Panel Reports). vi, 142p. 1992. pap. write for info. (*1-883712-17-3*, JTEC) Intl Tech Res.

Rich, Elaine & Knight, Kevin. Artificial Intelligence. 2nd ed. (Artificial Intelligence Ser.). 640p. (C). 1990. 90.63 (*0-07-052263-4*) McGraw.

Rich, Elaine S. Pondered in Her Heart: Hannah's Book: Inside & Outside. LC 98-84134. 136p. 1998. pap. 12.95 (*0-945530-20-X*) Wordsworth KS.

Rich, Elaine S., ed. Prayers for Everyday. LC 90-80749. 95p. 1990. pap. 6.95 (*0-87303-137-7*) Faith & Life.

Rich, Elizabeth H., ed. Funding in Aging: A Guide to Giving by Foundations, Corporations, & Charitable Organizations. LC 96-232388. 294p. 1996. 95.00 (*0-87954-663-8*, AGED) Foundation Ctr.

Rich, Everett. The Heritage of Kansas. 1960. pap. 8.95 (*0-686-14877-0*) Flint Hills.

Rich, Everett, ed. The Heritage of Kansas. 1960. pap. 5.00 (*0-686-00367-5*) AG Pr.

Rich, Foster. Prayers from the Heart. 144p. 1994. 19.00 (*0-06-062847-2*, Pub. by Harper SF) HarpC.

Rich, Frank. Avenging Angel. 1993. mass mkt. 3.50 (*0-373-63607-5*, 1-63607-5) Harlequin Bks.

— Boris Aronson: Stage Design as Visual Metaphor. (Illus.). 24p. 1989. 8.00 (*0-915171-14-7*) Katonah Gal.

— Day of Judgement. (Jake Strait Ser.). 1994. per. 3.50 (*0-373-63609-1*, 1-63609-1) Harlequin Bks.

— The Devil Knocks. (Jake Strait Ser.). 1993. mass mkt. 3.50 (*0-373-63608-3*, 1-63608-3) Harlequin Bks.

***Rich, Frank.** Ghost Light. 352p. 2000. 24.95 (*0-679-45299-0*) Random.

Rich, Frank. Hot Seat: Theater Criticism for the New York Times, 1980-1993. LC 98-22683. 800p. 1998. 39.95 (*0-679-45300-8*) Random.

— Twist of Cain. (Jake Strait Ser.). 1994. per. 4.99 (*0-373-63610-5*, 1-63610-9) Harlequin Bks.

Rich, Frederic C. The Ivy Club, 1879-1979. Snyder, Jon R. & Scheuch, W. Allen, II, eds. (Illus.). 1979. 9.95 (*0-934756-00-7*) Ivy Club.

Rich, Fredrick J., ed. Geology of the Black Hills, South Dakota & Wyoming. 2nd ed. (Illus.). 292p. 1986. pap. 31.25 (*0-913312-81-9*) Am Geol.

Rich, G. Proceedings of the 1st Oxford-Waterloo Research Seminar Vol. 2: Planning & Design in Britian & Canada. A Comparison of Education & Practice. (C). 1987. 40.00 (*0-7855-3826-7*, Pub. by Oxford Polytechnic) St Mut.

Rich, George. Common Bible Questions of Our Day. (New Life Ser.). 24p. (Orig.). 1991. teacher ed. 1.99 (*0-87227-164-1*, RBP5190); pap. text, student ed. 1.99 (*0-87227-160-9*, RBP5191) Reg Baptist.

— Famous Interviews with Jesus Christ. (New Life Ser.). 24p. (YA). 1991. teacher ed. 1.99 (*0-87227-165-X*, RBP5192); pap. text, student ed. 1.99 (*0-87227-157-9*, RBP5193) Reg Baptist.

— How to Have a Successful Marriage. (New Life Ser.). 22p. 1991. pap., teacher ed. 1.99 (*0-87227-163-3*, RBP5188) Reg Baptist.

— How to Have a Successful Marriage. (New Life Ser.). 22p. 1995. pap. text, student ed. 1.99 (*0-87227-154-4*, RBP5189) Reg Baptist.

— Important Things God Can Do for You. (New Life Ser.). 24p. 1991. pap., teacher ed. 1.99 (*0-87227-166-8*, RBP5194); pap., student ed. 1.99 (*0-87227-158-7*, RBP5195) Reg Baptist.

— The Professional Practice of Urban & Rural Planning in Canada. LC 92-41583. 172p. 1993. pap. 59.95 (*0-7734-1942-X*) E Mellen.

— What's Bothering You? (New Life Ser.). 28p. 1991. teacher ed. 1.99 (*0-87227-162-5*, RBP5186); pap. text, student ed. 1.99 (*0-87227-155-2*, RBP5187) Reg Baptist.

— You Can Make the Right Decision. (New Life Ser.). 24p. 1992. pap., teacher ed. 1.99 (*0-87227-168-4*, RBP5198); pap., student ed. 1.99 (*0-87227-159-5*, RBP5199) Reg Baptist.

— Your Relationship to God. (New Life Ser.). 24p. 1991. pap., teacher ed. 1.99 (*0-87227-167-6*, RBP5196); pap., student ed. 1.99 (*0-87227-156-0*, RBP5197) Reg Baptist.

Rich, Gerald. Toxic, Hazardous, & Title 3 Air Pollutants. 1995. 29.95 (*0-934165-55-6*, 6556X) Gulf Pub.

Rich, Gerald A. Hiring: Getting Hired in the Environmental Field. 228p. 1994. 19.95 (*0-934165-54-8*, 65549) Gulf Pub.

— Toxic, Hazardous, & Title 3 Air Pollutants. 320p. 1995. 29.95 (*0-934165-56-4*, 6556X) Gulf Pub.

Rich, Harry A., ed. & illus. see Hogan, Julia R.

Rich, Hilary. How to Be a Great Catch. 256p. (Orig.). 1995. mass mkt. 4.99 (*0-380-77841-6*, Avon Bks) Morrow Avon.

Rich, Hilary & Kravitz, Helaina. A Perfect Marriage. LC 97-71173. 326p. 1997. pap. 16.95 (*0-02-861729-0*, Alpha Ref) Macmillan Gen Ref.

Rich, Ivan N. & Lappin, Terence R., eds. Molecular, Cellular, & Developmental Biology of Erythropoietin & Erythropoiesis. LC 94-10689. (Annals Ser.: Vol. 718). 376p. 1994. pap. 100.00 (*0-89766-838-3*) NY Acad Sci.

Rich, J. David. Myths of the Tribe: When Religion, Economics, Government & Ethics Converge. LC 93-17732. 296p. (C). 1993. 32.95 (*0-87975-824-4*) Prometheus Bks.

Rich, J. W., ed. see Dio Cocceianus, Cassius.

Rich, Jack C. Materials & Methods of Sculpture. (Illus.). 512p. pap. 13.95 (*0-486-25742-8*) Dover.

— Sculpture in Wood. (Illus.). xvi, 155p. 1992. reprint ed. pap. 8.95 (*0-486-27109-9*) Dover.

Rich, Jacqueline & Coltman, Virginia. Summary & Recommendations: Clean Water Act Section 404 Discharge of Dredged & Fill Materials & Section 401 Water Quality Certification Programs in Arizona. 200p. 1991. spiral bd. 25.00 (*1-884320-05-8*) ASU Herberger Ctr.

***Rich, Jamie S.** Cut My Hair: An Illustrated Novel. (Illus.). 248p. 2000. pap. 14.95 (*0-9700387-0-4*) Crazyfish.

***Rich, Jamie S., ed.** Soulwind: The Kid from Planet Earth. 128p. 2000. pap. 8.50 (*0-9667127-4-9*, Pub. by Oni Pr Inc) LPC Group.

Rich, Jamie S., ed. see Bendis, Brian Michael.

Rich, Jamie S., ed. see Brereton, Dan.

Rich, Jamie S., ed. see Clugston-Major, Chynna.

Rich, Jamie S., ed. see Dini, Paul.

Rich, Jamie S., ed. see Gaiman, Neil.

Rich, Jamie S., ed. see Morse, Scott.

Rich, Jamie S., ed. see Rucka, Greg.

Rich, Jamie S., ed. see Watson, Andi.

Rich, Jamie S., ed. see Winick, Judd.

Rich, Jan G. & Hurlbut, David. Free Trade with Mexico: What's in It for Texas? (U. S. - Mexican Policy Reports: No. 1). 80p. 1992. pap. 10.00 (*0-89940-310-7*) LBJ Sch Pub Aff.

Rich, Jan Gilbreath. Planning the Border's Future: The Mexican - U. S. Integrated Border Environmental Plan. (U. S. - Mexican Occasional Papers: Vol. 1). 54p. (C). 1992. pap. 7.00 (*0-89940-584-3*) LBJ Sch Pub Aff.

Rich, Jane K., ed. see Kinsley, Jessie C.

Rich, Jason. Age of Empires Strategies & Secrets: Unofficial. LC 97-61894. 240p. 1997. pap. text 14.99 (*0-7821-2234-5*) Sybex.

— As If! The Not So Clueless Alicia Silverstone. LC 97-168750. 176p. 1997. mass mkt. 5.99 (*1-57297-265-3*) Blvd Books.

— Everything College Survival Book. LC 97-7844. (Illus.). x, 310 p. (YA). 1997. pap. text 12.95 (*1-55850-720-5*) Adams Media.

***Rich, Jason.** The Everything Ghost Book: True Stories of Haunted Houses, Phantom Spirits, Unexplained Mysteries & More. (Everything Ser.). (Illus.). 304p. 2000. pap. 12.95 (*1-58062-397-2*) Adams Media.

— The Everything Guide to Las Vegas: Hotels, Casinos, Restaurants, Major Family Attractions & More. (Everything Ser.). (Illus.). 304p. 2000. pap. 12.95 (*1-58062-438-3*) Adams Media.

— The Everything Guide to Walt Disney World, Universal Studio & Greater Orlando. LC 98-23289. (Illus.). xviii, 318p. 1999. 12.95 (*1-58062-053-1*) Adams Media.

— The Everything Guide to Walt Disney World, Universal Studios & Greater Orlando. 2nd ed. (Illus.). 304p. 2000. pap. 12.95 (*1-58062-404-9*) Adams Media.

Rich, Jason. First Job, Great Job: America's Hottest Business Leaders Share Their Secrets. 1996. 15.95 (*0-02-861285-X*) Macmillan.

***Rich, Jason.** Legend of Zelda: Ocarina of Time Pathways to Adventure. LC 98-89151. 112p. 1998. pap. 9.99 (*0-7821-2478-X*) Sybex.

Rich, Jason. Pokemon: Pathways to Adventure. LC 98-89150. (Illus.). 102p. (J). (gr. 3-7). 1998. pap. 9.99 (*0-7821-2503-4*) Sybex.

— Virtua Racing: Official Driver's Strategy Guide. (Illus.). 96p. (Orig.). 1994. pap. 9.95 (*0-614-06069-9*) Brady Pub.

Rich, Jason R. Civilization II Strategies & Secrets. 3rd ed. LC 96-68698. 312p. 1996. pap. text 16.99 (*0-7821-1922-0*) Sybex.

An Asterisk (*) at the beginning of an entry indicates that the title is appearing for the first time.

***Rich, Jason R.** Donkey Kong N64 Pathways to Adventure, 2 vols. (Illus.). (J). 1999. pap. 9.99 (*0-7821-2723-1*) Sybex.
Rich, Jason R. Job Hunting for the Utterly Confused. LC 97-44036. (Utterly Confused Ser.). 304p. 1998. pap. 14.95 (*0-07-052665-6*) McGraw.
— The Official Rocket Science Guide to Cadillacs & Dinosaurs. (LAN Times Ser.). (Illus.). 208p. 1995. pap. text 16.95 (*0-07-882134-7*) McGraw.
— Resident Evil 2: Ultimate Strategy Guide. LC 98-84016. 144p. 1998. pap. text 9.99 (*0-7821-2265-5*) Sybex.
***Rich, Jason R.** Unofficial Guide to Marketing Your Business Online. 2000. pap. 16.99 (*0-7645-6268-1*) IDG Bks.
Rich, Jillian, jt. auth. see Rawlins, George.
Rich, Jim. Photoshop B&W Scanners, & Curves. 16p. 1996. 9.00 (*0-9647627-2-2*) Rich & Assocs.
***Rich, Jim.** Photoshop Grayscale Book. 2000. pap. 25.00 (*0-9647627-3-0*) Rich & Assocs.
Rich, Jim, jt. auth. see Bozek, Sandy.
Rich, John. The City in Late Antiquity. 216p. (C). 1996. pap. 24.99 (*0-415-14431-0*) Routledge.
Rich, John & Shipley, Graham. War & Society in the Greek World. (Leicester-Nottingham Studies in Ancient Society). (Illus.). 288p. (C). 1995. pap. 27.99 (*0-415-12166-3*, C0202) Routledge.
— War & Society in the Roman World. (Leicester-Nottingham Studies in Ancient Society). 320p. (C). 1995. pap. 27.99 (*0-415-12167-1*, C0218) Routledge.
Rich, John & Shipley, Graham, eds. War & Society in the Roman World. LC 92-36698. (Leicester-Nottingham Studies in Ancient Society: Vol. 5). 320p. (C). (gr. 13). 1993. 80.00 (*0-415-06644-1*) Routledge.
Rich, John & Wallace-Hadrill, Andrew, eds. City & Country in the Ancient World. (Leicester-Nottingham Studies in Ancient Society). (Illus.). 324p. (C). 1992. pap. 27.99 (*0-415-08223-4*, A7623) Routledge.
Rich, John M. Chief Seattle's Unanswered Challenge. 61p. 1977. reprint ed. pap. 9.95 (*0-87770-072-9*) Ye Galleon.
— Innovations in Education: Reformers & Their Critics. 6th ed. 310p. (C). 1991. pap. text 55.00 (*0-205-13299-5*) Allyn.
Rich, John M. & DeVitis, Joseph L. Theories of Moral Development. 2nd ed. LC 94-21565. 164p. (C). 1994. 36.95 (*0-398-05924-1*); pap. 24.95 (*0-398-06061-4*) C C Thomas.
Rich, John M., jt. auth. see DeVitis, Joseph L.
Rich, John Martin. Foundations of Education. (C). 1991. text 55.60 (*0-675-21265-0*, Merrill Coll) P-H.
Rich-Jones, W., ed. Vetus Registrum Sarisberiense, Alias Dictum Registrum S. Osmundi Episcopi, Register of St. Osmund, 2 vols. (Rolls Ser.: No. 78). 1974. reprint ed. 140.00 (*0-8115-1148-0*) Periodicals Srv.
Rich, Katherine Russell. The Red Devil: To Hell with Cancer . . . And Back. LC 99-25516. 256p. 1999. 22.00 (*0-609-60321-3*) Random Hse Value.
***Rich, Katherine Russell.** The Red Devil: To Hell with Cancer--And Back. 256p. 2000. pap. 12.95 (*0-609-80324-7*) Crown Pub Group.
Rich, Kim. Johnny's Girl: A Daughter's Memoir of Growing up in Alaska's Underworld. LC 99-23087. (Illus.). 1999. pap. 15.95 (*0-88240-524-1*) Gr Arts Ctr Pub.
Rich, Laurie. Trying Again. Date not set. write for info. (*0-393-03515-8*) Norton.
Rich, Laurie A. When Pregnancy Isn't Perfect: A Layperson's Guide to Complications in Pregnancy. 3rd ed. 349p. 1996. reprint ed. pap. 12.00 (*0-9654985-0-6*) Larata Pr.
Rich, Laurie J. Apologia for Vietnam. LC 95-92675. (Illus.). 76p. (Orig.). 1995. pap. 20.00 (*0-9649071-0-0*) Sheephrdr Wom.
— Herding Sheep in Northern Utah. LC 96-92147. (Illus.). 152p. (Orig.). 1998. per. write for info. (*0-9649071-1-9*) Sheephrdr Wom.
Rich, Lawrence. The Narrative of Antonio Munoz Molina: Self-Conscious Realism & "El Desencanto" LC 98-4951. (Currents in Comparative Romance Languages & Literatures Ser.: Vol. 78). XII, 135p. (C). 1999. text 38.95 (*0-8204-4080-9*, 40809) P Lang Pubng.
Rich, Liddy. Odyssey Book of Houseplants. 1990. pap. 19.95 (*0-9625702-0-6*) Plant Odyssey Pr.
Rich, Linda G., et al. Neighborhood: A State of Mind. LC 81-5992. (Illus.). 152p. 1981. 30.00 (*0-8018-2558-X*); pap. 16.95 (*0-8018-2559-8*) Johns Hopkins.
Rich, Linvil G. High Performance Aerated Lagoon Systems. Anderson, William C., ed. LC 98-31902. (Illus.). 224p. 1998. 99.95 (*1-883767-27-X*) Am Acad Environ.
— Unit Operations of Sanitary Engineering. LC 61-15410. (C). 1961. pap. 20.00 (*0-686-11818-9*) Rich SC.
— Unit Processes of Sanitary Engineering. LC 63-14067. (C). 1963. pap. 20.00 (*0-686-15000-7*) Rich SC.
Rich, Liz, et al, eds. National Guide to Funding for the Environment & Animal Welfare. 4th ed. 527p. 1998. 95.00 (*0-87954-770-7*, FIE4) Foundation Ctr.
Rich, Lorraine S. Charleston in Poetry & Photographs. large type ed. Sirigos, Nancy S., ed. LC 98-211410. (Illus.). 46p. 1998. 18.95 (*0-9662776-0-0*) Pen to Paper.
Rich, Louise D. The Coast of Maine: An Informal History & Guide. LC 93-30612. (Illus.). 400p. 1993. reprint ed. pap. 14.95 (*0-89272-342-4*) Down East.
— Happy the Land. LC 98-8791. 264p. 1998. reprint ed. pap. 12.95 (*0-89272-452-8*) Down East.
— Innocence under the Elms. 286p. 1983. reprint ed. pap. 7.95 (*0-940160-22-6*) Parnassus Imprints.
— My Neck of the Woods. LC 98-28401. 256p. 1998. reprint ed. pap. 12.95 (*0-89272-453-6*) Down East.
— Start of the Trail. 21.95 (*0-89190-726-2*) Amereon Ltd.
— We Took to the Woods. 24.95 (*0-89190-858-7*) Amereon Ltd.
— We Took to the Woods. 250p. 1992. reprint ed. lib. bdg. 18.95 (*0-89966-913-1*) Buccaneer Bks.
— We Took to the Woods. (Illus.). 322p. 1975. reprint ed. pap. 10.95 (*0-89272-016-6*) Down East.
Rich, Lynne. Everything Changes: In Gods Time: Grief & Its Other Side. LC 97-76497. 180p. 1997. pap. 15.95 (*1-888207-01-9*) LghtHeart Bks.
— Once Around the Wheel: Want to Go Again? LC 95-81030. 90p. (Orig.). 1995. pap. 12.99 (*1-888207-00-0*) LghtHeart Bks.
***Rich, M. B.** History of the First 100 Years in Woolrich, PA., 1830-1930. fac. ed. 233p. 2000. reprint ed. 32.50 (*0-7404-0049-5*) Higginson Bk Co.
Rich, M. Robert, et al, eds. Contemporary Southwest Art. 52p. 1988. 5.00 (*0-942746-14-7*) SUNYP R Gibson.
Rich, Malcolm C. & Brucar, Wayne E. The Central Panel System for Administrative Law Judges: A Survey of Seven States. LC 82-74139. 99p. 1983. lib. bdg. 47.95 (*0-313-27084-8*, U7084, Greenwood Pr) Greenwood.
Rich, Maria F. Who's Who in Opera: An International Biographical Directory of Singers, Conductors, Directors, Designers & Administers. 1976. 12.95 (*0-405-06652-X*, 19119) Ayer.
Rich, Marion K. A Song for All Seasons: Harmony in the Inner Life. 100p. (Orig.). 1992. pap. 7.99 (*0-8341-1446-1*) Beacon Hill.
Rich, Mark. Lifting. (Illus.). 58p. 1990. pap. 7.95 (*1-877655-02-3*) Wordcraft Oregon.
***Rich, Mark.** 100 Greatest Baby Boomer Toys. LC 99-68134. (Illus.). 208p. 2000. pap. 24.95 (*0-87341-880-8*, BOOM) Krause Pubns.
Rich, Martin, jt. auth. see Waye, Jerome D.
Rich, Marvin A., ed. Leukemia Reviews International, 2 vols., Vol. 1. LC 88-659642. (Illus.). 367p. 1983. reprint ed. pap. 113.80 (*0-7837-0620-0*, 204096500001) Bks Demand.
— Leukemia Reviews International, 2 vols., Vol. 2. LC 88-659642. (Illus.). 201p. 1984. reprint ed. pap. 57.30 (*0-7837-0621-9*) Bks Demand.
Rich, Marvin A., et al, eds. Breast Cancer: Origins, Detection & Treatment. (Developments in Oncology Ser.). 1986. text 120.50 (*0-89838-792-2*) Kluwer Academic.
— Breast Cancer: Progress in Biology, Clinical Management & Prevention. (Developments in Oncology Ser.). (C). 1989. text 118.50 (*0-7923-0507-8*) Kluwer Academic.
— Breast Cancer: Scientific & Clinical Progress. (C). 1988. text 190.00 (*0-89838-387-0*) Kluwer Academic.
— Understanding Breast Cancer: Clinical & Laboratory Concepts. LC 83-18981. (Illus.). 415p. reprint ed. pap. 128.70 (*0-7837-0673-1*, 204100800019) Bks Demand.
Rich, Marvin A. & Furmanski, Philip, eds. Biological Carcinogenesis. LC 82-4996. (Illus.). 320p. reprint ed. pap. 99.20 (*0-7837-0886-6*, 204119200019) Bks Demand.
Rich, Mary & Jose, Carol. Evil Web: A True Story of Cult Abuse & Courage. 260p. 1996. 22.95 (*0-88282-139-3*) New Horizon NJ.
Rich, Mary L. Courting Kate. 304p. 1997. mass mkt. 5.99 (*0-515-12048-0*, Jove) Berkley Pub.
— Heart's Folly. 320p. 1996. mass mkt. 5.99 (*0-515-11846-X*, Jove) Berkley Pub.
— The Tomboy. 304p. (Orig.). 1996. mass mkt. 4.99 (*0-515-11810-9*, Jove) Berkley Pub.
Rich, Mary P., ed. see Brown, Fern G.
Rich, Mary Perrotta, ed. Book Poems: Poems from National Children's Book Week, 1959-1998. LC 99-158017. (Illus.). 96p. (J). 1998. pap. 20.00 (*0-933633-05-X*) Child Bk Coun.
Rich, Meredith. Tender Offerings. LC 93-42074. 1994. 22.00 (*0-671-78883-3*) S&S Trade.
— Tender Offerings. large type ed. (Black Satin Romance Ser.). 496p. 1996. 27.99 (*1-86110-012-4*) Ulverscroft.
Rich, Michael D., jt. auth. see Gandara, Arturo.
Rich, Michael J. Federal Policymaking & the Poor: National Goals, Local Choices, & Distributional Outcomes. LC 93-7298. (Illus.). 424p. (C). 1993. text 47.50 (*0-691-08652-4*, Pub. by Princeton U Pr) Cal Prin Full Svc.
***Rich, Morton D.** The Dynamics of Tonal Shift in the Sonnet. LC 99-88988. (Studies in Comparative Literature: Vol. 31). 164p. 2000. text 79.95 (*0-7734-7777-2*) E Mellen.
Rich, Nancy B. The Flowering Dream: The Historical Saga of Carson McCullers. (Illus.). 131p. 1999. text 25.00 (*1-880849-14-3*) Chapel Hill NC.
Rich, Nelson G. & Gilligan, Lawrence G. The TI-85 Reference Guide. (Illus.). 112p. (Orig.). 1993. pap. 18.95 (*0-9626661-6-5*) Gilmar Pub.
— The TI-86/85 Reference Guide. unabridged ed. (Illus.). 192p. (C). 1997. pap. text 23.95 (*1-888808-01-2*) Gilmar Pub.
Rich, Neysa. Florida Real Estate Closings. 450p. 1991. ring bd. 90.00 (*0-409-27142-X*, MICHIE) LEXIS Pub.
— Florida Real Estate Closings. 1993. suppl. ed. 40.00 (*0-685-74288-1*, MICHIE) LEXIS Pub.
— Florida Real Estate Closings. 450p. 1994. ring bd. 90.00 (*0-614-05822-8*, MICHIE) LEXIS Pub.
Rich, Norman M. Great Power Diplomacy, 1815-1914. 502p. (C). 1991. 53.75 (*0-07-052254-5*) McGraw.
Rich, Norman M., jt. auth. see Wind, Gary G.
***Rich, P.** A Manual of Nail Disorders. 2001. write for info. (*1-84214-035-3*) Prthnon Pub.
Rich, P. A., jt. auth. see Scher, R. K.
Rich, P. J. Elixir of Empire: The English Public Schools, Ritualism, Freemasonry & Imperialism. 152p. (C). 1988. 80.00 (*0-7212-0759-6*, Pub. by Regency Pr GBR) St Mut.
Rich, P. V. New World Vultures with Old World Affinities. (Contributions to Vertebrate Evolution Ser.: Vol. 5). (Illus.). 1979. pap. 34.00 (*3-8055-0280-X*) S Karger.
Rich, Pamela E. & Tussing, Arlon R. The National Park System in Alaska: An Economic Impact Study. LC 73-620004. (ISER Reports: No. 35). (Illus.). 88p. 1973. pap. 2.00 (*0-88353-008-2*) U Alaska Inst Res.
Rich, Pat Vickers, jt. auth. see Rich, Thomas H. V.
Rich, Paul, ed. Latin America & Policy Studies. (Policy Studies Review: Vol. 15:2/3). 274p. 1998. pap. write for info. (*0-944285-51-1*) Pol Studies.
Rich, Paul B. Hope & Despair: English-Speaking Intellectuals & South African Politics 1896-1976. 224p. 1993. text 69.50 (*1-85043-489-1*) I B T.
— Reaction & Renewal in South Africa. 320p. 1996. text 65.00 (*0-312-16149-2*) St Martin.
— State Power & Black Politics in South Africa, 1912-51. LC 95-14921. 208p. 1996. text 65.00 (*0-312-12756-1*) St Martin.
— Warlords in International Relations. LC 99-21571. 192p. 1999. text 65.00 (*0-312-22524-5*) St Martin.
Rich, Peggy B. & Whitehurst, Marion A., compiled by. The Pickens Sentinel Favorite Newspaper of Pickens County: Pickens Court House, South Carolina 1872-1893 Historical & Genealogical Abstracts. (Illus.). 755p. (Orig.). 1994. pap. text 70.00 (*1-55613-985-3*) Heritage Bk.
Rich, Peggy B., et al. Alexander Families of Upper South Carolina. (Illus.). 1100p. 1988. 45.00 (*0-9620691-0-8*) Rich SC.
Rich, Penny. Pamper Your Partner. 1990. per. 15.95 (*0-671-69526-6*) S&S Trade.
— Practical Aromatherapy: The Complete Beginner's Guide to Choosing, Massaging & Relaxing with Essential Oils. (Illus.). 128p. 1999. reprint ed. text 25.00 (*0-7881-6195-4*) DIANE Pub.
***Rich, Peter.** Principles of Element Design. 3rd ed. 168p. 1999. pap. text 32.95 (*0-7506-3113-9*) Buttrwrth-Heinemann.
Rich, Phil. Grief Journey. LC 98-22978. 264p. 1999. pap. 16.95 (*0-471-29565-5*) Wiley.
***Rich, Phil & Copans, Stuart.** The Healing Journey Through Addiction: Your Journal for Recovery & Self-Renewal. LC 99-88272. (Healing Journey Ser.). 272p. 2000. pap. 17.95 (*0-471-38209-4*) Wiley.
Rich, Phil & Copans, Stuart A. The Healing Journey: A Journal of Self-Discovery. LC 97-28988. (Illus.). 177p. 1998. pap. 16.95 (*0-471-24712-X*) Wiley.
— The Healing Journey for Couples: Your Journal of Mutual Discovery. LC 97-50262. (Illus.). 271p. 1998. pap. 16.95 (*0-471-25470-3*) Wiley.
***Rich, Phil & Linzer Schwartz, Lita.** The Healing Journey Through Divorce: Your Journal of Understanding & Renewal. LC 98-35238. 264p. 1999. pap. 16.95 (*0-471-29575-2*) Wiley.
Rich, Phil & Mervyn, Fran. The Healing Journey Through Menopause: Your Journal for Reflection & Renewal. LC 99-23142. 281p. 1999. pap. 16.95 (*0-471-32691-7*) Wiley.
***Rich, Phil, et al.** The Healing Journey for Retirement: Your Journal of Transition & Transformation. LC 99-16053. 283p. 1999. pap. 16.95 (*0-471-32693-3*) Wiley.
— The Healing Journey Through Job Loss: Your Journal for Reflection & Revitalization. LC 98-56175. 282p. 1999. pap. 16.95 (*0-471-32694-1*) Wiley.
Rich Publishing Company Staff, ed. see Blakely, James, et al.
Rich, Richard, ed. Urban Service Distributions. (Orig.). (C). 1981. pap. 15.00 (*0-918592-46-1*) Pol Studies.
Rich, Richard C., jt. auth. see Manheim, Jarol B.
Rich, Robert E., jt. auth. see Billoni, Michael J.
Rich, Robert F. Social Science Information & Public Policy Making. LC 79-92468. (Jossey-Bass Social & Behavioral Science Ser.). 231p. reprint ed. pap. 71.70 (*0-8357-6888-0*, 203794000009) Bks Demand.
Rich, Robert F. & White, William D. Health Policy, Federalism, & the American States. LC 96-33521. (Illus.). 350p. 1996. 69.50 (*0-87766-659-8*) U Pr of Amer.
— Health Policy, Federalism, & the American States. LC 96-33521. (Illus.). 350p. 1996. pap. 28.50 (*0-87766-660-1*) Urban Inst.
Rich, Robert R., ed. Clinical Immunology: Principles & Practice. (Illus.). 2912p. (C). (gr. 13). 1995. text 320.00 (*0-8016-7636-3*, 07636) Mosby Inc.
***Rich, Ronda.** What Southern Women Know (That Every Woman Should) Timeless Secrets to Get Everything You Want. 2000. pap. 12.00 (*0-399-52627-7*, Perigee Bks) Berkley Pub.
Rich, Ronda. What Southern Women Know (That Every Woman Should) Timeless Secrets to Get Everything You Want in Love, Life, & Work. LC 99-29355. 224p. 1999. 19.95 (*0-399-14575-3*, G P Putnam) Peng Put Young Read.
Rich, Ruby B. Chick Flicks: Theories & Memories of the Feminist Film Movement. LC 98-12052. 448p. 1998. 59.95 (*0-8223-2106-8*) Duke.
Rich, Russell R. Ensign to the Nations: A History of the Church from 1846 to the Present. LC 72-91730. (Illus.). xviii, 663p. (C). 1972. pap. text 14.95 (*0-8425-0671-3*, Friends of the Library) Brigham.
Rich, Ruth & D'Onofrio, Carol N. Decisions for Health. (Discover Ser.). (Illus.). 520p. (YA). (gr. 9-12). 1993. teacher ed. 41.95 (*0-7854-0050-8*, 15192); text 26.95 (*0-7854-0149-0*, 15191); 221.95 (*0-7854-0051-6*, 15193); audio 113.95 (*0-7854-0060-5*, 15190) Am Guidance.
Rich, S. G., jt. auth. see Marwick, J. S.
Rich, Sandra L. & Tucker, Roy W. Oregon Corporation Law & Practice. LC 91-30641. (National Corporation Law Ser.). 1991. ring bd. 126.00 (*0-13-640129-5*) Aspen Law.
Rich, Sandra L., jt. auth. see Burton, Robert E.
Rich, Scharlotte. Base: Vertical Adventure: Strengthening Teens' Spiritual Grip. 100p. (YA). (gr. 8-12). 1996. pap. text 5.99 (*1-57673-001-8*) Zondervan.
— Basics of the Christian Life-On Your Mark. (Runners Power Pak Ser.: No. 1). (J). 1996. pap. 5.99 (*0-88070-912-X*, Gold n Honey) Zondervan.
— Character Choices & God's Provision: Going the Distance. (Runners Power Pak Ser.: No. 4). (J). 1996. pap. 5.99 (*0-88070-926-X*) Zondervan.
— Edge: Vertical Adventures: Social Issues. 100p. (YA). (gr. 8-12). 1996. pap. text 5.99 (*1-57673-003-4*, Gold n Honey) Zondervan.
***Rich, Scharlotte.** Grandma's Gospel: Stories of Character, Told with Love. LC 99-47799. (Illus.). 256p. (J). (ps-2). 2000. 12.95 (*1-57856-153-1*) Waterbrook Pr.
Rich, Scharlotte. The Grip: Vertical Adventure: Strengthening Teens' Spiritual Grip. 100p. (YA). (gr. 8-12). 1996. pap. text 5.99 (*1-57673-002-6*, Gold n Honey) Zondervan.
— How to Live Setting the Pace. (Runners Power Pak Ser.: No. 2). (J). 1996. pap. 5.99 (*0-88070-924-3*) Zondervan.
— I Love My Mommy. (Love Ser.). (Illus.). 120p. (J). (ps-k). 1995. 9.99 (*0-88070-748-8*, Gold n Honey) Zondervan.
— The Nursery Quiet & Noisy Book. (Illus.). 48p. (J). 1995. 7.99 (*0-88070-770-4*, Gold n Honey) Zondervan.
— Relationships with Friends, Parents & Teachers: Team Spirit. (Runners Power Pak Ser.: No. 3). (J). 1996. pap. 5.99 (*0-88070-925-1*, Gold n Honey) Zondervan.
— The Summit: Strengthening Teens' Spiritual Grip. (Vertical Adventure Ser.: No. 4). 100p. (YA). (gr. 8-12). 1996. pap. text 5.99 (*1-57673-004-2*, Gold n Honey) Zondervan.
— Who Made the Wild Woods? 48p. (J). (ps-2). 1999. 14.95 (*1-57856-027-6*) Waterbrook Pr.
Rich, Sharon. Critically Reflective Groups: A Context for Learning. Kincheloe, Joe & Steinberg, Shirley R., eds. 200p. Date not set. pap. text 18.95 (*0-8153-2318-2*) Garland.
Rich, Sharon & Steinberg, Shirley R. Critically Reflective Groups: A Context for Learning. Kincheloe, Joe, ed. (Critical Education Practice Ser.). 200p. Date not set. text 30.00 (*0-8153-1164-8*) Garland.
Rich, Shebnah. Truro-Cape Cod: Landmarks & Seamarks. (Illus.). 580p. 1989. reprint ed. lib. bdg. 58.00 (*0-8328-0916-0*, MA0203) Higginson Bk Co.
Rich, Sheila. Fun & Fitness: A Step-by-Step Guide. LC 89-27393. (Be the Best! Ser.). (Illus.). 64p. (J). (gr. 4-8). 1990. lib. bdg. 15.85 (*0-8167-1949-7*) Troll Communs.
— Fun & Fitness: A Step-by-Step Guide. LC 89-27393. (Be the Best! Ser.). (Illus.). 64p. (J). (gr. 4-8). 1997. pap. 3.95 (*0-8167-1950-0*) Troll Communs.
Rich, Stanley R. & Gumpert, David E. Business Plans That Win $ Lessons from the MIT Enterprise Forum. LC 84-48617. (Illus.). 240p. 1987. pap. 13.00 (*0-06-091391-6*, PL 1391, Perennial) HarperTrade.
Rich, Steve & Edwards, Anthony. GCSE Technology: Mechanisms. 92p. 1998. pap. 25.50 (*0-7487-0150-8*) St Mut.
— GCSE Technology: Structures with Materials. 90p. 1998. pap. 25.50 (*0-7487-0151-6*) St Mut.
Rich, Steven H., Sr. High Desert Testament: What We Had, How We Lost It, How We Can Get It Back, & a Vision of a World Beyond Bull. 56p. 1992. pap. text 5.95 (*1-881753-00-X*) Buckskin Mtn.
Rich, Stuart, jt. ed. see Rubin, Lewis J.
Rich, Sue. Aim for the Heart. 1996. mass mkt. 5.99 (*0-671-89808-6*) PB.
— Amber. 304p. 1997. per. 5.99 (*0-671-00044-6*) PB.
— Jade. 1997. per. 5.99 (*0-671-00045-4*) PB.
— Mistress of Sin. 1994. mass mkt. 5.50 (*0-671-79408-6*) PB.
— Rawhide & Roses. Tolley, Carolyn, ed. 272p. (Orig.). 1993. mass mkt. 4.99 (*0-671-75914-0*) PB.
— The Scarlet Temptress. 336p. (Orig.). 1991. mass mkt. 5.50 (*0-671-73625-6*) PB.
— Shadowed Vows. Tolley, Carolyn, ed. 272p. (Orig.). 1992. mass mkt. 5.50 (*0-671-73626-4*) PB.
— The Silver Witch. Tolley, Carolyn, ed. 320p. (Orig.). 1995. mass mkt. 5.99 (*0-671-79409-4*) PB.
— Wayward Angel. 1995. mass mkt. 5.99 (*0-671-89807-8*) PB.
***Rich, Susan.** The Cartographer's Tongue. LC 99-44072. 107p. 2000. pap. 14.00 (*1-893996-06-9*, Pub. by White Pine) SPD-Small Pr Dist.
Rich, Susan. Kline Guide to Packaging. Deitsch, Marian, ed. (Illus.). 324p. 1980. pap. 70.00 (*0-685-02813-5*) Kline.
Rich, Susan, ed. Directory of Cosmetic & Toiletry Ingredients. 2nd ed. 365p. 1982. pap. 985.00 (*0-686-84482-3*) Kline.
— Kline Guide to the Paint Industry. 6th ed. LC 81-84942. (Illus.). 200p. 1981. pap. 97.00 (*0-917148-01-0*) Kline.
— Profiles of U. S. Chemical Distributors. LC 81-83812. 265p. 1981. pap. 277.00 (*0-917148-77-0*) Kline.
***Rich, Susan, et al.** Africa South of the Sahara: Understanding Geography & History trhough Art. LC 99-21171. (Artisans Around the World Ser.). (Illus.). 48p. (YA). (gr. 5 up). 1999. 25.69 (*0-7398-0118-X*) Raintree Steck-V.
Rich, Susan, jt. ed. see Curry, Susan.
Rich, Susanna. Flexible Writer. 3rd ed. LC 97-16434. 450p. 1997. pap. text 42.00 (*0-205-26599-5*) P-H.
Rich, Susanna L. The Flexible Writer: A Basic Guide. 3rd ed. (C). 1997. pap. text, teacher ed. write for info. (*0-205-27170-7*, T7170-8) Allyn.
— The Flexible Writer: A Basic Guide: Examination Copy. 3rd ed. 528p. (C). 1997. pap. text. write for info. (*0-205-27653-9*, T7653-3) Allyn.
Rich, Terrell D., jt. auth. see Saab, Victoria A.
Rich, Terry L. Your Opportunities in Accounting. (Illus.). 8p. 1994. pap. 2.50 (*1-884241-00-X*, OS100) Energeia Pub.

R

R

***Rich, Thomas H. V. & Rich, Pat Vickers.** Dinosaurs of Darkness. LC 00-25794. (Life of the Past Ser.). (Illus.). 2000. 35.00 (*0-253-33773-9*) Ind U Pr.

Rich, Thomas P., jt. ed. see Hudson, C. Michael.

Rich, Vera, jt. auth. see Blum, Jakub.

Rich, Vincent. International Lead Trade. (International Trade Ser.). (Illus.). 336p. 1994. 170.00 (*1-85573-103-7*, Pub. by Woodhead Pubng) Am Educ Systs.

Rich, Vincent, ed. International Scrap & Recycling Industry Handbook. 500p. 2000. 890.00 (*1-85573-248-3*, Pub. by Woodhead Pubng) Am Educ Systs.

Rich, Virginia. The Nantucket Diet Murders. 288p. 1986. mass mkt. 6.50 (*0-440-16264-5*) Dell.

***Rich, Virginia Moulton.** A Symphony of Lyrical Lines in Rhyme. LC 99-95038. 2000. pap. 12.95 (*0-533-13276-2*) Vantage.

***Rich, Wilbur, ed.** The Economics & Politics of Sports Facilities. LC 99-56365. 248p. 2000. 67.50 (*1-56720-317-5*, Quorum Bks) Greenwood.

Rich, Wilbur, ed. Sports Policy. (Policy Studies Review: Vol. 15:1). 135p. 1998. pap. write for info. (*0-944285-50-3*) Pol Studies.

Rich, Wilbur C. Black Mayors & School Politics: The Failure of Reforms in Detroit, Gary, & Newark. LC 95-51042. (Reference Library of Social Science: Vol. 1048). 240p. 1996. text 44.00 (*0-8153-2066-3*, SS1048); pap. text 20.95 (*0-8153-2340-9*, SS1048) Garland.

— Coleman Young & Detroit Politics: From Social Activist to Power Broker. LC 88-39480. (African American Life Ser.). 300p. (C). 1989. 34.95 (*0-8143-2093-7*); pap. 19.95 (*0-8143-2094-5*) Wayne St U Pr.

Rich, Wilbur C., ed. The Politics of Minority Coalitions: Race, Ethnicity & Shared Uncertainties. LC 96-10428. 288p. 1996. pap. 24.95 (*0-275-95489-7*, Praeger Pubs) Greenwood.

— The Politics of Minority Coaltions: Race, Ethnicity & Shared Uncertainties. LC 96-10428. 288p. 1996. 65.00 (*0-275-95488-9*, Praeger Pubs) Greenwood.

Rich, Wilbur C., jt. ed. see Bowers, James R.

Rich, Wiley D. Legal Responsibilities & Rights of Public Accountants. Brief, Richard P., ed. LC 80-1514. (Dimensions of Accounting Theory & Practice Ser.). 1980. reprint ed. lib. bdg. 28.95 (*0-405-13539-4*) Ayer.

Rich, William J., jt. auth. see Antieau, Chester James.

Richalet, J., et al. Identification des Processus par la Methode du Modele. (Theorie des Systemes Ser.). xviii, 362p. 1972. text 516.00 (*0-677-50740-2*) Gordon & Breach.

Richalton, James. James Richalton's Photographic Travelogue of Imperial India. Lucas, Christopher J., ed. LC 90-46220. (Studies in the Photographic Arts: Vol. 2). (Illus.). 308p. 1990. lib. bdg. 99.95 (*0-88946-509-6*) E Mellen.

Richan, Willard C. Beyond Altruism: Social Welfare Policy in American Society. 238p. 1987. pap. 19.95 (*0-86656-756-9*) Haworth Pr.

— Beyond Altruism: Social Welfare Policy in American Society. LC 86-29437. (Administration in Social Work Ser.: Supp. No. 3). 238p. 1987. 39.95 (*0-86656-633-3*) Haworth Pr.

— Lobbying for Social Change. (Social Administration Ser.). 255p. (C). 1990. pap. text 19.95 (*1-56024-074-1*) Haworth Pr.

— Lobbying for Social Change. (Social Administration Ser.). 255p. (C). 1991. text 39.95 (*1-56024-079-2*) Haworth Pr.

— Lobbying for Social Change. 2nd ed. LC 95-35019. 362p. (C). 1996. 49.95 (*0-7890-6002-7*); pap. 19.95 (*0-7890-6003-5*) Haworth Pr.

Richan, Willard C., ed. see Professional Symposium on Human Services & Profess.

Richani, Nazih. Dilemmas of Democracy & Political Parties in Multiethnic Societies: The Case of the PSP in Lebanon. LC 97-30288. 1998. text 49.95 (*0-312-17450-0*) St Martin.

Richard. Applied Calculus Today. (C). 1996. pap. text 27.00 (*0-03-020114-4*) Harcourt Coll Pubs.

— Applied Calculus Today: +TI-85 REV. (C). 1996. pap. text 27.00 (*0-03-020117-9*) Harcourt Coll Pubs.

— Gods Special Promises to Me. LC 97-169371. 1996. pap. 9.99 (*0-932081-47-9*) Victory Hse.

— Mine Forever. 1989. pap. 14.95 (*0-340-49641-X*, Pub. by Hodder & Stought Ltd) Trafalgar.

— Mini Prayers That Prevail. LC 97-150890. 1996. pap. text 5.99 (*0-932081-35-5*) Victory Hse.

— Today God Says. LC 99-163666. 1997. mass mkt. 7.99 (*0-932081-50-9*) Victory Hse.

Richard & Edwards. Copy Me, Copycub. LC 99-1175. 32p. (J). (ps-2). pap. 5.95 (*0-06-443603-9*) HarpC Child Bks.

Richard, ed. see Rousseau, Jean-Jacques.

Richard, Dan G. Real Estate Rainmaker: Successful Strategies for Real Estate Marketing. LC 99-23926. 318p. (C). 1999. 24.95 (*0-471-34554-7*) Wiley.

Richard A. Goodman & Associates Staff. Modern Organizations & Emerging Conundrums: Medium, Meaning & Method. 384p. 1998. 38.00 (*0-7879-4125-5*) Jossey-Bass.

Richard, Adrienne & Reiter, Joel. Epilepsy. 288p. 1995. pap. 14.95 (*0-8027-7465-2*) Walker & Co.

Richard-Akers, Nancy. Lady Sarah's Charade. 1992. mass mkt. 3.99 (*0-380-76531-4*, Avon Bks) Morrow Avon.

Richard, Albert & Searle, Cary. Career Decisions. 58p. 1994. teacher ed. 17.00 (*0-8273-5994-2*) Delmar.

Richard, Albert & Searle, Gary. Career Decisions. LC 93-40056. 151p. 1994. mass mkt. 17.00 (*0-8273-5993-4*) Delmar.

Richard, Alfred. Panama Canal in American National Consciousness, 1870-1990. LC 90-3045. (Foreign Economic Policy of the United States Ser.). 378p. 1990. reprint ed. text 10.00 (*0-8240-7471-8*) Garland.

Richard, Alfred C. Censorship & Hollywood's Hispanic Image: An Interpretive Filmography, 1936-1955, 14. LC 92-40161. (Bibliographies & Indexes in the Performing Arts Ser.: No. 14). 640p. 1993. lib. bdg. 85.00 (*0-313-28842-9*, GR8842, Greenwood Pr) Greenwood.

— Contemporary Hollywood's Negative Hispanic Image: An Interpretive Filmography, 1956-1993, 16. LC 94-10862. (Bibliographies & Indexes in the Performing Arts Ser.: No. 16). 680p. 1994. lib. bdg. 79.50 (*0-313-28841-0*, Greenwood Pr) Greenwood.

Richard, Alfred C., Jr. The Hispanic Image on the Silver Screen: An Interpretive Filmography from Silents into Sound, 1898-1935, 12. LC 92-8917. (Bibliographies & Indexes in the Performing Arts Ser.: No. 12). 624p. 1992. lib. bdg. 75.00 (*0-313-27832-6*, RHJ, Greenwood Pr) Greenwood.

Richard, Alison F. Behavioral Variation: Case Study of a Malagasy Lemur. LC 76-19837. (Illus.). 213p. 1978. 37.50 (*0-8387-1965-1*) Bucknell U Pr.

— Primates in Nature. LC 84-18802. (Illus.). 588p. (C). 1985. pap. text 38.95 (*0-7167-1647-X*) W H Freeman.

Richard-Allerdyce, Diane. Anais Nin & the Remaking of Self: Gender, Modernism, & Narrative Identity. LC 97-14215. 256p. 1997. lib. bdg. 32.00 (*0-87580-232-X*) N Ill U Pr.

Richard-Amato. Through Other Eyes. LC 98-121819. 1997. text 26.50 (*0-8384-4728-7*) Heinle & Heinle.

Richard-Amato, Patricia. Exploring Themes: A-W Version. 1993. pap. text 19.74 (*0-201-59261-4*) P-H.

Richard-Amato, Patricia A. Exploring Themes. 176p. 1994. pap. text 22.64 (*0-8013-1315-5*) Addison-Wesley.

— Exploring Themes: An Interactive Approach to Literature. LC 92-40536. (Illus.). 1993. pap. text 20.40 (*0-8013-0601-9*) Longman.

— Making It Happen: Interaction in the Second Language Classroom. 1988. pap. text 44.00 (*0-8013-0027-4*, 75692) Longman.

— Making It Happen: Interaction in the Second Language Classroom: from Theory to Practice. 2nd ed. LC 95-15297. 496p. 1995. pap. text 44.10 (*0-201-42018-X*) Addison-Wesley.

Richard-Amato, Patricia A. & Hansen, Wendy A. Worlds Together. 192p. 1995. pap. text 19.69 (*0-201-82386-1*) Addison-Wesley.

— Worlds Together Anthology. (Teachers Guide Ser.). 96p. 1995. pap. text 22.48 (*0-201-82389-6*) Addison-Wesley.

Richard, Andrew, et al. Business School Companion. (Princeton Review Ser.). 1995. pap. 15.00 (*0-679-76463-1*) Villard Books.

Richard B. Robinson. Federal Income Taxation of Real Estate: Forms & Analysis. 1989. ring bd. 110.00 (*0-7913-0297-0*); write for info. (*0-318-67194-8*) Warren Gorham & Lamont.

Richard, Birgit & Klanten, Robert. Icons. (Localizer 1.3 Ser.). (Illus.). 176p. (Orig.). 1998. pap. 44.00 (*3-931126-04-8*, Pub. by Die Gestalten) Consort Bk Sales.

***Richard, C.** My Story. 1998. text 29.95 (*0-233-99300-2*, Pub. by Andre Deutsch) Trafalgar.

Richard, Carl J. The Founders & the Classics: Greece, Rome & the American Enlightenment. LC 93-28468. 312p. 1994. text 44.50 (*0-674-31425-5*) HUP.

— The Founders & the Classics: Greece, Rome & the American Enlightenment. 312p. (C). 1994. pap. text 17.50 (*0-674-31426-3*) HUP.

— The Louisiana Purchase. LC 94-74141. (Louisiana Life Ser.: No. 7). (Illus.). 55p. (Orig.). 1995. pap. 5.00 (*0-940984-91-1*) Univ LA Lafayette.

Richard, Chait & Papirno, Ralph, eds. Compression Testing of Homogeneous Materials & Composites - STP 808. LC 82-73768. 294p. 1983. text 40.00 (*0-8031-0248-8*, STP808) ASTM.

Richard, Claude. American Letters. LC 98-9961. 216p. (C). 1998. 35.00 (*0-8122-3434-0*) U of Pa Pr.

Richard, David. Anoint Yourself with Oil for Radiant Health. LC 97-227138. (Illus.). 60p. 1997. pap. 7.95 (*1-890612-01-4*, 58601) Vital Health.

— Gathering the Wind. 64p. (Orig.). 1994. pap. 5.00 (*0-9637547-3-4*) Arbor Hill Pr.

— My Whole Food ABC's. LC 98-171176. (Illus.). 32p. (J). (gr. k-2). 1997. pap. 8.95 (*1-890612-07-3*) Vital Health.

— A Seed. 40p. (Orig.). 1996. pap. 5.95 (*0-9637547-8-5*) Arbor Hill Pr.

***Richard, David.** Stevia Rebandiana: Natures Sweet Secret. 3rd ed. 80p. 1999. pap. 7.95 (*1-890612-15-4*) Vital Health.

Richard, David A. The Tsar's Colonels: Professionalism, Strategy, & Subversion in Late Imperial Russia. LC 98-19400. (Illus.). 320p. 1998. 49.95 (*0-674-91111-3*) HUP.

Richard Dennis Publications Staff, jt. auth. see Watney, Bernard M.

Richard, Dinah. Has Sex Education Failed Our Teenagers? A Research Report. 112p. (Orig.). 1990. pap. text 7.95 (*0-929608-22-4*) Focus Family.

***Richard, Earl J.** Reading 1 Peter, Jude & 2 Peter: Literary & Theological. LC 99-56441. (Reading the New Testament Ser.). 384p. Date not set. pap. 25.00 (*1-57312-314-5*) Smyth & Helwys.

Richard, Earl J., ed. First & Second Thessalonians. (Sacra Pagina Ser.: No. 11). 432p. 1995. 29.95 (*0-8146-5813-X*, M Glazier) Liturgical Pr.

Richard Earl of Bradford. Stately Secrets: Behind-the-Scene Stories from the Stately Homes of Britain. 211p. 1995. 23.95 (*0-86051-917-1*, Robson-Parkwest) Parkwest Pubns.

— Stately Secrets: Behind-the-Scenes Stories from the Stately Homes of Britain. (Illus.). 212p. 1997. pap. 11.95 (*1-86105-035-6*, Robson-Parkwest) Parkwest Pubns.

Richard, Ellis. Lassen Volcanic: The Story Behind the Scenery. LC 88-80120. (Illus.). 48p. (Orig.). 1988. pap. 7.95 (*0-88714-020-3*) KC Pubns.

Richard, Etienne. The Collected Works. Gustafson, Bruce, ed. (Art of the Keyboard Ser.: Vol. 3). (Illus.). 1994. pap. 27.50 (*0-8450-7630-2*) Broude.

Richard, Frederick S. Writing Modern Spanish: A Project of the Modern Language Association. 3rd ed. 1973. pap. 21.00 (*0-15-504503-2*) Bk Sales Inc.

Richard, G., et al. Fluorescein Angiography: Textbook & Atlas. 2nd ed. Blodi, Frederick C., tr. from ENG. LC 97-34734. 1997. write for info. (*3-13-741902-6*) Thieme Med Pubs.

Richard, Gail J. Discovering Abilities Within the Disability of Autism. 1997. pap. 38.00 incl. audio (*1-58041-004-9*, 0112070) Am Speech Lang Hearing.

Richard, Ginger & McCleary, Linda, eds. International Health Data Reference Guide, 1997. 8th ed. (Illus.). 155p. (C). 1998. pap. text 35.00 (*0-7881-7331-6*) DIANE Pub.

Richard, Gisbert. Fluorescein Angiography. Blodi, Frederick C., tr. (Illus.). 231p. 1990. text 110.00 (*0-86577-336-X*) Thieme Med Pubs.

— Fluorescein Angiography: Textbook & Atlas. 2nd ed. Blodi, Frederick C., tr. LC 97-34734. (Illus.). 412p. 1997. 159.00 (*0-86577-712-8*) Thieme Med Pubs.

Richard, Herbert L. Following Jesus in the Hindu Context: The Intriguing Implications of N. V. Tilak's Life & Thought. LC 98-46314. 145p. 1999. pap. 14.25 (*0-87808-288-3*, 0-87808-288-3) William Carey Lib.

Richard, Herman G. The Relation of Accelerated Normal & Retarded Puberty to the Height & Weight of School Children. (SRCD M Ser.: Vol. 2, No. 1). 1937. pap. 25.00 (*0-527-01494-X*) Periodicals Srv.

Richard, J. A. Student's Guide to Better Grades. 1976. pap. 3.00 (*0-87980-152-2*) Wilshire.

Richard, J. E. Board Compensation Committee Manual. 3rd ed. (Illus.). 184p. 1995. 125.00 (*1-887434-00-3*) J Richard.

— Board Compensation Guide. 2nd ed. (Illus.). 242p. 1999. 115.00 (*1-887434-26-7*) J Richard.

— Compensation Committee Manual. 4th ed. (Illus.). 210p. 1998. 145.00 (*1-887434-01-1*) J Richard.

Richard, J. E., et al. Board Compensation Guide. 184p. 1995. 95.00 (*1-887434-25-9*) J Richard.

Richard, J. Fraise, et al. Families of Beaver County, Pennsylvania. 300p. 1997. reprint ed. pap. 28.50 (*0-8063-4724-4*) Clearfield Co.

Richard, J. L. & Thurston, J. R., eds. Diagnosis of Mycotoxicoses. (Current Topics in Veterinary Medicine & Animal Science Ser.). 1986. lib. bdg. 270.50 (*0-89838-751-5*) Kluwer Academic.

Richard, J. M., et al, eds. The Elementary Structure of Matter. (Proceedings in Physics Ser.: Vol. 26). (Illus.). 530p. 1988. 85.95 (*0-387-19013-9*) Spr-Verlag.

Richard, J. P. Onze Etudes sur la Poesie Moderne. (FRE.). 1981. pap. 18.95 (*0-7859-2686-0*) Fr & Eur.

— Poesie et Profondeur. (FRE.). 1976. pap. 14.95 (*0-7859-2673-9*) Fr & Eur.

***Richard, J. Ron.** While Tyler Sleeps. LC 99-63726. 211p. 1999. pap. 16.95 (*1-893652-57-2*, Writers Club Pr) iUniversecom.

Richard, Jack & Lowe, David. The City of Lace. (C). 1988. 60.00 (*0-7855-3795-3*, Pub. by Lace Centre) St Mut.

Richard, James W. The Confessional History of the Lutheran Church. LC 83-45672. reprint ed. 62.50 (*0-404-19861-9*) AMS Pr.

Richard, Jean. Le Comte de Tripoli Sous la Dynastie Toulousaine (1102-1187) LC 78-63365. (Crusades & Military Orders Ser.: Second Series). reprint ed. 47.50 (*0-404-17033-1*) AMS Pr.

— Croisades et Etats Latins d'Orient. 133p. 1992. 115.95 (*0-86078-340-5*, Pub. by Variorum) Ashgate Pub Co.

— Croises, Missionaires et Voyageurs: Perspectives Orientales du Monde Latin Medieval. (Collected Studies: No. CS182). (FRE.). 340p. (C). 1983. reprint ed. lib. bdg. 124.95 (*0-86078-130-5*, Pub. by Variorum) Ashgate Pub Co.

***Richard, Jean.** The Crusades, c. 1071-1291. Birrell, Jean, tr. LC 98-43850. (Medieval Textbks.). (Illus.). 540p. (C). 1999. 64.95 (*0-521-62369-3*); pap. 24.95 (*0-521-62566-1*) Cambridge U Pr.

Richard, Jean-Marc. Dictionnaire des Expressions Paillardes et Libertines de la Litterature Francaise. (FRE.). 271p. 1993. pap. 49.95 (*0-7859-8053-9*, 2850183806) Fr & Eur.

Richard, Jenny. Relaxation for Children. 2nd ed. 1995. pap. 60.00 (*0-86431-148-6*, Pub. by Aust Council Educ Res) St Mut.

Richard, Jimmy L. The Real Rules. 296p. 1998. pap. 13.95 (*1-881524-28-0*) Milligan Bks.

Richard, Joe. The Kingfish Bible. (Illus.). 112p. 1995. reprint ed. pap. 17.95 (*0-9649317-0-2*) Saltwater Spec.

— The Snapper Bible. (Illus.). 128p. (Orig.). 1996. pap. 17.95 (*0-9649317-1-0*) Saltwater Spec.

Richard, John, jt. ed. see Forster, Roger.

Richard, John D. & Dearden, Richard G., comments. The Canada-U. S. Free Trade Agreement: Commentary & Related Documents. LC 89-188756. vi, 132 p. 1987. write for info. (*0-88796-458-3*) CCH Canad.

Richard, Kevin, jt. auth. see Burdette, David.

Richard, L. Comprehensive Geography of the Chinese Empire & Dependencies. Kennelly, M., tr. 1978. reprint ed. 40.00 (*0-89986-339-6*) Oriental Bk Store.

Richard, Lionel. Encyclopedie de l'Expressionisme. (FRE.). 288p. 1977. 59.95 (*0-8288-5419-X*, M6485) Fr & Eur.

***Richard, Lucien.** Living the Hospitality of God. 2001. pap. 14.95 (*0-8091-3998-7*) Paulist Pr.

Richard, Lucien J. Christ: The Self-Emptying of God. LC 96-32526. 240p. (Orig.). 1996. pap. 18.95 (*0-8091-3668-6*) Paulist Pr.

— What Are They Saying about the Theology of Suffering? LC 92-21583. (What Are They Saying about...Ser.). 176p. 1993. pap. 7.95 (*0-8091-3347-4*) Paulist Pr.

Richard, M. The Complete Book of Ballroom Dancing. 256p. 1992. pap. 17.95 (*0-385-42416-7*) Doubleday.

Richard, Margaret C., jt. ed. see Kohl, Lawrence F.

Richard, Margaret Cosse, jt. ed. see Kohl, Lawrence F.

Richard, Mark. Charity. LC 98-10317. 160p. 1998. 19.95 (*0-385-42562-7*, N A Talese) Doubleday.

— Charity: Stories. 160p. 1999. pap. 11.00 (*0-385-42570-8*) Doubleday.

— Fishboy: A Ghost's Story. LC 93-46786. 240p. 1994. pap. 11.95 (*0-385-42568-6*, Anchor NY) Doubleday.

— The Ice at the Bottom of the World. 160p. 1991. pap. 9.95 (*0-385-41544-3*, Anchor NY) Doubleday.

— The Papermaker. 1999. write for info. (*0-385-42569-4*) Doubleday.

— Propositional Attitudes: An Essay on Thoughts & How We Ascribe Them. (Studies in Philosophy). (Illus.). 285p. (C). 1990. pap. text 26.95 (*0-521-38819-8*) Cambridge U Pr.

Richard, Mary M. Before & after School Programs: A Start-Up & Administration Manual. LC 91-60075. 108p. (Orig.). (C). 1991. pap. text 24.95 (*0-917505-05-0*) School Age.

***Richard, Matthew V.** St. Francis of Assisi. 140p. 1999. pap. 9.95 (*0-9672534-0-3*) Pro Ventures Ltd.

Richard, Michel P. Without Passport: The Life & Work of Paul Richard. (American University Studies: History: Ser. IX, Vol. 28). XXII, 281p. (C). 1987. text 44.95 (*0-8204-0444-6*) P Lang Pubng.

Richard, Nancy. Once upon a Rainbow. (Illus.). 31p. (Orig.). 1992. pap. 4.95 (*0-9631685-0-9*) N&R Enter.

Richard, Naomi N., ed. see Clark, Timothy, et al.

Richard, Naomi N., ed. see Lee, Sherman E.

Richard, Norma, jt. auth. see Britz, Joan.

Richard, Octavia, ed. Charlemagne Romances No. 10: Four Sonnes of Aymon, 1 pts., Pt. 1. (EETS, ES Ser.: Nos. 44). 1972. reprint ed. 54.00 (*0-527-00253-4*) Periodicals Srv.

— Charlemagne Romances No. 10: Four Sonnes of Aymon, 1 pts., Pt. 2. (EETS, ES Ser.: Nos. 44). 1972. reprint ed. 40.00 (*0-527-00254-2*) Periodicals Srv.

Richard of Campsall. Works Vol. 2: Minor Treaties; Logica Campsale Anglici, Vol. 2. Synan, Edward A., ed. (ENG & LAT.). viii, 450p. pap. text 38.29 (*0-88844-058-8*) Brill Academic Pubs.

Richard of St. Victor. Richard of St. Victor's "Treatise on the Study of Wisdom That Men Call Benjamin" As Adapted in Middle English by the Author of "The Cloud of Unknowing" Together with "Treatise on Discretion of Spirits" & "Epistle on Discretion of Stirrings" Barnes, Dick, tr. from LAT. LC 90-39519. (Studies in Medieval Literature: Vol. 7). 120p. 1990. lib. bdg. 59.95 (*0-88946-294-1*) E Mellen.

Richard of St. Victor, et al. Cell of Self-Knowledge. Gardner, E. G., ed. LC 66-25702. (Medieval Library). reprint ed. 42.00 (*0-8154-0188-4*) Cooper Sq.

***Richard, Oscar G., III.** Kriegie: An American POW in Germany. LC 99-88025. (Illus.). 184p. 2000. 29.95 (*0-8071-2562-8*) La State U Pr.

Richard, Pablo. Apocalypse: A People's Commentary on the Book of Revelation. LC 95-42970. (Bible & Liberation Ser.). 150p. (Orig.). 1995. pap. 18.00 (*1-57075-043-2*) Orbis Bks.

— Death of Christendoms, Birth of the Church: Historical Analysis & Theological Interpretation of the Church in Latin America. Berryman, Phillip, tr. from FRE. LC 87-14825. (Illus.). 223p. reprint ed. pap. 69.20 (*0-7837-9833-4*, 206056200005) Bks Demand.

— The Idols of Death & the God of Life: A Theology. Campbell, Barbara E. & Shepard, Bonnie, trs. from SPA. LC 83-6788.Tr. of La/Lucha de los Dioses: la Idolos de la Opresion y la Busqueda del Dios Liberador. 240p. (Orig.). reprint ed. pap. 74.40 (*0-8357-2689-4*, 204022500015) Bks Demand.

Richard, Pascale. Versailles: The American Story. 160p. 1999. 50.00 (*2-909838-44-7*, Pub. by A Gourcuff) Antique Collect.

***Richard, Patricia M.** Crucified for Christ: The Story of Joseph Richard. (Illus.). 500p. 2000. pap. 18.95 (*0-9700429-0-6*) Agape & Philia.

Richard, Patrick, jt. ed. see Stockli, Martin.

***Richard, Paul.** Poems for the Wretched Child & Pets for the Wretched Child. 2000. pap. write for info. (*1-58235-433-2*) Watermrk Pr.

Richard, Paul S. The Dollarplan: A Financial Education Course. (Illus.). 1985. teacher ed. 55.00 (*0-318-04706-3*) Natl Ctr Fin Ed.

— The Dollarplan: A Financial Education Course. (Illus.). 230p. 1994. ring bd. 24.00 (*0-935451-00-5*) Natl Ctr Fin Ed.

— The Dollarplan: Spending & Savings Techniques for the 1990s. 122p. 1990. 24.95 (*0-685-34772-9*) Natl Ctr Fin Ed.

— Financial Education One Hundred One: The Student Dollar Plan. (Illus.). 1986. 15.00 (*0-317-47155-4*) Natl Ctr Fin Ed.

***Richard, Petersen Ian, et al.** Roboust Control Design Using H-P8S Methods. LC 99-56302. (Communications & Control Engineering Ser.). 2000. write for info. (*1-85233-171-2*, Pub. by Spr-Verlag) Spr-Verlag.

Richard, Philippe, jt. auth. see Urban, Ivan.

Richard, Pierre-Maurice. Le Francais Familier et Argotique: Spoken French That Foreigners Should Understand. (FRE & ENG., Illus.). 192p. 1997. pap. 17.95 (*0-8442-1512-0*, 15120) NTC Contemp Pub Co.

Richard, Poor, jt. auth. see Fawthrop, Paul B.

Richard, Ramesh. Scripture Sculpture: A Do-It-Yourself Manual for Biblical Preaching. LC 94-34615. 224p. 1995. pap. 11.99 (*0-8010-7774-5*) Baker Bks.

An Asterisk (*) at the beginning of an entry indicates that the title is appearing for the first time.

— Mending Your Soul: 6 Spiritual Laws for Energized Living. LC 99-28735. 160p. 1999. pap. 12.99 (*0-8054-1834-2*) Broadman.

Richard, Reginald L. & Staley, Marlys J., eds. Burn Care & Rehabilitation: Principles & Practice. LC 93-8304. (Contemporary Perspectives in Rehabilitation Ser.: Vol. 12). (Illus.). 711p. (C). 1993. 99.00 (*0-8036-7361-2*) Davis Co.

Richard, Robert. Johnny Novel. LC 98-182089. 104p. 1998. pap. text 9.95 (*1-55128-052-3*, Pub. by Mercury Bk) LPC InBook.

Richard, Roy, ed. see Conrad, Chris.

Richard, S. Releasing Anger. 20p. 1985. pap. 2.00 (*0-89486-249-9*, 1420B) Hazelden.

Richard, Sandra C., jt. ed. see Gray, H. Peter.

Richard, Stephen, ed. British Government Publications: An Index to Chairmen & Authors, Vol. 1, 1800-1899. LC 76-377815. 196p. reprint ed. pap. 60.80 (*0-608-08873-0*, 206951200001) Bks Demand.

— British Government Publications: An Index to Chairmen & Authors, Vol. 3, 1941-1978. LC 76-377815. 160p. reprint ed. pap. 49.60 (*0-608-08874-9*, 206951200003) Bks Demand.

— British Government Publications: An Index to Chairmen & Authors, Vol. 4, 1979-1982. LC 76-377815. 103p. reprint ed. pap. 32.00 (*0-608-08875-7*, 206951200004) Bks Demand.

Richard, Stephen A., jt. ed. see Yocom, Margaret R.

Richard T. Ingram & Associates Staff. Governing Independent Colleges & Universities: A Handbook for Trustees, Chief Executives, & Other Campus Leaders. LC 93-19511. 515p. 1993. text 53.00 (*1-55542-567-4*) Jossey-Bass.

— Governing Public Colleges & Universities: A Handbook for Trustees, Chief Executives, & Other Campus Leaders. LC 93-19512. 509p. (C). 1993. 54.95 (*1-55542-566-6*) Jossey-Bass.

Richard, Terry. Inside Out Oregon: A Best Places Guide to the Outdoors. 656p. 1998. pap. 21.95 (*1-57061-124-6*) Sasquatch Bks.

Richard, Valliere T. Norman McLaren, Manipulator of Movement: The National Film Board Years, 1947-67. LC 80-53998. (Illus.). 128p. 1982. 28.50 (*0-87413-192-8*) U Delaware Pr.

Richard, Wesley. Guide-A-Write. (Illus.). 120p. 1982. pap. 5.95 (*0-933704-22-4*) Dawn Pr.

Richard, Willis J. An Introduction to Economics, Economists, & Economies. 114p. 1969. pap. text 12.95 (*0-8290-1095-5*) Irvington.

Richard, Yann. Shiite Islam: Polity, Ideology & Creed. Nevill, Antonia, tr. from FRE. LC 94-15820. (Studies in Social Discontinuity).Tr. of Islam Chiite. 256p. (C). 1995. text 71.95 (*1-55786-469-1*); pap. text 28.95 (*1-55786-470-5*) Blackwell Pubs.

Richard, Yann, jt. auth. see Keddie, Nikki R.

Richardin, A. Dactylology: Conversing with the Deaf & Dumb. 1973. 59.95 (*0-87968-990-0*) Gordon Pr.

Richards. Birds Bees & Babies. 1990. per. 4.25 (*0-373-48228-0*) Harlequin Bks.

— Bloody Circus: The Labour Movement & the Popular Press. LC 97-14416. 1997. 54.95 (*0-7453-1117-2*, Pub. by Pluto GBR); pap. 18.95 (*0-7453-1118-0*, Pub. by Pluto GBR) Stylus Pub VA.

— Darwin & the Descent of Women. 1992. 27.50 (*0-226-71204-7*) U Ch Pr.

— Every Woman in the Bible. LC 99-11282. (Everything in the Bible Ser.). 320p. 1999. pap. 14.99 (*0-7852-1441-0*) Nelson.

— French for Business Customers. 1997. pap. 19.69 (*0-07-052580-3*) McGraw.

— Fundamentals of Health Assisting. (Home Care Aide Ser.). Date not set. pap., teacher ed. 14.00 (*0-8273-6145-9*) Delmar.

— Fundamentals of Health Assisting. (Home Care Aide Ser.). 1997. pap. 28.95 (*0-8273-6143-2*); pap., wbk. ed. 16.95 (*0-8273-6144-0*) Delmar.

— Fundamentals of Health Assisting CTB. (Home Care Aide Ser.). 1997. 64.95 (*0-8273-6146-7*) Delmar.

— The House with the Cherry Tree in the Orchard. LC 96-7403. (J). 1999. mass mkt. 16.00 (*0-689-80110-6*) S&S Bks Yung.

— Introduction to Dynamics. (C). 1979. pap. text. write for info. (*0-582-55183-8*, Pub. by Addison-Wesley) Longman.

— The Language of Reason. 1978. text 44.00 (*0-08-021846-6*, Pergamon Pr); pap. text 22.00 (*0-08-021845-8*, Pergamon Pr) Elsevier.

— Let the Circle Be Unbroken: The Implications of African Spirituality in the Diaspora. 1994. per. 6.95 (*0-932415-25-3*) Red Sea Pr.

— Race & Ethnic Relations. 1997. 36.25 (*0-07-218918-5*) McGraw.

— Soft Tissue Reconstruction in the Upper Extremity. 1995. text 127.00 (*0-443-08926-4*) Harcourt.

— Tadhkirat Al-Muluk. (Gibb Memorial Trust Ser.: Vol. 16). 1943. 38.50 (*0-906094-12-7*, Pub. by Aris & Phillips) David Brown.

— Unknown Thirties: An Alternative History of the British Cinema, Vol. 1. LC 98-179337. 320p. 1998. text 49.50 (*1-86064-303-5*, Pub. by I B T) St Martin.

Richards, ed. Document Forms for Orders of Official Appointment in the Mughal Empire: Translation Notes & Text. (Gibb Memorial New Ser.: Vol. 29). 1986. 62.50 (*0-906094-14-3*, Pub. by Aris & Phillips) David Brown.

***Richards & Aldgate.** The Best of the British. 256p. 1999. pap. 22.50 (*1-86064-288-8*) I B T.

Richards, jt. auth. see Bruess.

Richards, jt. auth. see Deutsch, Lawrence J.

Richards, jt. auth. see Gough.

Richards, jt. auth. see Reynolds, Tom D.

Richards, jt. auth. see Richards, F. Robert.

***Richards, David AJ.** Identity & the Case for Gay Rights: Race, Gender & Religion as Analogies. LC 99-32745. 184p. 2000. lib. bdg. 35.00 (*0-226-71208-7*) U Ch Pr.

***Richards, Gola Wolfson.** The Way to See (W)hole: A Course in Wisdom for Conflict Resolution. unabridged ed. (Illus.). 72p. 1999. pap. 20.00 (*0-9673939-0-6*) Motto Citizens.

Richards, A. J. Plant Breeding Systems in Seed Plants. (Illus.). 320p. (C). 1986. text 100.00 (*0-04-581020-6*); pap. text 44.95 (*0-04-581021-4*) Routledge.

Richards, A. J., ed. An Iban-English Dictionary. (Illus.). 1982. 65.00 (*0-19-864325-X*) OUP.

Richards, Adrian F., ed. Marine Geotechnique: Proceedings. International Research Conference on Marine Geotechnique (1966: Allerton House) LC 67-27773. (Illus.). 335p. reprint ed. 103.90 (*0-8357-9688-4*, 201493600097) Bks Demand.

— Vane Shear Strength Testing in the Field & Laboratory. LC 88-7684. (Special Technical Publication Ser.: No. STP 1014). (Illus.). 450p. 1988. text 79.00 (*0-8031-1188-6*, STP1014) ASTM.

Richards-Akers, Nancy. The Heart & the Heather. 384p. (Orig.). 1994. mass mkt. 4.50 (*0-380-77519-0*, Avon Bks) Morrow Avon.

— The Heart & the Holly. 368p. (Orig.). 1996. mass mkt. 5.50 (*0-380-78002-X*, Avon Bks) Morrow Avon.

— The Heart & the Rose. 384p. (Orig.). 1995. mass mkt. 4.99 (*0-380-78001-1*, Avon Bks) Morrow Avon.

— The Lilac Garland. 224p. (Orig.). 1990. mass mkt. 3.95 (*0-446-34923-2*, Pub. by Warner Bks) Little.

— Lord Fortune's Prize. 224p. (Orig.). 1993. mass mkt. 3.99 (*0-380-77191-8*, Avon Bks) Morrow Avon.

— Miss Wickham's Betrothal. 224p. (Orig.). 1992. mass mkt. 3.99 (*0-380-76532-2*, Avon Bks) Morrow Avon.

— So Wild a Kiss. 384p. 1998. mass mkt. 5.99 (*0-380-78947-7*, Avon Bks) Morrow Avon.

— Wild Irish Skies. 384p. 1997. mass mkt. 5.99 (*0-380-78948-5*, Avon Bks) Morrow Avon.

Richards, Alan. Are You Thinking of Moving from the City to the Country. (Illus.). 205p. (Orig.). 1995. pap. text 12.95 (*0-9643911-0-4*) A Richards.

— Birds of Prey: Hunters of the Sky. (Illus.). 144p. 1998. 17.98 (*0-7624-0286-5*, Courage) Running Pr.

— Development & Modes of Production in Marxian Economics (a Critical Evaluation), Vol. 12. (Fundamentals of Pure & Applied Economics Ser.: Volume 12). viii, 152p. 1986. pap. text 71.00 (*3-7186-0332-2*) Gordon & Breach.

Richards, Alan & Waterbury, John. A Political Economy of the Middle East. 2nd ed. LC 96-24374. 464p. (C). 1996. pap. text 35.00 (*0-8133-2411-4*, Pub. by Westview) HarpC.

Richards, Alan, ed. see Changhua Sun Rich, et al.

Richards, Albert G. The Secret Garden - One Hundred Floral Radiographs. (Illus.). 114p. 1991. 40.00 (*0-9628791-0-X*) Almar MI.

Richards, Alison, jt. ed. see Wolpert, Lewis.

Richards, Allan. How to Get a 4.0, Easily: One Hundred Twenty-Seven Ways to Get A's. 64p. 1993. pap. text 7.95 (*0-9630737-0-2*) Vector NY.

Richards, Alun. Alun Richards: Selected Stories. 340p. 1996. pap. 17.95 (*1-85411-117-5*, Pub. by Seren Bks) Dufour.

Richards, Alun. Penguin Book of Welsh Short Stories, Vol. 2. 416p. 1994. pap. 15.95 (*0-14-016871-0*, Pub. by Pnguin Bks Ltd) Trafalgar.

Richards, Alun. Plays for Players. 367p. (C). 1975. text 75.00 (*0-85088-290-7*, Pub. by Gomer Pr) St Mut.

Richards, Amy, jt. auth. see Baumgardner, Jennifer.

Richards, Andrew J. Miners on Strike: Class Solidarity & Division in Britain. LC 96-34875. 256p. 1997. 55.00 (*1-85973-172-4*, Pub. by Berg Pubs); pap. 19.50 (*1-85973-177-5*, Pub. by Berg Pubs) NYU Pr.

Richards, Ann. Cosmic Exchange. (J). 1996. pap. text 2.95 (*0-8114-9328-8*) Raintree Steck-V.

Richards, Ann & Nobile, Peter. High Heels & Backwards. 1989. 18.95 (*0-318-42520-3*) S&S Trade.

Richards, Ann & Wanner, Glen. Bicycling Middle Tennessee: A Guide to Scenic Bicycle Rides in Nashville's Countryside. 3rd rev. ed. LC 93-86049. (Illus.). 192p. (Orig.). 1996. pap. 15.95 (*0-9637798-2-6*) Pennywell Pr.

Richards, Ann L., jt. auth. see Wiehe, Vernon R.

Richards, Anne. Caring for Our Lizard, Vol. 4144. Graves, Kimberlee, ed. (Science Ser.). (Illus.). 16p. (J). (gr. k-1). 1997. pap. 2.75 (*1-57471-307-8*, 4144) Creat Teach Pr.

Richards, Anne & Schumrum, Tiparat. Invitations to Dialogue: The Legacy of Sidney M. Jourard. 336p. per. 29.95 (*0-7872-6468-7*) Kendall-Hunt.

Richards, Annette, jt. ed. see Franko, Mark.

Richards, Arlene K. & Willis, Irene. How to Get It Together When Your Parents Are Coming Apart. 170p. (J). (gr. 5-12). 1986. reprint ed. pap. 14.95 (*0-9615349-0-7*, HQ536.R48) Willard Pr.

Richards, Arlene K. & Willis, Irene. Under 18 & Pregnant. LC 82-12698. (Illus.). 256p. (J). (gr. 7 up). 1983. mass mkt. 8.95 (*0-688-01044-X*, Wm Morrow) Morrow Avon.

Richards, Arnold & Tyson, Phyllis, eds. The Psychology of Women: Psychoanalytic Perpectives. LC 97-784. 580p. 2000. 69.95 (*0-8236-5588-1*, No. 05588) Intl Univs Pr.

— The Psychology of Women: Psychoanalytic Perspectives. 555p. 1997. pap. 45.00 (*0-8236-5587-3*) Intl Univs Pr.

Richards, Arnold D. The Spectrum of Psychoanalysis: Essays in Honor of Martin S. Bergmann. 378p. 1994. 60.00 (*0-8236-4505-3*) Intl Univs Pr.

Richards, Arnold D. & Willick, Martin S., eds. Psychoanalysis: The Science of Mental Conflict - Essays in Honor of Charles Brenner. (Essays in Honor of Chas Brenner Ser.). 439p. 1986. text 55.00 (*0-88163-054-3*) Analytic Pr.

Richards, Arthur. The End: Year 2287. 200p. 1989. per. 10.95 (*0-89697-296-8*) Intl Univ Pr.

Richards, Audrey. Chisungu: A Girl's Initiation Ceremony among the Bemba. 224p. 1982. pap. 14.95 (*0-422-78070-7*, NO. 3665, Pub. by Tavistock) Routldge.

— Chisungu: Girl's Initiation Ceremony Among the Bemba of Zambia. 224p. (C). 1982. pap. 24.99 (*0-415-03695-X*) Routledge.

Richards, Audrey I. Hunger & Work in a Savage Society. LC 84-22540. 238p. 1985. reprint ed. lib. bdg. 59.50 (*0-313-24688-2*, RIHW, Greenwood Pr) Greenwood.

— The Multicultural States of East Africa. LC 74-101260. (Centre for Developing-Area Studies, McGill University, Keith Callard Lectures: No. 3). 135p. reprint ed. pap. 41.90 (*0-7837-1160-3*, 204168900022) Bks Demand.

Richards, Audrey I. & Kuper, Adam, eds. Councils in Action. LC 76-160101. (Cambridge Papers in Social Anthropology: No. 6). 222p. reprint ed. pap. 63.30 (*0-608-13303-5*, 2025594) Bks Demand.

Richards, B., jt. ed. see Henry, Frank.

Richards, B. Stephens, ed. Orthopaedic Knowledge Update: Pediatrics. 352p. 1996. pap. 115.00 (*0-89203-159-X*) Amer Acad Ortho Surg.

Richards, Barbara. Barbie.com Kitty's Surprise. LC 98-88158. (Road to Reading Ser.). (Illus.). 32p. (J). (gr. 2-3). 1999. pap. 3.99 (*0-307-26326-6*, Goldn Books) Gldn Bks Pub Co.

Richards, Barbara & S. I. Artists Staff. Barbie.Com: The First Adventure. LC 98-86207. (Barbie Ser.). (Illus.). 48p. (ps-3). 1998. pap. 3.99 (*0-307-26306-1*, Goldn Books) Gldn Bks Pub Co.

Richards, Barry. Disciplines of Delight: The Psychoanalysis of Popular Culture. LC 95-137211. 200p. (C). 1994. pap. 25.00 (*1-85343-325-X*, Pub. by Free Assoc Bks) NYU Pr.

Richards, Barry, jt. auth. see Heny, Frank.

Richards, Barry M. Thriving after Surviving. LC 88-84104. 128p. (Orig.). 1989. pap. 9.95 (*0-9622787-0-X*) Hartley Commns.

Richards, Bartlett, Jr. & Van Ackeren, Ruth. Bartlett Richards: Nebraska Sandhills Cattleman. LC 79-92129. (Illus.). 289p. (Orig.). 1980. 5.00 (*0-933307-05-5*) Nebraska Hist.

Richards, Benjamin B., ed. see Davis, Stephen C.

Richards, Bernard, ed. see James, Henry.

Richards, Beth, jt. auth. see Simmerman, Jim.

Richards, Betty W. & Kaneko, Anne. Japanese Plants: Know Them & Use Them. (Illus.). 224p. 1988. pap. 14.95 (*4-07-975121-4*, Pub. by Shufunomoto Co Ltd) Tuttle Pubng.

Richards, Bill. History of Tourism in the U. K. 320p. 1999. 69.95 (*0-7506-3374-3*) Buttrwrth-Heinemann.

Richards, Bill. How to Market Tourist Attractions, Festivals & Special Events: A Practical Guide to Maximizing Visitor Attendance & Income. LC 93-197314. vi, 142p. 1992. spiral bd. write for info. (*0-582-10250-2*, Pub. by Addison-Wesley) Longman.

Richards, Bob. It's in the Fine Print. Kirsch, J. Allen, ed. 200p. 1999. 12.95 (*1-878569-62-7*) Badger Bks Inc.

Richards, Bob & Yasiri, Jeanan. Putting the Patient First: Up Front with Advocacy & Community Service. 149p. (Orig.). 1997. pap. 90.00 (*1-56829-082-9*, 5001) Med Group Mgmt.

Richards, Bradley W. The Savage View: Charles Savage, Pioneer Mormon Photographer. Chapman, Jean, ed. LC 94-77983. (Illus.). 182p. 1995. pap. 19.95 (*0-9621940-6-9*) C Mautz Pubng.

Richards, Brant. Fantastic Book of Mountain Biking. LC 97-35114. (Fantastic Book of . . . Ser.). (Illus.). 32p. (J). (gr. 2-6). 1998. 10.95 (*0-7613-0725-7*, Copper Beech Bks); lib. bdg. 22.40 (*0-7613-0718-4*, Copper Beech Bks) Millbrook Pr.

***Richards, Brant.** Introduction to Mountain Biking. (Illus.). 80p. 2000. 9.99 (*0-517-16165-6*) Random Hse Value.

***Richards, Brian.** Berlin. (Globetrotter Travel Guide Ser.). (Illus.). 128p. 2000. pap. 10.95 (*1-85974-317-X*) New5 Holland.

Richards, Brian. Early Elegies. (Bloody Twin Press Ser.). (Illus.). 30p. (Orig.). 1992. pap. 30.00 (*1-886350-28-0*) Bloody Twin Pr.

Richards, Brian, ed. see Canalos, David, et al.

Richards, Brian J. Language Development & Individual Differences: A Study of Auxiliary Verb Learning. (Illus.). 270p. (C). 1990. text 69.95 (*0-521-36253-9*) Cambridge U Pr.

Richards, Brian J., jt. auth. see Yamada-Yamamoto, Asako.

Richards, Bruce. Alien Obsession. LC 95-224927. 80p. (J). (gr. 5-9). 1995. pap. text 2.95 (*0-8114-9329-6*) Raintree Steck-V.

— Blind Date. (Freddy Krueger's Tales of Terror Ser.: No. 1). 164p. (YA). 1994. mass mkt. 3.99 (*0-8125-5168-0*, Pub. by Tor Bks) St Martin.

— Fatal Games. (Freddy Krueger's Tales of Terror Ser.: No. 2). (YA). (gr. 6 up). 1995. pap. 3.99 (*0-8125-5189-3*, Pub. by Tor Bks) St Martin.

— The Killing Game. 224p. 1994. pap. 3.50 (*0-8217-4640-5*) NAL.

Richards, Bruce, jt. auth. see Bergantino, David.

Richards, C. Dialogue with the Masters. Arledge, G., ed. 54p. (Orig.). 1994. pap. text 4.00 (*0-9625067-1-0*) Helpers Pr.

— The Helpers. Arledge, G., ed. 44p. (Orig.). 1989. 3.00 (*0-9625067-0-2*) Helpers Pr.

Richards, C., jt. ed. see Ford, J. M.

***Richards, Cara Elizabeth.** The Loss of Innocents: Child Killers & Their Victims. LC 99-39723. 280p. 2000. 55.00 (*0-8420-2602-9*, SR Bks); pap. 19.95 (*0-8420-2603-7*, SR Bks) Scholarly Res Inc.

Richards, Carl. Prey: Designing & Tying New Imitations of Fresh & Saltwater Forage Foods. (Illus.). 144p. 1995. 24.95 (*1-55821-332-5*) Lyons Pr.

Richards, Carl & Braendle, Bob. Caddis Super Hatches. LC 98-132821. 80p. 1997. pap. 24.95 (*1-57188-078-X*) F Amato Pubns.

Richards, Carl, jt. auth. see Pobst, Dick.

Richards, Carl, jt. auth. see Swisher, Doug.

Richards, Carmen, jt. auth. see Siles, Fernando.

Richards, Carol A., jt. auth. see McKasson, Stephen C.

Richards, Caroline, jt. ed. see Lonergan, Anne.

Richards, Caroline C. Village Life in America, 1852-1872. 1977. lib. bdg. 59.95 (*0-8490-2798-5*) Gordon Pr.

— Village Life in America, 1852-1872: Diary of a School Girl. 225p. 1972. reprint ed. 24.95 (*0-87928-029-8*) Corner Hse.

— Village Life in America, 1852-1872 ': Including the Period of the American Civil War As Told by a School-Girl. 3rd unabridged ed. Ackerson, Anne W., ed. (Illus.). 258p. 1997. reprint ed. pap. 16.95 (*0-87928-115-4*) Corner Hse.

Richards, Carolyn, ed. see Coleman, Richard.

***Richards, Cate.** Lotus Notes & Domino 5 Developer's Handbook. (Developer's Handbks.). 1104p. 1999. 54.99 (*0-7821-2424-0*) Sybex.

Richards, Cate. Sams Teach Yourself Lotus Notes 4.6 in 24 Hours. LC 97-81440. 400p. 1998. pap. 19.99 (*0-672-31256-5*) Mac USA.

— Special Edition Using Lotus Notes & Domino 4.6: Special Edition. LC 97-80538. (Using... Ser.). 1000p. 1998. 49.99 (*0-7897-1535-X*) Que.

Richards, Cate & Robinson, Laura. Lotus Notes & Domino R5 24Seven. 4th ed. (24seven Ser.). 704p. 2000. 34.99 (*0-7821-2518-2*) Sybex.

Richards, Cathy, jt. ed. see Coker, Annabel.

Richards, Ceri, tr. see Stuart-Smith, Stephen & Redden, Mary, eds.

***Richards, Charles W.** The Second Was First. LC 98-75082. (Illus.). 519p. 1999. 34.95 (*0-9675054-0-2*) C W Richards.

Richards, Charlotte, ed. see Tacoma Writers Club Staff.

Richards, CherylAnne, jt. auth. see Michrina, Barry P.

Richards, Chris. Debt Control: How to Get Out of Debt & Stay Out of Debt. (Illus.). 176p. 1998. pap. 19.95 (*1-885373-19-8*) Emerald Ink.

— Hombro con Hombro: Un Llamado Para Descubrir la Fuerza Que Existe En la Unidad Del Companerismo Masculino. (Hombre a Hombre Ser.). (SPA.). 114p. 1997. mass mkt. 3.00 (*1-885630-44-1*) HLM Producciones.

— Teen Spirits: Music & Identity in Media Education. LC 98-215023. (Media, Education & Culture Ser.). 230p. 1998. pap. write for info. (*1-85728-859-9*, Pub. by UCL Pr Ltd) Taylor & Francis.

Richards, Chris, ed. The Illustrated Encyclopedia of World Religions. LC 97-30752. (Illustrated Bks.). (Illus.). 256p. 1997. pap. 34.95 (*1-85230-997-0*, Pub. by Element MA) Penguin Putnam.

Richards, Chris & Australia. Gathering Momentum: Commercialisation in the Public Sector. LC 94-242638. vi, 111 p. 1990. write for info. (*0-642-15418-X*) Aust Inst Criminology.

Richards, Cinda. One from the Heart. large type ed. (Linford Romance Library). 320p. 1994. pap. 16.99 (*0-7089-7521-6*, Linford) Ulverscroft.

Richards, Claire E. Raffia. 1999. 29.95 (*1-86126-161-6*, Pub. by Crolwood) Trafalgar.

Richards, Clarice E. A Tenderfoot Bride: Tales from an Old Ranch. LC 88-14347. (Illus.). viii, 240p. 1988. pap. 7.95 (*0-8032-8930-8*, Bison Books) U of Nebr Pr.

Richards, Clay. Marble Jungle. 1961. 12.95 (*0-8392-1064-7*) Astor-Honor.

Richards, Cliff. Prayers That Prevail for Your Children. 1994. pap. 9.99 (*0-932081-39-8*) Victory Hse.

Richards, Clift. More Prayers That Prevail. LC 96-228293. (Believer's Manual of Prayers Ser.). 1995. pap. 8.99 (*0-932081-46-0*) Victory Hse.

Richards, Colin. How Shall We School Our Children? Primary Education & Its Future. LC 98-188412. 1998. 85.00 (*0-7507-0781-X*) Taylor & Francis.

— Sheriff Pat Garrett's Last Days: A History. LC 85-25020. (Illus.). 96p. (Orig.). 1986. pap. 8.95 (*0-86534-079-X*) Sunstone Pr.

Richards, Colin, ed. Primary Teacher Education: High Status? High Standards? LC 99-160750. 232p. 1998. 85.00 (*0-7507-0846-8*, Falmer Pr) Taylor & Francis.

Richards, Colin & Taylor, Philip H. How Shall We School Our Children? Primary Education & Its Future. LC 98-188412. (New Millennium Ser.). ix, 193p. 1998. 26.95 (*0-7507-0780-1*, Falmer Pr) Taylor & Francis.

Richards, Colin, jt. ed. see Pearson, Michael P.

Richards, Connie L., ed. see Gilman, Charlotte Perkins.

Richards, Constance. Making Books & Journals: 20 Great Weekend Projects. LC 98-45006. (Weekend Crafter Ser.). (Illus.). 80p. 1999. pap. 14.95 (*1-57990-092-5*) Lark Books.

Richards, Constance, jt. auth. see Pacher, Sara.

***Richards, Constance E.** Creative Giftwraps: Ideas & Inspirations, Tips & Techniques. LC 99-44190. (Illus.). 2000. 24.95 (*1-57990-154-9*) Lark Books.

***Richards, Constance S.** Transnational Feminism & Literature: Studies in Woolf, Wicomb & Walker. (Wellesley Studies in Critical Theory, Literary History & Culture: Vol. 20). 180p. 2000. 50.00 (*0-8153-3366-8*, H2156) Garland.

Richards, Cory L., jt. auth. see Gold, Rachel B.

Richards, Craig E. Microcomputer Applications for Strategic Management in Education: A Case Study Approach. 127p. (C). 1989. pap. text 22.95 (*0-582-28668-9*, 71684) Longman.

R

Richards, D. J., ed. Mikhail Lermontov: A Hero of Our Time. (Bristol Russian Texts Ser.). (RUS.). (C). 1992. reprint ed. pap. 20.95 (*1-85399-314-X*, Pub. by Brist Class Pr) Focus Pub-R Pullins.

Richards, D. J., tr. see Suetin, A. S.

***Richards, Dan.** Getting Clients Keeping Clients: The Essential Guide for Tomorrow's Financial Advisor. LC 99-46498. 400p. 2000. text 59.95 (*0-471-36329-4*) Wiley.

Richards, Daniel B. Hill Family History. (Illus.). 278p. 1998. reprint ed. pap. 42.00 (*0-8328-9132-0*); reprint ed. lib. bdg. 52.00 (*0-8328-9131-2*) Higginson Bk Co.

Richards, Daniel L. Building & Managing Your Private Practice. 268p. 1990. pap. text 32.95 (*1-55620-071-4*, 72031) Am Coun Assn.

Richards, Daniel T. & Eakin, Dottie. Collection Development & Assessment in Health Sciences Libraries. LC 96-31662. (Current Practice in Health Sciences Librarianship Ser.: Vol. 4). 340p. 1997. 47.50 (*0-8108-3201-1*) Scarecrow.

Richards, Dave. Globetrotter's Guide to Kenya. Globetrotter Staff, ed. (Globe Trotter Travel Guides Ser.). (Illus.). 128p. 1996. pap. 30.00 (*1-85368-363-9*, Pub. by New5 Holland) Globe Pequot.

Richards, David. Civil Service under the Conservatives, 1979-1997: Whitehall's Political Poodles. LC 97-9219. 300p. 1997. 59.95 (*1-898723-63-X*, Pub. by Sussex Acad Pr); pap. 24.95 (*1-898723-64-8*, Pub. by Sussex Acad Pr) Intl Spec Bk.

Richards, David. Hockey Dreams: Memories of a Man Who Couldn't Play. 248p. 1997. pap. 18.95 (*0-385-25648-5*) Bantam.

Richards, David. Masks of Difference: Cultural Representations in Literature, Anthropology & Art. (Cultural Margins Ser.: No. 2). (Illus.). 362p. (C). 1995. pap. text 22.95 (*0-521-47972-X*) Cambridge U Pr.

***Richards, David.** A Photographic Guide to the Birds of East Africa. 2nd ed. (Photographic Wildlife Pocket Guides Ser.). (Illus.). 144p. 2000. pap. 15.95 (*0-88359-054-9*, RCB-0549, R Curtis Bk) R Curtis Pubng.

Richards, David. Russian Rightists & the Revolution of Nineteen Hundred Five. LC 94-8850. (Cultural Margins Ser.: No. 2). (Illus.). 302p. (C). 1995. pap. text 29.95 (*0-521-48386-7*) Cambridge U Pr.

Richards, David, jt. auth. see Foglia, Leonard.

Richards, David, jt. ed. see Schulte, Hans.

Richards, David, tr. see Bunin, Ivan A.

***Richards, David A. J.** Free Speech & the Politics of Identity. LC 99-47143. 296p. 2000. write for info. (*0-19-829886-2*) OUP.

— Identity & the Case for Gay Rights: Race, Gender & Religion as Analogies. LC 99-32745. 217p. 2000. pap. 14.00 (*0-226-71209-5*) U Ch Pr.

Richards, David A. J. Italian American: The Racializing of an Ethic Identity. LC 98-53611. 273p. 1999. 35.00 (*0-8147-7520-9*) NYU Pr.

Richards, David Adams. Blood Ties. 7.95p. 1996. pap. 7.95 (*0-7710-9887-1*) McCland & Stewart.

— Coming of Winter. 1996. pap. text 7.95 (*0-7710-9885-5*) McCland & Stewart.

— Conscience & the Constitution: History, Theory, & the Law of the Reconstruction Amendments. LC 92-42895. 248p. (C). 1993. text 42.50 (*0-691-03231-9*, Pub. by Princeton U Pr) Cal Prin Full Svc.

— Evening Snow Will Bring Such Peace. 1990. 24.95 (*0-7710-7462-X*) McCland & Stewart.

— Evening Snow Will Bring Such Peace. 1991. mass mkt. 5.99 (*0-7710-7463-8*) McCland & Stewart.

— For Those Who Hunt the Wounded Down. 1994. pap. 14.95 (*0-7710-7464-6*) McCland & Stewart.

— Hope in the Desperate Hour. 224p. 1996. pap. 19.99 (*0-7710-7459-X*) McCland & Stewart.

Richards, David Adams. A Lad from Brantford & Other Essays. 1994. pap. 9.00 (*0-921411-25-1*) Genl Dist Srvs.

Richards, David Adams. Lines on the Water: A Fisherman's Life on the Miramichi. 1998. 29.95 (*0-385-25697-3*) Bantam.

— Lives of Short Duration. 1996. pap. 7.95 (*0-7710-9886-3*) McCland & Stewart.

— Nights Below Station Street. 1994. pap. 12.95 (*0-7710-7465-4*) McCland & Stewart.

Richards, David Adams. Nights Below Station Street. 224p. 1997. reprint ed. pap. 11.95 (*0-7710-7467-0*) McCland & Stewart.

Richards, David Adams. Sex, Drugs, Death & the Law: An Essay on Human Rights & Overcriminalization. LC 81-23392. (Philosophy & Society Ser.). 328p. 1982. 60.00 (*0-8476-7063-5*); pap. 24.50 (*0-8476-7525-4*) Rowman.

— Toleration & the Constitution. 368p. 1989. reprint ed. pap. text 24.95 (*0-19-505947-6*) OUP.

— Women, Gays & the Constitution: The Grounds for Feminism & Gay Rights in Culture & Law. LC 97-35339. 517p. 1998. pap. text 22.00 (*0-226-71207-9*); lib. bdg. 65.00 (*0-226-71206-0*) U Ch Pr.

Richards, David B. Goethe's Search for the Muse: Translation & Creativity. (German Language & Literature Monographs: No. 7). vi, 114p. 1979. 29.00 (*90-272-0967-7*) J Benjamins Pubng Co.

Richards, David G. Exploring the Divided Self: Hermann Hesse's "Steppenwolf" & Its Critics. (LCGERM Ser.). x, 169p. (C). 1996. 55.00 (*1-879751-77-1*) Camden Hse.

— The Hero's Quest for the Self: An Archetypal Approach to Hesse's Demian & Other Novels. LC 87-8167. (Illus.). 170p. (Orig.). (C). 1987. pap. text 19.50 (*0-8191-6316-3*, Pub. by McMaster Colloquium) U Pr of Amer.

***Richards, David K.** The Federal Reserve Needs to Raise Interest Rates Now. (New Ser.: Vol. 24). 10p. 1999. pap. 15.00 (*0-86682-110-4*) Ctr Intl Relations.

Richards, David P. How to Discover Your Personal Painting Style. LC 94-41902. (Illus.). 144p. 1995. 27.99 (*0-89134-593-0*, North Lght Bks) F & W Pubns Inc.

Richards, David R. Tea: The Gentle Brew. 44p. 1985. pap. text 9.95 (*0-9614431-0-3*) D R Richards.

Richards, Dean & Bills, Peter. Deano. (Illus.). 288p. 1996. pap. 13.95 (*0-575-60027-6*, Pub. by V Gollancz) Trafalgar.

— Deano. (Illus.). 256p. 1996. 39.95 (*0-575-06110-3*, Pub. by V Gollancz) Trafalgar.

Richards, Deanna, et al, eds. The Ecology of Industry: Sectors & Linkages. 150p. 1997. pap. 29.00 (*0-309-06355-8*) Natl Acad Pr.

Richards, Deanna J., ed. The Industrial Green Game: Implications for Environmental Design & Management. LC 96-40095. 280p. 1997. 39.95 (*0-309-05294-7*) Natl Acad Pr.

Richards, Deborah D., ed. see Ibrahim, Zafar Y.

Richards, Debra D., ed. see Ibrahim, Zafar Y.

Richards, Dee. Mini-Baccarat & Roulette Guide for Women. Frerichs, Debby, ed. 50p. 1996. 10.95 (*1-890244-02-3*) D&D Pubns.

Richards, Dell. Superstars: Twelve Lesbians Who Changed the World. 256p. 1993. pap. 12.95 (*0-88184-955-3*) Carroll & Graf.

Richards, Delphene & Bishop, Carolyn, eds. Home Decorating Guide. LC 73-11786. (Family Circle Bks.). (Illus.). 128p. 1977. 12.95 (*0-405-09843-X*) Ayer.

Richards, Delphine, jt. auth. see Newman, Peter.

Richards, Denis. An Illustrated History of Modern Europe. 7th ed. 1986. pap. text 20.49 (*0-582-33204-4*, 72074) Longman.

— An Illustrated History of Modern Europe 1789-1974. (Illus.). 369p. (Orig.). (gr. 9-12). 1977. pap. text 18.96 (*0-582-34106-X*) Longman.

Richards, Denise. Blackjack for Women. Frerichs, Debby, ed. 50p. (Orig.). 1996. per. 10.95 (*1-890244-01-5*) D&D Pubns.

— The Craps Advantage for Women. Frerichs, Debby, ed. 50p. 1996. 10.95 (*1-890244-03-1*) D&D Pubns.

— How to Open an Elegant Resale Boutique. 1977. pap. 5.50 (*0-9614714-1-7*) Pavillion Fashion.

— Let It Ride & Caribbean Stud Poker for Women. Frerichs, Debby, ed. 54p. (Orig.). 1996. per. 10.95 (*1-890244-04-X*) D&D Pubns.

— Searching for a New You. Media-Siegel Graphics, tr. LC 85-61014. (Illus.). 109p. 1985. pap. 7.95 (*0-9614714-0-9*) Pavillion Fashion.

— The Woman's Guide to Casino Gambling: Table Games. Frerichs, Debby, ed. 140p. (Orig.). 1996. per. 19.95 (*1-890244-00-7*) D&D Pubns.

Richards, Dennis, jt. auth. see Oleson, Keith W.

Richards, Diane. Angel Kisses. 70p. 1996. pap. 10.50 (*1-56770-346-1*) S Scheewe Pubns.

— Angels in My Stocking. (Illus.). 98p. 1992. pap. 10.50 (*1-56770-254-6*) S Scheewe Pubns.

— Forever in My Heart. 100p. 1988. pap. text 6.50 (*1-56770-188-4*) S Scheewe Pubns.

— Forever in My Heart, No. II. 100p. 1989. pap. text 10.50 (*1-56770-205-8*) S Scheewe Pubns.

***Richards, Diane.** Heavenly Treasures. (Illus.). 72p. 1999. pap. 10.50 (*1-56770-472-7*) S Scheewe Pubns.

Richards, Diane. Memories in My Heart. 100p. 1988. pap. text 6.50 (*1-56770-189-2*) S Scheewe Pubns.

— Nostalgic Dreams. 96p. 1993. pap. 10.50 (*1-56770-273-2*) S Scheewe Pubns.

Richards, Dick. Artful Work: Awakening Joy, Meaning & Commitment in the Workplace. LC 94-46161. (Illus.). 144p. 1995. 25.00 (*1-881052-63-X*) Berrett-Koehler.

— Artful Work: Awakening Joy, Meaning & Commitment in the Workplace. 144p. 1997. reprint ed. pap. 12.00 (*0-425-15914-0*) Berkley Pub.

***Richards, Dick.** Get It Across! Effective Communication at Work. 180p. 2000. pap. 6.95 (*0-7160-2120-X*, Pub. by Elliot RW Bks) Midpt Trade.

Richards, Dick. Setting Your Genius Free: How to Discover Your Spirit & Calling. LC 98-134195. 224p. 1998. pap. 12.95 (*0-425-16165-X*) Berkley Pub.

— South-East Asian Ceramics: Thai, Khmer, & Vietnamese from the Collection of the Art Gallery of South Australia, Adelaide. (Asia Collection). (Illus.). 210p. 1995. text 95.00 (*967-65-3075-1*) OUP.

Richards, Dick & Smyth, Susan. Assessing Your Team: Seven Measures of Team Success Team Leader's Package. LC 94-65546. 32p. 1994. pap. 15.00 (*0-88390-437-3*, Pfiffr & Co) Jossey-Bass.

— Assessing Your Team: Team Member's Manual. LC 94-65546. 32p. 1994. pap., student ed. 9.95 (*0-88390-420-9*, Pfiffr & Co) Jossey-Bass.

Richards, Dick, et al. Waste-to-Energy Commercial Facilities Profiles: Technical, Operational & Economic Perspectives. LC 89-70986. (Pollution Technology Review Ser.: No. 177). (Illus.). 423p. 1990. 58.00 (*0-8155-1226-0*) Noyes.

Richards, Dickinson W., jt. ed. see Fishman, Alfred P.

Richards, Dixie, ed. see Ward, J. Leroy & Levin, Ginger.

Richards, Dixie, ed. see Ward, J. LeRoy & Levin, Ginger.

Richards, Don L. Twilight. 289p. (Orig.). 1992. pap. 7.95 (*0-9632478-0-8*) R T Partners.

Richards, Donald E., jt. auth. see Wark, Kenneth.

Richards, Donald M. & Ratsoy, Eugene W. Introduction to the Economics of Canadian Education. 127p. (Orig.). (C). 1987. pap. text 17.95 (*0-920490-66-2*) Temeron Bks.

Richards, Donald S., ed. Hypergeometric Functions on Domains of Positivity, Jack Polynomials, & Applications: (Proceedings of an AMS Special Session Held May 22-23, 1991 in Tampa, Florida) LC 92-26610. (Contemporary Mathematics Ser.: Vol. 138). 259p. 1992. pap. 44.00 (*0-8218-5159-4*, CONM/138) Am Math.

Richards, Dorothy & Buyukmichi, Hope S. Beaversprite: My Years Building an Animal Sanctuary. 2nd ed. LC 77-24150. (Illus.). 192p. 1984. pap. 9.95 (*0-932334-67-9*, NY73054) Hrt of the Lakes.

Richards, Dorothy S. A Practical Guide to Selecting a Cat. (Illus.). 162p. 1995. 10.95 (*1-56465-150-9*, 16014) Tetra Pr.

Richards, Douglas. I'm on the Way to a Brighter Day: A Collection of Poems. LC 83-73535. 64p. 1984. pap. 7.95 (*0-88396-202-0*) Blue Mtn Art.

Richards, Douglas, ed. 42 Gifts I'd Like to Give to You. LC 95-23497. (Illus.). 64p. 1995. pap. 8.95 (*0-88396-420-1*) Blue Mtn Art.

Richards, Dusty. By the Cut of Your Clothes. Grad, Doug, ed. 224p. (Orig.). 1995. mass mkt. write for info. (*0-671-87242-7*) PB.

— From Hell to Breakfast. 1994. mass mkt. 3.99 (*0-671-87241-9*) PB.

***Richards, Dusty.** The Lawless Land. 264p. 2000. mass mkt. 5.99 (*0-312-97410-8*) St Martin.

— Servant of the Law. 2000. mass mkt. write for info. (*0-312-97687-9*) St Martin.

Richards, E. & Clough, Monica. Cromartie: Highland Life 1650-1914. 672p. 1989. text 59.00 (*0-08-037732-7*, Pub. by Aberdeen U Pr) Macmillan.

Richards, E. G. Mapping Time: The Calendar & Its History. LC 98-24957. (Illus.). 464p. 1999. 35.00 (*0-19-850413-6*) OUP.

***Richards, E. G.** Mapping Time: The Calendar & Its History. (Illus.). 460p. 2000. pap. 16.95 (*0-19-286205-7*) OUP.

Richards, E. J. & Mead, D. J., eds. Noise & Acoustic Fatigue in Aeronautics. LC 68-55813. (Illus.). 524p. reprint ed. pap. 162.50 (*0-608-11673-4*, 201614900098) Bks Demand.

Richards, E. M. Commercialization of Non-Timber Forest Products in Amazonia. 1993. pap. 30.00 (*0-85954-338-2*, Pub. by Nat Res Inst) St Mut.

Richards, E. Randolph. Secretary in the Letters to Paul. (WissUNT Neuen Testament Ser.). 280p. (Orig.). 1990. pap. 77.50 (*3-16-145575-4*, Pub. by JCB Mohr) Coronet Bks.

Richards, Earl J., ed. Christine de Pizan & Medieval French Lyric. LC 98-14268. 224p. 1998. 55.00 (*0-8130-1618-5*) U Press Fla.

***Richards, Edward P. & Rathbun, Katharine C.** Law & the Physician. 2nd ed. 560p. 1999. 99.00 (*0-8342-1380-X*) Aspen Pub.

Richards, Edward P., III & Rathbun, Katharine C. Law & the Physician. 2nd ed. LC 99-22815. 1999. write for info. (*0-8342-1603-5*) Aspen Pub.

— Medical Risk Management: Preventive Legal Strategies for Health Care Providers. LC 82-16346. 311p. 1983. 73.00 (*0-89443-840-9*) Aspen Pub.

Richards, Elaine, tr. see Klock, Peter.

Richards, Elijah. When I Am Weak Then I Am Strong. 67p. (Orig.). 1994. pap. write for info. (*0-913183-04-0*) Lantern Lght.

Richards, Elise. Cut Ups! Art Starts. 1996. pap. 6.95 (*0-8167-4236-7*) Troll Communs.

— Funky Junk. (Illus.). 16p. (J). (gr. 2-9). 1997. pap. 6.95 (*0-8167-4401-7*) Troll Communs.

— Hot New Friendship Bracelets. 1997. pap. 7.95 (*0-8167-4213-8*) Troll Communs.

— Inch Book. (J). 1997. pap. 6.95 (*0-8167-4297-9*) Troll Communs.

— The Money Book: Learn to Count & Use Money. (Illus.). (J). (ps-3). 1997. pap. 6.95 (*0-8167-4296-0*) Troll Communs.

— Turned on by Electricity. (J). 1997. pap. 7.95 (*0-8167-4254-5*) Troll Communs.

Richards, Elise & Kerr, A. Bare Bones. LC 98-164129. 16 p. 1997. write for info. (*0-8167-4507-2*) Troll Communs.

Richards, Elizabeth. Every Day: A Novel. LC 96-37231. 1997. 22.00 (*0-671-00155-8*) PB.

— Every Day: A Novel. 240p. 1999. pap. 12.00 (*0-671-00156-6*, PB Trade Paper) PB.

— The Ravishers. 1992. write for info. (*0-9633891-0-6*) B S Richards.

— Rescue. LC 98-43727. 276p. 1999. 22.00 (*0-671-02397-7*, PB Hardcover) PB.

— Rescue. 288p. 2000. reprint ed. per. 12.95 (*0-671-02398-5*) PB.

Richards, Ellen H. Euthenics: The Science of Controllable Environment: A Plea for Better Conditions As a First Step Toward Higher Human Efficiency. Rosenkrantz, Barbara G., ed. LC 76-40639. (Public Health in America Ser.). (Illus.). 1977. reprint ed. lib. bdg. 19.95 (*0-405-09827-8*) Ayer.

Richards, Emilie. Bayou Midnight. 1994. per. 3.59 (*0-373-45168-7*) Silhouette.

***Richards, Emilie.** Beautiful Lies. 539p. 1999. per. 5.99 (*1-55166-492-5*, 1-66492-9, Mira Bks) Harlequin Bks.

Richards, Emilie. A Classic Encounter. (Men at Work Ser.: Vol. 33). 1998. per. 4.50 (*0-373-81045-8*) Harlequin Bks.

— Duncan's Lady: (Heartbreakers, the Men of Midnight) (Intimate Moments Ser.). 1995. per. 3.75 (*0-373-07625-8*, 1-07625-6) Silhouette.

— Un Enfant Tant Desire. (Amours d'Aujourd'Hui Ser.: No. 308). (FRE.). 1998. mass mkt. 4.99 (*0-373-38308-8*, 1-38308-2) Harlequin Bks.

— Good Time Man. (Family Continuity Program Ser.: No. 33). 1999. per. 4.50 (*0-373-82181-6*, 1-82181-8) Harlequin Bks.

— Iain Ross's Woman. (Intimate Moments Ser.). 1995. per. 3.75 (*0-373-07644-4*, 1-07644-7) Silhouette.

Richards, Emilie. Iain Ross's Woman. large type ed. (Large Print Ser.). 384p. 1997. 20.95 (*0-373-59850-5*) Harlequin Bks.

Richards, Emilie. Iron Lace. (Mira Bks.). 480p. 1996. per. 5.99 (*1-55166-152-7*, 1-66152-9, Mira Bks) Harlequin Bks.

— MacDougall's Darling. (Intimate Moments Ser.). 1995. per. 3.75 (*0-373-07655-X*, 1-07655-3) Silhouette.

— MacDougall's Darling. large type ed. (Silhouette Romance Ser.). 1998. 20.95 (*0-373-59856-4*) Thorndike Pr.

— Mail-Order Matty. (Special Edition Ser.: No. 1113). 1997. per. 3.99 (*0-373-24113-5*, 1-24113-2) Silhouette.

***Richards, Emilie.** Mail-Order Matty. large type ed. (Romance Ser.). 2000. 22.95 (*0-373-59721-5*) Silhouette.

Richards, Emilie. Once More with Feeling. 384p. (Orig.). 1996. mass mkt. 5.99 (*0-380-78363-0*, Avon Bks) Morrow Avon.

— One Moment Past Midnight: Men in Blue. (Intimate Moments Ser.: No. 949). 1999. mass mkt. 4.25 (*0-373-07949-4*, 1-07949-0) Silhouette.

— One Perfect Rose. (Special Edition Ser.: No. 750). 1992. per. 3.39 (*0-373-09750-6*, 5-09750-6) Harlequin Bks.

— Outback Nights. (Here Come the Grooms Ser.: No. 29). 1996. per. 3.99 (*0-373-30129-4*, 1-30129-0) Harlequin Bks.

— Rising Tides. 1997. per. 5.99 (*1-55166-273-6*, 0-66273-4, Mira Bks) Harlequin Bks.

— Somewhere Out There. (Intimate Moments Ser.). 1993. mass mkt. 3.39 (*0-373-07498-0*, 5-07498-4) Silhouette.

— The Trouble with Joe. 1997. per. 5.50 (*1-55166-279-5*, 1-66279-0, Mira Bks) Harlequin Bks.

— The Trouble with Joe. 1994. mass mkt. 3.50 (*0-373-09873-1*, 5-09873-6) Silhouette.

— Twice upon a Time. 384p. 1997. mass mkt. 5.99 (*0-380-78364-9*, Avon Bks) Morrow Avon.

***Richards, Emilie.** Whiskey Island. 512p. 2000. per. 6.50 (*1-55166-570-0*, 1-66570-2, Mira Bks) Harlequin Bks.

Richards, Emilie. Woman Without a Name. 1996. per. 3.99 (*0-373-07751-3*, 1-07751-0) Silhouette.

***Richards, Emilie.** Woman Without a Name. (Silhouette Ser.). 1999. 21.95 (*0-373-59595-6*) Silhouette.

Richards, Emilie & Michaels, Kasey. A Funny Thing Happened on the Way to the Delivery Room. 1997. per. 5.99 (*0-373-48341-4*, 1-48341-1) Harlequin Bks.

Richards, Emilie, jt. auth. see Blake, Jennifer.

***Richards, Eric.** The Highland Clearances. 2000. pap. 19.95 (*1-84158-040-6*, Pub. by Birlinn Ltd) Dufour.

— Patrick Sellar & the Highland Clearances: Homicide, Eviction & the Price of Progress. 352p. 2000. pap. text 25.00 (*1-902930-13-4*) Col U Pr.

Richards, Eric L. Law for Global Business. LC 93-48202. (Legal Studies in Business). (Illus.). 496p. (C). 1994. text 68.95 (*0-256-11372-6*, Irwn McGrw-H) McGrw-H Hghr Educ.

Richards, Ernest, jt. auth. see Hodgson, John.

Richards, Ernie S. & Weller, Robert F. Shipwrecks Near Wabasso Beach. (Illus.). 96p. (Orig.). 1995. pap. 9.95 (*0-9628359-4-3*) Cross Anchor.

Richards, Ernie S., ed. see Weller, Robert F.

Richards, Eugene. Americans We. (Illus.). 132p. 1995. 60.00 (*0-89381-594-2*) Aperture.

— Aperture Issue No. 144: Shared Lives: The Communal Spirit Today. (Illus.). 80p. 1996. pap. 27.95 (*0-89381-683-3*) Aperture.

— Knife & Gun Club: Scenes from an Emergency Room. LC 88-39302. (Illus.). 240p. 1995. pap. 21.00 (*0-87113-624-4*, Atlntc Mnthly) Grove-Atltic.

— The Knife & Gun Club: Scenes from an Emergency Room. LC 88-39302. (Illus.). 240p. 1995. 35.00 (*0-87113-623-6*, Atlntc Mnthly) Grove-Atltic.

Richards, Eugene, photos by. Cocaine True, Cocaine Blue. (Illus.). 160p. 1994. 60.00 (*0-89381-543-8*) Aperture.

— Cocaine True, Cocaine Blue. (Illus.). 160p. 1996. pap. 44.95 (*0-89381-687-6*) Aperture.

Richards, F., ed. Coastal Upwelling. (Coastal & Estuarine Sciences Ser.: Vol. 1). (Illus.). 529p. 1981. 29.00 (*0-87590-250-2*) Am Geophysical.

Richards, F. M. & Wyckoff, H. W. Ribonuclease-S. (Atlas of Molecular Structures in Biology Ser.). (Illus.). 1974. pap. 13.50 (*0-19-854704-8*) OUP.

Richards, F. Robert & Richards. Once Around San Diego: The Essential Sights. (Illus.). 50p. 1997. pap. 12.95 incl. audio (*0-9661311-0-X*, 100) Comp Cir Tours.

Richards, Fiona V. Scarab Seals from a Middle to Late Bronze Age Tomb at Pella in Jordan. (Orbis Biblicus et Orientalis Ser.: Vol. 117). 138p. 1992. text 34.50 (*3-7278-0813-6*, Pub. by Presses Univ Fribourg) Eisenbrauns.

Richards, Francis A., ed. Coastal Upwelling Ecosystems Analysis Program. 1977. pap. 23.00 (*0-08-021375-8*, Pergamon Pr) Elsevier.

Richards, Francis A. & Armon, Cheryl. Beyond Formal Operations: Late Adolescent & Adult Cognitive Development. Commons, Michael L., ed. LC 83-21142. 463p. 1984. 65.00 (*0-275-91139-X*, C1139, Praeger Pubs) Greenwood.

Richards, Frank F., jt. auth. see Baumgarten, Alexander.

Richards, Fred & Welch, I. David, eds. Sightings: Essays in Humanistic Psychology. LC 72-96552. 228p. (C). 1973. pap. 6.95 (*0-88310-002-9*) Publishers Consult.

Richards, Fred, jt. ed. see Welch, I. David.

Richards, Frederic M., et al, eds. Advances in Protein Chemistry Vol. 51: Linkage Thermodynamics of Macromolecular Interactions. (Illus.). 473p. (C). 1998. boxed set 99.95 (*0-12-034251-0*) Acad Pr.

— Advances in Protein Chemistry Vol. 52: Cytokines. (Illus.). 310p. (C). 1998. boxed set 99.95 (*0-12-034252-9*) Acad Pr.

Richards, Frederick B. The Black Watch at Ticonderoga. (Illus.). 98p. 1997. reprint ed. pap. 17.00 (*0-8328-6260-6*) Higginson Bk Co.

— The Black Watch at Ticonderoga: And Major Duncan Campbell of Arverawe. (Illus.). 136p. 1999. pap. 16.00 (*0-7884-1106-3*, R310) Heritage Bk.

An Asterisk (*) at the beginning of an entry indicates that the title is appearing for the first time.

Richards, Frederick M., et al, eds. Advances in Protein Chemistry Vol. 50: Protein Misassembly, Vol. 50. (Illus.). 282p. 1997. text 99.00 (*0-12-034250-2*) Morgan Kaufmann.

Richards, G. Scattering Methods in Polymer Science. 2nd ed. 350p. (C). 1996. text 120.00 (*0-13-791567-5*) P-H.

***Richards, G., ed.** Cultural Attractions & European Tourism. (Cabi Publishing Ser.). (Illus.). 288p. 2000. text 75.00 (*0-85199-440-7*) OUP.

Richards, G., ed. Cultural Tourism in Europe. LC 97-108434. (CAB International Publication). (Illus.). 360p. 1996. text 90.00 (*0-85199-104-1*) OUP.

Richards, G. K., jt. auth. see Jones, R. N.

Richards, G. Wolfson. Hell Is a (W)Hole in Heaven: A Gift of Peace from the 21st Century. (Illus.). Date not set. pap. 20.00 (*0-9661267-0-X*) Humanity Inst.

Richards, Gary D., et al. Human Skeletal Biology. (Archives of California Prehistory Ser.: Vol. 24). (Illus.). 178p. (Orig.). (C). 1988. pap. text 19.38 (*1-55567-060-1*) Coyote Press.

Richards, Gavin. Die Kinder. LC 92-80846. 192p. (Orig.). 1993. pap. 6.95 (*0-563-36104-2*, BBC-Parkwest) Parkwest Pubns.

Richards, George. Horoscope for Each Day of the Month. 143p. 1997. pap. 12.00 (*0-89540-237-8*, SB-237, Sun Bks) Sun Pub.

Richards, George C. Cicero. LC 79-109830. 298p. 1970. reprint ed. lib. bdg. 55.00 (*0-8371-4321-7*, RCIC, Greenwood Pr) Greenwood.

Richards, Gertrude R., ed. see Davison, Ellen S.

Richards, Gertrude R., ed. see National Society of Colonial Dames of America Staf.

Richards, Gillian, jt. ed. see Osborn, M. Elizabeth.

Richards, Glyn. The Philosophy of Gandhi: A Study of His Basic Ideas. 192p. (C). 1996. pap. text 18.00 (*0-7007-0228-8*, Pub. by Curzon Pr Ltd) UH Pr.

— A Source-Book of Modern Hinduism. 228p. (Orig.). (C). 1996. pap. text 20.00 (*0-7007-0317-9*, Pub. by Curzon Pr Ltd) UH Pr.

— Studies in Religion. LC 95-5584. 260p. 1995. text 69.95 (*0-312-12676-X*) St Martin.

— Towards a Theology of Religions. 208p. 1989. 55.00 (*0-415-02450-1*) Routledge.

Richards, Graham. Human Evolution: An Introduction for the Behavioral Sciences. (Illus.). 448p. 1987. pap. text 32.50 (*0-7102-1381-6*, Routledge Thoemms) Routledge.

— Mental Machinery: The Origins & Consequences of Psychological Ideas, 1600-1850. LC 92-1552. 416p. (C). 1992. text 55.00 (*0-8018-4544-0*) Johns Hopkins.

— Putting Psychology in Its Place: An Introduction from a Critical Historical Perspective. 208p. (C). 1996. 70.00 (*0-415-12862-5*); pap. 24.99 (*0-415-12863-3*) Routledge.

— Race Racism & Psychology: Towards a Reflexive History. LC 98-117261. 392p. (C). 1997. 85.00 (*0-415-10140-9*) Routledge.

— Race, Racism & Psychology: Towards a Reflexive History. LC 98-117261. 392p. (C). 1997. pap. 27.99 (*0-415-10141-7*) Routledge.

Richards, Grant. Memories of a Misspent Youth, 1872-1896. LC 79-8073. reprint ed. 35.00 (*0-404-18383-2*) AMS Pr.

***Richards, Greg & Hall, Derek R.** Tourism & Sustainable Community Development. LC 99-42599. 296p. 2000. 90.00 (*0-415-22462-4*) Routledge.

Richards, Guy. Imperial Agent: The Goleniewski-Romanov Case. 1966. 9.95 (*0-8159-5804-8*) Devin.

— The Rescue of the Romanovs. LC 74-27953. (Illus.). 1975. 14.95 (*0-8159-6717-9*) Devin.

— Sibelius: 20th Century Composers. 1997. pap. text 19.95 (*0-7148-3581-1*, Pub. by Phaidon Press) Phaidon Pr.

***Richards, Guy.** World War Two Troop Type Parachutes: Axis: Germany Italy Japan. (Illus.). 144p. 2000. pap. 29.95 (*0-7643-1110-7*) Schiffer.

Richards, Guyon. The Chain of Life. 104p. 1954. pap. 11.95 (*0-85032-119-0*, Pub. by C W Daniel) Natl Bk Netwk.

— The Chain of Life. 3rd ed. 232p. pap. 17.95 (*0-8464-4202-7*) Beekman Pubs.

Richards, H. J. A Carol Service for Children. 20p. (J). 1988. pap. 2.95 (*0-8146-1548-1*) Liturgical Pr.

— A Way of the Cross for Children. 24p. (J). 1989. pap. 2.95 (*0-8146-1805-7*) Liturgical Pr.

Richards, H. M., Jr. Faith & Prayer. (Uplook Ser.). 32p. 1971. pap. 0.99 (*0-8163-0071-2*, 06010-3) Pacific Pr Pub Assn.

Richards, H. M. Weiser Family. (Illus.). 115p. 1992. reprint ed. pap. 18.50 (*0-8328-2761-4*); reprint ed. lib. bdg. 28.50 (*0-8328-2760-6*) Higginson Bk Co.

Richards, H. M. S., Jr. New Ways to Tell the Old, Old Story. Crosby, Tim, ed. 64p. 1991. pap. 1.49 (*0-8163-1074-2*) Pacific Pr Pub Assn.

Richards, Harold M. Practical Secrets of the Spiritual Life: How-To Revealed. LC 89-2198. 160p. (Orig.). 1989. pap. 9.00 (*0-922615-05-5*) Hampton Hill.

Richards, Hazel. Make a Treat with Wheat. 3rd ed. 67p. 1968. reprint ed. spiral bd. 6.95 (*0-9670776-0-5*) L G Richards.

Richards, Heidi S. Rose Marketing on a Daisy Budget: Learn the Secrets to Blooming Profits. LC 98-177697. 220p. 1998. pap. 19.95 (*0-9656797-0-5*) WUN Pubns.

— South Florida Network Directory of Women's Business Organizations, Vol. 2. 2nd rev. ed. 187p. 1998. pap. 24.95 (*0-9656797-1-3*) WUN Pubns.

— "Yes" Is Only the Beginning: The Ideal Wedding Planner. 60p. 1999. pap. 5.95 (*0-9656797-3-X*) WUN Pubns.

Richards, Helene, jt. auth. see Freeman, Sheila.

Richards, Henry J. Therapy of the Substance Abuse Syndromes. LC 92-48826. 496p. 1994. 70.00 (*0-87668-539-4*) Aronson.

Richards, Henry J., tr. see Bass, Nelson E.

Richards, Henry M. The Pennsylvania-German in the Revolutionary War, 1775-1783. (Illus.). 542p. 1991. reprint ed. 27.50 (*0-8063-0793-5*, 4890) Clearfield Co.

Richards, Herbert. A Beginner's Guide to Tropical Fish. (Beginner's Guide Ser.). (Illus.). 64p. 1986. 4.95 (*0-86622-704-0*, T-108) TFH Pubns.

— Dog Breeding for Professionals. (Illus.). 224p. 1978. 19.95 (*0-86622-655-9*, H969) TFH Pubns.

Richards, Horace G. Annotated Bibliography of Quaternary Shorelines (Second Supplement, 1970-1973) (Special Publication: No. 11). 214p. 1974. pap. 10.00 (*0-910006-45-8*) Acad Nat Sci Phila.

Richards, Horace G., compiled by. Catalogue of Invertebrate Fossil Types at the Academy of Natural Sciences of Philadelphia. (Special Publication: No. 8). 222p. (Orig.). 1968. pap. 7.00 (*0-910006-36-9*) Acad Nat Sci Phila.

Richards, Horace G. & Fairbridge, Rhodes W. Annotated Bibliography of Quaternary Shorelines (1945-1964) (Special Publication: No. 6). 280p. (Orig.). 1965. pap. 7.00 (*0-910006-34-2*) Acad Nat Sci Phila.

Richards, Horace G., et al. Annotated Bibliography of Quaternary Shorelines (Supplement, 1965-1969) (Special Publication: No. 10). 240p. 1970. pap. 7.00 (*0-910006-44-X*); lib. bdg. 9.00 (*0-910006-37-7*) Acad Nat Sci Phila.

Richards, Howard. Letters from Quebec: A Philosophy for Peace & Justice. LC 93-37945. 448p. 1994. 74.95 (*1-883255-17-1*); pap. 44.95 (*1-883255-16-3*) Intl Scholars.

Richards, Hoy A., et al. Highway-Rail Grade Crossing Surfaces. LC 97-69824. (Synthesis of Highway Practice Ser.). 159p. 1995. 30.00 (*0-309-06106-7*, CP005) Natl Acad Pr.

Richards, Hubert J. The Gospel According to St. Paul. 136p. (Orig.). (C). 1988. 45.00 (*0-85597-451-6*, Pub. by McCrimmon Pub) St Mut.

— Pilgrim to Rome. 216p. 1994. pap. 35.00 (*0-85597-532-6*) St Mut.

— Pilgrim to the Holy Land. 256p. 1993. 50.00 (*0-85597-321-8*) St Mut.

— Some Catholic Prayers. 48p. (Orig.). 1992. pap. text 3.95 (*0-8146-2196-1*) Liturgical Pr.

— Some Catholic Prayers. (Orig.). (C). 1993. 35.00 (*0-85597-483-4*, Pub. by McCrimmon Pub) St Mut.

— What Christians Believe. 72p. (Orig.). 1992. pap. text 4.95 (*0-8146-2198-8*) Liturgical Pr.

— What Christians Believe. 72p. (Orig.) (C). 1993. 40.00 (*0-85597-481-8*, Pub. by McCrimmon Pub) St Mut.

— What Jesus Taught. 48p. (Orig.). 1992. pap. text 3.95 (*0-8146-2197-X*) Liturgical Pr.

— What Jesus Taught. (Orig.). (C). 1993. 40.00 (*0-85597-482-6*, Pub. by McCrimmon Pub) St Mut.

***Richards, Hugh.** Life & Worklife Expectancies. LC 99-48922. 272p. 2000. 85.00 (*0-913875-36-8*, 5368-N) Lawyers & Judges.

Richards, Hugh T. Through Los Alamos, 1945: Memoirs of a Nuclear Physicist. (Illus.). 106p. (Orig.). 1993. pap. 15.00 (*0-9637521-1-1*) Arlington Pl.

Richards, Hull. Interchanging Britian's English Student, 2 vols. 1995. pap. text 13.95 (*0-521-44930-8*) Cambridge U Pr.

Richards, I. A. Mencius on the Mind: Experiments in Multiple Definition. 192p. (C). 1996. text 49.00 (*0-7007-0434-5*, Pub. by Curzon Pr Ltd) UH Pr.

— Poetries: Their Media & Ends. LC 73-93947. (De Proprietatibus Litterarum, Ser. Major: No. 30). 256p. 1974. pap. text 56.95 (*90-279-3482-7*) Mouton.

— Poetries & Sciences. LC 68-22862. (C). 1972. pap. 3.00 (*0-393-00652-2*) Norton.

— Richards on Rhetoric: Selected Essays, 1929-1974. Berthoff, Ann E., ed. (Illus.). 287p. (C). 1990. pap. text 27.95 (*0-19-506426-7*) OUP.

— Science & Poetry. LC 74-6484. (Studies in Poetry: No. 38). 1974. lib. bdg. 75.00 (*0-8383-1916-5*) M S G Haskell Hse.

— Selected Letters of I. A. Richards, CH. Constable, John, ed. (Illus.). 272p. 1990. text 65.00 (*0-19-818602-9*) OUP.

Richards, I. A., et al. Foundations of Aesthetics. LC 74-1364. (Studies in Philosophy: No. 40). 1974. lib. bdg. 75.00 (*0-8383-2046-5*) M S G Haskell Hse.

Richards, I. G., et al. The Reclamation of Former Coal Mines & Steelworks. (Studies in Environmental Science: Vol. 56). 740p. 1993. 299.50 (*0-444-81703-4*) Elsevier.

Richards, Ian. How to Give a Professional Presentation. rev. ed. (C). 1988. pap. text 17.50 (*1-85333-087-6*, Pub. by Graham & Trotman) Kluwer Academic.

— How to Use the Computer to Improve Your Business. (C). 1990. pap. text 23.50 (*1-85333-323-9*, Pub. by Graham & Trotman) Kluwer Academic.

— How to Use the Computer to Improve Your Business. (C). 1990. lib. bdg. 39.50 (*1-85333-324-7*, Pub. by Graham & Trotman) Kluwer Academic.

— To Bed at Noon: The Life & Art of Maurice Duggan. (Illus.). 496p. 1998. 35.00 (*1-86940-159-X*, Pub. by Auckland Univ) Paul & Co Pubs.

Richards, Ivor A. Complementarities: Uncollected Essays. Russo, John P., ed. LC 76-19044. (Illus.). 317p. reprint ed. pap. 98.30 (*0-7837-6087-6*, 205913300007) Bks Demand.

— Practical Criticism, a Study of Literary Judgment. LC 56-13740. 378p. 1956. pap. 9.95 (*0-15-673626-8*, Harvest Bks) Harcourt.

Richards, Ivor A., ed. see Coleridge, Samuel Taylor.

Richards, J. Dictionary of Language Teaching & Applied Linguistics. 2nd ed. 1995. pap. 32.90 (*0-582-07244-1*) Addison-Wesley.

***Richards, J.** Innocence of Roast Chicken. 1999. pap. 12.95 (*0-7472-5520-2*, Pub. by Headline Bk Pub) Trafalgar.

— Touching the Lighthouse. 1999. pap. 12.95 (*0-7472-5521-0*, Pub. by Headline Bk Pub) Trafalgar.

Richards, J., ed. Voices from the Big Thicket, Vol. II. 152p. (Orig.). 1995. pap. 8.00 (*1-887303-03-0*) Blu Lantern Pub.

Richards, J., jt. auth. see Milne, G.

Richards, J., ed. see Clark, William A.

Richards, J., ed. see Mayhar, Ardath.

Richards, J., ed. see Terry, Dale.

Richards, J. A. Remote Sensing: Digital Image Analysis. (Illus.). 320p. 1986. 69.00 (*0-387-16007-8*) Spr-Verlag.

— Remote Sensing Digital Image Analysis. 2nd enl. rev. ed. LC 94-29196. 330p. 1995. 59.95 (*0-387-58219-3*) Spr-Verlag.

— Remote Sensing Image Analysis: An Introduction. 2nd ed. LC 94-29196. 1994. write for info. (*3-540-58219-3*) Spr-Verlag.

Richards, J. D. One More Yesterday. 230p. 1999. pap. 15.95 (*0-7414-0057-X*) Buy Books.

Richards, J. F. Mughal Administration in Golconda. (Illus.). 1975. 55.00 (*0-19-821561-4*) OUP.

Richards, J. F., ed. Kingship & Authority in South Asia. LC 98-909288. 386p. 1998. text 35.00 (*0-19-564219-8*) OUP.

Richards, J. L., jt. auth. see Pour-El, M. B.

Richards, J. M. & Pevsner, Nikolaus, eds. The Anti-Rationalists. LC 72-95812. (Illus.). 216p. reprint ed. pap. 67.00 (*0-8357-5630-0*, 201433900090) Bks Demand.

Richards, J. P., jt. auth. see Gough, W.

Richards, Jack & Bycina, David. Person to Person: Communicative Speaking & Listening Skills, Bk. 2. 1985. teacher ed. write for info. (*0-318-59138-3*) OUP.

Richards, Jack & Hull, Jonathan. As I Was Saying: Conversation Tactics. (Illus.). 160p. (C). 1987. pap. text 22.41 (*0-201-06433-2*) Addison-Wesley.

Richards, Jack, et al. Longman Dictionary of Applied Linguistics. 324p. 1985. pap. text 25.95 (*0-582-55708-9*, 74434) Longman.

Richards, Jack, jt. auth. see Lowe, David.

Richards, Jack C. As I Was Saying. 1987. text 44.10 (*0-201-06435-9*) Addison-Wesley.

— Beyond Training: Perspectives on Language Teacher Education. LC 97-35705. (Language Teaching Library). (Illus.). 224p. (C). 1998. pap. text 20.95 (*0-521-62680-3*) Cambridge U Pr.

— The Context of Language Teaching. (Cambridge Language Teaching Library). 256p. 1985. pap. text 20.95 (*0-521-31952-8*) Cambridge U Pr.

— Developing Tactics for Listening. LC 94-38352. (Illus.). 80p. 1996. pap. text, student ed. 10.75 (*0-19-434654-4*) OUP.

— Developing Tactics for Listening. LC 94-38352. (Illus.). 128p. 1996. pap. text, teacher ed. 8.95 (*0-19-434655-2*) OUP.

Richards, Jack C. Developing Tactics for Listening. LC 94-38352. (Illus.). 1996. 35.95 (*0-19-434745-1*); 31.95 (*0-19-434658-7*) OUP.

Richards, Jack C. Expanding Tactics for Listening. LC 94-48348. (Illus.). 80p. 1996. pap. text, student ed. 10.75 (*0-19-434660-9*) OUP.

— Expanding Tactics for Listening. LC 94-48348. (Illus.). 128p. 1996. pap. text, teacher ed. 8.95 (*0-19-434661-7*) OUP.

Richards, Jack C. Expanding Tactics for Listening. LC 94-48348. (Illus.). 1997. 31.95 (*0-19-434662-5*) OUP.

— Expanding Tactics for Listening. LC 94-48348. (Illus.). 1997. 35.95 (*0-19-434746-X*) OUP.

Richards, Jack C. Interchange Level 2: English for International Communication: Video Activity Book. LC 96-140530. (Illus.). 69p. (C). 1995. pap. text 12.95 (*0-521-46805-1*) Cambridge U Pr.

— Interchange Level 2: English for International Communication: Video Teacher's Guide. (Illus.). 125p. (C). 1996. pap. text, teacher ed. 16.95 (*0-521-46804-3*) Cambridge U Pr.

— Interchange Intro: English for International Communication. (Illus.). 78p. (C). 1994. pap. text 7.95 (*0-521-47185-0*) Cambridge U Pr.

— Interchange Intro: English for International Communication. (Illus.). 144p. (C). 1994. pap. text 12.95 (*0-521-46744-6*) Cambridge U Pr.

— Interchange Intro: English for International Communication. (Illus.). 68p. (C). 1994. pap. text 7.50 (*0-521-46743-8*) Cambridge U Pr.

— Interchange Intro: English for International Communication. (Illus.). 182p. (C). 1995. pap. text 17.95 (*0-521-46742-X*) Cambridge U Pr.

— Interchange Introduction - English for International Communication: Student Book B. 74p. (C). 1994. pap. text 7.95 (*0-521-47186-9*) Cambridge U Pr.

— Interchange Introduction - English for International Communication: Workbook A. 36p. (C). 1994. pap. text 4.95 (*0-521-47187-7*) Cambridge U Pr.

— Interchange Introduction - English for International Communication: Workbook B. 35p. (C). 1994. pap. text 4.95 (*0-521-47188-5*) Cambridge U Pr.

— The Language Teaching Matrix: Curriculum, Methodology, & Materials. (Language Teaching Library). (Illus.). 197p. (C). 1990. pap. text 19.95 (*0-521-38794-9*) Cambridge U Pr.

— New Interchange Video Activity Book: English for International Communication, Vol. 1. (Interchange Ser.). (Illus.). 80p. (C). 1998. pap. text 12.95 (*0-521-62864-4*) Cambridge U Pr.

— New Interchange Video Activity Book: English for International Communication, Vol. 2. (Interchange Ser.). (Illus.). 72p. (C). 1998. pap. text 12.95 (*0-521-62846-6*) Cambridge U Pr.

— New Person to Person, Bk. 2. (Illus.). 128p. 1995. pap. text, student ed. 11.95 (*0-19-434681-1*) OUP.

— New Person to Person Pt. 2: Communicative Speaking & Listening Skills. (Illus.). 152p. 1996. teacher ed., spiral bd. 16.95 (*0-19-434682-X*) OUP.

— Springboard, Vol. 1. LC 97-11076. (Illus.). 80p. 1997. pap. text, student ed. 11.95 (*0-19-435350-8*) OUP.

— Springboard: Student Book 2. LC 97-11076. (Illus.). 82p. 1998. pap. text 11.95 (*0-19-435353-2*) OUP.

— Springboard: Teacher's Book, Vol. 1. (Illus.). 160p. 1997. pap. text, teacher ed. 12.95 (*0-19-435351-6*) OUP.

— Tactics for Listening. (Illus.). 78p. 1995. pap. text, student ed. 10.75 (*0-19-434587-4*) OUP.

— Tactics for Listening: Basic Tactics for Listening. 128p. 1996. pap. text, teacher ed. 8.95 (*0-19-434588-2*) OUP.

Richards, Jack C., ed. Teaching in Action: Case Studies from Second Language Classrooms. LC 97-61578. 426p. 1998. pap. 29.95 (*0-939791-73-0*) Tchrs Eng Spkrs.

Richards, Jack C. & Lockhart, Charles. Reflective Teaching in Second Language Classrooms. (Language Education Ser.). 256p. (C). 1994. pap. 18.95 (*0-521-45803-X*); text 49.95 (*0-521-45181-7*) Cambridge U Pr.

Richards, Jack C. & Nunan, David, eds. Second Language Teacher Education. (Cambridge Language Teaching Library). (Illus.). 352p. (C). 1990. pap. text 26.95 (*0-521-38779-5*) Cambridge U Pr.

Richards, Jack C. & Rodgers, Theodore S. Approaches & Methods in Language Teaching: A Description & Analysis. (Cambridge Language Teaching Library). (Illus.). 192p. 1986. pap. text 19.95 (*0-521-31255-8*) Cambridge U Pr.

Richards, Jack C. & Sandy, Chuck. Passages: An Upper-Level Multi-Skills Course - Student's Book 1, No. 1. LC 98-16239. (Illus.). 128p. (C). 1998. pap. text, student ed. 13.50 (*0-521-56472-7*) Cambridge U Pr.

— Passages Teacher's Manual: An Upper-Level Multi-Skills Fluency Course, No. 1. 288p. (C). 1998. pap. text, teacher ed. 17.95 (*0-521-56468-9*) Cambridge U Pr.

— Passages 2 Student's Book: An Upper-Level Multi-Skills Course. LC 99-58577. (Illus.). 128p. (C). 2000. pap., student ed. 13.95 (*0-521-56471-9*) Cambridge U Pr.

— Passages 2 Teacher's Manual: An Upper-Level Multi-Skills Course. 212p. (C). 2000. pap., teacher ed. 18.50 (*0-521-56467-0*) Cambridge U Pr.

— Passages Workbook: An Upper-Level Multi-Skills Fluency Course, No. 1. 76p. (C). 1999. pap. text, wbk. ed. 8.95 (*0-521-56470-0*) Cambridge U Pr.

***Richards, Jack C. & Sandy, Chuck.** Passages 2 Audio CD: An Upper-Level Multi-Skills Course. 2000. audio compact disk 40.95 (*0-521-56463-8*) Cambridge U Pr.

Richards, Jack C. & Sandy, Chuck. Passages 2 Workbook: An Upper-Level Multi-Skills Course. 80p. (C). 2000. pap., wbk. ed. 9.50 (*0-521-56469-7*) Cambridge U Pr.

Richards, Jack C., et al. Interchange: English for International Communication, Level 2. (Illus.). 144p. (C). 1990. pap. text, student ed. 12.95 (*0-521-37681-5*) Cambridge U Pr.

— Interchange: English for International Communication, Level 2. (Illus.). 64p. (C). 1991. pap. text, student ed. 7.95 (*0-521-37683-1*) Cambridge U Pr.

— Interchange: English for International Communication, Level 2. (Illus.). 208p. (C). 1991. pap. text, teacher ed. 17.95 (*0-521-37682-3*) Cambridge U Pr.

— Interchange: English for International Communication, Level 3. (Illus.). 144p. (C). 1991. pap. text, student ed. 12.50 (*0-521-37684-X*) Cambridge U Pr.

— Interchange: English for International Communication, Level 3. (Illus.). 64p. (C). 1991. pap. text, wbk. ed. 7.95 (*0-521-37686-6*) Cambridge U Pr.

— Interchange: English for International Communication, Level 3. (Illus.). 255p. (C). 1992. pap. text, teacher ed. 17.95 (*0-521-37685-8*) Cambridge U Pr.

— Interchange: English for International Communication, Level 3. (Illus.). 91p. (C). 1993. pap. text, student ed. 16.95 (*0-521-42222-1*) Cambridge U Pr.

— Interchange: English for International Communication, Level Intro. 80p. (C). 1994. audio 5.95 (*0-521-47189-3*) Cambridge U Pr.

— Interchange: English for International Communication, Level 1, Level 1. 144p. (C). 1990. pap. text, student ed. 12.95 (*0-521-35988-0*) Cambridge U Pr.

— Interchange: English for International Communication, Level 1, Level 1. 192p. (C). 1990. pap. text, teacher ed. 17.95 (*0-521-35989-9*); pap. text, student ed. 7.95 (*0-521-35990-2*) Cambridge U Pr.

— Interchange: English for International Communication, Level 1, Level 1. 95p. (C). 1992. pap. text, student ed. 16.95 (*0-521-42218-3*) Cambridge U Pr.

— Listen for It: Student Book. 2nd ed. (Illus.). 96p. 1995. pap. text, student ed. 11.95 (*0-19-434656-0*) OUP.

— Listen for It: Teacher's Guide. 2nd ed. (Illus.). 108p. 1995. pap. text, teacher ed. 9.50 (*0-19-434657-9*) OUP.

— New Interchange Student's Book: English for International Communication, Bk. 1. LC 97-17432. (Illus.). 152p. (C). 1998. pap. text, student ed. 13.50 (*0-521-62881-4*) Cambridge U Pr.

— New Interchange Student's Book: English for International Communication, Bk. 2. LC 97-27440. (Interchange Ser.). (Illus.). 152p. (C). 1997. pap. text, student ed. 13.50 (*0-521-62862-8*) Cambridge U Pr.

— New Interchange Student's Book: English for International Communication, Bk. 3. (Illus.). 152p. (C). 1998. pap. text, student ed. 13.50 (*0-521-62844-X*) Cambridge U Pr.

— New Interchange Teacher's Edition: English for International Communication, Bk. 1. (Illus.). 312p. 1997. pap. text, teacher ed. 26.95 (*0-521-62875-X*) Cambridge U Pr.

— New Interchange: English for International Communication, No. 3. (Illus.). 226p. (C). 1998. pap. text, teacher ed. 24.95 (*0-521-62838-5*) Cambridge U Pr.

R

R

— New Interchange: English for International Communication, Vol. 2. (Interchange Ser.). (Illus.). 304p. (C). 1998. pap. text, teacher ed. 26.95 (*0-521-62856-3*) Cambridge U Pr.

— New Interchange Video Teacher's Guide: English for International Communication, Vol. 1. (Interchange Ser.). (Illus.). 128p. (C). 1997. pap. text, teacher ed. 16.95 (*0-521-62863-6*) Cambridge U Pr.

— New Interchange Video Teacher's Guide: English for International Communication, Vol. 2. LC 98-141916. (Interchange Ser.). (Illus.). 118p. (C). 1998. pap. text, teacher ed. 16.95 (*0-521-62845-8*) Cambridge U Pr.

— New Interchange Workbook: English for International Communication, Level 3. (New Interchange Ser.). (Illus.). 100p. (C). 1998. pap. text, wbk. ed. 8.50 (*0-521-62841-5*) Cambridge U Pr.

— New Interchange Workbook: English for International Communication, Vol. 2. (Interchange Ser.). (Illus.). 100p. (C). 1998. pap. text, wbk. ed. 8.95 (*0-521-62859-8*) Cambridge U Pr.

— New Interchange Workbook 1: English for International Communication. (Interchange Ser.). (Illus.). 100p. (C). 1997. pap. text, wbk. ed. 8.95 (*0-521-62878-4*) Cambridge U Pr.

— New Person to Person, Vol. 1. (Illus.). 128p. 1995. pap. text, student ed. 11.95 (*0-19-434678-1*) OUP.

— New Person to Person: Teacher's Book. (Illus.). 150p. 1995. teacher ed., spiral bd. 16.95 (*0-19-434679-X*) OUP.

Richards, Jack C., jt. auth. see Homer.

Richards, Jack C., jt. auth. see Long, Michael H.

Richards, Jack C., jt. ed. see Freeman, Donald A.

Richards, Jackie. Charlie Dog Two & Mustard. LC 97-28557. (Illus.). 32p. (J). (gr. 1-4). 1997. lib. bdg. 15.95 (*1-55618-164-7*) Brunswick Pub.

Richards, James. Pascal. 2nd ed. 1986. pap. 37.50 (*0-12-587522-3*) Acad Pr.

— Preparing Morning & Evening Prayer. (Preparing for Liturgy Ser.). 48p. 1997. pap. 3.95 (*0-8146-2516-9*) Liturgical Pr.

Richards, James A., jt. auth. see Lark, Susan M.

Richards, James B. Escape from Codependent Christianity. 216p. (Orig.). 1996. pap. 12.95 (*0-924748-10-9*) Impact Ministries.

— The Gospel of Peace: The Message of the Cross. 2nd rev. ed. 142p. (Orig.). 1995. pap. 10.00 (*0-924748-08-7*) Impact Ministries.

— Grace the Power to Change. 2nd rev. ed. 179p. 1993. pap. 10.00 (*0-924748-07-9*) Impact Ministries.

— Leadership That Builds People, Vol. 1. 143p. (Orig.). 1993. pap. 12.95 (*0-924748-06-0*) Impact Ministries.

— Leadership That Builds People, 3 vols., Vol. II. 165p. (Orig.). 1999. pap. 19.95 (*0-924748-11-7*) Impact Ministries.

— My Church, My Family: How to Have a Healthy Relationship with the Church. 153p. (Orig.). 1995. pap. 9.00 (*0-924748-09-5*) Impact Ministries.

— The Prayer Organizer. rev. ed. 114p. 1990. ring bd. 20.00 (*0-924748-01-X*) Impact Ministries.

— Satan Unmasked. LC 99-168274. 163p. (Orig.). 1998. pap. 12.95 (*0-924748-12-5*) Impact Ministries.

— Supernatural Evangelism. 2nd rev. ed. 1997. pap. 12.00 (*0-924748-05-2*) Impact Ministries.

— Supernatural Ministry: Unleashing the Gifts Within You. 222p. 1999. pap. text 12.95 (*0-924748-14-1*) Impact Ministries.

— Taking the Limits off God. 2nd ed. 96p. 1997. reprint ed. pap. 8.00 (*0-924748-00-1*) Impact Ministries.

Richards, James H. How to Die Young at the Oldest Possible Age. (Illus.). 88p. (Orig.). (C). 1991. pap. text 9.95 (*1-880047-01-2*) Creative Des.

***Richards, James Henry & Richards, Patricia Lewis.** 1765 Judge John Richards, 1850: Historic Adirondac Surveyor. Meschinelli, Mark, tr. LC 00-101049. (Illus.). xvi, 276p. (YA). 2000. 39.50 (*0-9675623-7-6*) Richards Studio.

***Richards, James R.** Ask Dr. Richards: A Special Report from CatWatch. Watanabe, Myrna, ed. (Illus.). 77p. 2000. pap. 19.99 (*1-929942-07-9*) Torstar.

Richards, James R. Transnational Criminal Organizations, Cybercrime & Money Laundering. LC 98-8240. 344p. 1998. boxed set 64.95 (*0-8493-2806-3*, 2806) CRC Pr.

Richards, James R. & American Society for the Prevention of Cruelty to. ASPCA Complete Guide to Cats: Everything You Need to Know about Choosing & Caring for Your Pet. LC 99-12354. (Illus.). 368p. 1999. pap. 24.95 (*0-8118-1929-9*) Chronicle Bks.

Richards, James R., jt. ed. see Houpt, Katherine A.

Richards, Janet C. & Gipe, Joan P. Elementary Literacy Lessons: Cases & Commentaries from the Field. 256p. 1999. teacher ed. write for info. (*0-8058-3457-5*); pap. 24.50 (*0-8058-2988-1*) L Erlbaum Assocs.

***Richards, Janet E. & Van Buren, Mary.** Order, Legitimacy & Wealth in Ancient States. LC 99-56316. 2000. write for info. (*0-521-77212-5*); write for info. (*0-521-77671-6*) Cambridge U Pr.

Richards, Janet L. Richards on Tennessee Family Law: 1997 Edition. LC 97-72930. 705p. 1997. 95.00 (*1-55834-537-X*, 66671, MICHIE) LEXIS Pub.

— Richards on Tennessee Family Law: 1998 Supplement. 1998. write for info. (*0-327-00218-2*, 66672-10) LEXIS Pub.

— Richards on Tennessee Family Law, 1999 Cumulative Supplement. 150p. 1999. pap. write for info. (*0-327-01345-1*, 6667211) LEXIS Pub.

***Richards, Janet Radcliffe.** Human Nature after Darwin: A Philosophical Introduction. LC 00-42460. 2000. pap. write for info. (*0-415-21244-8*) Routledge.

***Richards, Jean & Thacker, Kat.** The First Olympic Games. LC 99-45146. (J). 2000. write for info. (*0-7613-1311-7*) Millbrook Pr.

Richards, Jeanette. The Crofter's Cottage. large type ed. (Dales Romance Ser.). 201p. 1993. pap. 18.99 (*1-85389-404-4*) Ulverscroft.

— In Love's Image. (Rainbow Romances Ser.: No. 889). 160p. 1994. 14.95 (*0-7090-4841-6*) Parkwest Pubns.

— In Love's Image. large type ed. (Linford Romance Library). 288p. 1995. pap. 16.99 (*0-7089-7669-7*, Linford) Ulverscroft.

— A Summer of Innocence. large type ed. (Linford Romance Library). 272p. 1996. pap. 16.99 (*0-7089-7905-X*) Ulverscroft.

Richards, Jef I. Deceptive Advertising: Behavioral Study of a Legal Concept. (Communication Ser.). 264p. (C). 1990. text 55.00 (*0-8058-0649-0*) L Erlbaum Assocs.

Richards, Jeff. Down from Above. (Christian Theatre Ser.). 40p. 1995. pap. 3.50 (*1-57514-141-8*, 1143) Encore Perform Pub.

Richards, Jeffrey. Diana, The Making of A Media Saint. 1999. pap. text 19.95 (*1-86064-388-4*) IBT Video.

Richards, Jeffrey. Films & British National Identity: From Dickens to Dad's Army. LC 96-53007. 1997. 79.95 (*0-7190-4742-0*, Pub. by Manchester Univ Pr) St Martin.

Richards, Jeffrey. Fire Island: In Color. (Illus.). 144p. (Orig.). 1991. 40.00 (*0-9628881-0-9*); pap. 30.00 (*0-9628881-1-7*) KYX Pr.

— Sex, Dissidence & Damnation: Minority Groups in the Middle Ages. 192p. (C). (gr. 13). 1997. pap. 20.99 (*0-415-07147-X*, C0428) Routledge.

— Swordsmen of the Screen: From Douglas Fairbanks to Michael York. (Cinema & Society Ser.). (Illus.). 312p. 1980. pap. 10.95 (*0-7100-0681-0*, Routledge Thoemms) Routledge.

— Thorold Dickinson & the British Cinema. (Filmmakers Ser.: No. 54). (Illus.). 256p. 1997. 49.00 (*0-8108-3279-8*) Scarecrow.

Richards, Jeffrey & MacKenzie, John M. The Railway Station: A Social History. (Illus.). 480p. 1986. teacher ed. write for info. (*0-318-60820-0*) OUP.

Richards, Jeffrey, jt. auth. see Low, Rachael.

Richards, Jeffrey H. Early American Drama. LC 96-49410. 608p. 1997. pap. 13.95 (*0-14-043588-3*) Viking Penguin.

— Mercy Otis Warren. (Twayne's United States Authors Ser.). 1995. 32.00 (*0-8057-4003-1*, Twyne) Mac Lib Ref.

— Theater Enough: American Culture & the Metaphor of the World Stage, 1607-1789. LC 90-47943. 359p. 1991. text 37.95 (*0-8223-1107-0*) Duke.

Richards, Jeffrey J. Contemporary Christian Options of the World's End: The Eschatology of Lewis Sperry Chafer. LC 93-33936. (Illus.). 256p. 1993. text 89.95 (*0-7734-9391-3*) E Mellen.

— The Cry at Salem. 80p. (Orig.). (C). 1992. pap. text 11.35 (*0-88252-153-5*) Paladin Hse.

— The Promise of Dawn: The Eschatology of Lewis Sperry Chafer. 280p. (C). 1991. pap. 28.00 (*0-8191-8197-8*); lib. bdg. 52.00 (*0-8191-8196-X*) U Pr of Amer.

— Twenty-One Who Speak: Powerful Voices of Christianity from the First Through the Twentieth Centuries. 123p. (Orig.). (C). 1992. pap. text 23.30 (*0-88252-154-3*) Paladin Hse.

***Richards, Jennifer & Knowles, James, eds.** Shakespeare's Late Plays: New Readings. 256p. 1999. 81.00 (*0-7486-1152-5*, Pub. by Edinburgh U Pr); pap. text 27.00 (*0-7486-1153-3*, Pub. by Edinburgh U Pr) Col U Pr.

Richards, Jennifer, jt. auth. see Keshner, Sherrie B.

Richards, Jerri S. A Decade of Down. (Illus.). 60p. (Orig.). 1997. pap. 8.50 (*1-887303-21-9*) Blu Lantern Pub.

Richards, Jerri S., ed. Ariesmar. LC 95-94119. (Illus.). 100p. (Orig.). 1995. pap. text 7.50 (*1-887303-01-4*) Blu Lantern Pub.

Richards, Jerri S., ed. see Dunn, Marylois.

Richards, Jerri S., ed. see Mayhar, Ardath & Dunn, Marylois.

Richards, Jerri S., ed. see Nelson, Hazel J.

Richards, Jerri S., ed. see Wyborny, Sheila.

Richards, Jerri S., ed. & illus. see Fields, Joy.

Richards, Jerrold. Nuclear War & You: Before, During, After. LC 84-70562. 272p. (Orig.). 1984. pap. 8.95 (*0-9613278-0-4*) CFPR Pubns.

***Richards, Jerry C.** Aisle Twelve. LC 99-93402. 228p. 1999. pap. 6.99 (*1-57579-165-X*) Pine Hill Pr.

— Sunset Survivor. 204p. 1999. pap. write for info. (*1-57579-170-6*, Pub. by Pine Hill Pr) Penmarch Pub.

Richards, Jill. The I Ching Companion: An Answer for Every Question. LC 99-30326. 96p. 1999. pap. 9.95 (*1-57863-130-0*, Pub. by Weiser) ACCESS Pubs Network.

***Richards, Joan.** Angels of Reflection: A Story of Motherhood & Mathematics. 272p. 2000. text 23.95 (*0-7167-3831-7*) W H Freeman.

Richards, Joanette. A Summer of Innocence. (Rainbow Romances Ser.). 160p. 1995. 14.95 (*0-7090-5497-1*, 925) Parkwest Pubns.

Richards, Joanne & Standley, Marianne V. Fun with Puns. (Illus.). 88p. (J). (gr. 3-5). 1999. pap. 10.95 (*0-88160-350-3*, LW389) Learning Wks.

— School Spirit & Self-Esteem Bulletin Boards. (Easy-To-Make-&-Use Ser.). (Illus.). 64p. (J). (gr. k-6). 1986. pap. text 7.95 (*0-86530-135-2*, IP-112-4) Incentive Pubns.

Richards, Joanne, jt. auth. see Blankenhorn, Kathy.

***Richards, John.** Altichiero: An Artist & His Patrons in the Italian Trecento. (Illus.). 354p. (C). 2000. 150.00 (*0-521-35649-0*) Cambridge U Pr.

Richards, John. Basic Bass. (Illus.). 32p. 1987. pap. 10.95 (*0-7119-1075-8*, AM64858) Music Sales.

— Hidden Country: Nature on Your Doorstep. LC 72-12745. (Illus.). 144p. (J). (gr. 5-8). 1973. lib. bdg. 26.95 (*0-87599-195-5*) S G Phillips.

— The Pigeon Factory. (Illus.). (Orig.). 1987. pap. 10.95 (*0-932274-40-4*) Cadmus Eds.

— Primulas of the British Isles. (Natural History Ser.: No. 38). (Illus.). 24p. 1989. pap. 5.25 (*0-7478-0020-0*, Pub. by Shire Pubns) Parkwest Pubns.

— Timber Frame Houses in the Scottish Countryside. (Illus.). vi, 65p. 1994. pap. 25.00 (*0-11-495191-8*, HM51918, Pub. by Statnry Office) Balogh.

— Time Management: A Manual for Trainers. Adair, John Eric, ed. 255p. (C). 1989. ring bd. 285.00 (*0-85171-088-3*, Pub. by IPM Hse) St Mut.

— Working Stiff. LC 96-76624. 224p. 1997. pap. 15.00 (*1-57650-098-5*) Hi Jinx Pr.

Richards, John, jt. auth. see Vaillant, Janet.

Richards, John, jt. ed. see Gunton, Thomas.

Richards, John A. Remote Sensing Digital Image Analysis: An Introduction. 2nd ed. LC 93-10179. (Illus.). 344p. 1993. 119.00 (*0-387-54840-8*) Spr-Verlag.

Richards, John A. & Jia, X. Remote Sensing Digital Image Analysis: An Introduction. 3rd ed. Ricken, D. E. & Gessner, W., eds. LC 98-53847. (Illus.). xxi, 356p. 1999. 89.95 (*3-540-64860-7*) Spr-Verlag.

Richards, John C., jt. ed. see Richards, Mary F.

Richards, John D. Uncreated Light. 32p. (Orig.). 1993. pap. 3.95 (*1-881692-05-1*) Trillium WV.

Richards, John E., ed. Cognitive Neuroscience of Attention: A Developmental Perspective. LC 97-35558. 374p. 1998. write for info. (*0-8058-2409-X*) L Erlbaum Assocs.

Richards, John F. The Mughal Empire. (New Cambridge History of India Ser.: I: 5). (Illus.). 338p. (C). 1993. text 59.95 (*0-521-25119-2*) Cambridge U Pr.

— The Mughal Empire. (New Cambridge History of India Ser.: Vol. I:5). (Illus.). 337p. 1996. pap. text 22.95 (*0-521-56603-7*) Cambridge U Pr.

— Power, Administration & Finance in Mughal India. (Collected Studies: Vol. CS419). 336p. 1993. 115.95 (*0-86078-366-9*, Pub. by Variorum) Ashgate Pub Co.

***Richards, John F., ed.** The Imperial Monetary System of Mughal India. (Oxford India Paperbacks Ser.). (Illus.). 392p. 2000. pap. 17.95 (*0-19-564979-6*) OUP.

Richards, John F. & Tucker, Richard P., eds. World Deforestation in the Twentieth Century. LC 87-31953. (Duke Press Policy Studies). x, 321p. 1989. reprint ed. pap. text 22.95 (*0-8223-1013-9*) Duke.

Richards, John T. Abraham Lincoln, the Lawyer-Statesman, 1916. LC 99-20587. 1999. 60.00 (*1-886363-94-3*) Lawbk Exchange.

— The Fool of Love. (Mandrake Saga Ser.). (Illus.). 176p. (Orig.). 1995. pap. 8.00 (*0-9605980-4-9*) J T Richards.

— Leah & the Witches. (Mandrake Saga Ser.). (Illus.). 203p. 1997. pap. 8.00 (*0-9605980-5-7*) J T Richards.

— Luminous Sanity: Literary Criticism Written by John G. Neihardt. 1973. pap. 5.00 (*0-9605980-0-6*) J T Richards.

— A Voice Against the Wind: John G. Neihardt As Critic & Reviewer. (Illus.). 161p. (Orig.). 1986. pap. 6.00 (*0-9605980-1-4*) J T Richards.

— The Year of the Sorrats, Vol. I. (Mandrake Saga Ser.). (Illus.). 242p. (Orig.). 1994. pap. 8.00 (*0-9605980-3-0*) J T Richards.

— The Year of the Sorrats, Vol. 2. (Mandrake Saga Ser.). (Illus.). 175p. (Orig.). 1994. pap. 8.00 (*0-9605980-2-2*) J T Richards.

***Richards, John W.** The Bluffer's Guide to Small Business: Bluff Your Way in Small Business. (Bluffer's Guides Ser.). 64p. 1999. pap. 5.95 (*1-902825-63-2*) Oval Bks.

***Richards, John Winterson.** The Xenophobe's Guide to the Welsh. (Xenophobe's Guides Ser.). 64p. 1999. pap. 5.95 (*1-902825-46-2*) Oval Bks.

***Richards, Jon.** Air & Flight. LC 98-49440. (Science Factory Ser.). (Illus.). 32p. (J). (gr. 1-4). 1999. lib. bdg. 21.90 (*0-7613-0918-7*, Copper Beech Bks) Millbrook Pr.

— Chemicals & Reactions. (Science Factory Ser.). (Illus.). 32p. (J). (gr. 1-4). 2000. 21.90 (*0-7613-1160-2*, Copper Beech Bks) Millbrook Pr.

Richards, Jon. Diggers: And Other Construction Equipment. LC 98-51882. (Cutaway Ser.). (Illus.). 40p. (J). (gr. k-3). 1999. 9.95 (*0-7613-0790-7*, Copper Beech Bks); lib. bdg. 23.90 (*0-7613-0905-5*, Copper Beech Bks) Millbrook Pr.

— Fantastic Cutaway Book of Flight. LC 97-43127. (Illus.). 40p. 1998. pap. 9.95 (*0-7613-0726-5*, Copper Beech Bks) Millbrook Pr.

***Richards, Jon.** The Fantastic Cutaway Book of Flight. LC 97-43127. (Illus.). 40p. (J). (gr. 3-6). 1998. lib. bdg. 23.90 (*0-7613-0719-2*, Copper Beech Bks) Millbrook Pr.

Richards, Jon. The Fantastic Cutaway Book of Speed. (Illus.). 40p. (J). (gr. 4-8). 1997. pap. 9.95 (*0-7613-0579-3*, Copper Beech Bks); lib. bdg. 23.90 (*0-7613-0554-8*, Copper Beech Bks) Millbrook Pr.

— Farm Machines. LC 99-11426. (Cutaway Bks.). (Illus.). 40p. (J). (gr. k-3). 1999. pap. 9.95 (*0-7613-0791-5*, Copper Beech Bks) Millbrook Pr.

— Farm Machines. LC 99-11426. (Cutaway Bks.). (Illus.). 40p. (J). (gr. 1-3). 1999. lib. bdg. 23.90 (*0-7613-0906-3*, Copper Beech Bks) Millbrook Pr.

— Firefighters. LC 97-24338. (Cutaway Bks.). (Illus.). 40p. (J). (gr. k-3). 1997. 9.95 (*0-7613-0642-0*, Copper Beech Bks); lib. bdg. 22.90 (*0-7613-0711-7*, Copper Beech Bks) Millbrook Pr.

***Richards, Jon.** Forces & Simple Machines. LC 99-58085. (Science Factory Ser.). (Illus.). 32p. (J). (gr. 1-4). 2000. 21.90 (*0-7613-1159-9*, Copper Beech Bks) Millbrook Pr.

Richards, Jon. Jetliner. LC 98-16919. (Cutaway Bks.). (Illus.). 40p. (J). (gr. k-3). 1998. 9.95 (*0-7613-0744-3*, Copper Beech Bks); lib. bdg. 22.90 (*0-7613-0850-4*, Copper Beech Bks) Millbrook Pr.

***Richards, Jon.** Light & Sight. LC 99-29704. (Science Factory Ser.). (Illus.). 32p. (J). (gr. 1-4). 1999. 21.90 (*0-7613-3255-3*, Copper Beech Bks) Millbrook Pr.

— Magnetism & Magnets. LC 99-31624. (Science Factory Ser.). (Illus.). 32p. (J). (gr. 1-4). 1999. 21.90 (*0-7613-3257-X*, Copper Beech Bks) Millbrook Pr.

Richards, Jon. Racing Cars. LC 97-46338. (Cutaway Bks.). (Illus.). 40p. (J). (gr. k-3). 1998. lib. bdg. 22.90 (*0-7613-0720-6*, Copper Beech Bks) Millbrook Pr.

***Richards, Jon.** Science Factory. LC 99-461964. (Illus.). 224p. (J). (gr. 2-4). 2000. pap. 16.95 (*0-7613-0832-6*, Copper Beech Bks) Millbrook Pr.

— Shapes & Structures. LC 99-88306. (Science Factory Ser.). (Illus.). 32p. (J). (gr. 1-4). 2000. 21.90 (*0-7613-1161-0*, Copper Beech Bks) Millbrook Pr.

— Sound & Music. LC 99-29424. (Science Factory Ser.). (Illus.). 32p. (J). (gr. 1-4). 1999. 21.90 (*0-7613-3254-5*, Copper Beech Bks) Millbrook Pr.

Richards, Jon. Space Vehicles. LC 97-47118. (Cutaway Bks.). (Illus.). 40p. (J). (gr. k-3). 1998. 9.95 (*0-7613-0728-1*, Copper Beech Bks); lib. bdg. 22.90 (*0-7613-0721-4*, Copper Beech Bks) Millbrook Pr.

— Trains. LC 98-16915. (Cutaway Bks.). (Illus.). 40p. (J). (gr. k-3). 1998. 9.95 (*0-7613-0743-5*, Copper Beech Bks); lib. bdg. 22.90 (*0-7613-0824-5*, Copper Beech Bks) Millbrook Pr.

***Richards, Jon.** Units & Measurements. LC 99-58084. (Science Factory Ser.). (Illus.). 32p. (J). (gr. 1-4). 2000. 21.90 (*0-7613-1158-0*, Copper Beech Bks) Millbrook Pr.

Richards, Jon. Water & Boats. LC 98-49446. (Science Factory Ser.). (Illus.). 32p. (J). (gr. 1-4). 1999. lib. bdg. 21.90 (*0-7613-0919-5*, Copper Beech Bks) Millbrook Pr.

— The Young People's Atlas of the World. (Illus.). 40p. (J). (gr. 3-6). 1997. 12.95 (*0-7613-0588-2*, Copper Beech Bks); lib. bdg. 22.40 (*0-7613-0563-7*, Copper Beech Bks) Millbrook Pr.

Richards, Jon & Roberts, Dave. Calculator Power! Profits in Discounted Notes. 5th ed. 260p. 1999. reprint ed. pap. text 39.95 (*1-885847-03-3*) Noteworthy Invest.

Richards, Jonathan. Facadism. LC 94-170205. (Illus.). 240p. (C). 1994. 90.00 (*0-415-08316-8*) Routledge.

Richards, Josephine E. Honor Roll of Litchfield Connecticut Revolutionary Soldiers. 233p. 1997. pap. 20.00 (*0-7884-0662-0*, R317) Heritage Bk.

Richards, Josiah B. God of Our Fathers: Advice & Prayers of Our Nation's Founders. (Illus.). 304p. (Orig.). 1994. pap. 12.00 (*0-9643679-1-2*) Reading Bks.

Richards, Joyce A., et al. Teaming for Tomorrow: A Mentoring Program That Introduces Girls to a World of Career Choices. (Illus.). 36p. (YA). (gr. 9-12). 1996. ring bd. 25.00 (*0-9651432-0-1*) Girl Scout Coun.

Richards, Judith. Summer Lightning. 6th ed. 271p. 1998. reprint ed. pap. 13.95 (*0-9668579-0-9*) Pierian Qual.

— Too Blue to Fly. LC 97-71956. 192p. 1997. 20.00 (*1-56352-383-3*) Longstreet.

Richards, Judith W. Fundamentals of Development Finance: A Practitioner's Guide. LC 82-18958. 210p. 1983. 57.95 (*0-275-91062-8*, C1062, Praeger Pubs) Greenwood.

Richards, Judy. Catering Start & Run a Money Making Business. 274p. 1998. reprint ed. lib. bdg. 34.95 (*0-7351-0033-0*) Replica Bks.

Richards, Justin. Demontage. 1999. mass mkt. 5.95 (*0-563-55572-6*) BBC Worldwide.

— Dragon's Wrath. (Orig.). 1997. mass mkt. 5.95 (*0-426-20508-1*, Pub. by Virgin Bks) London Brdge.

— Dreams of Empire. 1998. pap. 5.95 (*0-563-40598-8*) BBC.

***Richards, Justin.** Grave Matter. (Doctor Who Ser.). (Illus.). 288p. (J). 2000. mass mkt. 6.95 (*0-563-55598-X*) BBC Bks.

— The Joy Device. 1999. mass mkt. 6.95 (*0-426-20535-9*, Pub. by Virgin Bks) London Brdge.

Richards, Justin. The Medusa Effect. (New Adventures Ser.). 1998. mass mkt. 5.95 (*0-426-20524-3*, Pub. by Virgin Bks) London Brdge.

— Option Lock. (Doctor Who Ser.). 1998. pap. 5.95 (*0-563-40583-X*) BBC.

***Richards, Justin.** Tears of the Oracle. (New Adventures Ser.). 1999. mass mkt. 6.95 (*0-426-20533-2*) London Brdge.

Richards, Justin, jt. ed. see Lane, Andy.

***Richards, K.** Mighty Mini Mind Bogglers. LC 99-45675. 160p. 1999. pap. text 4.95 (*0-8069-1239-1*) Strlng Pub CA.

Richards, K. G. Fatigue Strength of Welded Structures. (Illus.). 32p. 1969. pap. 49.95 (*0-85300-035-2*, Pub. by Woodhead Pubng) Am Educ Systs.

— Weldability of Steel. 28p. 1967. pap. 45.00 (*0-85300-034-4*, Pub. by Woodhead Pubng) Am Educ Systs.

Richards, K. S., ed. Biology of the Integument: Invertebrates, Vol. 1. (Illus.). 800p. 1984. 334.95 (*0-387-13062-4*) Spr-Verlag.

Richards, K. S., jt. ed. see Anderson, M. G.

Richards, Karen B. & Fallon, Maureen O. Workbook for the Verbally Apraxic Adult. 138p. 1987. student ed. 33.50 (*0-7616-7367-9*) Commun Skill.

Richards, Karen C. Mulan Puzzlers. LC 99-158961. (Illus.). 176p. (J). (gr. 3-7). 1998. pap. 9.95 (*0-7868-4224-5*) Little.

Richards, Katie, jt. auth. see Nagle, Ami.

Richards, Keith. Rivers: Form & Process in Alluvial Channels. 272p. 1982. pap. 27.50 (*0-416-74910-0*, NO. 3739) Routledge.

— Tender Mercies: Inside the World of a Child Abuse Investigator. LC 91-50624. 192p. (Orig.). 1991. pap. 12.95 (*1-879360-07-1*) Noble Pr.

Richards, Keith, jt. ed. see Edge, Julian.

Richards, Keith N. Tender Mercies: Inside the World of a Child Abuse Investigator. rev. ed. LC 98-47358. 1998. 14.95 (*0-87868-738-6*, CWLA Pr) Child Welfare.

Richards, Kel, jt. auth. see Jensen, Phillip D.

Richards, Kenneth G. The Gettysburg Address. LC 91-43371. (Cornerstones to Freedom Ser.). (Illus.). 32p. (J). (gr. 4-7). 1992. lib. bdg. 19.50 (*0-516-06654-4*) Childrens.

An Asterisk (*) at the beginning of an entry indicates that the title is appearing for the first time.

— The Gettysburg Address. LC 91-43371. (Cornerstones to Freedom Ser.). (Illus.). 32p. (J). (gr. 4-7). 1993. pap. 5.95 (*0-516-46654-2*) Childrens.

Richards, Kent D. Isaac I. Stevens: Young Man in a Hurry. LC 79-13637. (Illus.). xiv, 484p. 1979. 5.95 (*0-8425-1697-2*, Friends of the Library) Brigham.

— Isaac I. Stevens: Young Man in a Hurry. LC 92-41393. (Washington State University Press Reprint Ser.). (Illus.). 484p. 1993. reprint ed. pap. 24.95 (*0-87422-094-7*) Wash St U Pr.

Richards, Kent H., jt. auth. see Petersen, David L.

Richards, Kent H., ed. see American Academy of Religion Staff.

Richards, Kent H., jt. ed. see Eskenazi, Tamara C.

Richards, Kent H., ed. see Society of Biblical Literature Staff.

Richards, Kitty. Angelica's Awesome Adventure with Cynthia! (Rugrats Ser.). (Illus.). 16p. (J). (ps-2). 1999. mass mkt. 3.99 (*0-689-82831-4*, Simon Spot) Litle Simon.

— Be Brave, Chuckie! (Rugrats Ser.). (Illus.). 16p. (J). (ps-2). 1999. pap. 3.99 (*0-689-82832-2*, Simon Spot) Litle Simon.

***Richards, Kitty.** The Bird Who Cried Wolf. LC 99-46901. (Wild Thornberrys Ready-to-Read Ser.: Vol. 1). (Illus.). 32p. (gr. k-4). 2000. pap. 3.99 (*0-689-83234-6*, Simon Spot) Litle Simon.

— Bowling Twins. (Rugrats Ser.). (Illus.). 16p. (J). (ps-3). 2000. pap. 3.99 (*0-689-83103-X*, Simon Spot) Litle Simon.

Richards, Kitty. Hang on to Your Diapies, Babies, We're Going In! Trivia from the Rugrats Movie. (Rugrats Ser.). (Illus.). 48p. (J). (ps-3). 1998. pap. 2.99 (*0-689-82276-6*) S&S Childrens.

— Ice Cream Fun Day. (Rugrats Ser.). (Illus.). 16p. (ps-3). 1999. pap. 3.99 (*0-689-82388-6*, 076714003996) S&S Childrens.

***Richards, Kitty.** It's About Time, Max! LC 98-51118. (Math Matters Ser.). (Illus.). 32p. (J). (gr. 1-3). 2000. pap. 4.95 (*1-57565-088-6*) Kane Pr.

— It's about Time, Max! (Math Matters Ser.). (Illus.). (J). 2000. 10.40 (*0-606-18219-5*) Turtleback.

— Lights, Camera, Dil! (Rugrats Ser.: Vol. 5). (Illus.). 16p. (J). (ps-3). 2000. pap. 3.99 (*0-689-83102-1*, Simon Spot) Litle Simon.

Richards, Kitty. Merry Christmas, Rugrats! (Rugrats Ser.). (Illus.). (J). (ps-3). 1997. 10.95 (*0-689-81807-6*) S&S Childrens.

***Richards, Kitty.** Merry Christmas, Rugrats! (Rugrats Ser.). (Illus.). (J). (ps-3). 1998. 10.95 (*0-689-82179-4*) S&S Childrens.

— Merry Christmas, Rugrats! (Rugrats Ser.). (Illus.). (J). (ps-3). 1999. per. 10.95 (*0-671-02941-X*) S&S Trade.

Richards, Kitty. Once Upon a Reptar. (Rugrats Ser.). (Illus.). 16p. (ps-3). 1999. pap. 3.99 (*0-689-82389-4*, 076714003996) S&S Childrens.

— Salem's Guide to Life with Sabrina the Teenage Witch: A Spellbinding Trivia Book with Stickers. (Illus.). 24p. (J). (gr. 1-6). 1997. pap. text 6.99 (*0-689-81745-2*) S&S Childrens.

— Star-Spangled Babies. (Rugrats Chapter Bks.: No. 3). (Illus.). 64p. (J). (gr. 2-5). 1999. mass mkt. 3.99 (*0-689-82891-8*, Simon Spot) Litle Simon.

— The Turkey Who Came to Dinner. (Rugrats (tv) Ser.). (Illus.). 32p. (J). (ps-3). 1998. 5.99 (*0-689-82143-3*) S&S Childrens.

***Richards, Kitty.** Yo ho ho & a Bottle of Milk. (Rugrats Files: Vol. 2). 144p. (J). (gr. 3-7). 2000. 3.99 (*0-689-83335-0*) S&S Trade.

Richards, Kris. New Ways with Polymer Clay: The Next Generation of Projects & Techniques. LC 96-42125. (Illus.). 112p. 1997. pap. 19.95 (*0-8019-8869-1*) Krause Pubns.

***Richards, Kristen.** Retail & Restaurant Spaces: Portfolios of 40 Interior Designers. (Illus.). 192p. 1999. 50.00 (*1-56496-488-4*) Rockport Pubs.

Richards, Larry. African American Films Through 1959: A Comprehensive, Illustrated Filmography. LC 97-23730. (Illus.). 320p. 1998. boxed set 65.00 (*0-7864-0307-1*) McFarland & Co.

— The Bible. LC 98-86026. (God's Word for the Biblically-Inept Ser.). (Illus.). 352p. 1998. pap. 16.95 (*0-914984-55-1*, Pub. by Starburst) Natl Bk Netwk.

— Every Covenant & Promise. LC 98-12176. (Everything in the Bible Ser.). 1998. 14.97 (*0-7852-1379-1*) Nelson.

— Every Covenant & Promise in the Bible. LC 98-12176. (Everything in the Bible Ser.). 320p. 1998. 19.99 (*0-7852-1266-3*) Nelson.

— Every Good & Evil Angel in the Bible. LC 97-14577. (Everything in the Bible Ser.). (Illus.). 320p. 1998. 19.99 (*0-7852-1263-9*) Nelson.

— Every Man in the Bible. LC 99-46499. (Everything in the Bible Ser.). 384p. 1999. pap. 14.99 (*0-7852-1439-9*) Nelson.

— Every Miracle & Wonder in the Bible. LC 97-39584. (Everything in the Bible Ser.). (Illus.). 320p. 1998. 19.99 (*0-7852-1264-7*) Nelson.

— Every Prayer & Petition. LC 98-12171. (Everything in the Bible Ser.). 1998. 14.97 (*0-7852-1380-5*) Nelson.

— Every Prayer & Petition in the Bible. LC 98-12171. (Everything in the Bible Ser.). 320p. 1998. 19.99 (*0-7852-1265-5*) Nelson.

— God's Promises for Women Daybreak. 1993. text 9.99 (*0-310-96203-X*) Zondervan.

— The Illustrated Bible Handbook. LC 97-23733. (Illus.). 864p. 1997. 24.99 (*0-7852-1248-5*) Nelson.

— 735 Baffling Bible Questions Answered. LC 99-48969. 2000. 9.99 (*0-517-20731-1*) Random Hse Value.

— 735 Baffling Bible Questions Answered. LC 97-21650. 392p. 1997. pap. 12.99 (*0-8007-5632-0*) Revell.

— Talkable Bible Stories: Helping Your Kids Apply God's Word to Their Lives. LC 91-12923. (Illus.). 256p. (J). (gr. k-3). 1994. pap. 9.99 (*0-8007-5505-7*) Revell.

— Teaching Youth. 156p. 1982. pap. 8.99 (*0-8341-0776-7*) Beacon Hill.

— The Three Hundred Sixty-Five Day Devotional Commentary. 1216p. 1990. text 37.99 (*0-89693-503-5*, 6-1503, Victor Bks) Chariot Victor.

— Wisdom for the Graduate. (For the Graduate Ser.). 128p. 1988. 6.99 (*0-310-39400-7*, 18303) Zondervan.

— Zondervan Dictionary of Christian Literacy: Key Concepts of the Faith. 384p. 1990. pap. 14.99 (*0-310-51981-0*) Zondervan.

Richards, Larry, ed. Canadian Center for Architecture: Building & Gardens. (Illus.). 156p. (Orig.). 1989. pap. text 17.95 (*0-262-68058-0*) MIT Pr.

Richards, Larry & Richards, Sue. NIV Teen Study Bible. LC 99-191932. (Illus.). 1664p. (YA). (gr. 7-10). 1998. 29.99 (*0-310-90096-4*) Zondervan.

— Three Hundred & Sixty Five Ways to Keep Your Love Alive 1995 Calendar. 1994. spiral bd. 7.99 (*0-310-96356-7*) Zondervan.

— Three Hundred Sixty Five Ways to Show Your Kids You Care 1995 Calendar. 1994. spiral bd. 7.99 (*0-310-96355-9*) Zondervan.

Richards, Larry, ed. see Baldinger, Kathleen O'Bannon.

Richards, Larry, jt. ed. see Baraness, Marc.

Richards, Larry, ed. see Bodmer, Judy.

Richards, Larry, ed. see Duck, Daymond R.

Richards, Larry, ed. see Gibson, Joyce.

Richards, Larry, ed. see Girard, Robert C.

Richards, Larry, ed. see Ling, Georgia Curtis.

Richards, Larry, ed. see Littleton, Mark R. & Littleton, Jeanette Gardner.

Richards, Larry, ed. see Martin, Gib.

Richards, Larry, ed. see Miller, D. Larry.

Richards, Larry, ed. see Miller, Kathy Collard.

Richards, Laura E. For Tommy & Other Stories. LC 79-110210. (Short Story Index Reprint Ser.). 1977. 19.95 (*0-8369-3361-3*) Ayer.

***Richards, Laura E.** Jiggle Joggle Jee! (J). 2001. 15.95 (*0-688-17832-4*, Grenwillow Bks); lib. bdg. 15.89 (*0-688-17833-2*, Grenwillow Bks) HarpC Child Bks.

Richards, Laura E. Julia Ward Howe, 1819 to 1910, 2 vols., Set. (BCL1-PS American Literature Ser.). 1992. reprint ed. lib. bdg. 150.00 (*0-7812-6745-5*) Rprt Serv.

Richards, Laura E. & Elliott, Maude H. Julia Ward Howe, 1819 to 1910. LC 90-47729. (Illus.). 826p. 1990. reprint ed. 39.95 (*0-87797-196-X*) Cherokee.

Richards, Laura E., ed. see Howe, Samuel G.

Richards, Laurence D. Constraint Theory: An Approach to Policy-Level Modeling. (Illus.). 424p. (C). 1984. pap. text 33.00 (*0-8191-3513-5*) U Pr of Amer.

Richards, Lawrence. International Children's Bible Handbook: Answering Questions Children Ask-Genesis to Revelation. (Illus.). 224p. (J). (gr. 3-7). 1997. pap. text 12.99 (*0-8499-1481-7*) Word Pub.

Richards, Lawrence O. The Believer's Guidebook from Aspirin to Zoos: The Christian Life. 528p. 1983. 7.70 (*0-310-43470-X*, 18163) Zondervan.

— The Believer's Praise Book. 1984. pap. 20.70 (*0-310-43512-9*, 18204P) Zondervan.

— The Believer's Prayer Book. 1984. pap. 20.70 (*0-310-43602-8*, 18213P) Zondervan.

Richards, Lawrence O. Believer's Promise Book. 80p. (Orig.). 1982. mass mkt. 20.70 (*0-310-43462-9*, 18144P) Zondervan.

Richards, Lawrence O. The Bible Reader's Companion. 936p. 1991. 36.99 (*0-89693-039-4*, 6-1039) Chariot Victor.

— Christian Education: Modeling the Gift of New Life. 336p. 1988. pap. 22.99 (*0-310-52081-9*, 18216P) Zondervan.

— The Christian Man's Promise Book. 1984. pap. 17.70 (*0-310-43582-X*, 18211P) Zondervan.

— The Christian Woman's Promise Book. 1984. pap. 17.70 (*0-310-43592-7*, 18212P) Zondervan.

— Creative Personal Bible Study. rev. ed. 215p. 1987. pap. 7.95 (*0-310-31891-2*, 10712P) Zondervan.

— The Dictionary of Basic Bible Truths. 528p. 1987. pap. 14.95 (*0-310-43521-8*, 18164P) Zondervan.

— The Expository Dictionary of Bible Words. 596p. 1985. 24.99 (*0-310-39000-1*, 18300) Zondervan.

***Richards, Lawrence O.** Global Concise Bible Dictionary. 705p. 1999. write for info. (*1-58558-001-5*) Global Pubs.

— How Far I Can Go. 1980. pap. 4.95 (*0-310-38951-8*) Zondervan.

Richards, Lawrence O. Illustrated Bible Handbook. (Illus.). 1997. 15.97 (*0-7852-1414-3*) Word Pub.

— It Couldn't Just Happen. 192p. (J). (gr. 3-9). 1994. pap. 14.99 (*0-8499-3583-0*) Tommy Nelson.

— Living in Touch with God. 128p. (Orig.). 1988. pap. 6.95 (*0-310-39141-5*, 18302P) Zondervan.

— Love Your Neighbour: A Woman's Workshop on Fellowship. (Woman's Workshop Ser.). 160p. (Orig.). 1981. pap. 2.95 (*0-310-43451-3*, 18139P) Zondervan.

— The New International Encyclopedia of the Bible. LC 98-51045. 2000. 24.99 (*0-310-22912-X*) Zondervan.

— Ninety-Nine Ways to Start a Study Group & Keep It Growing. 160p. (Orig.). 1987. pap. 6.95 (*0-310-31921-8*, 18145P) Zondervan.

— A Practical Theology of Spirituality. 288p. 1987. 19.95 (*0-310-39140-7*, 18301) Zondervan.

— Richard's Complete Bible Handbook. 1987. pap. 17.99 (*0-8499-3097-9*) Word Pub.

— Small Group Member's Commentary. 656p. 1992. pap. 18.99 (*0-89693-055-6*, 6-1055, Victor Bks) Chariot Victor.

— The Teacher's Commentary. 1200p. 1987. text 41.99 (*0-89693-810-7*, 6-2810, Victor Bks) Chariot Victor.

— A Theology of Christian Education. 320p. 1975. 22.95 (*0-310-31940-4*, 18135) Zondervan.

— The Victor Bible Background Commentary: New Testament. LC 93-27863. 640p. 1994. 29.99 (*0-89693-507-8*, 6-1507, Victor Bks) Chariot Victor.

— Youth Ministry: Its Renewal in the Local Church. rev. ed. 1986. 22.95 (*0-310-32010-0*, 18150) Zondervan.

Richards, Lawrence O., ed. The Revell Bible Dictionary. 2nd deluxe ed. LC 90-33022. (Illus.). 1168p. (gr. 13). 1994. 39.99 (*0-8007-1594-2*) Revell.

Richards, Lawrence O. & Bredfeldt, Gary. Creative Bible Teaching. expanded rev. ed. 1998. 29.99 (*0-8024-1644-6*) Moody.

Richards, Lawrence O. & Hoeldtke, Clyde. A Theology of Church Leadership. (Illus.). 352p. 1980. 22.95 (*0-310-31960-9*, 18136) Zondervan.

Richards, Lawrence O. & Martin, Gib. Lay Ministry: Empowering the People of God. 336p. 1988. pap. 17.99 (*0-310-52101-7*, 18218P) Zondervan.

— Theology of Personal Ministry. 272p. (C). 1981. 22.95 (*0-310-31970-6*, 18137) Zondervan.

Richards, Lawrence P. & Bock, Walter J. Functional Anatomy & Adaptive Evolution of the Feeding Apparatus in the Hawaiian Honeycreeper Genus Loxops (Drepanididae) 173p. 1973. 10.00 (*0-685-06251-1*) Am Ornithologists.

Richards, LeGrand. A Marvelous Work & a Wonder. LC 76-2237. xv, 424p. 1976. 12.95 (*0-87747-161-4*); pap. 4.95 (*0-87579-171-9*) Deseret Bk.

Richards, Leila. The Hills of Sidon: Journal of an American Doctor in Lebanon. 224p. 1988. 17.95 (*1-55774-015-1*) Lambda Pubs.

Richards, Lenore, jt. auth. see Treat, Nola.

Richards, Leonard, jt. auth. see Graebner, William.

Richards, Leonard, jt. ed. see Graebner, William.

***Richards, Leonard L.** The Slave Power: The Free North & Southern Domination, 1780-1860. (Illus.). 208p. 2000. 39.95 (*0-8071-2537-7*); pap. 19.95 (*0-8071-2600-4*) La State U Pr.

Richards, Leslie. Love's Deadly Silhouette, Vol. II. (Illus.). 1979. mass mkt. 1.95 (*0-89083-438-5*, Zebra Kensgtn) Kensgtn Pub Corp.

Richards, Leverett G. Elephants Don't Snore. (Illus.). 384p. (Orig.). 1996. pap. 16.95 (*0-9631232-4-6*) Rose Wind Pr.

Richards, Linda. Reminiscences of Linda Richards. (American Autobiography Ser.). 121p. 1995. reprint ed. lib. bdg. 69.00 (*0-7812-8624-7*) Rprt Serv.

Richards, Llyn. Best of Set: Families & School. 1995. pap. 40.00 (*0-7855-2773-7*, Pub. by Aust Council Educ Res) St Mut.

Richards, Llyn & Jeffery, Peter. Best of Set: Discipline. (C). 1990. 59.00 (*0-86431-000-5*) St Mut.

— Best of Set: Junior Classes. (C). 1992. 75.00 (*0-86431-222-9*) St Mut.

Richards, Llyn, et al. Best of Set: Writing. (C). 1990. 70.00 (*0-7855-7020-9*) St Mut.

Richards, Lori A. & Walsh, John. Compliance Inspections & Examinations by the Securities & Exchange Commission. LC 97-32953. 1997. write for info. (*1-57073-489-5*) Amer Bar Assn.

***Richards, Lori A., et al.** Preparing for SEC Inspections & Examinations. LC 98-207506. (Corporate Law & Practice Course Handbook Ser.). 576p. 1998. write for info. (*0-87224-493-8*) PLI.

Richards, Louise E., jt. auth. see Pillsbury, Edmund P.

Richards, Lyn. Nobody's Home: Dreams & Realities in a New Suburb. 336p. 1990. pap. 19.95 (*0-19-554761-6*) OUP.

Richards, Lyn, et al, eds. Intermission: Women, Menopause & Midlife. (Illus.). 254p. 1999. pap. text 19.95 (*0-19-553947-8*) OUP.

Richards, Lyn, ed. see Coner, Kenyetta.

Richards, Lynn B., et al. The Vaginal Birth after Cesarean (VBAC) Experience: Birth Stories by Parents & Professionals. LC 87-15107. (Illus.). 304p. 1987. pap. 22.95 (*0-89789-120-1*, Bergin & Garvey) Greenwood.

Richards, Lynne, tr. see De Baar, Mirjam, et al, eds.

Richards, Lynne M. Measure It, Manage It: Laying the Foundation for Benchmarking Health Care Foodservice Operations. LC 97-33559. 1997. write for info. (*0-88091-157-3*) Am Dietetic Assn.

Richards, Lysander S. History of Marshfield, Massachusetts, Vol. 2: Old Historic Families. 247p. 1993. reprint ed. lib. bdg. 32.50 (*0-8328-3142-5*) Higginson Bk Co.

Richards, M. Triumph TR4, 5 & 6 Autofolio. (Illus.). 72p. Date not set. 19.95 (*0-85429-816-9*, Pub. by GT Foulis) Haynes Manuals.

Richards, M. C. Imagine Inventing Yellow: New & Selected Poems. 158p. 1997. pap. text 12.95 (*1-886449-45-7*) Barrytown Ltd.

— Imagine Inventing Yellow: New & Selected Poems. (Illus.). 192p. 1991. 24.95 (*0-88268-102-8*) Station Hill Pr.

Richards, M. Fallon, ed. Deaths from the Delaware Gazette 1854-59, 61-64. (Delaware Genealogical Abstracts from Newspapers Ser.: Vol. 1). 314p. 1995. pap. text 27.50 (*1-887061-06-1*) DE Geneal Soc.

Richards, M. Fallon, jt. auth. see Hart, Matilda S.

Richards, M. Gregory. When Someone You Know Is Hurt. 2000. 4.99 (*0-310-22152-8*) Zondervan.

Richards, Marcos. La Nueva Era Del Ocultismo. (SPA.). 55p. 1998. pap. 1.50 (*1-885630-47-6*) HLM Producciones.

— Sexo y el Soltero. 40p. (YA). 1995. pap. text 1.15 (*1-885630-34-4*) HLM Producciones.

Richards, Margaret. Key Issues in Child Sexual Abuse: Some Lessons from Cleveland & Other Inquiries. (C). 1988. 35.00 (*0-7855-0095-2*, Pub. by Natl Inst Soc Work); pap. 21.00 (*0-902789-58-9*, Pub. by Natl Inst Soc Work) St Mut.

— Memories, Thoughts & Forget-Me-Nots. Holst, Richard, ed. (Illus.). 80p. (Orig.). 1996. pap. 12.00 (*0-9643280-1-1*) Cape Elizabeth.

Richards, Margaret, et al, eds. Towards a Practice Led Curriculum. (C). 1988. 45.00 (*0-7855-5897-7*, Pub. by Natl Inst Soc Work); 65.00 (*0-7855-0080-4*, Pub. by Natl Inst Soc Work); pap. 21.00 (*0-902789-52-X*, Pub. by Natl Inst Soc Work) St Mut.

Richards, Margaret & Righton, Peter. Social Work Education in Conflict. 1979. 25.00 (*0-7855-0544-X*, Pub. by Natl Inst Soc Work) St Mut.

Richards, Margaret, et al. Staff Supervision in Child Protection Work. (C). 1990. 95.00 (*0-7855-0072-3*, Pub. by Natl Inst Soc Work); pap. 38.00 (*0-902789-70-8*, Pub. by Natl Inst Soc Work) St Mut.

— Towards a Practice Led Curriculum. (C). 1988. 42.00 (*0-7855-3738-4*, Pub. by Natl Inst Soc Work) St Mut.

***Richards, Marilee.** A Common Ancestor. (New California Voices Series: Bk. V). 112p. 2000. pap. 12.50 (*0-917658-31-0*, Hip Pocket) BPW & P.

Richards, Marion K. Ellen Glasgow's Development As a Novelist. LC 70-110957. (Studies in American Literature: No. 24). 1971. text 65.40 (*90-279-1606-3*) Mouton.

Richards, Mark. The Cotswold Way. (C). 1988. pap. 45.00 (*0-904110-93-1*, Pub. by Thornhill Pr) St Mut.

— Through Welsh Border Country. (C). 1988. pap. 35.00 (*0-904110-53-2*, Pub. by Thornhill Pr) St Mut.

Richards, Mark, et al. Offa's Dyke Path North: Knighton to Prestatyn. (National Trail Guides Ser.). (Illus.). 168p. (Orig.). 1995. pap. 19.95 (*1-85410-016-5*, Pub. by Aurum Pr) London Brdge.

— Offa's Dyke Path South. (National Travel Guide Ser.). (Illus.). 168p. (Orig.). 1995. pap. 19.95 (*1-85410-017-3*, Pub. by Aurum Pr) London Brdge.

Richards, Mark, jt. auth. see Abbey, Robert.

Richards, Mark A., et al, eds. Rapid Prototyping of Application Specific Signal Processors. LC 96-53499. 204p. (C). 1997. text 121.00 (*0-7923-9871-8*) Kluwer Academic.

Richards, Mark B., jt. auth. see Abbey, Robert M.

Richards, Martin & Light, Paul Charles, eds. Children of Social Worlds: Development in a Social Context. 336p. 1986. 44.00 (*0-674-11622-4*) HUP.

Richards, Martin, jt. ed. see Marteau, Theresa.

Richards, Marty. Caregiving: Church & Family Together. (Older Adult Issues Ser.). 50p. 1999. pap. 4.50 (*0-664-50091-9*) Geneva Press.

Richards, Marty, ed. Eldercare: The Best Resources to Help You Help Your Aging Relatives. LC 99-60553. 260p. 1999. pap. 24.95 (*1-892148-07-2*) Res Pathways.

Richards, Marty & Richardson, Richard C. Love: A Philosophical Perspective. 2nd ed. 192p. (C). 1994. 41.00 (*0-536-58501-6*) Pearson Custom.

Richards, Marty, et al. A Guidebook for Trainers of Nursing Home Staff: Understanding Families. 130p. 1985. ring bd. 40.00 (*0-295-96283-6*) U of Wash Pr.

Richards, Marvin. Without Rhyme or Reason: "Gaspard de la Nuit" & the Dialectic of the Prose Poem. LC 97-40348. 160p. 1998. 32.50 (*0-8387-5358-2*) Bucknell U Pr.

Richards, Mary A. Amos Starr Cooke & Juliette Montague Cooke, Their Autobiographies Gleaned from their Journals & Letters. rev. ed. (Illus.). text 19.95 (*0-938851-03-9*) Daughters of HI.

Richards, Mary B. Camping Out in the Yellowstone, 1882. rev. ed. Slaughter, William W., ed. (Illus.). 120p. 1994. pap. 10.95 (*0-87480-449-3*) U of Utah Pr.

Richards, Mary C. Centering in Pottery, Poetry, & the Person. 2nd ed. LC 88-38316. 187p. 1989. pap. 16.95 (*0-8195-6200-9*, Wesleyan Univ Pr) U Pr of New Eng.

— No Ordinary Man: William Francis Quinn, His Role in Hawaii's History. (Illus.). xv, 354p. 1998. pap. 24.95 (*0-9648963-2-X*) Hawaii Educ Assn.

— Sweet Voices of Lahaina: Life Story of Maui's Fabulous Gardens. (Illus.). 91p. 1990. 9.95 (*0-89610-170-3*) Island Heritage.

— Toward Wholeness: Rudolf Steiner Education in America. LC 80-14905. 222p. 1980. pap. 17.95 (*0-8195-6062-6*, Wesleyan Univ Pr) U Pr of New Eng.

Richards, Mary C., tr. see Artaud, Antonin.

Richards, Mary Caroline. The Crossing Point: Selected Talks & Writings. LC 73-6010. (Illus.). 256p. 1973. pap. 19.95 (*0-8195-6029-4*, Wesleyan Univ Pr) U Pr of New Eng.

— Opening Our Moral Eye: Essays, Talks & Poems Embracing Creativity & Community. LC 96-41084. (Illus.). 206p. 1996. pap. 19.95 (*0-940262-78-9*, Lindisfarne) Anthroposophic.

Richards, Mary D., ed. see Kaup, Donna L.

Richards, Mary F. & Richards, John C., eds. Delaware Genealogical Abstracts from Newspapers Vol. 2: Marriages from the Delaware Gazette 1854-59, 1861-64. LC 96-70266. 122p. 1996. 21.50 (*0-89725-279-9*, 1769) Picton Pr.

— Delaware Marriages & Deaths from Newspapers, 1729-1853. (Delaware Genealogical Abstracts from Newspapers Ser.: No. 3). 288p. 1997. 24.50 (*1-887061-08-8*) DE Geneal Soc.

Richards, Mary P. Texts & Their Traditions in the Medieval Library of Rochester Cathedral Priory. LC 87-72869. (Transactions Ser.: Vol. 78, Pt. 3). (Illus.). 212p. (C). 1988. pap. 15.00 (*0-87169-783-1*, T783-RIM) Am Philos.

R

An Asterisk (*) at the beginning of an entry indicates that the title is appearing for the first time.

R

Richards, Mary P., ed. Anglo-Saxon Manuscripts: Basic Readings. LC 94-12990. (Basic Readings in Anglo-Saxon England Ser.: Vol. 2). 424p. 1994. text 72.00 (*0-8153-0100-6*, H1434) Garland.

Richards, Matt. Deerskins into Buckskins: How to Tan with Natural Materials. LC 97-93709. (Illus.). 160p. 1997. pap. 14.95 (*0-9658672-0-X*) Backcntry Pub.

***Richards, Matthias H.** The German Emigration from New York Province into Pennsylvania Vol. IX: Excerpted from Part V of Pennsylvania, the German Influence in Its Settlement & Development--a Narrative & Critical History. The Pennsylvania-German Society Proceedings & Addresses. (Illus.). 97p. 1999. reprint ed. pap. 16.00 (*0-8063-4853-4*) Clearfield Co.

Richards, Maura. Single Issue. LC 99-174399. 248 p. 1998. write for info. (*1-85371-872-6*) Poolbeg Pr.

Richards, Max D. Intermediate & Long-Term Credit for Small Corporations. Bruchey, Stuart & Carosso, Vincent P., eds. LC 78-18975. (Small Business Enterprise in America Ser.). (Illus.). 1979. lib. bdg. 25.95 (*0-405-11478-8*) Ayer.

***Richards, Maxwell J.** George & the Dragon. 268p. 2000. pap. 13.95 (*1-891929-36-4*) Four Seasons.

Richards, Maxwell J. George Suspected of Murder. 190p. 1999. pap. 9.95 (*1-891929-17-8*) Four Seasons.

— George to the Rescue. 201p. 1998. pap. 9.95 (*0-9656811-7-3*) Four Seasons.

***Richards, Maxwell J.** George's Hawaiian Adventure. 2000. pap. 12.95 (*1-891929-54-2*) Four Seasons.

Richards, Melissa, jt. auth. see Mulvey, Kate.

Richards, Michael. The Church of Christ. (C). 1988. 39.00 (*0-85439-203-3*, Pub. by St Paul Pubns) St Mut.

— The Church Two Thousand One. (C). 1988. 65.00 (*0-85439-202-5*, Pub. by St Paul Pubns) St Mut.

— Light One Candle: A Guidebook for the Bootstrapping. 140p. 1998. pap. 9.95 (*1-891594-00-1*) Innovat Press.

— Nature & Necessity of Christ's Church. LC 83-2596. 142p. 1983. pap. 7.95 (*0-8189-0458-5*) Alba.

— A Time of Silence: Civil War & the Culture of Repression in Franco's Spain, 1936-1945. LC 98-3444. (Studies in the Social & Cultural History of Modern Warfare: No. 4). (Illus.). 275p. (C). 1998. 59.95 (*0-521-59401-4*) Cambridge U Pr.

Richards, Michael, et al, eds. Communication & Development: The Freirean Connection. (Communication Alternatives Ser.). 288p. 1999. text 59.50 (*1-57273-243-1*); pap. text 27.50 (*1-57273-244-X*) Hampton Pr NJ.

Richards, Michael & Waibel, Paul. Twentieth-Century Europe: A Brief History. LC 98-29855. (Illus.). 225p. (C). 1999. pap. text 17.95 (*0-88295-946-8*) Harlan Davidson.

Richards, Michael, jt. ed. see French, David.

Richards, Michael, tr. see Rinpoche, Pabongka.

***Richards, Michael D. & Riley, Philip F.** Term Paper Resource Guide to Twentieth-Century World History. LC 99-88458. 352p. 2000. 49.95 (*0-313-30559-5*, Greenwood Pr) Greenwood.

***Richards, Michael D. & Waibel, Paul R.** Study Guide to Twentieth-Century Europe: A Brief History. 40p. (C). 1999. pap. text, student ed. Price not set. (*0-88295-988-3*) Harlan Davidson.

Richards, Michaela. The Best Style: Marion Hall Best & Australian Interior Design 1935-1975. (Illus.). 132p. 1994. text 39.00 (*976-8097-64-7*) Gordon & Breach.

Richards, Mildred P. For Grandchildren: Stories, Letters, Etc. (Illus.). 74p. (Orig.). 1994. pap. 5.00 (*0-9637521-2-X*) Arlington Pl.

— Releases: More Poems. (Illus.). 66p. (Orig.). 1996. pap. 5.00 (*0-9637521-4-6*) Arlington Pl.

— Second Thoughts: More Poems. (Illus.). (Orig.). 1995. pap. 5.00 (*0-9637521-3-8*) Arlington Pl.

— Twigs: Poems by Mildred P. Richards. (Illus.). 53p. (Orig.). 1992. pap. 5.00 (*0-9637521-0-3*) Arlington Pl.

Richards, Mose, jt. auth. see Costeau, Jean-Michel.

Richards, Myron. The Greatest Sound on Earth. LC 94-66243.Tr. of Eine Kleine Alte Fahrt Mit Orchester. (GER., Illus.). 128p. 1994. 20.00 (*0-9622337-4-9*) Perry Pub WA.

Richards, N. E. & Spimmler, J. F. U. S. Sailing Association Portsmouth Yardstick. 70p. 1998. ring bd. 28.00 (*1-882502-61-2*) US Sail Assn.

Richards, Nanci B. & Schneier, Betsy R. The Golden Horizons Retirement Guide: California Edition. (Orig.). 1988. pap. 19.95 (*0-944261-01-9*) Golden Horizons.

— The Golden Horizons Retirement Guide: Washington State Edition. LC 87-81652. (Orig.). 1987. pap. 18.95 (*0-944261-00-0*) Golden Horizons.

Richards, Nancy E., et al. New England Furniture at Winterthur: Queen Anne & Chippendale Periods. LC 94-46794. (Illus.). 534p. 1997. 85.00 (*0-912724-38-2*) Winterthur.

Richards, Naomi Noble, ed. see Rosenfield, John M. & Cranston, Fumiko E.

Richards, Nat. Otis Dunn-Manhunter. Young, Billie, ed. LC 73-83919. 150p. 1974. 21.95 (*0-87949-018-7*) Ashley Bks.

Richards, Neil. The Arrowhead: Three Art Play. 40p. 1998. pap. write for info. (*1-57502-979-0*, PO2677) Morris Pubng.

— Douglas Adams Starship Titanic: The Official Strategy Guide. LC 98-23662. 192p. 1998. pap. 19.95 (*0-609-80147-3*) Crown Pub Group.

Richards, Norman. Monticello. LC 94-35654. (Cornerstones to Freedom Ser.). (Illus.). 32p. (J). (gr. 3-6). 1995. lib. bdg. 19.50 (*0-516-06695-1*) Childrens.

— Monticello. (Cornerstones to Freedom Ser.). (Illus.). 32p. (J). 1995. pap. 5.95 (*0-516-46695-X*) Childrens.

Richards, Norvin. Humility. 240p. (C). 1992. 49.95 (*0-87722-927-9*) Temple U Pr.

Richards, P. G., ed. see Travers, Tony.

Richards, P. J., jt. ed. see Leonor, M. D.

Richards, P. J., jt. ed. see Van der Hoeven, R.

Richards, P. Scott & Bergin, Allen E. A Spiritual Strategy for Counseling & Psychotherapy. LC 97-8297. 391p. 1997. text 39.95 (*1-55798-434-4*) Am Psychol.

***Richards, P. Scott & Bergin, Allen E., eds.** Handbook of Psychotherapy & Religious Diversity. LC 99-46210. 518p. 1999. text 39.95 (*1-55798-624-X*, 431-7384) Am Psychol.

Richards, P. W. The Tropical Rain Forest: An Ecological Study. 2nd ed. LC 93-49019. (Illus.). 598p. (C). 1996. pap. text 52.95 (*0-521-42194-2*) Cambridge U Pr.

— The Tropical Rain Forest: An Ecological Study. 2nd ed. LC 93-49019. (Illus.). 598p. (C). 1996. text 135.00 (*0-521-42054-7*) Cambridge U Pr.

***Richards, Pamela.** Alcohol. LC 00-38913. (Just the Facts Ser.). 2000. lib. bdg. write for info. (*1-57572-253-4*) Heinemann Lib.

Richards, Pamela B., jt. auth. see Bates, Joseph D.

Richards, Pamela S. Scientific Information in Wartime: An Allied-German Rivalry, 1939-1945, 151. LC 93-25050. (Contributions in Military Studies Ser.: No. 151). 192p. 1994. 55.00 (*0-313-29062-8*) Greenwood.

Richards, Pat. The Christmas Stocking: Elegant Projects for the Holidays. LC 96-28410. (Pat Richards Craft Collection). 128p. 1996. 24.95 (*1-56799-369-9*, Friedman-Fairfax) M Friedman Pub Grp Inc.

— 101 Christmas Crafts: Ornaments, Decorations & Gifts. LC 96-28405. (Pat Richards Craft Collection). (Illus.). 160p. 1996. 27.95 (*1-56799-340-0*, Friedman-Fairfax) M Friedman Pub Grp Inc.

***Richards, Pat.** Pensativo: Poems & Watercolors. (Illus.). vi, 76p. 2000. pap. 16.95 (*0-9662263-1-3*) P Richards.

Richards, Pat. Self Expression No. 100: Poems & Watercolors. (Illus.). vii, 63p. 1996. pap. 16.95 (*0-9662263-0-5*) P Richards.

— Wonderful Baby Quilts to Make. LC 96-34083. (Pat Richards Craft Collection). 1997. write for info. (*1-56799-400-8*, Friedman-Fairfax) M Friedman Pub Grp Inc.

Richards, Patricia. Dark Knight. (Rainbow Romances Ser.). 160p. 1993. 14.95 (*0-7090-4900-5*) Parkwest Pubns.

Richards, Patricia Lewis, jt. auth. see Richards, James Henry.

Richards, Paul. Fighting for the Rain Forest: War, Youth & Resources in Sierra Leone. LC 96-51446. (African Issues Ser.). 182p. 1996. pap. 19.50 (*0-435-07406-7*) Heinemann.

Richards, Paul & Harris, Nicola, eds. African Environment: Problems & Perspectives. LC 76-371759. (African Environment: Special Reports: Vol. 1). 131p. reprint ed. pap. 40.70 (*0-8357-5232-1*, 205538900017) Bks Demand.

***Richards, Paul & Ruivenkamp, Guido.** Seeds & Survival: Crop Genetic Resources in War & Reconstruction in Africa. (Illus.). 61p. 2000. reprint ed. pap. text 25.00 (*0-7881-8598-5*) DIANE Pub.

Richards, Paul, et al. Indigenous Knowledge Systems for Agriculture & Rural Development: The CIKARD Inaugural Lectures. (Studies in Technology & Social Change: Vol. 13). 40p. (C). 1989. pap. 5.00 (*0-945271-18-2*) ISU-CIKARD.

Richards, Paul, ed. see Krigger, John T.

Richards, Paul, jt. ed. see Simpson, David W.

Richards, Paul B., ed. Recent Developments in Space Flight Mechanics, (AAS/AAAS Symposium), Dec. 29, 1965, Berkeley, CA: AAS/AAAS Symposium, Berkeley, CA, Dec. 29, 1965. (Science & Technology Ser.: Vol. 9). 280p. 1966. 25.00 (*0-87703-037-5*, Am Astronaut Soc) Univelt Inc.

Richards, Paul B., jt. ed. see Bolger, Philip H.

Richards, Paul G., jt. auth. see Aki, Keiiti.

Richards, Paul W. Successful Enjoyable Selling: How to Get the Best Out of Your Career. LC 95-92731. (Illus.). 152p. (Orig.). 1996. pap. 9.95 (*0-9649313-8-9*) Rainier Pub.

Richards, Paulette. Terry McMillan: A Critical Companion. LC 99-27177. 184p. 1999. 29.95 (*0-313-30504-8*, Greenwood Pr) Greenwood.

Richards, Penny. Desires & Deceptions. (Delta Justice Ser.). 1998. mass mkt. 4.50 (*0-373-82572-2*) Harlequin Bks.

— Eden. (Calloway Corners Ser.). 1993. per. 3.50 (*0-373-83281-8*, 1-83281-5) Harlequin Bks.

— Gabe. (Superromance Ser.). 1996. per. 3.99 (*0-373-70710-X*, 1-70710-8) Harlequin Bks.

***Richards, Penny.** Lara's Lover. 2001. mass mkt. 4.50 (*0-373-24366-9*, 1-24366-9) Silhouette.

— The No-Nonsense Nanny: That Special Woman! (Special Edition Ser.: No. 1279). 1999. per. 4.25 (*0-373-24279-4*, 1-24279-1) Silhouette.

Richards, Penny. Passionate Kisses. (Crystal Creek Ser.: Vol. 14). 1994. per. 3.99 (*0-373-82526-9*, 1-82526-4) Harlequin Bks.

— The Ranger & the Schoolmarm. 1997. per. 3.99 (*0-373-24136-4*, 1-24136-3) Silhouette.

— Sisters (That Special Woman!) LC 96-7334. 251p. 1996. per. 3.99 (*0-373-24015-5*, 1-24015-9) Silhouette.

***Richards, Penny.** Sophie's Scandal. (Special Edition Ser.: Bk. 1359). 2000. mass mkt. 4.50 (*0-373-24359-6*, 1-24359-1) Silhouette.

Richards, Penny. Their Child: That's My Baby! (Special Edition Ser.: No. 1213). 1999. mass mkt. 4.25 (*0-373-24213-1*, 0-24213-1) Silhouette.

— Unanswered Prayers. 1994. per. 3.99 (*0-373-82533-1*, 1-82533-0) Harlequin Bks.

— Unanswered Prayers. 1997. per. 4.50 (*0-373-87006-X*, 1-87006-2) Harlequin Bks.

— Where Dreams Have Been. (Special Edition Ser.). 1995. mass mkt. 3.75 (*0-373-09949-5*, 1-09949-8) Silhouette.

— Where Dreams Have Been. large type ed. (Silhouette Romance Ser.). 1996. 19.95 (*0-373-59748-7*) Thorndike Pr.

— Wildcatter's Kid: Switched at Birth. (Special Edition Ser.: No. 1155). 1998. per. 4.25 (*0-373-24155-0*, 1-24155-3) Silhouette.

Richards, Penny, jt. ed. see Munns, Jessica.

Richards, Peter. Learning Medicine, 1994. 12th ed. 120p. 1995. pap. text 12.00 (*0-7279-0999-1*, Pub. by BMJ Pub) Login Brothers Bk Co.

— Learning Medicine, 1993. (Illus.). 108p. 1992. pap. text 12.00 (*0-7279-0820-0*, Pub. by BMJ Pub) Login Brothers Bk Co.

***Richards, Peter.** The Medieval Leper & His Northern Heirs. (Illus.). 192p. 2000. pap. 24.95 (*0-85991-582-4*) Boydell & Brewer.

Richards, Peter & Stockill, Simon, contrib. by. The New Learning Medicine. 14th ed. 148p. 1997. pap. 19.00 (*0-7279-1155-4*, Pub. by BMJ Pub) Login Brothers Bk Co.

***Richards, Peter & Stockill, Simon, eds.** Learning Medicine. 15th ed. 141p. 2000. 35.95 (*0-7279-1462-6*) BMJ Pub.

Richards, Peter, jt. ed. see Godfrey, Martin.

Richards, Peter, ed. see New York City Planning Commission.

Richards, Peter, jt. ed. see Paukert, Liba.

***Richards, Pevsner.** Anti Rationalists & the Rationalists. 2000. 85.95 (*0-7506-4815-5*) Buttrwrth-Heinemann.

Richards, Phil. Leaving the Folks Home. Date not set. pap. 13.00 (*0-06-093039-X*) HarpC.

Richards, Phil & Banigan, John J. How to Abandon Ship. LC 88-18954. (Illus.). 160p. 1988. reprint ed. pap. 6.95 (*0-87033-388-7*) Cornell Maritime.

Richards, Philip. African American Literature. 288p. 1999. 59.95 (*0-631-20221-8*); pap. 27.95 (*0-631-20222-6*) Blackwell Pubs.

***Richards, Pierre E. & Gross, Howard I.** The Trustee's Guide: A Handbook for Individual Trustees, Beneficiaries & Advisors. 300p. 1999. pap. 24.95 (*1-881758-64-8*) Tower Pub ME.

Richards, R. A Slide Atlas of Strabismus Surgery. (Illus.). 240p. 1991. ring bd. 895.00 (*0-442-31557-0*) Chapman & Hall.

Richards, R. & Peace, S. Polymer Surfaces & Interfaces III. LC 98-37165. 316p. 1999. 200.00 (*0-471-98286-5*) Wiley.

Richards, R. J. Solving Problems Control. (C). 1993. pap. 38.95 (*0-582-03298-9*, Pub. by Addison-Wesley) Longman.

Richards, R. M., jt. ed. see Winfield, A. J.

Richards, R. R. How to Build an Effective Board. LC 98-179434. (Illus.). ix, 217 p. 1997. pap. 42.95 (*0-88034-126-2*) Am Soc Assn Execs.

Richards, R. T. & Sykes, A. B. Woollen Yarn Manufacture. (Manual of Textile Technology Ser.). 1994. pap. 63.00 (*1-870812-18-2*, Pub. by Textile Inst) St Mut.

Richards, R. W. Brothers in Gray. Boart, Jeff, ed. (Alternative History Trilogy Ser.: Bk. II). (Illus.). 313p. 1993. pap. 12.95 (*0-9625502-1-3*) RoKarn Pubns.

— A Southern Yarn. Bogart, Jeffrey, ed. LC 89-92811. (Illus.). (Orig.). (YA). 1990. pap. 12.95 (*0-9625502-0-5*) RoKarn Pubns.

— Survival. Bogart, Jeff, ed. (Story of the New Southland Ser.: Bk. I). (Illus.). 252p. (YA). 1995. pap. text 13.95 (*0-9625502-4-8*) RoKarn Pubns.

Richards, R. W. & Pethrick, Richard A. Static & Dynamic Properties of the Polymeric Solid State. 1982. text 184.00 (*90-277-1481-9*) Kluwer Academic.

Richards, Ralph. All about Wills & Trusts for Florida Residents. 11th rev. ed. Diamond, Sandra F. & Valentine, Laurie W., eds. LC 64-25300. 1994. pap. text 5.95 (*0-88251-085-1*) Trend Bk Div.

Richards, Ramona. A Moment with God for Single Parents: Prayers for Every Single Parent. LC 98-49919. 64p. 1999. pap. 5.00 (*0-687-97550-6*) Dimen for Liv.

Richards, Rand. The Complete San Francisco Bay Area Sightseeing Guide. LC 94-25847. (Illus.). 224p. (Orig.). 1994. pap. 12.95 (*1-879367-02-5*) Hrtage Hse.

— Historic San Francisco: A Concise History & Guide. LC 91-70670. (Illus.). 320p. (Orig.). 1991. reprint ed. pap. 15.95 (*1-879367-00-9*) Hrtage Hse.

Richards, Randal W., jt. auth. see Jones, Richard A.

Richards, Randolph A. History of Monroe County: Past & Present, Including an Account of the Cities, Towns & Villages of the County. (Illus.). 946p. 1995. reprint ed. lib. bdg. 95.00 (*0-8328-5148-5*) Higginson Bk Co.

Richards, Ray, ed. see Thakur, Bhaktivinoda.

Richards, Raymond. Closing the Door to Destitution: The Shaping of the Social Security Acts of the United States & New Zealand. 1994. 42.50 (*0-271-01060-6*) Pa St U Pr.

Richards, Raymond & Richards, Rose. The "Incredible" 100 Year Memory-Line Journal: (A Marvelous Innovation for Personal Notes & Family History Keeping!) deluxe ed. (Illus.). 310p. 1997. vinyl bd. 32.50 (*1-886197-04-0*) Joy Books.

Richards, Rebecca A., jt. auth. see Shapiro, Joan.

Richards, Regina & Oppenheim, Gary S. Visual Skills Appraisal (VSA) 80p. 1984. 65.00 (*0-685-42805-2*, 453-0A); 15.00 (*0-685-42807-9*); teacher ed. 19.00 (*0-87879-453-0*); 10.00 (*0-87879-454-9*); 10.00 (*0-87879-455-7*); 10.00 (*0-87879-456-5*); 10.00 (*0-87879-457-3*); 8.00 (*0-87879-458-1*); 10.00 (*0-685-42806-0*) Acad Therapy.

Richards, Regina & Smith, Jeralee A. Angling for Words-Memory Foundations for Reading: MFR Manual. (Angling for Words Ser.). 50p. 1983. student ed. 4.00 (*0-87879-371-2*); 6.00 (*0-87879-369-0*); 4.00 (*0-87879-372-0*) Acad Therapy.

— Angling for Words-Memory Foundations for Reading: Plates. (Angling for Words Ser.). 45p. 1983. 6.00 (*0-87879-370-4*) Acad Therapy.

Richards, Regina G. Classroom Visual Activities (CVA) Brownell, Rick, ed. (Illus.). 80p. (Orig.). 1988. pap. text 12.00 (*0-87879-657-6*) Acad Therapy.

— Dysgraphia: The Writing Dilemma. (Illus.). 64p. 1998. pap. 13.00 (*0-9661353-1-8*) Richards Educ.

***Richards, Regina G.** Dyslexia Testing: A Process, Not a Score. 31p. 2000. pap. 8.00 (*0-9661353-2-6*) Richards Educ.

Richards, Regina G. Memory Foundations for Reading: Visual Mnemonics for Sound-Symbol Relationships. (Illus.). 65p. (C). 1997. pap. 13.00 (*0-9661353-0-X*) Richards Educ.

***Richards, Regina G.** The Source for Dyslexia & Dysgraphia. 308p. 1999. spiral bd. 39.95 (*0-7606-0308-1*) LinguiSystems.

Richards, Rhys. American Whaling on the Chatham Grounds. (Illus.). 70p. 1971. 1.00 (*0-9607340-3-1*) Nantucket Hist Assn.

— Captain Simon Metcalfe, Pioneer Fur Trader on the Northwest Coast, 1787-1794. (Alaska History Ser.: No. 37). 1991. 18.00 (*0-919642-37-3*) Limestone Pr.

Richards, Robert A. Living & Working in Spain: How to Prepare for a Successful Stay, Be It Short, Long-Term, or Forever. 2nd ed. 144p. 2000. pap. 14.95 (*1-85703-278-0*, Pub. by How To Bks) Midpt Trade.

***Richards, Robert B.** Dividing the Fire. 32p. 1999. pap. 3.75 (*1-896647-15-4*) Genl Dist Srvs.

— Unfolding Fern. 15 p. 1998. pap. text 2.25 (*0-921411-98-7*) Genl Dist Srvs.

Richards, Robert C., jt. auth. see Lein, Laura.

Richards, Robert D. Freedom's Voice: The Perilous Present & Uncertain Future of the First Amendment. LC 98-9996. 192p. 1998. 23.95 (*1-57488-152-3*) Brasseys.

***Richards, Robert D.** Freedom's Voice: The Perilous Present & Uncertain Future of the First Amendment/Robert D. Richards. large type ed. LC 99-87988. (American History Ser.). 2000. 27.95 (*0-7838-8978-X*) Mac Lib Ref.

Richards, Robert D. Uninhibited, Robust & Wide Open: Mr. Justice Brennan's Legacy to the First Amendment. LC 94-4973. 163p. 1994. pap. 35.00 (*0-9635752-4-4*) Pkway Pubs.

Richards, Robert H., et al. Textbook of Ore Dressing. 3rd rev. ed. LC 40-10540. 624p. reprint ed. pap. 177.90 (*0-608-14435-5*, 2051848) Bks Demand.

Richards, Robert J. Darwin & the Emergence of Evolutionary Theories of Mind & Behavior. LC 87-10891. (Science & Its Conceptual Foundations Ser.). (Illus.). 718p. 1989. pap. text 25.00 (*0-226-71200-1*) U Ch Pr.

— Darwin & the Emergence of Evolutionary Theories of Mind & Behavior. LC 87-10891. (Science & Its Conceptual Foundations Ser.). (Illus.). 688p. 1994. 42.50 (*0-226-71199-4*) U Ch Pr.

— The Meaning of Evolution: The Morphological Construction & Ideological Reconstruction of Darwin's Theory. LC 91-19017. (Science & Its Conceptual Foundations Ser.). (Illus.). 222p. 1992. lib. bdg. 22.50 (*0-226-71202-8*) U Ch Pr.

— The Meaning of Evolution: The Morphological Construction & Ideological Reconstruction of Darwin's Theory. LC 91-19017. (Science & Its Conceptual Foundations Ser.). (Illus.). xvi, 222p. (C). 1993. pap. text 10.95 (*0-226-71203-6*) U Ch Pr.

Richards, Robert R. Alaska: Business & Industry. 1989. 34.95 (*0-89781-265-4*) Am Historical Pr.

Richards, Roberta & Z, Rachel. The Devil Next Door. LC 93-84894. 280p. (Orig.). 1993. pap. 10.00 (*0-931104-38-6*) SunInk Pubn.

***Richards, Roland P.** Out of the Back Forty. (Illus.). 366p. 1999. pap. 28.95 (*0-937816-42-6*) Tech Data.

Richards, Ron. A Director's Method for Film & Television. 282p. 1991. pap. 39.95 (*0-240-80119-9*, Focal) Buttrwrth-Heinemann.

Richards, Ronald, compiled by. A Guide to Sources for the History of South Western Australia. 45.00 (*1-875560-11-4*, Pub. by Staples) Intl Spec Bk.

Richards, Ronald W. Gray Visions. 1995. pap. text 14.95 (*0-9625502-2-1*) RoKarn Pubns.

Richards, Ronald W., et al. Building Partnerships: Educating Health Professionals for the Communities They Serve. (Health Ser.). 240p. 1995. text 36.95 (*0-7879-0150-4*) Jossey-Bass.

Richards, Roosevelt. A Long Ways from Where I've Been: An African-American's Journey from the Jim Crow South to Chicago's Gold Coast. 176p. 1994. pap. 10.95 (*1-879360-35-7*) Noble Pr.

Richards, Rose, jt. auth. see Richards, Raymond.

Richards, Roy. One Hundred One Science Surprises: Exciting Experiments with Everyday Materials. LC 92-32491. (Illus.). 104p. (J). 1993. 17.95 (*0-8069-8822-3*) Sterling.

— One Hundred One Science Surprises: Exciting Experiments with Everyday Materials. (Illus.). 104p. (J). 1994. pap. 10.95 (*0-8069-8823-1*) Sterling.

— One Hundred One Science Tricks: Fun Experiments with Everyday Materials. LC 91-13263. (Illus.). 104p. (J). (gr. 4-10). 1995. 16.95 (*0-8069-8388-4*) Sterling.

Richards, Roy, ed. see Bennett, Matthew.

Richards, Roy L., jt. auth. see Irvine, Leland K.

Richards, Ruth, ed. see Andreasen, Nancy C., et al.

Richards, Ruth M., jt. auth. see Israeli, Isaac.

Richards, S. A. & Fielden, P. S. Temperature Regulation. LC 73-77794. (Wykeham Science Ser.: No. 27). 212p. (C). 1973. pap. 18.00 (*0-8448-1335-4*, Crane Russak) Taylor & Francis.

Richards, S. K. Advanced Business Computer Applications. 88p. (C). 1998. 19.00 (*1-890033-31-6*) Grey Thistle.

An Asterisk (*) at the beginning of an entry indicates that the title is appearing for the first time.

— Business Computer Applications: Problems & Exercises Manual. 4th ed. 80p. (C). 1999. 14.96 (*1-890033-22-7*) Grey Thistle.

***Richards, Sally.** Ask Jeeves: How to Build a .Com Business? (Illus.). 2000. 19.99 (*0-07-212659-0*) Osborne-McGraw.

— Sand Dreams & Silicon Orchards: Silicon Valley's Past & its Boundless Future. LC 00-103658. (Illus.). 300p. (C). 2000. 49.95 (*1-886483-45-0*) Heritge Media.

Richards, Sandra L. Rise of the English Actress. LC 91-37873. 352p. 1993. text 39.95 (*0-312-07578-2*) St Martin.

Richards, Sandra L., ed. Ancient Songs Set Ablaze: The Theatre of Femi Osofisan. LC 95-26721. (C). 1996. text 29.95 (*0-88258-109-0*) Howard U Pr.

— Ancient Songs Set Ablaze: The Theatre of Femi Osofisan. LC 95-26721. (C). 1997. pap. 19.95 (*0-88258-121-X*) Howard U Pr.

Richards, Scott. Answers for the Skeptic. Smith, Chuck, ed. (Calvary Basics Ser.). 55p. 1996. pap. 3.50 (*0-936728-66-3*) Word for Today.

— Reasonable Doubts. 2nd rev. ed. Orig. Title: Myths the World Taught Me. 240p. 1996. pap. 9.99 (*0-936728-60-4*) Word for Today.

— Understanding Homosexuality: Perspectives from LDS Psychologists & Psychotherapists. 140p. 1995. pap. 10.95 (*1-55517-173-7*) CFI Dist.

Richards, Scott, ed. see Smith, Chuck.

Richards, Selena. Rebecca Goes Out. (Grandmother Days Ser.). (Illus.). 18p. (J). (ps). 1992. 3.50 (*1-56288-269-4*) Checkerboard.

— Rebecca Goes to the Country. (Grandmother Days Ser.). (Illus.). 18p. (J). (ps). 1992. 3.50 (*1-56288-270-8*) Checkerboard.

— Rebecca Goes to the Park. (Grandmother Days Ser.). (Illus.). 18p. (J). (ps). 1992. 3.50 (*1-56288-271-6*) Checkerboard.

— Rebecca's Rainy Day. (Grandmother Days Ser.). (Illus.). 18p. (J). (ps). 1992. 3.50 (*1-56288-272-4*) Checkerboard.

Richards, Shirley. Denmark. (Illus.). 32p. (J). (gr. 1-4). 1999. pap. 11.99 (*1-57532-273-0*) Press-Tige Pub.

Richards, Stanley. The Most Popular Plays of the American Theatre. LC 79-65112. (Illus.). 1979. 24.95 (*0-8128-2682-5*, Scrbrough Hse) Madison Bks UPA.

***Richards, Stephanie & Gershon, Samuel.** Maintenance Pharmacotherapies for Neuropsychiatric Disorders. LC 98-45218. 390p. 1999. text 59.95 (*0-87630-894-9*) Brunner-Mazel.

Richards, Stephen, tr. see Di Terlizzi, Maurizio.

Richards, Stephen B., et al. Single Subject Research & Design: Applications in Educational & Clinical Settings. LC 98-28028. (Illus.). 200p. 1998. pap. 39.95 (*1-56593-799-6*, 1562) Thomson Learn.

Richards, Stephen P. Numbers at Work & at Play. (Illus.). 213p. (Orig.). (YA). (gr. 10-12). 1987. pap. 8.95 (*0-9608224-2-9*) S P Richards.

Richards, Steve. Invisibility. 160p. 1992. pap. 12.00 (*1-85538-168-0*) Thorsons PA.

***Richards, Sue.** Music for the Heather Folk. 48p. 1998. pap. 8.95 (*0-7866-2543-0*, 96324) Mel Bay.

Richards, Sue & Hagemeyer, Stanley. Ministry to the Divorced: Guidance, Structure & Organization That Promote Healing in the Church. 112p. 1986. pap. 8.95 (*0-310-20051-2*, 9604P) Zondervan.

Richards, Sue, jt. see Richards, Larry.

Richards, Sue, jt. auth. see Metcalfe, Les.

Richards, Sue, jt. auth. see Richards, Larry.

Richards, Susan, jt. auth. see Ober, Stuart.

Richards, Susan C. Protect Your Parents & Their Financial Health... Talk with Them Before It's Too Late. LC 98-36975. 248p. 1999. pap. 19.95 (*0-7931-2762-9*, 56806701) Dearborn.

Richards, T. Military Jeeps, 1941 to 1945. 100p. 1985. pap. 17.95 (*0-946489-27-0*) Portrayal.

***Richards, Tad.** My Night with the Language Thieves. (Illus.). 150p. 1999. pap. 14.00 (*1-889289-31-0*) Ye Olde Font Shoppe.

Richards, Tad. The New Country Music Encyclopedia. 1993. 25.00 (*0-671-88294-5*) S&S Trade.

Richards, Tad, jt. auth. see Godfrey, Neale S.

Richards, Tamara, jt. ed. see Austen, Mark.

Richards, Tana M. & Misrack, Robert. Isle of Fantasies: Secrets for Creating the Love of Your Life. 216p. Date not set. pap., wbk. ed. 22.95 (*1-880732-01-7*) Strat for Success.

***Richards, Tazz, ed.** The Belly Dance Book: Rediscovering the Oldest Dance. (Illus.). 208p. 2000. pap. 18.50 (*0-9700247-0-3*) Backbeat Pr.

Richards, Terri, jt. auth. see Pendleton, Moses.

Richards, Tessa, ed. Medicine in Europe. 164p. 1992. pap. text 8.00 (*0-7279-0319-5*, Pub. by BMJ Pub) Login Brothers Bk Co.

Richards, Theodore W. & Behr, Gustavus E., Jr. The Electromotive Force of Iron under Varying Conditions, & the Effect of Occluded Hydrogen. LC 07-3935. (Carnegie Institution of Washington Publication Ser.: No. 61). 43p. reprint ed. pap. 30.00 (*0-608-14273-5*, 201569800095) Bks Demand.

Richards, Thomas. At Work with Grotowski on Physical Actions. LC 94-23889.Tr. of Al Lavoro con Grotowski sulle Azioni Fisiche. (ENG & ITA.). 160p. (gr. 13). 1995. pap. 25.99 (*0-415-12492-1*) Routledge.

— The Cold War Within American Higher Education - Rutgers University As a Case Study. LC 98-65628. 240p. 1999. pap. 15.95 (*1-57197-108-4*) Pentland Pr.

— The Commodity Culture of Victorian England: Advertising & Spectacle, 1851-1914. LC 89-37035. 320p. 1990. 42.50 (*0-8047-1652-8*) Stanford U Pr.

Richards, Thomas. Composting to Reduce the Waste Stream: A Guide to Small Scale Food & Yard Waste Composting. (NRAES Ser.: Vol. 43). (Illus.). 44p. 1991. pap. text 8.00 (*0-935817-59-X*, NRAES-43) NRAES.

Richards, Thomas. The Imperial Archive: Knowledge & the Fantasy of Empire. 224p. (C). 1993. pap. 19.00 (*0-86091-605-7*, B0538, Pub. by Verso) Norton.

— The Meaning of Star Trek: An Excursion into the Myth & Marvel of Star Trek Universe. LC 97-6845. 208p. 1999. pap. 12.95 (*0-385-48439-9*) Doubleday.

— Zero Tolerance. LC 96-15656. 288p. 1997. 23.00 (*0-374-29662-6*) FS&G.

Richards, Thomas J. Clausal Form Logic: An Introduction to the Logic of Computer Reasoning. (International Computer Science Ser.). (Illus.). (C). 1989. pap. text 38.33 (*0-201-12920-5*) Addison-Wesley.

Richards, Tim. Improvising Blues Piano. (Illus.). 262p. (YA). 1997. pap. 35.00 (*0-946535-97-3*, Pub. by Hollis Direct) Eur-Am Music.

Richards, Tim, jt. auth. see Kaltenbach, Donald F.

Richards, Tommy, ed. see Zike, Dinah.

Richards, Toni, et al. Prenatal & Obstetric Care in Los Angeles County, 1990. LC 93-20333. 1993. pap. text 9.00 (*0-8330-1343-2*, MR-182-NHF) Rand Corp.

Richards, V., ed. Current Cancer Immunology. (Progress in Experimental Tumor Research Ser.: Vol. 25). (Illus.). 1980. 126.25 (*3-8055-3033-1*) S Karger.

— Immunology of Cancer. (Progress in Experimental Tumor Research Ser.: Vol. 19). 416p. 1974. 128.75 (*3-8055-1762-9*) S Karger.

Richards, Val & Wilce, Gillian. Fathers, Families & the Outside World. LC 98-150794. (Illus.). 120p. 1997. pap. 22.00 (*1-85575-170-4*, Pub. by H Karnac Bks Ltd) Other Pr LLC.

— The Person Who Is Me: Contemporary Perspectives on the True & False Self. LC 98-152425. (Illus.). 112p. 1996. pap. 22.00 (*1-85575-130-5*, Pub. by H Karnac Bks Ltd) Other Pr LLC.

Richards, Vernon, ed. Spain, 1936-1939: Social Revolution & Counter-Revolution. (Centenary Ser.: Vol. 2). 270p. (Orig.). 1990. pap. 10.00 (*0-900384-54-9*) Left Bank.

— Why Work? Arguments for the Leisure Society. (Illus.). 210p. (Orig.). (C). 1983. pap. 8.75 (*0-900384-25-5*) Left Bank.

Richards, Vernon, ed. see Malatesta, Errico.

Richards, Vernon, tr. see Kropotkin, Peter.

Richards, Victor. El Hombre y Sus Relaciones Personales. (SPA.). 42p. 1997. pap. 1.50 (*1-885630-45-X*) HLM Producciones.

Richards, Victor, ed. see Damp, Dennis V.

Richards, Vikki, jt. auth. see Kirkpatrick, Douglas.

Richards, Vikki, ed. see Kirkpatrick, Douglas.

Richards, Vyvyan. Portrait of T. E. Lawrence. LC 75-22043. (English Biography Ser.: No. 31). 1975. lib. bdg. 75.00 (*0-8383-2093-7*) M S G Haskell Hse.

Richards, W. Graham. The Problems of Chemistry. (Illus.). 112p. (C). 1986. 24.95 (*0-19-219191-8*) OUP.

Richards, W. Graham, ed. Computer-Aided Molecular Design. (Illus.). 284p. 1989. 115.00 (*0-89573-738-8*, Wiley-VCH) Wiley.

Richards, W. Graham & Scott, Peter. Energy Levels in Atoms & Molecules. (Oxford Chemistry Primers Ser.: No. 26). (Illus.). 96p. (C). 1995. pap. text 12.95 (*0-19-855804-X*) OUP.

Richards, W. Graham, jt. auth. see Grant, Guy H.

Richards, W. Graham, jt. auth. see Grasser, Robert P.

Richards, W. H., jt. ed. see Peters, W.

Richards, W. Wiley. The Bible & Christian Traditons: Keys to Understanding the Allegorical Subplot of Nietzsche's "Zarathrustra" LC 90-33111. (American University Studies: Ser. XII, Vol. 75). 425p. (C). 1990. text 34.95 (*0-8204-1312-7*) P Lang Pubng.

— Winds of Doctrines: The Origin & Development of Southern Baptist Theology. 244p. 1991. 54.00 (*0-8191-8254-0*) U Pr of Amer.

Richards, Wallace F., jt. auth. see McClendon, Dennis E.

Richards, Whitman. Vision Research for Flight Simulation: A Report on a Workshop on Simulation of Low-Level Flight. LC TL0712.5.F55. 109p. reprint ed. pap. 33.80 (*0-8357-7689-1*, 203604000002) Bks Demand.

Richards, Whitman, jt. ed. see Knill, David C.

Richards, Whitman A., ed. Natural Computation: Selected Readings. 571p. (Orig.). 1988. pap. text 30.00 (*0-262-68055-6*, Bradford Bks) MIT Pr.

Richards, Willard. Fear, Faith, Courage: A Love Story. (Illus.). 205p. (Orig.). 1993. pap. 18.95 (*0-9641104-0-7*) W Richards.

Richards, William, tr. see Mookini, Esther T., ed.

Richards, William D., jt. ed. see Barnett, George.

Richards, William L. The Classification of the Greek Manuscripts of the Johannine Epistles. LC 77-23469. (Society of Biblical Literature. Dissertation Ser.: No. 35). 304p. reprint ed. pap. 94.30 (*0-7837-5456-6*, 204522100005) Bks Demand.

Richards, William R. The Zen of Empirical Research. LC 98-43366. (Communication Ser.). (Illus.). 280p. (C). 1998. pap. 27.95 (*1-57273-245-8*) Hampton Pr NJ.

Richards-Wilson, Stephani. Angel at War. LC 98-92802. 182p. 1998. mass mkt. 9.95 (*1-885516-04-5*) SD Writs Mnthly.

Richards, Wyn. The Far Away Hills. large type ed. 168p. 1992. 14.95 (*0-7451-1493-8*, G K Hall Lrg Type) Mac Lib Ref.

***Richards, Yevette.** Maida Springer: Pan-Africanist & International Labor Leader. (Biography Ser.). (Illus.). 350p. 2000. 29.95 (*0-8229-4139-2*) U of Pittsburgh Pr.

Richards, Yvette. Single Black Female. 192p. 1996. pap. 9.95 (*1-874509-10-7*) LPC InBook.

Richardsen, Cailen, jt. auth. see Caldwell, Stevhan.

Richardson. Administrative Law & Procedure. (C). 1996. text 39.95 (*0-8273-7977-3*) Delmar.

— Administrative Law & Procedure. (Paralegal Ser.). 96p. 1996. teacher ed. 12.95 (*0-8273-7469-0*) Delmar.

— AE: Business Ethics 96/97. 8th ed. 1996. (*0-697-31617-3*, WCB McGr Hill) McGrw-H Hghr Educ.

— Allozyme Electrophoresis. 1988. text 94.00 (*0-12-587840-0*) Acad Pr.

— American Drama Through W. W. I. 1997. pap. 18.00 (*0-8057-1618-1*, Twyne) Mac Lib Ref.

— Annual Editions: Marketing, 97-98. 19th annot. ed. 256p. (C). 1997. text. write for info. (*0-697-37316-9*, WCB McGr Hill) McGrw-H Hghr Educ.

— British Economy & Social History. 3rd ed. LC 96-154274. 384p. 1996. text 79.95 (*0-7190-3600-3*, Pub. by Manchester Univ Pr) St Martin.

— Business Calculus. (C). 1996. pap. text, lab manual ed. 23.50 (*0-03-016117-7*) Harcourt Coll Pubs.

— Business Calculus: Solutions Manual. (C). 1996. pap. text, teacher ed. 29.75 (*0-03-016113-4*) Harcourt Coll Pubs.

— Business Calculus today with Spreadsheets. (C). 1999. text 73.00 (*0-03-016042-1*) Harcourt.

— Business Calculus with Ti85. (C). 1999. text 73.00 (*0-03-016112-6*) Harcourt Coll Pubs.

— Business Ethics 1999-2000 Edition. 11th ed. 1999. pap., student ed. 16.56 (*0-07-041161-1*) McGraw.

— Business Ethics 94 & 95. 6th ed. 1994. 12.74 (*1-56134-266-1*) McGraw.

***Richardson.** Chemical Engineering, Vol. 2. 5th ed. 2000. pap. 56.95 (*0-7506-4445-1*) Buttrwrth-Heinemann.

— Chemical Engineering Vol. 1: Solutions Manual. 2000. pap. text 47.95 (*0-7506-4950-X*) Buttrwrth-Heinemann.

Richardson. The Child & Society. 5th ed. 2000. 27.00 (*0-07-232136-9*) McGraw.

— Civil Litigation for Paralegals. 128p. 1998. pap. text, teacher ed. 12.95 (*0-8273-8368-1*) Delmar.

***Richardson.** Close Relations. 2001. pap. 26.67 (*0-205-16645-8*) Allyn.

Richardson. CPSG Physics Lab Manual. 1996. 15.25 (*0-07-052500-5*) McGraw.

— Dictionary of Substances & Their Effects: Index. 311p. 1996. 89.00 (*0-85404-814-6*) CRC Pr.

— English Civil Wars. 1997. text 55.00 (*0-312-17778-X*) St Martin.

— Experimental Techniques in Condensed Matter Physics at Low Temperatures. 1993. pap. 56.00 (*0-201-62730-2*) Addison-Wesley.

***Richardson.** Farming as a Business. 144p. 1999. pap. text 34.95 (*0-7506-8938-2*) Buttrwrth-Heinemann.

Richardson. First Came the Owl. (J). Date not set. 14.95 (*0-8050-4605-4*) H Holt & Co.

— In the Garden. (Can You Find Ser.: No. 1). (J). (gr. k up). 1994. 2.95 (*0-671-89311-4*) Litle Simon.

— Industrial Plastics: Theory & Application. 2nd ed. (Mechanical Technology Ser.). 1989. pap., teacher ed. 22.00 (*0-8273-3393-5*) Delmar.

— Industrial Plastics: Theory & Applications. 3rd ed. (Mechanical Technology Ser.). 1995. teacher ed. 21.00 (*0-8273-6559-4*) Delmar.

— Introducing Art. 2nd ed. 1990. pap. text. write for info. (*0-582-87472-6*, Pub. by Addison-Wesley) Longman.

— IRM for Business Calculus Today. (C). 1995. text, teacher ed. 35.50 (*0-03-017549-6*) Harcourt Coll Pubs.

— MAC-AE: Business Ethics 96/97. 8th ed. 1996. (*0-697-31618-1*, WCB McGr Hill) McGrw-H Hghr Educ.

— Marketing. 16th ed. 1994. 12.74 (*1-56134-282-3*) McGraw.

— Marketing. 17th ed. 1995. 12.74 (*1-56134-362-5*) McGraw.

— Marketing 1999-2000 Edition. 21st ed. 1998. pap., student ed. 16.56 (*0-07-041175-1*) McGraw.

— Marketing 1996/97. 18th annot. ed. 1996. teacher ed. 13.12 (*0-697-31546-0*, WCB McGr Hill) McGrw-H Hghr Educ.

— McDonald's Collectibles. (Illus.). 1997. 22.98 (*0-7858-0803-5*) Bk Sales Inc.

— Music Every Day. 2000. 34.00 (*0-07-052396-7*) McGraw.

— Nitrification Inhibition in the Treatment of Sewage. 1989. 44.00 (*0-85186-596-8*) CRC Pr.

Richardson. Philosophy of John Rawls. 450.00 (*0-8153-2946-6*) Garland.

Richardson. Reading to Learn in Content Areas. (Education Ser.). 1990. mass mkt., teacher ed. write for info. (*0-534-11749-X*) Wadsworth Pub.

— Reading to Learn in Content Areas. 3rd ed. (Education Ser.). 1996. student ed. 15.25 (*0-534-50739-5*) Wadsworth Pub.

— A Selection of Folk Dances. 1981. pap. 18.25 (*0-08-026281-3*, Pergamon Pr) Elsevier.

— Statistical Computation. 1991. student ed. 31.50 (*0-07-831690-1*) McGraw.

— Tongue Thrust Book. 1985. 25.00 (*0-7616-7216-8*) Commun Skill.

— Type with One Hand. 2nd ed. (TA - Typing/Keyboarding Ser.). 1959. text 10.95 (*0-538-20090-1*) S-W Pub.

— Type with One Hand. 3rd ed. (Typing/Keyboarding Ser.). 1998. pap. 14.95 (*0-538-68275-2*) S-W Pub.

Richardson, ed. Using Soc Bicul Bint Cus. (C). 1995. text 45.00 (*0-673-99848-7*) Addison-Wesley.

Richardson & Lyons. Public Policy. (Political Science). 2000. mass mkt. 35.00 (*0-534-54882-2*) Wadsworth Pub.

***Richardson & Morgan.** Reading to Learn in the Content Areas. 4th ed. (Education Ser.). (C). 1999. text 80.95 (*0-534-50854-5*) Wadsworth Pub.

Richardson & Reader, G. T. Digital Electronics Circuit Analysis: Ellis Horwood Series in Electrical & Electronic Engineering. 200p. (C). 1995. text 34.00 (*0-13-211210-8*) P-H.

Richardson & Sisler. Inorganic Chemistry. 720p. 1996. write for info. (*0-8016-6562-0*) Mosby Inc.

Richardson & Smith. Low Temperature Techniques in Experimental Condensed Matter Physics. (Orig.). 1988. pap. 41.95 (*0-318-33228-0*, 15002) Addison-Wesley.

Richardson, jt. auth. see Bruess.

Richardson, jt. auth. see Ratcliffe.

Richardson, jt. auth. see Steinman.

Richardson, jt. auth. see Swihart, Ernest W.

Richardson, jt. ed. see Spenser.

Richardson, A., jt. auth. see Carter, Geoffrey W.

Richardson, A. G., jt. auth. see Reuther, Ruth E.

Richardson, A. Wayne, ed. Handbook of Copper Compounds & Applications. LC 96-51432. (Illus.). 448p. 1997. text 175.00 (*0-8247-8998-9*) Dekker.

Richardson, Adam L., Sr. New Life in Christ. 37p. (Orig.). 1995. pap. text 10.00 (*0-9657431-0-1*) Chrstian Life Bible.

***Richardson, Adele.** Australia. LC 98-4997. (Let's Investigate Ser.). 32p. (J). (gr. 1-4). 1998. lib. bdg. 19.95 (*0-88682-341-2*, Creat Educ) Creative Co.

Richardson, Adele. Beetles. LC 98-15345. (Bugbooks Ser.). (Illus.). 32p. (YA). (gr. 3 up). 1998. lib. bdg. 21.30 (*1-887068-30-9*) Smart Apple.

***Richardson, Adele.** Brazil. LC 98-46972. 1999. pap. write for info. (*0-88682-833-3*) Creative Co.

Richardson, Adele. Cockroaches. LC 98-15346. (Bugs Ser.). (Illus.). 32p. (J). 1998. lib. bdg. 21.30 (*1-887068-31-7*) Smart Apple.

***Richardson, Adele.** Covered Bridges. LC 98-43602. 2001. lib. bdg. 19.95 (*1-58341-004-X*, Creat Educ) Creative Co.

Richardson, Adele. Farms. LC 98-30294. (Let's Investigate Ser.). (J). 1999. 19.95 (*0-88682-353-6*, Creat Educ) Creative Co.

***Richardson, Adele.** Forts. LC 98-43606. (Let's Investigate Ser.). 2000. lib. bdg. 19.95 (*1-58341-005-8*, Creat Educ) Creative Co.

Richardson, Adele. Gems. LC 97-43738. (Let's Investigate Ser.). 32p. (J). (gr. 1-4). 1998. lib. bdg. 19.95 (*0-88682-993-3*, Creat Educ) Creative Co.

— Historic Mills. LC 99-10294. (Let's Investigate Ser.). 2001. lib. bdg. 19.95 (*1-58341-007-4*, Creat Educ) Creative Co.

— India. LC 99-10886. (Let's Investigate Ser.). (Illus.). 32p. (J). 2000. lib. bdg. 21.30 (*1-58341-031-7*, Creat Educ) Creative Co.

***Richardson, Adele.** Israel. LC 99-30514. (Let's Investigate Ser.). 2000. lib. bdg. 21.30 (*1-58341-033-3*, Creat Educ) Creative Co.

Richardson, Adele. Japan. LC 98-12253. (Let's Investigate Ser.). (Illus.). 32p. (J). (gr. 1-4). 1998. lib. bdg. 19.95 (*0-88682-983-6*, Creat Educ) Creative Co.

Richardson, Adele. Lighthouses. LC 98-43599. (Let's Investigate Ser.). lib. bdg. 19.95 (*1-58341-006-6*, Creat Educ) Creative Co.

Richardson, Adele. Mexico. LC 98-14261. (Let's Investigate Ser.). 32p. (J). (gr. 1-4). 1998. lib. bdg. 19.95 (*0-88682-984-4*, Creat Educ) Creative Co.

— Money, 28 vols. LC 98-36407. (Let's Investigate Economics Ser.). (Illus.). 32p. (YA). (gr. 2 up). 1999. lib. bdg. 19.95 (*0-88682-555-5*, Creat Educ) Creative Co.

— Moths. LC 98-14619. (Bugs Ser.). (Illus.). 32p. (J). 1998. lib. bdg. 21.30 (*1-887068-36-8*) Smart Apple.

***Richardson, Adele.** Orchards. LC 99-23825. (Let's Investigate Ser.). 2001. lib. bdg. write for info. (*1-58341-081-3*) Creative Co.

— Poultry. LC 99-36194. (Let's Investigate Ser.). 2001. lib. bdg. write for info. (*1-58341-082-1*, Creat Educ) Creative Co.

Richardson, Adele. Radio Astronomy. LC 98-20890. (Above & Beyond Ser.). (Illus.). 32p. (YA). (gr. 4 up). 1999. lib. bdg. 21.30 (*1-58340-051-6*) Smart Apple.

***Richardson, Adele.** Rain Forests. LC 00-9807. (Science Library). (Illus.). 2001. write for info. (*0-7368-0839-6*, Bridgestone Bks) Capstone Pr.

Richardson, Adele. Russia. LC 98-5883. (Let's Investigate Ser.). (Illus.). 32p. (J). (gr. 1-4). 1998. lib. bdg. 19.95 (*0-88682-986-0*, Creat Educ) Creative Co.

— Seashells. LC 97-43734. (Let's Investigate Ser.). 32p. (J). (gr. 1-4). 1998. lib. bdg. 19.95 (*0-88682-996-8*, Creat Educ) Creative Co.

— Silk. LC 98-30300. (Let's Investigate Ser.). (J). 1999. lib. bdg. 19.95 (*0-88682-963-1*, Creat Educ) Creative Co.

— Space Shuttle. LC 98-41869. (Above & Beyond Ser.). (Illus.). 32p. (YA). (gr. 4 up). 1999. lib. bdg. 21.30 (*1-58340-052-4*) Smart Apple.

— Walking Sticks. LC 98-15344. (Bugs Ser.). (Illus.). 32p. (J). 1998. lib. bdg. 21.30 (*1-887068-37-6*) Smart Apple.

***Richardson, Adele.** Wetlands. LC 00-9808. (Science Library). (Illus.). 2001. write for info. (*0-7368-0840-X*, Bridgestone Bks) Capstone Pr.

Richardson, Adele, jt. auth. see Gaines, Ann G.

Richardson, Adele, jt. auth. see Haffmann, Janet.

Richardson, Adele, jt. auth. see Halfmann, Janet.

Richardson, Adele, jt. auth. see Willard, Keith.

Richardson, Adele D. Astronauts. LC 98-41865. (Above & Beyond Ser.). (Illus.). 32p. (YA). (gr. 4 up). 1999. lib. bdg. 21.30 (*1-58340-046-X*) Smart Apple.

***Richardson, Adele D.** Cargo Ships. LC 00-22824. (Transportation Library). (Illus.). 24p. (J). (ps-3). 2000. lib. bdg. 15.93 (*0-7368-0606-7*, Bridgestone Bks) Capstone Pr.

— Delivery Trucks. LC 00-22827. (Transportation Library). (Illus.). 24p. (J). (ps-3). 2000. lib. bdg. 15.93 (*0-7368-0609-1*, Bridgestone Bks) Capstone Pr.

— Freight Trains. LC 00-22825. (Transportation Library). (Illus.). 24p. (J). (ps-3). 2000. lib. bdg. 15.93 (*0-7368-0607-5*, Bridgestone Bks) Capstone Pr.

— Transport Helicopters. LC 00-22826. 24p. (J). (ps-3). 2000. lib. bdg. write for info. (*0-7368-0608-3*, UXL) Gale.

Richardson, Adele D., jt. auth. see Hakkila, Jon Eric.

Richardson, Aileen, ed. Preparation to Care: A Foundation NVQ Text for Health Care Assistants. (Illus.). 246p. 1995. pap. write for info. (*0-7020-1793-0*, Pub. by W B Saunders) Saunders.

Richardson, Alan. The Auld Alliance: A Tale of the Napoleonic Times LC 81-132123. (Scottish Plays Ser.). 100p. 1979. write for info. (*0-85174-361-7*) Brown Son & Ferguson.

— Corporate & Organizational Video. (C). 1992. text 58.00 (*0-07-052334-7*) McGraw.

— Dancer to the Gods. pap. 9.95 (*0-85030-433-4*) Aqrn Pr.

— Earth God Rising: The Return of the Male Mysteries. LC 90-45552. (Men's Spirituality Ser.). (Illus.). 224p. (Orig.). 1999. pap. 9.95 (*0-87542-672-7*) Llewellyn Pubns.

— A Fine Gentleman. 32p. (Orig.). 1996. pap. 5.00 (*0-88734-355-4*) Players Pr.

— Individual Differences in Imaging: Their Measurement, Origins, & Consequences. LC 93-28218. (Imagery & Human Development Ser.). 223p. 1994. pap. 26.97 (*0-89503-117-5*); text 35.95 (*0-89503-116-7*) Baywood Pub.

— Literature, Education, & Romanticism: Reading As Social Practice, 1780-1832. LC 93-49343. (Cambridge Studies in Romanticism: No. 8). (Illus.). 345p. (C). 1995. text 64.95 (*0-521-46276-2*) Cambridge U Pr.

— Magical Gateways. LC 92-17844. (New Age Ser.). (Illus.). 208p. 1992. mass mkt. 4.95 (*0-87542-681-6*) Llewellyn Pubns.

— The Magical Life of Dion Fortune: Priestess of the Twentieth Century. (Illus.). 256p. 1991. pap. 14.00 (*1-85538-051-X*, Pub. by Aqrn Pr) Harper SF.

— A Mental Theater: Poetic Drama & Consciousness in the Romantic Age. LC 87-10922. 170p. 1988. lib. bdg. 35.00 (*0-271-00612-9*) Pa St U Pr.

— Nicht O' the Blunt Claymore: A Jacobean Farce LC 75-325713. (Scottish Plays Ser.). 95p. 1975. write for info. (*0-85174-220-3*) Brown Son & Ferguson.

— Platform Party. LC 98-55493. 1999. pap. 5.00 (*0-88734-829-7*) Players Pr.

— Science, History & Faith. LC 86-22863. 216p. 1986. reprint ed. lib. bdg. 59.50 (*0-313-25325-0*, RISHF, Greenwood Pr) Greenwood.

— A Tale of Two Undertakers. Landes, William-Alan, ed. 55p. (Orig.). 1996. pap. 5.00 (*0-88734-381-3*) Players Pr.

Richardson, Alan & Annwin, David. Inner Celtia. 1997. pap. 22.95 (*1-898307-52-0*, Pub. by Capall Bann Pubng) Holmes Pub.

Richardson, Alan & Bowden, John, eds. The Westminster Dictionary of Christian Theology. LC 83-14521. 632p. 1983. 39.95 (*0-664-21398-7*) Westminster John Knox.

Richardson, Alan & Hofkosh, Sonia, eds. Romanticism, Race & Imperial Culture, 1780-1834. LC 95-48392. (Illus.). 400p. 1996. text 39.95 (*0-253-33212-5*) Ind U Pr.

Richardson, Alan, jt. auth. see Battifarano, A. J.

Richardson, Alan, tr. see Erdman, Nikolai.

Richardson, Alan W. Carnap's Construction of the World: The Aufbau & the Emergence of Logical Empiricism. LC 97-8814. (Illus.). 252p. (C). 1997. text 49.95 (*0-521-43008-9*) Cambridge U Pr.

Richardson, Alan W., jt. ed. see Giere, Ronald N.

Richardson, Albert D. The Secret Service: The Field, the Dungeon, & the Escape. LC 70-37315. (Black Heritage Library Collection). 1977. reprint ed. 39.95 (*0-8369-8952-X*) Ayer.

— The Secret Service: The Field, the Dungeon, & the Escape. LC 77-173119. 1972. reprint ed. 39.95 (*0-405-08888-4*, Pub. by Blom Pubns) Ayer.

Richardson, Albert E. Georgian England: A Survey of Social Life, Trades, Industries & Art from 1700 to 1820. LC 67-23265. (Essay Index Reprint Ser.). 1977. 34.95 (*0-8369-0823-6*) Ayer.

— The Old Inns of England. LC 72-80704. (Illus.). 128p. 1972. reprint ed. lib. bdg. 18.95 (*0-405-08886-8*, Pub. by Blom Pubns) Ayer.

Richardson, Albert Levin, ed. see Maryland Original Research Society of Baltimore St.

Richardson, Alfred. Plants of Southernmost Texas. 298p. (Orig.). 1990. pap. text 13.00 (*0-9627293-0-2*) Gorgas Sci Fndtn.

— Plants of the Rio Grande Delta. (Gorgas Science Foundation, Inc., Treasures of Nature Ser.). (Illus.). 440p. (Orig.). 1995. pap. 24.95 (*0-292-77070-7*); text 45.00 (*0-292-77068-5*) U of Tex Pr.

Richardson, Alice M. Index to Stories of Hymns. LC 72-1690. reprint ed. 20.00 (*0-404-09911-4*) AMS Pr.

Richardson, Allen & Richardson, Owen. Prelude to the Dawn. 256p. 1997. pap. 12.95 (*1-890828-04-1*, 04-1, Pub. by Camden Ct) Origin Bk Sales.

Richardson, Allen F. Careers Without College: Sports. LC 93-4488. 112p. (YA). (gr. 10-12). 1993. pap. 7.95 (*1-56079-250-7*) Petersons.

Richardson, Alphyn P. Barnegat Ways. LC 79-166564. (Short Story Index Reprint Ser.). (Illus.). 1977. reprint ed. 19.95 (*0-8369-3994-8*) Ayer.

Richardson, Alphyn P. & Brief, Richard P., eds. The Influence of Accountants' Certificates on Commercial Credit. LC 80-1574. (Dimensions of Accounting Theory & Practice Ser.). 1980. reprint ed. lib. bdg. 17.95 (*0-405-13540-8*) Ayer.

***Richardson, Andrea.** Girl Director: Making Your Own Chick Flick. (Illus.). 128p. (YA). 2000. pap. 15.95 (*0-9659754-8-7*, Pub. by Girl Pr) LPC Group.

Richardson, Andrea, ed. The Research Tradition at UCSF: Conversations with Dr. Leslie Latty Bennett. (Oral History Ser.). (Illus.). 200p. (Orig.). 1992. pap. 20.00 (*1-881525-00-7*) Univ Calif SF.

Richardson, Andrew. The Mystery of the Treasure Map. LC 96-44839. (Publish-a-Book Clippers Ser.). (Illus.). (J). (gr. 1-6). 1997. lib. bdg. 22.83 (*0-8172-4435-2*) Raintree Steck-V.

Richardson, Andy. The Intranet: Opportunities Within the Corporate Environment. LC 97-28297. 1997. write for info. (*1-85617-331-3*) Elsevier.

Richardson, Andy, ed. see Waldstein, Mark.

***Richardson, Angelique, et al.** The New Woman in Fiction & in Fact: Fin de Si Ecle Feminisms. LC 00-27246. 2000. write for info. (*0-312-23490-2*) St Martin.

Richardson, Anna. Double Vision: A Travelogue of Recovery from Ritual Abuse. LC 97-60210. 331p. (Orig.). 1997. pap. 16.95 (*0-9623879-7-5*) Trilogy Bks.

Richardson, Anne, jt. ed. see Dick, John A.

Richardson, Antona H., ed. Directory of Churches & Religious Organizations in Minnesota: WPA 1942: New Format Reprint of 1942 WPA Listing with New & Expanded Index. LC 97-68536. xvi, 272p. 1997. reprint ed. otabind 35.00 (*0-9659271-0-5*, 971) Paduan Pr.

— Minnesotans in the Spanish American War & the Phillipine Insurrection. 232p. 1998. pap. 25.00 (*0-9659271-1-3*, 981) Paduan Pr.

Richardson, Antona H., ed. see Bowe, John.

Richardson, Antona H., ed. see Turner, T. A.

***Richardson, Antona Hawkins.** Roll of the Dead, 1886-1906, Department of Minnesota Grand Army of the Republic. 60p. 2000. pap. 12.00 (*0-9659271-2-1*) Paduan Pr.

***Richardson, Antona Hawkins, ed.** 1861-1910: Students & Faculty, Luther College, Decorah, Iowa. 44p. 1999. spiral bd. 8.95 (*0-9659271-5-6*) Paduan Pr.

Richardson, Arleen, jt. ed. see Fedoroff, Sergey.

Richardson, Arleigh D., 3rd, ed. see Alcott, Ron.

Richardson, Arlene Z. & Hannah, Sheila, eds. Introduction to Visual Resource Library Automation. (Visual Resources Association Guides). (Illus.). 178p. 1981. 17.00 (*0-938852-08-6*) Visual Resources Assn.

Richardson, Arlene Z. & Kuehn, Rosemary, eds. Guide to Copy Photography for Visual Resource Collections. (Visual Resources Association Guides). 122p. 1980. 10.00 (*0-938852-05-1*) Visual Resources Assn.

Richardson, Arleta. Across the Border. LC 95-53291. (Orphans' Journey Ser.: Bk. 4). 144p. (J). (gr. 4-7). 1996. 4.99 (*0-7814-0193-3*) Chariot Victor.

— At Home in North Branch. LC 88-9529. (Grandma's Attic Ser.). 160p. (J). (gr. 3-7). 1995. pap. 4.99 (*0-7814-0213-1*, Chariot Bks) Chariot Victor.

— Away from Home. LC 85-438. (Grandma's Attic Ser.). 160p. (J). (gr. 3-7). 1995. pap. 4.99 (*1-55513-669-9*, 59337, Chariot Bks) Chariot Victor.

***Richardson, Arleta.** Away from Home. (Grandma's Attic Ser.). (J). 2000. pap. text 5.99 (*0-7814-3290-1*) Chariot Victor.

Richardson, Arleta. A Day at the Fair. Davis, Catherine L., ed. (In Grandma's Attic Ser.). (Illus.). 32p. (J). (gr. k-3). 1995. 14.99 (*0-7814-0249-2*, Chariot Bks) Chariot Victor.

— Grandma's Attic: Wedding Bells Ahead. 1999. pap. text 5.99 (*0-7814-3292-8*) Chariot Victor.

— The Grandma's Attic Storybook. LC 92-33823. 256p. (J). 1993. pap. 10.99 (*0-7814-0070-8*, Chariot Bks) Chariot Victor.

— A Heart for God in India. Payne, Peggy & Yoder, Tamra, eds. (Illus.). 52p. (Orig.). (J). (gr. 4-6). 1989. pap. 2.50 (*0-89367-144-4*) Light & Life Comm.

— In Grandma's Attic. (J). 1999. pap. text 5.99 (*0-7814-3268-5*) Chariot Victor.

— Letters from Grandma's Attic. LC 96-102123. (In Grandma's Attic Ser.). (Illus.). 24p. (J). (gr. 3-6). 1995. 14.99 (*0-7814-0229-8*) Chariot Victor.

— Maria. 157p. 1998. pap. 5.95 (*0-89367-227-0*) Light & Life Comm.

***Richardson, Arleta.** More Stories from Grandma's Attic. (Grandma's Attic Ser.). (Illus.). (J). 1999. pap. 5.99 (*0-7814-3269-3*) Chariot Victor.

Richardson, Arleta. New Faces, New Friends. LC 88-34639. (Grandma's Attic Ser.). 160p. (J). (gr. 3-7). 1995. pap. 4.99 (*0-7814-0214-X*, Chariot Bks) Chariot Victor.

— Prairie Homestead. LC 94-27086. (Orphans' Journey Ser.: Vol. 3). 144p. (J). (gr. 1-8). 1994. pap. 4.99 (*0-7814-0091-0*) Chariot Victor.

— A School of Her Own. LC 85-29050. (Grandma's Attic Ser.). 173p. (J). (gr. 3-7). 1995. pap. 3.99 (*1-55513-670-2*, Chariot Bks) Chariot Victor.

***Richardson, Arleta.** School of Her Own. (Grandma's Attic Ser.). 2000. pap. 5.99 (*0-7814-3291-X*) Chariot Victor.

Richardson, Arleta. Still More Stories from Grandma's Attic, 1. (J). 1999. pap. text 5.99 (*0-7814-3270-7*) Chariot Victor.

— Stories from the Growing Years. LC 90-20123. (Grandma's Attic Ser.). 160p. (J). (gr. 3-7). 1995. pap. 4.99 (*0-7814-0212-3*, 38190, Chariot Bks) Chariot Victor.

— Treasures from Grandma's Attic. (J). 1999. pap. text 5.99 (*0-7814-3271-5*) Chariot Victor.

— Wedding Bells Ahead. LC 87-461. (Grandma's Attic Ser.). (Illus.). 156p. (J). (gr. 3-7). 1995. pap. 4.99 (*1-55513-668-0*, Chariot Bks) Chariot Victor.

— Whistle-Stop West. LC 92-46260. (Orphan Journey Ser.: Bk. 2). 144p. (J). 1993. pap. 4.99 (*0-7814-0922-5*, Chariot Bks) Chariot Victor.

Richardson, B. College Physics. 2001. 18.74 (*0-07-052407-6*) McGraw.

Richardson, B. A. Defects & Deterioration in Buildings. (Illus.). 220p. 1991. 72.95 (*0-442-31302-0*) Chapman & Hall.

Richardson, Barbara L. & Wirtenberg, Jeana, eds. Sex Role Research: Measuring Social Change. LC 83-2426. 274p. 1983. 36.95 (*0-275-91063-6*, C1063, Praeger Pubs) Greenwood.

***Richardson, Barry A.** Defects & Deterioration in Buildings. 2nd ed. LC 00-40055. 2001. write for info. (*0-419-25210-X*, E & FN Spon) Routledge.

Richardson, Barry A. Wood Preservation. 2nd ed. LC 92-30664. (Illus.). 240p. (C). 1993. 120.00 (*0-419-17490-7*, E & FN Spon) Routledge.

Richardson, Benjamin J., jt. ed. see Bosselmann, Klaus.

Richardson, Benjamin W., ed. see Pemberton, Robert.

Richardson, Bessie E. Old Age among the Ancient Greeks. LC 74-93775. (Illus.). reprint ed. 42.50 (*0-404-05289-4*) AMS Pr.

Richardson, Beth. Gardening with Children. LC 97-32697. (Illus.). 160p. 1998. pap. 19.95 (*1-56158-192-5*, 070319) Taunton.

***Richardson, Bill.** After Hamelin. 144p. (YA). (gr. 5-8). 2000. 18.95 (*1-55037-629-2*, Pub. by Annick Pr); per. 6.95 (*1-55037-628-4*, Pub. by Annick Pr) Firefly Bks Ltd.

Richardson, Bill. Bachelor Brothers' Bed & Breakfast. large type ed. LC 97-32625. 1997. 21.95 (*1-57490-131-1*, Beeler LP Bks) T T Beeler.

— Bachelor Brothers' Bed & Breakfast Pillow Book. (A Wyatt Bk.). 1997. pap. 10.95 (*0-312-17183-8*) St Martin.

— Bachelor Brothers' Bed & Breakfast Pillow Book. LC 97-14695. 1997. text 18.95 (*0-312-16779-2*) St Martin.

***Richardson, Bill.** Bachelor Brothers' Bed & Breakfast Pillow Book. 208p. 1998. pap. 10.95 (*0-312-19440-4*) St Martin.

Richardson, Bill & Richardson, Dana. Appaloosa Horse. 1979. pap. 7.00 (*0-87980-182-4*) Wilshire.

Richardson, Bob, Jr., jt. auth. see Richardson, Peter.

Richardson, Bonham C. The Caribbean in the Wider World, 1492-1992: A Regional Geography. (Geography of the World Economy Ser.). (Illus.). 251p. (C). 1992. text 59.95 (*0-521-35186-3*); pap. text 22.95 (*0-521-35977-5*) Cambridge U Pr.

— Caribbean Migrants: Environment & Human Survival on St. Kitts & Nevis. LC 82-7078. (Illus.). 224p. (C). 1983. text 31.00 (*0-87049-360-4*); pap. text 17.95 (*0-87049-361-2*) U of Tenn Pr.

— Economy & Environment in the Caribbean: Barbados & the Windwards in the Late 1800s. LC 97-28120. 294p. 1997. 39.95 (*0-8130-1539-1*) U Press Fla.

— Panama Money in Barbados, 1900-1920. LC 85-6127. (Illus.). 308p. 1986. text 34.00 (*0-87049-477-5*) U of Tenn Pr.

Richardson, Boyce. People of Terra Nullius: Betrayal & Rebirth in Aboriginal Canada. LC 94-11955. (Illus.). 408p. 1994. pap. 19.95 (*0-295-97391-9*) U of Wash Pr.

— Strangers Devour the Land: A Chronicle of the Assault upon the Last Coherent Hunting Culture in North America, the Cree Indians of Northern Quebec, & Their Vast Primeval Homelands. LC 90-26332. 392p. reprint ed. pap. 121.60 (*0-608-08582-0*, 206910500002) Bks Demand.

Richardson, Boyd. Moroni's Camp: Where Snakes Lurk. (Illus.). 174p. 1998. pap. 9.95 (*1-890828-08-4*, 08-4, Pub. by Camden Ct) Origin Bk Sales.

— White Thunder & Kokopelli. (Illus.). 180p. (Orig.). 1997. pap. 9.95 (*1-890828-02-5*, 02-5, Pub. by Camden Ct) Origin Bk Sales.

Richardson, Boyd C. Knife Thrower. 1996. pap. 8.95 (*1-55503-683-X*, 01111620) Covenant Comms.

— Voices in the Wind. 1992. pap. 7.95 (*1-55503-393-8*, 0111996) Covenant Comms.

Richardson, Bradley. Japanese Democracy: Power, Coordination, & Performance. LC 96-22203. 352p. 1997. 42.50 (*0-300-06258-3*); pap. 17.00 (*0-300-07664-9*) Yale U Pr.

— With a Little Help from My Friends. 2000. 13.95 (*0-06-095316-0*) HarpC.

***Richardson, Bradley G.** Daddy Smarts: A Guide for Rookie Fathers. LC 99-56764. 224p. 2000. pap. 14.95 (*0-87833-164-6*) Taylor Pub.

— JobSmarts 50 Top Careers. LC 97-20983. 400p. 1997. pap. 16.00 (*0-06-095220-2*, Perennial) HarperTrade.

Richardson, Bradley G. Jobsmarts for Twentysomethings. 1995. pap. 15.00 (*0-679-75717-1*) Vin Bks.

Richardson, Bradley M. & Flanagan, Scott C. Politics in Japan. (Comparative Politics Ser.). (C). 1984. pap. text 31.00 (*0-673-39472-7*) Addson-Wesley Educ.

Richardson, Bradley M., ed. see East Asian Studies Program-Ohio State University.

Richardson, Brenda. Andy Warhol: The Camouflage Paintings. Wingate, Ealan, ed. (Illus.). 100p. 1998. pap. 40.00 (*1-880154-26-9*) Gagosian Gallery.

— Brice Marden - Cold Mountain: The Way to Cold Mountain. LC 92-16791. 1992. 40.00 (*0-940619-09-1*) Houston Fine Art Pr.

— Brice Marden - Cold Mountain: The Way to Cold Mountain. LC 92-16791. 1992. 40.00 (*0-939594-30-7*, Menil Collection) Menil Found.

— Dr. Claribel & Miss Etta: The Cone Collection of the Baltimore Museum of Art. LC 85-70732. (Illus.). 204p. 1985. pap. 29.95 (*0-912298-58-8*) Baltimore Mus.

— Scott Burton. LC 86-22235. (Illus.). 92p. 1986. pap. 12.95 (*0-912298-61-8*) Baltimore Mus.

— What Mama Couldn't Tell Us About Love: Healing the Emotional Legacy of Racism by Celebrating Our Light. 272p. 2000. pap. 13.00 (*0-06-093079-9*, Perennial) HarperTrade.

Richardson, Brenda & Wade, Brenda. What Mama Couldn't Tell Us About Love: Healing the Emotional Legacy of Slavery, Celebrating Our Light. LC 99-12127. 272p. 1999. 24.00 (*0-06-019296-8*) HarpC.

Richardson, Brenda, jt. ed. see Baker, Malcolm.

Richardson, Brenda L. Chesapeake Song. LC 93-26412. 371p. 1994. pap. 10.95 (*1-56743-063-5*, Amistad) HarperTrade.

***Richardson, Brenda L.** Chesapeake Song. LC 93-26412. 371p. 1999. pap. 19.95 (*1-56743-040-6*, Amistad) HarperTrade.

Richardson, Brenda L. Chesapeake Song. 480p. 1996. mass mkt. 5.99 (*0-7860-0304-9*, Pinncle Kensgtn) Kensgtn Pub Corp.

Richardson, Brenda L., jt. auth. see Wade, Brenda.

***Richardson, Brenda Lane.** Guess Who's Coming to Dinner? Celebrating Interethnic, Interfaith & Interracial Relationships. LC 00-20554. 224p. 2000. pap. 14.95 (*1-885171-41-2*) Wldcat Canyon.

Richardson, Brian. Marketing For Artchitects & Engineers: New Approach. 152p. (C). (gr. 13). 1996. pap. 32.99 (*0-419-20290-0*) Chapman & Hall.

Richardson, Brian. Print Culture in Renaissance Italy: The Editor & the Vernacular Text, 1470-1600. LC 93-30907. (Studies in Publishing & Printing History: No. 8). 281p. (C). 1994. text 69.95 (*0-521-42032-6*) Cambridge U Pr.

***Richardson, Brian.** Printing, Writers & Readers in Renaissance Italy. LC 98-30354. (Illus.). 230p. (C). 1999. 59.95 (*0-521-57161-8*); pap. 22.95 (*0-521-57693-8*) Cambridge U Pr.

Richardson, Brian. The Secrets of Amusement Park Games...Revealed!, 1. (Illus.). 84p. 1999. pap. 3.95 (*0-9669659-0-6*) Silver Star.

— Unlikely Stories: Causality & the Nature of Modern Narrative. LC 96-30906. 224p. 1997. 36.00 (*0-87413-609-1*) U Delaware Pr.

Richardson, Brian A. About Juvenile Violence & Its Prevention. (Family Forum Library). 16p. 1992. 1.95 (*1-56688-046-7*) Bur For At-Risk.

Richardson, Bruce. Great Tea Rooms of Britain. (Illus.). 160p. 1997. 24.95 (*1-889937-09-6*) Crescent Hill Bks.

— Let No Man Deceive You: Responses to Objections about the Church of Jesus Christ of Latter-Day Saints. 308p. 1998. pap. 14.95 (*1-890828-09-2*, 09-2, Pub. by Camden Ct) Origin Bk Sales.

Richardson, Bruce, jt. auth. see Richardson, Shelley.

Richardson, Bruce G. Afghanistan: Ending the Reign of Soviet Terror. 2nd expanded rev. ed. Husseini, S. Noor & Husseini, S. Asrar, trs. (Illus.). 240p. (Orig.). 1998. pap. 15.95 (*0-9655813-0-6*) Bruce Richardson.

Richardson, Burton. Jeet Kune Do Unlimited. (Illus.). 140p. 1998. pap. 14.95 (*0-86568-167-8*, 440) Unique Pubns.

Richardson, Byron A., jt. auth. see Enloe, Stelle.

Richardson, C. Faith, tr. see Pettinato, Giovanni.

Richardson, C. James, jt. auth. see Himelfarb, Alexander.

Richardson, C. Joan, jt. ed. see Daeschner, C. William, Jr.

Richardson, Carl. Autopsy: An Element of Realism in Film Noir. LC 91-44181. (Illus.). 257p. 1992. 35.00 (*0-8108-2496-5*) Scarecrow.

Richardson, Carol. Por que luchamos tanto?Tr. of Why Do We Struggle So?. (SPA.). pap. 8.99 (*1-884369-93-6*) McDougal Pubng.

Richardson, Carol. Why Do We Struggle So? LC 99-165219. 168p. (Orig.). 1997. pap. 8.99 (*1-884369-44-8*, EBED Pubns) McDougal Pubng.

Richardson, Carol B. Communications Skills for the Military Family. (Family Forum Library). 16p. 1994. 1.95 (*1-56688-167-6*) Bur For At-Risk.

— Effective Child Discipline for Successful Military Families. (Family Forum Library). 16p. 1994. 1.95 (*1-56688-168-4*) Bur For At-Risk.

— Loss & Change in the Military Family. (Family Forum Library). 16p. 1993. 1.95 (*1-56688-074-2*) Bur For At-Risk.

— The Single Military Parent: Military Edition. (Family Forum Library). 16p. 1994. 1.95 (*1-56688-166-8*) Bur For At-Risk.

— Stress & the Military Family. (Family Forum Library). 16p. 1993. 1.95 (*1-56688-070-X*) Bur For At-Risk.

— Successful Parenting for the Military Family. (Family Forum Library). 16p. 1993. 1.95 (*1-56688-073-4*) Bur For At-Risk.

Richardson, Carol P., jt. auth. see Atterbury, Betty W.

Richardson, Chad. Batos, Bolillos, Pochos, & Pelados: Class & Culture on the South Texas Border. LC 98-38365. (Illus.). 284p. 1999. 35.00 (*0-292-77091-X*); pap. 17.95 (*0-292-77090-1*) U of Tex Pr.

Richardson, Charles. From Churchill's Secret Circle to the BBC: A Biography of Lieutenant General Sir Ian Jacob, GBE. 250p. 1991. 49.00 (*0-08-037692-4*, Pub. by Brasseys) Brasseys.

Richardson, Charles C., ed. Annual Review of Biochemistry, Vol. 64. LC 32-25093. 1995. text 49.00 (*0-8243-0864-6*) Annual Reviews.

— Annual Review of Biochemistry, Vol. 65. LC 32-25093. 1996. text 59.00 (*0-8243-0865-4*) Annual Reviews.

— Annual Review of Biochemistry, Vol. 66. LC 32-25093. 1997. text 68.00 (*0-8243-0866-2*) Annual Reviews.

— Annual Review of Biochemistry, Vol. 67. LC 32-25093. 970p. 1998. text 68.00 (*0-8243-0867-0*) Annual Reviews.

***Richardson, Charles C., ed.** Annual Review of Biochemistry, Vol. 68. LC 32-25093. 1186p. 1999. 136.00 (*0-8243-0868-9*) Annual Reviews.

Richardson, Charles C., et al, eds. Annual Review of Biochemistry, Vol. 53. LC 32-25093. (Illus.). 1984. text 41.00 (*0-8243-0853-0*) Annual Reviews.

— Annual Review of Biochemistry, Vol. 54. LC 32-25093. (Illus.). (C). 1985. text 41.00 (*0-8243-0854-9*) Annual Reviews.

— Annual Review of Biochemistry, Vol. 55. LC 32-25093. (Illus.). 1986. text 41.00 (*0-8243-0855-7*) Annual Reviews.

— Annual Review of Biochemistry, Vol. 56. LC 32-25093. (Illus.). 1987. text 41.00 (*0-8243-0856-5*) Annual Reviews.

— Annual Review of Biochemistry, Vol. 57. LC 32-25093. (Illus.). 1988. text 41.00 (*0-8243-0857-3*) Annual Reviews.

An Asterisk (*) at the beginning of an entry indicates that the title is appearing for the first time.

— Annual Review of Biochemistry, Vol. 58. LC 32-25093. 1989. text 41.00 (0-8243-0858-1) Annual Reviews.

— Annual Review of Biochemistry, Vol. 59. LC 32-25093. 1990. text 41.00 (0-8243-0859-X) Annual Reviews.

— Annual Review of Biochemistry, Vol. 60. LC 32-25093. 1991. text 41.00 (0-8243-0860-3) Annual Reviews.

— Annual Review of Biochemistry, Vol. 61. LC 32-25093. 1992. text 46.00 (0-8243-0861-1) Annual Reviews.

— Annual Review of Biochemistry, Vol. 62. LC 32-25093. (Illus.). 1993. text 46.00 (0-8243-0862-X) Annual Reviews.

— Annual Review of Biochemistry, Vol. 63. LC 32-25093. (Illus.). 1994. text 49.00 (0-8243-0863-8) Annual Reviews.

Richardson, Charles F. American Literature, 2 vols. LC 79-122461. (American Literature Ser.: No. 49). 1970. reprint ed. lib. bdg. 150.00 (0-8383-0901-1) M S G Haskell Hse.

Richardson, Cheryl. Life Makeovers: A Practical & Inspiring Way to Improve Your Life One Week at a Time. 224p. 12.00 (0-7679-0663-2) Broadway BDD.

Richardson, Cheryl. Take Time for Your Life. Marino, Lauren, ed. 272p. 1999. pap. 13.00 (0-7679-0207-6) Bantam.

— Take Time for Your Life: A Personal Coach's Seven Step Program for Creating the Life You Want. LC 98-20982. 272p. 1998. 23.00 (0-7679-0206-8) Broadway BDD.

Richardson, Chris E. Web Access Framework: C++ Objects for Internet Programming. (C). 2001. pap. 39.95 (0-13-494394-5) P-H.

Richardson, Christine, jt. auth. see Barlow, Jeffrey.

Richardson, Christine, jt. auth. see Johnston, Jackie.

Richardson, Christine, tr. see Manetti, Giovanni.

Richardson, Christopher D., jt. auth. see Pocock, Gillian.

Richardson, Chung, tr. see Perrolle, Pierre M., ed.

Richardson, Claire. I Want to Give up Smoking. 1999. pap. 6.95 (1-84024-065-2) Seven Hills Bk.

— Little Bathroom Book. 1998. pap. text 6.95 (1-84024-048-2, Pub. by Summers) Seven Hills Bk.

Richardson, Clive. The Fell Pony. 140p. 1990. 60.00 (0-85131-511-9, Pub. by J A Allen) St Mut.

— The Hackney. 1993. 40.00 (0-85131-613-1, Pub. by J A Allen) St Mut.

The Horsebreakers. 300p. 1998. text 80.00 (0-85131-722-7, Pub. by J A Allen) Trafalgar.

Richardson, Colin, jt. ed. see Burston, Paul.

Richardson, Craug R. & Ziebart, Geoff C. Red Tape in America: Stories from the Front Line. 120p. 1995. 14.95 (0-89195-059-1) Heritage Found.

Richardson, Cynthia C. Spring Fires Love. 1980. pap. 1.50 (0-373-58055-X) Harlequin Bks.

Richardson, Cyril C. Christianity of Ignatius of Antioch. LC 35-7948. reprint ed. 20.00 (0-404-05297-5) AMS Pr.

— The Church Through the Centuries. LC 72-6726. reprint ed. 34.50 (0-404-10645-5) AMS Pr.

— Early Christian. 1995. pap. text 14.00 (0-684-82951-7, Scribner Pap Fic) S&S Trade Pap.

Richardson, Cyril C., ed. Early Christian Fathers. (Library of Christian Classics: Vol. 1). 415p. (C). 1970. reprint ed. pap. 12.95 (0-02-088980-1) Macmillan.

Richardson, D. Hijo de Paz.Tr. of Peace Child. (SPA.). 1997. pap. text 8.99 (0-7899-0355-5, 498264) Editorial Unilit.

Richardson, D., et al. Cardiopulmonary System. (Integrated Medical Sciences Ser.). (C). 1997. pap. 22.95 (1-889325-30-9) Fence Crk Pubng.

Richardson, D. E. The Production of New Potato Varieties: Technological Advances. Jellis, G. J., ed. 384p. 1987. text 90.00 (0-521-32458-0) Cambridge U Pr.

Richardson, D. M., jt. ed. see Davis, G. W.

Richardson, D. R., jt. auth. see Baron, Robert A.

Richardson, Dale. Plutonian Phoenix. 168p. 1974. 12.00 (0-86690-145-0, R1398-014) Am Fed Astrologers.

Richardson, Dan. Moscow. 2nd ed. (Rough Guide Ser.). (Illus.). 416p. 1998. pap. text 16.95 (1-85828-322-1) Rough Guides.

Richardson, Dan & Hebbert, Charles. The Rough Guide to Hungary. 4th ed. (Rough Guide Ser.). (Illus.). 416p. 1998. pap. text 17.95 (1-85828-315-9, Pub. by Rough Guides) Penguin Putnam.

Richardson, Dan, jt. auth. see Bousfield, Jonathan.

Richardson, Dan, jt. auth. see Hebbert, Charles.

Richardson, Dan, jt. auth. see Humphreys, Rob.

Richardson, Dan K. The Cost of Environmental Protection: Regulating Housing Development in the Coastal Zone. 219p. 1976. pap. text 21.95 (0-87855-614-1) Transaction Pubs.

Richardson, Dana, jt. auth. see Richardson, Bill.

Richardson, Dana R., jt. auth. see Haidinger, Timothy P.

Richardson, Daniel. Logic, Language, Formalism, Informalism. (Illus.). 320p. 1995. mass mkt. 34.95 (1-85032-127-2) ITCP.

Richardson, Daniel R. Cardiopulmonary System. 1999. pap. text 19.95 (1-889325-43-0) Fence Crk Pubng.

Richardson, Daphne, ed. see Blue, Lionel.

Richardson, Darcy. Rainforests. (Bertinetti Ser.). (Illus.). 128p. 1992. reprint ed. 14.98 (0-8317-7342-1) Smithmark.

Richardson, David. Esperanto: Learning & Using the International Language. 2nd ed. LC 88-9858. (ESP., Illus.). 368p. 1990. reprint ed. 15.00 (0-939785-00-5, ESP046) Esperanto League North Am.

— Magic Islands: A Treasure-Trove of San Juan Islands Lore. rev. ed. (Illus.). 96p. 1995. reprint ed. pap. 4.95 (0-945742-08-8) Orcas Pub.

— Puget Sounds: A Nostalgic Review of Radio & TV in the Great Northwest. LC 80-26557. (Illus.). 192p. 1981. 14.95 (0-87564-636-0) Orcas Pub.

— Why Exports Really Matter! More. 1996. pap. 25.00 (0-88132-229-6) Inst Intl Eco.

Richardson, David, ed. Abolition & Its Aftermath: The Historical Context, 1790-1916. (Legacies of West Indian Slavery Ser.: No. 1). 224p. 1985. 57.50 (0-7146-3261-9, Pub. by F Cass Pubs) Intl Spec Bk.

Richardson, David & Richardson, Jane. The Kinemage Supplement & Introduction to Protein Structure: For Macintosh. 1993. 11.00 (0-8153-1607-0) Garland.

Richardson, David, jt. ed. see Eltis, David.

Richardson, David A., ed. Sixteenth Century British Non-Dramatic Writers: 3rd Series. (Dictionary of Literary Biography Ser.: Vol. 167). 400p. 1996. text 155.00 (0-8103-9362-X) Gale.

Richardson, David B. Pig War Islands: The San Juans of Northwest Washington. LC 70-149337. (Illus.). 416p. 1990. reprint ed. pap. 16.95 (0-945742-04-5) Orcas Pub.

Richardson, David G., jt. auth. see Simmonds, Peter T.

Richardson, David J. Distinctly Delicious: Favorite Recipes of the Distinctive Inns of Colorado. Richardson, Javana M., ed. LC 97-64873. (Illus.). 340p. (Orig.). 1997. pap. 17.95 (1-889120-07-3) StarsEnd Creations.

— The Star Dwarves Trilogy. 2nd rev. ed. LC 96-72269. Orig. Title: The Star Dwarves Travesty. 240p. 1996. pap. 12.95 (1-889120-06-5) StarsEnd Creations.

Richardson, David J. & Richardson, Javana M. Crackedweb, the Book. LC 96-70173. 220p. (Orig.). 1996. pap. 12.95 (1-889120-03-0) StarsEnd Creations.

Richardson, David J., jt. auth. see Richardson, Javana M.

Richardson, David M., ed. Ecology & Biogeography of Pinus. LC 97-11056. (Illus.). 546p. (C). 1998. text 155.00 (0-521-55176-5) Cambridge U Pr.

***Richardson, David M., ed.** Ecology & Biogeography of Pinus. (Illus.). 545p. (C). 2000. pap. text 54.95 (0-521-78910-9) Cambridge U Pr.

Richardson, David W., et al, eds. Frozen Human Semen: A Royal College of Obstetricians & Gynaecologists Workshop in the Cryobiology of Human Semen & Its Role on Artificial Insemination by Donor, March 22 & 23, 1979. (Developments in Obstetrics & Gynecology Ser.: No. 4). 280p. 1980. text 148.50 (90-247-2370-1) Kluwer Academic.

***Richardson, Dawn.** Building Blocks of Rock - Fundamentals. 96p. 1998. pap. 19.95 incl. audio compact disk (0-7866-4361-7, 97756BCD) Mel Bay.

— From the Heart of a Child: Meditations for Everyday Living. Law, Jennifer, ed. (Illus.). 99p. 1999. 10.99 (1-56309-747-8, N994142, New Hope) Womans Mission Union.

Richardson, Dawn. Smoke. 112p. (YA). (gr. 9-12). 1985. 7.95 (0-920806-73-2, Pub. by Penumbra Pr) U of Toronto Pr.

Richardson, Deborra A., jt. auth. see Hobson, Constance T.

Richardson, Delois, jt. auth. see Ramirez, Carl.

Richardson, Diana. The Love Keys: The Art of Magnetic Sex: A Unique Guide to Love & Sexual Fulfilment LC 98-55290. 1999. write for info. (1-86204-387-6) Element MA.

***Richardson, Diana.** Political Complexity: Nonlinear Models of Politics. 352p. (C). 2000. text 59.50 (0-472-10964-2, 10964) U of Mich Pr.

Richardson, Diana Edkins. Classic Landscapes of the Southwest. 1989. write for info. (0-8212-1636-8) Little.

Richardson, Diane. Women & AIDS. 160p. 1987. 29.95 (0-415-90175-8, A0762); pap. 11.95 (0-416-01751-7, A0766) Routledge.

— Women, Motherhood, & Childrearing. LC 92-19905. 1993. text 35.00 (0-312-08593-1) St Martin.

Richardson, Diane, ed. Theorizing Heterosexuality: Telling It Straight. 192p. 1996. pap. 28.95 (0-335-19503-2) OpUniv Pr.

Richardson, Diane, jt. auth. see Robinson, Victoria.

Richardson, Dick & Rootes, Chris, eds. The Green Challenge: The Development of Green Parties in Europe. LC 94-15095. 240p. (C). 1994. pap. 25.99 (0-415-10650-8) Routledge.

— The Green Challenge: The Development of Green Parties in Europe. LC 94-15095. 240p. (C). (gr. 13). 1994. 90.00 (0-415-10649-4) Routledge.

Richardson, Don. Acting Without Agony: An Alternative to the Method. 2nd ed. LC 93-24467. 1993. pap. text 33.00 (0-205-15165-9) Allyn.

Richardson, Don, ed. Conversations with Carter. LC 97-50176. 300p. 1998. lib. bdg. 48.00 (1-55587-801-6) L Rienner.

Richardson, Donald. Ghosts of Love. limited ed. (Illus.). 1987. 2.00 (0-932616-18-6) Brick Hse Bks.

— Great Zeus & All His Children. 318p. (C). 1993. pap. text 12.75 (1-57074-091-7) Greyden Pr.

— Knocking Them Dead. (Illus.). 50p. 1982. pap. 3.95 (0-932616-13-5) Brick Hse Bks.

— Stories of the Greeks & Romans: Introduction to Classical Mythology. (Illus.). (C). 1996. lib. bdg. 65.00 (0-89241-515-0) Caratzas.

— Stories of the Greeks & Romans: Introduction to Classical Mythology, 2 vols., Set. 2nd rev. ed. (Illus.). (C). 1996. pap. text 42.50 (0-89241-549-5) Caratzas.

— Stories of the Greeks & Romans: Introduction to Classical Mythology, Vol. I. 2nd rev. ed. (Illus.). (C). 1996. pap. text 22.50 (0-89241-575-4); pap. text 22.50 (0-89241-576-2) Caratzas.

Richardson, Donald V. & Caisse, Arthur J., Jr. Rotating Electric Machinery & Transformer Technology. 4th ed. LC 96-1816. 731p. (C). 1996. 74.20 (0-13-409640-1) P-H.

***Richardson, Donald W.** Birth Order & You. 2nd ed. 2000. pap. 9.95 (1-55180-245-7) Self-Counsel Pr.

Richardson, Donna. Visual Paraphrasing of Poetry: A Sourcebook for Teachers & Readers. 222p. (Orig.). (C). 1992. lib. bdg. 52.00 (0-8191-8819-0) U Pr of Amer.

Richardson, Donna. Visual Paraphrasing of Poetry: A Sourcebook for Teachers & Readers. 222p. (Orig.). (C). 1992. pap. text 26.50 (0-8191-8820-4) U Pr of Amer.

Richardson, Donna & Peden, David. Let's Get Real. LC 98-156081. 1998. per. 16.00 (0-671-53883-7, PB Trade Paper) PB.

Richardson, Donna L., ed. Youth Information Resources: An Annotated Guide for Parents, Professionals, Students, Researchers & Concerned Citizens, 10. LC 86-33492. (Bibliographies & Indexes in Sociology Ser.: No. 10). 371p. 1987. lib. bdg. 79.50 (0-313-25304-8, WYI/) Greenwood.

Richardson, Dorothy. The Long Day: The Story of a New York Working Girl. 320p. (C). 1990. reprint ed. pap. text 14.50 (0-8139-1289-X) U Pr of Va.

— Pilgrimage Vol. 1: Pointed Roofs, Backwater, Honeycomb. 496p. 1989. reprint ed. pap. 12.50 (0-252-06076-8) U of Ill Pr.

— The Quest of Simon Richardson. large type ed. (Illus.). 384p. 1987. 27.99 (0-7089-1714-3) Ulverscroft.

— Windows on Modernism: Selected Letters of Dorothy Richardson. Fromm, Gloria G., ed. LC 94-4170. (Illus.). 696p. 1995. 65.00 (0-8203-1659-8) U of Ga Pr.

Richardson, Dorothy & Ruta, Tina, eds. Arie Antiche. LC 90-62112. 150p. 1990. pap. text 18.95 (1-55725-017-0) Paraclete MA.

Richardson, Dorothy L. Half-Seen Face. LC 78-24600. 1979. 6.95 (0-87233-047-8) Bauhan.

— The Invisible Giant. LC 86-1032. 75p. 1986. 15.00 (0-87233-085-0) Bauhan.

Richardson, Dorsey. Constitutional Doctrines of Justice Oliver Wendell Holmes. LC 78-64115. (Johns Hopkins University. Studies in the Social Sciences. Thirtieth Ser. 1912: 3). reprint ed. 39.50 (0-404-61230-X) AMS Pr.

Richardson, Dot. Living the Dream. 192p. 1998. pap. 12.95 (1-57566-277-9, Knsington) Kensgtn Pub Corp.

Richardson, Dot & Yaeger, Don. Living the Dream. LC 97-71967. 256p. 1997. 19.95 (1-57566-203-5) Kensgtn Pub Corp.

Richardson, Doug. Dark Horse. 464p. 1998. mass mkt. 6.99 (0-380-78770-9, Avon Bks) Morrow Avon.

Richardson, Doug. True Believers. LC 99-21623. 400p. 1999. 24.00 (0-380-97315-4, Avon Bks) Morrow Avon.

***Richardson, Doug.** True Believers. 528p. 2000. mass mkt. 6.99 (0-380-78771-7, Avon Bks) Morrow Avon.

Richardson, Douglas. Big Cats. (Illus.). 124p. text 24.95 (0-905483-92-8, Pub. by Whittet Bks) Diamond Farm Bk.

Richardson, Douglass B. Networking. 224p. 1994. pap. 10.95 (0-471-31027-1) Wiley.

Richardson, Drew, jt. auth. see Guly, Ursula.

Richardson, Drew, ed. see Shreeves, Karl,

Richardson, Drew, ed. see Shreeves, Karl, et al.

Richardson, Drew, ed. see Wohlers, Bob, et al.

Richardson, Drew, ed. & pref. see Yakzan, Riad & Shreeves, Karl.

Richardson, E. History of Woonsocket, R. I. 264p. 1990. reprint ed. lib. bdg. 32.50 (0-8328-1630-2) Higginson Bk Co.

— Stream Stability & Scour at Highway Bridges Water Resources Engineering: Compendium of Stream Stability & Scour. LC 98-48489. 1040p. 1998. 85.00 (0-7844-0407-0) Am Soc Civil Eng.

Richardson, E. M. We Keep a Light. large type ed. 1990. 27.99 (0-7089-2227-9) Ulverscroft.

Richardson, Edgar P., et al. Charles Willson Peale & His World. (Illus.). 272p. 1983. 39.95 (0-8109-1478-6, Pub. by Abrams) Time Warner.

Richardson, Edward. Research Techniques for the Social Sciences Manual. LC 83-10749. 123p. 1983. pap. 5.00 (0-913480-58-4) Inter Am U Pr.

Richardson, Edward. To See a World in a Grain of Sand. 96p. 1972. 8.95 (0-8378-1789-7) Gibson.

Richardson, Edward P., Jr. & DeGirolami, Umberto. Pathology of the Peripheral Nerve. LC 94-20440. (Major Problems in Pathology Ser.: No. 32). 176p. 1994. text 64.00 (0-7216-3298-X, W B Saunders Co) Harcrt Hlth Sci Grp.

Richardson, Eleanor M. Andover: A Century of Change. LC 95-7906. 1995. write for info. (0-89865-938-8) Donning Co.

Richardson, Elisha R. An Atlas of Craniofacial Growth in Americans of African Descent. (Craniofacial Growth Ser.: Vol. 26). (Illus.). 1991. 69.00 (0-929921-22-4) UM CHGD.

Richardson, Elizabeth. Administrative Law & Procedure. LC 95-23056. (Paralegal Ser.). 496p. (C). 1995. mass mkt. 71.95 (0-8273-7468-2) Delmar.

Richardson, Elizabeth. Authority & Organization in the Secondary School LC 75-326004. (Schools Council Research Studies). x, 146p. 1975. write for info. (0-333-18065-8, Pub. by Macmillan) Macmillan.

Richardson, Elizabeth, ed. The Alaskan, November 1885 - March 1887: Newspaper Excerpts of Genealogical & Historical Interest. 156p. 1998. pap. 16.00 (0-9660396-0-2) E S Richardson.

Richardson, Elizabeth, ed. see Ellis, Robert E. & Ellis, Margaret R.

Richardson, Elizabeth C. & Regan, Milton C., Jr. Civil Litigation for Paralegals. 432p. 1992. write for info. (0-538-70399-7); teacher ed. write for info. (0-538-70373-3) S-W Pub.

Richardson, Elizabeth C. & Regan, Milton C. Civil Litigation for Paralegals. 2nd ed. LC 97-11013. (Paralegal). (C). 1997. 77.95 (0-8273-8367-3) Delmar.

Richardson, Elizabeth R., ed. A Bloomsbury Iconography. 384p. 1989. 40.00 (0-906795-63-X) Oak Knoll.

***Richardson, Elliot L.** Reflections of a Radical Moderate. LC 00-25626. 320p. 2000. pap. 19.00 (0-8133-9784-7) Westview.

Richardson, Elliot L., frwd. Arthur Flemming Crusader at Large. 371p. 1992. 25.00 (0-9628363-2-X) Caring Pub.

Richardson, Elliot L., jt. frwd. see Fasulo, Linda M.

Richardson, Ellis. The Battle of Trappers Pass: Short Vowel I Sequence. (Read Aloud Ser.: Bk. 5). 32p. (Orig.). 1988. pap. text 4.00 (1-56775-019-2, SVIS5-4) ISM Teach Systs.

— Becoming Friends: Introductory Sequence. (Read Aloud Ser.: Bk. 3). 24p. (Orig.). 1988. pap. text 4.00 (1-56775-014-1, INS3-5) ISM Teach Systs.

— Book of Lessons & Fun Book Level 1: Introductory Sequence. rev. ed. (Linguistic Pattern Ser.). 33p. (J). (gr. 2). 1993. pap. text 8.00 (1-56775-041-9) ISM Teach Systs.

— Book of Lessons & Fun Book, Level A: Beginner Sequence. rev. ed. (Linguistic Pattern Ser.). 21p. 1993. pap. text 8.00 (1-56775-037-0) ISM Teach Systs.

— Book of Lessons & Fun Book, Level B: Beginner Sequence. rev. ed. (Linguistic Pattern Ser.). 21p. 1993. pap. text 8.00 (1-56775-038-9) ISM Teach Systs.

— Book of Lessons & Fun Book, Level C: Beginner Sequence. rev. ed. (Linguistic Pattern Ser.). 21p. 1993. pap. text 8.00 (1-56775-039-7) ISM Teach Systs.

— Book of Lessons & Fun Book, Level D: Beginner Sequence. rev. ed. (Linguistic Pattern Ser.). 21p. 1993. pap. text 8.00 (1-56775-040-0) ISM Teach Systs.

— Book of Lessons & Fun Book, Level 2: Introductory Sequence. rev. ed. (Linguistic Pattern Ser.). 33p. 1993. pap. text 8.00 (1-56775-042-7) ISM Teach Systs.

— Book of Lessons & Fun Book, Level 3: Introductory Sequence. rev. ed. (Linguistic Pattern Ser.). 33p. 1993. pap. text 8.00 (1-56775-043-5) ISM Teach Systs.

— Book of Lessons & Fun Book, Level 4: Short Vowel I Sequence. rev. ed. (Linguistic Pattern Ser.). 33p. (J). (gr. 2-3). 1994. pap. text 8.00 (1-56775-054-0) ISM Teach Systs.

— Book of Lessons & Fun Book, Level 5: Short Vowel I Sequence. rev. ed. (Linguistic Pattern Ser.). 33p. 1994. pap. text 8.00 (1-56775-055-9) ISM Teach Systs.

— Book of Lessons & Fun Book, Level 6: Short Vowel I Sequence. rev. ed. (Linguistic Pattern Ser.). 33p. 1994. pap. text 8.00 (1-56775-056-7) ISM Teach Systs.

— Book of Lessons & Fun Book, Level 7: Short Vowel I Sequence. rev. ed. (Linguistic Pattern Ser.). 33p. (J). (gr. 2-3). 1994. pap. text 8.00 (1-56775-057-5) ISM Teach Systs.

— Book of Lessons, Level 1: Getting Ready Sequence. (Linguistic Pattern Ser.). (Illus.). 72p. (Orig.). 1989. pap., student ed. 7.00 (1-56775-000-1, GRIL1) ISM Teach Systs.

— Book of Lessons, Level 2: Getting Ready Sequence. (Linguistic Pattern Ser.). (Illus.). 72p. (Orig.). 1988. pap., student ed. 7.00 (1-56775-001-X, GRIL5) ISM Teach Systs.

— Book of Lessons, Levels 8-11: Short Vowell II Sequence. (Linguistic Pattern Ser.). 44p. (Orig.). 1989. pap., student ed. 5.00 (1-56775-024-9, SVIIL1) ISM Teach Systs.

— Common Short Vowel Syllables Level 9: Brown Sequence. rev. ed. (Linguistic Pattern Ser.). (Illus.). 64p. (YA). Date not set. pap. text. write for info. (1-56775-081-8) ISM Teach Systs.

— Flying on Wings: Beginner Sequence. (Read Aloud Ser.: Bk. D). 24p. (Orig.). 1988. pap. text 4.00 (1-56775-008-7, BGSD6) ISM Teach Systs.

— Fun Book Answer Key, Levels 4-7: Short Vowel I Sequence. (Linguistic Pattern Ser.). 12p. (Orig.). 1992. pap., teacher ed. 5.00 (1-56775-023-0, SVIFBA8) ISM Teach Systs.

— Learning to Teach by Learning to Read: A Primer for Teaching Teachers to Read. 6th ed. (Linguistic Pattern Ser.). (Illus.). 16p. 1997. pap. text. write for info. (1-56775-078-8) ISM Teach Systs.

— Misconduct & Mysteries: Short Vowel II Sequence. (Read Aloud Ser.: Bk. 9). 28p. (Orig.). 1990. pap. text 4.00 (1-56775-026-5, SVIIS9-4) ISM Teach Systs.

— Of Frocks & Frogs & Clogs in Bogs: Short Vowel I Sequence. (Read Aloud Ser.: Bk. 7). 32p. (Orig.). 1989. pap. text 4.00 (1-56775-021-4, SVIS7-6) ISM Teach Systs.

— Of Rams & Sacks & Tramps in Shacks: Short Vowel I Sequence. (Read Aloud Ser.: Bk. 4). 32p. (Orig.). 1988. pap. text 4.00 (1-56775-018-4, SVIS4-3) ISM Teach Systs.

— Of Seals & Jeeps & Steam That's Green: Introductory Sequence. (Read Aloud Ser.: Bk. 1). 28p. (Orig.). 1988. pap. text 4.00 (1-56775-012-5, INS1-2) ISM Teach Systs.

— Parte A Examen de Habilidad. (Linguistic Pattern Ser.). (SPA., Illus.). 4p. (J). (gr. 1-2). 1997. pap. text. write for info. (1-56775-075-3) ISM Teach Systs.

— Parte B Examen de Habilidad. (Linguistic Pattern Ser.). (SPA., Illus.). 4p. (J). (gr. 1-2). 1997. pap. text. write for info. (1-56775-076-1) ISM Teach Systs.

— Parte C Examen de Habilidad. (Linguistic Pattern Ser.). (SPA., Illus.). 4p. (J). (gr. 2-3). 1997. pap. text. write for info. (1-56775-077-X) ISM Teach Systs.

— The Rainmaker of Cullmans Bluff: Short Vowel II Sequence. (Read Aloud Ser.: Bk. 8). 32p. (Orig.). 1990. pap. text 4.00 (1-56775-025-7, SVIIS8-3) ISM Teach Systs.

— Reading Like Kings & Queens: Introductory Sequence. (Read Aloud Ser.: Bk. 2). 36p. (Orig.). 1988. pap. text 4.00 (1-56775-013-3, INS2-3) ISM Teach Systs.

— Resource Guide for Teaching Reading in Spanish. rev. ed. (Illus.). 85p. 1998. pap. text 25.00 (1-56775-084-2) ISM Teach Systs.

— Short a & Long e with ly & y Endings Level 5: Green Sequence. (Illus.). 1998. pap. text 9.00 (1-56775-087-7) ISM Teach Systs.

— Sound of Long E: Blue Sequence, Level I. (Illus.). 55p. 1998. pap. text 9.00 (1-56775-086-9) ISM Teach Systs.
— The Sound of Short A Level 4: Green Sequence. rev. ed. (Linguistic Pattern Ser.). (Illus.). 64p. (YA). Date not set. pap. text. write for info. (1-56775-079-6) ISM Teach Systs.
— The Sound of Short U Level 8: Brown Sequence. rev. ed. (Linguistic Pattern Ser.). (Illus.). 64p. (YA). Date not set. pap. text. write for info. (1-56775-080-X) ISM Teach Systs.
— We Can Sing: Beginner Sequence. (Read Aloud Ser.: Bk. A). (Illus.). 24p. (Orig.). 1988. pap. text 4.00 (1-56775-005-2, BGSA3) ISM Teach Systs.
— We Can Try to Fly Away: Beginner Sequence. (Read Aloud Ser.: Bk. C). 20p. (Orig.). 1988. pap. text 4.00 (1-56775-007-9, BGSC5) ISM Teach Systs.
— We May Ride Away: Beginner Sequence. (Read Aloud Ser.: Bk. B). 20p. (Orig.). 1988. pap. text 4.00 (1-56775-006-0, BGSB4) ISM Teach Systs.
— Wiggles & Giggles: Short Vowel I Sequence. (Read Aloud Ser.: Bk. 6). 32p. (Orig.). 1988. pap. text 4.00 (1-56775-020-6, SVIS6-5) ISM Teach Systs.
— Yellow Implementation Guide. rev. ed. (Illus.). 81p. 1998. pap. text 25.00 (1-56775-085-0) ISM Teach Systs.

Richardson, Ellis & DiBenedetto, Barbara. Book of Lessons, Levels 12-15: Long Vowel Sequence. (Linguistic Pattern Ser.). 44p. (Orig.). 1992. pap., student ed. 6.00 (1-56775-031-1, LVL1) ISM Teach Systs.
— Fun Book Answer Key for Levels 12-15: Long Vowel Sequence. (Linguistic Pattern Ser.). 12p. (Orig.). 1992. pap., teacher ed. 5.00 (1-56775-034-6, LV-FBA-8) ISM Teach Systs.
— Fun Book Answer Key, Levels 8-11: Short Vowel II Sequence. (Linguistic Pattern Ser.). 12p. (Orig.). 1992. pap., teacher ed. 5.00 (1-56775-029-X, SVIIFBA8) ISM Teach Systs.
— Fun Book, Levels 12-15: Long Vowel Sequence. (Linguistic Pattern Ser.). 64p. (Orig.). 1992. pap., student ed. 6.00 (1-56775-032-X, LVF2) ISM Teach Systs.
— Fun Book, Levels 8-11: Short Vowel Two Sequence. (Linguistic Pattern Ser.). 64p. (Orig.). 1989. pap., student ed. 6.00 (1-56775-035-4, SVII-F-2) ISM Teach Systs.
— Implementation Guide for Levels A-D: Beginner Sequence. (Linguistic Pattern Ser.). 52p. (Orig.). 1992. pap., teacher ed. 8.00 (1-56775-009-5, BGIG7) ISM Teach Systs.
— Implementation Guide for Levels I & II: Getting Ready Sequence. (Linguistic Pattern Ser.). 34p. (Orig.). 1989. pap., teacher ed. 8.00 (1-56775-002-8, GRIG9) ISM Teach Systs.
— Implementation Guide for Levels 1-3: Introductory Sequence. (Linguistic Pattern Ser.). 52p. (Orig.). 1992. pap., teacher ed. 8.00 (1-56775-015-X, INIG6) ISM Teach Systs.
— Implementation Guide for Levels 4-7: Short Vowel I Sequence. (Linguistic Pattern Ser.). 60p. (Orig.). 1992. pap., teacher ed. 8.00 (1-56775-022-2, SVIIG7) ISM Teach Systs.
— Implementation Guide for Levels 8-11: Short Vowel II Sequence. (Linguistic Pattern Ser.). 56p. (Orig.). 1992. pap., teacher ed. 8.00 (1-56775-030-3, SVIIIG7) ISM Teach Systs.
— Implementation Guide, Levels 12-15: Long Vowel Sequence. (Linguistic Pattern Ser.). 60p. (Orig.). 1992. pap., teacher ed. 8.00 (1-56775-033-8, LVIG7) ISM Teach Systs.
— The Integrated Skills Method (ISM) Manual: A Resource Guide for Teaching Reading. 150p. 1993. 25.00 (1-56775-036-2, TM-3) ISM Teach Systs.
— The Misfit: Short Vowel II Sequence. (Read Aloud Ser.: Bk. 10). 32p. (Orig.). 1991. pap. text 4.00 (1-56775-027-3, SVIIS10-5) ISM Teach Systs.
— More Short Vowel Syllables: Brown Sequence Level 11. (Linguistic Pattern Ser.). (Illus.). 64p. (J). 1997. pap. text 90.00 (1-56775-083-4) ISM Teach Systs.
— The Prom: Short Vowel II Sequence. (Read Aloud Ser.: Bk. 11). 32p. (Orig.). 1991. pap. text 4.00 (1-56775-028-1, SVIIS11-6) ISM Teach Systs.
— The Sound of Short E: Brown Sequence Level 10. (Linguistic Pattern Ser.). (Illus.). 64p. (J). Date not set. pap. text. write for info. (1-56775-082-6) ISM Teach Systs.

Richardson, Ellis & Freeman, Harold, Jr. Reading Progress Feedback System (RFFS) 86p. (Orig.). 1981. pap. 15.00 (0-939632-32-2) ILM.

Richardson, Elmo. David T. Mason: Forestry Advocate: His Role in the Application of Sustained Yield Management to Private & Public Forest Lands. LC 83-16533. (Illus.). xiii, 125p. 1983. pap. text 8.00 (0-89030-044-5) Forest Hist Soc.

Richardson, Elmo, jt. auth. see Pach, Chester J., Jr.

Richardson, Emeline H. The Etruscans, Their Art & Civilization. LC 76-381935. (Phoenix Bk.). (Illus.). 327p. reprint ed. pap. 101.40 (0-608-09513-3, 20543140005) Bks Demand.

Richardson, Emeline H., jt. ed. see Brown, Frank E.

Richardson Engineering Services, Inc. Staff. General Construction Estimating Standards: 1994, 3 vols., Set. 34th ed. (Illus.). 2438p. 1994. 227.00 (1-881386-09-0) Richardson Eng.
— General Construction Estimating Standards: 1994 - Masonry Metals Carpentry Doors Finishes Windows Specialties, Vol. 2. 34th ed. (Illus.). 754p. 1994. write for info. (1-881386-11-2) Richardson Eng.
— General Construction Estimating Standards: 1994 - Mechancial Electrical, Vol. 3. 34th ed. (Illus.). 762p. 1994. write for info. (1-881386-12-0) Richardson Eng.
— General Contruction Estimating Standards: 1994 - Sitework Piling Concrete, Vol. 1. 34th ed. (Illus.). 922p. 1994. write for info. (1-881386-10-4) Richardson Eng.
— Process Plant Construction Equipment Standards, 1994: Sitework Piling Concrete, Vol. 1. 34th ed. (Illus.). 950p. 1994. write for info. (1-881386-14-7) Richardson Eng.
— Process Plant Construction Estimating Standards: 1994 - Masonry, Metals, Carpentry, Doors, Finishes, Windows, Specialties, Vol. 2. 34th ed. (Illus.). 782p. 1994. write for info. (1-881386-15-5) Richardson Eng.
— Process Plant Construction Estimating Standards, 1994, 4 vols., Set. 33rd ed. (Illus.). 4048p. 1994. 457.00 (1-881386-13-9) Richardson Eng.
— Process Plant Construction Estimating Standards, 1994: Mechanical & Electrical, Vol. 3. 34th ed. (Illus.). 1026p. 1994. write for info. (1-881386-16-3) Richardson Eng.
— Process Plant Construction Estimating Standards, 1994: Process Equipment, Vol. 4. 34th ed. (Illus.). 1290p. 1994. write for info. (1-881386-17-1) Richardson Eng.

Richardson, Eric. Profitable Home Ownership: Building Wealth Through Home Ownership. Coleman, Margaret, ed. & illus. by. (Decisions/Decisions Ser.: No. 3). 256p. (Orig.). 1997. pap. 12.95 (0-9659992-0-3) Getting Ahead.
— Programming Web Server Applications. LC 96-70101. 480p. 1996. per. 40.00 (0-7615-0780-9) Prima Pub.

***Richardson, Eric.** Sams Teach Yourself E-Commerce Programming with ASP in 21 Days. (Teach Yourself... in 21 Days Ser.). (Illus.). 750p. 2000. pap. 39.99 (0-672-31898-9, Waite Grp Pr) Sams.

Richardson, Ethel. Howard - "The Lion & the Rose", the Great Howard Story: Norfolk Line, 957-1646; Suffolk Line, 1603-1917, 2 vols. in 1. (Illus.). 615p. 1994. reprint ed. 85.00 (0-8328-6565-6) Higginson Bk Co.

Richardson, Eugene S. Pennsylvanian Invertebrates of the Mazon Creek Area, Illinois. LC 56-969. (Chicago Natural History Museum, Publication 785, Fieldiana, Geology: Vol. 12, No. 14). 80p. reprint ed. pap. 30.00 (0-608-03775-3, 206461700009) Bks Demand.

Richardson, Eve, ed. see Rubin, David S. & Kiberd, James B.

***Richardson, Evelyn.** My Lady Nightingale. 224p. 1999. mass mkt. 4.99 (0-451-19858-1, Sig) NAL.

Richardson, Evelyn M. My Other Islands. large type ed. 1991. 27.99 (0-7089-2542-1) Ulverscroft.

Richardson, F. Breeding Cycles of Hawaiian Sea Birds. (BMB Ser.: No. 218). 1972. reprint ed. pap. 25.00 (0-527-02326-4) Periodicals Srv.

Richardson, F. & Macneill, Seumas. Piobaireachd & Its Interpretation. 144p. 1996. pap. 45.00 (0-85976-440-0, Pub. by J Donald) St Mut.

Richardson, F. E., ed. Sir Eglamour of Artois. (EETS Original Ser.: Vol. 256). 1965. 30.00 (0-19-722256-0, Pub. by EETS) Boydell & Brewer.

Richardson, F. L. & Walker, Charles E. Human Relations in an Expanding Company: Manufacturing Departments, Endicott Plant of the International Business Machines Corporation. Stein, Leon, ed. (Illus.). 1977. reprint ed. lib. bdg. 19.95 (0-405-10196-1, 77-70528) Ayer.

Richardson, Florence. A Study of Sensory Control in the Rat. (Psychology Monographs General & Applied: Vol. 12). 1974. reprint ed. pap. 55.00 (0-8115-1411-0) Periodicals Srv.

Richardson, Francis, ed. see McGarvey, Tracy.

Richardson, Frank C. Kleist in France. LC 62-64205. (North Carolina. University. Studies in the Germanic Languages & Literatures: No. 35). reprint ed. 27.00 (0-404-50935-5) AMS Pr.

***Richardson, Frank C., et al.** Re-Envisioning Psychology: Ethics & Values in Modern Practice. LC 98-40146. 1999. pap. 39.95 (0-7879-4384-3) Jossey-Bass.

Richardson, Frederick. Great Children's Stories: Classic Volland Edition. LC 72-83891. 160p. (J). (ps-3). 1938. 12.95 (1-56288-040-3) Checkerboard.
— Mother Goose. LC 72-161577. 160p. (J). (ps-4). 1915. 12.95 (1-56288-254-6) Checkerboard.
— Mother Goose: The Original Volland Edition. 128p. (J). (gr. k up). 1988. 9.99 (0-517-43619-1) Random Hse Value.

Richardson, G. B. The Economics of Imperfect Knowledge: Collected Papers of G. B. Richardson. LC 98-21067. (Economists of the Twentieth Century Ser.). 224p. 1998. 80.00 (1-85898-849-7) E Elgar.
— Information & Investment: A Study in the Working of the Competitive Economy. 2nd ed. (Illus.). 292p. 1991. text 55.00 (0-19-828728-3) OUP.
— Information & Investment: A Study in the Working of the Competitive Economy. 2nd ed. (Illus.). 292p. 1997. reprint ed. pap. text 29.95 (0-19-829243-0) OUP.

Richardson, G. J., et al. Worked Examples in Metalworking. 209p. 1985. pap. text 28.00 (0-904357-77-5, Pub. by Inst Materials) Ashgate Pub Co.

Richardson, Gail. Saving Water from the Ground Up: A Pilot Study of Irrigation Scheduling on Four California Fields. LC 85-60576. 69p. reprint ed. pap. 30.00 (0-7837-0335-X, 204065400017) Bks Demand.
— A Welcome for Every Child: How France Protects Maternal & Child Health - A New Frame of Reference for the United States. LC 94-74638. 62p. (Orig.). 1994. pap. text 10.00 (1-57285-011-6) Nat Ctr Educ.

Richardson, Gale, ed. see Graves, Lawrence L., et al.

Richardson, Gale, jt. ed. see Hanna, Paul.

Richardson, Gale, ed. see Newlin, Deborah L.

Richardson, Gale, ed. see Sullivan, Jerry M.

Richardson, Gale T. Anderson Island Poetry. 14p. 1989. 5.00 (0-9614337-3-6) Poetry Unltd.
— Serenity, Courage & Wisdom. 2p. (J). (ps). 1989. 3.50 (0-9614337-2-8) Poetry Unltd.
— The Wall. 9p. (Orig.). 1989. pap. write for info. (0-9614337-1-X) Poetry Unltd.
— The Wings. (YA). (gr. 9-12). 1989. write for info. (0-9614337-4-4) Poetry Unltd.

Richardson, Gary A., jt. auth. see Watt, Stephen.

Richardson, Gary H., ed. Standard Methods for the Examination of Dairy Products. 16th ed. 450p. 1992. 55.00 (0-87553-208-X); pap. 45.00 (0-87553-210-1) Am Pub Health.

Richardson, Gary L., et al. A Primer of Structured Program Design. 1980. pap. 15.00 (0-89433-110-8) Petrocelli.

Richardson, George P. Feedback Thought in Social Science & Systems Theory. LC 90-22746. (Illus.). 380p. (C). 1991. text 46.95 (0-8122-3053-1) U of Pa Pr.

***Richardson, George P.** Feedback Thought in Social Science & Systems Theory. LC 90-22746. (System Dynamics Ser.). (Illus.). 374p. 1999. reprint ed. pap. text 30.00 (1-883823-46-3, XFDBKP) Pegasus Comm.

Richardson, George P., ed. Modelling for Management: Simulation in Support of Systems Thinking, 2 vols., Set. (International Library of Management Ser.). (Illus.). 900p. 1995. text 389.95 (1-85521-697-3, Pub. by Dartmth Pub) Ashgate Pub Co.
— Modelling for Management Vols. I & II: Simulation in Support of Systems Thinking, 2 vols. (International Library of Management). (Illus.). 976p. 1997. pap. 89.95 (1-85521-888-7, Pub. by Ashgate Pub) Ashgate Pub Co.

Richardson, George P. & Pugh, Alexander L., III. Introduction to System Dynamics Modeling. LC 81-12371. (Illus.). 397p. 1981. pap. text 35.00 (1-883823-43-9, XINTRO) Pegasus Comm.

Richardson, Gerld, jt. auth. see Swihart, Juson.

Richardson, Gillian. Saskatchewan. LC 94-44842. (Hello Canada Ser.). (Illus.). 76p. (J). 1995. lib. bdg. 14.21 (0-8225-2760-X) Lerner Pub.

Richardson, Gladwell. Navajo Trader. Rulon, Philip R., ed. LC 86-11443. (Illus.). 235p. reprint ed. pap. 72.90 (0-608-08595-2, 206911800003) Bks Demand.

Richardson, Glenn & Felts, Michael. Health Enhancement Handbook. 310p. (Orig.). (C). 1990. pap. text 19.95 (0-89641-196-6) American Pr.

Richardson, Glenn, jt. auth. see Bruess, Clint E.

Richardson, Graham T. Illustrations: Everybody's Complete & Practical Guide. LC 85-735. 337p. 1985. 79.50 (0-89603-070-9); pap. 49.50 (0-89603-096-2) Humana.

Richardson, Graham T., jt. auth. see Camp, Mark J.

Richardson, Gregory, et al. Design, Operation, & Closure of Municipal Solid Waste Landfills: Seminar Publication. (Illus.). 86p. (Orig.). (C). 1994. pap. text 40.00 (0-7881-1419-0) DIANE Pub.

***Richardson, Gwendolyn, ed.** The Heritage of Monroe County, Alabama. (Heritage of Alabama Ser.: Vol. 50). 320p. 2001. 50.00 (1-891647-60-1) Herit Pub Consult.

Richardson, H. Rotuli Parliamentorum. (Camden Third Ser.). 63.00 (0-86193-051-7) David Brown.

Richardson, H. Edward. Cassius Marcellus Clay: Firebrand of Freedom. (Illus.). 192p. 1996. pap. 15.00 (0-8131-0861-6) U Pr of Ky.

Richardson, H. Edward, jt. auth. see Stuart, Jesse.

Richardson, H. L. The Shadows of Crazy Mountain. (Sam Dodd Western Mystery Ser.: No. 2). 320p. 1996. pap. 10.99 (0-8499-3856-2) Word Pub.
— Split Ticket. 256p. 1996. pap. 12.99 (0-8499-3933-X) Word Pub.

Richardson, Hamilton P. Journal of the Federal Convention of 1787 Analyzed: The Acts & Proceedings Thereof Compared; & Their Precedents Cited: In Evidence of the Making of the Constitution for Interpretation or Construction in the Alternative, According to Either the Federal Plan or the National Plan: That by the Latter Congress Have General Power to Provide for the Common Defense & General Welfare of the United States; Direct Taxes Are Taxes Direct to the Several State. 244p. 1985. reprint ed. 38.00 (0-8377-1042-1, Rothman) W S Hein.

Richardson, Harry V. Walk Together Children: The Story of the Birth & Growth of the Interdenominational Theological Center. 123p. (C). 1981. pap. 8.95 (0-614-08305-2) Jrnl Interdenom.

Richardson, Harry W., et al, eds. Analytical Urban Economics. LC 96-32413. (Modern Classics in Regional Science Ser.: No. 3). 720p. 1996. 280.00 (1-85898-110-7) E Elgar.

Richardson-Hawkins, Mary E. AJ's World. (J). 1995. 7.95 (0-533-11093-9) Vantage.

Richardson, Hazel. Water. LC 97-41598. (Against the Elements Ser.). (Illus.). 32p. (YA). (gr. 5 up). 1998. 22.40 (0-7613-0801-6, Copper Beech Bks) Millbrook Pr.

Richardson, Heather C. The Greatest Nation of the Earth: Republican Economic Policies During the Civil War. LC 96-46707. (Harvard Historical Studies). 336p. 1997. 35.00 (0-674-36213-6) HUP.

Richardson, Helen W., ed. see Murphy, Margaret D.

Richardson, Henry B. Outline of French Grammar with Vocabularies. rev. ed. (FRE.). 1950. text 15.50 (0-89197-327-3) Irvington.

Richardson, Henry G. The English Jewry under Angevin Kings. LC 83-18539. 313p. 1983. reprint ed. lib. bdg. 65.00 (0-313-24247-X, RIEJ, Greenwood Pr) Greenwood.

Richardson, Henry Handel. The Getting of Wisdom. LC 92-45021. (Illus.). 296p. 1993. 25.00 (1-56279-042-0) Mercury Hse Inc.

Richardson, Henry Handel. Maurice Guest. LC 82-12844. (Virago Modern Classic). 562 P. :p. 1983. reprint ed. 9.95 (0-385-27787-3) Delacorte.

***Richardson, Henry Handel, et al.** Maurice Guest LC 98-215770. (Academy Editions of Australian Literature Ser.). lxxi, 799p. 1998. write for info. (0-7022-3028-6, Pub. by Univ Queensland Pr) Intl Spec Bk.

Richardson, Henry S. Practical Reasoning about Final Ends. (Cambridge Studies in Philosophy). 342p. (C). 1994. text 69.95 (0-521-46472-2) Cambridge U Pr.
— Practical Reasoning about Final Ends. (Cambridge Studies in Philosophy). 340p. 1997. pap. text 21.95 (0-521-57442-0) Cambridge U Pr.

Richardson, Herbert W. Nun, Witch, Playmate: The Americanization of Sex. 2nd ed. xii, 147p. 1977. reprint ed. lib. bdg. 69.95 (0-88946-950-4) E Mellen.
— Symbols of the Spiritual Quest. 150p. 1991. pap. 24.95 (0-7734-9765-X) E Mellen.
— Toward an American Theology. 182p. 1967. lib. bdg. 79.95 (0-88946-028-0) E Mellen.
— What Do Religion, Politics & Science Contribute to the Good Society? Essays in Calvinist Social Theory. 239p. 1991. 89.95 (0-7734-9218-6) E Mellen.

Richardson, Herbert W., ed. Constitutional Issues in the Case of Rev. Moon: Amicus Briefs Presented to the United States Supreme Court. (Studies in Religion & Society: Vol. 10). 450p. 1989. 109.95 (0-88946-873-7) E Mellen.
— New Religions & Mental Health: Understanding the Issues. (Symposium Ser.: Vol. 5). 177p. (Orig.). (C). 1988. lib. bdg. 89.95 (0-88946-910-5) E Mellen.
— New Studies in Richard Wagner's "The Ring of the Nibelung" LC 91-38295. (Studies in the History & Interpretation of Music: Vol. 20). 200p. 1992. lib. bdg. 79.95 (0-88946-445-6) E Mellen.
— On the Problem of Surrogate Parenthood: Analyzing the Baby in Case. LC 87-24752. (Symposium Ser.: Vol. 25). 144p. 1987. lib. bdg. 69.95 (0-88946-717-X) E Mellen.

Richardson, Herbert W., et al, eds. Women & Religion: The Original Sourcebook of Women in Christian Thought. expanded rev. ed. LC 96-10959. 400p. 1997. pap. 22.00 (0-06-061409-9, Pub. by Harper SF) HarpC.

Richardson, Herbert W., et al. Truth in Advertising. LC 72-7241. 45p. 1984. reprint ed. 59.95 (0-88946-912-1) E Mellen.

Richardson, Herbert W., jt. auth. see Bryant, M. Darrol.

Richardson, Herbert W., ed. see Anselm, Saint of Canterbury.

Richardson, Herbert W., tr. see Anselm, Saint of Canterbury.

Richardson, Herbert W., tr. see Hopkins, Jasper, ed.

Richardson, Hester D. Side-Lights on Maryland History, Vols. 1 & 11. (Illus.). xxxiv, 960p. 1997. reprint ed. pap. 59.00 (0-7884-0693-0, R318) Heritage Bk.
— Side-Lights on Maryland History: With Sketches of Early Maryland Families, 2 vols., Set. (Illus.). 990p. 1995. 62.50 (0-8063-0296-8) Genealog Pub.

Richardson, Howard & Berney, William. Dark of the Moon. LC 56-9611. 82p. (Orig.). 1987. pap. 99.90 (0-87830-517-3, Thtre Arts Bks) Routledge.

Richardson, Howard D., jt. auth. see Masters, Lowell F.

Richardson, Hugh. High Peaks, Pure Earth: Collected Writings on Tibetan History & Culture. Aris, Michael, ed. LC 98-186837. (Illus.). 864p. 1998. pap. 40.00 (0-906026-46-6) Weatherhill.

Richardson, Hugh E. Ceremonies of the Lhasa Year. Aris, Michael, ed. (Illus.). 136p. (Orig.). 1994. pap. 24.95 (0-906026-29-6, Pub. by Serindia) Weatherhill.

Richardson, I. M. The Adventures of Eros & Psyche. LC 82-16057. (Illus.). 32p. (J). (gr. 4-8). 1983. pap. 3.95 (0-89375-862-0) Troll Communs.
— The Adventures of Hercules. LC 82-16557. (Illus.). 32p. (J). (gr. 4-8). 1997. pap. 3.95 (0-89375-866-3) Troll Communs.
— Charles Dickens' a Christmas Carol. (J). 1988. 7.70 (0-606-03559-1, Pub. by Turtleback) Demco.
— Demeter & Persephone: The Seasons of Time. LC 82-16023. (Illus.). 32p. (J). (gr. 4-8). 1983. lib. bdg. 18.60 (0-89375-863-9) Troll Communs.
— Demeter & Persephone: The Seasons of Time. LC 82-16023. (Illus.). 32p. (J). (gr. 4-8). 1997. pap. 3.95 (0-89375-864-7) Troll Communs.
— Prometheus & the Story of Fire. LC 82-15979. (Illus.). 32p. (J). (gr. 4-8). 1983. lib. bdg. 18.60 (0-89375-859-0) Troll Communs.
— Reluctant Dragon. (J). 1988. 7.70 (0-606-03643-1, Pub. by Turtleback) Demco.
— Story of the Christmas Rose. LC 87-13817. (Illus.). 32p. (J). (gr. k-4). 1988. lib. bdg. 15.85 (0-8167-1069-4) Troll Communs.
— Story of the Christmas Rose. LC 87-13817. (Illus.). 32p. (J). (gr. k-4). 1996. pap. 3.95 (0-8167-1070-8) Troll Communs.

Richardson, I. M., ed. see Dickens, Charles.

Richardson, I. M., ed. see Grimm, Jacob W. & Grimm, Wilhelm K.

Richardson, I. W. & Neergaard, Ejler B. Physics for Biology & Medicine. LC 76-180711. (Illus.). 257p. reprint ed. pap. 79.70 (0-608-18404-7, 203053800069) Bks Demand.

Richardson, Iain E., jt. auth. see Riley, Martyn J.

Richardson, Ilona E. Jesus, the Story. ix, 202p. 1998. pap. 14.95 (0-9669845-0-1) I E Richardson.

Richardson, Irv, jt. auth. see Grant, Jim.

Richardson, Irvine. Linguistic Survey of the Northern Bantu Borderland, Vol. 2. LC 57-2700. 98p. reprint ed. pap. 30.40 (0-8357-6967-4, 203902700009) Bks Demand.

Richardson, J. Roman Provincial Administration. (Inside the Ancient World Ser.). 88p. 1984. reprint ed. 16.95 (0-86292-128-7, Pub. by Brist Class Pr) Focus Pub-R Pullins.

Richardson, J. & Moon, Jeremy. Unemployment in the U. K. Politics & Policies. 240p. 1985. text 83.95 (0-566-00892-0, Pub. by Avebry) Ashgate Pub Co.

Richardson, J. & Reader, G. T. Electrical Circuit Analysis. 1990. text 82.95 (0-470-21615-8) P-H.

Richardson, J., jt. auth. see Coulson, J.

Richardson, J., jt. auth. see Kroeber, A. L.

Richardson, J., jt. ed. see Corlett, E. N.

An Asterisk (*) at the beginning of an entry indicates that the title is appearing for the first time.

Richardson, J. A. Falling Towers: The Trojan Imagination in The Waste Land, The Dunciad, & Speke Parott. LC 90-50984. 192p. 1992. 36.50 (*0-87413-419-6*) U Delaware Pr.

*Richardson, J. David & Lewis, Howard, III. Why Globalization Matters Most! 50p. 2000. pap. 12.95 (*0-88132-298-9*) Inst Intl Eco.

Richardson, J. David & Rindal, Karin. Why Exports Really Matter! What We Know. 1995. pap. 40.00 (*0-88132-221-0*) Inst Intl Eco.

This study appears in two parts. Part one, Why Exports Really Matter!, assesses the performance of US firms, plants & workers engaged in export activity, compared with their non exporting counterparts. It summarizes new statistical evidence, supported by case studies, on how exports have more value to more people than is commonly appreciated. Published in cooperation with the Manufacturing Institute, it relies on data from 1987 through 1993. Part two, Why Exports Matter More!, documents the superior performance of export plants & firms, as well as their workers in all skill categories, relying on data from 1992 through 1995. Among new findings are significantly stronger & more stable employment growth for exporters. The authors assess controversial questions such as whether export commitments cause superior performance or whether the two factors are merely correlated, whether imports & outsourcing are offset to the findings about exports & whether the role of small firms in exports has grown or declined. *Publisher Paid Annotation.*

Richardson, J. David, jt. auth. see Graham, Edward M.

Richardson, J. David, jt. auth. see Grossman, Gene M.

Richardson, J. David, jt. ed. see Arndt, Sven W.

Richardson, J. David, jt. ed. see Hooper, Peter.

Richardson, J. E. Great Known (1928) 382p. 1999. reprint ed. pap. 24.95 (*0-7661-0802-3*) Kessinger Pub.

— Self-Unfoldment: The Practical Application of Moral Principles to the Living of a Life (1929) 250p. 1999. reprint ed. pap. 17.95 (*0-7661-0754-X*) Kessinger Pub.

Richardson, J. F. A Selection of European Folk Dances, 5 vols., 1. 1965. pap. text 4.20 (*0-08-010833-4*) Elsevier.

— A Selection of European Folk Dances, 5 vols., 2. 1966. pap. text 4.20 (*0-08-010842-3*) Elsevier.

— A Selection of European Folk Dances, 5 vols., 3. 1966. pap. text 4.20 (*0-08-011926-3*) Elsevier.

— A Selection of European Folk Dances, 5 vols., 4. 1971. pap. text 4.20 (*0-08-016190-1*) Elsevier.

— A Selection of European Folk Dances, 5 vols., Vol. 5. 1978. pap. text 4.20 (*0-08-021589-0*, Pergamon Pr) Elsevier.

Richardson, J. F., jt. auth. see Chhabra, Raj.

Richardson, J. F., jt. auth. see Coulson, J. M.

Richardson, J. F., ed. see Coulson, J. M.

Richardson, J. G. Precast Concrete Production. 1977. pap. 50.00 (*0-7210-0912-3*, Pub. by C & CA) Scholium Intl.

Richardson, J. J., jt. auth. see Dudley, G. F.

Richardson, J. J., jt. auth. see Jordan, Grant.

Richardson, J. J., jt. auth. see Maloney, W. A.

Richardson, J. Jeffrey, ed. Artificial Intelligence in Maintenance. LC 85-15394. (Illus.). 485p. 1986. 48.00 (*0-8155-1042-X*) Noyes.

Richardson, J. M. Astrological Symbolism in Spenser's "The Shepheardes Calender" The Cultural Background of a Literary Text. LC 88-8436. (Studies in Renaissance Literature: Vol. 1). (Illus.). 1989. 119.95 (*0-88946-144-9*) E Mellen.

Richardson, J. S. The Romans in Spain. (History of Spain Ser.). (Illus.). 360p. (C). 1996. 82.95 (*0-631-17706-X*) Blackwell Pubs.

— The Romans in Spain. (History of Spain Ser.). 352p. 1998. reprint ed. pap. 26.95 (*0-631-20931-X*) Blackwell Pubs.

Richardson, J. T. Principles of Catalyst Development. (Fundamental & Applied Catalysis Ser.). (Illus.). 304p. (C). 1989. text 75.00 (*0-306-43162-9*, Kluwer Plenum) Kluwer Academic.

Richardson, J. T., ed. Cognition & the Menstrual Cycle. (Contributions to Psychology & Medicine Ser.). (Illus.). xi, 216p. 1991. 96.95 (*0-387-97612-4*) Spr-Verlag.

Richardson, J. W. Boxtime Charterparty: An Industry Report. 92p. 1990. pap. 240.00 (*1-85044-285-1*) LLP.

Richardson, Jabez. Monitor of Freemasonry. pap. 13.00 (*0-911164-25-1*) Powner.

*Richardson, Jabez. Richardson's Moniter of Freemasonry (1860) 194p. 1999. reprint ed. pap. 17.95 (*0-7661-0747-7*) Kessinger Pub.

Richardson, Jack. Gallows Humor. 1976. pap. 5.25 (*0-8222-0431-2*) Dramatists Play.

— Xmas in Las Vegas. 1966. pap. 5.25 (*0-8222-1282-X*) Dramatists Play.

Richardson, Jacques G., ed. Integrated Technology Transfer. LC 79-88170. 1979. 22.75 (*0-912338-19-9*); fiche 9.50 (*0-912338-20-2*) Lomond.

— Managing the Ocean: Resources, Research, Law. LC 88-50823. 407p. 1985. 28.95 (*0-912338-49-0*); fiche 19.50 (*0-912338-50-4*) Lomond.

— Models of Reality: Shaping Thought & Action. LC 83-80819. 328p. 1984. 32.95 (*0-912338-35-0*); fiche 15.00 (*0-912338-36-9*) Lomond.

— Windows on Creativity & Invention. LC 86-83428. 344p. 1988. 34.75 (*0-912338-57-1*); fiche 15.75 (*0-912338-58-X*) Lomond.

Richardson, James. As If: Poems. LC 91-43330. (National Poetry Ser.). 96p. (Orig.). 1992. pap. 9.95 (*0-89255-171-2*) Persea Bks.

— The God Who Shows Up. LC 81-47889. 55p. (Orig.). 1981. pap. 4.00 (*0-914520-16-4*) Insight Pr.

*Richardson, James. How Things Are. LC 99-72505. (Poetry Ser.). 88p. 2000. pap. 12.95 (*0-88748-327-5*, Pub. by Carnegie-Mellon) CUP Services.

Richardson, James. Misbegotten. LC 98-87020. 192p. 2000. pap. 11.95 (*1-56315-169-3*) SterlingHse.

— Narrative of a Mission to Central Africa, 1850-1851, 2 vols., Set. (Illus.). 704p. 1970. reprint ed. 95.00 (*0-7146-1848-9*, BHA-01848, Pub. by F Cass Pubs) Intl Spec Bk.

Richardson, James, III. People of the Andes. LC 94-22754. (Exploring the Ancient World Ser.). (Illus.). 176p. 1995. text 24.95 (*0-89599-041-5*) Smithsonian.

Richardson, James. Science Dictionary of Animals. LC 91-18826. (Science Dictionary Ser.). (Illus.). 48p. (YA). (gr. 3-7). 1997. pap. 3.95 (*0-8167-2440-7*) Troll Communs.

— Science Dictionary of Dinosaurs. LC 91-4110. (Science Dictionary Ser.). (Illus.). 48p. (YA). (gr. 3-7). 1997. pap. 3.95 (*0-8167-2441-5*) Troll Communs.

— Science Dictionary of the Human Body. LC 91-19162. (Science Dictionary Ser.). (Illus.). 48p. (YA). (gr. 3-7). 1992. pap. 3.95 (*0-8167-2442-3*) Troll Communs.

— Travels in the Great Desert of Sahara, 1845-1846, 2 vols. (Illus.). 1970. reprint ed. 125.00 (*0-7146-1850-0*, BHA-01850, Pub. by F Cass Pubs) Intl Spec Bk.

— Travels in the Great Sahara, Vol. 1. (C). 1988. 135.00 (*1-85077-192-8*, Pub. by Darf Pubs Ltd) St Mut.

— Travels in the Great Sahara, Vol. 2. (C). 1988. 135.00 (*1-85077-193-6*, Pub. by Darf Pubs Ltd) St Mut.

— Vanishing Lives: Style & Self in Tennyson, D. G. Rossetti, Swinburne, & Yeats. LC 87-25269. (Virginia Victorian Studies). 251p. 1988. reprint ed. pap. 77.90 (*0-608-01438-9*, 206220000002) Bks Demand.

— Wetlands Soils: Genesis, Hydrology, Landscapes, & Classification. 440p. 2000. ring bd. 89.95 (*1-56670-484-7*) Lewis Pubs.

— Wetlands Soils: Hydric Soils, 001. 2000. lib. bdg. 69.95 (*0-8493-4142-6*) CRC Pr.

— Willie Brown: A Biography. 282p. 1997. pap. text 17.95 (*0-520-21315-7*, Pub. by U CA Pr) Cal Prin Full Svc.

— Willie Brown: Style, Power, & a Passion for Politics. LC 96-16800. (Illus.). 282p. (C). 1996. 40.00 (*0-520-20456-5*, Pub. by U CA Pr) Cal Prin Full Svc.

Richardson, James, ed. Debt Recovery in Europe. 176p. 1993. pap. 34.00 (*1-85431-242-1*, Pub. by Blackstone Pr) Gaunt.

Richardson, James, et al. Quarterly Review of Literature Poetry Book Series Vol. XXXVII-XXXVIII. 287p. 1999. 20.00 (*1-888545-44-5*) Quarterly Rev.

Richardson, James, jt. auth. see Tonfoni, Graziella.

Richardson, James A., jt. ed. see Hildreth, W. Bartley.

Richardson, James B. The Jim Richardson Boat Book. 1985. (Illus.). pap. 12.95 (*0-9609772-2-8*) Ocean Wrld MD.

Richardson, James B., III, jt. ed. see Jacobs, Martina M.

Richardson, James E. Mastering Dollars & Sense on the Macintosh. 650p. (C). 1991. 27.66 (*0-673-38557-4*, Scott Frsmn) Addson-Wesley Educ.

Richardson, James E., jt. auth. see Tonfoni, Graziella.

Richardson, James H. Optical Microscopy for the Materials Science. LC 79-179481. (Monographs & Textbooks in Material Science: Vol. 3). 702p. reprint ed. pap. 200.00 (*0-608-30280-5*, 205501700007) Bks Demand.

*Richardson, James L. Contending Liberalisms in World Politics: Ideology, Power & World Order. 235p. (C). 2001. write for info. (*1-55587-915-2*) L Rienner.

Richardson, James L. Germany & the Atlantic Alliance: The Interaction of Strategy & Politics. LC 66-13184. 414p. reprint ed. pap. 128.40 (*0-608-30779-3*, 201654500004) Bks Demand.

Richardson, James M. Reflections on Life & Love. 112p. (Orig.). 1995. pap. 10.00 (*0-9647901-0-6*) Harmattan Pr.

Richardson, James T., ed. Money & Power in the New Religions. (Studies in Religion & Society: Vol. 22). 400p. 1990. 109.95 (*0-88946-852-4*) E Mellen.

Richardson, James T., et al, eds. The Satanism Scare. (Social Institutions & Social Change Ser.). 326p. 1991. pap. text 30.95 (*0-202-30379-9*); lib. bdg. 51.95 (*0-202-30378-0*) Aldine de Gruyter.

Richardson, James T., et al. Organized Miracles: A Study of a Contemporary, Youth, Communal, Fundamentalist Organization. LC 78-55937. 368p. 1979. 34.95 (*0-87855-284-7*) Transaction Pubs.

Richardson, James T., jt. ed. see Bromley, David G.

Richardson, James W., Jr., ed. Application & Performance of Structural Materials & Exterior Facades. LC 86-25910. 140p. 1986. pap. 5.00 (*0-87262-566-4*) Am Soc Civil Eng.

Richardson, Jan. Night Visions: Searching the Shadows of Advent & Christmas. LC 97-45177. 144p. (Orig.). 1998. 18.95 (*0-8298-1255-5*) Pilgrim OH.

Richardson, Jan L. Sacred Journeys: A Woman's Book of Daily Prayer. 448p. 1995. pap. 15.00 (*0-8358-0709-6*) Upper Room Bks.

Richardson, Jane. Law & Status among the Kiowa Indians. LC 84-45509. (American Ethnological Society Monographs: No. 1). 1988. reprint ed. 23.50 (*0-404-62901-6*) AMS Pr.

— Virgin Princess: An Historic Novel of Mewar (Udaipur, India) - The World's Oldest Dynasty. LC 90-90395. 434p. (Orig.). 1991. pap. 15.95 (*1-879403-09-9*) Thistle Pub.

Richardson, Jane, jt. auth. see Richardson, David.

Richardson, Jane M., ed. see Merton, Thomas.

Richardson, Janice K. & Iglarsh, Z. Annette. Clinical Orthopaedic Physical Therapy. LC 93-7209. (Illus.). 816p. 1993. text 75.00 (*0-7216-3257-2*, W B Saunders Co) Harcrt Hlth Sci Grp.

Richardson, Javana M. A Tribute to John Denver: Poems, Prayers & Promises. LC 98-90386. (Illus.). 100p. 1998. 16.95 (*1-889120-53-7*) StarsEnd Creations.

Richardson, Javana M. & Richardson, David J. Seasoned Greetings: Holiday Fare from the Distinctive Inns of Colorado. LC 98-66408. (Illus.). 325p. 1998. pap. 19.95 (*1-889120-13-8*) StarsEnd Creations.

Richardson, Javana M., jt. auth. see Richardson, David J.

Richardson, Javana M., ed. see Richardson, David J.

Richardson, Jean. The Bear Who Went to the Ballet. LC 95-14797. (Illus.). 32p. (J). (gr. k-3). 1995. 14.95 (*0-7894-0318-8*, 5-70668) DK Pub Inc.

— The Courage Seed. LC 93-20182. (Illus.). 76p. (J). (gr. 4-5). 1993. 14.95 (*0-89015-902-5*) Sunbelt Media.

— The Courage Seed. (ENG & NAV., Illus.). 76p. (J). 1997. pap. 8.95 (*1-57168-120-5*, Eakin Pr) Sunbelt Media.

— Dino, the Ding Bat Cat. LC 92-17736. (Illus.). 34p. (J). (gr. 3-4). 1992. 13.95 (*0-89015-869-X*) Sunbelt Media.

— Grumpy Granny Grumble's Book of Manners. LC 99-17525. 1999. 14.95 (*1-57168-306-2*, Eakin Pr) Sunbelt Media.

— The Return of the Dingbat Cat. (Illus.). 40p. (J). 1997. pap. 5.95 (*1-57168-020-9*, Eakin Pr) Sunbelt Media.

— Richardson: Plains Myths. 1988. pap. text 35.00 (*0-936598-03-4*) J Szoke Edns.

— Tag-Along Timothy Tours Alaska. Eakin, Edwin M., ed. (Illus.). 48p. (J). (gr. 2-3). 1989. 13.95 (*0-89015-706-5*) Sunbelt Media.

— Tag-Along Timothy Tours Alaska. (Illus.). 40p. (J). 1997. pap. 6.95 (*0-89015-997-1*, Eakin Pr) Sunbelt Media.

— Tag-Along Timothy Tours Texas. (Illus.). 40p. (J). 1997. pap. 7.95 (*1-57168-085-3*, Eakin Pr) Sunbelt Media.

— Thomas's Sitter. LC 90-13799. (Illus.). 32p. (J). (ps-1). 1991. lib. bdg. 13.95 (*0-02-776146-0*, Four Winds Pr) S&S Childrens.

— When Grandpa Had Fangs. LC 97-51132. (Illus.). 32p. (J). (gr. 2-3). 1997. 13.95 (*1-57168-175-2*, Eakin Pr) Sunbelt Media.

Richardson, Jeanne S. Here Lies Sioux Falls. LC 92-93393. (Illus.). 212p. 1992. pap. 12.95 (*0-9632542-1-9*) J S Richardson.

— Split Rock Influence. LC 96-92827. (Illus.). 140p. (Orig.). 1996. pap. 12.95 (*0-9632542-2-7*) J S Richardson.

Richardson, Jed J. The Ten Worst Frauds Against America's Seniors. LC 98-86013. 144p. 1998. pap. 6.95 (*0-9648635-2-9*) Srs Coalition.

Richardson, Jennifer J. Diary of Abuse, Diary of Healing. 128p. 1996. pap. 11.95 (*0-9615995-8-8*) Recovery.

Richardson, Jeremy J., ed. European Union: Power & Policy Making. LC 97-150456. 312p. (C). 1996. pap. 24.99 (*0-415-12917-6*) Routledge.

— European Union: Power & Policy Making. LC 97-150456. 312p. (C). 1996. 90.00 (*0-415-12916-8*) Routledge.

— Policy Styles in Western Europe. 224p. (C). 1982. text 49.95 (*0-04-350062-5*) Routledge.

— Pressure Groups. LC 92-42267. (Readings in Politics & Government Ser.). (Illus.). 282p. 1993. pap. text 18.95 (*0-19-878052-4*) OUP.

— Privatisation & Deregulation in Canada & Britain. (Illus.). 260p. 1990. text 72.95 (*1-85521-066-5*, Pub. by Dartmth Pub) Ashgate Pub Co.

Richardson, Jeremy J., et al, eds. Networks for Water Policy: A Comparative Perspective. 240p. 1995. 45.00 (*0-7146-4642-3*, Pub. by F Cass Pubs) Intl Spec Bk.

Richardson, Jeremy J., jt. ed. see Mazey, Sonia.

Richardson, Jerry. The Magic of Rapport. LC 87-63211. 1988. 16.95 (*0-916990-20-6*) META Pubns.

Richardson, Jessica. The Ring & I. McAlister, Jeffrey G. & Udd, Gary, eds. 225p. 1994. 16.95 (*0-9642398-0-9*); pap. 12.95 (*0-9642398-1-7*) Jessica Richardson.

Richardson, Jim. Classic Car Restorer's Handbook: General Restoration Tips & Techniques for Owners & Restorers of Classic Automobiles. LC 94-19094. 166p. (Orig.). 1994. pap. 17.95 (*1-55788-194-4*, HP Books) Berkley Pub.

*Richardson, Jim. Do-It-Yourself Guide to Engine & Chassis Detailing. (Do-it-Yourself Guides Ser.). (Illus.). 128p. 2000. pap. 18.95 (*1-884089-46-1*, Pub. by CarTech) Voyageur Pr.

— LPIC Linux Level I Cheat Sheet: Covers Test 1. (Cheat Sheet Ser.). 350p. 2000. pap. 24.99 (*0-7897-2289-5*) Que.

— Media Blasting. 128p. 2000. pap. 18.95 (*1-884089-48-8*, Pub. by CarTech) Voyageur Pr.

Richardson, Jim. Philippines. LC 90-156552. (World Bibliographical Ser.: Vol. 106). 404p. 1989. lib. bdg. 65.00 (*1-85109-077-0*) ABC-CLIO.

— Sustainable Farm Enterprises. (RRP Ser.). (Illus.). 144p. 1997. pap. text 36.95 (*0-7506-8939-0*, 31044) Buttrwrth-Heinemann.

— Tri-Five Chevy Handbook: Restoration & Upgrade How-Tos for 1955-1957 Chevrolets. LC 97-42424. 368p. 1998. pap. 17.95 (*1-55788-285-1*, HP Books) Berkley Pub.

Richardson, Jim, photos by. University of Colorado-Boulder. (Illus.). 112p. 1990. 39.00 (*0-916509-54-0*) Harmony Hse Pub.

Richardson, Jim, jt. auth. see Leaver, Richard.

Richardson, Jimmy. Doberman. 1991. 11.95 (*1-56465-189-4*) Tetra Pr.

— Doberman Pinschers Today. (Illus.). 160p. 1995. 27.95 (*0-87605-139-5*) Howell Bks.

— A Dog Owner's Guide to Doberman Pinschers. (Illus.). 118p. 10.95 (*3-923880-36-7*, 16044) Tetra Pr.

*Richardson, Jo. Home Sweet Home: Quick & Easy Creative Ideas for Every Room. 1999. pap. text 9.99 (*1-84100-252-6*) Quadrillion Pub.

Richardson, Joan. Relative to Relativity. 1999. pap. 22.00 (*0-670-83955-8*) Viking Penguin.

Richardson, Joan & Anderson, Edwin C., Jr. California Decedent Estate Practice Nos. 1 & 2: June 1995 Update. rev. ed. Tom, Janette, ed. LC 86-70193. 570p. 1995. ring bd. 60.00 (*0-88124-880-0*, ES-35667) Cont Ed Bar-CA.

Richardson, Joan, ed. see Stevens, Wallace.

Richardson, Joanna. Colette. LC 83-147615. xi, 276 p. 1983. write for info. (*0-413-48780-6*) Heinemann.

Richardson, Joe M., jt. auth. see Jones, Maxine D.

Richardson, Johanna, tr. see Verlaine, Paul M.

*Richardson, John. The Annals of London: A Year by Year Record of a Thousand Years of History. (Illus.). 408p. 2000. 37.50 (*0-520-22795-6*) U CA Pr.

Richardson, John. Arctic Searching Expedition: A Journal of a Boat Voyage Through Rupert's Land & the Arctic Sea, in Search of the Discovery Ships under Command of Sir John Franklin, 2 Vols, Set. LC 68-55214. 1851. reprint ed. lib. bdg. 75.00 (*0-8371-3858-2*, RIAS) Greenwood.

— The Birthday. (Can You Find Ser.: No. 2). 26p. (J). 1994. 2.95 (*0-671-89312-2*) Litle Simon.

*Richardson, John. Business Ethics 2000-2001. (Annual Editions Ser.). 240p. (C). 2000. pap. 16.56 (*0-07-236523-4*) McGrw-H Hghr Educ.

Richardson, John. Dictionary of the Persian Arabic: Arabic-English. (ARA, ENG & PER.). 1986. 150.00 (*0-8288-0546-6*, M 6600) Fr & Eur.

— Fauna Boreali-Americana, Pt. I. LC 73-17836. (Natural Sciences in America Ser.). (Illus.). 1974. 29.95 (*0-405-05759-8*) Ayer.

— Fauna Boreali-Americana: Zoology of the Northern Parts of British America, the Fish, Vol. 3. Sterling, Keir B., ed. LC 77-81088. (Biologists & Their World Ser.). (Illus.). 1978. reprint ed. lib. bdg. 34.95 (*0-405-10664-5*) Ayer.

Richardson, John, Jr. Government Information: Education & Research, 1928-1986, 2. LC 86-27086. (Bibliographies & Indexes in Library & Information Science Ser.: No. 2). 203p. 1987. lib. bdg. 55.00 (*0-313-25605-5*, RRV/, Greenwood Pr) Greenwood.

Richardson, John. A Life of Picasso, 1881-1906, Vol. 1. (Illus.). 560p. 1996. pap. 30.00 (*0-679-76421-6*) Random.

— Manet. (Color Library). (Illus.). (C). 1994. reprint ed. pap. 14.95 (*0-7148-2755-X*, Pub. by Phaidon Press) Phaidon Pr.

*Richardson, John. Marketing 2000-2001. 22nd ed. (Annual Editions Ser.). 240p. 1999. pap. 16.56 (*0-07-236400-9*) McGrw-H Hghr Educ.

Richardson, John. Nietzsche's System. 328p. 1996. 42.00 (*0-19-509846-3*) OUP.

— Old Growler's Last Match. (Illus.). 32p. (J). (gr. 1-3). 1997. 18.95 (*0-09-176675-3*, Pub. by Hutchnson) Trafalgar.

— The Polar Regions. LC 74-5869. reprint ed. 39.50 (*0-404-11676-0*) AMS Pr.

— Roman Provincial Administration, 227 BC to AD 117 LC 77-365902. 88p. 1976. write for info. (*0-333-18321-5*) Macmillan.

— Singing Archaeology: Philip Glass's "Akhnaten" LC 98-19454. (Music - Culture Ser.). (Illus.). 310p. 1999. pap. 19.95 (*0-8195-6342-0*, Wesleyan Univ Pr); text 45.00 (*0-8195-6317-X*, Wesleyan Univ Pr) U Pr of New Eng.

— The Sorcerer's Apprentice: Picasso, Provence & Douglas Cooper. LC 99-27200. 336p. 1999. 26.95 (*0-375-40033-8*) Knopf.

— Stories from the English Saints. 128p. 1996. pap. 39.95 (*0-85439-455-9*, Pub. by St Paul Pubns) St Mut.

— Ten Bears Go Marching: A Pop-Up Book. LC 95-81181. (Illus.). 24p. (J). (ps-3). 1996. 13.95 (*0-7868-0266-9*, Pub. by Hyprn Child) Little.

— Wacousta. 1996. pap. text 9.95 (*0-7710-9877-4*) McCland & Stewart.

— The World of the Little People. Date not set. 25.00 (*0-06-019316-6*); pap. 14.00 (*0-06-093131-0*) HarpC.

Richardson, John. Budgie at Bendick's Point. 40p. (J). (ps-1). 1996. pap. 5.99 (*0-689-80849-6*) S&S Bks Yung.

Richardson, John, Jr. & Ginsberg, Ralph B., eds. The Human Dimension of Foreign Policy: An American Perspective. LC 78-62597. (Annals Ser.: No. 442). 1979. 28.00 (*0-87761-234-X*); pap. 18.00 (*0-87761-235-8*) Am Acad Pol Soc Sci.

Richardson, John & Shaw, Alison, eds. The Body in Qualitative Research. (Cardiff Papers in Qualitative Research). 204p. 1998. text 59.95 (*1-84014-500-5*, Pub. by Ashgate Pub) Ashgate Pub Co.

Richardson, John & Swainson, William. Fauna Boreali-Americana: Pt. II, the Birds. Sterling, Keir B., ed. LC 73-17837. (Natural Sciences in America Ser.). (Illus.). 1974. reprint ed. lib. bdg. 54.95 (*0-405-05760-1*) Ayer.

Richardson, John, et al. Fauna Boreali-Americana: Zoology of the Northern Parts of British America, the Fish, Vol. 4. Sterling, Keir B., ed. LC 77-81108. (Biologists & Their World Ser.). 1978. reprint ed. lib. bdg. 35.95 (*0-405-10692-0*) Ayer.

Richardson, John, jt. ed. see Jaques, David.

Richardson, John A. Art: The Way It Is. 4th ed. 384p. (C). 1991. pap. text 57.33 (*0-13-040437-3*) P-H.

— From Pure Visibility to Virtual Reality in an Age of Estrangement. LC 98-10918. (Critical Perspectives on Culture & Society Ser.). 240p. 1998. 65.00 (*0-275-96088-9*, Praeger Pubs) Greenwood.

— Modern Art & Scientific Thought. LC 74-122914. (Illus.). 211p. reprint ed. pap. 65.50 (*0-608-08100-0*, 201489500093) Bks Demand.

Richardson, John E. Business Ethics, '98/'99. 10th ed. (Annual Ser.). (Illus.). 240p. 1998. pap. text 12.25 (*0-697-39131-0*, Dshkn McG-Hill) McGrw-H Hghr Educ.

R

— Marketing, 98-99. 20th ed. (Annual Ser.). (Illus.). 240p. 1998. pap. text 12.25 (*0-697-39180-9*, Dshkn McG-Hill) McGrw-H Hghr Educ.

Richardson, John E., ed. Annual Editions: Business Ethics, 95-96. 7th rev. ed. (Illus.). 256p. (C). 1995. text 12.95 (*1-56134-347-1*, Dshkn McG-Hill) McGrw-H Hghr Educ.

— Annual Editions: Business Ethics, 97-98. 9th ed. 256p. (C). 1997. text. write for info. (*0-697-37216-2*) Brown & Benchmark.

— Business Ethics: 1996-1997. annuals 8th ed. 256p. (C). 1996. text 13.57 (*0-697-31616-5*) Brown & Benchmark.

— Marketing, 1996-1997. annuals 18th ed. 256p. (C). 1995. text. write for info. (*0-697-31545-2*) Brown & Benchmark.

Richardson, John F., et al, eds. Proceedings: Papers from the Parasession on the Interplay of Phonology, Morphology & Syntax. LC 83-71958. 353p. 1983. pap. 8.00 (*0-914203-20-7*) Chicago Ling.

Richardson, John G. Common, Delinquent, & Special: The Institutional Shape of Special Education. LC 99-13736. (Studies in the History of Education: Vol. 9). (Illus.). 230p. 1999. 60.00 (*0-8153-3077-4*) Garland.

Richardson, John G., ed. Handbook of Theory & Research for the Sociology of Education. LC 85-931. (Illus.). 401p. 1986. lib. bdg. 79.50 (*0-313-23529-5*, RHT/, Greenwood Pr) Greenwood.

Richardson, John G. & National Center for State Courts. The Indian Child Welfare Act: A Cultural & Legal Education Program. LC 97-69655. 1997. write for info. (*0-89656-178-X*) Natl Ctr St Courts.

Richardson, John H. Economic Disarmament: A Study of International Cooperation. LC 75-41228. reprint ed. 34.50 (*0-404-14591-4*) AMS Pr.

Richardson, John H. & Barkley, W. Emmett, eds. Biosafety in Microbiological & Biomedical Laboratories. 2nd ed. (Illus.). 139p. (C). 1993. pap. text 35.00 (*1-56806-423-3*) DIANE Pub.

Richardson, John H., tr. see Petrov, Evgeni I. & Ilf.

Richardson, John M., ed. Making It Happen: A Positive Guide to the Future. 232p. 1982. 9.95 (*0-942718-00-3*) Roundtable Pr.

Richardson, John R. What Happens after Death? Some Musing on -- Is God Through with a Person After Death? LC 81-52115. 1981. 6.95 (*0-686-79843-0*) St Thomas.

Richardson, John T. Gender Differences in Human Cognition. LC 96-44115. (Counterpoints: Cognition, Memory, & Language Ser.). (Illus.). 192p. 1997. pap. text 19.95 (*0-19-511291-1*) OUP.

Richardson, John T., et al. Working Memory & Human Cognition. (Counterpoints Ser.). (Illus.). 176p. (C). 1996. pap. text 19.95 (*0-19-510100-6*) OUP.

***Richardson, John T. E.** Clinical & Neuropsychological Aspects of Closed Head Injury. 2nd ed. 360p. 1999. 54.95 (*0-86377-751-1*, Pub. by Psychol Pr) Taylor & Francis.

Richardson, John T. E. Imagery. (Cognitive Psychology Ser.). 176p. 1999. 44.95 (*0-86377-842-9*); pap. text 22.95 (*0-86377-843-7*) Taylor & Francis.

***Richardson, John T. E.** Researching Student Learning: Approaches to Studying in Campus-Based & Distance Education. LC 99-88223. 2000. write for info. (*0-335-20515-1*) Taylor & Francis.

Richardson, John V., Jr. The Gospel of Scholarship: Pierce Butler & a Critique of American Librarianship. LC 91-45695. (Illus.). 366p. 1992. 45.00 (*0-8108-2499-X*) Scarecrow.

Richardson, John V. Knowledge-Based Systems in General Reference Work: Applications, Problems, & Progress. LC 94-31851. (Library & Information Science Ser.). (Illus.). 355p. 1995. text 54.95 (*0-12-588460-5*) Acad Pr.

Richardson, Jonathan. Explanatory Notes & Remarks on Milton's Paradise Lost. LC 77-174317. reprint ed. 55.00 (*0-404-05298-3*) AMS Pr.

— The Works: Consisting of: The Theory of Painting; Essay on the Art of Criticism, So Far As It Relates to Painting; The Science of a Connoisseur. (Anglistica & Americana Ser.: No. 37). xix, 346p. 1969. reprint ed. 76.70 (*0-685-66510-0*, 05102433) G Olms Pubs.

Richardson-Jones, Tessa. Bear Prayers. (Paws for Thought Ser.). (Illus.). 5p. (J). (ps). 1999. 4.95 (*1-901881-66-0*, Pub. by Element Child) Penguin Putnam.

— Bunny Prayers. (Paws for Thought Ser.). (Illus.). 5p. (J). (ps). 1999. 4.95 (*1-901881-71-7*, Pub. by Element Child) Penguin Putnam.

— Lamb Prayers. (Paws for Thought Ser.). (Illus.). 5p. (J). (ps). 1999. 4.95 (*1-901881-76-8*, Pub. by Element Child) Penguin Putnam.

Richardson-Jones, Tessa. Puppy Prayers. (Paws for Thought Ser.). 5p. (J). (ps). 1998. bds. 4.95 (*1-901881-81-4*, Pub. by Element MA) Penguin Putnam.

Richardson, Joseph G. Long Life & How to Reach It. Rosenkrantz, Barbara G., ed. LC 76-40640. (Public Health in America Ser.). 1977. reprint ed. lib. bdg. 19.95 (*0-405-09828-6*) Ayer.

Richardson, Joseph R. & Mitchell, Ginger. Field Guide to Common Marine Algae of San Salvador Island, Bahamas. (Illus.). 89p. (Orig.). (C). 1994. pap. text 10.00 (*0-935909-49-4*) Bahamian.

Richardson, Joy. Air. LC 91-42612. (Picture Science Ser.). (Illus.). 32p. (J). (gr. 2-4). 1992. lib. bdg. 20.00 (*0-531-14201-9*) Watts.

— Airports. (Picture Science Ser.). (Illus.). 32p. (J). (gr. 2-4). 1994. lib. bdg. 20.00 (*0-531-14292-2*) Watts.

— Bridges. LC 93-30058. (Picture Science Ser.). (Illus.). 32p. (J). (gr. 2-4). 1994. lib. bdg. 20.00 (*0-531-14289-2*) Watts.

***Richardson, Joy.** How to Look at Art, 6 bks. Incl. Looking at Faces in Art. LC 99-52602. (Illus.). 32p. (J). 1999. lib. bdg. 19.93 (*0-8368-2624-8*); Showing Distance in Art. LC 99-52599. (Illus.). 32p. (J). 1999. lib. bdg. 19.93 (*0-8368-2627-2*); Showing Motion in Art. LC 99-54601. (Illus.). 32p. (J). 1999. lib. bdg. 19.93 (*0-8368-2626-4*); Telling Stories in Art. LC 99-52600. (Illus.). 32p. (YA). 1999. lib. bdg. 19.93 (*0-8368-2628-0*); Using Color in Art. LC 99-52598. (Illus.). 32p. (J). 1999. lib. bdg. 19.93 (*0-8368-2629-9*); Using Shadows in Art. LC 99-52597. (Illus.). 32p. (J). 1999. lib. bdg. 19.93 (*0-8368-2625-6*); Orig. Title: Looking at Pictures. (Illus.). (YA). (gr. 1 up). 1999. Set lib. bdg. 119.58 (*0-8368-2623-X*) Gareth Stevens Inc.

Richardson, Joy. Insects. LC 92-32189. (Picture Science Ser.). 32p. (J). (gr. 2-4). 1993. lib. bdg. 20.00 (*0-531-14248-5*) Watts.

— Inside the Museum: A Children's Guide to the Metropolitan Museum of Art. (Illus.). 72p. (J). 1993. pap. 12.95 (*0-8109-2561-3*, Pub. by Abrams) Time Warner.

— Joy for Living, Vol. 1. (Illus.). 267p. (Orig.). 1997. pap. 19.95 (*0-9681247-0-4*) Gordon Soules Bk.

— Looking at Pictures: An Introduction to Art for Young People. LC 96-86476. (Illus.). 80p. 1997. 17.95 (*0-8109-4252-6*, Pub. by Abrams) Time Warner.

— Mammals. LC 92-32913. (Picture Science Ser.). 32p. (J). 1993. lib. bdg. 20.00 (*0-531-14253-1*) Watts.

— Trains. LC 93-49731. (Picture Science Ser.). (Illus.). 32p. (J). 1994. lib. bdg. 20.00 (*0-531-14327-9*) Watts.

— Tunnels. LC 93-30057. (Picture Science Ser.). (Illus.). 32p. (J). (gr. 2-4). 1994. lib. bdg. 20.00 (*0-531-14290-6*) Watts.

Richardson, Judi, ed. see Junior League of Denver, Inc. Staff.

Richardson, Judith B. David's Landing. LC 84-22084. (Illus.). 150p. (J). (gr. 3-7). 1984. 10.95 (*0-9611374-1-X*) Woods Hole Hist.

— Mirrors Are Lonely. (Illus.). 95p. (YA). (gr. 6-9). 1992. 10.95 (*0-9611374-4-4*) Woods Hole Hist.

— Old Winter. LC 96-85. (Illus.). 32p. (J). (ps-2). 1996. lib. bdg. 16.99 (*0-531-08883-9*) Orchard Bks Watts.

— Old Winter. LC 96-85. (Illus.). 32p. (J). (ps-3). 1996. 15.95 (*0-531-09533-9*) Orchard Bks Watts.

— The Way Home. (Illus.). (J). (gr. k). 13.95 (*0-685-41406-X*) Macmillan.

***Richardson, Judith Benet.** First Came the Owl. 1998. 9.09 (*0-606-13387-9*, Pub. by Turtleback) Demco.

Richardson, Judith Knight & Richardson, Lloyd I. The Mathematics of Drugs & Solutions with Clinical Applications. 5th ed. (Illus.). 188p. (C). (gr. 13). 1993. pap. text 27.00 (*0-8016-7895-1*, 07895) Mosby Inc.

***Richardson, Judy S.** Read It Aloud! Using Literature in the Secondary Content Classroom. LC 99-49355. 118p. 2000. pap. 16.95 (*0-87207-256-8*, 256) Intl Reading.

Richardson, Judy S. & Morgan, Raymond F. Reading to Learn in the Content Areas. 544p. (C). 1989. pap. 45.95 (*0-534-11748-1*) Wadsworth Pub.

— Reading to Learn in the Content Areas. 2nd ed. 558p. 1994. pap. 42.75 (*0-534-20328-0*) Wadsworth Pub.

— Reading to Learn in the Content Areas. 3rd ed. LC 96-12029. (Education Ser.). 550p. (C). 1996. 65.95 (*0-534-50737-9*) Wadsworth Pub.

Richardson, Julia. Angel's Cove. large type ed. (Linford Romance Large Print Ser.). 288p. 1998. pap. 17.99 (*0-7089-5254-2*, Linford) Ulverscroft.

— 100 Keys to Great Fabric Painting. (One Hundred Keys Ser.). (Illus.). 64p. 1996. 17.99 (*0-89134-754-2*, North Lght Bks) F & W Pubns Inc.

Richardson, Julia, ed. Family Reunion. (So Weird Ser.: Vol. 1). (Illus.). 144p. (J). (gr. 1-6). 2000. pap. 4.99 (*0-7868-1397-0*, Pub. by Disney Pr) Time Warner.

Richardson, Julie, jt. ed. see Markandya, Anil.

Richardson, Justine. The Great British Art Search. (Illus.). 16p. (Orig.). (J). (gr. 2-6). 1993. pap., student ed. 2.50 (*0-685-70192-1*) Yale Ctr Brit Art.

Richardson, K. F., jt. auth. see Adlard, P. G.

Richardson, K. M., jt. auth. see Wheeler, Mortimer.

Richardson, Karen, ed. see Kimbell, Gordon.

Richardson, Karen, ed. see Van Osdol, Louise.

Richardson, Katherine, ed. see American Geophysical Union Staff.

Richardson, Katherine H. & Lee, Charles E. Pawley's Island: Historically Speaking. (Illus.). 132p. 1994. 35.00 (*0-9643909-0-6*) Pawleys Islnd.

Richardson, Katherine W. Salem Witchcraft Trials. 8th ed. LC 83-81118. (Illus.). 28p. (Orig.). 1997. reprint ed. pap. 5.95 (*0-88389-089-5*, PEMP101, Essx Institute) Peabody Essex Mus.

Richardson, Kathleen S., jt. auth. see Lowry, Thomas H.

Richardson, Kathy. Addition & Subtraction. 1998. pap. 22.95 (*0-7690-0059-2*) Seymour Pubns.

— Developing Number Concepts: Using Unifix Cubes. 1984. pap. text 24.95 (*0-201-06117-1*) Addison-Wesley.

— Developing Number Concepts Bk. 1: Counting, Comparing, & Pattern. (Illus.). 272p. 1998. pap. 22.95 (*0-7690-0058-4*) Seymour Pubns.

— Math Time: The Learning Environment. Antell, Karen, ed. (Illus.). 143p. (Orig.). 1996. pap. 19.95 (*1-888117-01-X*) Educ Enrich.

— Place Value, Multiplication & Division. LC 98-196536. 1998. pap. 22.95 (*0-7690-0060-6*) Seymour Pubns.

— Planning Guide for Developing Number Concepts. 2000. pap. 14.95 (*0-201-49524-4*) Addison-Wesley.

Richardson, Kay & Meinhof, Ulrike. Worlds in Common? Television Discourse in a Changing Europe. LC 98-30279. 17p. (C). 1999. 75.00 (*0-415-14060-9*); pap. 24.99 (*0-415-14061-7*) Routledge.

Richardson, Kay, jt. ed. see Meinho, Ulrike.

Richardson, Keith. Andy Lakey's Psychomanteum: Spiritual Journeys Guided by Art, Angels & Miracles. Embree, Mary, ed. 139p. 1998. pap. 12.95 (*0-9661555-0-5*) Ventura Pr CA.

***Richardson, Keith.** Developmental Psychology: How Nature & Nurture Interact. LC 99-44729. 1999. pap. write for info. (*0-8058-3625-X*) L Erlbaum Assocs.

***Richardson, Ken.** The Making of Intelligence. 2000. 24.95 (*0-231-12004-4*) Col U Pr.

— Models of Cognitive Development. 288p. 1998. 59.95 (*0-86377-852-6*, Pub. by Psychol Pr); pap. 29.95 (*0-86377-853-4*, Pub. by Psychol Pr) Taylor & Francis.

Richardson, Ken. The Origins of Human Potential: Evolution, Development, & Psychology. LC 97-14925. 240p. (C). 1998. write for info. (*0-415-17369-8*); pap. 24.99 (*0-415-17370-1*) Routledge.

— Reich Star Rulebook. Bell, Simon, ed. & illus. by. Hollighurst, Peter et al, illus. (Reich Star Ser.). 246p. (Orig.). 1990. pap. 19.95 (*0-9627428-0-5*) Creative Encounters.

— Understanding Intelligence. 192p. 1990. pap. 34.95 (*0-335-09397-3*) OpUniv Pr.

— Understanding Psychology. 160p. 1989. 110.00 (*0-335-09843-6*); pap. 30.95 (*0-335-09842-8*) OpUniv Pr.

Richardson, Kenneth, jt. auth. see Farmer, John.

Richardson-Koehler, Virginia, et al. School Children at Risk. 286p. 1989. 85.00 (*1-85000-514-1*, Falmer Pr); pap. 34.95 (*1-85000-515-X*, Falmer Pr) Taylor & Francis.

Richardson, Kristin K., ed. Total Quality Management in the Printing & Publishing Industry. 48p. 1992. 28.50 (*0-933505-23-X*) Graph Comm Assn.

Richardson, Kurt. James. LC 97-165601. (New American Commentary Ser.: Vol. 36). 1997. 27.99 (*0-8054-0136-9*, 4201-36) Broadman.

***Richardson, L.** A Catalog of Identifiable Figure Painters of Ancient Pompeii, Herculaneum & Stabiae. LC 99-33031. 272p. 1999. 49.95 (*0-8018-6235-3*) Johns Hopkins.

Richardson, L., Jr. A New Topographical Dictionary of Ancient Rome. (Illus.). 480p. 1992. text 65.00 (*0-8018-4300-6*) Johns Hopkins.

— Pompeii: An Architectural History. (Illus.). 445p. 1997. reprint ed. pap. text 24.95 (*0-8018-5661-2*) Johns Hopkins.

Richardson, Larry. Committed Aestheticism: The Poetic Theory & Practice of Gunter Eich. LC 83-48707. (American University Studies: Germanic Languages & Literature: Ser. I, Vol. 21). 246p. 1983. pap. text 25.25 (*0-8204-0034-3*) P Lang Pubng.

Richardson, Larry A. Diets & Weight Loss. LC 93-93661. (Illus.). 192p. (Orig.). 1993. pap. 17.95 (*0-9636840-1-9*) L A Richardson.

— Sir Cadian Weight Management: Sir Cadian...It's about Time. LC 93-92672. (Illus.). 198p. (Orig.). 1993. pap. text 20.00 (*0-9636840-0-0*) L A Richardson.

Richardson, Laurel W. Fields of Play: Constructing an Academic Life. LC 96-16174. 256p. (C). 1997. text 50.00 (*0-8135-2378-8*); pap. text 17.95 (*0-8135-2379-6*) Rutgers U Pr.

— The New Other Woman: Contemporary Single Women in Affairs with Married Men. 288p. (C). 1987. pap. 14.95 (*0-02-926891-5*) Free Pr.

— Writing Strategies: Reaching Diverse Audiences. (Qualitative Research Methods Ser.: Vol. 21). 88p. (C). 1990. 24.00 (*0-8039-3521-8*); pap. 10.50 (*0-8039-3522-6*) Sage.

Richardson, Laurel W., et al. Feminist Frontiers, Vol. 4. 4th ed. LC 96-20823. 1996. pap. text. write for info. (*0-07-052380-0*) McGraw.

— Feminist Frontiers, Vol. 4. 4th ed. LC 96-20823. 561p. (C). 1996. pap. 38.75 (*0-07-052379-7*) McGraw.

Richardson, Lawrence, ed. Yale Classical Studies, Vol. 19. LC PA0025.Y3. 292p. reprint ed. pap. 90.60 (*0-8357-8388-X*, 203387100087) Bks Demand.

Richardson, Lee, jt. ed. see Cateora, Philip R.

Richardson, Lee, ed. see Conference on Consumerism (1976: Baton Rouge, LA).

Richardson, Len. Coal, Class & Community: The United Mineworkers of New Zealand, 1880-1960. (Illus.). 344p. 1995. pap. 29.95 (*1-86940-113-1*, Pub. by Auckland Univ) Paul & Co Pubs.

Richardson, Lenore H., ed. see Hennessey, D. L.

Richardson, Leonard T. Lexique de la Langue des Oeuvres Burlesques de Scarron. lxv, 281p. 1976. reprint ed. write for info. (*3-487-05742-5*) G Olms Pubs.

Richardson, LeRoy. The Truth Shall Set Your Black Ass Free. 164p. 1998. pap. 14.95 (*1-57502-914-6*, PO2524) Morris Pubng.

Richardson, LeRoy W. International Organizations: U. S. Participation in the United Nations Development Program. (Illus.). 101p. 1998. pap. text 30.00 (*0-7881-3902-9*) DIANE Pub.

Richardson, Lewis F. Arms & Insecurity: A Mathematical Study of the Causes & Origins of War. Rashevsky, Nicolas & Trucco, Ernesto, eds. LC 78-27901. 335p. reprint ed. pap. 103.90 (*0-8357-5745-5*, 201700600006) Bks Demand.

— The Collected Works of Lewis Fry Richardson, 2 vols. Ashford, O. M. et al, eds. (Illus.). 1030p. (C). 1993. text 170.00 (*0-521-38297-1*) Cambridge U Pr.

— The Collected Works of Lewis Fry Richardson, Vol. 2. Ashford, O. M. et al, eds. (Illus.). 778p. (C). 1993. text 170.00 (*0-521-38298-X*) Cambridge U Pr.

— Statistics of Deadly Quarrels. Wright, Quincy & Lienau, C. C., eds. (Illus.). 1960. 45.00 (*0-910286-10-8*) Boxwood.

Richardson, Linda. Bankers in the Selling Role: A Consultative Guide to Cross-Selling Financial Services. 2nd ed. 177p. 1992. pap. 22.50 (*0-471-57265-9*) Wiley.

— Sales Coaching: Making the Great Leap From Sales Manager to Sales Coach. 130p. 1996. 19.95 (*0-07-052382-7*) McGraw.

— Selling by Phone: How to Reach & Sell to Customers in the Nineties. 288p. 1995. pap. 14.95 (*0-07-052376-2*) McGraw.

— Stop Telling, Start Selling: How to Use Customer-Focused Dialogue to Close Sales. rev. ed. LC 97-17550. (Illus.). 272p. 1997. pap. 16.95 (*0-07-052558-7*) McGraw.

— Winning Group Sales Presentations. 144p. 1991. text 17.50 (*1-55623-690-5*, Irwn Prfssnl) McGraw-Hill Prof.

— Winning Negotiation Strategies for Bankers. 150p. 1987. text 45.00 (*0-87094-990-X*, Irwn Prfssnl) McGraw-Hill Prof.

Richardson, Lloyd, tr. see Perrolle, Pierre M., ed.

Richardson, Lloyd I., jt. auth. see Richardson, Judith Knight.

Richardson, Lou, jt. auth. see Callahan, Genevieve A.

Richardson, Louise. When Allies Differ: Anglo-American Relations During the Suez & Falklands Crises. LC 95-38641. 352p. 1996. text 49.95 (*0-312-15852-1*) St Martin.

Richardson, Louvice F. & Callahan, Genevieve. How to Write for Homemakers. 2nd ed. LC 61-14205. 212p. reprint ed. pap. 65.80 (*0-608-13455-4*, 202276700029) Bks Demand.

Richardson, Lynn. APLIC Sixteenth Annual Conference: Proceedings. LC 76-643241. (Annual Report, APLIC Ser.). 153p. (Orig.). 1984. pap. text 15.00 (*0-933438-08-7*) APLIC Intl.

— Mostly Santa Barbara. (Illus.). 224p. 1998. 35.00 (*1-56474-301-2*) Fithian Pr.

Richardson, M. A., et al. Surveillance & Target Aquisition Systems. 2nd ed. LC 97-11874. (Land Warfare: Brassey's New Battlefield Weapons & Technology Ser.). (Illus.). 200p. 1997. 32.95 (*1-85753-137-X*, Pub. by Brasseys) Brasseys.

Richardson, M. D. Chess for Children. (J). 1990. pap. 14.95 (*0-08-029750-1*) S&S Trade.

Richardson, M. E., tr. see Koehler, Ludwig, et al.

Richardson, M. J. Modern Placer Mining. LC 92-90054. (Illus.). 315p. 1992. text 30.00 (*0-9665413-0-8*) Consol Placer.

Richardson, M. T., ed. Practical Blacksmithing, Vols. I & II, Pt. I. LC 98-163049. (Illus.). 262p. 1998. reprint ed. pap. 24.95 (*1-879335-81-6*) Astragal Pr.

— Practical Blacksmithing, Vols. III & IV, Pt. II. LC 98-163049. (Illus.). 284p. 1998. reprint ed. pap. 27.95 (*1-879335-82-4*) Astragal Pr.

— Practical Carriage Building, Set, Vols. I & II. LC 94-70620. (Illus.). 512p. 1994. reprint ed. pap. 24.95 (*1-879335-50-6*) Astragal Pr.

***Richardson, Malcolm & Johnson, Elizabeth.** Pocket Guide to Fungal Infection. (Illus.). 120p. 2000. pap. 29.95 (*0-632-05325-9*) Blackwell Sci.

Richardson, Malcolm D. & Warnock, D. W. Fungal Infection: Diagnosis & Management. 2nd ed. LC 97-5802. (Illus.). 256p. 1997. pap. text 49.95 (*0-86542-724-0*) Blackwell Sci.

Richardson, Margaret. Managing Worker Safety & Health for Excellence. LC 97-9095. (Illus.). 416p. 1997. 59.95 (*0-442-02393-6*, VNR) Wiley.

***Richardson, Margaret.** Preparing for the Voluntary Protection Programs: Building Your Star. LC 99-10454. 182p. 1999. pap. 59.95 (*0-471-32405-1*) Wiley.

Richardson, Margaret. Sketches by Edwin Luytens: Drawings from the Collection of the Royal Institute of British Artifacts. (Illus.). 120p. 1995. pap. 35.00 (*1-85490-377-2*, Pub. by Wiley) Wiley.

***Richardson, Margaret.** Type Graphics: The Power of Type in Graphic Design. 2000. 45.00 (*1-56496-714-X*) Rockport Pubs.

***Richardson, Margaret & Stevens, Mary Anne, eds.** John Soane, Architect: Master of Space & Light. (Illus.). 320p. 2000. 75.00 (*0-300-08195-2*) Yale U Pr.

Richardson, Margaret, tr. see De Oliveira Setubal, Paulo.

Richardson, Margaret R. Managing Worker Safety Health. (Occupational Health & Safety Ser.). 382p. 1997. 69.95 (*0-471-28801-2*, VNR) Wiley.

Richardson, Margot. Natural Style: Contemporary Soft Furnishings from Cotton, Linen, Silk & Wool. (Illus.). 128p. 1997. 27.95 (*0-7063-7582-3*, Pub. by WrLock) Sterling.

— Things to Wear. LC 97-13923. (Design & Create Ser.). (Illus.). 32p. (J). (gr. 2-5). 1998. lib. bdg. 22.83 (*0-8172-4888-9*) Raintree Steck-V.

Richardson, Margot, jt. auth. see Marshall, David.

Richardson, Marilyn, ed. Maria W. Stewart, America's First Black Woman Political Writer: Essays & Speeches. LC 86-43048. (Blacks in the Diaspora Ser.). (Illus.). 160p. 1987. 26.95 (*0-253-36342-X*); pap. 9.95 (*0-253-20446-1*, MB-446) Ind U Pr.

Richardson, Marion, jt. ed. see Hutcheon, Linda.

Richardson, Mark. The Ordeal of Robert Frost: The Poet & His Poetics. LC 96-51279. 288p. 1997. 24.95 (*0-252-02338-2*) U of Ill Pr.

***Richardson, Mark.** The Ordeal of Robert Frost: The Poet & His Poetics. 288p. 2000. reprint ed. pap. 16.95 (*0-252-06899-8*) U of Ill Pr.

Richardson, Mark. Otolaryngology: Pediatric Head & Neck Surgery, Vol. 3. (Illus.). 608p. (C). (gr. 13). 1998. text 150.00 (*0-8151-2135-0*, 29855) Mosby Inc.

Richardson, Mark, jt. auth. see DeLuca, Michael.

Richardson, Mark, ed. see Frost, Robert.

Richardson, Martha. Francisco Jose Goya: Spanish Painter. LC 93-2326. (Hispanics of Achievement Ser.). (Illus.). 120p. (YA). (gr. 5 up). 1993. lib. bdg. 19.95 (*0-7910-1780-X*) Chelsea Hse.

***Richardson, Martin, ed.** Globalisation & International Trade Liberalisation: Continuity & Change. LC 00-22626. 224p. 2000. 80.00 (*1-84064-350-1*) E Elgar.

Richardson, Martin J. Chess for Children. 1994. text 15.95 (*1-85744-078-1*, Pub. by Cadgn Bks) Macmillan.

An Asterisk (*) at the beginning of an entry indicates that the title is appearing for the first time.

R

Richardson, Mary. The Boy Jesus Goes A-Walking & Other Stories. (Illus.). 96p. 1988. pap. 2.95 (*0-8091-6575-9*) Paulist Pr.

— It Happened at Christmas & Other Stories. (Illus.). 96p. 1988. pap. 2.95 (*0-8091-6576-7*) Paulist Pr.

Richardson, Mary, jt. ed. see Ross, Austin.

Richardson, Mary A. Amino Acids in Psychiatric Disease. LC 89-18455. (Progress in Psychiatry Ser.). (Illus.). 210p. 1990. reprint ed. pap. 65.10 (*0-608-06657-5*, 206685400009) Bks Demand.

Richardson, Mary A. & Haugland, Gary, eds. Use of Neuroleptics in Children. (Clinical Practice Ser.: No. 37). 256p. 1995. text 36.00 (*0-88048-475-6*, 8475) Am Psychiatric.

***Richardson, Mathew.** The Tigers. (Illus.). 2000. 32.95 (*0-85052-719-8*, Pub. by Leo Cooper) Combined Pub.

Richardson, Matthew. Fathering. 1996. pap. 8.95 (*1-57008-253-7*) Bookcraft Inc.

— Whose Bright Idea Was That? Great Firsts of World History. LC 98-16847. 464p. 1998. pap. 16.95 (*1-56836-256-0*) Kodansha.

Richardson, Maureen. Grow Your Own Paper. LC 99-38589. (Illus.). 112p. 1999. pap. 21.95 (*1-56477-280-2*, DB400, PasTimes) Martingale & Co.

***Richardson, Megan & Hadfield, Gillian, eds.** The Second Ware of Law & Economics. 144p. 1999. pap. 45.00 (*1-86287-316-X*, Pub. by Federation Pr) Gaunt.

Richardson, Megan & Williams, Philip, eds. The Law & the Market. 235p. 1995. 64.00 (*1-86287-174-4*, Pub. by Federation Pr) Gaunt.

Richardson, Mervyn. Dictionary of Substances & Their Effects Vol. 5: I to M. 1000p. 1994. 350.00 (*0-85186-371-X*, R6371) CRC Pr.

— Effects of War on the Environment: Croatia. LC 95-67609. (Illus.). 256p. 1995. 129.95 (*0-419-19790-7*, E & FN Spon) Routledge.

— Environmental Toxicology Assessment: Birch Assessment Services for Information Chemicals (BASIC) 480p. 1995. 209.00 (*0-7484-0305-1*) Taylor & Francis.

Richardson, Mervyn, ed. Risk Reduction: Chemicals & Energy into the 21st Century. LC 97-108600. 612p. 1997. 199.00 (*0-7484-0398-1*, Pub. by Tay Francis Ltd) Taylor & Francis.

Richardson, Mervyn L. Risk Assessment of Chemicals in the Environment. 1988. 187.00 (*0-85186-118-0*) CRC Pr.

Richardson, Mervyn L., ed. Chemistry, Agriculture & the Environment. 1991. 198.00 (*0-85186-228-4*) CRC Pr.

***Richardson, Michael.** Amazing Faith: The Authorized Biography of Bill Bright. (Illus.). 320p. 2000. 19.95 (*1-57856-328-3*) Waterbrook Pr.

Richardson, Michael. Georges Bataille. LC 93-20940. 192p. (C). (gr. 13). 1994. 80.00 (*0-415-09841-6*) Routledge.

Richardson, MIchael. The Organization of Public Education in South Carolina. 408p. 1992. pap., per. 35.95 (*0-8403-8190-5*) Kendall-Hunt.

Richardson, Michael. Refusal of the Shadow: Surrealism & the Carribean. (Illus.). 256p. 1996. pap. 20.00 (*1-85984-018-3*, Pub. by Verso) Norton.

Richardson, Michael, ed. from CZE. The Dedalus Book of Surrealism: The Identity of Things. 2nd ed. 277p. 1999. reprint ed. pap. 14.99 (*1-873982-45-3*) Dedalus.

— Dedalus Book of Surrealism Pt. II: Myth of the World. 2nd ed. LC 93-223584. (Anthology Ser.). 320p. 1999. reprint ed. pap. 16.95 (*1-873982-36-4*, Pub. by Dedalus) Subterranean Co.

Richardson, Michael, et al, eds. Preparing to Study. 72p. 1979. pap. 33.95 (*0-335-00255-2*) OpUniv Pr.

Richardson, Michael, et al. Early Childhood Programs: Organization & Administration. LC 92-60849. 250p. 1996. pap. text 24.95 (*0-87762-881-5*) Scarecrow.

— Managing School Indebtedness: The Complete Guide to School Bonding. LC 94-60934. 245p. 1994. text 39.95 (*1-56676-180-8*) Scarecrow.

Richardson, Michael, jt. ed. see Costello, Neil.

Richardson, Michael, ed. & tr. see Bataille, Georges.

Richardson, Michael, tr. see Mirbeau, Octave.

Richardson, Michael D., et al. The Pursuit of Continuous Improvement in Educational Organizations. LC 97-30107. 280p. (C). 1997. 56.00 (*0-7618-0878-7*); pap. 34.50 (*0-7618-0879-5*) U Pr of Amer.

— School Principals & Change. LC 92-28436. (Source Books on Education: Vol. 33). 288p. 1993. text 51.00 (*0-8153-0383-1*, SS783) Garland.

Richardson, Mike. Aliens: Genocide. LC 99-211492. 1997. pap. text 16.95 (*1-56971-196-8*) Dark Horse Comics.

***Richardson, Mike.** Council of Blood. (Star Wars: Vol. 2). 1999. pap. 17.95 (*1-56971-410-X*) Dark Horse Comics.

Richardson, Mike, et al, eds. School Empowerment. LC 95-60051. 369p. 1995. text 39.95 (*1-56676-269-3*) Scarecrow.

Richardson, Mike & Richardson, Sue. Dinky Toys & Modelled Miniatures. 3rd ed. (Hornby Companion Ser.: Vol. 4). (Illus.). 384p. 1983. 60.00 (*0-904568-33-4*, Pub. by New Cavendish) Pincushion Pr.

Richardson, Mike & Richardson, Sue. Great Book of Dinky Toys. (Illus.). 342p. 75.00 (*1-872727-83-2*, Pub. by New Cavendish) Antique Collect.

— Wheels: Christie's World of Automotive Toys. (Illus.). 192p. 1999. pap. 24.95 (*0-8118-2320-2*) Chronicle Bks.

Richardson, Mike & Richardson, Susan. Christie's World of Automotive Toys. LC 98-44777. (Illus.). 192p. 1998. 39.95 (*0-7603-0569-2*) MBI Pubg.

Richardson, Mike, et al. Crimson Empire. (Star Wars: Vol. 1). 160p. (YA). (gr. 7 up). 1999. pap. 17.95 (*1-56971-355-3*) Dark Horse Comics.

— Indiana Jones & the Fate of Atlantis. (Illus.). 112p. 1992. pap. 13.95 (*1-878574-36-1*) Dark Horse Comics.

Richardson, Mike, jt. auth. see Duin, Steve.

Richardson, Mike, ed. see Cailleteau, Thierry & Vatine, Olivier.

Richardson, Miles. Cry Lonesome & Other Accounts of the Anthropologist's Project. LC 89-26240. (Illus.). 170p. (C). 1990. text 19.50 (*0-7914-0405-6*) State U NY Pr.

Richardson, Miles, ed. Place: Experience & Symbol. LC 83-83212. (Geoscience & Man Ser.: Vol. 24). (Illus.). 80p. 1984. pap. 10.00 (*0-938909-32-0*) Geosci Pubns LSU.

Richardson, Minni. Alpha Hand: Transcription & Review: Second Semester Textbook & Cassette. (Alpha Hand Ser.). 148p. 1989. 15.00 (*0-936862-47-5*, AH-22) DDC Pub.

Richardson, Mozelle. The Von Wegerer Skull 1980. 303p. mass mkt. 5.99 (*1-55197-764-8*) Picasso Publ.

***Richardson, N.** Breakfast in Brighton. 1998. text 35.00 (*0-575-06600-8*, Pub. by V Gollancz) Trafalgar.

Richardson, N. J. The Homeric Hymn to Demeter. 380p. 1979. reprint ed. text 55.00 (*0-19-814199-8*) OUP.

Richardson, Nan, jt. auth. see Hazzard, Shirley.

Richardson, Nan F. & Chermayeff, Ivan. Feathery Facts. LC 94-2479. (Illus.). 32p. (J). (ps-1). 1995. 11.00 (*0-15-200110-7*, Gulliver Bks) Harcourt.

Richardson, Nan Franks, jt. auth. see Steinman, Sarah O.

Richardson, Nancy A. The Golden Globe. (Star Wars: No. 1). (Orig.). (J). (gr. 4-7). 1995. mass mkt. 4.50 (*0-425-16825-5*) Berkley Pub.

— The Golden Globe. (Star Wars: No. 1). 128p. (Orig.). (J). (gr. 3-5). 1995. mass mkt. 4.50 (*1-57297-035-9*) Blvd Books.

— Lyric's World. (Star Wars: No. 2). (J). (gr. 4-7). 1998. pap. text 4.50 (*0-425-16762-3*) Berkley Pub.

— Lyric's World. (Star Wars: No. 2). 128p. (J). (gr. 3-5). 1996. mass mkt. 4.50 (*1-57297-068-5*) Blvd Books.

— Promises. (Star Wars: No. 3). (Orig.). (J). (gr. 4-7). 1999. mass mkt. 4.50 (*0-425-16955-3*) Berkley Pub.

— Promises. (Star Wars: No. 3). 128p. (Orig.). (J). (gr. 3-5). 1996. mass mkt. 4.50 (*1-57297-097-9*) Blvd Books.

Richardson, Nancy A., jt. auth. see Miller, Shannon.

Richardson, Neil. Paul's Language about God. LC 95-110006. (JSNT Supplement Ser.: Vol. 99). 371p. 1994. 85.00 (*1-85075-485-3*, Pub. by Sheffield Acad) CUP Services.

Richardson, Neil R. Foreign Policy & Economic Dependence. LC 78-6451. 224p. reprint ed. pap. 69.50 (*0-7837-1241-3*, 204137800020) Bks Demand.

Richardson, Nicholas, ed. see Homer.

Richardson, Noel. Summer Delights: Cooking with Fresh Herbs. (Illus.). 128p. 1986. spiral bd. 9.95 (*0-317-60787-1*) Aris Bks.

— Summer Delights: Growing & Cooking Fresh Herbs. (Illus.). 168p. 1994. pap. text 9.95 (*1-895099-47-1*) Gr Arts Ctr Pub.

— Winter Pleasures: Preserving & Cooking Herbs. (Illus.). 144p. pap. 9.95 (*1-895099-25-0*) Gr Arts Ctr Pub.

***Richardson, Nohel & Cameron, Jenny.** Herbal Celebrations Cookbook. 208p. 2000. 14.95 (*1-55110-835-6*) Whitecap Bks.

***Richardson, Norman, ed.** A Tapestry of Beliefs: Christian Traditions in Northern Ireland. 336p. 1999. pap. 21.00 (*0-85640-633-3*, Pub. by Blackstaff Pr) Dufour.

Richardson, Norman & Stubbs, Thomas. Plants, Agriculture & Human Society. LC 77-72644. 1978. pap. text 26.95 (*0-8053-8215-1*) Benjamin-Cummings.

Richardson, Owen, jt. auth. see Richardson, Allen.

Richardson, P. E., ed. see International Symposium on Electrochemistry in Min.

Richardson, P. E., jt. ed. see Woods, R.

Richardson, P. H. British Mining No. 44: Mining on Dartmoor & the Tamar Valley after 1913. 159p. 1990. 65.00 (*0-901450-38-3*, Pub. by Northern Mine Res) St Mut.

Richardson, P. J., ed. Archbold Criminal Pleading Evidence & Practice. 1994th ed. 1993. 317.00 (*0-421-47000-3*, Pub. by Sweet & Maxwll) Gaunt.

Richardson, P. J. & Darden, Robert. Wheels of Thunder. LC 96-37194. (Illus.). 192p. (Orig.). 1997. pap. 14.99 (*0-7852-7223-2*) Nelson.

Richardson, P. J., jt. auth. see Darden, Robert.

Richardson, P. Mick. Flowering Plants: Magic in Bloom. (Encyclopedia of Psychoactive Drugs Ser.: No. 1). (Illus.). 124p. (YA). (gr. 7 up). 1992. lib. bdg. 19.95 (*0-87754-757-2*) Chelsea Hse.

Richardson, Pam, ed. see Hoffman, Michael, et al.

Richardson, Paul. Computers: Manager's Guide. (Primary Health Care Management Advancement Programme (PHC MAP) Modules Ser.). 76p. 1993. pap. text. write for info. (*1-882839-20-X*) Aga Khan Fnd.

Richardson, Paul E. Russia Survival Guide: The Definitive Guide to Doing Business & Traveling in Russia. 7th ed. 260p. 1997. pap. 18.50 (*1-880100-30-4*) Russian Info Srvs.

Richardson, Paul E., et al, eds. Pollution Prevention for Process Engineers. (Engineering Foundation Conference Proceedings Ser.). 368p. 1996. 115.00 (*0-939204-53-3*, P-83) Eng Found.

Richardson, Pearl W. The Growth of Federal User Charges. (Illus.). 79p. (Orig.). (C). 1994. pap. text 30.00 (*0-7881-0653-8*) DIANE Pub.

Richardson, Peggy A., jt. auth. see Weinberg, Robert S.

Richardson, Peter. Herod: King of the Jews & Friend of the Romans. LC 99-22796. (Personalities of the New Testament Ser.). 400p. 1999. pap. text 23.00 (*0-8006-3164-1*, 1-3164, Fortress Pr) Augsburg Fortress.

— Herod: King of the Jews & Friend of the Romans. LC 96-25248. (Studies on Personalities of the New Testament). 360p. 1996. 34.95 (*1-57003-136-3*) U of SC Pr.

— Style. LC 97-15045. 113p. 1997. pap. text 25.00 (*0-205-19957-7*) P-H.

Richardson, Peter & Fischer, William. Como: Class Text Introductry Spanish Proficiency. 348p. (C). 1994. 35.00 (*0-536-58732-9*) Pearson Custom.

— Como: Introductory Spanish Proficiency Study Text. 202p. (C). 1994. 20.00 (*0-536-58731-0*) Pearson Custom.

Richardson, Peter & Granskou, David, eds. Anti-Judaism in Early Christianity Vol. 1: Paul & the Gospels. 240p. (C). 1986. pap. 18.95 (*0-88920-167-6*) W Laurier U Pr.

Richardson, Peter & Hurd, John C., Jr., eds. From Jesus to Paul: Studies in Honour of Francis Wright Beare. 233p. (C). 1984. pap. 15.95 (*0-88920-138-2*) W Laurier U Pr.

Richardson, Peter & Richardson, Bob, Jr. Great Careers for People Interested in How Things Work, 6 vols. LC 93-78076. (Career Connections Ser.: Vol. 5). (Illus.). 48p. (J). (gr. 6-9). 1993. text 23.00 (*0-8103-9389-1*, 102107, UXL) Gale.

— Great Careers for People Interested in Math & Computers, Vol. 1. LC 93-78079. (Career Connections Ser.: Series 1). (Illus.). 48p. (J). (gr. 6-9). 1993. text 23.00 (*0-8103-9385-9*, GML00597-102103, UXL) Gale.

Richardson, Peter & Westerholm, Stephen, eds. Law in Religious Communities in the Roman Period: The Debate over Torah & Nomos in Post-Biblical Judaism & Early Christianity. 152p. (C). 1991. pap. 16.95 (*0-88920-201-X*) W Laurier U Pr.

Richardson, Peter, jt. auth. see Wright, Patrick.

Richardson, Peter, jt. ed. see Donfried, Karl P.

Richardson, Peter, jt. ed. see Jervis, L. Ann.

Richardson, Peter D. Principles of Cell Adhesion. 400p. 1994. 157.95 (*0-8493-4559-6*) CRC Pr.

Richardson, Peter J., jt. ed. see Sekiguchi, Morie.

Richardson, Peter K. Style: A Pragmatic Approach. 32p. (C). 1997. pap. text, teacher ed. write for info. (*0-205-27934-1*, T7934-7) Allyn.

Richardson, Peter N., jt. auth. see Fischer, William B.

Richardson, Peter R. Cost Containment: The Ultimate Advantage. (Illus.). 304p. 1988. 35.00 (*0-02-926432-4*) Free Pr.

Richardson, Peter T. Four Spiritualities: Expressions of Self, Expressions of Spirit. LC 95-44375. 264p. 1996. pap. 16.95 (*0-89106-083-9*, 7684, Davies-Black Pub) Consulting Psychol.

Richardson, Phil. Bats. (Illus.). 128p. text 19.95 (*0-905483-41-3*, Pub. by Whittet Bks) Diamond Farm Bk.

***Richardson, Philip.** Economic Change in China, c. 1800-1950. LC 99-12835. (New Studies in Economic & Social History: No. 40). (Illus.). 100p. (C). 1999. 39.95 (*0-521-58396-9*); pap. 12.95 (*0-521-63571-3*) Cambridge U Pr.

Richardson, R. Business Planning - an Approach to Strategic Management. 236p. (C). 1989. 145.00 (*0-7855-5694-X*, Pub. by Inst Pur & Supply) St Mut.

Richardson, R. A. Facial Wrinkles. 1996. reprint ed. spiral bd. 11.50 (*0-7873-0714-9*) Hlth Research.

— Healthy Eyes Without Glasses: Increasing the Strength of the Eyes & the Eye Muscles Without the Aid of Glasses. 1996. reprint ed. pap. 16.00 (*0-7873-0715-7*) Hlth Research.

***Richardson, R. C.** The Changing Face of English Local History: Essays. LC 00-34852. 2000. write for info. (*1-84014-620-6*, Pub. by Ashgate Pub) Ashgate Pub Co.

Richardson, R. C. The Debate on the English Revolution. 2nd ed. (Illus.). 400p. 1989. pap. 25.00 (*0-415-01167-1*) Routledge.

***Richardson, R. C.** The Debate on the English Revolution. 3rd ed. LC 98-28825. 1998. pap. 24.95 (*0-7190-4740-4*) Manchester Univ Pr.

Richardson, R. C. The Debate on the English Revolution. 3rd ed. LC 98-28825. (Issues in Historiography Ser.). 1999. write for info. (*0-7190-4739-0*, Pub. by Manchester Univ Pr) St Martin.

Richardson, R. C. The Study of History: A Bibliographical Guide. 2nd ed. text. write for info. (*0-7190-5899-6*, Pub. by Manchester Univ Pr) St Martin.

Richardson, R. Dan. Comintern Army: The International Brigades & the Spanish Civil War. fac. ed. LC 80-5182. 240p. 1994. pap. 74.40 (*0-7837-7598-9*, 204735100007) Bks Demand.

Richardson, R. I. & Mead, G. C., eds. Poultry Meat Science, Vol. 25. (Poultry Science Symposium Ser.). (Illus.). 456p. 1999. text 120.00 (*0-85199-237-4*) OUP.

Richardson, R. T. Activation to Acquisition: Functional Aspects of the Basal Forebrain Cholinergic System. (Illus.). 392p. 1991. 108.00 (*0-8176-3467-3*) Birkhauser.

— Chucker Jones' Adventures in Shadowland: What's It All about Chucker? Dobie, Bruce, ed. (Illus.). 32p. (Orig.). (J). (gr. k-8). 1994. pap. 1.95 (*0-9643522-0-6*) R T Richardson.

Richardson, Ralph C., jt. auth. see Hahn, Kevin A.

Richardson, Ralph C., jt. ed. see Hahn, Kevin A.

Richardson, Ralph W. Historic Districts of America: New England. (Illus.). xvi, 182p. (Orig.). 1992. pap. 17.00 (*1-55613-550-5*) Heritage Bk.

— Historic Districts of America: The Mid-Atlantic. (Illus.). xviii, 309p. (Orig.). 1991. pap. 17.50 (*1-55613-395-2*) Heritage Bk.

— Historic Districts of America: The South. (Illus.). xvi, 223p. (Orig.). 1987. pap. text 12.50 (*1-55613-088-0*) Heritage Bk.

Richardson, Ray, jt. auth. see Rubin, Marcus.

Richardson, Recco. Teenagers Role in the Family Structure. Stokes, Tanya C., ed. 117p. (Orig.). 1991. pap. 8.00 (*0-9627849-7-4*) Temperance Pub Hse.

Richardson, Reed C. Collective Bargaining by Objectives: A Positive Approach. (Illus.). 1977. pap. 18.95 (*0-685-03794-0*) P-H.

Richardson, Richard C., Jr. Creating Effective Learning Environments. 56p. 1992. pap. 6.50 (*0-614-30588-8*, PS-92-4) Ed Comm States.

— Promoting Fair College Outcomes: Learning from the Experiences of the Past Decade. 50p. 1990. pap. 5.00 (*0-614-30587-X*, MP-90-4) Ed Comm States.

Richardson, Richard C., Jr. & Bender, Louis W. Students in Urban Settings: Achieving the Baccalaureate Degree. Fife, Jonathan D., ed. LC 85-73509. (ASHE-ERIC Higher Education Reports: No. 85-6). 90p. (Orig.). (C). 1985. pap. 24.00 (*0-913317-25-X*) GWU Grad Schl E&HD.

Richardson, Richard C., Jr. & Skinner, Elizabeth F. Achieving Quality & Diversity: Universities in a Multicultural Society. LC 96-23103. (ACE-Oryx Series on Higher Education). 288p. 1991. pap. 29.95 (*1-57356-089-8*) Oryx Pr.

Richardson, Richard C., et al. Literacy in the Open-Access College. LC 83-11999. (Jossey-Bass Higher Education Ser.). 207p. reprint ed. pap. 64.20 (*0-8357-4919-3*, 203784900009) Bks Demand.

Richardson, Richard C., jt. auth. see Richards, Marty.

Richardson, Richard W. Handbook of Human Blood Constituent. 357p. 1994. lib. bdg. 210.00 (*0-8493-8664-0*) CRC Pr.

Richardson, Richard W. & Haralz, Jonas H. Moving to the Market: The World Bank in Transition. LC 94-47640. (Policy Essay Ser.: Vol. 17). 1995. pap. 13.95 (*1-56517-023-7*) Overseas Dev Council.

***Richardson, Rick.** Evangelism Outside the Box. 2000. pap. 10.99 (*0-8308-2276-3*) InterVarsity.

Richardson, Rita C. Connecting with Others: Lessons for Teaching Social & Emotional Competence (Grades K-2) LC 96-69183. (Illus.). 336p. (Orig.). 1996. pap. text 39.95 (*0-87822-362-2*, 4917) Res Press.

— Connecting with Others: Lessons for Teaching Social & Emotional Competence (Grades 3-5) LC 96-69182. (Illus.). 336p. (Orig.). 1996. pap. text 39.95 (*0-87822-363-0*, 4918) Res Press.

Richardson, Rita C. & Evans, Elizabeth T. Connecting with Others: Lessons for Teaching Social & Emotional Competence (Grades 6-8) (Illus.). 408p. (Orig.). 1997. pap. text 39.95 (*0-87822-364-9*) Res Press.

Richardson, Robert. The Book of the Dead. large type ed. 296p. 1990. 20.95 (*0-7451-1094-0*, G K Hall Lrg Type) Mac Lib Ref.

— The Lazarus Tree. (WWL Mystery Ser.). 1995. per. 3.99 (*0-373-26166-7*, 1-26166-8) Harlequin Bks.

***Richardson, Robert.** Medicine: Through the Ages with Dr. Baldassare. 256p. 1999. 18.95 (*1-899163-47-6*) Cimino Pub Grp.

Richardson, Robert. Sleeping in the Blood. large type ed. 348p. 1992. 27.99 (*0-7505-0428-5*) Ulverscroft.

— Unlocking Inferno. 600p. 1997. 34.99 (*1-56205-667-0*) New Riders Pub.

Richardson, Robert, jt. ed. see Pratt, William.

Richardson, Robert C., jt. auth. see Bechtel, William.

Richardson, Robert D., Jr. Emerson: The Mind on Fire. LC 94-36008. (Illus.). 684p. 1995. 45.00 (*0-520-08808-5*, Pub. by U CA Pr) Cal Prin Full Svc.

— Emerson: The Mind on Fire. (Centennial Book Ser.). (Illus.). 684p. (C). 1996. pap. 18.95 (*0-520-20689-4*, Pub. by U CA Pr) Cal Prin Full Svc.

— Henry Thoreau: A Life of the Mind. LC 85-28845. (Illus.). 464p. 1986. 45.00 (*0-520-05495-4*, Pub. by U CA Pr); pap. 17.95 (*0-520-06346-5*, Pub. by U CA Pr) Cal Prin Full Svc.

Richardson, Robert D. Myth & Literature in the American Renaissance. LC 77-22638. 317p. reprint ed. pap. 98.30 (*0-8357-6684-5*, 205686300094) Bks Demand.

Richardson, Robert D., jt. auth. see Feldman, Burton.

Richardson, Robert D., ed. see De Beausobre, Isaac.

Richardson, Robert D., ed. see Jones, William.

Richardson, Robert D., jt. ed. see Mandelbaum, Allen.

Richardson, Robert H., ed. Chesapeake Bay Decoys: The Men Who Made & Used Them. LC 91-77999. (Illus.). 240p. 1992. 40.00 (*0-9631815-0-5*) Decoy Mag.

Richardson, Robert M. Disassembled Handbook for the TRS-80 Model 1 & 3: Advanced Baudot Radio Teletype for the TRS-80 Model 1 & 3, Vol. 5. Blevins, T. F., ed. 205p. 1983. 22.00 (*0-940972-06-9*) Richcraft Eng.

— Disassembled Handbook for TRS-80, Vol. 3. Abear, Gerald J., ed. 236p. 1981. 20.00 (*0-940972-03-4*) Richcraft Eng.

— Synchronous Packet Radio Using the Software Approach: AX.25 Protocal, Vol. 2. Belvins, T. F., ed. 280p. 1984. 22.00 (*0-940972-08-5*) Richcraft Eng.

— Synchronous Packet Radio Using the Software Approach: Vancouver Protocol, Vol. 1. Blevins, T. F., ed. 223p. 1983. 22.00 (*0-940972-07-7*) Richcraft Eng.

Richardson, Robert W. Chasing Trains. (Illus.). 432p. 1995. 55.00 (*0-913582-60-3*, 0253) Sundance.

— Robert W. Richardson's Narrow Gauge News. LC 70-102682. (Colorado Rail Annual Ser.: No. 21). (Illus.). 303p. 1994. 44.95 (*0-918654-21-1*) CO RR Mus.

Richardson, Robin. Daring to Be a Teacher. 180p. 1989. pap. 16.00 (*0-948080-32-9*, Trentham Bks) Stylus Pub VA.

— Enriching Literacy - Text, Talk & Tales in Today's Classroom. 76p. 1999. pap. 13.95 (*1-85856-163-9*, Trentham Bks) Stylus Pub VA.

***Richardson, Robin & Wood, Angela.** Inclusive Schools, Inclusive Society. 96p. 1999. pap. 15.95 (*1-85856-203-1*, Trentham Bks) Stylus Pub VA.

Richardson, Robin, jt. auth. see Wood, Angela.

Richardson, Ronald K. Moral Imperium: Afro-Caribbeans & the Transformation of British Rule, 1776-1838, 22. LC 86-3154. (Contributions in Comparative Colonial Studies: No. 22). 219p. 1987. 57.95 (*0-313-24724-2*, RMI/, Greenwood Pr) Greenwood.

Richardson, Ronald W. Creating a Healthier Church: Family Systems Theory, Leadership, & Congregational Life. LC 96-6369. (Creative Pastoral Care & Counseling Ser.). 184p. 1996. pap. 17.00 (*0-8006-2955-8*, 1-2955, Fortress Pr) Augsburg Fortress.

Richardson, Ronny. Dr. Batch File's Ultimate Collection. 1992. 39.95 (*0-07-052358-4*) McGraw.

— Dr. Batch File's Ultimate Collection. LC 92-9172. (Illus.). 432p. 1992. 39.95 (*0-8306-4112-2*, 4220, Windcrest) TAB Bks.
— Microsoft Office Essentials. LC 96-15538. 460p. 1996. pap. 24.95 (*1-884777-18-X*) Manning Pubns.
— Microsoft Office Essentials. 400p. (C). 1996. pap. text 24.95 (*0-13-262312-9*) P-H.
— MS-DOS Batch File Programming. 1988. pap. 19.95 (*0-8306-9328-9*) McGraw-Hill Prof.
— MS-DOS Batch File Programming. 1991. 24.95 (*0-8306-6663-X*) McGraw-Hill Prof.
— MS-DOS Utility Programs. 1991. 14.95 (*0-8306-5384-8*) McGraw-Hill Prof.
— MS-DOS Utility Programs (Five & One Quarter) 1991. 14.95 (*0-8306-5414-3*); 14.95 (*0-8306-5415-1*); 14.95 (*0-8306-5416-X*); 14.95 (*0-8306-5417-8*); 14.95 (*0-8306-5418-6*); 14.95 (*0-8306-5419-4*); 14.95 (*0-8306-5420-8*); 14.95 (*0-8306-5421-6*); 14.95 (*0-8306-5422-4*); 14.95 (*0-8306-5423-2*); 14.95 (*0-8306-5424-0*); 14.95 (*0-8306-5426-7*); 14.95 (*0-8306-5427-5*); write for info. (*0-8306-5444-5*) McGraw-Hill Prof.
— MS-DOS Utility Programs (Three & One Half) 1991. 14.95 (*0-8306-5428-3*); 14.95 (*0-8306-5430-5*); 14.95 (*0-8306-5431-3*); 14.95 (*0-8306-5432-1*); 14.95 (*0-8306-5433-X*); 14.95 (*0-8306-5434-8*); 14.95 (*0-8306-5435-6*); 14.95 (*0-8306-5436-4*); 14.95 (*0-8306-5437-2*); 14.95 (*0-8306-5438-0*); 14.95 (*0-8306-5439-9*); 14.95 (*0-8306-5440-2*); 14.95 (*0-8306-5441-0*); 14.95 (*0-8306-5442-9*); 14.95 (*0-8306-5443-7*); write for info. (*0-8306-5445-3*) McGraw-Hill Prof.
— Professional's Guide to Robust Spreadsheets: Using Examples in Lotus 1-2-3 & Microsoft Excel. LC 96-15537. xxi, 281 p. 1996. write for info. (*1-884777-19-8*) Manning Pubns.
— The Ultimate Batch File Book! 1995. 49.95 (*0-07-912050-4*) McGraw.
— Windows 95 Liferaft. LC 96-15536. 200p. (C). 1996. pap. text 14.95 (*0-13-492042-2*) P-H.
— Writing OS - 2 REXX Programs. LC 94-913. 1994. pap. text 39.95 (*0-07-052372-X*) McGraw.

Richardson, Ronny & Manning Publications Staff. Professional's Guide to Robust Spreadsheets. 400p. (C). 1996. pap. text 39.95 (*0-13-262320-X*) P-H.

Richardson, Ronny, et al. Java Applets & Channels: Without Programming. LC 97-23269. (Illus.). 377p. 1997. pap. 37.95 (*1-884777-39-2*) Manning Pubns.

Richardson, Rosalie & Fox, Larry L. Hancock County, Indiana: A Pictorial History. LC 93-13530. (Illus.). 1993. write for info. (*0-89865-869-1*) Donning Co.

Richardson, Rosamond. Country Ways & Wisdom: Over 400 Natural Tips & Traditions to Enhance Your Life. LC 98-2869. (Illus.). 192p. (gr. 11). 1999. 24.95 (*0-7370-0020-1*) T-L Custom Pub.
— Eileen's Story: An Inspirational Story of How One Woman Overcame Terminal Cancer. LC 97-175761. 192p. 1997. pap. 16.95 (*1-86204-057-5*, Pub. by Element MA) Penguin Putnam.
— The Great Green Cookbook. LC 97-19693. 224p. 1997. pap. 16.95 (*0-8092-2980-3*, 298030, Contemporary Bks) NTC Contemp Pub Co.

*__Richardson, Rosamund.__ Natural Superwoman: The Survival Guide for Women Who Have Too Much to Do. (Illus.). 208p. 2000. pap. 17.95 (*0-89087-981-8*) Celestial Arts.

Richardson, Rose & Yanovsky, Zal. Chez Piggy: Recipes from the Celebrated Restaurant & Bakery. (Illus.). 240p. 1998. pap. 24.95 (*1-55209-296-8*) Firefly Bks Ltd.

Richardson, Rosemund. Food from Green Places: Vegetarian Recipes from Garden & Countryside. (Illus.). 160p. 1998. 29.95 (*0-7892-0419-3*) Abbeville Pr.

Richardson, Roy, jt. auth. see Ames, Earline.

Richardson, Rufus B., ed. see Aeschines.

Richardson, Rupert N. The College Man & Our Rural Civilization. Clayton, Lawrence R., ed. (Illus.). 1989. write for info. (*0-910075-12-3*) Hardin-Simmons.
— Comanche Barrier: To the South Plains Settlement. 3rd ed. Jacobs, Kenneth R., ed. (Illus.). 278p. 1996. reprint ed. 29.95 (*1-57168-039-X*, Eakin Pr) Sunbelt Media.
— The Comanche Barrier to South Plains Settlement. 1993. reprint ed. lib. bdg. 75.00 (*0-7812-5948-7*) Rprt Serv.

Richardson, Rupert N. & Anderson, Adrian. Texas: The Lone Star State. 7th ed. 450p. (C). 1996. pap. text 47.00 (*0-13-487000-X*) P-H.

Richardson, Rupert N., et al. Texas: The Lone Star State. 4th ed. (Illus.). 464p. 1981. text 23.95 (*0-13-912444-6*) P-H.

*__Richardson, Rupert N., et al.__ Texas: The Lone Star State. 8th ed. 464p. 2000. pap. 32.00 (*0-13-028414-9*, Prentice Hall) P-H.

Richardson, Russell, jt. auth. see Stott, David.

Richardson, Ruth. Florencio Sanchez & the Argentine Theatre. 1974. 250.00 (*0-87968-227-2*) Gordon Pr.
— The Role of Women in the Life & Thought of the Early Schleiermacher (1768-1806) An Historical Overview. (Schleiermacher Studies & Translations: Vol. 7). 232p. 1991. 89.95 (*0-7734-9751-X*) E Mellen.

Richardson, Ruth & Thorne, Robert. The Builder Illustrations Index. (Illus.). 846p. 1995. 230.00 (*0-907101-06-2*, Pub. by Hutton Plus) Antique Collect.

Richardson, Ruth, ed. see Lange, Robert.

Richardson, Ruth, ed. see Schlegel, Dorothea.

Richardson, Ruth, tr. see Schlegel, Dorothea M.

Richardson, Ruth D., ed. Friedrich Schleiermacher's Toward a Theory of Sociable Conduct, & Essays on Its Intellectual-Cultural Context. LC 95-25509. (Publication of New Athenaeum-Neues Athenaeum Ser.: Vol. 4). 1995. 69.95 (*0-7734-8938-X*) E Mellen.
— New Atheneaum - Neues Athenaeum, 1992, Vol. 3. 226p. 1993. 49.95 (*0-7734-9274-7*) E Mellen.
— Schleiermacher in Context: Papers from the 1988 International Symposium on Schleiermacher at Herrnhut, the German Democratic Republic. LC 91-3611. (Schleiermacher Studies & Translations: Vol. 6). (Illus.). 472p. 1991. lib. bdg. 109.95 (*0-7734-9793-5*) E Mellen.

Richardson, S., jt. ed. see Shackel, B.

Richardson, S. D. Forests & Forestry in China: Changing Patterns of Resource Development. LC 89-24514. (Illus.). 352p. 1990. text 50.00 (*1-55963-023-X*); pap. text 32.00 (*1-55963-022-1*) Island Pr.

Richardson, S. M. Temporary Insanity. LC 96-90013. (Orig.). 1996. pap. 10.00 (*0-533-11861-1*) Vantage.

Richardson, Sally. A Circle of Life. 267p. 1998. pap. 14.95 (*0-913884-06-5*) Porphyrion Pr.

Richardson, Samuel. The Apprentice's Vade Mecum: or Young Man's Pocket-Companion, 3 pts. LC 92-2483. (Augustan Reprints Ser.: No. 169-170). 1975. reprint ed. 21.50 (*0-404-70169-8*, HD4885) AMS Pr.

Richardson, Samuel. Clarissa, 001. Sherburn, George, ed. LC 62-52256. (C). 1962. pap. 13.96 (*0-395-05164-9*, RivEd) HM.

Richardson, Samuel. Clarissa: Or the History of a Young Lady. Ross, Angus, ed. & intro. by. (Classics Ser.). 1,536p. 1986. pap. 24.95 (*0-14-043215-9*, Penguin Classics) Viking Penguin.
— Clarissa: Or, The History of a Young Lady - Comprehending the Most Important Concerns of Private Life; with a New Introduction to the AMS Edition by Florian Stuber & A Bibliographic Note by O M Brack, Jr, 8 vols., Set. LC 90-368. reprint ed. 765.00 (*0-404-64100-8*) AMS Pr.
— A Collection of the Moral & Instructive Sentiments, Maxims, Cautions, & Reflections, Contained in the Histories of Pamela, Clarissa, & Sir Charles Grandison. LC 92-9738. (Clarissa Project Ser.: Vol. 11). 1992. 76.50 (*0-404-64111-3*) AMS Pr.
— A Collection of the Moral & Instructive Sentiments, Maxims, Cautions & Reflexions, Contained in the Histories of Pamela, Clarissa, & Sir Charles Grandison. LC 80-22492. 448p. 1980. reprint ed. 75.00 (*0-8201-1357-3*) Schol Facsimiles.

*__Richardson, Samuel.__ The Complete Novels of Mr. Samuel Richardson, 19 vols. Incl. Pt. 1. History of Clarissa Harlowe. 272p. 1999. reprint ed. lib. bdg. 88.00 (*1-58201-131-1*); Pt. I. History of Sir Charles Gradison. 269p. 1999. reprint ed. lib. bdg. 88.00 (*1-58201-139-7*); Pt. 1. Pamela: or Virtue Rewarded. 280p. 1999. reprint ed. lib. bdg. 88.00 (*1-58201-127-3*); Pt. 2. History of Clarissa Harlowe. 326p. 1999. reprint ed. lib. bdg. (*1-58201-132-X*); Pt. 2. History of Sir Charles Gradison. 297p. 1999. reprint ed. lib. bdg. 88.00 (*1-58201-140-0*); Pt. 2. Pamela: or Virtue Rewarded. 330p. 1999. reprint ed. lib. bdg. 88.00 (*1-58201-128-1*); Pt. 3. History of Clarrisa Harlowe. 319p. 1999. reprint ed. lib. bdg. 88.00 (*1-58201-133-8*); Pt. 3. History of Sir Charles Gradison. 292p. 1999. reprint ed. lib. bdg. 88.00 (*1-58201-141-9*); Pt. 3. Pamela: or Virtue Rewarded. 332p. 1999. reprint ed. lib. bdg. 88.00 (*1-58201-129-X*); Pt. 4. History of Clarissa Harlowe. 333p. 1999. reprint ed. lib. bdg. 88.00 (*1-58201-134-6*); Pt. 4. History of Sir Charles Gradison. 304p. 1999. reprint ed. lib. bdg. 88.00 (*1-58201-142-7*); Pt. 4. Pamela: or Virtue Rewarded. 346p. 1999. reprint ed. lib. bdg. 88.00 (*1-58201-130-3*); Pt. 5. History of Clarissa Harlowe. 1999. reprint ed. lib. bdg. 88.00 (*1-58201-135-4*); Pt. 5. History of Sir Charles Gradison. 307p. 1999. reprint ed. lib. bdg. 88.00 (*1-58201-143-5*); Pt. 6. History of Clarissa Harlowe. 321p. 1999. reprint ed. lib. bdg. 88.00 (*1-58201-136-2*); Pt. 6. History of Sir Charles Gradison. 296p. 1999. reprint ed. lib. bdg. 88.00 (*1-58201-144-3*); Pt. 7. History of Clarissa Harlowe. 349p. 1999. reprint ed. lib. bdg. 88.00 (*1-58201-137-0*); Pt. 7. History of Sir Charles Gradison. 301p. 1999. reprint ed. lib. bdg. 88.00 (*1-58201-145-1*); Pt. 8. History of Clarissa Harlowe. 362p. 1999. reprint ed. lib. bdg. 88.00 (*1-58201-138-9*); 1999. reprint ed. Set lib. bdg. 1672.00 (*1-58201-126-5*) Classic Bks.

Richardson, Samuel. Correspondence of Samuel Richardson, 6 vols. Barbauld, Anna L., ed. LC 72-144675. reprint ed. write for info. (*0-404-05300-9*) AMS Pr.
— Letters & Passages Restored from the Original Manuscript of the History of Clarissa. LC 92-9737. (Clarissa Project Ser.: Vol. 10). 1992. 76.50 (*0-404-64110-5*) AMS Pr.
— Novels: Complete & Unabridged, 19 vols., Set. (BCL1-PR English Literature Ser.). 1992. reprint ed. lib. bdg. 1425.00 (*0-7812-7396-X*) Rprt Serv.
— Novels of Samuel Richardson, 19 vols. LC 75-114357. 1970. reprint ed. 1282.50 (*0-404-05310-6*) AMS Pr.

Richardson, Samuel. Pamela, 001. Duncan-Eaves, T. C. & Kimpel, B. D., eds. LC 71-134860. (Orig.). (C). 1971. pap. 13.96 (*0-395-11152-8*, RivEd) HM.

Richardson, Samuel. Pamela. 453p. (Orig.). 1991. pap. 7.95 (*0-460-87064-5*, Everyman's Classic Lib) Tuttle Pubng.
— Pamela: or Virtue Rewarded. Sabor, Petr, ed. (English Library). 544p. 1981. pap. 7.95 (*0-14-043140-3*) Viking Penguin.

Richardson, Samuel & Keymer, Tom. Samuel Richardson's Published Commentary on Clarissa, 1747-1765, 3 vols. Incl. Samuel Richardson's Published Commentary on Clarissa, 1747-1765. Brack, O. M. LC 97-17853. 1997. pap. (*1-85196-462-2*, Pub. by Pickering & Chatto); Samuel Richardson's Published Commentary on Clarissa, 1747-1765. LC 97-17853. 1997. (*1-85196-463-0*, Pub. by Pickering & Chatto); Samuel Richardson's Published Commentary on Clarissa, 1747-1765. LC 97-17853. 1997. (*1-85196-464-9*, Pub. by Pickering & Chatto); LC 97-17853. 1998. 360.00 (*1-85196-461-4*) Ashgate Pub Co.

Richardson, Sandy. The Girl Who Ate Chicken Feet & Other Stories. LC 97-9687. 144p. (J). 1998. 15.99 (*0-8037-2254-0*, Dial Yng Read) Peng Put Young Read.
— The Girl Who Ate Chicken Feet & Other Stories. LC 97-9687. (J). 1999. pap. 14.89 (*0-8037-2255-9*, Dial Yng Read) Peng Put Young Read.

Richardson, Sarah. Eighteenth-Century Ceramics: Products for a Civilized Society. (Illus.). 240p. 1999. text 59.95 (*0-7190-4464-2*) St Martin.

Richardson, Sarah, jt. auth. see Clark, Anna.

Richardson, Scott. MCSE Exam Notes: Proxy Server 2. LC 98-87585. (MCSE Exam Notes Ser.). 352p. 1998. pap. text 19.99 (*0-7821-2304-X*) Sybex.

Richardson, Selma K. Periodicals for School Media Programs. LC 77-25069. 419p. reprint ed. pap. 129.90 (*0-608-12590-3*, 202395200034) Bks Demand.

Richardson, Selma K., ed. Magazines for Children: A Guide for Parents, Teachers, & Librarians. 2nd ed. LC 90-45152. 139p. (C). 1991. pap. text 25.00 (*0-8389-0552-8*, 0552-8) ALA.
— Research about Nineteenth-Century Children & Books: Portrait Studies. LC 80-19165. (Monographs: No. 17). (Illus.). 145p. 1980. 8.00 (*0-87845-055-6*) U of Ill Grad Sch.

Richardson, Shannon, jt. auth. see Gunn, Brenda.

Richardson, Shawn. Biking Missouri's Rail-Trails. (Illus.). 96p. 1999. pap. text 8.95 (*1-885061-59-5*) Adventure Pubns.

*__Richardson, Shawn.__ Biking Ohio's Rail Trail. rev. ed. (Illus.). 2000. pap. 9.95 (*1-885061-86-2*) Adventure Pubns.

Richardson, Shawn. Biking Ohio's Rail Trails. (Illus.). 92p. (Orig.). 1996. pap. 8.95 (*1-885061-16-1*) Adventure Pubns.
— Biking Wisconsin's Rail-Trails. 168p. 1997. pap. text 9.95 (*1-885061-22-6*) Adventure Pubns.

Richardson, Shelley & Richardson, Bruce. A Tea for All Seasons: Celebrating Tea, Art, & Music at the Elmwood Inn. (Illus.). 116p. 1996. 19.95 (*1-889937-00-2*) Crescent Hill Bks.

Richardson, Stanley. Southeast Asian Management: Cases & Concepts. 302p. 1991. 42.50 (*9971-69-160-4*, Pub. by Sngapore Univ Pr) Coronet Bks.

Richardson, Stephen. The Eagle's Claw: Christians & the IRS. LC 96-77784. 208p. 1998. pap. 11.99 (*1-56384-128-2*) Huntington Hse.

Richardson, Stephen A. & Koller, Helene. Twenty-Two Years: Causes & Consequences of Mental Retardation. (Illus.). 416p. 1996. 46.95 (*0-674-21297-5*) HUP.

Richardson, Stephen C. Fluid Mechanics. (Illus.). 350p. (C). 1989. text 85.00 (*0-89116-671-8*) Hemisp Pub.

*__Richardson, Steve.__ Ricky Williams: Dreadlocks to Ditka. 200p. 1999. pap. 14.95 (*1-58261-144-0*, Pub. by Sprts Pubng) Partners-West.
— The Sweet Spot. 1998. mass mkt. 6.95 (*1-56333-628-6*) Masquerade.

*__Richardson, Steven H.__ Crossing the Chalk Line. 1999. pap. 12.95 (*1-890611-11-5*) Otter Crk Pr.

Richardson, Stewart, ed. see Bucholz, Barbara B. & Crane, Margaret.

Richardson, Stewart, ed. see Carr, Camilla.

Richardson, Stewart, ed. see Hanks, Stephen.

Richardson, Stewart, ed. see Hernon, Peter.

Richardson, Stewart, ed. see Midgley, Leslie.

Richardson, Stewart, ed. see Mitroff, Ian I. & Bennis, Warren G.

Richardson, Stewart, ed. see O'Faolain, Sean.

Richardson, Stewart, ed. see Parrish, Richard.

Richardson, Stewart, ed. see Silverman, Chip.

Richardson, Sue, ed. Reshaping the Labour Market: Regulation, Efficiency & Equality in Australia. LC 99-30802. (Reshaping Australian Institutions Ser.). (Illus.). 288p. (C). 1999. 64.95 (*0-521-65281-2*); pap. 34.95 (*0-521-65424-6*) Cambridge U Pr.

Richardson, Sue, jt. auth. see Richardson, Mike.

Richardson, Susan, jt. auth. see Richardson, Mike.

Richardson, Susan, jt. auth. see Travers, Peter.

Richardson, Sylvia O. The "D" Book: Doctors Ask Questions about Dyslexia: A Review of Medical Research. (Orton Emeritus Ser.). 1994. pap. 5.00 (*0-89214-007-0*) Intl Dyslexia.

Richardson, Ted. Wolf & the Cougar. large type ed. (Dales Large Print Ser.). (Illus.). 214p. 1996. pap. 18.99 (*1-85389-641-1*) Ulverscroft.

Richardson, Terry. Composites: A Design Guide. LC 87-609. (Illus.). 344p. 1987. 34.95 (*0-8311-1173-9*) Indus Pr.
— A Guide to Metrics. LC 78-61695. (Illus.). 1978. pap. 12.00 (*0-911168-38-9*) Prakken.
— Modern Industrial Plastics. LC 72-92621. 1974. 24.45 (*0-672-97657-9*, Bobbs) Macmillan.

*__Richardson, Terry.__ Son of Bob. (Illus.). 95p. 2000. pap. 35.00 (*4-947648-87-2*, Pub. by Little More) Dist Art Pubs.

Richardson, Terry. Total Quality Management. LC 96-16564. (Mechanical Technology Ser.). 448p. 1996. mass mkt. 63.95 (*0-8273-7192-6*) Delmar.

Richardson, Terry L. Industrial Plastics. 2nd ed. (Mechanical Technology Ser.). 1989. text 52.50 (*0-8273-3392-7*) Delmar.
— Total Quality Management Basics: A Primer for Technicians. 288p. 1997. teacher ed. write for info. (*0-8273-8210-3*) Delmar.

Richardson, Terry L. & Lokensgard, Erik. Industrial Plastics: Theory & Applications. 3rd ed. (Mechanical Technology Ser.). 544p. 1996. mass mkt. 77.95 (*0-8273-6558-6*) Delmar.

Richardson, Terry L. & Tolboldt, William K. Auto Body Repairing & Refinishing. rev. ed. LC 93-21748. Orig. Title: Auto Body Repairing & Repainting. (Illus.). 377p. 1993. text 37.28 (*0-87006-018-X*) Goodheart.

Richardson, Theresa R. & Fisher, Donald. Development of the Social Sciences in the United States & Canada: The Role of Philanthropy. LC 98-28084. (David C. Anchin Ser.). 1999. 73.25 (*1-56750-405-1*); pap. 24.95 (*1-56750-406-X*) Ablx Pub.

Richardson, Thomas J., jt. auth. see Peck, Merton J.

Richardson, Tim. Jump Starts: Wit & Wisdom to Super Charge Your Day LC 98-73460. 212 p. 1998. 12.00 (*0-9667386-0-8*) B Walter Melanoma.

Richardson, Tim, ed. see Wycoff, Joyce.

*__Richardson, Tim H.__ Functional Organic & Polymeric Materials. LC 99-31707. 1616p. 2000. text 175.00 (*0-471-98724-7*) Wiley.

*__Richardson, Tracey.__ Double Take Out. LC 98-48242. (Stevie Houston Mystery Ser.: No. 3). 224p. 1999. pap. 11.95 (*1-56280-244-5*) Naiad Pr.

Richardson, Tracey. Last Rites: A Stevie Houston Mystery. LC 96-45488. 1997. pap. 11.95 (*1-56280-164-3*) Naiad Pr.
— Over the Line: A Stevie Houston Mystery. LC 97-52740. 240p. (Orig.). 1998. pap. 11.95 (*1-56280-202-X*) Naiad Pr.

Richardson, Tracie, jt. auth. see Hooker, Monique.

Richardson-Tremble, Teedie. Just a Mother's Empty Soul. 1997. pap. write for info. (*1-57553-531-9*) Watermrk Pr.

Richardson, Trevor. The Chair: From Artifact to Object. Beesch, Ruth K., ed. (Illus.). 40p. 1991. pap. text 10.00 (*0-9627541-2-9*) UNC Greensboro.

Richardson, V. C. Diseases of Small Domestic Rodents. LC 97-6214. (Library of Veterinary Practice). (Illus.). 224p. 1997. write for info. (*0-632-04132-3*) Blackwell Sci.

*__Richardson, V. C. G.__ Diseases of Domestic Guinea Pigs. 2nd ed. LC 99-86938. (Library of Veterinary Practice). (Illus.). 162p. 2000. pap. text 36.95 (*0-632-05209-0*, Pub. by Blckwell Science) Iowa St U Pr.

*__Richardson, Virginia.__ Rabbits: Health, Husbandry & Diseases. LC 99-87566. (Illus.). 184p. 2000. pap. text 34.95 (*0-632-05221-X*, Pub. by Blckwell Science) Iowa St U Pr.

Richardson, Virginia, ed. Constructivist Teacher Education. LC 97-204749. 1997. pap. text 24.95 (*0-7507-0616-3*, Falmer Pr) Taylor & Francis.
— Teacher Change & the Staff Development Process. 240p. (C). 1994. text 40.00 (*0-8077-3361-X*); pap. text 18.95 (*0-8077-3360-1*) Tchrs Coll.

*__Richardson, Virginia & Association for Gerontology Education in Social Work Staff, compiled by.__ Teaching Gerontological Social Work: A Compendium of Model Syllabi. (Teaching Social Work Ser.). 157p. 1999. pap. text 14.00 (*0-87293-067-X*) Coun Soc Wk Ed.

Richardson, Virginia E. Retirement Counseling: A Handbook for Gerontology Practitioners. LC 92-48349. (Life Styles & Issues in Aging Ser.: Vol. 1). 224p. 1993. 31.95 (*0-8261-7020-X*) Springer Pub.

Richardson, W. J. Heidegger: Through Phenomenology to Thought. 3rd ed. (Phaenomenologica Ser.: No. 13). 797p. 1974. lib. bdg. 79.00 (*90-247-0246-1*, Pub. by M Nijhoff) Kluwer Academic.

Richardson, W. John. Marine Mammals & Noise. 1998. pap. text 39.95 (*0-12-588441-9*) Acad Pr.

Richardson, W. Mark & Wildman, Wesley, eds. Religion & Science: History, Method, Dialogue. LC 95-47045. 470p. (C). 1996. 75.00 (*0-415-91666-6*); pap. 29.99 (*0-415-91667-4*) Routledge.

Richardson, W. Mark, jt. auth. see McLain, F. Michael.

Richardson, Wade. Reading & Variant in Petronius: Studies in the French Humanists & Their Manuscript Sources. 187p. 1993. text 60.00 (*0-8020-2866-7*) U of Toronto Pr.

Richardson, Wally G. & Huett, Lenora. The Spiritual Value of Gem Stones. LC 79-54728. 176p. 1980. pap. 8.95 (*0-87516-383-1*) DeVorss.

Richardson, Wally G., et al. The Path to Illumination. LC 82-71211. (Illus.). 248p. (Orig.). 1982. pap. 9.95 (*0-87516-480-3*) DeVorss.

Richardson, Walter C. Report of the Royal Commission of 1552. LC 72-86893. 302p. 1974. 15.00 (*0-937058-08-4*) West Va U Pr.

Richardson, Wendy. The Link Between ADD & Addiction: Getting the Help You Deserve. LC 97-5122. 315p. (Orig.). 1997. pap. 16.00 (*1-57683-004-7*) Pinon Press.

Richardson, William. Anecdotes of the Russian Empire: In a Series of Letters, Written a Few Years Ago, from St. Petersburg. LC 79-115580. (Russia Observed, Series I). 1970. reprint ed. 26.95 (*0-405-03059-2*) Ayer.
— Essays on Shakespeare's Dramatic Character of Sir John Falstaff & on His Female Characters. LC 76-144676. reprint ed. 29.50 (*0-404-05307-6*) AMS Pr.
— Essays on Shakespeare's Dramatic Characters of Richard III, King Lear & Timon of Athens. LC 76-144676. reprint ed. 31.50 (*0-404-05308-4*) AMS Pr.
— Philosophical Analysis & Illustration of Some of Shakespeare's Remarkable Characters. rev. ed. LC 17-30453. 36.00 (*0-404-05309-2*) AMS Pr.

Richardson, William, jt. auth. see McCulloch, Gary.

Richardson, William B. & Moore, Gary. Working in Horticulture. (Career Preparation for Agriculture-Agribusiness Ser.). (Illus.). 1980. text 29.96 (*0-07-052285-5*) McGraw.

Richardson, William B., jt. auth. see Feldhusen, John F.

Richardson, William D. Democracy, Bureaucracy, & Character: Founding Thought. LC 96-51890. (Studies in Government & Public Policy). 198p. 1997. 29.95 (*0-7006-0824-9*); pap. 16.95 (*0-7006-0825-7*) U Pr of KS.
— Melville's "Benito Cereno" An Interpretation, with an Annotated Text & a Concordance. LC 86-70369. 246p. (C). 1987. lib. bdg. 35.00 (*0-89089-274-1*) Carolina Acad Pr.

Richardson, William D., et al, eds. Ethics & Character: The Pursuit of Democratic Virtues. LC 98-42285. 352p. 1999. pap. 28.00 (*0-89089-909-6*) Carolina Acad Pr.

An Asterisk (*) at the beginning of an entry indicates that the title is appearing for the first time.

Richardson, William D., jt. ed. see Jessen, Kristjan R.
Richardson, William F., tr. see Napier, John.
Richardson, William F., tr. see Vesalius, Andreas.
Richardson, William G., jt. auth. see Pritchett, Norman M.
*__Richardson, William J.__ Loving Obedience. LC 00-26977. 2000. pap. 12.99 (*1-881273-26-1*) Northfield Pub.
Richardson, William J., jt. auth. see Muller, John P.
Richardson, William J., jt. ed. see Muller, John P.
Richardson, Willis. Plays & Pageants from the Life of the Negro. 1990. 25.00 (*0-87498-028-3*) Assoc Pubs DC.
— Plays & Pageants from the Life of the Negro. abr. ed. LC 93-27075. (Illus.). 400p. 1993. text 40.00 (*0-87805-657-2*) U Pr of Miss.
— Plays & Pageants from the Life of the Negro. LC 93-27075. (Illus.). 400p. 1993. reprint ed. pap. 17.95 (*0-87805-658-0*) U Pr of Miss.
Richardson, Winifred L. Balance, Balance, Balance. (Illus.). 75p. 1996. pap. text 7.95 (*0-9655873-0-4*) W L Richardson.
Richardson, Wyman. The House on Nauset Marsh. (Illus.). 1980. reprint ed. pap. 7.95 (*0-85699-046-9*) Chatham Pr.
— The House on Nauset Marsh. LC 97-23726. (Illus.). 224p. 1997. reprint ed. pap. 12.00 (*0-88150-402-5*, Pub. by Countryman) Norton.
Richardus, Peter. Project Surveying: General Adjustment & Optimization Techniques with Applications to Engineering Surveying. 640p. (C). 1984. text 194.00 (*90-6191-519-8*, Pub. by A A Balkema); pap. text 110.00 (*90-6191-526-0*, Pub. by A A Balkema) Ashgate Pub Co.
Richardus, Peter, ed. Tibetan Lives: Three Himalayan Autobiographies. (Illus.). 210p. 1998. text 42.00 (*0-7007-1023-X*, Pub. by Curzon Pr Ltd) UH Pr.
Richardz, Klaus & Limbrunner, Alfred. World of Bats. (Illus.). 192p. 1993. 35.95 (*0-86622-540-4*, TS192) TFH Pubns.
Richardz, Robert. The Highest Price. 19p. (Orig.). 1995. pap., teacher ed. write for info. (*0-9636067-1-9*) Grace TX.
Richart, Robert W. Gyorgy Ligeti: A Bio-Bibliography, 30. LC 90-14022. (Bio-Bibliographies in Music Ser.: No. 30). 200p. 1990. lib. bdg. 55.00 (*0-313-25174-6*, RGL/, Greenwood Pr) Greenwood.
Richartz, Gisela. Einfluss Exogener und Endogener Faktoren Auf die Fruchtkoerperentwicklung des Basidiomyceten Pleurotus Ostreatus. (Bibliotheca Mycologica: Vol. 121). (GER., Illus.). 165p. 1988. 48.00 (*3-443-59022-5*, Pub. by Gebruder Borntraeger) Balogh.
Richarz, Monika, ed. Jewish Life in Germany: Memoirs from Three Centuries. Rosenfeld, Stella P. & Rosenfeld, Sidney, trs. LC 90-38733. (Modern Jewish Experience Ser.). (Illus.). 496p. 1991. 49.95 (*0-253-35024-7*) Ind U Pr.
Richarz, Sherrill. Understanding Children. (Psychology). 222p. 1980. mass mkt. 31.75 (*0-8299-0337-2*) West Pub.
Richason, Benjamin F. Introduction to Remote Sensing of the Environment. 2nd ed. LC 82-83014. (National Council for Geographic Education, Pacesetter Ser.). (Illus.). 594p. 1983. reprint ed. pap. 184.20 (*0-7837-9721-4*, 206045200005) Bks Demand.
*__Richburg, Keith B.__ Out of America: A Black Man Confronts Africa. LC 97-47710. 272p. (C). 1998. pap. 13.00 (*0-15-600583-2*) Harcourt.
Richburg, Shirley. Benny & the Grocer. (Illus.). (Orig.). (J). (gr. 2-5). 1998. pap. 4.95 (*0-9658432-2-X*) Peoples MD.
— Country Potatoes & Queens. LC 97-92646. iv, 50p. 1998. pap. 9.95 (*0-9658432-3-8*) Peoples MD.
— Just One of the Boas. (Orig.). 1998. pap. 14.95 (*0-9658432-1-1*) Peoples MD.
— Reflections. (Illus.). vii, 50p. 1997. pap. 9.95 (*0-9658432-0-3*) Peoples MD.
Richburg, Shirley, ed. see Acevedo, Judith & Tokarski, Henry J.
Richburg, Shirley, ed. see Cirino, Leonard J., et al.
Richburg, Shirley, ed. see White, Kelley J.
Richburg, Thomas J. Coming Out of the Dark: God's Will to Change the Way You Live!, 2 vols., Vol. 1. abr. ed. Johnson, P. M. & Cooke, Donna, eds. 255p. 1996. 34.99 (*1-889466-25-5*, HB001001); pap. 19.50 (*1-889466-26-3*, HB001001) One Way Intl.
— The Law vs. Grace. 4th ed. (Illus.). 100p. 1996. reprint ed. 14.95 (*1-889466-31-X*, HB001002); reprint ed. pap. 10.95 (*1-889466-32-8*, HB001002) One Way Intl.
— Ode to Yahshua: Collective Works of Thomas J. Richburg. large type ed. Johnson, P. M., ed. (Illus.). 75p. 1996. 15.95 (*1-889466-33-6*, PB001002); pap. 10.95 (*1-889466-34-4*, PB001002) One Way Intl.
Richbury, T. J. A Holy People in a Holy Land. Smith, Glen, ed. (Illus.). (J). (gr. 5-12). 1996. disk 24.95 (*1-889466-30-1*, PB001001) One Way Intl.
— A Holy People in a Holy Land. 3rd ed. Smith, Glen, ed. (Illus.). 150p. (YA). (gr. 5-12). 1996. reprint ed. 24.95 (*1-889466-27-1*, PB001001); reprint ed. pap. 19.95 (*1-889466-28-X*, PB001001) One Way Intl.
Richcreek, John. Structure of Intelligent Justice. LC 87-71747. (Illus.). 650p. (Orig.). 1988. pap. 21.50 (*0-9600434-1-1*) Camda.
Riche, Edward. Rare Birds. 272p. 1997. pap. write for info. (*0-385-25635-3*) Doubleday.
Riche, Pierre. The Carolingians: A Family Who Forged Europe. Allen, Michael I., tr. from FRE. LC 91-303532. (Middle Ages Ser.). 424p. (Orig.). (C). 1993. text 49.95 (*0-8122-3062-0*); pap. text 20.95 (*0-8122-1342-4*) U of Pa Pr.
— Daily Life in the World of Charlemagne. McNamara, Jo A., tr. from FRE. LC 78-53330. (Middle Ages Ser.). (Illus.). 352p. (C). 1978. pap. text 21.50 (*0-8122-1096-4*) U of Pa Pr.
— Education et Culture dans l'Occident Medieval. (Collected Studies: Vol. 420). 304p. 1993. 109.95 (*0-86078-391-X*, Pub. by Variorum) Ashgate Pub Co.
Riche, Robert. Poppy & Me. 220p. mass mkt. 4.99 (*1-896329-67-5*) Picasso Publ.
Riche, Robert. What Are We Doing in Latin America? A Novel about Connecticut. LC 90-53322. 208p. 1991. 22.00 (*1-877946-01-X*) Permanent Pr.
Riche, Robert, jt. auth. see Bauman, Lawrence.
Riche, William La, see La Riche, William.
Richeal, Kip, jt. auth. see Sandusky, Jerry.
Richeimer, Mary J. My Phoenix Song. 1997. pap. 56.95 (*1-57553-646-3*) Watermrk Pr.
Richek, Margaret A. Richek World of Words, 4 vols. 4th ed. (C). 1995. 43.16 (*0-395-78235-X*); 49.56 (*0-395-78236-8*) HM.
— The World of Words. (C). Date not set. write for info. (*0-395-77733-X*) HM.
— The World of Words. 1992. pap. text. write for info. (*0-318-68492-6*) HM.
— The World of Words, 4 vols. (C). 1995. pap. 35.56 (*0-395-75051-2*) HM.
— The World of Words. 2nd ed. 352p. 1988. write for info. (*0-318-63333-7*); pap. 23.56 (*0-685-44112-1*) HM.
— The World of Words, 3 vols. 3rd ed. (C). 1991. pap. text, teacher ed. 3.16 (*0-395-58912-6*) HM.
— The World of Words, 4 vols. 4th ed. (C). 1995. pap. text 34.36 (*0-395-71984-4*) HM.
*__Richek, Margaret A. & Caldwell, JoAnne S.__ Reading Problems: Assessment & Teaching Strategies. 4th ed. 416p. 2000. 65.00 (*0-205-33022-3*) Allyn.
Richek, Margaret A., jt. auth. see Caldwell, Joanne.
Richel, Veronica C. The German Stage, Seventeen Sixty-Seven to Eighteen Hundred & Ninety: A Directory of Playwrights & Plays, 7. LC 87-25155. (Bibliographies & Indexes in the Performing Arts Ser.: No. 7). 244p. 1988. lib. bdg. 59.95 (*0-313-24990-3*, RGS/) Greenwood.
Richelet, Pierre. Dictionnaire Francois, 2 vols. in 1. (FRE.). 1128p. 1973. reprint ed. write for info. (*3-487-04587-7*) G Olms Pubs.
Richelieu, Frank E. The Art of Being Yourself. LC 92-53722. 320p. (Orig.). 1992. pap. 12.95 (*0-917849-15-9*) Sci of Mind.
— Reincarnation: The Inheritance of a Soul. 32p. (Orig.). 1991. pap. 3.50 (*0-941992-25-X*) Los Arboles Pub.
Richelieu, Peter. A Soul's Journey. Orig. Title: From the Turret. (Illus.). 208p. 1989. pap. 12.00 (*0-85030-812-7*, Pub. by Aqrn Pr) Harper SF.
Richels, Richard, jt. auth. see Manne, Alan.
Richelson, Jeffrey T. American's Space Sentinels: DSP Satellites & National Security. LC 98-47339. (Modern War Studies). (Illus.). 328p. 1999. 35.00 (*0-7006-0942-3*) U Pr of KS.
— A Century of Spies: Intelligence in the Twentieth Century. (Illus.). 544p. 1995. 35.00 (*0-19-507391-6*) OUP.
— A Century of Spies: Intelligence in the Twentieth Century. (Illus.). 544p. 1997. reprint ed. pap. 19.95 (*0-19-511390-X*) OUP.
— Foreign Intelligence Organizations. 304p. 1988. text 45.00 (*0-88730-121-5*, HarpBusn) HarpInfo.
— Foreign Intelligence Organizations. 304p. 1988. pap. text 19.95 (*0-88730-122-3*, HarpBusn) HarpInfo.
— Social Choice Theory & Soviet National Security Decisionmaking. (CISA Working Papers: No. 37). 43p. (Orig.). 1982. pap. 15.00 (*0-86682-048-5*) Ctr Intl Relations.
— Sword & Shield: Soviet Intelligence & Security Apparatus. LC 85-15073. 304p. 1985. text 39.95 (*0-88730-035-9*, HarpBusn) HarpInfo.
— The U. S. Intelligence Community. 4th ed. LC 98-52830. 544p. 1999. pap. text 37.00 (*0-8133-6893-6*, Pub. by Westview) HarpC.
— United States Strategic Reconnaissance: Photographic - Imaging Satellites. (CISA Working Papers: No. 38). 51p. (Orig.). 1983. pap. 15.00 (*0-86682-050-7*) Ctr Intl Relations.
Richelson, Jeffrey T. & Ball, Desmond J. The Ties That Bind: Intelligence Co-operation Between the UKUSA Countries. (Illus.). 420p. 1986. text 34.95 (*0-04-327092-1*) Routledge.
— The Ties That Bind: Intelligent Cooperation Between the Ukusa Countries. rev. ed. 420p. (C). 1990. text 49.95 (*0-685-54061-8*) Routledge.
Richelson, Jeffrey T., ed. see National Security Archive Staff & Chadwyck-Healey Staff.
Richelson, Paul W., ed. The Permanent Collection of Twentieth Century Prints: Ohio University Gallery of Fine Art. LC 84-52582. (Illus.). 360p. (Orig.). 1985. pap. 14.95 (*0-933041-00-4*) Gallery Fine Art Ohio U.
Richelson, Paul W., ed. see Bunnell, Peter C.
Richemont, Enid. The Glass Bird. LC 92-54585. (Illus.). 112p. (J). (gr. 3-6). 1993. 14.95 (*1-56402-195-5*) Candlewick Pr.
— The Magic Skateboard. LC 92-53010. (Illus.). 80p. (J). (gr. 3-6). 1993. 14.95 (*1-56402-132-7*) Candlewick Pr.
— The Time Tree. (J). (gr. 3-7). 1990. 12.95 (*0-316-74452-2*) Little.
Richen, Geshe S. The Three Principal Aspects of the Path: An Oral Teaching by Geshe Sonam Rinchen on Tsongkhapa's Lam Gri Gtso Bo Rham Gsum. Sonam, Ruth, ed. & tr. by. from TIB. LC 99-25974. 200p. 1999. pap. 14.95 (*1-55939-116-2*) Snow Lion Pubns.
Richenbacher, Wayne E. Mechanical Cardiac Assistance. LC 99-33746. (Vademecum Ser.). 1999. spiral bd. 45.00 (*1-57059-530-5*) Landes Bioscience.
Richens, Calvin. Time Travelers & Other People. (Illus.). 69p. (Orig.). 1993. pap. 9.95 (*1-882892-01-1*) Creat Energies.
Richens, David T. The Chemistry of Aqua Ions. LC 96-30341. 604p. 1997. 320.00 (*0-471-97058-1*) Wiley.
Richens, Lane, jt. auth. see Talbot, Richard K.
Richens, Marvin G. Dreams of Reality. 54p. 1997. pap. 8.00 (*0-8059-4032-4*) Dorrance.
Richer, ed. see Nerval, Gerard De.
Richer, Cliff, ed. see Sequoia Audubon Society Staff.
Richer, Elaine, jt. auth. see Palmer, Ralph.
Richer, Jean. Sacred Geography of the Ancient Greeks: Astrological Symbolism in Art, Architecture, & Landscape. Rhone, Christine, tr. from FRE. LC 94-11960. (SUNY Series in Western Esoteric Traditions). (Illus.). 319p. (C). 1994. text 74.50 (*0-7914-2023-X*); pap. text 24.95 (*0-7914-2024-8*) State U NY Pr.
Richer, Lois. Baby on the Way. (Love Inspired Ser.: Vol. 73). 1999. mass mkt. 4.50 (*0-373-87073-6*, 1-87073-2) Harlequin Bks.
— Daddy on the Way: Brides of the Seasons. (Love Inspired Ser.: No. 79). 1999. per. 4.50 (*0-373-87079-5*, 1-87079-9) Harlequin Bks.
— Faithfully Yours: Faith, Hope & Charity. (Love Inspired Ser.). 1998. per. 4.50 (*0-373-87015-9*, 1-87015-3) Harlequin Bks.
*__Richer, Lois.__ His Answered Prayer. (Love Inspired Ser.: Bk. 115). 2000. mass mkt. 4.50 (*0-373-87121-X*, 1-87121-9, Steeple Hill) Harlequin Bks.
Richer, Lois. A Home, a Heart, a Husband. 1999. per. 4.50 (*0-373-87050-7*, 1-87050-0, Mira Bks) Harlequin Bks.
— Hopeful Heart. (Love Inspired Ser.). 1998. per. 4.50 (*0-373-87023-X*, Steeple Hill) Harlequin Bks.
*__Richer, Lois.__ Mother's Day Miracle. (Love Inspired Ser.: Vol. 101). 2000. per. 4.50 (*0-373-87107-4*) Harlequin Bks.
— Promise Given. (Castles of the Heart Ser.). 2000. pap. 12.99 (*0-8054-2182-3*) Broadman.
Richer, Lois. Sweet Charity: Faith,Hope& Charity. (Love & Laughter Ser.). 1998. per. 4.50 (*0-373-87032-9*, Steeple Hill) Harlequin Bks.
— This Child of Mine. (Love Inspired Ser.: Bk. 59). 1999. per. 4.50 (*0-373-87059-0*, 1-87059-1, Harlequin) Harlequin Bks.
*__Richer, Lois.__ Wedding on the Way. (Love Inspired Ser.: Bk. 85). 1999. per. 4.50 (*0-373-87085-X*, 1-87085-6) Harlequin Bks.
Richer, Lois. A Will & a Wedding. 1997. per. 4.50 (*0-373-87009-4*, 1-87009-6) Harlequin Bks.
Richer, Paul. Artistic Anatomy. Hale, Robert B., ed. (Illus.). 256p. 1986. pap. 24.95 (*0-8230-0297-7*) Watsn-Guptill.
Richer, Stephen & Weir, Lorna, eds. Beyond Political Correctness: Toward the Inclusive University. 232p. 1995. pap. text 17.95 (*0-8020-6010-2*) U of Toronto Pr.
— Beyond Political Correctness: Towards the Inclusive University. LC 95-178435. 1995. pap. text 19.95 (*0-8020-7748-X*) U of Toronto Pr.
Richer, Stephen, ed. see Barker, Arthur E.
Richeri, G., jt. ed. see Bianchi, A.
Richerson, jt. ed. see Cranmer.
Richerson, D., ed. Modern Ceramic Engineering: Properties, Processing, & Use in Design. 2nd ed. (Materials Engineering Ser.: Vol. 1). (Illus.). 880p. 1992. text 175.00 (*0-8247-8634-3*) Dekker.
Richerson, David W. The Magic of Ceramics. LC 99-56648. (Illus.). 250p. 2000. 45.00 (*1-57498-050-5*, G041) Am Ceramic.
*__Richerson, Margaret Settle & Jones, Mary Josephine.__ Diamonds, Rubies & Sand, the Story of Philip Arnold of the Great Diamond Fraud & His Connection with Elizabethtown, Kentucky. 26p. 1999. pap. 6.00 (*0-931244-16-1*) Hardin County Historical Society.
Richerson, Peter J., jt. auth. see Boyd, Robert.
Richert, Calvin M. & Richert, Carolyn H. The Think Space: A Low-Stress Behavior Management Technique, Especially for Early Childhood. LC 96-60311. (Illus.). xvi, 177p. (Orig.). 1996. pap. 14.95 (*0-9651971-9-0*) Take V Publns.
Richert, Carolyn H., jt. auth. see Richert, Calvin M.
Richert, Donald, jt. auth. see Kelley, John L.
Richert, E. Susanne & Feldhusen, John. Special Populations of Gifted Learners. Jenkins-Friedman, Reva C. et al, eds. 1991. pap. 14.99 (*0-89824-528-1*) Trillium Pr.
Richert, John P. West German Lay Judges: Recruitment & Representativeness. LC 82-20251. (Illus.). 233p. 1983. reprint ed. pap. 72.30 (*0-608-04504-7*, 206524900001) Bks Demand.
Richert, R. & Blumen, A., eds. Disorder Effects on Relaxation Processes. LC 93-39077. 1994. write for info. (*0-387-57327-5*) Spr-Verlag.
Richert, Sandy, ed. Cleveland As a Center of Regional American Art. 160p. (Orig.). (C). 1994. pap. 12.50 (*0-9639562-3-X*) Clevelnd Art.
Riches. First World Hunger: Food Security & Welfare Politics. 218p. 1998. pap. 22.95 (*0-312-21415-4*) St Martin.
Riches, jt. auth. see Keenan, K.
Riches, Catherine, jt. auth. see Diagram Group Staff.
Riches, B. E. Electric Circuit Theory. (Illus.). 288p. 1989. pap. 39.00 (*0-85274-041-7*); disk 270.00 (*0-7503-0080-9*) IOP Pub.
Riches, Brenda. Something to Madden the Moon. 1997. pap. 7.95 (*0-88801-156-3*, Pub. by Turnstone Pr) Genl Dist Srvs.
Riches, C., jt. auth. see Parker, C.
Riches, Colin R. & Morgan, Colin. Human Resource Management in Education. (Management in Education Ser.). 192p. 1990. 123.00 (*0-335-09251-9*); pap. 34.95 (*0-335-09250-0*) OpUniv Pr.
Riches, Collin. Developing Interviewing Skills in Education. 224p. 1988. lib. bdg. 35.00 (*0-415-00581-7*) Routledge.
Riches, Cromwell A. Unanimity Role & the League of Nations. LC 70-174318. reprint ed. 39.50 (*0-404-05330-0*) AMS Pr.
Riches, David. Northern Nomadic Hunter-Gatherer: A Humanistic Approach. (Studies in Anthropology). 1982. text 95.00 (*0-12-587620-3*) Acad Pr.
Riches, Francine, jt. auth. see Dann, Lucy.
*__Riches, Gordon & Dawson, Pam.__ An Intimate Loneliness: Supporting Bereaved Parents & Siblings. LC 99-29752. (Facing Death Ser.). 224p. 2000. 28.95 (*0-335-19972-0*) Taylor & Francis.
Riches, Graham. First World Hunger: Food Security & Welfare Politics. LC 96-15979. 218p. 1997. text 59.95 (*0-312-16107-7*) St Martin.
*__Riches, John.__ The Bible. LC 99-59056. (Very Short Introductions Ser.). (Illus.). 144p. 2000. pap. 8.95 (*0-19-285343-0*) OUP.
Riches, John E. A Century of New Testament Study. LC 93-23575. 256p. 1993. pap. 17.00 (*1-56338-064-1*) TPI PA.
— Matthew. (New Testament Guides Ser.: Vol. 1). 112p. 1996. pap. 12.50 (*1-85075-741-0*, Pub. by Sheffield Acad) CUP Services.
— The World of Jesus: First-Century Judaism in Crisis. (Understanding Jesus Today Ser.). 157p. (C). 1990. text 34.95 (*0-521-38505-9*); pap. text 10.95 (*0-521-38676-4*) Cambridge U Pr.
Riches, John E., ed. The Analogy of Beauty: The Theology of Hans Urs von Balthasar. 256p. 47.95 (*0-567-09351-4*, Pub. by T & T Clark) Bks Intl VA.
Riches, John E., ed. see Barclay, John M.
Riches, John E., ed. see Best, Ernest E.
Riches, John E., ed. see Hubner, Hans.
Riches, John E., ed. see Von Balthasar, Hans U.
Riches, Naomi. Agricultural Revolution in Norfolk. 2nd ed. (Illus.). 194p. 1967. reprint ed. 32.00 (*0-7146-1356-8*, BHA-01356, Pub. by F Cass Pubs) Intl Spec Bk.
Riches, Pamela, jt. ed. see Gore, Martin.
Riches, Pierre. Back to Basics. (C). 1988. 39.00 (*0-85439-227-0*, Pub. by St Paul Pubns) St Mut.
*__Riches, Pierre.__ Back to Basics: Catholic Faith in Today's World. 2000. pap. 16.00 (*1-930051-30-1*) Lantern Books.
*__Riches, Samantha.__ St. George: Hero Martyr & Myth. 2000. 27.95 (*0-7509-2452-7*, Pub. by Sutton Publng) Intl Pubs Mktg.
*__Riches, Sue & Riches, Victoria.__ Frigid Women. Medcalf, Gordon, ed. (Illus.). 240p. 2000. pap. 14.95 (*0-9530575-2-6*, Pub. by Travellerseye Ltd) Midpt Trade.
Riches, Victoria, jt. auth. see Riches, Sue.
Riches, Vivienne C. Everyday Social Interaction: A Program for People with Disabilities. LC 95-53994. (Illus.). 1996. 41.95 (*1-55766-258-4*) P H Brookes.
— Standards of Work Performance: A Functional Assessment & Training Manual for Training People with Disabilities for Employment. 304p. 1993. pap. 45.00 (*0-86433-090-1*, 0901, Pub. by MacLennan & Petty) P H Brookes.
Riches, Waine, ed. Utah Domestic Relations Manual. 3rd ed. (Utah Legal Services Manuals). 495p. 1992. ring bd. 175.00 (*1-891414-02-X*) Utah Legal.
Riches, William T. Civil Rights Movement. LC 96-40415. 176p. 1997. text 55.00 (*0-312-17403-9*) St Martin.
— Civil Rights Movement: Struggle & Resistance. LC 96-40415. 196p. 1997. pap. 19.95 (*0-312-17404-7*) St Martin.
Richesin, L. Dale & Bouchard, Larry D., eds. Interpreting Disciples: Practical Theology in the Disciples of Christ. LC 86-30072. 278p. (Orig.). 1987. pap. text 14.95 (*0-87565-072-4*) Tex Christian.
Richesin, L. Dale, jt. ed. see Mahan, Brian.
Richeson, jt. auth. see Marino.
Richeson, D. H., jt. auth. see Harrington, C. A.
Richeson, Hawley, ed. see Sanchez, Ray.
Richeson, J. David, jt. auth. see Marino, Michael F.
Richeson, J. David, jt. auth. see Marino, Michael F., III.
Richeson, Scott. Juvenile Deviance in Japan: Result of Culture, Institution, or Community? LC 97-66600. 60p. 1997. pap. 12.95 (*0-942511-72-7*) OICJ.
Richet, Charles. The Natural History of a Savant. Lodge, Oliver J., tr. from FRE. LC 74-26288. (History, Philosophy & Sociology of Science Ser.). 1975. reprint ed. 23.95 (*0-405-06614-7*) Ayer.
— Thirty Years of Psychical Research: Being a Treatise on Metaphysics. De Brath, Stanley, tr. from FRE. LC 75-7397. (Perspectives in Psychical Research Ser.). (Illus.). 1975. reprint ed. 54.95 (*0-405-07046-2*) Ayer.
Richet, Xavier. The Hungarian Model. Whitehouse, J. C., tr. (Cambridge Russian, Soviet & Post-Soviet Studies: No. 64). (Illus.). 224p. (C). 1989. text 69.95 (*0-521-34314-3*) Cambridge U Pr.
*__Richeters, Christian, photos by.__ Frank O. Gehry: Energie-Forum Innovation, Bad Oeynhausen. (Opus Ser.: Vol. 35). (GER & ENG., Illus.). 60p. 2000. 42.00 (*3-930698-35-8*) Edition A Menges.
Richetti, John, ed. The Cambridge Companion to the Eighteenth-Century Novel. (Cambridge Companions to Literature Ser.). 270p. (C). 1996. text 54.95 (*0-521-41908-5*); pap. text 18.95 (*0-521-42945-5*) Cambridge U Pr.
Richetti, John, ed. see Shakespeare, William.
Richetti, John J. The English Novel in History, 1700-1780. LC 98-8223. (Novel in History Ser.). 1999. 85.00 (*0-415-00950-2*); pap. 25.99 (*0-415-19030-4*) Routledge.
— Philosophical Writing: Locke, Berkeley, Hume. 304p. (C). 1983. 43.50 (*0-674-66482-5*) HUP.
Richetti, John J., et al, eds. The Columbia History of the British Novel. LC 92-35749. 1,200p. (C). 1994. 81.00 (*0-231-07858-7*) Col U Pr.
Richetti, John J., jt. ed. see Backsheider, Paula R.
Richetto. Interviewing 13 5587. 2nd ed. 1989. pap. text 26.00 (*0-02-399780-X*, Macmillan Coll) P-H.
Richey. Implement Activity Based Early Intervention Curriculum. (Special Education Ser.). 1995. text, teacher ed. 12.95 (*0-8273-6990-5*) Delmar.
Richey, A. G., jt. auth. see Hancock, W. N.

An Asterisk (*) at the beginning of an entry indicates that the title is appearing for the first time.

R

Richey, Charles R. Manual on Employment Discrimination & Civil Rights Actions in the Federal Courts: Attorneys' Edition. rev. ed. (Commercial Law Library). 610p. 1988. 85.00 (1-55834-010-6, MICHIE) LEXIS Pub.

— Manual on Employment Discrimination Law & Civil Rights Actions in the Federal Courts. LC 85-9640. 1985. ring bd. 100.00 (0-87632-465-0) West Group.

— Manual on Employment Discrimination Law & Civil Rights Actions in the Federal Courts. 2nd ed. 1994. 140.00 (0-318-72689-0) West Group.

— Manual on Employment Discrimination Law & Civil Rights Actions in the Federal Courts, 1988 Replacement Edition. 630p. 1988. 80.00 (0-685-28794-7, MICHIE) LEXIS Pub.

— Prisoner Litigation in the United States Courts. 2nd ed. LC 97-19989. 484p. 1997. pap. text. write for info. (0-314-22693-1) West Pub.

Richey, Cheryl, jt. auth. see Gambrill, Eileen.

Richey, Cynthia. Love's Masquerade. 1990. 19.95 (0-8027-1117-0) Walker & Co.

Richey, Cynthia K. Programming for Serving Children with Special Needs. LC 93-33365. (ALSC Program Support Publications). 19p. (Orig.). 1993. pap. text 8.00 (0-8389-5763-3) ALA.

Richey, D. Dean. Activity Based Early Intervention: Strategies for Families, Caregivers, & Interventionists. 288p. 1997. pap. 34.95 (0-8273-6700-7) Delmar.

Richey, Dave, ed. see Starr, Dwaine.

Richey, David & Richey, Fred. Empowerment How to Stay a Knight. Bianchi, Susan & Richey, Josephine, eds. (Illus.). 304p. (Orig.). 1993. 19.95 (0-930733-13-4); pap. 14.95 (0-930733-14-2) Quality Groups Pub.

Richey, David L., jt. auth. see Forrest, Judith M.

Richey, Esther G. The Politics of Revelation in the English Renaissance. LC 98-3089. 264p. 1998. 37.50 (0-8262-1166-6) U of Mo Pr.

Richey, Everett E. Christian Stewardship: Love in Action. 70p. 1997. pap. 10.95 (1-57438-020-6) Ed Ministries.

Richey, Franklin D., jt. auth. see Wells, Alexander T.

Richey, Fred, jt. auth. see Richey, David.

Richey, George, jt. auth. see Cosgrave, Patrick.

***Richey, H. G., ed.** Grignard Reagents: New Developments. 434p. 1999. 260.00 (0-471-99908-3) Wiley.

***Richey, James.** Journey of Rem. LC 99-90879. 1999. 25.00 (0-7388-0550-5); pap. 18.00 (0-7388-0551-3) Xlibris Corp.

***Richey, Jim.** Finishing. (Methods of Work Ser.). (Illus.). 224p. 2000. pap. 12.95 (1-56158-371-5) Taunton.

— Methods of Work, 4 vols. (Illus.). 2000. pap. 39.95 (1-56158-468-1) Taunton.

— Router. (Methods of Work Ser.). (Illus.). 256p. 2000. pap. 12.95 (1-56158-369-3) Taunton.

— Router Methods of Work: The Best Advice from 25 Years of Fine Woodworking. LC 00-37392. 2000. write for info. (1-56158-370-7) Taunton.

— Tablesaw. (Methods of Work Ser.). (Illus.). 256p. 2000. pap. 12.95 (1-56158-367-7) Taunton.

— Workshop. (Methods of Work Ser.). (Illus.). 256p. 2000. pap. 12.95 (1-56158-365-0) Taunton.

Richey, Jim, ed. Fine Woodworking on More Proven Shop Tips. LC 89-40573. 96p. 1990. pap. 9.95 (0-942391-43-8, 70109) Taunton.

— Fine Woodworking on Proven Shop Tips. LC 84-52095. (Illus.). 128p. 1985. pap. 9.95 (0-918804-32-9, 70038) Taunton.

Richey, Joseph. Riding the Big Earth: Poems, 1980-86. (Collected Poems Ser.). 64p. 1987. pap. 5.95 (0-915032-89-9) Natl Poet Foun.

Richey, Joseph, ed. see Blue, Sharkmeat, pseud.

Richey, Joseph, ed. see Sikelianos, Eleni.

Richey, Josephine, ed. see Richey, David & Richey, Fred.

Richey, Louis R. & Brody, Lawrence. Comprehensive Deferred Compensation: A Complete Guide to Nonqualified Deferred Compensation. 2nd rev. ed. LC 89-61882. 278p. 1993. pap. 35.00 (0-87218-119-7) Natl Underwriter.

***Richey, Mimi.** Genesis: The Rebirth. LC 99-67016. 128p. 2000. 15.95 (1-56167-562-8) Noble Hse MD.

Richey, Nancy, ed. see Young, Ross.

***Richey, Paul.** Fighter Pilot: A Personal Record of the Battle of France 1940. 2000. pap. 14.95 (1-902304-44-6) Grub St.

Richey, Paul. Fighter Pilot: A Personal Record of the Campaign in France 1939-1940. 237p. 1991. 22.95 (1-85089-550-3, Pub. by ISIS Lrg Prnt) Transaction Pubs.

Richey, Paul, jt. auth. see Franks, Norman.

Richey, Peter P. Counseling - Guidance, Interventions, Skills, Management & Sex Infections: Index of New Information & Bibliography. rev. ed. LC 96-3129. 157p. 1996. 47.50 (0-7883-0972-2); pap. 44.50 (0-7883-0973-0) ABBE Pubs Assn.

Richey, Russell E. Early American Methodism. LC 91-4373. (Religion in North America Ser.). 156p. Date not set. reprint ed. pap. 48.40 (0-608-20569-9, 205448300002) Bks Demand.

— Early American Methodism: A Reconsideration. LC 91-4373. (Religion in North America Ser.). 160p. 1991. 25.00 (0-253-35006-9) Ind U Pr.

— The Methodist Conference in America: A History. 320p. 1996. pap. 17.95 (0-687-02187-1) Abingdon.

Richey, Russell E., et al, eds. Connectionalism: Ecclesiology Mission & Identity. LC 97-38665. (United Methodism & American Culture Ser.: Vol. 1). 320p. 1997. pap. 19.95 (0-687-02189-8) Abingdon.

Richey, Russell E. & Jones, Donald G. American Civil Religion. 284p. 1990. 89.95 (0-7734-9997-0) E Mellen.

***Richey, Russell E., et al.** The Methodist Experience in America, Vol. 2. LC 00-42023. 2000. write for info. (0-687-24673-3) Abingdon.

Richey, Russell E., et al. Perspectives on American Methodism: Interpretive Essays. Schmidt, Jean M., ed. 384p. (Orig.). 1993. pap. 26.95 (0-687-30782-1) Abingdon.

***Richey, Terry.** Gould Evans: The Creative Spirit. 2000. pap. 40.00 (88-7838-080-6) L'Arca IT.

Richey, William. Blake's Altering Aesthetic. LC 96-31078. (Illus.). 216p. (C). 1996. 37.50 (0-8262-1077-5) U of Mo Pr.

Richey, William, jt. auth. see Dettmar, Kevin J. H.

Richey, William, jt. ed. see Dettmar, Kevin J.

Richey, Willie. Racism Is a Myth. 96p. 1996. pap. text, per. 19.95 (0-7872-2011-6) Kendall-Hunt.

— Will Creates Way. 112p. 1995. pap. text, per. 19.95 (0-7872-1371-3, 41137101) Kendall-Hunt.

Richfield, Patricia. Japanese Vegetarian Cookbook. 128p. 1995. text 21.95 (0-7499-1412-2) Genl Dist Srvs.

— Japanese Vegetarian Cooking: From Simple Soups to Sushi. (Vegetarian Cooking Ser.). (Illus.). 176p. (Orig.). 1996. 14.95 (0-89594-805-2) Crossing Pr.

Richgels, jt. auth. see McGee, Lea M.

Richharia. Satellite Communications System. 500p. 1999. 59.95 (0-07-134208-7) McGraw.

Richharia, M. Satellite Communication Systems: Design Principles. 1994. 55.00 (0-07-052374-6) McGraw.

Richie. The Japanese Tattoo. (Illus.). 120p. 1980. pap. 22.50 (0-8348-0149-3) Weatherhill.

Richie, Alexandra. Faust's Metropolis: A History of Berlin. LC 98-16802. (Illus.). 984p. 1998. 37.95 (0-7867-0510-8) Carroll & Graf.

— Faust's Metropolis: A History of Berlin. (Illus.). 1168p. 1999. pap. text 19.95 (0-7867-0681-3) Carroll & Graf.

Richie, Anne T., ed. see Thackeray, William Makepeace.

Richie, Beth, ed. see Refugee Women in Development Staff.

Richie, Beth E. Gender Entrapment: Life Stories of African American Battered Women in a New York City Jail. LC 95-18322. 192p. (C). (gr. 13). 1995. pap. 18.99 (0-415-91145-1) Routledge.

Richie, C. F. & Hager, R. A. The Chumash Canoe: The Structure & Hydrodynamics of a Model. (San Diego Museum of Man, Ethnic Technology Notes Ser.). (Illus.). 17p. (C). 1973. pap. text 2.19 (1-55567-736-3) Coyote Press.

Richie, D. Ryokan - The Japanese Inn. 1996. 31.95 (4-07-974222-3) Shufu No.

Richie, David. Health & Medicine. LC 94-17793. (Life in America 100 Years Ago Ser.). (Illus.). 100p. (YA). (gr. 5 up). 1994. lib. bdg. 19.95 (0-7910-2839-9) Chelsea Hse.

Richie, David S. Memories & Meditations of a Workcamper. LC 73-84213. 36p. (Orig.). 1973. pap. 4.00 (0-87574-190-8) Pendle Hill.

Richie, Donald. The Films of Akira Kurosawa. 3rd expanded rev. ed. LC 95-47804. (Illus.). 275p. (C). 1996. pap. 24.95 (0-520-20026-8, Pub. by U CA Pr) Cal Prin Full Svc.

***Richie, Donald.** The Films of Akira Kurosawa. 3rd expanded rev. ed. 280p. 1999. pap. 24.95 (0-520-22037-4, Pub. by U CA Pr) Cal Prin Full Svc.

Richie, Donald. The Inland Sea. Lancet, Barry, ed. 292p. 1993. pap. 9.00 (4-7700-1751-0) Kodansha.

— The Inland Sea. 1994. 21.00 (0-8446-6723-4) Peter Smith.

— Introducing Japan. (Illus.). 72p. 1990. 28.00 (0-87011-833-1) Kodansha.

— Introducing Tokyo. LC 86-40436. (Introducing Japan - Introducing Kyoto Ser.). (Illus.). 80p. 1987. 28.00 (0-87011-806-4) Kodansha.

— Introducing Tokyo. (Illus.). 80p. 1994. pap. 18.00 (4-7700-1798-7) Kodansha.

— Japanese Cinema: An Introduction. (Images of Asia Ser.). (Illus.). 112p. (C). 1990. text 16.95 (0-19-584950-7) OUP.

— Lafcadio Hearn's Japan: An Anthology of His Writings. LC 96-60931. 1997. pap. text 16.95 (0-8048-2096-1) Tuttle Pubng.

— A Lateral View: Essays on Culture & Style in Contemporary Japan. LC 91-47645. 248p. (Orig.). 1992. reprint ed. pap. 10.95 (0-9628137-4-5) Stone Bridge Pr.

— Memoirs of the Warrior Kumagai. 247p. 1999. 18.95 (0-8048-2126-7) Tuttle Pubng.

— Ozu: His Life & Films. (Illus.). 1974. pap. 16.95 (0-520-03277-2, Pub. by U CA Pr) Cal Prin Full Svc.

— Public People, Private People: Portraits of Some Japanese. 212p. 1997. reprint ed. pap. 12.00 (4-7700-2104-6) Kodansha.

— A Taste of Japan. (Illus.). 112p. 1993. pap. 19.95 (4-7700-1707-3) Kodansha.

— Temples of Kyoto. (Illus.). 136p. 1995. 29.95 (0-8048-2032-5) Tuttle Pubng.

— Tokyo: A View of the City. (Topographics Ser.). (Illus.). 143p. 1999. pap. 25.00 (1-86189-034-6, Pub. by Reaktion Bks) Consort Bk Sales.

— Tokyo Nights. 118p. 1994. pap. 9.95 (0-8048-1923-8) Tuttle Pubng.

— Zen Inklings: Some Stories, Fables, Parables & Sermons. 128p. (C). 1992. reprint ed. pap. 9.95 (0-8348-0230-9) Weatherhill.

Richie, Donald, ed. Rashomon. (Films in Print Ser.). 226p. (C). 1987. text 35.00 (0-8135-1179-8); pap. text 18.95 (0-8135-1180-1) Rutgers U Pr.

Richie, Donald, jt. auth. see Anderson, Joseph L.

Richie, Donald, jt. auth. see Buruma, Ian.

Richie, Donald, tr. see Kurosawa, Akira.

Richie, Donald A. The Young Oxford Companion to the Congress of the United States. LC 93-6466. (Illus.). 240p. (YA). (gr. 7 up). 1993. lib. bdg. 40.00 (0-19-507777-6) OUP.

***Richie, Elisavietta.** In Haste I Write You This Note. (Stories & Half Stories Ser.). 180p. 2000. 24.95 (0-931846-58-7); pap. 14.95 (0-931846-55-2) Wash Writers Pub.

Richie, Eugene. Island Light: Poems. LC 97-40859. 1998. write for info. (0-9651558-8-9) Painted Leaf.

Richie, Eugene, tr. see Manrique, Jaime.

***Richie, Jason.** Secretaries of State: Making Foreign Policy. Lerner, Mark, ed. (In the Cabinet Ser.: Vol. 1). (Illus.). 176p. (YA). (gr. 7-12). 2000. lib. bdg. 21.95 (1-881508-65-X) Oliver Pr MN.

— Secretaries of War, Navy, & Defense: Ensuring National Security. Lerner, Mark, ed. (In the Cabinet Ser.: Vol. 2). (Illus.). 176p. (YA). (gr. 7-12). 2000. lib. bdg. 21.95 (1-881508-64-1) Oliver Pr MN.

— Spectacular Space Travelers. Sterling, Denise, ed. (Profiles Ser.: No. 31). (Illus.). 160p. (YA). (gr. 5-12). 2001. lib. bdg. 18.95 (1-881508-71-4) Oliver Pr MN.

— Weapons: Designing the Tools of War. LC 98-53190. (Innovators Ser.). (Illus.). 144p. (YA). (gr. 5-12). 1999. lib. bdg. 19.95 (1-881508-60-9) Oliver Pr MN.

Richie, Jerome, jt. auth. see Oesterling, Joseph E.

Richie, Lionel. Lionel Richie Songbook. (Illus.). 144p. 24.95 (0-89524-220-6); pap. text 19.95 (0-89524-248-6, 9970) Cherry Lane.

Richie, Lloyd F. Table Top Lightning. 33p. 1992. 15.00 (0-914119-26-5) Tesla Bk Co.

Richie, Nicholas D. & Alperin, Diane E. Innovation & Change in the Human Services. (Illus.). 162p. 1992. pap. 24.95 (0-398-06400-8) C C Thomas.

— Innovation & Change in the Human Services. (Illus.). 162p. (C). 1992. text 38.95 (0-398-05763-X) C C Thomas.

Richie, Robert, jt. auth. see Hill, Steven.

Richie, Susan K. Your Opportunities in the Fashion World. (Illus.). 8p. 1993. pap. 2.50 (0-9626591-8-5, OS109) Energeia Pub.

Richier, Maurice, ed. see Nerval, Gerard De.

Richins, Paul, Jr. 50 Classic Backcountry Ski & Snowboard Summits in California: Mount Shasta to Mount Whitney. LC 99-6549. (Illus.). 240p. 1999. pap. 17.95 (0-89886-656-1) Mountaineers.

Richir, M. Au-Dela Du Renversement Copernicien. (Phaenomenologica Ser.: No. 73). 190p. 1977. lib. bdg. 141.50 (90-247-1903-8, Pub. by M Nijhoff) Kluwer Academic.

Richison, Marjorie W. Living Near to Nature's Heart: The History of the Pelican Lake Outing Club. 213p. 1992. 29.95 (1-880458-00-4) Kingswood.

***Richissin, Todd.** Fathers & Sons. (Illus.). 144p. 2000. 27.50 (0-7624-0697-6) Running Pr.

Richiusa, Gordon F., ed. see Classic, Carl.

Richler, Binyamin & Brody, Robert. Hebrew Manuscripts: A Treasured Legacy. Shoshana, Abraham, ed. LC 89-64170. 166p. (C). 1990. 29.95 (1-881255-05-0) OFEQ Inst.

Richler, Daniel. Kicking Tomorrow. 1992. mass mkt. 6.99 (0-7710-7470-0) McCland & Stewart.

Richler, Howard. A Bawdy Language: How a Second Rate Language Slept Its Way to the Top. 1999. pap. 15.95 (0-7737-6028-8) Stoddart Publ.

***Richler, Howard.** Bawdy Language: How a Second-Rate Language Slept Its Way to the Top. LC 99-488133. 1999. write for info. (0-7737-3186-5) Stoddart Publ.

Richler, Martha. National Gallery of Art, Washington: Ten Centuries of Art. LC 97-61688. (Illus.). 224p. 1998. 40.00 (1-85759-176-3) Scala Books.

Richler, Mordecai. The Apprenticeship of Duddy Kravitz. (New Canadian Library). 328p. 1989. mass mkt. 6.95 (0-7710-9972-X) McCland & Stewart.

— The Apprenticeship of Duddy Kravitz. 356p. 1999. 14.00 (0-671-02847-2, WSP) PB.

— Barney's Version. LC 97-37033. 384p. 1997. 25.00 (0-679-40418-X) Knopf.

— Barney's Version. 356p. 1999. 14.00 (0-671-02846-4, WSP) PB.

— Choice of Enemies. 268p. 1996. pap. text 6.95 (0-7710-9971-1) McCland & Stewart.

— Incomparable Atuk. 184p. 1996. pap. 7.95 (0-7710-9973-8) McCland & Stewart.

— Jacob Two-Two & the Dinosaur. (Illus.). 96p. 1998. pap. 6.99 (0-88776-425-8) Tundra Bks.

— Jacob Two-Two Meets the Hooded Fang. 96p. (J). 1982. pap. 2.50 (0-7704-2109-1, Skylark BDD) BDD Bks Young Read.

— Jacob Two-Two Meets the Hooded Fang. (Illus.). 96p. (J). (gr. 2-7). 1994. pap. 3.50 (0-685-71038-6) Random Bks Yng Read.

— Jacob Two-Two Meets the Hooded Fang. (Illus.). 96p. 1998. pap. 6.99 (0-88776-424-X) Tundra Bks.

***Richler, Mordecai.** Jacob Two-Two Meets the Hooded Fang. (Illus.). 96p. (J). (gr. 3-6). 1999. pap. 6.99 (0-88776-481-9) Tundra Bks.

Richler, Mordecai. Jacob Two-Two's First Spy Case. LC 95-26676. (Illus.). 152p. (J). (gr. 2-5). 1997. 16.00 (0-374-33659-8) FS&G.

Richler, Mordecai. Joshua Then & Now. 442p. 1997. pap. text 5.95 (0-7710-9864-2) McCland & Stewart.

Richler, Mordecai. The Modern Approach to the Christian Religion: The Truth. LC 98-90022. 1998. pap. 10.95 (0-533-12685-1) Vantage.

— Oh Canada! Oh Quebec! 1992. 20.00 (0-685-53593-2) Knopf.

***Richler, Mordecai.** On Snooker: A Brilliant Exploration of the Game & the Characters. 112p. 2000. 20.00 (1-58574-179-5) Lyons Pr.

Richler, Mordecai. Solomon Gursky Was Here: A Novel. 413p. 1998. pap. text 10.00 (0-7881-5262-9) DIANE Pub.

— Son of a Smaller Hero. 208p. 1996. pap. text 7.95 (0-7710-9970-3) McCland & Stewart.

— Title. 1986. pap. 6.98 (0-7710-7489-1) McCland & Stewart.

Richler, Nancy. Throwaway Angels. 264p. 1996. pap. 12.95 (0-88974-062-3, Pub. by Press Gang Pubs) LPC InBook.

Richleson. Wizards of Langley. 2000. 29.95 (0-8133-6699-2) HarpC.

***Richley, Pat.** The Everything Online Genealogy Book: Use the Web to Discover Long-Lost Relations, Trace Your Family Tree Back to Royalty & Share Your History with Far-Flung Cousins! (Everything Ser.). (Illus.). 304p. 2000. pap. 12.95 (1-58062-402-2) Adams Media.

Richlin, Amy. Juvenal Satira Six. (Latin Commentaries Ser.). 107p. (Orig.). (C). 1986. pap. text 6.00 (0-929524-42-X) Bryn Mawr Commentaries.

Richlin, Amy, ed. Pornography & Representation in Greece & Rome. (Illus.). 352p. (C). 1992. pap. text 27.95 (0-19-506723-1) OUP.

Richlin, Amy, jt. ed. see Rabinowitz, Nancy S.

Richlin-Klonsky, Judith, et al. A Guide to Writing Sociology Papers. LC 85-61301. 128p. (Orig.). (C). 1986. pap. text 8.00 (0-312-35307-3) St Martin.

Richlin, Laurie, ed. Preparing Faculty for the New Conceptions of Scholarship. LC 85-644763. (New Directions for Teaching & Learning Ser.: No. TL 54). 113p. 1993. pap. 22.00 (1-55542-726-X) Jossey-Bass.

Richlin, Laurie & Manning, Brenda. Improving A College/University Teaching Evaluation System: A Comprehensive Developmental Curriculum for Faculty & Administrators. 2nd rev. ed. (Curriculum for Change Ser.: Vol. 1). 336p. 1995. 53.00 (0-9645071-2-9) Allnce Pub.

Richlin, Laurie, jt. auth. see Grasha, Anthony F.

Richling, B., jt. ed. see Koos, Wolfgang T.

Richling, C. & Drewitz, I. Dictionary of Cable Engineering: English-German-French. (ENG, FRE & GER.). 610p. 1976. pap. 73.00 (3-87097-072-3) IBD Ltd.

Richling, Christel. Woerterbuch der Kabeltechnik. (ENG, FRE & GER.). 1976. pap. 95.00 (0-8288-5775-X, M6988) Fr & Eur.

***Richman.** Math for Liberal Arts. 394p. (C). 1998. pap. text 26.00 (0-536-01588-0) Pearson Custom.

Richman. Problems of Preschool Children. 1988. pap. text 84.44 (0-471-91932-2) Wiley.

***Richman, Alyson.** The Mask Carver's Son. 384p. 2000. 23.95 (1-58234-063-3) Bloomsbury Pubg.

Richman, Ann F., ed. The Plow Reader: Selections from an Appalachian Alternative Newsmagazine of the Late 1970's. (Illus.). xxiv, 328p. (Orig.). 1996. reprint ed. pap. 15.00 (1-885912-09-9) Sows Ear Pr.

Richman, Barry M. & Farmer, Richard N. Leadership, Goals & Power in Higher Education: A Contingency & Open-Systems Approach to Effective Management. LC 74-9112. (Jossey-Bass Higher Education Ser.). 380p. reprint ed. pap. 117.80 (0-608-12172-X, 202387800034) Bks Demand.

Richman, Beth & Hassol, Susan. Everyday Chemicals. 2nd ed. LC 89-51685. (Creating a Healthy World - 101 Practical Tips for Home & Work Ser.). (Illus.). 68p. 1989. pap. 3.95 (0-9622492-4-6) Windstar Foundation.

— Everyday Chemicals: Creating a Healthy World. Katzenberger, John, ed. (Illus.). 56p. 1989. write for info. (0-318-65067-3) Windstar Foundation.

Richman, Beth, jt. auth. see Hassol, Susan.

Richman, Brenda. From Disappointment to Joy: Studies in Ruth. 65p. (Orig.). 1993. pap. 3.95 (0-943167-22-1) Faith & Fellowship Pr.

Richman, C. The Light of Life: The Ohrhachayim on the Torah. (Adaptation of the Ohrhachayim Ser.: Vol. 1). (HEB.). 320p. 1995. 19.95 (1-888234-00-8) Rachav Commun.

Richman, Carol, jt. auth. see Kane, Katherine.

Richman, Dan. From Aaron to Zoe: Fifteen Thousand Great Baby Names. LC 92-44632. 288p. 1993. pap. 13.00 (0-316-74444-1) Little.

Richman, Daniel A. James E. Carter: 39th President of the United States. Young, Richard G., ed. LC 88-24562. (Presidents of the United States Ser.). (Illus.). (J). (gr. 5-9). 1989. lib. bdg. 21.27 (0-944483-24-0) Garrett Ed Corp.

Richman, Daniel C. Report of the Department of the Treasury on the Bureau of Alcohol, Tobacco & Firearms Investigation of Vernon Wayne Howell, Also Known as David Koresh, September 1993. 526p. 1993. per. 44.00 (0-16-042025-3) USGPO.

Richman, Darryl. Bock. (Classic Beer Style Ser.). (Illus.). 174p. (Orig.). 1994. pap. 11.95 (0-937381-39-X) Brewers Pubns.

Richman, David. Laughter, Pain, & Wonder: Shakespeare's Comedies & the Audience in the Theater. LC 89-40413. 200p. 1990. 36.50 (0-87413-388-2) U Delaware Pr.

***Richman, David.** Passionate Action: Yeats's Mastery of Drama. LC 00-23413. 2000. write for info. (0-87413-718-7) U Delaware Pr.

Richman, David P., ed. Myasthenia Gravis & Related Diseases: Disorders of the Neuromuscular Junction. LC 97-52826. (Annals of the New York Academy of Sciences Ser.: No. 841). 838p. 1998. pap. 160.00 (1-57331-120-0) NY Acad Sci.

— Myasthenia Gravis & Related Diseases: Disorders of the Neuromuscular Junction. LC 97-52826. (Annals of the New York Academy of Sciences Ser.: No. 841). 838p. 1998. 160.00 (1-57331-119-7) NY Acad Sci.

Richman, Douglas D., ed. Antiviral Drug Resistance. LC 96-13385. 324p. 1996. 159.95 (0-471-96120-5) Wiley.

Richman, Douglas D., et al. Clinical Virology. LC 96-48084. 1996. text 180.00 (0-443-07653-7) Church.

Richman, Ellen. Spotlight on Computer Literacy. (J). (gr. 6-8). 1984. pap. 14.00 (0-07-480653-X) McGraw.

Richman, Elliot. Blastin' Out of Abilene. 1988. 4.00 (0-685-25017-2) Windless Orchard.

***Richman, Elliot.** Franz Kafka's Daughter Meets the Evil Nazi Empire!!! The Heroism of Roaches: Holocaust-Tainted Poems. 80p. 1999. pap. 10.00 (1-878580-71-X) Asylum Arts.

An Asterisk (*) at the beginning of an entry indicates that the title is appearing for the first time.

Richman, Elliot. Honorable Manhood: Poems of Eros & Dust. LC 93-79281. 72p. (Orig.). 1994. pap. 8.95 (*1-878580-50-7*) Asylum Arts.

— The World Dancer: Poems. LC 93-71191. 112p. 1993. pap. 9.95 (*1-878580-44-2*) Asylum Arts.

Richman, Elliott. A Bucket of Nails. 20p. (Orig.). 1990. pap. 3.00 (*0-318-50052-3*) Samisdat.

Richman, Fred, et al. A Course in Constructive Algebra. 360p. 1987. 57.95 (*0-387-96640-4*) Spr-Verlag.

***Richman, Fred, et al.** Mathematics for the Liberal Arts Student. LC 99-26057. 386p. 1999. pap. 44.00 (*0-13-014547-5*) P-H.

Richman, Fred, jt. auth. see Bridges, Douglas.

Richman, Fred, jt. auth. see Johnston, Bernard L.

Richman, George J. History of Hancock County, Indiana. (Illus.). 815p. 1992. reprint ed. lib. bdg. 79.50 (*0-8328-2542-5*) Higginson Bk Co.

Richman, Howard. Fat & the Art of Focusing: Three Easy Non-Diet Steps to Permanently End the Yo-Yo Cycle. LC 94-68878. (Illus.). 150p. (Orig.). 1995. pap. 14.95 (*1-882060-76-8*) Sound Feelings.

— Pain-Free Typing Technique: Simple Solutions to Prevent Repetitive Strain Injuries from a Concert Pianist. (Illus.). 12p. 1999. pap. 4.95 (*1-882060-80-6*) Sound Feelings.

— Story of a Bill: Legalizing Homeschooling in Pennsylvania. 152p. (Orig.). 1989. pap. 6.95 (*0-929446-01-1*) PA Homeschoolers.

— Stutter Control Drill: Mastering Elements of Fluent Speech. 2nd rev. ed. 12p. 1999. pap. 4.95 (*1-882060-81-4*) Sound Feelings.

Richman, Howard, ed. Super Sight-Reading Secrets: An Innovative, Step-by-Step Program for Musical Keyboard Players of All Levels. 3rd rev. ed. LC 85-90522. 52p. (C). 1986. pap. 9.95 (*0-9615963-0-9*) Sound Feelings.

Richman, Howard B. & Richman, Susan P. The Three R's at Home. LC 88-90813. 228p. (Orig.). 1988. pap. 7.95 (*0-929446-00-3*) PA Homeschoolers.

Richman, Irving B. California under Spain & Mexico, 1535-1847. 1992. reprint ed. lib. bdg. 75.00 (*0-7812-5078-1*) Rprt Serv.

— From Discovery Through Kino: California under Spain & Mexico, 1535-1847. 75p. reprint ed. pap. 10.00 (*1-877959-00-6*) D Henson Bks.

— Rhode Island: A Study in Separatism. LC 72-3749. (American Commonwealths Ser.: No. 17). reprint ed. 42.50 (*0-404-57217-0*) AMS Pr.

Richman, Irving B., ed. History of Muscatine County: From the Earliest Settlement to the Present Time (1911), 2 vols. (Illus.). 1278p. 1997. reprint ed. lib. bdg. 119.00 (*0-8328-6694-6*) Higginson Bk Co.

Richman, Irwin. Borscht Belt Bungalows: Memories of Catskill Summers. LC 97-22662. 256p. 1998. 29.95 (*1-56639-585-2*) Temple U Pr.

***Richman, Irwin.** Catskills. (Images of America Ser.). 128p. 1999. pap. 18.99 (*0-7385-0308-8*) Arcadia Publng.

Richman, J. William. Pureed Foods with Substance & Style. LC 93-43913. 242p. 1994. 56.00 (*0-8342-0554-8*) Aspen Pub.

***Richman, Jack M. & Fraser, Mark W., eds.** The Context of Youth Violence: Resilience, Risk & Protection. LC 95-21762. 229p. 2000. 64.00 (*0-275-96724-7*, Praeger Pubs) Greenwood.

Richman, Jan. Because the Brain Can Be Talked into Anything: Poems. LC 94-37532. 64p. 1995. text 15.95 (*0-8071-1993-8*) La State U Pr.

Richman, Jan. Because the Brain Can Be Talked into Anything: Poems. LC 94-37532. 64p. 1995. pap. 10.95 (*0-8071-1994-6*) La State U Pr.

Richman, Jeffrey I. Brooklyn's Green-Wood Cemetery: New York's Buried Treasure. (Illus.). 256p. 1998. 50.00 (*0-9663435-0-6*) Green-Wood Cem.

Richman, Joseph. Family Therapy for Suicidal People. 224p. 1985. 33.95 (*0-8261-5030-1*) Springer Pub.

— Preventing Elderly Suicide: Overcoming Personal Despair, Professional Indifference, & Social Bias. LC 92-35995. (Death & Suicide Ser.: Vol. 11). 176p. 1993. 29.95 (*0-8261-7480-9*) Springer Pub.

Richman, Karin, tr. see Clahsen, Harald.

Richman, Kenneth, jt. auth. see Read, Rupert J.

Richman, Larry L. Project Management: A Strategic Approach. (Illus.). 152p. 1996. ring bd. 39.95 (*0-941846-04-0*) Centry Pub.

***Richman, Linda.** I'd Rather Laugh: How to Be Happy Even When Life Has Other Plans for You. 288p. 2001. 23.95 (*0-446-52676-2*) Warner Bks.

Richman, Linda G. Everybody's Doing It! (Illus.). 440p. (Orig.). 1992. spiral bd. 29.00 (*0-9609160-9-1*) Mayer-Johnson.

— Introduction to Kitchen Appliances. (Illus.). 144p. (Orig.). 1992. ring bd. 24.00 (*0-9609160-8-3*) Mayer-Johnson.

— Listen to These Nouns. (Illus.). 288p. (Orig.). 1994. spiral bd. 29.00 (*1-884135-01-3*) Mayer-Johnson.

— Listen to This. (Illus.). 294p. 1987. spiral bd. 29.00 (*0-9609160-2-4*) Mayer-Johnson.

— Listen to Verbs Those. (Illus.). 264p. (Orig.). 1994. spiral bd. 29.00 (*1-884135-02-1*) Mayer-Johnson.

— Playtime. (Illus.). 252p. 1995. spiral bd. 29.00 (*1-884135-18-8*) Mayer-Johnson.

— Stories about Me. (Illus.). 220p. 1989. spiral bd. 24.00 (*0-9609160-5-9*) Mayer-Johnson.

— This Is the One I Want. (Illus.). 172p. 1987. spiral bd. 24.00 (*0-9609160-3-2*) Mayer-Johnson.

Richman, Marcella. North Dakota...Where Food Is Love. 200p. 1994. pap. 10.95 (*0-9642215-0-0*) N Dakota Ckbook.

— Season's Eatings from North Dakota. 1999. spiral bd. 12.95 (*0-9642215-1-9*) N Dakota Ckbook.

Richman, Mark. How to Help Your Child Succeed in School: The Ultimate Guide for Parents. (Illus.). 184p. 1998. pap. 24.95 (*0-9649007-3-4*) M Richman.

Richman, Mark S. High Caliber Kids: A Book of Interdisciplinary Values Education. 1996. lib. bdg. 24.95 (*0-9649007-1-8*) M Richman.

— Just Let Me Survive Today: A Primer in Classroom Management & Motivation. (Illus.). 180p. 1995. lib. bdg., teacher ed. 24.95 (*0-9649007-0-X*) M Richman.

— The Ultimate Camp Counsellor Manual: How to Survive & Succeed Magnificently at Summer Camp. (Illus.). 150p. 1997. lib. bdg. 24.95 (*0-9649007-2-6*) M Richman.

Richman, Michael B., jt. auth. see Myers, Donald J.

Richman, Naomi. In the Midst of the Whirlwind: A Manual for Helping Refugee Children. 120p. 1998. pap. 17.95 (*1-85856-101-9*, Trentham Bks) Stylus Pub VA.

Richman, Naomi, et al. Pre-School to School: A Behavioural Study. (Behavioral Development Monographs). 1982. text 110.00 (*0-12-587940-7*) Acad Pr.

Richman, Naomi, jt. auth. see McGuire, Jacqueline.

***Richman, Nessa J.** The Natural Foods Market: A National Survey of Strategies for Growth. (Policy Studies Report: No. 12). (Illus.). 87p. 1999. pap. 150.00 (*1-893182-19-3*) H A Wallace Inst.

Richman, Paul. Diagnostic Cytopathology. 1994. vdisk 400.00 (*1-56815-031-8*) Mosby Inc.

Richman, Paula. Extraordinary Child: Poems from a South Indian Devotional Genre. LC 96-40072. (SHAPS Library of Translations). (Illus.). 280p. 1997. pap. text 27.00 (*0-8248-1063-5*) UH Pr.

— Women, Branch Stories, & Religious Rhetoric in a Tamil Buddhist Text. LC 87-31551. (Foreign & Comparative Studies Program, South Asian Ser.: No. 12). 288p. (Orig.). (C). 1988. 19.00 (*0-915984-90-3*) Syracuse U Foreign Comp.

Richman, Paula, ed. Many Ramayanas: The Diversity of a Narrative Tradition in South Asia. LC 91-7273. 280p. 1991. 50.00 (*0-520-07281-2*, Pub. by U CA Pr); pap. 18.95 (*0-520-07589-7*, Pub. by U CA Pr) Cal Prin Full Svc.

***Richman, Paula, ed.** Questioning Ramayanas: A South Asian Tradition. (Illus.). 400p. 2000. 50.00 (*0-520-22073-0*); pap. 19.95 (*0-520-22074-9*, Pub. by U CA Pr) Cal Prin Full Svc.

Richman, Peter. Insider's Guide to Growing Small Businesses: Straight Advice from One Who's Been There. LC 96-68536. 1996. 19.95 (*0-02-861176-4*) Macmillan.

Richman, Phyllis C. The Butter Did It: A Gastronomic Tale of Love & Murder. 384p. 1998. mass mkt. 5.99 (*0-06-109625-3*) HarpC.

— The Butter Did It: A Gastronomic Tale of Love & Murder. large type ed. LC 97-15101. (Cloak & Dagger Ser.). 459p. 1997. 24.95 (*0-7862-1183-0*) Thorndike Pr.

— Murder on the Gravy Train. LC 99-10192. 256p. 1999. 23.00 (*0-06-018390-X*) HarpC.

***Richman, Phyllis C.** Murder on the Gravy Train. 336p. 2000. mass mkt. 6.50 (*0-06-109783-7*, Avon Bks) Morrow Avon.

— Murder on the Gravy Train. large type ed. LC 99-41960. (Thorndike Mystery Ser.). 398p. 1999. 28.95 (*0-7862-2208-5*) Thorndike Pr.

Richman, Phyllis C. The Washington Post Dining Guide. Epstein, Noel, ed. (Illus.). iii, 248p. (Orig.). 1996. pap. 11.95 (*0-9625971-3-9*) Washington Post.

— The Washington Post Dining Guide, 1999-2000 Edition. Epstein, Noel, ed. 247p. 1998. pap. 10.95 (*0-9625971-8-X*) Washington Post.

Richman, Robert. Voice on the Wind: Poems. LC 96-47669. 60p. 1997. pap. 10.00 (*0-914278-72-X*) Copper Beech.

Richman, Robert J. Prolegomena to a Theory of Practical Reasoning. 208p. 1983. text 121.50 (*90-277-1548-3*, D Reidel) Kluwer Academic.

Richman, Sheldon. Bilingual Education: A Failed Experiment on the Children. (Issue Paper #6-97 Ser.). 23p. 1997. pap. text 8.00 (*1-57655-158-X*) Independ Inst.

— Separating School & State: How to Liberate America's Families. LC 94-72163. 150p. (Orig.). 1994. 22.95 (*0-9640447-1-4*); pap. 14.95 (*0-9640447-2-2*) Future of Freedom.

— Why Colorado Should Drop Out of Goals, 2000. (Issue Paper #2-96 Ser.). 17p. 1996. pap. write for info. (*1-57655-146-6*) Independ Inst.

— Your Money or Your Life: Why We Must Abolish the Income Tax. LC 97-60308. 135p. (Orig.). 1997. 22.95 (*0-9640447-8-1*); pap. 14.95 (*0-9640447-9-X*) Future of Freedom.

Richman, Sheldon & Kopel, David B. End Compulsory Schooling. (Issue Paper #1-96 Ser.). 16p. 1996. pap. 8.00 (*1-57655-145-8*) Independ Inst.

Richman, Susan P. Writing from Home: A Portfolio of Homeschooled Student Writing. (Illus.). 372p. (Orig.). 1990. 16.95 (*0-929446-02-X*); pap. 8.95 (*0-929446-03-8*) PA Homeschoolers.

Richman, Susan P., ed. Math by Kids: A Collection of Word Problems Written by Kids for Kids of All Ages. (J). (gr. k-12). 1996. wbk. ed. 6.95 (*0-929446-04-6*) PA Homeschoolers.

Richman, Susan P., jt. auth. see Richman, Howard B.

Richman, William, jt. auth. see Casad, Robert C.

Richman, William M. & Reynolds, William L. Understanding Conflict of Laws. 2nd ed. LC 92-45658. (C). 1993. pap. 30.00 (*0-8205-0062-3*) Bender.

Richmaria, M. Richmaria Mobile Satellite Communications. (C). 2000. text. write for info. (*0-201-33142-X*) Addison-Wesley.

Richmers, C. Mabel & Geiger, Wilhelm, trs. from PLI. Culavamsa, 2 vols. (C). 1930. 41.90 (*0-86013-013-4*, Pub. by Pali Text) Elsevier.

Richmond. AIDS & Other Sexually Transmitted Disease. 1993. text 65.00 (*0-7295-0351-8*, W B Saunders Co) Harcrt Hlth Sci Grp.

RICHMOND. National Policy & Naval Strength. 400p. 1993. 73.95 (*0-7512-0122-7*) Ashgate Pub Co.

— Navy in India 1763-1783. 448p. 1993. 79.95 (*0-7512-0123-5*) Ashgate Pub Co.

— Navy in the War of 1739-1748, Vol. 3. 968p. 1993. 192.95 (*0-7512-0121-9*) Ashgate Pub Co.

Richmond. Standing in the Light: A Lakota Way of Seeing. 1994. 30.00 (*0-939185-00-8*) General Communications Inc.

Richmond, ed. Ovidii, Nasonis: Ponto Libri Quattuor. (LAT.). 1990. 32.50 (*3-322-00669-7*, T1566, Pub. by B G Teubner) U of Mich Pr.

Richmond & McCrosskey. Communication: Apprehension, Avoidance, & Effectiveness. 5th ed. LC 99-162274. 152p. 1997. pap. text 24.00 (*0-205-27982-1*) P-H.

Richmond-Abbott, Marie. Masculine & Feminine: Gender Roles over the Life Cycle. 2nd ed. 448p. (C). 1991. 50.31 (*0-07-052357-6*) McGraw.

Richmond, Akasha. The Art of Tofu: Celebrated Vegetarian Recipes from Around the World. 88p. 1997. pap. 10.95 (*0-9664543-0-8*, Pub. by Morinaga) Book Pub Co.

Richmond, Al. Cowboys, Miners, Presidents & Kings: The Story of the Grand Canyon Railway. rev. ed. LC 89-80211. (Illus.). 230p. 1994. reprint ed. 19.95 (*0-933269-03-X*); reprint ed. pap. 14.95 (*0-933269-02-1*) Gd Canyon Railway.

— Rails to the Rim: Milepost Guide to the Grand Canyon Railway. 4th rev. ed. LC 94-75686. (Illus.). 136p. 1998. reprint ed. pap. 6.95 (*0-933269-32-3*) Gd Canyon Railway.

Richmond, Alan & Cox, Mark. HTML & CGI Unleashed. LC 95-69417. (Illus.). 864p. 1995. 49.99 (*0-672-30745-6*) Sams.

Richmond, Allen E. & Hecht, Gary. CALCULUS FOR ELECTRONICS 4E. 4th ed. 544p. (C). 1988. text 79.36 (*0-07-052355-X*) Glencoe.

Richmond, Amos. Handbook of Microalgal Mass Culture. 576p. 1986. 296.00 (*0-8493-3240-0*, SH389, CRC Reprint) Franklin.

Richmond, Anthony H. Global Apartheid: Refugees, Racism & The New World Order. (Illus.). 328p. 1995. pap. text 29.95 (*0-19-541013-0*) OUP.

Richmond, Arline L. Yenlo & the Mystic Brotherhood. 1996. reprint ed. spiral bd. 15.00 (*0-7873-0716-5*) Hlth Research.

— Yenlo & the Mystic Brotherhood. 140p. 1996. reprint ed. pap. 14.50 (*1-56459-824-1*) Kessinger Pub.

Richmond, Barbara. Recycled Nun. LC 97-69956. 128p. 1998. pap. 7.95 (*1-883928-25-7*) Longwood.

***Richmond, Barry.** The "Thinking" in Systems Thinking: Seven Essential Skills. (Toolbox Reprint Ser.). (Illus.). 25p. 2000. pap. 16.95 (*1-883823-48-X*, TRST02) Pegasus Comm.

Richmond, Ben, ed. see Coffin, Levi.

Richmond, Bert O. & Kicklighter, Richard H. Children's Adaptive Behavior Scale Cards: Administrator's Stimulus Manual. rev. ed. 42p. (Orig.). (C). 1983. pap. 14.95 (*0-89334-040-5*) Humanics Ltd.

— Children's Adaptive Behavior Scale Manual. 16p. (Orig.). 1982. pap. 10.95 (*0-89334-030-8*) Humanics Ltd.

Richmond, Bruce. Radio Frequency Data Communication for Warehouse Management. (Illus.). 72p. 1993. pap. 20.00 (*1-892663-10-4*) WERC.

Richmond, C. R., ed. Health & Ecological Implications of Radioactively Contaminated Environments. LC 91-10034. (Annual Meeting Proceedings Ser.: No. 12). 233p. (Orig.). 1991. pap. text 40.00 (*0-929600-14-2*) NCRP Pubns.

Richmond, C. R., et al, eds. Mammalian Cells: Probes & Problems, Proceedings. LC 75-600009. (ERDA Symposium Ser.). 324p. 1975. pap. 16.00 (*0-685-01478-9*, CONF-731007); fiche 6.00 (*0-87079-267-9*, CONF-731007) DOE.

Richmond, C. W. History of Dupage County, Illinois. 277p. 1999. reprint ed. pap. 23.50 (*0-7884-1197-7*, R319) Heritage Bk.

Richmond, C. W. & Vallette, H. F. A History of the County of Du Page, Illinois. 212p. 1994. reprint ed. lib. bdg. 29.50 (*0-8328-4015-7*) Higginson Bk Co.

Richmond, Carl. Twisted: One Drug Addict's Desperate Struggle for Recovery. LC 91-50641. 290p. 1991. pap. 11.95 (*1-879360-08-X*) Noble Pr.

Richmond, Carolyn, ed. see Clarin, Leopoldo A.

Richmond, Carolynn K., jt. auth. see Richmond, George H.

Richmond, Chandler S. Beyond the Spring: Cordelia Stanwood of Birdsacre. rev. ed. LC 88-83667. (Illus.). 176p. (Orig.). 1989. pap. 12.95 (*0-932448-03-8*) Latona Pr.

— Beyond the Spring: Cordelia Stanwood of Birdsacre. 2nd rev. ed. LC 88-83667. (Illus.). 176p. (Orig.). 1989. 24.95 (*0-932448-02-X*) Latona Pr.

Richmond, Charles & Smith, Paul, eds. The Self-Fashioning of Disraeli, 1818-1851. LC 97-52756. 224p. (C). 1999. text 49.95 (*0-521-49729-9*) Cambridge U Pr.

Richmond, Christina. Chemo Girl: Saving the World... (Nursing Ser.). 32p. 1996. 12.50 (*0-7637-0314-1*) Jones & Bartlett.

Richmond, Clare. Hawaiian Heat. (American Romance Ser.). 1993. per. 3.39 (*0-373-16476-9*, 1-16476-3) Harlequin Bks.

Richmond, Clint. Selena: The Phenomenal Life & Tragic Death of the Tejano Music Queen. 15p. 1995. mass mkt. 5.99 (*0-671-54522-1*) PB.

— VH-1 Behind the Music: Willie Nelson. (VH1 Behind the Music Ser.: Vol. 3). (Illus.). 144p. 2000. per. 12.95 (*0-671-03960-1*, MTV Bks) PB.

Richmond, Clint, jt. auth. see Forrest, Deborah A.

Richmond, Colin. The Paston Family in the 15th Century: Fastolf's Will, Vol. 2. LC 95-44017. (Illus.). 292p. (C). 1996. text 59.95 (*0-521-56238-4*) Cambridge U Pr.

Richmond, Colin, jt. auth. see Aston, Margaret.

***Richmond, Cora L. V.** The Soul in Human Embodiments. 128p. 1999. reprint ed. pap. 11.95 (*0-9671610-8-8*) Modern Am Spiritualism.

***Richmond, Cynthia.** Dream Power: How to Use Your Night Dreams to Change Your Life. LC 99-49573. 272p. 2000. 22.00 (*0-684-87094-0*) S&S Trade.

Richmond, Dick, ed. see Pinnock, Tom.

Richmond, Don. Some Conversations with an Old Man & Other Poems & Songs. (Illus.). 67p. 1987. pap. write for info. (*0-943909-02-3*) Gibbs Assocs.

Richmond-Donahue, Dick & Richmond-Donahue, Leigh. Blindsided. 172p. (Orig.). 1993. pap. 10.95 (*0-943975-03-4*) Interdimens Sci.

Richmond-Donahue, Leigh, jt. auth. see Richmond-Donahue, Dick.

Richmond, Dorothy. Practice Makes Perfect: Spanish Pronouns & Prepositions. LC 97-69977. (Practice Makes Perfect Ser.). (Illus.). 160p. 1998. pap. 9.95 (*0-8442-7311-2*, 73112) NTC Contemp Pub Co.

Richmond, Doug. How to Disappear Completely & Never Be Found. LC 94-17639. 120p. 1994. pap. 8.95 (*0-8065-1559-7*, Citadel Pr) Carol Pub Group.

Richmond, Douglas. Carlos Pellegrini & the Crisis of the Argentine Elites, 1880-1916. LC 88-34032. 206p. 1989. 49.95 (*0-275-93288-5*, C3288, Praeger Pubs) Greenwood.

Richmond, Douglas, jt. ed. see Francaviglia, Richard.

Richmond, Douglas W. Venustiano Carranza's Nationalist Struggle, 1893-1920. LC 83-3652. (Illus.). 347p. reprint ed. pap. 107.60 (*0-8357-2942-7*, 203919800011) Bks Demand.

Richmond, Douglas W., ed. Essays on the Mexican War. LC 86-5886. (Walter Prescott Webb Memorial Lectures: No. 20). (Illus.). 120p. 1986. 18.95 (*0-89096-291-X*) Tex A&M Univ Pr.

Richmond, Edmun B. A Comparative Survey of Seven Adult Functional Literacy Programs in Sub-Saharan Africa. (Illus.). 122p. (Orig.). (C). 1986. pap. text 17.00 (*0-8191-5521-7*) U Pr of Amer.

Richmond, Emma. Amante Temporal: His Temporary Mistress. (Bianca Ser.: No. 140).Tr. of Temporary Lover. 1999. mass mkt. 3.50 (*0-373-33490-7*, 1-33490-3) Harlequin Bks.

— The Bachelor Chase. (Romance Ser.). 1996. per. 3.25 (*0-373-03430-X*, 1-03430-5) Harlequin Bks.

— The Bachelor Chase. large type ed. (Holding Out for a Hero Ser.). 1996. per. 3.25 (*0-373-15676-6*) Harlequin Bks.

— The Bachelor Chase. large type ed. (Mills & Boon Large Print Ser.). 288p. 1996. 23.99 (*0-263-14670-7*, Pub. by Mills & Boon) Ulverscroft.

— Un Bonheur Oublie. (Azur Ser.: Bk. 739). 1999. mass mkt. 3.50 (*0-373-34739-1*, 1-37439-2) Harlequin Bks.

***Richmond, Emma.** The Boss's Bride: Marrying the Boss. (Romance Ser.: Bk. 3609). 2000. per. 3.50 (*0-373-03609-4*, 1-03609-4) Harlequin Bks.

Richmond, Emma. Casate Conmigo-A Wayward Love. 1996. per. 3.50 (*0-373-33358-7*) Harlequin Bks.

— Deliberate Provocation: Presents Plus. (Presents Ser.). 1994. per. 2.99 (*0-373-11624-1*, 1011624-3) Harlequin Bks.

— A Family Closeness. LC 95-13697. (Romance Ser.). 188p. 1995. per. 2.99 (*0-373-03374-5*, 1-03374-5) Harlequin Bks.

— First-Time Father. (Baby Boom Ser.). 1997. per. 3.25 (*0-373-03453-9*, 1-03453-7) Harlequin Bks.

— First-Time Father. large type ed. (Baby Boom Ser.). 1997. per. 3.25 (*0-373-15699-5*, 1-15699-1) Harlequin Bks.

— A Foolish Dream. (Presents Ser.: No. 461). 1992. per. 2.89 (*0-373-11461-3*, 1-11461-0) Harlequin Bks.

— A Foolish Dream. large type ed. 1995. 11.50 (*0-7505-0828-0*, Pub. by Mgna Lrg Print) Ulverscroft.

— The Gentle Trap. large type ed. 1990. reprint ed. lib. bdg. 18.95 (*0-263-12273-5*, G K Hall Lrg Type) Mac Lib Ref.

— Heart in Hiding. large type ed. 232p. 1996. 11.50 (*0-7505-0853-1*, Pub. by Mgna Lrg Print) Ulverscroft.

— Una Historia de Amor (A Love Story) (Bianca Ser.). (SPA.). 1998. per. 3.50 (*0-373-33447-8*, 1-33447-3) Harlequin Bks.

***Richmond, Emma.** A Husband for Christmas. large type ed. 1999. per. 3.50 (*0-373-15826-2*, Harlequin) Harlequin Bks.

Richmond, Emma. A Husband for Christmas. large type ed. (Mills & Boon Large Print Ser.). 288p. 1998. 24.99 (*0-263-15518-8*, Pub. by Mills & Boon) Ulverscroft.

***Richmond, Emma.** A Husband for Christmas: Daddy Boom. (Harlequin Romance Ser.). 1999. mass mkt. 3.50 (*0-373-03580-2*) Harlequin Bks.

Richmond, Emma. Instant Mother. (Romance Ser.: No. 415). 1999. mass mkt. 3.50 (*0-373-17415-2*, 1-17415-0) Harlequin Bks.

— Love of My Heart. LC 95-4593. (Romance Ser.). 185p. 1995. per. 2.99 (*0-373-03349-4*, 1-03349-7) Harlequin Bks.

***Richmond, Emma.** Matrimonsio por un Ano: Instant Mother. (Bianca Ser.: No. 152).Tr. of Marriage for a Year. (SPA.). 1999. per. 3.50 (*0-373-33502-4*, 1-33502-5) Harlequin Bks.

Richmond, Emma. More Than a Dream. (Presents Ser.). 1994. per. 2.99 (*0-373-11669-1*, 1-11669-8) Harlequin Bks.

— One Bride Required! (Romance Ser.). 1998. per. 3.50 (*0-373-03505-5*, 0-03505-5) Harlequin Bks.

— One Bride Required! large type ed. (Large Print Ser.). 1998. per. 3.50 (*0-373-15751-7*, Harlequin) Harlequin Bks.

— Por Primera Vez: First Time Father. (Bianca Ser.).Tr. of For the First Time. (SPA.). 1997. per. 3.50 (*0-373-33433-8*, 1-33433-3) Harlequin Bks.

R

— Printemps a Rome. (Azur Ser.: No. 746). (FRE.). 1999. mass mkt. 3.50 (0-373-34746-4, 1-34746-7) Harlequin Bks.
— The Reluctant Groom. 1999. mass mkt. 3.50 (0-373-17435-7, 1-17435-8) Harlequin Bks.
— A Stranger's Trust. (Presents Ser.). 1993. per. 2.99 (0-373-11582-2, 1-11582-3) Harlequin Bks.
Richmond, Emma, et al. Christmas Journeys. 1995. per. 4.99 (0-373-15271-X, 1-15271-9) Harlequin Bks.
***Richmond, Farley.** Theatre: The Collaborative Art: A Worktext with Readings. 328p. (C). 1999. pap. text 74.95 (0-7872-6008-8, 41600801) Kendall-Hunt.
Richmond, Farley P. Kutiyattam: Sanskrit Theater of India. LC 98-10879. (Illus.). (C). audio compact disk 89.95 (0-472-00263-5, 00263) U of Mich Pr.
Richmond, Farley P. Theatre: The Collaborative Art: A Worktext with Readings. 360p. (C). 1998. per. 44.95 (0-7872-5313-8, 41531301) Kendall-Hunt.
Richmond, Farley P., ed. see Miner, Allyn.
Richmond, Floyd, jt. auth. see Rudolph, Thomas.
Richmond, Frances J., jt. ed. see Peterson, Barry W.
Richmond, Frederick K. & Steketee, Martha W. State of the Child: A Profile of Pennsylvania's Children (A 1993 Factbook) (Illus.). 192p. (Orig.). 1993. pap. 20.00 (0-9637063-0-6) PA Ptnership.
— The State of the Child in Pennsylvania: A 1995 Kidscount Fact Book. 260p. 1995. pap. 29.00 (0-9645008-1-7) PA Ptnership.
Richmond, Frederick K., et al. Mathematics for Liberal Arts. (C). 2000. 20.00 (0-13-014932-2) S&S Trade.
Richmond, Frederick K., jt. auth. see Steketee, Martha W.
Richmond, G. L., ed. Second Harmonic Generation - Sum Frequency Generation at Surfaces. (Studies in Surface Science & Catalysis). 1996. text. write for info. (0-444-88893-4) Elsevier.
Richmond, Gail L. Federal Tax Research: Guide to Materials & Techniques. 4th ed. (University Textbook Ser.). 189p. 1990. pap. text 15.25 (0-88277-801-3) Foundation Pr.
— Federal Tax Research, Guide to Materials & Techniques. LC 98-137724. (University Casebook Ser.). 235p. 1997. pap. text. write for info. (1-56662-457-6) Foundation Pr.
Richmond, Gail L., jt. auth. see Llewellyn, Don W.
Richmond, Gary. Barnaby Goes Wild, No. 7. (J). (gr. 1-5). 1991. text 6.99 (0-8499-0914-7) Word Pub.
— Bears. (Illus.). (J). (ps). 1991. lib. bdg. 3.99 (0-8499-0860-4) Word Pub.
***Richmond, Gary.** Divorce Decision. 2000. pap. 21.00 (1-891833-56-1) Davidson Pr.
Richmond, Gary. The Forgotten Friend. (J). (gr. 1-5). 1991. text 6.99 (0-8499-0913-9) Word Pub.
— Successful Single Parenting. LC 97-42571. 258p. 1998. pap. 9.99 (1-56507-860-8) Harvest Hse.
Richmond-Garza, Elizabeth M. Forgotten Cites - Sights: Interpretation & the Power of Classical Citation in Renaissance English Tragedy. LC 93-37795. (Renaissance & Baroque Studies & Texts: Vol. 13). 248p. (C). 1995. text 58.95 (0-8204-2284-3) P Lang Pubng.
Richmond, George H. & Richmond, Carolynn K. The MicroSociety Handbook. Schweber, Lynn & Kharfen, Rachel, eds. LC 96-77961. (Illus.). 586p. 1996. ring bd. write for info. (0-9654262-0-3) MicroSociety.
Richmond, Grace. The Cottage in the Wood. large type ed. (Linford Romance Library). 1991. pap. 16.99 (0-7089-7120-2) Ulverscroft.
— Fugitive from Love. large type ed. (Linford Romance Library). 272p. 1992. pap. 16.99 (0-7089-7295-0) Ulverscroft.
— The Love Race. large type ed. (Linford Romance Library). 304p. 1992. pap. 16.99 (0-7089-7276-4, Linford) Ulverscroft.
— The Reluctant Heir. large type ed. (Linford Romance Library). 1990. pap. 16.99 (0-7089-6948-8) Ulverscroft.
— Yesterday's Love. large type ed. (Linford Romance Library). 1991. pap. 16.99 (0-7089-7052-4) Ulverscroft.
Richmond, Grace S. Mrs. Red Pepper. 25.95 (0-89190-493-X) Amereon Ltd.
— Red Pepper Burns. reprint ed. lib. bdg. 21.95 (0-89190-491-3, Rivercity Pr) Amereon Ltd.
— Red Pepper's Patients. reprint ed. lib. bdg. 23.95 (0-89190-492-1, Rivercity Pr) Amereon Ltd.
Richmond, H. I. Richmond Family Records Vol. I: Maryland, Virginia, New England, Ireland & Somerset. 232p. 1994. reprint ed. pap. 37.00 (0-8328-4134-X); reprint ed. lib. bdg. 47.00 (0-8328-4133-1) Higginson Bk Co.
— Richmond Family Records Vol. II: The Richmonds Alias Webb, of Wiltshire, England. 265p. 1994. reprint ed. pap. 42.00 (0-8328-4131-5); reprint ed. lib. bdg. 52.00 (0-8328-4132-3) Higginson Bk Co.
— Richmond Family Records Vol. III: The Richmonds of Wiltshire, England. 327p. 1994. reprint ed. pap. 49.50 (0-8328-4130-7); reprint ed. lib. bdg. 59.50 (0-8328-4129-3) Higginson Bk Co.
Richmond, H. M. Renaissance Landscapes: English Lyrics in a European Tradition. 1973. pap. text 33.85 (90-279-2470-8) Mouton.
Richmond, Herbert W. Sea Power in the Modern World. LC 72-4293. (World Affairs Ser.: National & International Viewpoints). 318p. 1972. reprint ed. 23.95 (0-405-04585-9) Ayer.
Richmond, Howard. Cockatiels As Pets: A Complete Authoritative Guide. (Illus.). 64p. 1998. 12.95 (0-7938-0342-X, WW101) TFH Pubns.
— Joy of Budgerigars. (Illus.). 96p. 1983. 11.95 (0-86622-082-8, PS-799) TFH Pubns.
— Joy of Cockatiels. (Illus.). 96p. 1984. 11.95 (0-87666-554-7, PS-797) TFH Pubns.
Richmond, Hugh M. King Henry VIII. LC 93-28156. (Shakespeare in Performance Ser.). 1994. text 79.95 (0-7190-3657-7, Pub. by Manchester Univ Pr) St Martin.
***Richmond, Hugh M.** Shakespeare & the Renaissance Stage: An Annotated Bibliography of Shakespeare Studies, 1604-1998. LC 99-49464. (Shakespeare Bibliographies Ser.). 130p. 2000. pap. 9.95 (1-889818-22-4) Pegasus Pr.
Richmond, Hugh M., adapted by. John Milton's Drama of Paradise Lost. LC 91-30191. (Illus.). 80p. (C). 1992. text 18.95 (0-8204-1719-X) P Lang Pubng.
Richmond, Hugh M., ed. Henry Fourth: Part One. LC 66-28232. 1967. pap. 2.05 (0-672-61092-2, Bobbs) Macmillan.
Richmond, Hugh M., ed. see Rosenberg, Marvin.
Richmond, Iain, jt. auth. see Cookson, John.
Richmond, Ian. Trajan's Army on Trajan's Column. (Illus.). 56p. 1982. pap. 9.00 (0-904152-05-7, Pub. by British Schl Rome) David Brown.
Richmond, Ian & Ball, Derek. SyBase SQL Anywhere Developer's Guide. LC 97-80451. (Illus.). 400p. 1997. mass mkt. 39.99 (1-85032-860-9) ITCP.
Richmond, Ian M., ed. Aspects of Internationalism: Language & Culture. (Papers of the Center for Research & Documentation on World Language Problems: No. 3). 162p. (C). 1992. lib. bdg. 42.50 (0-8191-8859-X) U Pr of Amer.
Richmond, J. A., jt. ed. see Martin, F. X.
Richmond, J. B. The Richmond Family, 1594-1896, & Pre-American Ancestry, 1040-1594. (Illus.). 633p. 1989. reprint ed. pap. 95.00 (0-8328-1023-1); reprint ed. lib. bdg. 103.00 (0-8328-1022-3) Higginson Bk Co.
Richmond, J. C. & DeWitt, D. P., eds. Applications of Radiation Thermometry- STP 895. LC 85-26709. (Illus.). 173p. 1985. text 28.00 (0-8031-0445-6, STP895) ASTM.
Richmond, James M., ed. Cationic Surfactants: Organic Chemistry. (Surfactant Science Ser.: Vol. 34). (Illus.). 320p. 1990. text 199.00 (0-8247-8381-6) Dekker.
Richmond, Jan. The Wealthy Tortoise: How to Get Rich Without Risk - Slowly. LC 96-69503. (Illus.). 120p. (Orig.). 1997. pap. 12.95 (0-9653237-7-3, 1456) Suntrak.
Richmond, Jessica, ed. see Romano, John.
Richmond, John C., et al. Sports Medicine for Primary Care. LC 95-32073. 608p. 1995. 79.95 (0-86542-348-2) Blackwell Sci.
Richmond, Jonathan Y. Anthology of Biosafety I: Perspectives on Laboratory Design. LC 99-60507. 273p. 1999. write for info. (1-882147-55-3) Am Art Therapy.
— Biosafety in Microbiological & Biomedical Laboratories. 183p. (Orig.). 1993. per. 8.00 (0-16-040585-8) USGPO.
Richmond, Jonathan Y., ed. Designing a Modern Microbiological/Biomedical Laboratory. LC 96-78611. 322p. (Orig.). 1997. pap. 65.00 (0-87553-231-4) Am Pub Health.
***Richmond, Jonathan Y. & McKinney, Robert W., eds.** Biosafety in Microbiological & Biomedical Laboratories. 4th ed. 250p. (Orig.). (C). 2000. pap. text 45.00 (0-7881-8513-6) DIANE Pub.
Richmond, Joy S., compiled by. Medical Reference Works, 1973-1974. LC 67-30664. 89p. 1975. pap. 3.50 (0-8108-2441-8) Scarecrow.
— Medical Reference Works, 1969-1972. LC 67-30664. 1973. pap. 5.00 (0-8108-2440-X) Scarecrow.
Richmond, Julius B. Currents in American Medicine: A Developmental View of Medical Care & Education. LC 69-12733. (Commonwealth Fund Publications). 150p. 1969. 18.00 (0-674-18015-1) HUP.
Richmond, Julius B., jt. ed. see Cheung, Lilian W.
Richmond, Julius B., jt. ed. see Walker, Deborah K.
Richmond, Katherine, jt. auth. see Clevely, Andi.
Richmond, Keith. Wanderings in Lower Dolpo: Reminiscences of a "Gonpa Thief", An Account of a Journey Through North West Nepal in the Last Quarter of 1995. (Illus.). 112p. 1998. 60.00 (0-930126-56-4) Typographeum.
Richmond, Keith, ed. see Norton, Rosaleen.
Richmond, Kent D. & Middleton, David L. The Pastor & the Patient. 144p. (Orig.). 1992. pap. 13.95 (0-687-30352-4) Abingdon.
Richmond, Leah. The Dairyman's Daughter. unabridged ed. (Children's Heritage Ser.). (Illus.). 86p. (J). (gr. 4-6). 1996. reprint ed. pap. 5.98 (1-58339-126-6, D26) Triangle Press.
— The Young Cottager. unabridged ed. (Children's Heritage Ser.). 95p. (J). (gr. 4-6). 1996. reprint ed. pap. 5.98 (1-58339-127-4, D27) Triangle Press.
Richmond, Lee. Hazmat Emergency: Leader's Guide. 2nd ed. Massingham, Gordon, ed. 1992. pap. 20.00 (0-945790-04-X) Detrick Lawrence.
Richmond, Lee J., jt. auth. see Bloch, Deborah P.
Richmond, Lee J., jt. ed. see Bloch, Deborah P.
Richmond, Leigh, jt. auth. see Richmond, Walter.
Richmond, Lewis. Work as a Spiritual Practice: A Practical Buddhist Approach to Inner Growth & Satisfaction. LC 98-30814. 320p. 1999. 25.00 (0-7679-0232-7) Broadway BDD.
***Richmond, Lewis.** Work as a Spiritual Practice: A Practical Buddhist Approach to Inner Growth & Satisfaction on. 272p. 2000. pap. 13.00 (0-7679-0233-5) Broadway BDD.
Richmond, Lewis H., jt. ed. see Azima, Fern J.
Richmond, M. A. Bid the Vassal Soar: Interpretive Essays on the Life & Poetry of Phillis Wheatley & George Moses Horton. LC 73-85493. 1974. 19.95 (0-88258-001-9) Howard U Pr.
Richmond, M. H., jt. ed. see Clarke, P. H.
Richmond, M. Temple. Sirius. LC 96-53578. 448p. (Orig.). 1997. pap. 19.95 (0-9635766-2-3) Source.
***Richmond, Mabel E.** Centennial of Decatur & Macon County. (Illus.). 479p. 1999. reprint ed. lib. bdg. 52.00 (0-8328-9794-9) Higginson Bk Co.
Richmond, Mardi, ed. Caring for a Person with Memory Loss & Confusion. (Illus.). 32p. 1995. 3.95 (1-56885-059-X) Journeyworks Pub.
Richmond, Mardi & Barash, Melanee L. Ruffing It: The Complete Guide to Camping with Dogs. Nelson, Dianne, ed. LC 98-36665. (Illus.). 224p. 1998. pap. 21.95 (1-57779-009-X) Alpine Pubns.
Richmond, Margie H., ed. Look What You Can Make with Tubes: Over 90 Pictured Crafts & Dozens of More Ideas. LC 96-80396. (Illus.). 48p. (J). (gr. k-7). 1997. pap., student ed. 5.95 (1-56397-677-3) Boyds Mills Pr.
Richmond, Marianne. The Gift of a Memory: A Keepsake to Commemorate the Loss of a Loved One. (Illus.). 48p. 1999. 15.95 (0-9652448-1-4) Marianne Richmond.
— The Gift of an Angel: For Parents Welcoming a New Child. LC 97-170991. (Illus.). 35p. 1997. 15.95 (0-9652448-0-6) Marianne Richmond.
Richmond, Marie L. Immigrant Adaptation & Family Structure Among Cubans in Miami, Florida. Cortes, Carlos E., ed. LC 79-6220. (Hispanics in the United States Ser.). (Illus.). 1981. lib. bdg. 23.95 (0-405-13168-2) Ayer.
Richmond, Marvin. Tornado! Eighty-Four Minutes, Ninety-Four Lives. LC 93-70976. 328p. 1993. VHS 19.95 (0-9636277-1-6) Chandler Hse.
Richmond, Marvin, jt. auth. see O'Toole, John.
Richmond, Mary. The Long View. (Russell Sage Foundation Reprint Ser.). (Illus.). 1971. reprint ed. lib. bdg. 37.00 (0-697-00209-8) Irvington.
Richmond, Mary E. Friendly Visiting among the Poor, a Handbook for Charity Workers. LC 69-16244. (Criminology, Law Enforcement, & Social Problems Ser.: No. 92). 1969. reprint ed. 18.00 (0-87585-092-8) Patterson Smith.
— Social Diagnosis. 512p. 1917. 45.00 (0-87154-703-1) Russell Sage.
— What Is Social Case Work? An Introductory Description. LC 70-137185. (Poverty U. S. A. Historical Record Ser.). 1977. reprint ed. 23.95 (0-405-03123-8) Ayer.
Richmond, Mary E. & Hall, Fred S. A Study of Nine & Eighty-Five Widows Known to Certain Charity Organization Societies in 1910. LC 74-3971. (Women in America Ser.). (Illus.). 84p. 1974. reprint ed. 16.95 (0-405-06119-6) Ayer.
Richmond, Mary E., jt. auth. see Ellsworth, Anzolette D.
Richmond, Michael D. How to Retire in 7 Years. 70p. 1996. pap. 7.00 (0-9656913-1-4) Eagle Pubns IL.
— This Is Your Life. 80p. 1998. pap. 10.00 (0-9656913-2-2) Eagle Pubns IL.
Richmond, Michael D. & Black, Rex E. God's Money in Caesar's Pocket. 87p. (Orig.). 1996. pap. 10.00 (0-9656913-7-3) Eagle Pubns IL.
Richmond, Naima & Cuneo, Marilyn M., eds. Seeing the World Through Women's Eyes. (Illus.). 183p. (Orig.). 1996. pap. 11.95 (0-9655569-0-5) Womens Intl Leag.
Richmond, Oliver P. Mediating in Cyprus: The Cypriot Communities & the United Nations. LC 98-11818. (Peacekeeping Ser.: No. 3). 320p. 1998. 54.50 (0-7146-4877-9, Pub. by F Cass Pubs) Intl Spec Bk.
— Mediating in Cyprus: The Cypriot Communities & the United Nations. LC 98-11818. (Peacekeeping Ser.: No. 3). xxxi, 282p. 1998. pap. 24.50 (0-7146-4431-5) Intl Spec Bk.
Richmond, Olney H. Card Interpretations: From "Mystic Test Book" McLaren-Owens, Iain, ed. & intro. by. (Astro-Cards Reprints Ser.). (Illus.). 130p. 1997. reprint ed. pap. text 9.00 (1-885500-17-3, AR:12) Astro-Cards.
— Mystic Test Book. Date not set. pap. text 14.95 (0-87877-245-6) Newcastle Pub.
— The Mystic Test Book: Magic of the Cards. 6th annot. ed. McLaren-Owens, Iain, ed. LC 97-77161. (Astro-Cards Reprints Ser.). (Illus.). 387p. 1998. reprint ed. pap. text 40.00 (1-885500-13-0, AR:11) Astro-Cards.
— The Mystic Test Book: The Magic of the Cards. 1997. reprint ed. pap. 17.50 (0-7873-0717-3) Hlth Research.
— Temple Lectures Pts. 1 & 2: Religion of the Stars; Evolutionism. McLaren-Owens, Iain, ed. & pref. by. (Astro-Cards Reprints Ser.). (Illus.). 263p. 1996. reprint ed. pap. text 26.00 (1-885500-14-9, AR9) Astro-Cards.
— Temple Lectures of the Order of the Magi. 1996. reprint ed. spiral bd. 16.50 (0-7873-0718-1) Hlth Research.
— Temple Lectures of the Order of the Magi (1892) 270p. 1996. reprint ed. pap. 14.95 (1-56459-801-2) Kessinger Pub.
Richmond, Pamela. Bookbinding: A Manual of Techniques. (Illus.). 160p. 1995. pap. 35.00 (1-85223-886-0, Pub. by Crolwood) Trafalgar.
Richmond, Pamela. Good Night, Sweet Prince. LC 98-67765. write for info. (1-57087-442-5) Prof Pr NC.
Richmond, Patricia J. Trail to Disaster. 1992. pap. 14.95 (0-87081-275-0) Univ Pr Colo.
Richmond, Peggy A. On the Road to Economic Development: Continuing Education Programs at Historically Black Colleges & Universities. 95p. 1997. pap. 13.00 (0-16-063605-1) USGPO.
Richmond, Peggy A. & Maramark, Sheilah. On the Road to Economic Development: A Guide for Continuing Education Programs at Historically Black Colleges & Universities. (Illus.). 89p. (Orig.). (C). 1997. pap. text 30.00 (0-7881-3996-7) DIANE Pub.
Richmond, Peter. Ballpark: Camden Yards & the Building of an American Dream. 288p. 1995. per. 13.00 (0-684-80048-9, Fireside) S&S Trade Pap.
Richmond, Peter, jt. auth. see Ali, Muhammad.
Richmond Publishing. Richmond Picture Dictionary: A Child's First Bilingual Dictionary, 1. 1998. pap. text 19.95 (1-58105-260-X) Santillana.
***Richmond, Ray.** South Park: The Tourist Guide to South Park. 1999. 25.00 (0-671-03634-3) PB.
— Tv Moms: None. 192p. 2000. pap. 14.95 (1-57500-130-6, Pub. by TV Bks) HarpC.
Richmond, Ray, ed. The Simpsons: A Complete Guide to Your Favorite Family. LC 98-141857. (Illus.). 256p. 1997. pap. 16.95 (0-06-095252-0, Perennial) HarperTrade.
Richmond, Ray & Goodman, David. South Park a Stickyforms Adventure: 4 C Hardcover. (Illus.). 96p. 1998. 25.00 (0-671-02599-6) PB.
Richmond, Raymond. My Greatest Day in Show Business: Screen Legends Share Their Fondest Memories. LC 99-18436. 1999. pap. 15.95 (0-87833-224-3) Taylor Pub.
Richmond, Robert H., ed. Proceedings of the Seventh International Coral Reef Symposium, 2 vols. Incl. Vol. 1. (Illus.). (C). 1994. (1-881629-01-5); Vol. 2. (Illus.). (C). 1994. (1-886129-02-9); 1993. 125.00 (1-881629-03-1) Univ Guam Pr.
Richmond, Robert W. Kansas: A Land of Contrasts. 4th ed. LC 98-49693. (Illus.). 411p. (C). 1999. text 31.95 (0-88295-949-2) Harlan Davidson.
— Kansas: A Pictorial History. rev. ed. LC 92-13822. (Illus.). xii, 276p. 1992. 35.00 (0-7006-0543-6) U Pr of KS.
Richmond, Robert W. & Mardock, Robert W., eds. A Nation Moving West: Readings in the History of the American Frontier. LC 66-10446. 376p. reprint ed. pap. 116.60 (0-7837-6013-2, 204582400008) Bks Demand.
Richmond, Robin. Animals in Art. LC 93-9766. (Story in a Picture Ser.). (Illus.). 48p. (J). (gr. 2-5). 1993. text 15.95 (0-8249-8613-X, Ideals Child); lib. bdg. 16.00 (0-8249-8626-1, Ideals Child) Hambleton-Hill.
— Children in Art. LC 92-7184. (Story in a Picture Ser.). (Illus.). 48p. (J). (gr. 2-5). 1992. 15.95 (0-8249-8552-4, Ideals Child); lib. bdg. 16.00 (0-8249-8588-5, Ideals Child) Hambleton-Hill.
— Michelangelo & the Creation of the Sistine Chapel. LC 95-14238. (Illus.). 160p. 1995. 14.99 (0-517-14194-9) Random Hse Value.
Richmond, Robyn L., ed. Interventions for Smokers: An International Perspective. LC 93-38968. (Illus.). 363p. 1994. 39.00 (0-683-07272-2) Lppncott W & W.
Richmond, Roe. Rio Grande Riptide. large type ed. (Linford Western Library). 368p. 1993. pap. 16.99 (0-7089-7359-0, Linford) Ulverscroft.
— Showdown at Fire Hill. (Orig.). 1979. mass mkt. 1.95 (0-89083-560-8, Zebra Kensgtn) Kensgtn Pub Corp.
Richmond, Rosemary. Rosie: Selected Works by Rosemary Richmond. 180p. (Orig.). 1995. pap. 10.95 (0-9646037-2-1) Rosehill Pr IL.
Richmond, Sally. Decorative Painting. 1995. 7.98 (0-7858-0320-3) Bk Sales Inc.
Richmond, Sandra. Shoot to Score, Vol. 31. (Sports Stories Ser.). 92p. (J). (gr. 3-7). 1999. text 5.50 (1-55028-642-0, Pub. by J Lorimer) Orca Bk Pubs.
— Wheels for Walking. Kroupa, Melanie, ed. LC 85-70855. 196p. (YA). (gr. 6 up). 1985. 13.95 (0-316-74439-5, Joy St Bks) Little.
Richmond, Scott. Fishing in Oregon's Best Fly Waters. LC 98-71182. 228p. 1998. pap. 24.95 (0-916473-13-9) Flying Pencil.
— Fishing in Oregon's Cascade Lakes. (Illus.). 192p. (Orig.). 1994. pap. 12.95 (0-914763-09-1) Educ Development.
— Fishing in Oregon's Cascade Lakes. LC 94-70896. (Illus.). 214p. (Orig.). 1994. pap. 14.95 (0-916473-09-0) Flying Pencil.
— Fishing in Oregon's Deschutes River. LC 93-70651. (Illus.). 176p. (Orig.). 1993. pap. 14.95 (0-916473-08-2) Flying Pencil.
— Fishing in Oregon's Endless Season. (Illus.). 218p. (Orig.). 1997. pap. 14.95 (0-916473-11-2) Flying Pencil.
— The Pocket Gillie: Fly Fishing Essentials. 224p. 1992. pap. 14.95 (0-9633067-0-7) Four Rivers Pr.
— River Journal - Crane Prairie & Deschutes Headwaters. (River Journal Ser.: Vol. 5, No. 4). (Illus.). 48p. 1999. pap. 15.95 (1-57188-095-X) F Amato Pubns.
***Richmond, Scott.** Rogue River Vol. 6, No. 2. (River Journal Ser.). 1999. pap. 15.95 (1-57188-171-9, JRG) F Amato Pubns.
Richmond, Simon, jt. auth. see Dodd, Jan.
Richmond, Steve. Aphrodite Rising. 66p. 1990. pap. 6.50 (0-9625349-2-7) Guerilla Poetics.
— Demon Notebook. 48p. (Orig.). 1988. pap. 6.95 (0-934953-21-X) Water Row Pr.
— Earth Rose. 249p. 1993. pap. 10.00 (1-883657-00-8) Earth Rose Pr.
— Five Point OL. Berlinski, Allen, ed. (Illus.). 32p. (Orig.). 1991. pap. 4.95 (0-941543-02-1) Sun Dog Pr.
— Hitler Painted Roses. (Illus.). 112p. 1994. pap. 12.00 (0-941543-05-6) Sun Dog Pr.
— Hitler Painted Roses. deluxe limited ed. (Illus.). 112p. 1994. pap. 20.00 (0-941543-06-4) Sun Dog Pr.
— Red Work, Black Widow. LC 76-15539. (Illus.). 1976. pap. 2.00 (0-916918-03-3) Duck Down.
— Santa Monica Poems. (Illus.). 48p. 1987. pap. 8.00 (0-941543-00-5) Sun Dog Pr.
— Spinning Off Bukowski. (Illus.). 144p. (Orig.). 1996. pap. 12.95 (0-941543-10-2) Sun Dog Pr.
— Spinning Off Bukowski. limited ed. (Illus.). 144p. (Orig.). 1996. pap. 20.95 (0-941543-11-0) Sun Dog Pr.
Richmond, Steven, jt. auth. see Greenblatt, Michael.
Richmond, Susan. Further Steps in Stagecraft. LC 98-41015. 80p. (Orig.). 1994. pap. 6.00 (0-88734-907-2) Empire Pub Srvs.
— A Junior Textbook of Stagecraft. LC 98-31675. 98p. (Orig.). 1994. pap. 6.00 (0-88734-906-4) Empire Pub Srvs.
— A Textbook of Stagecraft. LC 98-40826. 140p. (Orig.). 1994. pap. 6.00 (0-88734-908-0) Empire Pub Srvs.
Richmond, Susan, et al. Operational Parameters for Hazardous Waste Combustion Devices. (Illus.). 83p. (C). 1997. reprint ed. pap. text 30.00 (0-7881-4158-9) DIANE Pub.

An Asterisk (*) at the beginning of an entry indicates that the title is appearing for the first time.

R

Richmond, Ted, tr. see Babin, Ronald.

Richmond, Theo. Konin: One Man's Quest for a Vanished Jewish Community. 1996. pap. 15.00 (*0-679-75823-2*) Vin Bks.

Richmond, Velma B. The Legend of Guy of Warwick. LC 95-17168. (Studies in Medieval Literature: Vol. 14). (Illus.). 632p. 1995. text 109.00 (*0-8153-2085-X*, H1929) Garland.

— The Popularity of Middle English Romance. LC 75-21576. 1975. 14.95 (*0-87972-114-6*) Bowling Green Univ Popular Press.

Richmond, Virginia P. & McCroskey, James C. Nonverbal Communication. 4th ed. LC 99-45962. 356p. (C). 1999. pap. text 40.00 (*0-205-29577-0*, Longwood Div) Allyn.

— Organizational Communication for Survival: Making Work, Work. 168p. (C). 1991. pap. text 38.00 (*0-13-640079-5*) P-H.

Richmond, Virginia P. & McCroskey, James C., eds. Power in the Classroom: Communication, Control, & Concern. (Communication Ser.). 224p. 1992. text 45.00 (*0-8058-1027-7*) L Erlbaum Assocs.

Richmond, Virginia P., jt. auth. see McCroskey, James C.

Richmond, Virginia P., jt. ed. see McCroskey, James C.

Richmond, W. Edson. Ballad Scholarship: An Annotated Bibliography. LC 84-48017. 320p. 1989. text 20.00 (*0-8240-8932-4*, H499) Garland.

Richmond, W. Edson, ed. see Wolford, Leah J.

Richmond, Walter & Richmond, Leigh. The Lost Millennium. rev. ed. xviii, 172p. 1986. pap. 10.95 (*0-943975-00-X*) Interdimens Sci.

Richmond, Winthrop E., ed. Studies in Folklore: In Honor of Distinguished Service Professor Stith Thompson. LC 72-163547. (Illus.). 270p. 1972. reprint ed. lib. bdg. 15.00 (*0-8371-6208-4*, RISF, Greenwood Pr) Greenwood.

Richmond, Yale. From Da to Yes: Understanding the East Europeans. LC 95-3679. (InterAct Ser.). 320p. (Orig.). (C). 1995. pap. 18.95 (*1-877864-30-7*) Intercult Pr.

— From Nyet to Da: Understanding the Russians. 2nd rev. ed. LC 96-16004. (InterAct Ser.). 219p. 1996. pap. 18.95 (*1-877864-41-2*, 1408R) Intercult Pr.

Richmond, Yale & Gestrin, Phyllis. Into Africa: Intercultural Insights. LC 97-38933. (InterAct Ser.). 305p. 1998. pap. 17.95 (*1-877864-57-9*) Intercult Pr.

***Richmong, Velma B.** Shakespeare, Catholicism, & Romance. LC 99-40184. 208p. 1999. 34.50 (*0-8264-1209-2*) Continuum.

Richnak, Barbara. A River Flows: The Life of Robert Lardin Fulton. LC 83-51605. (Illus.). 210p. (Orig.). 1984. pap. 9.95 (*0-915933-00-4*) Comstock NV Pub Co.

— Silver Hillside: The Life & Times of Virginia City. (Illus.). 200p. 1985. 29.95 (*0-915933-01-2*) Comstock NV Pub Co.

Richner, Hans & Phillips, Peter, eds. The Radiosonde Intercomparison SONDEX: Spring, 1981, Payerne. (Contributions to Current Research in Geophysics Ser.: Vol. 11). 352p. 1984. text 79.95 (*3-7643-1614-4*) Birkhauser.

***Richo, David.** Catholic Means Universal: Integrating Spirituality & Religion. LC 99-39020. 1999. pap. 16.95 (*0-8245-1837-3*) Crossroad NY.

Richo, David. How to Be an Adult: A Handbook on Psychological & Spiritual Integration. 144p. 1991. pap. 8.95 (*0-8091-3223-0*) Paulist Pr.

— Shadow Dance: Liberating the Power & Creativity of Your Dark Side. LC 98-46478. 332p. 1999. pap. 15.95 (*1-57062-444-5*, Pub. by Shambhala Pubns) Random.

***Richo, David.** Unexpected Miracles: The Gift of Synchronicity & How to Open It. LC 97-32409. 192p. 1998. pap. 14.95 (*0-8245-1729-6*, Crsrd) Crossroad NY.

Richo, David. When Love Meets Fear: How to Become Defense-Less & Resource-Ful. LC 96-39729. 240p. (Orig.). 1997. pap. 12.95 (*0-8091-3702-X*) Paulist Pr.

Richstad, Jim & McMillan, Michael. Mass Communication & Journalism in the Pacific Islands: A Bibliography. LC 77-20695. 330p. reprint ed. pap. 102.30 (*0-7837-3975-3*, 204380500011) Bks Demand.

Richstatter, Thomas. Liturgical Law Today: New Style, New Spirit. LC 77-3008. 271p. reprint ed. pap. 84.10 (*0-608-13632-8*, 201910400011) Bks Demand.

— Liturgy & Worship: A Course on Prayer & Sacraments: Keystone Parish Edition. (Faith & Witness Program Ser.). (Illus.). 128p. (J). (gr. 7-9). 1999. pap. text 7.50 (*0-8215-5655-X*) Sadlier.

— Liturgy & Worship - A Course on Prayer & Sacraments: Keystone School Edition. (Faith & Witness Program Ser.). (Illus.). 192p. (J). (gr. 7-9). 1998. pap. text 11.40 (*0-8215-5604-5*) Sadlier.

— Sacraments: How Catholics Pray. LC 96-180331. 144p. 1995. pap. 7.95 (*0-86716-176-0*) St Anthony Mess Pr.

Richstatter, Thomas, jt. auth. see Blevins, Isabel F.

Richsteig, E. Libanius: Index Nominum Propriorum. 90p. 1963. reprint ed. write for info. (*0-318-72041-8*) G Olms Pubs.

Richstein, Kelly & Sachsel, Nan, eds. Dark Orchid: Anthology of Erotica. (Illus.). 80p. (Orig.). 1993. pap. 8.75 (*1-882300-02-5*) Willo Trees.

Richt, Adrian, ed. see Dunn, Robert W.

Richtarik, Marilynn J. Acting Between the Lines: The Field Day Theatre Company & Irish Cultural Politics, 1980-84. (English Monographs). 364p. 1995. text 65.00 (*0-19-818247-3*) OUP.

Richter. Borzoi Book of Short Fiction. 1983. teacher ed. 16.50 (*0-07-554436-9*) McGraw.

— Critical Tradition. 2nd ed. LC 97-74970. 1600p. 1997. pap. text 73.95 (*0-312-10106-6*) St Martin.

— Falling: Story. 4th ed. 2000. pap. text 39.15 (*0-312-13369-3*) St Martin.

— Falling into Theory. 2nd ed. 1999. pap. text 22.95 (*0-312-20156-7*) St Martin.

***Richter.** Ireland & Her Neighbours in the Seventh Century. 17th ed. LC 98-37332. 256p. 1999. text 55.00 (*0-312-22075-8*) St Martin.

Richter. Unix Systemverwalting. (GER.). (C). 1990. text. write for info. (*0-201-56206-5*) Addison-Wesley.

Richter, Stephen. Tapping Technique for Bass Guitar: From Beginner to Professional Level. (Progressive Ser.). 1997. pap. text 14.95 (*0-947183-16-7*) KLAP Records.

Richter, Ada. The Ada Richter Piano Course Bk. 1: For Individual or Class Instruction. 2nd ed. Flatau, Carole, ed. (Illus.). 40p. (J). (gr. 2-6). 1981. reprint ed. pap. text 5.95 (*0-7692-0093-1*, AR003) Wrner Bros.

Richter, Alan. The Investment Astrology Articles of Dr. Alan Richter. LC 96-84954. (Illus.). ii, 81p. (Orig.). 1996. pap. 21.00 (*0-9652424-3-9*) Catt Bks.

— Sexual Slang: A Compendium of Offbeat Words & Colorful Phrases, from Shakespeare to Today. 3rd ed. LC 94-34728. 1995. 12.00 (*0-602-72504-6*, Perennial) HarperTrade.

***Richter, Anne.** Jewelry of South East Asia. LC 00-36363. (Illus.). 304p. 2000. 75.00 (*0-8109-3528-7*, Pub. by Abrams) Time Warner.

Richter, Barbara. Eat Like a Horse: And Lose Weight. (Illus.). 192p. (Orig.). 1994. pap. 11.95 (*0-9641715-3-8*) Airplane Bks.

Richter, Benno. Breitling Timepieces: 1884 to the Present. Force, Edward, tr. LC 95-37218. (Illus.). 176p. 1995. 49.95 (*0-88740-864-8*) Schiffer.

***Richter, Benno.** Breitling Timepieces, 1884-Present. 2nd rev. ed. LC 99-86815. (Illus.). 176p. 2000. 49.95 (*0-7643-1006-2*) Schiffer.

Richter-Bernburg, Lutz. Persian Medical Manuscripts at the University of California, Los Angeles: A Descriptive Catalogue. LC 77-94986. (Humana Civilitas Ser.: Vol. 4). (Illus.). xxiv, 297p. 1978. 57.00 (*0-89003-026-X*) Undena Pubns.

Richter-Bernburg, Melanie, tr. see Von Westphalen, Joseph.

Richter, Bernd C. & Kreitler, Charles W. Geochemical Techniques for Identifying Sources of Ground-Water Salinization. 272p. 1993. lib. bdg. 85.00 (*1-56670-000-0*, L5000) Lewis Pubs.

***Richter, Bernd C. & Richter, Susan E.** Do Alaskans Live in Igloos? Show Me Your Alaska Home. (Illus.). 32p. (Orig.). (J). (ps-6). 1999. pap. 9.95 (*0-9663495-2-0*, Pub. by Saddle Pal Creat) Partners-West.

— How Alaska Got Its Flag. LC 99-97038. (Illus.). 32p. (J). (gr. 1-4). 2000. 9.95 (*0-9663495-4-7*) Saddle Pal Creat.

— Peek-a-Boo Alaska. (J). (ps). 2000. bds. 6.95 (*0-9663495-5-5*) Saddle Pal Creat.

— Uncover Alaska's Wonders. 24p. (J). (ps-1). 1999. 10.95 (*0-9663495-3-9*, Pub. by Saddle Pal Creat) Partners-West.

— When Grandma & Grandpa Visited Alaska They. . . (Illus.). 48p. (Orig.). (J). (ps-6). 1998. pap., boxed set 9.95 (*0-9663495-0-4*, Pub. by Saddle Pal Creat) Partners-West.

— When Grandma Visited Alaska She. . . (Illus.). 48p. (Orig.). (J). (ps-6). 1999. pap., boxed set 9.95 (*0-9663495-1-2*, Pub. by Saddle Pal Creat) Partners-West.

Richter, Bernice & Wenzel, Duane. The Museum of Science & Industry Basic List of Children's Science Books, 1973-1984. LC 85-18719. 167p. reprint ed. pap. 51.80 (*0-7837-5917-7*, 204571600007) Bks Demand.

— The Museum of Science & Industry Basic List of Children's Science Books, 1986. LC 86-22320. 83p. reprint ed. pap. 30.00 (*0-7837-5953-3*, 204575300007) Bks Demand.

— The Museum of Science & Industry Basic List of Children's Science Books, 1987. LC 87-641170. 85p. reprint ed. pap. 30.00 (*0-7837-5954-1*, 204575400007) Bks Demand.

Richter, Bertina. Fort Miller, California, 1851-1865. (American University Studies: Regional Studies: Ser. XX, Vol. 2). X, 154p. (C). 1988. text 27.00 (*0-8204-0703-8*) P Lang Pubng.

Richter, Betts. Something Special Within. 2nd ed. (Illus.). 48p. (J). (ps-5). 1982. reprint ed. pap. 7.95 (*0-87516-488-9*) DeVorss.

Richter, Brigitte. Precis de Bibliotheconomie. 5th rev. ed. (FRE.). ix, 298p. 1992. lib. bdg. 32.50 (*3-598-11077-4*) K G Saur Verlag.

Richter, C., et al, eds. Numerical Methods of Nonlinear Programming: Implementations. (Mathematical Research Ser.). 135p. 1991. 29.00 (*3-05-500883-9*, Pub. by Akademie Verlag) Wiley.

Richter, Carl, ed. see Crumb, R.

Richter, Charles F. Designing Flexible Object-Oriented Systems with UML. (Software Engineering Ser.). (Illus.). 404p. 1999. pap. 40.00 (*1-57870-098-1*) Macmillan Tech.

Richter, Conrad. Brothers of No Kin: And Other Stories. LC 72-10812. (Short Story Index Reprint Ser.). 1977. reprint ed. 24.95 (*0-8369-4225-6*) Ayer.

— Early Americana & Other Stories. 23.95 (*0-89190-857-9*) Amereon Ltd.

— The Fields. LC 90-20771. 161p. 1991. reprint ed. pap. 12.95 (*0-8214-0979-4*) Ohio U Pr.

— The Free Man. LC 98-39180. (Pennsylvania Paperbacks Ser.). 160p. 1998. pap. 13.95 (*0-8122-1679-2*) U of Pa Pr.

— The Lady. 20.95 (*0-89190-332-1*) Amereon Ltd.

— The Light in the Forest. 21.95 (*0-89190-333-X*) Amereon Ltd.

— The Light in the Forest. 1991. lib. bdg. 21.95 (*1-56849-064-X*) Buccaneer Bks.

— The Light in the Forest. 144p. (YA). 1994. mass mkt. 4.99 (*0-449-70437-8*) Fawcett.

Richter, Conrad. Light in the Forest. 1994. 10.09 (*0-606-06903-8*, Pub. by Turtleback) Demco.

Richter, Conrad. The Light in the Forest, Set. abr. ed. (J). 1992. audio 15.99 (*0-553-47047-7*, 391070) BDD Aud Pub.

— The Sea of Grass. 128p. 1984. mass mkt. 3.50 (*0-345-31778-5*, Ballantine) Ballantine Pub Grp.

— Sea of Grass. 138p. Date not set. 18.95 (*0-8488-2590-X*) Amereon Ltd.

— The Sea of Grass. LC 92-5181. 149p. (C). 1992. reprint ed. pap. 9.95 (*0-8214-1026-1*) Ohio U Pr.

— The Town. 1981. lib. bdg. 17.95 (*0-89967-048-2*, Harmony Rain) Buccaneer Bks.

— The Town. LC 90-20736. 300p. 1991. reprint ed. pap. 14.95 (*0-8214-0980-8*) Ohio U Pr.

— The Trees. LC 90-19936. 167p. 1991. reprint ed. pap. 12.95 (*0-8214-0978-6*) Ohio U Pr.

Richter, Conrad, jt. auth. see Center for Learning Network Staff.

***Richter, Curt P.** Portrait of Southern Writers. 2000. 45.00 (*1-892514-83-4*) Hill St Pr.

Richter, D., et al, eds. Advanced Psychosomatic Research in Obstetrics & Gynecology. (Illus.). xv, 262p. 1991. 107.00 (*0-387-52500-9*) Spr-Verlag.

— Dynamics of Disordered Materials. (Proceedings in Physics Ser.: Vol. 37). (Illus.). 320p. 1989. 70.95 (*0-387-50942-9*, 2789) Spr-Verlag.

— The Structure & Conformation of Amphiphilic Membranes: Proceedings of the International Workshop on Amphiphilic Membranes, Julich, Germany, September 16-18, 1991. LC 92-14296. (Proceedings in Physics Ser.: Vol. 66). (Illus.). xi, 298p. 1992. 90.95 (*0-387-55452-1*) Spr-Verlag.

Richter, D. & Springer, Timothy A., eds. Polymer Motion in Dense Systems. (Proceedings in Physics Ser.: Vol. 29). (Illus.). 305p. 1988. 70.00 (*0-387-19167-4*) Spr-Verlag.

***Richter, Dagmar.** X Y Z: The Architecture of Dagmar Richter. (Illus.). 192p. 2001. pap. 35.00 (*1-56898-248-8*) Princeton Arch.

Richter, Daniel K. The Ordeal of the Longhouse: The Peoples of the Iroquois League in the Era of European Colonization. LC 92-53621. (Institute of Early American History & Culture Ser.). (Illus.). xviii, 436p. (C). 1992. 59.95 (*0-8078-2060-1*); pap. 19.95 (*0-8078-4394-6*) U of NC Pr.

Richter, David. Collector's Guide to Tootsietoys. 2nd ed. (Illus.). 272p. 1995. pap. text 19.95 (*0-89145-676-7*, 4566) Collector Bks.

Richter, David H. The Borzoi Book of Short Fiction. 1439p. (C). 1982. pap. 41.25 (*0-07-554363-X*) McGraw.

— Fab 4 Chronicles: The Early Days of the Beatles. 1998. pap. text 12.95 (*1-901674-57-6*) Arrowhead.

— Fable's End: Completeness & Closure in Rhetorical Fiction. LC 74-10344. x, 214p. (C). 1995. lib. bdg. 24.00 (*0-226-71317-2*) U Ch Pr.

— Falling into Theory: Conflicting Views on Reading Literature. 297p. 1993. pap. text 22.95 (*0-312-08122-7*) St Martin.

— Kurt Cobain Files. 1998. pap. text 12.95 (*1-901674-61-4*) Arrowhead.

— Metallica Files. 1998. pap. text 12.95 (*1-901674-60-6*) Arrowhead.

— Oasis Chronicles. 1998. pap. text 12.95 (*1-901674-42-8*) Arrowhead.

Richter, David H., ed. Ideology & Form in Eighteenth-Century Literature. LC 99-13130. 288p. 1999. 39.95 (*0-89672-415-8*) Tex Tech Univ Pr.

— Narrative - Theory. LC 95-21302. 352p. (C). 1995. pap. 35.66 (*0-8013-1610-3*) Longman.

Richter, Detlev. Lacquered Boxes. LC 89-84171. (Illus.). 216p. 1989. 69.95 (*0-88740-197-X*) Schiffer.

Richter, Detlev K. Entstehung und Diagenese der Devonischen und Permotriassischen Dolomite in der Eifel: Text in German with English Summary. (Contributions to Sedimentology Ser.: No. 2). (GER., Illus.). ii, 101p. 1974. 26.00 (*3-510-57002-2*, Pub. by E Schweizerbartsche) Balogh.

Richter, Dieter. Aachen und Umgebung: Nordeifel und Nordardennen mit Vorland. (Sammlung Geologischer Fuehrer Ser.: Band 48). (GER., Illus.). xvi, 302p. 1985. spiral bd. 29.00 (*3-443-15044-6*, Pub. by Gebruder Borntraeger) Balogh.

— Allgauer Alpen. 3rd ed. (Sammlung Geologischer Fuehrer Ser.: Band 77). (GER., Illus.). x, 253p. 1984. spiral bd. 29.00 (*3-443-15038-1*, Pub. by Gebruder Borntraeger) Balogh.

— Ruhrgebiet und Bergisches Land: Zwischen Ruhr und Wupper. 3rd ed. (Sammlung Geologischer Fuehrer Ser.: Band 55). (GER., Illus.). x, 222p. 1996. spiral bd. 35.00 (*3-443-15063-2*, Pub. by Gebruder Borntraeger) Balogh.

— Stratigraphisch-Tektonische Analyse des Kristallinen Westlichen Fichtelgebirges Unter Besonderer Beruecksichtigung der Pravariscischen Magmatite. (Geotektonische Forschungen Ser.: Vol. 16). (GER.). ii, 120p. 1963. 35.00 (*3-510-50907-2*, Pub. by E Schweizerbartsche) Balogh.

Richter, Dietmar, ed. Lipmann Symposium: Energy, Regulation & Biosynthesis in Molecular Biology. 698p. (C). 1974. 138.50 (*3-11-004976-7*) De Gruyter.

Richter, Don, jt. ed. see Wyckoff, D. Campbell.

Richter, Donald. Chemical Soldiers: British Gas Warfare in World War I. LC 92-12329. (Modern War Studies). (Illus.). xii, 284p. 1992. 35.00 (*0-7006-0544-4*) U Pr of KS.

— Chemical Soldiers: British Gas Warfare in World War One. (Illus.). 286p. 1994. 43.50 (*0-85052-388-5*, Pub. by Leo Cooper) Trans-Atl Phila.

— Where the Sun Stood Still. LC 92-61189. 432p. 1992. text 19.95 (*0-9611696-3-X*) D Richter.

Richter, Donald C., ed. see Sotheby, Lionel.

Richter, Donald G. Lincoln: Twenty Years on the Eastern Prairie. (Illus.). 348p. 1999. 35.00 (*0-9654976-2-3*) Vermil.

***Richter, E.** Technical Dictionary: Machinery, Installation, Environment. (GER & ENG.). 706p. 1998. 195.00 (*0-320-02141-6*) Fr & Eur.

Richter, E. & Feyerabend, T. Normal Lymph Node Topography: A CT-Atlas. (Illus.). 120p. 1990. 165.00 (*0-387-52549-1*) Spr-Verlag.

Richter, Eberhardt. Woerterbuch Tibetisch-Deutsch. 3rd ed. (GER & TIB.). 444p. 1992. 115.00 (*0-7859-8301-5*, 3324002745) Fr & Eur.

Richter, Eileen W. & Montgomery, Patricia C. Sensorimotor Integration for Developmentally Disabled Children: A Handbook. 2nd ed. LC 76-62660. 100p. 1991. pap. 49.50 (*0-87424-142-1*, W-142A) Western Psych.

— The Sensorimotor Performance Analysis. (Illus.). 135p. (C). 1989. pap. 30.00 (*0-685-27007-6*) PDP Pr.

Richter, Elaine. Discovering Life after Divorce. (Master's Touch Bible Study Ser.). 63p. 1994. pap. 4.50 (*0-570-09438-0*, 20-2459) Concordia.

Richter, Erik A. & Saltin, Bengt, eds. Skeletal Muscle Metabolism in Exercise & Diabetes: Proceedings of the Copenhagen Muscle Research Center Symposium on Regulation of Skeletal Muscle Metabolism: Focus on Glucose Transport, Held in Copenhagen, Denmark, October 23-26, 1997. LC 98-26175. (Advances in Experimental Medicine & Biology Ser.: Vol. 441). (Illus.). 340p. 1998. 95.00 (*0-306-45920-5*, Kluwer Plenum) Kluwer Academic.

Richter, Eugene. Co-Operative Stores, Their History, Organization, & Management. LC 76-47885. reprint ed. 37.50 (*0-404-60088-3*) AMS Pr.

Richter, Eva, tr. see Neumann, Eckhard.

Richter, Frank, jt. auth. see Buttner, Manfred.

Richter, Frank J. Strategic Networks: The Art of Japanese Interfirm Cooperation. LC 99-14372. 206p. 1999. 49.95 (*0-7890-0725-8*, Intl Busn Pr) Haworth Pr.

Richter, Frank-Jurgen. The Dynamics of Japanese Organizations. LC 95-34232. (International Studies in Asian-Pacific Business Ser.: Vol. 1). 224p. (C). 1996. 85.00 (*0-415-13191-X*) Routledge.

***Richter, Frank-Jurgen.** The East Asian Development Model: Economic Growth Institutional. LC 99-45254. 2000. text 69.95 (*0-312-23305-1*) St Martin.

Richter, Frank-Jurgen, ed. Business Networks in Asia: Promises, Doubts & Perspectives. LC 98-48945. 320p. 1999. 75.00 (*1-56720-302-7*, Quorum Bks) Greenwood.

***Richter, Frank-Jurgen, ed.** The Dragon Millennium: Chinese Business in the Coming World Economy. LC 99-36601. (Illus.). 240p. 2000. 59.95 (*1-56720-353-1*, Q353, Quorum Bks) Greenwood.

Richter, Franz A., tr. see Holm, Bill.

Richter, G. Gazetteer of Coorg. (C). 1995. 16.00 (*81-86142-55-X*, Pub. by Low Price) S Asia.

— German-English - English-German Dictionary of Optics, Photography & Video. 429p. 1993. 93.00 (*3-88955-063-0*) IBD Ltd.

— German-English--English-German Dictionary of Optics, Photography & (ENG & GER.). 429p. 1993. 110.00 (*0-7859-8773-8*) Fr & Eur.

Richter, G., jt. ed. see Pecsi, M.

***Richter-Gebert, J. & Kortenkamp, U. H.** A User's Manual for the Interactive Geometry Software Cinderella. 150p. 2000. pap. 24.95 (*3-540-67139-0*) Spr-Verlag.

Richter-Gebert, Jurgen. Realization Spaces of Polytopes, Vol. 164. LC 96-51634. (Lecture Notes in Mathematics Ser.). 187p. 1996. pap. 35.00 (*3-540-62084-2*) Spr-Verlag.

Richter, George. The Consciousness of Earth. 195p. (Orig.). 1989. pap. 10.00 (*0-9622662-0-5*) Gaia Pr.

— Evolving Order: Critical Path to Human Survival. LC 94-61712. (Illus.). 260p. (Orig.). 1996. pap. 12.95 (*0-9643542-0-9*) Yin-Yang Bks.

***Richter, Gerard.** Photography & Painting in the Work of Gerard Richter. (Illus.). 2000. pap. 22.00 (*84-89771-91-X*) Actar.

Richter, Gergory C., tr. see Rank, Otto.

Richter, Gerhard. Abstract Painting. (Illus.). 1997. 19.95 (*3-931141-42-X*) Dist Art Pubs.

Richter, Gerhard. Catalogue Raisonne, 1962-1993, 3 vols. annot. ed. (GER., Illus.). 544p. 125.00 (*3-89322-574-9*, Pub. by Dr Cantz sche Druckerei GmbH) Dist Art Pubs.

Richter, Gerhard. The Daily Practice of Painting: Writings 1960-1993. Obrist, Hans-Ulrich, ed. Britt, David, tr. LC 95-9818. (ENG & GER., Illus.). 272p. 1995. pap. text 25.00 (*0-262-68084-X*) MIT Pr.

— Gerhard Richter: Atlas. (Illus.). 432p. 1997. 85.00 (*1-881616-88-6*) Dist Art Pubs.

— Gerhard Richter: Catalogue Raisome, 1962-1993. 1997. 125.00 (*3-89322-554-4*, Pub. by Edition Cantz) Dist Art Pubs.

***Richter, Gerhard.** Gerhard Richter: Drawings 1964-1999. Schwarz, Dieter, ed. & text by. Pelzer, Birgit, text. (Illus.). 320p. 2000. 80.00 (*3-933807-04-2*, Pub. by Richter Verlag) Dist Art Pubs.

Richter, Gerhard. Gerhard Richter: Landscapes. 1998. 45.00 (*3-89322-951-5*) Dist Art Pubs.

***Richter, Gerhard.** Gerhard Richter: Watercolors 1964-1997. (Illus.). 160p. 2000. 60.00 (*3-933807-05-0*, Pub. by Richter Verlag) Dist Art Pubs.

Richter, Gerhard. Gerhard Richter, 1998. (Illus.). 112p. 1999. 65.00 (*0-947564-78-0*) A D'Offay Gallery.

***Richter, Gerhard.** Gerhard Richter, 1998. (Illus.). 112p. 1999. pap. 40.00 (*0-947564-75-6*, Pub. by A D'Offay Gallery) Dist Art Pubs.

R

Richter, Gerhard. Theodoros Dukas Laskaris: Der Naturliche Zusammenhang: Ein Zeugnis vom Stand der Byzantinischen Philosophie in der Mitte des 13. Jahrhunderts. (GER.). viii, 258p. (Orig.). 1989. pap. 78.00 (*90-256-0944-9*, Pub. by AM Hakkert) BookLink Distributors.

***Richter, Gerhard.** Walter Benjamin & the Corpus of Autobiography. LC 99-48541. (Kritik Ser.). 307p. 2000. 34.95 (*0-8143-2880-6*) Wayne St U Pr.

Richter, Gernot, jt. auth. see Durchholz, Reiner.

Richter, Gerold, jt. auth. see Pecsi, Marton.

Richter, Gert. Lexikon der Kunstmotive: Antike und Christliche Welt. (GER.). 319p. 1993. 29.95 (*0-7859-8689-8*, 357200554x) Fr & Eur.

Richter, Gisela. The Portraits of the Greeks. Smith, R. R., ed. LC 83-73222. (Illus.). 272p. 1984. text 52.50 (*0-8014-1683-3*) Cornell U Pr.

Richter, Gisela M. Archaic Gravestones of Attica. (Illus.). 184p. 1988. reprint ed. pap. text 30.00 (*0-86516-189-5*) Bolchazy-Carducci.

— Catalogue of the Greek & Roman Antiquities in the Dumbarton Oaks Collection. LC 56-10351. (Illus.). 77p. 1956. 20.00 (*0-88402-002-9*) Dumbarton Oaks.

— A Handbook of Greek Art. 9th ed. (Quality Paperbacks Ser.). (Illus.). 431p. 1987. pap. text 22.50 (*0-306-80298-8*) Da Capo.

— Handbook of Greek Art: A Survey of the Visual Arts of Ancient Greece. (Illus.). 328p. (C). 1994. reprint ed. pap. 22.95 (*0-7148-2496-8*, Pub. by Phaidon Press) Phaidon Pr.

— Korai: Archaic Greek Maidens: A Study of the Development of the Kore Type in Greek Sculpture. LC 87-80026. (Illus.). xii, 327p. 1988. reprint ed. lib. bdg. 100.00 (*0-87817-318-8*) Hacker.

— Kouroi: Archaic Greek Youths: A Study of the Development of the Kouros Type in Greek Sculpture. LC 87-80047. (Illus.). xvi, 365p. 1988. reprint ed. lib. bdg. 100.00 (*0-87817-317-X*) Hacker.

Richter, Goetz W., et al, eds. International Review of Experimental Pathology Vol. 33: Progress in Hodgkins Disease. (Illus.). 368p. (C). 1992. text 104.00 (*0-12-366833-6*) Acad Pr.

Richter, Gregory C. The Gate of All Marvelous Things: A Guide to Reading the Tao Te Ching. (CHI & ENG.). 150p. 1998. pap. text 16.95 (*1-891688-00-6*) China Bks.

Richter, Gregory C., tr. see Rank, Otto.

Richter, Gunter. Nikon F5. LC 97-178221. (Magic Lantern Guides Ser.). (Illus.). 176p. (Orig.). (C). 1998. pap. 19.95 (*1-883403-24-3*, H 131, Silver Pixel Pr) Saunders Photo.

Richter, Gunter & Burian, Peter K. Nikon N70-F70. Ohlig, Hayley, tr. from GER. (Magic Lantern Guides Ser.). (Illus.). 176p. (Orig.). (C). 1998. pap. 19.95 (*1-883403-19-7*, H 141, Silver Pixel Pr) Saunders Photo.

Richter, Gunter, jt. auth. see Burian, Peter K.

Richter, Gunter, jt. auth. see Pollock, Steve.

Richter, H. J., ed. Thermodynamics & the Design, Analysis, & Improvement of Energy Systems 1993. LC 93-73595. 435p. pap. 80.00 (*0-7918-1042-9*) ASME.

Richter, H. P. & Schwan, W. Creighton. Wiring Simplified: Based on the 1999 National Electrical Code. 39th rev. ed. (Illus.). 224p. 1999. pap. 9.95 (*0-9603294-7-1*, QBI 99-221) Park Pub.

Richter, Hans. Dada: Art & Anti-Art. Britt, David, tr. from GER. LC 96-61461. (World of Art Ser.). (Illus.). 246p. 1997. reprint ed. pap. 14.95 (*0-500-20039-4*, Pub. by Thames Hudson) Norton.

— The World Between the Ox & the Swine: Dada Drawings by Hans Richter. (Illus.). 56p. 1971. pap. 2.00 (*0-911517-43-X*) Mus of Art RI.

***Richter, Hans-Gunther.** Sexueller Mi & Beta; Brauch Im Spiegel von Zeichnungen: Interpretationsansatze--Interpretationsversuche. 341p. 1999. 32.95 (*3-631-34977-7*) P Lang Pubng.

Richter, Hans P. Friedrich. LC 86-18702. (Novels Ser.). 149p. (J). (gr. 7-12). 1987. pap. 4.99 (*0-14-032205-1*, PuffinBks) Peng Put Young Read.

— Friedrich. (J). (gr. 6 up). 1992. 19.00 (*0-8446-6573-8*) Peter Smith.

— I Was There. (Novels Ser.). (J). (gr. 5-9). 1987. pap. 4.99 (*0-14-032206-X*, PuffinBks) Peng Put Young Read.

Richter, Hans P. I Was There. (J). 1987. 10.09 (*0-606-02170-1*, Pub. by Turtleback) Demco.

Richter, Hans Peter. Friedrich. 1987. 10.09 (*0-606-01812-3*, Pub. by Turtleback) Demco.

Richter, Harvena. The Innocent Island. Hunting, Constance, ed. 1999. pap. 9.95 (*0-913006-69-6*) Puckerbrush.

— Writing to Survive: The Private Notebooks on Conrad Richter. LC 87-34237. 289p. reprint ed. pap. 89.60 (*0-7837-5851-0*, 204557000006) Bks Demand.

Richter, Heinz. British Intervention in Greece from Varkiza to Civil War. 1985. 35.95 (*0-85036-301-2*, Pub. by MRLN) Paul & Co Pubs.

Richter, Helmut. Helmut Richter Buildings & Projects. LC 99-37069. (Illus.). 200p. 1999. 70.00 (*3-7643-5361-9*) Birkhauser.

Richter, Helmut, jt. ed. see Gibbon, Dafydd.

Richter, Herbert P. Gettering & Defect Engineering in Semiconductor Technology. 660p. 1992. text 200.00 (*0-87849-568-1*, Pub. by Trans T Pub) Enfield Pubs NH.

— Gettering & Defect Engineering in Semiconductor Technology: GADEST 93. (Solid State Phenomena Ser.: Vol. 32-33). (Illus.). 642p. (C). 1993. text 216.00 (*3-908450-00-4*, Pub. by Trans T Pub) Enfield Pubs NH.

— Gettering & Defect Engineering in Semiconductor Technology: GADEST '95. (Solid State Phenomena Ser.: Vol. 47-48). (Illus.). 640p. 1995. text 216.00 (*3-908450-11-X*, Pub. by Trans T Pub) Enfield Pubs NH.

Richter, Herbert P. & Schwan, W. Creighton. Practical Electrical Wiring: Residential, Farm & Industrial. 16th ed. LC 92-35995. 643p. 1992. 35.00 (*0-07-052394-0*) McGraw.

Richter, Herbert P., jt. auth. see Schwan, W. C.

Richter, Herbert W. & Rubenstein, Charles F. Electrical & Electronic Drafting. 2nd ed. LC 84-29191. 317p. 1985. text 44.95 (*0-471-05784-3*) P-H.

Richter, Ida. Compassion. 1973. pap. 2.95 (*0-686-16723-6*) Malcolm Hse.

Richter, Ingo, jt. ed. see Birch, Ian.

Richter, Irma A., ed. & selected by see da Vinci, Leonardo.

Richter, Irving. Labor's Struggles, 1945-1950: A Participant's View. (Illus.). 176p. (C). 1994. text 64.95 (*0-521-41412-1*) Cambridge U Pr.

***Richter, J. E., ed.** GERD: Current Issues & Controversies. (Digestive Diseases Ser.: Vol. 18, No. 1 (2000)). (Illus.). 48p. 2000. pap. 25.25 (*3-8055-7079-1*) S Karger.

Richter, James G. Khrushchev's Double Bind: International Pressures & Domestic Coalition Politics. LC 93-48702. 263p. 1994. text 45.00 (*0-8018-4814-8*) Johns Hopkins.

Richter, Jan, jt. auth. see Seiger, Lon H.

Richter, Jared H. Norway: Eighteen Seventy-One to Eighteen Seventy-Five Issue Skilling Denominations, Shaded Posthorn. (Illus.). 50p. (Orig.). 1984. pap. text 5.00 (*0-936493-07-0*) Scand Philatelic.

Richter, Jared H., ed. see Berntsen, Arnstein.

Richter, Jared H., ed. see Gellein, Per.

Richter, Jared H., ed. see Thune-Larsen, D.

Richter, Jean-Paul, ed. see da Vinci, Leonardo.

Richter, Jeffrey M. Advanced Windows. 3rd ed. 1996. pap. text 49.99 incl. cd-rom (*1-57231-548-2*) Microsoft.

***Richter, Jeffrey M.** Programming Applications for Microsoft Windows. LC 99-40456. 1999. pap. 59.99 (*1-57231-996-8*) Microsoft Pr.

Richter, Jeffrey M. Windows 3.1: A Developer's Guide. 2nd ed. LC 92-16517. 1995. 39.95 incl. disk (*1-55851-276-4*, M&T Bks) IDG Bks.

Richter, Jeffrey M., jt. auth. see Clark, Jason.

Richter, Jeffrey M., jt. auth. see Locke, Jonathan.

Richter, Jessica & Fraknoi, Andrew. Project ASTRO How-To Manual for Teachers & Astronomers. (Illus.). 42p. 1996. pap. 5.00 (*1-886733-99-6*) Astron Soc Pacific.

Richter, Joachim B. Hans Ferdinand Massmann: Altdeutscher Patriotismus im 19. Jahrhundert. (Quellen und Forschungen zur Sprach und Kulturgeschichte der Germanischen Voelker: NF Band 100, 224). (GER.). xiv, 482p. (C). 1992. lib. bdg. 175.40 (*3-11-012910-8*) De Gruyter.

Richter, Joachim F. Antique Enamels for Collectors. LC 90-61804. (Illus.). 176p. 1990. 59.95 (*0-88740-261-5*) Schiffer.

Richter, Jochen H. Die Knozeption Des "Neuen Menschen" In Ernst Barlachs Dramatischen Schaffen. LC 92-8238. (American University Studies: Germanic Languages & Literature: Ser. I, Vol. 95). 189p. (C). 1993. text 38.95 (*0-8204-1552-9*) P Lang Pubng.

Richter, Joel D. A Comparative Methods of Approach to the Study of Oocytes & Embryos. LC 98-13183. (Advances in Molecular Biology Ser.). (Illus.). 536p. 1999. pap. text 65.00 (*0-19-511594-5*) OUP.

Richter, Joel D., ed. Mrna Formation & Function. LC 97-33343. (Illus.). 395p. 1997. text 85.00 (*0-12-587545-2*) Morgan Kaufmann.

Richter, Joel E. Ambulatory Esophageal PH Monitoring: Practical Approach & Clinical Applications. 2nd ed. LC 97-2003. 1997. write for info. (*4-260-14343-3*); write for info. (*0-89640-343-2*) Igaku-Shoin.

— Ambulatory Esophageal PH Monitoring: Practical Approach & Clinical Applications. 2nd ed. LC 97-2003. 229p. 1997. 49.00 (*0-683-30335-X*) Lppncott W & W.

Richter, Joel E., ed. Ambulatory Esophageal PH Monitoring: Practical Approach & Clinical Applications. 2nd ed. (Illus.). 1997. write for info. (*0-614-23147-7*) Igaku-Shoin.

Richter, Joel E., jt. ed. see Castell, Donald O.

Richter, Johann P. Army Chaplain Schmelzle's Journey to Flaetz & Life of Quintus Fixlein. Carlyle, Thomas, tr. from GER. (GERM Ser.: Vol. 57). xxii, 310p. 1992. 60.00 (*0-938100-89-0*) Camden Hse.

Richter, John H., ed. Topical Time, Vol. 12-13. 2nd ed. (Illus.). 44p. 1970. reprint ed. pap. text 7.00 (*0-935991-26-3*) Am Topical Assn.

Richter, John T. & Richter, Vera M. Nature, the Healer. 1996. reprint ed. spiral bd. 23.50 (*0-7873-0719-X*) Hlth Research.

Richter, Judy. Pony Talk: A Complete Learning Guide for Young Riders. (Illus.). 192p. 1993. 22.00 (*0-87605-849-7*) Howell Bks.

Richter, Judy & Maynard, Sue. Horse & Rider: From Basics to Show Competition LC 78-11735. xiii, 146p. 1979. write for info. (*0-671-18369-9*) S&S Trade.

Richter, Julius. History of Protestant Missions in the Near East. LC 79-133822. reprint ed. 54.50 (*0-404-05331-9*) AMS Pr.

Richter, K. Atlas of Reptiles & Amphibians. 830p. 1988. 129.95 (*0-86622-958-2*, H-1102) TFH Pubns.

Richter, Karen, jt. auth. see Sandor, Bela I.

Richter, Kathleen. Shades of Gray. LC 95-91055. 75p. 1998. 10.95 (*0-533-11842-5*) Vantage.

Richter, Klaus C. The Cavalry of the Wehrmacht, 1941-1945. Johnston, David, tr. from GER. LC 95-68640. (Illus.). 208p. 1995. 29.95 (*0-88740-814-1*) Schiffer.

***Richter, Klaus C.** Semiclassical Theory of Mesoscopic Quantum Systems. LC 99-51337. (Tracts in Modern Physics Ser.: Vol. 161). (Illus.). ix, 219p. 2000. 129.00 (*3-540-66566-8*) Spr-Verlag.

Richter, Klaus C. Weapons & Equipment of the German Cavalry in World War II. Johnston, David, tr. from GER. (Illus.). 48p. 1995. pap. 9.95 (*0-88740-816-8*) Schiffer.

Richter, Klemens. The Meaning of the Sacramental Symbols: Answers to Today's Questions. Maloney, Linda M., tr. from GER. 132p. 1990. pap. 11.95 (*0-8146-1882-0*) Liturgical Pr.

Richter, Konrad. Wipe Your Feet, Santa Claus! 1985. 10.95 (*0-03-005739-6*) H Holt & Co.

Richter, L. Training Needs: Assessment & Monitoring. viii, 83p. (Orig.). 1990. pap. 15.75 (*92-2-105458-6*) Intl Labour Office.

Richter, L., jt. auth. see Mason, W.

***Richter, Laurence R.** Tchaikovsky's Complete Song Texts. (ENG & RUS.). xi, 146p. 1999. pap. text 20.00 (*1-878617-29-X*) Leyerle Pubns.

Richter, Linda K. Land Reform & Tourism Development: Policy Making in the Philippines. 240p. 1982. 22.95 (*0-87073-413-X*); pap. 15.95 (*0-87073-414-8*) Schenkman Bks Inc.

Richter, Linda M., jt. auth. see Barbarin, Oscar A.

Richter, Lydia. Beloved Kathe Kruse Dolls: Yesterday & Today. rev. ed. 112p. 1991. pap. 12.95 (*0-87588-210-2*) Hobby Hse.

— China, Parian & Bisque German Dolls. LC 94-152109. (Illus.). 184p. 1993. 39.95 (*0-87588-411-3*) Hobby Hse.

— Collecting Antique Dolls. (Illus.). 124p. (Orig.). 1991. pap. 12.95 (*0-87588-362-1*) Hobby Hse.

Richter, Lydia & Schmelcher, Karin. Heubach Character Dolls & Figurines. (Illus.). 144p. 1992. 29.95 (*0-87588-393-1*) Hobby Hse.

Richter, M. M., et al, eds. Computation & Proof Theory, Pt. 2. (Lecture Notes in Mathematics Ser.: Vol. 1104). viii, 475p. 1984. 59.95 (*0-387-13901-X*) Spr-Verlag.

Richter, M. M., jt. ed. see Muller, G. H.

Richter, Manfred, jt. auth. see Wotjak, Barbara.

Richter, Marga. Blackberry Vines & Winter Fruit for Orchestra. (Illus.). 1978. pap. 15.00 (*0-8258-0063-3*, 05073) Fischer Inc NY.

Richter, Maurice N., Jr. The Autonomy of Science: An Historical Comparative Analysis. LC 80-23534. 188p. 1981. text 18.95 (*0-87073-381-8*); pap. text 11.95 (*0-87073-382-6*) Schenkman Bks Inc.

— Science As a Cultural Process. 160p. 1972. pap. text 13.95 (*0-87073-073-8*) Schenkman Bks Inc.

— Society: A Macroscopic View. 122p. 1980. pap. text 11.95 (*0-87073-804-6*) Schenkman Bks Inc.

— Technology & Social Complexity. LC 82-5683. 120p. (C). 1983. text 64.50 (*0-87395-644-3*); pap. text 21.95 (*0-87395-645-1*) State U NY Pr.

Richter, Max. Vorarlberger Alpen. 2nd ed. (Sammlung Geologischer Fuehrer Ser.: Band 49). (GER., Illus.). x, 171p. 1978. spiral bd. 23.00 (*3-443-15023-3*, Pub. by Gebruder Borntraeger) Balogh.

Richter, Melvin. The History of Political & Social Concepts: A Critical Introduction. 224p. 1995. text 49.95 (*0-19-508826-3*) OUP.

— The Politics of Conscience: T. H. Green & His Age. Johnson, Peter, ed. (Idealism Ser.: No. 4). 415p. 1996. 72.00 (*1-85506-486-3*) Bks Intl VA.

Richter, Melvin. The Politics of Conscience: T. H. Green & His Age. Johnson, Peter, ed. (Idealism Ser.: No. 4). (Illus.). 415p. 1996. pap. 25.00 (*1-85506-487-1*) Bks Intl VA.

Richter, Melvin, tr. & intro. see Montesquieu.

Richter, Melvin, tr. & intro. see Montesquieu, Charles de Secondat.

Richter, Michael. The Formation of the Medieval West: Studies in the Oral Culture of the Barbarians. LC 94-29797. 1994. text 59.95 (*0-312-12402-3*) St Martin.

— Ireland & Her Neighbours in the Seventh Century. LC 99-194776. 272p. 1999. boxed set 55.00 (*1-85182-369-7*, Pub. by Four Cts Pr) Intl Spec Bk.

— Medieval Ireland: The Enduring Tradition. Stone, Brian & Keogh, Adrian, trs. from GAE. 224p. 1996. pap. 19.95 (*0-312-15812-2*) St Martin.

— Studies in Medieval Language & Culture. LC 95-225225. 250p. 1995. 49.50 (*1-85182-171-6*, Pub. by Four Cts Pr) Intl Spec Bk.

Richter, Michael, ed. see Hennig, John.

Richter, Michael M. Algorithmic Learning Theory: 9th International Conference, ALT'98, Otzenhausen, Germany, October 8-10, 1998, Proceedings, Vol. 150. Smith, C. H. et al, eds. LC 98-40480. (Lecture Notes in Computer Science Ser.: Vol. 1501). xi, 439p. 1998. pap. 67.00 (*3-540-65013-X*) Spr-Verlag.

***Richter, Michaela W.** The Party State & Democracy in Germany. 1999. text (*0-312-21461-8*) St Martin.

Richter, N., jt. auth. see Hoegner, W.

***Richter, Nelly.** Gestaltpadagogisches Lehren und Lernen im Deutsch Als Fremdsprache-Unterricht. (Werkstattreihe Deutsch als Fremdsprache Ser.). 174p. 1999. 35.95 (*3-631-34413-9*) P Lang Pubng.

Richter, O. & Sondgerath, D. Parameter Estimation in Ecology: The Link Between Data & Models. LC 89-25070. 218p. 1990. 142.00 (*3-527-27954-7*, Wiley-VCH) Wiley.

Richter, O., et al. Environmental Fate Modelling of Pesticides: From the Laboratory to the Field Scale. (Illus.). 320p. 1996. 175.00 (*3-527-30064-3*, Wiley-VCH) Wiley.

Richter, O. G., jt. auth. see Huchtmeier, W. K.

Richter, P. H., jt. auth. see Peitgen, Heinz-Otto.

Richter, Patricia & Duvivier, Roger. Midlife, Madness, or Menopause: Does Anyone Know What's Normal? 264p. 1995. pap. 12.95 (*1-56561-059-8*) Wiley.

Richter, Patricia, ed. see Matos, Candi & Matos, Chris.

Richter, Patricia J. Midlife, Madness, or Menopause: Does Anyone Know What's Normal? 264p. 1995. pap. 12.95 (*0-471-34685-3*) Wiley.

Richter, Paul. David Hume's Kausalitaetstheorie und Ihre Bedeutung Fuer die Begrundung der Theorie der Induktion. (Abhandlungen zur Philosophie und Ihrer Geschichte Ser.: Bd. 1). (GER.). iv, 51p. 1980. reprint ed. write for info. (*3-487-06768-4*) G Olms Pubs.

Richter, Paul, jt. ed. see Schwadron, Terry.

Richter, Peter-Cornell, ed. Nude Photography: Masterpieces from the Past 150 Years. LC 98-234099. (Illus.). 144p. 1998. pap. 29.95 (*3-7913-1998-1*) te Neues.

Richter, Peyton E. & Fogg, Walter L. Philosophy Looks to the Future: Confrontation, Commitment & Utopia. 2nd ed. 576p. (C). 1985. reprint ed. pap. text 31.95 (*0-88133-185-6*) Waveland Pr.

Richter, R., ed. Graphs & Algorithms. LC 89-216. (Contemporary Mathematics Ser.: Vol. 89). 197p. 1989. pap. 30.00 (*0-8218-5095-4*, CONM/89) Am Math.

Richter, R., jt. auth. see Assonyi, Cs.

Richter, R., jt. auth. see Elzer, P. F.

Richter, Ralph, photos by. Frank O. Gehry, Museo Guggenheim Bilbao. (Opus Ser.: Vol. 32). (Illus.). 56p. 1998. 39.00 (*3-930698-32-3*, Pub. by Edition A Menges) Natl Bk Netwk.

***Richter, Ralph A.** How Are Companies & Workers Preparing for the Workforce of the Future? 113p. 2000. per. 11.00 (*0-16-050289-6*) USGPO.

***Richter, Robert.** Cuauhtemoc Cardenas & the Roots of Mexico's New Democracy. (Contemporary Profiles & Policy Series for the Younger Reader). (YA). (gr. 8 up). 2000. write for info. (*0-934272-66-2*); pap. write for info. (*0-934272-65-4*) J G Burke Pub.

Richter, Robert. Something in Vallarta. LC 90-53330. 208p. 1991. 22.00 (*1-877946-09-5*) Permanent Pr.

Richter, Robert F. SEC Accounting & Reporting Manual, 2 vols. ring bd. 340.00 (*0-685-69600-6*, SAPM) Warren Gorham & Lamont.

Richter, Roland, tr. see Pflaum, Hans G.

Richter, Rudolf, jt. auth. see Furuboth, Eirik G.

Richter, Rudolf, jt. auth. see Furubotn, Eirik G.

Richter, Rudolf, jt. ed. see Furubotn, Eirik G.

Richter, Rudolf, jt. ed. see Haller, Max.

Richter, Scott E., et al. Securities Litigation: Forms & Analysis, 2 vols. 1989. ring bd. 250.00 (*0-685-44956-4*) West Group.

Richter, Stacey. My Date with Satan: Stories. LC 99-13146. 224p. 1999. 21.50 (*0-684-85701-4*) S&S Trade.

***Richter, Stacey.** My Date with Satan: Stories. 224p. 2000. pap. 11.00 (*0-684-85702-2*) Scribner.

Richter, Stephan. Bass Licks. (Progressive Ser.). 1997. pap. text 14.95 incl. cd-rom (*0-947183-72-8*) Koala Pubns.

— Blues Bass. (Progressive Ser.). (Illus.). 1997. pap. 14.95 incl. cd-rom (*1-875726-42-X*) Koala Pubns.

— Blues Bass Licks. (Progressive Ser.). (Illus.). 1997. pap. text 14.95 incl. cd-rom (*1-875726-44-6*) Koala Pubns.

— Heavy Metal Bass Licks. (Progressive Ser.: Vol. 2). 1997. pap. 14.95 incl. audio compact disk (*0-947183-62-0*) Koala Pubns.

— Heavy Metal Bass Licks, Vol. 1. 1997. pap. 14.95 (*0-947183-61-2*) Koala Pubns.

— Heavy Metal Method Bass Guitar. (Progressive Ser.). 1997. pap. text 14.95 incl. cd-rom (*0-947183-64-7*) Koala Pubns.

— Heavy Metal Techniques Bass Guitar. 1997. pap. 14.95 (*0-947183-65-5*) Koala Pubns.

— Introducing Bass. 1997. pap. 14.95 (*0-947183-88-4*) Koala Pubns.

— Rhythm Section Method for Bass & Drums. (Progressive Ser.). (Illus.). 1997. pap. text 14.95 incl. audio compact disk (*1-875726-06-3*) Koala Pubns.

— Rock Bass. (Progressive Ser.). (Illus.). 1997. pap. text 14.95 incl. audio compact disk (*1-875726-41-1*) Koala Pubns.

— Rock Bass Licks. (Progressive Ser.). (Illus.). 1997. pap. text 14.95 (*1-875726-43-8*) Koala Pubns.

— Tapping Technique for Bass Guitar. 1997. pap. 14.95 (*0-947183-17-5*) Koala Pubns.

Richter, Stephen B. & Fields, Scott J. Winning Lottery Combinations Vol. 1: Guaranteed Number Sets for All Pick 5, 6 & 7 Games. 137p. (Orig.). 1990. pap. 19.95 (*0-9625318-0-4*) Over Horizon.

Richter, Stephen B. & Moquin, Brian P. Book of Guaranteed Winning Pick 5 Lottery Combinations, Series 4, Series 4. 228p. Date not set. pap. 19.95 (*1-892896-48-6*) Buy Books.

— Book of Guaranteed Winning Pick 5 Lottery Combinations. 228p. 1998. pap. 19.95 (*1-892896-45-1*); pap. 19.95 (*1-892896-46-X*); pap. 19.95 (*1-892896-47-8*) Buy Books.

— Book of Guaranteed Winning Pick 6 Lottery Combinations, Series 1. 228p. 1998. pap. 19.95 (*1-892896-81-8*) Buy Books.

— Book of Guaranteed Winning Pick 6 Lottery Combinations, Series 2. 228p. 1998. pap. 19.95 (*1-892896-82-6*) Buy Books.

— Book of Guaranteed Winning Pick 6 Lottery Combinations, Series 3. 228p. 1998. pap. 19.95 (*1-892896-83-4*) Buy Books.

— Book of Guaranteed Winning Pick 6 Lottery Combinations, Series 4. 228p. 1998. pap. 19.95 (*1-892896-84-2*) Buy Books.

Richter, Stephen B. & Moquin, Brian P. Book of Guaranteed Winning Pick 4 Lottery Combinations, Series 1. 220p. 1998. pap. 19.95 (*1-892896-41-9*) Buy Books.

— Book of Guaranteed Winning Pick 4 Lottery Combinations, Series 2. 220p. 1998. pap. 19.95 (*1-892896-42-7*) Buy Books.

— Book of Guaranteed Winning Pick 4 Lottery Combinations, Series 3. 220p. 1998. pap. 19.95 (*1-892896-43-5*) Buy Books.

An Asterisk (*) at the beginning of an entry indicates that the title is appearing for the first time.

— Book of Guaranteed Winning Pick 4 Lottery Combinations, Series 4. 220p. 1998. pap. 19.95 (*1-892896-44-3*) Buy Books.

— Book of Guaranteed Winning Pick 7 Lottery Combinations, Series 1. 1998. pap. 19.95 (*1-892896-85-0*) Buy Books.

— Book of Guaranteed Winning Pick 7 Lottery Combinations, Series 2. 1998. pap. 19.95 (*1-892896-86-9*) Buy Books.

— Book of Guaranteed Winning Pick 7 Lottery Combinations, Series 3. 228p. 1998. pap. 19.95 (*1-892896-87-7*) Buy Books.

— Book of Guaranteed Winning Pick 7 Lottery Combinations, Series 4. 228p. 1998. pap. 19.95 (*1-892896-88-5*) Buy Books.

Richter, Sue, ed. see Tickle, Naomi R.

Richter, Susan, jt. auth. see Kaare, Christian.

Richter, Susan E., jt. auth. see Richter, Bernd C.

*__Richter, Thomas.__ Untersuchungen zu den lokalen Panthea Sud: Und Mittelbabyloniens in altbabylonischer Zeit. (Alter Orient und Altes Testament Ser.: Vol. 257). xxii, 518p. 1999. text 92.00 (*3-927120-64-2*, Pub. by Ugarit-Verlag) Eisenbrauns.

Richter, Thomas, ed. see Bock, Barbara.

Richter-Ushanas, Egbert. Indus Script & the Rg Veda. LC 97-902045. (C). 1997. 34.00 (*81-208-1405-3*, Pub. by Motilal Bnarsidass) S Asia.

Richter, Vera M. Mrs. Richter's Cook-Less Book with Scientific Food Chart. 15th ed. 1996. reprint ed. spiral bd. 11.00 (*0-7873-0720-3*) Hlth Research.

Richter, Vera M., jt. auth. see Richter, John T.

Richter Verlag Staff. Gunther Forg. (Illus.). 174p. 1996. 70.00 (*3-928762-56-7*, 620793, Pub. by Richter Verlag) Dist Art Pubs.

Richter, Walter, jt. auth. see Herring, Charles, Jr.

Richter, Will, ed. see Schwartz, Eduard.

Richter, William L. The ABC-CLIO Companion to American Reconstruction, 1862-1877. LC 96-46616. (Clio Companion Staff). 505p. 1997. lib. bdg. 60.00 (*0-87436-851-0*) ABC-CLIO.

— The ABC-CLIO Companion to Transportation in America. LC 95-13170. (ABC-CLIO Companions Ser.). (Illus.). 653p. (YA). (gr. 8 up). 1995. lib. bdg. 65.00 (*0-87436-789-1*) ABC-CLIO.

— The Army in Texas during Reconstruction, 1865-1870. LC 86-30056. (Military History Ser.: No. 3). 280p. 1987. 35.95 (*0-89096-282-0*) Tex A&M Univ Pr.

— Overreached on All Sides: The Freedmen's Bureau Administrators in Texas, 1865-1868. LC 91-15364. 448p. 1991. 49.50 (*0-89096-473-4*) Tex A&M Univ Pr.

Richter, William L., et al, eds. Combating Corruption - Encouraging Ethics. 350p. 1990. 29.95 (*0-936678-14-3*) Am Soc Pub Admin.

Richter, William L. & Reagan, Charles E., eds. The Landon Lectures: Perspectives from the First Twenty Years. LC 87-81227. (Illus.). 361p. 1987. 25.00 (*0-9616658-1-5*) Friends Lib KSU.

Richter, William L., jt. auth. see Smith, Ronald D.

Richter, Wolfgang, jt. ed. see Bauer, Gunther.

Richterich, Roland & Colombo, J. P. Clinical Chemistry: Theory, Practice, & Interpretation. LC 80-40286. (Illus.). 790p. reprint ed. pap. 200.00 (*0-608-17558-7*, 203053900069) Bks Demand.

Richterich, Roland, jt. ed. see Colombo, Jean-Pierre.

Richtermeyer, Mark & Entrepreneur Magazine Staff. Entrepreneur Magazine: Entrepreneurial Opportunities on the Internet. (Entrepreneur Magazine Ser.). 256p. 2000. pap. 19.95 (*0-471-17825-X*) Wiley.

Richters, Christian, photos by. Berger+Parkkinen, Die Botschaften der Nordischen Lander, Berlin: Opus 40. (GER & ENG., Illus.). 60p. 42.00 (*3-930698-40-4*) Edition A Menges.

— Heinz Tesar, Sammlung Essl, Klosterneuburg: Opus 38. (GER & ENG., Illus.). 60p. 42.00 (*3-930698-38-2*) Edition A Menges.

— Kisho Kurokawa, New Wing, Van Gogh Museum, Amsterdam: Opus 39. (Illus.). 60p. 42.00 (*3-930698-39-0*) Edition A Menges.

Richters, John E., et al, eds. Children & Violence. 144p. 1993. pap. text 20.00 (*0-89862-588-2*) Guilford Pubns.

Richthofen, Manfred. The Red Air Fighter. LC 98-49436. 1999. pap. 18.95 (*1-85367-362-5*) Stackpole.

Richthofen, Manfred F. Von, see Von Richthofen, Manfred F.

Richtik, Cyndy. Good Stranger, Bad Stranger, Bk. 2. (Luma Ser.). (Illus.). 48p. (J). (gr. 1-6). 1995. 16.95 (*0-9643318-1-0*) Vis Bks Intl.

— Pet-a-Luma. LC 94-96332. (Luma Ser.). (Illus.). 23p. (J). (gr. k-12). 1994. 14.95 (*0-9643318-0-2*) Vis Bks Intl.

Richtmyer, R. D. Principles of Advanced Mathematical Physics, Vol. 1. (Texts & Monographs in Physics). (Illus.). 1985. 75.95 (*0-387-08873-3*) Spr-Verlag.

— Principles of Advanced Mathematical Physics, Vol. II. (Texts & Monographs in Physics). (Illus.). 350p. 1986. 79.95 (*0-387-10772-X*) Spr-Verlag.

Richtmyer, Robert D. & Morton, K. W. Difference Methods for Initial-Value Problems. 2nd ed. 420p. (C). 1994. reprint ed. lib. bdg. 49.50 (*0-89464-763-6*) Krieger.

Richtmyer, Robert D., jt. auth. see Ramsay, Arlan.

Richtsteig, jt. ed. see Forster.

Richwine, Lynda F. Miracle in Bethlehem. 24p. 1969. pap. 4.50 (*0-8341-9725-1*) Nazarene.

Richwine, Lynda R. Miracle in Bethlehem. 1969. 4.99 (*0-685-68589-6*, MC-21) Lillenas.

Ricigliano. Melody & Harmony in Contemporary Songwriting. 1978. 30.00 (*0-935058-01-X*); student ed. 20.00 (*0-935058-02-8*) Donato Music.

Ricigliano, Daniel A. Popular & Jazz Harmony. 1967. 25.00 (*0-935058-03-6*) Donato Music.

Ricigliano, Lorraine. Austin Clarke: A Reference Guide. LC 92-42514. (Reference Publications in Literature). 180p. 1993. 50.00 (*0-8161-7384-2*, Hall Reference) Macmillan.

Rick, Abbott, tr. see Prevelakis, Pandelis.

Rick-Burge, L. Cortney. Bronski: United States Army Special Investigator. Nicholson, Jim & Napier, Jesse, eds. (Illus.). 250p. (Orig.). 1996. pap. 12.95 (*0-9653398-0-7*) Lucky Bear.

Rick, John W. Heat-Altered Cherts of the Lower Illinois Valley. LC 80-102085. (Prehistoric Records Ser.: No. 2). (Illus.). 83p. 1978. 12.00 (*0-942118-06-5*); pap. 8.00 (*0-942118-07-3*) Ctr Amer Arche.

Rick, Shoshana. Of Milk & Honey: A Workbook on Israel & the Bible. 56p. 1992. pap. 6.95 (*965-229-086-6*, Pub. by Gefen Pub Hse) Gefen Bks.

Rick, Stephanie. The Reflexology Workout. 1995. pap. 14.00 (*0-517-88485-2*) Random Hse Value.

Rickabaugh, Marilyn. Wounded Lovers. Eaton, Dave & Flessing, Greg, eds. 20p. 1988. 34.95 (*0-317-90947-9*); VHS 29.95 (*0-317-90948-7*) Flessing & Flessing.

Rickabaugh. Sex & Gender. 4th ed. 1997. pap., student ed. 21.56 (*0-07-052618-4*) McGraw.

Rickaby, Franz. Ballads & Songs of the Shanty-Boy. (Illus.). lvi, 244p. 1998. reprint ed. pap. 24.95 (*0-8063-1428-1*, 7780) Clearfield Co.

Rickaby, Glenys, jt. auth. see McConville, James.

Rickaby, Joseph J. Free Will & Four English Philosophers. LC 74-84333. (Essay Index Reprint Ser.). 1977. 17.95 (*0-8369-1103-2*) Ayer.

Rickard, Alan. A Book of Sonnets. 1990. pap. 7.00 (*0-936128-17-8*) De Young Pr.

— Collected Works of Alan Rickard. 1990. 24.49 (*0-936128-50-X*) De Young Pr.

— Green River Poems & Stories. (Australian Collection). 1990. pap. 7.00 (*0-936128-14-3*) De Young Pr.

— A Mountain Winter & Other Poems. (Australian Collection). 1984. pap. 7.00 (*0-936128-12-7*) De Young Pr.

— Snakes. 1991. pap. 7.00 (*0-936128-26-7*) De Young Pr.

— The Song of Joy & Other Poems. (Australian Collection). 1990. pap. 7.00 (*0-936128-13-5*) De Young Pr.

— Stories from the Outback. (Illus.). 35p. 1997. 12.50 (*0-936128-49-6*) De Young Pr.

— A Story of Lebanon & Other Poems & Stories. (Australian Collection). 1990. pap. 7.00 (*0-936128-15-1*) De Young Pr.

Rickard, Arelene D., ed. see Rickard, Glen L.

*__Rickard, Bob.__ Unexplained Phenomena. (Illus.). 2000. pap. 19.95 (*1-85828-589-5*, Pub. by Rough Guides) Penguin Putnam.

Rickard, Clinton. Fighting Tuscarora: The Autobiography of Chief Clinton Rickard. Graymont, Barbara, ed. LC 73-8208. (York State Bk.). 252p. reprint ed. pap. 78.20 (*0-8357-4965-7*, 203789800009) Bks Demand.

Rickard, Cole. God Damn the Union! large type ed. (Dales Large Print Ser.). 207p. 1997. pap. 18.99 (*1-85389-704-3*) Ulverscroft.

— Riders of the White Hell. large type ed. (Linford Western Library). 240p. 1993. pap. 16.99 (*0-7089-7363-9*, Linford) Ulverscroft.

— Sixgun Venus. large type ed. (Linford Western Large Print Ser.). 256p. 1998. pap. 17.99 (*0-7089-5204-6*, Linford) Ulverscroft.

*__Rickard, Cole.__ The Yankee Hangman. large type ed. 256p. 1999. pap. 18.99 (*0-7089-5499-5*, Linford) Ulverscroft.

Rickard, David, ed. see Royal Swedish Academy of Sciences Staff.

Rickard, Garth, jt. auth. see Cox, Heather.

Rickard, Glen L. Saint or Slaver. Rickard, Arelene D., ed. (Orig.). 1991. pap. 10.95 (*0-9627012-0-3*) G L Rickard Pub.

Rickard, Jack. Change in the Weather. 100p. 2000. pap. 10.00 (*1-883573-13-0*) Pride & Imprints.

— The House at the Edge of Winter. 1997. 5.00 (*0-932593-21-6*) Black Bear.

— Staining the Grass Red. 32p. 1997. pap. 7.95 (*0-944754-41-4*) Pudding Hse Pubns.

Rickard, Jack, jt. auth. see Silverstone, Lou.

Rickard, Jacqueline. Complete Premarital Contracting: Loving Communication for Today's Couples. LC 93-26893. 240p. 1993. pap. 8.95 (*0-87131-739-7*) M Evans.

Rickard, Joan & Bucman, Lamond. Whatever It Takes. 408p. Date not set. mass mkt. 4.99 (*1-55197-049-X*) Picasso Publ.

Rickard, John. Australia: A Cultural History. 2nd ed. LC 96-28652. 336p. (Orig.). (C). 1997. pap. 29.07 (*0-582-27605-5*) Longman.

— A Family Romance: The Deakins at Home. (Illus.). 192p. 1997. pap. 24.95 (*0-522-84740-4*, Pub. by Melbourne Univ Pr) Paul & Co Pubs.

— Longer-Term Issues in Transportation: Conference Papers. 400p. 1991. 112.95 (*1-85628-254-6*, Pub. by Avebry) Ashgate Pub Co.

Rickard, John Nelson. Patton at Bay. LC 98-36753. (Praeger Series in War Studies). 320p. 1999. 45.00 (*0-275-96354-3*, Praeger Pubs) Greenwood.

Rickard, John S. Irishness & (Post) Modernism. (Buckness Review Ser., Vol. 38: No. 1). (Illus.). 232p. 1994. 22.00 (*0-8387-5271-3*) Bucknell U Pr.

— Joyce's Book of Memory: The Mnemotechnics of Ulysses. LC 98-25721. 1999. 49.95 (*0-8223-2158-0*); pap. 17.95 (*0-8223-2170-X*) Duke.

Rickard-Lauri, Patricia, et al. Snow White: A Practical Guide to Child-Centered Musical Theatre. (Illus.). 172p. 1997. pap. text 54.00 incl. audio compact disk (*0-9624080-6-9*) Barcelona Pubs.

*__Rickard, Lawrence V.__ Eighteenth & Early Nineteenth Century Beckers of Eastern New York. 418p. 2000. 75.00 (*1-56012-166-1*) Kinship Rhinebeck.

— A Richtmyer, Rightmyer Genealogy. 362p. 1999. lib. bdg. 64.95 (*1-56012-159-9*, 166) Kinship Rhinebeck.

— Vital Records of Saint John's Evangelical Lutheran Church, Town of Seward, Schoharie County, NY: Baptisms 1801-1861, Marriages, 1847-1861. 106p. 2000. lib. bdg. 23.00 (*1-56012-163-7*, 175) Kinship Rhinebeck.

— Vital Records of Saint Peter's Evangelical Lutheran Church of New Rhinebeck: Town of Seward, Schoharie County, NY Baptisms, 1802-1867, Marriages, 1806-1848. 146p. 2000. lib. bdg. 34.00 (*1-56012-164-5*, 176) Kinship Rhinebeck.

— Vital Records of the Gilboa Reformed Church, Gilboa, Schoharie County, NY: Baptisms 1801-1882, Mamages, 1803-1884. 100p. 1999. pap. 17.00 (*1-56012-158-0*, 163) Kinship Rhinebeck.

— Vital Records of the Reformed Churches of Sharon Town of Sharon, Schoharie County, NY: Reformed Church of Sharon, the Reformed Dutch Church. 125p. 2000. lib. bdg. 31.00 (*1-56012-162-9*, 174) Kinship Rhinebeck.

— Vital Records of the Zion Evangelical Lutheran Church, Cobleskill, New York: Town of Cobleskill, Schokane County, NY, Baptisms, 1794-1871, Marriages, 1806-1871, Deaths, 1817-1858. 99p. 2000. lib. bdg. 22.00 (*1-56012-161-0*, 173) Kinship Rhinebeck.

Rickard, Lawrence V., ed. Vital Records of Lawyersville Reformed Church, Lawyersville, Schoharie County, New York: Baptisms 1790-1876, Marriages 1790-1882. 139p. 1995. lib. bdg. 30.00 (*1-56012-142-4*, 140) Kinship Rhinebeck.

Rickard, M. J., ed. Basement Tectonics Nine - Australia & Other Regions: Proceedings of the Ninth International Conference on Basement Tectonics, Held in Canberra, Australia, July, 1990. 272p. (C). 1992. text 166.50 (*0-7923-1559-6*) Kluwer Academic.

*__Rickard, Martin.__ The Plantfinder's Guide to Garden Ferns. LC 00-26329. (Illus.). 192p. 2000. 34.95 (*0-88192-476-8*) Timber.

Rickard, Michael. Lab Exercises in Microbiology. 3rd ed. 152p. (C). 1998. spiral bd. 28.95 (*0-7872-5624-2*, 41562401) Kendall-Hunt.

Rickard, Peter. The French Language in the Seventeenth Century: Contemporary Opinion in France. (ENG & FRE.). 563p. (C). 1992. 75.00 (*0-85991-353-8*, DS Brewer) Boydell & Brewer.

— History of the French Language. 2nd ed. LC 89-5562. (Illus.). 192p. (Orig.). (C). 1989. pap. 24.99 (*0-415-10887-X*) Routledge.

— A History of the French Language. 2nd ed. 192p. 1989. pap. text 18.95 (*0-04-445295-0*) Routledge.

Rickard, Philip & Bennett, Henry. Hawaiian Heirloom Jewelry: A Lasting Remembrance. 128p. 1992. 35.00 (*0-9635062-9-3*); pap. 22.95 (*0-9635062-8-5*) HI Heirloom.

Rickard, Scott T., jt. auth. see Clement, Linda M.

Rickard, Stanley. With All Purity: What You Need to Know about Sexual Ethics. rev. ed. LC 89-29357. 30p. 1989. pap. text 2.99 (*0-87227-139-0*, RBP5123) Reg Baptist.

Rickard, T. A. Across the San Juan Mountains. Benham, Jack L., ed. (Illus.). 178p. (Orig.). 1980. reprint ed. pap. 5.95 (*0-941026-03-5*) Bear Creek Pub.

Rickard, Thomas A. Man & Metals: A History of Mining in Relation to the Development of Civilization, 2 vols. LC 74-358. (Gold Ser.: Vol. 16). (Illus.). 1974. reprint ed. 81.95 (*0-405-05919-1*) Ayer.

Rickard, Verna. The Learning about Myself Handbook for Group Participants. LC 97-45067. 64p. 1998. pap. 14.95 (*0-7890-0471-2*, Hawrth Medical) Haworth Pr.

— The Learning about Myself (LAMS) Program for At-Risk Parents: Learning from the Past--Changing the Future. LC 97-45068. (Illus.). 196p. 1998. 39.95 (*0-7890-0107-1*, Maltreatment & Trauma Pr); pap. 24.95 (*0-7890-0474-7*, Maltreatment & Trauma Pr) Haworth Pr.

Rickard, Walter L. Rocky Goes Hunting. LC 96-27269. (J). 1997. write for info. (*1-56763-237-8*) Ozark Pub.

Rickard, Walter L. Rocky Goes Hunting. LC 96-27269. (Illus.). 17p. (J). (ps-3). 1997. pap. write for info. (*1-56763-238-6*) Ozark Pub.

Rickard, Wendy, jt. ed. see McMonus, Fran.

Rickards, Barrie. Freshwater Fishing. 1998. 19.99 (*0-7858-0993-7*) Bk Sales Inc.

Rickards, Barrie, jt. ed. see Palmer, Douglas.

Rickards, Debbie & Cheek, Earl H., Jr. Designing Rubrics for K-6 Classroom Assessment. 128p. 1998. pap. text 15.95 (*0-926842-86-2*) CG Pubs Inc.

Rickards, Denny. Fly-Fishing Stillwaters for Trophy Trout. 1998. pap. 34.95 (*0-9656458-0-0*) Stillwater Prods.

Rickards, Guy. Hindemith, Hartman, & Henze. (20th Century Composers Ser.). (Illus.). 240p. (Orig.). (C). 1995. pap. 19.95 (*0-7148-3174-3*, Pub. by Phaidon Press) Phaidon Pr.

Rickards, Jim. Fields of Light. large type ed. (Ulverscroft Large Print Ser.). (Illus.). 512p. 1997. 27.99 (*0-7089-3743-8*) Ulverscroft.

*__Rickards, Maurice.__ Encyclopedia of Ephemera: A Guide to the Fragmentary Documents of Everyday Life for the Collector, Curator & Historian. Twyman, Michael, ed. (Illus.). 2000. 62.00 (*0-415-92648-3*) Routledge.

Rickards, Peter. Popular Activities & Games for Blind, Visually Impaired & Disabled People. large type ed. (Illus.). 64p. 1986. pap. 19.95 (*0-9599747-8-4*) Am Foun Blind.

Rickards, Raymond R. The Path to True Health & Fulfillment. Trainer, Beverly, ed. (Illus.). 85p. (Orig.). 1995. pap. 15.95 (*0-9650288-0-1*) Sunburst Publns.

Rickards, Robert C. Managing the Metropolis in Japan & Texas: Sister City Relationships, Municipal Finance, & Urban Economic Development Projects. (Policy Research Project Report: No. 94). 92p. 1991. pap. 9.50 (*0-89940-702-1*) LBJ Sch Pub Aff.

— Socioeconomic & Political Influences on Industrial Production Decisions in East German Provinces. (Working Paper Ser.: No. 44). 36p. 1988. pap. 5.00 (*0-89940-525-8*) LBJ Sch Pub Aff.

Rickards, Robert C. & Lein, Laura. Child Care, Higher Education, & Pension System in Japan & the United States. (Special Project Reports). 84p. 1993. pap. 9.50 (*0-89940-901-6*) LBJ Sch Pub Aff.

Rickards, Robert C., et al. Sentencing Research in Texas: A Survey of Issues Relevant to Local Criminal Justice Officials. (Special Project Reports). 42p. 1991. pap. 9.50 (*0-89940-870-2*) LBJ Sch Pub Aff.

R

Rickards, Robert C., jt. auth. see Lein, Laura.

Rickards, Teresa. Dicionario Cambridge de Fisica. (POR.). 256p. 1988. 39.95 (*0-7859-5812-6*) Fr & Eur.

Rickards, Tudor. Creativity & Problem Solving at Work. 240p. 1997. pap. 34.95 (*0-566-07961-5*, Pub. by Gower) Ashgate Pub Co.

— Creativity & the Management of Change. LC 99-32756. (MBM Ser.). 1999. 64.95 (*0-631-21067-9*); pap. 32.95 (*0-631-21068-7*) Blackwell Pubs.

*__Rickards, Tudor & Moger, Susan.__ A Team Approach to Creativity. LC 98-27583. 125p. 1998. 71.95 (*0-566-08051-6*, Pub. by Gower) Ashgate Pub Co.

Rickart, Charles E. General Theory of Banach Algebras. LC 74-143. 406p. 1974. reprint ed. 45.50 (*0-88275-091-7*) Krieger.

— Natural Functions Algebras. (Universitext Ser.). 240p. 1979. 69.95 (*0-387-90449-2*) Spr-Verlag.

— Structuralism & Structures. LC 94-28563. (Series in Pure Mathematics: Vol. 21). 236p. 1995. text 48.00 (*981-02-1860-5*) World Scientific Pub.

Rickart, Eric A. Reproduction, Growth, & Development in Two Species of Cloud Forest Peromyscus from Southern Mexico. (Occasional Papers: No. 67). 22p. 1977. pap. 1.00 (*0-317-04907-0*) U KS Nat Hist Mus.

Ricke, Gaetane. Modern Taekwondo. LC 98-44565. 256p. 1999. 17.95 (*0-8069-3989-3*) Sterling.

Ricke, Helmut, et al, eds. Swedish Glass Factories: Production Catalogues, 1915-1960. (ENG, GER & SWE., Illus.). 442p. 1987. 185.00 (*3-7913-0804-1*, Pub. by Prestel) te Neues.

Ricke, Helmut & Schmitt, Eva, eds. Italian Glass: Murano - Milan, 1930-1970. LC 97-1902. (Illus.). 352p. 1997. 85.00 (*3-7913-1736-9*, Pub. by Prestel) te Neues.

Ricke, Herbert, et al. Ausgrabungen von Khor Dehmit bis Bet el-Wali. LC 68-15933. (Oriental Institute Nubian Expedition Publications: Vol. 2). (Illus.). 70p. 1968. lib. bdg. 36.00 (*0-226-62366-1*, OINE2) U Ch Pr.

— Beit El-Wali Temple of Ramesses Second. LC 67-18437. (Oriental Institute Nubian Expedition Publications: Vol. 1). (Illus.). 1995. lib. bdg. 36.00 (*0-226-62365-3*, OINE1) U Ch Pr.

*__Rickel, A. U. & Wise, T. N.__ Understanding Managed Care: An Introduction for Health Care Professionals. LC 99-42843. (Illus.). x, 122p. 1999. pap. 35.00 (*3-8055-6960-2*) S Karger.

Rickel, Annette U. Teen Pregnancy & Parenting. 225p. 1989. 48.95 (*0-89116-808-7*); pap. 29.95 (*0-89116-908-3*) Hemisp Pub.

Rickel, Annette U., et al, eds. Social & Psychological Problems of Women: Prevention & Crisis Intervention. LC 83-18423. (Clinical & Community Psychology Ser.). 352p. 1984. text 51.95 (*0-89116-330-1*) Hemisp Pub.

Rickel, Annette U. & Allen, La Rue. Preventing Maladjustment from Infancy Through Adolescence. (Developmental Clinical Psychology & Psychiatry Ser.: Vol. 11). 160p. 1987. text 42.00 (*0-8039-2868-8*); pap. text 18.95 (*0-8039-2869-6*) Sage.

Rickel, Annette U. & Becker, Evvie. Keeping Children from Harm's Way: How National Policy Affects Psychological Development. LC 97-20445. 334p. 1997. pap. 24.95 (*1-55798-443-3*) Am Psychol.

Rickel, Boyer. Arreboles. LC 91-7634. (Wesleyan New Poets Ser.). 64p. 1991. pap. 12.95 (*0-8195-1199-4*, Wesleyan Univ Pr); text 25.00 (*0-8195-2197-3*, Wesleyan Univ Pr) U Pr of New Eng.

— Taboo. LC 98-49498. (Living Out Ser.). 120p. 1999. 14.95 (*0-299-16260-5*) U of Wis Pr.

Rickels, Curtis E. The Three Ring Circus. 289p. 1992. pap. write for info. (*0-9637087-0-8*) Sunrise Track.

Rickels, Karl, jt. auth. see Freeman, Ellen W.

Rickels, Laurence A. The Case of California. LC 90-49952. (Parallax). 192p. 1991. pap. text 16.95 (*0-8018-4139-9*) Johns Hopkins.

— The Vampire Lectures. LC 99-30570. 376p. 1999. pap. 19.95 (*0-8166-3392-4*, Pub. by U of Minn Pr); lib. bdg. 49.95 (*0-8166-3391-6*, Pub. by U of Minn Pr) Chicago Distribution Ctr.

Rickels, Laurence A., ed. Acting Out in Groups. LC 99-45088. 216p. 1999. pap. 17.95 (*0-8166-3321-5*, Pub. by U of Minn Pr); lib. bdg. 44.95 (*0-8166-3320-7*, Pub. by U of Minn Pr) Chicago Distribution Ctr.

— Looking after Nietzsche. LC 89-4579. (SUNY Series, Intersections). 265p. (C). 1989. pap. text 21.95 (*0-7914-0157-X*) State U NY Pr.

Rickels, Milton. George Washington Harris. LC 65-24244. (Twayne's United States Authors Ser.). 1965. pap. 7.95 (*0-8290-0009-7*); lib. bdg. 17.95 (*0-89197-770-8*) Irvington.

Ricken, A. Vademecum fuer Pilzfreunde: Taschenbuch Zur Bequemen Bestimmung Aller in Mittel-Europa Vorkommenden Ansehnlichen Pilzkoerper. 1969. reprint ed. 32.00 (*3-7682-0603-3*) Lubrecht & Cramer.

— Vademekum Fuer Pilzfreunde. (GER.). 1969. 69.95 (*0-8288-6618-X*, M-7137) Fr & Eur.

Ricken, D. & Gessner, W., eds. Advanced Microsystems for Automotive Applications 98. 350p. 1998. 110.00 (*3-540-64091-6*) Spr-Verlag.

Ricken, D. E., et al, eds. Advanced Microsystems for Automotive Applications, 99. (Illus.). 350p. 1999. 129.00 (*3-540-65183-7*) Spr-Verlag.

Ricken, D. E., ed. see Richards, John A. & Jia, X.

R

Ricken, Friedo. Philosophy of the Ancients. Watkins, Eric, tr. LC 90-70852. 232p. (C). 1991. pap. text 17.50 (*0-268-01588-0*) U of Notre Dame Pr.

Ricken, Robert. Love Me When I'm Most Unlovable, Vol. II. 32p. (J). (gr. 6-9). 1987. pap. 4.00 (*0-88210-198-6*) Natl Assn Principals.

Ricken, Werner. Seidmentation As a Three-Component System: Organic Carbon, Carbonate, Noncarbonate. LC 93-34945. (Lecture Notes in Earth Sciences Ser.: Vol. 51). 1993. 65.95 (*0-387-57386-0*) Spr-Verlag.

Ricken, Werner & Seilacher, A. Adolf. Cycles & Events in Stratigraphy. (Illus.). 1040p. 1991. 98.95 (*0-387-52784-2*) Spr-Verlag.

Rickenbacker, Edward. Flying the Fighting Circus. (Great Commanders Ser.). 371p. 1995. reprint ed. 30.00 (*1-56515-005-8*) Collect Reprints.

Rickenbacker, Edward V. Rickenbacker. (Airlines History Project Ser.). (Illus.). reprint ed. 57.50 (*0-404-19332-3*) AMS Pr.

Rickenbacker, William F., ed. The Twelve-Year Sentence: Radical Views on Compulsory Education. 234p. 1999. reprint ed. 24.95 (*0-930073-30-4*); reprint ed. pap. 14.95 (*0-930073-29-0*) Fox & Wilkes.

Rickenbacker, William F., jt. auth. see Bridges, Linda.

Rickenbaker, Michael. Breaking into Prison. LC 92-62679. 176p. (Orig.). 1993. pap. 8.95 (*1-882673-00-X*) Spirit & Truth.

Ricker, Audrey. Backtalk: Four Steps to Ending Rude Behavior in Your Kids. 1998. 10.00 incl. audio (*0-671-58265-8*) S&S Audio.

Ricker, Audrey & Crowder, Carolyn. Backtalk: Four Steps to Ending Rude Behavior in Your Kids. LC 97-36549. 1998. pap. 10.00 (*0-684-84124-X*, Fireside) S&S Trade Pap.

***Ricker, Audrey, et al.** Whining: 3 Steps to Stop It Before the Tears & Tantrums Start. 160p. 2000. per. 11.00 (*0-684-85742-1*, Fireside) S&S Trade Pap.

Ricker, David T., jt. auth. see DeWolf, John T.

Ricker, Elizabeth M. Seppala - Alaskan Dog Driver. deluxe ed. (Illus.). 296p. 1995. 40.00 (*0-614-04553-3*) Donald R Hoflin.

Ricker, Jacquelyn L., ed. see Talcott, Alvan.

Ricker, Jeffrey. Managing Metadata with XML & RDF: Improving Workflow for Web Applications. 400p. 1998. pap. 39.99 (*0-471-31519-2*) Wiley.

Ricker, John, ed. see Khalsa, Waheguru S.

Ricker, John F. Yuraq Janka: Guide to the Peruvian Andes-Cordilleras: Blanca & Rosko. LC 77-82861. (Illus.). 192p. 1981. reprint ed. pap. 12.95 (*0-930410-05-X*) Amer Alpine Club.

Ricker, M. O. Bedside Bonus Years. 80p. (Orig.). 1996. pap. 5.95 (*1-886094-56-X*) Chicago Spectrum.

Ricker, Percy L. & Holland, Elwin R. A Genealogy of the Ricker Family, 2 vols., Set. 772p. (Orig.). 1996. pap. 53.50 (*0-7884-0461-X*, R315) Heritage Bk.

Ricker, Richard E., jt. ed. see Jones, Russell H.

Ricker, Ruth A. Smart Guide to Vitamins & Healing Supplements. LC 98-33835. (Smart Guides Ser.). 174p. 1998. pap. 10.95 (*0-471-29633-3*) Wiley.

***Ricker, Sarah M.** Milton & Milton Mills. (Images of America Ser.). 1999. pap. 18.99 (*0-7524-1267-1*) Arcadia Publng.

Ricker, Trent & Stevens, Michael. Fairways to Heaven: The Journeyman's Guide to the Best of American Golf. LC 96-72109. (Illus.). 320p. (Orig.). 1997. pap. 29.95 (*0-9655592-3-8*) Pin High.

***Ricker, Werner.** Operator Algebras Generated by Commuting Projections: A Vector Measure Approach. LC 99-42231. (Lecture Notes in Mathematics Ser.: Vol. 1711). (Illus.). i, 159p. 1999. pap. 37.00 (*3-540-66461-0*) Spr-Verlag.

Rickerby, D. S. & Matthews, A., eds. Advanced Surface Coatings: A Handbook of Surface Engineering. 320p. 1991. 145.00 (*0-412-02541-8*, A4219, Chap & Hall NY) Chapman & Hall.

Rickerby, D. S., jt. auth. see Matthews, A.

***Rickerby, David.G., et al.** Impact of Electron & Scanning Probe Microscopy on Materials Research. LC 99-42003. (NATO ASI Ser.). 1999. write for info. (*0-7923-5939-9*) Kluwer Academic.

Rickerby, Laura. Ulysses S. Grant & the Strategy of Victory. (History of the Civil War Ser.). (Illus.). 160p. (YA). (gr. 5 up). 1990. pap. 7.95 (*0-382-24053-7*) Silver Burdett Pr.

Rickerson, Don, Jr., ed. Rickerson. The Diary of Achsa M. Tubbs-Rickerson, 1876-1901, Spring Creek, Warren Co., Pa. (Illus.). 137p. 1996. reprint ed. pap. 19.00 (*0-8328-5392-5*); reprint ed. lib. bdg. 29.00 (*0-8328-5391-7*) Higginson Bk Co.

Rickerson, Jeff. Real Estate Investor's Master Guide to Real Estate Wealth & Success. Rickerson, Robert B., ed. LC 84-62753. 285p. 1985. 40.00 (*0-933001-00-2*); pap. 25.00 (*0-317-17995-0*) Intl Inst Fin Res.

Rickerson, Robert B., ed. see Rickerson, Jeff.

Rickert. The Fast Track to Vehicle Services Fact: A Motor Vehicle Regulations & Procedures. 188p. 1996. pap. text 50.00 (*0-7872-2116-3*) Kendall-Hunt.

Rickert, Blandine M. Introduction a l'Etude de la Stylistique Francaise. LC 93-14526. (FRE.). 208p. 1993. pap. 29.95 (*0-7734-1964-0*) E Mellen.

Rickert, Corinne H. The Case of John Darrell: Minister & Exorcist. LC 62-62828. (University of Florida Humanities Monographs: No. 9). 76p. reprint ed. pap. 30.00 (*0-7837-5006-4*, 204467300004) Bks Demand.

Rickert, Douglas E., ed. Toxicity of Nitroaromatic Compounds. LC 84-8937. (Chemical Industry Institute of Toxicology Ser.). (Illus.). 295p. 1985. 125.00 (*0-89116-304-2*) Hemisp Pub.

Rickert, Edith. Chaucer's World. Olson, Clair C. & Crow, Martin M., eds. LC 48-6059. (Illus.). 498p. reprint ed. pap. 154.40 (*0-608-17539-0*, 203071500070) Bks Demand.

Rickert, Edith, ed. The Romance of Emare. (EETS, ES Ser.: Vol. 99). 1974. reprint ed. 40.00 (*0-8115-3407-3*) Periodicals Srv.

Rickert, Edith & Paton, Jessie, eds. American Lyrics. LC 72-8289. (Granger Index Reprint Ser.). 1977. reprint ed. 37.95 (*0-8369-6393-8*) Ayer.

Rickert, Edith, jt. auth. see Manly, John M.

Rickert, Ellen, ed. see Altman, Joan, et al.

Rickert, Heinrich. The Limits of Concept Formation in Natural Science: A Logical Introduction to the Historical Sciences. abr. ed. Oakes, Guy, ed. & tr. by. from GER. (Texts in German Philosophy Ser.). 272p. 1986. pap. text 27.95 (*0-521-31015-6*) Cambridge U Pr.

***Rickert, Janet E.** Russ & the Apple Tree Surprise. LC 99-37700. (Illus.). 28p. (J). (ps-3). 1999. 14.95 (*1-890627-16-X*) Woodbine House.

***Rickert, Janet Elizabeth.** Russ & the Firehouse. LC 99-58178. (Day with Russ Ser.). (Illus.). 24p. (J). (ps-2). 2000. 14.95 (*1-890627-17-8*) Woodbine House.

Rickert, Jeanne M. Ohio Limited Liability Companies. LC 99-162663. (Baldwin's Ohio Handbook Ser.). 516p. 1999. write for info. (*0-8322-0750-0*) Banks-Baldwin.

— Ohio Limited Liability Companies, 1996-97. 470p. 1996. pap. 43.50 (*0-8322-0656-3*) Banks-Baldwin.

Rickert, Jessica A. Exploring Careers in Dentistry. rev. ed. (Careers in Depth Ser.). 154p. (gr. 7-12). 1988. lib. bdg. 16.95 (*0-8239-0801-1*) Rosen Group.

— Exploring Careers in Dentistry. rev. ed. (Careers in Depth Ser.). (Illus.). 154p. (YA). (gr. 8-12). 1996. lib. bdg. 16.95 (*0-8239-2246-4*, D2246-4) Rosen Group.

Rickert, Richard. Brush up Your Logic! The Citizen's Guide to Effective Thinking. (Illus.). 100p. 1997. 24.95 (*0-9663181-0-2*, GR-98-1) Gronvold Res.

Rickert, Robert R., contrib. by. Selecting & Evaluating a Referral Laboratory: Tentative Guideline (1991) 1991. 75.00 (*1-56238-139-3*, GP9-T) NCCLS.

Rickert, William E. & Bloomquist, Jane. Resources in Theatre & Disability. LC 88-5545. 208p. (Orig.). (C). 1988. pap. text 25.00 (*0-8191-5749-X*); lib. bdg. 47.00 (*0-8191-5748-1*) U Pr of Amer.

Rickes, Persis, ed. Special Planning for Special Spaces. (Illus.). 143p. 1997. pap. 34.95 (*0-9601608-5-X*) Soc Coll & Univ Planning.

Ricketson, Anna & Ricketson, Walton, eds. Daniel Ricketson & His Friends: Letter, Poems, Sketches, Etc. LC 80-2513. (Thoreau Ser.). (Illus.). 440p. reprint ed. 67.50 (*0-404-19061-8*) AMS Pr.

Ricketson, Jean C., jt. auth. see Ricketson, William F.

Ricketson, Walton, jt. ed. see Ricketson, Anna.

Ricketson, William, jt. auth. see Mufuka, Ken.

Ricketson, William F. & Ricketson, Jean C. Overview of Western Civilization: A Guide, Vol. I. 196p. (Orig.). (C). 1984. pap. text 22.00 (*0-8191-3968-8*) U Pr of Amer.

Ricketson, William F., jt. auth. see Wilson, Jerome D.

Rickett, Adele A., ed. Chinese Approaches to Literature from Confucius to Liang Chi-Chao. LC 77-7311. 282p. reprint ed. pap. 87.50 (*0-8357-6055-3*, 203465000090) Bks Demand.

Rickett, Adele A. & Lianli, Liu, eds. Selected Readings of Contemporary Chinese Short Stories. 503p. 1992. 19.95 (*0-8351-1923-8*) China Bks.

Rickett, Arthur. Vagabond in Literature. LC 68-8489. (Essay Index Reprint Ser.). 1977. reprint ed. 19.95 (*0-8369-0825-2*) Ayer.

***Rickett, Charles E. F. & Austin, Graeme W., eds.** International Intellectual Property & the Common Law World. 320p. 2000. 56.00 (*1-84113-179-2*, Pub. by Hart Pub) Intl Spec Bk.

Rickett, Charles E. F., jt. auth. see Grantham, Ross B.

Rickett, Daniel & Welliver, Dotsey, eds. Supporting Indigenous Ministries: With Selected Readings. (Monograph Ser.). 142p. 1997. pap. 10.95 (*1-879089-26-2*) B Graham Ctr.

Rickett, Harold W. Wild Flowers of the United States Vol. 1: Northeastern States. LC 66-17920. (Illus.). 559p. 1966. 70.00 (*0-89327-274-4*) NY Botanical.

Rickett, Harold W., intro. Wild Flowers of America. LC 92-40132. (Tiny Folios Ser.). (Illus.). 448p. 1996. pap. 11.95 (*1-55859-564-3*) Abbeville Pr.

Rickett, Harold W., ed. see Colden, J.

Rickett, W., tr. Guanzi: Political, Economic & Philosophical Essays from Early China. (Princeton Library of Asian Translations Ser.). 608p. 1998. text 99.50 (*0-691-04816-9*, Pub. by Princeton U Pr) Cal Prin Full Svc.

Rickett, W. Allyn, tr. see Kuan, Chung.

Ricketts. Energy & Environmental Visions for the New Millenium. 565p. (C). 1997. 98.00 (*0-13-916313-1*, Prentice Hall) P-H.

Ricketts & Rawlins. Introduction to Agribusiness. LC 99-40037. (Agriculture Ser.). 1999. mass mkt. 42.95 (*0-7668-0024-5*) Delmar.

Ricketts, Cliff. Leadership: Personal Dev & Career Success. (Agriculture Ser.). 96p. 1996. text, teacher ed. 12.75 (*0-8273-6754-6*) Delmar.

— Leadership: Personal Development & Career Success. LC 95-16642. 576p. 1995. mass mkt. 46.95 (*0-8273-6753-8*) Delmar.

Ricketts, David & Guasti, Carol A., eds. Family Circle Busy Cooks Book. 320p. 1988. 19.95 (*0-933585-09-8*) Family Circle Bks.

Ricketts, David & McQuillan, Susan. Simply Healthful Fish: Delicious New Low-Fat Recipes. LC 92-39978. (Simply Healthful Ser.). (Illus.). 96p. (Orig.). 1993. pap. 9.95 (*1-881527-05-0*, Chapters Bks) HM.

Ricketts, David, jt. auth. see Family Circle Editors.

Ricketts, David, ed. see Family Circle Editors.

Ricketts, Donald. Managerial Accounting, 2 vols. 2nd ed. (C). 1990. pap. text, teacher ed. 6.76 (*0-395-57193-6*) HM.

— Managerial Accounting, 2 vols. 2nd ed. (C). 1991. pap. text, teacher ed., suppl. ed. 3.96 (*0-395-57194-4*) HM.

Ricketts, Edward F., et al. Between Pacific Tides. 6th ed. LC 83-40620. (Illus.). 614p. (C). 1985. 59.50 (*0-8047-1229-8*); pap. 22.50 (*0-8047-2068-1*) Stanford U Pr.

Ricketts, Edward F., jt. auth. see Steinbeck, John.

***Ricketts, G. E.** Management Guidelines for Efficient Sheep Production. rev. ed. (Illus.). 63p. 1999. pap. text 25.00 (*0-7881-8286-2*) DIANE Pub.

***Ricketts, Harry.** Rudyard Kipling: A Life. 448p. 2000. 28.00 (*0-7867-0711-9*) Carroll & Graf.

Ricketts, Harry & Roberts, Hugh. How You Doing? A Selection of New Zealand Comic & Satiric Verse. LC 99-193520. write for info. (*0-909049-26-2*) Lincoln Univ Pr.

Ricketts, Ian W. Managing Your Software Project: A Student's Guide. LC 97-34671. xiii, 103p. (C). 1997. pap. 19.95 (*3-540-76046-6*) Spr-Verlag.

Ricketts, Jana. Energy Business & Technology Sourcebook. LC 96-61608. 710p. (C). 1997. pap. text 98.00 (*0-13-743253-4*) P-H.

— Exploring Energy & Facilities Management Opportunities in a Changing Marketplace. LC 98-73533. 528p. 1999. 98.00 (*0-13-012255-6*) P-H.

Ricketts, Jana, ed. Competitive Energy Management & Environmental Technologies. (Illus.). 684p. Date not set. 95.00 (*0-88173-203-6*, 0345) Fairmont Pr.

— Energy & Environmental Visions for the New Millennium. LC 97-77092. (Illus.). xiii, 579 p. 1998. 98.00 (*0-88173-289-3*) Fairmont Pr.

Ricketts, Jana, ed. Exploring Energy & Facilities Management Opportunities In A Changing Marketplace. LC 98-73533. (Illus.). 509p. 98.00 (*0-88173-308-3*) Fairmont Pr.

Ricketts, Jana, ed. & compiled by see Association of Energy Engineers Staff.

Ricketts, Jennifer, ed. see Macduff, Nancy.

Ricketts, Jill M. Visualizing Boccaccio. (Cambridge Studies in New Art History & Criticism). (Illus.). 224p. (C). 1997. text 64.95 (*0-521-49600-4*) Cambridge U Pr.

Ricketts, L. W. Fundamentals of Nuclear Hardening of Electronic Equipment. 586p. 1986. reprint ed. text 73.50 (*0-89874-941-7*) Krieger.

Ricketts, Mac L. Mircea Eliade: The Romanian Roots, 1907-1945, 2 vols., Set. (East European Monographs: No. 248). 1453p. 1988. text 276.00 (*0-88033-145-3*, Pub. by East Eur Monographs) Col U Pr.

Ricketts, Mac L., jt. ed. see Girardot, Norman J.

Ricketts, Mac L., ed. & tr. see Stanescu, Gabriel.

Ricketts, Mac L., tr. see Eliade, Mircea.

Ricketts, Mac L., tr. see Stanescu, Gabriel, ed.

Ricketts, Marijane, ed. see Writers League of Washington Staff.

Ricketts, Marijane G. Is It the Onions Making Life Pungent? Cameron, Dana, ed. (Orig.). (YA). (gr. 7 up). 1987. reprint ed. pap. 7.50 (*0-9618223-0-9*) M G Ricketts.

Ricketts, Marijane G. & Van den Broek, Gonny, eds. The Poets of Ellicott Street. (Illus.). 48p. (Orig.). 1989. pap. 5.00 (*0-9618223-1-7*) M G Ricketts.

Ricketts, Mark. Book of the Twilight Graphic Novel. (Illus.). 144p. 1994. 13.95 (*0-941613-63-1*) Stabur Pr.

Ricketts, Martin, ed. Neo-Classical Microeconomics, 2 vols., Set. (Schools of Thought in Economics Ser.: Vol. 3). 784p. 1989. text 335.00 (*1-85278-115-7*) E Elgar.

Ricketts, Martin & Shoesmith, Edward. British Economic Opinion: A Survey of a Thousand Economists. (Illus.). 100p. 1990. pap. 22.50 (*0-255-36233-1*, Pub. by Inst Economic Affairs) Coronet Bks.

Ricketts, Martin J., jt. auth. see Mudambi, Ram.

Ricketts, Max & Bien, Edwin. The Great Anxiety Escape: A Revolutionary Program to Escape Anxiety, Insomnia, Depression & Drug Dependency. (Illus.). 192p. (Orig.). Date not set. pap. 9.95 (*0-9626205-0-5*) Matulungin Pub.

Ricketts, Mitchell S. Bobcat Trapper's Guide. (Illus.). 116p. (Orig.). 1987. pap. 10.95 (*0-9617720-0-X*) Elk River Pr.

— Muskrat Trapper's Guide. LC 88-81827. (Illus.). 182p. (Orig.). 1988. pap. 13.95 (*0-9617720-1-8*) Elk River Pr.

Ricketts, Norma B. The Mormon Battalion: United States Army of the West, 1846-1848. LC 96-35706. (Illus.). 400p. 1996. pap. 22.95 (*0-87421-215-4*) Utah St U Pr.

Ricketts, R. Allan & Norton, Richard J., eds. National Security: Case Studies in Policy Making & Implementation, Vol. I. LC 94-18039. (Illus.). (C). 1994. pap., teacher ed. write for info. (*1-884733-02-6*) Naval War Coll.

Ricketts, Robert, tr. see Hayashi, Ryoichi.

Ricketts, Robert M. The Reappearing American. 360p. 1993. text 21.95 (*0-9635961-0-1*) Wright & Co.

Ricketts, Taylor H., et al. Terrestrial Ecoregions of North America: A Conservation Assessment. LC 99-18912. 558p. (C). 1999. pap. 75.00 (*1-55963-722-6*) Island Pr.

Ricketts, Thomas C., III, ed. Rural Health in the United States. (Illus.). 232p. 1999. pap. text 39.95 (*0-19-513128-2*) OUP.

Ricketts, Thomas C., et al, eds. Geographic Methods for Health Services Research: A Focus on the Rural-Urban Continuum. 396p. (Orig.). 1994. pap. text 38.50 (*0-8191-9533-2*); lib. bdg. 62.50 (*0-8191-9532-4*) U Pr of Amer.

Ricketts, Thomas C., III, jt. ed. see Gesler, Wilbert M.

Ricketts, Virginia. Then & Now in Southern Idaho. LC 98-74110. (Illus.). 250p. 1998. pap. 24.95 (*0-9667684-0-X*) Fall City Pubg.

Ricketts, Wendell. Lesbians & Gay Men As Foster Parents. (Orig.). 1991. pap. write for info. (*0-939561-09-3*) Univ South ME.

Ricketts, Wendell, et al, eds. Intimate Relationships: Some Social Work Perspectives on Love. LC 87-19729. (Journal of Social Work & Human Sexuality: Vol. 5, No. 2). 140p. 1987. text 39.95 (*0-86656-712-7*) Haworth Pr.

Rickey, Alfred J. Voyage to Destiny. 226p. (Orig.). 1989. pap. 8.95 (*0-9623077-0-X*) Aldarob Enterprises.

Rickey, Brad & Duffens, Kurt. FastAct Pocket First Aid Guide. (Illus.). 100p. 1999. pap. 7.95 (*0-9669933-0-6*) Fast Act.

Rickey, Carrie, jt. auth. see Friis-Hansen, Dana.

Rickey, Don, Jr. Forty Miles a Day on Beans & Hay: The Enlisted Soldier Fighting the Indian Wars. LC 62-9952. (Illus.). 1973. reprint ed. pap. 16.95 (*0-8061-1113-5*) U of Okla Pr.

***Rickey, Don, Jr.** $10 Horse, $40 Saddle. LC 99-18169. (Illus.). 135p. 1999. pap. 19.95 (*0-8032-8977-4*, Bison Books) U of Nebr Pr.

Rickey, George. Constructivism: Origins & Evolution. rev. ed. (Illus.). 306p. 1995. pap. 25.00 (*0-8076-1381-9*) Braziller.

— Constructivist Tendencies. (Illus.). 135p. 1970. pap. 8.00 (*0-942006-36-4*) U of CA Art.

Rickey Hawkins, Lamar, ed. see Heiskell Rickey, Ann.

Rickey, Kay, ed. see Krenzel, Karoleigh.

Rickey, Mary E. Rhyme & Meaning in Crashaw. LC 72-5491. (Studies in Poetry: No. 38). 1972. reprint ed. lib. bdg. 55.00 (*0-8383-1603-4*) M S G Haskell Hse.

Rickey, V. F., jt. ed. see Srzednicki, Jan T.

Rickford, Angela Marshall. I Can Fly: Teaching Narratives & Reading Comprehension to African American & Other Ethnic Minority. 328p. 1999. 57.00 (*0-7618-1279-2*); pap. 32.50 (*0-7618-1280-6*) U Pr of Amer.

Rickford, John R. African American Vernacular English: Features, Evolution, Educational Implications. LC 98-47775. (Language in Society Ser.). 416p. 1999. 59.95 (*0-631-21244-2*); pap. 26.95 (*0-631-21245-0*) Blackwell Pubs.

— Dimensions of a Creole Continuum: History, Texts, & Linguistic Analysis of Guyanese Creole. LC 87-10065. (Illus.). 368p. 1987. 49.50 (*0-8047-1377-4*) Stanford U Pr.

***Rickford, John R. & Rickford, Russell J.** Spoken Soul: The Story of Black English. LC 99-37796. 268p. 2000. 24.95 (*0-471-32356-X*) Wiley.

***Rickford, John R. & Romaine, Suzanne, eds.** Creole Genesis, Attitudes & Discourse: Studies Celebrating Charlene J. Sato. LC 99-14907. (Creole Language Library Ser.: Vol. 20). viii, 418p. 1999. 125.00 (*1-55619-667-9*) J Benjamins Pubng Co.

Rickford, Russell J., jt. auth. see Rickford, John R.

Rickgarn, Ralph L. Perspectives on College Student Suicide. LC 94-41. (Death, Value & Meaning Ser.). 244p. 1994. pap. 23.07 (*0-89503-154-X*); text 32.95 (*0-89503-153-1*) Baywood Pub.

Rickheit, Gert & Bock, Michael, eds. Psycholinguistic Studies in Language Processing. (Research in Text Theory Ser.: Vol. 7). viii, 305p. 1983. 112.35 (*3-11-008994-7*) De Gruyter.

Rickheit, Gert & Habel, Christopher, eds. Focus & Coherence in Discourse Processing. LC 95-22835. (Research in Text Theory Ser.: Vol. 22). xii, 300p. 1995. lib. bdg. 143.10 (*3-11-014466-2*) De Gruyter.

Ricking, Myrl. Personnel Utilization in Libraries: A Systems Approach. LC 74-8688. 168p. reprint ed. pap. 52.10 (*0-608-12591-1*, 202395300034) Bks Demand.

***Rickitt, Richard.** Special Effects: The History & Technique. (Illus.). 320p. 2000. 75.00 (*0-8230-7733-0*) Watsn-Guptill.

Ricklefs. Ecology. 4th ed. 1999. 160.00 (*0-7167-3418-4*) W H Freeman.

— Ecology. 4th ed. LC 99-18604. 1999. pap. text 80.95 (*0-7167-2829-X*) W H Freeman.

— Economy of Nature. 1997. write for info. (*0-7167-3189-4*) W H Freeman.

***Ricklefs.** Economy of Nature Scientific American Reader. 5th ed. 2000. pap. text. write for info. (*0-7167-3987-9*) W H Freeman.

Ricklefs & Scientific American Staff. The Economy of Nature. 2000. 50.00 (*0-7167-2596-7*) W H Freeman.

Ricklefs, M. C. A History of Modern Indonesia since c. 1300. 2nd ed. LC 92-85217. (Illus.). 380p. (C). 1993. 49.50 (*0-8047-2194-7*); pap. 16.95 (*0-8047-2195-5*) Stanford U Pr.

Ricklefs, Merle. War, Culture & Economy in Java, 1677-1726. 224p. 1993. pap. text 24.95 (*1-86373-380-9*, Pub. by Allen & Unwin Pty) Paul & Co Pubs.

***Ricklefs, Merle C.** The Seen & Unseen Worlds in Java, 1726-1749: History, Literature & Islam in the Court of Pakubuwana II. LC 97-42719. (Southeast Asia Publications Ser./Asian Studies Association of Australia). (Illus.). 408p. 1998. text 36.00 (*0-8248-2052-5*) UH Pr.

Ricklefs, Robert E. Ecology. 3rd ed. 896p. (C). 1989. pap. text 72.95 (*0-7167-2077-9*) W H Freeman.

Ricklefs, Robert E., ed. Audubon Conservation Report No. 6: Report of the Advisory Panel on the California Condor. (Audubon Conservation Report). (Illus.). 1978. pap. 3.00 (*0-930698-04-5*) Natl Audubon.

Ricklefs, Robert E. & Finch, Caleb E. Aging: A Natural History. LC 95-2334. (Illus.). 256p. 1995. pap. text 32.95 (*0-7167-5056-2*) W H Freeman.

Ricklefs, Robert E. & Schluter, Dolph, eds. Species Diversity in Ecological Communities: Historical & Geographical Perspectives. LC 93-16747. (Illus.). 432p. 1993. pap. text 34.00 (*0-226-71823-9*); lib. bdg. 98.00 (*0-226-71822-0*) U Ch Pr.

Ricklefs, Robert E., jt. ed. see Starck, J. Matthias.

Ricklefs, Roger, ed. see Stevenson, Robert Louis.

Ricklen, Neil. Los Amigos del Bebe. (Super Chubby Board Bks.).Tr. of Baby's Friends. (SPA., Illus.). 24p. (J). (ps-k). 1995. 4.95 (*0-689-80437-7*) Litle Simon.

An Asterisk (*) at the beginning of an entry indicates that the title is appearing for the first time.

— Baby Outside. (Super Chubby Board Bks.: No. 3). (Illus.). 12p. (J). (ps-k). 1996. reprint ed. 4.99 (0-689-81046-6) Litle Simon.
— Baby's Big & Little. (Super Chubby Board Bks.: No. 1). (Illus.). 24p. (J). (ps-k). 1996. reprint ed. 4.99 (0-689-81044-X) Litle Simon.
— Baby's Birthday. (Super Chubby Board Bks.). (Illus.). 12p. (J). (ps). 1998. 4.99 (0-689-81550-6) Litle Simon.
— Baby's Christmas. (Super Chubby Board Bks.: No. 2). (Illus.). 24p. (J). (ps up). 1996. reprint ed. 4.99 (0-689-81045-8) Litle Simon.
— Baby's Good Morning: A Super Chubby Board Book. (J). (ps). 1992. pap. 4.95 (0-671-76084-X) Litle Simon.
— Baby's Good Night: A Super Chubby Board Book. (Illus.). 24p. (J). (ps-k). 1992. pap. 4.95 (0-671-76085-8) Litle Simon.
— Baby's Neighborhood. (Illus.). 24p. (J). (ps up). 1994. 4.95 (0-671-89111-1) Litle Simon.
Ricklen, Neil. Baby's 1-2-3. (Illus.). 24p. (J). (ps up). 1997. 4.99 (0-689-81265-5) S&S Childrens.
Ricklen, Neil. Baby's Playtime. (J). 1994. 4.95 (0-671-89113-8) Litle Simon.
— Baby's Toys. (J). 1986. 4.95 (0-671-62078-9) S&S Trade.
— Baby's Zoo. (Super Chubby Board Bks.). (Illus.). 12p. (J). (ps). 1998. 4.99 (0-689-81547-6) Litle Simon.
***Ricklen, Neil.** Blue's Buttons. (Super Chubby Board Bks.: No. 6). (gr. k-3). 2000. bds. 4.99 (0-689-83379-2, Simon Spot) Litle Simon.
Ricklen, Neil. La Casa del Bebe.Tr. of Baby's Home. (SPA., Illus.). 24p. (J). (ps up). 1995. 4.95 (0-689-80438-5) Atheneum Yung Read.
— Grandpa & Me. (Super Chubby Board Bks.). (Illus.). 12p. (J). (ps). 1998. 4.99 (0-689-81549-2) Litle Simon.
— Los Juguetes del Bebe.Tr. of Baby's Toys. (SPA., Illus.). 24p. (J). (ps up). 1995. 4.95 (0-689-80439-3) Atheneum Yung Read.
— La Ropa del Bebe.Tr. of Baby's Clothes. (SPA., Illus.). 24p. (J). (ps up). 1995. 4.95 (0-689-80436-9) Atheneum Yung Read.
— Super Chubby Reissue Baby Toys. (Super Chubby Board Bks.). (Illus.). 24p. (J). (ps). 1997. 4.99 (0-689-81548-4) Litle Simon.
Rickles, Don A. Snappy Comebacks to Stop Hecklers. unabridged ed. Fife, Bruce, ed. LC 98-30230. (Illus.). 32p. 1998. pap. 10.00 (0-941599-39-6, Pub. by Piccadilly Bks) Empire Pub Srvs.
Ricklin, Thomas. Der Traum der Philosophie Im 12: Jahrhundert: Traumtheorien Zwischen Constantinus Africanus und Aristoteles. (Mittellateinisch Studien und Texte Ser.: Vol. 24). (GER.). 1998. 182.50 (90-04-11116-6) Brill Academic Pubs.
Ricklis, Robert A. The Karankawa Indians of Texas: An Ecological Study of Cultural Tradition & Change. LC 95-30404. (Texas Archaeology & Ethnohistory Ser.). (Illus.). (C). 1996. pap. 16.95 (0-292-77077-4); text 35.00 (0-292-77073-1) U of Tex Pr.
Rickman, Alan & Macdonald, Sharman. Winter Guest. 1998. pap. 13.95 (0-571-19479-6) Faber & Faber.
Rickman, David. California Missions Coloring Book. (Illus.). (J). (gr. k-3). 1992. pap. 2.95 (0-486-27346-6) Dover.
— Cowboys of the Old West Coloring Book. (Illus.). (J). (gr. k-3). 1985. pap. 2.95 (0-486-25001-6) Dover.
— Plains Indians Coloring Book. (Illus.). (J). (gr. 4-7). 1983. pap. 2.95 (0-486-24470-9) Dover.
Rickman, Geoffrey. The Corn Supply of Ancient Rome. 1980. 62.00 (0-19-814838-0) OUP.
— Roman Granaries & Store Buildings. LC 76-116843. 397p. reprint ed. pap. 113.20 (0-608-11033-7, 2013245) Bks Demand.
***Rickman, Gregg, ed.** The Film Comedy Reader. 400p. 2000. pap. 25.00 (0-87910-295-0) Limelight Edns.
Rickman, Gregg, jt. ed. see Kitses, Jim.
***Rickman, Gregg J.** Swiss Banks & Jewish Souls. LC 99-17332. (Illus.). 3p. 1999. 32.95 (1-56000-426-6) Transaction Pubs.
Rickman, H. & Valtonen, M. J., eds. Worlds in Interaction - Small Bodies & Planets of the Solar System: Proceedings of the Meeting "Small Bodies in the Solar System & Their Interactions with the Planets" Held in Mariehamn, Finland on August 8 - 12, 1994. LC 95-48428. 528p. (C). 1996. text 235.50 (0-7923-3930-4) Kluwer Academic.
Rickman, H. P. Dilthey Today: A Critical Appraisal of the Contemporary Relevance of His Work, 35. LC 87-31779. (Contributions in Philosophy Ser.: No. 35). 114p. 1988. 49.95 (0-313-25933-X, RDT/, Greenwood Pr) Greenwood.
— Philosophy in Literature. LC 96-3741. 1996. 36.50 (0-8386-3652-7) Fairleigh Dickinson.
Rickman, H. P., ed. The Adventure of Reason: The Uses of Philosophy in Sociology, 46. LC 83-5622. (Contributions in Sociology Ser.: No. 46). 172p. 1983. 52.95 (0-313-23871-5, RAR/, Greenwood Pr) Greenwood.
Rickman, Phil. Candlenight. 480p. 1995. mass mkt. 5.99 (0-515-11715-3, Jove) Berkley Pub.
— Curfew. Orig. Title: Crybbe. 640p. 1994. reprint ed. mass mkt. 7.50 (0-425-14334-1) Berkley Pub.
— December. 688p. 1996. mass mkt. 6.99 (0-425-15377-0) Berkley Pub.
Rickman, Rebecca, jt. auth. see Longhauser, Elsa.
Rickman, Seppo. Quasiregular Mappings. LC 93-4824. (Ergebnisse der Mathematik und Ihrer Grenzgebiete Ser.: Vol. 3). 1993. 118.95 (0-387-56648-1) Spr-Verlag.
Rickman, Sidney. Joker's Love Tune. LC 99-171537. 286p. 1998. 15.95 (1-885478-55-0, Pub. by Genesis Press) BookWorld.
Rickman, Stephen, jt. ed. see Travis, Jeremy.
Rickman, William S., ed. Handbook of Incineration of Hazardous Wastes. 1991. lib. bdg. 325.00 (0-8493-0557-8, QD96) CRC Pr.
Rickmers, A. D. & Todd, H. N. Statistics: An Introduction. 1967. text 54.50 (0-07-052616-8) McGraw.
Rickmers, C. Mabel. The Chronology of Indian History. 420p. reprint ed. text 27.50 (0-685-13325-7) Coronet Bks.
Ricks, jt. auth. see Armajani.
Ricks, Beatrice, compiled by. William Faulkner: A Bibliography of Secondary Works. LC 80-15251. (Author Bibliographies Ser.: No. 49). 684p. 1981. lib. bdg. 60.00 (0-8108-1323-8) Scarecrow.
Ricks, Betty R. Contemporary Supervision: Managing People & Technology. 2nd ed. 640p. (C). 1994. pap. 68.75 (0-07-052648-6) McGraw.
Ricks, Betty R. & Gow, Kay F. Business Communication: Systems & Applications. 1987. pap. text 19.50 (0-471-83873-X) P-H.
— Information Resource Management: A Records Systems Approach. 2nd ed. 654p. (C). 1988. text 51.95 (0-538-07511-2, G51) S-W Pub.
Ricks, Betty R. & Swafford. Information & Image Management. 3rd ed. (KI - P/S Record Management Ser.). (C). 1991. mass mkt. 41.00 (0-538-70068-8) S-W Pub.
Ricks, Betty R., et al. Contemporary Supervision: Managing People & Technology. 2nd ed. (C). 1994. pap., student ed. 24.69 (0-07-052650-8) McGraw.
Ricks, Betty R., jt. auth. see Swafford.
***Ricks, Byron.** Homelands: Kayaking the Inside Passage. LC 99-25357. 384p. 1999. pap. 13.50 (0-380-80918-4, Avon Bks) Morrow Avon.
Ricks, Christopher. Beckett's Dying Words: The Clarendon Lectures, 1990. LC 92-47234. 224p. (C). 1993. 45.00 (0-19-812358-2) OUP.
— Beckett's Dying Words: The Clarendon Lectures 1990. 224p. 1995. pap. text 15.95 (0-19-282407-4) OUP.
— Essays in Appreciation. LC 95-25050. 368p. (C). 1996. text 29.95 (0-19-818344-5, Clarendon Pr) OUP.
— Essays in Appreciation. 368p. 1998. reprint ed. pap. text 14.95 (0-19-288084-5) OUP.
— The Force of Poetry. 462p. 1995. pap. text 21.00 (0-19-818326-7) OUP.
— Keats & Embarrassment. 232p. 1984. reprint ed. pap. text 21.00 (0-19-812829-0) OUP.
— Milton's Grand Style. 164p. (C). 1978. pap. text 16.95 (0-19-812090-7) OUP.
— The Oxford Book of English Verse. LC 99-20831. 750p. 1999. 39.95 (0-19-214182-1) OUP.
Ricks, Christopher, ed. A. E. Housman: A Collection of Critical Essays. (Twentieth Century Views Ser.). 1968. 12.95 (0-13-395913-9, Spectrum IN); pap. 1.95 (0-13-395905-8, STC83, Spectrum IN) Macmillan Gen Ref.
— The New Oxford Book of Victorian Verse. LC 94-273. (Oxford Poets Ser.). 688p. 1990. pap. 17.95 (0-19-282778-2) OUP.
— The Tennyson Archive Vol. XI: The Manuscripts at Trinity College, Cambridge: Miscellaneous Manuscripts & Notebooks 13-17. LC 88-16352. 318p. 1988. text 81.50 (0-8240-4210-7) Garland.
Ricks, Christopher & Day, Aidan, eds. Tennyson, No. XVI. LC 88-31103. (Tennyson Archive Ser.). 316p. 1989. reprint ed. text 81.50 (0-8240-4215-8) Garland.
— Tennyson, No. XVII. LC 88-31103. (Tennyson Archive Ser.). 318p. 1989. reprint ed. text 81.50 (0-8240-4216-6) Garland.
— Tennyson, No. XVIII. LC 88-31103. (Tennyson Archive Ser.). 336p. 1989. reprint ed. text 81.50 (0-8240-4217-4) Garland.
— Tennyson, No. XIX. LC 88-31103. (Tennyson Archive Ser.). 324p. 1989. reprint ed. text 81.50 (0-8240-4218-2) Garland.
— Tennyson, No. XX. LC 88-31103. (Tennyson Archive Ser.). 306p. 1989. reprint ed. text 81.50 (0-8240-4219-0) Garland.
— Tennyson, No. XXI. LC 88-31103. (Tennyson Archive Ser.). 316p. 1989. reprint ed. text 81.50 (0-8240-4220-4) Garland.
— Tennyson, No. XXII. LC 88-31103. (Tennyson Archive Ser.). 336p. 1989. reprint ed. text 81.50 (0-8240-4221-2) Garland.
— Tennyson, No. XXIII. LC 88-31103. (Tennyson Archive Ser.). 302p. 1989. reprint ed. text 81.50 (0-8240-4222-0) Garland.
— Tennyson, The Manuscripts at the Victoria & Albert Museum, the Robert H. Taylor Collection of Princeton University, & the Alderman Library of the University of Virginia. LC 92-16236. (Tennyson Archive Ser.: Vol. 30). 316p. 1992. text 81.50 (0-8240-4229-8) Garland.
— Tennyson, the Manuscripts in the Minor Collections & the Indexes for the Tennyson Archive. LC 92-36298. 192p. 1993. text 55.00 (0-8240-4230-1) Garland.
Ricks, Christopher & Michaels, Leonard, eds. The State of the Language: 1990 Edition. 600p. 1989. 48.00 (0-520-05906-9, Pub. by U CA Pr) Cal Prin Full Svc.
Ricks, Christopher & Vance, William L., eds. The Faber Book of America. 467p. (C). 1998. reprint ed. pap. text 10.00 (0-7881-5213-0) DIANE Pub.
Ricks, Christopher, ed. see Eliot, T. S.
Ricks, Christopher, ed. see Tennyson, Alfred Lord.
Ricks, Christopher B., ed. see Eliot, T. S.
Ricks, Christopher B., ed. & intro. see Milton, John.
Ricks, David. Byzantine Heroic Poetry. (ENG & GRE.). 192p. (C). 1990. text 45.00 (0-89241-498-7) Caratzas.
— The Shade of Homer: A Study in Modern Greek Poetry. 208p. (C). 1990. text 54.95 (0-521-36663-1) Cambridge U Pr.
Ricks, David & Magdalino, Paul, eds. Byzantium & the Modern Greek Identity. LC 98-3288. (Centre for Hellenic Studies Ser.: Vol. 4). (Illus.). 208p. 1998. text 74.95 (0-86078-613-7, DF802.B98, Pub. by Ashgate Pub) Ashgate Pub Co.
Ricks, David, jt. auth. see Beaton, Roderick.
Ricks, David, jt. ed. see Silk, Michael.
***Ricks, David A.** Blunders in International Business. 3rd rev. ed. LC 99-33931. 176p. 2000. pap. 19.95 (0-631-21776-2) Blackwell Pubs.
Ricks, David A. International Business. 2nd ed. (Illus.). 600p. 1996. 66.95 (1-57718-004-6) Blackwell Pubs.
Ricks, David A., jt. auth. see Nicoleta, Lascu D.
Ricks, David A., ed. see Arpan, Jeffrey S. & AlHashim, Dhia D.
Ricks, David A., ed. see Phatak, Arvind V.
Ricks, David A., ed. see Terpstra, Vern.
Ricks, David F. & Dohrenwend, Barbara S., eds. Origins of Psychopathology: Problems in Research & Public Policy. LC 82-14638. 295p. reprint ed. pap. 84.10 (0-608-15605-1, 2031717) Bks Demand.
Ricks, Day, ed. The Tennyson Archive Vol. XII: The Manuscripts at Trinity College, Cambridge: Notebooks 18-25. LC 88-16352. 360p. 1988. text 81.50 (0-8240-4211-5) Garland.
— The Tennyson Archive Vol. XIII: The Manuscripts at Trinity College, Cambridge: Notebooks 26-29. LC 88-16352. 334p. 1988. text 81.50 (0-8240-4212-3) Garland.
— The Tennyson Archive Vol. XIV: The Manuscripts at Trinity College, Cambridge: Notebooks 30-36. LC 88-16352. 424p. 1988. text 81.50 (0-8240-4213-1) Garland.
— The Tennyson Archive Vol. XV: The Manuscripts at Trinity College, Cambridge: Notebooks 37-40 & Miscellaneous Manuscripts. LC 88-16352. 356p. 1988. text 81.50 (0-8240-4214-X) Garland.
Ricks, Delthia T., et al. Hysterectomy & You. (Illus.). 1994. pap. 3.60 (0-318-37516-8) Budlong.
Ricks, Eldin. Plan for a Daily Reading of the 4 Standard Works. 48p. 1997. reprint ed. pap. text 2.95 (1-57636-036-9) SunRise Pbl.
Ricks, Emma D. Look for the Lollipops. LC 98-91451. xii, 98p. 1998. pap. 9.95 (0-9664071-0-5) Lollipop Shoppe.
Ricks, Gary K., jt. auth. see Crispin-Little, Jan.
Ricks, George R. Some Aspects of the Religious Music of the United States Negro. Dorson, Richard M., ed. LC 77-70621. (International Folklore Ser.). 1979. reprint ed. lib. bdg. 40.95 (0-405-10123-6) Ayer.
Ricks, Howard, et al, compiled by. Ricks: History & Genealogy of the Ricks Family of America, Descendants of Isaac Ricks, born in England, 1638, & His Wife Kathren, & Allied Families. rev. ed. (Illus.). 767p. 1994. reprint ed. pap. 109.00 (0-8328-4089-0); reprint ed. lib. bdg. 119.00 (0-8328-4088-2) Higginson Bk Co.
Ricks, J. Brent. Kachinas: Spirit Beings of the Hopi. LC 92-8363. (Illus.). 200p. 1993. 50.00 (0-936755-21-0) Avanyu Pub.
Ricks, Jay & Wiley, Richard E. The Cable Communication Policy Act of 1984. 1985. 35.00 (0-317-29482-2, #CO3360) Harcourt.
Ricks, Lucille. A Buffalo Soldier's Legacy: "Ready & Forward" 10th ed. LC TX3569812. (Illus.). 127p. (Orig.). 1993. reprint ed. per. 12.00 (0-9664211-0-8) Buffalo Soldiers.
— For Love of My Dogs. 1998. pap. 10.00 (1-57553-737-0) Watermrk Pr.
Ricks, Mitchell. Yesterday's Visions. 5p. Date not set. 9.95 (1-887750-45-2) Rutledge Bks.
Ricks, Patricia W. The Christmas Spirit. Date not set. mass mkt. write for info. (0-449-22403-1, Crest) Fawcett.
Ricks, Robert C. & Fry, S. A., eds. The Medical Basis for Radiation Accident Preparedness. 548p. 1991. 175.00 (0-444-01585-X) P-H.
Ricks, Shirley S., ed. see Nibley, Hugh.
Ricks, Stephen D. & Welch, John W., eds. The Allegory of the Olive Tree. LC 93-36632. 624p. 1994. 28.95 (0-87579-767-9) Deseret Bk.
Ricks, Stephen D., jt. auth. see Parry, Donald W.
Ricks, Stephen D., jt. auth. see Welch, John W.
Ricks, Stephen D., jt. ed. see Parry, Donald W.
Ricks, Stephen David, jt. auth. see Parry, Donald W.
Ricks, Thomas, ed. Critical Perspectives on Modern Persian Literature. LC 81-51656. (Critical Perspectives Ser.). (Illus.). 510p. 1984. 40.00 (0-914478-95-8, Three Contnts) L Rienner.
***Ricks, Thomas E.** Making the Corps. (Illus.). 320p. 1998. pap. 13.00 (0-684-84817-1, Touchstone) S&S Trade Pap.
— Making the Corps. (Illus.). 320p. 2000. reprint ed. text 24.00 (0-7881-6994-7) DIANE Pub.
Ricks, Thomas E. Making the Corps: 61 Men Came to Paris Island to Become Marines, Not All of Them Made It. LC 97-25174. 320p. 1997. 24.00 (0-684-83109-0) S&S Trade.
Ricks, Truett A., et al. Principles of Security. 3rd ed. LC 93-71748. (Illus.). 462p. (C). 1993. pap. 34.95 (0-87084-746-5) Anderson Pub Co.
Rickson, Dun. Dun & Bradstreet's Business in a Box. (C). 1996. 99.00 (0-13-731283-0, Macmillan Coll) P-H.
Rickson, R. J., ed. Conserving Soil Resources: European Perspectives. (Illus.). 448p. 1994. text 120.00 (0-85198-948-9) OUP.
Rickson, Richard, ed. Asian & Australasian Companies: A Guide to Sources of Information. 334p. 1994. 94.95 (0-900246-61-8) CBD Res.
***Rickstad, Eric.** Reap. LC 99-34919. 272p. 2000. 23.95 (0-670-88517-7, Viking) Viking Penguin.
Rickwell, Robert & Moran, Richard. Classically Kiawah. (Illus.). 224p. 1996. 14.95 (0-9651792-2-2) Alternat SC.
Rickwood, D., jt. auth. see Graham, J. M.
Rickwood, D., jt. ed. see Hames, B. David.
Rickwood, David. Preparative Centrifugation: A Practical Approach. (Practical Approach Ser.: Vol. 113). (Illus.). 420p. 1993. pap. 55.00 (0-19-963211-1) OUP.
Rickwood, David, ed. Iodinated Density Gradient Media. (Practical Approach Ser.). 254p. 1983. pap. 39.00 (0-904147-51-7) OUP.
— Preparative Centrifugation: A Practical Approach. (Practical Approach Ser.: Vol. 113). (Illus.). 420p. 1993. 95.00 (0-19-963208-1) OUP.
Rickwood, David & Harris, J. Robin, eds. Cell Biology: Essential Techniques. LC 96-35033. 192p. 1997. pap. 49.95 (0-471-96315-1) Wiley.
Rickwood, David & Patel, Dipak. Cell & Molecular Biology: Essential Data. (Essential Data Ser.). 240p. 1995. pap. 39.95 (0-471-95568-X) Wiley.
Rickwood, David, jt. auth. see Jones, Paul.
Rickwood, David, jt. ed. see Chambers, J. A.
Rickwood, David, jt. ed. see Dealtry, G. B.
Rickwood, David, jt. ed. see Graham, John.
Rickwood, Edgell. Calendar of Modern Letters, 3 vols., Set. Garman, D., ed. 1966. reprint ed. 195.00 (0-7146-2104-8, Pub. by F Cass Pubs) Intl Spec Bk.
— Rimbaud: The Boy & the Poet. LC 72-163208. (Studies in French Literature: No. 45). 1971. reprint ed. lib. bdg. 75.00 (0-8383-1309-4) M S G Haskell Hse.
Ricles, James M., ed. Annual Technical Session Proceedings, 1993. 434p. (Orig.). 1993. pap. 40.00 (1-879749-54-8) Structural Stability.
— Is Your Structure Suitably Braced? 257p. (Orig.). 1993. pap. 40.00 (1-879749-55-6) Structural Stability.
— 1995 Annual Technical Session Proceedings. 240p. (Orig.). 1995. pap. 40.00 (1-879749-60-2) Structural Stability.
— SSRC 50th Anniversary Conference Proceedings, 1994: SSRC - Link Between Research & Practice. 407p. 1994. text 45.00 (1-879749-56-4) Structural Stability.
Ricles, James M., jt. ed. see Walsh, Diana.
Rico & Mano, Sandra. American Mosaic: Multicultural Readings in Context. 1991. write for info. (0-318-69200-7, 3-46985) HM Soft Schl Col Div.
Rico, A. G. & Boieau, J., eds. International Symposium on Food Toxicology: Proceedings of the International Symposium on Food Toxicology, France, October 1983. Vol. 1, No. 2. 164p. 1984. write for info. (0-318-65446-6) Taylor & Francis.
Rico, Armando B. Asiano - Banking: A Bilingual Word Guide of the English & Spanish Language - Banking. (ENG & SPA.). 42p. 1997. lib. bdg. 12.95 (1-879219-08-5) Veracruz Pubs.
— Asinano. (ENG & SPA.). 155p. 1990. lib. bdg. 9.50 (1-879219-00-X) Veracruz Pubs.
— Asinano: A Bilingual Word Guide of the English & Spanish Language. 2nd rev. ed. (ENG & SPA.). 273p. 1995. lib. bdg. 21.95 (1-879219-07-7) Veracruz Pubs.
— Asinano - Bilingual Word Guide of the English & Spanish Language Fruits & Vegetables. (ENG & SPA.). 42p. (J). (gr. k-12). 1997. pap. 12.95 (1-879219-09-3) Veracruz Pubs.
— Hay Roca en Tu Coca. (SPA., Illus.). 47p. (Orig.). (YA). 1992. pap. 2.75 (1-879219-05-0) Veracruz Pubs.
— Later with the Latex: AIDS. 44p. (Orig.). (YA). 1992. pap. 2.95 (1-879219-06-9) Veracruz Pubs.
— School Adventures: Aventuras Escolares. 27p. (Orig.). (J). 1989. pap. text 4.95 (1-879219-04-2) Veracruz Pubs.
— A Sound Mind in a Sound Body. 23p. (Orig.). (YA). 1990. pap. 16.00 (1-879219-03-4) Veracruz Pubs.
— There's a Rock in Your Coke. 47p. (Orig.). (YA). 1987. pap. 2.50 (1-879219-02-6) Veracruz Pubs.
— Three Coffins for Nino Lencho. 332p. 1987. lib. bdg. 12.00 (1-879219-01-8) Veracruz Pubs.
Rico, Barbara R. The American Mosaic, 2 vols. LC 94-76543. (C). Date not set. pap., teacher ed., suppl. ed. 30.36 (0-395-71899-6) HM.
— The American Mosaic. (C). 1990. pap. text, teacher ed. 2.76 (0-395-53691-X) HM.
— Rico You, the Writer. LC 96-76950. (C). 1997. pap. text 28.76 (0-395-68635-0) HM.
Rico, Barbara R. & Mano, Sandra. American Mosaic: Multicultural Readings in Context, 2 vols. (C). 1995. text, teacher ed. 11.96 (0-395-71591-1) HM.
Rico, Carlos, jt. ed. see Coatsworth, John H.
Rico, Daniel T., ed. see O'Halloran, Bethany J.
Rico, Don, jt. auth. see Hurst, Walter E.
Rico, Donato, jt. auth. see Hurst, Walter E.
Rico, Donato, ed. see Hurst, Walter E.
Rico, Gabriele. Writing the Natural Way: Turn the Task of Writing into the Joy of Writing. rev. ed. LC 99-49296. (Illus.). 320p. 2000. 16.95 (0-87477-961-8, Tarcher Putnam) Putnam Pub Group.
Rico, Gabriele L. Pain & Possibility. 288p. 1991. pap. 16.95 (0-87477-571-X, Tarcher Putnam) Putnam Pub Group.
Rico, Gabriele L. & Guth, Hans P. You the Writer: Reading, Writing, Thinking. (C). 1997. text, teacher ed. 11.96 (0-395-83836-3) HM.
Rico, Gabriele L., jt. auth. see Guth, Hans P.
***Rico-Godoy, Carmwn.** Como Ser una Mujer y No Morir en el Inteno. (SPA.). 1998. pap. 10.95 (84-7880-750-0) E Temas de Hoy.
Rico, Joe, ed. see Leinster, Murray.
Rico, Ul De, see De Rico, Ul.
Ricoeur, Paul. The Conflict of Interpretations: Essays on Hermeneutics. LC 73-91311. (Studies in Phenomenology & Existential Philosophy). 512p. 1974. pap. 24.95 (0-8101-0529-2) Northwestern U Pr.
Ricoeur, Paul. Essays on Biblical Interpretation. Mudge, Lewis S., ed. LC 80-8052. 192p. (Orig.). reprint ed. pap. 59.60 (0-608-18361-X, 203304500083) Bks Demand.
— Fallible Man: Philosophy of the Will. rev. ed. LC 65-16280. xxxvii, 146p. 1986. 35.00 (0-8232-1150-9); pap. 18.50 (0-8232-1151-7) Fordham.
— Figuring the Sacred: Religion, Narrative & Imagination.

An Asterisk (*) at the beginning of an entry indicates that the title is appearing for the first time.

R

Wallace, Mark I., ed. Pellauer, David, tr. from FRE. LC 95-5454. 352p. 1995. pap. 27.00 (0-8006-2894-2, Fortress Pr) Augsburg Fortress.
— Freedom & Nature: The Voluntary & the Involuntary. Kohak, Erazim V., tr. (Studies in Phenomenology & Existential Philosophy). 498p. 1966. 42.95 (0-8101-0208-0); pap. 22.95 (0-8101-0534-9) Northwestern U Pr.
— Freud & Philosophy: An Essay on Interpretation. Savage, Denis, tr. LC 70-89907. (Terry Lectures Ser.). 1977. pap. 19.00 (0-300-02189-5) Yale U Pr.
— From Text to Action. Blamey, Kathleen & Thompson, John B., trs. from FRE. (Studies in Phenomenology & Existential Philosophy). 346p. (Orig.). 1991. 49.95 (0-8101-0978-6); pap. 9.95 (0-8101-0992-1) Northwestern U Pr.
— Hermeneutics & the Human Sciences. Thompson, John B., ed. LC 80-41546. 324p. 1981. pap. text 35.95 (0-521-28002-8) Cambridge U Pr.
— History & Truth. Kelbley, C. A., tr. (Studies in Phenomenology & Existential Philosophy). 333p. 1965. pap. 26.95 (0-8101-0598-5) Northwestern U Pr.
Ricoeur, Paul. Husserl: An Analysis of His Phenomenology. Ballard, Edward G & Embree, Lester, trs. (Studies in Phenomenology & Existential Philosophy). 238p. 1967. pap. 22.50 (0-8101-0530-6) Northwestern U Pr.
Ricoeur, Paul. Interpretation Theory: Discourse & the Surplus of Meaning. LC 76-29604. 108p. (C). 1976. pap. 10.00 (0-912646-59-4) Tex Christian.
— Lectures on Ideology & Utopia. Taylor, George, ed. LC 86-6813. 384p. 1986. text 68.00 (0-231-06048-3) Col U Pr.
— Oneself As Another. Blamey, Kathleen, tr. LC 92-107. 374p. (C). 1999. 32.95 (0-226-71328-8) U Ch Pr.
— Oneself as Another. Blamey, Kathleen, tr. 374p. 1994. pap. 17.00 (0-226-71329-6) U Ch Pr.
— The Reality of the Historical Past. LC 84-60012. (Aquinas Lectures). 51p. 1984. 15.00 (0-87462-152-6) Marquette.
— A Ricoeur Reader: Reflection & Imagination. Valdes, Mario J., ed. 516p. 1991. text 60.00 (0-8020-5880-9); pap. text 24.95 (0-8020-6814-6) U of Toronto Pr.
— The Rule of Metaphor: Multi-Disciplinary Studies of the Creation of Meaning in Language. Czerny, Robert, tr. 1977. pap. text 22.50 (0-8020-6447-7) U of Toronto Pr.
— The Rule of Metaphor: Multi-Disciplinary Studies of the Creation of Meaning in Language. Czerny, Robert et al, trs. LC 77-5514. 394p. reprint ed. pap. 122.20 (0-8357-8313-8, 203402200088) Bks Demand.
— The Symbolism of Evil. LC 67-11506. 1969. reprint ed. pap. 20.00 (0-8070-1567-9, BPA18) Beacon Pr.
— Time & Narrative, Vol. 1. McLaughlin, Kathleen & Pellauer, David, trs. from FRE. LC 83-17995. (Illus.). 288p. 1984. 27.50 (0-226-71331-8) U Ch Pr.
— Time & Narrative, Vol. 1. Blamey, Kathleen & Pellauer, David, trs. LC 83-17995. 286p. 1990. pap. 15.95 (0-226-71332-6) U Ch Pr.
— Time & Narrative, Vol. 2. Blamey, Kathleen & Pellauer, David, trs. LC 83-17995. 216p. 1990. pap. 14.00 (0-226-71334-2) U Ch Pr.
— Time & Narrative, Vol. 2. McLaughlin, Kathleen & Pellauer, David, trs. viii, 216p. 1999. lib. bdg. 30.00 (0-226-71333-4) U Ch Pr.
— Time & Narrative, Vol. 3. Blamey, Kathleen & Pellauer, David, trs. 362p. 1988. lib. bdg. 36.00 (0-226-71335-0) U Ch Pr.
— Time & Narrative, Vol. 3. Blamey, Kathleen & Pellauer, David, trs. LC 83-17995. vi, 362p. 1990. pap. 17.00 (0-226-71336-9) U Ch Pr.
Ricoeur, Paul, ed. Tolerance Between Intolerance & the Intolerable. (Diogenes Library). 224p. 1997. pap. 15.00 (1-57181-136-2) Berghahn Bks.
Ricoeur, Paul & Lacocque, Andre. Thinking Biblically. Pellauer, David, tr. LC 97-44091. 441p. 1998. 30.00 (0-226-71337-7) U Ch Pr.
Ricoeur, Paul, jt. auth. see Changeux, Jean-Pierre.
Ricoeur, Paul, jt. auth. see MacIntyre, Alasdair C.
Ricolfi, T. & Scholz, J. Thermal Sensors. LC 90-22902. (Sensors Ser.). xii, 412p. 1990. write for info. (0-89573-676-4, Wiley-VCH) Wiley.
Ricon, Amado, jt. auth. see Davis, Thomas B.
Riconda, Andrew, ed. Gambling. (Reference Shelf Ser.: Vol. 67, No. 4). 1995. pap. 25.00 (0-8242-0871-4) Wilson.
Riconda, Margaret, ed. Finding: The Librarian's National Telephone Book. rev. ed. 453p. 1998. pap. 49.95 (0-935912-67-3, HF5801) LDA Pubs.
Ricord, Frederick W. General Index to the Documents Relating to the Colonial History of the State of New Jersey, 10 vols., Set. 198p. 1994. reprint ed. 14.50 (0-8063-4874-7) Genealog Pub.
Ricord, Frederick W. History of Union County, New Jersey. 556p. 1992. reprint ed. lib. bdg. 68.00 (0-8328-6544-3) Higginson Bk Co.
Ricotta, Kimberly, ed. see Redstone, P. G.
Ricotti, Lucio P. & Becchetti, Claudio. Automatic Speech Recognition Programming & Implementation. 428p. (C). 1999. pap. 125.00 incl. cd-rom, disk (0-471-97730-6) Wiley.
Ricou, L. Field Guide to Guide Dungeness Spit. LC 98-140846. 64p. 1997. pap. 12.95 (0-88982-165-8, Pub. by Oolichan Bks) Genl Dist Srvs.
Ricou, Laurence. Vertical Man, Horizontal World: Man & Landscape in Canadian Prairie Fiction. LC 73-80447. xii, 151p. 1973. write for info. (0-7748-0022-4) U BC Pr.
Ricouard, M. J. Formwork for Concrete Construction. rev. ed.Tr. of Constructions en Beton - Lecoffrage: Calculs, Applications, Formulaire. (Illus.). 195p. (C). 1983. text 65.00 (0-333-29360-6) Scholium Intl.
Ricouart, Janine. Ecriture Feminine et Violence: Une Etude de Marguerite Duras. LC 91-65035. (FRE.). 222p. 1991. lib. bdg. 32.95 (0-917786-82-3) Summa Pubns.
— Marguerite Duras Lives On. LC 98-24668. 256p. 1998. 39.50 (0-7618-1206-7) U Pr of Amer.
Ricouart, Janine, ed. Relectures de Madeleine Monette. LC 98-61741. (FRE.). 249p. 1999. lib. bdg. 42.95 (1-883479-23-1) Summa Pubns.
***Ricouer, Paul.** The Just. Pellauer, David, tr. from FRE. LC 99-40311. 2000. 20.00 (0-226-71339-3) U Ch Pr.
Ricour, Pierre. Lexique Anglais-Francais de la Banque et de la Monnaie: English - French Lexicon of Banking & Finance. (ENG & FRE.). 40p. 1974. pap. 9.95 (0-8288-6311-3, M-6486) Fr & Eur.
Ricoy, M. A. & Volakis, John L. Electromagnetic Scattering from Two-Dimensional Thick Material Junctions. LC QC0670.. (University of Michigan Reports: No. 835921-14-T). 178p. reprint ed. pap. 55.20 (0-8357-2933-8, 203917400011) Bks Demand.
Ricquier, W. J. & Heong, Stanley Y. Breaches of Trust in Singapore & Malaysia. 98p. 1984. pap. 44.00 (0-406-18115-2, MICHIE) LEXIS Pub.
R.I.C.S. Books Staff. The Contractor's Basis of Valuation for Rating Purposes - A Guidance Note. 1995. pap. 40.00 (0-85406-712-4, Pub. by R-I-C-S Bks) St Mut.
— An Elemental Analysis of Service Charges. 1995. pap. 27.00 (0-85406-696-9, Pub. by R-I-C-S Bks) St Mut.
— The Insurance of Managed Property. 1995. pap. 40.00 (0-85406-695-0, Pub. by R-I-C-S Bks) St Mut.
RICS Books Staff. The Mundic Problem: A Guidance Note Recommended Sampling, Examination & Classification Procedure for Suspect Concrete Building Materials in Devon & Cornwall. 1993. pap. 100.00 (0-85406-586-5, Pub. by R-I-C-S Bks) St Mut.
— Reinstatement Cost Assessment & Insurance Claims. 1995. pap. 33.00 (0-85406-685-3, Pub. by R-I-C-S Bks) St Mut.
— RICS Appraisal & Valuation Manual: The New Red Book. 300p. 1995. ring bd. 270.00 (0-85406-699-3, Pub. by R-I-C-S Bks) St Mut.
RICS Energy Efficience Office Staff. Energy Appraisal of Existing Buildings: A Handbook for Surveyors. 86p. 1993. 80.00 (0-85406-561-X, Pub. by R-I-C-S Bks) St Mut.
RICS Insurance Services Staff. Caveat Surveyor. (C). 1986. text 75.00 (0-85406-306-4, Pub. by R-I-C-S Bks) St Mut.
— Caveat Surveyor Eleven. (C). 1989. text 75.00 (0-85406-425-7, Pub. by R-I-C-S Bks) St Mut.
RICS Staff. Chartered Surveyors As a Management Consultant: An Emerging Market. 63p. 1995. pap. 75.00 (0-85406-686-1, Pub. by R-I-C-S Bks) St Mut.
— Cost Management in Engineering Construction Projects: Guidance Notes. (C). 1992. pap. text 90.00 (0-85406-524-5, Pub. by R-I-C-S Bks) St Mut.
— Directory of Planning & Development Consultants. 80p. (C). 1989. text 85.00 (0-85406-424-9, Pub. by Surveyors Pubns) St Mut.
— Directory of Research & Development: Activities in the U. K. in Land Survey & Related Fields. 100p. (C). 1987. text 65.00 (0-85406-356-0, Pub. by Surveyors Pubns) St Mut.
— Environmental Management & the Chartered Surveyor. 108p. 1995. pap. 75.00 (0-85406-662-4, Pub. by R-I-C-S Bks) St Mut.
— Flat Roof Covering Problems: A Guidance Note. 1995. pap. 35.00 (0-85406-711-6, Pub. by R-I-C-S Bks) St Mut.
— Guidance Note on the 1995 Agricultural Tenancies Act. 60p. 1995. pap. 60.00 (0-85406-692-6, Pub. by R-I-C-S Bks) St Mut.
— Guidance Notes on the Valuation of Assets. 174p. (C). 1989. text 125.00 (0-85406-423-0, Pub. by Surveyors Pubns) St Mut.
— A Guide to Life Cycle Costing for Construction. (C). 1986. text 45.00 (0-85406-322-6, Pub. by Surveyors Pubns) St Mut.
— Guidelines for the Preparation of Hydrographic Surveys for Dredging. (C). 1984. text 50.00 (0-85406-232-7, Pub. by Surveyors Pubns) St Mut.
— Guidelines for the Preparation of Specifications for Hydrographic Surveys. (C). 1984. text 50.00 (0-85406-185-1, Pub. by Surveyors Pubns) St Mut.
— Housing the Nation, Vols. 1 & 2. (C). 1992. pap. text 125.00 (0-85406-510-5, Pub. by R-I-C-S Bks) St Mut.
— Introductory Guidance to Insurance under Building Contracts. 1995. pap. 50.00 (0-85406-680-2, Pub. by R-I-C-S Bks) St Mut.
— Land Contamination Guidance for Chartered Surveyors. 1995. pap. 30.00 (0-85406-670-5, Pub. by R-I-C-S Bks) St Mut.
— The Making of Planning Applications. (C). 1991. text 90.00 (0-85406-497-4, Pub. by R-I-C-S Bks) St Mut.
— Property Insurance: Some Points to Consider in Relation to the Proper Cover of Risks. (C). 1985. text 39.00 (0-85406-288-2, Pub. by Surveyors Pubns) St Mut.
— Property Insurance: Some Points to Consider in Relation to the Property Cover of Risks. 1995. pap. 40.00 (0-85406-703-5, Pub. by R-I-C-S Bks) St Mut.
— Putting the Estate Agents Act 1979 & Its Order & Regulations into Practice. (C). 1991. pap. text 90.00 (0-85406-503-2, Pub. by R-I-C-S Bks) St Mut.
— QS-2000 the Future Role of the Chartered Quantity Surveyor. (C). 1991. pap. text 90.00 (0-85406-495-8, Pub. by R-I-C-S Bks) St Mut.
— Refurbishment & Alteration Work. (C). 1983. text 29.00 (0-85406-181-9, Pub. by Surveyors Pubns) St Mut.
— RICS Directory of International Practices. 120p. (C). 1986. text 75.00 (0-7855-5976-0, Pub. by Surveyors Pubns) St Mut.
— Shaping Britain for the Twenty-First Century. (C). 1991. pap. text 125.00 (0-85406-501-6, Pub. by R-I-C-S Bks) St Mut.
— Specification for Mapping at Scales Between 1:1,000 & 1:10,000. (C). 1988. text 90.00 (0-85406-375-7, Pub. by Surveyors Pubns) St Mut.
— Terms & Conditions of Contract for Land Surveying Services. (C). 1989. text 59.00 (0-85406-418-4, Pub. by Surveyors Pubns) St Mut.
RICS Staff, ed. Specification for Surveys of Land, Buildings & Utility Services at Scales of L:500 & Larger. (C). 1986. text 49.00 (0-85406-297-1, Pub. by Surveyors Pubns) St Mut.
RICS Staff & Building Design Partnership Staff. A Study of Quantity Surveying & Client Demand. (C). 1984. text 90.00 (0-7855-5977-9, Pub. by Surveyors Pubns) St Mut.
RICS Staff & Building Employers Confederation Staff. SMM7 - The Standard Method of Measurement of Building Works. LC 99-492084. 190p. (C). 1988. text 125.00 (0-85406-360-9, Pub. by R-I-C-S Bks) St Mut.
— SMM7 Measurement Code. (C). 1988. pap. text 75.00 (0-85406-361-7, Pub. by R-I-C-S Bks) St Mut.
RICS Staff, jt. auth. see ISUA Staff.
Ricucci, Betsy, jt. auth. see Ricucci, Gary.
Ricucci, Gary & Ricucci, Betsy. Love That Lasts: Making a Magnificent Marriage. Somerville, Greg, ed. 176p. 1992. pap. 8.99 (1-881039-02-1) PDI Ministries.
Ricuperati, Guisseppe & Carpanetto, Dino. Italy in the Age of Reason, 1685-1789. LC 86-15174. (Longman History of Italy Ser.: Vol. 5). 367p. 1987. reprint ed. pap. 113.80 (0-608-03613-7, 206443600009) Bks Demand.
Ricur, Paul, et al. Critique & Conviction: Conversations with Francois Azouvi & Marc De Launay. Blamey, Kathleen, tr. from FRE. LC 97-27567. 224p. 1998. 26.00 (0-231-10734-X) Col U Pr.
— A Key to Husserl's Ideas I. LC 96-10139. (Studies in Philosophy). 1996. 20.00 (0-87462-609-9) Marquette.
Rida, Muhammad R. The Muhammadan Revelation. DeLorenzo, Yusuf T., tr. from ARA. 160p. 1996. pap. text 9.95 (1-881963-55-1) Al-Saadawi Pubns.
Ridaeus, Barbro Norstrom, see Norstrom Ridaeus, Barbro.
Ridall, R. Clyde. Search the Scriptures, Old Testament Vol. 6: Judges, Ruth. 1965. pap. 1.99 (0-8341-0033-9) Beacon Hill.
Ridcon, G. T. History of the Millingas & Millanges, Milliken, Millikin, Family of Saxony & Normandy. 882p. 1994. reprint ed. pap. 106.00 (0-8328-3864-0); reprint ed. lib. bdg. 116.00 (0-8328-3863-2) Higginson Bk Co.
Ridd, Stephen, et al, eds. Julius Caesar in Gaul & Britain. LC 94-28699. (History Eyewitness Ser.). (Illus.). 48p. (J). (gr. 7-8). 1995. lib. bdg. 24.26 (0-8114-8283-9) Raintree Steck-V.
Riddall, J. G. Riddall: Introduction to Land Law. 5th ed. 592p. 1993. pap. 38.00 (0-406-00589-3, U.K., MICHIE) LEXIS Pub.
Riddall, John G. The Law of Trusts. 5th ed. 464p. 1996. pap. write for info. (0-406-00905-8, RLT5, MICHIE) LEXIS Pub.
— Riddall: Introduction to Land Law. 6th ed. 1997. pap. write for info. (0-406-99612-1, RILL6, MICHIE) LEXIS Pub.
Riddel, jt. auth. see Stamos.
Riddel, Diana, jt. auth. see O'Brien, Eileen.
Riddel, Frank S., jt. auth. see Coffey, William E.
Riddel, Joseph N. Clairvoyant Eye: The Poetry & Poetics of Wallace Stevens. LC 91-15505. 308p. 1991. pap. text 18.95 (0-8071-0716-6) La State U Pr.
— Inverted Bell: Modernism & the Counterpoetics of William Carlos Williams. LC 91-14721. 308p. 1991. pap. text 18.95 (0-8071-1697-1) La State U Pr.
— Purloined Letters: Originality & Repetition in American Literature. Bauerlain, Mark, ed. LC 94-30483. (Horizons in Theory & American Culture Ser.). 232p. (C). 1995. text 32.50 (0-8071-1872-9) La State U Pr.
— The Turning Word: American Literary Modernism & Continental Theory. 192p. 1996. text 36.50 (0-8122-3378-6); pap. text 16.50 (0-8122-1600-8) U of Pa Pr.
Riddel, Maria D. La Escritura Femenina el la Postguerra Espanola, Vol. 10. (Wor(l)ds of Change Ser.). (SPA.). 208p. (C). 1995. text 45.95 (0-8204-2619-9) P Lang Pubng.
Riddel, Roger C., et al. Manufacturing Africa: Performance & Prospects of Seven Countries in Sub-Saharan Africa. 419p. (C). 1990. pap. 30.00 (0-435-08050-4, 08050) Heinemann.
***Riddell.** Deep Stuff. 1999. pap. 20.95 (0-7459-4041-2, Pub. by Lion Pubng) Trafalgar.
***Riddell & Shackelford.** Understanding Society: Economics: A Tool for Critically Understanding Society. 5th ed. (C). 1999. text 46.66 (0-201-63587-9) Addison-Wesley.
Riddell, jt. auth. see Cave.
Riddell, Alan. Eclipse. pap. 10.95 (0-7145-0907-8) Riverrun NY.
Riddell, C. Avian Histopathology. (Illus.). (Orig.). 1987. pap. text 26.00 (0-915538-03-2) AAAP PA.
Riddell, Carol. The Findhorn Community: Creating a Human Identity for the 21st Century. (Orig.). 1991. pap. 14.95 (0-905249-77-1, Pub. by Findhorn Pr) Words Distrib.
— The Path to Love Is the Practice of Love: An Introduction to Spirituality. (Guidebooks for Growth Together). 144p. (Orig.). 1995. pap. 10.95 (1-899171-20-7, Pub. by Findhorn Pr) Words Distrib.
Riddell, Carol, jt. auth. see Coulson, Margaret.
Riddell, Cecilia, jt. auth. see Kleiner, Lynn.
Riddell, Chris. Ben & the Bear. LC 85-23899. (Illus.). 32p. (J). (ps-2). 1986. lib. bdg. 11.89 (0-397-32194-5) HarpC Child Bks.
— Buddhism for Bears. LC 99-22785. 1999. text 12.95 (0-312-20503-1) St Martin.
— Feng Shui for Cats. 1999. 9.95 (0-09-185421-0, Pub. by Ebury Pr) Trafalgar.
— Feng Shui for Dogs. 1999. 9.95 (0-09-186085-7) Ebury Pr.
— Mr. Underbed. (Illus.). 32p. (J). (ps-1). 1998. pap. 9.95 (0-86264-786-X, Pub. by Andersen Pr) Trafalgar.
— The Trouble with Elephants. LC 87-24963. (Illus.). 32p. (J). (ps-2). 1988. 12.95 (0-397-32272-0); lib. bdg. 12.89 (0-397-32273-9) HarpC Child Bks.
Riddell, Diana, jt. auth. see O'Brien, Eileen.
Riddell-Dixon, Elizabeth. Canada & the International Seabed: Domestic Determinants & External Constraints. 240p. (C). 1989. text 65.00 (0-7735-0694-2, Pub. by McG-Queens Univ Pr) CUP Services.
Riddell, Doug. From the Cab: Stories from A Locomotive Engineer. LC 99-19470. 1999. 14.95 (1-56342-010-4) Pentrex Media.
Riddell, Edwina. My First Ballet Class. LC 92-24450. (Illus.). 32p. (J). (ps-2). 1993. pap. 5.95 (0-8120-1674-2) Barron.
— My First Day at Preschool. LC 91-18374. (Illus.). 32p. (J). (ps). 1992. 9.95 (0-8120-6261-2) Barron.
— My First Day at Preschool. (Illus.). 32p. 1995. pap. 5.95 (0-8120-1878-8) Barron.
— One Hundred First Words. (Illus.). 32p. (J). (ps). 1991. pap. 4.95 (0-8120-4888-1) Barron.
Riddell, Edwina, jt. auth. see Smallman, Clare.
Riddell, Francis A. The Archaeology of the Karlo Site (LAS-7), California. fac. ed. (Reports of the University of California Archaeological Survey: No. 53). (Illus.). 137p. 1960. reprint ed. pap. 15.00 (1-55567-369-4) Coyote Press.
Riddell, Francis A. & Heizer, R. F. The Archaeology of Two Kern County Sites. fac. ed. (Reports of the University of California Archaeological Survey: No. 10). (Illus.). 40p. 1951. reprint ed. pap. 4.38 (1-55567-334-1) Coyote Press.
Riddell, Francis A. & Olsen, W. H. The Archeology of the Western Pacific Railroad Relocation, Oroville Project, Butte County, California. (Publications of the Department of Parks & Recreation: No. 7). (Illus.). 95p. (C). 1963. reprint ed. pap. text 10.63 (1-55567-459-3) Coyote Press.
— Salvage of the Rio Oso Site, Yuba County, California. (Publications of the Department of Parks & Recreation: No. 6). (Illus.). 29p. (C). 1962. reprint ed. pap. text 3.44 (1-55567-458-5) Coyote Press.
Riddell, Francis A., et al. Current Views on Great Basin Archaeology. fac. ed. (Reports of the University of California Archaeological Survey: No. 42). (Illus.). 137p. 1958. reprint ed. pap. 15.00 (1-55567-359-7) Coyote Press.
— Papers on California Archaeology, Nos. 34-36. fac. ed. (Reports of the University of California Archaeological Survey: No. 32). (Illus.). 48p. 1955. reprint ed. pap. 5.31 (1-55567-350-3) Coyote Press.
— Papers on California Archaeology, Nos. 44-46. fac. ed. (Reports of the University of California Archaeological Survey: No. 35). (Illus.). 69p. 1956. reprint ed. pap. 8.13 (1-55567-353-8) Coyote Press.
Riddell, Francis A., jt. auth. see Meighan, Clement W.
Riddell, Francis A., jt. ed. see Wallace, William J.
Riddell, Frank G., jt. ed. see Lambert, Joseph B.
Riddell, George A. More Things That Matter. LC 79-128299. (Essay Index Reprint Ser.). 1977. 21.95 (0-8369-1843-6) Ayer.
— Some Things That Matter. LC 74-37793. (Essay Index Reprint Ser). 1977. reprint ed. 20.95 (0-8369-2620-X) Ayer.
Riddell, James. Many, Many Times. LC 98-76192. 250p. 1999. write for info. (1-893766-03-9) Aeon Pub Co.
Riddell, James & Dickerman, Carol. Country Profiles of Land Tenure: Africa 1986. (LTC Papers: No. 127). 237p. (Orig.). (C). 1986. pap. text 12.00 (0-934519-42-0, LTC 127) U of Wis Land.
Riddell, James, jt. auth. see Fortmann, Louise.
Riddell, James, ed. see Plato.
Riddell, James A. & Stewart, Stanley. Jonson's Spenser: Evidence & Historical Criticism. LC 95-11767. (Duquesne Studies: Language & Literature Ser.: Vol. 18). (Illus.). 228p. (C). 1995. text 48.00 (0-8207-0263-3) Duquesne.
Riddell, Jennifer & Druckrey, Timothy. The Art of Detection: Surveillance in Society. unabridged ed. (Illus.). 48p. 1997. pap. 10.00 (0-938437-56-9) MIT List Visual Arts.
***Riddell, John.** Canadian National Color Guide to Freight & Passenger Equipment, Vol. 1. (Illus.). 128p. 1999. 54.95 (1-58248-033-8) Morning NJ.
Riddell, John. Canadian Pacific Color Guide to Freight & Passenger Equipment. LC 97-72728. (Illus.). 128p. 1998. 49.95 (1-878887-86-6) Morning NJ.
Riddell, John, ed. Founding the Communist International: Proceedings & Documents of the First Congress - March 1919. Cantrick, Bob & Dees, Robert, trs. LC 87-70239. (Communist International in Lenin's Time Ser.: Vol. 3). 424p. (Orig.). 1987. pap. 27.95 (0-913460-97-4); lib. bdg. 65.00 (0-913460-96-6) Pathfinder NY.
— The German Revolution & The Debate on Soviet Power Documents: 1918-1919. Cantrick, Bob et al, trs. LC 86-60845. (Communist International in Lenin's Time Ser.: Vol. 2). 540p. (Orig.). 1986. pap. 31.95 (0-937091-01-4); lib. bdg. 75.00 (0-937091-00-6) Pathfinder NY.
— Workers of the World & Oppressed Peoples Unite! Proceedings & Documents of the Second Congress, 1920, 2 vols. LC 91-66263. (Illus.). 1147p. (C). 1991. lib. bdg. 160.00 (0-937091-07-3) Pathfinder NY.
— Workers of the World & Oppressed Peoples Unite!

An Asterisk (*) at the beginning of an entry indicates that the title is appearing for the first time.

Proceedings & Documents of the Second Congress, 1920, 2 vols. LC 91-66263. (Illus.). 1147p. (C). 1992. pap. 65.00 (0-937091-06-5) Pathfinder NY.

— Workers of the World & Oppressed Peoples Unite! Proceedings & Documents of the Second Congress, 1920, 2 vols., 1. LC 91-66263. (Illus.). 587p. (C). 1991. pap. 35.95 (0-937091-08-1); lib. bdg. 85.00 (0-937091-09-X) Pathfinder NY.

— Workers of the World & Oppressed Peoples Unite! Proceedings & Documents of the Second Congress, 1920, 2 vols., 2. LC 91-66263. (Illus.). 560p. (C). 1991. pap. 35.95 (0-937091-10-3); lib. bdg. 85.00 (0-937091-11-1) Pathfinder NY.

Riddell, John, ed. To See the Dawn: Baku, Nineteen Twenty - First Congress of the Peoples of the East. LC 93-85321. (Communist International in Lenin's Time Ser.). (Illus.). 344p. (Orig.). 1993. pap. 19.95 (0-87348-769-9); lib. bdg. 55.00 (0-87348-768-0) Pathfinder NY.

Riddell, John, ed. see Lenin, Vladimir Il'ich.

Riddell, John, ed. see Trotsky, Leon & Marx, Karl.

Riddell, John, jt. ed. see Yell, Denis.

Riddell, Lee & Welsh, Stanley L. Wildflowers of Zion National Park. (Illus.). 136p. pap. 9.95 (0-915630-27-3) Zion.

***Riddell, Marjorie.** M for Mother. 2000. pap. 12.95 (0-552-99747-1, Pub. by Transworld Publishers Ltd) Trafalgar.

Riddell, Marjorie. M for Mother. large type ed. 1998. 23.95 (0-7531-5802-7, Pub. by ISIS Lrg Prnt) Transaction Pubs.

***Riddell, Marjorie.** M for Mother. large type unabridged ed. 109p. 1999. pap. 19.95 (0-7531-5814-0, 158140, Pub. by ISIS Lrg Prnt) ISIS Pub.

***Riddell, Mary.** The Duchess of Kent. LC 99-458599. 256p. 1999. write for info. (0-283-06329-7) Trafalgar.

Riddell, Michael. Threshold of the Future: Reforming the Church in the Post-Christian West. 160p. 1998. pap. text 21.95 (0-281-05055-4) Intl Pubs Mktg.

***Riddell, Neil.** Labour in Crisis: The Second Labour Government, 1929-31. 1999. 79.95 (0-7190-5084-7, Pub. by Manchester Univ Pr) St Martin.

Riddell, Newton N. Method: The Riddell Lectures on Applied Psychology & Vital Christianity (1913) 320p. 1998. reprint ed. pap. 24.95 (0-7661-0229-7) Kessinger Pub.

Riddell, Peter. Parliament under Pressure. 256p. 1998. 40.00 (0-575-06435-8, Pub. by V Gollancz) Trafalgar.

— Transferring a Tradition: C Abd Al Ra'uf Al-Singkili's Rendering into Malay of the Jalalayn. unabridged ed. (Monographs: Vol. 31). 320p. (Orig.). 1990. pap. text 25.00 (0-944613-10-1) UC Berkeley Ctrs SE Asia.

Riddell, Peter G., et al. Islam: Essays on Scripture, Thought, & Society: A Festschrift in Honour of Anthony H. Johns. LC 97-9661. (Islamic Philosophy, Theology, & Science Ser.). 1997. 124.50 (90-04-10692-8) Brill Academic Pubs.

Riddell, Robert H., ed. Dysplasia & Cancer in Colitis: Proceedings of the Symposium Held June 1-4, 1989, Baltimore, MD. 296p. 1991. 155.00 (0-444-01570-1) P-H.

— Pathology of Drug-Induced & Toxic Diseases. LC 82-4230. (Illus.). 696p. reprint ed. pap. 200.00 (0-7837-2584-1, 204274500006) Bks Demand.

Riddell, Roger, jt. auth. see Robinson, Mark.

Riddell, Roger C. Foreign Aid Reconsidered. LC 87-2949. (Johns Hopkins Studies in Development). 319p. reprint ed. pap. 98.90 (0-7837-4488-9, 204426500001) Bks Demand.

Riddell, Sheila, jt. ed. see Salisbury, Jane.

Riddell, Stephen. Motivation & Compensation. 200p. 1994. write for info. (0-936840-14-5) Tech Marketing.

Riddell, Stephen M. Selling Genius: Achieving Extraordinary Sales Results with Ordinary People. LC 94-60402. viii, 182p. 1994. write for info. (0-936840-17-X) Tech Marketing.

Riddell, Tom. Economics: A Tool for Understanding Society. 5th ed. LC 97-34257. (Illus.). 562p. (C). 1997. pap. text 72.00 (0-201-55714-2) Addison-Wesley.

— Economics No. 3: A Tool for Understanding Society & Economic Times Bundle. 4th ed. (C). 1995. text 50.00 (0-201-59457-9) Addison-Wesley.

Riddell, Tom, et al. Economics: A Tool for Understanding Society. 3rd ed. LC 86-14043. (Economics Ser.). (Illus.). 600p. (C). 1987. pap. text 37.75 (0-201-06368-9) Addison-Wesley.

Riddell, Walter A. Rise of Ecclesiastical Control in Quebec. (Columbia University. Studies in the Social Sciences: No. 174). reprint ed. 22.50 (0-404-51174-0) AMS Pr.

Riddell, William A. Regina: From Pile O' Bones to Queen City of the Plains. 1980. 24.95 (0-89781-029-5, 5040) Am Historical Pr.

Ridder, Chantal De, see De Ridder, Chantal.

Ridder, Geert, et al, eds. Panel Data & Labor Market Studies. (Contributions to Economic Analysis Ser.: No. 192). 336p. 1990. 131.50 (0-444-88461-0, North Holland) Elsevier.

Ridder, Herman. Membership in the Reformed Church. 1980. pap. 1.95 (0-686-23484-7) Rose Pub MI.

***Ridder, J. W. A. & De Kort, I., eds.** Mimosoideae of South-East Asia: MAC-WIN-Version. 2000. cd-rom 59.95 (3-540-14705-5) Spr-Verlag.

Ridder, Kathleen C. Shaping My Feminist Life: A Memoir. LC 98-24413. (Midwest Reflections Ser.). (Illus.). 199p. 1998. 24.95 (0-87351-364-9, 364-9); pap. 15.95 (0-87351-365-7, 365-7) Minn Hist.

Ridder, Klaus. Mittelhochdeutsche Minne - und Aventiureromane. 400p. 1998. 116.00 (3-11-015414-5) De Gruyter.

Ridder-Numan, J. Historical Biogeography of the Southeast Asian Genus Spatholobus (Legum.-Papilionoideae) & Its Allies. LC 97-213733. (Blumea Ser.: No. 10). (Illus.). 144p. 1996. 49.00 (90-71236-30-7, Pub. by Rijksherbarium) Balogh.

Ridder, Richard R. De, see Hofman, Leonard J. & De Ridder, Richard R.

***Ridderbos, Herman.** Pensamiento de Pablo. Casanova, Humberto & Pimentel, Alejandro, eds.Tr. of Paul: An Outline of His Theology. (SPA.). 2000. write for info. (1-55883-119-3) Libros Desafio.

Ridderbos, Herman N. Coming of the Kingdom. LC 62-15429. 1962. pap. 17.99 (0-87552-408-7) P & R Pubng.

— Paul: An Outline of His Theology. 1997. pap. text 30.00 (0-8028-4469-3) Eerdmans.

— Redemptive History & the New Testament Scriptures. Graffin, Richard B. & De Jongste, H., Jr., trs. LC 87-32875. Orig. Title: The Authority of the New Testament Scriptures. (DUT.). 110p. 1988. pap. 6.99 (0-87552-416-8) P & R Pubng.

Ridderbos, Herman N. & Jongste, H. De. The Gospel of John: A Theological Commentary. 735p. 1997. pap. text 42.00 (0-8028-0453-5) Eerdmans.

Ridderbos, J. Bible Student's Commentary: Deuteronomy. (Bible Student's Commentary Ser.). 336p. 1984. 19.95 (0-310-45260-0, 11760) Zondervan.

— Bible Student's Commentary: Isaiah. (Bible Student's Commentary Ser.). 528p. 1985. 20.95 (0-310-45270-8, 11761) Zondervan.

Ridderbos, N. H. Die Psalmen: Stilistische Verfahren und Aufbau mit besonderer Beruecksichtigung von Ps. 1-41. Mittring, Karl E., tr. from DUT. (Beiheft zur Zeitschrift fuer die Alttestamentliche Wissenschaft Ser.: No. 117). 305p. (C). 1972. 110.00 (3-11-001834-9) De Gruyter.

Ridderikhoff, J. Methods in Medicine. 240p. (C). 1989. lib. bdg. 148.50 (1-55608-080-8, Pub. by Kluwer Academic) Kluwer Academic.

Ridderstrale, Jonas. Global Innovation: Managing International Innovation Projects at ABB & Electrolux. LC 97-195719. (Institute of International Business Ser.). 422p. 1996. pap. 87.50 (91-971730-4-5, Pub. by Almqvist Wiksell) Coronet Bks.

Riddervold, Astri & Ropeid, Andreas, eds. Food Conservation: Ethnological Studies. 224p. (Orig.). 1988. pap. 28.00 (0-907325-40-8, Pub. by Prospect) Food Words.

Riddervold, Hans O. Easily Missed Fractures & Corner Signs in Radiology. (Illus.). 416p. 1991. 150.00 (0-87993-502-2) Futura Pub.

Riddick, Barbara. Living with Dyslexia. 248p. (C). 1996. pap. 24.99 (0-415-12501-4) Routledge.

— Toys & Play for the Handicapped Child. (Illus.). 224p. 1982. pap. 27.50 (0-7099-0292-1, Pub. by C Helm) Routldge.

Riddick, Barbara, et al. Students & Dyslexia: Growing up with a Specific Disability. 180p. 1997. 39.95 (1-56593-886-0, 1736) Singular Publishing.

Riddick, Carol & Russell, Ruth V. Evaluative Research in Recreation, Park & Sport Settings: Searching for Useful Information. (Illus.). 392p. 1999. 44.95 (1-57167-245-1) Sagamore Pub.

Riddick, John F. Who Was Who in British India. LC 98-23311. 464p. 1998. lib. bdg. 115.00 (0-313-29232-9) Greenwood.

Riddick, John F., compiled by. Glimpses of India: An Annotated Bibliography of Published Personal Writings by Englishmen, 1608-1947, 15. LC 88-37582. (Bibliographies & Indexes in World History Ser.: No. 15). 215p. 1989. lib. bdg. 55.00 (0-313-25661-6, RGI/) Greenwood.

— A Guide to Indian Manuscripts, 2. LC 93-4771. (Reference Guides to Archival & Manuscript Sources in World History Ser.: No. 2). 296p. 1993. lib. bdg. 75.00 (0-313-27501-7, RGA/, Greenwood Pr) Greenwood.

Riddick, Ruth. The Right to Choose. (C). 1989. 60.00 (0-946211-85-X) St Mut.

Riddick, Sarah. Pioneer Studio Pottery: Milner-White Collection. (Illus.). 176p. 1990. 60.00 (0-85331-590-6, Pub. by Lund Humphries) Antique Collect.

— Pioneer Studio Pottery: Milner-White Collection. (Illus.). 176p. (C). 1990. pap. 35.00 (0-85331-581-7, Pub. by Lund Humphries) Antique Collect.

Riddick, Tut A. If You Ain't Dyin' Get Up: An Ozzie Scrapbook. 56p. 1992. pap. 10.00 (1-883172-00-4) Heart Press.

Riddick, Walter E. & Stewart, Eva M. Workbook for Program Evaluation in the Human Services. 196p. (Orig.). 1981. pap. text 23.50 (0-8191-1783-8) U Pr of Amer.

Riddick, Wiley G. Thoughts Promotive of the Higher Life (1910) 294p. 1998. reprint ed. pap. 24.95 (0-7661-0525-3) Kessinger Pub.

Riddick, William. Charrette Processes: A Tool in Urban Planning. LC 74-14257. (Illus.). 110p. 1971. pap. 7.50 (0-87387-041-7) Shumway.

Ridding, Laura, ed. Travels of Macarius: Extracts from the Diary of the Travels of Macarius, Patriarch of Antioch. LC 77-115577. (Russia Observed Ser.). 1971. reprint ed. 15.95 (0-405-03089-4) Ayer.

Riddle. Analytic Geometry W Vectors 2nd. 2nd ed. (Math). 1976. 19.75 (0-534-00485-7) Brooks-Cole.

— Analytical Geometry W/vectors. (Math). 1972. 12.75 (0-534-00090-8) Brooks-Cole.

— Calculus & Analytic Geometry 2nd. 2nd ed. (Math). 1973. 26.00 (0-534-00301-X) Brooks-Cole.

— Nursing Care Studies. 1989. pap. text 11.00 (0-443-03939-9, W B Saunders Co) Harcrt Hlth Sci Grp.

— Nursing Care Studies. 1993. pap. text 58.95 (0-443-04995-5, W B Saunders Co) Harcrt Hlth Sci Grp.

— Nursing Care Studies, Vol. 3. 1988. pap. text 11.00 (0-443-03936-4, W B Saunders Co) Harcrt Hlth Sci Grp.

— Nursing Care Studies, Vol. 4. 1989. pap. text 11.00 (0-443-03937-2, W B Saunders Co) Harcrt Hlth Sci Grp.

— Nursing Care Studies, Vol. 5. 1989. pap. text 11.00 (0-443-03938-0, W B Saunders Co) Harcrt Hlth Sci Grp.

— Sol Anal Geometry W/vectors 2nd. 2nd ed. (Math). 1978. student ed. 7.50 (0-534-00620-5) Brooks-Cole.

— Sol F/stdt-calc & Anal Geo, 3rd. 3rd ed. (Math). 1980. student ed. 12.75 (0-534-00706-6) Brooks-Cole.

— Sol F/stdt-calc & Analy Geo ,2nd. 2nd ed. (Math). 1976. student ed. 6.00 (0-534-00501-2) Brooks-Cole.

— Solutions Manual, Analytic Geometry. 4th ed. (Math). 1987. student ed. 12.75 (0-534-07777-3) Brooks-Cole.

Riddle, Alfy. Applications of Electrical Engineering with Mathematica. (C). 1994. 42.95 (0-201-53477-0) Addison-Wesley.

***Riddle, Barbara.** The Girl Pretending to Read Rilke. LC 00-130339. 225p. 2000. pap. 15.95 (0-943485-06-1) Ren Sound Pubns.

***Riddle, Dan.** Crossword Review of A & P. 296p. 1999. 20.00 (1-886855-33-1) Tavenner Pub.

Riddle, Dana. The Captive Reef: A Concise Guide to Reef Aquaria in the Home. LC 96-164541. (Illus.). 297p. 1996. 39.95 (0-9640147-2-6) Energy Savers.

Riddle, Donald H. The Truman Committee: A Study in Congressional Responsibility. LC 63-16306. 217p. reprint ed. pap. 67.30 (0-608-30714-9, 205063800087) Bks Demand.

Riddle, Donald L., et al, eds. C. Elegans II. LC 96-86372. (Monographs: Vol. 33). (Illus.). 1248p. (C). 1997. text 175.00 (0-87969-488-2) Cold Spring Harbor.

— C. Elegans II. (Monograph Ser.: No. 33). (Illus.). 1222p. (C). 1998. pap. text 71.00 (0-87969-532-3) Cold Spring Harbor.

Riddle, Donald W. Congressman Abraham Lincoln. LC 79-11614. 280p. 1979. reprint ed. lib. bdg. 59.75 (0-8371-9307-9, RIAL, Greenwood Pr) Greenwood.

Riddle, Dorothy I. Service-Led Growth: The Role of the Service Sector in World Development. LC 85-16743. 304p. 1985. 79.50 (0-275-92041-0, C2041, Praeger Pubs) Greenwood.

Riddle, Douglas F. Analysis of Geological Materials. (Illus.). 480p. 1993. text 195.00 (0-8247-9132-0) Dekker.

Riddle, Douglas F. Analytic Geometry. 3rd ed. (Math). (C). 1982. mass mkt. 29.50 (0-534-01030-X) PWS Pubs.

— Analytic Geometry. 4th ed. (Math). 474p. (C). 1987. mass mkt. 41.75 (0-534-07776-5) PWS Pubs.

— Analytic Geometry. 5th ed. 445p. (C). 1992. text 52.00 (0-534-17274-1) PWS Pubs.

— Analytic Geometry. 6th ed. (Mathematics Ser.). 1995. mass mkt. 49.00 (0-534-94854-5) PWS Pubs.

— Calculus & Analytic Geometry. alternate ed. 1110p. (C). 1984. mass mkt. 76.50 (0-534-01198-5) PWS Pubs.

Riddle, Florence K., ed. see Reynolds, Harold R.

***Riddle, George & Wetlauffer, Brianna, eds.** The Unleashing of Evolutionary. (Illus.). 356p. 2000. 29.95 (0-9670428-9-5) Min Universal Wisdom.

***Riddle, George S.** Venuto the Venusian. deluxe ed. (Illus.). 278p. 2000. 32.95 (0-9670428-8-7) Min Universal Wisdom.

***Riddle, George S., ed.** When Stars Look Down. 203rd rev. ed. (Illus.). (YA). (gr. 9 up). 1999. pap. 15.95 (0-9670428-0-1) Min Universal Wisdom.

***Riddle, George S., ed.** The Proceedings of the College of Universal Wisdom: Journal of the Research from the Ministry of Universal Wisdom, 3 vols., Set. 2nd ed. 650p. 2000. 350.00 (0-9670428-6-0) Min Universal Wisdom.

***Riddle, George S., ed.** The Council of Seven Lights. 2nd ed. (Illus.). 156p. (YA). (gr. 9). 1999. pap. 15.95 (0-9670428-1-X) Min Universal Wisdom.

Riddle, Gordon. The Kestrel. (Natural History Ser.: No. 52). (Illus.). 24p. 5.25 (0-7478-0054-5, Pub. by Shire Pubns) Parkwest Pubns.

— The Kestrel. 1989. pap. 25.00 (0-7855-7040-3, Pub. by Shire Pubns) St Mut.

Riddle, Grant. Amputees & Devotees. 1989. 29.95 (0-8290-1824-7) Irvington.

Riddle, Gregory W. & Patel, Ashok, eds. Interactive Accounting: The Byzantium Workbook. LC 97-16960. 224p. 1997. pap. text 34.95 (0-631-20750-3) Blackwell Pubs.

Riddle, J. H. British & American Plans for International Currency Stabilization. (Occasional Papers: No. 16). 48p. 1943. reprint ed. 20.00 (0-87014-331-X) Natl Bur Econ Res.

Riddle, Janet T. Anatomy & Physiology Applied to Nursing. 6th ed. LC 84-21413. (Churchill Livingstone Nursing Text Ser.). (Illus.). 196p. 1985. pap. text 23.95 (0-443-03030-8) Church.

Riddle, Jeff C. The Indian History of the Modoc War. LC 74-78125. (Primary Source Bks.). (Illus.). 292p. 1975. reprint ed. 18.95 (0-913522-03-1); reprint ed. pap. 12.95 (0-913522-04-X) Urion Pr CA.

Riddle, Jesse L. The Guide to Free & Discount Travel. 110p. 1992. pap. 17.95 (0-9626583-2-4) Carriage Group.

— A Simple Guide to Courier Travel: How to Fly Free or at Discounted Prices to Cities Around the World. 50p. 1989. pap. text 9.95 (0-9626583-0-8) Carriage Group.

— A Simple Guide to Courier Travel: How to Fly Free or at Discounted Prices to Cities Around the World. 2nd ed. 72p. 1991. pap. 14.95 (0-9626583-1-6) Carriage Group.

Riddle, John. Fund Raising for Fun & Profit. large type ed. (For Fun & Profit Ser.). (Illus.). 350p. (Orig.). 1999. pap. 24.95 (1-56559-932-2) HGI-Over Fifty.

Riddle, John, et al. Sources in Electrical History 3: An International Guide to Corporate Records & Archives of Companies in the Electrical, Electronics, & Computer Industries. ix, 77p. (Orig.). 1995. pap. 15.00 (0-7803-9997-8) Inst Electrical.

Riddle, John . Contraception & Abortion from the Ancient World to the Renaissance. (Illus.). 256p. 1994. pap. 18.50 (0-674-16876-3) HUP.

Riddle, John I. The Six-Year Rural High School: A Comparative Study of Small & Large Units in Alabama. LC 70-177191. (Columbia University. Teachers College. Contributions to Education Ser.: No. 737). reprint ed. 37.50 (0-404-55737-6) AMS Pr.

Riddle, John M. Contraception & Abortion from the Ancient World to the Renaissance. (Illus.). 272p. (C). 1992. 48.95 (0-674-16875-5) HUP.

— Eve's Herbs: A History of Contraception & Abortion in the West. LC 96-40383. (Illus.). 384p. 1997. 42.00 (0-674-27024-X) HUP.

— Eve's Herbs: A History of Contraception & Abortion in the West. 1999. pap. text 18.95 (0-674-27026-6) HUP.

— Quid Pro Quo: Studies in the History of Drugs. (Collected Studies: No. CS367). 320p. 1992. 111.95 (0-86078-319-7, Pub. by Variorum) Ashgate Pub Co.

Riddle, Julie, ed. see Jones, Bruce.

***Riddle, Katharine P.** A Nourishing Life. LC 99-74223. (Illus.). 256p. 1999. pap. 16.95 (1-57197-183-1) Pentland Pr.

Riddle, Katharine P., jt. auth. see Taylor, Clara M.

Riddle, Kelley. The Art of Surveillance. 90p. 1997. pap. 19.95 (0-918487-00-5) Thomas Investigative.

Riddle, Kelly. Find Out Fast: The Instant Guide to Private Investigation. 1997. pap. 15.00 (1-891247-00-X) Thomas Investigative.

— The Internet Black Book. 180p. 1998. spiral bd. 19.95 (1-891247-13-1) Kelmar & Assocs.

— Nursing Home Abuse Investigations: New Trend in Private Investigative Practice Identified. 120p. 1997. 19.95 (1-891247-04-2) Kelmar & Assocs.

Riddle, Kelly E. The Art of Surveillance: Who's Who in America . . . & Where Are They? (Illus.). 109p. 1997. 19.95 (0-9653096-1-4) Kelmar & Assocs.

— Private Investigating Made Easy. 2nd ed. (Illus.). 127p. 1994. pap. 19.95 (1-881825-05-1) Hist Pubns TX.

— To Serve & Protect: The True Story. 122p. (Orig.). Date not set. 14.95 (0-9653096-0-6) Kelmar & Assocs.

Riddle, Kenneth W., ed. MicroStation 95 Productivity Book: Using MicroStation's Advanced Tools. (Illus.). 416p. (C). 1996. pap. 57.95 (1-56690-077-8) Thomson Learn.

Riddle, Lyn. Ashes to Ashes. 352p. 1997. mass mkt. 5.99 (0-7860-0410-X, Pinncle Kensgtn) Kensgtn Pub Corp.

Riddle, Margaret, jt. auth. see Fad, Kathleen.

Riddle, Marilyn R. Large Print Innovative Cookbook. large type ed. (Illus.). 64p. (Orig.). 1984. pap. 10.00 (0-9603748-3-3) Sandpiper OR.

— Poems from the Oregon Sea Coast. large type ed. (Illus.). 24p. 1979. pap. 10.00 (0-9603748-0-9) Sandpiper OR.

— Unicorns for Everyone. large type ed. (Illus.). 24p. (Orig.). 1980. pap. 10.00 (0-9603748-1-7) Sandpiper OR.

— Walk with Me: Prayers & Meditations. large type ed. (Illus.). 40p. (Orig.). 1982. pap. 10.00 (0-9603748-2-5) Sandpiper OR.

Riddle, Marilyn R., ed. Otherwhere . . . One Step Beyond: Anthology. large type ed. (Illus.). 48p. (Orig.). 1988. pap. 10.00 (0-9603748-5-X) Sandpiper OR.

— Physically Challenged Can-Do: Anthology. large type ed. 84p. (Orig.). 1989. pap., per. 10.00 (0-9603748-6-8) Sandpiper OR.

***Riddle, Mary E. & Kozak, Catherine.** Outer Banks Pocket Companion. (Insiders' Guide Travel Ser.). (Illus.). 160p. 1998. pap. 6.95 (1-57380-099-6, The Insiders' Guide) Falcon Pub Inc.

Riddle, Maxwell. The New Complete Brittany. 2nd ed. LC 87-3891. (Illus.). 304p. 1987. 25.95 (0-87605-090-9) Howell Bks.

— The New Complete Shetland Sheepdog. 2nd ed. (Illus.). 256p. 1992. 25.95 (0-87605-333-9) Howell Bks.

Riddle, Maxwell & Harris, Beth J. The New Complete Alaskan Malamute. 2nd ed. (Illus.). 256p. 1990. 25.95 (0-87605-008-9) Howell Bks.

Riddle, Michael R., jt. auth. see Clark, Michael B.

Riddle, Pauline, jt. auth. see Andrews, Mildred.

Riddle, Paxton. Lost River. 1999. mass mkt. 6.50 (0-425-16940-5) Berkley Pub.

Riddle, Peter H. America's Standard Gauge Electric Trains. LC 98-71062. (Illus.). 192p. 1998. pap. 26.95 (0-930625-22-6, Antique Trader) Krause Pubns.

— Easy Lionel Layouts You Can Build. LC 97-218845. (Illus.). 80p. 1997. pap. 15.95 (0-89778-408-1, 10-8030, Kalmbach Books) Kalmbach.

— Greenberg's Guide to Lionel Trains, 1901-1942 Vol. 3: Accessories. (Illus.). 160p. 1993. pap. 39.95 (0-89778-432-4, 10-8085, Greenberg Books) Kalmbach.

— Greenberg's Wiring Your Lionel Layout: A Primer for Lionel Train Enthusiasts. (Illus.). 80p. 1992. pap. 12.95 (0-89778-206-2, 10-7555, Greenberg Books) Kalmbach.

— Greenberg's Wiring Your Lionel Layout Vol. 2: Intermediate Techniques. (Illus.). 80p. 1993. pap. 14.95 (0-89778-372-7, 10-7560, Greenberg Books) Kalmbach.

— Greenberg's Wiring Your Lionel Layout Vol. 3: Advanced Technologies Made Easy. (Illus.). 96p. 1996. pap. 14.95 (0-89778-506-1, 10-7565, Greenberg Books) Kalmbach.

Riddle, Peter H. Tips & Tricks for Toy Train Operators. (Illus.). 1994. pap. 16.95 (0-89778-511-8) Kalmbach.

Riddle, Peter H. Trains from Grandfather's Attic. (Illus.). 144p. 1991. pap. text 22.95 (0-89778-215-1, 10-7585, Greenberg Books) Kalmbach.

Riddle, Rita S. Aluminum Balloons & Other Poems. (Appalachian Connection Ser.). 44p. 1996. pap. 5.50 (0-936015-65-9) Pocahontas Pr.

Riddle, Ronald. Flying Dragons, Flowing Streams: Music in the Life of San Francisco's Chinese, 7. LC 82-12005. (Contributions in Intercultural & Comparative Studies: No. 7). 349p. 1983. 65.00 (0-313-23682-8, RIF/, Greenwood Pr) Greenwood.

An Asterisk (*) at the beginning of an entry indicates that the title is appearing for the first time.

***Riddle, Tanya.** This Proud, Proud Land. 253p. 2000. pap. 15.95 (*0-7414-0356-0*) Buy Books.

Riddle, Thomas W. The Old Radicalism: John R. Rogers & the Populist Movement in Washington. LC 91-15137. (Modern American History Ser.). 336p. 1991. text 25.00 (*0-8240-1896-6*) Garland.

***Riddle, Tohby.** The Great Escape from City Zoo. LC 99-10645. (Illus.). 32p. (J). (ps-3). 1999. 16.00 (*0-374-32776-9*) FS&G.

Riddle, Tohby. A Most Unusual Dog. LC 93-38724. (Illus.). 32p. (J). (gr. 1 up). 1994. lib. bdg. 21.27 (*0-8368-1088-0*) Gareth Stevens Inc.

***Riddle, Waide.** All-American Texan. LC 99-93230. 148p. 1999. pap. 15.00 (*1-57579-159-5*) Pine Hill Pr.

***Riddle, William I.** The Magnolia Convalescent Center. LC 00-190927. 2000. 25.00 (*0-7388-2112-8*); pap. 18.00 (*0-7388-2113-6*) Xlibris Corp.

Riddleberger, Patrick W. Eighteen Sixty-Six: The Critical Year Revisited. (Illus.). 308p. 1984. reprint ed. pap. text 25.50 (*0-8191-4239-5*) U Pr of Amer.

— George Washington Julian: Radical Republican. 344p. 1966. 10.00 (*1-885323-22-0*) IN Hist Bureau.

Riddles, Libby. Storm Run. LC 96-71195. (Illus.). 48p. (J). (gr. 5-7). 1996. 13.95 (*0-934007-31-4*) Paws Four Pub.

Riddles, Libby & Jones, Tim. Race Across Alaska: First Woman to Win the Iditarod Tells Her Story. LC 87-25273. (Illus.). 240p. (Orig.). 1988. pap. 14.95 (*0-8117-2253-8*) Stackpole.

Riddlesperger, James W. & Jackson, Donald W., eds. Presidential Leadership & Civil Rights Policy, 356. LC 95-5268. (Contributions in Political Science Ser.: Vol. 356). 208p. 1995. 57.95 (*0-313-29624-3*, Greenwood Pr) Greenwood.

Riddlesperger, James W., jt. ed. see Jackson, Donald.

Riddlesperger, Kris, jt. auth. see Huber, Jeffrey T.

Riddoch, Mark. What's the Verdict? LC 93-24237. 1993. pap. 3.95 (*1-56420-000-0*) New Readers.

***Riddy, Felicity.** Prestige, Authority & Power in Late Medieval Manuscripts & Texts. LC 99-58712. (York Manuscripts Conference Ser.: No. 0955-9663). (Illus.). 192p. 2000. 75.00 (*0-9529734-6-4*) Boydell & Brewer.

Riddy, Felicity, ed. Regionalism in Late-Medieval Manuscripts & Texts: Essays Celebrating the Publication of a Linguistic Atlas of Late Medieval England. (York Manuscripts Conferences: II). 222p. (C). 1991. 75.00 (*0-85991-311-2*) Boydell & Brewer.

Riddy, Felicity, jt. ed. see Carley, James P.

Ride, Lindsay. Robert Morrison: The Scholar & the Man, & Illustrated Catalogue of the Exhibition Held at the University of Hong Kong, September 4-18, 1957, to Commemorate the 150th Anniversary of Robert Morrison's Arrival in China. LC 58-2866. 83p. 1957. reprint ed. pap. 30.00 (*0-608-01383-8*, 206214400002) Bks Demand.

***Ride, Lindsay & Ride, May.** The Voices of Macao Stones. Wordie, Jason, ed. (Illus.). 192p. 1999. 39.50 (*962-209-487-2*, Pub. by HK Univ Pr) Coronet Bks.

Ride, May, jt. auth. see Ride, Lindsay.

Ride, Sally. The Mystery of Mars. LC 98-52929. (Illus.). 48p. (gr. 3-5). 1998. lib. bdg. 20.99 (*0-517-70972-4*, Pub. by Crown Bks Yng Read) Random.

***Ride, Sally.** The Mystery of Mars. LC 98-52929. (Illus.). 48p. (gr. 3-5). 1998. 19.00 (*0-517-70971-6*, Pub. by Crown Bks Yng Read) Random.

Ride, Sally & Okie, Susan. To Space & Back. LC 85-23757. (Illus.). 96p. (J). (gr. 1 up). 1989. mass mkt. 12.95 (*0-688-09112-1*, Wm Morrow) Morrow Avon.

Ride, Sally & Okie, Susan. To Space & Back. LC 85-23757. (Illus.). 96p. (J). (gr. 2-6). 1986. reprint ed. 19.00 (*0-688-06159-1*) Lothrop.

Ride, W. D. & Younes, Talal, eds. Biological Nomenclature Today. (International Union of Biological Sciences Monograph Ser.: No. 2). 76p. 1987. pap. text 26.00 (*1-85221-016-8*) OUP.

Ride, W. D., jt. ed. see Groves, R. H.

Rideal, C. F. Charles Dickens' Heroines. LC 74-7273. (Studies in Dickens: No. 52). 1974. lib. bdg. 75.00 (*0-8383-1987-4*) M S G Haskell Hse.

Rideal, Liz. Double Take. (Illus.). 48p. 1991. pap. 14.95 (*0-9515642-5-0*) Antique Collect.

Rideau, S. Noel. Uncle Noel's Fun Fables Program. (Illus.). 80p. 1991. student ed. 8.95 (*0-9630734-0-0*) Aesop Systs.

Rideau, Wilbert. Life Sentences. 1992. pap. 16.00 (*0-8129-2048-1*, Times Bks) Crown Pub Group.

Riden, K., jt. auth. see Wilson, P.

Ridenhour, David E. I Was There: Good Friday Tenebrae Service. Sherer, Michael L., ed. (Orig.). 1988. pap. 1.95 (*1-55673-021-7*, 8808) CSS OH.

Ridenour, jt. auth. see Cox.

Ridenour, Alan. Offbeat Food: Adventures in an Omnivorous World. LC 99-59930. (Illus.). 240p. 2000. pap. 19.95 (*1-891661-09-4*, 1094) Snta Monica.

Ridenour, Austin. The Progressive Revelation of Jesus As Savior, Lord & King. LC 98-92241. 390p. 1998. pap. 14.95 (*0-7392-0027-5*, PO2787) Morris Pubng.

— Will My Doggie Go to Heaven. 50p. (Orig.). (J). 1996. pap. 3.25 (*1-57502-293-1*, P1004) Morris Pubng.

Ridenour, David A. & Almasi, David. Nicaragua's Continuing Revolution, 1977-1990: A Chronology. LC 90-61757. pap. 20.00 (*0-930095-12-X*) Signal Bks.

Ridenour, Fritz. Como Ser Cristiano Sin Ser Religioso.Tr. of How to Be Christian Without Being Religious. (SPA.). 144p. 1972. pap. write for info. (*0-614-27009-X*) Editorial Unilit.

— Como Ser Cristiano Sin Ser Religioso (How to Be a Christian Without Being Religious) rev. ed. (SPA.). 1986. 4.50 (*0-685-74919-3*, 490231) Editorial Unilit.

— How Do You Handle Life? LC 77-140941. 192p. 1976. pap. 3.95 (*0-8307-0430-2*, S104156, Regal Bks) Gospel Lght.

— How to Decide What's Really Important. LC 78-68146. 160p. 1978. 3.50 (*0-8307-0266-0*, S122154, Regal Bks) Gospel Lght.

***Ridenour, Fritz.** So What's the Difference. 2001. pap. 10.99 (*0-8307-1898-2*, Regal Bks) Gospel Lght.

Ridenour, Fritz, compiled by. The Marriage Collection: Keys to Make Your Marriage Better. 528p. 1989. pap. 14.99 (*0-310-20961-7*) Zondervan.

Ridenour, Fritz, jt. auth. see Smith, Michael W.

Ridenour, Hugh A. The Greens of Falls of Rough: A Kentucky Family Biography 1795-1965. LC 97-72131. (Illus.). 192p. 1997. 18.95 (*0-913383-54-6*) McClanahan Pub.

Ridenour, Nina. Mental Health in the United States: A Fifty-Year History. LC 61-11630. 160p. reprint ed. pap. 49.60 (*0-7837-4707-1*, 205905700002) Bks Demand.

Ridenour, Ron. Backfire: The CIA's Biggest Burn. 179p. 1991. pap. 9.95 (*0-9624975-1-7*) Infoservicios.

— Cuba at the Crossroads. 193p. 1994. pap. 9.95 (*0-9624975-7-6*) Infoservicios.

Rideout. Basic Newbury House Dictionary. (Miscellaneous/Catalogs Ser.). 1998. text 20.95 (*0-8384-8017-9*) Heinle & Heinle.

Rideout, Bonnie. Celtic Circles. 48p. 1996. pap. 7.95 (*0-7866-0666-5*, 95572); pap. 17.95 incl. audio (*0-7866-0668-1*, 95572P); pap. 22.95 incl. audio compact disk (*0-7866-0670-3*, 95572CDP) Mel Bay.

— A Scottish Christmas for Fiddle: Beginning-Intermediate Level. 64p. 1997. pap. 19.95 incl. audio (*0-7866-3003-5*, 96784P); pap. 24.95 incl. audio compact disk (*0-7866-3000-0*, 96784CDP) Mel Bay.

— A Scottish Christmas for Guitar: Beginning-Intermediate Level. 64p. 1997. pap. 9.95 (*0-7866-2997-5*, 96784) Mel Bay.

— Soft May Morn. 96p. (Orig.). 1997. pap. 12.95 (*0-7866-0661-4*, 95571); pap. 22.95 incl. audio (*0-7866-0663-0*, 95571P); pap. 27.95 incl. audio compact disk (*0-7866-0665-7*, 95571CDP) Mel Bay.

Rideout, Douglas B. & Hesseln, Hayley. Principles of Forest & Environmental Economics. rev. ed. LC 97-69028. (Illus.). 285p. 1997. pap. text 42.50 (*0-9659183-0-0*) Res & Environ Mgmt.

Rideout, Effie A. Cushing. Sketches from the History of the Cushing Family, Which Relate to Laban & Nancy Whitney Cushing, to Their Ancestors & Descendants. 63p. 1997. reprint ed. pap. 12.50 (*0-8328-8186-4*); reprint ed. lib. bdg. 22.50 (*0-8328-8185-6*) Higginson Bk Co.

Rideout, G. Bradley: Andestors & Descendants of Morris A. Bradley. (Illus.). 176p. 1991. reprint ed. pap. 28.00 (*0-8328-2102-0*); reprint ed. lib. bdg. 38.00 (*0-8328-2101-2*) Higginson Bk Co.

Rideout, Karen. Country Classics. (Illus.). 48p. 1997. pap. 10.50 (*1-56770-413-1*) S Scheewe Pubns.

Rideout, Nigel. First Steps Towards an Acting Career. 160p. 1996. pap. write for info. (*0-7136-4130-4*, Pub. by A & C Blk) Midpt Trade.

Rideout, Philip M. The Newbury House Basic English Dictionary. LC 98-152110. 550p. (J). 1998. mass mkt. 19.95 (*0-8384-6015-1*) Heinle & Heinle.

— Newbury House Dictionary: ELS Edition. (Miscellaneous/Catalogs Ser.). (J). 1996. pap. 13.95 (*0-8384-7069-6*) Wadsworth Pub.

— Newbury House Dictionary of American English. (College ESL Ser.). (J). 1995. pap. 17.95 (*0-8384-5532-8*) Heinle & Heinle.

— Newbury House Dictionary of American English. 2nd ed. LC 98-167539. 1024p. (J). 1998. pap. 19.95 (*0-8384-7812-3*) Heinle & Heinle.

— Newbury House Dictionary of American English: An Essential Reference for Learners of American English & Culture. (College ESL Ser.). Date not set. pap. 18.95 (*0-614-10351-7*) Heinle & Heinle.

— Newbury House Dictionary of American English: An Essential Reference for Learners of American English & Culture. (College ESL Ser.). 1031p. (J). 1996. mass mkt. 28.95 (*0-8384-5613-8*) Heinle & Heinle.

Rideout, R. W. The Right to Membership of a Trade Union, No. 5--5. LC 75-17201. (Univ. of London Legal Ser.: No. 5). 243p. 1975. reprint ed. lib. bdg. 65.00 (*0-8371-8295-6*, RIMTU, Greenwood Pr) Greenwood.

Rideout, R. W. & Hepple, Bob A. Current Legal Problems 1992 Vol. 45, Pt. 2: Collected Papers. 296p. 1993. text 49.95 (*0-19-825722-8*) OUP.

Rideout, Ralph, ed. see Timmons, Jonathan P.

Rideout, Sandy, jt. auth. see Collins, Yvonne.

Rideout, Steve. Don't Go Up a Windmill. LC 99-209024. (Illus.). 96p. (YA). (gr. 4-8). 1999. pap. 9.95 (*0-9670157-0-7*) Blue Windmill.

— Don't Go Up a Windmill. (Illus.). 96p. (gr. 4-10). 1999. lib. bdg. write for info. (*3-09-670157-1*) Blue Windmill.

Rideout, T. R. Practical Aspects of Tip Relief. (Technical Paper Ser.: Vol. P78). (Illus.). 22p. 1931. pap. 30.00 (*1-55589-177-2*) AGMA.

Rideout, Walter B. The Radical Novel in the U. S., 1900-1954: Some Interrelations of Literature & Society. 360p. 1992. pap. 18.50 (*0-231-08077-8*, Mrngside) Col U Pr.

Rideout, Walter B., ed. Sherwood Anderson: A Collection of Critical Essays. (Twentieth Century Views Ser.). 192p. 1974. 12.95 (*0-13-036558-0*, Spectrum IN); pap. 2.45 (*0-13-036533-5*, Spectrum IN) Macmillan Gen Ref.

Rideout, Walter B., jt. auth. see Robinson, James K.

Rider. Developments in European Company Law. 272p. 1997. 110.50 (*90-411-0671-5*) Kluwer Law Intl.

***Rider.** Our Voices: Psychology of Women. LC 99-28656. (Psychology Ser.). 544p. 1999. pap. 46.95 (*0-534-34681-2*) Wadsworth Pub.

Rider. Realm of Company Law. LC 98-177775. xxii, 273p. 1997. lib. bdg. 119.00 (*90-411-0733-9*) Kluwer Law Intl.

Rider, et al. Disaster Exercise Planning & Evaluation. 186p. 1991. ring bd. 25.00 (*0-913724-43-2*) Emerg Response Inst.

***Rider, Alan J.** The International Dictionary of Personal Finance. 96p. 1999. pap. 11.95 (*1-873668-54-6*, Pub. by Take That Bks) Trafalgar.

Rider, Amy. AbraVocabra: Sensible Approach to Teach Vocabulary. 176p. 1997. pap. text 21.95 (*1-877673-32-3*, ABRA) Cottonwood Pr.

***Rider, Amy.** Promise You Won't Get Mad: And Other Read-Aloud Plays for Young Adults. 80p. (YA). (gr. 7-10). 2000. pap. 15.95 (*1-877673-39-0*) Cottonwood Pr.

Rider, Anne. A Safe Place. LC 73-22656. 192p. 1974. 6.95 (*0-672-51992-5*, Bobbs) Macmillan.

Rider, B. A. & Ashe, Michael. Rider & Ashe: Financial Services Law. 1997. pap. write for info. (*0-406-04996-3*, RAFS, MICHIE) LEXIS Pub.

Rider, Barry A., ed. Corruption: The Enemy Within. LC 97-223673. 388p. 1997. 87.00 (*90-411-0712-6*) Kluwer Academic.

Rider, Barry A., et al, eds. Commercial Law in a Global Context: Some Perspectives in Anglo-Japanese Law. LC 98-28131. 384p. 1997. 146.00 (*90-411-0709-6*) Kluwer Academic.

Rider, Barry A., jt. auth. see Frommel, Stefan N.

***Rider, Barry A. K. & Andenas, Mads, eds.** The Quest for an Ideal Legal Form for Small Businesses, 1997. (Developments in European Company Law Ser.: Vol. 2). 192p. 1999. 87.00 (*90-411-9697-8*) Kluwer Law Intl.

Rider, Bevan. A More Expeditious Conveyance. 160p. 1990. 50.00 (*0-85131-394-9*, Pub. by J A Allen) St Mut.

Rider, Charles H. EDGAR Filer Hanbook: A Guide for Electronic Filing with SEC. 5th ed. LC 94-29188. 484p. 1998. ring bd. 150.00 (*0-13-340746-2*) Aspen Law.

— TSO - E CLISTs: The Complete Tutorial & Desk Reference. 1993. 54.99 (*0-471-58809-1*, GD4078) Wiley.

Rider, Christine. An Introduction to Economic History. LC 92-18279. (C). 1994. text. write for info. (*0-8013-0858-5*) Longman.

Rider, Christine & Thompson, Micheal, eds. The Industrial Revolution in Comparative Perspective. LC 99-15418. (Open Forum Ser.). 268p. (C). 2000. pap. text 24.50 (*0-89464-990-6*) Krieger.

Rider, Christine, jt. ed. see Knell, Mark.

Rider, D. Adventures with Bernard Shaw. LC 74-1152. (Studies in Shaw Ser.: No. 92). 1974. lib. bdg. 49.00 (*0-8383-2023-6*) M S G Haskell Hse.

Rider, David. Aircraft Maintenance & Services. (Transportation - Related Special Reports). 695.00 (*0-7106-1600-7*) Janes Info Group.

— Jane's Air Traffic Control, 1997-98: Evaluate Worldwide ATC Equipment Manufacturers & Their Systems. 4th ed. 1997. 320.00 (*0-7106-1532-9*) Janes Info Group.

— Jane's Airports, Equipment & Services, 1997-98: Stay Informed of the Latest Equipment Used in Airports Around the World. 1997. 320.00 (*0-7106-1534-5*) Janes Info Group.

Rider, David F. Jewelry Making: A Manual of Techniques. (Illus.). 160p. 1994. pap. 35.00 (*1-85223-813-5*, Pub. by Crolwood) Trafalgar.

Rider, David F., ed. Jane's Airports Equipment & Services, 1998-99. 1998. 350.00 (*0-7106-1787-9*) Janes Info Group.

Rider, Debra, jt. auth. see Blacke, Terry L.

Rider, Donald G. Effective Writing for Feds. (Illus.). 96p. 1992. pap. 9.95 (*0-936295-25-2*) FPMI Comns.

Rider, Frederick. The Dialectic of Selfhood in Montaigne. 128p. 1973. 19.50 (*0-8047-0830-4*) Stanford U Pr.

— The Dialectic of Selfhood in Montaigne. fac. ed. LC 72-91679. 127p. 1973. reprint ed. pap. 30.00 (*0-7837-7917-8*, 204767300008) Bks Demand.

Rider, Fremont. Rider's California: A Guidebook for Travelers. 1992. reprint ed. lib. bdg. 75.00 (*0-7812-5079-X*) Rprt Serv.

Rider, G. Ghosts of Door County Wisconsin. (Illus.). 186p. 1992. pap. 9.95 (*1-878488-41-4*) Quixote Pr IA.

Rider, Gail, jt. auth. see Faimann, Don.

Rider, Hope S. Valour Fore & Aft. LC 76-17516. (Illus.). 280p. 1987. 24.00 (*0-934943-12-5*) Thirteen Colonies Pr.

Rider, Janine. The Writer's Book of Memory: An Interdisciplinary Study for Writing Teachers. 152p. 1995. pap. 17.50 (*0-8058-1981-9*); text 34.50 (*0-8058-1980-0*) L Erlbaum Assocs.

— The Writer's Book of Memory: An Interdisciplinary Study for Writing Teachers. 146p. 1999. reprint ed. pap. text 15.00 (*0-7881-6026-5*) DIANE Pub.

Rider, Jeff, tr. Michel Zink - Medieval French Literature: An Introduction. (Medieval & Renaissance Texts & Studies: Vol. 110). 184p. (C). 1995. 25.00 (*0-86698-163-2*, MR110) MRTS.

Rider, Jeff, tr. see Zink, Michel.

Rider, Jesse. Torch Songs. LC 96-203614. (Illus.). 48p. (Orig.). 1995. pap. 3.00 (*1-888431-05-9*) ASGP.

Rider, Joanne. First Grade Valentines. LC 92-35388. (First Grade Is the Best! Ser.). (Illus.). 32p. (J). (gr. k-2). 1996. pap. 3.95 (*0-8167-3005-9*) Troll Communs.

Rider, Kate, ed. see Hildebrand, Ron, et al.

Rider, Nick. Yucatan & Southern Mexico. (Cadogan Guides). (Illus.). 320p. 1998. pap. text 19.95 (*1-86011-093-2*, Pub. by Cadgn Bks) Globe Pequot.

Rider, Pamela, ed. see Senseman, Laurence A.

Rider, Paul R. & Fischer, Carl H. Mathematics of Investment. (C). 1951. text 9.95 (*0-914004-02-6*) Ulrich.

Rider, Peter E., ed. Studies in History & Museums. LC 96-185729. (Mercury Ser.: History No. 47). (Illus.). 178p. 1994. pap. 24.95 (*0-660-14022-5*, Pub. by CN Mus Civilization) U of Wash Pr.

Rider, Raymond A. The Fearings & the Fearing Tavern with the Bumpus Family. (Illus.). 1977. 10.00 (*0-88492-021-6*) W S Sullwold.

Rider, Robert L. Alto Before the Dawn. LC 91-74091. (Illus.). 409p. 1992. 29.95 (*0-9634116-0-8*) Dawn Pub Co.

Rider, Robin E., compiled by. A Bibliography of Early Modern Algebra, 1500-1800. LC 81-51030. (Berkeley Papers in History of Science: No. 7). 171p. (Orig.). 1982. pap. 8.00 (*0-918102-08-1*) U Cal Hist Sci Tech.

Rider, Robin E. & Lowood, Henry E., compiled by. Guide to Sources in Northern California for History of Science & Technology. (Berkeley Papers in History of Science: No. 10). (Illus.). 194p. 1984. pap. text 12.00 (*0-918102-12-X*) U Cal Hist Sci Tech.

Rider, Rowland & Paulsen, Deirdre. The Roll Away Saloon: Cowboy Tales of the Arizona Strip. (Western Experience Ser.). 132p. 1985. pap. 12.95 (*0-87421-124-7*) Utah St U Pr.

Rider, Stephen. Queen - These Are the Days of Our Lives: The Essential Queen Biography. (Illus.). 240p. 1993. pap. 10.00 (*0-685-72583-9*, Pub. by Castle Communs) Viking Penguin.

***Rider, Stuart.** The Complete Idiot's Guide to Real Estate Investing. 2000. pap. 18.95 (*0-02-863976-6*, Alpha Ref) Macmillan Gen Ref.

Rider, Susan S. Journey to Genesee: From Zero to Sixty in Fifty-Five Years. (Illus.). 1998. 24.95 (*0-9669455-0-6*) Burr Oak.

Rider, Tracy, ed. see Bennett, Geraldine M.

Rider, William. An Historical & Critical Account of the Lives & Writings of the Living Authors of Great-Britain. LC 92-24818. (Augustan Reprints Ser.: No. 163). 1974. reprint ed. 14.50 (*0-404-70163-9*, PR443) AMS Pr.

Rider-Zerhire, Janet L. The Zoo-Hire Family Cookbook for Todd & Jamey, Made with Love, by Mom & the Cats. 344p. Date not set. pap. 22.95 (*0-9649010-0-5*) Zoo-Hire.

***Riders in the Sky Staff.** Riders in the Sky - Saddle Pals. 80p. 1998. pap. 16.95 (*0-7866-3845-1*, 97265) Mel Bay.

Riders, Leigh, jt. auth. see Authors, Mandy.

Ridge, Antonia. The Man Who Painted Roses: The Story of Pierre-Joseph Redoute. large type ed. 1976. 27.99 (*0-85456-496-9*) Ulverscroft.

— The Thirteenth Child. large type ed. 1978. 27.99 (*0-7089-0181-6*) Ulverscroft.

Ridge, Ardena, ed. & prod. see Ridge, Ben.

Ridge, Ben. Reproduce Almost Anything: Basic Silicone Mold Making, Vol. I. Ridge, Ardena, ed. & prod. by. (Illus.). 44p. (YA). (gr. 3-12). 1992. pap., wbk. ed. 39.95 (*0-9634267-0-2*) Cherokee Access.

Ridge, Bill, Jr. The Geometric Approach to Golf: A New Concept of Golf. (Illus.). 136p. 1991. 7.95 (*0-9622532-0-0*) Lauschen Co.

Ridge, C. H., ed. Index to Wills Proved in the Prerogative Court of Canterbury, Vol. 10: 1676-1685. (British Record Society Index Library: Vols. 71-72). 1969. reprint ed. 100.00 (*0-8115-1512-5*) Periodicals Srv.

Ridge, George R. Joris-Karl Huysmaus. 123p. 1968. 49.50 (*0-685-63211-3*) Elliots Bks.

Ridge, Holly & Ray, Beverly. Fluency at Your Fingertips: Pragmatic & Thematic Therapy Materials. (Illus.). 252p. 1991. pap. text 45.00 (*0-7616-7660-0*) Commun Skill.

Ridge, Irene. Plant Physiology: Biology: Form & Function. (Illus.). 372p. 1991. pap. 52.50 (*0-340-53186-X*, Pub. by Hodder & Stought Ltd) Lubrecht & Cramer.

Ridge, John D. Annotated Bibliographies of Mineral Deposits in the Western Hemisphere: Includes 1974 Supplementary References. LC 72-178773. (Geological Society of America, Memoir Ser.: No. 131). 705p. reprint ed. pap. 200.00 (*0-8357-5491-X*, 202545900044) Bks Demand.

— Selected Bibliographies of Hydrothermal & Magmatic Mineral Deposits. LC 59-1279. (Geological Society of America, Memoir Ser.: No. 75). 209p. reprint ed. pap. 64.80 (*0-608-11164-3*, 200439700062) Bks Demand.

Ridge, John D., ed. Ore Deposits of the United States, 1933-1967: The Graton-Sales Volume, Vol. 1. LC 68-24170. (Rocky Mountain Fund Ser.). (Illus.). 1023p. 1970. reprint ed. pap. 200.00 (*0-7837-9171-2*, 204987100001) Bks Demand.

— Ore Deposits of the United States, 1933-1967: The Graton-Sales Volume, Vol. 2. LC 68-24170. (Rocky Mountain Fund Ser.). (Illus.). 895p. 1970. reprint ed. pap. 200.00 (*0-7837-9172-0*, 204987100002) Bks Demand.

— Proceedings of the 5th Quadrennial Symposium, Snowbird, Utah, 1978. (International Association on the Genesis of Ore Deposits (IAGOD) Symposia Ser.). (Illus.). xii, 795p. 1980. text 58.00 (*3-510-65094-8*, Pub. by E Schweizerbartsche) Balogh.

Ridge, John R. Life & Adventures of Joaquin Murieta, the Celebrated California Bandit. (Western Frontier Library: No. 4). (Illus.). 1977. reprint ed. pap. 10.95 (*0-8061-1429-0*) U of Okla Pr.

Ridge, M. D. & Purtill, Mark. Good Guitar Stuff: A Practical Handbook for Pastoral Guitarists & Music Directors. (Illus.). 56p. 1997. pap. 6.95 (*1-57992-002-0*) OR Catholic.

Ridge, Martin. Ignatius Donnelly: Portrait of a Politician. LC 90-28170. (Illus.). xviii, 428p. 1991. reprint ed. pap. 17.50 (*0-87351-262-6*, Borealis Book) Minn Hist.

— The New Bilingualism: An American Dilemma. 272p. 1982. 39.95 (*0-88474-104-4*) Transaction Pubs.

Ridge, Martin, ed. Frederick Jackson Turner: Wisconsin's Historian of the Frontier. LC 86-5996. (Illus.). 80p. 1986. reprint ed. pap. 9.95 (*0-87020-246-4*, FRJA) State Hist Soc Wis.

Ridge, Martin, et al. Writing the History of the American West. (Illus.). 110p. 1991. pap. 12.95 (*0-944026-31-1*, 42179) Oak Knoll.

Ridge, Martin, jt. auth. see Billington, Ray A.

Ridge, Martin, jt. ed. see Billington, R. A.

Ridge, Martin, jt. ed. see Nugent, Walter.

Ridge, Peter M. The Book of SCSI: A Guide for Adventurers. LC 94-44670. 400p. 1995. pap. 34.95 (*1-886411-02-6*) No Starch Pr.

Ridge, Peter M., jt. auth. see Field, Gary.

Ridge, Terry, jt. auth. see Fawcett, Neil.

Ridge, Virginia. O-Ridge-Inals. 66p. 1998. pap. write for info. (*1-57502-934-0*, PO2573) Morris Pubng.

Ridge, Warren J. Value Analysis for Better Management. LC 75-96142. 207p. reprint ed. pap. 64.20 (*0-608-10879-0*, 205043900081) Bks Demand.

Ridge, Warren J. & Johnson, Leane E. How to Control Costs & Improve Profits Through The Effective Management of Computer Software. LC 73-82312. ix, 217p. 1973. write for info. (*0-87094-061-9*, Irwn Prfssnl) McGraw-Hill Prof.

***Ridgefield Archives Committee.** Ridgefield. (Images of America Ser.). 1999. pap. 18.99 (*0-7385-0187-5*) Arcadia Publng.

***Ridgefield Community Foundation, Inc., Staff, ed.** Ridgefield Kids Are Funny. (Illus.). 132p. 2000. pap. 15.00 (*0-9679742-0-8*) Ridgefield Comm Fdn.

Ridgefield Garden Club Coloring Book Committee Sta. Ridgefield to Color & Keep. Willis, Lillian, ed. (Illus.). 44p. (Orig.). 1988. pap. 3.75 (*0-317-91201-1*) Ridgefield Garden Club.

Ridgell, Reilly. Bending to the Trade Winds: Stories of the Peace Corps Experience in Micronesia. (Illus.). vi, 102p. (Orig.). (C). 1991. pap. 9.95 (*1-881629-00-7*) Univ Guam Pr.

— Pacific Nations & Territories. 1995. pap., teacher ed. 9.95 (*1-57306-003-8*) Bess Pr.

— Pacific Nations & Territories. LC 88-70787. (Illus.). 112p. 1995. pap., student ed. 8.95 (*1-57306-002-X*) Bess Pr.

— Pacific Nations & Territories. 3rd ed. (Illus.). 184p. 1995. pap. 34.95 (*1-57306-006-2*) Bess Pr.

— Pacific Nations & Territories. 3rd rev. ed. LC 88-70787. (Illus.). 176p. 1995. 44.95 (*1-57306-001-1*) Bess Pr.

Ridgell, Reilly, jt. auth. see Dunford, Betty.

Ridgely, Beverly S. & Eglaus, Gustavs E. Supplement to Birds of the World in Philately. (Illus.). 62p. 1986. pap. text 6.00 (*0-935991-00-X*) Am Topical Assn.

Ridgely, Beverly S. & Eqlajs, Gustavs E. Birds of the World in Philately, Vol. 1. (Illus.). 252p. (Orig.). 1984. pap. text 14.00 (*0-614-25040-4*) Am Topical Assn.

Ridgely, Frances S. The Condell Collection of Oriental Art. (Handbook of Collections: No. 1). (Illus.). 64p. 1963. pap. 1.25 (*0-89792-025-2*) Ill St Museum.

Ridgely, Frances S., jt. auth. see Holtz, Frederick C.

Ridgely, Joseph V., jt. ed. see Pollin, Burton R.

Ridgely, Joseph V., ed. see Simms, William Gilmore.

Ridgely-Nevitt, Cedric. American Steamships on the Atlantic. LC 78-66835. 360p. 1981. 85.00 (*0-87413-140-5*) U Delaware Pr.

Ridgely, Robert S. & Gwynne, John A., Jr. A Guide to the Birds of Panama, with Costa Rica, Nicaragua, & Honduras. enl. ed. (Illus.). 608p. (C). 1992. pap. text 37.50 (*0-691-02512-6*, Pub. by Princeton U Pr) Cal Prin Full Svc.

Ridgely, Robert S. & Tudor, Guy. Birds of South America Vol. 1: The Oscine Passerines. (Illus.). 562p. 1989. 70.00 (*0-292-70756-8*) U of Tex Pr.

— The Birds of South America Vol. 2: The Suboscine Passerines. (Illus.). 900p. (C). Date not set. write for info. (*0-19-857218-2*) OUP.

Ridgely, Roberta, ed. see Szekely, Deborah.

Ridgeon, Bob. The Economics of Pig Production. 275p. 1993. text 34.95 (*0-85236-269-2*, Pub. by Farming Pr) Diamond Farm Bk.

Ridgeon, Lloyd. Aziz Nasafi. LC 98-189785. 234p. 1998. 65.00 (*0-7007-1013-2*, Pub. by Curzon Pr Ltd); pap. 29.95 (*0-7007-1014-0*, Pub. by Curzon Pr Ltd) Paul & Co Pubs.

Ridgeon, Lloyd, tr. Persian Metaphysics & Mysticism: Selected Works of 'Aziz Nasafi. 228p. 1997. 75.00 (*0-7007-0666-6*, Pub. by Curzon Pr Ltd) Paul & Co Pubs.

***Ridgeon, Lloyd V. J.** Islamic Interpretations of Christianity. LC 00-34496. 2000. write for info. (*0-312-23854-1*) St Martin.

***Ridgeway & Wallace.** Empowering Change: The Role of People Management. 224p. 2000. pap. 59.95 (*0-8464-5045-3*) Beekman Pubs.

Ridgeway, jt. auth. see Wallace.

***Ridgeway, Andrei.** Psychic Living: Tap Into Your Psychic Potential, 1. 192p. 1999. pap. 12.00 (*1-57566-415-1*) Kensgtn Pub Corp.

Ridgeway, Brunhilde S., jt. auth. see Eiseman, Cynthia J.

Ridgeway, Burton S. The FECMA Conspiracy. LC 98-89516. 375p. 1998. text 25.00 (*0-7388-0217-4*); pap. text 15.00 (*0-7388-0218-2*) Xlibris Corp.

Ridgeway, C. L., ed. Gender, Interaction & Inequality. (Illus.). ix, 247p. 1991. 79.95 (*0-387-97578-0*) Spr-Verlag.

Ridgeway, Cecilia L. Dynamics of Small Groups. LC 82-60480. 352p. 1983. pap. text 65.00 (*0-312-22369-2*) St Martin.

***Ridgeway, Christopher.** Sir John Vanbrugh & Landscape Architecture in Baroque England, 1690-1730. (Illus.). 256p. 2000. 42.50 (*0-7509-2190-0*) Sutton Publng.

Ridgeway, Christopher & Wallace, Brian. Empowering Change: The Role of People Management. 160p. 1993. pap. 175.00 (*0-85292-548-4*, Pub. by IPM Hse) St Mut.

— Leadership for Strategic Change. 240p. 1996. pap. 76.00 (*0-85292-613-8*, Pub. by IPM Hse) St Mut.

***Ridgeway, Christie.** Wish You Were Here. LC 99-95333. 384p. 2000. mass mkt. 5.99 (*0-380-81255-X*, Avon Bks) Morrow Avon.

Ridgeway, James. Blood in the Face: The Ku Klux Klan, Aryan Nations, Nazi Skinheads & the Rise of a New White Culture. 2nd ed. (Illus.). 210p. 1995. pap. 19.95 (*1-56025-100-X*, Thunders Mouth) Avalon NY.

— Pocket Guide to Environmental Bad Guys: And a Few Ideas on How to Stop Them. LC 98-34022. (Illus.). 178p. 1998. pap. text 10.95 (*1-56025-153-0*, Thunders Mouth) Avalon NY.

— Red Light: Inside the Sex Industry. 1999. pap. 19.95 (*1-56025-197-2*, Thunders Mouth) Avalon NY.

— Red Light: Inside the Sex Industry. LC 95-73242. (Illus.). 256p. 1996. 39.95 (*1-57687-000-6*, pwerHse Bks) pwerHse Cultrl.

— Red Light: Inside the Sex Industry. limited ed. (Illus.). 256p. 1996. boxed set 135.00 (*1-57687-001-4*, pwerHse Bks) pwerHse Cultrl.

Ridgeway, James, ed. The March to War. LC 91-11607. 244p. 1991. pap. 9.95 (*0-941423-61-1*) FWEW.

Ridgeway, James, jt. ed. see Udovicki, Jasminka.

Ridgeway, James, jt. ed. see Udoviicki, Jasminka.

***Ridgeway, James M., Jr.** Little Mac: Demise of an American Hero. LC 99-91008. 1999. pap. 18.00 (*0-7388-0579-3*) Xlibris Corp.

Ridgeway, John. Flood Tide. large type ed. (Illus.). 1991. 27.99 (*0-7089-8620-X*) Ulverscroft.

Ridgeway, Judy. The Cheese Companion: The Connoisseur's Guide. (Illus.). 224p. 1999. 24.95 (*0-7624-0500-7*) Running Pr.

— The Vegetarian Gourmet. (Illus.). 176p. 1981. 14.95 (*0-13-941492-4*, Spectrum IN) Macmillan Gen Ref.

***Ridgeway, Rick.** Below Another Sky: A Tibetan Journey of Remembrance. (Illus.). 320p. 2001. text 26.00 (*0-8050-6284-X*) H Holt & Co.

Ridgeway, Rick. The Last Step: The American Ascent of K2. (Illus.). 304p. 1999. pap. 21.95 (*0-89886-632-4*) Mountaineers.

— The Shadow of Kilimanjaro: On Foot Across East Africa. LC 98-15970. (Illus.). 288p. 1998. 27.50 (*0-8050-5389-1*) H Holt & Co.

— The Shadow of Kilimanjaro: On Foot Across East Africa. 288p. 1999. pap. 14.95 (*0-8050-5390-5*) H Holt & Co.

Ridgeway, Roy. Natural Way: Asthma; A Comprehensive Guide to Gentle, Safe & Effective Treatment. (Natural Way Ser.). 128p. 1994. pap. 5.95 (*1-85230-492-8*, Pub. by Element MA) Penguin Putnam.

Ridgeway, Sam H. & Harrison, Richard J., eds. Handbook of Marine Mammals Vol. 1: The Walrus, Sea Lions, Fur Seals & Sea Otter. LC 80-42010. 1981. text 136.00 (*0-12-588501-6*) Acad Pr.

Ridgeway, William. The Dramas & Dramatic Dances of Non-European Races. LC 63-23187. (Illus.). 448p. 1972. reprint ed. 33.95 (*0-405-08889-2*, Pub. by Blom Pubns) Ayer.

— The Origin & Influence of the Thoroughbred Horse. LC 73-174446. (Illus.). 1972. reprint ed. 30.95 (*0-405-08890-6*, Pub. by Blom Pubns) Ayer.

— The Origin of Tragedy. LC 65-19621. (Illus.). 238p. 1972. 23.95 (*0-405-08891-4*, Pub. by Blom Pubns) Ayer.

Ridgley, Nancy. Parent Involvement in Education: Your Child Can Achieve. (Illus.). 136p. 1997. pap. 16.00 (*0-8059-4113-4*) Dorrance.

Ridgley, Robert S. The Birds of South America: The Suboscine Passerines, Vol. 2. (Illus.). 940p. (C). 1994. 85.00 (*0-292-77063-4*) U of Tex Pr.

***Ridgley, Stanley K., ed.** Start the Presses! 2nd ed. LC 00-100081. 127p. 2000. 14.95 (*1-882926-52-8*) ISI Books.

Ridgman, Jeremy. David Hare. Armstrong, Isobel & Loughrey, Bryan, eds. (Writers & Their Work Ser.). 1998. pap. 17.00 (*0-7463-0774-8*, Pub. by Northcote House) U Pr of Miss.

Ridgman, Jeremy & Arts Council of England Staff. Boxed Sets: Television Representations of Theatre. LC 98-185543. viii, 219 p. 1998. write for info. (*1-86020-519-4*) U of Luton Pr.

Ridgway. Hard Capsules: Development - Technology. 1987. 100.00 (*0-85369-159-2*, Pub. by Pharmaceutical Pr) Rittenhouse.

Ridgway, B. S. Greek Sculpture in the Art Museum, Princeton University: Greek Originals, Roman Copies & Variants. LC 93-74259. (Publications of the Department of Art & Archaeology Ser.). 360p. 1994. text 49.50 (*0-943012-16-3*, Pub. by Princeton U Pr); pap. text 24.95 (*0-943012-17-1*, Pub. by Princeton U Pr) Cal Prin Full Svc.

Ridgway, Brunhilde S. The Archaic Style in Greek Sculpture. 2nd rev. ed. (Illus.). xxviii, 497p. (C). 1993. pap. text 55.00 (*0-89005-516-5*) Ares.

— Classical Collection: Sculpture. LC 72-79496. 244p. 1972. 10.00 (*0-686-05424-5*) Mus of Art RI.

— Hellenistic Sculpture I: The Styles of Ca. 331-200 B. C. LC 89-40266. (Studies in Classics). (Illus.). 288p. (C). 1990. text 40.00 (*0-299-11820-7*) U of Wis Pr.

— Roman Copies of Greek Sculpture: The Problem of the Originals. (Jerome Lectures: No. 15). 200p. (C). 1984. text 57.50 (*0-472-10038-6*, 10038) U of Mich Pr.

Ridgway, Brunilde S. Fourth-Century Styles in Greek Sculpture. LC 96-41949. (Wisconsin Studies in Classics). (Illus.). xviii, 480p. 1997. 45.00 (*0-299-15470-X*) U of Wis Pr.

— Prayers in Stone: Greek Architectural Sculpture 600-100 BC. LC 98-3583. (Sather Classical Lectures: Vol. 63). 363p. 1999. 50.00 (*0-520-21556-7*, Pub. by U CA Pr) Cal Prin Full Svc.

***Ridgway, Brunilde Sismondo.** Hellenistic Sculpture II: The Styles of ca. 200-100 B. C. (Illus.). 2000. 45.00 (*0-299-16710-0*) U of Wis Pr.

Ridgway, Brunilde Sismondo, jt. auth. see De Grummond, Nancy Thomson.

Ridgway, Christie. Big Bad Dad. (Yours Truly Ser.). 1998. per. 3.50 (*0-373-52073-5*, 1-52073-3) Silhouette.

— Follow That Groom! (Yours Truly Ser.). 1997. per. 3.50 (*0-373-52038-7*, 1-52038-6) Silhouette.

— Have Baby, Will Marry. 1997. per. 3.50 (*0-373-52051-4*, 1-52051-9) Silhouette.

— Ready, Set . . . Baby! (Yours Truly Ser.). 1998. per. 3.50 (*0-373-52062-X*, 1-52062-6) Silhouette.

— The Wedding Date. (Yours Truly Ser.). 1996. mass mkt. 3.50 (*0-373-52012-3*, 1-52012-1) Silhouette.

— Yours Truly: The Millionaire & the Pregnant Pauper. 1999. per. 3.50 (*0-373-52084-0*, 1-52084-0) Harlequin Bks.

Ridgway, David. The Etruscans. 53p. 1981. pap. 6.00 (*0-614-21823-3*) David Brown.

Ridgway, Donald P. Introduction to Vascular Scanning: A Guide for the Complete Beginner. 2nd ed. 1998. pap. 59.95 (*0-941022-39-0*) Davies Pubng.

Ridgway, George J., ed. see Wright, James E., et al.

Ridgway, George S., ed. see Wourms, John P., et al.

***Ridgway, James M., Jr.** Little Mac: Demise of an American Hero. LC 99-91008. 1999. 25.00 (*0-7388-0578-5*) Xlibris Corp.

Ridgway, Judith. Practical Media Relations. 232p. 1996. pap. 26.95 (*0-566-07702-7*, Pub. by Gower) Ashgate Pub Co.

***Ridgway, Judy.** Aceite de Oliva. (Evergreens Ser.). 1998. 16.99 (*3-8228-7570-8*) Benedikt Taschen.

Ridgway, Judy. International Vegetarian Cooking. LC 97-11516. (Vegetarian Cooking Ser.). (Illus.). 192p. 1997. pap. 14.95 (*0-89594-854-0*) Crossing Pr.

— Quick After-Work Pasta & Sauces Cookbook. LC 96-2431. (Quick After-Work Ser.). (Illus.). 128p. 1996. pap. 12.95 (*1-55561-089-7*) Fisher Bks.

— Quick After-Work Vegetarian Cookbook. LC 96-2432. (Quick After-Work Ser.). (Illus.). 164p. 1996. pap. 12.95 (*1-55561-090-0*) Fisher Bks.

— Quick After-Work Winter Vegetarian Cookbook. 1998. pap. text 12.95 (*0-7499-1772-5*, Pub. by Piatkus Bks) London Brdge.

— Wine-Tasting Course. LC 97-104961. 1996. 40.00 (*0-517-70559-1*) Random.

Ridgway, Keith. The Long Falling. LC 97-45669. 320p. 1998. 22.00 (*0-395-90530-3*) HM.

— The Long Falling. 305p. 1999. pap. 13.00 (*0-395-95782-6*) HM.

Ridgway, Matthew. The Korean War. (Great Commanders Ser.). 290p. 1998. reprint ed. 30.00 (*1-56515-018-X*) Collect Reprints.

Ridgway, Matthew B. The Korean War. (Quality Paperbacks Ser.). (Illus.). 360p. 1986. pap. 13.95 (*0-306-80267-8*) Da Capo.

Ridgway, Merce. The Bayman: A Life on Barnegat Bay. LC 99-33064. (Illus.). 223p. 2000. 24.95 (*0-945582-62-5*) Down the Shore Pub.

Ridgway, Nino M., jt. auth. see Mahr, Daniel L.

Ridgway, Peggi. Jump-Start Your Job Search. LC 92-93451. (Illus.). 112p. (Orig.). 1994. pap. text 14.95 (*0-9635836-0-3*) Wordpictures.

— Romancing the Personals: How to Find Your Partner in the Classifieds. LC 96-90124. (Illus.). 112p. 1996. pap. 9.95 (*0-9635836-1-1*) Wordpictures.

Ridgway, Philip. Revenue Law. (Lecture Notes...Ser.). 350p. 1996. pap. 36.00 (*1-874241-89-9*, Pub. by Cavendish Pubng) Gaunt.

Ridgway, Philip, jt. auth. see Sanders, Tim.

Ridgway, Richard L., et al, eds. Mass-Reared Natural Enemies, Application, Regulation & Needs. (Proceedings, Thomas Say Publications in Entomology Ser.). 341p. 1998. pap. 35.00 (*0-938522-66-3*) Entomol Soc.

Ridgway, Richard L., ed. see Inscoe, et al.

Ridgway, Rick. Three Squirt Dog. 176p. 1994. pap. 12.95 (*0-312-11079-0*) St Martin.

Ridgway, Robert. Ornithology: United States Geological Exploration of the Fortieth Parallel. LC 73-17839. (Natural Sciences in America Ser.: Pt. 3). (Illus.). 370p. 1974. reprint ed. 28.95 (*0-405-05761-X*) Ayer.

Ridgway, Ronald S. Voltaire & Sensibility. LC 72-94539. 308p. reprint ed. pap. 95.50 (*0-608-14102-X*, 202384500034) Bks Demand.

Ridgway, S. H. & Harrison, R., eds. Handbook of Marine Mammals Vol. 6: The Second Book of Dolphins & Porpoises, Vol. 6. (Handbook of Marine Mammals Ser.). (Illus.). 448p. 1998. boxed set 99.95 (*0-12-588506-7*) Acad Pr.

Ridgway, Sam H. & Harrison, Richard J., eds. Handbook of Marine Mammals Vol. 4: River Dolphins & the Larger Toothed Whales. 442p. 1989. text 125.00 (*0-12-588504-0*) Acad Pr.

***Ridgway, Tom.** The Young Zillionaire's Guide to Buying Goods & Services. LC 00-27207. (Be a Zillionaire Ser.). 2000. write for info. (*0-8239-3263-X*) Rosen Group.

***Ridgway, Virginia.** After Tomorrow: Life, Love & Laughter in the Retirement World. large type ed. Smith, Kenneth Weldon, ed. 320p. 2000. pap. 18.00 (*0-9674241-3-5*) IZA Pubg.

Ridgway, Whitman H., jt. auth. see Melusky, Joseph A.

Ridgwell, Jenny. Bread. LC 97-44112. (Food in Focus Ser.). (Illus.). 32p. 1998. 14.95 (*1-57572-654-8*) Heinemann Lib.

— Fruit & Vegetables. LC 97-44111. (Food in Focus Ser.). (Illus.). 32p. (YA). (gr. 1-5). 1998. 14.95 (*1-57572-656-4*) Heinemann Lib.

— A Taste of Italy. (Food Around the World Ser.). 1993. 22.83 (*0-8172-4854-4*) Raintree Steck-V.

— A Taste of Italy. LC 93-25200. (Food Around the World Ser.). (Illus.). 48p. (J). (gr. 3-6). 1993. lib. bdg. 22.83 (*1-56847-098-3*) Raintree Steck-V.

Ridgwell, Jenny. Taste of Japan. LC 93-14148. (Food Around the World Ser.). (Illus.). 48p. (gr. 4-7). 1997. 22.82 (*0-8172-4851-X*) Raintree Steck-V.

Ridick, Joyce. Treasures in Earthen Vessels: The Vows. (C). 1988. 39.00 (*0-7855-3228-5*, Pub. by St Paul Pubns) St Mut.

Ridilla, Paul. Born to Build: A Parent's Guide to Academic Alternatives. LC 94-21564. 1994. 12.95 (*0-912524-93-6*) Busn News.

Riding, Alan. Distant Neighbors: A Portrait of the Mexicans. 352p. 1989. pap. 13.00 (*0-679-72441-9*) Vin Bks.

***Riding, Christine & Riding, Jacqueline, eds.** The Houses of Parliament. (Illus.). 240p. 2000. 50.00 (*1-85894-112-1*, Pub. by Merrell Holberton) Rizzoli Intl.

Riding, Don. Sub-Contracts DOM 1 & DOM 2: A Guide to Rights & Obligations. LC 96-26491. 247p. 1996. 79.95 (*0-632-04125-0*) Blackwell Sci.

***Riding, Jacqueline.** Theatre of State: The Art, Architecture & Ceremony of the Palace of Westminster. 224p. 1999. pap. 50.00 (*0-85331-787-9*, Pub. by Lund Humphries) Antique Collect.

Riding, Jacqueline, jt. ed. see Riding, Christine.

Riding, Laura. First Awakenings: The Early Poems of Laura Riding. Friedmann, Elizabeth et al, eds. LC 92-8585. 320p. 1992. 29.95 (*0-89255-179-8*) Persea Bks.

— Four Unposted Letters to Catherine. LC 93-3467. 80p. 1993. 15.00 (*0-89255-192-5*) Persea Bks.

— Modernistic Poetry. reprint ed. lib. bdg. 79.00 (*0-7812-0321-X*) Rprt Serv.

— A Pamphlet Against Anthologies. (BCL1-PR English Literature Ser.). 192p. 1992. reprint ed. lib. bdg. 69.00 (*0-7812-7082-0*) Rprt Serv.

— The Poems of Laura Riding. 420p. (C). 1985. reprint ed. pap. 14.95 (*0-89255-087-2*) Persea Bks.

— Progress of Stories: A New, Enlarged Edition with Commentary by Laura (Riding) Jackson. 414p. 1994. reprint ed. pap. 15.00 (*0-89255-203-4*) Persea Bks.

— Selected Poems: In Five Sets. 96p. 1993. reprint ed. pap. 9.95 (*0-89255-189-5*) Persea Bks.

— A Selection of Poems of Laura Riding. Nye, Robert, ed. & intro. by. 1997. pap. 12.95 (*0-614-29443-6*) Penguin Putnam.

— A Survey of Modernist Poetry. (BCL1-PR English Literature Ser.). 295p. 1992. reprint ed. lib. bdg. 79.00 (*0-7812-7073-1*) Rprt Serv.

Riding, Laura & Samuels, Lisa. Anarchism Is Not Enough LC 99-20038. 250p. 2000. pap. 16.95 (*0-520-21394-7*, Pub. by U CA Pr) Cal Prin Full Svc.

Riding, R., ed. Calcareous Algae & Stromatolites. (Illus.). 544p. 1990. 204.95 (*0-387-52373-1*) Spr-Verlag.

Riding, Richard. Cognitive Styles & Learning Strategies: Understanding Style Differences in Learning & Behavior. LC 98-149933. 1998. pap. 29.95 (*1-85346-480-5*, Pub. by David Fulton) Taylor & Francis.

Riding, Robvert, jt. ed. see Leadbeater, Barry S.

Ridinger, Gayle, et al, eds. Italian Poetry, 1950-1990: Bilingual Anthology. (ENG & ITA.). 500p. (Orig.). 1996. pap. 18.95 (*0-937832-34-0*) Dante U Am.

Ridinger, Johannes E. Kleine Reitschule: Vorstellung und Beschreibung derer Schul und Campagne Pferden nach ihren Lectionen. 35p. 1997. reprint ed. 115.00 (*3-487-08388-4*) G Olms Pubs.

Ridinger, Robert B. African Archaeology: A Selected Bibliography. (G. K. Hall Reference Ser.). 550p. 1993. 60.00 (*0-8161-9086-0*, Hall Reference) Macmillan.

— The Gay & Lesbian Movement: References & Resources. LC 96-30352. (Reference Publications on American Social Movements Ser.). 487p. 1996. 46.00 (*0-8161-7373-7*, G K Hall & Co) Mac Lib Ref.

— The Peace Corps: An Annotated Bibliography. 300p. (C). 1989. 40.00 (*0-8161-8912-9*, Hall Reference) Macmillan.

Ridinger, Robert B., compiled by. The Homosexual & Society: An Annotated Bibliography, 18. LC 90-31738. (Bibliographies & Indexes in Sociology Ser.: No. 18). 456p. 1990. lib. bdg. 69.50 (*0-313-25357-9*, RHO, Greenwood Pr) Greenwood.

***Ridinger, Robert B. & Awramik, S. M., eds.** Microbial Sediments. LC 99-52961. (Illus.). 345p. 2000. 206.00 (*3-540-61828-7*) Spr-Verlag.

***Ridinger, Robert B. & Zhuravlev, Andrey, eds.** The Ecology of the Cambrian Radiation. 576p. 2000. text 80.00 (*0-231-10612-2*); pap. text 40.00 (*0-231-10613-0*) Col U Pr.

***Ridinger, Robert B. Marks.** The Archaeology of the Indian Subcontinent & Sri Lanka: A Selected Bibliography. Vol. 10. 2000. lib. bdg. write for info. (*0-313-30001-1*) Greenwood.

Ridings, Daniel. The Attic Moses: The Dependency Theme in Some Early Christian Writers. LC 95-213005. (Studia Graeca et Latina Gothoburgensia: No. LIX). 270p. (Orig.). 1995. pap. 72.50 (*91-7346-275-6*) Coronet Bks.

Ridings, Donald, jt. auth. see Dungan, Christopher.

Ridings, Eugene. Business Interest Groups in Nineteenth Century Brazil. LC 93-32152. (Latin American Studies: No. 78). 395p. (C). 1994. text 74.95 (*0-521-45485-9*) Cambridge U Pr.

Ridings, Jean E., tr. see Lilie, Ralph-J.

Ridings, Jim. Ashpile, No. 1. (Illus.). 142p. (YA). (gr. 6 up). 1998. pap. 7.95 (*0-9664974-2-2*, Side Show Comics) Ink & Feathers.

— The Politically Incorrect Cheese Weasel. (Illus.). 200p. 1993. pap. 11.95 (*0-9664974-3-0*, Side Show Comics) Ink & Feathers.

Ridings, Jim, jt. auth. see Feinman, Myke.

Ridings, William J. Rating the Presidents: A Ranking of U. S. Leaders from the Great & Honorable to the Dishonest. (Illus.). 320p. 1998. pap. text 15.95 (*0-8065-1969-X*, Citadel Pr) Carol Pub Group.

— Rating the Presidents: A Ranking of U.S. Leaders, From the Great & Honorable to the Dishonest. 1999. pap. text 15.95 (*0-8065-2151-1*) Carol Pub Group.

R

R

Ridings, William J., Jr. & McIver, Stuart B. Rating the Presidents: A Ranking of the Most Influential Presidents in U. S. History. LC 95-50073. 1996. write for info. (*0-614-11712-7*) Carol Pub Group.
— Rating the Presidents: Every Chief Executive Ranked in Order of Influence. LC 95-50073. (Illus.). 304p. 1996. 22.95 (*0-8065-1799-9*, Citadel Pr) Carol Pub Group.
Ridington, Candace E. Rubicon: The Love Story of Emily Dickinson's Brother, Austin, & Mabel Todd, the Woman Who Saved Emily's Poetry. LC 97-6883. 496p. (Orig.). 1997. pap. 19.95 (*0-9656773-1-1*, 032398) Arlngton Pr.
Ridington, Jillian & Ridington, Robin. People of the Longhouse: How the Iroquoian Tribes Lived. (How They Lived Ser.). (Illus.). 48p. (J). (gr. 4-7). 1992. pap. 7.95 (*1-55054-221-4*) Firefly Bks Ltd.
Ridington, Jillian, jt. auth. see Ridington, Robin.
Ridington, Richard, ed. see DeLuca, Michael & Richardson, Mark.
Ridington, Richard W. Macro Engineer: A 1-2-3 Macro Developer's Toolkit-2 Disks Included. 1990. pap. 79.95 (*0-13-543331-2*) P-H.
Ridington, Robin. Little Bit Know Something: Stories in a Language of Anthropology. LC 89-48164. (Illus.). 299p. (C). 1990. pap. text 13.95 (*0-87745-286-5*) U of Iowa Pr.
— Trail to Heaven: Knowledge & Narrative in a Northern Native Community. LC 88-17098. (Illus.). 317p. 1992. reprint ed. pap. text 12.95 (*0-87745-391-8*) U of Iowa Pr.
Ridington, Robin & Hastings, Dennis. Blessing for a Long Time: The Sacred Pole of the Omaha Tribe. LC 97-6558. (Illus.). xxviii, 259p. 1997. text 60.00 (*0-8032-3925-4*) U of Nebr Pr.
— Blessing for a Long Time: The Sacred Pole of the Omaha Tribe. 259p. 2000. pap. 18.00 (*0-8032-8981-2*, Bison Books) U of Nebr Pr.
Ridington, Robin & Ridington, Jillian. People of the Trail: How the Northern Forest Indians Lived. (How They Lived Ser.). (Illus.). 40p. (J). (gr. 4-7). 1992. pap. 7.95 (*0-88894-412-8*) Firefly Bks Ltd.
Ridington, Robin, jt. auth. see Ridington, Jillian.
Ridini, Steven P. Health & Sexuality Education in Schools: The Process of Social Change. LC 98-9536. 224p. 1998. 59.95 (*0-89789-570-3*, Bergin & Garvey) Greenwood.
Ridjanovic, Midhat, tr. see Dizdarevic, Zlatko.
Ridjanovic, Midhat, tr. see Hukanovic, Rezak.
Ridker, Claire & Savage, Patricia. Railing Against the Rush of Years: A Personal Journey Through Aging Via Art Therapy, Poems, Paintings, & Prose. LC 96-24802. (Illus.). 87p. 1996. pap. 15.95 (*1-884206-02-6*) Unfinish Monumnt.
Ridker, Ronald G. Population & Development: The Search for Selective Interventions. LC 76-16806. (Resources for the Future Ser.). (Illus.). 467p. 1976. 37.50 (*0-8018-1884-2*, Pub. by Resources Future) Johns Hopkins.
— The World Bank's Role in Human Resource Development in Sub-Saharan Africa: Education, Training & Technical Assistance. LC 94-20212. (Operations Evaluation Studies). 138p. 1994. pap. 22.00 (*0-8213-2864-6*, 12864) World Bank.
Ridker, Ronald G., ed. Changing Resource Problems of the Fourth World. LC 75-42978. (Resources for the Future Ser.: Pd-1). (Illus.). 162p. 1976. pap. 8.00 (*0-8018-1847-8*) Johns Hopkins.
— Changing Resource Problems of the Fourth World. LC 75-42978. (RFF Working Paper Ser.: No. PD-1). 161p. reprint ed. pap. 50.00 (*0-608-18809-3*, 203021300067) Bks Demand.
Ridker, Ronald G. & Watson, William D., Jr. To Choose a Future. LC 79-3643. (Resources for the Future Ser.). 1980. 37.00 (*0-8018-2354-4*) Johns Hopkins.
Ridky, Jill & Sheldon, George F. Managing in Academics: A Health Center Model. LC 93-23854. (Illus.). 359p. 1993. pap. 30.00 (*0-942219-11-2*) Quality Med Pub.
Ridl, Jack. After School. 1988. pap. 1.50 (*0-318-37519-2*) Samisdat.
Ridl, Julie, jt. auth. see West, Larry.
***Ridland, John.** Life with Unkie. 40p. 1999. pap. 8.00 (*1-890887-12-9*) Mille Grazie.
***Ridlen, Susanne S.** Tree-Stump Tombstones: A Field Guide to Rustic Funerary Art in Indiana. (Illus.). 192p. 1999. 35.00i (*1-891598-03-1*); pap. 27.00i (*1-891598-02-3*) Old Richardville.
Ridler, Anne. A Matter of Life & Deth Death. (C). 1990. 60.00 (*0-906887-07-0*, Pub. by Greville Pr) St Mut.
Ridless, Glenn. Little Treasures. (Charming Petites Ser.). (Illus.). 80p. 1991. 4.95 (*0-88088-733-8*) Peter Pauper.
Ridley. Beginning Bioethics: A Text with Integrated Readings. LC 97-65376. 352p. 1997. pap. text 30.95 (*0-312-13291-3*) St Martin.
— Introduction to Programmable Logic Controllers. LC 97-148582. (Electrical Engineering Ser.). 224p. 1997. pap. 21.95 (*0-340-67666-3*, VNR) Wiley.
Ridley & Channing. Safety at Work. 5th ed. LC 99-191393. 800p. 1998. text 145.00 (*0-7506-4018-9*) Buttrwrth-Heinemann.
Ridley, Aaron. Music, Value, & the Passions. LC 98-29695. (Illus.). 216p. 1995. text 29.95 (*0-8014-3035-6*) Cornell U Pr.
— Nietzsche's Conscience: Six Character Studies from the "Genealogy" 208p. 1998. 39.95 (*0-8014-3557-9*); pap. 16.95 (*0-8014-8553-3*) Cornell U Pr.
Ridley, Aaron, ed. Arguing about Art: Topics in Contemporary Philosophical Aesthetics. LC 94-14036. 352p. (C). 1994. pap. 23.44 (*0-07-046191-0*) McGraw.
Ridley, Aaron, jt. auth. see Neill, Alex.
Ridley, Alison & Garfield, Curtis F. As Ancient Is This Hostelry: The Story of the Wayside Inn. (Illus.). 338p. (Orig.). (YA). (gr. 7 up). 1989. reprint ed. pap. 15.00 (*0-9621976-0-2*) Porcupine Enter.
— The Story of the Lygon Arms. (Illus.). 240p. 1992. pap. 17.50 (*0-9621976-1-0*) Porcupine Enter.
Ridley, Alison, et al. Journeys: Finding Life's Way in Spite of Obstacles. (Illus.). 184p. 1999. pap. 12.95 (*0-9621976-4-5*) Porcupine Enter.
Ridley, B. K. Electrons & Phonons in Semiconductor Multilayers. (Studies in Semiconductor Physics & Microelectronic Engineering: No. 5). (Illus.). 350p. (C). 1996. text 74.95 (*0-521-47492-2*) Cambridge U Pr.
— Time, Space & Things. 3rd ed. (Canto Book Ser.). (Illus.). 203p. (C). 1995. pap. 10.95 (*0-521-48486-3*) Cambridge U Pr.
Ridley, Bill & Ridley, Leora. Adventism: Delayed or Derailed? LC 98-86543. 328 p. 1998. 14.95 (*1-57258-140-9*) Teach Servs.
Ridley, Brian K. Quantum Processes in Semiconductors. 4th ed. LC 99-16185. (Illus.). 464p. 2000. text 110.00 (*0-19-850580-9*); pap. text 50.00 (*0-19-850579-5*) OUP.
Ridley, Bromfield L. Battles & Sketches of the Army of Tennessee 1861-65: Journal of B. L. Ridley, Lieut. General A. P. Stewart's Staff. unabridged ed. (Illus.). 672p. 1995. reprint ed. text 47.50 (*0-89029-047-4*) Morningside Bkshop.
***Ridley, C. M., et al.** Vulval Disease. (An Arnold Publication Ser.). 208p. 2000. pap. text 69.95 (*0-340-75890-2*) OUP.
***Ridley, C. Marjorie & Neill, Sarah M.** The Vulva. 2nd ed. LC 98-23209. (Illus.). 1999. 225.00 (*0-632-04768-2*) Blackwell Sci.
Ridley, Charles P., et al. Training for Selection Interviewing. 125p. (Orig.). 1998. pap. 189.00 incl. VHS (*1-889638-13-7*) ChurchSmart.
Ridley, Charles R. Overcoming Unintentional Racism in Counseling & Therapy: A Practitioner's Guide to International Action. (Multicultural Aspects of Counseling Ser.: Vol. 5). 120p. 1994. 42.00 (*0-8039-4869-7*); pap. 18.95 (*0-8039-4870-0*) Sage.
Ridley, Chas. Black Hole: Unexpected Tool for Joyous Living. 92p. 1994. pap. 15.00 (*1-890894-02-8*, 97003) Chas HotBooks.
— Lessons to Share: Workbook for a Healthy Family. 3rd rev. ed. (Illus.). 120p. 1987. pap. 15.00 (*1-890894-00-1*, 97001) Chas HotBooks.
— On Shifting Sands: And Other Poems of Transition. (Illus.). 92p. 1992. pap. 15.00 (*1-890894-01-X*, 97002) Chas HotBooks.
***Ridley, Chas.** Pioneer Lessons: 87 Things I Almost Wish We'd Known. (Illus.). 112p. 1999. pap. 15.00 (*1-890894-13-3*) Chas HotBooks.
Ridley, Chas. Sizzling Spells: How to Make Any Man Want to Talk to You. ix, 82p. 1997. pap. 4.95 (*1-890894-06-0*, 97015) Chas HotBooks.
Ridley, Chas, ed. see Brooks, Jennifer.
Ridley, Clarence H., et al. Computer Software Agreements. 1987. 175.00 (*0-88712-750-9*) Warren Gorham & Lamont.
— Computer Software Agreements: Forms & Commentary with Forms on Disk. rev. ed. 1993. ring bd. 195.00 incl. disk (*0-685-69655-3*, PLS) Warren Gorham & Lamont.
Ridley, Clifford. How to Grow Your Own Groceries for One Hundred Dollars a Year. 128p. 1974. pap. 3.95 (*0-89036-029-4*) Liahona Pub Trust.
Ridley, D. Scott & Walther, Bill. Creating Responsible Learners: The Role of a Positive Classroom Environment. LC 95-22563. (Psychology in the Classroom Ser.). 121p. 1996. pap. 17.95 (*1-55798-295-3*) Am Psychol.
Ridley, David W. Marching into Tyranny. LC 97-215875. x, 268p. (Orig.). 1997. pap. 12.95 (*0-9658784-2-2*) Ridley Assocs.
Ridley, Dennis. Fourcast. (Illus.). xi, 128p. 1984. pap. 35.00 (*0-9669838-0-7*) Engineering Mgmt.
Ridley, Edgar J. An African Answer: The Key to Global Productivity. LC 92-14518. 100p. (Orig.). 1992. 24.95 (*0-86543-358-5*); pap. 8.95 (*0-86543-359-3*) Africa World.
Ridley, Elizabeth. Rainey's Lament. LC 99-10507. 300p. 1999. 24.95 (*0-87951-949-5*, Pub. by Overlook Pr) Penguin Putnam.
— Throwing Roses. LC 92-34344. 131p. 1993. 22.00 (*1-877946-29-X*) Permanent Pr.
Ridley, F. A. The Assassins: A Study of the Cult of the Assassins in Persia & Islam. (Islam Ser.). 1980. lib. bdg. 59.95 (*0-8490-3077-3*) Gordon Pr.
Ridley, F. F. British Government & Politics since 1945: Changes in Perspective. 254p. 1995. pap. text 21.00 (*0-19-922239-8*) OUP.
— Sleaze: Politicians, Private Interests, & Public Reaction. 222p. 1996. pap. text 19.95 (*0-19-922273-8*) OUP.
Ridley, F. F. & Jordan, Grant, eds. Protest Politics: Cause Groups & Campaigns, Vol. 7. LC 99-185239. (Hansard Society Series in Government & Politics: 7). 188p. 1998. pap. text 26.00 (*0-19-922374-2*) OUP.
Ridley, F. F., jt. ed. see Thompson, Brian.
Ridley, Francis A. The Jesuits: A Study in Counter-Reformation. LC 83-45595. reprint ed. 35.00 (*0-404-19888-0*) AMS Pr.
— The Papacy & Fascism: The Crisis of the 20th Century. LC 72-180422. (Studies in Fascism: Ideology & Practice). reprint ed. 45.00 (*0-404-56156-X*) AMS Pr.
Ridley, Gustave. From Boredom to Bliss. Campbell, Jean, ed. (Illus.). 138p. (Orig.). 1983. pap. 8.95 (*0-9610544-0-9*) Harmonious Pr.
Ridley, Henry N. Spices: Book on Medicinal Plants. 449p. (C). 1983. reprint ed. pap. 325.00 (*81-7089-015-2*, Pub. by Intl Bk Distr) St Mut.
Ridley, Hugh. The Problematic Bourgeois: Twentieth-Century Criticism on Thomas Mann's Buddenbrooks & the Magic Mountain. (LCGERM Ser.). xiv, 194p. 1994. 55.00 (*1-879751-87-9*) Camden Hse.
Ridley, Ian, jt. auth. see Claridge, Steve.
***Ridley, Jane.** Intimacy in Crisis, 1. 1999. pap. text 34.95 (*1-86156-113-X*) Whurr Pub.
Ridley, Jason. Power Packing: Principles of Lightweight Long Distance Backpacking. ii, 68p. (Orig.). 1996. mass mkt. write for info. (*0-9655261-6-X*) TwoLB Ent.
Ridley, Jasper. Elizabeth I: The Shrewdness of Virtue. LC 88-29255. 391p. 1989. reprint ed. pap. 16.00 (*0-88064-110-X*) Fromm Intl Pub.
— The Law of Carriage of Goods by Land, Sea & Air. Whitehead, Geoffrey, ed. (C). 1982. pap. 110.00 (*0-7855-2308-1*, Pub. by Scientific) St Mut.
***Ridley, Jasper.** Mussolini: A Biography. (Illus.). 2000. pap. 19.95 (*0-8154-1081-6*, Pub. by Cooper Sq) Natl Bk Netwk.
Ridley, Jasper. Mussolini: A Biography. LC 98-37813. 448p. 1998. 27.50 (*0-312-19303-3*, Thomas Dunne) St Martin.
— The Tudor Age. LC 90-6884. (Illus.). 384p. 1990. 40.00 (*0-87951-405-1*, Pub. by Overlook Pr) Penguin Putnam.
— The Tudor Age. (Illus.). 385p. 1996. pap. 24.95 (*0-87951-684-4*, Pub. by Overlook Pr) Penguin Putnam.
Ridley, Jeffrey & Stephens, Krystyna. International Quality Standards: Implications for Internal Auditing. Campbell, Lee A., ed. LC 96-233495. 119p. 1996. pap. 65.00 (*0-89413-362-4*, A309) Inst Inter Aud.
Ridley, Jennifer. Reflection & Strategies in Foreign Language Learning: A Study of Four University-Level "Ab Initio" Learners of German. (Fremdsprachendidaktik Inhalts- und Lernerorientiert Ser.: Bd. 2). 260p. 1997. pap. 51.95 (*3-631-30445-5*) P Lang Pubng.
— Reflection & Strategies in Foreign Language Learning: A Study of Four University-Level "Ab Initio" Learners of German. (Fremdsprachendidaktik Inhalts- und Lernerorientiert Ser.: Bd. 2). (Illus.). 260p. 1997. pap. 51.95 (*0-8204-3206-7*) P Lang Pubng.
Ridley, Jessica. The Decorated Doll House: How to Design & Create Miniature Interiors. LC 90-3933. (Illus.). 128p. 1997. reprint ed. 35.00 (*0-8021-1232-3*, Grove) Grove-Atltic.
Ridley, Jo A. Looking for Eulabee Dix: The Illustrated Biography of an American Miniaturist. LC 97-29794. (Illus.). 304p. 1998. 45.00 (*0-940979-36-5*) Natl Museum Women.
— Looking for Eulabee Dix: The Illustrated Biography of an American Miniaturist (1878-1961) LC 97-29794. (Illus.). 1997. pap. write for info. (*0-940979-37-3*) Natl Museum Women.
Ridley, Jo A., jt. auth. see Kennedy, Arthur R.
***Ridley, John.** Everybody Smokes in Hell. 256p. 2000. pap. 14.00 (*0-345-42147-7*) Ballantine Pub Grp.
— Everybody Smokes in Hell. LC 99-23566. 240p. 1999. 23.00 (*0-375-40143-1*) Knopf.
Ridley, John. Everybody Smokes in Hell. 1999. 24.00 (*0-676-79020-8*) Random.
Ridley, John. Guarding of Machinery. (Illus.). 192p. Date not set. 72.95 (*0-7506-4830-9*) Buttrwrth-Heinemann.
Ridley, John. Love is a Racket. 1999. mass mkt. 6.99 (*0-345-43409-9*) Ballantine Pub Grp.
— Love Is a Racket: A Novel. LC 98-15879. 288p. 1998. 24.00 (*0-375-40142-3*) Random.
— U-Turn: The Shooting Script. LC 97-29130. (Shooting Script Ser.). (Illus.). 176p. 1997. pap. 16.95 (*1-55704-327-2*, Pub. by Newmarket) Norton.
Ridley, John E. Introduction to Programmable Logic Controllers: The Mitsubishi FX. LC 97-148582. Ep. 1997. pap. 64.95 (*0-470-23729-5*) Wiley.
Ridley, John R. Health & Safety... In Brief. LC 97-51507. (Made Simple Bks.). 256p. 1998. pap. text 29.95 (*0-7506-3765-X*) Buttrwrth-Heinemann.
— Safety at Work. 4th ed. LC 93-46862. (Illus.). 800p. 1994. 245.00 (*0-7506-0746-7*) Buttrwrth-Heinemann.
***Ridley, John R. & Channing, John.** Occupational Health & Hygiene. LC 99-35498. (Safety at Work Ser.). 241p. 1999. write for info. (*0-7506-4557-1*) Buttrwrth-Heinemann.
— Risk Management, Vol. 2. LC 99-26608. (Safety at Work Ser.). 221p. 1999. write for info. (*0-7506-4558-X*) Buttrwrth-Heinemann.
— Safety Law. LC 99-34600. (Safety at Work Ser.). 207p. 1999. write for info. (*0-7506-4559-8*) Buttrwrth-Heinemann.
— Workplace Safety LC 99-35497. (Safety at Work Ser.). 1999. 49.95 (*0-7506-4560-1*) Buttrwrth-Heinemann.
Ridley, Ken, jt. auth. see Morrison, Keith.
Ridley, Leora, jt. auth. see Ridley, Bill.
Ridley, Mark. Animal Behavior: An Introduction to Behavioral Mechanisms, Development, & Ecology. 2nd ed. (Illus.). 223p. 1994. pap. 39.95 (*0-86542-390-3*) Blackwell Sci.
— Evolution. 2nd ed. LC QH366.2.R524 1996. (Illus.). 1996. pap. 67.95 incl. cd-rom (*0-86542-495-0*) Blackwell Sci.
— The Explanation of Organic Diversity: The Comparative Methods of Adaptations for Mating. (Illus.). 1983. 45.00 (*0-19-857597-1*) OUP.
Ridley, Mark, ed. Evolution: An Oxford Reader. LC 97-28965. (Oxford Readers Ser.). (Illus.). 438p. (C). 1998. pap. 22.95 (*0-19-289287-8*) OUP.
Ridley, Mark, jt. auth. see Dawkins, Richard.
Ridley, Mark, ed. see Darwin, Charles.
Ridley, Mark, jt. ed. see Dawkins, Richard.
Ridley, Matt. Down to Earth: A Contrarian View of Environmental Problems. (IEA Studies on the Environment: No. 3). 80p. 1995. pap. 22.50 (*0-255-36345-1*, Pub. by Inst Economic Affairs) Coronet Bks.
— Down to Earth Vol. II: Combating Environmental Myths. (IEA Studies on the Environment: No. 7). 102p. 1996. pap. 26.50 (*0-255-36383-4*, Pub. by Inst Economic Affairs) Coronet Bks.
***Ridley, Matt.** The Future of Disease. LC 99-206565. (Predictions Ser.). 58p. 1999. pap. 3.95 (*0-297-84065-7*, Pub. by Weidenfeld & Nicolson) Trafalgar.
— Genome: The Autobiography of a Species in 23 Chapters, LC 99-40933. 352p. 2000. 26.00 (*0-06-019497-9*) HarpC.
Ridley, Matt. The Origins of Virtue: Human Instincts & the Evolution of Cooperation. (Illus.). 295p. 1997. text 24.95 (*0-670-86357-2*) Viking Penguin.
— The Origins of Virtue: Human Instincts & the Evolution of Cooperation. LC 96-44907. 295p. 1998. pap. 13.95 (*0-14-026445-0*) Viking Penguin.
— The Red Queen: Sex & the Evolution of Human Nature. 416p. 1995. pap. 14.95 (*0-14-024548-0*, Penguin Bks) Viking Penguin.
Ridley, Maurice R. Keats' Craftsmanship: A Study in Poetic Development. LC 63-14696. (Illus.). 328p. reprint ed. 101.70 (*0-8357-9707-4*, 201143700079) Bks Demand.
— Keats' Craftsmanship: A Study in Poetic Development. (BCL1-PR English Literature Ser.). 312p. 1992. reprint ed. lib. bdg. 89.00 (*0-7812-7574-1*) Rprt Serv.
— Studies in Three Literatures: English, Latin & Greek Contrasts & Comparisons. LC 78-42. 1977p. 1978. reprint ed. lib. bdg. 55.00 (*0-313-20189-7*, RISTL, Greenwood Pr) Greenwood.
Ridley, Maurice R., ed. see Shakespeare, William.
Ridley, Michael. The Art of World Religions: Buddhism. (Illus.). 184p. 1978. 49.95 (*0-7137-0886-7*) Asia Bk Corp.
Ridley, Michael A. Lowering the Cost of Emission Reduction: Joint Implementation in the Framework Convention on Climate Change. LC 97-49849. (Environment & Policy Ser.). 188p. 1998. 84.00 (*0-7923-4914-8*) Kluwer Academic.
Ridley, Norman, ed. Superplasticity: 60 Years after Pearson. 400p. 1995. 100.00 (*0-901716-77-4*, Pub. by Inst Materials) Ashgate Pub Co.
Ridley, Norman, jt. auth. see Pilling, John.
Ridley, Pauline. Modern Art. (Art & Artists Ser.). (Illus.). 64p. (J). (gr. 5-10). 1995. lib. bdg. 24.26 (*1-56847-356-7*) Raintree Steck-V.
Ridley, Philip. The American Dreams. LC 97-223098. (Screenplay Ser.). 1997. pap. 10.95 (*0-413-71140-4*) Methn.
Ridley, Philip. Apocalyptica. 1998. pap. 11.95 (*0-413-68870-4*) Heinemann.
Ridley, Philip. Dreamboat Zing. (Illus.). 64p. (J). (ps-3). 1997. pap. 7.95 (*0-14-037282-2*, Pub. by Pnguin Bks Ltd) Trafalgar.
Ridley, Philip. Ghost from a Perfect Place. LC 95-120372. 96p. 1995. pap. 11.95 (*0-413-68860-7*, Methuen Drama) Methn.
Ridley, Philip. The Krays. LC 97-226350. (Screenplay Ser.). 1997. pap. 10.95 (*0-413-71130-7*) Methn.
— Plays, No. 1. LC 97-223095. (Contemporary Dramatists Ser.). 1997. pap. 14.95 (*0-413-71100-5*) Methn.
Ridley, Philip, jt. auth. see Goetzee, Paul.
***Ridley, Randy.** SUSE Linux Bible. (Bible Ser.). (Illus.). 700p. 2000. pap. text 39.99 (*0-7645-4711-9*) IDG Bks.
Ridley, Rosalind M. & Baker, Harry F. Fatal Protein: The Story of CJD, BSE & Other Prion Diseases. (Illus.). 260p. 1998. text 54.50 (*0-19-852435-8*) OUP.
Ridley, Rosalind M., jt. ed. see Baker, Harry F.
Ridley, Ruth A. God's Love: Knowing God Through the Psalms. (Life Guide Bible Studies). 64p. 1998. pap. 4.99 (*0-8308-1085-4*, 1085) InterVarsity.
***Ridley, Ruth Ann.** Bach's Passion: The Life of Johann Sebastian Bach - A Novel. LC 98-89639. 400p. 1999. pap. 16.99 (*1-57921-170-4*, Pub. by WinePress Pub) BookWorld.
Ridley, RuthAnn. Every Marriage Is Different. (Tapestry Collection). 96p. (Orig.). 1993. pap. 6.50 (*1-56476-051-0*, 6-3051, Victor Bks) Chariot Victor.
Ridley, Sarah, jt. auth. see Merrill, Linda.
Ridley, W. N., jt. auth. see Picott, R.
***Ridley, Yvette.** God Sent Forty Motivational Poems for Lent. 92p. 2000. pap. 10.00 (*0-9678851-0-8*) Y Ridley.
Ridlington, Sandra S., jt. ed. see Good, James W.
Ridlington, Sandy, jt. ed. see Cone, Joseph.
Ridlon, Florence V. A Fallen Angel: The Status Insularity of the Female Alcoholic. LC 86-47992. 184p. 1988. 30.00 (*0-8387-5115-6*) Bucknell U Pr.
Ridlon, G. T. Early Settlers of Harrison, with an Historical Sketch of the Settlement, Progress & Present Condition of the Town. 138p. 1997. reprint ed. pap. 17.50 (*0-8328-5855-2*); reprint ed. lib. bdg. 27.50 (*0-8328-5854-4*) Higginson Bk Co.
— History of the Ancient Ryedales & Their Descendants in Normandy, Great Britain, Ireland, & America from 860 to 1884 Comprising the Genealogy & Biography, for about 1000 Years., of the Families of Riddell, Riddle, Ridlon, Ridley, Etc. (Illus.). 801p. 1994. pap. text 46.00 (*0-7884-0011-8*) Heritage Bk.
— History of the Ancient Ryedales & Their Descendants in Normandy, Great Britain, Ireland, & America from 860-1914, Comprising the Family of Riddell, Riddle, Ridlon, Ridley, Etc. (Illus.). 796p. 1989. reprint ed. pap. 119.00 (*0-8328-1025-8*); reprint ed. lib. bdg. 127.00 (*0-8328-1024-X*) Higginson Bk Co.
Ridlon, G. T., ed. see Gowdy, M. M.
Ridlon, Robert W. Understanding the Origin & Diversity of Life. (Illus.). 146p. 1998. pap. 10.00 (*1-57502-719-4*, PO2019) Morris Pubng.
Ridolfi, Carlo. The Life of Tintoretto. Enggass, Catherine & Enggass, Robert, trs. from ITA. LC 83-23829. 112p. 1984. 28.50 (*0-271-00369-3*) Pa St U Pr.
— The Life of Titian by Carlo Ridolfi. Bondanella, Julia C. et al, eds. Bondanella, Peter, tr. LC 95-38040. (Illus.). 168p. 1996. 45.00 (*0-271-01547-0*) Pa St U Pr.

An Asterisk (*) at the beginning of an entry indicates that the title is appearing for the first time.

Ridolfi, Ray. Shiatsu. (Tuttle Alternative Health Ser.). (Illus.). 128p. (Orig.). 1993. pap. 12.95 (*0-8048-1834-7*) Tuttle Pubng.

Ridolphi, Margaret, jt. auth. see Driscoll, Susan.

Ridomi, Marco. Lakota Healer. LC 99-11452. (Illus.). 96p. (Orig.). 1998. pap. 19.95 (*1-886449-66-X*, P966X, Pub. by Barrytown Ltd) Consort Bk Sales.

Ridout. All Round English, Bk. 1. Date not set. pap. text. write for info. (*0-582-18484-3*, Pub. by Addison-Wesley) Longman.

— All Round English, Bk. 2. 1975. pap. text. write for info. (*0-582-18485-1*, Pub. by Addison-Wesley) Longman.

— All Round English, Bk. 3. Date not set. pap. text. write for info. (*0-582-18486-X*, Pub. by Addison-Wesley) Longman.

— All Round English, Bk. 4. Date not set. pap. text. write for info. (*0-582-18487-8*, Pub. by Addison-Wesley) Longman.

— Your English, Bk. 1. Date not set. pap. text. write for info. (*0-582-18784-2*, Pub. by Addison-Wesley); pap. text, wbk. ed. write for info. (*0-582-18788-5*, Pub. by Addison-Wesley) Longman.

— Your English, Bk. 4. Date not set. pap. text. write for info. (*0-582-18787-7*, Pub. by Addison-Wesley); pap. text, wbk. ed. write for info. (*0-582-18791-5*, Pub. by Addison-Wesley) Longman.

Ridout, B. Timber Decay in Buildings: Conservation Approach to Treatment. (Illus.). 250p. 1997. 47.00 (*0-419-18820-7*, E & FN Spon) Routledge.

***Ridout, James W., IV.** Plantation Secrets. 376p. 2000. 23.95 (*0-9678838-0-6*) Pilot.

Ridout, Lucy, jt. auth. see Gray, Paul.

Ridout, Lucy, jt. auth. see Reader, Lesley.

Ridout, Orlando, jt. ed. see Miller, Marcia.

Ridpath. Norton's Star Atlas. 19th ed. 192p. (C). 1998. pap. text 31.88 (*0-582-35655-5*) Longman.

***Ridpath.** Nortons Star Atlas&Ref. 19th ed. (C). 1998. 62.81 (*0-582-31283-3*) Longman.

Ridpath, Ian. Collins Pocket Guide: Stars & Planets. 2nd ed. 384p. 1994. pap. 26.95 (*0-00-219979-3*, Pub. by HarpC) HarpC.

— The Facts on File Atlas of Stars & Planets: A Beginner's Guide to the Universe. LC 92-32463. (Illus.). 80p. (YA). (gr. 5 up). 1983. 18.95 (*0-8160-2926-1*) Facts on File.

***Ridpath, Ian.** Stars. (Collins Gem Ser.). (Illus.). 256p. 2000. pap. 7.95 (*0-00-472474-7*, Pub. by HarpC) Trafalgar.

Ridpath, Ian. Stars & Planets. LC 98-11961. (Eyewitness Handbooks Ser.). 224p. 1998. 29.95 (*0-7894-3560-8*) DK Pub Inc.

Ridpath, Ian, ed. A Dictionary of Astronomny. LC 97-14619. (Oxford Paperback Reference Ser.). (Illus.). 532p. 1998. pap. 14.95 (*0-19-211596-0*) OUP.

Ridpath, Ian & Murtagh, Terence. A Comet Called Halley. LC 85-18981. 48p. reprint ed. pap. 25.00 (*0-608-17097-6*, 2027290) Bks Demand.

***Ridpath, Ian & Tirion, Wil.** The Monthly Sky Guide. 5th ed. LC 99-21390. (Illus.). 64p. 1999. pap. 16.95 (*0-521-66771-2*) Cambridge U Pr.

Ridpath, Ian & Woodruff, John. Cambridge Astronomy Dictionary. LC 96-229055. (Illus.). 240p. (C). 1996. pap. 14.95 (*0-521-58991-6*); text 29.95 (*0-521-58007-2*) Cambridge U Pr.

Ridpath, John C. History of the United States: Prepared for Schools. LC 74-15750. (Popular Culture in America Ser.). 390p. 1975. reprint ed. 36.95 (*0-405-06384-9*) Ayer.

— World War I: A Comprehensive History. (Illus.). 530p. 1992. reprint ed. text 59.95 (*1-877767-80-8*) Univ Publng Hse.

Ridpath, John C., ed. see Taylor, William.

***Ridpath, Michael.** Final Venture. 2000. mass mkt. 6.99 (*0-451-19753-4*, Sig) NAL.

Ridpath, Michael. The Market Maker. 384p. 1999. mass mkt. 6.99 (*0-451-19752-6*) NAL.

Ridriguez, Michael W. Humidity Moon: Short Stories of the Vietnam War. 152p. 1998. pap. 15.00 (*1-877603-54-6*) Pecan Grove.

Ridsdale. Evidence Based on General Practice. 1995. pap. text 29.95 (*0-7020-1611-X*, W B Saunders Co) Harcrt Hlth Sci Grp.

Riduttori, Bonfiglioli, ed. Gear Motor Handbook. (Illus.). xxviii, 606p. 1996. 149.59 (*3-540-58988-0*) Spr-Verlag.

Ridwan, Ibn. Medieval Islamic Medicine. Dois, Michael W., tr. 200p. 1996. 39.95 (*0-614-21553-6*, 772) Kazi Pubns.

***Ridyard, Susan, ed.** Chivalry, Knighthood & War in the Middle Ages. 218p. 1999. pap. 20.00 (*0-918769-46-9*) Univ South Pr.

— Earthly Love, Spiritual Love, Love of the Saints. (Sewanee Mediaeval Studies: Vol. 8). 316p. 1999. pap. 20.00 (*0-918769-47-7*) Univ South Pr.

***Ridyard, Susan J., ed.** Death, Sickness & Health in Medieval Society & Culture. LC 82-50575. 248p. (C). 2000. pap. 20.00 (*0-918769-49-3*) Univ South Pr.

Ridyard, Susan J., jt. auth. see King, Edward B.

Ridzon, Leonard & Walters, Charles. The Carbon Cycle. LC 94-70735. 143p. 1994. pap. 15.00 (*0-911311-46-7*) Acres USA.

Ridzweski, Beate. Neuhebraische Grammatik Auf Grund Altester Handschriften und Inschriften. (Heidelberger Orientalistische Studien Ser.: Bd. 21). (GER.). XVIII, 201p. 1992. 44.80 (*3-631-43695-5*) P Lang Pubng.

Rie, K. T. & Portella, P. D. Low Cycle Fatigue & Elasto-Plastic Behaviour of Materials. LC 98-34273. 1998. 253.00 (*0-08-043326-X*) Elsevier.

Rie-mann, Bo, jt. ed. see Bjornsen, Peter K.

Riebel, Jim. Sanfords Guide to Nicodemus, His Pottery & His Art. Terhune, Maryanne & McGuire, Anne, eds. LC 98-206353. (Illus.). 100p. 1997. 25.00 (*0-9633531-4-4*) M S Sanford.

Riebel, John P. How to Write Reports, Papers, Theses, Articles. 2nd ed. LC 73-125893. xiii, 121p. 1972. write for info. (*0-668-02392-9*) Macmillan.

Rieben, Laurence & Perfetti, Charles A. Learning to Read: Basic Research & Its Implications. 224p. (C). 1991. text 49.95 (*0-8058-0564-8*) L Erlbaum Assocs.

***Rieben, Richard G.** Ethics for Earthlings, A Revolution in Values: How to Triumph over Morality. 210p. (YA). 2000. pap. 12.95 (*1-930187-03-3*) Berapa Pr Inter.

— Reciprocia - Natural Political Philosophy: Liberty, Law & Government - Common Sense for the New Millennium. LC 99-91476. 406p. 2000. pap. 24.95 (*1-930187-01-7*) Berapa Pr Inter.

Riebenstahl, Horst. The 1st Panzer Division, 1935-1945. LC 90-62980. (Illus.). 226p. 1991. 29.95 (*0-88740-283-6*) Schiffer.

— German Combat Engineers in World War II: A Photo Chronicle. LC 98-84757. (Illus.). 144p. 1998. 24.95 (*0-7643-0574-3*) Schiffer.

Riebenstahl, Horst & Scheibert, Horst. Panzer IV (Lang) LC 96-213586. (Illus.). 48p. 1996. pap. 9.95 (*0-7643-0094-6*) Schiffer.

Rieber, Alfred J. Merchants & Entrepreneurs in Imperial Russia. fac. ed. LC 80-28554. (Illus.). 490p. 1982. reprint ed. pap. 151.90 (*0-7837-8058-3*, 204781100008) Bks Demand.

— Merchants & Entrepreneurs in Imperial Russia. LC 80-28554. (Illus.). xxvi, 464p. (C). 1991. reprint ed. pap. 24.95 (*0-8078-4305-9*) U of NC Pr.

Rieber, Alfred J. & Rubinstein, Alvin Z., eds. Perestroika at the Crossroads. LC 90-8633. 400p. (C). (gr. 13). 1991. text 67.95 (*0-87332-741-1*) M E Sharpe.

Rieber, Alfred J. & Rubinstein, Alvin Z., eds. Perestroika at the Crossroads. LC 90-8633. 400p. (C). (gr. 13). 1991. pap. text 43.95 (*0-87332-742-X*) M E Sharpe.

Rieber, Hans, jt. auth. see Kuhn-Schnyder, Emil.

Rieber, J. E. & Lamb, V. R. Pogo User's Manual, General Aids to Graphic Programming. LC 70-131898. 191p. 1970. 25.00 (*0-403-04531-2*) Scholarly.

***Rieber, John N.** Books of Magic: Burning Girl. 192p. (YA). 2000. pap. text 17.95 (*1-56389-619-2*, Pub. by DC Comics) Time Warner.

Rieber, Lloyd J. Computers, Graphics, & Learning. 304p. (C). 1993. text. write for info. (*0-697-14894-7*) Brown & Benchmark.

Rieber, Ney. A Resource for the Study of Islam. 227p. 1993. pap. text 9.95 (*1-56794-045-5*, C-2326) Star Bible.

Rieber, R. W. The Psychology of War & Peace: The Image of the Enemy. (Illus.). 302p. (C). 1990. 52.50 (*0-306-43543-8*, Plenum Trade) Perseus Pubng.

Rieber, R. W., ed. Foundations of Neuropsychology: An Historical Reader. LC 78-72822. 1987. 32.50 (*0-404-60891-4*) AMS Pr.

— Handedness & Mental Abilities: An Historical Reader. LC 78-72823. 1987. 32.50 (*0-404-60892-2*) AMS Pr.

Rieber, R. W., jt. auth. see Vetter, Harold J.

Rieber, R. W., ed. see Goldstein, Kurt.

Rieber, Robert W. Manufacturing Social Distress: Psychopathy in Everyday Life. LC 96-52872. (PATH in Psychology Ser.). (Illus.). 238p. (C). 1928. 39.50 (*0-306-45346-0*, Plenum Trade) Perseus Pubng.

Rieber, Robert W., ed. Advances in Forensic Psychology & Psychiatry, Vol. 1. (Advances in Forensic Psych & Psychiatry Ser.). 196p. 1984. text 73.25 (*0-89391-191-7*) Ablx Pub.

Rieber, Robert W., ed. The Collected Works of L. S. Vygotsky Vol. 4: The History of the Development of Higher Mental Functions, Vol. 4. Hall, Marie J., tr. LC 87-7219. (Cognition & Language Ser.). (Illus.). 312p. (C). 1997. 59.50 (*0-306-45609-5*, Plenum Trade) Perseus Pubng.

Rieber, Robert W., ed. The Collected Works of L. S. Vygotsky Vol. 5: Child Psychology. (Cognition & Language Ser.). (Illus.). 380p. (C). 1998. 59.50 (*0-306-45707-5*, Kluwer Plenum) Kluwer Academic.

***Rieber, Robert W., ed.** The Collected Works of L. S. Vygotsky Vol. 6: Scientific Legacy. Hall, Marie J., tr. LC 87-7219. (Cognition & Language Ser.). 334p. 1999. 68.50 (*0-306-45913-2*, Kluwer Plenum) Kluwer Academic.

Rieber, Robert W., ed. Communication Disorders. LC 80-18394. (Applied Psycholinguistics & Communication Disorders Ser.). 366p. 1981. 65.00 (*0-306-40527-X*, Plenum Trade) Perseus Pubng.

— Dialogues on the Psychology of Language & Thought: Conversations with Noam Chomsky, Charles Osgood, Jean Piaget, Ulric Neisser, & Marcel Kinsbourne. LC 82-42850. (Cognition & Language Ser.). 174p. 1983. 42.50 (*0-306-41185-7*, Plenum Trade) Perseus Pubng.

— The Individual, Communication & Society: Essays in Memory of Gregory Bateson. (Studies in Emotion & Social Interaction). (Illus.). 357p. (C). 1990. text 69.95 (*0-521-26741-2*) Cambridge U Pr.

Rieber, Robert W. & Salzinger, Kurt D., eds. Psychology: Theoretical-Historical Perspectives. 2nd rev. ed. LC 98-28447. 509p. 1998. 49.95 (*1-55798-524-3*) Am Psychol.

Rieber, Robert W. & Vetter, Harold J., eds. The Psychological Foundations of Criminal Justice: Historical Perspectives on Forensic Psychology, Vol. 1. LC 78-18781. (Illus.). (C). 1978. 20.00 (*0-89444-009-8*); pap. 20.00 (*0-89444-012-8*) John Jay Pr.

Rieber, Robert W. & Wollock, Jeffrey, eds. The Collected Works of L. S. Vygotsky Vol. 3: Problems of the Theory & History of Psychology, Vol. 3. (Cognition & Language). (Illus.). 438p. (C). 1997. 59.50 (*0-306-45488-2*, Plenum Trade) Perseus Pubng.

Rieber, Robert W., jt. auth. see Mercier, Charles.

Rieber, Robert W., jt. ed. see Adler, Helmut E.

Rieber, Robert W., jt. ed. see Vetter, Harold J.

Riebesell, M., jt. ed. see Hausen, P.

Riebeth, Carolyn R. J. H. Sharp among the Crow Indians, 1902-1910: Personal Memories of His Life & Friendships on the Crow Reservation in Montana. LC 84-51553. (Montana & the West Ser.: Vol. 2). (Illus.). 178p. (Orig.). (C). 1985. 65.00 (*0-912783-01-X*) Upton & Sons.

Riebling, Barbara, jt. ed. see Easterlin, Nancy.

Riebold, Thomas W., et al. Large Animal Anesthesia: Principles & Techniques. LC 81-15609. 162p. reprint ed. pap. 50.30 (*0-7837-2174-9*, 204251200004) Bks Demand.

— Large Animal Anesthesia: Principles & Techniques. 2nd ed. LC 94-24471. (Illus.). 312p. 1995. text 46.95 (*0-8138-0774-3*) Iowa St U Pr.

Riebs, George E. Elkhart: A Pictorial History. 2nd ed. (Indiana Pictorial History Ser.). (Illus.). 1997. reprint ed. write for info. (*0-943963-17-6*) G Bradley.

Riebsame. Environmental Manual. 1999. pap. text 18.00 (*0-471-37191-2*) Wiley.

Riebsame, William E. & Robb, James J. Atlas of the New West: Portrait of a Changing Region. 192p. 1997. 35.00 (*0-393-04550-1*) Norton.

Riech, Emil. Hungarian Literature: An Historical & Critical Survey. 1977. lib. bdg. 69.95 (*0-8490-2028-X*) Gordon Pr.

Riechel, Rosemarie. Percival, the Homeless Parrot. (Illus.). 16p. (J). (gr. k-3). 1998. pap. 7.00 (*0-8059-4481-8*) Dorrance.

— Public Library Services to Business. LC 94-7018. 131p. 1994. pap. 45.00 (*1-55570-168-X*) Neal-Schuman.

— Reference Services for Children & Young Adults. LC 91-31973. xvi, 219p. (C). 1991. lib. bdg. 36.00 (*0-208-02290-2*, Lib Prof Pubns) Shoe String.

Riechel, Rosemarie, ed. Children's Nonfiction for Adult Information Needs: An Annotated Bibliography. LC 98-7141. 140p. 1998. lib. bdg. 30.00 (*0-208-02447-6*, Linnet Bks) Shoe String.

Riechenberger, jt. auth. see Regueiro.

Riechers, A. F. Complete Full Length Roof Framer. Date not set. lib. bdg. 15.95 (*0-8488-1765-6*) Amereon Ltd.

— Full Length Roof Framer. (Illus.). 116p. 1995. reprint ed. lib. bdg. 14.95 (*0-89966-907-7*) Buccaneer Bks.

Riechert, Richard. Effective DRE. 1998. pap. text 39.95 (*0-8294-1062-7*) Loyola Pr.

Riechmann, Donna. Team Performance Questionnaire: Facilitator's Guide. (Business Training Ser.). 48p. 1998. 24.95 (*0-7879-4164-6*) Jossey-Bass.

— Team Performance Questionnaire: Team Development Workbook. (Business Training Ser.). 24p. 1998. pap., wbk. ed. 12.95 (*0-7879-4163-8*) Jossey-Bass.

Rieck, Annette. Der Heilige Ivo von Helory: 1247-1303. (Rechtshistorische Reihe Ser.: Band 178). (GER., Illus.). 275p. 1998. 51.95 (*3-631-32907-5*) P Lang Pubng.

— The Oxford Color French Dictionary: French-English, English-French; Francais-Anglais, Anglais-Francais. rev. ed. 576p. 1998. pap. 7.95 (*0-19-860190-5*) OUP.

Rieck, Bill. A Guy Named Bill. (Illus.). 232p. (Orig.). 1995. pap. 7.50 (*0-9650330-3-1*) Worthwhile Pubs.

Rieck, Donald A., jt. auth. see Schmidt, William D.

Rieck, Horst. Before & After: Orthopedic Photography, Vol. 2. (Illus.). 120p. 1999. 45.00 (*3-929078-87-2*) G Kehayoff.

Rieck, Sondra & Rutledge, Carol. Move & Match Colors with Busy Bear. 22p. (J). (ps). 1990. 9.95 (*0-9634376-0-7*) Woodville Pr.

Rieck, Sondra & Stippel, Lori. Learn Basic Concepts with Cuddles Clown. 24p. (J). (ps). 1990. 9.95 (*0-9634082-0-8*) Woodville Pr.

***Rieck, William.** Teaching in Secondary Schools. 2nd ed. 290p. (C). 1999. per. 47.95 (*0-7872-6200-5*) Kendall-Hunt.

Riecke, Christiane. Feministische Filmtheorie in der Bundesrepublik Deutschland. Mohrmann, Renate, ed. (Studien Zum Theater, Film und Fernschen Ser.: Vol. 25). 116p. 1998. pap. 26.95 (*3-631-33160-6*) P Lang Pubng.

Riecken, E. O., et al, eds. Intestinal & Pancreatic Adaptation: Adaptational Response & Repair Mechanisms in the Entero Pancreatic System - Journal: Digestion, Vol. 46, Suppl. 2, 1990. (Illus.). vi, 478p. 1990. pap. 148.00 (*3-8055-5314-5*) S Karger.

— Malignancy & Chronic Inflammation in the Gastrointestinal Tract: New Concepts: Proceedings of the 81st Falk Symposium, Held in Berlin, Germany, November 3-5, 1994. LC 95-35759. 1995. text 73.50 (*0-7923-8889-5*) Kluwer Academic.

Riecken, Ernst-Otto. Mucosal Immunity in HIV Infection: Proceedings of the International Symposium, Berlin, June 6-7, 1997. Ullrich, Reiner et al, eds. (Pathobiology Ser.: Vol. 66, Nos. 3 & 4, 1998). (Illus.). 82p. 1998. pap. 55.75 (*3-8055-6739-1*) S Karger.

Riecken, Nancy. Today Is the Day. LC 95-23927. (Illus.). 32p. (J). (ps-3). 1996. 14.95 (*0-395-73917-9*) HM.

Riecken, Ted & Court, Deborah, eds. Dilemmas in Educational Change. 106p. (Orig.). (C). 1993. pap. text 17.95 (*1-55059-053-7*) Temeron Bks.

Riecker, G., ed. see Bohm, M. & Erdmann, Erland.

Riecker, R. E., ed. Rio Grande Rift: Tectonics & Magmatism. (Special Publications). (Illus.). 438p. 1979. 25.00 (*0-87590-214-6*) Am Geophysical.

Ried, Glenda E., jt. auth. see Gaylord, Gloria L.

Ried, J. L., ed. Pre-Harvest Sprouting in Cereals, 1992. LC 93-71502. (Illus.). xiv, 480p. 1993. pap. 99.00 (*0-913250-81-3*, BEF 2345) Am Assn Cereal Chem.

***Ried, Janine, Group, Inc. Staff.** Crisis Management: Planning & Media Relationships for the Design & Construction Industry. LC 99-88401. 250p. 2000. text 69.95 (*0-471-35419-8*) Wiley.

Ried, Sibylle & Beck-Managetta, Gertrud. Epilepsy, Pregnancy & the Child. 96p. (Orig.). 1996. pap. text 19.95 (*0-632-04164-1*) Blackwell Sci.

Riede, Anne M. BASIC Computer Literacy. (Illus.). 244p. 1984. 10.95 (*0-931983-01-0*) Basic Comp Lit.

— Coach's Clipboards. (Illus.). 306p. (Orig.). (J). (gr. 5-8). 1986. 10.95 (*0-931983-02-9*, BCLTXT-3) Basic Comp Lit.

Riede, David. Dante Gabriel Rossetti Revisited. (Twayne's English Authors Ser.). 160p. 1992. 32.00 (*0-8057-7027-5*, Twyne) Mac Lib Ref.

Riede, David C. & Baker, J. Wayne. Pagans, Christians & Jews. rev. ed. LC 73-166489. v, 149p. 1974. write for info. (*0-8403-0440-4*) Kendall-Hunt.

Riede, David G. Dante Gabriel Rossetti & the Limits of Victorian Vision. LC 82-22099. (Illus.). 288p. 1983. text 42.50 (*0-8014-1552-7*) Cornell U Pr.

— Matthew Arnold & the Betrayal of Language. LC 87-13693. (Virginia Victorian Studies). 253p. reprint ed. pap. 78.50 (*0-7837-4347-5*, 204405700012) Bks Demand.

— Oracles & Hierophants: Constructions of Romantic Authority. LC 91-55074. 288p. 1991. text 42.50 (*0-8014-2626-X*) Cornell U Pr.

Riedel, David T. Rhode Island Practice Vol. 3: Wills, Trusts & Gifts. 1993. ring bd., suppl. ed. 40.00 (*0-685-74272-5*, MICHIE) LEXIS Pub.

— Rhode Island Practice Vol. 3: Wills, Trusts & Gifts. 700p. 1994. boxed set 125.00 (*0-88063-724-2*, MICHIE) LEXIS Pub.

— Rhode Island Wills, Trusts & Gifts, Vol. 3. 2nd rev. ed. 700p. 1998. pap. 95.00 (*1-881758-42-7*) Tower Pub ME.

Riedel, Erwin. Allgemeine und Anorganische Chemie: Ein Lehrbuch fuer Studenten mit Nebenfach Chemie. 3rd ed. (GER., Illus.). x, 346p. 1985. pap. text 37.70 (*3-11-010269-2*) De Gruyter.

Riedel, F. Carl. Crime & Punishment in the Old French Romances. LC 39-8313. reprint ed. 20.00 (*0-404-05333-5*) AMS Pr.

***Riedel, Frank.** Imperfect Information & Investor Heterogeneity in the Bond Market. LC 99-53200. (Contributions to Economics Ser.). (Illus.). viii, 115p. 2000. pap. 56.00 (*3-7908-1247-1*, Pub. by Physica-Verlag) Spr-Verlag.

Riedel, H. Fracture at High Temperatures. (Materials Research & Engineering Ser.). (Illus.). 370p. 1987. 137.95 (*0-387-17271-8*) Spr-Verlag.

Riedel, Hermann. Originalmusik und Musikbearbeitung. 259p. 1971. 24.00 (*3-8059-0813-X*) Theodore Front.

Riedel, James. The Industrialization of Hong Kong. 168p. 1974. pap. text 33.50 (*3-16-335381-9*) Coronet Bks.

— Myths & Reality of External Constraints on Development. (Thames Essays Ser.: No. 47). 100p. 1987. text 19.95 (*0-566-05336-5*, Pub. by Avebry) Ashgate Pub Co.

***Riedel, Jaroslav, ed.** The Plastic People of the Universe. 185p. 1999. 17.00 (*80-86013-58-8*, Pub. by Mata) SPD-Small Pr Dist.

Riedel, Johannes, ed. see Regnart, Jacob, et al.

***Riedel, Marc.** Research Strategies for Secondary Data: A Perspective for Criminology & Criminal Justice. LC 99-6836. 1999. write for info. (*0-8039-5838-2*) Sage.

Riedel, Marc. Stranger Violence: A Theoretical Inquiry. LC 92-432. (Current Issues in Criminal Justice Ser.: Vol. 1). 208p. 1993. text 39.00 (*0-8153-0094-8*, SS753) Garland.

Riedel, Margit, jt. auth. see Kiefer, Klaus H.

Riedel-Michel, Madeleine. Spiritual Healing: As a Complement to the Art of Medicine. 216p. (C). 1988. 35.00 (*0-7212-0753-7*, Pub. by Regency Pr GBR) St Mut.

Riedel, Nicolai. Internationale Gunter-Kunert-Bibliographie. (Bibliographien Zur Deutschen Literature Ser.: Vol. 5). 584p. 1987. write for info. (*3-487-07950-X*) G Olms Pubs.

— Untersuchungen Zur Geschichte der Internationalen Rezeption Uwe Johnsons. (Germanistische Texte und Studien: Vol. 21). xiii, 672p. 1985. write for info. (*3-487-07624-1*) G Olms Pubs.

Riedel, Nicolai, jt. ed. see Gansel, Carsten.

***Riedel, Patty Hupfer.** Getting Started: 100 Icebreakers for Youth Gatherings. (Youth Ministry Resource Library Ser.). (Illus.). 97p. 1999. pap. 19.95 (*0-937997-59-5*) Hi-Time Pflaum.

***Riedel, Ralf, ed.** Handbook of Ceramic Hard Materials, 2 vols., Set. 1132p. 2000. 310.00 (*3-527-29972-6*) Wiley.

Riedel, Raymond T., ed. see Parker Hannifin Corporation Staff.

Riedel, Robert A. Hotel Air Quality Management. LC 95-18105. 1995. pap. write for info. (*0-86612-096-3*) Educ Inst Am Hotel.

Riedel, Sharon L., jt. auth. see Adelman, Leonard.

Riedel, Susan A., jt. auth. see Nelsson, James.

Riedel, T., jt. auth. see Sahoo, P. K.

Riedel, W. R., jt. ed. see Funnell, B. M.

Riedel, Walter E., ed. The Old World & the New: Literary Perspectives of German-Speaking Canadians. LC 85-135731. 199p. reprint ed. pap. 61.70 (*0-8357-6388-9*, 203574300096) Bks Demand.

Riedel, Werner, jt. ed. see Toft, Soren.

Riedel, Wolfgang. Homo Natura: Literarische Anthropoligie um 1900. (Quellen und Forschungen zur Literatur und Kulturgeschichte: Vol. 7(241)). (GER.). xxii, 327p. (C). 1996. lib. bdg. 87.40 (*3-11-015112-X*) De Gruyter.

Riedell, Edwin H. Babies by the Dozen: Free Home Delivery. LC 97-11656. 112p. (Orig.). 1998. pap. 10.95 (*1-56474-233-4*) Fithian Pr.

Rieder. Methods in Cell Biology. LC 99-172833. (C). 1998. text 99.95 (*0-12-544163-0*) Acad Pr.

Rieder, Grace, jt. auth. see Rieder, John.

Rieder, Helmut. Robust Asymptotic Statistics. LC 94-1070. (Series in Statistics). 416p. 1994. 65.95 (*0-387-94262-9*) Spr-Verlag.

R

R

Rieder, Helmut, ed. Robust Statistics, Data Analysis, & Computer Intensive Methods: In Honor of Peter Huber's 60th Birthday. LC 95-49239. (Lecture Notes in Statistics Ser.: Vol. 109). 429p. 1995. 54.95 (*0-387-94660-8*) Spr-Verlag.

Rieder, Ines, tr. see Galgoczi, Erzsebet.

Rieder, John. Wordsworth's Counterrevolutionary Turn: Community, Virtue, & Vision in the 1790s. LC 96-52719. 272p. 1997. 41.50 (*0-87413-610-5*) U Delaware Pr.

*__Rieder, John & Rieder, Grace.__ Jewels for His Crown. LC 99-98134. 111p. 2000. pap. 7.95 (*1-58597-015-8*) Leathers Pub.

Rieder, John & Smith, Larry R., eds. Changing Representation of Minorities East & West: Selected Conference Papers. (Literary Studies East & West: Vol. 11). 272p. 1996. pap. text 20.00 (*0-8248-1861-X*) Coll Lang Ling & Lit.

— Multiculturalism & Representation: Selected Essays. (Literary Studies East & West: Vol. 10). (Illus.). 248p. 1996. pap. text 20.00 (*0-8248-1860-1*) Coll Lang Ling & Lit.

Rieder, Jonathan. Canarsie: The Jews & Italians of Brooklyn Against Liberalism. LC 84-15660. (Illus.). 328p. 1985. 43.50 (*0-674-09360-7*); pap. 16.00 (*0-674-09361-5*) HUP.

Rieder, K. A., et al, eds. Nursing & Computers: An Anthology. (Computers & Medicine Ser.). (Illus.). 345p. 1989. 68.00 (*0-387-96937-3*) Spr-Verlag.

Rieder, Marge. Mission to Millboro. LC 93-6003. (Illus.). 208p. 1993. pap. 13.00 (*0-931892-59-7*) B Dolphin Pub.

— Return to Millboro: The Reincarnation Drama Continues. LC 95-41447. (Illus.). 256p. (Orig.). 1996. pap. 14.95 (*0-931892-28-7*) B Dolphin Pub.

Rieder, Ruth. Power Before the Throne. Sledge, Bethany, ed. (Illus.). 100p. 1999. pap. write for info. (*0-7392-0121-2*, PO3022) Morris Pubng.

*__Rieder, William.__ A Charmed Couple: The Art & Life of Walter & Matilda Gay. LC 00-26627. (Illus.). 240p. 2000. 45.00 (*0-8109-4561-4*, Pub. by Abrams) Time Warner.

Riederer, contrib. by. Parkinson's Disease: Experimental Models & Therapy. 350p. 1996. pap. 190.00 (*3-211-82749-8*) Spr-Verlag.

Riederer, Joe. Restoration in the Barren's: The Story of a Young Teen's Struggle to Rebuild His Life While Helping to Rebuild a Local Prairie. LC 99-62229. 144p. 1999. pap. 14.95 (*0-9671386-0-4*) Big Bluestem.

Riederer, P. Advances in Research on Neurodegeneration 5. LC 96-51004. (Journal of Neural Transmission). 1997. 113.00 (*3-211-82898-2*) Spr-Verlag.

Riederer, P. Advances in Research on Neurodegeneration 5. LC 96-51004. (Journal of Neural Transmission). 1997. 149.00 (*3-211-82933-4*) Spr-Verlag.

Riederer, P., et al, eds. Advances in Research on Neurodegeneration, I: Definitions, Clinical Features, & Morphology. (Advances in Research on Neurodegeneration Ser.). (Illus.). 280p. 1993. 109.50 (*0-8176-3631-5*) Birkhauser.

— Parkinson's Disease: From Clinical Aspects to Molecular Basis. (Key Topics in Brain Research Ser.). (Illus.). 240p. 1992. 91.95 (*0-387-82272-0*) Spr-Verlag.

Riederer, P. & Przuntek, H., eds. MAO-B-Inhibitor Selegiline (R-(-)-Deprenyl) (Journal of Neural Transmission: Suppl. 25). (Illus.). 220p. 1987. 69.95 (*0-387-82009-4*) Spr-Verlag.

Riederer, P. & Wesemann, W., eds. Pathobiology & Clinics of Basal Ganglia Disorders. (Journal of Nonprofit & Public Sector Marketing: Suppl. 38). (Illus.). 155p. 1993. 72.95 (*0-387-82425-1*) Spr-Verlag.

Riederer, P. & Youdim, M. B., eds. Amine Oxidases & Their Impact on Neurobiology. (Journal of Neural Transmission: Suppl. 32). xii, 491p. 1990. 192.00 (*0-387-82239-9*) Spr-Verlag.

— Iron in Central Nervous System Disorders: With Contributions by Numerous Experts. (Key Topics in Brain Research Ser.). (Illus.). 208p. 1994. 79.95 (*0-387-82520-7*) Spr-Verlag.

Riederer, P., et al. An Introduction to Neurotransmission in Health & Disease. (Illus.). 416p. 1990. 98.00 (*0-19-261431-2*) OUP.

Riederer, P., jt. auth. see Birkmayer, W.

Riederer, P., jt. ed. see Beckmann, H.

Riederer, Stephen J., ed. Medical Imaging. (Illus.). 144p. 1995. pap. 26.00 (*0-917853-57-1*, RB-65) Am Assn Physics.

Riedesel, C. Alan & Schwartz, James E. Teaching Elementary School Math. 6th ed. 517p. 1996. pap. text 75.00 (*0-205-15223-6*) Allyn.

Riedesel, C. Alan, et al. Essentials of Elementary Mathematics. 2nd ed. LC 98-17350. 232p. (gr. 2). 1998. pap. text 27.00 (*0-205-28750-6*) Allyn.

— Teaching Elementary School Mathematics. 6th ed. (C). 1996. pap., teacher ed. write for info. (*0-205-15638-X*, H5638-5) Allyn.

Riedesel, Frederick A. Letters & Journals Relating to the War of the American Revolution, & the Capture of the German Troops at Saratoga. LC 67-29035. (Eyewitness Accounts of the American Revolution Ser.). 1968. reprint ed. 19.95 (*0-405-01120-2*) Ayer.

Riedesel, Friedrich A. Memoirs & Letters & Journals of Major-General Riedesel, During His Residence in America, 2 vols., Set. Stone, William L., tr. LC 79-77109. (Eyewitness Accounts of the American Revolution Ser.). (Illus.). 1969. reprint ed. 34.95 (*0-405-01172-5*) Ayer.

— Memoirs & Letters & Journals of Major-General Riedesel, During His Residence in America, 2 vols., Vol. 1. Stone, William L., tr. LC 79-77109. (Eyewitness Accounts of the American Revolution Ser.). (Illus.). 1969. reprint ed. 15.95 (*0-405-01173-3*) Ayer.

— Memoirs & Letters & Journals of Major-General Riedesel, During His Residence in America, 2 vols., Vol. 2. Stone, William L., tr. LC 79-77109. (Eyewitness Accounts of the American Revolution Ser.). (Illus.). 1969. reprint ed. 15.95 (*0-405-01174-1*) Ayer.

Riediger, Carsten. Paul Wunderlich's Graphic Work, 1948-1982. (GER.). 456p. 1983. 150.00 (*1-55660-115-8*) A Wofsy Fine Arts.

Riedijk, Willem, ed. Appropriate Technology in Industrialized Countries. (Illus.). 372p. (Orig.). 1989. pap. 42.50 (*90-6275-284-5*, Pub. by Delft U Pr) Coronet Bks.

Riedinger, Edward A. Where in the World to Learn: A Guide to Library & Information Science for International Education Advisers. LC 94-42728. (Educators' Reference Collection). 176p. 1995. lib. bdg. 59.95 (*0-313-28703-1*, Greenwood Pr) Greenwood.

Riedinger, Jeffrey M. Agrarian Reform in the Philippines: Democratic Transitions & Redistributive Reform. LC 94-44005. 386p. 1995. 45.00 (*0-8047-2530-6*) Stanford U Pr.

Riedinger, Jeffrey M., jt. auth. see Prosterman, Roy L.

Riedinger-Johnson, Noel, ed. see Foster, Jeanne R.

Riedinger, Margaret, jt. auth. see Guidry, Mike.

Riedinger, Rudolf, ed. Acta Conciliorum Oecumenicorum Series Secunda, Pars Prima: Concilium Universale Constantinopolitanum Concilii Actiones I-IX. xiv, 513p. (C). 1990. pap. 400.00 (*3-11-011758-4*) De Gruyter.

— Acta Conciliorum Oecumenicorum Sub Auspiciis Academiae Scientiarum Bavaricae Edita Series Secunda, Volumen Secundum, Pars Tertia: Index Verborum Graecorum Quae un Actis Synodi Lateranensis a.649 et in Actis Concilii Oecumenici Sexti Continentur. (GRE & LAT.). viii, 258p. (C). 1995. pap. text 229.25 (*3-11-014538-3*) De Gruyter.

— Concilium Universale Constantinopolitanum Concilii Actiones XII-XVIII, Epistulae, Indices. (Acta Conciliorum Oecumenicorum Series Secunda, Volumen Secundum, Pars Secunda). (GRE & LAT.). xxxiv, 962p. (C). 1992. lib. bdg. 380.80 (*3-11-012935-3*) De Gruyter.

*__Riedinger, Susan Allin.__ Even Start: Facilitating Transitions to Kindergarten. 60p. 2000. reprint ed. pap. text 20.00 (*0-7881-8213-7*) DIANE Pub.

Riedjik, W. Technology for Liberation. 250p. (Orig.). 1986. pap. text 29.50 (*90-6275-244-6*, Pub. by Delft U Pr) Coronet Bks.

Riedl, A. & Winckler, G. Macroeconomic Policy Games. (Studies in Empirical Economics). (Illus.). xii, 123p. 1996. 70.00 (*3-7908-0857-1*) Spr-Verlag.

Riedl, Clare. Grosseteste: On Light. (Medieval Philosophical Texts in Translation Ser.). 1978. pap. 5.00 (*0-87462-201-8*) Marquette.

Riedl, Gerda. Modell Assisi. 344p. 1997. text 99.00 (*3-11-015814-0*) De Gruyter.

Riedl, Hermann. Zeichen und Herrlichkeit: Die Christologische Relevanz der Semeiaquelle in Den Kanawundern Joh 2, 1-11 und John 4, 46-54. (Regensburger Studien Zur Theologie Ser.: Bd. 51). (GER.). 362p. 1996. 63.95 (*3-631-30451-X*) P Lang Pubng.

Riedl, Joan. The Integrated Technology Classroom: Building Self-Reliant Learners. LC 94-42727. 272p. (C). 1995. pap. text 35.00 (*0-205-16157-X*, Longwood Div) Allyn.

Riedl, John C., tr. see Giles Of Rome.

Riedl, John O. University in Process. LC 65-19126. (Aquinas Lectures). 1965. 15.00 (*0-87462-130-5*) Marquette.

Riedl, Max J. Optical Design Fundamentals for Infrared Systems. LC 95-20201. (Tutorial Texts in Optical Engineering Ser.: Vol. TT 20). 1995. pap. 42.00 (*0-8194-1935-4*) SPIE.

Riedl, Richard. Die Industrie Osterreichs Wahrend des Krieges. (Wirtschafts-Und Sozialgeschichte des Weltkrieges (Osterreichische Und Ungarische Serie)). (GER.). 1932. 125.00 (*0-317-27476-7*) Elliots Bks.

Riedl, Rupert. Fauna und Flora des Mittelmeeres. Ein Systematischer Meeresfuehrer fuer Biologen und Naturfreunde (Fauna & Flora of the Mediteranean. A Systematic Guide for Biologists & Nature Lovers) 3rd expanded rev. ed. (Illus.). 836p. 1983. 117.00 (*3-8263-2613-X*, Pub. by Blckwell Wissenschafts) Balogh.

— Order in Living Organisms: A Systems Analysis of Evolution. Jefferies, R. P., tr. LC 77-28245. (Illus.). 333p. reprint ed. pap. 103.30 (*0-608-17654-0*, 203051300069) Bks Demand.

Riedlbauer, Jorg. Die Opern Von Tommaso Trajetta. (GER., Illus.). x, 586p. 1994. write for info. (*3-487-09798-2*) G Olms Pubs.

Riedler, Bill. Change & Become Yourself. rev. ed. 28p. 1968. reprint ed. 6.95 (*1-893404-04-8*) Global Relationship.

— Why I Couldn't Stay Married & How You Can. 26p. 1996. 7.95 (*1-893404-02-1*) Global Relationship.

Riedler, Isabella. Great Picture Puzzles. LC 98-199456. (Illus.). 96p. (J). 1998. pap. text 5.95 (*0-8069-9695-1*) Sterling.

Riedler, W., ed. Scientific Ballooning: Proceedings of a Symposium of the 21st Plenary Meeting of the Committee on Space Research, Innsbruck, Austria, May 29-June 10 1978. LC 78-41182. (Illus.). 226p. 1979. 76.00 (*0-08-023420-8*, Pergamon Pr) Elsevier.

Riedler, W. & Friedrich, M., eds. Scientific Ballooning II. (Advances in Space Research Ser.: Vol. 1, No. 11). (Illus.). 274p. 1981. pap. 42.00 (*0-08-028390-X*, Pergamon Pr) Elsevier.

Riedler, W. & Torkar, K. M. Scientific Ballooning. (Advances in Space Research Ser.). 122p. 1995. pap. 97.75 (*0-08-042653-0*, Pergamon Pr) Elsevier.

Riedler, W. & Torkar, K. M., eds. Balloon Technology & Observations: Proceedings of Symposium P3 of the COSPAR 29th Plenary Meeting Held in Washington, D. C., U. S. A., 28 August-5 September, 1992. (Advances in Space Research Ser.: Vol. 14). 220p. 1993. pap. 190.25 (*0-08-042473-2*, Pergamon Pr) Elsevier.

— Scientific Ballooning: Proceedings of Symposium 14 of the COSPAR Interdisciplinary Scientific Commission of the COSPAR 28th Plenary Meeting Held in The Hague, The Netherlands, 25 June-6 July, 1990. (Advances in Space Research Ser.: Vol. 13). 226p. 1992. pap. 165.00 (*0-08-042048-6*, Pergamon Pr) Elsevier.

— Scientific Ballooning: Proceedings of Symposium 7 of the COSPAR Twenty-Fifth Plenary Meeting Held in Graz, Austria, 25 June -7 July 1984, No. IV. (Illus.). 140p. 1985. pap. 54.00 (*0-08-032753-2*, Pub. by PPL) Elsevier.

Riedley, Mary P. And Where Were You, Dr. Spock? 1990. pap. 9.95 (*0-925928-08-9*) Tiny Thought.

*__Riedling, Ann Marlow.__ Reference Skills for the School Library Media Specialist: Tools & Tips. 152p. 2000. pap. 44.00 (*1-58683-000-7*) Linworth Pub.

Riedling, K. Ellipsometry for Industrial Applications. (Illus.). 99p. 1988. 44.95 (*0-387-82040-X*) Spr-Verlag.

Riedlinger, Thomas J., ed. see Moore, Julia A.

Riedlsperger, Max E. Lingering Shadow of Nazism. (East European Monographs: No. 42). 214p. 1978. text 54.50 (*0-914710-35-4*, Pub. by East Eur Monographs) Col U Pr.

Riedman, Marianne. The Pinnipeds: Seals, Sea Lions, & Walruses. (Illus.). 439p. 1991. reprint ed. pap. 27.50 (*0-520-06498-4*, Pub. by U CA Pr) Cal Prin Full Svc.

— Sea Otters. LC 90-6225. (Natural History Ser.). (Illus.). 80p. 1997. pap. 9.95 (*1-878244-03-5*) Monterey Bay Aquarium.

Riedman, Sarah R. Biological Clocks. LC 81-43873. (Illus.). 128p. (J). (gr. 5 up). 1982. 11.95 (*0-690-04182-9*); lib. bdg. 12.89 (*0-690-04183-7*) HarpC Child Bks.

Riedman, Sarah R. & Witham, Ross. Turtles: Extinction or Survival? LC 73-6188. (Illus.). 160p. (J). (gr. 5 up). 1963. 12.95 (*0-200-00126-4*) HarpC Child Bks.

Riedmann, jt. auth. see Lamanna.

Riedmann, Agnes. Science That Colonizes: A Critique of Fertility Studies in Africa. LC 92-26098. 256p. 1993. 49.95 (*1-56639-042-7*) Temple U Pr.

Riedmann, Agnes, jt. auth. see Lamanna.

Riedmann, Agnes, jt. auth. see Lamanna, Mary A.

Riedmatten, Henri De, see De Riedmatten, Henri.

Riedmiller, A., jt. auth. see Aas, G.

Riedner, Erwin. Token Creek. (Heritage Ser.). 1998. 25.00 (*1-878569-55-4*, Waubesa Pr); pap. 14.95 (*1-878569-57-0*, Waubesa Pr) Badger Bks Inc.

Riedner, Gunter. Die Kammer Fur Soziale Ordnung der Evangelischen Kirche in Deutschland: Uber Den Versuch, Aus Christlicher Verantwortung die Sozial- und Wirtschaftspolitik der Bundesrepublik Mitzugestalten. (Europaische Hochschulschriften Ser.: Bd. 510). (GER.). X, 483p. 1994. 61.95 (*3-631-47201-3*) P Lang Pubng.

Riedner, Ulrich & Rain, Patricia. Pea Soup Andersen's Scandinavian-American Cookbook. LC 88-70661. (Illus.). 180p. 1995. pap. 9.95 (*0-89087-523-5*) Celestial Arts.

Riedwyl, H., jt. auth. see Flury, Bernhard.

Riedwyl, Hans, jt. auth. see Henze, Norbert.

Rief, Linda. Seeking Diversity: Language Arts with Adolescents. LC 91-34800. 299p. (C). 1991. pap. text 24.00 (*0-435-08598-0*, 08598) Heinemann.

— Vision & Voice: Extending the Literacy Spectrum. LC 98-34180. 94p. 1999. pap. text. write for info. (*0-325-00097-2*) Heinemann.

Rief, Linda & Barbieri, Maureen, eds. All That Matters: What Is It We Value in School & Beyond? LC 95-6643. 256p. 1995. pap. text 24.00 (*0-435-08848-3*, 08848) Heinemann.

Rief, Linda, jt. ed. see Barbieri, Maureen.

Rief, Sandra. The ADD/ADHD Checklist: An Easy Reference for Parents & Teachers. LC 97-37991. 272p. (C). 1997. pap. text 11.95 (*0-13-762395-X*) P-H.

Rief, Sandra F. How to Reach & Teach ADD-ADHD Children: Practical Techniques & Strategies for Grades K-8. 256p. 1993. pap. text 27.95 (*0-87628-413-6*) Ctr Appl Res.

Rief, Sandra F. & Heimburge, Julie A. How to Reach & Teach All Children in the Inclusive Classroom: Ready-to-Use Strategies, Lessons, & Activities for Teaching Students with Diverse Learning Needs. LC 96-26633. 324p. 1996. pap. text 28.95 (*0-87628-385-7*); pap. text 28.50 (*0-87628-399-7*) Ctr Appl Res.

Riefe, Barbara. Against All Odds: The Lucy Scott Mitchum Story. 2000. mass mkt. 5.99 (*0-8125-5522-8*, Pub. by Forge NYC) St Martin.

— Amelia Dale Archer Story. LC 98-14629. 304p. (YA). (gr. 8 up). 1998. text 22.95 (*0-312-86077-3*) St Martin.

*__Riefe, Barbara.__ Barringer House. LC 99-54985. 2000. 26.95 (*0-7862-2337-5*) Five Star.

Riefe, Barbara. Desperate Crossing: The Jenny Sanders Pryor Story. LC 97-24762. 320p. 1997. text 22.95 (*0-312-86071-4*) St Martin.

— Desperate Crossings. 256p. 1999. mass mkt. 5.99 (*0-8125-5520-1*, Pub. by Forge NYC) St Martin.

— For Love of Two Eagles. 384p. 1996. mass mkt. write for info. (*0-614-05509-1*) Forge NYC.

— For Love of Two Eagles. 416p. 1996. mass mkt. 5.99 (*0-8125-3660-6*, Pub. by Tor Bks) St Martin.

— Mohawk Woman. 1996. mass mkt. 5.99 (*0-8125-4802-7*, Pub. by Tor Bks) St Martin.

*__Riefe, Barbara.__ Westward Hearts. 256p. 1999. mass mkt. 5.99 (*0-8125-5530-9*, Pub. by Forge NYC) St Martin.

Riefe, Barbara. The Woman Who Fell from the Sky. 384p. 1995. 5.99 (*0-8125-2377-6*) Forge NYC.

Riefenstahl, Leni. Leni Riefenstahl: A Memoir. LC 94-45089. 669p. 1995. pap. 16.00 (*0-312-11926-7*) St Martin.

Riefenstahl, Leni. People of Kau. (Illus.). 224p. 1997. text 40.00 (*0-312-16963-9*) St Martin.

*__Rieff, David.__ Going to Miami: Exiles, Tourists & Refugees in the New America. LC 99-53238. (Florida Sand Dollar Book Ser.). (Illus.). 248p. 1999. pap. 14.95 (*0-8130-1765-3*) U Press Fla.

Rieff, David. The New Europe. 2001. 25.00 (*0-684-80977-X*) Simon & Schuster.

— The Slaughterhouse: Bosnia & the Failure of the West. 240p. 1996. per. 12.00 (*0-684-81903-1*, Touchstone) S&S Trade Pap.

Rieff, David, ed. Humanities in Review, Vol. 1. LC 82-4589. 246p. reprint ed. pap. 70.20 (*0-608-15714-7*, 2031642) Bks Demand.

Rieff, David, jt. ed. see Gutman, Roy.

Rieff, Philip. The Feeling Intellect: Selected Writings. 430p. 1989. lib. bdg. 72.00 (*0-226-71641-4*) U Ch Pr.

— The Feeling Intellect: Selected Writings. 430p. 1990. pap. text 24.00 (*0-226-71642-2*) U Ch Pr.

— Fellow Teachers: Of Culture & Its Second Death, with a New Preface. LC 84-8910. (Illus.). xxviii, 244p. 1995. reprint ed. lib. bdg. 24.00 (*0-226-71643-0*) U Ch Pr.

— Fellow Teachers: Of Culture & Its Second Death, with a New Preface. LC 84-8910. (Illus.). xxviii, 270p. 1996. reprint ed. pap. 9.95 (*0-226-71644-9*) U Ch Pr.

— Freud: The Mind of the Moralist. 3rd ed. LC 78-69967. 464p. 1979. pap. text 25.00 (*0-226-71639-2*, P777) U Ch Pr.

— Triumph of the Therapeutic: Uses of Faith after Freud. xviii, 292p. (C). 1987. reprint ed. pap. text 25.00 (*0-226-71646-5*) U Ch Pr.

— Triumph of the Therapeutic Uses of Faith After Freud; With a New Preface. LC 86-24952. 1987. 13.95 (*0-226-71645-7*) U Ch Pr.

Rieff, Tana. The Road to Somewhere. (Illus.). 1992. mass mkt. 5.55 (*0-8224-7154-X*) Fearon Teacher Aids.

Rieffel, Alexis. The Role of the Paris Club in Managing Debt Problems. LC 85-23294. (Essays in International Finance Ser.: No. 161). 48p. 1985. pap. text 10.00 (*0-88165-068-4*) Princeton U Int Finan Econ.

Rieffel, Marc A. Deformation Quantization for Actions of Rd. LC 93-6114. (Memoirs Ser.: Vol. 106/506). 93p. 1993. pap. 29.00 (*0-8218-2575-5*, MEMO/106/506) Am Math.

Rieffel, Marc A., jt. auth. see Coburn, Lewis A.

Rieffler-Bonham, Phyllis M., tr. see Kaspar, Herbert & Shell, Bob.

Rieffler-Bonham, Phyllis M., tr. see Peterson, B. Moose & Huber, Michael.

Rieffler-Bonham, Phyllis M., tr. see Shell, Bob & Hennings, Heiner.

Rieffler-Bonham, Phyllis M., tr. see Shell, Bob & Hunecke, Richard.

*__Riefler, Erwin.__ Jahrbuch Fur Sozialmedizin, Sozialpsychiatrie, Medizinische Anthropologie Und Philosophische Reflexionen, Jahrgang 1: Teil I: Naturwissenschaftliche Beitrage. (Illus.). 132p. 1999. 28.95 (*3-631-31130-3*) P Lang Pubng.

Riefler, S., jt. auth. see Finn, J. L.

Riefling, Werner A., ed. see Urquhart, Sharon C.

Riefling, Werner A., ed. see Yarnell, Mark B.

Riefstahl, Elizabeth. Ancient Egyptian Glass & Glazes in the Brooklyn Museum. LC 68-57359. (Wilbour Monographs: No. 1). (Illus.). 1968. 15.00 (*0-913696-04-8*) Bklyn Mus.

*__Riegel & Moser.__ The Heart Failure Handbook. Orig. Title: An Interdisciplinary Approach to Improving Outcomes in Heart Failure. 2000. 79.00 (*0-8342-1644-2*) Aspen Pub.

Riegel, Anne, ed. see Mitchell, David & Livingston, Patricia H.

Riegel, Barbara J. & Ehrenreich, Donna. Psychological Aspects of Critical Care Nursing. 352p. 1989. 62.00 (*0-87189-799-7*, 89799) Aspen Pub.

Riegel, C. Fundamentals of Atmospheric Dynamics & Thermodynamics. 340p. 1992. text 59.00 (*9971-978-86-5*); pap. text 33.00 (*9971-978-87-3*) World Scientific Pub.

Riegel, Carl, jt. auth. see Dallas, Melissa.

Riegel, Carl D., jt. auth. see Reid, R. Dan.

Riegel, Carl R. & Reigle, James E. Riegell to Riggle: A Genealogy, 1390-1995. LC 96-67735. (Illus.). 664p. 1996. 49.50 (*0-89725-260-8*, 1740, Penobscot Pr) Picton Pr.

*__Riegel, David L.__ Understanding Loved Boys & Boylovers. 108p. 2000. pap. 9.95 (*0-9676997-0-3*) SafeHaven Found.

Riegel, E. B., compiled by. Gems of Thought for Fraternal Speakers in Poetry & Prose. rev. ed. viii, 183p. 1984. reprint ed. text 8.50 (*0-88053-309-9*, S-71) Macoy Pub.

Riegel, E. C. Flight from Inflation: The Monetary Alternative. MacCallum, Spencer H. & Morton, George, eds. LC 76-25381. (Illus.). 1978. 10.00 (*0-9600300-4-2*); pap. 6.00 (*0-9600300-8-5*) Heather Foun.

— The New Approach to Freedom. rev. ed. MacCallum, Spencer H., ed. LC 76-24987. (Illus.). 1976. 14.95 (*0-9600300-7-7*) Heather Foun.

Riegel, G. C. Case Hardening Large Gears with High Frequency Current. (Technical Papers: Vol. P237). (Illus.). 7p. 1943. pap. text 30.00 (*1-55589-344-9*) AGMA.

Riegel, Klaus F., ed. The Development of Dialectical Operations: Journal: Human Development, Vol. 18, Nos. 1 & 2. (Illus.). vii, 241p. 1976. 33.25 (*3-8055-2225-8*) S Karger.

Riegel, Klaus F. & Rosenwald, George C., eds. Structure & Transformation: Developmental & Historical Aspects. LC 75-15659. (Origins of Behavior Ser.: Vol. 3). 268p. reprint ed. pap. 83.10 (*0-608-30616-9*, 201647000004) Bks Demand.

An Asterisk (*) at the beginning of an entry indicates that the title is appearing for the first time.

Riegel, Martin P. California's Maritime Heritage. LC 87-62442. (California Heritage Ser.: Vol. I). (Illus.). 88p. (Orig.). (C). 1987. 15.00 (*0-944871-01-1*); pap. 9.00 (*0-944871-00-3*) Riegel Pub.

— Ghost Ports of the Pacific Vol. I: California. LC 89-90772. (Illus.). 52p. (Orig.). (YA). 1989. 11.00 (*0-944871-18-6*); pap. 4.95 (*0-944871-19-4*) Riegel Pub.

— Ghost Ports of the Pacific Vol. II: Oregon. LC 89-90772. (Illus.). 52p. (Orig.). (YA). 1989. 11.00 (*0-944871-20-8*); pap. 4.95 (*0-944871-21-6*) Riegel Pub.

— Ghost Ports of the Pacific Vol. III: Washington. LC 89-90772. (Illus.). 52p. (Orig.). (YA). 1989. 11.00 (*0-944871-22-4*); pap. 4.95 (*0-944871-23-2*) Riegel Pub.

— Historic Ships of California. LC 88-60111. (California Heritage Ser.: Vol. III). (Illus.). 105p. (Orig.). 1988. 16.00 (*0-944871-05-4*); pap. 9.95 (*0-944871-04-6*) Riegel Pub.

— Historic Ships of Hawaii. LC 88-92776. (Illus.). 44p. (Orig.). (YA). 1988. 11.00 (*0-944871-12-7*); pap. 4.95 (*0-944871-13-5*) Riegel Pub.

— Historic Ships of Oregon. LC 88-92771. (Illus.). 48p. (Orig.). (YA). 1988. 11.00 (*0-944871-14-3*); pap. 4.95 (*0-944871-15-1*) Riegel Pub.

— Historic Ships of Washington. LC 88-63929. (Illus.). 52p. (Orig.). (YA). 1988. 11.00 (*0-944871-16-X*); pap. 4.95 (*0-944871-17-8*) Riegel Pub.

— A Ship Lovers Guide to California. LC 88-60110. (California Heritage Ser.: Vol. II). (Illus.). 168p. (Orig.). 1988. 16.00 (*0-944871-03-8*); pap. 9.95 (*0-944871-02-X*) Riegel Pub.

— Ship Lovers Guide to the Pacific Northwest. (Illus.). 110p. (Orig.). 1990. 15.95 (*0-944871-30-5*); pap. 9.95 (*0-944871-31-3*) Riegel Pub.

— A Ship Lovers Guide to the Pacific Northwest, Vol. 1: Oregon. (Illus.). 52p. (Orig.). 1989. 11.00 (*0-944871-24-0*); pap. 4.95 (*0-944871-25-9*) Riegel Pub.

— A Ship Lovers Guide to the Pacific Northwest, Vol. 2: Washington. (Illus.). 52p. (Orig.). 1989. 11.00 (*0-944871-26-7*); pap. 4.95 (*0-944871-27-5*) Riegel Pub.

— The Ships of Catalina Island. LC 88-61279. (California Heritage Ser.: Vol. IV). (Illus.). 88p. (Orig.). 1988. 14.00 (*0-944871-07-0*); pap. 8.95 (*0-944871-06-2*) Riegel Pub.

— The Ships of the California Gold Rush. LC 88-92421. (Illus.). 48p. (Orig.). (YA). 1988. 11.00 (*0-944871-11-9*); pap. 4.75 (*0-685-24979-4*) Riegel Pub.

— The Ships of the Orange Coast. LC 88-92522. (Illus.). 40p. (Orig.). (YA). (gr. 9 up). 1988. pap. 4.75 (*0-944871-09-7*); lib. bdg. 11.00 (*0-944871-08-9*) Riegel Pub.

Riegel, Mayburt S. Early Ohioans Residences from the Land Grant Records. 1994. reprint ed. per. 9.00 (*0-935057-73-0*) OH Genealogical.

— Jackson. Descendants & Ancestors of William Jackson & His Wife Rachel Tomlinson Jackson. (Illus.). 159p. 1997. reprint ed. pap. 24.50 (*0-8328-9325-0*); reprint ed. lib. bdg. 34.50 (*0-8328-9324-2*) Higginson Bk Co.

Riegel, Oscar W. Mobilizing for Chaos: The Story of the New Propaganda. LC 72-4677. (International Propaganda & Communications Ser.). 231p. 1972. reprint ed. 20.95 (*0-405-04761-4*) Ayer.

Riegel, Robert E. American Feminists. LC 80-13163. (Illus.). 223p. 1980. reprint ed. lib. bdg. 65.00 (*0-313-22434-X*, RIAF, Greenwood Pr) Greenwood.

— American Women: A Story of Social Change. LC 78-99327. 376p. 1975. 35.00 (*0-8386-7615-4*) Fairleigh Dickinson.

— The Story of the Western Railroads: From 1852 Through the Reign of the Giants. LC 26-9772. xviii, 345p. 1964. pap. 11.95 (*0-8032-5159-9*, Bison Books) U of Nebr Pr.

Riegel, Udo. BMW Motorcycles: The New Generation. (Illus.). 128p. 1999. pap. 17.95 (*1-85532-933-6*, Pub. by Ospry) Motorbooks Intl.

Riegelman, Richard K. Minimizing Medical Mistakes. 1991. 32.95 (*0-316-74523-5*, Little Brwn Med Div) Lppncott W & W.

— Preventing Crime Package. 1988. 350.00 (*0-316-74522-7*, Aspen Law & Bus) Aspen Pub.

— Studying A Study & Testing A Test: How to Read the Health Science Literature. 4th ed. LC 99-56118. 356p. 1999. pap. text. write for info. (*0-7817-1860-0*) Lppncott W & W.

— Studying a Study & Testing a Test: How to Read the Medical Literature. 1981. pap. 19.50 (*0-316-74518-9*, Little Brwn Med Div) Lppncott W & W.

Riegelman, Richard K. & Hirsch, Robert P. Studying a Study & Testing a Test: How to Read the Health Science Literature. 3rd ed. 352p. 1996. pap. text 31.95 (*0-316-74521-9*, Little Brwn Med Div) Lppncott W & W.

Riegelman, Richard K. & Povar, Gail J. Putting Prevention into Practice: Problem Solving in Clinical Prevention. 432p. 1988. 32.95 (*0-316-74519-7*, Little Brwn Med Div) Lppncott W & W.

Riegelman, Richard K., jt. auth. see Hirsch, R.

Riegelman, Richard K., jt. auth. see Hirsch, R. P.

Riegelman, Richard K., jt. auth. see Schoth, S.

Rieger, Richard. An Inside Job: A Spiritual Approach to Finding Your Right Work. LC 98-41062. 155p. 1999. pap. 10.95 (*0-87159-227-4*) Unity Bks.

Rieger, Branimir, ed. Dionysus in Literature: Essays on Literary Madness. LC 93-74076. 237p. 1994. pap. 15.95 (*0-87972-650-4*) Bowling Green Univ Popular Press.

Rieger, Burkhard, jt. ed. see Schaeder, Burkhard.

Rieger, Daniel. Philosophical Thinkers: A Compendium of Primary Texts. 620p. (C). 1997. per. 68.95 (*0-7872-2680-7*) Kendall-Hunt.

Rieger, Erwin. Up Is the Mountain & Other Views. LC 73-89240. (Illus.). 200p. 1973. 12.95 (*0-8323-0235-X*) Binford Mort.

Rieger, Eva. Frau und Musik: Bibliographie, 1970-1996. (Studien und Materialien zur Musikwissenschaft Ser.: Bd. 14). (GER.). vi, 282p. 1999. 55.00 (*3-487-10320-6*, Pub. by G Olms Verlag) Lubrecht & Cramer.

Rieger, Fritz, jt. ed. see Wong-Rieger, Durhane.

Rieger, H. Multilingual Dictionary for Mechanics, Salesmen & Engineers in Metal-Working. (ENG, FRE, GER, ITA & POR.). 519p. 1981. 75.00 (*0-8288-0607-1*, M 15547) Fr & Eur.

Rieger, Heinz. The Alternating Current Circuit. LC TK1141. (Siemens Programmed Insturction Ser.: 13). 68p. reprint ed. pap. 30.00 (*0-8357-5330-1*, 205210300033) Bks Demand.

— Alternating Voltage & Current. LC TK1141. (Siemens Programmed Instruction Ser.: No. 12). 80p. reprint ed. pap. 30.00 (*0-8357-5331-X*, 205208900033) Bks Demand.

— The Magnetic Circuit. LC TK0454.4.M3R. (Siemens Programmed Instruction Ser.: 4). 69p. reprint ed. pap. 30.00 (*0-608-12360-9*, 205208100033) Bks Demand.

— Power & Energy in Alternating-Current Circuits. LC TK1141. (Siemens Programmed Instruction Ser.: No. 14). 68p. reprint ed. pap. 30.00 (*0-608-13139-3*, 205209000033) Bks Demand.

Rieger, James H., ed. see Shelley, Mary Wollstonecraft.

Rieger, James H., ed. & intro. see Shelley, Mary Wollstonecraft.

Rieger, Janusz A., ed. A Lexical Atlas of the Hutsul Dialects of the Ukrainian Language. LC 97-187357. (Illus.). 370p. 1996. pap. 39.95 (*83-86619-90-2*) Harvard Ukrainian.

***Rieger, Joerg.** God & the Excluded: Visions & Blindspots in Contemporary Theology. 2000. pap. 19.00 (*0-8006-3254-0*, Fortress Pr) Augsburg Fortress.

Rieger, Joerg. Remember the Poor: The Challenge to Theology in the Twenty-First Century. LC 98-42316. 240p. 1998. pap. 19.00 (*1-56338-256-3*) TPI PA.

***Rieger, Joerg.** Theology from the Belly of the Whale: A Frederick Herzog Reader. LC 99-26105. 400p. 1999. pap. 26.00 (*1-56338-265-2*) TPI PA.

Rieger, Joerg M., ed. Liberating the Future: God, Mammon & Theology. 160p. 1998. pap. 14.00 (*0-8006-3143-9*, 1-3143) Augsburg Fortress.

***Rieger, Loretta Metzger & Bajorek, Lagretta Metzger.** Children's Paper Premiums in American Advertising, 1890-1990s. LC 99-41588. 160p. 1999. pap. 29.95 (*0-7643-1012-7*) Schiffer.

Rieger, Martin M. Surfactant Encyclopedia. 2nd rev. ed. (Ingredient Resource Ser.). 52p. 1996. pap. 49.00 (*0-931710-49-9*) Allured Publishing Corp.

Rieger, Martin M., ed. Harry's Cosmeticology. 8th ed. (Illus.). 950p. 2000. 275.00 (*0-8206-0372-4*) Chem Pub.

— Surfactants in Cosmetics. LC 84-28718. (Surfactant Science Ser.: No. 16). (Illus.). 498p. reprint ed. pap. 154.40 (*0-7837-4775-6*, 204453000003) Bks Demand.

Rieger, Martin M., jt. ed. see Rhein, Linda D.

Rieger, Michael. Inkarnation: Christliches Heilsverstandnis Im Kontext Franzosischsprachiger Theologie der Menschwerdung. (Europaische Hochschulschriften Ser.: Reihe 23, Bd. 496). (GER.). 329p. 1993. 55.95 (*3-631-46589-0*) P Lang Pubng.

Rieger, N. F. Gear-Excited Torsional Vibrations of Machine Drive Systems. (Technical Papers: Vol. P109.20). (Illus.). 38p. 1968. pap. text 30.00 (*1-55589-373-2*) AGMA.

— Unbalance Response & Balancing of Flexible Rotors in Bearings. LC 72-92595. (Flexible Rotor-Bearing System Dynamics Ser.: Vol. 2). (Illus.). 33p. reprint ed. pap. 30.00 (*0-608-11694-7*, 201230500082) Bks Demand.

— Vibration Characteristics of Geared Transmission Systems. (Technical Papers: Vol. P109.14). (Illus.). 10p. 1964. pap. text 30.00 (*1-55589-372-4*) AGMA.

Rieger, N. F., ed. Rotordynamics Two Problems in Turbomachinery. (CISM International Centre for Mechanical Sciences Ser.: Vol. 297). (Illus.). viii, 586p. 1989. 111.95 (*0-387-82091-4*) Spr-Verlag.

Rieger, N. F. & Smalley, A. J. Dynamic Loads on Gear Teeth from Transient Shock. (Technical Papers: Vol. P229.14). (Illus.). 37p. 1970. pap. text 30.00 (*1-55589-281-7*) AGMA.

Rieger, Neville F., jt. ed. see Eshleman, Ronald L.

Rieger, Paula. Pocket Guide to Biotherapy. (Nursing Ser.). 200p. Date not set. pap. 31.25 (*0-7637-0543-8*) Jones & Bartlett.

Rieger, Paula T. Biotherapy: A Comprehensive Overview. (Nursing Ser.). 352p. 1995. 49.95 (*0-86720-707-8*) Jones & Bartlett.

***Rieger, Paula T.** Clinical Handbook for Biotherapy. (Illus.). 416p. (C). 1999. pap. text 33.75 (*0-7637-1152-7*) JB Pubns.

Rieger, Paula T. Clinical Handbook for Biotherapy. LC 98-42753. (Nursing Ser.). 18p. 1998. pap. 32.50 (*0-7637-0649-3*) Jones & Bartlett.

Rieger, Paula T., jt. auth. see Rumsey, Kimberly A.

Rieger, R. English & Spanish Dictionary of Genetics, Classical & Molecular Cytogenetics: Diccionario de Genetica y Citogenetica Clasica y Molecular. (ENG & SPA.). 538p. 1982. pap. 85.00 (*0-8288-0952-6*, S3212) Fr & Eur.

Rieger, R., et al. Glossary of Genetics: Classical & Molecular. 5th ed. (Illus.). vii, 546p. 1991. 69.95 (*0-387-52054-6*) Spr-Verlag.

— Glossary of Genetics & Cytogenetics. 4th rev. ed. LC 76-16183. (Illus.). 1976. pap. 25.00 (*3-540-07668-9*) Spr-Verlag.

Riegert, jt. auth. see Bruacher.

Riegert, Evelyn, ed. see Mohr-Stephens, Judy.

Riegert, Lillian, jt. auth. see Kunath, Anne.

***Riegert, Ray.** AAA Hidden Highways of Northern California. (Illus.). 2000. pap. 17.95 (*1-56975-236-2*) Ulysses Pr.

— Californie. (Travel Guide Ser.). (FRE.). 1998. pap. text 29.95 (*2-89464-046-3*) Edits Ulysse.

Riegert, Ray. Hidden Coast of California. 7th rev. ed. (Hidden Travel Ser.). (Illus.). 526p. 1999. pap. 17.95 (*1-56975-170-6*) Ulysses Pr.

— Hidden Hawaii. 10th ed. (Hidden Travel Ser.). (Illus.). 480p. 1998. reprint ed. pap. 17.95 (*1-56975-143-9*) Ulysses Pr.

***Riegert, Ray.** Hidden Hawaii. 11th ed. (Illus.). 2000. pap. 18.95 (*1-56975-218-4*) Ulysses Pr.

Riegert, Ray. Hidden Maui. 3rd rev. ed. (Hidden Travel Ser.). (Illus.). 224p. 1999. pap. 13.95 (*1-56975-195-1*, Pub. by Ulysses Pr) Publishers Group.

— Hidden Oahu. 2nd rev. ed. (Hidden Travel Ser.). (Illus.). 192p. 1999. pap. 13.95 (*1-56975-196-X*, Pub. by Ulysses Pr) Publishers Group.

— Hidden San Francisco & Northern California. 8th rev. ed. (Hidden Travel Guides Ser.). (Illus.). 520p. 1998. pap. 17.95 (*1-56975-129-3*) Ulysses Pr.

***Riegert, Ray.** Hidden San Francisco & Northern California. 9th rev. ed. (Hidden Travel Ser.). (Illus.). 520p. 2000. pap. 18.95 (*1-56975-207-9*, Pub. by Ulysses Pr) Publishers Group.

— Hidden Southern California. 7th rev. ed. (Hidden Travel Ser.). (Illus.). 560p. 2000. pap. 17.95 (*1-56975-206-0*, Pub. by Ulysses Pr) Publishers Group.

Riegert, Ray, et al. Hidden New England: The Adventurer's Guide LC 90-70261. 548 p. 1990. 13.95 (*0-86190-361-7*) S Asia.

Riegert, Ray, jt. auth. see Dart, John.

Riegert, Ray, jt. auth. see Harris, Richard.

Riegert, Ray, jt. ed. see Borg, Marcus.

Riegert, Ray, ed. see Hock, Ronald F.

Riegert, Ray, ed. see Vayda, William.

Riegert, Ray, tr. see Borg, Marcus & Powelson, Mark, eds.

Riegger, Hal. The Camas Prairie: Idaho's Railroad on Stilts. Pacific Fast Mail Staff, ed. (Illus.). 160p. 1986. 32.50 (*0-915713-13-6*) Pac Fast Mail.

Riegger, Michael H. Management for Results: A "How to" Workbook for Improving the Management of Your Veterinary Practice. 200p. 1992. pap. 59.95 (*0-929870-06-9*) Advanstar Commns.

— More Management for Results: A "How to" Workbook for Improving the Management of Your Veterinary Practice. 300p. 1995. pap. 59.95 (*0-929870-32-8*) Advanstar Commns.

Riegl, Alois. The Group Portraiture of Holland. Kain, Evelyn M., tr. from GER. LC 99-26062. (Texts & Documents Ser.). 448p. 1999. pap. 55.00 (*0-89236-548-X*, Pub. by J P Getty Trust) OUP.

— Problems of Style: Foundations for a History of Ornament. Kain, Evelyn, tr. (Illus.). 384p. 1993. text 57.50 (*0-691-04087-7*, Pub. by Princeton U Pr) Cal Prin Full Svc.

Riegle, Rod, jt. auth. see Rhodes, Dent M.

Riegle, Tim. Collected Readings in Science & Technology. 236p. (C). 1997. per. 36.95 (*0-7872-4461-9*, 41446101) Kendall-Hunt.

***Riegler, Alex, et al.** Understanding Representation in the Cognitive Sciences: Does Representation Need Reality? LC 99-86377. 320p. 2000. 125.00 (*0-306-46286-9*, Kluwer Plenum) Kluwer Academic.

Riegler, Gordon A. The Socialization of the New England Clergy Eighteen Hundred to Eighteen Sixty. LC 79-13027. (Perspectives in American History Ser.: No. 37). 187p. 1979. reprint ed. lib. bdg. 35.00 (*0-87991-361-4*) Porcupine Pr.

Riegler, Guenter R. & Blandford, Roger D., eds. The Galactic Center: AIP Conference Proceedings, No. 83, California Institute of Technology, Jan. 7-8, 1982. LC 82-71635. 216p. 1982. 30.25 (*0-88318-182-7*) Am Inst Physics.

Riehecky, Janet. Alosaurio (Allosaurus) LC 88-1693. (Libros Sobre Dinosaurios! Ser.). (SPA., Illus.). 32p. (J). (gr. k-4). 1994. lib. bdg. 21.36 (*1-56766-134-3*) Childs World.

— Anatosaurio (Anatosaurus) (Libros Sobre Dinosaurios! Ser.).Tr. of Anatosaurus. (SPA., Illus.). 32p. (J). (gr. k-4). 1994. lib. bdg. 21.36 (*1-56766-141-6*) Childs World.

— Anquilosaurio (Ankylosaurus) (Libros Sobre Dinosaurios! Ser.). (SPA., Illus.) 32p. (J). (gr. k-4). 1994. lib. bdg. 21.36 (*1-56766-126-2*) Childs World.

— Apatosaurio (Apatosaurus) LC 88-1694. (Libros Sobre Dinosaurios! Ser.). (SPA., Illus.). 32p. (J). (gr. k-4). 1994. lib. bdg. 21.36 (*1-56766-131-9*) Childs World.

— Baryonix (Baryonyx) (Libros Sobre Dinosaurios! Ser.). (SPA., Illus.). 32p. (J). (gr. k-4). 1994. lib. bdg. 21.36 (*1-56766-132-7*) Childs World.

— Braquiosaurio (Brachiosaurus) LC 89-22069. (Libros Sobre Dinosaurios! Ser.). (SPA., Illus.). 32p. (J). (gr. k-4). 1994. lib. bdg. 21.36 (*1-56766-135-1*) Childs World.

— The Child's World of Carefulness. LC 96-39558. (Child's World of Values Ser.). (Illus.). 24p. (J). (ps-2). 1997. lib. bdg. 18.50 (*1-56766-394-X*) Childs World.

— China. LC 98-21142. (Ticket to Ser.). 48p. (J). (gr. k-2). 1999. lib. bdg. 22.60 (*1-57505-140-0*, Carolrhoda) Lerner Pub.

— China. LC 98-6100. (Globe-Trotters Club Ser.). 48p. (J). (gr. 3-5). 1999. lib. bdg. 22.60 (*1-57505-115-X*, Carolrhoda) Lerner Pub.

— Cinco de Mayo. LC 93-13249. (Circle the Year with Holidays Ser.). (Illus.). 32p. (J). (ps-2). 1994. pap. 3.95 (*0-516-40681-7*) Childrens.

— Coelofisis (Coelophysis) (Libros Sobre Dinosaurios! Ser.). (SPA., Illus.). 32p. (J). (gr. k-4). 1994. lib. bdg. 21.36 (*1-56766-136-X*) Childs World.

— Compsognatus (Compsognathus) (Libros Sobre Dinosaurios! Ser.). (SPA., Illus.). 32p. (J). (gr. k-4). 1994. lib. bdg. 21.36 (*1-56766-133-5*) Childs World.

— Deinonichus (Deinonychus) (Libros Sobre Dinosaurios! Ser.). (SPA., Illus.). 32p. (J). (gr. k-4). 1994. lib. bdg. 21.36 (*1-56766-127-0*) Childs World.

— Descubriendo Dinosaurios (Discovering Dinosaurs) (Libros Sobre Dinosaurios! Ser.). (SPA., Illus.). 32p. (J). (gr. k-4). 1994. lib. bdg. 21.36 (*1-56766-137-8*) Childs World.

— Dinosaur Relatives. (Dinosaurs Bks.). (Illus.). 32p. (J). (gr. k-4). 1991. lib. bdg. 21.36 (*0-89565-626-4*) Childs World.

— Diplodoco (Diplodocus) (Libros Sobre Dinosaurios! Ser.). (SPA., Illus.). 32p. (J). (gr. k-4). 1994. lib. bdg. 21.36 (*1-56766-140-8*) Childs World.

— Estegosaurio (Stegosaurus) (Libros Sobre Dinosaurios! Ser.). (SPA., Illus.). 32p. (J). (gr. k-4). 1994. lib. bdg. 21.36 (*1-56766-124-6*) Childs World.

***Riehecky, Janet.** Greece. (Countries of the World Ser.). 24p. (J). (ps-3). 2000. lib. bdg. 15.93 (*0-7368-0628-8*, Bridgestone Bks) Capstone Pr.

Riehecky, Janet. Hipsilofodonte (Hypsilophodon) (Libros Sobre Dinosaurios! Ser.). (SPA., Illus.). 32p. (J). (gr. k-4). 1994. lib. bdg. 21.36 (*1-56766-128-9*) Childs World.

— Iguanodonte (Iguanodon) LC 89-15850. (Libros Sobre Dinosaurios! Ser.). (SPA., Illus.). 32p. (J). (gr. k-4). 1994. lib. bdg. 21.36 (*1-56766-143-2*) Childs World.

— Kwanzaa. LC 93-17076. (Circle the Year with Holidays Ser.). (Illus.). 32p. (J). (ps-2). 1993. pap. 3.95 (*0-516-40686-8*) Childrens.

— Mayasauria (Maiasaura) LC 89-22076. (Libros Sobre Dinosaurios! Ser.). (SPA., Illus.). 32p. (J). (gr. k-4). 1994. lib. bdg. 21.36 (*1-56766-147-5*) Childs World.

— The Mystery of the Dragon in the Dungeon Vol. 3: The Red Door Detective Club. (Red Door Detective Club Ser.: Bk. 3). (Illus.). 100p. (J). (gr. 3-6). 1999. lib. bdg. 12.95 (*1-56674-089-4*) Forest Hse.

— The Mystery of the Missing Money. (Illus.). 120p. (J). (gr. 3-6). 1996. pap. 6.95 (*1-56674-701-5*) Forest Hse.

— The Mystery of the Missing Money. LC 94-928. (Red Door Detective Club Ser.: Bk. 1). (Illus.). 120p. (J). (gr. 3-6). 1996. lib. bdg. 12.95 (*1-56674-087-8*) Forest Hse.

— The Mystery of the UFO. LC 94-929. (Red Door Detective Club Ser.: Bk. 2). (Illus.). 128p. (J). (gr. 3-6). 1996. lib. bdg. 12.95 (*1-56674-088-6*) Forest Hse.

— Oviraptor. (Libros Sobre Dinosaurios! Ser.). (SPA., Illus.). 32p. (J). (gr. k-4). 1994. lib. bdg. 21.36 (*1-56766-146-7*) Childs World.

— Pachycephalosaurus. (Dinosaurs Bks.). (Illus.). 32p. (J). (gr. k-4). 1991. lib. bdg. 21.36 (*0-89565-632-9*) Childs World.

— Paquicefalosaurio (Pachycephalosaurus) (Libros Sobre Dinosaurios! Ser.). (SPA., Illus.). 32p. (J). (gr. k-4). 1994. lib. bdg. 21.36 (*1-56766-129-7*) Childs World.

— Parasaurolophus. (Dinosaurs Bks.). (Illus.). 32p. (J). (gr. k-4). 1991. lib. bdg. 21.36 (*0-89565-633-7*) Childs World.

— Parasaurolophus. (Libros Sobre Dinosaurios! Ser.). (SPA., Illus.). 32p. (J). (gr. k-4). 1994. lib. bdg. 21.36 (*1-56766-130-0*) Childs World.

— Parientes de los Dinosaurios. (Libros Sobre Dinosaurios! Ser.). (SPA., Illus.). 32p. (J). (gr. k-4). 1994. lib. bdg. 21.36 (*1-56766-125-4*) Childs World.

— Protoceratops. (Dinosaurs Bks.). (Illus.). 32p. (J). (gr. k-4). 1990. lib. bdg. 21.36 (*0-89565-634-5*) Childs World.

— Protoceratops. (Libros Sobre Dinosaurios! Ser.). (SPA., Illus.). 32p. (J). (gr. k-4). 1994. lib. bdg. 21.36 (*1-56766-144-0*) Childs World.

— The Red Door Detective Club Mysteries, 4 vols., Set. (Illus.). (J). (gr. 3-6). Date not set. lib. bdg. 51.80 (*1-56674-900-X*) Forest Hse.

— Saltasaurio (Saltasaurus) (Libros Sobre Dinosaurios! Ser.). (SPA., Illus.). 32p. (J). (gr. k-4). 1994. lib. bdg. 21.36 (*1-56766-138-6*) Childs World.

— Stegosaurus. LC 88-15347. (Dinosaurs Bks.). (Illus.). 32p. (J). (gr. k-4). 1987. lib. bdg. 21.36 (*0-89565-385-0*) Childs World.

***Riehecky, Janet.** Sweden. LC 00-24191. (Countries of the World Ser.). (Illus.). 24p. (J). (ps-3). 2000. lib. bdg. 15.93 (*0-7368-0629-6*, Bridgestone Bks) Capstone Pr.

Riehecky, Janet. Thank-You. LC 88-16840. (Manners Matter Ser.). (Illus.). 32p. (J). (ps-2). 1988. lib. bdg. 18.50 (*0-89565-387-7*) Childs World.

— Tiranosaurio (Tyrannosaurus) LC 88-1692. (Libros Sobre Dinosaurios! Ser.). (SPA., Illus.). 32p. (J). (gr. k-4). 1994. lib. bdg. 21.36 (*1-56766-123-8*) Childs World.

— Triceratops. LC 88-508. (Dinosaurs Bks.). (Illus.). 32p. (J). (gr. k-4). 1988. lib. bdg. 21.36 (*0-89565-422-9*) Childs World.

— Triceratops. LC 88-508. (Libros Sobre Dinosaurios! Ser.). (SPA., Illus.). 32p. (J). (gr. k-4). 1994. lib. bdg. 21.36 (*1-56766-122-X*) Childs World.

— Troodon. (Dinosaurs Bks.). (Illus.). 32p. (J). (gr. k-4). 1991. lib. bdg. 21.36 (*0-89565-636-1*) Childs World.

— Troodonte (Troodon) (Libros Sobre Dinosaurios! Ser.). (SPA., Illus.). 32p. (J). (gr. k-4). 1994. lib. bdg. 21.36 (*1-56766-139-4*) Childs World.

Riehl, C. Luise. Family Nursing. (Illus.). 384p. (C). 1974. text 23.20 (*0-02-663760-X*) Glencoe.

Riehl, Dan. Desktop Guide to AS/400 Programmers' Tools. LC 94-48576. (News 3X/400 Technical Reference Ser.). 266p. (Orig.). 1995. pap. 34.95 (*1-882419-14-6*) News Four-Hund.

Riehl, Dan & Dick, Frederick, eds. NEWS 3X/400's Power Tools for the AS/400, Vol. II. 702p. 1995. pap. 129.00 incl. disk (*1-882419-08-1*) News Four-Hund.

Riehl, Dan & Ryan, Michael. TCP/IP & the AS/400. LC 98-58066. 350p. 1999. pap. 59.00 (*1-882419-72-3*) News Four-Hund.

Riehl, Dan, jt. auth. see Meyers, Bryan.

R

Riehl Foundation Staff. An Hour with Jesus, Vol. I. LC 94-65655. 120p. 1994. pap. 3.00 (*1-877678-27-9*) Queenship Pub.

Riehl, Heinz. Managing Risk in the Foreign Exchange, Money, & Derivative Markets. LC 98-6532. 300p. 1998. 60.00 (*0-07-052673-7*) McGraw.

Riehl, Heinz & Rodriguez, Rita M. Foreign Exchange & Money Markets: Managing Foreign & Domestic Currency Operations. 2nd ed. (Illus.). 416p. 1983. 50.00 (*0-07-052671-0*) McGraw.

Riehl, Herbert, et al. The Jet Stream. (Meteorological Monograph: Vol. 2, No. 7). (Illus.). 100p. (Orig.). 1954. pap. 17.00 (*0-933876-02-5*) Am Meteorological.

Riehl, Joseph. That Dangerous Figure: Charles Lamb & His Critics. LC 97-50538. (Literary Criticism in Perspective Ser.). 210p. 1998. 55.00 (*1-57113-040-3*) Camden Hse.

Riehl, Nikolaus. Stalin's Captive: Nikolaus Riehl & the Soviet Race for the Bomb. Seitz, Frederick, ed. (History of Modern Chemical Sciences Ser.). (Illus.). 242p. 1995. 34.95 (*0-8412-3310-1*) Am Chemical.

Riehl, Rudiger & Baensch, Hans. Aquarium Atlas. (Illus.). 994p. 39.95 (*3-88244-050-3*, 16050) Tetra Pr.

Riehl, Rudiger & Baensch, Hans A. Aquarium Atlas, Vol. 2. (Illus.). 1216p. 49.95 (*1-56465-114-2*, 16821) Tetra Pr.

— Aquarium Atlas, Vol. 3. Fischer, Gero W. & Borrer, Shellie E., trs. LC 95-21997. (Illus.). 1100p. 1996. 59.95 (*1-56465-185-1*) Tetra Pr.

— Baensch Aquarium Atlas, Vol. 1. rev. ed. (Illus.). 992p. 1997. 44.95 (*1-890087-12-2*); pap. 24.95 (*1-890087-05-X*) Microcosm Ltd.

— Baensch Aquarium Atlas, Vol. 2. (Illus.). 1216p. 1997. 44.95 (*1-890087-13-0*); pap. 29.95 (*1-890087-06-8*) Microcosm Ltd.

— Baensch Aquarium Atlas, Vol. 3. (Illus.). 1104p. 1997. 44.95 (*1-890087-14-9*); pap. 29.95 (*1-890087-07-6*) Microcosm Ltd.

Riehl, Wilhelm H. The Natural History of the German People. Diephouse, David J., ed. & tr. by. from GER. LC 89-12900. (Studies in German Thought & History: Vol. 13). 392p. 1990. lib. bdg. 99.95 (*0-88946-789-7*) E Mellen.

Riehle Foundation Staff, ed. The Gold Book of Prayers. LC 88-61907. 96p. 1988. pap. 3.00 (*0-9618840-4-5*) Queenship Pub.

Riehle Foundation Staff, ed. see Barbaric, Slavko.

Riehle Foundation Staff, ed. see Joseph, Albert & Shamon, Mary.

Riehle Foundation Staff, ed. see Kuharski, Mary A.

Riehle Foundation Staff, ed. see Shamon, Albert.

Riehle Foundation Staff, ed. & photos by see Brown, Michael H.

Riehle, Ginger, ed. see Marlette, Jerry.

Riehle, Ginger, ed. see McLellan, David P. & Warrick, Bill.

Riehle, Mary C. & Ready, Dolores. Happy Together, 1977. rev. ed. 1985. 5.44 (*0-86683-110-X*) Harper SF.

Riehle, Wolfgang. Shakespeare, Plautus & the Humanist Tradition. (Illus.). 319p. 1991. 90.00 (*0-85991-305-8*) Boydell & Brewer.

Riehm. Entrepreneurship. 1992. mass mkt. 27.25 (*0-314-92885-5*) West Pub.

Riehm, C. R., jt. ed. see Hambleton, I.

Riehm, H., ed. Malignant Neoplasms in Childhood & Adolescence. (Monographs in Pediatrics: Vol. 18). (Illus.). viii, 396p. 1986. 130.50 (*3-8055-4206-2*) S Karger.

Riehm, Sarah. 50 Great Businesses for Teens. LC 97-70047. 260p. 1997. pap. 14.95 (*0-02-861337-6*, Arc) IDG Bks.

— 50 Great Businesses for Teens. (YA). (gr. 7 up). 1997. pap. 14.95 (*0-614-27603-9*) Macmillan USA.

Riehm, Sarah L. Entrepreneurship. Date not set. pap. text, teacher ed. 21.95 (*0-314-01131-5*) West Pub.

Riehn, Richard K. 1812: Napoleon's Russian Campaign. LC 90-26018. 525p. 1991. pap. 19.95 (*0-471-54302-0*) Wiley.

— French Imperial Army, 1813, 1814 & Waterloo. 1959. pap. 8.00 (*0-912364-01-7*) Imrie-Risley.

— French Infantry & Artillery, 1795-1812. 1963. pap. 5.00 (*0-912364-02-5*) Imrie-Risley.

Rieke, Alison. The Senses of Nonsense. LC 92-10292. 295p. 1992. text 26.95 (*0-87745-384-5*) U of Iowa Pr.

Rieke, Fred, et al. Spikes: Exploring the Neural Code. LC 95-46161. (Computational Neuroscience Ser.). (Illus.). 413p. 1996. 49.50 (*0-262-18174-6*, Bradford Bks) MIT Pr.

— Spikes: Exploring the Neural Code. (Computational Neuroscience Ser.). (Illus.). 395p. 1999. reprint ed. pap. 55.00 (*0-262-68108-0*, Bradford Bks) MIT Pr.

Rieke, G. H. Detection of Light: From the Ultraviolet to the Submillimeter. 358p. 1996. pap. text 39.95 (*0-521-57674-1*) Cambridge U Pr.

Rieke, Mark L., jt. ed. see Conn, Steven R.

Rieke, P. C., et al, eds. Materials Synthesis Utilizing Biological Processes Vol. 174: Materials Research Society Symposium Proceedings. 294p. 1990. text 17.50 (*1-55899-062-3*) Materials Res.

Rieke, Richard D. Argumentation & Critical Decision Making. 5th ed. 352p. (C). 2000. pap. text 52.00 (*0-321-05563-2*) Addson-Wesley Educ.

Rieke, Richard D. & Stutman, Randall K. Communication in Legal Advocacy. LC 89-16759. (Studies in Communication Processes). 255p. (C). 1992. pap. text 21.95 (*0-87249-681-3*) U of SC Pr.

Rieke, Susan. Small Indulgences. LC 89-17928. (Target Poetry Ser.). 64p. (Orig.). 1990. pap. 6.50 (*0-933532-72-5*) BkMk.

Riekehof, Lottie L. The Joy of Signing. 2nd ed. LC 86-80173. (Illus.). 352p. 1987. teacher ed. 21.99 (*0-88243-520-5*, 02-0520) Gospel Pub. Illustrating over 1,500 signs, the best-selling The Joy of Signing, Second Edition is one of the most comprehensive guides available for mastering the current signs used in English American Sign Language. Rather than simply providing isolated words, this manual encourages signing fluency through the placement of words within the context of sentence formation. Such developments include the difference between a statement, command & question when identical signs are used; pluralization; tense; ordinal numbers; & introduction of the use of classifiers. Also included in the manual are sections on the history of sign language & fingerspelling, the art of signing, language patterns of signs, an illustrated guide for fingerspelling & a detailed index of every sign included in the book. This bestseller combines with The Joy of Signing Puzzle Book (0-88243-676-7, $3.95) & The Joy of Signing Puzzle Book 2 (0-88243-538-8. $7.95) & enhances the learning process through constructive enjoyment. Written by Lottie L. Riekehof who has been Professor of Sign Communications at Gallaudet University, the world's only liberal arts college for the deaf. Now retired, she is engaged in activities involving deaf children. Order your copy of The Joy of Signing, Second Edition from your local bookstore or Gospel Publishing House, 1445 N. Boonville Ave., Springfield, MO 65802; 800-641-4310. ***Publisher Paid Annotation.***

— Talk to the Deaf: A Manual of Approximately 1,000 Signs Used by the Deaf of North America. LC 63-17975. (Illus.). 149p. (J). (gr. k up). 1963. teacher ed. 12.99 (*0-88243-612-0*, 02-0612) Gospel Pub.

Riekehof, Lottie L., jt. auth. see Hillebrand, Linda L.

Riekehof, Lottie L., jt. auth. see Hillebrand, Linda Lascelle.

Rieken, Bill. Adventures in UNIX Network Applications Programming. 464p. 1992. pap. 49.99 (*0-471-52858-7*) Wiley.

Rieken, Elizabeth, ed. see Malm, Kiyoko.

Rieker, Hans-Ulrich. The Yoga of Light: The Classic Esoteric Handbook of Kundalini Yoga. Becherer, Elsy, tr. LC 79-167868. (Illus.). 203p. 1996. pap. 14.95 (*0-913922-07-2*) Dawn Horse Pr.

Rieker, Patricia P. & Carmen, Elaine H., eds. The Gender Gap in Psychotherapy. LC 84-11511. (Illus.). 392p. (C). 1984. 90.00 (*0-306-41657-3*, Plenum Trade) Perseus Pubng.

Rieker, Yvonne. Kindheiten. (Haskala Ser.: Bd. 17). 163p. 1997. 63.00 (*3-487-10243-9*) G Olms Pubs.

Riekerk, Marion. How to Give Children an Emotional Head Start: Filipino Translation. 1998. pap. 2.00 (*1-885357-73-7*) Rational Isl.

— How to Give Children an Emotional Head Start: Norwegian Translation. (NOR.). 1996. pap. 2.00 (*1-885357-58-3*) Rational Isl.

Riekerk, Marjon. Como Dar A Los Ninos Una Ventaja Emocional: Spanish Translation. 1989. pap. 2.00 (*0-913937-37-1*) Rational Isl.

— How to Give Children an Emotional Head Start. Karlsen, Torill E., tr. (Illus.). 13p. Date not set. pap. 2.00 (*82-91816-27-1*) Rational Isl.

— How to Give Children an Emotional Head Start. 1988. pap. 2.00 (*0-913937-33-9*) Rational Isl.

— How to Give Children an Emotional Head Start. (RUS.). 1996. pap. 2.00 (*1-885357-37-0*); pap. 2.00 (*1-885357-40-0*) Rational Isl.

— How to Give Children an Emotional Head Start: Arabic Translation. 1992. pap. 2.00 (*0-913937-67-3*) Rational Isl.

Riekerk, Marjon. How to Give Children an Emotional Head Start: Greek Translation. 1997. pap. 2.00 (*1-885357-47-8*) Rational Isl.

Riekerk, Marjon. How to Give Children an Emotional Head Start: Italian Translation. 1995. pap. 2.00 (*1-885357-25-7*) Rational Isl.

Riekes, et al. Conflict, Courts & Trials. 3rd ed. 1991. pap. 29.00 (*0-314-47361-0*) Thomson Learn.

Riekes, Linda. Conflict Court Trials. 3rd ed. Date not set. pap. text, teacher ed. 21.95 (*0-314-93776-5*) West Pub.

— Juvenile Problems & Law. 2nd ed. Date not set. pap. text 26.75 (*0-8299-1025-5*) West Pub.

— Juvinile Responsibility. 3rd ed. 1989. mass mkt. 26.75 (*0-314-47363-7*) West Pub.

— Law Enforcement. 2nd ed. Date not set. pap. text, teacher ed. 21.95 (*0-314-91103-0*) West Pub.

— Law Enforcement. 2nd ed. 1991. mass mkt. 26.75 (*0-314-47362-9*) West Pub.

— Young Consumers. 2nd ed. Ackerly, Sally M., ed. (Law in Action Ser.). (Illus.). 124p. (J). (gr. 5-9). 1980. pap. text 26.75 (*0-8299-1021-2*); pap. text, teacher ed. 26.75 (*0-8299-1022-0*) West Pub.

Riekes, Linda & Ackerly, Sally M. Courts & Trials. Olsen, Harry, ed. (Law in Action Series, Lessons in Law for Young People). (Illus.). 165p. (gr. 5-9). 1980. pap. text, student ed. 26.75 (*0-8299-1027-1*) West Pub.

— Courts & Trials. 2nd ed. Olsen, Harry, ed. (Law in Action Series, Lessons in Law for Young People). (Illus.). 165p. (gr. 5-9). 1980. teacher ed. write for info. (*0-8299-1028-X*) West Pub.

— Juvenile Problems & Law. 2nd ed. (Law in Action Ser.). (Illus.). 133p. 1980. pap. text 26.75 (*0-8299-1026-3*) West Pub.

— Lawmaking. 2nd ed. (Law in Action Ser.). (Illus.). 142p. (J). (gr. 5-9). 1980. pap. text 26.75 (*0-8299-1023-9*); pap. text, teacher ed. 26.75 (*0-8299-1024-7*) West Pub.

Riekes, Linda, et al. Citizenship Through Sports & Law. 2nd ed. LC 94-32063. 1994. pap. write for info. (*0-314-40118-0*) West Pub.

— Citizenship Through Sports & Law. 2nd ed. LC 94-32063. 1996. mass mkt. 26.75 (*0-314-01180-3*) West Pub.

Rieks, Craig. Fields of Fire. 96p. (Orig.). (J). (gr. 6-9). 1997. pap. 8.95 (*0-931209-71-4*) Mid-Prairie Bks.

Riekse, Robert J. & Holstege, Henry. Growing Older in America. LC 95-81850. 548p. (C). 1996. 65.63 (*0-07-052742-3*) McGraw.

Riel, Arthur. Object-Oriented Design Through Heuristics. 400p. (C). 1996. text 44.95 (*0-201-63385-X*) Addison-Wesley.

Riel, Gerd A., et al, eds. Iohannes Scottus Eriugena: The Bible & Hermeneutics; Proceedings of the Ninth International Colloquium, June 1995. (Ancient & Medieval Philosophy Ser.: No. 1, XX). 408p. 1996. 87.50 (*90-6186-736-3*, Pub. by Leuven Univ) Coronet Bks.

Riel, Louis. The Queen vs Louis Riel. LC 73-91562. (Social History of Canada Ser.: No. 19). 419p. reprint ed. pap. 129.90 (*0-7837-0377-5*, 204069700019) Bks Demand.

Riel, Marquita, jt. auth. see Lowenthal, David.

Riel, Steven. How to Dream. (Amherst Writers & Artists Chapbook Ser.). 36p. (Orig.). 1993. pap. 8.00 (*0-941895-10-6*) Amherst Wri Art.

Riele, T. Te, see Te Riele, T.

Rieley, James B. Total Quality Management in Higher Education. 48p. (Orig.). (C). 1994. pap. text 25.00 (*0-7881-1293-7*) DIANE Pub.

Riello, Cheryl. Sculpting Dolls in Super Sculpey. Shields, Kim, ed. (Illus.). 80p. (Orig.). 1995. pap. text 14.95 (*1-879825-20-1*) Jones Publish.

Rielly, E. J. The Furrow's Edge. (Haiku Ser.: No. 19). (Orig.). 1987. pap. 3.50 (*1-55780-097-9*) Juniper Pr ME.

Rielly, Edward J. The Breaking of Glass Horses & Other Poems. 40p. 1988. pap. 4.50 (*0-9613465-9-0*) Great Elm.

Rielly, Edward J., ed. Approaches to Teaching Swift's Gulliver's Travels. LC 88-13148. (Approaches to Teaching World Literature Ser.: No. 18). ix, 148p. 1988. pap. 18.00 (*0-87352-512-4*, AP18P); lib. bdg. 37.50 (*0-87352-511-6*, AP18C) Modern Lang.

***Rielly, Robin L.** Mighty Midgets at War: The Saga of the LCS(L) Ships from Iwo Jima to Vietnam. (Illus.). 2000. pap. 18.95 (*1-55571-522-2*, Hellgate Pr) PSI Resch.

— The Secrets of Shotokan Karate. LC 99-41593. (Illus.). 244p. 2000. pap. 24.95 (*0-8048-3229-3*, Periplus Eds) Tuttle Pubng.

Riely, Elizabeth. The Chef's Companion. 2nd ed. (Culinary Arts Ser.). 224p. 1996. text 41.95 (*0-442-02248-4*, VNR) Wiley.

— The Chef's Companion: A Concise Dictionary of Culinary Terms. 2nd expanded rev. ed. (Culinary Arts Ser.). 336p. 1996. 49.95 (*0-471-28759-8*, VNR) Wiley.

— A Feast of Fruits. 352p. 1996. 15.00 (*0-02-861019-9*) Macmillan.

Riely, John & Pillsbury, Edmund P. Rowlandson Drawings from the Paul Mellon Collection. LC 77-85174. (Illus.). 93p. (Orig.). 1977. pap. 10.00 (*0-930606-05-1*) Yale Ctr Brit Art.

Riely, Phyllis E., jt. ed. see Gall, Lorraine S.

Riely, Sara J., ed. Connecting Arizona: The Natural Yellow Pages. (Illus.). 120p. (Orig.). 1989. pap. 3.69 (*0-685-29362-9*) Hampshire Group.

Rieman, Bruce E. & McIntyre, John D. Demographic & Habitat Requirements for Conservation of Bull Trout. (Illus.). 40p. 1997. reprint ed. 10.00 (*0-89904-912-5*, Cascade Geog Soc); reprint ed. pap. 5.00 (*0-89904-913-3*, Cascade Geog Soc) Crumb Elbow Pub.

Rieman, Timothy D. Shaker: The Art of Craftmanship: the Mount Lebanon Collection. LC 94-36405. 1995. pap. 24.95 (*0-88397-109-7*) Art Srvc Intl.

Rieman, Timothy D. & Burks, Jean M. The Complete Book of Shaker Furniture. LC 92-47357. (Illus.). 400p. 1993. 75.00 (*0-8109-3841-3*, Pub. by Abrams) Time Warner.

Rieman, W. & Walton, H. Ion Exchange in Analytical Chemistry. LC 74-105870. 1970. 138.00 (*0-08-015511-1*, Pub. by Pergamon Repr) Franklin.

Riemann. Riemann, Musiklexikon. (GER.). 108p. 1967. 350.00 (*0-8288-6690-2*, M-7602) Fr & Eur.

Riemann, jt. auth. see Cliver.

Riemann, Bernhard. Gesammelte Mathematische Werke, Wissenschaftlicher Nachlass & Nachtrage: Collected Papers. (GER.). 888p. 1990. 175.00 (*0-387-50033-2*) Spr-Verlag.

Riemann, Gottfried, ed. see Schinkel, Karl F.

Riemann, Hans & Bryan, Frank L., eds. Food-Borne Infections & Intoxication. 2nd ed. LC 79-14935. (Food Science & Technology Ser.). 1979. text 146.00 (*0-12-588360-9*) Acad Pr.

Riemann, Hugo. Dictionary of Music. LC 75-125060. (Music Ser.). 1970. reprint ed. lib. bdg. 95.00 (*0-306-70025-5*) Da Capo.

— Opern-Handbuch. (GER.). 862p. 1979. reprint ed. write for info. (*3-487-06823-0*) G Olms Pubs.

Riemann, Hugo, jt. auth. see Mickelsen, William C.

Riemann, Othon. Etudes Sur la Langue et la Grammaire de Tite-Live. 326p. 1974. reprint ed. write for info. (*3-487-05226-1*) G Olms Pubs.

Riemann-Reyher, Marie-Ursula, jt. ed. see Keisch, Claude.

***Riemenschneider, Tilman, et al.** Tilman Riemenschneider: Master Sculptor of the Late Middle Ages. LC 99-25450. 1999. write for info. (*0-89468-244-X*) Natl Gallery Art.

***Riemer, Andrea K.** Griechenland und Turkei im neuen Millennium. 2000. 35.95 (*3-631-34486-4*, Pub. by P Lang) P Lang Pubng.

Riemer, Andrea K. Die Turkei an der Schwelle Zum 21. Jahrhundert. (Europaische Hochschulschriften Ser.: Reihe 31, Vol. 358). (Illus.). 252p. 1998. pap. 45.95 (*3-631-30721-7*) P Lang Pubng.

Riemer, Andrew. The Habsburg Cafe. 1995. 22.50 (*0-8446-6867-2*) Peter Smith.

Riemer, David R. The Prisoners of Welfare: Liberating America's Poor from Unemployment & Low Wages. LC 88-3926. 219p. 1988. 57.95 (*0-275-92705-9*, C2705, Praeger Pubs) Greenwood.

Riemer, Donald N. Introduction to Freshwater Vegetation. rev. ed. LC 92-38624. 218p. (C). 1993. reprint ed. lib. bdg. 49.50 (*0-89464-820-9*) Krieger.

***Riemer, Frances Julia.** Working at the Margins: Moving off Welfare in America. (C). 2001. pap. text. write for info. (*0-7914-4926-2*) State U NY Pr.

— Working at the Margins: Moving off Welfare in America. (C). 2001. text. write for info. (*0-7914-4925-4*) State U NY Pr.

Riemer, Jack, ed. Jewish Insights on Death & Mourning. 400p. 1996. pap. 15.00 (*0-8052-1035-0*) Schocken.

Riemer, Jack & Stampfer, Nathaniel, eds. So That Your Values Live On: Ethical Wills & How to Prepare Them. 272p. 1993. pap. 17.95 (*1-879045-34-6*) Jewish Lights.

Riemer, James D. From Satire to Subversion: The Fantasies of James Branch Cabell, 38. LC 89-1903. (Contributions to the Study of Science Fiction & Fantasy Ser.: No. 38). 128p. 1989. 47.95 (*0-313-25569-5*, RNT, Greenwood Pr) Greenwood.

Riemer, Jeremiah, tr. see Shandley, Robert R.

Riemer, John J., ed. Cataloging & Classification Standards & Rules. LC 96-12747. (Cataloging & Classification Quarterly Ser.: Vol. 21, Nos. 3 & 4). 235p. (C). 1996. 34.95 (*1-56024-806-8*) Haworth Pr.

Riemer, Judith, jt. auth. see Dreifuss, Gustav.

Riemer, Neal. Creative Breakthroughs in Politics. LC 96-2201. 192p. 1996. 57.95 (*0-275-95595-8*, Praeger Pubs) Greenwood.

— Karl Marx & Prophetic Politics. LC 86-30242. 177p. 1987. 55.00 (*0-275-92543-9*, C2543, Praeger Pubs); pap. 12.95 (*0-275-92635-4*, B2635, Praeger Pubs) Greenwood.

***Riemer, Neal.** Protection Against Genocide: Mission Impossible? LC 99-46405. 208p. 2000. write for info. (*0-275-96515-5*, Praeger Pubs); pap. write for info. (*0-275-96516-3*, Praeger Pubs) Greenwood.

Riemer, Neal, ed. Let Justice Roll: Prophetic Challenges in Religion, Politics, & Society. (Religious Forces in the Modern Political World). 244p. (C). 1996. pap. text 25.95 (*0-8476-8193-9*); lib. bdg. 66.00 (*0-8476-8192-0*) Rowman.

Riemer, Neal & Simon, Douglas. The New World of Politics: An Introduction to Political Science. 4th ed. (Illus.). 488p. (C). 1997. pap. text 41.75 (*0-939693-41-0*) Collegiate Pr.

Riemer, Neal & Thompson, Kenneth, eds. New Thinking & Developments in International Politics: Opportunities & Dangers, Vol. III. (Miller Center Series on a World in Change). 206p. (C). 1991. pap. text 23.50 (*0-8191-8309-1*); lib. bdg. 46.00 (*0-8191-8308-3*) U Pr of Amer.

Riemer, Otto. Journal of a Trucker. (Illus.). 86p. (Orig.). 1995. pap. 4.95 (*0-9646505-0-9*) O Riemer.

Riemer, Pamela C., jt. auth. see Bennett, John P.

Riemer, Pierce & Mills, Steve. Ford Based Kit Cars. (Illus.). 29.95 (*0-85429-623-9*, F623, Pub. by GT Foulis) Haynes Manuals.

Riemer, Robert J., jt. auth. see Kim, Kwan S.

Riemer, Ruth, jt. auth. see Bloom, Leonard.

Riemer, Seth D. National Biases in French & English Drama. LC 90-44653. (Studies in Comparative Literature). 184p. 1990. reprint ed. 15.00 (*0-8240-5471-7*) Garland.

Riemer, Shirley J. The German Research Companion. LC 97-70445. (Illus.). 672p. (Orig.). 1997. pap. 29.95 (*0-9656761-4-5*) Lorelei Pr.

Riemer, Shirley J. The German Research Companion. 2nd rev. ed. (Orig.). pap. 28.00 (*0-9656761-0-2*) Lorelei Pr.

***Riemer, Willy.** After Postmodernism: Austrian Literature & Film in Transition. LC 00-29275. 2000. write for info. (*1-57241-091-4*) Ariadne CA.

Riemer, Willy, tr. see Schlag, Evelyn & Tomalin, Claire.

Riemersma, R. A. Essential Fatty Acids & Eicosanoids: Invited Papers from the Third International Congress. LC 98-49623. 448p. 1998. write for info. (*0-935315-96-9*, AOCS Press) Am Oil Chemists.

Riempp, Gerold. Wide Area Workflow Management: Creating Partnerships for the 21st Century. LC 98-3622. (Computer Supported Cooperative Work Ser.). 1998. pap. write for info. (*3-540-76243-4*) Spr-Verlag.

Riemsdijk, Henk Van, see Corver, Norbert & Van Riemsdijk, Henk, eds.

Riemsdyk, H. V., ed. see Borer, H.

Riemsdyk, H. Van, see Van Riemsdyk, H., ed.

Riemslag, Tom. Crack Growth in Polyethylene. 138p. 1997. pap. 49.50 (*90-407-1453-3*, Pub. by Delft U Pr) Coronet Bks.

Rien, T. A., et al. Population & Fishery Statistics for Largemouth Bass, Smallmouth Bass, & Black Crappie, & Limnology of Owyhee Reservoir, Oregon, 1992. 64p. 1998. reprint ed. 12.40 (*0-89904-861-7*, Cascade Geog Soc); reprint ed. pap. 7.40 (*0-89904-862-5*, Cascade Geog Soc) Crumb Elbow Pub.

Rienas, Sabine. Teamarbeit Als Ausgehandelte Ordnung: Qualitative Analyse Von Teamentwicklungsprozessen auf Drogenzugsstationen. (Europaische Hochschulschriften Ser.: Reihe 6, Vol. 607). 365p. 1998. pap. 56.95 (*3-631-32925-3*) P Lang Pubng.

An Asterisk (*) at the beginning of an entry indicates that the title is appearing for the first time.

Riencourt, Amaury De, see De Riencourt, Amaury.

***Riendeau, Renee.** Angels in Prayer. LC 99-91208. 1999. 25.00 (*0-7388-0670-6*); pap. 18.00 (*0-7388-0671-4*) Xlibris Corp.

***Riendeau, Roger.** A Brief History of Canada. (Illus.). 336p. 2000. pap. 19.95 (*1-55041-555-7*) Fitzhenry & W Ltd.

Riendeau, Russell. Thinking on Your Seat - For the Recruiting Professional: A Catalyst to Create Respect, Results & Revenue. Telingator, Sue, ed. (Illus.). 228p. (Orig.). 1996. pap. 44.95 (*0-9654631-0-9*) R Riendeau.

Rienecker, Fritz. Lexicon of the Bible: Lexikon Zur Bibel. 10th ed. (GER.). 968p. 1985. 95.00 (*0-8288-2311-1*, M7192) Fr & Eur.

Riener, R., jt. auth. see Quintern, J.

Rienhoff, O. & Schneider, B., eds. Expert Systems & Decision Support in Medicine. (Lecture Notes in Medical Informatics Ser.: Vol. 36). xii, 591p. 1988. pap. 103.00 (*0-387-50317-X*) Spr-Verlag.

Rienhoff, O., ed. see O'Moore, R. R., et al.

Rienitz, Andrea. Diccionari Catala-Alemany, Alemany-Catala. (CAT & GER.). 288p. 1990. pap. 11.95 (*0-7859-6036-8*, 8440461976) Fr & Eur.

Rienow, Nonie. Unbottled Scotch. 1987. pap. 10.95 (*0-940168-06-5*) Boxwood.

Rienstra, Ellen W., jt. auth. see Wilson, Callie C.

Rienstra, M. Howard, ed. Jesuit Letters from China, 1583-1584. LC 85-8539. (Illus.). 57p. 1986. reprint ed. pap. 30.00 (*0-608-00843-5*, 206163400010) Bks Demand.

Rienzi, Leonard P. Narcotics Trial Manual for New York State. 2000. ring bd. 25.95 (*0-930137-78-7*) Looseleaf Law.

Rienzo, John S., jt. auth. see Ebert, Robert R.

Rienzo, Patricia G. Nursing Care of the Person Who Smokes. 216p. 1992. 33.95 (*0-8261-7620-8*) Springer Pub.

Rienzo, Paul De, see De Rienzo, Paul.

Riepe, Dale. Objectivity & Subjectivism in the Philosophy of Science with Special Reference to India. 232p. 1986. 27.50 (*0-8364-1655-4*, Pub. by KP Bagchi) S Asia.

Riepe, Dale, ed. Asian Philosophy Today. xviii, 304p. 1981. text 147.00 (*0-677-15490-9*) Gordon & Breach.

Riepe, Dale, et al, eds. Philosophy & Revolutionary Theory, Vol. 1. (Philosophical Currents Ser.: Vol. 32). 253p. (Orig.). (C). 1989. pap. write for info. (*90-6032-278-9*) B R Gruner.

Riepe, Dale M. The Naturalistic Tradition in Indian Thought. LC 82-9185. 308p. 1982. reprint ed. lib. bdg. 65.00 (*0-313-23622-4*, RINA, Greenwood Pr) Greenwood.

***Riepe, Jack.** Politically Correct Cigar Smoking for Social Terrorists. unabridged ed. Reilly, John J. & Marsh, Leslie, eds. LC 99-93281. (Illus.). xi, 177p. 1999. pap. 14.95 (*0-9672987-0-9*, A-01) Croften & Stone Pubs.

Riepe, Mark W., jt. auth. see Lummer, Scott L.

Riepen, Magdalena R. De, see De Riepen, Magdalena R.

Rieper, Bernd & Witte, Thomas. Grundwissen Produktion: Produktions- & Kostentheorie 3., Uberarbeitete Auflage. (GER.). 132p. 1995. 12.95 (*3-631-48214-0*) P Lang Pubng.

Rieper, Olaf, jt. ed. see Toulemonde, Jacques.

Riepl, Wolfgang. Das Nachrichtenwesen des Altertums Mit Besonderer Rucksicht Auf die Romer. xiv, 478p. 1972. reprint ed. write for info. (*3-487-04218-5*) G Olms Pubs.

Rieppel, Oliver C. Fundamentals of Comparative Biology. 250p. 1988. 48.50 (*0-8176-1956-9*) Birkhauser.

— The Phylogeny of Anguinomorph Lizards. 88p. 1980. 55.50 (*0-8176-1224-6*) Birkhauser.

Rieppel, Olivier, jt. ed. see Grande, Lance.

Rier, David C. Guide Lotus Hal. (Illus.). 188p. 1987. pap. 19.95 (*0-201-16827-8*) Addison-Wesley.

Rier, David C. & Fine, Edmund S. Orchestrating 1-2-3: Notes for Advanced Users. LC 84-20436. 1985. pap. write for info. (*0-201-16901-0*) Addison-Wesley.

***Riera, Carme.** A Matter of Self-Esteem & Other Stories. Caminals-Heath, Roser, ed. Cashman, Holly, tr. from SPA. Orig. Title: Contra l'Amor en Companyia i Altres Relats. 160p. 2000. 21.95 (*0-8419-1411-7*) Holmes & Meier.

Riera, Carme. Mirror Images: Carma Riera's Joc de Miralls. De la Torre, Cristina, tr. from CAT. LC 93-9535. (Catalan Studies: Vol. 9).Tr. of Joc de Miralls. 182p. 1993. 29.95 (*0-8204-2077-8*) P Lang Pubng.

Riera, Carmen. Te Dejo el Mar. Cotoner, Luisa, tr. & intro. by. (Nueva Austral Ser.: Vol. 211). (SPA.). 1991. pap. text 24.95 (*84-239-7211-9*) Elliots Bks.

Riera, Emilio L., jt. auth. see Horvath, Juan.

***Riera, J. D. & Davenport, A. G., eds.** Wind Effects on Buildings & Structures: Proceedings of the Jubileum Conference on Wind Effects & Structures, Porto Alegre, Brazil, 25-29 May 1998. (Illus.). 500p. 1998. 79.00 (*90-5410-959-9*, Pub. by A A Balkema) Ashgate Pub Co.

Riera, Michael. Surviving High School. LC 96-45273. (Illus.). 160p. (J). (gr. 8-12). 1997. pap. 10.95 (*0-89087-825-0*) Celestial Arts.

— Uncommon Sense for Parents with Teenagers. 250p. 1995. pap. 14.00 (*0-89087-749-1*) Celestial Arts.

***Riera, Michael & Di Prisco, Joseph.** Field Guide to the American Teenager: A Parent's Companion: Appreciating the Teenager You Live With. 320p. 2000. text 25.00 (*0-7382-0267-3*, Pub. by Perseus Pubng) HarpC.

Riera-Ojeda, Oscar. The New American Apartment: Innovations in Residential Design & Construction: 30 Case Studies. LC 97-23273. (Illus.). 264p. 1997. 55.00 (*0-8230-3166-7*) Watsn-Guptill.

Rierden, Andi. The Farm: Life Inside a Women's Prison. LC 96-51511. (Illus.). 232p. 1997. pap. 16.95 (*1-55849-080-9*) U of Mass Pr.

***Ries.** Positioning. 20th anniversary ed. 1999. pap. 24.95 (*0-07-135916-8*) McGraw.

Ries, A. C., jt. ed. see Coward, M. P.

***Ries, Al.** The 11 Immutable Laws of Internet Branding. LC 99-86018. Orig. Title: Branding on the Net. 192p. 2000. 21.00 (*0-06-019621-1*, HarpBusn) HarpInfo.

— Focus: The Future of Your Company Depends on It. 1999. 14.00 (*0-06-662032-5*) HarpC.

Ries, Al. Focus: The Future of Your Company Depends on It. 1997. pap. 14.00 (*0-88730-863-5*, HarpBusn) HarpInfo.

***Ries, Al.** Focus: The Future of Your Company Depends on It. 304p. 2000. reprint ed. text 25.00 (*0-7881-6857-6*) DIANE Pub.

— Focus: The Future of Your Company Depends on It, Set. abr. ed. 1996. audio 18.00 (*0-694-51628-7*, CPN 2552) HarperAudio.

Ries, Al. Refocusing the Corporation. 1996. 25.00 (*0-614-15438-3*, HarpBusn) HarpInfo.

***Ries, Al.** 22 Immutable Laws of Branding. 1998. audio 12.00 (*0-694-52047-0*) HarperAudio.

— The 22 Immutable Laws of Marketing: Violate Them at Your Own Risk! 1999. pap. 13.00 (*0-06-662030-9*, HarpBusn) HarpInfo.

Ries, Al & Kinni, Theodore B. Future Focus: How 21 Companies Are Capturing 21st Century Success. 288p. 1998. write for info. (*1-900961-65-2*, Pub. by Capstone Pub NH) LPC Group.

Ries, Al & Ries, Laura. 22 Immutable Laws of Branding: How to Build a Product or Service into a World-Class Brand. LC 98-21892. (Illus.). 176p. 1998. 23.00 (*0-88730-937-2*, HarpBusn) HarpInfo.

***Ries, Al & Ries, Laura.** The 22 Immutable Laws of Branding: How to Build a Product or Service into a World-Class Brand. 1999. 23.00 (*0-06-662031-7*, HarpBusn) HarpInfo.

Ries, Al & Trout, Jack. Bottom-up Marketing. 240p. 1990. pap. 13.95 (*0-452-26418-9*, Plume) Dutton Plume.

Ries, Al & Trout, Jack. Bottom-Up Marketing. 1988. 9.95 incl. audio (*0-07-052734-2*) McGraw.

Ries, Al & Trout, Jack. Marketing Warfare. (Illus.). 216p. 1986. 24.95 (*0-07-052730-X*) McGraw.

— Marketing Warfare. 216p. 1997. pap. 12.95 (*0-07-052726-1*) McGraw.

— Positioning: The Battle for Your Mind. rev. ed. 1985. text 24.95 (*0-07-065264-3*) McGraw.

— Positioning: The Battle for Your Mind. rev. ed. 224p. 1987. mass mkt. 6.99 (*0-446-34794-9*, Pub. by Warner Bks) Little.

Ries, Al & Trout, Jack. The 22 Immutable Laws of Marketing: Ries,&Al. abr. ed. 1993. audio 12.00 (*1-55994-760-8*, CPN 1980, Pub. by HarperAudio) Lndmrk Audiobks.

Ries, Al & Trout, Jack. The 22 Immutable Laws of Marketing: Violate Them at Your Own Risk! LC 92-53334. 128p. 1993. 22.00 (*0-88730-592-X*, HarpBusn) HarpInfo.

— The 22 Immutable Laws of Marketing: Violate Them at Your Own Risk! LC 92-53334. (Illus.). 143p. 1994. reprint ed. pap. 14.00 (*0-88730-666-7*, HarpBusn) HarpInfo.

Ries, Andrew. Positioning. 1993. 4.99 (*0-446-77692-0*) Warner Bks.

Ries, Andrew, et al. Shortness of Breath: A Guide to Better Living & Breathing. 5th ed. LC 95-24648. (Illus.). 128p. (C). (gr. 13). 1995. pap. text 9.95 (*0-8151-7339-3*, 25929) Mosby Inc.

***Ries, Andrew L.** Shortness of Breath: A Guide to Better Living & Breathing. 6th ed. LC 00-40197. (Illus.). 2000. pap. write for info. (*0-323-01064-4*, Mosby) Harcrt Hlth Sci Grp.

Ries, Arthur. The Pulsar Mission. 228p. 1988. pap. 8.95 (*0-89697-306-9*) Intl Univ Pr.

Ries, Celeste R., jt. ed. see Prelinger, Richard.

Ries, Christian. Uberblick Ueber die Ackerunkrautvegetation Oesterreichs und Ihre Entwicklung In Neuerer Zeit. (Dissertationes Botanicae Ser.: Band 187). (GER., Illus.). iv, 188p. 1992. pap. 71.00 (*3-443-64099-0*, Pub. by Gebruder Borntraeger) Balogh.

***Ries, Ed.** Fishing Barges of California, 1921-1998. (Illus.). 104p. 2000. pap. 14.95 (*0-9679247-0-7*) Monterey.

Ries, Ed. Tales of the Golden Years of California Ocean Fishing, 1900-1950. LC 97-60739. (Illus.). 128p. 1997. 24.95 (*0-9657547-0-7*); pap. 14.95 (*0-9657547-1-5*) Frnds of LA.

Ries, Eric, ed. The Dog Did It: And Other Classroom Stories from Vocational Educators. 118p. (Orig.). 1998. pap. 6.95 (*0-89514-001-2*) ACTE.

Ries, Eric, ed. see Amundson, Kristen.

Ries, Eric, ed. see Busch, Julie A.

Ries, Eric, ed. see Davis, Scott & Hunts, Holly.

Ries, Eric, ed. see Kaufmann, Barbara A. & Wills, Joan L.

Ries, Eric, ed. see Packer, Arnold & Brainard, Scott.

Ries, Estelle H. The Ingenuity of Man. LC 75-8726. (Illus.). 333p. 1975. reprint ed. lib. bdg. 65.00 (*0-8371-8041-4*, RIIM, Greenwood Pr) Greenwood.

Ries, Frank W. The Dance Theatre of Jean Cocteau. LC 85-19078. (Theater & Dramatic Studies: No. 33). 260p. reprint ed. pap. 80.60 (*0-8357-1994-4*, 207066100015) Bks Demand.

Ries, Howard. Pocket Dictionary of Guitar Chords. 1965. pap. 2.95 (*0-934286-22-1*) Kenyon.

Ries, Joanne B. & Leukefeld, Carl G. The Research Funding Guidebook: Getting It, Managing It & Renewing It. LC 97-4829. 272p. 1997. 46.00 (*0-7619-0230-9*); pap. 21.95 (*0-7619-0231-7*) Sage.

Ries, Joanne B. & Leukefeld, Karl G. Applying for Research Funding: Getting Started & Being Funded. 252p. 1994. 45.00 (*0-8039-5364-X*); pap. 21.00 (*0-8039-5365-8*) Sage.

Ries, John C. The Management of Defence: Organization & Control of the United States Armed Services. LC 64-18122. 247p. reprint ed. pap. 76.60 (*0-608-30729-7*, 200466100045) Bks Demand.

Ries, Judith. Ed O'Kelley: The Man Who Murdered. LC 94-67428. (Illus.). 120p. (Orig.). 1995. pap. 12.95 (*0-934426-61-9*) NAPSAC Reprods.

Ries, Karl. Mom, What Is Peace? unabridged ed. (Illus.). 200p. 1997. pap. 15.00 (*0-9659514-0-5*) K Ries Bks.

Ries, Karl & Ring, Hans. The Legion Condor, 1936-1939: A History of the Luftwaffe in the Spanish Civil War. rev. ed. Johnston, David, tr. from GER. LC 91-62741. (Illus.). 288p. 1992. 37.50 (*0-88740-339-5*) Schiffer.

Ries, Laura, jt. auth. see Ries, Al.

Ries, Linda A. Guide to Photographs at the Pennsylvania State Archives. 229p. 1992. 9.95 (*0-89271-049-7*) Pa Hist & Mus.

Ries, Marcella L. I'll See You Through: Messages for the Journey. (Illus.). 52p. (Orig.). 1990. pap. 6.50 (*0-9624543-0-3*) HeartSong Pub.

Ries, Margaret, tr. see Daniel, Ute.

Ries, Nancy. Russian Talk: Culture & Conversation During Perestroika. LC 97-10136. (Illus.). 1996. text 39.95 (*0-8014-3385-1*); pap. text 16.95 (*0-8014-8416-2*) Cornell U Pr.

***Ries, Philippe.** Asian Storm: The Economic Crisis Examined. Starr, Peter, tr. LC 99-42135. 208p. 2000. 24.95 (*0-8048-3235-8*) Tuttle Pubng.

Ries, Raul A. Hear What the Spirit Is Saying: A Practical Approach to the Seven Churches of Revelation. LC 93-78422. 156p. (Orig.). 1993. pap. 6.95 (*0-9637117-0-9*) Logos Media.

Ries, Richard. Assessment & Treatment of Patients with Coexisting Mental Illness & Alcohol & Other Drug Abuse. (Illus.). 114p. (C). 1996. reprint ed. pap. text 35.00 (*0-7881-3388-8*) DIANE Pub.

— Building Your Perfect Bike: From Bare Frame to Personalized Superbike. LC 96-84655. (Illus.). 128p. 1997. pap. 17.95 (*0-933201-77-X*, Bicycle Bks) MBI Pubg.

Ries, Richard & Shepard, Dave. Mountain Bike! The Midwest. 2nd rev. ed. (America by Mountain Bike Ser.). (Illus.). 1999. pap. write for info. (*0-89732-306-8*) Menasha Ridge.

— Mountain Bike! The Midwest. 2nd rev. ed. (America by Mountain Bike Ser.). 400p. 1999. pap. 15.95 (*0-89732-282-7*) Menasha Ridge.

***Ries, Shauna.** Quality of Life. 2000. pap. write for info. (*0-688-17804-9*, Wm Morrow) Morrow Avon.

Ries, Tim C. Trumpets Are Sounding. 120p. 1997. mass mkt. 4.99 (*1-55197-317-0*) Partners Pubs Grp.

Riesbeck, Christopher K. & Schank, Roger C. Inside Case-Based Reasoning. 448p. 1989. 79.95 (*0-89859-767-6*) L Erlbaum Assocs.

Riesbeck, Christopher K., jt. auth. see Schank, Roger C.

Riesbeck, Christopher K., jt. ed. see Kolodner, J. L.

Riesch, Craig. U. S. M1 Carbines: Wartime Production. 3rd ed. (For Collectors Only Ser.). (Illus.). 132p. (Orig.). 1998. pap. 16.95 (*1-882391-23-3*) N Cape Pubns.

Riesch, Craig, jt. auth. see Poyer, Joe.

***Rieschick, Kurt.** Who Am I? 2001. 7.99 (*0-517-16227-X*) Crown Pub Group.

Rieschick, Kurt. Who Am I: Test Your Biography I.Q. LC 98-37773. (Illus.). 160p. 1999. pap. 8.95 (*0-8362-7873-9*) Andrews & McMeel.

Riesco, Laura. Ximena at the Crossroads. Berg, Mary G., tr. LC 98-12694. (Secret Weavers Ser.). 269p. 1998. pap. text 14.00 (*1-877727-80-6*, Pub. by White Pine) SPD-Small Pr Dist.

Riese, Alexander. Geographi Latini Minores. (GER.). xlviii, 175p. 1995. reprint ed. 60.00 (*3-487-05026-9*) G Olms Pubs.

Riese, Alexander, ed. Geographi Latini Minores. xlviii, 175p. 1964. reprint ed. write for info. (*0-318-71125-7*) G Olms Pubs.

Riese, Alexander, ed. see Varro, Terentius.

Riese, Erika, jt. auth. see Pfeiffer, Ehrenfried.

Riese, Hans P., jt. auth. see Krane, Susan.

Riese, Herthe. Heal the Hurt Child: An Approach Through Educational Therapy with Special Reference to the Extremely Deprived Negro Child. LC 62-19623. 639p. reprint ed. pap. 198.10 (*0-608-12118-5*, 202406400035) Bks Demand.

Riese, Randall. Her Name Is Barbra. Set. abr. ed. Kaye, Jocelyn, ed. 1994. 15.95 incl. audio (*1-882071-48-4*) B&B Audio.

— Her Name is Barbra: An Intimate Portrait of the Real Barbra Streisand. LC 93-2521. (Illus.). 448p. 1993. 22.50 (*1-55972-203-7*, Birch Ln Pr) Carol Pub Group.

Riese, Uta. Gerhard Merz Dresden. 1999. pap. text 15.95 (*3-7757-0814-6*) Gerd Hatje.

Rieseberg, Barbara H., jt. auth. see McKinney, Betty.

Riesebrodt, Martin. Pious Passion: The Emergence of Modern Fundamentalism in the United States & Iran. Reneau, Don, tr. from GER. LC 92-32233. (Comparative Studies in Religion & Society: Vol. 6). 1993. 48.00 (*0-520-07463-7*, Pub. by U CA Pr) Cal Prin Full Svc.

— Pious Passion: The Emergence of Modern Fundamentalism in the United States & Iran. (Comparative Studies in Religion & Society). 1998. pap. text 18.95 (*0-520-07464-5*, Pub. by U CA Pr) Cal Prin Full Svc.

Riesel, Hans. Prime Numbers & Computer Methods for Factorization. (Progress in Mathematics Ser.: No. 57). 1987. 62.50 (*0-8176-3291-3*) Birkhauser.

— Prime Numbers & Computer Methods for Factorization. 2nd ed. LC 94-27688. xvi, 464p. 1994. 69.50 (*0-8176-3743-5*) Birkhauser.

Rieselbach, Helen F. Conrad's Rebels: The Psychology of Revolution in the Novels from Nostromo to Victory. LC 84-23917. (Studies in Modern Literature: No. 42). 162p. reprint ed. pap. 50.30 (*0-8357-1600-7*, 207057200001) Bks Demand.

Rieselbach, Leroy N. Congressional Politics. 2nd ed. 500p. (C). 1997. pap. text 13.00 (*0-673-97649-1*) Addson-Wesley Educ.

— Congressional Reform: The Changing Modern Congress. 232p. 1993. pap. text 21.95 (*0-87187-838-0*) Congr Quarterly.

— Roots of Isolationism: Congressional Voting & Presidential Leadership in Foreign Policy. (Orig.). (C). 1966. write for info. (*0-672-51169-X*, Bobbs) Macmillan.

Rieselbach, Leroy N., ed. Legislative Reform. 272p. (C). 1978. pap. 15.00 (*0-918592-21-6*) Pol Studies.

— Legislative Reform: The Policy Impact. 272p. 1985. reprint ed. lib. bdg. 42.00 (*0-8191-5157-2*) U Pr of Amer.

Rieselbach, Leroy N., jt. auth. see Unekis, Joseph K.

Rieselbach, Richard E. & Garnick, Marc B., eds. Cancer & the Kidney. LC 81-8277. (Illus.). 949p. reprint ed. pap. 200.00 (*0-8357-7654-9*, 205698000096) Bks Demand.

Rieselman, Brian. Dream Girl. 1997. mass mkt. 5.99 (*0-312-96091-3*) St Martin.

Rieseman, Steve, jt. ed. see Divine, M. J.

Riesemann, Oskar Von, see Von Riesemann, Oskar.

Riesen, A. H. & Thompson, R. F. Advances in Psychobiology, Vol. 3. LC 70-178148. 509p. reprint ed. 157.80 (*0-8357-9831-3*, 201517700098) Bks Demand.

Riesen, Beat. Thomas Hardy's Minor Novels. (European University Studies: Anglo-Saxon Language & Literature: Ser. 14, Vol. 208). 152p. 1990. pap. 26.00 (*3-261-04194-3*) P Lang Pubng.

Riesen, Janet. Un Gato Grandioso. Peinado, Monica, ed. LC 96-84465. (Illus.). 32p. (J). (ps up). 1996. 19.95 (*0-9626993-3-0*); 24.95 incl. audio (*0-614-29476-2*) Armadillo Niche.

Riesen, Janet & Grall, Eloise. He's Your Father Now! Facts, Figures & Fantasies. LC 92-81067. (Illus.). 65p. (Orig.). 1992. pap. 5.95 (*0-9626993-2-2*) Armadillo Niche.

— Mama, Your Slip is Showing! A How-It-Is Prescription Guide for Caregivers on Aging. 36p. (Orig.). 1990. pap. 5.95 (*0-9626993-0-6*) Armadillo Niche.

Riesen, Janet, see Mancebo, pseud.

Riesenberg, Felix. Cape Horn. LC 94-11744. (Illus.). xvi, 500p. 1994. reprint ed. 39.95 (*1-881987-04-3*) Ox Bow.

— Pacific Ocean. LC 79-128300. (Essay Index Reprint Ser.). 1977. 23.95 (*0-8369-2125-9*) Ayer.

— Yankee Skippers to the Rescue. LC 78-93374. (Essay Index Reprint Ser.). 1977. 23.95 (*0-8369-1313-2*) Ayer.

Riesenberg-Malcolm, Ruth. Bearing Unbearable States of Mind. LC 98-39629. (New Library of Psychoanalysis Ser.). 1999. write for info. (*0-415-20518-2*); pap. 29.99 (*0-415-20519-0*) Routledge.

Riesenberg, Peter. Citizenship in the Western Tradition Plato to Rousseau. LC 91-45807. 348p. (C). 1994. pap. text 19.95 (*0-8078-4459-4*) U of NC Pr.

Riesenberg, Peter, jt. auth. see Mundy, John H.

Riesenberg, Peter, jt. ed. see Agresto, John.

Riesenberger, John R. Global Challenge: Building the New World Enterprise. 1994. 26.95 (*0-07-709002-0*) McGraw.

Riesener, Ingrid. Der Stamm 'Abad in Alten Testament. (Beiheft zur Zeitschrift fuer die Alttestamentliche Wissenschaft Ser.: Vol. 149). (C). 1979. 165.40 (*3-11-007260-2*) De Gruyter.

Riesenfeld, Stefan A. Creditors' Remedies & Debtors' Protection: Cases & Materials. 4th ed. (American Casebook Ser.). 514p. (C). 1986. reprint ed. 57.50 (*0-314-30130-5*) West Pub.

— Creditors' Remedies & Debtors' Protection, 1990 Supplement. 4th ed. (American Casebook Ser.). 92p. (C). 1990. pap. 14.50 (*0-314-76484-4*) West Pub.

Riesenfeld, Stefan A., ed. Parliamentary Participation in the Making & Operation of Treaties: A Comparative Study. LC 93-13382. (Current Legal Issues in International & Comparative Law Ser.). 612p. (C). 1994. lib. bdg. 221.00 (*0-7923-1735-1*) Kluwer Academic.

***Riesenfeld, Stefan A. & Carnegie Endowment for International Peace Staff.** Protection of Coastal Fisheries under International Law. LC 99-48873. (Carnegie Endowment for International Peace Monograph Ser.: No. 5). 308p. 2000. reprint ed. 47.50 (*1-57588-562-X*, 323940) W S Hein.

Riesenfeld, Stefan A., jt. ed. see Krueger, Robert B.

Riesenkampff, Alexander & Lehr, Stefan. European Cartel Law. Date not set. pap. 50.00 (*0-86640-062-1*) German Am Chamber.

Riesenman, Steve, jt. ed. see Divine, M. J.

Rieser, A., et al, eds. Environmental Decisionmaking in a Transboundary Region. (Lecture Notes on Coastal & Estuarine Studies: Vol. 20). xiii, 209p. 1987. pap. 40.00 (*0-387-96446-0*) Spr-Verlag.

Rieser, Allan. Boy Meets Family: Manuscript Edition. 1938. pap. 13.00 (*0-8222-0141-0*) Dramatists Play.

Rieser, H., jt. ed. see Petoefi, J. S.

Rieser, Max. Analysis of Poetic Thinking. Schueller, Herbert M., tr. LC 69-11535. (Criticism Monograph Ser.: No. 1). 170p. reprint ed. pap. 52.70 (*0-7837-3641-X*, 204350900009) Bks Demand.

Riesgo, Rodolfo. Cuba: El Movimiento Obrero y Su Entorno Socio-Politico. (Realidades Ser.). (SPA.). 250p. (Orig.). 1985. pap. 10.00 (*0-917049-02-0*) Saeta.

Riesman, David. Abundance for What. rev. ed. 696p. (C). 1993. pap. 32.95 (*1-56000-599-8*) Transaction Pubs.

— Constraint & Variety in American Education. LC 56-13482. (Landmark Edition Ser.). 175p. reprint ed. pap. 54.30 (*0-8357-2945-1*, 203920100011) Bks Demand.

— On Higher Education: The Academic Enterprise in an Era

R

R

of Rising Student Consumerism. LC 98-9622. (Foundations of Higher Education Ser.). 421p. 1998. pap. text 27.95 (*0-7658-0438-7*) Transaction Pubs.

— On Higher Education: The Academic Enterprise in an Era of Rising Student Consumerism. LC 80-8007. (Carnegie Council Ser.). 459p. reprint ed. pap. 142.30 (*0-8357-4690-9*, 205234500008) Bks Demand.

— Thorstein Veblen. rev. ed. 248p. (C). 1994. pap. 24.95 (*1-56000-776-1*) Transaction Pubs.

Riesman, David & Glazer, Nathan. Faces in the Crowd: Individual Studies in Character & Politics. Coser, Lewis A. & Powell, Walter W., eds. LC 79-7015. (Perennial Works in Sociology). 1980. reprint ed. lib. bdg. 59.95 (*0-405-12114-8*) Ayer.

Riesman, David, et al. Lonely Crowd: A Study of the Changing American Character. abr. ed. (Studies in National Policy: No. 3). (C). 1961. reprint ed. pap. 18.00 (*0-300-00193-2*, Y41) Yale U Pr.

Riesman, David, jt. auth. see Grant, Gerald.

Riesman, David, jt. auth. see Jencks, Christopher.

Riesman, David, jt. auth. see McLaughlin, Judith B.

Riesman, Paul. First Find Your Child a Good Mother: The Construction of Self in Two African Communities. LC 91-18209. (Illus.). 260p. (C). 1992. text 40.00 (*0-8135-1767-2*); pap. text 16.95 (*0-8135-1768-0*) Rutgers U Pr.

— Freedom in Fulani Social Life: An Introspective Ethnography. Fuller, Martha, tr. LC 98-11166. 297p. 1998. pap. text 16.00 (*0-226-71743-7*) U Ch Pr.

Riesner, Dieter, jt. auth. see Schweik, R. C.

Riesner, Dieter, jt. auth. see Schweik, Robert C.

Riess, Curt, ed. They Were There. LC 70-134127. (Essay Index Reprint Ser.). 1977. 37.95 (*0-8369-2029-5*) Ayer.

Riess, Daniel M., jt. ed. see McGann, Jerome J.

Riess, Jonathan B. Luca Signorelli: The San Brizio Chapel, Orvieto. LC 93-21668. (Great Fresco Cycles of the Renaissance Ser.). (Illus.). 104p. 1995. 25.00 (*0-8076-1312-6*) Braziller.

— Political Ideals in Medieval Italian Art: The Frescoes in the Palazzo dei Priori, Perugia, 1297. LC 81-12950. (Studies in the Fine Arts: Iconography: No. 1). (Illus.). 201p. reprint ed. pap. 62.40 (*0-8357-1238-9*, 207025200065) Bks Demand.

— Renaissance Antichrist: Luca Signorelli's Orvieto Frescoes. LC 94-19396. 248p. (C). 1995. text 62.50 (*0-691-04086-9*, Pub. by Princeton U Pr) Cal Prin Full Svc.

Riess, Maryam. Night Notes. LC 96-222883. (Cliffs Notes Ser.). 72p. 1996. pap. text 4.95 (*0-8220-0893-9*, Cliff) IDG Bks.

Riess, Peter & Nygard, Thomas, eds. Native Faces: Winold Reiss. (Illus.). 67p. (Orig.). 1997. pap. 25.00 (*0-9620327-5-1*) Nygard Pub.

Riess, R. Dean, jt. auth. see Johnson, Lee W.

Riess, Steven A. The American Sporting Experience: A Historical Anthology of Sport in America. LC 84-7188. 400p. (Orig.). 1984. reprint ed. pap. 124.00 (*0-608-04289-7*, 206506800012) Bks Demand.

— City Games: The Evolution of American Urban Society & the Rise of Sports. (Sport & Society Ser.). (Illus.). 368p. 1991. pap. text 13.95 (*0-252-06216-7*) U of Ill Pr.

— Major Problems in American Sport History. LC 96-76951. (Major Problems in American History Ser.). 512p. (C). 1996. pap. text 29.16 (*0-669-35380-9*) HM Trade Div.

— Sport in the Industrial Age, 1850-1920. Eisenstadt, A. S. & Franklin, John H., eds. (American History Ser.). 150p. (C). 1995. pap. text 12.95 (*0-88295-916-6*) Harlan Davidson.

— Sports & the American Jew. LC 97-20930. (Sports & Entertainment Ser.). 342p. 1998. 49.95 (*0-8156-2754-8*); pap. 24.95 (*0-8156-2761-0*) Syracuse U Pr.

***Riess, Steven A.** Touching Base: Professional Baseball & American Culture in the Progressive Era. LC 98-58018. 288p. 1999. pap. 18.95 (*0-252-06775-4*) U of Ill Pr.

Riess, Steven A. Touching Base: Professional Baseball & American Culture in the Progressive Era, Revised. LC 98-58018. (Sport & Society Ser.). 288p. 1999. 49.95 (*0-252-02467-2*) U of Ill Pr.

Riess, Suzanne B. & Baum, Willa K., eds. Catalogue of the Regional Oral History Office: 1954-1979. (Illus.). 119p. (Orig.). (C). 1980. pap. text 6.50 (*0-9604164-0-4*) U CA Region Oral Hist.

Riess, Suzanne B., jt. auth. see Baum, Willa K.

Riesser, Ingeborg, jt. auth. see Bahar, Ann.

Riesser, J. The German Great Banks & Their Concentration in Connection with the Economic Development of Germany. Wilkins, Mira, ed. LC 76-29741. (European Business Ser.). (Illus.). 1977. reprint ed. lib. bdg. 74.95 (*0-405-09758-1*) Ayer.

Riessman, Catherine K. Divorce Talk: Women & Men Make Sense of Personal Relationships. LC 89-36065. 264p. (Orig.). (C). 1990. pap. text 16.95 (*0-8135-1503-3*) Rutgers U Pr.

— Narrative Analysis. (Qualitative Research Methods Ser.: Vol. 30). (Illus.). 96p. (C). 1993. text 24.00 (*0-8039-4753-4*); pap. text 10.50 (*0-8039-4754-2*) Sage.

Riessman, Catherine K., ed. Qualitative Studies in Social Work Research. (Illus.). 256p. (C). 1993. text 52.00 (*0-8039-5451-4*); pap. text 24.00 (*0-8039-5452-2*) Sage.

Riessman, Frank, jt. auth. see Gartner, Alan.

Riessman, Frank, jt. ed. see Gartner, Alan.

Riessmann, F., et al. Essays on New Careers: Social Implications for Adult Educators. LC 74-127038. (Notes & Essays Ser.: No. 65). (C). 1970. pap. text 2.50 (*0-87060-029-X*, NES 65) Syracuse U Cont Ed.

Riester, Albert E. & Kraft, Irvin A., eds. Child Group Psychotherapy: Future Tense. LC 86-10486. 1986. 45.00 (*0-8236-0765-8*, BN#00765) Intl Univs Pr.

Riestra, Miguel A. Fundamentos Filosoficos de la Educacion. (SPA.). 320p. 1992. pap. 9.00 (*0-8477-2724-6*) U of PR Pr.

— Fundamentos Filosoficos de la Educacion. 2nd ed. (SPA.). 320p. 1992. pap. 9.00 (*0-8477-2747-5*) U of PR Pr.

Riesz, C. H., et al. Improvement of Nickel Cracking Catalysts. (Research Bulletin Ser.: No. 20). iv, 28p. 1952. pap. 25.00 (*1-58222-026-3*) Inst Gas Tech.

— Pilot Plant Catalytic Gasification of Hydrocarbons. (Research Bulletin Ser.: No. 6). viii, 44p. 1953. pap. 25.00 (*1-58222-037-9*) Inst Gas Tech.

— Sulfur Poisoning of Nickel Catalysts. (Research Bulletin Ser.: No. 10). iv, 23p. 1951. pap. 25.00 (*1-58222-048-4*) Inst Gas Tech.

Riesz, Frigyes, jt. auth. see Sz.-Nagy, Bela.

Riesz, Marcel. Clifford Numbers & Spinors: With Riesz's Private Lectures to E. Folke Bolinder & a Historical Review by Pertti Lounesto. Bolinder, E. Folke & Lounesto, Pertti, eds. LC 93-1381. (Fundamental Theories of Physics Ser.: Vol. 54). 256p. (C). 1993. text 147.00 (*0-7923-2299-1*) Kluwer Academic.

Riet, V. D. & Burg, J. F., eds. Applications of Natural Language to Information Systems. LC 96-76771. 300p. (YA). (gr. 12). 1996. 94.00 (*90-5199-273-4*, 273-4) IOS Press.

Riet, Vernon Van De, see Van De Riet, Vernon.

Rietbergen-McCracken, Jennifer & Narayan, Deepa. Participation & Social Assessment: Tools & Techniques. LC 98-14646. 360p. 1998. 60.00 incl. VHS (*0-8213-4186-3*, 14186) World Bank.

Rietbergen-McCracken, Jennifer & World Bank Staff. Participation in Practice: The Experience of the World Bank & Other Stakeholders, Vol. 333. LC 96-22256. (Discussion Papers: No. 333). 112p. 1997. pap. 22.00 (*0-8213-3684-3*, 13684) World Bank.

Rietbergen, Peter. Europe: Cultural History. LC 98-22241. (Illus.). 512p. (C). 1999. 95.00 (*0-415-17229-2*); pap. 27.99 (*0-415-17230-6*) Routledge.

Rietbergen, Simon, ed. The Earthscan Reader in Tropical Forestry. 344p. 1993. per. 52.95 (*1-85383-127-1*) St Lucie Pr.

Rieter, Russel J., ed. The Pineal Gland: Extra-Reproductive Effects, Vol. III. 248p. 1982. 144.00 (*0-8493-5717-9*, QP188, CRC Reprint) Franklin.

Rieth, A. Suesswasserflora von Mitteleuropa Band 4: Xanthophyceae 2. Pascher, A. et al, eds. (GER., Illus.). 147p. 1980. lib. bdg. 44.50 (*3-437-30304-X*, Pub. by Gustav Fischer) Balogh.

Rieth, Elizabeth, jt. auth. see Johmann, Carol.

Rieth, Hamburg, ed. Proceedings: International Symposium on Bifonazole, Kopenhagen, June 1984. (Journal: Dermatologica: Vol. 169, Suppl. 1). iv, 148p. 1985. pap. 40.00 (*3-8055-4021-3*) S Karger.

***Rieth, John, et al.** Jersey Shore Fire Apparatus Vol. 1: Classics Thru the 60s. (Illus.). 100p. 1999. 39.95 (*0-9674511-0-8*) Jersey Shore Fire.

Rieth, Otto. Die Kunst Menanders in Den "Adelphen" Des Terenz. Gaiser, Konrad, ed. xii, 160p. 1964. write for info. (*0-318-70821-3*) G Olms Pubs.

Riethmueller, Richard H. Walt Whitman & the Germans. 1972. 59.95 (*0-8490-1273-2*) Gordon Pr.

***Riethmuller, A.** Morphologie, Okologie und Phylogenie Aquatischer Oomyceten. (Bibliotheca Mycologica Ser.: Band 185). viii, 344p. 2000. 90.00 (*3-443-59087-X*, Pub. by Gebruder Borntraeger) Balogh.

Rietkerk, Wim. If Only I Could Believe. xxii, 169p. 1997. reprint ed. pap. 11.99 (*1-900507-36-6*, Pub. by Solway) OM Literature.

Rietman, Edward. Experiments in Artificial Neural Networks. (Advanced Technology Ser.). (Illus.). 160p. 1988. 24.95 (*0-8306-0237-2*, 3037); pap. 16.95 (*0-8306-9337-8*) McGraw-Hill Prof.

***Rietman, Edward.** Molecular Nanotechnology: Current & Future Methodologies. (Illus.). 2000. 59.95 (*0-387-98988-9*) Spr-Verlag.

Rietman, Edward A. & Taylor-Smith, Ralph E. Intelligent Manufacturing: Computerized Factories for the 21st Century. 1998. 74.95 (*0-8493-2693-1*, 2693) CRC Pr.

Rietmann, Kearney. Upgrading & Fixing Macs for Dummies. LC 94-77184. 384p. 1994. pap. 19.95 (*1-56884-189-2*) IDG Bks.

Rietschel, E. T. & Wagner, H., eds. Current Topics in Microbiology & Immunology: Pathology of Septic Shock, Vol. 216. 344p. 1996. 159.50 (*3-540-61026-X*) Spr-Verlag.

Rietschel, Robert L. & Fowler, Joseph F., Jr. Fisher's Contact Dermatitis. 5th ed. 1000p. text 119.00 (*0-7817-2252-7*) Lppncott W & W.

Rietschel, Robert L. & Fowler, Joseph F., Jr., eds. Fisher's Contact Dermatitis. 4th ed. LC 94-26917. (Illus.). 1136p. 1995. 89.00 (*0-683-07282-X*) Lppncott W & W.

Rietschel, Robert L. & Spencer, Thomas S. Methods for Cutaneous Investigation. (Cosmetic Science & Technology Ser.: Vol. 9). (Illus.). 248p. 1990. text 145.00 (*0-8247-8264-X*) Dekker.

Rietstap, Johannes B. Armorial General, 2 vols. LC 65-21472. 2465p. 1998. reprint ed. pap. 150.00 (*0-8063-0442-1*) Clearfield Co.

Rietti, J. C. Military Annals of Mississippi: Military Organizations Which Entered the Service of the Confederate States of America, from the State of Mississippi. LC 75-45377. 196p. 1999. reprint ed. 25.00 (*0-87152-218-7*) Reprint.

Rietti, Mario. Money & Banking in Latin America. LC 79-4157. 295p. 1979. 69.50 (*0-275-90412-1*, C0412, Praeger Pubs) Greenwood.

Rietvel, Hillegonda C., ed. This Is Our House: House Music, Cultural Spaces & Technologies. 276p. 1998. text 65.95 (*1-85742-242-2*, ML3528.5.R54, Pub. by Ashgate Pub) Ashgate Pub Co.

Rietveld, A. C. & Van Hout, R. Statistical Techniques for the Study of Language & Language Behaviour. LC 92-35677. 1993. 44.65 (*3-11-013663-5*) Mouton.

Rietveld, Hillegonda C. This Is Our House: House Music, Cultural Spaces & Technologies. LC 97-46173. (Popular Culture Studies). 280p. 1998. pap. 33.95 (*1-85742-243-0*, ML3528.5.R54, Pub. by Ashgate Pub) Ashgate Pub Co.

Rietveld, Jeffrey, ed. see Pidgie, Sere W.

Rietveld, Jeffrey, ed. see Reese, Bernie, et al.

Rietveld, Jeffrey, ed. see Ross, Ellena & Champlin, Allen R., Sr.

Rietveld, M. T., ed. Active Experiments in Space Plasmas: Proceedings of the D4.1 Symposium of COSPAR Scientific Commission D, Held During the 30th COSPAR Scientific Assembly, Hamburg, Germany, 11-21 July, 1994. (Advances in Space Research Ser.: Vol. 15). 156p. 1995. pap. 97.75 (*0-08-042620-4*) Elsevier.

— Active Experiments in Space Plasmas (1996) Proceedings of the D0.6 Symposium of COSPAR Scientific Commission D Which Was Held During the 31st COSPAR Scientific Assembly, Birmingham, U. K. 14-21 July, 1996. (Advances in Space Research Ser.: Vol. 21, No. 5). 786p. 1998. pap. 123.50 (*0-08-043458-4*, Pergamon Pr) Elsevier.

***Rietveld, Piet & Bruinsma, Frank R.** Is Transport Infrastructure Effective? Transport Infrastructure & Accessibility Impacts on the Space Economy. LC 98-29661. (Advances in Spatial Science Ser.). (Illus.). xiv, 384p. 1998. 99.00 (*3-540-64542-X*) Spr-Verlag.

***Rietveld, Piet & Shefer, Daniel, eds.** Regional Development in an Age of Structural Economic Change. LC 99-76364. 267p. 1999. pap. text 69.95 (*1-84014-824-1*, Pub. by Ashgate Pub) Ashgate Pub Co.

Rietveld, Piet, jt. auth. see Nijkamp, Peter.

Rietveld, Piet, jt. ed. see Capineri, Cristina.

Rietveld, W. J., ed. Agroforestry & Sustainable Systems: Symposium Proceedings. (Illus.). 276p. (C). 1996. reprint ed. pap. text 50.00 (*0-7881-3562-7*) DIANE Pub.

Rietz, Helen L. & Manning, Marilyn. The One Stop-Guide to Workshops. LC 93-13299. 324p. 1993. 40.00 (*1-55623-938-6*, Irwn Prfssnl) McGraw-Hill Prof.

Rietz, Julius, ed. see Mendelssohn, Felix.

Rietz, Sandra A., jt. auth. see Livo, Norma J.

Rieu, Charles. Catalogus Codicum Manuscriptorum Orientalium Qui in Murso Britannico Asservantur: Supplement to the Catalogue of the Arabic Manuscripts in the British Museum. xv, 935p. reprint ed. write for info. incl. 3.5 hd (*0-318-71497-3*) G Olms Pubs.

— Supplement to the Catalogue of the Arabic Manuscripts in the British Museum. xvi, 935p. reprint ed. write for info. (*0-318-71556-2*) G Olms Pubs.

Rieu, Charles, jt. ed. see Cureton, W.

Rieu, E. V., tr. see Homer.

Rieu, Emil V., tr. see Homer.

Rieu, Emil V., tr. & intro. see Apollonius, Rhodius.

Rieu, Michel, ed. Physical Work Capacity in Organ Transplantation. LC 97-51463. (Medicine & Sport Science Ser.: Vol. 42, 1998). (Illus.). viii, 188p. 1998. 194.00 (*3-8055-6610-7*) S Karger.

Rieul, Roland. Escape into Espionage: The True Story of a French Patriot in World War Two. 1987. 15.95 (*0-8027-0959-1*) Walker & Co.

— Escape into Espionage: The True Story of a French Patriot in World War Two. (Illus.). 224p. 1989. reprint ed. mass mkt. 4.50 (*0-380-70551-6*, Avon Bks) Morrow Avon.

Rieuwerts, Sigrid, jt. ed. see Cheesman, Tom.

Rievaulx, Aelred. Life of St. Edward the Confessor. Bertram, Jerome, tr. (Illus.). 140p. 1997. pap. 16.95 (*1-901157-75-X*) St Austin.

Riew, C. Keith, ed. Rubber-Toughened Plastics: Developed from a Symposium Sponsored by the Division of Polymeric Materials: Science & Engineering of the American Chemical Society, at the 194th National Meeting of the American Chemical Society, New Orleans, LA, August 30-September 4, 1987. LC 89-14938. (Advances in Chemistry Ser.: No. 222). (Illus.). 456p. reprint ed. pap. 141.40 (*0-608-06787-3*, 206698400009) Bks Demand.

Riew, C. Keith & Gillham, John K., eds. Rubber-Modified Thermoset Resins. LC 84-21566. (Advances in Chemistry Ser.: No. 208). 374p. 1984. lib. bdg. 96.95 (*0-8412-0828-X*) Am Chemical.

— Rubber-Modified Thermoset Resins: Based on a Symposium Sponsored by the Division of Polymeric Materials Science & Engineering at the 186th Meeting of the American Chemical Society, Washington, DC, August 28-September 2, 1983. LC 84-21566. (Advances in Chemistry Ser.: No. 208). 384p. reprint ed. pap. 119.10 (*0-7837-1962-0*, 205244000001) Bks Demand.

Riew, C. Keith & Kinloch, Anthony J., eds. Toughened Plastics I: Science & Engineering. LC 92-34578. (Advances in Chemistry Ser.: Vol. 233). (Illus.). 589p. 1993. 150.00 (*0-8412-2500-1*, Pub. by Am Chemical) OUP.

Riew, C. Keith, ed. see American Chemical Society Staff, et al.

Riewald, J. G., ed. & notes see Beerbohm, Max.

Riewe, Rick, jt. auth. see Oakes, Jill.

Riewoldt, Otto. Hotel Design - Otto Riewoldt. (Illus.). 240p. 1998. 59.95 (*3-927258-62-8*) Gingko Press.

— Intelligent Spaces: Architecture for the Information Age. (Illus.). 240p. 1997. 65.00 (*1-85669-097-0*, Pub. by L King Pubng) Bks Nippan.

***Riewoldt, Otto.** Retail Design. (Illus.). 240p. 2000. 60.00 (*3-8238-5457-7*) te Neues.

***Riewoldt, Otto, ed.** Light Years: The Zumtobel Story 1950-2000. (Illus.). 600p. 2000. pap. 58.00 (*3-7643-6332-0*) Birkhauser.

Riezebos, E. P., et al, eds. Le Parc National de Tal, Cote D'Ivoire: Synthese des Connaissances. (Tropenbos Technical Ser.: No. 8). (Illus.). 322p. 1994. pap. 63.00 incl. disk (*90-5113-020-1*, Pub. by Backhuys Pubs) Balogh.

Riezler, Kurt. Uber Finanzen und Monopole Im Alten Griechenland: Zur Theorie und Geschichte der antiken Stadtwirtschaft. Finley, Moses, ed. LC 79-5002. (Ancient Economic History Ser.). (GER.). 1979. reprint ed. lib. bdg. 15.95 (*0-405-12391-4*) Ayer.

Riezman, Raymond G., jt. ed. see Neuefeind, Wilhelm.

Rifaat, Ahmed M. International Aggression: A Study of the Legal Concept. (Its Development & Definition in International Law Ser.). 359p. 1979. pap. 45.00 (*91-22-00298-7*) Coronet Bks.

Rifaat, Alifa. Distant View of a Minaret & Other Stories. (African Writers Ser.). 116p. (C). 1987. reprint ed. pap. 9.95 (*0-435-90912-6*, 90912) Heinemann.

Rifai, Nader, et al, eds. Handbook of Lipoprotein Testing. LC 97-13361. 598p. 1997. pap. 75.00 (*0-915274-92-2*, 202735) Am Assn Clinical Chem.

***Rifai, Nader, et al.** Handbook of Lipoprotein Testing. 2nd ed. LC 00-31313. (Illus.). 2000. write for info. (*1-890883-35-2*) Am Assn Clinical Chem.

Rifbjerg, Klaus. Anna (I) Anna. Taylor, Alexander, tr. from DAN. LC 82-5140. 254p. (Orig.). 1982. pap. 10.95 (*0-915306-30-1*) Curbstone.

— War. Murray, Steven T. & Nunnally, Tiina, trs. from DAN. LC 95-5738. (International Poetry Ser.: No. 3). 80p. 1995. 20.00 (*0-940242-67-2*); pap. 10.00 (*0-940242-66-4*) Fjord Pr.

— Witness to the Future. Murray, Steven T., tr. from DAN. LC 87-17359.Tr. of De Hellige Aber. 217p. (Orig.). 1987. 17.95 (*0-940242-21-4*) Fjord Pr.

Rife. Essentials in Chemistry. (C). 1993. text 86.00 (*0-03-030353-2*) Harcourt Coll Pubs.

— Returns Only-sg Essentials Of Chemistry. (C). 1993. pap. text 12.50 (*0-03-097767-3*) Harcourt.

Rife, Carl B. Bumper Sticker Religion: Seven Messages Unstuck from Bumper Stickers. 1992. pap. 5.50 (*1-55673-600-2*, 9320) CSS OH.

***Rife, Chuck & Rife, Eileen.** Marriage with an Attitude: How to Build an Exciting Marriage with a Fantastic Attitude. 150p. 2000. pap. text 10.00 (*0-7392-0504-8*) Morris Pubng.

Rife, Douglas M. Bill of Rights. Mitchell, Judy, ed. (Illus.). 48p. (Orig.). (J). (gr. 4-8). 1997. pap., teacher ed. 6.95 (*1-57310-079-X*) Teachng & Lrning Co.

— Declaration of Independence. Mitchell, Judy, ed. (Illus.). 32p. (Orig.). (J). (gr. 4-8). 1997. pap., teacher ed. 5.95 (*1-57310-077-3*) Teachng & Lrning Co.

— Gettysburg Address. Mitchell, Judy, ed. (Illus.). 32p. (Orig.). (J). (gr. 4-8). 1997. pap., teacher ed. 5.95 (*1-57310-078-1*) Teachng & Lrning Co.

— Pledge of Allegiance. Mitchell, Judy, ed. (Illus.). 32p. (J). (gr. 4-8). 1998. pap., teacher ed. 5.95 (*1-57310-128-1*) Teachng & Lrning Co.

— Preamble to the U. S. Constitution. Mitchell, Judy, ed. (Illus.). 32p. (J). (gr. 4-8). 1998. pap., teacher ed. 5.95 (*1-57310-129-X*) Teachng & Lrning Co.

— The Star-Spangled Banner. Mitchell, Judy, ed. (Illus.). 32p. (J). (gr. 4-8). 1998. pap., teacher ed. 5.95 (*1-57310-130-3*) Teachng & Lrning Co.

Rife, Eileen, jt. auth. see Rife, Chuck.

Rife, Janet M. Injured Mind, Shattered Dreams: Brian's Journey from Severe Head Injury to a New Dream. LC 93-43284. 182p. 1993. pap. 17.95 (*0-914797-95-6*) Brookline Bks.

Rife, Janet W. Germans & German-Russians in Nebraska: A Research Guide to Nebraska Ethnic Studies. Welsch, Roger, ed. (Nebraska Ethnic Resource Ser.). 238p. (Orig.). (C). 1980. pap. text 10.00 (*0-938932-01-2*) U Nebr CFGPS.

Rife, Joanne. Bicycling Country Roads: From San Jose to Santa Barbara. rev. ed. LC 81-52672. (Illus.). 124p. 1991. pap. 9.95 (*0-934136-45-9*) Good Life.

Rife, Joe, jt. auth. see Schulman, Karen.

Rife, John C., ed. Employment of the Elderly: An Annotated Bibliography, 23. LC 94-39775. (Bibliographies & Indexes in Gerontology Ser.: Vol. 23). 152p. 1995. lib. bdg. 65.00 (*0-313-29191-8*, Greenwood Pr) Greenwood.

Rife, Patricia. Lise Meitner & the Dawn of the Nuclear Age. LC 97-52076. (Illus.). 250p. 1997. 39.95 (*0-8176-3732-X*, Pub. by Birkhauser) Spr-Verlag.

Rife, Patricia & Meitner, Lise. Lise Meitner & the Dawn of the Nuclear Age. LC 97-52076. xviii, 432 p. 1998. 39.95 (*3-7643-3732-X*) Birkhauser.

Rife, William. Essentials of Chemistry. (C). 1991. pap. text, student ed. 30.50 (*0-03-074221-8*) Harcourt Coll Pubs.

— Essentials of Chemistry. (C). 1992. pap. text, teacher ed. 34.00 (*0-03-030344-3*) Harcourt Coll Pubs.

— Essentials of Chemistry. (C). 1992. pap. text, student ed. 31.50 (*0-03-030339-7*, Pub. by Harcourt Coll Pubs) Harcourt.

— Essentials of Chemistry. 560p. (C). 1992. pap. text 74.50 (*0-03-030337-0*) SCP.

— Essentials of Chemistry. 2nd ed. (C). 2000. pap. text 52.00 (*0-03-001382-8*); pap. text, student ed. 21.50 (*0-03-001418-2*) Harcourt Coll Pubs.

— Essentials of Chemistry. 2nd expanded ed. (C). 1999. pap. text 63.50 (*0-03-009227-2*) Harcourt.

— Essentials of Chemistry: Extended Education. (C). 1992. pap. text, teacher ed. 28.00 (*0-03-030359-1*) Harcourt Coll Pubs.

— Essentials of Chemistry: Test Bank. 2nd ed. (C). 2000. pap. text, suppl. ed. 33.00 (*0-03-001532-4*, Pub. by Harcourt Coll Pubs) Harcourt.

— SSM Essentials of Chem: Extended Ed. expanded ed. (C). 1992. pap. text, student ed. 30.50 (*0-03-043098-4*) Harcourt Coll Pubs.

An Asterisk (*) at the beginning of an entry indicates that the title is appearing for the first time.

Rifelj, Carol D. Reading the Other: Novels & the Problem of Other Minds. 264p. (C). 1993. text 44.50 (*0-472-10340-7*, 10340) U of Mich Pr.
— Word & Figure: The Language of Nineteenth-Century French Poetry. LC 87-1504. 220p. reprint ed. pap. 68.20 (*0-608-09869-8*, 206983400006) Bks Demand.
Rifenbary, Jay. No Excuse: Key Principles for Balancing Life & Achieving Success. 3rd rev. ed. Markowski, Mike & Markowski, Marjie, eds. LC 94-77875. (Personal Development Ser.). (Illus.). 336p. 2000. pap. 16.95 (*0-938716-22-0*, Possible Pr) Markowski Intl.
— No Excuse! The Workbook: Your Companion to the Book to Help You Live the "No Excuse!" Lifestyle. Markowski, Mike & Markowski, Marjie, eds. (Personal Development Ser.). (Illus.). 64p. 1996. per., wbk. ed. 9.95 (*0-938716-27-1*) Markowski Intl.
Rifert, V. G. Condensation Heat Transfer Enhancement. (Developments in Heat Transfer Ser.). 300p. 2000. 138.00 (*1-85312-538-5*, 5385, Pub. by WIT Pr) Computational Mech MA.
Riff, Michael. The Face of Survival: Jewish Life in Eastern Europe Past & Present. (Illus.). 224p. (C). 1993. text 35.00 (*0-85303-220-3*) NYU Pr.
Riffard, Pierre. Dictionnaire de l'Esoterisme. (FRE.). 396p. 1993. pap. 36.95 (*0-7859-5620-4*, 2228886548) Fr & Eur.
Riffaterre, Hermine, jt. ed. see Caws, Mary A.
Riffaterre, Michael. Fictional Truth. LC 89-45491. (Parallax). 144p. 1990. text 30.00 (*0-8018-3933-5*) Johns Hopkins.
— Semiotics of Poetry. LC 78-3245. (Advances in Semiotics Ser.). 223p. 1978. pap. 69.20 (*0-608-05039-3*, 205970000004) Bks Demand.
— Style des Pleiades de Gobineau. 239p. 1957. 23.95 (*0-8288-7498-0*) Fr & Eur.
Riffe, Andrew L., IV, jt. ed. see Reddy, Anne W.
Riffe, D. Mort Safety Assurance Systems. 2nd ed. (Occupational Safety & Health Ser.). Date not set. write for info. (*0-8247-9936-4*) Dekker.
Riffe, Daniel, et al. Quantitative Content Analysis. LC 97-47384. (LEA Communication Ser.). 150p. 1998. write for info. (*0-8058-2018-3*); pap. write for info. (*0-8058-2019-1*) L Erlbaum Assocs.
Riffe, Daniel, jt. auth. see Sneed, Don.
Riffe, Joyce. A Very Happy Day. (Great Big Bk. Ser.). (Illus.). 16p. (J). 1995. pap. 14.95 (*0-687-01448-4*) Abingdon.
Riffe, Joyce. A Very Happy Day: Leader's Guide. (J). 1.50 (*0-687-05347-1*) Abingdon.
Riffel, Anthony, jt. auth. see Levin, Benjamin.
Riffel, Herman. Dream Interpretation. 182p. (Orig.). 1993. pap. 10.99 (*1-56043-122-9*) Destiny Image.
— Dreams: Giants & Geniuses in the Making. 112p. (Orig.). 1996. pap. 8.99 (*1-56043-171-7*) Destiny Image.
Riffel, Herman. Dreams: Wisdom Within. 144p. 1990. text 9.99 (*1-56043-007-9*) Destiny Image.
Riffel, Herman. Growing in Christian Maturity. LC 97-65738. 210p. 1997. pap. 10.99 (*1-56043-191-1*) Destiny Image.
Riffel, Jim. Video Detective's 1997 Guide to the Top 1000 Films of All Time. LC 96-53493. 320p. 1997. pap. 5.95 (*0-88001-542-X*) HarpC.
Riffel, Paul. Reading Maps. LC 79-13628. (Illus.). (YA). (gr. 7 up). 1973. spiral bd. 11.05 (*0-8331-1300-3*, 440) Hubbard Sci.
Riffenburgh, Beau. The Myth of the Explorer. (Polar Research Ser.). (Illus.). 224p. 1993. text 59.00 (*1-85293-260-0*) St Martin.
Riffenburgh, R. H. Statistics in Medicine. (Illus.). 458p. 1999. 44.95 (*0-12-588560-1*) Acad Pr.
Riffert, George R. Great Pyramid Proof of God. 1932. 8.00 (*0-685-08804-9*) Destiny.
Riffig, T. T. A Sharper Edge. (Illus.). 154p. (Orig.). 1989. pap. text 5.95 (*0-9621755-0-1*) Metahomin Pub.
Riffle, Dave. The Greatest Hammerless Repeating Shotgun Ever Built: The Model 12, 1912-1964. 2nd ed. (Illus.). 288p. 1995. reprint ed. 49.95 (*0-9644281-0-5*) D Riffles.
Riffle, J., jt. auth. see Salamone, J. C.
Riffle, Robert L. The Tropical Look: An Encyclopedia of Dramatic Landscape Plants. LC 97-41819. (Illus.). 524p. 1998. 49.95 (*0-88192-422-9*) Timber.
Riffle, Timothy J., jt. auth. see Deer, Richard E.
Rifi, M. R. & Covitz, Frank H. Introduction to Organic Electrochemistry. LC 72-97484. (Techniques & Applications in Organic Synthesis Ser.). 429p. reprint ed. pap. 133.00 (*0-608-16643-X*, 202781200054) Bks Demand.
***Rifkin, Adrian.** Ingres Then & Now. LC 99-42448. 176p. 2000. pap. 21.95 (*0-415-06698-0*) Routledge.
— Ingres Then & Now. LC 99-42448. (Re/Visions: Critical Studies in the History & Theory of Art). 176p. (C). 2000. text 75.00 (*0-415-06697-2*) Routledge.
Rifkin, Adrian, ed. About Michael Baxandall. LC 99-17651. (Art History Special Issues Ser.: Vol. 21). (Illus.). vi, 138p. 1999. pap. 24.95 (*0-631-21191-8*) Blackwell Pubs.
Rifkin, Barry R. Biology & Physiology of the Osteoclast. 512p. 1992. lib. bdg. 199.00 (*0-8493-5437-4*, QP88) CRC Pr.
***Rifkin, Benjamin.** Hieronymus Bosch. (Essential Ser.). (Illus.). 2000. 12.95 (*0-8109-5810-4*, Pub. by Abrams) Time Warner.
— Hieronymus Bosch. (Essential Ser.). 2000. 12.95 (*0-7407-0726-4*, Abrams Essential) Andrews & McMeel.
Rifkin, Benjamin. START - A Program in Russian. (Illus.). 40p. (C). 1998. 25.95 incl. disk (*0-941051-93-5*) Focus Pub-R Pullins.
Rifkin, Benjamin A. Grammatika V Kontekste: Systematizing Russian in Literary & Nonliterary Texts. 398p. (C). 1995. pap. 44.69 (*0-07-052831-4*) McGraw.
— Grammatika V Kontekste: Systematizing Russian in Literary & Nonliterary Texts. 287p. (C). 1996. pap., wbk. ed. 23.44 (*0-07-052834-9*) McGraw.
— Grammatika V Kontekste: Systematizing Russian in Literary & Nonliterary Texts. LC 95-38613. (ENG & RUS.). 1996. write for info. (*0-614-08377-X*) McGraw.
— Semiotics of Narration in Film & Prose Fiction: Case Studies of Scarecrow & My Friend Ivan Lapshin. LC 92-25032. (Russian & East European Studies in Aesthetics & the Philosophy of Culture: Vol. 2). (Illus.). XII, 249p. (C). 1994. text 59.95 (*0-8204-1995-8*) P Lang Pubng.
Rifkin, Benjamin A., tr. see Amman, Jost & Sachs, Hans.
Rifkin, Daniel B. & Klagsbrun, Michael, eds. Angiogenesis: Mechanisms & Pathobiology. (Current Communications in Molecular Biology Ser.). (Illus.). 200p. 1987. pap. 30.00 (*0-87969-300-2*) Cold Spring Harbor.
Rifkin, Don. A Brief Period of Time & Two Eggs Scrambled Soft. 1989. pap. 5.25 (*0-8222-0151-8*) Dramatists Play.
— The Delusion of Angels. 1987. pap. 5.25 (*0-8222-0298-0*) Dramatists Play.
***Rifkin, Glenn & Matthews, Douglas.** The CEO Chronicles: Lessons from the Top about Inspiration & Leadership. 300p. 1999. 24.95 (*1-888232-23-4*) Knowldge Exchange.
Rifkin, Glenn & Matthews, Douglas. The CEO Chronicles: Personal Portraits of Leadership & Life at the Top. 220p. 1999. pap. write for info. (*1-888232-02-1*) Knwldg Univ.
Rifkin, Glenn, jt. auth. see Hill, Sam.
Rifkin, Harold & Raskin, Philip, eds. Diabetes Mellitus, Vol. 5. (Illus.). 391p. 1980. text 22.95 (*0-87619-747-0*) P-H.
Rifkin, J. F. Stegosaurus. 1999. pap. 4.50 (*0-451-45270-4*, Onyx) NAL.
***Rifkin, Jeremy.** The Age of Access: The New Culture of Hypercapitalism, Where All of Life Is a Paid-For Experience. LC 99-54028. 320p. 2000. 24.95 (*1-58542-018-2*, Tarcher Putnam) Putnam Pub Group.
Rifkin, Jeremy. Beyond Beef: The Rise & Fall of the Cattle Culture. LC 91-32285. 368p. 1993. pap. 14.95 (*0-452-26952-0*, Plume) Dutton Plume.
— The Biotech Century: Harnessing the Gene & Remaking the World. LC 97-44358. 288p. 1999. reprint ed. pap. 12.95 (*0-87477-953-7*, Tarcher Putnam) Putnam Pub Group.
— Declaration of a Heretic. 150p. 1985. pap. 8.95 (*0-7102-0710-7*, Routledge Thoemms) Routledge.
— The End of Work: The Decline of the Global Labor Force & the Dawn of the Post-Market Era. 368p. 1996. pap. 15.95 (*0-87477-824-7*, Tarcher Putnam) Putnam Pub Group.
Rifkin, Jeremy & Rossen, John, eds. How to Commit Revolution American Style: Bicentennial Declaration. LC 72-86167. 209p. 1973. 7.95 (*0-8184-0041-2*) Carol Pub Group.
Rifkin, Joshua. North European Baroque. rev. ed. (New Grove Ser.). Date not set. pap. write for info. (*0-393-31594-0*) Norton.
Rifkin, Joshua, et al. The New Grove North European Baroque Masters. (New Grove Composer Biography Ser.). (Illus.). 1985. pap. 9.95 (*0-393-30099-4*) Norton.
***Rifkin, Libbie.** Career Moves: Olson, Creeley, Zukofsky, Berrigan, & the American Avant-garde. LC 99-53743. 2000. pap. write for info. (*0-299-16844-1*) U of Wis Pr.
Rifkin, Lori & Obermeyer, Vera R. Finding a Preschool for Your Child in San Francisco: Public & Private Preschools. rev. ed. LC 95-81240. 152p. 1995. pap. text 14.95 (*0-9635882-0-6*) Lrning Assocs.
Rifkin, Mark, jt. auth. see Strasser, Todd.
Rifkin, Matthew D. Diagnostic Imaging of the Lower Genitourinary Tract. LC 84-42780. 352p. 1985. reprint ed. pap. 109.20 (*0-608-04698-1*, 206541900004) Bks Demand.
— Ultrasound of the Prostate. 2nd ed. LC 96-23896. 400p. 1996. text 142.00 (*0-397-51769-6*) Lppncott W & W.
Rifkin, Matthew D. & Waldroup, Larry. Pocket Atlas of Normal Ultrasound Anatomy. (Illus.). 72p. 1985. pap. text 16.95 (*0-88167-163-0*) Lppncott W & W.
Rifkin, Ned. Highlights from the Collection: Selected Paintings, Sculpture, Photographs & Decorative Art. LC 94-72752. (Illus.). 112p. 1994. pap. 25.00 (*0-939802-78-3*) High Mus Art.
— Made in Philadelphia VI. (Illus.). 38p. 1984. pap. 7.00 (*0-88454-035-9*) U of Pa Contemp Art.
Rifkin, Ned, jt. auth. see Gumpert, Lynn.
Rifkin, Paul. The God Letters. 240p. (Orig.). 1986. mass mkt. 5.95 (*0-446-38319-8*, Pub. by Warner Bks) Little.
Rifkin, S. B., jt. auth. see Annett, H.
Rifkin, Shepard. King Fisher's Road. 160p. 1979. pap. 1.50 (*0-449-14236-1*, GM) Fawcett.
— King Fisher's Road. large type ed. (Western Ser.). 1976. 27.99 (*0-85456-497-7*) Ulverscroft.
Rifkin, Sherri. Givin' It Their All. 1998. mass mkt. 5.50 (*0-345-42654-1*) Ballantine Pub Grp.
Rifkin, Sherri, jt. auth. see Valeria, Andrea.
Rifkin, Susan B. Community Participation in Maternal & Child Health - Family Planning Programmes: An Analysis Based on Case Study Materials. (CHI, ENG, FRE & SPA.). ix, 38p. 1990. pap. text 9.50 (*92-4-156135-1*, 1150338) World Health.
Rifkind, Basil M., ed. Drug Treatment of Hyperlipidemia. (Fundamental & Clinical Cardiology Ser.: Vol. 1). (Illus.). 280p. 1991. text 125.00 (*0-8247-8512-6*) Dekker.
— Lowering Cholesterol in High-Risk Individuals & Populations. LC 94-45081. (Fundamental & Clinical Cardiology Ser.: No. 24). (Illus.). 384p. 1995. text 145.00 (*0-8247-9412-5*) Dekker.
Rifkind, Carole. Field Guide to American Architecture. (Illus.). 1980. pap. 34.95 (*0-452-26269-0*, Z5224, Plume) Dutton Plume.
— Field Guide to American Architecture. rev. ed. LC 98-2716. 384p. 1998. 45.00 (*0-525-94008-1*) NAL.
Rifkind Center Staff. Bibliography of German Expressionism: Catalog of the Library of the Robert Gore Rifkind Center for German Expressionist Studies at the Los Angeles County Museum of Art. 500p. (C). 1990. 175.00 (*0-8161-0494-8*, G K Hall & Co) Mac Lib Ref.
Rifkind, D. The Medical Abacus: The Formulas of Clinical Practice & How to Use Them. LC 98-44811. (Illus.). 130p. 2000. pap. 21.95 (*1-85070-023-0*) Prthnon Pub.
Rifkind, Lawrence & Harper, Loretta F. Sexual Harassment in the Workplace: Men & Women in Labor. 224p. (C). 1993. per. 22.95 (*0-8403-8650-8*) Kendall-Hunt.
Rifkind, Lawrence, jt. auth. see Harper, Loretta F.
Rifkind, Marion, tr. see Anderson, Rickie W.
Rifkind, Simon H., et al. The Basic Equities of the Palestine Problem. Davis, Moshe, ed. LC 77-70736. (America & the Holy Land Ser.). 1977. reprint ed. lib. bdg. 19.95 (*0-405-10279-8*) Ayer.
Rifon, N. J., et al. Media Management: A Casebook Approach. (Communication Textbook Journalism Subseries). 28p. 1993. pap., teacher ed. write for info. (*0-8058-1452-3*) L Erlbaum Assocs.
Riforgiato, Leonard R. Missionary of Moderation: Henry Melchior Muhlenberg & the Lutheran Church in English America. LC 78-75203. 256p. 1970. 36.50 (*0-8387-2379-9*) Bucknell U Pr.
Riga, Alan T. & Neag, Michael, eds. Materials Characterization by Thermomechanical Analysis, STP 1136. (Special Technical Publication Ser.). (Illus.). 200p. 1991. text 61.00 (*0-8031-1434-6*, STP1136) ASTM.
Riga, Alan T. & Patterson, Gerald H., eds. Oxidative Behavior of Materials by Thermal Analytical Techniques. LC 97-39992. (STP Ser.: Vol. STP1326). (Illus.). 247p. 1997. 69.00 (*0-8031-2483-X*, STP1326) ASTM.
Riga, Carla L., jt. auth. see Federici, Carla.
Riga, Carla Larese, jt. auth. see Federici, Carla.
Rigal, Barry. Card Games for Dummies. LC 97-80305. (For Dummies Ser.). 384p. 1997. pap. 16.99 (*0-7645-5050-0*) IDG Bks.
Rigal, Jean, ed. Minor Surgical Procedures in Remote Areas. (Medecins Sans Frontieres - Hatier Ser.). 172p. 1989. vinyl bd. 23.95 (*2-218-02163-3*) Hatier Pub.
Rigal, Laura. The American Manufactory: Art, Labor, & the World of Things in the Early Republic. LC 98-7152. 250p. 1998. text 29.95 (*0-691-01558-9*, Pub. by Princeton U Pr) Cal Prin Full Svc.
***Rigalt, Carmen.** Mi Corazon Que Baila Con Espigas. (SPA.). 1998. 22.95 (*84-08-02081-1*, Pub. by Planeta Edit) Planeta.
Rigamer, Anna, ed. Airport Planning, Operation, & Management (TRR 1423) (Transportation Research Record Ser.). (Illus.). 68p. 1994. pap. text 22.00 (*0-309-05570-9*) Natl Res Coun.
— Field Performance of Subsurface Drainage (TRR 1425) (Transportation Research Record Ser.). (Illus.). 72p. 1994. pap. text 24.00 (*0-309-05572-5*) Natl Res Coun.
— Lightweight Artificial & Waste Materials for Embankments over Soft Soils (TRR 1422) (Transportation Research Record Ser.). (Illus.). 80p. 1994. pap. text 24.00 (*0-309-05569-5*) Natl Res Coun.
Rigamonti, Justin. The Pigs Went Marching Out! Thatch, Nancy R., ed. LC 98-13553. (Books for Students by Students). (Illus.). 29p. (J). (gr. k-3). 1998. lib. bdg. 15.95 (*0-933849-70-2*) Landmark Edns.
Rigante, Elodia. Italian Immigrant Cooking. LC 94-62213. (Illus.). 33p. 1996. 29.95 (*1-885440-02-2*) First Glance.
Riganti, R., jt. ed. see Bellomo, N.
Rigard, John. Medieval Framlingham: Select Documents, 1270-1524. 176p. (C). 1985. 45.00 (*0-85115-432-8*) Boydell & Brewer.
Rigas, Basil & Spiro, Howard M. Clinical Gastroenterology: Companion Handbook. 4th ed. (Illus.). 384p. 1995. pap. text 36.00 (*0-07-003341-2*) McGraw-Hill HPD.
Rigas, Doganis, jt. auth. see Bergstrand, Simon.
Rigatelli, Laura T. Evariste Galois (1811-1832) (Vita Mathematica Ser.). 1996. 29.50 (*3-7643-5410-0*) Birkhauser.
Rigau, Jorge. Puerto Rico Nineteen Hundred: Turn-of-the-Century Architecture in the Hispanic Caribbean 1890-1930. LC 91-11264. (Illus.). 232p. 1992. 50.00 (*0-8478-1400-9*, Pub. by Rizzoli Intl); pap. 35.00 (*0-8478-1430-0*, Pub. by Rizzoli Intl) St Martin.
Rigau, Jorge, jt. auth. see Stout, Nancy.
Rigaud, M. & Allaire, C. Advances in Refractories for the Metallurgical Industries. 1996. 110.00 (*0-919086-65-9*) CIM.
Rigaud, M. A., ed. Advances in Refractories for the Metallurgical Industries: Proceedings of the International Symposium, Winnipeg, August 1987. (CIM Ser.: No. 4). (Illus.). 327p. 1988. 26.25 (*0-08-035881-0*, Pergamon Pr); 45.00 (*0-08-035880-2*, Pergamon Pr) Elsevier.
Rigaud, M. A. & Landy, R. A. Pneumatic Steelmaking: Refractories, Vol. III. 180p. 1996. 75.00 (*1-886362-08-4*) Iron & Steel.
Rigaud, Milo. Secrets of Voodoo. 13.95 (*0-87286-178-3*) City Lights.
Rigaud, Milo. Secrets of Voodoo. Cross, Robert B., tr. from FRE. (Illus.). 256p. 1985. reprint ed. pap. 14.95 (*0-87286-171-6*) City Lights.
— Ve-Ve Diagrammes Rituels du Voudou. (ENG, FRE & SPA.). 583p. 1992. pap. 59.95 (*0-8288-0000-6*, S10043) Fr & Eur.
Rigaud, Stephen J. Correspondence of Scientific Men of the Seventeenth Century: Including Letters of Barrow, Flamsteed, Wallis, & Newton, Printed from the Originals in the Collection of the Right Honourable the Earl of Macclesfield, 2 vols., Set. 1965. reprint ed. 180.70 incl. 3.5 hd (*0-685-66511-9*, 05101097) G Olms Pubs.
Rigaudias-Weiss, Hilde. Las Enquetes Ouvrieres en France entre 1830 et 1848: The Working Class Surveys in France Between 1830 & 1848. LC 74-25777. (European Sociology Ser.). (FRE.). 270p. 1975. reprint ed. 26.95 (*0-405-06531-0*) Ayer.
Rigaudis, Marc. Ito-san. Kirkup, James, tr. from JPN. 135p. 1991. 29.00 (*0-7206-0818-X*, Pub. by P Owen Ltd) Dufour.
Rigauer, Bero. Sport & Work. Guttmann, Allen, ed. LC 81-793. (ENG.). 110p. 1981. text 38.50 (*0-231-05200-6*) Col U Pr.
Rigault, Andre & Charbonneau, Rene, eds. Proceedings of the Seventh International Congress of the Phonetic Sciences, Montreal, 22-28 August 1971-Actes Du Septieme Congres International Des Sciences Phonetiques. (Janua Linguarum, Series Major: No. 57). (Illus.). 1972. 346.15 (*90-279-2311-6*) Mouton.
Rigberg, Lynn R. Jane Austen's Discourse with New Rhetoric. LC 98-39074. (Studies in Nineteenth-Century British Literature: Vol. 14). 288p. 1999. text 54.95 (*0-8204-4257-7*, 42577) P Lang Pubng.
Rigbey, Liz A. Total Eclipse. 1996. pap., mass mkt. 5.99 (*0-671-79580-5*, PB Trade Paper) PB.
— Total Eclipse. large type ed. 876p. 1995. 26.95 (*0-7838-1503-4*, G K Hall Lrg Type) Mac Lib Ref.
Rigby. The May 30 Movement. (Australian National University Press Ser.). 1980. 37.00 (*0-08-033001-0*, Pergamon Pr) Elsevier.
***Rigby.** Technical Document Basics for Engineering Technicians & Technologists. 460p. 2000. pap. 26.67 (*0-13-490137-1*) P-H.
Rigby, Andrew. Initiation & Initiative: An Exploration into the Life & Ideas of Dimitrije Mitrinovic. 217p. 1984. text 55.50 (*0-88033-056-2*, Pub. by East Eur Monographs) Col U Pr.
— Living the Intifada. 240p. (C). 1991. text 62.50 (*1-85649-039-4*, Pub. by Zed Books); text 22.50 (*1-85649-040-8*, Pub. by Zed Books) St Martin.
Rigby, Bev, jt. auth. see Rigby, Geoff.
Rigby, Catherine, jt. auth. see Beinssen-Hesse, Silke.
Rigby, Cynthia L., ed. Power, Powerlessness, & the Divine: New Inquiries in Bible & Theology. LC 97-42124. (Studies in Theological Education). 314p. 1997. 39.95 (*0-7885-0422-3*, 000809); pap. 24.95 (*0-7885-0423-1*, 000809) Duke.
Rigby, D. Sue & Hanson, Robert N. Production Typing Projects. 1980. text 10.12 (*0-07-052836-5*) McGraw.
Rigby, D. Sue, jt. auth. see Hanson, Robert N.
***Rigby, Darrell K.** Management Tools & Techniques: An Executive's Guide. 69p. 2000. pap. 14.95 (*0-9656059-3-0*) Bain & Co.
Rigby, Darrell K. Management Tools & Techniques: An Executive's Guide. rev. ed. 69p. 1999. pap. 14.95 (*0-9656059-2-2*) Bain & Co.
— Management Tools & Techniques: An Executive's Guide, 1998. rev. ed. 69p. 1998. pap. 14.95 (*0-9656059-1-4*) Bain & Co.
Rigby, David. Wordworks Rule File. 464p. 2000. pap. text 26.67 (*0-13-490103-7*) P-H.
Rigby, David L., jt. auth. see Webber, Michael J.
Rigby, Dick, jt. auth. see Breen, Ann.
Rigby, Dornamae. How to Repair Restore & Maintain Your Credit. LC 96-92288. 136p. (Orig.). 1996. pap. 21.95 (*0-9652610-0-X*) Villa Books.
Rigby, Elizabeth. Letters from the Shores of the Baltic. LC 73-115533. (Russia Observed, Series I). 1970. reprint ed. 33.95 (*0-405-03023-1*) Ayer.
Rigby, Geoff & Rigby, Bev. Colour Your Garden with Australian Natives. (Illus.). 128p. 1993. 29.95 (*0-86417-492-6*, Pub. by Kangaroo Pr) Seven Hills Bk.
Rigby, Gwynneth, jt. ed. see Shattock, Michael.
Rigby, Hugh. Hardwear: The Art of Prevention. 176p. 1996. pap. 29.95 (*0-9696831-8-9*, Pub. by Quon Edns) Bks Nippan.
Rigby, Ida K. An Alle Kunstler-War-Revolution-Weimar: German Expressionist Prints, Drawings, Posters & Periodicals from the Robert Gore Rifkind Foundation. LC 83-60977. (Illus.). 118p. 1987. pap. 18.75 (*0-916304-62-0*) SDSU Press.
Rigby, Ida K., intro. Inner Visions: German Prints from the Age of Expressionism. (Illus.). 150p. 1992. pap. 24.95 (*0-295-97190-8*) U of Wash Pr.
Rigby, J. G., et al. The 1997 New Year's Floods in Western Nevada. (Special Publications: No. 23). (Illus.). 112p. 1998. pap. 24.95 (*1-888035-03-X*) Nev Bureau Mines & Geol.
Rigby, J. Keith & Hamblin, W. Kenneth, eds. Recognition of Ancient Sedimentary Environments. LC 72-194231. (Society of Economic Paleontologists & Mineralogists, Special Publication Ser.: No. 16). 350p. reprint ed. pap. 108.50 (*0-608-12940-2*, 202474100038) Bks Demand.
Rigby, J. Keith & Petersen, Morris S. Interpreting Earth History: A Manual in Historical Geology. 5th ed. 240p. (C). 1993. text 34.07 (*0-697-10171-1*, WCB McGr Hill) McGrw-H Hghr Educ.
Rigby, J. Keith, Jr., jt. ed. see Fassett, James E.
Rigby, James H., jt. auth. see Reich, Hans J.
Rigby, Jennifer A. Outdoor Science Education in Orange County, California: A Comprehensive Directory of Facilities & Programs. 35p. 1992. 7.95 (*1-881150-00-3*) Acorn Grp.
Rigby, John P., ed. Public Transport Planning in Shire Counties: An Evaluation of the Public Transport Plan As an Aid to Transport Policy Making. (C). 1980. 35.00 (*0-7855-3870-4*, Pub. by Oxford Polytechnic) St Mut.

R

An Asterisk (*) at the beginning of an entry indicates that the title is appearing for the first time.

R

Rigby, Julie. Sports. LC 94-15315. (Illus.). 96p. (J). 1994. 13.95 (*0-8442-4361-2*, 43612, VGM Career) NTC Contemp Pub Co.

Rigby, Keith J. & Webby, Barry D. Palaeontographica Americana Vol. 56: Late Ordovician Sponges from the Malongulli Formation of Central New South Wales, Australia. 147p. 1988. 50.00 (*0-87710-410-7*) Paleo Res.

Rigby, Ken. Bullying in Schools: And What to Do about It. 312p. 1997. pap. write for info. (*1-85302-455-4*, Pub. by Jessica Kingsley) Taylor & Francis.

Rigby, Ken, jt. auth. see Slee, Phillip T.

Rigby, Malcolm. Meteorological Abstracts & Bibliography Vols. 1-10: Cumulative Geographic Index, 1950-1959. 412p. (Orig.). 1963. pap. 210.00 (*0-933876-93-9*) Am Meteorological.

— Meteorological & Geoastrophysical Abstracts: Cumulative Author Index, 1970-1975, Vols. 21-26. 647p. 1978. text 205.00 (*0-933876-94-7*) Am Meteorological.

Rigby, Malcolm, ed. Meteorological Abstracts & Bibliography: Cumulative Index, Authors-L-Z (1950-1959), 3 vols., Set. 1724p. (Orig.). 1963. pap. write for info. (*0-933876-92-0*) Am Meteorological.

— Meteorological Abstracts & Bibliography Vols. 1-10: Cumulative Index, Authors-A-K, 3 vols., Set. 839p. (Orig.). 1963. pap. write for info. (*0-933876-91-2*) Am Meteorological.

Rigby, Michael, et al, eds. Management of Child Health Services. LC 97-68391. (Illus.). 208p. 1997. pap. text 45.00 (*0-412-59660-1*, Pub. by E A) OUP.

***Rigby, Mike.** European Trade Unions Change & Response. LC 98-48622. 1999. 90.00 (*0-415-17043-5*) Routledge.

Rigby, Mike, ed. see Borgia, Anthony.

Rigby, P. A. Contentious Costs. (Practice Notes Ser.). 90p. 1988. pap. write for info. (*0-85121-450-9*, Pub. by Cavendish Pubng) Gaunt.

Rigby, Peter. African Images: Racism & the End of Anthropology. Kapferer, Bruce & Gledhill, John, eds. (Global Issues Ser.). 156p. 1996. 49.50 (*1-85973-196-1*, Pub. by Berg Pubs) NYU Pr.

— African Images: Racism & the End of Anthropology. Kapferer, Bruce et al, eds. LC 97-191364. (Global Issues Ser.). 156p. 1996. pap. 19.50 (*1-85973-102-3*, Pub. by Berg Pubs) NYU Pr.

— Cattle, Capitalism & Class: Ilparakuyo Maasai Transformations. (Illus.). 272p. (C). 1992. text 59.95 (*0-87722-954-6*) Temple U Pr.

— Cattle, Capitalism & Class: Ilparakuyo Maasai Transformations. (Illus.). 272p. (C). 1994. pap. text 22.95 (*1-56639-204-7*) Temple U Pr.

Rigby, S. H. Chaucer in Context: Society, Allegory, & Gender. (Medieval Sources Ser.). 224p. 1997. text 27.95 (*0-7190-4236-4*, Pub. by Manchester Univ Pr) St Martin.

— English Society in the Later Middle Ages: Class, Status, & Gender. LC 94-43981. 1995. text 32.54 (*0-312-12544-5*) St Martin.

***Rigby, S H.** Marxism & History: A Critical Introduction. 2nd ed. 314p. 1999. pap. 27.95 (*0-7190-5612-8*, Pub. by Manchester Univ Pr) St Martin.

Rigby, Shirley L. Smaller Than Most. LC 85-42636. (Illus.). 32p. (J). (gr. k-3). 1985. 11.50 (*0-06-025027-5*) HarpC Child Bks.

Rigby, Stephen, tr. see Bessieres, Albert.

Rigby, Susan. Caves. LC 91-45082. (Our Planet Ser.). (Illus.). 32p. (J). (gr. 4-6). 1997. pap. 4.95 (*0-8167-2750-3*) Troll Communs.

***Rigby, Susan & Kipping, Peggy.** The Speech-language Pathologist's Guide to Managing the New Medicare. LC 99-55580. 2000. write for info. (*0-89079-847-8*) PRO-ED.

Rigby, Thomas H. Changing Soviet System: Mono-Organisational Socialism from Its Origins to Gorbachev's Restructuring. 264p. 1990. 90.00 (*1-85278-304-4*) E Elgar.

— Lenin's Government: Sovnarkom, 1917 to 1922. LC 78-18754. (Soviet & East European Studies). 336p. reprint ed. pap. 95.80 (*0-608-15606-X*, 2031718) Bks Demand.

— Political Elites in the U. S. S. R. Central Leaders & Local Cadres from Lenin to Gorbachev. 308p. 1990. text 95.00 (*1-85278-303-6*) E Elgar.

Rigby, Thomas H. & Miller, John D., eds. The Disintegrating Monolith: Pluralist Trends in the Communist World. LC 66-5402. xiii, 264p. 1965. 39.50 (*0-678-05188-7*) Kelley.

Rigby, William H. Computer Interfacing: A Practical Approach to Data Acquisition & Control. 256p. 1994. 63.00 (*0-13-288374-0*) P-H.

Rigby, William H. & Dalby, Terry L. Computer Interfacing: A Practical Approach. 176p. (C). 1995. pap. text, lab manual ed. 40.00 (*0-13-339797-1*) P-H.

— Microcontrollers: A Practical Approach to Embedded Control. (C). 2001. 62.00 (*0-13-190232-6*, Macmillan Coll) P-H.

Rigby, William H., jt. auth. see Dalby, Terry L.

Rigden, B. & Henry, L., eds. Water Quality & Management for Recreation & Tourism: Proceedings of IAWPRC Conference, Brisbane, Australia, 10-15 July 1988. (Water Science & Technology Ser.: No. 21). (Illus.). 318p. 1989. pap. 107.50 (*0-08-037383-6*, Pergamon Pr) Elsevier.

Rigden, Denis. Kill the Fuhrer: Section X & Operation Foxley. 2000. 35.00 (*0-7509-2195-1*) Sutton Pub Ltd.

Rigden, Diana W. & Waugh, Susan S. The Shape of This Century: Readings from the Disciplines. 738p. (C). 1990. pap. text 15.00 (*0-685-45686-2*); pap. text, teacher ed. 5.75 (*0-15-580841-9*) Harcourt Coll Pubs.

Rigden, Diane W. What Business Leaders Can Do to Help Change Teacher Education. 1997. pap. 5.00 (*0-89333-136-8*) AACTE.

Rigden, John S. Macmillan Encyclopedia, Vol. 4. 1997. 100.00 (*0-02-864589-8*) Macmillan.

— Physics & the Sound of Music. 2nd ed. LC 84-10401. 368p. 1985. text 89.95 (*0-471-87412-4*) Wiley.

***Rigden, John S.** Rabi: Scientist & Citizen. 320p. 2000. pap. 19.95 (*0-674-00435-3*) HUP.

Rigden, John S., jt. ed. see Brown, Laurie M.

Rigden, John S., jt. ed. see Redish, Edward F.

Rigden, John S., ed. see Suplee, Curt.

Rigdon, Charles. The Caramour Woman. 448p. 1983. mass mkt. 2.95 (*0-446-90227-6*, Pub. by Warner Bks) Little.

Rigdon, Elizabeth H. Never a Day Off: Surviving Single Parenthood. (Christian Living Ser.). 60p. 1990. pap. 3.50 (*0-8341-1376-7*) Beacon Hill.

Rigdon, Mark, jt. auth. see Hercik, Jeanette M.

Rigdon, Steve E., jt. auth. see Basu, Asit P.

Rigdon, Susan M. The Culture Facade: Art, Science, & Politics in the Work of Oscar Lewis. LC 87-19063. (Illus.). 352p. 1988. text 27.95 (*0-252-01495-2*) U of Ill Pr.

Rigeau. EEC Competence. pap. text 28.00 (*90-6544-664-8*) Kluwer Academic.

Rigelhof, R., jt. ed. see Herz, C.

Rigelhof, T. F. Badass on a Softail. LC 98-113607. 222p. 1998. pap. 14.95 (*0-86492-185-3*, Pub. by Goose Ln Edits) Genl Dist Srvs.

— The Education of J. J. Pass: A Novel. 200p. (C). 1989. 69.00 (*0-907839-02-9*, Pub. by Brynmill Pr Ltd); pap. text 35.00 (*0-907839-03-7*, Pub. by Brynmill Pr Ltd) St Mut.

— Je T'aime Cowboy. 200p. 1993. pap. 13.95 (*0-86492-144-6*) Goose Ln Eds.

Rigell, Elizabeth W., jt. auth. see Rigell, Joseph S.

Rigell, Joseph S. & Rigell, Elizabeth W. Fired Again & Again, Praise the Lord! 550p. 1992. pap. write for info. (*0-9632253-0-8*) Afikomen.

Rigelsford, Adrian. Carry on Laughing: A Celebration. LC 97-105658. (Illus.). 192p. 1996. text 19.95 (*1-85227-554-5*, Pub. by Virgin Bks) London Brdge.

— Classic Who: The Harper Classics - The Making of "The Caves of Androzani" & "Revelation of the Daleks" (Illus.). 127p. 1999. text 25.00 (*0-7881-6061-3*) DIANE Pub.

Rigelsford, Adrian, compiled by. Peter Sellers: A Celebration. (Illus.). 192p. 1997. text 23.95 (*1-85227-623-1*, Pub. by Virgin Bks) London Brdge.

Rigelsford, Adrian, intro. Dr. Who Postcard Collection. (Illus.). 21p. 1999. reprint ed. pap. text 15.00 (*0-7881-6060-5*) DIANE Pub.

Rigelsford, Adrian, et al. Are You Being Served? The Inside Story of Britain's Funniest - & Public Television's Favorite - Comedy Series. LC 95-1623. (Illus.). 224p. 1995. pap. 17.95 (*0-912333-04-9*, KQED Bks) BB&T Inc.

Riger, Robert, ed. Man in Sport. (Illus.). 1967. pap. 3.50 (*0-912298-10-3*) Baltimore Mus.

***Riger, Stephanie.** Transforming Psychology. LC 99-45366. 192p. 2000. 29.95 (*0-19-507466-1*) OUP.

Riger, Stephanie, jt. auth. see Gordon, Margaret T.

Rigg, A. G. Editing Medieval Texts: Papers Given at the Twelfth Annual Conference on Editorial Problems, University of Toronto, 5-6 November, 1976. LC 88-47820. (Conference on Editorial Problems Ser.: No. 12). 1987. 42.50 (*0-404-63662-4*) AMS Pr.

Rigg, A. G., et al, eds. Singing Early Music: The Pronunciation of European Languages in the Late Middle Ages & Renaissance. LC 95-22575. (Music: Scholarship & Performance Ser.). 1996. 49.95 (*0-253-32961-2*) Ind U Pr.

Rigg, A. G., jt. ed. see Brewer, Charlotte.

Rigg, A. G., ed. see Langland, William.

Rigg, A. G., jt. ed. see Mantello, F. A.

Rigg, A. George, ed. see Walter of Wimborne.

Rigg, Diana, compiled by. No Turn Unstoned: The Worst Ever Theatrical Reviews. LC 91-11430. (Illus.). 192p. 1991. reprint ed. pap. 13.95 (*1-879505-03-7*) Silman James Pr.

Rigg, J. Southeast Asia: A Region in Transition. 304p. 1989. pap. 18.95 (*0-04-445378-7*, A8311) Routledge.

Rigg, J. A., jt. ed. see Bliss, Anne M.

Rigg, J. C., et al. Compendium of Terminology & Nomenclature of Properties in Clinical Laboratory Sciences: The Silver Book. 304p. 1995. pap. 28.50 (*0-86542-612-0*) Blackwell Sci.

Rigg, Jacque C. Curing the Incurable: How to Use Your Body's Natural Self-Healing Ability to Overcome MS & Other Diseases. LC 98-73710. 320p. 1999. pap. 18.95 (*1-883697-17-4*) Hara Pub.

Rigg, Jennifer. Pencarnan. LC 76-45573. 1977. 8.95 (*0-672-52288-8*, Bobbs) Macmillan.

Rigg, Jonathan. Southeast Asia. LC 94-20444. (Country Fact Files Ser.). (J). 1995. lib. bdg. 24.26 (*0-8114-2788-9*) Raintree Steck-V.

— Southeast Asia: Human Landscape of Modernization & Development. LC 98-138110. (Illus.). 352p. (C). 1997. 85.00 (*0-415-13920-1*); pap. 25.99 (*0-415-13921-X*) Routledge.

Rigg, Lucy. Baby's Christmas. (Little Christmas Treasure Bks.). (J). 1990. 2.95 (*0-8378-1883-4*) Gibson.

— Little Christmas Treasure Books: Christmas Joys. (Illus.). (J). (gr. 2 up). 1989. 2.95 (*0-8378-1870-2*) Gibson.

— Wedding Memories. (Illus.). 64p. 1994. 21.00 (*0-614-01771-8*) Gibson.

— Welcome Baby. (Illus.). 1992. 18.50 (*0-8378-4154-2*) Gibson.

— We're Having a Party. (Tiny Touch Bks.). (Illus.). 1994. 7.50 (*0-8378-7624-9*) Gibson.

Rigg, Mary L. A Cat Tops the Tree. LC 96-69990. (Illus.). 48p. (Orig.). (J). (gr. k-5). 1996. pap. 7.95 (*1-882792-29-7*) Proctor Pubns.

Rigg, Pat & Allen, Virginia G., eds. When They Don't All Speak English: Integrating the ESL Student into the Regular Classroom. 176p. 1989. 12.95 (*0-8141-5693-2*) NCTE.

Rigg, Pat & Enright, D. S., eds. Children & ESL: Integrating Perspectives. 171p. 1986. pap. 13.95 (*0-939791-24-2*) Tchrs Eng Spkrs.

Rigg, Pat, et al. Approaches to Adult ESL Literacy Instruction. Crandall, Joann & Peyton, Joy K., eds. LC 93-30665. (Language in Education Ser.: Vol. 82). 98p. (Orig.). 1993. pap. text 13.50 (*0-937354-82-1*) Delta Systems.

Rigg, Pat, jt. auth. see Kazemek, Francis E.

Rigg, Patricia D. Robert Browning's Romantic Irony in the Ring & the Book. LC 98-35806. 1999. write for info. (*0-8386-3773-6*) Fairleigh Dickinson.

Rigg, Peter W. Words of Still Waters. 68p. 1980. pap. 4.00 (*0-910477-00-0*) LoonBooks.

Rigg, Phyllis, ed. see Hall, Tamara.

Rigg, Robert B. Red China's Fighting Hordes: A Realistic Account of the Chinese Communist Army by a U. S. Army Officer. LC 70-138177. (Illus.). 378p. 1971. reprint ed. lib. bdg. 35.00 (*0-8371-5634-3*, RIRC, Greenwood Pr) Greenwood.

***Riggans, Walter.** Hebrews. (Focus on the Bible Commentary Ser.). 1999. pap. 12.99 (*1-85792-328-6*) Christian Focus.

Riggans, Walter. Numbers. 264p. 1993. pap. 22.00 (*0-7152-0522-6*, Pub. by St Andrew) St Mut.

Riggar, T. F. Stress Burnout: An Annotated Bibliography. LC 84-5447. 319p. 1985. 21.95 (*0-8093-1186-0*) S Ill U Pr.

Riggar, T. F. & Matkin, R. E. Handbook for Management of Human Service Agencies. LC 85-26120. 184p. (Orig.). 1986. pap. text 17.95 (*0-8093-1285-9*) S Ill U Pr.

Riggar, T. F., jt. auth. see Crimando, William.

Riggar, T. F., jt. auth. see Matkin, Ralph E.

Riggar, T. F., jt. ed. see Crimando, William.

Riggar, T. F., jt. ed. see Maki, Dennis R.

Riggeman, Liz, ed. see Strong, Dina.

Riggen, Martinez. Luis Barragan, 1902-1988. (ITA., Illus.). 256p. 1997. 139.95 (*88-435-4866-2*, Pub. by Art Bks Intl) Partners Pubs Grp.

***Riggenbach.** Grammar Dimensions Platinum Book 2. 3rd ed. (C). 2000. pap. 30.95 (*0-8384-0268-2*) Heinle & Heinle.

Riggenbach, Heidi. Grammar Dimensions, Bk. 2. (College ESL Ser.). (J). 1994. mass mkt., wbk. ed. 36.95 (*0-8384-4358-3*) Wadsworth Pub.

— Grammar Dimensions, Bk. 2B. (College ESL Ser.). (J). 1994. mass mkt. 22.95 (*0-8384-5573-5*) Wadsworth Pub.

— Grammar Dimensions, Vol. 2. 2nd ed. (Miscellaneous/ Catalogs Ser.). (J). 1997. mass mkt., teacher ed. 7.95 (*0-8384-7372-5*) Heinle & Heinle.

— Grammar Dimensions 2A. (College ESL Ser.). (J). 1994. pap. 11.25 (*0-8384-5394-5*) Heinle & Heinle.

— Grammar Dimensions 2B. (College ESL Ser.). (J). 1994. pap. 11.25 (*0-8384-5395-3*) Heinle & Heinle.

***Riggenbach, Heidi, ed.** Perspectives on Fluency. LC 99-87225. (Illus.). 336p. (C). 2000. text 49.50 (*0-472-11028-4*, 11028); pap. text 29.95 (*0-472-08604-9*, 08604) U of Mich Pr.

Riggenbach, Heidi & Samuda, Virginia. Grammar Dimensions: Form, Meaning & Use, Bk. 2. (J). 1993. mass mkt. 25.00 (*0-8384-3969-1*) Heinle & Heinle.

— Grammar Dimensions: Form, Meaning & Use, Bk. 2. (J). 1993. pap., teacher ed. 8.25 (*0-8384-4128-9*) Heinle & Heinle.

— Grammar Dimensions: Form, Meaning, & Use, Bk. 2. 2nd ed. (J). 1997. 24.25 incl. audio (*0-8384-7408-X*) Heinle & Heinle.

— Grammar Dimensions: Form, Meaning, & Use, Bk. 2A. 2nd ed. 1997. 19.95 (*0-8384-7145-5*) Heinle & Heinle.

— Grammar Dimensions: Form, Meaning, & Use, Bk. 2B. 2nd ed. 1997. 19.95 (*0-8384-7181-1*) Heinle & Heinle.

Riggenbach, Jan. Midwest Gardener's Handbook. 432p. 1999. pap. 24.95 (*1-888608-13-7*) Cool Springs Pr.

Riggenbach, Jan, jt. auth. see Lovejoy, Ann.

Riggenbach, Jeff. In Praise of Decadence. LC 98-37930. 213p. 1998. 21.95 (*1-57392-246-3*) Prometheus Bks.

Riggenback, Heidi. Discourse Analysis in the Language Classroom: The Spoken Language. LC 98-40287. 232p. 1999. pap. text 24.95 (*0-472-08541-7*, 08541) U of Mich Pr.

***Rigger, Shelley.** Politics in Taiwan: Voting for Democracy. (Illus.). 256p. (Orig.). (C). 1999. text 90.00 (*0-415-17208-X*) Routledge.

Riggers, Shelley. Politics in Taiwan: Voting for Democracy. LC 99-22354. 1999. pap. 27.99 (*0-415-17209-8*) Routledge.

Riggiero, Timothy J., ed. see Curtiss, Allen, Jr.

***Riggin, J. D.** Lest We Forget: or Character Gems Gleaned from South Arkansas. (Illus.). 230p. 1999. reprint ed. pap. 18.00 (*1-56546-145-2*) Arkansas Res.

Riggin, Judith M. John Wayne: A Bio-Bibliography. LC 91-35218. (Popular Culture Bio-Bibliographies Ser.). 168p. 1992. lib. bdg. 49.95 (*0-313-22308-4*, RJW/, Greenwood Pr) Greenwood.

Riggin, Lauren, jt. auth. see Harvey, Pharis.

Riggin, W. Debra. Ex-Lover Weird Shit: A Collection of Short Fiction, Poetry, & Cartoons by Lesbians & Gay Men. 152p. 1994. pap. 10.95 (*0-9642803-3-7*) TOOTS.

Riggins, Elmer & Rathgeber, David. To Blanche from Elmer with Love. LC 95-92792. 46p. 1995. pap. 9.95 (*0-9635337-5-4*) Realty Res.

Riggins, J. H. Lest We Forget: or Character Gems Gleaned from South Arkansas. 224p. 1978. reprint ed. 20.00 (*0-89308-072-1*) Southern Hist Pr.

Riggins, John & Winter, Jack. Gameplan: The Language & Strategy of Pro Football. rev. ed. Halsey, Alexandra, ed. LC 84-40402. (Illus.). 240p. 1984. reprint ed. pap. 12.95 (*0-915643-08-1*) Santa Barb Pr.

Riggins, Robert E., et al, eds. Watershed Planning & Analysis in Action. 608p. 1990. pap. text 54.00 (*0-87262-767-5*) Am Soc Civil Eng.

Riggins, Stephen H., jt. ed. see Harold, Stephen.

Riggins, Stephen H., ed. Ethnic Minority Media: An International Perspective. (Communication & Human Values Ser.: Vol. 10). (Illus.). 304p. (C). 1992. 52.00 (*0-8039-4723-2*); pap. 24.95 (*0-8039-4724-0*) Sage.

— The Language & Politics of Exclusion: Other in Discourse. LC 97-4595. (Communication & Human Values Ser.). 336p. (C). 1997. 55.00 (*0-7619-0728-9*, 07289); pap. 24.95 (*0-7619-0729-7*, 07297) Sage.

— The Socialness of Things: Essays on the Socio-Semiotics of Objects. (Approaches to Semiotics Ser.: No. 115). 490p. (C). 1994. lib. bdg. 175.40 (*3-11-014133-7*, 226-94) Mouton.

Riggins, William, tr. see Steiner, Rudolf.

***Riggio.** Introduction to Industrial & Organizational Psychology Field. 1998. pap. text 78.00 (*0-673-78873-3*, GoodYrBooks) Addson-Wesley Educ.

Riggio, Anita. Beware the Brindlebeast. LC 93-70875. (Illus.). 32p. (J). (ps-1). 1994. 16.95 (*1-56397-133-X*) Boyds Mills Pr.

— A Moon in My Teacup. LC 91-77622. (Illus.). 32p. (J). (ps-3). 1993. lib. bdg. 14.95 (*1-56397-008-2*) Boyds Mills Pr.

— Secret Signs: Along the Underground Railroad. LC 95-80777. (Illus.). 32p. (J). (ps-3). 1997. 15.95 (*1-56397-555-6*) Boyds Mills Pr.

Riggio, Anita, retold by. Beware the Brindlebeast. LC 97-70875. (Illus.). 32p. (J). 1997. pap. text 8.95 (*1-56397-684-6*) Boyds Mills Pr.

Riggio, Milla C. The Play of Wisdom: Its Texts & Contexts. LC 86-47840. (Studies in the Middle Ages: No. 14). 32.50 (*0-404-61444-2*) AMS Pr.

***Riggio, Milla C.** Teaching Shakespeare Through Performance. LC 99-24092. (Options for Teaching Ser.). 500p. 1999. pap. text 22.00 (*0-87352-373-3*) Modern Lang.

Riggio, Milla C., ed. The Wisdom Symposium: Papers from the Trinity College Medieval Festival. LC 85-48070. (Studies in the Middle Ages: No. 11). (Illus.). 1986. 32.50 (*0-404-61441-8*) AMS Pr.

Riggio, Milla Cozart, ed. Teaching Shakespeare Through Performance. LC 99-24092. (Options for Teaching Ser.). x, 503p. (C). 1999. text 40.00 (*0-87352-372-5*, J214) Modern Lang.

Riggio, Ronald E. Introduction to Industrial-Organizational Psychology. (C). 1990. pap. text 75.00 (*0-673-38188-9*) Addson-Wesley Educ.

***Riggio, Ronald E. & Porter, Lyman W.** Introduction to Industrial-Organizational Psychology. 3rd ed. LC 99-13595. (Illus.). 586p. (C). 1999. 80.00 (*0-321-05687-6*) Addson-Wesley Educ.

Riggio, Thomas P., ed. see Dreiser, Theodore.

Riggio, Thomas P., ed. see Eastman, Yvette S. & Dreiser, Theodore.

***Riggle, Ellen D. & Tadlock, Barry L., eds.** Gays & Lesbians in the Democratic Process: Public Policy, Public Opinion & Political Representation. 384p. 1999. 49.50 (*0-231-11584-9*); pap. 24.50 (*0-231-11585-7*) Col U Pr.

Riggle, Ellen D., jt. ed. see Ellis, Alan L.

Riggle, H. M. Beyond the Tomb. 288p. 8.00 (*0-686-29100-X*) Faith Pub Hse.

— Christian Baptism, Feet Washing & the Lord's Supper. 264p. 8.00 (*0-686-29105-0*) Faith Pub Hse.

— Jesus Is Coming Again. 111p. pap. 2.50 (*0-686-29123-9*) Faith Pub Hse.

— The Kingdom of God & the 1000 Year Reign. 160p. pap. 3.50 (*0-686-29153-0*) Faith Pub Hse.

— The Sabbath & the Lord's Day. 160p. pap. 3.50 (*0-686-29165-4*) Faith Pub Hse.

— The Two Works of Grace. 56p. pap. 1.50 (*0-686-29168-9*); pap. 1.00 (*0-686-29169-7*) Faith Pub Hse.

Riggle, H. M., jt. auth. see Speck, Von S.

Riggle, H. M., jt. auth. see Warner, D. S.

Riggle, H. M., jt. compiled by see Speck, S. L.

Riggle, Jon, et al. Dating with Success: Proven Methods - Practical Suggestions. 58p. (Orig.). 1995. pap. 7.95 (*0-9650490-0-0*) J M J Pubns.

Riggle, Judith, jt. auth. see Barstow, Barbara.

Riggleman, Liz, jt. auth. see Strong, Dina.

Riggleman, Liz, ed. see Strong, Dina.

Riggott, Dean, photos by. Rochester: The Images. (Illus.). 88p. 1997. pap. 18.95 (*0-9659875-0-7*) D Riggott.

Riggs. Engineering Economics. 3rd ed. 1986. text, student ed. 28.12 (*0-07-052877-2*) McGraw.

— A Low-Budget Program for Multi-Ethnic Gifted Students. 1989. pap. 14.99 (*0-89824-133-2*) Trillium Pr.

— Teaching Global Past. 1998. pap. text, teacher ed. write for info. (*0-312-17188-9*) St Martin.

— The United Nations. 3rd ed. (C). 1999. pap. 53.00 (*0-15-507865-8*) Harcourt.

Riggs, jt. ed. see Zimmie.

Riggs, A. R. & Velk, Tom, eds. Canadian-American Free Trade (The Sequel) Historical, Political & Economic Dimensions. 113p. 1988. 18.00 (*0-88645-073-X*, Pub. by Inst Res Pub) Ashgate Pub Co.

Riggs, Alan, ed. see Anthony, Piers.

Riggs, Angela. When the Music Stopped I Kept on Dancing: A Story of Courage, Hope & the Magnificence of the Human Spirit. LC 94-78434. 184p. 1995. pap. 12.95 (*1-885221-19-3*) BookPartners.

Riggs, Ann, jt. ed. see Mott, Sarah.

Riggs, Anne, jt. auth. see Gibb, Heather.

An Asterisk (*) at the beginning of an entry indicates that the title is appearing for the first time.

Riggs, B. Lawrence & Melton, L. Joseph, III, eds. Osteoporosis: Etiology, Diagnosis & Management. 2nd ed. LC 95-7020. 560p. 1995. text 134.00 (0-7817-0275-5) Lppncott W & W.

Riggs-Bergesen, Catherine. Candle Therapy. (Illus.). 153p. (Orig.). 1992. pap. 16.95 (0-9640440-1-3) Other Worldly.

Riggs, Bob. My Best Defense. LC 96-60283. 208p. (Orig.). (J). (gr. 4-9). 1996. pap. 5.95 (1-886747-01-6) Ward Hill Pr.

Riggs, Brett H., jt. ed. see Duggan, Betty J.

Riggs, Bryan, et al, photos by. Charleston, SC: Walking Tour with Map. (Illus.). 16p. 1995. pap. 2.50 (0-9649686-1-4) Chrlstn Post Card.

Riggs, Bryan & McLemore, Joe, photos by. Charleston & Surrounding Barrier Islands. (Illus.). 56p. 1995. pap. 7.95 (0-9649686-0-6) Chrlstn Post Card.

— Patriots Point: Naval & Maritime Museum. (Illus.). 28p. 1996. pap. 4.95 (0-9649686-2-2) Chrlstn Post Card.

Riggs, Charles H. Criminal Asylum in Anglo-Saxon Law. LC 63-63598. (University of Florida Monographs: Social Sciences: No. 18). 67p. reprint ed. pap. 30.00 (0-7837-5001-3, 204466800004) Bks Demand.

Riggs, Charles T., tr. see Kritoboulos.

Riggs, Charlie. Learning to Walk with God. 208p. (Orig.). 1990. pap. 7.95 (0-89066-082-4) World Wide Pubs.

Riggs, Cheryl. Teaching "The Global Past", Vol. II. 1998. teacher ed. write for info. (0-312-17193-5) St Martin.

Riggs, Claude E. Flood Brothers. 270p. 1993. pap. text. write for info. (0-9631958-0-8) C E Riggs.

Riggs, D. Randy. Flat-Out Racing: An Insider's Look at the World of Stock Car Racing. LC 94-34798. 176p. 1995. text 17.98 (1-56799-165-3, MetroBooks) M Friedman Pub Grp Inc.

Riggs, David. Ben Jonson: A Life. (Illus.). 399p. 1989. pap. 19.50 (0-674-06626-X) HUP.

— Shakespeare's Heroical Histories: Henry VI & Its Literary Tradition. LC 75-152701. 206p. 1971. reprint ed. pap. 63.90 (0-7837-4183-9, 205903300012) Bks Demand.

Riggs, David A. & Robbins, Sharon L. The Executive's Guide to Supply Management Strategies: Building Supply Chain Thinking into Business Processes. LC 97-35490. 256p. 1997. 35.00 (0-8144-0385-9) AMACOM.

Riggs, David F. East of Gettysburg: Custer vs. Stuart. rev. ed. LC 85-61163. (Illus.). 1985. pap. 5.95 (0-88342-208-5) Old Army.

— Embattled Shrine: Jamestown in the Civil War. LC 97-24185. 208p. 1997. 24.95 (1-57249-075-6) White Mane Pub.

— Seventh Virginia Infantry. (Virginia Regimental Histories Ser.). (Illus.). 107p. 1982. 19.95 (0-930919-02-5) H E Howard.

— Thirteenth Virginia Infantry. (Virginia Regimental Histories Ser.). (Illus.). 158p. 1988. 19.95 (0-930919-65-3) H E Howard.

Riggs, David W. Nettles & Balsams. 28p. (Orig.). 1995. pap. write for info. (1-883331-13-7) Anderie Poetry.

Riggs, Donald E., ed. Creativity, Innovation & Entrepreneurship in Libraries. LC 89-33071. (Journal of Library Administration: Vol. 10, Nos. 2-3). (Illus.). 233p. 1989. text 49.95 (0-86656-940-5) Haworth Pr.

— Library Communication: The Language of Leadership. LC 91-34565. (Illus.). 198p. 1991. reprint ed. pap. 61.40 (0-608-01737-X, 206239400002) Bks Demand.

Riggs, Donald E. & Tarin, Patricia A. Cultural Diversity in Libraries. LC 94-17007. 226p. 1994. 45.00 (1-55570-139-6) Neal-Schuman.

Riggs, Donald E., jt. ed. see Aluri, Rao.

Riggs, E. H. & Riggs, H. E. Hynes: Our Pioneer Ancestors, being a Record of Available Information as to the Hynes, Chenault, Dunn, McKee, Anderson, Talylor, Finley, Letcher & Houston Families in the Direct Line of Ancestry of Samuel B. & Ellen M. Anderson Hynes. (Illus.). 207p. 1991. reprint ed. pap. 32.00 (0-8328-1922-0); reprint ed. lib. bdg. 42.00 (0-8328-1921-2) Higginson Bk Co.

***Riggs, Frank D., ed.** Bilingual Education Reform: Congressional Hearing. 120p. (C). 2000. reprint ed. pap. text 25.00 (0-7881-8752-X) DIANE Pub.

— Education & Technology: Meeting the Needs of Tomorrow: Congressional Hearing. (Illus.). 148p. (C). 2000. reprint ed. pap. text 30.00 (0-7881-8746-5) DIANE Pub.

— Public & Private School Choices in the District of Columbia: Congressional Hearing. 165p. (C). 2000. reprint ed. pap. text 30.00 (0-7881-8762-7) DIANE Pub.

— Technology & Education: Working Together for the Future: Congressional Hearing. (Illus.). 113p. (C). 2000. reprint ed. pap. text 25.00 (0-7881-8747-3) DIANE Pub.

Riggs, Fred W. Frontiers of Development Administration: American Society for Public Administration. LC 70-134010. (Comparative Administration Group Ser.). 647p. reprint ed. pap. 200.00 (0-608-15055-X, 202621400048) Bks Demand.

Riggs, H. E. Riggs: Our Pioneer Ancestors, Being a Record of Available Information As to the Riggs, Baldridge, Agnew, Earle, Kirkpatrick, Vreeland & Allied Families in the Ancestry of Samual Agnew Riggs & Catherine Doane Earle Riggs. (Illus.). 230p. 1993. reprint ed. pap. 37.00 (0-8328-3737-7); reprint ed. lib. bdg. 47.00 (0-8328-3736-9) Higginson Bk Co.

Riggs, H. E., jt. auth. see Riggs, E. H.

Riggs, Henry E. Financial & Cost Analysis for Engineering & Technology Management. (Series in Engineering & Technology Management). 488p. 1994. 99.00 (0-471-57415-5) Wiley.

Riggs, Henry H. Days of Tragedy in Armenia: Personal Experiences in Harpoot, 1915-1917. LC 96-77782. (Armenian Genocide Documentation Ser.). xviii, 220p. (Orig.). 1997. pap. 25.00 (1-884630-01-4) Gomidas Inst.

Riggs, J. B. Riggs Family of Maryland: A Genealogical & Historical Record Including Several of the Families in England. (Illus.). 534p. 1993. reprint ed. pap. 81.00 (0-8328-3735-0); reprint ed. lib. bdg. 91.00 (0-8328-3734-2) Higginson Bk Co.

Riggs, J. Rosemary. Materials & Components of Interior Architecture. 5th ed. LC 98-4590. 240p. 1998. pap. text 61.00 (0-13-923228-1) P-H.

Riggs, James B. An Introduction to Numerical Methods for Chemical Engineers. 2nd ed. (Illus.). 472p. (C). 1994. text 65.00 (0-89672-334-8) Tex Tech Univ Pr.

Riggs, James L. & West, Thomas. Engineering Economics. 3rd ed. (C). 1986. text. write for info. (0-07-052873-X) McGraw.

— Essentials of Engineering Economics. 2nd ed. (C). 1986. text 72.50 (0-07-052872-1) McGraw.

Riggs, James L., et al. Engineering Economics. 4th ed. LC 95-42896. (McGraw-Hill Series in Industrial Engineering & Management Science). 736p. (C). 1996. 93.75 (0-07-912248-5) McGraw.

Riggs, Jennifer. Under the Sea Activity Book. 32p. (J). (ps-3). 1993. pap. 1.95 (0-590-46297-0) Scholastic Inc.

Riggs, Jennifer, tr. Paintings. LC 94-49433. (First Discovery Book).Tr. of Tableaux. (ENG & FRE., Illus.). 28p. (J). (ps-2). 1996. 11.95 (0-590-55201-5, Cartwheel) Scholastic Inc.

— Portraits. LC 94-49121. (First Discovery Art Bk.).Tr. of Portraits. (ENG & FRE., Illus.). 24p. (J). (ps-2). 1995. 11.95 (0-590-55200-7, Cartwheel) Scholastic Inc.

Riggs, John A., tr. see Runci, Paul.

Riggs, John B. A Guide to Manuscripts. 293p. 1970. suppl. ed. 15.00 (0-914650-15-7) Hagley Museum.

— A Guide to the Manuscripts in the Eleutherian Mills Historical Library. 1205p. 1970. 15.00 (0-914650-02-5) Hagley Museum.

Riggs, John H. Respiratory Facts. LC 88-2057. (Illus.). 327p. (C). 1989. text 18.95 (0-8036-7333-7) Davis Co.

Riggs, John R. Cold Hearts & Gentle People. LC 94-25441. 272p. 1994. 17.95 (1-56980-021-9) Barricade Bks.

— Cold Hearts & Gentle People. large type ed. (Americana Series). 350p. 1995. 20.95 (0-7862-0317-X) Thorndike Pr.

— Dead Letter. LC 91-28339. 1992. 15.95 (0-942637-40-2) Barricade Bks.

— A Dragon Lives Forever. LC 92-17748. (Garth Ryland Mystery Ser.). 1992. 17.95 (0-942637-78-X) Barricade Bks.

— A Dragon Lives Forever. large type ed. LC 92-40988. (Cloak & Dagger Ser.). 350p. 1993. reprint ed. lib. bdg. 20.95 (1-56054-605-0) Thorndike Pr.

— He Who Waits: A Garth Ryland Mystery. LC 96-42559. (Garth Ryland Mystery Ser.). 288p. 1997. 17.95 (1-56980-096-0) Barricade Bks.

— Killing Frost: A Garth Ryland Mystery. LC 95-21901. 304p. 1995. 17.95 (1-56980-053-7) Barricade Bks.

— Let Sleeping Dogs Lie. 1993. mass mkt. 4.50 (0-515-11211-9, Jove) Berkley Pub.

— The Lost Scout: A Garth Ryland Mystery. LC 97-32233. 352p. 1998. 17.95 (1-56980-121-5) Barricade Bks.

— One Man's Poison. LC 90-35745. (Garth Ryland Mystery Ser.). 1991. 17.95 (0-942637-31-3, Dembner NY) Barricade Bks.

— One Man's Poison. large type ed. LC 92-11659. 315p. 1992. reprint ed. 16.95 (1-56054-424-4) Thorndike Pr.

— Snow on the Roses: A Garth Ryland Mystery. LC 95-51078. 272p. 1996. 17.95 (1-56980-072-3) Barricade Bks.

Riggs, Karen B. The Preppy Chef. rev. ed. LC 82-960707. (Illus.). 229p. 1982. reprint ed. 7.00 (0-9655657-0-X) Riggs.

Riggs, Karen E. Mature Audiences: Television & the Elderly. LC 97-49866. (Communications, Media & Culture Ser.). 224p. (C). 1998. pap. text 18.00 (0-8135-2540-3) Rutgers U Pr.

— Mature Audiences: Television in the Lives of Elders. LC 97-49866. (Communications, Media & Culture Ser.). xiv, 197p. (C). 1998. text 48.00 (0-8135-2539-X) Rutgers U Pr.

Riggs, L. Spencer, jt. auth. see Popely, Rick.

Riggs, Larry W. Moliere & Plurality: Decomposition on the Classicist Self. LC 89-31588. (Sociocriticism: Literature, Society & History Ser.: Vol. 1). 276p. (C). 1989. text 44.95 (0-685-46923-9) P Lang Pubng.

— Myths of Mastery & Drama of Decomposition in Moliere. (Sociocriticism: Literature, Society & History Ser.: Vol. 1). 275p. (C). 1989. text 44.95 (0-8204-0912-X) P Lang Pubng.

— Resistance to Culture in Moliere, Laclos, Flaubert, & Camus: A Post-Modernist Approach. LC 92-32474. (Studies in French Literature: Vol. 13). 228p. 1992. text 89.95 (0-7734-9159-7) E Mellen.

Riggs, Lawrence B., ed. Prevention & Treatment of Osteoporosis. LC 92-48734. (Illus.). 50p. 1993. 19.90 (0-88937-098-2) Hogrefe & Huber Pubs.

Riggs, Leland S., jt. auth. see Halpin, Daniel W.

Riggs, Lou E., jt. auth. see Epstein, Alan.

Riggs, Lynne E., tr. see Ashihara, Yoshinobu.

Riggs, Maida L., ed. A Small Bit of Bread & Butter: Letters from the Dakota Territory, 1832-1869. LC 96-83698. 350p. (Orig.). 1996. pap. 17.95 (1-886172-22-6) Ash Grove Pr.

Riggs, Marcia Y. Awake, Arise, & Act: A Womanist Call for Black Liberation. LC 94-23378. 168p. (Orig.). 1994. pap. 13.95 (0-8298-1009-9) Pilgrim OH.

Riggs, Marcia Y., ed. Can I Get a Witness? Prophetic Religious Voices of African-American Women. LC 96-29584. 250p. (Orig.). 1997. pap. 18.00 (1-57075-113-7) Orbis Bks.

Riggs, Maribeth. The Women's Home Remedy Kit: Simple Recipes for Treating Common Health Conditions. 146p. (Orig.). 1998. pap. text 12.00 (0-7881-5870-8) DIANE Pub.

Riggs, Michael, ed. see Ludel, Leonard.

Riggs, Olen L., Jr. & Locke, Carl E. Anodic Protection: Theory & Practice in the Prevention of Corrosion. LC 80-20412. 298p. 1981. 85.00 (0-306-40597-0, Plenum Trade) Perseus Pubng.

Riggs, Paul D. Una Nueva Oportunidad. (Deseo Ser.).Tr. of New Opportunity. (SPA.). 1999. per. 3.50 (0-373-35308-1, 1-35308-5) Harlequin Bks.

Riggs, Paula D. Baby by Design. 1997. per. 3.99 (0-373-07806-4, 1-07806-2) Silhouette.

— The Bachelor Party. (Intimate Moments Ser.). 1995. per. 3.75 (0-373-07656-8, 1-07656-1) Silhouette.

— Daddy by Accident. (Maternity Row Ser.). 1997. mass mkt. 3.50 (0-373-76073-6, 1-76073-5) Silhouette.

— Desperate Measures: New Mexico. 1997. per. 4.50 (0-373-47181-5, 1-47181-2) Harlequin Bks.

***Riggs, Paula D.** Firebrand. 2000. mass mkt. 4.50 (0-373-82235-9, 1-82235-2) Harlequin Bks.

Riggs, Paula D. Firebrand. (Intimate Moments Ser.). 1993. mass mkt. 3.39 (0-373-07481-6, 5-07481-0) Silhouette.

— Firebrand. large type ed. (Silhouette Romance Ser.). 380p. 1995. 18.95 (0-373-59625-1) Mac Lib Ref.

— Her Secret, His Child. 1995. per. 3.75 (0-373-07667-3, 1-07667-8) Silhouette.

— Mommy by Surprise. (Intimate Moments Ser.: No. 794). 1997. per. 3.99 (0-373-07794-7, 1-07794-0) Silhouette.

— Murdock's Family. (Desire Ser.). 1994. per. 2.99 (0-373-05898-5, 1-05898-1) Silhouette.

— No Easy Way Out. large type ed. (Silhouette Romance Ser.). 1995. 18.95 (0-373-59640-5) Mac Lib Ref.

— Once More a Family. (Intimate Moments Ser.: No. 933). 1999. per. 4.25 (0-373-07933-8, 1-07933-4) Silhouette.

— Once upon a Wedding: Romantic Traditions. (Intimate Moments Ser.). 1993. per. 3.50 (0-373-07524-3, 5-07524-7) Silhouette.

— The Parent Plan. (Thirty-Six Hours Ser.). 1998. per. 4.50 (0-373-65016-7, 1-65016-7) Harlequin Bks.

— A Perfect Hero: Whose Child? (Intimate Moments Ser.: No. 889). 1998. per. 4.25 (0-373-07889-7, 0-07889-9) Silhouette.

— Taming the Night. 1999. mass mkt. 5.99 (0-449-15019-4, GM) Fawcett.

Riggs, Peter J. Whys & Ways of Science: Introducing Philosophical & Sociological Theories of Science. 248p. (Orig.). (C). 1992. pap. 19.95 (0-522-84471-5, Pub. by Melbourne Univ Pr) Paul & Co Pubs.

Riggs, Peter J., ed. Natural Kinds, Laws of Nature & Scientific Methodology. LC 96-35782. (Australasian Studies in History & Philosophy of Science: Vol. 12). 272p. (C). 1996. text 137.50 (0-7923-4225-9) Kluwer Academic.

Riggs, R. Espiritu Mismo.Tr. of Spirit Himself. (SPA.). 224p. 1964. pap. 5.99 (0-8297-0551-1) Vida Pubs.

— Periodos Biblicos.Tr. of Dispensations. (SPA.). 160p. 1969. pap. 5.99 (0-8297-0590-2) Vida Pubs.

***Riggs, Ralph M.** The Life of Christ. (Discovery Ser.). 2000. pap. text. write for info. (1-891110-12-8, ATTS Pubns) Africa Theolog Trng.

— Periodos Biblicos. 1998. pap. 5.99 (0-8297-1578-9) Vida Pubs.

Riggs, Ralph M. The Spirit Himself. rev. ed. 224p. 1977. pap. 7.50 (0-88243-590-6, 02-0590) Gospel Pub.

***Riggs, Ricky & Wolfe, Angela.** Photo Album & Collectibles: Elementary Photo Album & Collectibles, Vols. 1-6. (Illus.). (J). (gr. k-5). 1999. mass mkt. 179.94 (1-930141-06-8) Priceless Bks.

— Photo Album & Collectibles: Fifth Grade Photo Album & Collectibles, Vol. 6. (Illus.). 22p. (J). (gr. 5). 1999. mass mkt. 29.99 (1-930141-05-X) Priceless Bks.

— Photo Album & Collectibles: First Grade Photo Album & Collectibles, Vol. 2. (Illus.). 22p. (J). (gr. 1). 1999. mass mkt. 29.99 (1-930141-01-7) Priceless Bks.

— Photo Album & Collectibles: Fourth Grade Photo Album & Collectibles, Vol. 5. (Illus.). 22p. (J). (gr. 4). 1999. mass mkt. 29.99 (1-930141-04-1) Priceless Bks.

— Photo Album & Collectibles: Kindergarten Photo Album & Collectibles, Vol. 1. (Illus.). 22p. (J). (gr. k). 1999. mass mkt. 29.99 (1-930141-00-9) Priceless Bks.

— Photo Album & Collectibles: Second Grade Photo Album & Collectibles, Vol. 3. (Illus.). 22p. (J). (gr. 2). 1999. mass mkt. 29.99 (1-930141-02-5) Priceless Bks.

— Photo Album & Collectibles: Third Grade Photo Album & Collectibles, Vol. 4. (Illus.). 22p. (J). (gr. 3). 1999. mass mkt. 29.99 (1-930141-03-3) Priceless Bks.

Riggs, Robert. Twelve Steps to a Never Union Company. 74p. (Orig.). 1995. pap. 19.95 (0-9645296-0-2) Fam Busn Bks.

Riggs, Robert D. & Wrather, J. Allen, eds. Biology & Management of the Soybean Cyst Nematode. LC 92-70943. (Illus.). 186p. (Orig.). 1992. pap. 39.00 (0-89054-125-6) Am Phytopathol Soc.

Riggs, Robert E. Politics in the United Nations: A Study of United States Influence in the General Assembly. LC 83-20164. 208p. 1984. reprint ed. lib. bdg. 59.50 (0-313-24298-4, RIP0, Greenwood Pr) Greenwood.

Riggs, Robert E. & Plano, Jack C. The United Nations: International Organization & World Politics. 2nd ed. 364p. (C). 1993. pap. text 53.00 (0-534-19704-3) Harcourt.

Riggs, Robert O., et al. Sexual Harassment in Higher Education: From Conflict to Community. Fife, Jonathan D., ed. & frwd. by. (ASHE-ERIC Higher Education Reports: No. 93-2). 89p. (Orig.). 1993. pap. 24.00 (1-878380-23-0) GWU Grad Schl E&HD.

Riggs, S. R., jt. ed. see Burnett, W. C.

Riggs, Seth. Singing for the Stars: A Complete Program for Training Your Voice. rev. ed. Carratello, John, ed. (Illus.). 1985. audio 45.00 (0-88284-472-5, 2535) Alfred Pub.

— Singing for the Stars: A Complete Program for Training Your Voice. rev. ed. Carratello, John, ed. (Illus.). 96p. 1987. pap. 45.00 incl. audio (0-88284-340-0, 2200) Alfred Pub.

— Singing for the Stars: A Complete Program for Training Your Voice. 5th rev. ed. Carratello, John, ed. (Illus.). 1992. pap. 45.00 incl. audio compact disk (0-88284-528-4, 3379) Alfred Pub.

Riggs, Sherry, jt. auth. see Pendergrass, Paula.

Riggs, Stephanie. Josh's First Day of School. (Illus.). 32p. (J). (ps-3). 1999. 15.95 (1-893815-00-5) Pie Sky.

Riggs, Stephen R. A Dakota-English Dictionary. 2nd ed. xvi, 665p. 1992. reprint ed. pap. 24.95 (0-87351-282-0, Borealis Book) Minn Hist.

— Dakota Grammar, Texts & Ethnography. LC 74-7998. reprint ed. 49.50 (0-404-11891-7) AMS Pr.

— Tah-Koo Wah-Kan: or The Gospel among the Dakotas. LC 78-38460. (Religion in America, Ser. 2). 534p. 1972. reprint ed. 36.95 (0-405-04081-4) Ayer.

Riggs, Susan A. Twenty-First Virginia Infantry. (Virginia Regimental Histories Ser.). (Illus.). 105p. 1991. 19.95 (1-56190-013-3) H E Howard.

Riggs, Thomas. St. James Guide to Black Artists. LC 97-3068. 625p. 1997. 155.00 (1-55862-220-9, 00155964) St James Pr.

Riggs, Thomas, contrib. by. Reference Guide to Short Fiction. 2nd ed. LC 98-35874. 1197p. 1999. 140.00 (1-55862-222-5, 00109209) St James Pr.

Riggs, Thomas, ed. Contemporary Poets, Vol. 1. 6th ed. 1336p. 1995. 160.00 (1-55862-191-1, 200208) St James Pr.

— Gale Business Strategies: Encyclopedia of Major Marketing Campaigns. LC 99-31858. 1700p. 1998. 250.00 (0-7876-3042-X) Gale.

***Riggs, Thomas, ed.** Reference Guide to American Literature. 4th ed. LC 99-31376. 1200p. 1999. 150.00 (1-55862-417-1, GML00299-200296, Pub. by St James Pr) Gale.

Riggs, Thomas L., et al. Sunset to Sunset: A Lifetime with My Brothers, the Dakotas. LC 97-35692. xxvi, 226p. 1997. pap. 14.95 (0-9622621-4-5) SD State Hist Soc.

Riggs, W. Webster, Jr. The You You Don't Know: Covert Influences on Your Behavior. LC 96-48012. 349p. 1997. 26.95 (1-57392-116-5) Prometheus Bks.

Riggs, William F., jt. ed. see Malhotra, Deepak.

Riggs, Wm. Bryan, et al, photos by. Low Country Scenes: Charleston, S. C. rev. ed. (Illus.). 24p. 1996. pap. 4.95 (0-9649686-3-0) Chrlstn Post Card.

Riggsbee, E. T., jt. auth. see Hashemian, H. M.

Riggsby, Andrew M. Crime & Community in Ciceronian Rome. LC 99-13718. 278p. 1999. pap. 19.95 (0-292-77099-5) U of Tex Pr.

***Riggsby, Andrew M.** Crime & Community in Ciceronian Rome. LC 99-13718. 278p. 1999. 40.00 (0-292-77098-7) U of Tex Pr.

Righetti, A., jt. ed. see Donath, A.

Righetti, Maggie. Crocheting in Plain English. 9th ed. (Illus.). 258p. 1988. pap. 15.95 (0-312-01412-0) St Martin.

— Knitting in Plain English. 13th ed. (Illus.). 224p. 1986. pap. 14.95 (0-312-45853-3) St Martin.

— Sweater Design in Plain English. (Illus.). 352p. (Orig.). 1990. pap. 17.95 (0-312-05164-6) St Martin.

Righetti, P. G. Immobilized pH Gradients: Theory & Methodology. (Laboratory Techniques in Biochemistry & Molecular Biology Ser.: Vol. 20). 398p. 1990. pap. 48.00 (0-444-81315-2) Elsevier.

Righetti, P. G. & Hancock, William, eds. Capillary Electrophoresis in Analytical Biotechnology. (Analytical Biotechnology Ser.). 576p. 1995. boxed set 189.95 (0-8493-7825-7, 7825) CRC Pr.

Righetti, Paolo. Alfred Wong Partnership: Innovation & Knowledge. 1999. pap. text 25.00 (88-7838-061-X) L'Arca IT.

Righi-Belkaoui, Ahmed. Handbook of Cost Accounting Theory & Techniques. LC 90-45142. 400p. 1991. 89.50 (0-89930-583-0, BTQ, Quorum Bks) Greenwood.

— The New Foundations of Management Accounting. LC 91-36667. 192p. 1992. 57.95 (0-89930-700-0, BKJ/, Quorum Bks) Greenwood.

Righi, Francois. Francois Righi. 186p. 1994. pap. 45.00 (2-908257-06-8, Pub. by F R A C) Dist Art Pubs.

Righini, Fernando & Papzzoni, Marco. The International Collectors' Book of Cigarette Packs. LC 97-80166. (Illus.). 176p. 1998. pap. 29.95 (0-7643-0448-8) Schiffer.

Righini, Giancarlo C., ed. Fiber Integrated Optics, Vol. 2954. (Europto Ser.). 212p. 1996. 66.00 (0-8194-2358-0) SPIE.

Righini, Giancarlo C., et al, eds. Integrated Optic Devices II, Vol. 3278. LC 98-171714. 362p. 1998. 80.00 (0-8194-2717-9) SPIE.

***Righini, Giancarlo C. & Najafi, S. Iraj, eds.** Integrated Optics Devices III. 408p. 1999. pap. text 92.00 (0-8194-3090-0) SPIE.

***Righini, Paul.** Thinking Architecturally: An Introduction to the Creation of Form & Place. (Illus.). 320p. 1999. pap. 69.95 (1-919713-29-8, U Pr W Africa) Intl Scholars.

Right Associates Staff. Lessons Learned: Dispelling the Myths of Downsizing. 84p. (Orig.). 1992. pap. 25.00 (0-9628438-1-4) Right Assocs.

— Severance: A Comprehensive Survey of Canadian Severance Practices. 121p. (Orig.). pap. 250.00 (0-9628438-2-2) Right Assocs.

Right, Bobby. Eternal Life. 432p. 1997. 23.95 (1-887750-49-5) Rutledge Bks.

R

An Asterisk (*) at the beginning of an entry indicates that the title is appearing for the first time.

Right, Zack. Everyone's Guide to Opening Doors by Telephone. 2nd ed. 352p. 1981. pap. 10.95 (*0-9604554-0-X*) Talmud Pr.

— Selling to Consumers: Complete Training Book. 350p. (Orig.). (C). 1984. pap. 9.95 (*0-9604554-1-8*) Talmud Pr.

Righteous Mother. Sex Her Right... Or Else! A Brother's Guide to Paradise. Clark, Gina, ed. LC 99-93947. (Illus.). 96p. 1999. pap. 4.95 (*0-9652540-3-8*) Swing St Pub.

Righteous Mother & Shakeefa, Sister. Get on Top! A Sister's Guide to Life, Love & Her Biggest Difficulty, the Black Man. LC 96-67612. (Illus.). 168p. (Orig.). 1997. pap. 9.95 (*0-9652540-0-3*) Swing St Pub.

Righteous Mother Staff & Shakeefa, Sister. Get on Top! A Sister's Guide to Life, Love & Her Biggest Difficulty... 2nd rev. ed. LC 98-60121. (Illus.). 176p. 1999. pap. 9.95 (*0-9652540-2-X*) Swing St Pub.

Righter, Anne, ed. see Shakespeare, William.

Righter, Carroll. Astrology & You. 1989. pap. 5.00 (*0-87980-422-X*) Wilshire.

Righter, Evie. The Best of Mexico: A Cookbook. LC 92-19622. (Illus.). 96p. 1992. 14.95 (*0-00-255148-9*) Collins SF.

Righter, Evie, ed. The Best of France: A Cookbook. (Best of Ser.). (Illus.). 96p. 1992. 16.95 (*0-00-255086-5*) Collins SF.

— The Best of Italy: A Cookbook. (Best of Ser.). (Illus.). 96p. 1992. 16.95 (*0-00-255085-7*) Collins SF.

Righter, Evie, jt. auth. see Downard, Georgia C.

Righter, R. W., jt. auth. see Krogg, A. J.

Righter, Robert W. Crucible for Conservation: The Creation of Grand Teton National Park. LC 81-69792. (Illus.). 202p. reprint ed. pap. 62.70 (*0-608-08864-1*, 206950300004) Bks Demand.

— Wind Energy in America: A History. LC 95-24686. (Illus.). 361p. 1996. 34.95 (*0-8061-2812-7*) U of Okla Pr.

Righter, Robert W., ed. A Teton Country Anthology. (Illus.). 208p. 1990. pap. 12.50 (*0-911797-73-4*) Roberts Rinehart.

Righter, Robert W., jt. auth. see Andrews, Robert.

Righter, Ron. Flex: The Total Offense. 64p. (Orig.). 1984. pap. 9.95 (*0-932741-99-1*) Championship Bks & Vid Prodns.

Righter, Rosemary. Utopia Lost: The United Nations & World Order. LC 94-33886. 421p. (C). 1995. 29.95 (*0-87078-358-0*) Century Foundation.

— Utopia Lost: The United Nations & World Order. LC 94-33886. 421p. (C). 1995. pap. 12.00 (*0-87078-359-9*) Century Foundation.

Righter, Walter C. A Pilgrim's Way. LC 97-49461. 1999. pap. 11.00 (*0-679-77655-9*) Knopf.

— Pilgrim's Way. LC 97-49461. 192p. 1998. 22.00 (*0-679-45442-X*) Knopf.

Righter, William. The Myth of Theory. LC 93-30388. 234p. (C). 1994. text 54.95 (*0-521-44544-2*) Cambridge U Pr.

Rightmire, Craig T., et al, eds. Coalbed Methane Resources of the United States. LC 84-45747. (AAPG Studies in Geology Ser.: No. 17). (Illus.). 386p. 1984. reprint ed. pap. 119.70 (*0-608-04230-7*, 206498700012) Bks Demand.

Rightmire, G. Phillip. The Evolution of "Homo Erectus" Comparative Anatomical Studies of an Extinct Human Species. (Illus.). 272p. (C). 1993. pap. text 29.95 (*0-521-44998-7*) Cambridge U Pr.

Rightmire, R. David. Sacraments & the Salvation Army: Pneumatological Foundations. LC 90-21325. (Studies in Evangelicalism: No. 10). 341p. 1990. 50.00 (*0-8108-2396-9*) Scarecrow.

— Salvationist Samurai: Gunpei Yamamuro & the Rise of the Salvation Army in Japan. LC 96-49240. (Pietist & Wesleyan Studies: No. 8). (Illus.). 216p. 1997. 51.50 (*0-8108-3270-4*) Scarecrow.

Righton, Caroline. Caroline Righton's Create It with Paint in an Evening. (Illus.). 80p. 1999. pap. 22.50 (*1-85486-174-3*) Trans-Atl Phila.

— Caroline Righton's Create It with Paper in an Evening. (Illus.). 80p. (Orig.). 1998. pap. 22.50 (*1-85486-175-1*, Pub. by Nexus Special Interests) Trans-Atl Phila.

— Caroline Righton's Create It with Thread in an Evening. (Illus.). 80p. (Orig.). 1998. pap. 22.50 (*1-85486-176-X*) Nexus Special Interests.

*__Righton, Caroline.__ Holiday & Festive Crafts. (Illus.). 80p. 1999. pap. 26.50 (*1-85486-191-3*, Pub. by Nexus Special Interests) Trans-Atl Phila.

Righton, Peter, jt. auth. see Richards, Margaret.

Rights, Douglas L. The American Indian in North Carolina. LC 57-9277. (Illus.). 298p. 1988. reprint ed. pap. 14.95 (*0-89587-066-5*) Blair.

Rights International Staff. International Human Rights, 2 vols., Set. 2250p. 1998. lib. bdg. 340.00 (*90-411-0608-1*) Kluwer Law Intl.

Rights International Staff, jt. auth. see Martin, Francisco F.

Rights, Lucille R. A Portrait of St. Lucie County, Florida. LC 94-32009. (Illus.). 1994. write for info. (*0-89865-917-5*) Donning Co.

Rights, R., jt. auth. see Ketzner, R.

Rights Watch of Asia Staff. Death by Default: A Policy of Fatal Neglect in China's State Orphanages. (Illus.). 406p. 1996. pap. 20.00 (*0-300-06894-8*) Yale U Pr.

*__Rigil, Jakob.__ Global Brothel: Survival & Post-Soviet Chaos. (Anthropology, Culture & Society Ser.). 2000. pap. text 22.50 (*0-7453-1597-6*) Pluto GBR.

Rigler, James. San Francisco Moon. (Illus.). 80p. 1998. 22.95 (*0-89087-871-4*); pap. 14.95 (*0-89087-856-0*) Celestial Arts.

— San Francisco Moon Postcard Book. (Illus.). 46p. 1998. pap. 8.95 (*0-89087-857-9*) Celestial Arts.

Rigler, Judyth W., jt. auth. see Rigler, Lewis C.

Rigler, Lewis C. & Rigler, Judyth W. In the Line of Duty: Reflections of a Texas Ranger Private. LC 95-16646. 204p. 1995. reprint ed. pap. 14.95 (*0-929398-99-8*) UNTX Pr.

Rigley, Kevin, jt. auth. see Harnett, Maggie.

Rigley, Steve. City of Gold: Impressions of Heaven. 55p. 1997. reprint ed. 16.99 (*1-900507-62-5*, Pub. by Solway) OM Literature.

Rigling, Walter S. Rigid-Flex Printed Wiring Design for Production & Readiness. (Electrical Engineering & Electronics Ser.: Vol. 47). (Illus.). 296p. 1988. text 155.00 (*0-8247-7707-7*) Dekker.

Rigmaiden, Paul. God Loves Us All. (Illus.). 32p. (Orig.). (J). (gr. k-4). 1988. pap. 5.00 (*0-9621598-0-8*) DADA Pubns.

Rigmant, Vladimir, jt. auth. see Gordon, Yefim.

Rignall, John, ed. George Eliot & Europe. LC 96-37220. (Warwick Studies in the European Humanities). 256p. 1997. text 61.95 (*1-85928-334-9*, Pub. by Scolar Pr) Ashgate Pub Co.

*__Rignall, John, ed.__ The Oxford Reader's Companion to George Eliot. (Illus.). 672p. 2000. 55.00 (*0-19-860099-2*) OUP.

Rignell, Gosta. The Peshitta to the Book of Job: Critically Investigated with Introduction, Translation, Commentary & Summary. 382p. (Orig.). 1994. pap. 59.50 (*91-88034-24-0*) Coronet Bks.

Rignell, L. G. The Old Testament in Syriac According to the Peshitta Version Pt. II, Fasc. 1a: Job. LC 78-339247. xix, 55p. 1993. reprint ed. 56.00 (*90-04-06342-0*) Brill Academic Pubs.

*__Rigney & Bayer.__ Wear of Materials '99. 1380p. 1999. text 302.00 (*0-08-043007-4*) Elsevier.

Rigney, jt. auth. see Derfler.

Rigney, Ann & Fokkema, Douwe, eds. Cultural Participation: Trends since the Middle Ages. LC 93-1451. (Utrecht Publications in General & Comparative Literature: Vol. 31). x, 261p. 1993. 47.00 (*1-55619-430-7*) J Benjamins Pubng Co.

Rigney, Ann, jt. ed. see Leerssen, Joep.

Rigney, Barbara. The Voices of Toni Morrison. LC 91-16092. 206p. 1991. text 47.50 (*0-8142-0554-2*) Ohio St U Pr.

— The Voices of Toni Morrison. LC 91-16092. 206p. (C). 1991. pap. text 14.95 (*0-8142-0555-0*) Ohio St U Pr.

Rigney, Barbara H. Lilith's Daughters: Women & Religion in Contemporary Fiction. LC 81-70012. 133p. reprint ed. pap. 41.30 (*0-608-20471-4*, 207172300002) Bks Demand.

— Madness & Sexual Politics in the Feminist Novel: Studies in Bronte, Woolf, Lessing & Atwood. LC 78-53291. 158p. reprint ed. pap. 49.00 (*0-608-09922-8*, 206926000003) Bks Demand.

— Margaret Atwood: A Critical Inquiry. LC 87-1370. (Women Writers Ser.). (C). 1987. pap. 19.50 (*0-389-20743-8*, N8301) B&N Imports.

Rigney, Barbara Hill, ed. see Schneider, Bronka.

Rigney, D. & Bayer, R. G., eds. Proceedings of the 11th International Conference on Wear of Materials, 1997. 740p. 1997. 281.00 (*0-08-042841-X*, Pergamon Pr) Elsevier.

Rigney, David A., ed. see American Society for Metals Staff.

Rigney, David A., ed. see ASM Materials Science Seminar Staff.

Rigney, Francis J. A Beginner's Book of Magic. (Illus.). (YA). (gr. 6 up). 1963. 9.95 (*0-8159-5103-5*) Devin.

Rigney, Francis J., jt. auth. see Murray, William D.

Rigney, H. M. Australian Business Taxation. 430p. 1990. pap. 69.00 (*0-409-30159-0*, Austral, MICHIE) LEXIS Pub.

Rigney, James, ed. & intro. see Shakespeare, William.

Rigney, Jim. Daniel Defoe. Armstrong, Isobel & Loughrey, Bryan, eds. (Writers & Their Work Ser.). 1998. pap. 17.00 (*0-7463-0848-5*, Pub. by Northcote House) U Pr of Miss.

Rigo, H. G., et al. The Relationship Between Chlorine in Waste Streams & Dioxin Emissions from Waste Combustor Stacks Vol. 36: The Relationship Between Chlorine in Waste Streams & Dioxin Emissions from Waste Combustor Stacks. (CRTD Ser.: Vol. 36). 716p. 1995. 100.00 (*0-7918-1222-7*, I00385) ASME.

Rigo, J. M. Geomembranes: Identification & Performance Testing. 4. 376p. (C). (gr. 13). 1990. write for info. (*0-412-38530-9*) Chapman & Hall.

Rigo, J. M., jt. ed. see Rollin, A. L.

Rigobello, L., jt. auth. see Andrioli, G.

Rigobon, Roberto, jt. ed. see Hausmann, Ricardo.

Rigol, Francese. My First Phone. (J). (ps up). 1996. 12.99 (*0-614-15713-7*) Random.

Rigola. Microsoft Word 6.0 for Windows: Easy Reference Guide. (DF - Computer Applications Ser.). 144-160p. 1996. mass mkt. 9.95 (*0-538-71462-X*) S-W Pub.

*__Rigole, Marc.__ Lisbon. 2nd ed. (Illus.). 2001. pap. 13.95 (*2-89464-233-4*) Ulysses Travel.

Rigole, Marc. Ulysses Due South Guide: Cartagena. (Illus.). 128p. 1998. pap. 9.95 (*2-89464-018-8*) Ulysses Travel.

*__Rigole, Marc & Langlois, Claude Victor.__ Acapulco. 2nd ed. Ulysses Travel Guide Staff, ed. (Due South Guide Ser.). (Illus.). 176p. 1999. pap. 9.95 (*2-89464-213-X*, Pub. by Ulysses Travel) Globe Pequot.

*__Rigole, Marc & Langlois, Claude-Victor.__ Portugal. 3rd ed. (Illus.). 448p. 2000. pap. 17.95 (*2-89464-245-8*, Pub. by Ulysses Travel) Globe Pequot.

— Ulysses Travel Guide: Panama. 3rd ed. (Illus.). 288p. 1999. 17.95 (*2-89464-129-X*, Pub. by Ulysses Travel) Globe Pequot.

*__Rigolosi, Steven A.__ Tools for Success: Soft Skill Construction Industry. (C). 2000. pap. 25.00 (*0-13-025927-6*) P-H.

Rigoni, Francine, et al. Des Roses Blanches pour Danielle, & Autres Histoires. (Serie Rouge). (Illus.). 63p. (C). 1994. pap. 7.50 (*0-521-44981-2*) Cambridge U Pr.

Rigoni Stern, Mario. The Sergeant in the Snow. Colquhoun, Archibald, tr. 158p. 1998. pap. text 15.95 (*0-8101-6055-2*, Marlboro) Northwestern U Pr.

Rigonistern, Mario. The Story of Tonle. Shepley, John, tr. from ITA. LC 98-9910. 128p. 1998. text 26.95 (*0-8101-6034-X*, Marlboro) Northwestern U Pr.

Rigopoulos, Antonio. Dattatreya: The Immortal Guru, Yogin, & Avatara: A Study of the Transformative & Inclusive Character of a Multi-Faceted Hindu Deity. LC 97-21244. (SUNY Series in Religious Studies). (Illus.). 342p. (C). 1998. text 89.50 (*0-7914-3695-0*); pap. text 29.95 (*0-7914-3696-9*) State U NY Pr.

— The Life & Teachings of Sai Baba of Shirdi. LC 91-40880. (SUNY Series in Religious Studies). 494p. (C). 1993. text 64.50 (*0-7914-1267-9*); pap. text 23.95 (*0-7914-1268-7*) State U NY Pr.

Rigopoulos, Antonio, jt. ed. see Mastromattei, Romano.

Rigopoulos, Antonio, tr. see Filippi, Gian Giuseppe.

Rigor, Benjamin M., jt. auth. see Schurr, Avital.

Rigor, Benjamin M., jt. ed. see Schurr, Avital.

Rigos, Sarah A., tr. see Averoff-Tossizza, Evangelos.

Rigotti, Paolo, et al, eds. European Society for Surgical Research (ESSR) Abstracts from 33rd Congress, Padua, Italy April 22 - 25, 1998. (European Surgical Research Ser.: Vol. 30, Suppl. 1). xii, 134p. 1998. pap. 44.50 (*3-8055-6699-9*) S Karger.

Rigsbee, David. A Skeptic's Notebook. 80p. (Orig.). 1996. pap. 10.00 (*1-879934-46-9*) St Andrews NC.

— Styles of Ruin: Joseph Brodsky & the Postmodernist Elegy, 93. LC 98-26454. (Contributions to the Study of World Literature Ser.: Vol. 93). 192p. 1999. 55.00 (*0-313-30419-X*, Greenwood Pr) Greenwood.

— Your Heart Will Fly Away. LC 92-80447. 80p. (Orig.). 1992. pap. 10.95 (*0-912292-97-0*) Smith.

Rigsbee, David, jt. auth. see Burch-Brown, Carol.

Rigsbee, Edwin Richard. Developing Strategic Alliances. Young, George & Atmore, Barbara, eds. LC 99-75083. (Illus.). 112p. 1999. pap. 16.95 (*1-56052-550-9*) Crisp Pubns.

*__Rigsbee, Edwin Richard.__ Partnershift: How to Profit from the Partnering Trend. 2nd ed. LC 00-36652. 288p. 2000. 29.95 (*0-471-38653-7*) Wiley.

Rigsbee, W. Lynn, II, jt. auth. see Allen, Calvin H.

Rigsby, Bruce, ed. see Smith, Harlan I.

Rigsby, David. The Hopper Light. (Poetry Ser.). 56p. (Orig.). (C). 1988. pap. 8.00 (*0-934332-45-2*) LEpervier Pr.

Rigsby, Gem. Herb Seed for Thought: Herbal Translations with Hearticulture. Rigsby, W. Terry, ed. (Illus.). 112p. 1998. 14.95 (*0-9664548-5-5*) Spur Ridge.

Rigsby, Gregory U. Alexander Crummell: Pioneer in Nineteenth-Century Pan-African Thought, 101. LC 86-15034. (Contributions in Afro-American & African Studies: No. 101). 249p. 1987. 59.95 (*0-313-25570-9*, RYC/, Greenwood Pr) Greenwood.

Rigsby, Kent J. Asylia: Territorial Inviolability in the Hellenistic World. LC 95-22410. (Hellenistic Culture & Society Ser.: Vol. XXII). (Illus.). 660p. (C). 1996. 100.00 (*0-520-20098-5*, Pub. by U CA Pr) Cal Prin Full Svc.

Rigsby, L. W. Historic Georgia Families. 258p. 1997. reprint ed. lib. bdg. 32.50 (*0-8328-6620-2*) Higginson Bk Co.

Rigsby, Lee, jt. auth. see Pruett, James.

Rigsby, Leo C., jt. auth. see McDill, Edward L.

Rigsby, Lewis W. Historic Georgia Families. LC 69-17128. (Illus.). 258p. 1998. reprint ed. pap. 25.00 (*0-8063-0298-4*) Clearfield Co.

Rigsby, Michael A. The Outer Bay. (Illus.). 24p. 1996. pap. 4.95 (*1-878244-12-4*) Monterey Bay Aquarium.

Rigsby, Michael A., ed. A Natural History of Monterey Bay National Marine Sanctuary. LC 97-7956. (Illus.). 300p. 1999. pap. 19.95 (*1-878244-11-6*) Monterey Bay Aquarium.

Rigsby, Olga, tr. see Rivera, Guadalupe & Colle, Marie-Pierre.

Rigsby, W. Terry, ed. see Rigsby, Gem.

Rigutini, Giuseppe & Bulle, Oscar. Italian-German - German-Italian Dictionary. (GER & ITA.). 1984p. 175.00 (*0-7859-8868-8*) Fr & Eur.

Rigutini, Guiseppe, jt. auth. see Bulle, O.

Rigzin, Tsepak. Tibetan-English Dictionary of Buddhist Terminology. (ENG & TIB.). 1987. 95.00 (*0-8288-2319-7*, F 140705) Fr & Eur.

Riha, Bob, Jr. & Handschuh, David. National Media Guide for Emergency & Disaster Incidents. (Illus.). 81p. 1998. pap. text 30.00 (*0-7881-3911-8*) DIANE Pub.

Riha, John, jt. auth. see Hodgson, Larry.

Riha, Karl. Dada Zurich: A Clown's Game for Nothing. 1996. 95.00 (*0-8161-7328-1*) Macmillan.

— Fundgrube Mediengeschichte: Texte und Kommentare. (GER.). 235p. 1997. 38.95 (*3-631-31898-7*) P Lang Pubng.

Riha, Karl, ed. see Delling, Manfred.

Riha, Karl, ed. see Viehoff-Kamper, Evelyn.

Riha, Susanne. Animal Journeys: Life Cycles & Migrations. (Animals in the Wild Ser.). (Illus.). 32p. (J). (gr. 3-5). 1999. lib. bdg. 16.95 (*1-56711-426-1*) Blackbirch.

— Animals at Rest: Sleeping Patterns & Habitats. LC 99-13894. (Animals in the Wild Ser.). (Illus.). 32p. (J). (gr. 3-5). 1999. lib. bdg. 16.95 (*1-56711-425-3*) Blackbirch.

*__Riha, Susanne.__ Animals & the Seasons: The Cycle of Nature. LC 99-59475. (Animals in the Wild Ser.). 32p. (J). (gr. 3-5). 2000. lib. bdg. 17.95 (*1-56711-429-6*) Blackbirch.

Riha, Thomas. A Russian European: Paul Miliukov in Russian Politics. LC 68-27582. 391p. reprint ed. pap. 121.30 (*0-608-15460-1*, 202931200060) Bks Demand.

Riha, Thomas, ed. Readings in Russian Civilization, 3 vols. rev. ed. Incl. Vol. 1. Russia Before Peter the Great, 900-1700. LC 69-14825. 1969. pap. text 15.95 (*0-226-71853-0*); Vol. 2. Imperial Russia, 1700-1917. LC 69-14825. 1969. pap. text 19.00 (*0-226-71855-7*); Vol. 3. Soviet Russia, 1917 - Present. LC 69-14825. 1969. pap. text 17.95 (*0-226-71857-3*); LC 69-14825. 1969. write for info. (*0-318-56069-0*) U Ch Pr.

Rihaczek, August W. Radar Resolution & Complex-Image Analysis. LC 96-11029. 524p. 1996. 115.00 (*0-89006-868-2*) Artech Hse.

Rihaldi, Enrico. Seed of the Divine Fruit. LC 86-91340. 1987. 18.95 (*0-87212-200-X*) Libra.

Rihani, Ameen A. Toukous-ul Maa! (Water Rituals) Letters to Serene. (ARA.). 224p. 1999. pap. 6.00 (*0-9634349-3-4*) Platform Intl.

*__Rihani, Ameen F.__ Critiques in Art. (Illus.). 200p. 1999. 16.00 (*0-9634349-5-0*, Pub. by Librairie Du Liban) Platform Intl.

Rihani, Ameen F. Maker of Modern Arabia. LC 83-1485. (Illus.). 370p. 1983. reprint ed. lib. bdg. 92.50 (*0-313-23854-5*, RIMA, Greenwood Pr) Greenwood.

*__Rihani, Ameen F. & Gibran, Kahlil.__ Book of Khalid. 6th ed. (Illus.). 364p. 2000. reprint ed. 18.00 (*0-9634349-8-5*, Pub. by Librairie Du Liban) Platform Intl.

Rihani, Serene. Awrak Samita: Serene's Diary. (ARA., Illus.). 112p. 1998. pap. 10.00 (*0-9634349-1-8*, Pub. by Dar Al-Ibda IE) Platform Intl.

— Silent Diary: Serene's Notes. (Illus.). 112p. 1998. pap. 10.00 (*0-9634349-2-6*, Pub. by Dar Al-Ibda IE) Platform Intl.

Riherd, jt. auth. see Reinhartsen.

Rihoit, Catherine. Les Abimes du Coeur. (FRE.). 1984. pap. 13.95 (*0-7859-4206-8*) Fr & Eur.

— Le Bal des Debutantes. (FRE.). 1982. pap. 11.95 (*0-7859-4168-1*) Fr & Eur.

— La Favorite. (FRE.). 1985. pap. 10.95 (*0-7859-4231-9*) Fr & Eur.

Rihova, Blanka & Vetvicka, Vaclav. Immunological Disorders in Mice. 280p. 1990. lib. bdg. 195.00 (*0-8493-5635-0*, QR188) CRC Pr.

*__Riichi, Yokomitsu.__ Shanghai. Washburn, Dennis, tr. from JPN. (Michigan Monograph Series in Japanese Studies: No. 33). 180p. 2000. 34.95 (*1-929280-00-9*, 52095, Pub. by U MI Japan); pap. 16.95 (*1-929280-01-7*, 52096, Pub. by U MI Japan) U of Mich Pr.

Riikonen, Eero & Smith, Gregory M. Re-Imagining Therapy: Living Conversations & Relational Knowing. (Inquiries in Social Construction Ser.). 192p. (C). 1997. 45.00 (*0-8039-7653-4*, 76534); pap. 14.99 (*0-8039-7654-2*, 76542) Sage.

Riikonen, Nancy. Industrial Wastewater Source Control: An Inspection Guide: The City of San Diego. LC 91-66930. 300p. (Orig.). 1991. pap. text 29.95 (*0-87762-855-6*) Technomic.

Riis. Small Animal Opthalmology, '94. 1994. text 32.95 (*0-7234-2003-3*) Wolfe Pubng AZ.

Riis, Jacob A. The Battle with the Slum. LC 98-10020. (Illus.). 480p. 1998. pap. 14.95 (*0-486-40196-0*) Dover.

— The Battle with the Slum. LC 69-16245. (Criminology, Law Enforcement, & Social Problems Ser.: No. 77). (Illus.). 1969. reprint ed. 25.00 (*0-87585-077-4*) Patterson Smith.

— The Battle with the Slum: A Ten Years War Rewritten. (Illus.). 1972. reprint ed. 14.00 (*0-8290-0653-2*) Irvington.

— Children of the Poor. LC 73-137186. (Poverty U. S. A. Historical Record Ser.). 1971. reprint ed. 25.95 (*0-405-03124-6*) Ayer.

— Children of the Tenements. LC 75-122732. (Short Story Index Reprint Ser.). (Illus.). 1977. 23.95 (*0-8369-3565-9*) Ayer.

— Children of the Tenements. LC 70-104549. (Illus.). reprint ed. lib. bdg. 22.00 (*0-8398-1757-6*) Irvington.

— How the Other Half Lives. (Illus.). 233p. 1971. pap. 10.95 (*0-486-22012-5*) Dover.

— How the Other Half Lives. 240p. 1996. text 39.95 (*0-312-12809-6*) St Martin.

— How the Other Half Lives. Sante, Luc, ed. 1997. pap. 9.95 (*0-14-118004-8*) Viking Penguin.

Riis, Jacob A. Making of an American. (Illus.). Date not set. reprint ed. 35.00 (*0-87556-811-4*) Saifer.

Riis, Jacob A. Making of an American, 1902. (Illus.). 443p. 1992. pap. 35.00 (*0-87556-121-7*) Saifer.

— Nibsy's Christmas. LC 71-90590. (Short Story Index Reprint Ser.). 1977. 15.95 (*0-8369-3073-8*) Ayer.

— Out of Mulberry Street. LC 74-104550. 279p. reprint ed. lib. bdg. 29.75 (*0-8398-1758-4*) Irvington.

— Ten Years' War: An Account of the Battle with the Slum in New York. LC 70-103655. (Select Bibliographies Reprint Ser.). 1977. 29.95 (*0-8369-5155-7*) Ayer.

— Theodore Roosevelt, the Citizen. LC 71-101270. reprint ed. 34.50 (*0-404-05335-1*) AMS Pr.

— Theodore Roosevelt, the Citizen. (History - United States Ser.). 471p. 1992. reprint ed. lib. bdg. 99.00 (*0-7812-6220-8*) Rprt Serv.

— Theodore Roosevelt, the Citizen. LC 77-108531. 1970. reprint ed. 15.00 (*0-403-00224-9*) Scholarly.

Riis, Jacob A. & Sante, Luc. How the Other Half Lives: Studies among the Tenements of New York. LC 97-8455. (Penguin Classics Ser.). 224p. 1997. pap. 9.95 (*0-14-043679-0*) Viking Penguin.

*__Riis, Jens Ove, et al.__ Games in Operations Management: IFIP TC5/WG5.7 Fourth International Workshop of the Special Interest Group on Integrated Production Management Systems & the European Group of University Teachers for Industrial Management EHTB: November 26-29, 1998, Ghent, Belgium. LC 00-28580. 2000. write for info. (*0-7923-7844-X*) Kluwer Academic.

Riis, Ole, jt. ed. see Pettersson, Thorleif.

An Asterisk (*) at the beginning of an entry indicates that the title is appearing for the first time.

R

An Asterisk (*) at the beginning of an entry indicates that the title is appearing for the first time.

R

RILEM Technical Committee 119, jt. auth. see Springenschmid, R.

RILEM Technical Committee 51-ALC Staff, jt. auth. see RILEM Technical Committee 78-MCA Staff.

RILEM Technical Committee 78-MCA Staff & RILEM Technical Committee 51-ALC Staff. Autoclaved Aerated Concrete: Properties, Testing, & Design: RILEM Recommended Practices. LC 93-6890. (Illus.). 424p. (C). 1993. 125.00 (0-419-17960-7, E & FN Spon) Routledge.

***Riles, Annelise.** The Network Inside Out. LC 99-87959. 304p. (C). 1999. text 44.50 (0-472-11071-3, 11071) U of Mich Pr.

Riley. Critical Thinking & Problem Solving. (C). 1998. pap. text 35.00 (0-536-01604-6) Pearson Custom.

— Dandy, Day & the Devil. (Orig.). pap. 17.95 (0-8488-1595-5) Amereon Ltd.

— Engineering Mechanics: Dynamics & Statics & Mechanics of Materials, Set. 2nd ed. 1360p. 1996. pap. text 203.90 (0-471-15247-1) Wiley.

— English Mechanical Dynamics Syllabus. 2nd ed. 1999. text 64.00 (0-471-37664-7) Wiley.

***Riley.** Fantastic Space Stories. 2000. pap. 6.95 (0-552-52767-X, Pub. by Transworld Publishers Ltd) Trafalgar.

Riley. Human Resource Management. 2nd ed. LC 97-145370. 264p. 1996. pap. text 36.95 (0-7506-2729-8) Buttrwrth-Heinemann.

— In God's Image. 32p. 1996. pap. text 2.95 (0-934134-21-9, LL0219) Sheed & Ward WI.

— Twelve Days of Christmas. (J). 1996. 15.00 (0-671-89202-9) S&S Bks Yung.

— Using Modula 2. 1987. pap., teacher ed. 12.25 (0-87835-237-6) PWS Pubs.

Riley & Moynes. The Money Coach: Your Game Plan for Growth & Security. 1992. pap. text. write for info. (0-7730-5265-8) Addison-Wes.

Riley, jt. auth. see Beveridge.

Riley, jt. auth. see Giarratano, Joseph C.

Riley, jt. auth. see Headington, Mark.

Riley, Alan J., et al, eds. Sexual Pharmacology. (Illus.). 248p. 1994. text 75.00 (0-19-262283-8) OUP.

Riley, Alice C. Slumber Boat. (Illus.). 24p. (J). (ps). 1995. 14.95 (0-9642944-2-7) Starry Night.

Riley, Anita M. Evaluating Acquired Skills in Communication (EASIC) rev. ed. 48p. 1991. 99.00 (0-7616-7788-7) Commun Skill.

Riley, Ann L. Restoring Streams in Cities: A Guide for Planners, Policymakers & Citizens. LC 97-42715. 1998. pap. text 35.00 (1-55963-042-6); pap. text 55.00 (1-55963-043-4) Island Pr.

Riley, Annabel. The Beginning. (Mini Pop-up Bible Stories Ser.). (Illus.). 8p. (J). 1995. 4.99 (0-7814-1521-7) Chariot Victor.

— The Birth of Jesus. (Mini Pop-Up Bible Stories Ser.). (Illus.). 6p. (J). (gr. k-2). 1994. 4.99 (0-7814-1520-9, Lion) Chariot Victor.

Riley, Anne. Help Me. (My First Prayers Bks.). (Illus.). (J). 1997. 2.50 (1-85608-021-8) Hunt GBR.

— I'm Sorry. (My First Prayers Bks.). (Illus.). (J). 1997. 2.50 (1-85608-016-1) Hunt GBR.

— Please, God. (My First Prayers Bks.). (Illus.). (J). 1997. 2.50 (1-85608-026-9) Hunt GBR.

— Thank You. (My First Prayers Bks.). (Illus.). (J). 1997. 2.50 (1-85608-011-0) Hunt GBR.

Riley, Anne W. & Zaccaro, Stephen J., eds. Occupational Stress & Organizational Effectiveness. LC 86-25250. 287p. 1987. 59.95 (0-275-92281-2, C2281, Praeger Pubs) Greenwood.

Riley, Anne W., jt. ed. see Frederiksen, Lee W.

Riley, B. F. History of Conecuh County: Embracing a Detailed Record of Events from the Earliest Period to the Present (1881); Biographical Sketches of Those Who Have Been Most Conspicuous in the Annals. 233p. 1997. reprint ed. lib. bdg. 29.50 (0-8328-6595-8) Higginson Bk Co.

Riley, Barbara. Preparing Your Child for Surgery: What a Family Can Do. 20p. 1998. pap. 5.95 (0-9666043-0-X) Team Surgery.

Riley, Barbara W. & Brokensha, David. The Mbeere in Kenya Vol. I: Changing Rural Ecology. LC 88-12108. (Illus.). 384p. (Orig.). (C). 1988. pap. text 29.00 (0-8191-6998-6); lib. bdg. 55.00 (0-8191-6997-8) U Pr of Amer.

Riley, Betty. A Veil Too Thin: Reincarnation Out of Control. LC 84-50090. 96p. 1984. pap. 2.95 (0-911842-37-3, B920) Valley Sun.

Riley, Bob. Evaluation of Therapeutic Recreation Through Quality Assurance. LC 87-50299. 103p. 1987. text 16.95 (0-910251-18-5) Venture Pub PA.

Riley, Bob, ed. Quality Management: Applications for Therapeutic Recreation. LC 91-66102. 242p. (C). 1991. text 23.95 (0-910251-47-9) Venture Pub PA.

Riley, Bruce T. The Psychology of Religious Experience in Its Personal & Institutional Dimensions. (American University Studies: Theology & Religion: Ser. VII, Vol. 49). XVI, 361p. (C). 1988. text 47.70 (0-8204-0862-X) P Lang Pubng.

Riley, C. J. The Encyclopedia of Trains & Locomotives. LC 94-1826. 224p. 1994. 19.98 (1-56799-087-8, MetroBooks) M Friedman Pub Grp Inc.

***Riley, C. J.** Encyclopedia of Trains & Locomotives. (Illus.). 224p. 2000. 14.98 (1-56799-982-4) M Friedman Pub Grp Inc.

Riley, C. J. The Golden Age of the Passenger Train: From Steam to Diesel & Beyond. LC 96-38290. 1997. 24.98 (1-56799-383-4, MetroBooks) M Friedman Pub Grp Inc.

Riley, C. J., jt. auth. see Solomon, Brian.

Riley, Caroline L. The Newsom Papers. 150p. 1988. 35.00 (0-9621609-0-3) C L Riley.

***Riley, Carroll L.** The Kachina & the Cross: Indians & Spaniards in the Early Southwest. LC 99-22274. (Illus.). 360p. 1999. 34.95 (0-87480-610-0) U of Utah Pr.

Riley, Carroll L. Rio Del Norte: People of the Upper Rio Grande from the Earliest Times to the Pueblo Revolt. (Illus.). 336p. (C). 1996. reprint ed. pap. text 15.95 (0-87480-496-5) U of Utah Pr.

Riley, Carroll L., jt. auth. see Lange, Charles H.

Riley, Carroll L., ed. see Bandelier, Adolph F.

Riley, Carroll L., jt. ed. see Schaafsma, Curtis F.

Riley, Charles A., II. Color Codes: Modern Theories of Color in Philosophy, Painting & Architecture, Literature, Music, & Psychology. LC 94-9733. (Illus.). 365p. 1995. pap. 25.00 (0-87451-742-7) U Pr of New Eng.

— High-Access Home: Design & Decoration for Barrier-Free Living. LC 99-14404. (Illus.). 160p. 1999. 40.00 (0-8478-2213-3, Pub. by Rizzoli Intl) St Martin.

Riley, Charles A., 2nd. Jaime Franco: New Paintings. (Illus.). 12p. (Orig.). 1994. pap. 5.00 (0-9626731-6-1) Yoshii Gallery.

Riley, Charles A., II. The Saints of Modern Art: The Ascetic Ideal in Painting, Sculpture, Architecture, Music, Dance, Literature, & Philosophy. LC 97-43017. (Illus.). 371p. 1998. 40.00 (0-87451-765-6) U Pr of New Eng.

Riley, Charles A. Small Business, Big Politics: What Entrepreneurs Need to Know to Use Their Growing Political... 271p. 1996. pap. text 14.95 (1-56079-707-X) Petersons.

Riley, Charles A., 2nd, ed. see Di Crescenzo, Casimiro.

Riley, Charles A., 2nd, ed. see Fabre, Josep P.

Riley, Charles V. Nine Annual Reports on the Noxious, Beneficial & Other Insects of the State of Missouri, 1869-1877: With a General Index & Supplement, 10 vols. Sterling, Keir B., ed. LC 77-81105. (Biologists & Their World Ser.). 1979. reprint ed. lib. bdg. 145.95 (0-405-10745-5) Ayer.

Riley, Christopher. Walter Kempowski's "Deutsche Chronik" A Study in Ironic Narration. LC 96-52753. (Historisch-Kritische Arbeiten zur Deutschen Literatur Ser.: Bd. 19). 191p. 1996. pap. 42.95 (0-8204-3228-8) P Lang Pubng.

— Walter Kempowski's "Deutsche Chronik" A Study in Ironic Narration. LC 96-52753. (Historisch-Kritische Arbeiten zur Deutschen Literatur Ser.: Bd. 19). 191p. 1997. pap. 42.95 (3-631-30975-9) P Lang Pubng.

Riley, Christopher, et al, eds. Releasing Resources to Achieve Health Gain. 1995. 79.95 (1-85775-018-7, Radcliffe Med Pr) Scovill Paterson.

Riley, Christopher M. Pharmaceutical & Biomedical Applications of Liquid Chromatography. Lough, W. John et al, eds. LC 94-20192. (Progress in Pharmacology & Clinical Pharmacology Ser.: No. 1). 380p. 1994. 155.00 (0-08-041009-X, Pergamon Pr) Elsevier.

Riley, Christopher M. & Rosanske, Thomas W., eds. Pharmaceutical & Biomedical Analysis: Development & Validation of Analytical Methods. LC 96-33800. (Progress in Pharmaceutical & Biomedical Analysis Ser.: No. 3). 352p. 1996. 86.50 (0-08-042792-8, Pergamon Pr) Elsevier.

Riley, Cole. Dark Blood Moon: Murder in New Orleans. 288p. 1995. mass mkt. 4.95 (0-87067-746-2) Holloway.

— The Devil to Pay. 224p. (Orig.). 1994. mass mkt. 3.95 (0-87067-742-X) Holloway.

— The Killing Kind. 288p. (Orig.). 1990. mass mkt. 3.50 (0-87067-548-6) Holloway.

— Rough Trade. 320p. (Orig.). 1987. mass mkt. 3.50 (0-87067-835-3) Holloway.

Riley, Corwin E. Selling's My Game: Riley's the Name. (Illus.). 96p. 1988. 6.95 (0-9621048-0-9) Corray Pub Co.

Riley, D., jt. auth. see Riley, P.

***Riley, D. N.** Aerial Archaeology in Britain. 2nd ed. LC 97-149884. (Archaeology Ser.: No. 22). (Illus.). 64p. 1999. pap. 10.50 (0-7478-0322-6, Pub. by Shire Pubns) Parkwest Pubns.

Riley, Dan, ed. The Red Sox Reader. 288p. 1999. pap. 13.00 (0-395-97999-4) HM.

Riley, Dan, jt. ed. see Weinberger, Miro.

Riley, David D. Using Pascal: An Introduction to Computer Science I. 608p. 1987. pap., teacher ed. 12.75 (0-87835-235-X) PWS Pubs.

Riley, David D., jt. auth. see Headington, Mark R.

Riley, David J. Descendants of Theodor Leonhard & Verena Setz of Passaic County, New Jersey. 2nd ed. (Illus.). 77p. (Orig.). 1995. write for info. (0-9651078-0-9) D J Riley.

— Diary of Gladys Terriberry: American Nurse, France, 1918. 16p. 1998. pap. write for info. (0-9651078-1-7) D J Riley.

Riley, David L., Sr. Business. LC 89-91725. (Illus.). 60p. (Orig.). 1989. pap. 12.50 (0-9618976-3-5) D L Riley.

— Loci, Memory-Minute: How to Improve Your Memory Fast. LC 87-90689. (Illus.). 75p. (Orig.). 1987. pap. 10.00 (0-9618976-0-0) D L Riley.

Riley, David L. Study, Study, Study, Study, Study, Study. (Illus.). 1995. 35.00 (0-9618976-4-3) D L Riley.

Riley, Denise. Am I That Name? Feminism & the Category of "Women" in History: Feminism & the Category of Women in History. LC 88-21640. vi, 126p. (Orig.). 1989. pap. 13.95 (0-8166-1731-7) U of Minn Pr.

— Quuneq.Tr. of Calm Weather. (ESK., Illus.). 12p. (J). (gr. k-3). 1998. pap. text 6.00 (1-58084-029-9) Lower Kuskokwim.

***Riley, Denise.** Words of Selves: Identification, Solidarity, Irony. 2000. 49.50 (0-8047-3672-3) Stanford U Pr.

— Words of Selves: Identification, Solidarity, Irony. 2000. pap. text 18.95 (0-8047-3911-0) Stanford U Pr.

Riley, Dennis D. Controlling the Federal Bureaucracy. LC 86-14469. 216p. 1987. 32.95 (0-87722-455-2) Temple U Pr.

— Controlling the Federal Bureaucracy. 216p. 1989. pap. 16.95 (0-87722-704-7) Temple U Pr.

Riley, Derrick, jt. auth. see Kennedy, David.

Riley, Diana. Perinatal Mental Health. 1994. 24.75 (1-870905-78-4, Radcliffe Med Pr) Scovill Paterson.

Riley, Diane, jt. auth. see Riley, Kerry.

***Riley, Dick & McAllister, Pam.** The Bedside, Bathtub & Armchair Companion to Sherlock Holmes. LC 82-40265. (Illus.). 288p. 1998. 29.95 (0-8264-1140-1) Continuum.

Riley, Dick & McAllister, Pam. The Bedside, Bathtub & Armchair Companion to Sherlock Holmes. LC 98-23376. (Illus.). 288p. (C). 1998. pap. 19.95 (0-8264-1116-9) Continuum.

Riley, Dick & McAllister, Pam, eds. The New Bedside, Bathtub & Armchair Companion to Agatha Christie. 362p. 1986. pap. text 15.95 (0-8044-6725-0) F Ungar Bks.

***Riley, Don.** Gallivan's Gang. LC 99-68124. (Illus.). 360p. 1999. 22.95 (0-931714-81-8, Pub. by Nodin Pr) Bookmen Inc.

Riley, Don, jt. auth. see Rudensky, Morris R.

Riley, Don, jt. auth. see Selvig, Dick.

Riley, Dorothy W. The Blackburn Affair. 25p. (YA). (gr. 4-12). 1986. pap. write for info. (1-880234-04-1) Winbush Pub.

— Complete Kwanzaa, The (RI) Celebrating Our Cultural Harvest. (Illus.). 400p. 1997. pap. 15.00 (0-06-092764-X, Perennial) HarperTrade.

— Family Reunion. 25p. (YA). 1986. pap. write for info. (1-880234-02-5) Winbush Pub.

— It's up to You. 25p. (YA). (gr. 4-12). 1986. pap. write for info. (1-880234-03-3) Winbush Pub.

— My Soul Looks Back, 'Less I Forget. 332p. (YA). 1991. write for info. (1-880234-06-8); pap. write for info. (1-880234-00-9) Winbush Pub.

— My Soul Looks Back, 'Less I Forget, Vol. 2. 332p. (YA). 1992. pap. write for info. (1-880234-01-7) Winbush Pub.

Riley, Dorothy W., ed. Black Men in the Image of God. LC 98-54156. (Illus.). 128p. 1999. 21.95 (0-8298-1256-3) Pilgrim OH.

— Black Women in the Image of God. LC 98-50324. (Illus.). 128p. 1999. text 21.95 (0-8298-1257-1) Pilgrim OH.

— My Soul Looks Back, 'Less I Forget. rev. ed. 512p. 1995. pap. 20.00 (0-06-272057-0, Harper Ref) HarpC.

Riley, Dorothy W. & Riley, Tiaudra. Dorothy Mae's Cornbread. 25p. (YA). 1992. pap. write for info. (1-880234-05-X) Winbush Pub.

Riley, Douglas. The Defiant Child: A Parent's Guide to Oppositional Defiant Disorder. LC 97-24358. 224p. (Orig.). 1997. pap. 12.95 (0-87833-963-9) Taylor Pub.

***Riley, Douglas A.** The Depressed Child: A Parent's Guide for Rescuing Kids. 2001. pap. 12.95 (0-87833-187-5) Taylor Pub.

Riley, Dru, ed. see Manns, William, et al.

Riley, E. Baxter. Among Papuan Headhunters. LC 75-35155. (Illus.). 344p. 1983. reprint ed. 52.50 (0-404-14170-6) AMS Pr.

Riley, E. Baxter, jt. auth. see Ray, Sidney H.

Riley, E. C. Cervantes's Theory of the Novel. (Documentacion Cervantina Ser.: No. 13). 244p. 1992. pap. 12.00 (0-936388-56-0) Juan de la Cuesta.

— Don Quixote. Rawson, Claude, ed. LC 85-11179. (Unwin Critical Library). 192p. 1986. text 44.95 (0-04-800009-4) Routledge.

Riley, E. C., jt. ed. see Avalle-Arce, J. B.

Riley, E. C., ed. & tr. see De Cervantes Saavedra, Miguel.

Riley, E. P. & Vorhees, C. V. Handbook of Behavioral Teratology. LC 86-20517. (Illus.). 542p. (C). 1986. 110.00 (0-306-42246-8, Plenum Trade) Perseus Pubng.

Riley, Edward. Riley's Flute Melodies, 2 vols. in 1. Hitchcock, H. Wiley, ed. & intro. by. LC 72-14213. (Earlier American Music Ser.: Vol. 18). 200p. 1973. reprint ed. lib. bdg. 27.50 (0-306-70565-6) Da Capo.

Riley, Edward M. Starting America: The Story of Independence Hall. rev. ed. (Illus.). 64p. (YA). 1990. reprint ed. pap. text 4.95 (0-939631-23-7) Thomas Publications.

***Riley, Edward T. & Cohen, Shelia E.** Obstetric Anesthesia Pocket Reference. (Illus.). 144p. 2000. pap. text 25.00 (0-7506-7166-1) Buttrwrth-Heinemann.

Riley, Eileen. Major Political Events in South Africa, 1948-1990. LC 90-22490. 256p. 1991. reprint ed. pap. 79.40 (0-608-02861-4, 206392500007) Bks Demand.

Riley, Elihu S. The "Ancient" City: History of Annapolis, in Maryland, 1649-1887. 396p. 1995. reprint ed. pap. 28.50 (0-8063-4587-X, Pub. by Clearfield Co) ACCESS Pubs Network.

Riley, Elizabeth, compiled by. Love Poems. LC 68-58827. (Granger Index Reprint Ser.). 1977. 15.95 (0-8369-6040-8) Ayer.

Riley-Elliott, Marcia. WIPE (Write in Plain English) 2nd ed. 92p. (Orig.). 1994. reprint ed. pap. 20.00 (0-9639075-2-2) EA Inc.

Riley, Eugene W. & Acuna, Victor E. Transmission Systems. 2nd ed. LC 76-15104. (ABC of the Telephone Ser.: Vol. 8). (Illus.). 55p. (C). 1984. pap. text 17.95 (1-56016-007-1) ABC TeleTraining.

— Understanding Transmission. 2nd ed. LC 73-85629. (ABC of the Telephone Ser.: Vol. 7). (Illus.). 48p. (C). 1988. spiral bd. 17.95 (1-56016-059-4) ABC TeleTraining.

Riley, Eugenia. Angel Flame. 1990. mass mkt. 4.95 (0-446-34938-0) Warner Bks.

— Bushwhacked Bride, 1 vol. (Love Spell Ser.). 400p. 1999. mass mkt. 5.99 (0-505-52320-5) Dorchester Pub Co.

— Ecstasy's Triumph. 1983. mass mkt. 3.50 (0-685-07869-8, Zebra Kensgtn) Kensgtn Pub Corp.

***Riley, Eugenia.** Lovers & Other Lunatics. (Time of Your Life Ser.). 400p. 2000. mass mkt. 5.99 (0-505-52371-X, Love Spell) Dorchester Pub Co.

Riley, Eugenia. Rogue's Mistress. 400p. (Orig.). 1991. mass mkt. 4.50 (0-380-76474-1, Avon Bks) Morrow Avon.

— Stellar Attraction. (Temptation Ser.: No. 391). 1992. mass mkt. 2.99 (0-373-25491-1, 1-25491-1) Harlequin Bks.

— Taming Kate. 384p. (Orig.). 1992. mass mkt. 4.50 (0-380-76475-X, Avon Bks) Morrow Avon.

— Timeswept Bride. 416p. (Orig.). 1995. mass mkt. 5.50 (0-380-77157-8, Avon Bks) Morrow Avon.

— Waltz in Time. 384p. 1997. mass mkt. 5.99 (0-380-78910-8, Avon Bks) Morrow Avon.

— Wanted Across Time. 1997. mass mkt. 5.99 (0-380-78909-4, Avon Bks) Morrow Avon.

***Riley, Eugenia, et al.** New Year's Babies. 400p. 1999. mass mkt. 5.99 (0-505-52345-0, Love Spell) Dorchester Pub Co.

Riley, Eugenia, jt. auth. see Raye, Kimberly.

Riley, Frances J. The King's Daughter Dances: The Susan Ray Story. LC 97-75447. (Illus.). 128p. 1997. pap. 11.95 (1-57736-081-8) Providence Hse.

Riley, Frank, jt. auth. see Clifton, Mark.

Riley, Frank, jt. auth. see Eshelman, Byron E.

Riley, Frank, jt. auth. see Riley, Natoma.

Riley, Frank, ed. see Riley, Natoma.

Riley, Frank J. Assembly Automation. 2nd ed. LC 96-33563. 320p. 1996. 48.95 (0-8311-3041-5) Indus Pr.

— Biblical Allegorism. 1991. lib. bdg. 79.95 (0-8490-5008-1) Gordon Pr.

— Biblical Allegorism: A Key to the Mysteries of the Kingdom of God. 1991. lib. bdg. 89.95 (0-87700-983-X) Revisionist Pr.

Riley, Frank J., ed. Electronic Assembly. (International Trends in Manufacturing Technology Ser.). (Illus.). 450p. 1987. 87.00 (0-387-17441-9) Spr-Verlag.

Riley, Frank L. The Bible of Bibles. 1996. reprint ed. spiral bd. 25.50 (0-7873-0355-0) Hlth Research.

— The Bible of Bibles: A Source Book of Religions Demonstrating the Unity of the Sacred Books of the World (1928) 432p. 1996. reprint ed. pap. 24.50 (1-56459-751-2) Kessinger Pub.

— Biblical Allegorism. 1996. reprint ed. spiral bd. 15.50 (0-7873-0724-6) Hlth Research.

— Biblical Allegorism: A Key to the Mysteries of the Kingdom of God. 258p. 1996. reprint ed. pap. 14.95 (1-56459-605-2) Kessinger Pub.

Riley, Frank L., ed. The Bible of Bibles: A Source Book of Religions Demonstrating the Unity of the Sacred Books of the World. 1991. lib. bdg. 250.00 (0-87700-960-0) Revisionist Pr.

Riley, Franklin L. School History of Mississippi. LC 76-68. (Illus.). 457p. 1976. reprint ed. 25.00 (0-87152-219-5) Reprint.

Riley, Franklin L., ed. General Robert E. Lee After Appomattox. LC 72-37353. (Select Bibliographies Reprint Ser.). 1977. reprint ed. 23.95 (0-8369-6700-3) Ayer.

Riley, Gail B. Censorship. LC 97-8382. (Library in a Book). 1998. 26.95 (0-8160-3373-0) Facts on File.

— Top 10 NASCAR Drivers. LC 94-32061. (Sports Top 10 Ser.). (Illus.). 48p. (J). (gr. 4-10). 1995. lib. bdg. 18.95 (0-89490-611-9) Enslow Pubs.

— Wah Ming Chang: Artist & Master of Special Effects. LC 95-15390. (Multicultural Junior Biographies Ser.). (Illus.). 112p. (J). (gr. 4-10). 1995. lib. bdg. 20.95 (0-89490-639-9) Enslow Pubs.

Riley, Gary, jt. auth. see Giarratano, Joseph C.

Riley, Gary L. & Baldridge, Victor J., eds. Governing Academic Organizations: New Problems, New Perspectives. LC 76-56995. 367p. (C). 1977. 37.50 (0-8211-1715-7) McCutchan.

Riley, Gay. The Pocket Personal Trainer: A Total Nutrition & Fitness Planner for Busy People. Rodriguez, Patricia, ed. 290p. 1994. pap. text 9.95 (0-9642204-0-7) Lipo-Visuals.

Riley, George R. Sound Systems: A Guide to Better Sound in Your Parish. (Worship Ser.). 1994. pap. text 10.95 (1-56929-017-2, Pastoral Press) OR Catholic.

Riley, Gillian. Feast for the Eyes: Evocative Recipes & Surprising Tales Inspired by Paintings in the National. 168p. 1998. 25.00 (0-300-07366-6) Yale U Pr.

— How to Stop Smoking & Stay Stopped for Good. 160p. 1997. pap. 15.95 (0-09-180969-X) Trafalgar.

Riley, Glenda. Building & Breaking Families in the American West. LC 95-41743. (Calvin P. Horn Lectures in Western History & Culture). 204p. 1996. pap. 17.95 (0-8263-1720-0) U of NM Pr.

— Divorce: An American Tradition. LC 97-12258. (Illus.). xiii, 262p. 1997. pap. 15.00 (0-8032-8969-3, Bison Books) U of Nebr Pr.

— The Female Frontier: A Comparative View of Women on the Prairie & the Plains. LC 87-32447. (Illus.). xii, 292p. 1988. pap. 14.95 (0-7006-0424-3) U Pr of KS.

— Inventing the American Woman Vol. I: An Inclusive History, Early America to 1877. 2nd rev. ed. (Illus.). 168p. (C). 1995. pap. text 16.95 (0-88295-922-0) Harlan Davidson.

— Inventing the American Woman Vol. II: An Inclusive History, 1877 to the Present. 2nd rev. ed. (Illus.). 176p. (C). 1995. pap. text 16.95 (0-88295-923-9) Harlan Davidson.

— The Life & Legacy of Annie Oakley. LC 94-10260. (Oklahoma Western Biographies Ser.: Vol. 7). (Illus.). 272p. 1994. write for info. (0-8061-2656-6) U of Okla Pr.

— A Place to Grow: Women in the American West. 325p. 1992. pap. text 21.95 (0-88295-886-0) Harlan Davidson.

— Women & Indians on the Frontier, 1825-1915. LC 84-13235. (Illus.). 336p. 1985. pap. 17.95 (0-8263-0780-9) U of NM Pr.

An Asterisk (*) at the beginning of an entry indicates that the title is appearing for the first time.

***Riley, Glenda.** Women & Nature: Saving the "Wild" West. LC 98-35168. (Women in the West Ser.). 368p. 1999. pap. 24.95 (*0-8032-8975-8*); text 60.00 (*0-8032-3932-7*) U of Nebr Pr.

Riley, Glenda, ed. Prairie Voices: Iowa's Pioneering Women. LC 96-24258. 300p. (Orig.). (C). 1996. pap. text 24.95 (*0-8138-2595-4*) Iowa St U Pr.

Riley, Glenda & Etulain, Richard W. By Grit & Grace: Eleven Women Who Shaped the American West. LC 97-25057. (Illus.). 240p. (Orig.). 1997. pap. 17.95 (*1-55591-259-1*) Fulcrum Pub.

Riley, Glenda, jt. auth. see Etulain, Richard W.

Riley, Glenda, jt. ed. see Etulain, Richard W.

Riley, Glyndon D. & Riley, Jeanna. Oral Motor Assessment & Treatment: Improving Syllable Production. 64p. (Orig.). 1985. pap. text 79.00 (*0-685-12077-5*, 2983) PRO-ED.

Riley, Gregory J. One Jesus, Many Christs. LC 97-3294. 1997. pap. 12.00 (*0-06-066798-2*) HarpC.

— One Jesus, Many Christs: The Truth about Christian Origins. LC 97-3294. 240p. 1997. 23.00 (*0-06-066799-0*, Pub. by Harper SF) HarpC.

***Riley, Gregory J.** One Jesus, Many Churches: How Jesus Inspired Not One True Christianity, but Many. 240p. 2001. pap. 16.00 (*0-8006-3242-7*) Augsburg Fortress.

Riley, Gregory J. Resurrection Reconsidered: Thomas & John in Controversy. 208p. 1995. pap. 19.00 (*0-8006-2846-2*, 1-2846, Fortress Pr) Augsburg Fortress.

Riley, H. T., tr. see De Hoveden, Roger.

Riley, H. T., tr. see Ingulf, Abbot.

Riley, Harlin & Vidacaich, Johnny. New Orleans Jazz & Second Line Drumming. Thress, Dan, ed. (Illus.). 120p. (Orig.). 1995. pap. text 24.95 (*0-89724-921-6*, MMBK0043CD) Wrner Bros.

Riley, Harold. The First Gospel. 220p. 1992. text 25.00 (*0-86554-409-3*, MUP/H332) Mercer Univ Pr.

— The Making of Mark: An Exploration. LC 89-37902. 275p. (C). 1989. 25.00 (*0-86554-359-3*, MUP/H297) Mercer Univ Pr.

Riley, Harold, jt. auth. see Orchard, Bernard.

Riley, Harvey. A Treatise on the Mule. (Illus.). 107p. 1967. reprint ed. pap. 5.00 (*0-9659312-3-4*) Am Donkey.

Riley, Helene M. Michael Kalteisen: Founder of the German Friendly Society. 1995. pap. 15.00 (*1-929751-02-8*) Sagas Pubg.

— Register of St. Johannes Lutheran Church, Charleston, SC. (GER.). 239p. (Orig.). 1992. pap. 35.00 (*1-929751-03-6*) Sagas Pubg.

Riley, Helene M. Weibliche Muse: Sechs Essays Uber Kunstlerisch Schaffende Frauen der Goethezeit. LC 81-69883. (GERM Ser.: Vol. 8). (GER., Illus.). 280p. 1986. 35.00 (*0-938100-05-X*) Camden Hse.

Riley, Helene M. Kastinger. Idee und Gestaltung: Das Konfigurative Strukturprinzip bei Ludwig Achim von Arnim. (GER.). 187p. 1977. pap. 35.00 (*1-929751-07-9*) Sagas Pubg.

— John Adam Treutlen: The European Heritage of Georgia's First Governor. (Illus.). 24p. 1999. pap. 14.95 (*1-929751-06-0*) Sagas Pubg.

— Ludwig Achim von Arnime Kritische Schriften: Erstdrucke und Unbekanntes. (GER.). 626p. 1989. 65.00 (*1-929751-00-1*) Sagas Pubg.

— Michael Kalteisen: Ein Deutscher in South Carolina. large type ed. (GER., Illus.). 42p. 1995. pap. 15.00 (*1-929751-01-X*) Sagas Pubg.

Riley, Henry T. Chronica Monasterii S. Albani, 7 works in 12 vols., Set. Incl. Vol. 1. Historia Anglicana., 12 vols. Walshingham, T. 1972. reprint ed. (*0-8115-1047-6*); Vol. 2. Chronica et Annales, 1259-1307. Rishanger, W. 1972. reprint ed. (*0-8115-1048-4*); Vol. 3. Johannis de Trokelowe et Henrici de Blaneforde - Chronica et Annales, 1259-96, 1307-24, 1392-1406. 1972. reprint ed. (*0-8115-1049-2*); Vol. 4. Gesta Abbatum Monasterii S. Albani a Thoma Walshingham, 793-1411., 3 vols. 1972. reprint ed. (*0-8115-1050-6*); Vol. 4. Gesta Abbatum Monasterii S. Albani a Thoma Walshingham, 793-1411., 3 vols. 1972. reprint ed. (*0-8115-1051-4*); Vol. 4. Gesta Abbatum Monasterii S. Albani a Thoma Walshingham, 793-1411., 3 vols. 1972. reprint ed. (*0-8115-1052-2*); Vol. 5. Johannis Amundesham Monachi Monasterii S. Albani., 2 vols. 1972. reprint ed. (*0-8115-1053-0*); Vol. 6. Registra Quorundam Abbatum Monasterii S. Albani Qui Saeculo XVMO Floruere., 2 vols. 1972. reprint ed. (*0-8115-1054-9*); Vol. 6. Registra Quorundam Abbatum Monasterii S. Albani Qui Saeculo XVMO Floruere., 2 vols. 1972. reprint ed. (*0-8115-1055-7*); Vol. 7. Ypodigma Neustriae, a Thoma Walsingham. 1972. reprint ed. (*0-8115-1056-5*); (Rolls Ser.: No. 28). 1972. reprint ed. 840.00 (*0-685-10001-4*) Periodicals Srv.

Riley, Henry T., ed. Munimenta Gildhallae Londoniensis: Liber Albus, Liber Custumarum, et Liber Horn, 3 vols., Set. Incl. Vol. 1. Liber Albus. 1974. (*0-8115-1015-8*); Vol. 2, Pts. 1 & 2. Liber Custumarum, with Extracts from the Cottonian Ms Claudius D II. 1974. (*0-8115-1016-6*); Vol. 3. Transcript of the Anglo-Norman Passages in Liber Albus, Glossaries, Appendices, & Index. 1974. (*0-8115-1017-4*); (Rolls Ser.: No. 12). 1974. reprint ed. 210.00 (*0-685-09995-4*) Periodicals Srv.

Riley, Herbert J., et al. Grades & Grading Practices: The Results of the 1992 AACRAO Survey. LC 94-3195. 80p. (C). 1994. pap. text 18.00 (*0-929851-20-X*) Am Assn Coll Registrars.

Riley, Hugh M. Christian Initiation: A Comparative Study of the Interpretation of the Baptismal Liturgy in the Mystagogical Writing of Cyril of Jerusalem, John Chrysostom, Theodore of Mopsuestia, & Ambrose of Milan. LC 74-11191. (Catholic University of America Studies in Christian Antiquity: No. 17). 515p. reprint ed. pap. 159.70 (*0-608-13264-0*, 202512600042) Bks Demand.

Riley, Hugh M., ed. see Auer, Johann.

Riley, J. L. What Matters: No Expanding Universe, No Big Bang. (Illus.). 227p. 1993. pap. 19.00 (*0-9636842-1-3*); lib. bdg. 29.00 (*0-9636842-0-5*) J L Riley.

***Riley, J. P.** Napoleon & the World War of 1813: Lessons in Coalition Warfighting. LC 99-16266. (Illus.). 512p. 2000. 57.50 (*0-7146-4893-0*, Pub. by F Cass Pubs) Intl Spec Bk.

Riley, J. P. Soldiers of the Queen: The History of the Queen's Regiment 1966-1992. 816p. 1990. 165.00 (*0-948251-65-4*, Pub. by Picton) St Mut.

Riley, J. R., jt. auth. see Reynolds, D. R.

Riley, J. T., jt. ed. see Vourvopoulos, G.

***Riley, James.** Sufferings in Africa: The Astonishing Account of a New England Sea Captain Enslaved by North Africa. 2000. pap. 14.95 (*1-58574-080-2*) Lyons Pr.

Riley, James & Schachle, Ted. Alaska Wilderness Trails: 23 Southcentral Trails. (ENG.). 84p. 1989. per. 17.00 (*1-878100-86-6*) Todd Commns.

Riley, James, et al. Helping Children with Mathematics. 144p. (Orig.). (J). (gr. 3-5). 1995. pap. 12.95 (*0-673-36155-1*, GoodYrBooks) Addson-Wesley Educ.

— Helping Your Child with Mathematics. (Illus.). 144p. (Orig.). (J). (ps-2). 1993. pap. 12.95 (*0-673-36061-X*, GoodYrBooks) Addson-Wesley Educ.

— Stand up Math: 180 Challenging Problems for Kids, Budding Genius Level, Ages 8-10. (Illus.). 184p. (Orig.). 1994. spiral bd. 9.95 (*0-673-36144-6*, GoodYrBooks) Addson-Wesley Educ.

— Stand up Math: 180 Challenging Problems for Kids, Genius Level, Ages 9-11. (Illus.). 184p. (Orig.). 1994. spiral bd. 9.95 (*0-673-36145-4*, GoodYrBooks) Addson-Wesley Educ.

— Stand up Math: 180 Challenging Problems for Kids, Super Genius Level, Ages 10 Up. (Illus.). 184p. (Orig.). 1994. spiral bd. 9.95 (*0-673-36146-2*, GoodYrBooks) Addson-Wesley Educ.

Riley, James A. The Biographical Encyclopedia of the Negro Baseball Leagues. (Illus.). 1998. 9.99 (*0-7628-0050-X*) Alva Pr.

— Dandy, Day & the Devil. (Orig.). 52.00 (*0-8488-1580-7*) Amereon Ltd.

— Dandy, Day & the Devil. LC 87-90021. (Illus.). 153p. (Orig.). 1987. 49.95 (*0-9614023-3-4*); pap. 12.95 (*0-9614023-2-6*) TK Pubs.

— The Negro Leagues. LC 95-46411. (African-American Achievers Ser.). 124p. (YA). (gr. 5 up). 1996. pap. 8.95 (*0-7910-2592-6*) Chelsea Hse.

— The Negro Leagues. LC 95-46411. (African-American Achievers Ser.). (Illus.). 124p. (YA). (gr. 5 up). 1996. lib. bdg. 19.95 (*0-7910-2591-8*) Chelsea Hse.

— Negro World Series of 1942. (Orig.). 1989. pap. write for info. (*0-9614023-4-2*) TK Pubs.

— Too Dark for the Hall. (Illus.). 175p. (Orig.). 1991. pap. 15.95 (*0-9614023-6-9*) TK Pubs.

Riley, James A., ed. Black Baseball Journal, Vol. 1, No. 1. (Illus.). 64p. (Orig.). (YA). 1990. pap. 6.95 (*0-9614023-5-0*) TK Pubs.

— Kentucky Voices: A Collection of Contemporary Kentucky Short Stories. LC 97-67129. (Illus.). 256p. 1997. 19.95 (*0-933302-00-2*) Pikeville Coll.

Riley, James A., et al, eds. Once upon a Midnight... New Dark Verse. (Unnameable Poetry Works Ser.). (Illus.). 87p. 1995. pap. 10.95 (*0-934227-16-0*) Unnameable Pr.

Riley, James A. & Leonard, Buck. Buck Leonard: The Black Lou Gehrig: The Hall of Famers's Story in His Own Words. 304p. 1995. 21.00 (*0-7867-0119-6*) Carroll & Graf.

Riley, James A. & Speer, Renwick W. The Hundred Years of Chet Hoff. 30p. (Orig.). 1991. pap. 10.00 (*0-9614023-7-7*) TK Pubs.

Riley, James A., jt. auth. see Irvin, Monte.

Riley, James C. The Dawn of Salvation: An Easter Service. 16p. (Orig.). 1978. reprint ed. pap. 2.25 (*0-89536-295-3*) CSS OH.

— International Government Finance & the Amsterdam Capital Market, 1740-1815. LC 79-152. 379p. reprint ed. pap. 108.10 (*0-608-17525-0*, 2030617) Bks Demand.

— The Seven Years War & the Old Regime in France: The Economic & Financial Toll. LC 86-42847. (Illus.). 280p. 1986. reprint ed. pap. 86.80 (*0-608-04518-7*, 206526300001) Bks Demand.

— Sick, Not Dead: The Health of British Workingmen During the Mortality Decline. LC 96-26961. 384p. 1997. text 58.00 (*0-8018-5411-3*) Johns Hopkins.

— Sickness, Recovery, & Death: A History & Forecast of Ill Health. LC 88-51148. (Illus.). 288p. 1989. text 36.95 (*0-87745-233-4*) U of Iowa Pr.

Riley, James Whitcomb. Afterwhiles. (Notable American Authors Ser.). 1999. reprint ed. lib. bdg. 125.00 (*0-7812-8782-0*) Rprt Serv.

— The Best of James Whitcomb Riley. Manlove, Donald C., ed. LC 82-47958. (Illus.). 224p. 1982. 20.00 (*0-253-10610-9*); pap. 10.95 (*0-253-20299-X*, MB-299) Ind U Pr.

— Book of Joyous Children. LC 79-98085. (Granger Index Reprint Ser.). 1977. 20.95 (*0-8369-6087-4*) Ayer.

— Book of Joyous Children. (Notable American Authors Ser.). 1999. reprint ed. lib. bdg. 125.00 (*0-7812-8789-8*) Rprt Serv.

— The Boss Girl: A Christmas Story, & Other Sketches. LC 76-160948. (Short Story Index Reprint Ser.). 1977. reprint ed. 20.95 (*0-8369-3927-1*) Ayer.

— A Child-World. LC 76-39403. (Granger Index Reprint Ser.). 1977. reprint ed. 22.95 (*0-8369-6350-4*) Ayer.

— Complete Poems. 1992. reprint ed. lib. bdg. 39.95 (*0-89968-289-8*, Lghtyr Pr) Buccaneer Bks.

— The Complete Poetical Works of James Whitcomb Riley. LC 92-28235. 920p. 1993. 39.95 (*0-253-34989-3*); pap. 24.95 (*0-253-20777-0*, MB-777) Ind U Pr.

— The Complete Works of James Whitcomb Riley. 6 vols., Set. LC 74-153347. (Illus.). reprint ed. 435.00 (*0-404-05340-8*) AMS Pr.

— The Gobble-Uns'll Git You Ef You Don't Watch Out! LC 74-23110. (Illus.). (J). (gr. 2-5). 1975. 13.95 (*0-397-31621-6*) HarpC Child Bks.

— Green Fields & Running Brooks. (Notable American Authors Ser.). 1999. reprint ed. lib. bdg. 125.00 (*0-7812-8786-3*) Rprt Serv.

— Letters of James Whitcomb Riley. Phelps, William L., ed. LC 78-153348. reprint ed. 49.50 (*0-404-05336-X*) AMS Pr.

— Letters of James Whitcomb Riley. (American Biography Ser.). 349p. 1991. reprint ed. lib. bdg. 79.00 (*0-7812-8323-X*) Rprt Serv.

— Little Orphan Annie & Other Poems. 80p. 1994. pap. text 1.00 (*0-486-28260-0*) Dover.

— Old Fashinoed Roses (London) (Notable American Authors Ser.). 1999. reprint ed. lib. bdg. 125.00 (*0-7812-8784-7*) Rprt Serv.

— The Old Swimmin' Hole. (Notable American Authors Ser.). 1999. reprint ed. lib. bdg. 125.00 (*0-7812-8781-2*) Rprt Serv.

— Pipes O' Pan at Zekesbury. (Notable American Authors Ser.). 1999. reprint ed. lib. bdg. 125.00 (*0-7812-8783-9*) Rprt Serv.

— Poems Here at Home. (Notable American Authors Ser.). 1999. reprint ed. lib. bdg. 125.00 (*0-7812-8787-1*) Rprt Serv.

— Rhymes of Childhood. (Notable American Authors Ser.). 1999. reprint ed. lib. bdg. 125.00 (*0-7812-8785-5*) Rprt Serv.

— Riley Child-Rhymes. LC 74-121933. (Granger Index Reprint Ser.). 1977. 22.95 (*0-8369-6174-9*) Ayer.

— Riley Child Rhymes. (Notable American Authors Ser.). 1999. reprint ed. lib. bdg. 125.00 (*0-7812-8788-X*) Rprt Serv.

— Riley Child Rhymes with Hoosier Pictures. (Illus.). 188p. (J). reprint ed. 20.00 (*1-878208-17-9*) Guild Pr IN.

— When the Frost Is on the Punkin. (Illus.). 32p. (J). 1991. 17.95 (*0-87923-912-3*) Godine.

— When the Frost Is on the Punkin. (Illus.). 32p. (J). 1993. pap. 9.95 (*0-87923-988-3*) Godine.

Riley, James Whitcomb, jt. auth. see Schachle, Ted.

Riley, Jan. The Bells: Donald Lipski. Robinson, Victoria, ed. (Illus.). 36p. 1991. pap. 60.00 (*0-917562-59-3*) Contemp Arts.

— The Bells: Donald Lipski. limited ed. Robinson, Victoria, ed. (Illus.). 36p. 1991. 300.00 (*0-685-59430-0*) Contemp Arts.

Riley, Jan & Burnham, Michael. Mechanika. (Illus.). 58p. (Orig.). 1991. pap. 20.00 (*0-917562-57-7*) Contemp Arts.

Riley, Jan, jt. auth. see Chambers, Kristin.

Riley, Jan, ed. see Rubinstein, Meyer R. & Schwabsky, Barry.

Riley, Jana. The Tarot Book: Basic Instruction for Reading Cards. (Orig.). 1997. pap. text 11.95 (*0-88079-722-3*, BK136) US Games Syst.

— The Tarot Book: Basic Instruction for Reading Cards. LC 91-29396. (Illus.). 212p. (Orig.). 1992. pap. 11.95 (*0-87728-723-6*) Weiser.

— Tarot Dictionary & Compendium. LC 95-8713. (Illus.). 320p. 1995. pap. text 14.95 (*0-87728-821-6*) Weiser.

Riley, Jane & Carlson, Mary. Help for Parents of Gifted & Talented Children. (Illus.). 64p. (J). (gr. k-6). 1984. student ed. 3.99 (*0-86653-190-4*, GA 539) Good Apple.

Riley, Janeway. Us And . . . Good Stuff. (Illus.). 176p. (J). 1993. 19.95 (*0-9637378-1-3*) Janeway Riley.

Riley, Jannelle M. Laurel Quarberg: Treading Water. (Illus.). 8p. (Orig.). 1994. pap. 8.00 (*1-885163-01-0*) Virginia Beach Ctr.

Riley, Jeanna, jt. auth. see Riley, Glyndon D.

Riley, Jeni. The Teaching of Reading: The Development of Literacy in the Early Years of School. (One-Off Ser.). (Illus.). 152p. 1996. pap. (*1-85396-307-0*) Corwin Pr.

— Teaching Reading: Key Stage 1 & Before. (Stanley Thornes Teaching Primary English Ser.). (Illus.). 224p. 1999. pap. 29.50 (*0-7487-3516-X*) S Thornes Pubs.

Riley, Jo. Chinese Theatre & the Actor in Performance. (Studies in Modern Theatre: Vol. 3). (Illus.). 360p. (C). 1997. text 64.95 (*0-521-57090-5*) Cambridge U Pr.

Riley, Joan. A Kindness to the Children. 312p. 1998. pap. 13.95 (*0-7043-4319-3*, Pub. by Womens Press) Trafalgar.

— Romance. 240p. 1998. pap. 13.95 (*0-7043-4508-0*, Pub. by Womens Press) Trafalgar.

— The Unbelonging. rev. ed. 144p. 1997. pap. 11.95 (*0-7043-3959-5*, Pub. by Womens Press) Trafalgar.

Riley, Joanne M. Crossing Without Daughters: Poems by Joanne Mokosh Riley. Bixby, Robert, ed. 34p. 1994. pap. text 6.00 (*1-882983-16-5*) March Street Pr.

— Pacing the Moon. LC 85-4159. 72p. 1985. pap. 5.95 (*0-941608-04-2*) Chantry Pr.

Riley, Jocelyn. America Fever: A Resource Guide. 114p. 1995. 45.00 (*1-877933-50-3*) Her Own Words.

— Audrey Handler: Glass Artist. 114p. (YA). (gr. 4 up). 1996. 45.00 incl. VHS (*1-877933-60-0*, 15002) Her Own Words.

— Belle Case la Follette 1859-1931: A Resource Guide. 114p. 1995. 45.00 (*1-877933-05-8*) Her Own Words.

— Big Sister, Little Sister: American Indian Women's Stories. 114p. 1995. 45.00 incl. VHS (*1-877933-57-0*, 16002); audio 45.00 (*1-877933-58-9*, 16003) Her Own Words.

— Ethel Kvalheim, Rosemaler: A Resource Guide. 114p. 1995. 45.00 incl. VHS (*1-877933-24-4*, 11002) Her Own Words.

— Her Mother Before Her: Winnebago Women's Stories of Their Mothers & Grandmothers: A Resource Guide. 114p. 1995. 20.00 (*1-877933-21-X*) Her Own Words.

— The Literature of Quilts: A Resource Guide. 114p. 1995. 45.00 (*1-877933-09-0*) Her Own Words.

— The Literature of the Prairie: A Resource Guide. 114p. 1995. 45.00 (*1-877933-14-7*) Her Own Words.

***Riley, Jocelyn.** Math at Work. (Women in Nontraditional Careers Ser.: Vol. 8). 114p. (J). (gr. 6-12). 2000. teacher ed. 45.00 (*1-877933-85-6*, 25002) Her Own Words.

Riley, Jocelyn. Mountain Wolf Woman, 1884-1960: A Resource Guide. 114p. (YA). (gr. 5 up). 1995. 45.00 incl. VHS (*1-877933-12-0*) Her Own Words.

— Norwegian Pioneer Women: A Resource Guide. 114p. 1995. 45.00 incl. VHS (*1-877933-16-3*) Her Own Words.

— Pioneer Women's Diaries: A Resource Guide. 114p. 1995. VHS 45.00 (*1-877933-07-4*) Her Own Words.

— Prairie Child, 1848. 114p. 1999. teacher ed. 45.00 (*1-877933-90-2*, 24002) Her Own Words.

— Seventy-Five Activities for Celebrating Seventy-Five Years of Votes for Women: A Resource Guide. 150p. 1995. 45.00 (*1-877933-55-4*) Her Own Words.

— Sewing Together: A Birthday Quilt. 114p. 1996. teacher ed. 45.00 incl. VHS (*1-877933-66-X*, 19001) Her Own Words.

— Sisters & Friends: A Resource Guide. 114p. 1995. 45.00 (*1-877933-45-7*) Her Own Words.

— Votes for Women?! A Resource Guide. 114p. 1995. 45.00 incl. VHS (*1-877933-10-4*) Her Own Words.

— Winnebago Songs & Stories: A Resource Guide. 114p. 1995. 45.00 (*1-877933-19-8*) Her Own Words.

— Women in Construction: A Resource Guide. rev. ed. 114p. 1995. 20.00 (*0-614-05258-0*) Her Own Words.

— Women in Dentistry. 114p. 1996. teacher ed. 45.00 (*1-877933-63-5*, 18002) Her Own Words.

***Riley, Jocelyn.** Women in Engineering: A Resource Guide. (Women in Nontraditional Careers Ser.: Vol. 9). 114p. 2000. 45.00 (*1-877933-93-7*, 27002) Her Own Words.

Riley, Jocelyn. Women in Firefighting. 114p. 1997. teacher ed. 45.00 (*1-877933-72-4*, 20002) Her Own Words.

— Women in Machining. 114p. (gr. 6-12). 1998. teacher ed. 45.00 (*1-877933-78-3*, 22002) Her Own Words.

— Women in Nontraditional Careers: An Introduction. 114p. teacher ed. 95.00 incl. VHS (*1-877933-68-6*, 23002) Her Own Words.

— Women in Policing: A Resource Guide. 114p. 1995. 45.00 (*1-877933-53-8*) Her Own Words.

***Riley, Jocelyn.** Women in Welding. 114p. 1999. teacher ed. 45.00 (*1-877933-75-9*, 21002) Her Own Words.

— Work Talk. (Women in Nontraditional Careers Ser.: No. 10). 114p. 2000. 45.00 (*1-877933-95-3*, 28002) Her Own Words.

Riley, Jocelyn. Writing on the Lakes, 1848. 114p. 1999. teacher ed. 45.00 (*1-877933-91-0*, 26002) Her Own Words.

— Zona Gale - Her Life & Writings: A Resource Guide. 114p. 1995. 45.00 incl. VHS (*1-877933-08-2*) Her Own Words.

Riley, Joe S. Bio Chemistry. 1996. reprint ed. pap. 8.00 (*0-7873-0721-1*) Hlth Research.

— Correspondence Course in Zone Therapy, Reflex Technique & Hook Work. 13p. 1996. reprint ed. spiral bd. 14.00 (*0-7873-1179-0*) Hlth Research.

— Iridology Simplified. 1996. reprint ed. spiral bd. 8.00 (*0-7873-0722-X*) Hlth Research.

Riley, Joe S. & Daglish, W. E. Zone Reflex Plus Translation Diet: Hydro-Therapy & Swedish Massage. 78p. 1996. reprint ed. spiral bd. 18.50 (*0-7873-1124-3*) Hlth Research.

Riley, Joe S., et al. Numerology & Vibration. 1996. reprint ed. spiral bd. 10.00 (*0-7873-0726-2*) Hlth Research.

***Riley, John.** Benjamin Franklin: A Photo-Biography. large type ed. LC 99-89222. (Illus.). 24p. (J). (gr. 1-3). 2000. lib. bdg. write for info. (*1-883846-64-1*) M Reynolds.

Riley, John. Beyond Bop. Thress, Dan, ed. (Illus.). 80p. (Orig.). 1997. pap. text 24.95 (*1-57623-609-9*, MMBK0070CD) Wrner Bros.

***Riley, John.** George Washington Carver: A Photo-Biography. large type ed. (Illus.). 24p. (J). (gr. 1-3). 2000. lib. bdg. write for info. (*1-883846-62-5*) M Reynolds.

— Jane Addams: A Photo-Biography. large type ed. LC 99-89221. (Illus.). 24p. (J). (gr. 1-3). 2000. lib. bdg. 15.95 (*1-883846-61-7*) M Reynolds.

— John D. Rockefeller: Oil Baron & Philanthropist. (American Business Tycoons Ser.). (Illus.). 112p. (YA). (gr. 5 up). 2000. lib. bdg. 19.95 (*1-883846-59-5*) M Reynolds.

— John Paul Jones: A Photo-Biography. large type ed. LC 99-89219. (Illus.). 24p. (J). (gr. 1-3). 2000. lib. bdg. write for info. (*1-883846-63-3*) M Reynolds.

Riley, John & Longville, Tim, trs. What I Own: Versions of Holderin & Mandelshtam. 128p. 1998. pap. 24.95 (*1-85754-175-8*, Pub. by Carcanet Pr) Paul & Co Pubs.

***Riley, John B.** J. P. Morgan: Banker to a Growing Nation. (American Business Tycoons Ser.). (Illus.). 112p. (YA). (gr. 5 up). 2000. lib. bdg. 19.95 (*1-883846-60-9*) M Reynolds.

Riley, John G., jt. auth. see Hirshleifer, Jack.

Riley, John J. A History of the American Soft Drink Industry: Bottled Carbonated Beverages, 1807-1957. LC 72-5071. (Technology & Society Ser.). (Illus.). 366p. 1975. reprint ed. 24.95 (*0-405-04721-5*) Ayer.

Riley, John P., ed. Chemical Oceanography, Vol. 9. 320p. 1989. text 151.00 (*0-12-588609-8*) Acad Pr.

Riley, John P., et al, eds. Chemical Oceanography Vol. 10: SEAREX: the Sea-Air Exchange Program. 404p. 1989. text 147.00 (*0-12-588610-1*) Acad Pr.

Riley, John W., Jr. & Johnson, Marilyn E. Aging & Society, Vol. 2: Aging & the Professions. Riley, Matilda W. et al, eds. LC 68-54406. 410p. 1969. 55.00 (*0-87154-719-8*) Russell Sage.

R

An Asterisk (*) at the beginning of an entry indicates that the title is appearing for the first time.

R

*__Riley, Jonathan.__ Napoleon & the World War of 1813: Lessons in Coalition Warfighting. LC 99-16266. 350p. 1999. write for info. (*0-7146-4444-7*, Pub. by F Cass Pubs) Intl Spec Bk.

__Riley, Jonathan.__ Mill on Liberty. LC 97-35429. (Routledge Philosophy Guidebooks Ser.). 256p. (C). 1998. pap. 12.99 (*0-415-14189-3*) Routledge.

— Mill on Liberty: Jonathan Riley. LC 97-35429. (Philosophy Guidebooks Ser.). 256p. (C). 1998. 50.00 (*0-415-14188-5*) Routledge.

__Riley, Jonathan, ed. & intro. see Mill, John Stuart.__

__Riley, Judith C.__ Ancient Peruvian Textiles: From the Chrysler Museum. (Illus.). 13p. 1980. pap. 3.50 (*0-940744-28-7*) Chrysler Museum.

*__Riley, Judith M.__ The Master of All Desires. LC 99-29828. 480p. 1999. 26.95 (*0-670-88450-2*, Viking) Viking Penguin.

— Master of All Desires. 2000. pap. 14.00 (*0-14-029653-0*) Penguin Putnam.

__Riley, Judith M.__ The Oracle Glass. 528p. 1995. pap. 12.50 (*0-449-91006-7*) Fawcett.

— The Serpent Garden. 480p. 1997. pap. 13.95 (*0-14-025880-9*) Viking Penguin.

__Riley, Judy, jt. auth. see DiSilvestro, J.__

__Riley, Julia B.__ Instant Teaching Tools for Health Care Teams. (Illus.). 376p. (C). (gr. 13). 1997. pap. text 36.95 (*0-8151-5589-1*, 29945) Mosby Inc.

__Riley, K., et al.__ Small Millets. (C). 1989. 50.00 (*81-204-0434-3*) S Asia.

__Riley, K., jt. auth. see Motta, Janice C.__

__Riley, K. F.__ Problems for Physics Students: With Hints & Answers. LC 82-4575. 190p. 1982. pap. text 29.95 (*0-521-27073-1*) Cambridge U Pr.

__Riley, K. F., et al.__ Mathematical Methods for Physics & Engineering: A Comprehensive Guide. LC 96-52942. (Illus.). 1028p. (C). 1998. pap. text 49.95 (*0-521-55529-9*) Cambridge U Pr.

__Riley, K. Jack.__ Crack, Powder Cocaine & Heroin: Drug Purchase & Use Patterns in Six U. S. Cities. (Illus.). 39p. (C). 1999. pap. text 15.00 (*0-7881-7627-7*) DIANE Pub.

__Riley, K. Jack, jt. ed. see Travis, Jeremy.__

__Riley, Kana, ed.__ See Us Hear Us: Voices of Breast Cancer. 128p. (Orig.). 1994. pap. 5.00 (*0-9644254-0-8*) NH Breast Cancer.

__Riley, Karen E., tr. see Kanafani, Ghassan.__

__Riley, Karl.__ Tracing EMFs in Building Wiring & Grounding. (Illus.). 126p. (Orig.). 1995. pap. 27.50 (*0-9646790-0-0*) Magnetic Sci.

__Riley, Katheryn A. & Nuttall, Desmond L., eds.__ Measuring Quality - Education Indicators: United Kingdom & International Perspectives. LC 94-2854. 176p. 1994. 85.00 (*0-7507-0260-5*, Falmer Pr); pap. 29.95 (*0-7507-0261-3*, Falmer Pr) Taylor & Francis.

__Riley, Kathryn.__ The Big Sale. LC 98-39620. (Real Kids Readers Ser.). (Illus.). 32p. (J). (gr. k-2). 1999. pap. 3.99 (*0-7613-2082-2*, Copper Beech Bks); lib. bdg. 16.90 (*0-7613-2057-1*, Copper Beech Bks) Millbrook Pr.

— Quality & Equality: Promoting Opportunities in Schools. Sayer, John, ed. (Educational Management Ser.). (Illus.). 160p. 1994. 95.00 (*0-304-32687-9*) Continuum.

— Whose School Is It Anyway? Power & Politics. LC 98-152445. 1998. 79.00 (*0-7507-0713-5*, Falmer Pr) Taylor & Francis.

__Riley, Kathryn, et al.__ Revising Professional Writing: In Science & Technology, Business & the Social Sciences. (Illus.). 170p. 1998. pap. text 21.95 (*0-9644636-6-0*) Parlay Enter.

— Revising Technical & Business Writing: Principles & Applications. 153p. 1992. pap. text 19.95 (*0-9644636-0-1*) Parlay Enter.

__Riley, Kathryn, jt. auth. see Parker, Frank.__

__Riley, Kathryn L. & Parker, Frank.__ Advanced English Grammar: Prescriptive, Descriptive, Generative & Performance. LC 98-12889. 324p. 1998. pap. text 48.00 (*0-205-20025-7*) Allyn.

__Riley, Kenneth, et al, eds.__ Advances in Small Millets. (Illus.). 575p. (C). 1994. text 85.00 (*1-881570-07-X*) Science Pubs.

*__Riley, Kerry & Riley, Diane.__ Sexual Secrets for Men: What Every Woman Will Want Her Man to Know. (Illus.). 256p. 2000. pap. 14.95 (*1-86204-838-X*) Element MA.

__Riley, Kevin J.__ Snow Job? On Controlling Cocaine at the Source. 252p. (C). 1996. text 34.95 (*1-56000-242-5*) Transaction Pubs.

__Riley, Kevin J. & Hoffman, Bruce R.__ Domestic Terrorism: A National Assessment of State & Local Preparedness. LC 94-47133. (Orig.). 1995. pap. text 13.00 (*0-8330-1627-X*, MR-505-NIJ) Rand Corp.

__Riley, L., Jr.__ Renal Pathophysiology. (Pathophysiology Ser.). 1998. pap. 24.95 (*1-889325-03-1*) Fence Crk Pubng.

__Riley, Laura & Riley, William.__ Guide to the National Wildlife Refuges. LC 92-15459. 684p. 1996. pap. 16.00 (*0-02-063660-1*) Macmillan.

__Riley, Laura H.__ The Coastal Cook of West Marin: Kitchen Conversations & Recipes. (Illus.). 240p. (Orig.). 1991. pap. text 12.95 (*0-9628426-0-5*) Riley & Co.

— The Fork Ran Away with the Spoon: More Kitchen Conversations & Recipes from the Folks Who Live on the Coast of Narin County, California. (Illus.). 336p. 1996. pap., per. write for info. (*0-9628426-1-3*) Riley & Co.

__Riley, Laurie.__ Basic Harp for Beginners. 80p. 1994. pap. 10.95 (*0-7866-0021-7*, 95109) Mel Bay.

*__Riley, Laurie.__ Body, Mind & Music: A Practical Guide to Musical Wholeness. 109p. 1999. pap. 15.00 (*0-9672779-0-6*, Pub. by L Riley) MMB Music.

__Riley, Laurie, jt. auth. see McMichael, Leslie.__

__Riley, Lavawan.__ The Love of God: Hymns of Faith & Assurance. 1998. pap. 8.99 (*0-8341-9768-5*) Nazarene.

__Riley, Lee H., jt. auth. see Anderson, Howard S.__

__Riley, Len.__ Harlem. 1998. mass mkt. 6.99 (*0-425-16343-1*) Berkley Pub.

— Harlem. LC 97-1363. 384p. 1997. 21.95 (*0-385-48508-5*) Doubleday.

__Riley, Lew.__ Where Was the Sexual Revolution When I Needed It? (Playscript) LC 92-56436. 68p. (Orig.). 1992. pap. 6.00 (*0-88734-204-3*) Players Pr.

*__Riley, Linda.__ The Call to Love: Living the Great Commandments. LC 00-37785. 2000. pap. 10.99 (*0-8423-3787-3*) Tyndale Hse.

__Riley, Linda, ed.__ Marius Barbeau's Photographic Collection: The Nass River. (Mercury Ser.: CES No. 109). (Illus.). 204p. 1988. pap. 16.95 (*0-660-10766-X*, Pub. by CN Mus Civilization) U of Wash Pr.

__Riley, Linda A., et al.__ Directory of New Mexico Manufacturers. 3rd rev. ed. 342p. 1992. pap. 50.00 (*1-884324-25-8*) NMSU Ctr Econ.

__Riley, Linda C.__ Elephants Swim. LC 94-42185. (Illus.). 40p. (J). (ps-2). 1995. 14.95 (*0-395-73654-4*) HM.

__Riley, Linda C., jt. auth. see Merbreier, Carter.__

__Riley, Linnea A.__ Mouse Mess. LC 96-49499. (Illus.). 32p. (J). (ps-2). 1997. 15.95 (*0-590-10048-3*) Scholastic Inc.

__Riley, Linnea A.__ The Twelve Days of Christmas. LC 95-14362. 32p. (J). (ps-2). 1995. 15.00 (*0-689-80275-7*) S&S Bks Yung.

__Riley, Loretta.__ The Best Fruits. 66p. 1999. pap. 14.95 (*0-7392-0070-4*, PO2915) Morris Pubng.

__Riley, Lori L., et al.__ Exploring Charlotte, 1998-99: Your Guide to Fun in the Queen City. (Illus.). 124p. 1998. pap. 6.99 (*0-9663796-0-8*) Back Pocket Bks.

__Riley, Lucy R.__ You've Been Down Too Long, It's Time to Get Up. 105p. 1998. pap. 10.00 (*0-9665811-0-5*) Prosperity & You.

__Riley, Lynn M.__ Shelter Hill: An Analysis of Faunal Remains & Artifacts from a Marin County Shellmound (04-MRN-14) xiv, 206p. (C). 1985. reprint ed. pap. text 23.13 (*1-55567-014-8*) Coyote Press.

__Riley, M. J., ed.__ Management Information Systems. 2nd ed. 425p. 1981. pap. text 23.95 (*0-8162-7190-9*) Holden-Day.

__Riley, Marcia.__ A Kid's Guide to Crafts: Threads Yarn & Fabric Projects. Yonick, Deborah, ed. LC 97-68269. (Illus.). 40p. (Orig.). (J). (gr. 2 up). 1997. pap. 6.95 (*1-881982-07-6*) Stackpole Mag.

*__Riley, Margaret.__ Guide to Internet Job Searching 2000-2001. 288p. 2000. pap. 14.95 (*0-658-00225-2*, 002252) NTC Contemp Pub Co.

__Riley, Margaret, et al.__ The Guide to Internet Job Searching. (Illus.). 192p. (Orig.). 1996. pap. 14.95 (*0-8442-8197-2*, VGM Career) NTC Contemp Pub Co.

— The Guide to Internet Job Searing: (1998-99 Edition) LC 98-16128. (Illus.). 224p. 1998. pap. 14.95 (*0-8442-8199-9*, VGM Career) NTC Contemp Pub Co.

__Riley, Margaret C.__ Whole Language Discovery Activities for the Primary Grades. 336p. 1992. pap. text 27.95 (*0-87628-616-3*) Ctr Appl Res.

__Riley, Margaret C. & Taylor, Donna L.__ Year Round Creative Thinking Activities for the Primary Classroom. 288p. (C). 1990. pap. text 26.95 (*0-87628-985-5*) P-H.

__Riley, Maria.__ Wisdom Seeks Her Way: Liberating the Power of Women's Spirituality. 86p. (Orig.). 1987. pap. text 5.95 (*0-934255-04-0*) Center Concern.

— Women Connecting: Facilitator's Guide. LC 94-223853. 40p. 1994. pap. 15.00 (*0-934255-11-3*) Center Concern.

— Women Connecting: Participant's Workbooks. (Illus.). 21p. (Orig.). 1994. pap. 3.50 (*0-934255-12-1*) Center Concern.

— Women Faithful for the Future. (Illus.). 32p. 1987. pap. text 2.95 (*1-55612-103-2*) Sheed & Ward WI.

__Riley, Maria & Sylvester, Nancy.__ Trouble & Beauty: Women Encounter Catholic Social Teaching. 64p. (Orig.). 1991. pap. text 3.95 (*0-934255-10-5*) Center Concern.

__Riley, Marilyn A., ed. see Citation Directories, Ltd., Inc. Staff.__

__Riley, Marilyn A., ed. see Citation Directories, Ltd. Inc. Staff.__

__Riley, Marjorie.__ The Wife of Riley, Vol. 1. 2nd ed. Riley, Wyman, ed. LC 88-886235. (Illus.). 173p. reprint ed. 16.95 (*0-9623624-0-9*) Levee Hse Bks.

__Riley, Martha, jt. auth. see Rathlev, Mary.__

__Riley, Martin.__ Boggart's Sandwich. (Illus.). 95p. (J). (gr. 7-9). 1992. pap. 3.95 (*0-563-20871-6*, Pub. by BBC) Parkwest Pubns.

__Riley, Martin, jt. auth. see Minardi, Henry.__

__Riley, Martyn J. & Richardson, Iain E.__ Digital Video Communications. LC 96-37127. (Communications Engineering Ser.). 215p. 1997. 79.00 (*0-89006-890-9*) Artech Hse.

__Riley, Mary A. & Beltran, Mary J.__ Clinical Nursing Interventions with Critical Elements. LC 85-20360. 385p. 1989. pap. text 28.50 (*0-8273-4338-8*) Delmar.

__Riley, Matilda W., ed.__ Social Change & the Life Course. (American Sociological Association Presidential Ser.). 560p. 1988. 74.95 (*0-8039-3432-7*) Sage.

— Social Change & the Life Course, Set, Vols. 1 & 2. (American Sociological Association Presidential Ser.). 560p. 1988. pap. 34.90 (*0-8039-3433-5*) Sage.

— Social Change & the Life Course Vol. 2: Sociological Lives. LC 87-37658. (American Sociological Association Presidential Ser.). 192p. 1988. reprint ed. pap. 59.60 (*0-608-01727-2*, 206238400002) Bks Demand.

— Sociological Lives, Vol. 2: Social Change & the Life Course. (American Sociological Association Presidential Ser.). 192p. (C). 1988. text 42.00 (*0-8039-3285-5*); pap. text 19.50 (*0-8039-3286-3*) Sage.

__Riley, Matilda W., et al, eds.__ Age & Structural Lag: Changes in Work, Family, Retirement, & Other Structures. 304p. 1994. 115.00 (*0-471-01678-0*) Wiley.

— The Aging Dimension: Perspectives in Behavioral Medicine. 208p. 1987. text 39.95 (*0-89859-927-X*) L Erlbaum Assocs.

— Aging in Society: Selected Reviews of Recent Research. 288p. (C). 1983. text 59.95 (*0-89859-267-4*) L Erlbaum Assocs.

— AIDS in an Aging Society: What We Need to Know. 240p. 1989. 32.95 (*0-8261-7060-9*) Springer Pub.

— Social Change & the Life Course Vol. 1: Social Structures & Human Lives. LC 87-37658. 368p. 1988. pap. 114.10 (*0-7837-8966-1*, 204974700001) Bks Demand.

— Social Structures & Human Lives, Vol. 1: Social Change & the Life Course. (American Sociological Association Presidential Ser.). 368p. (C). 1988. text 48.00 (*0-8039-3287-1*); pap. text 21.50 (*0-8039-3288-X*) Sage.

__Riley, Matilda W. & Foner, Anne.__ Aging & Society Vol. 1: An Inventory of Research Findings. LC 68-54406. 636p. 1968. 55.00 (*0-87154-718-X*) Russell Sage.

__Riley, Matilda W., et al.__ Aging & Society, Vol. 3: A Sociology of Age Stratification. LC 68-54406. 652p. 1972. 55.00 (*0-87154-720-1*) Russell Sage.

__Riley, Matilda W., jt. ed. see Merton, Robert K.__

__Riley, Matilda W., ed. see Riley, John W., Jr. & Johnson, Marilyn E.__

__Riley, Maurice W.__ The History of the Viola, Vol. I. LC 79-66348. (Illus.). 400p. 1980. 29.50 (*0-9603150-0-4*); pap. 24.50 (*0-9603150-1-2*) M W Riley.

— The History of the Viola, Vol. I. rev. ed. (Illus.). 400p. 1993. pap. 24.50 (*0-9603150-5-5*) M W Riley.

— The History of the Viola, Vol. I. 2nd rev. ed. (Illus.). 400p. 1993. 29.50 (*0-9603150-4-7*) M W Riley.

— The History of the Viola, Vol. II. (Illus.). 400p. 1991. 29.50 (*0-9603150-2-0*); pap. 24.50 (*0-9603150-3-9*) M W Riley.

__Riley, Michael.__ Estate Administration in Massachusetts: A Handbook with Forms. 2nd ed. 1995. ring bd. 105.00 (*0-327-03922-1*, 81517-10, MICHIE) LEXIS Pub.

*__Riley, Michael.__ Managing People. 2nd ed. 224p. 2000. pap. 29.95 (*0-7506-4536-9*) Buttrwrth-Heinemann.

__Riley, Michael.__ Managing People in the Hotel & Catering Industry. (Illus.). 240p. 1995. 29.95 (*0-7506-2289-X*) Buttrwrth-Heinemann.

__Riley, Michael, jt. auth. see Palmer, James.__

*__Riley, Michael D.__ Circling the Stones. 32p. (C). 2000. pap. text 7.95 (*1-881871-35-5*, Pub. by Creighton U Pr) Fordham.

__Riley, Michael D.__ How to Hear Better in 77 Steps: A Step-Wise Method to Help You Hear. (Illus.). 24p. 1997. pap. 2.95 (*0-9635378-1-4*) Listening Inst.

— How to Hear Better, Longer: The Owner's Manual for Ear Users. 310p. 1996. pap. 12.95 (*0-9635378-0-6*) Listening Inst.

— Speech Time-Frequency Representation. (C). 1988. text 77.50 (*0-89838-298-X*) Kluwer Academic.

__Riley, Michael H.__ Estate Administration in Massachusetts, Issue 6. 200p. 1999. ring bd. write for info. (*0-327-01382-6*, 8151816) LEXIS Pub.

— Estate Administration in Massachusetts: A Handbook with Forms. 2nd ed. LC 93-39830. 420p. 1994. spiral bd. 95.00 (*0-250-40726-4*, MICHIE) LEXIS Pub.

__Riley, Michael H. & Rice, Anne.__ Conversations with Anne Rice: An Intimate, Enlightening Portrait of Her Life & Work. 320p. 1996. 12.00 (*0-345-39636-7*) Ballantine Pub Grp.

__Riley, Michael O.__ Oz & Beyond: The Fantasy World of L. Frank Baum. LC 97-276. (Illus.). xiii, 286p. 1998. 29.95 (*0-7006-0832-X*) U Pr of KS.

*__Riley, Michael O.__ Oz & Beyond: The Fantasy World of L. Frank Baum. LC 97-276. (Illus.). 302p. 1998. pap. 15.95 (*0-7006-0933-4*) U Pr of KS.

__Riley, Mildred.__ Journey's End. 256p. 1995. mass mkt. 4.99 (*0-8217-0102-9*, Zebra Kensgtn); mass mkt. 4.99 (*0-7860-0102-X*, Pinncle Kensgtn) Kensgtn Pub Corp.

— Midnight Moon. 1995. mass mkt. 4.99 (*0-7860-0200-X*, Pinncle Kensgtn) Kensgtn Pub Corp.

*__Riley, Mildred.__ Trust in Love. 2000. mass mkt. 5.99 (*1-58314-110-3*) BET Bks.

__Riley, Mildred E.__ Love Always. 306p. 1997. pap. 10.95 (*1-885478-15-1*, Pub. by Genesis Press) BookWorld.

— No Regrets. LC 98-208436. (Indigo Love Stories). 295p. 1998. 15.95 (*1-885478-33-X*, Pub. by Genesis Press) BookWorld.

*__Riley, Mildred E.__ No Regrets. unabridged ed. 304p. 1999. pap. 8.95 (*1-885478-64-X*) Genesis Press.

__Riley, Miles O'Brien, see O'Brien Riley, Miles.__

__Riley, Mona, jt. auth. see Sargent, Brad.__

__Riley, Monica, jt. ed. see Drlica, Karl.__

__Riley, Natoma.__ Miracles in Natoma's Kitchen: Healthy Low Fat Downhome Cooking. 362p. 1995. 17.95 (*1-886246-04-1*) Alpha LifeSpan.

— Natoma's Low-Fat Home-Style Cooking. LC 95-103480. 260p. 1994. spiral bd. 16.95 (*1-886246-00-9*) Alpha LifeSpan.

— Natoma's Low-Fat Lifestyle Cooking: Down-Home Cooking at It's Best. Riley, Frank, ed. 264p. (Orig.). 1997. pap. 15.95 (*1-886246-08-4*) Alpha LifeSpan.

— Natoma's 28 Days to a Low-Fat Lifestyle: A Guide to Better Health & Weight Loss. rev. ed. Riley, Frank, ed. (Healthy Living Ser.). 110p. 1997. pap. 12.95 (*1-886246-06-8*) Alpha LifeSpan.

— The Trim-Down Version of Miracles in Natoma's Kitchen: Healthier Living with Low-Fat Homestyle Cooking. Riley, Frank, ed. 312p. 1997. pap. 14.95 (*1-886246-07-6*) Alpha LifeSpan.

__Riley, Natoma & Riley, Frank.__ Road Rage in the Kitchen: Woman-to-Woman Secrets for Permanent Weight Loss! 315p. 1999. 24.95 (*1-886246-09-2*) Alpha LifeSpan.

__Riley, Noel.__ Gifts for Good Children Pt. I: The History of Children's China 1790-1890. (Illus.). 310p. 1991. 60.00 (*0-903685-29-9*, Pub. by R Dennis) Antique Collect.

— A History of Decorative Tiles. 128p. 1997. 12.98 (*1-55521-146-1*) Bk Sales Inc.

— Tea Caddies. (Antique Pocket Guides Ser.). 1997. pap. text 6.95 (*0-7188-2598-5*, Lutterworth-Parkwest) Parkwest Pubns.

— Tea Caddies. (Antique Pocket Guides Ser.). (Illus.). 64p. 1985. pap. 6.95 (*0-911403-25-6*) Seven Hills Bk.

__Riley, Noel, jt. auth. see Rowland, Tom.__

__Riley, P. & Riley, D.__ Jack the Ripper: or When London Walked in Terror. 1996. 95.00 (*1-874712-29-8*, Pub. by P & D Riley) St Mut.

__Riley, Pat.__ Showtime: Inside the Lakers' Breakthrough Season. (Illus.). 312p. 1988. mass mkt. 5.95 (*0-446-35370-1*, Pub. by Warner Bks) Little.

— The Winner Within. 272p. 1994. pap. 12.95 (*0-425-14175-6*) Berkley Pub.

— The Winner Within: A Life Plan for Team Players. 224p. 1993. 22.95 (*0-399-13839-0*, G P Putnam) Peng Put Young Read.

__Riley, Pat.__ The Winner Within: A Life Plan for Team Players. 1993. 17.00 (*0-671-87476-4*) S&S Trade.

__Riley, Pat, jt. auth. see Borst, Bill.__

__Riley, Patricia.__ Growing up Native American. LC 92-46484. 1993. 17.10 (*0-606-06432-X*, Pub. by Turtleback) Demco.

*__Riley, Patricia.__ Weimaraner: An Owner's Guide to a Happy Healthy Pet. (Guide to a Happy Healthy Pet Ser.). (Illus.). 160p. 2000. write for info. (*1-58245-171-0*) Howell Bks.

__Riley, Patricia, ed.__ Growing Up Native Americ. LC 92-46484. 336p. 1995. pap. 12.50 (*0-380-72417-0*, Avon Bks) Morrow Avon.

__Riley, Patrick.__ The General Will Before Rousseau: The Transformation of the Divine into the Civic. LC 86-4859. (Studies in Moral, Political, & Legal Philosophy). 293p. 1988. reprint ed. pap. 90.90 (*0-608-02911-4*, 206397500008) Bks Demand.

— Leibniz' Universal Jurisprudence: Justice As the Charity of the Wise. 368p. 1996. 43.00 (*0-674-52407-1*) HUP.

*__Riley, Patrick.__ 1 Page Proposal. 2000. 14.95 (*0-06-039375-0*); pap. 12.00 (*0-06-098860-6*) HarpC.

__Riley, Patrick.__ Will & Political Legitimacy: A Critical Exposition of Social Contract Theory in Hobbes, Locke, Rousseau, Kant, & Hegel. 294p. 1982. 40.00 (*0-674-95316-9*) HUP.

— The X-Rated Videotape Guide, Vol. 7. (Illus.). 800p. 1998. pap. 24.95 (*1-57392-249-8*) Prometheus Bks.

— The X-Rated Videotape Guide VIII. 800p. 1999. pap. 24.95 (*1-57392-757-0*) Prometheus Bks.

— The X-Rated Videotape Guide V. LC 94-42854. (Illus.). 629p. 1995. pap. 21.95 (*0-87975-950-X*) Prometheus Bks.

— The X-Rated Videotape Guide VI. (Illus.). 629p. (Orig.). 1996. pap. 22.95 (*1-57392-102-5*) Prometheus Bks.

— X-Rated Videotape Guides, Vols. 4-6. (Illus.). 1998. pap. 49.95 (*1-57392-234-X*) Prometheus Bks.

— The X-Rated Videotape Star Index II. 2nd ed. LC 97-27750. 780p. 1997. pap. text 22.95 (*1-57392-168-8*) Prometheus Bks.

— The X-Rated Videotape Star Index, 1994. LC 94-3401. (Illus.). 526p. (Orig.). 1994. pap. 22.95 (*0-87975-916-X*) Prometheus Bks.

— The X-Rated Videotape Star Index III, Vol. III. LC 99-18434. (Illus.). 750p. 1999. pap. 22.95 (*1-57392-689-2*) Prometheus Bks.

__Riley, Patrick, ed.__ Essays on Political Philosophy. LC 92-4402. (Library of the History of Ideas: Vol. VI). 413p. 1992. 75.00 (*1-878822-08-X*) Univ Rochester Pr.

__Riley, Patrick & Shaw, Russell B., eds.__ Anti-Catholicism in the Media: An Examination of Whether Elite News Organizations Are Biased Against the Church. LC 92-61550. 256p. (C). 1993. text 16.95 (*0-87973-551-1*, 551) Our Sunday Visitor.

__Riley, Patrick, jt. auth. see Rimmer, Robert H.__

__Riley, Patrick, ed. see Bossuet, Jacques.__

__Riley, Patrick, ed. see Fenelon, Francois.__

__Riley, Patrick, ed. see Leibniz, Gottfried Wilhelm.__

__Riley, Patrick, tr. & intro. see Malebranche, Nicolas.__

__Riley, Paul.__ Flower Painting: How to Paint Free & Vibrant Watercolours. (Illus.). 160p. 1998. reprint ed. pap. 24.95 (*1-870586-10-7*, D Porteous-Parkwest) Parkwest Pubns.

— Watercolour Landscapes: How to Paint Close-Up Views in Watercolours. (Illus.). 160p. 1999. pap. 24.95 (*1-870586-34-4*, D Porteous-Parkwest) Parkwest Pubns.

__Riley, Paul, jt. auth. see Dix, Mark.__

__Riley, Peter.__ Distant Points Pt. 1: Excavations, Bks. 1 & 2. 64p. 1995. 10.95 (*1-874400-06-7*, Pub. by Reality St Edits) SPD-Small Pr Dist.

— Earth. LC 97-44632. (Cycles in Science Ser.). (J). 1998. 21.36 (*1-57572-620-3*) Heinemann.

— Electricity. (Straightforward Science Ser.). (Illus.). 32p. (J). (gr. 3-6). 1999. pap. text 6.95 (*0-531-15366-5*) Watts.

— Energy. LC 97-44654. (Cycles in Science Ser.). (Illus.). 32p. (J). (gr. 4-5). 1998. 21.36 (*1-57572-617-3*) Heinemann Lib.

— Food. LC 97-44655. (Cycles in Science Ser.). (J). 1998. (*1-57572-618-1*) Heinemann Lib.

— Food Chains. (Straightforward Science Ser.). (Illus.). 32p. (J). (gr. 3-6). 1999. pap. text 6.95 (*0-531-15367-3*) Watts.

— Light & Color. 1999. pap. text 6.95 (*0-531-15371-1*) Watts.

— Magnetism. (Straightforward Science Ser.). 1999. pap. text 6.95 (*0-531-15372-X*) Watts.

— Materials. LC 97-44653. (Cycles in Science Ser.). (J). 1998. (*1-57572-619-X*) Heinemann Lib.

— Materials & Processes. LC 97-45602. (Straightforward Science Ser.). (J). 1998. 18.00 (*0-531-11514-3*) Watts.

An Asterisk (*) at the beginning of an entry indicates that the title is appearing for the first time.

— Materials & Processes. (Straightforward Science Ser.). (Illus.). 32p. (J). (gr. 3-6). 1999. pap. text 6.95 (*0-531-15369-X*) Watts.

— Our Mysterious Ocean. LC 97-74769. (Windows on Science Ser.). (Illus.). 14p. (J). (gr. 4-6). 1998. 12.99 (*1-57584-058-8*) Rdrs Digest.

Riley, Peter, ed. Banking Course Supervision. (C). 1990. pap. 125.00 (*0-85297-250-4*, Pub. by Chartered Bank) St Mut.

Riley, Peter & Gerstein, Sherry. Nightwatch: Nightlife in the Tropical Rain Forest. LC 98-65524. (Windows on Science Ser.). (Illus.). 16p. (J). (gr. 3-7). 1999. 12.99 (*1-57584-251-3*, Pub. by Rdrs Digest) Random.

Riley, Peter & Snedden, Robert. Earth & Beyond. LC 98-49891. (Smart Science Ser.). (Illus.). 32p. (YA). 1999. 21.36 (*1-57572-867-2*) Heinemann Lib.

— Electricity & Magnetism. LC 98-49854. (Smart Science Ser.). (Illus.). 32p. (YA). 1999. 21.36 (*1-57572-868-0*) Heinemann Lib.

— Energy. LC 98-49860. (Smart Science Ser.). (Illus.). 32p. (YA). 1999. 21.36 (*1-57572-879-6*) Heinemann Lib.

— Forces & Motion. LC 98-49853. (Smart Science Ser.). (Illus.). 32p. (YA). 1999. 21.36 (*1-57572-869-9*) Heinemann Lib.

— Light & Sound. LC 98-49852. (Smart Science Ser.). (Illus.). 32p. (YA). 1999. 21.36 (*1-57572-870-2*) Heinemann Lib.

***Riley, Peter & Snedden, Robert.** Matter. LC 98-49823. (Smart Science Ser.). 32p. (YA). 1999. write for info. (*1-57572-871-0*) Heinemann Lib.

Riley, Peter, et al. Our Solar System. rev. ed. LC 98-65328. (Windows on Science Ser.). (Illus.). 16p. (J). (gr. 4-6). 1998. 12.99 (*1-57584-244-0*, Pub. by Rdrs Digest) Random.

***Riley, Peter D.** The Earth in Space. LC 98-34724. (Straightforward Science Ser.). 32p. 1999. lib. bdg. 6.95 (*0-531-15370-3*) Watts.

Riley, Peter D. The Earth in Space. LC 98-34724. (Straightforward Science Ser.). (J). 1999. 19.00 (*0-531-14504-2*) Watts.

***Riley, Peter D.** Electricity. (Illus.). (J). 1999. 12.40 (*0-606-18147-4*) Turtleback.

Riley, Peter D. Electricity. LC 97-45601. (Straightforward Science Ser.). (J). (gr. k-2). 1998. 18.00 (*0-531-11511-9*) Watts.

***Riley, Peter D.** Food Chains. (Illus.). (J). 1999. 12.40 (*0-606-18148-2*) Turtleback.

Riley, Peter D. Food Chains. LC 97-50345. (Straightforward Science Ser.). (J). 1998. 18.00 (*0-531-11512-7*) Watts.

— Forces & Motion. LC 99-12885. (Science Topics Ser.). 1999. write for info. (*1-57572-772-2*) Heinemann Lib.

— Forces of Movement. LC 97-53193. (Straightforward Science Ser.). (J). 1998. 18.00 (*0-531-11513-5*) Watts.

— Light & Colors. LC 98-18804. (Straightforward Science Ser.). (J). 1999. 19.00 (*0-531-14505-0*) Watts.

— Magnetism. LC 98-18300. (Straightforward Science Ser.). (J). 1999. 19.00 (*0-531-14506-9*) Watts.

***Riley, Peter D.** Plant Life. LC 98-34725. (Straightforward Science Ser.). 32p. 1999. lib. bdg. 6.95 (*0-531-15373-8*) Watts.

Riley, Peter D. Plant Life. LC 98-34725. (Straightforward Science Ser.). (J). 1999. 19.00 (*0-531-14507-7*) Watts.

— Straightforward Science, 4, Set. 1998. 72.00 (*0-531-19434-5*) Watts.

Riley, Phil M., jt. auth. see Cousins, Frank.

Riley, Philip & Candlin, C. N., eds. Discourse & Learning. 389p. (Orig.). (C). 1985. pap. text 24.11 (*0-582-55374-1*) Longman.

Riley, Philip B., jt. ed. see Fallon, Timothy P.

Riley, Philip F., et al. Global Experience: Readings in World History to 1500, Vol. 1. 3rd ed. LC 97-2038. Vol. 1. 359p. (C). 1997. pap. text 32.80 (*0-13-310798-1*) P-H.

Riley, Philip F., jt. auth. see Harding, Edith.

Riley, Philip F., jt. auth. see Richards, Michael D.

Riley, Philip J. A Blind Bargain. LC 88-90745. (Ackerman Archives Ser.: Vol. 2). (Illus.). 196p. 1995. 29.00 (*1-882127-00-5*) Magicimage Filmbooks.

— A Blind Bargain. deluxe limited ed. (Ackerman Archives Ser.). (Illus.). 1991. boxed set 49.00 (*1-882127-36-6*) Magicimage Filmbooks.

— House of Dracula: The Original Shooting Script. LC 93-20464. (Universal Filmscript Series: Classic Horror Films: Vol. 14). 192p. 1995. pap. 19.95 (*1-882127-19-6*) Magicimage Filmbooks.

— My Hollywood - When Both of Us Were Young: The Memories of Patsy Ruth Miller, 2 bks. in 1. (Illus.). 1991. 39.95 (*0-929127-01-3*) Magicimage Filmbooks.

— The Wolf Man: The Original Shooting Script. LC 93-32968. 262p. 1995. pap. 19.95 (*1-882127-21-8*) Magicimage Filmbooks.

Riley, Philip J. & Mank, Gregory W. Abbott & Costello Meet Frankenstein: The Original Shooting Script. Semler, Robert, ed. LC 89-63447. (Universal Filmscript Series: Vol. 1). (Illus.). 168p. 1994. pap. 19.95 (*1-882127-10-2*) Magicimage Filmbooks.

— Frankenstein Meets the Wolf Man: The Original Shooting Script. LC 90-61037. (Universal Filmscript Series: Classic Horror Films). 208p. 1995. pap. 19.95 (*1-882127-13-7*) Magicimage Filmbooks.

— The House of Frankenstein: The Original Shooting Script. LC 90-61039. (Universal Filmscript Series: Classic Horror Films). (Illus.). 200p. 1995. pap. 19.95 (*1-882127-17-X*) Magicimage Filmbooks.

Riley, Philip J. & Turner, George. Dracula: The Original 1931 Shooting Script. LC 90-61035. (Universal Filmscript Series: Classic Horror Films). 256p. 1990. pap. 19.95 (*1-882127-09-9*) Magicimage Filmbooks.

Riley, Philipe E., et al. Global Experience: Readings in World History since 1500, Vol. 2. 3rd ed. LC 97-2038. Vol. 2. 342p. (C). 1997. pap. text 32.80 (*0-13-317711-4*) P-H.

Riley, R. E-Z Rules & Reviews: Criminal Law. 125p. (C). 1998. pap. text 14.95 (*1-887426-37-X*) Law Rules.

— Easy Review for Administrative Law: With 2000 Supplement. 2nd ed. Rhea, A. & Ruderman, S., eds. 168p. 1999. pap. text 16.95 (*1-887426-51-5*) Law Rules.

— Easy Review for Constitutional Law: With 2000 Supplement. 2nd ed. Feist, G. et al, eds. 160p. 1999. pap. text 16.95 (*1-887426-52-3*) Law Rules.

— Easy Review for Criminal Law: With 2000 Supplement. Feist, G. et al, eds. 128p. 1999. pap. text 16.95 (*1-887426-53-1*) Law Rules.

— Easy Review for Criminal Procedure: With 2000 Supplement. Feist, G. et al, eds. 160p. 1998. pap. text 16.95 (*1-887426-36-1*) Law Rules.

— Easy Review for Family Law. Havlik, K., ed. 160p. 1998. pap. text 16.95 (*1-887426-41-8*) Law Rules.

— Easy Review for Professional Responsibility & Legal Ethics. Havlik, K., ed. 144p. 1999. pap. text 16.95 (*1-887426-54-X*) Law Rules.

— Easy Review for Property. Havlik, K. & Lombardi, R., eds. 144p. 1998. pap. text 16.95 (*1-887426-40-X*) Law Rules.

Riley, R., ed. see Gitlitz, A.

Riley, R., ed. see Hoch, A.

Riley, R. C. Belgium. LC 90-154434. (World Bibliographical Ser.: Vol. 104). 312p. 1989. lib. bdg. 70.00 (*1-85109-099-1*) ABC-CLIO.

Riley, Ralph & Lewis, K. R., eds. Chromosome Manipulation & Plant Genetics: The Contributions to a Symposium Held During the Tenth International Botanical Congress, Edinburgh, 1964. LC 66-71193. 134p. reprint ed. pap. 41.60 (*0-608-13804-5*, 202070100018) Bks Demand.

Riley, Ranny & Bark, Linda. Compass Vol. 1: Your Roadmap Through Menopause. Howard, Tracy A., ed. (Illus.). 136p. 1998. pap. 29.95 (*0-9666839-4-3*) Lifeline Inst.

Riley, Regina. Snowflakes & Fingerprints. 72p. 1992. pap. write for info. (*1-57579-080-7*) Pine Hill Pr.

Riley, Richard. Electric Guitar Handbook. (Illus.). 192p. 1997. pap. 17.95 (*1-878427-61-X*, XC8032) Cimino Pub Grp.

***Riley, Richard.** Teach Yourself C++ (Teach Yourself Ser.). (Illus.). 192p. 2000. pap. 14.95 (*0-658-00696-7*, 006967) NTC Contemp Pub Co.

Riley, Richard W. Breaking the Tyranny of Time: Voices from the Goals 2000 Teacher Forum, November 1994. 24p. 1996. pap. 1.75 (*0-16-048647-5*) USGPO.

Riley, Robert J. Unionism, International Trade, & Trade Policy. rev. ed. LC 94-35675. (Foreign Economic Policy of the United States Ser.). (Illus.). 208p. 1995. text 20.00 (*0-8153-1993-2*) Garland.

Riley, Robert Q. Alternative Cars in the 21st Century: A New Personal Transportation Paradigm. LC 94-19325. (Illus.). 400p. 1994. 39.00 (*1-56091-519-6*, R139) Soc Auto Engineers.

Riley, Robert T. Poker Expertise Through Probability. (Illus.). 186p. 1996. spiral bd. write for info. (*0-9701586-0-2*) R T Riley.

Riley, Robert T., jt. auth. see Lorenzi, Nancy M.

Riley, Robyn, jt. auth. see Wood, Carl.

Riley, Roger S., et al. Clinical Applications of Flow Cytometry. (Illus.). 928p. 1993. 125.00 (*0-89640-200-2*) Igaku-Shoin.

Riley, Ron. A Kid's Guide to Crafts: Cooking Projects. Yonick, Deborah, ed. LC 97-66161. (Illus.). 32p. (Orig.). (J). (gr. 2-8). 1997. pap. 9.95 (*1-881982-03-3*) Stackpole Mag.

Riley, Russell. Presidency & the Politics of Racial Inequality: Nation-Keeping from 1831 to 1965. LC 98-37018. (Power, Conflict, & Democracy Ser.). 480p. 1999. lib. bdg. 49.50 (*0-231-10722-6*) Col U Pr.

***Riley, Russell.** Presidency & the Politics of Racial Inequality: Nation-Keeping from 1831 to 1965. LC 98-37018. (Power, Conflict, & Democracy Ser.). 480p. 1999. pap. 22.50 (*0-231-10723-4*) Col U Pr.

Riley, Sam G. The American Newspaper Columnist. LC 98-4334. 272p. 1998. 65.00 (*0-275-95867-1*, Praeger Pubs) Greenwood.

— Biographical Dictionary of American Newspaper Columnists. LC 95-7185. 424p. 1995. lib. bdg. 85.00 (*0-313-29192-6*, Greenwood Pr) Greenwood.

— Gr8 Pl8s. (Illus.). 288p. (Orig.). 1991. pap. 6.95 (*0-942257-25-1*) New Chapter Pr.

— Index to Southern Periodicals. LC 85-27232. (Historical Guides to the World's Periodicals & Newspapers Ser.). 468p. 1986. lib. bdg. 65.00 (*0-313-24515-0*, RII/, Greenwood Pr) Greenwood.

— Magazines of the American South. LC 85-8012. (Historical Guides to the World's Periodicals & Newspapers Ser.). 359p. 1986. lib. bdg. 65.00 (*0-313-24337-9*, RPA/, Greenwood Pr) Greenwood.

Riley, Sam G., ed. American Magazine Journalists, 1850-1900. (Dictionary of Literary Biography Ser.: Vol. 79). 387p. 1988. text 155.00 (*0-8103-4557-9*, 006547-M99348) Gale.

— American Magazine Journalists, 1741-1850. (Dictionary of Literary Biography Ser.: Vol. 73). 430p. 1988. text 155.00 (*0-8103-4551-X*, 006541-M99348) Gale.

Riley, Sam G., ed. The Best of the Rest: Non-Syndicated Newspaper Columnists Select Their Best Work, 39. LC 92-36610. (Contributions to the Study of Mass Media & Communications Ser.: No. 39). 368p. 1993. 59.95 (*0-313-28508-X*, RBC, Greenwood Pr) Greenwood.

— Consumer Magazines of the British Isles. LC 92-19876. (Historical Guides to the World's Periodicals & Newspapers Ser.). 336p. 1993. lib. bdg. 85.00 (*0-313-28562-4*, RUZ, Greenwood Pr) Greenwood.

— Corporate Magazines of the United States. LC 91-33481. 296p. 1992. lib. bdg. 85.00 (*0-313-27569-6*, RCG, Greenwood Pr) Greenwood.

Riley, Sam G., ed. Dictionary of Literary Biography Vol. 91: American Magazine Journalists, 1900-1960, Vol. 91. LC 89-48356. (First Ser.). (Illus.). 416p. 1990. text 155.00 (*0-8103-4571-4*, 006559) Gale.

Riley, Sam G. & Selnow, Gary W., eds. Regional Interest Magazines of the United States: Historical Guides to the World's Periodicals & Newspapers. LC 90-36739. 432p. 1990. lib. bdg. 105.00 (*0-313-26840-1*, RRI, Greenwood Pr) Greenwood.

Riley, Sandra. Stone Poems & Wotai: Help on the Way, 2 bks. in 1. (Illus.). 200p. 1998. pap. 8.95 (*0-9665310-0-0*) Riley Hall.

***Riley, Scot A.** Releasing the Curse: A Study of the Generational Curse. LC 99-61669. 128p. 1999. pap. 9.99 (*1-56384-170-3*, Pub. by Huntington Hse) BookWorld.

Riley, Shawn S. Borrowed Blood: Victory over Leukemia. 118p. (Orig.). 1991. pap. 5.00 (*0-936635-06-1*) Lion Pr & Vid.

***Riley, Shirley.** Contemporary Art Therapy with Adolescents. LC 98-45881. 285p. 1999. 69.95 (*1-85302-636-0*, Pub. by Jessica Kingsley) Taylor & Francis.

Riley, Shirley. Contemporary Art Therapy with Adolescents. LC 98-45881. 1999. pap. 26.95 (*1-85302-637-9*) Jessica Kingsley.

Riley, Shirley & Malchiodi, Cathy A. Integrative Approaches to Family Art Therapy. LC 94-72843. (Illus.). 262p. (Orig.). (C). 1994. pap. text 29.95 (*0-9613309-5-3*) Magnolia St Pub.

Riley, Shirley, jt. auth. see Malchiodi, Cathy A.

Riley, Shirley E. On the Real Side. (Illus.). 56p. 1989. pap. 6.50 (*0-936073-05-5*) Gumbs & Thomas.

Riley-Smith, Jonathan. The Crusades: A Short History. 332p. (C). 1990. reprint ed. pap. 16.00 (*0-300-04700-2*) Yale U Pr.

— The First Crusade & the Idea of Crusading. LC 86-1608. (Middle Ages Ser.). 229p. (C). 1986. reprint ed. pap. text 19.95 (*0-8122-1363-7*) U of Pa Pr.

— The First Crusaders, 1095-1131. LC 96-36669. (Illus.). 316p. (C). 1997. text 49.95 (*0-521-59005-1*) Cambridge U Pr.

***Riley-Smith, Jonathan.** The First Crusaders, 1095-1131. (Illus.). 316p. (C). 1998. pap. text 19.95 (*0-521-64603-0*) Cambridge U Pr.

Riley-Smith, Jonathan, ed. Atlas of the Crusades. (Cultural Atlas Ser.). (Illus.). 192p. 1990. 40.00 (*0-8160-2186-4*) Facts on File.

— A History of the Crusades. 488p. 2000. pap. 16.95 (*0-19-285364-3*) OUP.

— The Oxford Illustrated History of the Crusades. (Oxford Illustrated Histories Ser.). (Illus.). 448p. (C). 1995. 49.95 (*0-19-820435-3*) OUP.

— The Oxford Illustrated History of the Crusades. LC 96-39343. (Illus.). 448p. 1997. pap. 24.95 (*0-19-285294-9*) OUP.

***Riley-Smith, Jonathan S.** Hospitallers: The History of the Order of St. John. LC 99-32132. 1999. write for info. (*1-85285-196-1*) Hambledon Press.

Riley, Stan. Don't Be Denied God's Power. 184p. 1997. pap. 10.00 (*0-939513-79-X*) Joy Pub SJC.

***Riley, Stan.** Don't Be Denied Your Authority: Using the Authority Given to Us by Jesus Christ. 182p. 2000. pap. 10.00 (*0-939513-38-2*) Joy Pub SJC.

Riley, Stanley R. Learning Process Skills. 128p. (Orig.). 1991. pap. text 15.00 (*0-87879-946-X*) Acad Therapy.

— Riley Inventory of Basic Learning Skills (RIBLS) 64p. 1991. pap. text 17.00 (*0-87879-932-X*); student ed., vinyl bd. 50.00 (*0-87879-931-1*); student ed., vinyl bd. 50.00 (*0-87879-935-4*); student ed. 20.00 (*0-87879-933-8*); student ed. 20.00 (*0-87879-938-9*); 10.00 (*0-87879-934-6*); 10.00 (*0-87879-939-7*) Acad Therapy.

Riley, Stephen, jt. auth. see Parfitt, Trevor.

Riley, Stephen T. & Hanson, Edward W., eds. The Papers of Robert Treat Paine, Vol. 1. (Collections of the Massachusetts Historical Society Ser.: Vol. 87). 1992. 50.00 (*0-934909-30-X*, Pub. by Mass Hist Soc) NE U Pr.

— The Papers of Robert Treat Paine, Vol. 2. (Collections of the Massachusetts Historical Society: Vol. 88). 1992. 50.00 (*0-934909-33-4*, Pub. by Mass Hist Soc) NE U Pr.

Riley, Sue S. How to Generate Values in Young Children: Integrity, Honesty, Individuality, Self-Confidence & Wisdom. LC 79-65310. 94p. 1984. pap. text 5.00 (*0-912674-88-1*, NAEYC #202) Natl Assn Child Ed.

***Riley, Susan L.** Afraid. LC 99-25376. (Thoughts & Feelings Ser.). (Illus.). 32p. (J). 1999. lib. bdg. 18.50 (*1-56766-666-3*) Childs World.

Riley, Susan L. Angry. LC 99-22626. (Thoughts & Feelings Ser.). (Illus.). 32p. (J). (ps-1). 1999. lib. bdg. 12.95 (*1-56766-667-1*) Childs World.

***Riley, Susan L.** Help. LC 99-28176. (Illus.). 32p. (J). 1999. lib. bdg. 18.50 (*1-56766-670-1*) Childs World.

— Sharing. LC 99-22908. (Thoughts & Feelings Ser.). (Illus.). 32p. (J). 1999. lib. bdg. 18.50 (*1-56766-674-4*) Childs World.

Riley, Susan L. Success. LC 99-22621. (Thoughts & Feelings Ser.). (Illus.). 32p. 1999. lib. bdg. 18.50 (*1-56766-676-0*) Childs World.

Riley, Susan L. & Colby, Peter W. Practical Government Budgeting: A Workbook for Public Managers. LC 89-26374. (SUNY Series in Public Administration). 138p. (C). 1990. pap. text 17.95 (*0-7914-0392-0*) State U NY Pr.

Riley, T. J., et al, eds. Rapid Thermal & Integrated Processing VI Vol. 470: Materials Research Society Symposium Proceedings. 435p. 1997. text 71.00 (*1-55899-374-6*) Materials Res.

Riley, Terence. The International Style: Exhibition 15 & the Museum of Modern Art. Perrella, Stephen, ed. (Illus.). 224p. (C). 1997. reprint ed. pap. text 25.00 (*0-7881-5088-X*) DIANE Pub.

— The International Style: Exhibition 15 & the Museum of Modern Art, Catalogue 3. Perrella, Stephen, ed. (Illus.). 224p. 1992. pap. 29.95 (*0-9623829-6-5*) CUGSA.

— Light Construction. LC 95-78626. (Illus.). 160p. 1995. pap. 29.95 (*0-8109-6154-7*) Abrams.

***Riley, Terence.** The Un-Private House. LC 99-74231. 144p. 1999. pap. text 29.95 (*0-8109-6199-7*, Pub. by Abrams) Time Warner.

— The Un-Private House. LC 99-74231. (Illus.). 152p. 1999. pap. 29.95 (*0-87070-097-9*, Pub. by Mus of Modern Art) Abrams.

Riley, Terence, et al. Fabrications. (Illus.). 140p. 1998. pap. 27.00 (*84-89698-73-2*, Pub. by Actar) Dist Art Pubs.

Riley, Terence, ed. see Wright, Frank Lloyd.

Riley, Terrence, ed. see Wright, Frank Lloyd.

Riley, Thomas A. Germany's Poet-Anarchist: The Life & Work of John Henry Mackay. (Illus.). 336p. 1972. 250.00 (*0-87700-101-4*) Revisionist Pr.

Riley, Thomas D. Celebrating Excellence, Creating Opportunity: A History of Florida International University. LC 98-31379. 1998. write for info. (*1-57864-054-7*) Donning Co.

Riley, Tiaudra, jt. auth. see Riley, Dorothy W.

Riley, Tim. Hard Rain: A Dylan Commentary. LC 98-54777. 400p. 1999. mass mkt. 15.95 (*0-306-80907-9*, Pub. by Da Capo) HarpC.

— I'm Lettin' Go... But I Ain't Givin' Up! A Simple Guide for Clearing the Clutter That's Dragging You Down. LC 98-96294. 120p. 1999. pap. 12.95 (*0-9664714-0-7*) Sugar Pine.

Riley, Tom. Proving Punitive Damages: The Complete Handbook. LC 81-2062. 347p. 1981. 37.50 (*0-13-731778-6*, Busn) P-H.

Riley, Tom & Tomlinson, Colin. Principles of Electroanalytical Methods. James, Arthur M., ed. LC 86-23397. (Analytical Chemistry by Open Learning Ser.). (Illus.). 273p. reprint ed. pap. 84.70 (*0-608-00194-5*, 206097700006) Bks Demand.

Riley, Tracy, jt. auth. see Karnes, Frances A.

Riley, V., ed. see International Pigment Cell Conference Staff.

Riley, Vera & Gass, Saul I. Linear Programming & Associated Techniques: A Comprehensive Bibliography on Linear, Nonlinear & Dynamic Programming. rev. ed. LC 58-3589. 623p. reprint ed. pap. 193.20 (*0-608-11401-4*, 201040600069) Bks Demand.

Riley, Vernon, ed. see International Pigment Cell Conference Staff.

Riley, W. F., jt. ed. see Thompson, D. O.

Riley, W. Willshire. Sequel to Riley's Narrative. 1979. reprint ed. lib. bdg. 49.00 (*0-403-00317-2*) Scholarly.

Riley, William. The Bible Group: An Owner's Manual. 154p. 1989. pap. 22.00 (*0-86217-098-2*, Pub. by Veritas Pubns) St Mut.

Riley, William. King & Cultus in Chronicles: Worship & the Reinterpretation of History. (JSOT Supplement Ser.: No. 160). 229p. 1993. 65.00 (*1-85075-397-0*, Pub. by Sheffield Acad) CUP Services.

Riley, William. The Spiritual Adventure of the Apocalypse. LC 97-60031. 160p. (Orig.). 1997. pap. 9.95 (*0-89622-720-0*) Twenty-Third.

— The Tale of Two Testaments. 150p. 1989. pap. 22.00 (*0-86217-180-6*, Pub. by Veritas Pubns) St Mut.

Riley, William, jt. auth. see Riley, Laura.

Riley, William B. The Antievolution Pamphlets of William Bell Riley. Trollinger, William V., Jr., ed. & intro. by. LC 94-43258. (Creationism in Twentieth-Century America Ser.: Vol. 4). 1995. write for info. (*0-8153-1801-4*) Garland.

***Riley, William B. & Adams, John W.** U. S. Expatriate Handbook, a Guide to Living & Working Abroad: China Edition. 144p. 2000. 29.95 (*0-9663171-1-4*) WVUC Busn & Econs.

Riley, William F. & Sturges, Leroy D. Engineering Mechanics: Dynamics, Vol. 2. 2nd ed. LC 95-46438. 656p. 1995. text 108.95 (*0-471-05339-2*) Wiley.

— Engineering Mechanics: Statics. 2nd ed. LC 95-40833. 704p. 1995. text 108.95 (*0-471-05333-3*) Wiley.

Riley, William F. & Zachary, Loren W. Introduction to Mechanics of Materials. LC 88-21587. 768p. 1989. pap. 106.95 (*0-471-84933-2*) Wiley.

Riley, William F., et al. Engineering Mechanics, 2 vols., Vol. 2. 2nd ed. 1996. text 93.00 (*0-471-13811-8*) Wiley.

— Mechanics of Materials. 5th ed. LC 98-16173. 720p. 1998. text 111.95 (*0-471-58644-7*) Wiley.

— Statics & Mechanics of Materials: An Integrated Approach. LC 95-4072. 672p. 1996. text 108.95 (*0-471-01334-X*) Wiley.

Riley, William F., jt. auth. see Dally, James W.

Riley, Wilma. Pies. (Illus.). 32p. 1991. pap. 7.95 (*1-55050-021-X*, Pub. by Coteau) Genl Dist Srvs.

Riley, Woodbridge. American Thought: From Puritanism to Pragmatism (1915) 384p. 1998. reprint ed. pap. 27.95 (*0-7661-0567-9*) Kessinger Pub.

Riley, Wyman, ed. see Riley, Marjorie.

Riling, Ray. Guns & Shooting: A Bibliography. (Illus.). 1981. 75.00 (*0-9603094-3-8*) Ray Riling.

— The Powder Flask Book. 496p. 1992. 70.00 (*1-884849-04-0*) R&R Bks.

Rilke, Clara, ed. see Rilke, Rainer Maria.

Rilke, Franco, ed. Cervical Neoplasia. (Journal: Applied Pathology: Vol. 5, No. 1). (Illus.). 76p. 1987. pap. 41.75 (*3-8055-4605-X*) S Karger.

Rilke, Ina, tr. see De Moor, Margriet.

Rilke, Ina, tr. see Nooteboom, Cees.

Rilke, Ina, tr. see Palmen, Connie.

Rilke, O., jt. auth. see Masera, M.

Rilke, Phia. Ephemeral Aphorisms. Mieder, Wolfgang & Scrase, David, trs. from GER. LC 98-3304. (Studies in Austrian Literature, Culture & Thought). 1998. 14.50 (*1-57241-063-9*) Ariadne CA.

R

An Asterisk (*) at the beginning of an entry indicates that the title is appearing for the first time.

Rilke, Rainer Maria. Ahead of All Parting: The Selected Poetry & Prose of Rainer Maria Rilke. large type ed. Mitchell, Stephen, tr. 960p. 1995. 20.00 (*0-679-60161-9*) Random.
— The Best of Rilke: 72 Form-True Verse Translations with Facing Originals, Commentary, & Compact Biography. Arndt, Walter, tr. LC 88-40345. (GER & ENG.). 213p. 1989. pap. 15.95 (*0-87451-461-4*) U Pr of New Eng.
— The Book of Fresh Beginnings: Selected Poems of Rainer Maria Rilke. Young, David, tr. from GER. & intro. by. (Field Translation Ser.: No. 20). 99p. 1994. 22.95 (*0-932440-68-1*); pap. 12.95 (*0-932440-67-3*) Oberlin Coll Pr.
— The Book of Images. Snow, Edward, tr. 288p. 1991. 25.00 (*0-86547-468-0*) N Point Pr.
— The Book of Images. Snow, Edward, tr. 280p. 1994. pap. 14.00 (*0-86547-477-X*) N Point Pr.
— Das Buch der Bilder. (GER.). (C). 1973. 10.95 (*0-8442-2835-4*, X2835-4) NTC Contemp Pub Co.
— The Complete French Poems of Rainer Maria Rilke. Poulin, A., Jr., tr. from FRE. LC 86-81786. 383p. (Orig.). 1986. pap. 16.00 (*0-915308-83-5*) Graywolf.
— Diaries of a Young Poet. Snow, Edward & Winkler, Michael, trs. 352p. 1997. 27.50 (*0-393-04553-6*) Norton.
— Diaries of a Young Poet. Snow, Edward & Winkler, Michael, trs. (Illus.). 336p. 1998. pap. 15.00 (*0-393-31850-8*, Norton Paperbks) Norton.
— Duino Elegies. Miranda, Gary, tr. from GER. LC 96-86070. 64p. 1996. pap. 10.95 (*1-885214-07-3*) Azul Edits.
— Duino Elegies. Oswald, David, tr. 178p. 1995. 14.95 (*3-85630-535-1*) Continuum.
***Rilke, Rainer Maria.** Duino Elegies. 2000. 15.95 (*3-85630-541-6*) Daimon Pubs.
— Duino Elegies. 105p. 1999. pap. 15.95 (*1-874320-26-8*, Pub. by Menard Pr.) SPD-Small Pr Dist.
Rilke, Rainer Maria. Duino Elegies. Jaeger, Sharon A. & Hammer, Louis, trs. from GER. LC 91-3842. 91p. 1991. pap. 9.95 (*0-937584-15-0*) Sachem Pr.
— Duino Elegies. MacIntyre, C. F., tr. 1961. pap. 11.95 (*0-520-01073-6*, Pub. by U CA Pr) Cal Prin Full Svc.
***Rilke, Rainer Maria.** The Duino Elegies. Waterfield, John, tr. from GER. LC 99-47958. (Studies in German Language & Literature: Vol. 24). 136p. 2000. text 69.95 (*0-7734-7889-2*) E Mellen.
— Duino Elegies: A Bilingual Edition. LC 99-45083. 112p. 1999. 20.00 (*0-86547-546-6*) N Point Pr.
Rilke, Rainer Maria. Duino Elegies: The Sonnets to Orpheus. Hunter, Robert, tr. from GER. (Illus.). 1993. pap. 19.95 (*0-938493-21-3*) Hulogosi Inc.
***Rilke, Rainer Maria.** Duino Elegies Bilingual Edition. Cohn, Stephen, tr. (European Poetry Classics Ser.). 102p. 1998. pap. text 12.95 (*0-8101-1648-0*) Northwestern U Pr.
Rilke, Rainer Maria. Dunio Elegies. David, Young, tr. 104p. 1992. pap. 8.95 (*0-393-30931-2*) Norton.
***Rilke, Rainer Maria.** The Essential Rilke Bilingual Edition. Kinnell, Galway & Liebmann, Hannah, trs. LC 98-55133. (ENG & GER.). 176p. 1999. 22.95 (*0-88001-676-0*) HarpC.
Rilke, Rainer Maria. Ewald Tragy. Halpert, Inge D., ed. LC 61-7867. (GER.). (Orig.). 1961. pap. text 6.95 (*0-89197-155-6*) Irvington.
— Geschichten vom Lieben Gott. Wunderlich, Eva C., ed. (Illus.). 1957. 29.50 (*0-8057-5272-2*) Irvington.
— Last Poems. limited ed. Mitchell, Stephen, tr. (ENG & GER., Illus.). 75p. 1989. 95.00 (*0-942067-01-0*) Okeanos Pr.
— Lay of the Love. Date not set. reprint ed. pap. write for info. (*0-393-31620-3*) Norton.
— Letters on Cezanne. Rilke, Clara, ed. Agee, Joel, tr. from GER. LC 85-16014. 98p. 1988. pap. 10.00 (*0-88064-107-X*) Fromm Intl Pub.
— Letters to a Young Poet. Mitchell, Stephen, tr. & frwd. by. 128p. 1986. pap. 9.00 (*0-394-74104-8*) Vin Bks.
— Letters to a Young Poet. Mitchell, Stephen, tr. from GER. & frwd. by. LC 93-20169. (Pocket Classics Ser.). 112p. 1993. reprint ed. pap. 6.00 (*0-87773-946-3*, Pub. by Shambhala Pubns) Random.
***Rilke, Rainer Maria.** Letters to a Young Poet. rev. ed. Burnham, Joan M., tr. LC 91-42157. 128p. 2000. 15.00 (*1-57731-155-8*, Pub. by New Wrld Lib) Publishers Group.
— Letters to a Young Poet. rev. ed. Norton, M. D., tr. LC 91-42157. 128p. 1993. pap. 7.95 (*0-393-31039-6*) Norton.
Rilke, Rainer Maria. New Poems. Cohn, Stephen, tr. Orig. Title: Neue Gedichte. (ENG & GER.). 296p. 1997. pap. 18.95 (*1-85754-323-8*, Pub. by Carcanet Pr) Paul & Co Pubs.
***Rilke, Rainer Maria.** New Poems: Bilingual Edition. Cohn, Stephen, tr. (European Poetry Classics Ser.). 295p. 1998. pap. text 16.95 (*0-8101-1649-9*) Northwestern U Pr.
Rilke, Rainer Maria. New Poems, 1908: The Other Part. Snow, Edward, tr. LC 86-62835. 224p. 1990. pap. 13.00 (*0-86547-416-8*) N Point Pr.
— New Poems, 1907. Snow, Edward, tr. from FRE. LC 84-60683. 224p. 1990. pap. 12.00 (*0-86547-415-X*) N Point Pr.
— The Notebooks of Malte Laurids Brigge. Norton, M. D., tr. 240p. 1992. pap. 12.00 (*0-393-30881-2*) Norton.
— The Notebooks of Malte Laurids Brigge. Mitchell, Stephen, tr. LC 90-50272. (Vintage International Ser.). 304p. 1990. pap. 14.00 (*0-679-73245-4*) Vin Bks.
Rilke, Rainer Maria. Oeuvres en Prose. deluxe ed. (FRE.). 1280p. 1992. 150.00 (*0-7859-0966-4*, 2070112551) Fr & Eur.
Rilke, Rainer Maria. Orpheus. Eurydice. Hermes: Notations on a Landscape. deluxe limited ed. Mitchell, Stephen, tr. (ENG & GER., Illus.). 35p. 1996. 500.00 (*0-89304-057-6*) Cross-Cultrl NY.
— Orpheus, Eurydice, Hermes: Notations on a Landscape. limited ed. Mitchell, Stephen, tr. (ENG & GER., Illus.). 35p. 1996. 150.00 (*0-89304-058-4*) Cross-Cultrl NY.
— Poems. Leishman, J. B. & Spender, Stephen, trs. 1996. 12.50 (*0-679-45098-X*) McKay.
— Poems from the Book of Hours. Deutsch, Babette, tr. & intro. by. LC 42-21208. 64p. 1975. pap. 6.95 (*0-8112-0595-9*, NDP408, Pub. by New Directions) Norton.
— Possibility of Being: Selected Poems. Leishman, J. B., tr. from GER. LC 77-4656. 122p. 1977. pap. 8.95 (*0-8112-0651-3*, NDP436, Pub. by New Directions) Norton.
— Prose & Poetry, 100 Vols. Schwarz, Egon, ed. LC 77-6951. (The German Library). 264p. 1984. 39.50 (*0-8264-0286-0*) Continuum.
— Prose & Poetry, 100 Vols., Vol. 7. LC 80-7563. (German Library). 264p. 1984. pap. 19.95 (*0-8264-0287-9*) Continuum.
— Rainer Maria Rilke: Aspects of His Mind & Poetry. Rose, William & Houston, G. Craig, eds. LC 73-114098. (Illus.). 189p. 1970. reprint ed. 50.00 (*0-87752-092-5*) Gordian.
— Rainer Maria Rilke: Selected Poems. Flemming, Albert E., tr. from GER. (Illus.). 224p. (Orig.). 1985. pap. 11.95 (*0-416-01191-8*) Routledge.
— Rilke & Benvenuta: An Intimate Correspondence. Von Hattingberg, Magda, ed. Agee, Joel, tr. from GER. LC 87-15660.Tr. of Briefwechsel Mit Benvenuta. 148p. 1987. 16.95 (*0-88064-072-3*) Fromm Intl Pub.
— Rilke's Book of Hours: Love Poems to God. Barrows, Anita & Macy, Joanna, trs. 176p. 1997. reprint ed. pap. 8.00 (*1-57322-585-1*, Riverhd Trade) Berkley Pub.
— Rilke's Duino Elegies. Keele, Alan F. & Norris, Leslie, trs. (GERM Ser.: Vol. 65). (Illus.). x, 66p. 1993. 35.00 (*1-879751-01-1*) Camden Hse.
— Rodin. LC 74-6405. (Studies in French Literature: No. 45). 1974. lib. bdg. 75.00 (*0-8383-1913-0*) M S G Haskell Hse.
Rilke, Rainer Maria. The Rose Window & Other Verses from New Poems. LC 97-26948. (Illus.). 152p. 1997. 22.95 (*0-8212-2364-X*, Pub. by Bulfinch Pr) Little.
Rilke, Rainer Maria. Selected Poems. MacIntyre, C. F., tr. (C). 1940. pap. 10.95 (*0-520-01070-1*, Pub. by U CA Pr) Cal Prin Full Svc.
— Selected Poems of Rilke. Bly, Robert, tr. & comment by. 240p. 1981. pap. 15.00 (*0-06-090727-4*, Perennial) HarperTrade.
— The Selected Poetry of Rainer Maria Rilke. Mitchell, Stephen, tr. (International Ser.). 1989. pap. 13.00 (*0-679-72201-7*) Vin Bks.
— Shadows on the Sundial. Barkan, Stanley H., ed. Krapf, Norbert, tr. (Review Chapbook Ser.: No. 21: Swiss (German) Poetry 1). (ENG & GER., Illus.). 48p. 1992. 15.00 (*0-89304-895-X*); pap. 5.00 (*0-89304-896-8*) Cross-Cultrl NY.
— Sonnets to Orpheus. Norris, Leslie & Keele, Alan F., trs. LC 88-63602. (GERM Ser.: Vol. 42). (GER., Illus.). xix, 60p. 1989. 35.00 (*0-938100-65-3*) Camden Hse.
— Sonnets to Orpheus. Wadden, Paul, tr. & intro. by. 77p. 1989. pap. 8.00 (*0-933704-78-X*) Dawn Pr.
— Sonnets to Orpheus. Norton, M. D., tr. 160p. 1992. pap. 9.95 (*0-393-30932-0*) Norton.
— Sonnets to Orpheus. Pitchford, Kenneth, tr. from GER. LC 81-84492. (Illus.). 68p. 1983. pap. 10.00 (*0-938266-01-2*) Purchase Pr.
— Sonnets to Orpheus. Mitchell, Stephen, tr. & intro. by. 1985. 13.70 (*0-671-55708-4*, Touchstone) S&S Trade Pap.
— Sonnets to Orpheus. MacIntyre, C. F., tr. (C). 1960. pap. 11.95 (*0-520-01069-8*, Pub. by U CA Pr) Cal Prin Full Svc.
— Sonnets to Orpheus. Young, David, tr. & intro. by. LC 87-6146. (Wesleyan Poetry in Translation Ser.). (ENG & GER.). 134p. 1987. pap. 14.95 (*0-8195-6165-7*, Wesleyan Univ Pr) U Pr of New Eng.
***Rilke, Rainer Maria.** Sonnets to Orpheus & Letters to a Young Poet. 192p. 2000. 19.95 (*1-85754-456-0*, Pub. by Carcanet Pr) Paul & Co Pubs.
Rilke, Rainer Maria. Stories of God. Norton, M. D., tr. 144p. 1992. pap. 8.95 (*0-393-30882-0*) Norton.
— Translations from the Poetry. Norton, M. D., tr. 256p. 1993. pap. 10.95 (*0-393-31038-8*) Norton.
— Two Stories of Prague: King Bohush, the Siblings. Esterhammer, Angela, tr. from GER. & intro. by. LC 93-35912. 151p. 1994. pap. 12.95 (*0-87451-789-3*) U Pr of New Eng.
— Uncollected Poems. Snow, Edward, tr. from GER. LC 94-24438. 266p. 1996. 22.00 (*0-86547-482-6*) N Point Pr.
— Uncollected Poems. Snow, Edward, tr. & selected by by. 288p. 1997. pap. 13.00 (*0-86547-513-X*) N Point Pr.
— The Unknown Rilke. enl. ed. Wright, Franz, tr. from GER. & intro. by. (Field Translation Ser.: No. 17). 176p. 1990. pap. 12.95 (*0-932440-56-8*) Oberlin Coll Pr.
— An Unofficial Rilke. Hamburger, Michael, tr. 116p. 1992. pap. 15.95 (*0-85646-077-X*, Pub. by Anvil Press) Dufour.
— Where Silence Reigns: Selected Prose. Houston, G. Craig, tr. from GER. LC 78-9079. 154p. 1978. pap. 9.95 (*0-8112-0697-1*, NDP464, Pub. by New Directions) Norton.
Rilke, Rainer Maria & Poulin, A., Jr. Duino Elegies & the Sonnets to Orpheus, 001. LC 76-47553. 224p. 1977. pap. 14.00 (*0-395-25058-7*) HM.
Rilke, Rainer Maria, et al. Letters, Summer 1926. Pasternak, Yevgeny et al, eds. Wettlin, Margaret & Arndt, Walter, trs. LC 85-865. (Helen & Kurt Wolff Bk.). (Illus.). 384p. 1985. 24.95 (*0-15-150871-2*) Harcourt.
— Rainer Maria Rilke: Aspects of His Mind & Poetry. Houston, G. C., ed. LC 72-6484. (Studies in German Literature: No. 13). (Illus.). 190p. 1972. reprint ed. lib. bdg. 39.95 (*0-8383-1617-4*) M S G Haskell Hse.
Rillema, James A., ed. Actions of Prolactin on Molecular Processes. LC 86-17138. 256p. 1987. 134.00 (*0-8493-5376-9*, QP572, CRC Reprint) Franklin.
Rillera, Mary J. Adoption Encounter: Hurt, Transition, Healing. 171p. (Orig.). 1991. pap. 15.95 (*0-941770-05-2*) Pure CA.
— The Adoption Searchbook: Techniques for Tracing People. 15.95 (*0-941770-02-8*) Triadoption Lib.
— The Adoption Searchbook: Techniques for Tracing People. 3rd rev. ed. 210p. 1991. reprint ed. pap. 18.95 (*0-910143-00-5*) Pure CA.
— The Family Book: Keepsake of Family Records for Children with Multiple Parents. 112p. (Orig.). 1991. pap. 13.95 (*0-910143-04-8*) Pure CA.
— The Reunion Book, Vol. 1. 216p. (Orig.). 1991. pap. 17.95 (*0-910143-05-6*) Pure CA.
— The Search & Support Directory. 216p. (Orig.). 1991. pap. 19.95 (*0-910143-01-3*) Pure CA.
Rillera, Mary J., ed. A Poem Is Where the Heart Is: A Chronicle of Verse. 226p. (Orig.). 1991. pap. 15.95 (*0-910143-03-X*) Pure CA.
Rillera, Mary J. & Kaplan, Sharon. Cooperative Adoption: A Handbook. 158p. 1985. pap. 14.95 (*0-941770-03-6*) Triadoption Lib.
— Cooperative Adoption: A Handbook. 2nd ed. 158p. 1991. pap. 14.95 (*0-685-54343-9*) Pure CA.
Rilliet, Albert. Calvin & Servetus: The Reformer's Share in the Trial of Michael Servetus Historically Ascertained. Tweedie, W. K., tr. from FRE. LC 83-45631. reprint ed. 31.50 (*0-404-19848-1*) AMS Pr.
Rilling, Helmuth. Johann Sebastian Bach's B-Minor Mass. Paine, Gordon, tr. LC 84-60301. 154p. 1984. reprint ed. pap. 19.95 (*0-911009-05-1*) Prestige Pubns.
Rillo. Finders Keepers. 32p. (Orig.). 1992. pap. 9.00 (*1-880516-04-7*) Left Hand Bks.
— Hymns. 32p. (Orig.). 1991. pap. 9.00 (*1-880516-00-4*) Left Hand Bks.
— Public Enemy. 48p. (Orig.). 1997. pap. 9.00 (*1-880516-21-7*) Left Hand Bks.
— Wolf's Clothing. 80p. 1994. pap. 9.00 (*1-880516-12-8*) Left Hand Bks.
***Rillo, Cary.** Barney's Play & Learn Book Set, 4 vols. 18p. (ps-k). 1999. 9.99 (*1-57064-754-2*, 97428, Barney Publ) Lyrick Pub.
Rillo, Cary. Bear: Bear Loves Food!, Vol. 1. 10p. (J). (gr. k-3). 1999. pap. 4.99 (*0-689-82416-5*, 076714004993, Simon Spot) Litle Simon.
— Bear Loves Water. 10p. (J). (ps-3). 1999. pap. 4.99 (*0-689-82417-3*, 076714004993, Simon Spot) Litle Simon.
Rilly, Cherly. Great Moments in Sex. 1999. pap. 15.00 (*0-609-80243-7*, Crown) Crown Pub Group.
Rilly, Thomas & Gillis, Robert P. Privacy in the Information Age. unabridged ed. 300p. (Orig.). 1996. pap. 195.00 (*1-890299-04-9*) Gov Technology.
Riloba, Fortunato, jt. tr. see Schmidt, J. J.
***Rilyeu, Gary.** Reference Handbook for Iowa's Property Tax System. Netcott, Rachel, ed. (Illus.). 90p. 1999. pap. 10.95 (*0-9676683-0-1*) INRE Pub.
***Rim, Byung Hee.** Hans Magnus Enzensberger: Ein Paradigma der deutschen Lyrik seit Mitte der 1950er Jahre. 2000. 34.95 (*3-631-35902-0*) P Lang Pubng.
Rim, Jong-Joo, see Hailji, pseud.
Rima, Ingrid H. Development of Economic Analysis. 5th ed. LC 95-47041. 624p. (C). 1996. pap. 32.99 (*0-415-14307-1*) Routledge.
***Rima, Ingrid H.** Development of Economic Analysis. 6th ed. LC 00-38255. 2000. pap. write for info. (*0-415-23297-X*) Routledge.
— Labor Markets in a Global Economy: An Introduction. LC 95-41943. (Illus.). 416p. (C). (gr. 13). 1996. text 79.95 (*0-87332-737-3*); pap. text 36.95 (*0-87332-738-1*) M E Sharpe.
Rima, Ingrid H., ed. The Classical Tradition in Economic Thought: Perspectives on the History of Economic Thought. LC 95-217437. (Perspectives on the History of Economic Thought Ser.: Vol. 11). 136p. 1995. 85.00 (*1-85898-141-7*) E Elgar.
— The Joan Robinson Legacy. LC 90-28932. 296p. (C). (gr. 13). 1991. text 85.95 (*0-87332-611-3*) M E Sharpe.
— The Political Economy of Global Restructuring Vol. 1: Economic Organization & Production. LC 93-12027. 256p. 1993. 85.00 (*1-85278-638-8*) E Elgar.
***Rima, Samuel D., Sr.** Leading from the Inside Out: The Art of Self-Leadership. 256p. 2000. pap. 14.99 (*0-8010-9104-7*) Baker Bks.
Rima, Samuel D., Sr., jt. auth. see McIntosh, Gary L.
Rimai, Don S., jt. auth. see Sharpe, Louis H.
Rimal, Rajiv N. 30 Days to the GRE. 2nd ed. 240p. 1998. pap. 11.95 (*0-02-862180-8*) Macmillan.
Rimal, Rajiv N. & Orton, Peter Z. 30 Days to the SAT. LC 96-16204. 240p. 1996. pap. 10.95 (*0-02-861262-0*, Arc) IDG Bks.
Rimal, Rajvin N. 30 Days to the GRE. LC 96-208603. 240p. 1996. 11.95 (*0-02-861261-2*, Arc) IDG Bks.
Rimane, R., et al, eds. Advances in Simulation 1997. 195p. 1997. 32.00 (*1-56555-109-5*); 32.00 (*1-56555-110-9*) Soc Computer Sim.
Rimanelli, David, contrib. by. Brice Marden: Paintings & Drawings. (Illus.). 120p. 1995. 24.95 (*1-880146-11-8*) M Marks.
Rimanelli, Giose. Accademia. LC 96-78720. (Prose Ser.: No. 38). 160p. 1997. pap. 12.00 (*1-55071-015-X*) Guernica Editions.
— Alien Cantica: An American Journey (1964-1993) Bonaffini, Luigi, tr. from ITA. LC 94-37736. (Studies in Southern Italian & Italian-American Culture: Vol. 7). XXXVII, 163p. (C). 1996. text 39.95 (*0-8204-2650-4*) P Lang Pubng.
— Moleseide: Songs & Ballads in the Molisan Dialect. Femminella, Francis X., ed. Bonaffini, Luigi, tr. (Studies in Southern Italian & Italian American Culture: Vol. 1). 333p. 1992. 61.95 (*0-8204-1722-X*) P Lang Pubng.
— Moliseide & Other Poems. Bonaffini, Luigi, tr. from ITA. LC 98-21632. (Italian Poetry in Translation Ser.: No. 3). 212p. 1998. pap. 20.00 (*1-881901-14-9*) LEGAS.
Rimanelli, Giose & Atchity, Kenneth J., eds. Italian Literature: Roots & Branches: Essays in Honor of Thomas Goddard Bergin. LC 75-18182. 471p. reprint ed. pap. 146.10 (*0-8357-8189-5*, 203387500087) Bks Demand.
Rimanelli, Giose & Fontanella, Luigi. Da G. a G. 101 Sonetti: From G to G: 101 Sonnets. LC 96-6887. (Studies in Southern Italian & Italian-American Culture Ser.: Vol. 8). XXVII, 207p. (C). 1996. text 46.95 (*0-8204-3125-7*) P Lang Pubng.
Rimanelli, Giose & Serrao, Achille. Viamerica: The Eyes. Bonaffini, Luigi & Vitiello, Justin, trs. from ITA. LC 98-73310. (Essential Poets Ser.: Vol. 86). 48p. 1999. pap. 10.00 (*1-55071-079-6*) Guernica Editions.
Rimanelli, Goise. Benedetta in Guysterland, Vol. 1. 194p. 1993. pap. 13.00 (*0-920717-88-8*) Guernica Editions.
Rimanelli, Marco. Comparative Democratization & Peaceful Change in Single-party-Dominant Countries. LC 99-23099. 2000. text 59.95 (*0-312-16595-1*) St Martin.
— Italy Between Europe & the Mediterranean: Diplomacy & Naval Strategy from Unification to NATO, 1800's-2000. LC 95-8449. (Studies in Modern European History: Vol. 21). XXVI, 1075p. (C). 1997. pap. text 69.95 (*0-8204-2852-3*) P Lang Pubng.
Rimanelli, Marco & Postman, Sheryl Lynn. The Eighteen Ninety-One New Orleans Lynchings & U. S.-Italian Relations: A Look Back. LC 91-32335. (Studies in Southern Italian & Italian American Culture: Vol. 2). 425p. (C). 1992. text 59.95 (*0-8204-1672-X*) P Lang Pubng.
Rimanich, Heidi. Observations - Thoughts - Feelings. (Orig.). 1997. pap. write for info. (*1-57553-466-5*) Watermrk Pr.
Rimanoczy, Richard S., jt. auth. see Wilkie, Leighton A.
Rimaschewskaja, Emilja. Deutsch-Russisches, Russiches-Deutsches Woerterbuch. 2nd ed. (GER & RUS.). 935p. 1991. 69.95 (*0-7859-8547-6*, 3894511109) Fr & Eur.
Rimbach, Harald. Gnade und Erkenntnis in Calvins Pradestinationslehre: Calvin Im Vergleich Mit Pighius, Beza und Melanchthon. (Kontexte Ser.: Bd. 19). (GER.). 473p. 1996. 76.95 (*3-631-49290-1*) P Lang Pubng.
Rimbach, Zane L. Medical Scientists Research on War & Wars in Active, Passive & Historic Military Operations: Index of New Information with Authors, Subjects & References. 150p. 1996. 47.50 (*0-7883-0810-6*); pap. 44.50 (*0-7883-0811-4*) ABBE Pubs Assn.
Rimbaud, Thom. Atonements: Screams & Whispers from the Tightrope Walk of Poetry. 64p. 1999. pap. 8.95 (*1-893172-18-X*) Epiphany Pr.
— Teachers' Tales. (Tales from the Trenches Ser.). 264p. 1999. pap. 12.95 (*1-886539-00-6*) Blue Prism Pr.
***Rimbaud, Arthur.** Arthur Rimbaud: Complete Works, LC 99-57064. (Perennial Classics Ser.). 384p. 2000. pap. 15.00 (*0-06-095550-3*, Perennial) HarperTrade.
Rimbaud, Arthur. Collected Poems. Bernard, Oliver, tr. & intro. by. 384p. 1987. pap. 13.95 (*0-14-042064-9*, Penguin Classics) Viking Penguin.
— Complete Works. Schmidt, Paul, tr. 336p. 1976. pap. 15.00 (*0-06-090490-9*, CN490, Perennial) HarperTrade.
— Complete Works with Selected Letters. Fowlie, Wallace, tr. LC 66-13885. 382p. 1967. reprint ed. pap. 14.00 (*0-226-71973-1*, P288) U Ch Pr.
— Correspondance, 1888-1891. (FRE.). 228p. 1965. pap. 18.95 (*0-7859-1303-3*, 2070254364) Fr & Eur.
— Illuminations. Sloate, Daniel, tr. 130p. pap. 10.00 (*0-920717-04-7*) Guernica Editions.
— Illuminations. Varese, Louise, tr. LC 56-13365. (ENG & FRE.). (C). 1957. pap. 9.95 (*0-8112-0184-8*, NDP56, Pub. by New Directions) Norton.
— Les Illuminations. Incl. Saison en Enfer. (FRE.). (Poesie Ser.). 7.50 (*0-685-34966-7*) Schoenhof.
— Illuminations: Coloured Plates. Osmond, Nick, ed. (French Poets Ser.). (FRE.). 186p. (C). 1976. pap. 12.50 (*0-485-12710-5*, Pub. by Athlone Pr) Humanities.
— Lettres de la Vie Litteraire. (Imaginaire Ser.). (FRE.). 1990. pap. 11.95 (*2-07-072009-8*) Schoenhof.
— Lettres de sa Vie Litteraire, 1870-1875. (FRE.). 236p. 1931. pap. 10.95 (*0-7859-1302-5*, 2070254356) Fr & Eur.
— Lettres du Voyant, 13 et 15 Mai 1871. Schaeffer, Gerard, ed. (FRE.). 195p. 1975. pap. 49.95 (*0-7859-5380-9*) Fr & Eur.
— Oeuvres Vol. 1: Poesies. (FRE.). pap. 3.95 (*0-7859-2992-4*) Fr & Eur.
— Oeuvres Vol. 2: Une Saison en Enfer; Verse Nouveaux. (FRE.). 1989. pap. 10.95 (*0-7859-2993-2*) Fr & Eur.
— Oeuvres Vol. 3: Illuminations - Correspondence, 1873-1891. (FRE.). 1989. pap. 10.95 (*0-7859-2995-9*) Fr & Eur.
— Oeuvres Completes. Adam, Antoine, ed. (FRE.). 1312p. 1972. lib. bdg. 105.00 (*0-7859-3785-4*, 2070104761) Fr & Eur.
— Oeuvres Completes. deluxe ed. Renneville & Moquet, eds. (Pleiade Ser.). (FRE.). 1946. 68.95 (*2-07-010476-1*) Schoenhof.
— Oeuvres Poetiques, 2 tomes, Set. (FRE., Illus.). 87.50 (*0-685-34968-3*) Fr & Eur.
— Poems. LC 94-2496. 288p. 1994. 12.50 (*0-679-43321-X*) Random.

An Asterisk (*) at the beginning of an entry indicates that the title is appearing for the first time.

— Poesies. (FRE.). pap. 5.95 (*2-87714-132-2*, Pub. by Bookking Intl) Distribks Inc.
— Poesies. (FRE.). 1984. pap. 10.95 (*0-7859-3122-8*) Fr & Eur.
— Poesies: Avec: Une Saison en Enfer, Illuminations. Forestier, Louis, ed. (FRE.). 157p. 1992. pap. 8.95 (*0-7859-1493-5*, 2277231533) Fr & Eur.
— Poesies: Edition Critique. (FRE.). 232p. 1966. pap. 24.95 (*0-7859-5381-7*) Fr & Eur.
— Poesies Completes. (FRE.). (C). 1984. pap. 7.95 (*0-8442-1957-6*, VF1957-6) NTC Contemp Pub Co.
— Poesies, Une Saison en Enfer, Illuminations. (Poesie Ser.). (FRE.). 318p. 1981. pap. 9.95 (*2-07-031955-5*) Schoenhof.
— A Season in Hell. Schmidt, Paul, tr. LC 97-70307. (Illus.). 95p. (gr. 8). 1998. 22.50 (*0-8212-2458-1*) Little.
— A Season in Hell. Peschel, Enid R., tr. (ENG & FRE., Illus.). 192p. 1974. pap. text 9.95 (*0-19-501760-9*) OUP.
— A Season in Hell & Illuminations. Mathieu, Bertrand, tr. (ENG & FRE.). 176p. 1991. 25.00 (*0-918526-88-4*); pap. 12.50 (*0-918526-89-2*) BOA Edns.
***Rimbaud, Arthur.** A Season in Hell & Illuminations. Treharne, Mark, tr. 164p. 2000. pap. 24.95 (*0-460-87984-7*, Pub. by J M Dent & Sons) Trafalgar.
Rimbaud, Arthur. A Season in Hell & The Drunken Boat. Varese, Louise, tr. LC 61-14900. (FRE.). 1961. pap. 8.95 (*0-8112-0185-6*, NDP97, Pub. by New Directions) Norton.
Rimbaud, Arthur, et al. A Season in Hell. 206p. 1994. 29.95 (*0-85646-219-5*, Pub. by Anvil Press); pap. 16.95 (*0-85646-220-9*, Pub. by Anvil Press) Dufour.
Rimbaud, Dee. The Bad Seed. LC 99-218175. 1998. write for info. (*1-900152-20-7*, Pub. by Stride Pubns) SPD-Small Pr Dist.
Rimbaud, Jean N. Four Poems by Rimbaud: The Problem of Translation. Belitt, Ben, tr. LC 77-11475. reprint ed. 32.50 (*0-404-16337-8*) AMS Pr.
— Oeuvres de Arthur Rimbaud. Berrichon, Paterne, ed. LC 77-11477. reprint ed. 41.50 (*0-404-16338-6*) AMS Pr.
— Prose Poems from Les Illuminations of Arthur Rimbaud. Rootham, Helen, tr. LC 77-11478. reprint ed. 29.50 (*0-404-16339-4*) AMS Pr.
Rimbaud, Penny. Shibboleth: My Revolting Life. 343p. 1997. pap. 10.95 (*1-873176-40-6*) AK Pr Dist.
Rimbaud, Penny & Ratter, J. J. Diamond Signature: A Novel in Four Books & the Death of the Imagination. 245p. 1997. pap. 10.95 (*1-873176-55-4*, Pub. by AK Pr) SPD-Small Pr Dist.
Rimbault, Edward F. The Early English Organ Builders & Their Work. 1977. lib. bdg. 75.00 (*0-8490-1740-8*) Gordon Pr.
— The Early English Organ Builders & Their Works: Fifteenth Century to the Great Rebellion. LC 74-24201. reprint ed. 31.50 (*0-404-12819-X*) AMS Pr.
— The Rounds, Catches & Canons of England: A Collection of Specimens of the Sixteenth, Seventeenth, & Eighteenth Centuries Adopted to Modern Use. LC 76-21067. (Music Reprint Ser.). 208p. 1976. 35.00 (*0-306-70823-X*) Da Capo.
Rimbault, Edward F., ed. The Old Cheque-Book: or Book of Rememberance of the Chapel Royal from 1561 to 1744. LC 65-23407. (Music Ser.). 1966. reprint ed. lib. bdg. 35.00 (*0-306-70911-2*) Da Capo.
Rimbault, Edward F., jt. auth. see Hopkins, Edward J.
Rimbault, Edward F., ed. see North, Roger.
Rimbeaux, B. C., jt. auth. see Cassidy, John.
Rimberg, John. The Motion Picture in the Soviet Union, 1918-1952: A Sociological Analysis. LC 72-559. (Dissertations on Film Ser.). 238p. 1974. reprint ed. 19.95 (*0-405-04102-0*) Ayer.
Rimboi, Nicholas R., jt. auth. see Kirk, Franklyn W.
Rime, Bernard, jt. ed. see Feldman, Robert S.
Rimell, Raymond L. Building & Painting Model Dinosaurs. LC 98-128162. (Illus.). 88p. 1998. pap. 15.95 (*0-89024-270-4*, 12167, Kalmbach Books) Kalmbach.
— Lancaster: Auro Lancaster B MK1. (Aeroguide Ser.: No. 3). 1986. pap. 6.00 (*0-918805-27-9*) Pac Aero Pr.
Rimell, Raymond L., jt. auth. see Chesneau, Roger.
Rimenhild, jt. auth. see Horn.
Rimer, J. Thomas. Modern Japanese Fiction & Its Traditions: An Introduction. LC 78-51188. 327p. reprint ed. pap. 101.40 (*0-8357-4287-3*, 207098600007) Bks Demand.
***Rimer, J. Thomas.** Reader's Guide to Japanese Literature. 1999. pap. 12.00 (*4-7700-2359-6*) Kodansha.
Rimer, J. Thomas, ed. The Blue-Eyed Tarokaja: A Donald Keen Anthology. LC 95-39337. 320p. 1996. 27.50 (*0-231-10340-9*) Col U Pr.
— A Hidden Fire: Russian & Japanese Cultural Encounters, 1868-1926. LC 94-38116. 312p. 1995. 45.00 (*0-8047-2513-6*) Stanford U Pr.
— Mask & Sword: Two Plays for the Contemporary Japanese Theater. (Modern Asian Literature Ser.). (Illus.). 1980. text 55.50 (*0-231-04932-3*) Col U Pr.
Rimer, J. Thomas, tr. The Way of Acting: The Theatre Writings of Tadashi Suzuki. LC 86-5894. (Illus.). 188p. 1985. reprint ed. pap. 9.95 (*0-930452-56-9*) Theatre Comm.
Rimer, J. Thomas, et al. Court & Samurai in an Age of Transition: Medieval Paintings & Blades from the Gotoh Museum, Tokyo. LC 89-63130. (Illus.). 128p. 1990. pap. 25.00 (*0-913304-28-X*) Japan Soc.
— Court & Samurai in an Age of Transition: Medieval Paintings & Blades from the Gotoh Museum, Tokyo. LC 89-63130. (Illus.). 127p. 1995. pap. 25.00 (*0-913304-29-8*, 298) Japan Soc.
— Kyoto Encounters. (Illus.). 112p. 1995. pap. 19.95 (*0-8348-0309-7*) Weatherhill.
— Shisendo: Hall of the Poetry Immortals. (Illus.). 224p. (Orig.). 1991. pap. 29.95 (*0-8348-0241-4*) Weatherhill.
Rimer, J. Thomas, jt. auth. see Takashina, Shuji.
Rimer, J. Thomas, jt. ed. see McDonald, Keiko.
Rimer, J. Thomas, ed. see Mori Ogai, pseud.
Rimer, J. Thomas, jt. ed. see Schlant, Ernestine.
Rimer, J. Thomas, tr. see Conant, Ellen P.
Rimer, J. Thomas, tr. see Konishi, Jin I., et al.
Rimer, J. Thomas, tr. see Senda Akihiko.
Rimington, Anthony. Technology & Transition: A Survey of Biotechnology in Russia, Ukraine & the Baltic States. LC 92-20948. 384p. 1992. 79.50 (*0-89930-804-X*, Q804, Quorum Bks) Greenwood.
***Rimington, Derek & Klinger, Ron.** Improve Your Bidding & Play. 96p. 1999. pap. 13.95 (*0-575-06742-X*, Pub. by V Gollancz) Trafalgar.
Rimini, jt. auth. see Mayer.
Rimini, Emanuele. Ion Implantation: Basics to Device Fabrication. (International Series in Engineering & Computer Science, Natural Language Processing & Machine Translation). 408p. (C). 1994. text 169.00 (*0-7923-9520-4*) Kluwer Academic.
Rimler, George W. & Humphreys, Neil J. Small Business: Developing the Winning Management Team. LC 79-54848. 190p. reprint ed. pap. 58.90 (*0-608-12830-9*, 202356200033) Bks Demand.
Rimler, George W., jt. auth. see Newcomb, Donald L.
***Rimler, Marlene.** All Star Quotes. 1999. pap. 6.50 (*1-56245-389-0*) Great Quotations.
Rimler, Marlene. Behold the Golfer. 64p. 1995. 6.50 (*1-56245-215-0*) Great Quotations.
— Best Friends. Caton, Patrick, ed. 365p. 1997. pap., spiral bd. 6.50 (*1-56245-315-7*) Great Quotations.
— Champion Quotes. 366p. (Orig.). 1995. pap., spiral bd. 6.50 (*1-56245-177-4*) Great Quotations.
— Commanders in Chief: Words & Wisdom from Twentieth Century American Presidents. Caton, Patrick, ed. LC 96-76129. 68p. 1996. 6.50 (*1-56245-270-3*) Great Quotations.
— First Ladies: The Women Who Helped Shape Our Nation. Caton, Patrick, ed. LC 96-76128. 68p. 1996. 6.50 (*1-56245-271-1*) Great Quotations.
— Generations: Sister, Mother, Daughter, Friend. Caton, Patrick, ed. 365p. 1996. 6.50 (*1-56245-233-9*) Great Quotations.
— I Thought of You Today. Caton, Patrick, ed. LC 96-78981. 68p. 1997. 6.50 (*1-56245-284-3*) Great Quotations.
***Rimler, Marlene.** My Friends & Me. (Illus.). 1999. pap. 6.50 (*1-56245-386-6*) Great Quotations.
Rimler, Marlene. My Husband, My Love. Caton, Patrick, ed. LC 96-78980. 68p. 1997. 6.50 (*1-56245-283-5*) Great Quotations.
— The Other Species: Observations by Women on the Study of Men. Caton, Patrick, ed. LC 96-78977. 168p. 1997. pap. 5.95 (*1-56245-281-9*) Great Quotations.
***Rimler, Marlene.** Winning Words: 365 Keys to Success. 1999. pap. 6.50 (*1-56245-390-4*) Great Quotations.
Rimler, Walter. A Cole Porter Discography. LC 94-69684. (Songwriter Discographies Ser.). 381p. 1995. 55.00 (*1-886385-25-4*) N C Sylvan.
— A Gershwin Companion: A Critical Inventory & Discography, 1916-1984. 500p. 1991. lib. bdg. 55.00 (*1-56075-019-7*) Popular Culture.
— Not Fade Away: A Comparison of Two Generations of Composers of Contemporary Popular Music. (Illus.). 240p. 1983. 40.00 (*0-87650-159-5*) Popular Culture.
Rimlinger, Frank S. Pregroups & Bass-Serre Theory. LC 86-32112. (Memoirs of the American Mathematical Society Ser.: No. 361). 73p. 1987. pap. 16.00 (*0-8218-2421-X*, MEMO/65/361C) Am Math.
Rimm, Sylvia. Raising Preschoolers: Parenting for Today. LC 97-18764. 128p. 1997. pap. 12.95 (*0-609-80163-5*) Crown Pub Group.
— See Jane Win: The Rimm Report on How 1,000 Girls Became Successful Women. LC 98-55295. 400p. 1999. 25.00 (*0-517-70666-0*, Crown) Crown Pub Group.
***Rimm, Sylvia.** See Jane Win: The Rimm Report on How 1000 Girls Became Successful Women. 2000. pap. 14.95 (*0-609-80560-6*, Three Riv Pr) Crown Pub Group.
Rimm, Sylvia B. Dr. Sylvia Rimm's Smart Parenting: How to Parent So Children will Learn. LC 97-8570. 1997. pap. 14.00 (*0-609-80121-X*) Random Hse Value.
— Gifted Kids Have Feelings Too: And Other Not-So-Fictitious Stories for & about Teenagers. LC 90-81442. (Illus.). 162p. (Orig.). (YA). (gr. 6-12). 1990. pap. text 15.00 (*0-937891-06-1*) Apple Pub Wisc.
— Keys to Parenting the Gifted Child. LC 94-6105. (Parenting Keys Ser.). 208p. (Orig.). 1994. pap. 6.95 (*0-8120-1820-6*) Barron.
— Sylvia Rimm on Raising Kids. (Illus.). 244p. (Orig.). 1992. pap. 15.00 (*0-937891-09-6*) Apple Pub Wisc.
— Why Bright Kids Get Poor Grades: And What You Can Do about It. 1996. pap. 15.00 (*0-517-88687-1*, Pub. by Crown Bks Yng Read) Random.
Rimm, Sylvia B. & Priest, Christine. Exploring Feelings: Discussion Book for Gifted Kids Have Feelings Too. LC 90-81442. (Illus.). 162p. (Orig.). (YA). (gr. 6-12). 1990. pap. text 15.00 (*0-937891-07-X*) Apple Pub Wisc.
Rimm, Sylvia B., jt. auth. see Davis, Gary A.
***Rimmele, T. R., et al, eds.** High Resolution Solar Physics: Theory, Observations & Techniques. (Conference Series Proceedings: Vol. 183). 568p. 1999. text 52.00 (*1-58381-009-9*) Astron Soc Pacific.
Rimmer, A. Cromford & High Peak Railway. (C). 1985. 45.00 (*0-85361-319-2*) St Mut.
Rimmer, Alfred. Ancient Stone Crosses of England. 1991. lib. bdg. 79.95 (*0-8490-4965-2*) Gordon Pr.
— Ancient Stone Crosses of England. 1996. reprint ed. spiral bd. 14.00 (*0-7873-0727-0*) Hlth Research.
— Ancient Stone Crosses of England (1875) 167p. 1996. reprint ed. pap. 13.95 (*1-56459-817-9*) Kessinger Pub.
Rimmer, Brenda M. International Guide to Official Industrial Property Publications. 3rd rev. ed. (Key Resources Ser.). 312p. 1992. pap. 69.95 (*0-7123-0791-5*, Pub. by SRIS) L Erlbaum Assocs.
Rimmer, Christine. Born Innocent. (Special Edition Ser.). 1993. per. 3.50 (*0-373-09833-2*, 5-09833-0) Silhouette.
— Cat's Cradle. (Desire Ser.). 1995. per. 3.25 (*0-373-05940-X*, 1-05940-1) Silhouette.
***Rimmer, Christine.** Cinderella's Big Sky Groom: Montana Mavericks: Return to Whitehorn. (Special Edition Ser.: No. 1280). 1999. per. 4.25 (*0-373-24280-8*, 1-24280-9) Silhouette.
Rimmer, Christine. Counterfeit Bride. (Desire Ser.). 1993. per. 2.99 (*0-373-05812-8*, 5-05812-8) Silhouette.
— Dr. Devastating: Prescription: Marriage. (Special Edition Ser.: No. 1215). 1998. per. 4.25 (*0-373-24215-8*, 1-24215-5) Silhouette.
— A Doctor's Vow: Prescription Marriage. 2000. mass mkt. 4.25 (*0-373-24293-X*, 1-24293-2) Silhouette.
— For the Baby's Sake: (That Special Woman!) (Special Edition Ser.). 1994. per. 3.50 (*0-373-09925-8*, 1-09925-8) Silhouette.
— A Hero for Sophie Jones. (Special Edition Ser.). 1998. per. 4.25 (*0-373-24196-8*, 1-24196-7) Silhouette.
— Un Hombre de Ensueno: The Midnight Rider Takes a Bride. (Silhouette Deseo Ser.: Vol. 237).Tr. of Dream Man. (SPA.). 1998. per. 3.50 (*0-373-35237-9*, 1-35237-6, Harlequin) Harlequin Bks.
— A Home for the Hunter. (Special Edition Ser.). 1994. mass mkt. 3.50 (*0-373-09908-8*, 1-09908-4) Harlequin Bks.
— Honeymoon Hotline. 1996. per. 3.99 (*0-373-24063-5*, 1-24063-9) Silhouette.
— Husband in Training (The Jones Gang) (Special Edition Ser.: No. 1233). 1999. per. 4.25 (*0-373-24233-6*, 1-24233-8) Harlequin Bks.
***Rimmer, Christine.** The M. D. She Had to Marry. (Special Edition Ser.: Vol. 1345). 2000. mass mkt. 4.50 (*0-373-24345-6*, 1-24345-0) Harlequin Bks.
Rimmer, Christine. Man of the Mountain. 1994. mass mkt. 3.50 (*0-373-09886-3*) Silhouette.
— The Man, the Moon & the Marriage Vow. 1996. per. 3.99 (*0-373-24010-4*, 1-24010-0) Silhouette.
— Marriage by Necessity. 1998. per. 4.25 (*0-373-24161-5*, 1-24161-1) Silhouette.
— Married by Accident: Conveniently Yours. (Special Edition Ser.: No. 1250). 1999. per. 4.25 (*0-373-24250-6*, 1-24250-2) Silhouette.
— The Midnight Rider Takes a Bride. 1997. per. 3.50 (*0-373-76101-5*, 1-76101-4) Silhouette.
***Rimmer, Christine.** The Millionaire She Married. 2000. mass mkt. 4.50 (*0-373-24322-7*) Harlequin Bks.
Rimmer, Christine. The Nine-Month Marriage: Conveniently Yours. (Special Edition Ser.: No. 1148). 1998. per. 3.99 (*0-373-24148-8*, 1-24148-8) Silhouette.
— No Less Than a Lifetime. (Special Edition Ser.: No. 1040). (Orig.). 1996. per. 3.99 (*0-373-24040-6*, 1-24040-7) Silhouette.
***Rimmer, Christine.** Une Nouvelle Chance de Bonheur. 1999. mass mkt. 3.99 (*0-373-39534-5*) Silhouette.
Rimmer, Christine. Practically Married. 1998. per. 4.25 (*0-373-24174-7*, 1-24174-4) Silhouette.
— Slow Larkin's Revenge. (Family Continuity Program Ser.: No. 15). 1999. per. 4.50 (*0-373-82163-8*, 1-82163-6) Harlequin Bks.
— Sunshine & the Shadowmaster: The Jones Gang & that Special Woman. 1995. per. 3.75 (*0-373-09979-7*) Harlequin Bks.
— Sweetbriar Summit. 1994. per. 3.50 (*0-373-09896-0*, 1-09896-1) Harlequin Bks.
— The Taming of Billy Jones. (Silhouette Promo Ser.). 1998. per. 5.99 (*0-373-48367-8*, 1-48367-6) Harlequin Bks.
— Wagered Woman. 1993. mass mkt. 3.39 (*0-373-09794-8*, 5-09794-4) Silhouette.
— Wife Wanted. (Fortune's Children Ser.). 256p. 1997. per. 4.50 (*0-373-50184-6*, 1-50184-0) Harlequin Bks.
Rimmer, Christine & Greene, Jennifer. Single Dad Seeks... Sweetbriar Summit & Heat Wave, 2 bks. in 1. (By Request 2's Ser.). 2000. per. 4.99 (*0-373-21707-2*, 1-21707-4) Harlequin Bks.
***Rimmer, Christine, et al.** Montana Mavericks: Big Sky Brides. 2000. per. 5.99 (*0-373-48381-3*) Harlequin Bks.
Rimmer, D. L., jt. ed. see Syers, J. K.
Rimmer, David. Album. 1981. pap. 5.25 (*0-8222-0013-9*) Dramatists Play.
Rimmer, Douglas, ed. Action in Africa: The Experience of People Involved in Government, Business & Aid. LC 93-38558. 192p. 1994. pap. 19.95 (*0-435-08098-9*, 08098) Heinemann.
— Rural Transformation in Tropical Africa. LC 89-212560. (Illus.). 187p. 1988. reprint ed. pap. 58.00 (*0-608-00190-2*, 206097300006) Bks Demand.
***Rimmer, Douglas, et al.** The British Intellectual Engagement with Africa in the Twentieth Century. LC 99-54954. 2000. 69.95 (*0-312-22950-X*) St Martin.
Rimmer, James D. Fitness & Rehabilitation Programs for Special Populations. 344p. (C). 1993. text. write for info. (*0-697-11619-0*) Brown & Benchmark.
***Rimmer, James H.** Achieving a Beneficial Fitness: A Program & a Philosophy in Mental Retardation. LC 00-35545. (Contemporary Issues in Health Ser.). 2000. write for info. (*0-940898-71-3*) Am Assn Mental.
Rimmer, Joan. The Irish Harp. 1984. pap. 7.95 (*0-85342-151-X*) Dufour.
Rimmer, Mary, ed. see Hardy, Thomas.
Rimmer, Mary, ed. & intro. see Hardy, Thomas.
Rimmer, Peter J. Pacific Rim Development: Integration & Globalisation in the Asia-Pacific Economy. LC 97-158825. 240p. 1997. pap. 24.95 (*1-86373-978-5*, Pub. by Allen & Unwin Pty) Paul & Co Pubs.
Rimmer, Peter J. & Allen, Lisa M., eds. The Underside of Malaysian History: The Pullers, Prostitutes, Plantation Workers. 308p. (Orig.). 1990. pap. 39.50 (*9971-69-127-2*, Pub. by Sngapore Univ Pr) Coronet Bks.
Rimmer, Robert H. The Harrad Experiment. rev. ed. LC 90-61598. 324p. (C). 1990. reprint ed. pap. 18.95 (*0-87975-623-3*) Prometheus Bks.
— Let's Really Make Love: Sex, the Family, & Education in the Twenty-First Century. LC 95-2877. 296p. 1995. pap. 18.95 (*0-87975-964-X*) Prometheus Bks.
— The Resurrection of Anne Hutchinson. LC 86-25472. 425p. 1987. 28.95 (*0-87975-370-6*) Prometheus Bks.
— X-Rated Videotape Guide, Vol. 1. LC 93-9742. 654p. 1993. pap. 21.95 (*0-87975-799-X*) Prometheus Bks.
— X-Rated Videotape Guide, 3 vols., Vol. 1, 2 & 3. 1993. pap. 49.95 (*0-87975-835-X*) Prometheus Bks.
— The X-Rated Videotape Guide II: More Than 1200 New Reviews & Ratings. LC 85-27062. (Illus.). 625p. 1991. pap. 21.95 (*0-87975-673-X*) Prometheus Bks.
Rimmer, Robert H. & Riley, Patrick. The X-Rated Videotape Guide, Vol. 3. LC 92-42911. (Illus.). 573p. (C). 1993. pap. 21.95 (*0-87975-818-X*) Prometheus Bks.
— The X-Rated Videotape Guide IV. LC 94-4535. (Illus.). 628p. 1994. pap. 21.95 (*0-87975-897-X*) Prometheus Bks.
Rimmer, Robert H., ed. see Butler, Jerry.
Rimmer, Russell. Income Distribution in a Corporate Economy. (New Directions in Modern Economics Ser.). 272p. 1993. 95.00 (*1-85278-695-7*) E Elgar.
Rimmer, Russell J. Generic Bifurications for Involutary Area Preserving Maps. LC 82-20615. (Memoirs Ser.: No. 41/272). 165p. 1982. pap. 19.00 (*0-8218-2272-1*, MEMO/41/272) Am Math.
Rimmer, Shane. Public Procurement, Vol. III-2. (Single Market Review Ser.). 1998. 90.00 (*0-7494-2325-0*) Kogan Page Ltd.
Rimmer, Steve W. Bit-Mapped Graphics. 1991. 24.95 incl. 5.25 hd (*0-8306-6750-4*); 24.95 incl. 3.5 hd (*0-8306-6751-2*) McGraw-Hill Prof.
— Canned Code for DOS & Windows. 1994. 39.95 (*0-07-053002-5*) McGraw.
— Graphic File Toolkit: Converting & Using Graphic Files. 352p. 1992. pap. 29.95 (*0-201-60846-4*) Addison-Wesley.
— Internet Graphics: VIP Tour to the Internet Graphics Toolkit. LC 95-52982. (Illus.). 304p. 1996. text 44.95 (*0-07-912183-7*) McGraw.
— Mondo Internet. LC 94-27583. 1994. text 36.95 (*0-07-053014-9*) McGraw.
— Supercharged Bit-Mapped Graphics. 1992. 34.95 (*0-07-052976-0*) McGraw.
— Windows & OS/2 Bitmapped Grahics. 2nd ed. LC 96-19103. (Illus.). 512p. 1996. pap. text 38.95 incl. disk (*0-07-911903-4*) McGraw.
— Windows & OS/2 Bitmapped Graphics. 2nd ed. LC 96-19103. (Illus.). 512p. 1996. text 49.95 incl. cd-rom (*0-07-911902-6*) McGraw.
— Windows Bit-Mapped Graphics. 1992. 38.95 (*0-07-052995-7*) McGraw.
— Windows Bitmapped Graphics. (Illus.). 448p. 1992. 38.95 incl. VHS (*0-8306-4207-2*, 4265, Windcrest) TAB Bks.
— Windows Graphics & Prepress/Book & Disk. LC 94-37380. 336p. 1994. pap. 34.95 (*0-201-62205-X*) Addison-Wesley.
— World Wide Web Explorer: A Planet Internet Guide. (Illus.). 256p. 1995. text 34.95 (*0-07-053026-2*) McGraw.
Rimmer, Steve W., jt. auth. see Cooke, LeRoy.
Rimmer, William. Art Anatomy. 153p. 1962. pap. 8.95 (*0-486-20908-3*) Dover.
Rimmer, Yvonne. Marie's Journey. LC 98-36364. 128p. 1998. pap. 6.99 (*1-56722-224-2*) Word Aflame.
Rimmerman, Craig A. The New Citizenship: Unconventional Politics, Activism & Service. LC 96-52120. (Dilemmas in American Politics Ser.). 176p. (C). 1997. pap. 17.00 (*0-8133-2267-7*, Pub. by Westview); text 69.00 (*0-8133-2266-9*, Pub. by Westview) HarpC.
Rimmerman, Craig A., ed. Gay Rights, Military Wrongs: Political Perspectives on Lesbians & Gays in the Military. LC 96-20929. (Illus.). 376p. 1996. pap. text 19.95 (*0-8153-2580-0*, SS1049) Garland.
— Gay Rights, Military Wrongs: Political Perspectives on Lesbians & Gays in the Military. LC 96-20929. (History-Reference Ser.). (Illus.). 376p. 1996. text 66.00 (*0-8153-2086-8*, SS1049) Garland.
***Rimmerman, Craig A., et al.** The Politics of Gay Rights. LC 99-55589. (Series on Sexuality, History & Society). (Illus.). 376p. 1998. pap. text 19.00 (*0-226-71999-5*) U Ch Pr.
Rimmerman, Harlan, ed. Resources in Cooperative Learning. (Illus.). 179p. 1996. pap. text 25.00 (*1-879097-31-1*) Kagan Cooperative.
Rimmington, Don. Chinese: An Essential Grammar. LC 95-52974. (Routledge Grammars Ser.). (CHI.). 240p. (C). 1997. pap. 22.99 (*0-415-13535-4*) Routledge.
Rimmington, Don, jt. auth. see Yip, Po-Ching.
Rimmington, Don, jt. auth. see Yip Po-ching.
Rimmington, Don, jt. auth. see Yip, Po-Ching.
Rimmington, Helen & Chambers, John. Echocardiography: A Practical Guide for Reporting. LC 97-35746. (Illus.). 96p. 1998. 28.00 (*1-85070-011-7*) Prthnon Pub.
Rimmington, Michael, jt. auth. see Morrison, Alison.
Rimmon-Kenan, Shlomith. A Glance Beyond Doubt: Narration, Representation, Subjectivity. LC 96-13704. (Theory & Interpretation of Narrative Ser.). 160p. 1996. text 40.00 (*0-8142-0706-5*) Ohio St U Pr.
— Narrative Fiction: Contemporary Poetics. (New Accents Ser.). 136p. (C). 1983. pap. 18.99 (*0-415-04294-1*) Routledge.

R

— Narrative Fiction: Contemporary Poetics. LC 82-18859. 173p. 1983. pap. 13.95 (*0-416-74230-0*, NO. 3817) Routledge.

Rimmon-Kenan, Shlomith, ed. Discourse in Psychoanalysis & Literature. 208p. (Orig.). 1987. pap. 13.95 (*0-416-00452-0*, A0394) Routledge.

Rimmon-Kenan, Shlomith, et al, eds. Rereading Texts - Rethinking Critical Presuppositions: Essays in Honor of H. M. Daleski. 350p. 1997. pap. 51.95 (*3-631-30686-5*) P Lang Pubng.

— Rereading Texts - Rethinking Critical Presuppositions: Essays in Honor of H. M. Daleski. LC 97-4480. 350p. 1997. pap. 51.95 (*0-8204-3213-X*) P Lang Pubng.

Rimo Publications Staff, et al. Sepia Tones (7 Short Stories) 2nd ed. 1986. pap. 6.95 (*0-918680-32-8*) Griffon House.

Rimoin, D. L., et al, eds. Emery & Rimoin's Principles & Practice of Medical Genetics, 2 vols. 3rd ed. LC 96-216363. (Illus.). 2756p. 1996. write for info. (*0-443-04851-7*) Church.

Rimoin, David L., ed. International Nomenclature of Constitutional Diseases of Bone with Bibliography, Vol. 15, No. 1. 1979. write for info. (*0-318-54283-8*) March of Dimes.

Rimoldi, Eleanor, jt. auth. see Rimoldi, Max.

Rimoldi, Max & Rimoldi, Eleanor. Hahalis & the Labour of Love: A Social Movement on Buka Island. 312p. 1992. 30.00 (*0-85496-704-4*) Berg Pubs.

Rimon, S. G. Fluids & Applied Mathematics. 1983. pap. 54.00 (*0-08-030531-8*, Pergamon Pr) Elsevier.

Rimpoche, L., jt. tr. see Hopkins, J.

Rimrott, F. P., jt. auth. see Tabarrok, B.

Rimrott, Friedrich P. & Schwaighofer, J., eds. Mechanics of the Solid State. LC 68-110059. 292p. reprint ed. pap. 90.60 (*0-608-30992-3*, 201438300090) Bks Demand.

Rimselis, Victoras, intro. Constitutions of the Marian Clerics under the Title of the Immaculate Conception of the Most Blessed Virgin Mary. 121p. 1991. pap. write for info. (*0-933820-07-0*) Marian Fathers.

Rimsky. Capriccio Espagnol & Other Concert. 1998. pap. 14.95 (*0-486-40249-5*, 884132Q) Dover.

Rimsky-Korsakov, Nikolay. Principles of Orchestration. 489p. 1922. pap. text 12.95 (*0-486-21266-1*) Dover.

— Principles of Orchestration: General Overview: Getting the Sounds in Your Head. 2nd rev. ed. (Rimsky-Korsakov Ser.: Vol. 1). (Illus.). 341p. (C). 1989. pap. text 34.95 (*0-939067-73-0*) Alexander Pub.

— Scheherazade in Full Score. 240p. 1984. pap. 11.95 (*0-486-24734-1*) Dover.

***Rimsky-Korsakov, Nikolay.** Scheherazade, Op. 35. 240p. 1999. pap. 5.95 (*0-486-40641-5*) Dover.

Rinaldi. Cast Two Shadows. LC 98-4770. 288p. (J). (gr. 5-9). 1998. 16.00 (*0-15-200881-0*) Harcourt.

***Rinaldi.** The Yellow Rose of Texas. 2001. write for info. (*0-15-202620-7*) Harcourt.

Rinaldi, Angelo. Les Dames de France. (FRE.). 1980. pap. 11.95 (*0-7859-4131-2*) Fr & Eur.

— La Derniere Fete de l'Empire. (FRE.). 1984. pap. 11.95 (*0-7859-4212-2*) Fr & Eur.

— L' Education de l'Oubli. (FRE.). 1979. pap. 11.95 (*0-7859-4089-8*) Fr & Eur.

— Les Jardins du Consulat. (FRE.). 280p. 1986. pap. 11.95 (*0-7859-4253-X*, 2070377717) Fr & Eur.

— La Maison des Atlantes. (FRE.). 1973. pap. 15.95 (*0-7859-4013-8*) Fr & Eur.

Rinaldi, Ann. An Acquaintance with Darkness. LC 96-51008. (Great Episodes Ser.). 304p. (J). (gr. 7). 1997. 16.00 (*0-15-201294-X*, Harcourt Child Bks) Harcourt.

— An Acquaintance with Darkness. LC 96-51008. (Great Episodes Ser.). 304p. 1999. pap. 6.00 (*0-15-202197-3*, Harcourt Child Bks) Harcourt.

— Amelia's War. LC 98-23286. 265p. (YA). (gr. 5-9). 1999. 15.95 (*0-590-11744-0*, Pub. by Scholastic Inc) Penguin Putnam.

— Blue Door. (Illus.). 288p. (gr. 6-12). 1999. mass mkt. 4.99 (*0-590-46052-8*) Scholastic Inc.

— The Blue Door: The Quilt Trilogy III. LC 95-39318. (Quilt Trilogy Ser.: No. 3). 272p. (YA). (gr. 7 up). 1996. 15.95 (*0-590-46051-X*) Scholastic Inc.

— A Break with Charity: A Story about the Salem Witch Trials. LC 92-8858. (Great Episodes Ser.). 256p. (YA). (gr. 5 up). 1992. 17.00 (*0-15-200353-3*, Gulliver Bks) Harcourt.

— A Break with Charity: A Story about the Salem Witch Trials. LC 92-8858. 256p. (YA). (gr. 5 up). 1994. pap. 6.00 (*0-15-200101-8*, Gulliver Bks) Harcourt.

Rinaldi, Ann. Break with Charity: A Story about the Salem Witch Trials. LC 92-8858. (Great Episodes Ser.). 1992. 11.10 (*0-606-06249-1*, Pub. by Turtleback) Demco.

— Broken Days. LC 94-17665. (Quilt Trilogy Ser.: Vol. 2). 288p. (YA). (gr. 7 up). 1995. 14.95 (*0-590-46053-6*, Scholastic Hardcover) Scholastic Inc.

— Broken Days. (Quilt Trilogy Ser.). 1997. 10.09 (*0-606-11167-0*, Pub. by Turtleback) Demco.

Rinaldi, Ann. Broken Days. (Quilt Trilogy Ser.: No. 3). (YA). (gr. 7 up). 1997. reprint ed. pap. 4.99 (*0-614-29043-0*, Point) Scholastic Inc.

— Broken Days, Vol. 2. (Quilt Trilogy Ser.). 1997. mass mkt. 4.99 (*0-590-46054-4*, Point) Scholastic Inc.

— Cast Two Shadows. 288p. (YA). (gr. 7 up). 2000. pap. 6.00 (*0-15-200882-9*) Harcourt.

***Rinaldi, Ann.** Cast Two Shadows: The American Revolution in the South. (Illus.). (J). 2000. 11.35 (*0-606-18805-3*) Turtleback.

Rinaldi, Ann. The Coffin Quilt: The Feud Between the Hatfields & the McCoys. LC 99-14455. (Great Episodes Ser.). 224p. (YA). (gr. 7 up). 1999. 16.00 (*0-15-202015-2*, Gulliver Bks) Harcourt.

***Rinaldi, Ann.** The Education of Mary: A Little Miss of Color of 1832. LC 99-57621. 192p. (YA). (gr. 5-9). 2000. 15.99 (*0-7868-0532-3*, Pub. by Hyprn Child) Time Warner.

Rinaldi, Ann. The Fifth of March: A Story of the Boston Massacre. LC 93-17821. (Great Episodes Ser.). (Illus.). 272p. (YA). (gr. 5 up). 1993. 12.00 (*0-15-200343-6*, Gulliver Bks); pap. 6.00 (*0-15-227517-7*, Gulliver Bks) Harcourt.

— Finishing Becca: A Story about Peggy Shippen & Benedict Arnold. LC 94-11255. (Great Episodes Ser.). 304p. (YA). (gr. 7 up). 1994. 12.00 (*0-15-200880-2*, Gulliver Bks); pap. 6.00 (*0-15-200879-9*, Gulliver Bks) Harcourt.

— Hang a Thousand Trees with Ribbons: The Story of Phillis Wheatley. LC 96-872. 352p. (YA). (gr. 4-9). 1996. 12.00 (*0-15-200876-4*); pap. 6.00 (*0-15-200877-2*) Harcourt.

— Hang a Thousand Trees with Ribbons: The Story of Phillis Wheatley. 1996. 11.10 (*0-606-10834-3*, Pub. by Turtleback) Demco.

— In My Father's House. LC 91-46839. (Illus.). 336p. (YA). (gr. 7-9). 1993. 14.95 (*0-590-44730-0*) Scholastic Inc.

— In My Father's House. 336p. (YA). (gr. 8-12). 1994. pap. 4.99 (*0-590-44731-9*) Scholastic Inc.

Rinaldi, Ann. In My Father's House. 1993. 10.09 (*0-606-07012-5*, Pub. by Turtleback) Demco.

Rinaldi, Ann. The Journal of Jasper Jonathan Pierce: A Pilgrim Boy, Plymouth Plantation, 1620. LC 99-26028. (My Name Is America Ser.). (Illus.). 208p. (J). (gr. 4-7). 2000. 10.95 (*0-590-51078-9*) Scholastic Inc.

— Keep Smiling Through. LC 95-31214. 188p. (J). (gr. 3-7). 1996. 12.00 (*0-15-200768-7*); pap. 6.00 (*0-15-201072-6*) Harcourt.

— The Last Silk Dress. 352p. (YA). 1990. mass mkt. 4.99 (*0-553-28315-4*) Bantam.

Rinaldi, Ann. The Last Silk Dress. 352p. 1990. mass mkt. 5.50 (*0-440-22861-1*) Bantam Dell.

— The Last Silk Dress. (J). 1988. 10.09 (*0-606-04464-7*, Pub. by Turtleback) Demco.

Rinaldi, Ann. Mine Eyes Have Seen. LC 97-10680. 288p. (J). (gr. 7-12). 1997. 16.95 (*0-590-54318-0*) Scholastic Inc.

— My Heart is on the Ground: The Diary of Nannie Little Rose, a Sioux Girl, Carlisle Indian School, Pennsylvania, 1880. LC 98-26767. (Dear America Ser.). (Illus.). 197p. (J). (gr. 4-9). 1999. 10.95 (*0-590-14922-9*) Scholastic Inc.

— A Ride into Morning: The Story of Tempe Wick. Grove, Karen, ed. LC 90-49481. (Great Episodes Ser.). 368p. (YA). (gr. 7 up). 1991. 15.95 (*0-15-200573-0*, Gulliver Bks) Harcourt.

— A Ride into Morning: The Story of Tempe Wick. LC 90-49481. (Great Episodes Ser.). 368p. (YA). (gr. 7 up). 1995. pap. 6.00 (*0-15-200673-7*, Gulliver Bks) Harcourt.

— Ride Into Morning: The Story of Tempe Wick. (Great Episodes Ser.). (J). 1995. 10.10 (*0-606-08074-0*) Turtleback.

— The Second Bend in the River. LC 96-25938. (J). 1997. 15.95 (*0-590-74258-2*) Scholastic Inc.

— The Secret of Sarah Revere. LC 95-5570. 352p. (YA). (gr. 7 up). 1995. 12.00 (*0-15-200393-2*, Gulliver Bks); pap. 5.00 (*0-15-200392-4*, Gulliver Bks) Harcourt.

— Secret of Sarah Revere. 1995. 11.10 (*0-606-09838-0*, Pub. by Turtleback) Demco.

***Rinaldi, Ann.** The Staircase. 2000. 16.00 (*0-15-202430-1*, Harcourt Child Bks) Harcourt.

Rinaldi, Ann. A Stitch in Time. (Quilt Trilogy Ser.). 320p. (J). (gr. 7-9). 1994. 13.95 (*0-590-46055-2*, Scholastic Hardcover) Scholastic Inc.

— A Stitch in Time. LC 93-8964. (Quilt Trilogy Ser.: Vol. 1). 320p. (J). (gr. 7 up). 1995. 3.99 (*0-590-46056-0*) Scholastic Inc.

— A Stitch in Time. (Quilt Trilogy Ser.). (J). 1994. 10.09 (*0-606-08206-9*, Pub. by Turtleback) Demco.

***Rinaldi, Ann.** Time Enough for Drums. 256p. (YA). (gr. 7-12). 2000. mass mkt. 4.50 (*0-440-22850-6*, LLL BDD) BDD Bks Young Read.

Rinaldi, Ann. Time Enough for Drums. (J). 1986. 9.05 (*0-606-04048-X*, Pub. by Turtleback) Demco.

— Wolf by the Ears. 272p. (J). (gr. 7-9). 1991. 13.95 (*0-590-43413-6*, Scholastic Hardcover) Scholastic Inc.

— Wolf by the Ears. LC 90-40563. 272p. (YA). (gr. 7-12). 1993. pap. 4.99 (*0-590-43412-8*) Scholastic Inc.

Rinaldi, Ann. Wolf by the Ears. (Point Ser.). (J). 1991. 10.09 (*0-606-02993-1*, Pub. by Turtleback) Demco.

Rinaldi, Fiori & Gillies, Peter. Narcotic Offences. xxx, 444p. 1991. 87.50 (*0-455-21025-X*, Pub. by LawBk Co) Gaunt.

Rinaldi, Giacomo. A History & Interpretation of the Logic of Hegel. LC 92-12222. (Studies in the History of Philosophy: Vol. 26). 512p. 1992. lib. bdg. 119.95 (*0-7734-9509-6*) E Mellen.

***Rinaldi, Mariangela & Vicini, Mariangela.** Buon Appetito, Your Holiness: The Secrets of the Papal Table. (Illus.). 2000. 24.95 (*1-55970-557-4*, Pub. by Arcade Pub Inc) Time Warner.

Rinaldi, Maura. Ceramics in Scholarly Taste. (Illus.). 152p. (C). 1995. pap. 34.95 (*981-00-4395-3*) Heian Intl.

— Kraak Porclain. (Illus.). 298p. 1989. 147.50 (*1-870076-09-5*, Pub. by Bamboo Pub) Antique Collect.

Rinaldi, Nicholas. The Luftwaffe in Chaos. 83p. 1985. 10.00 (*0-685-14614-6*) Negative Capability Pr.

— We Have Lost Our Fathers, & Other Poems. LC 80-22908. (Contemporary Poetry Ser.). (Illus.). 88p. 1982. reprint ed. pap. 30.00 (*0-608-04485-7*, 206523000001) Bks Demand.

***Rinaldi, Nicholas M.** The Jukebox Queen of Malta. LC 99-13322. 368p. 1999. 25.00 (*0-684-85612-3*) Simon & Schuster.

— Jukebox Queen of Malta: A Novel. 368p. 2000. pap. 13.00 (*0-684-86742-7*) Scribner.

***Rinaldi, Paolo.** Interiores de Toscana. (SPA.). 300p. 1998. 49.99 (*3-8228-7653-4*) Benedikt Taschen.

Rinaldi, Paolo. Tuscany Interiors. (Jumbo Ser.). (Illus.). 300p. 1998. 39.99 (*3-8228-7882-0*) Taschen Amer.

— Vietnam. (Places & History Ser.). 272p. 1998. 24.95 (*1-55670-694-4*) Stewart Tabori & Chang.

Rinaldi, Peter M. By Love Compelled: The Life of Blessed Philip Rinaldi, Third Successor of St. John Bosco. (Illus.). 242p. 1992. pap. 5.00 (*0-89944-377-X*) Salesiana Pubs.

— Man with a Dream: The Story of Saint John Bosco. (Illus.). 162p. 1978. reprint ed. pap. 5.00 (*0-89944-035-5*, 035-5) Salesiana Pubs.

Rinaldi, Roberto. The Great Barrier Reef Dive Guide. LC 98-28648. (Illus.). 168p. 1999. pap. 24.95 (*0-7892-0456-8*) Abbeville Pr.

Rinaldi, Sergio, jt. auth. see Farina, Loreza.

Rinaldi, Wendy, ed. see Schmuller, Joseph.

Rinaldis, Aldo De, see De Rinaldis, Aldo.

Rinaldo, Andrea, jt. auth. see Rodriguez-Iturbe, Ignacio.

Rinaldo, Dorothy W., ed. see Beach, Rachel Trout.

Rinaldo, John B. An Analysis of Culture Change in the Ackmen-Lowry Area. LC 51-2418. (Chicago Natural History Museum Anthropology Ser.: Vol. 36, No. 5, July 14, 1950). (Illus.). 14p. 1950. reprint ed. pap. 30.00 (*0-608-02722-7*, 206338700004) Bks Demand.

Rinaldo, John B., jt. auth. see Martin, Paul S.

***Rinaldo, Peter M. Atheists, Agnostics & Deists in America: A Brief History. LC 00-131022. 192p. 2000. 19.95 (*1-890849-03-0*) DorPete Pr.**

This is the FIRST history of religious disbelief in the United States covering the period from the American Revolution to the year 2000-from Thomas Jefferson to the American Humanist Association. It examines the influence on our Founding Fathers of the philosophers Epicurus, Marcus Aurellus & Voltaire & discusses the religious beliefs of Ralph Waldo Emerson, Henry David Thoreau, Ralph Ingersoll & Clarence Darrow, as well as the lives of lesser-known figures such as Fanny Wright, an atheist whom Jefferson invited to the White House & Walt Whitman praised. It also traces the history of Unitairans, Universalists, Ethical Culture, Buddhists & Humanists in the United States. Finally, the book examines why atheism has never become more than a fringe belief in this country, as contrasted with much greater popularity in Europe & whether it will have more influence in future years. The book includes a glossary, an index & eight-page bibliography. The author, Peter Rinaldo, has written twelve widely-praised books in the fields of history & sociology. Order over the internet, from your local bookstore, or directly from the publisher, DorPete Press, P. O. Box 238, Briarcliff Manor, NY 10510.
Publisher Paid Annotation.

Rinaldo, Peter M. The Five-Day Weekend: A Proposal for Calendar & Work Schedule Change. LC 89-50030. 122p. (C). 1989. 14.95 (*0-9622123-2-6*); pap. 6.95 (*0-9622123-3-4*) DorPete Pr.

— Full Employment: Is It Possible? LC 94-70583. 136p. 1994. 14.95 (*0-9622123-8-5*) DorPete Pr.

— The Great Reindeer Caper: The Missionary & the Miners. LC 97-66799. 120p. 1997. 14.95 (*1-890849-00-6*) DorPete Pr.

— Marrying the Natives: Love & Interracial Marriage. LC 95-92343. 120p. 1996. 14.95 (*0-9622123-9-3*) DorPete Pr.

— Nature, Nurture, & Chance. LC 97-66986. (Illus.). 140p. 1998. 14.95 (*1-890849-01-4*) DorPete Pr.

— The Trouts from London: William Trout Branch. LC 88-71508. (Illus.). 658p. (C). 1989. 45.00 (*0-9622123-1-8*) DorPete Pr.

— Trying to Change the World. LC 91-90387. 172p. (C). 1992. 14.95 (*0-9622123-6-9*) DorPete Pr.

— Unnecessary Wars? Causes & Effects of United States Wars from the Revolution to Vietnam. LC 93-70883. (Illus.). 168p. (C). 1993. 14.95 (*0-9622123-7-7*) DorPete Pr.

Rinaldo, Peter M., ed. see Beach, Rachel Trout.

Rinaman. Foundations of Probability. (C). 1993. pap. text, teacher ed. 28.00 (*0-03-096724-4*) Harcourt Coll Pubs.

Rinard, Judith E. Along a Rocky Shore. (Books for Young Explorers: Set 17, No. 1). (Illus.). (J). (gr. k-4). 1990. lib. bdg. 16.95 (*0-87044-823-4*) Natl Geog.

— Along a Rocky Shore. LC 90-5583. (Books for Young Explorers: Set 17, No. 1). (Illus.). (J). (gr. k-4). 1994. 8.00 (*0-87044-822-6*) Natl Geog.

— Creatures of the Night. (J). 1977. pap. write for info. (*0-87044-241-4*) Natl Geog.

Rinard, Judith E. Zoos Without Cages. LC 79-3243. (Books for World Explorers Series 2: No. 3). (Illus.). 104p. (J). (gr. 3-8). 1981. 8.95 (*0-87044-335-6*); lib. bdg. 12.50 (*0-87044-340-2*) Natl Geog.

Rinard, Judy. Amazing Animals of the Sea. Crump, Donald J., ed. LC 80-8796. (Books for World Explorers Series 3: No. 1). (Illus.). 104p. (J). (gr. 3-8). 1981. 8.95 (*0-87044-382-8*); lib. bdg. 12.50 (*0-87044-387-9*) Natl Geog.

Rinbochay, Denma L., jt. auth. see Rinbochay, Lati.

Rinbochay, Khetsun S. Tantric Practice in Nying-Ma. Hopkins, Jeffery & Klein, Anne C., eds. LC 86-3762. 240p. 1983. pap. 14.95 (*0-937938-14-9*) Snow Lion Pubns.

Rinbochay, Lati. Mind in Tibetan Buddhism. Napper, Elizabeth S., ed. LC 86-3799. 184p. (C). 1980. lib. bdg. 16.95 (*0-937938-02-5*) Snow Lion Pubns.

Rinbochay, Lati & Hopkins, Jeffrey. Death, Intermediate State & Rebirth: In Tibetan Buddhism. 93p. 1981. pap. 9.95 (*0-937938-00-9*) Snow Lion Pubns.

Rinbochay, Lati & Rinbochay, Denma L. Meditative States in Tibetan Buddhism. Zahler, Leah & Hopkins, Jeffrey, trs. LC 96-24298. (Illus.). 208p. 1996. pap. 15.95 (*0-86171-119-X*) Wisdom MA.

Rinchen, Geshe S. Atisha's Lamp for the Path to Enlightenment: An Oral Teaching by Geshe Sonam Rinchen. Sonam, Ruth, ed. & tr. by. from TIB. LC 97-27144. 217p. 1997. pap. 12.95 (*1-55939-082-4*) Snow Lion Pubns.

— The Six Perfections: An Oral Teaching by Geshe Sonam Rinchen. Sonam, Ruth, tr. LC 98-9466. 185p. 1998. pap. 14.95 (*1-55939-089-1*) Snow Lion Pubns.

— The Thirty-Seven Practices of Bodhisattvas: An Oral Teaching by Geshe Sonam Rinchen. Sonam, Ruth, tr. from TIB. 110p. 1997. pap. 12.95 (*1-55939-068-9*) Snow Lion Pubns.

Rinchen, Geshe S., tr. see Komito, David R.

***Rinchen, Geshe Sonam.** The Bodhisattva Vow. Sonam, Ruth, ed. & tr. by. 184p. 2000. pap. 14.95 (*1-55939-150-2*, BOVOW) Snow Lion Pubns.

***Rinck, Jane.** Vermont Mountain Air: For People Stuck Inside. (Illus.). 128p. 1999. pap. write for info. (*0-9672969-0-0*) AL-JO.

Rinck, Margaret. Can Christians Love Too Much? 192p. 1989. pap. 9.99 (*0-310-51471-1*) Zondervan.

— Christian Men Who Hate Women. 176p. 1990. pap. 12.99 (*0-310-51751-6*) Zondervan.

Rinck, Meg J., jt. auth. see Arterburn, Stephen.

Rinck, Peter A. Magnetic Resonance in Medicine. 3rd ed. 256p. 1993. 95.00 (*0-632-03781-4*) Blackwell Sci.

— The Rational Use of Magnetic Resonance Imaging. (Illus.). 300p. 1996. 135.00 (*0-86542-823-9*) Blackwell Sci.

Rinckart, Martin. Der Muntzerische Bawren-Krieg. (GER.). 359p. 1991. reprint ed. write for info. (*3-487-09312-X*) G Olms Pubs.

Rincon, Carlos, jt. auth. see Eich, Dieter.

Rincon Garcia, W. Ayuntamientos de Espana. (SPA., Illus.). 416p. 1993. 295.00 (*84-239-5279-7*) Elliots Bks.

Rincon, Jesus M. & Romero, M., eds. Characterization Techniques of Glasses & Ceramics. LC 98-32084. xii, 239p. 1998. 89.95 (*3-540-63657-9*) Spr-Verlag.

Rincover, Arnold. How to Use Sensory Extinction. (Teaching the Autistic Ser.). 34p. 1981. pap. 8.00 (*0-89079-062-0*, 1036) PRO-ED.

— The Parent-Child Connection: Your Guide to Baby & Child Behavior in the First Six Years. 208p. 1990. per. 8.95 (*0-671-68164-8*) PB.

— The Parenting Challenge: Your Child's Behavior from 6-12. Peters, Sally, ed. 256p. (Orig.). 1991. pap. 9.00 (*0-671-68163-X*) PB.

Rind & Marasa, Paul. The Video Courses for the Verbal & Math SAT. 1995. teacher ed. write for info. (*1-57004-024-9*) Lrning NJ.

Rind, Bruce & Marasa, Paul, eds. The SAT Video Course. 1993. student ed. 109.95 (*1-57004-010-9*); VHS 99.95 (*1-57004-008-7*); VHS 99.95 (*1-57004-011-7*) L Erlbaum Assocs.

— The SAT Video Course. 1993. pap., student ed., wbk. ed. 129.95 incl. audio (*1-57004-007-9*) L Erlbaum Assocs.

— The SAT Video Course: Math, Set. 1993. pap. text, teacher ed., wbk. ed. 149.95 incl. VHS (*1-57004-009-5*) Lrning NJ.

— The SAT Video Course: Verbal, Set. 1993. lib. bdg., teacher ed., wbk. ed. 169.95 incl. VHS (*1-57004-006-0*) Lrning NJ.

Rind, Sherry. Fall Out the Door. LC 94-71362. 72p. (Orig.). 1994. pap. 12.00 (*1-881090-09-4*) Confluence Pr.

— The Hawk in the Back Yard. 1985. pap. 8.00 (*0-938078-20-8*) Anhinga Pr.

***Rind, Sherry, ed.** To Aire Is Divine: Further Tips, Tricks & Tales about Airedale Terriers. 192p. 1999. pap. 15.00 (*0-9674729-0-3*) S Rind.

Rindal, Karin, jt. auth. see Richardson, J. David.

Rinden, David. Biblical Foundations. 3rd ed. 40p. 1988. reprint ed. pap. 3.95 (*0-943167-23-X*) Faith & Fellowship Pr.

— Directions: From the Word of God. 62p. 1992. pap. 4.95 (*0-943167-15-9*) Faith & Fellowship Pr.

— Living Faith: Studies in James. 75p. (Orig.). 1993. pap. 4.95 (*0-943167-25-6*) Faith & Fellowship Pr.

Rinden, David, ed. The Small Catechism: A Handbook of Basic Christian Instruction for the Family & Congregation. (Illus.). 51p. 1993. pap. text 6.95 (*0-943167-27-2*) Faith & Fellowship Pr.

Rinden, David, jt. auth. see Olsen, Warren.

Rinden, David, ed. see Atheosen, Curt, et al.

Rinden, David, ed. see Bardanouve, Venus E.

Rinden, David, ed. see Bardenouve, Venus E.

Rinden, David, ed. see Boe, Eugene.

Rinden, David, ed. see Foss, Allen J.

Rinden, David, ed. see Larsen, Per W.

Rinden, David, ed. see Larson, Luther & Olsen, Warren.

Rinden, David, jt. ed. see Olsen, Warren.

Rinden, David, ed. see Salmonson, Gunnar.

Rinden, David, ed. see Varborg, Dale & Varborg, Idella.

Rinden, David, ed. see Wisloff, Fredrik.

Rinden, David, ed. see Wisloff, H. E.

Rinden, Gracia. The Life in Jesus: Twelve Studies in John 12-21. annot. ed. 116p. (Orig.). 1992. pap. 4.95 (*0-943167-10-8*) Faith & Fellowship Pr.

— Triumphant Christian Living. 37p. (Orig.). 1991. pap. 4.95 (*0-943167-13-2*) Faith & Fellowship Pr.

— The Truth in Jesus: Twelve Studies in John 1-11. annot. ed. 116p. (Orig.). 1992. pap. 4.95 (*0-943167-09-4*) Faith & Fellowship Pr.

An Asterisk (*) at the beginning of an entry indicates that the title is appearing for the first time.

Rinden, Robert & Witke, Roxane. The Red Flag Waves: A Guide to the Hung-Ch'i p'iao-p'iao Collection. LC 68-65796. (China Research Monographs: No. 3). 159p. 1968. pap. 4.00 (*0-912966-04-1*) IEAS.

Rinder, Larry & Estrin, Jerry, eds. Self Evidence. (Illus.). (C). 1989. pap. 8.00 (*0-937335-05-3*) LA Contemp Exhib.

Rinder, Lawrence. Richard Burton. (Illus.). 46p. 1996. pap. 9.95 (*1-880146-14-2*) M Marks.

— Searchlight: Consciousness at the Millennium. LC 99-70859. (Illus.). 192p. 1999. pap. 39.95 (*0-500-28136-X*, Pub. by Thames Hudson) Norton.

Rinder, Lawrence & Humphrey, David. Beattie & Davidson. (Illus.). 88p. 1998. pap. 20.00 (*1-889195-21-9*) Smart Art Pr.

Rinder, Lawrence, jt. auth. see Bourgeois, Louise.

Rinder, Lawrence, jt. auth. see Merrill, Kathleen.

Rinder, Lenore. Bones & Skin. Oszkay, Zulay, tr.Tr. of Huesos y Piel. (J). (ps-7). Date not set. pap. 5.00 (*0-9678778-1-4*, 002) Child Scope.

***Rinder, Lenore & Moschea, Pat.** Star's Circus Parade. (Illus.). 16p. (J). (ps-4). 2000. pap. 5.00 (*0-9678778-0-6*, 001) Child Scope.

Rinder, Walter. World I Used to Know. LC 89-81211. 1990. pap. 7.95 (*0-89087-596-0*) Celestial Arts.

Rinderknecht, Carol. A Checklist of American Imprints, 1830-1839, Title Index, 2 vols. LC 64-11784. 830p. 1989. 92.00 (*0-8108-2208-3*) Scarecrow.

Rinderknecht, Carol, compiled by. A Checklist of American Imprints for 1835: Items 29894-35601. LC 64-11784. 545p. 1985. 60.00 (*0-8108-1828-0*) Scarecrow.

— A Checklist of American Imprints for 1836: Items 35602-42652. LC 64-11784. 617p. 1986. 70.00 (*0-8108-1839-6*) Scarecrow.

— A Checklist of American Imprints for 1837: Items 42653-48672. LC 64-11784. 514p. 1986. 55.00 (*0-8108-1841-8*) Scarecrow.

— A Checklist of American Imprints for 1838: Items 48673-53805. LC 64-11784. 261p. 1988. 50.00 (*0-8108-2123-0*) Scarecrow.

— A Checklist of American Imprints, 1830-1839: Author Index. LC 64-11784. 177p. 1989. 31.00 (*0-8108-2252-0*) Scarecrow.

Rinderknecht, Carol & Bruntjen, Scott. Checklist of American Imprints: 1845, Items 45-1 - 45-7137. 539p. 1996. 67.50 (*0-8108-3109-0*) Scarecrow.

— A Checklist of American Imprints for 1834: Items 22796-29893. LC 64-11784. 646p. 1982. reprint ed. 60.00 (*0-8108-1487-0*) Scarecrow.

— A Checklist of American Imprints for 1844: Items 44-1 - 44-6827. LC 64-11784. 524p. 1993. 71.00 (*0-8108-2654-2*) Scarecrow.

— Checklist of American Imprints 1846. 1997. 69.50 (*0-8108-3212-7*) Scarecrow.

Rinderknecht, Carol & Bruntjen, Scott, eds. A Checklist of American Imprints for 1842: Items 42-1 - 42-5379. LC 64-11784. 428p. 1992. 62.00 (*0-8108-2533-3*) Scarecrow.

— A Checklist of American Imprints 1843. LC 64-11784. 428p. 1992. 62.00 (*0-8108-2653-4*) Scarecrow.

Rinderle, Walter & Norling, Bernard. The Nazi Impact on a German Village. LC 92-10030. (Illus.). 296p. (C). 1993. text 34.95 (*0-8131-1794-1*) U Pr of Ky.

Rindfleisch, Jan. Coming Across: Art by Recent Immigrants. 64p. 1994. pap. 10.00 (*1-886215-00-6*) Euphrat Mus.

***Rindfleisch, Norval.** A Cliff of Fall: Selected Short Stories & Novellas. LC 99-91896. 262p. 2000. 25.00 (*0-7388-1390-7*); pap. 18.00 (*0-7388-1391-5*) Xlibris Corp.

Rindfleisch, Norval. The Season of Letting Go. 144p. (Orig.). 1995. pap. 10.50 (*0-9645843-7-9*) Claritas Imprints.

Rindfuss, Jill, ed. The Bentley Collection Guide: The Reference Tool for Consultants. 6th ed. (Illus.). 250p. 1998. pap. 23.95 (*0-9646280-3-1*) J Phillip Inc.

— The Bentley Collection Guide: The Reference Tool for Consultants. 7th ed. (Illus.). 250p. 1999. pap. 23.95 (*0-9646280-4-X*) J Phillip Inc.

***Rindfuss, Jull.** The Bentley Collection Guide: The Reference Tool for Consultant, Collectors & Enthyusiastics of Longaberger Baskets. 8th rev. ed. (The Bentley Collection Guide). (Illus.). 300p. 2000. pap. 24.95 (*0-9646280-5-8*) J Phillip Inc.

Rindge, R., et al. Ceramic Art Malibu Potteries. LC 88-62053. (Malibu Lagoon Museum Ser.). (Illus.). 136p. 1994. pap. 35.00 (*0-295-97372-2*) U of Wash Pr.

Rindhart, Carroll A., jt. auth. see March, Mary V.

Rindisbacher, Hans J. The Smell of Books: A Cultural-Historical Study of Olfactory Perception in Literature. 392p. (C). 1993. text 54.50 (*0-472-10383-0*, 10383) U of Mich Pr.

Rindlaub, Curtis. The Maine Coast Guide for Small Boats: Casco Bay. (Maine Coast Guide for Small Boats Ser.: Vol. 2). (Illus.). 288p. (Orig.). 1999. pap. write for info. (*0-9649246-2-5*) Diamond Pass.

Rindler, Wolfgang. Essential Relativity. 2nd rev. ed. (Texts & Monographs in Physics). (Illus.). 284p. 1995. 59.00 (*0-387-10090-3*) Spr-Verlag.

— Introduction to Special Relativity. 2nd ed. (Illus.). 184p. (C). 1991. 67.95 (*0-19-853953-3*); pap. text 37.95 (*0-19-853952-5*) OUP.

Rindler, Wolfgang, jt. auth. see Penrose, Roger.

Rindner, David. Form-Z Modeling: For Digital Effects & Animation. (Illus.). 450p. 2000. pap. 49.95 (*1-886801-97-5*, 1-88680-1-97-5) Chrles River Media.

Rindo, Ronald J. Secrets Men Keep. LC 94-67064. (Minnesota Voices Project Ser.: Vol. 71). 120p. 1995. pap. 11.95 (*0-89823-163-9*) New Rivers Pr.

— Suburban Metaphysics: A Collection of Stories. 97p. 1990. pap. 7.95 (*0-89823-114-0*) New Rivers Pr.

Rindone, Bruno. Life Chemistry Reports Vol. 10, No. 2: Proceedings of the Meeting Organised by the Italian Chemical Society, Vol. 10. (Life Chemistry Reports). 120p. 1994. pap. text 247.00 (*3-7186-5533-0*) Gordon & Breach.

Rindone, Willian R. Dusty Days & Distant Drums. deluxe ed. LC 84-81865. (Illus.). 316p. 37.50 (*0-9614007-3-0*) Game Flds Pr.

— Dusty Days & Distant Drums. deluxe limited ed. LC 84-81865. (Illus.). 316p. 95.00 (*0-317-14041-8*) Game Flds Pr.

Rindsberg, Steve. Using Microsoft Powerpoint 97. 1998. 29.99 (*0-7897-1601-1*, Que New Media) MCP SW Interactive.

Rine, David C., ed. Object-Oriented Systems & Applications (Readings In) LC 94-10044. 256p. 1994. 19.95 (*0-8186-6222-0*, BP06222) IEEE Comp Soc.

Rinear, Bernie. Moose Creek Charlie & the Quick Freeze: A Tall, Tall Tale by Bernie Rinear. (Illus.). 14p. (Orig.). 1982. pap. 2.00 (*1-878654-49-7*) Lit Coun AK.

***Rinear, Marilyn.** CLAST Language Arts - English - Writing. (FTCE Ser.). (C). 2000. spiral bd. 22.50 (*1-58197-070-6*) XAM.

— ExCet Educational Media Specialist. (ExCet Teacher Certification Ser.). (C). 1999. per. 22.50 (*1-58197-116-8*) XAM.

— PRAXIS Educational Media Specialist. abr. ed. (Praxis Ser.). 125p. (C). 2000. per. 22.50 (*1-58197-022-6*) XAM.

— PRAXIS I Language Arts - English - Writing. (Praxis Ser.). (C). 2000. per. 22.50 (*1-58197-053-6*) XAM.

Rinear, Sheila L. We're Doing Cinderella. 24p. (Orig.). (YA). (gr. 6-11). 1993. pap. 3.00 (*1-57514-127-2*) Encore Perform Pub.

Rinear, Sheila L. & Davis, Megan A. We've Got Something to Say: Algo Tenemos Que Decirles! (Scene Bks.). 42p. (YA). (gr. 7-12). 1994. pap. 8.95 (*1-57514-005-5*, 5014) Encore Perform Pub.

Rinearson, Peter M., et al. The Road Ahead. LC 96-220439. 320p. 1996. pap. 15.95 (*0-14-026040-4*) Viking Penguin.

— The Road Ahead. large type ed. 1996. 25.95 (*1-56895-306-2*) Wheeler Pub.

Rinebold, Albert F. Aware Tribe: Relating the Ancient Wisdom of the Seneca Indian Wolf Clan Present Day Living. (Illus.). 150p. (Orig.). 1989. pap. 15.00 (*0-9626135-0-9*) Aware Tribe.

Rinebold, Albert F. & Rinebold, Analo T. Amber Wolf Enters Fifth World & (History Wolf Clan Teaching Lodge) Amber Wolf's Aware Tribe for Kids. LC 92-97452. (Illus.). (Orig.). 1993. pap. 11.50 (*0-9626135-3-3*) Aware Tribe.

Rinebold, Albert F., jt. auth. see Rinebold, Analo T.

Rinebold, Albert F., ed. see Nitsch, Twylah H.

Rinebold, Analo T. & Rinebold, Albert F. Aware Tribe for Kids: Growing up among Native Americans. 50p. (Orig.). (YA). 1994. pap. 10.00 (*0-9626135-4-1*) Aware Tribe.

Rinebold, Analo T., jt. auth. see Rinebold, Albert F.

Rinefort, Foster C., ed. Readings in Cost Benefit-Cost Control. 88p. 1985. 10.00 (*0-939874-68-7*) ASSE.

Rinehardt, Mary R. The Case of Jennie Brice. 160p. 1997. mass mkt. 5.50 (*1-57566-135-7*, Knsington) Kensgtn Pub Corp.

Rinehart. Client/Server Clipper Programming. 1996. pap. write for info. (*0-201-40734-5*) Addison-Wesley.

Rinehart. Great Mistake. pap. text. write for info. (*0-8058-9014-9*) H Holt & Co.

— Red Lamp. pap. text. write for info. (*0-8058-9001-7*) H Holt & Co.

Rinehart. Windows 3.1 Survival Guide. (Management Information Systems Ser.). 1996. pap. 38.95 (*0-534-20706-5*) S-W Pub.

— Windows 3.1 Quick Course. (Management Information Systems Ser.). 1995. mass mkt., student ed. 15.95 (*0-538-65988-2*) S-W Pub.

Rinehart, Alice D. Mortals in the Immortal Profession: An Oral History of Teaching. LC 82-17200. 410p. 1983. pap. text 22.95 (*0-8290-1049-1*) Irvington.

Rinehart, Alice Duffy, jt. auth. see Leight, Robert L.

Rinehart, Bruce & Hudson, David. Rewired. LC 96-78514. 336p. 1997. 29.99 (*1-57870-003-5*) Macmillan Tech.

Rinehart, Carroll, jt. compiled by see Meske, Eunice B.

Rinehart, Constance, ed. Library Technical Services: A Selected, Annotated Bibliography. LC 76-27130. 238p. 1976. lib. bdg. 49.95 (*0-8371-9286-2*, MAB/, Greenwood Pr) Greenwood.

Rinehart, Dean, et al. Mammoth Lakes Sierra: A Handbook for Roadside & Trail. 6th ed. Smith, Genny, ed. LC 93-1250. (Illus.). 220p. 1993. pap. 14.95 (*0-931378-13-3*) Live Oak.

Rinehart, Frederick R., ed. Chronicles of Colorado. 2nd rev. ed. LC 83-62747. (Illus.). 222p. 1993. pap. 14.95 (*1-879373-65-3*) Roberts Rinehart.

Rinehart, Gray. Quality Education. (Illus.). 329p. 1993. text 21.95 (*0-87389-184-8*, Irwn Prfssnl) McGraw-Hill Prof.

Rinehart, J. S. Geysers & Geothermal Energy. (Illus.). 223p. 1980. 54.00 (*0-387-90489-1*) Spr-Verlag.

Rinehart, James, et al. Just Another Car Factory? Lean Production & Its Discontents. LC 97-4958. (ILR Press Book). (Illus.). 232p. 1996. text 37.50 (*0-8014-3373-8*); pap. text 14.95 (*0-8014-8407-3*) Cornell U Pr.

Rinehart, James F. Revolution & the Millennium: China, Mexico & Iran. LC 97-4228. 208p. 1997. 59.95 (*0-275-95931-7*, Praeger Pubs) Greenwood.

Rinehart, James R. & Lee, Jackson F. American Education & the Dynamics of Choice. LC 90-21312. 184p. 1991. 52.95 (*0-275-93823-9*, C3823, Praeger Pubs) Greenwood.

Rinehart, James R., jt. ed. see Hektoen, Faith H.

Rinehart, Janice S. & Cook, Sharon Touhy. Introduction to Personal Computing. Young, Natalie B., ed. 75p. 1997. student ed. 125.00 incl. audio (*0-917792-97-1*, 130) OneOnOne Comp Trng.

Rinehart, Joyce. Wonderful Raggedy Anns. LC 97-66783. (Schiffer Book for Collectors Ser.). (Illus.). 200p. 1997. pap. 29.95 (*0-7643-0277-9*) Schiffer.

Rinehart, Joyce Gerardi. The Bear Made Me Buy It: Product Advertising Bears. LC 98-89210. (Illus.). 160p. 1999. pap. 29.95 (*0-7643-0734-7*) Schiffer.

***Rinehart, Joyce Gerardi.** Bears with an Attitude; Promotional Advocate Toys. (Illus.). 160p. 2000. pap. 29.95 (*0-7643-1046-1*) Schiffer.

Rinehart, Julia R., jt. auth. see Heise, Jon O.

Rinehart, Kimberly. Greatest Gift of All. (Illus.). 72p. (J). 1997. 7.99 (*0-88486-185-6*, Inspirational Pr) Arrowood Pr.

Rinehart, Martin. Java Database Development. LC 98-114052. (Illus.). 848p. (Orig.). 1997. pap. text 39.99 incl. cd-rom (*0-07-882356-0*, Oracle Press) Osborne-McGraw.

Rinehart, Martin L. BLDNG DBASE VI 2 0 APPL. LC 93-35644. 432p. 1993. pap. text 34.95 (*0-201-62634-9*) Addison-Wesley.

— Client Serv Dbase Prgrm. 336p. 1994. pap. text 39.95 (*0-201-40640-3*) Addison-Wesley.

— Learn Visual dBASE Programming: A Hands-On Guide to Object-Oriented Database Programming, set. 400p. (C). 1995. pap. text 39.95 incl. disk (*0-201-60836-7*) Addison-Wesley.

Rinehart, Mary Roberts. After House. 23.95 (*0-8488-1140-2*) Amereon Ltd.

— After House. 1989. mass mkt. 3.99 (*0-8217-4242-6*, Zebra Kensgtn); mass mkt. 3.50 (*0-8217-2821-0*, Knsington) Kensgtn Pub Corp.

— Album. 384p. 1998. mass mkt. 5.99 (*1-57566-280-9*, Knsington) Kensgtn Pub Corp.

— Alibi for Isabel. reprint ed. lib. bdg. 23.95 (*0-89190-326-7*, Rivercity Pr) Amereon Ltd.

— Alibi for Isabel & Other Stories. large type ed. LC 93-33293. 316p. 1993. lib. bdg. 20.95 (*1-56054-464-3*) Thorndike Pr.

— Amazing Interlude. 24.95 (*0-8488-0311-6*) Amereon Ltd.

— Bat. 1989. mass mkt. 3.50 (*0-8217-2627-7*, Zebra Kensgtn) Kensgtn Pub Corp.

— The Bat. 288p. 1998. mass mkt. 5.99 (*1-57566-238-8*, Knsington) Kensgtn Pub Corp.

— The Bat. large type ed. LC 98-10152. 308p. 1998. 22.95 (*0-7838-8448-6*, G K Hall & Co) Mac Lib Ref.

— Best of Tish. 21.95 (*0-8488-0188-1*) Amereon Ltd.

— The Case of Jennie Brice. 1987. mass mkt. 2.95 (*0-8217-2193-3*, Zebra Kensgtn) Kensgtn Pub Corp.

— The Case of Jenny Brice. 15.95 (*0-8488-1460-6*) Amereon Ltd.

— The Case of Jenny Brice. 1976. lib. bdg. 16.95 (*0-89968-182-4*, Lghtyr Pr) Buccaneer Bks.

— The Circular Staircase. Date not set. lib. bdg. 20.95 (*0-8488-2159-9*) Amereon Ltd.

— The Circular Staircase. 1976. lib. bdg. 19.95 (*0-89968-181-6*, Lghtyr Pr) Buccaneer Bks.

— The Circular Staircase. 1985. mass mkt. 3.50 (*0-8217-1723-5*, Zebra Kensgtn); mass mkt. 3.95 (*0-8217-3528-4*, Zebra Kensgtn) Kensgtn Pub Corp.

— The Circular Staircase. 288p. 1997. mass mkt. 5.50 (*1-57566-180-2*, Knsington) Kensgtn Pub Corp.

— The Circular Staircase. LC 97-1445. (Dover Mystery Classics Ser.). (Illus.). 160p. 1997. reprint ed. pap. text 2.00 (*0-486-29712-5*) Dover.

— Dangerous Days. 27.95 (*0-8488-0312-4*) Amereon Ltd.

— The Door. 1986. pap. 3.95 (*0-8217-3526-8*) NAL

— Door. 384p. 1998. mass mkt. 5.99 (*1-57566-367-8*) Kensgtn Pub Corp.

— The Door. large type ed. LC 93-17774. 491p. 1993. lib. bdg. 21.95 (*1-56054-462-7*) Thorndike Pr.

***Rinehart, Mary Roberts.** Episode of the Wandering Knife. 2000. mass mkt. 5.99 (*1-57566-530-1*, Knsington) Kensgtn Pub Corp.

Rinehart, Mary Roberts. Episode of Wandering Knife. 1990. mass mkt. 3.50 (*0-8217-2874-1*, Zebra Kensgtn) Kensgtn Pub Corp.

— The Frightened Wife. 256p. 1988. mass mkt. 3.50 (*0-8217-2489-4*, Zebra Kensgtn) Kensgtn Pub Corp.

***Rinehart, Mary Roberts.** Frightened Wife. 2000. mass mkt. 5.99 (*1-57566-603-0*, Knsington) Kensgtn Pub Corp.

Rinehart, Mary Roberts. The Great Mistake. 368p. 1997. mass mkt. 5.50 (*1-57566-198-5*, Knsington) Kensgtn Pub Corp.

***Rinehart, Mary Roberts.** The Great Mistake. (Mystery Ser.). 2000. 27.95 (*0-7862-2480-0*) Thorndike Pr.

Rinehart, Mary Roberts. Haunted Ladu. 1995. 9.95 (*0-8050-0808-X*) H Holt & Co.

— Haunted Lady. Date not set. lib. bdg. 22.95 (*0-8488-2160-2*) Amereon Ltd.

***Rinehart, Mary Roberts.** Haunted Lady. 272p. 2000. mass mkt. 5.99 (*1-57566-567-0*) Kensgtn Pub Corp.

Rinehart, Mary Roberts. K. reprint ed. lib. bdg. 27.95 (*0-8488-0313-2*, Rivercity Pr) Amereon Ltd.

— K. 1992. reprint ed. lib. bdg. 19.95 (*0-89968-275-8*, Lghtyr Pr) Buccaneer Bks.

— A Light in the Window. 1986. mass mkt. 3.99 (*0-8217-4021-0*, Zebra Kensgtn) Kensgtn Pub Corp.

— Light in the Window, 1. 352p. 1999. text 11.00 (*1-57566-444-5*) Kensgtn Pub Corp.

— Lost Ecstasy. 400p. 1998. mass mkt. 5.99 (*1-57566-344-9*) Kensgtn Pub Corp.

— The Man in Lower Ten. 19.95 (*0-8488-0839-8*) Amereon Ltd.

— The Man in Lower Ten. 1976. lib. bdg. 19.95 (*0-89968-180-8*, Lghtyr Pr) Buccaneer Bks.

— Mary Roberts Rinehardt. 1995. pap. 13.00 (*1-57566-114-4*) Kensgtn Pub Corp.

— Miss Pinkerton. 272p. 1998. mass mkt. 5.99 (*1-57566-255-8*, Knsington) Kensgtn Pub Corp.

— Miss Pinkerton. reprint ed. lib. bdg. 24.95 (*0-89190-327-5*, Rivercity Pr) Amereon Ltd.

— More Tish. reprint ed. lib. bdg. 23.95 (*0-89190-328-3*, Rivercity Pr) Amereon Ltd.

— My Story. Baxter, Annette K., ed. LC 79-8806. (Signal Lives Ser.). (Illus.). 1980. reprint ed. lib. bdg. 69.95 (*0-405-12852-5*) Ayer.

— My Story. 1993. reprint ed. lib. bdg. 89.00 (*0-7812-5824-3*) Rprt Serv.

— My Story. (American Autobiography Ser.). 570p. 1995. reprint ed. lib. bdg. 109.00 (*0-7812-8625-5*) Rprt Serv.

— A Poor Wise Man. 27.95 (*0-8488-0314-0*) Amereon Ltd.

— The Red Lamp. 24.95 (*0-8488-1139-9*) Amereon Ltd.

— The Red Lamp. 336p. 1987. mass mkt. 3.50 (*0-8217-2017-1*, Zebra Kensgtn) Kensgtn Pub Corp.

— The Red Lamp. 352p. 1997. mass mkt. 5.99 (*1-57566-213-2*, Knsington) Kensgtn Pub Corp.

— The State vs. Elinor Norton. 21.95 (*0-8488-0618-2*) Amereon Ltd.

— The State vs. Elinor Norton. 288p. 1988. mass mkt. 3.50 (*0-8217-2412-6*, Zebra Kensgtn) Kensgtn Pub Corp.

— The Swimming Pool. 1985. mass mkt. 3.50 (*0-8217-1686-7*, Zebra Kensgtn) Kensgtn Pub Corp.

— The Swimming Pool. 1991. mass mkt. 3.95 (*0-8217-3679-5*, Zebra Kensgtn) Kensgtn Pub Corp.

— The Swimming Pool. 336p. 1997. mass mkt. 5.50 (*0-8217-5634-6*); mass mkt. 5.50 (*1-57566-157-8*, Knsington) Kensgtn Pub Corp.

— Through Glacier Park in 1915. LC 83-60777. 102p. 1983. pap. 6.95 (*0-911797-06-8*) Roberts Rinehart.

— Tish. reprint ed. lib. bdg. 26.95 (*0-89190-329-1*, Rivercity Pr) Amereon Ltd.

— Tish Returns. 24.95 (*0-8488-0713-8*) Amereon Ltd.

— The Wall. 352p. 1989. mass mkt. 3.99 (*0-8217-4017-2*, Zebra Kensgtn) Kensgtn Pub Corp.

— The Wall. 352p. 1998. mass mkt. 5.99 (*1-57566-310-4*) Kensgtn Pub Corp.

— When a Man Marries. 24.95 (*0-8488-0315-9*) Amereon Ltd.

— The Window at the White Cat. 24.95 (*0-8488-0316-7*) Amereon Ltd.

— The Window at the White Cat. 1990. mass mkt. 3.99 (*0-8217-4246-9*, Zebra Kensgtn) Kensgtn Pub Corp.

— The Window at the White Cat. 1992. reprint ed. lib. bdg. 19.95 (*0-89968-274-X*, Lghtyr Pr) Buccaneer Bks.

— Window at the White House. 1997. mass mkt. 5.99 (*0-8217-5794-6*) Kensgtn Pub Corp.

— The Yellow Room. Date not set. lib. bdg. 21.95 (*0-8488-2158-0*) Amereon Ltd.

— The Yellow Room. 352p. 1996. mass mkt. 5.50 (*1-57566-119-5*, Knsington) Kensgtn Pub Corp.

— The Yellow Room. LC 99-18838. 1999. 26.95 (*0-7862-1909-2*) Thorndike Pr.

Rinehart, Paula. Bumps in the Road: Sticker Studies. (Sticker Studies: No. 4). (Illus.). 64p. (Orig.). (J). (gr. 3-7). 1996. pap. 4.99 (*1-57673-009-3*, Gold n Honey) Zondervan.

— One of a Kind: Sticker Studies. (Sticker Studies: No. 2). (Illus.). 64p. (Orig.). (J). (gr. 3-7). 1996. pap. 4.99 (*1-57673-007-7*, Gold n Honey) Zondervan.

— Stuck Like Glue: Sticker Studies. (Sticker Studies). (Illus.). (Orig.). (J). (gr. 3-7). 1996. pap. 5.99 (*1-57673-006-9*, Gold n Honey) Zondervan.

Rinehart, Paula, jt. auth. see Rinehart, Stacy P.

Rinehart, Robert, ed. Under the North Star: Reflections of Finland. 136p. (C). 2000. pap. 38.50 (*0-8133-1303-1*) Westview.

Rinehart, Robert E. Players All: Performances in Contemporary Sport. LC 98-19008. (Drama & Performance Studies). 240p. 1998. 35.00 (*0-253-33426-8*); pap. 15.95 (*0-253-21223-5*) Ind U Pr.

Rinehart, Robert E., jt. auth. see Pope, S.

Rinehart, Ronald E. Radar for Meteorologists. (Illus.). 218p. (C). 1990. pap. text 15.95 (*0-9608700-5-9*) U NDak Pres.

— Radar for Meteorologists. 2nd ed. 334p. (C). 1991. pap. text 25.00 (*0-9608700-7-5*) U NDak Pres.

Rinehart, Ronald E. Radar for Meteorologists. 3rd ed. 428p. 1997. pap. 39.00 (*0-9658002-0-2*) Rinehart Pub.

Rinehart, Stacy. Upside Down: The Paradox of Servant Leadership. LC 98-10669. 1998. pap. 10.00 (*1-57683-079-9*) NavPress.

Rinehart, Stacy P. & Rinehart, Paula. Choices: Finding God's Way in Dating, Sex, Singleness & Marriage. (NavClassics Ser.). 1996. pap. 9.00 (*0-89109-943-3*) NavPress.

Rinehart, Stephen H., ed. see Freund, Norman C.

***Rinehart, Steven.** Kick in the Head: Stories. LC 99-55774. 228p. 2000. 22.00 (*0-385-49853-5*) Doubleday.

Rinehart, Sue T. Gender Consciousness & Politics. (Perspectives on Gender Ser.). (Illus.). 216p. (C). 1992. pap. 25.99 (*0-415-90685-7*, A9553) Routledge.

Rinehart, Theodore R., jt. ed. see Wittkofski, J. Mark.

Rinehart, William. How to Clear Your Adult & Juvenile Criminal Records. LC 96-78458. (Illus.). 112p. (Orig.). 1996. pap. 12.95 (*1-55950-158-8*, 76059) Loompanics.

Rinehold, Connie. Veil of Tears. (American Romance Ser.: No. 380). 1991. per. 2.95 (*0-373-16380-0*) Harlequin Bks.

Rinella, Bernard B. Illinois Domestic Relations Forms. 620p. 1994. spiral bd. 159.00 (*0-87189-797-0*, MICHIE) LEXIS Pub.

Rinella, Bernard B. & Rinella, Richard A. Illinois Domestic Relations Forms. 1993. ring bd., suppl. ed. 85.00 (*0-562-57353-4*, MICHIE) LEXIS Pub.

R

R

— Illinois Domestic Relations Forms, Issue 9. 150p. 1999. ring bd. write for info. (0-327-01497-0, 8110715) LEXIS Pub.

Rinella, Jack. The Master's Manual: A Handbook of Erotic Dominance. Bean, Joseph, ed. LC 93-74629. 200p. (Orig.). 1994. pap. 14.95 (1-881943-03-8) Daedalus Pub.

Rinella, Maureen. Be with Me: A Book of Prayers to Comfort Dying Persons & Their Loved Ones. LC 97-73788. 80p. 1997. pap. 4.95 (0-87029-304-4, 20143) Abbey.

Rinella, Richard A. Illinois Criminal Procedure, 2 vols., Set. 2nd ed. Ruebner, Ralph, ed. 800p. 1994. spiral bd., suppl. ed. 170.00 (0-250-40731-0, 81091-10, MICHIE) LEXIS Pub.

Rinella, Richard A., jt. auth. see Rinella, Bernard B.

Riner, contrib. by. Successful Teaching in the Elementary School. LC 99-26331. (Illus.). 432p. (C). 1999. pap. text 44.00 (0-02-401613-6, Macmillan Coll) P-H.

Rinere, Elissa, ed. New Law & Life: Sixty Practical Questions & Answers on the New Code of Canon Law. 103p. (Orig.). 1985. pap. 3.00 (0-943616-28-X) Canon Law Soc.

Rines, Edward. Old Historic Churches in America. 373p. 1993. reprint ed. lib. bdg. 89.00 (0-7812-5225-3) Rprt Serv.

Rines, J. E. & Hargraves, P. E. The Chaetoceros Ehrenberg (Bacillariophyceae) Flora of Narragansett Bay, Rhode Island, U. S. A. (Bibliotheca Phycologica Ser.: Vol. 79). (Illus.). 196p. 1988. 65.00 (3-443-60006-9, Pub. by Gebruder Borntraeger) Balogh.

Rines, Russell L., jt. auth. see Scouten, William H.

Riney, Bobye J., jt. auth. see Rubin, Rose M.

Riney, Deborah. The Good Health Journal. 112p. 1993. pap. 10.95 (0-9635454-0-X) DER Prods.

Riney, Hal, jt. auth. see Cederwall, Sandraline.

Riney-Kehrberg, Pamela. Rooted in Dust: Surviving Drought & Depression in Southwestern Kansas. (Illus.). 264p. 1997. reprint ed. pap. 14.95 (0-7006-0839-7) U Pr of KS.

Riney-Kehrberg, Pamela, ed. Waiting on the Bounty: The Dust Bowl Diary of Mary Knackstedt Dyck. LC 99-29217. (Illus.). 382p. 1999. text 37.95 (0-87745-694-1) U of Iowa Pr.

***Riney, Scott.** The Rapid City Indian School, 1898-1933. LC 99-25821. 288p. 1999. 29.95 (0-8061-3162-4) U of Okla Pr.

Ring, et al. The Early Virtuoso. 64p. (J). (gr. 3-12). 1974. pap. text 9.95 (0-87487-631-1) Summy-Birchard.

Ring, Carlyn & Ham, William C. Bitters Bottles. deluxe ed. LC 98-93507. (Illus.). x, 617p. 1998. 129.95 (0-9666255-0-1) William C Ham.

Ring, Alfred A. & Dasso, Jerome. Real Estate Principles & Practices. 9th ed. (Illus.). 752p. 1981. student ed. 29.95 (0-685-03905-6) P-H.

— Real Estate Principles & Practices. 10th ed. 768p. (C). 1985. 45.95 (0-13-765983-0) P-H.

Ring, Alfred A., jt. auth. see Boykin, James H.

Ring, Anne M. Read Easy: Large Print Libraries for Older Adults. 84p. (Orig.). 1991. ring bd. 19.95 (1-878866-13-3) CAREsource Prog.

Ring, B. Albert. The Neglected Cause of Stroke: Occlusion of the Smaller Intracranial Arteries & Their Diagnosis by Cerebral Angiography. LC 68-55659. (Illus.). 220p. 1969. 12.00 (0-87527-066-2) Green.

Ring, Betty J., jt. ed. see Plasa, Carl.

Ring, C. L. The Biology of Enterprise. LC 78-70432. 1979. 12.95 (0-87212-121-6) Libra.

Ring, Constance. Index to Fairfax County, Virginia & Fiduciary Records, 1742-1855. xi, 204p. 1996. pap. 18.00 (1-888265-02-7) Willow Bend.

Ring, Contance K. & Scott, Craig R. Index to the Fairfax County, Virginia Register of Marriages, 1853-1933. 208p. 1997. pap. 20.00 (1-888265-27-2) Willow Bend.

Ring, David. Just As I Am. 1996. reprint ed. pap. 10.99 (0-8024-1733-7, 193) Moody.

Ring, Elizabeth. Henry David Thoreau: In Step with Nature. LC 92-11559. (Gateway Greens Ser.). (Illus.). 48p. (J). (gr. 2-4). 1993. pap. 5.95 (1-56294-795-8); lib. bdg. 19.90 (1-56294-258-1) Millbrook Pr.

— Henry David Thoreau: In Step with Nature. 1994. 11.15 (0-606-12331-8, Pub. by Turtleback) Demco.

— Loon at Northwood Lake. (Smithsonian's Backyard Ser.). (Illus.). 32p. (J). (ps-2). 1997. 15.95 (1-56899-393-5); 19.95 incl. audio (1-56899-397-8, BC5013) Soundprints.

— Loon at Northwood Lake, Incl. large bk. & large toy. (Smithsonian's Backyard Ser.). (Illus.). 32p. (J). (ps-2). 1997. 32.95 (1-56899-395-1); 36.95 incl. audio (1-56899-399-4) Soundprints.

— Loon at Northwood Lake, Incl. Sm. & Lg. Plush Toy. LC 96-39101. (Smithsonian's Backyard Ser.). (Illus.). 32p. (J). (ps-2). 1997. 43.95 incl. audio (1-56899-640-3) Soundprints.

— Loon at Northwood Lake, Micro bk. (Smithsonian's Backyard Ser.). (Illus.). 32p. (J). (ps-2). 1997. 4.95 (1-56899-394-3) Soundprints.

— Loon at Northwood Lake: Micro Book & Toy. (Illus.). 32p. (J). (ps-2). 1997. 12.95 (1-56899-459-1) Soundprints.

— Lucky Mouse. LC 94-46948. (Illus.). 32p. (J). (gr. k-3). 1995. lib. bdg. 21.40 (1-56294-344-8) Millbrook Pr.

— Maine in the Making of the Nation, 1783-1870. (Illus.). 384p. 1991. pap. text. write for info. (0-933858-13-2) Kennebec River.

— Monarch Butterfly of Aster Way. (Smithsonian's Backyard Ser.: Vol. 17). (Illus.). 32p. (J). (ps-2). 1999. 15.95 (1-56899-568-7); 19.99 incl. audio (1-56899-570-9, BC5017); 43.95 (1-56899-571-7) Soundprints.

— Monarch Butterfly of Aster Way, Incl. toy. (Smithsonian's Backyard Ser.: Vol. 17). (Illus.). 32p. (J). (ps-2). 1999. 32.95 (1-56899-572-5); 36.95 incl. audio (1-56899-574-1) Soundprints.

— Monarch Butterfly of Aster Way: Micro Book. LC 98-42565. (Smithsonian's Backyard Ser.: No. 17). (Illus.). 32p. (J). (ps-2). 1999. 4.95 (1-56899-569-5) Soundprints.

— Monarch Butterfly of Aster Way: Micro Book, Incl. toy. (Smithsonian's Backyard Ser.: Vol. 17). (Illus.). 32p. (J). (ps-2). 1999. 12.95 (1-56899-573-3) Soundprints.

— Monarch Butterfly of Aster Way: Micro Edition, Incl. toy. (Smithsonian's Backyard Ser.: Vol. 17). (Illus.). 32p. (J). (ps-2). 1999. write for info. incl. audio (1-56899-575-X) Soundprints.

— Night Flier. LC 93-40115. (Illus.). 32p. (J). (gr. k-3). 1994. lib. bdg. 21.90 (1-56294-467-3) Millbrook Pr.

— Rachel Carson: Caring for the Earth. LC 91-37644. (Gateway Green Biography Ser.). (Illus.). 48p. (J). (gr. 2-4). 1992. pap. 5.95 (1-56294-798-2); lib. bdg. 19.90 (1-56294-056-2) Millbrook Pr.

— Ranch & Farm Dogs: Herders & Guards. LC 93-41529. (Good Dogs! Ser.). (Illus.). 32p. (J). (gr. 2-4). 1994. lib. bdg. 19.90 (1-56294-295-6, Copper Beech Bks) Millbrook Pr.

— A Reference List of Manuscripts Relating to the History of Maine (1938) (Illus.). 970p. 1992. reprint ed. lib. bdg. 89.00 (0-8328-2519-0) Higginson Bk Co.

— Search & Rescue Dogs: Expert Trackers & Trailers. LC 93-42278. (Good Dogs! Ser.). (Illus.). 32p. (J). (gr. 2-4). 1994. 19.90 (1-56294-294-8, Copper Beech Bks) Millbrook Pr.

— Some Stuff. LC 94-26196. (Illus.). 32p. (J). (gr. k-3). 1995. lib. bdg. 20.90 (1-56294-466-5) Millbrook Pr.

— Tiger Lilies & Other Beastly Plants. (Illus.). 32p. (J). 1996. pap. 6.95 (0-8027-7454-7) Walker & Co.

— What Rot! Natures's Mighty Recycler. LC 95-353. (Illus.). 32p. (J). (gr. k-3). 1996. lib. bdg. 23.40 (1-56294-671-4) Millbrook Pr.

Ring, Frances. A Western Harvest: Gatherings of an Editor. LC 90-13882. (Illus.). 192p. (Orig.). 1991. pap. 9.95 (0-936784-87-3) J Daniel.

Ring, Frances K. Against the Current. 160p. (Orig.). 1987. pap. 6.95 (0-88739-015-3) Creat Arts Bk.

— Against the Current: As I Remember F. Scott Fitzgerald. LC 84-47682. (Illus.). 160p. (C). 1985. 14.95 (0-88739-001-3) Creat Arts Bk.

Ring, Francis J. & Phillips, Barbara, eds. Recent Advances in Medical Thermology. LC 84-3366. 723p. 1984. 135.00 (0-306-41672-7, Plenum Trade) Perseus Pubng.

Ring, Gerhard. Werberecht der Rechtsanwalte. (GER.). 269p. 1990. pap. 44.00 (3-7890-1907-0, Pub. by Nomos Verlags) Intl Bk Import.

Ring, Grete. A Century of French Painting: Fourteen Hundred to Fifteen Hundred. LC 79-83857. (Illus.). 1979. reprint ed. lib. bdg. 50.00 (0-87817-249-1) Hacker.

Ring, Hans, jt. auth. see Ries, Karl.

Ring, Harry. Socialism & Individual Freedom. 22p. 1982. reprint ed. pap. 2.50 (0-87348-393-6) Pathfinder NY.

Ring, Henrik. Vibrations. 161p. (C). 1985. pap. 12.95 (0-942494-90-3) Coleman Pub.

Ring, I., jt. auth. see Van Konkelenberg, R.

***Ring, Irene, et al, eds.** Regional Sustainability: Applied Ecological Economics Bridging the Gap Between Natural & Social Sciences. LC 99-37886. (Contributions to Economics Ser.). (Illus.). viii, 229p. 1999. pap. 63.00 (3-7908-1233-1) Spr-Verlag.

Ring, J., jt. ed. see Manno, V.

***Ring, J. Michael.** The Ride Guide: America's Best Motorcycle Tours, Vol. 1. Ringwald, Barbara & Kunik, John, eds. (Illus.). 224p. 2000. spiral bd. 29.95 (1-890676-59-4, Pub. by Beavers Pond) Bookman Bks.

Ring, Jennifer. Modern Political Theory & Contemporary Feminism: A Dialectical Analysis. LC 90-46118. (SUNY Series in Feminist Political Theory). 229p. (C). 1991. text 21.50 (0-7914-0753-5) State U NY Pr.

— The Political Consequences of Thinking: Gender & Judaism in the Work of Hannah Arendt. LC 96-47278. (SUNY Series in Political Theory). 358p. (C). 1997. text 54.50 (0-7914-3483-4) State U NY Pr.

— The Political Consequences of Thinking: Gender & Judaism in the Work of Hannah Arendt. LC 96-47278. (SUNY Series in Political Theory). (C). 1998. pap. text 22.95 (0-7914-3484-2) State U NY Pr.

Ring, Jim. Erskine Childers: A Biography. LC 96-208312. (Illus.). 320p. 1997. 40.00 (0-7195-5681-3, Pub. by John Murray) Trafalgar.

Ring, Johannes, et al. New Trends in Allergy IV, Together with Environmental Allergy & Allergotoxicology III: Joint International Symposium, Hamburg, April 29-May 1, 1995. LC 96-42937. (Illus.). 280p. 1996. 199.00 (3-540-61120-7) Spr-Verlag.

Ring, Johannes, jt. ed. see Burg, G.

Ring, Johannes, jt. ed. see Kraft, Dietrich.

Ring, Johannes, jt. ed. see Przybilla, B.

***Ring, Ken & Romhany, Paul.** Pawmistry: How to Read Your Cat's Paws. LC 99-23384. (Illus.). 88p. 1999. pap. text 9.95 (1-58008-111-8) Ten Speed Pr.

***Ring, Kenneth.** Mindsight: Near-Death & Out-Of-Body Experiences in the Blind. 1999. pap. 12.95 (0-9669630-0-8) W James Ctr.

Ring, Kenneth & Kubler-Ross, Elizabeth. Heading Toward Omega: In Search of the Meaning of the Near-Death Experience. LC 85-62560. 348p. 1985. pap. 11.00 (0-688-06268-7, Quil) HarperTrade.

***Ring, Kenneth & Valarino, Evelyn Elsaesser.** Lessons from the Light: What We Can Learn from the Near-Death Experience. LC 99-59665. 364p. 2000. pap. 16.95 (0-9661327-8-5, Pub. by Moment Pt Pr) ACCESS Pubs Network.

***Ring, Laura.** The First Christmas: An ABC Book. Caldwell, Lise, ed. LC 99-70910. (Illus.). 24p. (ps-1). 1999. pap. 1.99 (0-7847-1087-2, 04283, Bean Sprouts) Standard Pub.

Ring, Laura. Jesus Lives! The Easter Story. (Happy Day Bks.). (Illus.). 24p. (J). (ps-2). 1999. pap. 1.99 (0-7847-0892-4, 04265) Standard Pub.

***Ring, Laura.** What Do Angels Do? Caldwell, Lise, ed. LC 99-70908. (Illus.). 24p. (ps-1). 1999. pap. 1.99 (0-7847-1045-7, 04275, Bean Sprouts) Standard Pub.

***Ring, Laura, ed.** Favorite Christmas Carols. (Illus.). 24p. (J). (ps-1). 1999. pap. 1.99 (0-7847-1085-6, 04281, Bean Sprouts) Standard Pub.

Ring, Laura, ed. Prayers for a Child's Day. (Happy Day Bks.). (Illus.). 24p. (J). (ps-2). 1999. pap. 1.99 (0-7847-0891-6, 04264) Standard Pub.

***Ring, Laura, ed.** Sing Praises. (Illus.). 24p. (J). (ps-1). 1999. pap. 1.99 (0-7847-1047-3, 04277, Bean Sprouts) Standard Pub.

Ring, Laura, ed. see Atchison, Beth.

Ring, Laura, ed. see Fischer, Jean.

Ring, Laura, ed. see Head, Heno, Jr.

Ring, Laura, ed. see Keener, Joan N.

Ring, Laura, ed. see Lingo, Susan L.

Ring, Laura, ed. see McConnaughhay, JoDee.

Ring, Laura, ed. see Mishica, Clare.

Ring, Laura, ed. see Mykowski, Michelle.

Ring, Laura, ed. see Senseman, Patricia A.

Ring, Laura, ed. see Wilkinson, Lisa.

Ring, Lawrence J. Decisions in Marketing. 2nd ed. (C). 1994. text 30.95 (0-256-17788-0, Irwn McGrw-H) McGrw-H Hghr Educ.

Ring, Layton, jt. auth. see Dolmetsch, Rudolph.

Ring, Malvin E. Dentistry: An Illustrated History. (Illus.). 320p. 1985. 75.00 (0-8109-1100-0) Abrams.

— Dentistry: An Illustrated History. (Illus.). 320p. 1992. pap. 39.98 (0-8109-8116-5, Pub. by Abrams) Time Warner.

— Dentistry: An Illustrated History. (Illus.). 331p. (C). (gr. 13). 1985. text 49.95 (0-8016-4146-2, 04146) Mosby Inc.

Ring, Merrill. Beginning with the Pre-Socratics. 2nd ed. LC 99-21502. 168p. 1999. pap. text 22.95 (0-7674-1338-5) Mayfield Pub.

Ring, Nancy. Walking on Walnuts: My Grandmothers' Recipes for Rugelach, Romance & Surviving the Real World. 352p. 1997. pap. 12.95 (0-553-37516-4) Bantam.

Ring, Nancy C. Doctrine Within the Dialectic of Subjectivity & Objectivity: A Critical Study of the Positions of Paul Tillich & Bernard Lonergan. LC 91-625. 304p. 1991. lib. bdg. 99.95 (0-7734-9948-2) E Mellen.

Ring, Peter. Strategic Alliances. 2000. pap. text 29.95 (0-538-88661-7) S-W Pub.

Ring, Peter S. Networked Organization: A Resource Based Perspective. (Studia Oeconomiae Negotiorum: Vol. 39). 52p. (Orig.). 1996. pap. 32.50 (91-554-3685-4) Coronet Bks.

Ring, Rolf, jt. auth. see Alfredsson, Gudmundur.

Ring, Susan. Design It! Build It! (Early Science Big Bks.). (Illus.). 16p. (J). (ps-2). Date not set. pap. 16.95 (1-58273-121-7) Newbridge Educ.

— The Fox & the Crow. (Between the Lions Ser.). (Illus.). (J). 2000. pap. 3.99 (0-307-25215-9, Goldn Books) Gldn Bks Pub Co.

Ring, Susan. Polar Babies. LC 98-49207. (Early Step into Reading Ser.). (Illus.). (J). 2000. lib. bdg. 11.99 (0-679-99387-8) Random.

Ring, Susan. What Is Technology? (Early Science Big Bks.). (Illus.). 16p. (J). (ps-2). Date not set. pap. 16.95 (1-58273-119-5) Newbridge Educ.

Ring, Terry. Fundamentals of Ceramic Powder Processing & Synthesis. LC 95-15418. (Illus.). 961p. 1996. text 150.00 (0-12-588930-5) Acad Pr.

Ring Theory Conference Staff. Ring Theory: Proceedings of the Oklahoma Conference, 1st, University of Oklahoma. fac. ed. McDonald, Bernard R. et al, eds. LC 73-90768. (Lecture Notes in Pure & Applied Mathematics Ser.: No. 7). 315p. 1974. pap. 97.70 (0-7837-7717-5, 204747900007) Bks Demand.

— Ring Theory & Algebra III: Proceedings of the Third Oklahoma Conference, University of Oklahoma, 1979. McDonald, Bernard R., ed. LC 80-17204. (Lecture Notes in Pure & Applied Mathematics Ser.: Vol. 55). 446p. 1980. reprint ed. pap. 138.30 (0-608-04566-7, 206530500001) Bks Demand.

— Ring Theory II: Proceedings of the Ring Theory Conference, 2nd, University of Oklahoma, 1975. McDonald, Bernard R. & Morris, Robert A., eds. LC 76-55134. (Lecture Notes in Pure & Applied Mathematics Ser.: Vol. 26). 315p. reprint ed. pap. 97.70 (0-608-30327-5, 201769300007) Bks Demand.

Ring, Thomasina. Time-Spun Treasure. 368p. 1997. mass mkt. 5.50 (0-505-52214-4, Love Spell) Dorchester Pub Co.

Ring, Tony & Clark, John. Tax Warranties & Indemnities. 2nd ed. 180p. 1990. boxed set 120.00 (0-614-05553-9, UK, MICHIE) LEXIS Pub.

— Tax Warranties & Indemnities (with Precedents) 2nd ed. 1990. 120.00 (0-406-51166-7, U.K., MICHIE) LEXIS Pub.

Ring, Trudy. Careers in Finance. (Illus.). 160p. 1994. pap. 13.95 (0-8442-4187-3, VGM Career) NTC Contemp Pub Co.

— Careers in Finance. (Illus.). 192p. 1994. 17.95 (0-8442-4186-5, VGM Career) NTC Contemp Pub Co.

Ring, Trudy. Careers in Finance. 2nd ed. LC 98-46768. (VGM Professional Careers Ser.). 176p. 1999. pap. 13.95 (0-8442-2070-1, 20701, VGM Career) NTC Contemp Pub Co.

***Ring, Trudy.** Careers in Finance. 2nd ed. LC 98-46768. (VGM Professional Careers Ser.). 176p. 1999. 17.95 (0-8442-2069-8, 20698, VGM Career) NTC Contemp Pub Co.

Ring, Trudy, et al, eds. International Dictionary of Historic Places, 5 vols. Incl. Americas. (Illus.). 900p. 1994. lib. bdg. 125.00 (1-884964-00-1); Asia & Oceania. LC 94-32327. 900p. 1996. lib. bdg. 125.00 (1-884964-04-4); Middle East & Africa. (Illus.). 900p. (YA). 1996. lib. bdg. 125.00 (1-884964-03-6); Northern Europe. LC 94-34327. (Illus.). 900p. (C). 1995. lib. bdg. 125.00 (1-884964-01-X); Southern Europe. LC 94-32327. (Illus.). 900p. (YA). (gr. 9 up). 1995. lib. bdg. 125.00 (1-884964-02-8); (Illus.). 1996. Set lib. bdg. 500.00 (1-884964-05-2) Fitzroy Dearborn.

***Ring, U., et al, eds.** Exhumation Processes: Normal Faulting, Ductile Flow & Erosion. 384p. 1999. 148.00 (1-86239-032-0, Pub. by Geol Soc Pub Hse) AAPG.

Ringblum, Jeri L. Miniature Perfume Bottles: Minis, Mates, & More. LC 96-6012. (Illus.). 264p. 1996. pap. 24.95 (0-7643-0038-5) Schiffer.

Ringbom, Hakan. The Role of the First Language in Foreign Language Learning. 1987. 69.00 (0-905028-81-3); pap. 24.95 (0-905028-80-5) Taylor & Francis.

Ringbom, Henrik, ed. Competing Norms in the Law of Marine Environmental Protection, Vol. IELP. LC 97-225169. (International Environmental Law & Policy Ser.: No. 46). 304p. 1997. 115.00 (90-411-0699-5) Kluwer Academic.

Ringbom, Nils-Eric. Jean Sibelius: A Master & His Work. De Courcy, G. I., tr. from SWE. LC 77-14425. (Illus.). 196p. 1978. reprint ed. lib. bdg. 49.75 (0-8371-9840-2, RIJS, Greenwood Pr) Greenwood.

Ringe, B. Leberchirurgie. 92p. 42.75 (3-8055-6670-0) S Karger.

Ringe, Buzz, jt. auth. see Hart, Gene.

Ringe, Don. On the Chronology of Sound Changes in Tocharian Vol. 1: From Proto-Indo-European to Proto-Tocharian. LC 96-171340. (Monographs: No. 80). xxv, 203p. 1996. 45.00 (0-940490-80-3) Am Orient Soc.

Ringe, Donald A. Charles Brockden Brown. rev. ed. (Twayne's United States Authors Ser.). 226p. 1991. 22.95 (0-8057-7606-0, TUSAS 98, Twyne) Mac Lib Ref.

— James Fenimore Cooper. (United States Authors Ser.: No. 11). 176p. 1988. 32.00 (0-8057-7527-7) Macmillan.

Ringe, Donald A., Jr. On Calculating the Factor of Chance in Language Comparison. LC 92-70402. (Transactions Ser.: Vol. 82, Pt. 1). 110p. (C). 1992. pap. 16.00 (0-87169-821-8, T821-RID) Am Philos.

Ringe, Donald A., ed. see Cooper, James Fenimore.

Ringe, Donald A., ed. & intro. see Cooper, James Fenimore.

Ringe, Mark. Electra & the Empty Urn: Metatheater & Role Playing in Sophocles. LC 97-24548. 272p. 1998. lib. bdg. 45.00 (0-8078-2391-0) U of NC Pr.

Ringe, Sharon H. Luke. Bartlett, David L. & Miller, Patrick D., eds. (Westminster Bible Companion Ser.). 291p. 1995. pap. 20.00 (0-664-25259-1) Westminster John Knox.

— Wisdom's Friends: Community & Christology in the Fourth Gospel. 176p. 1999. pap. 15.95 (0-664-25714-3) Westminster John Knox.

Ringe, Sharon H., jt. auth. see Tiffany, Frederick C.

Ringe, Sharon H., jt. ed. see Newsom, Carol A.

Ringe, Sharon H., tr. see Tamez, Elsa.

Ringeisen, Richard D., jt. ed. see Roberts, Fred S.

Ringeissen, Christophe, ed. see FroCoS 2000 Staff.

Ringel, Claus M. Tame Algebras & Integral Quadratic Forms. (Lecture Notes in Mathematics Ser.: Vol. 1099). xiii, 376p. 1985. 49.95 (0-387-13905-2) Spr-Verlag.

Ringel, Claus M. & Michler, G. O. Representation Theory of Finite Groups & Finite-Dimensional Algebras. (Progress in Mathematics Ser.: Vol. 95). 532p. 1991. 99.00 (0-8176-2604-2) Birkhauser.

Ringel, Claus M., jt. auth. see Dlab, Vlastimil.

Ringel, Eleanor. Star Gazing: Movies & Astrology. LC 98-66366. (Illus.). 160p. 1998. pap. 12.95 (1-56352-493-7) Longstreet.

Ringel, Faye. New England's Gothic Literature: History & Folklore of the Supernatural from the Seventeenth Through the Twentieth Centuries. LC 94-34973. 272p. 1995. text 89.95 (0-7734-9047-7) E Mellen.

Ringel, Fred. Suzanne. LC 98-90305. 1998. 19.95 (0-533-12753-X) Vantage.

Ringel, G. Map Color Theorem. LC 73-17986. (Grundlehren der Mathematischen Wissenschaften Ser.: Vol. 209). (Illus.). 220p. 1974. 86.95 (0-387-06548-2) Spr-Verlag.

Ringel, Harvey. History of the National Association of Teachers of Singing. (Illus.). 354p. (Orig.). 1990. pap. 33.00 (0-932761-01-1) NATS.

Ringel, J. Marine Motifs on Ancient Coins. (Illus.). 96p. 1984. lib. bdg. 25.00 (965-222-008-6) Maureen Mack.

Ringel, S. A., et al, eds. III-V & IV-IV Materials & Processing Challenges for Highly Integrated Microelectronics & Optoelectronics Vol. 535: Materials Research Society Symposium Proceedings. LC 99-38997. 308p. 1999. text 91.00 (1-55899-441-6) Materials Res.

Ringel, Steven P. Neuromuscular Disorders: A Guide for Patient & Family. LC 85-43509. 174p. 1987. reprint ed. pap. 54.00 (0-608-04667-1, 206538800004) Bks Demand.

Ringel, William E. & Pellis, Mark. Searches & Seizures, Arrests & Confessions, 3 vols., Set. 2nd ed. LC 79-22482. (Criminal Law Ser.). 1980. ring bd. 375.00 (0-87632-079-5) West Group.

Ringelberg, Joop, ed. Diel Vertical Migration of Zooplankton: Proceedings of an International Symposium Held at Lelystad, The Netherlands. (Advances in Limnology Ser.: Vol. 39). (GER., Illus.). x, 222p. 1993. pap. text 58.00 (3-510-47040-0, Pub. by E Schweizerbartsche) Balogh.

Ringelblum, Emmanuel. Polish-Jewish Relations During the Second World War. Allon, Dafna et al, trs. LC 76-1394. 330p. 1976. 35.00 (0-86527-155-0) Fertig.

An Asterisk (*) at the beginning of an entry indicates that the title is appearing for the first time.

— Polish-Jewish Relations During the Second World War. annot. ed. Krakowski, Shmuel, ed. Allon, Dafna et al, trs. from YID. 671p. 1992. reprint ed. pap. 19.95 (*0-8101-0963-8*) Northwestern U Pr.

***Ringeler, Frank.** Zur Konzeption der Protagonistenidentitat im deutschen Artusroman um 1200: Aspekte einer Gattungspoetik. 2000. 47.95 (*3-631-35379-0*) P Lang Pubng.

Ringelheim, Joan, compiled by. A Catalogue of Audio & Video Collections of Holocaust Testimony, 23. 2nd ed. LC 91-43368. (Bibliographies & Indexes in World History Ser.: No. 23). 232p. 1992. lib. bdg. 75.00 (*0-313-28221-8*, RAV/, Greenwood Pr) Greenwood.

Ringelstein, E. B., ed. Eighth International Symposium on Cerebral Hemodynamics, Muenster, September 1994: Abstracts. (Journal: Cerebrovascular Diseases Ser.: Vol. 4, Suppl. 3, 1994). xxii, 26p. 1994. pap. 21.00 (*3-8055-6065-6*) S Karger.

Ringen, Stein. Citizens, Families & Reform. (Illus.). 200p. 1997. text 55.00 (*0-19-829082-9*) OUP.

— Democracy, Science, & the Civic Spirit: An Inaugural Lecture Delivered Before the University of Oxford on 27 October, 1992. LC 93-18200. 1993. pap. 4.50 (*0-19-951359-7*, Clarendon Pr) OUP.

Ringen, Stein, jt. auth. see Wallace, Claire.

Ringenbach, Paul T. Tramps & Reformers, 1873-1916: The Discovery of Unemployment in New York, Vol. 27. LC 77-175610. (Contributions in American History Ser.: No. 27). (Illus.). 224p. 1973. 59.95 (*0-8371-6266-1*, RAT/, Greenwood Pr) Greenwood.

Ringenbach, Paul T. U. S. A. A. A Tradition of Service, 1922-1997. LC 97-11162. 1997. write for info. (*0-89865-993-0*) Donning Co.

Ringenbach, Paul T. & Melly, Peter J. The Battle for An Loc. 102p. 1993. reprint ed. pap. 12.50 (*0-923135-59-6*) Dalley Bk Service.

Ringenberg, Lawrence A. A Portrait of 2. (Illus.). 42p. (YA). (gr. 10-12). 1995. reprint ed. pap. 8.50 (*0-87353-414-X*) NCTM.

Ringenberg, Margaret J. & Roth, Jane L. Girls Can't Be Pilots: An Aerobiography. LC 98-70166. (Illus.). 320p. 1998. pap. 14.95 (*0-9661859-0-0*) Daedalus Pr IN.

Ringenberg, William C. Taylor University the First 150 Years. 2nd rev. ed. (Illus.). 272p. 1996. 25.00 (*0-9621187-2-9*); pap. 15.00 (*0-9621187-3-7*) Taylor Univ.

Ringer, Alexander. Early Romantic Era Between Revolutions: 1789 & 1848. 400p. (C). 1990. pap. write for info. (*0-318-65464-4*) P-H.

Ringer, Benjamin B. We the People & Others: Duality & America's Treatment of Its Racial Minorities. 1178p. 1985. pap. text 28.50 (*0-422-60160-8*, 9677, Pub. by Tavistock) Routldge.

— We the People & Others: Duality & America's Treatment of the Racial Minorities. 1165p. 1983. 75.00 (*0-422-78180-0*, NO. 3734, Pub. by Tavistock) Routldge.

Ringer, Benjamin B. & Lawless, Elinor R. Race, Ethnicity & Society. 256p. (C). 1989. pap. 21.99 (*0-415-90035-2*, A1591) Routledge.

Ringer, Bruce. New Zealand by Bike. 2nd ed. (Illus.). 240p. 1994. pap. 16.95 (*0-89886-409-7*) Mountaineers.

Ringer, Douglas L. Physicians' Guide to Nutriceuticals. 290p. 1998. 39.99 (*0-9665665-0-5*) Nutrtnl Data Resces.

***Ringer, Fritz K.** Max Weber's Methodology: The Unification of the Cultural & Social Sciences. 2000. pap. text 18.95 (*0-674-00183-4*) HUP.

Ringer, Fritz K. The Decline of the German Mandarins: The German Academic Community, 1890-1933. LC 90-50315. 548p. 1990. pap. text 35.00 (*0-8195-6235-1*, Wesleyan Univ Pr) U Pr of New Eng.

— Max Weber's Methodology: The Unification of the Cultural & Social Sciences. LC 97-21685. (Illus.). 256p. 1998. 35.00 (*0-674-55657-7*) HUP.

***Ringer, Fritz K.** Toward a Social History of Knowledge: Collected Essays. 2000. 49.95 (*1-57181-231-8*) Berghahn Bks.

Ringer, Gordon, tr. see Marcel, Gabriel.

Ringer, Gregory D. Destinations: Cultural Landscapes of Tourism. LC 97-44289. (Advances in Tourism Ser.). (Illus.). 200p. (C). 1998. 75.00 (*0-415-14919-3*) Routledge.

Ringer, Mark. Electra & the Empty Urn: Metatheater & Role Playing in Sophocles. LC 97-24548. 272p. 1998. pap. 19.95 (*0-8078-4697-X*) U of NC Pr.

Ringer, R. Jeffrey, ed. Queer Words, Queer Images: Communication & the Construction of Homosexuality. 400p. (C). 1994. text 50.00 (*0-8147-7440-7*); pap. text 18.50 (*0-8147-7441-5*) NYU Pr.

***Ringer, Robert.** Getting What You Want: The Seven Principles of Rational Living. 288p. 2000. 23.95 (*1-58542-050-6*, Tarcher Putnam) Putnam Pub Group.

***Ringer, Robert J.** Getting What You Want: The 7 Principles of Rational Living. (Illus.). (J). 2000. 23.95 (*0-399-14686-5*, G P Putnam) Peng Put Young Read.

Ringer, Robert J. Looking Out for #1. 352p. 1985. mass mkt. 6.99 (*0-449-21010-3*, Crest) Fawcett.

— Million Dollar Habits. 320p. 1991. mass mkt. 6.99 (*0-449-21878-3*, Crest) Fawcett.

— Winning Through Intimidation. 304p. 1984. mass mkt. 5.99 (*0-449-20786-2*, Crest) Fawcett.

— Wordasaurus Quick-Answer Guide: The System for Mastering Microsoft Word. LC 98-93369. (Illus.). 640p. (J). (gr. 6-12). 1998. spiral bd. 34.95 (*0-9665991-0-1*) North Pine Ltd.

Ringer, Virginia, tr. see Marcel, Gabriel.

Ringers, Joseph, Jr. & Decker, Larry E. School Community Centers: Guidelines for Interagency Planners. 96p. (Orig.). 1995. pap. 14.95 (*0-930388-11-9*) Comm Collaborators.

Ringertz, Hans, jt. auth. see Pettersson, H.

Ringertz, Nils. Nobel Lectures in Physiology or Medicine, 1991-1995. 300p. 1997. pap. text 19.00 (*981-02-3062-1*) World Scientific Pub.

Ringertz, Olof, et al. Sport Medicine: Pathology. LC 73-10369. (Sport Medicine Ser.: Vol. 3). 1973. 32.00 (*0-8422-7141-4*) Irvington.

Ringgold, Faith. Aunt Harriet's Underground Railroad in the Sky. LC 92-20072. (Illus.). 32p. (J). (ps-4). 1993. lib. bdg. 17.99 (*0-517-58768-8*, Pub. by Crown Bks Yng Read) Random.

— Aunt Harriet's Underground Railroad in the Sky. (J). (ps-4). 1995. pap. 6.99 (*0-517-88543-3*) Crown Pub Group.

— Aunt Harriet's Underground Railroad in the Sky. (J). 1995. 12.19 (*0-606-08478-9*, Pub. by Turtleback) Demco.

— Award Puzzles: The Coretta Scott King Collection - Tar Beach. (Illus.). 1993. 6.95 (*0-938971-92-1*) JTG Nashville.

— Bonjour, Lonnie. LC 95-41146. (Illus.). 32p. (J). (gr. k-4). 1996. 15.95 (*0-7868-0076-3*, Pub. by Hyprn Child); lib. bdg. 15.89 (*0-7868-2062-4*, Pub. by Hyprn Child) Little.

***Ringgold, Faith.** Cassie's Colorful Day. (Tar Beach Ser.). (Illus.). 12p. (J). 1999. bds. 6.99 (*0-517-80021-7*, Pub. by Crown Bks Yng Read) Random.

— Counting to Tar Beach. (Tar Beach Ser.). 12p. (J). 1999. bds. 6.99 (*0-517-80022-5*, Pub. by Crown Bks Yng Read) Random.

Ringgold, Faith. Dinner at Aunt Connie's House. LC 92-54871. (Illus.). 32p. (J). (gr. k-4). 1993. lib. bdg. 14.89 (*1-56282-426-0*, Pub. by Hyprn Child) Little.

— Dinner at Aunt Connie's House. LC 92-54871. (Illus.). 32p. (J). (ps-3). 1993. 14.95 (*1-56282-425-2*, Pub. by Hyprn Child) Time Warner.

— Dinner at Aunt Connie's House. LC 92-54871. (Illus.). 32p. (J). (gr. k-4). 1996. pap. 4.95 (*0-7868-1150-1*, Pub. by Hyprn Ppbks) Little.

Ringgold, Faith. Dinner at Aunt Connie's House. 1996. 10.15 (*0-606-10782-7*, Pub. by Turtleback) Demco.

Ringgold, Faith. If A Bus Could Talk: The Story of Rosa Parks. LC 98-22578. (Illus.). 32p. (J). (gr. k-4). 1999. 16.00 (*0-689-81892-0*) S&S Bks Yung.

***Ringgold, Faith.** The Invisible Princess. (J). 2001. pap. 6.99 (*0-440-41735-X*) BDD Bks Young Read.

Ringgold, Faith. The Invisible Princess. LC 98-14379. 32p. (J). 1998. 18.00 (*0-517-80024-1*); lib. bdg. 19.99 (*0-517-80025-X*, Crown) Crown Pub Group.

— My Dream of Martin Luther King. (Illus.). 32p. (J). (ps-4). 1995. 18.00 (*0-517-59976-7*) Crown Pub Group.

— My Dream of Martin Luther King. (J). 1998. pap. 6.99 (*0-517-88577-8*) Crown Pub Group.

— My Grandmother's Story Quilt. (J). 1998. lib. bdg. write for info. (*0-517-70948-1*) Crown Bks Yng Read.

— My Grandmother's Story Quilt. (J). 1999. write for info. (*0-517-70947-3*) Crown Bks Yng Read.

— Tar Beach. LC 90-40410. (Illus.). 32p. (J). (ps-3). 1991. 18.00 (*0-517-58030-6*, Pub. by Crown Bks Yng Read); lib. bdg. 18.99 (*0-517-58031-4*, Pub. by Crown Bks Yng Read) Random.

— Tar Beach. 1996. pap. 6.99 (*0-517-88544-1*) Random Hse Value.

— Tar Beach. LC 90-40410. (J). 1996. 12.19 (*0-606-10950-1*, Pub. by Turtleback) Demco.

Ringgold, Faith, et al. Talking to Faith Ringgold. LC 95-23455. (J). (gr. 3 up). 1996. pap. 11.99 (*0-517-88546-8*) Crown Pub Group.

Ringgold, Gene. The Complete Films of Bette Davis. (Illus.). 1990. pap. 15.95 (*0-8065-1177-X*, Citadel Pr) Carol Pub Group.

— The Complete Films of Rita Hayworth: The Legend & Career of a Love Goddess. (Illus.). 256p. 1992. pap. 15.95 (*0-8065-1260-1*, Citadel Pr) Carol Pub Group.

Ringgold, Gene & Bodeen, DeWitt. The Complete Films of Cecil B. Demille. (Illus.). 386p. 1985. reprint ed. pap. 12.95 (*0-8065-0956-2*, Citadel Pr) Carol Pub Group.

— Films of Cecil B. DeMille. 1969. pap. 6.95 (*0-8065-0207-X*, Citadel Pr) Carol Pub Group.

Ringgold, Nicolette P. Out of the Corner of My Eye: Living with Vision Loss in Later Life. large type ed. LC 91-3352. 120p. 1991. pap. 23.95 (*0-89128-193-2*) Am Foun Blind.

Ringgren, Helmer. The Faith of Qumran: Theology of the Dead Sea Scrolls. LC 95-67351. 324p. 1995. pap. 17.95 (*0-8245-1258-8*) Crossroad NY.

Ringgren, Helmer, jt. ed. see Botterweck, G. Johannes.

Ringgren, Helmer, ed. & tr. see Engnell, Ivan.

Ringham, Felizitas, jt. auth. see Martin, Bronwen.

Ringheim, Karin. At Risk of Homelessness: The Roles of Income & Rent. LC 90-34290. 280p. 1990. 62.95 (*0-275-93582-5*, C3582, Praeger Pubs) Greenwood.

Ringhofer, Kevin R. & Harding, Martha E. Coaches Guide to Drugs & Sport. LC 95-16965. (Illus.). 208p. (Orig.). 1995. pap. 19.95 (*0-87322-715-8*, PRIN0715) Human Kinetics.

Ringholtz, Rae C. Diggings & Doings in Park City. 1977. reprint ed. 3.50 (*0-914740-16-4*) Western Epics.

Ringholz, Raye C. On Belay! The Life of Legendary Mountaineer Paul Petzoldt. LC 97-41247. (Illus.). 272p. 1998. 24.95 (*0-89886-558-1*) Mountaineers.

***Ringholz, Raye C.** On Belay! The Life of Legendary Mountaineer Paul Petzoldt. (Illus.). 272p. 2000. pap. 16.95 (*0-89886-725-8*) Mountaineers.

Ringholz, Raye C. Paradise Paved: The Challenge of Growth in the New West. LC 96-15764. (Illus.). 216p. 1996. pap. 14.95 (*0-87480-511-2*) U of Utah Pr.

— Park City Trails. 1999. pap. 7.95 (*0-87480-634-8*) U of Utah Pr.

Ringholz, Raye C. Park City Trails. LC 84-60807. (Illus.). 104p. 1984. pap. 7.95 (*0-915272-26-1*) Wasatch Pubs.

Ringis, Rita. Elephants of Thailand: Myth, Art, & Reality. (Illus.). 206p. 1996. text 65.00 (*967-65-3068-9*) OUP.

— Thai Temples & Temple Murals. (Illus.). 192p. (C). 1990. text 60.00 (*0-19-588933-9*) OUP.

***Ringius, Lasse.** Radioactive Waste Disposal at Sea: Public Ideas, Transnational Policy Entrepeneurs & Environmental... (Global Environmental Accord Ser.). (Illus.). 337p. (C). 2001. 62.00 (*0-262-18202-5*); pap. 25.00 (*0-262-68118-8*) MIT Pr.

Ringkamp, Stephen H., et al. Missouri Approved Jury Instructions (mai) 5th ed. LC 96-61666. lxxvii, 783 p. 1996. write for info. (*0-314-21604-9*) West Pub.

Ringl & Dasso, Jerome. Real Estate Principles & Practices. 8th ed. Incl. Florida Supplement. 1977. pap. 7.95 (*0-13-765875-3*); Illinois Supplement. 8th ed. 1977. pap. 7.95 (*0-13-765867-2*); Texas Supplement. 1977. pap. 7.95 (*0-13-765883-4*); 1977. pap. write for info. (*0-318-54926-3*) P-H.

Ringlaben, Ravic, jt. ed. see Hilton, Alan.

Ringland, Elinor. Alzheimer's Disease from Care to Caring. rev. ed. LC 85-81657. (Illus.). 112p. 1988. pap. 12.00 (*0-9613775-3-4*) Healthcare Pr.

Ringland, Gill. Scenario Planning: Managing for the Future. LC 97-31194. (Illus.). 407p. 1998. 39.95 (*0-471-97790-X*) Wiley.

Ringle, Denis J. Life in Mr. Lincoln's Navy. LC 98-15352. 272p. 1998. 32.95 (*1-55750-736-8*) Naval Inst Pr.

Ringle, Martin H., jt. ed. see Lehnert, Wendy G.

Ringle, William J. Techedge: Using Computers to Present & Persuade. LC 98-167573. (Essence of Public Speaking Ser.). 186p. (C). 1997. pap. text 12.00 (*0-205-27305-X*, T7305-0) Allyn.

Ringle, William M. & Smith-Stark, Thomas C. A Concordance to the Inscriptions of Palenque, Chiapas, Maxico. LC 92-12571. (Publication Ser.: No. 62). 1997. 35.00 (*0-939238-93-4*) Tulane MARI.

Ringleb, jt. auth. see Meiners.

Ringleb, Al H., et al. Managing In The Legal Environmment. 2/e. 2nd ed. Fenton, ed. LC 92-30982. (SWC-Business Law). 700p. (C). 1992. text 65.75 (*0-314-01165-X*) West Pub.

Ringleben, Joachim. Aneignung: Die Spekulative Theologie Soren Kierkegaards. 509p. 1983. 123.10 (*3-11-008878-9*) De Gruyter.

— Hegels Theorie der Suende: Die Subjektivitaets-Logishe Umformung Eines Theologischen Begriffs. (Theologische Bibliothek Toepelmann Ser.: Vol. 31). 1977. 90.35 (*3-11-006650-5*) De Gruyter.

Ringleben, Joachim, ed. Christentumsgeschichte und Wahrheitsbewusstsein: Studien zur Theologie Emanuel Hirschs. (Theologische Bibliothek Toepelmann Ser.: Vol. 50). (GER.). vii, 254p. (C). 1991. lib. bdg. 86.15 (*3-11-012700-8*) De Gruyter.

Ringleben, Joachim & Meckenstock, Guenter, eds. Schleiermacher & die Wissenschaftliche Kultur des Christentums. (Theologische Bibliothek Toepelmann Ser.: Vol. 51). (GER.). xvi, 521p. (C). 1991. lib. bdg. 152.35 (*3-11-012857-8*) De Gruyter.

Ringler, Carol A. The New Complete Book of Food: A Nutritional, Medical, & Culinary. LC 99-21200. 448p. 1999. pap. 19.95 (*0-8160-3988-7*, Checkmark) Facts on File.

Ringler, D. L. American History on the Internet. (Young People's Internet Guides Ser.: No. 1). (Illus.). 200p. (J). (gr. 3-8). 1999. spiral bd. 19.95 (*0-9660286-2-7*) O S S Pub Co.

— Clear, Quick & Easy Word Processing: WordPerfect 6.1 for Windows 3.1 & 95. LC 98-91629. (Illus.). 323p. 1998. spiral bd. 24.95 (*0-9660286-1-9*) O S S Pub Co.

Ringler, D. L., ed. see Ringler, J. S.

Ringler, J. S. Exploring the World's Greatest Inventions on the Internet. Ringler, D. L., ed. (Young People's Internet Guides Ser.: No. 2). (Illus.). 150p. (J). (gr. 3-8). 1999. spiral bd. 17.95 (*0-9660286-3-5*) O S S Pub Co.

— The Family Guide to Classic Movies. LC 97-92522. (Illus.). 354p. 1997. spiral bd. 19.95 (*0-9660286-0-0*) O S S Pub Co.

Ringler, R., jt. auth. see Cassidy, F. J.

Ringler, Richard N., jt. ed. see Rothstein, Eric.

Ringler, Sara & Cotter, Louise. Mature Elegance: Styles & Techniques for Mature Clients. LC 97-14863. 160p. (C). 1997. pap. 31.95 (*1-56253-339-8*) Thomson Learn.

***Ringler, Stephen M.** A Dictionary of Cinema Quotations from Filmmakers & Critics: Over 3400 Axioms, Criticisms, Opinions & Witticisms from 100 Years of the Cinema. 240p. 2000. 45.00 (*0-7864-0849-9*) McFarland & Co.

Ringler, Susan J., ed. see Ringler, William A., Jr.

Ringler, Thor, jt. ed. see Wukas, Mark.

Ringler, William A. Bibliography & Index of English Verse Printed, 1476-1558. 448p. 1989. text 250.00 (*0-7201-1892-1*) Continuum.

Ringler, William A., Jr. Index of English Verse in Manuscript, 1501-1558. Rudick, Michael & Ringler, Susan J., eds. 344p. 1992. text 240.00 (*0-7201-2099-3*) Continuum.

Ringler, William A., Jr. & Flackmann, Michael, eds. Beware the Cat by William Baldwin: The First English Novel. LC 88-13057. (Illus.). 162p. (C). 1995. reprint ed. pap. text 7.95 (*0-87328-154-3*) Huntington Lib.

Ringler, William A., jt. intro. see Fox, Denton.

Ringling Bros. & Barnum & Bailey Combined Shows, I. Animals of the Circus. Self, Kathy A., ed. LC 90-62395. (Orig.). (J). 1990. pap. 3.50 (*1-878163-01-9*) Feld Entertainment.

— Circus Days Cookbook. Self, Kathy A., ed. LC 90-62393. (Orig.). (J). 1990. pap. 13.00 (*1-878163-00-0*) Feld Entertainment.

Ringlstetter, Maria, tr. see Perkins, Anne.

Ringlstetter, Maria, jt. tr. see Perkins, Anne T.

***Ringma, Charles R.** Dare to Journey with Henri Nouwen. 2000. pap. 10.00 (*1-57683-226-0*) Pinon Press.

— Resist the Powers with Jacques Ellul. 2000. pap. 10.00 (*1-57683-225-2*) Pinon Press.

— Seize the Day with Dietrich Bonhoeffer. 2000. pap. 10.00 (*1-57683-216-3*) Pinon Press.

Ringmar, Erik. Identity, Interest & Action: A Cultural Explanation of Sweden's Intervention in the Thirty Years' War. (Cultural Social Studies). 247p. (C). 1996. text 59.95 (*0-521-56314-3*) Cambridge U Pr.

Ringnalda, Don. Fighting & Writing the Vietnam War. LC 94-16059. 224p. 1994. text 37.50 (*0-87805-730-7*) U Pr of Miss.

Ringney, Steve. Network Planning & Management: Your Personal Consultant. 1995. pap. text 24.95 (*1-56276-309-1*, Ziff-Davis Pr) Que.

Ringo, Betty, ed. see Paull, Susan G.

Ringo, James. Uncle Theodor. LC 97-65967. 80p. 1997. 16.95 (*1-57197-058-4*) Pentland Pr.

***Ringo, John.** A Hymn Before Battle. 2000. write for info. (*0-671-31941-8*) PB.

Ringoir, S., et al, eds. Uremic Toxins. LC 87-25936. (Illus.). 308p. 1987. 85.00 (*0-306-42771-0*, Plenum Trade) Perseus Pubng.

Ringold, Dena, jt. auth. see Allison, Christine.

Ringold, Dena, jt. auth. see Laporte, Bruno.

Ringold, Francine, ed. Australia. 160p. 1993. pap. 6.95 (*0-685-65045-6*) Art & Human Council Tulsa.

— Awards, 4. (Nimrod Ser.). (Illus.). 112p. 1982. pap. 5.50 (*0-942374-09-6*) Art & Human Council Tulsa.

— Awards, 6. 119p. 1984. pap. 5.50 (*0-317-60711-1*) Art & Human Council Tulsa.

— Awards, 7. 107p. 1985. pap. 5.50 (*0-317-60726-X*) Art & Human Council Tulsa.

— Awards, 8. 144p. 1991. pap. 6.95 (*0-317-60728-6*) Art & Human Council Tulsa.

— Awards, 9. 152p. 1987. pap. 5.50 (*0-685-45298-0*) Art & Human Council Tulsa.

— Awards, 11. 148p. 1989. 6.50 (*0-685-34258-1*) Art & Human Council Tulsa.

— Awards, 12. 160p. 1990. pap. 6.90 (*0-685-37855-1*) Art & Human Council Tulsa.

— Awards, 13. 160p. 1991. 6.90 (*0-933031-54-8*) Art & Human Council Tulsa.

— Awards, 14. 160p. 1992. pap. 6.90 (*0-685-62340-8*) Art & Human Council Tulsa.

— Awards, 15. 160p. 1993. pap. 6.90 (*0-685-62356-4*) Art & Human Council Tulsa.

— Awards, 16. 168p. 1994. pap. 6.95 (*0-614-03086-2*) Art & Human Council Tulsa.

— Awards Tenth. 152p. 1988. 5.50 (*0-685-45299-9*) Art & Human Council Tulsa.

— Awards Third. (Nimrod Ser.). 109p. (Orig.). 1981. pap. text 5.50 (*0-942374-06-1*) Art & Human Council Tulsa.

— China Today. 132p. 1986. pap. 5.50 (*0-317-60731-6*) Art & Human Council Tulsa.

— From the Soviets. 160p. 1990. pap. 6.90 (*0-933031-52-1*) Art & Human Council Tulsa.

— Frontiers: Land, Space, & Mind. (Nimrod Ser.). 96p. 1982. pap. text 5.50 (*0-942374-08-8*) Art & Human Council Tulsa.

— India: A Wealth of Diversity. 160p. 1988. pap. 5.50 (*0-318-32886-0*) Art & Human Council Tulsa.

— Making Language: Thirty-Fifth Anniversary Issue. 144p. 1992. pap. 6.90 (*0-685-62341-6*) Art & Human Council Tulsa.

— O, Canada. 160p. 1994. pap. 6.95 (*0-685-66039-7*) Art & Human Council Tulsa.

— Oklahoma Indian Markings. 160p. 1989. 6.95 (*0-685-45300-6*) Art & Human Council Tulsa.

— Thirty-Thirty Three. 146p. 1987. pap. 5.50 (*0-318-32887-9*) Art & Human Council Tulsa.

— Tulsa-Tbilisi. 168p. 1985. pap. 5.50 (*0-317-60730-8*) Art & Human Council Tulsa.

Ringold, Jeanette K., tr. see Friedman, Carl.

Ringold, Jeannette K., tr. see Enquist, Anna.

Ringold, Jeannette K., tr. see Friedman, Carl.

Ringold, Jeannette K., tr. see Minco, Marga.

Ringold, Jennette K., tr. see Enquist, Anna.

Ringold, May S. The Role of the State Legislatures in the Confederacy. LC 66-27607. 149p. reprint ed. pap. 46.20 (*0-608-15799-6*, 203105100073) Bks Demand.

***Ringolsby, Tracy.** Vinny Castilla: Mexican Treasure. (Illus.). 200p. 2000. 22.95 (*1-58261-138-6*, Pub. by Sprts Pubng) Partners-West.

Ringquist, Evan J. Environmental Protection at the State Level: Politics & Progress in Controlling Pollution. LC 93-12298. (Bureaucracies, Public Administration & Public Policy Ser.). 256p. (C). (gr. 13). 1993. text 79.95 (*1-56324-203-6*) M E Sharpe.

Ringquist, Evan J. Environmental Protection at the State Level: Politics & Progress in Controlling Pollution. LC 93-12298. (Bureaucracies, Public Administration, & Public Policy Ser.). 256p. (C). (gr. 13). 1993. pap. text 39.95 (*1-56324-204-4*) M E Sharpe.

Ringquist, Neil A., jt. ed. see Carter, Mildred.

***Ringrose.** Expansion & Global Interaction 1200-1700. 1998. pap. text 16.80 (*0-201-45680-X*) Addison-Wesley.

***Ringrose, David R.** Expansion & Global Interaction: 1200-1700. 176p. 2000. pap. text 19.33 (*0-321-01125-2*) Longman.

Ringrose, David R. Spain, Europe, & the "Spanish Miracle", 1700-1900. LC 96-158113. (Illus.). 455p. (C). 1996. text 69.95 (*0-521-43486-6*) Cambridge U Pr.

— Spain, Europe, & the "Spanish Miracle", 1700-1900. (Illus.). 455p. (C). 1998. pap. text 22.95 (*0-521-64630-8*) Cambridge U Pr.

— Transportation & Economic Stagnation in Spain, 1750-1850. LC 78-101131. 213p. reprint ed. pap. 66.10 (*0-608-11971-7*, 202344100033) Bks Demand.

R

Ringrose, Hyacinthe. The Inns of Court: An Historical Description of the Inns of Court & Chancery of England. iv, 183p. 1997. reprint ed. 57.00 (*1-56169-326-X*) Gaunt.
— Inns of Court: An Historical Description of the Inns of Court & Chancery of England. (Illus.). iv, 183p. 1983. reprint ed. 42.00 (*0-8377-1040-5*, Rothman) W S Hein.
Ringrose, Hyacinthe, ed. Marriage & Divorce Laws of the World. 270p. 1988. reprint ed. 45.00 (*0-8377-2540-2*, Rothman) W S Hein.
Ringrose, J. S., jt. ed. see Baker, J. H.
Ringrose, John R., jt. auth. see Kadison, Richard V.
Ringrose, John R., jt. ed. see Kadison, Richard V.
Ringrose, Linda, jt. auth. see Rathbun, Linda.
Ringrose, Marjorie & Lerner, Adam, eds. Reimagining the Nation. LC 92-47424. 1993. 118.00 (*0-335-19150-9*) OpUniv Pr.
Ringrose-Voase, A. J. & Humphreys, G. S., eds. Soil Micromorphology: Studies in Managment & Genesis. LC 94-21731. (Development in Soil Science Ser.: 22). 900p. 1994. 264.25 (*0-444-89792-5*) Elsevier.
Rings, Guido, jt. auth. see Tenberg, Richard.
Rings, Lana, jt. auth. see Clausing, Gerhard.
Rings, Roy W., et al. The Owlet Moths of Ohio (Order Lepidoptera Family Noctuidae) LC 91-62768. (Bulletin New Ser.: Vol. 9, No. 2). (Illus.). 200p. 1992. pap. text 20.00 (*0-86727-110-8*) Ohio Bio Survey.
Ringskog, Klas, jt. auth. see Idelovitch, Emanuel.
Ringskog, Klas, jt. auth. see Simpson, Larry.
Ringsrud, Karen M. Urinalysis & Body Fluids. (Illus.). 272p. (gr. 13). 1994. pap. text 43.00 (*0-8016-7043-8*, 07043) Mosby Inc.
Ringsrud, Karen M., jt. auth. see Linne, Jean J.
Ringstad, M. Adventures on Library Shelves. LC 68-16398. (Illus.). 48p. (J). (gr. 2 up). 1967. ring bd. 12.35 (*0-87783-001-0*) Oddo.
Ringstad, Muriel. Eye of the Changer: A Northwest Indian Tale. LC 83-7121. (Illus.). 96p. (Orig.). (J). (gr. 4 up). 1984. pap. 9.95 (*0-88240-251-X*, Alaska NW Bks) Gr Arts Ctr Pub.
Ringsven, Bond. Gerontology & Leadership Skills for Nurses. 2nd ed. LC 96-18183. (LPN/LVN Nursing Ser.). 448p. (C). 1996. mass mkt. 50.95 (*0-8273-6778-3*) Delmar.
Ringsven, Mary K. Basic Community & Home Care Nursing. (LPN/LVN Nursing Ser.). 1988. pap. 29.95 (*0-8273-2969-5*); pap., teacher ed. 14.00 (*0-8273-2970-9*) Delmar.
— Gerontology: Leadership Skills for Nurses. 2nd ed. (LPN/LVN Nursing Ser.). 1997. 13.50 (*0-8273-6779-1*) Delmar.
— Gerontology & Leadership Skills - Nurses. 1991. pap. 32.95 (*0-8273-3450-8*) Delmar.
Ringsven, Mary K. & Bond, Donna. Gerontology & Leadership for Nurses: Instructor's Guide. 1991. 13.50 (*0-8273-3451-6*) Delmar.
Ringtved, Jytte, jt. ed. see Fabech, Charlotte.
Ringuest, Jeffery L. Multiobjective Optimization: Behavioral & Computational Considerations. 192p. (C). 1992. lib. bdg. 101.00 (*0-7923-9236-1*) Kluwer Academic.
Ringuet, Antoine S. Thirty Acres. 312p. 1996. pap. text 7.95 (*0-7710-9995-9*) McCland & Stewart.
Ringwald, Barbara & McRee, Nancy J. Know the U. S. A. 1991. 4.95 (*1-55708-362-2*, MCR642) McDonald Pub Co.
— Know Your State. 1991. 4.95 (*1-55708-361-4*, MCR641) McDonald Pub Co.
— Know Your World. 1991. 4.95 (*1-55708-363-0*, MCR643) McDonald Pub Co.
Ringwald, Barbara, ed. see Ring, J. Michael.
Ringwald, Christopher D. Faith in Words: Ten Writers Reflect on the Spirituality of Their Profession. (Orig.). 1997. pap. 12.95 (*0-87946-161-6*) ACTA Pubns.
Ringwald, Donald C. Steamboats for Rondout: Passenger Service Between New York & Rondout Creek, 1829-1863. LC 81-51099. (Illus.). 145p. 1981. 17.00 (*0-913423-00-9*) Steamship Hist Soc.
Ringwald, Lydia E. Blessings in Disguise. 36p. (Orig.). 1989. pap. 8.00 (*0-685-29073-5*) Creative Realities.
Ringwald, Richard. Means Heavy Construction Handbook. 1993. pap. 74.95 (*0-87629-283-X*, 67148) R S Means.
Ringwalt, J. L. Diller Family (of Pennsylvania) (Illus.). 56p. 1997. reprint ed. pap. 11.00 (*0-8328-8306-9*); reprint ed. lib. bdg. 21.00 (*0-8328-8305-0*) Higginson Bk Co.
Ringwood, A. E. Origin of the Earth & Moon. (Illus.). 1979. 73.00 (*0-387-90369-0*) Spr-Verlag.
Ringwood, Graem A., jt. auth. see Huntbach, Matthew M.
Rinhart, Floyd & Rinhart, Marion. America's Centennial Celebration. LC 75-38859. (Illus.). 1976. pap. 4.95 (*0-914042-08-4*) Laura Bks.
***Rinhart, Floyd, et al.** The American Tintype. LC 98-49828. (Illus.). 392p. 1999. text 75.00 (*0-8142-0806-1*) Ohio St U Pr.
Rinhart, Marion, jt. auth. see Rinhart, Floyd.
***Rini, Joel.** Exploring the Role of Morphology in the Evolution of Spanish. LC 99-31510. (Current Issues in Linguistic Theory Ser.: Vol. 179). xvi, 187p. 1999. 74.00 (*1-55619-956-2*) J Benjamins Pubng Co.
Rini, Joel. Motives for Lingustic Change in the Formation of the Spanish Object Pronouns. (Estudios Linguisticos Ser.). 152p. 1992. pap. 12.00 (*0-936388-52-8*) Juan de la Cuesta.
Rini, Kristiana S., jt. auth. see Woods, Paul.
Rini, Lisa, jt. auth. see Werner, Peter H.
Rini, Suzanne M. Beyond Abortion: A Chronicle of Fetal Experimentation. LC 92-82133. 197p. 1993. reprint ed. pap. 12.00 (*0-89555-487-9*) TAN Bks Pubs.
Rini, William A. The NYIF Vest-Pocket Guide to Stock Brokerage Math. LC 92-15201. 208p. (C). 1992. text 16.95 (*0-13-847690-X*) P-H.
***Riniker, Christian.** Die Gerichtsverkundigung Jesu. 487p. 1999. 62.95 (*3-906761-89-4*, Pub. by P Lang) P Lang Pubng.
Rinjiro, Shirata, jt. auth. see Stevens, John.
Rink. Teaching for Learning. 2nd ed. 1992. 14.06 (*0-697-40352-1*) McGraw.
— Teaching Physical Education 4th ed. 2001. text 36.50 (*0-07-232910-6*) McGraw.
Rink, David R., jt. auth. see Kaminski, Peter F.
Rink, Deane, jt. auth. see Wood, Linda.
Rink, Evald. Printing in Delaware, 1761-1800. (Illus.). 214p. 1969. 5.00 (*0-914650-01-7*) Hagley Museum.
Rink, Evald, ed. see Kool, Ferdinand.
Rink, Henry W., jt. auth. see Gallo, Joseph D.
Rink, Hinrich. Tales & Traditions of the Eskimo: With a Sketch of Their Habits, Religion, Language & Other Peculiarities. unabridged ed. LC 97-24234. (Illus.). 484p. 1998. reprint ed. pap. 11.95 (*0-486-29966-X*) Dover.
Rink, Hinrich J. Danish Greenland: Its People & Its Products. LC 74-5870. (Illus.). reprint ed. 64.50 (*0-404-11677-9*) AMS Pr.
— The Eskimo Tribes, 2 vols. in 1. LC 74-5871. reprint ed. 72.50 (*0-404-11678-7*) AMS Pr.
— Tales & Traditions of the Eskimo, with a Sketch of Their Habits, Religion, Language & Other Peculiarities. LC 74-5872. (Illus.). reprint ed. 67.50 (*0-404-11681-7*) AMS Pr.
Rink, John. Chopin: The Piano Concertos. LC 97-6905. (Music Handbks.). 150p. (C). 1998. text 39.95 (*0-521-44109-9*); pap. text 13.95 (*0-521-44660-0*) Cambridge U Pr.
Rink, John, ed. The Practice of Performance: Studies in Musical Interpretation. (Illus.). 304p. (C). 1996. text 69.95 (*0-521-45374-7*) Cambridge U Pr.
Rink, John & Samson, Jim, eds. Chopin Studies 2, No. 2. (Illus.). 263p. (C). 1995. text 69.95 (*0-521-41647-7*) Cambridge U Pr.
***Rink, Martin.** Vom Partheyganger/Zum Partisanen: Die Konzeption des Kleinen Krieges in Preu & Betaen, 1740-1813. (Europaische Hochschulschriften Geschichte und Ihre Hilfswissenschaften Ser.). (Illus.). XXXIII, 474p. 1999. 74.95 (*3-631-35109-7*) P Lang Pubng.
Rink, Oliver A. Holland on the Hudson: An Economic & Social History of Dutch New York. LC 86-2317. (Illus.). 288p. 1986. text 42.50 (*0-8014-1866-6*) Cornell U Pr.
Rinke, Hans. Woerterbuch der Seeschiffahrt: Dictionary of Merchant Shipping, Vol. 1. 2nd ed. (ENG & GER.). 1975. 59.95 (*0-8288-5967-1*, M6958) Fr & Eur.
— Woerterbuch der Seeschiffahrt: Dictionary of Merchant Shipping, Vol. 2. 2nd ed. (ENG & GER.). 59.95 (*3-19-006295-1*, M-6957) Fr & Eur.
Rinke, Lynn T. & Wilson, Alexis A., eds. Outcome Measures in Home Care: Research, Vol. I. 250p. (Orig.). 1987. pap. 22.95 (*0-88737-378-X*) Natl League Nurse.
Rinke, Wolf J. Make It a Winning Life: Success Strategies for Life, Love & Business. LC 91-75609. 283p. 1992. 24.95 (*0-9627913-8-5*) Achvmnt Pubs.
— The 6 Success Strategies for Winning at Life, Love & Business. 300p. 1996. pap. 12.95 (*1-55874-390-1*, 3901) Health Comm.
— The Winning Foodservice Manager: Strategies for Doing More with Less. 2nd ed. LC 90-84599. 261p. 1990. reprint ed. text 32.50 (*0-9627913-9-3*) Achvmnt Pubs.
— Winning Management: 6 Fail-Safe Strategies for Building High Performance Organizations. LC 95-83088. 300p. 1997. 24.95 (*0-9627913-7-7*) Achvmnt Pubs.
***Rinken, Sebastian.** The AIDS Crisis & the Modern Self: Biographical Self-Construction in the Awareness of Finitude. LC 00-33068. (International Library of Ethics, Law & the New Medicine). 2000. write for info. (*0-7923-6371-X*) Kluwer Academic.
Rinker, Eleanor. Writing with Sharpened Senses. (Illus.). (J). (gr. 6-8). 1994. pap. text, wbk. ed. 15.95 (*1-881641-05-8*) Pencil Point.
Rinker Enterprises Staff. Antiques & Collectibles. 17th ed. 1999. pap. 15.95 (*0-676-60178-2*) Hse Collectbls.
— Collector Plates, Offcial Price. 1999. pap. 17.00 (*0-676-60154-5*) Hse Collectbls.
***Rinker Enterprises Staff.** The Official Price Guide to Antiques & Collectibles. 18th ed. (Illus.). 784p. 2000. pap. 16.00 (*0-676-60185-5*) Hse Collectbls.
Rinker, Harry, jt. auth. see Moore, Connie.
Rinker, Harry L. Antique Trader Books Guide to Games & Puzzles. LC 97-75160. (Illus.). 224p. 1997. pap. 17.95 (*0-930625-62-5*) Krause Pubns.
Rinker, Harry L. Dinnerware of the 20th Century. 1997. pap. 29.95 (*0-676-60085-9*) Random.
Rinker, Harry L. Flea Market Treasures. 5th ed. 1999. pap. 22.95 (*0-676-60180-4*) Hse Collectbls.
***Rinker, Harry L.** Harry L. Rinker Collectibles. 3rd ed. 480p. 1999. pap. 19.95 (*0-676-60158-8*) Hse Collectbls.
Rinker, Harry L. Hopalong Cassidy: King of the Cowboy Merchandisers. LC 94-49645. (Illus.). 160p. (Orig.). 1995. pap. 29.95 (*0-88740-765-X*) Schiffer.
***Rinker, Harry L.** Official Price Guide to Collectibles. 4th ed. (Illus.). 480p. 2000. pap. 19.95 (*0-676-60159-6*) Hse Collectbls.
Rinker, Harry L. The Old Raging Erie . . . There Have Been Several Changes: A Postcard History of the Erie & Other New York State Canals, 1895-1915. (Illus.). 20.00p. (Orig.). 1984. pap. 20.00 (*0-9613675-0-4*) Canal Captains.
— Price Guide to Flea Market Treasures. 4th ed. LC 97-198430. (Illus.). 356p. 1997. pap. 19.95 (*0-87069-748-X*, Wllce-Homestd) Krause Pubns.
— Schuylkill Navigation: A Photographic History. LC 90-85567. (Illus.). 96p. 1991. pap. 16.00 (*0-9613675-2-0*) Canal Captains.
Rinker, Harry L. Silverware of the 20th Century: The Top 250 Patterns. 256p. 1997. pap. 24.95 (*0-676-60086-7*) Random.
Rinker, Harry L. Stemware in the 20th Century. (Illus.). 224p. 1997. pap. 24.95 (*0-676-60084-0*) Random.
Rinker, Harry L., jt. auth. see Morykan, Dana G.
Rinker, Robert A. Cooking Healthy with Wild Game: Delicious Healthy Game & Fish Recipes. Complete Guide from Field to Table. LC 97-69944. 140p. 1997. pap. 9.95 (*0-9645598-3-8*) Mulberry Hse Pub.
— Understanding Firearm Ballistics: Basic to Advanced Ballistics Simplified, Illustrated & Explained. 4th rev. ed. LC 98-68591. (Illus.). 427p. 1999. pap. 24.95 (*0-9645598-4-6*) Mulberry Hse Pub.
Rinker, Rosalind. Learning Conversational Prayer. 48p. (Orig.). 1992. pap. text 3.95 (*0-8146-2036-1*) Liturgical Pr.
Rinker, Rosalind. Prayer Conversing with God. 128p. 1986. mass mkt. 9.99 (*0-310-32171-9*) Zondervan.
Rinker, Rosalind. You Can Witness with Confidence. LC 91-72627. 72p. 1991. reprint ed. pap. 14.95 (*0-940232-44-8*) Seedsowers.
Rinkevich, B. & Muller, W. E. Invertebrate Immunology, Vol. 15. LC 95-24586. (Progress in Molecular & Subcellular Biology Ser.). 247p. 1996. 158.00 (*3-540-59239-3*) Spr-Verlag.
Rinkevich, Thomas E. A KWIC Concordance to Lucretius' De Rerum Natura, 2 Vols., Set. LC 93-85190. (LAT.). v, 1030p. 1995. 130.00 (*0-9644790-1-X*) Nonce NE.
— A KWIC Concordance to Lucretius' De Rerum Natura, Vol. 1. LC 93-85190. (LAT.). v, 482p. 1995. 65.00 (*0-9644790-0-1*) Nonce NE.
— A KWIC Concordance to Lucretius' De Rerum Natura, Vol. 2. LC 93-85190. (LAT.). 548p. 1995. 65.00 (*0-9644790-2-8*) Nonce NE.
Rinkevichius, B. S. Laser Diagnostics in Fluid Mechanics. LC 96-29931. 1997. write for info. (*1-56700-073-8*) Begell Hse.
Rinkevichius, Bronius S. Laser Diagnostics in Fluid Mechanics. LC 96-29931. 1998. 115.00 (*1-56700-109-2*) Begell Hse.
Rinkle, Max & Denber, H. C. Chemical Concepts of Psychosis. (Illus.). 1958. 24.95 (*0-8392-1012-4*) Astor-Honor.
Rinkoff, Barbara. Map Is a Picture. LC 65-11648. (Let's-Read-&-Find-Out Science Bks.). (Illus.). (J). (gr. k-3). 1965. lib. bdg. 10.89 (*0-690-51793-9*) HarpC Child Bks.
— The Remarkable Ramsey. (Illus.). (J). (gr. 2-6). 1990. 15.75 (*0-8446-6195-3*) Peter Smith.
Rinkwich, Randy. While Beyond the Forest. Barkan, Stanley H., ed. (Review Chapbook Ser.: No. 24: Yiddish Poetry 1). (ENG & YID.). 40p. 1991. 15.00 (*0-89304-762-7*); pap. 5.00 (*0-89304-763-5*) Cross-Cultrl NY.
— While Beyond the Forest: Mini Book. Barkan, Stanley H., ed. (Review Chapbook Ser.: No. 24: Yiddish Poetry 1). (ENG & YID.). 40p. 1991. 15.00 (*0-89304-764-3*); pap. 5.00 (*0-89304-765-1*) Cross-Cultrl NY.
Rinn, Ludwig A. The Polychromatic Layering Technique. (Illus.). 155p. 1990. text 88.00 (*0-86715-225-7*) Quint Pub Co.
Rinn, Miriam. Baseball Greats LC 98-205508. 64 p. 1999. write for info. (*0-8167-4934-5*) Troll Communs.
— Great Adventurers. LC 98-205510. (Real Lives Ser.). 64 p. 1999. write for info. (*0-8167-4932-9*, Troll Medallion) Troll Communs.
— Heroes & Idealists LC 98-205503. (Real Lives Ser.). 64 p. 1999. write for info. (*0-8167-4933-7*, Troll Medallion) Troll Communs.
— Leaders of the People. LC 98-205440. 64 p. 1999. 8.95 (*0-8167-4929-9*, Troll Medallion) Troll Communs.
— The Saturday Secret. LC 98-22138. (Illus.). 144p. (J). (gr. 3-8). 1999. pap. 7.95 (*1-881283-26-7*) Alef Design.
— Seekers of Truth: The Story of the Philalethes Society. LC 98-205448. (New York Practice Skills Course Handbook Ser.). 64 p. 1999. write for info. (*0-8167-4930-2*, Troll Medallion) Troll Communs.
— Women of Valor LC 98-205507. (Real Lives Ser.). 64 p. 1999. write for info. (*0-8167-4931-0*, Troll Medallion) Troll Communs.
Rinn, Roger C. & Markle, Allan. Positive Parenting. (Illus.). 1986. pap. text 8.95 (*0-89147-052-2*) CAS.
Rinne, Carl H. Excellent Classroom Management: Content Focused Controls. LC 96-32174. (Education Ser.). (Illus.). 800p. (C). 1997. 56.95 (*0-534-25074-2*) Wadsworth Pub.
Rinne, F. & Berek, M. Anleitung Zur Allgemeinen und Polarisations-Mikroskopie der Festkoerper im Durchlicht. xii, 323p. 1973. 29.00 (*3-510-65040-9*, Pub. by E Schweizerbartsche) Balogh.
Rinnen, Henri. Dictionnaire Francais-Luxembourgeois. (FRE.). 1170p. 1988. 95.00 (*0-7859-8664-2*, 287963007x) Fr & Eur.
***Rinner, Jill A.** Creative Lettering: The Secrets Revealed. (Scrapbooking Made Easy Ser.). 1998. pap. write for info. (*1-891520-26-1*) Red Pt Publ.
Rinner, Jill A. Designer Die Cuts. (Scrapbooking Made Easy Ser.). 1998. pap. write for info. (*1-891520-29-6*) Red Pt Publ.
***Rinner, Jill A.** Enhancing with Color. (Scrapbooking Made Easy Ser.). 1998. pap. text. write for info. (*1-891520-27-X*) Red Pt Publ.
— Finding Inspiration: Defining Your Personal Style. (Scrapbooking Made Easy Ser.). 1998. pap. write for info. (*1-891520-24-5*) Red Pt Publ.
Rinner, Jill A. Photo Journaling: Telling the Story. 1998. pap. 3.95 (*1-891520-28-8*) Red Pt Publ.
***Rinner, Jill A.** Principles of Design. (Scrapbooking Made Easy Ser.). 1998. pap. 3.95 (*1-891520-25-3*) Red Pt Publ.
— Scrapbooking Made Easy! LC 99-38593. 128p. (gr. 11). 1999. pap. 9.95 (*0-7370-0058-9*) T-L Custom Pub.
Rinner, Jill A. Terrific Titles: Getting Off to a Great Start. (Scrapbooking Made Easy Ser.). 1998. pap. write for info. (*1-891520-30-X*) Red Pt Publ.
***Rinner, Jill A.** Things You Should Know. (Scrapbooking Made Easy Ser.). 1998. pap. write for info. (*1-891520-23-7*) Red Pt Publ.
Rinnooy-Kan, A. H., jt. auth. see Kan, A. H.
Rinpoche, Dilgo K. The Excellent Path to Enlightenment: Oral Teachings on the Root Textof Jamyang Khyentse Wangpo. Padmakara Translation Group Staff, tr. from TIB. (Illus.). 128p. 1996. pap. 12.95 (*1-55939-064-6*) Snow Lion Pubns.
Rinpoche, H. H. Chetsang. The Practice of Mahamudra: The Teachings of His Holiness, the Drikung Kyabgon, Chetsang Rinpoche. Chodron, Ani T. & Emmerich, D., eds. Clark, Robert & Gyaltshen, Khenpo K., trs. from TIB. LC 99-27858. 135p. 1999. pap. 12.95 (*1-55939-124-3*) Snow Lion Pubns.
Rinpoche, Akong T. Taming the Tiger: Tibetan Teachings on Right Conduct, Mindfulness & Universal Compassion. LC 95-31532. (Illus.). 188p. 1996. pap. 12.95 (*0-89281-569-8*) Inner Tradit.
Rinpoche, Bokar. Chenrezig, Lord of Love: Principles & Methods of Deity Meditation. Jorgensen, Dan, ed. Buchet, Christiane, tr. from FRE. & intro. by. LC 91-73587. (Illus.). 112p. (Orig.). 1997. reprint ed. pap. text 12.95 (*0-9630371-0-2*) ClearPoint.
— The Day of a Buddhist Practitioner. Buchet, Christiane, tr. from FRE. LC 98-70366. 1998. pap. 8.95 (*0-9630371-9-6*) ClearPoint.
— Meditation: Advice to Beginners. Pessereau, Jennifer, ed. LC 92-75390. (Illus.). 160p. (Orig.). 1993. pap. 14.95 (*0-9630371-1-0*) ClearPoint.
— Opening the Door to Certainty. Buchet, Christiane, tr. from FRE. LC 96-96789. 64p. 1996. pap. 9.95 (*0-9630371-7-X*) ClearPoint.
— Profound Wisdom of the Heart Sutra: And Other Teachings. Buchet, Christiane, tr. from FRE. LC 94-68742. (Illus.). 96p. (Orig.). 1994. pap. text 10.95 (*0-9630371-3-7*) ClearPoint.
— Taking the Bodhisattva Vow. Buchet, Christiane, tr. from FRE. LC 97-77053. (Illus.). 128p. 1998. pap. 9.95 (*0-9630371-8-8*) ClearPoint.
***Rinpoche, Bokar.** Tara the Feminine Divine. Buchet, Christiane, tr. from FRE. LC 99-80111. (Illus.). 176p. 1999. pap. 18.95 (*1-930164-00-9*) ClearPoint.
Rinpoche, Chokyi N. Bardo Guidebook. 190p. 1996. pap. 14.95 (*962-7341-11-8*, Pub. by Rang Jung Yshe) Bookpeople.
— Indisputable Truth. 208p. 1996. pap. 18.00 (*962-7341-27-4*, Pub. by Rang Jung Yshe) Bookpeople.
— The Song of Karmapa. 128p. 1996. pap. 12.95 (*962-7341-14-2*, Pub. by Rang Jung Yshe) Bookpeople.
— The Union of Mahamudra & Dzogchen. 240p. 1996. pap. 18.00 (*962-7341-21-5*, Pub. by Rang Jung Yshe) Bookpeople.
Rinpoche, Dagyab. Buddhist Symbols in Tibetan Culture: An Investigation of the Nine Best-Known Groups of Symbols. Walshe, Maurice O., tr. from GER. LC 95-35742. (Illus.). 160p. 1995. pap. 15.95 (*0-86171-047-9*, Pub. by Wisdom MA) Natl Bk Netwk.
Rinpoche, Deshung K. The Three Levels of Spiritual Perception: An Oral Commentary on the Three Visions (Nang Sum) of Ngorchen Konchong Lhundrub. Scott, Victoria R., ed. Rhoton, Jared, tr. LC 95-1490.Tr. of Lam Bras Snon Groi Khrid Yig Snan Gsum Mdzes Rgyan. (ENG & TIB., Illus.). 620p. 1995. 39.95 (*0-86171-101-7*, Pub. by Wisdom MA) Natl Bk Netwk.
Rinpoche, Dilgo K. Enlightened Courage: An Explanation of Atisha's Seven Point Mind Training. Padmakara Translation Group Staff, tr. from TIB. LC 93-28462. 144p. 1993. pap. 12.95 (*1-55939-023-9*) Snow Lion Pubns.
— Guru Yoga: According to the Preliminary Practice of Longchen Nyingtik. Tenzin, Gelong K., tr. from TIB. LC 99-52039. 95p. 1999. pap. 12.95 (*1-55939-121-9*, Pub. by Snow Lion Pubns) Natl Bk Netwk.
Rinpoche, Dudjom & Dorje, Jigdrel Y. The Nyingma School of Tibetan Buddhism: Its Fundamentals & History, 2 vols., Set. Kapstein, Matthew & Dorje, Gyurme, eds. & trs. by. (Illus.). 1568p. 1991. 240.00 (*0-86171-087-8*) Wisdom MA.
Rinpoche, Gyatrul. Ancient Wisdom: Nyingma Teachings on Dream Yoga, Meditation & Transformation. Wallace, B. Alan & Khandro, Sangye, trs. LC 93-13992. 176p. 1993. pap. 14.95 (*1-55939-018-2*) Snow Lion Pubns.
— Generating the Deity. Khandro, Sangye, tr. 139p. 1996. pap. 14.95 (*1-55939-055-7*) Snow Lion Pubns.
Rinpoche, Gyutrul. The Secret Oral Teachings on Generating the Deity. Khandro, Sangye, tr. (Illus.). 164p. 1992. pap. 25.00 (*957-638-105-3*, PRE015, Pub. by SMC Pub) Antique Collect.
Rinpoche, Jigme, tr. see Dalai Lama.
Rinpoche, Kalu. Excellent Buddhism: An Exemplary Life. Buchet, Christiane, tr. from FRE. LC 95-78755. (Illus.). 200p. 1995. pap. text 15.95 (*0-9630371-4-5*) ClearPoint.
— Foundations of Tibetan Buddhism: The Gem Ornament of Manifold Oral Instructions Which Benefits Each & Everyone Accordingly. Orig. Title: Gem Ornament of Manifold Instructions. 200p. 1999. reprint ed. pap. 16.95 (*1-55939-117-0*) Snow Lion Pubns.
— Luminous Mind: The Way of the Buddha. LC 96-24689. (Illus.). 352p. 1996. pap. 18.95 (*0-86171-118-1*) Wisdom MA.
— Profound Buddhism: From Hinayana to Vajrayana. Buchet, Christiane, tr. from FRE. LC 95-78919. (Illus.). 200p. 1995. pap. text 15.95 (*0-9630371-5-3*) ClearPoint.
— Secret Buddhism: Vajrayana Practices. Buchet, Christiane, tr. from FRE. LC 95-78920. (Illus.). 200p. 1995. pap. text 15.95 (*0-9630371-6-1*) ClearPoint.

An Asterisk (*) at the beginning of an entry indicates that the title is appearing for the first time.

Rinpoche, Khamtul. Dzog Chen Meditation. Sparham, Gareth, tr. from TIB. (C). 1994. text 14.00 (*81-7030-407-5*, Pub. by Sri Satguru Pubns) S Asia.

Rinpoche, Khempo K. & Gampopa. The Instructions of Gampopa: A Precious Garland of the Supreme Path. Roth, Laura, ed. Gyamtso, Yeshe, tr. LC 95-52951. 213p. 1996. 14.95 (*1-55939-046-8*) Snow Lion Pubns.

Rinpoche, Khen, tr. see Tsongkapa.

Rinpoche, Khenchen P. & Rinpoche, Khenpo T. Lions Gaze: A Dzogchen Commentary on Three Statements of Garalo Dorje & the Special Teaching of the Wise & Glorious Sovereign by Patrol Rindpoche. Kaye, Joan, ed. Harding, Sarah, tr. from TIB. (Dzog-chen - The Clear Light Great Perfection Ser.). (Illus.). 240p. 1998. 90.00 (*1-880975-04-1*) Sky Dancer Pr.

Rinpoche, Khenpo P. Ceaseless Echoes of the Great Silence: A Commentary on the Heart Sutra Prajnaparamito. Taylor, Phyllis & Kaye, Joan, eds. Rinpoche, Khenpo T., tr. from TIB. (Illus.). 102p. (Orig.). (C). 1993. pap. text 17.00 (*1-880975-01-7*) Sky Dancer Pr.

— Door to Inconceivable Wisdom & Compassion. Bialick, Craig & Kaye, Joan, eds. Rinpoche, Khenpo T., tr. 176p. (Orig.). Date not set. pap. text 17.00 (*1-880975-03-3*) Sky Dancer Pr.

Rinpoche, Khenpo T., jt. auth. see Rinpoche, Khenchen P.

Rinpoche, Khenpo T., tr. see Rinpoche, Khenpo P.

Rinpoche, Khunu. Vast As the Heavens, Deep As the Sea: Verses in Praise of Bodhicitta. LC 98-40886. 151p. 1999. pap. 16.95 (*0-86171-146-7*, Pub. by Wisdom MA) Natl Bk Netwk.

Rinpoche, Kunga, tr. see Milarepa.

Rinpoche, Lama Kunga, jt. auth. see Carnahan, Sumner.

Rinpoche, Lama Thubten Zopa. The Door to Satisfaction: The Heart Advice of a Tibetan Buddhist Master. Cameron, Ailsa & Courtin, Robina, eds. LC 93-35945. 184p. 1994. pap. 12.50 (*0-86171-058-4*) Wisdom MA.

— Transforming Problems into Happiness. Cameron, Ailsa & Courtin, Robina, eds. LC 92-1423. 104p. 1994. pap. 11.95 (*0-86171-038-X*) Wisdom MA.

Rinpoche, Lama Thubten Zopa, jt. auth. see Yeshe, Lama Thubten.

Rinpoche, Lama Thubten Zopa, tr. see Dalai Lama XIV.

Rinpoche, Lama Zopa, jt. auth. see Yeshe, Lama Thubten.

Rinpoche, Nyshul K. Natural Great Perfection: Dzogchen Teachings & Vajra Songs. Das, Surya, ed. LC 95-15875. 204p. 1995. 14.95 (*1-55939-049-2*) Snow Lion Pubns.

Rinpoche, Orgyen T. The Life & Teachings of Chokgyur Lingpa. 62p. 1996. pap. 7.95 (*962-7341-03-7*, Pub. by Rang Jung Yshe) Bookpeople.

Rinpoche, Pabongka. Liberation in the Palm of Your Hand: A Concise Discourse on the Stages of the Path to Enlightenment. Rinpoche, Trijang, ed. Richards, Michael, tr. from TIB. LC 97-19285. 1997. pap. 24.95 (*0-86171-126-2*) Wisdom MA.

Rinpoche, Palden S. & Rinpoche, Tsewang D. Lion's Gaze: A Commentary on Tsig Sum Nedek. Kaye, Joan, ed. Harding, Sara, tr. from TIB. (Illus.). 216p. 1998. mass mkt. write for info. (*1-880975-05-X*) Sky Dancer Pr.

Rinpoche, Patrul. The Heart Treasure of the Enlightened Ones. LC 91-52593. 240p. (Orig.). 1993. pap. 17.00 (*0-87773-493-3*, Pub. by Shambhala Pubns) Random.

— The Words of My Perfect Teacher. 1994. pap. 26.95 (*0-7619-8996-X*) Sage.

— The Words of My Perfect Teacher. rev. ed. LC 98-22526. 1998. pap. 25.00 (*1-57062-412-7*, Pub. by Shambhala Pubns) Random.

— The Words of My Perfect Teacher. 2nd ed. LC 98-23830. (Sacred Literature Ser.). 512p. 1998. pap. 24.95 (*0-7619-9027-5*) AltaMira Pr.

— The Words of My Perfect Teacher. 2nd ed. LC 98-23830. (Sacred Literature Ser.). 512p. 1998. 69.00 (*0-7619-9026-7*) AltaMira Pr.

— The Words of My Perfect Teacher: Kunzang Lama'i Shelung. Association Padmakara Staff, tr. from TIB. LC 93-37175. (Sacred Literature Ser.). 1994. 32.00 (*0-06-066449-5*) Harper SF.

Rinpoche, Ringu T. The Boy Who Had a Dream: A Nomadic Folk Tale from Tibet. (Illus.). 32p. (Orig.). (J). 1995. pap. 10.95 (*1-899171-10-X*, Pub. by Findhorn Pr) Words Distrib.

Rinpoche, Sogyal. Glimpse After Glimpse: Daily Reflections on Living & Dying. Gaffney, Patrick, ed. LC 94-41924. 384p. 1995. pap. 13.00 (*0-06-251126-2*, Pub. by Harper SF) HarpC.

— Meditation. LC 94-13757. (Little Book of Wisdom Ser.). 96p. 1994. pap. 10.00 (*0-06-251114-9*, Pub. by Harper SF) HarpC.

— The Tibetan Book of Living & Dying: A New Spiritual Classic from One of the Foremost Interpreters of Tibetan Buddhism to the West. LC 90-56214. (Illus.). 448p. 1994. reprint ed. pap. 17.00 (*0-06-250834-2*, Pub. by Harper SF) HarpC.

— The Tibetan Book of Living & Dying: New Spiritual Classic from One of the Foremost Interpreters of Tibetan Buddhism. LC 90-56214. 448p. 1992. 28.00 (*0-06-250793-1*, Pub. by Harper SF) HarpC.

Rinpoche, Thrangu. Buddha Nature. 128p. 1996. pap. 14.00 (*962-7341-17-7*, Pub. by Rang Jung Yshe) Bookpeople.

— King of Samadhi. 192p. 1996. pap. 17.00 (*962-7341-19-3*, Pub. by Rang Jung Yshe) Bookpeople.

Rinpoche, Trijang, ed. see Rinpoche, Pabongka.

Rinpoche, Tsewang D., jt. auth. see Rinpoche, Palden S.

Rinpoche, Tulka T., et al. The Practice of Dzogchen. 2nd ed. Talbott, Harold, ed. LC 88-39545. Vol. 3. 488p. 1989. pap. 22.95 (*1-55939-054-9*) Snow Lion Pubns.

Rinpoche, Tulku U. Rainbow Painting. 192p. 1996. pap. 20.00 (*962-7341-22-3*, Pub. by Rang Jung Yshe) Bookpeople.

— Repeating the Words of the Buddha. 112p. 1996. pap. 12.95 (*962-7341-16-9*, Pub. by Rang Jung Yshe) Bookpeople.

Rinschler, Geri, ed. Cranbrook Reflections: A Culinary Collection. (Illus.). 208p. 1991. 19.95 (*0-9628714-0-0*) Cranbrook Hse.

Rinser, Luise. Abelard's Love (Abaelards Liebe) Snook, Jean M., tr. LC 97-14767. (European Women Writers Ser.). xvii, 154p. 1998. pap. 15.00 (*0-8032-8968-5*); text 40.00 (*0-8032-3914-9*) U of Nebr Pr.

— Bruder Feuer. (GER.). 128p. 1995. pap. 10.00 (*3-596-22124-2*, Pub. by Fischer Tasch) Intl Bk Import.

— Daniela. (GER.). 1995. pap. 13.50 (*3-596-21116-6*, Pub. by Fischer Tasch) Intl Bk Import.

— Prison Journal. LC 90-200783. viii, 151p. 1987. write for info. (*0-333-44968-1*) Macmillan.

Rinsky, Lee A. Vocabulary Strategies for Success. (C). 1995. pap. text 43.00 (*0-15-502134-6*, Pub. by Harcourt Coll Pubs) Harcourt.

— Vocabulary Strategies for Success. (C). 1996. pap. text, teacher ed. 28.00 (*0-15-502137-0*) Harcourt Coll Pubs.

Rinsky, Lee Ann. Teaching Word Recognition Skills. 6th ed. 220p. (C). 1996. pap. text 49.00 (*0-13-776865-6*) P-H.

Rinsland, Henry D. Analysis of Completion Sentences & Arithmetical Problems As Items for Intelligence Tests. LC 73-177192. (Columbia University. Teachers College. Contributions to Education Ser.: No. 666). reprint ed. 37.50 (*0-404-55666-3*) AMS Pr.

Rinsley, Donald B. Borderline & Other Self Disorders. LC 81-20538. 336p. 1982. 50.00 (*0-87668-447-9*) Aronson.

— Developmental Pathogenesis & Treatment of Borderline & Narcissistic Personalities. LC 89-17506. 192p. 1989. 35.00 (*0-87668-828-8*) Aronson.

— Treatment of the Severely Disturbed Adolescent. LC 80-66922. 368p. 1983. 45.00 (*0-87668-415-0*) Aronson.

— Treatment of the Severely Disturbed Adolescent. LC 80-66922. 364p. 1994. pap. 45.00 (*1-56821-222-4*) Aronson.

Rinsley, Donald B., jt. auth. see Grotstein, James S.

Rinsley, Donald B., jt. ed. see Grotstein, James S.

Rintala, J., et al, eds. Industrial Wastewaters '89-Nairobi: Proceedings of the First IAWPRC East African Regional Conference on Industrial Wastewaters, held in Nairobi, Kenya, 25-28 October 1989. (Water Science & Technology Ser.). (Illus.). 120p. 1991. pap. 65.00 (*0-08-041139-8*, Pergamon Pr) Elsevier.

Rintala, Marvin. The Constitution of Silence: Essays on Generational Themes. 25. LC 78-20018. (Contributions in Political Science Ser.: No. 25). 95p. 1979. 55.00 (*0-313-20723-2*, RCS/, Greenwood Pr) Greenwood.

— Lloyd George & Churchill: How Friendship Changed Politics. LC 94-27342. 1994. 27.95 (*1-56833-031-6*) Madison Bks UPA.

Rintelmann, William F. & Musiek, Frank E. Contemporary Perspectives in Hearing Assessment. 3rd ed. LC 98-55568. 518p. (C). 1999. pap. text 77.00 incl. audio compact disk, disk (*0-205-27457-9*, Macmillan Coll) P-H.

Rintels, David W. Andersonville: Screenplay by David W. Rintels. (Illus.). 240p. (Orig.). (C). 1996. pap. 14.95 (*0-8071-2088-X*) La State U Pr.

Rintoul. Ontario Estate Administration: A Guide for Legal Secretaries & Law Clerks. 2nd ed. 184p. 1991. spiral bd. 44.00 (*0-409-90377-9*, MICHIE) LEXIS Pub.

— The Solicitor's Guide to Estate Practice in Ontario. 2nd ed. 288p. 1990. 65.00 (*0-409-89336-6*, MICHIE) LEXIS Pub.

Rintoul, David. A Student's Companion T - A Molecular Cell Biology. (Illus.). 448p. (C). 1990. 18.40 (*0-7167-2110-4*) W H Freeman.

Rintoul, M. C. Dictionary of Real People & Places in Fiction. LC 92-46092. 1200p. (C). (gr. 13). 1993. 200.00 (*0-415-05999-2*, A6963) Routledge.

Rintoul, Mary & West, Bernard. Back in Ten Minutes: Easy Everyday Exercises to Keep Your Back Strong & Supple. 1995. pap. 13.95 (*0-14-023482-9*, Pub. by Pnguin Bks Ltd) Trafalgar.

Rintoul, R. F., ed. Farquharson's Textbook of Operative Surgery. 8th ed. LC 94-43499. 714p. 1995. text 189.00 (*0-443-04712-X*) Church.

Rintoul, William. Drilling Through Time: Seventy-Five Years with California's Division of Oil & Gas. Hodgson, Susan F., ed. LC 90-81141. (Illus.). 200p. 1990. 10.00 (*0-9627124-0-X*) CA Div Oil Gas.

***Rintoul, William.** Drilling Through Time: 75 Years with California's Division of Oil & Gas. Hodgson, Susan F., ed. (Illus.). 178p. 2000. reprint ed. 25.00 (*0-7881-8743-0*) DIANE Pub.

Rinvolucri. Q Book. Date not set. pap. text. write for info. (*0-582-79606-7*, Pub. by Addison-Wesley) Longman.

Rinvolucri, Mario. Anatomy of a Church: Greek Orthodoxy Today. LC 66-30071. 192p. reprint ed. pap. 59.60 (*0-7837-0468-2*, 204079100018) Bks Demand.

— Grammar Games: A Resource Book for Teachers. (Illus.). 144p. 1985. pap. text 19.95 (*0-521-27773-6*) Cambridge U Pr.

Rinvolucri, Mario & Morgan, John. Vocabulary. Maley, Alan, ed. (Illus.). 136p. 1987. pap. text 13.95 (*0-19-437091-7*) OUP.

Rinvolucri, Mario, jt. auth. see Davis, Paul.

Rinvolucri, Mario, jt. auth. see Morgan, John.

Rinvolucri, Mario, tr. see Spatharis, Sotiris.

Rinzema, J. The Sexual Revolution: Challenge & Response. Smedes, Lewis B., tr. LC 73-14712. 107p. reprint ed. pap. 33.20 (*0-608-10749-2*, 201284900083) Bks Demand.

Rinzler, Alan, jt. ed. see Brinton, William M.

Rinzler, Alan, jt. ed. see Ray, Michael.

Rinzler, Carol A. Are You at Risk? How to Identify & Reduce Your Risk for More Than 100 Diseases & Medical Conditions. LC 90-21071. 224p. 1991. reprint ed. pap. 69.50 (*0-608-02860-6*, 206392400007) Bks Demand.

— The Complete Book of Herbs, Spices & Condiments. (Illus.). 220p. 1997. 6.98 (*1-56731-184-9*, MJF Bks) Fine Comms.

— The Complete Book of Herbs, Spices, & Condiments: From Garden to Kitchen to Medicine Chest. (Illus.). 208p. (Orig.). 1995. pap. 12.00 (*0-8050-1618-X*, Owl) H Holt & Co.

— Estrogen & Breast Cancer: A Warning to Women. 2nd rev. ed. LC 96-33977. (Illus.). 240p. 1996. pap. 14.95 (*0-89793-198-X*) Hunter Hse.

— The New Complete Book of Food: A Nutritional, Medical & Culinary Guide. LC 99-21200. 464p. 1999. 40.00 (*0-8160-3987-9*, Checkmark) Facts on File.

— Nutrition for Dummies. 2nd ed. LC 97-70747. (For Dummies Ser.). (Illus.). 410p. 1996. pap. 19.99 (*0-7645-5032-2*) IDG Bks.

***Rinzler, Carol A.** Nutrition for Dummies. 2nd ed. (For Dummies Ser.). 416p. 1999. pap. 19.99 (*0-7645-5180-9*, Dummies Trade Pr) IDG Bks.

Rinzler, Carol A. Why Eve Doesn't Have an Adam's Apple: A Dictionary of Sex Differences. LC 95-43133. (Illus.). 208p. 1996. pap. 14.95 (*0-8160-3356-0*) Facts on File.

— Why Eve Doesn't Have an Adam's Apple: A Dictionary of Sex Differences. 208p. 1996. 27.95 (*0-8160-3352-8*) Facts on File.

— The Women's Health Products Handbook: Smart Buys for Healthy Bodies. 288p. 1996. 25.95 (*0-89793-210-2*); pap. 15.95 (*0-89793-209-9*) Hunter Hse.

***Rinzler, Carol Ann.** The New Complete Book of Herbs & Spices. LC 00-32164. (Illus.). 2001. write for info. (*0-8160-4152-0*) Facts on File.

— Quick & Healthy Cooking for Dummies. 384p. 2000. pap. 19.99 (*0-7645-5214-7*) IDG Bks.

— The Wordsworth Book of Herbs & Spices: A Tasty Guide for Cooks, Gardeners & All Healthy Eaters. (Illus.). 199p. 2000. reprint ed. pap. text 20.00 (*0-7881-9152-7*) DIANE Pub.

Rinzler, Michael. Public Sector Jobs. 1992. pap. write for info. (*0-201-52230-6*) Addison-Wesley.

Rinzler, Paul E. Jazz Arranging & Performance Practice: A Guide for Small Ensembles. (Illus.). 178p. 1989. 24.00 (*0-8108-2257-1*) Scarecrow.

***Rinzler, Paul E.** Jazz Arranging & Performance Practice: A Guide for Small Ensembles. (Illus.). 184p. 1999. pap. 26.50 (*0-8108-3689-0*) Scarecrow.

Rinzler, Susan, jt. auth. see Mair, Nancy.

Rio, A. del, see del Rio, A.

Rio, Carmen D. Jorge Luis Borges y la Ficcion: El Conocimiento Como Invencion. LC 82-84262. (SPA.). 192p. (Orig.). 1983. pap. text 12.95 (*0-89729-325-8*) Ediciones.

Rio, Eduardo Del, see RIUS Staff & Del Rio, Eduardo.

Rio, Fernando Del, see Del Rio, Fernando.

Rio Ignacio, Del, see Del Rio, Ignacio.

Rio, Michel. Parrot's Perch. Hafrey, Leigh, tr. from FRE. LC 85-744. 96p. 1985. 10.95 (*0-15-170964-5*) Harcourt.

***Rio, Nela.** Tunel de Proa Verde: Tunnel of the Green Prow. (SPA & ENG.). 1998. 10.95 (*0-921411-80-4*) Genl Dist Srvs.

Rio, Pablo Del, see Del Rio, Pablo.

***Rio, Raul.** Ingles en Action.Tr. of English in Action. (SPA.). xi, 405p. 1999. pap. 35.00 (*0-9675471-0-5*) English in Action.

Rioja, Jose A. Dictionary of Symbols & Myths: Diccionario de Simbolos y Mitos. 3rd ed. (ENG & SPA.). 436p. 1988. pap. 29.95 (*0-7859-4965-8*) Fr & Eur.

Riojas, Jesse R., jt. auth. see Featherstone, Robert.

Riolo, et al. An Atlas of Craniofacial Growth. (Craniofacial Growth Ser.: Vol. 2). (Illus.). 379p. 1979. reprint ed. 65.00 (*0-929921-01-1*) UM CHGD.

Riolo, Robert. Forty-Two Sure Ways to Become an Unsuccessful Actor. (Illus.). 37p. (Orig.). 1988. pap. 4.95 (*0-9620323-0-1*) WOW Enter.

Riols, Noreen. Before the Dawn. LC 96-7253. (House of Annanbrae Ser.: Bk. 3). 320ep. 1996. pap. 10.99 (*0-89107-872-X*) Crossway Bks.

— My Unknown Child. LC 99-12862. 208p. 1999. pap. text 10.99 (*1-57673-466-8*) Multnomah Pubs.

— Where Hope Shines Through. large type ed. LC 94-4323. (House of Annanbrae Ser.: Vol. 1). 320p. 1994. pap. 10.99 (*0-89107-790-1*) Crossway Bks.

— Where Hope Shines Through. large type ed. LC 97-18506. (Inspirational Ser.). 492p. 1997. lib. bdg. 21.95 (*0-7838-8225-4*, G K Hall Lrg Type) Mac Lib Ref.

— Where Love Endures. LC 97-27307. (House of Annanbrae Ser.: Vol. 4). 304p. 1997. pap. 10.99 (*0-89107-779-0*) Crossway Bks.

— Where Love Endures. 1998. 22.95 (*0-7862-1368-X*) Five Star.

Rion, Michael. Responsible Manager: Practical Strategies for Ethical Decision Making. 1996. pap. text 19.95 (*0-87425-351-9*) HRD Press.

Rion, Rosana, jt. auth. see Mott, Brian.

Rionero, S., ed. Waves & Stability in Continuous Media. 444p. (C). 1991. text 118.00 (*981-02-0554-6*) World Scientific Pub.

Rionero, S. & Ruggeri, T. Waves Stability in Continuous Media: Proceedings of the 7th International Conference. 448p. 1994. text 112.00 (*981-02-1878-8*) World Scientific Pub.

Rionero, S., jt. auth. see Flavin, M. N.

Rionero, S., jt. auth. see Galdi, Giovanni P.

Rioni, S. G., ed. Politics & Economics of Hong Kong. LC 93-103974. 247p. 1997. lib. bdg. 85.00 (*1-56072-497-8*) Nova Sci Pubs.

Riopedre, Jorge A. Cubanacan (Decimas Cubanas) LC 79-90276. (Coleccion Espejo de Paciencia). (Illus.). 1979. pap. 3.50 (*0-89729-238-3*) Ediciones.

Riopel, James. Organismal Biology. 222p. (C). 1998. spiral bd. 28.95 (*0-7872-5663-3*, 41566304) Kendall-Hunt.

***Riopelle, Christopher.** Brush with Nature: The Gere Collection of Landscape Oil. 168p. 1999. 40.00 (*0-300-07928-1*) Yale U Pr.

Riordan. Agayul/Our Way of Making Prayer: Kegginaqut, Kangiit-llu/Yup'ik Masks & the Stories They Tell. LC 95-25849. (ENG & ESK., Illus.). 272p. 1996. pap. 14.95 (*0-295-97509-1*) U of Wash Pr.

— The Coming of Night: A Yoruba Tale from West Africa. LC 98-24261. (Illus.). 32p. (J). (gr. k-3). 1999. lib. bdg. 21.40 (*0-7613-1358-3*, Copper Beech Bks) Millbrook Pr.

— Technical Report Writing, 6 vols. (C). 1995. pap., teacher ed., suppl. ed. 11.96 (*0-395-73053-8*) HM.

— Technical Report Writing, 6 vols. 6th ed. (C). 1995. pap. text 46.36 (*0-395-73052-X*) HM.

Riordan, ed. Equality & Achievement. (C). 1997. pap. text, wbk. ed. write for info. incl. disk (*0-673-99270-5*) Addson-Wesley Educ.

Riordan, jt. auth. see Pauley, Steven E.

Riordan, Barbara, jt. auth. see Riordan, Lee A.

Riordan, Barbara, ed. see Riordan, Lee.

Riordan, Colin. Contemporary German Writers. 200p. 1995. 14.95 (*0-7083-1289-6*, Pub. by Univ Wales Pr) Paul & Co Pubs.

— Green Thought in German Culture. 312p. 1998. 75.00 (*0-7083-1421-X*, Pub. by Univ Wales Pr) Paul & Co Pubs.

— Jurek Becker. Williams, Rhys, ed. LC 99-165380. (Contemporary German Writers Ser.). 154 p. 1998. pap. 16.95 (*0-7083-1456-2*, Pub. by Univ Wales Pr) Paul & Co Pubs.

Riordan, Colin, ed. see Schneider, Peter.

Riordan, Cornelius H. Equality & Achievement. LC 96-34352. 320p. (C). 1997. pap. text 61.33 (*0-673-99269-1*) Longman.

— Girls & Boys in School: Together or Separate? 200p. (C). 1989. text 14.95 (*0-8077-2993-0*) Tchrs Coll.

Riordan, Cornelius H., et al. Introductory Sociology Workbook & Disk. 2nd ed. 150p. 1997. pap. text 27.40 (*0-321-02272-6*) Addison-Wesley.

Riordan-Eva, Paul, jt. ed. see Acheson, James M.

Riordan, Francis E. Concept of Love in the French Catholic Literary Revival. LC 76-94183. (Catholic University of America. Studies in Romance Languages & Literatures: No. 42). reprint ed. 37.50 (*0-404-50342-X*) AMS Pr.

Riordan, Hugh D. Medical Mavericks, Vol. 1. LC 88-63321. 102p. (Orig.). 1988. pap. 7.95 (*0-942333-07-1*) Bio-Comns Pr.

— Medical Mavericks, Vol. 2. LC 88-63321. 120p. (Orig.). 1989. pap. 7.95 (*0-942333-09-8*) Bio-Comns Pr.

Riordan, J. Sport & International Politics. LC 98-189017. x, 227 p. 1998. 65.00 (*0-419-21440-2*, E & FN Spon) Routledge.

Riordan, James. Favorite Stories of the Ballet. LC 84-42778. (Illus.). 128p. (J). (gr. 4 up). 14.95 (*1-56288-252-X*) Checkerboard.

***Riordan, James.** Korean Folk-Tales. 144p. (YA). 2000. pap. 12.95 (*0-19-521673-3*) OUP.

Riordan, James. Little Bunny Bobkin. LC 98-15771. (Illus.). 32p. (J). (ps-1). 1999. 14.95 (*1-888444-38-X*) Little Tiger.

— My G-r-r-r-reat Uncle Tiger. LC 95-13109. (Illus.). (J). (ps-3). 1995. 14.95 (*1-56145-110-X*) Peachtree Pubs.

***Riordan, James.** My Gr-r-r-reat Uncle Tiger. (Illus.). 32p. (J). (ps-2). 2000. pap. 6.95 (*1-56145-228-9*) Peachtree Pubs.

Riordan, James. Russia & the Commonwealth of Independent States. (Countries Ser.). (Illus.). 48p. (J). (gr. 5 up). 1999. lib. bdg. 21.00 (*0-382-24378-1*) Silver Burdett Pr.

***Riordan, James.** Russian Myths & Legends. (Oxford Myths & Legends Ser.). (Illus.). 96p. (YA). 2001. 19.95 (*0-19-274536-0*) OUP.

Riordan, James. Stone: The Controversies, Excesses & Exploits of a Radical Filmmaker. LC 94-5661. (Illus.). 640p. (J). 1995. 24.95 (*0-7868-6026-X*, Pub. by Hyperion) Time Warner.

— The Sun Maiden & the Crescent Moon: Siberian Folk Tales. LC 90-42586. (International Folk Tale Ser.). 224p. 1991. 24.95 (*0-940793-66-0*); pap. 11.95 (*0-940793-65-2*) Interlink Pub.

— Tales from the Arabian Nights. LC 84-62456. (Illus.). 128p. (J). (gr. 4 up). 1985. 14.95 (*1-56288-258-9*) Checkerboard.

— Tales of King Arthur. LC 81-86152. (Illus.). 128p. (J). (gr. 4-7). 1982. 14.95 (*1-56288-251-1*) Checkerboard.

— Twelve Labors of Hercules. LC 97-10182. (Illus.). 64p. (J). (gr. 3 up). 1997. lib. bdg. 22.40 (*0-7613-0315-4*) Millbrook Pr.

Riordan, James, as told by. Korean Folk Tales. (Myths & Legends Ser.). (Illus.). 144p. (YA). (gr. 5-12). 1994. pap. 12.95 (*0-19-274160-8*) OUP.

Riordan, James, ed. Soviet Education: The Gifted & the Handicapped. 240p. (C). 1988. lib. bdg. 55.00 (*0-415-00574-4*) Routledge.

— Soviet Youth Culture. LC 88-13487. (Illus.). 158p. 1989. 31.50 (*0-253-35423-4*) Ind U Pr.

— Sport under Communism: A Comparative Study. 1978. 24.95 (*0-7735-0505-9*, Pub. by McG-Queens Univ Pr) CUP Services.

— Sport under Communism: The U.S.S.R., Czechoslovakia, the G.D.R., China, Cuba. 1982. pap. 27.95 (*0-7735-0533-4*, Pub. by McG-Queens Univ Pr) CUP Services.

Riordan, James, tr. Russian Gypsy Tales. LC 92-7316. (International Folk Tale Ser.). (Illus.). 160p. 1992. pap. 11.95 (*0-940793-97-0*) Interlink Pub.

***Riordan, James & Jones, Robin.** Sport & Physical Education in China. LC 98-51481. 1999. write for info. (*0-419-24750-5*, E & FN Spon) Routledge.

R

R

Riordan, James & Jones, Robin. Sport & Physical Education in China. LC 98-51481. (ISCPES Book Ser.). 1999. pap. write for info. (*0-419-22030-5*) Thomson Learn.

*__Riordan, James & Kruger, Arnd, eds.__ European Cultures in Sport: Examining the Nations & Regions. 192p. 2000. text 34.95 (*1-84150-014-3*, Pub. by Intellect) Cromland.

Riordan, James & Prochnicky, Jerry. Break on Through: The Life & Death of Jim Morrison. (Illus.). 544p. 1992. pap. 15.00 (*0-688-11915-8*, Quil) HarperTrade.

Riordan, James, jt. ed. see Kon, Igor S.

Riordan, James, jt. ed. see Kruger, Arnd.

Riordan, James, tr. see Tolstoy, Leo.

Riordan, James F., et al, eds. Metallobiochemistry, Pt. A. (Methods in Enzymology Ser.: Vol. 158). 464p. 1988. text 146.00 (*0-12-182059-9*) Acad Pr.

Riordan, Jan & Auerbach, Kathleen. Breastfeeding & Human Lactation. 2nd ed. LC 98-3502. (Nursing Ser.). 704p. Date not set. 89.95 (*0-7637-0545-4*) Jones & Bartlett.

*__Riordan, Jan & Auerbach, Kathleen G.__ Breastfeeding & Human Lactation. 2nd ed. (Illus.). (C). 1998. pap. text, student ed. 22.50 (*0-7637-0829-1*) JB Pubns.

Riordan, Jan & Auerbach, Kathleen G. Resource Guide to Accompany Breastfeeding & Human Lactation. LC 96-175925. 1996. pap. 40.00 (*0-7637-0220-X*) Jones & Bartlett.

Riordan, Janice, jt. auth. see Auerbach, Kathleen.

Riordan, Janice, jt. auth. see Auerbach, Kathleen G.

Riordan, Jim & Bridger, Sue, eds. Dear Comrade Editor: Readers' Letters to the Soviet Press. LC 91-20441. 251p. reprint ed. pap. 77.90 (*0-608-09359-9*, 205410500002) Bks Demand.

Riordan, Jim & Kruger, Arnd, eds. The International Politics of Sport In the 20th Century. LC 98-41234. (Illus.). 224p. 1996. pap. write for info. (*0-419-21160-8*, E & FN Spon) Routledge.

Riordan, Jim, tr. see Mikulsky, K.

Riordan, John. Clinical Audit in Mental Health: Toward a Multidisciplinary Approach. LC 96-48521. 182p. 1997. pap. 47.00 (*0-471-96332-1*) Wiley.

— An Introduction to Combinatorial Analysis. LC 80-337. (Illus.). 254p. 1978. reprint ed. pap. 78.80 (*0-608-07174-9*, 206739900009) Bks Demand.

Riordan, John & Cotliar, William. Complying with FDA Good Manufacturing Requirements: How to Develop Your Quality System Manual. 253p. 1991. pap. 195.00 (*0-910275-53-X*, GMP1-209) Assn Adv Med Instrn.

Riordan, John C. The Art Collection at Potsdam. (Illus.). 118p. (Orig.). 1982. pap. 10.00 (*0-942746-04-X*) SUNYP R Gibson.

Riordan, John J. & Cotliar, William. How to Develop Your GMP QC Manual. 253p. pap. write for info. (*0-914176-20-X*) Wash Busn Info.

*__Riordan-Karlson, Mary.__ Teaching Reading Across the Curriculum. (Illus.). 240p. (J). (gr. 3-8). 1999. pap., teacher ed. 24.95 (*1-57690-466-0*, TCM2466) Tchr Create Mat.

Riordan, Kevin. Misdirection. (Adventure Ser.: No. 1). (Orig.). 1994. pap. 10.00 (*1-888636-04-1*) Sara Ranchouse.

*__Riordan-Kirlsson, Mary.__ The Process of Writing. (Illus.). 76p. 1999. pap., teacher ed. 9.95 (*1-57690-473-3*, TCM2473) Tchr Create Mat.

Riordan, Lee. Jishin: Lives Shattered, Love Discovered amid the Great Tokyo Quake. Riordan, Barbara, ed. LC 96-61136. (Illus.). 278p. (Orig.). 1997. pap. 15.00 (*4-900737-40-2*, Pub. by Yen Bks) Tuttle Pubng.

Riordan, Lee A. & Riordan, Barbara. College Bred or a Four Year Loaf. LC 87-60675. 264p. (Orig.). 1987. pap. 6.95 (*0-9618266-0-6*); lib. bdg. 9.95 (*0-9618266-1-4*) L Riordan.

Riordan, M. Lepton & Photon Interaction at High Energies. 556p. (C). 1990. pap. 48.00 (*981-02-0216-4*); text 130.00 (*981-02-0104-4*) World Scientific Pub.

Riordan, M. Minette, ed. see Yochum, Mary H.

Riordan, Mark. Windows NT Power User's Toolkit. (Illus.). 448p. 1996. pap. text 49.95 incl. cd-rom (*0-07-912301-5*) McGraw.

Riordan, Michael. The Day after Midnight: The Effects of Nuclear War. LC 82-9538. (Illus.). 143p. (Orig.). 1982. reprint ed. pap. 44.40 (*0-7837-9010-4*, AU0046200004) Bks Demand.

— The Hunting of the Quark: A True Story of Modern Physics. LC 87-16530. (Touchstone Book Ser.). (Illus.). 400p. reprint ed. pap. 124.00 (*0-7837-3745-9*, AU0043300010) Bks Demand.

Riordan, Michael & Hoddeson, Lillian. Crystal Fire: The Birth of the Information Age. LC 96-47464. (Illus.). 352p. 1997. 27.50 (*0-393-04124-7*) Norton.

— Crystal Fire: The Invention of the Transistor & the Birth of the Information Age. (Illus.). 368p. 1998. pap. 15.00 (*0-393-31851-6*, Norton Paperbks) Norton.

Riordan, Michael, jt. auth. see Anderson, Bruce.

Riordan, nice, jt. auth. see Auerbach, Kathleen G.

Riordan, P. H., ed. Geology of Asbestos Deposits: Sponsored by Industrial Minerals Division of SME-AIME, Society of Economic Geologists. fac. ed. LC 80-52898. (Illus.). 126p. 1981. reprint ed. pap. 39.10 (*0-7837-7858-9*, 204761700007) Bks Demand.

Riordan, Patrick. The Practical Philosophy of Oswald Schwemmer. 128p. (Orig.). (C). 1991. pap. text 19.50 (*0-8191-8181-1*); lib. bdg. 44.00 (*0-8191-8180-3*) U Pr of Amer.

Riordan, Pauline & Bourget, Paul G. World Weather Extremes. (Illus.). 77p. (Orig.). (C). 1994. pap. text 25.00 (*0-7881-1537-5*) DIANE Pub.

*__Riordan, Rebecca.__ Designing Relational Database Systems. LC 99-40791. 525p. 1999. pap. 49.99 (*0-7356-0634-X*) Microsoft.

— Microsoft SQL Server 2000 Programming Step by Step. 400p. 2000. pap. 49.99 (*0-7356-1142-4*) Microsoft.

Riordan, Rick. Big Red Tequilla. 400p. 1997. mass mkt. 5.99 (*0-553-57644-5*) Bantam.

— The Gunman's Cantina. 2001. mass mkt. 5.99 (*0-553-57991-6*) Bantam.

*__Riordan, Rick.__ The Last King of Texas. LC 99-46460. 304p. 2000. 23.95 (*0-553-80156-2*) Bantam.

Riordan, Rick. The Widower's Two-Step. 416p. 1998. mass mkt. 5.99 (*0-553-57645-3*) Bantam.

Riordan, Robert M., ed. see Nature Conservancy Council Staff.

Riordan, Stephen J., IV. Government Advanced Open Water Diver Instructor Manual. 16p. 1994. pap. text. write for info. (*1-880229-18-8*) Concept Sys.

Riordan, Timothy. In a Fluid State: Poems. 135p. 1998. pap. 15.00 (*0-9625817-2-0*) In Hse Bks.

Riordan, Timothy M. Lesser Bird of Paradise: Selected Poems, 1979-1989. (Illus.). 115p. (Orig.). 1990. pap. 19.95 (*0-9625817-0-4*) In Hse Bks.

— Portfolio Breeches: A Poem. 21p. (Orig.). 1988. pap. 10.00 (*0-9625817-1-2*) In Hse Bks.

Riordan, William L. Plunkitt of Tammany Hall. 101p. reprint ed. lib. bdg. 17.95 (*0-88411-977-7*) Amereon Ltd.

— Plunkitt of Tammany Hall. 1993. reprint ed. lib. bdg. 14.95 (*1-56849-215-4*) Buccaneer Bks.

— Plunkitt of Tammany Hall: A Series of Very Plain Talks on Very Practical Politics. (C). 1995. mass mkt. 5.95 (*0-451-52620-1*) NAL.

— Plunkitt of Tammany Hall: A Series of Very Plain Talks On Very Practical Politics. McDonald, Terrence J., ed. LC 92-72221. (Books in American History). 160p. (C). 1993. text 35.00 (*0-312-09666-6*) St Martin.

— Plunkitt of Tammany Hall: A Series of Very Plain Talks On Very Practical Politics. McDonald, Terrence J., ed. LC 92-72221. (Books in American History). 148p. (C). 1993. pap. text 11.95 (*0-312-08444-7*) St Martin.

Riordon, William L. Honest Graft: The World of George Washington Plunkitt. rev. ed. Olson, James S. et al, eds. 176p. (C). 1997. pap. text 12.50 (*1-881089-58-4*) Brandywine Press.

Riordon, William L., ed. Honest Graft: The World of George Washington Plunkitt. (Illus.). 176p. (C). 1994. pap. text 12.50 (*1-881089-06-1*) Brandywine Press.

Rios, Alberto. The Curtain of Trees. 146p. 1999. pap. 14.95 (*0-8263-2071-6*) U of NM Pr.

*__Rios, Alberto.__ The Curtain of Trees. 146p. 1999. 29.95 (*0-8263-2070-8*) U of NM Pr.

Rios, Alberto. The Lime Orchard Woman: Poems. LC 88-18534. 94p. (Orig.). 1988. pap. 12.95 (*0-935296-77-8*, Pub. by Sheep Meadow) U Pr of New Eng.

— Whispering to Fool the Wind: Poems. LC 82-3269. 82p. (C). 1982. pap. 12.95 (*0-935296-31-X*, Pub. by Sheep Meadow) U Pr of New Eng.

*__Rios, Alberto A.__ Capirotada: A Nogales Memoir. LC 99-30583. 148p. 1999. 35.00 (*0-8263-2093-7*); pap. 15.95 (*0-8263-2094-5*) U of NM Pr.

Rios, Alberto Alvaro. The Iguana Killer: Twelve Stories of the Heart. LC 97-40680. 120p. 1998. pap. 12.95 (*0-8263-1922-X*) U of NM Pr.

— Teodoro Luna's Two Kisses. 96p. 1992. pap. 9.95 (*0-393-30809-X*) Norton.

Rios, Andres C. La Noche y la Poesia Tienen Algo Que Decir. (Aqui y Ahora Ser.). 48p. 1996. pap. 6.95 (*0-8477-0265-0*) U of PR Pr.

Rios, Asdrubal. Comentario Biblico Continente Nuevo: Mateo.Tr. of New Continent Bible Commentary: Matthew. (SPA.). 286p. 1994. 9.99 (*1-56063-757-9*, 498639); pap. 5.99 (*1-56063-756-0*, 498640) Editorial Unilit.

Rios, Barbara. Bible Pyramids. LC 97-81019. (Illus.). 112p. 1998. per. 9.95 (*1-57258-129-8*) Teach Servs.

Rios, Beatriz G., tr. see Fulbrook, Mary.

Rios-Bustamante, Antonio. Mexican Los Angeles: A Narrative & Pictorial History. (Illus.). 250p. 1990. 35.00 (*0-915745-19-4*) Floricanto Pr.

Rios-Bustamante, Antonio & Castillo, Pedro. An Illustrated History of Mexican Los Angeles, 1781-1985. (Monographs: No. 12). (Illus.). 196p. 1986. pap. 20.00 (*0-89551-053-7*) UCLA Chicano Studies.

Rios-Bustamante, Antonio & Marin, Christine, eds. Latinos in Museums: A Heritage Reclaimed. LC 97-26230. (Public History Ser.). (Illus.). 142p. (C). 1998. 19.50 (*0-89464-981-7*) Krieger.

Rios-Bustamante, Antonio, jt. auth. see Arroyo, Luis L.

Rios-Bustamante, Antonio, ed. see Anderson, Karen.

Rios-Bustamante, Antonio, ed. see Harris, Robert L., Jr.

Rios-Bustamante, Antonio, ed. see Hune, Shirley.

Rios-Bustamante, Antonio, ed. see Okihiro, Gary Y.

Rios-Bustamante, Antonio, ed. see Sanchez Korrol, Virginia.

Rios-Bustamante, Antonio, ed. see Wilson, Terry P.

Rios, Eduardo E. Life of Fray Antonio Margil De Jesus. (Illus.). 1959. 25.00 (*0-88382-254-7*) AAFH.

Rios, Emilio De Los, see De Los Rios, Emilio.

Rios-Font, Wadda C. Rewriting Melodrama: The Hidden Paradigm in Modern Spanish Theater. LC 96-47684. 240p. 1997. 36.50 (*0-8387-5342-6*) Bucknell U Pr.

Rios, Francisco A., ed. Teacher Thinking in Cultural Contexts. LC 95-51310. (SUNY Series, the Social Context of Education). 400p. (C). 1996. text 59.50 (*0-7914-2881-8*); pap. text 19.95 (*0-7914-2882-6*) State U NY Pr.

Rios, Francisco Giner De Los, see Giner de Los Rios, Francisco.

*__Rios-Insua, David & Ruggeri, Fabrizio.__ Robust Bayesian Analysis. LC 00-41912. (Lecture Notes in Statistics). 2000. pap. write for info. (*0-387-98866-1*) Spr-Verlag.

Rios, Julian. Kitaj: Pictures & Conversations. LC 95-21187. (Illus.). 228p. (Orig.). 1997. pap. 24.95 (*1-55921-148-2*) Moyer Bell.

— Larva: Midsummer Night's Babel. Francis, Richard A. & Levine, Suzanne J., trs. from SPA. LC 90-3773. (Illus.). 685p. 1990. 27.50 (*0-916583-66-X*) Dalkey Arch.

*__Rios, Julian.__ Loves That Bind: A Novel. (Vintage International Ser.). 256p. 1999. pap. 12.00 (*0-375-70060-9*) Vin Bks.

Rios, Julian. Poundemonium. Francis, Richard A., tr. from SPA. LC 96-7665. (Larva Ser.: No. 2). (Illus.). 160p. (Orig.). 1997. pap. 13.50 (*1-56478-138-0*) Dalkey Arch.

Rios, M. S. & Sastre, A., eds. Dairy Products in Human Health & Nutrition: Proceedings of the First World Congress, Madrid, Spain, June 1993. (Illus.). 700p. (C). 1994. text 128.00 (*90-5410-359-0*, Pub. by A A Balkema) Ashgate Pub Co.

Rios, Manual C., jt. auth. see Lamb, F. Bruce.

Rios, Manuel. Economics I. 5th ed. 330p. (C). 1992. pap. text 28.80 (*0-536-58270-X*) Pearson Custom.

— Economics II. 4th ed. 276p. (C). 1992. pap. text 27.00 (*0-536-58266-1*) Pearson Custom.

*__Rios, Reyna.__ Destination: Love. (Encanto Ser.). 2000. mass mkt. 3.99 (*0-7860-1155-6*, Pinncle Kensgtn); mass mkt. 3.99 (*0-7860-1159-9*, Pinncle Kensgtn) Kensgtn Pub Corp.

Rios, Sixto, et al, eds. Decision Theory & Decision Analysis: Trends & Challenges. LC 94-15768. 312p. (C). 1994. lib. bdg. 127.00 (*0-7923-9466-6*) Kluwer Academic.

Rios, Stevie. Playing for Keeps. 256p. 1995. pap. 10.99 (*1-883061-07-5*) Rising AZ.

*__Rios, Theodore & Sands, Kathleen Mullen.__ Telling a Good One: The Process of a Native American Collaborative Biography. LC 00-29920. (American Indian Lives Ser.). (Illus.). 352p. 2000. text 60.00 (*0-8032-4265-4*, Bison Books); pap. text 29.95 (*0-8032-9281-3*, Bison Books) U of Nebr Pr.

Riosley, Lane. The Attack of the Crab Nebula. (Lucky Hightops & the Cosmic Cat Patrol Ser.: No. 2). (Illus.). (Orig.). (J). (gr. 2-8). pap. 3.00 (*1-57514-268-6*, 1027) Encore Perform Pub.

— Captives of the Dog Star. (Lucky Hightops & the Cosmic Cat Patrol Ser.: No. 1). (Illus.). (J). (gr. 2-8). pap. 3.00 (*1-57514-267-8*, 1026) Encore Perform Pub.

— The Commedia Cinderella. (Commedia Plays Ser.). 26p. (Orig.). (J). 1993. pap. 3.00 (*1-57514-214-7*, 1152) Encore Perform Pub.

— Lady Elizabeth's Christmas. 29p. (Orig.). 1995. pap. 2.50 (*1-57514-220-1*, 3017) Encore Perform Pub.

— A Night at the Hotel Pyramid. 57p. (Orig.). 1993. pap. 4.00 (*1-57514-115-9*, 1151) Encore Perform Pub.

— Pecos Bill's Wild West Show. (Illus.). 22p. (Orig.). (J). (gr. k-8). 1992. pap. 3.00 (*1-57514-256-2*, 1060) Encore Perform Pub.

— Polaris, the Robot King. (Lucky Hightops & the Cosmic Cat Patrol Ser.: No. 3). (Illus.). (J). (gr. 2-8). pap. 3.00 (*1-57514-269-4*, 1028) Encore Perform Pub.

— Revenge of the Dog Robber. (Lucky Hightops & the Cosmic Cat Patrol Ser.: No. 4). (Illus.). (J). (gr. 2-8). pap. 3.00 (*1-57514-270-8*, 1116) Encore Perform Pub.

— Swords Beneath Camelot: The Quest for Excalibur. (Illus.). 23p. (Orig.). (J). (gr. 3 up). 1992. pap. 3.00 (*1-57514-264-3*, 1047) Encore Perform Pub.

Riosley, Lane & Byan, Rebecca. Game Quest. 23p. (Orig.). (J). (gr. k-6). 1993. pap. 3.00 (*1-57514-247-3*, 1136) Encore Perform Pub.

Riosley, Lane & Byars, Rebecca L. Shakespeare's Clowns. 28p. (Orig.). (J). 1994. pap. 3.00 (*1-57514-122-1*, 1078) Encore Perform Pub.

*__Riotta, Gianni.__ Prince of the Clouds. Sartarelli, Stephen, tr. from ITA. LC 99-55335. 288p. 2000. 24.00 (*0-374-23725-5*) FS&G.

Riotte, J. C. Annotated List of Ontario Lepidoptera. 1994. pap. write for info. (*0-88854-397-2*) Royal Ontario.

Riotte, Louise. Astrological Gardening: The Ancient Wisdom of Successful Planting & Harvesting by the Stars. LC 89-11987. (Illus.). 224p. 1989. pap. 11.95 (*0-88266-561-8*, Garden Way Pub) Storey Bks.

— Berries, Rasp- & Black. 1997. pap. 2.95 (*0-88266-207-4*) Storey Bks.

— Carrots Love Tomatoes: Secrets of Companion Planting for Successful Gardening. 2nd rev. ed. LC 97-31914. (Illus.). 240p. 1998. 14.95 (*1-58017-027-7*, Garden Way Pub) Storey Bks.

— Catfish Ponds & Lily Pads: Creating & Enjoying a Family Pond. LC 96-41127. (Illus.). 160p. (Orig.). 1997. pap. 12.95 (*0-88266-949-4*) Storey Bks.

— Grow the Best Strawberries. LC 98-41499. (Storey Country Wisdom Bulletin Ser.). 1998. pap. 2.95 (*1-58017-158-3*) Storey Bks.

— Planetary Planting. LC 98-5959. 1998. pap. 16.95 (*1-58017-066-8*) Storey Bks.

— Raising Animals by the Moon: Practical Advice on Breeding, Birthing, Weaning & Raising Animals in Harmony with Nature. LC 99-42376. (Illus.). 176p. 1999. pap. 14.95 (*1-58017-068-4*) Storey Bks.

— Roses Love Garlic: Companion Planting & Other Secrets of Flowers. 2nd rev. ed. LC 97-42029. (Illus.). 1998. 14.95 (*1-58017-028-5*, Garden Way Pub) Storey Bks.

— Sleeping with a Sunflower: A Treasury of Old-Time Gardening Lore. Burns, Deborah, ed. LC 87-45008. (Illus.). 224p. (Orig.). 1987. pap. 11.95 (*0-88266-502-2*, Garden Way Pub) Storey Bks.

— Successful Small Food Gardens. (Illus.). 200p. 1993. 21.95 (*0-88266-816-1*, Garden Way Pub) Storey Bks.

Riou, Ann. Paris Pas Cher '97. 874p. 1996. 24.95 (*0-7859-9363-0*) Fr & Eur.

*__Riou, Anne.__ Paris Pas Cher 2000. annuals (FRE.). 1999. pap. 39.95 (*0-320-03688-X*) Fr & Eur.

Rioux, Bernard, jt. auth. see Steed, John.

Rioux, David, ed. see Valla, Dianne.

Rioux, Frank & Foster, Judith C. Separating Selected Metal Cations by Paper Chromatography. Stanitski, C. L., ed. (Modular Laboratory Program in Chemistry Ser.). 12p. (C). 1998. pap. text 1.50 (*0-87540-498-7*, ANAL 498) Chem Educ Res.

Rioux, Jean-Pierre. The Fourth Republic, 1944-1958. Rogers, Godfrey, tr. (History of Modern France Ser.: No. 7). (Illus.). 548p. (C). 1989. pap. text 22.95 (*0-521-38916-X*) Cambridge U Pr.

— Renault. (Illus.). 600p. 1998. pap. 55.00 (*2-85025-600-5*) Gingko Press.

Rioux, Jean-Pierre, jt. auth. see Bernstein, Serge.

Rioux, Jean W., ed. Nature, the Soul, & God: A Philosopher's Approach. 152p. (C). 1995. pap. text 14.95 (*0-943025-76-1*) Cummngs & Hath.

— Plato, Aristotle, & Thomas Aquinas: An Introduction to Moral Philosophy. 118p. (Orig.). (C). 1995. pap. text 12.95 (*0-943025-77-X*) Cummngs & Hath.

Rioux, Marie-Claude, tr. see Biagi, Susan.

Rioux, Pierre. Repertoire des Deces et Seplutures Suppl. 12: Biencourt, 1932-1994, Esprit-Saint, 1937-1994, Lac-des-Aigles, 1932-1994, Saint-Guy, 1936-1994, Saint-Medard, 1929-1994, Trinite-des-Monts, 1939-1994. LC 96-22338. (FRE.). 110p. 1996. 18.00 (*2-921848-02-3*) SGEQ.

Rioux, Pierre, et al. Recensement, 1851 No. 11: District de Rimouski. (FRE.). 47p. 1996. 13.00 (*2-921848-01-5*) SGEQ.

Rip, A., ed. see Bottcher, C. J., et al.

Rip, Arie, et al, eds. Managing Technology in Society. LC 95-3879. 1995. write for info. (*1-85567-339-8*); pap. write for info. (*1-85567-340-1*) St Martin.

Ripa, Cesare. Iconologia. Mandowsky, E., ed. (Illus.). vii, 528p. 1970. reprint ed. write for info. (*3-487-02342-3*) G Olms Pubs.

Ripa, Louis W., jt. auth. see Mellberg, James R.

Ripa, Matteo. Memoirs of Father Ripa. LC 75-36239. reprint ed. 32.50 (*0-404-14487-X*) AMS Pr.

Ripamonti, Aldo, jt. auth. see Marshall, Norman F.

Riparetti, Star, ed. see Pry, Daniel J.

Ripellino, Angelo M. Magic Prague. Marinelli, David N., tr. from ITA. LC 92-11065. 1993. 40.00 (*0-520-07352-5*, Pub. by U CA Pr) Cal Prin Full Svc.

Riper, Craig Van, see Van Riper, Craig.

Riper, Frank Van, see Van Riper, Frank.

Riper, Guernsey V., Jr. Knute Rockne: Young Athlete. LC 86-10791. (Childhood of Famous Americans Ser.). (Illus.). 192p. (J). (gr. 3-7). 1986. reprint ed. per. 4.95 (*0-02-042110-9*, Pub. by Macmillan) S&S Trade.

Riper, Guernsey Van, see Van Riper, Guernsey, Jr.

Riper, Guernsey Van, see Van Riper, Guernsey.

Riper, K. A. Van, see Van Riper, K. A.

Riper, Robert Van, see Van Riper, Robert.

Ripert, Eric, jt. auth. see Le Coze, Maguy.

Riphagen, Dean. South African Fly-Fishing Handbook. 1999. 39.95 (*1-86872-147-7*) Struik Pubs.

Riphagen, Dean & Rutherford, Sally D. The South African Fly-by-Fishing Handbook. LC 99-162154. 192p. 1998. write for info. (*1-85974-101-0*, Pub. by New5 Holland) Sterling.

Riphahn, Anna. The Timekeeper. Thatch, Nancy R., ed. LC 96-12957. (Books for Students by Students). (Illus.). 29p. (J). (gr. 2-4). 1996. lib. bdg. 15.95 (*0-933849-62-1*) Landmark Edns.

Riphenburg, Carol J. Oman: Political Development in a Changing World. LC 97-33208. 264p. 1998. 59.95 (*0-275-96144-3*, Praeger Pubs) Greenwood.

Ripic, Carol S., jt. auth. see Oakley, Kenneth H.

Ripic, Carol S., ed. see Oakley, Ken.

Ripich, Danielle, et al. Dementia Grand Rounds. 150p. 1997. pap. 110.00 incl. VHS (*0-910329-98-2*, 0111023) Am Speech Lang Hearing.

Ripich, Danielle N., ed. Handbook of Geriatric Communication Disorders. LC 90-74311. 494p. 1991. text 41.00 (*0-89079-423-5*, 1944) PRO-ED.

Ripich, Danielle N. & Craighead, Nancy A., eds. School Discourse Problems. 2nd ed. LC 93-36789. (School-Age Children Ser.). 426p. (Orig.). 1994. 55.00 (*1-56593-096-7*, 0400) Thomson Learn.

Ripin, Edwin. Early Keyboard Instruments. Date not set. pap. write for info. (*0-393-30520-1*) Norton.

Ripin, Edwin M. Early Keyboard Instruments. (New Grove Musical Instrument Ser.). 1989. pap. 14.95 (*0-393-30515-5*) Norton.

Ripin, Kathy. Outsourcing Info Systems. 1997. pap. 28.95 (*0-201-63457-0*) Addison-Wesley.

Ripin, Kathy M., jt. auth. see Lugowski, Marek.

Ripin, Kevin, ed. see Carey, Diane.

Ripin, Rowena, tr. see Buhler, Charlotte M.

Ripinsky-Naxon, Michael. The Nature of Shamanism: Substance & Function of a Religious Metaphor. LC 92-5415. 289p. (C). 1993. pap. text 21.95 (*0-7914-1386-1*) State U NY Pr.

Ripka, Georges. Quarks Bound by Chiral Fields: The Quark Structure of the Vacuum & of Light Mesons & Baryons. LC 97-15622. (Oxford Studies in Nuclear Physics: No. 21). (Illus.). 222p. 1997. text 105.00 (*0-19-851784-X*) OUP.

Ripka, Georges, jt. auth. see Blaizot, Jean-Paul.

Ripka, Leslie V. Plumbing. LC 94-23444. (Illus.). 384p. 1994. 36.96 (*0-8269-0612-5*) Am Technical.

Ripke, Gustav. Beziehungen Zwischen Komplexem Denken und Kreativitat Bei Hochqualifizierten Forschern in der Chemischen Industrie. (Illus.). VIII, 123p. 1997. 32.95 (*3-631-31917-7*) P Lang Pubng.

Ripken, Cal, Jr. Cal Ripken, Jr. Play Ball! 96p. (J). (gr. 1-4). 1999. pap. 3.99 (*0-14-130184-8*, PuffinBks) Peng Put Young Read.

Ripken, Cal, Sr. The Ripken Way: A Manual for Baseball & Life. 2000. per. write for info. (*0-671-02776-X*) S&S Trade.

An Asterisk (*) at the beginning of an entry indicates that the title is appearing for the first time.

Ripken, Cal, Jr. & Brown, Greg. Count Me In. LC 95-31921. (Illus.). 40p. (J). (gr. 3-7). 1995. 14.95 (*0-87833-915-9*) Taylor Pub.

Ripken, Cal, Jr. & Bryan, Mike. The Only Way I Know. 320p. 1998. pap. 12.95 (*0-14-026626-7*) Viking Penguin.

Ripken, Cal, Sr. & Burke, Larry. The Ripken Way: A Manual for Baseball & Life. (Illus.). 234p. 1999. 22.00 (*0-671-02775-1*, PB Hardcover) PB.

***Ripken, Cal, Jr., et al.** Cal Ripken, Jr. My Story. Kane, Cindy, ed. LC 98-7799. (Illus.). 128p. (YA). (gr. 3-7). 1999. 16.99 (*0-8037-2348-2*, Dial Yng Read) Peng Put Young Read.

— Play Ball! Level 3. Wallenstein, Dena & Kane, Cindy, eds. LC 98-26366. (Illus.). 48p. (J). (gr. k-3). 1999. 13.99 (*0-8037-2415-2*, Dial Yng Read) Peng Put Young Read.

Ripkin, Don, jt. auth. see Brewer, Chris.

Ripley & Slotnick. Readings of American Government & Politcs. LC 98-13173. 442p. 1998. pap. text 36.00 (*0-205-18880-X*) Allyn.

Ripley, Alexandra. Charleston. 560p. 1982. mass mkt. 4.95 (*0-380-57729-1*, Avon Bks) Morrow Avon.

— Charleston. 560p. 1991. mass mkt. 6.50 (*0-446-36000-7*, Pub. by Warner Bks) Little.

— From Fields of Gold. 464p. 1996. mass mkt. 6.50 (*0-446-60249-3*, Pub. by Warner Bks) Little.

— From Fields of Gold. large type ed. LC 94-47560. 577p. 1995. lib. bdg. 24.95 (*0-7838-1237-X*, G K Hall Lrg Type) Mac Lib Ref.

— A Love Divine. 832p. 1997. mass mkt. 7.99 (*0-446-60472-0*, Pub. by Warner Bks); mass mkt. 215.73 (*0-446-16428-3*) Warner Bks.

— New Orleans Legacy. 496p. 1988. mass mkt. 6.99 (*0-446-34210-6*, Pub. by Warner Bks) Little.

— On Leaving Charleston. 576p. 1991. mass mkt. 6.50 (*0-446-36001-5*, Pub. by Warner Bks) Little.

Ripley, Alexandra. Scarlett: The Sequel to Margaret Mitchell's Gone with the Wind. 1991. 12.09 (*0-606-02212-0*, Pub. by Turtleback) Demco.

Ripley, Alexandra. Scarlett: The Sequel to Margaret Mitchell's Gone with the Wind. 896p. 1992. mass mkt. 6.99 (*0-446-36325-1*, Pub. by Warner Bks) Little.

— Scarlett: The Sequel to Margaret Mitchell's Gone with the Wind. deluxe limited ed. 1992. 100.00 (*0-446-51718-6*) Warner Bks.

— Scarlett: The Sequel to Margaret Mitchell's Gone with the Wind, Vol. 1. large type unabridged ed. 1992. lib. bdg. 11.97 (*0-8161-5535-6*, G K Hall Lrg Type) Mac Lib Ref.

— Scarlett: The Sequel to Margaret Mitchell's Gone with the Wind, Vol. 2. large type ed. (General Ser.). 1184p. 1992. pap. 21.95 (*0-8161-5528-3*, G K Hall Lrg Type) Mac Lib Ref.

— Scarlett: The Sequel to Margaret Mitchell's Gone with the Wind, Vol. 2. large type unabridged ed. 1992. lib. bdg. 11.97 (*0-8161-5536-4*, G K Hall Lrg Type) Mac Lib Ref.

— The Time Returns. 416p. 1996. mass mkt. 6.50 (*0-446-60258-2*, Pub. by Warner Bks) Little.

Ripley, Andy. Forfait Finance for Exporters. LC 96-44672. 208p. 1996. text 49.95 (*1-86152-036-0*) Thomson Learn.

Ripley, Ann. Death of a Garden Pest. LC 95-53296. (Louise Eldridge Mystery Ser.). 288p. 1996. text 22.95 (*0-312-14311-7*) St Martin.

— Death of a Political Plant: A Gardening Mystery. 336p. 1998. mass mkt. 5.99 (*0-553-57735-2*) Bantam.

***Ripley, Ann.** The Garden Tour Affair: A Gardening Mystery. 352p. 1999. mass mkt. 5.99 (*0-553-57736-0*) Bantam.

Ripley, Ann. Mulch. 304p. 1998. reprint ed. mass mkt. 5.99 (*0-553-57734-4*) Bantam.

Ripley, Ann. The Perennial Killer: A Gardening Mystery. LC 99-33254. 2000. 20.01 (*0-553-10694-5*) Bantam.

***Ripley, Ann.** The Perennial Killer: A Gardening Mystery. 352p. 2000. mass mkt. 5.99 (*0-553-57737-9*) Bantam Dell.

Ripley, Brian D. Spatial Statistics. LC 80-26104. (Probability & Mathematical Statistics Ser.). 272p. 1981. 159.95 (*0-471-08367-4*) Wiley.

— Stochastic Simulation. LC 86-15728. (Probability & Mathematical Statistics Ser.). 256p. 1987. 104.95 (*0-471-81884-4*) Wiley.

Ripley, Brian D. & Hjort, N. L. Pattern Recognition & Neural Networks. (Illus.). 415p. (C). 1996. text 57.95 (*0-521-46086-7*) Cambridge U Pr.

Ripley, Brian D. & Venables, W. N. Modern Applied Statistics with S-Plus, Vol. XII. rev. ed. Scott, D. W. & Sheather, S., eds. (Statistics & Computing Ser.). (Illus.). 462p. 1994. 44.95 incl. disk (*3-540-94350-1*) Spr-Verlag.

Ripley, Brian D., jt. auth. see Venables, W. N.

***Ripley, C. Peter.** Conversations with Cuba. LC 99-16371. (Illus.). 264p. 1999. 24.95 (*0-8203-2163-X*) U of Ga Pr.

Ripley, C. Peter. Richard Nixon. (World Leaders Past & Present Ser.). (Illus.). 120p. (YA). (gr. 5 up). 1987. lib. bdg. 19.95 (*0-87754-585-5*) Chelsea Hse.

— Slaves & Freedmen in Civil War Louisiana. fac. ed. LC 75-18043. 253p. 1976. reprint ed. pap. 78.50 (*0-7837-7819-8*, 204757500007) Bks Demand.

Ripley, C. Peter, ed. The Black Abolitionist Papers Vol. IV: The United States, 1847-1858. LC 84-13131. (Illus.). xxxvi, 444p. (C). 1991. 65.00 (*0-8078-1974-3*) U of NC Pr.

— Black Abolitionist Papers Vol. V: The United States, 1859-1865. LC 84-13131. (Illus.). xxviii, 436p. (C). 1992. 65.00 (*0-8078-2007-5*) U of NC Pr.

Ripley, C. Peter, et al, eds. The Black Abolitionist Papers Vol. 1: The British Isles, 1830-1865. LC 84-13131. (Illus.). xxx, 609p. 1985. 65.00 (*0-8078-1625-6*) U of NC Pr.

— The Black Abolitionist Papers Vol. II: Canada, 1830-1865. LC 84-13131. (Illus.). xviii, 560p. 1987. 65.00 (*0-8078-1698-1*) U of NC Pr.

— The Black Abolitionist Papers Vol. III: The United States, 1830-1846. LC 84-13131. (Illus.). xxx, 522p. (C). 1991. 65.00 (*0-8078-1926-3*) U of NC Pr.

— Witness for Freedom: African-American Voices on Race, Slavery, & Emancipation. LC 92-21591. (Illus.). xxvi, 306p. (C). 1993. pap. 16.95 (*0-8078-4404-7*) U of NC Pr.

Ripley, Catherine. Do the Doors Open by Magic? And Other Supermarket Questions. (Illus.). 32p. (YA). (ps-3). 1995. 14.95 (*1-895688-35-3*, Pub. by Owl Bks); pap. 5.95 (*1-895688-40-X*, Pub. by Owl Bks) Firefly Bks Ltd.

— Do the Doors Open by Magic? And Other Supermarket Questions. 1995. 11.15 (*0-606-09198-X*, Pub. by Turtleback) Demco.

— Two Dozen Dinosaurs: A First Book of Dinosaur Facts & Mysteries, Games & Fun. (Illus.). 32p. (YA). (gr. k up). 1992. pap. 5.95 (*0-920775-55-1*, Pub. by Owl Bks) Firefly Bks Ltd.

— Why Do Cows Moo? And Other Farm Animal Questions. (Questions & Answers Storybook Ser.). (Illus.). 32p. (YA). (ps up). 1998. 17.95 (*1-895688-77-9*, Pub. by Greey dePencier); pap. text 6.95 (*1-895688-78-7*, Pub. by Greey dePencier) Firefly Bks Ltd.

— Why Do Stars Twinkle? And Other Nighttime Questions. (Questions & Answers Storybook Ser.). (Illus.). 32p. (YA). (ps up). 1996. 17.95 (*1-895688-41-8*, Pub. by Owl Bks); pap. 6.95 (*1-895688-42-6*, Pub. by Owl Bks) Firefly Bks Ltd.

— Why Does Popcorn Pop? And Other Kitchen Questions. (Questions & Answers Storybook Ser.). (Illus.). 32p. (J). (gr. k up). 1997. pap. 6.95 (*1-895688-71-X*, Pub. by Owl Bks) Firefly Bks Ltd.

— Why Does Popcorn Pop? And Other Kitchen Questions. (Questions & Answers Storybook Ser.). (Illus.). 32p. (YA). (gr. k up). 1997. 17.95 (*1-895688-70-1*, Pub. by Owl Bks) Firefly Bks Ltd.

— Why Is Soap So Slippery? And Other Bathtime Questions. (Questions & Answers Storybook Ser.). (Illus.). 32p. (YA). (ps-3). 1995. 14.95 (*1-895688-34-5*, Pub. by Owl Bks) Firefly Bks Ltd.

— Why Is Soap So Slippery? And Other Bathtime Questions. (Questions & Answers Storybook Ser.). (Illus.). 32p. (YA). (ps up). 1995. pap. 5.95 (*1-895688-39-6*, Pub. by Owl Bks) Firefly Bks Ltd.

— Why Is Soap So Slippery? And Other Bathtime Questions. 1995. 11.15 (*0-606-10070-9*, Pub. by Turtleback) Demco.

— Why Is the Sky Blue? And Other Outdoor Questions, Vol. 4. (Questions & Answers Storybook Ser.). (Illus.). 32p. (YA). (ps up). 1997. 17.95 (*1-895688-43-4*, Pub. by Owl Bks); pap. 6.95 (*1-895688-44-2*, Pub. by Owl Bks) Firefly Bks Ltd.

Ripley, Clements & Ripley, Katharine B. Cities of Fear: And Other Adventure Stories. (Illus.). 380p. (Orig.). 1990. pap. 13.95 (*0-9626696-0-1*) W Ripley.

Ripley, Dillon S. A Naturalist's Adventure in Nepal: Search for the Spiny Babbler. 317p. (C). 1978. 90.00 (*0-89771-109-2*, Pub. by Ratna Pustak Bhandar) St Mut.

Ripley, Dorothy. Winter Barn. LC 93-32420. (Pictureback Ser.). (Illus.). 32p. (Orig.). (J). (ps-1). 1995. pap. 3.25 (*0-679-84472-4*, Pub. by Random Bks Yng Read) Random.

Ripley-Duggan, Edward, ed. Book Arts Collections: A Representative Selection. LC 88-15286. (Special Collections: Vol. 4, No. 1). 123p. 1989. text 3.95 (*0-86656-594-9*) Haworth Pr.

Ripley, E., jt. auth. see Barrots, W.

Ripley, E. A. & Redmann, R. E. Energy Exchange in Ecosystems. write for info. (*0-318-56694-X*) Elsevier.

Ripley, Earle A., et al. Environmental Effects of Mining. LC 95-210701. 36p. 1995. boxed set 84.95 (*1-884015-76-X*) St Lucie Pr.

Ripley, Edward H. Vermont General. Eisenschiml, Otto, ed. (Illus.). 1959. 12.50 (*0-8159-7101-X*) Devin.

Ripley, Eliza. Social Life in Old New Orleans: Being Recollections of My Girlhood. LC 75-1867. (Leisure Class in America Ser.). (Illus.). 1975. reprint ed. 26.95 (*0-405-06933-2*) Ayer.

Ripley Entertainment Editors, ed. see Mooney, Julie.

Ripley Entertainment Inc. Ripley's Believe It or Not: Wild Animals. 1992. pap. 3.50 (*0-8125-1289-8*, Pub. by Tor Bks) St Martin.

Ripley, Francis J. Mary, Mother of the Church: What Recent Popes Have Said about the Blessed Mother's Role in the Church. 1987. reprint ed. pap. 4.00 (*0-89555-094-6*) TAN Bks Pubs.

***Ripley, Francis J.** This Is the Faith. LC 98-61395. 405p. 1999. pap. 18.50 (*0-89555-642-1*, 1578) TAN Bks Pubs.

Ripley, George. The Bosom Book of George Ripley. 1998. reprint ed. pap. 5.95 (*0-916411-31-1*) Holmes Pub.

— The Compound of Alchemy. 87p. 1992. reprint ed. pap. 9.95 (*1-56459-077-1*) Kessinger Pub.

— The Compound of Alchemy. LC 77-7423. (English Experience Ser.: No. 887). 1977. reprint ed. lib. bdg. 35.00 (*90-221-0887-2*) Walter J Johnson.

— Five Preparations of the Philosopher's Mercury. 1989. reprint ed. pap. 3.95 (*1-55818-158-X*) Holmes Pub.

— The Marrow of Alchemy. Holmes, J. D., ed. 1994. reprint ed. pap. 6.95 (*1-55818-281-0*) Holmes Pub.

Ripley, J. R. Skulls of Sedona: A Tony Kozol Mystery. LC 99-21336. 188p. 2000. pap. 12.00 (*1-892339-07-2*) Bchfront Pubng.

— Stiff in the Freezer: A Tony Kozol Mystery. LC 98-6891. 72p. 1998. 19.95 (*1-892339-04-8*) Bchfront Pubng.

Ripley, Jill, ed. see Hunger, Bill.

Ripley, John. Coriolanus on Stage in England & America, 1609-1994. LC 97-36482. (Illus.). 432p. 1998. 57.50 (*0-8386-3741-8*) Fairleigh Dickinson.

Ripley, Jonathan G., jt. auth. see Greene, Michael.

Ripley, Jonathan G., jt. auth. see Greene, Michael T.

Ripley, Joseph M., Jr. The Practices & Policies Regarding Broadcasting of Opinions About Controversial Issues by Radio & Television Stations in the United States. Sterling, Christopher H., ed. LC 78-21734. (Dissertations in Broadcasting Ser.). 1980. lib. bdg. 20.95 (*0-405-11771-X*) Ayer.

Ripley, Kate, et al. Dyspraxia: Movement Development, Coordination, Organization, Sequencing, a Guide for Teachers & Parents. 112p. 1997. pap. 24.95 (*1-85346-444-9*, Pub. by David Fulton) Taylor & Francis.

Ripley, Katharine B. Sand in My Shoes: A Carolina Classic. rev. ed. 332p. 1995. pap. 13.95 (*1-878086-40-5*, Pub. by Down Home NC) Blair.

Ripley, Katharine B., jt. auth. see Ripley, Clements.

Ripley, M. M., tr. see Gautier, Theophile.

Ripley, Marie J. Your Child's Ages & Stages: 7 to 12 Year Old: Values Acquiring Stage. 1998. pap. 14.95 (*1-892794-00-4*) Carefree Pr.

Ripley, Marie J., jt. auth. see Ripley, Robert E.

Ripley, Mike. Angel Confidential. 256p. 1998. mass mkt. 8.95 (*0-00-649698-9*, Pub. by HarpC) Trafalgar.

***Ripley, Mike.** Family of Angels. unabridged large type ed. 2000. 25.95 (*0-7531-5801-9*, 158019, Pub. by ISIS Lrg Prnt) ISIS Pub.

Ripley, Mike. That Angel Look. LC 98-139581. (Bloodlines Ser.). 208p. 1998. pap. 16.95 (*1-899344-23-3*, Pub. by Do-Not Pr) Dufour.

Ripley, Mike & Jakubowski, Maxim, eds. Fresh Blood. LC 97-129992. 222p. 1997. pap. 13.95 (*1-899344-03-9*) Dufour.

— Fresh Blood II. LC 98-139596. (Bloodlines Ser.). 200p. 1998. pap. 16.95 (*1-899344-20-9*, Pub. by Do-Not Pr) Dufour.

***Ripley, Mike & Jakubowski, Maxim, eds.** Fresh Blood III. 2000. pap. 16.95 (*1-899344-52-7*, Pub. by Do-Not Pr) Dufour.

Ripley, R. Study Guide for Real Estate License Examinations. 1974. pap. 3.95 (*0-13-858753-1*, Reward) P-H.

Ripley, Randall B. American National Government & Public Policy. LC 73-10574. (Illus.). (Orig.). (C). 1974. pap. text 9.95 (*0-02-926540-1*) Free Pr.

— Congress: Process & Policy. 4th ed. (Illus.). (C). 1988. text 41.75 (*0-393-95617-2*) Norton.

— The Politics of Economic & Human Resource Development. LC 79-173977. (Policy Analysis Ser.). (C). 1972. write for info. (*0-672-51479-6*, Bobbs) Macmillan.

Ripley, Randall B. & Franklin, Grace A., eds. Policy-Making in the Federal Executive Branch. LC 74-33093. (Illus.). 1975. 27.95 (*0-02-926490-1*) Free Pr.

Ripley, Randall B. & Lindsay, James M., eds. Congress Resurgent: Foreign & Domestic Policy on Capitol Hill. LC 93-16033. (Mershon Center Series on International Security & Foreign Policy). 352p. (C). 1993. text 59.50 (*0-472-09533-1*, 09533); pap. text 20.95 (*0-472-06533-5*, 06533) U of Mich Pr.

— U. S. Foreign Policy after the Cold War. LC 97-4569. (Policy & Institutional Studies). 392p. 1997. pap. 22.95 (*0-8229-5625-X*); text 50.00 (*0-8229-3981-9*) U of Pittsburgh Pr.

Ripley, Randall B., jt. auth. see Franklin, Grace A.

Ripley, Richard. The Ridgerunner. (Orig.). 1987. pap. 11.95 (*0-9603566-4-9*) Backeddy Bks.

Ripley, Robert E. & Ripley, Marie J. How to Manage It All--Yourself, Your Company, Others. LC 88-71797. (Illus.). 290p. (C). 1988. pap. 12.95 (*0-9621133-1-X*) Carefree Pr.

— It Takes a Parent . . . to Raise a Child. 319p. 1997. pap. 29.95 (*0-9621133-9-5*, PE 104) Carefree Pr.

— Personal Empowerment - Taking Control of Your Life: Side-Roads & Main-Roads: A Trip for Discovering Your Personal Empowerment. LC 93-70693. (Illus.). 129p. 1993. pap. 19.95 (*0-9621133-2-8*, B006) Carefree Pr.

— Self-Managing Teams: Understanding Your Role As a Member Or a Leader. LC 93-70695. (Illus.). 100p. 1993. pap. 12.95 (*0-9621133-5-2*, WB011) Carefree Pr.

— Taking Control of Your Career & Quality Lifestyle: Taking Control of Your Ship on the Career Sea of Life. LC 93-70694. (Illus.). 191p. 1993. pap. 19.95 (*0-9621133-3-6*, B009) Carefree Pr.

— Training Adults: Life Long Learning. (Illus.). 180p. 1993. pap. 19.95 (*0-9621133-7-9*, WB011) Carefree Pr.

— Your Child's Ages & Stages: Ages 0 to 6. (Illus.). 161p. 1997. pap. 14.95 (*0-9621133-8-7*, PE101) Carefree Pr.

Ripley, S. Dillon. Cabinets, Lost & Found. (Connecticut Academy of Arts & Sciences Ser., Trans.: Vol. 46). 1975. pap. 29.50 (*0-685-22883-5*) Elliots Bks.

— Rails of the World: A Monograph of the Family Reunion. LC 75-619273. (Illus.). 432p. 1977. 100.00 (*0-87923-198-X*) Godine.

Ripley, S. Dillon. A Synopsis of the Birds of India & Pakistan: Together with Those of Nepal, Bhutan, Bangladesh & Sri Lanka. 2nd ed. (Illus.). 678p. 1988. text 35.00 (*0-19-562164-6*) OUP.

Ripley, S. Dillon, intro. Fire of Life: The Smithsonian Book of the Sun. (Illus.). 264p. 1981. 24.95 (*0-393-80006-7*) Norton.

Ripley, S. Dillon & Scribner, Lynette. Ornithological Books in the Yale University Library. (Illus.). 338p. 1993. reprint ed. 85.00 (*1-888262-61-3*) Martino Pubng.

Ripley, S. Dillon, jt. auth. see Ali, Salim.

Ripley, Sidney & Beenler, Bruce M. Rails of the World: A Compilation of New Information, 1975-1983 (Aves Hallidae) LC 84-600393. (Smithsonian Contribution to Zoology Ser.: No. 417). 32p. reprint ed. pap. 30.00 (*0-608-14828-8*, 202617800048) Bks Demand.

Ripley, Steve, ed. FDC Handbook for Junior Collector, AFDCS. (Illus.). 12p. 1998. pap. 1.00 (*1-879390-25-6*) AFDCS.

Ripley, Steven M. The Intermediate Handbook for First Day Cover Collectors: A Guide for the Intermediate Collector, Vol. 1. (Illus.). 100p. (Orig.). 1995. pap. 13.95 (*1-879390-04-3*) AFDCS.

Ripley, Theresa M., jt. auth. see Loughary, Jack.

Ripley, Theresa M., jt. auth. see Loughary, John W.

Ripley, Tim. Jane's Pocket Guide: C.H. LC 99-213832. (Illus.). 144p. 1999. pap. 15.00 (*0-00-472134-9*, Harper Ref) HarpC.

Ripley, Tom. Security Forces in Northern Ireland, 1969-92. (Elite Ser.: No. 44). (Illus.). 64p. pap. 12.95 (*1-85532-278-1*, 9459, Pub. by Ospry) Stackpole.

***Ripley, Virginia.** The Little Troll's Big Adventure. (Illus.). 32p. (J). (gr. k-2). 1999. pap. 12.00 (*0-9674612-0-0*) Strike Pubng.

Ripley, Warren, ed. Siege Train: The Journal of a Confederate Artilleryman in the Defense of Charleston. LC 86-7021. (Illus.). 386p. 1996. pap. 16.95 (*1-57003-127-4*) U of SC Pr.

Ripley, William E., jt. auth. see Roedel, Phil M.

Ripley, William Z. Financial History of Virginia 1609-1776. LC 78-127449. (Columbia Studies in the Social Sciences: No. 10). reprint ed. 24.50 (*0-404-51010-8*) AMS Pr.

— Main Street & Wall Street. LC 73-2531. (Big Business; Economic Power in a Free Society Ser.). 1973. reprint ed. 26.95 (*0-405-05109-3*) Ayer.

— Main Street & Wall Street. LC 72-93640. 1973. reprint ed. text 30.00 (*0-914348-07-8*) Scholars Bk.

— Railroads: Finance & Organization. Bruchey, Stuart, ed. LC 80-1699. (Railroads Ser.). (Illus.). 1981. reprint ed. lib. bdg. 60.95 (*0-405-13823-7*) Ayer.

— Railroads: Rates & Regulation. LC 73-2532. (Big Business; Economic Power in a Free Society Ser.). 1973. reprint ed. 42.95 (*0-405-05110-7*) Ayer.

Ripling, E., jt. auth. see Polakowski, N. H.

Riplinger, Gail. The Language of the King James Bible: An Introduction. (Illus.). 179p. 1998. pap. 10.00 (*0-9635845-1-0*) A V Pubns.

Riplinger, Gail A. New Age Bible Versions: An Exhaustive Documentation of the Message, Men, & Manuscripts Moving Mankind to the Antichrist's One World Religion. 10th ed. LC 93-92561. 700p. 1993. pap. 14.95 (*0-9635845-0-2*) A V Pubns.

— Which Bible Is God's Word? LC 96-197705. 118p. 1994. pap. 9.50 (*1-879366-81-9*) Hearthstone OK.

Ripman, Barbara. Basic Dressage. (Crowood Equestrian Guides Ser.). (Illus.). 96p. 1992. pap. 17.95 (*1-85223-535-7*, Pub. by Cro1wood) Trafalgar.

— Basic Training. (Crowood Equestrian Guides Ser.). (Illus.). 96p. 1992. pap. 17.95 (*1-85223-534-9*, Pub. by Cro1wood) Trafalgar.

Ripmaster, Terence M. Bucky Pizzarelli/A Life in Music. LC 98-172530. 208p. 1998. pap. 9.95 (*0-7866-3315-8*) Mel Bay.

Ripoli, Angeles S. Las Traducciones de Shakespeare en Espana: El Ejemplo de Othello. Editorial Arcos, Inc., Staff, ed. (Coleccion Interdisciplinar: No. 2). (SPA., Illus.). 302p. (C). 1988. lib. bdg. 25.00 (*0-937509-03-5*) Edit Arcos.

Ripoll, Carlos. Archivo Jose Marti: Repertorio Critico, Medio Siglo de Estudios Martianos. 1971. 14.50 (*0-88303-010-1*); pap. 11.50 (*0-685-73214-2*) E Torres & Sons.

— Conciencia Intelectual de America: Antologia del Ensayo Hispanoamericano. 3rd rev. ed. 1974. 9.50 (*0-88303-150-7*) E Torres & Sons.

— Escritos Desconocidos de Jose Marti. (SPA.). 1971. 10.50 (*0-88303-001-2*) E Torres & Sons.

— Harnessing the Intellectuals: Censoring Writers & Artists in Today's Cuba. 1985. 3.00 (*0-317-90494-9*) Cuban Amer Natl Fndtn.

— The Heresy of Words in Cuba. LC 85-20672. (Perspectives on Freedom Ser.: No. 4). 75p. 1985. 10.25 (*0-932088-07-4*) Freedom Hse.

— Jose Marti, Letras y Huellas Desconocidas. 1976. 10.95 (*0-88303-024-1*); pap. 6.50 (*0-685-73013-1*) E Torres & Sons.

— Jose Marti, the United States, & the Marxist Interpretaton of Cuban History. 95p. 1984. pap. 14.95 (*0-87855-976-0*) Transaction Pubs.

— Jose Marti Thoughts. 48p. 1994. pap. text 5.00 (*1-884619-02-9*) Endowment CAS.

— Marti Ideario. 94p. (C). 1994. pap. text 5.00 (*1-884619-03-7*) Endowment CAS.

— Patria: El Periodico de Jose Marti, Registro General, 1892-1895. 1971. 9.95 (*0-88303-011-X*); pap. 6.95 (*0-685-73215-0*) E Torres & Sons.

Ripoll, Jamie. How Our Senses Work. (Invisible World Ser.).Tr. of Como Funcionan Nuestros Sentidos. (Illus.). 32p. (J). (gr. 4 up). 1994. lib. bdg. 15.95 (*0-7910-2128-9*) Chelsea Hse.

Ripoll, Jose. The Future of International Trade in Services. (New Ser.: No. 10). 19p. 1996. pap. 15.00 (*0-86682-101-5*) Ctr Intl Relations.

Ripoll, Roger, ed. see Zola, Emile.

Riposa & Dersch. City of Angels. 224p. (C). 1992. per. 32.95 (*0-8403-8061-5*, 40806101) Kendall-Hunt.

Riposa, Gerry, jt. auth. see Andranovich, Gregory D.

Riposo, Joe. Jazz Improvisation: A Whole-Brain Approach. (Illus.). 240p. (Orig.). 1992. pap. 24.95 incl. audio (*0-9623694-0-3*) JR Pubs.

Ripp, Bobby. End Time Deceptions: An Expose on: Medjugorje (Marian Apparitions), the New Age Movement, UFO Phenomenon, & Others. LC 95-90610. 320p. (Orig.). 1996. pap. 14.95 (*0-9648952-0-X*) True Light.

Ripp, Charles H. When I Grow up I Want to Be a Doctor. (Illus.). 16p. (J). (gr. 3-6). 1996. pap. 6.00 (*0-8059-4056-1*) Dorrance.

R

Ripp, Victor. Crime & Punishment. 1999. pap. write for info. (*0-525-93776-5*) Viking Penguin.

Rippa, S. Alexander. Education in a Free Society: An American History. 6th ed. 496p. (C). 1989. pap. text 24.95 (*0-8013-0127-0*, 75791) Longman.

***Rippe, James.** Healthy Heart Cookbook for Dummies. (Illus.). 384p. 2000. pap. 19.99 (*0-7645-5222-8*) IDG Bks.

Rippe, James, jt. auth. see Dwyer, Johanna.

Rippe, James M. Fit over Forty: A Revolutionary Plan to Achieve Lifelong Physical & Spiritual Health & Well-Being. 1996. 23.00 (*0-614-96799-6*, Wm Morrow); 23.00 (*0-688-14708-9*, Wm Morrow) Morrow Avon.

— Fit over Forty: A Revolutionary Plan to Achieve Lifelong Physical & Spiritual Health & Well-Being. (Illus.). 348p. 1999. reprint ed. text 23.00 (*0-7881-6283-7*) DIANE Pub.

— Fit over Forty: A Revolutionary Plan to Achieve Lifelong Physical & Spiritual Health & Well-Being. (Illus.). 368p. 1997. reprint ed. pap. 14.00 (*0-688-15399-2*, Quil) HarperTrade.

***Rippe, James M.** The Healthy Heart for Dummies. 384p. 1999. pap. 19.99 (*0-7645-5199-X*) IDG Bks.

— Healthy Heart for Dummies. 2000. pap. 19.99 (*0-7645-5166-3*) IDG Bks.

— Lifestyle Medicine. LC 99-13000. (Illus.). 1999. 125.00 (*0-86542-294-X*) Blackwell Sci.

Rippe, James M. Manual ICU Asia, No. 2. 1989. 10.95 (*0-316-74714-9*) Little.

— Manual ICU ISE. 2nd ed. 1989. 15.95 (*0-316-74713-0*, Little Brwn Med Div) Lppncott W & W.

— Manual ICU Medicine. 2nd ed. 614p. 1989. spiral bd. 38.00 (*0-316-74712-2*) Lppncott W & W.

Rippe, James M., et al, eds. Intensive Care Medicine, 2 vols. 3rd ed. (Illus.). 2725p. 1996. text 185.00 (*0-316-74735-1*) Lppncott W & W.

— Intensive Care Medicine, Vols. 1 & 2. 3rd ed. LC 95-33188. 2592p. 1995. text 187.00 (*0-316-74728-9*) Lppncott W & W.

Rippe, James M. & Csete, Marie. Manual of Intensive Care Medicine. (Spiral Manual Ser.). 465p. 1983. spiral bd. 22.50 (*0-316-74708-4*, Little Brwn Med Div) Lppncott W & W.

Rippe, James M. & Curley, Frederick J., eds. Procedures & Techniques in Intensive Care Medicine. LC 94-29395. 336p. 1994. pap. text 65.00 (*0-316-74721-1*) Lppncott W & W.

Rippe, James M. & Kashiwa, Anne. Fitness Walking for Women. (Illus.). 176p. 1987. pap. 12.00 (*0-399-51407-4*, Perigee Bks) Berkley Pub.

Rippe, James M. & Ward, Carol A. The Rockport Walking Program. 1989. pap. 12.95 (*0-318-42596-3*) P-H.

Rippe, James M., jt. auth. see Alpert, Joseph S.

Rippe, James M., jt. auth. see Irwin, Richard S.

Rippe, James M., jt. auth. see Ward, Ann.

Rippe, Peter M. P. Buckley Moss: Painting the Joy of the Soul. Johnston, Becky, ed. (Illus.). 168p. 1997. 50.00 (*0-9646870-9-7*) Landauer Bks IA.

Rippeleau, Bruce E., jt. auth. see Funk, Robert E.

Rippen, Andrew & Knappert, Jan, eds. Textual Sources for the Study of Islam. (Textual Sources for the Study of Religion Ser.). (Illus.). xii, 222p. 1990. pap. text 18.00 (*0-226-72063-2*) U Ch Pr.

Rippen, B. Van, see Van Rippen, B.

Rippere, Vicky & Williams, Ruth, eds. Wounded Healers: Mental Health Workers' Experiences of Depression. LC 84-29118. 208p. 1987. pap. 108.95 (*0-471-90592-5*) Wiley.

Rippeteau, Bruce E., jt. auth. see Funk, Robert E.

Rippey, Elizabeth & Rowland, Barbara. Plants of the Perth Coast & Islands. LC 96-151372. (Illus.). 292p. 1995. 49.95 (*1-875560-46-7*, Pub. by Univ of West Aust Pr) Intl Spec Bk.

Rippey, J. Fred, ed. see Ugarte, Manuel.

Rippier, Jo S. Goodnight, Morning. 126p. 1977. 19.95 (*0-901072-54-0*, Pub. by Smyth) Dufour.

— Short Stories of Sean O'Faolain. 162p. 1976. 29.95 (*0-901072-30-3*, Pub. by Smyth) Dufour.

***Rippin.** Quran: Style & Contents. LC 99-58416. 2000. 117.95 (*0-86078-700-1*) Ashgate Pub Co.

Rippin, Andrew. Muslims: Their Religious Beliefs & Practices, Vol. 1, The Formative Period, Vol. 1. LC 89-10442. 192p. (C). (gr. 13). 1990. pap. 25.99 (*0-415-04519-3*, A4179) Routledge.

— Muslims Vol. 2: Their Religious Beliefs & Practices, Vol. 2. (Library of Religious Beliefs & Practices). 192p. (C). 1993. pap. 25.99 (*0-415-04528-2*) Routledge.

— Muslims Vols. 1 & 2: Their Religious Beliefs & Practices: The Formative Years & the Contemporary Period. 400p. 1996. pap. 36.00 (*0-614-21471-8*, 1434) Kazi Pubns.

***Rippin, Andrew, ed.** The Qur'an: Formative Interpretation. (Formation of the Classical Islamic World Ser.: 25). 420p. 1999. text 129.95 (*0-86078-701-X*, Pub. by Ashgate Pub) Ashgate Pub Co.

Rippin, D. W. & Hughes, R. R., eds. Computer Applications in Chemical Engineering: Proceedings of the 12th Symposium of the European Federation of Chemical Engineering, Montreux, April 1979. 636p. 1981. pap. 160.00 (*0-08-025022-X*, Pergamon Pr) Elsevier.

Rippin, Joanne. Aromatherapy: For Health, Relaxation & Well-Being. (Illus.). 96p. 1997. pap. text 12.95 (*1-85967-556-5*, Lorenz Bks) Anness Pub.

***Rippin, Joanne.** Oils, Essences & Creams. (Illus.). 2000. pap. 9.95 (*0-7548-0141-1*, Lorenz Bks) Anness Pub.

Rippin, Joanne. Potpourri & Scented Gifts: Gifts from Nature. (Illus.). 64p. 1997. 12.95 (*1-85967-499-2*, Lorenz Bks) Anness Pub.

Rippinger, Joel. The Benedictine Order in the United States: An Interpretive History. 299p. (Orig.). 1990. pap. text 19.95 (*0-8146-1817-0*) Liturgical Pr.

Rippinger, Joel, et al. Word & Spirit No. 18: Monastic Profession. LC 81-643362. 130p. 1998. pap. 8.00 (*1-879007-32-0*) St Bedes Pubns.

Ripple, Ezra H. Dancing along the Deadline: The Andersonville Memoir of a Prisoner of the Confederacy. Snell, Mark A., ed. LC 96-502. 192p. 1996. 19.95 (*0-89141-577-7*) Presidio Pr.

Ripple, G. Gary. Do It Write: How to Prepare A Great College Application. 8th ed. 1999. pap. text 6.00 (*1-57509-047-3*) Octameron Assocs.

Ripple, Gary. Campus Pursuit. 8th ed. 1999. pap. text 5.00 (*1-57509-049-X*) Octameron Assocs.

Ripple, Jeff. Florida: The Natural Wonders. LC 96-35226. (Illus.). 144p. 1997. 29.95 (*0-89658-324-4*) Voyageur Pr.

— Florida: The Natural Wonders. (Pictorial Discovery Guide Ser.). (Illus.). 144p. 1999. pap. 19.95 (*0-89658-424-0*) Voyageur Pr.

— The Florida Keys: The Natural Wonders of an Island Paradise. LC 94-29896. (Illus.). 128p. 1995. pap. 19.95 (*0-89658-262-0*) Voyageur Pr.

— Manatees & Dugongs of the World. LC 99-22721. (Illus.). 144p. 1999. 29.95 (*0-89658-393-7*) Voyageur Pr.

— Sea Turtles. LC 95-22059. (WorldLife Library). (Illus.). 84p. (YA). 1995. pap. 16.95 (*0-89658-315-5*) Voyageur Pr.

— Southwest Florida's Wetland Wilderness: Big Cypress Swamp & the Ten Thousand Islands. (Florida Sand Dollar Bk.). (Illus.). 112p. 1996. pap. 16.95 (*0-8130-1454-9*) U Press Fla.

Ripple, Jeff & Cerulean, Susan, eds. The Wild Heart of Florida: Florida Writers on Florida's Wildlands. LC 98-42184. 1999. 34.95 (*0-8130-1653-3*) U Press Fla.

— The Wild Heart of Florida: Florida Writers on Florida's Wildlands. LC 98-42184. 224p. 1999. pap. 19.95 (*0-8130-1656-8*) U Press Fla.

***Ripple, Wilhelminia.** Christmas Parties... What Do I Do? Lorang, Dianne, ed. (What Do I Do? Ser.). (Illus.). 192p. 2000. pap. 19.95 (*0-9649939-4-5*, Pub. by Oakbrook Pubng) IPG Chicago.

Ripple, Wilhelminia. Halloween School Parties . . . What Do I Do? LC 96-92239. 192p. 1996. pap. 19.95 (*0-9649939-8-8*) Oakbrook Pubng.

— Valentine Boxes . . . What Do I Do? Lorang, Dianne, ed. (What Do I Do? Ser.). (Illus.). 128p. 1999. pap. 12.95 (*0-9649939-3-7*) Oakbrook Pubng.

— Valentine School Parties . . . What Do I Do? LC 98-91455. (What Do I Do? Ser.). (Illus.). 192p. (Orig.). 1998. pap. 19.95 (*0-9649939-9-6*) Oakbrook Pubng.

Ripple, William J. Keiko the Whale, the Star of Free Willy. (Illus.). iv, 40p. (J). (ps-4). 1998. pap. write for info. (*0-9665844-0-6*) Nu Inc.

Ripple, William J., ed. Fundamentals of GIS: A Compendium. 248p. 1989. pap. 52.00 (*0-614-06096-6*, L332) Am Congrs Survey.

— Geographic Information Systems for Resource Management. 288p. 1986. pap. 52.00 (*0-614-06097-4*, L331) Am Congrs Survey.

Rippley, La Vern J. The Whoopee John Wilfahrt Old Time Dance Band: The German-Bohemian Roots of the Whoopee John Wilfahrt Dance Band. (Illus.). 22p. (Orig.). 1992. pap. write for info. (*0-9622931-1-3*) St Olaf German.

Rippley, Lavern. Of German Ways. 320p. 1992. pap. 12.00 (*0-06-092380-6*) HarpC.

Rippley, LaVern J. The Columbus Germans. (Illus.). 52p. 1999. reprint ed. pap. 3.75 (*1-880788-12-8*, Pub. by MKGAC & IGHS) NCSA Lit.

— Noble Women, Restless Men: The Rippley (Rieple, Ripley, Ripli, Rippli) Family in Wisconsin, North Dakota, Minnesota & Montana. LC 96-68411. (Illus.). 300p. 1996. 35.00 (*0-9622931-6-4*) St Olaf German.

Rippley, LaVern J. & Paulson, Robert J. German-Bohemians: The Quiet Immigrants. (Illus.). 1995. write for info. (*0-9622931-4-8*) St Olaf German.

Rippley, LaVern J., ed. see German-Bohemian Heritage Society Staff.

Rippley, LaVern J., tr. see Adams, Willi P.

Rippley, Vern, ed. see Roba, William, et al.

Rippon, Hugh. Discovering English Folk Dance. 1989. pap. 25.00 (*0-7478-0210-6*, Pub. by Shire Pubns) St Mut.

— Discovering English Folk Dance. (C). 1989. pap. 10.50 (*0-7478-0225-4*, Pub. by Shire Pubns) St Mut.

Rippon, John. A Memoir of the Life & Writings of Rev. John Gill, D. D. 1993. 15.99 (*0-87377-920-7*) GAM Pubns.

Rippon, John W., jt. ed. see Fromtling, Robert A.

Rippon, W. B., jt. auth. see Jamieson, A. M.

Ripps, Corinna, et al. Second Skin: Recent Work by University at Albany Graduate Program Alumni: Artists, Adidal Abou-Chamat, Luca Buvoli, James Charlton...[et Al.]. LC 98-60827. 40 p. 1998. 5.00 (*0-910763-18-6*) U Albany Art Mus.

Ripps, Susan. Sisters: Devoted or Divided. 320p. 1994. 22.50 (*0-8217-4679-0*, Zebra Kensgtn) Kensgtn Pub Corp.

***Rippy, Daniel S.** Sizing up a Start Up: Decoding the New Frontier of Career Opportunities. 304p. 2000. pap. text 16.00 (*0-7382-0353-X*) Perseus Pubng.

Rippy, J. Fred. British Investment in Latin America: 1822-1949. Wilkins, Mira, ed. LC 76-29755. (European Business Ser.). 1977. reprint ed. lib. bdg. 23.95 (*0-405-09771-9*) Ayer.

— The Capitalists & Colombia. Bruchey, Stuart & Bruchey, Eleanor, eds. LC 76-5031. (American Business Abroad Ser.). (Illus.). 1976. reprint ed. 26.95 (*0-405-09298-9*) Ayer.

Rippy, J. Fred, tr. see Henao, Jesus M. & Arrubla, Gerardo.

Rippy, James F. Joel R. Poinsett, Versatile American. (History - United States Ser.). 257p. 1993. reprint ed. lib. bdg. 79.00 (*0-7812-4826-4*) Rprt Serv.

— Rivalry of the United States & Great Britain over Latin America. (BCL1 - U. S. History Ser.). 322p. 1991. reprint ed. lib. bdg. 89.00 (*0-7812-6047-7*) Rprt Serv.

— United States & Mexico. rev. ed. LC 73-137281. reprint ed. 37.50 (*0-404-05337-8*) AMS Pr.

Rippy, Susan, jt. auth. see Brinkerhoff, Donna.

Rips, Lance J. The Psychology of Proof: Deductive Reasoning in Human Thinking. LC 93-5811. 463p. 1994. 55.00 (*0-262-18153-3*, Bradford Bks) MIT Pr.

Rips, Lance J., jt. ed. see Sloman, Steven A.

RIPS Staff. Asian Security, 1988-89. (Asian Security Ser.: No. 4). (Illus.). 200p. 1988. 31.95 (*0-08-036263-X*, Pergamon Pr); pap. 19.95 (*0-08-036703-8*, Pergamon Pr) Elsevier.

Ripski, J. Michael. Easter: A Lenten Study for Adults. LC 98-46456. 48p. 1999. pap. 3.95 (*0-687-08531-4*) Abingdon.

Ripskis, A. Louis. Cutting Loose: From Rat Race to Dream Lifestyles. LC 96-94139. (Illus.). 192p. (Orig.). 1996. pap. 23.90 (*0-9651892-0-1*) Impact Jrnl Pr.

Ripslinger, Jon. Triangle. LC 93-20983. 224p. (YA). (gr. 7 up). 1994. 10.95 (*0-15-200048-8*); pap. 3.95 (*0-15-200049-6*) Harcourt.

— Trust Me. 1997. 11.00 (*0-15-201474-8*); pap. 5.00 (*0-15-201475-6*) Harcourt.

***Ripstein, Arthur.** Equality, Responsibility & the Law. LC 98-3023. (Studies in Philosophy & Law). 368p. (C). 1999. 54.95 (*0-521-58452-3*) Cambridge U Pr.

Ripstein, Arthur, jt. ed. see Dyzenhaus, David.

Riquelme, John P. Harmony of Dissonances: T. S. Eliot, Romanticism, & Imagination. LC 90-4796. 368p. 1990. text 48.00 (*0-8018-4058-9*) Johns Hopkins.

— Teller & Tale in Joyce's Fiction: Oscillating Perspectives. LC 82-7805. 288p. 1983. reprint ed. pap. 89.30 (*0-608-03745-1*, 206457000009) Bks Demand.

Riquelme, John P., jt. auth. see Stoker.

Riquelme, John P., ed. see Hardy, Thomas.

Riquelme, John P., ed. see Senn, Fritz.

Riquer, Martin D., jt. intro. see Menendez Pidal, Ramon.

Riquer, Martin De, see De Riquer, Martin, ed.

Riquer, Martin De, see De Cervantes Saavedra, Miguel & De Riquer, Martin.

Riquer, Martin de, ed. see Luque Faxardo, Francisco de.

Riquier, Aline. The Cotton in Your T-Shirt. (Young Discovery Library). (Illus.). 40p. (J). (gr. k-6). 1993. lib. bdg. 2.99 (*1-56674-058-4*, HTS Bks) Forest Hse.

— The Cotton in Your T-Shirt. Bogard, Vicki, tr. from FRE. LC 91-45786. (Illus.). 38p. (J). (gr. k-5). 1992. 5.95 (*0-944589-40-5*) Young Discovery Lib.

***Riquier, Ann.** Voices of Tibetan Women. 2000. 24.95 (*1-56649-158-4*) Welcome Rain.

Rirdan, Daniel. Tucky Tum World Set: Essential Edition. Trail, Nubia & McDonough, Tom, eds. (Illus.). 150p. (J). (gr. 3-6). 1999. 29.95 (*0-9670889-0-9*) Tucky Tum.

Ririe, Robert L. Doin' Dutch Oven: Inside & Out. 130p. (Orig.). 1990. pap. 9.98 (*0-88290-368-3*) Horizon Utah.

— Let's Cook Dutch! A Complete Guide for the Dutch Oven Chef. LC 79-89360. (Illus.). 104p. 1979. pap. 8.98 (*0-88290-120-6*) Horizon Utah.

Ris. Palm Springs Lifestyle Cookbook. 1996. 13.95 (*0-9656813-1-9*) Haricot Verts.

Ris Allen, Joan de, jt. auth. see Allen, Paul M.

***Ris, Birgit, ed.** The Euro in Law & Practice. 152p. 1999. 42.00 (*87-16-13486-9*, Pub. by Copenhagen Busn Schl) Bks Intl VA.

— The Euro in Law & Practice. 152p. 1999. pap. 84.00 (*1-902558-16-2*, Pub. by Palladian Law) Gaunt.

Ris, Birgit, jt. auth. see Pullen, Mike.

Ris, R. C., jt. auth. see Meekes, J. A.

Risatti, Howard. Mountain Lake Workshop: Artists in Locale. (Illus.). (Orig.). 1996. pap. write for info. (*0-935519-21-1*) Anderson Gal.

— New Music Vocabulary: A Guide to Notational Signs for Contemporary Music. LC 73-81565. 235p. reprint ed. pap. 72.90 (*0-7837-5743-3*, 204540400006) Bks Demand.

— Postmodern Perspectives. 2nd ed. LC 97-36145. 318p. 1997. pap. text 36.80 (*0-13-614504-3*) P-H.

Risatti, Howard, et al. Dubuffet/Miro: Selections from the Acquavella Collection. High, Steven S., ed. LC 97-68531. 88p. 1997. 20.00 (*0-9658115-0-6*) NV Museum Art.

Risberg, Debra, contrib. by. Allan Sekula: Dismal Science. (Illus.). 212p. 1997. 70.00 (*0-945558-27-9*); pap. 35.00 (*0-614-17631-X*) ISU Univ Galls.

— Olive Branch: Photographs & Texts by Cedric Chatterley, 1987-1993. (Illus.). 32p. 1994. 10.00 (*0-945558-22-8*) ISU Univ Galls.

Risberg, Jarl, jt. ed. see Gustafson, Lars.

Risbrudt, Christopher D., jt. ed. see Royer, Jack P.

Risbud, Subhash H., jt. ed. see Bergeron, Clifton G.

Risby, Bonnie L. A Country Christmas. (Illus.). 96p. (Orig.). (J). (gr. 1-4). 1996. pap. 2.95 (*0-8167-4127-1*) Troll Communs.

Risby, Terence & Sehnert, Shelley. Chromatographic Analysis of the Environment. 3rd expanded rev. ed. (Chromatographic Science Ser.). (Illus.). Date not set. write for info. (*0-8247-9456-7*, 9456-7) Dekker.

Risby, Terence H., ed. Ultratrace Metal Analysis in Biological Sciences. LC 78-31903. (Advances in Chemistry Ser.: No. 172). 1979. 43.95 (*0-8412-0416-0*) Am Chemical.

— Ultratrace Metal Analysis in Biological Sciences & Environment. LC 78-31903. (Advances in Chemistry Ser.: Vol. 172). 272p. 1979. reprint ed. pap. 84.40 (*0-608-03868-7*, 206431500008) Bks Demand.

Risch, Franz X. Pseudo-Basilius: Adversus Eunomium IV-V: Einleitung, Ubersetzung und Kommentar. LC 91-37162. (Supplements to Vigiliae Christianae Ser.: Vol. 16). 234p. 1992. 74.50 (*90-04-09558-6*) Brill Academic Pubs.

Risch, Gail S., jt. ed. see Lawler, Michael G.

***Risch, Sara J. & Ho, Chi-Tang, eds.** Flavor Chemistry: Industrial & Academic Research. LC 99-58097. (ACS Symposium Ser.: 756). (Illus.). 192p. 2000. text 95.00 (*0-8412-3640-2*) OUP.

Risch, Sara J. & Hotchkiss, Joseph H., eds. Food & Packaging Interactions II. LC 91-31831. (Illus.). 265p. 1991. text 65.00 (*0-8412-2122-7*, Pub. by Am Chemical) OUP.

Risch, Sara J. & Reineccius, Gary A., eds. Encapsulation & Controlled Release of Food Ingredients. LC 95-2512. (ACS Symposium Ser.: No. 590). (Illus.). 226p. 1995. text 72.00 (*0-8412-3164-8*, Pub. by Am Chemical) OUP.

— Flavor Encapsulation. LC 88-10422. (ACS Symposium Ser.: No. 370). (Illus.). viii, 212p. 1988. 59.95 (*0-8412-1482-4*, Pub. by Am Chemical) OUP.

— Flavor Encapsulation. LC 88-10422. (ACS Symposium Ser.: Vol. 370). 216p. 1988. reprint ed. pap. 67.00 (*0-608-03283-2*, 206380100007) Bks Demand.

Risch, Sara J., ed. see American Chemical Society Staff.

Risch, Sarah J. New Developments in the Chemistry of Packaging Materials. LC 99-58687. (Illus.). 304p. 1999. text 95.00 (*0-8412-3617-8*, Pub. by Am Chemical) OUP.

Risch, Tore, jt. ed. see Litwin, Witold.

Rische, Jill M. & Martin, Walter. Through the Windows of Heaven: 100 Powerful Stories & Teachings from Walter Martin, the Original Bible-Answer-Man. LC 99-14348. 224p. 1999. pap. 14.99 (*0-8054-2031-2*) Broadman.

Rischel, Hans, jt. auth. see Ravn, Anders P.

Rischel, Jergen. Minor Mlabri: A Hunter-Gatherer Language of Northern Indochina. 350p. 1995. 98.00 (*87-7289-294-3*, Pub. by Mus Tusculanum) Paul & Co Pubs.

Rischer, ed. Discovering Biology. (C). 1998. text. write for info. (*0-321-01070-1*) Addson-Wesley Educ.

Rischin, Moses. Immigration & the American Tradition. (AHS Ser: No. 79). 512p. 1976. pap. 9.95 (*0-672-60130-3*, Bobbs) Macmillan.

— The Promised City: New York's Jews, 1870-1914. (Illus.). 342p. 1972. pap. 17.00 (*0-674-71501-2*) HUP.

Rischin, Moses, ed. The Jews of the West: The Metropolitan Years. (Illus.). 156p. 1975. pap. 5.95 (*0-943376-10-6*) Magnes Mus.

— Modern Jewish Experience, 59 vols., Set. 1975. 1630.50 (*0-405-06690-2*) Ayer.

— Yiddish Tales. Frank, Helena, tr. from YID. LC 74-29531. (Modern Jewish Experience Ser.). 1975. reprint ed. 52.95 (*0-405-06755-0*) Ayer.

Rischin, Moses, ed. The Jews of North America. LC 87-10110. 280p. 1987. 39.95 (*0-8143-1890-8*); pap. 18.95 (*0-8143-1891-6*) Wayne St U Pr.

Rischin, Moses & Livingston, John, eds. Jews of the American West. LC 90-44864. (American Jewish Civilization Ser.). (Illus.). 227p. reprint ed. pap. 70.40 (*0-608-10577-5*, 2071197) Bks Demand.

Rischin, Moses, jt. ed. see Brinner, William M.

Rischin, Moses, ed. see Hapgood, Hutchins.

Rischin, Moses, jt. ed. see Livingston, John.

***Rischpater, Ray.** Wireless Web Development. 250p. 2000. pap. text 34.95 (*1-893115-20-8*, Pub. by APress L P) Spr-Verlag.

Rischpater, Ray, jt. auth. see Mann, Steve.

Risden, E. L. Through a Glass Darkly. LC 95-8693. 68p. 1997. pap. 14.95 (*0-7734-2731-7*, Mellen Poetry Pr) E Mellen.

Risden, E. L., tr. Beowulf: A Student's Edition. xvi, 99p. (C). 1994. pap. text 12.50 (*0-87875-455-5*) Whitston Pub.

Risden, Edward L. Beasts of Time: Apocalyptic Beowulf. LC 93-37320. (Studies in the Humanities: Vol. 8). 165p. (C). 1994. text 41.95 (*0-8204-2334-3*) P Lang Pubng.

Rise, Elmer. Love among the Ruins: Manuscript Edition. 1963. pap. 13.00 (*0-8222-0917-9*) Dramatists Play.

Rise, Eric W. The Martinsville Seven: Race, Rape, & Capital Punishment. 256p. (C). 1995. 27.95 (*0-8139-1567-8*) U Pr of Va.

Rise, Eric W., jt. auth. see Hall, Kermit L.

Rise, Svein. The Christology of Wolfhart Pannenberg: Identity & Relevance. MacNeil, Brian, tr. LC 96-49241. 304p. 1997. 99.95 (*0-7734-2286-2*) E Mellen.

Risebero, Bill. Fantastic Form. (Illus.). 192p. 1992. 30.00 (*1-56131-057-3*, NAB) I R Dee.

— Modern Architecture & Design: An Alternative History. (Illus.). 256p. 1982. reprint ed. 32.00 (*0-262-18108-8*) MIT Pr.

— Modern Architecture & Design: An Alternative History. (Illus.). 256p. 1985. reprint ed. pap. text 17.50 (*0-262-68046-7*) MIT Pr.

— The Story of Western Architecture. rev. ed. LC 97-70118. (Illus.). 304p. 1997. pap. text 18.50 (*0-262-68095-5*) MIT Pr.

Riseborough, Donald J., ed. Canada & the French. LC 74-75155. 274p. reprint ed. pap. 85.00 (*0-8357-7989-0*, 202290100031) Bks Demand.

Riseborough, George, jt. auth. see Bates, Inge.

Riselman, Brian. Where Darkness Sleeps. 1995. mass mkt. 5.99 (*0-312-95682-7*) Tor Bks.

Risen, Celia. Some Jewels of Maine: Jewish Maine Pioneers. (Illus.). xiv, 184p. 1997. pap. 14.00 (*0-8059-4206-8*) Dorrance.

Risen, Jim & Thomas, Judy. Wrath of Angels: The American Abortion War. 416p. 1997. pap. 13.00 (*0-465-09273-X*, Pub. by Basic) HarpC.

— Wrath of Angels: The American Abortion War. LC 97-45936. (Illus.). 416p. 1997. 24.00 (*0-465-09272-1*, Pub. by Basic) HarpC.

Risener, Jeff. How to Raise Your Child in the World of Sports. LC 97-91376. 111p. 1998. pap. 10.95 (*0-533-12651-7*) Vantage.

Risenhoover, C. C. White Heat. LC 91-77072. 362p. 1992. 20.00 (*0-9627509-3-X*) Baskerville.

Risenhoover, C. C., ed. see Ivey, Don R.

Risenhoover, Morris & Blackburn, Robert T. Artists As Professors: Conversations with Musicians, Painters, Sculptors. LC 75-38681. 227p. 1976. text 24.95 (*0-252-00574-0*) U of Ill Pr.

Riser, Debra. The Child Within. (Orig.). 1996. pap. write for info. (*1-57553-248-4*) Watermrk Pr.

Riser, Howard. Aligning Pay & Results: Compensation Strategies That Work from the Boardroom to the Shop Floor. LC 99-25896. (Illus.). 320p. 1999. 35.00 (*0-8144-0458-8*) AMACOM.

Riser, Martin O. The Sternberg Family of Fossil-Hunters. LC 94-48127. (Illus.). 520p. 1995. text 119.95 (*0-7734-8985-1*) E Mellen.

Riser, Mel, jt. auth. see Shroeder, Rick.

Riser, Robert R., jt. auth. see Bailes, Gordon L.

Riser-Roberts, Eve. In Situ-On-Site Bioremediation of Refined Oils & Fuels. 496p. 1992. boxed set 104.95 (*0-87371-832-1*, TD879) Smoley.

— Remediation of Petroleum Contaminated Soils. LC 97-46784. 576p. 1998. boxed set 84.95 (*0-87371-858-5*, L858) Lewis Pubs.

Riser, Troy. Scissors Paper Rock: Stories by Troy Riser. 74p. (Orig.). 1993. per. 5.95 (*1-880649-31-4*) Writ Ctr Pr.

***Rish, Buck.** Sandbridge: Saga of an American Doctor. LC 98-55456. 1999. 23.00 (*1-883911-31-1*) Brandylane.

Rish West, Brana & Grohe, William. Talk Your Head Off... & Write, Too! 1996. teacher ed. 8.00 (*0-13-613605-2*) P-H.

Rish, William R. & Waite, David A. Mixed Waste Risk Assessment. Date not set. 65.00 (*0-87371-633-7*) Lewis Pubs.

Rishabchand. Sri Aurobindo: His Life Unique. (Illus.). 427p. 1981. 18.75 (*0-89071-326-X*, Pub. by SAA); pap. 15.00 (*0-89071-325-1*, Pub. by SAA) Acrpls Bks CO.

Rishabhchand. Sri Aurobindo: His Life Unique. 427p. (Orig.). 1982. pap. 14.95 (*0-89744-147-8*) Auromere.

Rishanger, William De, see De Rishanger, William.

Rishbeth, H., ed. EISCAT Science: Results from the First Year's Operation of the European Incoherent Scatter Radar: Papers from the EISCAT Workshop, Aussois, France, 5-8 September 1983. 184p. 1984. pap. 73.00 (*0-08-031440-6*, Pergamon Pr) Elsevier.

Rishbeth, H., jt. ed. see Thomas, L.

Rishe, Naphtali. Database Design: The Semantic Modeling Approach. 528p. 1992. 45.00 (*0-07-052955-8*) McGraw.

Rishel, James B. HVAC Pump Handbook. (Illus.). 529p. 1996. 69.95 (*0-07-053033-5*) McGraw.

Rishel, Jonas. The Indian Physician. 132p. 1980. 7.00 (*0-88215-048-0*) Friends Ohio St U Lib.

Rishel, Joseph F. Founding Families of Pittsburgh: The Evolution of a Regional Elite, 1760-1910. LC 89-39006. 253p. 1990. reprint ed. pap. 78.50 (*0-608-07700-3*, 206779000010) Bks Demand.

— The Spirit That Gives Life: The History of Duquesne University, 1878-1996. LC 97-4680. (Illus.). 330p. 1997. 39.95 (*0-8207-0268-4*) Duquesne.

Rishel, Joseph F., ed. American Cities & Towns: Historical Perspectives. LC 92-20597. 264p. (C). 1992. text 39.50 (*0-8207-0239-0*) Duquesne.

Rishel, Joseph J. Goya: Another Look. (Illus.). 64p. 1999. pap. 24.95 (*0-87633-131-2*) Phila Mus Art.

Rishel, Joseph J. & Lefton, Alice. The Henry P. McIlhenny Collection: An Illustrated History. LC 87-29196. (Illus.). 150p. (Orig.). 1987. pap. 10.00 (*0-87633-073-1*) Phila Mus Art.

Rishel, Joseph J., jt. auth. see Asperen de Boer, J. R. J. Van.

Rishel, R. W., jt. auth. see Fleming, Wendall H.

Rishel, Thomas, jt. auth. see Meier, John.

Rishell, Lyle. With a Black Platoon in Combat: A Year in Korea. LC 92-27918. (Military History Ser.: No. 29). (Illus.). 200p. 1993. 24.50 (*0-89096-526-9*) Tex A&M Univ Pr.

Risher, jt. auth. see Robinson, John W.

Risher, C. Craig & Wilcox, Christopher S., eds. Nephrology. 3rd ed. LC 94-27308. (House Officer Ser.). 324p. 1995. pap. 24.95 (*0-683-08277-9*) Lppncott W & W.

Risher, Carol, ed. see AAP Rights & Permissions Advisory Committee.

Risher, Howard W. Public Sector Compensation: An Overview of Present Practices & Emerging Trends. LC 98-116487. 1998. 34.65 (*1-57963-051-0*) Am Compensation.

Risher, Howard W. & Fay, Charles H. New Strategies for Public Pay: Rethinking Government Compensation Programs. LC 96-53433. (Jossey-Bass Public Administration Ser.). 1997. 34.95 (*0-7879-0826-6*) Jossey-Bass.

Risher, Howard W., jt. ed. see Fay, Charles.

Rishforth, Patti. 134 Sound-Loaded Scenes for Articulation. 135p. (J). (gr. k-5). 1997. spiral bd., wbk. ed. 25.95 (*1-58650-054-6*, BK-251) Super Duper.

— Say & Do Phonemic Awareness Stories & Activities. 226p. (J). (ps-2). 1998. spiral bd., wbk. ed. 34.95 (*1-58650-064-3*, BK-261) Super Duper.

Rishikesh, S. Ancient & Medieval Nepal. (C). 1990. 65.00 (*0-89771-058-4*, Pub. by Ratna Pustak Bhandar) St Mut.

Rishmawi, Mona A., ed. see International Commission of Jurists.

Risho, Ray. Risho's Registry. 130p. (Orig.). 1985. pap. 5.00 (*0-939872-03-X*) MRP.

Rishord, Norman K. Insights on American History, Vol. I. 292p. (C). 1988. pap. text 35.50 (*0-15-541445-3*, Pub. by Harcourt Coll Pubs) Harcourt.

— Insights on American History, Vol. II. 292p. (C). 1988. pap. text 35.50 (*0-15-541446-1*, Pub. by Harcourt Coll Pubs) Harcourt.

Rishworth, P., jt. auth. see Ladley, A.

Rising. Unified Mathematics. 1990. pap., teacher ed. 17.80 (*0-395-55064-5*) HM.

— Unified Mathematics. 1990. pap., student ed. 7.96 (*0-395-55066-1*) HM.

— Unified Mathematics, Vol. 2. 1990. pap., teacher ed. 17.80 (*0-395-55068-8*) HM.

— Unified Mathematics, Vol. 3. 1990. pap., teacher ed. 17.80 (*0-395-55070-X*) HM.

***Rising, Boardman.** Caryl's Game. 240p. 2000. pap. 16.95 (*1-57532-207-2*, Pub. by Press-Tige Pub) Am Wholesale.

Rising, Catharine. Darkness at Heart: Fathers & Sons in Conrad, 37. LC 89-29432. (Contributions to the Study of World Literature Ser.: No. 37). 224p. 1990. 57.95 (*0-313-26880-0*, RDH/, Greenwood Pr) Greenwood.

— Outside the Arch: Kohut & Five Modern Writers. LC 99-20581. 128p. 1999. 33.00 (*0-7618-1385-3*) U Pr of Amer.

Rising, David. Great Careers for People Interested in Film, Video & Photography, Vol. 1. 2nd ed. LC 94-60782. (Career Connections, Series 2: Communications, the Arts, & Entrepreneurship). 48p. 1994. text 23.00 (*0-8103-9968-7*, UXL) Gale.

Rising, David P. Switch Reference in Koasati Discourse. LC 92-80355. (Publications in Linguistics Ser.: Vol. 109). xii, 90p. 1992. pap. 8.00 (*0-88312-813-6*) S I L Intl.

Rising, Elmer. The Pen Renderings of Elmer Rising: New England in Black & White. LC 85-1463. (Illus.). 112p. 1985. 75.00 (*0-9614380-0-2*) FER Pub Co.

Rising, George. Clean for Gene: Eugene McCarthy's 1968 Presidential Campaign. LC 96-44684. 176p. 1997. 57.95 (*0-275-95841-8*, Praeger Pubs) Greenwood.

Rising, Gerald F., jt. auth. see Pieters, Richard S.

Rising, Gerald R., jt. auth. see Pieters, Richard S.

Rising, James D., ed. A Guide to the Identification & Natural History of the Sparrows of the United States & Canada. (Illus.). 384p. 1996. text 39.95 (*0-12-588970-4*); pap. text 24.95 (*0-12-588971-2*) Acad Pr.

***Rising, Linda.** The Pattern Almanac 2000. (Software Patterns Ser.). 448p. 2000. pap. 29.95 (*0-201-61567-3*) Addison-Wesley.

***Rising, Linda, ed.** Design Patterns in Communication Software. (SIGS Reference Library Ser.: Vol. 19). (Illus.). 500p. 2000. Price not set. (*0-521-79040-9*) Cambridge U Pr.

Rising, Linda, ed. The Patterns Handbook: Techniques, Strategies & Applications. (SIGS Reference Library: No. 13). 570p. 1998. pap. 44.95 (*0-521-64818-1*) Cambridge U Pr.

Rising, Trudy & Williams, Peter. Light Magic: And Other Science Activities about Energy. (Illus.). 64p. (YA). (gr. 3-7). 1994. 16.95 (*1-895688-15-9*, Pub. by Greey dePencier) Firefly Bks Ltd.

Rising, Trudy L. Light Magic: And Other Science Activities about Energy. (Owlet Bks.). (J). 1994. 15.15 (*0-606-06531-8*, Pub. by Turtleback) Demco.

Risinger, C. R., jt. ed. see Ethylene Producers' Committee of AIChE's Fuels & P.

Risingsun, Ted & Leman, Wayne. Let's Talk Cheyenne: An Audio Cassette Tape Course of Instruction in the Cheyenne Language. 57p. 1999. pap. 18.95 incl. audio (*0-9658014-1-1*) WinterSun Pr.

Risjord, Mark W. Woodcutters & Witchcraft: Rationality & Interpretive Change in the Social Sciences. LC 99-42500. (C). 2000. text 57.50 (*0-7914-4511-9*); pap. text 18.95 (*0-7914-4512-7*) State U NY Pr.

Risjord, Norman K. America: A History of the United States, 2 vols. (Illus.). (C). 1985. text 46.05 (*0-13-024340-X*) P-H.

— America: The Glorious Republic, 2 vols., Vol. 1 to 1877. 2nd ed. (Illus.). 450p. (C). 1987. pap. text 28.80 (*0-13-025156-9*) P-H.

— America: The Glorious Republic, 2 vols., Vol. 2 since 1865. 2nd ed. (Illus.). 400p. (C). 1987. pap. text 28.80 (*0-13-025198-4*) P-H.

— Builders of Annapolis: Enterprise & Politics in a Colonial Capital. LC 97-44607. 1998. pap. text 18.95 (*0-938420-61-5*) MD Hist.

— Chesapeake Politics, Seventeen Eighty One to Eighteen Hundred. LC 78-7996. 1978. text 92.50 (*0-231-04328-7*) Col U Pr.

— History of U.S. to 1877 83E. 1985. 57.00 (*0-03-061763-4*) Harcourt Schl Pubs.

— Jefferson's America, 1760-1815. (Illus.). 336p. 1991. text 34.95 (*0-945612-24-9*); pap. text 18.95 (*0-945612-25-7*) Madison Hse.

— Thomas Jefferson. LC 94-6614. (American Profiles Ser.). 1994. 29.95 (*0-945612-38-9*); pap. text 14.95 (*0-945612-39-7*) Madison Hse.

— Wisconsin: The Story of the Badger State. LC 95-61444. (Illus.). 240p. 1995. pap. 16.95 (*0-915024-49-7*) Trails Media.

***Risk & Reliability Division, ABS Group Inc. Staff.** Root Cause Analysis Handbook: A Guide to Effective Incident Investigation. LC 99-22515. 217p. 1999. pap. 89.00 (*0-86587-658-4*) Gov Insts.

Risk, Anna. The Poems of Theocritus. LC 77-20042. 264p. reprint ed. pap. 81.90 (*0-8357-3887-6*, 203661900004) Bks Demand.

Risk, Clifford, tr. see Todorov, I. T.

Risk, Louise B. House on the Hudson. 300p. 1993. pap. write for info. (*0-9633934-0-5*) L B Risk.

Risk Management Committee Staff. Risk Management for Newspapers. rev. ed. 40p. 1989. pap. 49.95 (*1-877888-10-9*) Intl Newspaper.

***Risk, Mary.** Hurry up, Molly. (I Can Read Bks.). (J). (ps-3). 2000. 6.95 (*0-7641-5286-6*) Barron.

— Hurry up, Molly. (I Can Read Bks.). (Illus.). (J). (ps-3). 2000. 6.95 (*0-7641-5287-4*) Barron.

— Puppy Finds a Friend. (I Can Read Bks.). (Illus.). 2000. 6.95 (*0-7641-5283-1*) Barron.

— Puppy Finds a Friend. (I Can Read Bks.). (Illus.). (J). (ps-3). 2000. 6.95 (*0-7641-5285-8*) Barron.

Risk, Mary. What's for Supper? (Que Hay de Almuerzo?) (ENG & SPA., Illus.). 28p. (J). (ps up). 1998. 6.95 (*0-7641-5127-4*) Barron.

— What's for Supper? (Qu'est-ce Qu'on Mange Ce Soir?) (ENG & FRE., Illus.). 28p. (J). (ps-3). 1998. 6.95 (*0-7641-5126-6*) Barron.

Risk, Mary & Jansen, Jacqueline. I Want My Banana: English-French Version: Je Veux Ma Banane. (I Can Read French Ser.). (ENG & FRE.). (J). (ps up). 1998. pap. 9.95 incl. audio (*0-7641-7190-9*) Barron.

— I Want My Banana (Je Veux Ma Banane) LC 95-53763. (I Can Read French Ser.). (FRE., Illus.). 28p. (J). (ps up). 1996. 6.95 (*0-8120-6579-4*) Barron.

Risk, Mary & Martin, Rosa. I Want My Banana: English-Spanish Version: Quiero Mi Platano. (I Can Read Spanish Ser.). (ENG & SPA.). (J). (ps up). 1998. pap. 9.95 incl. audio (*0-7641-7194-1*) Barron.

— I Want My Banana (Quiero Mi Platano) (I Can Read Spanish Ser.). (SPA., Illus.). 28p. (J). (ps up). 1996. 6.95 (*0-8120-6580-8*) Barron.

Risk, Mary, jt. auth. see Morton, Lone.

Risk, R. T. Four Private Presses: A Memoir. (Illus.). 60p. 1993. 45.00 (*0-930126-43-2*) Typographeum.

— Typographeum: Being Essays, Mainly Historical, on Printers & Printing, & Including A Remembrance of a Bookseller, along with a Personal Narrative. 48p. 1997. 50.00 (*0-930126-55-6*) Typographeum.

— Why Potocki? (Illus.). 60p. 1981. 50.00 (*0-930126-07-6*) Typographeum.

Risk, Richard B., Jr. Lang(e)land Family Reunion. unabridged ed. LC 97-78164. (Illus.). 240p. 1997. pap. 30.00 (*0-9662396-0-1*) AMROB Pub.

***Risk, William.** Dating & Waiting: Looking for Love in All the Right Places. 2000. pap. 10.99 (*0-8254-3581-1*) Kregel.

Riska, Elianne & Wegar, Katarina, eds. Gender, Work & Medicine: Women & the Medical Division of Labour. (International Sociology Ser.: Vol. 44). (Illus.). 224p. (C). 1993. text 55.00 (*0-8039-8902-4*); pap. text 19.95 (*0-8039-8903-2*) Sage.

Riska, Elianne, jt. auth. see Ettorre, Elizabeth.

Riskas, Thomas. Working Beneath the Surface: Attending to the Soul's "Hidden Agenda" for Wholeness, Fulfillment, & Deep Spiritual Healing. (Illus.). 280p. 1997. 24.95 (*1-890009-15-6*) Exec Excell.

RiskCare Staff. For the Record: Risk Management Issues in Medical Records & Documentation. 97p. 1997. pap. text 135.00 (*1-893929-01-9*) RiskCare.

— Medical-Legal Correspondence Course. 111p. 1980. reprint ed. pap. text 199.00 (*1-893929-02-7*) RiskCare.

— Medical Legal Issues in Long-Term Care: Regulations & Risk Management Safeguards Pennsylvania Physicians Need to Know. 75p. 1999. pap. text 79.00 (*1-893929-03-5*) RiskCare.

— Office Staff Risk Management Resource: Audio Cassette & Handbook. 38p. 1997. pap. text 29.00 incl. audio (*1-893929-09-4*) RiskCare.

— Risk Management Pointers: Practical Advice for Busy Physicians. 100p. 1998. pap. text 135.00 (*1-893929-00-0*) RiskCare.

***RiskCare Staff & Bartlett, Ed.** The Diagnostic Dilemma: Exploring Risk Management Solutions. 99p. 1999. pap. 150.00 (*1-893929-10-8*) RiskCare.

RiskCare Staff & Kollas, Chad D. The New Physician's Guide to Legal Medicine. 59p. 1997. pap. text 19.00 (*1-893929-06-X*) RiskCare.

***RiskCare Staff & Rozovsky, Fay.** Risk Management Strategies for Physicians in Managed Care. 100p. 1999. pap. 135.00 (*1-893929-11-6*) RiskCare.

Riske, Kris B. Astrometeorology: Planetary Power in Weather Forecasting. LC 98-127548. (Illus.). 191p. 1997. pap. 19.95 (*0-86690-476-X*, R3686-014) Am Fed Astrologers.

Riske, Milt. Those Magnificent Cowgirls. LC 83-71805. (Illus.). 130p. 1984. pap. 15.00 (*0-913701-00-9*) Wyoming Pub.

Riske, S. Bernadine. Chi-Chi Chipmunk & the Grapevine. large type ed. LC 95-94789. (Illus.). 20p. (Orig.). (J). (ps-12). 1995. pap. text 9.95 (*1-885981-06-6*, Brisk Pubns) Brisk Pubng.

— Chick-A-Dee-Dee-Dee & Ollie Owl View People. large type ed. LC 94-96365. (Illus.). 16p. (Orig.). (J). (ps-12). 1994. pap. 9.95 (*1-885981-00-7*) Brisk Pubng.

— Connie Cat & Molly Mouse. large type ed. LC 95-96223. (Illus.). 20p. (Orig.). (J). (ps-12). 1996. pap. text 9.95 (*1-885981-10-4*, Brisk Pubns) Brisk Pubng.

—**Dee-Dee Chickadee & Friends. LC 97-94301. (Dee-Dee Chickadee Ser.). (Illus.). 10p. (Orig.). (J). (ps-12). 1998. pap. 9.95 (*1-885981-16-3*) Brisk Pubng.**

Birds & animals view their problems in human terms through poetry. Smaller birds must wait for a drink of water beside the lake until larger creatures have drunk. Bear's sweet tooth tempts him to take chances on getting stung by angry bees. A chimp watches a TV window & envies acting dogs on television. Freda Frog tries to convert goslings to a frog's lifestyle. Horse envies poodle who lives royally on charm & good looks. Fos & Bobcat accuse each other of being thieves. Rooster decides crowing on TV would show his real talents when he retires from herding hens. Chimps watch a ballgame but say sport fans are in a rut! Who knows who loses or wins? "To catch a ball is fun for mutts. They would rather play for coconuts." Poetry. *Publisher Paid Annotation.*

— Dee-Dee Chickadee & Piggy Puzzles. large type ed. LC 97-94995. (Illus.). 20p. (J). (gr. 3-12). 1996. pap. 9.95 (*1-885981-17-1*) Brisk Pubng.

— Dee-Dee Chickadee & the Committee. large type ed. LC 96-85239. (Illus.). 18p. (Orig.). (J). (ps-12). 1996. pap. 9.95 (*1-885981-14-7*) Brisk Pubng.

— Dee-Dee Chickadee Crosses a Creek. large type ed. LC 96-85476. (Dee-Dee Chickadee's Friends Ser.). (Illus.). 20p. (Orig.). (J). (ps-12). 1996. pap. 9.95 (*1-885981-15-5*) Brisk Pubng.

— Dee-Dee Chickadee Gets Lost. large type ed. LC 95-94019. (Illus.). 20p. (Orig.). (J). (ps-12). 1995. pap. 9.95 (*1-885981-05-8*, Brisk Pubns) Brisk Pubng.

— Dee-Dee Chickadee Goes to School. large type ed. LC 95-96426. (Illus.). 20p. (Orig.). (J). (ps-12). 1995. pap. 9.95 (*1-885981-04-X*) Brisk Pubng.

— Dee-Dee Chickadee Goes to the Fair. large type ed. LC 95-96077. (Illus.). 20p. (Orig.). (J). (ps-12). 1996. pap. text 9.95 (*1-885981-11-2*, Brisk Pubns) Brisk Pubng.

— Dee-Dee Chickadee the Peacemaker. limited large type ed. LC 95-94955. (Illus.). 20p. (Orig.). (J). (ps-12). 1996. pap. 9.95 (*1-885981-13-9*) Brisk Pubng.

— Dee-Dee Chickadee Visits Beehives. large type ed. LC 95-96076. (Illus.). 20p. (Orig.). (J). (ps-12). 1996. pap. 9.95 (*1-885981-12-0*, Brisk Pubns) Brisk Pubng.

— Dee-Dee Chickadee Visits Neighbors. large type ed. LC 94-92383. (Illus.). 20p. (Orig.). (J). (ps-12). 1994. pap. 9.95 (*1-885981-01-5*) Brisk Pubng.

— Foxy Fox Sells Magic Berries. large type ed. LC 94-96447. (Illus.). 20p. (Orig.). (J). (ps-12). 1994. pap. 9.95 (*1-885981-03-1*) Brisk Pubng.

—**A Magic Flight. LC 98-93138. (Illus.). 20p. (J). (gr. 5-12). 1998. pap. 9.95 (*1-885981-18-X*, Brisk Pubns) Brisk Pubng.**

Molly Mouse & Ollie Owl lived in the famous Shobird Theater until Molly Mouse heard people talking about moving the theater to make room for a shopping mall. Molly called out to Ollie Owl in the rafters in the theater, "They want to move our house:. What can we do? Molly mouse called a meeting with her friends in the park & Ollie came up with a plan to move their theater home. They caught a big balloon on the roof of the Shobird & tied it to the theater. The balloon rose into the skies with Mollie, Ollie & their friends, birds & animals, dogs & cats riding in a basket with the balloon that flew them out to sea where they saw many strange creatures. The west wind finally blew the balloon & its menagerie back to its home on land in Minnesota. The story based on current interest in balloons & present remodeling early historic theaters with popular appeal for children & adults, grades K - 12, all ages. Poetry. *Publisher Paid Annotation.*

— The Musical Tree. large type ed. LC 94-96424. (Illus.). 20p. (Orig.). (J). (ps-12). 1994. pap. 9.95 (*1-885981-02-3*) Brisk Pubng.

— Polly Bumpkin Plants Pumpkins. large type ed. LC 95-94956. (Illus.). 15p. (Orig.). (J). (ps-12). 1995. pap. 9.95 (*1-885981-08-2*, Brisk Pubns) Brisk Pubng.

Risken, H. The Fokker-Planck Equation: Methods of Solution & Applications. 2nd ed. LC 96-33182. (Springer Series in Synergetics). 1996. 59.95 (*3-540-61530-X*) Spr-Verlag.

— The Fokker-Planck Equation: Methods of Solution & Applications. 2nd ed. Haken, H., ed. (Synergetics Ser.: Vol. 18). (Illus.). xiv, 472p. 1992. reprint ed. 69.00 (*0-387-50498-2*) Spr-Verlag.

Riski, John E. & Witzel, Mary A. The Oral Mechanism Examination for Children & Young Adults: What Comes after "Ahhh" 1997. 110.00 incl. VHS (*1-58041-015-4*, 0112088) Am Speech Lang Hearing.

Riski, Maureen C. & Klakow, Nikolas. Patrick Gets Hearing Aids. (Illus.). 48p. (Orig.). (J). 1994. pap. 8.95 (*0-9647691-0-7*) Phonak.

***Riskin, Carl, ed.** China Human Development Report 1999: Transition & the State. (Illus.). 124p. (C). 2000. pap. text 19.95 (*0-19-592586-6*) OUP.

***Riskin, Carl, et al, eds.** China's Retreat from Equality: Income Distribution & Economic Transition. (Asia & the Pacific Ser.). 388p. 2000. 85.00 (*0-7656-0690-9*, East Gate Bk) M E Sharpe.

***Riskin, Carl & Khan, Azizur Rahman.** Inequality & Poverty in China in the Age of Globalization. (Illus.). 240p. 2000. text 45.00 (*0-19-513649-7*) OUP.

Riskin, Karen, jt. auth. see Munson, Lulie.

Riskin, Leonard L. Transcript & Simulation Materials: To Accompany Tape II: Mediation, the Red Devil Dog Lease, Instructor's Manual with A. (Dispute Resolution & Lawyers Videotape Ser.). 68p. (C). 1992. pap. text. write for info. (*0-314-01009-2*) West Pub.

— Transcript & Simulation Materials, Tape II: Transaction Negotiation the Carton Contract, Instructor's Manual with A. (Dispute Resolution & Lawyers Videotape Ser.). 47p. (C). 1992. pap. text. write for info. (*0-314-01008-4*) West Pub.

— Transcript & Simulation Materials to Accompany Tape I: Dispute Negotiation Thompson vs. Decker, a Medical Malpractice Claim, Instructor's Manual with A. (Dispute Resolution & Lawyers Videotape Ser.). 78p. (C). 1992. pap. text. write for info. (*0-314-01007-6*) West Pub.

R

— Transcript & Simulation Materials to Accompany Tape IV: Overview of ADR: The Roark vs. Daily Bugle Libel Claim, Instructor's Manual with A. (Dispute Resolution & Lawyers Videotape Ser.). 74p. (C). 1992. pap. text. write for info. (0-314-01010-6) West Pub.

Riskin, Leonard L. & Westbrook, James E. Dispute Resolution & Lawyers. (American Casebook Ser.). 468p. (C). 1987. text 32.50 (0-314-36473-0) West Pub.

— Dispute Resolution & Lawyers. abr. ed. (American Casebook Ser.). 223p. (C). 1987. pap. text 20.50 (0-314-68963-X) West Pub.

— Dispute Resolution & Lawyers. 2nd ed. LC 97-18396. (American Casebook Ser.). 848p. (C). 1997. 57.50 (0-314-07211-X) West Pub.

— Dispute Resolution & Lawyers. 2nd abr. ed. LC 97-47667. (American Casebook Ser.). 300p. (C). 1998. pap. 31.50 (0-314-07212-8) West Pub.

— Dispute Resolution & Lawyers: 1993 Supplement to Abridged Edition. (American Casebook Ser.). 117p. 1992. pap. 11.00 (0-314-01921-9) West Pub.

— Dispute Resolution & Lawyers: 1993 Supplement to Hardcover Edition. (American Casebook Ser.). 276p. (C). 1992. pap. text 14.50 (0-314-01920-0) West Pub.

Riskin, M. & McKenna. Practice Development: Creating the Marketing Mindset. 224p. 1989. pap. 63.00 (0-409-80636-6, MICHIE) LEXIS Pub.

Riskin, Marci L., ed. New Mexico's Historic Places: The Guide to National & State Register Sites. LC 99-58985. (Adventure Roads Ser.). (Illus.). 160p. 2000. pap. 16.95 (0-943734-40-1, 1HIS) Ocean Tree Bks.

Riskin, Martin. Alien Fun Book. 64p. (Orig.). 1997. pap. 5.95 (1-889647-14-4) Boston Am.

Riskin, Michael. Stop in the Name of Love: Ejaculation Control for Life. 103p. (Orig.). 1994. pap. 14.95 (0-9619609-1-4) Choice Fullerton.

Riskin, Michael & Banker-Riskin, Anita. Simultaneous Orgasm: And Other Joys of Sexual Intimacy. LC 97-19824. (Illus.). 240p. 1997. 24.95 (0-89793-222-6); pap. 14.95 (0-89793-221-8) Hunter Hse.

Riskin, Robert. Six Screenplays by Robert Riskin: Platinum Bonde, American Madness, It Happened One Night, Mr. Deeds Goes to Town, Lost Horizon, Meet John. McGilligan, Patrick, ed. LC 96-34595. (Illus.). 771p. 1997. 68.00 (0-520-20305-4, Pub. by U CA Pr) Cal Prin Full Svc.

— Six Screenplays by Robert Riskin: Platinum Bonde, American Madness, It Happened One Night, Mr. Deeds Goes to Town, Lost Horizon, Meet John. McGilligan, Pat, ed. LC 96-34595. (Illus.). 771p. 1997. pap. 38.00 (0-520-20525-1, Pub. by U CA Pr) Cal Prin Full Svc.

Riskin, Robert D. Between Opportunities: A Survival Guide for Job Seekers & Career Changers. 332p. (Orig.). 1992. pap. 14.95 (0-9633781-0-4) Aar Dee Aar Pub.

Riskin, Shlomo. Passover Haggadah: Riskin Haggadah. 1986. pap. 7.95 (0-88125-014-7) Ktav.

***Riskin, Steven M., ed.** Three Dimensions of Peacebuilding in Bosnia: Findings from USIP--Sponsored Research & Field Projects. 54p. 2000. pap. text 20.00 (0-7881-8979-4) DIANE Pub.

Riskind, David H., jt. auth. see Burleson, Bob.

Riskind, Mary. Apple Is My Sign. LC 80-39746. 160p. (J). (gr. 5-9). 1993. pap. 5.95 (0-395-65747-4) HM.

***Riskind, Mary.** Apple Is My Sign. 1999. 19.50 (0-8446-7004-9) Peter Smith.

— Apple is My Sign. 1983. 11.05 (0-606-05125-2, Pub. by Turtleback) Demco.

Risko, Donald G. & Kozak, Jerzy. Electrochemical Machining Technology for Advanced Manufacturing. Date not set. write for info. (0-8247-9928-3) Dekker.

***Risko, Robert.** The Risko Book. (Illus.). 192p. 2000. pap. 29.95 (1-58093-072-7, Pub. by Monacelli Pr) Penguin Putnam.

Risler, J. J. Mathematical Methods for CAD. (Illus.). 198p. (C). 1993. text 100.00 (0-521-43100-X) Cambridge U Pr.

— Methematical Methods for CAD. (Illus.). 198p. 1993. pap. text 42.95 (0-521-43691-5) Cambridge U Pr.

Risler, J. J., jt. auth. see Bellaiche, Andre.

Risler, J. J., jt. ed. see Bellaiche, Andre.

Risley, Agnes F., compiled by. Miscellaneous Bible Records, Principally New Jersey Families. (Illus.). 151p. 1997. reprint ed. pap. 22.00 (0-8328-6031-X) Higginson Bk Co.

Risley, E. H. Risley: Family History. (Illus.). 318p. 1990. reprint ed. pap. 51.00 (0-8328-1619-1); reprint ed. lib. bdg. 59.00 (0-8328-1618-3) Higginson Bk Co.

Risley, Herbert H. Gazetteer of Sikhim. (C). 1993. 22.00 (81-85557-05-5, Pub. by Low Price) S Asia.

Risley, John S. & Geballe, Ronald, eds. Electronic & Atomic Collisions: Abstracts of Papers of the 9th International Conference on the Physics of Electronic & Atomic Collisions, 2 vols., Set. LC 75-15451. 1198p. 1975. pap. 50.00 (0-295-95456-6) U of Wash Pr.

— The Physics of Electronic & Atomic Collisions: Invited Lectures, Review Papers & Progress Reports of the Ninth International Conference on the Physics of Electronic & Atomic Collisions. LC 75-39962. 916p. 1976. 50.00 (0-295-95455-8) U of Wash Pr.

Risley, John S. & Redisch, Edward F., eds. Computers in Physics Instruction: Abstracts of Contributed Papers. 237p. (Orig.). (C). 1988. pap. text 25.00 (0-317-90354-3) NCSU Physics.

Risley, Michael D. & Young, Catherine Murr. Automobile Insurance Law in Kentucky. xi, 151p. 1995. pap. 40.00 (1-58757-007-6, PM020) Univ of KY.

Risley, S., jt. auth. see Adams, A.

Risley, Teena, jt. auth. see McCollum, Susan.

Risley, Theodore G., ed. Wabash County, Illinois. (Illus.). 828p. 1994. reprint ed. lib. bdg. 85.00 (0-8328-3986-8) Higginson Bk Co.

Risley, Todd R., jt. auth. see Hart, Betty.

Risley, Todd R., jt. auth. see Hart, Betty M.

***Risman, Barbara.** Gender Vertigo: American Families in Transition. LC 97-28857. (Illus.). 208p. 1999. 15.00 (0-300-08083-2) Yale U Pr.

Risman, Barbara, jt. auth. see Johnson, Jacqueline.

***Risman, Barbara J.** Gender Vertigo: American Families in Transition. LC 97-28857. 224p. 1998. 25.00 (0-300-07215-5) Yale U Pr.

Rismiller, Peggy. The Echidna: Australia's Enigma. (Illus.). 128p. 1999. 25.00 (0-88363-788-X, Pub. by H L Levin) Publishers Group.

Risner, Carl L. The Pilgrim Experience Ore Book. 40p. 1998. pap. write for info. (1-57502-991-X, PO2701) Morris Pubng.

Riso, Don R. Discovery Your Personality Type: The New Enneagram Questionnaire. rev. ed. 120p. 1994. pap. 10.00 (0-395-71092-8) HM.

— Enneagram Transformations: Releases & Affirmations for Healing Your Personality Type. LC 92-28727. 120p. 1993. pap. 10.00 (0-395-65786-5) HM.

— Understanding the Enneagram: The Practical Guide to Personality Types. (Illus.). 288p. 1990. pap. 14.00 (0-395-52148-3) HM.

Riso, Don R. & Hudson, Russ. Personality Types. rev. ed. 456p. 1996. pap. 14.00 (0-395-79867-1) HM.

Riso, Don Richard. The Power of the Enneagram: A New Technology of Self-Discovery. 1996. 18.00 incl. audio (0-671-56797-7) S&S Trade.

***Riso, Don Richard.** Understanding the Enneagram: The Practical Guide to Personality Types. rev. ed. 304p. 2000. pap. 14.00 (0-618-00415-7) HM.

Riso, Don Richard & Hudson, Russ. The Wisdom of the Enneagram: The Complete Guide to Psychological & Spirtual Growth for the Nine Personality Types. LC 98-50577. (Illus.). 400p. 1999. reprint ed. pap. 17.95 (0-553-37820-1) Bantam.

Riso, Michael J. Little Michael's Guide to Raising Good Parents: A Seven Year Old's View. (Illus.). 93p. 1999. pap. 9.95 (0-9668103-0-9) Continuous Lrning Pubs.

Risoli, Vincent & Grippo, Frank A. Empty Boxes Vol. 1: The Stories of My Loves. (Illus.). 68p. 1998. pap. 9.95 (0-9610404-3-2) Mogul Bk.

Risom, Ole, jt. auth. see Retan, Walter.

Risom, Ole, ed. see Zallinger, Peter.

Rison, A. D. TAAS Test Champion for Social Studies & Language Arts: Reading & Writing. (Illus.). 270p. (YA). 1994. pap. text 25.00 (0-9635870-3-X, Book 3) Sunbelt Theatre.

Rison, Alton D. Guide to Pass the TAAS: Test Language Arts, Reading & Writing. 2nd rev. ed. (Illus.). 190p. (J). (gr. 3-12). 1990. pap. text 20.00 (0-9635870-1-3, Book 1) Sunbelt Theatre.

— How to Teach Black Children. (Illus.). 251p. 1992. pap. 25.00 (0-9635870-0-5) Sunbelt Theatre.

— Math Professor: To Pass 185 Math Tests & Quizzes, Bk. 4. (Illus.). 280p. (J). (gr. 2-12). 1997. pap. text 25.00 (0-9635870-4-8, Book 4) Sunbelt Theatre.

Rison, Robert. Elevated Dining: Cuisine Art of Healing with Vegetables, Vitamins Minerals & Gems. Allen, Chris, ed. (Illus.). 88p. (Orig.). 1993. pap. 16.95 (0-9625706-3-X) ECLAT Bks.

— The Living Information: Subconscious Mind & Power. (Illus.). 61p. (Orig.). (C). 1988. pap. 7.95 (0-9625706-0-5) ECLAT Bks.

Rispens, Jan, et al, eds. Perspectives on the Classification of Specific Developmental Disorders. LC 97-32490. (Neuropsychology & Cognition Ser.). 286p. 1998. 130.50 (0-7923-4871-0) Kluwer Academic.

Rispin, C., jt. auth. see Parnham, P.

***Rispin, Karen.** African Skies. 2000. mass mkt. 6.99 (1-57673-626-1) Multnomah Pubs.

Rispin, Karen. Rustlers. LC 98-217434. 250p. 1998. pap. 9.99 (1-57673-292-4, Palisades OR) Multnomah Pubs.

— Summit. LC 98-49979. 384p. 1999. pap. 6.99 (1-57673-402-1) Multnomah Pubs.

Rispler-Chaim, Vardit. Islamic Medical Ethics in the Twentieth Century. LC 92-47108. (Social, Economic & Political Studies of the Middle East: Vol. 46). viii, 152p. 1993. 33.50 (90-04-09608-6) Brill Academic Pubs.

— Islamic Medical Ethics in the Twentieth Century. 150p. 1996. 59.00 (0-614-21550-1, 639) Kazi Pubns.

Riss-Fang, Josephine, et al, eds. World Guide to Libary & Information Science Education. 2nd ed. LC 96-119945. (IFLA: vol. 72/73). 600p. 1995. 130.00 (3-598-21799-4) K G Saur Verlag.

Riss, Kathryn, jt. auth. see Riss, Richard.

Riss, Richard & Riss, Kathryn. Images of Revival. LC 97-194952. 182p. 1997. pap. 10.99 (1-56043-687-5, Revival Pr) Destiny Image.

Riss, Richard M. A Survey of Twentieth Century Revival Movements in North America. 202p. 1988. pap. 9.95 (0-913573-72-8) Hendrickson MA.

Rissanen, J. Stochastic Complexity in Statistical Inquiry Theory. (Series in Computer Science: Vol. 15). 188p. (C). 1989. text 55.00 (9971-5-0859-1); pap. text 33.00 (981-02-0311-X) World Scientific Pub.

Rissanen, Matti, et al, eds. Early English in the Computer Age: Explorations Through the Helsinki Corpus. LC 93-27036. (Topics in English Linguistics Ser.: No. 11). x, 296p. (C). 1993. lib. bdg. 129.25 (3-11-013739-9) Mouton.

— English in Transition: Corpus-Based Studies in Linguistic Variation & Genre Styles. LC 97-25407. 371p. 1997. text 111.00 (3-11-015632-6) Mouton.

— Grammaticalization at Work: Studies on Long-Term Developments in English. LC 97-25408. 434p. 1997. text 124.00 (3-11-015631-8) Mouton.

— History of Englishes: New Methods & Interpretations in Historical Linguistics. LC 92-31358. (Topics in English Linguistics Ser.: Vol. 10). (Illus.). xi, 799p. (C). 1992. lib. bdg. 229.25 (3-11-013216-8) Mouton.

Risse, Guenter B. Mending Bodies, Saving Souls: A History of Hospitals. (Illus.). 752p. 1999. text 39.95 (0-19-505523-3) OUP.

Risse, Gunter B., tr. see Rothschuh, Karl E.

Risse, Joseph, jt. auth. see Wilson, J. Sam.

Risse, Joseph A., ed. Study Guide for the Associate CET Test. 4th ed. 72p. 1989. pap. 10.00 (0-317-04954-2) Intl Soc Cert Elect.

Risse, Joseph A. & Wilson, Sam. The CET Study Guide. 4th ed. LC 95-35539. (Illus.). 336p. 1995. student ed. 32.95 (0-07-053022-X) McGraw.

— The CET Study Guide. 4th ed. LC 95-35539. (Illus.). 336p. 1995. pap., student ed. 19.95 (0-07-052933-7) McGraw-Hill Prof.

Risse, Joseph A., jt. auth. see Wilson, J. Sam.

Risse, Joseph A., jt. auth. see Wilson, Sam.

Risse-Kappen, Thomas. Cooperation among Democracies: The European Influence on U. S. Foreign Policy. (Princeton Studies in International History & Politics). 260p. 1995. pap. text 18.95 (0-691-01711-5, Pub. by Princeton U Pr) Cal Prin Full Svc.

— Cooperation among Democracies: The European Influence on U. S. Foreign Policy. 264p. (C). 1995. text 39.50 (0-691-03644-6, Pub. by Princeton U Pr) Cal Prin Full Svc.

— Structure & Process in Superpower Arms Control: Lessons from INF. (CISA Working Papers: No. 69). 41p. (Orig.). 1989. pap. 15.00 (0-86682-085-X) Ctr Intl Relations.

Risse-Kappen, Thomas, ed. Bringing Transnational Relations Back In: Non-State Actors, Domestic Structures & International Institutions. (Studies in International Relations: No. 42). 341p. (C). 1995. text 59.95 (0-521-48183-X); pap. text 19.95 (0-521-48441-3) Cambridge U Pr.

Risse-Kappen, Thomas, jt. auth. see Lebow, Richard N.

Risse, Thomas, et al, eds. The Power of Human Rights: International Norms & Domestic Change. (Studies in International Relations: Vol. 66). (Illus.). 330p. 1999. pap. 19.95 (0-521-65882-9) Cambridge U Pr.

— The Power of Human Rights: International Norms & Domestic Change. (Studies in International Relations: Vol. 66). (Illus.). 330p. (C). 1999. 54.95 (0-521-65093-3) Cambridge U Pr.

Risse, Wilhelm. Bibliographia Logica, 4 vols., Pt. 1: Verzeichnis der Druckschriften Zur Logik mi. (Studien und Materialien Zur Geschichte der Philosophie Ser.: Vol. 1). 293p. 1979. write for info. (3-487-04532-X) G Olms Pubs.

— Bibliographia Logica, 4 vols., Pt. 2: Verzeichnis der Druckschriften Zur Logik mi. (Studien und Materialien Zur Geschichte der Philosophie Ser.: Vol. 1). 494p. 1979. write for info. (3-487-04531-1) G Olms Pubs.

— Bibliographia Logica, 4 vols., Pt. 3: Verzeichnis der Zeitschriftenartikel Zur Lo. (Studien und Materialien Zur Geschichte der Philosophie Ser.: Vol. 1). 412p. 1979. write for info. (3-487-06960-1) G Olms Pubs.

— Bibliographia Logica, 4 vols., Pt. 4: Verzeichnis der Handschriften Zur Logik. (Studien und Materialien Zur Geschichte der Philosophie Ser.: Vol. 1). 390p. 1979. write for info. (3-487-06961-X) G Olms Pubs.

— Bibliographia Philosophica Vetus: Repertorium Generale Systematicum Operum Philosophicorm Usque ad Annum MDCCC Typis Impressorum: De Anima. (Studien und Materialien Zur Geschichte Der Philosophie: Bd. 45, Pars 5). (GER.). viii, 300p. 1998. write for info. (3-487-10541-1) G Olms Pubs.

— Bibliographia Philosophica Vetus: Repertorium Generale Systematicum Operum Philosophicorm Usque ad Annum MDCCC Typis Impressorum: Doxoscopia (Geschichte der Philosophie) (Studien und Materialien Zur Geschichte Der Philosophie: Bd. 45, Pars 7). (GER.). viii, 252p. 1998. write for info. (3-487-10543-8) G Olms Pubs.

— Bibliographia Philosophica Vetus: Repertorium Generale Systematicum Operum Philosophicorm Usque ad Annum MDCCC Typis Impressorum: Ethica et Politica. (Studien und Materialien Zur Geschichte Der Philosophie: Bd. 45, Pars 4). (GER.). viii, 648p. 1998. write for info. (3-487-10540-3) G Olms Pubs.

— Bibliographia Philosophica Vetus: Repertorium Generale Systematicum Operum Philosophicorm Usque ad Annum MDCCC Typis Impressorum: Logica. (Studien und Materialien Zur Geschichte Der Philosophie: Bd. 45, Pars 2). (GER.). viii, 492p. 1998. write for info. (3-487-10538-1) G Olms Pubs.

***Risse, Wilhelm.** Bibliographia Philosophica Vetus: Repertorium Generale Systematicum Operum Philosophicorm Usque ad Annum MDCCC Typis Impressorum: Metaphysica. (Studien und Materialien Zur Geschichte Der Philosophie: Bd. 45, Pars 3). (GER.). viii, 145p. 1998. write for info. (3-487-10539-X) G Olms Pubs.

Risse, Wilhelm. Bibliographia Philosophica Vetus: Repertorium Generale Systematicum Operum Philosophicorm Usque ad Annum MDCCC Typis Impressorum: Philosophia Generalis. (Studien und Materialien Zur Geschichte Der Philosophie: Bd. 45, Pars 1). (GER.). x, 469p. 1998. write for info. (3-487-10537-3) G Olms Pubs.

— Bibliographia Philosophica Vetus: Repertorium Generale Systematicum Operum Philosophicorm Usque ad Annum MDCCC Typis Impressorum: Philosophia Naturalis. (Studien und Materialien Zur Geschichte Der Philosophie: Bd. 45, Pars 6). (GER.). viii, 458p. 1998. write for info. (3-487-10542-X) G Olms Pubs.

— Bibliographia Philosophica Vetus: Repertorium Generale Systematicum Operum Philosophicorm Usque ad Annum MDCCC Typis Impressorum: Syllabus Auctorum. (Studien und Materialien Zur Geschichte Der Philosophie: Bd. 45, Pars 9). (GER.). viii, 348p. 1998. write for info. (3-487-10547-0) G Olms Pubs.

— Bibliographia Philosophica Vetus: Repertorium Generale Systematicum Operum Philosophicorm Usque ad Annum MDCCC Typis Impressorum: Theses Academicae (Akademische Reden) (Studien und Materialien Zur Geschichte Der Philosophie: Bd. 45, Pars 8). viii, 1516p. 1998. write for info. (3-487-10546-2) G Olms Pubs.

— Bibliographia Philosophica Vetus: Repertorium Generale Systematicum Operum Philosophicorm Usque ad Annum MDCCC Typis Impressorum: Theses Academicae (Disputationen) (Studien und Materialien Zur Geschichte Der Philosophie: Bd. 45 Pars 8). (GER.). viiip. 1998. write for info. (3-487-10544-6) G Olms Pubs.

— Bibliographia Philosophica Vetus: Repertorium Generale Systematicum Operum Philosophicorm Usque ad Annum MDCCC Typis Impressorum: Theses Academicae (Programme) (Studien und Materialien Zur Geschichte Der Philosophie: Bd. 45, Pars 8). viii, 1516p. 1998. write for info. (3-487-10545-4) G Olms Pubs.

— Complutenses Discalceati - Collegii Complutensis Disputationes in Aristotelis Dialecticam Et Philosophiam Naturalem. vii. 338p. 1977. reprint ed. write for info. incl. 3.5 hd (3-487-06240-2) G Olms Pubs.

— Conimbricenses - Commentarii Collegii Conimbricensis...in Universam Dialecticam Aristotelis, 2 vols. in 1. 38p. 1976. reprint ed. write for info. incl. 3.5 hd (3-487-05906-1) G Olms Pubs.

Risseeuw, Carla. Gender Transformation, Power & Resistance among Women in Sri Lanka. (C). 1991. 34.00 (81-85425-68-X, Pub. by Manohar) S Asia.

Risseeuw, Carla, jt. ed. see Palriwala, Rajni.

Risseeux, Carla & Ganesh, Kamela, eds. Negotiation & Social Space: A Gendered Analysis of Changing Kin & Security Networks in South Asia & Sub-Saharan Africa. LC 98-24651. 360p. 1999. 44.95 (0-7619-9270-7) Sage.

Rissel, Dorothy A., et al. En Directo! A Beginning Course. 2nd ed. LC 93-20993. (C). 1994. pap., wbk. ed. 28.75 (0-07-006972-7) McGraw.

— En Directo! A Beginning Course. 2nd ed. (C). 1994. pap. text 26.87 (0-07-006975-1) McGraw.

Rissel, Hilda. Three Plays by Moreto & Their Adaptation in France, Vol. II. LC 93-40940. (Iberica Ser.). VII, 164p. (C). 1995. 42.95 (0-8204-2364-5) P Lang Pubng.

Risselada, Rodie. Imperatives & Other Directive Expressions in Latin: A Study in the Pragmatics of a Dead Language. (Amsterdam Studies in Classical Philology Ser.: Vol. 2). xii, 349p. 1993. 84.00 (90-5063-206-8, Pub. by Gieben) J Benjamins Pubng Co.

***Risselada, Rodie.** Latin in Use: Amerserdam Studies in the Pragmatics of Latin. LC 99-192394. (Amsterdam Studies in Classical Philology Ser.: Vol. 8). viii, 120p. 1999. 45.00 (90-5063-297-1, Pub. by Gieben) J Benjamins Pubng Co.

Risselada, Rodie, et al, eds. On Latin: Linguistic & Literary Studies in Honour of Harm Pinkster. 216p. 1996. lib. bdg. 54.00 (90-5063-137-1, Pub. by Gieben) J Benjamins Pubng Co.

Risser, Christy. Do Miracles Happen? Signs & Wonders in the Gospel of John. (Generation Why: Vol. 2:6). 36p. (YA). (gr. 9-12). 1997. pap. 12.95 (0-87303-269-1) Faith & Life.

Risser, James. Hermeneutics & the Voice of the Other: Re-Reading Gadamer's Philosophical Hermeneutics. LC 96-22787. (SUNY Series in Contemporary Continental Philosophy). 256p. (C). 1997. text 65.50 (0-7914-3257-2); pap. text 21.95 (0-7914-3258-0) State U NY Pr.

Risser, James, ed. Heidegger Toward the Turn: Essays on the Work of the 1930's. LC 99-26111. (SUNY Series in Contemporary Continental Philosophy). 416p. (C). 1999. pap. text 25.95 (0-7914-4302-7, Suny Pr) State U NY Pr.

— Heidegger Toward the Turn: Essays on the Work of the 1930's. LC 99-26111. (SUNY Series in Contemporary Continental Philosophy). 416p. (C). 1999. text 75.50 (0-7914-4301-9, Suny Pr) State U NY Pr.

Risser, James, jt. auth. see Brogan, Walter.

Risser, James, jt. ed. see Brogan, Walter.

Risser, Joy. OJT Traffic Clerk Resource Materials. 2nd ed. (Gregg Office Job Training Program Ser.). (Illus.). 112p. (gr. 11-12). 1981. pap. text 9.88 (0-07-052960-4) McGraw.

***Risser, Martha K.** Corinthian Conventionalizing Pottery. LC 00-25741. (Corinth Ser.). (Illus.). 200p. 2000. 60.00 (0-87661-075-0) Am Sch Athens.

Risser, Rita. Stay Out of Court: The Manager's Guide to Preventing Employee Lawsuits. LC 93-6799. (C). 1993. pap. text 19.95 (0-13-845561-9) P-H.

Risset, Jacqueline. The Translation Begins: Poems. Moxley, Jennifer, tr. from FRE. (Serie d'Ecriture: Vol. 10).Tr. of La Traduction Commence. 96p. 1996. pap. 10.00 (1-886224-09-9) Burning Deck.

Rissetto, Harry. A Light on the Hill: Tampa United Methodist Centers in the Modern Era. (Illus.). 152p. 1998. pap. 9.95 (0-9672198-0-9) Tampa Untd Meth.

Rissik, Dee. Culture Shock! South Africa. (Illus.). 240p. (Orig.). 1993. pap. 12.95 (1-55868-149-3) Gr Arts Ctr Pub.

***Rissik, Maureen.** Princess A Precious Gift to Unlock & Treasure. 1999. pap. text 9.95 (0-7624-0539-2) Running Pr.

— Tooth Fairy Box A Magical Gift to Unlock & Treasure. 1999. pap. text 9.95 (0-7624-0538-4) Running Pr.

***Rissinger, Matt.** Best School Jokes Ever. 1999. pap. text 4.95 (0-8069-9832-6) Sterling.

Rissinger, Matt & Yates, Philip. Biggest Joke Book in the World. (Illus.). 192p. (J). (gr. 3). 1996. pap. 6.95 (0-8069-0853-X) Sterling.

— Great Book of Zany Jokes. (Illus.). 96p. (J). (gr. 3-7). 1995. pap. 4.95 (0-8069-0471-2) Sterling.

Rissinger, Matt, jt. auth. see Yates, Philip.

An Asterisk (*) at the beginning of an entry indicates that the title is appearing for the first time.

Rissler, Jane & Mellon, Margaret. The Ecological Risks of Engineered Crops. (Illus.). 192p. (C). 1996. 32.00 (*0-262-18171-1*); pap. text 16.95 (*0-262-68085-8*) MIT Pr.

Rissman, Paul & Chitalwala, Y. M. Harappan Civilization & Oriyo Timbo. 1990. 30.00 (*81-204-0484-X*, Pub. by Oxford IBH) S Asia.

Risso, Giuseppe. Cospaia. Asselin, Claudette, tr. from ITA. LC 78-70626. (Illus.). 1979. pap. 7.95 (*0-915570-14-9*) Oolp Pr.

Risso, Mario. Safari Grammar. 128p. 1995. pap. 7.95 (*0-8442-5466-5*, 54665, Natl Textbk Co) NTC Contemp Pub Co.

— Safari Punctuation. 128p. 1994. pap. 7.95 (*0-8442-5467-3*, 54673, Natl Textbk Co) NTC Contemp Pub Co.

Risso, Mario & Grathwohl, J. David. To Will? Or to Trust? That Is the Question? (Illus.). 160p. (Orig.). 1992. pap. text 19.95 (*0-917035-01-1*) Chicken Little.

Risso, Mario & Risso, Nancy. Funny-Fax. (Illus.). 112p. (Orig.). 1992. pap. 9.95 (*0-917035-24-0*) Chicken Little.

Risso, Mario, jt. auth. see Collis, Harry.

Risso, Nancy, jt. auth. see Risso, Mario.

Risso, Patricia. Merchants & Faith: Muslim Commerce & Culture in the Indian Ocean. LC 94-42937. (New Perspectives on Asian History Ser.). 168p. (C). 1995. pap. 23.00 (*0-8133-8911-9*, Pub. by Westview) HarpC.

Rist. Platonism & Its Christian Heritage. 94.95 (*0-86078-169-0*) Ashgate Pub Co.

Rist, Carl & Friedman, Robert. Building the Ladder: Strategies for Economic Independence-Oriented Welfare Reform. 40p. 1996. pap. 15.00 (*1-883187-22-2*) Corp Ent Dev.

Rist, Carl & Sahay, Puchka. Community-Based Organizations & Business Networks: New Ideas for Creating Job Opportunities for Inner-City Residents. 49p. 1996. pap. 25.00 (*1-883187-12-5*) Corp Ent Dev.

Rist, Carl, jt. auth. see Clones, Daphne.

Rist, Charles. History of Monetary & Credit Theory: From John Law to the Present Day (1940 Edition) 442p. 1996. reprint ed. 75.00 (*1-85506-333-6*) Bks Intl VA.

— History of Monetary & Credit Theory from John Law to the Present Day. LC 66-21371. (Reprints of Economic Classics Ser.). 442p. 1966. reprint ed. 49.50 (*0-678-00161-8*) Kelley.

Rist, Gilbert. The History of Development: From Western Origins to Global Faith. LC 97-7618. 1997. pap. 25.00 (*1-85649-492-6*, Pub. by Zed Books) St Martin.

Rist, J. M. Human Value. 1982. pap. 42.00 (*90-04-06757-4*, PHA, 40) Brill Academic Pubs.

Rist, Johann, et al, eds. Saemtliche Werke. Incl. Vol. 1. Dramatische Dichtungen: Irenaromachia, Perseus. (Illus.). iv, 289p. 1967. 193.00 (*3-11-000346-5*); Vol. 2. Dramatische Dichtungen. 1972. 304.00 (*3-11-004125-1*); Vol. 4. Epische Dichtungen. 1972. 207.00 (*3-11-004124-3*); Vol. 5. Epische Dichtungen. Die Alleredelste Torheit. Die Alleredelste Belustigugh. 1974. 274.00 (*3-11-004591-5*); Vol. 6. Epische Dichtungen: Die alleredelste Erfindung, Die alleredelste Zeitverkuerzung. 1976. 296.00 (*3-11-006817-6*); Vol. 7. Philosophischer Phoenix, Rettung des Phoenix, Teutsche Hauptsprache, Alleredelste Hauswatter. 1982. 256.00 (*3-11-008659-X*); (Ausgaben Deutscher Literatur des XV bis XVIII Jahrhunderts Ser.). (GER.). (C). write for info. (*0-318-51643-8*) De Gruyter.

Rist, John M. Augustine: Ancient Thought Baptized. 356p. 1996. pap. text 22.95 (*0-521-58952-5*) Cambridge U Pr.

— Epicurus: An Introduction. LC 70-177939. 199p. reprint ed. pap. 56.80 (*0-608-12496-6*, 2024523) Bks Demand.

— Man, Soul & Body: Essays in Ancient Thoughts from Plato to Dionysius. (Collected Studies: No. CS549). 320p. 1996. 98.95 (*0-86078-547-5*, Pub. by Variorum) Ashgate Pub Co.

— The Mind of Aristotle: A Study in Philosophical Growth. (Phoenix Supplementary Volumes Ser.). 361p. 1989. text 60.00 (*0-8020-2692-3*) U of Toronto Pr.

***Rist, John M.** On Inoculating Moral Philosophy Against God. LC 99-50978. (Aquinas Lecture Ser.). 2000. write for info. (*0-87462-167-4*) Marquette.

Rist, Peter, jt. ed. see Barnard, Timothy.

Rist, Rachel A., jt. auth. see Thomasen, Eivind.

Rist, Ray C. The Invisible Children: School Integration in American Society. LC 77-24554. 301p. reprint ed. pap. 93.40 (*0-7837-2320-2*, 205740800004) Bks Demand.

Rist, Ray C., ed. The Democratic Imagination: Dialogues on the Work of Irving Louis Horowitz. 475p. (C). 1994. 49.95 (*1-56000-174-7*) Transaction Pubs.

— Policy Evaluation: Linking Theory to Practice. LC 94-32281. (Reference Collection: International Library of Comparative Public Policy: Vol. 3). 608p. 1995. 230.00 (*1-85278-946-8*) E Elgar.

— Policy Issues for the 1990s. (Policy Studies Review Annual: Vol. 9). 800p. 1988. 89.95 (*0-88738-265-7*) Transaction Pubs.

— Policy Studies Review Annual, Vol. 6. 776p. 1982. text 69.95 (*0-8039-1875-5*) Transaction Pubs.

— Policy Studies Review Annual, Vol. 7. 700p. (C). 1985. text 69.95 (*0-88738-008-5*) Transaction Pubs.

— Policy Studies Review Annual, Vol. 8. 726p. 1987. pap. 34.95 (*0-88738-673-3*); text 79.95 (*0-88738-116-2*) Transaction Pubs.

— Pornography Controversy: Changing Moral Standards in American Life. LC 73-92813. (Social Policy Ser.). 290p. 1974. pap. 21.95 (*0-87855-587-0*) Transaction Pubs.

— Program Evaluation & the Management of Government. 378p. 1989. 39.95 (*0-88738-297-5*) Transaction Pubs.

***Rist, Ray C., ed.** Program Evaluation & the Management of Government. 193p. 1999. pap. 24.95 (*0-7658-0600-2*) Transaction Pubs.

Rist, Ray C., ed. Restructuring American Education: Innovations & Alternatives. LC 75-186712. 250p. 1972. 39.95 (*0-87855-037-2*); pap. text 21.95 (*0-87855-533-1*) Transaction Pubs.

Rist, Ray C. & Anson, Ronald J., eds. Education, Social Science, & the Judicial Process. LC 77-962. 154p. reprint ed. pap. 47.80 (*0-608-18802-6*, 203018000067) Bks Demand.

Rist, Ray C., ed. see Fine, Doris.

Rist, Ray C., jt. ed. see Picciotto, Robert.

Rist, Robert, jt. ed. see Detienne, Francoise.

***Rist, Thomas.** Shakespeare's Romances & the Politics of Counter-Reformation. LC 99-24876. (Renaissance Studies: Vol. 3). 268p. 1999. text 89.95 (*0-7734-8033-1*) E Mellen.

— Shakespeare's Romances & the Politics of Counter-reformation. LC 99-24876. 1999. write for info. (*0-88946-880-X*) E Mellen.

Ristad, Eloise. A Soprano on Her Head: Right-Side-Up Reflections on Life - And Other Performances. LC 81-23369. 201p. 1982. 19.00 (*0-911226-20-6*); pap. 13.50 (*0-911226-21-4*) Real People.

Ristad, Eric S., ed. Language Computations. LC 94-28045. (DIMACS Series in Discrete Mathematics & Theoretical Computer Science: 17). 198p. 1994. text 60.00 (*0-8218-6608-7*, DIMACS/17) Am Math.

Ristad, Eric Sven. The Language Complexity Game. Bobrow, Daniel G. et al, eds. (Artificial Intelligence Ser.). (Illus.). 168p. 1993. 30.00 (*0-262-18147-9*) MIT Pr.

Ristaino, Marcia R. China's Art of Revolution: The Mobilization of Discontent, 1927-1928. LC 87-470. xv, 274p. (C). 1987. text 54.95 (*0-8223-0718-9*) Duke.

Ristau. Business Careers. 2nd ed. (CA - Career Development Ser.). 1984. mass mkt., wbk. ed. 18.95 (*0-538-25400-9*) S-W Pub.

— Mirror/Mirror - An International Office Simulation. (GB - Basic Business Ser.). 1994. mass mkt., wbk. ed. 16.95 (*0-538-62384-5*) S-W Pub.

Ristau, et al. Introduction to Business: The Economy & You. 3rd ed. (GB - Basic Business Ser.). 1996. mass mkt. 58.95 (*0-538-65688-3*) S-W Pub.

— Introduction to Business: The Economy & You, Un. 1-6. 3rd ed. (GB - Basic Business Ser.). 1996. pap., student ed. 16.95 (*0-538-65690-5*) S-W Pub.

— Introduction to Business Units 1-11: The Economy & You. 3rd ed. (GB - Basic Business Ser.). 1996. mass mkt., student ed. 27.95 (*0-538-65689-1*); mass mkt., student ed. 16.95 (*0-538-65691-3*) S-W Pub.

— Introduction to Business, Glossary: Economics & You. 3rd ed. (GB - Basic Business Ser.). (SPA.). 1996. mass mkt. 5.95 (*0-538-66670-6*) S-W Pub.

— Introduction to Business, Test/Exam Bank Pt. 1: Economics & You. 3rd ed. (GB - Basic Business Ser.). 1996. pap. 5.95 (*0-538-65695-6*) S-W Pub.

— Introduction to Business, Test/Exam Bank Pt. 2: Economics & You. 3rd ed. (GB - Basic Business Ser.). 1997. pap. 5.95 (*0-538-66211-5*) S-W Pub.

Ristau, jt. auth. see Daughtrey.

Ristau, Bruno A. International Judicial Assistance: Civil & Commercial, 2 vols. LC 84-63137. 900p. 1990. suppl. ed. 295.00 (*0-935328-30-0*) Intl Law Inst.

Ristau, Bruno A. & Abbell, Michael. International Judicial Assistance, 6 vols. 1985. ring bd. 790.00 (*90-411-0996-X*) Kluwer Law Intl.

— International Judicial Assistance: Civil & Commercial, 5 vols. LC 84-63137. 900p. 1990. suppl. ed. 560.00 (*0-935328-60-2*) Intl Law Inst.

— International Judicial Assistance: Civil & Commercial, 7 vols., Set, Vols. 1-6. rev. ed. LC 84-63137. 2000p. 1990. suppl. ed. 760.00 (*0-935328-61-0*) Intl Law Inst.

Ristau, Carolyn, ed. Cognitive Ethology: The Minds of Other Animals Essays in Honor of Donald R. Griffin. (Comparative Cognition & Neuroscience Ser.). 344p. 1990. pap. 45.00 (*0-8058-0252-5*); text 89.95 (*0-8058-0251-7*) L Erlbaum Assocs.

***Ristau, Debra A. & Renebome, Joyce.** Horse Whispers & Lies. (Illus.). 320p. 1999. pap. 18.95 (*1-929055-44-7*) Veracity Bks.

Ristau, Herbert. Kommunale Elektrizitatsversorgung in Den Neuen Bundeslandern: Unter Besonderer Berucksichtigung von Umweltbelangen. (Europaische Hochschulschriften Ser.: Reihe 5, Bd. 2133). (GER., Illus.). XXVI, 306p. 1997. 57.95 (*3-631-31813-8*) P Lang Pubng.

Ristau, Karen, ed. see Bartle, Pat.

Ristau, Karen, ed. see Ford, Judith E.

Ristau, Karen, ed. see Grace, Bill.

Ristau, Karen, ed. see McGinnis, James & McGinnis, Kathleen.

Ristau, Karen, ed. see Rord, Elinor R. & Durante, Sheila R.

Ristau, Karen, ed. see Wincek, Jean & O'Malley, Colleen.

Ristau, Karen, ed. see Zukowski, Angela A.

Ristau, Karen M. & Rogus, Joseph F. Leadership of & on Behalf of Catholic Schools. (National Congress Catholic Schools for the 21st Century Ser.). 45p. 1991. pap. 2.00 (*1-55833-067-4*) Natl Cath Educ.

***Ristau, Steve.** Realizing Packetswitch Technology. 1999. pap. 49.99 (*0-7897-2254-2*) Que.

Riste, Olav. The Norwegian Intelligence Service, 1945-1970: Northern Vigil. LC 99-23373. (Studies in Intelligence Ser.). 352p. 1999. pap. 24.50 (*0-7146-4455-2*, Pub. by F Cass Pubs) Intl Spec Bk.

***Riste, Olav.** The Norwegian Intelligence Service, 1945-1970: Northern Vigil. LC 99-23373. (Studies in Intelligence Ser.). 315p. 1999. 59.50 (*0-7146-4900-7*) F Cass Pubs.

Riste, Tormod, ed. Phase Transitions & Relaxation in Systems with Competing Energy Scales: Proceedings of the NATO Advance Study Institute, Geilo, Norway, 13-23 April 1993. LC 93-31136. (NATO Advanced Science Institutes Series C: Mathematical & Physical Sciences). 464p. (C). 1993. text 259.00 (*0-7923-2504-4*) Kluwer Academic.

Riste, Tormod & Sherrington, D., eds. Spontaneous Formation of Space-Time Structures & Criticality. 464p. (C). 1991. text 219.50 (*0-7923-1452-2*) Kluwer Academic.

Riste, Tormod, jt. ed. see Pynn, Roger.

Riste, Tormod, ed. see Sherrington, D. C.

Riste, Tormod, jt. ed. see Sherrington, D.

Risteau, Delores. 1996 American Payroll Association: Basic Guide to Payroll. 1995. 125.00 (*0-87622-678-0*) Aspen Pub.

***Risteau, Delores & Mitchell-George, Joanne.** 2000 American Payroll Association Basic Guide to Payroll. 750p. 2000. ring bd. 149.00 (*0-7355-1103-9*) Panel Pubs.

Ristelhueber, Rene. History of the Balkan Peoples. Spector, Sherman D., ed. & tr. by. from FRE. LC 78-147184. (Illus.). 470p. 1978. reprint ed. 50.50 (*0-8290-0176-X*); reprint ed. pap. text 19.95 (*0-8290-0177-8*) Irvington.

Ristelhueber, Sophie. Sophie Ristelhueber. (Illus.). 112p. 1998. 25.00 (*2-85025-610-2*, 821093) Hazan.

Ristenen, Elaine K., tr. see Popov, A. A.

Ristenin, Les. The Knives of Finland. 96p. 1990. pap. 14.95 (*0-9626839-0-6*) Suomi Shop.

Rister, Carl C. Comanche Bondage: Dr. John Charles Beale's Settlement of La Villa de Dolores on Las Moras Creek in Southern Texas of the 1830's with an Annotated Reprint of Sarah Ann Horn's Narrative of Her Captivity among the Comanches, Her Ransom by Traders in New Mexico & Return Via the Sante Fe Trail. LC 89-4943. (Illus.). 211p. reprint ed. pap. 65.50 (*0-608-20139-1*, 207141100011) Bks Demand.

— Land Hunger: David L. Payne & the Oklahoma Boomers. LC 75-118. (Mid-American Frontier Ser.). (Illus.). 1975. reprint ed. 23.95 (*0-405-06884-0*) Ayer.

***Rister, Chip.** Apache Gold. 168p. 1999. pap. 4.95 (*0-9666690-1-0*) Hidden Val.

Rister, M. Edward, et al, eds. Rice Economics Research & Extension Programs at Texas A & M University. (Illus.). 65p. (Orig.). (C). 1993. pap. text 30.00 (*1-56806-452-7*) DIANE Pub.

***Rister, Marie V.** In Christian Love: Poems from the Heart. (Illus.). 64p. 2000. pap. 8.95 (*0-9666690-2-9*) Hidden Val.

Rister, R., tr. see Blumenthal, Mark, et al, eds.

Rister, Robert. Japanese Herbal Medicine: The Healing Art of Kampo. LC 98-53401. 360p. 1999. pap. 19.95 (*0-89529-836-8*, Avery) Penguin Putnam.

— Prescription for Herbal Healing: A Practical A-Z Reference to Drug-Free Remedies Using Herbs & Herbal Preparations. 480p. 1999. pap. 19.95 (*0-89529-869-4*, Avery) Penguin Putnam.

***Rister, Robert & Balch, Phyllis.** Prescription for Herbal Healing. 2001. pap. 23.95 (*1-58333-094-1*, Avery) Penguin Putnam.

***Risterucci-Roudnicky, Danielle.** France - RDA Anatomie d'Un Transfert Litteraire 1949-1990. xxv, 464p. 1999. 60.95 (*3-906760-23-0*) P Lang Pubng.

Ristic, Ljubisa, ed. Sensor Technology & Devices. LC 94-2361. 524p. 1994. 109.00 (*0-89006-532-2*) Artech Hse.

Ristic, Miodrag. Diseases of Cattle in the Tropics. 1981. lib. bdg. 230.00 (*90-247-2399-X*) Kluwer Academic.

— Diseases of Cattle in the Tropics. 1981. pap. text 126.50 (*90-247-2495-3*) Kluwer Academic.

Ristic, Miodrag, ed. Babesiosis of Domestic Animals & Man, Vol. I. 176p. 1988. 152.00 (*0-8493-4908-7*, QR201, CRC Reprint) Franklin.

Ristic, Miodrag, et al, eds. Malaria & Barbesiosis. (New Perspectives in Clinical Microbiology Ser.). 1984. text 225.00 (*0-89838-675-6*) Kluwer Academic.

Ristic, Miodrag, jt. ed. see Woldehiwet, Zerai.

Ristich, Alberta. Color Me Love. Satchell, Alexis, ed. LC 84-91395. (Illus.). 50p. (Orig.). 1984. pap. 6.25 (*0-931841-01-1*) Satchells Pub.

Ristig, M. L., jt. auth. see Clark, J. W.

Ristinen, Robert A. & Kraushaar, Jack J. Energy & the Environment. LC 98-23071. 384p. 1998. pap. 67.95 (*0-471-17248-0*) Wiley.

Ristinen, Robert A., jt. auth. see Kraushaar, Jack J.

Ristiniemi, Jari. Experiential Dialectics: An Inquiry into the Epistemological Status & the Methodological Role of the Experiential Core in Paul Tillich's Systematic Thought. (Studia Philosophiae Religionis: No. 14). 215p. (Orig.). 1987. pap. text 41.00 (*91-22-00983-3*) Coronet Bks.

***Ristino, Robert J.** The Agile Manager's Guide to Managing Change. LC 00-102365. (Agile Manager Ser.). (Illus.). 112p. 2000. pap. 9.95 (*1-58099-019-3*) Velocity Busn.

Ristock, Janice L. & Pennell, Joan. Community Research As Empowerment: Feminist Links, Postmodern Interpretations. LC 97-139209. 152p. 1996. pap. text 21.00 (*0-19-541080-7*) OUP.

Ristock, Janice L. & Taylor, Catherine, eds. Inside the Academy & Out: Lesbian/Gay/Queer Studies & Social Action. LC 99-218294. 416p. 1998. text 50.00 (*0-8020-0860-7*); pap. text 24.95 (*0-8020-7848-6*) U of Toronto Pr.

Ristoff, Dilvo I. John Updike's "Rabbit at Rest" Appropriating History. (Modern American Literature Ser.: Vol. 18). XVII, 209p. (C). 1998. text 46.95 (*0-8204-3990-8*) P Lang Pubng.

Riston, Doug. The Great White Duck Hunter. 140p. 1998. pap. 12.95 (*0-9653340-3-1*) Green Lght.

Ristori, Adelaide. Memoirs & Artistic Studies. LC 74-81977. (Illus.). 279p. 1972. 24.95 (*0-405-08892-2*, Pub. by Blom Pubns) Ayer.

Ristori, Al. Fishing for Bluefish. 4th rev. ed. Barrett, Linda, ed. (Fisherman Library). (Illus.). 176p. 1995. reprint ed. 15.95 (*0-923155-03-1*) Fisherman Lib.

Ristori, Bridget. Patients in My Care. large type ed. (Non-Fiction Ser.). 1971. 27.99 (*0-85456-089-0*) Ulverscroft.

Ristovic, Aleksandar. Devil's Lunch: Selected Poems. Simic, Charles, tr. 96p. 2000. pap. 13.00 (*0-571-20008-7*) Faber & Faber.

— Some Other Wine & Light. Simic, Charles, tr. LC 89-60744. 1989. 10.00 (*0-910350-11-6*) Charioteer.

***Ristow, Gerald H.** Pattern Formation in Granular Materials. LC 99-56369. (Tracts in Modern Physics Ser.: Vol. 164). (Illus.). xiii, 161p. (C). 2000. 96.00 (*3-540-66701-6*) Spr-Verlag.

Ristow, W. W. Guide to the History of Cartography: An Annotated List of References in the History of Maps & Mapmaking. 100p. 1997. reprint ed. 30.00 (*1-57898-035-6*) Martino Pubng.

Ristow, Walter W. American Maps & Mapmakers: Commercial Cartography in the Nineteenth Century. LC 84-25798. (Illus.). 488p. reprint ed. pap. 151.30 (*0-608-20289-4*, 207154800001) Bks Demand.

— Emergence of Maps in Libraries. 358p. 1980. 100.00 (*0-7201-1620-1*) Elliots Bks.

Ristow, William, ed. San Francisco Bar Book. LC 81-66873. (Illus.). 128p. 1981. pap. 3.95 (*0-913192-03-1*) SF Bay Guardian.

— San Francisco Free & Easy. rev. ed. LC 80-66932. (Illus.). 352p. 1980. pap. 5.95 (*0-913192-02-3*) SF Bay Guardian.

Ristuccia, Angela M. & Cunha, Burke A., eds. Antimicrobial Therapy. LC 84-17843. (Handbook of Therapeutic Drug Monitoring Ser.). (Illus.). 636p. 1984. reprint ed. pap. 197.20 (*0-608-00627-0*, 206121400007) Bks Demand.

Risvik, Einar, jt. ed. see Naes, Tomrod.

Risvold, Floyd E. The Minnesota Territory in Postmarks, Letters & History. LC 85-73113. (Illus.). 329p. 1985. 65.00 (*0-916675-01-7*) L H Hartmann.

Rita, Corinne J., jt. auth. see Gallagher, Bernard J., III.

Rita, Emilio S. Tapping the Multicultural Roots of Success. 180p. (C). 1995. text 31.80 (*0-536-58719-1*) Pearson Custom.

Rita, Emilio S. Preparandose Para Triunfar. (SPA.). (C). 1991. pap. text 41.00 (*0-536-57965-2*) Pearson Custom.

Rita-Mess, Bela J. & Jozsa, R. Localization & Ontogeny of Peptidergic Neurons in Birds: Comparative Studies on the Releasing & Inhibiting Hormones in Birds & Mammals. 95p. 1993. pap. 295.00 (*963-05-6608-7*, Pub. by Akade Kiado) St Mut.

Rita, Suzanne, et al. Advanced Nursing Practice. unabridged ed. Larson, Linda & Egging, Darcy, eds. 113p. (Orig.). 1997. pap. 33.00 (*0-935890-09-2*) Emerg Nurses IL.

Ritacco, Rochelle & Carroll, Michael P. The Drinking Buddy: A Guide to the Nightspots of the Jersey Shore: South Monmouth Edition. (Illus.). (Orig.). 1997. pap. 6.95 (*0-9659418-0-9*, 2226661) Crossings NJ.

Ritajananda. Swami Turiananda. (Illus.). pap. 6.95 (*81-7120-721-9*) Vedanta Pr.

Ritamary, Sister, see Sister Ritamary.

Ritberger, Carol. What Color Is Your Personality? Red, Orange, Yellow, Green... LC 99-12898. 156p. 1999. pap. 15.95 (*1-56170-651-5*) Hay House.

***Ritberger, Carol.** Wisdom Without Boundaries: Initiation into Higher Consciousness. 256p. 2000. pap. 13.95 (*1-56170-711-2*, 5021) Hay House.

Ritberger, Carol. Your Personality, Your Health: Connecting Personality with the Human Energy System, Chakras & Wellness. LC 98-11819. 244p. 1998. pap. 12.95 (*1-56170-538-1*, 567) Hay House.

Ritcey, G. M. Tailings Management: Problems & Solutions in the Mining Industry. (Process Metallurgy Ser.: No. 6). 970p. 1989. 348.25 (*0-444-87374-0*) Elsevier.

Ritcey, G. M. & Ashbrook, A. W. Solvent Extraction: Principles & Applications to Process Metallurgy, Pt. 2. (Process Metallurgy Ser.: Vol. 1, Pt. 2). 738p. 1979. 258.25 (*0-444-41771-0*) Elsevier.

Ritch, Barbara A. & Ficke, Mary M. A History of Aphrodisiacs & Related Subjects: Yesterday & Today. Dinin, Denise, ed. (Illus.). 200p. (Orig.). 1985. pap. 9.95 (*0-9614846-0-8*) Gems N Gold Pub.

Ritch, Barbara F. Coal Camp Kids, Coming up Hard & Making It. 352p. 1991. 29.95 (*0-942407-12-1*) Father & Son.

Ritch, Van. Background Investigation for Law Enforcement. LC 97-67325. (Illus.). 176p. (C). 1997. pap. 20.00 (*0-89089-901-0*) Carolina Acad Pr.

Ritchart, Ronald E. Making Numbers Make Sense: A Sourcebook for Developing Numeracy in Grades K-8. 1993. pap. 15.00 (*0-201-81749-7*) Addison-Wesley.

***Ritchart, Ronald E.** Pythagora's Bow Tie: Pre-Algebra Investigations Using the 121-Pin Geoboard. (Illus.). 1999. pap. 18.95 (*1-57452-256-6*) Cuisenaire.

Ritchason, Jack. Hiatal Hernia: The Natural Approach to Overcoming Hiatal Hernia & Other Gastrointestinal ... 1997. pap. text 11.95 (*1-885670-34-6*) Woodland UT.

— Little Herb Encyclopedia. 126p. 1984. pap. 5.95 (*0-913923-18-4*) Woodland UT.

— Little Herb Encyclopedia. 2nd ed. 126p. 1994. pap. 9.95 (*0-913923-89-3*) Woodland UT.

— La Pequena Enciclopedia de Hierbas (Little Herb Encyclopedia) (SPA.). Date not set. pap. 7.95 (*1-885670-63-X*) Woodland UT.

— La Pequena Enciclopedia de Hierbas (Little Herb Encyclopedia) 228p. 1992. pap. text 6.95 (*0-913923-00-1*) Woodland UT.

— Vitamin & Health Encyclopedia. 129p. 1986. pap. 7.95 (*0-913923-92-3*) Woodland UT.

***Ritchee, Aileen.** Juju Girl. (Nick Hern Bks.). 2000. pap. 14.95 (*1-85459-462-1*) Theatre Comm.

Ritcher, Paul O. White Grubs & Their Allies: A Study of North American Scarabaeoid Larvae. LC 66-63008. (Illus.). 216p. 1966. 29.95 (*0-87071-054-0*) Oreg St U Pr.

Ritcheson, Charles R. Aftermath of Revolution: British Policy Toward the United States, 1783-1795. LC 77-86328. 519p. reprint ed. pap. 160.90 (*0-8357-8793-1*, 203342600086) Bks Demand.

— British Politics & the American Revolution. LC 81-1808. (Illus.). 320p. 1981. reprint ed. lib. bdg. 65.00 (*0-313-22953-8*, RIBP, Greenwood Pr) Greenwood.

Ritchey, Bill. The Statistical Imagination. LC 99-17717. 1999. 47.50 (*0-07-289123-8*) McGraw.

Ritchey, Brenda. The Christian Soldier's Sword: God's Word for Daily Victory. 208p. (Orig.). 1997. pap. 7.95 (*1-885729-12-X*) Toccoa Falls.

— Know the Happy Face. Durand-Gordon, Lara & Velazquez, Patty, eds. LC 97-94852. (Illus.). 218p. 1997. pap. 17.95 (*0-9660530-0-1*) ALASKA.

Ritchey, David, ed. A Guide to the Baltimore Stage in the Eighteenth Century: A History & Day Book Calendar. LC 81-13461. (Illus.). 342p. 1982. lib. bdg. 99.50 (*0-313-22589-3*, RBS/, Greenwood Pr) Greenwood.

Ritchey, Ferris J., jt. auth. see Cockerham, William C.

**Ritchey, Ferris Joseph.* Keys Statistical Imagination. 1999. pap. text 30.00 (*0-07-234198-X*) McGraw.

***Ritchey, Gail.** Making Miniature Villages in Polymer Clay. LC 99-36221. (Illus.). 128p. 2000. pap. 22.99 (*0-89134-956-1*, 31422, North Lght Bks) F & W Pubns Inc.

Ritchey, Gene. Biblical Christianity. (Illus.). 260p. 1998. 29.95 (*0-9661736-0-0*); pap. 29.95 (*0-9661736-1-9*) Sequoia Pub CA.

— Building a Lasting Relationship. (Illus.). 110p. 1999. 49.95 (*0-9661736-4-3*); pap. 29.95 (*0-9661736-5-1*) Sequoia Pub CA.

— Your Immune System & Your Health. (Illus.). 161p. 1999. 49.95 (*0-9661736-2-7*); pap. 29.95 (*0-9661736-3-5*) Sequoia Pub CA.

Ritchey, Joseph D. & Rumbaugh, James O., eds. Subsurface Fluid Flow (Ground-Water & Vadose Zone) Modeling, STP 1288. LC 96-38424. (Special Technical Publication: Vol. 128). (Illus.). 425p. 1996. text 69.00 (*0-8031-2021-4*, STP1288) ASTM.

Ritchey, Laurence, jt. auth. see Horton, Charles E.

Ritchey, Lee W. & Blankenhorn, James C. High Speed PCB Design. 110p. (C). 1992. text 299.95 (*1-882812-04-2*) SMT Plus.

Ritchey, Tim & Siyan, Karanjit S. Inside Java. 2nd ed. LC 96-54294. 800p. 1997. pap. text 55.00 (*1-56205-664-6*) New Riders Pub.

Ritchey, Timothy D. Java: Programming with Beta 2.0. LC 96-106244. (Illus.). 350p. (Orig.). 1995. pap. 35.00 incl. cd-rom (*1-56205-533-X*) New Riders Pub.

— JavaScript for the Macintosh. LC 96-75189. 336p. 1996. pap. text 40.00 incl. cd-rom (*1-56830-278-9*) Hayden.

Ritchey, Timothy D., jt. auth. see Meggitt, Ashley.

***Ritchhart, Lisa Ashley.** Start an Effective Nursery/Toddler Ministry. (But I Don't Know How to... Ser.). 2000. pap. 4.95 (*0-87162-866-X*) Warner Pr.

Ritchhart, Ron, ed. Through Mathematical Eyes: Exploring Functional Relationships in Math & Science. LC 97-5389. (Moving Middle Schools Ser.). 172p. 1997. pap. text 19.50 (*0-435-07217-X*, 07217) Heinemann.

***Ritchie.** Engineering Applications. 240p. (C). 1998. pap. text 39.95 (*0-7506-2577-5*) Buttrwrth-Heinemann.

Ritchie. First Steps in Latin. Date not set. pap. text. write for info. (*0-582-36267-9*, Pub. by Addison-Wesley) Longman.

— Handbook of Language Acquisition. 2nd ed. (C). 1998. text 139.95 (*0-12-589040-0*) Acad Pr.

— San Diego & Old Town (German) Geschichteu aus der Pionierzeit (1769-1927) (ENG & GER., Illus.). 110p. 1998. 12.50 (*1-889361-06-2*) Ruroanik.

Ritchie, Adrian. Media French: A Guide to Contemporary French Idiom. 268p. 1997. 39.95 (*0-7083-1399-X*, Pub. by Univ Wales Pr) Paul & Co Pubs.

***Ritchie, Adrian C., ed.** A Selection of the Political Journalism: With Introduction & Notes. 179p. (C). 1999. pap. 28.95 (*0-8204-4248-8*) P Lang Pubng.

Ritchie, Adrian C., ed. see Maupassant, Guy de.

Ritchie, Andrew. Major Taylor: The Extraordinary Career of a Champion Bicycle Racer. LC 95-44486. (Illus.). 336p. (C). 1996. reprint ed. pap. 15.95 (*0-8018-5303-6*) Johns Hopkins.

Ritchie, Andrew, jt. ed. see Lessing, Hans-Erhard.

Ritchie, Andrew C. Abstract Painting & Sculpture in America. LC 70-86432. (Museum of Modern Art Publications in Reprint). (Illus.). 1969. reprint ed. 24.95 (*0-405-01544-5*) Ayer.

— Edouard Vuillard. LC 79-86445. (Museum of Modern Art Publications in Reprint). (Illus.). 1969. reprint ed. 15.95 (*0-405-01545-3*) Ayer.

— English Painters, Hogarth to Constable. LC 68-57337. (Essay Index Reprint Ser.). 1977. 12.95 (*0-8369-0124-X*) Ayer.

— Sculpture of the Twentieth Century. LC 78-169311. (Museum of Modern Art Publications in Reprint). (Illus.). 288p. 1972. reprint ed. 42.95 (*0-405-01570-4*) Ayer.

Ritchie, Andrew C., jt. auth. see Museum of Modern Art Library Staff.

Ritchie, Andrew C., ed. see Haftmann, Werner, et al.

Ritchie, Andrew J. Sketches of Rabun County History, 1819-1948. (Illus.). 503p. 1997. reprint ed. lib. bdg. 53.00 (*0-8328-6627-X*) Higginson Bk Co.

Ritchie, Anna. Picts: An Introduction to the Life of the Picts & the Carved Stones in the Care of the Secretary of State for Scotland. Tabraham, Christopher, ed. (Historic Scotland Ser.). (Illus.). 64p. 1989. pap. 15.00 (*0-11-493491-6*, Pub. by Statnry Office) Seven Hills Bk.

— Shetland. (Exploring Scotland's Heritage Ser.). (Illus.). 176p. 1997. pap. 18.95 (*0-11-495289-2*, Pub. by Statnry Office) Seven Hills Bk.

***Ritchie, Anna, ed.** Neolithic Orkney in Its European Context. 300p. (C). 2000. 80.00 (*1-902937-04-X*, Pub. by McDonald Inst) David Brown.

Ritchie, Anna, et al, eds. The Ancient Monuments of Orkney. (Historic Scotland Ser.). 76p. 1995. 12.00 (*0-11-495734-7*, Pub. by Statnry Office) Balogh.

Ritchie, Anna & Ritchie, Graham. Scotland: An Oxford Archaeological Guide. (Oxford Archaeological Guides Ser.). (Illus.). 268p. 1998. pap. 16.95 (*0-19-288002-0*) OUP.

Ritchie, Anna, jt. auth. see Ritchie, Graham.

Ritchie, Anne I. Blackstick Papers. LC 71-76911. (Essay Index Reprint Ser.). 1977. 21.95 (*0-8369-0027-8*) Ayer.

— From the Porch. LC 70-152208. (Essay Index Reprint Ser.). (Illus.). 1977. reprint ed. 20.95 (*0-8369-2252-2*) Ayer.

— Madame de Sevigne. LC 77-37716. reprint ed. 29.50 (*0-404-56809-2*) AMS Pr.

— The Works of Miss Thackeray, 15 vols., Set. LC 70-37717. reprint ed. 525.00 (*0-404-56810-6*) AMS Pr.

Ritchie, Anne T. Mrs. Dymond (1885) (Pocket Classics Ser.). 272p. 1997. pap. 12.95 (*0-7509-1411-4*, Pub. by Sutton Pub Ltd) Intl Pubs Mktg.

— Records of Tennyson, Ruskin & Browning. LC 70-172549. 190p. 1972. reprint ed. 24.95 (*0-405-08893-0*, Pub. by Blom Pubns) Ayer.

Ritchie, Anne Thackeray. Anne Thackeray Ritchie: Journals & Letters. Maynard, John & Bloom, Abigail B., eds. LC 94-15018. (Studies in Victorian Life & Literature). 372p. 1995. text 65.00 (*0-8142-0638-7*) Ohio St U Pr.

Ritchie, B., ed. see Lindsay, P. A., et al.

Ritchie, Bill H. The Art of Selling Art: Between Production & Livelihood. 252p. (C). 1996. pap. 19.95 (*1-56235-117-6*) Ritchies Perfect Pr.

Ritchie, Branson W. Avian Viruses: Function & Control. LC 95-60930. (Illus.). 528p. (C). 1995. text 99.00 (*0-9636996-3-6*) Zoological Educ.

Ritchie, Branson W., et al, eds. Avian Medicine: Principles & Application. LC 93-60501. (Illus.). 1384p. (C). 1994. text 175.00 (*0-9636996-0-1*) Zoological Educ.

— Avian Medicine: Principles & Application. abr. ed. (Illus.). 800p. (C). 1997. pap. text 69.00 (*0-9636996-5-2*) Zoological Educ.

— Exotic Medicine Library. (Illus.). 2400p. (C). 1994. text 225.00 incl. cd-rom (*0-9636996-2-8*) Zoological Educ.

***Ritchie, Branson W. & Harrison, Greg J.** Avian Medicine: Principles & Application. Harrison, Linda R., ed. 1000p. 1999. reprint ed. text 100.00 (*0-9674066-0-9*) HBD Intl.

Ritchie, Branson W., jt. auth. see Mcconnell, Vicki C.

Ritchie, C. Operating Systems. 226p. 1995. pap. 59.95 (*1-85805-131-2*, Pub. by DP Publns) St Mut.

Ritchie, C. A. Physical Organic Chemistry: The Fundamental Concepts. 2nd expanded rev. ed. (Illus.). 376p. 1989. text 59.75 (*0-8247-8307-7*, 8307-7) Dekker.

Ritchie, Calvin D., jt. ed. see Coetzee, J. F.

***Ritchie, Carl & Dewsberry, Elise.** Any Body Home? 103p. 1999. pap. 5.60 (*0-87129-962-3*, A85) Dramatic Pub.

Ritchie, Carson I. Frontier Parish: An Account of the Society for the Propagation of the Gospel & the Anglican Church in America, Drawn from the Records of the Bishop of London. LC 75-3564. 210p. 1976. 18.50 (*0-8386-1735-2*) Fairleigh Dickinson.

— Q-Ships: Britain's Secret Weapon Against the U-Boats, 1914-1918. 236p. 1990. 48.00 (*0-86138-011-8*, Pub. by T Dalton) St Mut.

— Rock Art of Africa. LC 76-24614. (Illus.). 157p. 1978. 25.00 (*0-87982-024-1*) Art Alliance.

— Rock Art of Africa. 25.00 (*0-8453-1753-9*, Cornwall Bks) Assoc Univ Prs.

Ritchie, Charles M. Diplomatic Passport: More Undiplomatic Diaries. 200p. 1986. pap. 4.95 (*0-7715-9258-2*) Genl Dist Srvs.

— Gemini G. E. L. Recent Prints & Sculpture. LC 94-19078. (Illus.). 91p. 1994. reprint ed. pap. 30.00 (*0-608-00214-3*, 206100700006) Bks Demand.

— The Siren Years: A Canadian Diplomat Abroad. 216p. 1987. pap. 4.95 (*0-7715-9269-8*) Genl Dist Srvs.

Ritchie, D. F., et al, eds. Compendium of Stone Fruit Diseases. LC 95-77906. (Disease Compendium Ser.). (Illus.). 128p. (Orig.). 1995. pap. 42.00 (*0-89054-174-4*) Am Phytopathol Soc.

Ritchie, Daniel E., ed. Edmund Burke: Appraisals & Applications. 294p. (C). 1990. 44.95 (*0-88738-328-9*) Transaction Pubs.

Ritchie, Daniel E., ed. see Burke, Edmund.

Ritchie, David. Ballots & Bullets, No. 3. 1983. 5.50 (*0-394-53067-5*) Random.

— Encyclopedia of Earthquakes & Volcanoes. LC 93-7670. (Illus.). 240p. 1994. 40.00 (*0-8160-2659-9*) Facts on File.

— Frontier Life. (Life in America 100 Years Ago Ser.). (Illus.). 100p. (YA). (gr. 5 up). 1995. 19.95 (*0-7910-2842-9*) Chelsea Hse.

— Shipwrecks: An Encyclopedia of the World's Worst Disasters at Sea. LC 95-15664. (Illus.). 304p. 1996. 40.00 (*0-8160-3163-0*, Checkmark) Facts on File.

— Shipwrecks: An Encyclopedia of the World's Worst Disasters at Sea. (Illus.). 304p. 1999. pap. 18.95 (*0-8160-4056-7*, Checkmark) Facts on File.

— Sports & Recreation. (Life in America 100 Years Ago Ser.). (Illus.). 100p. (YA). (gr. 5 up). 1995. lib. bdg. 19.95 (*0-7910-2848-8*) Chelsea Hse.

— UFO: The Definitive Guide to Unidentified Flying Objects & Related Phenomena. LC 93-31037. (Illus.). 272p. 1994. 40.00 (*0-8160-2894-X*) Facts on File.

— UFO - the Definitive Guide to Unidentified Flying Objects & Related Phenomena. (Illus.). 276p. 1997. 9.98 (*1-56731-200-4*, MJF Bks) Fine Comms.

***Ritchie, David & Ritchie, Deborah.** Connecticut: Off the Beaten Path. 4th ed. LC 00-21209. (Off the Beaten Path Ser.). (Illus.). 256p. (Orig.). 2000. pap. 13.95 (*0-7627-0643-0*) Globe Pequot.

Ritchie, David, jt. auth. see Ritchie, Deborah.

Ritchie, David F. Four Years in the First New York Light Artillery: The Papers of David F. Ritchie. rev. ed. Ritchie, Norman L., ed. LC 97-30979. (Illus.). viii, 257p. 1997. 24.95 (*0-9622393-9-9*) Edmonston Publ.

Ritchie, David G. Plato: 1902 Edition. (Key Texts Ser.). 240p. 1996. reprint ed. pap. 19.95 (*1-85506-215-1*) Bks Intl VA.

— Principles of State Interference. LC 70-94282. (Select Bibliographies Reprint Ser.). 1977. 21.95 (*0-8369-5060-7*) Ayer.

Ritchie, Deborah & Ritchie, David. Connecticut - Off the Beaten Path: A Guide to Unique Places. 3rd ed. LC 98-15455. (Off the Beaten Path Ser.). (Illus.). 256p. 1998. pap. 12.95 (*0-7627-0170-6*) Globe Pequot.

Ritchie, Deborah, jt. auth. see Ritchie, David.

Ritchie, Dennis M., jt. auth. see Kernighan, Brian W.

***Ritchie, Donald A.** American History: The Modern Era since 1865 LC 99-202501. xxvxviii, 918 p. 1999. teacher ed. write for info. (*0-02-822433-7*) Glencoe.

— American History: The Modern Era since 1865. LC 99-202501. 1999. teacher ed. write for info. (*0-02-822438-8*) Glencoe.

Ritchie, Donald A. American Journalists: Getting the Story. LC 96-29208. (Oxford Profiles Ser.). (Illus.). 336p. (YA). (gr. 5 up). 1998. 35.00 (*0-19-509907-9*) OUP.

— Doing Oral History. (Twayne's Oral History Ser.). (Illus.). 288p. 1994. 29.95 (*0-8057-9124-8*, Twyne); per. 14.95 (*0-8057-9128-0*, Twyne) Mac Lib Ref.

— James M. Landis: Dean of the Regulators. LC 80-12828. 276p. 1980. 37.95 (*0-674-47171-7*) HUP.

— Press Gallery: Congress & the Washington Correspondents. LC 90-43676. (Illus.). 288p. 1991. 42.00 (*0-674-70375-8*, RITPRE) HUP.

— Press Gallery: Congress & the Washington Correspondents. (Illus.). 312p. 1992. pap. 18.00 (*0-674-70376-6*) HUP.

Ritchie, Donald A., jt. auth. see Manning, Diane K.

Ritchie, Donald A., jt. auth. see Pious, Richard M.

Ritchie, Donald A., ed. see Gluck, Sherna B.

Ritchie, Donald D. & Carola, Robert. Biology. 2nd ed. LC 82-11318. (Biology Ser.). (Illus.). 672p. (C). 1983. text. write for info. (*0-201-06356-5*); 8.00 (*0-201-06359-X*); sl. 120.00 (*0-201-06393-X*) Addison-Wesley.

— Biology: A Study Guide. 2nd ed. LC 82-11318. (Biology Ser.). (Illus.). 672p. (C). 1983. pap. text, student ed. 16.00 (*0-201-06358-1*) Addison-Wesley.

Ritchie, Donald J. Ball Lightning: A Collection of Soviet Research in English Translation. LC 61-15177. 70p. reprint ed. pap. 30.00 (*0-8357-5950-4*, 202470700038) Bks Demand.

Ritchie, Elisavietta. The Arc of the Storm. unabridged ed. LC 98-15049. 200p. 1998. pap. 15.00 (*0-930095-06-5*) Signal Bks.

— Elegy for the Other Woman. 63p. (Orig.). 1996. pap. 14.00 (*0-930095-20-0*) Signal Bks.

— Flying Time: Stories & Half-Stories. LC 92-37103. 1992. pap. 12.00 (*0-930095-14-6*) Signal Bks.

— Raking the Snow. LC 81-86642. 55p. 1982. pap. 7.00 (*0-931846-21-8*) Wash Writers Pub.

— Tightening the Circle over Eel Country. LC 74-17130. 110p. 1974. pap. 4.95 (*0-87491-390-X*) Signal Bks.

Ritchie, Elisavietta, ed. Finding the Name. 144p. 1983. pap. 5.95 (*0-9612158-0-1*) Wineberry Pr.

— A Wound-Up Cat & Other Bedtime Stories. pap. 4.95 (*1-895450-14-4*) Signal Bks.

Ritchie, Esther, tr. see Porter, Jack N., ed.

Ritchie, Esther, tr. see Porter, Jack N. & Merin, Yehuda, eds.

Ritchie, Ethel M., ed. see Fairburn, William A.

Ritchie, Evelyn. Hickory Sled. 64p. 1989. pap. 5.95 (*0-932616-24-0*) Brick Hse Bks.

Ritchie, Everett J., jt. auth. see Hehner, Nels E.

***Ritchie, Fern J.** Edible Herbs: And the Plants That Add Flavor. LC 97-95121. (Incredible Edibles Ser.: Vol. 4). (Illus.). 362p. 2000. pap. 79.95 (*0-939656-25-6*) Ritchie Unltd.

Ritchie, Fern J. Growing Vegetables from Seed Successfully: All the Information You Need for Planting Right at Your Fingertips. 1 vol. LC 97-95122. (Incredible Edible Ser.). viii, 38p. 1998. 39.95 (*0-939656-24-8*) Ritchie Unltd.

***Ritchie, Fern J.** Handbook of Edible Wild Plants & Weeds: Using Fruit, Nuts, Seeds & Flowers, Buds & Other Plant Parts from the Plants That Grow Nearby but Outside the Garden As Wilds or Weeds. LC 99-64725. (Incredible Edible Ser.: Vol. 2). (Illus.). 340p. 1999. pap. 44.95 (*0-939656-26-4*) Ritchie Unltd.

— Handbook of Edible Wild Plants & Weeds Vol. 2: Reference. LC 99-64725. (Incredible Edible Ser.: Vol. 3). 82p. 1999. pap. 8.95 (*0-939656-27-2*) Ritchie Unltd.

Ritchie, Fern J., jt. auth. see Ritchie, Ralph W.

Ritchie, G. J. Circuitos con Transistores, Technicas Discretas E Integradas. (SPA.). 272p. (C). 1994. pap. text 14.00 (*0-201-62556-3*) Addison-Wesley.

Ritchie, G. S. No Day too Long - An Hydrographer's Tale. 247p. (C). 1989. text 50.00 (*1-872795-63-3*, Pub. by Pentland Pr) St Mut.

Ritchie, George C., Jr. Ordered to Return: My Life after Dying. 2nd ed. LC 98-70607. 184p. 1998. reprint ed. pap. 12.95 (*1-57174-096-1*) Hampton Roads Pub Co.

Ritchie, George G. & Sherrill, Elizabeth. Return from Tomorrow. LC 91-25512. 128p. (gr. 10). 1981. mass mkt. 3.99 (*0-8007-8412-X*, Spire) Revell.

***Ritchie, George H. & Stauffer, George B.** Organ Technique: Modern & Early. (Illus.). 384p. 2000. pap. text 35.00 (*0-19-513745-0*) OUP.

Ritchie, Gordon J. Transistor Circuit Techniques. 2nd ed. 1987. pap. 34.95 (*0-278-00034-7*) Chapman & Hall.

Ritchie, Gordon J., et al. Principles & Practice of General Surgery: Essentials of Practice. (Illus.). 1200p. (C). 1994. text 162.00 (*0-397-51114-0*, Lippnctt) Lppncott W & W.

Ritchie, Graeme D. Computational Grammar: An Artificial Intelligence Approach to Linguistic Description. (Harvester Studies in Cognitive Science: No. 15). 254p. 1980. 42.00 (*0-389-20048-4*, N6819) B&N Imports.

Ritchie, Graeme D., et al. Computational Morphology: Practical Mechanisms for the English Lexicon. (ACL-MIT Press Ser.). (Illus.). 304p. 1991. 42.00 (*0-262-18146-0*, Bradford Bks) MIT Pr.

Ritchie, Graham, ed. The Archaeology of Argyll. LC 97-124416. (Illus.). 288p. 1996. pap. 30.00 (*0-7486-0645-9*, Pub. by Edinburgh U Pr) Col U Pr.

Ritchie, Graham & Harman, Mary. Argyll & the Western Isles. (Exploring Scotland's Heritage Ser.). 168p. 1985. 14.00 (*0-11-492429-5*, Pub. by Statnry Office) Balogh.

Ritchie, Graham & Ritchie, Anna. Scotland: Archaeology & Early History. (Illus.). 208p. 1992. pap. 25.00 (*0-7486-0291-7*, Pub. by Edinburgh U Pr) Col U Pr.

Ritchie, Graham, jt. auth. see Henshall, Audrey.

Ritchie, Graham, jt. auth. see Ritchie, Anna.

***Ritchie, Guy.** Lock, Stock & Two Smoking Barrels. (Illus.). 148p. 1999. mass mkt. 10.00 (*0-7472-6205-5*, Pub. by Headline Bk Pub) Trafalgar.

Ritchie, Harland D. Livestock Judging & Evaluation Manual. (Illus.). x, 259p. 1983. reprint ed. pap. 8.50 (*0-87013-152-4*) Mich St U Pr.

Ritchie, Harry. Last Pink Bits: Travels Through the Remnants of the British Empire. 230p. (J). 1999. mass mkt. (*0-340-66683-8*) Hodlder & Stoughton.

Ritchie, Harry, ed. Acid Plaid: New Scottish Writing. LC 97-25382. 256p. 1997. pap. 13.45 (*1-55970-398-9*, Pub. by Arcade Pub Inc) Time Warner.

***Ritchie, Hugh & Carnegie Endowment for International Peace Staff.** The Navicert System During the World War. LC 99-48867. (Carnegie Endowment for International Peace Monograph Ser.: No. 2). viii, 83p. 2000. reprint ed. 37.50 (*1-57588-559-X*, 323910) W S Hein.

Ritchie, Ian. Biggest Glass Palace in the World. 1998. pap. text 7.50 (*1-899858-21-0*, Pub. by Ellipsis) Norton.

Ritchie, Ingrid & Hayes, William. A Guide to Implementation of the ISO 14000 Series on Environmental Management. LC 97-10725. 512p. 1997. 75.00 (*0-13-541097-5*) P-H.

Ritchie, J. Thirty Families: Their Living Standards in Unemployment. (DSS Research Report Ser.). 1990. 13.00 (*0-11-761683-4*, Pub. by Statnry Office) Bernan Associates.

Ritchie, J., et al. GPs & IVB. A Qualitative Study of the Role of GPs in the Award of Invalidity Benefit. (DSS Research Report Ser.). 1993. write for info. (*0-11-762077-7*, Pub. by Statnry Office) Bernan Associates.

Ritchie, J. C. Past & Present Vegetation of the Far Northwest Canada. 272p. (C). 1984. text 37.50 (*0-8020-2523-4*) U of Toronto Pr.

— Post-Glacial Vegetation of Canada. (Illus.). 192p. 1987. text 105.00 (*0-521-30868-2*) Cambridge U Pr.

Ritchie, J. M. German Exiles: British Perspectives. LC 96-37491. (Exilstudien/Exile Studies: Vol. 6). X, 334p. (C). 1997. text 55.95 (*0-8204-3743-3*) P Lang Pubng.

Ritchie, J. M., jt. auth. see Hawksworth, D. L.

Ritchie, J. M., ed. & tr. see Al-Amin bin Ali al Mazru'i, Shaykh.

Ritchie, J. M., tr. see Raabe, Paul, ed.

Ritchie, J. Murdoch, jt. ed. see Waxman, Stephen G.

Ritchie, J. N., jt. auth. see Ritchie, W. F.

Ritchie, J. N. G. Brochs of Scotland. (Archaeology Ser.: Vol. 53). (Illus.). 64p. 1999. pap. text 10.50 (*0-7478-0389-7*, Pub. by Shire Pubns) Parkwest Pubns.

Ritchie, J. R., et al, eds. World Travel & Tourism Review: Indicators, Trends & Issues, Vol. 3. (Illus.). 320p. 1993. text 185.00 (*0-85198-853-9*) OUP.

Ritchie, J. R. & Goeldner, Charles R. Travel, Tourism, & Hospitality Research: A Handbook for Managers & Researchers. 2nd ed. 640p. 1994. 69.95 (*0-471-58248-4*) Wiley.

Ritchie, J. R. & Hawkins, D. F., eds. World Travel & Tourism Review: Indicators, Trends, & Issues, Vol. 2. (Illus.). 320p. 1992. text 185.00 (*0-85198-771-0*) OUP.

Ritchie, J. T. & Hanks, R. J. Modeling Plant & Soil Systems. (Agronomy Monograph Ser.: Vol. 31). 565p. 1991. 30.00 (*0-89118-106-7*) Am Soc Agron.

Ritchie, Jack. Tiger Island. 2nd ed. 1987. 4.95 (*0-932310-09-5*) U of Wis-Stevens Point.

Ritchie, James. Created by God. 10.00 (*0-687-07409-6*) Abingdon.

— Created by God: About Human Sexuality for Older Girls & Boys. (Illus.). (YA). 1999. teacher ed. 49.95 (*0-687-07408-8*) Abingdon.

Ritchie, James. FolkPsalms: A Musical Story Based on the Book of Psalms: Leader/Accompanist Edition. 72p. 1993. spiral bd. 14.95 (*0-687-13258-4*) Abingdon.

An Asterisk (*) at the beginning of an entry indicates that the title is appearing for the first time.

— FolkPsalms: A Musical Story Based on the Book of Psalms: PreviewPak. 1995. pap. 6.00 incl. audio (*0-687-06675-1*) Abingdon.

— FolkPsalms: A Musical Story Based on the Book of Psalms: Singer's Edition. 16p. 1993. pap. 2.95 (*0-687-13259-2*) Abingdon.

— Folkpsalms: Intro Pak - Both Books & Listening Tape. 1993. 19.95 (*0-687-13257-6*) Abingdon.

Ritchie, James. We & the Earth Are One. 1.50 (*0-687-06198-9*) Abingdon.

Ritchie, James A. Kerrigan. LC 93-8065. 1993. 19.95 (*0-8027-1276-2*) Walker & Co.

— Kerrigan. large type ed. LC 93-45624. 280p. 1994. lib. bdg. 19.95 (*0-7862-0164-9*) Thorndike Pr.

— The Last Free Range. 224p. 1995. 19.95 (*0-8027-4150-9*) Walker & Co.

Ritchie, James A. Over on the Lonesome Side. 192p. 1991. 19.95 (*0-8027-4118-5*) Walker & Co.

Ritchie, James A. Payback. 172p. 1992. 19.95 (*0-8027-1233-9*) Walker & Co.

— The Wagon Wars: A Sequel to "The Last Free Range" LC 96-43383. 190p. 1997. 20.95 (*0-8027-4157-6*) Walker & Co.

Ritchie, James L., ed. Thallium--201 Myocardial Imaging. fac. ed. LC 78-3004. (Illus.). 166p. pap. 51.50 (*0-7837-7357-9*, 204716600005) Bks Demand.

***Ritchie, Jean.** Abducted: The Remarkable Story of Alien Abduction. 1999. 35.00 (*0-7472-2121-9*, Pub. by Headline Bk Pub); pap. 19.95 (*0-7472-7516-5*, Pub. by Headline Bk Pub) Trafalgar.

Ritchie, Jean. The Dulcimer Book. (Illus.). 1963. pap. 12.95 (*0-8256-0016-2*, OK61465, Oak) Music Sales.

— Folk Songs of the Southern Appalachians As Sung by Jean Ritchie. 2nd ed. (Illus.). 112p. 1997. 30.00 (*0-8131-2021-7*); pap. 16.00 (*0-8131-0927-2*) U Pr of Ky.

— Jean Ritchie Celebration of Life: Her Songs . . . Her Poems. 128p. 1997. pap. 11.95 (*0-8256-9676-3*, JI10009) Music Sales.

***Ritchie, Jean.** Jean Ritchie's Swapping Song Book. (Illus.). 96p. 2000. pap. 14.95 (*0-8131-0973-6*) U Pr of Ky.

Ritchie, Jean. Singing Family of the Cumberlands. LC 88-17337. 264p. 1988. 30.00 (*0-8131-1679-1*); pap. 18.00 (*0-8131-0186-7*) U Pr of Ky.

Ritchie, Jean, ed. Jean Ritchie's Dulcimer People. (Illus.). pap. 14.95 (*0-8256-0142-8*, OK62968, Oak) Music Sales.

Ritchie, Jim. Shocco Tales: Southern Fried Sagas. 1991. 17.95 (*1-879034-07-7*) MS River Pub.

— Shocco Tales: Southern Fried Sagas. 2nd ed. (Illus.). 204p. 1991. reprint ed. 17.95 (*0-9656002-0-3*) Shocco Stories.

Ritchie, Joan, jt. auth. see Brooks, Maureen.

Ritchie, Joanne. Cartographies of Silence: An Annotated Bibliography of English Language Diaries & Reminiscences of New Brunswick Women, 1783-1980. LC 98-104152. 1997. write for info. (*0-919653-73-1*) CRIA.

Ritchie, John. Feasts of Jehovah. LC 82-182. 80p. 1982. reprint ed. pap. 5.99 (*0-8254-3613-3*, Kregel Class) Kregel.

— Five Hundred Bible Subjects. 1993. reprint ed. pap. 7.99 (*0-88019-301-8*) Schmul Pub Co.

— 500 Children's Sermon Outlines. LC 86-27396. (John Ritchie Sermon Outlines Ser.). 128p. 1987. reprint ed. pap. 6.99 (*0-8254-3623-0*) Kregel.

— 500 Evangelistic Sermon Outlines. LC 86-27200. (John Ritchie Sermon Outlines Ser.). 128p. 1987. reprint ed. pap. 6.99 (*0-8254-3619-2*) Kregel.

— 500 Gospel Sermon Outlines. LC 86-27760. (John Ritchie Sermon Outlines Ser.). 128p. 1987. reprint ed. pap. 6.99 (*0-8254-3621-4*) Kregel.

— 500 Sermon Outlines on Basic Bible Truths. LC 86-27541. (John Ritchie Sermon Outlines Ser.). 128p. 1987. reprint ed. pap. 6.99 (*0-8254-3618-4*) Kregel.

Ritchie, John. Martin Luther, Hero of the Reformation. (Illus.). 63p. 1996. pap. 4.99 (*0-88019-357-3*) Schmul Pub Co.

Ritchie, John. Our Glorious Lord. 1996. pap. 8.99 (*0-946351-08-2*, Pub. by John Ritchie) Loizeaux.

— The Tabernacle in the Wilderness. LC 82-178. 128p. (C). 1982. reprint ed. pap. 6.99 (*0-8254-3616-8*) Kregel.

— El Tabernaculo en el Desierto. Orig. Title: The Tabernacle in the Wilderness. (SPA., Illus.). 144p. 1987. pap. 4.99 (*0-8254-1616-7*, Edit Portavoz) Kregel.

— The Wentworths: Father & Son. (Illus.). 328p. 1998. 39.95 (*0-522-84751-X*, Pub. by Melbourne Univ Pr) Paul & Co Pubs.

Ritchie, John, ed. Australian Dictionary of Biography: 1940-1980 Di-Kel, Vol. 14. 652p. 1996. 75.00 (*0-522-84717-X*, Pub. by Melbourne Univ Pr) Paul & Co Pubs.

***Ritchie, John, ed.** Australian Dictionary of Biography Vol. 15: 1940-1980 Kem-Pie. 611p. 2000. 75.00 (*0-522-84843-5*, Pub. by Melbourne Univ Pr) Paul & Co Pubs.

Ritchie, John, III, et al. Cases & Materials on Decedents' Estates & Trusts. 8th ed. (University Casebook Ser.). 1424p. 1993. text. write for info. (*1-56662-066-X*) Foundation Pr.

Ritchie, John, jt. auth. see Garrahan, Philip.

Ritchie, John C., Jr. Fundamental Analysis: A Back-to-Basics Investment Guide to Selecting Quality Stocks, Revised Edition. 3rd rev. ed. LC 95-39277. 375p. 1995. 27.50 (*1-55738-866-0*, Irwn Prfssnl) McGraw-Hill Prof.

***Ritchie, John C., Jr.** The 3 Ps of Negotiating: Exploring the Dimensions. LC 99-51500. 112p. 2000. pap. 23.20 (*0-13-026333-8*) P-H.

Ritchie, Johnna M. & Ritchie, T. Dale. Guide to North Carolina Potters. (Illus.). 250p. (Orig.). 1996. pap. 12.95 (*0-9651220-1-8*) WtrMark Pubns.

Ritchie, Joshuas H., jt. auth. see Ritchie, Liliane.

***Ritchie, Joy S. & Wilson, David E.** Teacher Narrative as Critical Inquiry: Rewriting the Script. LC 00-23415. (Practitioner Inquiry Ser.). 2000. pap. write for info. (*0-8077-3960-X*) Tchrs Coll.

Ritchie, Judy. Stamp-a-Christmas Book & Kit. 1995. 25.00 (*0-88363-319-1*) H L Levin.

— Stamp-a-Christmas Book & Kit. (Illus.). 96p. 1995. pap. 25.00 (*0-88363-895-9*, Scribners Ref) Mac Lib Ref.

— Stamp-a-Greeting. 104p. 1996. 25.00 (*0-88363-896-7*) H L Levin.

Ritchie, Judy, et al. Stamp-a-Birthday: Book & Rubber Stamp Kit. (Illus.). 104p. 1998. pap. 25.00 (*0-88363-929-7*, Pub. by H L Levin) Publishers Group.

***Ritchie, Judy, et al.** Stamp-A-Christian Greeting: A Book & Rubber Stamp Kit. (Illus.). 104p. 1999. pap. 25.00 (*0-88363-930-0*, Pub. by H L Levin) Publishers Group.

Ritchie, Judy, et al. Stamp-a-Love Note: A Book & Rubber Stamp Kit. (Illus.). 1998. 25.00 (*0-88363-898-3*) H L Levin.

Ritchie, Karen. Marketing to Generation X: Strategies for a New Era. 1995. 25.00 (*0-02-926545-2*) Free Pr.

Ritchie, Kathy. Decorative Painting: Fruits, Vegetables & Berries. (Illus.). 128p. 1997. pap. 22.99 (*0-89134-796-8*, North Lght Bks) F & W Pubns Inc.

***Ritchie, Kathy F.** Stencilling. (Contemporary Crafts Ser.). (Illus.). 96p. 2000. pap. 14.95 (*1-85368-663-8*) New5 Holland.

Ritchie, Kathy F. Stencilling: How to Create Clever Paint Effects on Wood, Ceramics, Paper, & Fabric - 12 Projects. 89p. 1995. pap. 15.95 (*0-8050-4267-9*) H Holt & Co.

Ritchie, L. Carol, ed. My First Year in Television. (First Year Career Ser.). 160p. (J). 1995. pap. 9.95 (*0-8027-7424-5*) Walker & Co.

Ritchie, L. David. Information. (Communication Concepts Ser.: Vol. 2). 120p. (C). 1991. text 28.00 (*0-8039-3904-3*); pap. text 11.95 (*0-8039-3905-1*) Sage.

Ritchie, Leo. Reminiscences of Woodland Stalking. 174p. (C). 1989. 49.00 (*0-7223-2290-9*, Pub. by A H S Ltd) St Mut.

Ritchie, Lewis A. Naval Occasions, & Some Traits of the Sailorman. LC 70-130070. (Short Story Index Reprint Ser.). 1977. 23.95 (*0-8369-3651-5*) Ayer.

— Navy Eternal. LC 72-134977. (Short Story Index Reprint Ser.). 1977. 19.95 (*0-8369-3706-6*) Ayer.

Ritchie, Liliane & Ritchie, Joshuas H. A Gift of Love. (Illus.). 88p. (J). (gr. 4-7). 1985. pap. 19.95 (*0-942494-99-7*, NO. 135) Coleman Pub.

Ritchie, Malcolm. Village Japan. 1999. pap. 14.95 (*0-8048-2121-6*) Tuttle Pubng.

Ritchie, Malcolm L. Roy Cheville: The Graceland College Years. (Illus.). 356p. (Orig.). 1995. pap. 10.50 (*0-9636457-1-4*) Gracelnd Coll.

Ritchie, Mark A. God in the Pits: Confessions of a Commodities Trader. 271p. 1997. pap. 9.95 (*0-9646952-2-7*) Island Lake.

— God in the Pits: Confessions of a Commodities Trader. rev. ed. 271p. 1997. reprint ed. pap. 9.95 (*0-614-29855-5*) Island Lake.

Ritchie, Mark Andrew. Spirit of the Rainforest: A Yanomamo Shaman's Story. LC 95-80652. (Illus.). 288p. 1996. pap. 14.95 (*0-9646952-1-9*) Island Lake.

— Spirit of the Rainforest: A Yanomamo Shaman's Story. 2nd rev. ed. LC 99-73686. 288p. 1999. pap. 14.95 (*0-9646952-3-5*) Island Lake.

Ritchie, Michael. Please Stand By. 1995. 22.95 (*0-8050-1973-1*) H Holt & Co.

— Please Stand By: The Prehistory of Television. (Illus.). 247p. 1994. 23.95 (*0-87951-546-5*, Pub. by Overlook Pr) Penguin Putnam.

— Please Stand By: The Prehistory of Television. 280p. 1995. pap. 15.95 (*0-87951-615-1*, Pub. by Overlook Pr) Penguin Putnam.

Ritchie, Mildred H., ed. see Handy, Isaac W.

Ritchie, N. G. Brochs of Scotland. 1989. pap. 25.00 (*0-85263-928-7*, Pub. by Shire Pubns) St Mut.

***Ritchie, Nigel.** Communism. LC 00-33280. (Ideas of the Modern World Ser.). 2001. write for info. (*0-7398-3158-5*) Raintree Steck-V.

Ritchie, Nigel. Fire. LC 97-41600. (Against the Elements Ser.). (Illus.). 32p. (YA). (gr. 5 up). 1998. lib. bdg. 22.40 (*0-7613-0800-6*, Copper Beech Bks) Millbrook Pr.

Ritchie-Noakes, Nancy. Old Docks. 1989. pap. 25.00 (*0-85263-893-0*, Pub. by Shire Pubns) St Mut.

Ritchie, Norman L., ed. see Ritchie, David F.

Ritchie, Pat T., jt. auth. see Downs, Janet B.

Ritchie, Paul. Saint Honey & Oh David, Are You There? 124p. 1968. 16.95 (*0-910278-45-8*) Boulevard.

Ritchie, R. & Marshall, D. V. Business Risk Management. (Bus Press-Previous C&H). 376p. 1993. mass mkt. 34.95 (*0-412-43100-9*) Chapman & Hall.

Ritchie, R. O. & Lankford, J., eds. Small Fatigue Cracks: Proceedings of the Second Engineering Foundation International Conference. LC 86-19175. (Illus.). 677p. reprint ed. pap. 200.00 (*0-608-15986-7*, 205226800084) Bks Demand.

Ritchie, Ralph W. All That's Practical about Wood: Stoves, as a Fuel, Heating - Including Food Pellet Stoves. 2nd rev. ed. LC 98-66546. (Energy Conservation Ser.: Vol. 1). (Illus.). 138p. 1998. pap. 17.95 (*0-939656-23-X*) Ritchie Unltd.

— Electric Kiln Handbook: For the Professional Ceramist & Hobbiest, Schools. 2nd rev. ed. LC 95-92806. (Illus.). 190p. 1996. pap. 24.95 (*0-939656-22-1*) Ritchie Unltd.

— Emergency Procedures for Country Living: What to Do in Case of Fires, Floods, Earthquakes, Cold, Winds, Civil Disorders, Hazardous Spills. 2nd rev. ed. LC 95-42213. (Emergency Procedures Ser.: Vol. 6). (Illus.). 157p. 1996. pap. 24.95 (*0-939656-19-1*) Ritchie Unltd.

Ritchie, Ralph W. Emergency Procedures for Schools: A Guide & Disaster Plan Framework. LC 95-92431. (Emergency Procedures Ser.: No. 5). (Illus.). 169p. (Orig.). 1995. pap. 24.95 (*0-939656-20-5*) Ritchie Unltd.

Ritchie, Ralph W. Emergency Procedures for the Small Business & Shop: A Guide & Disaster Plan Framework. LC 95-92212. (Emergency Procedures Ser.: No. 5). 109p. 1997. pap. 19.95 (*0-939656-21-3*) Ritchie Unltd.

— First Aid for Disaster Stress Trauma Victims: A Guide & Self-Help Manual for the Lay Person Treating Disaster Stress Trauma Victims. LC 95-92032. (Emergency Procedures Ser.). 81p. (Orig.). 1995. pap. 11.95 (*0-939656-18-3*) Ritchie Unltd.

— Free Heat: How to Conserve, Recover & Re-Use Heat over & Over. (Illus.). 152p. 1993. pap. 11.95 (*0-939656-12-4*) Ritchie Unltd.

***Ritchie, Ralph W.** Gas Kiln Firing. (Illus.). 136p. 1999. reprint ed. pap. 24.95 (*0-939656-47-7*) Ritchie Unltd.

Ritchie, Ralph W. How to Find & Benefit from a "Passive Solar Collector" As a Space Heater. Orig. Title: Solar Space Heating for Free Heat. (Illus.). 64p. (Orig.). 1993. pap. 14.95 (*0-939656-15-9*) Ritchie Unltd.

***Ritchie, Ralph W.** How to Lift & Move Almost Anything: For Almost Anyone Who Finds the Need to Lift Or Move Heavy, Bulky, Or Massive Objects: For Sculptors, Independent Women, Individuals Working Alone, ... Applications rev. ed. LC 98-96602. 83p. 1998. write for info. (*0-939656-29-9*) Ritchie Unltd.

Ritchie, Ralph W. How to Make the Best Use of Fuels for Heating: A Guide to Efficient Combustion in Kilns & Furnaces. LC 95-92031. (Energy Conservation Ser.). (Illus.). 69p. 1994. pap. 11.95 (*0-939656-17-5*) Ritchie Unltd.

— How You Can Cope with Y2K, the Coming Computer Crisis; Whether You Know It or Not, the Computer Failure Problem Will. deluxe ed. LC 98-89611. (Emergency Procedures Ser.: Vol. 8). 72p. 1998. pap. 7.95 (*0-939656-31-0*) Ritchie Unltd.

— Solar Energy Owner's Guide, No. 1. (Energy & Ecology "Do It" Bks.). (Illus.). 100p. (Orig.). 1981. pap. 6.00 (*0-939656-07-8*) Ritchie Unltd.

— Survival Cooking: How to Cook in an Improvised Situation. deluxe ed. LC 98-89294. (Emergency Procedures Ser.: Vol. 7). 75p. 1999. pap. 11.95 (*0-939656-35-3*) Ritchie Unltd.

— User's Fuel Handbook. LC 81-90075. (Energy Conservation in the Crafts - Craft Monograph Ser.: No. 7). (Illus.). 1981. pap. 6.00 (*0-939656-06-X*) Ritchie Unltd.

***Ritchie, Ralph W.** Using Sunlight for Your Own Solar Electricity: Build Your Own System, Become Independent of the GEID, Domestic Photovoltaics. LC 99-61796. (Illus.). 152p. 1999. pap. text 24.95 (*0-939656-46-9*) Ritchie Unltd.

***Ritchie, Ralph W. & Ritchie, Fern J.** The Clay Book: Its Technology, Handling & Application in an Art Studio. LC 00-190625. (Craft Ser.: Vol. 7). (Illus.). 150p. 2000. pap. 39.95 (*0-939656-49-3*) Ritchie Unltd.

Ritchie, Ralph W. & Ritchie, Fern J. What? A Touch of Humor for Those Who Need or Wear Hearing Aids. (Illus.). 60p. 1992. pap. 9.95 (*0-939656-08-6*) Ritchie Unltd.

Ritchie, Rene. Yuen Kay-San Wing Chun Kuen. 1998. pap. 16.95 (*1-892515-03-2*, 275-1) Unique Pubns.

Ritchie, Rob, jt. auth. see Ataie, Iraj J.

Ritchie, Robert & Ritchie, Ruth. San Diego's Old Town, 1820-1885. (Illus.). 106p. 1996. reprint ed. 12.50 (*1-889361-00-3*) Ruroanik.

— San Diego's Past, 1769-1927. (Illus.). 105p. 1996. reprint ed. 12.50 (*1-889361-01-1*) Ruroanik.

Ritchie, Robert, et al. Information Systems in Business. 2nd ed. 448p. 1997. pap. 24.99 (*1-86152-053-0*) Thomson Learn.

Ritchie, Robert, jt. auth. see Ritchie, Ruth.

Ritchie, Robert C. Captain Kidd & the War Against the Pirates. (Illus.). 320p. 1986. reprint ed. pap. text 16.50 (*0-674-09502-2*) HUP.

— The Duke's Province: A Study of New York Politics & Society, 1664-1691. fac. ed. LC 77-681. 318p. 1977. reprint ed. pap. 98.60 (*0-7837-8057-5*, 204781000008) Bks Demand.

Ritchie, Robert C., jt. ed. see Hutton, Paul A.

Ritchie, Robert F., contrib. by. Assessing the Quality of Systems for Alpha-Fetoprotein (AFP) Assays Used in Frenatal Screening & Diagnosis of Open Neural Tube Defects: Approved Guideline (1996) 1996. 95.00 (*1-56238-202-0*, I/LA17-A) NCCLS.

Ritchie, Robert F., ed. Automated Immunoanalysis, 2 pts., Pt. 1. LC 77-28836. (Clinical & Biochemical Analysis Ser.: No. 7). (Illus.). 349p. reprint ed. pap. 108.20 (*0-7837-0817-3*, 204113200001) Bks Demand.

— Automated Immunoanalysis, 2 pts., Pt. 2. LC 77-28836. (Clinical & Biochemical Analysis Ser.: No. 7). (Illus.). 303p. reprint ed. pap. 94.00 (*0-7837-0818-1*, 204113200002) Bks Demand.

Ritchie, Robert L. The Normans in Scotland. LC 80-2216. reprint ed. 57.50 (*0-404-18783-8*) AMS Pr.

Ritchie, Robert L., jt. auth. see Ritchie, Ruth M.

Ritchie, Robert W. The Hell-Roarin' Forty-Niners. 1992. reprint ed. lib. bdg. 75.00 (*0-7812-5080-3*) Rprt Serv.

Ritchie, Ron. Primary Design & Technology: A Process for Learning. 192p. 1995. pap. text 23.00 (*1-85346-340-X*, Pub. by David Fulton) Taylor & Francis.

Ritchie, Ron, ed. Profiling in Primary Schools: A Handbook for Teachers. 176p. 1992. spiral bd. 50.00 (*0-304-32450-7*) Continuum.

Ritchie, Ron, jt. auth. see Bell, Derek.

Ritchie, Ron, jt. auth. see Ollerenshaw, Chris.

Ritchie, Roy & Stewart, Ron. Standard Guide to Razors: Identification & Values. 2nd ed. LC 99-166186. 160p. 1998. pap. 9.95 (*1-57432-091-2*) Collector Bks.

— The Standard Knife Collectors Guide. 3rd rev. ed. LC 97-120479. (Illus.). 688p. 1996. pap. 12.95 (*0-89145-737-2*, 4730) Collector Bks.

Ritchie, Roy, jt. auth. see Stewart, Ron.

Ritchie, Ruth & Ritchie, Robert. California's Stories of Past, 1769-1927. (Illus.). 104p. 1996. reprint ed. 12.50 (*1-889361-02-X*) Ruroanik.

— The Stronger Sex. 121p. 1996. pap. 9.50 (*1-889361-03-8*) Ruroanik.

Ritchie, Ruth & Wood, Sudie R. Garner-Keene Families of Northern Neck, Virginia. (Illus.). 240p. 1997. reprint ed. pap. 37.00 (*0-8328-8706-4*); reprint ed. lib. bdg. 47.00 (*0-8328-8705-6*) Higginson Bk Co.

Ritchie, Ruth, jt. auth. see Ritchie, Robert.

Ritchie, Ruth M. & Ritchie, Robert L. Short Stories from Around the World. 422p. 1998. pap. 19.50 (*1-889361-04-6*) Ruroanik.

Ritchie, Sandra S., et al. Mickey Unlimited Ultimate Cross Stitch Collection: 63 Projects! LC 98-67367. 96p. 1998. 19.95 (*1-57486-142-5*) Leisure AR.

Ritchie, Scot, jt. auth. see Wark, Laurie.

Ritchie, Sebastian. Industry & Air Power: The Expansion of British Aircraft Production, 1935-1941. Cox, Sebastian, ed. LC 96-43588. (Studies in Air Power: Vol. 5). (Illus.). 296p. (C). 1997. 57.50 (*0-7146-4724-1*, Pub. by F Cass Pubs); pap. 26.50 (*0-7146-4343-2*, Pub. by F Cass Pubs) Intl Spec Bk.

Ritchie, Sheila, ed. Modern Library Practice: A Manual & Textbook. 1982. 70.00 (*0-9505828-5-9*, Pub. by Elm Pubns) St Mut.

***Ritchie, Sheila & Martin, Peter.** Motivation Management. LC 98-40509. xviii, 293 p. 1999. 96.95 (*0-566-08102-4*) Ashgate Pub Co.

Ritchie, Sheri & Lavranos, Destini. Goodnight Little Reindeer. (Illus.). 2p. (J). (ps). 1993. 14.95 (*0-9638393-1-4*) Bedtime Bks.

Ritchie, Sheri, jt. auth. see Lavranos, Destini.

Ritchie, Simon. Work for a Dead Man. 1991. per. 3.50 (*0-373-26064-4*) Harlequin Bks.

Ritchie, Stephen G., jt. auth. see Hendrickson, Chris.

Ritchie, T. Dale, jt. auth. see Ritchie, Johnna M.

Ritchie, Thomas E., jt. auth. see Poplin, Robert L.

Ritchie, Tony. Dry Fly-Fishing for Trout. (Illus.). 80p. 1994. 25.95 (*0-86417-622-8*) Seven Hills Bk.

— Finding Feeding Trout. (Illus.). 48p. (Orig.). 1995. pap. 13.95 (*0-86417-632-5*) Seven Hills Bk.

Ritchie, Tori, jt. auth. see Hizer, Cynthia.

Ritchie, Tori, ed. see Hizer, Cynthia.

Ritchie, Tori, ed. see Worthington, Diane R.

Ritchie, W. & Stern, V., eds. Telecommunications Local Networks. 500p. 1992. 79.95 (*0-442-30883-3*) Chapman & Hall.

Ritchie, W., et al. Surveying Mapping Field Scientists. (Illus.). 192p. (C). 1996. pap. 69.00 (*0-582-30086-X*) Addison-Wesley.

Ritchie, W. F. & Ritchie, J. N. Celtic Warriors. (Archaeology Ser.: No. 41). (Illus.). 56p. 1989. pap. 10.50 (*0-85263-714-4*, Pub. by Shire Pubns) Parkwest Pubns.

Ritchie, Wallace. Advice to Violin Students. 110p. 1991. reprint ed. lib. bdg. 69.00 (*0-7812-9353-7*) Rprt Serv.

— Chats with Violinists. 112p. 1991. reprint ed. lib. bdg. 69.00 (*0-7812-9361-8*) Rprt Serv.

Ritchie, Wallace P., et al, eds. General Surgery. LC 94-15124. (Illus.). 1001p. reprint ed. pap. 200.00 (*0-608-09737-3*, 206990000007) Bks Demand.

Ritchie, Ward. Fine Printers: The New Generation in Southern California. (Illus.). 1988. pap. 15.00 (*0-929722-22-1*) CA State Library Fndtn.

— Fine Printing: The Los Angeles Tradition. LC 86-600279. 65p. 1987. 20.00 (*0-8444-0541-8*) Lib Congress.

— Growing up with Lawrence Clark Powell. 18p. 1987. pap. 3.95 (*0-929722-15-9*) CA State Library Fndtn.

— The Mystique of Printing: A Half Century of Books Designed by Ward Ritchie. 30p. 1984. pap. 2.50 (*0-929722-00-0*) CA State Library Fndtn.

— Of Bookmen & Printers. 189p. 1989. 50.00 (*0-87093-275-6*) Oak Knoll.

Ritchie, Ward, ed. see Powell, Lawrence C.

Ritchie, William A. The Archaeology of New York State. LC 94-12299. (Illus.). 400p. 1994. pap. 25.00 (*0-935796-52-5*) Purple Mnt Pr.

— Hammerstones, Anvils & Certain Pitted Stones. (New York Archeological Association Ser.: Vol. VII(2)). (Illus.). 32p. (C). 1929. pap. text 3.75 (*1-55567-725-8*) Coyote Press.

Ritchie, William A. A Prehistoric Fortified Village Site at Canandaigua, Ontario County, New York, No. 3. (Rochester Museum of Arts & Sciences of Research Records Ser.). 80p. (C). 1936. pap. text 9.06 (*1-55567-828-9*) Coyote Press.

Ritchie, William C. & Bhatia, Tej K., eds. Handbook of Child Language Acquisition. LC 98-85528. (Illus.). 768p. (C). 1999. text 99.95 (*0-12-589041-9*) Acad Pr.

— Handbook of Second Language Acquisition, Vol. 2. LC 94-44081. (Illus.). 758p. 1996. text 69.95 (*0-12-589042-7*) Acad Pr.

Ritchie, Wm. A. Traces of Early Man in the Northeast. fac. ed. (New York State Museum & Science Service Ser.: No. 358). (Illus.). 100p. (C). 1957. reprint ed. pap. text 12.19 (*1-55567-756-8*) Coyote Press.

Ritchin, Fred. Fred Ritchin: In Our Own Image. (Writers on Photography Ser.). 1999. text 24.95 (*0-89381-856-9*); pap. text 16.95 (*0-89381-857-7*) Aperture.

Ritchin, Fred, jt. auth. see Galeano, Eduardo.

Ritchin, Fred, jt. auth. see Naggar, Carole.

Ritchings, Joan D. Eva the Fair. LC 81-48147. (Illus.). 700p. 1982. 20.00 (*0-9608078-0-2*) Gray Moose.

— Wee Beasties. (Illus.). 48p. 2000. pap. write for info. (*0-9608078-2-9*) Gray Moose.

— Welcome, Jesus! 20p. 1988. pap. 5.00 (0-9608078-1-0) Gray Moose.

Ritchison, Gary. Downy Woodpecker. LC 98-39595. (Wild Bird Guides Ser.). 1999. 19.95 (0-8117-2724-6) Stackpole.

***Ritchison, Gary.** Eastern Bluebird. LC 99-47530. (Wild Bird Guides Ser.). (Illus.). 2000. pap. 19.95 (0-8117-2745-9) Stackpole.

Ritchison, Gary. Northern Cardinals. LC 96-44268. (Wild Bird Studies). (Illus.). 112p. 1997. pap. 19.95 (0-8117-3100-6) Stackpole.

Ritchken, Peter, ed. Derivative Markets. (C). 1996. pap. text, teacher ed. write for info. (0-321-40433-5) Addison-Wesley.

Ritchken, Peter, et al, eds. Advances in Futures & Options Research, Vol. 9. 296p. 1997. 78.50 (0-7623-0125-2) Jai Pr.

— Advances in Futures & Options Research: In Preparation, Spring, 1999, Vol. 10. 296p. 1998. 78.50 (0-7623-0326-3) Jai Pr.

Ritchken, Peter H., et al. Portfolio Risk Management: A Computer Simulation for Stock & Options. (Illus.). (C). 1989. pap. text 41.95 (0-201-06498-7) Addison-Wesley.

***Ritchotte, Louis.** Pierriche. (Illus.). 143p. 2000. pap. 11.95 (0-595-00251-X, Writers Showcase) iUniversecom.

Ritchre, Elisavietta, ed. The Dolphin's Arc: Poems on Endangered Creatures of the Sea. LC 89-60251. (SCOP Ser.: No. 12). 166p. 1989. pap. 10.95 (0-930526-11-2) Signal Bks.

Ritenour. Computer Applications in Diagnostic Radiology Study. 64p. (C). (gr. 13). 1985. text, wbk. ed. 20.95 (0-8016-1351-5, 01351) Mosby Inc.

— Principles of Magnetic Resonance Imaging: Student Workbook. (gr. 13). 1985. spiral bd. 13.95 (0-8016-4532-8, 04532) Mosby Inc.

— Radiation Protection & Biology. 128p. (C). (gr. 13). 1985. student ed., spiral bd., wbk. ed. 17.95 (0-8016-4013-X, 04013) Mosby Inc.

Riter, Tim. A Passionate Pursuit of God: How Knowing God Transforms Your Life. LC 99-18733. 150p. 1999. pap. 9.99 (0-8308-2205-4, 2205) InterVarsity.

Ritger, Dick. Dick Ritger Academy: Coaches-Instructors' Manual. (Illus.). 68p. (C). 1987. write for info. (0-318-63408-2) R Ritger.

Ritger, Dick & Allen, George. The Complete Guide to Bowling Spares: The Encyclopedia of Spares. LC 78-68659. (Encyclopedia of Bowling Instruction Ser.: Vol. 3). (Illus.). 240p. (C). 1979. 17.95 (0-933554-04-4); pap. 12.95 (0-933554-05-2) Tech-Ed Pub.

Ritger, Dick, jt. auth. see Allen, George.

***Ritger, Paul D.** Differential Equations with Applications. 2000. pap. 18.95 (0-486-41154-0) Dover.

Ritholz, Jules & London, Barry. Tax Return Preparer's Liability. LC 85-147123. 1985. 25.00 (0-13-885252-9) P-H.

Ritholz, Sophie. Children's Behavior. 1966. 16.95 (0-317-18406-7) NCUP.

Ritkin, Ned. Signs. LC 84-61734. (Illus.). 24p. 1985. pap. 4.00 (0-915557-46-0) New Mus Contemp Art.

Ritley, M. R., jt. auth. see Borsch, Frederick H.

Ritman, Erik L., et al. Imaging Physiological Functions: Experience with the Dynamic Spatial Reconstructor. LC 84-18247. 318p. 1985. 75.00 (0-275-91322-8, C1322, Praeger Pubs) Greenwood.

Ritmeyer, Kathleen, jt. auth. see Ritmeyer, Leen.

Ritmeyer, Leen & Ritmeyer, Kathleen. Secrets of Jerusalem's Temple Mount. LC 98-27110. 1998. 8.95 (1-880317-52-4) Biblical Arch Soc.

Ritner, Gary. Father's Liberation Ethics: A Holistic Ethical Advocacy for Active Nurturant Fathering. 306p. (Orig.). (C). 1992. pap. text 34.50 (0-8191-8466-7); lib. bdg. 56.50 (0-8191-8465-9) U Pr of Amer.

Ritner, George. Bankruptcy, How to Avoid It, How to Use It. write for info. (0-686-22992-4) G Ritner.

Ritner, Robert K. The Mechanics of Ancient Egyptian Magical Practice. LC 92-61830. (Studies in Ancient Oriental Civilization: No. 54). (Illus.). xviii, 322p. 1992. pap. 50.00 (0-918986-75-3) Orient Inst.

Rito, Daniele L. Bach Flower Massage. Calliope, Tami, tr. from ITA. LC 97-26253. (Illus.). 208p. 1997. pap. 14.95 (0-89281-736-4) Inner Tradit.

Ritsch, Margaret, jt. auth. see Solomon, Mary Jane.

Ritschel, Daniel. The Politics of Planning: The Debate on Economic Planning in Britain in the 1930's. LC 97-221670. (Oxford Historical Monographs). 378p. 1997. text 90.00 (0-19-820647-X) OUP.

Ritschel, Wolfgang A. GerontoKinetics. (Illus.). 225p. 1988. lib. bdg. 39.95 (0-936923-15-8) Telford Pr.

— GerontoKinetics: PharmacoKinetics of Drugs in the Elderly. 225p. 1988. 69.95 (0-936923-16-4) Telford Pr.

Ritschel, Wolfgang A. & Kearns, Gregory L. Handbook of Basic Pharmacokinetics: . . . Including Clinical Applications. 5th rev. ed. (Illus.). 563p. 1998. pap. text 49.00 (0-917330-73-0, T222) Am Pharm Assn.

Ritscher, Angelika V., tr. see Aeppli, Willi.

Ritschl, A. Prices & Production. (Contributions to Economics Ser.). (Illus.). v, 132p. 1989. 27.90 (0-387-50916-X) Spr-Verlag.

Ritschl, Albrecht B. Three Essays. Hefner, Philip, tr. & intro. by. LC 72-75654. 309p. reprint ed. pap. 95.80 (0-608-18694-5, 202688700053) Bks Demand.

Ritschl, Dietrich, ed. see Barth, Karl.

Ritschl, Friedrich. Opuscula Philologica, 5 vols., Set. lxxxiv, 4122p. 1978. reprint ed. write for info. (3-487-06642-4) G Olms Pubs.

***Ritsema, Alex.** Discover the Islands of Ireland. LC 99-198433. (Orig.). 1999. pap. 29.95 (1-898256-67-5, Pub. by Collins Press) Dufour.

Ritsema, Rudolf. I Ching: The Classic Chinese Oracle of Change, the First Complete Translation with Concordance. Karcher, Stephen, tr. 816p. 1995. pap. 19.95 (1-85230-669-6, Pub. by Element MA) Penguin Putnam.

Ritsema, Rudolf & Karcher, Stephen. I Ching: The Classic Chinese Oracle of Change, the First Complete Translation with Concordance. LC 95-199333. 816p. 1994. pap. 34.95 (1-85230-536-3, Pub. by Element MA) Penguin Putnam.

Ritson. Community Response to Alcohol-Related Problems: Review of an International Study. (Public Health Papers: No. 81). 58p. 1985. 8.00 (92-4-130081-7) World Health.

Ritson, Christopher, jt. ed. see Harvey, David R.

Ritson, Joseph. Cursory Criticism on the Edition of Shakespeare: Published by Edmond Malone Together with a Letter to the Rev. Richard Farmer, D.D. Relative to the Edition of Shakespeare, Published in 1790. 156p. 1970. reprint ed. 25.00 (0-7146-2516-7, Pub. by F Cass Pubs) Intl Spec Bk.

— Cursory Criticisms on the Edition of Shakespeare. LC 76-174322. xi, 104, 39 p. 1974. reprint ed. 34.50 (0-404-05338-6) AMS Pr.

— Fairy Tales, Legends & Romances, Illustrating Shakespeare & Other Early English Writers. LC 70-174323. reprint ed. 52.50 (0-404-05339-4) AMS Pr.

— Remarks, Critical & Illustrative, on the Text & Notes of the Last Edition of Shakspeare. LC 73-174324. reprint ed. 32.50 (0-404-05348-3) AMS Pr.

— Scottish Songs, 2 vols. in 1. 2nd ed. LC 77-144573. reprint ed. 74.50 (0-404-08688-8) AMS Pr.

Ritson, Joseph & Bewick, Thomas, eds. Robin Hood: Collection of Ancient Poems, 2 vols. (IRTP Library of Folklore & Popular Culture). (Illus.). 600p. (C). 1997. 200.00 (0-415-15383-2) Routledge.

Ritson, Joseph & Malone, Edmond. Cursory Criticisms on the Edition of Shakespeare Published by Edmond Malone, & a Letter to the Rev. Richard Farmer. LC 70-96366. (Eighteenth Century Shakespeare Ser.: No. 20). 1970. reprint ed. 24.50 (0-678-05132-1) Kelley.

Ritson, Phil & Andrisani, John. Total Golf: An Encyclopedic Guide to Better Golf. Orig. Title: Golf Your Way. (Illus.). 288p. 1999. pap. 17.95 (1-55821-890-4) Lyons Pr.

Ritson, Robert J., jt. auth. see Hart, James E.

Ritsos, Yannis. Erotica. Friar, Kimon, tr. from GRE. LC 82-17018. 96p. 1982. 13.50 (0-937584-05-3); pap. 6.95 (0-937584-06-1) Sachem Pr.

— Exile & Return. Keeley, Edmund, tr. from GRE. (Selected Poems, 1967-1974 Ser.). 199p. 1987. pap. 8.50 (0-88001-018-5) HarpC.

— The Fourth Dimension. Green, Peter & Bardsley, Beverly, trs. LC 92-27141. (Modern Greek Studies). (Illus.). 304p. (C). 1993. pap. 15.95 (0-691-02465-0, Pub. by Princeton U Pr) Cal Prin Full Svc.

— The Lady of the Vineyards. Athanassakis, Apostolos N., tr. from GRE. LC 80-84407. (ENG & GRE.). 77p. 1980. pap. text 7.00 (0-918618-10-X) Pella Pub.

— Late into the Night: The Last Poems of Yannis Ritsos. McKinsey, Martin, tr. from GRE. & intro. by. (Field Translation Ser.: No. 21). 121p. 1995. pap. 12.95 (0-932440-71-1) Oberlin Coll Pr.

— Monovasia & the Women of Monemvasia. Friar, Kimon & Myrsiades, Kostas, trs. from GRE. LC 87-62280. 67p. 1988. 20.00 (0-932963-04-8) Nostos Bks.

— The New Oresteia of Yannis Ritsos. Pilitsis, George & Pastras, Philip, trs. from GRE.Tr. of E Nea Oresteia. 168p. (Orig.). 1990. pap. text 12.00 (0-918618-45-2) Pella Pub.

— 3 x 111 Tristichs. Newton, Rick M., tr. from GRE. 173p. (Orig.). 1990. pap. text 12.00 (0-918618-46-0) Pella Pub.

— Yannis Ritsos: Selected Poems 1938-1988. Friar, Kimon & Myrsiades, Kostas, eds. & trs. by. 486p. 1989. 30.00 (0-918526-66-3) BOA Edns.

— Yannis Ritsos: Selected Poems 1938-1988. Friar, Kimon & Myrsiades, Kostas, eds. & trs. by. 486p. 1989. pap. 15.00 (0-918526-67-1) BOA Edns.

Ritstein, Charles. Executive Guide to Computer Viruses. (Illus.). 60p. (Orig.). (C). 1993. pap. text 35.00 (1-56806-251-6) DIANE Pub.

Ritt, Joseph F. Integration in Finite Terms: Liouville's Theory of Elementary. LC 48-2225. 110p. reprint ed. pap. 34.10 (0-608-30487-5, 205013700059) Bks Demand.

Ritt, Lawrence G., jt. ed. see Keller, Peter A.

Ritt, Michael J. A Lifetime of Riches. 304p. 1999. pap. 11.95 (0-452-27478-8, Plume) Dutton Plume.

Ritt, Michael J., Jr. & Hill, Napoleon. Napoleon Hill's Keys to Positive Thinking: 10 Steps to Health, Wealth & Success. 176p. 1999. pap. 11.95 (0-452-27905-4, Plume) Dutton Plume.

Ritt, Morey, ed. Four-Hand Piano Music by Nineteenth-Century Masters. 288p. 1980. pap. 14.95 (0-486-23860-1) Dover.

Ritt, Nikolaus. Quantity Adjustment: Vowel Lengthening & Shortening in Early Middle English. (Studies in Linguistics: Supplementary Volumes). (Illus.). 216p. (C). 1995. text 52.95 (0-521-46232-0) Cambridge U Pr.

Ritt, William B., et al. Child Welfare: HHS Begins to Assume Leadership to Implement National & State Systems. (Illus.). 44p. 1998. pap. text 20.00 (0-7881-4173-2) DIANE Pub.

Rittaler, Jan B., jt. auth. see Schmidt, Ingo L.

Rittaud-Hutinet, Chantal. La Phonopragmatique. (Sciences pour la Communication Ser.: Vol. 45). (FRE.). 312p. 1995. 47.95 (3-906754-25-1, Pub. by P Lang) P Lang Pubng.

Rittberger, Volker, ed. International Regimes in East-West Politics. 256p. 1990. text 49.00 (0-86187-868-X, Pub. by P P Pubs) Cassell & Continuum.

— International Regimes in East-West Politics. 272p. 1993. pap. 18.95 (1-85567-169-7) St Martin.

Rittelmeyer, Friedrich. Meditation: Guidance of the Inner Life. pap. 14.95 (0-86315-065-9, 359, Pub. by Floris Bks) Anthroposophic.

Rittelmeyer, Friedrich, jt. auth. see Easton, Stewart C.

Rittenberg, Larry & Nair, R. D. Improving the Effectiveness of Audit Committees. Barth, Claire, ed. 78p. (Orig.). 1993. pap. 20.00 (0-86641-217-4, 93279) Inst Mgmt Account.

Rittenberg, Larry E. Auditing: Concepts for a Changing Environment. 2nd ed. (C). 1997. pap. text, teacher ed. 70.00 (0-03-018714-1) Harcourt.

— Auditing: Concepts for a Changing Environment. 2nd ed. 1997. 101.50 (0-03-024089-1) Harcourt Coll Pubs.

— Auditing: Concepts for a Changing Environment. 3rd ed. (C). 2000. text. write for info. (0-03-026877-X) Harcourt.

— Study Guide Auditing. 2nd ed. (C). 1996. pap. text, student ed. 32.50 (0-03-018807-5) Harcourt Coll Pubs.

Rittenberg, Larry E. & Institute of Internal Auditors. Research Foundation. The Outsourcing Dilemma: What's Best for Internal Auditing. Campbell, Lee A., ed. LC 97-216324. (Illus.). 155p. 1997. pap. 95.00 (0-89413-384-5) Inst Inter Aud.

Rittenberg, Larry E. & Schwieger, Bradley J. Auditing: Concepts for a Changing Environment. 834p. (C). 1996. text. write for info. (0-03-018808-3) Harcourt Coll Pubs.

— AUDITING, 2E. 2nd ed. LC 96-20222. (Series in Accounting). 803p. (C). 1996. text 99.00 (0-03-018598-X) Dryden Pr.

— Solutions Manual to Accompany Auditing. 644p. (C). 1993. 33.25 (0-03-029918-7) Dryden Pr.

Rittenberg, Libby, ed. The Political Economy of Turkey in the Post-Soviet Era: Going West & Looking East? LC 97-26174. 240p. 1998. 59.95 (0-275-95596-6, Praeger Pubs) Greenwood.

Rittenberg, Libby, jt. ed. see Katz, Bernard S.

Rittenberg, Sidney & Bennett, Amanda. The Man Who Stayed Behind. LC 93-6541. (Illus.). 512p. 1993. 25.00 (0-671-73595-0) S&S Trade.

Rittenberg, Stephen. Ethnicity, Nationalism, & the Pakhtuns: The Independence Movement in India's North-West Frontier Province. LC 84-70181. (Illus.). 286p. 1988. lib. bdg. 34.95 (0-89089-277-6) Carolina Acad Pr.

Rittenberg, V. & Dietz, K., eds. Infinite Lie Algebras & Conformal Invariance in Condensed Matter & Particle Physics: Proceedings of the Johns Hopkins Workshop on Current Problems in Particle Theory, 10th, Bad Honnef, September 1-3, 1986. 212p. 1987. text 81.00 (9971-5-0240-2) World Scientific Pub.

Rittenberry, T. J., jt. auth. see Hart, Raymond G.

Rittenger, P. J. Allied Health Professional Jobs. (C). 1989. pap. 13.95 (0-13-023334-X) P-H.

Rittenhous. Guide Book to Highway 66. LC 89-4807. (Illus.). 128p. 1989. reprint ed. pap. 7.95 (0-8263-1148-2) U of NM Pr.

Rittenhouse Book Staff. Basic Science & Clinical Review: Study for Surgery Housestaff. 1997. 39.00 (0-01-570300-2) Rittenhouse.

Rittenhouse, Caroline. An Island Woman: Salome Sylvester Sellers, 1800-1909. LC 98-91632. (Illus.). 104p. 1998. pap. 14.95 (0-9665183-0-6) P Mitten Pr.

Rittenhouse, Don & Rittenhouse, Jane. You Are the Light of the World. (Illus.). 24p. (J). (ps-5). 1995. 4.00 (0-9646494-0-3) Memor-Eyes.

Rittenhouse, Jack D. Maverick Tales: True Stories of Early Texas. 22.95 (0-89190-867-6) Amereon Ltd.

— Trail of Commerce & Conquest: A Brief History of the Road to Santa Fe. (Illus.). 30p. (Orig.). 1987. pap. 1.95 (0-938463-03-9) Western Bks.

Rittenhouse, Jane, jt. auth. see Rittenhouse, Don.

Rittenhouse, Jessie B. Younger American Poets. LC 68-16971. (Essay Index Reprint Ser.). 1977. 23.95 (0-8369-0826-0) Ayer.

Rittenhouse, Jessie B., ed. Little Book of American Poets, 1787-1900. LC 74-149110. (Granger Index Reprint Ser.). 1977. 29.95 (0-8369-6235-4) Ayer.

— Little Book of Modern British Verse. LC 78-149111. (Granger Index Reprint Ser.). 1977. 21.95 (0-8369-6236-2) Ayer.

— Little Book of Modern Verse. LC 71-149112. (Granger Index Reprint Ser.). 1977. 18.95 (0-8369-6237-0) Ayer.

— Second Book of Modern Verse. LC 75-149113. (Granger Index Reprint Ser.). 1977. 18.95 (0-8369-6238-9) Ayer.

— Third Book of Modern Verse. LC 79-149114. (Granger Index Reprint Ser.). 1977. 23.95 (0-8369-6239-7) Ayer.

Rittenhouse, Jessie B., jt. compiled by see Scollard, Clinton.

Rittenhouse, Jessie B., jt. ed. see Scollard, Clinton.

Rittenhouse, Jonathan & Rose, Courtice G., eds. Journal of History & Politics (Journal d'Histoire et de Politique) Regionalism & Theory, Vol. IX, 1991. 176p. 1992. 79.95 (0-7734-8934-7) E Mellen.

Rittenhouse, Jonathan, jt. auth. see Whittaker, Herbert.

Rittenhouse, Michele Raper. Angel on My Shoulder. 39p. 1997. pap. 10.00 (0-929741-52-8) Playsmith.

Rittenhouse, Mignon. Amazing Nellie Bly. LC 74-148227. (Biography Index Reprint Ser.). 1977. 20.95 (0-8369-8074-3) Ayer.

Rittenhouse, Norman & Jeremiah. Gods in the Making: The New Solar System. 2nd ed. (Illus.). 307p. 1996. reprint ed. pap. 14.95 (0-9639053-2-5) Univ Truth Pr.

Rittenhouse, Robert K. Metaphor Stories for Deaf Children. LC 98-220813. (Illus.). 128p. (YA). (gr. 7-12). 1999. student ed., spiral bd. 14.95 (1-884362-33-8) Butte Pubns.

RittenHouse Staff. Recent Projects: Dynamic Equillibrium. 1994. pap. 29.95 (1-874056-06-4) Ellipsis.

Rittenhouse, Stan. For Fear of the Jews. LC 81-68608. (Illus.). 258p. 1982. 11.00 (0-9609260-0-3) Exhorters.

Ritter. EEC Competition. 1993. pap. text 96.50 (90-6544-687-7) Kluwer Academic.

— Introductory Biochemistry. (Chemistry Ser.). 1995. mass mkt. 110.95 (0-534-33865-8) Brooks-Cole.

— Nelson Biology. (UK - Science Ser.). 1992. pap., teacher ed. 54.95 (0-17-603861-2) S-W Pub.

— Neuronale Netze. 2nd ed. (GER.). (C). 1990. text. write for info. (0-201-55937-4) Addison-Wesley.

— Process Geomorphology. 4th ed. 1999. text 58.50 (0-697-34410-X) McGraw.

Ritter, et al. Nelson Biology Blue Text. (UK - Science Ser.). 1993. mass mkt. 61.95 (0-17-603870-1) S-W Pub.

Ritter, A. M., ed. see Metallurgical Society of AIME Staff.

Ritter, Abraham. Philadelphia & Her Merchants, As Constituted Fifty to Seventy Years Ago, As Illustrated by Diagrams of the River Front & Portraits of Some of Its Prominent Occupants, Together with Sketches of Character & Incidents & Anecdotes of the Day. (Illus.). 223p. 1998. reprint ed. lib. bdg. 32.00 (0-8328-9625-X) Higginson Bk Co.

Ritter, Adolf M., jt. ed. see Heil, Gunther.

Ritter, Agnes, ed. see Klinger, Karl.

Ritter, Alan, ed. see Rousseau, Jean-Jacques.

Ritter, Alexander, ed. Supplement Series - Materialien und Dokumente, 9 vols., Set. 760p. 1993. reprint ed. write for info. (3-487-09316-2) G Olms Pubs.

Ritter, Archibald R., et al, eds. Latin America in the Year 2000: Reactivating Growth, Improving Equity, Sustaining Democracy. LC 91-22939. 280p. 1992. 55.00 (0-275-93747-X, C3747, Praeger Pubs) Greenwood.

Ritter, Archibald R. & Kirk, John M., eds. Cuba in the International System: Normalization & Integration. LC 95-1328. (International Political Economy Ser.). 260p. 1995. text 59.95 (0-312-12653-0) St Martin.

Ritter, Archibald R. & Pollock, David H., eds. Latin American Prospects for the 1980's: Equity, Democratization & Development. LC 82-18039. 330p. 1983. 65.00 (0-275-91064-4, C1064, Praeger Pubs) Greenwood.

Ritter, Arthur B. & Reisman, Stanley. Introduction to Biomedical Engineering. (Illus.). Date not set. text. write for info. (0-8247-9616-0) Dekker.

Ritter, Artus. Ode to the Lost Dutchman Mine. unabridged ed. (Illus.). 72p. 1997. pap. 9.00 (0-9660719-0-5) A Ritter.

Ritter, Beverly L. Computer-Compatible Machine Shorthand for Expanding Careers Vol. 1: Theory. (Realtime Machine Shorthand Ser.). 271p. (C). 1991. pap. text, teacher ed. 33.25 (0-938643-00-2) Stenotype Educ.

— Computer-Compatible Machine Shorthand for Expanding Careers Vol. 1: Theory. rev. ed. (Realtime Machine Shorthand Ser.). 344p. (C). 1991. pap. text 48.00 (0-938643-01-0) Stenotype Educ.

— Dictionary of Briefs & Phrases. Rhyne, Patricia J., ed. (Realtime Machine Shorthand Ser.). 52p. (C). 1992. pap. text 8.00 (0-938643-26-6) Stenotype Educ.

— Professional Dictionary. (Realtime Machine Shorthand Ser.). 279p. (Orig.). (C). 1992. pap. text 40.00 (0-938643-12-6) Stenotype Educ.

— Reverse Dictionary. (Realtime Machine Shorthand Ser.). 228p. (Orig.). (C). 1992. pap. text 32.00 (0-938643-13-4) Stenotype Educ.

— StenEd's Realtime Professional Dictionary for Stenotypists LC 98-183224. viii, 388 p. 1998. write for info. (0-938643-72-X) Stenotype Educ.

— Student Cassette Series, Set C. rev. ed. (Realtime Machine Shorthand Ser.). 29p. (C). 1993. pap. text 30.00 incl. audio (0-938643-19-3, 703) Stenotype Educ.

— Student Cassette Series, Set D. rev. ed. (Realtime Machine Shorthand Ser.). 40p. (C). 1993. pap. text 31.25 incl. audio (0-938643-20-7, 704) Stenotype Educ.

— Student Cassette Series, Set A. rev. ed. (Realtime Machine Shorthand Ser.). 6p. (C). 1993. pap. text 27.50 incl. audio (0-938643-17-7, 701) Stenotype Educ.

— Student Cassette Series, Set B. rev. ed. (Realtime Machine Shorthand Ser.). 24p. (C). 1993. pap. text 28.75 incl. audio (0-938643-18-5, 702) Stenotype Educ.

— Student Cassette Series, Set E. rev. ed. (Realtime Machine Shorthand Ser.). 70p. (C). 1993. pap. text 32.50 incl. audio (0-938643-21-5, 705) Stenotype Educ.

— Student Cassette Series, Set F. (Realtime Machine Shorthand Ser.). 63p. (C). 1993. pap. text 35.00 incl. digital audio (0-938643-22-3) Stenotype Educ.

— Student Cassette Series, Set G. (Realtime Machine Shorthand Ser.). 73p. (C). 1993. pap. text 35.00 incl. digital audio (0-938643-23-1) Stenotype Educ.

— Student Theory Package. (Realtime Machine Shorthand Ser.). 458p. (C). 1991. pap. text 90.00 incl. digital audio (0-938643-36-3) Stenotype Educ.

— 10 Steps to Realtime Writing. (Realtime Machine Shorthand Ser.). 272p. (C). 1993. pap. text 43.25 (0-938643-34-7) Stenotype Educ.

— 10 Steps to Realtime Writing Package. (Realtime Machine Shorthand Ser.). 271p. (C). 1993. pap. text 82.00 incl. audio (0-938643-45-2) Stenotype Educ.

Ritter, Beverly L. & Andrews, George P. Medical Terminology for Stenotypists. (Realtime Machine Shorthand Ser.). 189p. (C). 1992. pap. text, teacher ed. 30.75 (0-938643-54-1) Stenotype Educ.

— Medical Terminology for Stenotypists. (Realtime Machine Shorthand Ser.). (Illus.). 675p. (C). 1994. pap. text 53.25 (0-938643-27-4) Stenotype Educ.

— Steno Tutorial User Manual. (Realtime Machine Shorthand Ser.). (C). 1992. pap. text 6.50 (0-938643-43-6) Stenotype Educ.

Ritter, Beverly L. & Antunovich, John D. Advanced Literacy Dictation. rev. ed. (Realtime Machine Shorthand Ser.). 188p. (C). 1992. teacher ed. 36.00 (0-938643-52-5, 620) Stenotype Educ.

An Asterisk (*) at the beginning of an entry indicates that the title is appearing for the first time.

— Advanced Literary Dictation. (Realtime Machine Shorthand Ser.). 163p. (C). 1992. pap. text 33.25 (*0-938643-30-4*) Stenotype Educ.

Ritter, Beverly L. & Davis, Kim C. Vocabulary Development Vol. II, Vol. I. rev. ed. (Realtime Machine Shorthand Ser.). 73p. (C). 1991. pap. text, teacher ed. 13.25 (*0-938643-08-8*) Stenotype Educ.

— Vocabulary Development Vol. II, Vol. I. rev. ed. (Realtime Machine Shorthand Ser.). 176p. (C). 1992. pap. text 25.00 (*0-938643-06-1*) Stenotype Educ.

Ritter, Beverly L. & LaBorde, Michael. Reporter on the Job. rev. ed. (Realtime Machine Shorthand Ser.: Vol. III). 276p. (C). 1992. pap. text 35.50 (*0-938643-09-6*) Stenotype Educ.

— Reporter on the Job, Vol. I. rev. ed. (Realtime Machine Shorthand Ser.: Vol. III). 160p. (C). 1992. pap. text, teacher ed. 26.75 (*0-938643-11-8*) Stenotype Educ.

Ritter, Beverly L. & Rhyne, Patricia J. Stenotype Theory for the Professional Scopist. (Realtime Machine Shorthand Ser.). 88p. (Orig.). (C). 1995. pap. text, teacher ed. 15.00 (*0-938643-65-7*) Stenotype Educ.

Ritter, Beverly L., et al. Reader Vol. 1: Theory. (Realtime Machine Shorthand Ser.). 114p. (C). 1992. pap. text 15.00 (*0-938643-31-2*) Stenotype Educ.

Ritter, Beverly L., jt. auth. see Andrews, George P.

Ritter, Beverly L., ed. see Floyd, Sally & Mathias, Dot.

Ritter, Beverly L., ed. see Mathias, Dot & Floyd, Sally.

Ritter, Beverly L., ed. see Nash, Jacqueline A. & Kinkaid, Joann.

Ritter, Bob, et al. Nelson Biology-Blue: Teacher's Resource Guide. (Illus.). 288p. (Orig.). pap., teacher ed. 49.75 (*0-17-603871-X*) Thomson Learn.

Ritter, Charles & Wakelyn, Jon L. American Legislative Leaders, 1850-1910, Vol. 2. Broussard, James H. et al, eds. LC 88-24734. 1156p. 1989. lib. bdg. 165.00 (*0-313-23943-6*, BLL02, Greenwood Pr) Greenwood.

Ritter, Charles F., et al, eds. Leaders of the Civil War: A Biographical & Historiographical Dictionary. LC 98-12156. 504p. 1998. lib. bdg. 85.00 (*0-313-29560-3*, Greenwood Pr) Greenwood.

Ritter, Constantin. Neue Untersuchungen Uber Platon. LC 75-13289. (History of Ideas in Ancient Greece Ser.). (GER.). 1976. reprint ed. 31.95 (*0-405-07332-1*) Ayer.

— Platon: Sein Leben, Seine Schriften, Seine Lehre, 2 vols., Vol. 1. LC 75-13291. (History of Ideas in Ancient Greece Ser.). (GER.). 1976. reprint ed. 51.95 (*0-405-07334-8*) Ayer.

— Platon: Sein Leben, Seine Schriften, Seine Lehre, 2 vols., Vol. 2. LC 75-13291. (History of Ideas in Ancient Greece Ser.). (GER.). 1976. reprint ed. 51.95 (*0-405-07335-6*) Ayer.

— Platon: Sein Leben, Seine Schriften, Seine Lehre, 2 vols., Vols. 1 [00ad] 2. LC 75-13291. (History of Ideas in Ancient Greece Ser.). (GER.). 1976. reprint ed. 101.95 (*0-405-07333-X*) Ayer.

— Die Quintilianischen Declamationen. xii, 275p. 1967. reprint ed. write for info. (*0-318-71217-2*) G Olms Pubs.

Ritter, Dale F. & Kochel, R. Craig. Process Geomorphology. 3rd ed. 560p. (C). 1994. text. write for info. (*0-697-07632-6*, WCB McGr Hill) McGrw-H Hghr Educ.

Ritter, Dale F., et al. Process Geomorphology. 3rd ed. LC 94-72474. 560p. (C). 1995. text. write for info. (*0-697-27127-7*, WCB McGr Hill) McGrw-H Hghr Educ.

Ritter, Darlene M. The Letters of Louise Ritter from 1893-1925. (Illus.). 178p. (Orig.). (C). 1980. pap. 10.00 (*0-9609372-0-X*) Siegenthaler-Ritter.

Ritter, Debbie. English Springer Spaniel: An Owner's Guide to a Happy Healthy Pet. 160p. 1996. 12.95 (*0-87605-482-3*) Howell Bks.

Ritter, Diane, jt. auth. see Brassard, Michael.

Ritter, Diane, jt. auth. see Peach, Robert.

Ritter, Dwight S. The Cross-Selling Toolkit: The Complete Guide to Cross-Selling Financial Products & Services. 250p. 1994. per. 24.95 (*1-55738-717-6*, Irwn Prfssnl) McGraw-Hill Prof.

— Cross-Selling Toolkit & Relationship Banking. 1994. text 55.00 (*1-55738-787-7*, Irwn Prfssnl) McGraw-Hill Prof.

— High Performance Branch Banking: A Manager's Guide to Maximizing Branch Profitability. 224p. (C). 1996. 50.00 (*1-55738-799-0*, Irwn Prfssnl) McGraw-Hill Prof.

— Pocket Guide to Financial Products & Services. 2nd ed. 240p. 1996. per. 12.95 (*0-7863-1110-X*, Irwn Prfssnl) McGraw-Hill Prof.

— The Pocket Guide to Financial Products & Services: Product Information/Customer Profile/Cross Selling Checklist. 2nd rev. ed. 48p. 1996. 50.00 (*0-7863-1109-6*, Irwn Prfssnl) McGraw-Hill Prof.

Ritter, E. A. Shaka Zula. (Nonfiction Ser.). 416p. 1985. pap. 13.95 (*0-14-004826-X*, Penguin Bks) Viking Penguin.

— Shaka Zulu: The Rise of the Zulu Empire. 412p. 1990. 35.00 (*0-947898-99-9*, 5588) Stackpole.

Ritter, Ed, jt. auth. see Biasiotto, Judd.

Ritter, Eileen. Life in the Real World: 5-Minute Devotions for Teens. LC 96-39219. 128p. (J). 1997. 6.99 (*0-570-04888-5*, 12-3305) Concordia.

— Life in the Real World 2: 5-Minute Devotions for Teens. LC 98-41223. 128p. (YA). 1999. 6.99 (*0-570-05348-X*, 12-3396GJ) Concordia.

Ritter, Eldon. Know Your Monthly Payments, Before You Buy, Borrow or Lend. 317p. 1992. pap. text 14.95 (*0-934739-06-4*) Pussywillow Pub.

Ritter, Ellen M., jt. ed. see Arntzen, Charles J.

Ritter, Eric. Archaeological Test Excavations at Spider Rockshelter (CA-Tch-1432) Lower Mill Creek Canyon, CA. fac. ed. (Bureau of Land Management, Cultural Resource, Nevada Ser.). (Illus.). 107p. (C). 1987. reprint ed. pap. text 10.95 (*1-55567-669-3*) Coyote Press.

***Ritter, Eric.** Rock Art Studies in the Great Basin. (Archives of Great Basin Prehistory Ser.: Vol. 1). (Illus.). 129p. (C). 1998. pap. text 15.63 (*1-55567-750-9*) Coyote Press.

Ritter, Erika. Automatic Pilot. 96p. 1997. pap. text 10.95 (*0-88754-473-8*) Playwrights.

Ritter, Ernst, jt. ed. see International Council on Archives Staff.

Ritter, Fanny R., ed. see Schumann, Robert.

***Ritter, Frank E. & Young, Richard M., trs.** Proceedings of the Second European Conference on Cognitive Modelling (ECCM-98) 215p. 1999. pap. 90.00 (*1-897676-67-0*, Pub. by Nottingham Univ Pr) St Mut.

Ritter, Frank N. & Fritsch, Michael H. Atlas of Paranasal Sinus Surgery. LC 91-7018. (Illus.). 296p. 1992. 115.00 (*0-89640-194-4*) Igaku-Shoin.

***Ritter, George Wenzel.** George Wenzel Ritter: Six Quarters for Bassoon & Strings. Lipori, Daniel, ed. (Recent Researches in Music of the Classic Era Ser.: Vol. RRC55). (Illus.). ix, 84p. 1999. pap. 40.00 (*0-89579-432-2*) A-R Eds.

Ritter, Gerhard A. Frederick the Great: A Historical Profile. Paret, Peter, tr. & intro. by. 268p. 1968. pap. 14.95 (*0-520-02775-2*, Pub. by U CA Pr) Cal Prin Full Svc.

— German Resistance. Clark, R. T., tr. LC 74-124253. (Select Bibliographies Reprint Ser.). 1977. 34.95 (*0-8369-5441-6*) Ayer.

— The Sword & the Scepter: The Problem of Militarism in Germany. Norden, Heinz, tr. Incl. Vol. 1. Prussian Tradition, 1740-1890. LC 68-31041. 338p. 1988. pap. 12.95 (*0-945726-13-9*); Vol. 2. European Powers & the Wilhelminian Empire, 1890-1914. LC 68-31041. 328p. 1970. pap. 12.95 (*0-945726-14-7*); Vol. 3. Tragedy of Statesmanship: Bethmann Hollweg As War Chancellor (1914-1917) LC 68-31041. 612p. 1988. lib. bdg. 35.00 (*0-945726-20-1*); Vol. 4. Reign of German Militarism & the Disaster of 1918. LC 68-31041. 496p. 1988. pap. 14.95 (*0-945726-16-3*); LC 68-31041. 1174p. 1988. reprint ed. Set pap. 49.95 (*0-945726-17-1*) Scholars Bookshelf.

— The Sword & the Scepter: The Problem of Militarism in Germany, Set. Norden, Heinz, tr. Incl. Vol. 1. Prussian Tradition, 1740-1890. LC 68-31041. 338p. 1988. lib. bdg. 25.00 (*0-945726-18-X*); Vol. 2. European Powers & the Wilhelminian Empire, 1890-1914. LC 68-31041. 328p. 1970. lib. bdg. 25.00 (*0-945726-19-8*); Vol. 3. Tragedy of Statesmanship: Bethmann Hollweg As War Chancellor (1914-1917) LC 68-31041. 612p. 1988. pap. 16.95 (*0-945726-15-5*); Vol. 4. Reign of German Militarism & the Disaster of 1918. LC 68-31041. 496p. 1988. lib. bdg. 35.00 (*0-945726-21-X*); LC 68-31041. 1174p. 1988. reprint ed. Set lib. bdg. 99.50 (*0-945726-22-8*) Scholars Bookshelf.

Ritter, Gerhard A. & Hart, B. Liddell. The Schlieffen Plan, Critique of a Myth. LC 78-9962. (Illus.). 195p. 1979. reprint ed. lib. bdg. 35.00 (*0-313-20757-7*, RISCH, Greenwood Pr) Greenwood.

***Ritter, Gerhard X.** Handbook of Computer Vision Algorithms in Image Algebra. 2nd ed. (Illus.). 2000. 89.95 (*0-8493-0075-4*) CRC Pr.

Ritter, Gretchen. Goldbugs & Greenbacks: The Antimonopoly Tradition & the Politics of Finance in America. 317p. (C). 1997. text 59.95 (*0-521-56167-1*) Cambridge U Pr.

— Goldbugs & Greenbacks: The Antimonopoly Tradition & the Politics of Finance, 1865-1896. 317p. (C). 1999. pap. text 19.95 (*0-521-65392-4*) Cambridge U Pr.

Ritter, H.-G., jt. ed. see Bauer, W.

Ritter, Harry. Alaska's History: The People, the Land, & Events of the North Country. LC 92-38364. (Pocket Guides Ser.). (Illus.). 144p. 1993. pap. 12.95 (*0-88240-432-6*, Alaska NW Bks) Gr Arts Ctr Pub.

— Dictionary of Concepts in History, 3. LC 85-27305. (Reference Sources for the Social Sciences & Humanities Ser.: No. 3). 511p. 1986. lib. bdg. 95.00 (*0-313-22700-4*, RCH/, Greenwood Pr) Greenwood.

***Ritter, Hartien S.** From the Banks of Loch Lomand to the Prairies of Kansas: The Ancestory of Charlotte Burtnett Ritter. 144p. 1999. 15.95 (*1-58244-037-9*) Rutledge Bks.

Ritter, Hartien S. History of the Ohio Genealogical Society, 1959-1984. 1984. 2.50 (*0-935057-09-9*) OH Genealogical.

Ritter, Irene. The Cobbler Crusade: Bringing an Old-Fashioned Dish to Modern Cooks. LC 92-12019. (Illus.). 144p. (Orig.). 1992. pap. 10.95 (*1-55561-044-7*) Fisher Bks.

Ritter, J. Representation Theory & Number Theory in Connection with the Local Langlands Conjecture. LC 88-39030. (Contemporary Mathematics Ser.: Vol. 86). 266p. 1989. pap. 36.00 (*0-8218-5093-8*, CONM/86) Am Math.

Ritter, J., jt. auth. see Appelrath, Hans-Jurgen.

Ritter, James M., et al. Multiple Choice Questions in Clinical Pharmacology. 168p. 1995. pap. text 15.95 (*0-340-55932-2*, Pub. by E A) OUP.

***Ritter, James M., et al.** A Textbook of Clinical Phamrmacology. 4th ed. LC 99-40626. (An Arnold Publication). (Illus.). 736p. 2000. pap. text 59.95 (*0-340-70593-0*, Pub. by E A) OUP.

Ritter, James M., et al. A Textbook of Clinical Pharmacology. 3rd ed. 736p. 1995. pap. text 39.95 (*0-340-55864-4*, Pub. by E A) OUP.

Ritter, Jim, tr. see Cartan, Elie.

Ritter, John E., ed. Erosion of Ceramic Materials. 220p. 1992. text 91.00 (*0-87849-637-8*, Pub. by Trans T Pub) Enfield Pubs NH.

Ritter, John H. Choosing up Sides. LC 97-39779. 163p. (J). (gr. 5-9). 1998. 15.99 (*0-399-23185-4*, Philomel) Peng Put Young Read.

***Ritter, John H.** Choosing up Sides. 176p. (gr. 5-9). 2000. pap. 4.99 (*0-698-11840-5*, PapStar) Peng Put Young Read.

— Over the Wall. LC 99-49911. (Illus.). 320p. (YA). (gr. 5-9). 2000. 17.99 (*0-399-23489-6*, Philomel) Peng Put Young Read.

***Ritter, Jorge Eduardo.** Panama Canal. 2000. 65.00 (*958-9393-82-9*) Villegas Ed.

Ritter, Judith, jt. ed. see Wholey, Mary L.

Ritter, Jurgen, jt. ed. see Frey, Gerhard.

Ritter, K. Comparative Geography of Palestine & the Sinaitic Peninsula, 4 Vols, Set, Vol. 1. LC 68-26367. (Reference Ser.: No. 44). 721p. 1969. reprint ed. lib. bdg. 159.95 (*0-8383-0180-0*) M S G Haskell Hse.

Ritter, Karl. Comparative Geography. LC 77-174325. reprint ed. 39.50 (*0-404-05349-1*) AMS Pr.

— The Comparative Geography of Palestine, 4 vols., Set. 1865. 65.00 (*0-403-03564-3*) Scholarly.

— Comparative Geography of Palestine & the Sinaitic Peninsula, 4 vols. Gage, William L., tr. LC 69-10151. 1969. reprint ed. lib. bdg. 195.00 (*0-8371-9946-8*, RISP) Greenwood.

— Comparative Geography of Palestine & the Sinaitic Peninsula, 4 vols., 1. Gage, William L., tr. LC 69-10151. 1971. reprint ed. lib. bdg. 19.50 (*0-685-02003-7*) Greenwood.

— The Comparative Geography of Palestine & the Sinaitic Peninsula, 4 vols., Vol. 1. LC 69-10151. (Illus.). 1969. lib. bdg. 65.00 (*0-8371-0638-9*, RISP, Greenwood Pr) Greenwood.

— Comparative Geography of Palestine & the Sinaitic Peninsula, 4 vols., Vol. 2. Gage, William L., tr. LC 69-10151. 1969. reprint ed. lib. bdg. 65.00 (*0-8371-0838-1*, RISB) Greenwood.

— Comparative Geography of Palestine & the Sinaitic Peninsula, 4 vols., Vol. 3. Gage, William L., tr. LC 69-10151. 1969. reprint ed. lib. bdg. 65.00 (*0-8371-0839-X*, RISC) Greenwood.

— Comparative Geography of Palestine & the Sinaitic Peninsula, 4 vols., Vol. 4. Gage, William L., tr. LC 69-10151. 1969. reprint ed. lib. bdg. 65.00 (*0-8371-0840-3*, RISD) Greenwood.

Ritter, Kathleen, jt. auth. see O'Neill, Craig.

Ritter, Kathleen Y. & O'Neill, Craig W., eds. Righteous Religion: Unmasking the Illusions of Fundamentalism & Authoritarian Catholicism. LC 96-4734. 212p. (C). 1996. 39.95 (*0-7890-6016-7*, Haworth Pastrl) Haworth Pr.

— Righteous Religion: Unmasking the Illusions of Fundamentalism & Authoritarian Catholicism. LC 96-4734. 212p. 1997. pap. 17.95 (*0-7890-6017-5*) Haworth Pr.

Ritter, Kim H. Quick Quilting: Rotary Cutting, Machine Piecing, Machine Applique & Machine Quilting. LC 97-15390. (Illus.). 128p. 1997. pap. 19.95 (*0-8442-2656-4*, Quilt Dgst Pr) NTC Contemp Pub Co.

***Ritter, Klaus.** Average-Case Analysis of Numerical Problems. LC 00-30799. (Lecture Notes in Mathematics). 2000. pap. write for info. (*3-540-67449-7*) Spr-Verlag.

Ritter, Kurt & Henry, David. Ronald Reagan: The Great Communicator, 13. LC 91-28148. (Great American Orators: Critical Studies, Speeches & Sources Ser.: No. 13). 248p. 1992. lib. bdg. 55.00 (*0-313-26069-9*, HRR/, Greenwood Pr) Greenwood.

Ritter, Lawrence S. Principles of Money: Banking & Financing (Study Guide) 9th ed. 320p. (C). 1997. pap. text, student ed. 28.00 (*0-673-98416-8*) Addison-Wesley.

***Ritter, Lawrence.** Accompany Principles of Money, Banking, & Financial Market. 10th ed. 384p. (C). 1999. pap. text 29.40 (*0-321-06469-0*) Addison-Wesley.

Ritter, Lawrence S. East Side, West Side: Tales of New York Sporting Life, 1910-1960. LC 98-84567. (Illus.). 224p. 1998. 34.95 (*0-9656949-6-8*) Total Sprts.

— The Glory of Their Times: The Story of the Early Days of Baseball Told by the Men Who Played It. LC 91-40203. (Illus.). 384p. 1992. pap. 11.00 (*0-688-11273-0*, Quil) HarperTrade.

— Leagues Apart. (Illus.). 40p. (J). (ps-3). 1999. mass mkt. 5.95 (*0-688-16693-8*, Wm Morrow) Morrow Avon.

— Leagues Apart: The Men & Times of the Negro Baseball Leagues. LC 94-17512. (Illus.). 40p. (J). (gr. 3 up). 1995. lib. bdg. 14.93 (*0-688-13317-7*, Wm Morrow) Morrow Avon.

— Leagues Apart: The Men & Times of the Negro Baseball Leagues. LC 94-17512. (Illus.). 40p. (J). (ps up). 1995. 15.00 (*0-688-13316-9*, Wm Morrow) Morrow Avon.

— Lost Ballparks: A Celebration of Baseball's Legendary Fields. (Illus.). 224p. 1994. pap. 19.95 (*0-14-023422-5*) Studio Bks.

— Principles of Money, Banking & Financial Markets. 10th ed. LC 99-28472. 640p. (C). 1999. 92.00 (*0-321-02020-0*) Addison-Wesley Educ.

***Ritter, Lawrence S.** The Story of Baseball. rev. ed. (Illus.). 210p. 2000. text 22.00 (*0-7881-9082-2*) DIANE Pub.

— The Story of Baseball. 2nd rev. ed. LC 89-48952. (Illus.). 224p. (J). (gr. 4-7). 1990. pap. 9.95 (*0-688-09057-5*, Wm Morrow) Morrow Avon.

Ritter, Lawrence S. The Story of Baseball. 3rd ed. LC 89-48952. 208p. (J). 1999. mass mkt. 7.95 (*0-688-16265-7*, Wm Morrow) Morrow Avon.

— The Story of Baseball: Third Revised & Expanded Edition. 3rd ed. LC 98-35456. (Illus.). 224p. (YA). (gr. 5-9). 1999. 16.95 (*0-688-16264-9*, Wm Morrow) Morrow Avon.

Ritter, Lawrence S. & Honig, Donald. Image of Their Greatness: An Illustrated History of Baseball from 1900 to the Present. 3rd ed. 448p. 1992. pap. 15.00 (*0-517-58728-9*, Crown) Crown Pub Group.

Ritter, Lawrence S. & Rucker, Mark. The Babe: A Life in Pictures. (Illus.). 288p. 1988. 40.00 (*0-89919-768-X*, Pub. by Ticknor & Fields) HM.

— The Babe: The Game That Ruth Built. 2nd rev. ed. LC 97-61736. (Illus.). xii, 296p. 1997. 40.00 (*0-9656949-0-9*) Total Sprts.

Ritter, Lawrence S. & Silber, William L. Principles of Money, Banking, & Financial Markets. 8th ed. LC 93-14741. 688p. (C). 1993. pap. 66.50 (*0-465-06367-5*) Basic.

Ritter, Lawrence S., jt. auth. see Kurz, Susanne.

Ritter, Lennart, et al. EEC Competition Law: A Practitioners Guide. 1200p. 1991. 185.00 (*90-6544-465-3*) Kluwer Law Intl.

***Ritter, Lennart, et al.** European Competition Law: A Practitioner's Guide. 2nd ed. 1352p. 1999. pap. 64.00 (*90-411-1334-7*); text 164.00 (*90-411-1267-7*) Kluwer Law Intl.

Ritter, M. & Crisp, N. The Thymus: In Focus. (In Focus Ser.). (Illus.). 96p. (C). 1992. pap. text 17.95 (*0-19-963144-1*) OUP.

Ritter, M. A., jt. ed. see Kendall, Marion D.

Ritter, Mark, tr. see Beck, Ulrich.

Ritter, Mark, tr. see Beck, Ulrich & Beck-Gernsheim, Elisabeth.

Ritter, Mark, tr. see Beck, Ulrick.

Ritter, Mark A., tr. see Beck, Ulrich.

Ritter, Marnie. Embroidery My Way: For Fabric & Canvas. (Illus.). 82p. (Orig.). 1993. pap. text. write for info. (*0-9635593-1-1*) Marnies Crewel.

— Marnie Ritter's Canvas Patterns, Bk. 2. 109p. 1992. pap. text 27.95 (*0-9635593-0-3*) Marnies Crewel.

— Marnie Ritter's Canvas Patterns, Bk. 2. (Illus.). 100p. 1994. pap. text 28.00 (*0-9635593-2-X*) Marnies Crewel.

Ritter, Mary, ed. see Reider, Barbara E.

Ritter, Mary A. & Ladyman, Heather M., eds. Monoclonal Antibodies: Production, Engineering & Clinical Application. (Postgraduate Medical Science Ser.: No. 2). (Illus.). 496p. (C). 1995. pap. text 47.95 (*0-521-42503-4*) Cambridge U Pr.

***Ritter, Merrill A. & Albohm, Marjorie J.** Your Injury: A Common Sense Guide to Sports Injuries. rev. ed. 189p. 2000. pap. 20.00 (*1-884125-79-4*) Cooper Pubng.

Ritter, Merrill A. & Gosling, Craig. The Knee: A Guide to the Examination & Diagnosis of Ligament Injuries. (Illus.). 32p. 1979. spiral bd. 12.95 (*0-398-03901-1*) C C Thomas.

Ritter, Michael. Great Women: And Their Words of Wisdom. 64p. 1995. 6.50 (*1-56245-212-6*) Great Quotations.

Ritter, Michael, ed. Fortune Cookies Without the Calories: A Proverbial Guide to Global Wisdom. (Day Riser Ser.). 366p. 1995. spiral bd. 6.50 (*1-56245-217-7*) Great Quotations.

Ritter, Michael E. Earth Online: An Internet Guide for Earth Science. (Earth Science Ser.). (Illus.). 300p. (C). 1996. 21.95 (*0-534-51707-2*) Wadsworth Pub.

Ritter, Nancy A., jt. ed. see der Hulst, Harry.

Ritter, Naomi. Art As Spectacle: Images of the Entertainer since Romanticism. LC 89-4844. (Illus.). 360p. 1989. text 37.50 (*0-8262-0719-7*) U of Mo Pr.

Ritter, Naomi, jt. auth. see Smith, Carl B.

Ritter, Naomi, ed. see Mann, Thomas.

Ritter, Nicole Rosenleaf, jt. ed. see Hubbs, Clayton A.

Ritter, O. & Fattorusso, V. Atlas der Elektrokardiographie. 5th ed. 1976. 48.75 (*3-8055-2416-1*) S Karger.

Ritter, Otto, jt. auth. see Fattorusso, V.

Ritter, P., jt. auth. see Fischer, Wilhelm.

Ritter, Peck. Biochemistry: A Foundation. teacher ed. write for info. (*0-534-33866-6*) Brooks-Cole.

Ritter, Priscilla & Fleishman, Thelma. Newton, Massachusetts, 1679-1779: A Biographical Directory. 152p. 1982. pap. 11.95 (*0-88082-001-2*) New Eng Hist.

***Ritter, R. M., ed.** The Oxford Dictionary for Writers & Editors. 2nd ed. 480p. 2000. 24.95 (*0-19-866239-4*) OUP.

Ritter, Rhoda. Michigan Riding & Hiking Trail Vol. 1: True Stories of the First Crossing & Further Adventures. LC 96-208917. (Illus.). 135p. (Orig.). 1996. pap., mass mkt. 14.95 (*0-9651614-0-4*) River Outpost.

Ritter, Rus. Managing Effectively in a Reinvented Government: The Federal Manager's Roadmap to Success. 2nd rev. ed. (Illus.). 133p. 1997. pap. text 14.95 (*0-936295-82-1*) FPMI Comns.

— Managing the Civilian Workforce: A Guide for the Military Manager. 3rd rev. ed. (Illus.). 119p. 1998. pap. text 14.95 (*0-936295-83-X*) FPMI Comns.

Ritter, Scott, jt. auth. see Ritter, William.

Ritter, Sue. Bethlem Royal & Maudsley Manual of Clinical Mental Health Nursing: Principles & Guidelines. 2nd ed. 400p. (C). 1996. pap. text 63.75 (*1-56593-186-6*, 0501) Singular Publishing.

— Neuroanatomy & Physiology of Abdominal Vagal Afferents. 336p. 1992. boxed set 127.95 (*0-8493-8881-3*, QM471) CRC Pr.

Ritter, Sue, et al, eds. Collaborative Community Mental Health Care. 320p. 1995. 38.25 (*1-56593-773-2*, 1504) Singular Publishing.

Ritter, Sue & Gournay, Kevin. Manual of Clinical Psychiatric Nursing. 2nd ed. (Illus.). 352p. 1999. pap. 42.50 (*0-7487-3299-3*) Standard Pub.

Ritter, Thomas J. & Denniston, George C. Say No to Circumcision! 40 Compelling Reasons. 2nd ed. (Illus.). 108p. (Orig.). 1996. pap. 9.95 (*0-934061-30-0*) Marketscope Bks.

Ritter, Ulrich. Grundwortschatz Wirtschaftswissenschaftlicher. 5th ed. (ENG & GER.). 272p. 1991. lib. bdg. 39.95 (*0-8288-3891-7*, M15083) Fr & Eur.

Ritter, Ulrich & Zinn, K. G. Grundwortschatz Wirtschaftswissenschaftlicher Begriffe. 4th ed. (ENG & GER.). 231p. 1987. 29.95 (*0-8288-0101-0*, M15083) Fr & Eur.

***Ritter v. Greiffen, Norberto Iblher.** Die Rezeption des Lombardischen Lehensrechts und Sein Einflu & Beta; Auf das Mittelalterliche Lehenswesen. (Europaische

An Asterisk (*) at the beginning of an entry indicates that the title is appearing for the first time.

Hochschulschriften Geschichte und Ihre Hilfswissenschaften Ser.). 396p. 1999. 56.95 (3-631-45972-6) P Lang Pubng.

Ritter Von Hohnel, Ludwig. Over Land & Sea: Memoir of an Austrian Rear Admiral's Life in Europe & Africa, 1857-1909. Coons, Ronald E. & Imperato, Pascal J., eds. LC 99-45080. (Illus.). 384p. 2000. 40.00 (0-8419-1390-0) Holmes & Meier.

Ritter-Walker, Eva, jt. ed. see Wurtman, R. J.

***Ritter, William & Ritter, Scott.** Endgame: Solving the Iraq Problem -- Once & For All. LC 99-21736. 192p. 1999. 22.00 (0-684-86485-1) S&S Trade.

Ritter, William F., ed. Irrigation & Drainage. LC 91-21084. 832p. 1991. pap. text 67.00 (0-87262-811-6) Am Soc Civil Eng.

Ritter, William Frederick & Shirmohammadi, Adel. Agriculture Nonpoint Source Pollution: Watershed Management & Pollution. 300p. 1999. 69.95 (1-56670-222-4, L1222) Lewis Pubs.

Ritter, Zofia. Kuchina Amerykanska: American Cooking. (POL., Illus.). 137p. (Orig.). 1989. reprint ed. pap. 8.95 (0-9617846-0-1) Scorpio IL.

Ritterband, Paul & Kosmin, Barry A., eds. Contemporary Jewish Philanthropy in America. 250p. (C). 1991. lib. bdg. 64.50 (0-8476-7647-1) Rowman.

Ritterband, Paul & Wechsler, Harold S. Jewish Learning in American Universities: The First Century. LC 93-48233. (Modern Jewish Experience Ser.). 384p. 1994. 35.00 (0-253-35039-5) Ind U Pr.

Ritterbusch, Dale. Lessons Learned. write for info. (1-885215-08-8, Viet Nam Gnrtn) Burning Cities Pr.

Ritterman, Michele. Using Hypnosis in Family Therapy. LC 83-48162. (Jossey-Bass Social & Behavioral Science Ser.). 375p. reprint ed. pap. 116.30 (0-7837-6525-8, 204563700007) Bks Demand.

Ritterman, Michelle K. Hope under Siege: State Terror vs. Family Support in Chile. Tick, Edward, ed. (Frontiers in Psychotherapy Ser.). 304p. 1991. pap. 39.50 (0-89391-801-6); text 73.25 (0-89391-758-3) Ablx Pub.

***Rittershausen, Brian & Rittershausen, Sara.** Orchids, a Care Manual. (Illus.). 2000. 19.95 (1-57145-676-7, Laurel Glen Pub) Advantage Pubs.

Rittershausen, Brian & Rittershausen, Wilma. Orchids: A Splendid Obsession. LC 99-35327. (Illus.). 224p. 1999. 50.00 (1-57959-054-3, SOMA) BB&T Inc.

— Popular Orchids. 224p. 1982. 40.00 (0-7223-0940-6, Pub. by A H S Ltd) St Mut.

Rittershausen, Brian, jt. auth. see Rittershausen, Wilma.

Rittershausen, Sara, jt. auth. see Rittershausen, Brian.

Rittershausen, Wilma. Success with Orchids. 1998. 16.98 (1-57717-063-6) Todtri Prods.

***Rittershausen, Wilma & Rittershausen, Brian.** Orchids: The Complete Grower's Guide. (Illus.). 176p. 2000. 49.50 (1-870673-34-4, Pub. by Garden Art Pr) Antique Collect.

Rittershausen, Wilma, jt. auth. see Rittershausen, Brian.

Ritterskamp, James J. Purchasing Manager's Deskbook of Purchasing Law Supplement. 210p. 1990. pap. text 35.00 (0-13-739210-9) P-H.

Ritterskamp, James J., Jr. & King, Donald. Purchasing Manager's Desk Book of Purchasing Law, 1999 Cumulative Supplement. 3rd ed. 272p. 1998. pap. 39.95 (0-13-959669-0) P-H.

Ritterskamp, James J., Jr., jt. auth. see King, Donald B.

Rittersporn, Gabor T. Simplifications Staliniennes et Complications Sovietiques. 2nd ed. 384p. 1991. pap. text 60.00 (2-88124-223-5) Gordon & Breach.

— Stalinist Simplications & Soviet Complications: Social Tensions & Political Conflicts in the U. S. S. R. 1933-1953, Vol. (Social Orders Ser.). xii, 334p. 1991. text 80.00 (3-7186-5107-6, Harwood Acad Pubs) Gordon & Breach.

Rittersporn, Gabor T., jt. ed. see Lampert, Nick.

Ritthaler, Pauline. Beans with Character: An Unofficial Guide to the Disney Mini Bean Bag Plush Collection. 1999. pap. text 18.95 (0-9659036-5-6) Dinomates.

Ritthaler, Shelly. Amanda. (American Dreams Ser.). (YA). (gr. 7 up). 1997. pap. 3.99 (0-614-28634-4, Avon Bks) Morrow Avon.

— Dinosaurs Alive! 96p. (J). (gr. 2 up). 1994. pap. 3.50 (0-380-77323-6, Avon Bks) Morrow Avon.

— Dinosaurs for Lunch. 80p. (Orig.). (J). (gr. 2). 1993. pap. 3.50 (0-380-76796-1, Avon Bks) Morrow Avon.

— Dinosaurs Wild! 96p. (Orig.). (J). 1994. pap. 3.50 (0-380-77322-8, Avon Bks) Morrow Avon.

— The Ginger Jar. LC 90-91540. 92p. (Orig.). 1990. pap. 7.00 (0-9625745-1-1) Raven Creek Pr.

— Heart of the Hills. (American Dreams Ser.). 1996. 9.09 (0-606-10210-8, Pub. by Turtleback) Demco.

— Heart of the Hills: American Dreams. 176p. (Orig.). (YA). 1996. mass mkt. 3.99 (0-380-78374-6, Avon Bks) Morrow Avon.

— With Love. (American Dreams Ser.). (YA). (gr. 7 up). 1997. pap. 3.99 (0-614-28633-6, Avon Bks) Morrow Avon.

— With Love, Amanda. (YA). 1997. mass mkt. 3.99 (0-380-78375-4, Avon Bks) Morrow Avon.

Ritthaler, Shelly. With Love, Amanda. (American Dreams Ser.). (YA). 1997. 9.09 (0-606-10976-5, Pub. by Turtleback) Demco.

Ritti, R. Richard. The Ropes to Skip & the Ropes to Know: Studies in Organizational Behavior. 5th ed. LC 97-41. (Management Ser.). 304p. 1997. pap. 36.95 (0-471-13304-3) Wiley.

Rittig, Dessa, jt. auth. see Borell, Brigitte.

Rittig, Falk R., jt. auth. see Ory, Robert L.

Rittig, Falk R., jt. ed. see Ory, Robert L.

Rittle, Emma Sansone, tr. see Usai, Paolo C.

Rittman, Sandra K., et al. Desktop Publishing Using PageMaker 5.0 Windows Version. 592p. (C). 1993. text 42.95 (0-697-21361-7) Bus & Educ Tech.

***Rittmann, B. E., ed.** Microbial Ecology of Biofilms. (Water Science & Technology Ser.). 280p. 1999. pap. 163.00 (0-08-043654-4, Pergamon Pr) Elsevier.

Rittmann, Bruce E., et al. In Situ Bioremediation. 2nd ed. LC 94-3867. (Illus.). 260p. 1994. 69.00 (0-8155-1348-8) Noyes.

Rittmayer, Jane F. Life, Time. LC RC0514.R57. 127p. reprint ed. pap. 39.40 (0-608-12396-X, 205557200031) Bks Demand.

Rittmueller, Jean, jt. auth. see Koch, John T.

Rittner, Barbara & Trudeau, Patricia. The Women's Guide to Surviving Graduate School. LC 97-21015. (Graduate Survival Skills Ser.: Vol. 2). 180p. 1997. 42.00 (0-7619-0389-5); pap. 19.95 (0-7619-0390-9) Sage.

Rittner, C., et al, eds. Proceedings of the Sixth Complement Genetics Workshop & Conference, Mainz, July 1989. (Illus.). vi, 142p. 1990. reprint ed. 113.25 (3-8055-5342-0) S Karger.

Rittner, C., jt. auth. see Ma.

Rittner, Carol. Elie Wiesel: Between Memory & Hope. 232p. (C). 1991. pap. text 17.50 (0-8147-7421-0) NYU Pr.

Rittner, Carol, ed. Anne Frank in the World: Essays & Reflections. LC 97-17605. 168p. (gr. 13). 1997. 58.95 (0-7656-0019-6) M E Sharpe.

— Anne Frank in the World: Essays & Reflections. LC 97-17605. 168p. (C). (gr. 13). 1997. pap. 21.95 (0-7656-0020-X) M E Sharpe.

***Rittner, Carol, et al, eds.** The Holocaust & the Christian World: Reflections on the Past, Challenges for the Future. 296p. 2000. 49.95 (0-8264-1298-X); pap. 24.95 (0-8264-1299-8) Continuum.

Rittner, Carol & Myers, Sondra. Courage to Care: Rescuers of Jews During the Holocaust. 176p. (C). 1989. pap. text 32.50 (0-8147-7406-7) NYU Pr.

Rittner, Carol & Roth, John K., eds. Different Voices: Women & the Holocaust. LC 92-28233. (Illus.). 435p. 1993. pap. 18.95 (1-55778-504-X) Paragon Hse.

Rittner, Carol A. & Roth, John K. From the Unthinkable to the Unavoidable: American Christian & Jewish Scholars Encounter the Holocaust, 48. LC 96-28057. (Contributions to the Study of Religion Ser.). 232p. 1997. 65.00 (0-313-29683-9) Greenwood.

Rittner, Carol A. & Roth, John K., eds. Memory Offended: The Auschwitz Convent Controversy. LC 90-47333. 312p. 1991. 62.95 (0-275-93606-6, C3606, Praeger Pubs); pap. 22.95 (0-275-93848-4, B3848, Praeger Pubs) Greenwood.

Rittner, Carol K. & Roth, John, eds. From the Unthinkable to the Unavoidable: American Christian & Jewish Scholars Encounter the Holocaust. LC 96-28057. 232p. 1997. pap. 22.95 (0-275-95764-0, Praeger Pubs) Greenwood.

Rittner, Debra, tr. see Kalechofsky, Roberta, ed.

***Rittner, Don.** Albany. (Images of America Ser.). 128p. 1999. pap. 18.99 (0-7385-0088-7) Arcadia Publng.

Rittner, Don. Hello, Goodbye: Disappearing Artifacts & Landscapes of the Hudson & Mohawk Valley. (Illus.). 36p. (Orig.). 1989. pap. 21.00 (0-9624263-0-X) Hardcopy News.

***Rittner, Don.** I-Mac, Ibook & G3 Troubleshooting Pocket Reference. (Illus.). 512p. 2000. pap. 19.99 (0-07-212468-7) McGraw.

— The iMac Book. LC 98-53324. 1999. pap. text 24.99 (1-57610-429-X) Coriolis Grp.

Rittner, Don. Imac Design Visual Insight. 1999. pap. text 24.99 (1-57610-505-9) Coriolis Grp.

***Rittner, Don.** Lansingburgh. (Images of America Ser.). (Illus.). 128p. (Orig.). 1999. pap. 18.99 (0-7385-0089-5) Arcadia Publng.

Rittner, Don. Rittners Field Guide to the Web Business & Finance Resources. 1996. pap. text 19.95 (0-937666-51-3) MNS Pub.

— Rittners Field Guide to the Web Environmental Resources. 1997. pap. text 19.95 (0-937666-52-1) MNS Pub.

— Rittner's Field Guide to Usenet. LC 96-51251. (Illus.). 132p. (Orig.). 1996. pap. 19.95 (0-937666-50-5) MNS Pub.

— Rittners Field Guide to Web: Medical & Public Health Resources. 1997. pap. text 19.95 (0-937666-53-X) MNS Pub.

— Troy. LC 98-88053. (Images of America Ser.). (Illus.). 128p. 1998. pap. 16.99 (0-7524-1266-3) Arcadia Publng.

— Usenet Starter Kit for Macintosh. (Illus.). 350p. (Orig.). 1995. pap. text 25.00 (1-56830-130-8) Hayden.

Rittner, Mindy N. & Abraham, Thomas. Iron & Iron Oxide Powders: Trends & Markets. LC 98-120907. (Report Ser.: No. GB-209). 168p. 1997. 3350.00 (1-56965-462-X) BCC.

Rittner, Roger. Traffic Incident. (Read-along Radio Dramas Ser.). (YA). (gr. 6-11). 1982. ring bd. 38.00 (1-878298-10-0) Balance Pub.

Rittrich-Dorenkamp, Sigrun. Canaries. LC 99-27198. 128p. 1999. 12.95 (0-7641-5208-4) Barron.

Ritts, Herb. Africa, Vol. 1. LC 94-71832. (Illus.). 136p. 1994. 85.00 (0-8212-2121-3, Pub. by Bulfinch Pr) Little.

— Duo. 64p. 1991. 45.00 (0-944092-17-9) Twin Palms Pub.

— Duo. limited ed. 64p. 1991. 150.00 (0-944092-18-7) Twin Palms Pub.

— Herb Ritts: Work. (Illus.). 396p. 1996. 135.00 (0-8212-2296-1, Pub. by Bulfinch Pr) Little.

— Men - Women. (Illus.). 208p. 1989. 65.00 (0-944092-11-X) Twin Palms Pub.

— Modern Souls. 1995. 50.00 (1-881616-61-4) Dist Art Pubs.

— Notorious. LC 92-53227. (Illus.). 168p. 1992. 125.00 (0-8212-1911-1, Pub. by Bulfinch Pr) Little.

— Work. 1996. pap. 75.00 (0-8212-2372-0, Pub. by Bulfinch Pr) Little.

Ritts, Herb, photos by. Herb Ritts: Pictures. (Illus.). 144p. 1988. 75.00 (0-944092-01-2) Twin Palms Pub.

— Stern Portfolio: Body Art - Herb Ritts. (Illus.). 96p. 1998. pap. 19.95 (3-570-19135-4) te Neues.

Ritums, John, ed. see Martin, Philip R.

Ritundo, R. L. Advances in Gene Technology: Molecular Neurobiology & Neuropharmacology. Bialy, Harvey et al, eds. (ICSU Short Series Reports: Vol. 9). (Illus.). 180p. 1989. pap. 50.00 (1-85221-205-5) OUP.

Ritvo, Edward, jt. auth. see Katz, Illana.

Ritvo, Harriet. The Animal Estate: The English & Other Creatures in the Victorian Age. LC 87-11848. (Illus.). 368p. 1987. text 44.00 (0-674-03706-5) HUP.

— The Animal Estate: The English & Other Creatures in the Victorian Age. (Illus.). 368p. 1987. reprint ed. pap. text 12.95 (0-674-03707-3) HUP.

— The Platypus & the Mermaid: And Other Figments of the Classifying Imagination. LC 97-405. (Illus.). 304p. 1997. 31.00 (0-674-67357-3) HUP.

— The Platypus & the Mermaid: And Other Figments of the Classifying Imagination. (Illus.). 304p. 1998. pap. 15.95 (0-674-67358-1) HUP.

Ritvo, Harriet, et al. An English Arcadia: Landscape & Architecture in Britain & America: Papers Delivered at a Huntington Symposium. LC 92-30971. (Illus.). 180p. 1992. pap. 20.00 (0-87328-139-X) Huntington Lib.

Ritvo, Harriet, jt. ed. see Arac, Jonathan.

Ritvo, Phyllis T. The World of Gouda Pottery. LC 97-27277. (Illus.). 192p. 1998. 49.95 (1-883280-11-7); pap. 39.95 (1-883280-10-9) Font & Ctr Pr.

Ritvo, Roger A., et al, eds. Managing in the Age of Change: Essential Skills to Manage Today's Diverse Workplace. LC 94-9331. 324p. 1994. text 25.00 (0-7863-0303-4, Irwn Prfssnl) McGraw-Hill Prof.

Ritvo, Roger A. & Plotkin, Diane M. Sisters in Sorrow: Voices of Care in the Holocaust. LC 97-46013. (Illus.). 368p. 1998. 35.95 (0-89096-810-1) Tex A&M Univ Pr.

***Ritvo, Roger A. & Plotkin, Diane M.** Sisters in Sorrow: Voices of Care in the Holocaust. (Illus.). 314p. 2000. pap. 16.95 (0-89096-970-1) Tex A&M Univ Pr.

Ritvo, Roger A., jt. ed. see Hokenstad, Merl C., Jr.

Ritvo, Roger A., ed. see Sargent, Alice G.

Ritz. Exploring Production Systems. (Technology & Industrial Education Ser.). (J). 1990. mass mkt. 19.95 (0-87192-244-4) S-W Pub.

***Ritz, Charles.** A Fly Fisher's Life: The Art & Mechanics of Fly Fishing. 256p. 1999. 7.98 (1-56731-264-0, MJF Bks) Fine Comms.

Ritz, Corinna. Harmonisierungsprobleme bei der Umsetzung der EG-Richtlinie 87/102 uber den Verbraucherkredit. (GER.). xx, 233p. 1996. 51.95 (3-631-49635-4) P Lang Pubng.

Ritz, David. Divided Soul: The Life of Marvin Gaye. (Quality Paperbacks Ser.). (Illus.). 367p. 1991. reprint ed. pap. 13.95 (0-306-80443-3) Da Capo.

— Family Blood. 448p. 1993. mass mkt. 4.99 (0-8217-4058-X, Zebra Kensgtn) Kensgtn Pub Corp.

— Ray Charles: The Musician Who Lost Sight at Age Seven. LC 93-30224. (Great Achievers Ser.). (Illus.). 120p. (YA). (gr. 5 up). 1994. lib. bdg. 19.95 (0-7910-2080-0) Chelsea Hse.

— Ray Charles, Voice of Soul. (Great Achievers Ser.). 1994. 14.05 (0-606-08058-9) Turtleback.

Ritz, David, et al. The Brothers Neville. (Illus.). 352p. 2000. 24.95 (0-316-73009-2) Little.

Ritz, David, jt. auth. see Charles, Ray.

Ritz, David, jt. auth. see James, Etta.

Ritz, David, jt. auth. see Wexler, Jerry.

Ritz, Deanna. Yellow Bird: The Saga of George Armstrong Custer's Daughter. 208p. 1997. 16.00 (0-8059-3981-4) Dorrance.

Ritz, Eberhard, ed. Issues in Gloerulonephritis & Renin System. (Contributions to Nephrology Ser.: Vol. 43). (Illus.). viii, 204p. 1984. 29.75 (3-8055-3912-6) S Karger.

— Nephropathy in Type 2 Diabetes. LC 99-26166. (Oxford Clinical Nephrology Ser.). (Illus.). 304p. 1999. text 145.00 (0-19-262945-X) OUP.

Ritz, Eberhard, jt. auth. see Massry, Shaul G.

Ritz, Eberhard, ed. see Heidelberg Seminars in Nephrology Staff.

Ritz, Eberhard, jt. ed. see Schaefer, K.

Ritz, Eberhard, jt. ed. see Zeier, Martin.

Ritz, George J. Total Construction Project Management. LC 93-27856. 432p. 1992. 64.95 (0-07-052986-8) McGraw.

Ritz, John M., et al. Exploring Production Systems. (Illus.). (J). 1990. mass mkt. 49.95 (0-87192-205-3) Delmar.

— Exploring Production Systems. (Illus.). 1991. teacher ed. 15.95 (0-87192-239-8) Delmar.

Ritz, Paul S., ed. see Ritz, Rudolph A.

Ritz, Randy. Act It Out! 20 Terrific Techniques for Teaching Any Bible Story. Caldwell, Lise, ed. LC 98-43150. (Illus.). 112p. (J). (gr. 1-6). 1999. teacher ed. 12.99 (0-7847-0919-X, 03390) Standard Pub.

Ritz, Richard E. An Architect Looks at Downtown Portland. 102p. 1991. pap. 19.95 (0-9629661-1-8) Greenhills.

— History of the Whitman College Campus & Its Buildings. 128p. 1992. 24.95 (0-9632955-0-0); 50.00 (0-9632955-2-7); pap. 15.95 (0-9632955-1-9) Whitman Coll.

***Ritz, Rudolph A.** Grains of Sand: Devotions by Rudolph A. Ritz. deluxe ed. Ritz, Paul S., ed. (Illus.). 112p. 1998. 21.95 (1-885309-10-4) SpellBound Pr.

***Ritz, Stacy.** Disney World. 3rd ed. (Travel Guide (French Guides) Ser.). (FRE.). 1998. pap. text 24.95 (2-89464-079-X) Ulysses Travel.

Ritz, Stacy. Disneyland & Beyond: Orlando's Family Attractions. 4th rev. ed. (Illus.). 336p. (Orig.). 1997. pap. 13.95 (1-56975-076-9) Ulysses Pr.

— Hidden Belize. (Hidden Travel Ser.). (Illus.). 264p. 1999. pap. 15.95 (1-56975-198-6, Pub. by Ulysses Pr) Publishers Group.

— Hidden Carolinas. 3rd rev. ed. (Hidden Travel Ser.). (Illus.). 456p. 1999. pap. 17.95 (1-56975-171-4) Ulysses Pr.

— The New Key to Belize. 3rd rev. ed. LC 97-60638. (New Key Guides Ser.). (Illus.). 232p. (Orig.). 1997. pap. 14.95 (1-56975-085-8) Ulysses Pr.

***Ritz, Stacy & Corbeil, Pierre.** Boston. (Travel Guide (French Guides) Ser.).Tr. of Hidden Boston & Cape Cod. (FRE.). 1998. pap. 17.95 (2-89464-103-6) Ulysses Travel.

***Ritz, Stacy & Oppenheimer, Lisa.** Hidden Walt Disney World, Orlando & Beyond. (Hidden Travel Ser.). (Illus.). 336p. 2000. pap. 13.95 (1-56975-202-8, Pub. by Ulysses Pr) Publishers Group.

Ritz, Susan. The Civil Rights Act of Nineteen Ninety-One: Its Impact on Employment Discrimination Litigation. (Litigation & Administrative Practice Ser.). 304p. 1992. pap. text 70.00 (0-685-56924-1, H4-5127) PLI.

Ritz, Wilfred J. Rewriting the History of the Judiciary Act of 1789: Exposing Myths, Challenging Premises & Using New Evidence. Holt, Wythe & LaRue, L. H., eds. LC 89-37863. 288p. 1990. 35.00 (0-8061-2239-0) U of Okla Pr.

Ritz, Wilfred J., compiled by. American Judicial Proceedings First Printed Before 1801: An Analytical Bibliography. LC 83-18605. (Illus.). 364p. 1984. lib. bdg. 59.95 (0-313-24057-4, RAJ/, Greenwood Pr) Greenwood.

Ritzdorf, Marsha, jt. ed. see Thomas, June M.

Ritzel, G., ed. Alkohol, Tabak und Drogen im Leben des jungen Mannes. (Sozialmedizinische und Paedagogische Jugendkunde Ser.: Band 14). (Illus.). 1976. 42.75 (3-8055-2381-5) S Karger.

Ritzel, G., ed. see Biener, K.

Ritzel, G., ed. see Mueller, Hans R.

Ritzel, Wolfgang. Immanuel Kant: Eine Biographie. (GER.). xiv, 738p. 1985. 161.55 (3-11-010634-5) De Gruyter.

Ritzema, H., et al. Drainage of Irrigated Lands. (Irrigation Water Management Training Manual Ser.: No. 9). 82p. 1996. pap. 11.00 (92-5-103779-5, F37795, Pub. by FAO) Bernan Associates.

Ritzen, Martin, ed. European Society for Pediatric Endocrinology (ESPE) & the Lawson Wilkins Pediatric Endocrine Society (LWPES) 5th Joint Meeting, Stockholm, June 1997: Abstracts. (Hormone Research Ser.: Vol. 48, Suppl. 2, 1997). xiv, 212p. 1997. pap. 98.25 (3-8055-6546-1) S Karger.

Ritzen, Martin, ed. see Karolinska Institute Nobel Conference Staff.

Ritzenberg, Edna. The Pinballs: A Study Guide. (Novel-Ties Ser.). (J). (gr. 4-6). 1984. pap. text, teacher ed., student ed. 15.95 (0-88122-090-6) Lrn Links.

— Sadako & the Thousand Paper Cranes: A Study Guide. (Novel-Ties Ser.). (J). (gr. 3-5). 1984. pap. text, teacher ed., student ed. 15.95 (0-88122-062-0) Lrn Links.

Ritzenhofen, Ute. Amerikas Italien: Deutsche Texasbilder des 19.Jahrhunderts. (Mainzer Studien zur Amerikanistik: No. 37). 302p. 1997. 57.95 (3-631-31640-2) P Lang Pubng.

Ritzenthaler, Mary L. Preserving Archives & Manuscripts. (Archival Fundamentals Ser.). 228p. 1993. 27.00 (0-931828-94-5) Soc Am Archivists.

Ritzenthaler, Mary L., et al. Archives & Manuscripts: Administration of Photo Collections. (Basic Manual Ser.). 176p. 1984. pap. text 23.00 (0-931828-61-9) Soc Am Archivists.

Ritzenthaler, Pat, jt. auth. see Ritzenthaler, Robert E.

Ritzenthaler, Robert E. & Quimby, George I. The Red Ocher Culture of the Upper Great Lakes & Adjacent Areas. LC 62-15263. (Chicago Natural History Museum Anthropology Ser.: Vol. 36, No. 11, March 27, 1962). (Illus.). 33p. 1962. reprint ed. pap. 30.00 (0-608-02706-5, 206337100004) Bks Demand.

Ritzenthaler, Robert E. & Ritzenthaler, Pat. The Woodland Indians of the Western Great Lakes. (Illus.). 160p. (C). 1991. reprint ed. pap. text 10.95 (0-88133-548-7) Waveland Pr.

Ritzenthaler, Tom. 1999-2000 Guide to Museum Studies & Training in the United States. 4th ed. Adams, Roxana, ed. 190p. 1999. pap. 21.50 (0-931201-59-4, 830) Am Assn Mus.

Ritzer. Contemporary Social Theory. 2002. pap. text 38.50 (0-07-234962-X) McGraw.

— Modern Sociological Theory. 5th ed. LC 99-44807. 648p. 1999. pap. 50.00 (0-07-229604-6) McGraw.

— Social Problems. 2nd ed. 1986. teacher ed. 28.12 (0-07-554987-5) McGraw.

— Sociology Theory. 5th ed. LC 99-33735. 792p. 1999. 61.56 (0-07-229605-4) McGraw.

Ritzer, George. Classical Sociological Theory. 2nd ed. LC 95-36203. (C). 1995. pap. text 38.25 (0-07-053017-3) McGraw.

***Ritzer, George.** Classical Sociological Theory. 3rd ed. LC 99-45912. 2000. write for info. (0-07-229606-2) McGrw-H Hghr Educ.

— El Encanto de un Mundo Desencantado. (SPA.). 224p. 2000. pap. 23.95 (84-344-1435-X) Planeta Edit.

Ritzer, George. Enchanting a Disenchanted World: Revolutionizing the Means of Consumption. 1999. pap. write for info. (0-7619-8511-5) Sage.

— Expressing America: A Critique of the Global Credit Card Society. LC 94-38142. 1995. pap. 17.95 (0-8039-9044-8) Pine Forge.

— Frontiers of Sociological Theory. 1991. pap. text 25.50 (0-231-07079-9) Col U Pr.

— The McDonaldization of Society. 240p. 1994. 29.95 (0-8039-9046-4) Sage.

— The McDonaldization of Society: An Investigation into the Changing Character of Contemporary Social Life. rev. ed. LC 95-16950. (Orig.). 1995. write for info. (0-8039-9076-6) Pine Forge.

An Asterisk (*) at the beginning of an entry indicates that the title is appearing for the first time.

— The McDonaldization of Society: An Investigation into the Changing Character of Contemporary Social Life. 2nd rev. ed. LC 95-16950. (Orig.). 1995. pap. 17.95 (*0-8039-9077-4*) Pine Forge.

— The McDonaldization Thesis: Explorations & Extensions. LC 97-68493. 256p. 1997. 75.00 (*0-7619-5539-9*); pap. 32.00 (*0-7619-5540-2*) Sage.

— Modern Sociological Theory. 4th rev. ed. LC 95-36202. Orig. Title: Contemporary Sociological Theory, 3rd ed.. (C). 1995. pap. text 36.00 (*0-07-053018-1*) McGraw.

— Postmodern Social Theory. LC 96-21073. 336p. (C). 1996. pap. 41.88 (*0-07-053019-X*) McGraw.

— Social Problems. 2nd ed. (Illus.). 544p. (C). 1986. pap. 67.50 (*0-07-554947-6*) McGraw.

— Sociological Beginnings for Beginners: On the Origins of Key Ideas in Sociology. LC 93-23915. 224p. (C). 1994. pap. 27.50 (*0-07-052974-4*) McGraw.

— Sociological Theory. 4th ed. LC 95-36204. (C). 1995. text 51.25 (*0-07-053016-5*) McGraw.

***Ritzer, George, ed.** A Companion to Major Social Theorists. LC 99-49624. (Companions to Social Theory Ser.). 700p. 1999. 99.95 (*0-631-20710-4*) Blackwell Pubs.

Ritzer, George, ed. Metatheorizing. LC 91-44206. (Key Issues in Sociological Theory Ser.: No. 6). 178p. 1992. reprint ed. pap. 55.20 (*0-608-04320-6*, 206509900012) Bks Demand.

— Metatheorizing: A Coming of Age. (Key Issues in Sociological Theory Ser.: Vol. 6). (Illus.). 200p. (C). 1992. 56.00 (*0-8039-3990-6*); pap. 26.00 (*0-8039-3991-4*) Sage.

Ritzer, George, jt. auth. see Kammeyer, Kenneth C.

Ritzer, George, jt. auth. see Vera, Hernan.

Ritzer, George, jt. ed. see Calhoun, Craig.

Ritzer, George, jt. ed. see Farganis, James.

Ritzer, George, ed. see Rogers, Mary F.

Ritzer, Mariann. An Evening on Mildred Street. 28p. 1995. pap. 6.00 (*0-9644333-0-3*) CrossplusRds.

— Once I Loved Him Madly. (Orig.). 1996. pap. 6.00 (*0-9644333-5-4*) CrossplusRds.

Ritzman, Carolyn T., jt. auth. see King, Claude V.

Ritzman, Larry P., et al, eds. Disaggregation: Problems in Manufacturing & Service Organizations. 1979. lib. bdg. 144.00 (*0-89838-003-0*) Kluwer Academic.

Ritzman, Larry P., jt. auth. see Krajewski, Lee J.

Ritzman, Marlene, jt. auth. see Moffet, Stanley N.

Ritzvi, S. N., et al. Practice in English Vol. I: The Art of Composition. 206p. 1996. pap. 35.00 (*81-209-0772-8*, Pub. by Pitambar Pub) St Mut.

— Practice in English Vol. II: The Art of Comprehension. 128p. 1996. pap. 25.00 (*81-209-0757-4*, Pub. by Pitambar Pub) St Mut.

— Practice in English Vol. III: Grammar, Usage & Vocabulary. 268p. 1996. pap. 25.00 (*81-209-0870-8*, Pub. by Pitambar Pub) St Mut.

Riu, Pere J. Electrical Bioimpedance Methods: Applications to Medicine & Biotechnology. LC 99-22308. (Annals of The New York Academy of Sciences Ser.). 1999. pap. write for info. (*1-57331-191-X*) NY Acad Sci.

Riu, Pere J., et al, eds. Electrical Bioimpedance Methods: Applications to Medicine & Biotechnology. LC 99-22308. 550p. 1999. 160.00 (*1-57331-190-1*) NY Acad Sci.

Riu, Xavier. Dionysism & Comedy. LC 99-11261. 304p. 1999. 63.00 (*0-8476-9441-0*); pap. 23.95 (*0-8476-9442-9*) Rowman.

Riu y Riu, M. Manual de Historia de Espana Vol. 2: Edad Media (711-1500) 644p. 1989. 125.00 (*84-239-5092-1*) Elliots Bks.

Rius. Cuba for Beginners. (Documentary Comic Bks.). (Illus.). 1981. 6.95 (*0-906495-29-6*) Writers & Readers.

— Devilishness. (Diabluras: Un Libro de Todos Los Diablos Ser.). 70p. 1987. pap. 9.00 (*0-910309-50-7*, 5438) Am Atheist.

Rius. Hitler Para Masoquistas. 1997. pap. text 8.98 (*968-419-358-0*) Grijalbo Edit.

— Interminable Conquista de Mexico. 1997. pap. text 10.98 (*968-419-391-2*) Grijalbo Edit.

Rius. Manual del Perfecto Ateo. 1997. pap. text 12.98 (*968-419-161-8*) Grijalbo Edit.

— Mao for Beginners. 176p. 1993. pap. 9.95 (*0-906386-07-1*) Writers & Readers.

— The Myth of the Virgin of Guadalupe. Orig. Title: El Mito Guadalupano. 69p. 1988. pap. 9.00 (*0-910309-52-3*, 5439) Am Atheist.

Rius, jt. auth. see Vendrell.

Rius de Riepen. Calor y Movimiento. (Ciencia Para Todos Ser.). (SPA.). pap. 6.99 (*968-16-4814-5*, Pub. by Fondo) Continental Bk.

Rius, Jorge. The Communist Manifesto in Cartoon Form. 3rd ed. Edelson, Morris, tr. from SPA. (Illus.). reprint ed. pap. 1.50 (*0-9600306-1-1*) Quixote.

Rius, Maria. A Child's Introduction to the Four Seasons: Spring, Summer, Fall, Winter, 4 vols. (Four Seasons Ser.). (Illus.). (J). 1998. pap. 23.95 (*0-7641-7167-4*) Barron.

— Las Cuatro Estaciones (The Four Seasons) El Invierno (Winter) (SPA., Illus.). 32p. (J). (ps-k). 1999. pap. 5.95 (*0-7641-0894-8*) Barron.

— Las Cuatro Estaciones (The Four Seasons) El Otono (Autumn) (SPA., Illus.). 32p. (J). (ps-k). 1999. pap. 5.95 (*0-7641-0892-1*) Barron.

— Las Cuatro Estaciones (The Four Seasons) El Verano (Summer) (SPA., Illus.). 32p. (J). (ps-k). 1999. pap. 5.95 (*0-7641-0891-3*) Barron.

— Las Cuatro Estaciones (The Four Seasons) La Primavera (Spring) (SPA., Illus.). 32p. (J). (ps-k). 1999. pap. 5.95 (*0-7641-0895-6*) Barron.

— Fall. LC 97-78311. (Four Seasons Ser.). (Illus.). 32p. (J). 1998. pap. 5.95 (*0-7641-0552-3*) Barron.

Rius, Maria. Grandparents. (Family Ser.). 1987. 12.15 (*0-606-08940-3*, Pub. by Turtleback) Demco.

Rius, Maria. Hearing. (Five Senses Ser.). 1985. 12.15 (*0-606-01072-6*, Pub. by Turtleback) Demco.

— El Oido. 2nd ed. (Cinco Sentidos Ser.). (SPA.). (J). 1986. 12.15 (*0-606-01519-1*, Pub. by Turtleback) Demco.

— Sight. (Five Senses Ser.). (J). 1985. 12.15 (*0-606-01122-6*, Pub. by Turtleback) Demco.

— Smell. (J). 1985. 12.15 (*0-606-01120-X*, Pub. by Turtleback) Demco.

— Spring. LC 97-78310. (Four Seasons Ser.). (Illus.). 32p. (J). 1998. pap. 5.95 (*0-7641-0555-8*) Barron.

— Summer. LC 97-78312. (Four Seasons Ser.). (Illus.). 32p. (J). 1998. pap. 5.95 (*0-7641-0556-6*) Barron.

— El Tacto. 2nd ed. (Cinco Sentidos Ser.). (SPA.). (J). 1986. 12.15 (*0-606-01528-0*, Pub. by Turtleback) Demco.

— Touch. (Five Senses Ser.). (J). 1985. 12.15 (*0-606-01129-3*, Pub. by Turtleback) Demco.

Rius, Maria. La Vista. 2nd ed. (SPA.). 1986. 12.15 (*0-606-02307-0*, Pub. by Turtleback) Demco.

Rius, Maria. Winter. (Four Seasons Ser.). (Illus.). 32p. (J). 1998. pap. 5.95 (*0-7641-0553-1*) Barron.

Rius, Maria & Parramon, J. M. Air. (Four Elements Ser.). (J). 1985. 6.95 (*0-8120-5741-4*) Barron.

— Fire. (Four Elements Ser.). (J). 1986. 6.95 (*0-8120-5743-0*) Barron.

Rius, Maria & Parramon, Josep M. El Campo (Countryside) (Let's Discover Ser.). (SPA., Illus.). 32p. (J). (ps-1). 1986. pap. 6.95 (*0-8120-3750-2*) Barron.

— La Ciudad (City) (Let's Discover Ser.). (SPA., Illus.). 32p. (J). (ps-1). 1986. pap. 7.95 (*0-8120-3753-7*) Barron.

— El Mar (Seaside) (Let's Discover Ser.). (SPA., Illus.). 32p. (J). (ps). 1986. pap. 7.95 (*0-8120-3751-0*) Barron.

— La Montana (Mountains) (Let's Discover Ser.). (SPA., Illus.). 32p. (J). (ps-1). 1986. pap. 6.95 (*0-8120-3752-9*) Barron.

Rius, Maria, et al. Fire. LC 85-6106. (Four Elements Ser.). (Illus.). 32p. (J). 1985. pap. 6.95 (*0-8120-3598-4*) Barron.

— Hearing. (Five Senses Ser.). (Illus.). 32p. (J). 1985. 6.95 (*0-8120-5736-8*) Barron.

— Sight. (Five Senses Ser.). (Illus.). 32p. (J). 1985. 6.95 (*0-8120-5737-6*) Barron.

— Smell. (Five Senses Ser.). (Illus.). 32p. (J). 1985. 6.95 (*0-8120-5738-4*) Barron.

— Taste. (Five Senses Ser.). (Illus.). 32p. (J). 1985. 6.95 (*0-8120-5739-2*) Barron.

— Touch. (Five Senses Ser.). (Illus.). 32p. (J). 1985. 6.95 (*0-8120-5740-6*) Barron.

Rius, Maria, jt. auth. see Parramon, J. M.

Rius, Maria A. El Gusto. (Cinco Sentidos Ser.). (SPA.). (J). 1983. 12.15 (*0-606-01513-2*, Pub. by Turtleback) Demco.

Rius, R. Hansel & Gretel. (Fairy Tale Theater Ser.). 32p. (J). (gr. k-3). 1998. pap. 8.95 (*0-7641-5113-4*) Barron.

— Hansel & Gretel. (Fairy Tale Theater Ser.). (SPA., Illus.). 32p. (J). (ps-3). 1998. pap. 8.95 (*0-7641-5145-2*) Barron.

— The Three Little Pigs. (Fairy Tale Theater Ser.). (Illus.). 32p. (J). (gr. k-3). 1998. pap. 8.95 (*0-7641-5115-0*); pap. 8.95 (*0-7641-5147-9*) Barron.

Rius, Roser. Peter Pan. (SPA.). 32p. (J). (ps-3). 1999. 8.95 (*0-7641-5154-1*) Barron.

— Peter Pan: Peter Pan. 32p. (J). (ps-3). 1999. 8.95 (*0-7641-5153-3*) Barron.

RIUS Staff & Del Rio, Eduardo. Cuba for Beginners. LC 70-108717. 153p. 1971. reprint ed. pap. 12.95 (*0-87348-128-3*); reprint ed. lib. bdg. 40.00 (*0-87348-193-3*) Pathfinder NY.

Riutort, Ana. Historia Breve del Arte Puertorriqueno. (SPA., Illus.). 264p. (C). 1994. pap. text 14.95 (*1-56328-059-0*) Edit Plaza Mayor.

Riva, Alessandro, et al, eds. Ultrastructure of Male Urogenital Glands: Prostrate, Semial Vesicles, Urethral, & Bulbourethral Glands. LC 94-11636. (Electron Microscopy in Biology & Medicine Ser.: EMBM 11). 224p. (C). 1994. text 247.00 (*0-7923-2800-0*) Kluwer Academic.

Riva, Alessandro & Motta, Pietro M., eds. Ultrastructure of the Extraparietal Glands of the Digestive Tract. (Electron Microscopy in Biology & Medicine Ser.). (C). 1989. text 246.50 (*0-7923-0303-2*) Kluwer Academic.

Riva, Anna. Art of Domination. 32p. (Orig.). 1995. pap. text 4.95 (*0-943832-23-3*) Intl Imports.

— Black & White Magic. 64p. (Orig.). 1994. pap. 4.95 (*0-943832-22-5*) Intl Imports.

— Candle Burning Magic. 96p. 1980. pap. 4.95 (*0-943832-06-3*) Intl Imports.

— The Colonial Laws of Massachusetts, 2 bks., Set. 1995. lib. bdg. 137.50 (*0-614-03187-7*) W S Hein.

— Devotions to the Saints. 112p. 1982. pap. 4.95 (*0-943832-08-X*) Intl Imports.

— Golden Secrets of Mystic Oils Revised. 178p. (Orig.). 1990. pap. 5.95 (*0-943832-16-0*) Intl Imports.

— How to Conduct a Seance. rev. ed. 24p. 1994. pap. 2.95 (*0-943832-20-9*) Intl Imports.

— Magic with Incense & Powders. 128p. (Orig.). 1985. pap. 4.95 (*0-943832-11-X*) Intl Imports.

— Modern Herbal Spellbook. (Illus.). 64p. 1974. pap. 4.95 (*0-943832-03-9*) Intl Imports.

— Modern Witchcraft Spellbook. (Illus.). 64p. (Orig.). 1973. pap. 4.95 (*0-943832-02-0*) Intl Imports.

— Powers of the Psalms. 128p. (Orig.). 1982. pap. 4.95 (*0-943832-07-1*) Intl Imports.

— Secrets of Magical Seals. (Illus.). 64p. 1975. pap. 4.95 (*0-943832-04-7*) Intl Imports.

— Six Lessons in Crystal Gazing. 32p. (Orig.). 1993. pap. text 2.95 (*0-943832-18-7*) Intl Imports.

— Spellcraft, Hexcraft & Witchcraft. (Illus.). 64p. 1977. pap. 4.95 (*0-943832-00-4*) Intl Imports.

— Voodoo Handbook of Cult Secrets. (Illus.). 48p. 1974. pap. 4.95 (*0-943832-01-2*) Intl Imports.

— Your Lucky Number Forever. 144p. (Orig.). 1993. pap. text 4.95 (*0-943832-17-9*) Intl Imports.

Riva, Anna, et al, eds. Prayer Book. 128p. (Orig.). 1984. pap. 4.95 (*0-943832-09-8*) Intl Imports.

Riva, Daria & Benton, Arthur. Localization of Brain Lesions & Developmental Functions. 168p. 68.00 (*0-86196-599-X*, Pub. by John Libby) Buttrwrth-Heinemann.

Riva, Douglas. 20 Minute Intermediate Piano Workout. 248p. (YA). pap. 19.95 (*0-943748-44-5*, PF0691) Ekay Music.

— The 20 Minute Piano Workout. 1990. pap. 15.95 (*0-943748-30-5*) Ekay Music.

Riva, G., ed. Virtual Reality in Neuro-Psycho-Physiology: Cognitive, Climical & Methodological Issues in Assessment & Treatment. LC 97-76731. (Studies in Health Technology & Informatics: Vol. 44). 209p. 1997. 78.00 (*90-5199-364-1*, 364-1) IOS Press.

Riva, Jim. The Champion of Reason. LC 99-218282. 368p. 1998. pap. 16.50 (*1-891262-00-9*) Soaring Sparrow.

— The Geographer. 168p. 1998. pap. 12.50 (*1-891262-01-7*) Soaring Sparrow.

***Riva, John.** Deathtone. Zagury, Carolyn, ed. LC 98-61855. 368p. 1999. pap. 18.95 (*1-880254-58-1*) Vista.

Riva, Joseph P., Jr. Exploration Opportunities in Latin America. 288p. 1992. 25.00 (*0-87814-371-8*) PennWell Bks.

Riva, Joseph P. Petroleum Exploration Opportunities in the Former Soviet Union. LC 94-201. 316p. 1994. 25.00 (*0-87814-414-5*, P4524) PennWell Bks.

***Riva, Pietro, ed.** Cancer Radioimmunotherapy: Present & Future. 530p. 1998. text 190.00 (*90-5702-309-1*, Harwood Acad Pubs) Gordon & Breach.

***Rivademar, Daniel.** Patagonia: The Last Wilderness. (Illus.). 160p. 1999. 39.95 (*1-894020-65-0*, Pub. by Warwick Publ) Firefly Bks Ltd.

Rivadeneyra, Antonio D. Solis Y, see Solis Y Rivadeneyra, Antonio D.

Rivadue, Barry. Alice Faye: A Bio-Bibliography, 10. LC 89-25631. (Bibliographies & Indexes in the Performing Arts Ser.: No. 10). 239p. 1990. lib. bdg. 49.95 (*0-313-26525-9*, RVA/, Greenwood Pr) Greenwood.

— Lee Remick: A Bio-Bibliography, 64. LC 95-12421. (Bio-Biographies in the Performing Arts Ser.: Vol. 64). 248p. 1995. lib. bdg. 55.00 (*0-313-28447-4*, Greenwood Pr) Greenwood.

— Mary Martin: A Bio-Bibliography, 18. LC 91-16233. (Bio-Bibliographies in the Performing Arts Ser.: No. 18). 272p. 1991. lib. bdg. 49.95 (*0-313-27345-6*, RMF, Greenwood Pr) Greenwood.

Rivage-Seul, D. Michael & Rivage-Seul, Marguerite K. Imagining a New Earth Order: Changing Paradigms. LC 95-3341. 176p. 1995. 55.00 (*0-275-95201-0*, Praeger Pubs) Greenwood.

Rivage-Seul, Marguerite K., jt. auth. see Rivage-Seul, D. Michael.

Rivail, Hippolytel., see Kardec, Allan, pseud.

Rivail, Hippolytel., tr. see Kardec, Allan, pseud.

Rivail, Jean-Louis, jt. ed. see Bernardi, Francesco.

Rival, Andre. Self Images: 100 Women. (Illus.). 152p. 1995. 49.95 (*3-905514-45-1*, Pub. by Edit Stemmle) Dist Art Pubs.

Rival, Ivan. Algorithms & Order. (C). 1988. text 251.00 (*0-7923-0007-6*) Kluwer Academic.

— Combinatorics & Ordered Sets. LC 86-8006. (Contemporary Mathematics Ser.: Vol. 57). 285p. 1986. pap. 38.00 (*0-8218-5051-2*, CONM/57) Am Math.

Rival, Ivan, ed. Combinatorics & Ordered Sets: Proceedings of the AMS - IMS - SIAM Joint Summer Research Conference, Held August 11-17, 1985, with Support from the National Science Foundation. LC 86-8006. (Contemporary Mathematics Ser.: No. 57). (Illus.). 205p. reprint ed. pap. 63.60 (*0-608-05983-8*, 205264900008) Bks Demand.

— Graphs & Order: The Role of Graphs in the Theory of Ordered Sets & Its Applications. 1985. text 329.00 (*90-277-1943-8*) Kluwer Academic.

— Ordered Sets. 1982. text 346.50 (*90-277-1396-0*) Kluwer Academic.

Rival, Laura, ed. The Social Life of Trees: Anthropological Perspectives on Tree Symbolism. LC 98-219504. (Materializing Culture Ser.). 256p. 1998. 55.00 (*1-85973-923-7*, Pub. by Berg Pubs); pap. 19.50 (*1-85973-928-8*, Pub. by Berg Pubs) NYU Pr.

Rival, Pierre, jt. auth. see Baudot, Francois.

***Rivara, Frederick P., et al, eds.** Injury Control: Research & Program Evaluation. (Illus.). 300p. (C). 2000. text Price not set. (*0-521-66152-8*) Cambridge U Pr.

Rivara, J. H. Da Cunha, see Da Cunha Rivara, J. H.

Rivard, Catherine W., jt. ed. see Diedrich, Marjorie H.

***Rivard, David.** Bewitched Playground. 72p. 2000. pap. 12.95 (*1-55597-302-7*, Pub. by Graywolf) SPD-Small Pr Dist.

Rivard, David. Wise Poison. LC 96-75791. 72p. 1996. pap. 12.95 (*1-55597-247-0*) Graywolf.

Rivard, Denis, ed. Ozone Layer Dictionary. (FRE.). 493p. (Orig.). 1993. pap. 36.95 (*0-660-58897-8*, Pub. by Canadian Govt Pub) Accents Pubns.

Rivard, Ken. Frankie's Desires. 88p. 1987. pap. 12.95 (*0-919627-54-4*, Pub. by Quarry Pr) LPC InBook.

— Maman, l'Ecole a Ete Inondee! (Mom, the School Flooded) (FRE., Illus.). 32p. (J). (ps-2). 1996. pap. 4.95 (*1-55037-478-8*, Pub. by Annick); lib. bdg. 15.95 (*1-55037-479-6*, Pub. by Annick) Firefly Bks Ltd.

— Mom, the School Flooded. (Illus.). 32p. (J). (ps-2). 1996. pap. 4.95 (*1-55037-474-5*, Pub. by Annick); lib. bdg. 15.95 (*1-55037-475-3*, Pub. by Annick) Firefly Bks Ltd.

Rivard, Paul E. Lion: The History of an 1846 Locomotive Engine in Maine. (Business & Technology Ser.). (Illus.). 64p. 1987. pap. text 6.50 (*0-913764-19-1*) Maine St Mus.

Rivas, Anabella, tr. see Stott, John.

Rivas De Jara, Orquidea, ed. & tr. see Aleshire, Daniel O.

Rivas, Duque de. Don Alvaro O la Fuerza del Sino. Ruiz Silva, Carlos, ed. (Nueva Austral Ser.: Vol. 162). (SPA.). 1991. pap. text 17.95 (*84-239-1962-5*) Elliots Bks.

— Don Alvaro o la Fuerza del Sino. (SPA.). pap. 12.95 (*84-376-0057-X*, Pub. by Ediciones Catedra) Continental Bk.

***Rivas, Duque de.** Don Alvaro O la Fuerza del 517. (SPA.). 1999. 13.00 (*84-481-0955-4*, McGrw-H College) McGrw-H Hghr Educ.

Rivas, Duque De, see De Rivas, Duque.

Rivas, Edelberto T., jt. ed. see Flora, Jan L.

Rivas, Garcia. 150 Biografias de Mexicanos Ilustres. (SPA.). 1997. pap. text 16.98 (*968-13-2562-1*) Edit Diana.

***Rivas, Hull.** Case Studies in Generalist Practice. 2nd ed. LC 99-46271. 1999. pap. text 50.95 (*0-534-36219-2*) Brooks-Cole.

Rivas, J. & Lopez-Quintela, M. A., eds. Noncrystalline & Nanoscale Materials: Proceedings of the 5th International Workshop on Noncrystalline Solids Santiago de Compostela, Spain 2-5 July, 1997. 600p. 1998. 128.00 (*981-02-3282-9*) World Scientific Pub.

Rivas, Jose L., tr. see Bosco, Henri.

***Rivas, Maite Suarez.** Latino Read-Aloud Stories. LC 00-20007. Vol. 7. (Illus.). 384p. (J). (gr. 4-7). 1999. 12.98 (*1-57912-091-1*) Blck Dog & Leventhal.

Rivas, Paul & Tremblay, E. A. If You're Fat It's Not Your Fault. 200p. Date not set. 19.95 (*0-9647675-0-3*) David-Paul.

Rivas, Robert F. & Hull, Grafton H. Case Studies in Generalist Practice. LC 95-23807. (Social Work Ser.). 450p. 1995. pap. 31.25 (*0-534-20232-2*) Brooks-Cole.

Rivas, Robert F., jt. auth. see Toseland, Ronald W.

Rivas Rodriguez, Manuel. La Solucion a la Productividad en Oficinas. (SPA.). 242p. 1993. pap. 23.50 (*84-7978-093-2*, Pub. by Ediciones Diaz) IBD Ltd.

***Rivas, Victoria.** Doing Laundry. 48p. 1999. pap. 5.00 (*1-889289-44-2*) Ye Olde Font Shoppe.

Rivas, Yolanda, tr. see Rogovin, Janice.

Rivasseau, Vincent. From Perturbative to Constructive Renormalization. Anderson, Philip W. et al, eds. (Physics Ser.). (Illus.). 337p. 1991. text 79.50 (*0-691-08530-7*, Pub. by Princeton U Pr) Cal Prin Full Svc.

Rivasseau, Vincent, et al, eds. Constructive Physics: Results in Field Theory, Statistical Mechanics & Condensed Matter Physics: Proceedings of the Conference Held at Palaiseau, France 25-27 July 1994. LC 95-12155. (Lecture Notes in Physics Ser.: Vol. 446). x, 337p. 1995. 85.95 (*3-540-59190-7*) Spr-Verlag.

Rivaz, R. C. Tail Gunner. large type ed. 1998. 24.95 (*0-7531-5047-6*) T T Beeler.

— Tail Gunner: Squadron Leader. LC 97-156864. (Illus.). 257p. 1996. 26.95 (*0-7509-1327-4*, Pub. by Sutton Pub Ltd) Intl Pubs Mktg.

***Rive Box, Bob De La, ed.** Encyclopedia of Classic Cars: Sports Cars, 1945-1995. 300p. 1999. pap. text 35.00 (*1-57958-118-8*) Fitzroy Dearborn.

Rive, Richard. Emergency Continued. 176p. 1991. 18.95 (*0-930523-87-3*); pap. 10.95 (*0-930523-88-1*) Readers Intl.

Rive, Richard & Couzens, Tim. Seme: The Founder of the ANC. LC 91-78313. 100p. 1992. 29.95 (*0-86543-312-7*); pap. 9.95 (*0-86543-313-5*) Africa World.

Rive-Rivera, David. Recursos Extraordinarios. 2nd rev. ed. (SPA.). 460p. 1997. pap. text 50.00 (*1-881711-03-X*) Univ Interamrcna.

Riveill, Michel. Object-Based Distributed Programming: ECOOP '93 Workshop, Kaiserslautern, Germany, July 1993, Proceedings. Guerraoui, Rachid et al, eds. LC 94-10103. (Lecture Notes in Computer Science Ser.: Vol. 791). 1994. 44.95 (*0-387-57932-X*) Spr-Verlag.

Rivele, Richard J. & Freeman, Kerry A., photos by. Chilton's GM Sub-Compacts, 1971-1980: Repair & Tune-Up Guide. LC 79-8303. (New Automotive Ser.). (Illus.). 280p. (C). 1980. pap. 17.95 (*0-8019-6935-2*) Thomson Learn.

— Chilton's Guide to Engine Rebuilding & Repair. LC 85-47925. (Illus.). 240p. (C). 1985. pap. 19.95 (*0-8019-7643-X*) Thomson Learn.

Rivele, Stephen, jt. auth. see Ramsey, Edwin P.

Rivele, Stephen J. A Booke of Days: A Journal of the Crusades. LC 96-36795. 448p. 1997. 24.00 (*0-7867-0348-2*) Carroll & Graf.

— A Booke of Days: A Novel of the Crusades. LC 97-27600. 448p. 1998. pap. 13.95 (*0-7867-0462-4*) Carroll & Graf.

Rivelles, V. O., jt. auth. see Peboli, O. J.

Rivelli, Pauline & Levin, Robert, eds. Giants of Rock Music. LC 81-9685. (Quality Paperbacks Ser.). (Illus.). 125p. 1981. reprint ed. pap. 7.95 (*0-306-80148-5*) Da Capo.

River Boat Books Staff, tr. see Gallimard.

River, Lindsay & Gillespie, Sally. The Knot of Time: Astrology & Female Experience. 320p. 1997. pap. 15.95 (*0-7043-3912-9*, Pub. by Womens Press) Trafalgar.

River, Liris-Garigliano, et al. Underwater Investigations at Roman Minturnae, Pt. 1. (Studies in Mediterranean Archaeology & Literature: No. 119). (Illus.). 260p. (Orig.). 1995. pap. 87.75 (*91-7081-058-3*, Pub. by P Astroms) Coronet Bks.

River Oaks Garden Club Staff, ed. Garden Book for Houston & the Gulf Coast. 4th ed. 396p. 1989. 27.50 (*0-88415-350-9*, 5350) Gulf Pub.

River, Sol. River: Plays. (Oberon Bks.). 56p. 1997. pap. 12.95 (*1-870259-82-3*) Theatre Comm.

River Watch Staff. Testing the Waters: Chemical & Physical Vital Signs of a River. 240p. 1997. per. 24.95 (0-7872-3492-3, 41349201) Kendall-Hunt.

Rivera, A. Ramon & Gruenbaum, Thelma. To Music & Children with Love! Reflections for Parents & Teachers. 133p. (C). 1979. pap. 6.95 (0-936190-03-5) ExPressAll.

Rivera, Alejandro Tapia y, see Tapia y Rivera, Alejandro.

Rivera, Alicia, et al. El Amor Nuestro de Cada Dia. (Marriage & Marriage Preparation Ser.). (Illus.). 154p. 1995. 4.75 (0-940679-05-1) CCOC.

Rivera, Alvarado. 2000 Pensamientos de Grandes Filosofos. (SPA.). 1997. pap. 20.98 (968-13-1862-5) Edit Diana.

Rivera, Andres. La Revolucion Es un Sueno Eterno. 192p. 1995. pap. 12.50 (0-679-76335-X) Vin Bks.

Rivera, Angel Quintero, see Quintero Rivera, Angel.

Rivera-Batiz, Francisco L. Political Economy. pap. 0.00 (0-691-00385-8) Princeton U Pr.

Rivera-Batiz, Francisco L. Reinventing Urban Education: Multiculturalism & the Social Context of Schooling. 300p. (C). 1994. pap. write for info. (0-9638459-0-X) IUME Pr.

Rivera-Batiz, Francisco L., et al, eds. U. S. Immigration Policy Reform in the 1980s: A Preliminary Assessment. LC 90-7377. 160p. 1991. 47.95 (0-275-93620-1, C3620, Praeger Pubs) Greenwood.

Rivera-Batiz, Francisco L. & Rivera-Batiz, Luis. International Finance & Open Economy Macroeconomics. 2nd ed. (Illus.). 704p. (C). 1993. 72.80 (0-02-400581-9, Macmillan Coll) P-H.

Rivera-Batiz, Francisco L. & Santiago, Carlos E. Island Paradox: Puerto Rico in the 1990s. (1990 Census Research Ser.: Vol. IV). 256p. 1998. pap. 16.95 (0-87154-751-1) Russell Sage.

— Island Paradox: Puerto Rico in the 1990s. LC 96-21094. (1990 Census Research Ser.: Vol. 4). (Illus.). 256p. (C). 1998. reprint ed. pap. 16.95 (0-87154-721-X) Russell Sage.

Rivera-Batiz, Luis, jt. auth. see Rivera-Batiz, Francisco L.

Rivera, Beatriz. Midnight Sandwiches at the Mariposa Express. LC 97-22187. 118p. 1997. pap. 11.95 (1-55885-216-6) Arte Publico.

***Rivera, Beatriz.** Playing with Light. 240p. 2000. pap. 12.95 (1-55885-310-3) Arte Publico.

Rivera, Benito V., jt. ed. see Mathiesen, Thomas J.

Rivera, Benito V., tr. & intro. see Burmeister, Joachim.

Rivera, Carlos & Eastman, P. D., trs. Are You My Mother? (Spanish Beginner Bks.: No. 4).Tr. of Eres Tu Mi Mama?. (ENG & SPA.). (J). (gr. 2-4). 1967. 9.95 (0-394-81596-3, Pub. by Random Bks Yng Read) Random.

Rivera, Carlos, tr. see Eastman, P. D.

Rivera, Carlos, tr. see Seuss, Dr., pseud.

Rivera, Charlene, ed. Communicative Competence Approaches to Language Proficiency Assessment: Research & Application. 150p. 1984. 74.00 (0-905028-22-8, Pub. by Multilingual Matters); pap. 25.00 (0-905028-21-X, Pub. by Multilingual Matters) Taylor & Francis.

— An Ethnographic-Sociolinguistic Approach to Language Assessment. 140p. 1983. 69.00 (0-905028-20-1, Pub. by Multilingual Matters); pap. 24.00 (0-905028-19-8, Pub. by Multilingual Matters) Taylor & Francis.

Rivera De Figueroa, Carmen A. Architecture for the Tropics: A Bibliographical Synthesis (from the Beginnings to 1972) LC 77-26261. (Illus.). 203p. 1980. pap. 12.00 (0-8477-2107-8) U of PR Pr.

Rivera de Hernandez, Hilda. Biologia Moderna: Serie de Modulos Para Laboratorio Primer Semestre. 2nd rev. ed. 265p. (C). 1991. text 24.95 (1-881375-07-2) Libreria Univ.

— Biologia Moderna: Serie de Modulos Para Laboratorio Segundo Semestre. 291p. (C). 1991. text 24.95 (1-881375-08-0) Libreria Univ.

Rivera De Otero, Consuelo. Mass Communication Services: An Analysis (Puerto Rican Government: Radio, Television, & Community Education) LC 76-2025. 153p. (Orig.). 1976. pap. 5.00 (0-8477-2731-9) U of PR Pr.

Rivera De Rosales, Jacinto. Sueno y Realidad: La Ontologia Poetica de Calderon de la Barca. Ecole, Jean & Theis, Robert, eds. (Studien und Texte zur Geschichte der Europaischen Ideen: Reihe I, Bd. 7). (GER.). ix, 332p. 1998. write for info. (3-487-10702-3) G Olms Pubs.

Rivera, Diana. Bird Language. LC 93-30723. 114p. 1994. 11.00 (0-927534-41-X) Biling Rev-Pr.

Rivera, Diane M., jt. auth. see Smith, Deborah D.

Rivera, Diane P. Mathematics Education for Students with Learning Disabilities: Theory to Practice. LC 97-38019. 318p. 1998. write for info. (0-89079-710-2) PRO-ED.

Rivera, Diane P. & Smith, Deborah D. Teaching Students with Learning & Behavior Problems. 3rd ed. LC 96-26089. 480p. 1996. pap. text 70.00 (0-205-16448-X) Allyn.

— Teaching Students with Learning & Behavior Problems. 3rd ed. (C). 1996. pap., teacher ed. write for info. (0-205-26314-3, T6314-3) Allyn.

Rivera, Diego. My Art, My Life: An Autobiography (with Gladys March) (Illus.). 224p. 1992. reprint ed. pap. 7.95 (0-486-26938-8) Dover.

Rivera, Diego, jt. auth. see Berliner, Isaac.

Rivera, Donald S. Hear-Say: Kid's Guide to Learning English. 32p. (J). 12.95 incl. audio (1-56015-679-1) Penton Overseas.

— Hear-Say: Kid's Guide to Learning French. (J). 1999. 12.95 incl. audio (1-56015-675-9) Penton Overseas.

— Hear-Say: Kid's Guide to Learning German. (J). (ps-3). 1999. 12.95 incl. audio (1-56015-676-7) Penton Overseas.

— Hear-Say: Kid's Guide to Learning Italian. (J). 12.95 incl. audio (1-56015-677-5) Penton Overseas.

— Hear-Say: Kid's Guide to Learning Spanish. (J). (ps-3). 1999. 12.95 incl. audio (1-56015-678-3) Penton Overseas.

— LinguaFun! Language Learning Card Games: French. (Travel Ser.). (ENG & FRE.). (J). 1996. pap. 12.95 incl. audio (1-56015-603-1) Penton Overseas.

— LinguaFun! Language Learning Card Games: French. unabridged ed. (Family Ser.). (FRE & ENG.). (J). (gr. 4 up). 1996. pap. 12.95 incl. audio (1-56015-591-4) Penton Overseas.

— LinguaFun! Language Learning Card Games: German. (Family Ser.). (ENG & GER.). (J). (gr. 4 up). 1996. pap. 12.95 incl. audio (1-56015-600-7) Penton Overseas.

— LinguaFun! Language Learning Card Games: German. (Travel Ser.). (ENG & GER.). (J). 1998. pap. 12.95 incl. audio (1-56015-605-8) Penton Overseas.

— LinguaFun! Language Learning Card Games: Ingles (English for Spanish-speakers) unabridged ed. (Family Ser.). (SPA & ENG.). (J). 1996. pap. 12.95 incl. audio (1-56015-592-2) Penton Overseas.

— LinguaFun! Language Learning Card Games: Italian. (Family Ser.). (ENG, ITA & SPA.). (J). (gr. 4 up). 1996. pap. 12.95 incl. audio (1-56015-601-5) Penton Overseas.

— LinguaFun! Language Learning Card Games: Italian. (Travel Ser.). (ENG & ITA.). 1998. pap. 12.95 incl. audio (1-56015-606-6) Penton Overseas.

— LinguaFun! Language Learning Card Games: Spanish. (Travel Ser.). (ENG & SPA.). (J). 1996. pap. 12.95 incl. audio (1-56015-602-3) Penton Overseas.

— LinguaFun! Language Learning Card Games: Spanish. unabridged ed. (Family Ser.). (SPA & ENG.). (J). 1996. pap. 12.95 incl. audio (1-56015-590-6) Penton Overseas.

Rivera, Edward. Family Installments: Memories of Growing up Hispanic. 304p. 1983. pap. 12.95 (0-14-006726-4, Penguin Bks) Viking Penguin.

***Rivera, Elena.** Unknowne Land. Dienstfiey, Patricia, ed. LC 00-27384. 55p. 2000. 10.00 (0-932716-53-9) Kelsey St Pr.

Rivera, Elizabeth. The Power of the Word: The Story of Dorcas Camacho Byrd. LC 98-176609. (Illus.). 118p. (YA). (gr. 7-12). 1998. pap. text 7.95 (1-56309-235-2, W986104) Womans Mission Union.

***Rivera, Elizabeth, contrib. by.** Evangelism Through Ministry.Tr. of En Bussqueda de Paz. (Illus.). 90p. 1999. pap. 12.99 (1-56309-301-4) Womans Mission Union.

Rivera, Elizabeth, ed. see Trevino, Margarita.

Rivera, Esteban R. & De Leon, Juana P., eds. Dream with No Name: Contemporary Fiction from Cuba. 304p. 1999. 30.00 (1-888363-72-X, Pub. by Seven Stories); pap. 16.95 (1-888363-73-8, Pub. by Seven Stories) Publishers Group.

***Rivera, Etnairis.** El Viaje de los Besos. LC 99-53527. (Colecibon Sinsonte). 2000. write for info. (0-8477-0088-7) U of PR Pr.

Rivera, Feliciano, jt. ed. see Meier, Matt S.

Rivera, Felix G. Suiseki: The Japanese Art of Miniature Landscape Stones. LC 96-38067. (Illus.). 192p. (Orig.). 1997. pap. 29.95 (1-880656-27-2) Stone Bridge Pr.

Rivera, Felix G. & Erlich, John. Community Organizing in a Diverse Society. 3rd ed. LC 97-18437. 288p. 1998. pap. text 42.00 (0-205-26834-X) Allyn.

Rivera, Felix J. La Muneca de Chocolate. (SPA., Illus.). 192p. 1995. pap. 8.95 (1-56328-106-6) Edit Plaza Mayor.

Rivera, Fernando L. Personalidades del Calvario.Tr. of Personalities at Calvary. (SPA.). 144p. (Orig.). 1996. pap. 11.99 (0-8272-2949-6) Chalice Pr.

— Personalidades del Pesebre. (SPA., Illus.). (Orig.). 1992. pap. 9.99 (0-8272-2943-7) Chalice Pr.

Rivera, Francisco P. & Hurtado, Mario. Introduccion a la Literatura Espanola. (YA). (gr. 11-12). 1976. pap. text 9.95 (0-88345-437-8) Prentice ESL.

Rivera, Francisco P., et al. Introductionn a la Literatura Espanola. (C). 1987. pap. text 29.00 (0-13-477225-3) Prentice ESL.

Rivera, Frank. Cuentos Cubanos. LC 92-73682. (Coleccion Caniqui). (SPA., Illus.). 75p. (Orig.). 1992. pap. 9.95 (0-89729-653-2) Ediciones.

***Rivera, Frank.** Inside TrueSpace 4. LC 98-89436. (Illus.). 674p. 1999. pap. 44.99 incl. cd-rom (1-56205-957-2) New Riders Pub.

Rivera, Frank. Varadero y Otros Cuentos Cubanos. LC 98-87605. (Coleccion Caniqui). (SPA., Illus.). 128p. (Orig.). 1998. pap. 13.00 (0-89729-883-7) Ediciones.

Rivera, Garcia I. Dictionary of Legal Terms. (ENG & SPA.). 704p. 1985. 75.00 (0-8288-7956-7, F36820) Fr & Eur.

Rivera, Gladys, ed. see De Mena, Juan.

Rivera Gonzalez, Melitina. Mi Diccionario: Primera Coleccion de Palabras-Educacion Primaria, Primer Ciclo. (SPA., Illus.). 223p. 1992. pap. 49.50 (84-207-4697-5) Elliots Bks.

— Mi Diccionario No. 2: Educacion Primaria, 8-12 Anos. (SPA., Illus.). 479p. 1993. pap. 69.50 (84-207-5003-4) Elliots Bks.

Rivera, Guadalupe & Colle, Marie-Pierre. Frida's Fiestas: Recipes & Recollections of Life with Frida Kahlo. Krabbenhoft, Kenneth & Rigsby, Olga, trs. LC 93-19284. (Illus.). 224p. 1994. 35.00 (0-517-59235-5) C Potter.

Rivera, Guadalupe, jt. auth. see Colle, M. P.

Rivera, Guadalupe, jt. auth. see Miller, Carol.

Rivera, Guillermo, tr. see Cano, Fray A.

Rivera, Guillermo, tr. see De Avendano y Loyola, Fray A.

Rivera, Hector J. Introduccion a la Moneda y la Banca. LC 76-967. 292p. 1975. pap. 5.00 (0-8477-2625-8) U of PR Pr.

Rivera, Illeana, jt. auth. see Colon, Doris E.

Rivera, Isidro J., jt. auth. see Nance, Kimberly A.

Rivera, Jaime Monge, see Monge Rivera, Jaime.

Rivera, John & Walker, Carol A. Wake up America - Regain Your American Heritage: Become Financially Fit Through Debt Elimination. Pluth, Tamara, ed. (Illus.). 250p. 1997. 19.95 (0-9657857-0-X) Financial Frdm Ent.

Rivera, Jose. Maricela de la Luz Lights the World. 52p. (J). (gr. 1 up). 1998. pap. 5.50 (0-87129-894-5, MB3) Dramatic Pub.

— Marisol & Other Plays. LC 97-5736. 240p. (Orig.). 1997. pap. 14.95 (1-55936-136-0) Theatre Comm.

Rivera, Jose A. Acequia Culture: Water, Land & Community in the Southwest. LC 98-23877. (Illus.). 243p. 1998. 50.00 (0-8263-1858-4); pap. 19.95 (0-8263-1859-2) U of NM Pr.

Rivera, Jose Eustasio. Promised Land/Tierra De Promisio'n: Hispanic Literature, No.45. Cobb, Carl W., tr. from SPA. LC 98-31827. 128p. 1999. 59.95 (0-7734-8277-6) E Mellen.

— La Voragine. (SPA.). pap. 13.95 (84-206-1838-1, Pub. by Alianza Editorial) Continental Bk.

— La Voragine. (SPA.). pap. 8.95 (968-432-131-7, Pub. by Porrua) Continental Bk.

Rivera, Juan, jt. auth. see Razin, Ehud.

Rivera, Juan M. Poemas de la Nieve Negra. LC 84-62597. (Serie de Poesia Guampara: No. 3). (SPA.). 96p. (Orig.). 1985. pap. text 5.95 (0-910235-09-0) Prisma Bks.

Rivera, Louis R. Who Pays the Cost? (Illus.). 40p. (Orig.). 1977. pap. 2.00 (0-917886-03-8) Shamal Bks.

Rivera, Louis R., et al. Poets in Motion. (Illus.). (Orig.). 1976. pap. text 3.00 (0-917886-00-3) Shamal Bks.

Rivera, Louis R., ed. see Ismaili, Rashidah, et al.

Rivera, Louis R., ed. see Killens, John O.

Rivera Lugo, Carlos, jt. auth. see Garcia Passalacqua, Juan.

Rivera Lugo, Carlos, jt. auth. see Garcia Passalacqua, Juan M.

Rivera, Margo. More Alike Than Different: Treating Severely Dissociative Trauma Survivors. 304p. 1996. text 50.00 (0-8020-0450-4); pap. text 24.95 (0-8020-7238-0) U of Toronto Pr.

***Rivera, Mario.** Enfrente Sus Conflictos. 1998. pap. text 8.99 (0-88113-501-1) Caribe Betania.

Rivera, Mario. Facing Unresolved Conflicts. LC 92-64448. 224p. (Orig.). 1992. pap. 9.95 (0-89221-230-6) New Leaf.

Rivera, Mario A. Decision & Structure: U. S. Refugee Policy & the Mariel Crisis. 278p. (C). 1991. lib. bdg. 48.00 (0-8191-8389-X) U Pr of Amer.

***Rivera, Mario A. & Woller, Gary M., eds.** Public Administration in a New Era: Postmodern & Critical Perspectives. LC 99-50927. (Illus.). xii, 210p. (C). 2000. pap. 24.95 (1-57420-071-2, JF1351.P8) Chatelaine.

Rivera, Mario E. Emotional Freedom. LC 92-81732. 128p. (Orig.). 1992. pap. 6.95 (0-89221-225-X) New Leaf.

— Por Favor, Ayudame a Cambiar. (Serie Guia de Bolsillo - Pocket Guides Ser.).Tr. of Free to Be Me. (SPA.). 1989. pap. 2.79 (0-945792-23-9, 498046) Editorial Unilit.

Rivera, Mark A. & Jacquart, Joanne. Touched by the Father's Hand. 138p. (Orig.). 1991. pap. 9.95 (0-9625097-2-8) Stonecrest FL.

Rivera, Mary, tr. see Maguire, Daniel C. & Maguire, Marjorie R.

Rivera-Medina, Eduardo & Ramirez, Rafael L. Del Canaveral a la Fabrica: Cambio Social en Puerto Rico. LC 85-80187. (Huracan Academia Ser.). (SPA.). 152p. 1985. pap. 8.25 (0-940238-78-0) Ediciones Huracan.

Rivera-Milan, Frank F., et al, eds. Management & Monitoring of Resident & Migratory Birds & Their Habitats in Latin America & the Caribbean: An Interamerican Perspective. (ENG & SPA.). 48p. (C). 1997. reprint ed. pap. text 30.00 (0-7881-4288-7) DIANE Pub.

***Rivera-Mills, Susana Victoria.** New Perspectives on Current Sociolinguistic Knowledge with Regard to Language Use, Proficiency & Attitudes among Hispanics in the U. S. The Case of a Rural Northern California Community. LC 99-46936. (Studies in Linguistics & Semiotics: Vol. 4). 196p. 1999. text 79.95 (0-7734-7906-6) E Mellen.

Rivera, Monte, jt. ed. see Jennings, James.

Rivera, Nelson. Visual Artists & the Puerto Rican Performing Arts, 1950-1990: The Works of Jack & Irene Delano, Antonio Martorell, Jaime Suarez, & Oscar Mestey-Villamil. LC 94-26758. (Wor(l)ds of Change: No. 9). (Illus.). XVII, 232p. (C). 1997. text 47.95 (0-8204-2620-2) P Lang Pubng.

Rivera, Nilda R. Programacion Estructurada, 4 Vol. Set, Vol. 1. (SPA., Illus.). 133p. (C). 1994. pap. text. write for info. (1-879185-02-4) CompuConsultants.

— Programacion Estructurada y Cobol, 4 vol. set. rev. ed. (Programacion Estructurada Ser.). (SPA., Illus.). 133p. 1994. pap. text 19.95 (1-879185-01-6) CompuConsultants.

Rivera, Nilda R. & Betancourt, Luiz. Disenos de Bordados: Para Bebe's. rev. ed. (SPA., Illus.). 60p. 1995. pap. text. write for info. (1-879185-04-0) Lubnir.

Rivera, Nilda R. & Betancourt, Luz. Disenos de Letras. rev. ed. (SPA., Illus.). 60p. 1995. pap. text. write for info. (1-879185-03-2) Lubnir.

Rivera, Norberto, tr. see Kuhn, Walter N., Jr.

Rivera Nunez, Diego, jt. auth. see Obon de Castro, Concepcion.

Rivera, Oswald. Fire & Rain: A Novel of Vietnam. LC 90-34078. 186p. 1990. 17.95 (0-941423-41-7) FWEW.

— Puerto Rican Cuisine in America: Nuyorican & Bodega Recipes. LC 92-41478. (Illus.). 294p. (Orig.). 1993. pap. 16.95 (0-941423-84-0) FWEW.

Rivera-Pagan, Luis N. Entre el Oro y la Fe. (SPA.). 128p. 1995. pap. 11.95 (0-8477-0241-3) U of PR Pr.

Rivera Pagan, Luis N. Mito, Exilio y Demonios. (SPA.). 138p. 1997. pap. write for info. (0-929441-99-0) Pubns Puertorriquenas.

Rivera, Paul C. Hydrodynamics, Sediment Transport & Light Extinction off Cape Bolinao, Philippines. (IHE Thesis Ser.: No. 11). (Illus.). 264p. (C). 1997. text 52.00 (90-5410-408-2, Pub. by A A Balkema) Ashgate Pub Co.

Rivera, Pedro A. Manos a la Obra: The Story Behind Operation Bootstrap. 25p. 1986. pap. 7.00 (1-878483-18-8) Hunter Coll CEP.

Rivera Perez, Efrain. Puerto Rico Tres Caminos Hacia un Futuro. (SPA.). 170p. 1991. pap. write for info. (0-929441-18-4) Pubns Puertorriquenas.

Rivera Porto, Eduardo. Computadoras en la Educacion. (SPA.). 310p. 1993. pap. write for info. (0-929441-47-8) Pubns Puertorriquenas.

Rivera, Rafael Valle, see Valle Rivera, Rafael.

Rivera, Ralph & Nieto, Sonia, eds. The Education of Latino Students in Massachusetts: Issues, Research, & Policy Implications. LC 93-32148. 280p. (Orig.). 1994. pap. 17.95 (0-87023-895-7) U of Mass Pr.

Rivera Ramos, Efren. Pequeno Canto a los Mios (Poemario) LC 87-25562. 72p. 1987. pap. 5.00 (0-8477-3236-3) U of PR Pr.

Rivera, Rhonda, jt. auth. see Whaley, Douglas J.

Rivera, Rhonda R. Sexual Orientation Law. 1996. text 70.00 (0-8133-8546-6) Westview.

Rivera, Rhonda R., et al. AIDS Law & Policy. 2nd ed. LC 94-72965. 562p. 1995. pap. 59.00 (0-916081-35-4) J Marshall Pub Co.

Rivera, Richard J. & Scherer, Andrew, contrib. by. Basic Landlord/tenant Law, 1998. LC 99-159981. (Real Estate Law & Practice, Course Handbook Ser. 1983-1984). 336 p. 1998. 129.00 (0-87224-540-3) PLI.

Rivera-Rodas, Oscar. El Metateatro y la Dramatica de Vargas Llosa: Hacia una Poetica del Espectador. LC 92-33765. (Purdue University Monographs in Romance Languages: Vol. 41). viii, 213p. 1992. 65.00 (1-55619-310-6); pap. 27.95 (1-55619-311-4) J Benjamins Pubng Co.

Rivera-Rodriguez, Juan C. Laws of Puerto Rico, 1994: 1998 Edition, 3 vols. 1222p. 1998. pap. write for info. (0-327-06209-6, 47579-15) LEXIS Pub.

Rivera-Rodriguez, Juan C., ed. Leyes de Puerto Rico, 1997, Vol. 1.Tr. of Laws of Puerto Rico, 1997. (SPA.). 990p. 1998. write for info. (0-327-05795-5, 8460314) LEXIS Pub.

— Leyes de Puerto Rico, 1997, Vol. 2.Tr. of Laws of Puerto Rico, 1997. (SPA.). 1082p. 1998. write for info. (0-327-05796-3, 8460414) LEXIS Pub.

— Leyes de Puerto Rico, 1997, Vol. 3.Tr. of Laws of Puerto Rico, 1997. (SPA.). 600p. 1998. write for info. (0-327-05797-1, 8460514) LEXIS Pub.

Rivera, Rudy, jt. auth. see Deutsch, Roger D.

Rivera, Scott. French in a Box, Set. (FRE & ENG.). 1998. boxed set 44.95 incl. audio (1-56015-667-8) Penton Overseas.

— Spanish in a Box, Set. unabridged ed. (SPA & ENG.). 1997. boxed set 44.95 incl. audio (1-56015-665-1) Penton Overseas.

— TravelTalk: Spanish (European) (ENG & SPA.). 1998. pap. 15.95 incl. audio (1-56015-637-6) Penton Overseas.

Rivera, Sergio. Neusa: 9,000 Anos de Presencia Humana en el Paramo. (SPA., Illus.). 144p. 1992. pap. 8.50 (1-877812-28-5, BR026) UPLAAP.

Rivera, Tomas. The Searchers: Collected Poetry. Olivares, Julian, ed. 112p. 1990. pap. 7.00 (1-55885-018-X) Arte Publico.

— Y No Se lo Trago la Tierra. rev. ed. (SPA.). 115p. (YA). (gr. 6-12). 1996. pap. 7.95 (1-55885-151-8, Pinata Bks) Arte Publico.

— Y No Se lo Trago la Tierra. 3rd ed. Vigil, Evangelina, tr. LC 87-70275. (SPA.). 208p. 1995. pap. 11.95 (1-55885-083-X) Arte Publico.

— Y No Se Lo Trago la Tierra (And the Earth Did Not Devour Him) 3rd ed. (SPA.). (J). 1995. 16.05 (0-606-04429-9, Pub. by Turtleback) Demco.

Rivera, Tulio D. Hechos y Legitimidades Cubanas: Un Planteamento. LC 86-82313. (Coleccion Cuba y sus Jueces). (SPA.). 96p. (Orig.). 1987. pap. 6.00 (0-89729-418-1) Ediciones.

***Rivera-Valdes, Sonia.** The Forbidden Stories of Marta Veneranda. 160p. 2000. 21.95 (1-58322-047-X) Seven Stories.

— Las Historias Prohibidas de Marta Veneranda. (SPA.). 160p. 2000. 21.95 (1-58322-053-4) Seven Stories.

Rivera-Valdes, Sonia, jt. auth. see Cocco-Defilippis, Daisy.

Rivera, Vestena R., jt. auth. see Kutash, Krista.

Rivera, W. M. Planning Adult Learning: Issues, Practices & Directions. 180p. (C). 1986. 33.00 (0-7099-4224-9, Pub. by C Helm) Routldge.

Rivera, W. M., ed. Agricultural Extension Worldwide: Factors for Success. (International Perspectives on Adult & Continuing Education Ser.). 272p. 1986. 35.00 (0-7099-4238-9, Pub. by C Helm) Routldge.

Rivera, W. M. & Gustafson, D. J. Agricultural Extension: Worldwide Institutional Evolution & Forces for Change. 312p. 1991. 195.25 (0-444-89239-7) Elsevier.

Rivera, William L. The Unmaking of the President, 1996. 238p. mass mkt. 5.95 (1-896329-69-1) Picasso Publ.

Rivera, William M., jt. ed. see Charters, Alexander N.

Rivera, Zwinda L., jt. auth. see Aponte, Maria A.

Rivere, E. W., jt. ed. see Irish, J. A.

Rivere, Richard, ed. Loyalty & Security in a Democratic State. LC 75-54570. (Great Contemporary Issues Ser.). 1977. lib. bdg. 27.95 (0-405-09864-2) Ayer.

Rivero, Albert J. Critical Essays on Henry Fielding. LC 97-34644. 1998. 49.00 (0-7838-0059-2) Mac Lib Ref.

— The Plays of Henry Fielding: A Critical Study of His Dramatic Career. LC 88-35304. 170p. 1989. text 30.00 (0-8139-1228-8) U Pr of Va.

Rivero, Albert J., ed. Augustan Subjects: Essays in Honor of Martin C. Battestin. LC 96-30529. 312p. 1997. 45.00 (0-87413-616-4) U Delaware Pr.

An Asterisk (*) at the beginning of an entry indicates that the title is appearing for the first time.

Rivero-De-La-Calle, Manuel, jt. auth. see Dacal-Moure, Ramon.

Rivero, Eliana S., jt. ed. see Rebolledo, Tey D.

***Rivero, Maria-Luisa & Ralli, Angela, eds.** Comparative Syntax of the Balkan Languages. LC 99-27575. (Oxford Studies in Comparative Syntax). 240p. 2000. text 55.00 (0-19-512951-2); pap. text 35.00 (0-19-512952-0) OUP.

Rivero, Piedad P. Sacerdotes y Comerciantes. (SPA.). pap. 12.99 (968-16-3299-0, Pub. by Fondo) Continental Bk.

Rivero-Potter, Alicia. Autor-Lector: Huidobro, Borges, Fuentes y Sarduy. LC 90-37640. (Latin American Literature & Culture Ser.). (SPA.). 184p. (C). 1990. text 32.95 (0-8143-2226-3) Wayne St U Pr.

— Autor-Lector: Huidobro, Borges, Fuentes y Sarduy. LC 90-37640. (Latin American Literature & Culture Ser.). 184p. reprint ed. pap. 57.10 (0-608-10537-6, 2071157) Bks Demand.

Rivero-Potter, Alicia, ed. Between the Self & the Void: Essays in Honor of Severo Sarduy. LC 97-62159. (Illus.). 136p. 1998. pap. 36.00 (0-89295-089-7) Society Sp & Sp-Am.

Rivero, Samuel. New Essays on Richardson. LC 96-28366. 229p. 1996. text 45.00 (0-312-12508-9) St Martin.

Rivero, Sonia. Patron de Asentamiento Rural en la Region de San Gregorio, Chiapas, para el Clasico Tardio. 380p. 1990. pap. 15.00 (968-6068-48-1, IN031) UPLAAP.

Riverol, A. R. Live from Atlantic City: The History of the Miss America Pageant Before, After & in Spite of Television. LC 92-81612. (Illus.). (C). 1992. 24.95 (0-87972-557-5); pap. 12.95 (0-87972-558-3) Bowling Green Univ Popular Press.

Riveron, Jose Luis, tr. see Young, Ed.

Riveros, F., jt. auth. see Skerman, P. J.

Riveros, Luis A., jt. ed. see Paredes, Ricardo.

Rivers, jt. auth. see Silverthistle.

Rivers, B. J., et al. The Bottles of Old Sacramento No. 20, Pt. I: A Study of Nineteenth-Century Glass & Ceramic Retail Containers. (Publications of the Department of Parks & Recreation: No. 20). (Illus.). 202p. (C). 1980. reprint ed. pap. text 21.88 (1-55567-469-0) Coyote Press.

***Rivers, Bo.** Rancho Snake-O. LC 98-38. 269p. 1999. pap. 15.95 (1-55212-219-0, Pub. by Tra3fford) Trafford Pub.

Rivers, Caryl. Camelot. LC 98-20796. 352p. 1998. 24.00 (0-944072-96-8) Zoland Bks.

— Slick Spins & Fractured Facts: How Cultural Myths Distort the News. LC 95-42313. 288p. 1996. 16.50 (0-231-10152-X) Col U Pr.

Rivers, Caryl, jt. auth. see Barnett, Rosalind.

Rivers, Caryl, jt. auth. see Barnett, Rosalind C.

***Rivers, Charles.** How to Become Your Spouse's Best Friend. LC 99-91407. 144p. 2000. pap. write for info. (1-56167-563-6, Five Star Spec Ed) Am Literary Pr.

Rivers, Chris H. & Wiles, Patricia L. Jonathon: How His Dying Brought Two Women Together. LC 95-41268. (Illus.). 212p. (Orig.). 1995. pap. 20.00 (0-86663-215-8) Ide Hse.

Rivers, Christopher. Face Value: Physiognomical Thought & the Legible Body in Marivaux, Lavatar, Balzac, Gautier & Zola. LC 94-14586. (Illus.). 288p. 1994. 55.00 (0-299-14390-2); pap. 24.95 (0-299-14394-5) U of Wis Pr.

Rivers, Clayton P. Alcohol & Human Behavior: Theory, Research & Practice. LC 93-33821. 324p. (C). 1993. pap. text 34.00 (0-13-019878-1) P-H.

Rivers, D. Wayne & Campbell, Thomas H. You Don't Have to Die to Win: Success & Succession for Family Businesses. 1996. pap. 21.95 (0-9653193-1-8) Fmly Busn.

Rivers, Dan. Addiction & Sigmund Freud: Freud's Psychology Applied to Addiction. LC 94-79564. 350p. (Orig.). 1995. pap. 29.95 (0-9644355-2-7) Mercie Pub.

Rivers, David A., ed. see Bingelis, Tony.

Rivers, Dennis. Communicating More Cooperatively: The Seven Challenges Workbook. 80p. 1999. pap. 12.00 (0-9669908-0-3) D Rivers Pub.

Rivers, Earl, jt. tr. see Wydeville, A.

Rivers, Elias L. Muses & Masks: Some Classical Genres of Spanish Poetry. (U. California, Irvine, Hispanic Studies: No. 1). 120p. 1992. 15.50 (0-936388-53-6) Juan de la Cuesta.

— Quixotic Scriptures: Essays on the Textuality of Hispanic Literature. LC 82-49300. 164p. 1983. pap. 50.90 (0-608-05040-7, 205970100004) Bks Demand.

Rivers, Elias L., ed. Renaissance & Baroque Poetry of Spain. 351p. (C). 1988. reprint ed. pap. text 15.95 (0-88133-363-8) Waveland Pr.

Rivers, Elias L., ed. & tr. see Alonso, Damaso.

Rivers, F. Un Eco en las Tinieblas, Vol. 2.Tr. of Echo in the Darkness. (SPA.). pap. 14.99 (0-7899-0088-2, 497469) Editorial Unilit.

Rivers, F. Tan Cierto Como el Amanecer.Tr. of As Sure as the Dawn. (SPA.). 14.99 (0-7899-0308-3, 497470) Editorial Unilit.

Rivers, F. Una Voz en el Viento.Tr. of Voice in the Wind. (SPA.). 526p. 14.99 (0-7899-0087-4, 497468) Editorial Unilit.

Rivers, Francine. As Sure As the Dawn. LC 95-1034. (Mark of the Lion Ser.: Vol. 3). 448p. 1995. pap. 11.99 (0-8423-3976-0) Tyndale Hse.

Rivers, Francine. The Atonement Child. LC 96-40212. 375p. 1997. pap. 12.99 (0-8423-0052-X) Tyndale Hse.

Rivers, Francine. An Echo in the Darkness. LC 94-5909. (Mark of the Lion Ser.: Vol. 2). 464p. 1994. pap. 12.99 (0-8423-1307-9) Tyndale Hse.

***Rivers, Francine.** A Just Cause. 2000. 12.99 (0-8423-1947-6) Tyndale Hse.

Rivers, Francine. The Last Sin Eater. 380p. 1999. pap. 12.99 (0-8423-3571-4) Tyndale Hse.

— The Last Sin Eater: A Novel. LC 98-19967. 324p. 1998. 16.97 (0-8423-3570-6) Tyndale Hse.

***Rivers, Francine.** Leota's Garden. LC 99-25963. 425p. 1999. 17.97 (0-8423-3572-2); audio 15.99 (0-8423-5211-2) Tyndale Hse.

Rivers, Francine. Leota's Garden LC 99-25963. 1999. pap. 12.99 (0-8423-3498-X) Tyndale Hse.

— Mark of the Lion Trilogy. 1998. pap. text 29.99 (0-8423-3952-3) Tyndale Hse.

— Redeeming Love. LC 97-14694. 464p. 1997. pap. text 13.99 (1-57673-186-3, Multnomah Bks) Multnomah Pubs.

— Redeeming Love. large type ed. LC 93-13563. 670p. 1993. lib. bdg. 23.95 (0-8161-5823-1, G K Hall Lrg Type) Mac Lib Ref.

— The Scarlet Thread. LC 96-3721. (Illus.). 462p. 1996. pap. 12.99 (0-8423-3568-4) Tyndale Hse.

***Rivers, Francine.** The Shoe Box. LC 99-34161. 1999. 12.99 (0-8423-1901-8) Tyndale Hse.

— Unashamed No. 2: A Lineage of Grace. 2000. 12.99 (0-8423-3596-X) Tyndale Hse.

Rivers, Francine. A Voice in the Wind. LC 93-16608. (Mark of the Lion Ser.: Vol. 1). 514p. 1993. pap. 12.99 (0-8423-7750-6) Tyndale Hse.

Rivers, Frank. The Way of the Owl: Succeeding with Integrity in a Conflicted World. LC 95-20645. 176p. 1997. pap. 12.00 (0-06-251397-4, Pub. by Harper SF) HarpC.

Rivers, Glenn & Brooks, Bruce. Those Who Love the Game: Glenn "Doc" Rivers on Life in NBA & Elsewhere. (Illus.). 89p. (YA). (gr. 6 up). 1995. 15.95 (0-8050-2822-6, Bks Young Read) H Holt & Co.

Rivers, Gloria R. Eight Keys to Cosmic Consciousness. White, Richard et al, eds. (Illus.). 32p. (Orig.). 1984. pap. 6.00 (0-918341-00-0) Temple Pubns.

Rivers, Ira La, see La Rivers, Ira.

Rivers, Isabel. Classical & Christian Ideas in English Renaissance Poetry. 1979. pap. text 15.95 (0-04-807003-3) Routledge.

— Classical & Christian Ideas in English Renaissance Poetry: A Student's Guide. 2nd ed. LC 94-12710. 240p. (C). 1994. pap. 22.99 (0-415-10647-8, B7073) Routledge.

— Reason, Grace & Sentiment Vol. 1: A Study of the Language of Religion & Ethics in England, 1660-1780: Whichcote to Wesley. (Studies in Eighteenth-Century English Literature & Thought: No. 8). 291p. (C). 1991. text 64.95 (0-521-38340-4) Cambridge U Pr.

***Rivers, Isabel.** Reason, Grace & Sentiment - A Study of the Language of Religion & Ethics in England, 1660-1780 Vol. 2: Shaftesbury to Hume. (Cambridge Studies in Eighteenth-Century English Literature & Thought: No. 37). 403p. 2000. text 69.95 (0-521-38341-2) Cambridge U Pr.

Rivers, J. W. The Place of Understanding: A Poem. 72p. (Orig.). 1994. pap. 14.95 (0-936044-06-3) Pikestaff Pr.

— When the Owl Cries, Indians Die. LC 85-47624. 112p. 1986. 14.95 (0-8453-4509-5) VA Ctr Creative Arts.

Rivers, Jerry. Dearly Beloved. LC 98-93562. xi, 211p. 1998. pap. 9.95 (0-9667556-1-8) Isador Pubg.

Rivers, Jerry, jt. auth. see Moore, Terry.

Rivers, Joan. Bouncing Back: I've Survived Everything--& I Mean Everything--& You Can Too! large type ed. LC 97-5829. (Americana Series). 305p. 1997. 26.95 (0-7862-0932-1) Thorndike Pr.

Rivers, Joan. Bouncing Back: I've Survived Everything...& I Mean Everything...& You Can Too! abr. ed. 1997. audio 18.00 (0-694-51719-4, CPN 2592) HarperAudio.

Rivers, Joan. Don't Count the Candles. 240p. 2000. mass mkt. 6.99 (0-06-109797-7, Torch) HarpC.

— Don't Count the Candles: Just Keep the Fire Lit. LC 99-11405. 208p. 1999. 25.00 (0-06-018383-7) HarpC.

— Don't Count the Candles: Just Keep the Fire Lit. LC 99-25616. 1999. 27.95 (0-7862-1993-9) Thorndike Pr.

***Rivers, Joan.** Don't Count the Candles: Just Keep the Fire Lit, Set. abr. ed. 1999. audio 18.00 (0-694-52081-0) HarperAudio.

Rivers, Joan. From Mother to Daughter. LC 98-42610. (Illus.). 96p. 1998. 12.95 (1-55972-493-5, Birch Ln Pr) Carol Pub Group.

— Having a Baby Can Be a Scream. 192p. 1978. pap. 3.50 (0-380-00292-2, Avon Bks) Morrow Avon.

— Still Talking. 328p. 1992. mass mkt. 5.99 (0-380-71992-4, Avon Bks) Morrow Avon.

Rivers, Johnny, jt. auth. see Chase, Leah.

Rivers, Judith. Weddings & Honeymoons in the Vineyards of Northern California. 1997. pap. 21.95 (1-890083-24-0) J R Pub.

Rivers, Judith A. Beautiful Marin to Mendocina & Coastal Weddings: Locations Guidance Professionals. 6th rev. ed. Hensley, Sandra, ed. 254p. (Orig.). 1998. pap. write for info. (1-890083-10-0) J & R Pub.

— Beautiful Napa Valley Events: Locations Guidance Management Professionals. rev. ed. Hensley, Sandra, ed. 299p. (Orig.). 1999. pap. write for info. (1-890083-08-9) J & R Pub.

— Beautiful Sonoma Wine Country Weddings: Locations Professionals Guidance, Vol. 9. 8th rev. ed. Hensley, Sandra, ed. 290p. (Orig.). 1998. pap. write for info. (1-890083-09-7) J & R Pub.

***Rivers, K. E.** Standing Rocks & Sleeping Rainbows: Mile by Mile Through Southeast Utah. (Illus.). 192p. 2000. pap. 18.95 (0-9658901-4-7) Great Vacations.

***Rivers, Karen.** Dream Water. LC 99-65170. 192p. (YA). (gr. 8-12). 2000. 14.95 (1-55143-160-2); pap. 6.95 (1-55143-162-9) Orca Bk Pubs.

Rivers, Karen. Waldorf Student Reading List. pap. 8.95 (0-9647832-0-7, 1642) Michaelmas Pr.

Rivers, Kathleen E. Idaho's Scenic Highways: A Mile-by-Mile Road Guide. LC 97-73991. (Illus.). 160p. (Orig.). 1997. pap. 25.00 (0-9658901-3-9) Great Vacations.

Rivers, Kenneth T. Transmutations: Understanding Literary & Pictorial Caricature. 330p. (Orig.). (C). 1991. pap. text 28.00 (0-8191-8329-6); lib. bdg. 49.00 (0-8191-8328-8) U Pr of Amer.

Rivers, Larry. Some American History: Slavery: The Black Man & the Man. LC 72-153088. 50p. (Orig.). (YA). 1971. pap. text 8.95 (0-939594-12-9, Menil Collection) Menil Found.

***Rivers, Larry Eugene.** Slavery in Florida: Territorial Days to Emancipation. 2000. 29.95 (0-8130-1813-7) U Press Fla.

Rivers, Laura, ed. Pigtails & Froglegs: A Family Cookbook from Neiman Marcus. (Illus.). 1993. 19.95 (0-9629473-1-8) Neiman-InCircle.

***Rivers, Lynn & McDonald, Sharon.** Pigs, Plants & Other Biological Wonders: An Investigative Approach. 2nd ed. 282p. (C). 1999. spiral bd. 32.95 (0-7872-6366-4, 41636603) Kendall-Hunt.

Rivers, Mark. Taggard Point: Shapes, Bk. 2. 208p. (Orig.). (YA). 1995. mass mkt. 3.99 (0-425-14726-6) Berkley Pub.

— Taggard Point: The Clown, Bk. 4. 176p. (Orig.). 1995. mass mkt. 3.99 (0-425-15016-X) Berkley Pub.

— Taggard Point Bk. 1: The Forever House. 176p. (Orig.). 1995. mass mkt. 3.99 (0-425-14567-0) Berkley Pub.

— Taggard Point Bk. 3: When the Dead Scream. 176p. (Orig.). (YA). 1995. mass mkt. 3.99 (0-425-14880-7) Berkley Pub.

Rivers, Michele. Time for Tea: Conversations with English Women. LC 93-42375. 1995. 22.00 (0-517-59219-3, Crown) Crown Pub Group.

***Rivers-Moore, Judith.** Beautiful Events 2000: Special Events Planning, Wedding Guidance & Management Concepts. rev. ed. Moore, Robert & Moore, Carol, eds. (Illus.). 2000. pap. text 10.95 (1-890083-15-1) J R Pub.

— Beautiful Marin-Mendocino Pacific Coast Events. 6th rev. ed. Moore, Robert & Purroy, Carol, eds. (Illus.). 2000. pap. text 10.95 (1-890083-14-3) J R Pub.

— Beautiful Napa Valley Wine Country Events. 6th rev. ed. Moore, Robert & Purroy, Carol, eds. (Illus.). 2000, pap. text 10.95 (1-890083-12-7) J R Pub.

— Beautiful Sonoma Wine Country Events 2000. 10th rev. ed. Moore, Robert & Purroy, Carol, eds. (Illus.). 2000. pap. 10.95 (1-890083-13-5) J R Pub.

Rivers, Nancy F. A New Life for Toby. LC 97-73252. 80p. (Orig.). (J). (gr. 3-4). 1997. pap. 9.95 (1-57736-052-4, Hillsboro Pr) Providence Hse.

Rivers, Nikki. Daddy's Little Matchmaker. LC 95-13710. (American Romance Ser.). 248p. 1995. per. 3.50 (0-373-16592-7, 1-16592-7) Harlequin Bks.

— For Better for Bachelor. 1999. per. 3.99 (0-373-16764-4, Harlequin) Harlequin Bks.

— Her Prince Charming. (American Romance Ser.). 1998. per. 3.99 (0-373-16723-7, 1-16723-8) Harlequin Bks.

— Romancing Annie. 1997. per. 3.75 (0-373-16664-8, 1-16664-4) Silhouette.

— Seducing Spencer. (American Romance Ser.). 1994. per. 3.50 (0-373-16550-1, 1-16550-5) Harlequin Bks.

Rivers, P. Clayton & Diensthier, Richard A., eds. Nebraska Symposium on Motivation, 1996: Alcohol & Addictive Behavior. LC 53-11655. (Nebraska Symposium on Motivation Ser.: No. 34). 346p. Date not set. text 45.00 (0-8032-3880-0); pap. text 25.00 (0-8032-8925-1) U of Nebr Pr.

Rivers, P. Clayton & Shore, Elsie R., eds. Substance Abuse on Campus: A Handbook for College & University Personnel. LC 97-18722. (Educator's Reference Collection). 296p. 1997. lib. bdg. 69.50 (0-313-29310-4, GR9310, Greenwood Pr) Greenwood.

Rivers, R. W. Speed Analysis for Traffic Accident Investigation. 2nd ed. LC 98-208762. 239p. 1997. write for info. (1-884566-25-1) Inst Police Tech.

— Technical Traffic Accident Investigators' Handbook: A Level 3 Reference, Training & Investigation Manual. 2nd ed. LC 96-47758. (Illus.). 504p. (Orig.). 1997. text 86.95 (0-398-06696-5); pap. text 66.95 (0-398-06697-3) C C Thomas.

— Traffic Accident Field Measurements & Scale Diagrams Manual. (Illus.). 154p. 1983. pap., spiral bd. 33.95 (0-398-04845-2) C C Thomas.

— Traffic Accident Investigators' & Reconstructionists' Book of Formulae & Tables. 2nd ed. LC 99-21209. (Illus.). 134p. 1999. spiral bd. 24.95 (0-398-06972-7) C C Thomas.

— Traffic Accident Investigator's Manual: A Levels 1 & 2 Reference, Training & Investigation Manual. 2nd ed. LC 94-40334. Orig. Title: On-Scene Traffic Accident Investigator's Manual. (Illus.). 238p. (C). 1995. text 62.95 (0-398-05967-5); pap. text 41.95 (0-398-05968-3) C C Thomas.

— Training & Reference Manual for Traffic Accident Investigation. 2nd rev. ed. (Illus.). 558p. (C). 1995. pap. text 45.00 (1-884566-18-9) Inst Police Tech.

Rivers, Susan. Tiny Talk: Level 1A. (Illus.). 48p. 1997. pap. text, student ed. 5.95 (0-19-435150-5) OUP.

— Tiny Talk: Level 1B. (Illus.). 48p. 1997. pap. text, student ed. 5.95 (0-19-435155-6) OUP.

— Tiny Talk: Level 2. 96p. 1998. pap. text, teacher ed. 8.95 (0-19-435280-3) OUP.

— Tiny Talk: Level 2A. (Illus.). 48p. 1997. pap. text, student ed. 5.95 (0-19-435160-2) OUP.

Rivers, Tammy W. What Goes on in This House Stays in This House: Echoes from the Children Whose "Tears Are Never Seen Whose Cries Are Never Heard" (Illus.). 189p. 1998. pap. 12.95 (1-881524-37-X) Milligan Bks.

Rivers, Theodore J. Contra Technologiam: The Crisis of Value in a Technological Age. 128p. (C). 1993. lib. bdg. 35.00 (0-8191-9090-X) U Pr of Amer.

Rivers, Theodore J., intro. Laws of the Salian & Ripuarian Franks. LC 85-48002. (Studies in the Middle Ages: No. 8). 1986. 42.50 (0-404-61438-8) AMS Pr.

Rivers, Thomas E. My Sixty Years in Recreation Working for Life Enrichment: An Autobiography: a Story of the Leisure Movement in the Twentieth Century. Douglass, Paul, ed. LC 83-61662. (Illus.). 108p. reprint ed. pap. 33.50 (0-7837-1548-X, 204183600024) Bks Demand.

Rivers, Victoria Z. The Shining Cloth: Dress & Adornment That Glitter. LC 99-70843. (Illus.). 192p. 1999. 50.00 (0-500-01951-7, Pub. by Thames Hudson) Norton.

Rivers, W. H. The Todas, 2 vols., Set. 1990. reprint ed. 78.00 (81-7033-014-9, Pub. by Rawat Pubns) S Asia.

Rivers, W. Napoleon, ed. see Dumas, Alexandre.

Rivers, Wilga M. Communicating Naturally in a Second Language: Theory & Practice in Language Teaching. LC 82-23620. (Cambridge Language Teaching Library). 256p. 1983. pap. text 20.95 (0-521-27417-6) Cambridge U Pr.

— Foreign Language Careers. LC 98-7380. (Opportunities in... Ser.). 160p. 1998. 14.95 (0-8442-6470-9, 64709); pap. 11.95 (0-8442-6471-7, 64717) NTC Contemp Pub Co.

— Opportunities in Foreign Language Careers. LC 92-15588. (Opportunities In . . . Ser.). (Illus.). 160p. pap. 12.95 (0-8442-4043-5, 297OIFL, VGM Career) NTC Contemp Pub Co.

— Opportunities in Foreign Language Careers. LC 92-15588. (Illus.). 160p. 1994. 14.95 (0-8442-4042-7, VGM Career) NTC Contemp Pub Co.

— The Psychologist & the Foreign Language Teacher. LC 64-15809. 1993. reprint ed. pap. text 4.95 (0-226-72094-2, P741) U Ch Pr.

— Teaching Foreign Language Skills. 2nd rev. ed. LC 80-24993. 576p. (C). 1981. reprint ed. pap. text 35.00 (0-226-72097-7) U Ch Pr.

— Teaching Languages in College: Curriculum & Content. 448p. 1993. pap. 31.95 (0-8442-9364-4, NTC Business Bks) NTC Contemp Pub Co.

Rivers, Wilga M., ed. L' Enseignement du Francais: (French Translation) 2nd ed. (Teaching . . . Ser.). (FRE.). 376p. (C). 1998. pap. 32.45 (0-8442-1264-4, VS1264-4) NTC Contemp Pub Co.

— Interactive Language Teaching. (Illus.). 252p. 1987. pap. text 20.95 (0-521-31108-X) Cambridge U Pr.

— Interactive Language Teaching. (Illus.). 258p. 1987. text 54.95 (0-521-32216-2) Cambridge U Pr.

Rivers, Wilga M. & Temperley, Mary S. A Practical Guide to the Teaching of English As a Second or Foreign Language. 416p. 1978. pap. text 15.95 (0-19-502210-6) OUP.

Rivers, William, et al, eds. Aspen Handbook on the Media, 1977-1979 Edition. 6.95 (0-686-25999-8) The Aspen Inst.

Rivers, William H. Kinship & Social Organization, Together with the Genealogical Method of Anthropological Enquiry. LC 68-108214. (London School of Economics. Monographs on Social Anthropology: No. 34). 124p. reprint ed. pap. 38.50 (0-608-18265-6, 203298500082) Bks Demand.

— Medicine, Magic & Religion. LC 76-44784. reprint ed. 32.50 (0-404-15967-2) AMS Pr.

— Social Organization. LC 76-44785. reprint ed. 29.50 (0-404-15968-0) AMS Pr.

Rivers, William L. The Opinionmakers. LC 83-18529. 207p. 1983. reprint ed. lib. bdg. 59.50 (0-313-24251-8, RIOP, Greenwood Pr) Greenwood.

— The Other Government: Power & the Washington Media. LC 81-40694. 210p. 1982. text 15.00 (0-87663-365-3, Pub. by Universe) St Martin.

Rivers, William L. & Atkins, Gary. Reporting with Understanding. LC 86-22808. (Illus.). 248p. 1987. reprint ed. pap. 76.90 (0-608-00061-2, 206082700006) Bks Demand.

Rivers, William L. & Harrington, Susan L. Finding Facts: Research Writing Across the Curriculum. 2nd ed. (Illus.). 256p. (C). 1987. pap. text 16.80 (0-13-316845-X) P-H.

Rivers, William L. & Rodriguez, Alison W. Journelist Guide to Grammar & Style. LC 94-27634. 352p. 1994. pap. text 37.00 (0-205-14633-3) Allyn.

Rivers, William L. & Work, Alison R. Free-Lancer & Staff Writer: Newspaper Features & Magazine Articles. 4th ed. 386p. (C). 1985. pap. write for info. (0-534-05292-4) Wadsworth Pub.

Rivers, William P., jt. auth. see Brecht, Richard D.

***Riverside, Diana.** The Erotic Way: Everything You Need, from Stories to Playthings, for an Amorous, Unforgettable Evening. LC 98-17303. (Illus.). 104p. 1999. 25.00 (0-684-84883-X) S&S Trade.

Riverside Reading Staff. OLTP Systems 1. (J). 1989. pap., teacher ed. 57.32 (0-8292-8526-1) HM.

— OLTP Systems 2, Vol. 2. (J). 1989. pap., teacher ed. 57.32 (0-8292-8527-X) HM.

— Riverside Reading Oral Language Development System: Defining Time. 1988. pap. 36.56 (0-8292-7758-7) HM.

— Riverside Reading Oral Language Development System: Story Time. 1989. pap., teacher ed. 36.56 (0-8292-8026-X) HM.

Riverso, Maurice. Italian: Language Survival Kit. (Illus.). 256p. 1998. pap. 5.95 (0-86442-456-6) Lonely Planet.

Riverson, John D., et al. Rural Roads in Sub-Saharan Africa: Lessons from World Bank Experience. (Technical Papers). (FRE.). 70p. 1992. pap. 22.00 (0-8213-2064-5, 12064) World Bank.

Riverson, L. Kwabena. Telecommunications Development: The Case of Africa. 130p. (C). 1995. lib. bdg. 38.00 (0-8191-9315-1) U Pr of Amer.

Riversong, Michael. Design Ecology. (Illus.). 94p. (Orig.). 1995. pap. 12.95 (0-945685-17-3) Borderland Sciences.

Riverstone. Thamara & Juda. (Illus.). 48p. 1997. pap. text 14.95 (0-86719-448-0) Last Gasp.

R

An Asterisk (*) at the beginning of an entry indicates that the title is appearing for the first time.

Riverview School Staff. Second Chance: A Guide to Post-Secondary Options for Young Adults with Severe Learning Disabilities. 224p. 1993. 15.95 (*0-9635773-0-1*) Riverview Sch.

***Riverwood Roundtable Writers Staff.** Once Around the Table: Recipes for the Body & Soul. 2000. 9.50 (*1-891609-06-8*) Home Brew Pr.

Rives, David. Walk Yourself Thin. rev. ed. 1998. 19.95 (*1-878143-00-X*); pap. 12.95 (*1-878143-01-8*) Moon River.

Rives, David A. Dying for a Smoke. 176p. 1991. 19.95 (*1-878143-06-9*) Moon River.

Rives, Elsie & Wahl, Dick. The Shoemakes: God's Helpers. (Meet the Missionary Ser.). 28p. (J). (gr. k-3). 1996. pap. text 5.99 (*1-56309-154-2*, W947129) Womans Mission Union.

Rives, Hallie E. Smoking Flax. LC 72-2026. (Black Heritage Library Collection). 1977. reprint ed. 26.95 (*0-8369-9057-9*) Ayer.

Rives, Hallie E. & Forbush, Gabrielle E. John Book. (Biography Index Reprint Ser.). 1977. reprint ed. 22.95 (*0-8369-8107-3*) Ayer.

Rives, J. B. Religion & Authority in Roman Carthage: From Augustus to Constantine. (Illus.). 348p. 1995. text 65.00 (*0-19-814083-5*) OUP.

Rives, James, ed. see Tacitus.

Rives, Janet M. & Yousefi, Mahmood, eds. Economic Dimensions of Gender Inequality: A Global Perspective. LC 97-5592. 256p. 1997. 59.95 (*0-275-95618-0*, Praeger Pubs) Greenwood.

Rives, Margaret R. Blue Ridge Parkway: The Story Behind the Scenery. LC 82-82578. (Illus.). 48p. (Orig.). 1982. pap. 7.95 (*0-916122-81-6*) KC Pubns.

Rives, Norfleet W., Jr. & Serow, William J. Introduction to Applied Demography: Data Sources & Estimation Techniques. (Quantitative Applications in the Social Sciences Ser.: Vol. 39). 96p. (C). 1984. pap. text 10.95 (*0-8039-2134-9*) Sage.

Rives, William C. History of the Life & Times of James Madison, 3 Vols, Set. LC 76-126253. (Select Bibliographies Reprint Ser.). 1977. reprint ed. 108.95 (*0-8369-5480-7*) Ayer.

Rivest, Ronald L. & Warmuth, Manfred K. Computational Learning Theory Proceedings of the 2nd Annual Workshop: Proceedings. 450p. (Orig.). (C). 1998. pap. text 19.95 (*1-55860-086-8*) Morgan Kaufmann.

Rivet, Mary M. Influence of the Spanish Mystics on the Works of Saint Francis De Sales. LC 79-115355. (Catholic University of America. Studies in Romance Languages & Literatures: No. 22). reprint ed. 37.50 (*0-404-50322-5*) AMS Pr.

Rivett, A. J., jt. auth. see Bittar, E. Edward.

Rivett, Bess Burrows. Looking Back. (Illus.). 96p. pap. (*0-9698752-8-2*) Sh1oreline.

Rivett, Darren, jt. auth. see Jones, Mark.

Rivett, Julie M., jt. ed. see Layman, Richard.

Rivett, Patrick. Model Building for Decision Analysis. LC 79-40739. (Illus.). 184p. reprint ed. pap. 57.10 (*0-8357-4687-9*, 205234200008) Bks Demand.

Rivett, Patrick & Ackoff, Russell L. A Manager's Guide to Operational Research. LC 63-14115. (Illus.). 117p. reprint ed. pap. 36.30 (*0-7837-6394-8*, 204610700010) Bks Demand.

Rivette, David A. Guidebook for California Seniors: Answers to Legal & Financial Problems of California Senior Citizens. 208p. (Orig.). 1989. pap. text 15.00 (*0-929913-00-0*) Darcal Pubns.

***Rivette, Kevin & Kline, David.** Rembrandts in the Attic: Unlocking the Hidden Value of Patents. LC 99-33756. 2000. 27.50 (*0-87584-899-0*) Harvard Busn.

Rivezzi, Rose & Trithart, David. Kids on the Trail! Hiking with Children in the Adirondacks. LC 97-36706. (Illus.). 192p. (Orig.). 1997. pap. 12.95 (*0-935272-91-7*) ADK Mtn Club.

Rivier. Principles of Practice of Plant Hormone Analysis, 2 vols. 1987. 210.00 (*0-12-198374-9*) Acad Pr.

Rivier, I. K. The Predatory Cladocera (Onychopoda: Podonidae, Polyphemidae, Cercopagidae) & Leptodorida of the World) Onychopoda: Podonidae, Polyphemidae, Ceropagidae & Leptodorida of the World. (Guides to the Identification of the Microinvertebrates of the Continental Waters of the World Ser.: Vol. 13). (Illus.). 214p. 1998. pap. 70.00 (*90-73348-85-4*, Pub. by Backhuys Pubs) Balogh.

Rivier, Jean E. & Marshall, Garland R., eds. Peptides - Chemistry, Structure & Biology: Proceedings of the 11th American Peptide Symposium, July 9-14, 1989, La Jolla, California, U. S. A. 1168p. (C). 1990. text 475.00 (*90-72199-06-5*, Pub. by Escom Sci Pubs) Kluwer Academic.

Rivier, Jean E., jt. ed. see Smith, John A.

Rivier, Laurent & Crozier, Alan, eds. Principles & Practice of Plant Hormone Analysis, Vol. 1. (Biological Techniques Ser.). 1987. text 104.00 (*0-12-198375-7*) Acad Pr.

— Principles & Practice of Plant Hormone Analysis, Vol. 2. (Biological Techniques Ser.). 1987. text 104.00 (*0-12-198376-5*) Acad Pr.

Rivier, N., jt. auth. see Sadoc, J. F.

Riviera Publications Staff. Children's Directory. Nelson, Elizabeth, ed. 1989. 4.95 (*0-317-93658-1*) Riviera Pubns.

— Orange County Children's Directory. Nelson, Elizabeth A., ed. 110p. 1990. pap. 4.95 (*1-877609-01-3*) Riviera Pubns.

— San Diego Children's Directory. Nelson, Elizabeth A., ed. 96p. 1990. pap. text 3.95 (*1-877609-03-X*) Riviera Pubns.

Riviere. Up & Down. 96p. 19.95 (*1-893263-01-0*) Ipso Facto.

Riviere & Myhra, eds. Handbook of Surface & Interface Analysis: Methods of Problem Solving. LC 97-46944. (Illus.). 1000p. 1998. text 225.00 (*0-8247-0080-5*) Dekker.

Riviere, ed. see Gilbert.

Riviere, Bill. The Open Canoe. (Illus.). 288p. 1985. pap. 12.95 (*0-316-74768-8*) Little.

Riviere, Diana, tr. see Jung, C. G., et al.

Riviere, Emmanuel, jt. ed. see Clarke, Velta J.

Riviere, Francois. In the Footsteps of Agatha Christie. (Illus.). 160p. 1997. 29.95 (*1-57076-069-1*) Trafalgar.

Riviere, Holliston L. Lab Manual of Normal Oral Histology. (Illus.). 34.00 (*0-86715-386-5*) Quint Pub Co.

Riviere, J. C. Surface Analytical Techniques. (Monographs on the Physics & Chemistry of Materials). (Illus.). 720p. 1990. 185.00 (*0-19-851370-4*) OUP.

Riviere, J. Edmond, et al, eds. Handbook of Comparative Pharmacokinetics & Tissue Residues of Veterinary Antimicrobial Drugs. 544p. 1991. boxed set 419.95 (*0-8493-3211-7*) CRC Pr.

Riviere, Jacques, jt. auth. see Proust, Marcel.

***Riviere, Jean-Louis.** Ecological Risk Evaluation of Polluted Sites. (Illus.). 236p. (C). 2000. text 58.50 (*90-5410-796-0*, Pub. by A A Balkema) Ashgate Pub Co.

— Ecological Risk Evaluation of Polluted Soils. 235p. 2000. 65.00 (*1-57808-124-6*) Science Pubs.

Riviere, Jean R. El Arte de la China. (Summa Artis Ser.: Vol. 20). 600p. 1989. 295.00 (*84-239-5220-7*) Elliots Bks.

— El Arte de la India. (Summa Artis Ser.: Vol. 19). 600p. 1989. 295.00 (*84-239-5219-3*) Elliots Bks.

Riviere, Jim. Comparative Pharmacokinetics: Principles, Techniques & Applications. LC 98-31926. (Illus.). 338p. 1999. text 94.95 (*0-8138-2931-3*) Iowa St U Pr.

Riviere, Jim E. Why Our Food Is Safer Through Science: Fallacies of the "Chemical Threat" LC 96-70835. 192p. (Orig.). 1997. pap. 12.95 (*1-884570-62-3*) Research Triangle.

Riviere, Jim Edmond. Handbook Comparative Pharmacokinetics & Residues: Pesticides & Environmental Contaminants - Animals. 592p. 1995. boxed set 224.95 (*0-8493-3213-3*) CRC Pr.

Riviere, Joan, jt. ed. see Klein, Melanie.

Riviere, Joan, tr. see Freud, Sigmund.

***Riviere, Marc Serge, ed.** The Governor's Noble Guest: Hyacinthe de Bougainville's Account of Port Jackson, 1825. (Illus.). 250p. 2000. 49.95 (*0-522-84852-4*, Pub. by Melbourne Univ Pr) Paul & Co Pubs.

Riviere, Nancy & Farley, Patricia, eds. Artists & Writers Market List, 1991: Greeting Card Creative Network's Artists & Writers' Market List. 50p. 1991. pap. 25.00 (*0-938369-12-1*) Greeting Card Assn.

Riviere, Nancy, jt. ed. see Albertson, Mila.

Riviere, Peter. Absent-Minded Imperialism: Britain & the Expansion of Empire in Nineteenth-Century Brazil. 224p. 1995. text 65.00 (*1-85043-913-3*) St Martin.

— Christopher Columbus. LC 99-207030. 1999. pap. text 9.95 (*0-7509-1876-4*) A Sutton.

Riviere, Sylvie, jt. auth. see Galat, Andrezj.

Riviere, T., jt. auth. see Pacard, Frank.

Riviere, Tristan, jt. auth. see Pacard, Frank.

Riviere, W. Echoes of War. mass mkt. 13.95 (*0-340-69607-9*, Pub. by Hodder & Stought Ltd) Trafalgar.

Riviere, William. Borneo Fire. 292p. 1996. mass mkt. 10.95 (*0-340-61853-1*, Pub. by Hodder & Stought Ltd) Trafalgar.

— Eros & Psyche. 246p. 1995. pap. 10.95 (*0-340-60967-2*, Pub. by Hodder & Stought Ltd) Trafalgar.

Riviere, Yves. Pierre Courtin. L'Oeuvre Grave, 1944-1972. 240p. 1973. 50.00 (*0-915346-18-4*) A Wofsy Fine Arts.

— Soulages: Etchings & Lithographs, 1952-1973. (FRE.). 146p. 1974. 175.00 (*1-55660-152-2*) A Wofsy Fine Arts.

Rivieres, Jim Des, see Kiczales, Gregor & Des Rivieres, Jim.

Rivierre. Dictionnaire Paici-Francais, Suivi d'un Lexique Francais-Paici. (FRE.). 372p. 1984. 39.95 (*0-8288-1628-X*, F37540) Fr & Eur.

Rivin, Eugene I. Stiffness & Damping in Mechanical Design LC 99-14998. (Illus.). 528p. 1999. text 195.00 (*0-8247-1722-8*) Dekker.

Rivington, Charles A. Samuel Pepys & the London Booksellers. 1999. pap. 23.00 (*1-85072-113-0*, Pub. by W Sessions) St Mut.

— Tyrant. 1999. pap. 48.00 (*1-85072-039-8*, Pub. by W Sessions) St Mut.

Rivington, H. Gibson. Law of Property in Land. 2nd ed. xxiv, 547p. 1999. reprint ed. 172.00 (*1-56169-519-X*) Gaunt.

Rivinus, Edward F., jt. auth. see Youssef, E. M.

Rivinus, Timothy M., intro. Alcoholism Chemical Dependency & the College Student. LC 88-9443. (Journal of College Student Psychotherapy: Vol. 2, Nos. 3-4). (Illus.). 257p. (Orig.). 1988. text 49.95 (*0-86656-734-8*) Haworth Pr.

— Alcoholism Chemical Dependency & the College Student. LC 88-9443. (Journal of College Student Psychotherapy: Vol. 2, Nos. 3-4). (Illus.). 257p. (Orig.). 1995. pap. text 14.95 (*0-86656-812-3*) Haworth Pr.

***Rivise, Charles W. & Caesar, A. D.** Interference Law & Practice, 4 vols. LC 99-46779. 2000. reprint ed. 395.00 (*1-57588-601-4*, 323500) W S Hein.

Rivius, Gualtherus H. & Ryff, Walther H. Der Furnehmbsten Notwendigsten der Gantzen Architectur Angehorigen Mathematischen und Mechanischen Kunst Eygentlicher Bericht und Unterrichtung. (GER.). 1997. reprint ed. 248.00 (*3-487-06946-6*) G Olms Pubs.

Rivkin, Allen & Kerr, Laura. The Farmer's Daughter. adapted ed. 1962. pap. 5.25 (*0-8222-0386-3*) Dramatists Play.

Rivkin, Arnold. Nation-Building in Africa: Problems & Prospects. Morrow, John H., ed. LC 74-96028. 320p. reprint ed. pap. 99.20 (*0-7837-5681-X*, 205910900005) Bks Demand.

Rivkin, Ellis. What Crucified Jesus? Messianism, Pharisaism & the Development of Christianity. LC 97-11698. 192p. 1997. pap. 10.00 (*0-8074-0630-9*, 571214) UAHC.

Rivkin, Julie. False Positions: The Representational Logics of Henry James' Fiction. LC 95-51566. (C). 1996. 35.00 (*0-8047-2617-5*) Stanford U Pr.

Rivkin, Julie & Ryan, Michael, eds. Literary Theory: An Anthology. LC 97-20348. (Illus.). 960p. (C). 1998. text 84.95 (*0-631-20028-2*); pap. text 42.95 (*0-631-20029-0*) Blackwell Pubs.

***Rivkin, Leonard L. & Silberfeld, Jeffrey.** May It Please the Court! From Auto Accidents to Agent Orange - Building a Storefront Practice into America's Largest Suburban Law Firm. LC 99-69959. 444p. 2000. 30.00 (*0-89089-915-0*) Carolina Acad Pr.

Rivkin, Mary, jt. auth. see Harlan, Jean.

Rivkin, Mary S. The Great Outdoors: Restoring Children's Right to Play Outside. 1995. pap. 8.00 (*0-935989-71-4*) Natl Assn Child Ed.

Rivkin, Nacha. Reishis Chochmah, Vol. 2. (Illus.). 1997. pap., teacher ed. 6.75 (*0-914131-56-7*, A030) Torah Umesorah.

— Reishis Chochmah Text. (Illus.). 64p. 1997. pap. 5.50 (*0-914131-54-0*, A010) Torah Umesorah.

Rivkin, Steve, et al. To the Point: Effective Communications for the Medical Staff. LC 97-159307. (Medical Staff Reengineering Ser.). vi, 28 p. 1996. 32.00 (*1-885829-25-6*) Opus Communs.

Rivkin, Steve, jt. auth. see Trout, Jack.

Rivkin, Y. The Metallurgy of Soviet High Speed Diesels. Jones, Steven, ed. 101p. (Orig.). 1984. pap. text 75.00 (*1-55831-041-X*) Delphic Associates.

Rivlin. Phase Equilibria in Iron Ternary Alloys. 1988. 199.00 (*0-901462-34-9*) Institute of Management Consultants.

Rivlin, Alice & Cox, Carol. Understanding Economic Policy: A Citizen's Handbook. 1990. 5.95 (*0-89959-417-4*, 896) LWVUS.

Rivlin, Alice M. Reviving the American Dream: The Economy, the States, & the Federal Government. 196p. (C). 1993. 14.95 (*0-8157-7476-1*) Brookings.

— Systematic Thinking for Social Action. LC 74-161600. 150p. 1971. 28.95 (*0-8157-7478-8*) Brookings.

Rivlin, Alice M., ed. Economic Choices 1984. LC 84-71381. 171p. 1984. 32.95 (*0-8157-7488-5*); pap. 12.95 (*0-8157-7487-7*) Brookings.

Rivlin, Alice M. & Timpane, P. Michael, eds. Planned Variation in Education: Should We Give up or Try Harder? LC 75-5151. (Brookings Institution Studies in Social Experimentation). 198p. reprint ed. pap. 61.40 (*0-608-12471-0*, 202540200043) Bks Demand.

Rivlin, Alice M. & Wiener, Joshua M. Caring for the Disabled Elderly: Who Will Pay? LC 88-10528. 318p. 1988. pap. 16.95 (*0-8157-7497-4*) Brookings.

Rivlin, Alice M., jt. ed. see Bosworth, Barry P.

Rivlin, Benjamin, ed. Ralph Bunche: The Man & His Times. LC 89-24666. (Illus.). 279p. (C). 1989. 39.50 (*0-8419-1145-2*) Holmes & Meier.

Rivlin, Benjamin & Gordenker, Leon, eds. The Challenging Role of the U. N. Secretary-General: Making "the Most Impossible Job in the World" Possible. LC 92-34949. 320p. 1993. 59.95 (*0-275-94466-2*, C4466, Praeger Pubs) Greenwood.

Rivlin, Elizabeth. Elmo's Little Glowworm. LC 93-38193. (Illus.). 16p. (J). (ps-1). 1994. pap. 5.99 (*0-679-85402-9*, Pub. by Random Bks Yng Read) Random.

Rivlin, Gary. Drive-By. 88p. 1995. 25.00 (*0-8050-2921-4*) H Holt & Co.

— Fire on the Prairie: Chicago's Harold Washington & the Politics of Race. (Illus.). 464p. 1995. pap. 14.95 (*0-8050-2698-3*, Owl) H Holt & Co.

***Rivlin, Gary.** Plot to Get Bill Gates: An Irreverent Investigation of the World's Richest Man. 2000. pap. 14.00 (*0-8129-9073-0*, Times Bks) Crown Pub Group.

Rivlin, Gary. The Plot to Get Bill Gates: An Irreverent Investigation of the World's Richest Man ... & the People Who Hate Him. LC 99-18228. 360p. 1999. 25.00 (*0-8129-3006-1*) Times Pub TX.

Rivlin, Gershon. Haganah Highlights. (Orig.). 1994. pap. 14.95 (*0-930832-05-1*) Herzl Pr.

Rivlin, Gideon. Guide to Organizing an International Scientific Conference. (Illus.). 94p. 1995. pap. 68.00 (*3-8055-6151-2*) S Karger.

Rivlin, Lilly & Gevirtz, Gila. Welcome to Israel! 128p. (J). (gr. 4-6). Date not set. pap. 12.95 (*0-87441-692-2*) Behrman.

Rivlin, Michael E. Manual of Gynecology ISE, No. 3. 1990. 15.95 (*0-316-74773-4*, Little Brwn Med Div) Lppncott W & W.

Rivlin, Michael E., et al. Manual of Clinical Problems in Obstetrics & Gynecology: With Annotated Key References. 2nd ed. 448p. 1986. 22.50 (*0-316-74769-6*, Little Brwn Med Div) Lppncott W & W.

Rivlin, Michel E. & Martin, Rick W., eds. Manual of Clinical Problems in Obstetrics & Gynecology. 4th ed. LC 93-35803. 544p. 1994. spiral bd. 34.95 (*0-316-74777-7*) Lppncott W & W.

Rivlin, Michel E., et al. Manual of Clinical Problems in Obstetrics & Gynecology. 5th ed. LC 99-25744. 512p. 1999. spiral bd. 34.95 (*0-7817-1723-X*) Lppncott W & W.

Rivlin, Paul. The Dynamics of Economic Policymaking in Egypt. LC 85-12190. 220p. 1985. 49.95 (*0-275-90156-4*, C0156, Praeger Pubs) Greenwood.

***Rivlin, Paul.** Economic Policy & Performance in the Arab World. 170p. 2000. lib. bdg. 49.95 (*1-55587-932-2*) L Rienner.

Rivlin, R. S., ed. see American Society of Mechanical Engineers Staff.

Rivlin, Robert & Gravelle, Karen. Deciphering the Senses. 1985. pap. 7.95 (*0-671-46124-9*, Touchstone) S&S Trade Pap.

Rivlin, Ronald S., et al. Collected Papers of R. S. Rivlin. LC 96-22080. 1200p. 1996. 129.00 (*0-387-94825-2*) Spr-Verlag.

Rivlin, Theodore J. Chebyshev Polynomials: From Approximation Theory to Algebra & Number Theory. 2nd ed. LC 89-22721. 249p. 1990. 140.00 (*0-471-62896-4*) Wiley.

— An Introduction to the Approximation of Functions. 160p. (C). 1998. reprint ed. pap. 5.95 (*0-486-64069-8*) Dover.

Rivoirard, Jacques. Introduction to Disjunctive Kriging & Non-Linear Geostatistics. (Spatial Information Systems Ser.). (Illus.). 190p. 1994. text 58.00 (*0-19-874180-4*) OUP.

Rivoire, Jeanne L., jt. ed. see Kidd, Aline H.

***Rivoli Design Group Staff.** Jay Jay the Jet Plane's COLORS. (Jay Jay Jet Plane's Spinner Bks.). 10p. (J). 2000. 6.95 (*1-58117-098-X*, Piggy Toes Pr) Intervisual Bks.

***Rivoli Group Staff.** Jay Jay the Jet Plane's Numbers. (Spinner Bks.). 10p. (J). 2000. 6.95 (*1-58117-099-8*, Piggy Toes Pr) Intervisual Bks.

— Jay Jay the Jet Plane's Opposites. (Peek-A-Boo Board Bks.). 12p. (J). 2000. bds. 6.95 (*1-58117-100-5*, Piggy Toes Pr) Intervisual Bks.

Rivolta, Marcelo N., jt. ed. see Holley, Matthew C.

***Rix, Alan.** The Australia-Japan Political Alignment: 1952 to the Present. LC 99-193809. 1999. write for info. (*0-415-19781-3*) Routledge.

Rix, Brian. Life in the Farce Lane. (Illus.). 256p. 1996. 45.00 (*0-233-98936-6*, Pub. by Andre Deutsch); pap. 24.95 (*0-233-98963-3*, Pub. by Andre Deutsch) Trafalgar.

Rix, Brian, ed. Gullible's Travails. (Illus.). 192p. 1996. 17.95 (*0-233-99010-0*, Pub. by Andre Deutsch) Trafalgar.

Rix, David, jt. tr. see King, Donald.

***Rix, Donna.** Doctor from the Past. large type ed. 320p. 1999. pap. 20.99 (*1-85389-953-4*, Dales) Ulverscroft.

— Nurse Courageous. large type ed. 320p. 2000. 20.99 (*1-84137-022-3*, Pub. by Mgna Lrg Print) Ulverscroft.

Rix, G. S. History & Genealogy of the Eastman Family of America: Containing Biographical Sketches & Genealogy of Both Males & Females. (Illus.). 1000p. 1989. reprint ed. pap. 150.00 (*0-8328-0511-4*); reprint ed. lib. bdg. 158.00 (*0-8328-0510-6*) Higginson Bk Co.

Rix, Guy S. Eastman: History & Genealogy of Dea. Jos. Eastman of Hadley, Ma., Grandson of Roger Eastman of Salisbury, Ma. Eastman, M. Emily, ed. (Illus.). 263p. 1997. reprint ed. pap. 39.50 (*0-8328-8412-X*); reprint ed. lib. bdg. 49.50 (*0-8328-8411-1*) Higginson Bk Co.

Rix, H. W., jt. ed. see Minniti, D.

Rix, Herbert. Tent & Testament: Camping Tour in Palestine with Some Notes on Scriptural Sites. Davis, Moshe, ed. LC 77-70737. (America & the Holy Land Ser.). (Illus.). 1977. reprint ed. lib. bdg. 33.95 (*0-405-10280-1*) Ayer.

Rix, Herbert D. Martin Luther: The Man & the Image. 335p. 1983. text 37.50 (*0-8290-0554-4*) Irvington.

Rix, J., jt. ed. see Teixeira, J. C.

Rix, Jamie. The Last Chocolate Cookie. LC 97-7303. (Illus.). 32p. (J). (ps-3). 1998. 4.99 (*0-7636-0411-9*) Candlewick Pr.

Rix, Jonathan. Some Hope. 228p. 1994. pap. 15.95 (*0-233-98834-3*, Pub. by Andre Deutsch) Trafalgar.

Rix, Judy. Welcome Home to Lenexa: Traditions. (Illus.). 100p. (Orig.). 1997. pap. write for info. (*0-9638542-3-2*) Geo Graphics.

Rix, Judy, intro. Welcome Home to Lenexa. (Illus.). 96p. 1993. write for info. (*0-9638542-0-8*) Geo Graphics.

Rix, K. J., jt. ed. see Mortimer, A. M.

Rix, Len, tr. see Szerb, Antal.

Rix, Martyn, jt. auth. see Phillips, R.

Rix, Martyn, jt. auth. see Phillips, Roger.

Rix, Martyn E. Art of Botanical Illustrations. 1990. 85.00 (*0-685-33410-4*) Random Hse Value.

Rix, Martyn E., jt. auth. see Phillips, Roger.

***Rix, Rebecca.** Sexual Abuse Litigation: A Practical Resource for Attorneys, Clinicians & Advocates. LC 00-40763. 2000. write for info. (*0-7890-1175-1*, Hawrth Medical) Haworth Pr.

Rix, Sara E. Older Workers. LC 90-46349. (Choices & Challenges: An Older Adult Reference Ser.). 243p. 1990. lib. bdg. 45.00 (*0-87436-259-8*) ABC-CLIO.

Rix, Sara E. & Fisher, Paul. Retirement-Age Policy: An International Perspective. (Policy Studies on Social Policy). (Illus.). 176p. 1982. 56.00 (*0-08-028840-5*, K110, L115, Pergamon Pr) Elsevier.

Rixen, Gail. Chicken Logic. iii, 25p. (Orig.). 1996. pap. 5.00 (*0-9656210-0-6*) Sidewalks.

***Rixford, Elizabeth M. Leach.** Families Directly Descended from All the Royal Families in Europe. 175p. 1999. pap. 23.50 (*0-8063-4945-X*) Clearfield Co.

— Three Hundred Colonial Ancestors & War Service: Their Part in Making American History from 495 to 1934. 425p. 1999. pap. 39.95 (*0-8063-4944-1*) Clearfield Co.

Rixom, M. R. & Mailvaganam, N. P. Chemical Admixtures for Concrete. 275p. 1986. text 47.50 (*0-419-12630-9*, 9571, E & FN Spon) Routledge.

***Rixom, M. R. & Mailvaganam, N. P.** Chemical Admixtures for Concrete. 3rd ed. LC 98-43377. 1999. write for info. (*0-419-22520-X*, E & FN Spon) Routledge.

***Rixon, Angela S.** The Faithful Dog. 96p. 2000. pap. 9.95 (*1-84215-332-3*) Anness Pub.

— The Noble Horse. 96p. 2000. pap. 9.95 (*1-84215-330-7*) Anness Pub.

— The Secret Cat. 96p. 2000. pap. 9.95 (*1-84215-331-5*) Anness Pub.

Rixon, Angelia. Illustrated Encyclopedia of Cat Breeds. 256p. 1995. 19.98 (*0-7858-0364-5*) Bk Sales Inc.

An Asterisk (*) at the beginning of an entry indicates that the title is appearing for the first time.

***Rixson, Denis.** Knoydart: The Last Wilderness. (Illus.). 128p. 1999. pap. 13.95 (*1-84158-019-8*, Pub. by Birlinn Ltd) Dufour.
Rixson, Denis. The West Highland Galley. (Illus.). 300p. 1998. 39.95 (*1-874744-86-6*, Pub. by Birlinn Ltd) Dufour.
Riza, Nebeel A. Selected Papers on Photonic Control Systems for Phased Array Antennas. LC 97-3308. (SPIE Milestone Ser.). 1997. write for info. (*0-8194-2613-X*) SPIE.
Rizack, Martin A. The Medical Letter Handbook of Adverse Drug Interactions, 1997. rev. ed. 347p. 1997. pap. 18.00 (*0-9660510-0-9*) Med Letter.
— The Medical Letter Handbook of Adverse Drug Interactions, 1998. rev. ed. 377p. 1998. 18.00 (*0-9660510-1-7*) Med Letter.
Rizack, Martin A., ed. The Medical Letter Handbook of Adverse Drug Interactions 1999. rev. ed. 404p. 1999. 18.00 (*0-9660510-4-1*) Med Letter.
Rizal, Jose. Noli Me Tangere. Locsin, Raul L., ed. Lacson-Locsin, Ma. S., tr. from SPA. (SHAPS Library of Translations). 472p. 1997. text 47.00 (*0-8248-1916-0*); pap. text 27.95 (*0-8248-1917-9*) UH Pr.
Rizer, Arden C., Jr. The American Spiritualist Ministry. American Spiritualist Assembly Directors, ed. 240p. (Orig.). 1987. pap. 20.00 (*0-939795-30-2*) Amer Spirit.
— American Spiritualist Psychology. 24p. 1987. pap. 9.00 (*0-939795-20-5*) Amer Spirit.
— Astral Projection (Out of Body Experience) A. S. A. Staff, ed. 25p. 1991. pap. 6.92 (*0-939795-41-8*) Amer Spirit.
— I Am the Power. (Illus.). 87p. (Orig.). (J). (gr. 7-12). 1992. pap. 10.00 (*0-939795-46-9*) Amer Spirit.
— A Metasciences Textbook. A. S. A. Educations & Research Staff, ed. (Orig.). 1987. pap. 23.50 (*0-939795-32-9*) Amer Spirit.
— Paths of Attainment. 82p. 1987. pap. 18.00 (*0-939795-13-2*) Amer Spirit.
— Spiritual Magic: Yi King Numerology. 180p. (Orig.). 1987. pap. 18.00 (*0-939795-29-9*) Amer Spirit.
Rizer, Arden C., Jr., pref. Catalogue of Numbers Vol. 4: Sexuality, Courtship, Marriage. (Orig.). pap. 20.00 (*0-939795-38-8*) Amer Spirit.
Rizer, Arden C., Jr., ed. see Berlinquette, Esther R.
Rizk, A., et al, eds. Hypertext: Concepts, Systems & Applications: Proceedings of the First European Conference on Hypertext, INRIA, France, November 1990. (Series on Electronic Publishing: No. 5). (Illus.). 383p. (C). 1991. text 80.00 (*0-521-40517-3*) Cambridge U Pr.
Rizk, Abdel-Fattah M. Naturally Occurring Pyrrolizidine Alkaloids. (Illus.). 224p. 1990. lib. bdg. 190.00 (*0-8493-4650-9*, QP801) CRC Pr.
— Poisonous Plant Contamination of Edible Plants. (Illus.). 192p. 1990. lib. bdg. 149.00 (*0-8493-6369-1*, RA1250) CRC Pr.
Rizk, Beatriz J. El Nuevo Teatro Latinoamericano: Una Lectura Historica. (Towards a Social History of Hispanic & Luso-Brazilian Literature Ser.). (SPA.). 144p. (Orig.). (C). 1987. pap. 9.95 (*0-910235-25-2*) Prisma Bks.
Rizk, Helen S., narrated by. Stories of the Christian Hymns. rev. ed. (Ichthus Ser.). 1986. pap. 4.95 (*0-687-18300-6*) Abingdon.
Rizk, Kim. The Hay Day Country Market Cookbook. LC 98-37983. 256p. 1998. 24.95 (*0-7611-1429-7*); pap. 13.95 (*0-7611-0025-3*) Workman Pub.
Rizk, Yvonne, jt. auth. see Sweeney, Joseph D.
Riznichenko, Yu V. Problems of Seismology: Selected Papers. (Illus.). xvii, 445p. 1992. 247.95 (*0-387-54230-2*) Spr-Verlag.
Riznik, Barnes. Waioli Mission House. (Illus.). pap. 14.95 (*0-9617174-1-6*) Grove Farm Homestead & Waioli.
Rizo, Felix. El Mundo Sin Clara. (SPA.). 1997. pap. 9.95 (*0-89729-824-1*) Ediciones.
Rizo, Luis. The Great Plains. LC 95-2947. (Amazing World of Plants Ser.). 32p. (J). (gr. 3-12). 1996. lib. bdg. 15.95 (*0-7910-3464-X*) Chelsea Hse.
— The Mysterious Jungles. LC 95-15155. 32p. (J). (gr. 3-12). 1996. lib. bdg. 15.95 (*0-7910-3465-8*) Chelsea Hse.
— Plants of the Desert. LC 95-10768. (Amazing World of Plants Ser.).Tr. of Plantas del Desierto. 32p. (J). (gr. 3-12). 1996. lib. bdg. 15.95 (*0-7910-3466-6*) Chelsea Hse.
— Plants under the Sea. LC 95-18261. (Incredible World of Plants Ser.).Tr. of Plantas del Mar. (ENG & SPA.). 32p. (J). (gr. 3 up). 1996. lib. bdg. 15.95 (*0-7910-3468-2*) Chelsea Hse.
— The Vegetation of Rivers, Lakes, & Swamps. LC 95-22431. (Incredible World of Plants Ser.).Tr. of Vegetacion en los Rios, Lagos y Plantanos. 32p. (J). (gr. 3 up). 1996. lib. bdg. 15.95 (*0-7910-3469-0*) Chelsea Hse.
Rizo, Luis, jt. auth. see Fite, Josep M.
Rizopatron, Marina, ed. see Asherman, Robyn.
Rizos, C., jt. auth. see Brunner, F. K.
Rizos, Chris, jt. auth. see Drane, Chris R.
***Rizutto.** Getting Started with JavaScript. (C). 1999. pap. text 35.00 (*0-03-022139-0*) Harcourt Coll Pubs.
Rizvi, Br. Balti: A Scheduled Tribe of Jammu & Kashmir. 1993. 14.00 (*81-212-0402-X*, Pub. by Gian Publng Hse) S Asia.
Rizvi, Fazal. Administrative Leadership & the Democratic Community As a Social Ideal. 119p. (C). 1986. 48.00 (*0-7300-0417-1*, Pub. by Deakin Univ) St Mut.
— Ethnicity, Class & Multicultural Education. 102p. (C). 1986. 51.00 (*0-7300-0401-5*, Pub. by Deakin Univ) St Mut.
— Multiculturalism As an Educational Policy. 120p. (C). 1985. 65.00 (*0-7300-0118-0*, Pub. by Deakin Univ) St Mut.
Rizvi, Fazal, jt. ed. see Gunew, Sneja.
Rizvi, Gowher. South Asia in a Changing International Order. LC 92-40699. 180p. 1993. 28.95 (*0-8039-9467-2*) Sage.
Rizvi, Hasan-Askari. The Military & Politics in Pakistan. 367p. 1989. text 30.00 (*81-220-0084-3*, Pub. by Konark Pubs Pvt Ltd) Advent Bks Div.
***Rizvi, Hasan Askari.** Military, State & Society in Pakistan. LC 99-55831. 2000. 79.95 (*0-312-23193-8*) St Martin.
Rizvi, Janet. Ladakh: Crossroads of High Asia. 2nd ed. (Illus.). 265p. 1998. reprint ed. pap. text 14.50 (*0-19-564546-4*) OUP.
— Trans-Himalayan Caravans: Merchant Princes & Peasant Traders in Ladakh. (Illus.). 320p. 2000. text 35.00 (*0-19-564855-2*) OUP.
Rizvi, M. Haseeb, ed. Modern Statistical Selection: Proceedings of the Conference "Statistical Ranking & Selection--Three Decades of Development", University of California at Santa Barbara, December 1984, Pt. 1. LC 86-71924. (Mathematical & Management Sciences Ser.: Vol. 13). 1986. 195.00 (*0-935950-13-3*) Am Sciences Pr.
— Modern Statistical Selection: Proceedings of the Conference "Statistical Ranking & Selection--Three Decades of Development", University of California at Santa Barbara, December 1984, Pt. II. LC 86-71924. (Mathematical & Management Sciences Ser.: Vol.14). 1987. 195.00 (*0-935950-14-1*) Am Sciences Pr.
Rizvi, S. A. A History of Sufism in India, Vol. 1. 467p. 1975. 34.95 (*0-318-37182-0*) Asia Bk Corp.
— Wonder That Was India, Vol. II. (C). 1993. 20.00 (*0-8364-2889-7*, Pub. by Rupa) S Asia.
Rizvi, S. H. & Roy, Shivani. In Search of Roots: A Study in Ethnogenesis. LC 94-900360. (C). 1994. 18.50 (*81-7018-760-5*, Pub. by BR Pub) S Asia.
Rizvi, S. H., jt. auth. see Roy, Shibani.
Rizvi, S. N. Learning English Through Arabic. 384p. 1992. lib. bdg. 60.00 (*81-209-0505-9*, Pub. by Pitambar Pub) St Mut.
— Medical Anthropology of the Jaunsaris. (C). 1991. text 16.00 (*81-7211-012-X*, Pub. by Northern Bk Ctr) S Asia.
— The Shompen. (Andaman & Nicobar Island Tribes Ser.). (C). 1990. 7.50 (*81-7046-075-1*, Pub. by Seagull Bks) S Asia.
Rizvi, S. N., jt. auth. see Dickens, Charles.
Rizvi, S. N., jt. auth. see Dumas, Alexandre.
Rizvi, S. N., jt. auth. see Fuste, Greg J.
Rizvi, S. N., jt. auth. see Fuste, J. M.
Rizvi, S. N., jt. auth. see Hammond, C. B.
Rizvi, S. S. Islamic Philosophy of Education. 1989. 19.95 (*1-56744-103-3*) Kazi Pubns.
***Rizvi, S. S. H.** Supercritical Fluid Processing of Food & Biomaterials. 257p. 1998. 159.00 (*0-8342-1356-7*) Aspen Pub.
Rizvi, S. S. H., jt. ed. see Rao, M. M.
Rizvi, S. T., jt. auth. see Jain, Subodh K.
Rizvi, S. Taria, jt. ed. see Jain, S. K.
Rizvi, Saiyid A. History of Sufism in India, 2 vols. (Illus.). 1983. 62.50 (*0-685-13690-6*) Coronet Bks.
— History of Sufism in India, 2 vols. 1986. 88.00 (*81-215-0038-9*, Pub. by M Manoharial) Coronet Bks.
— History of Sufism in India Vol. 1: Early Sufism & Its History, 2 vols. 1986. 44.00 (*81-215-0039-7*, Pub. by M Manoharial) Coronet Bks.
— History of Sufism in India Vol. 2: From Sixteenth Century to Modern Times, 2 vols. 1986. 44.00 (*81-215-0040-0*, Pub. by M Manoharial) Coronet Bks.
— Muslim Revivalist Movements in Northern India in the 16th & 17th Century: In the Sixteenth & Seventeenth Centuries. 376p. (C). 1995. reprint ed. 42.00 (*81-215-0590-9*, Pub. by M Manoharial) Coronet Bks.
— Socio-Intellectual History of the Isna Ashari Shi'is in India, 7th to 19th Century AD, Set, Vols. 1 & 2. 1986. 78.50 (*81-215-0004-4*, Pub. by M Manoharial) Coronet Bks.
Rizvi, Sayyid S., tr. The Holy Prophet: The Life of Prophet Muhammad. 250p. 1997. 20.00 (*1-879402-54-8*); pap. 12.00 (*1-879402-41-6*) Tahrike Tarsile Quran.
Rizvi, Syed A. Muslim Tradition in Psychotherapy & Modern Trends. 1995. 25.50 (*1-56744-160-2*) Kazi Pubns.
Rizvi, Syed S. Elements of Islamic Studies. Husnain, Syed T., ed. LC 89-51359. 100p. 1989. pap. 4.95 (*0-940368-99-4*, 84) Tahrike Tarsile Quran.
Rizwani, Raza H. Qur'an Made Easy. rev. ed. 130p. 1983. reprint ed. pap. 6.00 (*0-941724-09-3*) Islamic Seminary.
Rizwani, RAza H., ed. see Al-Sadr, Ayatullah B.
Rizwani, Raza H., ed. see Sadr, Muhammad B. & Murtaza, Mutahhery.
Rizza, Charles R. & Lowe, Gordon D., eds. Haemophilia & Other Inherited Bleeding Disorders. (Illus.). 521p. 1997. text 95.00 (*0-7020-1755-8*) W B Saunders.
***Rizza, Margaret M.** California Managed Care Directory: A Comprehensive Directory of HMO, PPO & POS Health Plans. 210p. 2000. pap. 150.00 (*0-9700562-0-6*, CA101) Ntnl Med.
Rizza, R. A., jt. ed. see Marshall, S. M.
***Rizza, Robert.** Getting Started with Pro/Engineer. 476p. (C). 1999. pap. text 49.00 (*0-13-040212-5*) P-H.
Rizza, Robert, jt. ed. see Draznin, Boris.
Rizza, Steve. Rudolf Kassner & Hugo von Hofmannsthal: Criticism As Art, the Reception of Pre-Raphaelitism in Fin de Siecle Vienna. (Tubinger Studien zur Deutschen Literatur: Bd. 16). 291p. 1997. pap. 54.95 (*3-631-31162-1*) P Lang Pubng.
— Rudolf Kassner & Hugo von Hofmannsthal: Criticism As Art, the Reception of Pre-Raphaelitism in Fin de Siecle Vienna. (Tubinger Studien zur Deutschen Literatur: Bd. 16). 291p. 1997. pap. 54.95 (*0-8204-3237-7*) P Lang Pubng.
Rizzardi, Fran, jt. auth. see Abrahams, D. Mark.
Rizzarelli, E. & Theophanides, Theophile M., eds. Chemistry & Properties of Biomolecular Systems. 248p. (C). 1991. text 146.50 (*0-7923-1393-3*) Kluwer Academic.
Rizzatti, Lorella. Butterfly. (Portable Pets Ser.). 1999. 5.95 (*0-8109-5631-4*) Abrams.
— Butterfly. (Portable Pets Ser.). (Illus.). 12p. 1999. bds. 5.95 (*0-8109-5630-6*, Pub. by Abrams) Time Warner.
— Kitten. (Portable Pets Ser.). (Illus.). 12p. 1999. bds. 5.95 (*0-8109-5633-0*, Pub. by Abrams) Time Warner.
— Kittens. (Portable Pets Ser.). 1999. 6.95 (*0-8109-5632-2*) Abrams.
— Ladybug/Crab/Turtle/Frog. (Portable Pets Ser.). (J). 1998. pap. 95.20 (*0-8109-5099-5*) Abrams.
— Lamb, 1. (Portable Pets Ser.). 1999. 5.95 (*0-8109-5641-1*) Abrams.
— Lamb. (Portable Pets Ser.). (Illus.). 12p. 1999. bds. 5.95 (*0-8109-5640-3*, Pub. by Abrams) Time Warner.
— The Moon. 1999. 5.95 (*0-8109-5636-5*) Abrams.
— The Moon. (Illus.). 12p. 1999. bds. 5.95 (*0-8109-5637-3*, Pub. by Abrams) Time Warner.
— Rabbit. (Portable Pets Ser.). (Illus.). 12p. 1999. bds. 5.95 (*0-8109-5645-4*, Pub. by Abrams) Time Warner.
— Rabbits. (Portable Pets Ser.). (Illus.). 12p. (ps-k). 1999. 6.95 (*0-8109-5646-2*) Abrams.
— The Sun. 1999. 5.95 (*0-8109-5649-7*) Abrams.
— The Sun. (Illus.). 12p. 1999. bds. 5.95 (*0-8109-5648-9*, Pub. by Abrams) Time Warner.
Rizzatti, Lorella. Crab. (Portable Pets Ser.). 12p. (J). 1998. bds. 5.95 (*0-8109-5626-8*, Pub. by Abrams) Time Warner.
— Frog. (Portable Pets Ser.). 12p. (J). 1998. bds. 5.95 (*0-8109-5627-6*, Pub. by Abrams) Time Warner.
— Ladybug. (Portable Pets Ser.). 12p. (J). 1998. bds. 5.95 (*0-8109-5628-4*, Pub. by Abrams) Time Warner.
— Turtle. (Portable Pets Ser.). 12p. (J). 1998. bds. 5.95 (*0-8109-5629-2*, Pub. by Abrams) Time Warner.
Rizzello, Salvatore. The Economics of the Mind. LC 99-34496. 224p. 1999. 80.00 (*1-84064-163-0*) E Elgar.
Rizzi, A., et al, eds. Advances in Data Science & Classification: Studies in Classification, Data Analysis, & Knowledge Organization. LC 98-35573. (Studies in Classification, Data Analysis, & Knowledge Organization). (Illus.). xvi, 682p. 1998. pap. 119.00 (*3-540-64641-8*) Spr-Verlag.
Rizzi, Alberto. Delloto in Dresden: Dresden, Vienna, Monaco. 1997. 125.00 (*88-86502-15-X*, Pub. by Canal & Stamperia) Antique Collect.
Rizzi, Cesare. Candrakirti. (C). 1988. 11.00 (*81-208-0401-5*, Pub. by Motilal Bnarsidass) S Asia.
Rizzi, James. James Rizzi: The New York Paintings. LC 97-194295. (Illus.). 128p. 1996. pap. 75.00 (*3-7913-1668-0*, Pub. by Prestel) te Neues.
— Three-D Constructions. (Illus.). 119p. 1988. 50.00 (*0-936598-02-6*) J Szoke Edns.
Rizzi, Luigi. Relativized Minimality. 160p. 1990. 27.50 (*0-262-18136-3*); pap. text 17.00 (*0-262-68061-0*) MIT Pr.
Rizzi, Luigi, jt. auth. see Friedemann, Marc-Ariel.
Rizzi, Luigi, jt. ed. see Belletti, Adriana.
Rizzi, Marcia S. Some Pictures from My Life: A Diary. LC 72-87034. (Illus.). 64p. (Orig.). 1972. pap. 3.25 (*0-87810-022-9*) Times Change.
Rizzi, Peter A. Microwave Engineering. (Illus.). 640p. (C). 1987. 70.60 (*0-13-586702-9*) P-H.
Rizzi, Silvio, et al. The Pasta Bible. LC 96-67512. 240p. 1996. 34.95 (*0-670-86996-1*, Viking) Viking Penguin.
Rizzi, Timothy. The Phalanx Dragon. 480p. 2000. reprint ed. mass mkt. 5.99 (*0-8439-3885-4*, Leisure Bks) Dorchester Pub Co.
— Strike of the Cobra. 480p. 2000. reprint ed. mass mkt. 5.99 (*0-8439-3630-4*, Leisure Bks) Dorchester Pub Co.
Rizzini, Carlos T., jt. auth. see Mors, Walter B.
Rizzo. Fundamentals of Anatomy & Physiology. (Anatomy & Physiology). (C). 2000. pap. 36.00 (*0-7668-0498-4*); pap., student ed. 16.00 (*0-7668-0527-1*) Delmar.
— Understanding Health Insurance: Guide to Uniform Billing. LC 99-49687. 318p. 2000. mass mkt. 38.95 (*0-8273-8223-5*) Delmar.
Rizzo, Ann-Marie & Mendez, Carmen. The Integration of Women in Management: A Guide for Human Resources & Management Development Specialists. LC 90-8422. 224p. 1990. 57.95 (*0-89930-475-3*, RON, Quorum Bks) Greenwood.
Rizzo, Betty & Mahony, Robert, eds. The Annotated Letters of Christopher Smart. 144p. (C). 1991. 26.95 (*0-8093-1609-9*) S Ill U Pr.
Rizzo, Betty, ed. see Scott, Sarah.
Rizzo, Cindy, et al, eds. All the Ways Home: Parenting & Children in the Lesbian & Gay Communities - A Collection of Short Fiction. LC 94-37031. 200p. (Orig.). 1995. 19.95 (*0-934678-68-5*); pap. 10.95 (*0-934678-65-0*) New Victoria Pubs.
Rizzo, David. Freeway Alternates: A Guide to Commuting in Los Angeles & Orange Counties. LC 90-83235. (Illus.). (Orig.). 1990. pap. 10.95 (*0-935182-45-4*) Gem Guides Bk.
Rizzo, Diurny. Magia Hecha en Casa. 1994. pap. 5.95 (*0-942272-38-2*) Original Pubns.
Rizzo, G., jt. auth. see Nicolaides, K. H.
Rizzo, Idle, jt. auth. see Hutter, Michael.
Rizzo, Ilde. The Hidden Debt. (C). 1990. lib. bdg. 114.50 (*0-7923-0610-4*) Kluwer Academic.
Rizzo, Ilde, jt. ed. see Peacock, Alan.
Rizzo, Jacques. Reading Jazz - Alto Sax: The New Method for Learning to Read Written Jazz Music. 2nd rev. ed. Clark, Larry, ed. (Reading Jazz Ser.). 76p. 1989. pap. 19.95 incl. audio compact disk (*0-7692-1425-8*, SB272CD) Wrner Bros.
— Reading Jazz - Trumpet: The New Method for Learning to Read Written Jazz Music. 2nd rev. ed. Clark, Larry, ed. (Reading Jazz Ser.). 76p. 1989. pap. 19.95 incl. audio compact disk (*0-7692-1422-3*, SB274CD) Wrner Bros.
Rizzo, Janis, jt. ed. see Banks, Carolyn.
Rizzo, Jeff, jt. auth. see Landes, William-Alan.
Rizzo, John. How Macs Work. 2nd ed. LC 96-200052. 240p. 1996. pap. 24.99 (*1-56276-401-2*, Ziff-Davis Pr) Que.
***Rizzo, John.** Mac OS X Clearly Explained. (Illus.). 2000. pap. 44.95 (*0-12-589327-2*) Morgan Kaufmann.
Rizzo, John. Macintosh Windows Integration: Integrating Your Macintosh with Windows 95 & Windows NT Environment. 400p. 1999. pap. text 44.95 incl. cd-rom (*0-12-589325-6*) Morgan Kaufmann.
— MacUser Guide to Connectivity. (Guide to...Ser.). (Illus.). 380p. (Orig.). 1992. pap. 27.95 (*1-56276-056-4*, Ziff-Davis Pr) Que.
Rizzo, John & Clark, Daniel. How Macs Work. (How It Works Ser.). (Illus.). 222p. 1993. pap. 24.95 (*1-56276-146-3*, Ziff-Davis Pr) Que.
Rizzo, John, jt. auth. see Poole, Lon.
Rizzo, John A., jt. ed. see Sato, Ryuzo.
Rizzo, John R. Management for Librarians: Fundamentals & Issues, 33. LC 79-8950. (Contributions in Librarianship & Information Science Ser.: No. 33). (Illus.). 339p. 1980. 55.00 (*0-313-21990-7*, RML/, Greenwood Pr) Greenwood.
Rizzo, Joseph V., jt. auth. see Suran, Bernard G.
Rizzo, Joyce A. Aboveground Storage Tank Management: A Practical Guide. 219p. 1990. pap. text 79.00 (*0-86587-202-3*) Gov Insts.
— Underground Storage Tank Management: A Practical Guide. 5th ed. LC 98-155010. 391p. 1998. pap. text 89.00 (*0-86587-607-X*, 607) Gov Insts.
***Rizzo, Kay D.** Abigail's Dream. LC 99-54907. (Serenity Inn Ser.: Vol. 5). 280p. 2000. pap. 7.99 (*0-8054-2131-9*) Broadman.
Rizzo, Kay D. Claims upon My Heart. LC 92-43931. 1993. pap. 9.99 (*0-8163-1133-1*) Pacific Pr Pub Assn.
Rizzo, Kay D. Face to Face with Forgiveness: Guilty, Hopeless, Condemned. Everything Changed When Mary Came. LC 96-43771. 191p. 1997. pap. 6.97 (*0-8163-1366-0*) Pacific Pr Pub Assn.
Rizzo, Kay D. Flee My Father's House. LC 92-33707. (Chloe Mae Chronicles Ser.: Vol. 1). 1993. pap. 9.99 (*0-8163-1134-X*) Pacific Pr Pub Assn.
— Josephine's Fortune. LC 98-49464. (Serenity Inn Ser.: No. 3). 256p. (Orig.). 1999. pap. 7.99 (*0-8054-1675-7*) Broadman.
— Lilia's Haven. LC 99-23956. (Serenity Inn Ser.: No. 4). 256p. 1999. pap. 7.99 (*0-8054-1685-4*) Broadman.
— Love's Cherished Refrain. LC 94-27523. (Chloe Celeste Chronicles Ser.: 4). 1994. pap. 9.99 (*0-8163-1222-2*) Pacific Pr Pub Assn.
Rizzo, Kay D. Love's Tender Prelude. LC 94-5442. (Chloe Celeste Chronicles Ser.: No. 1). 1994. pap. 9.99 (*0-8163-1219-2*) Pacific Pr Pub Assn.
Rizzo, Kay D. On Wings of Praise: How I Found Real Joy in a Personal Friendship with God. LC 95-49789. 176p. 1996. pap. 12.99 (*0-8280-1050-1*) Review & Herald.
Rizzo, Kay D. Praise a la Carte: Nourishment for Body & Soul from My Kitchen to Yours. LC 96-1940. 1997. 6.97 (*0-8163-1353-9*) Pacific Pr Pub Assn.
Rizzo, Kay D. The Secret Dreams of Dolly Spencer. LC 98-50934. (Chloe Family Chronicles Ser.). 1999. 12.99 (*0-8163-1689-9*) Pacific Pr Pub Assn.
***Rizzo, Kay D.** Serenity's Desire. LC 98-15560. (Serenity Inn Ser.: Vol. 1). 256p. 1998. pap. 7.99 (*0-8054-6373-9*) Broadman.
Rizzo, Kay D. Serenity's Quest. LC 98-20316. (Serenity Inn Ser.: Vol. 2). 256p. 1998. pap. 7.99 (*0-8054-1674-9*) Broadman.
Rizzo, Kay D. She Said No: But He Crossed the Line Between Passion & Violence. LC 93-28923. 189p. 1994. pap. 10.99 (*0-8163-1179-X*) Pacific Pr Pub Assn.
Rizzo, Kay D. Silence of My Love. LC 92-43132. 1993. pap. 9.99 (*0-8163-1135-8*) Pacific Pr Pub Assn.
— Still My Aching Heart. LC 92-43699. (Chloe Mae Chronicles Ser.: No. 4). 1993. pap. 9.99 (*0-8163-1136-6*) Pacific Pr Pub Assn.
— Sweet Strings of Love. LC 94-18538. (Chloe Celeste Chronicles Ser.: Vol. 3). 1994. pap. 9.99 (*0-8163-1221-4*) Pacific Pr Pub Assn.
— Winter's Silent Song. LC 94-7118. (Chloe Celeste Chronicles Ser.: No. 2). 1994. pap. 9.99 (*0-8163-1220-6*) Pacific Pr Pub Assn.
Rizzo, Kay D., jt. auth. see Huston, Todd.
Rizzo, Kay D., jt. auth. see Johnson, Terry.
Rizzo, Kenneth E. Total Production Maintenance. LC 97-70433. (Illus.). 224p. (C). 1997. text 75.00 (*0-88362-199-1*, 1543) GATFPress.
Rizzo, Leo. Automotive Cylinder Boring. LC 79-730978. 1979. student ed. 7.00 (*0-8064-0131-1*, 433) Bergwall.
— CNC Lathe. 1985. student ed. 7.00 (*0-8064-0255-5*, 519) Bergwall.
— Digital Codes & Numbering Systems. (Series 870). (Orig.). 1983. pap., student ed. 7.00 (*0-8064-0355-1*, 870) Bergwall.
— The Drill Press Explained. LC 81-730687. 1982. student ed. 7.00 (*0-8064-0249-0*, 516) Bergwall.
— The Four Cycle Diesel Engine. LC 79-730763. 1978. student ed. 7.00 (*0-8064-0189-3*, 470) Bergwall.
— The Horizontal Surface Grinder. LC 81-730686. 1982. student ed. 7.00 (*0-8064-0251-2*, 517) Bergwall.
— Lathe Cutting Explained. LC 79-730988. 1979. student ed. 7.00 (*0-8064-0243-1*, 513) Bergwall.
— The Lathe Explained. LC 72-737347. 1971. student ed. 7.00 (*0-8064-0219-9*, 501) Bergwall.
— Measuring Tools Explained. LC 73-732668. 1972. student ed. 7.00 (*0-8064-0223-7*, 503) Bergwall.
— Milling Machine Explained. LC 73-732667. 1984. student ed. 7.00 (*0-8064-0221-0*, 502) Bergwall.

An Asterisk (*) at the beginning of an entry indicates that the title is appearing for the first time.

— Pneumatics Explained. LC 84-730253. 1984. student ed. 7.00 (*0-8064-0038-2*, 530) Bergwall.
— Sheet Metal Machinery. LC 82-730275. 1982. student ed. 7.00 (*0-8064-0253-9*, 518) Bergwall.
— The Vertical Milling Machine Explained. LC 79-731074. (Orig.). 1978. student ed. 6.00 (*0-8064-0241-5*, 512); audio 319.00 (*0-8064-0242-3*) Bergwall.
Rizzo, Leonard J. The Key to Success in Running an Outdoor Festival. 3rd rev. ed. (Illus.). 87p. 1998. pap., wbk. ed. 18.00 (*0-9661912-1-8*, 0319) Saint Joseph Pub.
— The River Always Moves. 300p. 1998. pap. 23.00 (*0-9661912-0-X*, 0320) Saint Joseph Pub.
***Rizzo, Luigi & Fdida, Serge, eds.** Networked Group Communication: Proceedings of the 1st International COST 264 Workshop, NGC'99, Pisa, Italy, November 17-20, 1999. rev. ed. LC 99-56376. (Lecture Notes in Computer Science Ser.: Vol. 1736). xiii, 339p. 1999. pap. 62.00 (*3-540-66782-2*) Spr-Verlag.
Rizzo, Margaret, jt. auth. see Jweid, Rosann.
Rizzo, Mario J., jt. auth. see O'Driscoll, Gerald P., Jr.
Rizzo, Mario J., jt. ed. see Boettke, Peter J.
Rizzo, Mario J., jt. ed. see Cowan, Robin.
Rizzo, Matthew & Tranel, Daniel, eds. Head Injury & Postconcussive Syndrome. 533p. 1995. text 115.00 (*0-443-08964-7*) Church.
***Rizzo, Monica.** Meet the Stars of Roswell. (Illus.). 144p. (J). (gr. 7-12). 2000. mass mkt. 4.99 (*0-439-20758-4*) Scholastic Inc.
Rizzo, Monica, jt. auth. see Fishel, Danielle.
Rizzo, Philip A. Cambridge Brick Details. LC 83-63460. 128p. 1984. 13.95 (*0-9613164-0-3*) Rotunda Bks.
Rizzo, Rebecca K. Short & Scary Thrillers. LC 98-20581. (Illus.). 176p. 1998. pap. 10.95 (*0-7627-0319-9*) Globe Pequot.
Rizzo, Robert, jt. auth. see Jorajuria, Albert.
Rizzo, Sandy T., et al. Peacemaking Skills for Little Kids: Grade 1. Burke, James A., II et al, eds. (Illus.). 104p. 1997. pap. text, teacher ed. 23.95 (*1-878227-37-8*) Peace Educ.
— Peacemaking Skills for Little Kids: Student Activity Book. Burke, James A., II et al, eds. (Illus.). 56p. (Orig.). (J). (gr. 1). 1996. pap. text 2.79 (*1-878227-38-6*) Peace Educ.
Rizzo, Stephen R., Jr. & Trudeau, Michael D., eds. Clinical Administration in Audiology & Speech-Language Pathology. LC 93-25798. (Illus.). 306p. (Orig.). (C). 1993. pap. text 59.95 (*1-56593-088-6*, 0393) Thomson Learn.
Rizzo, Steve. Becoming a Humor Being: The Power to Choose a Better Way. LC 98-89961. 176p. 1999. 19.95 (*0-9669895-0-3*) Full Circle Pub.
Rizzo, Susan & Thompson, Sue. From the Heart of Harvest Cafe. (Illus.). 114p. (Orig.). 1994. pap. text 10.00 (*0-9645715-0-1*) Voyager Enter.
Rizzo, Thomas. Programming Microsoft Outlook & Microsoft Exchange, 1. LC 99-13555. (Illus.). 684p. 1999. pap. 49.99 (*0-7356-0509-2*) Microsoft.
— Speaking with Impact: T. A. R. G. E. T. Viewpoint. LC 94-72879. 144p. 1994. pap. text, per. 19.95 (*0-7872-0261-4*) Kendall-Hunt.
Rizzo, Thomas A. Friendship Development among Children in School. Wallat, Cynthia, ed. LC 88-24053. (Language & Learning for Human Service Professions Ser.: Vol. 6). 208p. (C). 1988. pap. 39.50 (*0-89391-548-3*); text 73.25 (*0-89391-503-3*) Ablx Pub.
Rizzo, Thomas R., jt. ed. see Myers, Anne B.
Rizzo, Tony. Rizzo's Unofficial Dictionary of the Disney Language. pap. 29.95 (*0-9701318-0-1*) A M Rizzo.
Rizzo, Tracey, jt. auth. see Mason, Laura.
Rizzoli, P. M. Botany Dictionary: Dizionario Di Botanica. (ITA.). 528p. 1984. 75.00 (*0-8288-1245-4*, M15663) Fr & Eur.
***Rizzoli, Renato.** Representation & Ideology in Jacobean Drama: The Politics of the Coup de Theatre. LC 99-38360. (Salzburg Studies in English Literature: Vol. 104). 212p. 1999. text 89.95 (*0-7734-1253-0*) E Mellen.
Rizzoli Staff. Christian Boltanski: Advent & Other Times. 1997. 50.00 (*84-343-0819-3*, Pub. by Rizzoli Intl) St Martin.
Rizzolo, Florence. Logan County, Colorado, War Book. (Illus.). 128p. 1992. 35.00 (*0-88107-213-3*) Curtis Media.
Rizzolo, Mary A., ed. Interactive Video: Expanding Horizons in Nursing. 200p. (C). 1994. 29.95 (*0-937126-27-6*) Am Journal Nurse.
— Interactive Video: Expanding Horizons in Nursing. LC 94-72215. 199p. 1994. reprint ed. pap. 61.70 (*0-608-00804-4*, 206158100010) Bks Demand.
Rizzolo, Robert S. The Office Supply Buyer's Guide: The Smart Person's Guide to Buying the Right Items at the Right Price. (Illus.). 186p. (Orig.). 1996. pap. 14.95 (*0-9651874-0-3*); spiral bd. 14.95 (*0-9651874-1-1*) Oscan Pr.
Rizzon, Beverly. Pearl S. Buck: The Final Chapter. LC 88-7002. (Illus.). 444p. 1989. 23.95 (*0-88280-120-1*) ETC Pubns.
***Rizzon, Roberto.** Grandmother's Footsteps: A Journey in Search of Penelope Betjeman. 1999. pap. text 3.99 (*0-85953-711-0*) Childs Play.
— Hunt The Thimble. 1999. pap. text 3.99 (*0-85953-710-2*) Childs Play.
— Moving Home. 1999. pap. text 3.99 (*0-85953-712-9*) Childs Play.
— Tug of War. 1999. pap. text 3.99 (*0-85953-713-7*) Childs Play.
Rizzoni, G., et al, eds. Transportation Systems, 1992. (DSC Ser.: Vol. 44). 464p. 1992. 72.50 (*0-7918-1119-0*, G00763) ASME.
Rizzoni, Giorgio. A Practical Introduction to Electronic Instrumentation. 3rd ed. 136p. (C). 1997. spiral bd. 29.95 (*0-7872-3576-8*, 41357601) Kendall-Hunt.
— Principles & Applications of Electrical Engineering. 2nd ed. LC 95-18650. 944p. (C). 1995. text 76.50 (*0-256-17770-8*, Irwn Prfssnl) McGraw-Hill Prof.
***Rizzoni, Giorgio.** Principles & Applications of Electrical Engineering. 3rd ed. LC 99-25420. 976p. 2000. 119.27 incl. audio compact disk (*0-256-26116-4*, Irwn McGrw-H) McGrw-H Hghr Educ.
Rizzoni, Giorgio, ed. Dynamic Systems & Control Division: Proceedings, ASME International Mechanical Engineering Congress & Exposition, Dallas, TX, 1997. LC 97-76704. (DSC Ser.: Vol. 61). 766p. 1997. pap. 210.00 (*0-7918-1824-1*, TJ151) ASME Pr.
Rizzoni, Giorgio & Utkin, Vadim I. Advances in Automotive Control, 1998: A Proceedings Volume from the 2nd IFAC Workshop, Mohican State Park, Loudonville, Ohio, U. S. A., 26 February-1 March, 1998. LC 98-21863. 1998. 75.50 (*0-08-043226-3*, Pergamon Pr) Elsevier.
***Rizzotti, Martino.** Early Evolution: From the Appearance of the First Life Cell to the First Modern Organisms. LC 99-88991. (Illus.). 184p. 1999. 49.95 (*3-7643-6191-3*, Pub. by Birkhauser) Spr-Verlag.
Rizzuto, Ana-Maria. The Birth of the Living God: A Psychoanalytic Study. LC 78-10475. (Illus.). 256p. 1981. pap. text 14.00 (*0-226-72102-7*) U Ch Pr.
— Why Did Freud Reject God? A Psychoanalytic Interpretation. LC 97-49877. (Illus.). 256p. 1998. 30.00 (*0-300-07525-1*) Yale U Pr.
Rizzuto, Anthony. Camus: Love & Sexuality. LC 98-5411. 240p. 1998. 49.95 (*0-8130-1589-8*) U Press Fla.
— Camus' Imperial Vision. LC 81-1370. 160p. 1981. 16.95 (*0-8093-1002-3*) S Ill U Pr.
Rizzuto, C., jt. ed. see Giuliano, S.
Rizzuto, Charlz, tr. see Balbin, Julius.
Rizzuto, James. How to Prepare for SAT II: Mathematics Level I & IC, Level IC. 7th rev. ed. LC 95-45228. (SAT II Subject Test Preparation Manuals Ser.). 1996. pap. 12.95 (*0-8120-9529-4*) Barron.
***Rizzuto, James J.** How to Prepare for the Sat II, Mathematics Level I. 8th ed. LC 99-11433. 480p. 2000. pap. text 13.95 (*0-7641-0770-4*) Barron.
Rizzuto, Jim. Fishing Hawaii Style, Vol. 1. pap. 12.95 (*0-944462-01-4*) Hawaii Fishing News.
— Fishing Hawaii Style, Vol. 2. pap. 14.95 (*0-681-02831-9*) Booklines Hawaii.
— Fishing Hawaii Style, Vol. 3. pap. 14.95 (*0-944462-03-0*) Hawaii Fishing News.
Rizzuto, Phil. O Holy Cow. 128p. 1997. reprint ed. pap. 10.00 (*0-88001-533-0*) HarpC.
— O Holy Cow! The Selected Verse of Phil Rizzuto. Seely, Hart & Peyer, Tom, eds. LC 92-40352. 1993. pap. 8.95 (*0-88001-325-7*) HarpC.
Rizzuto, Phil & Horton, Tom. The October Twelve. 320p. 1995. 5.99 (*0-8125-3480-8*, Pub. by Forge NYC) St Martin.
— The October Twelve: The Story of the Legendary Team. 288p. 1999. pap. 14.95 (*0-312-86991-6*, Pub. by Forge NYC) St Martin.
Rizzuto, R. Why She Left Us: A Novel. 304p. 2000. pap. 13.00 (*0-06-093182-5*) HarpC.
Rizzuto, Rahna Reiko. Why She Left Us: A Novel. LC 98-54634. 304p. 1999. 24.00 (*0-06-019370-0*) HarpC.
Rizzuto, Ronald J. & Wirth, Michael O. Costs & Benefits of Municipal Cable Overbuilds: Private vs. Public Costs & Benefits & Long-Term Sustainability. 85p. 1998. pap. 27.95 (*0-9666500-0-X*) GSA Pr Inc.
Rizzuto, Shirley. Fishwife: Fish Dishes of the Pacific. pap. 11.95 (*0-681-02828-9*) Booklines Hawaii.
— Fresh Catch of the Day . . . From the Fishwife. Johnston, Chuck, ed. LC 97-74326. (Illus.). 208p. 1997. pap. 19.95 (*0-944462-07-3*) Hawaii Fishing News.
Rjndt, Philippe Van, see Van Rjndt, Philippe.
RL, Stine. Graduate Guides, 1999. (Peterson's Graduate & Professional Program Ser.). 1998. 269.70 (*0-7689-0153-7*) Petersons.
— Guide to Understanding Sexual Harassment, the Amendment with Disabilities Act & the Family & Medical Leave Act. LC 99-168311. 80p. 1998. pap. 68.95 (*0-9668710-0-6*) Indiana Busn.
— Hocus-Pocus Horror. (Give Yourself Goosebumps Ser.: No. 35). 1999. pap. text 3.99 (*0-590-51673-6*) Scholastic Inc.
— Kristy at Bat. (Baby-Sitters Club Ser.: No. 129). 160p. (J). (gr. 3-7). 1999. pap. text 4.50 (*0-590-50352-9*) Scholastic Inc.
***RL, Stine.** Windows NT 4 Workstation for Dummies Quick Reference. 2nd ed. LC QA76.76.O63H5724. (For Dummies). 240p. 1999. spiral bd. 12.99 (*0-7645-0497-5*) IDG Bks.
***Rlegg, Arthur.** New Living, Hans Richter 1930. (Illus.). 160p. 2000. 60.00 (*3-907078-22-5*) Lars Muller.
Rlister, Paul. Digital Literacy. 276p. 1998. pap. 12.95 (*0-471-24952-1*) Wiley.
RMA Association Staff & First Manhattan Consulting Group Staff. Winning the Credit Cycle Game: Adding Shareholder Value Through Credit Portfolio Management. LC 97-50246. 1997. 395.00 (*1-57070-020-6*) Robt Morris Assocs.
RMG Consultants, Inc. Staff. Plans & Recommendations for Linking Automated Systems in Long Island Libraries. 84p. 1991. pap. 10.00 (*0-938435-21-3*) LI Lib Resources.
RMJM Staff. RMJM: A Progressive Tradition. 1999. pap. text 25.00 (*88-7838-058-X*) L'Arca IT.
RMT/Jones & Neuse, Inc. Staff. Guidelines for Safe Process Operations & Maintenance. LC 94-46233. 319p. 1995. 120.00 (*0-8169-0627-0*, G-29) Am Inst Chem Eng.
Rnad McNally Staff. Cosmopolitan World Atlas. 340p. 1996. 70.00 (*0-528-83809-1*) Rand McNally.
Ro. Surgical Pathology of the Prostate Gland. (C). 1999. text write for info. (*0-7216-6010-X*, W B Saunders Co) Harcrt Hlth Sci Grp.
Ro, Chung-Hyun. Public Administration & the Korean Transformation: Concepts, Policies, & Value Conflicts. LC 93-3592. (Library of Management for Development). (Illus.). 224p. 1993. 34.95 (*1-56549-023-1*); pap. 18.95 (*1-56549-022-3*) Kumarian Pr.
Ro, Jae Y., et al. Atlas of Surgical Pathology of the Male Reproductive Tract. Day, Lesley, ed. (Illus.). 240p. 1996. text 159.00 (*0-7216-5284-0*, W B Saunders Co) Harcrt Hlth Sci Grp.
Ro, Jung Soon, jt. auth. see Tenopir, Carol.
Ro, Ronin. Have Gun Will Travel: The Spectacular Rise & Violent Fall of Death Row Records. 384p. 1999. pap. 14.00 (*0-385-49135-2*) Doubleday.
Ro, Sigmund. Literary America: An Introduction to the Literature of the United States. 310p. (C). 1997. pap. 37.00 (*82-00-21954-2*, Pub. by Scand Univ Pr) IBD Ltd.
Ro, Young-chan. The Korean Neo-Confucianism of Yi Yulgok. LC 87-12172. (SUNY Series in Philosophy). 154p. (C). 1988. pap. text 21.95 (*0-88706-656-9*) State U NY Pr.
Ro, Young-chan. The Korean Neo-Confucianism of Yi Yulgok. LC 87-12172. (SUNY Series in Philosophy). 154p. (C). 1988. text 64.50 (*0-88706-655-0*) State U NY Pr.
***Roa, Alberto Saldarriaga.** Casa Republicana: Columbia's Belle Epoque. (Illus.). 260p. 2000. 55.00 (*958-9393-07-1*) Villegas Ed.
Roa, Anthony. Favorite Animals Masks: Six Punch-Out Designs. (Illus.). (J). (gr. k-3). 1993. pap. 2.95 (*0-486-27654-6*) Dover.
— Wild Animals Masks: Six Punch-Out Designs. (Illus.). (J). (gr. k-3). 1993. pap. 4.95 (*0-486-27653-8*) Dover.
Roa Bastos, Augusto. Hijo de Hombre - Son of Man. (SPA., Illus.). 320p. 1996. pap. 12.95 (*0-14-026083-8*, Penguin Bks) Viking Penguin.
— Son of Man. (Voices of Resistance Ser.). 288p. 1988. 24.00 (*0-85345-767-0*, Pub. by Monthly Rev); pap. 13.00 (*0-85345-733-6*, Pub. by Monthly Rev) NYU Pr.
Roa, Michael. Environmental Science Activities Kit: Lessons, Labs, & Worksheets for Secondary Students. LC 93-12227. (Illus.). 352p. 1993. spiral bd. 29.95 (*0-87628-304-0*) Ctr Appl Res.
Roa, Michael & Tinkelenberg, Donnell. Biology Teacher's Instant Vocabulary Kit with Ready to Use Crossword Puzzles & Word Searches. 368p. 1990. pap. text 29.95 (*0-13-083841-1*) P-H.
***Roa, Mohan & World Bank Staff.** Disinvesting in Health: The World Bank's Prescriptions for Health. LC 99-26781. 1999. write for info. (*0-7619-9348-7*) Sage.
Roa, S., et al, eds. Global Infrastructure Evolution. LC 96-77951. 700p. (gr. 12). 1996. 106.00 (*90-5199-290-4*, 290-4) IOS Press.
Roach. Evolution Equations. 1995. lib. bdg. 79.95 (*0-582-24669-5*, Pub. by Addison-Wesley) Longman.
Roach. Health Risks & Hazardous Substances at Work. 558p. 1992. text 173.00 (*0-08-040837-0*, Pergamon Pr) Elsevier.
Roach & Leddy. Basic College Chemistry. 2nd ed. (C). 1991. pap. text 37.40 (*0-536-58063-4*) Pearson Custom.
Roach & Williams. Troubleshooting Grammar Problems in Writing. 2nd ed. 264p. 1995. per. 25.95 (*0-8403-7337-6*) Kendall-Hunt.
Roach, Alfred J. Fire in My Belly. LC 98-231212. 224p. 1998. write for info. (*0-86327-678-4*) Wolfhound Press.
Roach, Abby M. Some Successful Marriages. LC 76-152956. (Short Story Index Reprint Ser.). (Illus.). 1977. reprint ed. 21.95 (*0-8369-3871-2*) Ayer.
Roach, Alicia. The Sexy Book. LC 98-24681. 280p. 1999. 15.95 (*1-58141-001-8*) Rivercross Pub.
Roach, Catharyn & Moore, JoAnne. Teaching Library Skills in Grades K Through 6: A How-to-Do-It Manual. (How-to-Do-It Ser.). 157p. 1993. 38.50 (*1-55570-126-4*) Neal-Schuman.
Roach, Clyde E. Confessions of an Airline Pilot. 160p. 1998. pap. 16.95 (*1-878853-67-8*) Venture Pr FL.
Roach, Colleen, ed. Communication & Culture in War & Peace. (Communication & Human Values Ser.: Vol. 11). (Illus.). 216p. (C). 1993. text 52.00 (*0-8039-5062-4*); pap. text 24.95 (*0-8039-5063-2*) Sage.
Roach, Donald B. & Beck, F. H. Performance & Reliability of Corrosion-Resistant Alloy Castings: Phase I, Causes of Unsatisfactory Performance. LC TA0462.R54. (MTI Manual Ser.: No. 5). (Illus.). 137p. 1981. reprint ed. pap. 42.50 (*0-608-06694-X*, 206689100009) Bks Demand.
— Performance & Reliability of Corrosion-Resistant Alloy Castings: Phase II, Casting Discontinuities. LC TA0479.S7R63. (MTI Manual Ser.: No. 6). (Illus.). 209p. 1981. reprint ed. pap. 64.80 (*0-608-06693-1*, 206689000009) Bks Demand.
Roach, Donald W. Complete Secondary Choral Music Guide. LC 89-48386. 320p. (C). 1990. pap. text 37.95 (*0-13-162538-1*) P-H.
Roach, Dudley, intro. National Conference on Bulk Materials Handling, 1993. (National Conference Publication Ser.: No. 93-8). (Illus.). 279p. (Orig.). 1993. pap. text 72.00 (*0-85825-578-2*, Pub. by Inst Engrs Aust-EA Bks) Accents Pubns.
Roach, E. S., et al. Sturge-Weber Syndrome. (Illus.). 175p. 1999. write for info. (*0-9670484-0-0*) Sturge Weber.
Roach, Eloise, tr. see Jimenez, Juan Ramon.
Roach, Emma, ed. The Gramophone Film Music Good CD Guide. 256p. (Orig.). 1996. pap. 15.95 (*0-902470-74-4*, GG 19963, Pub. by Gramophone) Music Sales.
Roach, G. Aspects of Nonlinear Scattering Theory. LC 93-19958. (Pitman Monographs & Surveys in Pure & Applied Mathematics). 1996. 70.00 (*0-582-09230-2*, Pub. by Addison-Wesley) Longman.
Roach, Gary, et al. Pro-Mo's Secrets for Finding Walleyes. (Illus.). 112p. (Orig.). 1988. pap. write for info. (*0-318-64036-8*) Fishing Pro-Mos Inc.
— Pro-Mo's Secrets to Jigging Walleyes. (Illus.). 112p. (Orig.). 1988. pap. write for info. (*0-318-64037-6*) Fishing Pro-Mos Inc.
— Pro-Mo's Secrets to Rigging Walleyes. (Illus.). 112p. (Orig.). 1988. pap. write for info. (*0-318-64035-X*) Fishing Pro-Mos Inc.
Roach, Gary F. Inverse Problems & Imaging. LC 90-49351. (Pitman Research Notes in Mathematics Ser.: Vol. 245). 279p. 1991. reprint ed. pap. 86.50 (*0-608-03625-0*, 206445200009) Bks Demand.
Roach, Geraldine. The Bullmastiff: Peerless Protector. LC 98-12385. 256p. 1998. 27.95 (*0-87605-081-X*) Howell Bks.
Roach, Gerry. Colorado's Fourteeners: From Hikes to Climbs. 2nd rev. ed. LC 98-50301. (Illus.). 4p. (Orig.). 1999. pap. 18.95 (*1-55591-412-8*) Fulcrum Pub.
— Colorado's Fourteeners: From Hikes to Climbs, Companion Map Package. 54p. 1999. pap. 14.95 (*1-55591-431-4*) Fulcrum Pub.
— Colorado's Indian Peaks Wilderness Areas. 2nd rev. ed. LC 97-49102. 1998. pap. 16.95 (*1-55591-404-7*) Fulcrum Pub.
— Rocky Mountain National Park: Classic Hikes & Climbs. LC 88-16307. (Fulcrum's Guide Ser.). 272p. 1988. pap. 14.95 (*1-55591-033-5*) Fulcrum Pub.
Roach, Hannah B. Taxables in the City of Philadelphia. (Special Publications: No. 4). 41p. 1990. reprint ed. pap. 6.00 (*1-887099-03-4*) Geneal Soc Pa.
Roach, Hannah B., compiled by. The Pennsylvania Militia in 1777. (Special Publications: No. 1). 80p. 1994. reprint ed. pap. 5.00 (*1-887099-00-X*) Geneal Soc Pa.
Roach, Harry. Gettysburg: Hour-by-Hour. (Illus.). 72p. (C). 1993. pap. text 7.95 (*0-939631-50-4*) Thomas Publications.
Roach, Helen P. History of Speech Education at Columbia College, 1754-1940. LC 70-177194. (Columbia University. Teachers College. Contributions to Education Ser.: No. 963). reprint ed. 37.50 (*0-404-55963-8*) AMS Pr.
***Roach, Hesta.** First Grade Again. (Illus.). 22p. 1998. pap. 7.95 (*0-9660583-1-3*) Sakura Pr.
Roach-Higgins, Mary E., et al. Dress & Identity. LC 94-61223. 511p. 1995. pap. 45.00 (*1-56367-057-7*) Fairchild.
Roach, Hildred. Black American Music. 2nd ed. 390p. 1994. reprint ed. 46.50 (*0-89464-870-5*) Krieger.
— Black American Music: Past & Present. 2nd ed. LC 82-25860. 390p. (C). 1992. 52.50 (*0-89464-580-3*) Krieger.
Roach, J. Ashley & Smith, Robert W. United States Responses to Excessive Maritime Claims. 2nd ed. LC 96-14669. 1996. lib. bdg. 174.00 (*90-411-0225-6*, Pub. by M Nijhoff) Kluwer Academic.
Roach, J. Michael. 10 Minute Guide to Microsoft Internet Explorer. LC 95-71044. (Illus.). 191p. (Orig.). 1995. 14.99 (*0-7897-0628-8*) Que.
Roach, Jerry V. The Gathering Storm. (Illus.). 288p. (Orig.). 1994. pap. 16.95 (*0-943639-20-4*) Anchor Pub Co.
— God's Healing Touch: The Natural & the Supernatural. Roach, Linda, ed. LC 96-84391. 160p. (Orig.). 1996. pap. 10.00 (*1-889281-00-X*) Faith Teaching.
— A New & Living Way. (Illus.). 123p. (Orig.). 1993. pap. text 11.95 (*0-943639-16-6*) Anchor Pub Co.
Roach, John. A Regional Study of Yorkshire Schools, 1500-1820. LC 98-30871. (Studies in Education: Vol. 39). 372p. 1998. text 99.95 (*0-7734-8250-4*) E Mellen.
— Surprizing Adventures of John Roach, Mariner of Whitehaven. 2nd ed. 864p. 1986. reprint ed. pap. 8.00 (*0-913129-14-3*) La Tienda.
Roach, John, ed. A Bibliography of Modern History. LC 67-11528. 412p. reprint ed. pap. 117.50 (*0-8357-7197-0*, 2051466) Bks Demand.
Roach, John C. Williamsburg: An Artist's Sketchbook. (Illus.). 80p. 1998. pap. write for info. (*1-884824-05-6*) Tryon Pubng.
Roach, John P., Jr. San Diego Trolley Guide. (Illus.). 124p. 1998. pap. 9.95 (*0-9662910-0-X*) Advant Publ CA.
Roach, Joseph. Cities of the Dead: Circum-Atlantic Performance. (Social Foundations of Aesthetic Forms Ser.). (Illus.). 328p. 1996. 55.00 (*0-231-10460-X*); pap. 18.50 (*0-231-10461-8*) Col U Pr.
Roach, Joseph R. The Player's Passion: Studies in the Science of Acting. LC 84-40059. (Illus.). 256p. 1986. 38.50 (*0-87413-265-7*) U Delaware Pr.
— The Player's Passion: Studies in the Science of Acting. (Theater & Dramatic Studies). 256p. (C). 1993. reprint ed. pap. text 17.95 (*0-472-08244-2*, 08244) U of Mich Pr.
Roach, Joseph R., jt. ed. see Reinelt, Janelle G.
Roach, Joyce G. C. L. Sonnichsen. LC 79-53653. (Western Writers Ser.: No. 40). (Illus.). 48p. (Orig.). 1979. pap. 4.95 (*0-88430-064-1*) Boise St U W Writ Ser.
— The Cowgirls. rev. ed. LC 90-39339. (Illus.). 282p. 1990. reprint ed. pap. 16.95 (*0-929398-15-7*) UNTX Pr.
Roach, Joyce G., ed. Collective Heart: Texans in WW II. LC 96-16139. (Illus.). 232p. (Orig.). 1996. pap. 15.95 (*1-57168-023-3*, Eakin Pr) Sunbelt Media.
— This Place of Memory: A Texas Perspective. LC 92-6890. (Illus.). 161p. (Orig.). 1992. pap. 8.95 (*0-929398-32-7*) UNTX Pr.
***Roach, Kent.** Criminal Law. 2nd ed. (Essentials of Canadian Law Ser.). xvi, 366p. 2000. pap. 31.95 (*1-55221-041-3*, Pub. by Irwin Law) Gaunt.
Roach, Kent. Due Process & Victims' Rights: The New Law & Politics of Criminal Justice. 416p. 1999. text 55.00 (*0-8020-0931-X*); pap. text 19.95 (*0-8020-7901-6*) U of Toronto Pr.
Roach, Lee S., jt. auth. see Ludwig, William B.

An Asterisk (*) at the beginning of an entry indicates that the title is appearing for the first time.

Roach, Linda, ed. see Roach, Jerry V.

Roach, M. Simone, ed. Caring from the Heart: The Convergence of Caring & Spirituality. LC 97-12485. 224p. (Orig.). 1997. pap. 14.95 (*0-8091-3717-8*) Paulist Pr.

Roach, Margaret. A Way to Garden: A Hands-On Primer for Every Season. LC 97-13997. 1998. 35.00 (*0-517-70733-0*) C Potter.

Roach, Margaret, ed. The Natural Lawn & Alternatives. (Illus.). 96p. 1993. pap. 7.95 (*0-945352-80-8*) Bklyn Botanic.

Roach, Margaret, jt. auth. see Druse, Ken.

Roach, Margaret, ed. see Druse, Ken.

Roach, Margaret J. I Love You, Charles Henry: Cats & Dogs in My Life. Moore, Susan J. & Craft, Page, eds. (Illus.). (J). (gr. 1-6). 1994. pap. 13.50 (*1-882666-02-X*) M Roach & Assocs.

— Mac & His Dog, Sir John.Tr. of Mac y Su Perro, Don Juan. (SPA., Illus.). (Orig.). (J). (gr. k-8). 1993. pap. 13.50 (*1-882666-01-1*); pap. 13.50 (*1-882666-00-3*) M Roach & Assocs.

— Mac & His Dog, Sir John.Tr. of Mac y Su Perro, Don Juan. (ITA., Illus.). (Orig.). (J). (ps-8). 1996. pap. 15.00 (*1-882666-03-8*) M Roach & Assocs.

Roach, Marilynne K. Encounters with the Invisible World: Being Ten Tales of Ghosts, Witches, & the Devil Himself in New England. LC 76-22186. (Illus.). (J). (gr. 5-9). 1977. 12.95 (*0-690-01277-2*) HarpC Child Bks.

— Encounters with the Invisible World Being Ten Tales of Ghosts, Witches & the Devil Himself in New England. 18.95 (*0-89190-874-9*) Amereon Ltd.

— In the Days of the Salem Witchcraft Trials. LC 94-32383. (Illus.). 96p. (YA). (gr. 5 up). 1996. 15.00 (*0-395-69704-2*, Pub. by Ticknor & Fields) HM.

Roach, Martin. The Prodigy: The Fat of the Land. (Illus.). 128p. (C). 1997. pap. 24.95 (*1-897783-12-4*, MR 55645, Pub. by Indep Music Pr) Music Sales.

***Roach, Michael.** The Diamond Cutter: The Buddha on Strategies for Managing Your Business & Your Life. LC 99-53059. 288p. 2000. 21.95 (*0-385-49790-3*) Doubleday.

— The Garden: A Parable. LC 99-46051. 208p. 2000. pap. 9.95 (*0-385-49789-X*, Image Bks) Doubleday.

Roach, Michael, tr. see Tsongkapa.

Roach, Michael T. Red Brigades. 312p. mass mkt. 4.99 (*1-55197-345-6*) Picasso Publ.

Roach, Paul, ed. see Castro, Fred.

Roach, Penelope. Political Socialization in the New Nations of Africa. LC 66-24873. (Columbia University, Center for Education in Asia, Publications). 41p. reprint ed. pap. 30.00 (*0-608-14831-8*, 202605800048) Bks Demand.

Roach, Peter. The Complete Book of Pet Care. (Illus.). 272p. 1995. 17.95 (*0-87605-484-X*) Howell Bks.

***Roach, Robert C., et al.** Hypoxia: Into the Next Millennium. LC 99-47777. (Advances in Experimental Medicine & Biology Ser.). 1999. write for info. (*0-306-46289-3*, Kluwer Plenum) Kluwer Academic.

Roach, Robert C., jt. ed. see Wood, Stephen C.

Roach, Ronald Russell. Armageddon Quest, Vol. 1. (Illus.). 296p. 1997. pap. 13.00 (*1-57989-006-7*) Sirius Ent.

— Armageddon Quest, Vol. 2. (Illus.). 304p. 1997. pap. 13.00 (*1-57989-007-5*) Sirius Ent.

— Armageddon Quest, Vol. 3. (Illus.). 296p. 1997. pap. 13.00 (*1-57989-008-3*) Sirius Ent.

Roach, Sally. Introductory Clinical Pharmacology. 5th ed. 224p. 1995. pap. text, student ed. 15.95 (*0-397-55246-7*) Lppncott W & W.

Roach, Sally S. Introductory Gerontological Nursing. 352p. pap. text 24.95 (*0-397-55479-6*) Lppncott W & W.

— Study Guide to Accompany Introductory Clinical Pharmacology. 6th ed. 256p. pap. text 15.95 (*0-7817-1751-5*) Lppncott W & W.

Roach, Sally S. & Nieto, Beatriz C. Healing & the Grief Process. LC 96-576. 240p. 1996. mass mkt. 21.95 (*0-8273-6968-9*) Delmar.

Roach, Sarah F. Libellus Fabularum Latinarum. 200p. 1997. 49.00 (*0-7618-0866-3*); pap. 29.50 (*0-7618-0867-1*) U Pr of Amer.

Roach, Susan. Bread Dough Creations. (Illus.). 68p. 1994. pap. 7.95 (*1-86351-102-4*, Pub. by Sally Milner) Sterling.

***Roach, Susan.** On My Way: The Arts of Sarah Albritton. LC 98-67413. (Illus.). 96p. 1998. pap. 15.00 (*1-57806-114-8*) U Pr of Miss.

Roach, Terrlyn R. & Williams, Dewilda M. What Makes Me Happy? (Byrant Series). (Illus.). 16p. (J). (gr. k-2). 1996. 10.95 (*1-886493-03-0*) NBC Study Pub.

Roach, Thomas R. Newsprint: Canadian Supply & American Demand. LC 94-6940. (Issues Ser.). viii, 56p. 1994. pap. 6.95 (*0-89030-050-X*) Forest Hist Soc.

Roach, Thomas R., jt. auth. see Gillis, Peter.

Roach, Virginia, et al. State Accountability Systems & Students with Disabilities. 2nd ed. 16p. 1997. pap. 7.00 (*1-58434-035-5*) NASBE.

— State Reforms in Teacher Preparation, Licensure, & Professional Development. 2nd ed. 24p. 1996. pap. 7.50 (*1-58434-027-4*) NASBE.

— Winning Ways: Creating Inclusive Schools, Classrooms, & Communities. 2nd ed. 48p. 1995. pap. 12.00 (*1-58434-005-3*) NASBE.

Roach, Virginia, jt. auth. see Raber, Suzanne.

Roach, William, ed. Continuations of the Old French Perceval of Chretien De Troyes - The First Continuation Vol. 1: Redaction of Manuscripts TVD. 1949. 12.00 (*0-87169-999-0*) Am Philos.

Roach, William, ed. Continuations of the Old French Perceval of Chretien De Troyes - The First Continuation Vol. 3, Pt. 1: Redaction of Manuscripts ALPRS. 1952. 12.00 (*0-87169-997-4*, AP3A-ROW) Am Philos.

Roach, William, ed. Continuations of the Old French Perceval of Chretien De Troyes - The Second Continuation, Vol. 4. 1971. 15.00 (*0-87169-995-8*) Am Philos.

Roach, William, ed. Continuations of the Old French Perceval of Chretien De Troyes - The Third Continuation, Vol. 5. LC 49-10414. 1983. 40.00 (*0-87169-994-X*, AP50-ROW) Am Philos.

Roach, William & Foulet, Lucien, eds. Continuations of the Old French Perceval of Chretien De Troyes - The First Continuation Vol. 3, Pt. 2: Glossary to Vols. 1-3. 1955. 10.00 (*0-87169-996-6*) Am Philos.

Roach, William & Ivy, Robert H., Jr., eds. Continuations of the Old French Perceval of Chretien De Troyes - The First Continuation Vol. 2: Redaction of Manuscripts EMQU. 1950. 12.00 (*0-87169-998-2*, AP20-ROW) Am Philos.

Roache, Catharine S. Old Children of God. (Illus.). 16p. 1973. 2.00 (*0-913478-00-8*) Hermosa.

— What Are Forests For? 44p. 1971. 2.00 (*0-913478-01-6*) Hermosa.

Roache, James. New Jerusalem. 217p. (Orig.). 1998. pap. 9.95 (*1-891929-00-3*, Manatee Publng) Four Seasons.

Roache, James D. Five-Eighty-Worst. 167p. 1997. pap. 8.95 (*0-9656811-0-6*) Four Seasons.

— Windsong. 317p. (Orig.). 1997. pap. 9.95 (*1-891929-02-X*) Four Seasons.

Roache, L. D., tr. see Plattard, Jean.

Roache, Patrick J. Computational Fluid Dynamics. rev. ed. vii, 446p. 1976. 26.50 (*0-913478-05-9*) Hermosa.

— Elliptic Marching Methods & Domain Decomposition. LC 95-18775. (Symbolic & Numeric Computation Ser.). 208p. 1995. boxed set 94.95 (*0-8493-7378-6*, 7378) CRC Pr.

— Fundamentals of Computational Fluids Dynamics. LC 98-96546. 13p. 1998. text 78.50 (*0-913478-09-1*) Hermosa.

— Verification & Validation in Computational Science & Engineering. LC 98-96214. xvi, 446p. 1998. text 88.50 (*0-913478-08-3*) Hermosa.

Roache, Patrick J., jt. auth. see Stweart-Roache, Catherine.

Roache-Selk, Evelyn. From the Womb of Earth: An Appreciation of Yoruba Bronze Art. LC 78-56919. (Illus.). 1978. pap. text 15.00 (*0-8191-0521-X*) U Pr of Amer.

Roadarmel, Paul. Beach House Seven. 320p. 1988. pap. 4.50 (*0-373-97077-3*) Harlequin Bks.

***Roadifer, Greg.** The Golden Guru: 10 Spiritually Based Principles to Success, Fulfillment & Wealth. (Illus.). 160p. 2000. pap. 14.95 (*0-9700414-3-8*, 101) GoldenHouse.

Roads & Transportation Association of Canada, Proj. Guide to Bridge Hydraulics. Neill, C. R., ed. LC 72-95811. 203p. reprint ed. pap. 63.00 (*0-608-16699-5*, 205611700050) Bks Demand.

Roads, C. H. The British Soldiers Firearm, 1850-1864. (Illus.). 336p. 1994. reprint ed. 53.00 (*1-884849-13-X*) R&R Bks.

Roads, Curtis, ed. The Music Machine: Selected Readings from Computer Music Journal. (Illus.). 740p. 1992. reprint ed. pap. text 35.00 (*0-262-68078-5*) MIT Pr.

Roads, Curtis, et al, eds. Musical Signal Processing. LC 97-2598. (Studies on New Music Research). 480p. 1997. pap. 39.00 (*90-265-1483-2*) Swets.

— Musical Signal Processing. LC 97-2598. (Studies on New Music Research). 480p. 1997. 99.00 (*90-265-1482-4*) Swets.

Roads, Curtis, et al. The Computer Music Tutorial. LC 94-19027. 1234p. 1996. pap. text 58.00 (*0-262-68082-3*) MIT Pr.

Roads, Michael J. Getting There. LC 98-71593. 376p. 1998. pap. 12.95 (*1-57174-104-6*) Hampton Roads Pub Co.

— Into a Timeless Realm: A Metaphysical Adventure. LC 95-21211. 276p. 1996. pap. 11.95 (*0-915811-66-9*) H J Kramer Inc.

— Journey into Nature: A Spiritual Adventure. Lipsett, Suzanne, ed. LC 89-80727. 228p. 1990. pap. 10.95 (*0-915811-19-7*) H J Kramer Inc.

— Journey into Oneness: A Spiritual Odyssey. Carleton, Nancy, ed. LC 93-38394. 252p. 1994. pap. 10.95 (*0-915811-54-5*) H J Kramer Inc.

— Talking with Nature: Sharing the Energies & Spirit of Trees, Plants, Birds & Earth. Armstrong, Gregory, ed. (Illus.). 156p. (Orig.). 1987. pap. 9.95 (*0-915811-06-5*) H J Kramer Inc.

Roads, Samuel, Jr. The History & Traditions of Marblehead. rev. ed. (Illus.). 595p. 1989. reprint ed. lib. bdg. 60.00 (*0-8328-0842-3*, MA0111) Higginson Bk Co.

Roadstrum, William H. Being Successful As an Engineer. LC 77-27435. 246p. (C). 1988. pap. text 16.95 (*0-910554-24-2*) Engineering.

Roadstrum, William H. & Wolaver, Dan H. Electrical Engineering: For All Engineers. 2nd ed. 736p. 1993. text 100.95 (*0-471-51043-2*) Wiley.

Roadway Committee. American National Standards Practice for Tunnel Lighting ANSI Approved: RP-22-96. rev. ed. (Recommended Practices Ser.). (Illus.). 31p. 1996. pap. 28.00 (*0-87995-130-3*, RP-22-96) Illum Eng.

Roaf, Caroline & Bines, Hazel, eds. Needs, Rights & Opportunities. (Education & Alienation Ser.). 250p. 1989. 65.00 (*1-85000-516-8*, Falmer Pr) Taylor & Francis.

Roaf, John, jt. auth. see Kalman, Harold D.

Roaf, Michael. Cultural Atlas of Mesopotamia & the Ancient Near East. Postgate, Nicholas, ed. (Cultural Atlas Ser.). (Illus.). 240p. 1990. 45.00 (*0-8160-2218-6*) Facts on File.

Roah, Kathy, ed. see Hilbert, Donna, et al.

Roake, Margaret. Essays in Kentish History. Whyman, John, ed. (Illus.). 315p. 1973. 30.00 (*0-7146-2956-1*, Pub. by F Cass Pubs) Intl Spec Bk.

Roakes, Susan L. & Zwolinski, Marie. The Land Trust As a Conservation Tool. LC 95-32068. (CPL Bibliographies Ser.: Vol. 323). 25p. 1995. pap. 10.00 (*0-86602-323-2*, Sage Prdcls Pr) Sage.

Roalf, Peggy. American Vision of Painting. 256p. (J). lib. bdg. write for info. (*0-7868-2099-3*) Hyperion.

Roalf, Peggy. Cats. (Looking at Paintings Ser.). 1992. 12.15 (*0-606-05441-3*, Pub. by Turtleback) Demco.

— Cats: Looking at Paintings. LC 91-73829. (Looking at Paintings Ser.). (Illus.). 48p. (J). (gr. 3-7). 1992. pap. 6.95 (*1-56282-091-5*, Pub. by Hyprn Child) Little.

— Circus: Looking at Paintings. LC 92-52983. (Looking at Paintings Ser.). (Illus.). 48p. (J). (gr. 3-7). 1993. pap. 6.95 (*1-56282-305-1*, Pub. by Hyprn Child) Time Warner.

— Dancers. (Looking at Paintings Ser.). (J). 1992. 12.15 (*0-606-05442-1*, Pub. by Turtleback) Demco.

— Dancers: Looking at Paintings. LC 91-73827. (Looking at Paintings Ser.). (Illus.). 64p. (J). (gr. 3-7). 1992. pap. 6.95 (*1-56282-089-3*, Pub. by Hyprn Child) Time Warner.

— Dogs. LC 93-10585. (Looking at Paintings Ser.). (Illus.). 48p. (J). (gr. 3-7). 1993. pap. 6.95 (*1-56282-530-5*, Pub. by Hyprn Child) Little.

— Dogs. (Looking at Paintings Ser.). (J). 1993. 12.15 (*0-606-05912-1*, Pub. by Turtleback) Demco.

— Flowers. LC 92-72015. (Looking at Paintings Ser.). (Illus.). 48p. (J). (gr. 3-7). 1993. pap. 6.95 (*1-56282-358-2*, Pub. by Hyprn Child) Time Warner.

— Flowers. (Looking at Paintings Ser.). (J). 1993. 12.15 (*0-606-05443-X*, Pub. by Turtleback) Demco.

— Horses. LC 92-52979. (Looking at Paintings Ser.). (Illus.). 64p. (J). (gr. 3-7). 1992. pap. 6.95 (*1-56282-307-8*, Pub. by Hyprn Child); lib. bdg. 14.89 (*1-56282-306-X*, Pub. by Hyprn Child) Little.

— Landscapes. LC 92-52980. (Looking at Paintings Ser.). (Illus.). 48p. (J). (gr. 3-7). 1992. lib. bdg. 14.89 (*1-56282-302-7*, Pub. by Hyprn Child) Little.

— Musicians. (Looking at Paintings Ser.). (J). 1993. 11.90 (*0-606-05911-3*, Pub. by Turtleback) Demco.

— Seascapes. LC 91-73828. (Looking at Paintings Ser.). (Illus.). 64p. (J). (gr. 3-7). 1992. pap. 6.95 (*1-56282-093-1*, Pub. by Hyprn Child) Time Warner.

— Self-Portraits. LC 92-72042. (Looking at Paintings Ser.). 1993. 12.15 (*0-606-05440-5*, Pub. by Turtleback) Demco.

Roalfe, William R., ed. How to Find the Law: With Special Chapters on Legal Writing. 6th ed. 313p. 1996. reprint ed. 98.00 (*1-56169-231-X*) Gaunt.

Roalman, Arthur R. Investor Relations That Work. LC 80-65707. 287p. reprint ed. pap. 89.00 (*0-608-11961-X*, 202350400033) Bks Demand.

Roalman, Arthur R., ed. Investor Relations Handbook. LC 73-85192. vi, 234 p. 1974. pap. 19.95 (*0-8144-5349-X*) AMACOM.

Roalson, Louise. Notably Norwegian: Recipes, Festivals, Folk Arts. LC 82-81569. (Illus.). 88p. 1982. pap. 8.95 (*0-941016-05-6*) Penfield.

***Roame, Anthony.** FreeHand 9 Authorized. 2nd ed. (Macromedia Press Authorized Ser.). 512p. 2000. pap. 39.99 incl. cd-rom (*0-201-70034-4*) Addison-Wesley.

Roan, jt. auth. see Kaiser.

Roan, Carol. Clues to American Dance. LC 93-18775. (Clues to American Arts Ser.). (Illus.). 80p. (Orig.). 1993. pap. 7.95 (*0-913515-83-3*, Starrhill Press) Black Belt Communs.

— Speak Easy: A Guide to Successful Performances, Presentations, Speeches, & Lectures. 96p. (Orig.). 1995. pap. 8.95 (*1-57359-000-2*, Starrhill Press) Black Belt Communs.

Roan, Carole E., jt. auth. see Buddin, Richard.

Roan, Donald, jt. auth. see Roan, Nancy.

Roan, N. & Gehret, E., eds. Goschenhoppen Historians Folk Festival Recipes. 72p. 1971. pap. 5.00 (*1-883801-01-X*) Goschenhopn Hist.

Roan, Nancy & Gehret, Ellen J. Just a Quilt: "Juscht en Deppich" A Folk Cultural Study. (Illus.). 40p. 1984. pap. 5.00 (*1-883801-00-1*) Goschenhopn Hist.

Roan, Nancy & Roan, Donald. Lest I Shall Be Forgotten: Anecdotes & Traditions of Quilts. LC 93-78780. (Illus.). 96p. 1993. per. 10.00 (*1-883801-02-8*) Goschenhopn Hist.

***Roan, Shari.** Our Daughters' Health: Practical & Invaluable Advice for Raising Confident Girls Ages 6-16. 2001. pap. 14.95 (*0-7868-8500-9*, Pub. by Disney Pr) Time Warner.

Roan, Sharon. Ozone Crisis: The Fifteen Year Evolution of a Sudden Global Emergency. 270p. 1990. pap. 9.95 (*0-471-52823-4*) Wiley.

— Postpartum Depression. 1993. write for info. (*0-471-54678-X*) Wiley.

Roane, Martha K., jt. ed. see Coyier, Duane L.

RoAne, Susan. How to Work a Room. 224p. 1989. mass mkt. 13.95 (*0-446-39065-8*, Pub. by Warner Bks) Little.

***RoAne, Susan.** How to Work a Room: Learn the Strategies of Savvy Socializing - For Business & Personal Success. rev. ed. 224p. 2000. pap. 11.99 (*0-446-67646-2*) Warner Bks.

— How to Work a Room: The Ultimate Guide to Savvy Socializing in Person & Online. 2000. pap. 14.00 (*0-06-095785-9*, Quil) HarperTrade.

RoAne, Susan. The Secrets of Savvy Networking: How to Make the Best Connections for Business & Personal Success. 224p. (Orig.). 1993. mass mkt. 13.99 (*0-446-39410-6*, Pub. by Warner Bks) Little.

— What Do I Say Next? Talking Your Way to Business & Social Success. 288p. 1999. mass mkt. 14.00 (*0-446-67426-5*, Pub. by Warner Bks) Little.

***Roanhaus, Arlene.** Threads of Memories: My Tragic but Fascinating Life. 470p. 1999. pap. text 16.95 (*0-7392-0451-3*, P-03749) Morris Pubng.

Roankin, Myron, ed. & intro. see Wolkinson, Benjamin W. & Block, Richard N.

Roanoke Bar Asssociation Staff, jt. auth. see Virginia Law Foundation Committee on Continuing Le.

***Roantree, M., et al, eds.** Engineering Federated Information Systems: Proceedings of the 3rd Workshop (EFIS 2000) June 19 - 20, 2000, Dublin (Ireland) 114p. 2000. pap. 42.00 (*1-58603-075-2*) IOS Press.

Roantree, T. C. Non-Metallic Material, What Part Will It Play in the Future of the Gear Industry? (AGMA Technical Paper: Vol. P72). (Illus.). 9p. 1928. pap. text 30.00 (*1-55589-319-8*) AGMA.

Roaring, Elena D. Upgrading Technological Capabilities of Small Industry. 168p. 1991. pap. text 15.00 (*92-833-2107-3*, 321073) Productivity Inc.

***Roark.** American Promise Compact. 1999. pap. text 42.95 (*0-312-19206-1*) St Martin.

— American Promotional Combination Mapworkbook, Vol. 1 & 2. 1997. pap. text 48.00 (*0-312-18454-9*) St Martin.

Roark. Sampler of American Promise. Date not set. pap. text. write for info. (*0-312-15722-3*) St Martin.

***Roark, Candice.** Adolescent God. LC 99-97781. 96p. (YA). (gr. 8 up). 1999. pap. 8.99 (*0-9677184-0-6*) C Roark.

***Roark, Carol.** Fort Worth's Legendary Landmarks. (Illus.). 36p. 2000. boxed set 29.95 (*0-87565-211-5*, Pub. by Tex Christian) Tex A&M Univ Pr.

Roark, Carol. Fort Worth's Legendary Landmarks. (Illus.). 234p. 1997. reprint ed. pap. 19.95 (*0-87565-176-3*) Tex Christian.

Roark, Carol E., et al. Catalogue of the Amon Carter Museum Photography Collection. LC 92-36173. (Illus.). 720p. 1993. 39.95 (*0-88360-063-3*) Amon Carter.

Roark, Derrie B., ed. see Association of College & Research Libraries.

Roark, James L. American Promise. 1999. pap. text 53.95 (*0-312-19199-5*) St Martin.

— American Promise, Vol. 2. Johnson, Michael P. & Cohen, Patricia C., eds. 1997. pap. text 36.90 (*0-312-18456-5*) St Martin.

— American Promise, Vol. 2. 1999. pap. text 42.95 (*0-312-19207-X*) St Martin.

— American Promise: The Autobiography of Ben Franklin, Vol. 1. 1998. pap. text 40.05 (*0-312-20210-5*) St Martin.

— American Promise Combination Document U. S., Vols. 1 & 2. 1997. pap. text 54.00 (*0-312-18458-1*) St Martin.

— American Promise Document, Vols. 1 & 2. 1997. pap. text 36.90 (*0-312-18455-7*) St Martin.

— American Promise Map Workbook, Vol. 1. 1997. pap. text 35.00 (*0-312-18452-2*) St Martin.

— American Promise Map Workbook, Vol. 2. 1997. pap. text 35.00 (*0-312-18453-0*) St Martin.

— Masters Without Slaves. (C). 1978. pap. 14.00 (*0-393-00901-7*) Norton.

Roark, James L., jt. auth. see Johnson, Michael P.

Roark, James L., jt. ed. see Johnson, Michael P.

Roark, Kelley. The Connecticut Outdoor Activity Guide. LC 93-47044. (Outdoor Activity Guide Ser.). (Illus.). 140p. (Orig.). 1994. pap. 9.95 (*1-56626-046-9*, Cntry Rds Pr) NTC Contemp Pub Co.

— Hiking Tennessee. LC 96-32563. (Illus.). 296p. 1996. pap. 15.95 (*1-56044-394-4*) Falcon Pub Inc.

Roark, Kelley, ed. Land for Housing: Developing a Research Agenda. LC HD0205.R627. (Monograph Ser.: No. 85-3). 81p. reprint ed. pap. 30.00 (*0-7837-2172-2*, 204249700004) Bks Demand.

Roark, Kimberly. Celebrating Christmas No. 4533: Christmas Decorations. Kupperstein, Joel, ed. (Illus.). 16p. (J). (ps-2). 1999. pap. 2.99 (*1-57471-578-X*) Creat Teach Pr.

— Celebrating Valentines Day No. 4525: My Special Valentines. Kupperstein, Joel, ed. (Illus.). 16p. (J). (ps-2). 1999. pap. 2.99 (*1-57471-570-4*) Creat Teach Pr.

Roark, Laurelee, jt. auth. see Normandi, Carol Emery.

Roark, Michael. Oklahoma: A Geography. 1996. text 35.00 (*0-86531-640-6*) Westview.

— Oklahoma: A Geography. (C). 1996. pap. text 20.00 (*0-86531-641-4*) Westview.

Roark, Randolph. Awakening Osiris. (Illus.). 80p. (Orig.). (C). 1996. pap. 8.00 (*1-882775-07-4*) Selva Edit.

***Roark, Randy.** Hymns. (Illus.). 24p. 2000. pap. 5.00 (*1-880743-15-9*, Pub. by Dead Metaphor) SPD-Small Pr Dist.

Roark, Sarah & Shomshak, Dean. The Time of Thin Blood. (Vampire Ser.). (Illus.). 120p. 1999. pap. 15.95 (*1-56504-245-X*, 2101) White Wolf.

***Roark, Thelma.** What Made the Difference? LC 99-63245. 1999. pap. 7.99 (*1-57921-187-9*) WinePress Pub.

Roarke, Mike. Silent Drums, Bk. 2. (First Frontier Ser.). 1994. mass mkt. 4.99 (*0-312-95224-4*) St Martin.

Roarty, Robert S., ed. & intro. see Ruttenber, Tim.

Roast, C. R. & Siddiqi, J. I. BCS-FACS Workshop on Formal Aspects of the Human Computer Interface: Proceedings of the BCS-FACS Workshop on Formal Aspects of the Human Computer Interface, Sheffield Hallam University, 10-12 September 1996. LC 96-44415. (Electronic Workshops in Computing Ser.). 1996. pap. 59.95 (*3-540-76105-5*) Spr-Verlag.

Roast, C. R., ed. see Johnson, H. & Nigay, L. M.

Roat, John C. Class 29 UDT Seal. unabridged limited ed. Grokenberger, Anna, ed. (Illus.). 116p. 1998. 50.00 (*0-9672406-0-3*) J Roat.

***Roat, John Carl.** Class-29: The Making of U. S. Navy SEALs. 2000. mass mkt. 6.99 (*0-8041-1893-0*) Ivy Books.

Roat, Paul & Marquis, Darcy. The Insiders' Guide to Sarasota & Bradenton. 3rd ed. (Insiders' Guide Travel Ser.). (Illus.). 1996. pap. 15.99 (*1-57380-005-8*, The Insiders Guide) Falcon Pub Inc.

An Asterisk (*) at the beginning of an entry indicates that the title is appearing for the first time.

Roat, Richard. Eco Design: Environmentally Sound Packaging & Graphic Design. (Illus.). 160p. 1994. 34.99 (*1-56496-083-8*) Rockport Pubs.

Roat, Ronald C. Close Softly the Doors. (Stuart Mallory Mystery Ser.). 148p. 1993. pap. 12.95 (*0-934257-96-5*) Story Line.

— Close Softly the Doors. 2nd ed. (Stuart Mallory Mystery Ser.). 160p. 1991. 18.95 (*0-934257-48-5*) Story Line.

— High Walk. (Stuart Mallory Mystery Ser.). 288p. (Orig.). 1996. 17.95 (*1-885266-16-2*) Story Line.

— A Still & Icy Silence. (Stuart Mallory Mystery Ser.). 303p. 1993. 21.95 (*0-934257-94-9*) Story Line.

Roath, Stuart. Aspects of Leukemia Treatment with Special Reference to Drug Development, 4 vols. 74p. 1990. text 141.00 (*3-7186-5077-0*) Gordon & Breach.

Roath, Stuart, ed. Raynaud's: A Guide for Health Professionals. (Illus.). 160p. 1990. pap. 22.95 (*0-412-33680-4*, A4442) Chapman & Hall.

Roath, Stuart & Huisman, Titus H., eds. Current Views on Thalassaemia: With Special Reference to Its Mediterranean Presence. LC 92-1571. 154p. 1992. text 85.00 (*3-7186-5262-5*) Gordon & Breach.

Roath, Stuart, jt. ed. see Corn, M.

Roath, Stuart, jt. ed. see Gross, Samuel.

Roath, Stuart, ed. see Mauri, C.

Roazen, P., ed. see Deutsch, Helene.

Roazen, Paul. Brother Animal: The Story of Freud & Tausk. 224p. (C). 1990. pap. 24.95 (*0-88738-851-5*) Transaction Pubs.

***Roazen, Paul.** Canada's King: An Essay in Political Psychology. LC 99-203117. 195p. 1998. pap. 18.95 (*0-88962-667-7*) Mosaic.

Roazen, Paul. Encountering Freud: The Politics & Histories of Psychoanalysis. 405p. 1989. 44.95 (*0-88738-295-9*) Transaction Pubs.

— Erik H. Erikson: The Power & Limits of a Vision. LC 97-19207. 258p. 1997. pap. text 40.00 (*0-7657-0094-8*) Aronson.

— Freud: Political & Social Thought. (Psychoanalysis: Examined & Re-Examined Ser.). xii, 332p. 1986. reprint ed. lib. bdg. 35.00 (*0-306-76294-3*) Da Capo.

— Freud & His Followers. (Illus.). 643p. 1992. reprint ed. pap. 17.95 (*0-306-80472-7*) Da Capo.

— Freud, Political & Social Thought. 3rd ed. LC 99-22508. 331p. 1999. 28.95 (*0-7658-0617-7*) Transaction Pubs.

— Helene Deutsch: A Psychoanalyst's Life. 384p. 1985. 19.95 (*0-671-25028-0*) S&S Trade.

— Helene Deutsch: A Psychoanalyst's Life. 384p. (C). 1991. pap. 24.95 (*1-56000-552-1*) Transaction Pubs.

***Roazen, Paul.** Historiography of Psychoanalysis. (Illus.). 2000. 39.95 (*0-7658-0019-5*) Transaction Pubs.

Roazen, Paul. How Freud Worked: First-Hand Accounts of Patients. LC 95-11733. 328p. 1995. 40.00 (*1-56821-556-8*) Aronson.

— Meeting Freud's Family. LC 93-22734. (Illus.). 256p. 1993. 30.00 (*0-87023-873-6*) U of Mass Pr.

***Roazen, Paul.** Oedipus in Britain: Edward Glover & the Struggle over Klein. LC 00-35661. 2000. write for info. (*1-892746-66-2*) Other Pr.

Roazen, Paul, ed. Sigmund Freud. (Series in Science). vi, 186p. 1987. reprint ed. pap. 9.95 (*0-306-80292-9*) Da Capo.

Roazen, Paul & Swerdloff, Bluma. Heresy: Sandor Rado & the Psychoanalytic Movement. LC 94-21882. 232p. 1995. 50.00 (*1-56821-321-2*) Aronson.

Roazen, Paul, jt. auth. see Dufresne, Todd.

Roazen, Paul, ed. see Deutsch, Helene.

Roazen, Paul, ed. see Hartz, Louis.

Roazen, Paul, ed. & intro. see Tausk, Victor.

***Roazzi, Vincent M.** The Spirituality of Success. LC 99-93590. 1999. 19.95 (*0-533-13075-1*) Vantage.

Rob. ACP: Big Blue Basic:ITT Technology. (General Business & Business Education Ser.). 1995. pap. 32.50 (*0-8273-9122-6*) Delmar.

— Database Design & Application Development. 256p. 1995. pap. 45.94 (*0-07-053051-3*) McGraw.

***Rob.** Database Systems: Design, Implementation & Management. 4th ed. (Miscellaneous/Catalogs Ser.). (C). 1999. pap. 69.95 (*0-7600-1090-0*) Thomson Learn.

***Rob, et al.** Database Systems: Design, Implementation & Management. 4th ed. (C). 1999. pap. 91.50 (*0-619-00074-0*) Course Tech.

Rob, Caroline & Reynolds, Janet. The Caregiver's Guide: Helping Older Friends & Relatives with Health & Safety Concerns. 320p. 1992. pap. 15.00 (*0-395-58780-8*) HM.

Rob McDonald Photography Staff, photos by. Sounds Delicious: Atlanta Symphony Associates. 192p. 1999. 27.95 (*0-9670854-0-3*, Pub. by Atlanta Symph) Ckbk Mrktplace.

Rob, Peter & Coronel, Carlos. Database Systems: Design, Implementation, & Management. 736p. (C). 1997. 49.95 (*0-7600-4905-X*) Course Tech.

— Database Systems: Design, Implementation, & Management. 2nd ed. LC 94-40216. 1995. pap. 49.95 (*0-7895-0052-3*) Course Tech.

— Database Systems: Design, Implementation & Management. 3rd ed. LC 98-104010. 736p. (C). 1997. pap. 49.00 (*0-7600-4904-1*) Course Tech.

— Database Systems: Implementation & Management. 643p. (C). 1993. pap. 56.95 (*0-534-17052-8*) Course Tech.

Rob, Peter & Williams, Treyton. Database Design & Application Development Using Access. (C). 1994. text. write for info. (*0-07-912020-2*) McGraw.

Rob Sharif, Muhammed Ali, see Ali Rob Sharif, Muhammed.

Rob Weisbach Books Editors, ed. Virgin Fiction. LC 98-2966. 432p. 1998. pap. 14.00 (*0-688-16081-6*, Wm Morrow) Morrow Avon.

***Rob Weisbach Books Staff.** Virgin Fiction 2, Vol. 2. LC 99-24081. 432p. 1999. pap. 14.00 (*0-688-17014-5*, Wm Morrow) Morrow Avon.

Roba, William, et al. Hans Reimer Claussen, 1804-1894: A Sketch of His Life - Eine Lebensskinzize. Rippley, Vern, ed. (Illus.). 1994. pap. 6.00 (*0-941947-03-3*) Hesperian Pr.

Roback, Abraham A. The Psychology of Character: With a Survey of Temperament. LC 73-2988. (Classics in Psychology Ser.). 1974. reprint ed. 37.95 (*0-405-05160-3*) Ayer.

— The Story of Yiddish Literature. 1972. 300.00 (*0-87968-084-9*) Gordon Pr.

Roback, Abraham A., ed. The Albert Schweitzer Jubilee Book. LC 79-97392. (Illus.). 508p. 1971. reprint ed. lib. bdg. 65.00 (*0-8371-2670-3*, ASJB, Greenwood Pr) Greenwood.

Roback, Charles W. The Mysteries of Astrology & the Wonders of Magic. 1996. reprint ed. spiral bd. 15.50 (*0-7873-0728-9*) Hlth Research.

— The Mysteries of Astrology & the Wonders of Magic, 1854. 239p. 1996. reprint ed. pap. 14.95 (*1-56459-799-7*) Kessinger Pub.

Roback, Edward A., jt. auth. see Guttman, Barbara.

Roback, Howard B., ed. Helping Patients & Their Families Cope with Medical Problems: A Guide to Therapeutic Group Work in Clinical Settings. LC 83-49267. (Joint Publication in the Jossey-Bass Social & Behavioral Science Series & the Jossey-Bass Health Ser.). 589p. reprint ed. pap. 182.60 (*0-7837-2522-1*, 204268100006) Bks Demand.

Roback, Jennifer. A Matter of Choice: A Critique of Comparable Worth by a Skeptical Feminist - A Twentieth Century Fund Paper. 53p. (Orig.). (C). 1986. pap. text 7.00 (*0-87078-172-3*) Century Foundation.

***Roback, Kekoa.** 'O Pa'ao. (HAW., Illus.). 21p. (J). (gr. 3-4). 1999. pap. 6.95 incl. audio (*1-58191-064-9*) Aha Punana Leo.

Roback, Mark G. Handbook of Pediatric Mock Codes. LC 97-37730. 1998. pap. text 25.00 (*1-55664-452-3*) Mosby Inc.

Roback, Rostyslaw. Primer for Today's Substance Abuse Counselors. 152p. 1991. 23.95 (*0-669-26935-2*) Lxngtn Bks.

Roback, Selwyn S. Adults of the Subfamily Tanypodinae (Pelopiinae) in North America (Diptera: Chironomidae) (Monograph: No. 17). (Illus.). 410p. (Orig.). 1971. pap. 8.00 (*0-910006-25-3*) Acad Nat Sci Phila.

ROBAIR, GINO. Making the Ultimate Demo. 2nd ed. LC 99-62486. 180p. 1999. pap. text 29.95 (*0-87288-728-6*) Intertec Pub.

Robak, Patricia. Dog Antiques & Collectibles. LC 98-89870. (Illus.). 160p. 1999. pap. 29.95 (*0-7643-0791-6*) Schiffer.

***Robalik, Nick.** TrueSpace F/X Creations. (Illus.). 400p. 2000. pap. 49.95 (*1-58450-012-3*) Chrles River Media.

***Roban, Whitney.** Forms for Helping the Oppositional Child. (Best Practices in Short-Term Therapy Ser.: Vol. 1). (Illus.). 114p. 1998. pap. 29.95 (*1-882732-74-X*, 61548) Childswork.

Robar, Neil F. Inspection of Motorcycles after Impact. LC 97-124918. (Illus.). 56p. 1996. pap. text 15.95 (*1-884566-20-0*) Inst Police Tech.

Robarchek. Waorani. LC 97-76877. (C). 1997. pap. text 23.50 (*0-15-503797-8*) Harcourt Coll Pubs.

Robarchek, C. An Intensive Archaeological Survey of Proposed Gravel Operations in Bicycle Lake Basin, Fort Irwin, California. fac. ed. (Fort Irwin Archaeology Project, Research Reports: No. 3). (Illus.). 33p. (C). 1982. reprint ed. pap. text 3.75 (*1-55567-525-5*) Coyote Press.

Robarchek, C., et al. An Archaeological Survey of the 1982 Gallant Eagle Exercise Area, Fort Irwin, San Bernardino County, California. fac. ed. (Fort Irwin Archaeology Project, Research Reports: No. 7). (Illus.). 281p. (C). 1984. reprint ed. pap. text 29.38 (*1-55567-531-X*) Coyote Press.

— Intensive Cultural Resource Survey of Portions of the Live Fire Maneuver Range, Fort Irwin, California. fac. ed. (Fort Irwin Archaeology Project, Research Reports: No. 5). (Illus.). 190p. (C). 1982. reprint ed. pap. text 20.63 (*1-55567-527-1*) Coyote Press.

Robards, Anthony W., et al, eds. Low Temperature Methods in Biological Electron Microscopy. (Practical Methods in Electron Microscopy Ser.: Vol. 10). 552p. 1986. pap. 108.75 (*0-444-80684-9*) Elsevier.

Robards, Anthony W., jt. ed. see Bald, W. B.

Robards, Anthony W., jt. ed. see Betts, W. B.

Robards, Anthony W., jt. ed. see Wilson, A. J.

Robards, Brooks. A Magical Place: Poems, Paintings & Photographs of Martha's Vineyard. (Illus.). 80p. 1998. pap. 19.95 (*0-9645250-2-X*) Smmrst Pr.

Robards, Brooks & Kaplan, Jim. Sweet & Sour: One Woman's Chinese Adventure, One Man's Chinese Torture. LC 95-67939. 200p. (Orig.). 1995. pap. 14.95 (*0-9645250-0-3*) Smmrst Pr.

***Robards, Hugh J.** Foxhunting in England, Ireland & North America: A Life in Hunt Service. LC 00-35838. (Illus.). 320p. 2000. 50.00 (*1-58667-036-0*) Derrydale Pr.

Robards, K., et al. Principles & Practice of Modern Chromatography. (Illus.). 495p. 1994. 59.00 (*0-12-589570-4*) Acad Pr.

Robards, Karen. Amanda Rose. 432p. 1984. reprint ed. mass mkt. 5.99 (*0-446-30617-7*, Pub. by Warner Bks) Little.

— Dark of the Moon. 416p. 1988. mass mkt. 5.99 (*0-380-75437-1*, Avon Bks) Morrow Avon.

— Dark Torment. 400p. 1985. mass mkt. 6.50 (*0-446-30618-5*, Pub. by Warner Bks) Little.

— Dark Torment. 400p. 1998. mass mkt. 3.99 (*0-446-60689-8*, Pub. by Warner Bks) Little.

— Desire in the Sun. 400p. 1988. mass mkt. 5.99 (*0-380-75554-8*, Avon Bks) Morrow Avon.

— Desire in the Sun. large type ed. LC 97-17723. 597p. 1997. 25.95 (*0-7862-1138-5*) Thorndike Pr.

— Forbidden Love. 384p. 1997. mass mkt. 6.50 (*0-440-22106-4*) Dell.

***Robards, Karen.** Ghost Moon. LC 99-47420. 368p. 2000. 24.95 (*0-385-31972-X*) Delacorte.

— Ghost Moon. LC 00-31961. 2000. write for info. (*0-7838-9114-8*, G K Hall & Co) Mac Lib Ref.

Robards, Karen. Green Eyes. 400p. 1993. lib. bdg. 20.00 (*0-7278-4390-7*) Severn Hse.

— Green Eyes. 400p. 1991. reprint ed. mass mkt. 5.99 (*0-380-75889-X*, Avon Bks) Morrow Avon.

— Heart Breaker. 400p. 1998. mass mkt. 6.99 (*0-440-21596-X*) Dell.

— Heartbreaker. large type ed. LC 96-52142. 1997. 20.00 (*0-7838-8092-8*, G K Hall Lrg Type) Mac Lib Ref.

— Heartbreaker. large type ed. 571p. 1997. 26.95 (*0-7862-1085-0*) Thorndike Pr.

— Hunter's Moon. 448p. 1996. mass mkt. 6.50 (*0-440-21593-5*) Dell.

— Hunter's Moon. large type ed. LC 95-8856. 1996. 25.95 (*1-56895-296-1*) Wheeler Pub.

— Island Flame. 352p. 1995. pap. 5.99 (*0-8349-3844-8*) Dorchester Pub Co.

***Robards, Karen.** Island Flame. large type ed. 448p. 2000. lib. bdg. 27.95 (*1-58547-025-2*) Ctr Point Pubg.

Robards, Karen. Island Flame. 384p. 1998. reprint ed. mass mkt. 6.50 (*0-440-22107-2*) Dell.

— Loving Julia. 384p. 1986. reprint ed. mass mkt. 6.99 (*0-446-30057-8*, Pub. by Warner Bks) Little.

— Maggy's Child. 416p. 1994. mass mkt. 6.99 (*0-440-20830-0*) Dell.

— Maggy's Child. large type ed. LC 93-47353. 1994. 25.95 (*1-56895-057-8*) Wheeler Pub.

— The Midnight Hour. LC 98-35730. 368p. 1999. 24.95 (*0-385-31971-1*) Delacorte.

— The Midnight Hour. 454p. 1999. mass mkt. 6.99 (*0-440-22504-3*) Dell.

— The Midnight Hour. LC 99-19339. (Wheeler Large Print Book Ser.). 1999. write for info. (*1-56895-719-X*, Wheeler) Wheeler Pub.

— Morning Song. large type ed. LC 97-13853. (Americana Series). 584p. 1997. 25.95 (*0-7862-1133-4*) Thorndike Pr.

— Morning Song. 400p. 1990. reprint ed. mass mkt. 5.99 (*0-380-75888-1*, Avon Bks) Morrow Avon.

— Night Magic. 1987. mass mkt. 3.95 (*0-446-30058-6*, Pub. by Warner Bks) Little.

— Night Magic. 384p. 1988. mass mkt. 6.99 (*0-446-35391-4*, Pub. by Warner Bks) Little.

— Nobody's Angel. 416p. 1992. mass mkt. 5.99 (*0-440-20828-9*) Dell.

— Nobody's Angel. large type ed. 575p. 1992. reprint ed. lib. bdg. 20.95 (*1-56054-449-X*) Thorndike Pr.

— One Summer. 400p. 1993. mass mkt. 6.99 (*0-440-20829-7*) Dell.

***Robards, Karen.** Paradise County. 352p. 2000. 24.95 (*0-671-78645-8*, PB Hardcover) PB.

Robards, Karen. Sea Fire. 480p. 1998. mass mkt. 6.99 (*0-440-22108-0*) Bantam.

— The Senator's Wife. 448p. 1999. mass mkt. 6.99 (*0-440-21599-4*) Dell.

— The Senator's Wife. large type ed. LC 98-29244. (Large Print Book Ser.). 1998. 26.95 (*1-56895-584-7*) Wheeler Pub.

— This Side of Heaven. 448p. 1991. mass mkt. 6.99 (*0-440-20827-0*) Dell.

— Tiger's Eye. 400p. (Orig.). 1989. mass mkt. 6.50 (*0-380-75555-6*, Avon Bks) Morrow Avon.

— To Love a Man. 384p. 1988. mass mkt. 6.50 (*0-446-35350-7*, Pub. by Warner Bks) Little.

— Walking after Midnight. 416p. 1995. mass mkt. 6.99 (*0-440-21590-0*) Dell.

— Wild Orchids. 384p. 1986. mass mkt. 6.99 (*0-446-32692-5*, Pub. by Warner Bks) Little.

— Wild Orchids. large type ed. LC 97-3572. 1997. 25.95 (*1-56895-421-2*, Compass) Wheeler Pub.

Robards, Terry. The New York Times Book of Wine. 480p. 1977. pap. 8.95 (*0-380-01720-2*, Avon Bks) Morrow Avon.

Robare, Lorie, jt. illus. see Gerrity, Peg.

***Robarge, David Scott.** A Chief Justice's Progress: John Marshall from Revolutionary Virginia to the Supreme Court , 185. LC 99-33829. (Contributions in American History Ser.). 400p. 2000. 65.00 (*0-313-30858-6*) Greenwood.

Robart, Rose. The Cake That Mack Ate. (Illus.). (J). (ps-3). 1991. pap. 5.95 (*0-316-74891-9*) Little.

Robarts, Sadie, jt. auth. see Stamp, Paddy.

Robartson, Linda. The Complete Kwanzaa Celebration Book. 60 p. 1993. pap. 9.95 (*0-9639026-9-5*) Creat Acrylic.

Robaton, John, jt. auth. see Smith, Harris.

Robaut, Alfred. L' Oeuvre Complet de Eugene Delacroix: Peintures, Dessins, Gravures Lithographies. LC 78-75310. (Graphic Arts, Painting & Sculpture Ser.). 1969. lib. bdg. 85.00 (*0-306-71628-3*) Da Capo.

Robb. Metals Databook. 1988. 90.00 (*0-904357-69-4*) Institute of Management Consultants.

— Unofficial Guide to Online Investing. (Unofficial Guides Ser.). 400p. 2000. pap. 15.95 (*0-02-863752-6*) Macmillan Gen Ref.

***Robb, Andy.** Betty Boat, 1. 1999. 4.00 (*0-570-05568-7*) Concordia.

— Bigger & Bigger Book of Bible Stories, 1. 1999. 9.99 (*0-570-05589-X*) Conceivable Concepts.

— Lost Sheep, 1. 1999. 6.00 (*0-570-05586-5*) Concordia.

— Lost Son, 1. (Illus.). 10p. (J). (ps). 1999. 6.00 (*0-570-05587-3*) Concordia.

— Polly Plane, 1. 1999. 4.00 (*0-570-05570-9*) Concordia.

— Rory Racer, 1. 1999. 4.00 (*0-570-05569-5*) Concordia.

— Tommy Tractor, 1. 1999. 4.00 (*0-570-05571-7*) Concordia.

— Who Made The World?, 1. 1999. 7.00 (*0-570-05577-6*) Concordia.

Robb, Betty J. And How Was Your Day? Dageforde, Linda J., ed. LC 98-71483. 112p. 1998. pap. 9.95 (*1-886225-31-1*, 1000) Dageforde Pub.

Robb, Beverly. Collectible Golfing Novelties. LC 92-60627. (Illus.). 160p. (Orig.). 1992. pap. 29.95 (*0-88740-423-5*) Schiffer.

***Robb, Bob.** Complete Book of Elk Hunting: Technques & Strategies of the World's Greatest Hunters. (Illus.). 2000. pap. 24.95 (*1-58574-180-9*) Lyons Pr.

Robb, Bob. The Field & Stream Bowhunting Handbook. LC 99-10281. (Field & Stream Fishing And Hunting Library). 1999. pap. 9.95 (*1-55821-914-5*) Lyons Pr.

— Hunting Wild Boar in California. LC 89-92684. (Illus.). 160p. (Orig.). 1989. pap. text 14.95 (*0-936513-09-8*) Larsens Outdoor.

Robb, Brian. Ewan McGregor: From Junkie to Jedi. 1999. pap. 16.95 (*0-85965-276-9*) Publishers Group.

— Nicolas Cage: Hollywood's Wild Talent. 144p. 1998. pap. text 16.95 (*0-85965-264-5*, Pub. by Plexus) Publishers Group.

Robb, Brian J. Brad Pitt: Hollywood Maverick. (Illus.). 160p. 1996. pap. text 15.95 (*0-85965-241-6*, Pub. by Plexus) Publishers Group.

***Robb, Brian J.** Brad Pitt: The Rise to Stardom. 2nd ed. (Illus.). 2000. pap. 16.95 (*0-85965-288-2*) Plexus.

Robb, Brian J. Johnny Depp: A Modern Rebel. (Illus.). 168p. 1996. pap. text 15.95 (*0-85965-236-X*, Pub. by Plexus) Publishers Group.

— Keanu Reeves: An Excellent Adventure. (Illus.). 144p. Date not set. pap. 15.95 (*0-85965-245-9*, Pub. by Plexus) Publishers Group.

— The Matt Damon Album. (Illus.). pap. 16.95 (*0-85965-278-5*) Plexus.

— River Phoenix: A Short Life. 2nd ed. 1997. pap. text 16.95 (*0-85965-214-9*, Pub. by Plexus) Publishers Group.

— Screams & Nightmares: The Films of Wes Craven. LC 98-48787. (Illus.). 192p. 1999. text 27.95 (*0-87951-918-5*, Pub. by Overlook Pr) Penguin Putnam.

***Robb, Brian J.** Screams & Nightmares: The Films of Wes Craven. 2000. pap. 18.95 (*1-58567-090-1*, Pub. by Overlook Pr) Penguin Putnam.

— William Smith: King of Cool. (Illus.). 96p. 1999. pap. 16.95 (*0-85965-281-5*, Pub. by Plexus) Publishers Group.

Robb, Cairo, et al, eds. International Environmental Law Reports Vol. I: Early Decisions. (Illus.). 750p. (C). 1999. text 130.00 (*0-521-64347-3*) Cambridge U Pr.

— International Environmental Law Reports Vol. 1: Early Decisions. (Illus.). 750p. (C). 1999. pap. text 59.95 (*0-521-64397-X*) Cambridge U Pr.

***Robb, Cairo A. R., ed.** Trade & Environment. (International Environmental Law Reports: Vol. 2). 800p. (C). 2001. write for info. (*0-521-65035-6*); pap. write for info. (*0-521-65967-1*) Cambridge U Pr.

Robb, Candace M. The Apothecary Rose: A Medieval Mystery. 1994. mass mkt. 5.99 (*0-312-95360-7*) St Martin.

— A Gift of Sanctuary: An Owen Archer Mystery. 304p. 1998. text 22.95 (*0-312-19266-5*) St Martin.

***Robb, Candace M.** A Gift of Sanctuary: An Owen Archer Mystery. 320p. 2000. mass mkt. 5.99 (*0-312-97477-9*, Minotaur) St Martin.

Robb, Candace M. A Gift of Sanctuary: An Owen Archer Mystery. LC 99-18841. 1999. 27.95 (*0-7862-1910-6*) Thorndike Pr.

***Robb, Candace M.** The King's Bishop. large type unabridged ed. 389p. 1999. 26.95 (*0-7531-5951-1*, 159511, Pub. by ISIS Lrg Prnt) ISIS Pub.

Robb, Candace M. The King's Bishop, Vol. 1. 1997. mass mkt. 5.99 (*0-312-96282-7*) St Martin.

— The Lady Chapel. 1995. mass mkt. 5.50 (*0-312-95460-3*) St Martin.

— The Riddle of St. Leonard's: An Owen Archer Mystery, Vol. 1. LC 97-16231. 304p. 1998. mass mkt. 5.99 (*0-312-96651-2*) St Martin.

Robb, Carol S. Equal Value: An Ethical Approach to Economics & Sex. LC 95-15090. 208p. 1997. pap. 14.00 (*0-8070-6505-6*) Beacon Pr.

Robb, Carol S., jt. ed. see Deats, Paul.

Robb, Carol S., ed. see Harrison, Beverly W.

Robb, Caroline M. Can the Poor Influence Policy? Responding to the Challenge of Inclusion Through Participatory Assessments. LC 97-45176. 148p. 1999. pap. 22.00 (*0-8213-4144-8*) World Bank.

***Robb, Charles.** God Speaks. 2000. 14.95 (*0-375-50427-3*) Villard Books.

***Robb, Christina.** This Changes Everything. 2000. text. write for info. (*0-374-27581-5*) FS&G.

Robb, D. A. & Pierpoint, S. Metals & Micronutrients: Uptake & Utilization by Plants. 1983. text 136.00 (*0-12-589580-1*) Acad Pr.

Robb, Dale. Love & Living Together. LC 77-15242. 110p. (Orig.). reprint ed. pap. 34.10 (*0-608-16313-9*, 202718000054) Bks Demand.

Robb, David. God's Fiction: Symbolism & Allegory in the Works of George MacDonald. 1989. pap. 8.95 (*0-940652-36-6*) Sunrise Bks.

Robb, David S. Collected Poems of Alexander Scott. 272p. 1989. pap. 40.00 (*1-873644-28-0*, Pub. by Mercat Pr Bks) St Mut.

***Robb, Don.** Hail to the Chief. LC 99-52350. (Illus.). 32p. (J). (ps-5). 2000. pap. 7.95 (*0-88106-393-2*) Charlesbridge Pub.

— Hail to the Chief: The American Presidency. LC 99-52350. (Illus.). 32p. (J). (ps-5). 2000. 16.95 (*0-88106-392-4*) Charlesbridge Pub.

Robb, Donald W., jt. auth. see Driscoll, William.

R

An Asterisk (*) at the beginning of an entry indicates that the title is appearing for the first time.

Robbie, Ken & Wright, Mike. Management Buy-Ins: Entrepreneurship, Active Investors, & Corporate Restructuring. LC 95-4959. (Studies in Finance). 330p. 1996. text 79.95 (*0-7190-4281-X*) Manchester Univ Pr.

Robbie, Ken, jt. ed. see Wright, Mike.

Robbie, Vic. Scotland's Golf Courses: The Complete Guide. (Illus.). 224p. 1997. 24.95 (*1-85158-945-7*, Pub. by Mainstream Pubng) Trafalgar.

Robbillard, Jean & Conley, Edgar, eds. Industrial Applications for Optical Data Processing & Holography. 224p. 1992. lib. bdg. 119.00 (*0-8493-0139-4*, TA1542) CRC Pr.

Robbin, Alexandra, et al, eds. Training Families to Do a Successful Intervention: A Professional's Guide. 152p. (Orig.). 1996. pap. 15.95 (*1-56246-116-8*, 3267, HazeldenJohnson Inst) Hazelden.

Robbin, Joel W. Matrix Algebra Using MINImal MATlab. LC 93-39372. (Illus.). 560p. (C). 1994. text 68.00 incl. disk (*1-56881-024-5*) AK Peters.

Robbin, Lynn E. The Recipe Book for 25. 416p. (C). 1994. pap. 125.00 (*1-888143-03-7*) Robbins Mgmt.

Robbin, Sallie. A Lighted Candle in Her Heart. 200p. 1985. 9.95 (*0-930061-15-2*) Interspace Bks.

Robbin, T. Engineering a New Architecture. LC 95-36222. 138p. 1996. 50.00 (*0-300-06116-1*) Yale U Pr.

***Robbins.** Allyn & Bacon Quick Guide to the Internet 2000 Edition: For Cultural Anthropology. 3rd ed. 1999. pap. 8.00 (*0-205-30961-5*) Allyn.

Robbins. Altered Reading. LC 98-37917. 1p. 1999. lib. bdg. 42.00 (*0-226-72112-4*) U Ch Pr.

***Robbins.** The Business of Writing & Speaking. 3rd ed. 1998. 34.00 (*0-07-230334-4*) McGraw.

Robbins. Fundamentals of Management. 2nd ed. 1998. pap. text, student ed. 13.05 (*0-13-646704-0*) P-H.

— Fundamentals of Management: Essential Concepts & Applications. (C). 1995. student ed. 20.00 (*0-13-307281-9*, Macmillan Coll) P-H.

— The House Hold Herbal. 311p. 1996. 29.95 (*0-593-03620-4*) Bantam.

— Household Herbal. (Illus.). 409p. 1997. pap. 15.99 (*0-553-40800-3*) Bantam.

— Integrating Managed Care & Ethics. 1997. 59.00 (*0-8342-0954-3*) Aspen Pub.

***Robbins.** Management Supplement. 6th ed. 2000. pap., student ed. 18.67 (*0-13-019854-4*) P-H.

Robbins. Managing Today. 2nd ed. LC 98-50314. (Illus.). 651p. 1999. text 96.00 incl. audio compact disk (*0-13-011672-6*) P-H.

— Organizational Behavior: Concepts, Controversies, Applications D-Cart. 8th ed. 1998. 77.00 (*0-13-011088-4*) P-H.

***Robbins.** Putting Healthcare Promises into Practice. 2000. 29.95 (*0-7668-1972-8*) Delmar.

Robbins. Railway Age. LC 98-2901. (Illus.). 1998. pap. 15.95 (*1-901341-09-7*) St Martin.

Robbins. Shakespeare: Interdisciplinary Thematic Unit. (Illus.). 176p. (J). (gr. 5-8). 1995. pap. text, wbk. ed. 15.95 (*1-55734-614-3*) Tchr Create Mat.

Robbins. Wellness, A Way of Life. 2nd ed. 1995. text (*0-697-33458-9*, WCB McGr Hill) McGrw-H Hghr Educ.

— Wellness Way of Life. 2nd ed. 1993. teacher ed. 45.93 (*0-697-12660-9*) McGraw.

Robbins & Stevens. American Experiences: Readings in Social & Political History. 204p. (C). 1992. pap. text 34.80 (*0-536-58310-2*) Pearson Custom.

Robbins & Taylor. Plains Indians. (Illus.). 48p. (J). (gr. 3-6). 1996. pap., teacher ed. 5.95 (*1-55799-576-1*, 545) Evan-Moor Edu Pubs.

Robbins, jt. auth. see Cotton.

***Robbins, Adreana.** New Adreana Robbins Novel. 2000. text 24.95 (*0-312-87280-1*) St Martin.

— Paris Never Leaves You. 2000. mass mkt. 6.99 (*0-8125-7078-2*) Forge NYC.

Robbins, Adreana. Paris Never Leaves You. 2nd ed. LC 99-21743. 384p. 1999. 25.95 (*0-312-86755-7*, Pub. by Forge NYC) St Martin.

Robbins, Alan. Final Run. (Illus.). 8p. (C). 1991. 20.00 (*0-922242-29-1*) Bepuzzled.

— Murder on the Rocks: A Mystery Jigsaw Puzzle Thriller. (BePuzzled Ser.). (Orig.). 1994. 20.00 (*0-922242-62-3*) Bepuzzled.

— Purrceptive Detective. (YA). (gr. 7 up). 1994. 20.00 (*0-922242-71-2*) Bepuzzled.

— To Kill a Boss: A Mystery Jigsaw Puzzle Thriller. (BePuzzled Ser.). (Orig.). (YA). (gr. 7 up). 1994. 20.00 (*0-922242-60-7*) Bepuzzled.

— To Kill a Lawyer: A Mystery Jigsaw Puzzle. (BePuzzled Ser.). (YA). (gr. 7 up). 1993. 20.00 (*0-922242-54-2*) Bepuzzled.

Robbins, Aldona. The ABCs of Social Security: Basic Questions & Answers about the Retirement Program. (Illus.). 37p. (Orig.). 1988. pap. 5.95 (*0-922623-00-7*) IRET.

Robbins, Aldona & Robbins, Gary. The Bush Savings Plan. 1990. pap. 10.00 (*0-943802-55-5*, 152) Natl Ctr Pol.

— Capital, Taxes & Growth. (Illus.). 45p. (C). 1992. pap. 10.00 (*0-943802-72-5*, 169) Natl Ctr Pol.

— The Case for IRAs. 1991. pap. 10.00 (*0-943802-66-0*, 163) Natl Ctr Pol.

— Paying People Not to Work: The Economic Cost of the Social Security Retirement Earnings Limit. 1989. pap. 10.00 (*0-943802-45-8*, 142) Natl Ctr Pol.

— A Strategy for Growth. (Illus.). 21p. (C). 1992. pap. 10.00 (*0-943802-73-3*, 170) Natl Ctr Pol.

— Why Bush Lost the Election: Ten Lessons for the Clinton Administration. (Illus.). 24p. 1993. pap. 5.00 (*1-56808-007-7*, BG 120) Natl Ctr Pol.

Robbins, Aldona, jt. auth. see Robbins, Gary.

Robbins, Allan H. Introductory Circuit Analysis. (Electronics Technology Ser.). 1995. teacher ed. 21.00 (*0-8273-5415-0*) Delmar.

— Introductory Circuit Analysis. (Electronics Technology Ser.). (C). 1995. lab manual ed. 24.75 (*0-8273-5422-3*) Delmar.

Robbins, Allan H., et al. Introduction to Troubleshooting Microprocessor Based Systems. (Illus.). 448p. (C). 1987. text 28.95 (*0-8359-3249-4*) P-H.

Robbins, Allan H., jt. auth. see Miller, Wilhelm.

Robbins, Allan H., jt. auth. see Miller, Wilhelm C.

Robbins, Allen. The Glenmore Haunting. 1993. 20.00 (*0-922242-32-1*) Bepuzzled.

— Swim at Your Own Risk: Adventure Mystery for Kids Ages 8-12. (Spider Tales Ser.). (Orig.). (J). (gr. 3-7). 1995. 14.00 (*0-922242-76-3*) Bepuzzled.

Robbins, Andrea & Becher, Max, photos by. Contact Sheet, 98: Andrea Robbins & Max Becher: Bavarian by Law - German Indians. (Contact Sheet Ser.). (Illus.). 32p. 1998. pap. 10.00 (*0-935445-05-6*) Light Work.

Robbins, Andy. The Very Thought of You: Poems. LC 98-39542. (Contemporary Poetry Ser.). 72p. (Orig.). 1999. pap. 15.95 (*0-8203-2099-4*) U of Ga Pr.

Robbins, Anita K. & Jackson, Sara. "Say & Do" Language Unit Worksheets Vol. 1: Animals, Around the Home, Clothing. (Illus.). 166p. (J). (ps-3). 1993. spiral bd., wbk. ed. 26.95 (*1-58650-032-5*, BK-223) Super Duper.

Robbins, Anita K. & Jackson, Sara M. "Say & Do" Holiday Unit Worksheets: Lots of Reproducible Activities, Poems & Stories for Each Holiday! Webber, Sharon G., ed. & illus. by. 179p. (J). (ps-2). 1988. spiral bd. 27.95 (*1-58650-017-1*, BK-207) Super Duper.

Robbins, Anita K., jt. auth. see Jackson, Sara.

Robbins, Anita K., jt. auth. see Jackson, Sara M.

Robbins, Ann R. Twenty-Five Vegetables Anyone Can Grow. 1974. pap. 6.95 (*0-486-23029-5*) Dover.

Robbins, Anthony. Awaken the Giant Within: How to Take Immediate Control of Your Mental, Emotional, Physical & Financial Destiny. LC 92-30041. (Illus.). 544p. 1992. per. 12.00 (*0-671-79154-0*) S&S Trade Pap.

Robbins, Anthony. Awaken the Giant Within: How to Take Immediate Control of Your Mental, Emotional, Physical & Financial Destiny. abr. ed. 1991. audio 12.00 (*0-671-75018-6*) S&S Audio.

Robbins, Anthony. Despertando Al Gigante Interior. 1997. pap. text 18.98 (*970-05-0448-4*) Grijalbo Edit.

— Giant Steps. 416p. 1994. per. 10.00 (*0-671-89104-9*) S&S Trade.

— Notes from a Friend: A Quick & Simple Guide to Taking Control of Your Life. LC 95-19436. 112p. 1995. per. 8.95 (*0-684-80056-X*) S&S Trade.

— On the Tropic of Time: Poems. LC 95-8286. 1995. write for info. (*0-89924-092-5*); pap. write for info. (*0-89924-091-7*) Lynx Hse.

— Poder Sin Limites La Nueva Ciencia Del Desarrollo Personal. 1997. pap. text 17.98 (*970-05-0202-3*) Grijalbo Edit.

— Public Health Reports Vol. 113, Suppl., 1, 1998: HIV Prevention with Drug-Using Populations - Current Status & Future Prospects. (DHHS Publication Ser.: Vol. 98-50193). (Illus.). 206p. 1998. pap. 17.00 (*0-16-049601-2*) USGPO.

Robbins, Anthony. Unlimited Power. 1996. pap. 12.50 (*0-449-45669-2*, Ballantine) Ballantine Pub Grp.

Robbins, Anthony. Unlimited Power. 1987. pap. 12.50 (*0-449-90280-3*) Fawcett.

— Unlimited Power: The New Science of Personal Achievement. LC 97-35403. (Illus.). 424p. 1997. pap. 13.00 (*0-684-84577-6*) S&S Trade.

— Unlimited Power, 1998. 1997. pap. 9.95 (*0-684-83326-3*, S&S Edns) Simon & Schuster.

***Robbins, Anthony.** Your Driving Force. 2000. 16.00 incl. audio (*0-671-57713-1*, A1253, Sound Ideas) S&S Trade.

Robbins, Anthony. Your Driving Force: Harnessing Your Six Inner Drives to Create an Extraordinary Quality of Life. (Illus.). 288p. 1999. 25.00 (*0-684-80902-8*) Simon & Schuster.

Robbins, Anthony, ed. Behavioral Science in HIV Prevention. (Illus.). 144p. (Orig.). (C). 1996. pap. text 35.00 (*0-7881-3721-2*) DIANE Pub.

Robbins, Anthony & McClendon, Joseph, III. Ebony Power Thoughts: Inspirational Thoughts from Outstanding African-Americans. LC 97-37090. 384p. 1997. pap. 10.00 (*0-684-82437-X*, Fireside) S&S Trade Pap.

— Unlimited Power: A Black Choice. LC 96-39232. 1997. 23.50 (*0-684-82436-1*) S&S Trade.

— Unlimited Power: A Black Choice. 432p. 1997. per. 13.00 (*0-684-83872-9*) S&S Trade.

***Robbins, Arnold.** Bash Reference Card. 26p. 1998. reprint ed. pap. text 4.95 (*1-57831-010-5*, Pub. by Specialized Sys) F Kasper Assocs.

— Hp-Ux: A Companion to Unix in a Nutshell. LC 99-86238. 2000. write for info. (*1-56592-760-5*) OReilly & Assocs.

— Sed, Awk & Regular Expressions Pocket Reference. Toporek, Chuck, ed. (Illus.). 56p. 1999. pap. 6.95 (*1-56592-729-X*) OReilly & Assocs.

— VI Editor Pocket Reference. Estabrook, Gigi, ed. (Illus.). 72p. 1999. reprint ed. pap. 7.95 (*1-56592-497-5*) OReilly & Assocs.

Robbins, Arnold, jt. auth. see Lamb, Linda.

Robbins, Arnold D. GAWK: The GNU Awk Users' Guide. 2nd ed. 324p. 1998. per. 25.00 (*1-882114-27-2*) Free Software.

— Korn Shell Reference. rev. ed. 28p. (Orig.). (C). 1995. pap. text 4.50 (*0-916151-72-7*) Specialized Sys.

— Sed & Awk. 2nd ed. Estabrook, Gigi, ed. (Illus.). 450p. 1997. pap. 29.95 (*1-56592-225-5*) Thomson Learn.

Robbins, Arthur. The Artist As Therapist. LC 86-10466. 226p. 1987. 42.95 (*0-89885-322-2*, Kluwer Acad Hman Sci); pap. 22.95 (*0-89885-439-3*, Kluwer Acad Hman Sci) Kluwer Academic.

— Between Therapists: The Processing of Transference - Countertransference Material. 227p. (C). 1988. 38.95 (*0-89885-373-7*, Kluwer Acad Hman Sci) Kluwer Academic.

— A Multi-Modal Approach to Creative Art Therapy. LC 94-236986. 250p. 1994. pap. 23.00 (*1-85302-262-4*) Taylor & Francis.

Robbins, Arthur, ed. Pratt Institute Creative Arts Therapy Review, Vol. 16. (Orig.). 1995. pap. text 8.00 (*1-884870-01-5*) Pratt Inst.

— Pratt Institute Creative Arts Therapy Review, Vol. 17. (Illus.). (Orig.). 1997. pap. text 8.00 (*1-884870-02-3*) Pratt Inst.

— Therapeutic Presence: Bridging Expression & Form. LC 97-223546. 275p. 1997. pap. 24.95 (*1-85302-559-3*, Pub. by Jessica Kingsley) Taylor & Francis.

***Robbins, Arthur D.** Greenfield for President. LC 99-76122. 224p. 2000. 23.95 (*0-9676127-5-6*) Acropolis Bks.

Robbins, Barbara H. Just for Fun: Nature Stories in Sign Language. (Illus.). 112p. (Orig.). (J). (gr. k-12). 1992. pap. 12.95 (*0-9630060-0-2*, Pub. by Robbinspring) Partners Pubs Grp.

***Robbins, Barbara H.** 2000 Wiley Medical Malpractice Update, 1. 440p. 1999. pap. text 165.00 (*0-7355-1291-4*) Aspen Pub.

Robbins, Barbara H. & Stahl, Kathryn M. Awful Abigail & Why She Changed. LC 95-62281. (Illus.). 64p. (J). (gr. k-12). 1995. pap. 8.95 (*0-9630060-1-0*) Robbinspring.

Robbins, Barbara H., et al. Wolf Country - A Mystery in Progress. (Illus.). (J). (gr. k-12). 1996. pap. 17.95 (*0-9630060-2-9*) Robbinspring.

Robbins, Beverly. Definite Article in English Transformations. 1968. pap. text 56.95 (*90-279-0082-5*) Mouton.

***Robbins, Brian.** Inclusive Mathematics. (Illus.). 2000. pap. 24.95 (*0-304-70703-1*) Continuum.

Robbins, Brian, jt. auth. see Rubin, Howard.

***Robbins, Bruce.** Feeling Global: Internationalism in Distress. LC 98-58005. (Cultural Front Ser.). 224p. 1999. pap. 17.95 (*0-8147-7514-4*); text 50.00 (*0-8147-7513-6*) NYU Pr.

Robbins, Bruce. Secular Vocations: Intellectuals, Professionalism, Culture. 256p. (C). 1993. pap. 19.00 (*0-86091-630-8*, B0530, Pub. by Verso) Norton.

— The Servant's Hand: English Fiction from Below. LC 85-14955. 256p. 1986. text 57.50 (*0-231-05966-3*) Col U Pr.

— The Servant's Hand: English Fiction from Below. LC 93-7141. 280p. (C). 1993. pap. text 16.95 (*0-8223-1397-9*) Duke.

Robbins, Bruce, ed. Intellectuals: Aesthetics, Politics, Academics. (Cultural Politics Ser.). 408p. (Orig.). 1990. pap. 18.95 (*0-8166-1831-3*) U of Minn Pr.

— The Phantom Public Sphere. LC 92-28619. (Cultural Politics Ser.: Vol. 5). 336p. (C). 1993. pap. 19.95 (*0-8166-2126-8*); text 49.95 (*0-8166-2124-1*) U of Minn Pr.

Robbins, Bruce, jt. auth. see Klenicki, Leon.

Robbins, Bryan, jt. auth. see Yates, Keith D.

Robbins, C. R. Chemical & Physical Behavior of Human Hair. (Illus.). 330p. 1988. 79.00 (*0-387-96660-9*) Spr-Verlag.

Robbins, Carol & Robbins, Clive. Music for the Hearing Impaired & Other Special Groups: A Resource Manual & Curriculum Guide. (Illus.). 480p. 1980. pap., spiral bd. 24.95 (*0-918812-11-9*, ST 027) MMB Music.

Robbins, Carol, jt. ed. see Robbins, Clive.

Robbins, Carol T., et al. Removing Regulatory Barriers to Affordable Housing: How States & Localities Are Moving Ahead. 84p. (Orig.). (C). 1993. pap. text 20.00 (*0-7881-0068-8*) DIANE Pub.

Robbins, Carol T., jt. auth. see Wolff, Herbert.

Robbins, Carolyn R. The Job Searcher's Handbook. 176p. 1996. pap. 33.33 incl. disk (*0-13-199621-5*) P-H.

Robbins, Carroll, ed. see Bustamante, Eduardo.

Robbins, Carroll, ed. see Rutstein, Nathan.

Robbins, Casey, jt. ed. see Cabarga, Leslie E.

Robbins, Casey, jt. ed. see Robbins, Trina.

Robbins, Ceila D., jt. auth. see Lurdang, Laurence.

Robbins, Ceila D., jt. auth. see Muccigrosso, Robert.

Robbins, Ceila D., jt. auth. see Spector, Robert.

Robbins, Ceila D., ed. see Blodgett, Richard.

Robbins, Ceila D., ed. see Cross, Wilbur.

Robbins, Ceila D., ed. see Evans, Glen.

Robbins, Ceila D., ed. see Filson, Brent.

Robbins, Ceila D., ed. see Harrington, Melissa.

Robbins, Ceila D., ed. see Hubbard, Ian.

Robbins, Ceila D., ed. see Naleid, James C.

Robbins, Ceila D., ed. see O'Hanlon, Tom.

Robbins, Ceila D., ed. see Yenne, William P.

Robbins, Cella D., ed. see Blodgett, Richard.

Robbins, Chandler S., ed. Atlas of the Breeding Birds of Maryland & the District of Columbia. LC 96-2425. (Pitt Series in Nature & Natural History). (Illus.). 504p. 1997. text 55.00 (*0-8229-3923-1*) U of Pittsburgh Pr.

Robbins, Charles E. Attorney's Master Guide to Expediting Top Dollar Case Settlements. 1975. 69.50 (*0-13-050526-9*) Exec Reports.

Robbins, Charles J., ed. see Cannon, Thomas H.

Robbins, Charles L. R. Madison Mitchell: His Life & Decoys. (Illus.). 1988. 24.95 (*0-9620028-0-1*) C L Robbins.

— Teachers in Germany in the Sixteenth Century: Conditions in Protestant Elementary & Secondary Schools. LC 74-177195. (Columbia University. Teachers College. Contributions to Education Ser.: No. 52). reprint ed. 37.50 (*0-404-55052-5*) AMS Pr.

Robbins, Charles T. Wildlife Feeding & Nutrition. 2nd ed. (Animal Feeding & Nutrition Ser.). (Illus.). 347p. 1994. pap. text 63.00 (*0-12-589383-3*) Acad Pr.

Robbins, Charles T., jt. auth. see Palo, R. Thomas.

Robbins, Christopher. The Earl of Wharton & Whig Party Politics, 1679-1715. LC 91-43272. (Studies in British History: Vol. 29). (Illus.). 484p. 1992. lib. bdg. 109.95 (*0-7734-9462-6*) E Mellen.

***Robbins, Christopher.** Test of Courage: The Michel Thomas Story. LC 00-37634. 2000. pap. write for info. (*0-7432-0263-5*) Free Pr.

Robbins, Christopher, jt. auth. see Polunin, Miriam.

Robbins, Clarence R. Chemical & Physical Behavior of Human Hair. LC 93-38111. 1997. 92.95 (*0-387-94191-6*) Spr-Verlag.

Robbins, Clive & Robbins, Carol, eds. Healing Heritage: Paul Nordoff Exploring the Tonal Language of Music. LC 99-171118. (Illus.). 240p. (C). 1998. pap. text 32.00 (*1-891278-06-1*) Barcelona Pubs.

Robbins, Clive, jt. auth. see Nordoff, Paul.

Robbins, Clive, jt. auth. see Robbins, Carol.

Robbins, Coy D. Indiana Negro Registers, 1852-1865. LC 94-184811. 185p. (Orig.). 1994. pap. text 30.00 (*1-55613-940-3*) Heritage Bk.

— Reclaiming African Heritage at Salem, Indiana. 234p. (Orig.). 1995. pap. 33.00 (*0-7884-0325-7*) Heritage Bk.

Robbins, Curt. Conducting Internet Research. Alcorn, Susan & Nichols, Holly, eds. (Illus.). 145p. 1997. pap. text 34.00 (*1-891976-04-4*) NetQuest Pubg.

— Exploring the Web. Alcorn, Susan & Nichols, Holly, eds. (Illus.). 141p. 1997. pap. text 29.00 (*1-891976-02-8*) NetQuest Pubg.

— HTML Fundamentals. Alcorn, Susan & Nichols, Holly, eds. 156p. 1996. pap. text 29.00 (*1-891976-03-6*) NetQuest Pubg.

— Internet Fundamentals. Alcorn, Susan & Nichols, Holly, eds. (Illus.). 141p. 1996. pap. text 29.00 (*1-891976-00-1*) NetQuest Pubg.

— Introduction to the Internet & Online Services. Alcorn, Susan, ed. (Illus.). 90p. 1996. pap. text 16.00 (*1-891976-06-0*) NetQuest Pubg.

— Navigating the Web. Alcorn, Susan & Nichols, Holly, eds. (Illus.). 141p. 1997. pap. text 29.00 (*1-891976-01-X*) NetQuest Pubg.

— Using the Internet in Business. Alcorn, Susan & Nichols, Holly, eds. (Illus.). 142p. 1997. pap. text 29.00 (*1-891976-05-2*) NetQuest Pubg.

Robbins, Curt, jt. auth. see DDC Publishing Staff.

Robbins, D. R. Count Us In. (Illus.). 24p. (J). (ps-4). 1996. 13.95 (*1-889506-03-6*) Kendar Pub.

Robbins, D. V. Embarrassed by the Light: A Terminal-Death Experience. (Illus.). 144p. 1995. pap. 8.95 (*0-9644907-5-7*) Raven Hse.

— God Left Town on a Tuesday: The Ravings of a Creator Gone Psycho. (Illus.). 1996. 12.00 (*0-9644907-4-9*) Raven Hse.

Robbins, D. W. Robbins. 221p. 1991. reprint ed. pap. 34.50 (*0-8328-2028-8*); reprint ed. lib. bdg. 44.50 (*0-8328-2027-X*) Higginson Bk Co.

Robbins, Dale A. What People Ask about the Church: Answers to Your Questions Concerning Today's Church. LC 95-90611. 212p. (Orig.). 1995. pap. 9.95 (*0-9648022-0-1*) Victorious Pubns.

Robbins, Dan. Whatever Happened to Paint-by-Numbers? A Humorous (Personal) Account of What It Took to Make Anyone an Artist. Weller, William, ed. (Illus.). 340p. 1998. pap. 16.95 (*0-9660693-4-X*) Possum Hill.

Robbins, Daniel. Beyond Minimalism, George Waterman Collection. LC 78-105670. (Illus.). 1969. pap. 2.00 (*0-911517-21-9*) Mus of Art RI.

— Edward Koren: Prints & Drawings, 1959-1981. Littlefield, Thomson, ed. LC 82-61087. (Illus.). 56p. (Orig.). 1982. pap. 10.00 (*0-910763-00-3*) U Albany Art Mus.

— Joaquin Torres-Garcia, 1874-1949. LC 74-130023. (Illus.). 137p. 1970. pap. 4.50 (*0-911517-23-5*) Mus of Art RI.

— Vintage Racing Machine: Cars from the Collection of George Waterman Jr. (Illus.). 1970. pap. 5.00 (*0-911517-41-3*) Mus of Art RI.

Robbins, Daniel & Downing, George, eds. Herbert & Nannette Rothschild Collection. LC 66-29131. (Illus.). 1966. pap. 7.50 (*0-911517-22-7*) Mus of Art RI.

Robbins, Daniel & Fayerweather, Eleanor. Mountain Artisans - Appalachia. (Illus.). 1970. pap. 3.00 (*0-911517-28-6*) Mus of Art RI.

Robbins, Daniel & Seitz, William, eds. Exchange Exhibition, Exhibition Exchange. LC 67-19406. (Illus.). 1967. pap. 5.00 (*0-911517-18-9*) Mus of Art RI.

Robbins, Daniel & Zinsser, John, texts. Larry Poons, 1963-1990. LC 90-60991. (Illus.). 113p. 1990. pap. 40.00 (*1-58821-060-X*) Salander OReilly.

Robbins, David. Driving South. 250p. 19.95 (*1-86812-467-3*) Menasha Ridge.

— The Fox Run. (Endworld Ser.: No. 1). 256p. 1991. pap. text, mass mkt. 3.50 (*0-8439-3105-1*) Dorchester Pub Co.

***Robbins, David.** Navy Diver. (Illus.). (J). 2000. mass mkt. 6.99 (*0-451-40974-4*, Onyx) NAL.

Robbins, David. The Return of the Virginian. large type ed. LC 94-10669. 535p. 1994. lib. bdg. 20.95 (*0-8161-5997-1*, G K Hall Lrg Type) Mac Lib Ref.

— Spartan Run - Madman Run. (Endworld Double Edition Ser.). 384p. 1993. pap. text, mass mkt. 4.50 (*0-8439-3484-0*) Dorchester Pub Co.

— Vampire Strike - Pipeline Strike, 2 vols. in 1. (Blade Double Edition Ser.). 384p. 1992. pap. 4.50 (*0-8439-3310-0*) Dorchester Pub Co.

An Asterisk (*) at the beginning of an entry indicates that the title is appearing for the first time.

Robbins, David, et al, eds. Rethinking Social Inequality. 272p. 1982. text 78.95 (*0-566-00557-3*) Ashgate Pub Co.

Robbins, David C., jt. ed. see Leslie, R. D.

Robbins, David E. Securities Arbitration Procedure Manual. 300p. 1994. ring bd. 125.00 (*0-614-05963-1*, MICHIE) LEXIS Pub.

— Securities Arbitration Procedure Manual. 2nd ed. LC 95-224449. 1990. spiral bd. 110.00 (*1-55834-266-4*, 82378, MICHIE) LEXIS Pub.

— Securities Arbitration Procedure Manual. 3rd ed. LC 98-84907. xviii, 1097 p. 1998. 120.00 (*1-55834-890-5*) LEXIS Pub.

— Securities Arbitration Procedure Manual, 1990-1993. 32p. 1994. ring bd., suppl. ed. 63.00 (*0-614-03168-0*, MICHIE) LEXIS Pub.

***Robbins, David L.** The End of War: A Novel of the Race for Berlin. 400p. 2000. 24.95 (*0-553-10830-1*, Spectra) Bantam.

Robbins, David L. A History of Suffolk University. (Illus.). 272p. (C). 1996. write for info. (*0-9652812-0-5*) Suffolk U Creative.

— Souls to Keep: A Novel. LC 97-43703. 400p. 1998. 23.00 (*0-06-101300-5*) HarpC.

— Souls to Keep: A Novel. 400p. 1999. mass mkt. 6.50 (*0-06-109791-8*) HarpC.

Robbins, David L. War of the Rats. LC 98-43918. 416p. 1999. 23.95 (*0-553-10817-4*) Bantam.

***Robbins, David L.** War of the Rats. 496p. 2000. mass mkt. 6.99 (*0-553-58135-X*) Bantam.

Robbins, Dawn Michelle, jt. auth. see Dreibrodt, Stacie Champlin.

Robbins, Dawn Michelle, ed. see Dreibrodt, Stacie Champlin.

Robbins, Dawn Michelle, ed. see Klar, Elizabeth.

Robbins, Dawn Michelle, ed. see Klar, Elizabeth & Trim, Cheryl Klar.

Robbins, Dawn Michelle, ed. see Mammen, Lori.

Robbins, Dawn Michelle, ed. see Watson, Pat.

Robbins, Debra L. Destination 2000, Level C. 1997. pap., student ed. 7.99 (*1-55743-456-5*) Raintree Steck-V.

— Destination 2000, Level D. 1997. pap., student ed. 7.99 (*1-55743-459-X*) Raintree Steck-V.

— Destination 2000, Level B. 1997. pap., student ed. 7.99 (*1-55743-453-0*) Raintree Steck-V.

— Destination 2000, Level E. 1997. pap., student ed. 7.99 (*1-55743-462-X*) Raintree Steck-V.

— Destination 2000, Level F. 1997. pap., student ed. 7.99 (*1-55743-465-4*) Raintree Steck-V.

— Destination 2000, Level G. 1997. pap., student ed. 7.99 (*1-55743-468-9*) Raintree Steck-V.

— Destino 2000. (SPA.). 1997. pap., student ed. 7.99 (*0-8114-9719-4*); pap., student ed. 7.99 (*0-8114-9721-6*); pap., student ed. 7.99 (*0-8114-9723-2*) Raintree Steck-V.

Robbins, Denise. Flame & the Frost. large type ed. (Ulverscroft Large Print Ser.). 592p. 1998. 29.99 (*0-7089-3909-0*) Ulverscroft.

Robbins, Dennis. Managed Care on Trial: Recapturing Trust, Integrity, & Accountability in Healthcare. LC 98-15938. (Illus.). 225p. 1998. 40.00 (*0-07-053099-8*) McGraw.

Robbins, Dennis & Sweatt, Jeremy, eds. Big Road Exit Guide, 1993. (Eastern Edition Ser.). (Illus.). 188p. (Orig.). 1993. pap. 9.95 (*1-880477-01-7*) Inter Am Pub.

Robbins, Dennis A. Integrating Managed Care & Ethics: Transforming Challenges into Positive Outcomes. LC 97-48804. (Illus.). 400p. 1998. 60.00 (*0-07-053083-1*) McGraw.

Robbins, Dennis A. & Mangum. Ethical & Legal Issues in Home Health & Long-Term Care: Challenges & Solutions. LC 96-5377. 254p. 1996. 52.00 (*0-8342-0783-4*) Aspen Pub.

Robbins, Deri. Christmas Fun: Great Things to Make & Do. LC 95-2454. (Illus.). 32p. (J). (gr. 1-6). 1995. pap. 6.95 (*1-85697-567-3*) LKC.

***Robbins, Don.** Living Beyond the Cycle of Defeat: How to Overcome Self Centeredness. LC 99-231254. 252p. 1998. pap. 12.99 (*1-884369-76-6*) McDougal Pubng.

Robbins, Don. The Preservation of Food by Irradiation. 128p. (C). 1991. 320.00 (*1-85271-149-3*, Pub. by IBC Tech Srvs) St Mut.

Robbins, Doren. Sympathetic Manifesto: Poems. LC 87-42791. (Illus.). 91p. (Orig.). 1987. pap. 7.95 (*0-912288-26-4*) Perivale Pr.

***Robbins, Dorothy.** Vygotsky's Psychology-Philosophy: A Metaphor for Language Theory & Learning. LC 00-34937. 2000. write for info. (*0-306-46423-3*) Kluwer Academic.

Robbins, Duffy. Going the Distance: How to Build Your Faith for the Long Haul. 176p. 1991. pap. 9.99 (*0-310-54051-8*) Zondervan.

— The Ministry of Nurture: How to Build Real-Life Faith into Your Kids. 192p. 1990. pap. 14.99 (*0-310-52581-0*) Zondervan.

— Nuts & Bolts: Youth Ministry Between the Meetings. 192p. 1991. pap. 12.99 (*0-310-52571-3*) Zondervan.

Robbins, Duffy, jt. auth. see Fields, Doug.

Robbins, Edward. Why Architects Draw. LC 93-39911. (Illus.). 323p. 1994. 50.00 (*0-262-18157-6*) MIT Pr.

— Why Architects Draw. (Illus.). 328p. 1997. reprint ed. pap. text 25.00 (*0-262-68098-X*) MIT Pr.

Robbins, Edward M. Poems for Ecumencity. 59p. 1985. 7.95 (*0-89697-236-4*) Intl Univ Pr.

Robbins, Edwin C. Railway Conductors. LC 76-127435. (Columbia University. Studies in the Social Sciences: No. 148). reprint ed. 32.50 (*0-404-51148-1*) AMS Pr.

Robbins, Fern. Eastern Cowgirl Fern Goes West. (Eastern Cowgirl Fern Ser.). (Illus.). 64p. 1994. pap. 7.95 (*0-9634541-0-2*) F Robbins ECF.

Robbins, Florence G. Educational Sociology: A Study in Child Youth, School & Community. LC 72-94592. 529p. 1970. reprint ed. lib. bdg. 79.50 (*0-8371-2573-1*, ROES, Greenwood Pr) Greenwood.

Robbins, Fred, jt. auth. see Schlessinger, Nathan.

Robbins, Frederick C., jt. ed. see Daniel, Thomas M.

Robbins, Gary. Taxing Capital Gains. 1989. pap. 10.00 (*0-943802-46-6*, 143) Natl Ctr Pol.

Robbins, Gary & Robbins, Aldona. Federal Budget Issue: Jerry Brown's Tax Plan. (Illus.). 15p. (C). 1992. pap. 5.00 (*0-943802-96-2*, BG117) Natl Ctr Pol.

— Federal Budget Issue: The Clinton Economic Plan. 1992. pap. 5.00 (*1-56808-003-4*, BG120) Natl Ctr Pol.

— Federal Budget Issue: The Perot Economic Plan. 1992. pap. 5.00 (*1-56808-005-0*, BG122) Natl Ctr Pol.

— Forecasting the Effects of the Clinton Health Plan. (Illus.). 38p. (Orig.). 1994. pap. 10.00 (*1-56808-044-1*) Natl Ctr Pol.

— Forecasting the Effects of the Mitchell Health Bill. 31p. 1994. pap. 10.00 (*1-56808-024-7*, 186) Natl Ctr Pol.

— If the Budget Summit Was a Success, Why Is the Five-Year Deficit Heading Toward One Trillion Dollars? 1991. pap. 5.00 (*0-943802-88-1*, BG109) Natl Ctr Pol.

— President Clinton's Economic Plan. (Illus.). 23p. 1993. pap. text 4.00 (*1-56808-008-5*, BG 125) Natl Ctr Pol.

— A Pro-Growth Budget Strategy: Vision for the 1990s. 1990. pap. 10.00 (*0-943802-57-1*, 154) Natl Ctr Pol.

— Reforming Medicare with Medical Savings Accounts. 16p. 1995. pap. 10.00 (*1-56808-060-3*, 195) Natl Ctr Pol.

— Tax Fairness: Myths & Reality. 1991. pap. 10.00 (*0-943802-63-6*, 160) Natl Ctr Pol.

— Taxes, Deficits & the Current Recession. 1991. pap. 10.00 (*0-943802-59-8*, 156) Natl Ctr Pol.

— What a Canadian-Style Health Care System Would Cost U. S. Employers & Employees. 1990. pap. 10.00 (*0-943802-48-2*, 145) Natl Ctr Pol.

— Will the New Budget Package Create a Recession? 1990. pap. 5.00 (*0-943802-87-3*, BG108) Natl Ctr Pol.

Robbins, Gary, et al. How Our Health Care System Works. (Illus.). 44p. (Orig.). 1993. pap. 10.00 (*1-56808-000-X*, 177) Natl Ctr Pol.

— Immigration Solution. 1992. pap. 10.00 (*0-943802-75-X*, 172) Natl Ctr Pol.

— Inefficiency in the U. S. Health Care System: What Can We Do. 26p. (Orig.). 1994. pap. text 10.00 (*1-56808-016-6*, 182) Natl Ctr Pol.

Robbins, Gary, jt. auth. see Robbins, Aldona.

Robbins, Georgia, jt. auth. see Perry, Charles E., Jr.

Robbins, Gregory A. Genesis 1-3 in the History of Exegesis. (Studies in Women & Religion: Vol. 27). 312p. 1988. write for info. (*0-88946-522-3*) E Mellen.

Robbins, Guy L. And in the Seventh Day. (American University Studies: Ser. VII, Vol. 36). 242p. (C). 1995. pap. text 32.95 (*0-8204-0504-3*) P Lang Pubng.

Robbins, Gwen. A Wellness Way of Life. 4th ed. LC 98-5963. 1998. pap. text 15.50 (*0-697-29578-8*) McGraw.

Robbins, Gwen, et al. A Wellness Way of Life. 2nd ed. 496p. (C). 1993. text. write for info. (*0-697-12659-5*) Brown & Benchmark.

— A Wellness Way of Life. 3rd ed. LC 95-83871. 448p. (C). 1996. text. write for info. (*0-697-25915-3*) Brown & Benchmark.

Robbins, H. Bryan, jt. auth. see Yates, Keith D.

Robbins, Harold. The Adventurers. 1993. mass mkt. 6.99 (*0-671-87482-9*) PB.

— The Adventurers. 1995. reprint ed. lib. bdg. 29.95 (*1-56849-642-7*) Buccaneer Bks.

— The Betsy. 1993. mass mkt. 6.99 (*0-671-87483-7*) PB.

— The Betsy. 1995. reprint ed. lib. bdg. 29.95 (*1-56849-641-9*) Buccaneer Bks.

— The Carpetbaggers. 1993. mass mkt. 6.99 (*0-671-87484-5*) PB.

— The Carpetbaggers. 1993. reprint ed. lib. bdg. 45.95 (*1-56849-141-7*) Buccaneer Bks.

***Robbins, Harold.** El Corcel. Nart, Inigo, tr. 411p. (Orig.). 1998. pap. text 12.95 (*84-08-02723-9*) Planeta.

Robbins, Harold. Descent from Xanadu. 1993. mass mkt. 6.99 (*0-671-87485-3*) PB.

— The Dream Merchants. 1993. per. 6.99 (*0-671-87486-1*) PB.

— The Dream Merchants. 1995. reprint ed. lib. bdg. 29.95 (*1-56849-640-0*) Buccaneer Bks.

— Dreams Die First. 1993. mass mkt. 6.99 (*0-671-87487-X*) PB.

— Goodbye, Janette. 1993. per. 6.99 (*0-671-87488-8*) PB.

— The Inheritors. 1993. pap. 6.99 (*0-671-87489-6*, Pocket Books) PB.

***Robbins, Harold.** Intrusos, Los. 1998. pap. 12.95 (*84-08-02207-5*) Planeta.

Robbins, Harold. The Lonely Lady. 1993. per. 6.99 (*0-671-87490-X*) PB.

— Memories of Another Day. 1993. per. 6.99 (*0-671-87491-8*, Pocket Books) PB.

— Never Leave Me. 224p. 1978. mass mkt. 4.99 (*0-380-00179-9*, Avon Bks) Morrow Avon.

***Robbins, Harold.** Never Leave Me. 2001. text. write for info. (*0-312-86610-0*) St Martin.

Robbins, Harold. Never Love a Stranger. 1993. per. 5.99 (*0-671-87492-6*) PB.

— Never Love a Stranger. 1995. reprint ed. lib. bdg. 29.95 (*1-56849-644-3*) Buccaneer Bks.

— The Piranhas. 1986. write for info. (*0-318-60976-2*) S&S Trade.

— The Piranhas. 1994. per. 6.99 (*0-671-87494-2*) S&S Trade.

— The Pirate. 1993. per. 6.99 (*0-671-87493-4*) PB.

— El Precio del Placer. (SPA.). 256p. 1992. pap. 3.95 (*1-56780-155-2*) La Costa Pr.

— The Predators. 407p. 1999. mass mkt. 6.99 (*0-8125-7178-9*, Pub. by Forge NYC) St Martin.

— The Predators. LC 98-5553. 348p. 1998. text 24.95 (*0-312-85294-0*) St Martin.

— The Raiders. 496p. 1995. per. 6.99 (*0-671-87293-1*, PB Trade Paper) PB.

— The Raiders. 1995. 23.00 (*0-671-87289-3*) S&S Trade.

— The Raiders. large type ed. 1995. 24.95 (*1-56895-262-7*, Compass) Wheeler Pub.

***Robbins, Harold.** The Secret. LC 00-23935. 352p. 2000. 25.95 (*0-312-86608-9*, Pub. by Forge NYC) St Martin.

Robbins, Harold. Seventy-Nine Park Avenue. 1993. pap. 6.99 (*0-671-87496-9*) PB.

— 79 Park Avenue. 1995. reprint ed. lib. bdg. 29.95 (*1-56849-643-5*) Buccaneer Bks.

— Spellbinder. 1993. per. 5.99 (*0-671-87495-0*) PB.

— The Stallion. 1997. mass mkt. 6.99 (*0-671-87294-X*) PB.

— Stiletto. LC 96-42517. 240p. 1997. pap. 21.95 (*1-55611-516-4*, Pub. by D I Fine) Penguin Putnam.

— Stiletto. 320p. 1999. mass mkt. 6.99 (*0-451-19743-7*, Sig) NAL.

— Stiletto. large type ed. 272p. 1983. 11.50 (*0-7089-8101-1*) Ulverscroft.

— A Stone for Danny Fisher. 1994. pap. 6.99 (*0-671-87497-7*) PB.

— The Storyteller. 1994. mass mkt. 5.99 (*0-671-87522-1*) PB.

— Tycoon. 426p. 1998. mass mkt. 7.99 (*0-671-87295-8*, Pocket Books) PB.

— Tycoon. LC 96-48523. 1997. 23.50 (*0-684-81068-9*) S&S Trade.

— Where Love Has Gone. 1994. mass mkt. 5.99 (*0-671-87498-5*) PB.

Robbins, Harvey. Why Change Doesn't Work. 232p. 1997. pap. text 14.95 (*1-56079-944-7*) Petersons.

Robbins, Harvey & Finley, Michael. Beyond Competition: From Competition & Collaboration to Transcompetition. LC 97-48492. 288p. 1998. 24.95 (*0-07-053082-3*, BusinessWeek Bks) McGraw.

***Robbins, Harvey & Finley, Michael.** The New Why Teams Don't Work: What Went Wrong & How to Make It Right. rev. ed. 270p. 2000. pap. 17.95 (*1-57675-110-4*, Pub. by Berrett-Koehler) Publishers Group.

Robbins, Harvey & Finley, Michael. Why Change Doesn't Work: Why Initiatives Go Wrong & How to Try Again & Succeed. 240p. 1996. 24.95 (*1-56079-675-8*, Petersons Pacesetter) Petersons.

— Why Teams Don't Work: What Went Wrong & How to Make It Right. LC 95-3270. 240p. 1995. 24.95 (*1-56079-497-6*, Petersons Pacesetter) Petersons.

Robbins, Harvey A. How to Speak & Listen Effectively. (AMA Worksmart Ser.). 90p. (Orig.). 1992. pap. 10.95 (*0-8144-7793-3*) AMACOM.

Robbins, Hayes, ed. see Gompers, Samuel.

Robbins, Ira A. The Trouser Press Guide to '90s Rock. Sprague, David, ed. LC 96-41087. 1997. pap. 24.95 (*0-684-81437-4*) S&S Trade.

Robbins, Ira P. Habeas Corpus Checklists, 1 vol. (Criminal Law Ser.). 1993. 75.00 (*0-87632-906-7*) West Group.

— Prisoners & the Law, 4 vols., Set. LC 85-16678. (Civil Rights Ser.). 1985. ring bd. 450.00 (*0-87632-478-2*) West Group.

Robbins, J. & Moscrop, J. E. Caring for the Dying Patient & the Family. 3rd ed. 304p. 1995. pap. 49.95 (*1-56593-328-1*, 0658) Singular Publishing.

Robbins, J., jt. ed. see Kankey, R.

Robbins, J. Albert. The Merrill Checklist of Edgar Allan Poe. LC 72-90037. (Charles E. Merrill Program in American Literature Ser.). iv, 44 p. 1969. write for info. (*0-675-09463-1*) Macmillan.

Robbins, J. Albert, ed. American Literary Scholarship: An Annual, 1968. LC 65-19450. xiv, 335p. 1970. text 60.00 (*0-8223-0235-7*) Duke.

— American Literary Scholarship: An Annual, 1969. LC 65-19450. xiv, 385p. 1971. text 60.00 (*0-8223-0248-9*) Duke.

— American Literary Scholarship: An Annual, 1970. LC 65-19450. xii, 434p. 1972. text 60.00 (*0-8223-0270-5*) Duke.

— American Literary Scholarship: An Annual, 1971. LC 65-19450. xiv, 418p. 1973. text 60.00 (*0-8223-0293-4*) Duke.

— American Literary Scholarship: An Annual, 1972. LC 65-19450. xvi, 448p. 1974. text 60.00 (*0-8223-0324-8*) Duke.

— American Literary Scholarship: An Annual, 1976. LC 65-19450. xv, 490p. 1978. text 60.00 (*0-8223-0406-6*) Duke.

— American Literary Scholarship: An Annual, 1978. LC 65-19450. xviii, 528p. 1980. text 60.00 (*0-8223-0443-0*) Duke.

— American Literary Scholarship: An Annual, 1985. LC 65-19450. 536p. (C). 1987. text 60.00 (*0-8223-0720-0*) Duke.

— American Literary Scholarship: An Annual, 1988. LC 65-19450. 616p. (C). 1990. text 60.00 (*0-8223-1033-3*) Duke.

— American Literary Scholarship, 1980. LC 65-1950. xix, 625p. 1982. text 60.00 (*0-8223-0464-3*) Duke.

— American Literary Scholarship, 1984. LC 65-19450. 613p. 1986. text 60.00 (*0-8223-0666-2*) Duke.

Robbins, Jack, jt. auth. see Gosselin, Raymond A.

Robbins, Jack A., ed. The Complete Poetry of John Reed. LC 82-21915. 102p. (Orig.). 1983. lib. bdg. 40.50 (*0-8191-2931-3*) U Pr of Amer.

Robbins, James G. & Jones, Barbara S. Effective Communication for Today's Manager. LC 74-79216. (Illus.). 174p. 1989. pap. 28.95 (*0-912016-36-1*) Lebhar Friedman.

Robbins, James M., ed. see Huffstickler, Albert.

Robbins, James M., ed. see King, Willie J.

Robbins, James M., jt. ed. see Kirmayer, Laurence J.

Robbins, James M., ed. see Norwood, Ben.

Robbins, James M., ed. see Scofield, James.

Robbins, Jane & Zweizig, Douglas L. Are We There Yet? Evaluating Library Collections, Reference Services, Programs & Personnel. 152p. 1988. pap. 8.00 (*0-936442-12-3*) U Wis Sch Lib.

Robbins, Jane, et al. Evaluation Strategies & Techniques for Public Library Children's Services: A Sourcebook. 302p. 1990. pap. 18.00 (*0-936442-14-X*) U Wis Sch Lib.

— Libraries: Partners in Adult Literacy. Hernon, Peter & McClure, Charles R., eds. (Information Management, Policies & Services Ser.: Vol. 15). 248p. 1991. text 73.25 (*0-89391-614-5*) Ablx Pub.

— The Tell It! Manual: The Complete Program for Evaluating Library Performance. LC 95-26323. (Illus.). 272p. 1996. pap. 35.00 (*0-8389-0679-6*, 0-6796-2045) ALA.

Robbins, Jeffrey, ed. see Feynman, Richard Phillips, et al.

Robbins, Jeffrey M., ed. Primary Care Podiatry. LC 93-17926. 1994. text 69.00 (*0-7216-4363-9*, W B Saunders Co) Harcrt Hlth Sci Grp.

Robbins, Jenni L., ed. Quality Program: Quality Plan Manual. LC 94-27478. (Illus.). (C). 1994. ring bd. 175.00 (*1-56395-040-5*) Am Assn Blood.

— Quality Program: Self-Assessment Manual. LC 94-27478. (Illus.). (C). 1994. ring bd. 175.00 (*1-56395-039-1*) Am Assn Blood.

Robbins, Jeremy. The Challenges of Uncertainty: An Introduction to Seventeenth-Century Spanish Literature. 160p. 1998. 49.00 (*0-8476-9327-9*); pap. 22.95 (*0-8476-9328-7*) Rowman.

***Robbins, Jerry.** For Love & Liberty LC 98-96478. 224p. 1998. write for info. (*1-892358-00-X*) Medea Pubng.

— Provocables! Dramatic Readings for Faith & Life. LC 99-55436. 2000. pap. 17.50 (*0-7880-1591-5*) CSS OH.

Robbins, Jill. Altered Reading: Levinas & Literature. LC 98-37917. 216p. 1999. pap. text 16.00 (*0-226-72113-2*) U Ch Pr.

— Prodigal Son - Elder Brother: Interpretation & Alterity in Augustine, Petrarch, Kafka, Levinas. LC 90-19722. (Religion & Postmodernism Ser.). 190p. 1991. 29.95 (*0-226-72110-8*) U Ch Pr.

Robbins, Jim. Crappie! 1991. 21.95 (*1-879034-02-6*) MS River Pub.

***Robbins, Jim.** A Symphony in the Brain: The Evolution of the New Brain Wave Biofeedback. LC 99-86648. 256p. 2000. 24.00 (*0-87113-807-7*, Pub. by Grove-Atltic) Publishers Group.

Robbins, Jo. High Impact Presentation: A Multimedia Approach. LC 97-28025. 245p. 1997. pap. 19.95 (*0-471-15781-3*) Wiley.

Robbins, Joan H. & Siegel, Rachel J., eds. Women Changing Therapy: New Assessments, Values, & Strategies in Feminist Therapy. LC 83-12643. (Women & Therapy Ser.: Vol. 2, Nos. 2-3). 240p. 1983. text 39.95 (*0-86656-239-7*); pap. text 14.95 (*0-86656-240-0*) Haworth Pr.

— Women Changing Therapy: New Assessments, Values & Strategies in Feminist Therapy. LC 84-19276. 240p. 1985. pap. text 14.95 (*0-918393-07-8*, Harrington Park) Haworth Pr.

Robbins, Joan W., ed. see Clark, Gordon H.

Robbins, Joel, ed. High Performance Futures Trading: Power Lessons for the Masters. 1991. text 45.00 (*1-55738-149-6*, Irwn Prfssnl) McGraw-Hill Prof.

Robbins, Joel & Clarke, Peter S. The Bankers Compliance Credit & Loan Administration: Developing & Monitoring a Cost-Effective Quality Control Program. 1994. per. 60.00 (*1-55738-733-8*, Irwn Prfssnl) McGraw-Hill Prof.

Robbins, Joel, jt. ed. see Akin, David.

Robbins, John. Diet for a New America. 2nd ed. LC 98-10195. (Illus.). 448p. 1998. pap. 14.95 (*0-915811-81-2*) H J Kramer Inc.

— May All Be Fed: Diet for a New World. 416p. 1993. reprint ed. pap. 14.00 (*0-380-71901-0*, Avon Bks) Morrow Avon.

— Reclaiming Our Health: Exploding the Medical Myth & Embracing the Source of True Healing. (Illus.). 432p. 1998. pap. 14.95 (*0-915811-80-4*) H J Kramer Inc.

— Strings: The Miracle of Life. 220p. 1998. 23.95 (*1-880823-17-9*) N Star Pubns.

Robbins, John & Mitgang, Susan, eds. The ABC's of Parent Involvement in Education: Preparing Your Child for Success--Parent Involvement Tips for Lifelong Learning. (Illus.). 160p. 1998. pap. text 0.99 (*0-9663119-0-6*) Natl Parents Day.

Robbins, John & Mortifee, Ann. The Awakened Heart: Finding Harmony in a Changing World. 2nd rev. ed. LC 96-40536. (Inner Light Ser.: Bk. 3). (Illus.). 120p. 1997. 14.00 (*0-915811-74-X*) H J Kramer Inc.

— Le Coeur en Eveil: Meditations pour Trouver l'Harmonie dans un Monde en Changement. (FRE.). 1998. 19.95 (*2-89466-014-6*) Edns Roseau.

Robbins, John, jt. ed. see Fink-Hafner, Danica.

Robbins, John B., et al, eds. Bacterial Vaccines. LC 86-9523. 589p. 1987. 115.00 (*0-275-92157-3*, C2157, Praeger Pubs) Greenwood.

Robbins, John W. Cornelius Van Til: The Man & the Myth. 42p. (Orig.). 1986. pap. 2.45 (*0-94093l-15-X*) Trinity Found.

— Ecclesiastical Megalomania: The Economic & Political Thought of the Roman Catholic Church. 350p. 1999. 29.95 (*0-940931-78-8*); pap. 19.95 (*0-940931-52-4*) Trinity Found.

— Without a Prayer: Ayn Rand & the Close of Her System. (Trinity Papers: Vol. 50). 350p. 1997. 27.95 (*0-940931-50-8*) Trinity Found.

Robbins, John W., ed. Gordon H. Clark: Personal Recollections. 150p. (Orig.). 1989. pap. 6.95 (*0-940931-27-3*) Trinity Found.

R

An Asterisk (*) at the beginning of an entry indicates that the title is appearing for the first time.

R

Robbins, John W. & Spangler, Mark, eds. A Man of Principle: Essays in Honor of Hans F. Sennholz. 571p. (C). 1992. 30.00 (0-9631818-0-7) Grove City Coll.

***Robbins, John W., et al.** The Church Effeminate: And Other Essays. 500p. (C). 2000. pap. 19.95 (0-940931-54-0) Trinity Found.

Robbins, John W., ed. see Clark, Gordon H.

Robbins, John W., ed. see Clark, Gordon H., et al.

Robbins, John W., ed. see Machen, J. Gresham.

Robbins, John W., ed. see Warfield, Benjamin B., et al.

Robbins, John W., ed. & frwd. see Clark, Gordon H.

Robbins, John W., ed. & intro. see Bonar, Horatius.

Robbins, John W., ed. & intro. see Carranza, Elihu.

Robbins, John W., ed. & intro. see Clark, Gordon H.

Robbins, John W., ed. & intro. see Clark, Gordon H. & Augustine, Aurelius.

Robbins, John W., ed. & intro. see Clark, Gordon H. & Warfield, Benjamin B.

Robbins, John W., ed. & intro. see Crampton, W. Gary.

Robbins, John W., ed. & intro. see Hodge, Charles.

Robbins, John W., ed. & intro. see Hoeksema, Herman.

Robbins, John W., ed. & intro. see Machen, J. Gresham.

Robbins, Jon G., et al, eds. Basic & Clinical Perspectives in Vision Research: A Celebration of the Career of Hisako Ikeda. (Illus.). 244p. 1996. 85.00 (0-306-45202-2, Kluwer Plenum) Kluwer Academic.

Robbins, Joyce. Cats. 1995. 7.98 (0-7858-0413-7) Bk Sales Inc.

— Kittens. 1995. 7.98 (0-7858-0412-9) Bk Sales Inc.

— Wildlife. 1995. 7.98 (0-7858-0416-1) Bk Sales Inc.

Robbins, Judd. Lotus 1-2-3: Step by Step. 1990. pap. 24.95 (0-672-22712-6, MICHIE) LEXIS Pub.

— SAT Flash Card Set: Mathematics. unabridged ed. (SAT Flash Card Study Materials Ser.). 101p. (YA). 1997. pap. 15.00 (0-9614937-5-5) Present Dynam.

— SAT Flash Card Set: The Complete Collection. unabridged ed. (SAT Flash Card Study Materials Ser.). 816p. (YA). 1997. pap. 49.00 (0-9614937-7-1) Present Dynam.

— SAT Flash Card Set: The Overall SAT I. unabridged ed. (SAT Flash Card Study Materials Ser.). 101p. (YA). 1997. pap. 15.00 (0-9614937-3-9) Present Dynam.

— SAT Flash Card Set: Verbal. unabridged ed. (SAT Flash Card Study Materials Ser.). 101p. (YA). 1997. pap. 15.00 (0-9614937-4-7) Present Dynam.

— SAT Flash Card Set: Vocabulary. unabridged ed. (SAT Flash Card Study Materials Ser.). 101p. (YA). 1997. pap. 15.00 (0-9614937-6-3) Present Dynam.

***Robbins, Judd & Miller, Alan R.** Circuit Analysis: Theory & Practice. 2nd ed. LC 99-37574. (Instructor Material TV Ser.). 1113p. (C). 1999. pap. text 95.95 (0-7668-0626-X) Delmar.

Robbins, Judd, ed. see Cohn, Steven M.

Robbins, Judd, ed. see Pilates, Joseph H.

Robbins, Judd, ed. see Pilates, Joseph H. & Miller, William J.

Robbins, Judith R. Sun Priestess. 416p. 1998. mass mkt. 6.99 (0-451-40787-3, Onyx) NAL.

Robbins, Juliette, jt. auth. see Collins, Brad.

Robbins, K. Thomas. Advances in Head & Neck Oncology. LC 97-36322. (Illus.). 300p. 1998. pap. 99.95 (1-56593-840-2, 1640) Thomson Learn.

Robbins, K. Thomas & Murry, Thomas. Head & Neck Cancer: Organ Preservation, Function, & Rehabilitation. (Illus.). 140p. 1998. pap. 75.00 (1-56593-972-7, 1924) Thomson Learn.

Robbins, Karen. Divide the Child. 1999. pap. 9.95 (1-886699-18-6) Five Corners.

Robbins, Kay A. & Robbins, S. The Cray X-MP - Model 24. (Lecture Notes in Computer Science Ser.: Vol. 374). iv, 165p. 1989. 32.95 (0-387-97089-4, 3132) Spr-Verlag.

Robbins, Kay A. & Robbins, Steven. Practical UNIX Programming: A Guide to Concurrency, Communication, & Multithreading. LC 95-39618. 672p. 1996. 62.00 (0-13-443706-3) P-H.

Robbins, Kay A., jt. auth. see Gonzales, Mario J.

Robbins, Keith. Appeasement. 2nd rev. ed. LC 96-44376. (Historical Association Studies). 144p. (C). 1997. pap. text 14.95 (0-631-20326-5) Blackwell Pubs.

— Bibliography of Writings on British History, 1914-1989. LC 96-233104. 958p. 1996. text 160.00 (0-19-822496-6) OUP.

— Churchill. (Profiles in Power Ser.). (C). 1992. text 42.50 (0-582-03137-0, Pub. by Addison-Wesley) Longman.

Robbins, Keith. Churchill. LC 91-46364. (Profiles in Power Ser.). 208p. (C). 1995. pap. text 34.80 (0-582-03136-2) Addison-Wesley.

Robbins, Keith. Churchill. (Profiles In Power Ser.). 1993. pap. text 19.95 (0-685-72550-2, 79372) Longman.

— Eclipse Great 1870 1992. 2nd ed. LC 94-841. (Foundations of Modern Britain Ser.). (C). 1994. text 68.95 (0-582-09612-X, 76707, Pub. by Addison-Wesley) Longman.

— Eclipse Great Power. LC 81-18608. (Illus.). 304p. (C). 1983. pap. text 29.95 (0-582-48972-5, 73420) Longman.

— The First World War. (Illus.). 208p. 1985. pap. text 15.95 (0-19-289149-9) OUP.

— Great Britain: Identities, Institutions & the Idea of Britishness. LC 96-53505. (Present & Past Ser.). (Illus.). 377p. (C). 1998. pap. text 26.25 (0-582-03119-2, Pub. by Addison-Wesley) Longman.

— History, Religion, & Identity in Modern Britain. LC 93-17978. 312p. 1993. 60.00 (1-85285-101-5) Hambledon Press.

— Nineteenth-Century Britain: Integration & Diversity. (Ford Lectures 1986-1987). 212p. 1995. pap. text 21.00 (0-19-820585-6) OUP.

— Politicians, Diplomacy & War in Modern British History. LC 94-2354. 336p. 1994. 60.00 (1-85285-111-2) Hambledon Press.

***Robbins, Keith.** The World Since 1945: A Concise History. LC 98-3706. 288p. 1998. pap. 17.95 (0-19-219234-5) OUP.

Robbins, Keith, ed. see Pope, Stephen & Wheal, Elizabeth-Anne.

Robbins, Keith, ed. see Tan, Richard & Warnke, Cheryl.

Robbins, Ken. Air. (Elements Ser.). (Illus.). 88p. (J). (gr. 4-6). 1995. 16.95 (0-8050-2292-9) H Holt & Co.

— Autumn Leaves. LC 97-43895. (Illus.). 32p. (J). (ps-k). 1998. 15.95 (0-590-29879-8, Pub. by Scholastic) Scholastic Inc.

— Earth. (Elements Ser.). (Illus.). 88p. (J). 1995. 16.95 (0-8050-2294-5) H Holt & Co.

— Fire. LC 95-25209. (Elements Ser.). (Illus.). 88p. (J). (gr. 4-6). 1995. 16.95 (0-8050-2293-7) H Holt & Co.

— Make Me a Peanut Butter Sandwich & a Glass of Milk. (Illus.). 32p. (J). (ps up). 1992. 14.95 (0-590-43550-7, 023, Scholastic Hardcover) Scholastic Inc.

— Power Machines. 1997. pap. text 6.95 (0-8050-5297-6) H Holt & Co.

***Robbins, Ken.** Thunder on the Plains: The Story of the American Buffalo. LC 00-21426. (Illus.). (J). 2001. write for info. (0-689-83025-4) Atheneum Yung Read.

— Tools. 1999. 24.99 (0-590-07881-X, Blue Sky Press) Scholastic Inc.

Robbins, Ken. Trucks: Giants of the Highway. LC 98-47640. (Illus.). 32p. (J). 1999. 16.00 (0-689-82664-8) Atheneum Yung Read.

Robbins, Ken, photos by. Power Machines. LC 92-30649. (Illus.). 32p. (J). (gr. k-3). 1995. 15.95 (0-8050-1410-1, Bks Young Read) H Holt & Co.

Robbins, Kenn. Buttermilk Bottoms: A Novel. LC 87-4997. 268p. reprint ed. pap. 83.10 (0-7837-1625-7, 204191800024) Bks Demand.

Robbins, Kenneth. A Good & Dandy World. 1980. pap. 1.75 (0-686-38380-X) Eldridge Pub.

Robbins, Kevin C. City on the Ocean Sea: La Rochelle 1530-1650: Urban Society, Religion, & Politics on the French Atlantic Frontier. LC 97-24830. (Studies in Medieval & Reformation Thought: Vol. 64). (Illus.). xviii, 466p. 1997. 159.00 (90-04-10880-7) Brill Academic Pubs.

Robbins, L. Pearne. One Shahaptan Gathering Fuel. (Illus.). 118p. (Orig.). 1994. pap. 8.00 (1-883501-01-6) R Lodges Pub.

— One Shahapton Stirring Ashes. rev. ed. (Illus.). 135p. 1993. pap. 8.00 (1-883501-00-8) R Lodges Pub.

Robbins, Larry M. The Business of Writing & Speaking: A Managerial Communication Manual. 2nd rev. ed. LC 95-37232. 256p. 1995. pap. 28.13 (0-07-053091-2) McGraw.

Robbins, Laura. The Bride's Guide to Writing Thank You Notes. 52p. (Orig.). 1996. pap. 9.95 (0-9657555-0-9) Notations.

***Robbins, Lawrence.** Headache Help: A Complete Guide to Understanding Headaches & the Medications That Relieve Them. (Illus.). 288p. 2000. pap. 15.00 (0-618-04436-1) HM.

Robbins, Lawrence & Lang, Susan S. Headache Help: A Complete Guide to Understanding Headaches & the Medicines That Relieve Them. LC 94-43494. 224p. 1995. pap. 12.00 (0-395-70751-X) HM.

Robbins, Lawrence D. Management of Headache & Headache Medications. LC 93-19226. 217p. 1994. 75.00 (0-387-94040-5) Spr-Verlag.

***Robbins, Lawrence D.** Management of Headache & Headache Medications. 2nd ed. LC 99-46474. 224p. 2000. pap. 49.00 (0-387-98944-7) Spr-Verlag.

Robbins, Lawrence H. Stones, Bones & Ancient Cities: Great Discoveries in Archaeology & the Search for Human. 1992. pap. 10.95 (0-312-07848-X) St Martin.

***Robbins, Lionel.** History of Economic Thought: The LSE Lectures. (Illus.). 393p. 2000. pap. 18.95 (0-691-07014-8) Princeton U Pr.

Robbins, Lionel, et al. A History of Economic Thought: The LSE Lectures. LC 97-51808. 393p. 1998. text 39.95 (0-691-01244-X, Pub. by Princeton U Pr) Cal Prin Full Svc.

Robbins, Lionel, ed. see Wicksell, Knut.

Robbins, Lionel C. Economic Planning & International Order. LC 72-4294. (World Affairs Ser.; National & International Viewpoints). 348p. 1972. reprint ed. 23.95 (0-405-04586-7) Ayer.

— Great Depression. LC 75-150198. (Select Bibliographies Reprint Ser.). 1977. reprint ed. 25.95 (0-8369-5711-3) Ayer.

Robbins, Louise S. Censorship & the American Library: The American Library Association's Response to Threats to Intellectual Freedom, 1939-1969, 89. LC 96-8429. (Contributions in Librarianship & Information Science: Vol. 89). 272p. 1996. 59.95 (0-313-29644-8, Greenwood Pr) Greenwood.

***Robbins, Louise S.** The Dismissal of Miss Ruth Brown: Civil Rights, Censorship, & the American Library. LC 99-38926. (Illus.). 256p. 2000. 29.95 (0-8061-3163-2) U of Okla Pr.

Robbins, Lynn, ed. see Bouldin, Carol Walker.

Robbins, Lynn E. The Administrative Handbook. 364p. 1995. lib. bdg. 80.00 (1-888143-11-8) Robbins Mgmt.

— The Food Service Handbook. 140p. 1995. pap. 45.00 (1-888143-13-4) Robbins Mgmt.

— The Menu Book. 356p. (C). 1995. pap. 125.00 (1-888143-10-X) Robbins Mgmt.

— The Recipe Book for 50. 416p. (C). 1994. pap. 125.00 (1-888143-04-5) Robbins Mgmt.

— The Recipe Book for 100. 416p. (C). 1994. pap. 125.00 (1-888143-05-3) Robbins Mgmt.

— The Recipe Book for 10. 416p. (C). 1994. pap. 125.00 (1-888143-02-9) Robbins Mgmt.

— The Recipe Book for 200. 416p. (C). 1994. pap. 125.00 (1-888143-06-1) Robbins Mgmt.

— The Sing-Along Book. 68p. 1993. pap. 8.00 (1-888143-07-X) Robbins Mgmt.

— The Staff Training Manual. 324p. 1995. lib. bdg. 80.00 (1-888143-12-6) Robbins Mgmt.

Robbins, M. North London Railway. (C). 1985. 39.00 (0-85361-074-6) St Mut.

Robbins, M. S. Amelie. (Illus.). 1986. pap. 5.00 (0-941240-07-X) Ommation Pr.

Robbins, Manuel. Fluorescence: Gems & Minerals under Ultraviolet Light. LC 93-77811. (Illus.). 400p. 1994. 40.00 (0-945005-13-X) Geoscience Pr.

Robbins, Marc L. & McIver, D. W. Precision-Guided Logistics: Flexible Support for the Force-Projection Army's High-Technology Weapons. LC 94-30295. 1994. pap. 15.00 (0-8330-1574-5, MR-437-A) Rand Corp.

***Robbins, Marc L., et al.** Measurement of USMC Logistics Processes: Creating a Baseline to Support Precision Logistics Implementation. LC 98-168088. xx, 139p. 1998. pap. 10.00 (0-8330-2613-5) Rand Corp.

Robbins, Marc L., jt. auth. see Fricker, Ronald D.

Robbins, Margaret. AppWare: A Developers Guide. LC 95-9910. 450p. 1995. pap. 39.95 incl. disk (1-55851-403-1, M&T Bks) IDG Bks.

— Evaluating Palliative Care: Establishing the Evidence Base. (Illus.). 192p. 1998. pap. text 32.50 (0-19-262621-3) OUP.

Robbins, Mari. Medical Receptionists & Secretaries Handbook. LC 95-48411. 254p. 1996. pap. 23.00 (1-85775-084-5, Radcliffe Med Pr) Scovill Paterson.

Robbins, Mari L. Adam of the Road. (Literature Unit Ser.). (Illus.). 48p. 1994. pap., teacher ed. 7.95 (1-55734-444-2) Tchr Create Mat.

— Anne Frank: The Diary of a Young Girl. (Literature Unit Ser.). (Illus.). 48p. 1995. pap., teacher ed. 7.95 (1-55734-559-7) Tchr Create Mat.

— Dicey's Song: A Literature Unit. (Literature Units Ser.). (Illus.). 48p. (Orig.). 1993. pap., student ed. 7.95 (1-55734-422-1) Tchr Create Mat.

— Dragonwings: A Literature Unit. (Literature Units Ser.). (Illus.). 48p. 1993. student ed. 7.95 (1-55734-429-9) Tchr Create Mat.

— From the Mixed up Files of Mrs. Basil E. Frankweiler. (Literature Unit Ser.). (Illus.). 48p. 1994. pap., teacher ed. 7.95 (1-55734-448-5) Tchr Create Mat.

— I Heard the Owl Call My Name: Literature Unit. Cain, Janet, ed. (Illus.). 48p. (Orig.). 1994. pap., student ed. 7.95 (1-55734-520-1) Tchr Create Mat.

— Native American Tales & Activities: Creative Kids. (Creative Kids Ser.). (Illus.). 160p. (J). (gr. 2 up). 1996. pap., wbk. ed. 14.95 (1-55734-677-1) Tchr Create Mat.

— The People Could Fly. (Literature Unit Ser.). (Illus.). 48p. 1995. pap., teacher ed. 7.95 (1-55734-524-4) Tchr Create Mat.

— The Red Pony: A Literature Unit. (Literature Units Ser.). (Illus.). 48p. (Orig.). (J). (gr. 6-8). 1993. pap., student ed. 7.95 (1-55734-443-4) Tchr Create Mat.

— Sounder: Literature Unit. Cain, Janet, ed. (Illus.). 48p. (Orig.). 1994. pap., student ed. 7.95 (1-55734-530-9) Tchr Create Mat.

— Writing Simulations. (Illus.). 96p. (J). 1998. pap., teacher ed. 11.95 (1-57690-121-1, TCM2121) Tchr Create Mat.

Robbins, Mari L. & Teacher Created Materials Staff. Writing Simulations: Intermediate. 96p. (J). (gr. 3-5). 1997. pap. 11.95 (1-57690-098-3) Tchr Create Mat.

Robbins, Mari L., jt. auth. see Bruce, Kathy.

Robbins, Mari L., jt. auth. see Herweck, Dona.

***Robbins, Mari Lu.** How to Write a Research Report: Grades 6-8. (Illus.). 48p. 1999. pap., teacher ed. 7.95 (1-57690-492-X, TCM 2492) Tchr Create Mat.

Robbins, Mari Lu. Internet Activities for Language Arts: TechKnowledgey. Hill, Char-Lee L., ed. 144p. (J). (gr. 5-8). 1997. pap., teacher ed. 14.95 (1-57690-408-3, TCM2408) Tchr Create Mat.

— Romeo & Juliet. (Literature Units Ser.). 48p. (J). (gr. 5-8). 1997. pap. 7.95 (1-57690-135-1) Tchr Create Mat.

— Sing down the Moon. (Literature Unit Ser.). 48p. (J). (gr. 5-8). 1997. pap. 7.95 (1-55734-432-9) Tchr Create Mat.

Robbins, Mari Lu, jt. auth. see Teacher Created Materials Staff.

Robbins, Maria. One Dish Vegetarian. LC 98-29938. 182p. 1998. text 24.95 (0-312-18151-5) St Martin.

***Robbins, Maria.** One-dish Vegetarian. (Illus.). 192p. 2000. pap. 14.95 (0-312-25403-2) St Martin.

Robbins, Maria P. Baking for Christmas: 50 of the Best Cookie, Bread, & Cake Recipes for Holiday Gift Giving, Decorating, & Eating. LC 95-21292. (Illus.). 144p. 1995. pap. 6.95 (0-312-13432-0) St Martin.

— Blue Ribbon Cookies. 144p. 1988. 11.95 (0-312-01738-3); pap. 7.95 (0-312-01739-1) St Martin.

— Cookies for Christmas: Fifty of the Best Cookie Recipes for Holiday Gift Giving, Decorating, & Eating. (Illus.). 144p. (Orig.). 1993. pap. 6.95 (0-312-09775-1) St Martin.

— A Gardener's Bouquet of Quotations. 1999. pap. 8.95 (0-452-27232-7, Plume) Dutton Plume.

— Puss in Boots. (J). 1999. pap. 9.95 (0-452-27538-5, Plume) Dutton Plume.

Robbins, Maria P., ed. The Cook's Quotation Book: A Literary Feast. 2nd ed. LC 97-17324. (Illus.). 96p. 1997. 19.00 (0-88001-573-X) HarpC.

Robbins, Maria P. & Van Waerebeek, Ruth. Everybody Eats Well in Belgium Cookbook. (Illus.). 384p. 1996. 24.95 (0-7611-0106-3, 10106) Workman Pub.

Robbins, Maria P., jt. auth. see Fischer, Leah.

Robbins, Maria P., jt. auth. see Fischer, Leah L.

Robbins, Maria P., jt. auth. see Van Waerebeek, Ruth.

Robbins, Maria Polushkin, ed. Puss in Books. LC 97-22656. 1998. 19.00 (0-88001-588-8) HarpC.

Robbins, Mark B. & Easterla, David A. Birds of Missouri: Their Distribution & Abundance. (Illus.). 416p. (C). 1991. text 59.95 (0-8262-0791-X) U of Mo Pr.

Robbins, Mark D., jt. auth. see Simonsen, William.

Robbins, Martin. A Year with Two Winters. 74p. (Orig.). 1989. pap. 10.00 (0-932662-85-4) St Andrews NC.

Robbins, Mary S., ed. Against the Vietnam War: Writing by Activists. LC 98-45027. 256p. 1999. pap. 24.95 (0-8156-2797-1) Syracuse U Pr.

***Robbins, Mary S. & Zinn, Howard, eds.** Against the Vietnam War: Writing by Activists. LC 98-45027. 3p. 1999. 49.95 (0-8156-2796-3) Syracuse U Pr.

Robbins, Mary S., et al. To a Different Drummer: Helping Children with Learning Disabilities. 2nd rev. ed. (Illus.). 124p. 1999. pap. 14.95 (0-9668751-0-9) Tadd Instruct.

Robbins, Merry B. Mr. Fidgit's Big Day. LC 96-27666. (Illus.). (J). 1997. write for info. (1-56763-293-9); pap. write for info. (1-56763-294-7) Ozark Pub.

***Robbins, Michael.** Brooklyn: A State of Mind. 480p. 2000. 29.95 (0-7611-2203-6) Workman Pub.

Robbins, Michael. Conceiving of Personality. LC 95-47043. 256p. 1996. 35.00 (0-300-06422-5) Yale U Pr.

— Experiences of Schizophrenia: An Integration of the Personal, Scientific, & Therapeutic. LC 92-48311. 511p. 1993. lib. bdg. 60.00 (0-89862-997-7) Guilford Pubns.

***Robbins, Michael.** Smart Guide to Planning for Retirement. LC 99-32349. (Smart Guides Ser.). (Illus.). 240p. 1999. pap. 12.95 (0-471-35359-0) Wiley.

***Robbins, Michael & Palitz, Wendy, eds.** Brooklyn: A State of Mind. (Illus.). 480p. 2000. pap. 19.95 (0-7611-1635-4) Workman Pub.

Robbins, Michael D. Infinitization of Selfhood: A Treatise Consecrated to the Destruction of the Ego. LC 96-53563. (Illus.). 992p. (Orig.). 1997. pap. 49.95 (0-9621869-4-5) Univ Seven Rays Pub.

— The Tapestry of the Gods: Psychological Transformation & the Seven Rays, 2 vols., Vol. I. 400p. (Orig.). 1988. pap. write for info. (0-9621869-0-2) Univ Seven Rays Pub.

— The Tapestry of the Gods: Psychological Transformation & the Seven Rays, 2 vols., Vol. II. 400p. (Orig.). 1988. pap. write for info. (0-9621869-1-0) Univ Seven Rays Pub.

— The Tapestry of the Gods: Psychological Transformation & the Seven Rays, 2 vols., Vols. I-II. LC 88-51065. 1207p. (Orig.). 1996. pap. 65.00 (0-9621869-2-9) Univ Seven Rays Pub.

***Robbins, Molly.** Behind the Black Robe. 93p. 2000. 17.95 (0-7541-1026-5, Pub. by Minerva Pr) Unity Dist.

Robbins, Morgan. Morgan Robbins' Tarot. 1983. pap. 12.00 (0-88079-028-8, MG88) US Games Syst.

Robbins, Nancy, ed. Fan Fare. (Illus.). 324p. reprint ed. 14.50 (0-9612176-0-X) Rochester Philharmonic.

Robbins, Naomi C., jt. auth. see Herstein, Sheila R.

Robbins, Neal. Contemporary Chinese Fiction: Four Short Stories. (CHI.). 225p. (Orig.). 1986. pap. text 15.95 (0-88710-140-2) Yale Far Eastern Pubns.

Robbins, Neal E. Ronald W. Reagan: Fortieth President of the United States. Young, Richard G., ed. LC 89-39955. (Presidents of the United States Ser.). (Illus.). 128p. (J). (gr. 5-9). 1990. lib. bdg. 21.27 (0-944483-66-6) Garrett Ed Corp.

— Rutherford B. Hayes: Nineteenth President of the United States. Young, Richard G., ed. LC 88-24565. (Presidents of the United States Ser.). (Illus.). (J). (gr. 5-9). 1989. lib. bdg. 21.27 (0-944483-23-2) Garrett Ed Corp.

Robbins, O. B. Jackson: History of the Jackson Family of Hempstead, Long Island, Ohio & Indiana: Descendants of Robert & Agnes Washburn Jackson. (Illus.). 356p. 1995. reprint ed. pap. 55.00 (0-8328-4794-1); reprint ed. lib. bdg. 65.00 (0-8328-4793-3) Higginson Bk Co.

Robbins, Ocean & Solomon, Sol. Choices for Our Future: A Generation Rising for Life on Earth. LC 94-29060. (Illus.). 192p. (Orig.). (J). 1994. pap. 9.95 (1-57067-002-1) Book Pub Co.

Robbins, P. D., jt. ed. see Evans, C. H.

Robbins, Pam. How to Plan & Implement a Peer Coaching Program. LC 91-27082. 69p. 1991. pap. 8.95 (0-87120-184-4, 611-91149) ASCD.

— Laughing Matters: Selected Columns by Humorist Pam Robbins. LC 98-88047. 90p. (Orig.). 1998. pap. 10.00 (0-9667357-0-6) Global Busn Persp.

Robbins, Pam & Alvy, Harvey B. The Principal's Companion: Strategies & Hints to Make the Job Easier. (Illus.). 304p. 1995. pap. 32.95 (0-8039-6197-9) Corwin Pr.

— The Principal's Companion: Strategies & Hints to Make the Job Easier. 304p. 1995. 65.95 (2-8106-6196-0); pap. 29.95 (2-8106-6197-9) NEA.

Robbins, Pam & Herndon, Lynne E. Thinking Inside the Block: The Teacher's Day-Planner. (Illus.). 192p. 1998. pap. 24.95 (0-8039-6780-2) Corwin Pr.

Robbins, Pam, et al. Thinking Inside the Block Schedule: Strategies for Teaching in Extended Periods of Time. (One-Off Ser.). 212p. 2000. 67.95 (0-8039-6782-9); pap. 30.95 (0-8039-6783-7) Corwin Pr.

Robbins, Pamela & Alvy, Harvey B. The Principal's Companion: Strategies & Hints to Make the Job Easier. Gingell, Susan, ed. LC 95-7976. (Illus.). 304p. 1995. 69.95 (0-8039-6196-0) Corwin Pr.

Robbins, Pamela, jt. auth. see Alvy, Harvey B.

Robbins, Paul D. Gene Therapy Protocols. LC 96-42147. (Methods in Molecular Medicine Ser.: Vol. 7). (Illus.). 448p. 1996. 89.50 (0-89603-307-4) Humana.

Robbins, Paul D., ed. Gene Therapy Protocols. LC 96-42147. (Methods in Molecular Medicine Ser.: Vol. 7). 448p. 1996. 120.00 (0-89603-484-4) Humana.

Robbins, Paul R. Adolescent Suicide. LC 97-23810. 172p. 1997. pap. 30.00 (0-7864-0414-0) McFarland & Co.

***Robbins, Paul R.** Anger, Aggression & Violence: An Interdisciplinary Study. 208p. 2000. pap. 35.00 (0-7864-0903-7) McFarland & Co.

Robbins, Paul R. Anorexia & Bulimia. LC 97-34157. (Diseases & People Ser.). 128p. (YA). (gr. 6 up). 1998. lib. bdg. 20.95 (0-7660-1047-3) Enslow Pubs.

An Asterisk (*) at the beginning of an entry indicates that the title is appearing for the first time.

— Crack & Cocaine Drug Dangers. LC 98-30271. (Drug Dangers Ser.). (Illus.). 64p. (YA). (gr. 4-10). 1999. lib. bdg. 19.95 (*0-7660-1155-0*) Enslow Pubs.

*__Robbins, Paul R.__ Crack & Cocaine Drug Dangers. LC 98-30271. (Drug Dangers Ser.). (Illus.). 64p. (YA). (gr. 4-10). 1999. pap. 10.95 (*0-7660-1736-2*) Enslow Pubs.

Robbins, Paul R. Designer Drugs. LC 94-16314. (Drug Library Ser.). (Illus.). 104p. (YA). (gr. 6 up). 1995. lib. bdg. 20.95 (*0-89490-488-4*) Enslow Pubs.

— Hallucinogens. LC 95-39240. (Drug Library Ser.). (Illus.). 112p. (YA). (gr. 6 up). 1996. lib. bdg. 20.95 (*0-89490-743-3*) Enslow Pubs.

— Marijuana: A Short Course Updated for the Eighties. LC 75-22753. 80p. 1983. pap. 11.95 (*0-8283-1856-5*) Branden Bks.

— The Psychology of Dreams. LC 87-29889. (Illus.). 184p. 1988. lib. bdg. 29.95 (*0-89950-270-9*) McFarland & Co.

— Romantic Relationships: A Psychologist Answers Frequently Asked Questions. LC 96-24583. 211p. 1996. pap. 28.50 (*0-7864-0192-3*) McFarland & Co.

— Understanding Depression. LC 92-56685. 200p. 1993. lib. bdg. 28.50 (*0-89950-878-2*) McFarland & Co.

Robbins, Paula I. Nights of Summer, Nights of Autumn. (Illus.). 195p. (C). 1992. pap. 12.95 (*0-9632975-0-3*) Sampo Pub.

— Nights of Summer, Nights of Autumn: Self-Care for Bodyworkers. (Illus.). 195p. (Orig.). (C). 1992. spiral bd. 12.95 (*0-9632875-0-8*) Sampo Pub.

Robbins, Peter, jt. auth. see Warren, Larry.

Robbins, R., jt. auth. see Keirans, J.

Robbins, R. H., ed. see Browne, Thomas.

Robbins, R. Laurie. Field & Laboratory Biology for Elementary Teaching Majors. 256p. (C). 1994. 27.95 (*0-8403-9648-1*) Kendall-Hunt.

Robbins, R. Robert, et al. Discovering Astronomy & Activities Kit. 3rd ed. 802p. 1994. text 48.00 (*0-471-11667-X*) Wiley.

Robbins, R. Robert, jt. auth. see Hemenway, Mary K.

Robbins, Rae G. The Bloomsbury Group: A Selective Bibliography. 219p. 1978. 17.00 (*0-685-04148-4*) Price Guide.

Robbins, Ray K. Criminal Investigation Procedures. LC 93-77666. 350p. (C). 1993. text 38.00 (*0-8211-1752-1*) McCutchan.

— The Florida Law Enforcement Officer: The Basic Recruit Training Course. LC 91-66586. (Illus.). 269p. (C). 1992. pap. text 25.00 (*0-8211-1727-0*) McCutchan.

Robbins, Ray K. & Nichols, Larry. The California Peace Officer: The Basic Training Course, 3 vols., Set. 3rd ed. LC 91-66585. (Illus.). (Orig.). (C). 1992. pap. text 80.00 (*0-8211-1520-0*) McCutchan.

Robbins, Ray K., et al. The Texas Peace Officer, 2 vols. 7th ed. LC 00-101988. 707p. 2000. 80.00 (*0-8211-1762-9*) McCutchan.

Robbins, Rebecca. A Guardian for Angel. 288p. 1996. mass mkt. 4.50 (*0-8217-5197-2*, Zebra Kensgtn) Kensgtn Pub Corp.

— An Irresistible Pursuit. 2403p. (Orig.). 1995. mass mkt. 3.99 (*0-380-77671-5*, Avon Bks) Morrow Avon.

— Lucky in Love. 224p. (Orig.). 1994. mass mkt. 3.99 (*0-380-77485-2*, Avon Bks) Morrow Avon.

— The Mischievous Maid. 256p. (Orig.). 1993. mass mkt. 3.99 (*0-380-77336-8*, Avon Bks) Morrow Avon.

— An Unusual Inheritance. 224p. (Orig.). 1994. mass mkt. 3.99 (*0-380-77670-7*, Avon Bks) Morrow Avon.

Robbins, Rhea C. Wednesday's Child. 2nd rev. ed. LC 98-92339. (Illus.). 89p. (C). 1999. pap. 12.50 (*0-9668536-0-1*) Rheta Pr.

*__Robbins, Richard.__ Famous Persons We Have Known. (Illus.). 80p. 2000. 23.95 (*0-910055-65-3*); pap. 13.95 (*0-910055-66-1*) East Wash Univ.

Robbins, Richard. The Invisible Wedding: Poems. LC 83-16930. (Breakthrough Ser.: No. 44). 80p. 1984. pap. 12.95 (*0-8262-0438-4*) U of Mo Pr.

— Sidelines Activist: Charles S. Johnson & the Struggle for Civil Rights. LC 96-14472. 224p. 1996. text 45.00 (*0-87805-904-0*); pap. text 17.00 (*0-87805-932-6*) U Pr of Miss.

Robbins, Richard G., Jr. Famine in Russia, Eighteen Ninety-One to Eighteen Ninety-Two: The Imperial Government Responds to a Crisis. LC 74-8528. (Studies of the Russian Institute of Columbia University). 1975. text 57.50 (*0-231-03836-4*) Col U Pr.

— The Tsar's Viceroys: Russian Provincial Governors in the Last Years of the Empire. LC 87-47700. 328p. 1987. 42.50 (*0-8014-2046-6*) Cornell U Pr.

Robbins, Richard G. The Tsar's Viceroys: Russian Provincial Governors in the Last Years of the Empire. LC 87-47700. (Illus.). 288p. reprint ed. pap. 89.30 (*0-608-20942-2*, 207204100003) Bks Demand.

Robbins, Richard H. Cultural Anthropology: A Problem-Based Approach. 2nd ed. LC 96-69327. (Illus.). 240p. (C). 1997. pap. text 32.50 (*0-87581-404-2*, CA2) F E Peacock Pubs.

Robbins, Richard Howard. Global Problems & the Culture of Capitalism. LC 98-23668. 422p. 1998. pap. 45.00 (*0-205-19337-4*) P-H.

Robbins, Richard J., jt. ed. see Olefsky, Jerrold M.

Robbins, Richard L. The Automated Law Firm: A Complete Guide to Software & Systems. 254p. 1989. ring bd. 76.00 (*0-13-051038-6*) P-H.

— The Automated Law Firm: A Complete Guide to Software & Systems. 2nd ed. 590p. 1992. ring bd. 110.00 (*0-13-291352-6*) Aspen Law.

Robbins, Richard L., jt. auth. see O'Connor, Thomas J.

Robbins, Riki. Betrayed! How You Can Restore Sexual Trust & Rebuild Your Life. LC 97-46386. 192p. 1998. pap. 9.95 (*1-55850-848-1*) Adams Media.

Robbins, Riki, jt. auth. see Klein, Marty.

Robbins, Robert, et al. Discovering Astronomy. 3rd ed. 640p. 1994. pap. 70.95 (*0-471-58437-1*) Wiley.

Robbins, Robert, jt. auth. see Parker, Bruce.

Robbins, Robert K. Evolution, Comparative Morphology, & Identification of the Eumaeine Butterfly Genus Rekoa Kaye: Lycaenidae: Theclinae. LC 89-600292. (Smithsonian Contributions to Zoology Ser.: No. 498). 68p. reprint ed. pap. 30.00 (*0-7837-0269-8*, 204057800017) Bks Demand.

Robbins, Robin. Animals: A BBC Fact Finders Book. (Illus.). 48p. (J). 1996. pap. text 8.95 (*0-563-35539-5*, BBC-Parkwest) Parkwest Pubns.

— Looking at Nature: A Fact Finder Book. (Illus.). 48p. (J). (gr. 7-9). 1992. pap. 8.95 (*0-563-34499-7*, BBC-Parkwest) Parkwest Pubns.

Robbins, Roland. Mantracking: Introduction to the Step-by-Step Method. Anderson, Elizabeth et al, eds. LC 77-77680. (Illus.). 1977. pap. 39.00 (*0-9603392-0-5*) Search & Rescue.

Robbins, Ronald. The Rhythmic Cycle of Change. LC 88-25446. 306p. (Orig.). 1989. pap. 24.95 (*0-9620928-1-9*) Neshama Pubns.

— Rhythmic Integration: Finding Wholeness in the Cycle of Change. 1990. pap. 13.95 (*0-88268-099-4*) Station Hill Pr.

Robbins, Rossell H., jt. auth. see Brown, Carleton F.

*__Robbins-Roth, Cynthia.__ From Alchemy to IPO: The Business of Biotechnology. 272p. 2000. text 26.00 (*0-7382-0253-3*, Pub. by Perseus Pubng) HarpC.

Robbins-Roth, Cynthia, ed. Alternative Careers in Science: Leaving the Ivory Tower. LC 97-80573. (Illus.). 267p. 1998. pap. text 29.95 (*0-12-589375-2*) Morgan Kaufmann.

Robbins, Roy M. Our Landed Heritage: The Public Domain, 1776-1970. LC 75-3569. (Illus.). 517p. reprint ed. 160.30 (*0-8357-9712-0*, 201911600010) Bks Demand.

— Our Landed Heritage: The Public Domain, 1776-1970 2nd ed. LC 75-3569. xii, 503p. 1976. write for info. (*0-8032-0866-9*) U of Nebr Pr.

Robbins, Rudy, jt. auth. see Field, Shirley.

Robbins, Ruth. Baboushka & the Three Kings, 001. LC 60-15036. (Caldecott Medal Ser.). (Illus.). 32p. (J). (ps up). 1960. 16.00 (*0-395-27673-X*) HM.

— Baboushka & the Three Kings. LC 60-15036. (Illus.). 32p. (J). (ps-3). 1986. pap. 6.95 (*0-395-42647-2*) HM.

*__Robbins, Ruth.__ Literary Feminisms. LC 99-43176. 2000. pap. 19.95 (*0-312-22808-2*); text 55.00 (*0-312-22807-4*) St Martin.

— Victorian Gothic: Death, Dis-Ease, Desire & Doubling in Nineteenth Century Literature & Culture. 264p. 2000. text 69.95 (*0-312-23169-5*) St Martin.

Robbins, S., jt. auth. see Robbins, Kay A.

Robbins, Sabin. A Hundred Summers: An Affectionate History of Northport Point. (Illus.). 144p. 1999. 50.00 (*0-9651442-1-6*) Bayshore Prtnrs.

Robbins, Sally F. Porches: Structure & Design. LC 95-12221. 144p. 1995. 15.95 (*1-56799-208-0*, Friedman-Fairfax) M Friedman Pub Grp Inc.

Robbins, Samuel D., Jr. Wisconsin Birdlife: Population & Distribution Past & Present. LC 90-50095. 720p. 1991. 75.00 (*0-299-10260-2*) U of Wis Pr.

*__Robbins, Sandra.__ Big Annie: An American Tall Tale. (See-More's Stories Ser.). (Illus.). 32p. (ps-4). 1998. pap. 6.95 (*1-882601-25-4*); pap. 11.95 incl. audio (*1-882601-27-0*) See-Mores Wrkshop.

Robbins, Sandra. The Firefly Star: A Hispanic Folk Tale. (Illus.). 32p. (J). (gr. k-4). 1995. pap. 11.95 incl. audio (*1-882601-21-1*); pap. 6.95 (*1-882601-23-8*) See-Mores Wrkshop.

— The Growing Rock: A Native American Tale. (See-More's Stories Ser.). (Illus.). 32p. (Orig.). (J). (ps-4). 1993. pap. 9.98 incl. audio (*1-882601-15-7*); pap. 4.95 (*1-882601-16-5*) See-Mores Wrkshop.

— How the Turtle Got Its Shell: An African Tale. (See-More's Stories Ser.). (Illus.). 32p. (J). (ps-4). 1993. pap. 4.95 (*1-882601-10-6*); pap. 9.98 incl. audio (*1-882601-04-1*) See-Mores Wrkshop.

— Lumpy Bumpy Pumpkin: A Halloween Tale. (See-More's Stories Ser.). (Illus.). 32p. (Orig.). (J). (ps-4). 1993. pap. 9.98 incl. audio (*1-882601-18-1*); pap. 4.95 (*1-882601-19-X*) See-Mores Wrkshop.

— Ring Around a Rainbow: A Health Adventure. (See-More's Stories Ser.). (Illus.). 32p. (Orig.). (J). (gr. k-5). 1993. pap. 4.95 (*1-882601-08-4*); pap. 9.98 incl. audio (*1-882601-05-X*) See-Mores Wrkshop.

— See-More's Stories: A Series of Six Read-Aloud Books & Read-Along/Move-Along Tapes. (See-More's Stories Ser.). (Illus.). 32p. (Orig.). (J). (ps-4). 1993. pap. 54.95 incl. audio (*1-882601-22-X*) See-Mores Wrkshop.

— Tobias Turkey. (See-More's Stories Ser.). (Illus.). 32p. (J). (ps-3). 1998. pap. 6.95 (*1-882601-26-2*) See-Mores Wrkshop.

*__Robbins, Sandra.__ Tobias Turkey: A Thanksgiving Tale. (See-More's Stories Ser.). (Illus.). 32p. (Orig.). (ps-3). 1998. pap. 11.95 incl. audio (*1-882601-28-9*) See-Mores Wrkshop.

Robbins, Sara. Baby M Case: A Collection of the Complete Trial Transcripts, 6 vols. LC 88-80607. 1988. lib. bdg. 475.00 (*0-89941-637-3*, 305470) W S Hein.

— Surrogate Parenting: An Annotated Review of the Literature. LC 84-1824. (CompuBibs Ser.: No. 3). 40p. 1984. pap. 10.00 (*0-914791-04-4*) Vantage Info.

Robbins, Sara, jt. auth. see Levy, Charlotte L.

Robbins, Sarah F. & Yentsch, Clarice. Sea Is All about Us: A Guide to Marine Environments of Cape Ann & Other Northern New England Waters. 1973. pap. 10.95 (*0-87577-046-0*, PEMP152, Peabody Museum) Peabody Essex Mus.

Robbins, Scott, jt. auth. see Duston, Robert L.

Robbins, Serena. Isle of Rapture. large type ed. (Romance Ser.). 592p. 1984. 27.99 (*0-7089-1145-5*) Ulverscroft.

Robbins, Sharon L., jt. auth. see Riggs, David A.

Robbins, Shawn. Shawn Robbins' Prophecies for the End of Time. 240p. (Orig.). 1995. mass mkt. 4.99 (*0-380-77694-4*, Avon Bks) Morrow Avon.

Robbins, Shawn & Susman, Edward. More Prophecies for the Coming Millennium. 224p. (Orig.). 1996. mass mkt. 5.99 (*0-380-78455-6*, Avon Bks) Morrow Avon.

Robbins, Sheila. Get a Life! Start Your Home-Based Business Now: One Action Step at a Time. LC 96-92692. (Illus.). 256p. (Orig.). 1997. 17.95 (*0-9654971-2-7*) Small Bus Develop.

Robbins, Stanley L. Patologia Estructural y Funcional. 4th ed. 1990. text 99.00 (*0-07-104001-3*) McGraw.

Robbins, Stanley L., et al. Pocket Companion to Pathologic Basis of Disease. 5th ed. (Illus.). 630p. 1995. pap. text 26.95 (*0-7216-5742-7*, W B Saunders Co) Harcrt Hlth Sci Grp.

*__Robbins, Stephen P.__ Essentials of Organizational Behavior. 6th ed. LC 99-47893. (Illus.). 303p. 1999. pap. text 49.00 (*0-13-083572-2*) P-H.

Robbins, Stephen P. Managing Today! LC 96-19873. 584p. (C). 1996. text 84.00 (*0-13-233313-9*) P-H.

*__Robbins, Stephen P.__ Organizational Behavior: Concepts, Controversies, Applications. 9th ed. LC 99-49448. 750p. 2000. 96.00 (*0-13-016680-4*) P-H.

— Self-Assessment Library: Insights Into Your Skills Abilities & Interests. 1999. 15.00 (*0-13-021212-1*, Prentice Hall) P-H.

— The Self-assessment Library: Print Version. 95p. 1999. pap. 13.33 (*0-13-026925-5*, Prentice Hall) P-H.

Robbins, Stephen P. & Coulter, Mary K. Management. 6th ed. LC 98-10502. 645p. 1998. text 80.00 (*0-13-921503-4*) P-H.

*__Robbins, Stephen P. & DeCenzo, David A.__ Fundamentals of Management. 3rd ed. LC 99-57549. 592p. 2000. pap. 61.33 (*0-13-017601-X*) P-H.

Robbins, Stephen P. & Decenzo, David A. Fundamentals of Management: Essential Concepts & Applications. 2nd ed. LC 96-45064. 516p. 1997. pap. text 61.33 (*0-13-578600-2*) P-H.

— Supervision Today. 2nd ed. LC 97-3146. 601p. 1997. pap. text 72.00 (*0-13-608630-6*) P-H.

Robbins, Stephen P. & Hunsaker, Phillip L. Training in Interpersonal Skills: TIPS for Managing People at Work. 2nd ed. 305p. 1995. pap. text 42.00 (*0-13-435827-9*) P-H.

— Training in Managerial Skills. (C). Date not set. write for info. (*0-13-955014-3*, Macmillan Coll) P-H.

*__Robbins, Stephen P., et al.__ Supervision Today! 3rd ed. LC 00-36760. 576p. 2000. pap. 60.00 (*0-13-025441-X*) P-H.

Robbins, Stephen P., jt. auth. see DeCenzo, David A.

Robbins, Stephen P., jt. auth. see Wright, Penny L.

Robbins, Stephens. Essentials of Organizational Behavior. 5th ed. LC 96-21277. 336p. (C). 1996. pap. text 42.00 (*0-13-520305-8*) P-H.

Robbins, Stephens P. Organization Theory: Structures, Designs, & Applications. 3rd ed. 560p. 1990. 84.00 (*0-13-642471-6*) P-H.

— Organizational Behavior: Concepts, Controversies, Applications, Vol. 2. 8th ed. LC 97-5407. 675p. 1997. 90.67 (*0-13-857459-6*, Pub. by P-H) S&S Trade.

Robbins, Stephens P. & Chatterjee. Contemporary Human Behavior Theory. LC 97-18279. 465p. 1997. 63.00 (*0-205-14920-0*) P-H.

Robbins, Stephens P. & Decenzo, David A. Supervision Today. 2nd ed. 160p. (C). 1997. pap. text, student ed. 28.00 (*0-13-634684-7*) P-H.

Robbins, Sterling. Auyana: Those Who Held onto Home. LC 81-2707. (Anthropological Studies in the Eastern Highlands of New Guinea: No. 6). (Illus.). 274p. 1982. 40.00 (*0-295-95788-3*) U of Wash Pr.

Robbins, Steven, jt. auth. see Robbins, Kay A.

Robbins, Susan P., et al. Contemporary Human Behavior Theory: A Critical Perspective for Social Work: Instructor's Manual & Test Bank. 416p. 1998. text, teacher ed. write for info. (*0-205-58053-X*, T8055-0) Allyn.

Robbins, Thomas. Cults, Converts, & Charisma: The Sociology of New Religious Movements. 288p. (C). 1988. text 45.00 (*0-8039-8158-9*); pap. text 22.50 (*0-8039-8159-7*) Sage.

*__Robbins, Thomas.__ Professional Visual Basic 6 MTS Programming. 500p. 1998. pap. text 49.99 (*1-86100-244-0*) Wrox Pr Inc.

Robbins, Thomas & Anthony, Dick. In Gods We Trust: New Patterns of Religious Pluralism in America. 2nd rev. ed. 500p. 1989. pap. 29.95 (*0-88738-800-0*) Transaction Pubs.

Robbins, Thomas & Lance, Victory. Victory: By Victory Lance, Poet, Philosopher, Private Eye. LC 96-30515. (Illus.). 137p. 1996. pap. 9.95 (*0-87714-182-7*) Denlingers.

Robbins, Thomas & Palmer, Susan J., eds. Millenium, Messiahs & Mayhem: Contemporary Apocalyptic Movements. LC 97-12408. 332p. (C). 1997. 75.00 (*0-415-91648-8*); pap. 19.99 (*0-415-91649-6*) Routledge.

Robbins, Thomas & Robertson, Roland, eds. Church-State Relations: Tensions & Transitions. 380p. 1986. 44.95 (*0-88738-108-1*) Transaction Pubs.

*__Robbins, Tim.__ Cradle Will Rock: The Movie & the Moment. LC 99-52093. (Newmarket Pictorial Moviebook Ser.). (Illus.). 160p. 1999. text 32.95 (*1-55704-399-X*, Pub. by Newmarket) Norton.

Robbins, Tim. Dead Man Walking: The Shooting Script. LC 96-47471. (Illus.). 176p. 1997. pap. 15.95 (*1-55704-300-0*, Pub. by Newmarket) Norton.

Robbins, Tom. Another Roadside Attraction. 352p. 1990. pap. 11.95 (*0-553-34948-1*) Bantam.

— Even Cowgirls Get the Blues. 384p. 1990. pap. 11.95 (*0-553-34949-X*) Bantam.

*__Robbins, Tom.__ Fierce Invalids Home from Hot Climates. LC 99-51683. 432p. 2000. 27.50 (*0-553-10775-5*) Bantam.

Robbins, Tom. Half Asleep in Frog Pajamas. LC 94-11549. 386p. (J). 1995. reprint ed. pap. 11.95 (*0-553-37787-6*) Bantam.

— Jitterbug Perfume. 352p. 1990. pap. 11.95 (*0-553-34898-1*) Bantam.

— Still Life with Woodpecker. LC 81-103498. (Illus.). 277p. (Orig.). 1990. pap. 11.95 (*0-553-34897-3*) Bantam.

Robbins, Tom, et al. Skinny Legs & All. 432p. 1995. reprint ed. pap. 11.95 (*0-553-37788-4*) Bantam.

Robbins, Tom, jt. auth. see Van Sant, Gus.

Robbins, Trina. A Century of Women Cartoonists. deluxe limited ed. Schreiner, Dave, ed. (Illus.). 176p. 1993. 39.95 (*0-87816-206-2*) Kitchen Sink.

— From Girls to Grrrlz: A History of Women's Comics from Teens to Zines. LC 98-24966. (Illus.). 144p. (Orig.). 1999. pap. 17.95 (*0-8118-2199-4*) Chronicle Bks.

— The Great Women Superheroes. LC 96-22413. (Illus.). 288p. 1996. 31.95 (*0-87816-482-0*) Kitchen Sink.

— The Great Women Superheroes. deluxe limited ed. (Illus.). 288p. 1996. 39.95 (*0-87816-483-9*) Kitchen Sink.

— Great Women Superheros. LC 96-22413. (Illus.). 288p. 1998. reprint ed. pap. 21.95 (*0-87816-481-2*) Kitchen Sink.

— Strip AIDS U. S. A. A Collection of Cartoon Art to Benefit People with AIDS. (Illus.). 140p. 1988. pap. text 9.95 (*0-86719-373-5*) Last Gasp.

— Tomorrow's Heirlooms: Fashions of the '60's & '70's. LC 97-20315. 160p. 1997. pap. 29.95 (*0-7643-0354-6*) Schiffer.

— Wonder Woman: The Once & Future Story. (Illus.). 48p. 1998. pap. 4.95 (*1-56389-373-8*) DC Comics.

Robbins, Trina, ed. 930 Matchbook Advertising Cuts of the Twenties & Thirties. LC 96-40194. (Clip-Art Ser.). 80p. 1997. pap. 8.95 (*0-486-29564-8*) Dover.

Robbins, Trina & Robbins, Casey, eds. Travel & Vacation Advertising Cuts from the '20s & '30s. LC 94-13334. (Pictorial Archive Ser.). (Illus.). 96p. 1994. pap. 8.95 (*0-486-28199-X*) Dover.

Robbins, Vernon K. Exploring the Texture of Texts: A Guide to Socio-Rhetorical Interpretations. LC 96-42945. 144p. (Orig.). 1996. pap. 15.00 (*1-56338-183-4*) TPI PA.

— New Boundaries in Old Territory: Forms & Social Rhetoric in Mark. LC 93-21579. (Emory Studies in Early Christianity: Vol. 3). XX, 270p. (C). 1994. text 39.95 (*0-8204-1911-7*) P Lang Pubng.

— The Tapestry of Early Christian Discourse: Rhetoric, Society, & Ideology. 296p. (C). 1996. 85.00 (*0-415-13997-X*); pap. 27.99 (*0-415-13998-8*) Routledge.

Robbins, Vernon K., ed. Ancient Quotes & Anecdotes: From Crib to Crypt. LC 88-12583. 512p. 1989. 29.95 (*0-944344-02-X*); pap. 21.95 (*0-944344-03-8*) Polebridge Pr.

Robbins, Vesta O. No Coward Soul. LC 74-7399. 119p. reprint ed. pap. 36.90 (*0-608-16268-X*, 202666000051) Bks Demand.

Robbins, Virginia C. Southern Gourmet: Upscale Southern Dining for the Down-Home Kitchen. 1995. 13.95 (*0-9649067-0-8*) Precision Foods.

Robbins, W. Hard Times in Paradise: Coos Bay, Oregon, 1850-1986. LC 87-37180. (Illus.). 208p. 1988. pap. 16.95 (*0-295-96617-3*) U of Wash Pr.

Robbins, Warren M., jt. auth. see Elisofon, Eliot.

Robbins, Wendy H. The Portable College Adviser: A Guide for High School Students. LC 95-47026. (Illus.). 160p. (YA). (gr. 9-12). 1996. lib. bdg. 24.00 (*0-531-11257-8*) Watts.

— The Portable College Adviser: A Guide for High School Students. LC 95-47026. (Illus.). 160p. (YA). (gr. 9-12). 1996. pap. 9.00 (*0-531-15790-3*) Watts.

Robbins, Wendy H., jt. auth. see Options, Inc. Staff.

Robbins, Wilfred W. Ethnobotany of the Tewa Indians. (Bureau of American Ethnology Bulletins Ser.). 124p. 1995. lib. bdg. 79.00 (*0-7812-4055-7*) Rprt Serv.

Robbins, William. Landscapes of Promise: The Oregon Story, 1800-1940. LC 97-16531. (Weyerhaeuser Environmental Bks.). (Illus.). 416p. 1997. 40.00 (*0-295-97632-2*) U of Wash Pr.

Robbins, William. Newman Brothers: An Essay in Comparative Intellectual Biography. LC 66-4976. (Illus.). 214p. 1966. 26.50 (*0-674-62200-6*) HUP.

Robbins, William G. American Forestry: A History of National, State, & Private Cooperation. LC 84-28122. 359p. 1985. reprint ed. pap. 111.30 (*0-608-01541-5*, 205958500002) Bks Demand.

— Colony & Empire: The Capitalist Transformation of the American West. LC 94-11029. (Development of Western Resources Ser.). 274p. (Orig.). (C). 1994. 29.95 (*0-7006-0645-9*) U Pr of KS.

— Colony & Empire: The Capitalist Transformation of the American West. LC 94-11029. (Development of Western Resources Ser.). xviii, 256p. (Orig.). (C). 1995. pap. 15.95 (*0-7006-0750-1*) U Pr of KS.

*__Robbins, William G.__ Land in the American West: Private Claims & the Common Good. (Illus.). 224p. 2000. pap. 17.50 (*0-295-98020-6*) U of Wash Pr.

— Landscapes of Promise: The Oregon Story, 1800-1940. (Illus.). 416p. 1999. pap. text 19.95 (*0-295-97901-1*) U of Wash Pr.

Robbins, William G., et al, eds. Regionalism & the Pacific Northwest. LC 83-2416. 256p. 1983. 24.95 (*0-87071-337-X*); pap. 15.95 (*0-87071-338-8*) Oreg St U Pr.

Robbins, William G., ed. & intro. see Best, Norman.

Robbis, Miles, et al. Lonely Planet Walking in Spain. 2nd ed. 384p. 1999. pap. 17.95 (*0-86442-543-0*) Lonely Planet.

Robboy. Social Interaction. 5th ed. 2000. pap. text 26.95 (*0-312-18260-0*) St Martin.

Robboy, Anita, jt. auth. see Ginsburg, Edward M.

Robboy, Howard, jt. auth. see Clark, Candace.

R

Robbrecht, E. Kawa, les Secrets du Cafe: Du Cafeier a la Tasse. (FRE., Illus.). 127p. 1995. pap. 45.00 (1-878762-80-X, Pub. by Natl Botanic Grdn Belgium) Balogh.

Robbrecht, E., ed. Advances in Rubiaceae Macrosystematics. (Opera Botanica Belgica Ser.: Vol. 6). 200p. 1994. 58.00 (90-72619-14-5, Pub. by Natl Botanic Grdn Belgium) Balogh.

— De Relaties Tussen Botanische Collecties en de Tuinbouw. (Scripta Botanica Belgica Ser.: Vol. 7). 78p. 1994. 21.00 (90-72619-13-7, Pub. by Natl Botanic Grdn Belgium) Balogh.

Robbrecht, E., et al. The Second International Rubiaceae Conference. (Opera Botanica Belgica Ser.: Vol. 7). 432p. 1996. 109.00 (90-72619-29-3, Pub. by Natl Botanic Grdn Belgium) Balogh.

— Second International Rubiaceae Conference, Programme & Abstracts. (Scripta Botanica Belgica Ser.: Vol. 11). 100p. 1995. 20.00 (90-72619-25-0, Pub. by Natl Botanic Grdn Belgium) Balogh.

Robe, jt. auth. see Harben, Peter W.

Robe, Jacqueline M., jt. auth. see Robe, James T.

Robe, James T. & Robe, Jacqueline M. Illustrated Florida History. (Illus.). 87p. 1997. lib. bdg. 11.95 (0-9658971-0-9) J T Robe.

Robe, Sophie. Modelling Nonlinearities in the German Stock Market. LC 99-32380. (European University Studies: Vol. 2472, No. 5). (Illus.). XII, 165p. 1999. pap. text 39.95 (0-8204-4330-1) P Lang Pubng.

Robe, Stanley L. Hispanic Folktales from New Mexico: Narratives from the R. D. Jameson Collection. LC 76-52036. (University of California Publications, Folklore Studies: No. 30). 234p. reprint ed. pap. 72.60 (0-608-13905-X, 202120900021) Bks Demand.

Robe, Stanley L., ed. Antologia del Saber Popular: A Selection from Various Genres of Mexican Folklore Across Borders. (Monographs: No.2). 75p. 1971. pap. 9.95 (0-89551-001-4) UCLA Chicano Studies.

— Hispanic Legends from New Mexico: Narratives from the R. D. Jameson Collection. LC 79-64490. (University of California Publications Folklore & Mythology Studies: No. 31). 560p. reprint ed. pap. 173.60 (0-608-14172-0, 202121000021) Bks Demand.

Robe-Terry, Anna L. Bootstraps & Biscuits. LC 97-92831. 1997. pap. 17.98 (0-87012-587-7) McClain.
Set in the hills of West Virginia on her family land, Anna Lee Robe-Terry forages for wild foods & describes their preparation & uses. In her own colorful language, Anna Lee shares a rural family heritage in a narrative generously laced with anecdotes about life in the mountains. The result is a rich, compilation of hundreds of delicious recipes the ingredients available & ripe for picking. From paw paw pudding to mincemeat pie using wild meat a reader will find fulfillment for the soul, pallet & pocketbook. . *Publisher Paid Annotation.*

Robeck, Mildred C. & Wallace, Randall R. The Psychology of Reading: An Interdisciplinary Approach. 2nd ed. 1990. pap., teacher ed. write for info. (0-8058-0885-X) L Erlbaum Assocs.

Robeck, Mildred C., jt. ed. see Wallace, R. R.

Robeck, Mildred Coen, jt. auth. see Coen, Oscar Hoffman.

Robek, Mary E., et al. Information & Records Management: Document-Based Information Systems. 4th ed. 1995. teacher ed. 9.27 (0-02-801794-3) Glencoe.

Robek, Mary F., et al. Information & Records Management: Document-Based Information Systems. 4th ed. LC 94-31467. 1995. 51.50 (0-02-801793-5) Glencoe.

Robel, tr. see Bakhtine.

Robel, Nicole. Sam & Violet's Get Well Book. 1985. pap. 2.50 (0-380-89821-7, Avon Bks) Morrow Avon.

*Robel-Nolan, Allia. Little Chick. (Fluffy Tales Ser.). (Illus.). 10p. (J). (ps-k). 2000. bds. 5.99 (0-7847-0889-4, 03699) Standard Pub.

Robell, Victor, ed. see Bechard, Matthew.

Robenek, Horst. Ultrastructure, Membrane & Cell Interactions. Severs, Nicholas J., ed. 336p. 1992. lib. bdg. 229.00 (0-8493-5505-2, RC692) CRC Pr.

Robens, Alfred. Managing Great Britain Limited. LC 77-370608. (Lecture Ser.). 20p. 1977. write for info. (0-903542-14-5) Ashridge Manag College.

Robens, Erich, jt. auth. see Mikhail, Raouf S.

Robens, Erich, ed. see Conference on Vacuum Microbalance Techniques (9th:.

Robensen, Graham. Classic Convertibles. 1996. 6.98 (0-7858-0549-4) Bk Sales Inc.

Robequain, Charles. The Economic Development of French Indo-China. Ward, Isabel A., tr. LC 71-179238. reprint ed. 38.50 (0-404-54864-4) AMS Pr.

— Malaya, Indonesia, Borneo & the Philippines: A Geographical, Economic, & Political Description of Malaya, the East Indies, the Philippines. Laborde, E. D., tr. LC 75-30078. reprint ed. 37.00 (0-404-59555-3) AMS Pr.

Roberage, Pierre R., jt. ed. see Trethewey, Kenneth R.

Roberdeau, Thomas. Michael Strogoff: A Screenplay. 248p. (Orig.). 1995. pap. 10.95 (1-55713-098-1) Sun & Moon CA.

Roberege, Lawrence. The Cost of Abortion. 96p. (Orig.). 1995. pap. 6.95 (1-885857-16-0) Four Wnds Pubng.

Roberfroid, M. B. Free Radicals & Oxidation Phenomena in Biological Systems. (Illus.). 280p. 1994. text 150.00 (0-8247-9587-3) Dekker.

Roberfroid, M. B. & Preat, V., eds. Experimental Hepatocarcinogenesis. LC 87-35725. (Illus.). 332p. 1988. 85.00 (0-306-42797-4, Plenum Trade) Perseus Pubng.

Roberfroid, M. B., jt. contrib. by see Gibson, Glenn R.

Roberg, Alex, jt. ed. see Ottensoser, Max.

Roberg, Jeffrey L. Soviet Science under Control: The Struggle for Influence. LC 97-26036. 169p. 1998. text 65.00 (0-312-17736-4) St Martin.

Roberg, Roy R. Police Management & Organizational Behavior: A Contingency Approach. (Criminal Justice Ser.). (Illus.). 348p. 1979. pap. text, teacher ed. write for info. (0-314-44225-1) West Pub.

— Police Organization & Management: Behavior, Theory & Processes. 2nd ed. 480p. 1996. 37.95 (0-534-51418-9) Wadsworth Pub.

Roberg, Roy R. & Kuykendall, Jack. Police & Society. LC 92-35788. 484p. 1993. 43.25 (0-534-19872-4) Wadsworth Pub.

— Police Management. 2nd ed. LC 96-46541. (Illus.). 440p. (C). 1997. text. write for info. (0-935732-85-3) Roxbury Pub Co.

Roberg, Roy R., et al. Police & Society. 2nd rev. ed. LC 99-35450. (Illus.). 490p. (C). 2000. pap. text. write for info. (1-891487-17-5) Roxbury Pub Co.

Roberge, Earl. Timber Country Revisited: Managing Our Renewable Resource. 1991. 39.95 (0-9631295-0-3) WA Contract Log.

Roberge, Gaston. Mediation: The Action of the Media in Our Society. 1980. 24.00 (0-8364-0604-4, Pub. by Manohar) S Asia.

— Subject of Cinema. (C). 1990. 22.50 (0-685-49100-5, Pub. by Seagull Bks) S Asia.

— Ways of Film Studies: Film Theory & the Interpretation of Film. (C). 1992. 26.00 (81-202-0348-8, Pub. by Ajanta) S Asia.

Roberge, James. Data Structure C++ Lab Course. (Computer Science Ser.). 352p. 1997. pap. 27.50 (0-7637-0313-3) Jones & Bartlett.

— Data Structure Pascal Lab Course. (Computer Science Ser.). 284p. 1994. pap. 23.75 (0-669-29523-X) Jones & Bartlett.

— Data Structures in C++ A Laboratory Course. (Computer Science Ser.). 326p. (C). 1995. pap. 27.50 (0-669-34947-X) Jones & Bartlett.

— Data Structures in Pascal 3.5: A Laboratory Course. (Computer Science Ser.). 284p. (C). 1994. pap. 26.25 (0-669-29524-8) Jones & Bartlett.

— Data Structures in Pascal 5.25: A Laboratory Course. (Computer Science Ser.). 284p. (C). 1994. pap. 23.75 (0-669-29525-6) Jones & Bartlett.

Roberge, James, jt. auth. see Smith.

Roberge, James K., jt. auth. see Wedlock, Bruce D.

Roberge, Marc-Andre. Ferruccio Busoni: A Bio-Bibliography, 34. LC 90-22927. (Bio-Bibliographies in Music Ser.: No. 34). 432p. 1991. lib. bdg. 75.00 (0-313-25587-3, RFB, Greenwood Pr) Greenwood.

Roberge, P. R., jt. auth. see Mayor, P.

*Roberge, Pierre R. Corrosion Engineering Handbook. LC 99-35898. 1072p. 1999. 99.00 (0-07-076516-2) McGraw.

Roberge, W. G. & Whillet, D. C., eds. Polarimetry of the Interstellar Medium, Vol. 97. (ASP Conference Series Proceedings). 632p. 1996. 34.00 (1-886733-18-X) Astron Soc Pacific.

Roberge, Yves. The Syntactic Recoverability of Null Arguments. 224p. (C). 1990. text 65.00 (0-7735-0732-9, Pub. by McG-Queens Univ Pr) CUP Services.

Robergs. Excercise Physiology. 2nd ed. 1999. pap. text 55.62 (0-07-235392-9) McGraw.

*Robergs. Fundamental Principles of Exercise Physiology. 160p. 1999. 10.31 (0-07-236103-4) McGraw.

*Robern Publishing Staff. Dore Bible Gallery: Nineteenth Century Biblical Engravings in Postcards. (Illus.). 30p. 1999. pap. 8.95 (1-893262-06-5) Robern Pubg.

— Dore Masterpieces: Nineteenth Century Engravings Illustrating Classic Literary Works in Postcards. (Illus.). 30p. 1999. pap. 8.95 (1-893262-07-3) Robern Pubg.

Roberson. Criminal Procedure Today. LC 99-14676. (Illus.). 482p. 1999. 71.00 (0-13-080520-3) P-H.

Roberson. Engineering Fluid Mechanics. 6th ed. 429p. 1997. pap. text 45.00 (0-471-17306-1) Wiley.

Roberson. Texas Criminal Law pap., teacher ed. write for info. (0-7619-0218-X) Sage.

Roberson, et al. Learning in the Natural Laboratory: An Introductory Geology Lab Manual University of North Carolina. 146p. (C). 1998. spiral bd., lab manual ed. 38.95 (0-7872-5631-5, 41563102) Kendall-Hunt.

Roberson, B. A. The Middle East & Europe. LC 98-18945. 1998. write for info. (0-415-14044-7); pap. write for info. (0-415-14045-5) Routledge.

Roberson, B. A., ed. International Society & the Development of International Relations Theory. LC 97-27669. 278p. 1998. 65.00 (1-85567-403-3) Bks Intl VA.

Roberson, C. W. & Driscoll, C. F., eds. Non-Neutral Plasma Physics. LC 88-72275. (AIP Conference Proceedings Ser.: No. 175). 311p. 1988. lib. bdg. 65.00 (0-88318-375-7) Am Inst Physics.

Roberson, Cliff. Aviation: A Complete Legal Guide. 210p. 1987. 19.95 (0-8306-9414-5, 2414) McGraw-Hill Prof.

— The Businessperson's Legal Advisor. 2nd ed. (Illus.). 352p. 1990. pap. 19.95 (0-8306-3547-5, 3547) McGraw-Hill Prof.

— The Complete Book of Business Forms & Agreements. LC 93-24204. 525p. 1992. 79.95 (0-07-911611-6) McGraw.

*Roberson, Cliff. Criminal Codes, California. LC 97-67724. 500p. 2000. pap. 31.95 (0-942728-98-X) Copperhouse.

— Criminal Justice Reader. LC 99-69691. 438p. 2000. pap. text 19.95 (1-928916-07-4) Copperhouse.

Roberson, Cliff. Hire Right - Fire Right: A Manager's Guide to Employment Practices That Avoid Lawsuits. 259p. 1992. 39.95 (0-07-053114-5) McGraw.

— Introduction to Corrections. LC 97-65247. (Illus.). 545p. (C). 1997. pap. 37.95 (0-942728-78-5) Copperhouse.

— Introduction to Criminal Justice. 2nd ed. LC 93-73918. (Illus.). 562p. (C). 1996. pap. 37.95 (0-942728-71-8) Copperhouse.

— Juvenile Justice, Exploring. LC 95-83952. (Illus.). 310p. (Orig.). (C). 1996. pap. 31.95 (0-942728-70-X) Copperhouse.

— The McGraw-Hill Complete Book of Purchasing Forms & Agreements. LC 97-39552. 371p. 1998. pap. 79.95 (0-07-053117-X) McGraw-Hill Prof.

— Small Business Lawyer. 1996. pap. text 29.95 (0-07-852865-8) McGraw.

— The Small Business Tax Advisor: Understanding the New Tax Law. 176p. (Orig.). 1987. pap. 12.95 (0-8306-3024-4, 30024) McGraw-Hill Prof.

— Texas Criminal Law. 1995. 59.95 (0-8039-7364-0); pap. 24.95 (0-8039-7365-9) Sage.

— Vietnam Medic: What Am I Doing Here? (Illus.). 192p. (Orig.). 1996. pap. 6.95 (0-9647256-0-6) CSR Indus.

Roberson, Cliff & Wallace, Harvey. Introduction to Criminology. 500p. (C). 1998. pap. 37.95 (0-942728-84-X) Copperhouse.

— Written & Interpersonal Communication. 182p. (C). 1996. pap. text 43.00 (0-13-335472-5) P-H.

Roberson, Cliff, jt. auth. see Bayens, Geralo J.

Roberson, Cliff, jt. auth. see Wallace, Harvey.

Roberson, Clifford, jt. auth. see Wallace, Harvey.

Roberson, Dave. Casting Your Cares. 28p. 1997. pap. 1.00 (1-929339-01-1) D Roberson Min.

— Four Steps Out of Tribulation. 48p. 1999. pap. 1.00 (1-929339-06-2) D Roberson Min.

— Grace Illustrated. 28p. 1997. pap. 1.00 (1-929339-02-X) D Roberson Min.

— The Journey Back to God. 48p. 1999. pap. 1.00 (1-929339-07-0) D Roberson Min.

— Marriage, Divorce & the Children. 28p. 1997. pap. 1.00 (1-929339-03-8) D Roberson Min.

— Standing in the Gap. 48p. 1999. pap. 1.00 (1-929339-08-9) D Roberson Min.

— Transformation of the Soul. 28p. 1997. pap. 1.00 (1-929339-04-6) D Roberson Min.

— Unmasking Satan's Tactics. 72p. 1992. pap. 4.00 (1-929339-00-3) D Roberson Min.

— The Unpardonable Sin. 48p. 1999. pap. 1.00 (1-929339-09-7) D Roberson Min.

— The Walk of the Spirit - The Walk of Power: The Vital Role of Praying in Tongues. 409p. 1999. pap. 15.00 (1-929339-10-0) D Roberson Min.

— Worship Defeats Poverty. 28p. 1997. pap. 1.00 (1-929339-05-4) D Roberson Min.

Roberson, Davey G. Soul Seachers: The First Mission. LC 97-132852. (Illus.). (Orig.). 1997. pap. 10.99 (0-9656344-0-X) Destiny Pubg.

— Soul Searchers: Battle of Darkness. (Illus.). 100p. (Orig.). 1997. pap. 9.95 (0-9656344-1-8) Destiny Pubg.

*Roberson, Dennis. Winning 42. 2000. pap. 13.95 (0-89672-443-3) Tex Tech Univ Pr.

Roberson, Dennis. Winning 42: Strategy & Lore of the National Game of Texas. LC 97-8291. (Illus.). 192p. (Orig.). 1997. pap. 12.95 (0-89672-384-4) Tex Tech Univ Pr.

Roberson, Don. Rare Birds of the West Coast of North America. LC 80-51054. (Illus.). 548p. 1980. 24.95 (0-9605352-0-9) Woodcock.

Roberson, E. Wayne, ed. Educational Accountability Through Evaluation. LC 72-155346. 128p. 1971. pap. 24.95 (0-87778-017-X) Educ Tech Pubns.

*Roberson, Ed. Atmospheric Conditions, No. 35. 1999. pap. text 10.95 (1-55713-392-1, Pub. by Sun & Moon CA) Consort Bk Sales.

Roberson, Ed. Voices Cast Out to Talk Us In. LC 95-1031. (Iowa Poetry Prize Ser.). 166p. (Orig.). 1995. pap. 10.95 (0-87745-510-4) U of Iowa Pr.

Roberson, Elisa, et al. The Beauty of Creation: Inspiration for Pregnancy & Childbirth. LC 98-40575. (Illus.). 250p. 1998. pap. 14.95 (0-9644932-3-3) Kujichagulia Pr.

Roberson, Elizabeth W. Weep Not for Me, Dear Mother. LC 98-164863. (Illus.). 168p. 1998. text 19.95 (1-56554-389-0) Pelican.

Roberson, Elizabeth W. & Ivy, Alice S. Weep Not for Me, Dear Mother. 64p. 1998. text, teacher ed. 9.95 (1-56554-392-0) Pelican.

Roberson, Elizabeth W., ed. see Landers, Eli P.

Roberson, Erriel D. The Maafa & Beyond: Remembrance, Ancestral Connections & Nation Building for the African Global Community. LC 94-74578. 200p. (Orig.). 1995. pap. 15.00 (0-9644932-0-9) Kujichagulia Pr.

— Reality Revolution: Return to the Way. LC 96-75530. 352p. (Orig.). 1996. pap. 18.50 (0-9644932-1-7) Kujichagulia Pr.

Roberson, Frances, jt. auth. see Hazelip, Linda.

Roberson, Gail, ed. see Galie, Carl V.

Roberson, Geoffrey, jt. auth. see Meyler, John.

Roberson, Glenda F. & Johnson, Mary A. Century Early Childhood: History, Trend & Issue. 650p. (C). 1995. text 51.00 (0-536-58761-2) Pearson Custom.

— Century Early Childhood: History, Trends & Issue. 394p. (C). 1995. text 28.20 (0-536-58745-0) S&S Trade.

Roberson, Glenda F. & Johnson, Mary A., eds. Leaders in Education: Their Views on Controversial Issues. LC 88-19918. (Illus.). 228p. (Orig.). (C). 1988. pap. text 22.50 (0-8191-7123-9) U Pr of Amer.

Roberson, Gloria G., jt. auth. see Schroeder, Carol F.

Roberson, J. Conrad, et al. Instrumental Data for Drug Analysis, Set. 2nd ed. (Forensic & Police Science Ser.). 631p. 1991. 425.00 (0-444-01630-9) CRC Pr.

— Instrumental Data for Drug Analysis, Vol. 5. 2nd ed. (Forensic & Police Science Ser.). 631p. 1991. 120.00 (0-444-01626-0) CRC Pr.

Roberson, J. Conrad, jt. auth. see Mills, Terry, III.

Roberson, James E. Japanese Working Class Lives: An Ethnographic Study of Factory Workers. LC 97-27162. 240p. (C). 1998. 85.00 (0-415-17212-8) Routledge.

Roberson, James T., jt. auth. see Harris, Forrest E., Sr.

Roberson, Jennifer. Daughter of the Lion. (Chronicles of the Cheysuli Ser.: Bk. 6). 384p. (Orig.). 1989. mass mkt. 5.99 (0-88677-324-5, Pub. by DAW Bks) Penguin Putnam.

— Flight of the Raven. (Chronicles of the Cheysuli Ser.: Bk. 7). 384p. 1990. mass mkt. 5.99 (0-88677-422-5, Pub. by DAW Bks) Penguin Putnam.

— Highlander: Scotland the Brave. 224p. (Orig.). 1996. reprint ed. mass mkt. 5.99 (0-446-60286-8, Pub. by Warner Bks) Little.

— Highwaymen. 1997. pap. 5.99 (0-88677-732-1, Pub. by DAW Bks) Penguin Putnam.

*Roberson, Jennifer. Lady of Sherwood. 384p. 1999. 24.00 (1-57566-475-5, Knsington) Kensgtn Pub Corp.

— Lady of Sherwood. 384p. 2000. pap. 14.00 (1-57566-587-5) Kensgtn Pub Corp.

Roberson, Jennifer. Lady of the Forest. 768p. 1993. mass mkt. 5.99 (0-8217-4284-1, Zebra Kensgtn) Kensgtn Pub Corp.

— Lady of the Forest. 608p. 1995. pap. 12.00 (0-8217-4891-2, Knsington) Kensgtn Pub Corp.

— Lady of the Glen. 1997. pap. 14.95 (1-57566-129-2) Kensgtn Pub Corp.

— Lady of the Glen. 576p. 1998. mass mkt. 6.99 (1-57566-289-2) Kensgtn Pub Corp.

— Legacy of the Sword. (Chronicles of the Cheysuli Ser.: Bk. III). (Orig.). 1986. mass mkt. 4.99 (0-88677-316-4, Pub. by DAW Bks) Penguin Putnam.

— A Pride of Princes. (Chronicles of the Cheysuli Ser.: Bk. 5). 464p. (Orig.). 1988. pap. 6.99 (0-88677-261-3, Pub. by DAW Bks) Penguin Putnam.

— Shapechangers. (Chronicles of the Cheysuli Ser.: Bk. 1). (Orig.). 1984. mass mkt. 5.99 (0-88677-140-4, Pub. by DAW Bks) Penguin Putnam.

— The Song of Homana. (Chronicles of the Cheysuli Ser.: Bk. 2). 352p. 1985. mass mkt. 5.99 (0-88677-434-9, Pub. by DAW Bks) Penguin Putnam.

— Sword-Born: A Novel of Tiger & Del. LC 98-150408. 416p. (YA). 1998. 24.95 (0-88677-776-3, Pub. by DAW Bks) Penguin Putnam.

— Sword-Born: A Novel of Tiger & Del. 432p. 1999. mass mkt. 6.99 (0-88677-827-1, Pub. by DAW Bks) Penguin Putnam.

— Sword-Breaker. (Novels of Tiger & Del: No. 4). 464p. 1991. mass mkt. 5.99 (0-88677-476-4, Pub. by DAW Bks) Penguin Putnam.

— Sword Dancer, Bk. 1. 288p. 1986. mass mkt. 5.99 (0-88677-376-8, Pub. by DAW Bks) Penguin Putnam.

— Sword-Maker. 464p. 1989. mass mkt. 5.99 (0-88677-379-2, Pub. by DAW Bks) Penguin Putnam.

— Sword-Singer, Bk. 2. 384p. 1988. mass mkt. 5.99 (0-88677-447-0, Pub. by DAW Bks) Penguin Putnam.

— A Tapestry of Lions. (Chronicles of the Cheysuli Ser.: Bk. 8). 464p. (Orig.). 1992. mass mkt. 6.99 (0-88677-524-8, Pub. by DAW Bks) Penguin Putnam.

— Track of the White Wolf. (Chronicles of the Cheysuli Ser.: Bk. 4). 1987. mass mkt. 5.99 (0-88677-193-5, Pub. by DAW Bks) Penguin Putnam.

Roberson, Jennifer, ed. Return to Avalon. 400p. 1996. mass mkt. 5.99 (0-88677-679-1, Pub. by DAW Bks) Penguin Putnam.

Roberson, Jerry L., ed. see Lauderdale, Kathi & Bonilla, Carlos A.

Roberson, John A. & Crowe, Clayton T. Engineering Fluid Mechanics, 4 vols. 4th ed. (C). 1990. pap. text 9.16 (0-395-52693-0) HM.

— Engineering Fluid Mechanics. 6th ed. LC 96-32538. 752p. 1996. text 100.95 (0-471-14735-4) Wiley.

Roberson, John A., et al. Hydraulic Engineering. 2nd ed. LC 97-44580. 672p. 1998. text 106.95 (0-471-12466-4) Wiley.

Roberson, John R. Japan Meets the World: The Birth of a Super Power. LC 98-6071. (J). 1998. 24.90 (0-7613-0407-X) Millbrook Pr.

Roberson, Kristine, ed. see Hamilton, Kirk.

Roberson, Lee. Are You Tired of Living? 208p. 1986. pap. 4.95 (0-931117-06-2) Univ Pub.

— Fireworks Don't Last. 265p. 1987. pap. 6.95 (0-931117-07-0) Univ Pub.

*Roberson, Lee. Preaching to America. 213p. 1999. pap. write for info. (0-87398-667-9) Sword of the Lord.

Roberson, Lee. Start the Fire. 385p. 1986. pap. 7.95 (0-931117-04-6) Univ Pub.

*Roberson, Linda, et al. The Marital Property Classification Handbook. 80p. 1999. pap. 29.00 (1-57862-025-2) State Bar WI.

Roberson, Mary-Russell. Guide to the National Zoological Park. Lumpkin, Susan & Weinberg, Susan, eds. LC 89-80422. (Illus.). 56p. (Orig.). 1989. pap. 3.95 (0-9622062-0-2) Friends Natl Zoo.

Roberson, Mitch, ed. see Rice, Anne, et al.

Roberson, N., et al, eds. Tests of Time Reversal Invariance in Neutron Physics: Proceedings of the Aqueduct Conference Center, N. C. 216p. (C). 1987. text 97.00 (9971-5-0463-4) World Scientific Pub.

Roberson, Nancy, jt. auth. see Walker, Pam.

*Roberson, Noma. Year 2000 & Beyond. xvii, 80p. 1999. pap. 7.99 (0-9677350-0-9) N Roberson.

Roberson, R. E. & Schwertassek, R. Dynamics of Multibody Systems. (Illus.). 480p. 1988. 147.95 (0-387-17447-8) Spr-Verlag.

An Asterisk (*) at the beginning of an entry indicates that the title is appearing for the first time.

Roberson, Rae Anne. Writing Grade 5. Pedigo, Patricia & DeSanti, Roger, eds. (Kelley Wingate Ser.). (Illus.). 130p. 1996. pap. text 10.95 (*0-88724-438-6*, CD-3720) Carson-Dellos.

— Writing Grade 4. Pedigo, Patricia & DeSanti, Roger, eds. (Kelley Wingate Ser.). (Illus.). 131p. 1996. pap. text 10.95 (*0-88724-437-8*, CD-3719) Carson-Dellos.

— Writing Grade 1. Pedigo, Patricia & DeSanti, Roger, eds. (Kelley Wingate Ser.). (Illus.). 132p. 1996. pap. text 10.95 (*0-88724-434-3*, CD-3716) Carson-Dellos.

— Writing Grade 3. Pedigo, Patricia & DeSanti, Roger, eds. (Kelley Wingate Ser.). (Illus.). 129p. 1996. pap. text 10.95 (*0-88724-436-X*, CD-3718) Carson-Dellos.

— Writing Grade 2. Pedigo, Patricia & DeSanti, Roger, eds. (Kelley Wingate Ser.). (Illus.). 130p. 1996. pap. text 10.95 (*0-88724-435-1*, CD-3717) Carson-Dellos.

Roberson, Ruth H., ed. North Carolina Quilts. LC 88-10598. (Illus.). xviii, 214p. (C). 1988. 39.95 (*0-8078-1811-9*) U of NC Pr.

Roberson, Sheila F. & Drawe, Lynn, intros. Deer-Proof Fencing. (Illus.). 41p. (Orig.). 1985. pap. 1.50 (*0-912229-10-1*) CK Wildlife Res.

Roberson, Sheila F., jt. ed. see Beasom, Sam L.

***Roberson, Steven Henry.** Lili Kraus: Hungarian Pianist, Texas Teacher & Personality Extraordinaire. LC 99-46975. (Illus.). 160p. 2000. 21.95 (*0-87565-216-6*, Pub. by Tex Christian) Tex A&M Univ Pr.

Roberson, Susan L. Emerson in His Sermons: A Man-Made Self. 240p. 1994. text 39.95 (*0-8262-0983-1*) U of Mo Pr.

Roberson, Susan L., ed. Women, America, & Movement: Narratives of Relocation. LC 98-6619. 304p. 1998. 37.50 (*0-8262-1176-3*) U of Mo Pr.

Roberson, Virginia L. Careers in Graphic Arts. rev. ed. (Careers in Depth Ser.). (Illus.). (YA). (gr. 7-12). 1993. pap. 9.95 (*0-8239-1715-0*) Rosen Group.

Roberson, Whitney. The Mass: Remembering Our Story. (Catholic Home Library). (Illus.). 128p. 1989. 4.95 (*1-55944-002-3*) Franciscan Comns.

Roberson, William. The Ironic Space: Philosophy & Form in the Nineteenth Century Novel. LC 93-20208. (American University Studies: Vol. 46). 128p. (C). 1993. text 47.95 (*0-8204-1927-3*) P Lang Pubng.

Roberson, William H. James Wright: An Annotated Bibliography. LC 95-1504. (Author Bibliographies Ser.: No. 94). 314p. 1995. 61.00 (*0-8108-3000-0*) Scarecrow.

— Robert Bly: A Primary & Secondary Bibliography. Lee, Barbara, ed. LC 86-939. (Author Bibliographies Ser.: No. 75). 419p. 1986. 41.50 (*0-8108-1879-5*) Scarecrow.

Roberson, William H. & Battenfeld, Robert L. Walter M. Miller, Jr. A Bio-Bibliography, 3. LC 92-7335. (Bio-Bibliographies in American Literature Ser.: No. 3). 176p. 1992. lib. bdg. 49.95 (*0-313-27651-X*, RWA, Greenwood Pr) Greenwood.

Roberston, Merle G. & Benson, Elizabeth P., eds. Fourth Palenque Round Table, Nineteen Eighty. LC 85-61556. (Palenque Round Table Ser.: Vol. VI). (Illus.). 290p. (Orig.). 1985. pap. 55.00 (*0-934051-03-8*) Pre-Columbian Art.

Robert. Automotive Handbook. 4th ed. 892p. 1996. 39.00 (*1-56091-918-3*, BOSCH-4) Soc Auto Engineers.

Robert. Dictionnaire des Grandes Oeuvres de la Litterature Francaise. (FRE.). 720p. 1992. 95.00 (*0-7859-9220-0*) Fr & Eur.

— Petit Robert de la Langue Francaise. (FRE.). 2551p. 1997. 150.00 (*0-320-00418-X*) Fr & Eur.

Robert. Petit Robert Langue Francaise - Grand Format. large type ed. (FRE.). 2592p. 1997. 195.00 (*0-320-00447-3*) Fr & Eur.

— Petit Robert Noms Propres Grand Format. large type ed. (FRE.). 1998. write for info. (*0-320-00390-6*) Fr & Eur.

— Power of Strategic Thinking. 206p. 1999. 24.95 (*0-07-135777-7*) McGraw.

Robert. Robert & Collins du Management Commercial Financier Economique Juridique: Fran-Ang-Fran. (ENG & FRE.). 1044p. 1994. 150.00 (*0-7859-9202-2*) Fr & Eur.

— Robert College Dictionnaire du Francais. (FRE.). 1478p. 1997. 59.95 (*0-320-00460-0*) Fr & Eur.

— Robert D'Aujourd'Hui. (FRE.). 1716p. 1994. 89.95 (*0-7859-9203-0*) Fr & Eur.

— Robert de Poche: Langue Francaise & Noms Propres. (FRE.). 928p. 1995. 24.95 (*0-7859-9194-8*) Fr & Eur.

***Robert.** Robert Dictionary Historique Langue Francaise Compact, Vol. 3. (FRE.). 4336p. 1998. 195.00 (*0-320-02285-4*) Fr & Eur.

Robert. Robert Pour Tous. 1277p. 1994. 49.95 (*0-7859-8751-7*); 59.95 (*0-7859-9191-3*) Fr & Eur.

— Robert Quebecois d'Aujourd'hui. (FRE.). 343p. 1992. 95.00 (*0-7859-9355-X*) Fr & Eur.

— Robert Quotidien. (FRE.). 2181p. 1996. 99.00 (*0-320-00513-5*) Fr & Eur.

***Robert.** Roberts Rules of Order. 10th ed. 802p. 2000. pap. text 17.00 (*0-7382-0307-6*, Pub. by Perseus Pubng) HarpC.

Robert. Shogakukan-Robert: Grand Dictionnaire Francais-Japonais. (FRE & JPN.). 2597p. 1990. 895.00 (*0-7859-9214-6*) Fr & Eur.

Robert, ed. Dictionnaire Universel des Noms Propres: Nouvelle Edition, 5 vols. (FRE.). 3054p. 1991. 1495.00 (*0-7859-9224-3*) Fr & Eur.

— Le Robert et Collins Super Senior - French-English - English-French, 2 vols. (ENG & FRE.). 2712p. 1995. 175.00 (*0-7859-9221-9*) Fr & Eur.

Robert, Hervbe, jt. auth. see Montignac, Michel.

Robert, A. M. & Robert, L., eds. Biology & Pathology of Elastic Tissues. (Frontiers of Matrix Biology Ser.: Vol. 8). (Illus.). viii, 232p. 1980. 108.00 (*3-8055-3078-1*) S Karger.

Robert, Adolphe & Cougny, Gaston. Dictionnaire des Parlementaires Francais Comprenant Tous les Membres des Assemblees Francaises et Tous les Ministres Francais depuis le Ler Mai 1789 Jusqu'au Ler Mai 1889, 5 vols. (FRE.). xvi, 3189p. reprint ed. write for info. (*0-318-71403-5*) G Olms Pubs.

***Robert, Alain.** A Course in P-Adic Analysis. LC 99-44784. (Graduate Texts in Mathematics Ser.: Vol. 198). (Illus.). 400p. 2000. 49.95 (*0-387-98669-3*) Spr-Verlag.

Robert, Barbara, ed. see International Colloquium of Dermo-Chemistry on Aging Staff.

Robert Bentley, Inc., Staff. BMW 5-Series Service Manual, 1989-1995: 525I, 530I, 535I, 540I, Including Touring: 1989, 1990, 1991, 1992, 1993, 1994, 1995. LC 98-4621. (Illus.). 672p. 1998. pap. 69.95 (*0-8376-0319-6*) Bentley Pubs.

***Robert Bentley Inc. Staff.** BMW 7 Series Service Manual: 1988-1994. LC 99-35696. (Illus.). 990p. 1999. pap. 119.95 (*0-8376-0328-5*, B794) Bentley Pubs.

Robert Bentley, Inc., Staff. BMW 3 Series Service Manual, 1992-1998. LC 99-17179. (Illus.). 760p. 1999. pap. 69.95 (*0-8376-0326-9*) Bentley Pubs.

— BMW Z3 Service Manual, 1996-1998. LC 98-34627. 520p. 1998. pap. 54.95 (*0-8376-0327-7*) Bentley Pubs.

Robert Bentley Inc. Staff. BMW 5-Series Service Manual: 1982-1988. (Illus.). 548p. 1991. 59.95 (*0-8376-0318-8*) Bentley Pubs.

Robert Bentley, Inc. Staff. Toyota Pickup, 4Runner Service Manual: 1978-1987 Including Gasoline, Diesel, & Turbo Diesel, 4-Cylinder & 6-Cylinder Engines. (Illus.). 752p. 29.95 (*0-8376-0258-0*) Bentley Pubs.

— Volkswagen Cabriolet, Scirocco Service Manual, 1985-1993: Including 16V. (Illus.). 520p. 49.95 (*0-8376-0362-5*) Bentley Pubs.

Robert Bentley Inc. Staff. Volkswagen Jetta, Golf, GTI, Cabrio Service Manual, 1993-1999: Including Jetta III, Golf III, VRG & TDI. LC 99-14513. (Illus.). 832p. 1999. pap. text 59.95 (*0-8376-0366-8*, V699) Bentley Pubs.

***Robert Bentley, Inc., Staff.** Volkswagen Jetta, Golf, GTI, 1999, 2000: Service Manual, 2.0L Gasoline, 1.9L TDI Diesel, 2.8L VR6, 1.8L Turbo. LC 00-28918. (Illus.). 992p. 2000. 69.95 (*0-8376-0386-2*) Bentley Pubs.

Robert Bentley, Inc. Staff. Volkswagen Passat: Official Factory Repair Manual, 1995, 1996, 1997:Gasoline, Turbo Diesel & TDI, Including Wagon. LC 97-24306. (Illus.). 2332p. 1997. 144.95 (*0-8376-0380-3*) Bentley Pubs.

***Robert Bentley, Inc. Staff.** Volkswagen Workshop Manual: Types 11, 14 & 15, 1958-1960. LC 00-40329. (Illus.). 2000. write for info. (*0-8376-0392-7*) Bentley Pubs.

Robert Bentley Publishers Staff. Volkswagen Fox Service Manual, 1987-1993: Including GL, GL Sport, & Wagon. (Illus.). 440p. 1993. pap. 39.95 (*0-8376-0363-3*) Bentley Pubs.

***Robert Bentley Publishers Staff, ed.** Porsche 911 Carrera Service Manual, 1984-1989: Coupe, Targa & Cabriolet. LC 00-23006. (Illus.). 750p. 2000. pap. 119.95 (*0-8376-0291-2*, P989) Bentley Pubs.

Robert Bentley Publishers Staff, ed. Volkswagen New Beetle Service Manual, 1998-1999. LC 99-22856. (Illus.). 640p. 1999. pap. 54.95 (*0-8376-0385-4*, VB99) Bentley Pubs.

— Volkswagen Workshop Manual, Types 11, 14 & 15, 1952-1957. (Illus.). 704p. 1998. pap. 84.95 (*0-8376-0389-7*) Bentley Pubs.

Robert Bentley Staff. Volkswagen Eurovan: Official Factory Repair Manual: 1992, 1993, 1994, 1995, 1996, 1997, 1998: Gasoline, Diesel, TDI, 5-Cylinder, & VR6, Including Multivan & CV Camper. LC 97-31787. (Illus.). 2420p. 1997. 169.95 (*0-8376-0335-8*) Bentley Pubs.

Robert, Bently. Volvo 240 Service Manual 1983 Through 1993. (Illus.). 572p. 1993. 49.95 (*0-8376-0285-8*) Bentley Pubs.

Robert, Bernard-Paul. Le Surrealisme Desocculte: Manifeste du Surrealisme, 1924. LC 76-469238. (FRE.). 195p. 1975. reprint ed. pap. 60.50 (*0-608-02192-X*, 206286200003) Bks Demand.

Robert, C. At Home in Paris: Your Guide to Living in the French Capital. 390p. 1993. pap. 39.95 (*0-7859-9043-7*) Fr & Eur.

Robert, Carl. Archaeologische Hermeneutik: Anleitung Zur Deutung Klassischer Bildwerke. LC 75-10652. (Ancient Religion & Mythology Ser.). (GER., Illus.). 1976. reprint ed. 32.95 (*0-405-07276-7*) Ayer.

— Bild und Lied: Archaologische Beitrage Zur Geschichte der Griechischen Heldensage. LC 75-10653. (Ancient Religion & Mythology Ser.). (GER., Illus.). 1976. reprint ed. 18.95 (*0-405-07277-5*) Ayer.

Robert, Carl, ed. see Eratosthenes.

Robert, Cavett, jt. auth. see McCants, Louise.

Robert, Charles E. Negro Civilization in the South. LC 70-173614. (Black Heritage Library Collection). 1977. reprint ed. 17.95 (*0-8369-8906-6*) Ayer.

Robert, Christi. One Baby, Two Baby, Three Baby, Four! (Illus.). 16p. (J). (ps). 1998. pap. 5.95 (*1-891846-00-0*) Busn Word.

Robert, Christian P. The Bayesian Choice: A Decision-Theoretic Motivation. LC 94-10781. (Texts in Statistics Ser.). 436p. 1997. 59.95 (*0-387-94296-3*) Spr-Verlag.

— Discretization & MCMC Convergence Assessment. Bickel, P. et al, eds. LC 98-8676. (Lecture Notes in Statistics Ser.: Vol. 135). 208p. 1998. pap. 39.95 (*0-387-98591-3*) Spr-Verlag.

Robert, Christian P. & Casella, George. Monte Carlo Statistical Methods. LC 98-55413. (Texts in Statistics Ser.). 528p. 1999. 79.95 (*0-387-98707-X*) Spr-Verlag.

Robert, Craig. Combat Medic: Vietnam. 288p. 1991. mass mkt. 5.99 (*0-671-73691-4*) PB.

Robert Crown Center for Health Education, Womens A. An Invitation to Dine. (Illus.). 254p. 1977. 10.95 (*0-9613700-0-9*) R Crown Ctr.

Robert, Dan & Gillcrist, Paul. Spindrift: Sea Stories from the U. S. Navy. LC 98-84393. 272p. 1998. 24.95 (*0-7643-0590-5*) Schiffer.

Robert, Dana L. American Women in Mission: A Social History of Their Thought & Practice. LC 97-6439. 458p. 1997. pap. text 30.00 (*0-86554-549-9*, MUP/P158) Mercer Univ Pr.

Robert, Dana L., et al. Evangelism as the Heart of Mission, No. 1. (Mission Evangelism Ser.). 26p. 1997. pap. 3.00 (*1-890569-06-2*, 2744) Gnl Brd Glbl Minis.

Robert, E. B. Footnotes Not in the Book: Humor - Education in L. A. 2nd ed. 1969. 10.00 (*0-87511-664-7*) Claitors.

— Footnotes Not in the Book: Humor - Education in L. A. 3rd ed. 1969. pap. 10.00 (*0-87511-665-5*) Claitors.

Robert, Emile A., Jr., jt. auth. see Glacel, Barbara P.

Robert, F. Discrete Iterations. Rokne, J., tr. from FRE. (Computational Mathematics Ser.: Vol. 6). (Illus.). 195p. 1986. 129.95 (*0-387-13623-1*) Spr-Verlag.

***Robert, Francois & Robert, Jean.** Faces. LC 99-54704. (Illus.). 2000. pap. 16.95 (*0-8118-2793-3*) Chronicle Bks.

Robert Gore Rifkind Center Staff. German Expressionist Prints & Drawings, Vol. 2. (Illus.). 846p. 1997. 268.00 (*3-7913-0975-7*) Prestel.

Robert Haber & Co., Staff, intro. Gods, Beasts & Men: Images from Antiquity. LC 91-66769. (Illus.). 48p. 1991. pap. 15.00 (*0-935037-43-8*) G Peters Gallery.

Robert, Harvey. George Washington Swept Here: A Quickie in Z Acts. 32p. (J). (gr. 2 up). 1975. pap. 3.50 (*0-88680-068-4*) I E Clark.

— George Washington Swept Here: Directors Script. 32p. (J). (gr. 2 up). 1975. pap. 10.00 (*0-88680-069-2*) I E Clark.

Robert, Henry M. Parliamentary Law. 610p. (C). 1975. lib. bdg. 46.50 (*0-8290-0874-8*) Irvington.

— Parliamentary Practice: An Introduction to Parliamentary Law. 209p. (C). 1975. 15.95 (*0-8290-0875-6*) Irvington.

Robert, Henry M. Robert Rule of Order. 1971. reprint ed. pap. 7.95 (*0-688-05306-8*, Quil) HarperTrade.

Robert, Henry M. Robert's Rules of Order. Vixman, Rachel, ed. 1986. mass mkt. 4.50 (*0-515-09032-8*, Jove) Berkley Pub.

— Robert's Rules of Order. 192p. 1993. mass mkt. 5.99 (*0-8007-8610-6*, Spire) Revell.

— Robert's Rules of Order. 1989. 9.60 (*0-606-04527-9*, Pub. by Turtleback) Demco.

— Robert's Rules of Order. 1993. reprint ed. lib. bdg. 21.95 (*1-56849-216-2*) Buccaneer Bks.

— Robert's Rules of Order. rev. ed. 21.95 (*0-89190-990-7*) Amereon Ltd.

— Robert's Rules of Order. rev. ed. 160p. 1993. pap. 8.95 (*0-425-13928-X*) Berkley Pub.

— Robert's Rules of Order: Modern Edition. 155p. 1996. 8.97 (*1-55748-884-3*) Barbour Pub.

***Robert, Henry M., III, et al, eds.** Robert's Rules of Order. 10th rev. ed. 2000. 35.00 (*0-7382-0384-X*) Perseus Pubng.

Robert, Henry M. & Evans, William J., eds. Robert's Rules of Order. 9th rev. enl. ed. LC 21-8. 706p. 1991. 30.00 (*0-06-275002-X*, Harper Ref) HarpC.

Robert, Henry M. & Evans, William J., eds. Robert's Rules of Order. 9th rev. enl. ed. LC 89-10220. 706p. 1991. pap. 16.00 (*0-06-276051-3*, Harper Ref) HarpC.

Robert, Henry M., et al. Robert's Rules of Order. rev. ed. 1981. 16.95 (*0-673-15472-6*, Scott Frsmn) Addison-Wesley Educ.

— Robert's Rules of Order: 1990 Edition. 9th enl. rev. ed. Cleary, James W., ed. 800p. (*0-673-38736-4*) Addison-Wesley.

Robert, Henry Martyn. Robert's Rules of Order. rev. ed. 155p. 1989. mass mkt. 4.99 (*0-425-11690-5*) Berkley Pub.

Robert Herrick Memorial Conference, University of. Trust to Good Versus: Herrick Tercentenary Essays, Dearborn, 1974. Rollin, Roger B. & Patrick, J. Max, eds. LC 77-74547. 297p. reprint ed. pap. 92.10 (*0-7837-2147-1*, 204243300004) Bks Demand.

Robert, Howard. Conan of the Isles. (Conan Ser.: No. 12). 192p. 1986. reprint ed. mass mkt. 4.50 (*0-441-11623-X*) Ace Bks.

Robert, J., jt. auth. see Le Doeuff, R.

Robert, J. M. Genetique. (De la Biologie a la Clinique Ser.). (FRE., Illus.). 452p. 1983. lib. bdg. 37.00 (*0-318-04484-6*) S M P F Inc.

Robert, Jacques, jt. ed. see Anghileri, Leopold J.

Robert, Jean. Dictionnaire des Citations du Monde Entier. (FRE.). 45.00 (*0-317-45621-0*) Fr & Eur.

— Dictionnaire des Difficultes du Francais. (FRE.). 45.00 (*0-317-45622-9*) Fr & Eur.

— Dictionnaire des Expressions & Locutions Figurees. (FRE.). 45.00 (*0-317-45624-5*) Fr & Eur.

— Dictionnaire des Idees par le Mots. (FRE.). 45.00 (*0-317-45630-X*) Fr & Eur.

— Dictionnaire des Structures du Vocabulaire Savant. (FRE.). 45.00 (*0-317-45634-2*) Fr & Eur.

— Dictionnaire des Synonymes. (FRE.). 45.00 (*0-317-45635-0*) Fr & Eur.

— Dictionnaire Etymologique. (FRE.). 45.00 (*0-317-45625-3*) Fr & Eur.

— Grand Robert Vert, 9 vols. 995.00 (*0-317-45638-5*) Fr & Eur.

— Robert & Signorelly. French-Italian. (FRE & ITA.). 3008p. 1981. 175.00 (*0-8288-4675-8*, M9403) Fr & Eur.

Robert, Jean, et al. Face to Face. (Illus.). 128p. 1997. pap. 16.95 (*1-56898-111-2*) Princeton Arch.

Robert, Jean, jt. auth. see Mongredien, Georges.

Robert, Jean, jt. auth. see Robert, Francois.

Robert, Jean-Louis, jt. ed. see Winter, Jay.

Robert, Joseph C. Ethyl: A History of the Corporation & the People Who Made It. LC 83-6620. (Illus.). 467p. reprint ed. pap. 144.80 (*0-7837-4226-6*, 204391300012) Bks Demand.

— Road from Monticello: A Study of the Virginia Slavery Debate of 1832. LC 70-109912. (Duke University. Trinity College Historical Society. Historical Papers: No. 24). reprint ed. 30.00 (*0-404-51774-9*) AMS Pr.

Robert, K. Q., ed. see Symposium on Cotton Dust: Sampling, Monitoring, &.

Robert, Katherine. Kids on the Go: The Charleston Area Guide to Great Places to Take Kids. Funcik, Christine D., ed. (Illus.). 188p. 1997. pap. 11.95 (*1-887077-05-7*) Kids on the Go.

— Song Quest. 236p. (J). (gr. 5-7). 1999. 16.95 (*1-902618-28-9*, Pub. by Element Childrns) Penguin Putnam.

Robert Koch Gallery, Inc. Staff, ed. Lloyd Ullberg: A Structuralist's Overview, Catalogue. (Illus.). 16p. 1988. 10.00 (*0-929196-00-7*) R Koch Gallery.

Robert, L. Les Gladiateurs dans l'Orient Grec. (Illus.). 372p. 1940. reprint ed. lib. bdg. 67.50 (*0-685-13622-1*, Pub. by AM Hakkert) Coronet Bks.

Robert, L., ed. Adipose Tissue. (Frontiers of Matrix Biology Ser.: Vol. 2). (Illus.). 200p. 1976. 79.25 (*3-8055-2223-1*) S Karger.

— Studies on the Biology & Pathology of the Skin. (Frontiers of Matrix Biology Ser.: Vol. 4). (Illus.). 220p. 1977. 118.50 (*3-8055-2666-0*) S Karger.

Robert, L., et al, eds. Burkitt Lymphoma, Hemostasis & Intercellular Matrix: Barbara Robert Memorial. (Frontiers of Matrix Biology Ser.: Vol. 3). (Illus.). 1976. 155.75 (*3-8055-2326-2*) S Karger.

— Methods of Connective Tissue Research. (Frontiers of Matrix Biology Ser.: Vol. 10). (Illus.). xiv, 250p. 1985. 142.75 (*3-8055-3899-5*) S Karger.

— Structural Glycoproteins in Cell-Matrix Interactions. (Frontiers of Matrix Biology Ser.: Vol. 11). (Illus.). viii, 184p. 1986. 123.50 (*3-8055-4318-2*) S Karger.

Robert, L., ed. see Garrone, R.

Robert, L., ed. see International Colloquium of Dermo-Chemistry on Aging Staff.

Robert, L., ed. see International Colloquium, Paris Staff.

Robert, L., jt. ed. see Robert, A. M.

Robert L. Humphrey, J. D., & Associates Staff. Paradigm Shift: Teach the Universal Values. LC 83-83386. (Illus.). 100p. 1984. pap. 7.95 (*0-915761-00-9*) Life Values Pr.

Robert, Ladislas & Hornebeck, William, eds. Elastin & Elastases, Vol. II. 272p. 1989. lib. bdg. 225.00 (*0-8493-6429-9*, QP552) CRC Pr.

Robert, Lee E., jt. auth. see Tingley, Judith C.

Robert, Louis. Noms Indigenes Dans l'Asie-Mineure Greco-Romaine: Premiere Partie. (Bibliotheque Archeologique Et Historique De L'Institut Francais D'Archeologie D'Istanbul Ser.: No. XIII). (FRE.). 659p. 1991. pap. 130.00 (*0-685-50578-2*, Pub. by AM Hakkert) BookLink Distributors.

Robert, Louis, ed. Le Martyre de Pionios, Pretre de Smyrne. LC 93-24110. 152p. 1994. 35.00 (*0-88402-217-X*) Dumbarton Oaks.

Robert, M. Entomology for Introductory Courses. 629p. 1985. pap. 175.00 (*0-7855-0351-X*, Pub. by Intl Bks & Periodicals) St Mut.

Robert, M. How to Make Love to a Single Woman. 1977. reprint ed. pap. 19.95 (*0-914094-07-6*) Symphony Pr.

Robert, M., ed. see Cavalli-Sforza, L. L. & Feldman, Marcus W.

Robert, Martin, jt. auth. see Parrott, Thomas M.

***Robert-McComb, Jacalyn J.** The Management of Stress & Eating Disorders for Women & Children. LC 00-39759. (Series in Modern Nutrition). 2000. write for info. (*0-8493-2027-5*) CRC Pr.

Robert, Michel. The Essence of Leadership: Strategy, Innovation & Decisiveness. LC 91-17356. 136p. 1991. 42.95 (*0-89930-655-1*, REJ, Quorum Bks) Greenwood.

— Innovation Formula. 1990. pap. 14.95 (*0-88730-400-1*, HarpBusn) HarpInfo.

— Product Innovation Strategy, Pure & Simple: How Winning Companies Outpace Their Competitors. LC 95-11855. 174p. 1995. 24.95 (*0-07-053132-3*) McGraw.

— The Strategist CEO: How Visionary Executives Build Organizations. LC 87-10945. 149p. 1988. 45.00 (*0-89930-268-8*, RST/, Quorum Bks) Greenwood.

— Strategy Pure & Simple: How to Out Think & Outsmart Your Competition. LC 97-39581. (Illus.). 269p. 1997. 24.95 (*0-07-053133-1*) McGraw.

Robert, Michel & Weiss, Alan. The Innovation Formula: How to Turn Change into Opportunity. 144p. 1988. text 27.95 (*0-88730-352-8*, HarpBusn) HarpInfo.

Robert Miller Gallery Staff. Tina Modotti Photographs. 66p. 1997. pap. text 40.00 (*0-944680-52-6*) R Miller Gal.

Robert Moore School of Education, University of Nottingham Staff. Community & Conflict in Eastwood: A Study from the Nottinghamshire Coalfield before 1914. 92p. 1998. pap. 26.00 (*1-85041-080-1*, Pub. by U of Nottingham) St Mut.

Robert, Nicolas. Producers' English: English-French Vocabulary of the Cinema & Audiovisual. (ENG & FRE.). 292p. 1995. 95.00 (*0-7859-9941-8*) Fr & Eur.

Robert of Flamborough. Liber Poenitentialis. Firth, J. J., ed. (ENG & LAT.). xxx, 364p. 51.43 (*0-88844-018-9*) Brill Academic Pubs.

Robert of Orkney. St. Magnus. MacDonald, Iain, ed. (Celtic Studies Ser.). 62p. 1994. pap. 4.95 (*0-86315-164-7*) Dufour.

Robert of Thornton. Morte Arthure: An Alliterative Poem of the Fourteenth Century. Banks, Mary M., ed. LC 71-178545. reprint ed. 37.50 (*0-404-56648-0*) AMS Pr.

R

Robert, P. C. Precision Agriculture. Rust, R. H. & Larson, W. E., eds. LC 96-80281. 1222p. 1996. 42.00 (*0-89118-132-6*) Am Soc Agron.

Robert, P. C., et al, eds. Site-Specific Management for Agricultural Systems. LC 96-103620. 993p. 1995. pap. 39.00 (*0-89118-127-X*) Am Soc Agron.

— Soil Specific Crop Management: A Workshop on Research & Development Issues. LC 93-12790. 395p. 1993. 20.00 (*0-89118-116-4*) Am Soc Agron.

Robert Parker & Associates Book Staff, ed. see Haverstock, Henry W.

Robert, Paul. Le Micro-Robert, Dictionnaire du Francais Primordial. (FRE.). 1988. 49.95 (*0-8288-1949-1*, M6487) Fr & Eur.

— Organic Metamorphism & Geothermal History. (C). 1987. pap. text 104.50 (*90-277-2501-2*) Kluwer Academic.

Robert, Paul, et al. Micro Robert en Poche: Dictionnaire du Francais Primordial. (FRE.). 1210p. 1988. pap. 29.95 (*0-8288-1948-3*, M4519) Fr & Eur.

— Le Nouveau Micro Robert. (FRE.). 1376p. 1988. 69.95 (*0-8288-1947-5*, M4457) Fr & Eur.

Robert, Pierre-Edmond, ed. Paris, Page a Page. (FRE.). 191p. 1992. pap. 16.95 (*2-278-04201-7*, Pub. by Edns Didier) Hatier Pub.

— Toutes Latitudes. (FRE.). 159p. 1993. pap. 17.95 (*2-278-04307-2*, Pub. by Edns Didier) Hatier Pub.

Robert, Robert J. & Remick, Jack. The Weekend Novelist Writes a Mystery. LC 96-42991. 272p. 1998. pap. 11.95 (*0-440-50658-1*, Dell Trade Pbks) Dell.

***Robert Rose Editors.** Beans, Lentil & Tofu Gourmet. (Illus.). 192p. 2000. pap. 18.95 (*0-7788-0023-7*, Pub. by R Rose Inc) Firefly Bks Ltd.

Robert Seaman Elementary School Staff. Reflections Journal, 1999. (Illus.). 120p. 1999. pap. text. write for info. (*0-940429-22-5*) M B Glass Assocs.

***Robert Seaman School Students Staff.** Reflections Journal 2000. (Illus.). 252p. (J). 2000. pap. text. write for info. (*0-940429-24-1*) M B Glass Assocs.

Robert, Stephane, ed. Langage et Sciences Humaines: Propos Croises: Actes du Colloque "Langues et Langages" en Hommage a Antoine Culioli (Ecole Normale Superieure, Paris, 11 Decembre 1992) (Sciences pour la Communication Ser.: Vol. 46). (FRE.). x, 166p. 1995. 28.95 (*3-906754-22-7*, Pub. by P Lang) P Lang Pubng.

Robert, Stephane, jt. ed. see Fuchs, Catherine.

Robert, Thomas J. & Waterman, Robert H. In Search of Excellence. large type ed. LC 97-5605. 576p. 1997. 25.95 (*0-7838-8114-2*, G K Hall Lrg Type) Mac Lib Ref.

Robert, Tom. Goldilocks. (Illus.). 40p. (J). (gr. k-3). 1995. 10.95 incl. audio (*0-689-80057-6*) S&S Trade.

Robert, Ulysse. Bullaire Du Pape Calixte the Second, 2 vols. in 1. (Illus.). c, 931p. 1979. reprint ed. write for info. (*3-487-06765-X*) G Olms Pubs.

***Robert V. Fullerton Art Museum Staff.** Portraits from L. A. Don Bachardy, Dan McCleary, John Sonsini: Robert V. Fullerton Art Museum, California State University, San Bernardino, November 20, 1999-January 23, 2000. LC 99-52096. (Illus.). 1999. write for info. (*0-945486-15-4*) CSU SBRVFAM.

Robert Ventre Assoc. Staff. Mastering Reading, Food Service Book, Bk. 1. (YA - Adult Education Ser.). 1991. pap. 12.95 (*0-538-70997-9*) S-W Pub.

— Mastering Reading, Food Service Book, Bk. 2. (YA - Adult Education Ser.). 1991. pap. 12.95 (*0-538-70996-0*) S-W Pub.

— Mastering Reading, Food Service Book, Bk. 3. (YA - Adult Education Ser.). 1991. pap. 12.95 (*0-538-70995-2*) S-W Pub.

— Mastering Reading, Food Service Book, Bk. 4. (YA - Adult Education Ser.). 1991. pap. 12.95 (*0-538-70994-4*) S-W Pub.

— Mastering Reading, Health Care Book, Bk. 1. (YA - Adult Education Ser.). 1990. pap. 12.95 (*0-538-71002-0*) S-W Pub.

— Mastering Reading, Health Care Book, Bk. 2. (YA - Adult Education Ser.). 1990. pap. 12.95 (*0-538-71001-2*) S-W Pub.

— Mastering Reading, Health Care Book, Bk. 3. (YA - Adult Education Ser.). 1990. pap. 12.95 (*0-538-71000-4*) S-W Pub.

— Mastering Reading, Health Care Book, Bk. 4. (YA - Adult Education Ser.). 1990. pap. 12.95 (*0-538-70999-5*) S-W Pub.

Robert, Yves, et al, eds. Parallel Processing: CONPAR 92 - VAPP V, Second Joint International Conference of Vector & Parallel Processing, Lyon, France, September 1992, Proceedings. LC 92-27828. (Lecture Notes in Computer Science Ser.: Vol. 634). xvii, 853p. 1992. 120.95 (*0-387-55895-0*) Spr-Verlag.

Robert, Zack, jt. auth. see Joyer, Mike.

Roberta, Egan. High Jinks with This Ring. (Illus.). 300p. 1988. 19.95 (*0-9619233-0-X*) Four Leaf Clover.

Roberta, Robert. Outerspace, Innerspace: The Start of a Personal Journey. LC 97-181120. (Illus.). 184p. (Orig.). 1996. pap. 12.95 (*0-9654252-5-8*) Pearly Everlast.

Robertazzi, T. G. Computer Networks & Computer Systems: Queueing Theory & Performance Evaluation. Gerla, M. et al, eds. (Telecommunications Networks & Computer Systems Ser.). (Illus.). 328p. 1990. text 49.50 (*0-387-97393-1*) Spr-Verlag.

***Robertazzi, T. G.** Computer Networks & System: Queueing Theory & Performance Evaluation. 3rd ed. (Illus.). 388p. (C). 2000. text 59.95 (*0-387-95037-0*) Spr-Verlag.

Robertazzi, Thomas G. Computer Networks & Systems: Queuing Theory & Performance Evaluation. 2nd ed. LC 93-36469. (Illus.). 376p. 1995. 54.95 (*0-387-94170-3*) Spr-Verlag.

— Performance Evaluation of High-Speed Switching Fabrics & Networks: ATM, Broadband ISDN, & MAN Technology. LC 92-44950. (Illus.). 480p. 1993. text 79.95 (*0-7803-0436-5*, PC03335) Inst Electrical.

Robertazzi, Thomas G. & IEEE Communications Society Staff. Planning Telecommunication Networks. LC 98-38908. 208p. 1999. 79.95 (*0-7803-4702-1*) Inst Electrical.

Roberti, L., jt. ed. see Chiabo, Maria.

Roberti, Mark. The Fall of Hong Kong: Britain's Betrayal & China's Triumph. rev. ed. LC 96-22592. 368p. 1996. pap. 16.95 (*0-471-15961-1*) Wiley.

Roberti, Paolo. Financial Markets & Capital Income Taxation in a Global Economy. LC 97-52664. (Advances in Finance, Investment, & Banking Ser.). 428p. 1998. 129.50 (*0-444-82206-2*) Elsevier.

Roberti, Paolo, jt. ed. see Baldassarri, Mario.

***Robertie, Bill.** Advanced Backgammon Vol. 1: Positional Play. 288p. 2000. pap. 40.00 (*1-880604-11-6*) Gammon Pr.

— Advanced Backgammon Vol. 2: Technical Play. 288p. 2000. pap. 40.00 (*1-880604-12-4*) Gammon Pr.

Robertie, Bill. Backgammon for the Serious Player. LC 96-85062. (Illus.). 200p. 1996. pap. 14.95 (*0-940685-68-X*) Cardoza Pub.

— Backgammon for Winners. 2nd ed. LC 95-69039. (Illus.). 136p. 1995. pap. 9.95 (*0-940685-58-2*) Cardoza Pub.

— Basic Endgame Strategy: Kings, Pawns & Minor Pieces. LC 97-67064. (Illus.). 168p. 1998. pap. 12.95 (*0-940685-81-7*) Cardoza Pub.

— Basic Endgame Strategy - Queen & Rooks. LC 97-94720. (Illus.). 144p. 1998. pap. 12.95 (*0-940685-89-2*) Cardoza Pub.

— Beginning Chess Play. LC 94-70604. (Illus.). 144p. 1995. pap. 9.95 (*0-940685-50-7*) Cardoza Pub.

***Robertie, Bill.** 501 Essential Backgammon Problems. LC 98-74316. 384p. 2000. pap. 19.95 (*1-58042-019-2*) Cardoza Pub.

Robertie, Bill. Master Checkmate Strategy. LC 96-85084. (Road to Chess Mastery Ser.). (Illus.). 152p. 1997. pap. 9.95 (*0-940685-66-3*) Cardoza Pub.

— Winning Chess Openings. LC 94-70603. (Illus.). 144p. 1994. pap. 9.95 (*0-940685-51-5*) Cardoza Pub.

— Winning Chess Tactics. LC 95-71954. (Illus.). 128p. 1996. pap. 9.95 (*0-940685-63-9*) Cardoza Pub.

Robertiello, Jack, jt. auth. see Mohin, Andrea.

Robertiello, Richard C. & Schoenewolf, Gerald. One Hundred One Common Therapeutic Blunders: Countertransference & Counterresistance in Psychotherapy. LC 87-1406. 294p. 1987. 50.00 (*0-87668-960-8*) Aronson.

Robertis, E. D. De, see De Robertis, E. D.

Robertis, E. M. De, see De Robertis, E. D. & De Robertis, E. M., Jr.

Robertis, Eduardo D. De, see De Robertis, Eduardo D.

Robertis, Francesco M. De, see De Robertis, Francesco M.

Roberto, Calasso. The Marriage of Cadmus Harmony Tent Card. 1994. pap. 1.00 (*0-394-25870-3*) Random.

Roberto, D. The Love of Mary. LC 83-51545. 240p. 1985. reprint ed. pap. 8.00 (*0-89555-235-3*) TAN Bks Pubs.

Roberto, Eduardo L., jt. auth. see Kotler, Philip.

Roberto, J. B., et al, eds. Advanced Photon & Particle Techniques for the Characterization of Defects in Solids, Vol. 41. (Materials Research Society Symposium Proceedings Ser.). 1985. text 17.50 (*0-931837-06-5*) Materials Res.

Roberto, Jerry T., jt. auth. see Heindel, Lee E.

Roberto, Karen A. The Elderly Caregiver: Research & Practice. (Focus Editions Ser.: Vol. 160). (Illus.). 240p. (C). 1993. text 59.95 (*0-8039-5020-9*); pap. text 26.00 (*0-8039-5021-7*) Sage.

Roberto, Karen A., ed. Relationships Between Women in Later Life. LC 96-30653. (Journal of Women & Aging Ser.: Vol. 8, Nos. 3/4). 204p. (C). 1996. pap. 14.95 (*1-56023-091-6*, Harrington Park) Haworth Pr.

— Relationships Between Women in Later Life. LC 96-30653. (Journal of Women & Aging: Vol. 8, Nos. 3/4). 204p. (C). 1996. 34.95 (*0-7890-0009-1*, Haworth Pastrl) Haworth Pr.

Roberto, Karen A., ed. Older Women with Chronic Pain. LC 94-27471. (Journal of Women & Aging). (Illus.). 128p. 1994. lib. bdg. 39.95 (*1-56024-706-1*) Haworth Pr.

— Older Women with Chronic Pain. LC 94-27471. (Journal of Women & Aging Ser.). (Illus.). 119p. 1994. pap. 9.95 (*1-56023-061-4*, Harrington Park) Haworth Pr.

Roberto, Laura G. Transgenerational Family Therapies. LC 92-1530. (Family Therapy Ser.). 219p. 1992. lib. bdg. 30.00 (*0-89862-107-0*) Guilford Pubns.

Roberto, Vito, ed. Intelligent Perceptual Systems: New Directions in Computational Perception. LC 93-33441. (Lecture Notes in Computer Science, Lecture Notes in Artificial Intelligence Ser.: Vol. 745). 1993. 55.95 (*0-387-57379-8*) Spr-Verlag.

Roberton, D. M., jt. auth. see Robinson, M. J.

Roberton, N. R., ed. Textbook of Neonatology. 2nd ed. (Illus.). 1329p. 1992. text 315.00 (*0-443-04088-5*) Church.

Roberton, Reginald S., jt. ed. see Young, William C.

Roberts. Advanced Telephone Program. LC 98-45641. 672p. 1998. pap. text 39.99 (*0-13-080360-X*) P-H.

— Beginning Algebra. 2nd ed. 1996. pap. text, student ed. 29.33 (*0-13-568403-X*) P-H.

— Biomechanics: Problem Solving for Functional Activity. (Illus.). 216p. (gr. 13). 1991. pap. text 29.95 (*0-8016-4047-4*, 04047) Mosby Inc.

Roberts. Catalysts for Fine Chemical System. text. write for info. (*0-471-49054-7*) Wiley.

Roberts. Chemistry of Natural Waters. 1997. 1.20 (*0-7167-9201-X*) W H Freeman.

— Chemistry Oxygen: Basic/Acidic Oxide, Vol. 1. 1997. pap. write for info. (*0-7167-9177-3*) St Martin.

— Complete Pec Asia. 3rd ed. 1989. 10.95 (*0-316-74991-5*) Little.

— Construction Surveying & Layout. (Construction & Building Trades Ser.). 32p. 1995. teacher ed. 14.95 (*0-8273-5724-9*) Delmar.

— Cross Curricular Reader. 2000. pap. text 31.95 (*0-312-16758-X*) St Martin.

— A Cycle of Copper Reactions. 1997. 1.20 (*0-7167-9175-7*) St Martin.

— Data Analysis for Quality Management. (Business Statistics Ser.). (C). 1998. pap., teacher ed. 40.00 (*0-87709-884-0*) PWS Pubs.

Roberts. Data Visualization. pap. text. write for info. (*0-471-48931-X*) Wiley.

Roberts. Effective Study Skills: Maximiaing Your Academic Potential. LC 98-13861. 308p. (C). 1998. pap. text 28.00 (*0-13-095061-0*) P-H.

— Electrochemical Cells. 1997. 1.20 (*0-7167-9211-7*) W H Freeman.

— European Politics Today. LC 96-17959. 1997. pap. 22.95 (*0-7190-4363-8*, Pub. by Manchester Univ Pr); text 64.95 (*0-7190-4362-X*, Pub. by Manchester Univ Pr) St Martin.

***Roberts.** Fitness Supplement. (Illus.). (C). 1998. pap. text 11.25 (*0-7637-0816-X*) JB Pubns.

— Focus on Russia & Republics. (J). 1992. write for info. (*0-237-60308-X*) EVN1 UK.

Roberts. For the Love of the Rockies. 1989. pap. 6.95 (*0-9620621-1-1*) Earth Images.

***Roberts.** Forward Soviet. 256p. 1999. text 59.50 (*1-86064-282-9*) I B T.

Roberts. Foundations of Parasitology. 6th ed. LC 99-21380. 688p. 1999. 84.38 (*0-697-42430-8*) McGraw.

— General Chemistry in the Labor. 4th ed. 498p. (C). 1997. pap. text 42.95 (*0-7167-3028-6*) W H Freeman.

— Guide to Teaching American History with Film: Democracy Challenged. (C). 1997. pap. text 13.00 (*0-673-99798-7*) Addson-Wesley Educ.

— Heat Capacity of Metals. 1997. 1.50 (*0-7167-9185-4*) W H Freeman.

— The Home Care Aide's Quick Reference Guide. LC 98-36102. 176p. 1998. pap. text 15.20 (*0-8359-5321-1*) P-H.

***Roberts.** House of Blue Lights. 2000. 25.95 (*0-593-03525-9*, Pub. by Transworld Publishers Ltd) Trafalgar.

Roberts. Instructor's Manual for General Chemistry in the Lab. 3rd ed. (C). 1991. pap. text 14.40 (*0-7167-2212-7*) W H Freeman.

— Intermediate Algebra. 2nd ed. 1994. pap. text, student ed. 29.33 (*0-13-475336-4*) P-H.

— International Directory of Telecommunications. 4th ed. Date not set. pap. text. write for info. (*0-582-04738-2*, Pub. by Addison-Wesley) Longman.

— International Practice of Anaesthesia Update. 448p. Date not set. pap. text 60.00 (*0-7506-4216-5*) Buttrwrth-Heinemann.

— Ionic Bonds & Compounds. 1997. 1.50 (*0-7167-9190-0*) W H Freeman.

— Leadership Secrets. 1993. 8.95 (*0-446-77806-0*) Warner Bks.

— Linear Algebra: Theory & Application. (C). 1998. text 69.50 (*0-03-097169-1*) Harcourt Coll Pubs.

— Literature: An Introduction to Reading & Writing, Compact. 1504p. (C). 1998. pap. text 39.20 (*0-13-275926-8*, Prentice Hall) P-H.

— Living Without Procrastination. 152p. 1999. 6.98 (*1-56731-307-8*, MJF Bks) Fine Comms.

— Loony Laws & Other Strange Happenings. LC 98-56202. 1998. pap. 5.95 (*0-8069-2056-4*) Sterling.

— Manual of Complete Pediatrics ISE, No. 3. 1989. 15.95 (*0-316-74992-3*, Little Brwn Med Div) Lppncott W & W.

***Roberts.** Narrative & Voice in Post-War Poetry. LC 98-37694. 216p. (C). 1999. 65.95 (*0-582-23352-6*) Addison-Wesley.

Roberts. Nelson Balanced Science: Living World. (UK - Science Ser.). 1995. mass mkt. 35.95 (*0-17-438665-6*) S-W Pub.

— Nutrition Throughout the Lifecycle. 5th ed. 2002. 48.00 (*0-07-231615-2*) McGraw.

— Online College Handbook. 4th ed. 1993. text 21.00 incl. 5.25 hd (*0-07-832291-X*) McGraw.

— Online College Handbook: MAC. 4th ed. 1992. 21.25 (*0-07-832292-8*) McGraw.

— Optimize Your Cruising Sailboat. LC 00-22835. (Illus.). 192p. 2000. 25.95 (*0-07-134114-5*) McGraw.

— Polymers & Plastics. 1997. 1.20 (*0-7167-9216-8*) W H Freeman.

— The Principles & Art of Cure by Homeopathy. 1996. 25.95 (*1-869975-19-7*, Pub. by C W Daniel) Natl Bk Netwk.

— Privatising Electricity: The Politics of Power. 1991. pap. text 65.00 (*0-471-94761-X*) Wiley.

— Professional Liability: Guidelines in Obstetrics & Gynecology. 1991. 275.00 (*0-8016-3357-5*) Mosby Inc.

***Roberts.** Quick Consult to Diagnosing & Treating Ocular Disease. 2001. pap. 39.95 (*0-7506-7297-8*) Buttrwrth-Heinemann.

Roberts. Rate of Chemical Reaction. 1997. 1.20 (*0-7167-9198-6*) W H Freeman.

***Roberts.** REBOL for Dummies. 408p. 2000. pap. 24.99 incl. cd-rom (*0-7645-0745-1*) IDG Bks.

Roberts. Reel Leadership. 2000. text 24.00 (*0-7352-0118-8*) PH Pr.

***Roberts.** Religion in Sociological Perspective. 4th ed. 2001. pap. 34.00 (*0-534-57951-5*) Thomson Learn.

Roberts. Roberts on Competition-Antitrust: Canada & the United States. 2nd ed. 552p. 1992. 153.00 (*0-409-80890-3*, MICHIE) LEXIS Pub.

— Scientific Measurements. 1997. 1.20 (*0-7167-9171-4*) W H Freeman.

— Selected Errors: Writings on Art & Politics, 1981-90. 292p. (C). 59.95 (*0-7453-0498-2*, Pub. by Pluto GBR); pap. 19.95 (*0-7453-0497-4*, Pub. by Pluto GBR) Stylus Pub VA.

— Shane Wright or Wrong. (Clipper Fiction Ser.). 1994. pap. text. write for info. (*0-582-80269-5*, Pub. by Addison-Wesley) Longman.

— Sourcebook for Teachers on Writing. 13th ed. (C). 1997. pap. text. write for info. (*0-15-508158-6*) Harcourt Coll Pubs.

— The Soviet Union & the Second World War. 1995. pap. text 30.95 (*0-312-13259-X*) St Martin.

— Sport Lei: Sport, Leisure, Hospitality & Tourism. Date not set. pap. 8.95 (*0-7453-0931-3*, Pub. by Pluto GBR) Stylus Pub VA.

— Systems Perspective of Parenting. (Psychology Ser.). 1994. teacher ed. write for info. (*0-534-15547-2*) Wadsworth Pub.

— Taxation &Business Decisions. 2001. pap. 6250.00 (*0-324-02400-2*) Thomson Learn.

— Understanding Soil Mechanics. (Agriculture Ser.). 32p. 1996. text, teacher ed. 12.95 (*0-8273-6870-4*) Delmar.

— Writing Lewis Structures. 1997. 1.50 (*0-7167-9191-9*) W H Freeman.

Roberts, ed. Richard M. Nixon. (L.A.B. Ser.). (C). 1999. text. write for info. (*0-321-01029-9*) Addison-Wesley.

Roberts & Berger. Direct Marketing Management. 2nd ed. LC 99-10509. 447p. (C). 1999. 53.00 (*0-13-080434-7*) P-H.

Roberts & Cusimano. Alabama Tort Law Handbook: 1991 Supplement. 172p. 1991. pap. text. write for info. (*0-87473-762-1*, 66646-10, MICHIE) LEXIS Pub.

— Alabama Tort Law Handbook: 1992 Cumulative Supplement. 1992. write for info. (*0-87473-972-1*, 66647-10, MICHIE) LEXIS Pub.

— Alabama Tort Law, 1996. 2nd ed. LC 96-79134. 1600p. 1996. text 105.00 (*1-55834-443-8*, 66645-11, MICHIE) LEXIS Pub.

Roberts & DeWitt. Racquetball: Learning the Fundamentals. 4th ed. LC 97-207782. 146p. (C). 1997. per. 21.95 (*0-7872-4178-4*, 41417801) Kendall-Hunt.

***Roberts & Grantley, Darryl.** Christopher Marlowe & English Renaissance Cult. 296p. 1999. pap. 27.95 (*0-7546-0025-4*) Ashgate Pub Co.

Roberts & Jacobs. Literature: MLA '98. 5th rev. ed. 1998. pap. text 57.00 (*0-13-010076-5*) P-H.

Roberts & Monroe, eds. Simulation Applications in Business Management & MIS. 124p. 1993. pap. 50.00 (*1-56555-023-4*, MC93-3) Soc Computer Sim.

Roberts & Scheinmann, Feodor. Chemistry & Biochemistry of Proteins. 1979. 50.00 (*0-08-023811-4*, Pergamon Pr) Elsevier.

Roberts & Walters. Dermal Absorption & Toxicity Assessment. (Illus.). 792p. 1998. text 225.00 (*0-8247-0154-2*) Dekker.

Roberts & Weinstein. Aesthetic Laser Surgery, Resurfacing - Blepharoplasty Set. 160p. 1996. text. write for info. incl. VHS (*0-8151-8651-7*) Mosby Inc.

Roberts, et al. Hot Mix Asphalt Materials, Mixture Design & Construction. 2nd ed. 575p. 1996. text 60.00 (*0-914313-01-0*) Natl Asphalt Pavement.

Roberts, jt. auth. see Cook, Robert.

Roberts, jt. auth. see Mann.

Roberts, jt. auth. see Muraskin.

Roberts, jt. auth. see Reaves.

Roberts, jt. auth. see Thornley.

Roberts, jt. ed. see Beaumariage, Robert.

Roberts, jt. ed. see Hilber, Joseph.

Roberts, Stacey L. When the Breast Fairy Comes: A Parent's Survival Guide to Raising Girls. LC 98-83069. 160p. 1999. pap. 10.95 (*0-9669970-0-X*) Postv Image.

Roberts, A. & Donaldson, J., eds. Ante-Nicene Fathers Vol. 1: Apostolic Fathers. (Early Church Fathers Ser.). 1950. 30.00 (*0-8028-8087-8*) Eerdmans.

Roberts, A. & Donaldson, J., eds. Ante-Nicene Fathers Vol. 2: Second Century. (Early Church Fathers Ser.). 1951. 30.00 (*0-8028-8088-6*) Eerdmans.

— Ante-Nicene Fathers Vol. 3: Latin Christianity. (Early Church Fathers Ser.). 1951. 30.00 (*0-8028-8089-4*) Eerdmans.

— Ante-Nicene Fathers Vol. 4: Third Century. (Early Church Fathers Ser.). 1951. 30.00 (*0-8028-8090-8*) Eerdmans.

— Ante-Nicene Fathers Vol. 5: Third Century. (Early Church Fathers Ser.). 1951. 30.00 (*0-8028-8091-6*) Eerdmans.

— Ante-Nicene Fathers Vol. 6: Third Century, 3 vols. (Early Church Fathers Ser.). 1951. 30.00 (*0-8028-8092-4*) Eerdmans.

— Ante-Nicene Fathers Vol. 8: Third & Fourth Centuries, 2 vols. (Early Church Fathers Ser.). 1951. 30.00 (*0-8028-8094-0*) Eerdmans.

— Ante-Nicene Fathers Vol. 9: Bibliography, Synopsis, Index. (Early Church Fathers Ser.). 1951. 30.00 (*0-8028-8095-9*) Eerdmans.

— Ante-Nicene Fathers Vol. 10: Original Supplement. (Early Church Fathers Ser.). 1951. 30.00 (*0-8028-8096-7*) Eerdmans.

— The Early Church Fathers: Ante-Nicene Fathers, 10 vols. 1990. 275.00 (*0-8028-8097-5*) Eerdmans.

Roberts, A. B. Applied Geotechnology: A Text for Students & Engineers on Rock Excavation & Related Topics. (Illus.). 416p. 1981. text 148.00 (*0-08-024015-1*, Pub. by Pergamon Repr) Franklin.

Roberts, A. B., jt. ed. see Sporn, Michael B.

Roberts, A. C., et al, eds. The Prefrontal Cortex: Executive & Cognitive Functions. LC 97-51746. (Illus.). 256p. 1998. text 95.00 (*0-19-852442-0*); pap. text 45.00 (*0-19-852441-2*) OUP.

An Asterisk (*) at the beginning of an entry indicates that the title is appearing for the first time.

Roberts, A. D., ed. Frontiers of Tribology: Proceedings of the International Conference on Frontiers of Tribology, Stratford-upon-Avon, U. K. 15-17 April 1991. (Illus.). 354p. 1992. 221.00 (*0-7503-0190-2*) IOP Pub.

Roberts, A. Hood. Statistical Linguistic Analysis of American English. (Janua Linguarum, Series Practica: No. 8). 1965. text 89.25 (*90-279-0627-0*) Mouton.

Roberts, A. J. A One-Dimensional Introduction to Continuum Mechanics. LC 94-30315. 172p. 1994. text 28.00 (*981-02-1913-X*) World Scientific Pub.

Roberts, A. M., et al, eds. The Geometry of Normal Faults. (Geological Society Special Publications: No. 56). (Illus.). 264p. 1991. 115.00 (*0-903317-59-1*, 258, Pub. by Geol Soc Pub Hse) AAPG.

Roberts, A. M. & Walker, M. R. Allergic Mechanisms & Ummonotherapeutic Strategies. LC 96-35332. 212p. 1997. 135.00 (*0-471-96999-0*) Wiley.

Roberts, A. W. Breeze for a Bargeman. 144p. 1990. pap. 22.00 (*0-86138-007-X*, Pub. by T Dalton) St Mut.

Roberts, A. Wayne. Elementary Linear Algebra. 2nd ed. 1985. text 34.95 (*0-8053-8305-0*) Addison-Wesley.

— Faces Mathematics. 3rd ed. LC 94-2399. 484p. (C). 1997. 87.00 (*0-06-501069-8*); text, teacher ed. 24.00 (*0-06-502130-4*) Addson-Wesley Educ.

— Faces of Mathematics: An Introductory Course for College Students. 3rd ed. (C). 1997. pap., student ed. 28.00 (*0-06-502129-0*) Addson-Wesley Educ.

Roberts, A. Wayne. Faces of Mathematics: An Introductory Course for College Students. 3rd ed. (C). 1997. 67.00 (*0-06-502131-2*) S&S Trade.

Roberts, A. Wayne. S/M Elementary Linear Algebra. 2nd ed. 1985. pap. text, teacher ed. 9.95 (*0-8053-8306-9*) Addison-Wesley.

Roberts, A. Wayne, ed. Calculus: The Dynamics of Change. LC 95-81631. (MAA Notes Ser.: No. 39). 172p. 1995. pap. 34.95 (*0-88385-098-2*, NTE-39) Math Assn.

Roberts, Ada L. Sourdough Breads & Coffee Cakes from Lane Farm: Worth 104 Recipes. (Cookery, Wine, Nutrition Ser.). (Illus.). 192p. 1983. reprint ed. pap. 4.95 (*0-486-24529-2*) Dover.

Roberts, Adam. Civil Resistance in the East European & Soviet Revolutions. (Einstein Institution Monograph Ser.). 43p. 1991. 3.00 (*1-880813-04-1*) A Einstein Inst.

***Roberts, Adam.** Fredric Jameson. 2000. 50.00 (*0-415-21522-6*); pap. write for info. (*0-415-21523-4*) Routledge.

Roberts, Adam. Humanitarian Action in War: Aid, Protection & Impartiality in a Vacuum. (Adelphi Papers: No. 300). 96p. 1997. pap. text 32.00 (*0-19-828093-9*) OUP.

— Robert Browning Revisited. LC 96-3324. 1996. 28.95 (*0-8057-4590-4*, Twyne) Mac Lib Ref.

— Romantic & Victorian Long Poems: A Guide. Holloway, Royal, ed. LC 99-18600. 223p. 1999. text 59.95 (*1-85928-156-7*, Pub. by Ashgate Pub) Ashgate Pub Co.

***Roberts, Adam.** Science Fiction. LC 99-87223. 176p. 1999. pap. 14.99 (*0-415-19205-6*) Routledge.

— Science Fiction. LC 99-87223. (New Critical Idiom Ser.). 176p. 2000. 50.00 (*0-415-19204-8*) Routledge.

***Roberts, Adam, ed.** Alfred Tennyson. LC 99-46095. 688p. 2000. 60.00 (*0-19-210016-5*) OUP.

Roberts, Adam & Guelff, Richard, eds. Documents on the Laws of War. 3rd ed. 680p. 2000. text 90.00 (*0-19-876389-1*); pap. text 35.00 (*0-19-876390-5*) OUP.

Roberts, Adam & Kingsbury, Benedict. Presiding over a Divided World: Changing U. N. Roles, 1945-1993. LC 94-4467. (International Peace Academy Occasional Paper Ser.). 95p. 1994. pap. text 9.95 (*1-55587-519-X*) L Rienner.

Roberts, Adam & Kingsbury, Benedict, eds. United Nations, Divided World: The U. N.'s Roles in International Relations. 2nd ed. 606p. 1994. pap. text 22.00 (*0-19-827926-4*) OUP.

Roberts, Adam, et al. Academic Freedom under Israeli Military Occupation: Report of WUS-ICJ Mission of Enquiry into Higher Education in the West Bank & Gaza. LC LB2332.. 87p. reprint ed. pap. 30.00 (*0-8357-5028-0*, 202773400056) Bks Demand.

Roberts, Adam, ed. see Browning, Robert.

Roberts, Adam, ed. see Tennyson, Alfred Lord.

Roberts, Adrian C. Arthur Schnitzler & Politics. LC 89-6678. (Studies in Austrian Literature, Culture & Thought). 214p. 1989. pap. 23.00 (*0-929497-14-7*) Ariadne CA.

Roberts, Alan. Lowly Manger Empty Tomb. LC 98-68273. 80p. 1999. pap. 9.95 (*1-57197-152-1*) Pentland Pr.

— The Self-Managing Environment. 189p. 1980. 29.00 (*0-8476-6211-X*) Rowman.

***Roberts, Alan.** Unix & Windows 2000: Interoperability Guide. 500p. 2000. pap. 44.99 (*0-13-026332-X*) P-H.

Roberts, Alan & Bush, B. M., eds. Neurones Without Impulses. LC 79-42572. (Society for Experimental Biology Seminar Ser.: No. 6). (Illus.). 304p. 1981. pap. text 35.95 (*0-521-29935-7*) Cambridge U Pr.

***Roberts, Alan & Fareed, Dylan.** 123 Instructions 4 Microsoft PowerPoint 2000. (One Two Three Instructions 4 Learning Guides Ser.). (Illus.). 212p. 2000. pap. 19.95 (*0-9678053-1-7*) OneTwoThr Inst.

***Roberts, Alan & Grimaldi, Guido.** 123 Instructions 4 Microsoft Word 2000. (One Two Three Instructions 4 Learning Guides Ser.). (Illus.). 178p. 2000. pap. 19.95 (*0-9678053-0-9*) OneTwoThr Inst.

— 123 Instructions 4 Microsoft Windows 98. (One Two Three Instructions 4 Learning Guides Ser.). 160p. 2000. pap. 19.95 (*0-9678053-2-5*) OneTwoThr Inst.

— 123 Instructions 4 the Internet & Microsoft Outlook 2000. (One Two Three Instructions 4 Learning Guides Ser.). 172p. 2000. pap. 19.95 (*0-9678053-3-3*) OneTwoThr Inst.

Roberts, Alan, jt. auth. see Gonzalez, Jean.

Roberts, Alan P., jt. auth. see Allen, Thomas O.

Roberts, Alan W., contrib. by. Bulk Materials Storage, Handling & Transportation, 5th International Conference, 1995, 2 vols. (National Conference Proceedings 95 Ser.: Vol. 4). (Illus.). 532p. 1995. pap. 144.00 (*0-85825-627-4*, Pub. by Inst Engrs Aust-EA Bks) Accents Pubns.

Roberts, Alasdair. Midges. (Illus.). 126p. 1998. pap. 9.95 (*1-874744-79-3*, Pub. by Birlinn Ltd) Dufour.

— Out to Play: The Middle Years of Childhood. 175p. 1980. text 13.00 (*0-08-025719-4*, Pergamon Pr); pap. text 13.00 (*0-08-025718-6*, Pergamon Pr) Elsevier.

***Roberts, Alasdair.** Tales of the Braes of Glenlivet. 172p. 2000. pap. 13.95 (*1-84158-028-7*, Pub. by Birlinn Ltd) Dufour.

Roberts, Alasdair & Robertson, Barbara. Midges. 126p. 1998. pap. 9.95 (*1-874744-63-7*, Pub. by Birlinn Ltd) Dufour.

Roberts, Albert R. Helping Crime Victims: Research, Policy, & Practice. 256p. 1990. text 52.00 (*0-8039-3468-8*); pap. text 24.00 (*0-8039-3469-6*) Sage.

— Social Work in Juvenile & Criminal Justice Settings. 2nd ed. LC 96-19014. (Illus.). 474p. 1997. 87.95 (*0-398-06758-9*); pap. 69.95 (*0-398-06759-7*) C C Thomas.

Roberts, Albert R., ed. Battered Women & Their Families: Intervention Strategies & Treatment Programs. 2nd ed. LC 97-40907. (Series on Social Work). (Illus.). 552p. 1998. 49.95 (*0-8261-4591-4*) Springer Pub.

— Crisis Intervention & Time-Limited Cognitive Treatment. 320p. 1995. 54.00 (*0-8039-5629-0*); pap. 24.95 (*0-8039-5630-4*) Sage.

***Roberts, Albert R., ed.** Crisis Intervention Handbook: Assessment, Treatment & Research. 2nd ed. LC 99-48950. 584p. 2000. 49.95 (*0-19-513365-X*) OUP.

Roberts, Albert R., ed. Crisis Management & Brief Treatment: Theory, Technique, & Applications. LC 95-40746. 228p. (C). 1996. pap. text 38.95 (*0-8304-1429-0*) Thomson Learn.

— Critical Issues in Crime & Justice. 328p. (C). 1994. text 52.00 (*0-8039-5497-2*); pap. text 24.00 (*0-8039-5498-0*) Sage.

— Helping Battered Women: New Perspectives & Remedies. (Illus.). 272p. (C). 1996. pap. text 27.95 (*0-19-509587-1*) OUP.

— Juvenile Justice: Policies, Programs, & Services. 2nd rev. ed. LC 97-40390. 494p. (C). 1998. pap. text 42.95 (*0-8304-1423-1*) Thomson Learn.

Roberts, Albert R., jt. auth. see McNeece, C. Aaron.

Roberts, Albert R., jt. compiled by see Van Wormer, Katherine.

Roberts, Alexa, et al. Bits'iis Nineezi (The River of Neverending Life) Navajo History & Cultural Resources of the Grand Canyon. (Illus.). 181p. 1995. pap. write for info. (*0-9639162-1-1*) Navajo Nation.

Roberts, Alexander & Donaldson, James, eds. Early Church Fathers, the Ante-Nicene Fathers, 10 vols., Set. 1994. 299.00 (*1-56563-082-3*) Hendrickson MA.

Roberts, Alexander, et al. Early Church Fathers, 38 vols., Set. 22,800p. 1994. 1100.00 (*1-56563-081-5*) Hendrickson MA.

Roberts, Alexander, jt. tr. see Donaldson, James.

Roberts, Alexander, tr. see Jahangir.

Roberts, Alexnder, tr. see Origen, et al.

Roberts, Alfred R. Selected Papers of Earle C. King. Brief, Richard P., ed. LC 80-1464. (Dimensions of Accounting Theory & Practice Ser.). 1980. lib. bdg. 25.95 (*0-405-13486-X*) Ayer.

Roberts, Alina. Prairie Summer. (Great Escapes Ser.). 1994. per. 1.99 (*0-373-83274-5*, 1-83274-0) Harlequin Bks.

Roberts, Alison. Hathor Rising: The Power of the Goddess in Ancient Egypt. LC 97-6130. (Illus.). 192p. 1997. pap. 16.95 (*0-89281-621-X*) Inner Tradit.

***Roberts, Alison.** Mum's the Word. large type ed. 288p. 1999. 25.99 (*0-263-16025-4*, Pub. by Mills & Boon) Ulverscroft.

Roberts, Alison, jt. auth. see MacDonald, Fiona.

Roberts, Allen. Robert Francis Kennedy: The Biography of a Compulsive Politician. 1984. 19.95 (*0-8283-1890-5*) Branden Bks.

Roberts, Allen, jt. auth. see Sillitoe, Linda.

Roberts, Allen, ed. & illus. see Luedi, Marcus.

Roberts, Allen D., jt. auth. see Antrei, Albert C. T.

Roberts, Allen E. Craft & Its Symbols. 8th ed. LC 73-89493. (Illus.). xii, 90p. 1995. reprint ed. text 9.50 (*0-88053-058-8*, M 321) Macoy Pub.

— The Diamond Years: The Story of Babcock Lodge No. 322, AF&AM. (History of Babcock Lodge Ser.: No. 322). (Illus.). 315p. 1987. 18.00 (*0-935633-04-9*) Anchor Comm.

— La Francmasoneria y Sus Simbolos. Callejas, Roger F., tr. (SPA.). 188p. 1986. 9.50 (*0-88053-084-7*, M 330) Macoy Pub.

— Freemasonry in American History. (Illus.). xxx, 462p. 1985. text 19.50 (*0-88053-078-2*, M 317) Macoy Pub.

— G. Washington: Master Mason. LC 76-16296. (Illus.). xiv, 208p. 1976. 11.50 (*0-88053-060-X*, M-323) Macoy Pub.

— House Reunited: Civil War * Aftermath * Brotherhood. 98p. (Orig.). 1996. pap. 6.00 (*0-935633-15-4*) Anchor Comm.

— House Undivided: The Story of Freemasonry & the Civil War. xx, 356p. 1990. reprint ed. 22.95 (*0-88053-056-1*, M 319) Macoy Pub.

— How to Conduct a Leadership Seminar. 12p. 1995. pap. 3.50 (*0-88053-013-8*, M 057) Macoy Pub.

— Masonic Lifeline: Leadership. Orig. Title: More Light in Masonry. (Illus.). 160p. 1992. pap. 6.00 (*0-935633-11-1*) Anchor Comm.

— Masonic Trivia (And Facts) 209p. 1994. 18.00 (*0-935633-13-8*) Anchor Comm.

— The Mystic Tie. xvi, 296p. 1994. 16.50 (*0-88053-086-3*, M331) Macoy Pub.

— The Search for Leadership. 236p. 1987. 18.00 (*0-935633-05-7*) Anchor Comm.

— Seekers of Truth: The Story of the Philalethes Society. (History of the Philalethes Society Ser.). (Illus.). 269p. 1988. 18.00 (*0-935633-06-5*) Anchor Comm.

Roberts, Allen E., ed. Who Is Who in Freemasonry, Vol. 1. 188p. 1984. 36.00 (*0-935633-00-6*) Anchor Comm.

— Who Is Who in Freemasonry, Vol. 2. 203p. 1986. 36.00 (*0-935633-02-2*) Anchor Comm.

— Who Is Who in Freemasonry, Vol. 3. 300p. 1996. 36.00 (*0-935633-16-2*) Anchor Comm.

Roberts, Allen E. & Hunt, Bruce H. Brother Truman: The Masonic Life & Philosophy of Harry S. Truman. (Illus.). 313p. 1985. 18.00 (*0-935633-01-4*) Anchor Comm.

Roberts, Allen F. Animals in African Art: From the Familiar to the Marvelous. LC 94-73442. (Illus.). 192p. 1995. pap. 32.00 (*0-945802-17-X*) Museum African.

— Threshold: African Art on the Verge. (Illus.). 96p. 1994. pap. 19.95 (*3-7913-1369-X*) Mus African Art.

Roberts, Allen F., et al. Animals in African Art: From the Familiar to the Marvelous. (Illus.). 192p. 1995. 65.00 (*3-7913-1455-6*, Pub. by Prestel) te Neues.

Roberts, Allen F., jt. auth. see Maurer, Evan M.

Roberts, Allen F., jt. auth. see Nooter, M.

Roberts, Allen F., jt. auth. see Roberts, Mary N.

Roberts, Allen F., ed. see Childs, S. Terry & De Maret, Pierre.

Roberts, Allen F., jt. ed. see Roberts, Mary N.

Roberts, Allene. The Curiosity Club: Kids' Nature Activity Book. 192p. (J). 1992. pap. 14.95 (*0-471-55589-4*) Wiley.

Roberts, Alma, ed. New Breezes: An Anthology of African American Literary Voices. 51p. 1993. pap. 7.95 (*0-9638191-0-0*) New Breezes.

Roberts, Alvin. Coping with Blindness: Personal Tales of Blindness Rehabilitation. LC 98-12837. 144p. 1998. pap. text 12.95 (*0-8093-2160-2*) S Ill U Pr.

Roberts, Amanda. Pregnancy Week-by-Week. LC 97-177472. (Illus.). 96p. 1997. pap. 18.00 (*0-06-273483-0*, Perennial) HarperTrade.

Roberts, Amanda, ed. Reader's Digest Guide to Love & Sex. LC 97-40448. (Illus.). 320p. 1998. 29.95 (*0-7621-0043-5*, Pub. by RD Assn) Penguin Putnam.

Roberts, Andrew. The Eminent Churchillians. (Illus.). 354p. 1995. 27.50 (*0-684-80403-4*) S&S Trade.

— Eminent Churchillians. 1995. 27.50 (*0-671-76940-5*) Simon & Schuster.

— A History of the Bemba: Political Growth & Change in Northeastern Zambia Before 1900. LC 73-5813. (Illus.). 454p. 1973. reprint ed. pap. 140.80 (*0-608-07444-6*, 206767100009) Bks Demand.

— A History of Zambia. LC 76-40923. (Illus.). 288p. (C). 1976. 39.50 (*0-8419-0291-7*, Africana); pap. 25.00 (*0-8419-0490-1*, Africana) Holmes & Meier.

***Roberts, Andrew & Clarke, Rachel.** Double Down No. 1: Tar & Strange Place. (Illus.). 32p. 1999. pap. 3.00 (*0-9676085-0-3*) Epicenter Press.

***Roberts, Andrew, et al.** Public House & Beverage Management: Key Principles & Issues. 224p. 2000. pap. 36.95 (*0-7506-4678-0*) Buttrwrth-Heinemann.

Roberts, Andrew M. Joseph Conrad. LC 97-44495. (Critical Readers Ser.). 296p. (C). 1998. 76.00 (*0-582-24599-0*) Longman.

***Roberts, Andrew Michael.** Conrad & Masculinity. LC 99-42654. 2000. text 49.95 (*0-312-22782-5*) St Martin.

Roberts, Andy, jt. auth. see Clarke, David.

Roberts, Ann. Spokane County Cemetery Guide. (Illus.). 105p. 1990. pap. 12.95 (*0-945433-07-7*) Herit Quest.

Roberts, Ann, jt. auth. see Barnes, Althemese.

Roberts, Ann R. Mr. Rockefeller's Roads: The Untold Story of Acadia's Carriage Roads & Their Creator. LC 90-84029. (Illus.). 184p. 1990. pap. 14.95 (*0-89272-296-7*) Down East.

Roberts, Ann V. Louisa Elliott. 800p. 1990. mass mkt. 5.95 (*0-380-70991-0*, Avon Bks) Morrow Avon.

— Morning's Gate. 640p. 1993. reprint ed. mass mkt. 5.99 (*0-380-70992-9*, Avon Bks) Morrow Avon.

Roberts, Anna, ed. Violence Against Women in Medieval Texts. LC 97-48732. (Illus.). 304p. 1998. 49.95 (*0-8130-1566-9*) U Press Fla.

***Roberts, Anne.** Health & Illness in Retirement. 160p. 2000. pap. 30.00 (*0-86242-251-5*, Pub. by Age Concern Eng) St Mut.

Roberts, Anne F. & Cockrell, Marcia W., eds. Historic Albany: Its Churches & Synagogues. (Illus.). 415p. (Orig.). 1986. pap. 15.00 (*0-941237-00-1*) Libr Commns Servs.

Roberts, Anne F., ed. see Burkett, Lucille F.

Roberts, Anne F., ed. see Findlay, Lois P.

Roberts, Anne R. The Rockefeller Family Home: Kykuit. LC 97-39464. (Illus.). 192p. 1998. 49.95 (*0-7892-0222-0*) Abbeville Pr.

Roberts, Annette, jt. auth. see Hill, Stephen.

Roberts, Annie L. Cornucopia: The Lore of Fruits & Vegetables. (Illus.). 96p. 1998. 16.95 (*1-57715-036-8*) Knckerbocker.

Roberts, Annie L., jt. auth. see Ziga, Charles J.

Roberts, Anthony, tr. Living with Ghosts: Eleven Extraordinary Tales, Vol. 2. (Illus.). 192p. 1996. 25.00 (*0-393-03952-8*) Norton.

Roberts, Anthony, tr. see Modin, Yuri.

Roberts, Anthony, tr. see Patin, Sylvie.

Roberts, Arch E. Rakkasan! The 187th Regimental Combat Team. (Airborne Ser.: No. 8). (Illus.). 1981. 29.95 (*0-89839-008-7*) Battery Pr.

Roberts, Archibald E. America in Crisis Survival Portfolio. 100p. 1992. pap. 14.95 (*0-934120-23-4*) Comm Restore Const.

— Emerging Struggle for State Sovereignty. 300p. 1979. 9.95 (*0-318-13711-9*); pap. 5.95 (*0-318-13712-7*) Comm Restore Const.

— The Most Secret Science. LC 84-70100. (Illus.). 200p. 1984. pap. 12.00 (*0-934120-08-0*) Betsy Ross Pr.

— The Most Secret Science. 1984. pap. write for info. (*0-318-61784-6*) Comm Restore Const.

— Peace: By the Wonderful People Who Brought You Korea & Viet Nam. 377p. 1972. 6.95 (*0-318-13713-5*) Comm Restore Const.

— The Republic: Decline & Future Promise. 1975. write for info. (*0-318-61783-8*) Comm Restore Const.

— Victory Denied. 300p. 1966. pap. 2.00 (*0-318-13714-3*) Comm Restore Const.

Roberts, Art. The New Learning Tool I for Little Learners: Easy Adding & Subtracting Tables. (Illus.). (J). (gr. 1-2). 1995. text 7.99 (*1-887252-04-5*) Kids Success Learn.

— The New Learning Tool II for Young Learners: Easy Multiplying & Dividing Tables. (Illus.). 2p. (J). (gr. 3-5). 1995. text 7.99 (*1-887252-05-3*) Kids Success Learn.

Roberts, Arthur C. Head Trauma Cases: Law & Medicine, 2, Vol. 2. 2nd ed. LC 96-14331. (Personal Injury Library). 816p. 1996. boxed set 260.00 (*0-471-12182-7*) Wiley.

Roberts, Arthur D. & Cawelti, Gordon. Redefining General Education in the American High School. fac. ed. LC 84-71655. (Illus.). 168p. (Orig.). 1984. reprint ed. pap. 52.10 (*0-608-01033-2*, 208250900011) Bks Demand.

Roberts, Arthur J., ed. Coronary Artery Surgery: Application of New Technologies. LC 82-23905. (Illus.). 495p. reprint ed. pap. 153.50 (*0-8357-7630-1*, 205695300096) Bks Demand.

— Myocardial Protection in Cardiac Surgery. (Cardiothoracic Surgery Ser.: Vol. 3). (Illus.). 640p. 1987. text 250.00 (*0-8247-7638-0*) Dekker.

Roberts, Arthur J., jt. ed. see Adams, Ann S.

Roberts, Arthur O. Back to Square One: Turning Losses into Spiritual Gain. 40p. 1990. pap. 3.95 (*0-913342-67-X*) Barclay Pr.

— Drawn by the Light: Autobiographical Reflections of Arthur O. Roberts. LC 93-74582. 241p. 1993. 16.95 (*0-913342-77-7*) Barclay Pr.

— Look Closely at the Child: Christmas Poems. LC 97-76793. 70p. 1997. 17.00 (*0-913342-87-4*) Barclay Pr.

— Messengers of God: The Sensuous Side of Spirituality. 216p. (Orig.). 1996. pap. 14.95 (*0-913342-80-7*) Barclay Pr.

— Move over, Elijah: Sermons in Poetry & Prose. LC 67-24903. 161p. 1967. 7.95 (*0-913342-11-4*) Barclay Pr.

— Sunrise & Shadow: A Collection of Poems. LC 84-62861. 112p. 1985. pap. 7.95 (*0-913342-48-3*) Barclay Pr.

Roberts, Arthur O., ed. Faith & Practice: A Book of Christian Discipline. LC 87-73151. 114p. 1987. pap. 6.00 (*0-913342-62-9*) Barclay Pr.

Roberts, Arthur O., jt. ed. see Oliver, John W.

Roberts, Arthur W., ed. see O'Neill, Eugene.

Roberts, Aubrey C. & Wallis, James F. Concepts of Accounting Theory. (Orig.). 1979. pap. 9.98 (*0-89894-013-3*) Advocate Pub Group.

Roberts, Audrey. Bibliography of Commissions of Enquiry & Other Government-Sponsored Reports on the Commonwealth Caribbean, 1900-1975. (Bibliography & Reference Ser.: No. 14). 89p. (Orig.). 1985. pap. 15.00 (*0-917617-06-1*) SALALM.

Roberts, Audrey, jt. ed. see Thompson, Irene.

***Roberts, Audrey Jeanne.** Heart of a Loving Family: A Treasury of Devotions & Scripture. 2000. 9.99 (*0-310-98271-5*) Zondervan.

— Heart of a Loving Friendship: A Treasury of Devotions & Scripture. 2000. 9.99 (*0-310-98270-7*) Zondervan.

Roberts, Augustine. Centered on Christ: An Introduction to Monastic Profession. rev. ed. LC 93-7100. 173p. 1993. pap. 18.95 (*0-932506-99-2*) St Bedes Pubns.

Roberts, Augustine, tr. see Olivera, Bernardo.

Roberts, B. A., ed. see Proctor, J.

Roberts, B. Ellen & White, Jack E. Roberts vs. Texaco: A True Story of Race & Corporate America. LC 97-52303. 1998. mass mkt. 25.00 (*0-380-97627-7*, Avon Bks) Morrow Avon.

***Roberts, B. H.** The Essential B. H. Roberts. Madsen, Brigham D., ed. & intro. by. LC 99-41026. Vol. 6. 407p. 2000. text 29.95 (*1-56085-128-7*) Signature Bks.

Roberts, B. H. The Life of John Taylor. 11.95 (*0-88494-106-X*) Bookcraft Inc.

— The Mormon Doctrine of Deity: The Roberts-Van der Donckt Discussion. LC 98-4089. (Mormon Classics: No. 3). 328p. 1998. reprint ed. pap. 14.95 (*1-56085-111-2*) Signature Bks.

— A Scrap Book, Vol. II. 578p. 1991. 34.95 (*0-9622545-9-2*) L Pulsipher.

— Seventy's Course in Theology. 1000p. (C). 1995. 49.95 (*0-910523-16-9*) Grandin Bk Co.

— Studies of the Book of Mormon. 2nd ed. Madsen, Brigham D., ed. LC 92-22758. (Illus.). 416p. 1992. pap. 14.95 (*1-56085-027-2*) Signature Bks.

— The Truth, the Way, the Life: An Elementary Treatise on Theology: the Masterwork of B. H. Roberts. 2nd ed. Larson, Stan, ed. LC 94-14856. (Illus.). 800p. 1995. pap. 19.95 (*1-56085-077-9*, Smith Res) Signature Bks.

Roberts, B. H., intro. History of the Church, 7 vols. Incl. Vol. 7 (period 2, The Apostolic Interregnum). 640p. 1980. 15.95 (*0-87747-080-4*); 15.95 (*0-87747-291-2*) Deseret Bk.

Roberts, B. T. Holiness Teachings. pap. 11.99 (*0-88019-190-2*) Schmul Pub Co.

— Ordaining Women. rev. ed. LC 98-129481. 106p. 1992. reprint ed. pap. 5.95 (*0-89367-176-2*) Light & Life Comm.

Roberts, Barbara. Face Reading: What Does Your Face Say? 2nd ed. 1994. pap. text 22.95 (*0-9642727-0-9*) Insight & Healing.

***Roberts, Barbara.** Quilts for Girls & Boys. LC 00-24945. (Illus.). 80p. 2000. pap. write for info. (*1-56477-315-9*, B443, Pub. by Martingale & Co) F & W Pubns Inc.

R

Roberts, Barbara. A Reconstructed World: A Feminist Biography of Gertrude Richardson. (Illus.). 416p. 1996. 60.00 (*0-7735-1394-9*, Pub. by McG-Queens Univ Pr) CUP Services.

Roberts, Barbara, jt. auth. see Jaffe, Charlotte.

Roberts, Barbara A. Phoebe Flower's Adventures: That's What Kids Are For. LC 98-7706. (Phoebe Flower's Adventures Ser.). (J). 1998. 5.95 (*0-9660366-2-X*) Advantage Books.

***Roberts, Barbara A.** Phoebe's Lost Treasure. LC 99-39427. (Phoebe Flower's Adventures Ser.). (Illus.). (J). 1999. write for info. (*0-9660366-6-2*) Advantage Books.

Roberts, Bari-Ellen & White, Jack E. Roberts vs. Texaco: A True Story of Race & Corporate America. LC 97-52303. 304p. 1999. pap. 13.50 (*0-380-79639-2*, Avon Bks) Morrow Avon.

***Roberts, Barrie.** Sherlock Holmes & the Devil's Grail. 2000. pap. 9.95 (*0-7490-0470-3*, Pub. by Allison & Busby) Intl Pubs Mktg.

— Sherlock Holmes & the Man from Hell. large type ed. 312p. 2000. pap. 18.99 (*0-7089-5675-0*, Linford) Ulverscroft.

***Roberts, Barry.** Practice Safe Stress: A Guide to Using Your Inner Sense of Humor to Minimize Day to Day Stress. (Illus.). 88p. 2000. pap. 12.00 (*0-9700246-0-6*) HAHA.

Roberts, Barry J. & Upton, Kevin. The Compleat Facilitator: A Guide. (Illus.). 96p. (Orig.). 1994. pap. 29.95 (*0-9646972-0-3*) Howick Assocs.

Roberts, Barry S., jt. auth. see Mann, Richard A.

Roberts, Ben. In-Line Skating. (Extreme Sports Ser.). (Illus.). 32p. (YA). (gr. 5-9). 1999. pap. 6.95 (*0-7641-0798-4*) Barron.

***Roberts, Ben.** The Manic Street Preachers: Prole Art Threat. (Illus.). 2000. pap. 18.95 (*0-946719-25-X*, Pub. by SAF Pub) Interlink Pub.

Roberts, Benjamin C. Labour in the Tropical Territories of the Commonwealth. LC 64-25334. 444p. reprint ed. 137.70 (*0-8357-9110-6*, 201792500010) Bks Demand.

Roberts, Bernadette. The Experience of No-Self: A Contemplative Journey. rev. ed. 213p. (C). 1993. pap. text 19.95 (*0-7914-1694-1*) State U NY Pr.

— The Path to No-Self: Life at the Center. LC 91-30833. 214p. (C). 1991. pap. text 19.95 (*0-7914-1142-7*) State U NY Pr.

— What Is Self? A Study of the Spiritual Journey in Terms of Consciousness. 2nd ed. LC 89-91249. 216p. (Orig.). 1996. reprint ed. pap. 17.00 (*0-9623993-0-2*) M Goens Pub.

Roberts, Bernadette, et al. The Path to No-Self: Life at the Center. LC 91-30833. 214p. (C). 1991. text 42.50 (*0-7914-1141-9*) State U NY Pr.

Roberts, Bethany. Follow Me! LC 97-48304. (Illus.). (J). (ps-1). 1998. 15.00 (*0-395-82268-8*, Clarion Bks) HM.

— Halloween Mice! LC 93-17192. (Illus.). 32p. (J). (ps-1). 1995. 13.00 (*0-395-67064-0*, Clarion Bks) HM.

— Halloween Mice! (Illus.). 32p. (J). (ps-1). 1997. pap. 5.95 (*0-395-86619-7*, Clarion Bks) HM.

— Monster Manners. LC 94-23219. (Illus.). 32p. (J). (ps-3). 1997. pap. 5.95 (*0-395-86622-7*, Clarion Bks) HM.

— Monster Manners: A Guide to Monster Etiquette. LC 94-23219. (Illus.). 32p. (J). (ps-3). 1996. 15.00 (*0-395-69850-2*, Clarion Bks) HM.

— A Mouse Told His Mother. (Illus.). 32p. (J). (gr. k-3). 1997. 14.95 (*0-316-74982-6*) Little.

***Roberts, Bethany.** A Mouse Told His Mother. (Illus.). 32p. (J). (ps-2). 1999. pap. 5.95 (*0-316-74958-3*) Little.

— Ruby to the Rescue. 2001. text 15.95 (*0-8050-6486-9*) St Martin.

Roberts, Bethany. Valentine Mice! LC 96-50889. (Illus.). 32p. (J). (ps-1). 1997. 13.00 (*0-395-77518-3*, Clarion Bks) HM.

***Roberts, Bethany.** Valentine Mice! (Illus.). 32p. (J). (ps-k). 2001. pap. 5.95 (*0-618-05152-X*, Clarion Bks) HM.

Roberts, Bethany. Waiting for Christmas. (Illus.). 32p. (ps-1). 1996. pap. 5.95 (*0-395-79728-4*) HM.

Roberts, Bethany. Waiting-for-Christmas Stories. LC 93-11480. 1994. 11.15 (*0-606-10355-4*, Pub. by Turtleback) Demco.

Roberts, Bethany. Waiting for Christmas Stories. unabridged ed. 32p. (J). (ps-3). 1997. pap. 9.95 incl. audio (*0-395-85813-5*, 111213, Clarion Bks) HM.

— Waiting-for-Papa Stories. LC 89-36589. (Illus.). 32p. (J). (ps-3). 1990. 12.95 (*0-06-025050-X*) HarpC Child Bks.

***Roberts, Bethany.** Wind's Garden. LC 99-47348. 2001. text 15.95 (*0-8050-6367-6*) St Martin.

Roberts, Bethany & Hubbell, Patricia. Eleven Elephants Going Up! LC 95-30691. (Illus.). 32p. (J). (ps-2). 1996. 14.95 (*1-879085-61-5*, Whispering Coyote) Charlesbridge Pub.

Roberts, Bette B. Anne Rice. LC 93-40509. (Twayne's United States Authors Ser.: No. 644). 192p. 1994. 32.00 (*0-8057-3961-0*, Twyne) Mac Lib Ref.

— Anne Rice. 1995. pap. 14.95 (*0-8057-9231-7*) Mac Lib Ref.

— The Gothic Romance: Its Appeal to Women Writers & Readers in Late Eighteenth-Century England. Varma, Devendra P., ed. LC 79-8474. (Gothic Studies & Dissertations). 1980. lib. bdg. 31.95 (*0-405-12658-1*) Ayer.

Roberts, Bill. Stories on the Orift. LC 87-63108. (Illus.). 220p. 1988. pap. 8.00 (*0-944100-02-3*) Pirogue Pub.

Roberts, Bill, tr. see Hunt, Ann Dorian Brice.

***Roberts, Billy.** Educate Your Memory: Improvement Techniques for Students of All Ages. 2000. pap. text 10.95 (*1-902809-23-8*) Allison & Busby.

Roberts, Billy. Master Your Psychic Powers. LC 98-194388. 128p. 1998. 12.95 (*0-7137-2716-0*, Pub. by Blandford Pr) Sterling.

***Roberts, Billy.** Working Memory: Improving Your Memory for the Workplace. 159p. 1999. pap. 12.95 (*1-902809-06-8*, London House) Allison & Busby.

Roberts, Bob. Coasting Bargemaster. 168p. 1990. pap. 24.00 (*0-904623-95-5*) St Mut.

— A Slice of Suffolk. 112p. 1990. pap. 30.00 (*0-86138-020-7*, Pub. by T Dalton) St Mut.

Roberts, Bobby & Moneyhon, Carl H. Portraits of Conflict: A Photographic History of Arkansas in the Civil War. LC 87-5869. (Illus.). 256p. 1987. pap. 34.00 (*0-938626-84-1*) U of Ark Pr.

— Portraits of Conflict: A Photographic History of Louisiana in the Civil War. (Illus.). 370p. 1990. 75.00 (*1-55728-158-0*); pap. 34.00 (*1-55728-159-9*) U of Ark Pr.

— Portraits of Conflict: A Photographic History of Mississippi in the Civil War. LC 92-21637. (Illus.). 424p. (C). 1993. 75.00 (*1-55728-260-9*) U of Ark Pr.

Roberts, Bobby, jt. auth. see Moneyhon, Carl.

***Roberts, Bonita K. & Schlueter, Linda L.** Legal Research Guide: Patterns & Practice. 4th ed. LC 99-87993. 2000. 18.00 (*0-8205-4378-0*) Bender.

Roberts, Bonnie. To Hide in the Light. LC 98-72665. viii, 96p. 1998. pap. 12.00 (*0-9659751-2-6*) Elk River.

Roberts, Brad. Weapons Proliferation & World Order: After the Cold War. LC 96-1818. 416p. 1996. 115.00 (*90-411-0205-1*) Kluwer Law Intl.

Roberts, Brad, ed. Biological Weapons: Weapons of the Future? LC 92-47356. (Significant Issues Ser.: Vol. 15, No. 1). 113p. 1993. pap. 15.00 (*0-89206-210-X*) CSIS.

— The Chemical Weapons Convention: Implementation Ideas. LC 92-43724. (Significant Issues Ser.). 48p. 1993. pap. text 6.95 (*0-89206-207-X*) CSIS.

— The New Democracies: Global Change & U. S. Policy. 264p. 1990. 30.00 (*0-262-18137-1*); pap. text 16.50 (*0-262-68062-9*) MIT Pr.

— Order & Disorder after the Cold War. LC 95-35117. (Washington Quarterly Reader Ser.). 457p. 1995. pap. text 22.00 (*0-262-68088-2*) MIT Pr.

— Ratifying the Chemical Weapons Convention. LC 94-17403. (Significant Issues Ser.). 138p. (Orig.). (C). 1994. pap. 9.00 (*0-89206-264-9*) CSIS.

— Terrorism with Chemical & Biological Weapons: Calibrating the Risks & Responses. 140p. (Orig.). 1997. pap. 12.95 (*0-9656168-0-0*) Chemical & Biological.

— U. S. Foreign Policy after the Cold War. (Illus.). 378p. 1992. 35.00 (*0-262-18148-7*) MIT Pr.

— U. S. Security in an Uncertain Era. (Illus.). 428p. 1993. 40.00 (*0-262-18155-X*); pap. text 20.00 (*0-262-68080-7*) MIT Pr.

— Weapons Proliferation in the 1990s. (Washington Quarterly Reader Ser.). (Illus.). 473p. 1995. pap. text 22.00 (*0-262-68086-6*) MIT Pr.

Roberts, Brad & Preeg, Ernest, eds. New Forces in the World Economy. (Washington Quarterly Reader Ser.). (Illus.). 447p. 1996. pap. text 22.00 (*0-262-68089-0*) MIT Pr.

Roberts, Brady M., et al. Grant Wood: An American Master Revealed. LC 95-24186. (Illus.). 128p. 1995. pap. 26.95 (*0-87654-485-5*) Pomegranate Calif.

Roberts, Brandon D. Competition Across the Atlantic: The States Face Europe '92. Hurley, Larry, ed. (Illus.). 48p. 1991. pap. text 15.00 (*1-55516-805-1*, 3909) Natl Conf State Legis.

— Investment Across the Atlantic: New Competition & Challenges for States. 48p. 1992. pap. text 15.00 (*1-55516-806-X*, 3911) Natl Conf State Legis.

Roberts, Brenda. Collector's Encyclopedia of Hull Pottery. 1996. 19.95 (*0-89145-149-8*, 1276) Collector Bks.

— The Companion Guide to Roberts' Ultimate Encyclopedia of Hull Pottery. LC 91-68347. (Illus.). 308p. 1992. 24.95 (*0-9632136-1-X*) Cntry Side Antiques.

— Roberts' Ultimate Encyclopedia of Hull Pottery. LC 91-68348. (Illus.). 340p. 1992. 41.95 (*0-9632136-0-1*) Cntry Side Antiques.

Roberts, Brendan, jt. ed. see Bonavita, Mark.

Roberts, Brendan, ed. see Sporting News Editors.

***Roberts, Brian.** American Alchemy: The California Gold Rush & Middle-Class Culture. LC 99-48082. (Illus.). 400p. 2000. pap. 19.95 (*0-8078-4856-5*); lib. bdg. 49.95 (*0-8078-2543-3*) U of NC Pr.

Roberts, Brian. Land Care Manual. 1992. pap. 26.95 (*0-86840-053-X*, Pub. by New South Wales Univ Pr) Intl Spec Bk.

— The Quest for Sustainable Agriculture & Land Use. 1995. pap. 29.95 (*0-86840-374-1*, Pub. by New South Wales Univ Pr) Intl Spec Bk.

Roberts, Brian K. Landscapes of Settlement: Prehistory to the Present. LC 95-22435. (Illus.). 200p. (C). 1996. pap. 27.99 (*0-415-11968-5*) Routledge.

Roberts, Brigham H. The Autobiography of B. H. Roberts. Bergera, Gary J., ed. LC 90-39781. 284p. (Orig.). 1990. pap. 14.95 (*1-56085-005-1*) Signature Bks.

— Mormon Doctrine of Deity: The Roberts-Van der Donckt Discussion. 296p. 1975. 17.98 (*0-88290-058-7*) Horizon Utah.

Roberts, Bruce. Lighthouses: The Life & History of America's Waterways Boxed Set. 1999. 239.60 (*0-7910-5482-9*) Chelsea Hse.

— Plantation Homes of the James River. LC 89-39204. (Illus.). xii, 116p. (C). 1990. pap. 19.95 (*0-8078-4278-8*) U of NC Pr.

Roberts, Bruce, photos by. Western Great Lakes Lighthouses: Michigan & Superior. LC 95-53718. (Lighthouse Ser.). (Illus.). 112p. 1996. pap. 19.95 (*1-56440-954-6*) Globe Pequot.

Roberts, Bruce & Feiner, Susan, eds. Radical Economics. (Recent Economic Thought Ser.). 272p. (C). 1991. lib. bdg. 94.50 (*0-7923-9178-0*) Kluwer Academic.

Roberts, Bruce & Jones, Ray. American Lighthouses. LC 98-3958. (Illus.). 320p. 1998. pap. 21.95 (*0-7627-0324-5*) Globe Pequot.

— California Lighthouses: Point St. George to the Gulf of Santa Catalina. LC 99-26343. (Lighthouse Ser.). (Illus.). 112p. 1999. 29.95 (*0-7910-5485-3*) Chelsea Hse.

***Roberts, Bruce & Jones, Ray.** Eastern Great Lakes Lighthouses: Ontario, Erie & Huron. LC 99-15007. (Lighthouse Ser.). (Illus.). 112p. 1999. 29.95 (*0-7910-5487-X*) Chelsea Hse.

— Gulf Coast Lighthouses: Florida Keys to the Rio Grande. LC 99-15013. (Lighthouse Ser.). (Illus.). 112p. 1999. 29.95 (*0-7910-5484-5*) Chelsea Hse.

Roberts, Bruce & Jones, Ray. Mid-Atlantic Lighthouses: Hudson River to Chesapeake Bay. LC 99-26342. (Lighthouse Ser.). (Illus.). 112p. 1999. 29.95 (*0-7910-5489-6*) Chelsea Hse.

***Roberts, Bruce & Jones, Ray.** New England Lighthouses: Bay of Fundy to Long Island Sound. LC 99-15006. (Illus.). 112p. (YA). (gr. 5 up). 1999. 29.95 (*0-7910-5488-8*) Chelsea Hse.

Roberts, Bruce & Jones, Ray. New England Lighthouses: Bay of Fundy to Long Island Sound. LC 96-18770. (Lighthouses Ser.). (Illus.). 112p. 1996. pap. 19.95 (*1-56440-944-9*) Globe Pequot.

— Pacific Northwest Lighthouses: Oregon, Washington, Alaska & British Columbia. LC 99-26351. (Lighthouse Ser.). (Illus.). 112p. 1999. 29.95 (*0-7910-5490-X*) Chelsea Hse.

— Southeastern Lighthouses: Outer Banks to Cape Florida. LC 99-15012. (Lighthouse Ser.). (Illus.). 112p. 1999. 29.95 (*0-7910-5483-7*) Chelsea Hse.

— Southeastern Lighthouses: Outer Banks to the Florida Keys. LC 98-4831. (Illus.). 96p. 1998. pap. 19.95 (*0-7627-0217-6*) Globe Pequot.

***Roberts, Bruce & Jones, Ray.** Western Great Lakes Lighthouses: Michigan & Suprior. LC 99-15005. (Illus.). 112p. (YA). (gr. 5 up). 1999. 29.95 (*0-7910-5486-1*) Chelsea Hse.

Roberts, Bruce, jt. auth. see Elizabeth, Norma.

Roberts, Bruce, jt. auth. see Jones, Ray.

Roberts, Bruce, jt. auth. see Shelton-Roberts, Cheryl.

Roberts, Bruce B., jt. auth. see Thorsheim, Howard I.

Roberts, Bruce R. Water Management in Desert Environments: A Comparative Analysis. LC 93-12681. (Lecture Notes in Earth Sciences Ser.: Vol. 48). 1993. 103.95 (*0-387-56562-0*) Spr-Verlag.

Roberts, Bryan. The Making of Citizens: Cities of Peasants Revisited. (Arnold Publications). (Illus.). 272p. 1995. pap. text 39.95 (*0-340-60478-6*, B4020) OUP.

Roberts, Bryan R. Cities of Peasants: The Political Economy of Urbanization in the Third World. LC 79-87589. (Explorations in Urban Analysis Ser.: No. 1). 215p. reprint ed. pap. 66.70 (*0-8357-8505-X*, 203478600091) Bks Demand.

— Organizing Strangers: Poor Families in Guatemala City. LC 72-3513. (Texas Pan-American Ser.). 378p. reprint ed. pap. 117.20 (*0-8357-7759-6*, 203611700002) Bks Demand.

Roberts, Bryan R., et al, eds. The Sociology of Development, 2 vols. Set. LC 95-24272. (International Library of Critical Writings in Sociology: No. 2). 1232p. 1995. 455.00 (*1-85278-914-X*) E Elgar.

Roberts, Brynley F. Studies on Middle Welsh Literature. LC 91-36558. (Welsh Studies: Vol. 5). 160p. 1992. lib. bdg. 69.95 (*0-7734-9641-6*) E Mellen.

Roberts, C. New Mexico. LC 87-30086. (Illus.). 220p. 1989. pap. 16.95 (*0-8263-1145-8*) U of NM Pr.

Roberts, Carey. Pray God to Die. 320p. 1994. mass mkt. 4.99 (*0-380-72259-3*, Avon Bks) Morrow Avon.

Roberts, Carey & Seely, Rebecca. Tidewater Dynasty: A Biographical Novel of the Lees of Stratford Hall. LC 80-8758. 1981. 19.95 (*0-15-190294-1*) Harcourt.

Roberts, Carl W., ed. Text Analysis for the Social Sciences: Methods for Drawing Statistical Inferences from Texts & Transcripts. LC 96-40299. (Communication Ser.). 320p. (C). 1997. text 74.50 (*0-8058-1734-4*); pap. text 39.95 (*0-8058-1735-2*) L Erlbaum Assocs.

Roberts, Carla A., ed. see Lippard, Lucy R., et al.

Roberts, Carol. Timothy Findley: An Annotated Bibliography. 150p. (C). 1990. text 30.00 (*1-55022-112-4*, Pub. by ECW) Genl Dist Srvs.

— Timothy Findley: Stories from a Life. LC 94-165099. (Illus.). 180p. 1994. pap. 9.95 (*1-55022-195-7*, Pub. by ECW) LPC InBook.

Roberts, Carol, ed. see Boyd, Jeanne F. & Stricker, Gregory L.

Roberts, Carol, ed. see Hoekzema, Virginia.

Roberts, Carol A. & Burke, Sharon O. Nursing Research: A Quantitative & Qualitative Approach. 400p. 1989. 46.25 (*0-86720-415-X*) Jones & Bartlett.

Roberts, Carol E., jt. auth. see Wiley, D. Eugene.

Roberts, Carol E., ed. see Grin, Oliver D. & Bouwman, Dorothy L.

Roberts, Caroline, jt. ed. see Allan, J. W.

Roberts, Carolyn S. & Gorman, Martha. Euthanasia: A Reference Handbook. LC 96-28833. (Contemporary World Issues Ser.). 349p. 1996. lib. bdg. 45.00 (*0-87436-831-6*) ABC-CLIO.

Roberts, Cary M. Separate Peace Notes. (Cliffs Notes Ser.). 64p. 1965. pap. 4.95 (*0-8220-1183-2*, Cliff) IDG Bks.

Roberts, Casey. Shenanigans. (Superromance Ser.). 1993. mass mkt. 3.39 (*0-373-70547-6*, 1-70547-4) Harlequin Bks.

— Walking on Air. (Superromance Ser.: No. 493). 1992. per. 3.39 (*0-373-70493-3*, 1-70493-1) Harlequin Bks.

Roberts, Catherine. Science, Animals & Evolution: Reflections on Some Unrealized Potentials of Biology & Medicine, 14. LC 79-52322. (Contributions in Philosophy Ser.: No. 14). 221p. 1980. 49.95 (*0-313-21479-4*, RSA/, Greenwood Pr) Greenwood.

— Scientific Conscience: Reflections on the Modern Biologist & Humanism. 1974. pap. 22.95 (*0-8464-0819-8*) Beekman Pubs.

Roberts, Cathy, ed. see Cress, Eric.

Roberts, Celia, jt. auth. see Sarangi, Srikant.

Roberts, Celia, jt. ed. see Sarangi, Srikant.

Roberts, Chalmers M. In the Shadow of Power: The Story of the Washington Post. Gold, Jane, ed. LC 89-10274. 544p. (Orig.). 1989. pap. 16.95 (*0-932020-71-2*) Seven Locks Pr.

Roberts Chapman. Perspectives on Regional Planning & Development. 56.95 (*1-85972-527-9*) Ashgate Pub Co.

Roberts, Charles. New Card Games for You to Play. 160p. 1995. pap. 7.95 (*0-572-01381-7*, Pub. by Foulsham UK) Assoc Pubs Grp.

— An Olive Branch for the Conquered. 64p. 1990. pap. 6.95 (*0-932616-31-3*) Brick Hse Bks.

Roberts, Charles, et al. Mirrors of Mind: An Introduction to Humanities. 2nd ed. 320p. 1991. pap. text 24.95 (*0-88725-158-7*) Hunter Textbks.

Roberts, Charles, jt. auth. see Zazarine, Paul.

Roberts, Charles, jt. ed. see Rosenfeld, Ron G.

Roberts, Charles, ed. see Witt, Bill.

Roberts, Charles A., et al. Primary Prevention of Psychiatric Disorders. Chalke, F. C. R. & Day, John J., eds. LC 77-364638. (Clarence M. Hincks Memorial Lectures). viii, 168 p. 1968. write for info. (*0-8020-3205-2*) U of Toronto Pr.

Roberts, Charles G. By the Marshes of Minas. LC 74-178456. (Short Story Index Reprint Ser.). 1977. reprint ed. 21.95 (*0-8369-4057-1*) Ayer.

— Earth's Enigmas. LC 72-94742. (Short Story Index Reprint Ser.). 1977. 20.95 (*0-8369-3122-X*) Ayer.

— The Kindred of the Wild: A Book of Animal Life. 1977. 26.95 (*0-8369-4253-1*, 6062) Ayer.

— Selected Poetry & Critical Prose. LC 73-91558. (Literature of Canada, Poetry & Prose in Reprint Ser.: No. 9). 366p. reprint ed. pap. 113.50 (*0-608-12871-6*, 202366200033) Bks Demand.

Roberts, Charles S. Sand Patch: Clash of Titans (B&O-PRR) LC 93-90583. (Cumberland to Connellsville & Branches 1837-1993 Ser.). (Illus.). 224p. 1993. 50.00 (*0-934118-20-5*) Barnard Roberts.

— Stoking the Fire: A Surgical Memoir of London. LC 98-36943. (Illus.). 200p. 1998. 40.00 (*0-87993-422-0*) Futura Pub.

Roberts, Charles S., jt. auth. see Hollis, Jeffrey R.

Roberts, Charles S., ed. see Harwood, Herbert H., Jr.

Roberts, Charles S., ed. see Messer, David W.

Roberts, Charles V. & Watson, Kittie W., eds. Intrapersonal Communication Processes: Original Essays. (Illus.). 580p. (C). 1989. 39.95 (*0-89787-336-X*) SPECTRA Inc.

Roberts, Charles W. & Hirsch, Mary, eds. Treasures of Iowa. (Illus.). 76p. (Orig.). 1987. pap. 4.95 (*0-317-61645-5*) Mid Am Pub.

Roberts, Charlotte. Health & Disease in Britain From Prehistory to the Present Day. 1999. 36.00 (*0-7509-1844-6*) Bks Intl VA.

Roberts, Charlotte & Manchester, Keith. The Archeology of Disease. 2nd ed. 256p. 1997. pap. 22.50 (*0-8014-8448-0*) Cornell U Pr.

Roberts, Chell, et al, eds. Object-Oriented Simulation Conference: Mission Earth: Modeling & Simulation for a Sustainable Global System. 256p. 1996. pap. 100.00 (*1-56555-086-2*, OOS-96) Soc Computer Sim.

Roberts, Cheryl, ed. see Tucker, Louise E.

Roberts, Chris. Fugees. 1998. pap. text 11.95 (*0-7535-0173-2*, Pub. by Virgin Bks) London Brdge.

— Newnes Z80 Pocket Book. LC 92-225477. 191p. 1992. pap. 59.30 (*0-608-04988-3*, 206560600004) Bks Demand.

— Pow Wow Country. LC 92-29966. (Illus.). 128p. (Orig.). 1992. pap. 19.95 (*1-56037-025-4*) Am Wrld Geog.

— Powwow Country: People of the Circle. 128p. 1998. pap. text 21.95 (*1-56037-124-2*) Am Wrld Geog.

***Roberts, Christa.** Turning Seventeen: For Real, No. 3. LC 00-100946. (Turning Seventeen Ser.: No. 3). 208p. (YA). (gr. 7 up). 2000. mass mkt. 4.95 (*0-06-447239-6*, HarpTrophy) HarpC Child Bks.

Roberts, Christine, et al. Simply Delicious Recipes for Diabetics: 150 Easy to Make Dishes from Appetizers to Desserts. (Illus.). 206p. 1996. pap. 15.95 (*0-89529-688-8*, Avery) Penguin Putnam.

Roberts, Chrles S. Triumph I: Altoona to Pitcairn 1846-1996 PRR/PC/CR. LC 95-78455. (Illus.). 400p. 1997. 65.00 (*0-934118-23-X*) Barnard Roberts.

Roberts, Churchill L., jt. auth. see Becker, Samuel L.

Roberts, Cindy. Food Safety Sourcebook. (Illus.). 312p. 2001. 52.50 (*1-57356-305-6*) Oryx Pr.

***Roberts, Clare & Dong-hwa, Huh, eds.** Rapt in Color: Korean Textiles & Costumes of the Choson Dynasty. (Illus.). 110p. 2000. pap. 32.95 (*1-86317-074-X*) Museum Applied Arts.

Roberts, Clare B., jt. ed. see Adams, Carol A.

Roberts, Clarence V. Early Friends Families of Upper Bucks: With Some Account of Their Descendants. (Illus.). 680p. 2000. reprint ed. pap. 30.00 (*0-8063-0668-8*, 4960, Pub. by Clearfield Co) ACCESS Pubs Network.

Roberts, Clayton. History of England Vol. 2: Sixteen Eighty-Eight to the Present, Vol. 2. 3rd ed. Vol. II. 496p. (C). 1990. pap. text 57.33 (*0-13-390410-5*) P-H.

— The Logic of Historical Explanation. 328p. 1995. 55.00 (*0-271-01442-3*); pap. 19.95 (*0-271-01443-1*) Pa St U Pr.

— Schemes & Undertakings: A Study of English Politics in the Seventeenth Century. LC 84-25572. 347p. reprint ed. pap. 107.60 (*0-608-09870-1*, 2069835) Bks Demand.

An Asterisk (*) at the beginning of an entry indicates that the title is appearing for the first time.

Roberts, Clayton & Roberts, David. History of England Vol. 1: Prehistory to 1714, Vol. 1. 3rd ed. LC 90-7370. Vol. I. 464p. (C). 1990. pap. text 57.33 (*0-13-390394-X*) P-H.

***Roberts, Cokie.** We Are Our Mothers' Daughters. LC 98-14816. 256p. 2000. pap. 11.00 (*0-688-16967-8*, Quil) HarperTrade.

Roberts, Cokie. We Are Our Mothers' Daughters. LC 98-14816. 128p. (YA). 1998. 19.95 (*0-688-15198-1*, Wm Morrow) Morrow Avon.

— We Are Our Mothers' Daughters. large type ed. LC 98-28012. 1998. 27.95 (*0-7862-1626-3*) Thorndike Pr.

***Roberts, Cokie & Roberts, Steven.** From This Day Forward. LC 99-56708. 368p. 2000. 24.00 (*0-688-16891-4*, Wm Morrow) Morrow Avon.

— From This Day Forward. large type ed. LC 00-23475. 579p. 2000. write for info. (*0-7862-2575-0*) Thorndike Pr.

Roberts, Cokie & Sono, Ayako. Democracy & Discontent: Questions Facing the Political Process of Japan & the United States. 140p. 1992. pap. write for info. (*0-9635265-0-2*) U MT Mansfld.

Roberts, Colin. Chiens Perdue s.c.-La Cle'sur la Porte, Cesbron-Cardinal: Critical Monographs in English. 64p. 1993. pap. 32.00 (*0-85261-249-4*, Pub. by Univ of Glasgow) St Mut.

Roberts, Colin H. & Skeat, T. C. The Birth of the Codex. (Illus.). 88p. 1987. pap. text 35.00 (*0-19-726061-6*) OUP.

Roberts, Colin J. & David Hume Institute Staff. Deep Water: Fisheries Policy for the Future. LC 98-206520. (Hume Papers on Public Policy). 78p. 1997. write for info. (*0-7486-0995-4*, Pub. by Edinburgh U Pr) Col U Pr.

Roberts, Cory, ed. Harmonization Whys & Wherefores. 136p. (C). 1985. 50.00 (*0-85292-348-1*, Pub. by IPM Hse) St Mut.

Roberts, Courtney, jt. ed. see Somers, Ray.

Roberts, Craig. Kill Zone: A Sniper Looks at Dealey Plaza. (Illus.). 252p. (Orig.). 1994. pap. 11.95 (*0-9639062-0-8*) Consol Pr Intl.

— The Medusa File: Crimes & Coverups of the U. S. Government. 507p. 1997. reprint ed. pap. text 24.95 (*0-9639062-4-0*, Pub. by Consol Pr Intl) ACCESS Pubs Network.

— Police Sniper. Tobias, Eric, ed. 320p. (Orig.). 1993. mass mkt. 5.99 (*0-671-79459-0*) PB.

Roberts, Craig & Appel, Allen. Hellhound. 352p. (Orig.). 1994. mass mkt. 4.99 (*0-380-76783-X*, Avon Bks) Morrow Avon.

Roberts, Craig & Sasser, Charles W. The Walking Dead: A Marine's Story of Vietnam. 1989. mass mkt. 5.99 (*0-671-65777-1*) PB.

Roberts, Craig, jt. auth. see Sasser, Charles W.

Roberts, Craig, ed. & intro. see McGuire, Gary.

***Roberts, Craig S.** Ten Consecutive Years Living in Cars: Living, Traveling, Camping, Attending College, & Performing Surveillance in Cars--And Loving It! (Illus.). 209p. 1999. pap. 42.00 (*0-9676248-0-0*) Extreme Prods.

Roberts, Cynthia S. An End to Summer. 1994. lib. bdg. 22.00 (*0-7278-4667-1*) Severn Hse.

— Parents' Guide to the Delaware Valley. LC 88-15021. 270p. (Orig.). 1989. pap. 12.95 (*0-940159-04-X*) Camino Bks.

— The Running Tide. large type ed. (Romance Suspense Ser.). 624p. 1989. 27.99 (*0-7089-1998-7*) Ulverscroft.

— The Savage Shore. 448p. 1993. lib. bdg. 22.00 (*0-7278-4477-6*) Severn Hse.

— The Savage Shore. large type ed. (Charnwood Large Print Ser.). 1995. 27.99 (*0-7089-8841-5*, Charnwood) Ulverscroft.

— The Storms of Fate. 288p. 1992. lib. bdg. 19.00 (*0-7278-4337-0*) Severn Hse.

— Upon Stormy Downs. large type ed. (Romance Suspense Ser.). 1990. 27.99 (*0-7089-2256-2*) Ulverscroft.

— A Wind from the Sea. large type ed. (Romance Suspense Ser.). 1991. 27.99 (*0-7089-2351-8*) Ulverscroft.

Roberts, D. A Beginner's Guide to HTML: Learning HTML 4.0. 60p. (C). 1998. pap. 32.95 incl. disk (*1-57555-167-5*) Cedar Bay Pr.

Roberts, D., jt. auth. see Duncan, R. M.

Roberts, D. B., ed. Drosophila: A Practical Approach. 2nd ed. (The Practical Approach Ser.: No. 191). (Illus.). 414p. 1998. pap. text 60.00 (*0-19-963660-5*) OUP.

Roberts, D. F., ed. Human Variation & Natural Selection. (Symposia of the Society for the Study of Human Biology Ser.: Vol. 13). 220p. 1975. 36.00 (*0-85066-080-7*) Taylor & Francis.

Roberts, D. F., et al, eds. Isolation, Migration & Health. (Society for the Study of Human Biology Symposium Ser.: No. 33). (Illus.). 279p. (C). 1992. text 80.00 (*0-521-41912-3*) Cambridge U Pr.

Roberts, D. F. & De Stefano, G. F., eds. Genetic Variation & Its Maintenance. (Society for the Study of Human Biology Symposium Ser.: No. 27). (Illus.). 300p. 1986. text 69.95 (*0-521-33257-5*) Cambridge U Pr.

Roberts, D. F. & Sunderland, Eric, eds. Genetic Variation in Britain. (Symposia of the Society for the Study of Human Biology Ser.: Vol. 12). 314p. 1973. 36.00 (*0-85066-062-9*) Taylor & Francis.

Roberts, D. F., jt. ed. see Barron, S. Leonard.

Roberts, D. F., jt. ed. see Collins, K. J.

Roberts, D. F., tr. see Bernal, J. E.

Roberts, D. Jeanne. Taking Care of Caregivers: For Families & Others Who Care for People with Alzheimer's Disease & Other Forms of Dementia. (Illus.). 200p. (Orig.). 1991. pap. 14.95 (*0-923521-09-7*) Bull Pub.

Roberts, D. M., et al, eds. Evolution of Microbial Life. (Society for General Microbiology Symposium Ser.: No. 54). (Illus.). 308p. (C). 1996. text 115.00 (*0-521-56432-8*) Cambridge U Pr.

Roberts, D. W., et al, eds. American Society for Stereotactic & Functional Neurosurgery Pt. I: Proceedings of the Meeting of the American Society, Marina del Rey, Calif., March 1995. (Journal Ser.: Vol. 65, Nos. 1-4, 1995). (Illus.). x, 212p. 1996. pap. 144.50 (*3-8055-6364-7*) S Karger.

— American Society for Stereotactic & Functional Neurosurgery Pt. II: Proceedings of the Meeting of the American Society, Marina del Rey, Calif., March 1995. (Journal Ser.: Vol. 66, Nos. 1-3, 1996). (Illus.). viii, 160p. 1996. pap. 108.00 (*3-8055-6365-5*) S Karger.

Roberts, D. W., jt. auth. see Roberts, Dan W.

Roberts, Daffyd R., tr. see Serres, Michel, ed.

Roberts, Dafydd Lloyd, jt. auth. see Buchan, John.

Roberts, Dan W. & Roberts, D. W. Rangers & Sovereignty. LC 87-42527. (Illus.). 259p. 1987. reprint ed. 21.95 (*0-938349-16-3*); reprint ed. 60.00 (*0-938349-14-7*); reprint ed. pap. 12.95 (*0-938349-15-5*) State House Pr.

Roberts, Daniel K. & Terry, Jack E. Ocular Diseases: Diagnosis & Treatment. 2nd ed. (Illus.). 637p. 1996. text 99.95 (*0-7506-9062-3*) Buttrwrth-Heinemann.

***Roberts, Daniel Sanjiv.** Revisionary Gleam: De Quincey, Coleridge & the High Romantic Argument. 320p. 1999. 53.95 (*0-85323-794-8*, Pub. by Liverpool Univ Pr); pap. 24.95 (*0-85323-804-9*, Pub. by Liverpool Univ Pr) Intl Spec Bk.

Roberts, Dannel. Me & Uncle Mike & the 3-Toed Bear. (Illus.). 36p. (J). (gr. k-5). 1999. 14.95 (*1-893459-00-4*) Lions & Tigers.

***Roberts, Darrell.** Physical Geography: Laboratory Manual. 92p. (C). 1999. spiral bd., lab manual ed. 18.95 (*0-7872-6484-9*, 41648401) Kendall-Hunt.

Roberts, Darrell, ed. Human Factors. LC 91-75708. (Quality Instruction Materials Ser.). 272p. 1991. student ed. 54.25 (*0-929355-18-0*, M1591) Am Soc Ag Eng.

***Roberts, Darryl.** X Rated Wines. (Illus.). 2000. pap. 12.00 (*0-609-80632-7*, Crown) Crown Pub Group.

Roberts, Darryl, jt. auth. see Rollins, Thomas.

Roberts, Darryl J. Profits of Death: An Insider Exposes the Death Care Industries; Learn How to Cut Funeral Costs in Half. Howey, Paul M., ed. LC 96-53657. 224p. 1997. pap. 19.95 (*1-877749-21-4*) Five Star AZ.

Roberts, Dave. Designing for the User with OVID: Object-Oriented User Interface Development. LC 98-85558. 1998. pap. 45.00 (*1-57870-101-5*) Macmillan Tech.

— Internet Protocols Black Book: The Most Complete Reference to Internet Communications Logic. 1997. pap. text 49.99 (*1-57610-210-6*) Coriolis Grp.

— Pipe & Excavation Contracting. 400p. (Orig.). 1987. pap. 29.00 (*0-934041-22-9*) Craftsman.

Roberts, Dave, jt. auth. see Richards, Jon.

Roberts, Dave, jt. auth. see Walker, Robin.

Roberts, David. Art & Enlightenment: Aesthetic Theory after Adorno. LC 90-35508. (Modern German Culture & Literature Ser.). xx, 250p. 1991. text 50.00 (*0-8032-3897-5*) U of Nebr Pr.

— David Roberts: The Mountain of My Fear; Deborah: A Wilderness Narrative. LC 90-28126. (Illus.). 368p. 1991. pap. 16.95 (*0-89886-270-1*) Mountaineers.

— Deaths Reported by the Long Islander, 1878-1890. 332p. 1998. pap. 26.00 (*0-7884-0950-6*, R501) Heritage Bk.

— Escape Routes: Further Adventure Writings of David Roberts. LC 96-52175. 272p. 1997. 22.95 (*0-89886-509-3*) Mountaineers.

— Escape Routes: Further Adventure Writings of David Roberts. 256p. 1998. pap. 16.95 (*0-89886-601-4*) Mountaineers.

— A Field Guide to Geology of Eastern North America. Peterson, Roger T., ed. & notes by. (Illus.). 416p. 1996. 27.95 (*0-395-66326-1*, Field Guides); pap. 17.95 (*0-395-66325-3*) HM.

***Roberts, David.** The Holy Land & Egypt & Nubia. deluxe ed. (Illus.). 2000. boxed set 250.00 (*0-8478-2312-1*) Rizzoli Intl.

Roberts, David. Iceland: Land of the Sagas. LC 98-24618. (Illus.). 160p. 1998. pap. 19.95 (*0-375-75267-6*) Villard Books.

— In Search of the Old Ones: Exploring the Anasazi World of the Southwest. (Illus.). 272p. 1995. 24.00 (*0-684-81078-6*) S&S Trade.

— Jean Stafford: A Biography. 1988. 24.95 (*0-316-74998-2*) Little.

— Jerusalem & the Holy Land Rediscovered: The Prints of David Roberts (1796-1864) (Illus.). 392p. 1996. 89.95 (*0-614-26145-7*) Duke.

***Roberts, David.** Kosovo War Poetry: With Background Notes. 64p. 2000. pap. 7.95 (*0-9528969-2-3*, Pub. by Saxon Bks) Trans-Atl Phila.

Roberts, David. The Ladies: Female Patronage of Restoration Drama. (Oxford English Monographs). 198p. 1989. text 65.00 (*0-19-811743-4*) OUP.

— Moments of Doubt & Other Mountaineering Writings of David Roberts. LC 86-16357. 256p. (Orig.). 1986. pap. 12.95 (*0-89886-118-7*) Mountaineers.

— A Newer World: Kit Carson, John C. Fremont & the Claiming of the American West. LC 99-41816. 320p. 2000. pap. text 25.00 (*0-684-83482-0*) S&S Trade.

— Once They Moved Like the Wind: Cochise, Geronimo, & the Apache Wars. LC 93-7112. (Illus.). 320p. 1993. 24.00 (*0-671-70221-1*) S&S Trade.

— Once They Moved Like the Wind: Cochise, Geronimo, & the Apache Wars. LC 93-7112. 386p. 1994. per. 14.00 (*0-671-88556-1*, Touchstone) S&S Trade Pap.

***Roberts, David.** Outside Magazine's the Ascent Calendar 2000: Legendary Climbs of the Twentieth Century. (Illus.). 28p. 1999. 9.95 (*1-56512-228-3*, 72228) Algonquin Bks.

— True Summit: What Really Happened on the Legendary Ascent of Annapurna. (Illus.). 256p. 2000. 24.00 (*0-684-86757-5*) Simon & Schuster.

Roberts, David, ed. Minds at War: The Poetry & Experience of the First World War. (Illus.). 412p. 1996. pap. 28.50 (*0-9528969-0-7*, Pub. by Saxon Bks) Trans-Atl Phila.

— Out in the Dark: Poetry of the First World War in Context & with Basic Notes. (Illus.). 192p. 1998. pap. 20.00 (*0-9528969-1-5*, Pub. by Saxon Bks) Trans-Atl Phila.

— Points Unknown: A Century of Great Exploration. 500p. 2000. 29.95 (*0-393-05000-9*) Norton.

Roberts, David, ed. Reconstructing Theory: Gadamer, Habermas, Luhmann. LC 96-139447. (Interpretations Ser.). 144p. 1995. pap. 14.95 (*0-522-84570-3*, Pub. by Melbourne Univ Pr) Paul & Co Pubs.

***Roberts, David.** Ghoul School. 10p. (J). (ps-3). 2000. 17.95 (*0-8109-4140-6*, Pub. by Abrams) Time Warner.

Roberts, David. The Holy Land: Yesterday & Today - Lithographs & Diaries. LC 95-72934. 270p. 1996. 60.00 (*1-55670-462-3*) Stewart Tabori & Chang.

— Holy Land I Love. LC 99-64017. 40p. 1999. pap. 10.99 (*0-89221-517-8*) New Leaf.

Roberts, David & Thomson, Philip, eds. The Modern German Historical Novel: Paradigms, Problems, Perspectives. LC 89-18380. (Berg European Studies). 240p. 1991. 19.50 (*0-85496-667-6*) Berg Pubs.

Roberts, David, jt. auth. see Anker, Conrad.

Roberts, David, jt. auth. see Mancoff, Debra N.

Roberts, David, jt. auth. see Roberts, Clayton.

Roberts, David, jt. auth. see Ronald, Nick.

Roberts, David, jt. auth. see Washburn, Bradford.

Roberts, David, ed. see Chesterfield, Lord.

Roberts, David D. Nothing but History: Reconstruction & Extremity after Metaphysics. LC 94-43786. 342p. 1995. 45.00 (*0-520-20080-2*, Pub. by U CA Pr) Cal Prin Full Svc.

Roberts, David D. & Mecham, Robert P., eds. Cell Surface & Extracellular Glycoconjugates: Structure & Function. (Biology of Extracellular Matrix Ser.). (Illus.). 314p. 1993. text 90.00 (*0-12-589630-1*) Acad Pr.

Roberts, David D., jt. auth. see Kostelnick, Charles.

Roberts, David E. Psychotherapy & a Christian View of Man. LC 88-21391. 162p. 1990. reprint ed. lib. bdg. 55.00 (*0-313-25326-9*, RPSY, Greenwood Pr) Greenwood.

Roberts, David L. Sage Street: A Collection of Stories. LC 91-66153. 108p. (Orig.). (YA). (gr. 9 up). 1991. pap. 6.95 (*0-914767-20-8*) Skyline West Pr.

Roberts, David O. Mandan. (Cops of Discovery Ser.: Vol. 1). (Illus.). 400p. 1998. pap. 15.00 (*0-9668531-0-5*) Hoka Hey Pr.

***Roberts, David W.** Political Transition in Cambodia, 1991-1999: Power, Elitism & Democracy. LC 00-40451. 2000. write for info. (*0-312-23855-X*) St Martin.

Roberts, David W., ed. see Allen, Timothy F. & Hoekstra, Thomas W.

Roberts, David W., jt. ed. see Reeves, Alexander G.

Roberts, Debbie. It's about Life. 240p. (Orig.). 1996. pap. write for info. (*1-886094-44-6*) Chicago Spectrum.

— Rejoice: A Biblical Study of Dance. 112p. 1982. pap. 8.99 (*0-938612-02-6*) Destiny Image.

— The Super Studio: The Guide to a Successful Dance Studio! (Illus.). 160p. (Orig.). 1992. pap. 14.95 (*1-879260-07-7*) Evanston Pub.

— The Ultimate Guide to a Successful Dance Studio: Plus 120 Ideas That Will Transform Your Life. (Illus.). 312p. 1999. pap. 49.95 (*1-886094-93-4*) Chicago Spectrum.

***Roberts, Deborah D. & Taylor, Andy.** Flavor Release: Linking Experiments, Theory & Reality. (ACS Symposium Ser.: No. 763). (Illus.). 464p. 2000. text 150.00 (*0-8412-3692-5*, Pub. by Am Chemical) OUP.

Roberts, Deborah H., et al. Classical Closure: Reading the End in Greek & Latin Literature. LC 96-44439. 328p. 1997. text 39.50 (*0-691-04452-X*, Pub. by Princeton U Pr) Cal Prin Full Svc.

Roberts, Deborah H., tr. see Bovie, Palmer, ed.

Roberts-DeGennaro, Maria & Weil, Marie, eds. Diversity & Development in Community Practice. LC 93-39428. (Journal of Community Practice). (Illus.). 144p. 1993. lib. bdg. 39.95 (*1-56024-611-1*) Haworth Pr.

— Diversity & Development in Community Practice. LC 93-39428. (Journal of Community Practice). (Illus.). 144p. 1994. pap. text 12.95 (*1-56024-612-X*) Haworth Pr.

Roberts, Delno, ed. see Halbert, D. S.

Roberts, Dennis. Data Analysis for the Social Sciences. 372p. (C). 1995. spiral bd. 46.95 (*0-7872-1973-8*) Kendall-Hunt.

Roberts, Dennis C., ed. Designing Campus Activities to Foster a Sense of Community. LC 85-644751. (New Directions for Student Services Ser.: No. SS 48). 1989. pap. 22.00 (*1-55542-857-6*) Jossey-Bass.

Roberts, Dennis L., 2nd, ed. Planning Urban Education: New Techniques to Transform Learning in the City. LC 73-160895. 384p. 1972. 47.95 (*0-87778-024-2*) Educ Tech Pubns.

Roberts, Denton L. Able & Equal: A Gentle Path to Peace. 162p. 1987. 15.95 (*0-9613559-0-5*) Human Esteem Pub.

— Able & Equal: A Gentle Path to Peace. 2nd rev. ed. (Illus.). 150p. 1987. pap. 9.95 (*0-9613559-9-9*) Human Esteem Pub.

— Find Purpose - Find Power: Sing the Song in Your Heart. (Illus.). ii, 134p. 1997. pap. 15.95 (*0-9613559-1-3*) Human Esteem Pub.

— Lumps & Bumps: A Children's Book for Parents & a Parent's Book for Children. (Illus.). 22p. 1997. pap. 7.50 (*0-9613559-2-1*) Human Esteem Pub.

Roberts, Derek. British Longcase Clocks. LC 89-64089. (Illus.). 400p. 1990. 95.00 (*0-88740-230-5*) Schiffer.

— British Skeleton Clocks. 272p. 1987. 79.50 (*1-85149-059-0*) Antique Collect.

— Carriage & Other Traveling Clocks. LC 93-85224. (Illus.). 368p. 1993. 99.95 (*0-88740-454-5*) Schiffer.

— Collecting Clocks. 128p. 10.99 (*1-57215-245-1*, JG2451) World Pubns.

— Collector's Guide to Clocks. 1992. 12.98 (*1-55521-778-8*) Bk Sales Inc.

— Continental & American Skeleton Clocks. LC 89-62600. (Illus.). 288p. 1989. 79.95 (*0-88740-182-1*) Schiffer.

— Mystery, Novelty & Fantasy Clocks. LC 99-30136. (Illus.). 256p. 1999. 150.00 (*0-7643-0873-4*) Schiffer.

— Skeleton Clocks, Britain, 1800-1914. (Illus.). 272p. 79.50 (*1-85149-256-9*) Antique Collect.

Roberts, Derek, ed. Miller's Clocks & Barometers: Buyer's Guide. (Illus.). 320p. 1997. 29.95 (*1-85732-990-2*, Pub. by Millers Pubns) Antique Collect.

Roberts, Derrick P. & Smith, Nigel L. Radiographic Imaging: A Practical Approach. (Illus.). 368p. (Orig.). 1988. pap. write for info. (*0-443-03061-8*) Church.

— Radiographic Imaging: A Practical Approach. 2nd ed. LC 94-4029. (Orig.). 1994. text 61.00 (*0-443-04397-3*) Church.

Roberts, Dewi. Christmas in Wales. LC 98-232073. 160p. 1998. pap. 14.95 (*1-85411-186-8*, Pub. by Seren Bks) Dufour.

Roberts, Dewi & Roberts, Pamela. A-Z of North Wales. 56p. 1997. pap. 3.50 (*1-871083-95-8*, Pub. by J Jones Pub) Intl Spec Bk.

Roberts, Diana, ed. see Anderson, Alex.

Roberts, Diana, ed. see Armstrong, Carol.

Roberts, Diana, ed. see Brackman, Barbara.

Roberts, Diana, ed. see Collins, Sally.

Roberts, Diana, ed. see Montano, Judith B.

Roberts, Diana, ed. see Walner, Hari.

Roberts, Diane. Faulkner & Southern Womanhood. LC 93-9957. (C). 1995. pap. text 18.00 (*0-8203-1741-1*) U of Ga Pr.

— For Women Only: Accept No Substitutes. Harlan, Roberta & Hamilton, Vivian, eds. LC 95-225194. (Illus.). 87p. (Orig.). 1995. student ed. 7.00 (*1-879619-12-1*) East Hill Church.

— The Myth of Aunt Jemima: Representations of Race & Religion. LC 93-50574. 208p. (C). 1994. pap. 24.99 (*0-415-04919-9*, B4245) Routledge.

Roberts, Diane & Schroeder, Bonnie. Calc - Spreadsheet Planner: Lab Pack. (Illus.). 199.95 (*1-56177-095-7*, L394-3); 199.95 (*1-56177-047-7*, L194-3); disk 8.95 (*1-56177-094-9*, D394-3); Apple II 8.95 (*1-56177-046-9*, D194-3) CES Compu-Tech.

— Computer Applications: Calc - Spread Sheet Planner: Course Code S94-3. (Illus.). 81p. (J). (gr. 8). 1989. reprint ed. pap. text 8.95 (*0-917531-56-6*) CES Compu-Tech.

Roberts, Diane, et al. Calc - Spreadsheet Planner: Lab Pack. (Illus.). 1990. teacher ed., student ed. 179.95 incl. disk (*1-56177-145-7*, L494-3) CES Compu-Tech.

Roberts, Diane, jt. auth. see Hobbs, Betty C.

Roberts, Diane, jt. auth. see Mossman, Marilyn.

Roberts, Diane H. Down the Dirt Road. 47p. (Orig.). 1986. pap. 5.00 (*0-932662-63-3*) St Andrews NC.

Roberts, Dick. American Railroads: The Case for Nationalization. LC 80-80795. (Illus.). 108p. 1980. pap. 11.95 (*0-87348-600-5*); lib. bdg. 35.00 (*0-87348-601-3*) Pathfinder NY.

Roberts, Dione. Cozy Corners. (Illus.). 32p. 1996. pap. 14.95 (*0-935133-60-7*, 20133607) CKE Pubns.

***Roberts, Dione.** A Mosaic Christmas. 1999. pap. 14.95 (*0-935133-78-X*, 2013378X) CKE Pubns.

Roberts-Dominguez, Jan. The Mustard Book: How to Make Your Own - From Dijon to Creole - At Home. 176p. 1997. pap. text 12.95 (*0-02-861856-4*) Macmillan.

— Sandwich Cuisine - Oregon Style. Battrick, Craig J., ed. LC 90-82414. (Illus.). 188p. 1991. pap. 15.95 (*0-9626441-0-2*) Drift Creek Pr.

Roberts, Don. Rap to Live By. 128p. (J). (gr. 2-12). 1993. pap. 8.95 (*1-878901-55-9*) Hampton Roads Pub Co.

— Two Hundred Twenty-two BASIC Computer Programs for Home, School & Office. 288p. 1984. 18.95 (*0-86668-039-X*) ARCsoft.

Roberts, Don & Boyle, Dierdre, eds. Mediamobiles: Views from the Road. fac. ed. LC 79-18488. (Public Library Reporter: No. 19). 126p. 1994. pap. 39.10 (*0-7837-7321-8*, 204724800007) Bks Demand.

Roberts, Don & Roberts, Susan. Things That Scratch: The Story of Abrasives. (Illus.). 60p. (YA). (gr. 8 up). pap. 24.95 (*1-57555-169-1*); pap. 14.95 (*1-57555-170-5*) Cedar Bay Pr.

Roberts, Don, ed. see Twain, Mark, pseud.

Roberts, Don D. Existential Graphs of Charles S. Peirce. LC 73-85776. (Approaches to Semiotics Ser.: Vol. 27). (Illus.). 168p. 1973. text 41.55 (*90-279-2523-2*) Mouton.

Roberts, Don D., et al. Studies in the Logic of Charles Sanders Peirce. Houser, Nathan, ed. LC 96-3853. (Illus.). 704p. 1997. text 49.95 (*0-253-33020-3*) Ind U Pr.

Roberts, Don W. Renters' Revenge: (A Landlord's Nightmare) LC 91-65693. (Illus.). 112p. (Orig.). 1991. pap. 6.95 (*0-9629979-0-0*) Tower Pub GA.

Roberts, Donald F., jt. auth. see Christenson, Peter G.

Roberts, Donald G., jt. auth. see John, Martha T.

Roberts, Donald L., ed. Remedies, Potions & Razzmatazz. (Illus.). 510p. (Orig.). 1991. reprint ed. pap. 15.95 (*0-9628676-0-8*) Nostalgia CA.

Roberts, Donna & McMinn, Andrew. Diatoms of the Saline Lakes of the Vestfold Hills, Antarctica. (Bibliotheca Diatomologica Ser.: Band 44). (Illus.). 83p. 1999. 37.00 (*3-443-57035-6*) Gebruder Borntraeger.

Roberts, Donovan. Stubborn Ounces - Just Scales. 1992. pap. 14.95 (*1-55673-417-4*, 7900, Fairway Pr) CSS OH.

Roberts, Doreen. Broken Wings. (Intimate Moments Ser.: No. 422). 1992. per. 3.39 (*0-373-07422-0*, 5-07422-4) Harlequin Bks.

— A Cowboy's Heart. (Intimate Moments Ser.). 1996. per. 3.99 (*0-373-07705-X*, 1-07705-6) Silhouette.

R

— Every Waking Moment. 1997. per. 3.99 (*0-373-07783-1*, 1-07783-3) Silhouette.

— A Forever Kind of Cowboy: Rodeo Men. (Intimate Moments Ser.: No. 927). 1999. per. 4.25 (*0-373-07927-3*, 1-07927-6) Silhouette.

— Home Is Where the Cowboy Is: Rodeo Men. 1999. per. 4.25 (*0-373-07909-5*, Harlequin) Harlequin Bks.

— In Love with the Boss. (Romance Ser.: No. 1271). 1998. per. 3.25 (*0-373-19271-1*, 1-19271-5) Silhouette.

— The Marriage Beat: He's My Hero. (Romance Ser.: Bk. 1380). 1999. per. 3.50 (*0-373-19380-7*, 1-19380-4) Silhouette.

— The Maverick's Bride: Rodeo Man. (Intimate Moments Ser.: No. 945). 1999. per. 4.25 (*0-373-07945-1*, 1-07945-8) Silhouette.

— The Mercenary & the Marriage. (Intimate Moments Ser.). 1998. per. 4.25 (*0-373-07861-7*, 1-07861-7) Silhouette.

— A Mom for Christmas. 1996. per. 3.25 (*0-373-19195-2*, 1-19195-6) Silhouette.

— Only a Dream Away. (Intimate Moments Ser.). 1993. per. 3.50 (*0-373-07513-8*, 5-07513-0) Silhouette.

— So Little Time. (Intimate Moments Ser.). 1995. per. 3.75 (*0-373-07653-3*, 1-07653-8) Silhouette.

*__Roberts, Doreen.__ A Very...Pregnant New Year's. 2001. mass mkt. 4.50 (*0-373-27117-4*, 1-27117-0) Silhouette.

Roberts, Doreen. Where There's Smoke. 1994. per. 3.50 (*0-373-07567-7*) Silhouette.

Roberts, Doris L., jt. ed. see Krout, Anne M.

Roberts, Doris Parker, jt. auth. see Brown, Margaret.

Roberts, Dorothy. In the Flight of Stars. 85p. 1991. 16.95 (*0-86492-097-0*, Pub. by Goose Ln Edits) Genl Dist Srvs.

— Killing the Black Body. 1999. pap. 14.00 (*0-679-75869-0*) Vin Bks.

— Killing the Black Body: Race, Reproduction & the Meaning of Liberty. LC 97-2383. 384p. 1997. 26.00 (*0-679-44226-X*) McKay.

— Women, Pregnancy & Substance Abuse. (Law & Pregnancy Ser.). 21p. (C). 1991. pap. 8.00 (*1-877966-09-6*) Ctr Women Policy.

*__Roberts, Dorothy James.__ Kinsmen of the Grail. 320p. 2000. pap. 14.95 (*1-928999-07-7*) Green Knight.

Roberts, Douglas A. & Ostman, Leif. Problems of Meaning in Science Curriculum. LC 97-46462. (Ways of Knowing in Science Ser.). 1998. 48.00 (*0-8077-3709-7*); pap. 23.95 (*0-8077-3708-9*) Tchrs Coll.

Roberts, Dwight J. Use of Landfarming to Remediate Soil Contaminated by Pesticides. (Illus.). 42p. (Orig.). (C). 1995. pap. text 25.00 (*0-7881-2615-6*) DIANE Pub.

Roberts, E. Vegetable Materia Medica of India & Ceylon. 437p. (C). 1984. 60.00 (*0-7855-3298-6*, Pub. by Scientific) St Mut.

Roberts, E. C. English, Indiana: Memories of Main Street. LC 91-6301. (Illus.). 160p. 1991. 19.95 (*0-253-35032-8*) Ind U Pr.

Roberts, E. Kirk. Principles of Physical Chemistry. (C). 1984. pap. text 51.00 (*0-205-08011-1*, H80112); teacher ed. 7.00 (*0-685-07782-9*, H80120) P-H.

Roberts, E. M. A Flying Fighter: An American Above the Lines in France. 352p. 1989. pap. 19.95 (*0-947898-98-0*) Stackpole.

Roberts, E. S. & Gardner, E. A. An Introduction to Greek Epigraphy, Vol. I. LC 97-165241. 1996. 40.00 (*0-89005-553-X*) Ares.

— An Introduction to Greek Epigraphy, Vol. II. 1996. 40.00 (*0-89005-554-8*) Ares.

Roberts, E. Stanton, et al, eds. Reprints of Welsh Manuscripts, 7 vols., Set. Incl. Manuscript 49. Peniarth. LC 78-72656. 24.50 (*0-404-18246-1*); Manuscript 53. Peniarth. LC 78-72656. 24.50 (*0-404-18245-3*); Manuscript 57. Peniarth. LC 78-72656. 24.50 (*0-404-18243-7*); Manuscript 67. Peniarth. LC 78-72656. 24.50 (*0-404-18242-9*); Manuscript 76. Peniarth. LC 78-72656. 24.50 (*0-404-18244-5*); Vol. 1. Llanstephan, Ms. 6. LC 78-72656. 24.50 (*0-404-18241-0*); Vol. 7. Gwyneddon, Ms. 3. LC 78-72656. 24.50 (*0-404-18247-X*); LC 78-72656. (Celtic Language & Literature Ser.: Goidelic & Brythonic). reprint ed. 171.50 (*0-404-18240-2*) AMS Pr.

Roberts, Earl J. Unpublished Activities of World War II. LC 87-61783. (Illus.). 341p. 1988. 16.95 (*0-940553-00-7*) Scanly Pr.

Roberts, Earl W. Overcurrents & Undercurrents - All about GFCLs: Electrical Safety Advances Through Electronics. (Illus.). ix, 145p. 1996. pap. 15.00 (*0-9674323-0-8*) Reptec.

Roberts, Earle, jt. auth. see Roberts, Katie.

Roberts, Ed, ed. see Okun, James D. & Goodmere, Evangilita.

Roberts, Eddie, ed. see Briggs, Frank M., Sr.

*__Roberts, Edgar V.__ Literature: An Introduction to Reading & Writing with MLA. rev. ed. 1472p. 1998. pap. text 49.33 (*0-13-012123-1*) P-H.

Roberts, Edgar V. Writing about Literature. 9th ed. LC 98-17503. 400p. 1998. pap. text 32.20 (*0-13-081430-X*) P-H.

— Writing about Literature. 9th abr. ed. LC 98-17517. 274p. 1998. pap. text 24.20 (*0-13-081429-6*) P-H.

Roberts, Edgar V. & Jacobs, Henry E. Fiction: An Introduction to Reading & Writing. 3rd ed. 816p. (C). 1991. pap. text 49.00 (*0-13-319260-1*) P-H.

Roberts, Edgar V., ed. see Fielding, Henry.

Roberts, Edgar V., ed. see Gay, John.

Roberts, Edith A. & Rehmann, Elsa. American Plants for American Gardens: Plant Ecology - The Study of Plants in Relation to Their Environment. LC 96-11362. 144p. 1996. 27.95 (*0-8203-1851-5*) U of Ga Pr.

Roberts, Edmund B. & Onishenko, Gary. Fundamentals of Men's Fashion Design: A Guide to Casual Clothes. 2nd ed. LC 85-70375. (Illus.). 230p. (C). 1985. pap. 47.00 (*0-87005-514-3*) Fairchild.

Roberts, Edward, et al, eds. Biomedical Innovation. (Illus.). 368p. 1981. 44.00 (*0-262-18103-7*) MIT Pr.

Roberts, Edward, jt. auth. see Bishop, William H.

Roberts, Edward B. Entrepreneurs in High Technology: Lessons from MIT & Beyond. (Illus.). 400p. 1991. 35.00 (*0-19-506704-5*) OUP.

Roberts, Edward B., ed. Generating Technological Innovation. (Executive Bookshelf-Sloan Managament Review Ser.). (Illus.). 316p. 1987. text 30.00 (*0-19-505023-1*) OUP.

— Managerial Applications of System Dynamics. LC 77-26952. (Illus.). 669p. 1978. pap. text 25.00 (*1-883823-42-0*, XMNGAP) Pegasus Comm.

— Managerial Applications of System Dynamics. 562p. (C). reprint ed. pap. text 25.00 (*0-915299-59-3*) Productivity Inc.

Roberts, Edward F. Andersonville Journey. LC 97-32642. 278p. 1998. 29.95 (*1-57249-059-4*, Burd St Pr) White Mane Pub.

*__Roberts, Edward F.__ Andersonville Journey: The Civil War's Greatest Tragedy. LC 97-32642. 278p. 2000. pap. 17.95 (*1-57249-180-9*) White Mane Pub.

Roberts, Edward F. Ireland in America. LC 74-22756. (Labor Movement in Fiction & Non-Fiction Ser.). 1976. reprint ed. 39.50 (*0-404-58509-4*) AMS Pr.

Roberts, Edwards. The City of Denver, 1888. Jones, William R., ed. (Illus.). 24p. 1977. reprint ed. pap. 3.95 (*0-89646-006-1*) Vistabooks.

— Etymological Dictionary of Indoeuropean Spanish Language. (SPA.). Date not set. 79.95 (*0-7859-9590-0*) Fr & Eur.

Roberts, Edwin A. The Anglo-Marxists: A Study in Ideology & Culture. LC 96-34974. 320p. 1996. 71.00 (*0-8476-8395-8*); pap. 26.95 (*0-8476-8396-6*) Rowman.

Roberts, Elaine & Templeton, Betty. Home Care Services. (Skills for Caring Ser.). (Illus.). 48p. 1992. pap. 9.95 (*0-443-04623-9*) Church.

Roberts, Elda M. The Stubborn Fisherman. 2nd ed. LC 86-71820. (Illus.). 234p. 1997. pap. 16.95 (*0-9617139-0-9*) Creighton Pub.

Roberts, Elfed V., et al. Historical Dictionary of Hong Kong & Macau. LC 92-20816. (Asian Historical Dictionaries Ser.: No. 10). (Illus.). 406p. 1992. 58.00 (*0-8108-2574-0*) Scarecrow.

Roberts, Eli M. Distant Desire. LC 97-90686. 1998. 20.95 (*0-533-12460-3*) Vantage.

Roberts, Elisabeth, tr. see Roberts, William Owen.

Roberts, Elizabeth. Earth Prayers/Earth Songs: Book & CD Set, The. LC 90-55790. 480p. 1991. pap. 15.00 (*0-06-250746-X*, Pub. by Harper SF) HarpC.

— Georgia, Armenia, & Azerbaijan. LC 92-2242. (Former Soviet States Ser.). (Illus.). 32p. (J). (gr. 4-6). 1992. lib. bdg. 21.90 (*1-56294-309-X*) Millbrook Pr.

— Women & Families: An Oral History, 1940-1970. (Family, Sexuality & Social Relations in Past Times Ser.). (Illus.). 272p. 1995. pap. 28.95 (*0-631-19613-7*) Blackwell Pubs.

— A Women's Place: An Oral History of Working-Class Women 1890-1940. 256p. 1986. pap. text 28.95 (*0-631-14754-3*) Blackwell Pubs.

— Women's Work, 1840-1940. (New Studies in Economic & Social History: No. 6). 92p. (Orig.). (C). 1995. text 34.95 (*0-521-55265-6*); pap. text 10.95 (*0-521-55788-7*) Cambridge U Pr.

Roberts, Elizabeth, ed. Childhood Sexual Learning: The Unwritten Curriculum. 304p. 1980. text 29.95 (*0-88410-374-9*, HarpBusn) HarpInfo.

Roberts, Elizabeth & Amidon, Elias L., eds. Life Prayers: From Around the World: 365 Prayers, Blessings, & Affirmations to Celebrate the Human Journey. LC 96-385. 464p. 1996. pap. 17.00 (*0-06-251377-X*, Pub. by Harper SF) HarpC.

— Prayers for a Thousand Years: Blessings & Expressions of Hope for the New Millennium. LC 98-43252. 384p. 1999. pap. 15.00 (*0-06-066875-X*, Pub. by Harper SF) HarpC.

Roberts, Elizabeth, jt. ed. see Amidon, Elias L.

Roberts, Elizabeth, ed. see Men, Alexander.

Roberts, Elizabeth Maddox. Black Is My Truelove's Hair. Hardwick, Elizabeth, ed. LC 76-51675. (Rediscovered Fiction by American Women Ser.). 1977. reprint ed. lib. bdg. 33.95 (*0-405-10053-1*) Ayer.

— The Great Meadow. LC 91-67520. (Southern Classics Ser.). 356p. 1992. reprint ed. pap. 10.95 (*1-879941-07-4*) J S Sanders.

— The Haunted Mirror. LC 76-2121. reprint ed. 39.50 (*0-404-15236-8*) AMS Pr.

— Not by Strange Gods. LC 76-12119. reprint ed. 39.50 (*0-404-15237-6*) AMS Pr.

Roberts, Elizabeth Madox. The Time of Man. 288p. Date not set. 23.95 (*0-8488-2630-2*) Amereon Ltd.

— The Time of Man. LC 99-89766. 304p. 2000. reprint ed. pap. 18.00 (*0-8131-0981-7*) U Pr of Ky.

Roberts, Ellen E. M., ed. see Haddad, Charles S.

Roberts, Elliot, jt. auth. see Jensen, Lin.

Roberts, Ellis H. New York: The Planting & the Growth of the Empire State, 2 vols. LC 72-3763. (American Commonwealths Ser.: Nos. 8-9). reprint ed. 76.50 (*0-404-57221-9*) AMS Pr.

— New York: The Planting & the Growth of the Empire State, 2 vols., Set. 1993. reprint ed. lib. bdg. 99.00 (*0-7812-5197-4*) Rprt Serv.

Roberts, Ellis W. The Breaker Whistle Blows: Mining Diasters & Labor Leaders in the Anthracite Region. LC 85-147902. (Illus.). 166p. 1984. pap. 6.95 (*0-917445-03-1*) Anthracite.

Roberts, Ellwood. Biographical Annals of Montgomery County, Pennsylvania, 2 vols., Set. (Illus.). 1994. reprint ed. lib. bdg. 110.00 (*0-8328-4009-2*) Higginson Bk Co.

— Old Richland Families, Including Descendants of Edward Roberts, Thomas Roberts, Thomas Lancaster, Peter Lester (et al) Historical & Genealogical Data Being Derived from the Records of Friends & Other Original Sources. (Illus.). 246p. 1997. reprint ed. lib. bdg. 34.00 (*0-8328-6444-7*) Higginson Bk Co.

Roberts, Emma, jt. auth. see Morris, Edward.

Roberts, Eric S. Accounting Information Systems. 179p. 1986. pap. 46.95 (*0-471-81652-3*) Wiley.

— The Art & Science of C: An Introduction to Computer Science. LC 94-16744. (Illus.). 704p. (C). 1994. pap. text 65.00 (*0-201-54322-2*) Addison-Wesley.

— Programming Abstractions. LC 97-15248. 819p. (C). 1997. pap. text 73.00 (*0-201-54541-1*) Addison-Wesley.

Roberts, Ernest H. Treasures from near Eastern Looms. LC 81-68474. (Illus.). 1981. pap. 10.00 (*0-916606-02-3*) Bowdoin Coll.

Roberts, Erwin. The Complete Manual for Exhibiting in Trade Shows. LC 96-96501. (Illus.). 128p. 1996. ring bd. 95.00 (*1-889481-00-9*) A-Way-With-Words.

Roberts, Esther L. Sam Gets Ready for School. (Illus.). 24p. (Orig.). (J). (ps-6). 1996. pap. 5.00 (*0-9655120-1-0*) Starlight Farm.

— Sam the Horse. (Illus.). 24p. (Orig.). (J). (ps). 1996. pap. 5.00 (*0-9655120-0-2*) Starlight Farm.

Roberts, Eugene, et al, eds. GABA in Nervous System Function. LC 74-21983. (Kroc Foundation Ser.: Vol. 5). 568p. 1976. reprint ed. pap. 176.10 (*0-608-00352-2*, 206106800007) Bks Demand.

Roberts, Eunice. Memoirs of Eunice Irene Tutor Roberts. (Wisdom of the Ages Ser.). 34p. (Orig.). 1996. pap. 20.00 (*0-936390-07-7*, Wisdom of the Ages) Dialog Pr.

Roberts, Evan, jt. auth. see Penn-Lewis, Jessie.

Roberts, Evan H. The Big Picture: Self-Help. 90p. 1995. write for info. (*0-9649844-9-0*); pap. write for info. (*0-9649844-0-7*) Big Picture UT.

Roberts, F., et al. Reliability of Computer & Communication Networks. LC 91-9953. (DIMACS Ser.: Vol. 5). 259p. 1991. text 45.00 (*0-8218-6592-7*, DIMACS/5) Am Math.

Roberts, F. Barry. Confusion to Confidence: Informed Parenting. (Illus.). 210p. 1988. 16.95 (*0-9620695-0-7*) F B Roberts.

Roberts, F. Morgan. Are There Horses in Heaven? & Other Thoughts. LC 95-82040. 176p. 1996. 20.00 (*0-9637966-4-X*) Lghthse Pt Pr.

Roberts, F. W., ed. see Lawrence, D. H.

Roberts, F. Warren, ed. & intro. see Lawrence, D. H.

Roberts, F. X. & Rhine, C. D., eds. James A. Michener: A Checklist of His Works, with a Selected, Annotated Bibliography, 20. LC 94-42118. (Bibliographies & Indexes in American Literature Ser.: No.20). 152p. 1995. lib. bdg. 55.00 (*0-313-29453-4*, Greenwood Pr) Greenwood.

Roberts, Faye. Hey, Lord, Can Angels Type? 5-Minute Devotions for Working Women. 1996. 10.99 (*0-570-04844-3*, 12-3281) Concordia.

Roberts, Felicia. Talking about Treatment: Recommendations for Breast Cancer Adjuvant Treatment. (Oxford Studies in Sociolinguistics). 144p. 1999. text 35.00 (*0-19-512191-0*) OUP.

Roberts, Fitzmahan & Associates Staff, jt. auth. see Developmental Research & Programs, Inc. Staff.

Roberts, Fletcher, ed. see Cotter, Holland, et al.

Roberts, Frances J. Angel in the Fire. 1979. pap. 4.75 (*0-932814-31-X*) Kings Farspan.

— Christmas Reflections. 1982. pap. 3.25 (*0-932814-28-X*) Kings Farspan.

— Come Away, My Beloved. 1970. pap. 10.99 (*0-932814-02-6*) Kings Farspan.

— Come Away, My Beloved. 1970. 13.99 (*0-932814-01-8*) Kings Farspan.

— Come Away, My Beloved. deluxe ed. 1970. 17.99 (*0-932814-05-0*) Kings Farspan.

— Dialogues with God. 1968. pap. 6.50 (*0-932814-08-5*) Kings Farspan.

— Dialogues with God. 1968. 9.99 (*0-932814-07-7*) Kings Farspan.

— Launch Out! 1964. pap. 3.25 (*0-932814-21-2*) Kings Farspan.

— Learn to Reign. 1963. pap. 3.25 (*0-932814-22-0*) Kings Farspan.

— Listen to the Silence. 1964. pap. 3.25 (*0-932814-23-9*) Kings Farspan.

— Living Water. 1965. pap. 3.25 (*0-932814-20-4*) Kings Farspan.

— Lovest Thou Me? 1967. pap. 3.25 (*0-932814-19-0*) Kings Farspan.

— Make Haste, My Beloved. 1978. 11.99 (*0-932814-25-5*); pap. 8.50 (*0-932814-26-3*) Kings Farspan.

— On the Highroad of Surrender. 1973. pap. 8.50 (*0-932814-15-8*) Kings Farspan.

— On the Highroad of Surrender. 1973. 11.99 (*0-932814-14-X*) Kings Farspan.

— Progress of Another Pilgrim. 1970. 11.99 (*0-932814-10-7*); pap. 8.50 (*0-932814-11-5*) Kings Farspan.

— Sounding of the Trumpet. 1966. pap. 3.25 (*0-932814-24-7*) Kings Farspan.

— Total Love. 1983. 14.29 (*0-932814-32-8*); pap. 10.99 (*0-932814-33-6*) Kings Farspan.

— When the Latch Is Lifted. deluxe ed. 1970. pap. 4.99 (*0-932814-18-2*) Kings Farspan.

Roberts, Francine M. The Therapy Sourcebook. LC 97-45880. 352p. Date not set. pap. 17.00 (*0-7373-0011-6*, 00116W) NTC Contemp Pub Co.

Roberts, Frank, Jr. Archeological Remains in the Whitewater District, Eastern Arizona. (Bureau of American Ethnology Bulletins Ser.). 276p. 1995. lib. bdg. 89.00 (*0-7812-4121-9*); lib. bdg. 79.00 (*0-7812-4126-X*) Rprt Serv.

— River Basin Surveys Papers, No. 25. (Bureau of American Ethnology Bulletins Ser.). 447p. 1995. lib. bdg. 109.00 (*0-7812-4182-0*) Rprt Serv.

— River Basin Surveys Papers, Nos. 9-14. (Bureau of American Ethnology Bulletins Ser.). 392p. 1995. lib. bdg. write for info. (*0-7812-4169-3*) Rprt Serv.

— River Basin Surveys Papers, Nos. 15-20. (Bureau of American Ethnology Bulletins Ser.). 337p. 1995. lib. bdg. 99.00 (*0-7812-4176-6*) Rprt Serv.

— River Basin Surveys Papers, Nos. 21-24. (Bureau of American Ethnology Bulletins Ser.). 337p. 1995. lib. bdg. 99.00 (*0-7812-4179-0*) Rprt Serv.

— River Basin Surveys Papers, Nos. 26-32. (Bureau of American Ethnology Bulletins Ser.). 344p. 1995. lib. bdg. 99.00 (*0-7812-4185-5*) Rprt Serv.

— River Basin Surveys Papers, Nos. 33-38. (Bureau of American Ethnology Bulletins Ser.). 405p. 1995. lib. bdg. 109.00 (*0-7812-4189-8*) Rprt Serv.

— Ruins at Kiatuthlanna, Eastern Arizona. (Bureau of American Ethnology Bulletins Ser.). 195p. 1995. lib. bdg. 79.00 (*0-7812-4100-6*) Rprt Serv.

— Shabik'eshchee Village: A Late Basket Maker Site in the Chaco Canyon, New Mexico. (Bureau of American Ethnology Bulletins Ser.). 164p. 1995. lib. bdg. 79.00 (*0-7812-4092-1*) Rprt Serv.

Roberts, Frank, Jr., ed. Early Pueblo Ruins in the Piedra District, Southwestern Colorado. (Bureau of American Ethnology Bulletins Ser.). 190p. 1995. lib. bdg. 79.00 (*0-7812-4096-4*) Rprt Serv.

Roberts, Frank, ed. Songs of Joyful Praise. 1975. pap. 2.00 (*0-88027-060-8*) Firm Foun Pub.

Roberts, Frank, Jr., ed. Village of the Great Kivas on the Zuni Reservation, New Mexico. (Bureau of American Ethnology Bulletins Ser.). 197p. 1995. lib. bdg. 79.00 (*0-7812-4111-1*) Rprt Serv.

Roberts, Frank C. A Todas las Generaciones. (SPA.). 285p. pap. 9.95 (*1-55883-090-1*, 6704-6900C) Libros Desafio.

Roberts, Frank C., ed. Obituaries for the London Times, 1961-1970. 951p. 1977. lib. bdg. 235.00 (*0-313-28138-6*, ROK/, Greenwood Pr) Greenwood.

— Obituaries from the London Times, 1971-1975. 647p. 1978. lib. bdg. 175.00 (*0-313-28137-8*, ROG/, Greenwood Pr) Greenwood.

— Obituaries from The Times, 1951-1960. 896p. 1979. lib. bdg. 195.00 (*0-313-28136-X*, ROE/, Greenwood Pr) Greenwood.

Roberts, Frank D. & Clarke, C. G. History of the Town of Perry. (Illus.). 385p. 1997. reprint ed. lib. bdg. 42.00 (*0-8328-6203-7*) Higginson Bk Co.

Roberts, Frank H. Ceramic Sequence in the Chaco Canyon, New Mexico, & Its Relation to the Cultures of the San Juan Basin. LC 91-20404. (Evolution of North American Indians Ser.). 350p. 1991. text 10.00 (*0-8240-2513-X*) Garland.

Roberts, Frank H., Jr. Shabik Eschee Village: A Late Basket Maker Site in the Chaco Canyon, New Mexico. (Smithsonian Institution, Bureau of American Ethnology Ser.: No. 92). (Illus.). 173p. (C). 1929. pap. text 18.75 (*1-55567-732-0*) Coyote Press.

Roberts, Frank H., Jr. & Stewart, T. D. Archaeological Remains in the Whitewater District Eastern Arizona. fac. ed. (Smithsonian Institution, Bureau of American Ethnology Ser.: No. 126). (Illus.). 237p. (Orig.). (C). 1940. reprint ed. pap. text 25.00 (*1-55567-760-6*) Coyote Press.

Roberts, Frank H. H., Jr. Early Pueblo Ruins in the Piedra District, Southwestern Colorado. fac. ed. (Smithsonian Institution, Bureau of American Ethnology, Bulletins Ser.: No. 96). (Illus.). 199p. (C). 1930. reprint ed. pap. text 21.25 (*1-55567-858-0*) Coyote Press.

Roberts, Fred M. Guide to the Ricoh Hi-Color 35 & Marine Capsule. (Illus.). (Orig.). 1972. pap. 8.95 (*0-912746-05-X*) F M Roberts.

— Living With a Hearing Problem: Coping Strategies & Devices for the Hearing Impaired. (Illus.). 184p. 1990. pap. 16.95 (*0-912746-10-6*) F M Roberts.

— Tales of a Dakota Pilot, the Way It Was, 1929-1937. (Illus.). 112p. 1991. pap. 8.95 (*0-912746-09-2*) F M Roberts.

Roberts, Fred S. Applied Combinatorics. (Illus.). 672p. (C). 1984. text 56.00 (*0-685-07641-5*) P-H.

— Applied Combinatorics. LC 83-19052. 640p. 1984. 92.00 (*0-13-039313-4*) P-H.

— Discrete Mathematical Models with Applications to Social, Biological & Environmental Problems. (Illus.). 560p. 1976. text 49.00 (*0-13-214171-X*) P-H.

— Graph Theory & Its Applications to Problems of Society. LC 78-6277. (CBMS-NSF Regional Conference Ser.: No. 29). v, 122p. 1978. pap. text 32.50 (*0-89871-026-X*) Soc Indus-Appl Math.

Roberts, Fred S., ed. Applications of Combinatorics & Graph Theory to the Biological & Social Sciences. (IMA Volumes in Mathematics & Its Applications Ser.: Vol. 17). (Illus.). ix, 345p. 1989. 65.95 (*0-387-97046-0*, 2990) Spr-Verlag.

Roberts, Fred S. & Ringeisen, Richard D., eds. Applications of Discrete Mathematics. LC 87-51542. (Proceedings in Applied Mathematics Ser.: No. 33). x, 230p. 1988. 40.75 (*0-89871-219-X*) Soc Indus-Appl Math.

*__Roberts, G.__ Cracker Best Boys. 256p. 2000. text 22.95 (*0-312-20498-1*) St Martin.

Roberts, G. Langmuir-Blodgett Films. LC 89-72111. (Illus.). 434p. (C). 1990. text 115.00 (*0-306-43316-8*, Kluwer Plenum) Kluwer Academic.

— Pay: Strategy, Design & Negotiation. 1996. pap. 129.00 (*1-85953-086-9*, Pub. by Tech Comm) St Mut.

Roberts, G. & Cary, R. Tool Steels. 4th ed. 820p. 1980. 120.00 (*0-87170-096-4*, 6280) ASM.

Roberts, G., jt. auth. see Laidlaw, Andrew.

Roberts, G., jt. auth. see Roberts, R.

Roberts, G. D. The Collected Letters of Sir Charles. Boone, Laurel, ed. 664p. 1989. 34.95 (*0-86492-094-6*, Pub. by Goose Ln Edits) Genl Dist Srvs.

Roberts, G. Humphreys, tr. see Brod, Max.

An Asterisk (*) at the beginning of an entry indicates that the title is appearing for the first time.

Roberts, G. M., et al. Clinical Radiology for Medical Students. 3rd ed. LC 98-2712. 160p. 1998. pap. text 40.00 (*0-7506-1408-0*) Buttrwrth-Heinemann.

Roberts, G. N., jt. ed. see Pourzanjani, M. M.

Roberts, G. N., jt. ed. see Vukic, Z.

Roberts, Gareth. Designing & Managing a Pay Structure. (Financial Times Management Briefings Ser.). 1997. pap. 89.50 (*0-273-63189-6*, Pub. by F T P-H) Trans-Atl Phila.

Roberts, Gareth. The Faerie Queene. (Open Guides to Literature Ser.). 144p. 1992. 102.50 (*0-335-09036-2*); pap. 27.95 (*0-335-09037-0*) OpUniv Pr.

— The Mirror of Alchemy: Alchemical Ideas & Images in Manuscripts & Books from Antiquity to the 17th Century. (Illus.). 128p. 1995. pap. text 24.95 (*0-8020-7660-2*) U of Toronto Pr.

— The Mirror of Alchemy: Alchemical Ideas & Images in Manuscripts & Books from Antiquity to the 17th Century. (Illus.). 128p. 1995. text 55.00 (*0-8020-0710-4*) U of Toronto Pr.

***Roberts, Gareth.** Recruitment & Selection: A Competency Approach. 264p. 2000. pap. 56.95 (*0-8464-5139-5*) Beekman Pubs.

Roberts, Gareth. Recruitment & Selection: A Competency Approach. LC 98-183223. 240p. 1997. pap. 72.00 (*0-85292-707-X*, Pub. by IPM Hse) St Mut.

Roberts, Gareth & Russell, Gary. I Can't Believe It's an Unofficial Simpsons Guide. (Virgin Ser.). 1997. mass mkt. 5.95 (*0-7535-0166-X*, Pub. by Virgin Bks) London Brdge.

Roberts, Gareth, jt. ed. see Harrison, Paul.

Roberts, Gareth, jt. ed. see Normand, Lawrence.

Roberts, Gareth W. & Polak, Julia M., eds. Molecular Neuropathology. (Postgraduate Medical Science Ser.: No. 4). (Illus.). 199p. (C). 1995. pap. text 47.95 (*0-521-42558-1*) Cambridge U Pr.

Roberts, Gary B. Ancestors of American Presidents: First Definitive Edition. 473p. 1995. 35.00 (*0-936124-19-9*) C Boyer.

— Notable Kin. LC 97-78404. 288p. 1998. 35.00 (*0-936124-17-2*) C Boyer.

— Notable Kin, Vol. 2. LC 97-78404. 300p. 1998. lib. bdg. 30.00 (*0-936124-20-2*) C Boyer.

Roberts, Gary B., intro. Genealogies of Rhode Island Families from the New England Historical & Genealogical Register Vol. II: N-W & Source Records. 804p. 1989. 50.00 (*0-8063-1217-3*, 4883) Genealog Pub.

Roberts, Gary L., jt. ed. see Henderson, Harold P.

Roberts, Gary R. & Weiler, Paul C. Cases, Materials & Problems on the Law of Sports. 2nd ed. LC 98-3339. (American Casebook Ser.). 900p. 1998. 62.50 (*0-314-23128-5*) West Pub.

Roberts, Gary R., jt. auth. see Weiler, Paul C.

Roberts, Garyn G. A Cent a Story! The Best from Ten Detective Aces. LC 86-70384. 179p. 1986. 22.95 (*0-87972-353-X*) Bowling Green Univ Popular Press.

— Dick Tracy & American Culture: Morality & Mythology, Text & Context. LC 92-56687. (Illus.). 350p. 1993. lib. bdg. 45.00 (*0-89950-880-4*) McFarland & Co.

Roberts, Garyn G., et al, eds. Old Sleuth's Freaky Female Detectives. LC 89-85966. (Dime Novels Ser.). 118p. 1986. 31.95 (*0-87972-475-7*) Bowling Green Univ Popular Press.

***Roberts, Garyn G. & Prentice-Hall Publishing Staff.** The Prentice Hall Anthology of Science Fiction & Fantasy. LC 00-26411. 1000p. 2000. pap. 44.00 (*0-13-021280-6*) P-H.

Roberts, Gaye B. & Twitchett, John. The Raven Mason Collection: A Catalogue of the Collection at Keele University. (Illus.). 128p. 1998. 60.00 (*1-85331-225-8*, Pub. by Edinburgh U Pr) Col U Pr.

Roberts, Geessien J. Intelligence - "Beyond the Universe" 1998. pap. 8.95 (*0-533-12739-4*) Vantage.

Roberts, Gemma. Cavilaciones: Poesias. LC 99-60994. (Coleccion Espejo de Paciencia Ser.). (SPA.). 59p. 1999. pap. 7.95 (*0-89729-896-9*) Ediciones.

— Unamuno: Afinidades y Coincidencias Kierkegaardianas. LC 86-60967. (SPA.). 144p. 1986. pap. 30.00 (*0-89295-041-2*) Society Sp & Sp-Am.

Roberts, Gemma, ed. Analisis Existencial de Abaddon, El Exterminador de Ernesto Sabato. LC 90-60873. (SPA.). 98p. 1990. pap. 15.00 (*0-89295-061-7*) Society Sp & Sp-Am.

Roberts, Gene, Jr., jt. auth. see Nelson, Jack.

***Roberts, Geoffrey.** German Politics Today. 2000. pap. write for info. (*0-7190-4961-X*, Pub. by Manchester Univ Pr) St Martin.

Roberts, Geoffrey. Party Politics in Germany. LC 97-16322. (New Germany Ser.). 220p. 1996. pap. 24.95 (*1-85567-311-8*) Bks Intl VA.

— Party Politics in Germany. LC 97-16322. (New Germany Ser.). 220p. 1997. 75.00 (*1-85567-029-1*) Bks Intl VA.

— The Soviet Union & the Origins of Second World War: Russo-German Relations & the Road to War. LC 94-46862. (Making of the Twentieth Century Ser.). 208p. 1995. text 45.00 (*0-312-12603-4*) St Martin.

Roberts, Geoffrey & Edwards, Alistair. A New Dictionary of Political Analysis. LC 91-26692. 192p. 1995. pap. text 16.95 (*0-340-52860-5*, A6837, Pub. by E A) St Martin.

Roberts, Geoffrey, ed. see Girvin, Brian.

***Roberts, Geoffrey K.** German Politics Today. LC 99-56210. 2000. write for info. (*0-7190-4960-1*, Pub. by Manchester Univ Pr) St Martin.

Roberts, Geoffrey K. The Soviet Union in World Politics: Coexistence, Revolution, & Cold War, 1945-1991. LC 98-28013. (Making of the Contemporary World Ser.). xiv, 125 p. 1999. pap. 15.99 (*0-415-14435-3*) Routledge.

— The Soviet Union in World Politics: Coexistence, Revolution & Cold War, 1945-1991. LC 98-28013. (Making of the Contemporary World Ser.). 1999. 50.00 (*0-415-19246-3*) Routledge.

— Superwahljahr: The German Elections in 1994. LC 95-30140. 203p. (C). 1995. text 39.50 (*0-7146-4682-2*, Pub. by F Cass Pubs) Intl Spec Bk.

Roberts, George. Dire Wolf & Other Fierce & Fanciful Works by Sculptor George Roberts. LC 95-7063. 152p. (Orig.). 1995. pap. 25.00 (*0-89301-182-7*) U of Idaho Pr.

— Night Visits to a Wolf's Howl. 1979. 12.50 (*0-933114-03-6*); pap. 3.50 (*0-933114-02-8*) Oyster Pr.

— Quality Assurance in Research & Development. (Industrial Engineering Ser.: Vol. 8). (Illus.). 152p. 1983. text 75.00 (*0-8247-7071-4*) Dekker.

— Scrut: Poems. LC 82-81349. 60p. 1983. pap. 4.00 (*0-930100-10-7*) Holy Cow.

Roberts, George & Roberts, Jan. Discover Historic California. 5th ed. LC 99-71725. (Illus.). 576p. 1999. pap. 13.95 (*1-889786-03-9*) Gem Guides Bk.

— Discover Historic Washington State: A Travel Guide to Hundreds of Historical Places in the Evergreen State. (Illus.). 556p. 1999. pap. 13.95 (*1-889786-07-1*) Gem Guides Bk.

Roberts, George, et al. Tool Steels. 5th ed. LC 98-141358. 364p. 1998. 190.00 (*0-87170-599-0*, 6590) ASM.

Roberts, George, ed. see Yonge, Walter.

Roberts, George C. Paul M. Butler: Hoosier Politician & National Political Leader. LC 87-6275. (Illus.). 210p. (Orig.). (C). 1987. pap. text 22.50 (*0-8191-6296-5*) U Pr of Amer.

Roberts, George E. Illegal Police Surveillance. LC 98-129843. (Illus.). 152p. 1997. pap. 24.95 (*0-9657785-1-7*) Comet Press.

— Illegal Police Surveillance. 2nd rev. ed. LC 98-92670. (Illus.). 207p. 1999. pap. 24.75 (*0-9657785-2-5*) Comet Press.

Roberts, George M. Druse Genealogy (Descendants of Stephen Druse of RI & NY) 204p. 1997. reprint ed. pap. 32.00 (*0-8328-8360-3*); reprint ed. lib. bdg. 42.00 (*0-8328-8359-X*) Higginson Bk Co.

Roberts, George M. & Lovelace, Jayne P. Montgomery, Hampden Co., Massachusetts Families from the Early Times to about 1900: From the Manuscript Notes of George McKenzie Roberts. LC 98-183806. 270p. 1997. pap. 40.00 (*1-878545-24-8*) ACETO Bookmen.

Roberts, George O. The Anguish of Third World Independence: The Sierra Leone Experience. LC 81-48679. (Illus.). (Orig.). 1982. pap. text 34.50 (*0-8191-2396-X*) U Pr of Amer.

Roberts, George S. Historic Towns of the Connecticut River Valley. (Illus.). 494p. 1992. reprint ed. pap. 30.00 (*1-55613-614-5*) Heritage Bk.

— Old Schenectady. (Illus.). 296p. 1997. reprint ed. lib. bdg. 37.00 (*0-8328-6228-2*) Higginson Bk Co.

Roberts, George V. A Fly Fisher's Guide to Saltwater Naturals & Their Imitation. (Illus.). 192p. 1994. 34.95 (*0-07-053166-8*, Ragged Mntain) McGraw-Hill Prof.

***Roberts, George V., Jr.** A Fly-Fisher's Guide to Saltwater Naturals & Their Imitation. (Illus.). 163p. 1999. pap. 22.95 (*0-07-135325-9*) McGraw.

Roberts, George W. Total Quality Management for Research & Development. (Quality & Reliability Ser.). Date not set. write for info. (*0-8247-9358-7*) Dekker.

Roberts, George W., ed. Quality Planning, Control & Improvement in Research & Development. LC 94-39690. (Quality & Reliability Ser.: Vol. 44). (Illus.). 384p. 1994. text 125.00 (*0-8247-9585-7*) Dekker.

Roberts, Gerald, ed. Gerard Manley Hopkins. 448p. 1987. 88.50 (*0-7102-0414-0*, 04140, Routledge Thoemms) Routledge.

***Roberts, Gerrylynn K.** American Cities & Technology: Wilderness to Wired City. 272p. 2000. pap. 27.99 (*0-415-20084-9*) Routledge.

Roberts, Gerrylynn K. The American Cities & Technology Reader: Wilderness to Wired City. LC 98-42028. (Cities & Technology Ser.). 1999. write for info. (*0-415-20085-7*) Routledge.

Roberts, Gerrylynn K., ed. see Steadman, Philip.

Roberts, Gilda, tr. see De Van.

Roberts, Gilda, tr. see Van, Gilles De, et al.

***Roberts, Gillian.** Adam & Evil. LC 99-14225. 178p. (YA). 1999. 22.95 (*0-345-42934-6*) Ballantine Pub Grp.

— Adam & Evil. 240p. 2000. mass mkt. 6.50 (*0-345-42935-4*, Ballantine) Ballantine Pub Grp.

— Adam & Evil. large type ed. (Mystery Ser.). 2000. 25.95 (*1-57490-292-X*) T T Beeler.

Roberts, Gillian. The Bluest Blood. LC 98-93672. 285p. 1999. mass mkt. 5.99 (*0-345-42315-1*) Ballantine Pub Grp.

— The Bluest Blood, No. 8. Date not set. write for info. (*0-345-40325-8*, Ballantine) Ballantine Pub Grp.

— Caught Dead in Philadelphia. 1988. mass mkt. 5.99 (*0-345-35340-4*) Ballantine Pub Grp.

***Roberts, Gillian.** Helen Hath No Fury: An Amanda Pepper Mystery. 240p. 2000. 23.00 (*0-345-42933-8*) Ballantine Pub Grp.

Roberts, Gillian. How I Spent My Summer Vacation. 1995. mass mkt. 5.99 (*0-345-38594-2*) Ballantine Pub Grp.

— Philly Stakes. 1990. mass mkt. 5.99 (*0-345-36266-7*) Ballantine Pub Grp.

— Time & Trouble. LC 98-4768. 384p. 1998. text 24.95 (*0-312-18673-8*) St Martin.

— Time & Trouble. 336p. 1999. mass mkt. 5.99 (*0-312-96996-1*, St Martins Paperbacks) St Martin.

***Roberts, Gillian.** Where's the Harm?, Vol. 1. LC 99-31278. 1999. 21.95 (*0-7862-2036-8*, Five Star MI) Mac Lib Ref.

Roberts, Gillian. You Can Write a Mystery. LC 99-14776. (You Can Write It! Ser.). 128p. 1999. pap. 12.99 (*0-89879-863-9*, 10634, Wrtrs Digest Bks) F & W Pubns Inc.

Roberts, Gillian & Foster, Alan Dean. With Friends Like These... LC 92-97480. 256p. 1994. mass mkt. 4.99 (*0-345-37784-2*) Ballantine Pub Grp.

Roberts, Glen E. Interpretive Handbook for the Roberts Apperception Test for Children. 261p. 1994. spiral bd. write for info. (*0-87424-288-6*, W-288) Western Psych.

Roberts, Glenda S. Staying on the Line: Blue-Collar Women in Contemporary Japan. LC 93-27346. 1994. pap. text 17.00 (*0-8248-1579-3*) UH Pr.

Roberts, Glenda S., jt. auth. see Douglass, Mike.

Roberts, Glenn & Holmes, Jeremy, eds. Healing Stories: Narrative in Psychiatry & Psychotherapy. LC 98-19457. (Illus.). 248p. 1999. text 89.95 (*0-19-262827-5*) OUP.

***Roberts, Glenn L.** Maalstrom. 244p. 1999. pap. 12.00 (*0-9675809-0-0*) Dark Lotus.

— The Selk King. 303p. 1999. pap. 12.00 (*0-9675809-1-9*) Dark Lotus.

Roberts, Gloria A. A Family Planning Library Manual. 5th enl. rev. ed. LC 93-84534. (Illus.). 148p. (Orig.). 1994. pap. text 15.00 (*0-934586-72-1*) Plan Parent.

Roberts, Glyn, et al. Learning Experiences in Sport Psychology. 2nd rev. ed. LC 98-30815. 200p. (C). 1998. pap. text, student ed. 25.00 (*0-88011-932-2*, BROB0932) Human Kinetics.

Roberts, Glyn C. Psychology of Motor Behavior & Sport, 1978. Newell, Karl M., ed. LC 78-641529. 309p. 1979. reprint ed. pap. 95.80 (*0-608-10452-3*, 202953100061) Bks Demand.

Roberts, Glyn C., ed. Motivation in Sport & Exercise. LC 91-22864. (Illus.). 288p. (Orig.). 1995. reprint ed. pap. text 25.00 (*0-87322-876-6*, BROB0876) Human Kinetics.

Roberts, Glyn C., et al. Social Science of Play, Games & Sport: Learning Experiences. LC 79-89695. 110p. reprint ed. pap. 34.10 (*0-608-15282-X*, 202953200061) Bks Demand.

Roberts, Glyn C., ed. see North American Society for the Psychology of Sport & Physical Activity Staff.

Roberts, Godfrey, ed. Population Policy: Contemporary Issues. LC 89-36160. 232p. 1990. 59.95 (*0-275-93039-4*, C3039, Praeger Pubs) Greenwood.

Roberts-Goodson, Bruce. Boatbuilding. (Orig.). 1996. pap. 44.95 (*1-898307-06-7*, Pub. by Capall Bann Pubng) Holmes Pub.

— Choosing for Cruising: How to Select & Equip the Perfect Cruising Yacht. LC 97-28825. (Illus.). 192p. 1998. 29.95 (*1-57409-037-2*) Sheridan.

***Roberts-Goodson, Bruce.** Complete Guide to Metal Boats: Building, Maintenance & Repair. (Illus.). 320p. 2000. 34.95 (*0-07-136444-7*) McGraw.

— Metal Boats: Steel, Aluminum, Copper Nickel Building, Maintenance, & Repair. (Illus.). 1998. pap. 44.95 (*1-86163-031-X*, Pub. by Capall Bann Pubng) Holmes Pub.

Roberts-Goodson, R. Bruce. Spray: The Ultimate Cruising Boat. (Illus.). 224p. 1995. 29.95 (*0-924486-87-2*) Sheridan.

Roberts, Gordon, jt. auth. see Viscione, Jerry A.

Roberts, Gordon C., ed. NMR of Macromolecules: A Practical Approach. LC 93-17466. (Practical Approach Ser.: Vol. 134). (Illus.). 418p. 1993. pap. text 55.00 (*0-19-963224-3*) OUP.

***Roberts, Gordon W. & Leung, Vincent W.** Design & Analysis of Integrator-Based Log-Domain Filter Circuits. LC 99-47409. 1999. write for info. (*0-7923-8699-X*) Kluwer Academic.

Roberts, Gordon W. & Lu, Albert K. Analog Signal Generation for Built-in-Self-Test of Mixed-Signal Integrated Circuits. LC 95-989. (The Kluwer International Series in Engineering & Computer Science: 312). 136p. (C). 1995. text 91.00 (*0-7923-9564-6*) Kluwer Academic.

Roberts, Gordon W., jt. auth. see Sedra, Adel S.

***Roberts, Graham.** The Financial Services Industry & the Law. 456p. 1999. pap. 120.00 (*0-85297-539-2*, Pub. by Chartered Bank) St Mut.

Roberts, Graham. The Last Soviet Avant-Garde: OBERIU--Fact, Fiction, Metafiction. (Cambridge Studies in Russian Literature). 290p. (C). 1997. text 64.95 (*0-521-48283-6*) Cambridge U Pr.

— Law Relating to Banking Services. 3rd ed. 350p. 1998. pap. 105.00 (*0-85297-491-4*, Pub. by Chartered Bank) St Mut.

— Law Relating to International Banking. (Gresham Bks.). 192p. 1997. boxed set 210.00 (*1-85573-330-7*, Pub. by Woodhead Pubng) Am Educ Systs.

Roberts, Graham & Longhurst, Peter. Oral & Dental Trauma in Children & Adolescents. (Illus.). 112p. (C). 1996. text 115.00 (*0-19-262055-X*); pap. text 59.95 (*0-19-262049-5*) OUP.

Roberts, Graham, jt. auth. see Laidlaw, L.

Roberts-Gray, Cynthia, jt. ed. see Conrad, Kendon J.

Roberts, Greg. Tailgating in the Big Ten: A Users Guide Around the Conference. (Illus.). 128p. (Orig.). 1997. pap. 9.45 (*0-9642371-4-8*) Backroads Pr.

Roberts, Gregory & Roberts, Mark E. American Ancestors of Stephen. (Illus.). write for info. (*0-9616192-1-X*) Roberts CA.

Roberts, Guy B. Question Of Music. 1999. pap. text 15.95 (*0-572-02308-1*) Foulsham UK.

Roberts, Gwenda, jt. auth. see Butler, Ian.

Roberts, Gwilym R. New Lives in the Valley: Slate Quarries & Quarry Villages in North Wales, New York, & Vermont. (Illus.). x, 470p. 1998. 23.95 (*0-9668292-0-4*) RM Dist.

Roberts, H. Doing Feminist Research. 208p. (C). 1981. pap. 27.99 (*0-415-02547-8*) Routledge.

— Forest Insects in Nigeria. 1969. 55.00 (*0-85074-006-1*) St Mut.

— Homeopathic Medicine: Principles & Art of Cure. 1974. lib. bdg. 250.00 (*0-685-51361-0*) Revisionist Pr.

Roberts, H., ed. Photography & Art History. ix, 290p. 1990. text 30.00 (*2-88124-459-9*) Gordon & Breach.

Roberts, H., jt. auth. see Wallis, W.

Roberts, H. E., et al, eds. Reports on the Iconclass Workshop, November 1987 at Santa Monica, CA: A Special Issue of the Journal Visual Resources. x, 70p. 1988. text 16.00 (*2-88124-371-1*) Gordon & Breach.

— Visual Resources Vol. IV, No. 3: A Special Issue of the Journal Visual Resources. viii, 90p. 1987. text 24.00 (*2-88124-370-3*) Gordon & Breach.

Roberts, H. J. Aspartame (NutraSweet) Is It Safe? LC 89-81086. 328p. 1990. pap. 16.95 (*0-914783-58-0*); text 26.95 (*0-914783-37-8*) Charles.

— Breast Implants or Aspartame (Nutrasweet) Disease? The Suppressed Opinion about a Perceived Medicolegal Travesty. LC 98-91122. 62p. 1999. pap. 12.00 (*1-884243-10-X*) Sunshine Sentinel.

— The Cacof Conspiracy: Lessons of the New Millennium. LC 96-68073. 239p. 1998. pap. 17.95 (*1-884243-05-3*) Sunshine Sentinel.

— Defense Against Alzheimer's Disease: A Rational Blueprint for Prevention. LC 93-86995. (Illus.). 236p. 1995. 27.95 (*1-884243-00-2*) Sunshine Sentinel.

— Health & Wealth, Palm Beach Style: Diseases, Behavior & Sexuality of the Rich. LC 96-92351. 292p. (Orig.). 1997. pap. 21.95 (*1-884243-07-X*) Sunshine Sentinel.

— Is Vasectomy Worth the Risk? A Physician's Case Against Vasectomania. LC 92-64348. (Illus.). 125p. 1993. pap. 16.95 (*0-9633260-2-3*) Sunshine Sentinel.

— Mega Vitamin E: Is It Safe? LC 93-85653. (Illus.). 130p. 1994. pap. 17.95 (*0-9633260-8-2*) Sunshine Sentinel.

— My Wife, the Politician: A Play in Three Acts. 137p. 1993. pap. 17.95 (*0-9633260-5-8*) Sunshine Sentinel.

— Princess Diana, the House of Windsor & Palm Beach: America's Fascination with "The Touch of Royalty" LC 98-158451. (Illus.). 120p. 1998. pap. 24.95 (*1-884243-06-1*) Sunshine Sentinel.

— Sweet'ner Dearest: Bittersweet Vignettes about Aspartame (NutraSweet) LC 92-64347. (Illus.). 300p. 1992. pap. 19.95 (*0-9633260-1-5*) Sunshine Sentinel.

— West Palm Beach: Centennial Reflections. LC 94-68705. (Illus.). 300p. 1994. 25.95 (*1-884243-02-9*) Sunshine Sentinel.

Roberts, H. L., ed. see Campbell, W. A.

Roberts, Hadley B. Birds of East Central Idaho. (Illus.). 128p. (Orig.). (C). 1993. pap. text 9.95 (*0-9634903-0-3*) H B Roberts.

Roberts, Harold R., ed. New Aspects of Haemophilia Treatment. (Journal Ser.: Vol. 26, No. 1, 1996). (Illus.). vi, 166p. 1996. pap., suppl. ed. 53.25 (*3-8055-6279-9*) S Karger.

Roberts, Harold R., jt. ed. see High, Katherine A.

Roberts, Harold S. Roberts' Dictionary of Industrial Relations. rev. ed. LC 78-175029. 615p. reprint ed. pap. 190.70 (*0-608-16709-6*, 202679800052) Bks Demand.

Roberts, Harry. Backpacking. 2nd ed. Hall, Adrienne, ed. LC 99-25246. (Basic Essentials Ser.). (Illus.). 64p. (Orig.). 1999. pap. text 7.95 (*0-7627-0476-4*) Globe Pequot.

***Roberts, Harry.** Canoe Paddling. 2nd ed. (Basic Essentials Ser.). (Illus.). 80p. 2000. pap. text 7.95 (*0-7627-0662-7*) Globe Pequot.

— Capture at Arnhem: A Diary of Disaster & Survival. 1999. pap. 18.95 (*1-900624-27-3*) Windrush Pr.

Roberts, Harry. Movin' Out: Equipment & Technique for Hikers. rev. ed. LC 78-26618. (Illus.). 160p. 1979. pap. 9.95 (*0-913276-29-4*) Stone Wall Pr.

Roberts, Harry H. Field Guidebook to the Reefs & Geology of Grand Cayman Island, B.W.I. (Third International Symposium on Coral Reefs Ser.). (Illus.). 44p. 1977. pap. 5.00 (*0-932981-39-9*) Univ Miami A R C.

Roberts, Harry V. Data Analysis for Managers with MINITAB 7.0. 2nd ed. 510p. (C). 1993. text, mass mkt. 54.75 incl. 3.5 hd (*0-89426-193-2*) Course Tech.

— Data Analysis for Quality Improvement: A Supplementary Textbook for Statistics Courses. (Dimensions in Total Quality Ser.: Vol. 6). 375p. (C). Date not set. pap. text 31.95 (*1-55786-552-3*) Blackwell Pubs.

Roberts, Harry V., ed. Academic Initiatives in Total Quality for Higher Education. 607p. 1995. 50.00 (*0-87389-326-3*, H0881) ASQ Qual Pr.

Roberts, Harry V. & Sergesketter, Bernard F. Quality Is Personal: A Foundation for Total Quality Management. LC 93-21723. 192p. 1993. 29.95 (*0-02-926626-2*); per. 22.95 (*0-02-926625-4*) Free Pr.

Roberts, Hayden. Community Development: Learning & Action. LC 78-12986. (Canadian University Paperbooks Ser.: No. 224). 219p. reprint ed. pap. 67.90 (*0-608-16729-0*, 205612500050) Bks Demand.

Roberts, Helen. The Acrylic Watercolor Book. (Illus.). 32p. 1986. pap. 8.95 (*0-941284-35-2*) J Shaw Studio.

— Destiny of the Soul. rev. ed. Loehr, Franklin, ed. LC 83-82485. Orig. Title: The Soul That Sinneth--It Shall Die. 1987. pap. 9.95 (*0-915151-13-8*) Religious Res Pr.

— Karma, the Great Teacher. rev. ed. LC 93-85317. 328p. (Orig.). 1993. pap. 12.95 (*0-915151-19-7*) Religious Res Pr.

Roberts, Helen, ed. Doing Feminist Research. 224p. (Orig.). 1981. pap. 13.95 (*0-7100-0772-8*, Routledge Thoemms) Routledge.

Roberts, Helen, et al. Children at Risk? Safety As a Social Value. LC 95-9567. 120p. 1995. pap. 31.95 (*0-335-19210-6*) OpUniv Pr.

Roberts, Helen, ed. see Church of Religious Research, Inc. Staff.

R

R

Roberts, Helen H. Ancient Hawaiian Music. (BMB Ser.: No. 29). 1972. reprint ed. pap. 60.00 (0-527-02132-6) Periodicals Srv.

— Basketry of the San Carlos Apache Indians. LC 72-10331. (American Museum of Natural History Anthropological Papers: Vol. XXXI, Pt. II). (Illus.). 104p. 1985. reprint ed. pap. 10.00 (0-87380-147-4) Popular E Commerce.

Roberts, Helen R., et al. Teaching in the Multicultural Classroom. (Survival Skills for Scholars Ser.: Vol. 12). 128p. 1994. 37.00 (0-8039-5613-4); pap. 16.50 (0-8039-5614-2) Sage.

Roberts, Helene E. Art History Through the Camera's Lens. LC 95-167468. 328p. 1995. pap. text 28.00 (2-88124-643-5) Gordon & Breach.

— Art History Through the Camera's Lens Vol. II: Documenting the Image. LC 95-167468. 328p. 1995. text 66.00 (2-88124-642-7) Gordon & Breach.

— Iconographic Index to Old Testament Paintings Represented in Photographs & Slides of Paintings in the Visual Collections, Fine Arts Library, Harvard University. LC 86-25830. (Illus.). 224p. 1987. text 64.00 (0-8240-8345-8) Garland.

Roberts, Helene E., ed. Encyclopedia of Comparative Iconography: Themes Depicted in Works of Art, 2 vols. LC 98-163033. (Illus.). 1600p. 1998. lib. bdg. 250.00 (1-57958-009-2) Fitzroy Dearborn.

Roberts, Helene E. & Hall, Rachael. Iconographic Index to Narrative New Testament Subjects in the Italian School: Represented in Photographs & Slides of Paintings in the Visual Collections, Fine Arts Library, Harvard University. LC 91-36350. 266p. 1992. text 20.00 (0-8240-4385-5, H1154) Garland.

Roberts, Henry. The Complete Prophecies of Nostradamus: The Most Definitive & Accurately Translated & Interpreted Collection of the Seer's Prophecies. 384p. 1999. pap. 12.00 (0-609-80351-4, Crown) Crown.

Roberts, Henry C. Complete Prophecies of Nostradamus. Date not set. pap. write for info. (0-517-88603-0, Crown) Crown Pub Group.

— Nostradamus: Prophesies. 15.00 (0-685-22062-1) Wehman.

Roberts, Henry E. On Becoming the Person You Want to Be LC 97-73790. 152 p. 1997. write for info. (1-888676-04-3) Ardara Hse.

Roberts, Henry L. Rumania: Political Problems of an Agrarian State. 1951. 89.50 (0-685-45660-9) Elliots Bks.

Roberts, Henry M. Robert's Rules of Order: Classic Man. 224p. 1988. 5.99 (0-517-25920-6) Random Hse Value.

Roberts, Herbert A. The Principles & Art of Cure by Homoeopathy. 286p. (C). 1942. pap. 38.95 (0-8464-1042-7) Beekman Pubs.

— Sensations "As If -" 1976. 10.00 (0-685-76571-7) Formur Intl.

Roberts, Herrell B. The Inner World of the Black Juvenile Delinquent: Three Case Studies. 168p. 1987. text 29.95 (0-89859-895-8) L Erlbaum Assocs.

Roberts-Herrick, Lyn. The Good Remembering: A Message for Our Times, a Guide for Seekers. Bickford, Gail H., ed. 95p. (Orig.). 1995. pap. 9.95 (0-945069-06-5) Freedom Pr Assocs.

Roberts, Hewitt. ISO 14000 Implementation Handbook. LC 99-163007. 432p. 1998. pap. text 59.95 (0-7506-4020-0) Buttrwrth-Heinemann.

Roberts, Howard. Chord Directory. (Illus.). 108p. 1998. write for info. (0-318-69299-6) Playback Mus Pub.

— Plectrum Picking. (Illus.). 1998. 9.98 (0-89915-025-X) Playback Mus Pub.

Roberts, Howard & Hagberg, Garry. The Jazz Improviser: Technique, Musicianship, Theory, Performance. Palmer, Evie, ed. (Illus.). 328p. 1992. write for info. (0-89915-047-0) Playback Mus Pub.

— The Praxis System: Guitar Compendium, Vol. 1: Technique, Improvisation, Musicianship & Theory. (Illus.). 163p. (C). 1989. 35.00 (3-89221-019-5, Pub. by Advance Mus); pap. text 19.95 (0-317-04756-6, Pub. by Advance Mus) McClelland & Stewart.

— The Praxis System: Guitar Compendium, Vol. 2: Technique, Improvisation, Musicianship & Theory. (Illus.). 237p. 1989. 40.00 (3-89221-021-7, Pub. by Advance Mus); pap. text 19.95 (0-317-04626-8, Pub. by Advance Mus) McClelland & Stewart.

— The Praxis System: Guitar Compendium, Vol. 3: Technique, Improvisation, Musicianship & Theory. (Illus.). 227p. 1989. 40.00 (3-89221-020-9, Pub. by Advance Mus); pap. text 24.95 (0-317-04757-4, Pub. by Advance Mus) McClelland & Stewart.

Roberts, Howard R., ed. Food Safety. LC 80-25335. 355p. 1981. reprint ed. pap. 110.10 (0-608-17421-1, 205645700067) Bks Demand.

Roberts, Howard W. Doc. LC 86-90702. (Illus.). 176p. 1987. 11.95 (0-9617971-0-X) Circuit Writer.

— Faith & Ethics: Tough Choices for the 21st Century. LC 97-50021. Orig. Title: Approaching the Third Millennium. 192p. 1998. reprint ed. pap. 18.00 (1-880837-04-8) Smyth & Helwys.

— Pastoral Care Through Worship. 192p. 1995. pap. 15.00 (1-880837-74-9) Smyth & Helwys.

— Praying Like Jesus. LC 98-45513. 160p. 1999. pap. 15.95 (0-8298-1326-8) Pilgrim OH.

— Sins That Crucify. 112p. 1994. pap. 11.00 (1-880837-84-6) Smyth & Helwys.

Roberts, Hugh. Shelley & the Chaos of History: A New Politics of Poetry. LC 96-20029. (Literature & Philosophy Ser.). 512p. 1997. 75.00 (0-271-01640-X); pap. 25.00 (0-271-01641-8) Pa St U Pr.

Roberts, Hugh, jt. auth. see Ricketts, Harry.

Roberts, Humberto Casanova. Los Pastores y el Rebano. (SPA.). 222p. 10.95 (1-55883-105-3, 6724-0301C) Libros Desafio.

Roberts, I. A. & Murray, N. A. Haematology in the Newborn. 250p. 1997. 48.00 (981-02-3098-2) World Scientific Pub.

Roberts, Ian. Comparative Syntax. 320p. 1996. pap. text 29.95 (0-340-59286-9, Pub. by E A) OUP.

— Eine Rechnung, die Nicht Aufgeht: Identity & Ideology in the Fiction of Wolfdietrich Schnurre. (Historisch-kritische Arbeiten zur Deutschen Literatur Ser.: Bd. 20). (GER., Illus.). 258p. 1997. pap. 54.95 (3-631-31120-6) P Lang Pubng.

— Eine Rechnung, die Nicht Aufgeht: Identity & Ideology in the Fiction of Wolfdietrich Schnurre. LC 97-24804. (Historisch-Kritische Arbeiten zur Deutschen Literatur Ser.: Bd. 20). (Illus.). 258p. 1997. pap. 54.95 (0-8204-3239-3) P Lang Pubng.

Roberts, Ian, ed. see Battye, Adrian.

Roberts, Ian, jt. ed. see Battye, Adrian.

Roberts, Ian D. A Harvest of Hope: Jesuit Collegiate Education in England, 1794-1914. LC 95-81838. (Original Studies Composed in English: Series III, Vol. 12). (Illus.). xviii, 243p. (Orig.). 1996. pap. 27.95 (1-880810-16-6) Inst Jesuit.

Roberts, Ian G. Comparative Syntax. 352p. 1996. text 60.00 (0-340-67659-0, Pub. by E A) St Martin.

— Verbs & Diachronic Syntax: A Comparative History of English & French. (Studies in Natural Language & Linguistic Theory). 372p. (C). 1993. lib. bdg. 157.50 (0-7923-1705-X) Kluwer Academic.

— Verbs & Diachronic Syntax: A Comparative History of English & French. (Studies in Natural Language & Linguistic Theory). 388p. (C). 1993. pap. text 59.50 (0-7923-2495-1) Kluwer Academic.

Roberts, Ian G. & Borsley, Robert D., eds. The Syntax of the Celtic Languages: A Comparative Perspective. 368p. (C). 1996. text 59.95 (0-521-48160-0) Cambridge U Pr.

Roberts, Ian P. Craft, Class, & Control: The Sociology of a Shipbuilding Community. 224p. 1993. text 60.00 (0-7486-0395-6, Pub. by Edinburgh U Pr) Col U Pr.

Roberts, Ida M. Corley, see Corley Roberts, Ida M.

***Roberts, Irene.** Kingdom of the Sun. large type ed. 416p. 1999. pap. 20.99 (1-85389-879-1, Dales) Ulverscroft.

— Moonpearl. large type ed. 368p. 1999. pap. 20.99 (1-85389-882-1) Ulverscroft.

— Sea Jade. large type ed. 352p. 1999. pap. 20.99 (1-85389-881-3, Dales) Ulverscroft.

Roberts, Isaac P. Autobiography of a Farm Boy. (American Biography Ser.). 207p. 1991. reprint ed. lib. bdg. 69.00 (0-7812-8324-8) Rprt Serv.

Roberts, Ivanka, tr. see Maniguet, Xavier.

***Roberts, Ivor & Springer, Beverly.** Social Policy in the European Union: Between Harmonization & National Autonomy. 180p. 2001. 49.95 (1-55587-977-2) L Rienner.

Roberts, J. Art of Interruption: Photography, Realism & the Everyday. LC 97-12650. (Photography, Critical Views Ser.). (Illus.). 208p. 1998. 74.95 (0-7190-3560-0, Pub. by Manchester Univ Pr) St Martin.

Roberts, J. & Whitehouse, D. G. Practical Plant Physiology. LC 75-46566. 171p. reprint ed. pap. 53.10 (0-608-13081-8, 202521300043) Bks Demand.

Roberts, J., et al. Caldecotte: Excavations & Fieldwork 1966-1991. LC 95-134691. (Milton Keynes Archaeological Reports). (Illus.). 247p. 1995. pap. 45.00 (0-949003-14-X) David Brown.

Roberts, J., jt. auth. see Goldberg, P.

***Roberts, J. A.** A Concise History of China. (Illus.). 341p. 1999. text 45.00 (0-674-00074-9) HUP.

Roberts, J. A. Modern China: An Illustrated History. LC 98-191000. (Illus.). 320p. 1998. 39.95 (0-86299-847-6, Pub. by Sutton Pub Ltd) Intl Pubs Mktg.

Roberts, J. A. & Pembrey, M. E. Introduction to Medical Genetics. 8th ed. (Illus.). 400p. 1985. pap. 29.95 (0-19-261409-6) OUP.

Roberts, J. A., jt. auth. see Marshall, Bruce.

***Roberts, J. A. G.** China: Prehistory to the 19th Century. 2000. reprint ed. pap. 19.95 (0-7509-2564-7, Pub. by Sutton Publng) Intl Pubs Mktg.

Roberts, J. A. G. A Concise History of China. (Illus.). 341p. 1999. pap. 16.95 (0-674-00075-7) HUP.

***Roberts, J. A. G.** Modern China: An Illustrated History. 2000. reprint ed. pap. 19.95 (0-7509-2570-1, Pub. by Sutton Publng) Intl Pubs Mktg.

Roberts, J. Aelwyn. Holy Ghostbuster. 192p. 1996. pap. 12.95 (1-85230-913-X, Pub. by Element MA) Penguin Putnam.

— Yesterday's People: A Parson's Search for the Answers to Life after Death. LC 97-16945. 192p. 1997. pap. 12.95 (1-86204-000-1, Pub. by Element MA) Penguin Putnam.

Roberts, J. B., jt. auth. see Casciati, Fabio.

Roberts, J. B., jt. ed. see Casciati, Fabio.

Roberts, J. C. Neutral Sizing: A Literature Review. (Pira Reviews of Pulp & Paper Technology Ser.). 57p. 1995. reprint ed. pap. 95.00 (0-902799-83-5, TS1120, Pub. by Pira Internatl) Bks Intl VA.

Roberts, J. C., ed. Paper Chemistry. 288p. 1991. pap. 195.95 (0-412-02511-6, A4216, Chap & Hall NY) Chapman & Hall.

Roberts, J. C., jt. auth. see Lynch, M.

Roberts, J. D., tr. see Otera, Corazon.

Roberts, J. D., tr. see Otero, Corazon.

***Roberts, J. Deotis.** Africentric Christianity: A Theological Appraisal for Ministry. LC 99-32820. 128p. 2000. pap. 14.00 (0-8170-1321-0) Judson.

Roberts, J. Deotis. Black Theology in Dialogue. LC 86-15665. 132p. (Orig.). 1987. pap. 17.95 (0-664-24022-4) Westminster John Knox.

— Liberation & Reconciliation: A Black Theology. rev. ed. LC 93-38133. 150p. 1994. reprint ed. pap. 18.00 (0-88344-951-X) Orbis Bks.

— The Prophethood of Black Believers: An African-American Political Theology for Ministry. LC 93-32901. 192p. (Orig.). 1994. pap. 19.95 (0-664-25488-8) Westminster John Knox.

Roberts, J. E. Pioneers in Medical Physics: A History of Hospital Physics. LC 99-19619. (Illus.). 180p. 1998. 65.00 (0-7503-0494-4) IOP Pub.

Roberts, J. H. Angle Modulation: The Theory of System Assessment. LC 78-317398. (IEE Telecommunications Ser.: Vol. 5). (Illus.). 294p. reprint ed. pap. 91.20 (0-8357-5478-2, 203225300079) Bks Demand.

Roberts, J. Hatcher, jt. auth. see Wijeyaratne, P.

Roberts, J. J. Nahum, Habakkuk & Zephaniah: A Commentary. LC 90-24082. (Old Testament Library). 224p. 1991. text 24.95 (0-664-21937-3) Westminster John Knox.

Roberts, J. J., et al. Concrete Masonry Designer's Handbook. (Viewpoint Ser.). (Illus.). 1983. 90.00 (0-86310-013-9, Pub. by Palladian) Scholium Intl.

Roberts, J. J, et al. Handbook on BS 5628: The Structural use of Reinforced & Prestressed Masonry, Pt. 2. (Illus.). 207p. 1987. text 75.00 (0-86310-020-1, Pub. by Palladian) Scholium Intl.

Roberts, J. J., jt. ed. see Goedicke, Hans.

Roberts, J. M. Antiquity Unveiled: Ancient Voices from the Spirit Realms Proving Christianity to Be of Heathen Origin (1892) 621p. 1996. reprint ed. pap. 33.50 (1-56459-771-7) Kessinger Pub.

— Antiquity Unveiled: The Heathen Origins of Christianity. 1992. lib. bdg. 89.00 (0-8490-8747-3) Gordon Pr.

— A Concise History of the World. (Illus.). 632p. 1995. 39.95 (0-19-521151-0) OUP.

— Europe: Divided & United. 1994. pap. text. write for info. (0-582-22669-4, Pub. by Addison-Wesley) Longman.

— Europe 1880-1945. 2nd ed. LC 87-22524. (General History of Europe Ser.). 648p. (C). 1989. pap. 45.00 (0-582-49414-1, 73612) Longman.

— The French Revolution. 2nd ed. LC 97-10821. 192p. (C). 1997. pap. 19.95 (0-19-289292-4) OUP.

— A History of Europe. LC 99-159846. 832p. 1998. pap. 17.95 (0-14-026561-9) Viking Penguin.

— The Illustrated History of the World, 10 vols. (Illus.). 1920p. (YA). 2000. 275.00 (0-19-521529-X) OUP.

***Roberts, J. M.** The Illustrated History of the World, 11 vols. (Illus.). 1968p. (YA). 2000. text 290.00 (0-19-521698-9) OUP.

Roberts, J. M. The Illustrated History of the World: Eastern Asia & Classical Greece, 10 vols., Vol. 2. (Illus.). 192p. (YA). 2001. text 24.95 (0-19-521520-6) OUP.

— The Illustrated History of the World: Emerging Powers, 10 vols., Vol. 9. (Illus.). 192p. (YA). 2001. text 24.95 (0-19-521527-3) OUP.

— The Illustrated History of the World: Rome & the Classical West, 10 vols., Vol. 3. (Illus.). 192p. (YA). 2001. text 24.95 (0-19-521521-4) OUP.

— The Illustrated History of the World: The Age of Diverging Traditions, 10 vols., Vol. 4. (Illus.). 192p. (YA). 2001. text 24.95 (0-19-521522-2) OUP.

— The Illustrated History of the World: The Age of Revolution, 10 vols., Vol. 7. (Illus.). 192p. (YA). 2001. text 24.95 (0-19-521525-7) OUP.

— The Illustrated History of the World: The European Empires, 10 vols., Vol. 8. (Illus.). 192p. (YA). 2001. text 24.95 (0-19-521526-5) OUP.

— The Illustrated History of the World: The Far East & a New Europe, 10 vols., Vol. 5. (Illus.). 192p. (YA). 2001. text 24.95 (0-19-521523-0) OUP.

— The Illustrated History of the World: The Making of the European Age, 10 vols. , Vol. 6. (Illus.). 192p. (YA). 2001. text 24.95 (0-19-521524-9) OUP.

— The Illustrated History of the World: The New Global Era, 10 vols., Vol. 10. (Illus.). 192p. (YA). 2001. text 24.95 (0-19-521528-1) OUP.

***Roberts, J. M.** The Illustrated History of the World Vol. 11, 10 vols. 48p. (YA). 2000. text 16.95 (0-19-521697-0) OUP.

Roberts, J. M. The Illustrated History of the World Volume 1: Prehistory & the First Civilizations, 10 vols. (Illus.). 192p. (YA). 2001. text 24.95 (0-19-521519-2) OUP.

— The Penguin History of the World. rev. ed. (Illus.). 1152p. 1995. pap. 17.95 (0-14-015495-7, Penguin Bks) Viking Penguin.

— Shorter Illustrated History of the World. 616p. Date not set. pap. write for info. (1-85986-053-2) OUP.

— The Twentieth Century: The History of the World, 1901 to 2000. LC 99-41833. 857p. 1999. 39.95 (0-670-88456-1, Viking) Viking Penguin.

***Roberts, J. M.** Twentieth Century: The History of the World, 1901-2000. (Illus.). 2000. pap. 18.00 (0-14-029656-5) Penguin Putnam.

Roberts, J. M., ed. History of the World. (Illus.). 992p. 1993. 49.95 (0-19-521043-3) OUP.

Roberts, J. M., jt. auth. see Miller, Patrick D.

***Roberts, J. R.** Ambush at Black Rock. (Gunsmith Ser.: Vol. 217). 2000. mass mkt. 4.99 (0-515-12735-3, Jove) Berkley Pub.

Roberts, J. R. Ambush Moon. (Gunsmith Ser.: No. 148). 192p. (Orig.). 1994. mass mkt. 3.99 (0-515-11358-1, Jove) Berkley Pub.

— Apache Raid. (Gunsmith Ser.: Vol. 197). 1998. mass mkt. 4.99 (0-515-12293-9, Jove) Berkley Pub.

***Roberts, J. R.** Barnum & Bullets, (Gunsmith Ser.: Vol. 5). 2000. mass mkt. 5.99 (0-515-12908-9, Jove) Berkley Pub.

— Baron of Crime. (Gunsmith Ser.: Vol. 223). 2000. mass mkt. 4.99 (0-515-12873-2, Jove) Berkley Pub.

— Borton Family Gang, Vol. 214. 1999. mass mkt. 4.99 (0-515-12661-6, Jove) Berkley Pub.

— Brothel Inspector. (Gunsmith Ser.: Vol. 219). 2000. mass mkt. 4.99 (0-515-12771-X, Jove) Berkley Pub.

Roberts, J. R. Buried Pleasures. (Gunsmith Ser.: No. 117). 1996. mass mkt. 4.99 (0-515-11943-1, Jove) Berkley Pub.

— The Caliente Gold Robbery. (Gunsmith Ser.: No. 128). 192p. (Orig.). 1992. mass mkt. 3.99 (0-515-10903-7, Jove) Berkley Pub.

— The Challenge. (Gunsmith Ser.: No. 181). 192p. (Orig.). 1997. mass mkt. 4.99 (0-614-17459-7, Jove) Berkley Pub.

— Challenge, Vol. 181. (Gunsmith Ser.: No. 181). 192p. 1997. mass mkt. 4.99 (0-515-11999-7, Jove) Berkley Pub.

— Chinatown Assassin. (Gunsmith Ser.: No. 180). 192p. 1996. mass mkt. 4.99 (0-515-11984-9, Jove) Berkley Pub.

***Roberts, J. R.** The Cleveland Connection, 218. (Gunsmith Ser.: No. 218). 2000. mass mkt. 4.99 (0-515-12756-6, Jove) Berkley Pub.

Roberts, J. R. The Counterfeit Clergyman. (Gunsmith Ser.: Vol. 196). 1998. mass mkt. 4.99 (0-515-12279-3, Jove) Berkley Pub.

— Criminal Kin. (Gunsmith Ser.: Vol. 195). 1998. mass mkt. 4.99 (0-515-12266-1, Jove) Berkley Pub.

— Dakota Guns. (Gunsmith Ser.: No. 156). 192p. (Orig.). 1994. mass mkt. 3.99 (0-515-11507-X, Jove) Berkley Pub.

***Roberts, J. R.** Dangerous Breed. (Gunsmith Ser.: Vol. 221). 192p. 2000. mass mkt. 4.99 (0-515-12809-0) Berkley Pub.

— Dead Horse Canyon. (Gunsmith Ser.: Vol. 224). 2000. mass mkt. 4.99 (0-515-12891-0) Berkley Pub.

Roberts, J. R. Dead Man's Bluff, Vol. 203. (Gunsmith Ser.). 1998. mass mkt. 4.99 (0-515-12414-1, Jove) Berkley Pub.

Roberts, J R. Death Times Five, 1 vol., Vol. 209. (Gunsmith Ser.). 1999. mass mkt. 4.99 (0-515-12520-2, Jove) Berkley Pub.

Roberts, J. R. Denver Desperadoes. (Gunsmith Ser.). 1998. mass mkt. 4.99 (0-515-12341-2, Jove) Berkley Pub.

***Roberts, J. R.** End of the Trail. (Gunsmith Ser.: Vol. 220). 2000. mass mkt. 4.99 (0-515-12791-4, Jove) Berkley Pub.

***Roberts, J R.** Family Feud, , Vol. 212. 1999. mass mkt. 4.99 (0-515-12573-3, Jove) Berkley Pub.

Roberts, J. R. The Flying Machine. (Gunsmith Ser.: No. 183). 192p. 1997. mass mkt. 4.99 (0-515-12032-4, Jove) Berkley Pub.

— The Gambler, Vol. 201. (Gunsmith Ser.: No. 201). 192p. 1998. pap. 4.99 (0-515-12373-0, Jove) Berkley Pub.

— Gambler's Girl, 1 vol., Vol. 205. (Gunsmith Ser.). 1999. mass mkt. 4.99 (0-515-12451-6, Jove) Berkley Pub.

— Golden Gate Killers. (Gunsmith Ser.: No. 129). 192p. (Orig.). 1992. mass mkt. 3.99 (0-515-10931-2, Jove) Berkley Pub.

— Gunquick. (Gunsmith Ser.: No. 174). 192p. 1996. mass mkt. 4.99 (0-515-11880-X, Jove) Berkley Pub.

— The Gunsmith: Champion with a Gun. (Gunsmith Ser.: No. 151). 192p. (Orig.). 1994. mass mkt. 3.99 (0-515-11409-X, Jove) Berkley Pub.

— The Gunsmith: Ghost Town. unabridged ed. 1993. pap. 12.95 incl. audio (1-882071-41-7) B&B Audio.

— The Gunsmith: Hands of the Strangler. unabridged ed. 1993. pap. 12.95 incl. audio (1-882071-40-9) B&B Audio.

— The Gunsmith: Legbreakers & Heartbreakers. (Gunsmith Ser.). 192p. 1997. mass mkt. 4.99 (0-515-12105-3, Jove) Berkley Pub.

— The Gunsmith: Night of the Wolf. (Gunsmith Ser.: No. 150). 192p. (Orig.). 1994. mass mkt. 3.99 (0-515-11393-X, Jove) Berkley Pub.

— The Gunsmith: Spanish Gold. (Gunsmith Ser.: No. 149). 192p. (Orig.). 1994. mass mkt. 3.99 (0-515-11377-8, Jove) Berkley Pub.

— The Gunsmith: The Orient Express, Vol. 188. (Gunsmith Ser.). 192p. 1997. mass mkt. 4.99 (0-515-12133-9, Jove) Berkley Pub.

— The Gunsmith No. 154: Orphan Train, No. 154. 192p. (Orig.). 1994. mass mkt. 3.99 (0-515-11478-2, Jove) Berkley Pub.

— The Gunsmith No. 158: The Ransom. 192p. (Orig.). 1995. mass mkt. 3.99 (0-515-11553-3, Jove) Berkley Pub.

— The Gunsmith No. 159: The Huntsville Trip. 192p. (Orig.). 1995. mass mkt. 3.99 (0-515-11571-1, Jove) Berkley Pub.

— The Gunsmith No. 163: The Wild Women of Glitter Gulch. 192p. (Orig.). 1995. mass mkt. 3.99 (0-515-11656-4, Jove) Berkley Pub.

— The Gunsmith No. 170: The Elliott Bay Murder. 192p. (Orig.). 1996. mass mkt. 4.50 (0-515-11918-0, Jove) Berkley Pub.

— The Gunsmith No. 184: Homestead Law. (Gunsmith Ser.: No. 184). 192p. 1997. mass mkt. 4.99 (0-515-12051-0, Jove) Berkley Pub.

— The Gunsmith No. 185: The Biloxi Queen, Vol. 185. (Gunsmith Ser.). 192p. 1997. mass mkt. 4.99 (0-515-12071-5, Jove) Berkley Pub.

— The Gunsmith No. 186: Six for the Money. (Gunsmith Ser.). 192p. 1997. mass mkt. 4.99 (0-515-12082-0, Jove) Berkley Pub.

— The Gunsmith No. 189: The Posse from Elsinore. 192p. 1997. mass mkt. 4.99 (0-515-12145-2, Jove) Berkley Pub.

— The Gunsmith No. 190: Lady on the Run. 192p. 1997. mass mkt. 4.99 (0-515-12163-0, Jove) Berkley Pub.

— The Gunsmith No. 191: Outbreak. 192p. 1997. mass mkt. 4.99 (0-515-12179-7, Jove) Berkley Pub.

— The Gunsmith No. 193. 192p. 1998. mass mkt. 4.99 (0-515-12231-9, Jove) Berkley Pub.

— The Gunsmith No. 206: Legend of the Piasa Bird. (Gunsmith Ser.: 206). 192p. 1999. mass mkt. 4.99 (0-515-12469-9, Jove) Berkley Pub.

— The Gunsmith No. 207: Kansas City Killing. 192p. 1999. 4.99 (0-515-12486-9, Jove) Berkley Pub.

An Asterisk (*) at the beginning of an entry indicates that the title is appearing for the first time.

— Gunsmith Vol. 173: Jersey Lily. 192p. 1996. mass mkt. 4.99 (*0-515-11862-1*, Jove) Berkley Pub.
— Gunsmith Giant: Life & Times of Clint Adams, No. 2. 288p. (Orig.). 1995. mass mkt. 4.99 (*0-515-11728-5*, Jove) Berkley Pub.
— Gunsmith Giant Edition, No. 1: Trouble in Tombstone. 1993. mass mkt. 4.50 (*0-515-11212-7*, Jove) Berkley Pub.
— Gunsmith Massacre at Rock Springs. (Gunsmith Ser.). 1998. mass mkt. 4.99 (*0-515-12245-9*, Jove) Berkley Pub.
— Gunsmith, No. 1: Macklin's Women. 192p. 1988. mass mkt. 3.99 (*0-515-10145-1*, Jove) Berkley Pub.
— Gunsmith, No. 121: The Deadly Derringer. 192p. 1992. mass mkt. 3.50 (*0-515-10755-7*, Jove) Berkley Pub.
— Gunsmith, No. 139: Vigilante Hunt. 192p. (Orig.). 1993. mass mkt. 3.99 (*0-515-11138-4*, Jove) Berkley Pub.
— Gunsmith, No. 141: Gambler's Blood. 192p. (Orig.). 1993. mass mkt. 3.99 (*0-515-11196-1*, Jove) Berkley Pub.
— Gunsmith, No. 142: Wyoming Justice. 192p. 1993. mass mkt. 3.99 (*0-515-11218-6*, Jove) Berkley Pub.
— Gunsmith, No. 145: Gillett's Rangers. LC 94-130939. 192p. 1994. mass mkt. 3.99 (*0-515-11285-2*, Jove) Berkley Pub.
— The Gunsmith #200: The James Boys. (Gunsmith Ser.: Vol. 200). 181p. 1998. mass mkt. 4.99 (*0-515-12357-9*, Jove) Berkley Pub.
***Roberts, J. R.** Justice in Rimfire, (Gunsmith Ser.: Vol. 225). 192p. 2000. mass mkt. 4.99 (*0-515-12911-9*, Jove) Berkley Pub.
Roberts, J. R. Lady Killers. (Gunsmith Ser.: Vol. 198). 1998. mass mkt. 4.99 (*0-515-12303-X*, Jove) Berkley Pub.
— Last Bounty. (Gunsmith Ser.: No. 135). 192p. (Orig.). 1993. pap. 3.99 (*0-515-11063-9*, Jove) Berkley Pub.
***Roberts, J. R.** Last Bounty, 1 vol., Vol. 208. (Gunsmith Ser.). (Orig.). 1999. mass mkt. 4.99 (*0-515-12512-1*, Jove) Berkley Pub.
Roberts, J. R. The Last Great Scout. (Gunsmith Ser.: No. 162). 192p. (Orig.). 1995. mass mkt. 3.99 (*0-515-11635-1*, Jove) Berkley Pub.
***Roberts, J. R.** Lynched Man. (Gunsmith Ser.: Vol. 222). 192p. 2000. mass mkt. 4.99 (*0-515-12840-6*, Jove) Berkley Pub.
Roberts, J. R. The Magician. (Gunsmith Ser.: No. 155). 192p. (Orig.). 1994. mass mkt. 3.99 (*0-515-11495-2*, Jove) Berkley Pub.
***Roberts, J R.** Man from Peculiar, Vol. 216. (Gunsmith Ser.). 1999. mass mkt. 4.99 (*0-515-12708-6*, Jove) Berkley Pub.
Roberts, J. R. Maximilion's Treasure, 209. (Gunsmith Ser.). 1999. mass mkt. 4.99 (*0-515-12534-2*, Jove) Berkley Pub.
— Money Town. (Gunsmith Ser.: No. 192). 192p. 1997. mass mkt. 4.99 (*0-515-12192-4*, Jove) Berkley Pub.
— Outlaw Women. (Gunsmith Ser.: No. 134). 192p. (Orig.). 1993. mass mkt. 3.99 (*0-515-11045-0*, Jove) Berkley Pub.
— The Queensville Temptress. (Gunsmith Ser.: No. 179). 192p. 1996. mass mkt. 4.99 (*0-515-11969-5*, Jove) Berkley Pub.
— Return to Deadwood. (Gunsmith Ser.: No. 146). 192p. (Orig.). 1994. pap. 3.99 (*0-515-11315-8*, Jove) Berkley Pub.
— The Road to Testimony. (Gunsmith Ser.: No. 130). 192p. (Orig.). 1992. mass mkt. 3.99 (*0-515-10957-6*, Jove) Berkley Pub.
— Seminole Vengeance. (Gunsmith Ser.: No. 157). 192p. (Orig.). 1995. mass mkt. 3.99 (*0-515-11530-4*, Jove) Berkley Pub.
***Roberts, J R.** Showdown at Daylight, 215. 1999. mass mkt. 4.99 (*0-515-12688-8*, Jove) Berkley Pub.
Roberts, J. R. Showdown at Little Misery No. 3. (Gunsmith Ser.). 256p. 1998. mass mkt. 5.99 (*0-515-12210-6*, Jove) Berkley Pub.
— Son of a Gunsmith, 211. (Gunsmith Ser.). 1999. mass mkt. 4.99 (*0-515-12557-1*, Jove) Berkley Pub.
Roberts, J R. Strangler's Vendetta, Vol. 213. (Gunsmith Ser.). 1999. mass mkt. 4.99 (*0-515-12615-2*, Jove) Berkley Pub.
Roberts, J. R., Jr. Triple Cross. (Gunsmith Ser.: No. 176). 192p. 1996. mass mkt. 4.99 (*0-515-11926-1*, Jove) Berkley Pub.
Roberts, J. R. Vigilante Justice. (Gunsmith Ser.: No. 202). 192p. 1998. pap. 4.99 (*0-515-12393-5*, Jove) Berkley Pub.
***Roberts, J. R.** Wanted: Clint Adams. (Gunsmith Ser.: Vol. 226). 2000. mass mkt. 4.99 (*0-515-12933-X*, Jove) Berkley Pub.
Roberts, J. R. Wild Bull, Vol. 178. (Gunsmith Ser.: No. 178). 1996. mass mkt. 4.99 (*0-515-11957-1*, Jove) Berkley Pub.
— Winning Streak. (Gunsmith Ser.: No. 182). 192p. 1997. mass mkt. 4.99 (*0-515-12017-0*, Jove) Berkley Pub.
— Women on the Run, 204. (Gunsmith Ser.: Vol. 204). 186p. 1999. mass mkt. 4.99 (*0-515-12438-9*, Jove) Berkley Pub.
Roberts, J. S., pseud. 1933: The Devil Comes to Henry County. limited ed. Long, Robert, ed. (Illus.). 571p. 1989. 29.95 (*0-938650-48-3*) Thinkers Pr.
Roberts, J. T. Two French Language Teaching Reformers Reassessed-Claude Marcel & Francois Gouin. LC 99-26218. (Studies in Linguistics & Semiotics: Vol. 2). 196p. 1999. text 79.95 (*0-7734-7988-0*) E Mellen.
Roberts, J. T., ed. Structural Materials in Nuclear Power Systems. LC 81-1883. (Modern Perspectives in Energy Ser.). 500p. 1981. 89.50 (*0-306-40669-1*, Plenum Trade) Perseus Pubng.
***Roberts, J. Timmons & Hite, Amy, eds.** From Modernization to Globalization: Perspectives on Development & Social Change. LC 99-16942. (Readers in Sociology Ser.). 400p. 1999. text 62.95 (*0-631-21096-2*); pap. text 27.95 (*0-631-21097-0*) Blackwell Pubs.
Roberts, J. W. The Letter of James. LC 76-51637. 1984. 12.95 (*0-915547-35-X*) Abilene Christ U.
— The Letters of John. 1984. 12.95 (*0-915547-37-6*) Abilene Christ U.
— Looking Within: The Misleading Tendencies of Looking Backward Made Manifest. LC 78-154459. (Utopian Literature Ser.). 1976. reprint ed. 24.95 (*0-405-03541-1*) Ayer.
— Richard Boleslavsky: His Life & Work in the Theatre. LC 81-16411. (Theater & Dramatic Studies: No. 7). (Illus.). 298p. reprint ed. pap. 92.40 (*0-8357-1250-8*, 207027900065) Bks Demand.
Roberts, J. W., et al. Unto Us a Child Is Born. 126p. (Orig.). 1982. pap. 2.95 (*0-88027-109-4*) Firm Foun Pub.
Roberts, Jack. Construction Surveying: Layout & Dimension Control. LC 94-28591. 372p. (C). 1994. pap. 72.95 (*0-8273-5723-0*) Delmar.
— Nelson Mandela: Determined to Be Free. LC 94-21519. (Gateway Biographies Ser.). (Illus.). 48p. (J). (gr. 2-4). 1994. lib. bdg. 21.90 (*1-56294-558-0*) Millbrook Pr.
***Roberts, Jack L.** Garth Brooks. LC 99-31951. (People in the News Ser.). (Illus.). 144p. (YA). (gr. 6-9). 2000. lib. bdg. 23.70 (*1-56006-549-4*) Lucent Bks.
Roberts, Jack L. Oskar Schindler. LC 95-11712. (Importance of Ser.). (Illus.). 112p. (YA). (gr. 7 up). 1996. lib. bdg. 22.45 (*1-56006-079-4*) Lucent Bks.
— Ruth Bader Ginsburg: Supreme Court Justice. LC 93-39015. (Gateway Biographies Ser.). (Illus.). 48p. (J). (gr. 2-4). 1994. pap. 6.95 (*1-56294-744-3*) Millbrook Pr.
— Ruth Bader Ginsburg: Supreme Court Justice. (Gateway Biography Ser.). 1994. 12.15 (*0-606-12502-7*, Pub. by Turtleback) Demco.
Roberts, Jackie, ed. see Rose, Tui.
***Roberts-Jackson, Sheila.** Christina. LC 99-63205. 112p. 2000. pap. 12.95 (*1-56167-543-1*, Five Star Spec Ed) Am Literary Pr.
Roberts, Jacqueline A., et al. CITES Orchid Checklist for the Genera Cattleya, Cypripedium, Laelia, Paphiopedilum, Phalaenopsis, Phragmipedium, Pleione & Sophronitis, & Including Accounts of Constantia, Paraphalaenopsis & Sophronitella. viii, 136p. 1995. pap. 20.00 (*0-947643-87-7*, Pub. by Royal Botnic Grdns) Balogh.
Roberts, James. Bud's Easy How to Take Notes in Class & from Textbooks. 75p. pap. 7.00 (*1-891707-00-0*) Lawrence Hse.
— Curious Creatures Bats. 1997. pap. 12.43 (*0-7609-0123-6*) Curriculum MA.
— Curious Creatures Spiders. 1997. pap. 12.43 (*0-7609-0120-1*) Curriculum MA.
— Curious Creatures Wolves. 1997. pap. text 12.43 (*0-7609-0121-X*) Curriculum MA.
***Roberts, James.** How to Take Great Notes in Class & from Textbooks. 2nd rev. ed. 50p. (gr. 7 up). 1999. pap. 7.00 (*1-891707-03-5*) Lawrence Hse.
Roberts, James. The Revelation of John. LC 73-20857. 1984. 12.95 (*0-915547-38-4*) Abilene Christ U.
Roberts, James, et al. Broadband Network Teletraffic: Performance Evaluation & Design of Broadband Multiservice Networks: Final Report of Action Cost 242, Vol. 115. LC 96-41833. (Lecture Notes in Computer Science Ser.). xxii, 584p. 1996. pap. 94.00 (*3-540-61815-5*) Spr-Verlag.
Roberts, James, tr. see Bouquiaux, Luc & Thomas, Jacqueline M.
Roberts, James A. Just What Is EIR? 1991. write for info. (*0-9630515-0-4*) Global Env Mgmt.
Roberts, James A., ed. New York in the Revolution As Colony & State: These Records Were Discovered, Arranged & Classified 1895, 1896-1897 & 1898. 534p. 1993. reprint ed. lib. bdg. 53.50 (*1-56012-127-0*, 124) Kinship Rhinebeck.
Roberts, James A. & Mather, Frederick G. New York in the Revolution: As Colony & State, 2 vols. in 1. (Illus.). 900p. 1996. reprint ed. 60.00 (*0-8063-1489-3*) Genealog Pub.
Roberts, James D. Black Theology Today: Liberation & Contextualization. LC 83-17246. (Toronto Studies in Theology: Vol. 12). 218p. 1984. lib. bdg. 99.95 (*0-88946-755-2*) E Mellen.
— Liberation & Reconciliation: A Black Theology. rev. ed. LC 93-38133. 141p. reprint ed. pap. 43.80 (*0-608-20270-3*, 207152900012) Bks Demand.
Roberts, James L. Absalom, Absalom! Notes. (Cliffs Notes Ser.). 64p. 1964. pap. 4.95 (*0-8220-0110-1*, Cliff) IDG Bks.
— The Adventures of Huckleberry Finn Notes. (Cliffs Notes Ser.). 80p. 1971. pap. 4.95 (*0-8220-0606-5*, Cliff) IDG Bks.
— The American Notes. (Cliffs Notes Ser.). 80p. (Orig.). 1965. pap. 4.50 (*0-8220-0164-0*, Cliff) IDG Bks.
— As I Lay Dying Notes. (Cliffs Notes Ser.). 72p. 1964. pap. 4.95 (*0-8220-0210-8*, Cliff) IDG Bks.
— The Bear Notes. (Cliffs Notes Ser.). 88p. (Orig.). 1986. pap. text 4.95 (*0-8220-0222-1*, Cliff) IDG Bks.
— Crime & Punishment Notes. (Cliffs Notes Ser.). 88p. 1963. pap. 4.95 (*0-8220-0328-7*, Cliff) IDG Bks.
— Daisy Miller & the Turn of the Screw Notes. (Cliffs Notes Ser.). 64p. 1965. pap. 4.95 (*0-8220-0355-4*, Cliff) IDG Bks.
— Death of a Salesman Notes. (Cliffs Notes Ser.). 72p. 1964. pap. 4.95 (*0-8220-0382-1*, Cliff) IDG Bks.
— Dr. Jekyll & Mr. Hyde Notes. (Cliffs Notes Ser.). 64p. (Orig.). (C). 1984. pap. 4.95 (*0-8220-0408-9*, Cliff) IDG Bks.
— A Farewell to Arms, Notes. (Cliffs Notes Ser.). 64p. 1964. pap. 4.95 (*0-8220-0461-5*, Cliff) IDG Bks.
— Faulkner's Short Stories Notes. (Cliffs Notes Ser.). 72p. 1998. pap. text 4.95 (*0-8220-0477-1*, Cliff) IDG Bks.
— The Glass Menagerie & a Streetcar Named Desire Notes. (Cliffs Notes Ser.). 88p. 1965. pap. 4.95 (*0-8220-0533-6*, Cliff) IDG Bks.
— Go Down, Moses Notes. (Cliffs Notes Ser.). 104p. (Orig.). (C). 1985. pap. text 4.95 (*0-8220-0537-9*, Cliff) IDG Bks.
— The Grapes of Wrath Notes. (Cliffs Notes Ser.). 80p. 1965. pap. 4.95 (*0-8220-0542-5*, Cliff) IDG Bks.
***Roberts, James L.** Hemingway's Short Stories. (Cliffs Notes Ser.). 96p. 2000. pap. 4.95 (*0-7645-8552-5*) IDG Bks.
Roberts, James L. Light in August Notes. (Cliffs Notes Ser.). 72p. 1964. pap. 4.95 (*0-8220-0744-4*, Cliff) IDG Bks.
— Madame Bovary Notes. (Cliffs Notes Ser.). 80p. 1964. pap. 4.95 (*0-8220-0780-0*, Cliff) IDG Bks.
— Moby Dick, Notes. (Cliffs Notes Ser.). 104p. 1961. pap. 4.95 (*0-8220-0852-1*, Cliff) IDG Bks.
— Notes from the Underground Notes. (Cliffs Notes Ser.). 72p. 1970. pap. 4.95 (*0-8220-0900-5*, Cliff) IDG Bks.
— Of Mice & Men Notes. (Cliffs Notes Ser.). 56p. 1966. pap. 4.95 (*0-8220-0939-0*, Cliff) IDG Bks.
— Portrait of a Lady Notes. (Cliffs Notes Ser.). 80p. 1965. pap. 4.95 (*0-8220-1066-6*, Cliff) IDG Bks.
— Sound & the Fury Notes. (Cliffs Notes Ser.). 72p. 1963. pap. 4.95 (*0-8220-1219-7*, Cliff) IDG Bks.
— Three Musketeers Notes. (Cliffs Notes Ser.). 88p. (Orig.). 1989. pap. text 4.95 (*0-8220-1300-2*, Cliff) IDG Bks.
— The Unvanquished Notes. (Cliffs Notes Ser.). 88p. (Orig.). (C). 1980. pap. text 4.95 (*0-8220-1316-9*, Cliff) IDG Bks.
Roberts, James L., jt. auth. see Allen, L. David.
Roberts, James L., jt. auth. see Calandra, Denis M.
Roberts, James L., jt. auth. see Fisher, Jeffrey.
Roberts, James L., jt. auth. see Inness, Jeanne.
***Roberts, James P.** Bourland. (Other Door -- Science Fiction -- Macabre Ser.). 268p. 1999. 30.00 (*1-55246-162-9*); pap. 18.00 (*1-55246-163-7*) Battered Silicon.
Roberts, James R. & Hedges, Jerrie R. Clinical Procedures in Emergency Medicine. 3rd ed. Fletcher, Judy, ed. LC 96-37054. (Illus.). 1184p. 1997. text 150.00 (*0-7216-6055-X*, W B Saunders Co) Harcrt Hlth Sci Grp.
Roberts, James R. & Skutt, Alexander G. The Boxing Register: International Boxing Hall of Fame Official Record Book. 2nd rev. ed. LC 98-23771. (Illus.). 528p. 1998. pap. 22.95 (*0-935526-46-3*) McBooks Pr.
Roberts, James T., ed. Clinical Management of the Airway. LC 93-12115. (Illus.). 512p. 1994. text 84.00 (*0-7216-3670-5*, W B Saunders Co) Harcrt Hlth Sci Grp.
Roberts, Jan. Beverly Hills International Party Planner. 1994. 29.95 (*0-9634398-9-8*); pap. 19.95 (*0-9634398-4-7*) J Roberts Pubns.
Roberts, Jan, jt. auth. see Roberts, George.
Roberts, Jan B., ed. Godefroi de Buillon, Vol. X. LC 95-264456. (Old French Crusade Cycle Ser.). (FRE.). 176p. 1996. text 29.95 (*0-8173-0855-5*) U of Ala Pr.
Roberts, Jane. Adventures in Consciousness. 1994. lib. bdg. 24.95 (*1-56849-496-3*) Buccaneer Bks.
— Adventures in Consciousness: An Introduction to Aspect Psychology. 1978. 7.95 (*0-13-013953-X*) P-H.
— Adventures in Consciousness: An Introduction to Aspect Psychology. LC 97-10325. 1997. pap. write for info. (*1-889828-00-9*) SethNet Pub.
— Adventures in Consciousness: An Introduction to Aspect Psychology. 2nd ed. (Illus.). 276p. 1999. pap. 14.95 (*0-9661327-3-4*, Pub. by Moment Pt Pr) ACCESS Pubs Network.
— The Coming of Seth. (Orig.). 1993. reprint ed. lib. bdg. 29.95 (*1-56849-243-X*) Buccaneer Bks.
— Dialogues of the Soul & Mortal Self in Time. 1979. pap. 4.95 (*0-685-03831-9*) P-H.
Roberts, Jane. Dreams, Evolution & Value Fulfillment Vol. 1: A Seth Book, Vol. 1. LC 97-11965. 288p. 1997. pap. 17.95 (*1-878424-27-0*) Amber-Allen Pub.
Roberts, Jane. Dreams, Evolution & Value Fulfillment Vol. 2: A Seth Book, Vol. 2. LC 97-11965. 272p. 1997. pap. 16.95 (*1-878424-28-9*) Amber-Allen Pub.
***Roberts, Jane.** Emir's Education in the Proper Use of Magical Powers. (Illus.). 144p. (YA). (gr. 3 up). 2000. pap. 12.95 (*1-57174-142-9*) Hampton Roads Pub Co.
— Fell's Official Know-It-All Guide to ESP Power. (Illus.). 224p. 2000. pap. 16.95 (*0-88391-016-0*) F Fell Pubs Inc.
Roberts, Jane. The Further Education of Oversoul Seven. 198p. 1984. pap. 6.95 (*0-685-07788-8*) P-H.
***Roberts, Jane.** The God of Jane: A Psychic Manifesto. 2nd ed. LC 99-59125. 264p. 2000. pap. 15.95 (*0-9661327-5-0*) Moment Pt Pr.
Roberts, Jane. The Individual & the Nature of Mass Events. (Seth Bk.). 336p. (Orig.). 1995. reprint ed. pap. 16.95 (*1-878424-21-1*) Amber-Allen Pub.
— The Magical Approach: Seth Speaks about the Art of Creative Living. (Seth Bk.). 192p. 1995. pap. 12.95 (*1-878424-09-2*) Amber-Allen Pub.
— The Nature of Personal Reality. 1993. reprint ed. lib. bdg. 21.95 (*1-56849-244-8*) Buccaneer Bks.
— The Nature of Personal Reality: Specific, Practical Techniques for Solving Everyday Problems & Enriching the Life You Know. LC 94-10677. (Seth Bk.). 480p. 1994. reprint ed. pap. 17.95 (*1-878424-06-8*) Amber-Allen Pub.
— The Nature of the Psyche: Its Human Expression. (Seth Bk.). 256p. 1996. reprint ed. pap. 15.95 (*1-878424-22-X*) Amber-Allen Pub.
— The Oversoul Seven Trilogy: The Education of Oversoul Seven; The Further Education of Oversoul Seven; Oversoul Seven & the Museum of Time. 560p. 1995. pap. 19.95 (*1-878424-17-3*) Amber-Allen Pub.
***Roberts, Jane.** Psychic Politics: An Aspect Psychology Book. LC 99-48400. (Classics in Consciousness Ser.). 336p. 1999. pap. 15.95 (*0-9661327-4-2*, Pub. by Moment Pt Pr) ACCESS Pubs Network.
Roberts, Jane. Royal Landscape: The Royal Gardens & Parks of Windsor. LC 97-15718. 596p. 1997. 125.00 (*0-300-07079-9*) Yale U Pr.
— The Seth Material. 1995. reprint ed. lib. bdg. 35.95 (*1-56849-185-9*) Buccaneer Bks.
— Seth Speaks: The Eternal Validity of the Soul. LC 94-10678. (Seth Bk.). 480p. 1994. reprint ed. pap. 17.95 (*1-878424-07-6*) Amber-Allen Pub.
— The Unknown Reality Vol. I: A Seth Book, Vol. 1. 304p. (Orig.). 1996. reprint ed. pap. 17.95 (*1-878424-25-4*) Amber-Allen Pub.
— The Unknown Reality Vol. II: A Seth Book. 576p. 1996. reprint ed. pap. 19.95 (*1-878424-26-2*) Amber-Allen Pub.
— Views of Windsor: Watercolours by Thomas & Paul Sandby. LC 96-141564. (Illus.). 144p. 1995. 40.00 (*1-85894-020-6*, Pub. by Merrell Holberton) U of Wash Pr.
— The Way Toward Health: A Seth Book. LC 97-18255. 392p. (Orig.). 1997. pap. 17.95 (*1-878424-30-0*) Amber-Allen Pub.
— World View of Paul Cezanne. 1994. lib. bdg. 37.95 (*1-56849-495-5*) Buccaneer Bks.
Roberts, Jane, et al, eds. Alfred the Wise: Studies in Honor of Janet Bately on the Occasion of Her 65th Birthday. LC 96-38094. (Illus.). 304p. 1997. 90.00 (*0-85991-515-8*, DS Brewer) Boydell & Brewer.
Roberts, Jane & Roberts, Richard. A Seth Reader. 339p. (Orig.). 1993. pap. 15.95 (*0-942380-15-0*) Vernal Equinox.
***Roberts, Jane & Sylvester, Louise, eds.** Middle English Word Studies: A Word & Author Index. 240p. 2000. 60.00 (*0-85991-606-5*) Boydell & Brewer.
Roberts, Jane, et al. Privatising Electricity: The Politics of Power. 256p. 1991. text 55.00 (*1-85293-180-9*) St Martin.
Roberts, Jane, jt. ed. see Kraemer, Sebastian.
Roberts, Jane W., jt. auth. see Roberts, Kenneth D.
***Roberts, Jane Wright.** Homespun Poetry from the Mountains of North Caroline. (Illus.). 88p. 1999. pap. 9.95 (*1-893651-04-5*) Fern Creek Pr.
Roberts, Janet H., jt. auth. see Kitts, Jennifer.
Roberts, Janet Hatcher & Vlassoff, Carol. The Female Client & the Health-Care Provider. LC 97-702861. 172p. 1995. pap. 19.95 (*0-88936-773-6*, Pub. by IDRC Bks) Stylus Pub VA.
Roberts, Janet W., et al. City Kids & City Critters. (Illus.). 153p. (J). (gr. 3-8). 1996. pap. 15.95 (*0-07-053201-X*) McGraw.
Roberts, Janetta, ed. see Keller, Jan.
Roberts, Janette, jt. auth. see Naish, Francesca.
Roberts, Janice & Johnson, Joy. Thank You for Coming: A Book to Help Children Be a Part of the Funeral Rituals. (Illus.). 48p. 1994. pap. 5.95 (*1-56123-071-5*) Centering Corp.
Roberts, Janine. Tales & Transformation: Stories in Families & Family Therapy. 220p. (C). 1994. 27.00 (*0-393-70174-3*) Norton.
— Tales & Transformations: Stories in Families & Family Therapy. (Illus.). 230p. 1999. reprint ed. text 27.00 (*0-7881-6431-7*) DIANE Pub.
Roberts, Janine, jt. auth. see Imber-Black, Evan.
Roberts, Janret Hatcher, jt. auth. see Kitts, Jennifer.
Roberts, Jason. Director 6 Demystified: The Official Guide to Macromedia Director, Lingo, & Shockwave. LC 98-113421. 1136p. (C). 1997. pap. 49.95 incl. cd-rom (*0-201-68884-0*) Peachpit Pr.
Roberts, Jason, ed. Learn2 Guide: Burp a Baby, Carve a Turkey & 108 Other Things. LC 98-24550. 448p. 1999. pap. 17.95 (*0-375-75255-2*) Villard Books.
Roberts, Jason & Gross, Phil. Director Seven Demystified: The Official Guide to Macromedia Director, Lingo & Shockwave. 4th ed. (Illus.). 1200p. (C). 1999. pap. text 49.99 (*0-201-35445-4*) Peachpit Pr.
Roberts, Jason, jt. auth. see Gross, Phil.
Roberts, Jason C. How to Lose Your Ex-Wife (Financially) Forever: Gain Financial Freedom from Your Ex, Escape the Bondage of Excessive Child Support & Alimony. Jorgensen, Ron, ed. LC 90-61343. (Illus.). 182p. (Orig.). 1990. per. 17.95 (*0-922507-05-8*) Liberty UT.
Roberts, Jay, Jr., jt. ed. see Snyder, David L.
Roberts, Jean, tr. see Giono, Jean.
Roberts, Jeanie, jt. auth. see Roberts, Royston M.
Roberts, Jeanne A. The Shakespearean Wild: Geography, Genus & Gender. LC 90-13037. (Illus.). x, 214p. 1991. text 50.00 (*0-8032-3899-1*) U of Nebr Pr.
— The Shakespearean Wild: Geography, Genus & Gender. LC 90-13037. (Illus.). x, 214p. 1991. reprint ed. pap. text 14.00 (*0-8032-8950-2*, Bison Books) U of Nebr Pr.
— Shakespeare's English Comedy: "The Merry Wives of Windsor" in Context. LC 78-24239. 189p. 1979. reprint ed. pap. 58.60 (*0-608-03477-0*, 206418700008) Bks Demand.
Roberts, Jeanne A., jt. auth. see McManaway, James G.
Roberts, Jeff. How to be a Champion Through Faith Forgiveness Fellowship & Have the Power to Succeed. 218p. (Orig.). 1991. pap. 8.95 (*0-9628406-7-X*) Chrstian Pub Netwrk.
Roberts, Jeffrey D. You Too Can Have Fun in South Bend (And It's Neighbors) 79p. 1994. pap. 5.00 (*0-9649858-0-2*) Having Fun.
Roberts, Jeffrey W. Rattlesnake Pete. 50p. (Orig.). 1996. mass mkt. 2.99 (*0-9654318-0-0*) Atomic Wstrn.
Roberts, Jennifer, jt. tr. see Blanco, Walter.

R

R

Roberts, Jennifer D. Norman Bel Geddes: An Exhibition of Theatrical & Industrial Designs. (Illus.). 60p. 1979. pap. 10.00 (*0-87959-092-0*) U of Tex H Ransom Ctr.

Roberts, Jennifer T. Accountability in Athenian Government. LC 81-69827. (Wisconsin Studies in Classics). 283p. 1982. reprint ed. pap. 87.80 (*0-608-07445-4*, 206767200009) Bks Demand.

— Athens on Trial: The Antidemocratic Tradition in Western Thought. LC 93-24553. 432p. 1994. text 49.50 (*0-691-05697-8*, Pub. by Princeton U Pr); pap. text 16.95 (*0-691-02919-9*, Pub. by Princeton U Pr) Cal Prin Full Svc.

Roberts, Jennifer T., ed. The Peloponnesian War. Blanco, Walter, tr. LC 97-30006. (C). 1998. pap. 20.25 (*0-393-97167-8*) Norton.

Roberts, Jenny. Bible Places Then & Now. 1996. 35.00 (*0-614-21983-3*) Macmillan.

— Bible Then & Now. 144p. 1996. 29.95 (*0-02-861347-3*) Macmillan Info.

— Bibles Places Then & Now. 1996. 29.95 (*0-614-20420-8*) Macmillan USA.

— Introduction to the Bible. 1991. 12.98 (*1-55521-751-6*) Bk Sales Inc.

Roberts, Jeremy. Finger-Lickin' Strange. (Eerie Indiana Ser.: No. 10). 144p. (J). (gr. 3-7). 1998. pap. 3.99 (*0-380-79786-0*, Avon Bks) Morrow Avon.

***Roberts, Jeremy.** Joan of Arc. LC 99-33498. (A&E Biography Ser.). (Illus.). 128p. (YA). (gr. 6-12). 2000. 25.26 (*0-8225-4981-6*, Lerner Publctns) Lerner Pub.

— Joseph Goebbels. LC 00-26019. (Holocaust Biographies Ser.). 2000. write for info. (*0-8239-3309-1*) Rosen Group.

— King Arthur. LC 00-8875. (Illus.). (J). 2001. lib. bdg. write for info. (*0-8225-4891-7*) Lerner Pub.

— Oskar Schindler. LC 00-27846. (Holocaust Biographies Ser.). 2000. write for info. (*0-8239-3310-5*) Rosen Group.

Roberts, Jeremy A. & Tucker, Gregory A., eds. Plant Hormone Protocols. LC 99-58889. (Methods in Molecular Biology Ser.: Vol. 141). (Illus.). 216p. 2000. 69.50 (*0-89603-577-8*) Humana.

Roberts, Jeremy K. Differential Diagnosis in Neuropsychiatry. LC 83-23289. (Wiley Medical Publication). (Illus.). 397p. 1984. reprint ed. pap. 123.10 (*0-608-01633-0*, 206221800002) Bks Demand.

***Roberts, Jerry.** American Rain Forest Bibliography: An Annotated Guide to over 1600 Nonfiction Books about Central & South American Jungles. annot. ed. LC 99-26061. 320p. 1999. lib. bdg. 48.50 (*0-7864-0717-4*) McFarland & Co.

Roberts, Jerry. Robert Mitchum: A Bio-Bibliography, 32. LC 92-23784. (Bio-Bibliographies in the Performing Arts Ser.: No. 32). 448p. 1992. lib. bdg. 55.00 (*0-313-27547-5*, RRM, Greenwood Pr) Greenwood.

***Roberts, Jerry, ed.** Mitchum: In His Own Words. (Illus.). 240p. 2000. 28.95 (*0-87910-292-6*) Limelight Edns.

Roberts, Jerry & Gaydos, Steven, eds. Movie Talk from the Front Lines: Filmmakers Discuss Their Works with the Los Angeles Film Critics Association. LC 94-29998. (Illus.). 311p. 1995. lib. bdg. 39.95 (*0-7864-0005-6*) McFarland & Co.

Roberts, Jerry, jt. auth. see Marshall, John.

Roberts, Jessica F., jt. ed. see Spengemann, William C.

Roberts, Jill, ed. Pennsylvania German Fraktur & Printed Broadsides: A Guide to the Collections in the Library of Congress. LC 88-600044. 48p. 1988. 9.95 (*0-8444-0600-7*) Lib Congress.

Roberts, Jim. North Wales Transport. (Illus.). 160p. 1998. pap. 21.95 (*0-7509-1722-9*) Sutton Pub Ltd.

— Strutter's Complete Guide to Clown Make-up. LC 90-52814. (Illus.). 96p. 1991. pap. 24.00 (*0-941599-10-8*, Pub. by Piccadilly Bks) Empire Pub Srvs.

— Strutter's Complete Guide to Clown Makeup. LC 90-52814. (Illus.). (Orig.). 1991. 30.00 (*0-88734-607-3*) Players Pr.

Roberts, Jim, Jr. Warren County Running: An In-Depth Race History. (Illus.). 144p. (Orig.). 1995. pap. 13.00 (*0-9645729-2-3*, 500) J W Roberts.

Roberts, Jim, jt. auth. see Hitches, Mike.

Roberts, Jo. Internal Gravity Waves in the Ocean. LC 74-78969. (Marine Science Ser.: No. 2). (Illus.). 289p. reprint ed. pap. 89.60 (*0-7837-0773-8*, 204108700019) Bks Demand.

Roberts, Jo-Anna. Alligator & the Toothfairy. (Illus.). 56p. (J). (ps-2). 1991. 11.50 (*1-879212-00-5*) Desert Star Intl.

Roberts, Joan, jt. auth. see Hickman, Dwayne.

Roberts, Joan D. Caring for Those with Alzheimer's: A Pastoral Approach. LC 90-26574. 94p. (Orig.). 1991. pap. 4.95 (*0-8189-0593-X*) Alba.

Roberts, Joan I. Feminism & Nursing: An Historical Perspective on Power, Status, & Political Activism. LC 94-33756. 400p. 1995. pap. 27.95 (*0-275-95120-0*, Praeger Pubs) Greenwood.

Roberts, Joan I. & Group, Thetis M. Feminism & Nursing: An Historical Perspective on Power, Status & Political Activism. LC 94-33756. 400p. 1995. 75.00 (*0-275-94916-8*, Praeger Pubs) Greenwood.

Roberts, Joan L., jt. ed. see Harbert, Anita S.

Roberts, JoAnn. Art & Illusion Vol. 1: A Guide to Crossdressing: Face & Hair. 3rd ed. (Illus.). 40p. 1994. pap. 15.00 (*1-880715-05-8*) Creat Des Srvs.

— Art & Illusion Vol. 2: A Guide to Crossdressing: Fashion & Style. 3rd ed. (Illus.). 40p. 1994. pap. 15.00 (*1-880715-08-2*) Creat Des Srvs.

— Coping with Crossdressing. 2nd ed. 80p. (Orig.). 1992. pap. 12.00 (*1-880715-10-4*) Creat Des Srvs.

— Coping with Crossdressing. 3rd rev. ed. 84p. (Orig.). 1995. pap. 12.00 (*1-880715-12-0*) Creat Des Srvs.

Roberts, JoAnn, ed. see Van Maris, Delia.

Roberts, Joanne. Multinational Business Service Firms: The Development of Multinational Organization Structures in the U. K. Business Service Sector. LC 97-76945. (Illus.). 320p. 1998. text 67.95 (*1-84014-154-9*, Pub. by Ashgate Pub) Ashgate Pub Co.

Roberts, Joanne E., et al. Otitis Media in Young Children: Medical, Developmental & Educational Considerations. LC 96-42315. 1997. 48.95 (*1-55766-278-9*) P H Brookes.

Roberts, Jody, jt. auth. see Blank, Carla.

Roberts, John. Amele. 400p. 1987. 72.50 (*0-7099-4254-0*, Pub. by C Helm) Routldge.

— The Art of Interruption: Photography, Realism & the Everyday. LC 97-12650. (Photography, Critical Views Ser.). (Illus.). 208p. 1998. text 29.95 (*0-7190-3561-9*) Manchester Univ Pr.

— Battlecruisers. LC 98-135824. (Chatham Shipshape Ser.). (Illus.). 128p. 1998. 49.95 (*1-55750-068-1*) Naval Inst Pr.

— Caspian Pipelines. 60p. 1996. pap. text 12.95 (*1-899658-20-3*, Pub. by Royal Inst Intl Affairs) Brookings.

— City of Sokrates: Introduction to Classical Athens. 2nd ed. LC 97-32520. 320p. (C). 1998. pap. 25.99 (*0-415-16778-7*) Routledge.

— City of Sokrates: Introduction to Classical Athens. 2nd ed. LC 97-32520. (Illus.). 288p. (C). 1998. 75.00 (*0-415-16777-9*) Routledge.

— Collins Illustrated Dictionary of Trout Flies. (Illus.). 1998. 10.99 (*0-7858-0892-2*) Bk Sales Inc.

— A Guide to River Trout Flies. (Illus.). 240p. 1991. 45.00 (*1-85223-167-X*, Pub. by Crolwood) Trafalgar.

— The Gulf, Integration, & OPEC: Overseas Downstream Activities. 20p. 1988. pap. 10.00 (*0-918714-14-1*) Intl Res Ctr Energy.

— The Moth Comes to the Flame: Conversations Between Seekers & Sage. Lyons, Carol, ed. LC 98-92078. 368p. 1998. pap. 20.00 (*1-878682-03-2*) Roaring Lion Pub.

— The Moth Comes to the Flame Vol. 2: Conversations Between Seeker & Sage. Lyons, Carol, ed. LC 98-92155. 488p. 1998. pap. 25.00 (*1-878682-04-0*) Roaring Lion Pub.

— Noise Control in the Built Environment. 352p. 1989. text 86.95 (*0-566-09001-5*) Ashgate Pub Co.

— Ondina: A Narrative Poem. (Illus.). 136p. 1986. 18.00 (*0-9615617-0-X*); pap. 12.00 (*0-9615617-1-8*) Cloud Ridge Pr.

— OPEC & Non-OPEC Relations. 20p. 1989. pap. 10.00 (*0-918714-18-4*) Intl Res Ctr Energy.

— Reform & Retribution: An Illustrated History of American Prisons. LC 96-39441. (Illus.). 264p. 1997. 54.95 (*1-56991-054-5*) Am Correctional.

— The Team That Wouldn't Die. 224p. 1998. pap. 17.95 (*0-575-60270-8*, Pub. by V Gollancz) Trafalgar.

— To Rise a Trout. (Illus.). 224p. (Orig.). 1989. pap. 24.95 (*0-88317-151-1*) Stoeger Pub Co.

— Trailmen's Truce. large type ed. (Dales Large Print Ser.). 203p. 1997. pap. 18.99 (*1-85389-734-5*, Dales) Ulverscroft.

— The Unauthorized Grease Trivia Book. 1998. pap. text 12.95 (*1-888842-23-7*) J Robert Pub.

— Visions & Mirages: The Middle East in a New Era. LC 96-132516. (Illus.). 322p. 1996. 35.00 (*1-85158-429-3*, Pub. by Mainstream Pubng) Trafalgar.

— A War for Oil? Energy Issues & the Gulf War of 1991. 20p. 1991. pap. 10.00 (*0-918714-28-1*) Intl Res Ctr Energy.

— Warship, Vol. V. LC 78-55455. (Illus.). 288p. 1982. 41.95 (*0-87021-980-4*) Naval Inst Pr.

Roberts, John, ed. Art Has No History! Critical Essays on Contemporary Art. LC 94-4882. 288p. (C). 1994. pap. 19.00 (*0-86091-457-7*, Pub. by Verso) Norton.

— Escaping Prison Myths: Selected Topics in the History of Federal Corrections. LC 94-17502. 212p. (Orig.). 1994. lib. bdg. 69.50 (*1-879383-27-6*) Am Univ Pr.

Roberts, John, ed. Escaping Prison Myths: Selected Topics in the History of Federal Corrections. LC 94-17502. 212p. (Orig.). 1994. pap. text 31.50 (*1-879383-28-4*) Am Univ Pr.

Roberts, John, ed. Reinhard Keiser, Vol. 3. (Handel Sources Ser.). 372p. 1987. text 30.00 (*0-8240-6477-1*) Garland.

— Warship, Vol. III. LC 78-55455. (Illus.). 288p. 1981. 41.95 (*0-87021-977-4*) Naval Inst Pr.

— Warship, Vol. IV. LC 78-55455. (Illus.). 286p. 1981. 41.95 (*0-87021-979-0*) Naval Inst Pr.

— Warship, 1995. (Illus.). 256p. 1995. 41.95 (*0-85177-654-X*) Naval Inst Pr.

Roberts, John & Roberts, Nedra P. Excellence in English. (J). 1987. pap. text 12.00 (*0-8013-0134-3*; 75798) Longman.

Roberts, John & Roberts, Susan. Why Didn't I Think of That? 1,198 Hints from 222 Cruisers on 120 Boats from 9 Countries. LC 97-5422. 215p. 1997. pap. 19.95 (*0-07-053221-4*) McGraw.

— Why Didn't I Think of That? 1,198 Hints from 222 Cruisers on 120 Boats from 9 Countries. LC 97-5422. (Illus.). 224p. 1997. text 24.95 (*0-07-053222-2*) McGraw.

Roberts, John, jt. auth. see Milgrom, Paul.

Roberts, John A. The Fruit of Your Thoughts: Explore Mind, Money & Enlightenment. Jones, Josephine, ed. LC 96-93130. (Illus.). 256p. (Orig.). 1997. pap. 20.00 (*1-878682-02-4*) Roaring Lion Pub.

Roberts, John A., jt. auth. see Kirby, Ronald E.

Roberts, John B. & Spanos, P. D. Random Vibration & Statistical Linearization. LC 89-24807. (Illus.). 421p. 1990. reprint ed. pap. 130.60 (*0-608-05305-8*, 206584300001) Bks Demand.

Roberts, John C. World Citizenship & Mundialism. LC 98-25618. 176p. 1999. 55.00 (*0-275-96401-9*, Praeger Pubs) Greenwood.

***Roberts, John C. Q.** Speak Clearly into the Chandelier: Cultural Politics Between Britain & Russia. (Illus.). 316p. 2000. 49.95 (*0-7007-1296-8*, Pub. by Curzon Pr Ltd) Paul & Co Pubs.

Roberts, John D. The Right Place at the Right Time. (Illus.). 299p. 1990. text 36.00 (*0-8412-1766-1*, Pub. by Am Chemical) OUP.

Roberts, John G., jt. auth. see Davis, Glenn.

Roberts, John H. The Wesleyan Maori Mission in Te Upoko O Te Ika: Wellington District, 1839-1885 LC 93-187399. 95 p. 1992. write for info. (*0-473-01679-6*) The Bradbury Hse.

Roberts, John H., ed. Gasparini & Porta. (Handel Sources Ser.). 264p. 1987. text 30.00 (*0-8240-6478-X*) Garland.

Roberts, John H., et al, eds. Duke Mathematical Journal: Index 1-22. 60p. 1957. pap. text 10.00 (*0-8223-0629-8*) Duke.

Roberts, John J. As I Did See. (Illus.). 80p. 1997. pap. 9.00 (*0-8059-4026-X*) Dorrance.

***Roberts, John L.** Clan, King & Covenant: The History of the Highland Clans from the Civil War to the Glencoe Massacre. 272p. 2000. pap. text 23.00 (*0-7486-1393-5*) Col U Pr.

— Feuds, Forays & Rebellions: History of the Higland Clans, 1475-1625. 256p. 1999. pap. text 27.00 (*0-7486-1250-5*, Pub. by Edinburgh U Pr) Col U Pr.

— Highland Geology Trail. 120p. 2000. pap. 9.95 (*0-946487-36-7*) Luath Pr Ltd.

Roberts, John L. The Macmillan Field Guide to Geological Structures. (Illus.). 256p. 1996. reprint ed. pap. 29.50 (*0-333-66295-4*, Pub. by Macmillan) Trans-Atl Phila.

Roberts, John M. Cloak of Illusion. 288p. (Orig.). 1985. 2.95 (*0-8125-5202-4*, Pub. by Tor Bks) St Martin.

— Conan & the Amazon. 288p. 1995. 4.99 (*0-8125-2493-4*, Pub. by Tor Bks) St Martin.

— Conan & the Manhunters. 320p. 1994. mass mkt. 4.99 (*0-8125-2489-6*, Pub. by Tor Bks) St Martin.

— Conan & the Treasure of Python. (Orig.). 1993. pap. 7.99 (*0-8125-1415-7*, Pub. by Tor Bks) St Martin.

— Conan & the Treasure of Python. 288p. (Orig.). 1994. mass mkt. 4.99 (*0-8125-5000-5*, Pub. by Tor Bks) St Martin.

— Conan the Marauder. LC 95-4390. 228p. 1996. mass mkt. 4.50 (*0-8125-3149-3*, Pub. by Tor Bks) St Martin.

— Murder in Tarsis. LC 95-62207. (DragonLance Ser.). 1996. 18.99 (*0-7869-0500-X*, Pub. by TSR Inc) Random.

— Queens of Land & Sea, Vol. 5. 320p. (Orig.). 1994. mass mkt. 4.99 (*0-8125-2307-5*) Tor Bks.

— The Sacrilege: An SPQR Mystery. 224p. (Orig.). 1992. mass mkt. 4.50 (*0-380-76627-2*, Avon Bks) Morrow Avon.

***Roberts, John M.** Saturnalia. LC 99-22250. 288p. 1999. text 23.95 (*0-312-20582-1*) St Martin.

Roberts, John M. A Short History of the World. LC 96-49811. 560p. 1997. reprint ed. pap. 15.95 (*0-19-511504-X*) OUP.

— SPQR. 224p. 1990. mass mkt. 3.99 (*0-380-75993-4*, Avon Bks) Morrow Avon.

***Roberts, John M.** Temple of the Muses. LC 99-38764. 240p. 1999. pap. 13.95 (*0-312-24698-6*) St Martin.

— SPQR III: The Sacrilege. LC 99-26640. 1999. pap. 13.95 (*0-312-24697-8*) St Martin.

Roberts, John M. SPQR 2: The Catiline Conspiracy. 224p. 1991. mass mkt. 3.50 (*0-380-75995-0*, Avon Bks) Morrow Avon.

— Stormlands No. 1: The Islander. 1990. pap. 3.95 (*0-8125-0627-8*) Tor Bks.

— The Temple of the Muses: An SPQR Mystery. 224p. (Orig.). 1992. mass mkt. 4.50 (*0-380-76629-9*, Avon Bks) Morrow Avon.

— Zuni Daily Life. LC 67-2866. (Monographs). 174p. 1965. reprint ed. pap. 15.00 (*0-87536-810-7*) HRAFP.

Roberts, John M., jt. auth. see Nutini, Hugo G.

Roberts, John Mack, jt. ed. see Weinberg, Scott.

Roberts, John Maddox. Murder in Tarsis. 1999. pap. 5.99 (*0-7869-1587-0*) TSR Inc.

— Total Recall. 256p. 1999. mass mkt. 5.99 (*0-312-97070-6*) St Martin.

— A Typical American Town. large type ed. 480p. 1996. 27.99 (*0-7089-3507-9*) Ulverscroft.

Roberts, John Maddox, jt. auth. see Kotani, Eric.

Roberts, John R. George Herbert: An Annotated Bibliography of Modern Criticism, 1905-1984. rev. ed. LC 87-19095. 456p. 1988. text 42.00 (*0-8262-0487-2*) U of Mo Pr.

— John Donne: An Annotated Bibliography of Modern Criticism, 1912-1967. LC 72-913760. 336p. 1973. text 37.50 (*0-8262-0136-9*) U of Mo Pr.

— John Donne: An Annotated Bibliography of Modern Criticism, 1968-1978. LC 72-913760. 448p. 1982. text 44.00 (*0-8262-0364-7*) U of Mo Pr.

— Richard Crashaw: An Annotated Bibliography of Criticism, 1632-1980. LC 84-52264. 488p. 1985. text 45.00 (*0-8262-0468-6*) U of Mo Pr.

Roberts, John R., ed. New Perspectives on the Life & Art of Richard Crashaw. LC 84-52264. (Illus.). 248p. 1990. text 32.50 (*0-8262-0739-1*) U of Mo Pr.

— New Perspectives on the Seventeenth-Century English Religious Lyric. (Illus.). 336p. (C). 1994. text 47.50 (*0-8262-0909-2*) U of Mo Pr.

Roberts, John S. Black Music of Two Worlds. LC 74-6472. 282p. (C). 1982. reprint ed. pap. 12.95 (*0-9614458-0-7*) Original Music.

— The Latin Tinge: The Impact of Latin American Music on the United States. LC 78-26543. (Illus.). 246p. 1985. pap. 12.95 (*0-9614458-1-5*) Original Music.

— The Life & Explorations of David Livingstone. 1988. reprint ed. lib. bdg. 75.00 (*0-7812-0204-3*) Rprt Serv.

Roberts, John Storm. The Latin Tinge: The Impact of Latin American Music on the United States. 2nd ed. LC 98-19580. (Illus.). 304p. 1999. pap. 14.95 (*0-19-512101-5*) OUP.

Roberts, John T. Seasons: Kalidasa's Ritusamhara. LC 89-82402. (Monograph Ser.: No. 25). 180p. 1990. pap. 10.00 (*0-939252-22-8*) ASU Ctr Asian.

Roberts, John T., tr. from SAN. The Homely Touch: Folk Poetry of Old India. (Indo-Aryan Languages & Literature Ser.). 80p. (Orig.). (C). 1986. pap. text 7.95 (*0-939214-33-4*); lib. bdg. 12.00 (*0-939214-32-6*) Mazda Pubs.

Roberts, John W. City of Sokrates. 1984. pap. 13.95 (*0-7102-1102-3*, Routledge Thoemms) Routledge.

— From Hucklebuck to Hip Hop: Social Dance in the African-American Community in Philadelphia. (Illus.). 123p. 1997. reprint ed. pap. text 30.00 (*0-7881-3786-7*) DIANE Pub.

— From Trickster to Badman: The Black Folk Hero in Slavery & Freedom. LC 88-20804. 234p. (C). 1989. reprint ed. pap. text 17.95 (*0-8122-1333-5*) U of Pa Pr.

Roberts, John W., ed. From Hucklebuck to Hip Hop: Social Dance in the African American Community in Philadelphia. (Illus.). 134p. (Orig.). pap. text. write for info. (*1-885066-11-2*) Four-G Pubs.

Roberts, John W., jt. auth. see Phillips, Richard L.

Roberts, John W., ed. see Das, Jagannath.

Roberts, Jon. Language Teacher Education. LC 97-25919. (An Arnold Publication). (Illus.). 356p. 1997. reprint ed. pap. text 19.95 (*0-340-64625-X*) OUP.

— Language Teacher Education: The Reflective Trainer. LC 97-25919. (Illus.). 356p. 1998. text 75.00 (*0-340-64626-8*, Pub. by E A) OUP.

— Steps to Fluency: A Short Course in Communication LC 83-25048. (Materials for Language Practice Ser.). vii, 67p. 1985. pap. write for info. (*0-08-031094-X*, Pergamon Pr) Elsevier.

Roberts, Jon, jt. auth. see Weir, Cyril.

Roberts, Jon H. Darwinism & the Divine in America: Protestant Intellectuals & Organic Evolution, 1859-1900. LC 87-40374. (History of American Thought & Culture Ser.). 368p. (C). 1988. text 27.95 (*0-299-11590-9*) U of Wis Pr.

***Roberts, Jon H. & Turner, James.** The Sacred & the Secular University. LC 99-55426. 2000. 24.95 (*0-691-01556-2*) Princeton U Pr.

Roberts, Jonathan M. Antiquity Unveiled: Ancient Voices from the Spirit Realms. 1996. reprint ed. spiral bd. 34.50 (*0-7873-0729-7*) Hlth Research.

Roberts, Jonathan N. & Spearman, Gretta, eds. There Was No Jesus: The Teacher of the New Testament Was Apollonius of Tyana. 1996. reprint ed. pap. 19.00 (*0-7873-0730-0*) Hlth Research.

***Roberts-Jones, Philippe.** Brussels: Fin de Siecle. (Illus.). 280p. 1999. 29.99 (*3-8228-7023-4*) Taschen Amer.

Roberts, Joseph. The Lure of the Integers. LC 91-62053. (MAA Spectrum Ser.). 300p. 1992. pap. text 12.00 (*0-88385-502-X*, LURE) Math Assn.

Roberts, Joseph K. In the Shadow of Empire: Canada for Americans. LC 98-13459. 160p. 1998. 43.00 (*0-85345-996-7*, Pub. by Monthly Rev); pap. 15.00 (*0-85345-997-5*, Pub. by Monthly Rev) NYU Pr.

***Roberts, Joseph P.** The Ideology of Life: The Foundation of Political Revolution & 21st Century Sustainability. 171p. 1999. mass mkt. 9.95 (*1-890456-04-7*) Popl Rev Bks.

Roberts, Joseph S. & Welsch, Harold P. Building Your Dream Vol. 1: Business Plan Essentials. 320p. (Orig.). 1997. pap. 29.95 (*0-9658214-5-5*) MidAmerica Lrdship.

Roberts, Joseph S., jt. auth. see Welsch, Harold P.

Roberts, Josephine A., ed. Lady Mary Wroth: The First Part of the Countess of Montgomery's Urania. LC 95-2654. (Renaissance English Text Society Series, Medieval & Renaissance Texts & Studies: Vol. 140). 994p. 1995. 60.00 (*0-86698-176-4*, MR140) MRTS.

Roberts, Josephine A., ed. The Poems of Lady Mary Wroth. LC 82-20843. (Illus.). 304p. (C). 1992. pap. text 17.95 (*0-8071-1799-4*) La State U Pr.

Roberts, Josephine A. & Travitsky, Betty S. The Early Modern Englishwoman Vol. 10, Pt. 1: A Facsimile Library of Essential Works: Printings Writings, 1500-1640: Mary Wroth. 612p. 1996. 135.95 (*1-85928-101-X*, Pub. by Scolar Pr) Ashgate Pub Co.

Roberts, Joy. The Joy of Horses. LC 97-30269. (Illus.). 288p. 1997. pap. 16.95 (*0-8092-3065-8*, 306580, Contemporary Bks) NTC Contemp Pub Co.

***Roberts, J.R.** Death in Dodge City, 1 vol., Vol. 4. (Gunsmith Ser.). 1999. mass mkt. 5.99 (*0-515-12509-1*, Jove) Berkley Pub.

Roberts, Judith T. Chrysanthemums I Once Thought Sweet. LC 98-223551. (Illus.). 77p. 1998. pap. 10.00 (*0-910479-02-X*) Mid-America Pr.

Roberts, Judy G. Fine Line Design: Christmas. Booher, Jerry, ed. (Design Bks.: No. 8). (Illus.). 38p. 1995. pap. 14.95 (*1-883083-07-9*) Roberts Studio.

— Fine Line Design: Circus & Clowns. Booher, Jerry, ed. (Design Bks.: No. 7). (Illus.). 37p. 1995. pap. 14.95 (*1-883083-06-0*) Roberts Studio.

— Fine Line Design: Dog Breeds. Booher, Jerry, ed. (Design Bks.: Vol. 9). (Illus.). 48p. 1999. pap. 16.95 (*1-883083-08-7*) Roberts Studio.

— Fine Line Design: General. (Design Bks.: No. 1). 32p. 1992. pap. 14.95 (*1-883083-00-1*) Roberts Studio.

— Fine Line Design: Great Outdoors. (Design Bks.: No. 3). 35p. 1992. pap. 14.95 (*1-883083-02-8*) Roberts Studio.

— Fine Line Design: Pets & People. Booher, Jerry, ed. (Design Bks.: No. 6). (Illus.). 37p. 1994. pap. 14.95 (*1-883083-05-2*) Roberts Studio.

— Fine Line Design: Rural America. Booher, Jerry, ed. (Design Bks.: No. 5). (Illus.). 37p. 1993. pap. 14.95 (*1-883083-04-4*) Roberts Studio.

An Asterisk (*) at the beginning of an entry indicates that the title is appearing for the first time.

— Fine Line Design: Sports Book. Booher, Jerry, ed. (Design Bks.: No. 4). (Illus.). 42p. 1993. pap. 14.95 (*1-883083-03-6*) Roberts Studio.

— Fine Line Design: Western - South Western. (Design Bks.: No. 2). 37p. 1992. pap. 16.95 (*1-883083-01-X*) Roberts Studio.

— Intarsia: Easy to Make Inlay Wood Projects. 2nd ed. (Illus.). 147p. 1995. pap. 19.95 (*1-56523-055-8*) Fox Chapel Pub.

***Roberts, Judy G. & Booher, Jerry.** Easy to Make Inlay Wood Projects: Intarsia: Complete Patterns & Techniques. 3rd ed. 188p. 2000. pap. text 19.95 (*1-56523-126-0*) Fox Chapel Pub.

Roberts, Judy G. & Booher, Jerry. Intarsia Artistry in Wood: 12 Projects for Every Occasion. (Illus.). 62p. 1997. pap. 14.95 (*1-56523-096-5*) Fox Chapel Pub.

— Small Intarsia: Woodworking Projects You Can Make. (Illus.). 65p. 1996. pap. 14.95 (*1-56523-062-0*) Fox Chapel Pub.

Roberts, Judy G., jt. auth. see Booher, Jery.

Roberts, Julian. The Logic of Reflection: German Philosophy in the Twentieth Century. 256p. (C). 1992. 37.50 (*0-300-05207-3*) Yale U Pr.

Roberts, Julian L., Jr., et al. Chemistry in the Laboratory: Instructor's Manual. 4th ed. 1997. pap., teacher ed. 15.98 (*0-7167-3029-4*) W H Freeman.

***Roberts, Julian L., Jr., et al.** General Chemistry in the Laboratory. 5th ed. 2000. pap. text 47.95 (*0-7167-3547-4*) W H Freeman.

Roberts, Julian V. & Cole, David P., eds. Making Sense of Sentencing. 432p. 1999. pap. 27.95 (*0-8020-7644-0*); text 65.00 (*0-8020-0686-8*) U of Toronto Pr.

Roberts, Julian V. & Mohr, Renate M., eds. Sexual Assault in Canada: A Decade of Legal & Social Change. 384p. (C). 1994. text 50.00 (*0-8020-5928-7*); pap. text 19.95 (*0-8020-6868-5*) U of Toronto Pr.

***Roberts, Julian V. & Stalans, Loretta J.** Public Opinion, Crime & Criminal Justice. (Crime & Society Ser.). 352p. 1999. pap. 30.00 (*0-8133-6793-X*) Westview.

Roberts, June C. Born in the Spring: A Collection of Spring Wildflowers. LC 75-36979. (Illus.). 159p. 1976. reprint ed. pap. 21.95 (*0-8214-0226-9*) Ohio U Pr.

— Season of Promise: Wild Plants in Winter, Northeastern United States. (Illus.). 336p. (C). 1992. 49.95 (*0-8214-1022-9*); pap. 24.95 (*0-8214-1023-7*) Ohio U Pr.

Roberts, K. & Jung, B. Poland's First Post-Communist Generation. 240p. 1995. pap. 72.95 (*1-85628-897-8*, Pub. by Avebry) Ashgate Pub Co.

Roberts, K. F., ed. Advanced Technology in Water Management. 257p. 1991. text 76.00 (*0-7277-1638-7*, Pub. by T Telford) RCH.

Roberts, K. K., jt. auth. see Costello, Rick.

***Roberts, Karen.** The Flower Boy. LC 99-54470. 336p. 2000. 24.95 (*0-375-50316-1*) Random.

Roberts, Karen & Wilson, Mark, eds. Policy Choices: NAFTA & Michigan's Future. LC 96-26073. (Policy Choices Ser.: Vol. 3). (Illus.). 230p. 1996. pap. 21.95 (*0-87013-415-9*) Mich St U Pr.

Roberts, Karlene H., et al. Developing an Interdisciplinary Science of Organizations. LC 78-62568. (Jossey-Bass Social & Behavioral Science Ser.). 191p. reprint ed. pap. 59.30 (*0-8357-6889-9*, 203794100009) Bks Demand.

Roberts, Karon. Bright...& Behind: A Book for Children & Parents Learning to Cope with Reading & Attention. 1998. pap. text 9.95 (*0-9663817-3-4*) Edgeworth Comm.

Roberts, Kate. Feet in Chains. Jones, John I., tr. from WEL. 140p. 1998. pap. 14.95 (*0-8464-4882-3*) Beekman Pubs.

— Feet in Chains. Jones, John I., tr. from WEL. 134p. 1996. pap. 12.99 (*1-871083-80-X*, Pub. by J Jones Pub) Intl Spec Bk.

— Tea in the Heather. Griffith, Wyn, tr. from WEL. 280p. 1998. pap. 14.95 (*0-8496-4486-5*) Beekman Pubs.

— Tea in the Heather. Griffiths, Wyn, tr. from WEL. LC 97-228861. 134p. 1997. pap. 6.95 (*1-871083-85-0*, Pub. by J Jones Pub) Intl Spec Bk.

***Roberts, Katherine.** Song Quest. (Illus.). (J). 2000. pap. 5.95 (*1-902618-94-7*, Pub. by Element Childrns) Penguin Putnam.

Roberts, Katherine E. Persistence & Change in Personality Patterns. (SRCD M Ser.: Vol. 8, No. 3). 1943. 25.00 (*0-527-01528-8*) Periodicals Srv.

Roberts, Katherine J. Fair Ladies: Sir Philip Sydney's Female Characters. LC 93-20209. (Renaissance & Baroque Studies & Texts: Vol. 9). 136p. 1993. 42.95 (*0-8204-2145-6*) P Lang Pubng.

Roberts, Kathleen & Ludvigsen, Carol. Project Management for Health Care Professionals. LC 98-213326. (Illus.). 224p. 1998. pap. text 35.00 (*0-7506-3405-7*) Buttrwrth-Heinemann.

Roberts, Kathleen, jt. auth. see Ludvigsen, Carole.

Roberts, Kathleen H., jt. auth. see Flynn-Nason, Theresa.

***Roberts, Kathryn, ed.** A Dictionary for the Petroleum Industry. 3rd ed. 286p. 1999. pap. text 35.00 (*0-88698-187-5*) PETEX.

Roberts, Kathryn, ed. Orientation for Offshore Crane Operations. 2nd ed. LC 97-18616. (Rotary Drilling Ser.: Unit V, Lesson 8). (Illus.). 80p. 1997. pap. text 16.00 (*0-88698-179-4*, 2.50820) PETEX.

Roberts, Kathryn, ed. see Van Dyke, Kate.

Roberts, Kathy, jt. auth. see Ketola, Jeanne.

Roberts, Katie & Roberts, Earle. Our Florida Cranes & Their Neighbors - A Love Story. (Illus.). 56p. (Orig.). (J). (gr. 4-8). 1995. pap. 8.48 (*0-9647812-0-4*) K & E Roberts.

Roberts, Katrina. How Late Desire Looks. LC 97-740. (Peregrine Smith Poetry Competition Ser.). 80p. 1997. pap. 9.95 (*0-87905-815-3*) Gibbs Smith Pub.

Roberts, Keith. Anita. (Illus.). 195p. 1990. reprint ed. 20.25 (*0-913896-27-6*) Owlswick Pr.

— Bruegel. (Color Library). (Illus.). 128p. (C). 1988. reprint ed. pap. 18.95 (*0-7148-2239-6*, Pub. by Phaidon Press) Phaidon Pr.

— Degas. (Color Library). (Illus.). 128p. (C). 1994. reprint ed. pap. 14.95 (*0-7148-2757-6*, Pub. by Phaidon Press) Phaidon Pr.

— Soldiers of the English Civil War Vol. 1: Infantry. (Elite Ser.: No. 25). (Illus.). 64p. pap. 12.95 (*0-85045-903-6*, 9425, Pub. by Ospry) Stackpole.

Roberts, Keith & Michels, Leo. Introductory Mathematics for Industry Science, & Technology. LC 85-7714. (Mathematics Ser.). 315p. (C). 1985. mass mkt. 48.50 (*0-534-05148-0*) Brooks-Cole.

— Mathematics for Health Sciences. LC 81-12234. (Mathematics Ser.). 423p. (C). 1996. mass mkt. 41.25 (*0-8185-0478-1*) Brooks-Cole.

Roberts, Keith A. Religion in Sociological Perspective. 450p. (C). 1984. pap. write for info. (*0-534-10816-4*) Wadsworth Pub.

— Religion in Sociological Perspective. 2nd ed. 400p. (C). 1989. pap. 42.95 (*0-534-12102-0*) Wadsworth Pub.

— Religion in Sociological Perspective. 3rd ed. 465p. 1994. 72.95 (*0-534-20466-X*) Wadsworth Pub.

Roberts, Keli. Keli Roberts' Fitness Hollywood: The Trainer to the Stars Shares Her Body-Shaping Secrets. 320p. 1994. 19.95 (*1-56530-147-1*, Pub. by Summit TX) BookWorld.

Roberts, Kelsey. The Baby Exchange. (Intrigue Ser.). 1996. per. 3.75 (*0-373-22374-9*, 1-22374-2) Harlequin Bks.

— The Baby Exchange. (Promo Ser.). 1999. per. 4.50 (*0-373-21964-4*, 1-21964-1) Harlequin Bks.

— Her Mother's Arms. (Intrigue Ser.: No. 455). 1998. per. 3.99 (*0-373-22455-9*, 1-22455-9) Harlequin Bks.

— His Only Son: The Landry Brothers. (Intrigue Ser.: No. 535). 1999. per. 3.99 (*0-373-22535-0*, 1-22535-8) Harlequin Bks.

— In the Bride's Defense. (Delta Justice Ser.). 1997. per. 4.50 (*0-373-82564-1*) Harlequin Bks.

— Landry's Law: The Landry Brothers. (Intrigue Ser.: Bk. 545). 1999. per. 3.99 (*0-373-22545-8*, 1-22545-7) Harlequin Bks.

— Legal Tender. (Intrigue Ser.). 1993. mass mkt. 2.99 (*0-373-22248-3*, 1-22248-8) Harlequin Bks.

— The Silent Groom: The Rose Tattoo. (Intrigue Ser.). 1997. per. 3.75 (*0-373-22412-5*, 1-22412-0) Harlequin Bks.

— Someone to Watch over Her. (Delta Justice Ser.). 1998. per. 4.50 (*0-373-82568-4*, 1-82568-6) Harlequin Bks.

— Stolen Memories. (Intrigue Ser.). 1994. per. 2.99 (*0-373-22276-9*) Harlequin Bks.

***Roberts, Kelsey.** Stolen Memories. 2000. mass mkt. 4.50 (*0-373-82201-4*, 1-82201-4) Harlequin Bks.

Roberts, Kelsey. The Tall, Dark Alibi. 1996. per. 3.75 (*0-373-22395-1*, 1-22395-7) Harlequin Bks.

— Things Remembered. LC 97-10568. 250p. 1994. per. 2.99 (*0-373-22294-7*, 1-22294-2) Harlequin Bks.

— Undying Laughter. LC 96-582. (Intrigue Ser.). 248p. 1995. per. 3.50 (*0-373-22334-X*, 1-22334-6) Harlequin Bks.

— Unforgettable Night: Rose Tattoo. (Intrigue Ser.: Vol. 477). 1998. per. 3.99 (*0-373-22477-X*, 1-22477-3) Harlequin Bks.

— Unlawfully Wedded. LC 96-656. (Intrigue Ser.). 251p. 1995. per. 3.50 (*0-373-22330-7*, 1-22330-4) Harlequin Bks.

— Unspoken Confessions. LC 95-15847. (Intrigue Ser.). 251p. 1995. mass mkt. 3.50 (*0-373-22326-9*, 1-22326-2) Harlequin Bks.

— Wanted: Cowboy: Rose Tattoo. (Intrigue Ser.: Bk. 522). 1999. per. 3.99 (*0-373-22522-9*, 1-22522-6) Harlequin Bks.

— The Wrong Man. 1997. per. 3.75 (*0-373-22429-X*, 1-22429-4) Harlequin Bks.

Roberts, Kelsey, et al. Wish upon a Star: Sky's the Limit; The Perfect Match; The Arrangement. 1998. per. 5.99 (*0-373-83373-3*, 1-83373-0, Mira Bks) Harlequin Bks.

Roberts, Kelsey, jt. auth. see Delinsky, Barbara.

Roberts, Kelsey, jt. auth. see York, Rebecca.

Roberts, Ken. E. Ingraham & Company, 1880. 1972. pap. 5.00 (*0-9600264-5-2*) Am Clock & Watch.

— The Hollywood Principle: How to Use the "Magic" of Movies to Make Your Dreams Come True. LC 91-90145. (Illus.). 256p. (Orig.). (C). 1991. pap. text 17.95 (*0-9629127-7-8*) Four Star Pub.

— Leisure in Contemporary Society. LC 99-22426. (CABI Publishing Ser.). 256p. 1999. text 30.00 (*0-85199-338-9*) OUP.

— A Rich Man's Secret: An Amazing Formula for Success. LC 95-6490. 216p. 1999. pap. 9.95 (*1-56718-580-0*) Llewellyn Pubns.

— Stephanie Kaye. (Degrassi Book Ser.). 160p. (J). (gr. 6-9). 1995. mass mkt. 4.95 (*1-55028-109-7*); bds. 16.95 (*1-55028-111-9*) Formac Dist Ltd.

— Youth & Employment in Modern Britain. (Oxford Modern Britain Ser.). (Illus.). 160p. 1995. text 49.95 (*0-19-827965-5*) OUP.

Roberts, Ken, ed. Guide to the Free Trade Area of the Americas Negotiations. (Illus.). 48p. 1999. pap. 9.95 (*0-9670515-1-7*) World City.

— Who's Who in International Business in Miami & South Florida: A Publicaiton of World City Business. (Illus.). 180p. 1999. pap. 19.95 (*0-9670515-0-9*) World City.

***Roberts, Ken, ed.** Who's Who in International Business in Miami & South Florida - 2000 Edition Vol. 2: A Publication of WorldCity Business. (Illus.). 180p. 2000. pap. 19.95 (*0-9670515-2-5*) World City.

Roberts, Ken, jt. auth. see Castellarin, Loretta.

Roberts, Kenneth. Arundel. LC 95-15964. (Illus.). 496p. 1995. reprint ed. pap. 16.95 (*0-89272-364-5*) Down East.

— The Battle of Cowpens. 17.95 (*0-89190-967-2*) Amereon Ltd.

— The Battle of Cowpens. 111p. 1981. pap. 3.50 (*0-915992-05-1*) Eastern National.

— Boon Island: Including Contemporary Accounts of the Wreck of the Nottingham Galley. 1996. pap. text 15.95 (*0-07-053220-6*) McGraw.

— Boon Island: Including Contemporary Accounts of the Wreck of the "Nottingham Galley" rev. ed. Bales, Jack & Warner, Richard, eds. LC 95-43292. (Illus.). 385p. 1995. pap. 15.95 (*0-87451-744-3*) U Pr of New Eng.

— Captain Caution. 224p. Date not set. 21.95 (*0-8488-2382-6*) Amereon Ltd.

— Captain Caution. LC 99-17850. (Chronicles of Arundel Ser.: Vol. 4). 224p. 1999. reprint ed. pap. 15.95 (*0-89272-467-6*) Down East.

— The Kenneth Roberts Reader. 460p. 1976. reprint ed. lib. bdg. 29.95 (*0-89190-444-1*, Rivercity Pr) Amereon Ltd.

— Leisure. 2nd ed. LC 80-42055. (Aspects of Modern Sociology: the Social Structure of Modern Britain Ser.). 146p. reprint ed. pap. 45.30 (*0-608-13118-0*, 202522300043) Bks Demand.

— Northwest Passage. 1983. write for info. (*0-318-56616-8*) Haas Ent NH.

— Oliver Wiswell. LC 99-17851. 836p. 1999. reprint ed. pap. 24.95 (*0-89272-468-4*) Down East.

— Rabble in Arms. LC 96-19617. (Illus.). 592p. 1996. reprint ed. pap. 17.95 (*0-89272-386-6*) Down East.

— School Leavers & Their Prospects: Youth & the Labor Market in the 1980's. 169p. 1984. pap. 25.00 (*0-335-10418-5*) OpUniv Pr.

— The Working Class. LC 77-26300. (Aspects of Modern Sociology Ser.). 216p. reprint ed. pap. 67.00 (*0-608-13079-6*, 202521200043) Bks Demand.

Roberts, Kenneth. Youth & Employment in Modern Britain. (Illus.). 148p. 1995. pap. text 20.00 (*0-19-827964-7*) OUP.

Roberts, Kenneth. Youth & Leisure. (Leisure & Recreation Studies: No. 3). 240p. 1985. pap. text 18.95 (*0-04-301204-3*) Routledge.

***Roberts, Kenneth, et al.** Surviving Post-Communism: Young People in the Former Soviet Union. LC 99-53194. (Studies of Communism in Transition). 256p. 2000. 95.00 (*1-84064-103-7*) E Elgar.

Roberts, Kenneth B. Manual of Clinical Problems in Pediatrics. 2nd ed. 1985. spiral bd. 22.50 (*0-316-74990-7*, Little Brwn Med Div) Lppncott W & W.

Roberts, Kenneth B., ed. Manual of Clinical Problems in Pediatrics: With Annotated Key References. 4th ed. LC 94-22643. (Illus.). 600p. 1995. spiral bd. 35.95 (*0-316-75006-9*, Little Brwn Med Div) Lppncott W & W.

Roberts, Kenneth B., jt. auth. see Tunnessen, Walter W.

Roberts, Kenneth D. Agrarian Structure & Labor Migration in Rural Mexico. fac. ed. (Research Reports: No. 30). 46p. (Orig.). (C). 1981. pap. 5.00 (*0-935391-29-0*, RR-30) UCSD Ctr US-Mex.

— Introduction to Rule Collecting. (Illus.). 22p. (Orig.). 1982. pap. text 3.00 (*0-913602-52-3*) K Roberts.

— Some 19th Century English Woodworking Tools. rev. ed. (Illus.). 500p. 1991. 42.50 (*0-913602-68-X*) K Roberts.

— The Stanley Combination Plane. rev. ed. (Illus.). 80p. 1989. pap. 10.00 (*0-9618088-3-7*) Astragal Pr.

— Wooden Planes in Nineteenth Century America, Vol. II. (Illus.). 472p. 1983. 40.00 (*0-913602-59-0*) K Roberts.

Roberts, Kenneth D., ed. Belcher Brothers & Co.'s Eighteen Sixty Price List of Boxwood & Ivory Rules Vol. I. (Illus.). 40p. 1982. reprint ed. pap. text 5.00 (*1-879335-06-9*) Astragal Pr.

— Eighteen Hundred Eighty-Seven Catalogue of Millers Falls Co. (Illus.). 72p. 1981. reprint ed. pap. 7.50 (*1-879335-27-1*) Astragal Pr.

Roberts, Kenneth D. & Roberts, Jane W. Planemakers & Other Edge Tool Enterprises in New York State in the Nineteenth Century. 2nd rev. ed. (Illus.). 244p. 1989. reprint ed. pap. text 30.00 (*0-913602-66-3*) K Roberts.

Roberts, Kenneth D. & Taylor, Snowden. Eli Terry & the Connecticut Shelf Clock. 2nd rev. ed. (Illus.). 384p. 1994. 40.00 (*0-913602-71-X*) K Roberts.

— Forestville Clockmakers. (Illus.). 177p. (Orig.). 1992. pap. 24.00 (*0-913602-67-1*) K Roberts.

— Jonathan Clark Brown & the Forestville Manufacturing Co. (Illus.). 120p. 1988. pap. 18.75 (*0-913602-64-7*) K Roberts.

Roberts, Kenneth D., ed. see Ryan, E. Scott.

Roberts, Kenneth J. The Evangelizers. Waters, Anna M., ed. (Illus.). 100p. (Orig.). 1984. pap. text 3.50 (*0-9610984-2-2*) PAX Tapes.

— Mary, the Perfect Prayer Partner. Waters, Anna M., ed. LC 83-61151. (Illus.). 128p. (Orig.). 1983. pap. 3.95 (*0-9610984-1-4*) PAX Tapes.

— Pray It Again, Sam. Ruskin, Anna Marie, ed. LC 83-61243. 116p. (Orig.). 1983. pap. 3.95 (*0-9610984-0-6*) PAX Tapes.

— The Rest of the Week. LC 73-87984. 191p. 1988. reprint ed. pap. text 5.95 (*0-318-37581-8*) PAX Tapes.

— Up on the Mountain. LC 92-64000. 171p. 1992. pap. 11.95 (*1-55725-053-7*, 930-031, Pub. by Paraclete MA) BookWorld.

Roberts, Kenneth J. & Waters, Anna M. Shepherd's Pie. 217p. (Orig.). Date not set. pap. 9.95 (*0-9610984-4-9*) PAX Tapes.

Roberts, Kenneth L. Why Europe Leaves Home: A True Account of the Reasons Which Cause Central Europeans to Overrun America. Grob, Gerald N., ed. LC 76-46100. (Anti-Movements in America Ser.). 1977. reprint ed. lib. bdg. 34.95 (*0-405-09971-1*) Ayer.

Roberts, Kenneth Lewis. Arundel. 1930. 15.95 (*0-385-04024-5*) Doubleday.

Roberts, Kenneth Lewis. The Lively Lady: A Chronicle of Arundel, of Privateering, & of the Circular Prison on Dartmoor. 282p. Date not set. 23.95 (*0-8488-2591-8*) Amereon Ltd.

— The Lively Lady: A Chronicle of Arundel, of Privateering, & of the Circular Prison on Dartmoor. large type ed. 1994. write for info. (*0-318-72724-2*, G K Hall Lrg Type); lib. bdg. 20.95 (*0-8161-5996-3*, G K Hall Lrg Type) Mac Lib Ref.

— The Lively Lady: A Chronicle of Arundel, of Privateering, & of the Circular Prison on Dartmoor. LC 97-24404. 288p. 1997. reprint ed. pap. 15.95 (*0-89272-425-0*) Down East.

Roberts, Kenneth M. Deepening Democracy? The Modern Left & Social Movements in Chile & Peru. LC 98-16557. 1999. write for info. (*0-8047-3193-4*); pap. 19.95 (*0-8047-3194-2*) Stanford U Pr.

Roberts, Kevin. Automotive Heating, Ventilation, & Air Conditioning Systems. (Illus.). 456p. 1999. pap. 49.00 (*1-57932-114-3*) Chek-Chart.

Roberts, Kim. The Wishbone Galaxy. LC 94-4232. 1994. 10.00 (*0-931846-45-5*) Wash Writers Pub.

Roberts, L., jt. ed. see Crouch, M. A.

Roberts, L. E., et al. Power Generation & the Environment. (Science, Technology, & Society Ser.: No. 6). (Illus.). 224p. 1990. 55.00 (*0-19-858338-9*) OUP.

Roberts, L. M., jt. ed. see Murrell, J. C.

Roberts, L. R., jt. ed. see Skalny, J. P.

***Roberts, L. Shannon.** Ghost Gallery: Their Photos, Their Stories. 64p. 1999. spiral bd. 17.95 (*0-9673247-2-6*) TwinTwo Commn Inc.

— Ghost World: Featuring Celebrity Ghosts. (Illus.). 80p. 1999. spiral bd. 18.95 (*0-9673247-3-4*) TwinTwo Commn Inc.

Roberts, L. W., et al. Vascular Differentiation & Plant Growth Regulators. (Wood Science Ser.). (Illus.). x, 154p. 1988. 137.95 (*0-387-18989-0*) Spr-Verlag.

Roberts, Lamar, jt. auth. see Penfield, Wilder.

Roberts, Larenda L. Dallas Uncovered. 2nd ed. LC 97-48673. 1998. pap. text 16.95 (*1-55622-618-7*, Seaside Pr) Wordware Pub.

— New Orleans Uncovered. LC 98-22264. 1998. pap. text 16.95 (*1-55622-620-9*) Wordware Pub.

— San Francisco Uncovered. LC 95-36591. 296p. 1996. pap. 16.95 (*1-55622-395-1*, Seaside Pr) Wordware Pub.

Roberts, Larry S., et al. Foundations of Parasitology. 5th ed. 736p. (C). 1995. text. write for info. (*0-697-26071-2*, WCB McGr Hill) McGrw-H Hghr Educ.

Roberts, Larry S., jt. auth. see Hickman, Cleveland P.

Roberts, Larry S., jt. auth. see Hickman, Cleveland P., Jr.

Roberts, Larry S., jt. auth. see Hickman, Cleveland P.

Roberts, Launey F., Jr., ed. Individualizing Instruction in Educational Administration: A Performance-Based Worktext. 256p. 1976. pap. text 11.25 (*0-8422-0531-4*) Irvington.

Roberts, Laura, jt. auth. see Kirby, Colleen.

***Roberts, Laura Peyton.** The Diaries. (Clearwater Crossing Special Edition Ser.). 256p. (J). (gr. 7-12). 2000. mass mkt. 4.50 (*0-553-49334-5*) BDD Bks Young Read.

— Dream On. (Clearwater Crossing Ser.). 224p. (YA). (gr. 5-8). 2000. mass mkt. 3.99 (*0-553-49298-5*) BDD Bks Young Read.

Roberts, Laura Peyton. Get a Life. (Clearwater Crossing Ser.). 240p. (YA). (gr. 5-8). 1998. mass mkt. 3.99 (*0-553-57118-4*) BDD Bks Young Read.

***Roberts, Laura Peyton.** Get a Life. (Clearwater Crossing Ser.). (YA). (gr. 5-8). 1998. 9.09 (*0-606-13282-1*, Pub. by Turtleback) Demco.

— Ghost of a Chance. 192p. (YA). (gr. 5 up). 1999. pap. 3.99 (*0-440-41534-9*) BDD Bks Young Read.

Roberts, Laura Peyton. Ghost of a Chance. LC 97-6151. 192p. (YA). (gr. 7). 1997. 14.95 (*0-385-32508-8*) Delacorte.

— Heart & Soul. (Clearwater Crossing Ser.). 224p. (YA). (gr. 7 up). 1998. mass mkt. 3.99 (*0-553-57124-9*) BDD Bks Young Read.

***Roberts, Laura Peyton.** Heart & Soul. (Clearwater Crossing Ser.). (YA). (gr. 5-8). 1998. 9.09 (*0-606-13280-5*, Pub. by Turtleback) Demco.

Roberts, Laura Peyton. Hope Happens. 224p. 1999. mass mkt. 3.99 (*0-553-49297-7*) Bantam.

— Just Friends. (Clearwater Crossing Ser.). (YA). (gr. 5-8). 1998. mass mkt. 3.99 (*0-553-49258-6*) BDD Bks Young Read.

— Keep the Faith. (Clearwater Crossing Ser.). 240p. (YA). (gr. 5-8). 1998. mass mkt. 3.99 (*0-553-49259-4*) BDD Bks Young Read.

***Roberts, Laura Peyton.** Love Hurts. (Clearwater Crossing Ser.). (YA). (gr. 5-8). 2000. mass mkt. 3.99 (*0-553-49299-3*) BDD Bks Young Read.

Roberts, Laura Peyton. More Than This. (Clearwater Crossing Ser.). 224p. (YA). (gr. 5-8). 1999. mass mkt. 3.99 (*0-553-49296-9*) Bantam.

— New Beginnings. (Clearwater Crossing Ser.). 224p. (YA). (gr. 5-8). 1999. mass mkt. 3.99 (*0-553-49256-X*) BDD Bks Young Read.

— No Doubt. (Clearwater Crossing Ser.). 208p. (YA). (gr. 5-8). 1999. mass mkt. 3.99 (*0-553-49261-6*) BDD Bks Young Read.

— One Real Thing. (Clearwater Crossing Ser.). (YA). (gr. 5-8). 1999. mass mkt. 3.99 (*0-553-49257-8*) BDD Bks Young Read.

— Promises, Promises. (Clearwater Crossing Ser.). 224p. (YA). (gr. 7 up). 1998. mass mkt. 3.99 (*0-553-57127-3*) BDD Bks Young Read.

***Roberts, Laura Peyton.** Promises, Promises. (Clearwater Crossing Ser.). (YA). (gr. 5-8). 1998. 9.09 (*0-606-13281-3*, Pub. by Turtleback) Demco.

Roberts, Laura Peyton. Reality Check. (Clearwater Crossing Ser.). 224p. (YA). (gr. 5-8). 1998. mass mkt. 3.99 (*0-553-57121-4*) BDD Bks Young Read.

An Asterisk (*) at the beginning of an entry indicates that the title is appearing for the first time.

R

— Reality Check. (Clearwater Crossing Ser.). (YA). (gr. 5-8). 1998. 9.09 (0-606-13283-X, Pub. by Turtleback) Demco.

— Skin Deep. (Clearwater Crossing Ser.). (YA). (gr. 5-8). 1999. mass mkt. 3.99 (0-553-49260-8) BDD Bks Young Read.

***Roberts, Laura Peyton.** Tried & True. (Clearwater Crossing Ser.). (YA). (gr. 5-8). 2000. mass mkt. 4.50 (0-553-49331-0) BDD Bks Young Read.

— What Goes Around. (Clearwater Crossing Ser.). (YA). (gr. 5-8). 2000. mass mkt. 4.50 (0-553-49330-2) BDD Bks Young Read.

Roberts, Laura V. First Thessalonians 5:21: The Resurrection, the Jews, & the Hebrew Calendar. 2nd expanded large type ed. LC 94-76999. (Illus.). 176p. 1994. spiral bd. 14.95 (0-9632387-6-0) LVI Pubns.

Roberts, Laurence P. Dictionary of Japanese Artists. LC 76-885. 1977. 32.50 (0-8348-0113-2) Weatherhill.

Roberts, Lawrence D. How Reference Works: Explanatory Models for Indexicals, Descriptions, & Opacity. LC 92-31942. (SUNY Series, Scientific Studies in Natural & Artificial Intelligence). 202p. (C). 1993. text 59.50 (0-7914-1575-9); pap. text 19.95 (0-7914-1576-7) State U NY Pr.

Roberts, Lawrence D., ed. Approaches to Nature in the Middle Ages: Papers of the 10th Annual Conference of CEMERS. LC 82-8264. (Medieval & Renaissance Texts & Studies: Vol. 16). (Illus.). 240p. 1982. 25.00 (0-86698-051-2, MR16) MRTS.

Roberts, Lawrence G., jt. auth. see Kenney, John B.

Roberts, Lee. Praying God's Will for My Daughter. 320p. 1998. 4.99 (0-7852-7543-6) Nelson.

— Praying God's Will for My Husband. 320p. 1998. 4.99 (0-7852-7544-4) Nelson.

— Praying God's Will for My Marriage. LC 93-34311. 1994. pap. 11.99 (0-8407-9223-9) Nelson.

— Praying God's Will for My Son. 320p. 1998. 4.99 (0-7852-7545-2) Nelson.

Roberts, Leigh. Built to Last. (Superromance Ser.). 1993. mass mkt. 3.39 (0-373-70543-3, 1-70543-3) Harlequin Bks.

Roberts, Leigh M., ed. see Symposium on Comprehensive Mental Health Staff.

Roberts, Lemuel. Memoirs of Captain Lemuel Roberts. Decker, Peter, ed. LC 70-79945. (Eyewitness Accounts of the American Revolution Ser.). 1969. reprint ed. 15.95 (0-405-01175-X) Ayer.

Roberts, Len. Counting the Black Angels: Poems. LC 93-30476. 96p. 1994. 12.95 (0-252-06381-3) U of Ill Pr.

— Dangerous Angels. LC 93-12261. 64p. (Orig.). 1993. pap. 9.95 (0-914278-61-4) Copper Beech.

— Learning about the Heart. 28p. 1992. pap. 5.00 (1-878851-03-9) Silverfish Rev Pr.

— Sweet Ones: Poems. LC 87-63529. (Illus.). 72p. (Orig.). 1988. pap. 6.95 (0-915943-24-7) Milkweed Ed.

— The Trouble-Making Finch: Poems. LC 97-21189. 128p. 1998. 14.95 (0-252-06693-6) U of Ill Pr.

Roberts, Len, tr. & intro. see Csoori, Sandor.

Roberts, Leon. The Coming Choral Book. 103p. 1997. pap. 9.95 (0-915531-62-3) OR Catholic.

— Mass of St. Martin de Porres (Choral Book) 79p. 1997. pap. 8.95 (0-915531-56-9) OR Catholic.

Roberts, Leonard & Wildman, Stephen. Arthur Hughes: His Life & Works. (Illus.). 304p. 1997. 89.50 (1-85149-262-3) Antique Collect.

Roberts, Leonard W. South from Hell-fer-Sartin: Kentucky Mountain Folk Tales. LC 87-30039. 296p. 1988. 32.00 (0-8131-1637-6) U Pr of Ky.

— South from Hell-fer-Sartin: Kentucky Mountain Folk Tales. LC 87-30039. 296p. 1988. pap. 17.00 (0-8131-0175-1) U Pr of Ky.

— Up Cutshin & down Greasy: Folkways of a Kentucky Mountain Family. LC 87-29600. (Illus.). 176p. 1997. pap. 16.00 (0-8131-0176-X) U Pr of Ky.

Roberts, Les. The Best-Kept Secret. LC 99-22962. 336p. 1999. text 23.95 (0-312-20499-X) St Martin.

***Roberts, Les.** The Best-Kept Secret. (Milan Jacovich Mystery Ser.). 320p. 1999. mass mkt. 5.99 (0-312-97126-5) St Martin.

Roberts, Les. The Cleveland Connection. 1997. mass mkt. 5.99 (0-312-96218-5); mass mkt. 5.99 (0-614-27786-8) St Martin.

— Cleveland Local. LC 97-20581. (Milan Jacovich Mystery Ser.). 288p. 1997. text 22.95 (0-312-16801-2) St Martin.

— Cleveland Local, Vol. 1. 288p. Date not set. 5.99 (0-312-96678-4, Pub. by Tor Bks) St Martin.

— Collision Bend. (Milan Jacovich Mystery Ser.). 288p. 1997. mass mkt. 5.99 (0-312-96399-8, St Martins Paperbacks) St Martin.

***Roberts, Les.** Indian Sign. (Milan Jacovich Mystery Ser.). 2000. mass mkt. 23.95 (0-312-97646-1) St Martin.

Roberts, Les. The Lake Effect. LC 94-31315. 352p. 1994. text 21.95 (0-312-11537-7) St Martin.

***Roberts, Les.** The Lake Effect. 2000. pap. 5.99 (0-312-97823-5, St Martins Paperbacks) St Martin.

— Laughter of Children. mass mkt. write for info. (0-312-97642-9) St Martin.

— Laughter of Children. LC 00-24136. 320p. 2000. text 23.95 (0-312-25217-X) St Martin.

Roberts, Les. A Shoot in Cleveland. LC 98-12135. 368p. 1998. text 23.95 (0-312-18663-0) St Martin.

— A Shoot in Cleveland. 336p. 1999. 5.99 (0-312-96694-6, Pub. by Tor Bks) St Martin.

Roberts, Leslie. Cancer Today: Origins, Prevention & Treatment. LC 84-19031. (Illus.). 144p. reprint ed. pap. 44.70 (0-8357-6647-0, 203531400094) Bks Demand.

— The Mackenzie. LC 73-20906. 276p. 1974. reprint ed. lib. bdg. 65.00 (0-8371-5864-8, ROMR, Greenwood Pr) Greenwood.

Roberts, Lewes. The Marchants Mapp of Commerce. LC 74-80203. (English Experience Ser.: No. 689). 468p. 1974. reprint ed. 126.00 (90-221-0689-6) Walter J Johnson.

Roberts, Lewis & Wheale, Albert, eds. Innovation & Environmental Risk. 224p. 1992. text 57.95 (1-85293-156-6, Pub. by P P Pubs) CRC Pr.

Roberts, Lewis E. The By-Name Index to the Centennial History of Arkansas. 1994. pap. 28.50 (0-941765-97-0) Arkansas Res.

Roberts, Lillian. Riding for a Fall. 1996. mass mkt. 5.50 (0-449-14985-4) Fawcett.

Roberts, Lillian M. Almost Human. 1998. mass mkt. 5.99 (0-449-00228-4, GM) Fawcett.

Roberts, Linda. Achieving the Goals - Goal 5: First in the World in Math & Science: Technology Resources. 132p. 1998. reprint ed. pap. text 40.00 (0-7881-4239-9) DIANE Pub.

Roberts, Lindsell. The Secretary's Quick Reference Handbook. 4th ed. 1995. pap. 8.00 (0-671-89918-X) S&S Trade.

Roberts, Linleigh J. Let Us Make Man. 168p. (Orig.). (C). 1988. pap. 11.99 (0-85151-525-8) Banner of Truth.

Roberts, Lisa C. From Knowledge to Narrative: Educators & the Changing Museum. LC 96-37617. (Illus.). 272p. (Orig.). 1997. pap. text 18.95 (1-56098-706-5) Smithsonian.

***Roberts, Lisa J.** E-Prime SigmaEOS & the General Semantics Paradigm: Revolution, Devolution or Evolution? LC 99-41592. (ISGS Monographs: No. 1). (Illus.). 80p. (C). 1999. pap. text 11.95 (0-918970-48-2) Intl Gen Semantics.

***Roberts, Lisa J., et al.** Overcoming Addictions. LC 99-13341. 240p. 1999. pap. 25.00 (0-393-70299-5) Norton.

Roberts, Lisa M. How to Raise a Family & a Career under One Roof: A Parent's Guide to Home Business. Olson, Marla, ed. LC 96-4078. (Illus.). 224p. (Orig.). 1997. pap. 15.95 (0-943641-17-9) Bookhaven Pr.

Roberts, Liz, jt. auth. see Ganeri, Anita.

Roberts, Lois J. Archaeological Investigations on the San Antonio Terrace, Vandenberg Air Force Base, California, in Connection with MX Facilities Construction No. II: Historical Overview of the Study Area. (Illus.). 204p. (C). 1984. reprint ed. pap. text 21.88 (1-55567-445-3) Coyote Press.

— San Miguel Island: Santa Barbara's Fourth Island West. LC 91-73715. 216p. 1992. pap. 9.95 (0-9630370-0-5) Cal Rim.

Roberts, Lon. Process Reengineering: The Key to Achieving Breakthrough Success. LC 93-45264. 195p. 1994. text 33.00 (0-87389-274-7, H0830) ASQ Qual Pr.

Roberts, Lora. Murder Bone by Bone. 1997. mass mkt. 5.50 (0-449-14946-3) Fawcett.

— Murder Crops Up. 240p. 1998. mass mkt. 5.99 (0-449-15048-8, GM) Fawcett.

***Roberts, Lora.** Murder Follows Money. (Liz Sullivan Mysteries Ser.). 240p. 2000. mass mkt. 6.50 (0-449-00539-9) Fawcett.

Roberts, Lora. Murder in a Nice Neighborhood. LC 94-94033. (Northern California Mysteries Ser.). (Orig.). 1994. mass mkt. 4.99 (0-449-14891-2, GM) Fawcett.

— Murder in the Marketplace. 1995. mass mkt. 5.50 (0-449-14890-4) Fawcett.

— Murder Mile High. 1996. mass mkt. 5.50 (0-449-14947-1) Fawcett.

Roberts, Lorin W. Cytodifferentiation in Plants: Xylogenesis as a Model System. LC 75-10041. (Developmental & Cell Biology Ser.). 174p. reprint ed. pap. 49.60 (0-608-12495-8, 2024522) Bks Demand.

Roberts, Lorin W., jt. auth. see Dodds, John H.

Roberts, Lorraine. Henderson's Hill. 354p. 1997. pap. 16.95 (1-57502-626-0, PO1781) Morris Pubng.

Roberts, Louis. The Theological Aesthetics of Hans Urs von Balthasar. LC 86-28321. 272p. 1987. reprint ed. pap. 84.40 (0-7837-9118-6, 204991900004) Bks Demand.

Roberts, Louis, ed. Latin Texts from the Fourth to the Fifteenth Centuries. (Sources for the History of Cyprus Ser.: Vol. VIII). 300p. 1999. pap. 70.00 (0-9651704-8-9) Greece & Cyprus Res.

Roberts, Luis A. & Cabre, Xavier. Fully Nonlinear Elliptic Equations. LC 95-15024. (Colloquium Publications: Vol. 43). 104p. 1995. pap. 29.00 (0-8218-0437-5, COLL/43) Am Math.

Roberts, Luke S. Mercantilism in a Japanese Domain: The Merchant Origins of Economic Nationalism in 18th-Century Tosa. LC 97-18070. (Illus.). 280p. (C). 1998. text 59.95 (0-521-62131-3) Cambridge U Pr.

***Roberts, Lung Cheng.** The Heritage of Hong Kong: Its History, Architecture & Culture. (Illus.). 80p. 1999. 26.00 (962-7283-24-X, Pub. by FormAsia) Weatherhill.

Roberts, Lydia J. The Dona Elena Project. 113p. 1963. pap. 3.00 (0-8477-2420-4) U of PR Pr.

Roberts, Lydia J. & Stefani, Rosa L. Patterns of Living in Puerto Rican Families. LC 74-14247. (Puerto Rican Experience Ser.). (Illus.). 440p. 1975. reprint ed. 35.95 (0-405-06233-8) Ayer.

Roberts, Lynda S. Mitt Magic: Finger Plays for Finger Puppets. (Illus.). 89p. (Orig.). (ps-1). 1986. pap. 12.95 (0-87659-111-X) Gryphon Hse.

Roberts, Lynette & Pikoulis, John. Collected Poems. 180p. 1997. pap. 25.95 (1-85411-189-2, Pub. by Seren Bks) Dufour.

Roberts, Lynn S. & Turner, Eric. English Silver: Masterpieces by Omar Ramsden from the Campbell Collection. 60p. 1992. pap. 15.00 (0-9632870-0-1) D A Hanks.

Roberts, Lynn S., jt. auth. see Wardropper, Ian.

Roberts, M. Ezra, Nehemiah, Esther. (Mastering the Old & New Testament Ser.: Vol. 11). pap. 14.99 (0-8499-3550-4) Word Pub.

— Mishnah-Nezikin: Bava Basra. Danziger, Y., ed. (ArtScroll Mishnah Ser.). (Illus.). 240p. 1986. 22.99 (0-89906-293-8) Mesorah Pubns.

— Mishnah-Nezikin: Sanhedrin. Danzinger, Y., ed. (ArtScroll Mishnah Ser.). (Illus.). 206p. 1987. 22.99 (0-89906-295-4) Mesorah Pubns.

— Spiders of Britain & Europe. (Illus.). 320p. 1998. 32.95 (0-00-219981-5, Pub. by HarpC) HarpC.

— Swedish Diplomats at Cromwell's Court. (Camden Fourth Ser.: No. 36). 336p. 27.00 (0-86193-117-3) David Brown.

Roberts, M. & Arem, T. Z. Mishnah-Nashim: Gittin-Kiddushin. (ArtScroll Mishnah Ser.). (Illus.). 314p. 1986. 22.99 (0-89906-283-0) Mesorah Pubns.

Roberts, M., ed. see Grimmer, Glenna.

Roberts, M., ed. see Kahrimanis, Leola.

Roberts, M., ed. see Kerr, Rita.

Roberts, M., ed. see Liles, Maurine W.

Roberts, M., ed. see Pamplin, Laurel J.

Roberts, M B. The Honky Tonk Truth: The Brooks & Dunn Story. 160p. Date not set. 29.50 (1-57223-216-1) Willow Creek Pr.

Roberts, M. B., jt. auth. see Modra, Ronald C.

Roberts, M. F. & Wink, M. Alkaloids: Biochemistry, Ecology & Medicinal Applications. LC 98-17602. (Illus.). 452p. (C). 1998. text 115.00 (0-306-45465-3, Kluwer Plenum) Kluwer Academic.

Roberts, M. I. Managing a Shoot. (Illus.). 112p. 1990. 29.95 (0-948253-43-6, Pub. by Sportmans Pr) Trafalgar.

Roberts, M. L. World's Weirdest Bats. LC 96-8323. (Illus.). 32p. (J). (ps-3). 1996. pap. 3.95 (0-8167-4133-6, Whistlstop) Troll Communs.

— World's Weirdest Bats. LC 96-8323. 1996. 8.15 (0-606-10372-4, Pub. by Turtleback) Demco.

— World's Weirdest Birds. LC 95-17781. (Illus.). 32p. (J). (gr. k-3). 1995. pap. 3.95 (0-8167-3734-7, Whistlstop) Troll Communs.

— World's Weirdest Birds. (J). 1995. 7.70 (0-606-08401-0, Pub. by Turtleback) Demco.

— World's Weirdest Bugs & Other Creepy Crawlies. LC 94-18027. (Illus.). 32p. (J). (ps-2). 1997. pap. 3.95 (0-8167-3537-9, Whistlstop) Troll Communs.

— World's Weirdest Dinosaurs. LC 95-42215. (World's Weirdest Ser.). (Illus.). 32p. (J). (gr. k-3). 1996. pap. 3.95 (0-8167-3865-3, Whistlstop) Troll Communs.

— World's Weirdest Dinosaurs. LC 95-42215. 1996. 7.70 (0-606-10087-3, Pub. by Turtleback) Demco.

— World's Weirdest Dinosaurs. (Illus.). 32p. (J). (gr. 1-2). 1997. reprint ed. pap. text 3.50 (0-7881-3957-6) DIANE Pub.

— World's Weirdest Reptiles. LC 93-8493. (Illus.). 32p. (YA). (gr. 2-9). 1994. pap. 3.95 (0-8167-3221-3) Troll Communs.

— World's Weirdest Reptiles. LC 93-8493. (Illus.). 32p. (J). (gr. 2-9). 1997. lib. bdg. 18.60 (0-8167-3229-9) Troll Communs.

— World's Weirdest Sea Creatures. 1997. pap. 3.95 (0-8167-3689-8) Troll Communs.

— World's Weirdest Sea Creatures. (J). 1995. 8.15 (0-606-08402-9, Pub. by Turtleback) Demco.

— World's Weirdest Underwater Creatures. LC 93-21053. (J). 1993. pap. 3.95 (0-8167-3222-1) Troll Communs.

Roberts, M. S. Genealogy of the Descendants of John Kirk, 1660-1705. Cope, G., ed. (Illus.). 729p. reprint ed. pap. 99.50 (0-8328-0736-2); reprint ed. lib. bdg. 107.50 (0-8328-0735-4) Higginson Bk Co.

Roberts, M. Susan. Living Without Procrastination: How to Stop Postponing Your Life. LC 95-69484. 168p. 1995. pap. 12.95 (1-57224-026-1) New Harbinger.

Roberts, M Susan & Jansen, Gerard J. Living with ADD: A Workbook for Adults with Attention Deficit Disorder. LC 96-71152. 176p. (Orig.). 1997. pap., wbk. ed. 17.95 (1-57224-063-6) New Harbinger.

Roberts, M. W. Chemistry of the Metal-Gas Interface. McKee, C. S., ed. (Monographs on the Physics & Chemistry of Materials). (Illus.). 1979. 125.00 (0-19-851339-9) OUP.

— Interfacial Science. LC 97-7683. (IUPAC Chemical Data Ser.). (Illus.). xi, 302p. 1997. 95.00 (0-632-04219-2) Blackwell Sci.

Roberts, Madge T. Star of Destiny: The Private Life of Sam & Margaret Houston. LC 92-31587. (Illus.). 432p. 1993. 29.50 (0-929398-51-3) UNTX Pr.

Roberts, Madge T., ed. The Personal Correspondence of Sam Houston, 1839-1845, Vol. 1. LC 95-36738. 448p. 1996. 32.50 (1-57441-000-8) UNTX Pr.

— The Personal Correspondence of Sam Houston, 1846-1848, Vol. II. 390p. 1998. 32.50 (1-57441-031-8) UNTX Pr.

— The Personal Correspondence of Sam Houston, 1848-1852, Vol. III. LC 95-36738. 508p. 1999. 32.50 (1-57441-063-6) UNTX Pr.

Roberts, Malcolm B. The Wit & Wisdom of Wally Hickel. 2nd ed. LC 94-93929. (Illus.). 240p. 1995. reprint ed. text 24.95 (0-9644316-1-0); reprint ed. pap. text 14.95 (0-9644316-0-2) Searchers Pr.

Roberts, Marc. Neue Lexikon der Esoterik. (GER.). 461p. 1993. 75.00 (0-7859-8426-7, 3552045015) Fr & Eur.

Roberts, Marc J. & Bluhm, Jeremy S. The Choices of Power: Utilities Face the Environmental Challenge. LC 80-20729. 472p. reprint ed. pap. 146.40 (0-7837-4110-3, 205793300011) Bks Demand.

Roberts, Marcus. Analytical Marxism: A Critique. LC 96-48950. (C). 1997. pap. 20.00 (1-85984-116-3) Norton.

— Analytical Marxism: A Critique. LC 96-48950. (C). 1997. text 65.00 (1-85984-855-9, Pub. by Verso) Norton.

Roberts, Margaret. Pioneer California: Tales of Explorers, Indians, & Settlers. LC 81-22543. (Illus.). 296p. (J). (gr. 6 up). 1982. 12.95 (0-914598-42-2) Bear Flag Bks.

— Pot-Pourri Making. LC 94-5873. (Illus.). 96p. 1994. pap. 10.95 (0-8117-2590-1) Stackpole.

— Summer Cooking with Herbs. LC 94-8636. (Illus.). 104p. 1994. pap. 10.95 (0-8117-3070-0) Stackpole.

— Trial Psychology: Communication & Persuasion in the Courtroom. 490p. 1987. text 95.00 (0-327-01041-X, 82475, MICHIE) LEXIS Pub.

— Winter Cooking with Herbs. LC 94-9077. (Illus.). 96p. 1994. pap. 10.95 (0-8117-3096-4) Stackpole.

Roberts, Margaret C. Trial Psychology: Communication & Persuasion in the Courtroom. 490p. 1987. boxed set 95.00 (0-409-25105-4, 82475-10, MICHIE) LEXIS Pub.

Roberts, Marian. Mediation in Family Disputes: Principles in Practice. 2nd ed. LC 97-70319. 249p. 1997. pap. 31.95 (1-85742-315-1, Pub. by Arena) Ashgate Pub Co.

Roberts, Marie & Ormsby-Lennon, Hugh, eds. Secret Texts: The Literature of Secret Societies. LC 91-13789. (Studies in Cultural History: No. 1). 349 p. 1995. 55.00 (0-404-64251-9) AMS Pr.

Roberts, Marie M. The Artist's Design: Probing the Hidden Order. (Illus.). 260p. (Orig.). 1993. pap. 49.00 (0-9639758-0-3) Fradema Pr.

Roberts, Marie M., ed. For Her Own Good: A Series of Conduct Books. 1996. 120.00 (1-85506-378-6) Bks Intl VA.

— Her Write His Name Series, 5 vols., Set. 1996. 135.00 (1-85506-384-0) Bks Intl VA.

— Sources of British Feminism. 2017p. (C). 1993. 745.00 (0-415-10164-6) Routledge.

— Subversive Women Series. 1996. pap. 120.00 (1-85506-261-5) Bks Intl VA.

— The Young Lady's Pocket Library, or Parental Monitor: 1790 Edition. LC 95-222844. (For Her Own Good Ser.). 352p. 1996. reprint ed. pap. 29.95 (1-85506-382-4) Bks Intl VA.

Roberts, Marie M. & Mizuta, Tamae. Controversies in the History of British Feminism, 6 vols., Set. (History of British Feminism Ser.). 2955p. (C). (gr. 13). 1995. text, boxed set 700.00 (0-415-11873-5, C0434) Routledge.

Roberts, Marie M. & Mizuta, Tamae, eds. Perspectives on the History of British Feminism, 6 vols., Set. (History of British Feminism Ser.). 2301p. (C). (gr. 13). 1994. text, boxed set 700.00 (0-415-10352-5, B4783) Routledge.

Roberts, Marie M. & Zephaniah, Benjamin, eds. Out of the Night: Writings from Death Row. (Illus.). 192p. 1994. 45.00 (1-873797-10-9, Pub. by New Clarion); pap. 17.95 (1-873797-09-5, Pub. by New Clarion) Paul & Co Pubs.

Roberts, Marie M., ed. see Arnold, Ethel.

Roberts, Marie M., ed. see Collier, Jane.

Roberts, Marie M., ed. see Grand, Sarah.

Roberts, Marie M., ed. see James, Alice.

Roberts, Marie M., ed. see More, Hannah.

Roberts, Marie M., ed. see Parsons, Elsie C.

Roberts, Marie M., jt. ed. see Porter, Roy.

Roberts, Marie M., ed. see Shelley, Mary Wollstonecraft.

Roberts, Marie M., ed. see Swetnam, Joseph, et al.

Roberts, Marie M., ed. see Swift, Jonathan.

Roberts, Marie M., ed. see Thackeray, Anne I.

Roberts, Marie M., ed. see Wordsworth, Dorothy.

Roberts, Marie M., ed. & intro. see Lytton, Rosina B.

Roberts, Marie M., ed. & intro. see Thompson, W. & Wheeler, A.

Roberts, Marilyn, ed. Proceedings of the Conference of the American Academy of Advertising, 1999. 1999. pap. 25.00 (0-931030-22-6) Am Acad Advert.

Roberts, Marion. Mediation in Family Disputes: A Guide to Practice. (Community Care Practice Handbook Ser.). 120p. 1988. pap. text 15.95 (0-7045-0585-1, Pub. by Gower) Ashgate Pub Co.

— Mediation in Family Disputes: Principles in Practice. 2nd ed. 249p. 1997. text 64.95 (1-85742-318-6, Pub. by Arena) Ashgate Pub Co.

Roberts, Mark. Ezra & Nehemiah. (Communicator's Commentary Ser.: Vol. 11). 22.99 (0-8499-0416-1) Word Pub.

Roberts, Mark, jt. auth. see Pitts, Michael.

Roberts, Mark, jt. auth. see Watson, James, Jr.

Roberts, Mark, tr. see Lorenzi, Lorenzo.

Roberts, Mark E., jt. auth. see Roberts, Gregory.

Roberts, Mark J. Khomeini's Incorporation of the Iranian Military. 111p. 1996. per. 6.00 (0-16-061182-2) USGPO.

Roberts, Mark J. Khomeini's Incorporation of the Iranian Military. (Illus.). 107p. (C). 2000. reprint ed. pap. text 35.00 (0-7881-3678-X) DIANE Pub.

Roberts, Mark J. & Tybout, James R., eds. Industrial Evolution in Developing Countries: Micro Patterns of Turnover, Productivity, & Market Structure. LC 96-14987. (A World Bank Publication). (Illus.). 360p. 1997. text 60.00 (0-19-521110-3, 61110) OUP.

Roberts, Mark K. Gallow Riders. 240p. 1986. mass mkt. 2.50 (0-8217-1934-3, Zebra Kensgtn) Kensgtn Pub Corp.

— The Liberty Corps No. 5: Poisoned Paradise. 224p. (Orig.). 1988. mass mkt. 3.95 (0-445-20725-6, Pub. by Warner Bks) Little.

— The Liberty Corps No. 6: Costa Rican Chaos. 208p. 1988. mass mkt. 3.95 (0-445-20727-2, Pub. by Warner Bks) Little.

— Prairie Fire. LC 94-121842. 288p. 1993. mass mkt. 3.50 (0-8217-4167-5, Zebra Kensgtn) Kensgtn Pub Corp.

— Warrior Outlaws. 256p. 1993. mass mkt. 3.50 (0-8217-4374-0, Zebra Kensgtn) Kensgtn Pub Corp.

Roberts, Mark R., jt. auth. see Muir, Jeff.

Roberts, Mark S., jt. auth. see Allison, David B.

Roberts, Mark S., ed. see Lyotard, Jean-Francois.

Roberts, Mark S., tr. see Lyotard, Jean-Francois.

Roberts, Marta. Tumbleweeds. LC 74-22805. reprint ed. 37.50 (0-404-58461-6) AMS Pr.

Roberts, Martha D., jt. auth. see Roberts, Mervin F.

R

Roberts, Martin. Change Management Excellence: Putting NLP to Work in the 21st Century. 280p. 1999. 45.00 (*1-899836-14-4*, Pub. by Crown Hse) LPC Group.
— Italian Renaissance. (Longman Origin Ser.). 1992. pap. text 10.64 (*0-582-08252-8*) Longman.
— Machines & Liberty, a Portrait of Europe, 1789-1914. (Portrait of Europe Ser.). (Illus.). 360p. 1972. pap. 19.95 (*0-19-913040-X*) OUP.
— Michel Tournier: "Bricolage" & Cultural Mythology. (Stanford French & Italian Studies: No. 79). 192p. 1995. pap. 56.50 (*0-915838-95-8*) Anma Libri.

Roberts, Martin, tr. see Taibo, Paco Ignacio, II.

Roberts, Martin M., tr. see Taibo, Paco I.

Roberts, Martin Michael, tr. see Taibo, Paco Ignacio, II.

Roberts, Marvin F. All about Breeding Canaries. 128p. 9.95 (*0-86622-129-8*) TFH Pubns.

Roberts, Marvin L. & Stuckey, Ronald L. Bibliography of Theses & Dissertations on Ohio Floristics & Vegetation in Ohio Colleges & Universities. (Informative Circular Ser.: No. 7). 1974. pap. text 2.00 (*0-86727-074-8*) Ohio Bio Survey.

Roberts, Mary. The Creeper. LC 93-134. (Illus.). (J). 1994. write for info. (*0-383-03684-4*) SRA McGraw.

Roberts, Mary, jt. ed. see Johnson, Susan.

Roberts, Mary, ed. see Scherer, Bonnie L.

Roberts, Mary Beth. Yo, Blacken This! Hell's Kitchen Meets the French Quarter at the Delta Grill. LC 99-40955. (Illus.). 128p. 1999. 24.50 (*1-57223-280-3*) Willow Creek Pr.

Roberts, Mary J. Write with Your Ears. (Illus.). 158p. 1983. student ed. 14.95 (*0-913609-01-3*); pap. 19.95 (*0-913609-00-5*) Hse of Tomorrow.

Roberts, Mary K. & Bergner, Raymond M., eds. Advances in Descriptive Psychology Vol. 6: Clinical Topics: Adolescent-Family Problems, Bulimia, Chronic Mental Illness, & Mania. 316p. (C). 1991. 70.00 (*0-9625661-1-X*) Descriptive Psych Pr.

Roberts, Mary L. Civilization Without Sexes: Reconstructing Gender in Postwar France, 1917-1927. LC 93-26899. (Women in Culture & Society Ser.). 352p. 1994. pap. text 18.95 (*0-226-72122-1*); lib. bdg. 48.00 (*0-226-72121-3*) U Ch Pr.

Roberts, Mary L. & Berger, Paul. Direct Marketing Management. 440p. (C). 1989. text 84.00 (*0-13-214784-X*) P-H.

Roberts, Mary L. & Berger, Paul D. Direct Marketing Management. 2nd ed. LC 99-10509. 1999. 55.01 (*0-13-084084-X*) P-H.

Roberts, Mary Lou, jt. auth. see Long, Lorraine.

***Roberts, Mary M., et al.** Employment Law Compliance for New Businesses - 10/99 Update. Peyerwold, David, ed. LC 97-77814. (California Business Start-Up Ser.). 362p. 1999. ring bd. 60.00 (*0-7626-0365-8*, BU-32912) Cont Ed Bar-CA.

Roberts, Mary N. & Roberts, Allen F. A Sense of Wonder: African Art from the Faletti Family Collection. LC 97-18380. (Illus.). 144p. 1998. pap. 29.95 (*0-910407-33-9*) Phoenix Art.

Roberts, Mary N. & Roberts, Allen F., eds. Memory: Luba Art: The Making of History. (Illus.). 258p. 1996. 75.00 (*3-7913-1677-X*, Pub. by Prestel) te Neues.

Roberts, Mary N., et al. African Masterworks in the Detroit Institute of Arts. LC 95-6169. (Illus.). 192p. 1995. pap. 34.95 (*1-56098-602-6*) Smithsonian.
— Exhibition-ism: Museums & African Art. LC 94-78064. (Illus.). 1994. pap. 19.95 (*0-945802-16-1*) Museum African.

Roberts, Mary N., ed. see Childs, S. Terry & De Maret, Pierre.

Roberts, Matis. Mishnah-Kodashim Vol. 1B: Menachos. Kempler, Naftali & Danziger, Yehezkel, eds. (ArtScroll Mishnah Ser.). 302p. 1989. 22.99 (*0-89906-303-9*) Mesorah Pubns.
— Trei Assar/The Twelve Prophets: Hoshea, Yoel, Amos, Ovadiah. 22.99 (*0-89906-017-X*, TW1H); pap. 18.99 (*0-89906-018-8*, TW1P) Mesorah Pubns.

Roberts, Matt & Etherington, Don. Bookbinding & the Conservation of Books: A Dictionary of Descriptive Terminology. LC 81-607974. (Illus.). x, 296p. 1982. 27.00 (*0-8444-0366-0*, 030-000-00126-5) Lib Congress.

Roberts, Matthew W. Export Processing Zones in Jamaica & Mauritius: Evolution of an Export-Oriented Development Model. LC 92-30975. 200p. 1992. text 79.95 (*0-7734-9837-0*) E Mellen.
— The Impact of the World Bank & IMF on Political Developments in Sub-Saharan Africa: Examples from Ghana & Kenya. (Graduate Student Term Papers). 33p. 1986. pap. text 2.00 (*0-941934-50-0*) Indiana Africa.

Roberts, Maurice. The Thought of God. 232p. 1993. pap. 8.99 (*0-85151-658-0*) Banner of Truth.

Roberts, Maurice, ed. & photos by see Harithas, James & Poole, Claire.

Roberts, Maxine B., compiled by. The Cousin Finder Directory: A Related Line Locating Aid, Vol. 1. 146p. (Orig.). 1985. pap. text 10.00 (*0-9616192-0-1*) Roberts CA.

Roberts, Maxine B., ed. The Cousin Finder Directory: A Related Line Locating Aid, Vol. 2. (Orig.). 1988. pap. text. write for info. (*0-9616192-1-X*) Roberts CA.

Roberts, Maxwell J. & Russo, Riccardo. A Student's Guide to Analysis of Variance. LC 98-27699. 1999. write for info. (*0-415-16564-4*); pap. write for info. (*0-415-16565-2*) Routledge.

Roberts, Meg L., et al. A Home for All Seasons. LC 98-3500. (Illus.). 128p. 1998. 29.95 (*0-8109-3429-9*, Pub. by Abrams) Time Warner.

Roberts, Meg-Lynn. Lord Diablo's Demise. 1996. mass mkt. 4.50 (*0-8217-5338-X*, Zebra Kensgtn) Kensgtn Pub Corp.
— A Midnight Masquerade. 320p. 1996. mass mkt. 3.99 (*0-8217-4336-8*, Zebra Kensgtn) Kensgtn Pub Corp.
— A Perfect Match. 320p. 1993. mass mkt. 3.99 (*0-8217-4140-3*, Zebra Kensgtn) Kensgtn Pub Corp.
— Rake's Gambit. 224p. 1997. mass mkt. 4.99 (*0-8217-5687-7*, Zebra Kensgtn) Kensgtn Pub Corp.

Roberts, Melinda A. Child vs. Childmaker: Future Persons & Present Duties in Ethics & the Law. LC 98-13911. 256p. 1998. 65.00 (*0-8476-8900-X*); pap. 24.95 (*0-8476-8901-8*) Rowman.

Roberts, Melissa, ed. see Beverley, Mary F.

Roberts, Melissa, ed. see Bradshaw, Thomas I. & Clark, Marsha.

Roberts, Melissa, ed. see Charles, H. Robert.

Roberts, Melissa, ed. see Clendenin, Mary J.

Roberts, Melissa, ed. see Donaly, E. Brice.

Roberts, Melissa, ed. see Kerr, Rita.

Roberts, Melissa, ed. see Matthews, Billie P. & Chichester, A. Lee.

Roberts, Melissa, ed. see O'Neal, Bill.

Roberts, Melissa, ed. see Parnell, Ben.

Roberts, Melissa, ed. see Sharpe, George.

Roberts, Melissa, ed. see Swendson, Patsy.

Roberts, Melissa, ed. see Wade, Mary D.

Roberts, Melissa, ed. see Westmoreland, Ronald P.

Roberts, Melissa, ed. see Wiggs, Susan.

Roberts, Melissa, ed. see Wilkins, Frederick.

Roberts, Mervin F. All about Breeding Budgerigars. (Illus.). 96p. 1989. 11.95 (*0-86622-997-3*, PS-804) TFH Pubns.
— All about Breeding Lovebirds. (Illus.). 96p. 1983. 11.95 (*0-86622-695-8*, PS-800) TFH Pubns.
— All about Chameleons & Anoles. (Illus.). 96p. 1989. 8.95 (*0-86622-795-4*, PS-310) TFH Pubns.
— All about Ferrets. (Illus.). 64p. 1977. 4.95 (*0-87666-914-3*, PS-754) TFH Pubns.
— Chameleons. (Illus.). 32p. 1977. pap. 1.79 (*0-87666-188-6*, A-304) TFH Pubns.
— A Complete Introduction to Hamsters. (Illus.). 128p. 1987. pap. 8.95 (*0-86622-282-0*, CO-020S) TFH Pubns.
— Hamsters As Pets. (Hamsters As Pets). 32p. pap. 1.79 (*0-87666-202-5*) TFH Pubns.
— Mice. (Mice). 32p. pap. 1.79 (*0-87666-209-2*) TFH Pubns.
— Pearl Makers: The Tidemarsh Guide to Clams, Oysters, Mussels & Scallops. LC 84-50701. (Tidemarsh Guides Ser.). (Illus.). 168p. 1984. 6.95 (*0-917941-00-4*) M Roberts.
— Snakes. (Illus.). 80p. 1990. pap. 6.95 (*0-86622-784-9*, PB126) TFH Pubns.
— Starting Right with Rabbits. (Illus.). 112p. 1983. 11.95 (*0-87666-814-7*, PS-796) TFH Pubns.
— Terrariums for Your New Pet. (Illus.). 64p. (Orig.). 1990. pap. 6.95 (*0-86622-525-0*, TU-017) TFH Pubns.
— The Tidemarsh Guide. LC 79-63522. (Tidemarsh Guides Ser.). (Illus.). 240p. 1979. 5.95 (*0-933614-19-5*) M Roberts.
— The Tidemarsh Guide to Fishes. LC 85-90364. (Tidemarsh Guides Ser.). (Illus.). 370p. (Orig.). 1985. 10.95 (*0-9615047-0-6*) M Roberts.
— Turtles. (Illus.). 96p. 1980. 9.95 (*0-87666-928-3*, KW-051) TFH Pubns.
— Zebra Finches. (Illus.). 96p. 1981. 9.95 (*0-86622-762-8*, KW-055) TFH Pubns.

Roberts, Mervin F. & Roberts, Martha D. All about Iguanas. (Illus.). 96p. (Orig.). 1976. 11.95 (*0-86622-747-4*, PS-311) TFH Pubns.

Roberts, Michael. British Diplomacy & Swedish Politics, 1758-1773. LC 80-11499. (Nordic Ser.: No. 1). 553p. reprint ed. pap. 171.50 (*0-7837-2925-1*, 205752900006) Bks Demand.
— Gustavus Adolphus. 2nd ed. (Profiles in Power Ser.). 216p. (C). 1992. text 52.95 (*0-582-09001-6*, 79385) Longman.
— The Jeweled Style: Poetry & Poetics in Late Antiquity. LC 88-47941. (Illus.). 199p. reprint ed. pap. 61.70 (*0-608-20943-0*, 207204200003) Bks Demand.
— Jungle ABC. LC 97-33404. (Illus.). 64p. (J). (ps-3). 1998. 19.45 (*0-7868-0398-3*, Pub. by Hyperion) Time Warner.
— Modern Mind. LC 68-29241. (Essay Index Reprint Ser.). 1977. reprint ed. 19.95 (*0-8369-0827-9*) Ayer.

***Roberts, Michael.** Parisian Home Cooking: Conversations, Recipes, And Tips From The Cooks And Food Merchants Of Paris. LC 98-41750. (Illus.). 352p. 1999. 25.00 (*0-688-13868-3*, Wm Morrow) Morrow Avon.

Roberts, Michael. Poetry & the Cult of the Martyrs: The Liber Peristephanon of Prudentius. (Recentiores: Later Latin Texts & Contexts Ser.). 232p. 1993. text 52.50 (*0-472-10449-7*, 10449) U of Mich Pr.
— T. E. Hulme. LC 72-169106. (English Biography Ser.: No. 31). 1971. reprint ed. lib. bdg. 75.00 (*0-8383-1342-6*) M S G Haskell Hse.
— Whig Party, 1807-1812. 453p. 1965. 45.00 (*0-7146-1512-9*, Pub. by F Cass Pubs) Intl Spec Bk.

Roberts, Michael, ed. Exploring Confrontations: Sri Lanka Politics, Culture & History, Vol. 14. LC 95-214589. (Studies in Anthropology & History). 400p. 1995. pap. text 32.00 (*3-7186-5692-2*, Harwood Acad Pubs) Gordon & Breach.
— Exploring Confrontations: Sri Lanka Politics, History & Culture, Vol. 14. LC 95-214589. (Studies in Anthropology & History). 335p. 1995. text 58.00 (*3-7186-5506-3*, Harwood Acad Pubs) Gordon & Breach.
— New Country: Prose & Poetry by the Authors of New Signatures. LC 78-178457. (Short Story Index Reprint Ser.). 1977. reprint ed. 20.95 (*0-8369-4058-X*) Ayer.

Roberts, Michael, et al, eds. Readings in Pediatric Psychology. LC 93-7736. (Illus.). 402p. (C). 1993. pap. 54.00 (*0-306-44423-2*, Plenum Trade) Perseus Pubng.

***Roberts, Michael & Clarke, Simone, eds.** Women & Gender in Early Modern Wales. (Illus.). 224p. 2000. 65.00 (*0-7083-1580-1*, Pub. by U Wales Pr); pap. 29.95 (*0-7083-1550-X*, Pub. by U Wales Pr) Paul & Co Pubs.

Roberts, Michael & Wallander, Jan L., eds. Family Issues in Pediatric Psychology. 288p. 1992. pap. text 32.50 (*0-8058-0854-X*) L Erlbaum Assocs.

Roberts, Michael, jt. auth. see Konstan, David.

Roberts, Michael, tr. see Ahnlund, Nils G.

Roberts, Michael C., ed. Handbook of Pediatric Psychology. 2nd ed. LC 95-8536. 814p. 1995. lib. bdg. 75.00 (*0-89862-156-9*) Guilford Pubns.
— Handbook of Pediatric Psychology. 2nd ed. 814p. 1998. pap. text 39.00 (*1-57230-366-2*) Guilford Pubns.
— Model Practices in Service Delivery in Child & Family Mental Health. 456p. 1996. text 79.95 (*0-8058-1651-8*) L Erlbaum Assocs.
— Model Practices in Service Delivery in Child & Family Mental Health. 456p. 1996. pap. text 45.00 (*0-8058-1652-6*) L Erlbaum Assocs.

Roberts, Michael C., et al, eds. Publishing Child-Oriented Articles in Psychology: A Compendium of Publication Outlets. LC 82-45067. 178p. (Orig.). (C). 1982. pap. text 20.50 (*0-8191-2661-6*); lib. bdg. 52.50 (*0-8191-2660-8*) U Pr of Amer.

Roberts, Michael C. & Hurley, Linda K. Managing Managed Care. LC 97-33280. (Clinical Child Psychology Library). (Illus.). 206p. (C). 1997. 45.00 (*0-306-45670-2*, Kluwer Plenum) Kluwer Academic.
— Managing Managed Care. LC 97-33280. (Clinical Child Psychology Library). 188p. 1997. pap. 21.50 (*0-306-45671-0*, Kluwer Plenum) Kluwer Academic.

Roberts, Michael C. & Walker, C. Eugene, eds. Casebook of Child & Pediatric Psychology. LC 88-37197. 468p. 1989. lib. bdg. 55.00 (*0-89862-739-7*) Guilford Pubns.

Roberts, Michael C., jt. auth. see Hidore, John J.

Roberts, Michael C., jt. auth. see Walker, C. Eugene.

Roberts, Michael D., ed. see Kamm, Christian P.

Roberts, Michael J. The Jeweled Style: Poetry & Poetics in Late Antiquity. LC 88-47941. (Illus.). 192p. 1989. 35.00 (*0-8014-2265-5*) Cornell U Pr.
— The Spiders of Great Britain & Ireland, 3 vols., Set. (Illus.). 1985. 400.00 (*90-04-07658-1*) Lubrecht & Cramer.
— The Spiders of Great Britain & Ireland, 3 vols., Vol. I. (Illus.). 229p. 1985. write for info. (*0-318-64516-5*) Lubrecht & Cramer.
— The Spiders of Great Britain & Ireland, 3 vols., Vol. II. (Illus.). 204p. 1985. write for info. (*0-318-64517-3*) Lubrecht & Cramer.
— The Spiders of Great Britain & Ireland, 3 vols., Vol. III. (Illus.). 1985. write for info. (*0-318-64518-1*) Lubrecht & Cramer.

Roberts, Michael L. U. S. Naval Aviation Patches Vol. I: Aircraft Carriers, Carrier Air Wings, Support Establishment. LC 95-67278. (Illus.). 160p. 1995. 29.95 (*0-88740-753-6*) Schiffer.
— United States Naval Aviation Patches Vol. II: Aircraft/Attack Squadrons/Helicopter Squadrons. LC 95-67624. (United States Naval Aviation Patches Ser.). (Illus.). 144p. 1995. 29.95 (*0-88740-801-X*) Schiffer.
— United States Navy Patches Vol. IV: Amphibious Forces/Seal Teams, Fleets, Flotillas/Groups. (Illus.). 160p. 1996. 29.95 (*0-7643-0068-7*) Schiffer.
— United States Navy Patches Vol. V: Ships: Battleships/Cruisers/Destroyers/LSTs/Etc. LC 96-69998. (Illus.). 208p. 1997. 39.95 (*0-7643-0144-6*) Schiffer.
— United States Navy Patches Vol. VI: Submarines. LC 96-69997. (Illus.). 176p. 1997. 35.00 (*0-7643-0186-1*) Schiffer.

Roberts, Michael L. & Cusimano, Gregory S. Alabama Tort Law Handbook. 1065p. 1994. suppl. ed. 105.00 (*0-87473-581-5*, MICHIE) LEXIS Pub.

Roberts, Michael L., jt. auth. see Cusimano, Gregory S.

Roberts, Michele. Daughters of the House. 224p. 1994. reprint ed. pap. 10.00 (*0-380-72139-2*, Avon Bks) Morrow Avon.
— Impossible Saints. LC 99-12591. 1999. pap. 13.00 (*0-15-600659-6*, Harvest Bks) Harcourt.
— Impossible Saints. LC 97-36318. 320p. 1998. text 24.00 (*0-88001-597-7*) HarpC.
— The Visitation. 192p. 1997. pap. 13.95 (*0-7043-3903-X*, Pub. by Womens Press) Trafalgar.

Roberts, Michele & Schlueter. Legal Research Guide, 1996. 3rd ed. 134p. 1996. pap. text 18.00 (*1-55834-381-4*, 12991-11, MICHIE) LEXIS Pub.

Roberts, Michele S., ed. see Palmer Memorial Episcopal Churchwomen, Houston, Te.

Roberts, Michelle. How to Draw Cars & Trucks & Other Vehicles. (Illus.). 32p. (J). (gr. k-3). 1999. pap. 2.50 (*0-486-28114-0*) Dover.
— How to Draw Dinosaurs. LC 94-40101. (J). 1999. pap. 2.50 (*0-486-28460-3*) Dover.

Roberts, Miles, et al, eds. The Biology & Management of Australasian Carnivorous Marsupials. (Illus.). 158p. 1993. pap. text 20.00 (*0-9638408-1-9*) C & RC Nat Zool.

Roberts, Millard F. History of Remsen. 2nd ed. LC 84-52801. 453p. 1985. 15.00 (*0-317-19605-7*) Licht Pubns.
— Narrative History of Remsen, N. Y. 397p. 1993. reprint ed. lib. bdg. 42.50 (*0-8328-2884-X*) Higginson Bk Co.

Roberts, Millard F., compiled by. Historical Gazetteer of Steuben County, with Memoirs & Illustrations: Part I: Historical & Biographical; Part II: Directory of Individuals & Business. (Illus.). 946p. 1995. reprint ed. lib. bdg. 100.00 (*0-8328-5084-5*) Higginson Bk Co.

Roberts-Miller, Patricia. Voices in the Wilderness: Public Discourse & the Paradox of Puritan Rhetoric. LC 98-25394. 1999. 34.95 (*0-8173-0939-X*) U of Ala Pr.

Roberts, Mirvin F. Turtles. (Illus.). 96p. 1988. 9.95 (*0-86622-834-9*, KW-051) TFH Pubns.

***Roberts, Molly.** Site Design & Management with Microsoft FrontPage 98: A4, Version 2.07. Lane, Susan M. & McKenna, Jill, eds. (CIW Site Designer A4 Ser.). (Illus.). 1999. pap. write for info. (*1-58143-072-8*) Prosoft I-net.

Roberts, Molly & Willett, Steve. Empowering the Enterprise with Microsoft Internet Explorer 4.0. McKenna, Jill, ed. (Illus.). 272p. 1997. spiral bd. 29.95 (*1-58143-001-9*) Prosoft I-net.

***Roberts, Molly J.** Site Design & Management with FrontPage 98. Lane, Susan M. & McKenna, Jill, eds. (Illus.). 1999. pap. write for info. (*1-58143-013-2*, PSG2SDMFP98) Prosoft I-net.
— Site Design & Management with Microsoft FrontPage 98: Version 2.07. Lane, Susan M. & McKenna, Jill, eds. (CIW Site Designer Track Ser.). (Illus.). 1999. pap. write for info. (*1-58143-036-1*) Prosoft I-net.
— Visual Site Design & Management Using NetObjects Fusion 2.0. McKenna, Jill et al, eds. (Illus.). 1999. pap. write for info. (*1-58143-014-0*, PSGVSDMNOF) Prosoft I-net.

***Roberts, Monica.** Tempted. 368p. (Orig.). 1999. mass mkt. 5.50 (*0-505-52353-1*, Love Spell) Dorchester Pub Co.

Roberts, Monty. The Man Who Listens to Horses. 1999. mass mkt. 6.99 (*0-345-42705-X*) Ballantine Pub Grp.
— The Man Who Listens to Horses. 1998. mass mkt. write for info. (*0-449-00384-1*, Crest) Fawcett.
— The Man Who Listens to Horses. 304p. 1997. 23.00 (*0-679-45689-9*) Random.
— The Man Who Listens to Horses. 304p. 1997. 23.00 (*0-09-180206-7*) Random.
— The Man Who Listens to Horses. large type ed. LC 97-32699. 464p. 1998. 32.00 (*0-7862-1302-7*) Mac Lib Ref.

***Roberts, Monty.** Shy Boy: The Horse That Came in from the Wild. LC 99-22393. (Illus.). 256p. 1999. 30.00 (*0-06-019433-2*) HarpC.
— Shy Boy: The Horse That Came in from the Wild. 256p. 2000. pap. 16.00 (*0-06-093289-9*, Perennial) HarperTrade.

Roberts, Monty. Shy Boy: The Horse That Came in from the Wild. 1999. (*0-375-50308-0*) Random House.

***Roberts, Monty.** Shy Boy: The Horse That Came In from the Wild. large type ed. (Americana Series). 2000. pap. 25.95 (*0-7862-2210-7*) Thorndike Pr.
— Shy Boy: The Horse That Came in from the Wild. large type ed. LC 99-43256. (Thorndike Americana Ser.). 1999. 27.95 (*0-7862-2209-3*) Thorndike Pr.
— Shy Boy: The Horse That Came in from the Wild, Set. 1999. audio 24.00 (*0-694-52211-2*, 495741, Pub. by HarperAudio) Lndmrk Audiobks.

Roberts, Monty & Grealy, Lucy. The Man Who Listens to Horses. LC 97-17318. 258p. 1997. 23.00 (*0-679-45658-9*) Random.

Roberts, Morgan J. Classical Deities & Heroes. LC 94-10307. (Myths of the World Ser.). (Illus.). 112p. 1994. 15.98 (*1-56799-089-4*, MetroBooks) M Friedman Pub Grp Inc.
— Norse Gods & Heroes. LC 94-10323. (Myths of the World Ser.). (Illus.). 112p. 1994. 15.98 (*1-56799-090-8*) M Friedman Pub Grp Inc.

Roberts, Morley. Blue Peter: Sea Yarns. LC 71-178458. (Short Story Index Reprint Ser.). 1977. reprint ed. 20.95 (*0-8369-4059-8*) Ayer.

Roberts, Morris. Henry James' Criticism. LC 65-26463. (Studies in Henry James: No. 17). 1969. reprint ed. lib. bdg. 75.00 (*0-8383-0614-4*) M S G Haskell Hse.

Roberts, Morton S., ed. Astronomy & Astrophysics. LC 85-13380. 384p. (C). 1986. 51.00 (*0-87168-311-3*, 85-04S) AAAS.
— Astronomy & Astrophysics. LC 85-13380. (AAAS Miscellaneous Publications: No. 84-5). (Illus.). 407p. reprint ed. pap. 126.20 (*0-7837-6742-0*, 204637000011) Bks Demand.

Roberts, Moss, ed. Chinese Fairy Tales & Fantasies. (Fairy Tale & Folklore Library). (Illus.). 288p. 1980. pap. 16.00 (*0-394-73994-9*) Pantheon.

***Roberts, Moss, tr.** Three Kingdoms, Vol. 1. (Illus.). 562p. 2000. pap. 17.95 (*0-520-22478-7*) U CA Pr.
— Three Kingdoms, Vol. 2. (Illus.). 574p. 2000. pap. 17.95 (*0-520-22503-1*) U CA Pr.
— Three Kingdoms, Vol. 3. (Illus.). 554p. 2000. pap. 17.95 (*0-520-22505-8*) U CA Pr.

Roberts, Moss, jt. auth. see Lo Kuan-Chung.

Roberts, Moss, tr. see Tse-Tung, Mao.

Roberts, Myrna L., ed. see Roberts, Myrna P.

Roberts, Myrna P. Recipes from My Mom's Kitchen. Roberts, Myrna L., ed. 150p. (Orig.). 1990. pap. 12.95 (*0-9627075-0-3*) Conch Shell Pubns.

Roberts, Nancy. America's Most Haunted Places. LC 86-22577. (Illus.). 128p. (J). (gr. 4 up). 1987. reprint ed. pap. 8.95 (*0-87844-074-7*) Sandlapper Pub Co.
— Animal Ghost Stories. (American Storytelling Ser.). (Illus.). 128p. (YA). (gr. 6 up). 1995. 14.95 (*0-87483-401-5*) August Hse.
— Blackbeard & Other Pirates of the Atlantic Coast. LC 93-698. 222p. 1993. 13.95 (*0-89587-098-3*) Blair.

***Roberts, Nancy.** Blackbeard's Cat. LC 98-68229. (Cat of Nine Tales Ser.: Vol. I). (J). 1998. pap. text 9.95 (*1-886391-41-6*, Shipwreck Pr) Narwhal Pr.

Roberts, Nancy. Civil War Ghost Stories & Legends. LC 92-10411. (Illus.). 192p. 1992. pap. 12.95 (*0-87249-852-2*) U of SC Pr.
— Georgia Ghosts. LC 97-13697. (Orig.). 1997. pap. 9.95 (*0-89587-172-6*) Blair.
— Ghosts & Specters of the Old South. LC 84-14153. (Illus.). 93p. (J). (gr. 3 up). 1984. reprint ed. pap. 8.95 (*0-87844-058-5*) Sandlapper Pub Co.
— Ghosts of the Southern Mountains & Appalachia. rev. ed. LC 88-20836. (Illus.). 156p. 1989. reprint ed. pap. 9.95 (*0-87249-598-1*) U of SC Pr.

— The Gold Seekers: Gold, Ghosts & Legends from Carolina to California. LC 89-22563. (Illus.). 283p. 1989. pap. 9.95 (*0-87249-658-9*) U of SC Pr.

— Haunted Houses. 3rd ed. LC 98-24362. (Illus.). 224p. 1998. pap. 10.95 (*0-7627-0320-2*) Globe Pequot.

— The Haunted South: Where Ghosts Still Roam. LC 88-26096. 152p. 1988. reprint ed. pap. 9.95 (*0-87249-589-2*) U of SC Pr.

— North Carolina Ghosts & Legends. LC 91-14469. (Illus.). 133p. 1991. reprint ed. pap. 9.95 (*0-87249-765-8*) U of SC Pr.

— Recognitions: Images of a Woman Artist. LC 88-51097. 96p. 1989. pap. 15.95 (*0-944072-03-8*) Zoland Bks.

— Schools of Sympathy: Gender & Identification Through the Novel. LC 98-212932. 192p. 1997. text 60.00 (*0-7735-1668-9*, Pub. by McG-Queens Univ Pr); pap. text 22.95 (*0-7735-1685-9*, Pub. by McG-Queens Univ Pr) CUP Services.

— South Carolina Ghosts: From the Coast to the Mountains. (Illus.). 152p. 1984. pap. 9.95 (*0-87249-429-2*) U of SC Pr.

— Southern Ghosts. LC 86-21955. (Illus.). 72p. (J). (gr. 4 up). 1987. reprint ed. pap. 7.95 (*0-87844-075-5*) Sandlapper Pub Co.

— Women & Other Bodies of Water. 150p. 1987. 14.00 (*0-937872-38-5*) Dragon Gate.

Roberts, Nancy, et al. Integrating Computers into the Elementary & Middle School. (Illus.). 240p. 1988. pap. text 26.00 (*0-13-468794-9*) P-H.

— Introduction to Computer Simulation: Systems Dynamics Modeling Approach. 570p. 1997. pap. 35.00 (*1-56327-170-2*) Productivity Inc.

Roberts, Nancy, jt. auth. see Feurzeig, W.

Roberts, Nancy, ed. see Craig, Sharyn S.

Roberts, Nancy C. & King, Paula J. Transforming Public Policy: Dynamics of Policy Entrepreneurship & Innovation. (Public Administration Ser.). 302p. 1996. 30.95 (*0-7879-0202-0*) Jossey-Bass.

Roberts, Nancy L. American Peace Writers, Editors, & Periodicals: A Dictionary. LC 90-23169. 408p. 1991. lib. bdg. 75.00 (*0-313-26842-8*, RPB, Greenwood Pr) Greenwood.

— Dorothy Day & the Catholic Worker. LC 84-8492. 226p. (C). 1985. text 49.50 (*0-87395-938-8*); pap. text 16.95 (*0-87395-939-6*) State U NY Pr.

Roberts, Nancy L., jt. ed. see Klejment, Anne.

Roberts, Nancy L., ed. see O'Neill, Eugene.

Roberts, Nancy L., intro. see Silka, Henry P.

Roberts, Nancy N., tr. see Samman, Ghada.

Roberts, Ned. Muzzle-Loading Caplock Rifle. 1991. 30.00 (*0-935632-96-4*) Wolfe Pub Co.

Roberts, Nedra P. The Play's the Thing: An Introduction to Drama. 417p. (Orig.). (gr. 9-12). 1981. pap. text 10.50 (*0-88334-141-7*) Longman.

Roberts, Nedra P., jt. auth. see Roberts, John.

Roberts, Neil. The Changing Global Environment. LC 92-35490. 1993. pap. 38.95 (*1-55786-272-9*) Blackwell Pubs.

— The Holocene: An Environmental History. (Illus.). 320p. 1989. pap. 28.95 (*0-631-16178-3*) Blackwell Pubs.

— The Holocene: An Environmental History. 2nd ed. LC 97-43339. 260p. 1998. 73.95 (*0-631-18637-9*); pap. 36.95 (*0-631-18638-7*) Blackwell Pubs.

— Meredith & the Novel. LC 96-3208. 224p. 1997. text 55.00 (*0-312-16535-8*) St Martin.

Roberts, Nick. The Big Playstation Book. LC 97-69924. 384p. 1997. per. 14.99 (*0-7615-1332-9*) Prima Pub.

— Nintendo 64 Pocket Power Guide: Unauthorized. LC 96-70916. 96p. 1997. pap. 7.99 (*0-7615-0971-2*) Prima Pub.

— The Official Guide to Authorware 4. LC 97-204052. 704p. 1997. pap. 54.95 incl. cd-rom (*0-201-68899-9*) Addison-Wesley.

Roberts, Nick, ed. Nintendo 64 Player's Choice Pocket Power Guide. LC 98-65313. 96p. 1998. per. 7.99 (*0-7615-1565-8*) Prima Pub.

Roberts, Nickie. Whores in History. (Illus.). 384p. 1992. 28.00 (*0-246-13234-5*, Pub. by HarpC) HarpC.

Roberts, Nina, ed. A Guide to Women's Studies in the Outdoors: Review of Literature & Research with Annotated Bibliography. 96p. 1997. pap. text 19.50 (*0-536-00782-9*) Pearson Custom.

Roberts, Nora. All the Possibilities. 1992. mass mkt. 3.59 (*0-373-51015-2*, 5-51015-1) Harlequin Bks.

***Roberts, Nora.** The Art of Deception. LC 00-38892. 2000. write for info. (*0-7838-9055-9*, G K Hall & Co) Mac Lib Ref.

Roberts, Nora. The Art of Deception. (NR Flowers Ser.: No. 27). 1993. mass mkt. 3.59 (*0-373-51027-6*, 1-51027-0) Silhouette.

— Blithe Images. (NR Flowers Ser.: No. 38). 1993. per. 3.59 (*0-373-51038-1*, 1-51038-7) Silhouette.

— Born in Fire. 416p. 1994. mass mkt. 7.50 (*0-515-11469-3*, Jove) Berkley Pub.

— Born in Ice. 371384p. (YA). 1995. mass mkt. 7.50 (*0-515-11675-0*, Jove) Berkley Pub.

— Born in Ice. 352p. 1995. reprint ed. 22.00 (*0-7278-4832-1*) Severn Hse.

— Born in Shame. 368p. 1996. mass mkt. 7.50 (*0-515-11779-X*, Jove) Berkley Pub.

— Boundary Lines. (NR Flowers Ser.: No. 47). 1994. per. 3.59 (*0-373-51047-0*, 1-51047-8) Silhouette.

— Brazen Virtue. 259p. 1988. mass mkt. 7.50 (*0-553-27283-7*) Bantam.

— The Calhoun Women, 4 vols., Set. 1996. per. 12.99 (*0-373-48332-5*, 1-48332-0) Harlequin Bks.

— The Calhoun Women: Catherine & Amanda. (Silhouette Promo Ser.: Vol. I). 1998. per. 5.99 (*0-373-48354-6*, 1-48354-4) Silhouette.

— The Calhoun Women Vol. II: Lilah & Suzanna, 2 bks. in 1. (Silhouette Promo Ser.). 1998. per. 5.99 (*0-373-48355-4*, 1-48355-1) Silhouette.

— Captivated. 1992. mass mkt. 3.39 (*0-373-09768-9*, 5-09768-8) Silhouette.

— Captivated. large type ed. LC 93-620. 316p. 1993. pap. 19.95 (*1-56054-714-6*) Thorndike Pr.

***Roberts, Nora.** Captive Star. large type ed. (Romance Ser.). 2000. 22.95 (*0-373-59723-1*) Silhouette.

Roberts, Nora. Captive Star: The Stars of Mithra. (Intimate Moments Ser.: No. 823). 1997. per. 3.99 (*0-373-07823-4*, 1-07823-7) Harlequin Bks.

— Carnal Innocence. 512p. 1991. mass mkt. 7.50 (*0-553-29597-7*) Bantam.

— Carnal Innocence. LC 98-54920. 391p. 1999. 19.95 (*0-553-11094-2*) Bantam.

***Roberts, Nora.** Carolina Moon. LC 99-47968. 448p. 2000. 24.95 (*0-399-14592-3*) Putnam Pub Group.

— Carolina Moon. large type ed. LC 00-20641. (Basic Ser.). 674p. 2000. 31.95 (*0-7862-2287-5*) Thorndike Pr.

— Carolina Moon. large type ed. (Basic Ser.). 2000. pap. 29.95 (*0-7862-2288-3*) Thorndike Pr.

Roberts, Nora. Charmed. large type ed. LC 93-613. 315p. 1993. lib. bdg. 16.95 (*1-56054-716-2*) Thorndike Pr.

— Command Performance. (NR Flowers Ser.: No. 37). 1993. mass mkt. 3.59 (*0-373-51037-3*, 1-51037-9) Silhouette.

— Convincing Alex. 1994. mass mkt. 3.50 (*0-373-09872-3*, 5-09872-8) Silhouette.

— Dance of Dreams. (NR Flowers Ser.: No. 8). 1992. mass mkt. 3.59 (*0-373-51008-X*, 5-51008-6) Harlequin Bks.

***Roberts, Nora.** Dance of Dreams. large type ed. 235p. 2000. 29.95 (*0-7838-9043-5*) Mac Lib Ref.

Roberts, Nora. Dance to the Piper. 256p. 1994. per. 4.99 (*1-55166-007-5*, 1-66007-5, Mira Bks) Harlequin Bks.

— Dance to the Piper. (Mira Bks.). 1998. per. 5.99 (*1-55166-321-X*, 1-66321-0, Mira Bks) Harlequin Bks.

Roberts, Nora. Daring to Dream. 373p. 1996. mass mkt. 7.50 (*0-515-11920-2*, Jove) Berkley Pub.

Roberts, Nora. Daring to Dream. 384p. 1998. 25.00 (*0-7278-5310-4*) Severn Hse.

— Daring to Dream. large type ed. LC 96-36484. (Romance Ser.). 527p. 1996. lib. bdg. 25.95 (*0-7862-0894-5*) Thorndike Pr.

— Divine Evil. 512p. 1992. mass mkt. 7.50 (*0-553-29490-3*) Bantam.

***Roberts, Nora.** The Donovan Legacy. 1999. per. 14.95 (*0-373-48397-X*) Harlequin Bks.

Roberts, Nora. Dual Image. (Language of Love Ser.: No. 29). 1993. per. 3.59 (*0-373-51029-2*, 1-51029-6) Silhouette.

***Roberts, Nora.** Dual Image. LC 00-37796. (Illus.). 2000. pap. write for info. (*0-7862-2605-6*) Thorndike Pr.

— Enchanted: The Donovan Legacy. 1999. per. 4.25 (*0-373-07961-3*, 1-07961-5) Harlequin Bks.

— Enchanted: The Donovan Legacy. large type ed. LC 00-37701. 306p. 2000. write for info. (*0-7862-2599-8*) Thorndike Pr.

Roberts, Nora. Entranced. large type ed. LC 93-618. 318p. 1993. pap. 19.95 (*1-56054-715-4*) Thorndike Pr.

— The Fall of Shane Mackade: The Mackade Brothers. 1996. per. 3.99 (*0-373-24022-8*, 1-24022-5) Silhouette.

— The Fall of Shane MacKade: The MacKade Brothers. large type ed. (Silhouette Romance Ser.). 1998. 20.95 (*0-373-59863-7*) Thorndike Pr.

— Falling for Rachel. 1993. per. 3.39 (*0-373-09810-3*, 5-09810-8) Silhouette.

— Finding the Dream. 352p. 1997. mass mkt. 7.50 (*0-515-12087-1*, Jove) Berkley Pub.

— Finding the Dream. 368p. 1999. 26.00 (*0-7278-2295-0*, Pub. by Severn Hse) Chivers N Amer.

— Finding the Dream. large type ed. LC 97-40433. 544p. 1997. 27.95 (*0-7862-1130-X*) Thorndike Pr.

— First Impressions. (NR Flowers Ser.: No. 5). 1992. per. 3.59 (*0-373-51005-5*, 1-51005-2) Harlequin Bks.

— For Now, Forever. (NR Flowers Ser.: No. 19). 1992. mass mkt. 3.59 (*0-373-51019-5*, 5-51019-3) Harlequin Bks.

— For the Love of Lilah. (Special Edition Ser.: No. 685). 1991. mass mkt. 3.25 (*0-373-09685-2*) Harlequin Bks.

— From the Heart. 560p. 1996. mass mkt. 7.50 (*0-515-11965-2*, Jove) Berkley Pub.

Roberts, Nora. From the Heart. large type ed. 1997. 20.00 (*0-7862-0941-0*) Thorndike Pr.

— From the Heart. 595p. 2000. reprint ed. pap. 14.95 (*0-425-17616-9*) Berkley Pub.

Roberts, Nora. From This Day. (NR Flowers Ser.: No. 14). 1992. per. 3.59 (*0-373-51014-4*) Harlequin Bks.

— Gabriel's Angel. (Language of Love Ser.: No. 32). 1993. per. 3.59 (*0-373-51032-2*, 1-51032-2) Silhouette.

— Genuine Lies. large type ed. (Large Print Book Ser.). 1998. 26.95 (*1-56895-678-9*) Wheeler Pub.

— Genuine Lies. 521p. 1991. reprint ed. mass mkt. 7.50 (*0-553-29078-9*) Bantam.

— The Heart of Devin Mackade. LC 96-7306. (Intimate Moments Ser.). 242p. 1996. per. 3.99 (*0-373-07697-5*, 1-07697-5) Silhouette.

— The Heart of Devin Mackade. large type ed. (Silhouette Romance Ser.). 1998. 20.95 (*0-373-59859-9*) Harlequin Bks.

— Heart's Victory. 1992. per. 3.59 (*0-373-51016-0*, 5-51016-9) Harlequin Bks.

— Her Mother's Keeper. (NR Flowers Ser.: No. 20). 1992. per. 3.59 (*0-373-51020-9*, 5-51020-1) Harlequin Bks.

— Hidden Riches. 470p. 1995. mass mkt. 7.50 (*0-515-11606-8*, Jove) Berkley Pub.

— Hidden Riches. large type ed. LC 94-25466. 648p. 1994. lib. bdg. 24.95 (*0-7862-0272-6*) Thorndike Pr.

***Roberts, Nora.** Hidden Star. large type ed. (Romance Ser.). 2000. 22.95 (*0-373-59712-6*) Silhouette.

Roberts, Nora. Hidden Star: The/Star of Mithra. 1997. per. 3.99 (*0-373-07811-0*, 1-07811-2) Silhouette.

— Holding the Dream. 352p. 1999. 26.00 (*0-7278-2215-2*, Pub. by Severn Hse) Chivers N Amer.

— Holding the Dream. large type ed. 356p. 1997. mass mkt. 7.50 (*0-515-12000-6*, Jove) Berkley Pub.

— Holding the Dream. large type ed. LC 97-5023. 552p. 1997. 25.95 (*0-7862-1053-2*) Thorndike Pr.

— Home for Christmas. 1986. per. 4.99 (*0-373-48251-5*, 5-48251-8) Harlequin Bks.

— Homeport. LC 97-28912. 448p. 1998. 23.95 (*0-399-14387-4*, G & D) Peng Put Young Read.

— Homeport. large type ed. LC 98-12775. 1998. 28.95 (*0-7862-1426-0*) Thorndike Pr.

— Homeport. large type ed. LC 98-12775. 1998. pap. 20.00 (*0-7862-1427-9*) Thorndike Pr.

— Homeport. 484p. 1999. reprint ed. mass mkt. 7.50 (*0-515-12489-3*, Jove) Berkley Pub.

— Honest Illusions. 512p. 1993. mass mkt. 7.50 (*0-515-11097-3*, Jove) Berkley Pub.

— Hot Ice. 288p. (Orig.). 1987. mass mkt. 7.50 (*0-553-26461-3*) Bantam.

***Roberts, Nora.** Inner Harbor. 342p. 1998. mass mkt. 7.50 (*0-515-12421-4*, Jove) Berkley Pub.

Roberts, Nora. Inner Harbor. large type ed. LC 99-18685. 515p. 1999. 28.95 (*0-7862-1442-2*) Mac Lib Ref.

***Roberts, Nora.** Irish Hearts: Irish Thoroughbred & Irish Rose, 2 bks. in 1. 2000. mass mkt. 7.99 (*0-373-48400-3*, 1-48400-5) Harlequin Bks.

— Irish Rebel. (Special Edition Ser.: Bk. 1328). 2000. mass mkt. 4.50 (*0-373-24328-6*, 1-24328-6) Silhouette.

Roberts, Nora. Irish Rose. (NR Flowers Ser.: No. 3). 1992. mass mkt. 3.59 (*0-373-51003-9*, 5-51003-7) Harlequin Bks.

— Irish Thoroughbred. (NR Flowers Ser.: No. 1). 1992. per. 3.59 (*0-373-51001-2*, 5-51001-1) Harlequin Bks.

— Island of Flowers. (NR Flowers Ser.: No. 10). 1992. per. 3.59 (*0-373-51010-1*, 5-51010-2) Harlequin Bks.

***Roberts, Nora.** Jewels of the Sun. 384p. 1999. mass mkt. 7.50 (*0-515-12677-2*, Jove) Berkley Pub.

— Jewels of the Sun. LC 00-23949. 2000. write for info. (*0-7838-8990-9*, G K Hall & Co) Mac Lib Ref.

— Jewels of the Sun. large type ed. (Core Ser.). 2000. 30.95 (*0-7838-8989-5*, G K Hall Lrg Type) Mac Lib Ref.

Roberts, Nora. The Last Honest Man. 248p. 1995. per. 4.99 (*1-55166-020-2*, Mira Bks) Harlequin Bks.

— The Last Honest Woman. (O'Hurley's Ser.). 1990. pap. 2.95 (*0-373-48231-0*) Harlequin Bks.

— The Last Honest Woman. 1999. per. 5.99 (*1-55166-507-7*, 1-66507-4) Silhouette.

— The Law Is a Lady. (NR Flowers Ser.: No. 2). 1992. per. 3.59 (*0-373-51002-0*, 5-51002-9) Harlequin Bks.

— Lessons Learned. (NR Flowers Ser.: No. 25). 1993. per. 3.59 (*0-373-51025-X*, 1-51025-4) Silhouette.

— Local Hero. (NR Flowers Ser.: No. 48). 1994. per. 3.59 (*0-373-51048-9*, 1-51048-6) Silhouette.

— Loving Jack. (Language of Love Ser.: No. 42). 1994. mass mkt. 3.59 (*0-373-51042-X*, 1-51042-9) Silhouette.

— The MacGregor Brides. 384p. 1997. per. 6.99 (*0-373-48350-3*) Harlequin Bks.

— The MacGregor Grooms. 384p. 1998. per. 6.99 (*0-373-48369-4*, 1-48369-2) Silhouette.

***Roberts, Nora.** The MacGregors: Alan & Grant. 512p. 1999. pap. 6.99 (*0-373-48389-9*, 1-48389-0) Silhouette.

— The MacGregors: Ian & Daniel. 1999. per. 6.99 (*0-373-48390-2*, 1-48390-8, Harlequin) Harlequin Bks.

Roberts, Nora. The MacGregors: Serena-Caine Playing the Odds; Tempting Fate. (Silhouette Promo Ser.). 1998. per. 6.99 (*0-373-48388-0*, 1-48388-2, Harlequin) Harlequin Bks.

— Megan's Mate. 1996. per. 3.99 (*0-373-07745-9*, 1-07745-2) Silhouette.

***Roberts, Nora.** Megan's Mate, Vol. 1. (Silhouette Ser.). 1999. pap. 21.95 (*0-373-59990-0*) Harlequin Bks.

— Mind over Matter. LC 00-37795. 2000. pap. write for info. (*0-7862-2604-8*) Thorndike Pr.

Roberts, Nora. Montana Sky. 467p. 1997. mass mkt. 7.99 (*0-515-12061-8*, Jove) Berkley Pub.

— Montana Sky. large type ed. 707p. 1996. 26.95 (*0-7862-0672-1*) Thorndike Pr.

— Night Moves. (NR Flowers Ser.: No. 7). 1992. mass mkt. 3.59 (*0-373-51007-1*, 5-51007-8) Harlequin Bks.

— Night Shadow. large type ed. 329p. 1991. reprint ed. lib. bdg. 19.95 (*1-56054-175-X*) Thorndike Pr.

***Roberts, Nora.** Night Shield. (Intimate Moments Ser.: Vol. 1027). 2000. mass mkt. 4.50 (*0-373-27097-6*, 1-27097-4) Silhouette.

Roberts, Nora. Night Smoke. 1994. per. 3.50 (*0-373-07595-2*, 1-07595-1) Harlequin Bks.

— Night Smoke, Vol. 595. (Intimate Moments Ser.). 1998. 21.95 (*0-373-59929-3*) Silhouette.

***Roberts, Nora.** Night Tales: Night Shift; Night Shadow; Nightshade; Night Smoke, 4 bks. in 1. (Silhouette Promo Ser.). 768p. 2000. pap. 14.95 (*0-373-48410-0*, 1-48410-4) Harlequin Bks.

Roberts, Nora. Nightshade: American Hero, Night Tales. (Intimate Moments Ser.). 1993. mass mkt. 3.50 (*0-373-07529-4*, 5-07529-6) Silhouette.

— Once More with Feeling. LC 95-21497. 251p. 1995. mass mkt. 5.99 (*0-373-15311-2*, 1-15311-3) Harlequin Bks.

— One Man's Art. (NR Flowers Ser.: No. 17). 1992. mass mkt. 3.59 (*0-373-51017-9*, 5-51017-7) Harlequin Bks.

— One Summer. (Language of Love Ser.: No. 31). 1993. per. 3.59 (*0-373-51031-4*, 1-51031-8) Silhouette.

— Opposites Attract. (NR Flowers Ser.: No. 9). 1992. per. 3.59 (*0-373-51009-8*, 5-51009-4) Harlequin Bks.

— Partners. (NR Flowers Ser.: No. 21). 1992. per. 3.59 (*0-373-51021-7*, 5-51021-9) Harlequin Bks.

***Roberts, Nora.** Partners. LC 00-37751. 2000. write for info. (*0-7862-2612-9*) Thorndike Pr.

Roberts, Nora. The Perfect Neighbor: The MacGregors. (Silhouette Special Ser.: No. 1232). 251p. 1999. per. 4.25 (*0-373-24232-8*, 1-24232-0) Harlequin Bks.

— The Playboy Prince. (NR Flowers Ser.: No. 39). 1994. per. 3.59 (*0-373-51039-X*, 1-51039-5) Silhouette.

— Playing the Odds. (NR Flowers Ser.: No. 12). 1992. mass mkt. 3.59 (*0-373-51012-8*) Harlequin Bks.

— The Pride of Jared Mackade. Vol. 1000. 1995. per. 3.75 (*0-373-24000-7*, 1-24000-1) Silhouette.

— Prime Evil. 256p. 1995. mass mkt. 5.99 (*0-553-56437-4*, Fanfare) Bantam.

— Private Scandals. 501p. 1994. mass mkt. 7.50 (*0-515-11400-6*, Jove) Berkley Pub.

— Private Scandals. unabridged ed. 1993. 25.95 incl. audio (*1-56100-509-6*, Bkcassette) Brilliance.

— Public Secrets. 512p. 1998. mass mkt. 7.50 (*0-553-28578-5*) Bantam.

— Rebellion. (Promo Ser.). 1998. mass mkt. 5.99 (*0-373-83403-9*, 1-83403-5) Harlequin Bks.

— Rebellion. 298p. 1999. per. 6.99 (*0-373-83428-4*, 1-83428-2) Harlequin Bks.

***Roberts, Nora.** The Reef. 1999. mass mkt. 7.50 (*0-515-12608-X*) Berkley Pub.

— The Reef. LC 98-21329. 448p. 1998. 23.95 (*0-399-14441-2*, G P Putnam) Peng Put Young Read.

— The Reef. large type ed. LC 98-41611. 670p. 1998. 30.00 (*0-7862-1699-9*) Mac Lib Ref.

Roberts, Nora. The Reef. large type ed. LC 98-41611. 1999. 30.00 (*0-7862-1698-0*) Thorndike Pr.

— Reflections. (NR Flowers Ser.: No. 6). 1992. mass mkt. 3.59 (*0-373-51006-3*, 5-51006-0) Harlequin Bks.

— The Return of Rafe Mackade. (Intimate Moments Ser.). 1995. per. 3.75 (*0-373-07631-2*, 1-07631-4) Silhouette.

— The Right Path. (NR Flowers Ser.: No. 26). 1993. per. 3.59 (*0-373-51026-8*, 1-51026-2) Silhouette.

— Rising Tides. large type ed. LC 98-4340. 1999. 30.00 (*0-7862-1441-4*) Thorndike Pr.

— Rising Tides, Bk. 2. (Quinn Brothers Trilogy: No. 2). 352p. 1998. mass mkt. 7.50 (*0-515-12317-X*, Jove) Berkley Pub.

***Roberts, Nora.** River's End. 461p. 2000. mass mkt. 7.99 (*0-515-12783-3*, Jove) Berkley Pub.

Roberts, Nora. River's End. LC 98-36160. 432p. 1999. 23.95 (*0-399-14470-6*) Putnam Pub Group.

— River's End. large type ed. LC 99-10428. (Paperback Bestsellers Ser.). 664p. 1950. 28.95 (*0-7862-1862-2*) Thorndike Pr.

— River's End. large type ed. LC 99-10428. 1999. pap. 30.00 (*0-7862-1861-4*) Thorndike Pr.

— Rules of the Game. (NR Flowers Ser.: No. 18). 1992. per. 3.59 (*0-373-51018-7*, 5-51018-5) Harlequin Bks.

— Sacred Sins. 336p. 1987. mass mkt. 7.50 (*0-553-26574-1*) Bantam.

***Roberts, Nora.** Sacred Sins. 304p. 2000. 18.95 (*0-553-80116-3*, Spectra) Bantam.

— Sacred Sins. 2000. 18.95 (*0-375-43066-0*) Random Hse Lrg Prnt.

Roberts, Nora. Sanctuary. 1998. pap. text 7.50 (*0-515-12273-4*, Jove) Berkley Pub.

— Sanctuary. LC 96-31986. 1997. 23.95 (*0-399-14240-1*, G P Putnam) Peng Put Young Read.

— Sea Swept. 352p. 1998. mass mkt. 7.50 (*0-515-12184-3*, Jove) Berkley Pub.

— Sea Swept. large type ed. LC 98-14829. 1998. 27.95 (*0-7862-1433-3*) Thorndike Pr.

— Search for Love. (NR Flowers Ser.: No. 11). 1992. per. 3.59 (*0-373-51011-X*) Harlequin Bks.

— Second Nature. (Language of Love Ser.: No. 30). 1993. per. 3.59 (*0-373-51030-6*, 5-51030-0) Silhouette.

***Roberts, Nora.** Secret Star. large type ed. 2000. 22.95 (*0-373-59733-9*) Harlequin Bks.

Roberts, Nora. Secret Star: The Stars of Mithra. (Intimate Moments Ser.: No. 835). 1998. per. 4.25 (*0-373-07835-8*, 1-07835-1) Silhouette.

— Skin Deep. LC 95-21962. 248p. 1995. per. 4.99 (*1-55166-050-4*, 1-66050-5, Mira Bks) Harlequin Bks.

***Roberts, Nora.** The Stanislaski Brothers. 2000. 7.50 (*0-373-48422-4*) Silhouette.

Roberts, Nora. The Stanislaski Sisters: Taming Natasha, Falling for Rachel. 1997. per. 5.99 (*0-373-20134-6*, 1-20134-2) Harlequin Bks.

— Storm Warning. (NR Flowers Ser.: No. 4). 1992. per. 3.59 (*0-373-51004-7*, 5-51004-5) Harlequin Bks.

— Sullivan's Woman. (NR Flowers Ser.: No. 22). 1992. per. 3.59 (*0-373-51022-5*, 5-51022-7) Harlequin Bks.

— Summer Desserts. (NR Flowers Ser.: No. 23). 1993. per. 3.59 (*0-373-51023-3*, 5-51023-5) Silhouette.

— Sweet Revenge. 376p. 1997. mass mkt. 7.50 (*0-553-27859-2*) Bantam.

— Sweet Revenge. large type ed. LC 97-47200. (Compass Press Large Print Book Ser.). 1998. 25.95 (*1-56895-531-6*) Wheeler Pub.

***Roberts, Nora.** Tears of the Moon. 2000. mass mkt. 7.99 (*0-515-12854-6*, Jove) Berkley Pub.

— Tears of the Moon. LC 00-39678. (Illus.). 2000. pap. write for info. (*0-7838-8992-5*, G K Hall & Co) Mac Lib Ref.

Roberts, Nora. Tempting Fate. (NR Flowers Ser.: No. 13). 1992. mass mkt. 3.59 (*0-373-51013-6*) Silhouette.

— This Magic Moment. (NR Flowers Ser.: No. 24). 1993. per. 3.59 (*0-373-51024-1*, 5-51024-3) Silhouette.

***Roberts, Nora.** Three Complete Novels. LC 97-33363. 768p. 1998. 12.98 (*0-399-14388-2*, G P Putnam) Peng Put Young Read.

Roberts, Nora. Three Complete Novels. LC 98-50630. (Dream Ser.). 757p. 1999. 12.98 (*0-399-14480-3*) Putnam Pub Group.

***Roberts, Nora.** Three Complete Novels: Honest Illusions, Private Scandals & Hidden Riches. LC 00-28058. 800p. 2000. 12.98 (*0-399-14627-X*, G P Putnam) Peng Put Young Read.

An Asterisk (*) at the beginning of an entry indicates that the title is appearing for the first time.

— Traiciones (Haven's Call) 1998. pap. 8.50 (84-01-51902-0) Lectorum Pubns.

Roberts, Nora. Treasures Lost, Treasures Found. (NR Flowers Ser.: No. 40). 1994. per. 3.59 (0-373-51040-3, 1-51040-3) Silhouette.

— True Betrayals. 422p. 1996. mass mkt. 7.50 (0-515-11855-9, Jove) Berkley Pub.

— Unfinished Business. (Intimate Moments Ser.: No. 433). 1992. mass mkt. 3.39 (0-373-07433-6, 5-07433-1) Harlequin Bks.

— Unfinished Business. large type ed. (Popular Ser.). 294p. 1993. reprint ed. lib. bdg. 16.95 (1-56054-634-4) Thorndike Pr.

— Untamed. (NR Flowers Ser.: No. 28). 1993. mass mkt. 3.59 (0-373-51028-4, 1-51028-8) Silhouette.

— Waiting for Nick. (Special Edition Ser.). 1997. per. 3.99 (0-373-24088-0, 1-24088-6) Silhouette.

***Roberts, Nora.** Waiting for Nick. large type ed. (Silhouette Romance Ser.). 1999. 21.95 (0-373-59651-0) Harlequin Bks.

— The Winning Hand: MacGregors. (Special Edition Ser.: No. 1202). 1998. per. 4.25 (0-373-24202-6, 1-24202-3) Harlequin Bks.

Roberts, Nora. Without a Trace. LC 96-7351. 249p. 1996. per. 5.99 (1-55166-059-8, 1-66059-6, Mira Bks) Harlequin Bks.

Roberts, Nora, et al. Birds, Bees & Babies - 1994. 1994. mass mkt. 4.99 (0-373-48285-X, 5-48285-6) Silhouette.

— Forever Mine. (Promo Ser.). 1998. per. 9.99 (0-373-83400-4, 1-83400-1) Harlequin Bks.

— Jingle Bells, Wedding Bells: All I Want for Christmas; A Very Merry Step-Christmas; Jack's Ornament; The Forever Gift. 1994. per. 4.99 (0-373-48331-7, 1-48331-2) Harlequin Bks.

— Once upon a Castle. 1998. mass mkt. 6.99 (0-515-12241-6, Jove) Berkley Pub.

— Once Upon a Castle. large type ed. LC 98-22097. 1998. 20.00 (0-7862-1507-0) Thorndike Pr.

***Roberts, Nora, et al.** Once upon a Star. 1999. mass mkt. 5.99 (0-515-12700-0, Jove) Berkley Pub.

Roberts, Nora, et al. Silhouette Summer Sizzlers, 1989. 1989. mass mkt. 3.95 (0-373-48217-5) Harlequin Bks.

Roberts, Nora, see Robb, J. D., pseud.

Roberts, Nora Ruth. Four Working Class Writers: A Materialist Deconstructionist Reading. 250p. 1997. text 50.00 (0-8153-2008-6) Garland.

— Ripe Tomatoes: A Novel. 108p. 1999. pap. 9.00 (1-887128-39-5, Pub. by Soft Skull Pr) SPD-Small Pr Dist.

— Three Radical Women Writers: Class & Gender in Meridel le Sueur, Tillie Olsen, & Josephine Herbst. LC 95-43538. (Gender & Genre in Literature Ser.: Vol. 06). (Illus.). 224p. 1996. text 44.00 (0-8153-0330-0, H1452) Garland.

Roberts, Norma J. Masterpieces of Impressionism & European Modernism from the Columbus Museum of Art, Columbus Museum of Art & TG Concepts, Inc. LC 92-83841. (Illus.). 1993. pap. 29.95 (0-685-72344-5) Columbus Mus Art.

Roberts, Norma J., ed. The Quest for Self-Expression: Painting in Moscow & Leningrad, 1965-1990. LC 90-81953. (Illus.). 192p. (Orig.). 1990. pap. 29.95 (0-918881-25-0) Columbus Mus Art.

Roberts, Norma J., ed. see Columbus Museum of Art Staff.

Roberts, Norma J., ed. see Griffith, Dennison W.

Roberts, Norma J., ed. see Maciejunes, Nannette V., et al.

Roberts, Norma J., ed. see Robertson, Jean.

Roberts, Norma J., ed. see Schwindler, Gary.

Roberts, Norma J., ed. see Selz, Peter H. & Brettel, Richard.

***Roberts, Norman.** Steel & Velvet. LC 99-64397. 439p. 1999. 25.00 (0-7388-0506-8); pap. 18.00 (0-7388-0507-6) Xlibris Corp.

Roberts, Norman & Konn, Tania. Librarians & Professional Status: Continuing Professional Development & Academic Libraries. LC 91-230493. 222p. Date not set. reprint ed. pap. 68.90 (0-608-20729-2, 207182700002) Bks Demand.

Roberts, Norman C. Baja California Plant Field Guide. (Illus.). 324p. (Orig.). 1989. pap. 24.95 (0-9603144-1-5) Nat Hist Pub Co.

Roberts, Oral. Expect a Miracle: My Life & Ministry. (Illus.). 400p. 1998. pap. 14.99 (0-7852-7465-0) Nelson.

— Something Good Is Going to Happen to You. LC 97-158488. 160p. 1996. pap. 6.99 (1-880089-28-9, AP-928, Pub. by Albury Pub) Appalach Bk Dist.

— Unleashing the Power of Praying in the Spirit. 160p. 1993. pap. 8.99 (0-89274-678-5, HH-678) Harrison Hse.

Roberts, Oran M. A Description of Texas, Its Advantages & Resources. 2000. reprint ed. lib. bdg. 79.00 (0-7812-5898-7) Rprt Serv.

Roberts, Orlando W. Narrative of Voyages & Excursions on the East Coast & in the Interior of Central America: Describing a Journey up the River San Juan, & Passage Across the Lake of Nicaragua to the City of Leon. LC 65-28696. (Latin American Gateway Ser.). 331p. 1965. reprint ed. pap. 102.70 (0-608-04473-3, 206521800001) Bks Demand.

Roberts, P., jt. auth. see Mather, J.

Roberts, P., ed. see Goorney, Howard.

Roberts, P. A. Neuroanatomy. (Oklahoma Notes Ser.). (Illus.). ix, 84p. (C). 1989. pap. 11.95 (0-387-96335-9) Spr-Verlag.

— Neuroanatomy. (Oklahoma Notes Ser.). (Illus.). xi, 100p. 1991. pap. 13.95 (0-387-97477-6) Spr-Verlag.

— Neuroanatomy. 3rd ed. (Oklahoma Notes Ser.). (Illus.). 128p. 1992. 13.95 (0-387-97777-5) Spr-Verlag.

Roberts, P. C. Modelling Large Systems. 120p. 1978. 31.00 (0-85066-170-6) Taylor & Francis.

Roberts, P. D. & Ellis, J. E., eds. Large Scale Systems: Theory & Applications, 1995: A Postprint Volume from the 7th IFAC/IFORS/IMACS Symposium, London, U. K., 11-13 July, 1995. LC 95-47896. 962p. 1995. pap. write for info. (0-08-042365-5) Elsevier.

Roberts, P. H., ed. see European Geophysical Society Staff.

Roberts, P. J., et al, eds. Glutamate: Transmitter in the Central Nervous System. LC 80-42300. (Wiley-Interscience Publications). 250p. reprint ed. pap. 77.50 (0-608-13130-X, 205209300033) Bks Demand.

Roberts, P. J., ed. see Workshop on Biochemistry of the Dementias Staff.

Roberts, P. V., jt. ed. see McCarty, Perry L.

Roberts, Pam. Camera Work - The Complete Illustrations, 1903-1917, Alfred Stieglitz. (Klotz Ser.). 793p. 1997. pap. 29.99 (3-8228-8072-8) Taschen Amer.

***Roberts, Pam.** PhotoHistorica, Landmarks in Photography: Rare Images from the Collection of the Royal Photographic Society. LC 00-38615. (Illus.). 336p. 2000. 60.00 (1-57965-169-0, 85169) Artisan.

Roberts, Pam, jt. auth. see Gibson, Robin.

Roberts, Pamela. Teaching the Child Rider. 102p. (C). 1990. pap. 21.00 (0-85131-195-4, Pub. by J A Allen) Trafalgar.

— Teaching the Child Rider. 1987. 10.00 (0-87556-302-3) Saifer.

Roberts, Pamela, jt. auth. see Roberts, Dewi.

Roberts, Pasco. Book of Florida Gardening. LC 62-52630. 104p. (Orig.). 1962. pap. 3.95 (0-8200-0402-2) Great Outdoors.

Roberts, Pat, jt. auth. see Roberts, Ralph.

Roberts, Pat H., ed. see McCready, Jack.

Roberts, Pat H., ed. see Terrell, Bob.

***Roberts, Patricia.** Family Values Through Children's Literature. (School Library Media). 256p. (J). (gr. k-3). 2000. pap. text 32.50 (0-8108-3682-3) Scarecrow.

— Literature-Based History Activities for Children. LC 96-53228. 236p. (C). 1997. pap. text 29.00 (0-205-27090-5) Allyn.

Roberts, Patricia. Multicultural Friendship Stories & Activities for Children Ages 5-15. LC 97-15975. (School Library Media Ser.). 243p. (gr. k-9). 1998. pap. 22.50 (0-8108-3359-X) Scarecrow.

— Tender Prey. 256p. 1984. mass mkt. 2.95 (0-345-31781-5) Ballantine Pub Grp.

Roberts, Patricia, jt. auth. see Henderson, Daniel.

Roberts, Patricia, jt. auth. see Kelly, Thomas L.

Roberts, Patricia L. Alphabet: A Handbook of ABC Books & Book Extensions for the Elementary Classroom. 2nd ed. LC 93-42444. 1994. 34.50 (0-8108-2823-5) Scarecrow.

— Alphabet Books As a Key to Language Patterns: An Annotated Action Bibliography. LC 87-3216. ix, 263p. (C). 1988. lib. bdg. 36.00 (0-208-02151-5, Lib Prof Pubns) Shoe String.

— A Red, White, & Blue Day: Literature-Based History Activities for Children, Grades 4-8. LC 95-48955. 241p. (C). 1996. pap. text 29.00 (0-205-14737-2) Allyn.

— Taking Humor Seriously in Children's Literature: Literature-Based Mini-Units & Humorous Books for Children, Ages 5-12. LC 97-15547. (School Library Media Ser.: No. 11). 256p. 1997. pap. 35.00 (0-8108-3209-7) Scarecrow.

***Roberts, Patricia L., ed.** A Guide to Developing Interdisciplinary Thematic Units. 2nd ed. LC 99-25371. (Illus.). 277p. (C). 1999. pap. text 26.00 (0-13-921164-0) P-H.

Roberts, Patricia L., ed. Language Arts & Environmental Awareness: 100+ Integrated Books & Activities for Children. LC 97-32638. 295p. 1998. lib. bdg. 35.00 (0-208-02427-1, Linnet Bks) Shoe String.

Roberts, Patricia L. & Cecil, Nancy L. Developing Multicultural Awareness Through Children's Literature: A Guide for Teachers & Librarians, Grades K-8. LC 93-15144. 224p. 1993. pap. 29.95 (0-89950-879-0) McFarland & Co.

Roberts, Patricia L., et al. Integrating Language Arts & Social Studies for Kindergarten & Primary Children. LC 95-33302. 491p. (C). 1995. pap. text 45.00 (0-02-408460-3, Macmillan Coll) P-H.

Roberts, Patricia L., jt. auth. see Cecil, Nancy L.

***Roberts, Paul.** From This Hill, My Hand, Cynthiana's Wine. Dunphy, Alicia, ed. LC 99-64945. 200p. 1999. pap. 16.95 (0-9668716-2-6) Resonant Pubg.

Roberts, Paul. Images: The Piano Music of Claude Debussy. LC 95-11283. (Illus.). 396p. 1996. 39.95 (0-931340-97-7, Amadeus Pr) Timber.

Roberts, Paul, et al. Points in Time: Building a Life in Western Pennsylvania. LC 80-80284. (Illus.). 124p. (Orig.). 1998. pap. 30.95 (0-936340-00-2) Hist Soc West PA.

Roberts, Paul, ed. see James, Henry.

Roberts, Paul A. The Rasherhouse. LC 97-164203. 178p. 1997. pap. 14.95 (1-898256-21-7) Dufour.

Roberts, Paul C. Alienation & the Soviet Economy: The Collapse of the Socialist Era. rev. ed. 148p. 1990. pap. 16.95 (0-945999-63-1, 1340); lib. bdg. 29.95 (0-945999-64-X, 6073) Independent Inst.

— Marx's Theory of Exchange. LC 83-19136. 127p. 1983. 49.95 (0-275-91065-2, C1065, Praeger Pubs) Greenwood.

— Multiplicities & Chern Classes in Local Algebra. LC 97-46135. (Tracts in Mathematics Ser.: No. 133). 316p. (C). 1998. text 59.95 (0-521-47316-0) Cambridge U Pr.

— The Supply-Side Revolution: An Insider's Account of Policymaking in Washington. (Illus.). 328p. 1984. 41.50 (0-674-85620-1) HUP.

— The Supply-Side Revolution: An Insider's Account of Policymaking in Washington. (Illus.). 328p. 1984. pap. text 14.00 (0-674-85621-X) HUP.

Roberts, Paul C. & Araujo, Karen L. The Capitalist Revolution in Latin America. LC 96-25073. 224p. 1997. 35.00 (0-19-511176-1) OUP.

Roberts, Paul C. & LaFollette, Karen. Meltdown: Inside the Soviet Economy. 152p. 1990. pap. 19.95 (0-932790-80-1) Cato Inst.

Roberts, Paul C. & Stratton, Lawrence M. The New Color Line: How Quotas & Privilege Destory Democracy. (Illus.). 247p. 1997. pap. 12.95 (0-89526-423-4) Regnery Pub.

Roberts, Paul C. & Stratton, Lawrence M., Jr. The New Color Line: How Quotas & Privilege Destroy Democracy. 247p. 1995. 24.95 (0-89526-462-5) Regnery Pub.

Roberts, Paul C., ed. see Simpson, Judith.

***Roberts, Paul Craig & Stratton, Lawrence M.** The Tyranny of Good Intentions: How Prosecutors & Bureaucrats Are Trampling the Constitution. LC 99-54459. 240p. 2000. 24.95 (0-7615-2553-X) Prima Pub.

Roberts, Paul H. An Introduction to Magnetohydrodynamics. LC 67-88253. 274p. reprint ed. pap. 85.00 (0-608-30446-8, 205532000016) Bks Demand.

Roberts, Paul M. Review Text in United States History. 2nd ed. (YA). (gr. 7-9). 1989. pap. text 16.67 (0-87720-857-3) AMSCO Sch.

Roberts, Paul V., et al, eds. Adsorption Techniques in Drinking Water Treatment, Vol. 3. (Journal of Environmental Pathology, Toxicology & Oncology Ser.: Vol. 7, No. 7/8, 1987). 438p. 1987. 43.50 (0-685-34725-7) Chem-Orbital.

Roberts, Paul W. Empire of the Soul: Some Journeys in India. 384p. 1997. reprint ed. pap. 14.95 (1-57322-635-1, Riverhd Trade) Berkley Pub.

Roberts, Paul W., ed. Useful Procedures in Medical Practice. LC 85-4534. (Illus.). 632p. reprint ed. pap. 196.00 (0-7837-1495-5, 205719100023) Bks Demand.

Roberts, Paul William. The Demonic Comedy. LC 98-20558. 320p. 1998. 24.00 (0-374-13823-0) FS&G.

***Roberts, Paula.** Love Letters: How to Unlock the Secrets in Your Lover's Handwriting. 2000. pap. 9.95 (1-86204-693-X, Pub. by Element MA) Penguin Putnam.

Roberts, Paula. Women, Poverty, & Child Support. (Illus.). 166p. (Orig.). 1986. pap. 15.00 (0-941077-15-2, 41,980) NCLS Inc.

Roberts, Paula, jt. auth. see Junior League of Galveston County, Inc. Staff.

Roberts, Peggy. Just in Time. 480p. 1993. mass mkt. 4.50 (0-8217-4188-8, Zebra Kensgtn) Kensgtn Pub Corp.

— Whispers at Midnight. 352p. 1994. mass mkt. 4.50 (0-8217-4529-8, Zebra Kensgtn) Kensgtn Pub Corp.

Roberts, Peggy, ed. The Source, 1996-1997: The Greater Boston Theatre Resource Guide. 4th rev. ed. 424p. (Orig.). 1996. pap. 19.95 (0-9624740-3-7) StageSource.

Roberts, Penny. A City in Conflict: Troyes During the French Wars of Religion. LC 95-23334. (Illus.). 280p. 1996. text 79.95 (0-7190-4694-7) Manchester Univ Pr.

Roberts, Penny, jt. ed. see Levene, Mark.

Roberts, Perry L., et al. The Brooks Museum Bulletin. Bladon Lawrence, Patricia, ed. (Essays on the Collection: Vol. 3). (Illus.). 50p. 1999. write for info. (0-915525-05-4) Memphis Brooks Museum.

Roberts, Peter. Anthracite Coal Communities: A Study of the Demography, the Social, Educational & Moral Life of the Anthracite Regions. LC 75-129410. (American Immigration Collection. Series 2). (Illus.). 1970. reprint ed. 26.95 (0-405-00564-4) Ayer.

— Birdwatchers Guide to the Sydney Region. (Illus.). 204p. (Orig.). 1994. pap. 15.95 (0-86417-565-5, Pub. by Kangaroo Pr) Seven Hills Bk.

***Roberts, Peter.** Education, Literacy, & Humanization: An Introduction to the Work of Paulo Freire. LC 99-55889. (Critical Studies in Education & Culture Ser.). 192p. 2000. 59.95 (0-89789-571-1, Bergin & Garvey) Greenwood.

Roberts, Peter. Environmentally Sustainable Business: A Local & Regional Perspective. LC 96-127649. (Illus.). 288p. 1995. pap. 29.95 (1-85396-240-6, Pub. by P Chapman) Taylor & Francis.

— Granny's Incredible Edibles Cookbook. LC 94-76784. (Illus.). 160p. (Orig.). 1994. pap. 8.95 (0-9641565-5-5) Goldtree Pr.

— I Escaped the Holocaust. 49p. 1999. pap. 7.00 (0-8059-4528-8) Dorrance.

— Message of Astrology. 1990. pap. 12.95 (0-85030-823-2, Pub. by Aqrn Pr) Harper SF.

— The New Immigration: A Study of the Industrial & Social Life of Southeastern Europeans in America. LC 79-129411. (American Immigration Collection. Series 2). (Illus.). 1970. reprint ed. 26.95 (0-405-00565-2) Ayer.

— The New Immigration: A Study of the Industrial & Social Life of Southeastern Europeans in America. LC 78-145490. (American Immigration Library). xxii, 418p. 1971. reprint ed. lib. bdg. 49.95 (0-89198-023-7) Ozer.

— OJ - 101 Theories, Conspiracies & Alibis: Guilty or Innocent? You Be the Judge. LC 95-163333. 160p. (Orig.). 1995. pap. 9.95 (0-9641565-9-8) Goldtree Pr.

— Rhizoctonia-Forming Fungi: A Taxonomic Guide. (Illus.). 238p. 1999. pap. 70.00 (1-900347-69-5, Pub. by Royal Botnic Grdns) Balogh.

— Shakespeare & the Moral Curriculum: Rethinking the Secondary School Shakespeare Syllabus. LC 91-66911. 266p. (Orig.). 1992. pap. text 17.95 (0-9631311-0-9) Pripet Pr.

Roberts, Peter, ed. The Best of Plays & Players: 1969-1983, Vol. 2. (Illus.). 272p. (C). 1989. write for info. (0-413-62150-2, A0391, Methuen Drama); pap. write for info. (0-413-53720-X, A0494, Methuen Drama) Methn.

— The Best of Plays & Players, Vol. I: 1953-1968. (Illus.). 253p. (C). 1988. write for info. (0-413-52960-6, A0022, Methuen Drama) Methn.

— The Best of Plays & Players, Vol. One: 1953-1968. (Illus.). 254p. (Orig.). (C). 1990. pap. write for info. (0-413-52970-3, A0392, Methuen Drama) Methn.

Roberts, Peter, et al, eds. Managing the Metropolis: New Life for Old City Regions. 368p. 1993. 88.95 (1-85628-383-6, Pub. by Avebry) Ashgate Pub Co.

Roberts, Peter, jt. auth. see Gouldson, Andrew.

Roberts, Peter, jt. ed. see Bradshaw, Brendan.

Roberts, Peter, jt. ed. see Gouldson, Andrew.

Roberts, Peter, jt. ed. see Grantley, Darryl.

Roberts, Peter, tr. see Thrangu, Khenchen.

Roberts, Peter D. Modernism in Russian Piano Music: Skriabin, Prokofiev, & Their Russian Contemporaries, 2 vols. LC 91-32124. (Russian Music Studies). 1993. 89.95 (0-253-34992-3) Ind U Pr.

***Roberts-Phelps, Graham.** Customer Service Games for Trainers. 240p. 2000. 84.95 (0-566-08205-5) Ashgate Pub Co.

Roberts-Phelps, Graham. Display Screen Equipment. (Gower Health & Safety Workbook Ser.). 80p. 1998. pap., wbk. ed. 29.95 (0-566-08064-8, Pub. by Gower) Ashgate Pub Co.

— Environmental Awareness. (Gower Health & Safety Workbook Ser.). 80p. 1998. pap., wbk. ed. 29.95 (0-566-08063-X, Pub. by Gower) Ashgate Pub Co.

***Roberts-Phelps, Graham.** 50 Ways to Liven up Your Meetings. 192p. 2000. 79.95 (0-566-08392-2) Ashgate Pub Co.

Roberts-Phelps, Graham. Fire Safety. (Gower Health & Safety Workbook Ser.). 80p. 1998. pap., wbk. ed. 29.95 (0-566-08059-1, Pub. by Gower) Ashgate Pub Co.

— Flip Chart Games for Trainers. LC 97-32769. 192p. 1998. 72.95 (0-566-08025-7, Pub. by Gower) Ashgate Pub Co.

— Hazardous Substances. (Gower Health & Safety Workbook Ser.). 80p. 1998. pap., wbk. ed. 29.95 (0-566-08065-6, Pub. by Gower) Ashgate Pub Co.

— Health & Safety Games for Trainers. LC 98-53696. 200p. 1999. 86.95 (0-566-08202-0, Pub. by Ashgate Pub); ring bd. 131.95 (0-566-08203-9, Pub. by Ashgate Pub) Ashgate Pub Co.

— Office Safety. (Gower Health & Safety Workbook Ser.). 80p. 1998. pap., wbk. ed. 29.95 (0-566-08068-0, Pub. by Gower) Ashgate Pub Co.

— Personal Protective Equipment. (Gower Health & Safety Workbook Ser.). 80p. 1998. pap., wbk. ed. 29.95 (0-566-08061-3, Pub. by Gower) Ashgate Pub Co.

— Risk Assessment. (Gower Health & Safety Workbook Ser.). 80p. 1998. pap., wbk. ed. 29.95 (0-566-08066-4, Pub. by Gower) Ashgate Pub Co.

— Safe Manual Handling. (Gower Health & Safety Workbook Ser.). 80p. 1998. pap., wbk. ed. 29.95 (0-566-08062-1, Pub. by Gower) Ashgate Pub Co.

— Safety at Work. (Gower Health & Safety Workbook Ser.). 80p. 1998. wbk. ed. 29.95 (0-566-08067-2, Pub. by Gower) Ashgate Pub Co.

— Safety for Managers. (Gower Health & Safety Workbook Ser.). 80p. 1998. pap., wbk. ed. 29.95 (0-566-08060-5, Pub. by Gower) Ashgate Pub Co.

***Roberts-Phelps, Graham.** Sales Training Games. LC 99-40395. 1999. 86.95 (0-566-08206-3) Ashgate Pub Co.

Roberts-Phelps, Graham. Training Event Planning Guide. LC 99-187152. 196p. 1998. ring bd. 86.95 (0-566-08084-2, Pub. by Gower) Ashgate Pub Co.

Roberts-Phelps, Graham & McDougall, Anne. 50 Brain-Teasers: For Meetings, Presentations & Training Sessions. 256p. 1998. pap. 27.95 (0-566-07978-X, Pub. by Gower) Ashgate Pub Co.

— 90 Brain-Teasers for Trainers. 362p. 1997. 72.95 (0-566-07979-8, Pub. by Gower) Ashgate Pub Co.

Roberts, Phil. The Fifty-Two Best Hospitality Incentives, Contests & Rewards. (Illus.). 160p. 1994. pap. 19.95 (1-879239-02-7) Pencom.

— El Servicio Que Vende! El Arte de la Hospitalidad Rentable. Mendoza, Marcela, tr. (SPA., Illus.). 208p. 1995. pap. 16.95 (1-879239-06-X) Pencom.

— Work Smarter, Not Harder: The Service That Sells Workbook for Family Dining. (Illus.). 128p. 1995. pap. 9.95 (1-879239-04-3) Pencom.

Roberts, Phil, ed. Readings in Wyoming History: Issues in the History of the Equality State. (Wyoming History Ser.). 120p. (Orig.). 1994. pap. 6.95 (0-914767-22-4) Skyline West Pr.

Roberts, Phil & O'Donnell, Christopher. Quick Service That Sells! (Illus.). 132p. 1997. pap. 16.95 (1-879239-13-2) Pencom.

— Slam Dunk Marketing: From Rim Shots to Results. (Illus.). 196p. (Orig.). 1997. 19.95 (1-879239-15-9); pap. 16.95 (1-879239-14-0) Pencom.

Roberts, Phil & Stewart, Andrea. Turn the Tables on Turnover: 52 Ways to Find, Hire & Keep the Best Hospitality Employees. (Illus.). 123p. 1995. pap. 19.95 (1-879239-05-1) Pencom.

Roberts, Phil, et al. Wyoming Almanac. 3rd rev. ed. LC 94-66659. 460p. (Orig.). (YA). (gr. 9 up). 1994. pap. 11.95 (0-914767-21-6) Skyline West Pr.

— Wyoming Almanac. 4th rev. ed. 496p. (Orig.). 1996. pap. 12.95 (0-914767-24-0) Skyline West Pr.

Roberts, Phil, jt. auth. see Sullivan, Jim.

***Roberts, Philip.** The Royal Court Theatre & the Modern Stage. LC 98-53258. (Cambridge Studies in Modern Theatre). 267p. (C). 1999. 59.95 (0-521-47438-8); pap. 22.95 (0-521-47962-2) Cambridge U Pr.

Roberts, Philip, compiled by. Bond on File. (Methuen Writer-Files Ser.). 96p. (C). 1985. pap. write for info. (0-413-54040-5, A0034, Methuen Drama) Methn.

Roberts, Philip, jt. auth. see Hay, Malcolm.

Roberts, Philip A. Technology Transfer: A Policy Model. (Illus.). 86p. (C). 1998. reprint ed. pap. text 20.00 (0-7881-4823-0) DIANE Pub.

R

R

Roberts, Philip J. Valuation of Development Land in Hong Kong. LC 76-369546. 97p. reprint ed. pap. 30.10 (*0-608-13263-2*, 202512800042) Bks Demand.

Roberts, Philip M. The Gift of Tongues: An Evaluation. LC 91-70592. 50p. 1991. pap. 7.95 (*0-944788-96-3*) IBRI.

Roberts, Philip S. & Thomason, Ivan J. Sugarbeet Pest Management: Nematodes. (Illus.). 30p. 1981. pap. text 3.00 (*0-931876-52-4*, 3272) ANR Pubns CA.

Roberts, Phyllis A. Beyond Operating Room Doors. (Illus.). (Orig.). 1997. pap. 15.95 (*0-9657819-0-9*) P Roberts.

Roberts, Preston, jt. auth. see Terrell, Bob.

***Roberts, Priscilla.** The Cold War. 2001. pap. 9.95 (*0-7509-2437-3*, Pub. by Sutton Publng) Intl Pubs Mktg.

Roberts, R., ed. The Molecular Basis of Cardiology. (Molecular Basis of Clinical Medicine Ser.). (Illus.). 544p. 1992. pap. 49.95 (*0-86542-196-X*) Blackwell Sci.

Roberts, R. & Roberts, G. To Fight Better: A Biography of J. Oswald Sanders. 1989. pap. 6.95 (*0-946616-58-2*) OMF Bks.

Roberts, R., jt. auth. see Majapuria, M.

Roberts, R. E. Henrik Ibsen: A Critical Study. LC 73-21628. (Studies in Ibsen: No. 63). 1974. lib. bdg. 75.00 (*0-8383-1834-7*) M S G Haskell Hse.

Roberts, R. H. & Good, J. M., eds. The Recovery of Rhetoric: Persuasive Discourse & Disciplinarity in the Human Sciences. LC 92-39541. (Knowledge, Disciplinarity & Beyond Ser.). 278p. (C). 1993. pap. text 20.00 (*0-8139-1456-6*) U Pr of Va.

Roberts, R. J. & Shepherd, C. J. Handbook Trout & Salmon Diseases. LC 97-14109. 288p. (Orig.). 1997. pap. text 69.95 (*0-85238-244-8*) Blackwell Sci.

Roberts, R. J., jt. auth. see Bromage, Niall R.

Roberts, R. J., jt. auth. see Rowe, R. C.

Roberts, R. J., ed. see Qualben, Lois.

Roberts, R. M., jt. ed. see Stewart, I. A.

***Roberts, R. O. & Hall, J. Elizabeth.** The Building Industry in the Upper Swansea Valley & Its Economic & Social Ramifications, C. 1750-1975. LC 99-59019. (Welsh Studies: Vol. 16). 200p. 2000. text 79.95 (*0-7734-7788-8*) E Mellen.

Roberts, R. Philip. Mormonism Unmasked: Confronting the Contradictions Between Mormonism Beliefs & True Christianity. LC 98-12749. 120p. 1998. pap. 8.99 (*0-8054-1652-8*) Broadman.

Roberts, R. Phillip. Continuity & Change: London Calvinistic Baptists & the Evangelical Revival, 1760-1820. 282p. 1989. lib. bdg. 30.00 (*0-940033-30-5*) R O Roberts.

Roberts, Rachel. Library Development in Central & Eastern Europe - From Assistance to Cooperation. 139p. 1994. pap. 25.00 (*92-826-2657-1*, CD-NA-15660-ENC, Pub. by Comm Europ Commun) Bernan Associates.

Roberts, Ralph. Auction Action! A Survival Companion for Any Auction Goer. (Illus.). 192p. 1986. pap. 12.95 (*0-8306-2752-9*, NO. 2752) McGraw-Hill Prof.

— Chatting with Ben Hur: Featuring the Vocal Stylings of Mr. Perry Como. (Illus.). 64p. 1999. pap. 9.95 (*1-56664-152-7*) WorldComm.

— E. Y. Ponder: High Sheriff of the Kingdom of Madison. (Illus.). (Orig.). 1999. pap. 7.95 (*1-56664-043-1*) WorldComm.

— Excursion into the Endless Caves. (Illus.). 96p. (Orig.). 1993. pap. 9.95 (*1-56664-025-3*) WorldComm.

— Genealogy Via the Internet: Trace Your Family Roots Quickly & Easily Using the Worldwide Web. 2nd ed. 288p. 2000. pap. 16.95 (*1-57090-093-0*, Pub. by Alexander Dist) Midpt Trade.

— Genealogy Via the Internet: Tracing Your Family Roots Quickly & Easily Computerized. 1997. pap. text 12.95 (*1-57090-009-4*) Alexander Dist.

Roberts, Ralph. How the South Won the War & Perserved the Union. LC 97-120217. 1997. 9.95 (*1-57090-052-3*, Farthest Star) Alexander Dist.

Roberts, Ralph. How to Get Published: And Published & Published. (Illus.). 208p. (Orig.). 1999. pap. 12.95 (*1-56664-003-2*) WorldComm.

— Leo White: Rocket Man. LC 96-61839. (Illus.). 112p. (Orig.). 1996. pap. 9.95 (*1-56664-042-3*) WorldComm.

— The Pepsi Challenge: From 12 Full Ounces to a New Generation, 100 Years of Pepsi History. LC 96-31414. (Illus.). 320p. 1998. pap. text 14.95 (*1-57090-008-6*) Alexander Dist.

— The Power of Turbo Prolog: The Natural Language of Artificial Intelligence. (Illus.). 256p. 1987. 22.95 (*0-8306-0782-X*, 2782); pap. 14.95 (*0-8306-2782-0*) McGraw-Hill Prof.

***Roberts, Ralph.** Sell It Yourself. LC 99-28274. 256p. 1999. pap. 12.95 (*1-58062-204-6*) Adams Media.

***Roberts, Ralph & Roberts, Pat.** Cooking with Pepsi, Uh Huh! (Illus.). 208p. (Orig.). 1998. pap. 14.95 (*1-888295-05-8*) Elephant Books.

— The Great American Steak Book. (Illus.). 208p. 1998. pap. 14.99 (*1-888295-02-3*) Elephant Books.

— The Official Mr. Potatohead Cookbook. (Illus.). 208p. (Orig.). Date not set. pap. 14.99 (*1-888295-04-X*) Elephant Books.

— The Recovering Vegetarian Cookbook: 12 Easy Steps to Eating Meat Again. (Illus.). 208p. (Orig.). 1998. pap. 14.99 (*1-888295-03-1*) Elephant Books.

Roberts, Ralph, jt. auth. see Graham, Elizabeth C.

Roberts, Ralph, jt. auth. see Hall, Betty L.

Roberts, Ralph, ed. see Boone, Don.

Roberts, Ralph, ed. see Mashburn, Joseph L.

Roberts, Ralph, ed. see Wellman, Manly Wade.

Roberts, Ralph G. Tick Creek Cave: An Archaic Site in the Gasconade River Valley of Missouri. Bray, Robert T., ed. (Missouri Archaeologist Ser.: Vol. 27, No. 2). (Illus.). 52p. (Orig.). 1965. pap. 2.00 (*0-943414-44-X*) MO Arch Soc.

***Roberts, Ralph R.** Walk Like a Giant, Sell Like a Madman. 1999. pap. 13.50 (*0-06-662034-1*, HarpBusn) HarpInfo.

Roberts, Ralph R. Walk Like a Giant, Sell Like a Madman: America's #1 Salesman Shows You How to Sell Anything. LC 97-8008. 224p. 1998. pap. 13.50 (*0-88730-930-5*) HarpC.

— Walk Like a Giant, Sell Like a Madman: America's #1 Salesperson Shows You How to Sell Anything! LC 97-8008. 288p. 1997. 25.00 (*0-88730-843-0*, HarpBusn) HarpInfo.

Roberts, Ralph R. Walk Like a Giant, Sell Like a Madman: Roberts,&Ralph R. unabridged ed. 1997. audio 12.00 (*0-694-51896-4*, CPN 10121) HarperAudio.

Roberts, Ralph R. & Gallagher, John. 52 Weeks of Sales Success: America's #1 Salesman. LC 98-43026. 224p. 1999. 21.00 (*0-88730-963-1*, HarpBusn) HarpInfo.

***Roberts, Ralph R. & Gallagher, John.** Walk Like a Giant, Sell Like a Madman. 207p. 2000. reprint ed. text 25.00 (*0-7881-6858-4*) DIANE Pub.

Roberts, Randal, ed. Lessons in Leadership: Fifty Respected Evangelical Leaders Share Their Wisdom on Ministry. 288p. 1998. pap. text 13.99 (*0-8254-3630-3*) Kregel.

Roberts, Randy. But They Can't Beat Us: Oscar Robertson's & the Crispus Attacks Tigers. Indiana Historical Society Staff, ed. (Illus.). 200p. 1999. 19.95 (*1-57167-257-5*) Sports Pub.

— Jack Dempsey: The Manassa Mauler. LC 83-27514. (Illus.). 344p. 1984. pap. 14.95 (*0-8071-1161-9*) La State U Pr.

— Muhammad Ali. 1999. pap. write for info. (*0-14-010063-6*, Viking) Viking Penguin.

Roberts, Randy, ed. American Experience, Vol. 2. 4th ed. LC 97-34459. Vol. 2. (Illus.). 338p. (C). 1997. pap. text 37.00 (*0-321-01031-0*) Addson-Wesley Educ.

— American Experiences, Vol. 1. 4th ed. LC 97-34459. 365p. (C). 1997. pap. text 37.00 (*0-321-01030-2*) Addson-Wesley Educ.

***Roberts, Randy, ed.** Pittsburgh Sports: Stories from the Steel City. (Sports History Ser.). (Illus.). 238p. 2000. 29.95 (*0-8229-4143-0*) U of Pittsburgh Pr.

***Roberts, Randy & Garrison, J. Gregory.** Heavy Justice: The Trial of Mike Tyson. LC 99-86456. 336p. 2000. pap. 20.00 (*1-55728-600-0*) U of Ark Pr.

Roberts, Randy & Olson, James. Winning Is the Only Thing: Sports in America since 1945. LC 89-1689. (Illus.). 208p. 1989. 38.95 (*0-8018-3830-4*) Johns Hopkins.

— Winning Is the Only Thing: Sports in America since 1945. LC 89-1689. (American Moment Ser.). (Illus.). 208p. 1991. reprint ed. pap. 14.95 (*0-8018-4240-9*) Johns Hopkins.

***Roberts, Randy & Olson, James N.** A Line in the Sand: The Alamo in Blood & Memory. 1999. write for info. (*0-684-00982-X*) Free Pr.

— A Line in the Sand: The Alamo in Blood & Memory. 352p. 2000. 25.50 (*0-684-83544-4*) Free Pr.

Roberts, Randy & Olson, James S. John Wayne: American. LC 95-12536. (Illus.). 752p. 1995. 27.00 (*0-02-923837-4*) Free Pr.

— John Wayne: American. LC 97-20010. (Illus.). x, 762p. 1997. pap. 25.00 (*0-8032-8970-7*) U of Nebr Pr.

Roberts, Randy, jt. auth. see Olson, James S.

Roberts, Randy, jt. ed. see Mintz, Steven.

Roberts, Ransom. How to Have a Happier Year: Take a Number (Nonsense Numerology) LC 81-90709. (Illus.). 128p. (Orig.). 1982. pap. 5.95 (*0-9607834-0-7*) Uptown Bks.

Roberts, Ray. John Updike: A Biographical Checklist. 12.50 (*0-89679-011-8*); pap. text 4.50 (*0-89679-010-X*) Moretus Pr.

— Paper Airplanes from Around the World, Vol. 1. 4th enl. rev. ed. (Illus.). 260p. (YA). (gr. 6 up). 1995. reprint ed. 28.00 (*0-929995-00-7*) AIR Burbank.

Roberts, Ray, ed. see Goebel, Julius L., Jr.

Roberts, Renee, jt. auth. see Craddock, Jim.

Roberts, Rhia, jt. auth. see Mather, Nancy.

Roberts, Richard. Dance unto Death. LC 92-60330. 315p. (Orig.). 1992. pap. 10.95 (*0-942380-14-2*) Vernal Equinox.

— Faith to Try Again. LC 97-150935. 160p. 1996. pap. 6.99 (*1-880089-27-0*, AP-927, Pub. by Albury Pub) Appalach Bk Dist.

— From Eden to Eros: Origins of the Putdown of Women. (Illus.). 167p. (Orig.). 1985. pap. 8.95 (*0-942380-05-3*) Vernal Equinox.

— The Original Tarot & You. 210p. (Orig.). 1987. pap. 8.95 (*0-942380-06-1*) Vernal Equinox.

— Save the Whales! (Illus.). (Orig.). 1991. pap. 10.95 (*0-942380-12-6*) Vernal Equinox.

— Tales for Jung Folk: Original Fairytales for Persons of All Ages Dramatizing C. G. Jung's Archetypes of the Collective Unconscious. (Illus.). 120p. 1983. pap. 8.95 (*0-942380-01-0*); lib. bdg. 15.95 (*0-942380-02-9*) Vernal Equinox.

— Two Worlds of Cotton: Colonialism & the Regional Economy in the French Soudan, 1800-1946. LC 95-26213. 1996. write for info. (*0-8047-2652-3*) Stanford U Pr.

— The Wind & The Wizard, 2 vols., Vol. 1. (Illus.). 256p. 1990. pap. 15.95 (*0-942380-07-X*) Vernal Equinox.

— The Wind & the Wizard, Vol. 2. (Illus.). 177p. 1990. pap. 15.95 (*0-942380-09-6*) Vernal Equinox.

Roberts, Richard, ed. Global Financial Centres Vol. 2: London, New York, Tokyo. (International Financial Centres Ser.). 584p. 1994. 200.00 (*1-85898-153-0*) E Elgar.

— International Financial Centers Series, 4 vols. (Elgar Mini Ser.). 2432p. 1994. 830.00 (*1-85278-758-9*) E Elgar.

— International Financial Centres: Concepts, Development & Dynamics. (International Financial Centres Ser.: No. 1). 584p. 1994. 200.00 (*1-85898-152-2*) E Elgar.

— International Financial Centres of Europe, North America & Asia. (International Financial Centres Ser.: Vol. 3). 624p. 1994. 200.00 (*1-85898-154-9*) E Elgar.

— Offshore Financial Centres, Vol. 4. (International Financial Centres Ser.). 640p. 1994. 200.00 (*1-85898-155-7*) E Elgar.

Roberts, Richard & Kynaston, David, eds. The Bank of England: Money, Power & Influence, 1694-1994. (Illus.). 334p. 2000. reprint ed. pap. 24.95 (*0-19-829284-8*) OUP.

Roberts, Richard & Kynaston, David, eds. The Bank of England 1694-1994: Money, Power & Influence. (Illus.). 328p. 1995. text 45.00 (*0-19-828952-9*) OUP.

Roberts, Richard, jt. auth. see Campbell, Joseph.

Roberts, Richard, jt. auth. see Mann, Kristin.

Roberts, Richard, jt. auth. see Roberts, Jane.

Roberts, Richard, jt. ed. see Isaacman, Allen.

Roberts, Richard A. & Mullis, Clifford T. Digital Signal Processing. (Electrical Engineering Ser.). (Illus.). 578p. (C). 1987. 100.00 (*0-201-16350-0*) Addison-Wesley.

Roberts, Richard A., jt. auth. see Gabel, Robert A.

Roberts, Richard B. Studies of Macromolecular Biosynthesis. LC 64-21763. (Carnegie Institution of Washington Publication Ser.: Vol. 624). (Illus.). 718p. reprint ed. pap. 200.00 (*0-608-06224-3*, 206655300008) Bks Demand.

Roberts, Richard B., et al. Studies of Biosynthesis in Escherichia Coli. LC QH0086.S77R6. (Carnegie Institution of Washington Publication Ser.: Vol. 607). (Illus.). 537p. reprint ed. pap. 166.50 (*0-608-06222-7*, 206655100008) Bks Demand.

Roberts, Richard C., et al. A History of Weber County. LC 97-60679. (Illus.). write for info. (*0-913738-14-X*) Utah St Hist Soc.

Roberts, Richard C., jt. auth. see Sadler, Richard W.

Roberts, Richard H. A Theology on Its Way? Essays on Karl Barth. 256p. 1991. text 47.95 (*0-567-09585-1*, Pub. by T & T Clark) Bks Intl VA.

Roberts, Richard H., ed. Religion & the Transformations of Capitalism: Comparative Approaches. LC 94-28913. 344p. (C). 1995. 100.00 (*0-415-11917-0*, B4332) Routledge.

Roberts, Richard H., ed. see Ewald, William P., et al.

Roberts, Richard J., et al, eds. Nucleases, Monograph 25. 2nd ed. (Illus.). 300p. (C). 1994. pap. 38.00 (*0-87969-426-2*) Cold Spring Harbor.

Roberts, Richard J., jt. ed. see Linn, Stuart M.

Roberts, Richard J., jt. ed. see Varney, Nils R.

Roberts, Richard L. Warriors, Merchants, & Slaves: The State & the Economy in the Middle Niger Valley, 1700-1914. LC 86-23138. 305p. 1987. 45.00 (*0-8047-1378-2*) Stanford U Pr.

Roberts, Richard L., et al. Freeze Fracture Images of Cells & Tissues. (Illus.). 416p. 1991. text 79.00 (*0-19-505228-5*) OUP.

Roberts, Richard L., jt. ed. see Miers, Suzanne.

Roberts, Richard N. & Magrab, Phyllis R. Where Children Live: Solutions for Serving Young Children & Their Families. LC 98-55758. (Advances in Applied Developmental Psychology Ser.: Vol. 17). 1999. pap. 39.50 (*1-56750-441-8*) Ablx Pub.

Roberts, Richard N., et al. Strengthening the Family-Professional Partnership in Services for Young Children. LC 97-28101. 1997. 29.95 (*1-55766-319-X*) P H Brookes.

Roberts, Richard O. Revival. rev. ed. 159p. (C). 1991. reprint ed. pap. 8.95 (*0-940033-36-4*) R O Roberts.

— Revival. 2nd rev. ed. 159p. (C). 1991. reprint ed. lib. bdg. 12.95 (*0-940033-37-2*) R O Roberts.

— Revival Literature: An Annotated Bibliography with Biographical & Historical Notices. xxxii, 575p. 1987. lib. bdg. 60.00 (*0-940033-27-5*) R O Roberts.

— Sanctify the Congregation: A Call to the Solemn Assembly & to Corporate Repentance. LC 93-80173. xiv, 338p. (Orig.). 1994. pap. text 18.95 (*0-926474-10-3*) Intl Awakening Pr.

— Whitefield in Print: A Bibliographic Record. xlii, 765p. 1988. lib. bdg. 75.00 (*0-940033-28-3*) R O Roberts.

Roberts, Richard O., ed. Salvation in Full Color: Twenty Sermons by Great Awakening Preachers. LC 93-80172. xxii, 362p. (Orig.). 1994. pap. text 17.95 (*0-926474-12-X*) Intl Awakening Pr.

— Salvation in Full Color: Twenty Sermons by Great Awakening Preachers. LC 93-80172. xxii, 362p. (Orig.). 1994. pap. text 17.95 (*0-940033-46-1*) R O Roberts.

— Sanctify the Congregation: A Call to the Solemn Assembly & to Corporate Repentance. LC 93-80173. xiv, 338p. (Orig.). 1994. pap. text 18.95 (*0-940033-47-X*) R O Roberts.

— Scotland Saw His Glory: A History of Revivals in Scotland. LC 95-78264. 1995. lib. bdg. 21.95 (*0-926474-16-2*) Intl Awakening Pr.

Roberts, Richard O., ed. see Couper, W. J., et al.

Roberts, Richard O., ed. see Neprash, Ivan V., et al.

Roberts, Richard O., ed. see Orr, J. Edwin.

Roberts, Richard P. Alton, New Hampshire Vital Records, 1890-1997. 624p. 1999. pap. 45.00 (*0-7884-1145-4*, R510) Heritage Bk.

***Roberts, Richard P.** New Castle, New Hampshire, Vital Records, 1891-1997. 311p. 2000. pap. 26.00 (*0-7884-1454-2*, 1454) Heritage Bk.

Roberts, Richard P. New Hampshire Name Changes, 1768-1923. LC 96-228059. 333p. 1996. pap. 28.00 (*0-7884-0500-4*, R507) Heritage Bk.

***Roberts, Richard P.** Vital Records of New Durham & Middleton, New Hampshire, 1887-1998. 407p. 1999. pap. 33.50 (*0-7884-1246-9*) Heritage Bk.

— Vital Records of Wakefield, New Hampshire, 1887-1998. 623p. 2000. pap. 35.50 (*0-7884-1411-9*, R512) Heritage Bk.

Roberts Rinehart Publishers. Celtic Illustrations: A Prayer Journal. gif. ed. 176p. 1999. pap. 12.95 (*1-57098-308-9*) Roberts Rinehart.

Roberts, Robert. Classic Slum: Salford Life. 1990. pap. 13.95 (*0-14-013624-X*, Penguin Bks) Viking Penguin.

— The House Servant's Directory: Comprising Hints on the Arrangement & Performance of Servants' Work. Hodges, Graham R., ed. LC 97-24310. 240p. (C). (gr. 13). 1997. text 44.95 (*0-7656-0114-1*) M E Sharpe.

— The House Servant's Directory: or A Monitor for Private Families: A Monitor for Private Families: Comprising Hints on the Arrangement & Performance of Servants' Work. Hodges, Graham R., ed. LC 97-24310. 240p. (C). (gr. 13). 1997. pap. text 21.95 (*0-7656-0115-X*) M E Sharpe.

— A Ragged Schooling. 218p. 1997. pap. 16.95 (*1-901341-01-1*) St Martin.

— Roberts' Guide for Butlers & Household Staff. LC 93-19131. 180p. 1988. reprint ed. pap. 9.95 (*1-55709-120-X*) Applewood.

— The Social Laws of the Qoran: Considered & Compared with Those of the Hebrew & Other Ancient Codes. LC 89-27402. 136p. 1990. pap. 15.00 (*0-391-03661-0*) Humanities.

Roberts, Robert, jt. ed. see Suzuki, Shosuke.

Roberts, Robert B. New York's Forts in the Revolution. LC 77-74395. 500p. 1979. 38.50 (*0-8386-2063-9*) Fairleigh Dickinson.

Roberts, Robert C. & Talbot, Mark R., eds. Limning the Psyche: Explorations in Christian Psychology. LC 97-14456. 382p. 1997. pap. 24.00 (*0-8028-4331-X*) Eerdmans.

Roberts, Robert J., jt. auth. see Leff, Richard D.

Roberts, Robert N. White House Ethics: The History of the Politics of Conflict of Interest Regulation, 204. LC 87-24962. (Contributions in Political Science Ser.: No. 204). 215p. 1988. 57.95 (*0-313-25934-8*, RWH/, Greenwood Pr) Greenwood.

Roberts, Robert N. & Doss, Marion T. From Watergate to Whitewater: The Public Integrity War. LC 96-53616. 232p. 1997. 55.00 (*0-275-95597-4*, Praeger Pubs) Greenwood.

Roberts, Robert N., jt. ed. see Eksterowicz, Anthony J.

Roberts, Robert W. & Nee, Robert H., eds. Theories of Social Casework. LC 70-123358. 1995. lib. bdg. 29.00 (*0-226-72105-1*) U Ch Pr.

Roberts, Robert W. & Northen, Helen. Theories for Social Work with Groups. LC 76-4967. 400p. 1976. text 46.50 (*0-231-03885-2*) Col U Pr.

Roberts, Robert W., jt. ed. see Taylor, Samuel H.

Roberts, Robin. Anne McCaffrey: A Critical Companion. LC 95-40029. (Critical Companions to Popular Contemporary Writers Ser.). 208p. 1996. 29.95 (*0-313-29450-X*, Greenwood Pr) Greenwood.

***Roberts, Robin.** Basketball the Right Way. LC 00-25350. (Get in the Game! Ser.). (Illus.). (J). 2000. lib. bdg. 6.95 (*0-7613-1285-4*) Millbrook Pr.

— Basketball Year. LC 99-46223. (Get in the Game! Ser.). 5p. 2000. pap. 6.95 (*0-7613-1028-2*) Millbrook Pr.

— Basketball Year: What It's Like to Be a Woman Pro. LC 99-46223. (Get in the Game! Ser.). 48p. (J). (gr. 4-8). 2000. 21.90 (*0-7613-1406-7*) Millbrook Pr.

— Careers for Women Who Love Sports. (Get in the Game! Ser.). 5p. (J). 2000. pap. 6.95 (*0-7613-1282-X*) Millbrook Pr.

— Careers for Women Who Love Sports. LC 99-46221. (Get in the Game! Ser.). 48p. (J). (gr. 4-8). 2000. 21.90 (*0-7613-1408-3*) Millbrook Pr.

— Careers for Women Who Love Sports. (Illus.). (J). 2000. 12.30 (*0-606-18281-0*) Turtleback.

Roberts, Robin. Ladies First: Women in Music Videos. LC 96-14969. (Studies in Popular Culture). 184p. 1996. text 45.00 incl. Beta (*0-87805-933-4*); pap. text 22.50 incl. Beta (*0-87805-934-2*) U Pr of Miss.

— A New Species: Gender & Science in Science Fiction. LC 92-25385. (Illus.). 200p. (C). 1993. text 29.95 (*0-252-01983-0*); pap. text 12.95 (*0-252-06284-1*) U of Ill Pr.

— Sexual Generations: Star Trek, the Next Generation & Gender. LC 98-58090. (Orig.). 1999. write for info. (*0-252-02455-9*) U of Ill Pr.

***Roberts, Robin.** Sexual Generations: Star Trek, the Next Generation & Gender. LC 98-58090. 208p. (Orig.). 1999. pap. text 15.95 (*0-252-06810-6*) U of Ill Pr.

— Sports for Life: How Athletes Have More Fun. LC 00-24920. (Get in the Game! Ser.). (Illus.). (J). 2000. pap. 6.95 (*0-7613-1027-4*) Millbrook Pr.

***Roberts, Robin & Rogers, C. Paul, III.** The Whiz Kids & the 1950 Pennant. (Baseball in America Ser.). (Illus.). 390p. 2000. pap. 18.95 (*1-56639-790-1*) Temple U Pr.

Roberts, Robin & Rogers, C. Paul, 3rd. The Whiz Kids & the 1950 Pennant. (Baseball in America Ser.). (Illus.). 390p. (C). 2000. 59.50 (*1-56639-466-X*) Temple U Pr.

Roberts, Ron & Sammut, Judy. Asthma: An Alternative Approach. LC 96-52334. 232p. (Orig.). 1997. pap. 14.95 (*0-87983-771-3*, 37713K, Keats Publng) NTC Contemp Pub Co.

Roberts, Ron E. Social Problems. 310p. 1978. pap. 12.95 (*0-8016-4143-8*) Schenkman Bks Inc.

Roberts, Ron E. & Brintnall, Douglas. Reinventing Inequality. 339p. 1983. text 22.95 (*0-87073-793-7*); pap. text 18.95 (*0-87073-794-5*) Schenkman Bks Inc.

Roberts, Ronald. Iowa's Ethnic Roots. 192p. (C). 1993. pap. text 23.95 (*0-8403-8421-1*) Kendall-Hunt.

— John L. Lewis: Hard Labor & Wild Justice. LC 94-230993. 240p. (C). 1994. per. 29.95 (*0-8403-9297-4*) Kendall-Hunt.

Roberts, Ronald, jt. auth. see Muir, J. E.

Roberts, Ronald J. & Shepherd, C. Jonathan. Handbook of Trout & Salmon Diseases. 1978. 90.00 (*0-7855-6929-4*) St Mut.

An Asterisk (*) at the beginning of an entry indicates that the title is appearing for the first time.

Roberts, Ronald R. The Ditches of Edison County. LC 93-37206. 1993. write for info. (*0-525-27256-9*, Plume) Dutton Plume.
— The Ditches of Edison County. 1999. pap. write for info. (*0-451-18266-9*, Sig) NAL.
Roberts, Ronald S. Clarence Thomas & the Tough Love Crowd: Counterfeit Heroes & Unhappy Truths. 221p. (C). 1994. text 45.00 (*0-8147-7454-7*) NYU Pr.
— Clarence Thomas & the Tough Love Crowd: Counterfeit Heroes & Unhappy Truths. 221p. (C). 1996. pap. text 19.00 (*0-8147-7481-4*) NYU Pr.
Roberts, Roy R. Life in the Pressure Cooker: Studies in James. pap. 5.99 (*0-88469-036-9*) BMH Bks.
Roberts, Royston & Khalaf. Friedel-Crafts Alkylation Chemistry: A Century of Discovery. (Studies in Organic Chemistry: Vol. 10). 800p. 1984. text 275.00 (*0-8247-6433-1*) Dekker.
Roberts, Royston M. Serendipity: Accidental Discoveries in Science. LC 88-33638. (Illus.). 288p. 1989. pap. 16.95 (*0-471-60203-5*) Wiley.
Roberts, Royston M. & Roberts, Jeanie. Lucky Science: Accidental Discoveries from Gravity to Velcro, with Experiments. LC 94-10373. 128p. (gr. 4-7). 1994. pap. 12.95 (*0-471-00954-7*) Wiley.
Roberts, Rozella. Mind Assassins. large type ed. 201p. (Orig.). 1992. pap. 9.95 (*0-9633452-0-6*) Roxanne Unltd.
Roberts, Rozella, jt. auth. see Chiaverini, Evelyn.
Roberts, Russell. All about Blue Crabs: And How to Catch Them. 88p. 1993. pap. 8.95 (*1-882418-07-7*) Centenn Pubns.
***Roberts, Russell.** Ancient Egyptian Rulers. LC 98-35271. (History Makers Ser.). (Illus.). 144p. (YA). (gr. 4-12). 1998. lib. bdg. 23.70 (*1-56006-438-2*) Lucent Bks.
Roberts, Russell. Discover the Hidden New Jersey. (Illus.). 300p. (C). 1995. pap. 18.95 (*0-8135-2252-8*) Rutgers U Pr.
— Endangered Species. LC 98-15038. (Overview Ser.). (Illus.). (YA). (gr. 4-12). 1998. lib. bdg. 23.70 (*1-56006-191-X*) Lucent Bks.
***Roberts, Russell.** Lincoln & the Abolition of Slavery (Civil War) LC 99-23477. (American War Library). (Illus.). 144p. (YA). (gr. 6-9). 2000. lib. bdg. 23.70 (*1-56006-580-X*) Lucent Bks.
— Stolen! A History of Base Stealing. LC 98-53595. (Illus.). 240p. 1999. pap. 26.50 (*0-7864-0650-X*) McFarland & Co.
Roberts, Russell & Youmans, Richard. Down the Jersey Shore: A Historical Tour. LC 92-44337. (Illus.). 275p. (C). 1993. pap. 14.95 (*0-8135-1996-9*); text 29.95 (*0-8135-1995-0*) Rutgers U Pr.
Roberts, Russell D. Case Studies in Modern Corporate Finance: A Fable of Free Trade & Protectionism. LC 93-44899. 644p. 1994. text 65.00 (*0-13-288341-4*) P-H.
— The Choice: A Fable of Free Trade & Protectionism. (Illus.). 128p. (C). 1993. pap. text 11.95 (*0-13-083008-9*) P-H.
***Roberts, Russell D.** 101 Best Businesses to Start. 3rd ed. 2000. pap. 19.95 (*0-7679-0659-4*) Broadway BDD.
Roberts, Russell D. Primer to International Trade. (C). 1994. pap. 10.60 (*0-13-101650-4*, Macmillan Coll) P-H.
***Roberts, Ruth.** Apoptosis in Toxicology. LC 99-34776. 239p. 1999. 72.00 (*0-7484-0815-0*) Tay Francis Ltd.
Roberts, Ruth E., jt. auth. see Walsh, John T.
Roberts, S. PC-XT-AT-386 Hardware Reference: Concise Explanations of Hardware Elements, with Illustrations. (Info Compact Ser.). (Illus.). 100p. (C). 1991. pap. 5.00 (*0-911827-07-2*) Elcomp.
— PC-XT-AT-386 Technical Pocket Reference for IBM-PC & Compatibles Pt. 2: Important Information, Tables, Technical Data, 2. (Info Compact Ser.). (Illus.). 100p. (C). 1991. pap. 5.00 (*0-911827-08-0*) Elcomp.
— Windows 3 Pocket Reference: Concise Explanations of All Windows 3 Commands, Illustrated with Examples. (Info Compact Ser.). (Illus.). 100p. (C). 1991. pap. 5.00 (*0-911827-06-4*) Elcomp.
Roberts, S., ed. Law & the Family in Africa. 1977. 33.85 (*90-279-7663-5*) Mouton.
Roberts, S., jt. auth. see Hawthorn, P.
Roberts, S. C. Doctor Watson. 32p. 1977. reprint ed. lib. bdg. 20.00 (*0-910278-63-6*) Boulevard.
— Holmes & Watson: A Miscellany. LC 78-157958. 137p. 1972. reprint ed. lib. bdg. 35.00 (*0-8371-6172-X*, ROHW, Greenwood Pr) Greenwood.
— Holmes & Watson: A Miscellany. LC 94-8931. 144p. 1994. reprint ed. per. 8.00 (*1-883402-96-4*) S&S Trade.
Roberts, S. C., ed. see Piozzi, Hester Lynch.
Roberts, S. C., ed. & intro. see Doyle, Arthur Conan.
Roberts, S. D. Forth Applications: Ready to Run Programs. (Illus.). 149p. (Orig.). 1990. pap. 9.95 (*0-911827-00-5*, 61) Elcomp.
— Forth Quick Start: Introduction to Forth. (Illus.). 59p. (Orig.). 1990. pap. 5.00 (*0-911827-01-3*, 65) Elcomp.
— The Great Book of Batch Jobs: Introduction to Batch Programming on PC - XT - AT. (Illus.). 98p. (Orig.). 1990. pap. 9.95 (*0-911827-05-6*, 71) Elcomp.
***Roberts, S. Gary.** Masterful Woodturning: Projects & Inspiration for the Skilled Turner. LC 00-37290. (Illus.). 2000. write for info. (*0-8069-8709-X*) Sterling.
Roberts, S. Lowell. Back to Buck Lake. LC 93-71649. 304p. (YA). (gr. 7 up). 1993. 14.95 (*0-9636894-0-1*) Estrn Itascan.
Roberts, S. M., et al. Introduction to Biocatalysis Using Enzymes & Microorganisms. (Illus.). 207p. (C). 1995. text 64.95 (*0-521-43070-4*); pap. text 24.95 (*0-521-43685-0*) Cambridge U Pr.
Roberts, S. M., jt. ed. see Ganellin, C. R.
***Roberts, Sally A.** The Legend of Crystal Lake. LC 99-49996. 2000. write for info. (*1-57168-369-0*, Eakin Pr) Sunbelt Media.
Roberts, Sally-Ann. Going Live: An Anchorwoman Reports Good News. LC 97-47661. (Illus.). 112p. 1998. 14.95 (*1-56554-304-1*) Pelican.
Roberts, Sam. Christian Economics. (Extensions Adult Elective Bible Study Ser.). 56p. pap. 9.00 (*1-57312-112-6*) Smyth & Helwys.
Roberts, Sam D. Games for the Atari. 1982. pap. 7.95 (*0-936200-36-7*) Blue Cat.
— How to Program Your Atari in 6502 Machine Language. 106p. 1982. 9.95 (*0-936200-37-5*) Blue Cat.
— Statistics on the IBM: Introduction, Practial Applications, Ready to Run Programs. (Illus.). 200p. 1985. pap. 12.95 (*3-88963-047-2*) Elcomp.
— Tricks for VICs. 1984. 9.95 (*3-88963-176-2*) Blue Cat.
— UNIX, XENIX & VENIX: Introduction, Applications Tips & Tricks. (Illus.). 206p. 1985. pap. 12.95 (*3-88963-064-2*) Elcomp.
— UNIXV Pocket Reference. (Info Compact Ser.). 88p. 1992. pap. 5.00 (*0-911827-14-5*) Elcomp.
Roberts, Samuel J. Survival of Hegemony? The Foundations of Israeli Foreign Policy. LC 73-8134. (Studies in International Affairs: No. 20). 175p. reprint ed. pap. 49.90 (*0-608-14705-2*, 2025852); reprint ed. pap. 54.30 (*0-608-10344-6*, 202585200046) Bks Demand.
***Roberts, Samuel K., ed.** Born to Preach: Essays in Honor of the Ministry of Henry & Ella Mitchell. 160p. (YA). 2000. pap. 15.00 (*0-8170-1368-7*) Judson.
Roberts, Samuel K., jt. auth. see Bakke, Raymond J.
Roberts, Samuel R., III. Existence, Faith & Responsibility: Carl Michalson's Christian Ethics. (Contemporary Existentialism Ser.: Vol. 2). XVIII, 280p. (C). 1990. text 57.95 (*0-8204-0875-1*) P Lang Pubng.
Roberts, Sara R., jt. auth. see Lafo, Rachel R.
Roberts, Sarah, ed. see Hoppins, Charles.
Roberts, Sarah R. Observation & Fantasy: The Art of Arthur Spear. LC 94-74016. (Illus.). 40p. (Orig.). Date not set. pap. write for info. (*0-945506-18-X*) DeCordova Mus.
Roberts, Sasha. Romeo & Juliet. (Writers & Their Work Ser.). 96p. (Orig.). 1996. pap. 15.00 (*0-7463-0812-4*, Pub. by Northcote House) U Pr of Miss.
Roberts, Sasha, jt. auth. see Thompson, Ann.
***Roberts, Scott.** Programming Microsoft Internet Explorer 5. LC 99-27216. 1999. pap. text 49.99 (*0-7356-0781-8*) Microsoft.
Roberts, Scott, et al. Strength & Weight Training for Young Athletes. (Illus.). 192p. 1994. pap. 15.95 (*0-8092-3697-4*, 369740, Contemporary Bks) NTC Contemp Pub Co.
Roberts, Scott O., ed. The Business of Personal Training. LC 95-19815. (Illus.). 152p. (Orig.). 1995. pap. text 24.00 (*0-87322-605-4*, BROB0605) Human Kinetics.
Roberts, Scott O., et al, eds. Clinical Exercise Testing & Prescription: Theory & Application. LC 96-24940. 336p. 1997. boxed set 94.95 (*0-8493-4593-6*) CRC Pr.
Roberts, Scott O., jt. auth. see Pillarella, Debi.
***Roberts, Scott W.** Health Wellness: An Introductory Approach. 3rd ed. 350p. 1998. pap. 28.95 (*0-945483-72-4*) E Bowers Pub.
Roberts, Shane. The Art & Science of Making Money: Earning, Investing, & Spending Your Way to Greater Personal Wealth. LC 92-61032. 288p. 1993. 22.95 (*0-9633122-9-4*) McMahon Pub.
Roberts, Sharon. Backflips. 184p. (Orig.). 1997. pap. 11.95 (*0-9656439-0-5*) Greenlght Pub.
***Roberts, Sharon.** Selling to Women & Couples: Secrets of Selling in the New Millennium. (Illus.). viii, 96p. 1999. pap. 20.00 (*0-9700619-0-0*) Rob & Rob Assocs.
Roberts, Sharon L. Critical Care Nursing: Assessment & Intervention. 800p. (C). 1995. pap. text 49.95 (*0-8385-3604-2*, A3604-4, Apple Lange Med) McGraw.
— Somebody Lives Inside: The Holy Spirit. (Concept Books for Children). (Illus.). 24p. (J). (gr. k-4). 1986. pap. 3.99 (*0-570-08530-6*, 56-1557) Concordia.
Roberts, Shauna S., jt. auth. see Hansen, Barbara.
Roberts, Shawn & Williams, Jody. After the Guns Fall Silent: The Enduring Legacy of Landmines. LC 96-153171. (Illus.). 538p. (C). 1995. pap. 19.95 (*0-85598-337-X*, Pub. by Oxfam Pub) Stylus Pub VA.
Roberts, Sheila, ed. Still the Frame Holds: Essays on Women Poets & Writers. LC 87-823. (I. O. Evans Studies in the Philosophy & Criticism of Literature: No. 10). 216p. 1993. pap. 23.00 (*0-89370-404-0*) Millefleurs.
***Roberts, Shelley.** Remaining & Becoming: Cultural Crosscurrents in an Hispano School. (A Volume in the Sociocultural, Political & Historical Studies in Education Series). 192p. 2000. write for info. (*0-8058-2521-5*); pap. write for info. (*0-8058-2522-3*) L Erlbaum Assocs.
***Roberts, Shelly.** Baby Dykes. (Illus.). 110p. 2001. pap. 12.95 (*1-55583-525-2*, Pub. by Alyson Pubns) Consort Bk Sales.
Roberts, Shelly. The Dyke Detector: How to Tell the Real Lesbians from Ordinary People. LC 92-61205. (Illus.). 96p. (Orig.). 1992. pap. 7.95 (*0-9628595-6-7*) Paradigm San Diego.
— Hey Mom, Guess What! One Hundred Fifty Ways to Tell Your Mother. LC 93-84467. (Illus.). 160p. 1993. pap. 8.95 (*0-9628595-9-1*) Paradigm San Diego.
— Make News & Make Noise! How to Get Publicity for Your Book. LC 93-87210. 64p. (Orig.). 1994. pap. 5.95 (*1-882587-03-0*) Paradigm San Diego.
— Roberts' Rules of Lesbian Break-Ups. LC 97-238. (Roberts' Rules Ser.: Vol. 2). 175p. (Orig.). 1997. pap. 5.95 (*1-883523-19-2*) Spinsters Ink.
— Roberts' Rules of Lesbian Dating. LC 98-18496. (Roberts' Rules Ser.: Vol. 3). 196p. 1998. pap. 5.95 (*1-883523-25-7*) Spinsters Ink.
— Roberts' Rules of Lesbian Living. 192p. (Orig.). 1996. pap. 5.95 (*1-883523-09-5*) Spinsters Ink.
Roberts, Sherry. Maud's House. LC 94-715. 216p. 1994. 18.00 (*0-918949-32-7*) Roberts.
— Maud's House. LC 94-715. 216p. 1995. pap. 11.00 (*0-918949-28-9*) Roberts.
Roberts, Sherry, jt. auth. see Thompson, Deanna L.
Roberts, Sherry, ed. see Lenoir, Anna.
Roberts, Shirley. Harness The Future: The 9 Keys To Emerging Consumer Behaviour. 288p. 1998. reprint ed. 34.95 (*0-471-64235-5*) Wiley.
— Sophia Jex-Blake: A Woman Pioneer in Nineteenth Century Medical Reform. LC 93-14890. (Wellcome Institute Series in the History of Medicine). (Illus.). 176p. (C). 1993. 85.00 (*0-415-08753-8*, B0865) Routledge.
Roberts, Sidney I. Legislative History of United States Tax Conventions, 18 vols., Set. (Roberts & Holland Collection). 1986. ring bd. 2295.00 (*0-89941-379-X*, 303850) W S Hein.
Roberts, Sidney I., et al. Annotated Tax Forms. write for info. (*0-318-57361-X*) P-H.
***Roberts, Simon.** Complete Java 2 Certification Study Guide. 912p. 1999. pap. 49.99 (*0-7821-2700-2*) Sybex.
Roberts, Simon. Java 1.1 Certification. 1998. pap., student ed. 54.99 (*0-7821-2330-9*) Sybex.
Roberts, Simon & Heller, Philip. Java 1.1 Certification Study Guide. LC 97-69201. 752p. 1997. pap. text, student ed. 44.99 incl. cd-rom (*0-7821-2069-5*) Sybex.
Roberts, Simon & Palmer, Michael. Dispute Processes: Text & Materials. LC 98-198176. (Law in Context Ser.). 270p. 1998. pap. 35.00 (*0-406-89774-3*, Pub. by Buttrwrth Co Ltd) Northwestern U Pr.
***Roberts, Simon, et al.** The Complete Java 2 Certification Study Guide. LC 99-61816. (Certification Study Guide Ser.). 960p. 1999. 49.99 incl. cd-rom (*0-7821-2463-1*) Sybex.
Roberts, Simon, jt. auth. see Comaroff, John L.
Roberts, Simon, jt. auth. see Heller, Philip.
Roberts Staff. The Boer War Afrikaaners P. O. W. Roll. (C). 1993. 295.00 (*1-873058-16-0*, Pub. by Roberts) St Mut.
— British South Africa Company's Medal: The 1890 Mashonsland Medal. (C). 1989. 95.00 (*1-873058-45-4*, Pub. by Roberts) St Mut.
— British South Africa Company's Medal: The 1893 Metabeleland Medal. (C). 1989. 105.00 (*1-873058-50-0*, Pub. by Roberts) St Mut.
— British South Africa Company's Medal: The 1896 Rhodesia Medal. (C). 1989. 95.00 (*1-873058-55-1*, Pub. by Roberts) St Mut.
— British South Africa Company's Medal: The 1897 Mashonsland Medal. (C). 1989. 95.00 (*1-873058-60-8*, Pub. by Roberts) St Mut.
— British South Africa Company's Medal Complete Roll. (C). 1989. 360.00 (*1-873058-40-3*, Pub. by Roberts) St Mut.
— The Cape Cooper Company Limited Medal for the Defence of O'Kiep. (C). 1989. 90.00 (*1-873058-30-6*, Pub. by Roberts) St Mut.
— Cape of Good Hope Medal 1880-1897. (C). 1993. 90.00 (*1-873058-25-X*, Pub. by Roberts) St Mut.
— Colonial Auxiliary Forces Long Service Medal. (C). 1989. 90.00 (*1-873058-56-X*, Pub. by Roberts) St Mut.
— Decorations Awarded to Natal, Cape Colony & Union Defence Forces 1877-1961. (C). 1989. 90.00 (*1-873058-51-9*, Pub. by Roberts) St Mut.
— Defenders of Mafeking. (C). 1993. 90.00 (*1-873058-06-3*, Pub. by Roberts) St Mut.
— The Efficiency Decoration-The Union of South Africa. (C). 1989. 90.00 (*1-873058-70-5*, Pub. by Roberts) St Mut.
— Etonians Who Served in the Boer War. (C). 1989. 100.00 (*1-873058-21-7*, Pub. by Roberts) St Mut.
— The Jameson Raiders, 1896. (C). 1989. 120.00 (*1-873058-85-3*, Pub. by Roberts) St Mut.
— Kings Commendations-Union Forces, 1939-1945. (C). 1989. 100.00 (*1-873058-80-2*, Pub. by Roberts) St Mut.
— The Matabele Rebellion, 1896. (C). 1989. 95.00 (*1-873058-05-5*, Pub. by Roberts) St Mut.
— Die Medaljerol. (C). 1989. 125.00 (*1-873058-01-2*, Pub. by Roberts) St Mut.
— Medals for Gallantry & Distinguished Conduct Award to Natal, Cape Colony & Union Defence Forces 1877-1961. (C). 1989. 110.00 (*1-873058-95-0*, Pub. by Roberts) St Mut.
— The Officers, Men & Women of the Australian Imperial Forces, Vol. 6. (C). 1989. 130.00 (*1-873058-66-7*, Pub. by Roberts) St Mut.
— The Officers, Men & Women of the Merchant Navy & Mercantile Fleet Auxiliary, Vol. 5. (C). 1989. 125.00 (*1-873058-41-1*, Pub. by Roberts) St Mut.
— The Officers, Men & Women of the New Zealand Expeditionary Forces, Vol. 8. (C). 1989. 125.00 (*1-873058-76-4*, Pub. by Roberts) St Mut.
— The Officers, Men & Women of the South African Forces, Vol. 7. (C). 1989. 125.00 (*1-873058-71-3*, Pub. by Roberts) St Mut.
— Officers Who Died in the Service of British, Indian & East African Regiments & Corps 1914-1919, Vol. 1. (C). 1989. 125.00 (*1-873058-26-8*, Pub. by Roberts) St Mut.
— Officers Who Died in the Service of the Royal Navy, Royal Naval Reserve, Royal Naval Volunteer Reserve, Royal Marines, Royal Marines Reserve, Royal Navy Air Service & Royal Air Force, Vol. 2. (C). 1989. 125.00 (*1-873058-31-4*, Pub. by Roberts) St Mut.
— Roll of Honour South Africa 1939-1945 European, Natives & Coloured. (C). 1993. 95.00 (*1-873058-86-1*, Pub. by Roberts) St Mut.
— South African Mounted Irregular Forces, 1899-1902: A Multinational Force in the Boer War. (C). 1993. 90.00 (*1-873058-65-9*, Pub. by Roberts) St Mut.
— South African War Medal, 1877-89 the Medal Roll. (C). 1989. 90.00 (*1-873058-20-9*, Pub. by Roberts) St Mut.
— South Africa's Roll of Honour, 1914-1918. (C). 1989. 95.00 (*1-873058-75-6*, Pub. by Roberts) St Mut.
— The Transport Medal Roll. (C). 1989. 95.00 (*1-873058-15-2*, Pub. by Roberts) St Mut.
— The Zulu Rebellion, 1906. rev. ed. (C). 1989. 90.00 (*1-873058-00-4*, Pub. by Roberts) St Mut.
Roberts Staff, ed. Defenders of Kimberley. (C). 1989. 90.00 (*1-873058-35-7*, Pub. by Roberts) St Mut.
— Female Officers, Nurses, Enlisted Women & Civilians, Vol. 9. (C). 1989. 125.00 (*1-873058-81-0*, Pub. by Roberts) St Mut.
— Non-Commissioned Officers & Men of the Royal Navy & Commonwealth & Colonial Revies Who Died in Service 1914-1919, Vol. 4. (C). 1989. 125.00 (*0-7855-2660-9*, Pub. by Roberts) St Mut.
— Officers Who Died in the Service of Commonwealth & Colonial Regiments & Corps, Vol. 3. (C). 1989. 125.00 (*1-873058-36-5*, Pub. by Roberts) St Mut.
— Orders of Chivalry, Foreign Decorations & Awards to Natal, Cape Colony & Union Defence Forces. (C). 1989. 90.00 (*1-873058-90-X*, Pub. by Roberts) St Mut.
Roberts, Stanley. The Beginner's Guide to Winning Blackjack. (Illus.). (Orig.). 1983. pap. 10.00 (*0-89746-014-6*) Gambling Times.
— Gambling Times Guide to Blackjack. (Illus.). (Orig.). 1983. pap. text 5.95 (*0-685-01828-8*) Carol Pub Group.
— Gambling Times Guide to Blackjack, 1990. (Illus.). (Orig.). 1984. pap. 9.95 (*0-89746-015-4*) Gambling Times.
Roberts, Stanley, jt. auth. see Chambers, Alec.
***Roberts, Stanley M.** Biocatalysis for Fine Chemecial Synthesis. Casy, G., ed. LC 98-48782. 848p. 1999. 550.00 (*0-471-97901-5*) Wiley.
Roberts, Stanley M., ed. Molecular Recognition: Chemistry & Biochemistry Problems, No. 78. 1989. 109.00 (*0-85186-796-0*) CRC Pr.
Roberts, Stephanie, jt. auth. see Diamond, Lynn.
Roberts, Stephanie, ed. see Meister, Jeanne.
Roberts, Stephanie, ed. see Meister, Jeanne C.
Roberts, Stephen. The House That Hitler Built. 1975. 250.00 (*0-87968-338-4*) Gordon Pr.
— Radical Politicians & Poets in Early Victorian Britain: The Voices of Six Chartist Leaders. LC 93-50810. (Studies in British History: Vol. 27). 160p. 1994. text 69.95 (*0-7734-9126-0*) E Mellen.
— Telephone Installation Handbook. LC 99-495097. (Illus.). 160p. 1997. pap. text 37.95 (*0-7506-3427-8*, Newnes) Buttrwrth-Heinemann.
Roberts, Stephen, jt. auth. see Ashton, Owen R.
Roberts, Stephen A. Financial Cost Management for Library & Information Services. 2nd ed. LC 97-30611. 250p. 1997. 55.00 (*1-85739-089-X*) Bowker-Saur.
Roberts, Stephen G.H., ed. see Unamuno, Miguel de.
Roberts, Stephen H. Population Problems of the Pacific. LC 71-99884. reprint ed. 55.00 (*0-404-00599-3*) AMS Pr.
Roberts, Stephen M., et al. Hazardous Waste Incineration Evaluating the Human Health & Environmental Risks. LC 98-28649. 448p. 1998. 69.95 (*1-56670-250-X*, L1250) Lewis Pubs.
***Roberts, Stephen Morris.** A Space Inside a Space. 75p. 1999. pap. 11.95 (*1-879934-61-2*) St Andrews NC.
Roberts, Stephen O. B., et al. A Clinician's Guide to Fungal Disease. LC 84-14932. (Infectious Diseases & Antimicrobial Agents Ser.: Vol. 5). (Illus.). 264p. 1984. text 135.00 (*0-8247-7190-7*) Dekker.
Roberts, Stephen R. A Slash of Waking. Sherman, Alana, ed. 20p. (Orig.). 1995. pap. text 5.95 (*0-939689-19-7*) Alms Hse Pr.
Roberts, Stephen R., et al. West Wind Review, Vol. 14. 204p. 1995. pap. write for info. (*0-9630694-4-6*) So Oregon.
Roberts, Stephen S., jt. auth. see Bauer, K. Jack.
Roberts, Stephen S., jt. auth. see Stone, Jack L.
Roberts, Stephen S., ed. see Ropp, Theodore.
Roberts, Steven. Cul-de-Sac Cowboy. (Illus.). x, 65p. 1996. pap. 11.95 (*0-9660385-0-9*) Mustard Tree.
Roberts, Steven, jt. auth. see Roberts, Cokie.
Roberts, Steven K. The Complete Guide to Microsystem Management. 192p. (C). 1984. 26.00 (*0-13-160556-9*) P-H.
— Computing Across America: The Bicycle Odyssey of a High-Tech Nomad. (Illus.). 368p. 1988. pap. 9.95 (*0-938734-18-0*) Info Today Inc.
— Creative Design with Microcomputers. (Illus.). 400p. 1984. 16.95 (*0-13-189317-3*) P-H.
***Roberts, Steven K.** From Behemoth to Microship: A Detailed Look at Two Platforms for Technomadic Adventure. 3rd ed. (Monographs: Vol. NRL-401). (Illus.). 94p. 1999. pap. 12.50 (*1-929470-00-2*) Nomadic Research.
Roberts, Steven K. Industrial Design with Microcomputers. (Illus.). 416p. (C). 1982. 41.00 (*0-13-459461-4*) P-H.
***Roberts, Steven K.** The Nomadness Journals: Tales of the Behemoth Era. 2nd ed. (NRL Adventure Tales Ser.: Vol. NRL-217). (Illus.). 144p. 1999. pap. 12.95 (*1-929470-03-7*) Nomadic Research.
— Sexbar Design Package: A Serial Crossbar Switching Network. (NRL Technical Monographs: Vol. NRL-601). (Illus.). 45p. 1999. pap. 19.95 (*1-929470-01-0*) Nomadic Research.
— Video Turret Design Package: The Complete Design of a Microprocessor-Controlled Video Turret. 2nd ed. (NRL Technical Monographs: NRL-605). (Illus.). 80p. 1999. pap. 24.95 (*1-929470-02-9*) Nomadic Research.
Roberts, Sue N. & Bunker, Dorothy. Ginny Doll Encyclopedia. LC 95-157979. (Illus.). 176p. 1994. 29.95 (*0-87588-419-9*) Hobby Hse.
Roberts, Susan. Stanza. 1997. pap. 19.95 (*1-85224-423-2*, Pub. by Bloodaxe Bks) Dufour.
Roberts, Susan, jt. auth. see Roberts, Don.
Roberts, Susan, jt. auth. see Roberts, John.
Roberts, Susan A., et al. A History of New Mexico. 2nd rev. ed. 406p. 1997. 30.00 (*0-8263-1792-8*) U of NM Pr.

R

An Asterisk (*) at the beginning of an entry indicates that the title is appearing for the first time.

R

Roberts, Susan B., et al. Feeding Your Child for Lifelong Health: Birth Through Age Six. LC 99-20253. (Illus.). 353p. (Orig.). 1999. pap. 15.95 (0-553-37892-9) Bantam.

Roberts, Susan L., jt. auth. see Greene, David P.

***Roberts, Suzanne.** Coping in New Territory: A Guide for Adult Children of Aging Parents. unabridged ed. Osa, Nancy, ed. 160p. 2000. pap. 16.95 (0-9678161-0-6) Cheltenham Pr OR.

Roberts, T., jt. ed. see Brooks, G. T.

Roberts, T., jt. ed. see Narayanan, R.

Roberts, T. A. Painting the Cows: Twenty Years of Wildlife Conservation in California & the West. LC 98-14508. 176p. 1998. pap. 14.95 (1-880284-29-4) J Daniel.

Roberts, T. D. Understanding Balance: The Mechanics of Posture & Locomotion. 360p. 1995. pap. 47.99 (1-56593-416-4, 1082) Singular Publishing.

***Roberts, T. J.** The Butterflies of Pakistan. (Illus.). 300p. 2000. text 50.00 (0-19-577995-9) OUP.

— The Mammals of Pakistan. LC 97-930912. (Illus.). 1997. write for info. (0-19-577852-9) OUP.

Roberts, T. J., et al, eds. Wild Flowers of Pakistan. LC 95-930651. (Illus.). 332p. 1996. text 65.00 (0-19-577584-8) OUP.

Roberts, T. R. Eminent Welshmen: A Short Biographical Dictionary of Welshmen Who Have Obtained Distinction from the Earliest Times to the Present. 613p. 1995. reprint ed. pap. 45.00 (0-8063-4594-2, Pub. by Clearfield Co) ACCESS Pubs Network.

— Metabolism of Agrochemicals in Plants LC 99-16222. (Series in Agrochemicals & Plant Protection). 314p. 2000. 175.00 (0-471-80150-X) Wiley.

Roberts, T. R. & Kearney, Philip C., eds. Progress in Pesticide Biochemistry & Toxicology: Environmental Behaviour of Agrochemicals, Vol. 9, Environmental Behaviour of Agrochemicals. LC 83-647760. (Progress in Pesticide Biochemistry & Toxicology Ser.: Vol. 9). 418p. 1995. 305.00 (0-471-95301-6) Wiley.

Roberts, T. R., ed. see Greenhlagh.

Roberts, T. R., jt. ed. see Hutson, D. H.

Roberts, Tara. Am I the Last Virgin? (J). 1997. mass mkt. 3.99 (0-689-81254-X) S&S Childrens.

— Am I the Last Virgin? And Other Tales about Young Adult Black Female Sexuality. LC 96-23793. 112p. (J). (gr. 6 up). 1997. per. 15.00 (0-689-80449-0) S&S Childrens.

— Son of Darkness. (Illus.). 400p. 1997. pap. 10.00 (1-57502-659-7, PO1874) Morris Pubng.

***Roberts, Tatheena.** Macdougal Alley: A Novel. 288p. 2001. pap. 11.95 (1-55583-540-6, Pub. by Alyson Pubns) Consort Bk Sales.

Roberts, Ted. For Men Only: The Courageous Fight for Healthy Sexuality. Harlan, Roberta, ed. (Illus.). 132p. (Orig.). 1993. student ed. 7.00 (1-879619-09-1) East Hill Church.

— A Place of Hope, Place of Healing. LC 99-11351. 300p. 1999. pap. 11.99 (0-8307-2335-8, Regal Bks) Gospel Lght.

Roberts, Ted E. Practical Radio Promotions. (Electronic Media Guide Ser.). 104p. 1992. pap. 24.95 (0-240-80090-7, Focal) Buttrwrth-Heinemann.

Roberts, Terence A., et al, eds. Psychrotrophic Microorganisms in Spoilage & Pathogenicity. LC 81-67902. 552p. 1982. text 157.00 (0-12-589720-0) Acad Pr.

Roberts, Teresa Noelle. Digging up the Bones. 70p. 1994. pap. 7.00 (0-944920-12-8) Bellowing Ark Pr.

Roberts, Terry. Self & Community in the Fiction of Elizabeth Spencer. LC 93-26078. (Southern Literary Studies). 176p. 1994. text 30.00 (0-8071-1879-6) La State U Pr.

Roberts, Terry & Billings, Laura. The Paideia Classroom: Teaching for Understanding. LC 98-29063. 170p. 1999. pap. 26.95 (1-883001-60-9) Eye On Educ.

Roberts, Terry & National Paideia Center Staff. The Power of Paideia Schools: Defining Lives Through Learning. LC 98-9049. 125p. 1998. pap. 17.95 (0-87120-303-0, 198034) ASCD.

Roberts, Terry, jt. auth. see Kearney, P. C.

Roberts, Thom. Atlantic Free Balloon Race. (J). (gr. 3-7). 1986. pap. 2.50 (0-380-89868-3, Avon Bks) Morrow Avon.

— Summerdog. (Illus.). 128p. (Orig.). (J). (gr. 1 up). 1978. pap. 2.25 (0-380-01950-7, Avon Bks) Morrow Avon.

Roberts, Thomas, jt. ed. see Kramutschke, Eleanor.

Roberts, Thomas, jt. ed. see Rex, David.

Roberts, Thomas B. & Hruby, Paula J., eds. Religion & Psychoactive Sacraments: A Bibliographic Guide. (Entheogen Project Ser.: Vol. 1). 327p. 1995. spiral bd. 46.95 (1-889725-00-5) Coun Sprtal Pract.

Roberts, Thomas E., jt. auth. see Juergensmeyer, Julian C.

Roberts, Thomas P. Living with Your Living Trust: A Complete Guide to Funding & Managing Your Living Trust. LC 96-85010. 175p. (Orig.). 1996. ring bd. 39.95 (0-9652592-1-8) Daybreaker.

Roberts, Thomas S. Manual for the Identification of the Birds of Minnesota & Neighboring States. rev. ed. LC QL0684.M6R47. (Illus.). 295p. 1955. reprint ed. pap. 91.50 (0-608-00840-0, 206163100010) Bks Demand.

Roberts, Thomas W. A Systems Perspective of Parenting: The Individual, the Family, & the Social Network. LC 93-41870. 414p. 1994. mass mkt. 36.50 (0-534-15546-4) Brooks-Cole.

***Roberts, Timothy E., et al.** Historical Iowa Settlement in the Grand River Basin of Missouri & Iowa. (Missouri Archaeologist Ser.: Vol. 57). (Illus.). 102p. 1999. pap. 7.50 (0-943414-86-5, 115700) MO Arch Soc.

Roberts, Timothy R. Ancient Civilizations: Great Empires at Their Heights. (Illus.). 176p. 1997. 24.98 (0-7651-9328-0) Smithmark.

***Roberts, Timothy R.** Ancient Rome. LC 99-462290. (Illus.). 176p. 1999. 24.98 (1-56799-724-4, MetroBooks) M Friedman Pub Grp Inc.

Roberts, Timothy R. The Celts in Myth & Legend. (Myths of the World Ser.). (Illus.). 112p. 1995. text 15.98 (1-56799-092-4) M Friedman Pub Grp Inc.

— Central & South America. (Myths of the World Ser.). (Illus.). 112p. 1996. 15.98 (1-56799-351-6) M Friedman Pub Grp Inc.

— Gift of the Nile: Chronicles of Ancient Egypt. LC 98-22429. (Illus.). 176p. 1998. 24.98 (1-56799-585-3, MetroBooks) M Friedman Pub Grp Inc.

Roberts, Timothy R., et al. Mythology: Tales of Ancient Civilizations. LC 97-53045. (Illus.). 448p. 1998. 29.98 (1-56799-664-7, Friedman-Fairfax) M Friedman Pub Grp Inc.

Roberts, Tom. Friends & Villains. large type ed. (Non-Fiction Ser.). (Illus.). 384p. 1989. 27.99 (0-7089-2045-4) Ulverscroft.

— Friends & Villains: An Autobiography. (Illus.). 192p. 1988. text 22.95 (0-340-41150-3, Pub. by Hodder & Stought Ltd) Trafalgar.

— Funding Revolution: New Routes to Project Fundraising. LC 99-158348. 127p. 1998. 79.00 (0-7507-0822-0); pap. text 26.95 (0-7507-0821-2) Taylor & Francis.

— Goldilocks. LC 93-6679. (Illus.). (J). (ps-6). 1993. 9.95 incl. audio (0-88708-322-6, Picture Book Studio) S&S Childrens.

— Goldilocks & the Three Bears. LC 90-7166. (Illus.). 32p. (J). (ps-3). 1991. 14.95 (0-88708-146-0, Rabbit Ears) Litle Simon.

— Red Riding Hood. LC 93-12152. (Illus.). (J). (ps-6). 1993. 9.95 incl. audio (0-88708-320-X, Rabbit Ears) Litle Simon.

— Red Riding Hood. (Illus.). 40p. (J). (ps up). 1995. mass mkt. 10.95 incl. audio (0-689-80203-X, Rabbit Ears) Litle Simon.

— The Three Billy Goats Gruff. LC 93-6678. (Illus.). (J). (ps-6). 1993. 9.95 (0-88708-319-6, Picture Book Studio) S&S Childrens.

— The Three Little Pigs. abr. ed. LC 89-70097. (Storybook Classics Ser.). (Illus.). 32p. (J). (ps up). 1991. pap. 19.95 incl. audio (0-88708-133-9, Rabbit Ears) Litle Simon.

— The Three Little Pigs. (Illus.). 40p. (J). (gr. k-3). 1993. reprint ed. 9.95 incl. audio (0-88708-299-8, Rabbit Ears) Litle Simon.

Roberts, Tom, ed. see Andersen, Hans Christian.

Roberts, Tom J. The Birds of Pakistan, 1. (Illus.). 654p. (C). 1992. text 85.00 (0-19-577405-1) OUP.

— The Birds of Pakistan: Regional Studies & Non-Passeriformes, 1. (Illus.). 640p. 1991. text 85.00 (0-19-577404-3, 8452) OUP.

Roberts, Tomi-Ann, ed. The Lanahan Readings in the Psychology of Women. (Illus.). 574p. (Orig.). (C). 1997. pap. text 28.75 (0-9652687-2-1) Lanahan Pubs.

Roberts, Tony. Cycling along the Waterways of France. LC 98-10282. (Illus.). 192p. 1998. pap. 14.95 (0-933201-90-7) MBI Pubg.

Roberts, Tris. Equestrian Technique. 265p. (C). 1990. 80.00 (0-85131-555-0, Pub. by J A Allen) St Mut.

Roberts, Tristan D. Neurophysiology of Postural Mechanisms. 2nd ed. LC 77-30548. (Illus.). 430p. reprint ed. pap. 133.30 (0-608-18009-2, 205631800058) Bks Demand.

Roberts, Tyler T. Contesting Spirit: Nietzsche, Affirmation, Religion. LC 98-14875. 256p. 1998. text 59.50 (0-691-05937-3, Pub. by Princeton U Pr); pap. text 16.95 (0-691-00127-8, Pub. by Princeton U Pr) Cal Prin Full Svc.

Roberts, Tyson R. The Freshwater Fishes of Western Borneo (Kalimantan Barat, Indonesia) LC 88-70981. (Memoirs of the California Academy of Sciences Ser.: No. 14). (Illus.). 1989. 20.00 (0-940228-21-1) Calif Acad Sci.

— An Ichthyological Survey of the Fly River in Papua New Guinea: With Descriptions of New Species. LC 78-606184. (Smithsonian Contributions to Zoology Ser.: No. 281). 78p. reprint ed. pap. 30.00 (0-608-14439-8, 205185900011) Bks Demand.

Roberts, Ursula. Living in Two Worlds: The Autobiography of Ursula Roberts. Regency Press, Ltd. Staff, ed. 200p. 1984. 39.00 (0-7212-0629-8, Pub. by Regency Pr GBR) St Mut.

— Reminiscences: A Lifetime of Spiritualism. 115p. 1985. 35.00 (0-7212-0726-X, Pub. by Regency Pr GBR) St Mut.

Roberts, V. Flutophone & Tonette for Beginners (Also Song Flute) 32p. 1986. pap. 3.95 (0-7935-5413-6, 50394330) H Leonard.

***Roberts, Vaughan.** Turning Points. 214p. 1999. reprint ed. mass mkt. 9.99 (1-85078-336-5, Pub. by O M Pubng) OM Literature.

Roberts, Vega Z., jt. auth. see Foster, Angela.

Roberts, Verne L. Machine Guarding: A Historical Perspective. LC 80-84798. (Illus.). 282p. 1980. text 39.95 (0-938830-00-7) Inst Product.

Roberts, Victoria. British Poultry Standards: Complete Specifications & Judging Points of All Standardized Breeds & Varieties of Poultry As Compiled by the Specialist Breed Clubs & Recognized by the Poultry Club of Great Britain. 5th rev. ed. LC 96-9548. (Illus.). 384p. 1997. 89.95 (0-632-04052-1) Blackwell Sci.

— Poultry For Anyone. 1998. 38.95 (1-873580-38-X) Whittet Bks.

Roberts, Virginia C. With Their Own Blood: A Saga of Southwestern Pioneers. LC 91-15195. (Illus.). 288p. (C). 1991. 24.95 (0-87565-090-2) Tex Christian.

Roberts, Virginia F. Mountain Lake Remembered: In Memory of the Late Mary Moody Northern & Our Friend the Late Molly Malloy Brooks. LC 97-25366. 1997. write for info. (1-57168-901-X, Eakin Pr) Sunbelt Media.

Roberts, W. The Caribbean. 1976. lib. bdg. 59.95 (0-8490-1574-X) Gordon Pr.

Roberts, W., ed. N* Physics: Proceedings of the 4th CEBAF/INT Workshop. 300p. 1997. 56.00 (981-02-3138-5) World Scientific Pub.

Roberts, W. Adolphe. French in the West Indies. LC 70-147313. (Illus.). 1971. reprint ed. 53.50 (0-8154-0377-1) Cooper Sq.

— Lake Pontchartrain. (American Lakes Ser.). lib. bdg. 26.95 (0-8488-2021-5) Amereon Ltd.

Roberts, W. Dayton. Patching God's Garment: Environment & Mission in the 21st Century. 180p. 1994. pap. 5.95 (0-912552-85-9) MARC.

***Roberts, W. Dayton & Pretiz, Paul E.** Down-to-Earth Christianity: Creation-Care in Ministry. 200p. (C). 2000. pap. 19.95 (0-9678717-0-0) Evanglcls Social.

Roberts, W. G. Rental Management Made Easy. (Illus.). 150p. 1992. pap. 14.95 (0-9629979-1-9) Tower Pub GA.

Roberts, W. H. Drums & Guns Around Petersburg, Bk. 1. LC 96-119866. 133p. (Orig.). 1995. pap. 14.00 (0-7884-0345-1) Heritage Bk.

Roberts, W. H., III & Cordell, Robert J., eds. Problems of Petroleum Migration. LC 80-80879. (AAPG Studies in Geology: No. 10). (Illus.). 283p. reprint ed. pap. 87.80 (0-7837-2597-3, 204276100006) Bks Demand.

Roberts, W. Rhys & Fyfe, W. Hamilton, trs. The Poetics. (Loeb Classical Library: No. 199). 15.50 (0-674-99219-9) HUP.

Roberts, W. Rhys, ed. & tr. see Dionysius Of Halicarnassus.

Roberts, Wally. Happy Shoes. (C). 1990. 23.00 (0-947333-13-4, Pub. by Pascoe Pub) St Mut.

Roberts, Walter A. Mayor Harding of New York. LC 73-18602. reprint ed. 42.50 (0-404-11412-1) AMS Pr.

— The Mind Reader: A Mystery. LC 73-18600. reprint ed. 42.50 (0-404-11410-5) AMS Pr.

— The Moralist. LC 73-18601. reprint ed. 42.50 (0-404-11411-3) AMS Pr.

— Royal Street, a Novel of Old New Orleans. LC 73-18605. reprint ed. 42.50 (0-404-11415-6) AMS Pr.

— The Strange Career of Bishop Sterling. LC 73-18603. reprint ed. 42.50 (0-404-11413-X) AMS Pr.

— The Top-Floor Killer. LC 73-18604. reprint ed. 42.50 (0-404-11414-8) AMS Pr.

— U. S. Navy Fights. (Essay Index Reprint Ser.). 1977. 23.95 (0-8369-2068-6) Ayer.

Roberts, Walter O. & Friedman, Edward J. Living with the Changed World Climate. 38p. (Orig.). 1982. pap. text 10.50 (0-8191-5884-4) U Pr of Amer.

Roberts, Walter R. Tito, Mihailovic, & the Allies. LC 87-5357. (Illus.). xxi, 406p. 1987. pap. text 24.95 (0-8223-0773-1) Duke.

Roberts, Warren. A Bibliography of D. H. Lawrence. 2nd ed. LC 81-10149. 644p. reprint ed. pap. 180.00 (0-8357-7181-4, 2024582) Bks Demand.

— Jacques-Louis David & Jean-Louis Prieur, Revolutionary Artists: The Public, the Populace & Images of the French Revolution. LC 99-37078. (Illus.). 384p. (C). 1999. text 73.50 (0-7914-4287-X, Suny Pr); pap. text 24.95 (0-7914-4288-8, Suny Pr) State U NY Pr.

— Jane Austen & the French Revolution. 240p. (C). 1995. pap. 25.00 (0-485-12110-7, Pub. by Athlone Pr) Humanities.

— Morality & Social Class in 18th Century French Literature & Painting. LC 74-187951. (Toronto University Romance Ser.: No. 25). (Illus.). 204p. reprint ed. pap. 63.30 (0-608-11322-0, 202051400018) Bks Demand.

Roberts, Warren E. Log Buildings of Southern Indiana. LC 85-51209. (Illus.). 231p. (Orig.). 1984. pap. 10.00 (0-915305-00-3) Trickster Pr.

Roberts, Warren E. Log Buildings of Southern Indiana. rev. ed. (Illus.). 228p. (Orig.). 1996. pap. 14.95 (0-915305-06-2) Trickster Pr.

Roberts, Warren E. The Tale of the Kind & the Unkind Girls: AA-Th 480 & Related Tales. LC 93-27257. (Classics in Folklore Ser.). 178p. (C). 1994. reprint ed. pap. text 17.95 (0-8143-2490-8) Wayne St U Pr.

— Viewpoints on Folklife: Looking at the Overlooked. Bronner, Simon J., ed. LC 87-22710. (American Material Culture & Folklife Ser.). (Illus.). 331p. reprint ed. pap. 102.70 (0-8357-1849-2, 207075800004) Bks Demand.

Roberts, Wayne, et al. Get a Life! How to Make a Good Buck, Dance Around the Dinosaurs & Save the World. 344p. 1997. pap. 19.95 (0-9697755-1-2) Get A Life.

Roberts, Wayne, jt. auth. see Ehring, George.

Roberts, Wendy H. Celebrating Her: Feminist Ritualizing Comes of Age. LC 98-14596. 160p. (Orig.). 1998. pap. 15.95 (0-8298-1258-X) Pilgrim OH.

Roberts, Wes. Support Your Local Pastor: Practical Ways to Encourage Your Minister. LC 95-38505. 1995. pap. 9.00 (0-89109-923-9) NavPress.

Roberts, Wes, jt. auth. see Wright, Norman.

Roberts, Wess. Leadership Secrets of Attila the Hun. LC 88-27739. 110p. 1990. mass mkt. 12.95 (0-446-39106-9, Pub. by Warner Bks) Little.

— Victory Secrets of Attila the Hun. 160p. 1994. pap. 13.95 (0-440-50591-7) Dell.

Roberts, Wess & Ross, Bill. Make It So: Leadership for the Next Generation. 1996. pap. 12.00 (0-614-12596-0, PB Trade Paper) PB.

— Make It So: Leadership Lessons from Star Trek: The Next Generation. 256p. 1996. pap. 12.00 (0-671-52098-9) S&S Trade.

Roberts, William. An Account of the First Discovery, & Natural History of Florida: A Facsimile Reproduction of the 1763 Edition with an Introduction & Index by Robert L. Gold. LC 76-1971. 189p. reprint ed. pap. 58.60 (0-7837-0598-0, 204094600019) Bks Demand.

— The Earlier History of English Bookselling. 1972. 59.95 (0-8490-0064-5) Gordon Pr.

— How to Save Money on Just about Everything. 256p. 1996. pap. 20.00 (0-87364-870-6) Paladin Pr.

— Prophet in Exile: Joseph Mazzini in England, 1837-1868. (Studies in Modern European History). IX, 153p. (C). 1989. text 37.50 (0-8204-1051-9) P Lang Pubng.

— Treatise on the Construction of the Statutes, 13 Eliz. c.5 & 27 Eliz, c.4: Relating to Voluntary & Fraudulent Conveyances & on the Nature & Force of Different Considerations to Support Deeds & Other Legal Instruments, in the Courts of Law & Equity. 2nd ed. xv, 667p. 1979. reprint ed. 48.00 (0-8377-1028-6, Rothman) W S Hein.

Roberts, William A. Principles of Animal Cognition. LC 97-5653. 480p. 1997. 59.38 (0-07-053138-2) McGraw.

Roberts, William C. Cardiology 1994. 504p. 1994. text 115.00 (0-7506-9591-9) Buttrwrth-Heinemann.

***Roberts, William C.** Facts & Ideas from Anywhere. 192p. 2000. 39.00 (0-87993-463-8) Futura Pub.

Roberts, William C., jt. auth. see Sammartino, Peter.

Roberts, William C., jt. compiled by see Coppa, Frank J.

Roberts, William C., ed. see American Federation of Labor Staff.

Roberts, William C., ed. see Willerson, James T.

Roberts, William H. About Language: A Reader for Writers, 3 vols. (C). Date not set. pap., teacher ed., suppl. ed. 30.36 (0-395-71730-2) HM.

— About Language: A Reader for Writers. 2nd ed. 1989. teacher ed. write for info. (0-318-63334-5) HM.

***Roberts, William H.** Uss New Ironsides in the Civil War William H. Roberts. LC 98-45721. 1999. 49.95 (1-55750-695-7) Naval Inst Pr.

Roberts, William H. & Turgeon, Gregoire. About Language: A Reader for Writers, 4 vols. 4th ed. (C). 1995. text, teacher ed. 11.96 (0-395-68637-7); pap. text 30.36 (0-395-68636-9) HM.

Roberts, William H., jt. auth. see Rome, Edwin P.

Roberts, William L. Cold Rolling of Steel. (Manufacturing Engineering & Materials Processing Ser.: Vol. 2). (Illus.). 808p. 1978. text 245.00 (0-8247-6780-2) Dekker.

Roberts, William L. Flat Processing of Steel. (Manufacturing Engineering & Materials Processing Ser.: Vol. 24). (Illus.). 928p. 1987. text 275.00 (0-8247-7780-8) Dekker.

— Hot Rolling of Steel. (Manufacturing Engineering & Materials Processing Ser.: Vol. 10). (Illus.). 1024p. 1983. text 250.00 (0-8247-1345-1) Dekker.

Roberts, William O., Jr. Crossing the Soul's River: A Rite of Passage for Men. LC 98-10499. 154p. (Orig.). 1998. pap. 15.95 (0-8298-1259-8) Pilgrim OH.

***Roberts, William Owen.** Pestilence. Roberts, Elisabeth, tr. 214p. 2000. pap. 17.95 (1-85411-198-1, Pub. by Seren Bks) Dufour.

Roberts, William P., ed. Divorce & Remarriage: Religious & Psychological Perspectives. LC 89-63115. 168p. (Orig.). (C). 1990. pap. 13.95 (1-55612-231-4) Sheed & Ward WI.

Roberts, William P., jt. ed. see Lawler, Michael G.

Roberts, William R., tr. Dionysius of Halicarnassus, on Literary Composition. xiii, 358p. 1910. write for info. (0-318-70914-7) G Olms Pubs.

Roberts, William R., jt. ed. see Hagan, Kenneth J.

Roberts, William R., tr. & comment see Dionysius of Halicarnassus.

Roberts, William T., Jr. Sketches from Hickory Hill. LC 96-36999. (Illus.). 168p. 1997. 16.95 (1-883911-13-3) Brandylane.

Roberts, Willo D. Caught! LC 93-14422. 160p. (J). (gr. 3-7). 1994. 16.00 (0-689-31903-7) Atheneum Yung Read.

— Don't Hurt Laurie! LC 76-46569. (Illus.). 176p. (J). (gr. 4-6). 1977. 16.00 (0-689-30571-0) Atheneum Yung Read.

— Don't Hurt Laurie! 2nd ed. LC 87-21742. (Illus.). 176p. (J). (gr. 4-7). 1988. reprint ed. mass mkt. 3.95 (0-689-71206-5) Aladdin.

— Expendable. 20.95 (0-89190-855-2) Amereon Ltd.

— The Girl with the Silver Eyes. LC 80-12391. 208p. (J). (gr. 4-7). 1991. pap. 4.50 (0-590-44248-1) Scholastic Inc.

— The Girl with the Silver Eyes. (J). 1980. 9.60 (0-606-03099-9, Pub. by Turtleback) Demco.

— Hostage. LC PZ7.R54465HO 2000. 144p. (J). (gr. 4-6). 2000. 16.00 (0-689-81669-3) Atheneum Yung Read.

— Inherit the Darkness. reprint ed. lib. bdg. 21.95 (0-89190-865-X, Rivercity Pr) Amereon Ltd.

— Jo & the Bandit. LC 91-4100. 192p. (J). (gr. 4-7). 1992. 16.00 (0-689-31745-X) Atheneum Yung Read.

— Megan's Island. LC 89-18457. 192p. (J). (gr. 4-7). 1990. mass mkt. 4.50 (0-689-71387-8) Aladdin.

— Megan's Island. LC 87-17505. 192p. (J). (gr. 3-7). 1988. lib. bdg. 14.95 (0-689-31397-7) Atheneum Yung Read.

— Nightmare. LC 89-7038. 192p. (J). (gr. 5-9). 1989. 16.00 (0-689-31551-1) Atheneum Yung Read.

— Pawns. LC 97-36505. 154p. (J). (gr. 6-8). 1998. 16.00 (0-689-81668-5) S&S Trade.

— Pet-Sitting Peril. (J). 1983. 10.09 (0-606-00381-9, Pub. by Turtleback) Demco.

— The Pet-Sitting Peril. 2nd ed. LC 89-77696. 192p. (J). (gr. 4-6). 1990. reprint ed. mass mkt. 4.99 (0-689-71427-0) Aladdin.

— Scared Stiff. LC 90-37732. 192p. (J). (gr. 3-7). 1991. 16.00 (0-689-31692-5) Atheneum Yung Read.

— Secrets at Hidden Valley. (J). (gr. 4-8). 1997. 16.00 (0-614-29094-5) Atheneum Yung Read.

— Secrets at Hidden Valley. LC 96-17576. 160p. (J). (gr. 4-8). 1997. 16.00 (0-689-81166-7) S&S Childrens.

— Sugar Isn't Everything: A Support Book, in Fiction Form, for the Young Diabetic. LC 88-3358. 192p. (J). (gr. 3-7). 1988. mass mkt. 4.95 (0-689-71225-1) Aladdin.

An Asterisk (*) at the beginning of an entry indicates that the title is appearing for the first time.

R

— Sugar Isn't Everything: A Support Book, in Fiction Form, for the Young Diabetic. LC 86-17275. 208p. (J). (gr. 4 up). 1987. 16.00 (*0-689-31316-0*) Atheneum Yung Read.
— To Grandmother's House We Go. LC 94-466. 192p. (J). 1994. pap. write for info. (*0-689-71838-1*) Aladdin.
— To Share a Dream. (Orig.). 1986. pap. 4.50 (*0-373-97028-5*) Harlequin Bks.
— To Share a Dream. (Historical Ser.). (Orig.). 1994. per. 3.99 (*0-373-28831-X*, 1-28831-5) Harlequin Bks.
— Twisted Summer. LC 95-585. 160p. (J). (gr. 3-7). 1996. 16.00 (*0-689-80459-8*) Atheneum Yung Read.
— Twisted Summer. 1998. 9.09 (*0-606-13089-6*, Pub. by Turtleback) Demco.
— The View from the Cherry Tree. rev. ed. 192p. 1998. 16.00 (*0-689-82051-8*) S&S Bks Yung.
— The View from the Cherry Tree. 2nd ed. LC 93-31170. 192p. (J). (gr. 5 up). 1994. reprint ed. mass mkt. 3.95 (*0-689-71784-9*) Aladdin.
— What Are We Going to Do about David? LC 92-4726. 176p. (J). (gr. 3-7). 1993. 16.00 (*0-689-31793-X*) Atheneum Yung Read.
— What Could Go Wrong? LC 88-27484. 176p. (J). (gr. 3-7). 1989. 15.00 (*0-689-31438-8*) Atheneum Yung Read.
Roberts, Willo D. What Could Go Wrong? (J). 1993. 9.05 (*0-606-05692-0*, Pub. by Turtleback) Demco.
Roberts, Willo D. What Could Go Wrong? LC 92-26177. 176p. (J). (gr. 3-6). 1993. reprint ed. mass mkt. 3.95 (*0-689-71690-7*) Aladdin.
Roberts, Willo Davis. The Absolutely True Story . . . How I Visited Yellowstone Park with the Terrible Rupes. LC 94-14436. 160p. (J). (gr. 3-7). 1997. per. 3.99 (*0-689-81464-X*) Atheneum Yung Read.
— The Absolutely True Story . . . How I Visited Yellowstone Park with the Terrible Rupes. LC 94-14436. 160p. (J). (gr. 3-7). 1994. 15.00 (*0-689-31939-8*, Mac Bks Young Read) S&S Childrens.
— The Absolutely True Story...How I Visited Yellowstone Park with the Terrible Rupes. (J). 1997. 9.09 (*0-606-10994-3*, Pub. by Turtleback) Demco.
— Baby-Sitting is a Dangerous Job. 192p. (J). (gr. 4-6). 1996. per. 3.95 (*0-689-80657-4*) Aladdin.
— Baby-Sitting is a Dangerous Job. 144p. (J). 1987. mass mkt. 4.50 (*0-449-70177-8*, Juniper) Fawcett.
Roberts, Willo Davis. Baby-Sitting is a Dangerous Job. (J). 1987. 9.60 (*0-606-01206-0*, Pub. by Turtleback) Demco.
Roberts, Willo Davis. Baby-Sitting is a Dangerous Job. 1996. 9.05 (*0-606-09044-4*, Pub. by Turtleback) Demco.
***Roberts, Willo Davis.** Buddy is a Stupid Name for a Girl. LC 99-87471. (J). 2001. write for info. (*0-689-81670-7*) Atheneum Yung Read.
Roberts, Willo Davis. Don't Hurt Laurie! 1988. 9.05 (*0-606-12262-1*, Pub. by Turtleback) Demco.
— The Kidnappers. LC 96-53677. 144p. (J). (gr. 4-6). 1998. 15.00 (*0-689-81394-5*) Atheneum Yung Read.
— The Kidnappers: A Mystery. 128p. (J). (gr. 4-6). 1999. per. 3.99 (*0-689-81393-7*) Aladdin.
— Megan's Island. 1990. 9.60 (*0-606-12600-7*, Pub. by Turtleback) Demco.
***Roberts, Willo Davis.** Megans Island. (2000 Kids Picks Ser.). 192p. (J). (gr. 4-7). 2000. mass mkt. 2.99 (*0-689-83867-0*) Aladdin.
Roberts, Willo Davis. Nightmare. 1992. 9.60 (*0-606-00881-0*, Pub. by Turtleback) Demco.
— Pawns. (Illus.). 160p. (YA). (gr. 4-6). 2000. per. 4.99 (*0-689-83320-2*) Aladdin.
— Sugar Isn't Everything: A Support Book, in Fiction Form for the Young Diabetic. (J). 1987. 10.05 (*0-606-03661-X*, Pub. by Turtleback) Demco.
— Twisted Summer. 160p. (YA). (gr. 7 up). 1998. per. 3.99 (*0-689-80600-0*) Aladdin.
— View from the Cherry Tree. 3rd ed. LC 93-31170. (J). 1993. 9.05 (*0-606-03500-1*, Pub. by Turtleback) Demco.
Roberts, Willo Davis & Davis. Secrets at Hidden Valley. LC 96-17576. 160p. (J). (gr. 5-9). 1998. per. 4.50 (*0-689-81167-5*) S&S Childrens.
Roberts, Willow. Stokes Carson: Twentieth-Century Trading on the Navajo Reservation. LC 86-19207. (Illus.). 246p. 1987. reprint ed. pap. 76.30 (*0-608-04143-2*, 206487600011) Bks Demand.
Roberts, Willow D. In Search of the Old Ones. 272p. 1997. per. 12.00 (*0-684-83212-7*, Touchstone) S&S Trade Pap.
***Roberts Winsor, Ann.** A King Is Bound in the Tresses: Allusions to the Song of Songs in the Fourth Gospel. LC 97-31543. (Studies in Biblical Literature: Vol. 6). 111p. (C). 1999. text 41.00 (*0-8204-3931-2*) P Lang Pubng.
Roberts, Yvonne. Animal Heroes: True Stories from Around the World. 128p. 1991. 19.95 (*1-85089-510-4*, Pub. by ISIS Lrg Prnt) Transaction Pubs.
***Roberts, Yvonne.** Jean-Antoine de Baif & the Valois Court. 231p. 2000. pap. 37.95 (*0-8204-5056-1*) P Lang Pubng.
Robertshaw, Andrew. Soldier's Life. LC 96-44309. (J). (gr. 5-9). 1997. 16.99 (*0-525-67550-7*) NAL.
— Soldier's Life: A Visual History of Soldiers Through the Ages. (Picture Puffin Ser.). (Illus.). (J). (gr. 5-9). 1998. pap. 7.99 (*0-14-130076-0*, PuffinBks) Peng Put Young Read.
Robertshaw, Gregory A. Understanding Antennas for Radar, Communication & Avionics. (Illus.). 336p. 1987. text 79.95 (*0-442-27772-5*, VNR) Wiley.
Robertshaw, Joseph E. & Mecca, Stephen J. Problem Solving: A System Approach. 1991. 3.00 (*0-89433-119-1*) Petrocelli.
Robertshaw, Joseph E., jt. auth. see Mecca, Stephen J.
Robertshaw, P. Early Pastoralists of South-Western Kenya. (Illus.). 318p. 1990. 46.00 (*1-872566-01-4*, Pub. by Brit Inst Estrn Africa) David Brown.
Robertshaw, P., jt. ed. see Mack, John.
Robertshaw, Paul. The Jury & Judge. (Illus.). 232p. 1995. text 87.95 (*1-85521-430-X*, Pub. by Dartmth Pub) Ashgate Pub Co.
— Rethinking Legal Need: The Case of Criminal Justice. 259p. 1991. text 78.95 (*1-85521-207-2*, Pub. by Dartmth Pub) Ashgate Pub Co.
— Summary Justice: Judges Address Juries. LC 97-27668. 160p. 1998. 75.00 (*0-304-33701-3*) Continuum.
Robertshaw, Peter, ed. A History of African Archaeology. LC 89-26733. (Illus.). 378p. (Orig.). (C). 1990. pap. 30.00 (*0-435-08041-5*) Heinemann.
Robertshaw, Stuart. Dear Dr. Humor: A Collection of Humorous Stories for All Occasions. 155p. (Orig.). 1995. pap. 10.00 (*0-9645793-0-8*) NAHI.
Robertson. Auditing. 9th ed. 208p. 1998. pap., student ed. 35.00 (*0-07-303779-6*) McGraw.
— Basic College Math: Models, Concepts & Skills. (Mathematics Ser.). 2002. pap. 57.95 (*0-534-34984-6*) Brooks-Cole.
— Book of Humorous Quotations. (Reference Library). 256p. 1998. pap. 6.95 (*1-85326-759-7*, 7597WW, Pub. by Wrdsworth Edits) NTC Contemp Pub Co.
— Bridge to College Success. 445p. (J). 1991. 26.95 (*0-8384-2907-6*) Heinle & Heinle.
— Career Planning. LC 99-38200. (Illus.). 318p. 1999. pap. text 33.33 (*0-13-081227-7*) P-H.
— Diccionario Ingles-Espanol, Espanol-Ingles. (ENG & SPA.). 894p. 12.25 (*84-303-0107-0*, S-50396); pap. 49.95 (*84-303-0108-9*, S-50397) Fr & Eur.
— Dictionary of Quotations. (Reference Library). 1997. pap. 6.95 (*1-85326-379-6*, 3796WW, Pub. by Wrdsworth Edits) NTC Contemp Pub Co.
— Dictionary of Superstitions. (Classics Library). 352p. 1998. pap. 6.95 (*1-85326-756-2*, 7562WW, Pub. by Wrdsworth Edits) NTC Contemp Pub Co.
— Hal Leonard Banjo Method, Bk. 2. 64p. 1980. pap. 6.95 (*0-7935-2813-5*, 00699502) H Leonard.
— Human Rights in the World. 4th ed. LC 97-145376. 320p. 1997. text 24.95 (*0-7190-4923-7*) Manchester Univ Pr.
— Hypertension for the Clinician. (C). 1995. text 70.00 (*0-7020-1812-0*) Harcourt.
— Intermediate Algebra: Models, Concepts & Skills. (Mathematics Ser.). 2002. pap. 60.95 (*0-534-34985-4*) Brooks-Cole.
— International Law & Arms Control. 1999. text. write for info. (*0-312-05595-1*) St Martin.
— Introductory Algebra. Date not set. pap. 18.95 (*0-534-35135-2*) Brooks-Cole.
— Introductory Algebra: Models & Concepts. (Mathematics Ser.). 2000. pap. 57.95 (*0-534-34983-8*) Brooks-Cole.
***Robertson, Jr.** Lady of Kynachan. 2000. pap. 9.95 (*0-552-14298-0*, Pub. by Transworld Publishers Ltd) Trafalgar.
Robertson. Lotus 1-2-3 (2.4 Dos) Made Simple. 160p. Date not set. pap. text 19.95 (*0-7506-2066-8*) Buttrwrth-Heinemann.
— New Economics of Sustainable Development. LC 99-15905. (Forward Studies Ser.). 184p. 1999. text 39.95 (*0-312-22697-7*) St Martin.
***Robertson.** Painting As a Language. (C). 1999. pap. text 54.50 (*0-15-505600-X*, Pub. by Harcourt Coll Pubs) Harcourt.
Robertson. Quality Assurance for Nurses. 1992. pap. text. write for info. (*0-582-20904-8*, Pub. by Addison-Wesley) Longman.
— Quality Assurance for Nurses. 1994. pap. text. write for info. (*0-582-22977-4*, Pub. by Addison-Wesley) Longman.
— Safety, Nutrition & Health. LC 97-41064. (Early Childhood Education Ser.). 528p. (C). 1998. mass mkt. 58.95 (*0-8273-7329-5*) Delmar.
— Safety, Nutrition & Health. (Early Childhood Education Ser.). 64p. 1998. teacher ed. 12.00 (*0-8273-7330-9*) Delmar.
— Society. 2nd ed. 2000. student ed. 37.60 (*1-57259-737-2*) Worth.
Robertson, Jr. Society Reader. pap. text 23.95 (*1-57259-741-0*) Worth.
Robertson. Sociology. 4th ed. 2001. pap. text. write for info. (*1-57259-161-7*) W H Freeman.
— Sopena Robertson English-Spanish, Spanish-English Dictionary: Robertson Diccionario Ingles-Espanol-Ingles. (ENG & SPA.). 900p. 1984. 35.00 (*0-8288-2327-8*, S50396) Fr & Eur.
— Study of Industrial Fluctuations: London School of Economics. (LSE Scarce Tracts in Economics Ser.). 350p. (C). 1997. 90.00 (*0-415-14393-4*) Routledge.
— Teaching the Cat to Water-Ski. (Clipper Fiction Ser.). 1991. pap. text. write for info. (*0-582-87516-1*, Pub. by Addison-Wesley) Longman.
— Three Stuffed Owls, 2 vols. large type ed. (J). (gr. 6-7). reprint ed. 10.00 (*0-318-65701-5*) NAVH.
— Topics in Computational Group Theory. (C). (gr. 13). 1997. text. write for info. (*0-412-31000-7*) Chapman & Hall.
— Zondervan Bible Storybook. 1988. pap. 12.99 (*0-310-44431-4*, 11394P) Zondervan.
Robertson, Jr. & Cooper. Psychology Personnel Selection. 1995. pap. write for info. (*1-86152-612-1*, Pub. by ITBP) Thomson Learn.
Robertson & Mishra. Forced to Plough-Bonded Labour in Napal's Agricultural Economy. 1997. pap. 21.00 (*0-7855-7398-4*, Pub. by Ratna Pustak Bhandar) St Mut.
***Robertson, Jr. & Storla.** Preliminary Edition Introduction to Algebra: Models, Concepts & Skills. 1999. pap. 37.95 (*0-534-36894-8*) Thomson Learn.
Robertson, jt. see Klein.
Robertson, jt. auth. see Starr.
Robertson, Cheryl. Frank Lloyd Wright & George Mann Niedecken: Prairie School Collaborators. LC 99-198129. (Illus.). 116p. (C). 1999. pap. 18.95 (*1-889541-01-X*) Mus Our Natl Hertge.
Robertson, A. Offshore Disposal - Results of the 106-Mile Dumpsite Study, Vol. 3. 604p. 1997. pap. text 84.00 (*90-5699-059-4*) Gordon & Breach.
— Offshore Disposal - Results of the 106-Mile Dumpsite Study: Biological Fates & Effects, Vol. 3. 228p. 1996. pap. text 36.00 (*90-5699-034-9*) Gordon & Breach.
— Selection Experiments in Laboratory & Domestic Animals. 245p. (Orig.). 1980. pap. text 55.00 (*0-85198-461-4*) OUP.
***Robertson, A.** Simple Program Design. 3rd ed. (Programming Language Ser.). (C). 1999. text 30.95 (*0-619-01590-X*) Course Tech.
Robertson, A., ed. Offshore Disposal - Results of the 106-Mile Dumpsite Study: Transport Processes, Vol. 2. 180p. 1997. pap. text 26.00 (*2-919875-17-5*) Gordon & Breach.
— Offshore Disposal - Results of the 106-Mile Dumpsite Study: Water Column & Sediment Fates, Vol. 2. 196p. 1997. pap. text 26.00 (*90-5699-033-0*) Gordon & Breach.
Robertson, A. F. Beyond the Family: The Social Organization of Human Reproduction. LC 91-9381. 250p. 1991. 55.00 (*0-520-07518-8*, Pub. by U CA Pr); pap. 16.95 (*0-520-07721-0*, Pub. by U CA Pr) Cal Prin Full Svc.
— The Big Catch: A Practical Introduction to Development. 176p. (C). 1995. pap. 25.00 (*0-8133-2522-6*, Pub. by Westview) HarpC.
Robertson, A. F., ed. Fire Standards & Safety - STP 614. 343p. 1986. 27.75 (*0-8031-0352-2*, STP614) ASTM.
Robertson, A. F., jt. ed. see Friedland, Roger.
Robertson, A. H. Human Rights in the World: An Introduction to the Study of the International Protection of Humans. 1996. text 79.95 (*0-7190-4223-2*, Pub. by Manchester Univ Pr) St Martin.
Robertson, A. H., ed. European Yearbook, Vol. 24. 1978. lib. bdg. 178.50 (*90-247-2043-5*) Kluwer Academic.
— European Yearbook - Annuaire Europeen (1979). Vol. 27. 710p. 1981. lib. bdg. 255.00 (*90-247-2458-9*) Kluwer Academic.
— European Yearbook-Annuaire Europeen, Vol. XXV. 1979. lib. bdg. 212.50 (*90-247-2161-X*) Kluwer Academic.
— European Yearbook-Annuaire Europeen, Vol. XXVI. (ENG & FRE.). 696p. 1980. lib. bdg. 234.00 (*90-247-2298-5*) Kluwer Academic.
Robertson, A. H., et al, eds. The Geology & Tectonics of the Oman Region. (Geological Society Special Publications: No. 49). (Illus.). 864p. (C). 1990. 165.00 (*0-903317-46-X*, 200, Pub. by Geol Soc Pub Hse) AAPG.
Robertson, A. H. & Merrills, J. G. Human Rights in Europe: A Study of the European Convention on Human Rights. 3rd ed. 448p. 1995. text 29.95 (*0-7190-4613-0*) Manchester Univ Pr.
Robertson, A. Haeworth. The Big Lie: What Every Baby Boomer Should Know about Social Security & Medicare. LC 96-93007. (Illus.). xviii, 142p. 1997. 24.95 (*0-9632345-6-0*) Retire Policy.
— Social Security: What Every Taxpayer Should Know. LC 92-80166. (Illus.). 352p. 1992. 40.00 (*0-9632345-4-4*) Retire Policy.
— Social Security: What Every Taxpayer Should Know. 352p. 1992. pap. 14.95 (*0-9632345-5-2*) Retire Policy.
Robertson, A. J., ed. The Laws of the Kings of England from Edmund to Henry I. LC 80-2210. reprint ed. 57.50 (*0-404-18784-6*) AMS Pr.
Robertson, A. T. Armonia Anotada y Act los Evangelios. rev. ed.Tr. of A Revised Harmony of the Gospels. (SPA.). pap. write for info. (*0-311-04303-8*) Casa Bautista.
— Una Armonia De los Cuatro Evangelios. Patterson, W. F., tr. from ENG.Tr. of Harmony of the Four Gospels. (SPA.). 259p. 1963. reprint ed. pap. 12.99 (*0-311-04302-X*) Casa Bautista.
***Robertson, A. T.** The Glory of the Ministry: Paul's Exultation in Preaching. 244p. 1998. pap. 18.00 (*1-57910-177-1*) Wipf & Stock.
— A Harmony of the Gospels. 352p. 1932. 22.00 (*0-06-066890-3*, Pub. by Harper SF) HarpC.
Robertson, A. T. Life & Letters of John A. Broadus. 1996. 22.99 (*0-87377-916-9*) GAM Pubns.
***Robertson, A. T.** The Pharisees & Jesus: The Stone Lectures for 1915-1916. 202p. 1999. pap. 18.00 (*1-57910-289-1*) Wipf & Stock.
***Robertson, A. T. & Swanson, James A.** Word Pictures in the New Testament. LC 00-25658. (Illus.). 2000. 19.99 (*0-8054-9055-8*) Broadman.
Robertson, Adam, et al. Forced to Plough: Bonded Labour in Nepal's Agricultural Economy : a Report for Informal Sector Service Centre & Anti-Slavery International. LC 98-125055. (Illus.). 1997. write for info. (*0-900918-37-3*) Anti-Slavery Intl.
Robertson, Adele C. The Orchard: A Memoir. 256p. 1997. pap. 11.95 (*0-553-37859-7*) Bantam.
— The Orchard: A Memoir. LC 95-17187. 234p. 1995. 20.00 (*0-8050-4092-7*) H Holt & Co.
Robertson, Agnes. The Chestnut Tree. 90p. 1987. pap. 6.00 (*0-940584-13-1*) Gull Bks.
— The Me Inside of Me. 72p. 1987. pap. 6.00 (*0-940584-14-X*) Gull Bks.
Robertson, Agnes J. Anglo-Saxon Charters. 2nd ed. LC 85-81803. (Cambridge Studies in English Legal History). 580p. 1986. reprint ed. 135.00 (*0-912004-51-7*) Gaunt.
***Robertson, Aidan & Green, Nicholas, eds.** The Europeanisation of U. K. Competition Law. 144p. 1999. 45.00 (*1-84113-036-2*, Pub. by Hart Pub) Intl Spec Bk.
Robertson, Alec. Dvorak: Music Book Index. 234p. 1993. reprint ed. lib. bdg. 79.00 (*0-7812-9596-3*) Rprt Serv.
— Requiem: Music of Mourning & Consolation. LC 75-32462. 300p. 1976. reprint ed. lib. bdg. 35.00 (*0-8371-8552-1*, RORE, Greenwood Pr) Greenwood.
Robertson, Alexander. Atkinson Grimshaw. (Illus.). 128p. 1996. reprint ed. pap. 24.95 (*0-7148-3575-7*, Pub. by Phaidon Press) Phaidon Pr.
***Robertson, Alice W. & Smith, Barbara, eds.** Teaching in the 21st Century: Adapting Writing Pedagogies to the College Curriculum. LC 99-32108. (Cultural Studies in the Classroom: Vol. 1). 336p. 1999. 65.00 (*0-8153-3152-5*, SS1189) Garland.
Robertson, Alistair, jt. ed. see Alongi, Daniel.
Robertson, Alistar & Watts, Robyn, eds. Preserving Rural Australia: Issues & Solutions. 168p. (Orig.). pap. 39.95 (*0-643-06388-9*, Pub. by CSIRO) Accents Pubns.
Robertson, Alistar, jt. ed. see Pratley, Jim.
Robertson, Allen & Hutera, Donald, eds. The Dance Handbook. (Monograph Ser.). 278p. 1990. 18.95 (*0-8161-1829-9*, Hall Reference) Macmillan.
Robertson, Allen B. John Wesley's Nova Scotia Businessmen: Halifax Methodist Merchants. LC 94-15262. (American University Studies IX: Vol. 163). 192p. 2000. 47.95 (*0-8204-2484-6*) P Lang Pubng.
Robertson, Andrew C. The Military Investor's Handbook. LC 85-70435. 179p. 1985. pap. 9.95 (*0-935871-00-4*) Global Man.
Robertson, Andrew W. The Language of Democracy: Political Rhetoric in the United States & Britain, 1790-1900. (Illus.). 240p. 1995. text 37.50 (*0-8014-2899-8*) Cornell U Pr.
Robertson, Andy & McPherson, John. The Church You've Always Longed For: Church Resource Manual. (Nineteen Ninety-Seven 50-Day Spiritual Adventure Ser.). 312p. 1994. ring bd. 69.00 (*1-57849-007-3*) Chapel of Air.
Robertson, Andy & McPherson, John. Untapped Miracles for Tapped-Out Christians: Church Resource Manual. (Nineteen Ninety-Eight Fifty-Day Spiritual Adventure Ser.). 327p. 1997. 69.00 (*1-57849-070-7*) Mainstay Church.
— Untapped Miracles for Tapped-Out Christians: Church Resource Manual (with Samples) (Nineteen Ninety-Eight Fifty-Day Spiritual Adventure Ser.). 327p. 1997. 69.00 (*1-57849-048-0*) Mainstay Church.
Robertson, Ann, ed. & illus. see Burns, Eleanor B.
Robertson, Anne S. Roman Imperial Coins in the Hunter Coin Cabinet Vol. IV: Valerian I to Allectus, Vol. 4. (Glasgow University Publications). (Illus.). 1978. 98.00 (*0-19-713307-X*) OUP.
— Roman Imperial Coins in the Hunter Coin Cabinet, University of Glasgow, Vol. V: Diocletian (Reform) to Zeno, Vol. 5. (Illus.). 1982. 155.00 (*0-19-713310-X*) OUP.
— Roman Imperial Coins in the Hunter Coin Cabinet, University of Glasgow, Vol. 3: Pertinax to Aemilian, Vol. 3. (Illus.). 1977. 98.00 (*0-19-713306-1*) OUP.
Robertson, Anne W. The Service Books of the Royal Abbey of Saint-Denis: Images of Ritual & Music in the Middle Ages. (Oxford Monographs on Music). (Illus.). 584p. 1991. text 155.00 (*0-19-315254-1*) OUP.
Robertson, Archibald. Archibald Robertson, Lieutenant-General Royal Engineers. LC 70-140879. (Eyewitness Accounts of the American Revolution Ser.). 1971. reprint ed. 20.95 (*0-405-01224-1*) Ayer.
Robertson, Archibald T. Grammar of the Greek New Testament in the Light of Historical Research. (C). 1947. 59.99 (*0-8054-1308-1*, 4213-08) Broadman.
— Morals in World History. LC 74-6354. (World History Ser.: No. 48). (C). 1974. lib. bdg. 75.00 (*0-8383-1918-1*) M S G Haskell Hse.
***Robertson, Archibald T.** The Teaching of Jesus Concerning God the Father. 210p. 1998. pap. 20.00 (*1-57910-171-2*) Wipf & Stock.
Robertson, Archibald T. That Old-Time Religion. LC 78-24159. 282p. 1979. reprint ed. lib. bdg. 65.00 (*0-313-20823-9*, ROOT, Greenwood Pr) Greenwood.
Robertson, Archibald T., jt. auth. see Plummer, Alfred.
Robertson, Arlene. The Moon in Your Life. LC 84-71623. 245p. 1986. 19.95 (*0-86690-283-X*, R2604-014) Am Fed Astrologers.
Robertson, Arlene, ed. see Linares, Enrique.
Robertson, Arlene, ed. see Sandbach, John.
Robertson, Arlene, ed. see Starck, Marcia.
Robertson, Arthur. Listen for Success: A Guide to Effective Listening. LC 93-14441. 216p. 1993. 19.95 (*1-55623-830-4*, Irwn Prfsnl) McGraw-Hill Prof.
— Mateo. (Comentario Biblico Portavoz Ser.). (SPA.). 168p. 1994. pap. 6.99 (*0-8254-1620-5*, Edit Portavoz) Kregel.
Robertson, Arthur H. Characterization in the Conflict of Laws. LC 40-10604. (Harvard Studies in the Conflict of Laws: Vol. 4). xxix, 301p. 1978. reprint ed. lib. bdg. 45.00 (*0-89941-129-0*, 301350) W S Hein.
Robertson, Arthur K. & Proctor, William. Work a 4-Hour Day. 160p. 1996. mass mkt. 4.99 (*0-380-72627-0*, Avon Bks) Morrow Avon.
Robertson, Audrey, jt. auth. see Redleaf, Rhoda.
Robertson, B., et al, eds. Experimental & Clinical Aspects of Surfactant Replacement. (Journal: Biology of the Neonate: Vol. 61, Suppl. 1, 1992). (Illus.). vi, 66p. 1992. pap. 22.75 (*3-8055-5644-6*) S Karger.
Robertson, Barbara. Sir Wilfrid Laurier: The Great Conciliator. (Illus.). 164p. 1991. pap. 12.95 (*0-919627-95-1*, Pub. by Quarry Pr) LPC InBook.
Robertson, Barbara, jt. auth. see Roberts, Alasdair.
Robertson, Barbara, jt. auth. see Whyte, Hamish.
Robertson, Barbara A. A Yankee Cook in a Confederate Kitchen Vol. 1: With the Best of "Sportsman's Skillet" Bozka, Larry, ed. (Illus.). (Orig.). 1988. pap. write for info. (*0-318-64026-0*) TX Fish & Game.
Robertson, Barbara A., ed. see Becker, A. C., Jr.
Robertson, Ben. Red Hills & Cotton: An Upcountry Memory. (Southern Classics Ser.). 341p. 1973. reprint ed. pap. 12.95 (*0-87249-306-7*) U of SC Pr.
Robertson, Ben, jt. auth. see Von Nida, Norman.

R

Robertson, Bengt. Surfactant Therapy for Lung Disease. Taeusch, H. William, ed. (Lung Biology in Health & Disease Ser.: Vol. 84). (Illus.). 736p. 1995. text 215.00 (*0-8247-9502-4*) Dekker.

Robertson, Bengt D. Surfactant in Clinical Practice: Proceedings of an International Symposium, Parma, June 4-5, 1990. Parmigiani, Stefano et al, eds. LC 93-5629. 240p. 1993. text 64.00 (*3-7186-5279-X*) Gordon & Breach.

Robertson, Bengt D., et al, eds. Pulmonary Surfactant: From Molecular Biology to Clinical Practice. LC 92-48791. 754p. 1992. 337.25 (*0-444-89475-6*) Elsevier.

Robertson, Benjamin W. Just As He Promised. LC 98-65877. (Illus.). 128p. 1998. 16.95 (*1-57736-096-6*) Providence Hse.

Robertson, Bernard & Vignaux, G. A. Interpreting Evidence: Evaluating Forensic Science in the Courtroom. LC 95-221605. 262p. 1995. 67.50 (*0-471-96026-8*) Wiley.

Robertson, Beth, jt. auth. see Howren, Suzanne.

Robertson, Betty & Shaffer, Barbara. How to Handle Hurt. 1998. 3.95 (*0-9642707-2-2*) C C M Pub.

Robertson, Betty B. Bible Teaching Ideas That Work: For Grades 4, 5 & 6. (Illus.). 56p. 1989. pap. 8.99 (*0-8341-1313-9*) Beacon Hill.

— TLC for Aging Parents: A Practical Guide. 104p. (Orig.). 1992. pap. 9.99 (*0-8341-1456-9*, 85018) Beacon Hill.

Robertson, Beverly. Nursing Assistants: A Basic Study Guide. 5th rev. ed. (Illus.). 184p. 1998. pap. text 13.95 (*1-880246-09-0*) First Class Bks.

Robertson, Bill. How to Play Better Golf. (Illus.). 160p. 1992. pap. 16.95 (*0-7063-6995-5*, Pub. by WrLock) Sterling.

Robertson, Bob. The Inscrutable Dr. Hare: A Legend of Grass Valley. (Illus.). vi, 200p. (Orig.). 1997. 19.95 (*0-9656321-0-5*); pap. 12.95 (*0-9656321-1-3*) H & H Pubns AZ.

Robertson, Boyd & Taylor, Iain. Teach Yourself Gaelic. (GAE., Illus.). 224p. 1995. pap. 14.95 (*0-8442-3776-0*, Teach Yrslf) NTC Contemp Pub Co.

— Teach Yourself Gaelic Complete Course. (GAE., Illus.). 224p. 1994. pap. 27.95 incl. audio (*0-8442-3861-9*, Teach Yrslf) NTC Contemp Pub Co.

Robertson, Bozena-Eva. Alcohol Disabilities Primer: A Guide to Physical & Psychological Disabilities Caused by Alcohol Use. LC 93-22609. 208p. 1993. lib. bdg. 69.95 (*0-8493-8966-6*, RC565, CRC Reprint) Franklin.

***Robertson, Brewster Milton.** Rainy Days & Sundays. LC 00-26801. 400p. 2000. write for info. (*1-891799-12-6*, 640-006, Pub. by Harbor Hse) BookWorld.

Robertson, Brian. Brian Robertson's Favorite Texas Tales. (Illus.). 112p. 1997. pap. 7.95 (*1-57168-079-9*, Eakin Pr) Sunbelt Media.

— Handbook of Child Psychiatry for Primary Care. LC 98-145634. (Illus.). 376p. 1997. pap. 34.50 (*0-19-571372-9*) OUP.

— Little Blues Book. LC 96-19571. (Illus.). 160p. 1999. pap. 9.95 (*1-56512-137-6*) Algonquin Bks.

***Robertson, Brian C.** There's No Place Like Work: How Business, Government, & Our Obsession with Work Have Driven Parents from Home. LC 99-46792. xvi, 208p. 2000. 24.95 (*1-890626-18-X*) Spence Pub.

Robertson, Bridget M. Angels in Africa: A Memoir of Colonial Nursing. 200p. 1993. text 39.50 (*1-85043-527-8*, Pub. by I B T) St Martin.

Robertson, Bruce. Bombing Colours: British Bomber Camouflage & Markings, 1914-1937. LC 73-165369. 176p. 1972. write for info. (*0-85059-093-0*, Pub. by P Stephens) Haynes Manuals.

— The Ebsworth Collection: Twentieth-Century Art in America. (Illus.). 312p. 2000. 49.50 (*0-8109-6699-9*, Pub. by Abrams) Time Warner.

Robertson, Bruce. How to Draw Charts & Diagrams. (Illus.). 192p. 1999. reprint ed. pap. text 25.00 (*0-7881-6353-1*) DIANE Pub.

***Robertson, Bruce.** Learn to Draw Countryside. (Learn to Draw Ser.). (Illus.). 64p. 1999. pap. 14.95 (*0-00-413357-9*, Pub. by HarpC) Trafalgar.

— Marguerite Makes a Book. LC 98-31222. (Getty Trust Publications). (Illus.). 48p. (YA). (gr. 2-5). 1999. 18.95 (*0-89236-372-X*, Pub. by J P Getty Trust) OUP.

Robertson, Bruce. Marsden Hartley. LC 93-46820. (Illus.). 160p. 1995. 45.00 (*0-8109-3416-7*, Pub. by Abrams) Time Warner.

— Reckoning with Winslow Homer: His Late Paintings & Their Influence. LC 90-31989. 212p. 1990. 40.00 (*0-940717-02-6*); pap. 29.95 (*0-940717-03-4*) Cleveland Mus Art.

— You Can Draw. (Illus.). 192p. 1986. 22.95 (*0-13-972621-7*) P-H.

***Robertson, Bruce, et al.** The Ebsworth Collection: 20th Century American Art. LC 99-57007. (Illus.). 2000. write for info. (*0-89468-247-4*) Natl Gallery Art.

Robertson, Bruce, jt. auth. see White, Antony.

Robertson, Bruce C. Ram Mohan Ray: The Father of Modern India. (Illus.). 228p. 1995. 17.95 (*0-19-563417-9*) OUP.

Robertson, Bruce Carlisle. Raja Rammohan Ray: The Father of Modern India. (Illus.). 224p. 2000. pap. text 13.95 (*0-19-564853-6*) OUP.

Robertson, Bruce Carlisle, ed. see Roy, Raja Rammohun.

Robertson, Bryan. Elisabeth Frink: Sculpture & Drawings, 1950-1990. LC 90-60050. (Illus.). 80p. 1990. 32.95 (*0-940979-12-8*) Natl Museum Women.

Robertson, C. Alton. Meditations for the Six Days of Holy Week. 28p. (Orig.). 1997. pap. 5.75 (*0-7880-0731-9*) CSS OH.

Robertson, C. alton. The Moravians, the Miskitu & the Sandinistas on Nicaragua's Atlantic Coast, 1979-90. LC 98-65183. 96p. 1998. pap. 16.00 (*1-878422-37-5*) Moravian Ch in Amer.

Robertson, C. Alton. Prelude to Black Saturday: A Play for Good Friday. 24p. (Orig.). 1997. pap. 5.25 (*0-7880-0732-7*) CSS OH.

Robertson, C. C. On the Track of the Exodus. LC 89-82327. (Illus.). 120p. 1990. reprint ed. pap. 8.00 (*0-934666-40-7*) Artisan Pubs.

Robertson, C. Grant, et al. Humanism & Technology & Other Essays. LC 68-22099. (Essay Index Reprint Ser.). 1977. 17.95 (*0-8369-0553-9*) Ayer.

Robertson, C. M., jt. auth. see Polunin, N. V. C.

Robertson, C. P., et al. Nitrogen Cycling in Ecosystems of Latin America & the Caribbean. 1982. text 211.50 (*90-247-2719-7*) Kluwer Academic.

Robertson, C. Warren. The Secret Garden. 60p. 1996. pap. 4.00 (*1-57514-173-6*, 1073) Encore Perform Pub.

Robertson, Carleton J. Robby's Revelry. Vernon, Sidney, ed. (Illus.). (Orig.). pap. 7.00 (*0-943150-12-4*) Rovern Pr.

Robertson, Carol. Health Visiting in Practice. 2nd ed. (Illus.). 1991p. 1991. pap. text 34.95 (*0-443-04137-7*) Church.

— Portuguese Cooking: The Authentic & Robust Cuisine of Portugal. LC 93-1684. (Illus.). 166p. (Orig.). 1993. 24.95 (*1-55643-158-9*) North Atlantic.

— Turkish Cooking: A Culinary Journey Through Turkey. LC 95-18912. (Illus.). 225p. 1996. 24.95 (*1-883319-38-2*) Frog Ltd CA.

Robertson, Carol E., ed. Musical Repercussions of 1492: Encounters in Text & Performance. LC 92-6895. (Illus.). 496p. (C). 1992. text 65.00 (*1-56098-183-0*) Smithsonian.

***Robertson, Carolyn, et al.** Anatomy & Physiology Laboratory Manual. 3rd ed. 226p. (C). 1999. spiral bd. 47.95 (*0-7872-6335-4*, 41633501) Kendall-Hunt.

Robertson, Carolyn, jt. auth. see Robertson, James.

Robertson, Carolyn C. Anatomy & Physiology Laboratory Manual. 256p. (C). 1996. pap. text, spiral bd., lab manual ed. 29.95 (*0-8403-9466-7*) Kendall-Hunt.

***Robertson, Carra.** Meditations for Actors: For the Actor Within Us All. LC 00-90361. (Illus.). vi, 82p. 2000. pap. 10.00 (*0-9679837-0-3*) Dablond.

Robertson, Cary N. Prostate Cancer: A Guide for Men. Webster, G. D., ed. (Urology Ser.). (Illus.). 24p. (Orig.). 1996. pap. 2.95 (*1-885274-27-0*) Health InfoNet Inc.

Robertson, Catherine, ed. see Welch, C. W.

Robertson, Charles. History of Morgan County, with Portraits & Biographical Sketches of Some of the Pioneers & Prominent Men. (Illus.). 538p. 1995. reprint ed. lib. bdg. 57.00 (*0-8328-5096-9*) Higginson Bk Co.

Robertson, Charles B. How to Deal on an Automobile. 90p. (Orig.). 1988. pap. write for info. (*0-318-64785-0*) Blue Mountain Pub.

— How To Deal on An Automobile. 2nd rev. ed. 96p. (Orig.). 1990. pap. 7.95 (*0-9622155-1-1*) Blue Mountain Pub.

Robertson, Charles K. South Africa. 128p. 1986. pap. 3.95 (*0-88144-072-8*) Christian Pub.

Robertson, Charles L. The International Herald Tribune: The First Hundred Years. (Illus.). 380p. 1987. text 61.00 (*0-231-06562-0*) Col U Pr.

— International Politics since World War II: A Short History. 3rd ed. LC 96-46431. 400p. (C). (gr. 13). 1997. text 74.95 (*0-7656-0026-9*); pap. text 30.95 (*0-7656-0027-7*) M E Sharpe.

***Robertson, Charles L., ed.** Private Pilot Test Prep: Study & Prepare for Recreational & Private... FAA Exams. (Two Thousand Test Prep Ser.). (Illus.). 326p. 1999. pap. 14.95 (*1-56027-341-0*) ASA Inc.

***Robertson, Charles L., et al, eds.** Airline Transport Pilot Test Prep, 2000: Study & Prepare for the Airline Transport Pilot & Aircraft Test. (Two Thousand Test Prep Ser.). (Illus.). 494p. 1999. pap. 34.95 (*1-56027-342-9*) ASA Inc.

***Robertson, Charles T., II & Haman, Edward A.** How to File for Divorce in Georgia. 3rd ed. LC 98-12162. (Legal Survival Guides Ser.). 160p. 1998. pap. 19.95 (*1-57071-376-6*) Sourcebks.

Robertson, Charles T. & Warda, Mark. How to Start a Business in Georgia: With Forms. (Legal Survival Guides Ser.). 140p. 1999. pap. 16.95 (*1-57248-076-9*, Sphinx Pubng) Sourcebks.

Robertson, Cheryl D., ed. see Kaufman, Betty R.

Robertson, Chimp. POW-MIA: "The Men We Left Behind" LC 94-66614. 304p. 1995. 19.95 (*0-914984-64-0*) Starburst.

Robertson, Chip, ed. see Schorr, Daniel.

Robertson, Chris. Exceeding Expectations: The Strategy of Personal & Organizational Excellence. 104p. 1996. pap. text, per. 19.95 (*0-7872-2720-X*) Kendall-Hunt.

Robertson, Chris, jt. auth. see McCloskey, Moya.

Robertson, Christopher R. Electrical & Electronic Principles. (Electrical Engineering Ser.). 216p. (C). (gr. 13). 1994. pap. text 26.50 (*0-340-59231-1*) Chapman & Hall.

— Electrical & Electronic Principles. (C). 1994. pap. text 29.95 (*0-340-57918-8*, Pub. by E A) Routldge.

Robertson, Claire C. Trouble Showed the Way: Women, Men, & Trade in the Nairobi Area, 1890-1990. LC 97-40099. (Illus.). 384p. 1997. 49.95 (*0-253-33360-1*); pap. 24.95 (*0-253-21151-4*) Ind U Pr.

Robertson, Claire C. & Berger, Iris, eds. Women & Class in Africa. LC 85-17568. 300p. (C). 1986. pap. 19.95 (*0-8419-1187-8*) Holmes & Meier.

Robertson, Claire C., jt. auth. see Ndambuki, Berida.

Robertson, Claire C., jt. ed. see Berger, Iris.

Robertson, Clare. Il Grand Cardinale: Alessandro Farnese, Patron of the Arts. (Illus.). 256p. (C). 1992. 50.00 (*0-300-05045-3*) Yale U Pr.

Robertson, Clare & Whistler, Catherine. Drawings by the Carriccifrom British Collections. (Illus.). 160p. (Orig.). 1996. pap. 29.50 (*1-85444-092-6*, 092-6, Pub. by Ashmolean Mus) A Schwartz & Co.

Robertson, Claude E., Jr., ed. see Hayes, Dan.

Robertson, Clive, jt. auth. see Shaw, Jackie.

Robertson, Colin E. & Little, Keith, eds. A Manual of Accident & Emergency Resuscitation. LC 83-1290. (Wiley-Medical Publication). (Illus.). 191p. reprint ed. pap. 59.30 (*0-8357-3927-9*, 203666200004) Bks Demand.

Robertson, Colin E. & Redmond, Anthony D. The Management of Major Trauma. 2nd ed. (Hardbooks in Emergency Medicine Ser.: Vol. 9). (Illus.). 208p. 1994. 59.95 (*0-19-262448-2*); pap. text 27.50 (*0-19-262447-4*) OUP.

Robertson, D. B., ed. Power & Empowerment in Higher Education: Studies in Honor of Louis Smith. LC 77-76333. 167p. reprint ed. pap. 51.80 (*0-7837-5792-1*, 204545800006) Bks Demand.

Robertson, D. B., ed. see Niebuhr, Reinhold.

Robertson, D. J., jt. auth. see Hunter, Lawrence C.

Robertson, D. R., jt. auth. see Allen, Gerald R.

Robertson, D. Ross & Glynn, Peter W. Field Guidebook to the Reefs of San Blas Island, Panama. (Third International Symposium on Coral Reefs Ser.). (Illus.). 16p. 1977. pap. 3.00 (*0-932981-42-9*) Univ Miami A R C.

Robertson, D. W. Chaucer's London. LC 68-30920. (New Dimensions in History Ser.). x, 241p. 1968. write for info. (*0-471-72730-X*) Wiley.

Robertson, Dale, ed. Development & Dependency in the Pacific Islands. 224p. (C). 2000. pap. text 15.00 (*0-939154-63-3*) Inst Polynesian.

***Robertson, Dale N.** The Biblical Ciphers Unsealed: A Revival of the Hebrew Goddess. 672p. 2001. pap. 24.95 (*1-55778-797-2*) Paragon Hse.

Robertson, Dan & Taylor, Ron. Huntin' Humor I. (Illus.). 96p. 1990. 3.95 (*0-9627332-0-2*) DRT-Ink.

Robertson, Darick, et al. Transmetropolitan: Back on the Street. Moore, Stuart, ed. (Illus.). 72p. 1998. pap. text 7.95 (*1-56389-445-9*, Pub. by DC Comics) Time Warner.

Robertson, Darrel M. The Chicago Revival, Eighteen Seventy-Six: Society & Revivalism in a Nineteenth-Century City. LC 88-34865. (Studies in Evangelicalism: No. 9). 239p. 1989. 30.00 (*0-8108-2181-8*) Scarecrow.

Robertson, David. Booth: A Novel. LC 97-35654. (Illus.). 336p. 1997. 23.95 (*0-385-48706-1*, Anchor NY) Doubleday.

— Booth: A Novel. (Illus.). 336p. 1998. pap. 12.00 (*0-385-48707-X*) Doubleday.

— Denmark Vesey: The Buried History of America's Largest Slave Rebellion & the Man Who Led It. LC 98-31825. (Illus.). 202p. (YA). (gr. 9-12). 1999. 23.00 (*0-679-44288-X*) Knopf.

— Denmark Vesey: The Buried History of America's Largest Slave Rebellion & the Man Who Led It. 240p. 2000. 13.00 (*0-679-76218-3*) Vin Bks.

***Robertson, David.** Designing Complex Software. LC 99-12088. 240p. (C). 1999. 49.95 (*0-201-39819-2*) Addison-Wesley.

Robertson, David. A Dictionary of Human Rights. LC 97-204122. 300p. 1996. 85.00 (*1-85743-023-9*, Pub. by EurP) Taylor & Francis.

— Disorders of the Autonomic Nervous System. xvi, 434p. 1995. text 132.00 (*3-7186-5146-7*, Harwood Acad Pubs) Gordon & Breach.

— Judicial Discretion in the House of Lords. 440p. 1998. text 95.00 (*0-19-827442-4*) OUP.

***Robertson, David.** Narrow Way to Nearby. (Western Writers Ser: Vol. 141). (C). 1999. pap. 5.95 (*0-88430-140-0*) Boise St U W Writ Ser.

— Photo & Word. LC 97-70324. (Western Writers Ser: Vol. 128). (Illus.). 1997. pap. 4.95 (*0-88430-127-3*) Boise St U W Writ Ser.

Robertson, David. Real Matter. LC 96-50029. 182p. 1997. 39.95 (*0-87480-533-3*); pap. 15.95 (*0-87480-534-1*) U of Utah Pr.

— West of Eden: A History of Art & Literature of Yosemite. (Illus.). 174p. 1984. 15.95 (*0-939666-40-5*); pap. 9.95 (*0-939666-41-3*) Yosemite Assn.

Robertson, David, ed. East Asian Trade after the Uruguay Round. LC 96-9562. (Trade & Development Ser.). 308p. (C). 1997. text 64.95 (*0-521-58318-7*) Cambridge U Pr.

Robertson, David, et al, eds. Primer on the Autonomic Nervous System. (Illus.). 343p. 1996. text 79.95 (*0-12-589760-X*); pap. text 47.00 (*0-12-589761-8*) Acad Pr.

Robertson, David, et al. Eco-Logic: Logic-Based Approaches to Ecological Modelling. (Logic Programming - Ehud T. Shapiro Ser.). (Illus.). 272p. 1991. 40.00 (*0-262-18143-6*) MIT Pr.

Robertson, David, jt. auth. see Davis, Richard.

Robertson, David A., et al. Ecce Agnus Dei: Sacrificial Imagery of Christ 1350-1750 from the Collection of Loyola University. 1994. pap. 15.00 (*1-884936-00-8*) Loyola U Chicago.

***Robertson, David B.** Capital, Labor & State: The Battle for American Labor Markets from the Civil War to the New Deal. LC 99-87953. 320p. 2000. pap. 22.95 (*0-8476-9729-0*) Rowman.

Robertson, David B. A Theory of Party Competition. LC 74-23542. 220p. reprint ed. pap. 68.20 (*0-608-17677-X*, 203039400069) Bks Demand.

Robertson, David B., ed. Loss of Confidence: Politics & Policy in the 1970s. LC 98-26747. (Issues in Policy History Ser.: No. 8). 184p. 1998. pap. 16.95 (*0-271-01845-3*) Pa St U Pr.

***Robertson, David Brian.** Capitol, Labor, & State: The Battle for American Labor Markets from the Civil War to the New Deal. LC 99-87953. 320p. 2000. 65.00 (*0-8476-9728-2*) Rowman.

Robertson, David E., ed. Nuclear Waste Instrumentation Engineering, Vol. 3536. 192p. 1999. 59.00 (*0-8194-2997-X*) SPIE.

Robertson, David M., jt. ed. see Davis, Richard L.

Robertson, David P., jt. auth. see Lowstuter, Clyde C.

Robertson, David W. & Meyer, Robin, eds. Correspondence Between Leon Green & Charles McCormick, 1927-1962. annot. ed. x, 222p. 1988. 32.50 (*0-8377-1046-4*, Rothman) W S Hein.

Robertson, David W., et al. Cases & Materials on Torts. 2nd ed. LC 98-5636. (Paralegal). 1000p. 1998. text 40.50 (*0-314-21141-1*) West Pub.

— Cases & Materials on Torts: Cases & Materials. (American Casebook Ser.). 932p. (C). 1989. reprint ed. text 45.00 (*0-314-50709-4*) West Pub.

— Torts Cases & Materials on, Teachers Manual to Accompany. (American Casebook Ser.). 201p. 1989. pap. text. write for info. (*0-314-55687-7*) West Pub.

Robertson, Debbie. Blast off with Book Reports. (Illus.). 64p. (J). (gr. 3-8). 1985. student ed. 8.99 (*0-86653-327-3*, GA 682) Good Apple.

Robertson, Debbie & Barry, Patricia. Super Kids Publishing Company. xiii, 354p. 1990. pap. text 25.00 (*0-87287-704-3*) Teacher Ideas Pr.

Robertson, Debora. Making the Most of Storage. LC 95-71192. (Illus.). 80p. 1996. 19.95 (*0-8478-1937-X*, Pub. by Rizzoli Intl) St Martin.

Robertson, Deborah. Proudflesh. 1997. pap. 16.95 (*1-86368-205-8*, Pub. by Fremantle Arts) Intl Spec Bk.

Robertson, Debra. Portraying Persons with Disabilities: An Annotated Bibliography of Fiction for Children & Teenagers. (Serving Special Needs Ser.). 482p. 1992. 39.95 (*0-8352-3023-6*) Bowker.

Robertson, Denise. Act of Oblivion. large type ed. (Magna Large Print Ser.). 419p. 1997. 27.99 (*0-7505-1083-8*, Pub. by Mgna Lrg Print) Ulverscroft.

— The Anxious Heart. large type ed. 516p. 1995. 11.50 (*0-7505-0652-0*) Ulverscroft.

***Robertson, Denise.** Flower, Wreaths & Garlands in Cross Stitch. (Cross Stitch Ser.). (Illus.). 40p. 1999. pap. 6.95 (*1-85391-769-9*) Merehurst Ltd.

Robertson, Denise. Illusion. 336p. 2000. 22.50 (*0-684-86839-3*) S&S Trade.

— A Relative Freedom. large type ed. (Magna Large Print Ser.). 468p. 1997. 27.50 (*0-7505-1082-X*) Thorndike Pr.

— Remember the Moment. large type ed. 485p. 1993. 27.99 (*0-7505-0271-1*) Ulverscroft.

— Wait for the Day. 400p. 2000. 22.50 (*0-684-86828-8*) S&S Trade.

Robertson, Denise A. The Stars Burn On. large type ed. (Magna General Fiction Ser.). 575p. 1992. 27.99 (*0-7505-0300-9*) Ulverscroft.

— Towards Jeruslem. large type ed. (Magna Large Print Ser.). 1994. 27.99 (*0-7505-0617-2*, Pub. by Mgna Lrg Print) Ulverscroft.

Robertson, Dennis H. Banking Policy & the Price Level: An Essay in the Theory of the Trade Cycle. rev. ed. LC 50-3461. (Reprints of Economic Classics Ser.). xvii, 103p. 1989. reprint ed. 27.50 (*0-678-00675-X*) Kelley.

Robertson, Dominique, et al. Manipulation & Expression of Recombinant DNA: A Laboratory Manual. LC 97-195982. (Illus.). 224p. 1997. spiral bd. 45.00 (*0-12-589765-0*) Morgan Kaufmann.

Robertson, Don. Barb. 164p. 1988. 14.95 (*0-939738-93-7*) Zubal Inc.

— The Forest of Arden. 354p. 1986. 17.95 (*0-685-17070-5*) Zubal Inc.

— Harv. 170p. 1985. 11.95 (*0-939738-69-4*) Zubal Inc.

— The Ideal Genuine Man. deluxe ed. 1987. 50.00 (*0-318-23786-5*) Philtrum Pr.

Robertson, Donald. Mexican Manuscript Painting of the Early Colonial Period: The Metropolitan Schools. LC 94-12120. 234p. (Orig.). 1994. pap. 31.95 (*0-8061-2675-2*) U of Okla Pr.

Robertson, Donald B. Encyclopedia of Western Railroad History: Oregon & Washington, Vol. III. LC 86-9611. (Illus.). 340p. 1995. 34.95 (*0-87004-366-8*) Caxton.

— Encyclopedia of Western Railroad History: The Desert States. LC 86-9611. (Illus.). 334p. 1986. reprint ed. pap. 103.60 (*0-7837-7138-X*, 205916500004) Bks Demand.

— Encyclopedia of Western Railroad History Vol. IV: California. Cornell, Wayne, ed. (Illus.). 340p. 1998. 42.95 (*0-87004-385-4*) Caxton.

Robertson, Donald R., jt. auth. see Robertson, Douglas F.

Robertson, Donald S. Greek & Roman Architecture. 2nd ed. (Illus.). 432p. 1969. reprint ed. pap. text 34.95 (*0-521-09452-6*) Cambridge U Pr.

Robertson, Dougal. Survive the Savage Sea. (Illus.). 224p. 1994. pap. 14.95 (*0-924486-73-2*) Sheridan.

— Survive the Savage Sea. large type ed. (Non-Fiction Ser.). 448p. 1986. 15.95 (*0-7089-1409-8*) Ulverscroft.

Robertson, Dougal, ed. see Greenwald, Michael.

Robertson, Douglas F. & Robertson, Donald R. Using Microcomputer Applications: A Computer Lab Manual with DOS, WordPerfect 5.1, Lotus 1-2-3, & dBASE IV. 475p. (C). 1992. teacher ed. 10.75 (*0-685-70051-8*) Dryden Pr.

Robertson, Douglas S. The New Renaissance: Computers & the Next Level of Civilization. LC 97-31239. 208p. 1998. 25.00 (*0-19-512189-9*) OUP.

Robertson, Duncan. The Medieval Saints' Lives: Spiritual Renewal & Old French Literature. (Edward C. Armstrong Monographs on Medieval Literature: No. 8). 267p. (Orig.). 1995. pap. 24.95 (*0-917058-90-9*) French Forum.

Robertson, Durant W. Chaucer's London. LC 68-30920. (New Dimension in History Ser.). 256p. reprint ed. pap. 79.40 (*0-608-30169-8*, 201340900086) Bks Demand.

— Essays in Medieval Culture. LC 80-13130. (Illus.). 427p. 1980. reprint ed. pap. 132.40 (*0-7837-9433-9*, 206017500004) Bks Demand.

Robertson, Dwight & Estes, E. Harvey. Textbook of Family Practice. 1991. write for info. (*0-8151-7407-1*) Mosby Inc.

An Asterisk (*) at the beginning of an entry indicates that the title is appearing for the first time.

Robertson, E. Bruce. Art of Paul Sandby. LC 85-40260. (Illus.). 112p. (Orig.). 1985. pap. 12.95 (*0-930606-47-7*) Yale Ctr Brit Art.

Robertson, E. F., jt. auth. see Blyth, T. S.

Robertson, E. F., jt. ed. see Campbell, C. M.

Robertson, E. S., ed. see Birrell, Augustine.

Robertson, Ed. Customer Service in Communication: Achieving & Measuring Outstanding Results. (Strategic Communicator Ser.). 133p. 1999. 185.00 (*1-888015-15-2*) IABC.

— The Fugitive Recaptured: The Thirtieth Anniversary Companion to a Television Classic. (Illus.). 208p. (Orig.). 1993. pap. 17.95 (*0-938817-34-5*) Pomegranate Pr.

— Maverick: Legend of the West. (Illus.). 208p. (Orig.). 1994. pap. 17.95 (*0-938817-35-3*) Pomegranate Pr.

— This Is Jim Rockford: The Rockford Files. (Illus.). 208p. 1995. pap. 19.95 (*0-938817-36-1*) Pomegranate Pr.

Robertson, Edna E., jt. auth. see Nestor, Sarah.

Robertson, Edna W. Fundamentals of Document Examination. (Illus.). 500p. 1991. text 57.95 (*0-8304-1238-7*) Burnham Inc.

Robertson, Edward D., Jr. Personal Autonomy & Substituted Judgment: Legal Issues in Medical Decisions for Incompetent Patients. (Orig.). 1991. pap. 5.99 (*0-685-50296-1*) Diocesan Pr.

Robertson, Edwin H. The Biblical Bases of Healing. (C). 1990. pap. 35.00 (*0-85305-287-5*, Pub. by Arthur James) St Mut.

— Taking the Word to the World. LC 97-101373. (Illus.). 352p. 1996. 22.99 (*0-7852-7232-1*) Nelson.

— Wycliffe: Morning Star of the Reformation. 127p. 1987. pap. 3.70 (*0-310-55232-X*, 19023P) Zondervan.

Robertson, Edwin H., tr. see Lange, Ernst.

Robertson, Edwin H., tr. see Lochman, Jan M.

Robertson, Elizabeth. Early English Devotional Prose & the Female Audience. LC 89-24836. 240p. 1990. 33.00 (*0-87049-641-7*) U of Tenn Pr.

Robertson, Elizabeth B., ed. Rural Substance Abuse: State of Knowledge & Issues. (Illus.). 544p. (C). 1999. reprint ed. pap. text 45.00 (*0-7881-7744-3*) DIANE Pub.

Robertson, Ellen H. Magic Menu. (Illus.). (Orig.). 1954. pap. 2.00 (*0-87505-136-7*) Borden.

Robertson, Ellison. In Love with Then. 220p. 1992. pap. 12.95 (*0-86492-137-3*, Pub. by Goose Ln Edits) Genl Dist Srvs.

***Robertson, Eric.** Whatever Comes of Not Knowing. Clarke, Ben & Costello, Kitty, eds. 64p. 2000. pap. 11.95 (*0-9625153-9-6*) Freedom Voices Pubns.

Robertson, Eugene C. Interior of the Earth. 7p. 1994. pap. 1.00 (*0-16-061620-4*) USGPO.

Robertson, Everett, ed. Puppet Scripts for Use at Church. LC 78-72843. 96p. 1978. pap. 7.99 (*0-8054-7516-8*, 4275-16) Broadman.

— Puppet Scripts for Use at Church, No. 2. LC 78-72843. 96p. (J). (gr. k up). 1980. pap. 7.99 (*0-8054-7519-2*, 4275-19) Broadman.

Robertson, Everette. Puppet Scripts for Use, Set. 1979. pap. 12.99 incl. audio (*0-8054-7925-2*) Broadman.

Robertson, F. E. A Practical Treatise on Organ - Building, 2 vols. (Illus.). 370p. 1997. reprint ed. pap. 75.00 (*0-913746-04-5*) Organ Lit.

Robertson, F. L. Keene. Keayne - Keene(e) - Keeney - Kinne(y) - Kenney & Allied Families. (Illus.). 183p. 1997. reprint ed. pap. 27.00 (*0-8328-9383-8*); reprint ed. lib. bdg. 37.00 (*0-8328-9382-X*) Higginson Bk Co.

Robertson, Fiona. Legitimate Histories: Scott, Gothic & the Authorities of Fiction. LC 93-27024. (Oxford English Monographs). 336p. 1994. text 60.00 (*0-19-811224-6*, Clarendon Pr) OUP.

Robertson, Fiona, ed. see Crane, Stephen.

Robertson, Fiona, ed. & intro. see Scott, Sir Walter.

Robertson, Fleur. Little Book of Love. 1995. 4.98 (*0-7858-0294-0*) Bk Sales Inc.

— Little Book of Thoughtful Moments. 1994. 4.98 (*1-55521-992-6*) Bk Sales Inc.

— Remembered Kisses: An Illustrated Anthology of Irish Love Poetry. (Illus.). 1997. 12.95 (*1-85833-715-1*, Pub. by CLib Bks) Whitecap Bks.

Robertson, Florance K. Kinne. Genealogy of Henry & Ann Kinne, Pioneers of Salem, Mass. (Illus.). 218p. 1997. reprint ed. pap. 33.50 (*0-8328-9433-8*); reprint ed. lib. bdg. 43.50 (*0-8328-9432-X*) Higginson Bk Co.

***Robertson, Florence H.** The Marassa Concept. 182p. (C). 1999. per. 33.95 (*0-7872-6373-7*, 41637301) Kendall-Hunt.

Robertson, Florence H. Shadow Land: Stories of the South. LC 72-3188. (Black Heritage Library Collection). 1977. reprint ed. 19.95 (*0-8369-9077-3*) Ayer.

Robertson, Frank C. A Ram in the Thicket: The Story of a Roaming Homesteader Family on the Mormon Frontier. (Idaho Yesterdays Ser.). 350p. (C). 1995. reprint ed. pap. 15.95 (*0-89301-173-8*) U of Idaho Pr.

— Squatter's Rights. large type ed. (Linford Western Library). 352p. 1985. pap. 16.99 (*0-7089-6184-3*) Ulverscroft.

— Trouble at Topaz. large type ed. (Western Ser.). 1975. 27.99 (*0-85456-324-5*) Ulverscroft.

Robertson, Frank S. In the Saddle with Stuart: The Story of Frank Smith Robertson of Jeb Stuart's Staff. Trout, Robert J., ed. LC 98-34333. (Illus.). 168p. 1998. pap. 16.95 (*1-57747-029-X*) Thomas Publications.

Robertson, G. C. Butterworths Student Companions: Industrial Law. 2nd ed. 104p. 1994. pap. 18.00 (*0-409-30864-1*, Austral, MICHIE) LEXIS Pub.

Robertson, G. Croom, ed. see Grote, George.

Robertson, G. D., ed. Miguel de Unamuno's Political Writings, 1918-1924 Vol. 1: La Anarquia Reinante (1918-1920) LC 95-36709. (Hispanic Literature Ser.: Vol. 31). 448p. 1996. text 109.95 (*0-7734-8846-4*) E Mellen.

— Miguel de Unamuno's Political Writings, 1918-1924 Vol. 2: El Absolutismo en Acecho (1921-1922) LC 95-36709. (Hispanic Literature Ser.: Vol. 32). 520p. 1999. text 119.95 (*0-7734-8848-0*) E Mellen.

Robertson, G. D., ed. see Unamuno, Miguel de.

***Robertson, G. L.** Food Packaging: Principles & Practice. (Packaging & Converting Technology Ser.: 6). (Illus.). 688p. 1998. pap. text 69.75 (*0-8247-0175-5*) Dekker.

Robertson, G. Leo. Happiness & Many Things: Reflections on Happiness. 32p. 1987. pap. 5.00 (*0-9618775-1-0*) G L Robertson.

— Loving Is Many Things: Reflections on Love. 32p. 1987. pap. 5.00 (*0-9618775-0-2*) G L Robertson.

Robertson, G. Philip, et al, eds. Standard Soil Methods for Long-Term Ecological Research. LC 98-28545. (Long-Term Ecological Research Network Ser.). (Illus.). 480p. 1999. text 85.00 (*0-19-512083-3*) OUP.

***Robertson, Geoffrey.** Crimes Against Humanity: The Struggle for Global Justice. 2000. 30.00 (*1-56584-597-8*, Pub. by New Press NY) Norton.

— Freedom: The Individual & the Law. 1994. pap. 29.95 (*0-14-017264-5*, Pub. by Pnguin Bks Ltd) Trafalgar.

Robertson, Geoffrey. Obscenity: An Account of Censorship Laws & Their Enforcement in England & Wales. (Law in Context Ser.). xviii, 364p. 1979. 40.50 (*0-297-77213-9*) W S Hein.

***Robertson, Geoffrey & Andrew, Nicol.** Media Law. 1998. pap. 50.00 (*0-14-013866-8*, Pub. by Pnguin Bks Ltd) Trafalgar.

Robertson, George, et al, contrib. by. The Block Reader in Visual Culture. LC 95-44712. 360p. (C). 1996. pap. 24.99 (*0-415-13989-9*) Routledge.

— The Block Reader in Visual Culture. LC 95-44712. (Illus.). 360p. (C). 1996. 80.00 (*0-415-13988-0*) Routledge.

Robertson, George, et al, eds. FutureNatural: Nature, Science, Culture. LC 95-25912. (Futures, New Perspectives for Cultural Analysis Ser.). 328p. (C). 1996. 90.00 (*0-415-07013-9*); pap. 20.99 (*0-415-07014-7*) Routledge.

Robertson, George & Charteris, Henry. De Vita et Morte Roberti Rollok. Lee, John, ed. LC 77-172040. (Bannatyne Club, Edinburgh. Publications: No. 16). reprint ed. 45.00 (*0-404-52716-7*) AMS Pr.

Robertson, George, et al. Travellers' Tales: Narratives of Home & Displacement. LC 93-23698. (Futures, New Perspectives for Cultural Analysis Ser.). (Illus.). 272p. (C). 1994. pap. 22.99 (*0-415-07016-3*, B3899) Routledge.

— Travellers' Tales: Narratives of Home & Displacement. LC 93-23698. (Futures, New Perspectives for Cultural Analysis Ser.). (Illus.). 272p. (C). (gr. 13). 1994. 80.00 (*0-415-07015-5*, B3895) Routledge.

Robertson, George, jt. auth. see Kuske, Albrecht.

Robertson, George C. Elements of Psychology. Davids, C. A., ed. LC 78-72820. (Brainedness, Handedness, & Mental Abilities Ser.). reprint ed. 39.50 (*0-404-60889-2*) AMS Pr.

— Hobbes. LC 70-137283. reprint ed. 22.50 (*0-404-05359-9*) AMS Pr.

— Hobbes. 1971. reprint ed. 7.00 (*0-403-00251-6*) Scholarly.

Robertson, George L., ed. Buyer Beware: Evaluating Environmental Liabilities in Oil & Gas Transactions. LC 95-37191. 1995. 99.95 (*0-87814-453-6*) PennWell Bks.

Robertson, George S. Chitral: The Story of a Minor Siege. (Illus.). 1978. text 14.95 (*0-19-577248-2*) OUP.

— The Kafirs of the Hindu-Kush. (Asia Historical Reprints Ser.). (Illus.). 548p. 1986. 39.95 (*0-19-577127-3*) OUP.

Robertson, Georgia D. The Harvest of Hate. limited ed. viii, 586p. 1986. 26.00 (*0-930046-08-0*) CSUF Oral Hist.

Robertson, Gordon. A House Divided: Meech Lake, Senate Reform & the Canadian Union. 98p. 1989. 17.95 (*0-88645-096-9*, Pub. by Inst Res Pub) Ashgate Pub Co.

Robertson, Gordon L. Food Packaging: Principles & Practice. LC 92-25591. (Packaging & Converting Technology Ser.: Vol. 6). (Illus.). 688p. 1992. text 215.00 (*0-8247-8749-8*) Dekker.

Robertson, Graham, jt. auth. see Dell, Susanne.

Robertson, Greg. Hands on HTML. (Hands on Ser.). 576p. 2000. pap. 40.00 (*0-7615-1885-1*) Prima Pub.

Robertson, H. Thomas, jt. ed. see Hlastala, Michael P.

Robertson, Harry A., jt. ed. see Leslie, Ron A.

Robertson, Harry S. Statistical Thermophysics. LC 92-17052. 592p. (C). 1992. text 70.60 (*0-13-845603-8*) P-H.

Robertson, Heather. Beaute Tragique: Les Deux Conflicts Mondiaux Vus par des Artistes Canadiens. Dunlop-Hebert, Carol & Beaulieu, Michel, trs. 240p. 1978. text 49.95 (*0-88862-186-8*, Pub. by J Lorimer) Formac Dist Ltd.

Robertson, Heather. Driving Force: The McLaughlin Family & the Age of the Car. (Illus.). 384p. 1996. 34.99 (*0-7710-7556-1*) McCland & Stewart.

— Driving Force: The McLaughlin Family & the Age of the Car. (Illus.). 400p. 1997. pap. text 19.99 (*0-7710-7557-X*) McCland & Stewart.

Robertson, Heather. Grass Roots. 369p. 1973. 29.95 (*0-88862-045-4*, Pub. by J Lorimer); pap. 1.99 (*0-88862-099-3*, Pub. by J Lorimer) Formac Dist Ltd.

— Salt of the Earth. 224p. 1974. 29.95 (*0-88862-075-6*, Pub. by J Lorimer) Formac Dist Ltd.

Robertson, Heather. Writing from Life: A Guide for Writing True Stories. LC 98-168594. 272p. 1998. pap. text 15.95 (*0-7710-7558-8*) McCland & Stewart.

Robertson, Heather-Jane. No More Teachers, No More Books: The Commercialization of Canada's Schools. 304p. 1998. 24.95 (*0-7710-7575-8*) McCland & Stewart.

***Robertson, Heather-Jane.** No More Teachers, No More Books: The Commercialization of Canada's Schools. 360p. 1999. pap. 17.95 (*0-7710-7576-6*) McClelland & Stewart.

Robertson, Hector M. Aspects of the Rise of Economic Individualism: A Criticism of Max Weber & His School. LC 73-17059. (Reprints of Economic Classics Ser.). xvi, 223p. 1973. reprint ed. 37.50 (*0-678-00867-1*) Kelley.

— South Africa: Economic & Political Aspects. LC 57-8817. (Duke University, Commonwealth-Studies Center, Publication Ser.: No. 2). 204p. reprint ed. pap. 63.30 (*0-608-11970-9*, 202344200033) Bks Demand.

***Robertson, Hilary.** Boudoir: Creating the Bedroom of Your Dreams. (Illus.). 2000. 24.95 (*1-84222-067-5*) Carlton Bks Ltd.

Robertson, Howard W. To the Fierce Guard in the Assyrian Saloon. Trusky, Tom, ed. LC 86-71904. (Ahsahta Press Modern & Contemporary Poets of the West Ser.). 65p. (Orig.). 1987. pap. 6.95 (*0-916272-33-8*) Ahsahta Pr.

Robertson, Hugh, jt. auth. see Heather, Barrie.

Robertson, Hugh D., et al, eds. Plant Infectious Agents: Viruses, Viroids, Virusoids & Satellites. (Current Communications in Molecular Biology Ser.). 230p. 1983. pap. text 28.00 (*0-87969-159-X*) Cold Spring Harbor.

Robertson, Ian. Austria. 3rd rev. ed. (Blue Guide Ser.). (Illus.). 428p. 1992. pap. 22.95 (*0-393-30836-7*) Norton.

— Blue Guide: Spain. 6th ed. 508p. 1993. pap. 23.00 (*0-393-31053-1*) Norton.

— Blue Guide: Switzerland. 5th ed. (Illus.). 384p. 1992. pap. 21.95 (*0-393-30890-1*) Norton.

— France. 4th ed. (Blue Guide Ser.). (Illus.). 864p. 1997. pap. 29.95 (*0-393-31640-8*) Norton.

***Robertson, Ian.** A Guide to the Peninsular War, 1808-1814. 2000. pap. 19.95 (*0-85052-660-4*, Pub. by Pen & Sword) Combined Pub.

— Mind Sculpture: Unlocking Your Brain's Untapped Potential. 272p. 2000. 27.00 (*0-88064-221-1*) Fromm Intl Pub.

Robertson, Ian. Portugal. 4th ed. (Blue Guide Ser.) (Illus.). 320p. 1996. pap. 19.95 (*0-393-31416-2*, Norton Paperbks) Norton.

— Society: A Brief Introduction. 416p. (Orig.). (C). 1988. pap. text 30.95 (*0-87901-412-1*) Worth.

— Society: A Brief Introduction. 264p. (Orig.). (C). 1989. pap. text, student ed. 12.95 (*0-87901-415-6*) Worth.

— Society: A Brief Introduction. xvii, 416p. (Orig.). (C). 1990. text 35.95 (*0-87901-548-9*) Worth.

— Sociology. 3rd ed. 715p. (C). 1987. text 47.95 (*0-87901-245-5*) Worth.

— Sociology. 3rd ed. 558p. (C). 1987. pap. text, student ed. 12.95 (*0-87901-246-3*) Worth.

— Sociology: Social World Reader. 3rd ed. 360p. (C). 1987. 20.95 (*0-87901-330-3*) Worth.

Robertson, Ian, ed. MMIC Design. (Circuits & Systems Ser.: No. 7). 502p. 1995. boxed set 95.00 (*0-85296-816-7*, CS007) INSPEC Inc.

— Rugby World Cup '95: In Association with Scottish Life. (Illus.). 192p. 1995. 35.00 (*0-340-64953-4*, Pub. by Hodder & Stought Ltd) Trafalgar.

Robertson, Ian & Whitten, Phillip, eds. Race & Politics in South Africa. LC 76-50334. 274p. 1978. text 34.95 (*0-87855-137-9*) Transaction Pubs.

Robertson, Ian, jt. auth. see Gray-Durant, Delia.

Robertson, Ian, jt. auth. see Heather, Nick H.

Robertson, Ian, jt. auth. see McDonagh, Bernard.

Robertson, Ian, jt. auth. see Rothery, Brian.

Robertson, Ian, ed. see Saraiva, Jose H.

***Robertson, Ian H.** Spatial Neglect: A Clinical Handbook for Diagnosis & Treatment. 192p. 1999. 34.95 (*0-86377-809-7*) L Erlbaum Assocs.

Robertson, Ian M., et al, eds. Microstructure Evolution During Irradiation. LC 97-6963. (Materials Research Society Symposium Proceedings Ser.: No. 439). 733p. 1997. text 75.00 (*1-55899-343-6*) Materials Res.

— Microstructure of Irradiated Materials. (MRS Symposium Proceedings Ser.: Vol. 373). 569p. 1995. 76.00 (*1-55899-275-8*) Materials Res.

Robertson, Ian R. The Tenant League of Prince Edward Island, 1864-1867: Leasehold Tenure in the New World. (Illus.). 480p. 1996. text 60.00 (*0-8020-0769-4*); pap. text 24.95 (*0-8020-7138-4*) U of Toronto Pr.

Robertson, Ian W., tr. see Barth, Karl.

Robertson, Ina. France. 3rd ed. (Blue Guide Ser.). 1994. pap. 29.95 (*0-393-31055-8*) Norton.

Robertson, Irvine G. Que Creen las Sectas?Tr. of What Do the Sects Believe?. (SPA.). 1993. pap. 11.50 (*0-311-05768-3*) Casa Bautista.

— What the Cults Believe. expanded rev. ed. pap. 10.99 (*0-8024-9414-5*, 321) Moody.

Robertson, Isabel. Jehanne. 341p. (C). 1990. 79.00 (*1-85634-979-9*, Pub. by Excalibur) St Mut.

***Robertson, Ivan T.** Jack & the Leprechaun. LC 99-29845. (Pictureback Ser.). (Illus.). 24p. (J). (gr. k-3). 2000. pap. 3.25 (*0-375-80328-9*, Pub. by Random Bks Yng Read) Random.

Robertson, Ivan T. Theodore & the Stormy Day. (Jellybean Bks.). (Illus.). 24p. (J). (ps-k). 1999. 1.99 (*0-375-80076-X*, Pub. by Random Bks Yng Read) Random.

***Robertson, Ivan T.** Theodore & the Stormy Day. (Jellybean Bks.). (Illus.). 24p. (J). (ps-k). 1999. lib. bdg. 7.99 (*0-375-90076-4*, Pub. by Random Bks Yng Read) Random.

Robertson, Ivan T., et al, eds. Motivation: Strategy, Theory & Practice. 200p. (C). 1992. pap. 75.00 (*0-85292-488-7*, Pub. by IPM Hse) St Mut.

Robertson, Ivan T. & Cooper, Dominic. The Psychology of Personnel Selection: A Quality Approach. LC 95-7748. (Essential Business Psychology Ser.). 224p. (C). 1995. pap. 24.95 (*0-415-10326-6*) Thomson Learn.

— The Psychology of Personnel Selection: A Quality Approach. LC 95-7748. (Essential Business Psychology Ser.). 224p. (C). (gr. 13). 1995. pap. 43.95 (*0-415-13081-6*) Thomson Learn.

Robertson, Ivan T. & Smith, Mike. Motivation & Job Design: Theory, Research & Practice. 176p. (C). 1985. 70.00 (*0-85292-346-5*) St Mut.

Robertson, Ivan T., jt. auth. see Smith, Mike.

Robertson, Ivan T., jt. ed. see Cooper, C. L.

Robertson, Ivan T., jt. ed. see Cooper, Cary L.

Robertson, J., ed. Handbook of Clinical Nursing Research. (Illus.). 200p. 1994. pap. write for info. (*0-443-04866-5*) Church.

***Robertson, J., et al, eds.** Amorphous & Nanostructured Carbon Vol. 593: Materials Research Society Symposium Proceedings. LC 00-26819. 553p. 2000. text 95.00 (*1-55899-501-3*) Materials Res.

Robertson, J., jt. auth. see Harpp, D. N.

Robertson, J. A. List of Documents in Spanish Archives Relating to the History of the United States. (Carnegie Institute Ser.: Vol. 19). 1910. 40.00 (*0-527-00699-8*) Periodicals Srv.

Robertson, J. D. A Glossary of Dialect & Archaic Words Used in the County of Gloucester. Moreton, ed. (English Dialect Society Publications: No. 61). 1969. reprint ed. pap. 30.00 (*0-8115-0481-6*) Periodicals Srv.

Robertson, J. Daniel, jt. auth. see Delavigne, Kenneth T.

Robertson, J. G. & Tango, W. J., eds. Very High Angular Resolution Imaging: Proceedings of the 158th Symposium of the International Astronomical Union Held at the Women's College, University of Sydney, Australia, 11-15 January 1993. LC 93-23649. 524p. (C). 1994. pap. text 88.50 (*0-7923-2633-4*); lib. bdg. 181.00 (*0-7923-2632-6*) Kluwer Academic.

Robertson, J. H. & Robertson, J. T. Cranial Base Surgery. (Illus.). 800p. 2000. text. write for info. (*0-443-05685-4*, W B Saunders Co) Harcrt Hlth Sci Grp.

Robertson, J. I. Clinical Hypertension. (Handbook of Hypertension Ser.: Vol. 15). 812p. 1992. 405.00 (*0-444-81294-6*) Elsevier.

Robertson, J. Ian, et al, eds. Comparative Studies in Hypertension: Journal: Nephron, Vol. 47, suppl. 1. (Illus.). vi, 152p. 1987. pap. 48.00 (*3-8055-4710-2*) S Karger.

— Renovascular Hypertension. (Journal: Nephron: Vol. 44, Suppl. 1, 1986). (Illus.). iv, 116p. 1986. pap. 36.75 (*3-8055-4387-5*) S Karger.

Robertson, J. Ian & Janssen, Herwig, eds. Wound Healing. 232p. 1991. 75.00 (*1-871816-10-6*, Pub. by Wrightson Biomed) Taylor & Francis.

Robertson, J. Logie, ed. see Campbell, Thomas.

Robertson, J. M. Collected Works. 1973. 400.00 (*0-87968-896-3*) Gordon Pr.

Robertson, J. M., ed. Courses of Study: Clues to the Independent Study of Important Subjects. 1977. lib. bdg. 59.95 (*0-8490-1680-0*) Gordon Pr.

Robertson, J. M. & Wislicenus, G. F., eds. Cavitation State of Knowledge: Presented at the ASME Fluids Engineering & Applied Mechanics Conference, Northwestern University, Evanston, Ill., June 16-18, 1969. LC 73-173121. 247p. reprint ed. pap. 76.60 (*0-608-14418-5*, 205171300005) Bks Demand.

Robertson, J. M., jt. auth. see Dummer, Geoffrey W.

Robertson, J. M., ed. see American Society of Mechanical Engineers Staff.

Robertson, J. N., tr. see Orthodox Eastern Church Staff.

Robertson, J. Roy. Management of Drug Users in the Community. LC 98-232704. (Arnold Publications). (Illus.). 432p. (Orig.). 1998. pap. text 32.50 (*0-340-70013-0*) OUP.

Robertson, J. T., jt. auth. see Robertson, J. H.

***Robertson, Jack & Louwers, Timothy J.** Auditing: Internet Resource Guide. 9th ed. 60p. (C). 1998. pap. 14.38 (*0-07-365650-X*) McGrw-H Hghr Educ.

— Auditing with Internet Resource Guide. 9th ed. (C). 1998. pap., student ed. 90.31 (*0-07-561886-9*) McGrw-H Hghr Educ.

Robertson, Jack & Webb, William. Cake-Cutting Algorithms. LC 97-41258. (Illus.). 177p. 1998. text 38.00 (*1-56881-076-8*) AK Peters.

Robertson, Jack C. Auditing. 8th ed. LC 95-20776. (Irwin Series in Undergraduate Accounting). 1995. write for info. (*0-614-08000-2*, Irwn McGrw-H) McGrw-H Hghr Educ.

— Auditing. 8th ed. (C). 1995. text, student ed. 28.12 (*0-256-21160-4*, Irwn McGrw-H) McGrw-H Hghr Educ.

— Auditing. 8th ed. 1,104p. (C). 1995. text 75.40 (*0-256-18800-9*, Irwn McGrw-H) McGrw-H Hghr Educ.

— Fraud Examination for Managers & Auditors: 1996 Edition. 600p. 1996. pap. 42.95 (*1-889277-00-2*) Assn Certified Fraud.

Robertson, Jack C. & Louwers, Timothy J. Auditing. 9th ed. LC 98-17617. 1998. 91.43 (*0-07-290695-2*) McGraw.

Robertson, Jack C. & Nigrini, Mark. Fraud Examination for Managers & Auditors: 2000 Edition. rev. ed. (Illus.). 575p. 1999. pap. 49.00 (*0-9656785-1-2*) Viesca Bks.

Robertson, Jack M., jt. auth. see McKennon, Kelly.

Robertson, Jack S. Twentieth Century Artists on Art: An Index to Artists' Writings, Statements, & Interviews. 2nd ed. LC 95-33700. 1996. 95.00 (*0-8161-9059-3*, G K Hall Lrg Type) Mac Lib Ref.

Robertson, Jacqueline L. Pesticide Bioassays with Arthropods. 144p. 1991. lib. bdg. 129.00 (*0-8493-6463-9*, QH545) CRC Pr.

Robertson, James. Any Fool Can Be a Dairy Farmer. 176p. 1989. reprint ed. pap. 12.95 (*0-85236-195-5*, Pub. by Farming Pr) Diamond Farm Bk.

— Any Fool Can Be a Pig Farmer. 156p. 1989. reprint ed. pap. 12.95 (*0-85236-196-3*, Pub. by Farming Pr) Diamond Farm Bk.

— Beyond the Dependency Culture: People, Power & Responsibility in the 21st Century. LC 97-53213.

R

(Praeger Studies on the 21st Century). 240p. 1998. 59.95 (*0-275-96315-2*, Praeger Pubs); pap. 19.95 (*0-275-96316-0*, Praeger Pubs) Greenwood.

— Future Wealth: A New Economics for the 21st Century. LC 90-831. (TOES Bks.). 190p. (Orig.). 1990. pap. 14.50 (*0-942850-25-4*) Bootstrap Pr.

— The Hidden Cinema: British Film Censorship in Action. (Cinema & Society Ser.). 200p. (C). 1993. pap. 24.99 (*0-415-09034-2*, B0329) Routledge.

***Robertson, James.** New Economics of Sustainable Development. 2000. pap. 22.50 (*0-7494-3093-1*) Kogan Page Ltd.

Robertson, James. Transforming Economic Life: A Millennial Challenge. (Schumacher Briefings Ser.: No. 1). 80p. 1999. pap. 10.95 (*1-870098-72-2*, Pub. by Green Bks) Chelsea Green Pub.

Robertson, James, ed. Hospitals & Children. 160p. 1963. 27.50 (*0-8236-2360-2*) Intl Univs Pr.

Robertson, James & Robertson, Carolyn. The Small Towns Book: Show Me the Way to Go Home. LC 76-23813. 208p. reprint ed. pap. 64.50 (*0-608-14420-7*, 205172200002) Bks Demand.

Robertson, James & Robertson, Suzanne. Complete Systems Analysis: The Workbook, the Textbook, the Answers. (Illus.). 624p. 1998. reprint ed. pap. 57.95 (*0-932633-50-1*) Dorset Hse Pub Co.

Robertson, James, jt. compiled by see Cran, Angela.

***Robertson, James A.** A Bibliography of the Philippine Islands: Printed & Manuscript. 437p. 1998. reprint ed. 70.00 (*1-57898-095-X*) Martino Pubng.

Robertson, James A., ed. Louisiana under the Rule of Spain, France & the United States, 1785-1807, 2 vols, Set. LC 72-102254. (Select Bibliographies Reprint Ser.). 1977. 68.95 (*0-8369-5139-5*) Ayer.

Robertson, James A., tr. see Gentlemen of Elvias.

Robertson, James B., jt. auth. see Van Soest, Peter J.

Robertson, James B., jt. ed. see Johnston, William R.

Robertson, James B., tr. see Schlegel, Friedrich von.

Robertson, James Burton, tr. see Mohler, Johann A.

Robertson, James C. The Casablanca Man: The Career of Michael Curtiz. LC 92-33281. (Illus.). 208p. (C). (gr. 13). 1993. 65.00 (*0-415-06804-5*, B0722) Routledge.

— The Casablanca Man: The Cinema of Michael Curtiz. (Illus.). 208p. (C). (gr. 13). 1994. pap. 24.99 (*0-415-11577-9*, B4536) Routledge.

— The Hidden Cinema: British Film Censorship in Action, 1913-1972. (Cinema & Society Ser.). 208p. 1989. 58.00 (*0-415-03291-1*) Routledge.

— Introduction to Fire Prevention. 4th ed. LC 94-205423. 320p. 1995. 70.00 (*0-02-402241-1*, Macmillan Coll) P-H.

***Robertson, James C.** Introduction to Fire Prevention. 5th ed. LC 99-47209. 272p. 1999. 73.00 (*0-13-013916-5*) P-H.

Robertson, James C. & Sheppard, J. B., eds. Materials for the History of Thomas Becket, 7 vols. (Rolls Ser.: No. 67). 1969. reprint ed. 490.00 (*0-8115-1135-9*) Periodicals Srv.

Robertson, James C., jt. auth. see Jacob, Naomi.

Robertson, James C., ed. see Bargrave, John.

Robertson, James D. A Beer Drinkers Guide to Australia & New Zealand. (Illus.). 88p. 1994. pap. 9.95 (*0-9635332-6-6*) Bosak Pub.

— A Beer Drinkers Guide to Southern Germany. (Illus.). 96p. 1994. per. 9.95 (*0-9635332-3-1*) Bosak Pub.

— The Beer Log. (Illus.). 408p. 1992. ring bd. 37.50 (*0-9635332-0-7*) Bosak Pub.

— The Beer Log. (Illus.). 384p. 1994. per. 39.75 (*0-9635332-5-8*) Bosak Pub.

— The Beer Log, 1993 Update. (Illus.). 182p. 1993. ring bd. 16.00 (*0-9635332-1-5*) Bosak Pub.

— The Beer Log, 1994 Update. (Illus.). 224p. 1995. ring bd. 16.00 (*0-9635332-2-3*) Bosak Pub.

— The Beer Log, 1995 Update. (Illus.). 192p. 1995. ring bd. 16.00 (*0-9635332-7-4*) Bosak Pub.

— The Beer-Tasters Log: A World Guide to More Than 6000 Beers. LC 96-15284. (Illus.). 624p. (Orig.). 1996. pap. 24.95 (*0-88266-939-7*) Storey Bks.

Robertson, James E. The Birth of Humanity Being. LC 74-79179. 114p. 1974. 5.90 (*0-9600756-1-5*); pap. 3.90 (*0-9600756-2-3*) J E Robertson.

Robertson, James I., Jr. Civil War! America Becomes One Nation. LC 91-19177. (Illus.). 192p. (J). (gr. 4-7). 1992. lib. bdg. 16.99 (*0-394-92996-9*, Pub. by Knopf Bks Yng Read) Random.

— Civil War Sites in Virginia: A Tour Guide. LC 81-7426. (Illus.). 108p. 1982. pap. 7.95 (*0-8139-0907-4*) U Pr of Va.

— Civil War Virginia: Battleground for a Nation. (Illus.). 197p. (C). 1993. pap. 11.95 (*0-8139-1457-4*) U Pr of Va.

Robertson, James I. Common Soldier of the Civil War. (Civil-Structural Inspection Ser.). 52p. 1994. pap. 4.95 (*0-915992-65-5*) Eastern National.

— Eighteenth Virginia Infantry. (Virginia Regimental Histories Ser.). (Illus.). 96p. 1984. 19.95 (*0-930919-07-6*) H E Howard.

— Fourth Virginia Infantry. (Virginia Regimental Histories Ser.). (Illus.). 87p. 1982. 19.95 (*0-930919-00-9*) H E Howard.

Robertson, James I., Jr. Jackson & Lee: Legends in Grey. LC 95-34556. (Illus.). 180p. 1995. 34.95 (*1-55853-333-8*) Rutledge Hill Pr.

— Soldiers Blue & Gray. LC 98-220508. (Studies in American Military History). (Illus.). 288p. 1998. reprint ed. pap. 14.95 (*1-57003-299-8*) U of SC Pr.

***Robertson, James I.** Standing Like a Stone Wall: The Life of General Thomas J. Jackson. LC 00-36253. (Illus.). 2001. write for info. (*0-689-82419-X*) Atheneum Yung Read.

Robertson, James I., Jr. The Stonewall Brigade. LC 63-9648. (Illus.). xiii, 272p. 1977. pap. 16.95 (*0-8071-0396-9*) La State U Pr.

Robertson, James I. Stonewall Jackson: The Man, the Soldier, the Legend. LC 96-17042. (Illus.). 976p. 1997. 40.00 (*0-02-864685-1*) Mac Lib Ref.

***Robertson, James I., Jr.** Stonewall Jackson: The Man, the Soldier, the Legend. (Illus.). 950p. (C). 2000. reprint ed. text 40.00 (*0-7881-9226-4*) DIANE Pub.

Robertson, James I., Jr., ed. Civil War Letters of General Robert McAllister. LC 98-24587. (Illus.). 664p. 1998. pap. 24.95 (*0-8071-2325-0*) La State U Pr.

— The Medical & Surgical History of the Civil War, 15 vols., Set. Orig. Title: The Medical & Surgical History of the War of the Rebellion. (Illus.). 1992. reprint ed. 1400.00 (*0-916107-86-8*) Broadfoot.

— The Medical & Surgical History of the Civil War Index, 3 vols., Set. 1400p. 1992. 400.00 (*0-916107-95-7*) Broadfoot.

— Proceedings of the Advisory Council of the State of Virginia, April 21-June 19, 1861. LC 76-27470. (Illus.). xxiv, 182p. 1977. 15.00 (*0-88490-007-X*) Library of VA.

Robertson, James I., jt. auth. see Kunstler, Mort.

Robertson, James I., Jr., jt. auth. see Taylor, Walter H.

Robertson, James J., Jr. Civil War. 1996. pap. 15.95 (*0-679-88111-5*) Random.

Robertson, James L. In Scottish Fields. LC 73-144469. reprint ed. 39.50 (*0-404-08525-3*) AMS Pr.

Robertson, James R. A Kentuckian at the Court of the Tsars. (Illus.). 286p. 1989. reprint ed. 12.50 (*0-935680-23-3*) Kentucke Imprints.

— Petitions of the Early Inhabitants of Kentucky to the General Assembly of Virginia, 1769 to 1792. LC 74-146415. (First American Frontier Ser.). 1971. reprint ed. 31.98 (*0-405-02879-2*) Ayer.

— Petitions of the Early Inhabitants of Kentucky to the General Assembly of Virginia, 1769 to 1792. 292p. 1981. reprint ed. 25.00 (*0-89308-206-6*) Southern Hist Pr.

Robertson, James Rood. Petitions of the Early Inhabitants of Kentucky to the General Assembly of Virginia, 1769 to 1792. LC 97-77490. 261p. 1998. reprint ed. 25.00 (*0-8063-1553-9*) Genealog Pub.

Robertson, James S., ed. Compartmental Distribution of Radiotracers. 208p. 1983. 118.00 (*0-8493-6010-2*, R895, CRC Reprint) Franklin.

Robertson, James T. & Nowak, Thaddeus S., Jr., eds. Frontiers in Cerebrovascular Disease: Mechanisms, Diagnosis, & Treatment. LC 97-26376. (American Heart Association Monograph Ser.). (Illus.). 384p. 1997. 98.00 (*0-87993-674-6*) Futura Pub.

Robertson, James W., jt. auth. see Alhashim, Dhia D.

Robertson, Jamie, jt. auth. see Kline, David.

Robertson, Jane L. & Hughes, Deborah L. Metaphysical Primer: A Guide to Understanding Metaphysics. 2nd rev. ed. (Illus.). 138p. 1996. pap. 12.95 (*1-879203-02-2*) MetaGnosis.

Robertson, Janet. Betsy Cowles Partridge: Mountaineer. LC 97-48725. (Illus.). 232p. 1998. 29.95 (*0-87081-480-X*) Univ Pr Colo.

— Colorado Traveler: Day Hikes on the Colorado Trail. (American Traveler Ser.: Vol. 12). (Illus.). 48p. 1991. pap. 4.95 (*1-55838-116-3*) R H Pub.

— The Magnificent Mountain Women: Adventures in the Colorado Rockies. LC 89-14717. (Illus.). xxiii, 274p. 1990. pap. 12.00 (*0-8032-8933-2*, Bison Books) U of Nebr Pr.

— Oscar's Spots. LC 93-22199. (Illus.). 32p. (J). (ps-2). 1996. pap. 3.95 (*0-8167-3134-9*, Troll Medallion) Troll Communs.

Robertson, Jean. Matter Mind Spirit: Twelve Contemporary Indiana Women Artists. LC 98-48198. (Distributed for the Indiana Committee, National Museum of Women in the Arts Ser.). (Illus.). 56p. 1999. pap. 19.95 (*0-253-21322-3*); text. write for info. (*0-253-33556-6*) Ind U Pr.

— Modern Sculpture. Roberts, Norma J., ed. LC 86-73072. (Illus.). 32p. 1986. pap. 3.50 (*0-918881-17-X*) Columbus Mus Art.

Robertson, Jeanette. Painting Greeting Cards for Fun & Profit. LC 99-19203. (Illus.). 128p. 1999. pap. 23.99 (*0-89134-907-3*, 31444, North Lght Bks) F & W Pubns Inc.

Robertson, Jeanie. Thoughts in Rhyme. 128p. (Orig.). 1992. pap. 9.95 (*0-9632312-0-0*) Thoughts Rhyme.

Robertson, Jeanne. Don't Let the Funny Stuff Get Away. LC 98-67045. 156p. 1998. per. 15.00 (*0-927577-03-8*) Rich Pub Co.

— Humor: The Magic of Genie: Seven Potions for Developing a Sense of Humor. (Illus.). 232p. 1990. 14.95 (*0-9607256-9-5*) Rich Pub Co.

— Mayberry Humor Across the U. S. A. 349p. 1995. 19.95 (*0-927577-02-X*) Rich Pub Co.

Robertson, Jeffrey D. & Keavy, William T. Plastic Surgery Malpractice & Damages, 1. (Medico-Legal Library Ser.). 512p. 1993. boxed set 145.00 (*0-471-60831-9*) Wiley.

Robertson, Jennifer. Native & Newcomer: Making & Remaking a Japanese City. (Illus.). 252p. (C). 1994. pap. 16.95 (*0-520-08655-4*, Pub. by U CA Pr) Cal Prin Full Svc.

Robertson, Jennifer E. Takarazuka: Sexual Politics & Popular Culture in Modern Japan. LC 97-38671. 320p. 1998. 40.00 (*0-520-21150-2*, Pub. by U CA Pr); pap. 15.95 (*0-520-21151-0*, Pub. by U CA Pr) Cal Prin Full Svc.

Robertson, Jenny. Bible Storybook. Orig. Title: Ladybird Bible Storybook. (Illus.). 377p. 1993. 15.99 (*0-310-44430-6*) Zondervan.

— Enciclopedia de Historias Biblicas. LaValle, Maria T., tr.Tr. of Encyclopedia of Bible Stories. (SPA., Illus.). 272p. (J). (gr. 3-5). 1984. 17.99 (*0-311-03671-6*) Casa Bautista.

Robertson, Jenny & Parry, Alan. Jesus the Child. LC 80-22222. (Ladybird Bible Bks.). 1980. write for info. (*0-310-42820-3*) Zondervan.

Robertson, Jo, ed. see Benzel, David.

Robertson, Jo, ed. see Kjellander, Mike.

Robertson, Jo, ed. see Klarich, Tony.

Robertson, Jo, ed. see McMillan, Kent.

Robertson, Jo, ed. see Waterski Magazine Staff.

***Robertson, Joan.** My Life in Verse & Rhyme. 129p. 2000. 19.95 (*0-7541-1148-2*, Pub. by Minerva Pr) Unity Dist.

Robertson, Joan, jt. auth. see Graeme, E.

Robertson, Joan F., jt. ed. see Bengtson, Vern L.

Robertson, Joanne. The Harvest Queen. (Northern Lights Books for Children Ser.). (Illus.). 32p. (J). (gr. k-4). 1997. text 15.95 (*0-88995-134-9*, Pub. by Red Deer) Genl Dist Srvs.

Robertson, Joe E. On Kilroy's Trail: A World of Travel. LC 99-206945. (Illus.). 344p. 1998. pap. 22.95 (*0-89745-226-7*) Sunflower U Pr.

Robertson, Joel, jt. auth. see Opalewski, Dave.

Robertson, Joel C. Ayudese Usted Mismo.Tr. of Help Yourself. (SPA.). 375p. 1997. 15.99 (*0-88113-148-2*, B001-1482) Caribe Betania.

Robertson, Joel C. & Monte, Tom. Natural Prozac: Leaning to Release Your Body's Own Anti-Depressants. LC 96-33513. 240p. 1998. pap. 13.00 (*0-06-251354-0*, Pub. by Harper SF) HarpC.

Robertson, John. Aerosmith: The Complete Guide. pap. 8.95 (*0-7119-5598-0*, OP47830) Omnibus NY.

— Art & Music of John Lennon. 1991. 17.95 (*1-55972-076-X*, Birch Ln Pr) Carol Pub Group.

— Art & Music of John Lennon. 232p. 1993. pap. 12.95 (*0-8065-1438-8*, Citadel Pr) Carol Pub Group.

— Beach Boys. pap. 8.95 (*0-7119-5595-6*, OP 47827) Omnibus NY.

— The Beatles. (Complete Guides to the Music Of...Ser.). (Illus.). 138p. (Orig.). pap. 8.95 (*0-7119-3548-3*, OP 47368, Pub. by Omnibus Press) Omnibus NY.

— Block the Chesapeake. LC 97-92834. 136p. 1997. pap. 11.95 (*1-57502-676-7*, PO1899) Morris Pubng.

— Elvis Presley. (Complete Guides to the Music Of...Ser.). (Illus.). 118p. (Orig.). pap. 8.95 (*0-7119-3549-1*, OP 47376, Pub. by Omnibus Press) Omnibus NY.

— Jimi Hendrix. (Complete Guides to the Music Of...Ser.). (Illus.). 130p. (Orig.). 1995. pap. 8.95 (*0-7119-4304-4*, OP 47738, Pub. by Omnibus Press) Omnibus NY.

Robertson, John. John Lennon. (Illus.). 162p. (Orig.). pap. 8.95 (*0-7119-5599-9*, OP47831) Omnibus NY.

Robertson, John. John Lennon: A Day by Day Journey Through His Life in Words & Pictures. (Illus.). 160p. (Orig.). (C). pap. 19.95 (*0-7119-4981-6*, OP 47775) Omnibus NY.

— Neil Young: The Visual Documentary. LC 95-179908. (Illus.). 160p. pap. 21.95 (*0-7119-3816-4*, OP 47568) Omnibus NY.

— Paul Simon. (Illus.). 136p. (Orig.). pap. 8.95 (*0-7119-5597-2*, OP47829) Omnibus NY.

***Robertson, John.** A Pictorial History of Chevrolet, 1955-1957. (Illus.). 288p. 1999. 24.95 (*1-880524-35-X*, 128442AP) Cars & Parts.

Robertson, John. Van Morrison. (Illus.). 146p. (Orig.). pap. 8.95 (*0-7119-5600-6*, OP47832) Omnibus NY.

— The Velvet Underground. (Illus.). 1997. pap. 8.95 (*0-7119-5596-4*, OP 47828) Omnibus NY.

Robertson, John, ed. A Union for Empire: Political Thought & the British Union of 1707. 388p. (C). 1995. text 69.95 (*0-521-43113-1*) Cambridge U Pr.

Robertson, John & McCarthy, John. Australian War Strategy, 1939-1949: A Documentary History. 612p. 1985. text 49.95 (*0-7022-1924-X*, Pub. by Univ. Queensland Pr) Intl Spec Bk.

Robertson, John, ed. see Fletcher, Andrew.

Robertson, John, jt. ed. see Miller, Patricia C.

Robertson, John, jt. ed. see Rutherford, Brett.

Robertson, John, tr. see Haich, Elisabeth.

Robertson, John A. Children of Choice: Freedom & the New Reproductive Technologies. LC 93-35880. 296p. 1994. text 42.50 (*0-691-03353-6*, Pub. by Princeton U Pr); pap. text 16.95 (*0-691-03665-9*, Pub. by Princeton U Pr) Cal Prin Full Svc.

— Children of Choice: Freedom & the New Reproductive Technologies. (C). 1996. pap. 16.95 (*0-614-12622-3*) Princeton U Pr.

Robertson, John C., Jr. The Loss & Recovery of Transcendence: The Will to Power & the Light of Heaven. LC 95-5874. (Princeton Theological Monographs: Vol. 39). 1995. 14.00 (*1-55635-027-9*) Pickwick.

Robertson, John C. Mixed Company. LC 77-107735. (Essay Index Reprint Ser.). 1977. 20.95 (*0-8369-1533-X*) Ayer.

Robertson, John D. Pictorial History of Chevrolet, 1940-1954. (Illus.). 256p. 1998. boxed set 24.95 (*1-880524-29-5*) Cars & Parts.

— A Pictorial History of Chevrolet, 1929-1939, Vol. 1. (Illus.). 270p. 1998. boxed set 24.95 (*1-880524-25-2*) Cars & Parts.

Robertson, John G. The Babe Chases 60: That Fabulous 1927 Season, Home Run by Home Run. (Illus.). 188p. 1998. pap. 24.50 (*0-7864-0503-1*) McFarland & Co.

— Baseball's Greatest Controversies: Rhubarbs, Hoaxes, Blown Calls, Ruthian Myths, Managers' Miscues & Front-Office Flops. LC 94-48265. 206p. 1995. lib. bdg. 26.50 (*0-7864-0107-9*) McFarland & Co.

— Essays & Addresses on Literature. LC 68-26471. (Essay Index Reprint Ser.). 1977. reprint ed. 20.95 (*0-8369-0828-7*) Ayer.

— Goethe. LC 74-16295. (Studies in Goethe: No. 61). 1974. lib. bdg. 75.00 (*0-8383-2036-8*) M S G Haskell Hse.

— Goethe & the Twentieth Century. LC 72-3678. (Studies in German Literature: No. 13). 1972. reprint ed. lib. bdg. 59.00 (*0-8383-1581-X*) M S G Haskell Hse.

— The Life & Work of Goethe, 1749-1832. LC 79-179536. (Select Bibliographies Reprint Ser.). 1977. reprint ed. 23.95 (*0-8369-6665-1*) Ayer.

— The Life & Work of Goethe, 1749-1832. LC 72-8646. (Studies in German Literature: No. 13). 1973. reprint ed. lib. bdg. 75.00 (*0-8383-1671-9*) M S G Haskell Hse.

Robertson, John G., ed. Lessing's Dramatic Theory. LC 63-14713. (Illus.). 1972. 36.95 (*0-405-08894-9*) Ayer.

Robertson, John H. William Ernest Henley. 1972. 59.95 (*0-8490-1303-8*) Gordon Pr.

Robertson, John L., jt. auth. see Rooney, James R.

Robertson, John M. Baconian Heresy. LC 74-109660. (Select Bibliographies Reprint Ser.). 1977. 35.95 (*0-8369-5269-3*) Ayer.

— The Baconian Heresy, a Confutation. (BCL1-PR English Literature Ser.). 612p. 1992. reprint ed. lib. bdg. 149.00 (*0-7812-7290-4*) Rprt Serv.

— Croce As Shakespearean Critic. (Studies in Shakespeare: No. 24). 1978. lib. bdg. 49.00 (*0-8383-1810-X*) M S G Haskell Hse.

— Did Shakespeare Write "Titus Andronicus"? LC 77-39875. reprint ed. 31.50 (*0-404-05361-0*) AMS Pr.

— The Genuine in Shakespeare. LC 72-3656. (Studies in Shakespeare: No. 24). 1972. reprint ed. lib. bdg. 75.00 (*0-8383-1568-2*) M S G Haskell Hse.

— Introduction to the Study of the Shakespeare Canon. LC 70-109659. (Select Bibliographies Reprint Ser.). 1977. 34.95 (*0-8369-5268-5*) Ayer.

— Modern Humanists Reconsidered. LC 72-3443. (English Literature Ser.: No. 33). 1972. reprint ed. lib. bdg. 75.00 (*0-8383-1556-9*) M S G Haskell Hse.

— Montaigne & Shakespeare & Other Essays on Cognate Questions. LC 68-24914. (Studies in Comparative Literature: No. 35). 1969. reprint ed. lib. bdg. 75.00 (*0-8383-0234-3*) M S G Haskell Hse.

— Montaigne & Shakespeare & Other Essays on Cognate Questions. (BCL1-PR English Literature Ser.). 358p. 1992. reprint ed. lib. bdg. 89.00 (*0-7812-7291-2*) Rprt Serv.

— The Problems of the Shakespeare Sonnets. LC 72-8700. (Studies in Shakespeare: No. 24). 1973. reprint ed. lib. bdg. 75.00 (*0-8383-1676-X*) M S G Haskell Hse.

— Shakespeare & Chapman: A Thesis of Chapman's Authorship of a Lover's Complaint, & His Origination of Timon of Athens. (BCL1-PR English Literature Ser.). 302p. 1992. reprint ed. lib. bdg. 89.00 (*0-7812-7293-9*) Rprt Serv.

— A Short History of Freethought, Ancient & Modern. LC 74-169215. (Atheist Viewpoint Ser.). 464p. 1972. reprint ed. 29.95 (*0-405-03804-6*) Ayer.

Robertson, John P. Letters on South America Comprising Travels on the Banks of the Parana & the Rio De la Plata, 3 vols., Set. LC 70-128428. reprint ed. 145.00 (*0-404-05380-7*) AMS Pr.

Robertson, John P. & Robertson, W. P. Letters on Paraguay Comprising an Account of a Four Years' Residence in That Republic, under the Government of the Dictator Francia, 3 vols. 2nd ed. LC 74-128429. reprint ed. 155.00 (*0-404-05390-4*) AMS Pr.

Robertson, John S. Engineering Math with Mathematica. LC 94-77980. 272p. (C). 1994. pap. 24.06 (*0-07-053171-4*) McGraw.

— Engineering Mathematics with Maple. LC 95-11318. (International Series in Pure & Applied Mathematics). (Illus.). 278p. (C). 1995. pap. 22.81 (*0-07-053120-X*) McGraw.

— Engineering Mathematics with Maple. 1996. pap. text. write for info. (*0-07-053210-9*) McGraw.

— The History of Tense - Aspect - Mood - Voice in the Mayan Verbal Complex. 261p. (C). 1992. text 35.00 (*0-292-72075-0*) U of Tex Pr.

Robertson, John W. Edgar Allan Poe. LC 71-117583. (Studies in Poe: No. 23). 1970. reprint ed. lib. bdg. 75.00 (*0-8383-1016-8*) M S G Haskell Hse.

Robertson, Jon. The Birthplace. (Orig.). 1995. pap. 11.95 (*0-9647402-0-6*) Inkhorn VA.

— The Golden Thread of Oneness: A Journey Inward to the Universal Consciousness. LC 97-16705. (ARE Membership Ser.). 118p. 1998. pap. 7.95 (*0-87604-392-9*) ARE Pr.

Robertson, Jon, jt. auth. see Robertson, Robin.

Robertson, Jon, ed. see Frejer, B. Ernest.

Robertson, Jon, ed. see Gershom, Yonassan.

Robertson, Jon, ed. see Howard, Jane M.

Robertson, Jon, ed. see Lane, Barbara.

Robertson, Jon, ed. see McClure, Michael R.

Robertson, Jon H. & Clark, W. Craig, eds. Lasers in Neurosurgery. (Foundations in Neurological Surgery Ser.). (C). 1988. text 150.00 (*0-89838-966-6*) Kluwer Academic.

Robertson, Joseph, ed. Concilia Scotiae, 2 vols. LC 77-39875. (Bannatyne Club, Edinburgh. Publications: No. 113). reprint ed. 65.00 (*0-404-52866-X*) AMS Pr.

— Inuentaires de la Royne Descosse Douairiere de France. LC 78-172847. (Bannatyne Club, Edinburgh. Publications: No. 111). reprint ed. 47.50 (*0-404-52865-1*) AMS Pr.

— Liber Collegii Nostre Domine: Registrum Ecclesie B. V. Marie et S. Anne Infra Muros Civitatis Glasguensis. LC 71-168165. (Maitland Club, Glasgow. Publications: No. 65). reprint ed. 40.00 (*0-404-53073-7*) AMS Pr.

Robertson, Joseph, jt. ed. see Innes, Cosmos.

Robertson, Joseph F. The Magic of Film Editing. (Illus.). 352p. (Orig.). 1984. pap. 16.50 (*0-8306-1267-X*, 1267P) McGraw-Hill Prof.

Robertson, Josephine. Prayers for the Later Years. LC 74-187591. 60 p. 1972. write for info. (*0-687-33628-7*) Abingdon.

Robertson, Joy. Sentenced to Death. 120p. 1998. pap. 10.00 (*0-9667562-0-7*) Magnolia Pubg.

An Asterisk (*) at the beginning of an entry indicates that the title is appearing for the first time.

— Terror in the Streets: A Drug War. Valentino, Michael, ed. 1999. 19.95 (*0-9667562-1-5*) Magnolia Pubg.

*__Robertson, Judith P., ed.__ Teaching for a Tolerant World, Grades K-6: Essays & Resources. LC 99-16881. 475p. 1999. pap. 29.95 (*0-8141-5183-3*, 51833) NCTE.

Robertson, Judy. No Regrets: How I Found My Way Out of Mormonism. LC 97-218415. 224p. (Orig.). 1997. pap. 10.99 (*0-89367-222-X*) Light & Life Comm.

Robertson, Juliet T. Cooking with Jazz New Orleans Style. (Illus.). viii, 48p. 1998. 23.98 incl. audio compact disk (*0-9664497-0-3*) Ayo Inc.

Robertson, K. G. 1992: The Security Implications. (C). 1990. 35.00 (*0-907967-11-6*, Pub. by Inst Euro Def & Strat) St Mut.

*__Robertson, K. G.__ War, Resistance & Intelligence: Collected Essays in Honour of MRD Foot. 2000. 39.95 (*0-85052-689-2*, Pub. by Pen & Sword) Combined Pub.

Robertson, Karen. Raising Kids Right. LC 97-52250. 112p. (Orig.). 1998. pap. 8.99 (*0-8280-1295-4*) Review & Herald.

Robertson, Karen, jt. ed. see Frye, Susan.

Robertson, Karen, jt. ed. see Levin, Carole.

Robertson, Karen A. Get Ready: A Step-by-Step Handbook for Preparedness & Personal Survival in the 1990's. 175p. 1989. pap. 10.00 (*0-9623177-1-3*) Paragon Dallas.

Robertson, Kayo. Signs along the River: Learning to Read the Natural Landscape. 64p. 1986. pap. 6.95 (*0-911797-22-X*) Roberts Rinehart.

Robertson, Keith. Henry Reed, Inc. (Illus.). 240p. (J). (gr. 4-6). 1989. pap. 4.99 (*0-14-034144-7*, PuffinBks) Peng Put Young Read.

— Henry Reed, Inc. (J). 1989. 10.09 (*0-606-04244-X*, Pub. by Turtleback) Demco.

Robertson, Keith. Henry Reed, Inc. abr. ed. (J). (gr. 4-7). pap. 15.95 incl. audio (*0-670-36801-6*) Live Oak Media.

— Henry Reed, Inc., Set. abr. ed. (J). (gr. 4-7). 24.95 incl. audio (*0-670-36800-8*) Live Oak Media.

Robertson, Keith. Henry Reed's Baby-Sitting Service. (Illus.). 208p. (J). (gr. 4-6). 1989. pap. 4.99 (*0-14-034146-3*, PuffinBks) Peng Put Young Read.

Robertson, Keith. Henry Reed's Baby-Sitting Service. (J). 1989. 10.09 (*0-606-04245-8*, Pub. by Turtleback) Demco.

Robertson, Kell. Bear Crossing. Jacobsen, Steven, ed. & illus. by. 33p. 1990. pap. text 4.00 (*0-9625349-0-0*) Guerilla Poetics.

Robertson, Kell, et al. Five Card Stud. 1978. pap. 3.00 (*0-916918-09-2*) Duck Down.

*__Robertson, Ken.__ Work Transformation: Planning & Implementing the New Workplace. LC 99-207057. (Illus.). 306p. 1998. pap. 19.95 (*0-9664286-0-9*) HNB Pubg.

Robertson, Ken, jt. auth. see Aguilar, Dave.

Robertson, Kent A. Pedestrian Malls & Skywalks: Traffic Separation Strategies in American Downtown. LC 94-8723. 1994. 61.95 (*1-85628-687-8*, Pub. by Avebry) Ashgate Pub Co.

Robertson, Kevin. Leader: The Full Story. (Illus.). 288p. 1996. 39.95 (*0-7509-1003-8*, Pub. by Sutton Pub Ltd) Intl Pubs Mktg.

— Steam Around Eastleigh. LC 98-134111. (Illus.). 160p. 1998. pap. 19.95 (*0-7509-1650-8*, Pub. by Sutton Pub Ltd) Intl Pubs Mktg.

— Steam Around Reading. LC 99-187400. (Sutton's Photographic History of Railways Ser.). (Illus.). 128p. 1998. pap. 19.95 (*0-7509-1863-2*, Pub. by Sutton Pub Ltd) Intl Pubs Mktg.

Robertson, Kim. Arranging for Folk Harp. 40p. 1983. pap. 9.95 (*0-7866-0298-8*, 95346) Mel Bay.

— Kim Robertson - Celtic Harp Solos. 88p. 1995. pap. 14.95 (*0-7866-0297-X*, 95345) Mel Bay.

— Kim Robertson - Treasures of the Celtic Harp. 64p. 1999. pap. 12.95 (*0-7866-4037-5*, 97226); pap. 27.95 incl. audio compact disk (*0-7866-4039-1*, 97226CDP) Mel Bay.

— Tender Shepherd. 56p. 1995. pap. 9.95 (*0-7866-0901-X*, 94887); pap. 19.95 incl. audio (*0-7866-0902-8*, 94887P); pap. 24.95 incl. audio compact disk (*0-7866-0903-6*, 94887CDP) Mel Bay.

Robertson, Kirk. Ar-Ti-Facts. Gordon, Coco, ed. 20p. (Orig.). 1985. pap. 12.00 (*0-931956-17-X*) Water Mark.

— CETA & the Arts in Santa Barbara. (Illus.). 1978. pap. 3.00 (*0-916918-10-6*) Duck Down.

— Drinking Beer at Twenty-Two Below. 1976. 2.50 (*0-917554-04-3*) Maelstrom.

— Driving to Vegas: New & Selected Poems 1969-87. (Sun Lizard, Desert Southwest Bk.). (Illus.). 296p. (Orig.). 1989. pap. 14.95 (*0-933313-10-1*) SUN Gemini Pr.

— Just Past Labor Day: Selected & New Poems, 1969-1996. (Western Literature Ser.). 336p. 1996. pap. 16.00 (*0-87417-284-5*) U of Nev Pr.

— Music. (Illus.). 56p. 1995. pap. 10.00 (*0-912449-51-9*) Floating Island.

— Origins, Initiations. (Illus.). 1980. 100.00 (*0-918824-19-2*) Turkey Pr.

— Reasons & Methods: Poems by Kirk Robertson, with Constellations, Typoglifs by Karl Kempton. (Illus.). 20p. (Orig.). (C). 1981. pap. 2.50 (*0-916918-15-7*) Duck Down.

— Two Weeks Off. (Illus.). 48p. (Orig.). 1984. pap. 5.00 (*0-912449-11-X*) Floating Island.

Robertson, Kirk, ed. New Works: An Anthology of Ten Contemporary Poets. LC 81-65314. (Windriver Ser.). (Illus.). (Orig.). (C). 1981. pap. 5.95 (*0-916918-13-0*) Duck Down.

Robertson, Kirk & Barker, David. High Fallon, Southern Comfort. 1980. 3.00 (*0-917554-11-6*) Maelstrom.

Robertson, Kirk, jt. auth. see De Serpa, Valeria.

Robertson, Kirk, jt. auth. see Weidman, Phil.

Robertson, Kirk, ed. see Allen, Jo Harvey.

Robertson, Kirk, ed. see Bennett, John.

Robertson, Kirk, ed. see Fox, William L.

Robertson, Kirk, ed. see Haslam, Gerald.

Robertson, Kirk, ed. see Hogan, Michael.

Robertson, Kirk, ed. see Krapt, Norbert.

Robertson, Kirk, ed. see Masarik, Al.

Robertson, Kirk, ed. see Matte, Robert, Jr.

Robertson, Kirk, ed. see Northsun, Nila & Sagel, Jim.

Robertson, Kirk, ed. see Short, Gary.

Robertson, Kirk, ed. see Wagner, D. R.

Robertson, L. R., ed. see Minns, Michael L.

Robertson, Lamar, jt. auth. see Eisen, Ann.

Robertson, Lamar, jt. auth. see Eisen, Ann M.

Robertson, Laura F. Corpus of Cypriote Antiquities: The Brock University Collection of Cypriote Antiquities. (Studies in Mediterranean Archaeology: Vol. XX: 11). (Illus.). 77p. (Orig.). 1986. pap. 49.50 (*91-85058-32-7*, Pub. by P Astroms) Coronet Bks.

Robertson, Laura P. Robertson, Purcell, & Related Families. (Illus.). 242p. 1993. reprint ed. pap. 38.00 (*0-8328-3395-9*); reprint ed. lib. bdg. 48.00 (*0-8328-3394-0*) Higginson Bk Co.

Robertson, Laurel. The Laurel's Kitchen Bread Book. 1994. 29.50 (*0-8446-6748-X*) Peter Smith.

— The Laurel's Kitchen Bread Book. 448p. 1985. pap. 21.95 (*0-394-72434-8*) Random.

— Laurel's Kitchen Caring: Whole-Food Recipes for Everyday Home Caregiving. LC 97-22618. (Illus.). 160p. (Orig.). 1997. pap. 12.95 (*0-89815-951-2*) Ten Speed Pr.

— Number Power: A Cooperative Approach to Mathematics & Social Development. (J). (gr. 2). 1993. pap. text 21.95 (*0-201-45520-X*) Addison-Wesley.

— Number Power: A Cooperative Approach to Mathematics & Social Development. (J). (gr. 3). 1993. pap. text 21.95 (*0-201-45522-6*) Addison-Wesley.

— Number Power: A Cooperative Approach to Mathematics & Social Development. (J). (gr. 4). 1993. pap. text 21.95 (*0-201-45523-4*) Addison-Wesley.

— Number Power: A Cooperative Approach to Mathematics & Social Development. LC 95-127107. 1994. pap. text 21.95 (*0-201-45525-0*) Addison-Wesley.

— Number Power: A Cooperative Approach to Mathematics & Social Development. (J). (gr. 5). 1994. pap. text 21.95 (*0-201-45524-2*) Addison-Wesley.

— Number Power: A Cooperative Approach to Mathematics & Social Development. (J). (gr. k). 1995. teacher ed. 29.00 (*0-201-49320-9*) Addison-Wesley.

— Number Power: A Cooperative Approach to Mathematics & Social Development. (J). (gr. 1). 1996. pap. text 21.95 (*0-201-49323-3*) Addison-Wesley.

Robertson, Laurel, et al. Laurel's Kitchen Recipes. (Illus.). 352p. 1993. pap. 12.95 (*0-89815-537-1*) Ten Speed Pr.

— The New Laurel's Kitchen. 2nd ed. LC 86-14330. (Illus.). 511p. 1986. pap. 19.95 (*0-89815-166-X*) Ten Speed Pr.

*__Robertson, Laurel, et al.__ Number Power: A Cooperative Approach to Mathematics & Social Development: Grade 1. 214p. 1999. pap. 19.95 (*1-57621-197-5*, NPT011) Develop Studies.

— Number Power: A Cooperative Approach to Mathematics & Social Development: Grade 4. 208p. 1999. pap. 19.95 (*1-57621-202-5*, NPT041) Develop Studies.

— Number Power: A Cooperative Approach to Mathematics & Social Development: Grade 5. 212p. 1999. pap. 19.95 (*1-57621-203-3*, NPT051) Develop Studies.

— Number Power: A Cooperative Approach to Mathematics & Social Development: Grade 6. 222p. 1999. pap. 19.95 (*1-57621-204-1*, NPT061) Develop Studies.

— Number Power: A Cooperative Approach to Mathematics & Social Development: Kindergarten. 208p. 1999. pap. 19.95 (*1-57621-196-7*, NPT0K1) Develop Studies.

— Number Power Vol. 1: A Cooperative Approach to Mathematics & Social Development: Grade 2. 192p. 1999. pap. 19.95 (*1-57621-198-3*, NPT021) Develop Studies.

— Number Power Vol. 1: A Cooperative Approach to Mathematics & Social Development: Grade 3. 226p. 1999. pap. 19.95 (*1-57621-200-9*, NPT031) Develop Studies.

— Number Power Vol. 2: A Cooperative Approach to Mathematics & Social Development: Grade 2. 192p. 1999. pap. 19.95 (*1-57621-199-1*, NPT022) Develop Studies.

— Number Power Vol. 2: A Cooperative Approach to Mathematics & Social Development: Grade 3. 196p. 1999. pap. 19.95 (*1-57621-201-7*, NPT032) Develop Studies.

Robertson, Laurie. Fraction Fun Through Cooperative Learning. (Illus.). 94p. 1992. pap. text 20.00 (*1-879097-15-X*) Kagan Cooperative.

Robertson, Laurie & Kagan, Spencer. Co-op Across the Curriculum. (Illus.). 150p. 1992. pap. text 25.00 (*1-879097-12-5*) Kagan Cooperative.

Robertson, Laurie S. The Night Sea Sky. Iddings, Kathleen, ed. (Illus.). 29p. (Orig.). 1988. pap. text 6.00 (*0-931721-09-1*) La Jolla Poets.

Robertson, Lawrence D. Year of the Goddess. 1990. pap. 12.95 (*0-85030-859-3*, Pub. by Aqn Pr) Harper SF.

Robertson, Lawrence R., ed. Russia & Eurasia: Facts & Figures. 468p. 77.00 (*0-87569-185-4*) Academic Intl.

Robertson, Lee. Field Guide to Reality & Other Poems. 133p. (Orig.). 1989. pap. 15.00 (*0-685-26247-2*) Thermopylae.

— Mind Like a Mirror. Lansford, Kim D., ed. LC 92-61739. (Illus.). (Orig.). pap. 15.00 (*0-9623377-8-1*) Thermopylae.

Robertson, Leigh & Rocky Mountain Nature Association Staff. Southern Rocky Mountain Wildflowers: Including Rocky Mountain National Park. (Illus.). 272p. 1998. pap. 15.95 (*1-56044-624-2*) Falcon Pub Inc.

Robertson, Leon S. Injury Epidemiology. (Illus.). 256p. 1992. text 38.50 (*0-19-506956-0*) OUP.

— Injury Epidemiology: Research & Control Strategies. 2nd ed. (Illus.). 288p. 1998. text 48.50 (*0-19-512202-X*) OUP.

Robertson, Leon S., jt. auth. see Mazur, Allan.

Robertson, Leroy J., ed. Hymns from the Crossroads. (Illus.). 51p. 1965. pap. 8.50 (*0-8258-0137-0*, 0-4516) Fischer Inc NY.

Robertson, Lesley A. Simple Program Design. 2nd ed. 208p. (C). 1994. pap. 18.00 (*0-87709-283-4*, BF2834) S-W Pub.

— Simple Program Design: A Step by Step Approach. 2nd ed. (C). 1994. mass mkt., teacher ed. 49.95 (*0-87709-412-8*) Course Tech.

Robertson, Linda. The Complete Kwanzaa Celebration Book. rev. ed. LC 94-92261. (Illus.). 80p. 1994. pap. 9.95 (*0-9639026-8-7*) Creat Acrylic.

Robertson, Linda K. The Power of Knowledge: George Eliot & Education. LC 96-33035. (University of Kansas Humanistic Studies: No. 61). VII, 191p. (C). 1997. text 43.95 (*0-8204-3064-1*) P Lang Pubng.

Robertson, Lisa. Debbie: An Epic. LC 98-138531. 96p. 1997. pap. 11.00 (*0-921586-61-2*, Pub. by New Star Bks) Genl Dist Srvs.

— XEclogue. 2nd rev. ed. 96p. 2000. pap. (*0-921586-72-8*) New Star Bks.

Robertson-Lorant, Laurie. Melville: A Biography. LC 98-4899. (Illus.). 736p. 1998. reprint ed. pap. 22.95 (*1-55849-145-7*) U of Mass Pr.

*__Robertson, Lorenzo C.__ Detached. 206p. 1999. pap. 14.00 (*1-892096-35-8*) Ishai Creat.

— Eclectic Essence. 98p. 1999. pap. 12.00 (*1-892096-36-6*) Ishai Creat.

Robertson, Lori & Wadell, Brian C. Virtual Realty: A Guide to the Internet for Real Estate & Ancillary Professionals. LC 96-47851. (Orig.). 1996. pap. 34.00 (*1-884186-04-1*) Hollis Pub.

Robertson, Lynn, jt. ed. see Mack, Charles R.

Robertson, Lynn C., jt. auth. see Ivry, Richard B.

Robertson, Lynn C., jt. ed. see Knapp, Terry.

Robertson, Lynne N. Productivity in Foodservice. LC 90-46631. (Illus.). 96p. 1991. reprint ed. pap. 30.00 (*0-608-07180-3*, 206740500009) Bks Demand.

— Purchasing for Foodservice. 2nd ed. LC 94-5798. (Illus.). 160p. 1994. pap. text 21.95 (*0-8138-1463-4*) Iowa St U Pr.

Robertson, M. Hal Leonard Banjo Method: Easy Banjo Solos. 360p. 1982. pap. 6.95 (*0-7935-2333-8*, 00699515) H Leonard.

Robertson, M., jt. auth. see Katona, Cornelius L.

Robertson, M. J. & Greenblatt, M., eds. Homelessness: A National Perspective. (Topics in Social Psychiatry Ser.). (Illus.). 376p. (C). 1992. text 55.00 (*0-306-43789-9*, Kluwer Plenum) Kluwer Academic.

Robertson, M. M. & Katona, Cornelius L. Depression & Physical Illness. LC 96-37003. 576p. 1997. 189.95 (*0-471-96148-5*) Wiley.

*__Robertson, M. P.__ The Egg. LC 99-88352. (J). 2001. write for info. (*0-8037-2546-9*) Peng Put Young Read.

Robertson, Mac & Jackson, Don. The Sun upon the Lake Is Low. (ps up). 1997. pap. 10.00 (*0-9649164-2-8*) Lyric Prtnrs.

Robertson, Malcolm. Directory of Listed Derivative Contracts 1996/97. LC 95-53705. 416p. 1996. 395.00 (*0-471-96368-2*) Wiley.

Robertson, Malcolm H. Psychotherapy Education & Training: An Integrative Perspective. LC 95-6412. 181p. 1995. 27.50 (*0-8236-5402-8*) Intl Univs Pr.

Robertson, Malcolm H. & Woody, Robert H. Theories & Methods for Practice of Clinical Psychology. LC 96-25085. 300p. 1997. 45.00 (*0-8236-6518-6*, BN06518) Intl Univs Pr.

Robertson, Malcolm H., jt. auth. see Woody, Robert H.

Robertson, Marc. Cosmopsychology: Engine of Destiny. 98p. 1976. 13.95 (*0-86690-147-7*, R1402-014) Am Fed Astrologers.

— Eighth House. 80p. 1976. 13.00 (*0-86690-146-9*, R1401-014) Am Fed Astrologers.

— Not a Sign in the Sky, but a Living Person. 32p. 1975. 9.00 (*0-86690-219-8*, R1403-014) Am Fed Astrologers.

— Sex, Mind & Habit Compatibility. 56p. 1975. 10.00 (*0-86690-148-5*, R1404-014) Am Fed Astrologers.

— Time Out of Mind. 44p. 1972. 10.00 (*0-86690-220-1*, R1405-014) Am Fed Astrologers.

— Transit of Saturn. 74p. 1976. 12.50 (*0-86690-149-3*, R1406-014) Am Fed Astrologers.

*__Robertson, Margaret & Gerber, Rod.__ The Child's World. 300p. 2000. pap. 22.50 (*0-86431-301-2*, Pub. by Aust Council Educ Res) Stylus Pub VA.

*__Robertson, Mark.__ Seven Ways to Catch the Moon. (Illus.). 36p. (J). (ps-1). 1999. 18.99 (*0-7112-1417-4*) F Lincoln.

Robertson, Mark. A Treasury of Dragon Stories. LC 97-198943. (Treasury of Stories Ser.). 160p. (J). (gr. k-4). 1997. pap. 6.95 (*0-7534-5114-X*) LKC.

Robertson, Marta. Aaron Copland: A Guide to Research. Marco, Guy A., ed. LC 99-89420. (Composer Resource Manuals Ser.). 300p. Date not set. text 45.00 (*0-8153-2178-3*) Garland.

Robertson, Martha. Night-Scented Stock in Bloom? (C). 1989. pap. text 49.00 (*1-85821-035-6*, Pub. by Pentland Pr) St Mut.

Robertson, Martha B. Mexican Indian Manuscript Painting: A Catalog of the Tulane University Collection. (Illus.). 20p. (Orig.). 1991. pap. 7.50 (*0-87409-100-4*) Tulane Univ.

Robertson, Martha O., jt. ed. see Klaus, Marshall H.

Robertson, Martin. The Art of Vase-Painting in Classical Athens. (Illus.). 362p. (C). 1992. text 100.00 (*0-521-33010-6*) Cambridge U Pr.

— The Art of Vase-Painting in Classical Athens. (Illus.). 362p. (C). 1994. pap. text 38.95 (*0-521-33881-6*) Cambridge U Pr.

— History of Greek Art, 2 vols., Set. LC 73-79317. 1200p. 1976. text 190.00 (*0-521-20277-9*) Cambridge U Pr.

— A Shorter History of Greek Art. (Illus.). 256p. 1981. pap. text 35.95 (*0-521-28084-2*) Cambridge U Pr.

Robertson, Martyn, et al, eds. Toward the Twenty-First Century: The Challenges for Small Business. (U. K. Enterprise Management & Research Association Ser.). 295p. 1992. 88.00 (*0-9519230-0-5*, Pub. by P Chapman) Taylor & Francis.

Robertson, Mary. The Diana I Knew. 288p. 1999. mass mkt. 5.50 (*0-06-092939-1*) HarpC.

— The Diana I Knew. large type ed. LC 98-30799. 1998. 30.00 (*0-7862-1653-0*) Thorndike Pr.

Robertson, Mary, ed. Guide to Literary Manuscripts in the Huntington Library. LC 79-84369. 552p. 1979. 35.00 (*0-87328-102-0*) Huntington Lib.

Robertson, Mary, et al. Guide to British Historical Manuscripts in the Huntington Library. LC 81-17129. (Huntington Library Manuscript Guide). 450p. 1982. 35.00 (*0-87328-117-9*) Huntington Lib.

Robertson, Mary D., ed. A Confederate Lady Comes of Age: The Journal of Pauline DeCaradeuc Heyward, 1863-1888. LC 91-25091. 181p. 1997. pap. 12.95 (*1-57003-228-9*) U of SC Pr.

— Lucy Breckinridge of Grove Hill: The Journal of a Virginia Girl, 1862-1864. rev. ed. LC 93-46329. (Women's Diaries & Letters of the Nineteenth-Century South Ser.). (Illus.). 267p. (C). 1994. reprint ed. pap. text 15.95 (*0-87249-999-5*) U of SC Pr.

Robertson, Mary D., jt. auth. see Breckinridge, Lucy Gilmer.

Robertson, Mary D., ed. see Breckinridge, Lucy.

Robertson, Mary E. Family Life. large type ed. (Americana Series). 37p. 1988. lib. bdg. 7.95 (*0-89621-137-1*) Thorndike Pr.

— Meditations for Working Men. (Illus.). 72p. (Orig.). 1988. pap. 5.00 (*0-9620614-2-5*) Spirit Connect.

— Meditations for Working Women. rev. ed. (Illus.). 64p. 1988. reprint ed. pap., spiral bd. 5.00 (*0-9620614-5-X*) Spirit Connect.

Robertson, Mary E., ed. see Golliday, Mary.

Robertson, Mary M. & Baron-Cohen, Simon. Tourette's Syndrome: The Facts. 2nd ed. (The Facts Ser.). (Illus.). 122p. 1998. pap. 19.95 (*0-19-852398-X*) OUP.

Robertson, Mary M. & Eapen, Valsamma, eds. Movement & Allied Disorders in Childhood. LC 95-9400. 342p. 1996. 215.00 (*0-471-95324-5*) Wiley.

Robertson, Matra. Starving in the Silences: An Exploration of Anorexia Nervosa. LC 92-16188. 125p. (C). 1992. pap. text 15.00 (*0-8147-7435-0*) NYU Pr.

*__Robertson, Matthew.__ Insects & Spiders. LC 99-36390. (Pathfinders Ser.). (Illus.). 64p. (gr. 3-9). 2000. 16.99 (*1-57584-375-7*) Rdrs Digest.

Robertson, Matthew. Insects & Spiders. LC 99-36390. (Illus.). 64p. (J). (gr. 3-9). 2000. lib. bdg. 18.99 (*1-57584-381-1*) Rdrs Digest.

Robertson, Matthew, ed. The Big Book of Bugs. LC 99-29014. (Illus.). 448p. (gr. 4-7). 1999. 29.95 (*0-941807-33-9*) Welcome Enterprises.

Robertson, Merle G. Sculpture of Palenque, Vol. 5. (Illus.). 0.00 (*0-691-03573-3*) Princeton U Pr.

Robertson, Merle G. The Sculpture of Palenque Vol. 2: The Early Buildings of the Palace & the Wall Paintings. LC 82-341. 302p. 1985. reprint ed. pap. 93.70 (*0-608-04646-9*, 2065333) Bks Demand.

— The Sculpture of Palenque Vol. 3: The Late Buildings of the Palace. LC 82-341. 325p. 1985. reprint ed. pap. 100.80 (*0-608-04647-7*, 2065333) Bks Demand.

Robertson, Merle G., ed. Sixth Palenque Round Table, 1986. LC 90-12171. (Illus.). 368p. 1990. 70.00 (*0-8061-2277-3*) U of Okla Pr.

Robertson, Merle G., et al, eds. Eighth Palenque Round Table, 1993. (Palenque Round Table Ser.: Vol. X). (ENG & SPA., Illus.). 600p. Date not set. 80.00 (*0-614-10356-8*) Pre-Columbian Art.

Robertson, Merle G. & Fields, Virginia M., eds. Fifth Palenque Round Table, 1983. LC 85-60786. (Palenque Round Table Ser.: Vol. VII). (Illus.). 290p. (Orig.). 1985. pap. 48.00 (*0-934051-00-3*) Pre-Columbian Art.

Robertson, Michael. Stephen Crane, Journalism, & the Making of Modern American Literature. LC 97-15068. (Illus.). 272p. 1997. pap. 17.50 (*0-231-10969-5*) Col U Pr.

Robertson, Michael & Simpson, Ron. The Official MP3.Com Guide to MP3. pap. 19.95 (*0-9670574-0-X*) MPThreecom.

Robertson, Michael, jt. auth. see Wiggerhaus, Rolf.

Robertson, Michael, tr. see Moeller, Torsten B., et al.

Robertson, Michael J., jt. auth. see Dennis, Marshall W.

Robertson, Morgan. Down to the Sea. LC 71-101289. (Short Story Index Reprint Ser.). 1977. 20.95 (*0-8369-3226-9*) Ayer.

— Futility: The Wreck of the Titan. 60p. 1998. reprint ed. mass mkt. 6.95 (*0-9665458-1-X*) Virtual Ink.

— Futility: or The Wreck of the Titan. 120p. 1991. reprint ed. lib. bdg. 20.95 (*0-89966-821-6*) Buccaneer Bks.

— Futility: or The Wreck of the Titan: 100th Anniversary Edition. 72p. 1998. reprint ed. pap. 6.95 (*0-9665458-2-6*) Virtual Ink.

— Land Ho! LC 76-101290. (Short Story Index Reprint Ser.). 1977. 23.95 (*0-8369-3227-7*) Ayer.

— Spun-Yarn. LC 76-98592. (Short Story Index Reprint Ser.). 1977. 19.95 (*0-8369-3166-1*) Ayer.

— Three Laws & the Golden Rule. LC 70-86152. (Short Story Index Reprint Ser.). 1977. 20.95 (*0-8369-3058-4*) Ayer.

— Where Angels Fear to Tread, & Other Tales of the Sea. LC 79-122733. (Short Story Index Reprint Ser.). 1977. 19.95 (*0-8369-3566-7*) Ayer.

— Wreck of the Tian: or Futility & Morgan Robertson the Man. 19.95 (*0-8488-1461-4*) Amereon Ltd.

R

R

— Wreck of the Titan. LC 71-132125. (Short Story Index Reprint Ser.). 1977. 27.95 (0-8369-3682-5) Ayer.
*Robertson, Murdoch. A Touch of Murder Now & Then. 264p. 1999. pap. 18.95 (0-920576-75-3) Caitlin Pr.
Robertson, N. R. A Manual of Neonatal Intensive Care. 3rd ed. 416p. 1993. pap. text 24.95 (0-340-55572-6, Pub. by E A) OUP.
— A Manual of Normal Neonatal Care. 2nd ed. (Arnold Publication). 368p. 1996. pap. 27.95 (0-340-61375-0) OUP.
Robertson, Narelle. Australian Cattle Dogs, AKC Rank No. 63. (KW Dog Ser.). (Illus.). 1996. pap. 9.95 (0-7938-2351-X, KW198S) TFH Pubns.
*Robertson, Narelle. A New Owner's Guide to Australian Cattle Dogs. LC 99-461780. (New Owner's Guide to Ser.). (Illus.). 160p. 1999. 12.95 (0-7938-2808-2) TFH Pubns.
Robertson, Neil & Seymour, Paul, eds. Graph Structure Theory: Proceedings of the Joint Summer Research Conference on Graph Minors, Held June 22-July 5, 1991 at the University of Washington, Seattle, With Support from the National Science Foundation & the Office of Naval Research. LC 93-18553. (Contemporary Mathematics Ser.: Vol. 147). 688p. 1993. pap. 81.00 (0-8218-5160-8, CONM/147) Am Math.
Robertson, Neil, et al. Excluding Infinite Clique Minors, Vol. 566. LC 95-34453. (Memoirs of the American Mathematical Society Ser.: No. 566). 103p. 1995. pap. 34.00 (0-8218-0402-2, MEMO/118/566) Am Math.
Robertson, Noel. Festivals & Legends: The Formation of Greek Cities in the Light of Public Ritual. (Phoenix Supplementary Volumes Ser.: No. XXXI). 336p. 1992. text 75.00 (0-8020-5988-0) U of Toronto Pr.
Robertson, Noel, jt. auth. see Blaxter, Kenneth A.
Robertson, O. Prophet of the Coming Day. 1995. pap. 8.99 (0-85234-335-3, Pub. by Evangelical Pr) P & R Pubng.
Robertson, O. D. Sold on Sunday School. (Orig.). 1984. pap. text 3.95 (0-87148-808-6) Pathway Pr.
Robertson, O. H., et al. Endocrines & Aging. 232p. 1972. text 49.50 (0-8422-7029-9) Irvington.
Robertson, O. Palmer. The Christ of the Covenants. 1981. pap. 11.99 (0-87552-418-4) P & R Pubng.
— The Final Word. 150p. 1993. pap. 7.99 (0-85151-659-9) Banner of Truth.
*Robertson, O. Palmer. The Israel of God: Yesterday, Today & Tomorrow. 246p. 2000. pap. 12.99 (0-87552-398-6) P & R Pubng.
Robertson, O. Palmer. Jonah: A Study in Compassion. 64p. 1990. pap. 3.99 (0-85151-575-4) Banner of Truth.
— Nahum, Habakkuk & Zephaniah. (New International Commentary on the Old Testament Ser.). 384p. 1990. 34.00 (0-8028-2532-X) Eerdmans.
Robertson, O. Palmer. Psalms in Congregational Celebration. 1995. pap. 14.99 (0-85234-338-8, Pub. by Evangelical Pr) P & R Pubng.
Robertson, O. Palmer. Understanding the Land of the Bible: A Biblical-Theological Guide. LC 96-33675. (Illus.). 160p. (Orig.). 1996. pap. 9.99 (0-87552-399-4) P & R Pubng.
Robertson, Olga J. The Men in My Life. Steele, M. B., ed. (Illus.). 160p. (Orig.). 1992. pap. 6.95 (0-939497-30-1) Promise Pub.
Robertson, Oscar & O'Daniel, Michael. The Art of Basketball: A Guide to Self-Improvement in the Fundamentals of the Game. LC 98-84041. (Illus.). 96p. (YA). (gr. 5 up). 1998. pap. 12.95 (0-9662483-0-9) O R Media Vent.
Robertson, P. A. The Pheasant. (Natural History Ser.: No. 29). (Illus.). 24p. 1989. pap. 5.25 (0-85263-950-3, Pub. by Shire Pubns) Parkwest Pubns.
— Poplars of the British Isles. (Natural History Ser.: No. 58). (Illus.). 24p. 1989. pap. 5.25 (0-7478-0093-6, Pub. by Shire Pubns) Parkwest Pubns.
Robertson, P. J. Criticism & Creativity. 84p. (C). 1989. 60.00 (0-907839-22-3, Pub. by Brynmill Pr Ltd) St Mut.
Robertson, P. K. & Mayne, P. W., eds. Geotechnical Site Characterization: Proceedings of the 1st International Conference, Atlanta, Georgia, 19-22 April, 1998, 2 vols. LC 99-496419. (Illus.). 1471p. (C). 1998. text 154.00 (90-5410-939-4, Pub. by A A Balkema) Ashgate Pub Co.
Robertson, Pamela. Flowers: Charles Rennie Mackintosh. (Illus.). 112p. 1995. 24.95 (0-8109-3333-0, Pub. by Abrams) Time Warner.
— Guilty Pleasures: Feminist Camp from Mae West to Madonna. LC 95-45942. (Illus.). 208p. 1996. pap. 16.95 (0-8223-1748-6); text 49.95 (0-8223-1751-6) Duke.
Robertson, Pamela, ed. Charles Rennie Mackintosh: The Architectural Papers. (Illus.). 240p. 1998. 45.00 (0-9513124-1-3, Pub. by White Cockade) Paul & Co Pubs.
Robertson, Pat. Collected Works of Pat Robertson, 3 vols. in 1. 736p. 1994. 14.99 (0-88486-106-6) Arrowood Pr.
— End of the Age. 384p. 1996. mass mkt. 6.99 (0-8499-3966-6) Word Pub.
— End of the Age. 1998. mass mkt. 6.99 (0-8499-3713-2) Word Pub.
— The End of the Age. 384p. 1996. pap. 12.99 (0-8499-3979-8) Word Pub.
— Inspirational Writings of Pat Robertson. 1989. 12.98 (0-88486-029-9) Arrowood Pr.
— Inspirational Writings of Pat Robertson. 1991. 12.98 (0-88486-052-3, Inspirational Pr) Arrowood Pr.
— The New World Order. 1992. mass mkt. 5.99 (0-8499-3394-3) Word Pub.
— Le Royaume Secret. Cosson, Annie L., ed. Gimenez, Anne, tr.Tr. of Secret Kingdom. (FRE.). 261p. 1985. mass mkt. 5.95 (0-8297-1277-1) Vida Pubs.
— Secret Kingdom. 1992. 17.99 (0-8499-1004-8) Word Pub.
— The Secret Kingdom. large type ed. (Large Print Inspirational Ser.). 352p. 1986. pap. 14.95 (0-8027-2534-1) Walker & Co.
Robertson, Pat & Buckingham, Jamie. The Autobiography of Pat Robertson: Shout It from the Housetops! LC 72-76591. 369p. (Orig.). 1995. pap. text 5.99 (0-88270-097-9) Bridge-Logos.
Robertson, Patricia. City of Orphans. LC 94-210337. 160p. 1994. pap. write for info. (0-88984-176-4) Porcup Quill.
— Daily Meditations (with Scripture) for Busy Moms. LC 93-72793. (Illus.). 368p. 1993. pap. 9.95 (0-87946-085-7, 147) ACTA Pubns.
Robertson, Patrick. Guinness Book of Movie Facts. 1991. pap. text 19.95 (0-85112-908-0) Abbeville Pr.
Robertson, Patrick. Guinness Book of Movie Facts & Feats. 5th ed. (Illus.). 256p. 1993. pap. 19.95 (1-55859-697-6) Abbeville Pr.
— The New Shell Book of Firsts. (Illus.). 674p. 1996. pap. 19.95 (0-7472-7818-0, Pub. by Headline Bk Pub) Trafalgar.
Robertson, Paul, jt. auth. see Langlois, Richard N.
Robertson, Paul, jt. auth. see Pollard, Sidney.
Robertson, Paul B. & Musser, Guy G. A New Species of Peromyscus: Rodentia: Cricetidae, & a New Specimen of P. Simulatus from Southern Mexico, with Comments on Their Ecology. (Occasional Papers: No. 47). 8p. 1976. pap. 1.00 (0-317-04909-7) U KS Nat Hist Mus.
Robertson, Paul D. Firewalls Clearly Explained. (Clearly Explained Ser.). (Illus.). 350p. 1999. pap. text 34.95 (0-12-045598-6) Morgan Kaufmann.
*Robertson, Paul D., et al. Dynamic Object Technology Clearly Explained. (Clearly Explained Ser.). 350p. (C). 2000. pap. 49.95 (0-12-490340-1) Acad Pr.
Robertson, Paul L., jt. auth. see Foss, Nicolai J.
Robertson, Paul M. Authority & Control in Modern Industry: Theoretical & Empirical Perspectives. LC 98-25902. (Routledge Studies in Business Organization & Net: Vol. 5). 256p. (C). 1999. 75.00 (0-415-13212-6) Routledge.
Robertson, Pauline D. Borrowed Moccasins: Poems from Other Viewpoints. 64p. 1987. 10.95 (0-942376-12-9) Paramount TX.
— Field Notes: Poems on Late Light. 64p. 1987. 10.95 (0-942376-14-5) Paramount TX.
— Fringe Benefits: Light Verse from Living. 64p. 1987. 9.95 (0-942376-13-7) Paramount TX.
Robertson, Pauline D. & Robertson, R. L. Goodnight: A Pictorial History of the Pioneer Cattleman. (Illus.). 280p. 2001. 39.95 (0-942376-09-9) Paramount TX.
— Mystery Woman of Old Tascosa: The Legend of Frenchy McCormick. 2nd ed. (Illus.). 1995. pap. 3.95 (0-942376-16-1) Paramount TX.
— Panhandle Pilgrimage: Illustrated Tales Tracing History in the Texas Panhandle. 5th ed. LC 78-68222. (Illus.). 400p. 1989. 34.95 (0-942376-00-5) Paramount TX.
— Tascosa: Historic Site in the Texas Panhandle. 2nd rev. ed. (Illus.). 72p. 1995. pap. 6.95 (0-942376-15-3) Paramount TX.
Robertson, Pauline D., et al. Eve's Version: One Hundred Fifty Women of the Bible Speak Through Modern Poets. (Illus.). 1983. 13.95 (0-942376-11-0) Paramount TX.
Robertson, Pauline Durrett. Poetry Writing Self-Taught. (Illus.). 204p. 2000. pap. 17.95 (0-942376-10-2) Paramount TX.
Robertson, Pauline Durrett & Robertson, R. L. Quanah: Pictorial History of the Last Comanche Chief. unabridged ed. (Illus.). 230p. 2000. 39.95 (0-942376-08-0) Paramount TX.
Robertson, Peter. Beyond Southern Skies: Radio Astronomy & the Parkes Telescope. (Illus.). 369p. (C). 1992. text 80.00 (0-521-41408-3) Cambridge U Pr.
— Pheasants. LC 97-1859. (Illus.). 160p. 1997. 29.95 (0-89658-361-9) Voyageur Pr.
Robertson, Piedad, et al. Secrets of Cuban Entertaining: A Menu Cookbook. 133p. 1981. 9.95 (0-941072-00-2) Southern Herit.
Robertson, Priscilla. Revolutions of 1848: A Social History. 480p. 1952. pap. text 19.95 (0-691-00756-X, Pub. by Princeton U Pr) Cal Prin Full Svc.
Robertson, R., ed. Heine: Poems. (Bristol German Texts Ser.). (GER.). 142p. 1993. pap. 18.95 (1-85399-335-2, Pub. by Brist Class Pr) Focus Pub-R Pullins.
*Robertson, R. G. Competitive Struggle: America's Western Fur Trading Posts, 1764-1865. (Illus.). 356p. 1999. pap. 18.95 (1-886609-19-5) Tamarack Bks.
Robertson, R. G. Idaho Echoes of Time. LC 99-172633. (Illus.). 200p. 1998. pap. 15.95 (1-886609-12-8) Tamarack Bks.
Robertson, R. Garcia. Atlantis Found. 288p. 1997. mass mkt. 5.99 (0-380-78678-8, Avon Bks) Morrow Avon.
Robertson, R. Garcia, jt. auth. see Garcia, R.
Robertson, R. L., jt. auth. see Hughes, Richard T.
Robertson, R. L., jt. auth. see Robertson, Pauline D.
Robertson, R. L., jt. auth. see Robertson, Pauline Durrett.
*Robertson, Ralph A., ed. Reproductions of Etchings of Niagara River & Falls by Amos W. Sangster 1886. ii, 86p. 2000. pap. 22.00 (0-9679068-0-6) RAR.
Robertson, Ralston S., jt. auth. see Holzman, Eric L.
Robertson, Ray. Home Movies: A Novel. 228p. 1997. pap. text 15.95 (1-896951-02-3) Cormor Bks.
Robertson, Raymond. B-Trees for BASIC. 1992. disk 25.00 (0-89496-007-5, Baldar) Ross Bks.
— B-Trees for Basics: Create Your Own Lightning-Fast Database. 242p. (C). 1999. pap. 9.95 (0-89496-008-3) Ross Bks.
Robertson, Rhoda. Romantic Crochet: Thirty Beautiful Projects for Your Home. LC 98-84036. (Illus.). 108p. 1999. 24.95 (1-57076-119-1, Trafalgar Sq Pub) Trafalgar.
Robertson, Richard G., ed. Robertson's Practical English-Thai Dictionary. LC 79-87787. (ENG & THA.). 320p. 1969. pap. 14.95 (0-8048-0706-X) Tuttle Pubng.
Robertson, Richard J. & Powers, William T., eds. Introduction to Modern Psychology: The Control Theory View. 238p. (C). 1990. reprint ed. pap. text 25.00 (0-9647121-6-4) Benchmark CT.
Robertson, Ritchie. The Jewish Question in German Literature, 1749-1939: Emancipation & its Discontents. LC 99-22780. 544p. 1999. text 99.00 (0-19-818631-2) OUP.
— Kafka: Judaism, Politics, & Literature. 336p. 1987. pap. text 28.00 (0-19-815814-9) OUP.
Robertson, Ritchie, ed. The German-Jewish Dialogue: An Anthology of Literary Texts, 1749-1993. LC 98-47079. (Oxford World's Classics Ser.). 424p. 1999. pap. 13.95 (0-19-283910-1) OUP.
*Robertson, Ritchie & Beniston, Judith, eds. Catholicism & Austrian Culture: Austrian Studies 10. 240p. 1999. (0-7486-1310-2) Polygon.
Robertson, Ritchie & Timms, Edward. Theodor Herzl & the Origins of Zionism. 1997. 70.00 (0-7486-0944-X, Pub. by Edinburgh U Pr) Col U Pr.
Robertson, Ritchie & Timms, Edward, eds. The Austrian Enlightenment & Its Aftermath. 256p. 1991. pap. text 28.00 (0-7486-0236-4, Pub. by Edinburgh U Pr) Col U Pr.
— Gender & Politics in Austrian Fiction. (Austrian Studies). 320p. 1996. 63.00 (0-7486-0838-9, Pub. by Edinburgh U Pr) Col U Pr.
— The Habsburg Legacy: National Identity in Historical Perspective. (Austrian Studies: No. 5). (Illus.). 256p. 1994. 50.00 (0-7486-0487-1, Pub. by Edinburgh U Pr) Col U Pr.
— Theatre & Performance in Austria: From Mozart to Jelinek. LC 93-239291. (Austrian Studies: No. 4). 218p. 1994. 55.00 (0-7486-0436-7, Pub. by Edinburgh U Pr) Col U Pr.
Robertson, Ritchie, ed. see Freud, Sigmund.
Robertson, Ritchie, ed. see Hoffmann, E. T. A.
Robertson, Ritchie, jt. ed. see Timms, Edward.
Robertson, Ritchie, ed. & tr. see Hoffmann, E. T. A.
Robertson, Ritchie, tr. see Bitterli, Urs.
Robertson, Robert, jt. auth. see Noble, Bruce.
Robertson, Robert E., ed. Welfare Reform: State & Local Responses to Restricting Food Stamp Benefits. (Illus.). 53p. (C). 1999. reprint ed. pap. text 20.00 (0-7881-7718-4) DIANE Pub.
*Robertson, Robert E. & Cheston, Richard. Sugar Program: Changing the Method for Setting Import Quotas Could Reduce Cost to Users. (Illus.). 51p. (C). 2000. pap. text 20.00 (0-7881-8887-9) DIANE Pub.
Robertson, Robert J. Her Majesty's Texans: Two English Immigrants in Reconstruction Texas. LC 98-19819. (Centennial Series of the Association of Former Students, Texas A&M University: Vol. 78). (Illus.). 224p. 1998. 25.95 (0-89096-841-1) Tex A&M Univ Pr.
Robertson, Robin. Beginner's Guide to Jungian Psychology. LC 92-1772. (Illus.). 240p. (Orig.). 1992. pap. 12.95 (0-89254-022-2) Nicolas-Hays.
— Beginner's Guide to Revelation: A Jungian Interpretation. rev. ed. LC 94-18306. (Illus.). 288p. 1994. reprint ed. pap. 12.95 (0-89254-030-3) Nicolas-Hays.
— Jungian Archetypes: Jung, Godel & the History of the Archetypes. LC 95-19454. (Illus.). 320p. 1995. pap. 16.00 (0-89254-029-X) Nicolas-Hays.
*Robertson, Robin. Mining the Soul: From the Inside Out. (Illus.). 288p. 2000. pap. 18.95 (0-89254-055-9, Pub. by Nicolas-Hays) Weiser.
Robertson, Robin. A Painted Field. LC 97-27711. 108p. (C). 1998. 22.00 (0-15-100366-1) Harcourt.
— A Painted Field. LC 97-27711. 89p. (C). 1999. pap. 13.00 (0-15-600647-2) Harcourt.
*Robertson, Robin. Pasta for All Seasons: 125 Vegetarian Pasta Recipes for Family & Friends. (Illus.). 192p. 2000. 24.95 (1-55832-174-8); pap. 12.95 (1-55832-175-6) Harvard Common Pr.
— Rice & Spice: 100 Vegetarian One-Dish Dinners Made with the World's Most Versatile Grain. LC 99-57901. (Illus.). 162p. 2000. 19.95 (1-55832-159-4, Pub. by Harvard Common Pr); pap. 12.95 (1-55832-160-8) Harvard Common Pr.
Robertson, Robin. Some Like it Hot: 200 Spicy Vegetarian Recipes from Around the World. LC 98-10362. (Illus.). 288p. 1998. pap. 15.95 (0-452-27869-4, Plume) Dutton Plume.
— The Soy Solution: 75 Delicious & Healthful Soy Protein Recipes. LC 97-43378. 160p. 1998. pap. 11.95 (0-452-27922-4) NAL.
— 366 Healthful Ways to Cook Tofu & Other Meat Alternatives. LC 95-41517. 396p. 1996. pap. 16.95 (0-452-27597-0, Plume) Dutton Plume.
— 366 Healthful Recipes for Soy Milk. LC 96-27542. 1997. pap. 16.95 (0-452-27623-3, Plume) Dutton Plume.
— The Vegetarian Chili Cookbook: 80 Deliciously Different One-Dish Meals. LC 98-35574. (Illus.). 160p. 1998. pap. 10.95 (1-55832-148-9, Pub. by Harvard Common Pr) Natl Bk Netwk.
*Robertson, Robin. The Vegetarian Chili Cookbook: 80 Deliciously Different One-Dish Meals. LC 98-35574. (Illus.). 160p. 1998. 21.95 (1-55832-147-0, Pub. by Harvard Common Pr) Natl Bk Netwk.
Robertson, Robin. Your Shadow. LC 97-16808. (Illus.). 198p. (Orig.). 1997. pap. 12.95 (0-87604-391-0, 489) ARE Pr.
Robertson, Robin & Combs, Allan, eds. Chaos Theory in Psychology & the Life Sciences. 408p. 1995. text 79.95 (0-8058-1736-0); pap. text 39.95 (0-8058-1737-9) L Erlbaum Assocs.
Robertson, Robin & Robertson, Jon. The Sacred Kitchen: Higher-Consciousness Cooking for Health & Wholeness. LC 98-52992. (Illus.). 208p. 1999. pap. 16.95 (1-57731-092-6) New Wrld Lib.
Robertson, Robin, jt. auth. see Shestor, Michael.
Robertson, Robin, jt. auth. see Shestov, Michael.
Robertson, Roderick, jt. auth. see Smithee, Alan.
Robertson, Roland. Globalization: Social Theory & Global Culture. (Theory, Culture & Society Ser.). 240p. (C). 1992. 62.00 (0-8039-8186-4); pap. 22.95 (0-8039-8187-2) Sage.
Robertson, Roland & Garrett, William P., eds. Religion & Global Order. LC 90-44569. 1990. 29.95 (0-89226-090-4); pap. 14.95 (0-89226-091-2) Paragon Hse.
Robertson, Roland, jt. ed. see Robbins, Thomas.
Robertson, Ronald, ed. Talcott Parsons: Theorist of Modernity. (Theory, Culture & Society Ser.). 272p. (C). 1991. 59.95 (0-8039-8513-4); pap. 22.95 (0-8039-8514-2) Sage.
Robertson, S., jt. ed. see Suci, G. J.
Robertson, S. A. Flowering Plants of Seychelles. (Illus.). xvi, 327p. 1989. pap. 25.00 (0-947643-14-1, Pub. by Royal Botnic Grdns) Balogh.
Robertson, S. A., ed. Contemporary Ergonomics 1994. 518p. 1994. pap. text 95.00 (0-7484-0203-9, Pub. by Tay Francis Ltd) Taylor & Francis.
— Contemporary Ergonomics 1995. 512p. 1995. pap. 95.00 (0-7484-0328-0, Pub. by Tay Francis Ltd) Taylor & Francis.
— Contemporary Ergonomics 1996. 600p. 1996. pap. 89.95 (0-7484-0549-6, Pub. by Tay Francis Ltd) Taylor & Francis.
— Contemporary Ergonomics 1997. 600p. 1997. pap. 89.00 (0-7484-0677-8, Pub. by Tay Francis Ltd) Taylor & Francis.
Robertson, S. Ian. Types of Thinking. LC 98-48941. (Psychology Focus Ser.). 1999. write for info. (0-415-19105-X); pap. write for info. (0-415-19106-8) Routledge.
Robertson, Sandra. Lorca, Alberti, & the Theater of Popular Poetry. LC 91-17755. (American University Studies: Romance Languages & Literature: Ser. II, Vol. 170). 267p. 1992. 44.95 (0-8204-1565-0) P Lang Pubng.
Robertson, Sandra J. & Thomson, Fay. Working with Dysarthric Clients. 107p. 1987. pap. text 29.00 (0-7616-7444-6) Commun Skill.
Robertson, Sandy. The Aleister Crowley Scrapbook. LC 88-13101. (Illus.). 128p. 1988. pap. 19.95 (0-87728-689-2) Weiser.
Robertson, Sarah A., ed. see Underwood, Paula.
Robertson, Scot. The Development of RAF Strategic Bombing Doctrine, 1919-1939. LC 94-22654. (Studies in Diplomacy & Strategic Thought). 224p. 1995. 59.95 (0-275-94997-4, Praeger Pubs) Greenwood.
Robertson, Scott. Historic Model Ships from Scratch. (Illus.). 136p. (Orig.). 1998. pap. 33.50 (1-85486-187-5) Nexus Special Interests.
— Model Ships from Scratch. (Illus.). 190p. 1994. 34.95 (1-55750-589-6) Naval Inst Pr.
Robertson, Scott, ed. see Pattak, Evan M. & Wilson, Andrew G.
Robertson, Scott A., jt. auth. see Srikanth, Mokshagundam L.
Robertson-Scott, John W. Story of the Pall Mall Gazette. LC 73-141266. (Illus.). 470p. 1971. reprint ed. lib. bdg. 79.50 (0-8371-5826-5, ROPM, Greenwood Pr) Greenwood.
Robertson, Seona & Wilson, Leslie. Scotland's War. (Illus.). 192p. 1996. 35.00 (1-85158-700-4, Pub. by Mainstream Pubng) Trafalgar.
Robertson, Sharon E. & Brown, Roy I., eds. Rehabilitation Counselling: Approaches in the Field of Disability. LC 92-26462. (Rehabilitation Education Ser.: Vol. 5). 322p. 1992. 44.75 (1-56593-017-7, 0260) Singular Publishing.
Robertson, Shirley. Lou Who? The Odyssey of a French Poodle in England & America. LC 93-84751. (Illus.). 216p. (Orig.). 1993. pap. text 13.95 (1-880222-16-7) Red Apple Pub.
Robertson, Sidney, jt. ed. see Black, Eleanor.
*Robertson, Stacey M. Parker Pillsbury: Radical Abolitionist, Male Feminist. LC 99-46230. 2000. 35.00 (0-8014-3634-6) Cornell U Pr.
Robertson, Stephen L., jt. auth. see Diller, Daniel C.
Robertson, Struan. The Cold Choice: Pictures of a South African Reality. 1991. 24.95 (0-86543-217-1) Africa World.
— The Cold Choice: Pictures of a South African Reality. LC DT1758.R62. 128p. reprint ed. pap. 39.70 (0-7837-6567-3, 204613200011) Bks Demand.
Robertson, Susan & Smaller, Harry, eds. Teachers' Political Activism In The 1990'S. (Our Schools/Our Selves Ser.). 218p. pap. 19.95 (1-55028-538-6, Pub. by J Lorimer) Formac Dist Ltd.
*Robertson, Susan L. A Class Act: Changing Teachers' Work, the State & Globalisation. LC 00-22491. (Reference Library of Social Science). 2000. pap. write for info. (0-8153-3578-4) Garland.
Robertson, Susanne M. Programme: Lowell Musicale & Musical Portrait of the Spindle City. (Illus.). 131p. (Orig.). 1986. pap. 8.95 (0-9616315-0-3) Euterpe Pr.
Robertson, Suzanne. Mastering the Requirements Process. 416p. (C). 2000. 44.95 (0-201-36046-2) Addison-Wesley.
Robertson, Suzanne, jt. auth. see Robertson, James.
Robertson, Sylvia. Teach Yourself German Verbs. (GER., Illus.). 272p. 1994. pap. 7.95 (0-8442-3635-7, Teach Yrslf) NTC Contemp Pub Co.
Robertson, T. W., ed. see Ward, Artemus, pseud.
Robertson, Theodosia S., tr. see Fiut, Aleksander.
Robertson, Thomas, see Thomas, Roberta, pseud.
Robertson, Thomas Dolby & Van Rensburg, Chris. Thomas Dolby's Guide to Web Site Sound Design. 400p. 1997. 39.99 (1-56276-547-7, Ziff-Davis Pr) Que.
Robertson, Thomas S. Human Ecology, 2 vols. 560p. 1973. 600.00 (0-87968-340-6) Gordon Pr.

An Asterisk (*) at the beginning of an entry indicates that the title is appearing for the first time.

Robertson, Thomas S., et al. Televised Medicine Advertising & Children. LC 79-4280. 175p. 1979. 52.95 (*0-275-90413-X*, C0413, Praeger Pubs) Greenwood.

Robertson, Thomas S., jt. auth. see Tucker, Benjamin R.

Robertson, Thomas William. The Graduation Gift: A Love Story. 119p. (Orig.). 1996. pap. 12.95 (*0-9655350-0-2*) Willards Farm.

Robertson, Thyrele, et al, eds. Evaluating Natural Resources in Agriculture. LC 97-28592. 360p. 1997. 59.95 (*0-8138-2958-5*) Iowa St U Pr.

Robertson, Tom G., jt. auth. see Great American Opportunities Staff.

Robertson, Tomas. Baja California & Its Missions. 1978. pap. 4.50 (*0-87505-418-8*) Borden.

***Robertson, Una A.** Coming Out of the Kitchen: Women Beyond the Home. LC 00-34489. 2000. write for info. (*0-312-23824-X*) St Martin.

— Illustrated History of The Housewife, 1650-1950. 1999. pap. 18.95 (*0-312-22248-3*) St Martin.

Robertson, Veronica. Brain Quest Extra Black Heritage. (Illus.). 140p. (J). (gr. 1-7). 1996. pap. 10.95 (*0-7611-0534-4*, 10534) Workman Pub.

Robertson, Victoria. Breeding Rottweilers. (Illus.). 192p. 1993. 9.95 (*0-86622-816-0*, KW229) TFH Pubns.

***Robertson, Vonceil Rust.** Entwined: Robertson & Ruff Family History. 491p. 1999. 84.50 (*0-8328-9983-6*); pap. 74.50 (*0-8328-9984-4*) Higginson Bk Co.

Robertson, W. Augustine: On Christian Doctrine. 192p. (C). 1958. pap. text 8.40 (*0-02-402150-4*, Macmillan Coll) P-H.

— Francisco de Miranda & the Revolutionizing of South America. 1976. lib. bdg. 59.95 (*0-8490-1862-5*) Gordon Pr.

— Pocahontas: Alias Matoaka, & Her Descendants Through Her Marriage at Jamestown, Virginia, with John Rolfe, Gentleman. 84p. 1993. reprint ed. pap. 10.00 (*0-8328-3385-1*); reprint ed. lib. bdg. 20.00 (*0-8328-3384-3*) Higginson Bk Co.

Robertson, W., jt. auth. see Hill, C.

Robertson, W. L. Lubrication in Practice. 2nd ed. (Mechanical Engineering Ser.: Vol. 27). (Illus.). 240p. 1984. text 125.00 (*0-8247-7204-0*) Dekker.

Robertson, W. P., jt. auth. see Robertson, John P.

Robertson, Wallace J. Black Street. 1972. 4.00 (*0-685-67932-2*) Windless Orchard.

Robertson, Wayne & Koop, Edward C. Integrating Windows & Netware: A Professional's Guide. 1996. pap. 42.95 (*0-07-912126-8*) McGraw.

— Windows 95 & NT Networking: A Guide for Professionals. LC 96-30569. (Illus.). 389p. 1996. pap., pap. text 49.95 incl. cd-rom (*0-07-912983-8*) McGraw.

Robertson, Wendy. Cruelty Games. 224p. 1996. 22.00 (*0-7278-5177-2*) Severn Hse.

— A Dark Light Shining. 480p. 1996. mass mkt. 10.95 (*0-7472-4799-4*, Pub. by Headline Bk Pub) Trafalgar.

— Kitty Rainbow. 320p. 1997. pap. 11.95 (*0-7472-5183-5*, Pub. by Headline Bk Pub) Trafalgar.

— The Self-Made Woman. 288p. 1999. 25.00 (*0-7278-5408-9*, Pub. by Severn Hse) Chivers N Amer.

Robertson, William. Adult Language Warning. 80p. 1991. pap. 9.95 (*0-919626-52-1*, Pub. by Brick Bks) Genl Dist Srvs.

— K. D. Lang: Carrying the Torch. LC 93-227387. (Illus.). 112p. (Orig.). 1993. pap. 9.95 (*1-55022-158-2*, Pub. by ECW) LPC InBook.

— The Progress of Society in Europe: A Historical Outline from the Subversion of the Roman Empire to the Beginning of the 16th Century. Gilbert, Felix & Krieger, Leonard, eds. LC 75-190283. (Classic European Historians Ser.). 224p. 1994. lib. bdg. 14.00 (*0-226-72133-7*) U Ch Pr.

— Soldiers & Statesmen, 2 vols., Set. (Modern Revivals in Military History Ser.). 685p. 1992. 89.95 (*0-7512-0035-2*, Pub. by Gregg Revivals) Ashgate Pub Co.

— Somewhere Else. 96p. 1997. pap. 10.95 (*1-55050-111-9*, Pub. by Coteau) Genl Dist Srvs.

— Tin: Its Production & Marketing, 51. LC 82-9269. (Contributions in Economics & Economic History Ser.: No. 51). (Illus.). 212p. 1982. 55.00 (*0-313-23637-2*, RTN/, Greenwood Pr) Greenwood.

Robertson, William, et al, eds. Disinfection Dilemma: Microbiological Control vs. By-Products. (Illus.). 448p. 1993. 47.00 (*0-89867-709-2*, 20314) Am Water Wks Assn.

Robertson, William B., Jr. Everglades - The Park Story. rev. ed. LC 89-80983. (Illus.). 64p. (C). 1989. pap. 6.95 (*0-945142-01-3*) FL Natl Parks.

Robertson, William B., ed. The Cardiovascular System: General Considerations & Congenital Malformations, Pt. A. 3rd ed. LC 92-20957. (Systemic Pathology Ser.: Vol. 10, Pt. A). 1993. text 163.00 (*0-443-03096-0*) Church.

Robertson, William E. The Woodstock & Sycamore Traction Company. LC 85-4886. (Illus.). 56p. 1985. pap. 10.00 (*0-933449-00-3*) Transport Trails.

Robertson, William G. Back Door to Richmond: The Bermuda Hundred Campaign, April-June 1864. LC 85-41048. (Illus.). 284p. 1991. pap. 16.95 (*0-8071-1672-6*) La State U Pr.

— Back Door to Richmond: The Bermuda Hundred Campaign, April-June 1864. LC 85-41048. (Illus.). 288p. 1987. 42.50 (*0-87413-303-3*) U Delaware Pr.

— The Battle of Chickamauga. (Civil War Ser.). (Illus.). 52p. 1995. pap. 4.95 (*0-915992-77-9*) Eastern National.

— The Petersburg Campaign the Battle of Old Men & Young Boys June 9, 1864. (Virginia Civil War Battles & Leaders Ser.). (Illus.). 143p. 1989. 19.95 (*0-930919-70-X*) H E Howard.

Robertson, William J. A Century of French Verse: Brief Biographical & Critical Notices of Thirty-Three French Poets of the Nineteenth Century. LC 77-11481. (Symbolists Ser.). 392p. reprint ed. 52.50 (*0-404-16342-4*) AMS Pr.

Robertson, William M. Optoelectronic Techniques for Microwave & Millimeter-Wave Engineering. LC 95-21286. 244p. 1995. 93.00 (*0-89006-711-2*) Artech Hse.

Robertson, William O. Medical Malpractice: A Preventive Approach. LC 84-40322. 212p. 1985. text 20.00 (*0-295-96162-7*) U of Wash Pr.

Robertson, William P. & Cooke, Tricia. The Big Lebowski: The Making of a Coen Brothers Film. 1998. pap. 13.95 (*0-571-19335-8*) Faber & Faber.

— The Big Lebowski: The Making of a Coen Brothers Film. LC 97-37949. 192p. 1998. pap. 17.00 (*0-393-31750-1*) Norton.

Robertson, William S., ed. see De Miranda, Francisco.

Robertson, Wilmot. The Dispossessed Majority. rev. ed. LC 71-167649. 364p. 1981. 25.00 (*0-914576-15-1*) Howard Allen.

— The Dispossessed Majority. rev. ed. LC 71-167649. 364p. 1986. pap. 15.95 (*0-914576-16-X*) Howard Allen.

— The Ethnostate. 233p. (Orig.). 1993. pap. 12.00 (*0-914576-22-4*) Howard Allen.

— Ventilations. rev. ed. LC 74-20120. 115p. 1982. pap. 12.00 (*0-914576-06-2*) Howard Allen.

Robertson, Wilmot, ed. Best of Instauration 1977. 127p. 1982. pap. 12.00 (*0-914576-19-4*) Howard Allen.

— Best of Instauration 1978. 119p. 1986. pap. 12.00 (*0-914576-20-8*) Howard Allen.

Robertssen, Lowell. Remembering the Women of the Vietnam War. LC 89-52195. 197p. 1990. 19.95 (*0-9623029-2-9*); pap. 14.95 (*0-9623029-1-0*) St Johns Pub.

Robertus, Polly M. The Dog Who Had Kittens. LC 90-39174. (Illus.). 32p. (J). (gr. k-3). 1991. lib. bdg. 16.95 (*0-8234-0860-4*) Holiday.

— The Dog Who Had Kittens. LC 90-39174. (Illus.). 32p. (J). (gr. k-3). 1991. pap. 6.95 (*0-8234-0974-0*) Holiday.

— The Dog Who Had Kittens. unabridged ed. (Illus.). (J). (gr. k-3). 1992. 24.95 incl. audio (*0-87499-285-0*); pap. 15.95 incl. audio (*0-87499-284-2*) Live Oak Media.

— The Dog Who Had Kittens, Set. unabridged ed. (Illus.). (J). (gr. k-3). 1992. pap. 37.95 incl. audio (*0-87499-286-9*) Live Oak Media.

Roberty, Marc. Eric Clapton. (Complete Guides to the Music Of...Ser.). (Illus.). 152p. 1995. pap. 8.95 (*0-7119-4305-2*, OP 47739, Pub. by Omnibus Press) Omnibus NY.

— Eric Clapton: In His Own Words. (In Their Own Words Ser.). (Illus.). 96p. 1995. pap. 15.95 (*0-7119-3215-8*, OP 47175) Omnibus NY.

— Eric Clapton: The Complete Recording Sessions. 192p. 1995. pap. 15.95 (*0-312-13776-1*, St Martin Griffin) St Martin.

— Eric Clapton Scrapbook. (Illus.). 160p. 1993. pap. 16.95 (*0-8065-1454-X*, Citadel Pr) Carol Pub Group.

Robesin, Marga, jt. ed. see Gebers, Betty.

***Robeson, Bonnie & Mienville, Lisa.** Elder Care for the Millennium: A Practical & Compassionate Guide for Caregiving. large type ed. Loden, James M., ed. & tr. by. (SPA.). 164p. 1999. spiral bd. 19.95 (*0-9678591-0-7*) Graphix Third.

***Robeson, Carol & Robeson, Jerry.** Strongman's His Name II. (Illus.). 168p. 2000. pap. 11.99 (*0-88368-603-1*) Whitaker Hse.

Robeson, Carol, jt. auth. see Robeson, Jerry.

Robeson, Cheryl, jt. ed. see Evans, Sian.

Robeson, Ed. Just In: Word of Navigational Change: New & Selected Work. 136p. 1998. 32.95 (*1-883689-80-5*) Talisman Hse.

— Just In: Word of Navigational Change: New & Selected Work. 144p. 1998. pap. 11.95 (*1-883689-79-1*) Talisman Hse.

Robeson, Eslanda. African Journey. LC 73-164468. (Illus.). 154p. 1972. reprint ed. lib. bdg. 35.00 (*0-8371-6222-X*, ROAJ, Greenwood Pr) Greenwood.

Robeson, James F., jt. ed. see Copacino, William C.

***Robeson, Jerry & Robeson, Carol.** Strongman's His Name, What's His Game? (Illus.). 168p. 2000. wbk. ed. 13.99 (*0-88368-601-5*) Whitaker Hse.

Robeson, Jerry & Robeson, Carol. Strongman's His Name What's His Game Vol. I: An Authoritative Biblical Approach to Spiritual Warfare. (Illus.). 1998. pap. 13.95 (*1-891879-02-2*) Shiloh Pub.

Robeson, Jerry, jt. auth. see Robeson, Carol.

Robeson, Jerry, ed. see Allen, Jim.

Robeson, Jerry, ed. see Robeson, Randy.

Robeson, Kenneth. Monsters. 144p. Date not set. 18.95 (*0-8488-2621-3*) Amereon Ltd.

Robeson, Mari M. Magical Moments: A New Mother's Journal. (Illus.). 140p. 1998. spiral bd. 15.95 (*0-9670065-0-3*, LS-1-J) Le Sol Studio.

Robeson, Paul. Here I Stand. LC 87-47882. 160p. 1998. reprint ed. pap. 12.00 (*0-8070-6445-9*) Beacon Pr.

— Paul Robeson, Jr. Speaks to America. LC 92-36164. 225p. (C). 1993. 25.00 (*0-8135-1985-3*) Rutgers U Pr.

Robeson, Paul, Jr. Paul Robeson, Jr. Speaks to America: The Politics of Multiculturalism. (C). 1996. 15.95 (*0-8135-2322-2*) Rutgers U Pr.

Robeson, Paul & Karttunen, Frances. Between Worlds: Interpreters, Guides, & Survivors. LC 93-8366. (Illus.). 225p. (C). 1996. pap. text 18.00 (*0-8135-2031-2*) Rutgers U Pr.

Robeson, Paul & Werning, David H. The Paul Robeson Collection: Manuscript Collections from the Schomburg LC 92-7993. (Black Studies Research Sources). 9 p. 1991. write for info. (*1-55655-375-7*) U Pubns Amer.

Robeson, Paul, tr. see Skobel'tsyn, D. V., ed.

Robeson, Randy. Knee Deep in the Soup: And Other Stupid Stories. Robeson, Jerry, ed. (Illus.). 128p. (YA). 1998. pap. 10.95 (*1-891879-00-6*) Shiloh Pub.

Robeson, Susan. The Whole World in His Hands: A Pictorial Biography of Paul Robeson. (Illus.). 256p. 1981. 17.95 (*0-8065-0754-3*, Citadel Pr) Carol Pub Group.

— The Whole World in His Hands: A Pictorial Biography of Paul Robeson. (Illus.). 256p. 1998. reprint ed. pap. 21.95 (*0-8065-0977-5*, Citadel Pr) Carol Pub Group.

Robeson, Theresa. Wolfrider's Guide: Revised ed. 1999. pap. 16.95 (*0-936861-63-0*, Pub. by Warp Graphics) Midpt Trade.

***Robetaler, Elke.** Intertextualitat und Rezeption: Linguistische Untersuchungen Zur Rolle von Text-Text-Kontakten im Textverstehen Aktueller Zeitungstexte. (Sprache - System und Tatigkeit Ser.). 289p. 1999. 45.95 (*3-631-35131-3*) P Lang Pubng.

Robey. Late Lark. 1999. pap. write for info. (*0-316-75120-0*) Little.

Robey, Cora L. The New Handbook of Basic Writing. 4th ed. (C). 1996. pap. text, teacher ed. 28.00 (*0-15-503693-9*) Harcourt Coll Pubs.

Robey, Cora L., et al. The New Handbook of Basic Writing Skills. 4th ed. LC 96-75218. 432p. (C). 1996. pap. text 31.00 (*0-15-503694-7*, Pub. by Harcourt Coll Pubs) Harcourt.

— New Workbook of Basic Writing Skills. 4th ed. 240p. (C). 1996. teacher ed. 19.50 (*0-15-503706-4*, Pub. by Harcourt Coll Pubs) Harcourt.

Robey, Daniel. Designing Organizations. (C). 1981. 62.95 (*0-256-02513-4*, Irwn McGrw-H) McGrw-H Hghr Educ.

— Designing Organizations. 5th ed. 2000. text 69.74 (*0-256-23885-5*) McGraw.

— Designing Organizations: A Macro Perspective. 3rd ed. (C). 1990. 46.50 (*0-685-38299-0*, Irwn McGrw-H) McGrw-H Hghr Educ.

Robey, David & Sales, Carol A. Designing Organizations. 4th ed. LC 93-3727. 560p. (C). 1994. text 71.35 (*0-256-11699-7*, Irwn McGrw-H) McGrw-H Hghr Educ.

Robey, Jim. Ohio Fishing Guide. (Illus.). 164p. (Orig.). 1991. pap. 5.50 (*0-9616347-1-5*) Dayton Newspapers.

Robey, Jim & Morris, Jim. Ohio Fishing Guide. LC 97-211563. (Illus.). 164p. (Orig.). 1997. pap. 9.95 (*0-9656649-0-2*) Cox Custom.

Robey, John S., ed. The Analysis of Public Policy: A Bibliography of Dissertations, 1977-1982. LC 83-22556. 225p. 1984. lib. bdg. 55.00 (*0-313-23957-6*, RPU/, Greenwood Pr) Greenwood.

Robey, Melvin J. African Violets: Gifts from Nature. LC 84-45563. (Illus.). 320p. 1988. 45.00 (*0-8453-4766-7*, Cornwall Bks) Assoc Univ Prs.

Robey, Randall R. & Schultz, Martin C. Optimizing Theory & Experiments. LC 92-25260. (Illus.). 186p. (Orig.). (C). 1993. pap. text 34.95 (*1-56593-078-9*, 0382) Thomson Learn.

Robey, Richard C., ed. Research Library of Colonial Americana, 54 bks. 1972. 2012.00 (*0-405-03270-6*) Ayer.

Robey, Tom. Gringo's Guide to Mexican Whitewater. 1992. pap. 9.95 (*0-910467-10-2*) Heritage Assocs.

Robey, William G., Jr. Robey, Roby, Robie: The Family History from Early England to America. 1078p. (Orig.). 1994. pap. text 80.00 (*0-7884-0032-0*) Heritage Bk.

Robi, Diana M., jt. auth. see Cereta, Laura.

Robi, James M., jt. ed. see Monastersky, Glenn M.

Robichaud, Beryl & Buell, Murray F. Vegetation of New Jersey: A Study of Landscape Diversity. LC 72-4205. (Illus.). 352p. 1983. reprint ed. pap. 109.20 (*0-7837-9210-7*, 204996000004) Bks Demand.

Robichaud, Beryl, et al. Data Processing Work Kit. 2nd ed. 96p. (gr. 9-12). 1983. text 13.56 (*0-07-053207-9*) McGraw.

— Introduction to Data Processing. 3rd ed. Orig. Title: Understanding Modern Business Data Processing. 368p. (gr. 9-12). 1983. text 21.12 (*0-07-053194-3*) McGraw.

Robichaud, Heidi. Alaska over the Rainbow: A Colorable Journey Thru the North, Saddlestitch. (Illus.). 40p. 1994. 7.95 (*0-9644019-0-8*) Goode River.

Robichaux, Kabriel & Woolworth, Derrick. Laura Lemay's Web Workshop Net Object Fusion: NetObjects Fusion 2. LC 96-72265. 488p. 1997. 39.99 (*1-57521-278-1*) Sams.

Robichaux, Paul. Managing Microsoft Exchange Server. Denn, Robert, ed. 450p. 1999. pap. text 34.95 (*1-56592-545-9*) OReilly & Assocs.

— Managing the Windows NT Registry. LC 98-178655. (Illus.). 384p. 1998. pap. 39.95 (*1-56592-378-2*) OReilly & Assocs.

***Robichaux, Paul.** Managing the Windows 2000 Registry. Denn, Robert, ed. (Illus.). 500p. 2000. pap. 39.95 (*1-56592-943-8*) OReilly & Assocs.

— MCSE: Windows 2000 Network Administration Exam Notes. 2000. pap. 24.99 (*0-7821-2761-4*) Sybex.

Robichaux, Paul. Remote Access. 3rd ed. (24x7 Ser.). 448p. 1999. pap. text 34.99 (*0-7821-2531-X*) Sybex.

***Robichaux, Paul.** Windows 2000 Network Administration Study Guide. (MCSE Ser.). (Illus.). 704p. 2000. 49.99 (*0-7821-2755-X*, Network Pr) Sybex.

***Robichaux, Paul & Glenn, Walter.** Microsoft Exchange Server 6.0 Administrator's Companion. (gr. 8). 2000. pap. 59.99 (*0-7356-0938-1*) Microsoft.

Robichaux, Paul E. Jazz up Your Web Site: In a Weekend. LC 97-66856. (Illus.). 430p. 1997. pap. 24.99 incl. cd-rom (*0-7615-1137-7*) Prima Pub.

— Laura Lemay's Web Workshop: Creating Webcasting Channels. 1997. 39.99 (*1-57521-328-1*) Sams.

***Robichaux, Paul E.** Windows 2000 Server Administrator's Guide. 800p. 1998. 50.00 (*0-7615-1395-7*) Prima Pub.

Robichaux, Paul E. & Glenn, Walter J. Exchange Server 5.5 MCSE Study Guide. LC QA76.3.R634 1998. (MCSE Certification Ser.). 816p. 1998. student ed. 49.99 incl. cd-rom (*0-7645-3111-5*) IDG Bks.

Robichaux, Robert H. Ecology of Sonoran Desert Plants & Plant Communities. LC 98-40107. 312p. 1999. 45.00 (*0-8165-1869-6*) U of Ariz Pr.

***Robichaux, Robert H. & Yetman, David A.** The Tropical Deciduous Forest of Alamos: Biodiversity of a Threatened Ecosystem in Mexico. LC 99-50867. 260p. 2000. 50.00 (*0-8165-1922-6*) U of Ariz Pr.

Robicheaux, Jack & Jons, John A. Basic Narcotic Detection Dog Training. (Illus.). 52p. (Orig.). 1990. pap. text 15.00 (*0-9623099-1-5*) J Jons LA.

Robichek, A. Alexander, ed. Financial Research & Management Decisions. LC 67-22552. 248p. reprint ed. pap. 76.90 (*0-8357-9890-9*, 201484600093) Bks Demand.

Robichez, ed. see Verlaine, Paul M.

Robideaux, Sharon, jt. auth. see Agnew, Eleanor.

Robidoux, Barbara, ed. see Warschauer, Faye A.

Robie, Dave & Robie, Sharon. Bill & Hillary's Little Book of Promises: With Narration by Socks the Cat. LC 96-70116. (Illus.). 160p. (Orig.). 1996. pap. 6.95 (*0-914984-90-X*) Starburst.

Robie, Diane C. Searching in Florida: A Reference Guide to Public & Private Records. (ISC State Search Bks.: No. 2). (Orig.). 1982. 10.95 (*0-942916-01-8*) ISC Pubns.

Robie, Joan H. If I Only Knew... What Would Jesus Do? LC 98-51043. 224p. 1999. mass mkt. 9.99 (*0-446-67557-1*, Pub. by Warner Bks) Little.

— If I Only Knew, What Would Jesus Do? for Women: Over 100 Ways to "Walk the Walk" & "Talk the Talk" (If I Only Knew What Jesus Would Do? Ser.). 208p. 1999. pap. 9.95 (*1-892016-08-7*) Starburst.

— Reverse the Curse in Your Life. LC 90-70124. 176p. 1991. pap. 7.95 (*0-914984-24-1*) Starburst.

— Teenage Mutant Ninja Turtles Exposed. LC 91-66361. 80p. 1991. pap. 5.95 (*0-914984-31-4*) Starburst.

— The Truth about Dungeons & Dragons. LC 91-66238. 1992. audio 7.95 (*0-914984-25-X*) Starburst.

— The Truth about Dungeons & Dragons. LC 91-66238. 80p. 1992. pap. 5.95 (*0-914984-37-3*) Starburst.

— Turmoil in the Toy Box II. LC 86-60428. 224p. 1989. pap. 9.95 (*0-914984-20-9*) Starburst.

— Turmoil in the Toybox II. 1989. audio 7.95 (*0-914984-26-8*) Starburst.

Robie, Joan Hake. Devotion in Motion. LC 80-83298. 160p. 1981. pap. 5.95 (*0-914984-00-4*) Starburst.

Robie, Sharon, jt. auth. see Robie, Dave.

Robie, William. For the Greatest Achievement: A History of the Aero Club of America & the National Aeronautic Association. LC 92-31823. (Illus.). 416p. 1993. 35.00 (*1-56098-187-3*) Smithsonian.

Robiette, A. G. Electric Smelting Processes. (Illus.). 276p. 1973. text 50.00 (*0-85264-096-X*, Pub. by Hodder & Stought Ltd) Lubrecht & Cramer.

***Robieux, J.** High Power Laser Interactions: Isotopes Separation, Nuclear Fusion Control, Elementary Particles Selective Creation. (Illus.). 1160p. 2000. 199.00 (*1-898298-67-X*, Pub. by Intercept UK) Spr-Verlag.

Robigne, Bennett M. De, see De Robigne, Bennett M.

Robilio, Victor. The Red Neck Guide to Wine Snobbery. Storey, Thomas B. & Bedwell, Randall, eds. LC 98-67167. 128p. 1998. pap. 6.95 (*1-887654-31-3*) Premium Pr TN.

***Robillard, Veronica.** 15 Reproducible Spanish Write-&-Read Books: Instant Patterns for Easy Predictable Books for Students, 1 vol. (Illus.). 96p. 1999. pap. text 12.95 (*0-439-05176-2*) Scholastic Inc.

— Month-by-Month Write & Read Books: 15 Reproducible Predictable Books That Your Students Help Write. (Illus.). 96p. 1999. pap. 12.95 (*0-590-98360-1*) Scholastic Inc.

Robillard, Albert B. Meaning of a Disability: The Lived Experience of Paralysis. LC 98-36637. 208p. 1999. 59.50 (*1-56639-675-1*); pap. 19.95 (*1-56639-676-X*) Temple U Pr.

Robillard, Albert B., ed. Social Change in the Pacific Islands. 320p. (C). 1990. text 74.00 (*0-7103-0400-5*, A5632) Routledge.

Robillard, David A. Public Space Design in Museums. (Publications in Architecture & Urban Planning: No. R84-7). (Illus.). iv, 73p. 1984. 12.50 (*0-938744-36-4*) U of Wis Ctr Arch-Urban.

Robillard, Dianne. The Great Songs Sing along Coloring Book. large type ed. 44p. (Orig.). (J). (gr. k-6). 1997. 14.95 (*0-9659139-0-2*, StD001) Sing & Draw.

Robillard, Douglas. Melville & the Visual Arts: Ionian Form, Venetian Tint. LC 97-6780. (Illus.). 1997. 32.00 (*0-87338-575-6*) Kent St U Pr.

Robillard, Douglas, ed. American Supernatural Fiction: From Edith Wharton to the "Weird Tales" Writers. LC 95-42208. (Studies in Nineteenth-Century American Literature: Vol. 6). 280p. 1995. text 55.00 (*0-8153-1735-2*, H1855) Garland.

Robillard, Douglas, jt. auth. see Melville, Herman.

Robillard, Douglas, ed. see London, Jack & Strunsky, Anna B.

Robillard, Edmond. Reincarnation: Illusion or Reality. Whitehead, K. D., tr. from FRE. LC 82-1638. 190p. (Orig.). 1982. pap. 9.95 (*0-8189-0432-1*) Alba.

Robillard, Jane A., jt. ed. see Rice, Patricia O.

Robillard, Jean & Caulfield, H. John, eds. Industrial Applications of Holography. (Illus.). 224p. 1990. text 60.00 (*0-19-505855-0*) OUP.

Robillard, Jean J., jt. ed. see Allan, Graham G.

Robillard, Linda, jt. auth. see Long, Paula.

Robillard, Paula A., jt. contrib. by see Dougherty, Jayne H.

Robillard, V. E. 15 Reproducible Write-&-Read Books. 64p. 1998. pap. text 10.95 (*0-590-49890-8*) Scholastic Inc.

R

An Asterisk (*) at the beginning of an entry indicates that the title is appearing for the first time.

R

Robillard, Valerie & Jongeneel, Els. Painted Words. 200p. 1997. pap. 27.50 (*90-5383-523-7*, Pub. by VU Univ Pr) Paul & Co Pubs.

Robillard, Walter G. & Bouman, Lane J. Clark on Surveying & Boundaries. 1148p. 1993. suppl. ed. 95.00 (*1-55834-022-X*, MICHIE) LEXIS Pub.

— Clark on Surveying & Boundaries. 7th ed. LC 97-75905. 1217 p. 1997. 95.00 (*1-55834-816-6*) LEXIS Pub.

— Clark on Surveying & Boundaries, 1998 Supplement. 7th ed. 60p. 1998. write for info. (*0-327-00861-X*, 6089614) LEXIS Pub.

Robiller, Franz. Birds Throughout the World. 262p. 1980. 65.00 (*0-905418-39-5*, Pub. by Gresham Bks) St Mut.

Robilliard, David & Zalopany, Michele. Baby Lies Truthfully. Igliori, Paola, ed. (Illus.). 150p. 1990. pap. 15.00 (*0-9625119-5-1*) Inanout Pr.

Robilotta, Peter, jt. auth. see Bird, Stewart.

Robilotta, Peter T., jt. auth. see Bird, Stewart.

Robimzeva, Irina M., ed. Treasures of the Czars: From the State Museums of the Moscow, Kremlin. (Illus.). 256p. 1998. pap. text 30.00 (*0-7881-5902-X*) DIANE Pub.

Robin. Digital Television Fundamentals: Design & Installation of Video & Audio Systems. 2nd ed. 600p. 2000. pap. text 69.00 (*0-07-135581-2*) McGraw-Hill Prof.

— Neurogenic Disorders of Language. 2001. 40.00 (*1-56593-703-1*) Thomson Learn.

Robin & Henry. Lab Manual Workbook Golosary, Bk. 2. 2nd ed. 1998. pap. text, wbk. ed., lab manual ed. 21.33 (*0-13-895129-2*) P-H.

Robin, jt. auth. see Henry.

Robin, A., ed. see Osho.

Robin, Abbe. New Travels Through North America. Decker, Peter, ed. Freneau, Philip, tr. LC 73-77110. (Eyewitness Accounts of the American Revolution Ser.). 1969. reprint ed. 16.95 (*0-405-01176-8*) Ayer.

Robin, Anand, ed. see Osho.

Robin, Arthur L. ADHD in Adolescents: Diagnosis & Treatment. LC 98-36026. 461p. 1998. lib. bdg. 46.95 (*1-57230-391-3*) Guilford Pubns.

***Robin, Arthur L.** ADHD in Adolescents: Diagnosis & Treatment. 461p. 1999. pap. text 24.95 (*1-57230-545-2*, C0545) Guilford Pubns.

Robin, Arthur L. & Foster, Sharon L. Negotiating Parent-Adolescent Conflict: A Behavioral-Family Systems Approach. LC 87-31502. (Family Therapy Ser.). 338p. 1989. lib. bdg. 39.95 (*0-89862-072-4*) Guilford Pubns.

Robin, Bernard, et al, eds. Technology & Teacher Education Annual, 1996: Proceedings of Site, '96. (Illus.). 1080p. (Orig.). 1996. pap. 45.00 (*1-880094-20-7*) Assn Advan Comput Educ.

***Robin, Diana.** Women & Print Culture Italy. 1999. pap. text 18.00 (*0-226-72157-4*); lib. bdg. 50.00 (*0-226-72156-6*) U Ch Pr.

Robin, Diana & Jaffe, Ira, eds. Redirecting the Gaze: Gender, Theory, & Cinema in the Third World. LC 98-3355. (Suny Series, Cultural Studies in Cinema/Video). (Illus.). 384p. (C). 1998. text 71.50 (*0-7914-3993-3*); pap. text 23.95 (*0-7914-3994-1*) State U NY Pr.

Robin, Diana M. Filelfo in Milan: Writings, 1451-1477. LC 91-6546. (Illus.). 283p. 1991. reprint ed. pap. 87.80 (*0-608-02551-8*, 206319500004) Bks Demand.

Robin, Diana M., jt. auth. see Cereta, Laura.

Robin, Diana M., jt. auth. see Fedele, Cassandra.

Robin, Doris, et al. In a Faraway Galaxy: A Literary Approach to a Film Saga. (Illus.). 149p. (Orig.). 1984. pap. 6.95 (*0-935892-07-9*) Extequer.

Robin, Eugene D., ed. Claude Bernard & the Internal Environment: A Memorial Symposium. LC 79-23206. (Illus.). 319p. reprint ed. pap. 98.90 (*0-8357-6056-1*, 203456300090) Bks Demand.

— Extrapulmonary Manifestations of Respiratory Disease. LC 78-1279. (Lung Biology in Health & Disease Ser.: No. 8). (Illus.). 536p. reprint ed. pap. 166.20 (*0-7837-0733-9*, 204105700019) Bks Demand.

Robin, Gerald D. Violent Crime & Gun Control. LC 91-70555. (ACJS - Anderson Monographs). 98p. (C). 1991. pap. 14.95 (*0-87084-747-3*) Anderson Pub Co.

— Waging the Battle Against Drunk Driving: Issues, Countermeasures, & Effectiveness. LC 91-2505. (Contributions in Criminology & Penology Ser.: No. 32). 160p. 1991. pap. 18.95 (*0-275-94040-3*, B4040, Praeger Pubs) Greenwood.

— Waging the Battle Against Drunk Driving: Issues, Countermeasures, & Effectiveness, 32. LC 91-8235. (Contributions in Criminology & Penology Ser.: No. 32). 160p. 1991. 55.00 (*0-313-27856-3*, RWB, Greenwood Pr) Greenwood.

Robin, Gordon C., ed. Aetiology - Idiopathic Scoliosis. 1990. 83.00 (*0-8493-6722-0*, R) CRC Pr.

Robin, Gordon C., ed. see Muscular Dystrophy Symposium Staff.

Robin, Harry. I, Morgain: A Novella. Caso, Adolfo, ed. LC 94-42544. 192p. 1995. 17.95 (*0-8283-2004-7*) Branden Bks.

Robin, J. B., jt. ed. see Schanzlin, David J.

Robin, Jean. Elmdon: Continuity & Change in a North-West Essex Village, 1861-1964. LC 79-12964. 294p. reprint ed. pap. 83.80 (*0-608-15607-8*, 2031720) Bks Demand.

Robin, Jeffrey. Mental Health Care & Substance Abuse: A Review of Evidence on Insurance Coverage & Utilization. (Illus.). 69p. (Orig.). (C). 1992. pap. text 25.00 (*1-56806-131-5*) DIANE Pub.

Robin, Jennifer. Bouzi. LC 98-71179. 128p. 1999. pap. 13.50 (*0-88739-175-3*) Creat Arts Bk.

— Clothe Your Spirit: Dressing for Self-Expression. LC 87-23494. (Illus.). 176p. (Orig.). 1988. pap. 15.95 (*0-944296-03-3*) Spirit Pr.

Robin, Joanna & Henry, Katheryn. Golosa Book 2: A Basic Course in Russian, Bk. 2. 1994. pap. text, wbk. ed., lab manual ed. 22.67 (*0-13-293184-2*) P-H.

Robin, Joanna, et al. Golosa, Bk. 1. 2nd ed. LC 97-17336. Vol. 1. 384p. (C). 1997. 48.00 (*0-13-895038-5*) P-H.

Robin, Joanna, tr. see Glad, John, ed.

Robin, Lee. Gentlemen Prefer Blondes: Vocal Selections. (Illus.). 96p. 1992. pap. 15.95 (*0-8256-1245-4*, AM80201) Music Sales.

Robin, Leon. Aristotle. Mayer, J. P., ed. LC 78-67380. (European Political Thought Ser.). (FRE.). 1980. reprint ed. lib. bdg. 25.95 (*0-405-11730-2*) Ayer.

— La Theorie Platonicienne des Idees et des Nombres d'Apres Aristote. xvii, 702p. 1984. reprint ed. write for info. (*3-487-00344-9*) G Olms Pubs.

***Robin, Lia.** All about Numerology. 240p. 2000. pap. 14.95 (*965-494-109-0*) Astrolog Pub.

Robin, Lia. Basic Numerology. (Little Big Book Ser.). 72p. 1998. pap. 4.95 (*965-494-045-0*) Astrolog Pub.

— Day-by-Day Numerology. (Astrology Complete Guide Ser.). (Illus.). 128p. 1998. pap. 6.95 (*965-494-057-4*, Pub. by Astrolog Pub) Assoc Pubs Grp.

***Robin, Libby.** Defending the Little Desert: The Rise of Ecological Consciousness in Australia. 224p. 1999. pap. 24.95 (*0-522-84831-1*, Pub. by Melbourne Univ Pr) Paul & Co Pubs.

Robin, Libby, jt. ed. see Griffiths, Tom.

Robin, M. Canadian Provincial Politics. 2nd ed. 1978. pap. 12.50 (*0-13-113233-4*) P-H.

— Farewell to Innocence: Freud & Psychoanalysis. xii, 458p. 1989. 59.00 (*0-935016-73-2*, Assoc Sci Pubs) Zinn Pub Grp.

Robin, Marc C. Handbook of Sexually Transmitted Diseases: A Clinical Approach. LC 94-78412. (Illus.). 240p. 1995. pap. text 34.95 (*0-929894-15-4*) K-W Pubns.

Robin, Marcy, jt. auth. see Resch, Kathleen.

***Robin, Marie Monique.** Century in Pictures: 100 Historic Moments. (Illus.). 1999. 19.99 (*3-8228-6512-5*) Benedikt Taschen.

Robin, Martin. Shades of Right: Nativist & Fascist Politics in Canada, 1920-1940. (Illus.). 384p. (Orig.). 1992. text 60.00 (*0-8020-5962-7*); pap. text 16.95 (*0-8020-6892-8*) U of Toronto Pr.

Robin, Michael, ed. Assessing Child Maltreatment Reports: The Problem of False Allegations. LC 91-20799. (Child & Youth Services Ser.). (Illus.). 297p. 1991. pap. text 19.95 (*1-56024-161-6*) Haworth Pr.

— Assessing Child Maltreatment Reports: The Problem of False Allegations. LC 91-20799. (Child & Youth Services Ser.). (Illus.). 297p. 1991. lib. bdg. 49.95 (*0-86656-931-6*) Haworth Pr.

Robin, Michael & Poulin, Michel. Digital Television Fundamentals: Design & Installation of Video & Audio Systems. LC 97-17381. (Illus.). 571p. 1997. 60.00 (*0-07-053168-4*) McGraw.

— McGraw-Hill Circuit Encyclopedia & Troubleshooting Guide. (Illus.). 448p. 1997. pap. 39.95 (*0-07-038117-8*) McGraw.

— McGraw-Hill Circuit Encyclopedia & Troubleshooting Guide, Vol. 4. (Illus.). 448p. 1997. 69.50 (*0-07-038116-X*) McGraw.

Robin, Mitchell W. & Balter, Rochelle. Performance Anxiety. 240p. 1994. pap. 12.00 (*1-55850-441-9*) Adams Media.

Robin, Noel I. Clinical Handbook of Endocrinology & Metabolic Disease. LC 95-30949. (Clinical Handbook Ser.). 506p. 1996. pap. text 26.95 (*1-85070-637-9*) Prthnon Pub.

Robin, Peggy. Bottlefeeding Without Guilt: A Reassuring Guide for Loving Parents. LC 95-885. (Illus.). 304p. 1995. pap. 14.95 (*0-7615-0001-4*) Prima Pub.

— Fertility Patient Ho. LC 92-41043. 447p. 1993. pap. 15.00 (*0-688-11732-5*, Quil) HarperTrade.

— The Safe Nanny Handbook: Everything You Need to Know to Have Peace of Mind While Your Child Is in Someone Else's Care. LC 98-23462. (Illus.). 224p. 1998. pap. 14.00 (*0-688-16214-2*, Quil) HarperTrade.

— The Starfleet Academy Entrance Exam: Tantalizing Trivia from Classic Star Trek to Star Trek Voyager. rev. ed. LC 97-49028. 192p. 1998. pap. text 12.00 (*0-8065-1983-5*, Citadel Pr) Carol Pub Group.

— When Breastfeeding Is Not an Option: A Reassuring Guide for Loving Parents. LC 98-26018. 304p. 1998. per. 14.95 (*0-7615-1449-X*) Prima Pub.

Robin, Peggy, jt. auth. see Adler, Bill, Jr.

Robin, Peggy, jt. ed. see Adler, Bill, Jr.

Robin, Regine. Socialist Realism: An Impossible Aesthetic. Porter, Catherine, tr. from FRE. 376p. 1992. 47.50 (*0-8047-1655-2*) Stanford U Pr.

— The Wanderer. Aronoff, Phyllis, tr. from FRE. LC 98-111623. 184p. 1997. pap. 17.95 (*1-896743-00-5*, Pub. by Alter Ego Editions) Genl Dist Srvs.

Robin, Richard. Russian Listening Comprehension II, Pt. A, Units 45-49 Scripts. (OSU Foreign Language Publications: No. 73D). (RUS.). 86p. (C). 1994. pap. text 9.00 (*0-87415-275-5*, 73D) Foreign Lang.

Robin, Richard M., tr. see Glad, John, ed.

Robin, Richard S., jt. ed. see Moore, Edward C.

Robin, Robert. Above the Law. 1992. 20.00 (*0-671-74425-9*) PB.

— Above the Law. Rosenman, Jane, ed. 384p. 1993. reprint ed. mass mkt. 5.50 (*0-671-74424-0*, Pocket Star Bks) PB.

Robin, Ron. Enclaves of America: The Rhetoric of American Political Architecture Abroad, 1900-1965. 221p. 1992. pap. text 16.95 (*0-691-02618-1*, Pub. by Princeton U Pr) Cal Prin Full Svc.

— Signs of Change: Urban Iconographies in San Francisco, 1880-1915. LC 90-3506. (European Immigrants & American Society Ser.). 184p. 1990. reprint ed. text 15.00 (*0-8240-0317-9*) Garland.

Robin, Stanley & Wagenfeld, Morton O., eds. Paraprofessionals in the Human Services. LC 80-18011. (Community Psychology Ser.: Vol. VI). 368p. 1981. 45.95 (*0-87705-490-8*, Kluwer Acad Hman Sci) Kluwer Academic.

Robin, Stanley S., jt. ed. see Bosco, James J.

Robin, Thomas J. & Ward, Michael K. The AutoCAD R14 Workbook for Windows: A Complete Educational & Training Guide for Mastering 2D Applications of AutoCAD R14. (Illus.). 426p. (C). 1997. spiral bd. 29.95 (*0-87563-778-7*) Stipes.

— The AutoCAD R13 Workbook for Windows: A Complete Educational & Training Guide for Mastering 2D Applications of AutoCAD R13 for Windows. (Illus.). 426p. (C). 1995. spiral bd., wbk. ed. 29.80 (*0-87563-621-7*) Stipes.

Robin, Vicki, jt. auth. see Dominguez, Joe.

Robine, J. M., et al, eds. Longevity: To the Limits & Beyond. LC 98-100706. (Research & Perspectives in Longevity Ser.). (Illus.). 148p. 1997. 89.95 (*3-540-62945-9*) Spr-Verlag.

Robine, Jean-Marie, et al, eds. The Paradoxes of Longevity. LC 99-10782. (Research & Perspectives in Longevity Ser.). vi, 128p. 1999. 95.00 (*3-540-65544-1*) Spr-Verlag.

Robine, Marc. Anthologie de la Chanson Francaise: Des Trouveres aux Grands Auteurs du XIX Siecle. (FRE.). 1994. 95.00 (*0-7859-9240-5*) Fr & Eur.

Robine, Sylvie. The Art of Decorative Matting. LC 97-6176.Tr. of Lavis d'Encadrement. (Illus.). 96p. 1997. 29.95 (*1-55821-569-7*) Lyons Pr.

Robineault, Manfred J. Psychology & Health: Index of Modern Information with Bibliography. LC 89-78054. 150p. 1990. 47.50 (*1-55914-228-6*); pap. 44.50 (*1-55914-229-4*) ABBE Pubs Assn.

Robiner, Linda G. Reverse Fairy Tale. 34p. 1997. pap. 7.95 (*0-944754-44-9*) Pudding Hse Pubns.

Robinet. Mississippi Chariot. (J). 1998. pap. 3.99 (*0-87628-571-X*) Ctr Appl Res.

Robinet, Andre, jt. auth. see Descartes, Rene.

Robinet, Andre, ed. see Rousseau, Jean-Jacques.

Robinet, B., ed. International Symposium on Programming. (Lecture Notes in Computer Science Ser.: Vol. 83). 341p. 1980. 27.00 (*0-387-09981-6*) Spr-Verlag.

Robinet, B. & Wilhelm, R., eds. ESOP '86. (Lecture Notes in Computer Science Ser.: Vol. 213). vi, 374p. 1986. 42.00 (*0-387-16442-1*) Spr-Verlag.

Robinet, B., jt. ed. see Paul, M.

Robinet, Bill. By the Skin of My Teeth: A Cropduster's Story. LC 97-93260. (Illus.). 380p. 1997. 28.95 (*0-9657473-0-1*) Billville Pr.

Robinet, Harriet Gillem. Mississippi Chariot. 1997. 9.09 (*0-606-11629-X*, Pub. by Turtleback) Demco.

***Robinet, Harriette.** Children of the Haymarket Struggle. LC 99-88710. 2001. write for info. (*0-689-83895-6*) Atheneum Yung Read.

Robinet, Harriette. The Twins, the Pirates & the Battle of New Orleans. LC 96-22028. 144p. (J). (gr. 3-7). 1997. 15.00 (*0-689-81208-6*) S&S Childrens.

— Walking to the Bus Rider Blues. LC 99-29054. (Illus.). (J). 2000. 16.00 (*0-689-83191-9*) Atheneum Yung Read.

Robinet, Harriette G. Children Of The Fire. LC 91-9484. 144p. (J). (gr. 3-7). 1991. 16.00 (*0-689-31655-0*) Atheneum Yung Read.

— Forty Acres & Maybe a Mule. LC 97-39169. 132p. (J). (gr. 4-6). 1998. 16.00 (*0-689-82078-X*) S&S Childrens.

— Forty Acres & Maybe a Mule. 144p. (J). (gr. 4-6). 2000. reprint ed. per. 4.99 (*0-689-83317-2*) Aladdin.

— If You Please, President Lincoln! 160p. (J). (gr. 4-6). 1995. 16.00 (*0-689-31969-X*) Atheneum Yung Read.

— Mississippi Chariot. LC 94-11092. 128p. (J). (gr. 4-7). 1994. 14.95 (*0-689-31960-6*) Aladdin.

— Mississippi Chariot. 128p. (J). 1997. per. 3.99 (*0-689-80632-9*) Aladdin.

— Washington City Is Burning. LC 95-33382. 160p. (J). (gr. 3-7). 1996. 16.00 (*0-689-80773-2*) Atheneum Yung Read.

Robinet, Isabelle. Taoism: Growth of a Religion. Brooks, Phyllis, tr. LC 96-30127. 1996. write for info. (*0-8047-2838-0*); pap. 15.95 (*0-8047-2839-9*) Stanford U Pr.

— Taoist Meditation: The Mao-shan Tradition of Great Purity. Pas, Julian F. & Girardot, Norman J., trs. from FRE. LC 92-23086. (SUNY Series in Chinese Philosophy & Culture). (Illus.). 285p. (C). 1993. pap. text 21.95 (*0-7914-1360-8*) State U NY Pr.

Robinet, J. F., et al. Dictionnaire Historique et Biographique de la Revolution et de l'Empire: 1789-1815, 2 vols. (FRE.). 1899. 260.00 (*0-8115-4841-4*) Periodicals Srv.

Robinet, Jean F. Le Mouvement Religieux a Paris Pendant la Revolution, 1798-1801, 2 vols., Set. LC 70-174331. (Collection de documents relatifs a l'histoire de Paris pendant la Revolution francaise). reprint ed. 270.00 (*0-404-52567-9*) AMS Pr.

Robinett, et al. Solutions Manual for Quantum Mechanics: Classical Results, Modern Systems & Visualized Examples. 256p. 1997. pap., student ed. write for info. (*0-19-511564-3*) OUP.

Robinett, Betty W. Easy Latin Crossword Puzzles: Quid Pro Quo. (Easy...Word Games & Ser.). 64p. 1998. pap. text 5.95 (*0-8442-8446-7*, 84467, Passprt Bks) NTC Contemp Pub Co.

— Teaching English to Speakers of Other Languages: Substance & Technique. LC 78-11448. 335p. reprint ed. pap. 103.90 (*0-8357-3334-3*, 203955900013) Bks Demand.

Robinett, Betty W. & Schachter, Jacquelyn. Second Language Learning: Contrastive Analysis, Error Analysis & Related Aspects. 488p. 1983. pap. text 18.95 (*0-472-08033-4*, 08033) U of Mich Pr.

Robinett, Betty W., jt. auth. see Prator, Clifford H., Jr.

Robinett, Jane. This Rough Magic Vol. 13: Technology in Latin American Fiction. LC 92-17509. (Worcester Polytechnic Institute Studies in Science, Technology & Culture: Vol. 13). XII, 284p. (C). 1995. text 53.95 (*0-8204-1889-7*) P Lang Pubng.

Robinett, Joseph & Chauls, Robert. Trial of Goldilocks - Musical. 40p. 1991. pap. 5.95 (*0-87129-030-8*, T08) Dramatic Pub.

Robinett, Richard W. Quantum Mechanics: Classical Results, Modern Systems & Visualized Examples. (Illus.). 600p. (C). 1996. text 74.95 (*0-19-509202-3*) OUP.

Robinett, Stephen. Final Option. 256p. 1990. pap. 3.50 (*0-380-75848-2*, Avon Bks) Morrow Avon.

— Unfinished Business. 1990. mass mkt. 3.50 (*0-380-75849-0*, Avon Bks) Morrow Avon.

Robinett, Terri L. Frameworks for Teachers: A Self-Paced Internet Training Program & Resource Guide Specifically Designed for Teachers. (Frameworks Ser.). (Illus.). 132p. 1997. spiral bd. 29.95 (*0-9660226-0-2*) NetQuest.

Robinette, Danny R. & Scrivner, Louise M. Guide to Oral Interpretation: Solo & Group Performance. 2nd ed. 1980. pap. write for info. (*0-318-51113-4*) Macmillan.

Robinette, Diane, jt. auth. see Taraschi, Rosaria.

Robinette, Gary O. Local Landscape Ordinances. (Community Landscape Development Ser.). 348p. 1992. pap. text 24.95 (*1-882240-00-6*) Agora Comms.

— Parking Lot Landscape Development. 2nd ed. (Community Landscape Development Ser.). (Illus.). 200p. 1994. pap. text 29.95 (*1-882240-01-4*) Agora Comms.

Robinette, Gary O., ed. see Lofgren, Devid E.

Robinette, Hillary M. Burnout in Blue: Managing the Police Marginal Performer. LC 87-14571. 173p. 1987. 59.95 (*0-275-92687-7*, C2687, Praeger Pubs); pap. 24.95 (*0-275-92688-5*, B2688, Praeger Pubs) Greenwood.

Robinette, Joseph. ABC (America Before Columbus) Who Really Discovered America? 40p. (J). (gr. k-8). 1984. pap. 4.50 (*0-88680-212-1*) I E Clark.

— Ashes, Ashes, All Fall Down. 1982. pap. 5.50 (*0-87129-251-3*, A29) Dramatic Pub.

— Beanstalk! A Musical Comedy. (Illus.). 44p. (J). (gr. 2 up). 1985. pap. 4.50 (*0-88680-236-9*) I E Clark.

— Dorothy Meets Alice or Wizard of Wonderland: Musical. 1991. pap. 5.95 (*0-87129-079-0*, D51) Dramatic Pub.

— The Fabulous Fable Factory Musical. 1975. pap. 5.95 (*0-87129-348-X*, F01) Dramatic Pub.

— Get Bill Shakespeare Off the Stage! 1981. pap. 5.50 (*0-87129-309-9*, G36) Dramatic Pub.

— Once upon a Shoe - Straight. 1979. 3.50 (*0-87129-491-5*, O29) Dramatic Pub.

— Once upon a Shoe: Or The Rhymes & Mimes of Mother Goose & Her Traveling Troubadours - The Musical. 1988. pap. 4.95 (*0-87129-322-6*, O04) Dramatic Pub.

— Penny & the Magic Medallion: A Musical Play. (Illus.). 44p. (J). (gr. k up). 1987. pap. 4.50 (*0-88680-283-0*) I E Clark.

— Planet of the Perfectly Awful People. 40p. (YA). (gr. 7 up). 1979. pap. 3.00 (*0-87129-889-9*, P46) Dramatic Pub.

— Showdown at the Sugar Cane Saloon - Musical. 74p. 1979. pap. 5.95 (*0-87129-871-6*, S05) Dramatic Pub.

— Trial of Goldilocks - Straight. 34p. 1990. pap. 5.50 (*0-87129-003-0*, T81) Dramatic Pub.

— The Trial of the Big Bad Wolf. 54p. (J). (gr. 1 up). 1999. pap. 5.25 (*0-87129-905-4*, TB3) Dramatic Pub.

— The Trumpet of the Swan. 1992. pap. 5.50 (*0-87129-206-8*, T85) Dramatic Pub.

Robinette, Joseph, adapted by. The Adventures of Beatrix Potter & Her Friends - Musical. 1995. 5.95 (*0-87129-523-7*, A56) Dramatic Pub.

Robinette, Joseph, adapted by. Anne of Green Gables: A Musical in Two Acts. LC 98-192407. (Illus.). 98p. (YA). (gr. 7 up). 1997. pap. 5.95 (*0-87129-760-4*, A08) Dramatic Pub.

Robinette, Joseph & Chauls, Robert. The Phantom of the Opera Musical: Based upon the novel by Gaston Leroux. 1992. pap. 5.95 (*0-87129-173-8*, P08) Dramatic Pub.

Robinette, Joseph & Jurman, Karl. Kiddlewinks! 66p. 1983. pap. 5.95 (*0-87129-982-8*) Dramatic Pub.

Robinette, Joseph & Osborn, John J., Jr. The Paper Chase. 1981. 5.50 (*0-87129-398-6*, P54) Dramatic Pub.

Robinette, Joseph, jt. auth. see Faulkner, William.

Robinette, Joseph, jt. auth. see White, E. B.

Robinette, Martin, jt. auth. see Priever, Beth.

Robinette, Martin S. & Glattke, Theodore J. Otoacoustic Emissions: Clinical Applications. (Illus.). 368p. 1997. 49.00 (*0-86577-579-6*) Thieme Med Pubs.

Robinette, Michelle. Clarisworks Reference for Teachers. 2nd ed. LC 97-80740. 400p. 1997. pap. 24.99 (*0-7645-0142-9*) IDG Bks.

— Macs for Teachers. 384p. 1995. pap. 19.99 (*1-56884-601-0*) IDG Bks.

— Macs for Teachers. 3rd ed. LC 97-80224. 384p. 1997. pap. 24.99 (*0-7645-0226-3*) IDG Bks.

Robinette, Michelle & Dummies Technical Press Staff. Windows 95 for Teachers. LC 96-80222. (Illus.). 384p. 1997. pap. 24.99 (*0-7645-0081-3*) IDG Bks.

***Robinette, Scott.** Emotion Marketing: The Hallmark Way of Winning Customers for Life. 256p. 2000. 24.95 (*0-07-136414-5*) McGraw.

Robinovitz, Judith. Math Skills for College Students. LC 97-43600. (Learning Express Basic Skills for College Students Ser.). 212p. 1997. pap. text 20.40 (*0-13-080257-3*) P-H.

An Asterisk (*) at the beginning of an entry indicates that the title is appearing for the first time.

— Practical Math Success in 20 Minutes a Day. LC 98-6120. (Skill Builders Ser.). 208p. 1998. pap. 15.95 (*1-57685-129-X*) LrningExprss.

Robinowitz, C., jt. auth. see Spurlock, J.

Robinowitz, Carolyn B., et al, eds. Directory of Psychiatry Residency Training Programs. 3rd ed. LC 88-659060. 647p. reprint ed. pap. 200.00 (*0-8357-3038-7*, 203928700011) Bks Demand.

Robinowitz, Carolyn B., jt. ed. see Talbott, John A.

Robins. American Way. 1985. pap. text. write for info. (*0-582-35534-6*, Pub. by Addison-Wesley) Longman.

— Banking in Transition LC 99-41754. 1999. text 72.00 (*0-312-22392-7*) St Martin.

— For the Sake of Love. large type ed. 1995. pap. 18.99 (*1-85389-562-8*, Dales) Ulverscroft.

— Half Century British Politics. LC 96-51815. 272p. 1997. pap. 24.95 (*0-7190-4840-0*, Pub. by Manchester Univ Pr) St Martin.

***Robins.** Point of Honor. 1999. write for info. (*0-8125-7647-0*) Tor Bks.

Robins, Adrienne. The Analytical Writer: A College Rhetoric. 2nd rev. ed. LC 95-69716. (Illus.). 594p. (C). 1996. pap. text 42.75 (*0-939693-35-6*) Collegiate Pr.

Robins, Anna G. Modern Art in Britain, 1910-1919. LC 97-181018. (Illus.). 192p. 1997. 45.00 (*1-85894-032-X*, Pub. by Merrell Holberton) U of Wash Pr.

— Walter Sickert: Drawings. LC 96-14107. (Illus.). 1996. text 69.95 (*1-85928-310-1*, Pub. by Scolar Pr) Ashgate Pub Co.

Robins, Arthur. The Teeny Tiny Woman. LC 97-32302. (Illus.). 24p. (J). (ps-1). 1998. 3.29 (*0-7636-0452-6*) Candlewick Pr.

— The Teeny Tiny Woman. LC 97-32302. (Illus.). 24p. (J). (ps-3). 1998. 10.99 (*0-7636-0444-5*) Candlewick Pr.

Robins, Arthur, jt. auth. see Anholt, Laurence.

Robins, Arthur J. Alcohol Detoxification Manual: A Guide to Administering Comprehensive Services. 120p. 1988. 29.95 (*0-89885-402-4*, Kluwer Acad Hman Sci) Kluwer Academic.

Robins, Ashley H. Biological Perspectives on Human Pigmentation. (Studies in Biological Anthropology: No. 7). (Illus.). 267p. (C). 1991. text 80.00 (*0-521-36514-7*) Cambridge U Pr.

Robins, Auther, jt. auth. see Pratt Institute Art Therapy Staff.

Robins, C. Richard, et al. Common & Scientific Names of Fishes from the United States & Canada. 5th ed. LC 90-86052. (Special Publication Ser.: No. 20). 183p. 1991. 43.00 (*0-913235-70-9*, 510.16C); pap. 34.00 (*0-913235-69-5*, 510.16P) Am Fisheries Soc.

— World Fishes Important to North Americans Exclusive of Species from the Continental Waters of the United States & Canada. (Special Publication Ser.: No. 21). 243p. 1991. pap. 39.00 (*0-913235-53-9*, 510.17P); text 47.00 (*0-913235-54-7*, 510.17C) Am Fisheries Soc.

Robins, Corinne. Art in the Seventh Power. (Illus.). 72p. (Orig.). 1984. pap. 5.00 (*0-930557-00-X*) Pratt Press.

— Facing It. 62p. 1996. 9.00 (*0-930557-01-8*) Pratt Press.

***Robins, Corinne.** Marble Goddesses with Technicolor Skins. 108p. 2000. pap. 11.95 (*0-937804-84-3*, Pub. by Segue NYC) SPD-Small Pr Dist.

Robins, David. Tarnished Vision: Crime & Community Action in the Inner City. LC 92-22144. 160p. 1993. 45.00 (*0-19-825751-1*); pap. 16.95 (*0-19-825816-X*) OUP.

Robins, Denise. Bride of Doom. large type ed. (Ulverscroft Large Print Ser.). 544p. 1998. 29.99 (*0-7089-3897-3*) Ulverscroft.

— The Changing Years. large type ed. (Dales Large Print Ser.). 391p. 1997. pap. 18.99 (*1-85389-769-8*, Dales) Ulverscroft.

— Dark Corridor. large type ed. 416p. 1996. 27.99 (*0-7089-3491-9*) Ulverscroft.

— Dark, Secret Love. large type ed. (Dales Large Print Ser.). 325p. 1997. pap. 18.99 (*1-85389-702-7*) Ulverscroft.

— The Gilded Cage. 192p. 1998. 24.00 (*0-7278-5366-X*) Severn Hse.

— The Gilded Cage. large type ed. LC 98-33781. (Romance Ser.). 291p. 1999. write for info. (*0-7540-3533-6*) Chivers N Amer.

— The Gilded Cage. large type ed. LC 98-33781. 1999. 30.00 (*0-7838-0362-1*, G K Hall Lrg Type) Mac Lib Ref.

— Gold for the Gay Masters. large type ed. 640p. 1996. 27.99 (*0-7089-3522-2*) Ulverscroft.

— Heart of Paris. large type ed. (Ulverscroft Large Print Ser.). 464p. 1997. 27.99 (*0-7089-3744-6*) Ulverscroft.

— Infatuation. large type ed. (Dales Large Print Ser.). 334p. 1998. pap. 19.99 (*1-85389-767-1*, Dales) Ulverscroft.

— The Marriage Bond. large type ed. (Dales Large Print Ser.). 352p. 1998. pap. 19.99 (*1-85389-768-X*, Dales) Ulverscroft.

— Moment of Love. large type ed. 432p. 1995. 27.99 (*0-7089-3397-1*) Ulverscroft.

— Only My Dreams. large type ed. (Dales Large Print Ser.). 435p. 1997. pap. 18.99 (*1-85389-701-9*) Ulverscroft.

***Robins, Denise.** The Other Love. large type ed. 352p. 1999. pap. 20.99 (*1-85389-957-7*, Dales) Ulverscroft.

Robins, Denise. The Other Side of Love. large type ed. 432p. 1995. 27.99 (*0-7089-3437-4*) Ulverscroft.

— Set Me Free. large type ed. 1993. 17.95 (*0-7505-0479-X*, Pub. by Mgna Lrg Print) Ulverscroft.

— Set the Stars Alight. large type ed. 288p. 1995. 27.99 (*0-7089-3352-1*) Ulverscroft.

— The Strong Heart. large type ed. (Ulverscroft Large Print Ser.). 432p. 1997. 27.99 (*0-7089-3727-6*) Ulverscroft.

Robins, Deri. The Great Pirate Activity Book. LC 94-43140. (Illus.). 1995. 7.95 (*1-85697-578-9*, Kingfisher) LKC.

— Kids' Around the World Cookbook. LC 93-42504. (Illus.). 40p. (J). (gr. 3-7). 1994. pap. 8.95 (*1-85697-997-0*) LKC.

— Mystery of the Monster Party. LC 97-14745. (Gamebook Preschool Puzzles Ser.). (Illus.). 32p. (Orig.). (J). 1998. pap. 5.99 (*0-7636-0300-7*) Candlewick Pr.

— Papier Mache. LC 92-41102. (Step-by-Step Ser.). (Illus.). 40p. (J). (gr. 3-7). 1993. pap. 7.95 (*1-85697-926-1*, Kingfisher) LKC.

— Papier Mache. LC 92-41102. (Step-by-Step Ser.). (Illus.). 40p. (J). (gr. 3-7). 1995. 13.90 (*1-85697-692-0*, Kingfisher) LKC.

Robins, Deri & Robins, Jim. Stone in the Sword: The Quest for the Missing Emerald. LC 97-24065. (Gamebook Ser.). (Illus.). 32p. (J). (ps-4). 1998. 12.99 (*0-7636-0313-9*) Candlewick Pr.

Robins, Deri & Stowell, Charlotte. Making Books. LC 93-48560. (Illus.). (J). 1994. pap. 7.95 (*1-85697-518-5*) LKC.

Robins, Deri, et al. The Kids Can Do It Book: Fun Things to Make & Do. LC 92-43345. (Illus.). 80p. (J). (gr. k-4). 1993. pap. 12.95 (*1-85697-860-5*, Kingfisher) LKC.

Robins, E. Ibsen & the Actress. LC 73-10253. (Studies in Drama: No. 39). 1973. reprint ed. lib. bdg. 75.00 (*0-8383-1718-9*) M S G Haskell Hse.

Robins, Eleanor. Meg Parker, 5 in each set, Set 1 & 2. (Illus.). (J). (gr. 2-7). 1984. pap. 17.00 (*0-87879-439-5*) High Noon Bks.

— Meg Parker, 5 in each set, Set 2. (Illus.). (J). (gr. 2-7). 1985. pap. write for info. (*0-87879-472-7*) High Noon Bks.

Robins, Elizabeth. The Convert. LC 96-19635. 320p. 1996. pap. 12.95 (*1-55861-162-2*) Feminist Pr.

— The Magnetic North. LC 72-96893. reprint ed. lib. bdg. 22.50 (*0-8398-1760-6*) Irvington.

Robins, Elizabeth, et al. The Alaska-Klondike Diary of Elizabeth Robins, 1900. Moessner, Victoria J. & Gates, Joanne E., eds. LC 98-10019. (Illus.). xx, 370p. 1999. pap. 22.95 (*0-912006-99-4*) U of Alaska Pr.

Robins, Gay. The Art of Ancient Egypt. LC 97-19458. (Illus.). 288p. 1997. 39.95 (*0-674-04660-9*) HUP.

***Robins, Gay.** The Art of Ancient Egypt. (Illus.). 2000. pap. 24.95 (*0-674-00376-4*) HUP.

Robins, Gay. Egyptian Painting & Relief. (Shire Egyptology Ser.). (Illus.). 62p. 1990. pap. 10.50 (*0-85263-789-6*, Pub. by Shire Pubns) Lubrecht & Cramer.

— Proportion & Style in Ancient Egyptian Art. LC 93-65. (Illus.). 296p. (Orig.). 1994. pap. 19.95 (*0-292-77064-2*); text 40.00 (*0-292-77060-X*) U of Tex Pr.

— Reflections of Women in the New Kingdom: Ancient Egyptian Art from the British Museum. (EUMILOP Ser.: No. 7). 24p. 1995. pap. 10.00 (*0-9638169-6-9*) M C Carlos Mus.

— Women in Ancient Egypt. 208p. 1993. pap. text 19.95 (*0-674-95469-6*) HUP.

— Women in Ancient Egypt. LC 92-38221. 205p. 1993. reprint ed. pap. 18.95 (*0-674-95468-8*) HUP.

Robins, Gay, ed. Beyond the Pyramids: Egyptian Regional Art from the Museo Egizio, Turin. (EUMILOP Ser.: No. 4). (Illus.). 95p. 1995. pap. text 24.95 (*0-9638169-2-6*) M C Carlos Mus.

Robins, Gertrud, jt. auth. see Hartley, Paul.

Robins, Gina, pseud. Forbidden Kiss. 1995. pap. 4.99 (*0-8217-5161-1*) NAL.

Robins, Howard, jt. auth. see Null, Gary.

Robins, Jan. Honey for the Devil. large type ed. (Linford Romance Library). 288p. 1994. pap. 16.99 (*0-7089-7547-X*, Linford) Ulverscroft.

Robins, Jim, jt. auth. see Robins, Deri.

Robins, Joan. Addie Meets Max. (I Can Read Bks.). (Illus.). 32p. (J). (gr. 1-3). 1985. 9.95 (*0-06-025063-1*) HarpC Child Bks.

— Addie Meets Max. LC 84-48329. (I Can Read Bks.). (Illus.). 32p. (J). (ps-3). 1985. lib. bdg. 15.89 (*0-06-025064-X*) HarpC Child Bks.

— Addie Meets Max. (I Can Read Bks.). (Illus.). 32p. (J). (gr. 1-3). 1988. pap. 3.95 (*0-06-444116-4*, HarpTrophy) HarpC Child Bks.

Robins, Joan. Addie Meets Max. (I Can Read Bks.). (J). (gr. 1-3). 1988. 8.95 (*0-606-03540-0*, Pub. by Turtleback) Demco.

Robins, Joan. Addie Runs Away. LC 88-24350. (I Can Read Bks.). (Illus.). 32p. (J). (ps-3). 1989. 10.95 (*0-06-025080-1*); lib. bdg. 10.89 (*0-06-025081-X*) HarpC Child Bks.

— Addie's Bad Day. LC 92-13101. (I Can Read Bks.). (Illus.). 32p. (J). (ps-3). 1993. pap. 3.95 (*0-06-444183-0*, HarpTrophy) HarpC Child Bks.

Robins, Joan. Addie's Bad Day. (I Can Read Bks.). (J). (gr. 1-3). 1994. 8.95 (*0-606-06159-2*, Pub. by Turtleback) Demco.

Robins, Joyce. Natural Wonders of the World. 1992. 16.98 (*1-55521-760-5*) Bk Sales Inc.

— World's Greatest Disasters. 1990. 14.98 (*1-55521-566-1*) Bk Sales Inc.

Robins, Kay C. Come with Me to Grandma's House. LC 96-90129. (Illus.). 16p. (Orig.). (J). (ps-2). 1996. pap. 4.65 (*0-9652177-0-1*) Whispering Oaks.

Robins, Kevin. Into the Image: Culture & Politics in the Field of Vision. LC 95-52813. (Illus.). 208p. (C). 1996. pap. 22.99 (*0-415-14577-5*) Routledge.

***Robins, Kevin.** Times of Technoculture: From Information Society to Virtual Life. LC 99-20329. 1999. pap. 22.99 (*0-415-16116-9*) Routledge.

Robins, Kevin, ed. Understanding Information: Business, Technology & Geography. LC 91-40511. 288p. 1994. text 100.00 (*0-471-94763-6*) Wiley.

Robins, Kevin & Webster, Frank. Information Technology: A Luddite Analysis. Voigt, Melvin J., ed. LC 85-46065. (Communication & Information Science Ser.). 400p. 1986. text 78.50 (*0-89391-343-X*) Ablx Pub.

***Robins, Kevin & Webster, Frank.** Times of Technoculture: From Information Society to Virtual Life. (Comedia Ser.). 336p. (C). 1999. text 75.00 (*0-415-16115-0*) Routledge.

Robins, Kevin, jt. auth. see Morley, David.

Robins, Kikanza N. Unspoken Visions: An Inner Journey. LC 95-29996. (Illus.). 128p. (Orig.). 1996. pap. 12.95 (*0-918949-88-2*) Martz.

Robins, L. Introduction to Political Science. Date not set. pap. text. write for info. (*0-582-35493-5*, Pub. by Addison-Wesley) Longman.

Robins, L. J., jt. auth. see Pyper, Robert.

Robins, Lawrence R., jt. auth. see Petrini, Julie O.

Robins, Lee N. & Barrett, James E., eds. The Validity of Psychiatric Diagnosis. LC 87-43322. (American Psychopathological Association Ser.). 350p. 1989. reprint ed. pap. 108.50 (*0-608-03441-X*, 206414200008) Bks Demand.

Robins, Lee N. & Regier, Darrel A., eds. Psychiatric Disorders in America. 400p. 1990. 60.00 (*0-02-926571-1*) Free Pr.

Robins, Lee N. & Rutter, Michael, eds. Straight & Devious Pathways from Childhood to Adulthood. (Illus.). 411p. (C). 1990. text 80.00 (*0-521-36408-6*) Cambridge U Pr.

— Straight & Devious Pathways from Childhood to Adulthood. (Illus.). 411p. (C). 1992. pap. text 25.95 (*0-521-42739-8*) Cambridge U Pr.

Robins, Leonard S., jt. auth. see Litman, Theodor J.

Robins, Lewis, jt. auth. see Sackheim, George I.

Robins, Lynton, et al, eds. Britain's Changing Party System. LC 94-13743. 240p. (C). 1994. pap. text 21.95 (*0-7185-1505-6*) Bks Intl VA.

— Britain's Changing Party System. LC 94-13743. 240p. (C). 1994. 89.95 (*0-7185-1494-7*) Bks Intl VA.

Robins, Lynton, jt. ed. see Pyper, Robert.

Robins, Madeleine. My Dear Jenny. 224p. 1980. pap. 1.75 (*0-449-50041-1*, Coventry) Fawcett.

— The Stone War. LC 99-26075. 320p. 1999. 23.95 (*0-312-85486-2*, Pub. by Tor Bks) St Martin.

***Robins, Madeleine E.** Stone War. 2000. mass mkt. 6.99 (*0-8125-2431-4*) Tor Bks.

Robins, Madeline E. Daredevil: The Cutting Edge. 1999. mass mkt. 6.50 (*0-425-16938-3*) Blvd Books.

Robins, Marc. Pulse-to-Tone Conversion Technology: Promises & Pitfalls. 40p. (Orig.). 1996. pap. 85.00 (*0-9624360-7-0*) Robins Pr.

— Speech Recognition Reference Manual & Buyer's Guide. 4th ed. 305p. 1996. pap. 85.00 (*0-9624360-5-4*) Robins Pr.

— Voice & Fax Processing Printed Circuit Cards: A Sourcebook of Suppliers & Products. 188p. (Orig.). 1996. pap. 85.00 (*0-9624360-8-9*) Robins Pr.

— Voice & Fax Processing System Application Generators. 247p. (Orig.). 1996. pap. 85.00 (*0-9624360-6-2*, SR302) Robins Pr.

— The Voice Mail Reference Manual & Buyer's Guide. 6th ed. 465p. (C). 1996. pap. 75.00 (*0-9624360-0-3*) Robins Pr.

— A Voice Processing Primer. 210p. (Orig.). 1996. pap. 24.95 (*0-9624360-2-X*) Robins Pr.

— The Voice Response Reference Manual & Buyer's Guide. 5th ed. (Illus.). 375p. (C). 1996. pap. 85.00 (*0-9624360-1-1*) Robins Pr.

Robins, Melinda, ed. see Rhodes, Naomi.

Robins, Melinda Beth. Intersecting Places, Emancipatory Spaces: Women Journalists in Tanzania LC 99-27159. 1999. write for info. (*0-86543-761-0*) Africa World.

Robins, Mike, jt. auth. see Gilbert, Robert N.

Robins, Monty. The Manuscript of Jow Smithwitz. 323p. (C). 1989. text 50.00 (*1-872795-58-7*, Pub. by Pentland Pr) St Mut.

Robins-Mowry, Dorothy. Conversations Between Jews & Japanese: Exploring the Mindset of the Peoples of the East & West. 224p. (Orig.). 1995. pap. 19.50 (*1-883223-08-3*) Pacific NY.

— Taiwan Independence & Limitations to the Nation-State Concept. 176p. 1997. pap. 29.00 (*1-883223-12-1*) Pacific NY.

— What's Wrong with Japan, Anyway? 112p. (Orig.). 1993. pap. text 9.95 (*1-883223-00-8*) Pacific NY.

Robins-Mowry, Dorothy, ed. Canada-U. S. Relations: Perceptions & Misperceptions. 64p. (Orig.). (C). 1988. pap. text 9.00 (*0-8191-6873-4*) U Pr of Amer.

— Is a Korea-Japan Symbiosis Possible? 88p. 1996. pap. 29.00 (*1-883223-09-1*) Pacific NY.

— What's Wrong with the U. S. A., Anyway? LC 93-47930. 1994. 9.50 (*1-883223-03-2*) Pacific NY.

***Robins, Natalie.** The Girl Who Died Twice: Every Patient's Nightmare - The Libby Zion Case & the Hidden Hazards of Hospitals. (Illus.). 350p. 1999. reprint ed. text 23.00 (*0-7881-6599-2*) DIANE Pub.

Robins, Natalie. Living in the Lightning: A Cancer Journal. LC 98-37622. 120p. 1999. pap. 14.00 (*0-8135-2665-5*); text 31.00 (*0-8135-2664-7*) Rutgers U Pr.

Robins, Nicholas A. El Mesianismo y la Rebelion Indigena: La Rebelion de Oruro en 1781. (SPA.). 218p. (Orig.). 1997. pap. 6.00 (*0-9659015-0-5*) N Robins.

Robins, Nick, ed. Groundwater Pollution, Aquifer Recharge & Vulnerability. (Geological Society Special Publication: No. 130). 234p. 1998. 99.00 (*1-897799-98-5*, Pub. by Geol Soc Pub Hse) AAPG.

Robins, Owen H. With Love & Better Health, Onward Christian Soldiers! LC 91-90518. 160p. 1995. 16.95 (*0-9630319-0-2*) Larksdale.

Robins, P. Advanced Accounting Practice Book 1. 288p. 1988. pap. 31.95 (*0-278-00014-2*) Thomson Learn.

Robins, Patricia. The Constant Heart. large type ed. (Dales Large Print Ser.). (Illus.). 265p. 1996. pap. 18.99 (*1-85389-630-6*) Ulverscroft.

— Forbidden. 160p. 1992. reprint ed. 18.00 (*0-7278-4325-7*) Severn Hse.

***Robins, Patricia.** Forever. large type ed. 256p. 2000. 31.99 (*0-7089-4175-3*) Ulverscroft.

Robins, Patricia. Forsaken. 1993. 19.00 (*0-7278-4527-6*) Severn Hse.

— Forsaken. large type ed. 1994. 27.99 (*0-7089-3192-8*) Ulverscroft.

— Fulfillment. 224p. 1993. lib. bdg. 18.00 (*0-7278-4389-3*) Severn Hse.

— The Legend. large type ed. (Dales Large Print Ser.). 343p. 1997. pap. 18.99 (*1-85389-677-2*) Ulverscroft.

— The Long Wait. large type ed. (Dales Large Print Ser.). 300p. 1996. pap. 18.99 (*1-85389-629-2*, Dales) Ulverscroft.

— Love Me Tomorrow. large type ed. (Dales Large Print Ser.). 254p. 1996. pap. 18.99 (*1-85389-679-9*, Dales) Ulverscroft.

— Love Must Wait. large type ed. (Dales Large Print Ser.). 326p. 1997. pap. 18.99 (*1-85389-678-0*, Dales) Ulverscroft.

— No Stone Unturned. large type ed. 280p. 1989. pap. 12.95 (*0-8161-4438-9*, G K Hall Lrg Type) Mac Lib Ref.

— None but He. large type ed. (Dales Large Print Ser.). 1995. pap. 18.99 (*1-85389-461-3*, Dales) Ulverscroft.

— Return to Love. large type ed. 271p. 1994. pap. 18.99 (*1-85389-460-5*) Ulverscroft.

— Topaz Island. large type ed. (Dales Large Print Ser.). 1994. pap. 18.99 (*1-85389-462-1*, Pub. by Mgna Lrg Print) Ulverscroft.

Robins, Perry. Play It Safe in the Sun. (Illus.). 40p. (J). 1994. pap. 9.95 (*0-9627688-1-2*) Skin Cancer Fndtn.

— Sun Sense: A Complete Guide to the Prevention, Early Detection, & Treatment of Skin Cancer. (Illus.). 272p. 1990. pap. 109.95 (*0-9627688-0-4*) Skin Cancer Fndtn.

Robins, Perry & Perez, Maritza. Understanding Melanoma: What You Need to Know. (Illus.). 80p. (Orig.). 1996. mass mkt. 10.00 (*0-9627688-2-0*) Skin Cancer Fndtn.

Robins, Perry, et al. Dermatologic Surgery: Textbook & Atlas. LC 96-3794. (Illus.). 1996. write for info. (*0-387-59453-1*) Spr-Verlag.

— Dermatologic Surgery: Textbook & Atlas. Burgdorf, W. H., tr. (Illus.). 189p. 1996. 250.00 (*3-540-59453-1*) Spr-Verlag.

Robins, Peter. Doves for the Seventies: Poems for Those Who Choose to Care. LC 72-516001. 142p. 1969. write for info. (*0-552-08323-2*) Corgi Bks Ltd.

Robins, R. J. & Rhodes, M. J., eds. Manipulating Secondary Metabolism in Culture. (Illus.). 324p. (C). 1989. text 69.95 (*0-521-36254-7*) Cambridge U Pr.

Robins, R. J., jt. ed. see Tomas-Barberan, F. A.

Robins, R. S., et al. Psychopathology & Political Leadership, Vol. 16. LC 77-85747. 1977. pap. text 11.00 (*0-930598-16-4*) Tulane Stud Pol.

Robins, Richard. Texas Discovery Forms. 1991. ring bd. 115.00 (*0-327-00946-2*, 82546, MICHIE) LEXIS Pub.

— Texas Special Issues Forms, 2 vols. 2nd ed. 1995. ring bd. 120.00 (*0-327-00948-9*, 82647-11, MICHIE) LEXIS Pub.

Robins, Richard, ed. see Steves, Sterling W.

***Robins, Richard C.** Local Rules of the District Courts in Texas, Issue 6. 600p. 1999. ring bd. write for info. (*0-327-01387-7*, 8267217) LEXIS Pub.

Robins, Richard C. Texas Civil Appeals Forms. 420p. 1991. ring bd. 115.00 (*0-409-25502-5*, MICHIE) LEXIS Pub.

— Texas Discovery Forms, Issue 9. 150p. 1999. ring bd. write for info. (*0-327-01354-0*, 8254715) LEXIS Pub.

— Texas Discovery Forms, 1991-1992. 360p. Date not set. ring bd. 115.00 (*0-409-25534-3*, 82546, MICHIE) LEXIS Pub.

***Robins, Richard C.** Texas Special Issues Forms, Issue 4. 150p. 1999. ring bd. write for info. (*0-327-01479-2*, 9385816) LEXIS Pub.

Robins, Richard C. Texas Special Issues Forms, 1988-1993. LC 88-2589. 640p. 1994. ring bd., suppl. ed. 65.00 (*0-685-44084-2*, MICHIE) LEXIS Pub.

— Texas Special Issues Forms, 1988-1993. 2nd ed. LC 88-2589. 640p. Date not set. ring bd. 120.00 (*0-409-25339-1*, 82647-11, MICHIE) LEXIS Pub.

Robins, Robert H. The Byzantine Grammarians: Their Place in History. LC 92-47496. (Trends in Linguistics, Studies & Monographs: Vol. 70). xi, 278p. (C). 1993. lib. bdg. 129.25 (*3-11-013574-4*) Mouton.

Robins, Robert S., ed. Psychopathology & Political Leadership. LC 77-85747. (Tulane Studies in Political Science: Vol. 16). 212p. 1977. reprint ed. pap. 65.80 (*0-608-00824-9*, 206161300010) Bks Demand.

Robins, Robert S. & Post, Jerrold M. Political Paranoia: The Psychopolitics of Hatred. LC 96-40336. 353p. 1997. 30.00 (*0-300-07027-6*) Yale U Pr.

Robins, Robert S., jt. auth. see Post, Jerrold M.

Robins, Ron. The Barbed-Wire College: Educating German POWs in the United States During World War II. LC 94-21161. 224p. 1995. text 35.00 (*0-691-03700-0*, Pub. by Princeton U Pr) Cal Prin Full Svc.

Robins, Sam, jt. auth. see Crandall, Richard L.

Robins, Sander J. Management of Lipid Disorders: A Basis & Guide for Therapeutic Intervention. LC 97-181155. 136p. 1997. pap. 18.95 (*0-683-30350-3*) Lppncott W & W.

— Management of Lipid Disorders: A Basis & Guide for Therapy. (Illus.). 112p. (Orig.). 1997. pap. text. write for info. (*0-89640-337-8*) Igaku-Shoin.

Robins, Sandy. They Do Remember: A Story of Soul Survival. 200p. (Orig.). 1996. pap. 13.95 (*0-9649105-0-0*) Home Ofc Pub.

Robins, Scott, jt. auth. see Duston, Robert L.

Robins, Seymour. The Armillary Sphere. 16p. 1973. pap. 3.95 (*0-87663-908-2*) Universe.

Robins, Suki, jt. ed. see Hennessy, James E.

Robins, Tony, jt. contrib. by see Mayne, Thom.

R

R

Robins, W. P. Phase Noise in Signal Sources: Theory & Applications. rev. ed. (Telecommunications Ser.: No. 9). 336p. 1984. pap. 69.00 (*0-86341-026-X*, TE009) INSPEC Inc.

Robins, Wayne. VH-1 Behind the Music, 1968. 2000. per. 12.95 (*0-671-03961-X*, MTV Bks) PB.

Robinsn, Chase, ed. A Medieval Islamic City Reconsidered: An interdisciplinary Approach to Samarra. (Oxford Studies in Islamic Art: No. 14). (Illus.). 250p. 2000. text 70.00 (*0-19-728024-2*) OUP.

Robinson. African American Studies. LC 96-76952. (C). 1998. pap. text 9.16 (*0-395-79688-1*) HM.

Robinson. Anthropology of Marxism. 68.95 (*1-84014-700-8*) Ashgate Pub Co.

Robinson. The Artist & the Quilt. 1983. 12.95 (*0-07-544275-2*) McGraw.

— The Best Halloween Ever. 128p. (J). (gr. 3 up). Date not set. lib. bdg. 14.89 (*0-06-027863-3*) HarpC.

***Robinson.** The Best Halloween Ever. 128p. (J). (gr. 3 up). 2000. 14.95 (*0-06-027862-5*) HarpC Child Bks.

Robinson. Biochemistry & Nutrition Value. 1987. pap. text. write for info. (*0-582-49506-7*, Pub. by Addison-Wesley) Longman.

— Conflict & Change in the Countryside. 1990. pap. text 42.00 (*0-471-94765-2*) Wiley.

— Corporate Personality in Ancient Israel. 1992. pap. 14.95 (*0-567-29109-X*, Pub. by T & T Clark) Bks Intl VA.

— Counseling Children: A Developmental Approach. 592p. (C). 1998. 35.00 (*0-02-402441-4*, Macmillan Coll) P-H.

— Criminal Law. 2nd ed. 864p. 1995. 58.00 (*0-316-75111-1*, Aspen Law & Bus) Aspen Pub.

— Cultural Nationalism. LC 88-18804. 240p. 1989. pap. 30.00 (*0-295-96600-9*) U of Wash Pr.

Robinson. Current Protocols in Cytology on CD-Rom with User's Guide. 1997. pap. text 450.00 incl. cd-rom (*0-471-16132-2*) Wiley.

Robinson. Current Protocols in Cytometry. LC 96-47214. 500p. 1997. 395.00 (*0-471-16131-4*) Wiley.

— Diversity in Counseling the Convergence of Race Gender & Culture. LC 99-26332. (Illus.). 338p. (C). 1999. pap. text 37.00 (*0-02-402481-3*, Macmillan Coll) P-H.

— Encyclopedia of Food Microbiology. (C). 1999. text 310.00 (*0-12-227071-1*) Acad Pr.

— 15th Century Persian Painting. (C). 1993. pap. text 21.00 (*0-8147-7446-6*) NYU Pr.

— Free Lunch. 2000. text 22.95 (*0-312-86524-4*) St Martin.

— Gender & Healthcare Leaders. LC 98-58078. 1999. text 39.95 (*0-7879-0933-5*) Jossey-Bass.

Robinson. The Growing of America, 1789-1848. 2nd ed. (Forum's American History Ser.). 14.95 (*0-88295-171-8*) Forum Pr IL.

— Handbook of Language & Social Psychology. text. write for info. (*0-471-49096-2*) Wiley.

— Keyboarding: Formating/Document Processing. 5th ed. 1991. pap. 10.00 (*0-538-60502-2*) Sth-Wstrn College.

Robinson. Keyboarding for Computer Success. 1999. pap. 44.95 (*0-538-68585-9*) S-W Pub.

Robinson. Leave It to Chance: Shaman's Rain. 104p. pap. 9.95 (*1-56389-586-2*, Pub. by DC Comics) Time Warner.

Robinson. Maid Marian & Her Merry Men. 1992. pap. text. write for info. (*0-582-09554-9*, Pub. by Addison-Wesley) Longman.

— Managed Healthcare U. S. Evidence: U. S. Evidence & Lessons for the National Health Service. LC 97-13906. (State of Health Ser.). 206p. 1997. 105.00 (*0-335-19949-6*); pap. 29.95 (*0-335-19948-8*) OpUniv Pr.

— Open Learning for Nurses. 1989. pap. text. write for info. (*0-582-04616-5*, Pub. by Addison-Wesley) Longman.

— The Physical Environment of Canada & the Evolution of Settlement Patterns. (NFS Canada Ser.). 1993. pap. 8.95 (*0-88922-203-7*) Genl Dist Srvs.

— Physical Geology Customs. 2nd ed. 1999. pap. 12.80 (*0-07-235581-6*) McGraw.

Robinson. Planting Design. 312p. 1994. pap., student ed. 43.95 (*0-566-07545-8*) Ashgate Pub Co.

Robinson. Practical Pediatrics. 3rd ed. 1994. pap. text 66.00 (*0-443-04869-X*, W B Saunders Co) Harcrt Hlth Sci Grp.

— Practical Writing Techniques. 7th ed. 330p. 1998. pap. text 24.00 (*0-536-01225-3*) Pearson Custom.

— Primary Care Challenge. (C). 1999. pap. text. write for info. (*0-443-05634-X*) Church.

— Privacy. (Ethics & Behavior Ser.: Vol. 7, No. 3). 1997. pap. 20.00 (*0-8058-9854-9*) L Erlbaum Assocs.

— Texts & Contexts. (Adaptable Courseware-Softside Ser). Date not set. mass mkt. 18.50 (*0-534-15958-3*) Wadsworth Pub.

— Texts & Contexts. 1990. teacher ed. write for info. (*0-534-13045-3*) Wadsworth Pub.

— Texts & Contexts. 4th ed. LC 99-34177. (Developmental Study/Study Skill Ser.). 1999. pap. 34.75 (*0-534-50773-5*) Wadsworth Pub.

— Traplines. 1998. pap. 12.00 (*0-8050-5588-6*, Owl) H Holt & Co.

— Unread Runes. 2000. 29.95 (*0-07-135743-2*) McGraw.

Robinson & Cutis. Odysseus Goes Through Hell. (Illus.). (J). 1996. mass mkt. 8.95 (*0-340-66498-3*, Pub. by Hodder & Stought Ltd) Trafalgar.

— Odysseus Superhero. (Illus.). (J). 1996. mass mkt. 8.95 (*0-340-66497-5*, Pub. by Hodder & Stought Ltd) Trafalgar.

— Theseus Monster Killer. (Illus.). (J). 1996. mass mkt. 8.95 (*0-340-66499-1*, Pub. by Hodder & Stought Ltd) Trafalgar.

Robinson & Hewison. Southeast Asia in 1980s. 1989. pap. text 14.95 (*0-04-176012-3*, Pub. by Allen & Unwin Pty) Paul & Co Pubs.

Robinson & Jackson. People on Earth. Date not set. pap. text. write for info. (*0-582-33081-5*, Pub. by Addison-Wesley) Longman.

Robinson & Miller. Colby, Kerr, & Robinson's Color Atlas of Oral Pathology. 5th ed. (Illus.). 198p. 1990. text 63.00 (*0-397-51043-8*) Lppncott W & W.

***Robinson, et al.** Applied Computer Keyboarding. 4th ed. (Keyboarding/Typesetting-1st Yr Ser.). 1998. pap. 29.95 (*0-538-68759-2*); pap. 25.25 (*0-538-68760-6*) S-W Pub.

Robinson, et al. Basic Keyboarding & Typewriting Applications. 2nd ed. (TA - Typing/Keyboarding Ser.). 1988. mass mkt. 20.50 (*0-538-20390-0*) S-W Pub.

— Century 21 Keyboard & Information Processing. 6th ed. LC 95-69844. (TA - Typing/Keyboarding Ser.). 1996. pap. 64.95 (*0-538-64892-9*) S-W Pub.

— Century 21 Keyboarding & Information Processing, Book 1. 6th ed. LC 97-116089. (TA - Typing/Keyboarding Ser.). 1996. mass mkt. 51.95 (*0-538-64893-7*) S-W Pub.

— Century 21 Keyboarding & Information Processing, Style Manual. 6th ed. (TA - Typing/Keyboarding Ser.). 1997. mass mkt. 4.00 (*0-538-64938-0*) S-W Pub.

— Century 21 Keyboarding & Information Processing, Placement & Performance Tests, Vol. 1. 6th ed. (TA - Typing/Keyboarding Ser.). 1996. mass mkt. 4.75 (*0-538-64931-3*) S-W Pub.

— Century 21 Keyboarding & Information Processing, Placement & Performance Tests, Vol. 2. 6th ed. (TA - Typing/Keyboarding Ser.). 1996. mass mkt. 4.75 (*0-538-64932-1*) S-W Pub.

— Century 21 Keyboarding & Information Processing, Collaborative Simulation. 6th ed. (TA - Typing/Keyboarding Ser.). 1996. mass mkt. 11.25 (*0-538-64925-9*) S-W Pub.

— Century 21 Keyboarding, Formatting & Document Processing, Complete Course. 5th ed. (Keyboarding/ Typesetting-1st Yr Ser.). 1991. mass mkt. 53.95 (*0-538-60073-X*) S-W Pub.

— Century 21 Keyboarding, Formatting & Document Processing, Style Manual. 5th ed. (Keyboarding/ Typesetting-1st Yr Ser.). 1992. mass mkt. 4.95 (*0-538-60511-1*) S-W Pub.

— Century 21 Keyboarding, Placement Test 2. 5th ed. (Keyboarding/Typesetting-1st Yr Ser.). 1991. 2.95 (*0-538-60510-3*) S-W Pub.

— Century 21 Keyboarding, Formatting, Document Processing, Book 1. 5th ed. (TA - Typing/Keyboarding Ser.). 1991. mass mkt. 30.50 (*0-538-60074-8*) S-W Pub.

— Contemporary Climatology. 2nd ed. 384p. (C). 1999. pap. 41.00 (*0-582-27631-4*) Addison-Wesley.

— History & Genealogy of Morrill, Maine. LC 83-62231. (Illus.). 800p. 1983. 55.00 (*0-89725-044-3*) Picton Pr.

— Word Processing Application Guide 2: Century 21 Keyboarding, Formatting & Document Processing. 5th ed. (Keyboarding/Typesetting-1st Yr Ser.). 1992. mass mkt. 7.50 (*0-538-60949-4*) S-W Pub.

Robinson, jt. auth. see Dispirito, Mary Ann.

Robinson, jt. auth. see Fine Creative Staff.

Robinson, jt. auth. see Rowell.

Robinson, jt. auth. see Ryan.

Robinson & Cole Land Use, Staff, jt. auth. see Marine Law Institute, Staff.

Robinson, A. Vehicle Body Refinishing. 192p. 1995. pap. text 18.95 (*0-7506-2270-9*) Buttrwrth-Heinemann.

***Robinson, A. & Katzman, J.** Cracking the SAT 2001. 672p. 2000. pap. 18.00 (*0-375-75621-3*, Pub. by PRP NY) Random.

***Robinson, A. & Livesey, A.** Repair of Vehicle Bodies. 4th ed. LC 99-88583. (Illus.). 2000. pap. 39.95 (*0-7506-4517-2*) Buttrwrth-Heinemann.

Robinson, A. D., jt. ed. see Czernichow, P.

Robinson, A. G., ed. Regional & Petroleum Geology of the Black Sea & Surrounding Region. LC 97-42045. (Memoir Ser.: Vol. 68). (Illus.). vi, 385p. 1997. 149.00 (*0-89181-348-9*, 557) AAPG.

Robinson, A. G., jt. ed. see Horbury, A. D.

Robinson, A. L., jt. auth. see Robinson, Antony M.

Robinson, A. P. The Design & Development of a Suspension Burner for Forestry & Agricultural Residues. 1991. pap. 25.00 (*0-85954-289-0*, Pub. by Nat Res Inst) St Mut.

Robinson, A. P., et al, eds. A Timber-Drying System Fuelled by Sawdust. 1993. pap. 25.00 (*0-85954-328-5*, Pub. by Nat Res Inst) St Mut.

Robinson, A. P. & Breag, G. R. Heat Production from Sawdust: Construction & Operation of a Suspension Burner to Applications in Forest Industries. 1992. pap. 40.00 (*0-85954-300-5*, Pub. by Nat Res Inst) St Mut.

Robinson, A. P., et al. The Construction & Operation of a Rice Husk Burner. 1993. pap. 40.00 (*0-85954-357-9*, Pub. by Nat Res Inst) St Mut.

Robinson, A. P., jt. ed. see Williams, E. A.

Robinson, A. R. Theodor Fontane: An Introduction to the Man & His Work. LC 76-383573. (ENG & GER.). 219p. reprint ed. pap. 67.90 (*0-7837-5190-7*, 204492400004) Bks Demand.

Robinson, A. R. B., ed. The Counting House. 1992. pap. 35.00 (*1-85072-102-5*, Pub. by W Sessions) St Mut.

Robinson, A. S. & Hooper, G., eds. Fruit Flies Vols. A & B: Their Biology, Natural Enemies & Control, Vol. A. (World Crop Pests Ser.: Vols. 3A & 3B). 372p. 1990. 273.00 (*0-444-42763-5*) Elsevier.

— Fruit Flies Vols. A & B: Their Biology, Natural Enemies & Control, Vol. B. (World Crop Pests Ser.: Vols. 3A & 3B). 448p. 1990. 282.25 (*0-444-42750-3*) Elsevier.

Robinson, A. T., jt. auth. see Marks, R.

Robinson, Abraham. Non-Standard Analysis. rev. ed. LC 95-43750. (Landmarks in Mathematics & Physics Ser.). 308p. (C). 1996. pap. text 19.95 (*0-691-04490-2*, Pub. by Princeton U Pr) Cal Prin Full Svc.

— Numbers & Ideals. LC 65-16747. (Illus.). 1965. 16.00 (*0-8162-7234-4*) Holden-Day.

Robinson, Abraham & Laurmann, J. A. Wing Theory. LC 57-601. (Cambridge Aeronautical Ser.: No. 2). 579p. reprint ed. pap. 165.10 (*0-608-11489-8*, 2051692) Bks Demand.

Robinson, Adam. Princeton Review: GRE. 1989. pap. 10.95 (*0-394-75684-3*) Random.

— The Princeton Review: The Student Access Guide to College Admissions. 176p. 1993. pap. 12.00 (*0-679-74590-4*) Villard Books.

— Princeton Review: Word Smart 2. 1994. 25.00 incl. audio (*0-517-59761-6*) Liv Lang.

— What Smart Students Know: Maximum Grades Optimum Learning, Minimum Time. LC 93-20437. 1993. pap. 16.00 (*0-517-88085-7*, Crown) Crown Pub Group.

Robinson, Adam & Fleisher, Julian. The Princeton Review: Word Smart. 1993. 25.00 incl. audio (*0-517-59355-6*) Liv Lang.

Robinson, Adam & Katzman, J. Cracking the GRE 1999. (Princeton Review Ser.). 1998. pap. 18.00 (*0-375-75161-0*) Random.

Robinson, Adam & Katzman, John. The Princeton Review - Word Smart: Building an Educated Vocabulary. LC 87-40580. (Illus.). 256p. 1988. 10.00 (*0-394-75686-X*) Villard Books.

Robinson, Adam & Princeton Review Publishing Staff. Word Smart: Building an Educated Vocabulary. rev. ed. LC 87-40580. (Princeton Review Ser.). 320p. 1993. pap. 12.00 (*0-679-74589-0*) Villard Books.

— Word Smart II: How to Build a More Educated Vocabulary. 304p. 1992. pap. 12.00 (*0-679-73863-0*) Villard Books.

Robinson, Adam & Tallia, Rob. Cracking the LSAT: 2000 Edition. 1999. pap. 20.00 (*0-375-75409-1*) Random.

— Cracking the LSATwith Sample Tests on CD-ROM: 2000 Edition. 1999. pap. 34.95 incl. cd-rom (*0-375-75410-5*) Random.

Robinson, Adam, jt. auth. see Katzman, John.

Robinson, Adele J., ed. Portland Symphony Cookbook. 5th ed. LC 74-84052. 336p. 1974. 9.95 (*0-9601266-1-9*) Friends Portland Symphony.

Robinson, Alan. Clouds of Glory. 94p. 1994. pap. 45.00 (*0-85439-480-X*, Pub. by St Paul Pubns) St Mut.

— Enfoques Modernos Para la Mejora En la Fabricacion: El Sistema Shingo. Shingo, Shigeo, ed. (SPA., Illus.). 432p. (Orig.). 1992. pap. 25.00 (*84-87022-77-4*) Productivity Inc.

— Jesus According to John. 176p. 1996. pap. 39.95 (*0-85439-530-X*, Pub. by St Paul Pubns) St Mut.

— Malaysia 2020. (Euromoney Country Guide Ser.). 219p. 1997. 170.00 (*1-85564-595-5*, Pub. by Euromoney) Am Educ Systs.

— Mystic Rose. 112p. 1996. pap. 39.95 (*0-85439-525-3*, Pub. by St Paul Pubns) St Mut.

— The Repair of Vehicle Bodies. 2nd ed. 1989. pap. 27.95 (*0-7506-0159-0*) Buttrwrth-Heinemann.

— The Repair of Vehicle Bodies. 4th ed. (Illus.). 580p. 2000. pap. text 46.95 (*0-7506-0955-9*) Buttrwrth-Heinemann.

— Tongues of Angels. 190p. 1996. pap. 39.95 (*0-85439-471-0*, Pub. by St Paul Pubns) St Mut.

— The Treasures of Jesus: A Meditation on the Sermon on the Mount. 144p. 1996. pap. 30.00 (*0-85439-466-4*, Pub. by St Paul Pubns) St Mut.

— The Treasures of St. Paul: Selected Themes from Paul's Theology & Ethics. 220p. 1996. pap. 30.00 (*0-85439-500-8*, Pub. by St Paul Pubns) St Mut.

— Vehicle Body Fitting & Repair: NVQ Levels 2 & 3. 320p. 1995. pap. text 24.95 (*0-7506-2271-7*) Buttrwrth-Heinemann.

— Words for Worship. 160p. 1994. pap. 35.00 (*0-85439-509-1*, Pub. by St Paul Pubns) St Mut.

Robinson, Alan, ed. Continuous Improvement in Operations: A Systematic Approach to Waste Reduction. LC 90-21651. (Illus.). 406p. 1991. 35.00 (*0-915299-51-8*); pap. text 22.95 (*0-915299-86-0*) Productivity Inc.

— Modern Approaches to Manufacturing Improvement: The Shingo System. LC 89-43673. 420p. 1990. pap. 23.00 (*0-915299-64-X*) Productivity Inc.

— The Six Chaplet Rosary. 80p. 1994. pap. 30.00 (*0-85439-473-7*, Pub. by St Paul Pubns) St Mut.

Robinson, Alan G. & Stern, Sam. Corporate Creativity: How Innovation & Improvement Actually Happen. LC 97-24838. 300p. 1997. 29.95 (*1-57675-009-4*) Berrett-Koehler.

— Corporate Creativity: How Innovation & Improvement Actually Happen. LC 97-24838. 300p. 1998. pap. 17.95 (*1-57675-049-3*) Berrett-Koehler.

Robinson, Alan H. Virgin Islands National Park: The Story Behind the Scenery. LC 74-81560. (Illus.). 48p. 1974. pap. 7.95 (*0-916122-14-X*) KC Pubns.

Robinson, Alan J. An Odd Bestiary. LC 86-6941. 160p. 1986. 29.95 (*0-252-01353-0*) U of Ill Pr.

***Robinson, Alan James, ed.** Ode to Bass & Trout: An Illustrated Treasury of the Best Angling Literature. LC 98-47631. (Illus.). 160p. 1999. 14.98 (*0-7651-0909-3*) Smithmark.

Robinson, Alan S., jt. auth. see Block, Julian.

Robinson, Albert G. Cuba & the Intervention. 1976. lib. bdg. 59.95 (*0-8490-1690-8*) Gordon Pr.

Robinson, Aletha. The Lao Handbook of Maternal & Child Health. 1980. pap. 1.95 (*0-9602790-1-6*) Hlth Frontiers.

***Robinson, Alex.** Amazon. (Guides Bks.). (Illus.). 2000. pap. 24.95 (*1-86011-983-2*) Cadgn Bks.

Robinson, Alfred. Life in California Before the Conquest. LC 68-30553. (American Scene Ser.). (Illus.). 1969. reprint ed. lib. bdg. 39.50 (*0-306-71142-7*) Da Capo.

— Life in California Before the Conquest. 1992. reprint ed. lib. bdg. 75.00 (*0-7812-5081-1*) Rprt Serv.

Robinson, Alfred S. Hartford Numismatist. 28p. 1968. reprint ed. 3.00 (*0-940748-55-X*) Conn Hist Soc.

***Robinson, Alice A.** Poetry for Bouncers, Straphangers, Teenagers & Lovers. LC 98-91119. 1999. pap. 10.95 (*0-533-13055-7*) Vantage.

Robinson, Alice M. Betty Comden & Adolph Green: A Bio-Bibliography, 45. LC 93-21050. (Bio-Bibliographies in the Performing Arts Ser.: No. 45). 384p. 1993. text 69.50 (*0-313-27659-5*, Greenwood Pr) Greenwood.

Robinson, Alice M., et al, eds. Notable Women in the American Theatre: A Biographical Dictionary. LC 89-17065. 1008p. 1989. lib. bdg. 135.00 (*0-313-27217-4*, RNW/, Greenwood Pr) Greenwood.

Robinson, Allan R. & Brink, Kenneth H. The Sea: The Global Coastal Ocean: Processes & Methods. (Ideas & Observations on Progress in the Study of the Seas Ser.). 1080p. 1998. 300.00 (*0-471-11545-2*) Wiley.

Robinson, Allan R. & Lee, Ping. Oceanography & Acoustics: Prediction & Propagation Models. (AIP Series on Modern Acoustics & Signal Processing). (Illus.). 300p. 1994. text 69.95 (*1-56396-203-9*, AIP Pr) Spr-Verlag.

Robinson, Allan R., jt. auth. see Brink, Kenneth H.

Robinson, Allan R., jt. ed. see Malanotte-Rizzoli, Paola.

Robinson, Amanda, ed. The Creepy Crawly Critters Bugs & Bees Book. LC 97-72033. (Illus.). 32p. (J). (ps-2). 1997. 5.95 (*1-890570-00-1*) Huckleberry CT.

— How Do You Really Make a Rainbow? A Language Arts Learning Kit. (J). (ps-k). 1997. bds. 29.95 (*1-890570-06-0*) Huckleberry CT.

— Let's Create a Story. (J). (gr. 4-7). 1997. wbk. ed. 9.95 (*0-9653035-0-0*) Huckleberry CT.

Robinson, Ambrose & Hubbard, Steve. David Robinson. (Today's Heroes Ser.). 112p. (J). 1996. pap. 4.99 (*0-310-20906-4*) Zondervan.

Robinson, Aminah B. The Teachings: Drawn from African-American Spirituals. LC 92-18614. 1992. 26.95 (*0-15-188126-X*) Harcourt.

Robinson, Andrew. The Art of Rabindranath Tagore. (Illus.). 224p. 1989. 110.00 (*0-233-98359-7*, Pub. by Andre Deutsch) Trafalgar.

— Challenges for Champions. Bell, Rob, ed. (Champions Ser.). (Illus.). 64p. (Orig.). (C). 1989. pap. 9.00 (*1-55806-046-4*, 404) Hero Games.

— Earthshock. LC 93-60201. (Illus.). 304p. 1993. pap. 22.50 (*0-500-27738-9*, Pub. by Thames Hudson) Norton.

— The Story of Writing: Alphabets, Hieroglyphs, & Pictograms. LC 95-60276. (Illus.). 224p. 1999. pap. 19.95 (*0-500-28156-4*, Pub. by Thames Hudson) Norton.

— The Story of Writing: Alphabets, Hieroglyphs, & Pictographs. LC 95-60276. (Illus.). 224p. 1995. 29.95 (*0-500-01665-8*, Pub. by Thames Hudson) Norton.

Robinson, Andrew, et al, eds. Vaccine Protocols. LC 96-6818. (Methods in Molecular Medicine Ser.: Vol. 4). (Illus.). 328p. 1996. 99.00 (*0-89603-334-1*) Humana.

Robinson, Andrew & Hammond, Mark. Python Programming on Win32. Denn, Robert, ed. (Illus.). 450p. 1999. pap. 34.95 (*1-56592-621-8*) OReilly & Assocs.

Robinson, Andrew & Terlevich, Roberto J., eds. The Nature of Compact Objects in Active Galactic Nuclei. (Illus.). 455p. (C). 1994. text 74.95 (*0-521-46480-3*) Cambridge U Pr.

Robinson, Andrew, et al. Business & Macroeconomics. LC 94-42204. (Elements of Business Ser.). 304p. (C). (gr. 13). 1995. pap. 75.95 (*0-415-12399-2*) Thomson Learn.

Robinson, Andrew, jt. auth. see Berthon, Simon.

Robinson, Andrew, jt. auth. see Emery, Dominic.

Robinson, Andrew, jt. ed. see Dutta, Krishna.

Robinson, Andrew, tr. see Montalban, Manuel V.

***Robinson, Andrew J.** A Stitch in Time. (Star Trek Ser.: Vol. 27). 432p. 2000. per. 6.50 (*0-671-03885-0*, Star Trek) PB.

Robinson, Andrew J., jt. auth. see Snyder-Mackler, Lynn.

Robinson, Andy. Grassroots Grants: An Activist's Guide to Proposal Writing. LC 96-83387. 211p. (Orig.). 1996. pap. 25.00 (*0-9620222-5-X*) Chardon Pr.

Robinson, Anette. Key Art Works: Picasso. LC 99-462600. (Illus.). 125p. 1999. pap. 12.95 (*2-86656-201-1*) Scala Edit.

***Robinson, Anette.** Louvre. 1998. pap. text 12.95 (*2-86656-121-X*) Scala Edit.

Robinson, Anette. Matisse: Selected Works. 1999. pap. 12.95 (*2-86656-199-6*) Scala Edit.

Robinson, Ann. Cappy Claus. (Illus.). 32p. (J). (ps-6). 1992. pap. 4.95 (*0-9633373-0-0*) Chameleon FL.

— Parliament & Public Spending. LC 79-307097. 1978. text 77.95 (*0-435-83750-8*) Ashgate Pub Co.

Robinson, Ann L. Backward Glances: Growing up in the 30s. LC 97-94563. (Illus.). 64p. 1997. pap. 6.95 (*0-9633373-1-9*) Chameleon FL.

Robinson, Ann M., ed. see Pichard, J. Brent.

Robinson, Ann R. Childress: Touched Many One Man. Harkless, Necia D., ed. (Illus.). 5p. 1998. 19.99 (*0-9655079-1-2*) H To H Assocs.

Robinson, Anne, jt. auth. see Hall, Nigel.

Robinson, Anne, jt. auth. see Hammond, Bob.

Robinson, Anne, jt. ed. see Hall, Nigel.

Robinson, Anne M., jt. auth. see Cynkin, Simme.

Robinson, Anthony. In the Cockpit. 1991. 19.98 (*1-55521-743-5*) Bk Sales Inc.

— The Whole Truth. 480p. 1992. mass mkt. 5.99 (*0-8217-3792-9*, Zebra Kensgtn) Kensgtn Pub Corp.

Robinson, Antony M. & Robinson, A. L. Systematic Bibliography: A Practical Guide to the Work of Compilation. 4th rev. ed. LC 79-40542. 135p. reprint ed. pap. 41.90 (*0-7837-5325-X*, 204506400005) Bks Demand.

***Robinson, Armitage, tr.** Acts of the Scillitan Martyrs. 1999. pap. 0.50 (*0-89981-223-6*) Eastern Orthodox.

Robinson, Armstead L. & Sullivan, Patricia, eds. New Directions in Civil Rights Studies. (Carter G. Woodson Institute Series in Black Studies). 240p. 1991. text 29.50 (*0-8139-1319-5*) U Pr of Va.

An Asterisk (*) at the beginning of an entry indicates that the title is appearing for the first time.

Robinson, Arthur. Clinical Genetics Handbook. 2nd ed. 624p. 1993. pap. 44.95 (*0-86542-194-3*, 93-010567) Blackwell Sci.

Robinson, Arthur, et al, eds. Sex Chromosome Aneuploidy: Prospective Studies on Children. LC 78-13921. (Alan R. Liss Ser.: Vol. 15, No. 1). 1979. 38.00 (*0-685-03298-1*) March of Dimes.

Robinson, Arthur & North, Gary. Fighting Chance: Ten Feet to Survival. LC 86-71490. (Illus.). 289p. (Orig.). 1986. pap. 5.95 (*0-930462-10-6*) Oregon Inst Sci Med.

Robinson, Arthur E. The Professional Education of Elementary Teachers in the Field of Arithmetic. LC 78-177196. (Columbia University. Teachers College. Contributions to Education Ser.: No. 672). reprint ed. 37.50 (*0-404-55672-8*) AMS Pr.

Robinson, Arthur H. Early Thematic Mapping in the History of Cartography. LC 81-11516. (Illus.). 288p. 1982. 47.95 (*0-226-72285-6*) U Ch Pr.

Robinson, Arthur H. The Look of Maps: An Examination of Cartographic Design. LC 85-22647. (Illus.). 119p. 1952. reprint ed. pap. 36.90 (*0-608-07546-9*, 206776100009) Bks Demand.

Robinson, Arthur H., et al. Elements of Cartography. 6th ed. LC 94-33102. 688p. 1995. text 87.95 (*0-471-55579-7*) Wiley.

Robinson, Arthur H., jt. auth. see Hsu, Mei-Ling.

Robinson, B. Fletcher & Fraser, Malcolm. The Adventures of Addington Peace & the Trail of the Dead. (Illus.). 1995. pap. 18.00 (*1-896032-33-8*, Pub. by Grg A Vanderburgh) Battered Silicon.

Robinson, B. Fletcher & Traser, Malcolm. The Adventures of Addington Peace & the Trail of the Dead. (Illus.). 250p. 1995. 28.00 (*1-896032-32-X*, Pub. by Grg A Vanderburgh) Battered Silicon.

Robinson, B. V., et al. PVP: A Critical Review of the Kinetics & Toxicology of Polyvinylpyrrolidone (Povidone) (Illus.). 232p. 1990. lib. bdg. 159.00 (*0-87371-288-9*, L288) Lewis Pubs.

Robinson, B. W. Fifteenth-Century Persian Painting: Problems & Issues. (Hagop Kevorkian Series on Near Eastern Art & Civilization). (Illus.). 120p. (C). 1991. text 55.00 (*0-8147-7417-2*) NYU Pr.

— Japanese Sword-Fittings & Associated Metalwork. (Baur Collection Geneva: Vol. 7). (Illus.). 448p. 1981. 265.00 (*2-88031-003-2*, Pub. by Baur Foundation) Routldge.

— Japanese Sword-Fittings & Associated Metalwork. (Baur Collection Catalogues). 448p. 1994. 255.00 (*0-7103-0398-X*) Routledge.

— Persian Painting & the National Epic. (Individual Papers). 1983. 3.98 (*0-85672-455-6*) David Brown.

Robinson, B. W., jt. auth. see Khalili, Nasser D.

Robinson, Barbara. The Best Christmas Pageant Ever. LC 72-76501. (Illus.). 96p. (J). (gr. 3-7). 1972. lib. bdg. 15.89 (*0-06-025044-5*) HarpC Child Bks.

— The Best Christmas Pageant Ever. LC 72-76501. (Illus.). 96p. (J). (gr. 3-7). 1988. pap. 4.95 (*0-06-440275-4*); mass mkt. 4.95 (*0-06-447044-X*, HarpTrophy) HarpC Child Bks.

— The Best Christmas Pageant Ever. (J). 1988. 10.15 (*0-606-03963-5*, Pub. by Turtleback) Demco.

— The Best Christmas Pageant Ever. 25th anniversary ed. LC 72-76501. (Illus.). 96p. (J). (gr. 3-7). 1997. 15.95 (*0-06-025043-7*) HarpC Child Bks.

Robinson, Barbara. The Best Christmas Pageant Ever, Class Set. unabridged ed. (J). (gr. 5). 1997. pap., boxed set 89.30 incl. audio (*0-7887-2258-1*, 46104) Recorded Bks.

— The Best Christmas Pageant Ever, Set. unabridged ed. (J). (gr. 5). 1997. pap., boxed set 32.20 incl. audio (*0-7887-1839-8*, 40619) Recorded Bks.

— The Best Christmas Pageant Ever Audio. unabridged ed. (J). (gr. 3-7). 1991. audio 11.95 (*1-55994-497-8*, 395818) HarperAudio.

Robinson, Barbara. The Best School Year Ever. LC 93-50891. 128p. (J). (gr. 3-7). 1994. 14.95 (*0-06-023039-8*) HarpC Child Bks.

— The Best School Year Ever. LC 93-50891. 128p. (YA). (gr. 3-7). 1994. lib. bdg. 14.89 (*0-06-023043-6*) HarpC Child Bks.

— The Best School Year Ever. LC 93-50891. (Trophy Bk.). 128p. (J). (gr. 3-7). 1997. pap. 4.95 (*0-06-440492-7*, HarpTrophy) HarpC Child Bks.

— Focus: Interactive Grammar for Students of ESL. 2nd ed. 383p. (C). 1995. pap. text 22.95 (*0-521-65754-7*) Cambridge U Pr.

— Focus: Interactive Grammar for Students of ESL: Instructor's Manual. 2nd ed. 176p. (C). 1995. pap., teacher ed. 6.00 (*0-521-65753-9*) Cambridge U Pr.

— Focus: Interactive Grammar for Students of ESL: Workbook. 2nd ed. 80p. (C). 1995. wbk. ed. 15.95 (*0-521-65752-0*) Cambridge U Pr.

— My Brother Louis Measures Worms: And Other Louis Stories. LC 87-45302. (Charlotte Zolotow Bk.). 160p. (J). (gr. 3-7). 1988. lib. bdg. 15.89 (*0-06-025083-6*) HarpC Child Bks.

— My Brother Louis Measures Worms: And Other Louis Stories. LC 87-45302. (Charlotte Zolotow Bk.). 160p. (J). (gr. 3-7). 1991. pap. 4.95 (*0-06-440362-9*, HarpTrophy) HarpC Child Bks.

— Temporary Times, Temporary Places. LC 81-47732. (Charlotte Zolotow Bk.). 128p. (YA). (gr. 7 up). 1982. 9.95 (*0-06-025039-9*) HarpC Child Bks.

— Worst Best School Year Ever. 1997. 10.09 (*0-606-11006-2*, Pub. by Turtleback) Demco.

Robinson, Barbara & Prior, Mary. Systems Analysis Techniques. (Illus.). 288p. 1995. mass mkt. 27.95 (*1-85032-183-3*) ITCP.

Robinson, Barbara & Wolfson, Evelyn. Environmental Education: A Manual for Elementary Educators. LC 82-741. (Illus.). 233p. reprint ed. pap. 72.30 (*0-7837-1198-0*, 204172800023) Bks Demand.

Robinson, Barbara, jt. auth. see Blotnick, Elihu.

Robinson, Barbara A. And Still, I Cry. LC 90-86221. 220p. (Orig.). 1992. pap. 13.95 (*1-878647-01-6*) APU Pub Grp.

***Robinson, Barbara A.** Eyes of the Beholder. 2000. 21.95 (*1-878647-54-7*) APU Pub Grp.

Robinson, Barbara A. Yes You Can: How to Start, Operate & Grow a Business While Developing Yourself & Pursuing Your Personal Goals. LC 98-73356. 265p. 1999. pap. 18.00 (*1-878647-53-9*) APU Pub Grp.

Robinson, Barbara J., ed. Artistic Representation of Latin American Diversity: Sources & Collections. (Illus.). xviii, 518p. (Orig.). 1993. pap. 50.00 (*0-917617-32-0*) SALALM.

Robinson, Barbara J. & Robinson, J. Cordell. The Mexican American: A Critical Guide to Research Aids. Stueart, Robert D., ed. LC 76-5643. (Foundations in Library & Information Science: Vol. 1). 287p. 1980. 78.50 (*0-89232-006-0*) Jai Pr.

Robinson, Barrie W., jt. auth. see Nelson, Adie.

Robinson, Bart. Columbia Icefield: A Solitude of Ice. (Illus.). 112p. 1981. 29.95 (*0-89886-035-0*) Mountaineers.

***Robinson, Betsy.** Plan Z by Leslie Kove. 2000. pap. 14.00 (*0-922811-48-2*) Mid-List.

Robinson, Betty. A Guide to Arkansas Horse Trails. 2nd ed. (Illus.). 100p. (Orig.). 1995. pap. 12.95 (*0-929183-04-5*) Equestrian Unlimited.

— Horse Trails of Oklahoma. LC 97-60877. (Illus.). 120p. (Orig.). 1997. pap. 16.95 (*0-929183-05-3*) Equestrian Unlimited.

***Robinson, Betty.** Yesterday's Tomorrow. 1999. 12.99 (*1-57921-159-3*) WinePress Pub.

Robinson, Betty J. Up on Melody Mountain. 1997. 14.99 (*0-88419-453-1*) Creation House.

Robinson, Bettye W., jt. auth. see Calhoun, Calfrey C.

Robinson, Beverly J. Aunt Phyllis. 42p. 1989. pap. 14.95 (*0-916147-10-X*) Regent Pr.

Robinson, Bill. Destruction at Noonday. 224p. 1992. 22.95 (*0-924486-21-X*) Sheridan.

— The Sailing Mystique: The Challenges & Rewards of a Life under Sail. (Illus.). 250p. 1994. pap. 14.95 (*0-924486-63-5*) Sheridan.

— A Winter in the Sun. (Illus.). 180p. 1995. pap. 17.95 (*0-924486-69-4*) Sheridan.

***Robinson, Bill & Morris, Ceridwen.** Its All Your Fault: Everything the Hollywood Assistant Needs to Know about Breaking into & Moving up in the Movie Business. 224p. 2001. per. 11.00 (*0-684-86958-6*, Fireside) S&S Trade Pap.

Robinson, Blackwell P. Five Royal Governors of North Carolina, 1729-1775. (Illus.). 1968. reprint ed. pap. 4.00 (*0-86526-076-1*) NC Archives.

Robinson, Blake. The College Power Course: The Guide for Academic & Spiritual Success in College. Labrozzi, Douglas, ed. (Illus.). 160p. (Orig.). (C). 1996. pap. 22.95 (*1-888648-00-7*) Revltnry Pr Pubng.

Robinson, Blake, tr. see Fromentin, Eugene.

Robinson, Bradley. Dark Companion: The Story of Matthew Henson. 4th deluxe large type rev. ed. Robinson, Verne, ed. (Illus.). 1997. spiral bd. 45.00 (*0-9665762-0-9*) Widget Magic.

— Dark Companion: The Story of Matthew Henson. 4th large type rev. ed. Robinson, Verne, ed. (Illus.). 300p. 1997. 24.95 (*0-9665762-8-4*) Widget Magic.

Robinson, Brenda, jt. auth. see Mack, Angela.

Robinson, Brian. Dialysis, Transplantation, Nephrology: Proceedings, European Dialysis & Transplant Association. (Illus.). 1978. 65.00 (*0-8464-0329-3*) Beekman Pubs.

— The Fischer Indole Synthesis. LC 81-14749. (Illus.). 939p. reprint ed. pap. 200.00 (*0-8357-8643-9*, 203506700092) Bks Demand.

— Silver Pennies & Linen Towels - The Story of the Royal Maundy. (Illus.). 1992. lib. bdg. 80.00 (*0-907605-35-4*) S J Durst.

Robinson, Brian, ed. Dialysis, Transplantation, Nephrology: Proceedings European Dialysis & Transplant Assoc. Volume 13. (Illus.). 1977. 65.00 (*0-8464-0328-5*) Beekman Pubs.

— Dialysis, Transplantation, Nephrology: Proceedings, European Dialysis & Transplant Association, Vol. 15. (Illus.). 662p. 1979. 65.00 (*0-8464-1087-7*) Beekman Pubs.

Robinson, Brian S. The Nelson Island & Seabrook Marsh Sites Pt. 1: Late Archaic, Marine Oriented People on the Central New England Coast. (Ocassional Publications in Northeastern Anthropology: No. 9). (Illus.). xii, 107p. 15.00 (*0-318-32508-X*) F Pierce College.

Robinson, Brian S., et al. Early Holocene Occupation in Northern New England. (Occasional Publications in Maine Archaeology). 200p. (C). 1992. pap. text 15.00 (*0-935447-10-5*) ME Hist Preserv.

Robinson, Bruce. The Cyberts. (Illus.). 128p. 1999. pap. 8.95 (*0-9666956-7-4*, Pub. by Berco Pubng) ACCESS Pubs Network.

— Good Medicine. LC 98-96761. (Illus.). 132p. 1998. pap. 8.95 (*0-9666956-0-7*) Berco Pubng.

— The Peculiar Memories of Thomas Penman. 256p. 1998. 29.95 (*0-7475-3614-7*) Chronicle Bks.

***Robinson, Bruce.** The Peculiar Memories of Thomas Penman. LC 99-53449. 288p. 2000. pap. 13.00 (*0-06-095540-6*, Perennial) HarperTrade.

Robinson, Bruce. The Peculiar Memories of Thomas Penman. LC 98-47730. 278p. 1999. 24.95 (*0-87951-914-2*, Pub. by Overlook Pr) Penguin Putnam.

— Withnail & I: The Screenplay. 10th anniversary ed. 129p. 1996. pap. 12.95 (*0-87951-658-5*, Pub. by Overlook Pr) Penguin Putnam.

Robinson, Bruce, jt. auth. see Kradin, Richard.

Robinson, Bruce, ed. see Hamilton, Barbara S.

Robinson, Bryan & McCullers, Jamey. 611 Ways to Boost Your Self Esteem: Accept Your Love Handles & Everything about Yourself. LC 95-214832. 160p. (Orig.). 1994. pap. 8.95 (*1-55874-297-2*, 2972) Health Comm.

Robinson, Bryan E. Chained to the Desk: A Guidebook for Workaholics, Their Partners & Children, & the Clinicians Who Treat Them. LC 97-45349. 280p. 1998. 24.95 (*0-8147-7480-6*) NYU Pr.

***Robinson, Bryan E.** Don't Let Your Mind Stunt Your Growth: Stories, Fables & Techniques That Will Change the Ways You Think. 150p. 2000. pap. 10.95 (*1-57224-193-4*) New Harbinger.

Robinson, Bryan E. Heal Your Self Esteem: Recovery from Addictive Thinking. 1991. pap. 9.95 (*1-55874-119-4*) Health Comm.

Robinson, Bryan E. & Barret, Robert L. The Developing Father: Emerging Roles in Contemporary Society. LC 86-4637. 224p. 1986. pap. text 23.00 (*0-89862-905-5*) Guilford Pubns.

***Robinson, Bryan E. & Chase, Nancy D.** High Performing Families: Causes, Consequences & Clinical Solutions. LC 00-40156. 2000. write for info. (*1-55620-183-4*) Am Coun Assn.

Robinson, Bryan E. & Rhoden, J. Lyn. Working with Children of Alcoholics: The Practitioner's Handbook. 2nd ed. LC 97-33805. 248p. 1997. 30.00 (*0-7619-0756-4*) Sage.

Robinson, Bryan E. & Rhoden, J. Lyn. Working with Children of Alcoholics: The Practitioner's Handbook. 2nd ed. LC 97-33805. 248p. 1997. pap. 13.99 (*0-7619-0757-2*) Sage.

Robinson, Bryan E., jt. auth. see Lamorey, Suzanne.

Robinson, Bryan V. MCQs in Pharmacology. 286p. 1980. reprint ed. pap. text 26.00 (*0-443-03873-2*) Church.

Robinson, Bud. Honey in the Rock. 1988. pap. 13.99 (*0-88019-235-6*) Schmul Pub Co.

— Mountain Peaks. unabridged ed. 121p. 1994. reprint ed. pap. 7.99 (*0-88019-330-1*) Schmul Pub Co.

— A Pitcher of Cream. 110p. 1996. reprint ed. pap. 8.99 (*0-88019-354-9*) Schmul Pub Co.

Robinson, Buddy, jt. auth. see Hanna, Mark G.

Robinson, Byron F., jt. auth. see Bakeman, Roger.

Robinson, C. Dynamical Systems: Stability, Symbolic Dynamics & Chaos. 2nd ed. LC 98-34470. (Studies in Advanced Mathematics). 1998. 89.95 (*0-8493-8495-8*) CRC Pr.

Robinson, C., jt. ed. see Church, Martin K.

Robinson, C. A. Alexander the Great: Translation of the Extant Historians. LC 97-169063. 1996. 40.00 (*0-89005-555-6*) Ares.

Robinson, C. Clough. A Glossary of Words Pertaining to the Dialect of Mid-Yorkshire: With Others Peculiar to Lower Nidderdale. (English Dialect Society Publications: No. 14). 1969. reprint ed. pap. 25.00 (*0-8115-0446-8*) Periodicals Srv.

***Robinson, C. Kelly.** Not All Dogs. LC 99-95221. 349p. 1999. pap. 14.99 (*0-9673208-0-1*) Against the Grain.

***Robinson, C. Snelling.** 200,000 Miles Aboard the Destroyer Cotten. LC 99-21394. 320p. 1999. text 35.00 (*0-87338-645-0*) Kent St U Pr.

Robinson, C. W., jt. ed. see Moo-Young, M.

Robinson, Carey. The Fighting Maroons of Jamaica. LC 79-469853. 160 p. 1969. write for info. (*0-00-211273-6*) Collins SF.

Robinson, Carl. Australia. 3rd ed. (Odyssey Passport Ser.). 1999. pap. text 19.95 (*962-217-612-7*) Norton.

***Robinson, Carl.** Australia. 4th rev. ed. (Passport Ser.). (Illus.). 2000. pap. 19.95 (*962-217-671-2*) China Guides.

Robinson, Carl D. Dr. Carl Robinson's Basic Baby Care: A Guide for New Parents for the First Year. LC 97-75474. (Illus.). 160p. 1998. pap. 10.95 (*1-57224-105-5*) New Harbinger.

Robinson, Carlan M. Breaking up? Moving On . . . LC 89-92013. (Illus.). 54p. 1989. pap. 14.95 (*0-9623896-0-9*) Cable Pub.

Robinson, Carol. Growing up with Disability, 1. LC 98-213929. 1998. pap. text 28.95 (*1-85302-568-2*) Taylor & Francis.

— My Life with Thomas Aquinas. (Integrity Magazine Anthology Ser.: Vol. 1). (Illus.). 307p. (Orig.). 1992. pap. text 13.50 (*0-935952-83-7*) Angelus Pr.

— The Role of Children's Hospices in the Provision of Respite Care. 76p. 1998. pap. 17.00 (*1-900990-26-1*, Pub. by Natl Childrens Bur) Paul & Co Pubs.

Robinson, Carol, et al. Raising Your Children. Angelus Press Editors, ed. (Integrity Magazine Anthology Ser.: No. 2). 256p. 1995. pap. 13.50 (*0-935952-27-6*) Angelus Pr.

Robinson, Caroline H. Seventy Birth Control Clinics: A Survey & Analysis Including the General Effects of Control on Size & Quality of Population. LC 71-169398. (Family in America Ser.). 380p. 1972. reprint ed. 18.95 (*0-405-03875-5*) Ayer.

Robinson, Carolyn & Robinson, Ed. The Have-More Plan: A Little Land-A Lot of Living. LC 90-50353. (Illus.). 72p. 1983. pap. 9.95 (*0-88266-024-1*, Garden Way Pub) Storey Bks.

Robinson, Catherine & Ker, Phil. Understanding Accounting Principles. 338p. 1993. pap. 65.00 (*0-409-79000-1*, NZ, MICHIE) LEXIS Pub.

Robinson, Catherine & Rowekamp, Jenise. Speaking up at Work. (Illus.). 192p. 1985. pap. text, student ed. 10.95 (*0-19-434196-8*) OUP.

— Speaking up at Work. (Illus.). 48p. 1985. pap. text, teacher ed. 6.95 (*0-19-434197-6*) OUP.

Robinson, Catherine A. Tradition & Liberation: The Hindu Tradition in the Indian Women's Movement. 256p. (C). 1999. text 48.00 (*0-7007-1143-0*, Pub. by Curzon Pr Ltd) UH Pr.

***Robinson, Catherine A.** Tradition & Liberation: The Hindu Tradition in the Indian Women's Movement. LC 99-31639. 1999. text 55.00 (*0-312-22718-3*) St Martin.

Robinson, Cecil. Mexico & the Hispanic Southwest in American Literature. LC 76-24082. 391p. 1977. pap. 19.95 (*0-8165-0593-4*) U of Ariz Pr.

— No Short Journeys: The Interplay of Cultures in the History & Literature of the Borderlands. LC 91-28170. 148p. 1992. 39.95 (*0-8165-1270-1*) U of Ariz Pr.

Robinson, Cedric J. Black Marxism: The Making of the Black Radical Tradition. LC 99-30995. 436p. 2000. pap. 24.95 (*0-8078-4829-8*) U of NC Pr.

— Black Movements in America. LC 96-21986. (Revolutionary Thought & Radical Movements Ser.). 179p. (C). 1997. pap. 17.99 (*0-415-91222-9*) Routledge.

Robinson, Celeste. Access 97 - No Experience Required. LC 97-61720. 464p. 1997. pap. text 29.99 (*0-7821-2150-0*) Sybex.

— Access 2000. LC 98-89346. (No Experience Required Ser.). 512p. 1999. pap. 24.99 (*0-7821-2485-2*) Sybex.

— Access X in Record Time. 400p. 1998. 29.99 (*0-7821-2325-2*) Sybex.

***Robinson, Celeste.** Mastering Microsoft Works Suite 2000. (Mastering Ser.). 608p. 2000. pap. 29.99 (*0-7821-2655-3*) Sybex.

Robinson, Celeste & Simpson, Alan. Mastering WordPerfect Office 2000. LC 99-60026. (Mastering Ser.). (Illus.). 1067p. 1999. pap. 39.99 (*0-7821-2198-5*) Sybex.

Robinson, Celeste, jt. auth. see Simpson, Alan.

Robinson, Cervin. Cervin Robinson - Cleveland, Ohio. LC 89-22050. (Published in Association with the Cleveland Museum of Art Ser.). 124p. 1989. 44.95 (*0-910386-98-6*); pap. 21.95 (*0-910386-99-4*) Cleveland Mus Art.

Robinson, Cervin & Herschmann, Joel. Architecture Transformed: A History of the Photography of Buildings from 1839 to the Present. (Illus.). 224p. 1990. reprint ed. pap. text 37.50 (*0-262-68064-5*) MIT Pr.

Robinson, Charles. The Indian Trial: The Complete Story of the Warren Wagon Train Massacre & the Fall of the Kiowa Nation. LC 96-32479. (Illus.). 210p. 1997. 27.50 (*0-87062-262-5*) A H Clark.

Robinson, Charles, III. The Men Who Wear the Star: The Story of the Texas Rangers. LC 99-27160. 432p. 2000. 29.95 (*0-679-45649-X*) Random.

Robinson, Charles. Nonnegotiable. LC 99-62089. 112p. 1999. pap. 8.95 (*1-56167-492-3*) Am Literary Pr.

Robinson, Charles & Demattos, Frank. Rehoboth, Swansea, & Dighton. (Images of America Ser.). 128p. 1998. pap. 18.99 (*0-7524-0562-4*) Arcadia Publng.

Robinson, Charles A., Jr. Alexander the Great: The Meeting of East & West in World Government & Brotherhood. LC 84-10951. 252p. 1984. reprint ed. lib. bdg. 52.50 (*0-313-24572-X*, ROGR, Greenwood Pr) Greenwood.

— Athens in the Age of Pericles. (Centers of Civilization Ser.: Vol. 1). (Illus.). 180p. 1971. pap. 9.95 (*0-8061-0935-1*) U of Okla Pr.

Robinson, Charles B. How to Make the Most of Every Audit: An Etiquette Handbook for Auditing. 126p. 1992. pap. 23.00 (*0-87389-158-9*, H0696) ASQ Qual Pr.

Robinson, Charles B., ed. see ASQ Quality Audit Technical Committee.

Robinson, Charles E., ed. Lord Byron & His Contemporaries: Essays from the 6th International Byron Seminar. LC 80-66848. (Illus.). 256p. 1982. 35.00 (*0-87413-180-4*) U Delaware Pr.

— Mary Shelley: Collected Tales & Stories. (Illus.). 399p. 1990. reprint ed. pap. text 19.95 (*0-8018-4062-7*) Johns Hopkins.

Robinson, Charles E., ed. see Shelley, Mary Wollstonecraft.

Robinson, Charles E., tr. & comment see Shelley, Mary Wollstonecraft.

Robinson, Charles J. & Ginder, Andrew P. Implementing TPM: The North American Experience. (Illus.). 250p. 1995. text 45.00 (*1-56327-087-0*) Productivity Inc.

Robinson, Charles K., jt. auth. see Nicholson, Kenyon.

Robinson, Charles M. Bad Hand: A Biography of General Ranald S. Mackenzie. LC 93-5330. (Illus.). 410p. 1993. pap. 17.95 (*1-880510-02-2*) State House Pr.

Robinson, Charles M., III. The Buffalo Hunters. LC 95-7590. 192p. 1995. 29.95 (*1-880510-18-9*); pap. 19.95 (*1-880510-19-7*) State House Pr.

— The Buffalo Hunters. deluxe ed. LC 95-7590. 192p. 1995. 75.00 (*1-880510-20-0*) State House Pr.

— A Good Year to Die: The Story of the Great Sioux War. LC 96-21423. (Illus.). 464p. 1996. pap. 16.95 (*0-8061-2890-9*) U of Okla Pr.

Robinson, Charles M., 3rd. Hurricane of Fire: The Union Assault on Fort Fisher. LC 97-46090. (Illus.). 272p. 1998. 29.95 (*1-55750-720-1*) Naval Inst Pr.

Robinson, Charles M. The Kansas Conflict. LC 70-37599. (Black Heritage Library Collection). reprint ed. 29.95 (*0-8369-8975-9*) Ayer.

— Modern Civic Art: or The City Made Beautiful. 4th ed. LC 79-112570. (Rise of Urban America Ser.). (Illus.). 1978. reprint ed. 29.95 (*0-405-02473-8*) Ayer.

— Satanta: The Life & Death of a War Chief. LC 97-37009. 254p. 1998. 27.95 (*1-880510-55-3*) State House Pr.

— Satanta: The Life & Death of a War Chief. LC 97-37009. 254p. 1998. denim 60.00 (*1-880510-57-X*) State House Pr.

— Satanta: The Life & Death of a War Chief. LC 97-37009. 254p. 1998. pap. 18.95 (*1-880510-56-1*) State House Pr.

Robinson, Charles M., III. Shark of the Confederacy: The Story of the CSS Alabama. (Illus.). 212p. 1995. 39.50 (*0-85052-435-0*, Pub. by Leo Cooper) Trans-Atl Phila.

— Shark of the Confederacy: The Story of the CSS Alabama. LC 94-13816. (Illus.). 230p. 1994. 27.95 (*1-55750-728-7*) Naval Inst Pr.

Robinson, Charles M. & Shepherd, Charles. Philosophy of Health & Beauty. 100p. 1998. reprint ed. pap. 11.50 (*0-7661-0680-2*) Kessinger Pub.

R

An Asterisk (*) at the beginning of an entry indicates that the title is appearing for the first time.

R

Robinson, Charles N. British Tar in Fact & Fiction. (Illus.). 1968. reprint ed. 43.00 (*1-55888-938-8*) Omnigraphics Inc.

Robinson, Charles S. The Pharaohs of the Bondage & the Exodus (1887) 150p. 1998. reprint ed. pap. 14.95 (*0-7661-0129-0*) Kessinger Pub.

Robinson, Charles T. Ghosts: True New England Hauntings. (Illus.). 64p. 2000. 4.95 (*1-58066-001-0*, Covered Brdge Pr) Douglas Charles Ltd.

— The New England Ghost Files. LC 95-126. (Illus.). 256p. 1994. pap. 14.95 (*0-924771-48-8*, Covered Brdge Pr) Douglas Charles Ltd.

***Robinson, Charles T.** New England Ghost Files Vol. II: The Sequel. (Illus.). 256p. (C). 1999. pap. 14.95 (*1-58066-030-4*, Covered Brdge Pr) Douglas Charles Ltd.

Robinson, Charles T. New England's Notable Dead: A Guide to the Final Resting Places of the Famous & Infamous. (New England Gift Bks.: Vol. 6). (Illus.). 64p. Date not set. 4.95 (*1-58066-009-6*, Covered Brdge Pr) Douglas Charles Ltd.

— True New England Mysteries, Ghosts, Crimes & Oddities. LC 97-24786. (Illus.). 192p. (Orig.). 1997. pap. 12.95 (*0-924771-97-6*, Covered Brdge Pr) Douglas Charles Ltd.

***Robinson, Chase F.** Empire & Elites after the Muslim Conquest: The Transformation of Northern Mesopotamia. (Cambridge Studies in Islamic Civilization). (Illus.). 227p. (C). 2000. text Price not set. (*0-521-78115-9*) Cambridge U Pr.

Robinson, Cheri. Official Excite Yellow Pages. 912p. 1998. pap. 34.99 (*0-7645-3145-X*) IDG Bks.

Robinson, Chris. Collegiate Reader. rev. ed. 250p. (C). 1990. pap. text 21.99 (*1-56226-021-9*) CAT Pub.

— Internet for Free. 100p. (C). 1998. pap. text 18.50 (*1-56226-391-9*) CAT Pub.

— Plotting Directions: An Activist's Guide. LC 82-80105. (Illus.). 68p. 1982. pap. 5.00 (*0-916894-02-9*) Recon Pubns.

— Power Paragraphs: Buildings Blocks for Eloquent Essays. 80p. 1997. pap. text 16.50 (*1-56226-372-2*) CAT Pub.

Robinson, Christine, et al, eds. Transitions: Exeter Remembered. 195p. 1990. 15.95 (*0-939618-06-0*); pap. 9.95 (*0-939618-07-9*) Phillips Exeter.

Robinson, Christine A. Collegiate Reader. 250p. (C). 1995. pap. text 15.25 (*1-56226-228-9*) CAT Pub.

— Good Grief Grammar. rev. ed. 90p. (C). 1990. pap. text 15.75 (*1-56226-022-7*) CAT Pub.

— Say It with Style. rev. ed. (Plus Ser.). 328p. (C). 1991. pap. text 42.16 (*1-56226-088-X*) CAT Pub.

Robinson, Christopher. C. P. Cavafy. (Studies in Modern Greek: No. 1). xiv, 112p. (C). 1988. 25.00 (*0-89241-469-3*); pap. text 16.00 (*0-89241-470-7*) Caratzas.

— Lucian & His Influence in Europe. LC 79-16580. (Illus.). 258p. reprint ed. pap. 80.00 (*0-7837-3758-0*, 204357500010) Bks Demand.

Robinson, Chuck & Robinson, Debbie. The Art of Shelling: A Complete Guide to Finding Shells & Other Beach Collectibles at Shelling Locations from Florida to Maine. LC 95-69822. (Illus.). 152p. (Orig.). 1995. pap. 14.95 (*0-9647267-6-9*) Old Squan Vill Pub.

***Robinson, Chuck & Robinson, Debbie.** The Art of Shelling: A Complete Guide to Finding Shells & Other Ceach Collectibles. 2nd ed. LC 00-190216. (Illus.). 176p. 2000. pap. 14.95 (*0-9647267-8-5*) Old Squan Vill Pub.

Robinson, Chuck & Robinson, Debbie. Treasure for Our Sand Castle. LC 96-72259. (Illus.). 24p. (J). (gr. k-3). 1997. 16.95 (*0-9647267-7-7*) Old Squan Vill Pub.

Robinson, Claire. Bears. LC 97-12301. (Science All Around Me Ser.). (Illus.). 24p. 1998. write for info. (*1-57572-134-1*) Heinemann Lib.

— Chimpanzees. LC 97-12313. (Science All Around Me Ser.). (Illus.). 24p. 1998. write for info. (*1-57572-136-8*) Heinemann Lib.

***Robinson, Claire.** Crocodiles. LC 97-12300. (In the Wild Ser.). (Illus.). 24p. (J). (ps-2). 1998. 18.50 (*1-57572-133-3*) Heinemann Lib.

— Dolphin. LC 98-34529. (In the Wild Ser.). (Illus.). 24p. (J). 1999. write for info. (*1-57572-862-1*) Heinemann Lib.

Robinson, Claire. Elephants: Solids, Liquids, & Gases. LC 97-12311. (Science All Around Me Ser.). (Illus.). 24p. 1998. write for info. (*1-57572-135-X*) Heinemann Lib.

***Robinson, Claire.** In the Wild Series, 6 bks. 24p. 1999. 119.52 (*1-57572-131-7*) Heinemann Lib.

Robinson, Claire. Lions. LC 97-12310. (In the Wild Ser.). (Illus.). 24p. (J). (ps-2). 1998. 18.59 (*1-57572-132-5*) Heinemann Lib.

— Penguins. LC 97-12312. (In the Wild Ser.). (Illus.). 24p. (J). (ps-2). 1998. 18.50 (*1-57572-137-6*) Heinemann Lib.

— Shark. LC 98-34034. (In the Wild Ser.). 24p. (J). 1999. write for info. (*1-57572-863-X*) Heinemann Lib.

— Snake. LC 98-34029. (In the Wild Ser.). 24p. (J). 1999. write for info. (*1-57572-864-8*) Heinemann Lib.

***Robinson, Claire.** Whale. LC 98-34530. (In the Wild Ser.). 24p. (J). 1999. lib. bdg. 13.95 (*1-57572-865-6*) Heinemann Lib.

Robinson, Clara L. Psychology & Preparation of the Teacher for the Elementary School. LC 71-177197. (Columbia University. Teachers College. Contributions to Education Ser.: No. 418). reprint ed. 37.50 (*0-404-55418-0*) AMS Pr.

Robinson, Clarence & Brooks, Kenneth. The Impossible Dream: One Man's Drive to End Racial Oppression. LC 98-70509. 1998. pap. 9.95 (*0-9639042-9-9*) Amper Pubng.

Robinson, Clarie. Penguin. LC 91-44727. (Life Story Ser.). (Illus.). 32p. (J). (gr. 4-6). 1997. pap., teacher ed. 4.95 (*0-8167-2772-4*) Troll Communs.

Robinson, Clark. Dynamical Systems: Stability, Symbolic Dynamics, & Chaos. LC 94-24456. (Studies in Advanced Mathematics). 480p. (C). 1994. boxed set 104.95 (*0-8493-8493-1*, 8493) CRC Pr.

Robinson, Claude E. Straw Votes, a Study of Political Prediction. LC 75-41231. reprint ed. 29.50 (*0-404-14697-X*) AMS Pr.

Robinson, Clay, jt. auth. see Gibson, L. Tucker.

Robinson, Clement. A Handful of Pleasant Delights. Rollins, Hyder E., ed. 145p. 1965. pap. 4.95 (*0-486-21382-X*) Dover.

Robinson, Cliff. Walk with Me: To the Light. 76p. (Orig.). 1997. pap. 6.00 (*1-57502-402-0*, PO1246) Morris Pubng.

Robinson, Clinton D. Language Choice in Rural Development. LC 92-60918. (International Museum of Cultures Ser.: Vol. 26). x, 52p. 1992. pap. 5.00 (*0-88312-180-8*) S I L Intl.

— Language Use in Rural Development: An African Perspective. LC 95-50533. (Contributions to the Sociology of Language Ser.: Vol. 70). x, 327p. (C). 1996. lib. bdg. 117.05 (*3-11-014687-8*) Mouton.

Robinson, Clive. Lipid Mediators in Allergic Diseases of the Respiratory Tract. 268p. 1994. lib. bdg. 225.00 (*0-8493-5416-1*, RC859) CRC Pr.

Robinson, Colin. Effective Negotiating. 1997. pap. text 19.95 (*0-7494-2020-0*) Kogan Page Ltd.

Robinson, Colin, et al, eds. Dental Enamel: Formation to Destruction. LC 95-1383. 336p. 1995. lib. bdg. 205.00 (*0-8493-4589-8*, 4589) CRC Pr.

***Robinson, Colin, et al.** Chemistry & Biology of Mineralized Tissues: Proceedings of the Sixth International Conference, Vittel, France. LC 00-29973. 2000. pap. write for info. (*0-89203-225-1*) Amer Acad Ortho Surg.

Robinson, Colin, jt. auth. see Blundell, John.

Robinson, Colin, jt. auth. see Marshall, Eileen.

Robinson, Conway. The Wild White Shepherd. (J). (gr. 6-9). 1994. pap. 9.99 (*0-88092-091-2*) Royal Fireworks.

Robinson, Conway, ed. see Virginia Company of London, 1619-1624 Staff.

Robinson, Corinne H. Normal & Therapeutic Nutrition. 17th rev. ed. 784p. (C). 1990. text 75.00 (*0-02-402605-0*, Macmillan Coll) P-H.

Robinson, Courtland. D & C: A Guide for Women. Wallach, Edward E., ed. (Women's Health Ser.). (Illus.). 24p. (Orig.). 1996. pap. 2.95 (*1-885274-17-3*) Health InfoNet Inc.

Robinson, Craig. Exposed: Service Bureau Tips & Techniques for Desktop Publishing Success. (Illus.). iv, 78p. 1996. spiral bd. 19.95 (*0-9653154-0-1*) Stroft Communs.

Robinson Crowley, Christine B. Understanding Patient Financial Services. LC 97-25029. 350p. 1997. 65.00 (*0-8342-0916-0*, 20916) Aspen Pub.

Robinson-Cutler, Marjory L., jt. auth. see Cutler, Maxwell.

Robinson, Cynny. Much Love, Cynny-san. 200p. 1994. 19.95 (*1-878208-49-7*) Guild Pr IN.

Robinson, Cynthia, jt. ed. see Grabar, Oleg.

Robinson, Cyril D. Legal Rights, Duties, & Liabilities of Criminal Justice Personnel: History & Analysis. 2nd ed. 516p. 1992. pap. 58.95 (*0-398-06405-9*) C C Thomas.

— Legal Rights, Duties, & Liabilities of Criminal Justice Personnel: History & Analysis. 2nd ed. 516p. (C). 1992. text 79.95 (*0-398-05779-6*) C C Thomas.

Robinson, Cyril D. & Scaglion, Richard. Police in Contradiction: The Evolution of the Police Function in Society, 44. LC 93-25071. (Contributions in Criminology & Penology Ser.: No. 44). 216p. 1993. 62.95 (*0-313-28891-7*, GM8891, Greenwood Pr) Greenwood.

Robinson, Cyril E. Everyday Life in Ancient Greece. LC 75-41232. reprint ed. 45.00 (*0-404-14592-2*) AMS Pr.

— Everyday Life in Ancient Greece. LC 77-27627. 159p. 1978. reprint ed. lib. bdg. 55.00 (*0-8371-9078-9*, ROEL, Greenwood Pr) Greenwood.

— The Genius of the Greek Drama. 96p. 1977. 11.95 (*0-8369-8217-7*) Ayer.

— A History of Greece. 9th ed. (Illus.). 1957. pap. 16.50 (*0-423-71290-X*, NO. 2411) Routledge.

— A History of Rome from Seven Hundred Fifty-Three B.C. to A.D. Four Hundred Ten. (Illus.). 1950. pap. 17.95 (*0-423-87420-9*, NO. 2412) Routledge.

Robinson, D. Interracial Communication & So. LC 97-47446. (Race, Health, & Social Care Ser.). 1998. pap. 89.00 (*0-335-19551-2*) OpUniv Pr.

Robinson, D. People Sharing Jesus. 1995. VHS 159.99 (*0-7852-7762-5*) Nelson.

***Robinson, D., ed.** Immunological Mechanisms in Asthma & Allergic Diseases: Symposium Held on the Occasion of Prof. A. Barry Kay's 60th Birthday & 20th Year as Head of Department, London, June 1999. (Chemical Immunology Ser.: 78). (Illus.). xii, 200p. 2000. 174.00 (*3-8055-7112-7*) S Karger.

Robinson, D. & Hall, M., eds. Neurobiology & the Human Brain Package. (Illus.). 370p. (C). 1998. pap. 59.95 incl. cd-rom (*3-540-63778-8*) Spr-Verlag.

Robinson, D. & Robinson, Lena. Interracial Communication & So. LC 97-47446. (Race, Health, & Social Care Ser.). 160p. 1998. pap. 26.95 (*0-335-19550-4*) OpUniv Pr.

Robinson, D., et al. Susan Hiller: Wild Talents. (Illus.). 56p. 1998. spiral bd. 12.00 (*0-88454-087-1*) U of Pa Contemp Art.

Robinson, D., jt. ed. see Hall, M.

Robinson, D., jt. ed. see Paukert, F.

Robinson, D. A. & Williams, R. B., eds. Rock Weathering & Landform Evolution. LC 94-4636. (British Geomorphological Research Group Symposia Ser.). 544p. 1994. 185.00 (*0-471-95119-6*) Wiley.

Robinson, D. G., et al, eds. Methods of Preparation for Electron Microscopy: An Introduction for the Biomedical Sciences. (Illus.). 200p. 1987. pap. 55.00 (*0-387-17592-X*) Spr-Verlag.

Robinson, D. H. 1999: Apocalypse Maybe. LC 97-74722. 256p. 1997. pap. 12.95 (*0-9658820-0-4*) Kalos Pr.

Robinson, D. J. Course in Linear Algebra with Applications: Solutions to the Exercises. 208p. 1992. pap. text 21.00 (*981-02-1048-5*) World Scientific Pub.

— A Course in the Theory of Groups. (Graduate Texts in Mathematics Ser.: Vol. 80). 480p. 1982. 59.00 (*0-387-90600-2*) Spr-Verlag.

— A Course in the Theory of Groups. Ewing, J. H. et al, eds. (Graduate Texts in Mathematics Ser.: Vol. 80). (Illus.). 502p. 1994. reprint ed. pap. 42.50 (*0-387-94092-8*) Spr-Verlag.

— A Course in the Theory of Groups. 2nd ed. (Graduate Texts in Mathematics Ser.: Vol. 80). (Illus.). 500p. 1993. pap. text. write for info. (*3-540-94092-8*) Spr-Verlag.

— Finiteness Conditions & Generalized Soluble Groups, Pt. 1. (Ergebnisse der Mathematik und Ihrer Grenzgebiete Ser.: Vol. 62). (Illus.). 240p. 1972. 49.95 (*0-387-05620-3*) Spr-Verlag.

Robinson, D. Keith, jt. auth. see Bevington, Philip R.

Robinson, D. M., jt. auth. see Jamieson, G. A.

Robinson, D. N. & Mos, Leendert P. Annals of Theoretical Psychology, Vol. 6. LC 84-644088. (Illus.). 254p. (C). 1990. 95.00 (*0-306-43588-8*, Plenum Trade) Perseus Pubng.

Robinson, D. R., jt. auth. see Bowman, A. W.

Robinson, D. W. & Reid, G. T., eds. Interferogram Analysis: Digital Fringe Pattern Measurement Techniques. (Illus.). 302p. 1993. 147.00 (*0-7503-0197-X*) IOP Pub.

Robinson, D. W., jt. auth. see Bratteli, O.

Robinson, D. W., jt. ed. see Cavalloro, R.

Robinson, Dale & Fernandes, David. The Definitive Andy Griffith Show Reference: Episode-by-Episode, with Cast & Production Biographies & a Guide to Collectibles. LC 96-4042. (Illus.). 336p. 1996. lib. bdg. 45.00 (*0-7864-0136-2*) McFarland & Co.

Robinson, Dale, jt. auth. see Fernandes, David.

Robinson, Dale G. Intersecting Lives: Road Maps for Ministry to Young Adults. 180p. 1998. pap. 11.00 (*0-9661778-0-0*) CA So Bapt.

Robinson, Dan. Fundamentals of Structured Program Design. LC 99-19395. (Illus.). 326p. (C). 1999. pap. text 84.00 (*0-13-927930-X*) P-H.

Robinson, Dan & McKean, S., eds. Shifting Cultivation & Alternatives: An Annotated Bibliography, 1974-1989. 280p. (Orig.). 1992. pap. text 50.50 (*0-85198-680-3*) C A B Intl.

Robinson, Dan, jt. auth. see Coverdale, Andrew.

Robinson, Dana G. & Robinson, James C. Performance Consulting: Moving Beyond Training. LC 94-47066. (Illus.). 320p. 1996. reprint ed. pap. 24.95 (*1-881052-84-2*) Berrett-Koehler.

— Training for Impact: How to Link Training to Business Needs & Measure the Results. LC 88-46088. (Management Ser.). 336p. 1989. text 36.95 (*1-55542-153-9*) Jossey-Bass.

Robinson, Daniel. Lonely Planet Vietnam. 3rd ed. (FRE.). 1998. 27.95 (*2-84070-079-4*) Lonely Planet.

Robinson, Daniel, ed. The Mind. LC 98-11810. (Oxford Readers Ser.). 400p. (Orig.). (C). 1998. pap. text 22.95 (*0-19-289308-4*) OUP.

Robinson, Daniel & Wheeler, Tony. Lonely Planet Paris: City Guide. 2nd ed. (Lonely Planet City Guides). (Illus.). 264p. 1998. pap. text 14.95 (*0-86442-622-4*) Lonely Planet.

Robinson, Daniel, jt. auth. see Fallon, Steve.

Robinson, Daniel, jt. auth. see Feldman, Paula R.

Robinson, Daniel, jt. ed. see Feldman, Paula R.

Robinson, Daniel J. The Measure of Democracy: Polling, Market Research, & Public Life, 1930-1945. LC 99-222936. 272p. 1999. text 55.00 (*0-8020-4274-0*) U of Toronto Pr.

— The Measure of Democracy: Polling, Market Research, & Public Life, 1930-1945. LC 99-222936. (Illus.). 272p. 1999. pap. text 21.95 (*0-8020-8109-6*) U of Toronto Pr.

Robinson, Daniel J., jt. ed. see Taylor, William J.

Robinson, Daniel N. Aristotle's Psychology. 144p. 1999. pap. 17.95 (*0-9672066-0-X*) DNMRobinson.

— The Industrial Revolution. 416p. write for info. (*0-340-66212-3*, Pub. by E A) Routldge.

— An Intellectual History of Psychology. 3rd ed. LC 95-5697. 390p. 1995. pap. 21.95 (*0-299-14844-0*) U of Wis Pr.

— Mind Unfolded: Essays on Psychology's Historic Texts. LC 78-58510. 539p. 1978. pap. 19.95 (*0-313-27077-5*, P7077); lib. bdg. 85.00 (*0-313-27076-7*, U7076) Greenwood.

— Philosophy of Psychology. 176p. 1989. pap. text 18.00 (*0-231-05923-X*) Col U Pr.

— Toward a Science of Human Nature: Aspirations of Nineteenth Century Psychology. LC 81-38458. 256p. 1982. text 61.50 (*0-231-05174-3*) Col U Pr.

— Toward a Science of Human Nature: Aspirations of Nineteenth Century Psychology. LC 81-38458. 256p. 1982. pap. text 26.50 (*0-231-05175-1*) Col U Pr.

— Wild Beasts & Idle Humours: The Insanity Defense from Antiquity to the Present. 320p. 1996. 32.50 (*0-674-95289-8*) HUP.

— Wild Beasts & Idle Humours: The Insanity Defense from Antiquity to the Present. 320p. 1998. pap. text 15.95 (*0-674-95290-1*) HUP.

Robinson, Daniel N., ed. Social Discourse & Moral Judgment. (Illus.). 260p. 1992. text 49.95 (*0-12-590155-0*) Acad Pr.

Robinson, Daniel S., ed. The Story of Scottish Philosophy: A Compendium of Selections from the Writings of Nine Pre-Eminent Scottish Philosophers, with Biobibliographical Essays. LC 78-12114. (Illus.). 290p. 1979. reprint ed. lib. bdg. 38.50 (*0-313-21082-9*, ROST) Greenwood.

Robinson, Daniel S., ed. see Hoernle, Reinhold F.

Robinson, Danielle. Simple Guide to France: Customs & Etiquette. 2nd ed. (Simple Guides Ser.). 1997. pap. text. write for info. (*1-86034-006-7*, Pub. by Global Bks) Midpt Trade.

Robinson, Darrell W. People Sharing Jesus. LC 94-45172. 252p. 1995. pap. 9.99 (*0-7852-7929-6*) Nelson.

— El Pueblo Que Testifica de Cristo.Tr. of People Sharing Jesus. (SPA.). 272p. 1996. student ed. 10.99 (*0-89922-339-7*, C001-3397) Caribe Betania.

— El Pueblo Que Testifica de Cristo.Tr. of People Sharing Jesus. (SPA.). 1996. teacher ed. 10.99 (*0-89922-310-9*, C001-3109) Caribe Betania.

— Total Church Life. rev. ed. 224p. 1997. pap. 10.99 (*0-8054-6371-2*) Broadman.

Robinson, Dave. Introducing Descartes. 176p. 1998. pap. 10.95 (*1-874166-99-4*, Pub. by Totem Bks) Natl Bk Netwk.

— Introducing Philosophy, 1. (Illus.). 176p. 1999. pap. 10.95 (*1-84046-002-4*, Pub. by Totem Bks) Natl Bk Netwk.

***Robinson, Dave.** Introducing Plato. (Introducing Ser.). 2000. pap. 10.95 (*1-84046-113-6*) Totem Bks.

Robinson, David. Das Cabinet des Dr. Caligari. (BFI Film Classics). (Illus.). 80p. 1998. pap. 10.95 (*0-85170-645-2*, Pub. by British Film Inst) Ind U Pr.

— Chaplin: His Life & Art. (Illus.). 896p. 1994. reprint ed. pap. 21.95 (*0-306-80600-2*) Da Capo.

— Charlie Chaplin: Comic Genius. (Discoveries Ser.). (Illus.). 144p. 1996. pap. text 12.95 (*0-8109-2884-1*, Pub. by Abrams) Time Warner.

— Encyclopedia of Pet Rabbits. (Illus.). 320p. 1979. 19.95 (*0-87666-911-9*, H-984) TFH Pubns.

***Robinson, David.** The Family Cloister: Benedictine Wisdom for the Home. LC 99-16156. 192p. 2000. pap. 14.95 (*0-8245-1827-6*, Pub. by Crossroad NY) Natl Bk Netwk.

— Forensic Nursing & Multidisciplinary Care of the Mentally Disordered Offender, Vol. 14. LC 99-42863. (Forensic Focus Ser.). 1999. 34.95 (*1-85302-754-5*) Jessica Kingsley.

Robinson, David. From Drinking to Alcoholism: A Sociological Commentary. LC 75-26597. 223p. reprint ed. pap. 69.20 (*0-608-13128-8*, 205209400033) Bks Demand.

— From Peep Show to Palace: The Birth of American Film. (Illus.). 213p. 1996. 42.00 (*0-231-10338-7*) Col U Pr.

— From Peepshow to Palace: The Birth of American Film. (Illus.). 213p. 1997. pap. 18.50 (*0-231-10339-5*) Col U Pr.

— Introducing Ethics. LC 96-61108. 1997. pap. 10.95 (*1-874166-40-4*, Pub. by Totem Bks) Natl Bk Netwk.

— Laricollaguas: Ecology, Economy & Demography in a Seventeenth-Century Peruvian Village, Vol. 29. LC 91-16672. 400p. (C). 1998. pap. 55.00 (*0-8133-8022-7*) Westview.

— Neurobiology. LC 97-37177. 1997. write for info. (*0-7492-8151-0*) Spr-Verlag.

***Robinson, David.** Paths of Accommodation: Muslim Societies & French Colonial Authorities In Senegal & Mauritania, 1880-1920. (Western African Studies). 408p. (C). 2000. text 65.00 (*0-8214-1353-8*); pap. text 26.95 (*0-8214-1354-6*) Ohio U Pr.

Robinson, David. Saving Graces. LC 95-4069. (Illus.). 128p. 1999. pap. 15.95 (*0-393-31333-6*, Norton Paperbks) Norton.

— The Unitarians & the Universalists. LC 84-9031. (Denominations in America Ser.: No. 1). 368p. 1985. pap. 39.95 (*0-313-24893-1*, RUNPB) Greenwood.

— The Unitarians & the Universalists, 1. LC 84-9031. (Denominations in America Ser.: No. 1). 368p. 1985. lib. bdg. 45.00 (*0-313-20946-4*, RUN/) Greenwood.

Robinson, David, ed. Experimentation & Reconstruction in Environmental Archaeology. (Association for Environmental Archaeology Symposia Ser.: No. 9). (Illus.). 278p. 1990. pap. 40.00 (*0-946897-23-9*, Pub. by Oxbow Bks) David Brown.

— Neurobiology. LC 97-37177. (Illus.). 372p. (C). 1998. pap. 39.95 (*3-540-63546-7*) Spr-Verlag.

— William Ellery Channing: Selected Writings. LC 84-62567. (Sources of American Spirituality Ser.: Vol. 2). 320p. 1985. 12.95 (*0-8091-0359-1*) Paulist Pr.

Robinson, David & Reed, Val. The A-Z of Social Research Jargon. LC 97-49326. 128p. 1998. pap. 20.95 (*1-85742-388-7*, H49.5.A9, Pub. by Ashgate Pub) Ashgate Pub Co.

Robinson, David & Smith, Douglas. Sources of the African Past. LC 79-5399. 203p. 1979. 47.95 (*0-8419-0337-9*, Africana) Holmes & Meier.

Robinson, David, et al. Thailand: Adjusting to Success: Current Policy Issues. (Occasional Paper Ser.: No. 85). viii, 50p. (Orig.). 1991. pap. 10.00 (*1-55775-221-4*) Intl Monetary.

Robinson, David, jt. auth. see Jonash, Ronald.

Robinson, David, ed. see Aranda, Francisco.

Robinson, David, jt. ed. see Godfrey, Christine.

***Robinson, David A.** Understanding & Preventing Employee Lawsuits in Massachusetts: A Guide for Employers. 378p. 1999. pap. 95.00 (*0-9674688-0-9*) D Robinson.

Robinson, David B., ed. see Johnson, Adelaide M.

Robinson, David E. & Dispirito, Mary Ann. Burlington. LC 98-103731. (Images of America Ser.). 1997. pap. 16.99 (*0-7524-0456-3*) Arcadia Publng.

An Asterisk (*) at the beginning of an entry indicates that the title is appearing for the first time.

Robinson, David F. All about Internet FTP: Learning & Teaching to Transfer Files on the Internet. (Internet Workshop Ser.: Vol. 2). 1994. spiral bd. 30.00 (*1-882208-04-8*) Library Solns.

Robinson, David F., ed. Living on the Earth. 320p. 1988. 29.95 (*0-87044-734-3*); 41.95 (*0-87044-735-1*); lib. bdg. 31.95 (*0-87044-736-X*) Natl Geog.

Robinson, David G. Plant Membranes: Endo & Plasma Membranes. LC 84-7539. (Cell Biology: A Series of Monographs: Vol. 3). 352p. 1985. text 83.95 (*0-471-86210-X*) Krieger.

***Robinson, David G. & Rogers, John C., III.** Vacuolar Compartments. LC 00-29764. 2000. write for info. (*0-8493-0500-4*) CRC Pr.

Robinson, David J. Mexican Colonial Parish Registers, 1981, set only. 288p. 1981. 22.50 (*0-940764-22-9*) Genealog Inst.

— Studying Latin America: Essays in Honor of Preston E. James. LC 80-12413. (Dellplain Latin American Studies: No. 4). 289p. 1980. reprint ed. pap. 89.60 (*0-8357-0515-3*, 202259100028) Bks Demand.

Robinson, David J., ed. Migration in Colonial Spanish America. (Cambridge Studies in Historical Geography: No. 16). (Illus.). 416p. (C). 1990. text 69.95 (*0-521-36281-4*) Cambridge U Pr.

Robinson, David J., ed. Social Fabric & Spatial Structure in Colonial Latin America. LC 79-15744. (Dellplain Latin American Studies: No. 1). 496p. 1979. reprint ed. pap. 153.80 (*0-608-13425-2*, 202258900028) Bks Demand.

Robinson, David J., jt. auth. see Fox, David John.

Robinson, David J., ed. see Delson, Roberta M.

Robinson, David K. & Reed, Val. Measuring Forensic Psychiatric & Mental Health Nursing Interactions. LC 96-84008. (Developments in Nursing & Health Care Ser.). 252p. 1996. 72.95 (*1-85972-221-0*, Pub. by Avebry) Ashgate Pub Co.

Robinson, David L. Brain, Mind & Behavior: A New Perspective on Human Nature. LC 95-43765. 192p. 1996. 55.00 (*0-275-95468-4*, Praeger Pubs) Greenwood.

Robinson, David M. Emerson's Pragmatic Turn. LC 93-156. (Studies in American Literature & Culture: No. 70). 246p. (C). 1993. text 54.95 (*0-521-44497-7*) Cambridge U Pr.

— World of Relations: The Achievement of Peter Taylor. LC 97-32640. 224p. (C). 1998. 29.95 (*0-8131-2063-2*) U Pr of Ky.

Robinson, David M. & Fluck, Edward J. A Study of the Greek Love Names. Vlastos, Gregory, ed. LC 78-19375. (Morals & Law in Ancient Greece Ser.). 1979. reprint ed. lib. bdg. 23.95 (*0-405-11569-5*) Ayer.

Robinson, David W. Deconstructing East Germany: Christoph Hein's Literature of Dissent. LC 99-27607. (Studies in German Literature, Linguistics & Culture). 240p. 1999. 55.00 (*1-57113-163-9*, Pub. by Camden Hse) Boydell & Brewer.

Robinson, David W., ed. No Man's Land: East German Drama after the Wall. (Contemporary Theatre Review Ser.: Vol. 4, Pt. 2). 220p. 1996. pap. text 24.00 (*3-7186-5786-4*, ECU31, Harwood Acad Pubs) Gordon & Breach.

Robinson, Davis Rider. The Physical Comedy Handbook. LC 99-19681. 1999. pap. text 16.95 (*0-325-00114-6*) Heinemann.

Robinson, Davis S., jt. auth. see Eskin, N. A.

Robinson, Dawn, jt. auth. see Bragg, B. J.

Robinson, Dean. Seaforth. (Illus.). 84p. (Orig.). 1991. pap. 10.95 (*0-919783-53-8*, Pub. by Boston Mills) Genl Dist Srvs.

Robinson, Deanna, et al. Music at the Margins: Popular Music & Cultural Diversity. (Communication & Human Values Ser.: Vol. 8). (Illus.). 320p. 1991. 52.00 (*0-8039-3192-1*); pap. 24.95 (*0-8039-3193-X*) Sage.

Robinson, Debbie, jt. auth. see Bird, Doni.

Robinson, Debbie, jt. auth. see Robinson, Chuck.

Robinson, Debbie S., jt. auth. see Bird, Doni.

Robinson, Deborah W. The Collaborative Articulation & Assessment Project Training Manual (CAAP) No. 137: Foreign Language Publications. (Illus.). 212p. (Orig.). 1996. pap., teacher ed. 17.50 (*0-87415-314-X*, 137) Foreign Lang.

Robinson, Deidre. Open Hands, Open Heart: The Story of Biddy Mason. (Illus.). 48p. (YA). (gr. 4 up). 1997. 15.95 (*0-9660618-0-2*) Sly Fox Pub.

***Robinson, Denise.** PrayerStarters on the Way to Forgiveness. LC 00-100740. (Prayerstarters Ser.). 72p. 2000. pap. 4.95 (*0-87029-340-0*) Abbey.

***Robinson, Denise & Kidd, Pamela.** Primary Care Across the Life Span. LC 99-37349. (Illus.). 1300p. 1999. write for info. (*0-323-00148-3*) Mosby Inc.

Robinson, Denise L. Clinical Decision Making for Nurse Practitioners: A Case Study Approach. LC 97-17251. (Illus.). 464p. 1997. pap. text 37.95 (*0-397-55459-1*) Lppncott W & W.

Robinson, Dennis, jt. auth. see Coombs, Richard.

Robinson, Dennis M., jt. auth. see Robinson, Jacqueline.

Robinson, Dennis W., jt. ed. see Lam, Alven H. S.

Robinson, Derek. Artillery of Lies. large type ed. 1993. 39.95 (*0-7066-1018-0*, Pub. by Remploy Pr) St Mut.

— Civil Service Pay in Africa. xi, 220p. (Orig.). 1990. lib. bdg. 24.75 (*92-2-106459-X*) Intl Labour Office.

***Robinson, Derek.** Hornet's Sting. 2000. 26.00 (*1-86046-793-8*) Harvill Press.

Robinson, Derek. Monetarism & the Labour Market. (Library of Political Economy). 456p. 1986. pap. 19.95 (*0-19-877192-4*) OUP.

***Robinson, Derek.** Rugby Players Guide to the Laws. 3rd ed. 1999. pap. 13.95 (*0-00-218863-5*, Pub. by HarpC) Trafalgar.

Robinson, Derek J. A Course in the Theory of Groups. 2nd ed. Axler, S. et al, eds. LC 95-4025. (Graduate Texts in Mathematics Ser.: Vol. 80). (Illus.). 499p. 1995. 59.95 (*0-387-94461-3*) Spr-Verlag.

Robinson, Derek J., ed. A Course in Linear Algebra with Applications. 436p. (C). 1991. text 78.00 (*981-02-0567-8*); pap. text 44.00 (*981-02-0568-6*) World Scientific Pub.

Robinson, Deronta C. Behind My Eyes. (Illus.). 32p. 1999. pap. 4.95 (*0-9666100-1-6*) Black Ink.

Robinson, Diana M. To Stretch a Plank: A Survey of Psychokinesis. LC 80-12335. 282p. 1981. 32.95 (*0-88229-404-0*) Burnham Inc.

Robinson, Dianne P., jt. auth. see Poole, Lisa I.

Robinson, Dindy. World Cultures Through Art Activities. 200p. 1996. pap. text 23.00 (*1-56308-271-3*) Teacher Ideas Pr.

Robinson, Donald L. To the Best of My Ability. (C). 1988. pap. 14.00 (*0-393-95781-0*) Norton.

Robinson, Donald S., jt. ed. see Prien, Robert F.

***Robinson, Doreen.** Nevada State Children's Home, 1870-1920: Admission Records. 346p. 2000. pap. 35.00 (*1-58211-229-0*) Quintin Pub RI.

— Ross Burke Funeral Home Records, 1904-1919. 42p. 2000. pap. 15.00 (*1-58211-233-9*) Quintin Pub RI.

— Territorial Enterprise: Vital Record Announcements, 1886-1892. 83p. 2000. pap. 10.00 (*1-58211-230-4*) Quintin Pub RI.

— Walker River Valley Paiute Rolls, 1897-1920; Mason Valley Paiute Rolls, 1915-1920. 314p. 2000. pap. 30.00 (*1-58211-222-3*) Quintin Pub RI.

Robinson, Doris, ed. Fine Arts Periodicals: An International Directory of the Visual Arts. 570p. (Orig.). 1992. pap. 89.00 (*1-879796-03-1*) Peri Press.

— Music & Dance Periodicals: An International Directory & Guidebook. (Orig.). 1989. pap. 65.00 (*0-9617844-4-X*) Peri Press.

— Stamps, Coins, Postcards & Related Materials: A Directory of Periodicals. 150p. (Orig.). 1991. pap. text 29.00 (*0-9617844-7-4*) Peri Press.

Robinson, Doris & Mopsik, Wendy. Decision Making: A Program Designed for Students with a Variety of Handicapping Conditions. (Illus.). 28p. (Orig.). (J). (gr. k-6). 1993. pap. 7.95 (*1-57543-009-6*) Mar Co Prods.

— Mainstreaming - Inclusion: A Program Designed for Students with a Variety of Handicapping Conditions. LC 93-79191. (Special Student Book). 30p. (J). (gr. 3-8). 1993. 7.95 (*1-884063-07-1*) Mar Co Prods.

— Self Esteem: A Program Designed for Students with a Variety of Handicapping Conditions. (Illus.). 28p. (Orig.). (J). (gr. k-6). 1990. pap. 7.95 (*1-57543-007-X*) Mar Co Prods.

— Socialization & Interaction: A Program Designed for Students with a Variety of Handicapping Conditions. (Illus.). 28p. (Orig.). (J). (gr. k-6). 1991. pap. 7.95 (*1-57543-008-8*) Mar Co Prods.

Robinson, Doug. A Night on the Ground, a Day in the Open: A Mountain Vagabond Hard at Work. LC 96-887. (Illus.). 320p. 1996. pap. 19.00 (*1-879415-14-3*) Mtn n Air Bks.

Robinson, Doug & Frey, Martin. Low-Grade Metamorphism. LC 98-18900. (Illus.). 8p. 1998. pap. 75.00 (*0-632-04756-9*) Blackwell Sci.

Robinson, Douglas. American Apocalypses: The Image of the End of the World in American Literature. LC 84-28865. 304p. reprint ed. pap. 94.30 (*0-7837-4402-1*, 204414200012) Bks Demand.

— Becoming a Translator: An Accelerated Course. LC 97-7057. (Illus.). 344p. (C). 1997. 75.00 (*0-415-14860-X*); pap. 24.99 (*0-415-14861-8*) Routledge.

— No Less a Man: Masculist Art in a Feminist Age. LC 93-72885. 308p. (C). 1994. 45.95 (*0-87972-637-7*); pap. 18.95 (*0-87972-638-5*) Bowling Green Univ Popular Press.

— Translation & Taboo. LC 95-39478. 250p. 1996. pap. 18.50 (*0-87580-571-X*); lib. bdg. 35.00 (*0-87580-209-5*) N Ill U Pr.

— The Translator's Turn. LC 90-4629. (Parallax: Re-Visions of Culture & Society Ser.). 368p. 1991. text 52.00 (*0-8018-4046-5*); pap. text 16.95 (*0-8018-4047-3*) Johns Hopkins.

— What Is Translation? Centrifugal Theories, Critical Interventions. LC 97-11216. (Translation Studies). 235p. 1997. 32.00 (*0-87338-573-X*) Kent St U Pr.

***Robinson, Douglas.** Who Translates? Translator Subjectivities Beyond Reason. (C). 2001. pap. text 19.95 (*0-7914-4864-9*) State U NY Pr.

— Who Translates? Translator Subjectivities Beyond Reason. (C). 2001. text 59.50 (*0-7914-4863-0*) State U NY Pr.

Robinson, Douglas. The Zeppelin in Combat: A History of the German Naval Airship Division, 1912-1918. LC 93-84500. (Illus.). 410p. 1994. 49.95 (*0-88740-510-X*) Schiffer.

Robinson, Douglas, tr. Aleksis Kivi's Heath Cobblers (Nummisuutarit) & Kullervo. LC 93-20724. 1993. pap. 14.95 (*0-87839-081-2*) North Star.

Robinson, Douglas, ed. see Starr, Walter A., Jr.

Robinson, Douglas H. Ring Lardner & the Other. (Illus.). 336p. 1992. text 70.00 (*0-19-507600-1*) OUP.

Robinson, Douglas H., jt. auth. see Dick, Harold G.

Robinson, Douglas H., tr. see Eckener, Hugo.

Robinson, Douglas J. & James, Stephen E., eds. Anodes for Electrowinning: Proceedings of the Sessions. LC 84-60151. (Illus.). 119p. reprint ed. pap. 36.90 (*0-8357-5619-X*, 203259200080) Bks Demand.

***Robinson, Dow F.** Wind of the Son: The Story of God's Mighty Outpouring among the Descendants. 116p. 1999. pap. 5.95 (*1-58169-021-5*, Gazelle Pr) Genesis Comm Inc.

Robinson, Duke. Good Intentions: The Nine Unconscious Mistakes of Nice People. LC 96-34866. 272p. 1997. 22.00 (*0-446-52085-3*, Pub. by Warner Bks) Little.

— Good Intentions: The 9 Unconscious Mistakes of Nice People: A Discussion Guide for Small Groups. Dobson, David, ed. LC 98-30947. 48p. 1998. 7.95 (*1-57895-070-8*) Bridge Resources.

— Too Nice for Your Own Good: How to Stop Making 9 Self-Sabotaging Mistakes. 288p. 2000. pap. write for info. (*0-446-67386-2*) Warner Bks.

Robinson, Duncan & Bell, Keith. Stanley Spencer. abr. ed. (Illus.). 544p. (C). 1993. pap. 24.95 (*0-7148-2810-6*, Pub. by Phaidon Press) Phaidon Pr.

Robinson, Duncan & Kahn, Louis. The Yale Center for British Art at Twenty: A Living Tribute to Louis Kahn. LC 97-5923. 80p. 1997. pap. 16.00 (*0-300-06972-3*) Yale U Pr.

Robinson, Duncan, et al. Acquisitions: The First Decade. LC 86-51189. (Illus.). 40p. (Orig.). 1986. pap. 5.95 (*0-930606-54-X*) Yale Ctr Brit Art.

— British Art. (Mead Art Museum Monographs: Vols. 6 & 7). (Illus.). 63p. (Orig.). 1986. pap. text 5.00 (*0-914337-07-6*) Mead Art Mus.

Robinson, E., jt. ed. see Musson, A. E.

***Robinson, E. A.** Dual-Sensor Technology: Pt. B. (Handbook of Geophysical Exploration Ser.). (Illus.). 348p. 1999. 129.50 (*0-08-043627-7*, Pergamon Pr) Elsevier.

Robinson, E. A. Tilbury Score: Centennial Edition. 1987. reprint ed. pap. 5.00 (*0-912156-05-8*) Masterwork Pr.

***Robinson, E. John.** Paint the Sea in Oils Using Special Effects. Dodd, Terri, ed. (Illus.). 128p. 1999. write for info. (*1-929834-00-4*) Intl Artist Pubg.

— Paint the Sea in Oils Using Special Effects. (Illus.). 2000. 24.99 (*1-929834-04-7*) Intl Artist Pubg.

Robinson, E. L., jt. ed. see Dancy, T. E.

Robinson, E. S. Basic Physical Geology. 3rd ed. (Illus.). 595p. (C). 1991. reprint ed. text 138.00 (*1-878907-21-2*) TechBooks.

Robinson, E. S. & Mattingly, Harold B. The Date of the Roman Denarius & Other Landmarks in Early Roman Coinage. (Illus.). 59p. 1974. pap. 10.00 (*0-916710-17-3*) Obol Intl.

Robinson, Earl. The Bible Fact or Fiction? 1992. pap. 4.99 (*0-88019-296-8*) Schmul Pub Co.

— Marks of a Christian. pap. 2.99 (*0-88019-179-1*) Schmul Pub Co.

Robinson, Earl & Gordon, Eric A. Ballad of an American: The Autobiography of Earl Robinson. LC 97-33023. (American Folk Music & Musicians Ser.: No. 3). 512p. 1997. 49.50 (*0-8108-3433-2*) Scarecrow.

Robinson, Earl, jt. auth. see McEwen, Alex.

Robinson, Earl, jt. ed. see Bentley, Eric.

Robinson, Ed. Not Ashamed. 32p. 1992. pap. 3.99 (*0-8341-1438-0*) Beacon Hill.

***Robinson, Ed.** Old Timer's Motorcycle Tall Tales. (Illus.). 182p. 1999. pap. write for info. (*0-9673116-0-8*) WordPro Pr.

Robinson, Ed & Mowry, Kathryn L. Preteen Ministry: Between a Rock & a Hard Place. 95p. (Orig.). 1993. pap. 7.99 (*0-8341-1409-7*) Beacon Hill.

Robinson, Ed, jt. auth. see Robinson, Carolyn.

***Robinson, Eddie & Lapchick, Richard.** Never Before, Never Again: The Autobiography of Eddie Robinson. LC 99-36158. 320p. 1999. text 24.95 (*0-312-24224-7*) St Martin.

***Robinson, Eden.** Monkey Beach. 384p. 2000. 24.00 (*0-618-07327-2*) HM.

Robinson, Eden. Monkey Beach. 1950. text. write for info. (*0-8050-4839-1*) St Martin.

Robinson, Edgar E. The Roosevelt Leadership, 1933-1945. LC 75-146154. (American Scene Ser.). 1972. reprint ed. lib. bdg. 49.50 (*0-306-70202-9*) Da Capo.

Robinson, Edgar E. & Bornet, Vaughn D. Herbert Hoover: President of the United States. (Publication Ser.: No. 149). 398p. 1975. 14.95 (*0-8179-1491-9*) Hoover Inst Pr.

Robinson, Edgar L. Evolution of Buckley (Washington) Story of a Backwoods Town. (Illus.). 38p. 1984. reprint ed. pap. 5.00 (*0-945433-09-3*) Herit Quest.

Robinson, Edna M. Tennyson's Use of the Bible. 119p. (C). 1968. reprint ed. 40.00 (*0-87752-093-3*) Gordian.

Robinson, Edward. Biblical Researches in Palestine, Mount Sinai, & Arabic Petraea. (Notable American Authors Ser.). 1999. reprint ed. lib. bdg. 125.00 (*0-7812-8791-X*) Rprt Serv.

— Biblical Researches in Palestine: Mount Sinai & Arabia Petraea: A Journal of Travels in the Year 1838, 3 vols., 1. Davis, Moshe, ed. LC 77-70738. (America & the Holy Land Ser.). 1977. reprint ed. lib. bdg. 58.95 (*0-405-10282-8*) Ayer.

— Biblical Researches in Palestine: Mount Sinai & Arabia Petraea: A Journal of Travels in the Year 1838, 3 vols., Set. Davis, Moshe, ed. LC 77-70738. (America & the Holy Land Ser.). 1977. reprint ed. lib. bdg. 173.95 (*0-405-10281-X*) Ayer.

— Biblical Researches in Palestine: Mount Sinai & Arabia Petraea: A Journal of Travels in the Year 1838, 3 vols., Vol. 2. Davis, Moshe, ed. LC 77-70738. (America & the Holy Land Ser.). 1977. reprint ed. lib. bdg. 58.95 (*0-405-10283-6*) Ayer.

— Biblical Researches in Palestine: Mount Sinai & Arabia Petraea: A Journal of Travels in the Year 1838, 3 vols., Vol. 3. Davis, Moshe, ed. LC 77-70738. (America & the Holy Land Ser.). 1977. reprint ed. lib. bdg. 58.95 (*0-405-10284-4*) Ayer.

— Calmet's Dictionary of the Holy Bible. (Notable American Authors Ser.). 1999. reprint ed. lib. bdg. 125.00 (*0-7812-8796-0*) Rprt Serv.

— A Dictionary of the Holy Bible, for General Use in the Study of the Scriptures. (Notable American Authors Ser.). 1999. reprint ed. lib. bdg. 125.00 (*0-7812-8793-6*) Rprt Serv.

— A Dictionary of the Holy Bible for the Use of Schools & Young. (Notable American Authors Ser.). 1999. reprint ed. lib. bdg. 125.00 (*0-7812-8790-1*) Rprt Serv.

— A Greek & English Lexicon of the New Testament. (Notable American Authors Ser.). 1999. reprint ed. lib. bdg. 125.00 (*0-7812-8799-5*) Rprt Serv.

— A Greek Gramer (From the German of P. Buttmann) (Notable American Authors Ser.). 1999. reprint ed. lib. bdg. 125.00 (*0-7812-8800-2*) Rprt Serv.

— A Harmony of the Gospels in Greek. (Notable American Authors Ser.). 1999. reprint ed. lib. bdg. 125.00 (*0-7812-8797-9*) Rprt Serv.

— A Hebrew & English Lexicon of the Old Testament. (Notable American Authors Ser.). 1999. reprint ed. lib. bdg. 125.00 (*0-7812-8801-0*) Rprt Serv.

Robinson, Edward. Icons of the Present. (Illus.). 1993. pap. 19.00 (*0-334-02548-6*) TPI PA.

Robinson, Edward. Later Biblical Researches in Palestine & in Adjacent Regions: Journal of Travels in the Year 1852. Davis, Moshe, ed. LC 77-70739. (America & the Holy Land Ser.). 1977. reprint ed. lib. bdg. 58.95 (*0-405-10285-2*) Ayer.

— Later Biblical Researches in Palestine & the Adjacent Regions. (Notable American Authors Ser.). 1999. reprint ed. lib. bdg. 125.00 (*0-7812-8792-8*) Rprt Serv.

— Memoir of the Rev. William Robinson. (Notable American Authors Ser.). 1999. reprint ed. lib. bdg. 125.00 (*0-7812-8794-4*) Rprt Serv.

— The Original Vision: A Study of the Religious Experience of Childhood. 192p. (Orig.). 1984. 7.95 (*0-8164-2439-X*) Harper SF.

— Physical Geography of the Holy Land. (Notable American Authors Ser.). 1999. reprint ed. lib. bdg. 125.00 (*0-7812-8795-2*) Rprt Serv.

— Translator - A Greek Grammar of the New Testament (With Moses Stuart) (from the German of G.B. Winer) (Notable American Authors Ser.). 1999. reprint ed. lib. bdg. 125.00 (*0-7812-8798-7*) Rprt Serv.

Robinson, Edward, tr. see Gesenius, William.

Robinson, Edward A. Atoms, Molecules & Reactions. 1994. pap. text, student ed. 34.80 (*0-13-129446-6*) P-H.

Robinson, Edward E., jt. auth. see Ash, Peter F.

Robinson, Edward S., ed. & intro. see Melton, Arthur W.

Robinson, Edward S., tr. see Jaeger, Werner W.

Robinson, Edwin Arlington. Children of the Night. 1974. 200.00 (*0-87968-186-1*) Gordon Pr.

— Edwin Arlington Robinson's Letters to Edith Brower. Cary, Richard, ed. LC 68-17623. (Illus.). 242p. 1968. text 33.50 (*0-674-24035-9*) Belknap Pr.

— The Essential Robinson. LC 93-14493. (Essential Poets Ser.: Vol. 19). 1999. pap. 8.00 (*0-88001-336-2*) HarpC.

— Miniver Cheevy & Other Poems. LC 95-8708. (Thrift Editions Ser.). 64p. (Orig.). 1995. reprint ed. pap. text 1.00 (*0-486-28756-4*) Dover.

— The Poetry of E. A. Robinson. LC 98-31800. 256p. 1999. 19.95 (*0-679-60262-3*) Modern Lib NY.

— Selected Letters of Edwin Arlington Robinson. LC 79-15514. (Illus.). 191p. 1980. reprint ed. lib. bdg. 39.75 (*0-313-21266-X*, ROSL, Greenwood Pr) Greenwood.

— Selected Poems. Faggen, Robert, ed. & intro. by. LC 97-13727. 288p. 1997. pap. 12.95 (*0-14-018988-2*) Viking Penguin.

— Untriangulated Stars. (American Autobiography Ser.). 348p. 1995. reprint ed. lib. bdg. 89.00 (*0-7812-8626-3*) Rprt Serv.

— Van Zorn: A Comedy in Three Acts. LC 72-97890. reprint ed. 29.50 (*0-404-05363-7*) AMS Pr.

Robinson, Edwin Arlington, ed. see Perry, Thomas S.

Robinson, Edwin S. & Coruh, Cahit. Basic Exploration Geophysics. 99th ed. 576p. 1988. text 108.95 (*0-471-87941-X*) Wiley.

Robinson, Edythe. A Long Lonely Time: A Woman's Search for Justice. (Illus.). 160p. (Orig.). 1990. pap. 8.95 (*0-936101-11-3*) RBH.

Robinson, Elie. The Monster in Our Midst: Will You Be Spared by the Monster. 184p. 1997. pap. 15.00 (*0-8059-4229-7*) Dorrance.

Robinson, Elizabeth. Bed of Lists. Rosenwasser, Rena & Dienstfrey, Patricia, eds. LC 90-39994. (Illus.). 48p. (Orig.). (C). 1990. pap. text 8.00 (*0-932716-25-3*) Kelsey St Pr.

— Eight Etudes. (Orig.). 1988. pap. 3.50 (*0-945926-00-6*) Paradigm RI.

— In the Sequence of Falling Things. 96p. 1990. 10.00 (*0-945926-20-0*) Paradigm RI.

— In the Sequence of Falling Things. deluxe ed. 96p. 1990. 25.00 (*0-945926-21-9*) Paradigm RI.

— My Name Happens Also: Poems. deluxe limited ed. (Poetry Chapbooks). 32p. 1987. pap. 15.00 (*0-930901-44-4*) Burning Deck.

***Robinson, Ella.** A Guide to Literary Sites of the South. 2nd rev. ed. LC PS144.S67R63 2000. (Illus.). 280p. 1999. 17.95 (*1-885219-15-6*) Vision AL.

Robinson, Ella. Women on Mission Journal. Hansen, Susan, ed. (Illus.). 64p. (Orig.). 1995. pap. text 3.95 (*1-56309-111-9*, W953122) Womans Mission Union.

Robinson, Elwyn B. History of North Dakota. LC 95-68420. (Illus.). 610p. (C). 1995. pap. 25.00 (*0-911042-43-1*) NDSU Inst Reg.

Robinson, Emmet. How to Prosper in Business Regardless of the Economy. LC 96-179488. 307p. (Orig.). 1996. pap. 19.95 (*1-888873-00-0*) King Street.

Robinson, Enders A. Salem Witchcraft & Hawthorne's "House of the Seven Gables" (Illus.). 388p. (Orig.). 1992. pap. 29.50 (*1-55613-515-7*) Heritage Bk.

Robinson, Enders A. & Osman, Osman M., eds. Deconvolution 2. (Geophysics Reprints Ser.: Vol. 17). (Illus.). 726p. (Orig.). 1996. pap. 69.00 (*1-56080-039-9*, 191A) Soc Expl Geophys.

R

Robinson, Enders A. & Silvia, Manual T. Digital Foundations of Time Series Analysis: Wave-Equation Space-Time Processing. 464p. 1981. 49.95 (*0-8162-7270-0*); text 49.95 (*0-8162-7271-9*) Holden-Day.

Robinson, Enders A. & Silvia, Manuel T. Digital Signal Processing & Time Series Analysis. 1978. 49.95 (*0-8162-7264-6*) Holden-Day.

Robinson, Enders A., jt. ed. see Osman, Osman M.

Robinson, Eric. One Dark Mile: A Widower's Story. LC 89-32046. 200p. 1990. 30.00 (*0-87023-684-9*) U of Mass Pr.

Robinson, Eric, et al, eds. John Clare (1793-1864) Cottage Tales. pap. write for info. (*1-85754-032-8*, Pub. by Carcanet Pr) Paul & Co Pubs.

Robinson, Eric, ed. see Clare, John.

Robinson, Eric W. Metaphysics for Christians: Towards a Pluralistic Unity of Humankind. (Illus.). 118p. (Orig.). 1996. pap. 9.95 (*1-57502-118-8*) Morris Pubng.

Robinson, Erma. Never Turn Back. 236p. 1998. pap. 8.00 (*1-57502-772-0*, P02129) Morris Pubng.

Robinson, Eugene. Coal to Cream: A Black Man's Journey Beyond Color to an Affirmation of Race. LC 99-22037. 272p. 1999. 23.50 (*0-684-85722-7*) Free Pr.

— Eugene Robinson: Diary of a Super Bowl Season. LC 98-160976. (Illus.). 240p. 1998. pap. 19.95 (*0-87341-619-8*, SAFI) Krause Pubns.

— It Takes Endurance, Bk. 7. LC 98-36325. 160p. 1998. pap. 11.99 (*1-57673-454-4*) Multnomah Pubs.

Robinson, Eugene, et al. Papers on California Archaeology: 27-29. (University of California Archaeology Survey, Department of Anthropology Berkeley, CA Ser.: No. 28). (Illus.). 45p. (C). 1955. reprint ed. pap. text 5.00 (*1-55567-629-4*) Coyote Press.

Robinson, Eugene, jt. auth. see Jewell, Donald P.

Robinson, Eva C. Greening at the Grassroots: Alternative Forestry Strategies in India. LC 97-32064. 144p. 1997. 26.50 (*0-7619-9218-9*); pap. write for info. (*0-7619-9219-7*) Sage.

Robinson, F. Having It Both Ways: Self-Subversion in Western Popular Classics. 158p. 1996. pap. 12.95 (*0-8263-1750-2*) U of NM Pr.

Robinson, F. K. A Glossary of Words Used in the Neighbourhood of Whitby. (English Dialect Society Publications: Nos. 9, 13). 1969. reprint ed. pap. 30.00 (*0-8115-0442-5*) Periodicals Srv.

Robinson, F. M., ed. see Russell, Enid.

Robinson, F. R. Valentine's Checkup: Big Book. large type ed. (Little Books & Big Bks.). (Illus.). 8p. (J). (ps-1). 1998. pap. text 19.89 (*0-8215-0873-3*) Sadlier.

Robinson, F. Willard. Beverly Hills Principal. 176p. 1998. 19.95 (*1-885101-72-4*) Writers Pr ID.

Robinson, Famous. Brandon's First Baseball Game. LC 90-63290. (I Promise to Do My Best Ser.). 37p. (Orig.). (J). (ps-6). 1990. pap. text 5.00 (*0-9627951-0-0*) JRBB Pubs.

***Robinson, Fanny.** Country Flowers Of A Victorian Lady. 96p. 2000. 15.00 (*0-06-019703-X*) HarpC.

Robinson, Fay. Airport. LC 97-900. (Field Trips Ser.). (Illus.). 32p. (J). (gr. 1-4). 1997. lib. bdg. 21.36 (*1-56766-292-7*) Childs World.

— Amazing Lizards! LC 98-9171. (Hello Reader! Ser.). (Illus.). 32p. (J). (gr. k-2). 1999. 3.99 (*0-590-33073-X*) Scholastic Inc.

— Designs. (Let Me Read Ser.). (J). 1996. 2.95 (*0-673-36338-4*, GoodYrBooks) Addson-Wesley Educ.

***Robinson, Fay.** A Dinosaur Named Sue: The Find of the Century. (Hello Reader! Ser.). 1999. mass mkt. 3.99 (*0-439-09983-8*) Scholastic.

Robinson, Fay. Fantastic Frogs! LC 98-22398. (Hello Reader! Ser.). (Illus.). 32p. (J). (ps-2). 2000. mass mkt. 3.99 (*0-590-52269-8*) Scholastic Inc.

***Robinson, Fay.** Fantastic Frogs! (Hello, Reader! Ser.). (Illus.). (J). 2000. 9.44 (*0-606-18542-9*) Turtleback.

Robinson, Fay. Great Snakes! LC 95-10531. (Hello Readers! Ser.: Level 2). (Illus.). 32p. (J). (ps-3). 1996. pap. 3.50 (*0-590-26243-2*, Cartwheel) Scholastic Inc.

— Great Snakes! (Hello, Reader! Ser.). 1996. 8.70 (*0-606-09361-3*, Pub. by Turtleback) Demco.

***Robinson, Fay.** A Man Like Mac. (Superromance Ser.: Bk. 911). 2000. per. 4.50 (*0-373-70911-0*, 1-70911-2) Harlequin Bks.

Robinson, Fay. Meet My Mouse. (Let Me Read Ser.). (J). 1996. 2.95 (*0-673-36344-9*, GoodYrBooks) Addson-Wesley Educ.

— Mighty Spiders! LC 95-10530. (Hello Reader! Ser.: Level 2). (Illus.). 32p. (J). (gr. k-2). 1996. pap. 3.50 (*0-590-26262-9*, Cartwheel) Scholastic Inc.

— Mighty Spiders! (Hello, Reader! Ser.). 1996. 8.70 (*0-606-09613-2*, Pub. by Turtleback) Demco.

— Pilots Fly Airplanes. LC 96-7199. (Community Helpers Ser.). (Illus.). 32p. (J). (gr. k-3). 1996. lib. bdg. 21.36 (*1-56766-308-7*) Childs World.

***Robinson, Fay.** Singing Robins. LC 99-16244. (Pull Ahead Ser.). (Illus.). 32p. (J). (gr. k-2). 2000. 21.27 (*0-8225-3641-2*, Lerner Publctns); pap. 6.95 (*0-8225-3643-9*, First Ave Edns) Lerner Pub.

Robinson, Fay. Too Much Trash! LC 95-5560. (Rookie Read-About Science Ser.). (Illus.). 32p. (J). (ps-3). 1995. lib. bdg. 18.50 (*0-516-06042-2*) Childrens.

— The Upside-Down Sloth. LC 93-18981. (Rookie Read-About Science Ser.). (Illus.). 32p. (J). (gr. 1-2). 1993. pap. 4.95 (*0-516-46018-8*) Childrens.

— Vegetables, Vegetables. LC 94-14075. (Rookie Read-About Science Ser.). (Illus.). 32p. (J). (gr. 1-2). 1994. pap. 4.95 (*0-516-46030-7*); lib. bdg. 18.50 (*0-516-06030-9*) Childrens.

— We Love Fruit! LC 92-13312. (Rookie Read-About Science Ser.). (Illus.). 32p. (J). (ps-3). 1992. lib. bdg. 18.50 (*0-516-06006-6*) Childrens.

— We Love Fruit! LC 92-13312. (Rookie Read-About Science Ser.). (Illus.). 32p. (J). (ps-3). 1993. pap. 4.95 (*0-516-46006-4*) Childrens.

— Where Did All the Dragons Go? LC 95-3620. (Illus.). 32p. (J). (gr. 1-4). 1996. 15.95 (*0-8167-3808-4*) BrdgeWater.

— Where Did All the Dragons Go? (Illus.). 32p. (J). (ps-2). 1997. pap. 4.95 (*0-8167-3809-2*) Troll Communs.

— Where Do Puddles Go? LC 94-35629. (Rookie Read-About Science Ser.). (Illus.). 32p. (J). (gr. 1-2). 1995. lib. bdg. 18.50 (*0-516-06036-8*) Childrens.

— Where Do Puddles Go? (Rookie Read-About Science Ser.). (Illus.). 32p. (J). (gr. 1-2). 1995. pap. 4.95 (*0-516-46036-6*) Childrens.

Robinson, Fay, compiled by. A Frog Inside My Hat: A First Book of Poems. (J). 1993. 11.40 (*0-606-07549-6*) Turtleback.

***Robinson, Fay & Cassels, Jean.** Creepy Beetles. LC 99-41767. (Hello Reader! Ser.). (Illus.). (J). 2000. pap. 3.99 (*0-439-06754-5*) Scholastic Inc.

Robinson, Fay, jt. auth. see Fowler, Allan.

Robinson, Fay, jt. auth. see Mathews, Judith.

Robinson, Fay, jt. auth. see Matthews, Judith.

Robinson, Fayette & Street, Franklin. The Gold Mines of California: Two Guidebooks. LC 72-9445. (Far Western Frontier Ser.). 230p. 1973. reprint ed. 18.95 (*0-405-05002-X*) Ayer.

Robinson, Ferris. The Gorgeless Gourmet's Cookbook: Practically Fat Free Recipes for Super Busy People. 200p. (Orig.). 1996. pap. 16.95 (*0-9656481-0-9*) Peach Pub.

Robinson, Fiona. Globalizing Care: Ethics, Feminist Theory & International Relations. LC 98-41072. (Feminist Theory & Politics Ser.). 192p. 1999. 65.00 (*0-8133-3356-3*, Pub. by Westview); pap. 25.00 (*0-8133-3357-1*, Pub. by Westview) HarpC.

Robinson, Forbes & Kilpack, Gilbert. An Inward Legacy. (C). 1956. pap. 7.00 (*0-87574-092-8*) Pendle Hill.

Robinson, Forrest. After the Fire. 45p. (Orig.). 1988. pap. 7.00 (*0-935153-10-1*) Stormline Pr.

Robinson, Forrest, jt. ed. see Gillman, Susan.

Robinson, Forrest G. In Bad Faith. LC 86-4668. 272p. 1986. 37.95 (*0-674-44527-9*) HUP.

— In Bad Faith: The Dynamics of Deception in Mark Twain's America. 272p. (C). 1992. pap. 18.00 (*0-674-44528-7*) HUP.

— Love's Story Told: A Life of Henry A. Murray. LC 92-8705. 490p. 1992. 29.95 (*0-674-53928-1*) HUP.

— Love's Story Told: A Life of Henry A. Murray. (Illus.). 496p. (C). 1995. pap. 18.95 (*0-674-53929-X*) HUP.

Robinson, Forrest G., ed. The Cambridge Companion to Mark Twain. (Cambridge Companions to Literature Ser.). 282p. (C). 1995. pap. text 18.95 (*0-521-44593-0*) Cambridge U Pr.

— The Cambridge Companion to Mark Twain. LC 94-24658. (Cambridge Companions to Literature Ser.). 283p. (C). 1995. text 64.95 (*0-521-44036-X*) Cambridge U Pr.

— The New Western History. LC 98-19251. 220p. 1998. 40.00 (*0-8165-1915-3*) U of Ariz Pr.

— The New Western History: An Assessment. LC 98-19251. 220p. 1998. pap. 17.95 (*0-8165-1916-1*) U of Ariz Pr.

Robinson, Frances, jt. auth. see Brass, Paul.

Robinson, Frances M., jt. auth. see Harris, Kenneth B.

Robinson, Frances R. Antonio & His Enchanted Watering Can. 48p. (J). (gr. 3-4). 1994. pap. text 6.95 (*1-886114-01-3*) Arrow Pubns.

Robinson, Francesca, jt. auth. see Berkhout, Monique.

Robinson, Francis. Atlas of the Islamic World since 1500. (Cultural Atlas Ser.). (Illus.). 240p. 1982. 45.00 (*0-87196-629-8*) Facts on File.

***Robinson, Francis.** Islam & Muslim History in South Asia. 336p. 2000. text 29.95 (*0-19-564967-2*) OUP.

Robinson, Francis. Separatism among Indian Muslims: The Politics of the United Provinces' Muslims. (Illus.). 494p. 1993. reprint ed. pap. text 18.95 (*0-19-563126-9*) OUP.

— Separatism among Indian Muslims: The Politics of the United Provinces' Muslims, 1860-1923. LC 73-93393. (Cambridge South Asian Studies: No. 16). 487p. reprint ed. pap. 138.80 (*0-608-12494-X*, 2024521) Bks Demand.

Robinson, Francis, ed. The Cambridge Illustrated History of the Islamic World. (Illustrated Histories Ser.). (Illus.). 351p. (C). 1996. 39.95 (*0-521-43510-2*) Cambridge U Pr.

***Robinson, Francis, ed.** Islamic World. (Cambridge Illustrated History Ser.). (Illus.). 352p. 1999. pap. 27.95 (*0-521-66993-6*) Cambridge U Pr.

Robinson, Francis, jt. auth. see Harcourt, Freda.

Robinson, Francis T. & Dennis, Roger D. Preventing Pain & Injury from Your Computer. LC 93-93633. (Illus.). 50p. (Orig.). 1993. pap. write for info. (*0-9638697-0-1*) R&D Pubng.

Robinson, Frank K., compiled by. Edgar Lee Masters: An Exhibition in Commemoration of the Centenary of His Birth. LC 71-31042. (Illus.). 1970. pap. 8.00 (*0-87959-015-7*) U of Tex H Ransom Ctr.

Robinson, Frank K., ed. The Harmony of Deeper Music: Posthumous Poems of Edgar Lee Masters. LC 79-108963. (Tower Poetry Ser.: No. 10). 1976. 15.00 (*0-87959-091-2*) U of Tex H Ransom Ctr.

— The Harmony of Deeper Music: Posthumous Poems of Edgar Lee Masters. anniversary ed. LC 79-108963. (Tower Poetry Ser.: No. 10). 1976. 25.00 (*0-87959-021-1*) U of Tex H Ransom Ctr.

Robinson, Frank M. The Dark Beyond the Stars. 1997. pap. 14.95 (*0-312-86624-0*) St Martin.

— The Dark Beyond the Stars. 1992. mass mkt. 4.99 (*0-8125-1383-5*, Pub. by Tor Bks) St Martin.

— The Power. 224p. 2000. pap. 12.95 (*0-312-86654-2*, Pub. by Tor Bks) St Martin.

— Science Fiction of the 20th Century: An Illustrated History. Bennett, Ann G., ed. LC 99-27614. (Illus.). 256p. 1999. text 59.95 (*1-888054-29-8*, Pub. by Collectors Pr) Universe.

— Science Fiction of the 20th Century: An Illustrated History. limited ed. Bennett, Ann G., ed. LC 99-27614. (Illus.). 256p. 1999. 89.95 (*1-888054-30-1*, Pub. by Collectors Pr) Universe.

Robinson, Frank M. Waiting. LC 98-47183. 304p. 1999. 23.95 (*0-312-86652-6*, Pub. by Forge NYC) St Martin.

***Robinson, Frank M.** Waiting. LC 98-47183. 356p. 2000. mass mkt. 7.99 (*0-8125-4164-2*, Pub. by Tor Bks) St Martin.

***Robinson, Frank M. & Hull, Paul.** Death of a Marionette. 320p. 2000. pap. 13.95 (*0-312-87287-9*) Forge NYC.

Robinson, Frank M. & Smith, Joe. Death of a Marionette. 1995. 22.95 (*0-614-03855-3*) Forge NYC.

— Death of a Marionette. 1995. 22.95 (*0-614-08652-3*) Tor Bks.

Robinson, Frank M., et al. Coping+Plus: Dimensions of Disability. LC 94-22650. 280p. 1995. 59.95 (*0-275-94544-8*, Praeger Pubs) Greenwood.

Robinson, Frank S. Machine Politics: A Study of Albany's O'Connells. LC 76-3785. Orig. Title: Albany's O'Connell Machine. (Illus.). 262p. 1977. reprint ed. 39.95 (*0-87855-147-6*) Transaction Pubs.

Robinson, Franklin, ed. The Illustrated Bartsch Vol. 5: Netherlandish Artists. LC 79-50679. 1979. lib. bdg. 149.00 (*0-89835-005-0*) Abaris Bks.

Robinson, Franklin, jt. auth. see Shapiro, Robert.

Robinson, Franklin A., Jr. St. Thomas' Parish Register: Croome, Prince George's County, Maryland, 1849-1906. LC 98-154640. 290p. 1998. pap. 23.50 (*0-7884-0841-0*, R504) Heritage Bk.

Robinson, Franklin E., jt. auth. see Plochmann, George K.

Robinson, Franklin L., jt. auth. see Stigum, Marcia L.

Robinson, Franklin W. Gabriel Metsu, the Letter. (Focus Exhibition Catalogues Ser.). (Illus.). 16p. (Orig.). 1985. pap. text 1.50 (*0-9610866-3-7*) Putnam Found.

Robinson, Franklin W. & Nichols, Stephen G., Jr., eds. The Meaning of Mannerism. LC 71-189512. (Illus.). 142p. reprint ed. pap. 44.10 (*0-608-11309-3*, 202232700026) Bks Demand.

Robinson, Franklin W., et al. A Handbook of the Collection: Herbert F. Johnson Museum of Art. (Illus.). 224p. 1998. write for info. (*0-9646042-7-2*) Cornell U H F Johnson.

— The Herbert F. Johnson Museum of Art, Cornell University: A Handbook of the Collection. (Illus.). 216p. 1998. 50.00 (*0-9646042-8-0*); pap. write for info. (*0-9646042-6-4*) Cornell U H F Johnson.

***Robinson, Frazier & Bauer, Paul.** Catching Dreams: My Life in the Negro Baseball Leagues. (Illus.). 256p. 2000. pap. 16.95 (*0-8156-0658-3*) Syracuse U Pr.

Robinson, Frazier, jt. auth. see Bauer, Paul D.

Robinson, Fred, et al, eds. Economic Development Policies: An Evaluative Study of the Newcastle Metropolitan Region. (ESRC Inner Cities Research Programme Ser.). (Illus.). 168p. 1987. pap. 18.95 (*0-19-823271-3*) OUP.

Robinson, Fred C. Old English Literature: A Select Bibliography. LC 76-464039. (Toronto Medieval Bibliographies Ser.: No. 2). 86p. reprint ed. pap. 30.00 (*0-608-16237-X*, 202647000049) Bks Demand.

— The Tomb of Beowulf & Other Essays. LC 92-27331. 1993. 69.95 (*0-631-17328-5*) Blackwell Pubs.

Robinson, Fred C., jt. auth. see Greenfeld, Stanley B.

Robinson, Fred C., jt. auth. see Mitchell, Bruce.

Robinson, Fred M. The Comedy of Language: Studies in Modern Comic Literature. LC 80-125. 200p. 1980. lib. bdg. 30.00 (*0-87023-297-5*) U of Mass Pr.

— The Man in the Bowler Hat: His History & Iconography. LC 92-37188. (Illus.). xvi, 199p. (C). 1993. 29.95 (*0-8078-2073-3*) U of NC Pr.

— The Man in the Bowler Hat: His History & Iconography. LC 92-37188. 215p. reprint ed. pap. 66.70 (*0-608-08615-0*, 206913800003) Bks Demand.

Robinson, Fred M., jt. ed. see Heath, Mary.

Robinson, Freddie. Bible Quizzes with Humor. 80p. 1998. pap. text 9.95 (*0-9640487-4-4*) Transfig Prod.

— The Book of Daniel Unsealed. pap. 12.95 (*0-9640487-2-8*) Transfig Prod.

— Cloning & Christianity. LC 94-61772. 1998. 19.95 (*0-9640487-3-6*) Transfig Prod.

— A Voice Crying Out. LC 94-60333. 1994. pap. 8.95 (*0-9640487-0-1*) Transfig Prod.

Robinson, G. & Stringer, Peter, eds. Social Attitudes in Northern Ireland: The Third Report, 1992-93, Vol. 3. 177p. 1993. pap. 40.00 (*0-85640-512-4*, Pub. by Blackstaff Pr) Dufour.

Robinson, G. Alan, jt. ed. see Greengard, Paul.

Robinson, G. D., jt. auth. see Nelson, Jay.

Robinson, G. Frederick & Wheeler, Ruth R. Great Little Watertown, Mass., 1630-1930, a Tercentary History. (Illus.). 202p. 1996. reprint ed. lib. bdg. 32.00 (*0-8328-5208-2*) Higginson Bk Co.

Robinson, G. H., ed. Coordination Chemistry of Aluminum. 234p. 1993. pap. 159.00 (*0-471-18795-X*, Wiley-VCH) Wiley.

***Robinson, G. K.** Practical Strategies for Experimenting. LC 00-27336. (Series in Probability & Statistics). 2000. write for info. (*0-471-49055-5*) Wiley.

Robinson, G. W., et al. Water in Biology, Chemistry & Physics: Experimental Overviews & Computational Methodologies. (Series in Contemporary Chemical Physics: Vol. 8). 500p. 1996. text 84.00 (*981-02-2451-6*, CPcBPYg-B2923) World Scientific Pub.

Robinson, Gabrielle. A Private Mythology: The Manuscripts & Plays of John Whiting. LC 87-47983. (Illus.). 160p. 1989. 29.50 (*0-8387-5140-7*) Bucknell U Pr.

Robinson, Gail E., jt. ed. see Stewart, Donna E.

***Robinson, Gail K., ed.** Managed Care Tracking System: State Profiles on Public Sector Managed Behavioral Health Care & Other Reforms. (Illus.). 280p. 1999. pap. text 45.00 (*0-7881-8175-0*) DIANE Pub.

Robinson, Gary. The Effect of Futures Trading on Cash Market Volatility: Evidence from the London Stock Exchange. LC HG6024.G73. (Bank of England, Working Paper Ser.: No. 19). (Illus.). 38p. reprint ed. pap. 30.00 (*0-608-10643-7*, 207126500009) Bks Demand.

Robinson, Gary, jt. auth. see Pesaran, Bahram.

Robinson, Gary C., jt. ed. see Linebaugh, Donald W.

Robinson, Geoffrey. The Dark Side of Paradise: Political Violence in Bali. (Illus.). 376p. 1998. pap. text 17.95 (*0-8014-8172-4*) Cornell U Pr.

— Marriage, Divorce & Nullity: A Guide to the Annulment Process in the Catholic Church. 96p. 1988. pap. 8.95 (*0-8146-1570-8*) Liturgical Pr.

— Yorkshire Smiles. (C). 1989. text 40.00 (*0-948929-26-X*) St Mut.

Robinson, Geoffrey B. The Dark Side of Paradise: Political Violence in Bali. (Asia East by South Ser.). (Illus.). 376p. 1995. text 45.00 (*0-8014-2965-X*) Cornell U Pr.

***Robinson, George.** Essential Judaism: A Complete Guide to Beliefs, Customs & Rituals. LC 99-55288. 672p. 2000. 27.95 (*0-671-03480-4*, PB Hardcover) PB.

Robinson, George. Essential Judaism: A Complete Guide to Beliefs, Customs & Rituals. 1999. per. write for info. (*0-671-03481-2*) S&S Trade.

— Sequoia & Kings Canyon National Parks. (Pocket Portfolio Ser.: Vol. 6). (Illus.). 32p. 1997. pap. 5.95 (*0-939365-63-4*) Panorama Intl.

Robinson, George, jt. auth. see Moulton, Janice.

Robinson, George B. Glacier National Park. Nicholas, Jeff & Leach, Nicky, eds. (Pocket Portfolio Ser.: Vol. 12). (Illus.). 32p. 1998. pap. 5.95 (*0-939365-64-2*) Panorama Intl.

— Sequoia & Kings Canyon National Parks. Nicholas, Jeff & Leach, Nicky, eds. (Pocket Portfolio Ser.: Vol. 6). (GER., Illus.). 32p. 1997. pap. 6.95 (*0-939365-91-X*); pap. 6.95 (*0-939365-92-8*) Panorama Intl.

— Yellowstone National Park. Nicholas, Jeff & Leach, Nicky, eds. (Pocket Portfolio Ser.: Vol. 8). (Illus.). 32p. 1998. pap. 5.95 (*0-939365-61-8*) Panorama Intl.

— Yellowstone National Park: The Cycle of the Seasons. Leach, Nicky, ed. (Wish You Were Here Ser.). (Illus.). 96p. (Orig.). 1994. 24.95 (*0-939365-32-4*); pap. 14.95 (*0-939365-31-6*) Panorama Intl.

Robinson, George B., photos by. Vermont: A Harvest of Color. LC 90-60429. (Illus.). 32p. 1990. pap. 9.95 (*0-933050-81-X*) New Eng Pr VT.

— Vermont Scenes & Seasons. LC 89-63661. (Illus.). 80p. 1989. pap. 14.95 (*0-933050-65-8*) New Eng Pr VT.

Robinson, George B. & Chisholm-Robinson, Sandra. Discover a Watershed Vol. 1: The Everglades. (Illus.). 278p. (Orig.). 1996. pap. text, teacher ed. 15.95 (*1-888631-00-7*) Watercourse.

Robinson, George B. & Robinson, Sandra C. In Pictures Yellowstone: The Continuing Story. LC 90-60040. (Illus.). 48p. (Orig.). 1990. pap. 7.95 (*0-88714-047-5*) KC Pubns.

Robinson, George B., jt. auth. see Kesselheim, Alan S.

Robinson, George B., jt. auth. see Robinson, Sandra C.

Robinson, George C., jt. auth. see Cowdery, Ray.

Robinson, George F. History of Greene County, Ohio. 927p. 1993. reprint ed. lib. bdg. 92.50 (*0-8328-3123-9*) Higginson Bk Co.

***Robinson, George L.** Work Overseas: How to Find a High Paying Tax Free Job. LC 99-66906. (Illus.). 200p. 2000. pap. 24.95 (*1-885003-32-3*, Pub. by R D Reed Pubs) Midpt Trade.

Robinson, George M., jt. auth. see Moulton, Janice.

Robinson, George W. Minerals. LC 94-6344. (Illus.). 208p. 1994. 40.00 (*0-671-88002-0*) S&S Trade.

Robinson, George W., ed. Bert Combs the Politician: An Oral History. LC 90-19970. (Kentucky Remembered: An Oral History Ser.). 240p. 1991. text 32.00 (*0-8131-1740-2*) U Pr of Ky.

Robinson, Gerald, jt. auth. see James, Charles.

Robinson, Gerald, jt. auth. see Pagnoni, Mario.

Robinson, Gerald A., jt. auth. see Turner Publishing Company Staff.

Robinson, Gerald J. Federal Income Taxation of Real Estate: Forms & Checklists. 1989. ring bd. 115.00 (*0-685-69562-X*, FREF) Warren Gorham & Lamont.

***Robinson, Gerald J.** The Professional's Guide to Retirement Financial Management. (Illus.). 381p. 1999. pap. 139.00 incl. cd-rom (*0-15-606757-9*) Harcourt.

Robinson, Gerald J. Quicken for Windows in One Hour for Lawyers. LC 96-80096. 80p. 1996. pap. 29.95 (*1-57073-385-6*, 511-0380) Amer Bar Assn.

***Robinson, Gerald J.** 2001 Professional's Guide to Retirement Financial Management. 400p. 2000. pap. 139.00 (*0-15-607210-6*) Harcourt.

Robinson, Gerald S. Federal Income Taxation of Real Estate, No. 1. 1992. suppl. ed. 63.00 (*0-7913-0567-8*) Warren Gorham & Lamont.

— Federal Income Taxation of Real Estate, No. 3. 1992. suppl. ed. 66.00 (*0-7913-0957-6*) Warren Gorham & Lamont.

— Federal Income Taxation of Real Estate, No.6. 1996. suppl. ed. 135.00 (*0-7913-2273-4*, FRF) Warren Gorham & Lamont.

— Federal Income Taxation of Real Estate, Set. 1988th ed. 1992. ring bd. 110.00 (*0-88712-990-0*, FIRE) Warren Gorham & Lamont.

Robinson, Gershon & Steinman, Mordechai. The Obvious Proof. LC 92-76188. (Illus.). 141p. (C). 1993. 13.95 (*1-56062-175-3*) CIS Comm.

Robinson, Gertrude. David Urquhart: Some Chapters in the Life of a Victorian Knight Errant of Justice & Liberty. LC 78-110120. xii, 329p. 1970. reprint ed. 45.00 (0-678-00609-1) Kelley.

Robinson, Gertrude J. Constructing the Quebec Referendum: French & English Media Voices. LC 98-229697. (Illus.). 304p. 1998. text 50.00 (0-8020-0909-3); pap. text 18.95 (0-8020-7890-7) U of Toronto Pr.

Robinson, Gertrude J., ed. see Lukic, Sveta.

Robinson, Gilbert. Representation Theory of the Symmetric Group. LC 63-424. (Mathematical Expositions Ser.: No. 12). 214p. reprint ed. pap. 66.40 (0-608-10193-1, 201438500095) Bks Demand.

Robinson, Gillian. Sketch-Books: Explore & Store. 160p. 1996. pap., pap. text 19.00 (0-435-07018-5) Heinemann.

Robinson, Gillian. The Slow Reign of Calamity Jane. (Illus.). 96p. 1995. pap. 10.95 (1-55082-117-2) LPC InBook.

Robinson, Gillian, et al, eds. Social Attitudes in Northern Ireland: The Seventh Report. 220p. 1998. text 59.95 (1-84014-094-1, Pub. by Ashgate Pub) Ashgate Pub Co.

Robinson, Gillian & Rundell, John, eds. Rethinking Imagination: Culture & Creativity. LC 93-17209. 240p. (C). (gr. 13). 1993. text 69.95 (0-415-09192-6) Routledge.

Robinson, Gillian & Stringer, Peter. Social Attitudes in Northern Ireland. (Illus.). 240p. (Orig.). 1992. pap. 24.00 (0-85640-483-7, Pub. by Blackstaff Pr) Dufour.

Robinson, Gillian, jt. ed. see Stringer, Peter.

Robinson, Glen. The Case of the Secret Code. LC 94-23914. (Shoebox Kids Ser.: Vol. 2). (J). 1995. pap. 6.99 (0-8163-1249-4) Pacific Pr Pub Assn.

Robinson, Glen. The Clue in the Secret Passage. LC 97-10454. (Shoebox Kids Ser.: Vol. 7). (Illus.). (J). 1997. pap. 6.99 (0-8163-1386-5) Pacific Pr Pub Assn.

— Fifty-Two Things to Do on Sabbath. Wheeler, Gerald, ed. (Illus.). (Orig.). (J). 1983. pap. 2.99 (0-8280-0199-5) Review & Herald.

***Robinson, Glen.** If Tomorrow Comes: When the World Fell Apart, All They Had Was Hope. Lale, Tim, ed. LC 99-56582. 320p. 2000. pap. 14.99 (0-8163-1766-6) Pacific Pr Pub Assn.

Robinson, Glen & Thomas, Jerry D. The Broken Dozen Mystery. LC 96-15961. (Shoebox Kids Ser.: Vol. 5). 1996. 6.99 (0-8163-1332-6) Pacific Pr Pub Assn.

Robinson, Glen, ed. see Mansell, Donald E.

Robinson, Glen, ed. see Mosley, Steven.

Robinson, Glen, ed. see Vandeman, George E.

Robinson, Glen, ed. see Walker, Celeste P. & Stoffle, Eric.

Robinson, Glen O. American Bureaucracy: Public Choice & Public Law. 256p. (C). 1991. text 49.50 (0-472-10243-5, 10243) U of Mich Pr.

— The Forest Service: A Study in Public Land Management. LC 75-11352. (Resources for the Future Ser.). (Illus.). 358p. 1975. 28.50 (0-8018-1723-4) Johns Hopkins.

Robinson, Glen O., et al. The Administrative Process. 4th ed. (American Casebook Ser.). 803p. (C). 1993. 57.50 (0-314-02377-1) West Pub.

— The Administrative Process: 1995 Supplement. (American Casebook Ser.). 53p. (C). 1995. pap. 12.50 (0-314-06720-5) West Pub.

Robinson, Glenn. The Mysterious Treasure Map. LC 94-46118. (Shoebox Kids Ser.: Vol. 1). (J). 1995. pap. 6.99 (0-8163-1256-7) Pacific Pr Pub Assn.

Robinson, Glenn, ed. see Watts, Ron & Watts, Dorothy E.

Robinson, Glenn E. Building a Palestinian State: The Incomplete Revolution. LC 96-24708. (Indiana Series in Arab & Islamic). 1997. 29.95 (0-253-33217-6); pap. 14.95 (0-253-21082-8) Ind U Pr.

Robinson, Gloria, ed. Preludes to Genetics. 1979. 25.00 (0-87291-127-6) Coronado Pr.

Robinson, Gordon. The Forest & the Trees: Guide to Excellent Forestry. LC 88-9011. (Illus.). 252p. (C). 1988. pap. text 27.00 (0-933280-40-8) Island Pr.

Robinson, Gordon, jt. auth. see Callan, Lou.

Robinson, Grace. Older Child Adoption. LC 97-37545. 229p. 1998. pap. 17.95 (0-8245-1707-5, Crsrd) Crossroad NY.

Robinson, Grace I., jt. auth. see McCully, Brian J.

Robinson, Grady J. Did I Ever Tell You about the Time... Using the Power of Stories to Persuade & Captivate Any Audience. 241p. 2000. pap. 14.95 (0-07-134214-1) McGraw.

Robinson, Graham, jt. auth. see Lee, Stan.

Robinson, Granville H. Inside Ajas Cottage: Bermuda. (Illus.). 272p. 1999. pap. 18.00 (0-8059-4586-5) Dorrance.

Robinson, Gregory H., ed. Coordination Chemistry of Aluminum. LC 93-12703. 1993. 115.00 (1-56081-059-9, Wiley-VCH); pap. 49.50 (1-56081-656-2, Wiley-VCH) Wiley.

***Robinson, Gregory K.** Street Pieces. unabridged ed. 68p. 2000. pap. 7.00 (0-9675939-1-3, 2) Westron Pr.

***Robinson, Guy.** Australia & New Zealand: Economy, Society & Environment. 352p. 2000. text 80.00 (0-340-72032-8, Pub. by E A) OUP.

— Australia & New Zealand: Economy, Society & Environment. (Illus.). 352p. 2000. pap. text 35.00 (0-340-72033-6, Pub. by E A) OUP.

Robinson, Guy. Philosophy & Mystification. LC 97-18223. 312p. (C). 1998. 75.00 (0-415-17851-7) Routledge.

Robinson, Guy M. Quantitative & Qualitative Techniques in Human Geography. LC 97-43766. 572p. 1998. 175.00 (0-471-96231-7); pap. 54.95 (0-471-96232-5) Wiley.

Robinson, H. Flora of Ecuador No. 190(2) Compositae-Liabeae. (Opera Botanica Series B). 62p. 1978. pap. 15.00 (91-546-0237-8, Pub. by Coun Nordic Pubs) Balogh.

Robinson, H. Alan. Meeting Individual Differences in Reading. LC 64-24978. (Supplementary Education Monographs). 1992. lib. bdg. 6.50 (0-226-72176-0, SEM94) U Ch Pr.

Robinson, H. Alan & Thomas, Ellen L., eds. Fusing Reading Skills & Content. LC 70-21420. 233p. reprint ed. pap. 72.30 (0-608-17956-6, 202794400057) Bks Demand.

Robinson, H. Alan, et al. Reading Comprehension Instruction, 1783-1987: A Review of Trends & Research. Fitzgerald, Jill, ed. LC 89-38010. 212p. 1990. reprint ed. pap. 65.80 (0-608-03473-8, 206418300008) Bks Demand.

Robinson, H. Alan, ed. see Conference on Reading - University Of Chicago.

Robinson, H. Basil. Diefenbaker's World: A Populist in Foreign Affairs. (Illus.). 352p. 1991. pap. text 19.95 (0-8020-6922-3) U of Toronto Pr.

— Diefenbaker's World: A Populist in World Affairs. 1989. 35.00 (0-8020-2678-8) U of Toronto Pr.

Robinson, H. C., jt. auth. see Annandale, Nelson.

Robinson, H. D., tr. see d'Holbach, Baron P.

Robinson, H. E. Grant: American Ancestry of U. S. Grant. 17p. 1993. reprint ed. pap. 7.50 (0-8328-3326-6) Higginson Bk Co.

Robinson, H. L. History of Pittsfield in the Great Rebellion. (Illus.). 217p. 1997. reprint ed. lib. bdg. 29.00 (0-8328-6020-4) Higginson Bk Co.

Robinson, H. Lukin. Canada's Crippled Dollar: An Analysis of International Trade & Our Troubled Balance of Payments. 204p. 1980. 29.95 (0-88862-274-0, Pub. by J Lorimer); pap. 19.95 (0-88862-275-9, Pub. by J Lorimer) Formac Dist Ltd.

Robinson, H. P. Redemption, Conceived & Revealed. pap. 2.95 (0-911866-89-2) LifeSprings Res.

Robinson, H. Russell, ed. see Hakuseki, Arai.

Robinson, H. Wheeler. The Life & Faith of the Baptists. 158p. 1985. reprint ed. pap. 9.95 (0-913029-09-2) Stevens Bk Pr.

Robinson, H. Wheeler & Payne, Ernest A. British Baptists: An Original Anthology. Gaustad, Edwin S., ed. LC 79-52583. (Baptist Tradition Ser.). 1980. lib. bdg. 33.95 (0-405-12450-3) Ayer.

Robinson, Haddon W. Biblical Preaching: The Development & Delivery of Expository Messages. LC 80-66776. 264p. 1980. 17.99 (0-8010-7700-1) Baker Bks.

— Decision Making by the Book. 168p. 1991. 15.99 (0-89693-913-8, 6-1913, Victor Bks) Chariot Victor.

— Decision-Making by the Book: How to Choose Wisely in an Age of Options. LC 97-4944. 160p. 1998. pap. 12.99 (1-57293-021-7) Discovery Hse Pubs.

— Grief. 24p. 1976. reprint ed. pap. 4.99 (0-310-32261-8, 9772P) Zondervan.

— Grief: Comfort for Those Who Grieve & Those Who Help. LC 95-50812. 48p. 1996. pap. 7.99 (1-57293-010-1) Discovery Hse Pubs.

— Making a Difference in Preaching. LC 99-37518. 160p. 1999. 16.99 (0-8010-9092-X) Baker Bks.

— What Jesus Said about Successful Living: Principles from the Sermon on the Mount for Today. 300p. 1991. pap. 12.99 (0-929239-43-1) Discovery Hse Pubs.

Robinson, Haddon W., ed. Biblical Sermons: How Twelve Preachers Apply the Principles of Biblical Preaching. LC 89-248. 264p. 1997. pap. 14.99 (0-8010-9044-X) Baker Bks.

Robinson, Haddon W., et al, eds. The IVP New Testament Commentary Series, 11 vols., Set. 1996. 169.00 (0-8308-8046-1, 8046) InterVarsity.

Robinson-Hammerstein, Helga. European Universities in the Age of Reformation & Counter Reformation. rev. ed. LC 98-162635. 224p. 1998. boxed set 50.00 (1-85182-318-2, Pub. by Four Cts Pr) Intl Spec Bk.

Robinson-Hammerstein, Helga, ed. The Transmission of Ideas in the Lutheran Reformation. 240p. 1988. 39.50 (0-7165-2376-0, Pub. by Irish Acad Pr) Intl Spec Bk.

Robinson, Harlow, ed. from RUS. Selected Letters of Sergei Prokofiev. LC 98-9604. 448p. 1998. text 40.00 (1-55553-347-7) NE U Pr.

Robinson, Harold. A Generic Review of the Tribe Liabeae (Asteraceae) LC 82-10807. (Smithsonian Contributions to Botany Ser.: No. 54). 73p. reprint ed. pap. 30.00 (0-608-13789-8, 202033700017) Bks Demand.

Robinson, Harold, jt. auth. see Mohamed, Haji.

Robinson, Harold E. A Palynological Study of the Liabeae (Asteraceae) LC 86-600032. (Smithsonian Contributions to Botany Ser.: No. 64). 54p. reprint ed. pap. 30.00 (0-608-15314-1, 202955200061) Bks Demand.

Robinson, Harriet H. Loom & Spindle. LC 75-46389. 144p. (C). 1976. pap. 7.95 (0-916630-02-1) Pr Pacifica.

Robinson-Harris, Tracey & Savin-Williams, Ritch C. Beyond Pink & Blue: Exploring Our Stereotypes of Sexuality & Gender. 80p. 1994. pap. 20.00 (1-55896-322-7) Unitarian Univ.

Robinson, Harry. Men Born Equal. LC 74-22806. 384p. 1983. reprint ed. 45.00 (0-404-58462-4) AMS Pr.

— Write It on Your Heart: The Epic World of an Okanagan Story Teller. Wickwire, Wendy, ed. LC 90-104726. 320p. (ps up). 1989. pap. 16.95 (0-88922-273-8, Pub. by Talonbks) Genl Dist Srvs.

Robinson, Harry G., III & Edwards, Hazel R. The Long Walk: The Placemaking Legacy of Howard University. Battle, Thomas C. & Muse, Clifford L., eds. LC 96-76220. (Illus.). xviii, 264p. 1996. 250.00 (0-9652091-0-5); pap. 50.00 (0-9652091-1-3); lthr. 1500.00 (0-9652091-2-1) Howard Univ.

Robinson, Helen. Heal Thyself: For Health & Longevity. Plata, Sababu N., ed. LC 91-72476. 204p. 1993. reprint ed. pap. 9.95 (1-881316-01-7) A&B Bks.

Robinson, Helen, ed. see Carlson, Glenn E.

Robinson, Helen, ed. see Kelly, Jack.

Robinson, Helen M. Sequential Development of Reading Abilities. LC 60-14354. (Supplementary Educational Monographs). (Illus.). 1977. reprint ed. pap. text 11.00 (0-226-72188-4, SEM 90) U Ch Pr.

— Why Pupils Fail in Reading. LC 46-5912. 1992. lib. bdg. 6.75 (0-226-72210-4) U Ch Pr.

Robinson, Helja A. The Ethnography of Empowerment: The Transformative Power of Classroom Interaction. LC 94-24726. 150p. 1994. 75.00 (0-7507-0367-9, Falmer Pr); pap. 24.95 (0-7507-0368-7, Falmer Pr) Taylor & Francis.

Robinson, Henrietta F. & Williams, Carolyn C. Dedicated to Music: The Legacy of African American Church Musicians & Music Teachers in Southern New Jersey, 1915-1990. LC 97-10285. 1997. 24.95 (0-9653308-4-2) Africana Homestead.

Robinson, Henry. The Little Pearls of Wisdom Book: For the Successful Dental Team. LC 95-1025. 1995. 19.95 (0-87814-442-0) PennWell Bks.

Robinson, Henry C. Blake, Coleridge, Wordsworth, Lamb, Etc., Being Selections from the Remains of Henry Crabb Robinson. Morley, Edith J., ed. LC 23-6630. reprint ed. 24.50 (0-404-05364-5) AMS Pr.

— Diary, Reminiscences, & Correspondence, 3 vols., Set. (BCL1-PR English Literature Ser.). 1992. reprint ed. lib. bdg. 270.00 (0-7812-7622-5) Rprt Serv.

— Diary, Reminiscences, & Correspondence of Henry Crabb Robinson, 2 vols. Sadler, Thomas, ed. LC 28-15241. reprint ed. 115.00 (0-404-05365-3) AMS Pr.

— Henry Crabb Robinson on Books & Their Writers, 3 vols. Morley, Edith J., ed. LC 75-182705. reprint ed. 155.00 (0-404-05410-2) AMS Pr.

— Henry Crabb Robinson on Books & Their Writers, 3 vols., Set. Morley, Edith J., ed. 1136p. 1938. 69.50 (0-614-01807-2) Elliots Bks.

Robinson, Henry M. Fantastic Interim. LC 77-148895. (Select Bibliographies Reprint Ser.). 1977. 25.95 (0-8369-5658-3) Ayer.

Robinson, Henry M., jt. auth. see Campbell, Joseph.

Robinson, Henry P. The Elements of a Pictorial Photograph. LC 72-9228. (Literature of Photography Ser.). 1978. reprint ed. 12.95 (0-405-04934-X) Ayer.

— Letters on Landscape Photography. LC 72-9229. (Literature of Photography Ser.). 1973. reprint ed. 17.95 (0-405-04935-8) Ayer.

— Picture-Making by Photography. 5th ed. LC 72-9230. (Literature of Photography Ser.). 1973. reprint ed. 18.95 (0-405-04936-6) Ayer.

— The Studio: And What to Do in It. LC 72-9231. (Literature of Photography Ser.). 1973. reprint ed. 18.95 (0-405-04937-4) Ayer.

Robinson, Henry P. & Abney, W. D. The Art & Practice of Silver Printing. LC 72-9227. (Literature of Photography Ser.). 1973. reprint ed. 18.95 (0-405-04933-1) Ayer.

Robinson, Henry S. Great Britain & the Franco-Russian Alliance, 1894-1904 LC 87-1991. 1987. write for info. (0-8191-6143-8) U Pr of Amer.

Robinson, Henry W. Corporate Personality in Ancient Israel. rev. ed. LC 79-8887. 64p. reprint ed. pap. 30.00 (0-608-15294-3, 202960300061) Bks Demand.

— Inspiration & Revelation in the Old Testament. LC 78-9891. 298p. 1979. reprint ed. lib. bdg. 65.00 (0-313-21068-3, ROIR, Greenwood Pr) Greenwood.

Robinson, Henry W., ed. The Bible in Its Ancient & English Version. LC 76-109832. 337p. 1970. lib. bdg. 65.00 (0-8371-4323-3, ROBI, Greenwood Pr) Greenwood.

— Record & Revelation. LC 76-29395. reprint ed. 35.50 (0-404-15354-2) AMS Pr.

Robinson, Herbert S. Myths & Legends of All Nations. 1976. 17.05 (0-606-02094-2, Pub. by Turtleback) Demco.

Robinson, Herbert S. & Wilson, Knox. Myths & Legends of All Nations. (Quality Paperback Ser.: No. 319). 244p. 1978. reprint ed. pap. 11.95 (0-8226-0319-5) Littlefield.

Robinson, Herbert W. The Challenge to Government: Management of a Capitalist Economy. (Illus.). 300p. 1991. 39.95 (0-9628558-1-2) IMS Press.

— Election Issues, 1976. 194p. (Orig.). 1976. pap. 9.95 (0-9628558-0-4) IMS Press.

— In on the Ground Floor of the 20th Century Automation Revolution: An Autobiography by Herbert W. Robinson. 568p. 1996. 29.95 (0-9628558-2-0) IMS Press.

Robinson, Hilary, jt. auth. see Buckley, Jonathan.

Robinson, Hoggatt. Performance Tests. 5th ed. 1991. pap. text 2.75 (0-538-60505-7) Sth-Wstrn College.

Robinson, Hoke, ed. Proceedings of the Eighth International Kant Congress, Vol. 1, Pt. 1, Sections 1-2. LC 94-80267. 1995. 40.00 (0-87462-479-7) Marquette.

— Proceedings of the Eighth International Kant Congress, Vol. 1, Pt. 2, Sections 3A-3L. LC 94-80267. 1995. 40.00 (0-87462-480-0) Marquette.

— Proceedings of the Eighth International Kant Congress, Vol. 1, Pt. 3, Sections 3M - 3S, 4, 5. LC 94-80267. 1995. 40.00 (0-87462-481-9) Marquette.

— Proceedings of the Eighth International Kant Congress Vol. II, Vol. 2, Pt. 1, Sec. 1-9. LC 94-80267. 1995. pap. 40.00 (0-87462-477-0) Marquette.

— Proceedings of the Eighth International Kant Congress Vol. II, Vol. 2, Pt. 2, Sec. 10-18. LC 94-80267. 1995. pap. 40.00 (0-87462-478-9) Marquette.

Robinson, Hoke, tr. see Kamlah, Wilhelm & Lorenzen, Paul.

Robinson, Howard. British Post Office: A History. LC 76-88930. 467p. 1970. reprint ed. lib. bdg. 75.00 (0-8371-3142-1, ROPO, Greenwood Pr) Greenwood.

— Perception. LC 93-49381. (Problems of Philosophy Series: Their Past & Present). 272p. (C). (gr. 13). 1994. 75.00 (0-415-03364-0, B4651) Routledge.

Robinson, Howard, ed. Objections to Physicalism. (Illus.). 332p. 1997. reprint ed. pap. text 24.95 (0-19-823677-8) OUP.

Robinson, Howard, ed. see Berkeley, George.

Robinson, Howard, jt. ed. see Blumenthal, Henry.

Robinson, Howard, jt. ed. see Foster, John.

Robinson, I. Satellite Oceanography: An Introduction for Oceanographers & Remote-Sensing Scientist. LC 84-25142. (Marine Science Ser.). 455p. 1985. text 71.95 (0-470-20148-7) P-H.

Robinson, I., ed. Waltham Book Human-Companion Animal Interaction. LC 95-21317. (Waltham Centre for Pet Nutrition Ser.: No. 4). 1995. text 65.00 (0-08-042284-5, Pergamon Pr); pap. text 40.00 (0-08-042285-3, Pergamon Pr) Elsevier.

Robinson, I. K., jt. ed. see Zabel, H.

Robinson, I. S. The Papacy, 1073-1198: Continuity & Innovation. (Cambridge Medieval Textbooks Ser.). 571p. (C). 1990. text 80.00 (0-521-26498-7); pap. text 27.95 (0-521-31922-6) Cambridge U Pr.

Robinson, Ian. Chaucer & the English Tradition. (C). 1986. 125.00 (0-907839-29-0, Pub. by Brynmill Pr Ltd) St Mut.

— Chaucer & the English Tradition. LC 79-163179. 308p. reprint ed. pap. 87.80 (0-608-12501-6, 2024530) Bks Demand.

— The Establishment of Modern English Prose in the Reformation & the Enlightenment: The Art of Prose Writing from the Middle Ages to the Enlightenment. LC 97-35275. 302p. (C). 1998. 59.95 (0-521-48088-4) Cambridge U Pr.

— The New Grammarian's Funeral. LC 75-6009. (Illus.). 190p. 1978. pap. text 21.95 (0-521-29316-2) Cambridge U Pr.

— Skilful Squash. pap. write for info. (0-7136-5749-9, 91943, Pub. by A & C Blk) Midpt Trade.

***Robinson, Ian & Frost, Lee.** Dartmoor. (Illus.). 72p. 1999. pap. 16.95 (1-84107-039-4, Pub. by Colin Baxter Ltd) Voyageur Pr.

Robinson, Ian & Hunter, Margaret. Motor Neurone Disease. LC 97-32221. 160p. (C). 1998. pap. 22.99 (0-415-09711-8) Routledge.

Robinson, Ian & Mencher, Elaine, eds. The Market Bell. 322p. (C). 1989. 95.00 (0-907839-42-8, Pub. by Brynmill Pr Ltd) St Mut.

Robinson, Ian & Sims, David, eds. The Decline & Fall of Mr. Heath: Essays in Criticism of Recent British Politics. 78p. (C). 1989. 50.00 (0-9502723-4-5, Pub. by Brynmill Pr Ltd) St Mut.

Robinson, Ian, jt. auth. see Heather, Nick.

Robinson, Ian, jt. ed. see Knight, Roger.

Robinson, Ian S. Henry IV of Germany. 418p. (C). 2000. 69.95 (0-521-65113-1) Cambridge U Pr.

Robinson, Ira. Moses Cordovero's Introduction to Kabbalah: An Annotated Translation of His Or Neerav. LC 93-45501. 1993. 35.00 (0-88125-439-8) Ktav.

Robinson, Ira, ed. Cyrus Adler - Selected Letters. 1985. 50.00 (0-317-64460-2) Jewish Sem.

Robinson, Ira, et al, eds. The Thought of Moses Maimonides: Philosophical & Legal Studies. (Studies in the History of Philosophy: Vol. 17). (ENG & FRE.). 424p. 1991. lib. bdg. 109.95 (0-88946-286-0) E Mellen.

Robinson, Ira & Butovsky, Mervin, eds. Renewing Our Days: Montreal Jews in the Twentieth Century. 192p. 1995. pap. 16.95 (1-55065-062-9, Pub. by Vehicule Pr) Genl Dist Srvs.

Robinson, Ira & Rabkin, Yakov M., eds. The Interaction of Scientific & Jewish Cultures in Modern Times. LC 94-9910. 272p. 1994. 89.95 (0-7734-9063-9) E Mellen.

Robinson, J., ed. see Valery, Paul.

Robinson, J. Alan, ed. see Arbib, Michael A., et al.

Robinson, J. B., ed. Diagnosis of Mineral Disorders in Plants. 1984. 75.00 (0-8206-0311-2) Chem Pub.

Robinson, J. B., jt. ed. see Reuter, D. J.

Robinson, J. Bradford, tr. see Dahlhaus, Carl.

Robinson, J. Bradford, tr. see Luz, Ulrich.

Robinson, J. C. Bananas & Plantains: Crop Production Science in Horticulture. LC 96-214375. (Crop Production Science in Agriculture Ser.: No. 5). 256p. 1996. text 45.00 (0-85198-985-3) OUP.

Robinson, J. Cordell, jt. auth. see Robinson, Barbara J.

Robinson, J. E., ed. Abnormal Load on Power Systems: Report on the Symposium on Transient, Fluctuating & Distorting Loads & Their Effects on Power Systems & Communications, 25th & 26th February. LC 65-63212. (Institution of Electrical Engineers Conference Report Ser.: No. 8). 192p. reprint ed. pap. 59.60 (0-8357-5011-6, 205083000060) Bks Demand.

Robinson, J. Gregg, jt. auth. see McIlwee, Judith S.

Robinson, J. H., et al, eds. Dialysis, Transplantation, Nephrology: Proceedings, European Dialysis & Transplant Association, Vol. 16. (Illus.). 785p. 1979. 65.00 (0-8464-1067-2) Beekman Pubs.

Robinson, J. Hedley, ed. God & the Universe. 70p. (C). 1989. pap. 40.00 (0-7223-2220-8, Pub. by A H S Ltd) St Mut.

Robinson, J. Jill. Lovely in Her Bones. 188p. 1993. per. 12.95 (0-88978-260-1, Pub. by Arsenal Pulp) LPC InBook.

— Saltwater Trees. 160p. 1991. pap. 11.95 (0-88978-241-5, Pub. by Arsenal Pulp) LPC InBook.

Robinson, J. Lewis. Concepts & Themes in the Regional Geography of Canada. rev. ed. LC 89-216656. 272p. 1990. pap. 26.95 (0-88922-264-9) Genl Dist Srvs.

Robinson, J. Lewis, ed. British Columbia. LC 72-197301. (Studies in Canadian Geography Ser.). 149p. reprint ed. pap. 46.20 (0-8357-7420-1, 202653600050) Bks Demand.

Robinson, J. Lewis & Hardwick, Walter G. British Columbia: One Hundred Years of Geographic Change. LC 72-197301. 64p. 1993. pap. 16.95 (0-88922-048-4) Genl Dist Srvs.

Robinson, J. O. The Psychology of Visual Illusion. unabridged ed. LC 98-24691. (Illus.). 288p. 1998. pap. 9.95 (*0-486-40449-8*) Dover.

Robinson, J. Paul. Phagocyte Function for Research & Clinical Evaluation. LC 98-12095. 400p. 1998. 109.95 (*0-471-12364-1*) Wiley.

Robinson, J. Paul, et al, eds. Handbook of Flow Cytometry Methods. 260p. 1993. pap. 89.95 (*0-471-59634-5*) Wiley.

— Methods in Cell Biology Vol. 41: Flow Cytometry, Pt. A. 2nd ed. (Illus.). 591p. 1994. text 125.00 (*0-12-564142-7*); pap. text 59.95 (*0-12-203051-6*) Acad Pr.

Robinson, J. Paul, jt. auth. see Durack, Gary.

Robinson, J. Paul, jt. auth. see Matsudaira, Paul T.

Robinson, J. Russell. Radical Systems Development: An Introduction to Rapid Application Development. 152p. 1995. pap. 34.95 (*1-57087-105-1*) Prof Pr NC.

Robinson, J. S., ed. Extrusion of Plastics. LC 82-62311. 270p. (Orig.). 1982. pap. 45.00 (*0-942378-01-6*) Polymers & Plastics Tech Pub Hse.

— Hazardous Chemical Spill Cleanup. LC 79-16362. (Pollution Technology Review Ser.: No. 59). (Illus.). 406p. 1980. 48.00 (*0-8155-0767-4*) Noyes.

— Plastics Molding: Equipment, Processes, & Materials. LC 81-90745. x, 299p. 1981. pap. 42.00 (*0-942378-00-8*) Polymers & Plastics Tech Pub Hse.

Robinson, J. T., jt. auth. see Broom, Robert.

Robinson, J. W. Handbook of Spectroscopy, Vol. 3. 560p. 1981. 309.00 (*0-8493-0333-8*, QD95, CRC Reprint) Franklin.

— Studies in Fifteenth-Century Stagecraft. (Early Drama, Art & Music Monograph: No. 14). 1990. pap. 16.95 (*0-918720-39-7*); boxed set 26.95 (*0-918720-38-9*) Medieval Inst.

Robinson, Jack. Free Fall: The Story of the Needless Destruction of Eastern Airlines & Those Who Valiantly Struggled to Save It. LC 91-58510. 288p. 1992. 22.00 (*0-88730-556-3*, HarpBusn) HarpInfo.

— North Carolina - Robinson on Corporation Law: 1991 Supplement. 81p. 1996. write for info. (*0-87473-864-4*, 66662-10, MICHIE) LEXIS Pub.

— Teardrops on My Drum. 173p. (Orig.). 1997. reprint ed. pap. 12.95 (*0-85449-261-5*, Pub. by Gay Mens Pr) LPC InBook.

Robinson, Jack F. History of the Illinois Conference, United Church of Christ. LC 90-81374. 57p. 1990. pap. text 5.50 (*0-913552-43-7*) Exploration Pr.

Robinson, Jack H. John Calvin & the Jews. LC 91-34889. (American University Studies: Theology & Religion: Ser. VII, Vol. 123). 152p. (C). 1992. text 35.95 (*0-8204-1752-1*) P Lang Pubng.

Robinson, Jack W., Sr. & Mobley, Jeff. Pritchard on the Law of Wills & Administration of Estates, 3 vols. 5th ed. LC 94-79590. 1994. 225.00 (*1-55834-201-X*, 66040-11, MICHIE) LEXIS Pub.

— Pritchard on the Law of Wills & Administration of Estates. 5th ed. 1995. suppl. ed. 40.00 (*0-614-25256-3*, 66035-11, MICHIE) LEXIS Pub.

Robinson, Jack W., Sr. & Mobley, Jeffrey. Pritchard on Wills & Administration of Estates Vols. 1-3: 1998 Cumulative Supplement. 5th ed. 120p. 1998. suppl. ed. 85.00 (*0-327-00306-5*, 6603514) LEXIS Pub.

Robinson, Jack W., Jr., et al. Tennessee Forms, 4 vols., Set. 1991. 300.00 (*0-87473-714-1*, 66656-10, MICHIE) LEXIS Pub.

*__Robinson, Jack W., Jr., et al.__ Tennessee Forms, 4 vols., Vol. 3. 2nd ed. 650p. 1999. write for info. (*0-327-04932-4*, 6665911) LEXIS Pub.

Robinson, Jack W., Jr., et al. Tennessee Forms, 1998 Cumulative Supplement, 4 vols. Incl. Vol. 1. Tennessee Forms, 1998 Cumulative Supplement., 4 vols. 460p. 1998. (*0-327-00898-9*, 665513); Vol. 3. Tennessee Forms, 1998 Cumulative Supplement., 4 vols. 460p. 1998. (*0-327-00899-7*, 6665513); Vol. 4. Tennessee Forms, 1998 Cumulative Supplement., 4 vols. 460p. 1998. (*0-327-00900-4*, 6665513); 460p. 1998. write for info. (*0-327-00897-0*, 6665513) LEXIS Pub.

Robinson, Jackie. Dining Dazzle. 68p. 1993. pap. text 16.00 (*1-885156-04-9*) Animas Quilts.

— I Never Had It Made: The Autobiography of Jackie Robinson. 304p. 1990. pap. 14.00 (*0-88001-544-6*) HarpC.

Robinson, Jackie. I Never Had It Made: The Autobiography of Jackie Robinson. LC 94-45279. 320p. 1995. 24.00 (*0-88001-419-9*) HarpC.

Robinson, Jackie. Quilts in the Tradition of Frank Lloyd Wright. LC 96-107155. 80p. 1994. pap. text 19.00 (*1-885156-13-8*) Animas Quilts.

— Tessellations. 46p. 1992. pap. text 12.00 (*1-885156-03-0*) Animas Quilts.

— Weaver Fever. 14p. 1991. pap. text 6.50 (*1-885156-01-4*) Animas Quilts.

Robinson, Jacob. Palestine & the United Nations: Prelude to Solution. LC 71-147221. 269p. 1971. reprint ed. lib. bdg. 65.00 (*0-8371-5986-5*, ROPU, Greenwood Pr) Greenwood.

Robinson, Jacob, ed. The Holocaust & After: Sources & Literature in English. 353p. 1973. boxed set 39.95 (*0-87855-186-7*) Transaction Pubs.

Robinson, Jacob S. A Journal of the Santa Fe Expedition under Colonel Doniphan. LC 75-87634. (American Scene Ser.). (Illus.). 96p. 1972. reprint ed. lib. bdg. 15.00 (*0-306-71798-0*) Da Capo.

Robinson, Jacqueline. Modern Dance in France, 1920-1970: An Adventure. (Choreography & Dance Studies). (Illus.). 478p. 1998. text 98.00 (*90-5702-015-7*, Harwood Acad Pubs); pap. text 39.00 (*90-5702-016-5*, Harwood Acad Pubs) Gordon & Breach.

Robinson, Jacqueline & Robinson, Dennis M. Everything You Need to Score High on the SSAT & ISEE: High School Entrance Exams. 7th ed. 496p. 1998. 13.95 (*0-02-862405-X*, Arc) IDG Bks.

Robinson, Jacqueline, et al. High School Entrance Exams. 6th ed. 528p. 1996. 13.95 (*0-02-861085-7*) Macmillan.

Robinson, James. The Art of Curing, Pickling & Smoking Meat & Fish. 1973. 250.00 (*0-87968-053-9*) Gordon Pr.

— Batman/Deadman: Death & Glory. Kahan, Bob, ed. (Illus.). 96p. 1997. pap. 12.95 (*1-56389-228-6*, Pub. by DC Comics) Time Warner.

— Better Speeches in Ten Simple Steps. 2nd rev. ed. LC 94-39592. 144p. 1995. pap. 9.95 (*1-55958-691-5*) Prima Pub.

— A Cup Running Over. (Orig.). 1987. pap. 6.55 (*0-89536-873-0*, 7859) CSS OH.

— The Golden Age. Kahan, Bob, ed. (Illus.). 200p. 1995. mass mkt. 19.95 (*1-56389-203-0*, Pub. by DC Comics) Time Warner.

— Grendel Tales Bk. 1: Four Devils, One Hell. (Illus.). 168p. 1994. pap. 17.95 (*1-56971-027-9*) Dark Horse Comics.

— Illegal Alien. (Illus.). 80p. 1994. pap. 9.95 (*0-87816-297-6*) Kitchen Sink.

*__Robinson, James.__ Justice Be Done. (Justice Society of America Ser.). (Illus.). 144p. (J). 2000. pap. text 14.95 (*1-56389-620-6*, Pub. by DC Comics) Time Warner.

— Leave It to Chance: Monster Madness. 104p. Date not set. pap. text 12.95 (*1-56389-536-6*) DC Comics.

— Leave It to Chance No. II: Trick or Treat & Other Stories. 104p. pap. 12.95 (*1-56389-559-5*) DC Comics.

Robinson, James. Leave It to Chance No. II: Trick or Treat & Other Stories. (Illus.). 104p. 1998. pap. 12.95 (*1-58240-041-5*) Image Comics.

— Starman: A Wicked Inclination. LC 98-153212. (Illus.). 240p. 1998. pap. text 17.95 (*1-56389-409-2*, Pub. by DC Comics) Time Warner.

— Starman: Night & Day. (Illus.). 240p. 1997. mass mkt. 14.95 (*1-56389-270-7*, Pub. by DC Comics) Time Warner.

— Starman: Sins of the Father. Kahan, Bob, ed. LC 96-166359. (Illus.). 160p. 1996. mass mkt. 12.95 (*1-56389-248-0*, Pub. by DC Comics) Time Warner.

Robinson, James & Nielson, Nancy. Natural Healing & Prevention Secrets. pap. 19.95 (*0-9638596-1-7*) Amer Pubng.

Robinson, James, jt. auth. see Lobdell, Scott.

Robinson, James, jt. auth. see Ron, Marz.

Robinson, James, ed. see Spear, Robert K. & Moak, D. Michael.

Robinson, James, tr. see Abhayadatta.

Robinson, James A. Congress & Foreign Policy-Making: A Study in Legislative Influence & Initiative. LC 80-20372. 262p. (C). 1980. reprint ed. lib. bdg. 65.00 (*0-313-22706-3*, ROCF, Greenwood Pr) Greenwood.

— The House Rules Committee. LC 83-18495. 142p. 1983. reprint ed. lib. bdg. 55.00 (*0-313-24300-X*, R0H0, Greenwood Pr) Greenwood.

— Political Science Annual: An International Review, Vol. 3. annuals LC 66-29710. 1972. 17.95 (*0-672-51743-4*, Bobbs) Macmillan.

Robinson, James C. The Corporate Practice of Medicine: Competition & Innovation in Health Care. LC 99-14072. (California/milbank Ser. on Health & the Public: Vol. 1). 306p. 1999. 45.00 (*0-520-22075-7*, Pub. by U CA Pr); pap. 18.95 (*0-520-22076-5*, Pub. by U CA Pr) Cal Prin Full Svc.

— Peter Taylor. (Study of the Short Fiction Ser.: No. 3). 192p. 1988. 23.95 (*0-8057-8303-2*, Twyne) Mac Lib Ref.

— Toil & Toxics: Workplace Struggles & Political Strategies for Occupational Health. LC 90-20986. 253p. 1991. 40.00 (*0-520-07164-6*, Pub. by U CA Pr); pap. 14.95 (*0-520-08448-9*, Pub. by U CA Pr) Cal Prin Full Svc.

Robinson, James C., et al, eds. Moving from Training to Performance: A Practical Guidebook. LC 98-21647. 300p. 1998. pap. 29.95 (*1-57675-039-6*) Berrett-Koehler.

Robinson, James C., jt. auth. see Robinson, Dana G.

Robinson, James H. Essays in Intellectual History, Dedicated to James Harvey Robinson by His Former Seminar Students. LC 68-14903. (Essay Index Reprint Ser.). 1977. 23.95 (*0-8369-0425-7*) Ayer.

— Humanizing of Knowledge. LC 72-165742. (American Education Ser., No. 2). 1972. reprint ed. 11.95 (*0-405-03613-2*) Ayer.

— New Life for Your Sunday School. 78p. (Orig.). 1995. pap. 19.99 (*0-8100-0564-6*, 09N0935) Northwest Pub.

Robinson, James H., tr. & intro. see Petrarca, Francesco.

Robinson, James K. & Collins, Lynn M., eds. Introducing Evidence: A Practical Guide for Michigan Lawyers. LC 88-81316. 260p. 1991. ring bd., suppl. ed. 80.00 (*0-685-22722-7*, 88-010) U MI Law CLE.

— Introducing Evidence, 1990: A Practical Guide for Michigan Lawyers. LC 88-81316. 260p. 1988. suppl. ed. 35.00 (*0-685-44339-6*) U MI Law CLE.

— Introducing Evidence, 1991: A Practical Guide for Michigan Lawyers. LC 88-81316. 260p. 1988. suppl. ed. 35.00 (*0-685-22723-5*, 90-024) U MI Law CLE.

Robinson, James K. & Rideout, Walter B. A College Book of Modern Verse. 1977. 24.95 (*0-8369-6406-3*, 7470) Ayer.

Robinson, James K., ed. see Hardy, Thomas.

Robinson, James M., ed. The Nag Hammadi Library in English: Revised Edition. rev. ed. LC 88-45154. 576p. 1990. reprint ed. pap. 21.00 (*0-06-066935-7*, Pub. by Harper SF) HarpC.

Robinson, James M., et al. The Fifth Gospel: The Gospel of Thomas Comes of Age. 128p. 1998. 15.00 (*1-56338-249-0*) TPI PA.

Robinson, James M., jt. auth. see Eisenman, Robert H.

Robinson, James M., ed. see Knierim, Rolf P., et al.

*__Robinson, James McConkey, et al.__ The Critical Edition of Q: A Synopsis Including the Gospels of Matthew & Luke & Thomas with English, German & French Translations of Q & Thomas. LC 00-22716. (ENG, FRE & GER.). 2000. 60.00 (*0-8006-3149-8*, Fortress Pr) Augsburg Fortress.

Robinson, James R. Four Voices - One Gospel: The Synergistic Gospel of the New Testament - King James Edition. 608p. 1992. pap. 29.95 (*1-881426-00-9*) Quest Pub AZ.

Robinson, James Roper. Reflections on Renal Function. 2nd ed. LC 88-212127. ix, 310 p. 1988. write for info. (*0-632-02102-0*) Blackwell Sci.

Robinson, James W. Atomic Absorption Spectroscopy. 2nd rev. ed. LC 75-328457. (Illus.). 197p. reprint ed. pap. 61.10 (*0-7837-0896-3*, 204120100019) Bks Demand.

— Atomic Spectroscopy. LC 90-3452. (Illus.). 309p. reprint ed. pap. 95.80 (*0-608-08979-6*, 206961400005) Bks Demand.

— Atomic Spectroscopy. 2nd ed. (Illus.). 384p. 1996. text 165.00 (*0-8247-9742-6*) Dekker.

— Better Speeches in Ten Simple Steps. 136p. 1989. pap. 7.95 (*0-914629-86-7*) Prima Pub.

— Doing Business in Vietnam. LC 94-13044. 304p. 1994. 24.95 (*1-55958-591-9*) Prima Pub.

— Empire of Freedom: The Amway Story. 272p. 1996. 20.00 (*0-7615-0675-6*) Prima Pub.

— Empire of Freedom: The Amway Story & What It Means to You. 224p. 1997. per. 14.00 (*0-7615-1088-5*) Prima Pub.

— The Excel Phenomenon: The Astonishing Success Story of the Faster-Growing Communications Company. LC 97-23828. 256p. 1997. 20.00 (*0-7615-1171-7*) Prima Pub.

*__Robinson, James W.__ The New Excel Phenomenon. 5th ed. 2000. 22.00 (*0-7615-2525-4*) Prima Pub.

Robinson, James W. Practical Handbook Spectroscopy. (Illus.). 944p. 1991. boxed set 147.95 (*0-8493-3708-9*, QD95) CRC Pr.

— Prescription for Success: The Rexall Showcase Story & What It Means to You. LC 98-56030. 256p. 1999. pap. 15.00 (*0-7615-1981-5*, Frum) Prima Pub.

— Undergraduate Instrumental Analysis. 5th expanded rev. ed. LC 94-21455. (Illus.). 888p. 1994. text 65.00 (*0-8247-9215-7*) Dekker.

Robinson, James W. & Colliau, Russ. After the Revolution: A Citizen's Guide to the First Republican Congress in Forty Years. LC 94-47409. 208p. 1995. pap. 9.95 (*0-7615-0072-3*) Prima Pub.

Robinson, James W., et al. The Grievance Procedure & Arbitration: Text & Cases. LC 77-18573. 1978. pap. text 27.00 (*0-8191-0411-6*) U Pr of Amer.

Robinson, Jan. Sea to Shore. (Illus.). 288p. 1989. pap. 14.95 (*0-9612686-3-8*) Ship-Shore.

— Ship to Shore, Vol. II. (Illus.). 288p. 1986. pap. 14.95 (*0-9612686-1-1*) Ship-Shore.

— Sip to Shore. (Illus.). 128p. 1986. pap. 10.95 (*0-9612686-2-X*) Ship-Shore.

— Slim to Shore: Recipes for a Healthy Lifestyle. Martin, Jan, ed. (Illus.). 288p. 1994. pap. 14.95 (*0-9612686-5-4*) Ship-Shore.

— Sweet to Shore. (Illus.). 288p. 1990. pap. 14.95 (*0-9612686-4-6*) Ship-Shore.

Robinson, Jan, compiled by. Ship to Shore: Caribbean Charter Yacht Recipes. (Illus.). 448p. (Orig.). 1987. reprint ed. pap. 15.95 (*0-13-808932-9*) P-H.

Robinson, Jan & Fowler, Cheryl A., eds. Ship to Shore, Vol. I. (Illus.). 336p. 1983. pap. 14.95 (*0-9612686-0-3*) Ship-Shore.

Robinson, Jancis. Jancis Robinson's Guide to Wine Grapes. (Illus.). 240p. 1996. 13.95 (*0-19-860098-4*) OUP.

— Jancis Robinson's Wine Course. (Illus.). 320p. 1996. 29.95 (*0-7892-0256-5*) Abbeville Pr.

— The Oxford Companion to Wine. (Illus.). 1,102p. 1994. 60.00 (*0-19-866159-2*) OUP.

— The Oxford Companion to Wine. 2nd ed. (Illus.). 848p. 1999. 65.00 (*0-19-866236-X*) OUP.

— Tasting Pleasure: Confessions of a Wine Lover. 342p. 1999. pap. 15.95 (*0-14-027001-9*, PuffinBks) Peng Put Young Read.

— Vines, Grapes & Wines: The Wine Drinker's Guide to Grape Varieties. LC 73-29996. (Illus.). 280p. 1997. pap. 27.95 (*1-85732-999-6*, Pub. by Mitchell Beazley) Antique Collect.

Robinson, Jancis, jt. ed. see Cass, Bruce.

Robinson, Jane. Angels of Albion: Women of the Indian Mutiny. 320p. 1997. pap. 17.95 (*0-14-017308-0*, Pub. by Pnguin Bks Ltd) Trafalgar.

Robinson, Jane. The Whale in Lowell's Cove. LC 91-77670. (Illus.). 48p. (J). (ps-3). 1992. 14.95 (*0-89272-308-4*) Down East.

*__Robinson, Jane, ed.__ Parrot Pie for Breakfast: An Anthology of Women Pioneers. LC 99-25636. 177p. 2000. pap. 16.95 (*0-19-288020-9*) OUP.

Robinson, Jane, et al, eds. Policy Issues in Nursing. 192p. 1991. pap. 37.95 (*0-335-09466-X*) OpUniv Pr.

Robinson, Jane, selected by. Unsuitable for Ladies: An Anthology of Women Travelers. LC 93-34644. (Illus.). 496p. 1994. 35.00 (*0-19-211681-9*) OUP.

— Unsuitable for Ladies: An Anthology of Women Travelers. (Illus.). 490p. 1995. pap. 14.95 (*0-19-282489-9*) OUP.

Robinson, Jane & Elkan, Ruth. Health Needs Assessment: Theory & Practice. LC 96-5331. 250p. 1996. pap. text 29.95 (*0-443-05233-6*) Church.

Robinson, Jane, ed. see Seabrook, Peter.

Robinson, Jane W. A Birder's Guide to Japan. (Illus.). 358p. 1998. pap. 19.00 (*0-7881-5460-5*) DIANE Pub.

— A Birder's Guide to Japan. (Illus.). 358p. 1988. reprint ed. 17.95 (*0-934797-02-1*) Cornell U Pr.

Robinson, Janet E. Underground Storage Tank Management: Closure & Financial Assurance. 320p. 1993. lib. bdg. 79.95 (*0-87371-402-4*, L402) Lewis Pubs.

Robinson, Janice. Pride & Joy: African American Baby Celebrations. 1999. pap. write for info. (*0-446-67412-5*) Warner Bks.

Robinson, Janice & Successful Black Parenting Magazine Staff. A Blessed Event: The African-American Baby Book. 1999. pap. write for info. (*0-446-67413-3*) Warner Bks.

Robinson, Jay L. Conversations on the Written Word: Essays on Language & Literacy. LC 89-35894. 335p. (Orig.). (C). 1990. pap. text 27.00 (*0-86709-252-1*, 0252, Pub. by Boynton Cook Pubs) Heinemann.

Robinson, Jayme, ed. see Rice, Jayne.

Robinson, Jayne, jt. ed. see Dorsey, Tina.

Robinson, Jean L. How to Survive in Spite of Your Family: This Story Has Never Been Told. 325p. 1996. 25.00 (*0-9652487-0-4*) Topaz Pr PA.

Robinson, Jeanette. The Pleasure Program: The Lifestyle & Weight Management Guide for Busy People. 250p. 1996. pap. text, per. 19.95 (*0-7872-2457-X*) Kendall-Hunt.

Robinson, Jeanne, jt. auth. see Robinson, Spider.

Robinson, Jeanne M. Alienated: A Quest to Understand Contact. LC 97-74545. (Illus.). 212p. 1997. pap. 18.95 (*1-883729-05-X*) Greenleaf Tenn.

Robinson, Jeffrey. The Ginger Jar. large type ed. (Mystery Ser.). 560p. 1988. 11.50 (*0-7089-1905-7*) Ulverscroft.

— The Laundrymen: Inside Money Laundering, The World's Third-Largest Business. LC 96-8626. 1997. pap. 13.45 (*1-55970-385-7*, Pub. by Arcade Pub Inc) Time Warner.

— The Laundrymen: Money Laundering: The World's Third-Largest Business. 368p. 1996. 25.45 (*1-55970-330-X*, Pub. by Arcade Pub Inc) Time Warner.

*__Robinson, Jeffrey.__ Merger: The Conglomeration of International Organized Crime. 2000. 27.95 (*1-58567-030-8*, Pub. by Overlook Pr) Penguin Putnam.

Robinson, Jeffrey. Rainier & Grace. 1990. mass mkt. 4.95 (*0-380-71310-1*, Avon Bks) Morrow Avon.

Robinson, Jeffrey & McCann, Brian, eds. High on Hope: Gwyn Thomas. 120p. (C). 1989. 40.00 (*0-905928-40-7*, Pub. by D Brown & Sons Ltd) St Mut.

Robinson, Jeffrey C. The Current of Romantic Passion. LC 91-6580. 214p. (Orig.). (C). 1991. pap. 16.95 (*0-299-12964-0*) U of Wis Pr.

— Radical Literary Education: A Classroom Experiment with Wordsworth's "Ode" LC 86-23366. 224p. 1986. pap. text 14.95 (*0-299-11064-8*) U of Wis Pr.

— Romantic Presences: Living Images from the Age of Wordsworth & Shelley. 232p. (Orig.). 1998. pap. 17.95 (*1-886449-68-6*, P9686, Pub. by Barrytown Ltd) Consort Bk Sales.

— Spliced Romanticism. LC 97-354. 84p. 1997. pap. 14.95 (*0-7734-2814-3*, Mellen Poetry Pr) E Mellen.

— The Walk: Notes on a Romantic Image. LC 88-37876. (Illus.). 160p. 1989. 27.95 (*0-8061-2181-5*) U of Okla Pr.

Robinson, Jeffrey C., ed. & rev. see Van Ghent, Dorothy B.

Robinson, Jen. For Conifer Fanatics. 37p. 1996. pap. write for info. (*1-887128-18-2*) Soft Skull Pr.

Robinson, Jenefer, ed. Music & Meaning. LC 96-50450. (Illus.). 296p. 1996. pap. text 16.95 (*0-8014-8367-0*) Cornell U Pr.

Robinson, Jennifer. The Power of Apartheid: State, Power, & Space in South African Cities. LC 95-39072. (Policy, Planning, & Critical Theory Ser.). (Illus.). 192p. 1996. pap. 29.95 (*0-7506-2689-5*) Buttrwrth-Heinemann.

Robinson, Jennifer, ed. Music & Meaning. LC 96-50450. (Illus.). 296p. 1997. text 49.95 (*0-8014-3299-5*) Cornell U Pr.

Robinson, Jerome. The Complete Plays of Gilbert & Sullivan. 711p. 1991. reprint ed. text 119.00 (*0-7812-9326-X*) Rprt Serv.

Robinson, Jerome B. The Field & Stream Deer Hunting Handbook. LC 98-43471. (Field & Stream Fishing & Hunting Library). 1999. pap. 9.95 (*1-55821-911-0*) Lyons Pr.

— Hunt Close! A Realistic Guide to Training Close-Working Gun Dogs for Today's Tight Cover Condition. (Illus.). 221p. Date not set. 22.95 (*1-55821-264-7*) Lyons Pr.

*__Robinson, Jerome B.__ In the Deer Woods. 2000. 24.95 (*1-58574-149-3*) Lyons Pr.

Robinson, Jerome B. In the Turkey Woods. LC 98-4725. 1998. 24.95 (*1-55821-695-2*) Lyons Pr.

— Training the Hunting Retriever. 232p. 1993. 22.95 (*1-55821-263-9*) Lyons Pr.

— Training the Hunting Retriever. LC 99-33157. 1999. pap. text 18.95 (*1-55821-936-6*) Lyons Pr.

*__Robinson, Jerome B.__ Ultimate Guide to Bird Dog Training. 2000. 24.95 (*1-58574-126-4*) Lyons Pr.

Robinson, Jerry. Something's Out There: A Newspaperman's Columns from Days Gone By. 248p. 1992. pap. 16.95 (*0-9635444-9-7*) Robinson Comm.

— Syner Abs II. (Illus.). 46p. 1990. pap. 14.95 (*0-944831-27-3*) Health Life.

— The Weightless Workout. (Illus.). 158p. (Orig.). 1990. pap. 19.95 (*0-944831-26-5*) Health Life.

Robinson, Jerry & Carrino, Frank. MAXO2. LC 93-73083. (Illus.). 222p. 1993. pap. 19.95 (*0-944831-30-3*) Health Life.

Robinson, Jerry & Horrigan, Joseph. The Seven-Minute Rotator Cuff Solution. (Illus.). 64p. (Orig.). 1990. pap. 16.95 (*0-944831-25-7*) Health Life.

Robinson, Jerry & Miller, Robert. The Transfigure System Two. (Illus.). 132p. (Orig.). 1990. pap. 19.95 (*0-944831-24-9*) Health Life.

*__Robinson, Jerry W.__ Keyboarding for Computer Success. LC 98-164806. xvi, 80 p. 1998. 23.95 (*0-538-68584-0*) S-W Pub.

An Asterisk (*) at the beginning of an entry indicates that the title is appearing for the first time.

R

Robinson, Jerry W. & Hoggart, Jack P. Applied Keyboarding. LC 93-7454. 1994. 46.50 (*0-614-09622-7*, L-85823-00) Am Printing Hse.

Robinson, Jerry W., et al. Applied Keyboarding. 3rd ed. LC 93-7454. 80p. (YA). 1994. pap. 19.50 (*0-538-62297-0*) S-W Pub.

Robinson, Jerry W., et al. Applied Keyboarding. 3rd ed. LC 93-7454. (YA). 1994. mass mkt. 23.25 (*0-538-62298-9*) S-W Pub.

— Basic Information Keyboarding Skills: A Collegiate Course. 2nd ed. (C). 1987. mass mkt. 26.75 (*0-538-26160-9*, Z16) S-W Pub.

— Key Boarding & Computer Applications: Includes Commands & Directions for WordPerfect 5.1, Lotus 1-2-3, 2.3 MS-DOS, Microsoft Works 2.0 & 3.0 MS-DOS, Microsoft Works 2.0 Macintosh. large type ed. 1995. 123.00 (*0-614-20559-X*, L-85327-00 APHB) Am Printing Hse.

— Keyboarding & Computer Applications: Includes Commands & Directions for Wordperfect 5.1 MS-DOS, Microsoft Works 2.0 & 3.0 MS-DOS, Microsoft. LC 93-32416. 1995. mass mkt. 46.95 (*0-538-62193-1*) S-W Pub.

Robinson, Jerry W., jt. ed. see Christenson, James A.

Robinson, Jesse S. The Amalgamated Association of Iron, Steel & Tin Workers. LC 74-22757. reprint ed. 49.50 (*0-404-58510-8*) AMS Pr.

Robinson, Jessie B. & Abramson, Lillian S. Alef Bet Fun. LC 96-22922. 1996. pap. 5.95 (*0-8197-0621-3*) Bloch.

Robinson, Jessie B., jt. auth. see Eisenberg, Azriel.

***Robinson, Jill.** Falling in Love When You Thought. 2000. 24.00 (*0-06-019864-8*); pap. 12.00 (*0-06-095824-3*) HarpC.

Robinson, Jill. Past Forgetting: My Memory Lost & Found. LC 99-34975. 288p. 1999. 24.00 (*0-06-019430-8*, Cliff Street) HarperTrade.

— Past Forgetting: My Memory Lost & Found. 288p. 2000. pap. 13.00 (*0-06-093234-1*, Cliff Street) HarperTrade.

Robinson, Jill, et al. Design & Make It! Food Technology. 160p. 1998. pap. 30.00 (*0-7487-2472-9*) St Mut.

Robinson, Jim. Roggy Lived on Planet Sun. 288p. 1992. 22.00 (*0-9634367-0-8*) Swallows In-Hse.

Robinson, Jim, photos by. Morehouse College - Then & Now. (First Edition Ser.). (Illus.). 112p. 1992. 39.95 (*0-916509-86-9*) Harmony Hse Pub.

Robinson, Jo & Staeheli, Jean C. Unplug the Christmas Machine: A Complete Guide to Putting Love & Joy Back into the Season. rev. ed. 256p. 1991. pap. 10.00 (*0-688-10961-6*, Quil) HarperTrade.

Robinson, Jo, jt. auth. see Allen, Marvin.

Robinson, Jo, jt. auth. see Love, Patricia.

Robinson, Jo, jt. auth. see Reiter, Russel J.

Robinson, Jo A. A. J. Muste: Pacifist & Prophet. Mather, Eleanore P., ed. LC 81-80219. 31p. 1981. pap. 1.00 (*0-87574-235-1*) Pendle Hill.

Robinson, Jo A. The Montgomery Bus Boycott & the Women Who Started It. Garrow, David J., ed. LC 86-14684. (Illus.). 208p. 1987. pap. 16.50 (*0-87049-527-5*) U of Tenn Pr.

Robinson, Joan (Maurice). The Accumulation of Capital. 3rd ed. LC 85-12465. xvi, 440p. 1986. reprint ed. pap. 24.95 (*0-87991-260-X*); reprint ed. lib. bdg. 45.00 (*0-87991-266-9*) Porcupine Pr.

— Aspects of Development & Underdevelopment. LC 78-25610. (Modern Cambridge Economics Ser.). 170p. 1979. pap. text 18.95 (*0-521-29589-0*) Cambridge U Pr.

— Collected Economic Papers of Joan Robinson, 5 vols. 1980. 20.00 (*0-262-18098-7*) MIT Pr.

— Collected Economic Papers of Joan Robinson, 5 vols., 2. 293p. 1980. 37.50 (*0-262-18094-4*) MIT Pr.

— Collected Economic Papers of Joan Robinson, 5 vols., 5. 305p. 1980. 37.50 (*0-262-18097-9*) MIT Pr.

— An Essay on Marxian Economics. 2nd ed. xxiv, 104p. 1991. reprint ed. pap. 12.95 (*0-87991-270-7*) Porcupine Pr.

Robinson, Joan (Maurice). Notes from China. LC 64-23734. 46p. reprint ed. pap. 30.00 (*0-608-30848-X*, 200170700004) Bks Demand.

Robinson, Joan (Maurice). The Roots of Language Set, 3 bks., Set. (J). (gr. 4-9). 28.99 (*1-56417-729-7*, FE0005) Fearon Teacher Aids.

Robinson, Joan (Maurice). What Are the Questions? And Other Essays. LC 80-28062. 244p. (gr. 13). 1981. pap. text 40.95 (*0-87332-200-2*) M E Sharpe.

Robinson, Joan (Maurice). WordBuilding. (Roots of Language Ser.). (J). (gr. 4-8). 1989. pap. 10.99 (*0-8224-7450-6*) Fearon Teacher Aids.

— WordStrength. (Roots of Language Ser.). (J). (gr. 4-8). 1989. pap. 10.99 (*0-8224-7451-4*) Fearon Teacher Aids.

— WordWise. (Roots of Language Ser.). (J). (gr. 4-8). 1989. pap. 10.99 (*0-8224-7452-2*) Fearon Teacher Aids.

***Robinson, Joan G.** Dear Teddy Robinson. 1999. 16.95 (*0-7540-6075-6*) Chivers N Amer.

— Teddy Robinson Storybook. LC 99-58603. 224p. (J). 2000. 14.95 (*1-85697-494-4*, Kingfisher) LKC.

Robinson, Joan S., et al. Chihuly: Seaforms. Johnson, Diana, ed. LC 96-113980. (Illus.). 112p. 1997. 30.00 (*0-9608382-5-2*) Portland Pr.

Robinson, JoAnn G. The Montgomery Bus Boycott & the Women Who Started It. Garrow, David J., ed. LC 86-14684. (Illus.). 208p. 1987. text 36.00 (*0-87049-524-0*) U of Tenn Pr.

***Robinson, Joanne Maguire.** Nobility & Annihilation in Marguerite Porete's Mirror of Simple Souls. (C). 2001. pap. text. write for info. (*0-7914-4968-8*) State U NY Pr.

— Nobility & Annihilation in Marguerite Porete's Mirror of Simple Souls. (C). 2001. text. write for info. (*0-7914-4967-X*) State U NY Pr.

Robinson, Joe E. Stop! & Think. 28p. 1996. pap. 7.00 (*0-8059-4030-8*) Dorrance.

Robinson, John. Coach to Coach: Business Lessons from the Locker Room. LC 95-40337. (Warren Bennis Executive Briefing Ser.). 128p. 1995. 22.50 (*0-89384-274-5*, Pfffr & Co) Jossey-Bass.

— Destroying New Zealand: The Tragedy of the 21th Century LC 97-139158. 154p. 1996. write for info. (*0-473-03655-X*) The Bradbury Hse.

— How Americans Use Time: A Social-Psychological Analysis of Everyday Behavior. LC 76-58838. (Special Studies). 209p. 1977. 40.95 (*0-275-90273-0*, C0273, Praeger Pubs) Greenwood.

— A Justification of Separation from the Church of England. LC 77-7427. (English Experience Ser.: No. 888). 1977. reprint ed. lib. bdg. 65.00 (*90-221-0888-0*) Walter J Johnson.

— Legends of the Lost. 160p. (Orig.). 1989. pap. 12.95 (*1-882021-07-X*) Summer.

***Robinson, John.** Motorcycle Fuel Systems TechBook. (Illus.). 256p. 2000. 23.95 (*1-85960-514-1*, 130364AM, Pub. by Haynes Manuals) Motorbooks Intl.

Robinson, John. Motorcycle Tuning: Chassis. (Illus.). 259p. 1994. pap. text 36.95 (*0-7506-1840-X*) Buttrwrth-Heinemann.

— Motorcycle Tuning: Four-Stroke. 2nd ed. 160p. 1994. pap. text 36.95 (*0-7506-1805-1*) Buttrwrth-Heinemann.

— Motorcycle Tuning: Two-Stroke. 2nd ed. 144p. 2000. pap. text 36.95 (*0-7506-1806-X*) Buttrwrth-Heinemann.

— My Own Story. (American Autobiography Ser.). 172p. 1995. reprint ed. lib. bdg. 69.00 (*0-7812-8627-1*) Rprt Serv.

***Robinson, John.** Ordinary Enlightenment. 175p. 2000. pap. 12.95 (*0-87159-261-4*) Unity Bks.

***Robinson, John & Bennett, Elizabeth, eds.** Hunting for Sustainability in Tropical Forests. (Biology & Resource Management Ser.). (Illus.). 1000p. 1999. pap. 29.50 (*0-231-10977-6*) Col U Pr.

Robinson, John, tr. see Cecchini, Paolo, et al.

Robinson, John A. Exploration into God. LC 67-26529. x, 166p. 1967. 11.95 (*0-8047-0322-1*) Stanford U Pr.

Robinson, John B. Kilimanjaro Burning. (Illus.). 124p. 1998. 25.00 (*0-913559-38-5*) Birch Brook Pr.

— Pictures of Slavery & Anti-Slavery. LC 70-83875. (Black Heritage Library Collection). 1977. 20.95 (*0-8369-8646-6*) Ayer.

— Rebuilding the World. 1972. 250.00 (*0-8490-0934-0*) Gordon Pr.

Robinson, John B., et al. Life in 2030: Exploring a Sustainable Future in Canada. LC 97-121139. 224p. 1996. pap. 25.95 (*0-7748-0569-2*) U of Wash Pr.

Robinson, John B., jt. ed. see Dale, Ann.

Robinson, John B., ed. see Proudhon, Pierre-Joseph.

Robinson, John C. An Annotated Checklist of the Birds of Tennessee. LC 89-77251. 288p. 1990. 32.00 (*0-87049-642-5*) U of Tenn Pr.

— But Where Is God? Psychotherapy & the Religious Search. 246p. 1999. pap. 18.95 (*1-56072-504-4*, Nova Troitsa Bks) Nova Sci Pubs.

— Death of a Hero - Birth of the Soul: Answering the Call of Midlife. LC 97-37. 352p. 1997. reprint ed. pap. 16.95 (*1-57178-043-2*) Coun Oak Bks.

— Secret of the Snow Leopard. LC 98-67918. 304p. 1999. pap. 16.95 (*1-882897-29-3*) Lost Coast.

***Robinson, John G. & Bennett, Elizabeth L.** Hunting for Sustainability in Tropical Forests. LC 99-20178. (Biology & Resource Management Ser.). 1000p. 1999. 80.00 (*0-231-10976-8*) Col U Pr.

Robinson, John G. & Redford, Kent H., eds. Neotropical Wildlife Use & Conservation: With 47 Contributors. LC 90-44430. (Illus.). 538p. 1991. lib. bdg. 74.50 (*0-226-72258-9*) U Ch Pr.

— Neotropical Wildlife Use & Conservation: With 47 Contributors. LC 90-44430. (Illus.). 538p. 1997. pap. text 29.95 (*0-226-72259-7*) U Ch Pr.

Robinson, John H. A Reason to Live. (American Heroes Ser.). (Illus.). 446p. 1989. 19.95 (*0-916693-12-0*) Castle Bks.

***Robinson, John H., et al.** A Health Law Reader: An Interdisciplinary Approach. LC 98-28630. 848p. 1998. pap. 60.00 (*0-89089-907-X*) Carolina Acad Pr.

Robinson, John J. Born in Blood: The Lost Secrets of Freemasonry. LC 89-23703. 396p. 1989. 19.95 (*0-87131-602-1*) M Evans.

— Dungeon, Fire & Sword: The Knights Templar in the Crusades. LC 91-27495. 508p. 1992. 24.95 (*0-87131-657-9*) M Evans.

— A Pilgrim's Path: Freemasonry & the Religious Right. LC 93-9178. 192p. 1993. 17.95 (*0-87131-732-X*) M Evans.

Robinson, John L., jt. ed. see Levy, Maurice.

Robinson, John M., jt. auth. see Erdos, Paul.

Robinson, John M., jt. auth. see Rowell, Christopher.

Robinson, John M., jt. auth. see Woodcock, Thomas.

Robinson, John Martin, jt. auth. see Woodcock, Thomas.

Robinson, John P. Time for Life: The Surprising Ways Americans Use Their Time. 2nd ed. LC 99-37479. 1999. pap. 20.00 (*0-271-01970-0*) Pa St U Pr.

Robinson, John P., ed. Social Science & the Arts Nineteen Eighty-Four: A State-of-the-Arts Review from the Tenth Annual Conference on Social Theory, Politics & the Arts University of Maryland, College Park, October 12-14, 1984. (Illus.). 190p. (Orig.). 1986. pap. text 20.00 (*0-8191-4926-8*); lib. bdg. 46.00 (*0-8191-4925-X*) U Pr of Amer.

Robinson, John P., et al, eds. Measures of Personality & Social Psychological Attitudes, Vol. 1. LC 90-91. (Measure of Social Psychological Changes Ser.). 753p. 1990. pap. text 69.95 (*0-12-590244-1*) Acad Pr.

Robinson, John P. & Godbey, Geoffrey C. Time for Life: The Surprising Ways Americans Use Their Time. LC 96-52500. 288p. 1997. 24.95 (*0-271-01652-3*) Pa St U Pr.

Robinson, John P. & Levy, Mark R. The Main Source: Learning from Television News. LC 85-22195. (People & Communication Ser.: No. 17). (Illus.). 272p. (Orig.). 1986. reprint ed. pap. 84.40 (*0-7837-4559-1*, 204408700003) Bks Demand.

Robinson, John P., et al. Measures of Political Attitudes. LC 98-84427. (Measures of Social Psychological Attitudes Ser.). (Illus.). 816p. (C). 1999. text 125.00 (*0-12-590242-5*); pap. text 75.00 (*0-12-590245-X*) Acad Pr.

Robinson, John R. The Last Earls of Barrymore, 1769-1824. LC 72-80506. 286p. 1972. reprint ed. 24.95 (*0-405-08895-7*, Pub. by Blom Pubns) Ayer.

— The Octopus: A History of the Construction, Conspiracies, Extortions, Robberies & Villainous Acts of Subsidized Railroads. Bruchey, Stuart, ed. LC 80-1340. (Railroads Ser.). 1981. reprint ed. lib. bdg. 15.95 (*0-405-13812-1*) Ayer.

Robinson, John T. Early Hominid Posture & Locomotion. LC 72-77306. 384p. 1994. lib. bdg. 31.00 (*0-226-72230-9*) U Ch Pr.

Robinson, John W. Mines of the East Fork. 1980. pap. 4.50 (*0-87505-417-X*) Borden.

— Mines of the San Bernardino. 1986. pap. 4.50 (*0-87505-415-3*) Borden.

— Mines of the San Gabriels. 1986. pap. 4.50 (*0-87505-416-1*) Borden.

— San Bernardino Mountain Trails. 4th ed. LC 85-41027. (Illus.). 272p. 1986. pap. 14.95 (*0-89997-063-X*) Wilderness Pr.

— The San Bernardinos. 256p. 32.95 (*0-9615421-2-8*) Big Santa Hist.

— The San Gabriels. 311p. 34.95 (*0-9615421-5-2*) Big Santa Hist.

— Trails of the Angeles: 100 Hikes in the San Gabriels. 7th rev. ed. LC 98-15475. (Illus.). 264p. 1998. pap. 14.95 (*0-89997-232-2*) Wilderness Pr.

Robinson, John W. & Risher. The San Jacintos. 251p. 32.95 (*0-9615421-6-0*) Big Santa Hist.

Robinson, John W., jt. auth. see Green, Jon W.

Robinson, John W., ed. see American Society of Mechanical Engineers Staff.

Robinson, Jon. Property Valuation & Investment Analysis: A Cash Flow Approach. vii, 161p. 1989. pap. 36.50 (*0-455-20830-1*, Pub. by LawBk Co) Gaunt.

Robinson, Jonathan. Communication Miracles for Couples: Easy & Effective Tools to Create More Love & Less Conflict. LC 97-7473. 178p. (Orig.). 1997. pap. 10.95 (*1-57324-083-4*) Conari Press.

***Robinson, Jonathan.** The Complete Idiot's Guide Awakening Your Spirituality. (Complete Idiot's Guide Ser.). 336p. 2000. pap. 16.95 (*0-02-863826-3*) Macmillan.

Robinson, Jonathan. Duty & Hypocrisy in Hegel's Phenomenology of Mind: An Essay in the Real & Ideal. LC 78-300950. 164p. reprint ed. pap. 50.90 (*0-8357-6402-8*, 203576000096) Bks Demand.

— Instant Insight: The Not-So-Little Book of Life's Questions. 160p. (Orig.). 1996. pap. 8.95 (*1-55874-436-3*, 4363) Health Comm.

— The Little Book of Big Questions: 200 Ways to Explore Your Spiritual Nature. 120p. (Orig.). 1995. pap. 8.95 (*1-57324-014-1*) Conari Press.

— On the Lord's Appearing: An Essay on Prayer & Tradition. LC 96-36924. 280p. 1997. pap. text 19.95 (*0-8132-0887-4*) Cath U Pr.

— On the Lord's Appearing: An Essay on Prayer & Tradition. LC 96-36924. 280p. 1997. text 39.95 (*0-8132-0886-6*) Cath U Pr.

— Real Wealth: A Spiritual Approach to Money & Work. LC 97-33512. 176p. 1998. pap. text 12.95 (*1-56170-455-5*) Hay House.

— Shortcuts to Bliss: The 50 Best Ways to Improve Relationships, Connect with Spirit, & Make Dreams Come True. LC 98-24238. 256p. 1998. pap. 11.95 (*1-57324-137-7*) Conari Press.

***Robinson, Jonathan.** Shortcuts to Success: The Absolute Best Ways to Master Your Money, Time, Health & Relationships. LC 99-42066. 224p. 2000. pap. 12.95 (*1-57324-188-1*) Conari Press.

Robinson, Jonathan, ed. The Experience of God: How 40 Well-Known Seekers Encounter the Sacred. 2nd rev. ed. LC 97-33458. Orig. Title: Bridges to Heaven. (Illus.). 256p. 1997. pap. 12.95 (*1-56170-469-5*, 861) Hay House.

— Faith & Reform: A Reinterpretation of Aggiornamento. LC 70-75039. 182p. reprint ed. pap. 56.50 (*0-7837-0469-0*, 204079200018) Bks Demand.

Robinson, Jontyle Theresa & Powell, Richard. The Art of Ronald Burns. (Illus.). 25p. 1994. write for info. (*0-9621349-1-0*) Spelman Coll Art.

Robinson, Jontyle Theresa, et al. Bearing Witness: Contemporary Works by African American Women Artists. LC 96-4294. (Illus.). 176p. 1996. 45.00 (*0-8478-1962-0*, Pub. by Rizzoli Intl); pap. 27.50 (*0-8478-1963-9*, Pub. by Rizzoli Intl) St Martin.

Robinson, Jontyle Theresa, jt. auth. see Greenhouse, Wendy.

Robinson, Joseph A. Gilbert Crispin, Abbot of Westminster: A Study of the Abby under Norman Rule. LC 80-2211. reprint ed. 37.50 (*0-404-18785-4*) AMS Pr.

Robinson, Joseph K., jt. auth. see Martinex, Javier.

Robinson, Joseph R. & Lee, H. L. Vincent. Controlled Drug Delivery: Fundamentals & Applications. 2nd ed. (Drugs & the Pharmaceutical Sciences Ser.: Vol. 29). (Illus.). 744p. 1987. text 299.00 (*0-8247-7588-0*) Dekker.

Robinson, Josephine D. The Circus Lady. Baxter, Annette K., ed. LC 79-8808. (Signal Lives Ser.). (Illus.). 1980. reprint ed. lib. bdg. 35.95 (*0-405-12854-1*) Ayer.

Robinson, Joseph D. Moving Questions: A History of Membrane Transport & Bioenergetics. LC 96-48139. (People & Ideas Ser.). (Illus.). 392p. 1997. text 85.00 (*0-19-510564-8*) OUP.

Robinson, Joy M. Antoine de Saint-Exupery. (World Authors Ser.: No. 705). 200p. 1984. 23.95 (*0-8057-6552-2*, Twayne) Mac Lib Ref.

Robinson, Joyce H. Musical Notes by Honore Daumier: Prints from the Collection of Egon & Belle Gartenberg. (Illus.). 24p. 1998. pap. 6.00 (*0-911209-47-6*) Palmer Mus Art.

— Red Grooms & the Heroism of Modern Life. (Illus.). 20p. 1998. pap. 9.00 (*0-911209-48-4*) Palmer Mus Art.

Robinson, Joyce M., ed. see Schwartz, Eugene M.

Robinson, Judith. The Hearsts: An American Dynasty. LC 89-40768. (Illus.). 1991. 55.00 (*0-87413-383-1*) U Delaware Pr.

— The Hearsts: An American Dynasty. 432p. 1992. reprint ed. pap. 15.00 (*0-380-71947-9*, Avon Bks) Morrow Avon.

— You're in Your Mother's Arms: The Life & Legacy of Congressman Phil Burton. LC 94-92365. (Illus.). 700p. (Orig.). 1994. pap. 35.00 (*0-9643382-0-3*) M J Robinson.

Robinson, Judith, ed. see Valery, Paul.

Robinson, Judith S., ed. Tapping the Government Grapevine: The User-Friendly Guide to U. S. Government Information Sources. 3rd ed. LC 98-20618. (Illus.). 296p. 1998. pap. 45.50 (*1-57356-024-3*) Oryx Pr.

Robinson, Judith S., jt. auth. see Hardy, Gayle J.

Robinson, Judy L. Scholastic Journalism in the Sunshine State: The History of the Florida Scholastic Press Association, 1946-1996. Dodd, Julie E., ed. (Illus.). 65p. (YA). (gr. 6 up). 1996. pap. 20.00 (*0-9660379-0-1*) Fla Scholastic.

Robinson, Julia & Feferman, Solomon. The Collected Works of Julia Robinson, Vol. 6. LC 96-22866. 338p. 1996. text 69.00 (*0-8218-0575-4*, CWORKS/6) Am Math.

Robinson, Julian. Body Packaging - A Guide to Human Sexual Display. LC 88-6888. (Illus.). 208p. (C). 1988. 32.95 (*1-55599-027-4*) Elysium.

— The Quest for Human Beauty: An Illustrated History. LC 97-19491. 320p. 1998. 39.95 (*0-393-04004-6*) Norton.

Robinson, Julian, jt. auth. see Langner, Lawrence.

Robinson, Julian P., ed. Chemical & Biological Warfare Development, 1985. (SIPRI Chemical & Biological Warfare Studies). (Illus.). 110p. 1986. pap. text 45.00 (*0-19-829110-8*) OUP.

Robinson, Julian P., ed. see Stockholm International Peace Research Institute S.

Robinson, Julie, jt. auth. see Lauer, Keith.

Robinson, June K., et al. Cutaneous Medicine & Surgery: An Integrated Program in Dermatology, 2 vols., Set. LC 94-6429. (Illus.). 1600p. 1995. text 260.00 (*0-7216-4852-5*, W B Saunders Co) Harcrt Hlth Sci Grp.

Robinson, K., jt. auth. see Greenough, C.

Robinson, Kate & Shakespeare, Pam. Open Learning in Nursing, Health & Welfare Education. LC 94-43323. 160p. 1995. 114.95 (*0-335-19075-8*); pap. 36.95 (*0-335-19074-X*) OpUniv Pr.

Robinson, Kate, jt. auth. see Vaughan, Barbara.

Robinson, Kathleen. Heaven's Only Daughter. large type ed. LC 94-2966. 476p. 1994. reprint ed. lib. bdg. 22.95 (*0-8161-5961-0*, G K Hall Lrg Type) Mac Lib Ref.

Robinson, Kathleen & Luckett, Pete. Vegetarian's A to Z Guide to Fruits & Vegetables. LC 96-5413. (Illus.). 224p. 1996. reprint ed. pap. 12.95 (*1-55561-091-9*) Fisher Bks.

Robinson, Kathleen M., jt. auth. see DeGrandpre, Charles A.

Robinson, Kathleen Q. Help! I'm Just a Parent: Parenting the Child Who Learns Differently. 256p. 1997. pap. write for info. (*1-880976-13-7*) Brookshire Pubns.

Robinson, Kathryn. The Other Puerto Rico. (Illus.). 164p. (Orig.). 1984. pap. 11.95 (*0-915393-19-0*) Perm Pr.

— Where Dwarfs Reign: A Tropical Rain Forest in Puerto Rico. LC 96-22091. (Illus.). 242p. 1997. 29.95 (*0-8477-0255-3*) U of PR Pr.

Robinson, Kathryn & Irving, Stephanie, eds. Seattle Cheap Eats: Three Hundred Terrific Bargain Eateries. 5th rev. ed. (Illus.). 208p. 1993. pap. 9.95 (*0-912365-72-2*) Sasquatch Bks.

Robinson, Kathryn M. Stepchildren of Progress: The Political Economy of Development in an Indonesian Mining Town. LC 86-5847. (SUNY Series in the Anthropology of Work). 315p. (Orig.). (C). 1986. text 24.50 (*0-88706-119-2*) State U NY Pr.

Robinson, Kathy. My Many Faces. Date not set. per. 16.00 (*0-9673326-0-5*) K L Robinson.

— Weeds to Wildflowers. 1998. reprint ed. per. 16.00 (*0-9673326-1-3*) K L Robinson.

Robinson, Kathy, ed. see Houston, Yvonnia M.

Robinson, Kay. Model Plan for Implementation of Title I of the Americans with Disabilities Act: The Human Resource Perspective. (ADA Practice Ser.). 24p. 1994. pap. 9.00 (*0-934753-90-3*) LRP Pubns.

Robinson, Keith & Lehman, Fred. South Fork of the American River: From Chili Bar Dam to Salmon Falls Road. (Whitewater Ser.). (Illus.). 1982. pap. 3.95 (*0-941838-00-5*) Lore Unlim.

— Stanislaus River: From Camp Nine to Parrots Ferry. (Whitewater Ser.). (Illus.). 1982. pap. 3.95 (*0-941838-01-3*) Lore Unlim.

— Tuolumne River: From Lumsden Bridge to Ward's Ferry. (Whitewater Ser.). (Illus.). 1982. pap. 3.95 (*0-941838-02-1*) Lore Unlim.

***Robinson, Keith A.** Growing Older with Your Teeth: Or Something Like Them. large type ed. (Anthology on Aging Ser.). (Illus.). 155p. 1998. pap. 14.95 (*1-891151-00-2*) Synergy Publ.

Robinson, Kellie, jt. auth. see Toporek, Chuck.

Robinson, Ken, ed. The Arts & Higher Education: SRHE Leverhulme V. 220p. 1982. pap. 21.00 (*0-900868-89-9*) OpUniv Pr.

Robinson, Ken, ed. see Oldham, John.

Robinson, Kenneth. The Way & the Wilderness. 248p. 1994. text 30.00 (*1-85821-083-6*) World Scientific Pub.

Robinson, Kenneth & Madden, Frederick, eds. Essays in Imperial Government: Presented to Margery Perham by Kenneth Robinson & Frederick Madden. LC 84-12970. 295p. 1984. reprint ed. lib. bdg. 89.50 (*0-313-24226-7*, REIG, Greenwood Pr) Greenwood.

Robinson, Kenneth A. Thoreau & the Wild Appetite. LC 80-2682. (Thoreau Ser.). (Illus.). reprint ed. 29.50 (*0-404-19079-0*) AMS Pr.

***Robinson, Kenneth D.** Responsible Living: An MRT-Based Workbook. Little, Gregory L., ed. 26p. 1999. wbk. ed. 10.00 (*0-940829-26-6*) Eagle Wing Bks.

Robinson, Kenneth D., jt. auth. see Little, Gregory L.

Robinson, Kenneth D., ed. see Little, Gregory L.

Robinson, Kenneth G. Building a Global Information Society. (Communications & Society Program Book Ser.). 69p. 1996. pap. 10.00 (*0-89843-189-1*) The Aspen Inst.

Robinson, Kenneth J., jt. auth. see Short, Genie D.

Robinson, Kenneth L., jt. auth. see Tomek, William G.

Robinson, Kerry A., ed. The Catholic Funding Guide: A Directory of Resources for Catholic Activities. LC 97-77629. 370p. 1997. pap. 45.00 (*1-891646-00-1*) FADICA.

— Foundation Guide for Religious Grant Seekers. 6th ed. LC 94-48790. (Handbook Ser.: Vol. 9). 383p. 1995. pap. 19.95 (*0-7885-0090-2*, 00 15 09) Duke.

***Robinson, Kevin.** The Actor Sings: Discovering a Musical Voice for the Stage. LC 99-86171. 128p. 2000. pap. 13.95 (*0-325-00177-4*) Heinemann.

Robinson, Kevin. Mall Rats: A Stick Foster Mystery. 202p. 1992. 19.95 (*0-8027-3215-1*) Walker & Co.

— A Matter of Perspective. LC 93-15674. (Stick Foster Mystery Ser.). 1993. 19.95 (*0-8027-3242-9*) Walker & Co.

— Split Seconds. 208p. 1991. 18.95 (*0-8027-5785-5*) Walker & Co.

Robinson, Kidd, et al. Family Nurse Practitioner Certification Review. LC 98-23492. (Illus.). 768p. (C). (gr. 13). 1998. pap. text 54.95 (*0-8151-5581-6*, 31784) Mosby Inc.

***Robinson, Killian.** Homocysteine & Vascular Disease. 468p. 2000. 180.00 (*0-7923-6248-9*, Kluwer Plenum) Kluwer Academic.

Robinson, Killian, ed. Preventive Cardiology: A Guide for Clinical Practice. LC 98-6277. (Illus.). 432p. 1998. 69.00 (*0-87993-692-4*) Futura Pub.

Robinson, Kim Stanley. Antarctica. LC 97-41701. 528p. 1998. 24.95 (*0-553-10063-7*) Bantam.

— Antarctica. 672p. 1999. reprint ed. mass mkt. 6.99 (*0-553-57402-7*) Bantam.

— The Blind Geometer. deluxe limited ed. (Illus.). 96p. 1986. boxed set 150.00 (*0-941826-13-9*) Cheap St.

— Blue Mars. 784p. 1997. mass mkt. 6.99 (*0-553-57335-7*) Bantam.

Robinson, Kim Stanley. Blue Mars. (Illus.). (J). 1997. 12.34 (*0-606-17993-3*) Turtleback.

— Escape from Kathmandu. 320p. 2000. pap. 14.95 (*0-312-87499-5*, Pub. by Tor Bks) St Martin.

Robinson, Kim Stanley. The Gold Coast. 1988. 18.95 (*0-685-20156-2*) St Martin.

— The Gold Coast. 416p. 1988. pap. 3.95 (*0-8125-5239-3*) Tor Bks.

— The Gold Coast. 400p. 1995. pap. 13.95 (*0-312-89037-0*, Pub. by Tor Bks) St Martin.

— Green Mars. 640p. 1995. mass mkt. 6.99 (*0-553-57239-3*) Bantam.

Robinson, Kim Stanley. Green Mars. 1994. 12.09 (*0-606-07601-8*, Pub. by Turtleback) Demco.

Robinson, Kim Stanley. Icehenge. LC 98-23487. 288p. 1998. pap. 13.95 (*0-312-86609-7*) St Martin.

— The Martians. LC 99-13115. 352p. 1999. 24.95 (*0-553-80117-1*, Spectra) Bantam.

***Robinson, Kim Stanley.** The Martians. 2000. mass mkt. 6.99 (*0-553-57401-9*) Bantam.

Robinson, Kim Stanley. The Memory of Whiteness: A Scientific Romance. LC 95-30043. 352p. 1996. pap. 13.95 (*0-312-86143-5*) Orb NYC.

— The Novels of Philip K. Dick. Scholes, Robert, ed. LC 84-2621. (Studies in Speculative Fiction: No. 9). 162p. reprint ed. pap. 50.30 (*0-8357-1589-2*, 207062300008) Bks Demand.

— Pacific Edge. 336p. 1995. pap. 13.95 (*0-312-89038-9*, Pub. by Tor Bks) St Martin.

— The Planet on the Table. 256p. 1987. reprint ed. pap. 3.50 (*0-8125-5237-7*) Tor Bks.

— Red Mars. 1993. 12.09 (*0-606-08066-X*) Turtleback.

— Red Mars, No. 1. 592p. 1993. mass mkt. 6.99 (*0-553-56073-5*, Spectra) Bantam.

— Remaking History & Other Stories. 528p. 1994. pap. 14.95 (*0-312-89012-5*) Orb NYC.

— A Short, Sharp Shock. 160p. 1990. 18.00 (*0-929480-18-X*) Mark Ziesing.

— A Short, Sharp Shock. limited ed. 160p. 1990. 45.00 (*0-929480-19-8*) Mark Ziesing.

— A Short, Sharp Shock. 176p. 1996. reprint ed. mass mkt. 5.99 (*0-553-57461-2*, Spectra) Bantam.

— The Wild Shore. 384p. 1995. pap. 13.95 (*0-312-89036-2*, Pub. by Tor Bks) St Martin.

Robinson, Kim Stanley, ed. Future Primitive: The New Ecotopias. 352p. 1997. pap. 15.95 (*0-312-86350-0*) St Martin.

Robinson, Kim Stanley, jt. auth. see Vance, Jack.

Robinson, Kimberly. Bubbles: A Thematic Unit. (Thematic Units Ser.). (Illus.). 80p. (gr. 1-3). 1991. student ed. 9.95 (*1-55734-275-X*) Tchr Create Mat.

***Robinson, Kimberly P.** Wake up & Waterski. (Illus.). 34p. (J). (ps-3). 2000. spiral bd. 9.95 (*1-892216-33-7*) Bristol Fash.

Robinson, Kit. Balance Sheet. LC 93-85180. (Roof Bks.). 111p. (Orig.). 1993. pap. 9.95 (*0-937804-52-5*) Segue NYC.

— The Champagne of Concrete. 104p. (Orig.). 1990. pap. 9.00 (*0-937013-32-3*) Potes Poets.

— Counter Meditation. 42p. 1991. pap. 7.00 (*84-87467-09-1*) SPD-Small Pr Dist.

— Covers. 1988. 4.00 (*0-935724-37-0*) Figures.

— Democracy Boulevard. 104p. 11.95 (*0-937804-76-2*) Segue NYC.

— Down & Back. 1978. pap. 7.50 (*0-935724-83-4*) Figures.

— Ice Cubes. LC 87-63136. (Roof Bks.). 90p. 1988. pap. 10.00 (*0-937804-27-4*) Segue NYC.

Robinson, Kit, tr. see Kutik, Ilya, ed.

Robinson, Kris, jt. auth. see Provey, Joe.

Robinson-Kurpius, Sharon E., jt. auth. see Weiner, Neil.

Robinson, L. Strata Title Units in New South Wales. 4th ed. 230p. 1989. pap. 44.00 (*0-409-30248-1*, A.T., MICHIE) LEXIS Pub.

Robinson, L., jt. auth. see Marks, T.

Robinson, L. Louis. Poetic Ventures Vol. 1: Introspection of a Poet. LC 90-92023. 138p. (Orig.). 1991. pap. text 12.95 (*0-9628034-0-5*) L L Robinson.

Robinson, Lady S. & Corbett, Tom. The Dreamer's Dictionary. 384p. 1986. mass mkt. 6.50 (*0-446-34296-3*, Pub. by Warner Bks) Little.

Robinson, Lafayette. Penmanship from A to Z. (Illus.). 72p. (J). (gr. 3-4). 1988. student ed. 7.95 (*0-9621081-1-1*) Educ Graphics.

— Rite Easy from A to Z. Gonzalez, Inez, tr. (ENG & SPA., Illus.). 48p. (J). (gr. 1-3). 1993. lib. bdg. write for info. (*0-9621081-0-3*) Educ Graphics.

Robinson, Lana. The Best of Little Spouse on the Prairie. 1993. pap. 9.95 (*0-9636248-0-6*) Bedford Hse.

Robinson, Larry. The Art of Inlay: Contemporary Design & Technique. LC 94-12076. (Illus.). 112p. 1994. text 24.95 (*0-87930-332-8*) Miller Freeman.

***Robinson, Larry.** The Art of Inlay: Design & Technique for Fine Woodworking. (Illus.). 112p. 1999. pap. 19.95 (*0-87930-595-9*) Miller Freeman.

***Robinson, Larry C.** Training Basketball Officials: A Critical Analysis of the National College Associations. (Illus.). 102p. 2000. pap. text 20.00 (*1-55605-303-7*) Wyndham Hall.

Robinson, Larry M. & Adler, Roy D., eds. Marketing Megaworks: The Top 150 Books & Articles. LC 86-25248. 224p. 1987. 57.95 (*0-275-92318-5*, C2318, Praeger Pubs) Greenwood.

Robinson, Larry M., jt. auth. see Cooper, Philip D.

Robinson, Laura. Crossing the Line: Sexual Assault in Canada's National Sport. LC 99-161083. 256p. 1998. pap. 14.95 (*0-7710-7560-X*) McCland & Stewart.

***Robinson, Laura.** William & the Christmas Moon. (Illus.). 32p. (YA). (gr. k up). 2000. 27.50 (*0-87846-596-0*) Mus Fine Arts Boston.

Robinson, Laura, jt. auth. see Richards, Cate.

***Robinson, Laurie, frwd.** The Challenge of Crime in a Free Society: Looking Back Looking Forward: Research Forum. (Illus.). 218p. 2000. reprint ed. pap. text 35.00 (*0-7881-8805-4*) DIANE Pub.

Robinson, Leah R. Blood Run. LC 88-10172. 352p. 1999. mass mkt. 6.99 (*0-380-79113-7*, Avon Bks) Morrow Avon.

— First Cut. LC 96-28358. 384p. 1998. reprint ed. mass mkt. 6.99 (*0-380-79124-2*, Avon Bks) Morrow Avon.

***Robinson, Leah R.** Unnatural Causes. 384p. 2000. mass mkt. 6.99 (*0-380-79125-0*, HarpTorch) Morrow Avon.

***Robinson, Leah Ruth.** Unnatural Causes. LC 99-25043. 384p. 1999. 24.00 (*0-380-97459-2*, Avon Bks) Morrow Avon.

Robinson, Lee. Gateway. LC 95-17064. 176p. (J). (gr. 5-9). 1996. 14.95 (*0-395-72772-3*) HM.

— Gateway. 1998. 9.60 (*0-606-13413-1*, Pub. by Turtleback) Demco.

— Gateway. 176p. (YA). (gr. 7 up). 1998. reprint ed. mass mkt. 4.50 (*0-440-22700-3*, LLL BDD) BDD Bks Young Read.

Robinson, Lee, tr. see DuoDuo Staff.

Robinson, Lee A., jt. auth. see Hill, Steven C.

Robinson, Leif J. Outdoor Optics. (Illus.). 160p. 1990. pap. 13.95 (*1-55821-065-2*) Lyons Pr.

Robinson, Leif J., ed. see Harrington, Philip S.

Robinson, Leif J., ed. see Scagell, Robin.

Robinson, Leigh. The Eviction Book for California. 8th ed. (Illus.). 256p. (Orig.). 1997. pap. 23.95 (*0-932956-22-X*) ExPress.

— Landlording: A Handy Manual for Scrupulous Landlords & Landladies Who Do It Themselves. 8th ed. LC 97-77003. (Illus.). 526p. 1997. pap. 24.95 (*0-932956-21-1*) ExPress.

Robinson, Leland R. Foreign Credit Facilities in the United Kingdom. LC 68-57579. (Columbia University. Studies in the Social Sciences: No. 244). reprint ed. 20.00 (*0-404-51244-5*) AMS Pr.

Robinson, Lena. Psychology for Social Workers: Black Perspectives. LC 95-8131. 208p. (C). 1995. pap. 25.99 (*0-415-10108-5*) Routledge.

— Psychology for Social Workers: Black Perspectives. LC 95-8131. 208p. (C). (gr. 13). 1995. 75.00 (*0-415-10107-7*) Routledge.

Robinson, Lena, jt. auth. see Robinson, D.

Robinson, Lennox. Irish Theatre. LC 79-92980. (Studies in Drama: No. 39). 1969. reprint ed. lib. bdg. 75.00 (*0-8383-1201-2*) M S G Haskell Hse.

— Selected Plays. Murray, Christopher, ed. LC 82-71455. (Irish Drama Selections Ser.: No. 1). (Illus.). 296p. (C). 1982. 27.95 (*0-8132-0574-3*); pap. 16.95 (*0-8132-0575-1*) Cath U Pr.

— Towards an Appreciation of the Theatre. LC 74-6447. (Studies in Drama: No. 39). (C). 1974. lib. bdg. 75.00 (*0-8383-1915-7*) M S G Haskell Hse.

Robinson, Lennox, jt. auth. see Ohaodha, M.

Robinson, Lennox, jt. auth. see Yeats, John B.

Robinson, Lenton. Banish Your Belly. LC 97-2482. (Illus.). 384p. 1997. pap. 19.95 (*0-87596-501-6*) Rodale Pr Inc.

Robinson, Lenwood, Jr. Skins & Grins: The Plight of the Black American Golfer. LC 97-93130. (Illus.). 144p. 1997. pap. 14.95 (*1-886094-67-5*) Chicago Spectrum.

Robinson, Leon, et al. Eighteen by Thirteen. 144p. 1998. pap. 12.95 (*1-887750-91-6*) Rutledge Bks.

***Robinson, Leonard.** Winter Sea: The Development of an Image. 1999. pap. 60.00 (*1-85072-197-1*, Pub. by W Sessions) St Mut.

***Robinson, Leonard, Jr. & Noland, Thomas.** The Neglected Few. LC 00-130311. 130p. 2000. pap. 24.95 (*0-9678948-0-8*, 1003) Make-Do Prod.

Robinson, Leonard W. In the Whale. LC 83-70061. 80p. 1983. pap. 6.95 (*0-935306-21-8*) Barnwood Pr.

Robinson, Les. Field Guide to the Native Plants of Sydney. 2nd ed. (Illus.). 448p. 1995. pap. 19.95 (*0-86417-639-2*) Seven Hills Bk.

Robinson, Lesley, jt. auth. see Cousins, Jill.

Robinson, Lila W. & Armagost, James. Comanche Dictionary & Grammar. (Publications in Linguistics: No. 92). 360p. 1990. pap. 26.00 (*0-88312-715-6*) S I L Intl.

Robinson, Lillian. Sex, Class & Culture. 388p. 1986. pap. text 13.95 (*0-416-01241-8*, 9874) Routledge.

Robinson, Lillian H., ed. Psychiatry & Religion: Overlapping Concerns. LC 85-28728. (Clinical Insights Ser.). 190p. reprint ed. pap. 58.90 (*0-8357-7841-X*, 203621600002) Bks Demand.

Robinson, Lillian S. In the Canon's Mouth: Dispatches from the Culture Wars. LC 97-1670. 1997. 35.00 (*0-253-33309-1*); pap. 13.95 (*0-253-21134-4*) Ind U Pr.

— Murder Most Puzzling: A Literary Mystery. LC 98-4888. 320p. 1998. write for info. (*0-941968-09-X*) Wildcat Pubs.

— Sex, Class, & Culture. LC 77-15762. 373p. reprint ed. pap. 115.70 (*0-608-13212-8*, 205605200044) Bks Demand.

Robinson, Lillian S., jt. auth. see Bishop, Ryan.

Robinson, Lillie M. Hire & Keep Child Care Staff. 108p. (Orig.). 1997. pap. 10.95 (*0-9637908-0-3*) Readers Press.

— Start & Operate a Child Care Center. 2nd rev. ed. 171p. 1997. pap. 24.95 (*0-9637908-1-1*) Readers Press.

— Starting & Operating a Child Care Center: A Guide. 1994. 29.95 (*0-9637908-6-2*) Readers Press.

Robinson, Linton H. Mexican Slang: A Guide. 156p. (YA). 1998. reprint ed. pap. 6.95 (*0-9627080-7-0*) In One EAR.

Robinson, Linton H., et al. Mexican Slang Plus Graffiti. rev. ed. Reid, B. A., ed. Orig. Title: Mexican Slang: A Guide. (Illus.). 128p. 1999. pap. 9.95 (*1-881791-10-6*, Bueno Bks) In One EAR.

Robinson, Lisa. Psychiatric Nursing As a Human Experience. 3rd ed. (Illus.). 1983. text 58.00 (*0-7216-7622-7*, W B Saunders Co) Harcrt Hlth Sci Grp.

— Substitute Teachers Step-by-Step Survival Handbook: Elementary Level. (Illus.). 24p. (Orig.). 1994. teacher ed. 6.00 (*1-878276-34-4*) Educ Systs Assocs Inc.

Robinson, Lisa S., jt. auth. see McLaughlin, Kenneth, Jr.

Robinson, Lorraine, jt. auth. see Luthert, Joanna M.

Robinson, Lorraine, ed. see Tayloe, Deborah C.

Robinson, Lou. Extremes of High & Low Regard. 32p. 1988. pap. 3.00 (*0-917061-27-6*) Top Stories.

— Napoleon's Mare. 177p. 1991. 18.95 (*0-932511-47-3*); pap. 8.95 (*0-932511-48-1*) Fiction Coll.

Robinson, Lou & Norton, Camille, eds. Resurgent: New Writing by Women. 264p. 1992. text 39.95 (*0-252-01835-4*); pap. text 13.95 (*0-252-06203-5*) U of Ill Pr.

Robinson, Lou, ed. see Kelly, Mary B.

Robinson, Louis N. History & Organization of Criminal Statistics in the United States. LC 69-16246. (Criminology, Law Enforcement, & Social Problems Ser.: No. 83). 1969. reprint ed. 18.00 (*0-87585-083-9*) Patterson Smith.

Robinson, Louise, ed. see Windsor, Mary L. & Windsor, Rudolph R.

Robinson, Ludmilla. Handbook for Legal Interpreters. 1994. pap. write for info. (*0-455-21225-2*, Pub. by LawBk Co) Gaunt.

Robinson, Luther E., ed. Historical & Biographical Record of Monmouth & Warren County, 2 vols. (Illus.). 1565p. 1997. reprint ed. lib. bdg. 58.50 (*0-8328-5773-4*) Higginson Bk Co.

Robinson, Lynda S. Drinker of Blood. LC 98-16322. 304p. 1998. 22.00 (*0-89296-673-4*, Pub. by Mysterious Pr) Little.

— Easter of Souls, Vol. 4. 4th ed. 1998. mass mkt. 5.99 (*0-345-39533-6*) Ballantine Pub Grp.

— Eater of Souls: A Lord Meren Mystery. LC 96-46828. 228p. 1997. 21.95 (*0-8027-3294-1*) Walker & Co.

— Murder at the Feast of Rejoicing: A Lord Meren Mystery. 240p. (YA). 1996. 20.95 (*0-8027-3274-7*) Walker & Co.

— Murder at the Feast of Rejoicing: A Lord Meren Mystery, Vol. 3. 3rd ed. LC 96-97154. 248p. 1997. mass mkt. 5.99 (*0-345-39532-8*) Ballantine Pub Grp.

— Murder at the God's Gate. 1996. mass mkt. 5.99 (*0-345-39531-X*) Ballantine Pub Grp.

— Murder at the God's Gate. LC 94-28806. 248p. 1995. 19.95 (*0-8027-3198-8*) Walker & Co.

— Murder in the Place of Anubis. 192p. 1995. mass mkt. 4.99 (*0-345-38922-0*) Ballantine Pub Grp.

— Murder in the Place of Anubis. 203p. 1994. 18.95 (*0-8027-3249-6*) Walker & Co.

Robinson, Lynn A. & Carlson-Finnerty, Lavonne. Complete Idiot's Guide to Being Psychic. 384p. 1998. 16.95 (*0-02-862904-3*) Macmillan Gen Ref.

Robinson, Lynn B. Coming Out of Your Psychic Closet: How to Unlock Your Naturally Intuitive Self. 176p. (Orig.). 1994. 20.95 (*0-9626531-7-9*); pap. 11.95 (*0-9626531-6-0*) Factor Pr.

Robinson, Lynne & Lowther, Richard. Stencilling: Projects, Techniques Over 30 Stencil Designs. (Illus.). 102p. 1995. pap. 22.95 (*1-57076-028-4*, Trafalgar Sq Pub) Trafalgar.

Robinson, Lynne & Thomson, Gordon. Body Control: Using Techniques Developed by Joseph Pilates. LC 98-70508. (Illus.). 127p. 1998. pap. 19.95 (*1-891696-00-9*) BainBridgeBooks.

Robinson, Lynne, jt. auth. see Lowther, Richard.

***Robinson, Lynne A.** Directions from God. 224p. 2000. pap. 13.95 (*0-7894-6768-2*) DK Pub Inc.

Robinson, M., ed. The Concise Scots Dictionary: A Comprehensive One-Volume Dictionary of the Scots Language from the 12th Century to the Present Day. 928p. 1987. 22.75 (*0-685-11462-7*, Pub. by Aberdeen U Pr); pap. 20.50 (*0-08-028492-2*, Pub. by Aberdeen U Pr); lib. bdg. 85.00 (*0-08-032447-9*, Pub. by Aberdeen U Pr) Macmillan.

Robinson, M., ed. see International Conference on Chemical Vapor Deposit.

Robinson, M. A., jt. auth. see Allen, T. G.

Robinson, M. B., jt. auth. see Porter, B. E.

Robinson, M. J., ed. Practical Paediatrics. 2nd ed. (Illus.). 668p. 1990. pap. text 52.00 (*0-443-04053-2*) Church.

Robinson, M. J. & Roberton, D. M. Practical Paediatrics. 4th ed. LC 97-42805. 1998. text 70.00 (*0-443-05893-8*) Church.

Robinson, M. S. The Paintings of the Willem van de Veldes. (Illus.). 1136p. 1990. 395.00 (*0-85667-389-7*, Pub. by P Wilson) Hoovers TX.

Robinson, Maggie G. 21 Days to Better Fitness: A Proven Plan for Beginning New Habits. (Twenty-One Days Ser.). 128p. 1998. pap. 6.99 (*0-310-21750-4*) Zondervan.

Robinson, Maggie G., jt. auth. see Kleiner, Susan M.

Robinson, Mansel. Colonial Tongues. LC 95-218083. 96p. 1997. pap. text 11.95 (*0-88754-538-6*) Playwrights.

Robinson, Mansell. Heart As It Lived. 96p. 1998. pap. 13.95 (*0-88754-554-8*) Theatre Comm.

Robinson, Marc. Altogether Elsewhere. 444p. 1996. pap. 16.00 (*0-15-600389-9*) Harcourt Coll Pubs.

— Basics of Investing: It's Just What You Need to Know. LC 95-43386. (Your Money Matters Ser.). (Illus.). 40p. (gr. 11). 1999. 4.95 (*0-7835-4792-7*) Time-Life.

— Buying a Home: It's Just What You Need to Know. (Your Money Matters Ser.). (Illus.). 40p. (gr. 11). 1999. 4.95 (*0-7835-4790-0*) Time-Life.

***Robinson, Marc.** Buying the Best Home: The Quick & Easy Route to Finding Your New Home. 2000. pap. 6.95 (*0-7894-6320-2*) DK Pub Inc.

— Choosing the Right Stocks: The Clear Understanding & Instant Insight Insights. 72p. 2000. pap. 6.95 (*0-7894-6318-0*) DK Pub Inc.

Robinson, Marc. Cock-a-Doodle Doo! What Does It Sound Like to You? LC 92-30961. (Illus.). 32p. (J). (ps-3). 1993. 6.50 (*1-55670-267-1*) Stewart Tabori & Chang.

— Credit Basics: It's Just What You Need to Know. Time-Life Books Editors, ed. LC 96-20267. (Your Money Matters Ser.). (Illus.). 40p. (gr. 11). 1999. 4.95 (*0-7835-4794-3*) Time-Life.

***Robinson, Marc.** Divorce & Finances: Know Your Rights Clearly & Quickly. 72p. 2000. pap. 6.95 (*0-7894-6319-9*) DK Pub Inc.

Robinson, Marc. Estate Planning: It's Just What You Need to Know. LC 96-3237. (Your Money Matters Ser.). (Illus.). 40p. (gr. 11). 1999. 4.95 (*0-7835-4811-7*) Time-Life.

***Robinson, Marc.** Financial Aid for College: Understand & Plan Your Funding Options. 72p. 2000. pap. write for info. (*0-7894-6317-2*, Pub. by DK Pub Inc) Pub Resources Inc.

— Investing Basics: Make Smart Decisions Without Being an Expert. 72p. 2000. pap. 6.95 (*0-7894-6315-6*) DK Pub Inc.

Robinson, Marc. Mammals. LC 95-50116. (Nature Company 2-in-1 Poster Pack Ser.). (Illus.). 14p. (gr. k-7). 1999. pap. 9.95 (*0-7835-4795-1*) Time-Life.

***Robinson, Marc.** Managing Credit: What You Need to Know to Boost Your Buying Power. 72p. 2000. pap. 6.95 (*0-7894-6316-4*) DK Pub Inc.

Robinson, Marc. Managing Your 401(k) It's Just What You Need to Know. LC 96-40388. (Your Money Matters Ser.). (Illus.). 40p. (gr. 11). 1997. 4.95 (*0-7835-4812-5*) Time-Life.

— The Other American Drama. LC 96-53224. 216p. 1997. pap. 14.95 (*0-8018-5630-2*) Johns Hopkins.

— The Theater of Maria Irene Fornes. LC 99-21138. (PAJ Bks.). 264p. 1999. pap. 19.95 (*0-8018-6154-3*) Johns Hopkins.

***Robinson, Marc, ed.** The Theater of Maria Irene Fornes. LC 99-21138. (PAJ Bks.). 264p. 1999. 49.95 (*0-8018-6153-5*) Johns Hopkins.

Robinson, Marc & Time-Life Books Editors. Saving for College: It's Just What You Need to Know. LC 96-34250. (Your Money Matters Ser.). (Illus.). 40p. (gr. 11). 1999. 4.95 (*0-7835-4793-5*) Time-Life.

Robinson, Marcel. Fingerpicking Cat Stevens. (Illus.). 32p. 1988. pap. 14.95 (*0-8256-2549-1*, AM71358) Music Sales.

An Asterisk (*) at the beginning of an entry indicates that the title is appearing for the first time.

— Fingerpicking Dylan. (Illus.). 56p. 1990. pap. 14.95 (*0-8256-1281-0*, AM79740) Music Sales.
— Fingerpicking Leonard Cohen. (Illus.). 56p. 1989. pap. 14.95 (*0-8256-2586-6*, AM76621) Music Sales.
— Fingerpicking Paul Simon. (Illus.). 40p. 1988. pap. 14.95 (*0-8256-3304-4*, PS10909) Music Sales.
— Fingerpicking Paul Simon, No. 2. (Illus.). 64p. 1993. pap. 14.95 (*0-8256-3312-5*, PS11311) Music Sales.
***Robinson, Marcel.** Tori Amos for Fingerstyle Guitar: With Tablature. 176p. 1999. pap. 29.95 (*0-8256-1694-8*, AM948618) Music Sales.
Robinson, Marcel, selected by. Paul Simon: Themes & Variations, Clarinet. (Illus.). 48p. 1988. pap. 12.95 (*0-8256-2553-X*, PS10917) Music Sales.
— Paul Simon: Themes & Variations, Flute. (Illus.). 48p. 1988. pap. 12.95 (*0-8256-2554-8*, PS10925) Music Sales.
— Paul Simon: Themes & Variations, Trumpet. (Illus.). 48p. 1988. pap. 12.95 (*0-8256-2555-6*, PS10933) Music Sales.
Robinson, Marcus S. One Song Hero: The Inward Journey of an Urban Shaman. (Illus.). (Orig.). 1994. pap. 38.95 incl. cd-rom (*0-9639703-6-4*, Wetware New Media) Wetware.
— One Song Hero: The Inward Journey of an Urban Shaman. 2nd ed. Lyons, Charles et al, eds. (Illus.). (Orig.). Date not set. pap. 12.95 (*0-9639703-5-6*, Wetware New Media) Wetware.
— Quest of the One Song Hero: The Inward Journey of an Urban Shaman. (Illus.). 184p. 1994. pap. 12.95 (*0-9963970-3-5*) Wetware.
Robinson, Marcus S. & Kammer, Murray P. The Quest for Excellence. 158p. (Orig.). 1993. student ed. 8.95 (*0-9639703-1-3*); pap. 12.95 (*0-9639703-0-5*); audio 8.95 (*0-9639703-2-1*) Wetware.
Robinson, Mare. Time Life Books: Estate Planning. 1996. 4.95 (*0-7835-4791-9*) Time-Life.
Robinson, Margaret. Divorce as Family Transition: When Private Sorrow Becomes a Public Matter. LC 98-151029. 96p. 1997. pap. 22.00 (*1-85575-148-8*, Pub. by H Karnac Bks Ltd) Other Pr LLC.
Robinson, Margaret. Family Transformation During Divorce & Remarriage: A Systematic Approach. LC 92-39942. 368p. (C). (gr. 13). 1993. pap. 25.99 (*0-415-05228-9*, B0223) Routledge.
Robinson, Margaret, jt. auth. see Singh, Virendra.
Robinson, Margaret A. A Woman of Her Tribe. 160p. (YA). 1992. mass mkt. 4.50 (*0-449-70405-X*, Juniper) Fawcett.
— A Woman of Her Tribe. LC 90-31534. 144p. (YA). (gr. 7 up). 1990. mass mkt. 13.95 (*0-684-19223-3*) Scribner.
— The Woman of Her Tribe. 1992. 9.60 (*0-606-01209-5*, Pub. by Turtleback) Demco.
Robinson, Margot. The Peaceful Soul Within: Reflective Steps Toward Awareness. (Illus.). 97p. (Orig.). 1996. per. 14.95 (*0-7872-2221-6*) Kendall-Hunt.
Robinson, Marguerite S. Local Politics: The Law of the Fishes: Development Through Political Change in Medak District, Andhra Pradesh (South India) 364p. 1989. 18.95 (*0-19-561992-7*) OUP.
Robinson, Marian D. Meaningful Counseling: A Guide for Students, Counselors, & Clergy. 204p. 1988. 32.95 (*0-89885-385-0*, Kluwer Acad Hman Sci) Kluwer Academic.
Robinson, Marileta. Mr. Goat's Bad Good Idea: Three Stories. LC 77-26601. (J). (gr. 1-4). 1979. 11.50 (*0-690-03862-3*) HarpC Child Bks.
Robinson, Marilyn. Batavia Places & the People Who Called Them Home. LC 95-92614. 214p. 1996. per. 24.95 (*0-923889-21-3*) Inquisitors Pub.
— Holiday Windows: Pillows with Zippered Vinyl Pockets. Holmes, Sharon, ed. (Illus.). 28p. 1992. pap. 8.95 (*1-880972-00-X*) Pssblts Denver.
— Little Town in a Big Woods. rev. ed. 1996. 14.95 (*0-923889-20-5*) Inquisitors Pub.
— Window Zips: Zippered Vinyl Pockets in Memory Pillows. Holmes, Sharon, ed. (Illus.). 28p. 1992. pap. 8.95 (*0-9622477-9-0*) Pssblts Denver.
Robinson, Marilyn & Bisignano, Judith. Creating Your Future: Level 2. (Illus.). 72p. 1982. 6.95 (*0-9607366-8-9*, KP108) Kino Pubns.
Robinson, Marilyn & Schielke, Jeff, eds. John Gustafson's Historic Batavia. 464p. 1998. 24.95 (*0-923889-06-X*); per. 19.95 (*0-923889-08-6*) Inquisitors Pub.
Robinson, Marilyn, jt. ed. see Coldwell, Lynn.
Robinson, Marilyn, illus. see Simonich, Junanita & Phillips, Toni.
Robinson, Marilyn, tr. see Smith, Nancy J. & Milligan, Lynda S.
Robinson, Marilynne. The Death of Adam: Essays on Modern Thought. LC 98-18021. 254p. 1998. 24.00 (*0-395-92692-0*) HM.
***Robinson, Marilynne.** The Death of Adam: Essays on Modern Thought. 256p. 2000. pap. 14.00 (*0-618-00206-5*, Mariner Bks) HM.
Robinson, Marilynne. Housekeeping. LC 80-24061. 224p. 1997. pap. text 12.00 (*0-374-52518-8*) FS&G.
— Mother Country. 1989. 18.95 (*0-374-21361-5*) FS&G.
— Puritans & Prigs. 1999. 22.50 (*0-8050-4919-3*) H Holt & Co.
Robinson, Marion & Thurston, Rozetta L. Poetry for Men to Speak Chorally. 148p. 3.00 (*0-686-15465-7*) Expression.
***Robinson, Mark.** Against Design. 56p. 2000. pap. 18.00 (*0-88454-094-4*) U of Pa Contemp Art.
Robinson, Mark, ed. Corruption & Development. LC 98-16986. 166p. 1998. 39.50 (*0-7146-4902-3*, Pub. by F Cass Pubs); pap. 22.50 (*0-7146-4458-7*, Pub. by F Cass Pubs) Intl Spec Bk.
Robinson, Mark & Riddell, Roger. Working for the Poor: NGOs & Rural Poverty Alleviation. (Illus.). 316p. 1996. text 65.00 (*0-19-823330-2*) OUP.
Robinson, Mark & White, Gordon, eds. Democratic Developmental State: Political & Institutional Design. LC 98-35998. (Oxford Studies in Democratization). 368p. 1999. text 79.00 (*0-19-829382-8*) OUP.
Robinson, Mark, et al. The Role of Civic Organizations in the Provision of Social Services: Towards Synergy LC 98-213893. (Research for Action Ser.). vii, 52p. 1997. write for info. (*952-9520-61-1*) UN.
Robinson, Mark, jt. auth. see Shaffer, Jan.
Robinson, Mark A. Rough Water Power Boating. 268p. (C). 1990. 90.00 (*0-7316-4701-7*, Pub. by Pascoe Pub) St Mut.
Robinson, Marlene M. Grow Your Own Crystals: Discover the World of Crystals & How to Grow Them! (Illus.). 80p. (J). (gr. 2-8). 1996. 18.95 (*1-56138-600-6*) Running Pr.
Robinson, Marlyn & Simoni, Christopher, eds. The Flag & the Law: A Documentary History of the Treatment of the American Flag by the Supreme Court & Congress, 3 vols., Set. LC 93-12055. 7410p. 1993. ring bd. 395.00 (*0-89941-834-1*, 306430) W S Hein.
Robinson, Marsha. Hamlet in the 1980s: An Annotated Bibliography. Godshalk, William L., ed. (Garland Shakespeare Bibliographies Ser.). 600p. Date not set. text 90.00 (*0-8153-1161-3*) Garland.
Robinson, Marsha, jt. auth. see Jarest, Jackie.
Robinson, Martha. The Zoo at Night. LC 94-12773. (Illus.). 32p. (J). (ps-3). 1995. mass mkt. 16.00 (*0-689-50608-2*) McElderry Bks.
Robinson, Martha H. Helen Erskine. LC 74-164574. (American Fiction Reprint Ser.). 1977. reprint ed. 24.95 (*0-8369-7051-9*) Ayer.
Robinson, Martin. Old Letter Boxes. 1989. pap. 25.00 (*0-85263-846-9*, Pub. by Shire Pubns) St Mut.
— Sacred Places, Pilgrim Paths: An Anthology of Pilgrimage. 1997. 14.00 (*0-551-03101-8*, Pub. by M Pickering) Harper SF.
Robinson, Martin, jt. auth. see Isbister, Nick.
Robinson, Martin, tr. see Drieu La Rochelle, Pierre.
***Robinson, Martyn.** A Field Guide to Frogs of Australia: From Port Augusta to Fraser Island Including Tasmania. 112p. 1998. pap. 19.95 (*1-876334-19-3*) New Holland.
Robinson, Mary. The Amazing Valvano & the Mystery of the Hooded Rat. 160p. (J). (gr. 5). 1990. pap. 2.75 (*0-380-70713-6*, Avon Bks) Morrow Avon.
— Beloved, Notes. (Cliffs Notes Ser.). 104p. 1993. pap. 4.95 (*0-8220-0227-2*, Cliff) IDG Bks.
— Give It up, Mom. 144p. (J). (gr. 4). 1992. pap. 2.99 (*0-380-71126-5*, Avon Bks) Morrow Avon.
— I Know Why the Caged Bird Sings Notes. (Cliffs Notes Ser.). (Illus.). 72p. (Orig.). 1992. pap. text 4.95 (*0-8220-0641-3*, Cliff) IDG Bks.
— Letter to the Women of England on the Injustice of Mental Subordination 1799. LC 97-28632. (Revolution & Romanticism Ser.). 116p. 1998. 55.00 (*1-85477-211-2*) Continuum.
***Robinson, Mary.** Mary Robinson: Selected Poems. Pascoe, Judith, ed. 1999. text 24.95 (*1-55111-317-1*) Broadview.
Robinson, Mary. Mary Robinson: Selected Poems. Pascoe, Judith, ed. (Literary Texts Ser.). 450p. 1999. pap. 12.95 (*1-55111-201-9*) Broadview Pr.
— Poems, 1791. LC 94-29215. (Revolution & Romanticism Ser.). 262p. 1994. 55.00 (*1-85477-191-4*) Continuum.
— Sappho & Phaon: In a Series of Legitimate Sonnets (1796) fac. ed. LC 95-14726. (Scholars' Facsimiles & Reprints Ser.: Vol. 494). 122p. 1995. 50.00 (*0-8201-1494-4*) Schol Facsimiles.
— Two, But Not Two: Inspired Poems. 24p. 1996. pap. 7.00 (*0-8059-3860-5*) Dorrance.
Robinson, Mary, frwd. A Women's World: Beyond the Headlines. 128p. 1996. pap. 12.95 (*0-85598-349-3*, Pub. by Oxfam Pub) Stylus Pub VA.
Robinson, Mary A. Alpines: Step by Step to Growing Success. (Crowood Gardening Guides Ser.). (Illus.). 128p. 1992. pap. 17.95 (*1-85223-669-8*, Pub. by Cro1wood) Trafalgar.
— Primulas: The Complete Guide. (Illus.). 272p. 1994. pap. 22.95 (*1-85223-811-9*, Pub. by Cro1wood) Trafalgar.
— War of 1812. LC 97-77858. (Perspectives on History Ser.: Pt. III). 64p. (YA). (gr. 5-12). 1998. pap. 6.95 (*1-57960-007-7*) Disc Enter Ltd.
Robinson, Mary A., ed. The French & Indian War: Prelude to American Independence. LC 96-86734. (Perspectives on History Ser.: Pt. II). (Illus.). 64p. 1996. pap. 6.95 (*1-878668-82-X*) Disc Enter Ltd.
Robinson, Mary Alice B., ed. The Spanish American War: America Emerges As a World Power. LC 97-78305. (Perspectives on History Ser.: Pt. III). (Illus.). 64p. pap. 6.95 (*1-57960-015-8*) Disc Enter Ltd.
Robinson, Mary E. Newell D. Goff: The Life of a Young Entrepreneur at the Turn of the Twentieth Century. LC 92-27885. (Illus.). 1992. 9.95 (*0-914659-57-X*) Phoenix Pub.
Robinson-Masters, Nancy. Kansas. LC 99-12210. (America the Beautiful Ser.). 144p. (YA). (gr. 5-8). 1999. 32.00 (*0-516-20993-0*) Childrens.
Robinson, Matthew, jt. auth. see Vorobiev, Pavel.
***Robinson, Matthew J.** Making the Games Happen: Profiles of Sport Management Professionals. LC 00-40605. 2000. write for info. (*0-8342-1796-1*) Aspen Pub.
***Robinson, Maureen K.** The Chief Executive's Role in Developing the Board. (Nonprofit Governance Ser.: No. 201). 16p. 1998. pap. 12.00 (*0-925299-85-5*) Natl Ctr Nonprofit.
Robinson, Maureen K. Developing the Nonprofit Board: Strategies for Educating & Motivating Board Members. 16p. 1994. pap. text 12.00 (*0-925299-33-2*) Natl Ctr Nonprofit.
***Robinson, Maureen K.** Nonprofit Boards That Work: The End of One-Size-Fits All Governance. 224p. 2000. text 29.95 (*0-471-35432-5*) Wiley.
Robinson, Maxx. It Will Soon Be Dark: How Parent's Words Create Life Scripts. large type ed. (Illus.). x, 288p. (Orig.). 1997. mass mkt. 24.95 (*1-891014-02-1*) Cardinal Books.
— New Secrets for Acquiring Wealth - & Keeping It! It's Your Personality, Stupid! LC 97-69566. (Illus.). 256p. (Orig.). 1999. mass mkt. 19.95 (*1-891014-03-X*) Cardinal Books.
— So, You Want to Go into Real Estate? The Source of All Wealth. Armstrong, Milton, ed. LC 97-92406. (Illus.). 288p. (Orig.). 1998. 29.95 (*1-891014-06-4*, Birdie) Cardinal Books.
— So, You Want to Go into Real Estate? The Source of All Wealth. Armstrong, Milton, ed. LC 97-92406. (Illus.). 304p. (Orig.). 1999. per. 24.95 (*1-891014-01-3*, Birdie) Cardinal Books.
— This, You Won't Believe! Adventures of an Entrepreneur. LC 97-92408. (Illus.). ix, 288p. (Orig.). 1998. per. 19.95 (*1-891014-00-5*, 1) Cardinal Books.
Robinson, Maxx, jt. auth. see Benson, Floyd.
Robinson, Mei Li. The Kitchen God's Wife Notes. (Cliffs Notes Ser.). (Illus.). 104p. (C). 1996. pap. text, student ed. 4.50 (*0-8220-0712-6*, Cliff) IDG Bks.
Robinson, MeiLi. Farewell to Manzanar Notes. (Cliffs Notes Ser.). 80p. (Orig.). 1994. pap. 4.95 (*0-8220-0463-1*, Cliff) IDG Bks.
Robinson, Michael. Giovanni Paisiello (1740-1816) Vol. II: A Thematic Catalogue of His Music, Non-Dramatic Works by Michael Robinson & Ulrike Hoffman. (Thematic Catalogues Ser.). 1994. lib. bdg. 86.00 (*0-945193-60-2*) Pendragon NY.
***Robinson, Michael.** Nordic Letters, 1870-1910. 422p. 2000. 59.95 (*1-870041-39-9*, Pub. by Norvik Pr) Dufour.
Robinson, Michael. Strindberg & Autobiography: Writing & Reading Life. LC 87-62756. 192p. (Orig.). 1986. pap. 23.00 (*1-870041-00-3*, Pub. by Norvik Pr) Dufour.
Robinson, Michael, ed. Strindberg & Genre. (Norvik Press Series A: No. 9). 297p. 1991. 45.00 (*1-870041-18-6*, Pub. by Norvik Pr) Dufour.
Robinson, Michael & Hofmann, Ulrike. Giovanni Paisiello (1740-1816) A Thematic Catalogue of His Music Vol. I: The Dramatic Works. LC 90-7273. (Thematic Catalogues Ser.: No. 15). (Illus.). 400p. 1991. lib. bdg. 120.00 (*0-918728-75-4*) Pendragon NY.
Robinson, Michael, ed. see Strindberg, August.
Robinson, Michael, ed. & tr. see Strindberg, August.
Robinson, Michael, tr. see Behne, Adolf.
Robinson, Michael C., ed. see Stewart, J. David & Buehler, Dan Y.
Robinson, Michael D. Eternity & Freedom: A Critical Analysis of Divine Timelessness As a Solution to the Foreknowledge - Free Will Debate. LC 95-3456. 266p. (C). 1995. lib. bdg. 48.00 (*0-8191-9895-1*) U Pr of Amer.
Robinson, Michael E., jt. auth. see Shin, Gi-Wook.
Robinson, Michael H. & Challinor, David. Zoo Animals: A Smithsonian Guide. LC 94-48288. (Illus.). 256p. (J). 1995. 24.95 (*0-02-860406-7*); 18.00 (*0-02-860407-5*) Macmillan.
Robinson, Michael J., et al. Over the Wire & on TV: CBS & UPI in Campaign '80. LC 81-66977. 350p. 1983. 17.50 (*0-87154-722-8*) Russell Sage.
Robinson, Mike. Fighting Skills of the SAS. 1998. 22.95 (*0-9666771-2-9*) Lewis Intl Inc.
***Robinson, Mike & Boniface, Priscilla.** Tourism & Cultural Conflicts. LC 98-8604. 328p. 1999. 85.00 (*0-85199-272-2*) OUP.
Robinson, Minnie M. Minnie Mae: My Story. LC 96-17295. (Life Stories Ser.). 62p. (Orig.). 1996. pap. 3.95 (*1-56212-181-2*) CRC Pubns.
Robinson-Mitzel, Edith. Mother's Recipes Seasoned with Memories. (Seasoned with Memories Ser.: Vol. 1). (Illus.). 120p. 1991. 12.50 (*0-9628852-0-7*) Twinberry.
Robinson, Morgan P. Virginia Counties: Those Resulting from Virginia Legislation. (Illus.). 283p. 1992. reprint ed. 18.00 (*0-8063-1335-8*, 4985) Genealog Pub.
***Robinson, Morgan P.** Virginia Counties: Those Resulting from Virginia Legislation. 292p. 1999. reprint ed. pap. 24.50 (*0-7884-1244-2*, R511) Heritage Bk.
Robinson, Muriel. Children Reading Print & Television Narrative: It Always Ends at the Exciting Bit. LC 97-207991. 208p. 1997. 79.95 (*0-7507-0682-1*, Falmer Pr); pap. 27.95 (*0-7507-0636-8*, Falmer Pr) Taylor & Francis.
Robinson, Myles & Pace, Kathleen. Biology Start Up. 2nd ed. 8p. (C). 1995. text. write for info. (*0-697-27227-3*, WCB McGr Hill) McGrw-H Hghr Educ.
Robinson, N. Edward. Current Therapy in Equine Medicine. 4th ed. Bralow, Lisette, ed. (Illus.). 736p. 1997. text 95.00 (*0-7216-2633-5*, W B Saunders Co) Harcrt Hlth Sci Grp.
Robinson, N. Edward, ed. Current Therapy in Equine Medicine, Vol. 3. (Illus.). 881p. 1991. text 126.00 (*0-7216-3475-3*, W B Saunders Co) Harcrt Hlth Sci Grp.
Robinson, N. F. Monasticism in the Orthodox Church. LC 72-131506. reprint ed. 27.50 (*0-404-05375-0*) AMS Pr.
— Montasticism in the Orthodox Churches. 175p. 1998. reprint ed. pap. 15.95 (*1-886412-25-1*) Preserv Press.
***Robinson, Nancy A., ed.** Touched by Adoption: Stories, Letters & Poems. xi, 352p. 2000. pap. 19.95 (*0-9673363-0-9*) Grn River Pr.
Robinson, Nancy K. Angela & the Broken Heart. 144p. (J). (gr. 4-6). 1991. 12.95 (*0-590-43212-5*, Scholastic Hardcover) Scholastic Inc.
— Countess Veronica. 176p. (J). (gr. 4-6). 1994. 13.95 (*0-590-44485-9*, Scholastic Hardcover) Scholastic Inc.
— Countess Veronica. (J). 1996. pap. text 3.50 (*0-590-44486-7*) Scholastic Inc.
Robinson, Nancy K. Countess Veronica. LC 93-1801. (J). 1994. 8.60 (*0-606-09163-7*, Pub. by Turtleback) Demco.
Robinson, Nancy K. The Ghost of Whispering Rock. (J). (gr. 2-5). 1996. pap. 3.50 (*0-671-86952-3*) PB.
— Ghost of Whispering Rock. LC 92-52856. 1996. 8.60 (*0-606-09317-6*, Pub. by Turtleback) Demco.
— Just Plain Cat. LC 82-18258. 128p. (Orig.). (J). (gr. 3-6). 1984. lib. bdg. 13.95 (*0-02-777350-7*, Four Winds Pr) S&S Childrens.
— Just Plain Cat. 128p. (Orig.). (J). (gr. 4-6). 1992. pap. 3.50 (*0-590-45850-7*, Apple Paperbacks) Scholastic Inc.
— Mom, You're Fired! 112p. (Orig.). (J). (gr. 4-6). 1992. pap. 3.50 (*0-590-44903-6*, Apple Paperbacks) Scholastic Inc.
— Wendy on the Warpath. LC 93-32739. (J). (gr. 3 up). 1994. 13.95 (*0-590-45571-0*) Scholastic Inc.
Robinson, Natalie M., jt. auth. see Hardy, Edward.
Robinson, Neal. Christ in Islam & Christianity. LC 90-36383. 248p. (C). 1991. text 21.50 (*0-7914-0558-3*) State U NY Pr.
Robinson, Neal. Discovering the Qur'an: A Contemporary Approach to a Veiled Text. 1997. pap. 30.00 (*0-334-02649-0*) TPI PA.
Robinson, Neal. Islam: A Concise Introduction. 256p. 1998. 75.00 (*0-7007-1103-1*, Pub. by Curzon Pr Ltd); pap. 29.95 (*0-7007-1100-7*, Pub. by Curzon Pr Ltd) Paul & Co Pubs.
— Islam: A Concise Introduction. LC 98-54856. (Illus.). 197p. 1999. pap. 18.95 (*0-87840-224-1*) Georgetown U Pr.
— Simple Guide to Islam. pap. write for info. (*1-86034-013-X*, Pub. by Global Bks) Midpt Trade.
Robinson, Neal, ed. The Saying Of Muhammad. LC 98-4318. 64p. 1998. reprint ed. pap. 5.95 (*0-88001-641-8*) HarpC.
Robinson, Neil. Ideology & the Collapse of the Soviet System: A Critical History of Soviet Ideological Discourse. LC 94-48418. (Studies of Communism in Transition). 240p. 1995. 95.00 (*1-85898-167-0*) E Elgar.
***Robinson, Neil.** Institutions & Political Change in Russia LC 99-44142. 2000. text 65.00 (*0-312-22925-9*) St Martin.
— Lion of Scotland. (Illus.). 156p. 1999. pap. 13.95 (*1-84158-009-0*, Pub. by Birlinn Ltd) Dufour.
Robinson, Nicholas A. Environmental Law Lexicon. 300p. 1992. ring bd. 75.00 (*0-317-05396-5*, 00618) NY Law Pub.
— Environmental Regulation of Real Property. 1200p. 1986. reprint ed. 98.00 (*0-318-21431-8*, 00575) NY Law Pub.
Robinson, Nicholas A., ed. Comparative Environmental Law & Regulation, 2 vols. LC 96-48259. 1996. ring bd. 300.00 (*0-379-01251-0*) Oceana.
— New York Environmental Law. LC 92-53528. 1000p. 1992. 110.00 (*0-942954-48-3*) NYS Bar.
Robinson, Nicholas A., et al, eds. Agenda Twenty-One & the UNCED Proceedings, 6 vols., Set. LC 92-61109. (International Protection of the Environment, 3rd Ser.). 1993. 450.00 (*0-379-10350-8*) Oceana.
Robinson, Nicholas A., jt. ed. see Burhenne, Wolfgang E.
Robinson, Nicholas A., ed. see New York State Bar Association Staff.
Robinson, Nicholas K. Edmund Burke: A Life in Caricature. LC 96-9817. (Illus.). 240p. 1996. 50.00 (*0-300-06801-8*) Yale U Pr.
Robinson, Nick. Absolute Beginner's Origami: The Simple Three-Stage Guide to Creating Expert Origami. (Illus.). 96p. 1999. pap. text 22.50 (*0-8230-0054-0*) Watsn-Guptill.
— Paper Airplanes. 1991. 12.98 (*1-55521-724-9*) Bk Sales Inc.
— The Planting Design Handbook. 1992. 87.95 (*0-566-09008-2*, Pub. by Gower) Ashgate Pub Co.
— Super Simple Paper Airplanes: Step-by-Step Instructions to Make Paper Planes That Really Fly. LC 98-214522. (Illus.). 128p. (J). (gr. 3-7). 1998. pap. 12.95 (*0-8069-3779-3*) Sterling.
Robinson, Nina H. Aunt Dice: The Story of a Faithful Slave. LC 72-2036. (Black Heritage Library Collection). 1977. reprint ed. 17.95 (*0-8369-9058-7*) Ayer.
Robinson North, Norma & Gillette, M. L. Studying the pH of Strong Acid, Weak Acid, Salt, & Buffer Solutions. Stanitski, C. L., ed. (Modular Laboratory Program in Chemistry Ser.). 12p. (C). 1998. pap. text 1.50 (*0-87540-499-5*, EQUL 499) Chem Educ Res.
Robinson, O., ed. see R. C. C. Pilotage Foundation/SHOM Staff.
Robinson, O. A. The Pretty Good, Really Cheap Paperback Logic Book. 1998. pap. 6.50 (*0-934135-03-7*) Klare Ltd.
Robinson, O. A. & Bien, Joseph, eds. Contemporary Social Thought. (Orig.). (C). 1989. pap. write for info. (*0-934135-02-9*) Klare Ltd.
— Leviathan. (Orig.). 1986. pap. write for info. (*0-934135-00-2*) Klare Ltd.
Robinson, O. F. Ancient Rome: City Planning & Administration. 264p. (C). 1992. 75.00 (*0-415-02234-7*, A6063) Routledge.
— Ancient Rome: City Planning & Administration. (Illus.). 272p. (C). 1994. pap. 25.99 (*0-415-10618-4*, B3813) Routledge.
— The Criminal Law of Ancient Rome. LC 95-24849. 212p. (C). 1996. text 40.00 (*0-8018-5318-4*) Johns Hopkins.
— The Sources of Roman Law: Problems & Methods for Ancient Historians. LC 96-7551. (Approaching the Ancient World Ser.). 168p. (C). 1996. 60.00 (*0-415-08994-8*); pap. 20.99 (*0-415-08995-6*) Routledge.
Robinson, O. F., ed. The Register of Walter Bronescombe, Bishop of Exeter, 1258-1280, No. I. (Canterbury & York Society Ser.: Vol. 82). 208p. (C). 1995. 45.00 (*0-907239-51-X*, Canterbury & York Soc) Boydell & Brewer.

R

An Asterisk (*) at the beginning of an entry indicates that the title is appearing for the first time.

R

***Robinson, O. F., ed.** The Register of Walter Bronescombe, Bishop of Exeter, 1258-80, Vol. 2. (Canterbury & York Society Ser.). 192p. 1999. 45.00 (0-907239-57-9, Canterbury & York Soc) Boydell & Brewer.

Robinson, O. F., jt. intro. see Gaius, Gordon W.

Robinson, Olive, ed. The Peachtree Garden Book: Gardening in the Southeast. 5th rev. ed. LC 96-38994. (Illus.). 112p. 1997. 7.95 (1-56145-144-4) Peachtree Pubs.

Robinson, Orrin W. Old English & Its Closest Relatives: A Survey of the Earliest Germanic Languages. (Illus.). 304p. (C). 1992. 47.50 (0-8047-1454-1) Stanford U Pr.

— Old English & Its Closest Relatives: A Survey of the Earliest Germanic Languages. 304p. (C). 1993. pap. 16.95 (0-8047-2221-8) Stanford U Pr.

Robinson, Osborne. Vocabulary Development for Science & Technology. 112p. 1989. spiral bd. 13.95 (0-8403-5292-1) Kendall-Hunt.

Robinson, Oz. Atlantic Spain & Portugal: La Coruna to Gibraltar. 448p. 1996. 125.00 (0-9503742-8-8, Pub. by Cruising Assn) St Mut.

— Atlantic Spain & Portugal: La Coruna to Gibraltar. 230p. 2000. 125.00 (0-85288-405-2, Pub. by Laurie Norie & Wilson Ltd) St Mut.

***Robinson, Oz, ed.** Chile: Africa Desert to Tierra del Fuego. 200p. 1999. pap. 150.00 (0-85288-408-7, Pub. by Laurie Norie & Wilson Ltd) St Mut.

Robinson, Oz, ed. see R. C. C. Pilotage Foundation Staff.

Robinson, P. & Rawnsley, J. The Metaplectic Representation, MPC Structures & Geometric Quantization. LC 89-15191. (Memoirs Ser.: Vol. 81/410). 93p. 1989. pap. 18.00 (0-8218-2473-2, MEMO/81/410) Am Math.

Robinson, P. C. Declan's Night. 224p. (Orig.). 1992. pap. 12.95 (1-881333-01-9) White Mount Pubns.

Robinson, P. J., jt. auth. see Henderson-Sellers, A.

Robinson, P. K. Organizational Strategies for Older Workers. (Work in America Institute Studies in Productivity: No. 31). (Illus.). 36p. pap. 39.00 (0-317-66850-1, Pergamon Pr) Elsevier.

Robinson, P. Neville & Hall, George M., eds. How to Survive in Anaesthesia. 172p. 1997. pap. 35.00 (0-7279-1066-3, Pub. by BMJ Pub) Login Brothers Bk Co.

Robinson, P. Stuart. The Politics of International Crisis Escalation. LC 95-62324. 224p. 1996. text 65.00 (1-86064-064-8, Pub. by I B T) St Martin.

Robinson, Pam. A Manual of Bedfordshire Lace. 74p. 1987. pap. 24.50 (0-903585-20-0) Robin & Russ.

***Robinson, Pamela & Schiff, Nadine.** Career Project. 2001. pap. 14.95 (0-7434-0783-0, PB Trade Paper) PB.

Robinson, Pamela & Zim, Rivkah. Of the Making of Books: Medieval Manuscripts, Their Scribes & Readers. LC 96-51680. 344p. 1997. text 118.95 (1-85928-079-X, Pub. by Scolar Pr) Ashgate Pub Co.

Robinson, Pamela, jt. auth. see Smithers, Alan.

Robinson, Pashonia S. Bad by Myself. 130p. 1999. pap. 11.95 (0-9666100-0-8, 0-000-1) Black Ink.

***Robinson, Pashonia S.** The Other Woman. (Illus.). 152p. 1999. pap. 11.95 (0-9666100-2-4) Black Ink.

Robinson, Patricia. Living Life Well: New Strategies for Hard Times. (Illus.). 109p. (Orig.). 1996. pap., wbk. ed. 19.95 (1-878978-27-6) Context Pr.

— Love & Death in Charleston. LC 98-96228. 192p. 1998. 18.95 (0-8034-9306-1, Avalon Bks) Bouregy.

Robinson, Patricia, et al. Treating Depression in Primary Care: A Manual for Primary Care & Mental Health Providers. (Illus.). 265p. (Orig.). (C). 1996. pap. 42.95 (1-878978-26-8) Context Pr.

Robinson, Patricia, tr. see Mori, Takeo & Milenkovic, Dragen.

***Robinson, Patricia A. & Etter, Ryn.** Writing & Designing Manuals: Operator Manuals, Service & Maintenance Manuals for International Markets. 3rd ed. LC 99-86267. (Illus.). 224p. 2000. boxed set 59.95 (1-56670-378-6) Lewis Pubs.

Robinson, Patricia A., jt. auth. see Schoff, Gretchen H.

Robinson, Patrick. H. M. S. Unseen. LC 98-42775. 448p. 1999. 25.00 (0-06-019315-8) HarpC.

— H. M. S. Unseen. 528p. 2000. mass mkt. 7.50 (0-06-109801-9) HarpC.

***Robinson, Patrick.** HMS Unseen: Mccallum,&David, Set. 1999. audio 25.00 (0-694-52133-7) HarperAudio.

Robinson, Patrick. Kilo Class. LC 97-51172. 484p. 1998. 25.00 (0-06-019129-5) HarpC.

— Kilo Class. 519p. 2000. mass mkt. 7.50 (0-06-109685-7) HarpC.

***Robinson, Patrick.** Kilo Class: Lang,&Stephen, Set. abr. ed. 1998. audio. write for info. (0-694-51978-2, AD15R, Pub. by HarperAudio) Lndmrk Audiobks.

Robinson, Patrick. Nimitz Class. 2000. mass mkt. 6.99 (0-06-109594-X, Harp PBks) HarpC.

***Robinson, Patrick.** Nimitz Class: Export Edition. 528p. 1998. mass mkt. 6.99 (0-06-109684-9) HarpC.

— Nimitz Class: Sanders,&Jay O. abr. ed. 1997. audio 18.00 (0-694-51799-2, CPN 2641) HarperAudio.

— U.S.S. Seawolf. 448p. 2000. 25.00 (0-06-019630-0) HarpC.

— U.S.S. Seawolf. large type ed. (Illus.). 592p. 2000. pap. 25.00 (0-06-019707-2) HarpC.

Robinson, Patrick, jt. auth. see Woodward, Sandy.

Robinson, Paul. Gay Lives: Homosexual Autobiography from John Addington Symonds to Paul Monette. LC 98-24460. (Illus.). 428p. 1999. 30.00 (0-226-72180-9) U Ch Pr.

— Instant Print Estimator: Offset Prices That Reflect Your Costs. rev. ed. (Illus.). 550p. 1981. ring bd. 69.95 (0-9607084-0-5) Cushman Pubs.

— Ludwig Van Beethoven: Fidelio. (Cambridge Opera Handbooks Ser.). 202p. (C). 1996. text 59.95 (0-521-45221-X) Cambridge U Pr.

— Ludwig Van Beethoven: Fidelio. (Cambridge Opera Handbooks Ser.). (Illus.). 202p. (C). 1996. pap. text 18.95 (0-521-45852-8) Cambridge U Pr.

— Operas & Ideas: From Mozart to Strauss. LC 86-47637. 288p. 1986. pap. text 15.95 (0-8014-9428-1) Cornell U Pr.

***Robinson, Paul.** Tooth Extraction - A Practical Guide. (Illus.). 144p. 2000. pap. 30.00 (0-7236-1071-1) Buttrwrth-Heinemann.

Robinson, Paul, jt. auth. see Plymen, Roger.

Robinson, Paul A. The Freudian Left: Wilhelm Reich, Geza Roheim, Herbert Marcuse. fac. ed. LC 89-28749. 274p. 1990. reprint ed. pap. 85.00 (0-608-01018-9, 206187600012) Bks Demand.

Robinson, Paul H. Criminal Law. (Textbook Ser.). 880p. 1997. boxed set 40.95 (1-56706-495-7, 64957) Panel Pubs.

— Criminal Law Defenses, Vol. 1 & 2. 784p. 1984. write for info. (0-318-57626-0); text 115.00 (0-314-81513-9) West Pub.

— Fundamentals of Criminal Law. 2nd ed. 864p. 1995. teacher ed. write for info. (0-316-75135-9, 51359) Aspen Law.

— Justice, Liability & Blame: Community Views & the Criminal Law. (New Directions in Social Psychology Ser.). 328p. (C). 1996. pap. text 26.00 (0-8133-3281-8, Pub. by Westview) HarpC.

— Structure & Function in Criminal Law. LC 97-8004. (Oxford Monographs on Criminal Law & Justice). 286p. 1997. text 85.00 (0-19-825886-0) OUP.

— Would You Convict? 17 Cases That Challenged the Law. LC 99-6451. 320p. 1999. 28.95 (0-8147-7530-6) NYU Pr.

Robinson, Paul W. Freud & His Critics. LC 92-12935. (C). 1993. 35.00 (0-520-08029-7, Pub. by U CA Pr) Cal Prin Full Svc.

Robinson, Pauline K. Organizational Strategies for Older Workers. (Studies in Productivity: Vol. 31). 88p. 1983. pap. 55.00 (0-08-030954-2) Work in Amer.

Robinson, Pearl T. & Skinner, Elliott P., eds. Transformation & Resiliency in Africa. LC 82-23211. 336p. 1982. 21.95 (0-88258-054-X) Howard U Pr.

Robinson, Percy. Handel & His Orbit. LC 79-13828. (Music Reprint Ser.). 1979. reprint ed. lib. bdg. 35.00 (0-306-79522-1) Da Capo.

Robinson, Percy J., tr. see Du Creux, Francois.

Robinson, Peter. The American Horticultural Society Complete Guide to Water Gardening: Design Construction, Planting, Maintenance. LC 96-30989. (AHS Practical Guides Ser.). 216p. 1997. 34.95 (0-7894-1478-3) DK Pub Inc.

— Blood at the Root: An Inspector Banks Mystery. (Inspector Banks Mystery Ser.: No. 9). 320p. 1998. mass mkt. 5.99 (0-380-79476-4, Avon Bks) Morrow Avon.

Robinson, Peter. Caedmons Song. pap. write for info. (0-14-013290-2) Penguin Putnam.

Robinson, Peter. Caedmon's Song. large type ed. 419p. 1993. 27.99 (0-7505-0347-5, Pub. by Mgna Lrg Print) Ulverscroft.

***Robinson, Peter.** Cold Is the Grave: A Novel of Suspense. LC 00-37231. 384p. 2000. 24.00 (0-380-97808-3, Wm Morrow) Morrow Avon.

Robinson, Peter. Containers. LC 98-41492. (AHS Practical Guides Ser.). (Illus.). 80p. 1999. pap. 8.95 (0-7894-4152-7) DK Pub Inc.

Robinson, Peter. Dead Right. 336p. mass mkt. write for info. (0-14-026716-6) Penguin Putnam.

— A Dedicated Man. 352p. 1999. mass mkt. 6.99 (0-380-71645-3, Avon Bks) Morrow Avon.

— A Dedicated Man. pap. write for info. (0-14-009665-5) Penguin Putnam.

Robinson, Peter. Final Account: An Inspector Banks Mystery. LC 95-1381. 320p. 1995. pap. 21.95 (0-425-14935-8, Prime Crime) Berkley Pub.

Robinson, Peter. Final Account: An Inspector Banks Mystery. mass mkt. write for info. (0-14-024185-X) Penguin Putnam.

Robinson, Peter. Final Account: An Inspector Banks Mystery. large type ed. 502p. 1996. pap. 20.95 (0-7862-0611-X) Thorndike Pr.

— Final Account: An Inspector Banks Mystery. 352p. 1996. reprint ed. mass mkt. 5.99 (0-425-15382-7) Berkley Pub.

— Full Employment in Britain in the Nineteen Nineties: Lessons from Other Industrial Nations. (Campaign for Work Ser.). 235p. 1991. text 82.95 (1-85628-124-8, Pub. by Avebry) Ashgate Pub Co.

— Gallows View: An Inspector Banks Mystery. 320p. 1997. mass mkt. 5.99 (0-425-15672-9, Prime Crime) Berkley Pub.

***Robinson, Peter.** Gallows View: An Inspector Banks Mystery. 336p. 2000. mass mkt. 6.99 (0-380-71400-0) Morrow Avon.

— Gallows View: An Inspector Banks Mystery. pap. write for info. (0-14-009663-9) Penguin Putnam.

Robinson, Peter. The Hanging Valley. 1994. mass mkt. 4.99 (0-425-14196-9) Berkley Pub.

Robinson, Peter. The Hanging Valley. pap. write for info. (0-14-011544-7) Penguin Putnam.

Robinson, Peter. The Hanging Valley. large type ed. (Magna Mystery Ser.). 406p. 1992. 25.99 (0-7505-0345-9) Ulverscroft.

— In a Dry Season. LC 98-47391. 432p. 1999. 24.00 (0-380-97581-5, Avon Bks) Morrow Avon.

***Robinson, Peter.** In a Dry Season. 480p. 2000. mass mkt. 6.99 (0-380-79477-2, Avon Bks) Morrow Avon.

Robinson, Peter. In the Circumstances: About Poems & Poets. 272p. 1992. text 90.00 (0-19-811248-3) OUP.

Robinson, Peter. Innocent Graves: An Inspector Banks Mystery. 336p. mass mkt. write for info. (0-14-025689-X) Penguin Putnam.

Robinson, Peter. Innocent Graves: An Inspector Banks Mystery. 400p. 1997. reprint ed. mass mkt. 5.99 (0-425-15779-2, Prime Crime) Berkley Pub.

***Robinson, Peter.** It's My Party: A Republican's Messy Love Affair with the GOP. 256p. 2000. 24.95 (0-446-52665-7, Pub. by Warner Bks) Little.

Robinson, Peter. A Necessary End. 320p. 1992. text 19.95 (0-684-19385-X, Scribners Ref) Mac Lib Ref.

— A Necessary End. LC 91-24521. (Inspector Banks Mystery Ser.). 352p. 2000. mass mkt. 6.99 (0-380-71946-0, Avon Bks) Morrow Avon.

Robinson, Peter. A Necessary End. pap. write for info. (0-14-011545-5) Penguin Putnam.

Robinson, Peter. A Necessary End. large type ed. 466p. 1992. 25.99 (0-7505-0343-2, Pub. by Mgna Lrg Print) Ulverscroft.

Robinson, Peter. No Cure for Love. mass mkt. write for info. (0-14-025187-1) Penguin Putnam.

Robinson, Peter. Not Safe after Dark & Other Stories. LC 99-167275. 227p. 1998. pap. 16.00 (1-885941-29-3) Crippen & Landru.

— Past Reason Hated: An Inspector Banks Mystery. (Inspector Banks Mystery Ser.). 320p. 1994. mass mkt. 5.99 (0-425-14489-5, Prime Crime) Berkley Pub.

***Robinson, Peter.** Past Reason Hated: An Inspector Banks Mystery. 384p. 2000. mass mkt. 6.99 (0-380-73328-5) Morrow Avon.

— Past Reason Hated: An Inspector Banks Mystery. mass mkt. write for info. (0-14-014842-6) Penguin Putnam.

— Pond Basics: A Step-by-Step Guide for Water Gardeners. (Illus.). 2000. pap. 11.95 (0-8069-2287-7) Sterling.

Robinson, Peter. Ponds & Water Features. LC 98-37316. (AHS Practical Guides Ser.). 80p. 1999. 8.95 (0-7894-4156-X) DK Pub Inc.

— School Days: An Essay on the Hoover Institution Conference "Choice & Vouchers - The Future of American Education?" LC 93-35680. (Essays in Public Policy Ser.: No. 45). 1993. pap. 5.00 (0-8179-5502-X) Hoover Inst Pr.

— Snapshots from Hell: The Making of an MBA. 304p. 1995. mass mkt. 12.95 (0-446-67117-7, Pub. by Warner Bks) Little.

— Unemployment & Local Labour Markets. (Campaign for Work Ser.). 125p. 1991. text 82.95 (1-85628-125-6, Pub. by Avebry) Ashgate Pub Co.

— The Water Garden: A Practical Guide to Planning & Planting. (Illus.). 128p. 1997. pap. 16.95 (0-8069-0846-7) Sterling.

— Wednesday's Child. 320p. 1995. mass mkt. 5.99 (0-425-14834-3, Prime Crime) Berkley Pub.

Robinson, Peter. Wednesday's Child. mass mkt. write for info. (0-14-017474-5) Penguin Putnam.

Robinson, Peter. Wednesday's Child. 352p. 1994. 20.00 (0-684-19644-1) S&S Trade.

— Wednesday's Child. large type ed. LC 94-19361. 476p. 1994. pap. 18.95 (0-7862-0276-9) Thorndike Pr.

Robinson, Peter, ed. Can Congress Be Fixed? (And Is It Broken?) Five Essays on Congressional Reform. LC 95-58553. (Publication Ser.: No. 428). 96p. (Orig.). (C). 1995. pap. 14.95 (0-8179-9362-2) Hoover Inst Pr.

— Liverpool Accents: Seven Poets & a City. 224p. 1997. pap. 14.95 (0-85323-671-2, Pub. by Liverpool Univ Pr) Intl Spec Bk.

Robinson, Peter, jt. auth. see Dillon, Helen.

Robinson, Peter, jt. auth. see Hesp, Paul.

Robinson, Peter, jt. ed. see Kerrigan, John.

Robinson, Peter B. & Tambunlertchai, Somsak. Africa & Asia: Can High Rates of Economic Growth be Replicated? LC 93-10021. (Occasional Papers - International Center for Economic Growth: No. 40). 1993. pap. 9.95 (1-55815-261-X) ICS Pr.

Robinson, Peter G. Marine Engineer's Guide to Fluid Flow. LC 75-25933. (Illus.). 88p. 1975. reprint ed. pap. 30.00 (0-7837-9066-X, 204981500003) Bks Demand.

Robinson, Peter J. Consciousness, Rules & Instructed Second Language Acquisition. (Theoretical Studies in Second Language Acquisition: Vol. 7). XIV, 291p. (C). 1996. text 52.95 (0-8204-3040-4) P Lang Pubng.

Robinson, Peter J., Jr. & Powell, Jonathan. Exporting with the Internet. (Business Technology Ser.). 320p. (Orig.). 1997. pap. 39.95 (0-442-02571-8, VNR) Wiley.

Robinson, Peter M. Practical Fungal Physiology. LC 78-4243. 131p. reprint ed. pap. 40.70 (0-608-18821-2, 203047300069) Bks Demand.

Robinson, Phil. Apple IIe: Step-by-Step Programming Guides, 2 Vols., I. 64p. 1984. 19.95 (0-685-08723-9) P-H.

Robinson, Philip. Perspectives on the Sociology of Education. 250p. (C). 1981. write for info. (0-318-55559-X); pap. 15.95 (0-7100-0787-6) Routledge.

Robinson, Philip E., jt. ed. see Breen, Joseph J.

Robinson, Philip J., jt. auth. see Harding, L. K.

Robinson, Phillip R. Personal Finance on Your Computer: A Starter Kit. 352p. 1995. pap., pap. text 29.95 incl. cd-rom (1-55828-420-6, MIS Pr) IDG Bks.

— Using QEMM 7.0. 2nd ed. LC 93-44151. 482p. 1994. pap. 26.95 (1-55828-349-8, MIS Pr) IDG Bks.

— Welcome to Memory Management. LC 94-17282. 89p. 1994. pap. 19.95 (1-55828-343-9, MIS Pr) IDG Bks.

— Welcome to Personal Finance on Your Computer: A Guide to Saving, Spending, Taxing & Investing with Your Computer. LC 94-37872. 350p. 1994. pap. 19.95 (1-55828-372-2, MIS Pr) IDG Bks.

Robinson, Phillip R. & McLaughlin, Brenda. Expert Systems Using Turbo Prolog. 320p. 1987. text 21.95 (0-07-881267-4) Osborne-McGraw.

Robinson, Phillip R. & Walkenbach, John. PC World 1-2-3 for Windows Complete Handbook. LC 91-75964. 680p. 1991. pap. 29.95 (1-878058-21-5) IDG Bks.

Robinson, Phyllis S. & Wickham, Randi E. Cartwheels, Therapist Guide. 5th ed. 13p. (Orig.). (C). 1993. reprint ed. pap. 4.95 (0-9627375-2-6) Jalice Pubs.

Robinson Publishing Staff. Science Fiction Stories. (J). 1997. pap. 9.99 (0-679-88527-7) Random.

Robinson, R. Gene Mapping in Laboratory Animals. Incl. Pt. A. 160p. 1972. 32.50 (0-306-37551-6, Kluwer Plenum); 1972. write for info. (0-318-55320-1, Plenum Trade) Perseus Pubng.

Robinson, R. & Stott, R. Medical Emergencies. 6th ed. 320p. 1993. pap. text 45.00 (0-7506-0897-8) Buttrwrth-Heinemann.

Robinson, R., et al. Africa & the Victorians: The Official Mind of Imperialism. 2nd ed. (C). 1997. text 25.95 (0-333-31006-3, Pub. by Macmillan) Humanities.

Robinson, R., jt. auth. see Astbury, R.

Robinson, R., jt. auth. see Schwartz, B.

Robinson, R., jt. auth. see Sporn, Philip.

Robinson, R., jt. auth. see Ulbricht, T.

Robinson, R., tr. see Van Meteren, Emanuel.

***Robinson, R. K.** Modern Dairy Technology: Advances in Milk Processing, Vol. 1. 2nd ed. 504p. 1998. 160.00 (0-8342-1357-5) Aspen Pub.

Robinson, R. K. & Tamime, A. Y., eds. Feta & Related Cheeses. 272p. 1991. 171.00 (1-85573-278-5) Am Educ Systs.

Robinson, R. K., jt. auth. see Tamime, A. Y.

Robinson, R. W., et al, eds. Glycosaminoglycans & Arterial Diseases. (Monographs on Atherosclerosis: Vol. 5). (Illus.). viii, 134p. 1975. 60.00 (3-8055-2089-1) S Karger.

Robinson, R. W. & Decker-Walters, Deena. Curcurbits. LC 96-48885. (Crop Production Science in Horticulture: No. 6). (Illus.). 240p. 1997. pap. text 40.00 (0-85199-133-5) OUP.

Robinson, R. W., jt. auth. see Likar, I. V.

Robinson, Rachael, ed. Nephrology. (Illus.). lv, 1756p. 1984. 367.00 (0-387-96072-4) Spr-Verlag.

Robinson, Rachael & Pyrus, Victoria. Live & Work in Spain & Portugal. (Live & Work Abroad Guides Ser.). 256p. (Orig.). 1997. pap. 16.95 (1-85458-061-2, Pub. by Vac Wrk Pubns) Seven Hills Bk.

Robinson, Rachel. Jackie Robinson: An Intimate Portrait. (Illus.). 240p. 1998. pap. 14.95 (0-8109-8189-0, Pub. by Abrams) Time Warner.

— Sources for the History of Greek Athletics. 289p. 1980. pap. 20.00 (0-89005-297-2) Ares.

Robinson, Rachel S. The Size of the Slave Population of Athens, No. 3--3. LC 73-10760. 136p. 1974. reprint ed. lib. bdg. 57.50 (0-8371-7034-6, ROSP, Greenwood Pr) Greenwood.

Robinson, Ralph E. & Beswick, Barbara A. Success Oriented Schools: An Educator's Handbook for the 21st Century. 328p. (Orig.). (C). 1996. pap. text 37.50 (0-7618-0255-X) U Pr of Amer.

Robinson, Randal. Unlocking Shakespeare's Language: Help for the Teacher & Student. 86p. 1988. pap. 10.95 (0-8141-5568-5) NCTE.

***Robinson, Randall.** The Debt: What America Owes to Blacks. LC 99-45728. 272p. 2000. 23.95 (0-525-94524-5, Dutt) Dutton Plume.

Robinson, Randall. Defending the Spirit: A Black Life in America. 320p. 1999. pap. 12.95 (0-452-27968-2, Plume) Dutton Plume.

Robinson, Randall N. Chemical Engineering Practice Exam Set. 3rd ed. LC 96-16474. 136p. 1996. pap. 35.95 (0-912045-94-9) Prof Pubns CA.

— Chemical Engineering Reference Manual for the PE Exam. 5th ed. LC 96-16476. 408p. 1996. 69.95 (0-912045-92-2) Prof Pubns CA.

— Solutions Manual for the Chemical Engineering Reference Manual. 5th ed. LC 96-16477. 64p. 1996. pap. 29.95 (0-912045-93-0) Prof Pubns CA.

Robinson, Randy J. It's a Wonderful Life . . . Sometimes: Answers to Other People's Problems That Sound Like Your Own. LC 96-92350. (Illus.). 364p. (Orig.). 1996. pap. 12.95 (0-9654138-0-2) R&R Publns.

Robinson, Raoul A. Return to Resistance: Breeding Crops to Reduce Pesticide Dependence. LC 95-24667. 480p. 1996. pap. 29.95 (0-932857-17-5, Pub. by Ag Access) Fertile Ground Bks.

Robinson, Ray. American Original: A Life of Will Rogers. (Illus.). 320p. 1996. 30.00 (0-19-508693-7) OUP.

— Chronicles of the Westminster Years, 1969-1987. 1988. text 25.00 (0-911009-08-6) Prestige Pubns.

— Iron Horse: Lou Gehrig in His Time. LC 90-56212. 304p. 1991. pap. 13.50 (0-06-097408-7, Perennial) HarperTrade.

— Iron Horse: Lou Gehrig in His Time. 1990. 22.50 (0-393-02857-7) Norton.

— Iron Horse: Lou Gehrig in His Time. large type ed. 478p. 1991. reprint ed. lib. bdg. 22.95 (1-56054-133-4) Thorndike Pr.

— John Finley Williamson: A Centennial Appreciation. (Orig.). 1988. pap. text 25.00 (0-911009-07-8) Prestige Pubns.

— Krzysztof Penderecki: A Guide to His Works. 35p. (Orig.). (C). 1983. pap. text 9.95 (0-911009-02-7) Prestige Pubns.

Robinson, Ray, ed. Choral Music: Norton Historical Anthology. (C). 1978. pap. text 57.00 (0-393-09062-0) Norton.

Robinson, Ray & Le Grand, Julia. Evaluating the National Health Service Reforms. (Reshaping the Public Sector Ser.: Vol. 8). 275p. (C). 1994. 34.95 (1-56000-194-1); pap. 24.95 (1-56000-796-6) Transaction Pubs.

Robinson, Ray, et al. Up Front! Becoming the Complete Choral Conductor. (Illus.). 304p. (Orig.). (C). 1994. pap. 27.95 (0-911318-19-4) E C Schirmer.

Robinson, Ray, jt. auth. see Winold, Allen.

Robinson, Ray, jt. ed. see Le Grand, Julian.

An Asterisk (*) at the beginning of an entry indicates that the title is appearing for the first time.

Robinson, Raymond A. The Alien Intent: A Dire Warning. LC 99-231736. (Illus.). 256p. 1998. pap. 12.95 (*0-7137-2732-2*) Sterling.

Robinson, Raymond H. The Growing of America, 1789-1848. 2nd ed. (Illus.). 256p. (C). 1991. pap. text 14.95 (*0-88273-171-8*) Forum Pr IL.

— Rockne of Notre Dame: The Making of a Football Legend. LC 99-13712. (Illus.). 304p. 1999. 25.00 (*0-19-510549-4*) OUP.

Robinson, Raymond S., jt. auth. see Kaufman, Harold R.

Robinson, Rebecca Y. & Petrek, Jeanne A. A Step by Step Guide to Dealing with Your Breast Cancer. LC 94-18102. (Illus.). 236p. 1994. 18.95 (*1-55972-257-6*, Birch Ln Pr) Carol Pub Group.

— Step-by-Step Guide to Dealing with Your Breast Cancer. 256p. 1996. pap. 12.95 (*0-8065-1763-8*, Citadel Pr) Carol Pub Group.

— A Step-by-Step Guide to Dealing with Your Breast Cancer. rev. ed. LC 99-20383. 304p. 1999. pap. 14.95 (*0-8065-2106-6*, Citadel Pr) Carol Pub Group.

Robinson, Reuel. History of Camden & Rockport. (Illus.). 647p. 1997. reprint ed. lib. bdg. 67.00 (*0-8328-5821-8*) Higginson Bk Co.

— History of Camden & Rockport, Maine. (Illus.). 644p. 1995. reprint ed. lib. bdg. 65.00 (*0-8328-4669-4*) Higginson Bk Co.

Robinson, Richard. Encyclopedia of Food Microbiology. (C). 1999. text 310.00 (*0-12-227072-X*); text 310.00 (*0-12-227073-8*) Acad Pr.

Robinson, Richard. Light All Night. 165p. mass mkt. 4.99 (*1-55197-015-5*) Picasso Publ.

Robinson, Richard. Light All Night. unabridged ed. 143p. 1998. pap. 11.95 (*1-892896-63-X*) Buy Books.

— "Maul" the Wilderness Creature. unabridged ed. 82p. 1998. pap. 10.95 (*0-9665678-7-0*) Buy Books.

— The Sun Dogs. unabridged ed. 182p. 1998. pap. 16.95 (*1-892896-00-1*) Buy Books.

Robinson, Richard, et al, eds. Encyclopedia of Food Microbiology, 3 vols. LC 98-87954. (Illus.). 2467p. 2000. 925.00 (*0-12-227070-3*) Acad Pr.

Robinson, Richard & Pearce, John A. Strategic Management: Formulation, Implementation & Control. 4th ed. (C). 1990. text 60.95 (*0-256-08323-1*, Irwn McGrw-H) McGrw-H Hghr Educ.

Robinson, Richard & Weiss, Arthur. Tax Planning for S Corporations. 1988. 210.00 (*0-8205-1496-9*) Bender.

Robinson, Richard, jt. auth. see Pybus, Victoria.

Robinson, Richard, tr. see Bataille, Georges.

Robinson, Richard, tr. see Jaeger, Werner W.

Robinson, Richard, tr. & comment see Aristotle.

Robinson, Richard, tr. & intro. see Aristotle.

Robinson, Richard A., ed. Treatise on Invertebrate Paleontology Pt. G: Bryoza, Vol. 1. rev. ed. 641p. 1983. 52.00 (*0-8137-3107-0*) Geol Soc.

— Treatise on Invertebrate Paleontology Pt. W, Suppl. 2: Conodonta. LC 53-12913. (Illus.). 230p. 1982. 22.00 (*0-8137-3028-7*) Geol Soc.

Robinson, Richard B., Jr. Business History of the World: A Chronology. LC 93-25476. 576p. 1993. lib. bdg. 79.50 (*0-313-26094-X*, Greenwood Pr) Greenwood.

— United States Business History, 1602-1988: A Chronology. LC 90-34102. 656p. 1990. lib. bdg. 75.00 (*0-313-26095-8*, RUB/, Greenwood Pr) Greenwood.

Robinson, Richard B., jt. auth. see Pearce, John A.

Robinson, Richard B., Jr., jt. auth. see Pearce, John A., II.

Robinson, Richard B., jt. auth. see Pearce, John A.

Robinson, Richard B., Jr., jt. auth. see Pearce, John A., II.

Robinson, Richard B., jt. auth. see Pearce, John A.

Robinson, Richard B., Jr., jt. auth. see Perce, John A., II.

Robinson, Richard D. Cases on International Technology Transfer. 369p. (Orig.). (C). 1989. teacher ed. 15.00 (*0-317-93733-2*); pap. text 27.50 (*0-317-93732-4*) Hamlin Pubns.

— Direct Foreign Investment: Costs & Benefits. LC 87-17750. 244p. 1987. 67.95 (*0-275-92717-2*, C2717, Praeger Pubs) Greenwood.

— The First Turkish Republic: A Case Study in National Development. LC 63-17210. (Harvard Middle Eastern Studies: No. 9). 379p. reprint ed. pap. 117.50 (*0-7837-2321-0*, 205740900004) Bks Demand.

— High-Level Manpower in Economic Development: The Turkish Case. LC 67-25400. (Middle Eastern Monographs: No. 17). 147p. 1967. 8.95 (*0-674-39050-4*) HUP.

— International Business Policy. LC 82-970. (Modern Management Ser.). 252p. 1982. lib. bdg. 65.00 (*0-313-23356-X*, ROINT, Greenwood Pr) Greenwood.

— The International Transfer of Technology. 280p. 1988. text 27.95 (*0-88730-139-8*, HarpBusn) HarpInfo.

— Performance Requirements for Multinational Corporations: U. S. Management Response. LC 82-22469. 200p. 1983. 57.95 (*0-275-91066-0*, C1066, Praeger Pubs) Greenwood.

— Teacher Effectiveness & Reading Instruction. LC 91-31023. (Illus.). 100p. (Orig.). (C). 1991. pap. text 14.95 (*0-927516-25-X*) ERIC-REC.

— Teaching Notes for Cases on International Technology Transfer. (Illus.). 107p. (Orig.). (C). 1988. pap. text 15.00 (*0-317-93295-0*) Hamlin Pubns.

Robinson, Richard D., ed. Foreign Capital & Technology in China. LC 87-2450. 228p. 1987. 59.95 (*0-275-92716-4*, C2716, Praeger Pubs) Greenwood.

***Robinson, Richard D., ed.** Historical Sources in U. S. Reading Education 1900-1970: An Annotated Bibliography. 2000. pap., teacher ed. 17.95 (*0-87207-271-1*, 271) Intl Reading.

Robinson, Richard D., ed. The International Communication of Technology. (International Business & Trade Ser.: Vol. 1). 288p. 1991. 58.00 (*0-8448-1655-8*, Pub. by Tay Francis Ltd) Taylor & Francis.

Robinson, Richard D., et al, eds. Issues & Trends in Literacy Education: A Source Book. 2nd ed. LC 99-17011. 342p. (C). 1999. pap. 38.00 (*0-205-29651-3*, Longwood Div) Allyn.

Robinson, Richard D., jt. auth. see McKenna, Michael C.

Robinson, Richard E. Don't Buy a Used Car! Until You Read This! (Illus.). 44p. 1986. pap. 2.95 (*0-9618898-0-2*, 73291) RER Servs.

Robinson, Richard H. The Buddhist Religion. 4th ed. LC 96-9605. (Religion Ser.). 1996. 34.95 (*0-534-20718-9*) Wadsworth Pub.

Robinson, Richard H. & Johnson, Willard L. The Buddhist Religion: A Historical Introduction. 3rd ed. 290p. (C). 1982. mass mkt. 19.50 (*0-534-01027-X*) Wadsworth Pub.

Robinson, Richard H., tr. see Cranmer-Byng, J. L., ed.

***Robinson, Richard W.** Fairbanks Cabbies. 152p. 2000. pap. 13.95 (*0-7414-0359-5*) Buy Books.

Robinson, Rick E., jt. auth. see Csikszentmihalyi, Mihaly.

Robinson, Rita. Color Your World: Using the Power of Color & Light in Your Life. Misiroglu, Gina, ed. 192p. (Orig.). 1994. pap. 10.95 (*0-87877-189-1*) Newcastle Pub.

Robinson, Rita. Friendship Book: The Art of Making & Keeping Friends. 1992. pap. 12.95 (*0-87877-173-5*) Newcastle Pub.

— Health in Your Hands: A New Look at Modern Palmistry & Your Health. Gross, Gina R., ed. (Illus.). 204p. (Orig.). 1993. pap. 12.95 (*0-87877-181-6*) Newcastle Pub.

— The Palm: A Guide to Your Hidden Potential. 128p. 1988. pap. 10.95 (*0-87877-133-6*) Newcastle Pub.

— Survivors of Suicide. (Orig.). 1992. pap. 9.95 (*0-87877-174-3*) Newcastle Pub.

— When Women Choose to Be Single. (Orig.). 1992. pap. 9.95 (*0-87877-170-0*) Newcastle Pub.

Robinson, Rita & Rutledge, Don. Center of the World: Native American Spirituality. 136p. 1992. pap. 12.95 (*0-87877-172-7*) Newcastle Pub.

Robinson, Rita & Ummel, Christine. Grand Old Hotels of Southern & Central California. LC 97-116800. (Umbrella Guides Ser.). (Illus.). 160p. 1996. pap. 12.95 (*0-945397-47-X*, Umbrella Bks) Epicenter Pr.

Robinson, Rita, ed. see Neumann, Jeff & Ruth, Romy.

Robinson, Robb. Trawling: The Rise & Fall of British Trawl Fishery. (Illus.). 272p. 1996. 59.95 (*0-85989-480-0*, Pub. by Univ Exeter Pr) Northwestern U Pr.

— Trawling: The Rise & Fall of the British Trawl Fishery. (Illus.). 230p. 1999. pap. 24.95 (*0-85989-628-5*, Pub. by Univ Exeter Pr) Northwestern U Pr.

Robinson, Robbie. F-100 Super Sabre in Color. (Fighting Colors Ser.). (Illus.). 32p. 1992. pap. 9.95 (*0-89747-284-5*, 6565) Squad Sig Pubns.

— USAFE in Color, Vol. 2. (Fighting Colors Ser.). (Illus.). 32p. 1990. pap. 9.95 (*0-89747-250-0*, 6563) Squad Sig Pubns.

Robinson, Robby, jt. ed. see Badham, Mike.

Robinson, Robert, jt. auth. see Smith, Helen.

Robinson, Robert, jt. ed. see Chao, K. C.

Robinson, Robert, ed. see Kirsch, Sylvia J.

Robinson, Robert, tr. see Montaner, Carlos.

Robinson, Robert A. Consolidated Farm Service Agency: Update on the Farm Loan Portfolio. (Illus.). 88p. (C). 1996. reprint ed. pap. text 25.00 (*0-7881-3662-3*) DIANE Pub.

— ECA Benefit Communications. (ECA Employee Benefit Communications Ser.). (Illus.). 140p. 1990. ring bd. 679.00 (*1-884780-00-8*) Phoenix Pubng.

— ECA Prospecting Kit. (ECA Benefit Communications Ser.). 19p. 1992. student ed. 24.95 (*1-884780-01-6*) Phoenix Pubng.

— ELA Salesmaker Kit. abr. ed. (ECA Benefit Communications Ser.). 82p. 1991. student ed. 89.95 (*1-884780-10-5*) Phoenix Pubng.

— Employee Enrollment Presentation. Campbell, John, ed. (ECA Benefit Communications Ser.). 1990. pap. text 10.95 incl. audio (*1-884780-09-1*) Phoenix Pubng.

— The Hidden Paycheck: Employer Sales Presentation. abr. ed. Campbell, John, ed. (ECA Benefit Communications Ser.). 1991. pap. text 10.95 incl. audio (*1-884780-08-3*) Phoenix Pubng.

— Manifesting the Life of Your Dreams. abr. ed. (Magic Magnifying Mind Ser.). 1991. pap. text 8.95 incl. audio (*1-884780-02-4*) Phoenix Pubng.

— Positive Power Thinking. abr. ed. (Magic Magnifying Mind Ser.). 1991. pap. text 7.95 incl. audio (*1-884780-03-2*) Phoenix Pubng.

Robinson, Robert B., 3rd, ed. Roanoke Rapids: The First Hundred Years, 1897-1997. LC 97-9929. 1997. 34.95 (*1-55618-160-4*) Brunswick Pub.

Robinson, Robert E., jt. auth. see Prichard, Robert W.

Robinson, Robert G. The Clinical Neuropsychiatry of Stroke: Cognitive, Behavioral & Emotional Disorders Following Vascular Brain Injury. LC 97-26484. (Illus.). 503p. (C). 1998. text 95.00 (*0-521-44234-6*) Cambridge U Pr.

Robinson, Robert G. & Yates, William R. Psychiatric Treatment of the Medically Ill. LC 99-25213. (Medical Psychiatry Ser.). (Illus.). 576p. 1999. text 195.00 (*0-8247-1958-1*) Dekker.

Robinson, Robert G., jt. ed. see Starkstein, Sergio E.

Robinson, Robert H. Clambake Sans Sand in Pots & Woks. 1983. pap. 2.95 (*0-911145-04-4*) Sussex Prints.

— The Craft of Dismantling Crabs & Other Shellfish. 96p. (Orig.). 1982. pap. 4.95 (*0-685-08789-1*) Sussex Prints.

— The Essential Book of Shellfish. LC 82-184274. (Illus.). 160p. 1983. pap. 6.95 (*0-89709-040-3*) Liberty Pub.

Robinson, Robert H., ed. see Walthers, Lynette L.

Robinson, Robert J., jt. auth. see Van Osnabrugge, Mark.

Robinson, Robert L., Jr. Blinded Veterans of the Vietnam Era. LC 74-191191. 39p. reprint ed. pap. 30.00 (*0-8357-7321-3*, 202734200055) Bks Demand.

Robinson, Robert L. Complete Course in Professional Locksmithing. LC 73-174584. (Illus.). 414p. 1973. text 68.95 (*0-911012-15-X*) Burnham Inc.

Robinson, Robert L., Jr., jt. ed. see Chao, K. C.

Robinson, Robert L., Jr., jt. ed. see Kwang Chu Chao.

Robinson, Robert R. Issues in Security Management: Thinking Critically about Security. LC 98-39732. 208p. 1999. 29.95 (*0-7506-7078-9*) Buttrwrth-Heinemann.

Robinson, Robyn & Murdoch, Patricia. Guidelines for Establishing & Maintaining Peer Support Programs in Emergency Services. 2nd ed. 84p. 1998. pap. text 12.00 (*1-883581-08-7*, ROB1) Chevron Pub.

Robinson, Rodney P., jt. auth. see Tacitus.

***Robinson, Roger.** Bangladesh: Progress Through Partnership. LC 98-36252. (Operations Evaluation Studies). 80p. 1999. pap. 22.00 (*0-8213-4293-2*, 14293) World Bank.

Robinson, Roger. Brazil. LC 98-52759. (Country Studies Ser.). 64p. 1999. 27.07 (*1-57572-892-3*) Heinemann Lib.

Robinson, Roger, ed. Katherine Mansfield: In from the Margin. LC 93-25541. 224p. (C). 1994. text 30.00 (*0-8071-1865-6*) La State U Pr.

Robinson, Roger & Wattie, Nelson, eds. The Oxford Companion to New Zealand Literature. LC 99-200843. 624p. 1999. 72.00 (*0-19-558348-5*) OUP.

Robinson, Roger J., intro. Collected Works of James Beattie, 10 vols. 4779p. (C). 1996. 1400.00 (*0-415-13326-2*) Routledge.

Robinson, Roland I. Postwar Market for State & Local Government Securities. (Studies in Capital Formation & Financing: No. 5). 251p. 1960. reprint ed. 65.30 (*0-87014-103-1*) Natl Bur Econ Res.

Robinson, Ron. Cats Are from Saturn, Dogs Are from Pluto. LC 98-92430. (Illus.). 107p. 1998. 15.95 (*0-944287-21-2*); pap. 10.95 (*0-944287-20-4*) Ex Machina.

***Robinson, Ronald.** Diamond Trump: Events Surrounding the Great Powder-House Blowup by the Man Who Lit the Fuse. Rose, Margaret, ed. LC 99-51767. 262p. 2000. 19.95 (*0-944287-24-7*) Ex Machina.

Robinson, Ronald. Tumours That Secrete Catecholamines: Their Detection & Clinical Chemistry. LC 79-41731. 144p. reprint ed. pap. 44.70 (*0-608-14064-3*, 202403400035) Bks Demand.

Robinson, Ronald, ed. see Egan, C. John, Jr.

Robinson, Ronald, ed. see Tamal Krishna Goswami & Svarupa Dasa, Ravindra.

Robinson, Ronald D., jt. auth. see Hubbard, Elaine.

Robinson, Ronald F., jt. auth. see Haniford, Beatrice.

Robinson, Ronald L., ed. see Freeman, Jerome W.

Robinson, Ronald W. Prison Hostage: The Siege of the Walls Prison in Huntsville, Texas. LC 97-42275. (Criminology Studies: Vol. 2). (Illus.). 164p. 1997. 79.95 (*0-7734-8564-3*) E Mellen.

— Stanley, the Talking Parrot. LC 89-60801. (Illus.). 22p. (Orig.). (J). (gr. 3-4). 1989. 12.95 incl. audio, flmstrp (*0-9622692-2-0*); 8.95 incl. audio (*0-9622692-1-2*); pap. 4.95 (*0-9622692-0-4*) R W Robinson.

Robinson, Rony. The Beano. 176p. 1988. 16.95 (*0-15-111229-0*) Harcourt.

Robinson, Rosa L. The Etchings of God. LC 97-72211. (Illus.). 88p. 1997. 12.95 (*0-913383-55-4*, Commwlth Bk Co) McClanahan Pub.

Robinson, Rowan. El Gran Libro del Cannabis: Guia Completa Para el Uso Ecologico, Comercial y Edicinal de la Planta Mas Extraordinaria del Mundo.Tr. of Great Book of Hemp. (SPA., Illus.). 256p. 1997. pap. 19.95 (*0-89281-585-X*, Inner Trad) Inner Tradit.

— The Great Book of Hemp: The Complete Guide to the Environmental, Commercial, & Medicinal Uses of the World's Most Extraordinary Plant. (Illus.). 256p. 1995. pap. 19.95 (*0-89281-541-8*, Park St Pr) Inner Tradit.

— The Hemp Manifesto: 101 Ways That Hemp Can Save Our World. LC 97-20759. 112p. 1997. pap. 5.95 (*0-89281-728-3*) Inner Tradit.

Robinson, Rowena. Conversion, Continuity & Change: Lived Christianity in Southern Goa. LC 97-45133. 236p. 1998. 39.95 (*81-7036-683-6*) Sage.

— Conversion, Continuity & Change: Lived Christianity in Southern Goa. LC 97-45133. 236p. (C). 1998. 39.95 (*0-7619-9229-4*) Sage.

Robinson, Rowland E. Danvis Tales: Selected Stories. Budbill, David, ed. LC 95-13841. (Hardscrabble Bks.). (Illus.). 316p. 1995. 24.95 (*0-87451-718-4*) U Pr of New Eng.

— Sam Lovel's Boy, with Forest & Stream Fables. Perkins, Llewellyn R., ed. LC 70-160949. (Short Story Index Reprint Ser.). 1977. reprint ed. 20.95 (*0-8369-3928-X*) Ayer.

— Sam Lovel's Camps: And Other Stories, Including 'In the Green Wood' Perkins, Llewellyn R., ed. LC 77-37558. (Short Story Index Reprint Ser.). 1977. reprint ed. 21.95 (*0-8369-4117-9*) Ayer.

— Uncle Lisha's Shop: Life in a Corner of Yankeeland. LC 79-96892. 187p. reprint ed. lib. bdg. 22.00 (*0-8398-1761-4*) Irvington.

— Uncle Lisha's Shop: Life in a Corner of Yankeeland. 187p. (C). 1986. reprint ed. pap. text 6.95 (*0-8290-2045-4*) Irvington.

— Vermont: A Study of Independence. LC 72-3751. (American Commonwealths Ser.: No. 14). reprint ed. 39.50 (*0-404-57214-6*) AMS Pr.

Robinson, Roxana. Georgia O'Keeffe: A Life. LC 89-45061. (Illus.). 496p. 1989. pap. 12.95 (*0-685-25760-6*, E Burlingame Bks) HarpC.

— Georgia O'Keeffe: A Life. LC 98-30944. (Illus.). 647p. 1999. reprint ed. pap. 19.95 (*0-87451-906-3*) U Pr of New Eng.

— Short Stories. 1999. pap. 17.95 (*0-670-82792-4*); pap. write for info. (*0-14-012147-1*) Viking Penguin.

— Summer Light. LC 95-32560. (Hardscrabble Bks.). 211p. 1995. reprint ed. pap. 13.95 (*0-87451-738-9*) U Pr of New Eng.

— This Is My Daughter. LC 97-34452. 416p. 1998. 25.00 (*0-679-43901-3*) Random.

***Robinson, Roxana.** This Is My Daughter: A Novel. LC 99-27173. 416p. 1999. pap. 13.00 (*0-684-86436-3*, Scribner Pap Fic) S&S Trade Pap.

Robinson, Roy. Genetics for Cat Breeders. 2nd ed. LC 77-120591. 1977. text 36.00 (*0-08-021209-3*, Pergamon Pr) Elsevier.

— Genetics for Cat Breeders. 3rd ed. (Illus.). 220p. 1991. text 47.50 (*0-08-037506-5*, Pergamon Pr) Elsevier.

— Genetics for Dog Breeders. LC 81-15891. (Illus.). 272p. 1982. text 32.00 (*0-08-025917-0*, H235, Pergamon Pr) Elsevier.

***Robinson, Roy.** Genetics for Dog Breeders. 2nd ed. 280p. 1999. text 63.00 (*0-7506-4612-8*) Buttrwrth-Heinemann.

Robinson, Roy. Genetics for Dog Breeders. 2nd ed. 1990. text 47.50 (*0-08-037492-1*, Pergamon Pr) Elsevier.

***Robinson, Roy.** The Right Way to Keep Rabbits. 128p. 2000. pap. 6.95 (*0-7160-2117-X*, Pub. by Elliot RW Bks) Midpt Trade.

***Robinson, Roy & Baglin, David.** The Right Way to Keep Hamsters. 4th ed. (Illus.). 128p. 2001. pap. 6.95 (*0-7160-2128-5*, Pub. by Elliot RW Bks) Midpt Trade.

Robinson, Roy, jt. auth. see Vella, Carolyn M.

Robinson, Russell & Althouse, Jay. Complete Choral Warm-Up Book. 1995. pap. 19.95 (*0-88284-657-4*) Alfred Pub.

Robinson, Russell & Gammond, Peter. Bluff Your Way in Music. (Bluffers Ser.). 77p. (Orig.). 1993. pap. 4.95 (*1-57143-006-7*) RDR Bks.

Robinson, Russell D. The Empowerment Cookbook: Recipes for Creating, Sustaining, or Refocusing Empowered Work Teams. LC 96-47631. 120p. 1997. text 21.95 (*0-7863-1193-2*, Irwn Prfssnl) McGraw-Hill Prof.

— An Introduction to Dynamics of Group Leadership & Organizational Change. 5th rev. ed. 316p. 1995. pap. text 27.95 (*1-877837-02-4*, Pub. by Bible Study Pr) Omnibook Co.

— An Introduction to Helping Adults Learn & Change. rev. ed. LC 95-155437. 180p. (C). 1994. pap. text 22.95 (*1-877837-28-8*, Pub. by Bible Study Pr) Omnibook Co.

— Jerusalem Journey & Other Poems. 68p. 1985. reprint ed. pap. 7.95 (*1-877837-18-0*) Bible Study Pr.

— Teaching the Scriptures: A Study Guide for Bible Students & Teachers. 6th rev. ed. (Illus.). 220p. 1993. pap. text 19.95 (*1-877837-11-3*) Bible Study Pr.

Robinson, Russell L. Getting Started with Jazz - Show Choir. (Getting Started Ser.). 44p. (Orig.). 1994. pap. 11.00 (*1-56545-044-2*, 1630) MENC.

Robinson, Russell L., ed. Preparing to Teach Music in Today's Schools: The Best of MEJ. LC 94-234103. (Illus.). 72p. reprint ed. pap. 30.00 (*0-608-20275-4*, 207153400012) Bks Demand.

Robinson, Russell M., II. Robinson on North Carolina Corporation Law. 5th ed. LC 95-81834. 1,000p. 1995. 95.00 (*1-55834-287-7*, 6660-11, MICHIE) LEXIS Pub.

— Robinson on North Carolina Corporation Law, 1998 Cumulative Supplement. 5th ed. 75p. 1998. pap. write for info. (*0-327-00619-6*, 6666315) LEXIS Pub.

***Robinson, Ruth-Ann.** Enlightened Self Interest Guide to Successful Parenting Workbook: Raising the Responsible Adults for the New Millennium. (Illus.). 53p. 1999. pap. 20.00 (*1-929010-00-1*) Epiphany IL.

— My Heavenly Happys & My Secretly Sads: A Childs Workbook. (Illus.). 56p. (J). (gr. 3-10). 1999. pap. 20.00 (*1-929010-01-X*) Epiphany IL.

Robinson, Ruth E. Buy Books Where - Sell Books Where, 1992-1993: A Directory of Out of Print Booksellers & Collectors & Their Author-Subject Specialties. 8th rev. ed. 308p. (Orig.). 1992. pap. 29.75 (*0-9603556-9-3*) Robinson Bks.

— Buy Books Where - Sell Books Where, 1994-1995: A Directory of Out of Print Booksellers & Collectors & Their Author-Subject Specialties. 9th rev. ed. 329p. (Orig.). 1994. pap. 34.95 (*0-930284-53-4*) Robinson Bks.

Robinson, Ruth E. & Farudi, Daryush. Buy Books Where - Sell Books Where, 1988-1989: A Directory of Out of Print Booksellers & Their Author-Subject Specialties. 6th rev. ed. 270p. (Orig.). 1988. pap. 29.75 (*0-317-67852-3*) Robinson Bks.

— Buy Books Where-Sell Books Where. 6th ed. 1988. 29.75 (*0-9603556-7-7*) Robinson Bks.

Robinson, Ryan J. Worlds of Eternity. 60p. 1998. pap. write for info. (*0-9663328-9-X*) R O Robinson.

Robinson, S. El Malpais, Mt. Taylor & Zuni Mountains: A Hiking Guide & History. LC 94-18694. (Coyote Bks.). (Illus.). 276p. 1994. pap. 13.95 (*0-8263-1527-5*) U of NM Pr.

Robinson, S. & Marks, T. Woven Cloth Construction. 178p. 1973. 70.00 (*0-7855-7236-8*) St Mut.

Robinson, S. & Thomson, A. M., eds. Midwives, Research & Childbirth, Vol. 3. 1994. 45.00 (*1-56593-043-6*, 0291) Singular Publishing.

— Midwives, Research & Childbirth, Vol. 4. 288p. 1995. 44.75 (*1-56593-289-7*, 0613) Singular Publishing.

Robinson, S. Betram. In Pursuit of His Glory: Maturing in the Image of Christ. 254p. 1997. pap. 12.99 (*1-56043-289-6*, Treasure Hse) Destiny Image.

Robinson, S. J., jt. auth. see Urwin, J.

Robinson, S. Scott. The Law of Game, Salmon & Freshwater Fishing in Scotland. 336p. 1990. boxed set 124.00 (*0-406-11201-0*, U.K., MICHIE) LEXIS Pub.

— The Law of Interdict. 2nd ed. LC 96-152379. 208p. 1994. boxed set 90.00 (*0-406-01485-X*, UK, MICHIE) LEXIS Pub.

R

Robinson, Sallie. Buddie & I. 56p. 1987. reprint ed. pap. 2.99 (*0-8341-1216-7*) Beacon Hill.

Robinson, Sally. Engendering the Subject: Gender & Self-Representation in Contemporary Women's Fiction. LC 90-10249. (SUNY Series in Feminist Criticism & Theory). 240p. (C). 1991. text 21.50 (*0-7914-0727-6*) State U NY Pr.

***Robinson, Sally.** Marked Men: White Masculinity in Crisis. LC 00-25916. 2000. pap. 17.50 (*0-231-11293-9*); text 49.50 (*0-231-11292-0*) Col U Pr.

Robinson, Sam. Winning Against the Odds. LC 92-29120. (Illus.). 256p. 1993. 17.50 (*0-912526-58-0*) Lib Res.

Robinson, Sandra, et al. Water, a Gift of Nature: The Story Behind the Scenery. LC 93-77028. (Illus.). 48p. (Orig.). 1993. pap. 7.95 (*0-88714-077-7*) KC Pubns.

Robinson, Sandra C. The Everywhere Bear. (Wonder Ser.). (Illus.). 64p. (J). (gr. 4-6). 1992. pap. 7.95 (*1-879373-07-6*) Roberts Rinehart.

— Expedition Yellowstone: A Mountain Adventure. (Illus.). 173p. (J). (gr. 3-7). 1986. 25.00 (*0-911797-23-8*); pap. 12.50 (*0-911797-25-4*) Roberts Rinehart.

— Last Bit Bear: A Fable. (Illus.). 48p. 1991. pap. 4.95 (*0-911797-09-2*) Roberts Rinehart.

— Mountain Lion: Puma, Panther, Painter, Cougar. (Wonder Ser.). (Illus.). 64p. (J). (gr. 4-6). 1991. pap. 7.95 (*1-879373-00-9*) Roberts Rinehart.

— The Rainstick: A Fable. LC 94-21587. (Illus.). 40p. (Orig.). (J). (gr. 2 up). 1994. pap. text 9.95 (*1-56044-284-0*) Falcon Pub Inc.

— Sea Otter, River Otter: A Story & Activity Book. LC 92-62078. (Wonder Ser.). (Illus.). 64p. (Orig.). (J). (gr. 1-6). 1993. pap. 7.95 (*1-879373-41-6*) Roberts Rinehart.

— The Wonder of Wolves: A Story & Activities. 2nd expanded rev. ed. (Illus.). 56p. 1997. pap. text 8.95 (*1-57098-123-X*) Roberts Rinehart.

Robinson, Sandra C. & Robinson, George B. In Pictures Yellowstone: The Continuing Story. (GER., Illus.). 48p. 1990. pap. 8.95 (*0-88714-762-3*) KC Pubns.

— In Pictures Yellowstone: The Continuing Story. Le Bras, Yvon, tr. (FRE., Illus.). 48p. 1990. pap. 8.95 (*0-88714-763-1*) KC Pubns.

— In Pictures Yellowstone: The Continuing Story. Petzinger, Saori, tr. (JPN., Illus.). 48p. 1990. pap. 8.95 (*0-88714-764-X*) KC Pubns.

— In Pictures Yellowstone: The Continuing Story. Marapodi, Carlos, tr. (SPA., Illus.). 48p. 1990. pap. 8.95 (*0-88714-765-8*) KC Pubns.

— In Pictures Yellowstone: The Continuing Story. Lee, Frances Y., tr. (CHI., Illus.). 48p. 1993. pap. 8.95 (*0-88714-766-6*) KC Pubns.

— In Pictures Yellowstone: The Continuing Story. (KOR., Illus.). 48p. 1993. pap. 8.95 (*0-88714-767-4*) KC Pubns.

Robinson, Sandra C., jt. auth. see Robinson, George B.

Robinson, Sara T. Kansas: Its Interior & Exterior Life. LC 77-160991. (Select Bibliographies Reprint Ser.). 1977. reprint ed. 25.95 (*0-8369-5859-4*) Ayer.

Robinson, Sarah & Thomson, Ann, eds. Midwives, Research & Childbirth, Vol. 2. 256p. 1990. pap. 34.95 (*0-412-31650-1*, A4455) Chapman & Hall.

Robinson, Scott. History Confirms Christianity: The Story of Jesus As Told by Non-Christian Writers. 42p. 1996. reprint ed. pap. 2.95 (*1-56794-129-X*, C-2146) Star Bible.

Robinson, Scott K., jt. ed. see Rothstein, Stephen I.

Robinson, Scott R., jt. ed. see Smotherman, William P.

Robinson, Serjeant. Bench & Bar: Reminiscences of One of the Last of an Ancient Race. (Illus.). xi, 327p. 1988. reprint ed. 45.00 (*0-8377-2537-2*, Rothman) W S Hein.

Robinson, Sharon P. Building Knowledge for a Nation of Learners: A Framework for Education Research 1997. (Illus.). 112p. (Orig.). (C). 1997. pap. text 35.00 (*0-7881-3997-5*) DIANE Pub.

Robinson, Sharon P. Building Knowledge for a Nation of Learners: A Framework for Education Research 1997. 118p. (Orig.). 1997. pap. 12.00 (*0-16-048944-X*) USGPO.

Robinson, Sharon P., et al. Reimagining Professional Development. 46p. 1994. pap. 12.00 (*1-56377-039-3*, SC9401) Am Assn Higher Ed.

Robinson, Sheila, jt. auth. see Wood, Frank.

Robinson, Sheila C. Along the Lewis & Clark Trail in North Dakota. 142p. 1993. pap. 8.50 (*0-9643057-0-4*) Dakota Trails.

Robinson, Sheila K. How to Open a Family Child Care Home in Rhode Island: A Practical Guide on How to Become a Family Child Care Provider & How to Start a Family Child Care Home in Rhode Island. 175p. 1994. pap. 9.95 (*0-9637673-1-3*) Napa Sonoma.

— Stanford House Staff Auxiliary Guidebook to the Bay Area: A Guide for Finding Your Way Around the Bay from Napa to Monterey. LC 93-86355. (Illus.). 170p. (Orig.). 1994. pap. 9.95 (*0-9637673-3-X*) Napa Sonoma.

Robinson, Shelagh. Huskies in Harness: A Love Story in Antarctica. 1996. pap. text 24.95 (*0-86417-726-7*, Pub. by Kangaroo Pr) Seven Hills Bk.

Robinson, Shepard D. How to Turn-Around a Troubled Company. (Illus.). 100p. (Orig.). 1979. pap. 15.00 (*0-9603502-0-9*) Ingleside.

Robinson, Shepard D., ed. Manufactured Housing: What It Is, Where It Is, How It Operates. 1988. pap. 60.00 (*0-9603502-1-7*) Ingleside.

***Robinson, Sherry.** Apache Voices: Their Stories of Survival As Told to Eve Ball. LC 99-50769. 2000. 32.95 (*0-8263-2162-3*) U of NM Pr.

Robinson, Sidney K. The Architecture of Alden B. Dow. LC 82-24737. (Illus.). 168p. reprint ed. pap. 52.10 (*0-608-10534-1*, 2071154) Bks Demand.

— The Continuous Present of Organic Architecture. (Illus.). 80p. (Orig.). 1991. pap. 25.00 (*0-917562-56-9*) Contemp Arts.

— Inquiry into the Picturesque. LC 90-20338. 196p. 1991. 22.95 (*0-226-72251-1*) U Ch Pr.

Robinson, Sidney K., jt. ed. see Wilson, Richard G.

Robinson, Simon, jt. auth. see Wrox Development Staff.

Robinson, Sinclair & Smith, Donald, eds. NTC's Dictionary of Canadian French. LC 97-51184. 300p. 1995. 17.95 (*0-8442-1486-8*, 14868, Natl Textbk Co) NTC Contemp Pub Co.

Robinson, Solon. Solon Robinson, Pioneer & Agriculturist. Kellar, Herbert A., ed. LC 74-145268. (Illus.). 1971. reprint ed. 59.00 (*0-403-01183-3*) Scholarly.

Robinson, Spider. Callahan Chronicals. LC 97-204064. (Callahan Ser.). 1997. mass mkt. 9.99 (*0-8125-3937-0*, Pub. by Tor Bks) St Martin.

— The Callahan Touch. 240p. 1995. mass mkt. 5.99 (*0-441-00133-5*) Ace Bks.

***Robinson, Spider.** Callahan's Crosstime Saloon. 224p. 1999. mass mkt. 6.99 (*0-8125-7227-0*, Pub. by Tor Bks) St Martin.

— Callahan's Key. LC PS3568.O3156C34 2000. 352p. 2000. 23.95 (*0-553-11163-9*, Spectra) Bantam.

Robinson, Spider. Callahan's Legacy. 224p. 1996. 20.95 (*0-312-85776-4*) St Martin.

— Callahan's Legacy. 1997. mass mkt. 6.99 (*0-8125-5035-8*, Pub. by Tor Bks) St Martin.

— Deathkiller. 480p. 1996. mass mkt. 5.99 (*0-671-87722-4*) Baen Bks.

— Lady Slings the Booze. 272p. 1993. mass mkt. 5.99 (*0-441-46929-9*) Ace Bks.

— Lifehouse. 288p. 1997. per. 5.99 (*0-671-87777-1*) Baen Bks.

— Off the Wall at Callahan's. 160p. 1994. pap. 9.95 (*0-312-85661-X*, Pub. by Tor Bks) St Martin.

— User Friendly. 1998. per. 5.99 (*0-671-87864-6*) PB.

Robinson, Spider & Robinson, Jeanne. The Star Dancers. 416p. 1997. per. 5.99 (*0-671-87802-6*) Baen Bks.

— Starmind. LC 94-33374. 304p. (Orig.). 1995. pap. 21.95 (*0-441-00209-9*) Ace Bks.

— Starmind. (Orig.). 1996. mass mkt. 5.99 (*0-441-00305-2*) Ace Bks.

— Starseed. 256p. 1992. mass mkt. 4.99 (*0-441-78360-0*) Ace Bks.

Robinson, Stanley. The Property Law Act Victoria. 616p. 1992. 157.50 (*0-455-21050-0*, Pub. by LawBk Co) Gaunt.

Robinson, Stanley L. How to Avoid Old Age. LC 90-91721. (Illus.). 152p. 1990. write for info. (*0-9626830-0-0*) Remington NJ.

Robinson, Stanley L. & Miller. Automated Inspection & Quality Assurance. (Quality & Reliability Ser.: Vol. 16). (Illus.). 272p. 1989. text 75.00 (*0-8247-8002-7*) Dekker.

Robinson, Stephen E. Are Mormons Christians? 1998. pap. 8.95 (*1-57008-409-2*) Bookcraft Inc.

— Believing Christ: The Parable of the Bicycle & Other Good News. LC 92-20924. 131p. 1992. 14.95 (*0-87579-634-6*) Deseret Bk.

— Following Christ: The Parable of the Divers & Other Good News. LC 95-683. ix, 166p. 1995. 14.95 (*1-57345-059-6*) Deseret Bk.

— The Testament of Adam: An Examination of the Syriac & Greek Traditions. LC 80-12209. (Society of Biblical Literature. Dissertation Ser.: No. 52). 208p. reprint ed. pap. 64.50 (*0-7837-5440-X*, 204520500005) Bks Demand.

***Robinson, Stephen E. & Garrett, H. Dean.** A Commentary on the Doctrine & Covenants. LC 00-40441. 2000. write for info. (*1-57345-784-1*) Deseret Bk.

Robinson, Stephen E., jt. auth. see Blomberg, Craig L.

Robinson, Stephen T., jt. auth. see Gray, Rhonda.

Robinson, Steve. A Handbook of Financial Management. (Financial Times Management Ser.). 256p. 1994. 67.50 (*0-273-60338-8*, Pub. by Pitman Pub) Trans-Atl Phila.

Robinson, Steve & Hogan, Stephen. Starting Your Own Successful Indian Business. 160p. 1991. pap. 45.00 (*0-945253-08-7*) Thornsbury Bailey Brown.

Robinson, Stewart. Successful Simulation: A Practical Approach to Simulation Projects. LC 94-12966. 1994. write for info. (*0-07-707622-2*) McGraw.

***Robinson, Stuart.** Positioning for Power: Kneeling Low in Prayer, Standing Tall in God. 1998. pap. 12.99 (*1-85240-228-8*) SOV5.

Robinson, Sue. Amendment. 1990. 17.95 (*1-55972-018-2*, Birch Ln Pr) Carol Pub Group.

— The Amendment. 256p. 1991. pap. 4.50 (*0-8216-2501-2*, Carol Paperbacks) Carol Pub Group.

— The Complete Idiot's Guide to Bargain Hunting. 352p. Date not set. pap. 16.95 (*0-02-861742-8*) Macmillan.

— The Smart Shopper's Guide to the Best Buys for Kids. LC 96-68534. 174p. 1996. 12.95 (*0-02-861287-6*) Macmillan.

Robinson, Sue & Tobin-Singer, Joan F. First Steps: A Divorce Information Guidebook, Arizona Edition. 86p. (Orig.). 1986. pap. text 9.95 (*0-9617332-0-9*) Sue Robinson.

Robinson, Sugar Ray. Sugar Ray. 31.95 (*0-8488-1537-8*) Amereon Ltd.

Robinson, Sugar Ray & Anderson, Dave. Sugar Ray. (Illus.). 400p. 1994. reprint ed. pap. 14.95 (*0-306-80574-X*) Da Capo.

Robinson, Susan. Whatcha Gonna Do If the Grid Goes Down? Preparing Your Household for the Year 2000. 2nd ed. Evans, Stephany, ed. (Illus.). 140p. 1999. pap. 22.95 (*0-9667625-1-7*) Virtual Sage.

Robinson, Susan B. & Pirog, John. Mabel Dwight: A Catalogue Raisonne of the Lithographs. LC 95-48281. (Illus.). 344p. 1996. 65.00 (*1-56098-646-8*) Smithsonian.

Robinson, Suzanne. The Engagement. 293p. 1996. mass mkt. 5.50 (*0-553-56346-7*) Bantam.

***Robinson, Suzanne.** Just Before Midnight. (Meet Me at Midnight Ser.). 320p. 2000. mass mkt. 5.99 (*0-553-57961-4*) Bantam Dell.

Robinson, Suzanne. Lady Defiant. 320p. 1992. mass mkt. 5.50 (*0-553-29574-8*) Bantam.

— Lady Gallant. 368p. 1991. mass mkt. 5.99 (*0-553-29430-X*) Bantam.

— Lady Hellfire. 336p. 1992. mass mkt. 5.99 (*0-553-29678-7*) Bantam.

— Lady Valiant. 336p. 1993. mass mkt. 5.50 (*0-553-29575-6*) Bantam.

— Lord of Enchantment. 336p. 1994. mass mkt. 5.50 (*0-553-56344-0*) Bantam.

— Lord of the Dragon. 352p. 1995. mass mkt. 5.50 (*0-553-56345-9*, Fanfare) Bantam.

— The Rescue. 274p. 1998. mass mkt. 5.99 (*0-553-56347-5*) Bantam.

— The Treasure. 320p. 1999. mass mkt. 5.99 (*0-553-57958-4*) Bantam.

Robinson, Sylvia. HomeWork Coach Student Workbook. (HomeWork Coach Ser.). 1988. wbk. ed. 17.95 (*0-88671-353-6*, 4972) Am Guidance.

— HomeWork Coach Teacher's Guide. (HomeWork Coach Ser.). 1988. teacher ed. 16.95 (*0-88671-352-8*, 4971) Am Guidance.

Robinson, T. The Life & Death of Mary Magdalene. Sommer, H. Oskar, ed. (EETS, ES Ser.: Vol. 78). 1969. reprint ed. 30.00 (*0-8115-3401-4*) Periodicals Srv.

Robinson, T. E. & Justice, J. B., Jr. Microdialysis in the Neurosciences. (Techniques in the Behavioral & Neural Sciences Ser.: Vol. 7). 450p. 1991. 203.25 (*0-444-81194-X*); pap. 89.00 (*0-444-89375-X*) Elsevier.

Robinson, T. F. & Kinnel, R. K., eds. Cardiac Myocyte - Connective Tissue Interactions in Health & Disease. (Issues in Biomedicine Ser.: Vol. 13). (Illus.). x, 150p. 1990. 128.75 (*3-8055-5028-6*) S Karger.

Robinson, T. H. Decline & Fall of the Hebrew Kingdoms. LC 74-137284. reprint ed. 39.50 (*0-404-05376-9*) AMS Pr.

Robinson, T. H., et al, eds. Megilloth. (Biblia Hebraica Stuttgartensia Ser.). x, 62p. 1975. pap. 9.99 (*3-438-05213-X*, 104092) Untd Bible Soc.

Robinson, T. H. & Brockington, L. H., eds. Paradigms & Exercises in Syriac Grammar. 4th ed. 176p. 1982. pap. text 21.00 (*0-19-815458-5*) OUP.

Robinson, T. H., et al. Palestine in General History. (British Academy, London, Schweich Lectures on Biblical Archaeology Series, 1930). 1974. reprint ed. pap. 25.00 (*0-8115-1268-1*) Periodicals Srv.

Robinson, T. M. Plato's Psychology. LC 76-465044. 215p. reprint ed. pap. 66.70 (*0-608-31002-6*, 205121600093) Bks Demand.

Robinson, T. M. Plato's Psychology. 2nd rev. ed. (Phoenix Supplementary Volumes Ser.). 264p. 1995. text 60.00 (*0-8020-0635-3*); pap. text 22.95 (*0-8020-7590-8*) U of Toronto Pr.

Robinson, T. M., ed. Heraclitus: Fragments: A Text & Translation with a Commentary. (Phoenix Supplementary Volumes Ser.: No. XXII: Pre-Socratics II). 228p. 1991. pap. text 19.95 (*0-8020-6913-4*) U of Toronto Pr.

***Robinson, T. S.** Battle-Chasers. LC 99-61931. 128p. 1999. 25.00 (*0-7388-0360-X*); pap. 18.00 (*0-7388-0361-8*) Xlibris Corp.

Robinson, Tara. How to Catch Really Big Fish. (Illus.). 64p. (Orig.). 1983. pap. 6.95 (*0-88839-967-7*) Hancock House.

Robinson, Ted, jt. auth. see Woodley, Jeremy D.

Robinson, Terry. Purchasing Oil & Gas. 99p. (C). 1989. 210.00 (*0-7855-4613-8*, Pub. by Inst Pur & Supply) St Mut.

Robinson, Terry, ed. see Axiom Information Resources Staff.

Robinson, Terry E. Behavioral Approaches to Brain Research. (Illus.). 352p. 1983. text 40.00 (*0-19-503258-6*) OUP.

Robinson, Thelma S. Creatures of Habit. 28p. (Orig.). 1989. pap. text 5.00 (*0-685-28348-8*) In Tradition Pub.

Robinson, Therese A. Historical View of the Languages & Literatures of the Slavic Nations. 1980. lib. bdg. 79.95 (*0-8490-3165-6*) Gordon Pr.

Robinson, Thomas. The Schoole of Musicke, Wherein Is Taught the Perfect Method of True Fingering of the Lute, Pandora, Orpharion & Viol da Gamba. LC 73-6122. (English Experience Ser.: No. 589). 1973. reprint ed. 25.00 (*90-221-0589-X*) Walter J Johnson.

***Robinson, Thomas & Daniel, John.** Oregon: Then & Now. (Illus.). 184p. 2000. 60.00 (*1-56579-380-3*) Westcliffe Pubs.

Robinson, Thomas, jt. auth. see Mason, Steve.

Robinson, Thomas A. The Bauer Thesis Examined: The Geography of Heresy in the Early Christian Church. LC 87-28288. (Studies in the Bible & Early Christianity: Vol. 11). 240p. 1988. lib. bdg. 89.95 (*0-88946-611-4*) E Mellen.

— Mastering Greek Vocabulary. 2nd rev. ed. 178p. (Orig.). 1991. pap. 9.95 (*0-943575-85-0*) Hendrickson MA.

Robinson, Thomas A. & Greenshields, Malcolm, eds. North American Religion: The Journal of the Centre for the Study of North American Religion, Vol. 1. 1992. write for info. (*0-7734-9066-3*) E Mellen.

— North American Religion: The Journal of the Centre for the Study of North American Religion, Vol. 2. 1993. 69.95 (*0-7734-9416-2*); pap. 29.95 (*0-7734-9418-9*) E Mellen.

Robinson, Thomas A. & St. David's University Press Staff. Greek Verb Endings. LC 86-31268. 96p. 1986. pap. text 39.95 (*0-88946-206-2*) E Mellen.

Robinson, Thomas A., et al. The Early Church: An Annotated Bibliography of Literature in English. LC 93-34350. (American Theological Library Association Monograph: No. 33). 522p. 1993. 62.00 (*0-8108-2763-8*) Scarecrow.

Robinson, Thomas A., jt. ed. see Greenshields, Malcolm R.

Robinson, Thomas E., 2nd. Portraying Older People in Advertising: Magazine, Television, & Newspapers. (Garland Studies on the Elderly in America). 106p. 1998. 33.00 (*0-8153-3215-7*) Garland.

Robinson, Thomas G., jt. ed. see Lin Zhiling.

Robinson, Thomas H. Robinson. Thomas Robinson & His Descendants. rev. ed. 233p. 1996. reprint ed. pap. 36.00 (*0-8328-5332-1*); reprint ed. lib. bdg. 46.00 (*0-8328-5331-3*) Higginson Bk Co.

Robinson, Thomas M. Contrasting Arguments. Connor, W. R., ed. LC 78-18598. (Greek Texts & Commentaries Ser.). (ENG & GRE., Illus.). 1979. lib. bdg. 28.95 (*0-405-11439-7*) Ayer.

Robinson, Thomas M., jt. ed. see Westra, Laura.

Robinson, Thomas P. Radio Networks & the Federal Government. Sterling, Christopher H., ed. LC 78-21735. (Dissertations in Broadcasting Ser.). 1980. reprint ed. lib. bdg. 23.95 (*0-405-11772-8*) Ayer.

Robinson, Thomas W. The Chinese & Their Future: Beijing, Taipei, & Hong Kong. LC 93-21227. 554p. 1994. 39.75 (*0-8447-3805-0*, AEI Pr) Am Enterprise.

Robinson, Thomas W. & Shambaugh, David, eds. Chinese Foreign Policy: Theory & Practice. (Studies on Contemporary China). (Illus.). 660p. 1996. reprint ed. pap. text 39.95 (*0-19-829016-0*) OUP.

Robinson, Tim. Economic Theories of Exhaustible Resources. 288p. 1988. lib. bdg. 59.95 (*0-415-00988-X*) Routledge.

— Setting Foot on the Shores of Connemara & Other: Writings. 218p. 1997. 45.00 (*1-874675-79-1*); pap. 19.95 (*1-874675-74-0*) Dufour.

— Stones of Aran: Labyrinth. LC 95-225231. (Illus.). 504p. 1996. 19.95 (*1-874675-50-3*, Pub. by Lilliput Pr) Dufour.

Robinson, Tim. Stones of Aran Labyrinth. 512p. pap. 17.95 (*0-14-011566-8*, Pub. by Pnguin Bks Ltd) Trafalgar.

— Tobias, the Quig & the Rumplenut Tree. LC 99-36451. (Illus.). 32p. (J). (ps-3). 2000. 16.95 (*1-890817-20-1*, Pub. by Winslow Pr) Publishers Group.

Robinson, Tim. The View from the Horizon. (Illus.). 63p. 1998. pap. 18.95 (*0-906630-07-X*, Pub. by Coracle Pr) Dist Art Pubs.

Robinson, Tim, ed. & intro. see Synge, John Millington.

***Robinson, Timothy.** Good Things Jesus Did. (Missions & Me Ser.). 16p. 1999. 7.99 (*1-56309-285-9*) Womans Mission Union.

Robinson, Timothy A. Aristotle in Outline. LC 94-46137. 134p. (C). 1995. pap. text 6.95 (*0-87220-314-X*); lib. bdg. 24.95 (*0-87220-315-8*) Hackett Pub.

Robinson, Timothy A., ed. God. LC 96-31850. (Readings in Philosophy Ser.). 272p. (C). 1996. pap. text 10.95 (*0-87220-222-4*); lib. bdg. 27.95 (*0-87220-223-2*) Hackett Pub.

***Robinson, Timothy M.** Three Days Without Light. LC 00-21840. 2000. write for info. (*1-57345-567-9*) Deseret Bk.

***Robinson, Timothy M. & Madsen, James A.** A Night Without Darkness LC 99-33984. 1999. write for info. (*1-57345-504-0*) Deseret Bk.

Robinson, Timothy W. History of the Town of Morrill in the County of Waldo & State of Maine. Morse, Theoda M., ed. (Illus.). 253p. 1997. reprint ed. lib. bdg. 32.00 (*0-8328-5877-3*) Higginson Bk Co.

***Robinson, Tom.** Book Ends. 2000. pap. 7.95 (*0-533-13288-6*) Vantage.

Robinson, Tom. The Longcase Clock. rev. ed. (Illus.). 468p. 1995. 79.50 (*1-85149-232-1*) Antique Collect.

Robinson, Tom, ed. Connemara after the Famine, 1853: Journal of a Survey of the Martin Estate by Thomas Colville Scott. LC 95-237947. (Illus.). 126p. (Orig.). 1995. pap. 11.95 (*1-874675-69-4*, Pub. by Lilliput Pr) Irish Bks Media.

Robinson, Tom, jt. ed. see Hawkin, David J.

Robinson, Tom H. Arkansas Merchant Tokens. Schenkman, David E., ed. LC 85-51498. (Illus.). 259p. 1985. 32.50 (*0-918492-07-6*) TAMS.

Robinson, Tommy. Frank Wood's Business Accounting Multiple Choice Question Book. 160p. 1998. pap. 27.50 (*0-273-62545-4*, Pub. by Pitman Pub) Trans-Atl Phila.

Robinson, Tommy & Wood, Frank. Business Accounting - Irish Edition. 736p. 1998. pap. 54.00 (*0-273-63153-5*, Pub. by Pitman Pub) Trans-Atl Phila.

Robinson, Trevor. The Amateur Wind Instrument Maker. rev. ed. LC 80-5381. (Illus.). 128p. 1981. pap. 13.95 (*0-87023-312-2*) U of Mass Pr.

— The Organic Constituents of Higher Plants. 6th ed. (Illus.). iv, 346p. 1991. 18.50 (*0-935118-03-9*) Cordus Pr.

Robinson, Valencia, ed. see Thaxton-Mathis, Andreia.

Robinson-Valery, Judith, ed. see Valery, Paul.

Robinson, Vaughan. Transients, Settlers, & Refugees. (Illus.). 264p. 1986. 55.00 (*0-19-878009-5*) OUP.

Robinson, Vaughan, ed. Geography & Migration. LC 96-5694. (International Library of Studies on Migration: Vol. 2). 616p. (C). 1996. text 225.00 (*1-85898-117-4*) E Elgar.

***Robinson, Vaughan, ed.** Migration & Public Policy. LC 99-17120. (International Library of Studies on Migration: No. 8). 680p. 1999. 245.00 (*1-85898-922-1*) E Elgar.

Robinson, Vaughan, jt. ed. see Black, Richard.

Robinson, Vera M. Humor & the Health Professions: The Therapeutic Use of Humor in Health Care. 2nd ed. LC 89-43106. 256p. 1990. pap. 25.00 (*1-55642-141-9*) SLACK Inc.

An Asterisk (*) at the beginning of an entry indicates that the title is appearing for the first time.

Robinson, Verne, ed. see Robinson, Bradley.

Robinson, Victor. William Godwin & Mary Wollstonecraft. 1972. 250.00 (*0-8490-1304-6*) Gordon Pr.

Robinson, Victoria & Richardson, Diane. Introducing Women's Studies: Feminist Theory & Practice. LC 97-11592. 1997. text 55.00 (*0-8147-7493-8*); pap. text 20.00 (*0-8147-7494-6*) NYU Pr.

Robinson, Victoria, ed. see Riley, Jan.

Robinson, Vincent B. & Tom, Henry, eds. Towards SQL Database Language Extensions for Geographic Information Systems. (Illus.). 148p. (C). 1998. pap. text 25.00 (*0-7881-4765-X*) DIANE Pub.

— Towards SQL Database Language Extensions for Geographic Information Systems. LC 94-24762. 1994. write for info. (*0-929306-19-8*) Silicon Pr.

Robinson, Vincent W. Engine & Drivetrain Performance: Mathematics & Theory. LC 94-92239. (Illus.). 106p. (Orig.). 1995. pap. 16.95 (*0-9643024-0-3*) Robinson.

Robinson, Vinnie. Devil in Disguise. 145p. 1982. 9.95 (*0-9610404-0-8*) Mogul Bk.

— Ex-- the Unknown. 92p. 1987. pap. 3.95 (*0-9610404-2-4*) Mogul Bk.

— Too. 64p. 1985. 5.95 (*0-9610404-1-6*) Mogul Bk.

Robinson, Virginia P. The Development of a Professional Self: Teaching & Learning in Professional Helping Processes, Selected Writings, 1930-1968. LC 77-78322. (Studies in Modern Society: Political & Social Issues: No. 12). 42.50 (*0-404-16015-8*) AMS Pr.

Robinson, Viviane. Problem Based Methodology: Research for the Improvement of Practice. LC 92-36833. 290p. 1993. text 68.00 (*0-08-041925-9*, Pergamon Pr) Elsevier.

Robinson, W. Christ in Islam & Christianity. 234p. 1996. pap. 21.95 (*0-614-21661-3*, 1438) Kazi Pubns.

Robinson, W. Courtland. Terms of Refuge. LC 98-27305. 322p. 2000. text 69.95 (*1-85649-609-0*, Pub. by Zed Books); text 27.95 (*1-85649-610-4*, Pub. by Zed Books) St Martin.

Robinson, W. Douglas. Southern Illinois Birds: An Annotated List & Sight Guide. LC 95-14767. (Illus.). 480p. (C). 1996. 39.95 (*0-8093-2032-0*) S Ill U Pr.

Robinson, W. H., jt. auth. see Skinner, R. I.

Robinson, W. Heath. The Adventures of Uncle Lubin. (Illus.). 128p. (J). (ps-3). 1992. 15.95 (*0-87923-884-4*) Godine.

Robinson, W. I. The Relationship of the Tetracoralla to the Hexacoralla. (Connecticut Academy of Arts & Sciences Ser., Trans.: Vol. 21). 1917. pap. 49.50 (*0-685-22842-8*) Elliots Bks.

Robinson, W. P. Deceipt, Delusion, & Deception. LC 95-41791. (Language & Language Behaviors Ser.: Vol. 7). 370p. 1996. 58.00 (*0-8039-5260-0*); pap. 26.95 (*0-8039-5261-9*) Sage.

Robinson, W. Peter. Social Groups & Identities: Developing the Legacy of Henri Tajfel. LC 96-7631. (International Series in Social Psychology). 256p. 1996. pap. 31.95 (*0-7506-3083-3*) Buttrwrth-Heinemann.

Robinson, W. Stitt. James Glen: From Scottish Provost to Royal Governor of South Carolina, 165. LC 95-501. (Contributions in American History Ser.: Vol. 165). 192p. 1996. 55.00 (*0-313-29760-6*, Greenwood Pr) Greenwood.

Robinson, W. Stitt, Jr. Mother Earth: Land Grants in Virginia, 1607-1699. (Illus.). 77p. 1957. pap. text 5.95 (*0-8139-0136-7*) U Pr of Va.

Robinson, W. W. Los Angeles from the Days of the Pueblo. 2nd ed. Nunis, Doyce B., Jr., ed. (Illus.). 128p. 1981. pap. 7.95 (*0-910312-45-1*) Calif Hist.

Robinson, W. Wright. How Birds Build Their Amazing Homes. LC 99-26008. (Animal Architects Ser.). (Illus.). 64p. (J). (gr. 5-8). 1999. lib. bdg. 19.95 (*1-56711-376-1*) Blackbirch.

— How Insects Build Their Amazing Homes. LC 98-47975. (Animal Architects Ser.). (Illus.). 64p. (YA). (gr. 5-9). 1999. lib. bdg. 19.95 (*1-56711-375-3*) Blackbirch.

— How Mammals Build Their Amazing Homes. LC 99-14385. (Animal Architects Ser.). (Illus.). 64p. (J). (gr. 5-8). 1999. lib. bdg. 19.95 (*1-56711-381-8*) Blackbirch.

— How Shellmakers Build Their Amazing Homes. LC 99-20259. (Animal Architects Ser.). (Illus.). 64p. (J). (gr. 5-8). 1999. lib. bdg. 19.95 (*1-56711-379-6*) Blackbirch.

— How Spiders & Other Silkmakers Build Their Amazing Homes. LC 98-52800. (Animal Architects Ser.). (Illus.). 64p. (YA). (gr. 5-8). 1999. lib. bdg. 19.95 (*1-56711-378-8*) Blackbirch.

— Incredible Facts about the Ocean: How We Use It, How We Abuse It, Vol. 3. (Ocean World Library). (Illus.). 128p. (J). (gr. 4 up). 1990. lib. bdg. 13.95 (*0-87518-435-9*, Dillon Silver Burdett) Silver Burdett Pr.

— Incredible Facts about the Ocean: The Land Below, the Life Within, Vol. 2. LC 85-25430. (Ocean World Library). (Illus.). 120p. (J). (gr. 4 up). 1987. lib. bdg. 13.95 (*0-87518-358-1*, Dillon Silver Burdett) Silver Burdett Pr.

Robinson, Walter. Instant Art History: From Cave Art to Pop Art. (Illus.). 256p. (Orig.). 1995. pap. 10.00 (*0-449-90698-1*) Fawcett.

Robinson, Walter, jt. auth. see Gleason, Mat.

Robinson, Walter M. Eve, It Is Not Your Fault! LC 97-90415. (Illus.). 100p. (Orig.). (YA). (gr. 7 up). 1997. pap. 8.00 (*0-9658208-0-7*) F & D Pub.

Robinson, Wayne C. The African American Travel Guide. 98th ed. (Illus.). 280p. (Orig.). 1997. pap. 15.95 (*1-55650-797-6*) Hunter NJ.

Robinson, Wayne F. & Huxtable, Clive R., eds. Clinicopathologic Principles for Veterinary Medicine. (Illus.). 448p. 1988. text 74.95 (*0-521-30883-6*) Cambridge U Pr.

Robinson, Wendy. Gentle Giant: The Inspiring Story of an Autistic Child. LC 98-42682. 192p. 1999. pap. 16.95 (*1-86204-304-3*, Pub. by Element MA) Penguin Putnam.

Robinson, Willard B. American Forts: Architectural Form & Function. LC 76-25130. (Illus.). 244p. reprint ed. 75.70 (*0-8357-9662-0*, 201113800074) Bks Demand.

— The People's Architecture: Texas Courthouses, Jails & Municipal Buildings. (Illus.). xxii, 365p. 1983. 35.00 (*0-87611-060-X*) Tex St Hist Assn.

— Reflections of Faith: Houses of Worship in the Lone Star State. LC 94-20796. (Illus.). 268p. (Orig.). 1994. 45.00 (*0-918954-57-6*) Baylor Univ Pr.

Robinson, William. The Biblical Doctrine of the Church. 235p. 1997. pap. 20.00 (*0-9653517-7-7*) Wipf & Stock.

Robinson, William. The English Flower Garden. rev. ed. LC 95-3742. (Illus.). 734p. 1984. 35.00 (*0-89831-031-8*) Sagapr.

— An Exhibition of Drawings & Watercolors by John Groth. (Illus.). 12p. 1970. pap. 5.00 (*0-87959-116-1*) U of Tex H Ransom Ctr.

— Gravetye Manor or Twenty Years' Work Round an Old Manor House. limited ed. Thomas, Graham S. & Ingwersen, Will, eds. LC 84-22168. (Illus.). 159p. 1984. 125.00 (*0-89831-001-6*) Sagapr.

— The Wild Garden. 5th ed. LC 93-44917. (Illus.). 318p. 1994. reprint ed. 24.95 (*0-88192-284-6*) Sagapr.

Robinson, William & Hauri, Christine. Promotional Marketing. 2nd ed. Knudsen, Anne, ed. (Illus.). 192p. (Orig.). 1995. pap. 23.95 (*0-8442-3151-7*, NTC Business Bks) NTC Contemp Pub Co.

Robinson, William & Steinberg, David. Transformations in Cleveland Art, 1796-1946: Community & Diversity in Early Modern America. LC 96-11969. (Illus.). 304p. 1996. pap. 29.95 (*0-940717-33-6*); text 50.00 (*0-940717-34-4*) Cleveland Mus Art.

Robinson, William, et al. General Chemistry. 7th ed. 928p. (C). 1984. text 87.16 (*0-669-06335-5*) HM Trade Div.

Robinson, William, jt. auth. see Brezen-Block, Tamara.

Robinson, William, jt. ed. see Cikovsky, Nicolai.

Robinson, William A. Best Sales Promotions. 6th ed. 384p. 1994. 29.95 (*0-8442-3122-3*, NTC Business Bks) NTC Contemp Pub Co.

— Jeffersonian Democracy in New England. LC 68-57637. (Illus.). 190p. 1969. reprint ed. lib. bdg. 55.00 (*0-8371-0639-7*, ROJE, Greenwood Pr) Greenwood.

***Robinson, William A.** Practicing California Judicial Arbitration - 12/99 Update. Compton, Linda A., ed. LC 82-74525. 216p. 1999. pap. text 58.00 (*0-7626-0376-3*, CP-30666) Cont Ed Bar-CA.

Robinson, William A. Thomas B. Reed, Parliamentarian. (History - United States Ser.). 423p. 1992. reprint ed. lib. bdg. 99.00 (*0-7812-6200-3*) Rprt Serv.

Robinson, William A. & Hauri, Christine. Promotional Marketing: Ideas & Techniques for Success in Sales Promotion. Orig. Title: Strategic Sales Promotion. (Illus.). 192p. 1992. 39.95 (*0-8442-3150-9*, NTC Business Bks) NTC Contemp Pub Co.

Robinson, William A. & Schultz, Don E. Sales Promotion Essentials. 2nd ed. (Illus.). 208p. 1994. 39.95 (*0-8442-3366-8*, NTC Business Bks) NTC Contemp Pub Co.

Robinson, William A., jt. auth. see Schofield, Jill R.

Robinson, William A., jt. ed. see Brezen-Block, Tamara.

Robinson, William B., jt. auth. see Skvarcius, Romualdas.

***Robinson, William C.** Elements of American Jurisprudence. lviii, 401p. 1999. 140.00 (*1-56169-525-4*) Gaunt.

Robinson, William C. Elements of American Jurisprudence. lviii, 401p. 1985. reprint ed. 46.00 (*0-8377-1041-3*, Rothman) W S Hein.

— Forensic Oratory: A Manual for Advocates. xxix, 357p. 1993. reprint ed. 48.00 (*0-8377-2548-8*, Rothman) W S Hein.

— The Law of Patents for Useful Inventions, 3 vols., Set. LC 12-38173. 1972. reprint ed. lib. bdg. 130.00 (*0-89941-350-1*, 500480) W S Hein.

Robinson, William D., ed. The Solid Waste Handbook: A Pratical Guide. LC 85-12454. 848p. 1986. 225.00 (*0-471-87711-5*) Wiley.

Robinson, William H. Black New England Letters: The Uses of Writing in Black New England. 1977. 3.00 (*0-89073-051-2*, 195) Boston Public Lib.

— Parliamentary Libraries & Research Services in Central & Eastern Europe: Building More Effective Legislatures. (IFLA Publications: 87). x, 238p. 1998. write for info. (*3-598-21813-3*) K G Saur Verlag.

Robinson, William H., et al. A Brush with Light: Watercolor Painters of Northeast Ohio. Korneitchouk, Ursula, ed. LC 98-73711. (Illus.). 90p. 1998. pap. write for info. (*0-9639562-6-4*) Clevelnd Art.

Robinson, William H., jt. auth. see Shearer, Christine Fowler.

Robinson, William I. Promoting Polyarchy: Globalization, US Intervention, & Hegemony. (Cambridge Studies in International Relations: No. 48). 481p. (C). 1996. text 64.95 (*0-521-56203-1*) Cambridge U Pr.

Robinson, William L. Fool Hen: The Spruce Grouse on the Yellow Dog Plains. LC 79-3962. (Illus.). 243p. reprint ed. pap. 75.40 (*0-608-20472-2*, 207172400002) Bks Demand.

Robinson, William L., jt. auth. see Bolen, Eric G.

Robinson, William M. The Confederate Privateers. LC 89-25081. 388p. 1994. pap. 15.95 (*1-57003-005-7*) U of SC Pr.

— Justice in Grey: A History of the Judicial System of the Confederate States of America. LC 91-55437. xxi, 713p. 1991. reprint ed. 165.00 (*0-912004-94-0*) Gaunt.

Robinson, William R., ed. Man & the Movies. LC 67-24549. (Illus.). 387p. reprint ed. 120.00 (*0-8357-9389-3*, 205166000004) Bks Demand.

Robinson, William R., et al. Chemistry: Concepts & Models. 753p. (C). 1992. text 67.96 (*0-669-32800-6*); teacher ed. 2.66 (*0-669-28949-3*); teacher ed. 24.76 (*0-669-28950-7*); student ed. 25.16 (*0-669-28948-5*); trans. write for info. (*0-318-70089-1*) HM Trade Div.

— Essentials of General Chemistry. 10th ed. (C). 1996. text 83.16 (*0-669-35484-8*) HM Trade Div.

— Essentials of General Chemistry. 10th ed. (C). 1997. pap. text, student ed. 29.16 (*0-669-35485-6*) HM Trade Div.

— Essentials of General Chemistry. 10th ed. (C). 1997. pap. text, teacher ed. 11.96 (*0-669-35486-4*) HM Trade Div.

— Essentials of General Chemistry, 10 Vols. 10th ed. (C). 1997. pap. text, student ed. 33.96 (*0-669-35488-0*) HM Trade Div.

— Essentials of General Chemistry, 10 Vols. 10th ed. (C). 1997. pap. text, teacher ed. 27.96 (*0-669-35487-2*) HM Trade Div.

Robinson, William R., jt. auth. see Holtzclaw, Henry F., Jr.

Robinson, William S. Computers, Minds, & Robots. 230p. 1993. pap. 22.95 (*1-56639-082-6*) Temple U Pr.

— Texts & Contexts: A Contemporary Approach to College Writing. 3rd ed. LC 96-24955. (Developmental Study/Study Skill Ser.). 1996. 31.00 (*0-534-52335-8*) Wadsworth Pub.

Robinson, William S. & Tucker, Stephanie. Texts & Contexts: A Contemporary Approach to College Writing. 412p. (C). 1990. pap. 24.95 (*0-534-13044-5*) Wadsworth Pub.

Robinson, William W. Land in California: The Story of Mission Lands, Ranchos, Squatters, Mining Claims, Railroad Grants, Land Scrip, Homesteads. (Illus.). 1979. pap. 16.95 (*0-520-03875-4*, Pub. by U CA Pr) Cal Prin Full Svc.

— Land in California: The Story of Mission Lands, Ranchos, Squatters, Mining Claims, Railroad Grants, Land Scrip, Homesteads. Bruchey, Stuart, ed. LC 78-56665. (Management of Public Lands in the U. S. Ser.). (Illus.). 1979. reprint ed. lib. bdg. 23.95 (*0-405-11352-8*) Ayer.

— Seventeenth-Century Dutch Drawings: A Selection from the Maida & George Abrams Collection. (Illus.). 234p. 1991. pap. 39.95 (*0-685-63136-2*) Pierpont Morgan.

— Seventeenth-Century Dutch Drawings: A Selection from the Maida & George Abrams Collection. (Pierpont Morgan Library). (Illus.). 236p. 1994. pap. 39.95 (*0-87598-107-0*) Pierpont Morgan.

Robinson, William W., et al, eds. Shop Talk: Studies in Honor of Seymour Slive: Presented on His Seventy-Fifth Birthday. LC 95-40406. (Illus.). 1995. 65.00 (*0-916724-85-9*) Harvard Art Mus.

Robinson, William W., et al. Harvard's Art Museums: 100 Years of Collecting. LC 95-52347. (Illus.). 363p. 1996. pap. 35.00 (*0-916724-87-5*) Harvard Art Mus.

Robinson, Zan D. A Semiotic & Psychoanalytic Interpretation of Herman Melville's Fiction. LC 91-30813. 220p. 1991. lib. bdg. 89.95 (*0-7734-9957-1*) E Mellen.

— The Workplace. 209p. (Orig.). 1992. pap. text 15.00 (*0-9603888-7-7*) Labor Arts.

Robinson, Zan Dale. Practical Writing Techniques. 4th ed. 218p. (C). 1994. text 34.00 (*0-536-58565-2*) Pearson Custom.

— Practical Writing Techniques. 5th ed. 218p. (C). 1995. text 34.00 (*0-536-58887-2*) Pearson Custom.

Robinson, Zan Dale & Bothwell, Roberta. Spirit of November: Psychosemiotic & Dialectic. 92p. (C). 1996. text 20.40 (*0-536-59291-8*) Pearson Custom.

Robiquet, Paul. Le Personnel Municipal de Paris Pendant la Revolution. LC 73-174332. (Collection de documents relatifs a l'histoire de Paris pendant la Revolution francaise). reprint ed. 135.00 (*0-404-52557-1*) AMS Pr.

Robiscoe, James. Nick & Peter: The Fire Island Murder. 186p. (Orig.). 1995. pap. 10.95 (*0-9642911-1-8*) Tanner Long.

Robishaw, Sue. Carlos's Ma's Friends: A Novella. LC 97-74741. 56p. 1997. pap. 6.00 (*0-9652036-2-X*) ManyTracks.

***Robishaw, Sue.** Frost Dancing: Tips from a Northern Gardener. 3rd rev. ed. 40p. 2000. pap. 6.00 (*0-9652036-6-2*) ManyTracks.

Robishaw, Sue. Homesteading Adventures: A Guide for Doers & Dreamers. LC 97-72380. (Illus.). 303p. (Orig.). 1997. pap. 16.98 (*0-9652036-1-1*) ManyTracks.

— The Last Lamp. LC 96-94137. 256p. 1996. pap. 14.95 (*0-9652036-0-3*) ManyTracks.

— Rosita & Sian Search for a Great Work of Art. LC 98-89599. 160p. (J). (gr. 3-12). 1999. 16.98 (*0-9652036-3-8*) ManyTracks.

Robisheaux, Thomas. Rural Society & the Search for Order in Early Modern Germany. (Illus.). 320p. (C). 1989. text 80.00 (*0-521-35626-1*) Cambridge U Pr.

Robisheaux, Thomas, tr. see Imhof, Arthur E.

***Robison.** Why Did I Ever. 2000. 22.00 (*1-58243-060-8*, Pub. by Counterpt DC) HarpC.

Robison, jt. auth. see Moore.

Robison, John O., ed. see Klemm, Johann.

Robison, Andrew. Building a Collection. LC 97-32255. 1997. pap. 2.99 (*0-89468-234-2*) Natl Gallery Art.

— Piranesi: Early Architectural Fantasies: A Catalog Raisonne of the Etchings. (Illus.). x, 206p. 1996. pap. text 48.00 (*0-226-72320-8*, 72319-4) U Ch Pr.

Robison, Andrew, ed. The Glory of Venice: Art in the Eighteenth Century. LC 94-61010. (Illus.). 432p. 1995. 70.00 (*0-300-06185-4*) Yale U Pr.

Robison, Andrew, jt. ed. see Martineau, Jane.

Robison, B. C. Birds of Houston. 2nd ed. LC 97-28348. (Illus.). 141p. 1997. reprint ed. pap. 12.95 (*0-292-77082-0*) U of Tex Pr.

Robison, Betty B. Tomorrow's Troubles. LC 97-60733. 240p. (Orig.). 1997. pap. 11.99 (*1-57921-024-4*) WinePress Pub.

***Robison, Brice E.** Raus Mit Du (Make it Snappy) LC 99-96669. 2000. pap. 14.95 (*0-533-13319-X*) Vantage.

Robison, Bruce H., et al. The Deep Sea. LC 98-47557. (Natural History Ser.). 1999. pap. 9.95 (*1-878244-25-6*) Monterey Bay Aquarium.

***Robison, Carley.** Galesburg, Illinois: In Vintage Postcards. (Postcard History Ser.). (Illus.). 128p. 2000. 18.99 (*0-7385-0762-8*) Arcadia Publng.

Robison, Cathy A. Archaeological Excavations at the Fitzgibbons Site, Gallatin County, Illinois. LC 86-72024. (Center for Archaeological Investigations Research Paper Ser.: No. 53). (Illus.). xxi, 294p. 1986. pap. 18.50 (*0-88104-061-4*) Center Archaeol.

Robison, Clarence F., et al. Modern Techniques of Track & Field. LC 74-850. (Health Education, Physical Education, & Recreation Ser.). 357p. reprint ed. pap. 110.70 (*0-608-12689-6*, 205600700043) Bks Demand.

Robison, Clay, jt. auth. see Gibson, L. Tucker.

Robison, Dale W. Wisconsin & the Mentally Ill. Grob, Gerald N., ed. LC 78-22588. (Historical Issues in Mental Health Ser.). 1980. lib. bdg. 28.95 (*0-405-11939-9*) Ayer.

Robison, David. Alternative Work Patterns: Changing Approaches to Work Scheduling. LC 76-42369. 40p. 1976. pap. text 5.00 (*0-89361-001-1*) Work in Amer.

Robison, Debra. The Storm Within. LC 94-71755. 1994. pap. 4.95 (*1-55673-934-6*) CSS OH.

Robison, Elwin C. The First Mormon Temple: Design, Construction, & Historic Context of the Kirtland Temple. LC 97-21115. (Illus.). xvi, 216p. 1997. 21.95 (*0-8425-2333-2*, Friends of the Library) Brigham.

Robison, Esther, jt. auth. see Stern, Raphael.

Robison, Esther, jt. ed. see Stern, Raphael.

Robison, G. A., jt. auth. see Cehovic, G.

Robison, G. Alan, jt. ed. see Greengard, Paul.

Robison, Gordon. Lonely Planet Arab Gulf States. 2nd ed. (Illus.). 528p. 1996. pap. 19.95 (*0-86442-390-X*) Lonely Planet.

***Robison, Gordon & Greenway, Paul.** Lonely Planet Bahrain, Kuwait & Qatar. (Travel Guides Ser.). (Illus.). 24.95p. 2000. pap. 15.99 (*1-86450-132-4*) Lonely Planet.

Robison, Henry W. & Allen, Robert T. Only in Arkansas: A Study of the Endemic Plants & Animals of the State. (Illus.). 184p. 1995. text 42.00 (*1-55728-326-5*) U of Ark Pr.

Robison, Henry W. & Buchanan, Thomas M. Fishes of Arkansas. LC 87-10757. 544p. 1988. pap. 34.00 (*1-55728-001-0*) U of Ark Pr.

Robison, Henry W., et al. Fishes of Arkansas. LC 87-10757. 544p. 1988. text 54.00 (*1-55728-000-2*) U of Ark Pr.

Robison, James. My Father's Face: Entrusting Our Lives to a God Who Loves Us. LC 97-6733. 224p. 1997. 18.99 (*1-57673-030-1*, Multnomah Bks) Multnomah Pubs.

Robison, Jay D. Life after Death? Christian Interpretation of Personal Eschatology. LC 92-32236. (American Univ. Studies, VII: Vol. 137). XI, 234p. (C). 1998. text 43.95 (*0-8204-1959-1*) P Lang Pubng.

Robison, Jim. Large Scale Ceramics. 1997. 26.00 (*1-889250-05-8*) Gentle Br.

Robison, Jim. Large-Scale Ceramics. (Illus.). 112p. 1997. text. write for info. (*90-5703-551-0*, Harwood Acad Pubs) Gordon & Breach.

Robison, Jim & Andrews, Mark. Flashbooks: The Story of Central Florida's Past. LC 94-48818. 1995. write for info. (*1-56943-051-9*) NTC Contemp Pub Co.

Robison, John. Inside Atlantic City Slot Clubs. 10.00 (*0-9670810-0-9*) Syst Masters.

Robison, John. Proofs of a Conspiracy. 1979. lib. bdg. 59.95 (*0-8490-2987-2*) Gordon Pr.

Robison, John. Proofs of a Conspiracy. unabridged ed. 304p. reprint ed. pap. 12.00 (*0-945001-32-0*) GSG & Assocs.

***Robison, Korey.** Ghost Writer. 231p. 2000. pap. 15.95 (*0-7414-0380-3*) Buy Books.

***Robison, Lee.** Dazed Part of Light. v, 72p. 1999. pap. 11.00 (*0-9674291-0-2*) L Robison.

Robison, Lindon J. & Barry, Peter J. Present Value Models & Investment Analysis. 690p. (C). 1996. text 49.00 (*0-945704-00-3*) Genesis Comns.

— Present Value Models & Investment Analysis. (Illus.). 661p. (C). 1998. text 49.00 (*0-87013-488-4*) Mich St U Pr.

Robison, Lyn. Sams Teach Yourself Database Programming with Visual C++ in 21 Days. LC 98-85225. 1998. 39.99 (*0-672-31350-2*) Sams.

Robison, Lynda C. Boys Who Became Prophets. LC 98-37299. (Illus.). (J). 1998. 14.95 (*1-57345-083-9*) Deseret Bk.

Robison, Margaret. The Naked Bear. LC 77-83730. 70p. 1977. pap. 6.00 (*0-89924-011-9*) Lynx Hse.

— Red Creek: A Requiem. (Illus.). (Orig.). 1992. pap. 10.00 (*0-941895-08-4*) Amherst Wri Art.

Robison, Nancy. Dear Daughter about Your Wedding: A Guide for the Bride-to-Be. LC 98-50235. (Illus.). 64p. 1999. per. 9.95 (*0-684-84836-8*) S&S Trade.

— Dear Son, about Your Wedding: A Guide for the Groom-to-Be. LC 99-217334. (Illus.). 64p. 1999. per. 9.95 (*0-684-85968-8*) S&S Trade.

— Dear Son, about Your Wedding: A Guide for the Groom-to-Be. 64p. 1989. per. 6.95 (*0-671-67329-7*, Fireside) S&S Trade Pap.

Robison, Olin, et al, eds. The Arts in the World Economy: Public Policy & Private Philanthropy for a Global Cultural Community. LC 94-21200. 197p. 1994. 30.00 (*0-87451-698-6*) U Pr of New Eng.

Robison, Pamela L. Living with Chronic Illness. 1988. pap. 1.00 (*0-8309-0507-3*) Herald Pub Hse.

Robison, Richard. Indonesia: The Rise of Capital. 440p. (C). 1987. pap. 24.95 (*0-04-909024-0*, Pub. by Allen & Unwin Pty) Paul & Co Pubs.

— The New Rich in Asia. LC 96-178419. 224p. (C). 1996. pap. 24.99 (*0-415-11336-9*) Routledge.

Robison, Richard, ed. Pathways to Asia: The Politics of Engagement. LC 96-185109. 288p. 1997. pap. text 24.95 (*1-86448-102-1*, Pub. by Allen & Unwin Pty) Paul & Co Pubs.

***Robison, Richard, et al, eds.** Politics & Markets in Wake of the Asian Crisis. LC 99-31669. 304p. (C). 1999. text. write for info. (*0-415-22056-4*) Routledge.

Robison, Richard, et al, eds. Southeast Asia in the 1990s: Authoritarianism, Democracy & Capitalism. 240p. pap. 22.95 (*1-86373-230-6*, Pub. by Allen & Unwin Pty) Paul & Co Pubs.

***Robison, Richard, et al.** Politics & Markets in the Wake of the Asian Crisis. LC 99-31669. (Asian Capitalisms Ser.). 1999. pap. write for info. (*0-415-22057-2*) Routledge.

Robison, Richard A. & Tiechert, Curt, eds. Treatise on Invertebrate Paleontology Pt. A: Introduction: Fossilization (Taphonomy), Biogeography, & Biostratigraphy. LC 53-12913. 1979. 47.50 (*0-8137-3001-5*) Geol Soc.

Robison, Rita, jt. auth. see Bettigole, Neal H.

Robison, Samuel S. A History of Naval Tactics from 1530-1930: The Evolution of Tactical Maxims. LC 75-41234. reprint ed. 52.50 (*0-404-14698-8*) AMS Pr.

Robison, Sophia. Can Delinquency Be Measured? LC 75-129307. (Criminology, Law Enforcement, & Social Problems Ser.: No. 129). (Illus.). 312p. 1972. reprint ed. 24.00 (*0-87585-129-0*) Patterson Smith.

Robison, Susan D., ed. see Children & Youth Program Staff.

Robison, Wade L. Decisions in Doubt: The Environment & Public Policy. LC 94-20549. (Nelson A. Rockefeller Series in Social Science & Public Policy). 277p. 1994. text 40.00 (*0-87451-695-1*) U Pr of New Eng.

Robison, Wade L., et al, eds. Profits & Professions: Essays in Business & Professional Ethics. LC 82-23399. (Contemporary Issues in Biomedicine, Ethics, & Society Ser.). 343p. 1983. 49.50 (*0-89603-039-3*) Humana.

Robison, Wade L. & Pritchard, Michael S., eds. Medical Responsibility: Paternalism, Informed Consent & Euthanasia. LC 79-87656. (Contemporary Issues in Biomedicine, Ethics, & Society Ser.). 230p. 1979. 49.50 (*0-89603-007-5*) Humana.

***Robison, Wade L. & Reeser.** Ethics Decision Making in Social Work. LC 99-36052. 336p. 1999. pap. text 36.00 (*0-205-30779-5*) Allyn.

Robison, William. Sams Teach Yourself Microsoft SQL Server 7 in 10 Minutes. 1999. pap. 12.99 (*0-672-31663-3*) Sams.

Robison, William B., jt. auth. see Fritze, Ronald H.

Robison, Willis Eugene. As Life Passes: Selected Poetry of America's Western Frontier. LC 97-75400. 256p. 1997. 19.95 (*1-888125-21-7*) Publ Consult.

Robitaille. Writer's Resources. (C). 1999. pap. text 34.50 (*0-15-504148-7*) Harcourt.

Robitaille, Dianne, ed. see DiVecchio, Don.

***Robitaille, Louis-Bernard.** And God Created the French: Value Edition. rev. ed. Sinkler, Donald, tr. 288p. 2000. pap. 9.99 (*1-55207-028-X*) R Davies Multimed.

Robitaille, P.-M., jt. ed. see Berliner, Lawrence J.

Robitaille, Raymond, tr. see Gelinas.

***Robitille, Melissa A.** Blackstone Gate. LC 00-190443. 232p. 2000. 25.00 (*0-7388-1746-5*); pap. 18.00 (*0-7388-1747-3*) Xlibris Corp.

— In One Year's Time. LC 99-90698. 364p. 1999. 25.00 (*0-7388-0462-2*); pap. 18.00 (*0-7388-0463-0*) Xlibris Corp.

Robitiz, Kathie, ed. see Ross, Sharon.

Robitiz, Kathie, ed. see Strom, Karin.

Robitz, Kathie, ed. see Creative Homeowner Press Editors.

Robitz, Kathie, ed. see Maney, Susan.

Robl, Ernest H., ed. see Special Libraries Association Staff.

Robledo Galvan, Carmen De Monserrat, see Cuadriello, Jaime.

Robledo, Juan. The Elusive Knowledge. 187p. 1987. pap. 9.95 (*0-9633822-1-7*) J Robledo.

— Fox: An Ancient Tale. 49p. 1986. pap. 7.95 (*0-9633822-0-9*) J Robledo.

Roblee, Charles L. The Investigation of Fires. 2nd ed. (C). 1999. write for info. (*0-89303-643-9*) Appleton & Lange.

Roblee, Richard D. Interdisciplinary Dentofacial Therapy: A Comprehensive Approach to Optimal Patient Care. LC 94-20093. (Illus.). 236p. 1995. text 128.00 (*0-86715-188-9*) Quint Pub Co.

Robles, Al. Rapping with Ten Thousand Carabao in the Dark. Leong, Russell, ed. (Illus.). 140p. (Orig.). 1995. pap. 10.00 (*0-934052-25-5*) UCLA Asian Am Studies Ctr.

Robles, Albert G., jt. auth. see Levy, Sidney J.

Robles, Alfredo C., Jr. French Theories of Regulation & Concepts of the International Division of Labour. 1994. text 65.00 (*0-312-10744-7*) St Martin.

Robles Correa, Federico C. De, see De Robles Correa, Federico C.

Robles, Eduardo A. Legend of the Sun Stone: In Search of the Lost City. LC 98-94026. 193p. 1997. write for info. (*0-9661738-0-5*) Sun King.

Robles, Felix R. De los Gallos De Pelea y De Otros Temas. (Illus.). 402p. (Orig.). 1991. pap. 20.00 (*0-685-51538-9*) Saeta.

Robles-Garcia, Nelly M. Las Canteras de Mitla, Oaxaca Tecnologia para la Arquitectura Monumental. (Vanderbilt University Publications in Anthropology: Vol. 47). (SPA., Illus.). 66p. (Orig.). 1994. pap. 12.00 (*0-935462-38-4*) VUPA.

Robles, Harold E., compiled by. Reverence for Life: The Words of Albert Schweitzer. 212p. Date not set. 15.00 (*0-88365-927-1*) Galahad Bks.

***Robles, Jaime.** Unseen Stream. limited ed. 16p. 1998. pap. 15.00 (*1-889589-02-0*, Pub. by Em Pr) SPD-Small Pr Dist.

Robles, Jaime, et al, eds. Beginnings, Birth/Rebirth, & the New World: Five Fingers Review. (Review Ser.: No. 17). 184p. 1998. pap. 9.50 (*1-880627-06-X*) Five Fingers.

***Robles, Janice, ed.** The Neighborhood No. 18: Cadence of the Numerous: Five Fingers Review. (Illus.). 224p. (C). 1999. pap. 9.50 (*1-880627-08-6*) Five Fingers.

Robles, Jose F. Cartilla Espanola. (SPA., Illus.) (Orig.). 1935. pap. text 12.95 (*0-89197-064-9*) Irvington.

— La Secuencia Ceramica de la Region de Coba, Quintana Roo. 278p. 1990. pap. 11.00 (*968-6068-75-9*, IN028) UPLAAP.

Robles, Laureano, ed. see Unamuno, Miguel de.

Robles, Mariana, tr. see Salem, Lynn & Stewart, Josie.

Robles, Mariana, tr. see Worthington, Denise.

Robles, Martha. Mujeres, Mitos y Diosas (Women, Myths & Goddesses) (SPA.). 337p. 1996. pap. 29.99 (*968-16-4915-X*, Pub. by Fondo) Continental Bk.

Robles, Mireya. Hagiografia de Narcisa la Bella. (SPA.). 155p. 1985. pap. 10.00 (*0-910061-24-6*, 1113) Ediciones Norte.

— Hagiography of Narcisa the Beautiful. Diegel, Anna, tr. from SPA. LC 96-67376. 225p. 1996. pap. text 12.95 (*1-887378-03-0*) Readers Intl.

— Profecia y Luz en la Poesia de Maya Islas. Cardenas, Juan, ed. (SPA.). 40p. (Orig.). 1987. pap. 6.00 (*0-913983-05-5*) M & A Edns.

— Tiempo Artesano. (SPA.). 85p. 1973. pap. 7.00 (*0-317-46767-0*, 3402) Ediciones Norte.

Robles, Ruben, tr. see Kerri, Kenneth D.

Robles, Sainz De, see De Robles, Sainz.

Robleto, Adolfo. Catecismo Biblico y Doctrinal para el Nuevo Creyente.Tr. of Biblical Doctrinal Catechism for the New Believer. (SPA.). 164p. 1977. reprint ed. pap. 4.99 (*0-311-09088-5*) Casa Bautista.

— Conozca Quienes Son.Tr. of Know Who They Are. (SPA.). 112p. 1986. pap. 6.99 (*0-311-05764-0*) Casa Bautista.

Robleto, Adolfo. Dramas y Poemas para Dias Especiales, No. 1.Tr. of Dramas & Poems for Special Days. (SPA.). 94p. 1985. reprint ed. pap. 6.00 (*0-311-07004-3*, Edit Mundo) Casa Bautista.

— Dramas y Poemas para Dias Especiales, No. 2.Tr. of Dramas & Poems for Special Days. 96p. 1972. reprint ed. 6.00 (*0-311-07008-6*, Edit Mundo) Casa Bautista.

Robleto, Adolfo. Dramas y Poemas para Dias Especiales, Vol. 3.Tr. of Dramas & Poems for Special Days. (SPA.). 96p. 1992. pap. 7.99 (*0-311-07012-4*) Casa Bautista.

— Sermones para Dias Especiales, Vol. I.Tr. of Sermons for Special Days. (SPA.). 112p. 1989. reprint ed. 7.99 (*0-311-07009-4*) Casa Bautista.

— Sermones para Dias Especiales, Vol. II.Tr. of Sermons for Special Days. (SPA.). 96p. 1979. reprint ed. 7.99 (*0-311-07011-6*) Casa Bautista.

Robleto, Adolfo, compiled by. Quinientas una Ilustraciones Nuevas: 501 New Illustrations. 320p. 1980. reprint ed. pap. 13.50 (*0-311-42062-1*) Casa Bautista.

Robleto, Adolfo, tr. see Conner, T.

Robleto, Adolfo, tr. see Cowman, Lettie B.

Robleto, Adolfo, tr. see Dana, H. E.

Robleto, Adolfo, tr. see Dana, H. E. & Mantey, J. R.

Robleto, Jose J. Navas, see Navas Robleto, Jose J.

Robley, Grace & Robley, Rob. The Spirit Led Family. 160p. 1974. mass mkt. 5.99 (*0-88368-033-5*) Whitaker Hse.

Robley, H. G. Moko: The Art & History of Maori Tattooing. (Illus.). 216p. 1999. reprint ed. text 20.00 (*0-7881-6306-X*) DIANE Pub.

Robley, Rob, jt. auth. see Robley, Grace.

Robley, T. F. History of Bourbon County, Kansas: To the Close of 1865. 1976. reprint ed. pap. 15.00 (*0-9601568-4-4*) Historic Pres Bourbon.

Roblin, Ann. Easy Russian Phrasebook & Dictionary. LC 95-149492. (RUS & ENG., Illus.). 280p. 1994. pap. 12.95 (*0-8442-4279-9*, 42799) NTC Contemp Pub Co.

Roblin, Ronald. The Thinking Man's Guide to Success at the Trotters. 2nd rev. ed. 218p. 1995. pap. 29.95 (*1-891561-18-9*) Harness Handicappers.

Roblin, Ronald, ed. The Aesthetics of the Critical Theorists: Studies on Benjamin, Adorno, Marcuse, & Habermas. LC 90-30955. (Problems in Contemporary Philosophy Ser.: Vol. 23). 532p. 1990. lib. bdg. 119.95 (*0-88946-368-9*) E Mellen.

Roblin, Ronald, ed. see Dickie, George & Sclafani, Richard J.

Roblot, R. French Business Taxation. (European Commercial Law Library: No. 2). 1974. pap. 24.00 (*0-8464-0429-X*) Beekman Pubs.

Roblyer. Annotated Database Technology. 1999. cd-rom 18.00 (*0-13-755190-8*) P-H.

***Roblyer.** Ten First Steps on the Internet: A Learning Journey for Teachers. 2nd ed. 96p. 2000. pap. 10.00 (*0-13-030502-2*) P-H.

Roblyer, M. D. & Edwards, Jack. Integrating Educational Technology into Teaching. 2nd ed. LC 99-33275. 355p. 1999. pap. text 56.00 incl. audio compact disk (*0-13-974387-1*) P-H.

Roblyer, M. D., et al. Assessing the Impact of Computer-Based Instruction: A Review of Recent Research. LC 88-24377. (Computers in the Schools Ser.: Vol. 5, Nos. 3-4). (Illus.). 149p. 1988. text 39.95 (*0-86656-893-X*) Haworth Pr.

Roblyer, Margaret D,. Integrating the Internet into Your Classroom: Teaching with a CCC Internet Curriculum. LC 97-108316. 72p. (C). 1996. pap. text 17.00 (*0-13-700253-X*) P-H.

Robnett, Belinda. How Long? How Long? African American Women & the Struggle for Civil Rights. LC 97-2263. 272p. (C). 1997. 35.00 (*0-19-511490-6*) OUP.

— How Long? How Long? African American Women & the Struggle for Freedom & Justice. 272p. 2000. reprint ed. pap. 17.95 (*0-19-511491-4*) OUP.

Robnett, George W. Conquest Through Immigration: How Zionism Turned Palestine into a Jewish State. unabridged ed. 407p. 1968. reprint ed. pap. 14.00 (*0-945001-39-8*) GSG & Assocs.

Robnett, Regula H., jt. auth. see Chop, Walter.

Robinson, Jeffrey. The Hotel: Backstairs at the World's Most Exclusive Hotel. LC 97-71066. 320p. 1997. 24.45 (*1-55970-377-6*, Pub. by Arcade Pub Inc) Time Warner.

Robock, Stefan H. Brazil's Developing Northeast: A Study of Regional Planning & Foreign Aid. LC 79-26655. (Illus.). 213p. 1980. reprint ed. lib. bdg. 59.50 (*0-313-22295-9*, ROBD, Greenwood Pr) Greenwood.

Robock, Stefan H. & Simmonds, Kenneth. International Business & Multinational Enterprises. 4th ed. 800p. (C). 1988. text 68.50 (*0-256-03634-9*, Irwn McGrw-H) McGrw-H Hghr Educ.

Robock, Stefan H. & Simmonds, Kenneth R. International Business & Multinational Enterprises. 4th ed. 800p. (C). 1988. per. 35.50 (*0-256-07346-5*, Irwn McGrw-H) McGrw-H Hghr Educ.

***Robotham, Anne & Sheldrake, Doreen.** Health Visiting: Specialist & Higher Level Practice. LC 99-53179. (Illus.). 2000. text. write for info. (*0-443-06203-X*) Harcrt Hlth Sci Grp.

Robotham, F. P., jt. auth. see Tame, Adrian.

***Robotham, Robert.** The Last Years of the "Wee Donegal" The County Donegal Railways in Colour, 1950-59. LC 99-176252. (Illus.). 290p. 1998. 24.95 (*1-898392-42-0*, Pub. by Colourpoint) Irish Bks Media.

Robotham, Rosemarie. The Bluelight Corner: Black Women Writing on Passion, Sex & Romantic Love. 320p. 1999. 25.00 (*0-609-60223-3*, Crown) Crown Pub Group.

— The Bluelight Corner: Black Women Writing on Passion, Sex & Romantic Love. LC 98-28877. 320p. 1998. pap. 14.00 (*0-609-80354-9*) Random Hse Value.

— Zachary's Wings. 288p. 1999. pap. 12.00 (*0-684-85736-7*) S&S Trade.

Robotham, Rosemarie. Zachary's Wings. LC 98-23802. 288p. 1998. 22.00 (*0-684-84726-4*) Scribner.

Robotham, Tom. The Civil War. (Illus.). 304p. 19.99 (*1-57215-239-7*, JG2397) World Pubns.

— Edward S. Curtis. 1995. 15.98 (*0-7858-0410-2*) Bk Sales Inc.

— Varga. 1990. 15.98 (*1-57145-222-2*) Advantage Pubs.

Robotham, Tom. Varga. (Illus.). 112p. 1993. 15.98 (*0-7924-5599-1*, Thunder Bay) Advantage Pubs.

— Varga. 1995. 6.98 (*0-7858-0217-7*) Bk Sales Inc.

Robotic Industries Association, Robot Safety Subco. ANSI-RIA Robot Safety Standard. 2nd rev. ed. 22p. (Orig.). 1992. pap. 24.00 (*0-317-39388-X*) Robot Inst Am.

Robots 12 & Vision '88 Conference (1988: Detroit,. Robots 12 & Vision '88: Conference Proceedings, June 5-9, 1988, Detroit, MI, Vol. 2. LC 88-61194. (Illus.). 806p. reprint ed. pap. 200.00 (*0-8357-6501-6*, 203587200002) Bks Demand.

Robotti, Frances D. Indexing Books & Periodicals: Guidelines for Authors & Indexers. write for info. (*0-935497-01-3*) Fountainhead.

— Tracing Your Family Roots: The Ancestor Hunt. write for info. (*0-935497-03-X*) Fountainhead.

— Whaling & Old Salem: A Chronicle of the Sea. (Illus.). 292p. 1983. reprint ed. 17.95 (*0-685-41738-7*) Fountainhead.

Robotti, Frances D. & Vescovi, James. The U. S. S. Essex & the Birth of the American Navy. LC 98-52334. 304p. 1999. 22.95 (*1-58062-112-0*) Adams Media.

***Robotti, Frances Diane & Vescovi, James.** The U. S. S. Essex. 320p. 2000. pap. 10.95 (*1-58062-282-8*) Adams Media.

Robotti, Suzanne B. & Inman, Margaret A. Childbirth Instructor Magazine's Guide to Careers in Birth: How to Find a Fulfilling Job in Pregnancy, Labor & Parenting Support Without a Medical Degree. LC 97-16996. 214p. 1998. pap. 16.95 (*0-471-16230-2*) Wiley.

Robottom. Social & Economic History of Industrial Britain. Date not set. pap. text. write for info. (*0-582-22332-6*, Pub. by Addison-Wesley) Longman.

Robottom & Leake. Tutorial Topics. 1993. pap. text. write for info. (*0-582-33119-6*, Pub. by Addison-Wesley) Longman.

***Robottom, David, frwd.** Marketing Without Frontiers: The Royal Mail Guide to International Direct Marketing. 4th ed. (Illus.). 330p. 2000. reprint ed. pap. text 65.00 (*0-7881-8911-5*) DIANE Pub.

Robottom, Ian & Andrew, Jennifer. Creatures from the Other Side. 1996. pap. 50.00 (*0-949823-59-7*, Pub. by Deakin Univ) St Mut.

Robottom, Ian M. Environmental Education: Practice & Possibility. 122p. (C). 1995. pap. 34.00 (*0-7300-0543-7*, ECT317, Pub. by Deakin Univ) St Mut.

— Science Education: Exploring the Tension. 70p. (C). 1988. 41.00 (*0-7300-0562-3*, Pub. by Deakin Univ) St Mut.

Robottom, Ian M., jt. auth. see Hart, Paul.

Robottom, John. Castles & Cathedrals. (Longman Origin Ser.). 1991. pap. text 10.64 (*0-582-08250-1*) Longman.

Robottom, John, jt. auth. see Claypole, William.

Robowski, J. Dictionary of Papermaking English-Polish (P-E Index) (ENG & POL.). 491p. 1991. 48.50 (*83-85001-92-1*, Pub. by Sigma-NOT) IBD Ltd.

Roboz. Mass Spectrometry in Cancer Research. 1995. write for info. (*0-8493-0167-X*) CRC Pr.

Roboz, Helga, tr. see Marion-Wild, E. C.

Roboz, Steven, ed. Christian Rosenkreutz: From the Works of Rudolf Steiner. 20p. 1982. pap. 3.25 (*0-919924-16-6*, Pub. by Steiner Book Centre) Anthroposophic.

Roboz, Steven & Steiner, Rudolf. Islam: Study Notes. 33p. 1980. pap. 2.95 (*0-88010-050-8*, Pub. by Steiner Book Centre) Anthroposophic.

Roboz, Steven, tr. see Marion-Wild, E. C.

Robrock, K. H. Mechanical Relaxation of Interstitials in Irradiated Metals. (Tracts in Modern Physics Ser.: Vol. 118). (Illus.). 112p. 1990. 71.95 (*0-387-51090-7*) Spr-Verlag.

Robshaw, Brandon. Georgina & the Dragon. (Illus.). 96p. (J). pap. 7.95 (*0-14-038370-0*, Pub. by Pnguin Bks Ltd) Trafalgar.

Robsky, Paul, jt. auth. see Fraley, Oscar.

***ROBSON.** Lozen. 1999. mass mkt. write for info. (*0-8125-7609-8*) Tor Bks.

Robson. Man & His Seven Principles. 1986. 10.95 (*0-8356-7309-X*) Theos Pub Hse.

— Mishkat al-Masabih, 2 vols. 1994. 59.00 (*1-56744-141-6*) Kazi Pubns.

Robson. Quality Circles Members. 1982. student ed. 13.95 (*0-566-02344-X*) Ashgate Pub Co.

Robson, A. D., ed. Zinc in Soils & Plants: Proceedings of the International Symposium Held at the University of Western Australia, Perth, Western Australia, 27-28 September, 1993. LC 93-40339. (Developments in Plants & Soil Sciences Ser.: Vol. 55). 220p. (C). 1994. text 119.00 (*0-7923-2631-8*) Kluwer Academic.

Robson, A. D. & Abbott, L. K., eds. Management of Mycorrhizas in Agriculture, Horticulture & Forestry: Proceedings of an International Symposium, Held in Perth, Western Australia, September 28-October 2, 1992. LC 94-685. (Developments in Plant & Soil Sciences Ser.). 248p. (C). 1994. text 136.00 (*0-7923-2700-4*) Kluwer Academic.

Robson, A. Diedre. Prestige, Profit & Pleasure: The Market for Modern Art in New York in the 1940s & 1950s. LC 94-40929. (Garland Publications in the Fine Arts). (Illus.). 392p. 1995. text 83.00 (*0-8153-1364-0*) Garland.

Robson, Adrian P. Programmer's Guide to C++ LC 96-36943. 296p. 1997. pap. 34.50 (*0-8058-2681-5*) L Erlbaum Assocs.

Robson, Andrew J. Designing & Building Business Models Using Microsoft Excel. LC 95-6597. 1995. pap. write for info. (*0-07-709058-6*) McGraw.

— Thinking Globally. LC 96-33227. 672p. (C). 1997. pap. 37.19 (*0-07-053398-9*) McGraw.

Robson, Ann P. & Robson, John M., eds. Newspaper Writings, 4-vols. (Collected Works of John Stuart Mill: Vols. 22-25). (Illus.). 1986. text 195.00 (*0-8020-2602-8*) U of Toronto Pr.

Robson, Ann P., ed. see Mill, John Stuart, et al.

Robson, B. Pre-School Provision for Children with Special Needs. Mittler, Peter, ed. (Special Needs in Ordinary Schools Ser.). 208p. 1989. pap. text 29.95 (*0-304-31559-1*) Continuum.

Robson, B. A., jt. ed. see Burden, C. J.

Robson, Brian. Fuzzy Wuzzy: The Campaigns in the Eastern Sudan, 1884-85. (Illus.). 264p. 1994. 24.95 (*1-885119-05-4*) Sarpedon.

— Those Inner Cities: Reconciling the Social & Economic Aims of Urban Policy. (Illus.). 264p. 1989. 65.00 (*0-19-874148-0*) OUP.

Robson, Brian, ed. Fuzzy Wuzzy: The Campaigns in the Eastern Sudan 1884-85. 264p. 1997. 80.00 (*1-873376-15-4*, Pub. by Spellmnt Pubs) St Mut.

Robson, Brian, ed. Roberts in India: The Military Papers of Field Marshall Lord Roberts, 1876-1893. LC 93-26403. (Publications of the Army Records Society: Vol. 9). 1993. 72.00 (*0-7509-0401-1*, Pub. by Sutton Pub Ltd) Intl Pubs Mktg.

Robson, Brian, jt. auth. see Kershaw, Ronald.

Robson, Brian T., ed. Managing the City: The Aims & Impacts of Urban Policy. LC 87-1827. 240p. 1987. 57.00 (*0-389-20731-4*, N8289) B&N Imports.

***Robson, Charles & European Foundation for the Improvement of Living and Working Conditions Staff.** Employment & Sustainability: Digest Report. LC 99-196386. 10p. 1998. write for info. (*92-828-5026-9*, Pub. by Comm Europ Commun) Bernan Associates.

Robson, Cheryl, ed. Seven Plays by Women: Female Voices Fighting Lives. 272p. 1999. pap. 14.95 (*0-9515877-1-4*, Pub. by Theatre Comm) Consort Bk Sales.

— A Touch of the Dutch. LC 97-181984. 230p. 1999. pap. 19.95 (*0-9515877-7-3*, Pub. by Theatre Comm) Consort Bk Sales.

Robson, Cliff, jt. ed. see Sterling, Chris M.

Robson, Clive, jt. auth. see Cossali, Paul.

Robson, Colin. Drawing. LC 97-31118. 44p. 1997. 14.95 (*0-8230-5631-7*) Watsn-Guptill.

Robson, Colin. Experiment Design & Statistics in Psychology. 3rd ed. 1994. pap. 16.95 (*0-14-017648-9*, Pub. by Pnguin Bks Ltd) Trafalgar.

Robson, Colin. Real World Research: A Resource for Social Scientists & Practitioner-Researchers. LC 92-21782. 512p. 1993. pap. 33.95 (*0-631-17689-6*) Blackwell Pubs.

***Robson, Craig.** A Guide to the Birds of Southeast Asia: Thailand, Peninsular Malaysia, Singapore, Myanmar, Laos, Vietnam, Cambodia. (Illus.). 504p. 2000. 59.50 (*0-691-05012-0*, Pub. by Princeton U Pr) Cal Prin Full Svc.

***Robson, David.** Skydancing: Aerobatic Flight Techniques. LC 00-40626. (Illus.). 2000. write for info. (*1-56027-389-5*) ASA Inc.

Robson, David, et al. Homes for the Third Age: A Design Guide for Extra Care Sheltered Housing. LC 98-167578. (Illus.). 192p. (C). (gr. 13). 1998. 70.00 (*0-419-23120-X*, D5736, E & FN Spon) Routledge.

Robson, David, jt. auth. see Goldberg, Adele.

Robson, David, jt. auth. see Rees, Mike.

An Asterisk (*) at the beginning of an entry indicates that the title is appearing for the first time.

Robson, David W. Educating Republicans: The College in the Era of the American Revolution, 1750-1800, 15. LC 84-22436. (Contributions to the Study of Education Ser.: No. 15). (Illus.). 272p. 1985. 65.00 (*0-313-24606-8*, RER/) Greenwood.
Robson, Deb, ed. Socks on a Rooster: Louisiana's Earl K. Long. LC 93-47978. 56p. 1994. pap. 7.95 (*0-934026-94-7*) Interweave.
***Robson, Deborah.** Spin-Off Magazine Presents Handspun Treasures from Rare Wools: Collected Works from the Save the Sheep Project. LC 00-33602. (Illus.). 2000. pap. write for info. (*1-883010-84-5*) Interweave.
Robson, Douglas S., jt. auth. see Skalski, John R.
Robson, E. & Wendt, Larry. Shadows of the Voice. 1982. pap. 14.00 (*0-934982-09-0*) Primary Pr.
— Shadows of the Voice. deluxe limited ed. 1982. 35.00 (*0-934982-08-2*) Primary Pr.
Robson, E. & Wimp, J., eds. Against Infinity: An Anthology of Contemporary Mathematical Poetry. LC 79-90106. 1979. 17.00 (*0-934982-00-7*); pap. 8.95 (*0-934982-01-5*) Primary Pr.
Robson, E. H., et al, eds. Integration & Management of Technology for Manufacturing. (Management of Technology Ser.: No. 11). 466p. 1991. 99.00 (*0-86341-206-8*, MT011) INSPEC Inc.
Robson, E. H., jt. auth. see Moscardini, A. O.
Robson, E. W. & Robson, M. M. Film Answers Back: An Historical Appreciation of the Cinema. LC 73-169350. (Arno Press Cinema Program Ser.). (Illus.). 402p. 1972. reprint ed. 24.95 (*0-405-03923-9*) Ayer.
***Robson, Eleanor.** Mesopotamian Mathematics, 2100-1600 B. C. Technical Constants in Bureaucracy & Education, Vol. XIV. LC 98-38018. (Oxford Editions of Cuneiform Texts Ser.). (Illus.). 352p. 1999. pap. text 105.00 (*0-19-815246-9*) OUP.
Robson, Ellen & Halicki, Dianne. Haunted Highway: The Spirits of Route 66. LC 99-24786. (Illus.). 192p. 1999. pap. 12.95 (*1-885590-43-1*) Golden West Pub.
Robson, Eric & Lello, Ronald. The Beatitudes: Living with Blessings, Meditations & Prayer. LC 97-37800. (Illus.). 128p. 1997. 14.95 (*1-86204-154-7*, Pub. by Element MA) Penguin Putnam.
Robson, Ernest M. Freedom, Cannibalism, Creative Love & the Values of Cosmic Nonsense: A Philosophical Manifesto. LC 86-62122. (Illus.). 1986. 14.00 (*0-934982-11-2*) Primary Pr.
— Thomas Onetwo. (Illus.). 1971. 6.95 (*0-87110-074-6*) Primary Pr.
— Thomas Onetwo. (Illus.). 1971. 20.00 (*0-89366-258-5*) Ultramarine Pub.
— Transcualisticas: Bilingual Edition. Lopez De Thorgood, Lucy, tr. LC 78-65323. (ENG & SPA., Illus.). 1978. pap. 8.95 (*0-934982-04-X*) Primary Pr.
— Transcualisticas: Bilingual Edition. deluxe ed. Lopez De Thorgood, Lucy, tr. LC 78-65323. (ENG & SPA., Illus.). 1978. 25.00 (*0-934982-03-1*) Primary Pr.
— Transwhichics. LC 74-121306. 1970. 17.00 (*0-8023-1249-7*); pap. 8.95 (*0-8023-1250-0*) Primary Pr.
Robson, Ernest M., jt. auth. see Wendt, Larry.
Robson, Frank. The Basics of Gravure Printing. (Illus.). (Orig.). 1995. write for info. (*1-880290-01-4*) Gravure Assn.
Robson, G., jt. auth. see Langworth, R.
***Robson, Garry.** No One Likes Us, We Don't Care: The Myth & Reality of Millwall Fandom. (Illus.). 192p. 2000. 65.00 (*1-85973-367-0*, Pub. by Berg Pubs); pap. 19.50 (*1-85973-372-7*, Pub. by Berg Pubs) NYU Pr.
Robson, George D. Continuous Process Improvement: Simplifying Work Flow Systems. 352p. 1991. 37.50 (*0-02-926645-9*) Free Pr.
Robson, Graham. The Big Healey's: Collector's Guide. (Collector's Guide Ser.). (Illus.). 128p. 1982. 27.95 (*0-900549-55-6*, Pub. by Motor Racing) Motorbooks Intl.
***Robson, Graham.** BMW 3-Series, 1991-1999. (Illus.). 128p. 2000. pap. 19.95 (*1-899870-48-2*, 130538AE, Pub. by Motor Racing) Motorbooks Intl.
— The Cars of BMC. (Illus.). 302p. 1999. pap. 39.95 (*1-899870-41-5*, Pub. by Motor Racing) Motorbooks Intl.
Robson, Graham. Cars of the Roots Group: Hillman, Humber, Singer, Sunbeam & Sunbeam Talbot. (Illus.). 240p. 1990. 39.95 (*0-947981-35-7*, Pub. by Motor Racing) Motorbooks Intl.
— Cortina - Ford's Best Seller. (Illus.). 144p. 1998. 32.95 (*1-874105-98-7*, Pub. by Vloce Pub) Motorbooks Intl.
— Cosworth Story. 1990. 29.95 (*1-85260-238-4*, Pub. by P Stephens) Haynes Manuals.
— Fiat Sports Cars: From 1945 to the X1/9. LC 84-130222. 192 p. 1984. write for info. (*0-85045-558-8*) Ospry.
— The Lotus. (Album Ser.: no. 294). (Illus.). 32p. (C). 1989. pap. 4.75 (*0-7478-0217-3*, Pub. by Shire Pubns) Parkwest Pubns.
— Lotus since the 70's Vol. 2: Esprit, Etna & V8 Engines Collector's Guide. (Collector's Guide Ser.). (Illus.). 128p. 1993. 27.95 (*0-947981-69-1*, Pub. by Motor Racing) Motorbooks Intl.
— MG T-Series. (Illus.). 192p. 1998. 35.95 (*1-86126-179-9*, Pub. by Cro1wood) Motorbooks Intl.
***Robson, Graham.** The MGA, MGB & MGC: A Collector's Guide. 2000. pap. 19.95 (*1-899870-43-1*, 129756AE, Pub. by Motor Racing) Motorbooks Intl.
Robson, Graham. Prop Perfection: Restored Propliners & Warbirds. LC 97-52134. (Illus.). 112p. 1997. pap. 24.95 (*0-7603-0511-0*) MBI Pubg.
— Rallying: The 4 Wheel Drive Revolution. LC 88-81752. 207p. 1989. write for info. (*0-85429-723-5*) GT Foulis.
— Rallying - The 4 Wheel Drive Revolution. LC 86-82147. (Foulis Motoring Bk.). (Illus.). 192p. 34.95 (*0-85429-547-X*, F723, Pub. by GT Foulis) Haynes Manuals.
***Robson, Graham.** Rolls-Royce & Bentley Collector's Guide, Vol. 3. (Illus.). 144p. 2000. pap. 19.95 (*1-899870-44-X*, 129757AE, Pub. by Motor Racing) Motorbooks Intl.
Robson, Graham. Rolls-Royce & Bentley Collector's Guide: V4, 1980-98: Silver Spirit to Azure. (Illus.). 130p. 1999. 29.95 (*1-899870-30-X*, 127108AE) Motorbooks Intl.
***Robson, Graham.** Rolls-Royce Silver Cloud. 2000. 34.95 (*1-86126-322-8*) Cro1wood.
Robson, Graham. The Sporting Fords Vol. 4: Sierras. (Illus.). 128p. 1991. 27.95 (*0-947981-55-1*, Pub. by Motor Racing) Motorbooks Intl.
— Sunbeam Alpine & Tiger: The Complete Story. (Illus.). 208p. 1996. 35.95 (*1-85223-941-7*) MBI Pubg.
— Triumph Herald & Vitesse: The Complete Story. (Illus.). 200p. 1997. 35.95 (*1-86126-050-4*, Pub. by Cro1wood) Motorbooks Intl.
— Triumph Spitfire GT-6. (Illus.). 128p. 1991. 27.95 (*0-947981-60-8*, Pub. by Motor Racing) Motorbooks Intl.
— TVR's Vol. 1: Grantura to Taimar Collector's Guide, 1. (Collector's Guide Ser.). (Illus.). 128p. 1994. 27.95 (*0-947981-80-2*, Pub. by Motor Racing) Motorbooks Intl.
— TVR's Vol. 2: Tasmin to Chimaera Collector's Guide, 2. (Collector's Guide Ser.). (Illus.). 128p. 1994. 27.95 (*0-947981-81-0*, Pub. by Motor Racing) Motorbooks Intl.
— The World's Most Powerful Cars. 1990. 12.98 (*1-55521-563-7*) Bk Sales Inc.
Robson, Harry E., jt. ed. see Occelli, Mario L.
Robson, J., et al. After Abuse: Papers on Caring & Planning for a Child Who Has Been Sexually Abused. (C). 1989. 400.00 (*0-903534-82-7*, Pub. by Brit Ag for Adopt & Fost) St Mut.
Robson, J. C., jt. auth. see Gordon, Robert.
Robson, J. K. R., ed. Food, Ecology & Culture: Readings in the Anthropology of Dietary Practices, Vol. 1. x, 144p. 1980. text 168.00 (*0-677-16090-9*) Gordon & Breach.
Robson, J. M., ed. see Mill, John Stuart.
Robson, J. R. Famine: Its Causes, Effects & Management, Vol. 2. (Food & Nutrition in History & Anthropology Ser.). x, 170p. 1981. text 141.00 (*0-677-16180-8*) Gordon & Breach.
Robson, J. S. How a One-Legged Rebel Lives. 21.95 (*0-8488-1141-0*) Amereon Ltd.
Robson, J. T., ed. see Meares, L. G. & Hymowitz, C. E.
Robson, James C., jt. auth. see McConnell, J. C.
Robson, Janet. Growing As a Single Parent: Growing As a Single Parent. (Family Life Issues Ser.). 1995. pap. 4.50 (*0-570-09495-X*, 20-2707) Concordia.
Robson, Jenny. Winner's Magic. (Junior African Writers Ser.). (Illus.). 80p. (J). (gr. 3 up). 1992. pap. 3.88 (*0-7910-2906-9*) Chelsea Hse.
Robson, Jocelyn. Girls' Own Stories: Australian & New Zealand Women's Films. 1997. pap. text 16.95 (*1-85727-053-3*, Pub. by Scarlet Pr) LPC InBook.
Robson, Jocelyn, ed. The Professional F. E. Teacher: Staff Development & Training in the Corporate College. 160p. 1996. 66.95 (*1-85972-113-3*, Pub. by Avebry) Ashgate Pub Co.
***Robson, John.** Captain Cook's World: Maps of the Life & Voyages of James Cook R. N. (Illus.). 208p. 2000. 40.00 (*0-295-98019-2*) U of Wash Pr.
— One Man in His Time: The Biography of the Laird of Torosay Castle: Traveller, Wartime Escaper & Distinguished Politician. 240p. 1997. 100.00 (*1-86227-036-8*, Pub. by Spellmnt Pubs) St Mut.
Robson, John. The Pilgrim Goes Forth. 276p. (Orig.). 1986. pap. 8.75 (*0-685-17666-5*) Lake Crest Hse.
Robson, John, ed. A Guide to Growing Up. (Illus.). 45p. (Orig.). (gr. 4-6). 1982. pap. 2.50 (*0-936098-32-5*) Intl Marriage.
— Me & You. (Illus.). 48p. (Orig.). (J). (gr. 6-9). 1982. pap. 2.50 (*0-936098-33-3*) Intl Marriage.
— Origin & Evolution of the Universe: Evidence for Design? 318p. 1987. 65.00 (*0-7735-0617-9*, Pub. by McG-Queens Univ Pr); pap. 22.95 (*0-7735-0618-7*, Pub. by McG-Queens Univ Pr) CUP Services.
— Parents, Children & Sex. (Illus.). (Orig.). 1981. pap. 2.50 (*0-936098-31-7*) Intl Marriage.
— Parents, Teenagers & Sex. (Illus.). 40p. (Orig.). 1982. pap. 2.50 (*0-936098-34-1*) Intl Marriage.
— Three Early English Metrical Romances. (Camden Society, London. Publications, First Ser.: No. 18). reprint ed. 42.50 (*0-404-50118-4*) AMS Pr.
— You & Your Family. (Illus.). 30p. (Orig.). (J). (gr. 2-4). 1981. pap. 2.50 (*0-936098-30-9*) Intl Marriage.
Robson, John, jt. ed. see Carpenter, Roger.
Robson, John A. Wyclif & the Oxford Schools: The Relation of the "Summa de Ente" to Scholastic Debates at Oxford in the Later Fourteenth Century. LC 61-16171. (Studies in Medieval Life & Thought: Vol. 8). 282p. reprint ed. pap. 80.40 (*0-608-30565-0*, 2051448) Bks Demand.
Robson, John M. The Improvement of Mankind: The Social & Political Thought of John Stuart Mill. LC 68-140051. (University of Toronto, Department of English Studies & Texts: No. 15). 306p. reprint ed. pap. 94.90 (*0-608-12865-1*, 202367100037) Bks Demand.
— James & John Stuart Mill: Papers of the Centenary Conference. Laine, Michael, ed. LC 76-16177. 172p. reprint ed. pap. 53.40 (*0-8357-8190-9*, 203405800088) Bks Demand.
— Marriage or Celibacy? The Daily Telegraph on a Victorian Dilemma. 366p. 1996. pap. text 29.95 (*0-8020-7798-6*) U of Toronto Pr.
Robson, John M., ed. Editing Nineteenth-Century Texts: Papers Given at the Editorial Conference, University of Toronto, November, 1966. (Conference on Editorial Problems Ser.: No. 2). 1987. 42.50 (*0-404-63652-7*) AMS Pr.
— Editing Nineteenth Century Texts: Papers Given at the Editorial Conference, University of Toronto, November 1966. LC 67-108888. 155p. reprint ed. pap. 48.10 (*0-8357-3772-1*, 203650100003) Bks Demand.
Robson, John M., ed. see Mill, John Stuart.
Robson, John M., ed. see Mill, John Stuart, et al.
Robson, John M., jt. ed. see Robson, Ann P.
Robson, John M., ed. & intro. see Mill, John Stuart.
Robson, John R. K., jt. compiled by see Elias, Joel N.
Robson, Julien. David Levinthal: Die Nibelungen. (Illus.). 1994. pap. 15.00 (*1-881616-41-X*) Dist Art Pubs.
Robson, K. & University of Southampton Hartley Library Staff. MS 200, Papers of the International Military Tribunal & the Nuremberg Military Tribunals, 1945-49. LC 93-182980. (Library Archive Lists, Catalogues & Guides Ser.). vi, 61 p. 1993. write for info. (*0-85432-464-X*) Univ of Southampton.
Robson, K. G. Robson's Annotated Corporations Law, 2 vols. 2nd ed. LC 97-179402. 1700p. 1997. pap. 52.00 (*0-455-21494-8*, Pub. by LawBk Co) Gaunt.
Robson, Ken. Riley's Annotated Bills of Exchange Act & Cheques & Payment Orders Act. 4th ed. 320p. 1994. pap. 65.00 (*0-455-21294-5*, Pub. by LawBk Co) Gaunt.
Robson, Kenneth, ed. see Giamatti, A. Bartlett.
Robson, Kenneth, ed. see Skies, G. E.
Robson, Kenneth S. Manual of Clinical Child Psychiatry. LC 85-26869. 334p. 1986. reprint ed. pap. 103.60 (*0-608-02023-0*, 206267900003) Bks Demand.
Robson, Kenneth S., ed. Manual of Clinical Child & Adolescent Psychiatry. 2nd rev. ed. Orig. Title: Manual of Clinical Child Psychiatry. 497p. 1994. spiral bd. 44.50 (*0-88048-528-0*, 8528) Am Psychiatric.
Robson, L. L. The Convict Settlers of Australia. (Illus.). 257p. 1994. pap. 29.95 (*0-522-84585-1*, Pub. by Melbourne Univ Pr) Paul & Co Pubs.
Robson, Larry J. & Bouwman, Dorothy L. Carotid Artery Disease. Grin, Oliver D., ed. (Patient Education Ser.). (Illus.). 26p. (Orig.). 1990. pap. text 4.00 (*0-929689-39-9*) Ludann Co.
Robson, Lloyd. The First AIF: A Study of Its Recruitment,1914-1918. (Illus.). 240p. 1995. reprint ed. pap. 19.95 (*0-522-84237-2*, Pub. by Melbourne Univ Pr) Paul & Co Pubs.
— A Short History of Tasmania. 2nd rev. ed. LC 98-228449. (Illus.). 208p. 1998. pap. text 19.95 (*0-19-554199-5*) OUP.
Robson, Lloyd L. A History of Tasmania Vol. 1: Van Diemen's Land from the Earliest Times to 1855, Vol. 1. (Illus.). 640p. 1983. text 74.00 (*0-19-554364-5*) OUP.
— A History of Tasmania Vol. 2: Colony & State from 1856 to the 1980s. (Illus.). 674p. 1991. text 98.00 (*0-19-553031-4*) OUP.
Robson, Lucia St. Clair. Mary's Land. 1996. mass mkt. 5.99 (*0-345-40628-1*) Ballantine Pub Grp.
Robson, Lucia St. Claire. Fearless: A Novel of Sarah Bowman. LC 98-5396. 400p. 1998. 24.95 (*0-345-39771-1*, Ballantine Epiphany) Ballantine Pub Grp.
— Ride the Wind. 1985. mass mkt. 5.99 (*0-345-32522-2*) Ballantine Pub Grp.
Robson, M., jt. auth. see France, R.
Robson, M. M., jt. auth. see Robson, E. W.
Robson, Martin C., jt. auth. see Heggers, John P.
Robson, Meredith, jt. auth. see France, Richard.
Robson, Michael. Opium: The Poisoned Poppy. (Illus.). 85p. 1994. 38.00 (*962-7283-08-8*, Pub. by FormAsia) Weatherhill.
— Rona the Distant Island. 180p. (C). 1999. 56.00 (*0-86152-867-0*, Pub. by Acair Ltd); pap. 38.50 (*0-86152-823-9*, Pub. by Acair Ltd) St Mut.
***Robson, Michael.** St. Francis of Assisi: The Legend & the Life. 2000. pap. text 19.95 (*0-225-66876-9*) G Chapman.
Robson, Michelle & Clarke, Tim. LPC Case Study: Civil Litigation. 239p. 1994. pap. 24.00 (*1-85431-388-6*, Pub. by Blackstone Pr) Gaunt.
— LPC Case Study: Civil Litigation, 1995/96. 266p. 1995. 9.95 (*1-85431-476-9*, Pub. by Blackstone Pr) Gaunt.
— LPC Case Study: Civil Litigation, 1996/97. 3rd ed. 264p. 1996. pap. 26.00 (*1-85431-579-X*, Pub. by Blackstone Pr) Gaunt.
— LPC Case Study: Civil Litigation, 1997/98. 4th rev. ed. 285p. 1997. pap. 28.00 (*1-85431-697-4*, Pub. by Blackstone Pr) Gaunt.
— LPC Case Study: Civil Litigation, 1998-99. 5th ed. (Legal Practice Course Guides Ser.). 304p. 1998. pap. 36.00 (*1-85431-789-X*) Gaunt.
Robson, Michelle, jt. auth. see Khan, Malcolm.
Robson, Mike. Facilitating. 219p. 1995. 65.95 (*0-566-07449-4*, Pub. by Gower) Ashgate Pub Co.
— Problem Solving in Groups. 2nd ed. 160p. 1993. 61.95 (*0-566-07414-1*, Pub. by Gower); pap. 29.95 (*0-566-07415-X*, Pub. by Gower) Ashgate Pub Co.
— Quality Circles: A Practical Guide. 2nd ed. 256p. 1988. text 69.95 (*0-566-02748-8*, Pub. by Gower) Ashgate Pub Co.
— Quality Circles in Action. LC 84-4095. 176p. 1984. text 65.95 (*0-566-02433-0*, Pub. by Gower) Ashgate Pub Co.
Robson, Mike & Ullah, Philip. A Practical Guide to Business Process Re-Engineering. LC 95-40204. 169p. 1996. 74.95 (*0-566-07577-6*, Pub. by Gower) Ashgate Pub Co.
Robson, N. K., et al. Flora of Tropical East Africa: Celastraceae. 78p. 1994. pap. 19.50 (*90-6191-365-9*) Ashgate Pub Co.
Robson, N. K., ed. see Sivarajan, V. V.
Robson, Nigel, jt. auth. see Cyrus, Digby.
Robson, Pam. Banana. LC 97-6502. (What's for Lunch? Ser.). 32p. (J). 1998. lib. bdg. 20.00 (*0-516-20826-8*) Childrens.
— Banana. Cohen, Helaine, ed. LC 97-6502. (What's for Lunch? Ser.). (Illus.). 32p. (J). (ps-2). 1998. pap., student ed. 6.95 (*0-516-26217-3*) Childrens.
— Body Language. LC 97-3784. (Hello Out There! Ser.). (J). (gr. 2-5). 1997. 19.00 (*0-531-14468-2*) Watts.
— Body Language. (Hello Out There Ser.). (Illus.). 32p. (J). 1998. pap. 6.95 (*0-531-15349-5*) Watts.
— Corn. LC 97-6910. (What's for Lunch? Ser.). 32p. (J). 1998. 20.00 (*0-516-20823-3*) Childrens.
— Corn. LC 97-6910. (What's for Lunch? Ser.). (Illus.). 32p. (J). (ps). 1998. pap., student ed. 6.95 (*0-516-26219-X*) Childrens.
— Honey. LC 97-6503. (What's for Lunch? Ser.). 32p. (J). (gr. k-2). 1998. 20.00 (*0-516-20825-X*) Childrens.
— Honey. LC 97-6503. (What's for Lunch? Ser.). (Illus.). 32p. (J). (gr. k-2). 1998. pap., student ed. 6.95 (*0-516-26220-3*) Childrens.
— Rice. LC 97-6041. (What's for Lunch? Ser.). 32p. (J). 1997. 20.00 (*0-516-20824-1*) Childrens.
— Rice. Cohen, Helaine, ed. (What's for Lunch? Ser.). (Illus.). 32p. (J). 1998. pap., student ed. 6.95 (*0-516-26224-6*) Childrens.
Robson, Pam, jt. auth. see Chapman, Gillian.
Robson, Pat. The Celtic Heart. LC 99-63837. 232p. 1999. pap. 14.95 (*1-57098-309-7*) Roberts Rinehart.
Robson, Pat. Oil. (Butterfly Bks.). 32p. (J). (gr. 3-5). 1985. 9.95 (*0-86685-449-5*) Intl Bk Ctr.
— Rain. (Butterfly Bks.). 32p. (J). (gr. 3-5). 1985. 9.95 (*0-86685-451-7*) Intl Bk Ctr.
Robson, Patrick. Structural Appraisal of Traditional Buildings. 200p. 1990. text 74.95 (*0-566-09081-3*, Pub. by Gower) Ashgate Pub Co.
***Robson, Patsy.** Bangkok Magic. 272p. 2000. pap. 12.95 (*0-9700492-4-2*) Steel Pr Pubng.
Robson, Peter. Economic Integration in Africa. LC 68-25582. 320p. reprint ed. pap. 99.20 (*0-8357-9455-5*, 201477500093) Bks Demand.
— The Economics of International Integration. 4th ed. LC 97-29570. 1151p. (C). 1998. pap. 29.99 (*0-415-14877-4*) Routledge.
— The Economics of International Integration. 4th ed. LC 97-29570. 336p. (C). 1998. 99.99 (*0-415-14876-6*) Routledge.
— Integration, Development & Equity: Economic Integration in West Africa. (Illus.). 192p. (C). 1983. text 39.95 (*0-04-338109-X*) Routledge.
Robson, Peter, ed. Sunshine & Salt Air. 3rd rev. ed. (Illus.). 208p. 1997. pap. 17.95 (*1-55017-143-7*) Harbour Bks.
— Transnational Corporations & Regional Economic Integration. LC 93-18758. (United Nations Library on Transnational Corporations: Vol. 9). 1993. write for info. (*0-415-08542-X*) Routledge.
— Welfare Law. (International Library of Essays in Law & Legal Theory). 550p. (C). 1992. lib. bdg. 150.00 (*0-8147-7426-1*) NYU Pr.
Robson, Peter & Watchman, Paul, eds. Justice, Lord Denning & the Constitution. 272p. 1981. text 87.95 (*0-566-00399-6*, Pub. by Dartmth Pub) Ashgate Pub Co.
Robson, Philip. Forbidden Drugs. (Illus.). 160p. (C). Date not set. write for info. (*0-19-262430-X*) OUP.
— Forbidden Drugs. 2nd ed. LC 99-32331. (Illus.). 208p. 1999. pap. 21.95 (*0-19-262955-7*) OUP.
Robson, R. Thayne, ed. Employment & Training R&D: Lessons Learned & Future Directions. LC 84-7584. 133p. 1984. pap. text 12.00 (*0-88099-018-X*) W E Upjohn.
Robson Rhodes Financial Services Ltd., Personal Fi. Robson Rhodes: Personal Financial Planning Manual 1994-95. 10th ed. 1994. pap. 29.95 (*0-406-03597-0*, MICHIE) LEXIS Pub.
Robson, Robert. The Attorney in Eighteenth-Century England. LC 85-48164. (Cambridge Studies in English Legal History). 194p. 1986. reprint ed. 55.00 (*0-912004-34-7*) Gaunt.
— Using the STL: The C++ Standard Template Library. LC 97-8921. 440p. 1997. pap. 44.95 (*0-387-98204-3*) Spr-Verlag.
***Robson, Robert.** Using the STL: The C++ Standard Template Library. 2nd ed. LC 99-26377. 592p. 1999. pap. 54.95 (*0-387-98857-2*) Spr-Verlag.
Robson, Roy R. Old Believers in Modern Russia. LC 95-22663. (Illus.). 250p. 1996. lib. bdg. 30.00 (*0-87580-205-2*) N Ill U Pr.
Robson, Ruthann. A/K/A: A Novel. LC 97-7200. 1997. text 23.95 (*0-312-15469-0*) St Martin.
— A/K/A: A Novel. LC 98-52074. (Stonewall Inn Editions Ser.). 1998. pap. 12.95 (*0-312-19825-6*) St Martin.
— Cecile. LC 91-29775. 168p. (Orig.). 1991. pap. 8.95 (*1-56341-001-X*); lib. bdg. 18.95 (*1-56341-002-8*) Firebrand Bks.
— Eye of a Hurricane. LC 89-23603. 130p. (Orig.). 1989. pap. 8.95 (*0-932379-64-8*); lib. bdg. 18.95 (*0-932379-65-6*) Firebrand Bks.
— Gay Men & Lesbians & the Law. Duberman, Martin, ed. (Issues in Gay & Lesbian Life Ser.). (Illus.). 154p. (YA). (gr. 9 up). 1995. 24.95 (*0-7910-2612-4*); pap. 12.95 (*0-7910-2963-8*) Chelsea Hse.
— Lesbian (Out) Law: Survival under the Rule of Law. LC 92-8333. 188p. (Orig.). 1992. pap. 9.95 (*1-56341-012-5*); lib. bdg. 20.95 (*1-56341-013-3*) Firebrand Bks.
— Masks. LC 98-25138. 160p. 1999. pap. 14.00 (*0-9654578-5-0*, Pub. by Leapfrog Pr) Consort Bk Sales.
— Sappho Goes to Law School: Fragments in Lesbian Legal Theory. LC 97-52686. 320p. 1998. 49.50 (*0-231-10560-6*); pap. 17.50 (*0-231-10561-4*) Col U Pr.
***Robson, Ruthann.** The Struggle for Happiness. LC 99-87935. 240p. 2000. 22.95 (*0-312-25219-6*) St Martin.
Robson, S. O., jt. ed. see Ras, J. J.

R

An Asterisk (*) at the beginning of an entry indicates that the title is appearing for the first time.

Robson, Scott. Old Nova Scotian Quilts. LC 96-119200. (Illus.). 128p. 1998. pap. text 24.95 (*1-55109-118-6*) Nimbus Publ.

Robson-Scott, Elaine, tr. see Freud, Sigmund & Andreas-Salome, Lou.

Robson-Scott, William, tr. see Freud, Sigmund & Andreas-Salome, Lou.

Robson, Stephani, jt. ed. see Stipanuk, David M.

Robson, Stuart. The First World War. LC 98-13297. (Seminar Studies in History). 144p. (C). 1998. pap. 15.93 (*0-582-31556-5*) Longman.

Robson, Sucia St. Clair. Fearless: A Novel of Sarah Bowman. 1999. mass mkt. 6.99 (*0-345-39770-3*) Ballantine Pub Grp.

Robson, Sue & Smedley, Sue. Education in Early Childhood: First Things First. LC 96-210340. (Roehampton Teaching Studies). 208p. 1996. pap. 24.95 (*1-85346-385-X*, Pub. by David Fulton) Taylor & Francis.

***Robson, Terry.** The State & Community Action. LC 99-38284. 1999. write for info. (*0-7453-1479-1*) Pluto GBR.

— State & Community Action. 2000. pap. 22.50 (*0-7453-1474-0*) Pluto GBR.

Robson, Thomas D. Entree to Asia: A Culinary Adventure with Thomas Robson. LC 99-34567. 1999. 24.95 (*962-593-543-6*) Periplus.

Robson, Tom. Musical Wisdom: Songs & Drawings for the Child in Us All. (Illus.). 88p. (Orig.). (J). (gr. k-6). 1992. pap. 16.95 (*0-9633332-0-8*) Laughing Cat.

Robson, Vivian E. A Beginner's Guide to Practical Astrology. 184p. 1991. pap. 17.00 (*0-89540-123-1*, SB-123, Sun Bks) Sun Pub.

— Fixed Stars & Constellations in Astrology. 264p. 1995. pap. 22.00 (*0-89540-281-5*, SB-281, Sun Bks) Sun Pub.

— A Students' Text-Book of Astrology. 243p. 1981. pap. 18.50 (*0-89540-117-7*, SB-117, Sun Bks) Sun Pub.

Robson, Vivian E., jt. auth. see Leo, Alan.

Robson, W., tr. see Michaud, Joseph F.

Robson, W. W. Critical Essays. 240p. 1993. text 45.00 (*0-312-09612-7*) St Martin.

Robson, W. W., ed. & intro. see Doyle, Arthur Conan.

Robson, W. W., ed. & intro. see Kipling, Rudyard.

Robson, Walter. An English View of American Quakerism: The Journal of Walter Robson, 1842-1929 Written During the Fall of 1877, While Traveling among American Friends. Bronner, Edwin B., ed. LC 71-107345. (American Philosophical Society, Memoirs Ser.: Vol. 79). 175p. reprint ed. pap. 54.30 (*0-608-13252-7*, 202513500042) Bks Demand.

Robson, Wendy. Strategic Management & Information Systems: An Integrated Approach. 2nd ed. (Illus.). 400p. (Orig.). 1997. pap. 62.50 (*0-273-61591-2*, Pub. by Pitman Pub) Trans-Atl Phila.

Robson, William. James Chalmers: Pioneer Missionary to Papua New Guinea, Vol. 9. 1988. pap. 6.99 (*0-88019-236-4*) Schmul Pub Co.

Robson, William A. Civilisation & the Growth of Law: A Study of the Relations Between Men's Ideas about the Universe & the Institutions of Law & Government. xv, 354p. 1997. reprint ed. 110.00 (*1-56169-250-6*) Gaunt.

— Civilization & the Growth of Law: Study of Relations Between Men's Ideas About the Universe & the Institutions of Law & Government. LC 74-25779. (European Sociology Ser.). 374p. 1975. reprint ed. 31.95 (*0-405-06532-9*) Ayer.

— Governors & the Governed. LC 64-15876. (Edward Douglass White Lectures). 68p. reprint ed. pap. 30.00 (*0-8357-9385-0*, 201363900087) Bks Demand.

— Justice & Administrative Law: A Study of the British Constitution. 3rd ed. LC 72-98792. 674p. 1970. reprint ed. lib. bdg. 38.50 (*0-8371-3143-X*, ROJU, Greenwood Pr) Greenwood.

— Welfare State & Welfare Society: Illusion & Reality LC 76-368932. 184 p. 1976. write for info. (*0-04-360040-9*) Allen & Unwin Pty.

Robson, William A., ed. The Civil Service in Britain & France. LC 75-26777. 191p. 1975. reprint ed. lib. bdg. 35.00 (*0-8371-8347-2*, ROCSB, Greenwood Pr) Greenwood.

Robson, William A. & Crick, Bernard, eds. China in Transition. LC 75-11135. (Sage Contemporary Social Science Issues Ser.: No. 17). 120p. reprint ed. pap. 37.20 (*0-608-11651-3*, 202194500026) Bks Demand.

Robson, William B., jt. ed. see Lemco, Jonathan.

***Robson Wright, Margaret.** Fundamental C. 1999. pap. 45.00 (*1-898563-60-8*) Horwood Pub.

Robuchon, Joel, frwd. Eyewitness Handbook: French Cheeses. 1996. 17.95 (*0-614-19888-7*) DK Pub Inc.

Robuck, J. E. My Own Personal Experience & Observation As a Soldier in the Confederate Army During the Civil War, 1861-1865, Also During the Period of Reconstruction. (Illus.). 136p. 1977. reprint ed. 14.00 (*0-937130-03-6*) Burkes Bk Store.

Robustelli, Cecelia, jt. auth. see Maiden, Martin.

Robutti, Andreina, jt. auth. see Nissim-Momigliano, Luciana.

Roby, Kimberla Lawson. Here & Now. LC 98-65260. 288p. 1999. 22.00 (*1-57566-336-8*) Kensgtn Pub Corp.

***Roby, Kimberla Lawson.** Here & Now. 289p. 2000. pap. 13.00 (*1-57566-494-1*) Kensgtn Pub Corp.

Roby, Cynthia. When Learning Is Tough: Kids Talk about Learning Disabilities. LC 93-6532. (Illus.). (J). (gr. 2-7). 1994. lib. bdg. 13.95 (*0-8075-8892-X*) A Whitman.

Roby, George A. & Green, Lisle R. Mechanical Methods of Chaparral Modification. (Illus.). 60p. 1998. reprint ed. 13.00 (*0-89904-514-6*, Ecosytems Resrch); reprint ed. pap. 7.00 (*0-89904-515-4*, Ecosytems Resrch) Crumb Elbow Pub.

Roby, H. J. Roby: Pedigree of Roby of Castle Donington, County Leicester. 69p. 1993. reprint ed. pap. 14.00 (*0-8328-3741-5*); reprint ed. lib. bdg. 24.00 (*0-8328-3740-7*) Higginson Bk Co.

Roby, Henry J. Roman Private Law in the Times of Cicero & of the Antonines, 2 vols. 1977. lib. bdg. 195.00 (*0-8490-2533-8*) Gordon Pr.

— Roman Private Law in the Times of Cicero & of the Antonines, Vols. 1 & 2. 1103p. 1998. reprint ed. 295.00 (*1-56169-361-8*) Gaunt.

***Roby, Henry John.** An Introduction to the Study of Justinian's Digest: Containing an Account of Its Composition & of the Jurists Used or Referred to Therein. fac. ed. LC 99-59331. cclxxixp. 2000. 65.00 (*1-58477-073-2*) Lawbk Exchange.

— Roman Private Law in the Times of Cicero & of the Antonines, 1902, 2 vols., Set. fac. ed. LC 99-59270. 2000. 180.00 (*1-58477-074-0*) Lawbk Exchange.

Roby, James. Commitment. 1997. mass mkt. 5.99 (*0-345-40979-5*, Del Rey) Ballantine Pub Grp.

Roby, Kimberla L. Behind Closed Doors. LC 96-94608. x, 250p. 1997. pap. 12.00 (*0-9653470-4-4*) Lenox Pr.

— Behind Closed Doors. LC 96-94608. 244p. 1997. reprint ed. pap. 12.00 (*1-57478-005-0*) Black Classic.

***Roby, Kimberla L.** Casting the First Stone. 320p. 2000. 23.00 (*1-57566-489-5*, Knsington) Kensgtn Pub Corp.

Roby, Mary L. This Land Turns Evil Slowly. 1982. mass mkt. 2.50 (*0-451-11696-8*, AE1696, Sig) NAL.

Roby, Norman. Connoisseurs' Handbook of the Wines of California & the Pacific Northwest. LC 98-6375. 1998. pap. 19.95 (*0-375-70329-2*) Knopf.

Roby, Norman S. & Olken, Charles E. The New Connoisseurs' Handbook of California Wines. 3rd ed. LC 95-21554. 448p. 1995. 27.50 (*0-679-44486-6*) Knopf.

Roby, Pamela. Creating a Just World: Leadership for the Twenty-First Century. 59p. 1998. pap. 3.00 (*1-885357-74-5*) Rational Isl.

— Women in the Workplace. 138p. 1981. 18.95 (*0-87073-172-6*); pap. 11.95 (*0-87073-173-4*) Schenkman Bks Inc.

Roby, Pamela A. Women in the Workplace: Proposals for Research & Policy Concerning the Conditions of Women in Industrial & Service Jobs. LC 80-24605. 146p. 1981. reprint ed. pap. 45.30 (*0-608-05340-6*, 206504500012) Bks Demand.

Roby, Paul, jt. auth. see Huang, Samuel J.

Roby, Tom, ed. see Cornwell, Don M.

Roby, William C., jt. auth. see Dorris, Michael.

Robyn, Abby E. & Hanser, Lawrence M. JROTC Career Academies' Guidebook: With Materials from the California Partnership Academies Handbook: a Guide to Success. 37p. 1995. pap. text 13.00 (*0-8330-1664-4*, MR-573-OSD) Rand Corp.

Robyn, Abby E., jt. auth. see Devin, Phillip D.

Robyn, Abby E., jt. auth. see Hanser, Lawrence M.

Robyn, Donald, jt. auth. see Daphne, Clair.

Robyn, Dorothy L. Braking the Special Interests: Trucking Deregulation & the Politics of Policy Reform. LC 86-16015. (Illus.). xii, 308p. (C). 1987. 29.95 (*0-226-72328-3*) U Ch Pr.

Robynson, Ralph, tr. see More, Thomas.

Robyt, John F. Essentials of Carbohydrate Chemistry. LC 97-19019. (Advanced Texts in Chemistry Ser.). (Illus.). 336p. 1997. 54.95 (*0-387-94951-8*) Spr-Verlag.

Robyt, John F. & White, Bernard J. Biochemical Techniques: Theory & Practice. LC 86-26874. (Chemistry). 400p. 1987. 35.25 (*0-534-07944-X*) Brooks-Cole.

— Biochemical Techniques: Theory & Practice. (Illus.). 407p. (C). 1990. reprint ed. text 37.95 (*0-88133-556-8*) Waveland Pr.

Robyt, John F., ed. see Choi, Yang-Do.

Roc, John. Fire! A Play. LC 69-15511. 181p. 1969. 16.95 (*0-910278-46-6*) Boulevard.

Roc, Margaret. Little Koala Finds a Friend. (Illus.). 32p. (J). 1998. 16.00 (*0-207-19121-2*) HarpC.

Roca, A. Oshanahan, see Oshanahan Roca, A.

Roca, Alexander. Crusader: The Story of the Shelton Flying Wing. LC 89-91607. (Illus.). 184p. (C). 1989. text 59.50 (*0-9622886-0-8*) Rare Birds Pub.

***Roca, Ana.** Cuaderno Para Estudiantes Bilingues: Nuevos Mundos. 160p. 1999. pap. text 31.95 (*0-471-19200-7*) Wiley.

— Nuevos Mundos: Lectura, Cultura y Comunicacion: Curso de Espanol Para Estudiates Bilingues. (SPA.). 254p. 1998. pap. 40.95 (*0-471-19205-8*) Wiley.

— Teaching Spanish as a Heritage Language. pap. text. write for info. (*0-471-24200-4*) Wiley.

Roca, Ana & Jensen, John, eds. Spanish in Contact: Issues in Bilingualism. LC 96-44936. xi, 226p. 1996. pap. 23.95 (*1-57473-008-8*) Cascadilla Pr.

Roca, Ana & Jensen, John B., eds. Spanish in Contact: Issues in Bilingualism. (Illus.). xi, 226p. 1996. lib. bdg. 53.95 (*1-57473-108-4*) Cascadilla Pr.

Roca, Ana & Lipski, John M., eds. Spanish in the United States: Linguistic Contact & Diversity. LC 93-14956. (Studies in Anthropological Linguistics: No. 6). viii, 212p. (C). 1993. lib. bdg. 106.15 (*3-11-013204-4*) Mouton.

Roca, Castells A., et al. Enciclopedia de la Salud. 6th ed. (SPA.). 1043p. 1974. 70.00 (*0-7859-0868-4*, S-13678) Fr & Eur.

Roca, Empar. Saltapinos Ha Perdido los Calcetines.Tr. of Saltapinos Lost His Socks. (SPA., Illus.). 23p. (J). (gr. 2-4). 1997. 8.95 (*84-246-5406-4*, Pub. by SM Ediciones) IBD Ltd.

Roca, Iggy. A Workbook in Phonology. LC 99-12252. 100p. 1999. pap. 22.95 (*0-631-21394-5*) Blackwell Pubs.

Roca, Iggy & Johnson, Wyn. A Course in Phonology. LC 98-51941. 480p. 1999. 69.95 (*0-631-21345-7*); pap. 34.95 (*0-631-21346-5*) Blackwell Pubs.

Roca, Iggy M. Generative Phonology. LC 93-4066. (Linguistic Theory Guides Ser.). 256p. (C). 1994. pap. 29.99 (*0-415-04141-4*) Routledge.

Roca, Iggy M., ed. Derivations & Constraints in Phonology. LC 96-53307. (Illus.). 614p. 1997. text 135.00 (*0-19-823689-1*); pap. text 49.95 (*0-19-823690-5*) OUP.

— Logical Issues in Language Acquisition. (Linguistic Models Ser.: No. 15). xxiii, 298p. (Orig.). (C). 1990. pap. text 92.35 (*3-11-013373-3*) Mouton.

***Roca, Josep, et al.** Pulmonary & Peripheral Gas Exchange in Health & Disease. LC 00-31585. (Lung Biology in Health & Disease Ser.). 2000. write for info. (*0-8247-0335-9*) Dekker.

Roca Muntanola, Julio. Dictionary of Parapsychology: Diccionario de Parapsicologia. (ENG & SPA.). 272p. 1979. 29.95 (*0-8288-4761-4*, S50093) Fr & Eur.

Roca, Muria Bosch & Serrano, Marta. Cells, Genes, & Chromosomes. (Invisible World Ser.). (Illus.). 32p. (J). (gr. 4 up). 1995. lib. bdg. 15.95 (*0-7910-3154-3*) Chelsea Hse.

— The Nervous System & the Brain. (Invisible World Ser.). (Illus.). 32p. (YA). (gr. 4 up). 1995. lib. bdg. 15.95 (*0-7910-3152-7*) Chelsea Hse.

Roca, Paul M. Spanish Jesuit Churches in Mexico's Tarahumara. LC 78-14467. 394p. 1979. reprint ed. pap. 122.20 (*0-608-02360-4*, 206300200004) Bks Demand.

Roca, Philippe, jt. auth. see Davis, Wayne H.

Roca, Roberto, et al. Wings from Afar: An Ecoregional Approach to Conservation of Neotropical Migratory Birds in South America. Davis, Norah D., ed. LC 96-68384. (America Verde Ser.). (Illus.). 180p. (Orig.). (C). 1996. pap. text 29.95 (*1-886765-03-0*) Nature VA.

Roca, Roberto L. Oil Birds of Venezuela: Ecology & Conservation. (Publications of the Nuttall Orinth©lgical Club: No. 24). (Illus.). 83p. 1994. 11.00 (*1-877973-35-1*) Nuttall Ornith.

Roca, Ruben A., intro. Market Research for Shopping Centers. LC 79-92292. 210p. (Orig.). 1988. pap. 28.95 (*0-685-68040-1*) Intl Coun Shop.

— Market Research for Shopping Centers. LC 79-92292. 210p. (Orig.). 1988. pap. 39.95 (*0-913598-11-9*, 504) Intl Coun Shop.

Rocamona, Mary, jt. auth. see Koertge, Ron.

***Rocamora, Carol, ed.** Chekhov: Letters about the Theatre. 224p. 2000. pap. 19.95 (*1-57525-257-0*) Smith & Kraus.

Rocamora, Carol, tr. see Chekhov, Anton.

Rocard, Marcienne. The Children of the Sun: Mexican-Americans in the Literature of the United States. Brown, Edward G., Jr., tr. from FRE. LC 88-39772. 393p. 1989. 50.95 (*0-8165-0992-1*) U of Ariz Pr.

Rocawich, Linda. Our Food, Our Common Ground. (Southern Exposure Ser.). (Illus.). 112p. (Orig.). 1983. pap. 4.00 (*0-943810-16-7*) Inst Southern Studies.

Rocca, A. J. De, see De Rocca, A. J.

Rocca, Al M. The Shasta Dam Boomtowns: Community Building in the New Deal Era. LC 93-84961. (Illus.). 180p. (Orig.). 1993. pap. 12.95 (*1-884055-00-1*) Redding Mus.

Rocca, Al M. & Capener, J. Paul. America's Shasta Dam: A History of Construction, 1936-1945. (Illus.). 165p. (Orig.). 1994. pap. 15.95 (*0-9643378-0-0*) Renown Pubng.

Rocca, Alessandro. Ian Ritchie. LC 98-86725. 96p. 1999. pap. 29.95 (*0-8230-2508-X*) Watsn-Guptill.

Rocca, Carlos A. & Sahota, Gian S. Income Distribution: Theory, Modeling, & Case Study of Brazil. LC 84-8963. (Illus.). 246p. 1985. reprint ed. pap. 76.30 (*0-608-00179-1*, 206096100006) Bks Demand.

Rocca, Jorge J. & Da Silva, Luiz B., eds. Soft X-Ray Lasers & Applications II, Vol. 3156. LC 98-122612. 356p. 1997. 80.00 (*0-8194-2578-8*) SPIE.

***Rocca, Jorge J. & Da Silva, Luiz B., eds.** Soft X-Ray Lasers & Applications III. 1999. pap. text 84.00 (*0-8194-3262-8*) SPIE.

Rocca, Lawrence. Nomo! 1996. pap. 14.95 (*1-56931-052-1*) Viz Commns Inc.

Rocca, Michael Della, see Della Rocca, Michael.

Rocca, Robert C. Della, see Lemke, Bradley N.

Rocca, Robert C. Della, see Lemke, Bradley N. & Della Rocca, Robert C.

Roccapriore, Maria. Anointing of the Sick & Elderly. LC 80-65722. (Illus.). 144p. (Orig.). 1980. pap. 2.95 (*0-8189-1160-3*, 160, Pub. by Alba Bks) Intl Spec Bk.

Roccasalvo, Joan L. The Eastern Catholic Churches: An Introduction to Their Worship & Spirituality. (American Essays in Liturgy Ser.). 64p. (Orig.). 1992. pap. 4.95 (*0-8146-2047-7*) Liturgical Pr.

— The Ignatian Influence on the Spirituality of the Sisters of St. Joseph. (Illus.). 111p. (Orig.). 1993. pap. write for info. (*0-9638407-0-3*) Congreg St Joseph.

— The Plainchant Tradition of Southwester Rus. 185p. 1986. text 52.50 (*0-88033-096-1*, Pub. by East Eur Monographs) Col U Pr.

Roccasalvo, Joseph. Portrait of a Woman: A Novel. LC 94-73066. 253p. (Orig.). pap. 12.95 (*0-89870-545-2*) Ignatius Pr.

Roccatagliata, Giuseppe. A History of Ancient Psychiatry, 16. LC 84-15721. (Contributions in Medical Studies: No. 16). 304p. 1986. 75.00 (*0-313-24419-7*, RHI/, Greenwood Pr) Greenwood.

Roccella, Edward J. Working Group Report on Primary Prevention of Hypertension: National High Blood Pressure Education Program. (Illus.). 49p. 1998. reprint ed. pap. text 20.00 (*0-7881-4226-7*) DIANE Pub.

***Roccella, Edward J., ed.** Churches As an Avenue to High Blood Pressure Control. (Illus.). 97p. (C). 2000. reprint ed. pap. text 20.00 (*0-7881-8610-8*) DIANE Pub.

Rocchi, Marc, ed. High-Speed Digital IC Technologies. (Artech House Microwave Library). 320p. 1990. text 92.00 (*0-89006-326-5*) Artech Hse.

Rocchiccio. Clinical Leadership in Nursing. (C). 1998. pap. text 4.00 (*0-8089-2103-7*, Grune & Strat) Harcrt Hlth Sci Grp.

Rocchiccioli, Judith T. & Tilbury, Mary S. Clinical Leadership in Nursing. Eoyang, Thomas, ed. LC 97-34010. (Illus.). 320p. 1998. pap. text 29.95 (*0-7216-5442-8*, W B Saunders Co) Harcrt Hlth Sci Grp.

Rocchio. Reel Racism. 2000. 59.00 (*0-8133-6709-3*); pap. 20.00 (*0-8133-6710-7*) Westview.

Rocchio, Vincent F. Cinema of Anxiety: A Psychoanalysis of Italian Neorealism. LC 99-6046. 220p. 1999. pap. 17.95 (*0-292-77101-0*) U of Tex Pr.

***Rocchio, Vincent F.** Cinema of Anxiety: A Psychoanalysis of Italian Neorealism. LC 99-6046. 220p. 1999. 35.00 (*0-292-77100-2*) U of Tex Pr.

Rocco, Christopher. Tragedy & Enlightenment: Athenian Political Thought & the Dilemmas of Modernity. LC 96-11600. (Classics & Contemporary Thought Ser.: Vol. 4). 240p. (C). 1997. 45.00 (*0-520-20494-8*, Pub. by U CA Pr) Cal Prin Full Svc.

***Rocco, David.** Avventura: Journeys in Italian Cuisine. LC 00-23613. (Illus.). 192p. 2000. pap. 21.95 (*1-57959-510-3*, Pub. by BB&T Inc) Publishers Group.

Rocco, Ellen, ed. European Accountancy Yearbook, 1992. 1992. pap. text 235.00 (*1-85333-610-6*, Pub. by Graham & Trotman) Kluwer Academic.

Rocco, John, ed. see Cummings, E. E.

Rocco, K. On Campaign. (Illus.). 1995. 25.00 (*1-883476-01-1*, Pub. by Emperors Pr) Combined Pub.

Rocco, Mary E. A Collection of Poems. 1998. pap. write for info. (*1-57553-547-5*) Watermrk Pr.

Rocco, Michael P. Painting Realistic Watercolor Textures. (Illus.). 128p. 1996. 27.99 (*0-89134-659-7*, North Lght Bks) F & W Pubns Inc.

Rocco, Nola. The Hollywood Facelift: Facelifting, Cosmetic Surgery & the New You. 1995. pap. 19.95 (*0-935016-32-5*) Zinn Pub Grp.

Rocco, Pasquale. Pastillage: Executive Chef. LC 98-92180. (Illus.). 112p. 1998. pap. write for info. (*1-57502-976-6*, PO2669) Morris Pubng.

Rocco, Sha. The Masculine Cross & Ancient Sex Worship. 65p. 1993. pap. 6.00 (*0-89540-210-6*, SB-210) Sun Pub.

— The Masculine Cross & Ancient Sex Worship (1874) 65p. 1996. reprint ed. pap. 5.00 (*1-56459-723-7*) Kessinger Pub.

— The Musculine Cross & Ancient Sex Worship. 65p. 1994. reprint ed. spiral bd. 10.00 (*0-7873-1117-0*) Hlth Research.

— Sex Mythology. (Illus.). 55p. (C). 1982. reprint ed. 6.00 (*0-911826-34-3*, 5440) Am Atheist.

Rocco, Thomas M. & Murphy, Lawrence R., eds. Institutional & Staff Structures for Nontraditional Programs. LC 84-23655. (Alliance Manual Ser.: No. 2). 128p. 1985. 13.50 (*0-8108-1772-1*) Scarecrow.

Rocek, Thomas R. Navajo Multi-Household Social Units: Archaeology on Black Mesa, Arizona. LC 94-33277. 237p. 1995. 51.00 (*0-8165-1472-0*) U of Ariz Pr.

Rocek, Thomas R. & Bar-Yosef, Ofer, eds. Seasonality & Sedentism: Archaeological Perspectives from Old & New World Sites. LC 97-69904. (Peabody Museum Bulletin Ser.: Vol. 6). (Illus.). 230p. 1998. pap. 30.00 (*0-87365-956-2*, B6) Peabody Harvard.

Rocek, Thomas R. & Speth, John D. The Henderson Site Burials: Glimpses of a Late Prehistoric Population in the Pecos Valley. (Technical Reports Ser.: No. 18). (Illus.). xx, 348p. (Orig.). 1986. pap. 13.00 (*0-915703-08-4*) U Mich Mus Anthro.

Roceric, Alexandra. Memento. 1982. 5.00 (*0-917944-06-2*) Am Inst Writing Res.

— Romanian Textbook. LC 89-85238. 356p. 1990. 48.00 (*0-931745-57-8*) Dunwoody Pr.

Roceric, Alexandra, contrib. by. Interval - Opal Ocean. LC 97-93524. 50p. 1997. pap. 5.00 (*0-9623183-3-7*) Moonfall Pr VA.

Roceric, Alexandra, jt. auth. see Juilland, Alphonse.

Roces, Alfredo & Roces, Grace. Culture Shock! Philippines. LC 91-77245. (Illus.). 248p. 1992. 12.95 (*1-55868-089-6*) Gr Arts Ctr Pub.

Roces, Grace, jt. auth. see Roces, Alfredo.

Roces, Mina. Women, Power & Kinship Politics: Female Power in Post-War Philippines. LC 97-35136. 232p. 1998. 59.95 (*0-275-96006-4*, Praeger Pubs) Greenwood.

Roces, Mina, jt. auth. see Edwards, Louise.

Roch, Edward. Eating Out in Provence & the Cote D'Azur: A Personal Guide to Over 220 Restaurants. LC 92-4803. (Illus.). 192p. 1992. pap. 12.95 (*0-940793-93-8*) Interlink Pub.

Roch, Maria Teresa Soler, ed. see Academic Committee on European Tax Law Staff.

Roch, Patrick A. Minority Access to Higher Education: An Analysis of a Pipeline Approach Through Neighborhood Learning Centers - the Minnestoa Experiment. LC 94-4719. 156p. (Orig.). (C). 1994. lib. bdg. 48.00 (*0-8191-9496-4*) U Pr of Amer.

Rocha, A., jt. ed. see Catto, S.

Rocha, Adriana & Jorde-Rocha, Kristi. Child of Eternity. LC 94-26633. 336p. 1995. 23.00 (*0-345-38945-X*) Ballantine Pub Grp.

Rocha, Antonio F. Goncalves Da, see Harbert, John C. & Goncalves Da Rocha, Antonio F.

Rocha, Arturo Menchaca, see Menchaca Rocha, Arturo.

Rocha, Barbara. Getting over Yourself: A Guide to Public Speaking. Zaragoza, Luis, ed. (Illus.). 196p. (Orig.). 1998. pap. 19.95 (*0-9660001-2-9*, JDC0117) Bouldin Hill.

An Asterisk (*) at the beginning of an entry indicates that the title is appearing for the first time.

Rocha, Bolivar. Development Financing & Changes in Circumstances: The Case for Adoption Clauses. LC 97-50134. 224p. 1997. 110.00 (*0-7103-0590-7*, Pub. by Kegan Paul Intl) Col U Pr.

Rocha, Carlos, tr. see Trout, Susan S.

Rocha, Guy L., jt. auth. see Kintop, Jeffrey M.

Rocha, Guy L., jt. auth. see Zanjani, Sally.

***Rocha, Jan.** Brazil. 80p. 2000. pap. 9.95 (*0-85598-433-3*, Pub. by Oxfam Pub) Stylus Pub VA.

Rocha, Jan. Brazil: A Guide to the People, Politics & Culture. 2nd ed. (In Focus Guides Ser.). 96p. 1999. pap. text 12.95 (*1-56656-328-3*) Interlink Pub.

— Brazil in Focus: A Guide to the People, Politics & Culture. LC 97-9939. (In Focus Guides Ser.). (Illus.). 88p. 1997. pap. 12.95 (*1-56656-261-9*) Interlink Pub.

— Colombia in Focus: A Guide to the People, Politics & Culture. (In Focus Ser.). (Illus.). 80p. (Orig.). Date not set. pap. 12.00 (*0-85345-970-3*, Pub. by Lat Am Bur) Monthly Rev.

Rocha, Laurie A., jt. auth. see Lang, Andrew S.

Rocha, Mercedes Gonzalez De la, see Gonzalez de la Rocha, Mercedes, ed.

Rocha, Patricia K. Esthetic Denistry & Ceramic Restoration. (Illus.). 424p. 1998. 199.95 (*1-85317-159-X*) Thieme Med Pubs.

Rocha, Patricia K., jt. auth. see Tarantino, John A.

Rocha-Pereira, ed. Pausaniae Vol. I: Libri I-IV. (GRE.). 1989. 57.50 (*3-322-00508-9*, T1700, Pub. by B G Teubner) U of Mich Pr.

— Pausaniae Vol. II: Libri V-VIII. (GRE.). 1990. 49.50 (*3-322-00213-6*, T1576, Pub. by B G Teubner) U of Mich Pr.

— Pausaniae Vol. III: Libri IX-X Indices. (GRE.). 1989. 53.50 (*3-322-00509-7*, T1577, Pub. by B G Teubner) U of Mich Pr.

Rocha, Tina, ed. see Mayhew, Stephen.

Rochaix, J. D. & Goldschmidt-Clermont, M. The Molecular Biology of Chloroplasts & Mitochondria in Chlamydomonas. LC 98-35404. (Advances in Photosynthesis Ser.). 1998. 320.00 (*0-7923-5174-6*) Kluwer Academic.

Rochambeau, Jean B. De, see De Rochambeau, Jean B.

Rochard, Henri. For the Love of Kate. 1963. 18.00 (*0-614-29670-6*) Maple Mont.

— I Was a Male War Bride No. I. (Illus.). 1977. reprint ed. lib. bdg. 12.00 (*0-686-21179-0*) Maple Mont.

— I Was a Male War Bride No. II: For the Love of Kate. 1963. reprint ed. 18.00 (*0-686-21177-4*, 41132) Maple Mont.

— Pensees. (Illus.). 1977. reprint ed. pap. 5.00 (*0-686-21180-4*) Maple Mont.

***Rochat, H. & Martin-Eauclaire, M. F., eds.** Animal Toxin: Principles & Applications. (Methods & Tools in Biosciences & Medicine Ser.). 350p. 1999. 128.00 (*3-7643-5983-8*, Pub. by Birkhauser); pap. 98.00 (*3-7643-6020-8*, Pub. by Birkhauser) Spr-Verlag.

***Rochat, Hervbe. & Martin-Eauclaire, Marie-France.** Animal Toxins: Facts & Protocols. LC 00-23625. 2000. write for info. (*0-8176-6020-8*) Birkhauser.

Rochat, Philippe, ed. Early Social Cognition: Understanding Others in the First Months of Life. LC 98-24653. 352p. 1999. 79.95 (*0-8058-2829-X*) L Erlbaum Assocs.

— The Self in Infancy: Theory & Research. LC 95-35838. (Advances in Psychology Ser.: Vol.112). 496p. Date not set. 154.50 (*0-444-81925-8*) Elsevier.

Rochau, Elisabeth, ed. James Rizzi: The New York Paintings (Postcard Book) (ENG & GER., Illus.). 20p. 1996. pap. text 13.00 (*3-7913-1746-6*, Pub. by Prestel) te Neues.

Rochberg, Francesca. Babylonian Horoscopes. LC 97-44943. (Transactions Ser.: Vol. 88, Pt. 1). (Illus.). xi, 164p. 1998. pap. 20.00 (*0-87169-881-1*, T881-rof) Am Philos.

Rochberg-Halton, Eugene. Meaning & Modernity: Social Theory in Pragmatic Attitude. LC 86-7060. (Illus.). 320p. (C). 1995. lib. bdg. 48.00 (*0-226-72330-5*) U Ch Pr.

— Meaning & Modernity: Social Theory in Pragmatic Attitude. LC 86-7060. (Illus.). 314p. (C). 2000. pap. text 18.00 (*0-226-72331-3*) U Ch Pr.

Rochberg-Halton, Eugene, jt. auth. see Csikszentmihalyi, Mihaly.

Rochberg-Halton, Francesca, ed. Language, Literature, & History: Philological & Historical Studies Presented to Erica Reiner. (American Oriental Ser.: Vol. 67). (Illus.). xii, 439p. (C). 1987. 35.00 (*0-940490-67-6*, #PJ3189: L35) Am Orient Soc.

Roche. The International Banana Trade. 1998. 149.95 (*1-85573-405-2*, Pub. by Woodhead Pubng) Am Educ Systs.

— International Banana Trade. 1998. ring bd. 149.95 (*0-8493-0545-4*) CRC Pr.

— Mathematics of Measurement: A Critical History. (C). Date not set. text. write for info. (*0-485-11473-9*, Pub. by Athlone Pr) Humanities.

Roche, jt. auth. see Estrin.

Roche, Alex F. Growth, Maturation, & Body Composition: The Fels Longitudinal Study, 1929-1991. (Studies in Biological Anthropology: No. 9). (Illus.). 296p. (C). 1992. text 69.95 (*0-521-37449-9*) Cambridge U Pr.

Roche, Alex F., ed. Predicting Adult Stature for Individuals. (Monographs in Pediatrics: Vol. 3). 1975. 42.75 (*3-8055-1843-9*) S Karger.

Roche, Alex F., et al, eds. Human Body Composition. LC 95-21397. (Illus.). 376p. 1996. text 65.00 (*0-87322-638-0*, BROC0638) Human Kinetics.

Roche, Alex F. & Malina, Robert M., eds. Manual of Physical Status & Performance in Childhood Vol. 1: Physical Status, Set with Vol. 2. LC 82-16515. 1456p. 1983. 195.00 (*0-306-41136-9*, Plenum Trade) Perseus Pubng.

— Manual of Physical Status & Performance in Childhood Vol. 2: Physical Performance. LC 82-16515. 814p. 1983. 145.00 (*0-306-41137-7*, Plenum Trade) Perseus Pubng.

Roche, Alex F., et al. Assessing the Skeletal Maturity of the Hand-Wrist: FELS Method. (Illus.). 348p. (C). 1988. text 82.95 (*0-398-05452-5*) C C Thomas.

— Serial Changes in Subcutaneous Fat Thicknesses of Children & Adults. (Monographs in Pediatrics: Vol. 17). (Illus.). x, 110p. 1982. pap. 68.75 (*3-8055-3496-5*) S Karger.

Roche, Alphonse V. Alphonse Daudet. LC 75-25549. (Twayne's World Authors Ser.). (C). 1976. lib. bdg. 17.95 (*0-317-38183-0*) Irvington.

— Provencal Regionalism. LC 74-128942. (Northwestern University. Humanities Ser.: No. 30). reprint ed. 37.50 (*0-404-50730-1*) AMS Pr.

Roche, Anne, jt. auth. see Peguy, Charles.

Roche, Anthony. Contemporary Irish Drama: From Beckett to McGuinness. LC 94-22566. (C). 1994. text 45.00 (*0-312-12325-6*) St Martin.

Roche, Anthony, ed. see Martin, Augustine.

Roche, Billy. Tumbling Down. 144p. 1997. pap. 9.95 (*0-86327-431-5*, Pub. by Wolfhound Press) Irish Amer Bk.

— The Wexford Trilogy. 192p. 1993. pap. 19.95 (*1-85459-265-3*, Pub. by N Hern Bks) Theatre Comm.

Roche, Brien A. Virginia Domestic Relations Case Finder. 2nd ed. 273p. 1991. 90.00 (*0-87473-765-6*, MICHIE) LEXIS Pub.

— Virginia Domestic Relations Case Finder. 3rd ed. LC 96-76204. 390p. 1996. 90.00 (*1-55834-325-3*, 66607-11, MICHIE) LEXIS Pub.

— Virginia Domestic Relations Case Finder: 1998 Cumulative Supplement. 3rd ed. 1998. suppl. ed. 35.00 (*0-327-00217-4*, 66609-15) LEXIS Pub.

— Virginia Domestic Relations Case Finder with 1992 Supplement. 2nd ed. 273p. 1991. 70.00 (*0-685-59626-5*, MICHIE) LEXIS Pub.

— Virginia Domestic Relations Case Finder, 1999 Cumulative Supplement. 3rd ed. 60p. 1999. pap. write for info. (*0-327-01346-X*, 6660916) LEXIS Pub.

— Virginia Torts Case Finder. 3rd ed. 863p. 1994. 90.00 (*1-55834-161-7*, 66603-11, MICHIE) LEXIS Pub.

***Roche, Brien A.** Virginia Torts Case Finder. 4th ed. LC 99-62378. 943p. 1999. 110.00 (*0-327-01300-1*, 6660312) LEXIS Pub.

Roche, Brien A. Virginia Torts Case Finder: 1998 Cumulative Supplement. 3rd ed. LC 94-76780. 1998. 45.00 (*0-327-00118-6*, 66604-14) LEXIS Pub.

Roche, Catherine De La, see Dickinson, Thorold & De La Roche, Catherine.

Roche, Charles. Football's Stunting Defenses. LC 82-6321. 181p. 1982. 16.95 (*0-13-324020-7*, Parker Publishing Co) P-H.

Roche, Chris. A Boy, a Ball, a Dream: The Amazing Life of the World's Most Devoted Basketball Junkie, Tom J. "Toody" Cirincione. LC 92-72559. (Illus.). 1993. 21.95 (*0-8158-0488-1*) Chris Mass.

***Roche, Chris.** Impact Assessment for Development Agencies: Learning to Value Change. 160p. 2000. 39.95 (*0-85598-424-4*, Pub. by Oxfam Pub); pap. 15.95 (*0-85598-418-X*, Pub. by Oxfam Pub) Stylus Pub VA.

Roche, Chris, jt. auth. see Rogaly, Ben.

Roche, Christine, jt. auth. see Gilbert, Harriett.

Roche, Daniel. The Culture of Clothing: Dress & Fashion in the Ancien Regime. Birrell, Jean, tr. (Past & Present Publications). (Illus.). 548p. 1997. pap. text 21.95 (*0-521-57454-4*) Cambridge U Pr.

***Roche, Daniel.** France in the Enlightenment, 130. Goldhammer, Arthur, tr. (Harvard Historical Studies). 2000. pap. 24.95 (*0-674-00199-0*) HUP.

Roche, Daniel. France in the Enlightenment, Vol. 130. Goldhammer, Arthur, tr. from FRE. LC 97-42550. (Harvard Historical Studies). 736p. 1998. 39.95 (*0-674-31747-5*) HUP.

***Roche, Daniel.** A History of Everyday Things: The Birth of Consumption in France, 1600-1800. Pearce, Brian, tr. from FRE. LC 99-23258. 319p. (C). 2000. 59.95 (*0-521-63329-X*); pap. 22.95 (*0-521-63359-1*) Cambridge U Pr.

— Love's Labors: A Memoir of a Young Marriage & Divorce. 288p. 1999. pap. 13.00 (*1-57322-775-7*, Riverhd Trade) Berkley Pub.

Roche, Daniel. Love's Labors: A Story of Marriage & Divorce. LC 98-45432. (Illus.). 304p. 1999. 23.95 (*1-57322-067-1*, Riverhead Books) Putnam Pub Group.

— The People of Paris. LC 86-24506. (Studies on the History of Society & Culture: No. 2). 300p. 1987. pap. 17.95 (*0-520-06031-8*, Pub. by U CA Pr) Cal Prin Full Svc.

Roche, Daniel, jt. ed. see Darnton, Robert.

Roche, Daniel, ed. see Menetra, Louis.

Roche, David M., et al. Speed of Light: The 1996 World Solar Challenge. 336p. 1998. pap. 35.00 (*0-7334-1527-X*, Pub. by New South Wales Univ Pr) Intl Spec Bk.

Roche de Coppens, Peter. Apocalypse Now: The Challenges of Our Times. LC 87-45742. (Spiritual Sciences Ser.). 304p. (Orig.). 1999. pap. 9.95 (*0-87542-677-8*) Llewellyn Pubns.

— The Invisible Temple. LC 87-45111. (Spiritual Sciences Ser.). (Illus.). 304p. (Orig.). 1999. pap. 9.95 (*0-87542-676-X*) Llewellyn Pubns.

— The Sociological Adventure: A Holistic Perspective. 348p. (C). 1996. pap. text, per. 31.50 (*0-7872-2002-7*) Kendall-Hunt.

Roche, Denis. Art Around the World! Loo-Loo, Boo, & More Art You Can Do. LC 97-24556. (Illus.). 32p. (J). (gr. k-4). 1998. 15.00 (*0-395-85597-7*) HM.

— Brave Georgie Goat: Three Little Stories about Growing Up. LC 96-54000. (Illus.). 32p. (J). 1997. lib. bdg. 17.99 (*0-517-70965-1*) Crown Pub Group.

***Roche, Denis.** Brave Georgie Goat: 3 Little Stories about Growing Up. (Illus.). (J). 2000. pap. 6.99 (*0-375-81006-4*) Random.

Roche, Denis. Loo-Loo, Boo & Art You Can Do. LC 95-21971. (Illus.). 32p. (J). (ps-4). 1996. 14.95 (*0-395-75921-8*) HM.

— Ollie All Over. LC 96-21359. (Illus.). 14p. (J). 1997. 4.95 (*0-395-81124-4*) HM.

— Only One Ollie. LC 96-2851. (Illus.). 14p. (J). 1997. 4.95 (*0-395-81123-6*) HM.

Roche, Diana E. A Handbook for Group Dream Analysis. 36p. 1998. pap. 3.98 (*0-9659247-1-8*) Trefoil Pubns.

— The Sabian Symbols: A Screen of Prophecy. 430p. 1998. pap. 32.95 (*1-55212-217-4*, 98-0036) Trafford Pub.

Roche, Douglas, jt. auth. see Muller, Robert.

Roche, Edward, et al, eds. Global Information Technology & Systems Management: Key Issues & Trends. LC 95-77455. 635p. 1996. text 79.00 (*0-9648382-0-6*) Ivy Leag Pub.

Roche, Edward F. De, see De Roche, Edward F.

Roche, Edward J., Jr. & Poulson, Barry W. How to Keep the Lid on State Income Taxes: A Four-Step Plan for the Legislature. (Issue Papers: No. 2-87). 19p. 1987. pap. text 8.00 (*1-57655-007-9*) Independ Inst.

Roche, Edward M. & Bakis, Henry, eds. Developments in Telecommunications: Between Global & Local. LC 97-61063. (Illus.). 372p. 1997. text 83.95 (*1-85972-418-3*, Pub. by Ashgate Pub) Ashgate Pub Co.

Roche, Edward M. & Blain, Michael J. Information Technology, Development & Policy: Theoretical Perspectives & Practical Challenges. LC 96-84012. 336p. 1996. 78.95 (*1-85972-234-2*, Pub. by Avebry) Ashgate Pub Co.

Roche, Edward Mosley, jt. ed. see Blaine, Michael J.

Roche, Elizabeth. Motets, 1600-1650: Alessandro Grandi, Works from 1610-1616. Schnoebelen, Anne, ed. (Seventeenth-Century Italian Sacred Music: Vol. 21). 280p. 1996. text 99.00 (*0-8153-2361-1*) Garland.

— Motets, 1600-1650: Alessandro Grandi, Works from 1619-1630. Schnoebelen, Anne, ed. (Seventeenth-Century Italian Sacred Music Ser.: Vol. 22). 280p. 1996. text 99.00 (*0-8153-2362-X*) Garland.

Roche, Elizabeth, jt. auth. see Roche, Jerome.

Roche, Emmanuel & Shabes, Yves, eds. Finite-State Language Processing. LC 96-48159. (Language, Speech & Communication Ser.). (Illus.). 472p. 1997. 52.00 (*0-262-18182-7*, Bradford Bks) MIT Pr.

Roche, Francis X. Pension & Profit Sharing Plans for Small & Medium Size Businesses. LC 79-92397. 1984. 150.00 (*0-916592-48-0*) Panel Pubs.

Roche, George, 3rd. America by the Throat: The Stranglehold of Federal Bureaucracy. LC 82-12793. 200p. 1982. 14.95 (*0-8159-6844-2*) Devin.

Roche, George. The Fall of the Ivory Tower: Government Funding, Corruption & the Bankrupting of Higher Education. LC 93-47561. 320p. 1994. 24.00 (*0-89526-487-0*) Regnery Pub.

— Free Markets, Free Men: Frederic Bastiat, 1801-1850. LC 93-78834. 178p. 1993. pap. 14.95 (*0-916308-73-1*) Hillsdale Coll Pr.

— A Reason for Living. LC 89-36663. 156p. 1990. 17.95 (*0-89526-545-1*) Regnery Pub.

— A World Without Heroes: The Modern Tragedy. LC 87-80235. 368p. 1987. pap. 12.95 (*0-916308-89-8*) Hillsdale Coll Pr.

Roche, George, et al. The Book of Heroes: Great Men & Women in American History. LC 98-10025. (Illus.). 256p. (YA). (gr. 7 up). 1998. 24.95 (*0-89526-381-5*) Regnery Pub.

Roche, George C. Going Home. LC 86-3559. (Illus.). 192p. 1987. 14.95 (*0-915463-34-2*) Jameson Bks.

Roche, H. Have You Ever Picked a Dandelion? LC 98-196839. (Illus.). (J). (ps). 1998. spiral bd. 10.95 (*1-84089-005-3*, 868223Q) Zero to Ten.

— Have You Ever Seen a Chicken Hatch? LC 98-196840. (Illus.). (J). (ps). 1998. spiral bd. 10.95 (*1-84089-004-5*, 868221Q) Zero to Ten.

— My Dads a Wizard. LC 99-166908. (Illus.). (J). (ps). 1998. pap. 4.95 (*1-84089-013-4*, 868236Q) Zero to Ten.

— My Grandma Is Great. LC 99-166963. (Illus.). (J). (ps). 1998. pap. 4.95 (*1-84089-014-2*, 868237Q) Zero to Ten.

— My Mom Is Magic. LC 99-166958. (Illus.). (J). (ps). 1998. pap. 4.95 (*1-84089-012-6*, 868235Q) Zero to Ten.

— My Sister Is Super. LC 99-166916. (Illus.). (J). (ps). 1998. pap. 4.95 (*1-84089-015-0*, 868238Q) Zero to Ten.

Roche, Hannah. Corey's Kite. LC 98-60351. (My First Weather Bks.). (J). (ps up). 1998. 8.95 (*1-84089-033-9*) Zero to Ten.

— Pete's Puddles. LC 98-60350. (My First Weather Bks.). (J). (ps-2). 1998. 8.95 (*1-84089-031-2*) Zero to Ten.

— Sandra's Sunhat. LC 98-60353. (My First Weather Bks.). (J). (ps-2). 1998. 8.95 (*1-84089-032-0*) Zero to Ten.

— Su's Snowgirl. LC 98-60352. (My First Weather Bks.). (J). (ps-2). 1998. 8.95 (*1-84089-034-7*) Zero to Ten.

Roche, Hannah & Pratt, Pierre. Have You Ever Seen a Frog Leap? LC 98-46337. 16p. (J). 1999. 8.95 (*1-84089-158-0*) LKC.

— Have You Ever Seen a Frog Leap? LC 98-47426. 16p. (J). 1999. 8.95 (*1-84089-159-9*) Zero to Ten.

Roche, Henri-Pierre. Jules et Jim. (FRE.). 1979. pap. 10.95 (*0-7859-4115-0*) Fr & Eur.

— Jules et Jim. (Folio Ser.: No. 1096). (FRE.). 242p. 1953. pap. 8.95 (*2-07-037096-8*) Schoenhof.

Roche, Henri-Pierre. Jules et Jim. Evans, Patrick, tr. from FRE. LC 92-19043. 256p. 1993. reprint ed. pap. 14.95 (*0-7145-2958-3*) M Boyars Pubs.

Roche, J. The Mathematics of Measurement. (Illus.). 422p. 1998. 79.95 (*0-387-91581-8*) Spr-Verlag.

Roche, J., ed. Physicists Look Back: Studies in the History of Physics. LC 91-148368. (Illus.). 404p. 1990. 143.00 (*0-85274-001-8*) IOP Pub.

Roche, J. F. & O'Callaghan, D., eds. Follicular Growth & Ovulation Rate in Farm Animals. (Current Topics in Veterinary Medicine & Animal Science Ser.). 1987. text 176.50 (*0-89838-855-4*) Kluwer Academic.

— Manipulation of Growth in Farm Animals. (Current Topics in Veterinary Medicine & Animal Science Ser.). 316p. 1984. text 115.00 (*0-685-08511-2*) Kluwer Academic.

Roche, J. G. Product Liability. (Illus.). xxviii, 200p. 1990. 70.95 (*0-387-51819-3*) Spr-Verlag.

Roche, Jeff. Restructured Resistance: The Sibley Commission & the Politics of Desegregation in Georgia. LC 98-2660. 264p. (C). 1998. text 40.00 (*0-8203-1979-1*) U of Ga Pr.

Roche, Jenny. Teach Yourself Comedy Writing. (Teach Yourself Ser.). 192p. 1999. pap. 12.95 (*0-8442-2683-1*) NTC Contemp Pub Co.

Roche, Jeremy & Tucker, Stanley, eds. Youth in Society: Contemporary Theory, Policy & Practice. 304p. 1997. 75.00 (*0-7619-5372-8*); pap. 23.95 (*0-7619-5373-6*) Sage.

Roche, Jerome. The Flower of the Italian Madrigal, 3 vols. Incl. Vol. I. 224p. 1988. pap. 18.00 (*1-888471-02-6*); Vol. II. 256p. 1988. pap. 18.00 (*1-888471-03-4*); Vol. III. 198p. 1988. pap. 25.00 (*1-888471-04-2*); (Renaissance Voices). 60.85 (*1-888471-01-8*) Gaudia Mus & Arts.

— Introduction to the Italian Madrigal. (Renaissance Voices Ser.). 176p. 1989. pap. 15.00 (*1-888471-00-X*) Gaudia Mus & Arts.

Roche, Jerome & Roche, Elizabeth. A Dictionary of Early Music. (Illus.). 208p. 1981. 30.00 (*0-19-520255-4*) OUP.

Roche, John F. Joseph Reed: A Moderate in the American Revolution. LC 68-59259. (Columbia University. Studies in the Social Sciences: No. 595). reprint ed. 37.50 (*0-404-51595-9*) AMS Pr.

Roche, John P. The History & Impact of Marxist-Leninist Organizational Theory. LC 84-4582. (Foreign Policy Reports). 73p. 1984. 11.95 (*0-89549-059-5*) Inst Foreign Policy Anal.

Roche, Jorg & Webber, Mark. Fur- und Wider- Spruche: Ein integriertes Text-Buch fur Colleges und Universitaten. (Illus.). 512p. (C). 1995. pap. 37.50 (*0-300-05769-5*) Yale U Pr.

Roche, Joseph De, see De Roche, Joseph.

***Roche, Jude.** Split Ends. 150p. 1999. pap. write for info. (*0-7392-0260-X*) Morris Pubng.

Roche, Judith. Myrrh. 100p. (Orig.). 1993. pap. 11.00 (*0-930773-30-6*) Black Heron Pr.

Roche, Judith, ed. Ergo! The Bumbershoot Literary Magazine, Vol. 3, No. 1. (Illus.). 100p. (Orig.). 1988. pap. 5.00 (*0-929696-00-X*) Bumbershoot.

— Ergo! The Bumbershoot Literary Magazine, Vol. 4, No. 1. (Illus.). 100p. (Orig.). 1989. pap. 5.00 (*0-929696-01-8*) Bumbershoot.

— Ergo! Vol. IX: The Bumbershoot 1994 Literary Magazine. (Illus.). 112p. 1994. pap. 8.00 (*0-929696-06-9*) Bumbershoot.

Roche, Judith & Mchutchison, Meg. First Fish, First People: Salmon Tales of the North Pacific Rim. LC 98-18055. (Illus.). 204p. 1998. pap. 24.95 (*0-295-97739-6*) U of Wash Pr.

Roche, Julian. Forecasting Commodity Markets: Using Technical, Fundamental & Econometric Analysis. 450p. 1996. 45.00 (*1-55738-899-7*, Irwn Prfssnl) McGraw-Hill Prof.

— The International Cotton Trade. (International Trade Ser.). (Illus.). 384p. 1994. 170.00 (*1-85573-104-5*, Pub. by Woodhead Pubng) Am Educ Systs.

— The International Rice Trade. (International Trade Ser.). (Illus.). 240p. 1993. 170.00 (*1-85573-098-7*, Pub. by Woodhead Pubng) Am Educ Systs.

— The International Wool Trade. (International Trade Ser.). (Illus.). 240p. 1995. 170.00 (*1-85573-191-6*, Pub. by Woodhead Pubng) Am Educ Systs.

— Property Futures & Securitisation: The Way Ahead. 208p. 1995. 155.00 (*1-85573-180-0*, Pub. by Woodhead Pubng) Am Educ Systs.

Roche, Julie A. & Del-Debbio, Andy. The Rock: A History of Pebble Creek Ski Area. Chuen, Lam Kam, ed. LC 98-96878. (Illus.). 96p. (Orig.). 1998. pap. 12.95 (*0-9668815-0-8*) Rocheworks.

Roche, Lissa, ed. Still the Law of the Land? Essays on Changing Interpretations of the Constitution. LC 86-81686. 140p. 1989. pap. 5.00 (*0-916308-92-8*) Hillsdale Coll Pr.

Roche, Lissa, jt. ed. see Ebeling, Richard M.

Roche, Lorin. Meditation Made Easy. LC 98-22600. (Illus.). 208p. 1998. pap. 16.00 (*0-06-251542-X*, Pub. by Harper SF) HarpC.

***Roche, Lorin.** Meditation Made Easy: Roche,&Lorin. abr. ed. 1998. audio 12.00 (*0-694-52069-1*, CPN10168) HarperAudio.

Roche, Luane. The Promise: The Sequel to the Proud Tree. LC 96-82112. (Illus.). 64p. (J). (gr. 3-5). 1996. pap. 3.95 (*0-89243-877-0*) Liguori Pubns.

— The Proud Tree. LC 98-38862. (Illus.). 48p. (J). 1999. pap. 11.95 (*0-7648-0377-8*) Liguori Pubns.

— Proud Tree. rev. ed. LC 94-73019. (Illus.). 64p. 1995. pap. 3.95 (*0-89243-769-3*) Liguori Pubns.

Roche, Lyn. Coping with Caring: Daily Reflections for Alzheimer's Caregivers. 1995. 11.95 (*0-943873-29-0*) Elder Bks.

Roche, M. F. Dictionary of Surface Water Hydrology. (ENG, FRE, GER & SPA.). 288p. 1986. pap. 68.25 (*2-225-80739-6*, Pub. by Masson) IBD Ltd.

Roche, Marcel F. French, English, Spanish & German Dictionary of Surface Hydrology. (ENG, FRE, GER & SPA.). 288p. 1986. pap. 69.95 (*0-8288-0962-3*, F46020) Fr & Eur.

Roche, Marilyn. ARL - RLG Interlibrary Loan Cost Study. 64p. 1993. 10.00 (*0-918006-70-8*) ARL.

An Asterisk (*) at the beginning of an entry indicates that the title is appearing for the first time.

Roche, Mark W. Gottfried Benn's Static Poetry: Aesthetic & Intellectual-Historical Interpretations. LC 90-40007. (Germanic Languages & Literatures Ser.: No. 112). xi, 123p. (C). 1991. lib. bdg. 29.95 (*0-8078-8112-0*) U of NC Pr.

— Tragedy & Comedy: A Systematic Study & a Critique of Hegel. LC 97-986. (SUNY Series in Hegelian Studies). 450p. (C). 1997. pap. text 21.95 (*0-7914-3546-6*) State U NY Pr.

— Tragedy & Comedy: A Systematic Study & a Critique of Hegel. LC 97-986. (SUNY Series in Hegelian Studies). 450p. (C). 1997. text 65.50 (*0-7914-3545-8*) State U NY Pr.

Roche, Mary E., jt. auth. see Sahlem, James R.

Roche, Maurice. Compact. Polizzatti, Mark, tr. from FRE. & intro. by. LC 88-14194. 153p. 1988. 19.95 (*0-916583-29-5*) Dalkey Arch.

— Rethinking Citizenship: Welfare, Ideology, & Change in Modern Society. LC 92-20497. 280p. 1992. pap. 26.95 (*0-7456-0307-6*) Blackwell Pubs.

— Sport, Popular Culture & Identity, 1. 1998. pap. text 17.95 (*3-89124-468-1*) Meyer & Meyer.

Roche, Maurice & Van Berkel, Rik, eds. European Citizenship & Social Exclusion. LC 97-73459. (Research in Ethnic Relations Ser.). (Illus.). 304p. 1997. text 73.95 (*1-85972-659-3*, Pub. by Ashgate Pub) Ashgate Pub Co.

Roche, Nan. The New Clay: Techniques & Approaches to Jewelry Making. 2nd ed. Bress, Seymour, ed. (Illus.). 160p. 1992. pap. 24.95 (*0-9620543-4-8*) Flower Valley Pr.

***Roche, Nancy McGuire, ed.** Adoption Is Another Word for Love. (Charming Petites Ser.). (Illus.). 80p. 2000. 4.95 (*0-88088-329-4*) Peter Pauper.

Roche, Orion. Anarclaw. 92p. 1972. pap. 14.95 (*0-912282-04-5*) Pulse-Finger.

Roche, Patrick. Fishermen of the Coromandel: The Social Study of the Paravas of the Coromandel. 1985. 18.50 (*0-8364-1345-8*, Pub. by Manohar) S Asia.

Roche, Patrick A. Minority Access to Higher Education: An Analysis of a Pipeline Approach Through Neighborhood Learning Centers - the Minnesota Experiment. LC 94-4719. 156p. (Orig.). (C). 1994. pap. text 24.50 (*0-8191-9497-2*) U Pr of Amer.

Roche, Patrick J. & Barton, Brian. The Northern Ireland Question: Myth & Reality. 225p. 1991. text 77.95 (*1-85628-147-7*, Pub. by Avebry) Ashgate Pub Co.

***Roche, Patrick J. & Barton, Brian, eds.** The Northern Ireland Question: Nationalism, Unionism & Partition. 206p. (C). 1999. text 69.95 (*1-84014-490-4*) Ashgate Pub Co.

Roche, Patrick J., jt. ed. see Barton, Brian.

Roche, Paul. Aeschylus: Prometheus Bound. (Illus.). 148p. 1990. reprint ed. 9.00 (*0-86516-238-7*) Bolchazy-Carducci.

— Bible's Greatest Stories. 1990. mass mkt. 6.99 (*0-451-62779-2*) NAL.

— Three Plays by Plautus. 1984. pap. 9.00 (*0-86516-035-X*) Bolchazy-Carducci.

Roche, Paul, ed. Three Plays of Euripides: Alcestis, Medea, The Bacchae. 126p. (C). 1974. pap. 11.25 (*0-393-09312-3*) Norton.

Roche, Paul, tr. The Oedipus Plays of Sophocles. 1996. pap. 10.95 (*0-452-01167-1*, Plume) Dutton Plume.

— Orestes: Plays of Aeschylus. 1996. pap. 10.95 (*0-452-01166-3*, Plume) Dutton Plume.

Roche, Paul, tr. see Euripides.

Roche, Paul, tr. see Sappho.

Roche, Philip. The Criminal Mind: A Study of Communication Between the Criminal Law & Psychiatry. LC 76-28524. 299p. 1976. reprint ed. lib. bdg. 38.50 (*0-8371-9056-8*, ROCM, Greenwood Pr) Greenwood.

Roche, Regina M. Nocturnal Visit: A Tale, 2 vols. Varma, Devendra P., ed. LC 77-2045. (Gothic Novels III Ser.). 1977. reprint ed. lib. bdg. 91.95 (*0-405-10143-0*) Ayer.

Roche, Richard. The Call of the Wood Pigeon: A Day in the Life of a Monk in Pre-Viking Ireland. 1989. pap. 30.00 (*0-7855-6981-2*, Pub. by Veritas Pubns) St Mut.

— The Call of the Wood Pigeon - Glaoch an Choluir Choille: A Day in the Life of a Monk in Pre-Viking Ireland. (Illus.). (Orig.). (J). (gr. 1-8). 1990. pap. 5.95 (*1-85390-047-8*, Pub. by Veritas Pubns) Irish Bks Media.

— The Norman Invasion of Ireland. 134p. 1995. pap. 19.95 (*0-947962-81-6*, Pub. by Anvil Books Ltd) Irish Bks Media.

Roche, Ruth A., ed. see Shelley, Mary Wollstonecraft.

Roche, Ruth L. The Child & Science: Wondering, Exploring, Growing. LC 76-55313. (Illus.). 48p. reprint ed. pap. 30.00 (*0-7837-0547-6*, 204087700019) Bks Demand.

Roche, Sinclair & Temperley, eds. Repossession of Aircraft & Insolvency in the European Community. 162p. 1993. text 350.00 (*1-85044-471-4*) LLP.

***Roche, Susan E., et al.** Contesting Boundaries in Education: A Liberatory Approach to Cooperative Learning & Teaching. LC 99-39481. 175 p. 1999. pap. 16.00 (*0-87293-072-6*) Coun Soc Wk Ed.

Roche, Ted, jt. auth. see Granor, Tamar E.

Roche, Ted, jt. auth. see Hentzen, Whil.

Roche, Ted, ed. see Granor, Tamar E. & Martin, Della.

***Roche, Thomas.** Noirotica: An Anthology of Erotic Crime stories. 240p. 2000. reprint ed. pap. 15.00 (*1-892723-04-2*) Black Books.

— Noirotica: Stolen Kisses, 4, 3. 240p. (Orig.). 2000. pap. 15.00 (*1-892723-03-4*) Black Books.

— Noirotica 2, 4. 240p. (Orig.). 2001. reprint ed. pap. 15.00 (*1-892723-05-0*) Black Books.

Roche, Thomas, ed. Dark Matter. (Orig.). 1997. mass mkt. 6.95 (*1-56333-484-4*, Rhinoceros) Masquerade.

— Noirotica. (Orig.). 1996. mass mkt. 6.95 (*1-56333-390-2*, Rhinoceros) Masquerade.

Roche, Thomas, jt. ed. see Rowe, Michael.

Roche, Thomas P., Jr. Petrarch & the English Sonnet Tradition. LC 85-48062. (Studies in the Renaissance: No. 18). 1990. 57.50 (*0-404-62288-7*) AMS Pr.

Roche, Thomas P., Jr., jt. ed. see Cullen, Patrick.

Roche, Thomas P., ed. see Spenser, Edmund.

Roche, Thomas S., ed. Noirotica 2. (Orig.). 1997. mass mkt. 7.95 (*1-56333-584-0*, Rhinoceros) Masquerade.

Roche, Thomas S., jt. ed. see Kilpatrick, Nancy.

Roche, William. A Conversion of Manners: The Spiritual Legacy of Saint Benedict. LC 97-90593. (Illus.). vi, 306p. 1998. write for info. (*0-9659247-0-X*) Trefoil Pubns.

— The Roots of Sabian Philosophy. 64p. 1999. pap. 5.95 (*0-9659247-2-6*) Trefoil Pubns.

Rochecouste, Gabrielle M. The Role of Parallel Catamorphic Systems in the Structure of Zola's "Rougon-Maquart" (Romanistische Texte und Studien: Vol. 2). (Illus.). 276p. 1988. 35.10 (*3-487-07964-X*) G Olms Pubs.

Rochefort. Les Petits Enfants du Siecle: B Level. text 8.95 (*0-8219-1451-0*) EMC-Paradigm.

Rochefort, Christiane. Archaos du Jardin Etincelant. (FRE.). 448p. 1984. pap. 11.95 (*0-7859-1465-X*, 2253001074) Fr & Eur.

— C'Est Bizarre l'Ecriture. (FRE.). 160p. 1970. pap. 27.95 (*0-7859-5436-8*) Fr & Eur.

— Encore Heureux Qu'On Va Vers l'Ete. (FRE.). 218p. 1977. pap. 10.95 (*0-7859-1469-2*, 2253015741); pap. 26.95 (*0-686-55222-9*) Fr & Eur.

— L' Enfants d'Abord. (FRE.). 192p. 1976. pap. 28.95 (*0-7859-5437-6*) Fr & Eur.

— Les Petits Enfants du Siecle. 159p. 1969. 14.95 (*0-686-55224-5*); pap. 24.95 (*0-686-55225-3*) Fr & Eur.

— La Porte du Fond. (FRE.). 1990. pap. 12.95 (*0-7859-3154-6*, 2253052779) Fr & Eur.

— Printemps Au Parking. (FRE.). 192p. 1971. pap. 9.95 (*0-7859-5564-X*); pap. 3.95 (*0-686-55227-X*) Fr & Eur.

— Quand Tu Vas Chez les Femmes. (FRE.). 1983. pap. 4.95 (*0-7859-3112-0*) Fr & Eur.

— Le Repos du Guerrier. (Idees Ser.). 280p. 1958. 12.50 (*0-686-55228-8*) Fr & Eur.

— Une Rose pour Morrison. 1966. 18.95 (*0-686-55230-X*) Fr & Eur.

— Les Stances a Sophie. (FRE.). 250p. 1978. 11.95 (*0-686-55231-8*, 2246005892); pap. 24.95 (*0-7859-1452-8*) Fr & Eur.

Rochefort, David A. From Poorhouse to Homelessness: Policy Analysis & Mental Health Care. 2nd ed. LC 97-26771. 344p. 1997. pap. 24.95 (*0-86569-274-2*, Auburn Hse) Greenwood.

— From Poorhouses to Homelessness: Policy Analysis & Mental Health Care. 2nd ed. LC 97-26771. 344p. 1997. 69.50 (*0-86569-270-X*, Auburn Hse) Greenwood.

Rochefort, David A., ed. Handbook of Mental Health Policy in the United States. LC 88-32052. 563p. 1989. lib. bdg. 99.50 (*0-313-25009-X*, RHM, Greenwood Pr) Greenwood.

Rochefort, David A. & Cobb, Roger W., eds. The Politics of Problem Definition: Shaping the Policy Agenda. LC 94-11031. (Studies in Government & Public Policy). 240p. 1994. 29.95 (*0-7006-0646-7*); pap. 14.95 (*0-7006-0647-5*) U Pr of KS.

Rochefort, Harriet Welty. French Toast: An American in Paris Celebrates the Maddening Mysteries of the French. LC 98-31419. 128p. 1998. text 18.95 (*0-312-19978-3*) St Martin.

Rochegude, Alain, jt. auth. see Elbow, Kent.

Rocheleau, Corinne. Heritage of Peace: Land of Hope & Glory. Lind, Louise, ed. LC 97-211168. (Illus.). 250p. 1997. pap. 19.95 (*0-9655311-0-4*, JDS102) Jemtec Digital.

Rocheleau, David N., jt. auth. see Dally, James W.

Rocheleau, Diane E., jt. auth. see Thomas-Slayter, Barbara P.

Rocheleau, Dianne, et al, eds. Feminist Political Ecology: Global Issues & Local Experience. (International Studies of Women & Places). 352p. (C). 1996. 85.00 (*0-415-12026-8*); pap. 25.99 (*0-415-12027-6*) Routledge.

Rocheleau, Paul. Radio on Wheels: Eastern Edition. 1991. pap. 8.95 (*0-425-12860-1*) Berkley Pub.

— Radio on Wheels: Western Edition. 1991. pap. 8.95 (*0-425-12861-X*) Berkley Pub.

Rocheleau, Paul & Sprigg, June. Shaker Built: The Form & Function of Shaker Architecture. Larkin, David, ed. LC 94-76580. (Illus.). 272p. 1994. 60.00 (*1-885254-03-2*, Pub. by Monacelli Pr) Penguin Putnam.

Rocheleau, Paul, jt. auth. see Beveridge, Charles.

Rocheleau, Paul, jt. auth. see Thorne-Thomsen, Kathleen.

Rocheleau, Paul, jt. auth. see Wiencek, Henry.

Rochelle, Belinda. When Jo Louis Won the Title. (Illus.). 32p. (J). (ps-3). 1996. pap. 5.95 (*0-395-81657-2*) HM.

— When Jo Louis Won the Title. 1994. 11.15 (*0-606-10968-4*, Pub. by Turtleback) Demco.

— Witness to Freedom. (J). (gr. 3-7). 1997. pap. 5.99 (*0-614-28897-5*; PuffinBks) Peng Put Young Read.

Rochelle, Belinda. Witness to Freedom, Young People Who Fought for Civil Rights. (J). 1997. 11.19 (*0-606-12109-9*, Pub. by Turtleback) Demco.

Rochelle, Belinda. Witnesses to Freedom. 112p. 1997. pap. 6.99 (*0-14-038432-4*) Viking Penguin.

Rochelle, Belinda. Words with Wings. 48p. (J). 2001. 15.95 (*0-688-16415-3*, Wm Morrow) Morrow Avon.

***Rochelle, Belinda.** Words with Wings. (J). 2001. lib. bdg. 15.89 (*0-06-029363-2*, Wm Morrow) Morrow Avon.

***Rochelle, Belinda & Wolfe, Leslie R.** Building a Woman-Focused Response to HIV-AIDS: Policy Recommendations from the Metro DC Collaborative for Women with HIV-AIDS. 1999. pap. 15.00 (*1-877966-70-3*) Ctr Women Policy.

Rochelle, Belinda, et al. Building a National Policy Agenda: Ten Principles for Woman-Focused HIV/AIDS Prevention. 28p. (Orig.). 1996. pap. 8.00 (*1-877966-28-2*) Ctr Women Policy.

— Managed Care: Serving the Needs of Women? 116 Recommended Consumer Protections. 74p. 1998. pap. 10.00 (*1-877966-40-1*) Ctr Women Policy.

Rochelle, C., jt. ed. see Metcalfe, R.

Rochelle, D. P. The Real World of Alternate ID Acquisition. 28p. 1987. pap. 10.00 (*0-87364-440-9*) Paladin Pr.

Rochelle, Gary T., jt. ed. see Hudson, John L.

Rochelle, Gerald. Behind Time: The Incoherence of Time & McTaggart's Atemporal Replacement. (Avebury Series in Philosophy). 230p. 1998. text 63.95 (*1-84014-373-8*, Pub. by Ashgate Pub) Ashgate Pub Co.

— I Confess! 1998. pap. text 9.95 (*1-897809-51-4*) Silver Moon.

— The Life & Philosophy of J. McT. E. McTaggart, 1866-1925. LC 91-27674. (Studies in the History of Philosophy: Vol. 22). (Illus.). 268p. 1991. lib. bdg. 89.95 (*0-7734-9692-0*) E Mellen.

Rochelle, Gerald, ed. see Keeling, Stanley V.

Rochelle, Gerald, intro. see McTaggart, J. E.

***Rochelle, James A., et al.** Forest Fragmentation. LC 99-23815. 325p. 1999. 95.00 (*90-04-11388-6*) Brill Academic Pubs.

Rochelle, Jay C. An Attender of the Altar. LC 88-62023. (Orig.). 1988. pap. 4.00 (*0-87574-280-7*) Pendle Hill.

— What Wonderous Love: Devotions for the Home Lent-Holy Week- Easter. LC 96-44814. 64p. 1996. pap. 5.99 (*0-8066-2983-5*, 10-29835) Augsburg Fortress.

Rochelle, Jay C., tr. see Bonhoeffer, Dietrich.

Rochelle, Marion & Emmel, Ruth. Step by Step Math: Grade 5. Muffoletto, Mary L., ed. (Illus.). 64p. 1996. pap., teacher ed. 6.95 (*1-889369-07-1*, TI0012) Teaching Ink.

— Step by Step Math: Grade 6. Muffoletto, Mary L., ed. (Illus.). 64p. 1996. pap., teacher ed. 6.95 (*1-889369-08-X*, TI0013) Teaching Ink.

— Step by Step Math: Grades 3-4. Muffoletto, Mary L., ed. (Illus.). 64p. 1996. pap., teacher ed. 6.95 (*1-889369-06-3*, TI0011) Teaching Ink.

Rochelle, Marion & Muffoletto, Mary Lu. Childside Economics: Grades 4-6. (Illus.). 64p. 1997. pap., teacher ed. 6.95 (*1-889369-20-9*, TI0070) Teaching Ink.

***Rochelle, Marion, et al.** Research Revelations: Grades 4-6. (Illus.). 64p. 1998. pap., teacher ed. 6.95 (*1-889369-32-2*, TI0500) Teaching Ink.

Rochelle, Marion, jt. auth. see Muffoletto, Mary Lu.

Rochelle, Mercedes. Post-Biblical Saints Art Index: A Locator of Paintings, Sculptures, Mosaics, Icons, Frescoes, Manuscripts, Illuminations, Sketches, Woodcuts & Engravings Created from the 4th Century to 1950, with a Directory of the Institutions Holding Them. LC 94-10155. 367p. 1994. lib. bdg. 75.00 (*0-89950-942-8*) McFarland & Co.

Rochelson, Meri-Jane, jt. ed. see Manos, Nikki L.

Rochemont, Richard De, see Root, Waverley & De Rochemont, Richard.

Rochemont, Richard De, see Root, Waverly & De Rochemont, Richard.

Rocher, A., ed. see Sixth International Conference on Intergranular &.

Rocher, Daniel, jt. auth. see Clediere, J.

Rocher, Daniel, jt. auth. see Clediere, Jean.

Rocher, Francois & Smith, Miriam, eds. New Trends in Canadian Federalism. 380p. 1995. pap. 29.95 (*1-55111-019-9*) Broadview Pr.

Rocher, Francoise De, see Hagiwara, Peter M. & De Rocher, Francoise, eds.

Rocher, Gergory D. Rabelais's Laughers & Joubert's Traite du Ris. LC 78-15341. (Illus.). 176p. 1979. pap. 54.60 (*0-608-05123-3*, 206568200005) Bks Demand.

Rocher, Gregory D. De, see Joubert, Laurent.

Rocher, Gregory D. De, see De Rocher, Gregory D., tr.

Rocher, Ludo, ed. Ezourvedam: A French Veda of the Eighteenth Century. LC 84-6308. (University of Pennsylvania Studies of South Asia: No. 1). vii, 214p. 1984. 55.00 (*0-915027-05-4*); pap. 24.00 (*0-915027-06-2*) J Benjamins Pubng Co.

Rocher, Ludo, tr. & intro. see Paulinus, A. S. & Paulinus, A. S. Bartholomaeo.

Rocher, Marie-Paule. The French Connection. LC 88-17247. (Illus.). 90p. (Orig.). (C). 1988. pap. text 15.00 (*0-8191-7075-5*) U Pr of Amer.

Rocher, Rosane. Alexander Hamilton (1762-1824) A Chapter in the Early History of Sanskrit Philology. (American Oriental Ser.: Vol. 51). xii, 128p. 1968. pap. 8.00 (*0-940490-51-X*) Am Orient Soc.

— Orientalism, Poetry & Millenium. 1983. 44.00 (*0-8364-0870-5*) S Asia.

Rocher, Rosane, jt. auth. see Furber, Holden.

Rocher, Rosane, ed. see Brown, W. Norman.

Rochere, Martine Hennard Dutheil de la, see de la Rochere, Martine Hennard Dutheil.

Rocherolle, Eugenie. Tis the Season. 6.95 (*0-7692-9107-4*) Wrner Bros.

Roches, Brian des, see Des Roches, Brian.

Rochester, Anne. Why Farmers Are Poor: The Agricultural Crisis in the United States. McCurry, Dan C. & Rubenstein, Richard E., eds. LC 74-30649. (American Farmers & the Rise of Agribusiness Ser.). 1975. reprint ed. 31.95 (*0-405-06821-2*) Ayer.

Rochester Civic Music Guild Staff. Recipes of Note. (Illus.). 215p. (Orig.). 1988. write for info. (*0-318-63718-9*) Rochester Civic Mus Guild.

— Recipes of Note for Entertaining. 346p. (Orig.). 1994. 18.00 (*0-9621066-1-5*) Rochester Civic Mus Guild.

Rochester, Colin, jt. auth. see Harris, Margaret.

Rochester, Colin H., jt. ed. see Parfitt, Geoffrey D.

Rochester Community & Technical College Staff, jt. auth. see Murray, Steve.

Rochester Conference on Coherence & Quantum Optics. Coherence & Quantum Optics; Proceedings. Mandel, L. & Wolf, E., eds. LC 73-76700. (Illus.). 927p. 1973. reprint ed. pap. 200.00 (*0-608-05500-X*, 206596900006) Bks Demand.

Rochester, David, Jr. Contractor's Information "Sourcebook" The Building Code Simplified. Rene, Wendy, ed. (Illus.). 170p. (Orig.). (C). 1988. pap. 35.00 (*0-685-19928-2*); text 45.00 (*0-685-19927-4*) CIS Pub.

Rochester, Eugene W. Landscape Irrigation Design. LC 95-75549. (Illus.). 220p. 1995. spiral bd. 44.00 (*0-929355-61-X*, MO695) Am Soc Ag Eng.

Rochester Folk Art Guild Staff. Little Shooter of Birds & the Great Sun. (J). (ps-7). 1981. 9.50 (*0-686-33125-7*) Rochester Folk Art.

— More Simple Dishes. 1977. 4.50 (*0-686-21777-2*) Rochester Folk Art.

— Sunlight in the Morning: Songs from the Farm. (Illus.). 40p. (J). (gr. k-6). 1983. 13.00 (*0-686-40298-7*); audio 6.00 (*0-317-00393-3*) Rochester Folk Art.

Rochester Forth Applications Conference, et al. 1996 Rochester FORTH Conference: Open Systems, June 19-22, 1996, Ryerson Polytechnic University, Toronto, Ontario, Canada. LC 97-191662. (Illus.). 1997. write for info. (*0-914593-16-1*) Inst Appl Forth.

Rochester General Hospital Laser Group Staff. Color Atlas of CO2 Laser Surgical Techniques. Lanzafame, Raymond, ed. (Illus.). 300p. 1988. 145.00 (*0-912791-34-9*, Ishiyaku EuroAmerica) Med Dent Media.

Rochester, Helen. Helen Rochester's Guide to Montreal Restaurants. 240p. (Orig.). 1994. pap. 13.95 (*1-55065-059-9*, Pub. by Vehicule Pr) Genl Dist Srvs.

Rochester, J. Martin. Waiting for the Millennium: The United Nations & the Future of World Order. LC 92-45145. (Studies in International Relations). 361p. (C). 1993. text 39.95 (*0-87249-882-4*) U of SC Pr.

Rochester, J. Martin, jt. auth. see Coplin, William D.

Rochester, J. Martin, jt. auth. see Pearson, Frederic S.

Rochester, Jack B. Using Computers & Information. annot. ed. 1996. pap. text, teacher ed. 80.00 (*1-57576-060-6*) Que Educ & Trng.

— Using Computers & Information: Tools for Knowledge Workers. 1996. pap. text, student ed. 72.00 (*1-57576-059-2*) Que Educ & Trng.

— Using Computers & Information Study Guide. 1996. student ed. 32.00 (*1-57576-329-X*) Macmillan USA.

Rochester, Jack B. & Rochester, Jon. Computers for People. 2nd ed. LC 93-3703. 280p. (C). 1993. text 34.50 (*0-256-10777-7*, Irwn McGrw-H) McGrw-H Hghr Educ.

Rochester, Jack B., jt. auth. see Rochester, Jon.

Rochester, John W. Collected Works. (BCL1-PR English Literature Ser.). 407p. 1992. reprint ed. lib. bdg. 99.00 (*0-7812-7398-6*) Rprt Serv.

— The Complete Poems of John Wilmot, Earl of Rochester. LC 68-27768. 325p. reprint ed. pap. 100.80 (*0-8357-8077-5*, 203391000087) Bks Demand.

— The Letters of John Wilmot, Earl of Rochester. Treglown, Jeremy, ed. LC 80-20592. (Illus.). 292p. reprint ed. pap. 90.60 (*0-608-09552-4*, 205435400005) Bks Demand.

Rochester, John W. & James, Gomer R. Getting & Spending: An Introduction to the Market Economy. 4th ed. LC 72-175548. x, 253p. 1971. write for info. (*0-582-35049-2*) Addison-Wesley.

Rochester, Jon & Rochester, Jack B. Computers for People: Basic Programming. 88p. (C). 1991. text 12.50 (*0-256-10214-7*, Irwn McGrw-H) McGrw-H Hghr Educ.

Rochester, Jon, jt. auth. see Rochester, Jack B.

Rochester, Junius. Lakelore: A Tale of Medina, WA. 1993. pap. 11.00 (*0-9648950-0-5*) Tommie Pr.

— Little St. Simons Island on the Coast of Georgia. LC 93-44483. 1994. 30.00 (*0-913720-90-9*) Beil.

Rochester, Junius & SAS Staff. Thirty Years over the Top: Scandinavian Airlines System Polar Flights, Seattle-Copenhagen, 1966-1996. 33p. (Orig.). 1996. pap. write for info. (*0-9648950-1-3*) Tommie Pr.

Rochester, Junius, jt. auth. see Buerge, David M.

Rochester, Maxine K. Education for Librarianship in Australia. (Education of Library & Information Professionals). (Illus.). 272p. (C). 1996. text 99.50 (*0-7201-2216-3*) Continuum.

— Foreign Students in American Library Education: Impact on Home Countries, 55. LC 85-12675. (Contributions in Librarianship & Information Science Ser.: No. 55). (Illus.). 218p. 1986. 55.00 (*0-313-24201-1*, ROF/) Greenwood.

Rochester, Myrna B. Rene Crevel: Le Pays des Miroirs Absolus. (Stanford French & Italian Studies: No. 12). x, 174p. 1979. pap. 56.50 (*0-915838-25-7*) Anma Libri.

Rochester, Myrna B. & Convert-Chalmers, Claudine. Entree en Scene: Cours Premier de Langue et de Culture. (FRE.). (C). 1985. text 55.25 (*0-07-554525-X*) McGraw.

— Entree en Scene: Cours Premier de Langue et de Culture. (FRE.). (C). 1985. pap. text, wbk. ed. 22.00 (*0-07-554526-8*); pap. text, lab manual ed. 23.50 (*0-07-554527-6*) McGraw.

Rochester, Myrna B., et al. Bonjour, Ca Va? An Introductory Course. 3rd ed. 480p. (C). 1991. 74.06 (*0-07-557441-1*); pap. write for info. (*0-07-053402-0*); text, teacher ed. write for info. (*0-07-053403-9*) McGraw.

— Bonjour, Ca Va? An Introductory Course. 3rd ed. (C). 1991. pap., wbk. ed. 30.63 (*0-07-557443-8*); pap., lab manual ed. 25.94 (*0-07-557445-4*) McGraw.

An Asterisk (*) at the beginning of an entry indicates that the title is appearing for the first time.

— Bonjour, Ca Va? An Introductory Course. 3rd ed. 1991. audio. write for info. (*0-07-053401-2*) McGraw.

Rochester N.Y. Staff. Cuba: Culture & History. LC 98-178113. xi, 130 p. 1993. 26.00 (*1-56256-067-0*) Peoples Pub Grp.

— Dominican Republic: Culture & History. LC 98-178667. (People's Voice Ser.). xi, 100 p. 1993. 26.00 (*1-56256-030-1*) Peoples Pub Grp.

— Puerto Rico: Culture & History. LC 98-178668. (The Peoples' Voice Ser.). ix, 117p. 1993. 26.00 (*1-56256-095-6*) Peoples Pub Grp.

***Rochester, Stuart I.** Honor Bound: The History of American Prisoners of War in Southeast Asia, 1961-1973. 720p. 1998. boxed set 46.00 (*0-16-061137-7*) USGPO.

***Rochester, Stuart I. & Kiley, Frederick.** Honor Bound: The History of American Prisoners of War in Southeast Asia, 1961-1973. (Illus.). 704p. (C). 1999. text 65.00 (*0-7881-7745-1*) DIANE Pub.

Rochester, Stuart I. & Kiley, Frederick T. Honor Bound: The History of American Prisoners of War in Southeast Asia, 1961-1973. LC 98-39818. 706p. 1998. 36.95 (*1-55750-694-9*) Naval Inst Pr.

Rochet, Jean-Charles, jt. auth. see Freixas, Xavier.

Rochetta, Mario Incisa Della, see Incisa della Rochetta, Mario.

Rochette, Edward. Southwest Traveler: Lost Mines & Buried Treasure - A Guide to Sites & Legends of the Southwest. (American Traveler Ser.: Vol. 22). (Illus.). 48p. 1992. pap. 6.95 (*1-55838-130-9*) R H Pub.

Rochette, Edward C. Making Money (Counterfeiting) Rogues & Rascals Who Made Their Own. LC 86-22120. (Illus.). 150p. (Orig.). 1987. pap. 10.00 (*0-939650-25-8*) S J Durst.

— The Other Side of the Coin. LC 85-24442. (Illus.). 200p. (Orig.). 1986. pap. 10.00 (*0-939650-24-X*) S J Durst.

— The Romance of Coin Collecting. (Illus.). 184p. (Orig.). 1991. pap. text 12.95 (*0-943161-28-2*) Bowers & Merena.

Rochette, Joe. Smoke. Brimm, Mark, ed. (Royal Vagrant Chapbook Collection: Vol. 1). (Illus.). 28p. 1997. 4.00 (*1-889717-00-2*, RVP2) Royal Vagrant.

***Rochford, Bailey.** Bailey's Tale. (Illus.). (YA). 1999. pap. text. write for info. (*1-886618-01-1*) Rochford.

Rochford, Deidre. Rights for Animals? LC 96-2134. (Viewpoints Ser.). (J). 1997. lib. bdg. 22.00 (*0-531-14414-3*) Watts.

Rochford, E. Burke. Hare Krishna in America. (Illus.). 300p. (C). 1985. 40.00 (*0-8135-1113-5*) Rutgers U Pr.

Rochford, Joni. Is This House Safe? A Complete Guide to Identifying Household Hazards. 107p. (Orig.). 1996. pap. 5.00 (*1-886618-00-3*) Rochford.

Rochford, Pamela. Writing Erotic Fiction: How to Write a Successful Erotic Novel. 128p. 1997. pap. 19.95 (*1-85703-246-2*, Pub. by How To Bks) Trans-Atl Phila.

Rochford, Regina. An Approach to English Grammar for the Advanced ESL Student. 248p. (C). 1998. per. 36.95 (*0-7872-5141-0*, 41514101) Kendall-Hunt.

***Rochford, Tim.** Kickboxing. American Council on Exercise Staff, ed. (Illus.). 75p. 2000. pap. 14.95 (*1-890720-04-6*) Am Coun Exer.

Rochfort, Desmond. Mexican Muralists: Orozco, Rivera, Siqueiros. LC 97-27544. 239p. 1998. 27.50 (*0-8118-1928-0*) Chronicle Bks.

— Mexican Muralists: Orozco, Rivera, Siqueiros. (Illus.). 240p. 1994. 50.00 (*0-87663-626-1*, Pub. by Universe) St Martin.

Rochfort, Luke & Anderson, Lawrence. The Genealogie of Protestants. LC 79-304200. 199p. 1978. write for info. (*0-85967-480-0*) Scolar Pr.

***Rochin, Refugio & Valdes, Dennis, eds.** Voices of a New Chicana - O History. 275p. 2000. pap. 25.95 (*0-87013-523-6*) Mich St U Pr.

Rochin, Refugio I., ed. Immigration & Ethnic Communities: A Focus on Latinos. (C). 1996. pap. text. write for info. (*0-9650557-0-1*) MSU J Samora Res.

Rochinski, S. The Jazz Style of Tal Farlow: The Elements of Beebop. 128p. 1994. per. 19.95 (*0-7935-3384-8*, 00673245) H Leonard.

Rochkind-Dubinsky, Melissa L. Microbiological Decomposition of Chlorinated Aromatic Compounds. (Microbiology Ser.: Vol. 18). (Illus.). 336p. 1986. text 150.00 (*0-8247-7527-9*) Dekker.

Rochkind, Marc J. Advanced UNIX Programming. 265p. 1985. 35.95 (*0-13-011800-1*) P-H.

Rochlin, Fred. Old Man in a Baseball Cap: A Memoir of World War II. LC 99-21421. 160p. 1999. 20.00 (*0-06-019426-X*) HarpC.

— Old Man in a Baseball Cap: A Memoir of World War II. 160p. 2000. pap. 12.00 (*0-06-093227-9*, Perennial) HarperTrade.

***Rochlin, Fred.** Old Man in a Baseball Cap: A Memoir of World War II. large type ed. LC 99-57453. (Americana Series). 2000. 28.95 (*0-7862-2371-5*) Thorndike Pr.

Rochlin, Gene I. Trapped in the Net: The Unanticipated Consequences of Computerization. 310p. 1997. pap. 17.95 (*0-691-00247-9*, Pub. by Princeton U Pr) Cal Prin Full Svc.

— Trapped in the Net: The Unanticipated Consequences of Computerization. LC 96-41003. 293p. 1997. text 29.95 (*0-691-01080-3*, Pub. by Princeton U Pr) Cal Prin Full Svc.

Rochlin, Gene I. & Demchak, Chris C. Lessons of the Gulf War: Ascendant Technology & Declining Capability. LC 91-77818. (Policy Papers in International Affairs: No. 39). 42p. (Orig.). (C). 1991. pap. text 5.50 (*0-87725-539-3*) U of Cal IAS.

Rochlin, Gene I. & Socolow, Robert H. Efficient Use of Energy: A Physics Perspective. LC 75-18227. (AIP Conference Proceedings Ser.: No. 25). 305p. 1975. 20.00 (*0-88318-124-X*) Am Inst Physics.

Rochlin, Harriet. First Lady of Dos Cacahuates: A Novel. LC 97-44159. 256p. 1998. 19.95 (*1-56474-265-2*); pap. 11.95 (*1-56474-264-4*) Fithian Pr.

— The Reformer's Apprentice: A Novel of Old San Francisco. 224p. 1996. 19.95 (*1-56474-167-2*) Fithian Pr.

— The Reformer's Apprentice: A Novel of Old San Francisco. 222p. 1997. reprint ed. pap. 11.95 (*1-56474-237-7*) Fithian Pr.

Rochlin, James F. Redefining Mexican "Security" Society, State, & Region under NAFTA. LC 97-13585. 217p. 1997. 49.95 (*1-55587-569-6*) L Rienner.

Rochlin, Jay. Race & Class on Campus: Conversations with Ricardo's Daughter. LC 96-45817. 175p. 1997. 24.95 (*0-8165-1670-7*) U of Ariz Pr.

Rochlin, Michael J. Away Game. (Exposition Park Exiles Ser.: Vol. 1). (Illus.). 160p. (Orig.). (YA). (gr. 9 up). 1997. pap. 12.95 (*0-9648304-0-X*) Unreinforced Mason.

Rochlin, Michael Jacob. Ancient L. A. And Other Essays. (Illus.). 240p. 1999. pap. write for info. (*0-9648304-1-8*) Unreinforced Mason.

***Rochlin, Michael Jacob.** Mate Next Move. (Illus.). 80p. 2000. write for info. (*0-9648304-4-2*); pap. write for info. (*0-9648304-3-4*) Unreinforced Mason.

Rochlitz, Rainer. The Disenchantment of Art: The Philosophy of Walter Benjamin. Todd, Jane M., tr. LC 96-26. (Illus.). 298p. 1995. lib. bdg. 35.00 (*0-89862-408-8*, 2408) Guilford Pubns.

— The Disenchantment of Art: The Philosophy of Walter Benjamin. Todd, Jane M., tr. LC 96-26. 298p. 1998. pap. text 18.95 (*0-89862-407-X*, 2407) Guilford Pubns.

Rochlitz, Steve. Why Do Music Conductors Live into Their '90s? The Simple, Revolutionary Discovery that Can Make You Live Longer, Increase Your Stamina & Stretch & Normalize Your Blood Pressure in Minutes. LC 93-33432. (Illus.). 140p. (Orig.). 1994. pap. 12.95 (*0-945262-42-6*) HEBS.

Rochlitz, Steven. Allergies & Candida: With the Physicist's Rapid Solution. 3rd limited ed. LC 91-3199. (Towards a Science of Healing Ser.: Vol. I). (Illus.). 272p. (Orig.). 1991. text 50.00 (*0-945262-20-5*) HEBS.

— Allergies & Candida: With the Physicist's Rapid Solution. 3rd rev. ed. LC 91-3199. (Towards a Science of Healing Ser.: Vol. I). (Illus.). 272p. (Orig.). 1995. pap. text 19.95 (*0-945262-21-3*) HEBS.

— Towards a Science of Healing Vol. II: Advanced Human Ecology & Energy Balancing Sciences. deluxe ed. (Illus.). 100p. (C). 1991. spiral bd. 59.95 (*0-945262-40-X*) HEBS.

***Rochman, David I.** Rorschach Tests: Index of New Information for Reference & Research. rev. ed. 135p. 1999. 47.50 (*0-7883-2192-7*); pap. 44.50 (*0-7883-2193-5*) ABBE Pubs Assn.

Rochman, Hazel. Against Borders: Promoting Books for a Multicultural World. LC 93-17840. 288p. (Orig.). 1993. pap. text 25.00 (*0-8389-0601-X*) ALA.

— Clinical Pathology in the Elderly: A Textbook of Laboratory Interpretations. (Illus.). xiv, 222p. 1988. 77.50 (*3-8055-4694-7*) S Karger.

***Rochman, Hazel.** Leaving Home: Stories. LC 96-28979. (Illus.). 240p. (J). (gr. 12 up). 1998. pap. 11.00 (*0-06-440706-3*) HarpC.

Rochman, Hazel. Tales of Love & Terror: Booktalking the Classics, Old & New. LC 86-32285. 128p. 1987. pap. text 22.00 (*0-8389-0463-7*) ALA.

— Who Do You Think You Are? Stories of Friends & Enemies. (J). 1997. 13.05 (*0-606-13913-3*, Pub. by Turtleback) Demco.

Rochman, Hazel, ed. Somehow Tenderness Survives: Stories of Southern Africa. LC 88-916. (Charlotte Zolotow Bk.). 160p. (YA). (gr. 7 up). 1988. 12.95 (*0-06-025022-4*) HarpC Child Bks.

— Somehow Tenderness Survives: Stories of Southern Africa. LC 88-916. (Charlotte Zolotow Bk.). 208p. (YA). (gr. 7 up). 1990. mass mkt. 4.95 (*0-06-447063-6*, HarpTrophy) HarpC Child Bks.

Rochman, Hazel, ed. Somehow Tenderness Survives: Stories of Southern Africa. 1990. 9.60 (*0-606-04802-2*, Pub. by Turtleback) Demco.

Rochman, Hazel & McCampbell, Darlene, selected by. Who Do You Think You Are? Stories of Friends & Enemies. 176p. (J). (gr. 7 up). 1997. reprint ed. pap. 8.95 (*0-316-75320-3*) Little.

Rochman, Hazel & McCampbell, Darlene Z. Leaving Home: Stories. LC 96-28979. 240p. (YA). (gr. 7 up). 1997. lib. bdg. 16.89 (*0-06-024874-2*) HarpC Child Bks.

Rochman, Hazel & McCampbell, Darlene Z., eds. Leaving Home: Stories. LC 96-28979. 240p. (YA). (gr. 12 up). 1997. 16.95 (*0-06-024873-4*) HarpC Child Bks.

Rochman, Hazel & McCampbell, Darlene Z., selected by. Bearing Witness: Stories of the Holocaust. LC 95-13352. 144p. (YA). (gr. 7 up). 1995. 15.95 (*0-531-09488-X*); lib. bdg. 16.99 (*0-531-08788-3*) Orchard Bks Watts.

— Bearing Witness: Stories of the Holocaust. LC 95-13352. (Illus.). 144p. (YA). (ps-2). 1999. pap. 8.95 (*0-531-07115-4*) Orchard Bks Watts.

Rochman, Leyb. The Pit & the Trap: A Chronicle of Survival. Friedling, Sheila, ed. Kohn, O., tr. from YID. (Illus.). 288p. (Orig.). 1983. 11.95 (*0-89604-046-1*, Holocaust Library); pap. 6.95 (*0-89604-047-X*, Holocaust Library) US Holocaust.

Rochmis, Jon, ed. see Bernstein, Gary.

Rochmis, Jon, ed. see Dobbins, Dick & Twichell, Jon.

Rochmis, Jon, ed. see Lott, Ronnie.

Rochmis, Jon, ed. see Morgan, Joe.

Rochon, Kenneth. King Tuk Tuk & the Festival. (Illus.). 32p. (J). (gr. 2-4). 1999. pap. 11.99 (*1-57532-146-7*) Press-Tige Pub.

***Rochon, Louis-Philippe & Monroe, Stephen B.** Credit, Money & Production: An Alternative Post-Keynesian Approach. LC 99-27516. 352p. 2000. 95.00 (*1-85898-895-0*) E Elgar.

Rochon, T. R. Culture Moves: Ideas, Activism, & Changing Values. 280p. 1998. text 39.50 (*0-691-01157-5*, Pub. by Princeton U Pr) Cal Prin Full Svc.

***Rochon, Thomas R.** Culture Moves. (Illus.). 280p. 2000. pap. 16.95 (*0-691-07033-4*, Pub. by Princeton U Pr) Cal Prin Full Svc.

Rochon, Thomas R. Mobilizing for Peace: The Antinuclear Movements in Western Europe. LC 88-9876. (Illus.). 254p. 1988. reprint ed. pap. 78.80 (*0-608-07155-2*, 206738000009) Bks Demand.

***Rochon, Thomas R.** The Netherlands: The Politics of Internationalism. LC 99-21633. (Nations of the Modern World Ser.). 288p. 1999. text 65.00 (*0-8133-2880-2*, Pub. by Westview) HarpC.

Rochon, Thomas R. & Meyer, David S. Coalitions & Political Movements: The Lessons of the Nuclear Freeze. LC 97-10773. (Political Behavior & Participation Ser.). 1997. 55.00 (*1-55587-744-3*) L Rienner.

Rochow, Eugene G. Silicon & Silicones. (Illus.). 190p. 1987. 20.95 (*0-387-17565-2*) Spr-Verlag.

Rochow, T. G. & Tucker, P. A. Introduction to Microscopy by Means of Light, Electrons, X-Rays or Acoustics. 2nd ed. (Illus.). 476p. (C). 1994. text 55.00 (*0-306-44684-7*, Kluwer Plenum) Kluwer Academic.

Rochow, Theodore G. Light-Microscopical Resinography, Vol. 47. LC 83-61635. (Illus.). 1983. 30.00 (*0-904962-10-5*) Microscope Pubns.

Rochowanski, L. W., ed. Der Formwille der Zeit in der Angewandten Kunst. (Bauhaus Ser.). 1990. reprint ed. 40.00 (*3-601-00288-4*) Periodicals Srv.

Rochoz, I. Etude Paleoecologique du Lac de Seedorf (Fribourg, Suisse) Histoire de la Vegetation et du Milieu Durant l'Holocene - Le Ole de l'Homme et du Climat. (Dissertationes Botanicae Ser.: Band 293). 1998. pap. write for info. (*3-443-64205-5*, Pub. by Gebruder Borntraeger) Balogh.

Rochussen, Alan. Complete Next Generation. 320p. 1999. pap. 16.00 (*0-06-105350-3*, HarperPrism) HarpC.

Rochut, Joannes, ed. Melodious Etudes for Trombone, Bk. 1. (Illus.). 88p. 1928. pap. 11.95 (*0-8258-0149-4*, 0-1594) Fischer Inc NY.

Rochvarg, Arnold. Watergate Victory: Mardian's Appeal. LC 95-5695. 280p. (C). 1995. lib. bdg. 36.00 (*0-8191-9916-8*) U Pr of Amer.

Rochwarger, Arnold, jt. auth. see Miskovitz, Paul F.

Rocine, Victor G. Building a New Stomach. (Nutrition Ser.). 1991. lib. bdg. 75.00 (*0-8490-4260-7*) Gordon Pr.

— Building a New Stomach. 1996. reprint ed. pap. 12.00 (*0-7873-0732-7*) Hlth Research.

— Eating for Beauty. 1996. reprint ed. spiral bd. 12.00 (*0-7873-0731-9*) Hlth Research.

— Mind Training: A Practical System for Developing Self Confidence, Memory, Mental Concentration & Character. 1996. reprint ed. spiral bd. 18.50 (*0-7873-0734-3*) Hlth Research.

— Secrets of Eternal Youth. (Orig.). 1996. reprint ed. spiral bd. 14.00 (*0-7873-0733-5*) Hlth Research.

— Secrets of Eternal Youth: Why Diet Should Be Based upon Bio-Chemical Food Analysis for Health & Long Life. (Longevity Ser.). 1991. lib. bdg. 79.95 (*0-8490-4103-1*) Gordon Pr.

Rocissano, Lorraine & Fitzpatrick, Jean G. Helping Baby Talk: A Pressure-Free Approach to Your Child's First Words from Birth to 3 Years. 224p. 1990. mass mkt. 4.95 (*0-380-75681-1*, Avon Bks) Morrow Avon.

Rock. Christmas: The Complete Kit. 1997. pap. 7.50 (*0-7459-3788-8*, Pub. by Lion Pubng) Trafalgar.

Rock. Diagnostic Picture Tests in Pediatric Dentistry. LC 87-23472. 1988. 19.95 (*0-8151-7381-4*) Mosby Inc.

Rock. Discovering Churches. 1995. 16.95 (*0-7459-2920-6*, Pub. by Lion Pubng) Trafalgar.

— Discovering Churches. 1996. pap. 11.95 (*0-7459-3608-3*, Pub. by Lion Pubng) Trafalgar.

— Easter: Action Pack For Cool Chicks. 1998. pap. 3.50 (*0-7459-3879-5*, Pub. by Lion Pubng) Trafalgar.

— Easter: Fun & Festive Things To Make. 1999. pap. 4.95 (*0-7459-4050-1*, Pub. by Lion Pubng) Trafalgar.

— Festivals & Christian Year. 1996. pap., teacher ed. 11.95 (*0-7459-3736-5*, Pub. by Lion Pubng) Trafalgar.

— Festivals of the Christian Year. 1996. 16.95 (*0-7459-3456-0*, Pub. by Lion Pubng) Trafalgar.

— First Festivals: Harvest. 1999. 16.95 (*0-7459-3908-2*, Pub. by Lion Pubng) Trafalgar.

— Little Angels Joyful Christmas. 1997. pap. 2.95 (*0-7459-3787-X*, Pub. by Lion Pubng) Trafalgar.

— Little Chick's Easter Surprise. (J). 1997. pap. 2.95 (*0-7459-3730-6*, Pub. by Lion Pubng) Trafalgar.

— Little Fir Trees Busy for Xmas Book. (J). 1996. pap. 5.95 (*0-7459-3426-9*, Pub. by Lion Pubng) Trafalgar.

Rock. Mary Jane & Bud Wiser. LC 96-92297. 206p. (Orig.). 1996. pap. 11.95 (*0-9652562-0-0*) Rock.

***Rock.** Rock This! 256p. (YA). 2000. pap. 12.95 (*0-7868-8560-2*, Pub. by Hyperion) Time Warner.

Rock, jt. auth. see Rosenshein.

Rock, Jack P. The Practical Management of Low-Grade Primary Brain Tumors. LC 98-44542. 1999. write for info. (*0-7817-1101-0*) Lppncott W & W.

Rock & Learn, Inc. Staff. Nursery Rhymes. unabridged ed. (Rock n' Learn Ser.). (Illus.). 30p. (J). (ps-k). 1995. pap. 12.99 incl. audio (*1-878489-53-4*, RL953) Rock N Learn.

Rock & Roll Hall of Fame & Museum Staff. I Want to Take You Higher: The Psychedelic Era, 1965-1969. Henke, James, ed. LC 96-52197. (Illus.). 1997. pap. 24.95 (*0-8118-1700-8*) Chronicle Bks.

— I Want to Take You Higher: The Psychedelic Era, 1965-1969. Henke, James, ed. LC 96-52197. (Illus.). 1997. 45.00 (*0-8118-1725-3*) Chronicle Bks.

Rock, Bobby. Hypothetical Erotica: Provocative Scenarios for Your Contemplation & Discussion. (Illus.). 205p. 1999. 29.95 (*0-9668599-0-1*) Zen Man Publishing.

Rock, Calvin B. Seeing Christ: Windows on His Saving Grace. LC 93-40955. 1994. pap. 9.99 (*0-8280-0794-2*) Review & Herald.

***Rock, Chris.** Rock This! 202p. 2000. text 20.00 (*0-7881-9075-X*) DIANE Pub.

Rock, Chris. Rock This! 242p. (J). 1998. mass mkt. 6.99 (*0-7868-8941-1*, Pub. by Hyperion) Time Warner.

Rock Creek Research Staff. China Statistical Handbook, 1987. Keidel, Albert, ed. 25p. (Orig.). (C). 1987. pap. text 4.50 (*0-943085-02-0*) Rock Creek Res.

Rock, David. Argentina, Fifteen-Sixteen to Nineteen Eighty-Two: From Spanish Colonization to the Falklands War. LC 83-17948. 1985. pap. 19.95 (*0-520-06178-0*, Pub. by U CA Pr) Cal Prin Full Svc.

— Authoritarian Argentina: The Nationalistic Movement, Its History & Its Impact. 320p. (C). 1993. 45.00 (*0-520-07920-5*, Pub. by U CA Pr) Cal Prin Full Svc.

— Authoritarian Argentina: The Nationalistic Movement, Its History & Its Impact. LC 92-108. 320p. (C). 1995. pap. 16.95 (*0-520-20352-6*, Pub. by U CA Pr) Cal Prin Full Svc.

***Rock, David.** Jurek Becker: A Jew Who Became a German? 224p. 2000. 65.00 (*1-85973-332-8*, Pub. by Berg Pubs) NYU Pr.

Rock, David, ed. Latin America in the 1940's: War & Postwar Transitions. LC 93-29798. 285p. 1994. pap. 17.95 (*0-520-08417-9*, Pub. by U CA Pr) Cal Prin Full Svc.

***Rock, David, ed.** Voices in Times of Change: The Role of Writers, Opposition Movements & the Churches in the Transformation of East Germany. (Culture & Society in Germany Ser.: Vol. 4). 160p. 2000. 45.00 (*1-57181-959-2*) Berghahn Bks.

Rock, David & Brumbaugh, Douglas. Problem Solving with the CFX 9850 G-9850 GA Plus Color Graphing Calculator. unabridged ed. 50p. 1997. pap. text 10.95 (*0-9659710-2-3*) Paragon Publns.

Rock, David, jt. auth. see Brumbaugh, Douglas.

Rock, David, jt. ed. see Horrocks, D.

Rock-Evans, Rosemary. Analysis Within the Systems Development Life-Cycle: Activity Analysis - the Deliverables. (RRES Ser.: No. 3). (Illus.). 600p. 1987. pap. 59.95 (*0-08-034107-1*, Pergamon Pr) Elsevier.

— Analysis Within the Systems Development Life-Cycle: Data Analysis - the Methods. (RRES Ser.: No. 2). (Illus.). 360p. 1987. pap. 59.95 (*0-08-034106-3*, Pergamon Pr) Elsevier.

Rock-Evans, Rosemary, ed. Analysis Within the Systems Development Life-Cycle: Data Analysis - the Deliverables, Bk. 1. (RRES Ser.: No. 1). (Illus.). 300p. 1987. pap. 59.95 (*0-08-034105-5*, Pergamon Pr) Elsevier.

Rock, Gail A. & Decary, F., eds. The Platelet Membrane in Transfusion Medicine. (Current Studies in Hematology & Blood Transfusion: No. 54). (Illus.). viii, 156p. 1988. 126.25 (*3-8055-4657-2*) S Karger.

Rock, Gail A., jt. auth. see Seghatchian, M. J.

Rock, Gail A., jt. ed. see Decary, Francine.

***Rock, Helen.** Helen Rock's Irish Gardening. (Illus.). 224p. 1999. pap. 17.95 (*1-901866-24-6*, Pub. by Lilliput Pr) Irish Bks Media.

Rock, Howard B., et al, eds. American Artisans: Crafting Social Identity, 1750-1850. LC 95-1296. (Illus.). 272p. 1995. text 45.00 (*0-8018-5029-0*); pap. text 16.95 (*0-8018-5030-4*) Johns Hopkins.

Rock, Howard B., jt. auth. see Gilje, Paul A.

Rock, Ian, tr. see Chevalier, Jean-Marie.

Rock, Irvin. Indirect Perception. (Cognitive Psychology Ser.). (Illus.). 424p. (C). 1997. 46.00 (*0-262-18177-0*, Bradford Bks) MIT Pr.

— Perception. (Illus.). 243p. 1995. pap. text 19.95 (*0-7167-6011-8*) W H Freeman.

Rock, Irvin, ed. The Legacy of Solomon Asch: Essays in Cognition & Social Psychology. 320p. 1990. text 69.95 (*0-8058-0440-4*) L Erlbaum Assocs.

Rock, Irvin, jt. auth. see Mack, Arien.

Rock, J. F. A Monographic Study of the Hawaiian Species of the Tribe Lobelioideae, Family Campanulaceae. (BMB Ser.). (Orig.). 1919. 128.00 (*0-527-01651-9*) Periodicals Srv.

Rock, Jim. A Brief Commentary on Cans. (Illus.). 125p. (C). 1987. reprint ed. pap. text 13.75 (*1-55567-407-0*) Coyote Press.

Rock, Joe & Patterson, David. Thomas Begbie's Edinburgh. 200p. (C). 1996. 96.00 (*0-85976-337-4*, Pub. by J Donald) St Mut.

***Rock, John.** Key Account Management: Maximizing Profitability from Major Customers. 2nd ed. (Illus.). 258p. 1999. pap. 29.95 (*1-875680-59-4*) Woodslane.

Rock, John A. & Thompson, John D., eds. Te Linde's Operative Gynecology. 8th ed. LC 96-4875. 1,680p. 1996. text 142.00 (*0-397-51399-2*) Lppncott W & W.

Rock, John A., et al. Female Reproductive Surgery. (Illus.). 416p. 1992. 90.00 (*0-683-07317-6*) Lppncott W & W.

Rock, John A., jt. auth. see Carpenter, Sue Ellen Koehler.

Rock, John A., ed. see Advances in Obstetrics & Gynecology Staff.

Rock, John A., jt. ed. see Carpenter, Sue E.

Rock, John A., jt. ed. see Thomas, Eric J.

Rock, John P. Earl & Pearl, the Christmas Squirrels. LC 98-93580. (Illus.). 24p. (J). (gr. 1-6). 1998. pap. 4.95 (*0-9665625-3-4*, 0024) Habitat Pubns.

Rock, Joseph W. & Duncan, Barry L. Let's Face It, Men Are @$$#$$ What Women Can Do about It. LC 98-34228. 300p. 1998. pap. 12.95 (*1-55874-625-0*) Health Comm.

Rock, Judith. Terpsichore at Louis-le-Grand: Baroque Dance on the Jesuit Stage in Paris. unabridged ed. LC 96-79049. (Original Studies Composed in English: No. 15). viii, 212p. (Orig.). 1996. pap. 22.95 (*1-880810-22-0*) Inst Jesuit.

— Theology in the Shape of Dance: Using Dance in Worship & Theological Process. 1977. pap. 3.00 (*0-941500-16-0*) Sharing Co.

Rock, Judith, jt. auth. see Adams, Doug.

Rock, Judith, jt. auth. see Mealy, Norman.

Rock, Leo P. Making Friends with Yourself: Christian Growth & Acceptance. 144p. 1990. pap. 7.95 (*0-8091-3155-2*) Paulist Pr.

— Making Friends with Yourself: Christian Growth & Self-Acceptance. 144p. (C). 1996. pap. 39.95 (*0-85439-333-1*, Pub. by St Paul Pubns) St Mut.

Rock, Leon. Preparation & Pursuance of Civil Litigation. LC 76-24398. (Illus.). ix, 753p. 1983. 37.50 (*0-317-00679-7*) Natl Ctr PT.

Rock, Lois. All Year Long. LC 98-137233. (Nightlights Ser.: No. 3). 32p. (J). (ps-2). 1998. 7.99 (*0-7459-3732-2*, Lion) Chariot Victor.

— Before the Stars Were Made. LC 97-164431. (J). 1997. pap. text 7.99 (*0-7459-3635-0*) Lion USA.

— Best-Loved Prayers. (Illus.). 48p. (J). (gr. 2-6). 1998. 12.99 (*0-8499-5819-9*) Tommy Nelson.

— Bible Words about Happiness. 32p. (J). 1996. 8.90 (*0-7459-3345-9*) Lion USA.

— Discover the Bible. (Illus.). 32p. (J). (gr. k-2). 1997. 15.99 (*0-7459-3344-0*, Lion) Chariot Victor.

— A First Look: God. (Illus.). 32p. (J). (gr. k-2). 1997. pap. 3.99 (*0-7459-3747-0*, Lion) Chariot Victor.

— A First Look: Jesus. (Illus.). 32p. (J). (gr. k-2). 1997. pap. 3.99 (*0-7459-3748-9*, Lion) Chariot Victor.

— A First Look: Prayer. (Illus.). 32p. (J). (gr. k-2). 1997. pap. 3.99 (*0-7459-3751-9*, Lion) Chariot Victor.

— A First Look: The Bible. (Illus.). 32p. (J). (gr. k-2). 1997. pap. 3.99 (*0-7459-3749-7*, Lion) Chariot Victor.

— Gentle Carpenter. LC 97-164421. (J). 1997. pap. text 7.99 (*0-7459-3636-9*) Lion USA.

— Jesus All Alone. 32p. (J). 1996. mass mkt. 3.99 (*0-7459-3111-1*) Lion USA.

— Jesus & the Man Who Was Rescued. 32p. (J). 1996. mass mkt. 3.99 (*0-7459-3107-3*) Lion USA.

— Jesus Important Message. 32p. (J). 1996. mass mkt. 3.99 (*0-7459-3103-0*) Lion USA.

— Jesus New Beginning. 32p. (J). 1996. 3.99 (*0-7459-3112-X*) Lion USA.

— Jesus Shares a Picnic. 32p. (J). 1996. mass mkt. 3.99 (*0-7459-3105-7*) Lion USA.

— Jesus Story of the Lost Sheep. 32p. (J). 1996. mass mkt. 3.99 (*0-7459-3109-X*) Lion USA.

— A Little Life of Jesus. 346p. (J). (gr. k-2). 1997. pap. 9.99 (*0-7459-3796-9*, Lion) Chariot Victor.

— The Lord's Prayer for Children, 1 vol. (J). 1999. 9.99 (*0-7459-4092-7*) Lion USA.

— Lords Prayer for Children. 1999. 6.99 (*0-88486-232-1*, Inspirational Pr) Arrowood Pr.

— My Very First Christmas Story. (J). 1999. 10.99 (*0-7459-4096-X*) Lion USA.

— Sad News, Glad News. LC 99-173088. (Nightlights Ser.: No. 4). 32p. (J). (ps-2). 1998. 7.99 (*0-7459-3733-0*, Lion) Chariot Victor.

— Safe This Night. LC 99-173098. (Illus.). 32p. (J). (gr. k-2). 1997. 7.99 (*0-7459-3616-4*, Lion) Chariot Victor.

***Rock, Lois.** Ten Commandments for Children. (Illus.). (J). 2000. 9.99 (*0-7459-4093-5*) Lion USA.

— Time of Jesus. LC 99-201448. 64 p. 1999. 12.99 (*0-7459-4080-3*) Lion USA.

***Rock, Lois, retold by.** The Lord's Prayer: The Prayer That Jesus Taught Two Thousand Years Ago. (Illus.). 32p. (J). (gr. k-3). 2000. 8.95 (*0-8091-6679-8*) Paulist Pr.

***Rock, Lois & Newey, Gail.** Best-Loved Parables: Stories Jesus Told. (Illus.). 48p. 1999. 16.99 (*0-8066-3951-2*, Augsburg) Augsburg Fortress.

***Rock, Lois & Wilson, Anne.** I Wish Tonight. LC 00-30843. (Illus.). 28p. (J). 2000. 16.00 (*1-56148-315-X*) Good Bks PA.

Rock, Louise, ed. see Allen, Robert A.

Rock, Marcia, jt. auth. see Sanders, Marlene.

Rock, Maxine. Kishina: A True Story of Gorilla Survival. LC 95-45789. (Illus.). 96p. (Orig.). (YA). (gr. 4-7). 1996. pap. 12.95 (*1-56145-107-X*) Peachtree Pubs.

***Rock, Maxine.** Totally Fun Things to Do with Your Cat. LC 97-49027. (Play with Your Pet Ser.). (Illus.). 122p. (J). (gr. 3 up). 1998. pap. 12.95 (*0-471-19575-8*) Wiley.

Rock, Maxine. Totally Fun Things to Do with Your Dog. LC 97-35862. (Play with Your Pet Ser.). (Illus.). 122p. (J). (gr. 4-7). 1998. pap. 12.95 (*0-471-19574-X*) Wiley.

Rock Mechanics Symposium Staff. Applications of Rock Mechanics: Proceedings - 15th Symposium on Rock Mechanics Held at the State Game Lodge, Custer State Park, South Dakota, Sept. 17-19, 1973. LC 78-307544. (Symposium on Rock Mechanics Proceedings Ser.: Vol. 15). (Illus.). 670p. reprint ed. pap. 200.00 (*0-8357-5672-6*, 201953400013) Bks Demand.

— Design Methods in Rock Mechanics: Proceedings - 16th Symposium on Rock Mechanics, University of Minnesota, Sept. 22-24, 1975. Fairhurst, Charles P. & Crouch, Steven L., eds. LC TA0706.S9. (Illus.). 427p. reprint ed. pap. 132.40 (*0-608-30736-X*, 201954000013) Bks Demand.

— Rock Mechanics - Theory & Practice: Proceedings of the Symposium, 11th, University of California, Berkeley, 1969. Somerton, Wilbur H., ed. LC 73-103203. (Illus.). 772p. reprint ed. pap. 200.00 (*0-608-11612-2*, 200432600042) Bks Demand.

— Rock Mechanics Symposium: Presented at the Winter Annual Meeting of the American Society of Mechanical Engineers, Detroit, Michigan, November 11-15, 1973. Sikarskie, D. L., ed. LC 73-87731. (AMD Ser.: Vol. 3). (Illus.). 134p. reprint ed. pap. 41.60 (*0-8357-2880-3*, 203911700011) Bks Demand.

— Stability of Rock Slopes: Proceedings of the Symposium on Rock Mechanics, 13th, University of Illinois, Urbana, August 30-September 1, 1971. Cording, Edward J., ed. LC 76-380975. (Illus.). 922p. reprint ed. pap. 200.00 (*0-608-30732-7*, 201955300013) Bks Demand.

***Rock, Mick.** Raw Power: Iggy & the Stooges 1972. (Illus.). 160p. 2000. pap. 24.95 (*1-84068-050-4*, Pub. by Creation Books) Subterranean Co.

Rock, Milton L. Mergers & Acquisitions Handbook. 2nd ed. 608p. 1992. 84.95 (*0-07-053353-9*) McGraw.

Rock, Milton L. & Berger, Lance A. The Compensation Handbook: A State-of-the-Art Guide to Compensation Strategy & Design. 3rd ed. 704p. 1991. 89.50 (*0-07-053352-0*) McGraw.

Rock 'N Learn, Inc. Staff. Alphabet. unabridged ed. (Rock 'N Learn Ser.). (Illus.). 34p. (J). (ps-k). 1995. pap. 12.99 incl. audio (*1-878489-57-7*, RL957) Rock N Learn.

— Dinosaur Rap. unabridged ed. (Rock 'n Learn Ser.). (Illus.). 32p. (J). (gr. 1 up). 1996. pap. 12.99 incl. audio (*1-878489-59-3*, RL959) Rock N Learn.

Rock 'N Learn, Inc. Staff, et al. Colors, Shapes & Counting. unabridged ed. (Rock n' Learn Ser.). (Illus.). 32p. (J). (ps-k). 1994. pap. 12.99 incl. audio (*1-878489-32-1*, RL932) Rock N Learn.

Rock, N. M. Lamprophyres. 288p. (gr. 13). 1991. mass mkt. 161.95 (*0-442-30396-3*) Chapman & Hall.

— Numerical Geology. (Lecture Notes in Earth Sciences Ser.: Vol. 18). xi, 427p. 1988. 52.95 (*0-387-50070-7*) Spr-Verlag.

Rock, N. P. Diagnostic Picture Tests in Pediatric Dentistry. (C). (gr. 13). 1988. 16.00 (*0-7234-0984-6*, Pub. by Wolfe Pub) Mosby Inc.

Rock, N. P., jt. auth. see Budras.

Rock, Nicholas L., et al. Rehabilitation Methods in Neuropsychiatry. LC 95-48870. (Illus.). 314p. (Orig.). 1996. pap. 49.95 (*1-56593-632-9*, 1310) Thomson Learn.

Rock, Pamela A. Going off on Her Own. Warren, Shirley, ed. 24p. (Orig.). 1989. pap. 4.95 (*1-877801-01-1*) Still Waters.

Rock, Paul. After Homicide: Practical & Political Responses to Bereavement. (Clarendon Studies in Criminology). 384p. 1998. text 82.00 (*0-19-826795-9*, Clarendon Pr) OUP.

Rock, Paul, jt. auth. see Downes, David.

Rock, Paul, jt. ed. see Holdaway, Simon.

Rock, Paul E. Helping Victims of Crime: The Home Office & the Rise of Victim Support in England & Wales. (Oxford Socio-Legal Studies). 464p. 1991. text 98.00 (*0-19-825422-9*) OUP.

— Reconstructing a Women's Prison: The Holloway Redevelopment Project, 1968-88. (Clarendon Studies in Criminology). (Illus.). 378p. 1996. text 75.00 (*0-19-826095-4*, Clarendon Pr) OUP.

— The Social World of an English Crown Court: Witness & Professionals in the Crown Court Centre at Wood Green. LC 93-16309. (Oxford Socio-Legal Studies). (Illus.). 400p. 1993. text 72.00 (*0-19-825843-7*) OUP.

— A View from the Shadows: The Mystery of the Solicitor General of Canada & the Making of Justice for Victims of Crime Initiative. LC 86-16143. (Oxford Socio-Legal Studies). 416p. 1987. text 69.00 (*0-19-825523-3*, Clarendon Pr) OUP.

Rock, Paul E., ed. Drugs & Politics. LC 76-1766. (Society Bks.). 333p. 1977. 39.95 (*0-87855-076-3*); pap. text 24.95 (*0-87855-572-2*) Transaction Pubs.

— History of Criminology. 666p. 1994. 231.95 (*1-85521-331-1*, Pub. by Dartmth Pub) Ashgate Pub Co.

— Victimology: International Library of Criminology & Criminal Justice. 324p. 1994. 139.95 (*1-85521-405-9*, Pub. by Dartmth Pub) Ashgate Pub Co.

Rock, Paul E., jt. auth. see Holdaway, Simon.

Rock, Paul E., ed. see Davis, John.

Rock, Peter. Carnival Wolves: A Novel. LC 97-44208. 288p. 1998. pap. 12.95 (*0-385-49209-X*, Anchor NY) Doubleday.

— This Is the Place. LC 96-33606. 256p. 1997. pap. 12.00 (*0-385-48598-0*, Anchor NY) Doubleday.

Rock, Peter A. Chemical Thermodynamics. LC 82-51233. (Physical Chemistry Ser.). (Illus.). 548p. (C). 1983. 62.00 (*0-935702-12-1*) Univ Sci Bks.

Rock River Valley Girl Scout Council Staff. River Valley Recipes. LC 88-24663. 1987. 12.50 (*0-87197-242-5*) Favorite Recipes.

Rock, Robert C., jt. auth. see Noe, Dennis A.

Rock, Robert T. The Influence upon Learning of the Quantitative Variation of After-Effects. LC 79-177199. (Columbia University. Teachers College. Contributions to Education Ser.: No. 650). reprint ed. 37.50 (*0-404-55650-7*) AMS Pr.

Rock, Roger O., compiled by. The Native American in American Literature: A Selectively Annotated Bibliography, 3. LC 84-27972. (Bibliographies & Indexes in American Literature Ser.: No. 3). 211p. 1985. lib. bdg. 59.95 (*0-313-24550-9*, RKN/, Greenwood Pr) Greenwood.

***Rock, Stephen R.** Appeasement in International Politics. LC 99-87216. 256p. 2000. 29.95 (*0-8131-2160-4*) U Pr of Ky.

Rock, Stephen R. Why Peace Breaks Out: Great Power Rapprochement in Historical Perspective. LC 88-33824. xii, 220p. (C). 1989. 39.95 (*0-8078-1857-7*) U of NC Pr.

Rock, Susan. Teach Yourself Machine Embroidery: Easy Decorative Stitching Using Any Sewing Machine. LC 96-17853. (Illus.). 144p. 1996. pap. 19.95 (*0-8019-8522-6*) Krause Pubns.

***Rock, Tim.** Diving & Snorkeling Chuuk Lagoon, Pohnpei & Kosrae. (Pisces Bks.). (Illus.). 160p. 2000. pap. 17.95 (*1-86450-029-8*) Lonely Planet.

Rock, Tim. Lonely Planet Diving & Snorkeling Guide to Bali & the Komodo Region. (Diving & Snorkeling Guides Ser.). (Illus.). 96p. 1996. pap. 14.95 (*1-55992-086-6*, 2086, Pisces Books) Lonely Planet.

— Lonely Planet Diving & Snorkeling Guide to Guam & Yap. 2nd ed. LC 99-462601. (Diving & Snorkeling Guides Ser.). 128p. 1999. pap. text 15.95 (*0-86442-744-1*) Lonely Planet.

— Lonely Planet Diving & Snorkeling Guide to Truk Lagoon. LC 93-30789. (Diving & Snorkeling Guides Ser.). 96p. 1994. pap. 14.95 (*1-55992-069-6*, Pisces Books) Lonely Planet.

Rock, Tim & Toribiong, Francis. Lonely Planet Diving & Snorkeling Guide to Palau. LC 93-27894. (Diving & Snorkeling Guides Ser.). (Illus.). 96p. 1994. pap. 14.95 (*1-55992-068-8*, Pisces Books) Lonely Planet.

Rock, Tim, jt. auth. see Halstead, Bob.

Rock, Victoria, ed. see Knight, Joan MacPhail.

Rock, W. P., jt. auth. see Andlaw, R. J.

Rockafellar, Henry O., ed. Rockefeller, Vol. II: Transactions of the Rockefeller Family Assoc. (Illus.). 338p. 1992. reprint ed. lib. bdg. 56.50 (*0-8328-2203-5*) Higginson Bk Co.

Rockafellar, R. Tyrell. Network Flows & Monotropic Optimization. LC 98-72723. 634p. (C). 1998. text 49.50 (*1-886529-06-X*) Athena Scientific.

Rockafellar, R. Tyrrell. Conjugate Duality & Optimization. (CBMS-NSF Regional Conference Ser.: No. 16). vi, 74p. 1974. pap. text 21.50 (*0-89871-013-8*) Soc Indus-Appl Math.

— Convex Analysis. 469p. 1969. pap. text 22.95 (*0-691-01586-4*, Pub. by Princeton U Pr) Cal Prin Full Svc.

— Convex Analysis. LC 68-56318. (Mathematical Ser.: No. 28). 470p. 1969. text 89.50 (*0-691-08069-0*, Pub. by Princeton U Pr) Cal Prin Full Svc.

— Monotone Processes of Convex & Concave Type. LC 52-42839. (Memoirs Ser.: No. 1/77). 74p. 1967. pap. 16.00 (*0-8218-1277-7*, MEMO 1/77) Am Math.

Rockafellar, R. Tyrrell & Wets, Roger J. Variational Analysis. Chern, S. S. et al, eds. LC 97-35520. (Grundelehren der Mathematischen Wissenschaften Ser.: Vol. 317). 725p. 1997. text 129.00 (*3-540-62772-3*) Spr-Verlag.

Rockafeller, R. Tyrrell, tr. see Gol'Stein, E. G.

Rockafeller, Henry O., ed. Rockefeller, Vol. II: Transactions of the Rockefeller Family Assoc. (Illus.). 338p. 1992. reprint ed. pap. 46.50 (*0-8328-2204-3*) Higginson Bk Co.

Rockas, Lee. Style in Writing: A Prose Reader. 431p. (C). 1992. pap. text 32.76 (*0-669-20878-7*); teacher ed. 33.96 (*0-669-28172-7*) HM Trade Div.

Rockaway, Robert A. But - He Was Good to His Mother: The Lives & Crimes of Jewish Gangsters. LC 99-59148. (Illus.). 264p. (Orig.). 1994. pap. 12.95 (*965-229-092-0*) Gefen Bks.

***Rockaway, Robert A.** But He Was Good to His Mother: The Lives & Crimes of Jewish Gangsters. 2000. 14.95 (*965-229-249-4*) Gefen Pub Hse.

Rockaway, Robert A. Words of the Uprooted: Jewish Immigrants in Early 20th Century America. LC 97-52123. (Documents in American Social History Ser.). (Illus.). 256p. 1998. text 45.00 (*0-8014-3455-6*); pap. text 16.95 (*0-8014-8550-9*) Cornell U Pr.

Rockbridge Area Genealogical Society Staff. Rockbridge County, Virginia Heritage Book, 1778-1997. LC 97-62086. (Illus.). 478p. 1997. 75.00 (*0-9671723-3-0*) Legacy VA.

Rockcastle, Mary, ed. Remembering the Dance: Writing by Older Minnesotans. (Illus.). 224p. (Orig.). 1989. pap. 7.00 (*0-927663-00-7*) COMPAS.

Rockcastle, Mary F. Rainy Lake. 278p. 1994. 22.50 (*1-55597-218-7*) Graywolf.

— Rainy Lake. LC 94-29928. 278p. 1996. pap. 14.00 (*1-55597-242-X*) Graywolf.

Rockcastle, Verne N., jt. auth. see Schmidt, Victor E.

Rockdale Temple Sisterhood Staff. Beginning Again: More Hors D'oeuvres for Cooks Who Love in the Beginning. (Illus.). 200p. (Orig.). 1981. pap. 10.95 (*0-9602338-1-4*) Rockdale Ridge.

— Beginning Again: More Hors D'oeuvres for Cooks Who Love in the Beginning. braille ed. (Illus.). 200p. (Orig.). 1981. pap. write for info. (*0-318-55537-9*) Rockdale Ridge.

— In the Beginning: A Collection of Hors d'Oeuvres. braille rev. ed. 1982. pap. write for info. (*0-318-56779-2*) Rockdale Ridge.

— In the Beginning: A Collection of Hors d'Oeuvres. rev. ed. 1982. pap. 21.90 (*0-9602338-2-2*); pap. 8.95 (*0-9602338-3-0*) Rockdale Ridge.

— In the Beginning: A Collection of Hors d'Oeuvres, Set. rev. ed. 1982. boxed set 17.90 (*0-685-06087-X*) Rockdale Ridge.

Rocke, Adam. Atomic Bodyslams to Whiskey Zippers: A Bartender's Guide for the 21st Century. LC 97-969. 150p. 1997. pap. 9.95 (*1-57284-010-2*) Surrey Bks.

***Rocke, Adam.** Tiki Drinks. 70p. (C). 2000. 12.95 (*1-57284-036-6*) Surrey Bks.

Rocke, Alan J. Chemical Atomism in the Nineteenth Century: From Dalton to Cannizzaro. LC 83-25082. 404p. reprint ed. pap. 125.30 (*0-608-09871-X*, 206983600006) Bks Demand.

***Rocke, Alan J.** Nationalizing Science: Adolphe Wurtz & the Battle for French Chemistry. (Transformations Studies on the History of Science & Technology). (Illus.). 448p. (C). 2001. 39.95 (*0-262-18204-1*) MIT Pr.

Rocke, Alan J. The Quiet Revolution: Hermann Kolbe & the Science of Organic Chemistry. LC 92-28190. (California Studies in the History of Science: No. 11). 1993. 55.00 (*0-520-08110-2*, Pub. by U CA Pr) Cal Prin Full Svc.

Rocke, David M., jt. auth. see Downs, George W.

Rocke, Herman H. Check Your Panoply. 240p. 1977. pap. text 7.00 (*0-910424-71-3*) Concordant.

Rocke, Jennifer & McCoy, Peggy, contrib. by. A Chapter in Thornton's History: Compiled by Students on Team 7-2, York Middle School. 240p. 1998. pap. 10.00 (*1-57502-799-2*, PO2213) Morris Pubng.

Rocke, Lora. Easy Traditional Quilting. LC 96-117142. 92p. 1994. pap. 15.00 (*1-885156-15-4*) Animas Quilts.

Rocke, Michael. Forbidden Friendships: Homosexuality & Male Culture in Renaissance Florence. (Studies in the History of Sexuality). (Illus.). 384p. 1998. reprint ed. pap. 19.95 (*0-19-512292-5*) OUP.

***Rockefeller, Barbara.** The Global Electronic Trader. 224p. 2000. 29.95 (*0-471-38475-5*) Wiley.

Rockefeller, Barbara, jt. auth. see CNBC Staff.

***Rockefeller, Benjamin W.** Using SAP R/3 F1: Beyond Business Process Reengineering. LC 97-4236. 512p. 1998. 105.00 (*0-471-17996-5*) Wiley.

Rockefeller, Edwin S. Antitrust Questions & Answers. LC 73-93042. 703p. reprint ed. pap. 200.00 (*0-8357-5643-2*, 202430200037) Bks Demand.

Rockefeller, Henry O. Rockefeller Genealogy. (Illus.). 401p. 1996. reprint ed. pap. 61.00 (*0-8328-5394-1*); reprint ed. lib. bdg. 71.00 (*0-8328-5393-3*) Higginson Bk Co.

Rockefeller, John D. Random Reminiscences of Men & Events. (Illus.). 124p. 1984. 12.95 (*0-912882-58-1*) Sleepy Hollow.

— Random Reminiscences of Men & Events. LC 73-2533. (Big Business; Economic Power in a Free Society Ser.). 1979. reprint ed. 22.95 (*0-405-05111-5*) Ayer.

Rockefeller, John D., et al. Papers of John D. Rockefeller, Sr. LC 92-23427. 66 p. 1991. write for info. (*1-55655-397-8*) U Pubns Amer.

Rockefeller-MacArthur, Elizabeth, et al. From Petroglyphs to Hypertext: American Indian Library Services in Perspective. LC 98-10296. (Illus.). 162p. 1998. lib. bdg. 32.50 (*0-7864-0308-X*) McFarland & Co.

Rockefeller, R. D. Nobel Prize Winning Investment Strategies. 1992. pap. 12.95 (*0-9632572-1-8*) MDMI Int Pubns.

Rockefeller, R. D. & Chen, Gerald H. World Famous Investors Advice for 1993-2000: The Greatest Investors of All Time & Their Favorite Stocks, Bonds, Mutual Funds, Income & New Strategies for 1993-2000. Folder, M. Michael, ed. LC 93-77404. 96p. 1993. pap. 12.95 (*0-9632572-2-6*) MDMI Int Pubns.

Rockefeller, Ruth, ed. see Murdock, Dick.

Rockefeller, Steven C. John Dewey: Religious Faith & Democratic Humanism. 584p. 1991. text 61.50 (*0-231-07348-8*) Col U Pr.

— John Dewey: Religious Faith & Democratic Humanism. LC 90-28619. 683p. 1994. pap. 27.00 (*0-231-07349-6*) Col U Pr.

Rockefeller, Steven C. & Elder, John C. Spirit & Nature: Visions of Interdependence. (Illus.). 94p. (Orig.). 1990. pap. 15.00 (*0-9625262-1-5*) Middlebury Coll Mus.

Rockefeller, Steven C. & Elder, John C., eds. Spirit & Nature: Why the Environment Is a Religious Issue - An Interfaith Dialogue. LC 91-37116. (Illus.). 240p. 1992. pap. 18.50 (*0-8070-7709-7*) Beacon Pr.

Rockefeller University Staff, et al. Technological Trajectories & the Human Environment. Ausubel, Jessee H. & Langford, H. Dale, eds. LC 96-48427. 230p. (C). 1997. text 42.95 (*0-309-05133-9*) Natl Acad Pr.

Rockenbauch, Ralk. Verkehrskonzeptionen fur die Zukunft unter Besonderer Berucksichtigung des Fahrradverkehrs: Eine Okonomisch-Politische Analyse. (Europaische Hochschulschriften: Reihe 5: Bd. 1976). (GER., Illus.). 362p. 1996. pap. 61.95 (*3-631-30475-7*) P Lang Pubng.

Rockenstein, Zoa. Training the Creative/Intuitive Mind. 123p. 1994. pap. 14.95 (*0-943456-33-9*) Bearly Ltd.

Rockenwagner, Hans. Rockenwagner. LC 96-37455. (Illus.). 208p. 1997. 29.95 (*0-89815-875-3*) Ten Speed Pr.

Rocker, Bob, jt. auth. see Stanaway, John.

Rocker, Robert L. Life Flight. 56p. (Orig.). 1997. pap. 4.95 (*0-916155-34-X*) Trout Creek.

Rocker, Rudolf. Anarchism & Anarcho-Syndicalism. rev. ed. (Anarchist Classics Ser.). 48p. 1988. reprint ed. pap. 3.50 (*0-900384-45-X*) Left Bank.

— Anarcho-Syndicalism. 1972. 250.00 (*0-87968-038-5*) Gordon Pr.

— Anarcho-Syndicalism. 93p. (C). 1993. pap. 9.95 (*0-948984-05-8*, Pub. by Phoenix Pr) AK Pr Dist.

— Anarcho-Syndicalism. 1995. pap. 14.95 (*1-85305-077-6*, Pub. by Pluto GBR) Stylus Pub VA.

— Anarcho-Syndicalism. (Pluto Classic Ser.). 1998. pap. 18.95 (*0-7453-1387-6*, Pub. by Pluto GBR) Stylus Pub VA.

— Anarcho-Syndicalism. (C). 1989. pap. text 16.95 (*0-685-68138-6*) Westview.

— Bolshevism & Anarchism. 1976. lib. bdg. 250.00 (*0-8490-1522-7*) Gordon Pr.

— Nationalism & Culture. 592p. 1997. 57.99 (*1-55164-095-3*, Pub. by Black Rose); pap. 28.99 (*1-55164-094-5*, Pub. by Black Rose) Consort Bk Sales.

— Nationalism & Culture. Chase, Ray E., tr. from GER. LC 78-5960. 1978. 20.00 (*0-9602574-1-1*) M E Coughlin.

— Socialism & State. 1972. 250.00 (*0-8490-1069-1*) Gordon Pr.

— Spain: Tragedy & Truth. 1972. 250.00 (*0-8490-1098-5*) Gordon Pr.

Rocker, Stephen. Hegel's Rational Religion: The Validity of Hegel's Argument for the Identity in Content of Absolute Religion & Absolute Philosophy. LC 95-16686. 224p. 1995. 35.00 (*0-8386-3637-3*) Fairleigh Dickinson.

Rocker, Willard. Marriages & Obituaries from the Macon Messenger, 1818-1865. 588p. 1988. 47.50 (*0-89308-340-2*, GA 65) Southern Hist Pr.

Rockerbie, Russell A. Alcohol & Drug Intoxication. LC 99-6. 320p. 1999. 64.35 (*1-55212-239-5*) Trafford Pub.

An Asterisk (*) at the beginning of an entry indicates that the title is appearing for the first time.

Rockers, Colleen. Making a Difference: Listening, Loving & Serving. Coffey, Kathy, ed. (Crossings : Vol. 2). 80p. (YA). 1998. pap. 3.95 (*1-889108-28-6*) Liv Good News.

Rocket, Howard & Sklar, Rachel. Stroke of Luck: Life, Crisis & Rebirth of a Stroke Survivor, 1. 2nd ed. 196p. 1998. 24.95 (*0-9696106-3-7*, Pub. by Parnassus Comm) Assoc Pubs Grp.

***Rocket, Howard & Sklar, Rachel.** A Stroke of Luck: Life, Crisis & Rebirth of a Stroke Survivor. 2nd rev. ed. 1999. write for info. (*0-9696106-4-5*) Parnassus Comm.

Rocket, Kevin, ed. see British Film Institute Staff.

Rockets Redglare Staff. Users Manual. 246p. 1998. pap. 14.00 (*0-9656535-8-7*) Consafos Pr.

Rockett, jt. auth. see Miller.

Rockett, A. M. & Szusz, P. Continued Fractions. 200p. 1994. text 55.00 (*981-02-1047-7*); pap. text 25.00 (*981-02-1052-3*) World Scientific Pub.

Rockett, James M. & Ungles, Keith D. Bank Sales of Nondeposit Investment Products: A Compliance Guide. LC 95-136234. 600p. (Orig.). 1994. pap. 130.00 (*0-8366-0028-2*) West Group.

Rockett, Kevin & Finn, Eugene. Still Irish: A Century of the Irish in Film. (Illus.). 154p. 1999. reprint ed. text 27.00 (*0-7881-6145-8*) DIANE Pub.

Rockett, Rocky L. Ethnic Nationalities in the Soviet Union: Sociological Perspectives on an Historical Problem. LC 81-304. 171p. 1981. 45.00 (*0-275-90711-2*, C0711, Praeger Pubs) Greenwood.

Rockett, Susan, jt. auth. see Owens, Martha.

Rockett, Will H. Devouring Whirlwind: Terror & Transcendence in the Cinema of Cruelty, 21. LC 88-10254. (Contributions to the Study of Popular Culture Ser.: No. 21). 221p. 1988. 55.00 (*0-313-25998-4*, RCY/, Greenwood Pr) Greenwood.

Rockey, Arlaine. Ocean Court. LC 98-83190. 365p. 1999. 25.00 (*0-7388-0351-0*); pap. 15.00 (*0-7388-0352-9*) Xlibris Corp.

Rockey, Edward H. Communicating in Organizations. (Illus.). 168p. 1984. reprint ed. pap. text 20.50 (*0-8191-3751-0*) U Pr of Amer.

Rockey, J. L., et al, eds. History of New Haven County, Connecticut, 2 vols. (Illus.). 1567p. 1997. reprint ed. lib. bdg. 159.00 (*0-8328-5670-3*) Higginson Bk Co.

Rockey, J. L. & Bancroft, R. J. History of Clermont County, Ohio. (Illus.). 557p. 1993. reprint ed. lib. bdg. 57.00 (*0-8328-3614-1*) Higginson Bk Co.

Rockey, Linda D., jt. auth. see Kitzinger, Beth.

Rockford, Doris E. Sexology Encyclopedia Vol. 5: Intra-Uterine Devices: Index & Reference Books of New Information. Bartone, John C., ed. (Illus.). 151p. 1996. pap. 39.95 (*0-7883-0859-9*) ABBE Pubs Assn.

— Sexology Encyclopedia Vol. 5: Intra-Uterine Devices: Index & Reference Books of New Information, 25 vols., Set. Bartone, John C., ed. (Illus.). 170p. 1996. 49.95 (*0-7883-0858-0*) ABBE Pubs Assn.

Rockford Morning Star Staff. Rockford Today: Historical, Descriptive, Biographical. (Illus.). 179p. 1997. reprint ed. lib. bdg. 26.50 (*0-8328-5792-0*) Higginson Bk Co.

Rockhill, Kathleen. Academic Excellence Versus Public Service: The Development of Adult Higher Education in California. 320p. 1983. 34.95 (*0-87855-491-2*) Transaction Pubs.

Rockhill, William W. The Land of the Lamas: Notes of a Journey Through China, Mongolia & Tibet. (C). 1988. reprint ed. 32.00 (*81-206-0354-0*, Pub. by Asian Educ Servs) S Asia.

Rockin, Donna, jt. auth. see Rockin, Jan.

Rockin, Jan & Rockin, Donna. The Determined Dieter's Diary. (Illus.). 78p. (Orig.). 1985. pap. 3.25 (*0-9616081-0-2*) Rockin Enter.

Rockis. Solid State Fundamentals for Electricians: Instructor's Guide. 2nd ed. (Illus.). 232p. teacher ed. 9.96 (*0-8269-1633-3*) Am Technical.

Rockis, Gary. Solid State Fundamentals for Electricians. 2nd ed. LC 93-5537. (Illus.). 232p. 1993. 36.96 (*0-8269-1631-7*) Am Technical.

Rockis, Gary & Mazur, Glen A. Electrical Motor Controls. LC 96-31168. 1996. 52.96 (*0-8269-1671-6*) Am Technical.

Rockis, Gary & Mazur, Glen A. Electrical Motor Controls Manual. (Illus.). 490p. 1995. 14.96 (*0-8269-1668-6*) Am Technical.

Rockis, Gary, jt. auth. see Proctor, Thomas E.

Rockit, Johnny. Kolinar: The Rock 'n' Roll State of Mind. unabridged ed. (Illus.). 270p. 1998. pap. 13.00 (*1-892654-13-X*) Bayshore Ent.

Rockitter, Nate. Person to Person: A Group Approach to Peer Counseling. unabridged ed. LC 93-77665. 132p. 1993. pap. text 12.95 (*0-932446-04-3*) Jacqueline Enter.

Rockland, K. S., jt. auth. see Peters, A.

Rockland, Kathleen S., et al, eds. Cerebral Cortex Vol. 12: Extrastriate Cortex in Primates, Vol. 12. (Illus.). 870p. (C). 1998. text 191.00 (*0-306-45530-7*, Kluwer Plenum) Kluwer Academic.

Rockland, Lawrence H. Supportive Therapy: A Psychodynamic Approach. LC 89-42801. 320p. (C). 1989. pap. 45.00 (*0-465-08337-4*, Pub. by Basic) HarpC.

— Supportive Therapy for Borderline Patients: A Psychodynamic Approach. LC 92-1538. (Diagnosis & Treatment of Mental Disorders Ser.). 308p. 1992. lib. bdg. 40.00 (*0-89862-182-8*) Guilford Pubns.

Rockland, Louis B., jt. auth. see Beuchat, Larry R.

Rockland, Michael A. A Bliss Case. LC 89-36392. 176p. (Orig.). (C). 1989. pap. 9.95 (*0-918273-55-2*) Coffee Hse.

— Snowshoeing: Adventures in New York City, New Jersey, & Philadelphia. LC 94-10145. 165p. (C). 1994. 21.95 (*0-8135-2115-7*) Rutgers U Pr.

Rockland, Michael A., jt. auth. see Gillespie, Angus K.

Rockland, Michael A., tr. & intro. see Sarmiento, Domingo Faustino.

Rockliff, B. J. Crackerjack. large type ed. (General Fiction Ser.). 432p. 1992. 27.99 (*0-7089-2701-7*) Ulverscroft.

Rockliff, V. Saturday Bloody Saturday. 1987. 39.00 (*0-7223-2097-3*, Pub. by A H S Ltd) St Mut.

Rockliffe, N. J., jt. ed. see Castro, I. P.

Rocklin. Grandmaman the Hockey Fan. (J). 1995. 15.95 (*0-8050-2322-4*) H Holt & Co.

— This Book Is Haunted. 48p. (J). (gr. k-3). Date not set. pap. 3.95 (*0-06-444261-6*) HarpC Child Bks.

— This Book Is Haunted. 48p. (J). (gr. k-3). 2001. 14.95 (*0-06-028456-0*); lib. bdg. 14.89 (*0-06-028457-9*) HarpC Child Bks.

Rocklin, jt. auth. see Walton.

Rocklin, Joanne. The Case of the Missing Birthday Party. (Hello Math Reader Ser.). 1997. 9.19 (*0-606-11195-6*, Pub. by Turtleback) Demco.

Rocklin, Joanne. The Case of the Shrunken Allowance, Level 4. LC 97-43664. (Hello Reader! Math Ser.). (Illus.). 48p. (J). (gr. 2-4). 1999. pap. 3.99 (*0-590-12006-9*, Pub. by Scholastic Inc) Penguin Putnam.

— For Your Eyes Only. LC 95-39532. 112p. (J). (gr. 3-7). 1997. 14.95 (*0-590-67447-1*) Scholastic Inc.

— How Much Is That Guinea Pig in the Window? LC 95-13231. (Hello Math Reader Ser.: Level 4). (Illus.). 48p. (J). (ps-3). 1995. pap. 3.50 (*0-590-22716-5*, Cartwheel) Scholastic Inc.

— How Much Is That Guinea Pig in the Window? (Hello Math Reader Ser.). 1995. 8.70 (*0-606-07675-1*, Pub. by Turtleback) Demco.

— Jake & the Copycats. LC 97-28799. (Illus.). 48p. (J). (gr. k-3). 1998. pap. 4.50 (*0-440-41408-3*, YB BDD) BDD Bks Young Read.

— Just Add Fun! LC 98-20849. (Hello Reader! Math Ser.). (Illus.). 48p. (J). (ps-3). 2000. pap. 3.99 (*0-590-64399-1*) Scholastic Inc.

***Rocklin, Joanne.** Just Add Fun! (Hello, Reader! Ser.). (Illus.). (J). 2000. 9.44 (*0-606-18572-0*) Turtleback.

Rocklin, Joanne. Not Enough Room! (Hello Math Reader Ser.). (J). 1998. 8.70 (*0-606-13669-X*, Pub. by Turtleback) Demco.

— One Hungry Cat. LC 96-23043. (Hello Math Reader Ser.). (Illus.). (J). 1997. pap. 3.99 (*0-590-93972-6*) Scholastic Inc.

— One Hungry Cat. (Hello Math Reader Ser.). 1997. 9.19 (*0-606-11708-3*, Pub. by Turtleback) Demco.

— Sonia Begonia. 112p. (J). (gr. 3-7). 1987. pap. 2.50 (*0-380-70307-6*, Avon Bks) Morrow Avon.

***Rocklin, Joanne.** Strudel Stories. (Illus.). 144p. (J). (gr. 3-7). 2000. pap. 4.50 (*0-440-41509-8*, Yearling) BDD Bks Young Read.

Rocklin, Joanne. Strudel Stories. LC 98-23141. 144p. (J). (gr. 3-7). 1999. 14.95 (*0-385-32602-5*) Delacorte.

***Rocklin, Joanne.** Strudel Stories. LC 00-41183. (Illus.). (J). 2000. write for info. (*0-7862-2770-2*) Thorndike Pr.

Rocklin, Joanne. Three Smart Pals. LC 93-34156. (Hello Reader! Ser.). (Illus.). 48p. (J). (ps-3). 1994. pap. 3.99 (*0-590-47431-6*, Cartwheel) Scholastic Inc.

Rocklin, Joanne. Three Smart Pals. (Hello, Reader! Ser.). 1994. 9.19 (*0-606-06811-2*, Pub. by Turtleback) Demco.

— The Very Best Hanukkah Gift. LC 99-10726. 128p. 1999. 14.95 (*0-385-32656-4*) Bantam.

***Rocklin, Joanne & Burns, Marilyn.** The Incredibly Awesome Box. LC 99-33967. (Hello Math Reader Ser.). (Illus.). (J). 2000. pap. 3.99 (*0-439-09955-2*) Scholastic Inc.

Rocklin, Joanne & Burns, Marilyn. Not Enough Room! LC 97-12853. (Hello Math Reader Ser.). (Illus.). (J). 1998. 3.50 (*0-590-39962-4*) Scholastic Inc.

Rocklin, Joanne, et al. The Case of the Backyard Treasure. LC 97-11462. (Hello Math Reader Ser.). (Illus.). (J). 1998. 3.99 (*0-590-30872-6*) Scholastic Inc.

— The Case of the Missing Birthday Party. LC 96-14841. (Hello Math Reader Ser.: Level 4). (Illus.). 48p. (J). (gr. 2-4). 1997. 3.99 (*0-590-67359-9*, Cartwheel) Scholastic Inc.

Rockmaker, Gordon, jt. auth. see Adams, J.

Rockman, Alexis & Dion, Mark, eds. Concrete Jungle. LC 96-45940. 224p. (Orig.). 1997. pap. 24.95 (*0-9651042-2-2*) Juno Bks.

Rockman, Alexis, et al. Alexis Rockman: Second Nature. (Illus.). 96p. 1999. pap. 19.95 (*0-945558-23-6*) ISU Univ Galls.

Rockman, Bert A., jt. auth. see Aberbach, Joel D.

Rockman, Bert A., jt. auth. see Campbell, Colin.

Rockman, Bert A., jt. ed. see Campbell, Colin.

Rockman, Bert A., jt. ed. see Linden, Ronald H.

Rockman, Bert A., jt. ed. see Peters, B. Guy.

Rockman, Bert A., jt. ed. see Weaver, R. Kent.

***Rockman, Deborah A.** The Art of Teaching Art: A Guide for Teaching & Learning the Foundations of Drawing-based Art. LC 99-37642. 352p. 2000. 35.00 (*0-19-513079-0*) OUP.

Rockman, Richard G., Jr. Rainbow Man. Ouellette, Dean C., ed. (Illus.). 200p. (Orig.). 1991. pap. 9.95 (*0-9630916-0-3*) R G Rockman.

— Rainbow Man. rev. ed. Ouellette, Dean C., ed. (Illus.). 201p. (Orig.). 1992. pap. 9.95 (*0-9630916-1-1*) R G Rockman.

Rockman, Robert. Monarch Notes on Shaw's Plays. 4.25 (*0-671-00646-0*, Arco) Macmillan Gen Ref.

Rockmore, Tom. Before & after Hegel: A Historical Introduction to Hegel's Thought. LC 93-9719. 1993. 45.00 (*0-520-08205-2*, Pub. by U CA Pr); pap. 16.95 (*0-520-08206-0*, Pub. by U CA Pr) Cal Prin Full Svc.

— Cognition: An Introduction to Hegel's "Phenomenology of Spirit" LC 96-33059. 216p. 1997. 40.00 (*0-520-20661-4*, Pub. by U CA Pr) Cal Prin Full Svc.

— Habermas on Historical Materialism. LC 88-45449. (Studies in Phenomenology & Existential Philosophy). 216p. 1989. 37.50 (*0-253-32709-1*); pap. 5.95 (*0-253-20504-2*, MB-504) Ind U Pr.

— Hegel's Circular Epistemology. LC 85-45037. (Studies in Phenomenology & Existential Philosophy). 220p. (C). 1986. 27.50 (*0-253-32713-X*) Ind U Pr.

— Heidegger & French Philosophy: Humanism, Antihumanism, & Being. LC 93-47961. 304p. (C). (gr. 13). 1994. 90.00 (*0-415-11180-3*, B4728) Routledge.

— Heidegger & French Philosophy: Humanism, Antihumanism, & Being. LC 93-47961. 304p. (C). 1995. pap. 25.99 (*0-415-11181-1*, B4732) Routledge.

— Heidegger, German Idealism & Neo-Kantianism. LC 99-58576. 325p. 2000. 79.95 (*1-57392-737-6*, Humanity Bks) Prometheus Bks.

— Irrationalism: Lukacs & the Marxist View of Reason. (C). 1991. 59.95 (*0-87722-867-1*) Temple U Pr.

— On Hegel's Epistemology & Contemporary Philosophy. LC 95-32854. 320p. (C). 1996. text 60.00 (*0-391-03918-0*) Humanities.

— On Heidegger's Nazism & Philosophy. LC 91-22072. (C). 1992. 55.00 (*0-520-07711-3*, Pub. by U CA Pr) Cal Prin Full Svc.

— On Heidegger's Nazism & Philosophy. 1997. pap. text 19.95 (*0-520-20898-6*, Pub. by U CA Pr) Cal Prin Full Svc.

Rockmore, Tom, ed. Lukacs Today. 284p. (C). 1988. text 153.00 (*90-277-2661-2*, D Reidel) Kluwer Academic.

***Rockmore, Tom, ed.** New Essays on the Precritical Kant. 270p. 2001. 59.95 (*1-57392-871-2*) Prometheus Bks.

— Proceedings of the Twentieth World Congress of Philosophy Vol. II: Metaphysics. LC 99-66878. 256p. (C). 1999. 45.00 (*1-889680-06-0*) Philos Document.

Rockmore, Tom & Margolis, Joseph, eds. The Heidegger Case: On Philosophy & Ethics. 500p. (C). 1992. 69.95 (*0-87722-907-4*); pap. 32.95 (*0-87722-908-2*) Temple U Pr.

Rockmore, Tom & Singer, Beth J., eds. Antifoundationalism Old & New. (C). 1992. 69.95 (*0-87722-881-7*) Temple U Pr.

Rockmore, Tom & Zeman, Vladimir, eds. Transcendental Philosophy & Everyday Experience. LC 96-37869. 224p. (C). 1997. text 55.00 (*0-391-04024-3*) Humanities.

Rockmore, Tom, et al. Marxism & Alternatives: Towards the Conceptual Interaction among Soviet Philosophy, NeoThomism, Pragmatism, & Phenomenology. 325p. 1981. text 162.50 (*90-277-1285-9*) Kluwer Academic.

Rockmore, Tom, jt. ed. see Breazeale, Daniel.

Rockmore, Tom, jt. ed. see Margolis, Joseph.

Rockmuller, Seth. School Law in New York State: A Manual for Parents. 2nd rev. ed. LC 96-78424. 156p. (Orig.). 1996. pap. 14.95 (*0-9636096-7-X*) Longview NY.

Rockne, C. L. Little Daniel & Revelation. 248p. 1996. spiral bd. 14.95 (*0-9656048-2-9*) Little Garden.

Rockne, Cynthia. Growing a Garden of Love. 3rd unabridged ed. LC 97-24323. (Illus.). 190p. 1998. spiral bd. 16.95 (*0-9656048-1-0*) Little Garden.

Rockne, Jon, tr. see Alefeld, Gotz & Herzberger, Jurgen.

Rockner, Michael. A Dirichlet Problem for Distributions & Specifications for Random Fields. LC 84-29009. (Memoirs of the AMS Ser.: No. 54/324). 76p. 1988. reprint ed. pap. 18.00 (*0-8218-2325-6*, MEMO/54/324) Am Math.

Rockner, Michael & Ma, Zhi-Ming. Introduction to the Theory of (Non-Symmetric) Dirichlet Forms. LC 92-28120. (Universitext Ser.). 1992. 54.95 (*0-387-55848-9*) Spr-Verlag.

Rockness, Howard D., jt. auth. see Zmud, Robert W.

Rockness, Miriam H. Home - God's Design: Celebrating a Sense of Place. 240p. 1990. pap. 9.99 (*0-310-59081-7*) Zondervan.

***Rockness, Miriam H.** A Passion for the Impossible: The Life of Lilias Trotter. LC 98-26140. (Illus.). 288p. 1999. pap. 14.99 (*0-87788-512-5*, H Shaw Pubs) Waterbrook Pr.

Rockoff, Hugh. Drastic Measures: A History of Wage & Price Controls in the United States. LC 83-21019. (Studies in Economic History & Policy: The United States in the Twentieth Century). 232p. 1984. text 57.95 (*0-521-24496-X*) Cambridge U Pr.

— The Free Banking Era: A Re-Examination. LC 75-2593. (Dissertations in American Economic History Ser.). (Illus.). 1979. 21.95 (*0-405-07215-5*) Ayer.

Rockoff, Hugh, ed. Price Controls. (International Library of Macroeconomic & Financial History: Vol. 6). 404p. 1992. 170.00 (*1-85278-431-8*) E Elgar.

Rockoff, Hugh, jt. auth. see Walton, Gary M.

Rockoff, Hugh, jt. ed. see Goldin, Claudia D.

Rockoff, Hugh, jt. ed. see Mills, Geofrey T.

Rockort. Great Movie Graphics. (Illus.). 128p. 1995. 34.99 (*1-56496-178-8*) Rockport Pubs.

Rockowitz, Murrary, et al. GED Computer Study Program. 1996. pap. 29.95 incl. 3.5 hd, mac hd (*0-8120-8462-4*) Barron.

***Rockowitz, Murray.** How to Prepare for the GED High School Equivalency Exam. 11th ed. LC 00-41384. 2001. write for info. incl. cd-rom (*0-7641-7458-4*) Barron.

— Pass Key to the GED High School Equivalency Exam. 4th ed. LC 00-41383. 2001. write for info. (*0-7641-1372-0*) Barron.

Rockowitz, Murray, et al. Como Prepararse para el GED: How to Prepare for the GED. 2nd ed. Vendrell, Montserrat, tr. (SPA.). 896p. 1997. pap. text 14.95 (*0-8120-9363-1*) Barron.

— How to Prepare for the High School Equivalency Exam-GED. 10th rev. ed. LC 98-27424. 800p. 1998. pap. 14.95 (*0-7641-0433-0*) Barron.

— Pass Key to the GED. 3rd rev. ed. LC 98-38864. 400p. 1998. pap. 7.95 (*0-7641-0457-8*) Barron.

Rockport - Allworth Editions Staff. Signs & Spaces: International Survey of the Leading Environmental Design Firms. (Illus.). 200p. 1993. 49.99 (*1-56496-031-5*, 30509) Rockport Pubs.

Rockport Book Editors. Letterhead & Logo Designs 2: Creating the Corporate Image. (Illus.). 256p. 1995. pap. 29.99 (*1-56496-121-4*) Rockport Pubs.

Rockport Publisher Staff. Digital Design: The New Computer Graphics. (Illus.). 160p. 1998. pap. 34.99 (*1-56496-372-1*) Rockport Pubs.

— Layout. (Graphic Idea Resource Ser.). (Illus.). 96p. 1998. pap. 15.99 (*1-56496-373-X*) Rockport Pubs.

— Type. (Graphic Idea Resource Ser.). (Illus.). 96p. 1998. pap. 15.99 (*1-56496-374-8*) Rockport Pubs.

Rockport Publishers Editorial Staff. Business Card. (Design Library). (Illus.). 80p. 1996. pap. 14.99 (*1-56496-292-X*) Rockport Pubs.

— Graphic Design on a Limited Budget: Cutting Costs Creatively for the Client. 160p. 1995. pap. 29.99 (*1-56496-175-3*) Rockport Pubs.

Rockport Publishers Editorial Staff, compiled by. Best New Animation Design. (Illus.). 120p. 1995. 34.99 (*1-56496-166-4*) Rockport Pubs.

— The Best of Brochure Design, No. II. (Illus.). 192p. 1997. pap. 29.99 (*1-56496-226-1*) Rockport Pubs.

— Digital Graphics. (Design Library). (Illus.). 80p. 1996. pap. 19.99 (*1-56496-336-5*) Rockport Pubs.

— Direct Mail. (Design Library). 80p. 1996. pap. 19.99 (*1-56496-337-3*) Rockport Pubs.

— Illustration. (Design Library). (Illus.). 80p. 1995. pap. 19.99 (*1-56496-246-6*) Rockport Pubs.

— Music Graphics. (Design Library). (Illus.). 80p. 1996. pap. 14.99 (*1-56496-291-1*) Rockport Pubs.

— Poster Art. (Design Library). (Illus.). 80p. 1996. pap. 14.99 (*1-56496-290-3*) Rockport Pubs.

— Restaurant Graphics, No. 2. (Illus.). 160p. 1996. 34.99 (*1-56496-255-5*) Rockport Pubs.

— Retail & Restaurant. (Design Library). (Illus.). 80p. 1996. pap. 19.99 (*1-56496-338-1*) Rockport Pubs.

— T-Shirt. (Design Library). (Illus.). 80p. 1995. pap. 19.99 (*1-56496-245-8*) Rockport Pubs.

Rockport Publishers Editorial Staff, ed. The Best of Brochure Design. (Illus.). 240p. 1992. 49.99 (*1-56496-004-8*, 30455) Rockport Pubs.

— The Best of Business Card Design. LC 95-155922. (Illus.). 160p. 1994. 34.99 (*1-56496-045-5*, 30583) Rockport Pubs.

— The Best of Business Card Design, No. 2. (Illus.). 160p. 1996. 34.99 (*1-56496-206-7*) Rockport Pubs.

— The Best of Colored Pencil 3. (Illus.). 160p. 1996. 24.99 (*1-56496-209-1*) Rockport Pubs.

— Complete Process Color Finder: For Desktop Publishers & Graphics Designers. (Illus.). 180p. 1995. 24.99 (*1-56496-134-6*) Rockport Pubs.

— Computer Graphics: The Best of Computer Art & Design. (Illus.). 160p. 1993. pap. 34.99 (*1-56496-015-3*, 30395) Rockport Pubs.

— Computer Graphics III: More of the Best of Computer Art & Design, No. 3. (Illus.). 160p. 1996. pap. 29.99 (*1-56496-204-0*) Rockport Pubs.

— Computer Graphics 2: More of the Best of Computer Art & Design. (Illus.). 160p. 1994. pap. 34.99 (*1-56496-090-0*) Rockport Pubs.

— Cyber Design: Illustration: The Best Computer Generated Design. (Illus.). 144p. 1996. 24.99 (*1-56496-258-X*) Rockport Pubs.

— CyberDesign: Computer-Manipulated Photography. 144p. 1996. 24.99 (*1-56496-218-0*) Rockport Pubs.

— Guild 9: The Architect's Source of Artists & Artisans. (Illus.). 320p. 1994. 34.99 (*1-56496-094-3*, 30604) Rockport Pubs.

— Label Design Vol. 4: The Best New U. S. & International Design. (Illus.). 240p. 1994. 49.99 (*1-56496-069-2*, 30600) Rockport Pubs.

— Letterhead & Logo Design, No. 4. (Illus.). 192p. 1996. 44.99 (*1-56496-257-1*) Rockport Pubs.

— Shopping Bag Design, No. 2. (Illus.). 160p. 1997. 34.99 (*1-56496-299-7*) Rockport Pubs.

— Society of Publication Designers' Best of Magazine Publication Design, No. 29. (Illus.). 240p. 1995. 49.99 (*1-56496-152-4*) Rockport Pubs.

— Three-Dimensional Illustrator's Awards Annual, Vol. 3. (Illus.). 256p. 1993. 59.99 (*1-56496-024-2*, 30456) Rockport Pubs.

Rockport Publishers Editors. The Best of Brochure Design. (Illus.). 192p. 1996. 39.99 (*1-56496-256-3*) Rockport Pubs.

— The Best of Brochure Design, No. 2. LC 97-103384. (Illus.). 192p. 1994. 39.95 (*1-56496-092-7*) Rockport Pubs.

— Creative Inspirations: A Collection of Drawing & Painting Ideas for Artists. (Inspirations Ser.). (Illus.). 96p. 1997. pap. 12.99 (*1-56496-386-1*, Quarry Bks) Rockport Pubs.

— Digital Type. (Illus.). 144p. 1997. 34.99 (*1-56496-259-8*) Rockport Pubs.

***Rockport Publishers Editors.** Digital Type. 2000. pap. 25.00 (*1-56496-697-6*) Rockport Pubs.

Rockport Publishers Editors. Floral Inspirations: A Collection of Drawing & Painting Ideas for Artists. (Inspirations Ser.). (Illus.). 96p. 1997. pap. 12.99 (*1-56496-385-3*, Quarry Bks) Rockport Pubs.

— Great T-Shirt Graphics, Vol. 3. (Motif Design Ser.). (Illus.). 160p. 1997. 44.99 incl. cd-rom (*1-56496-368-3*) Rockport Pubs.

— Landscape Inspirations: A Collection of Drawing & Painting Ideas for Artists. (Inspirations Ser.). (Illus.). 96p. 1997. pap. 12.99 (*1-56496-384-5*, Quarry Bks) Rockport Pubs.

— Package & Label Design. (Motif Design Ser.). (Illus.). 160p. 1997. 44.99 incl. cd-rom (*1-56496-354-3*) Rockport Pubs.

R

— Portrait Inspirations: A Collection of Drawing & Painting Ideas for Artists. (Inspirations Ser.). (Illus.). 96p. 1997. pap. 12.99 (*1-56496-383-7*, Quarry Bks) Rockport Pubs.

— Shopping Bag Design. LC 95-155918. (Illus.). 160p. 1994. 34.95 (*1-56496-077-3*) Rockport Pubs.

Rockport Publishers Editors, compiled by. The Best of Brochure Design. 1994. pap. 34.99 (*1-56496-123-0*) Rockport Pubs.

— The Best of Business Card Design. (Illus.). 160p. 1997. pap. 24.99 (*1-56496-416-7*) Rockport Pubs.

— Designer Posters. (Illus.). 160p. 1996. 34.99 (*1-56496-247-4*) Rockport Pubs.

— Direct Response. (Design Library). (Illus.). 80p. 1998. pap. 14.99 (*1-56496-480-9*) Rockport Pubs.

— Great Sporting Graphics. (Illus.). 160p. 1995. 34.99 (*1-56496-179-6*) Rockport Pubs.

— Great T-Shirt Graphics. 160p. 1994. 34.99 (*1-56496-048-X*, 30554) Rockport Pubs.

— Great T-Shirt Graphics 3. (Illus.). 160p. 1997. bds. 34.99 (*1-56496-404-3*) Rockport Pubs.

— Great T-Shirt Graphics 2. (Illus.). 160p. 1995. 34.99 (*1-56496-180-X*) Rockport Pubs.

— Hotel Design: International Portfolio of the Finest Contemporary Designs. 160p. 1994. 39.95 (*1-56496-064-1*) Rockport Pubs.

— Labels & Tags. (Design Library). (Illus.). 80p. 1998. pap. 14.99 (*1-56496-508-2*) Rockport Pubs.

— Letterhead & Logo Design 4. (Illus.). 192p. 1997. pap. 34.99 (*1-56496-398-5*) Rockport Pubs.

— Package & Label Design. (Illus.). 1997. cd-rom 34.99 (*1-56496-403-5*) Rockport Pubs.

— Publications. (Design Library). (Illus.). 80p. 1998. pap. write for info. (*1-56496-543-0*) Rockport Pubs.

Rockport Publishers Editors & Visual Merchandising & Store Design Magazine Staff. Great Store Design. (Illus.). 160p. 1994. 34.95 (*1-56496-113-3*) Rockport Pubs.

Rockport Publishers Staff. The Best of Brochure Design 3. (Illus.). 192p. 1998. pap. 29.99 (*1-56496-556-2*) Rockport Pubs.

— Best Invitation, Card, & Announcement Design. (Motif Design Ser.). (Illus.). 160p. 1998. 34.99 (*1-56496-363-2*) Rockport Pubs.

— Hospitality & Leisure Architecture of Wimberly Allison Tong. 1995. pap. 29.99 (*1-56496-330-6*) Rockport Pubs.

— Hotel & Resort Interiors. (Interior Design Library). (Illus.). 80p. 1998. pap. 14.99 (*1-56496-484-1*, Pub. by Rockport Pubs) F & W Pubns Inc.

— Interiors in Blue. (Interiors Ser.). (Illus.). 96p. 1998. pap. 14.99 (*1-56496-441-8*) Rockport Pubs.

— Interiors in Red. (Interiors Ser.). (Illus.). 96p. 1998. pap. 14.99 (*1-56496-442-6*) Rockport Pubs.

— More Brochures. (Design Library Ser.). (Illus.). 80p. 1998. pap. text 14.99 (*1-56496-437-X*) Rockport Pubs.

— More Business Cards. (Design Library Ser.). (Illus.). 80p. 1998. pap. text 14.99 (*1-56496-438-8*) Rockport Pubs.

— More Logos & Letterheads. (Design Library Ser.). (Illus.). 80p. 1998. pap. text 14.99 (*1-56496-439-6*) Rockport Pubs.

— Package & Label Design No. 2. 192p. 1999. 40.00 (*1-56496-567-8*) Rockport Pubs.

— Restaurant Interiors. (Interior Design Library). (Illus.). 80p. 1998. pap. 14.99 (*1-56496-485-X*, Pub. by Rockport Pubs) F & W Pubns Inc.

— Retail Interiors. (Interior Design Library). (Illus.). 80p. 1998. pap. 14.99 (*1-56496-509-0*, Pub. by Rockport Pubs) F & W Pubns Inc.

Rockport Publishers Staff, compiled by. Best Direct Response Design. (Motif Design Ser.). (Illus.). 160p. 1998. pap. 34.99 (*1-56496-364-0*) Rockport Pubs.

— Best of Brochure Design, Vol. 4. (Illus.). 192p. 1998. pap. 39.99 (*1-56496-406-X*); pap. text 49.99 incl. cd-rom (*1-56496-376-4*) Rockport Pubs.

— Best of Business Card Design, Vol. 3. (Motif Design Ser.). (Illus.). 160p. 1997. pap. text 44.99 incl. cd-rom (*1-56496-365-9*) Rockport Pubs.

— Best of Business Card Design, Vol. 3. (Illus.). 160p. 1998. pap. 34.99 (*1-56496-402-7*) Rockport Pubs.

— Design Library: Animation. (Design Library). (Illus.). 80p. 1998. pap. 14.99 (*1-56496-479-5*) Rockport Pubs.

— Design Library: Publication. (Design Library Ser.). 80p. 1999. pap. 14.99 (*1-56496-554-6*) Rockport Pubs.

— Letterhead & Logo Design Vol. 3: Creating the Corporate Image. (Illus.). 256p. 1998. pap. 35.00 (*1-56496-228-8*) Rockport Pubs.

— Letterhead & Logo Design 5. (Illus.). 192p. 1998. pap. text 39.99 (*1-56496-405-1*) Rockport Pubs.

— Letterhead & Logo Design 5, Vol. 5. (Illus.). 192p. 1998. pap. 49.99 incl. cd-rom (*1-56496-366-7*) Rockport Pubs.

— Postcard Graphics: Designs from Around the World. (Motif Design Ser.). (Illus.). 160p. 1997. 34.99 (*1-56496-334-9*) Rockport Pubs.

Rockport Publishers Staff, ed. Best of Brochure Design 5. 208p. 1999. 45.00 (*1-56496-592-9*) Rockport Pubs.

— Design Library: More Packaging. (Design Library). (Illus.). 80p. 1998. pap. 14.99 (*1-56496-541-4*) Rockport Pubs.

— Design Library: More Promotion. (Design Library). (Illus.). 80p. 1998. pap. 14.99 (*1-56496-542-2*) Rockport Pubs.

— Interiors in Yellow. (Interiors Ser.). (Illus.). 96p. 1998. pap. 14.99 (*1-56496-444-2*) Rockport Pubs.

Rockport Publishers Staff, ed. see Cullen, Cheryl Dangel.

Rockport Publishers Staff, ed. see Hall, Mary Ann.

Rockport Publishers Staff, ed. see Sawahata, Lesa.

Rockport Publishers Staff, ed. see Singer, Alan.

Rockport Publishers Staff, ed. see Turkel Schwartz & Partners Staff.

***Rockport Publishing Staff, ed.** Package & Label Design. (Illus.). 2000. pap. 19.99 (*1-56496-682-8*) Rockport Pubs.

Rocks & Minerals (magazine) Staff, ed. Special Issue on Utah: Reprint of Rocks & Minerals Utah Special. (Public Information Ser.: Vol. 26). (Illus.). 62p. 1994. pap. 3.50 (*1-55791-359-5*, PI-26) Utah Geological Survey.

Rocks, Burton, jt. auth. see King, Clyde.

Rocks, David T. W. C. Fields - An Annotated Guide: Chronology, Bibliographies, Discography, Filmographies, Press Books, Cigarette Cards, Film Clips & Impersonators. LC 92-56688. (Illus.). 143p. 1993. lib. bdg. 32.50 (*0-89950-794-8*) McFarland & Co.

Rocksby, Rikky, ed. Fast Forward: Blues Guitar. (Illus.). 60p. (YA). 1998. pap. text 14.95 incl. audio compact disk (*0-7119-7041-6*, AM951160) Omnibus NY.

Rockstroh, Phil, jt. auth. see Chandler, Chris.

***Rockswold.** College Algebra. (C). 1999. text 26.40 (*0-321-03551-8*) Addson-Wesley Educ.

Rockswold. College Algebra: Student's Solutions Manual. (C). 1999. pap. text. write for info. (*0-321-01596-7*) Addson-Wesley Educ.

— College Algebra & Trigonometry Through Modeling & Visualization. LC 99-32639. 812p. (C). 1999. 91.00 (*0-321-04334-0*) Addson-Wesley Educ.

***Rockswold.** College Algebra Through Modeling Visualization. (C). 1999. text 26.40 (*0-321-03552-6*) Addson-Wesley Educ.

Rockswold. College Algebra Through Modeling Visualization. (C). 1999. text 71.00 (*0-321-03553-4*) Addson-Wesley Educ.

***Rockswold.** Graphing Calculator Manual: Rockwold's College Algebra & Trigonometry Through Modeling & Visualization. 2000. pap. 25.00 (*0-321-06667-7*) Addison-Wesley.

Rockswold. Graphing Calculator Manual for College Algebra Through Modeling & Visualization. 208p. (C). 1998. pap. text 16.00 (*0-321-02419-2*) Addson-Wesley Educ.

***Rockswold.** Precalculus Through Modeling & Visualization. LC 99-35868. 936p. (C). 1999. 91.00 (*0-321-05777-5*) Addson-Wesley Educ.

Rockswold. Rockswold's College Algebra & Trigonometry through Modeling & Visualization. (C). 2000. pap. text, teacher ed. 24.00 (*0-321-06668-5*) Addson-Wesley Educ.

***Rockswold.** Student's Solutions Manual for College Algebra Through Modeling & Visualization. (Illus.). 256p. (C). 1998. pap. 25.00 (*0-321-02861-9*) Addison-Wesley.

***Rockswold & Hornsby.** College Algebra Through Modeling & Visualization. rev. ed. 1999. 86.00 (*0-321-08028-9*) Addson-Wesley Educ.

Rockswold, E. Palmer. Per-Immigrant & Pioneer. 1982. pap. 6.95 (*0-934860-22-X*) Adventure Pubns.

Rockswold, Gary K. College Algebra Through Modeling & Visualization. LC 98-36379. 672p. (C). 1998. 79.00 (*0-321-01595-9*) Addson-Wesley Educ.

Rockway, John W. & Logan, James C. MININEC Broadcast Professional for Windows. 187p. 1995. pap. 390.00 incl. 3.5 hd (*1-887438-00-9*) EM Scientific.

— MININEC Broadcast Professional for Windows. LC 96-85405. (Illus.). 239p. 1996. pap. 790.00 (*1-887438-01-7*) EM Scientific.

— MININEC Broadcast Professional for Windows. 1997. pap. 125.00 incl. 3.5 hd (*1-887438-02-5*) EM Scientific.

***Rockwell.** Bugs Are Insects. (Let's-Read-&-Find-Out Science Bks.). 40p. (J). (ps-1). 2000. 15.95 (*0-06-028568-0*); lib. bdg. 15.89 (*0-06-028569-9*) HarpC Child Bks.

— Honey in a Hive. 40p. (J). (gr. k-4). 15.95 (*0-06-028566-4*); lib. bdg. 15.89 (*0-06-028567-2*) HarpC Child Bks.

— My Pet Hamster & Gerbils. 40p. (J). (ps-1). 15.95 (*0-06-028564-8*); lib. bdg. 15.89 (*0-06-028565-6*) HarpC Child Bks.

— Norman Rockwell's American Memories. (Illus.). 1999. 7.98 (*1-56731-352-3*, MJF Bks) Fine Comms.

Rockwell. Once upon a Saturday Morning. (J). 1996. 13.00 (*0-689-80525-X*) S&S Childrens.

Rockwell & Hurlburt. Educating the Horse. (Illus.). 227p. 1984. pap. 15.00 (*0-87556-355-4*) Saifer.

***Rockwell & Jenkins.** Bugs Are Insects. 40p. (J). (ps-1). 2000. pap. 4.95 (*0-06-445203-4*) HarpC Child Bks.

***Rockwell, Barbara.** Sarah's Gold: A Woman Pioneer of Vision. LC 00-190561. 289p. 2000. 25.00 (*0-7388-1828-3*); pap. 18.00 (*0-7388-1829-1*) Xlibris Corp.

Rockwell, A. D., ed. see Beard, George M.

Rockwell, Anne. The Acorn Tree & Other Folktales. LC 94-29277. (Illus.). 40p. (J). (ps-3). 1995. 16.00 (*0-688-10746-X*, Grenwillow Bks) HarpC Child Bks.

— Alligators. LC 99-44805. 40p. (J). (gr. k-4). Date not set. 15.95 (*0-06-028530-3*) HarpC Child Bks.

***Rockwell, Anne.** Alligators. LC 99-44805. 40p. (J). (gr. k-4). 2000. lib. bdg. 15.89 (*0-06-028531-1*) HarpC Child Bks.

Rockwell, Anne. Alligators. LC 99-44805. 40p. (J). (gr. k-4). 2001. pap. 4.95 (*0-06-445200-X*, HarpTrophy) HarpC Child Bks.

— Apples & Pumpkins. LC 94-629. (Illus.). 24p. (J). (ps-1). 1994. per. 4.99 (*0-689-71861-6*) Aladdin.

— Apples & Pumpkins. LC 88-22628. (Illus.). 24p. (J). (ps-1). 1989. lib. bdg. 15.00 (*0-02-777270-5*) S&S Childrens.

— At the Beach. LC 86-2943. (Illus.). 24p. (J). (ps-1). 1987. text, lib. bdg. 14.00 (*0-02-777940-8*, Mac Bks Young Read) S&S Childrens.

— At the Beach. LC 90-45620. (Illus.). 24p. (J). (ps-1). 1991. reprint ed. mass mkt. 4.95 (*0-689-71494-7*) Aladdin.

— Bear Child's Book of Hours. 1999. pap. 4.50 (*0-14-055291-X*) NAL.

— Big Boss. 64p. (J). 1996. per. 14.00 (*0-689-80883-6*) S&S Bks Yung.

— Big Boss. (Illus.). 64p. (J). (gr. k-3). 1996. mass mkt. 3.99 (*0-689-80884-4*) S&S Bks Yung.

— Big Boss, Ready-To-Read, Level 2. (Ready-to-Read Ser.). 1996. 9.19 (*0-606-11121-2*, Pub. by Turtleback) Demco.

— Boats. (Illus.). 24p. (J). 1993. pap. 5.99 (*0-14-054988-9*, PuffinBks) Peng Put Young Read.

— Bumblebee, Bumblebee, Do You Know Me. LC 97-28795. (Illus.). 24p. (J). (ps-2). 1999. lib. bdg. 14.89 (*0-06-028212-6*) HarpC Child Bks.

— Bumblebee, Bumblebee, Do You Know Me: A Garden Guessing Game. LC 97-28795. (Illus.). 24p. (J). (ps-2). 1999. 14.95 (*0-06-027330-5*) HarpC Child Bks.

— Cars. (J). 1992. pap. 5.99 (*0-14-054741-X*, PuffinBks) Peng Put Young Read.

Rockwell, Anne. Clouds. 40p. (ps-1). pap. 15.95 (*0-06-029101-X*); pap. 4.95 (*0-06-445220-4*); lib. bdg. 15.89 (*0-06-029102-8*) HarpC.

Rockwell, Anne. Come to Town. LC 86-6217. (Illus.). 32p. (J). (ps-1). 1991. pap. 4.95 (*0-06-107411-X*) HarpC Child Bks.

— Disobedient Servant Boy. LC 99-15201. (J). 2000. lib. bdg. 15.89 (*0-688-14882-4*, Grenwillow Bks) HarpC Child Bks.

Rockwell, Anne. Ducklings & Pollywogs. LC 93-16600. (Illus.). 32p. (J). (ps-2). 1994. pap. 14.95 (*0-02-777452-X*, Mac Bks Young Read) S&S Childrens.

Rockwell, Anne. Ferryboat Ride. LC 98-28827. (Illus.). 40p. (J). (ps-3). 1999. 17.00 (*0-517-70959-7*, Pub. by Crown Bks Yng Read) Random.

***Rockwell, Anne.** Ferryboat Ride. (Illus.). 40p. (J). (gr. k-3). 2000. pap. 6.99 (*0-517-88598-0*, Pub. by Crown Bks Yng Read) Random.

Rockwell, Anne. Ferryboat Ride! LC 98-28827. (Illus.). (J). (ps-3). 1999. lib. bdg. 18.99 (*0-517-70960-0*, Pub. by Crown Bks Yng Read) Random.

***Rockwell, Anne.** Ferryboat Ride! (Illus.). (J). 1999. 12.44 (*0-606-18088-5*) Turtleback.

Rockwell, Anne. Fire Engines. LC 86-4464. (Illus.). 24p. (J). (ps-1). 1986. 13.99 (*0-525-44259-6*, Dutton Child) Peng Put Young Read.

— First Comes Spring. LC 84-45331. (Illus.). 32p. (J). (ps-1). 1985. 14.95 (*0-694-00106-6*) HarpC Child Bks.

Rockwell, Anne. Honey in a Hive. 40p. (gr. k-4). pap. 4.95 (*0-06-445204-2*) HarpC.

— How Kittens Grow. 40p. (ps-1). pap. 15.95 (*0-06-029103-6*); pap. 4.95 (*0-06-445219-0*); lib. bdg. 14.89 (*0-06-029104-4*) HarpC.

Rockwell, Anne. Hugo at the Park. LC 89-2417. (Illus.). 32p. (J). (ps-k). 1990. lib. bdg. 13.95 (*0-02-777301-9*, Mac Bks Young Read) S&S Childrens.

Rockwell, Anne. I Fly. LC 94-29278. (J). 1997. lib. bdg. 0.17 (*0-517-59684-9*, Pub. by Crown Bks Yng Read) Random.

Rockwell, Anne. I Fly. LC 94-29278. (Illus.). (J). 1997. 16.00 (*0-517-59683-0*, Pub. by Crown Bks Yng Read) Random.

— I Fly. 32p. 1998. pap. 6.99 (*0-517-88569-7*) Crown Pub Group.

Rockwell, Anne. Katie Swims. LC 99-39893. (Illus.). 32p. (J). (ps-1). 5.95 (*0-06-446740-6*) HarpC.

— Katie Swims. LC 99-39893. (Illus.). 32p. (J). (ps-1). 2001. 14.89 (*0-06-028445-5*) HarpC.

— Katie Swims. LC 99-39893. (Illus.). 32p. (J). (ps-1). 2001. 14.95 (*0-06-028441-2*) HarpC Child Bks.

Rockwell, Anne. Long Ago Yesterday. LC 98-35267. (Illus.). 24p. (J). (ps up). 1999. 16.00 (*0-688-14411-X*, Grenwillow Bks) HarpC Child Bks.

— Mr. Panda's Painting. LC 92-9220. (Illus.). 32p. (J). (ps-1). 1993. lib. bdg. 14.95 (*0-02-777451-1*, Mac Bks Young Read) S&S Childrens.

Rockwell, Anne. Morgan Plays Soccer. LC 99-39894. (Illus.). 32p. (J). (ps-1). 5.95 (*0-06-446739-2*) HarpC.

— Morgan Plays Soccer. LC 99-39894. (Illus.). 32p. (J). (ps-1). 2000. 14.89 (*0-06-028444-7*) HarpC.

— Morgan Plays Soccer. LC 99-39894. (Illus.). 32p. (J). (ps-1). 2000. 14.95 (*0-06-028440-4*) HarpC Child Bks.

— My Pet Hamster. 40p. (ps-1). pap. 4.95 (*0-06-445205-0*) HarpC.

Rockwell, Anne. My Spring Robin. (Illus.). 24p. (J). (ps-1). 1996. per. 4.95 (*0-689-80447-4*) Aladdin.

— No! No! No! (Illus.). 32p. (J). (ps-1). 1995. mass mkt. 14.00 (*0-02-777782-0*, Mac Bks Young Read) S&S Childrens.

— The Old Woman & Her Pig & Ten Other Stories. LC 78-13901. (Illus.). (J). (gr. 1 up). 1979. 13.95 (*0-690-03927-1*); lib. bdg. 13.89 (*0-690-03928-X*) HarpC Child Bks.

— Once upon a Time This Morning. LC 96-6349. (Illus.). 24p. (J). (ps up). 1997. 15.00 (*0-688-14706-2*, Grenwillow Bks); lib. bdg. 14.93 (*0-688-14707-0*, Grenwillow Bks) HarpC Child Bks.

— One Bean. LC 97-36249. (Illus.). 32p. (J). (gr. k-1). 1999. 14.95 (*0-8027-8648-0*); lib. bdg. 15.85 (*0-8027-8649-9*) Walker & Co.

— The One-Eyed Giant. LC 95-12326. (Illus.). 32p. (J). (ps-3). 1996. 16.00 (*0-688-13809-8*, Grenwillow Bks) HarpC Child Bks.

— The One-Eyed Giant & Other Monsters from the Greek Myths. LC 95-12326. (Illus.). 32p. (J). (ps up). 1996. lib. bdg. 15.93 (*0-688-13810-1*, Grenwillow Bks) HarpC Child Bks.

Rockwell, Anne. 100 Days. 40p. (ps). pap. 14.95 (*0-06-029144-3*) HarpC.

— 100 Days. 40p. (ps-1). pap. 5.95 (*0-06-443727-2*); lib. bdg. 14.89 (*0-06-029145-1*) HarpC.

Rockwell, Anne. Our Earth. 24p. (J). 2000. pap. 6.00 (*0-15-202383-6*, Voyager Bks) Harcourt.

— Our Stars. LC 97-49518. (Illus.). 24p. (J). 1999. 13.00 (*0-15-201868-9*) Harcourt.

— Our Yard Is Full of Birds. LC 90-30436. (Illus.). 32p. (J). (ps-2). 1992. lib. bdg. 14.00 (*0-02-777273-X*, Mac Bks Young Read) S&S Childrens.

— Planes. (J). (ps-3). 1993. pap. 5.99 (*0-14-054782-7*, PuffinBks) Peng Put Young Read.

— Pots & Pans. LC 91-4976. (Illus.). 32p. (J). (ps-1). 1993. lib. bdg. 13.95 (*0-02-777631-X*, Mac Bks Young Read) S&S Childrens.

Rockwell, Anne. The Robber Baby: Stories from the Greek Myths. LC 90-39560. (Illus.). 80p. (J). (ps-3). 1994. lib. bdg. 17.93 (*0-688-09741-3*, Grenwillow Bks) HarpC Child Bks.

Rockwell, Anne. Romulus & Remus. (Illus.). (J). (gr. k-4). 1997. per. 3.99 (*0-689-81290-6*) S&S Childrens.

— Romulus & Remus. LC 96-25565. (Illus.). 40p. (J). (gr. k-3). 1997. 15.00 (*0-689-81291-4*) S&S Childrens.

Rockwell, Anne. Romulus & Remus. (Ready-to-Read Ser.). 1997. 9.19 (*0-606-13748-3*, Pub. by Turtleback) Demco.

Rockwell, Anne. Show & Tell Day. LC 95-26349. (Illus.). 32p. (J). (ps-k). 1997. 14.95 (*0-06-027300-3*); lib. bdg. 14.89 (*0-06-027301-1*) HarpC Child Bks.

— Show & Tell Day. LC 95-26349. (Illus.). 40p. (J). (ps-k). 2000. pap. 5.95 (*0-06-443624-1*) HarpC Child Bks.

***Rockwell, Anne.** Sojourner Truth. (J). 2000. lib. bdg. 16.99 (*0-679-99186-7*) Random.

— Sojourner Truth. 2000. 16.95 (*0-679-89186-2*) Random.

Rockwell, Anne. The Storm. LC 93-40976. (Illus.). 32p. (J). (ps-3). 1994. 15.95 (*0-7868-0017-8*, Pub. by Hyprn Child); lib. bdg. 15.89 (*0-7868-2013-6*, Pub. by Hyprn Child) Little.

— The Story Snail. LC 96-19215. (Illus.). 48p. (J). 1997. per. 3.99 (*0-689-81220-5*) S&S Childrens.

— The Story Snail. LC 96-19215. (Illus.). 48p. (J). (gr. k-4). 1997. per. 15.00 (*0-689-81221-3*) S&S Childrens.

— The Story Snail. LC 87-1097. (Ready-to-Read Ser.). (Illus.). 64p. (J). (gr. 1-4). 1987. reprint ed. pap. 3.95 (*0-689-71164-6*) Aladdin.

— Sweet Potato Pie. LC 94-34990. (Early Step into Reading Ser.). (Illus.). (J). (ps-3). 1996. pap. 3.99 (*0-679-86440-7*) Random.

— Sweet Potato Pie. LC 94-34990. (Early Step into Reading Ser.). (Illus.). (J). (ps-3). 1996. lib. bdg. 11.99 (*0-679-96440-1*) Random.

Rockwell, Anne. Sweet Potato Pie. (Early Step into Reading Ser.). (J). (ps-k). 1996. 9.19 (*0-606-08884-9*, Pub. by Turtleback) Demco.

Rockwell, Anne. Thanksgiving Day. LC 97-39290. (Illus.). 40p. (J). (ps-k). 1999. lib. bdg. 14.89 (*0-06-028388-2*) HarpC Child Bks.

— Things That Go. (J). 1995. pap. 5.99 (*0-14-054788-6*, Dutton Child) Peng Put Young Read.

— El Toro Pinto: And Other Songs in Spanish. (Illus.). 64p. (J). (gr. k-3). 1995. mass mkt. 5.95 (*0-689-71880-2*) Aladdin.

— Trucks. (J). (ps-3). 1992. pap. 5.99 (*0-14-054790-8*, Viking Child) Peng Put Young Read.

— Valentine's Day. LC 97-17492. (Illus.). 40p. (J). (ps-k). 1999. 14.95 (*0-06-027794-7*) HarpC Child Bks.

— Valentine's Day. 8th ed. LC 97-17492. (Illus.). 40p. (J). (ps-k). 2001. lib. bdg. 14.89 (*0-06-028515-X*) HarpC Child Bks.

— What We Like. LC 91-4990. (Illus.). 24p. (J). (ps-1). 1992. mass mkt. 13.95 (*0-02-777274-8*, Mac Bks Young Read) S&S Childrens.

Rockwell, Anne & Rockwell, Harlow. The First Snowfall. LC 86-23712. (Illus.). 24p. (J). (ps-1). 1987. lib. bdg. 13.95 (*0-02-777770-7*, Mac Bks Young Read) S&S Childrens.

— The First Snowfall. LC 91-41247. (Illus.). 24p. (J). (ps-1). 1992. reprint ed. mass mkt. 3.95 (*0-689-71614-1*) Aladdin.

Rockwell, Anne, jt. auth. see Walker & Company.

Rockwell, Anne F. Apples & Pumpkins. LC 94-629. 1994. 10.19 (*0-606-06181-9*, Pub. by Turtleback) Demco.

Rockwell, Anne F. The Boy Who Wouldn't Obey: A Mayan Legend. LC 99-15201. (Illus.). 24p. (J). (gr. k-3). 2000. 15.95 (*0-688-14881-6*, Grenwillow Bks) HarpC Child Bks.

— Career Day. LC 97-20999. (Illus.). 40p. (J). (ps-k). 2000. 14.95 (*0-06-027565-0*); lib. bdg. 14.89 (*0-06-027566-9*) HarpC Child Bks.

— Cars. (J). 1986. 10.19 (*0-606-03319-X*, Pub. by Turtleback) Demco.

— Fire Engines. (Picture Puffin Ser.). (Illus.). (J). 1993. 9.70 (*0-606-05287-9*, Pub. by Turtleback) Demco.

Rockwell, Anne F. First Snowfall. (J). 1992. 9.15 (*0-606-02002-0*, Pub. by Turtleback) Demco.

Rockwell, Anne F. Halloween Day. LC 96-36680. Orig. Title: Halloween. (Illus.). 40p. (J). (ps-k). 1997. 15.95 (*0-06-027567-7*) HarpC.

— Halloween Day. LC 96-36680. Orig. Title: Halloween. (Illus.). 40p. (J). (ps-k). 1999. pap. 5.95 (*0-06-443589-X*) HarpC Child Bks.

— I Fly. 1998. 12.19 (*0-606-13502-2*, Pub. by Turtleback) Demco.

— My Spring Robin. LC 88-13333. (J). 1996. 10.85 (*0-606-09656-6*, Pub. by Turtleback) Demco.

— Our Earth. LC 97-1247. (Illus.). 24p. (J). (gr. k-1). 1998. 13.00 (*0-15-201679-1*) Harcourt.

***Rockwell, Anne F.** Pumpkin Day, Pumpkin Night. LC 98-48370. (Illus.). 32p. (J). (gr. k-2). 1999. 15.95 (*0-8027-8696-0*) Walker & Co.

— Pumpkin Day, Pumpkin Night. LC 98-48370. (Illus.). 32p. (J). (ps-2). 1999. lib. bdg. 16.85 (*0-8027-8697-9*) Walker & Co.

Rockwell, Anne F. The Story Snail. (Ready-to-Read Ser.). (J). 1997. 9.19 (*0-606-11923-X*, Pub. by Turtleback) Demco.

— Thanksgiving Day. LC 97-39290. (Illus.). 40p. (J). (ps-k). 1999. 14.95 (*0-06-027795-5*) HarpC Child Bks.

An Asterisk (*) at the beginning of an entry indicates that the title is appearing for the first time.

Rockwell, Anne I. Our Seas. LC 98-27797. (J). 2001. 20.01 (*0-15-202023-3*) Harcourt.
Rockwell, Barry. Why the Leopard has Spots. LC 97-23069. 32p. (J). (gr. k-3). 1998. 19.97 (*0-8172-5156-1*) Raintree Steck-V.
Rockwell, Bart. The World's Strangest Baseball Stories. LC 92-10120. (Illus.). 96p. (J). (gr. 3-7). 1992. pap. 2.95 (*0-8167-2850-X*) Troll Communs.
— World's Strangest Baseball Stories. (J). 1993. 8.05 (*0-606-02994-X*, Pub. by Turtleback) Demco.
— World's Strangest Basketball Stories. LC 92-25676. (J). 1996. pap. 2.95 (*0-8167-2852-6*) Troll Communs.
— World's Strangest Basketball Stories. (J). 1993. 8.05 (*0-606-02995-8*, Pub. by Turtleback) Demco.
— The World's Strangest Football Stories. LC 92-10121. (Illus.). 96p. (J). (gr. 3-7). 1992. lib. bdg. 15.85 (*0-8167-2934-4*) Troll Communs.
— The World's Strangest Football Stories. LC 92-10121. (Illus.). 96p. (J). (gr. 3-7). 1996. pap. 2.95 (*0-8167-2851-8*) Troll Communs.
— World's Strangest Football Stories. (J). 1993. 8.05 (*0-606-02996-6*, Pub. by Turtleback) Demco.
— World's Strangest Hockey Stories. LC 92-25992. (Illus.). 96p. (J). (gr. 3-7). 1996. pap. 2.95 (*0-8167-2853-4*) Troll Communs.
— World's Strangest Hockey Stories. (J). 1993. 8.05 (*0-606-02997-4*, Pub. by Turtleback) Demco.
Rockwell, Browning. Using the Web to Compete in a Global Marketplace. LC 98-24483. 336p. 1998. pap. 29.99 (*0-471-25262-X*) Wiley.
***Rockwell, Bruce A. & Gossen, Thomas R.** The Cottage Meeting Commitment Workbook. 1998. wbk. ed. 9.95 (*0-8192-1792-1*, 1210) Morehouse Pub.
Rockwell, Bruce A., jt. auth. see Gossen, Thomas R.
Rockwell, Charles. The Catskill Mountains & the Region Around. 351p. 1993. reprint ed. lib. bdg. 89.00 (*0-7812-5134-6*) Rprt Serv.
Rockwell, Coralie J. Kagok, a Traditional Korean Vocal Form. LC 72-87568. (Asian Music Publications: Vol. D/3). (Illus.). 302p. (Orig.). (C). 1972. pap. 15.00 (*0-913360-05-8*) Theodore Front.
Rockwell, David. The Nature of North America: A Handbook to the Continent; Rocks, Plants & Animals. LC 98-27182. 560p. 1998. 29.95 (*0-425-16587-6*); pap. 15.00 (*0-425-16548-5*) Berkley Pub.
***Rockwell, David L.** At the Controls: F-14 Tomca. 96p. 1999. pap. 18.00 (*0-00-472254-X*, HarpRes) HarpInfo.
Rockwell, David L. Giving Voice to Bear: Native American Indian Myths, Rituals, & Images of the Bear. LC 92-61908. (Illus.). 240p. 1993. pap. 18.95 (*1-879373-48-3*) Roberts Rinehart.
— Glacier National Park: A Natural History Guide. LC 95-6058. (National Parks Natural History Ser.). (Illus.). 240p. 1995. pap. 14.00 (*0-395-69981-9*) HM.
Rockwell, David L. & Dorsey, Megan. Financing Residential Real Estate. 12th rev. ed. (Illus.). 366p. 1997. pap. text 34.95 (*1-887051-06-6*) Rockwell WA.
Rockwell, David L., et al. Oregon Real Estate Law. 4th ed. (Illus.). 245p. (Orig.). 1995. pap. 32.95 (*0-915799-96-0*) Rockwell WA.
— Oregon Real Estate Practices. 4th ed. (Illus.). 296p. (Orig.). 1995. pap. 32.95 (*0-915799-97-9*) Rockwell WA.
Rockwell, David L., jt. auth. see Dorsey, Megan.
Rockwell, David L., jt. auth. see Haupt, Kathryn J.
***Rockwell, Dean.** Antique Knife Rests: History, Manufacture & Illustrations of American, English & Continental Knife Rests in Metal, Glass & Ceramic. (Illus.). 80p. 2000. 49.95 (*1-882792-95-5*) Proctor Pubns.
Rockwell, Elsie. La Escuela Cotidiana. (SPA.). pap. 12.99 (*968-16-4524-3*, Pub. by Fondo) Continental Bk.
Rockwell, George L. White Power. unabridged ed. (Illus.). 482p. 1996. reprint ed. 25.00 (*0-9656492-8-8*) J McLaughlin.
— White Power. 2nd ed. 466p. 1994. reprint ed. pap. 9.95 (*0-937944-10-6*) Natl Vanguard.
Rockwell, Harlow. My Dentist. LC 75-6974. (Illus.). 32p. (J). (ps-3). 1975. 16.00 (*0-688-80011-4*, Wm Morrow) Morrow Avon.
Rockwell, Harlow. My Dentist. LC 75-6974. (Illus.). 32p. (J). (ps up). 1987. mass mkt. 4.95 (*0-688-07040-X*, Wm Morrow) Morrow Avon.
Rockwell, Harlow, jt. auth. see Rockwell, Anne.
Rockwell, Jack A., jt. auth. see Stocking, Stephen K.
Rockwell, James R., Jr., jt. auth. see Goldman, Leon.
Rockwell, Jeanne & Noonan, Thomas E., eds. Good Company: Poets at Michigan. LC 77-91403. 1977. 10.00 (*0-9602934-0-X*) Noon Rock.
Rockwell, Jeanne, ed. see Noonan, Thomas E.
***Rockwell, Jerry.** Blackbird & the Beggerman. 40p. 1998. pap. 24.95 incl. audio compact disk (*0-7866-1669-5*, 95701CDP); pap. 9.95 (*0-7866-1667-9*, 95701) Mel Bay.
Rockwell, Joan. Life & Old Age: A Commonplace Book. 234p. 1999. 42.50 (*1-85776-306-8*) Trans-Atl Phila.
Rockwell, Lizzy. Good Enough to Eat: A Kid's Guide to Food & Nutrition. LC 97-32145. 40p. (J). (gr. k-4). Date not set. pap. 5.95 (*0-06-445174-7*) HarpC Child Bks.
— Good Enough to Eat: A Kid's Guide to Food & Nutrition. LC 97-32145. (Illus.). 40p. (J). (gr. k-4). 1999. lib. bdg. 14.89 (*0-06-027435-2*) HarpC Child Bks.
— Good Enough to Eat: A Kid's Guide to Food & Nutrition. LC 97-32145. (Illus.). 40p. (J). (gr. k-4). 1999. 14.95 (*0-06-027434-4*) HarpC Child Bks.
— Hello Baby. LC 98-7339. (J). 1999. lib. bdg. 16.99 (*0-517-80012-8*, Pub. by Crown Bks Yng Read) Random.
***Rockwell, Lizzy.** Hello Baby. (Illus.). 32p. (J). (ps-k). 2000. pap. 6.99 (*0-517-80074-8*, Pub. by Crown Bks Yng Read) Random.
Rockwell, Lizzy. Hello Baby! LC 98-7339. 32p. (J). 1999. 15.00 (*0-517-80011-X*, Pub. by Crown Bks Yng Read) Random.
Rockwell, Llewellyn H., Jr., ed. Murray N. Rothbard: In Memoriam. 132p. (Orig.). 1995. pap. 14.95 (*0-945466-19-6*) Ludwig von Mises.
Rockwell, Llewellyn H., Jr., intro. The Economics of Liberty. 392p. (Orig.). 1990. pap. text 14.95 (*0-945466-08-0*) Ludwig von Mises.
— The Gold Standard: Perspectives in the Austrian School. 147p. (Orig.). 1992. reprint ed. pap. text 9.95 (*0-945466-11-0*) Ludwig von Mises.
Rockwell, Margaret. Davy's Lake. (Orig.). 1995. pap. text 10.95 (*0-9608496-1-0*) Caribou Pr.
***Rockwell, Margaret.** Norman Rockwell Christmas. (Illus.). 80p. 2000. 7.98 (*1-58663-073-3*) M Friedman Pub Grp Inc.
Rockwell, Margaret. Norman Rockwell's Chronicles of America. 120p. 1996. 17.98 (*1-56799-344-3*, MetroBooks) M Friedman Pub Grp Inc.
— Norman Rockwell's Growing up in America. LC 99-18036. 120p. 1998. 17.98 (*1-56799-598-5*, Friedman-Fairfax) M Friedman Pub Grp Inc.
Rockwell, Mark, ed. see McDaniel, Nello & Thorn, George.
Rockwell, Molly, ed. Norman Rockwell's Christmas Book. LC 93-9925. (Illus.). 222p. 1993. pap. 12.98 (*0-8109-8121-1*, Pub. by Abrams) Time Warner.
Rockwell Museum Staff. Great Paintings of the Old West. 1987. pap. 4.95 (*0-486-25360-0*) Dover.
— Remington Drawings. 1998. pap. text 4.95 (*0-486-25774-6*) Dover.
Rockwell, Norm. Badger Digs. 104p. (Orig.). 1980. pap. 3.95 (*0-9612002-0-0*) Moonlight Press.
— Murder in Menomonie. 120p. (Orig.). 1984. pap. 3.95 (*0-9612002-3-5*) Moonlight Press.
— Twin City Slickers. rev. ed. 104p. (Orig.). 1983. pap. 3.95 (*0-9612002-1-9*) Moonlight Press.
Rockwell, Norman. My School Days: A Keepsake Album. (Illus.). 42p. 1994. 16.95 (*0-8109-4450-2*, Pub. by Abrams) Time Warner.
— Norman Rockwell: My Adventures As an Illustrator. (Illus.). 432p. 1995. pap. 19.95 (*0-8109-2596-6*, Pub. by Abrams) Time Warner.
— Norman Rockwell: The Artist & His Work. 1999. 19.98 (*1-56799-760-0*) M Friedman Pub Grp Inc.
— Norman Rockwell's American Children: A Postcard Book. (Postcard Bks.). (Illus.). 64p. (Orig.). 1993. pap. 8.95 (*1-56138-258-2*) Running Pr.
— Norman Rockwell's American Christmas Postcard Book. (Postcard Bks.). (Illus.). 64p. (Orig.). 1990. pap. text 8.95 (*0-89471-894-0*) Running Pr.
— Old Fashioned Norman Rockwell Christmas. 96p. 1997. 14.99 (*1-57866-010-6*) Galahad Bks.
— Saturday Evening Post, Vol. 1. (Illus.). 120p. 1995. pap. 49.95 (*4-8457-0955-4*, Pub. by Treville) Bks Nippan.
— Willie Was Different. LC 94-8785. (Illus.). 32p. (J). 1994. 16.95 (*0-936399-61-9*) Berkshire Hse.
— Willie Was Different. (J). 1997. pap. 5.99 (*0-679-88262-6*) McKay.
— Willie Was Different. 1997. 11.19 (*0-606-12101-3*, Pub. by Turtleback) Demco.
— Willie Was Different. (J). (ps-3). 1997. reprint ed. pap. 5.99 (*0-614-28952-1*) Random Bks Yng Read.
Rockwell, Norman. An American Family Album. 40p. 1993. 6.95 (*0-8362-4711-6*) Andrews & McMeel.
— American Memories. 40p. 1993. 6.95 (*0-8362-4710-8*) Andrews & McMeel.
— The Art of Norman Rockwell. 80p. 1993. 4.95 (*0-8362-3033-7*) Andrews & McMeel.
— The Best of Norman Rockwell: A Celebration of 100 Years. 144p. 1988. 19.98 (*1-56138-637-5*, Courage) Running Pr.
— Norman Rockwell Postcard Book. (Postcard Bks.). 64p. (Orig.). 1987. pap. text 8.95 (*0-89471-554-2*) Running Pr.
— Romance. 40p. 1993. 6.95 (*0-8362-4709-4*) Andrews & McMeel.
— Wit & Humor of Norman Rockwell. 40p. 1993. 6.95 (*0-8362-4708-6*) Andrews & McMeel.
Rockwell, Norman & Murray, Stuart. Norman Rockwell's Four Freedoms. LC 97-48769. 176p. 1998. 12.99 (*0-517-20213-1*) Random Hse Value.
Rockwell, P. J. & Davis, R. A. An Introduction to Time Series & Forecasting. LC 96-11743. (Texts in Statistics Ser.). (Illus.). 420p. 1996. 64.95 (*0-387-94719-1*) Spr-Verlag.
Rockwell, Paul V. Rewriting Resemblance in Medieval French Romance: Ceci N' Est Pas un Graal. LC 95-13705. (Garland Studies in Medieval Literature: Vol. 13). 264p. 1995. text 55.00 (*0-8153-2035-3*, H1908) Garland.
Rockwell, Robert, et al. Linking Language: Simple Language & Literacy Activities Throughout the Curriculum. LC 99-28325. (Illus.). 256p. (J). 1999. pap. 19.95 (*0-87659-202-7*, 17561, Pub. by Gryphon Hse) Consort Bk Sales.
Rockwell, Robert E. Everybody Has a Body: Science from Head to Toe. 214p. 1992. pap. 16.95 (*0-87659-158-6*) Gryphon Hse.
Rockwell, Robert E., et al. Hug a Tree & Other Things to Do Outdoors with Young Children. 109p. (ps-1). 1983. pap. 9.95 (*0-87659-105-5*) Gryphon Hse.
— Mudpies to Magnets: A Preschool Science Curriculum. (Illus.). 156p. (J). (ps-1). 1987. pap. 14.95 (*0-87659-112-8*) Gryphon Hse.
— Parent & Teacher As Partners: Issues & Challenges. LC 95-75403. 336p. (C). 1995. pap. text 35.00 (*0-15-500483-2*, Pub. by Harcourt Coll Pubs) Harcourt.
— The Wonders of Water. Anderson, Catherine & Apple, Mali, eds. (Discovery Science Ser.). (Illus.). 76p. (Orig.). (J). 1996. pap. text 11.95 (*0-201-49661-5*, 36839) Seymour Pubns.
Rockwell, Robert E., jt. auth. see Endres, Jeanette.
Rockwell, S., jt. auth. see Woll, P.
Rockwell, S. P. Practical Metallography. (Technical Papers: Vol. P79). (Illus.). 6p. 1924. pap. text 30.00 (*1-55589-320-1*) AGMA.
— Rockwell Dilatometer. (Technical Papers: Vol. P85). (Illus.). 3p. 1925. pap. text 30.00 (*1-55589-321-X*) AGMA.
— Spark Tests for Steel. (Technical Papers: Vol. P88A). (Illus.). 2p. 1923. pap. text 30.00 (*1-55589-322-8*) AGMA.
Rockwell, Stephen, jt. auth. see Woll, Peter.
Rockwell, Sylvia. Back off, Cool down, Try Again: Teaching Students How to Control Aggressive Behavior. 144p. 1995. pap. text 29.95 (*0-86586-263-X*, P5120) Coun Exc Child.
— Tough to Reach, Tough to Teach: Students with Behavior Problems. LC 92-43363. 106p. 1993. pap. text 26.40 (*0-86586-235-4*, P387) Coun Exc Child.
Rockwell, Sylvia, et al. Developing Personal & Interpersonal Responsibility in Children & Youth with Emotional/Behavioral Disorders. 48p. 1997. pap. text 11.40 (*0-86586-306-7*) Coun Exc Child.
Rockwell, Theodore. The Rickover Effect: How One Man Made a Difference. LC 92-3909. (Illus.). 411p. 1992. 32.95 (*1-55750-702-3*) Naval Inst Pr.
— The Rickover Effects: The Inside Story of how Adm. Human Rickover Built the Nuclear Navy. LC 95-19843. 411p. 1995. pap. 19.95 (*0-471-12296-3*) Wiley.
Rockwell, Theodore, 3rd, ed. see AEC Technical Information Center Staff.
Rockwell, Thomas. How to Eat Fried Worms. LC 73-4262. (Illus.). 128p. (J). (gr. 4-7). 1953. pap. 4.99 (*0-440-44545-0*, YB BDD) BDD Bks Young Read.
Rockwell, Thomas. How to Eat Fried Worms. 179p. (J). (gr. 3-5). pap. 4.99 (*0-8072-1395-0*) Listening Lib.
— How to Eat Fried Worms. (Illus.). (J). (gr. 4-7). 2000. mass mkt. 2.99 (*0-375-80678-4*, Pub. by Random Bks Yng Read) Random.
Rockwell, Thomas. How to Eat Fried Worms. (J). 1973. 10.09 (*0-606-03537-0*, Pub. by Turtleback) Demco.
— How to Eat Fried Worms. LC 73-4262. (Illus.). 116p. (J). (gr. 4-6). 1973. lib. bdg. 24.00 (*0-531-02631-0*) Watts.
— How to Eat Fried Worms: Literature Unit. (J). 1953. mass mkt. 3.75 (*0-440-70004-3*) Doubleday.
— How to Eat Fried Worms: Literature Unit. 1997. pap. text 7.95 (*1-55734-816-2*) Tchr Create Mat.
— How to Fight a Girl. 112p. (J). (gr. k-6). 1988. pap. 3.99 (*0-440-40111-9*, YB BDD) BDD Bks Young Read.
— How to Fight a Girl. (J). 1987. 9.09 (*0-606-04097-8*, Pub. by Turtleback) Demco.
Rockwell, Thomas. How to Fight A Girl. 112p. (J). (gr. 3-5). pap. 3.99 (*0-8072-1452-3*) Listening Lib.
Rockwell, Thomas. How to Get Fabulously Rich. (Illus.). 128p. (J). (gr. 5-8). 1990. lib. bdg. 24.00 (*0-531-10877-5*) Watts.
***Rockwell, Tom.** Best of Norman Rockwell. (Illus.). 2000. 19.98 (*0-7624-0913-4*) Running Pr.
— Best of Norman Rockwell: A Celebration of 100 Years. (Illus.). 2000. 19.98 (*0-7624-0879-0*) Running Pr.
Rockwell, W. J., jt. ed. see Talley, Joseph E.
Rockwell, Willard F. Rebellious Colonel Speaks. 1964. text 4.95 (*0-07-053362-8*) McGraw.
***Rockwell, Wilson.** Sunset Slope. 2nd rev. ed. LC 98-83236. (Illus.). 290p. (Orig.). 1999. pap. 16.95 (*1-890437-25-5*) Western Reflections.
— Uncompahgre Country. 2nd ed. LC 65-28810. (Illus.). 310p. 1999. reprint ed. pap. 19.95 (*1-890437-38-7*) Western Reflections.
Rockwell, Wilson. The Utes: A Forgotten People. LC 98-60766. 307p. 1998. reprint ed. pap. 19.95 (*1-890437-23-9*) Western Reflections.
Rockwood. The Shoulder, Vol. 1. 1990. text. write for info. (*0-7216-2829-X*) Bailliere Tindall.
— The Shoulder, Vol. 2. 1990. text. write for info. (*0-7216-2830-3*) Bailliere Tindall.
Rockwood, Elizabeth. When Prayers Are Not Answered: Finding Peace When God Seems Silent. 125p. 1999. 12.95 (*1-56563-088-2*) Hendrickson MA.
Rockwood, Alyn & Chambers, Peter. Interactive Curves & Surfaces. LC 96-31279. 217p. (Orig.). 1996. pap. text 49.95 incl. disk (*1-55860-405-7*) Morgan Kaufmann.
Rockwood, Bruce, ed. Law & Literature Perspectives. 2nd ed. (Critic of Institutions Ser.: Vol. 9). 450p. (C). 1998. reprint ed. pap. text 45.95 (*0-8204-4044-2*) P Lang Pubng.
Rockwood, C. H. Atlas of Cheshire County, New Hampshire, 1877. 1982nd ed. LC 82-62166. (Illus.). 53p. 1982. reprint ed. pap. 15.95 (*0-911653-01-5*) Old Maps.
Rockwood, Charles A., Jr., ed. Rockwood & Green's Fractures in Adults, 2 vols., Set. 4th ed. 2405p. 1996. text 310.00 (*0-397-51602-9*) Lppncott W & W.
— Rockwood & Green's Fractures in Adults, Vol. 1. 4th ed. 1996. write for info. (*0-397-51510-3*) Lppncott W & W.
— Rockwood & Green's Fractures in Adults, Vol. 2. 4th ed. 1996. write for info. (*0-397-51511-1*) Lppncott W & W.
Rockwood, Charles A., Jr., et al, eds. Fractures in Children, Vol. 3. 4th ed. 1,232p. 1996. text 165.00 (*0-397-51512-X*) Lppncott W & W.
— Rockwood & Green's Fractures in Adults, 3 vols., Set. 4th ed. 4,100p. 1996. text 395.00 (*0-397-51509-X*) Lppncott W & W.
Rockwood, Charles A., Jr. & Matsen, III, Frederick A., 3rd. The Shoulder, 2. 2nd ed. Reines, Lew, ed. (Illus.). 1472p. (C). 1998. text 225.00 (*0-7216-8134-4*, W B Saunders Co) Harcrt Hlth Sci Grp.
Rockwood, Charles A., Jr., et al. Fractures, 3 vols., Three Vol. Set. 4th ed. 4,152p. 525.00 incl. cd-rom (*0-397-51776-9*) Lppncott W & W.
Rockwood, D. Stephen, jt. ed. see Miller, William.
Rockwood Hudson, Joyce. Consciousness & the Unconscious. (Wisdom Ser.: Vol. 2). (Illus.). iii, 53p. 1998. pap. 2.00 (*1-893383-02-4*) JRH Pubns.
— Dreams & Synchronicity. (Wisdom Ser.: Vol. 3). iii, 34p. 1998. pap. 2.00 (*1-893383-03-2*) JRH Pubns.
— Feminine Wholeness & Psyche & Eros. (Wisdom Ser.: Vol. 5). (Illus.). iii, 45p. 1998. pap. 2.00 (*1-893383-05-9*) JRH Pubns.
— Masculine Wholeness & the Beatles. (Wisdom Ser.: Vol. 4). (Illus.). iii, 52p. 1998. pap. 2.00 (*1-893383-04-0*) JRH Pubns.
Rockwood-Hudson, Joyce. Nature & Spirit in Christianity Today. (Wisdom Ser.: Vol. 1). iii, 36p. 1998. pap. 2.00 (*1-893383-01-6*) JRH Pubns.
Rockwood Hudson, Joyce, jt. auth. see Bowditch, Kevin E.
Rockwood, Jerome. The Craftsmen of Dionysus: An Approach to Acting. LC 92-25206. (Acting Ser.). 256p. 1992. pap. 19.95 (*1-55783-155-6*) Applause Theatre Bk Pubs.
Rockwood, Patricia, ed. see Wolak, Marsha.
Rockwood, Roy. The Jungle Boy. 208p. 1991. reprint ed. lib. bdg. 18.95 (*0-89966-825-9*) Buccaneer Bks.
Rocky Mountain Elk Foundation Staff, ed. Elk Hunting Secrets: 330 Tips & Tactics from the Rocky Mountain Elk Foundation. LC 99-39645. 192p. 1999. pap. 9.95 (*1-56044-938-1*) Falcon Pub Inc.
***Rocky Mountain Institute Staff.** Green Development: Integrating Ecology & Real Estate. LC 97-28995. (Series in Sustainable Design). 552p. 1998. 69.95 (*0-471-18878-6*) Wiley.
Rocky Mountain Institute Staff & Sardinsky, Robert. The Efficient House Sourcebook: Reviews of Selected Books & Directory of Organizations Devoted to Resource Efficient Housing. rev. ed. 180p. 1992. pap. 15.00 (*1-881071-00-6*) Rocky Mtn Inst.
Rocky Mountain Institute Water Program Staff. Water Efficiency: A Resource for Utility Managers, Community Planners, & Other Decisionmakers. 114p. (Orig.). 1991. pap. text 15.00 (*1-881071-02-2*, W91-27) Rocky Mtn Inst.
Rocky Mountain Mathematics Consortium Staff. Studies on Composition Operators: Proceedings of the Rocky Mountain Mathematics Consortium, July 8-19, 1996, University of Wyoming, Vol. 213. Jafari, Farhad et al, eds. LC 97-30687. (Contemporary Mathematics Ser.: Vol. JAFARI). 256p. 1997. pap. 49.00 (*0-8218-0768-4*) Am Math.
Rocky Mountain Mineral Foundation Staff. Federal & Indian Oil & Gas Royalty Valuation & Management, II, 1998, Bk. 2. (Mineral Law Ser.). 300p. 1998. text 82.50 (*0-929047-74-5*) Rocky Mtn Mineral Law Found.
Rocky Mountain Mineral Law Foundation Staff. International Resources Law II: A Blueprint for Mineral Development. (Mineral Law Ser.). 1995. student ed. 125.00 (*0-929047-52-4*) Rocky Mtn Mineral Law Found.
— Oil & Natural Gas Pipelines: Wellhead to End User. (Mineral Law Ser.). 1995. student ed. 125.00 (*0-929047-51-6*) Rocky Mtn Mineral Law Found.
Rocky Mountain Mineral Law Staff & Reid, Joan A. Law of Federal Oil & Gas Leases, 2 vols. 1964. ring bd. 390.00 (*0-8205-1515-9*) Bender.
Rocky Mountain Nature Association Staff, jt. auth. see Robertson, Leigh.
Rocky Mountain News Staff. El-Yea! LC 98-232815. 95 p. 1998. write for info. (*0-914807-16-1*) Denver Pub Co.
Rocky Mountain Translators Staff, tr. see Buttner-Janz, Karin.
Rocmans, P., jt. ed. see Houtte, P. Van.
Roco, M. C., ed. Particulate Two-Phase Flow. 1002p. 1993. text 115.00 (*0-7506-9275-8*) Buttrwrth-Heinemann.
Roco, M. C., et al, eds. Liquid-Solid Flows, 1994. LC 93-75377. (Fluid Engineering Division Conference Ser.: Vol. 189). 257p. 1994. pap. 45.00 (*0-7918-1372-X*) ASME.
***Roco, Mihail C., et al.** Nanotechnology Research Directions: Vision for Nanotechnology in the Next Decade. 360p. 2000. 149.00 (*0-7923-6220-9*) Kluwer Academic.
***Rocpsoreanu, C., et al.** The Fitzhugh-Nagumo Model: Bifurcation & Dynamics. LC 00-42667. (Mathematical Modelling Ser.). 2000. write for info. (*0-7923-6427-9*) Kluwer Academic.
Rocque, G. La, see La Rocque, G.
Rocques, Margaret, tr. see Cassis, Youssef.
Rocquet, Claude-Henri. Bruegel, or the Workshop of Dreams. Scott, Nora, tr. (Illus.). 220p. 1991. 24.95 (*0-226-72342-9*) U Ch Pr.
Rod, Aime Von, see Von Rod, Aime.
Rod, David L., jt. ed. see Bates, Larry M.
Rod, F., et al, eds. Ecology of Mediterranean Evergreen Oak Forests. LC 98-44830. (Ecological Studies: Vol. 137). (Illus.). 368p. 1999. 149.00 (*3-540-65019-9*) Spr-Verlag.
Rod Grantham Printing Staff, tr. see Diede, Pauline N.
Roda, Aldo. Aldo Roda. (Illus.). 152p. 1999. pap. 35.00 (*88-8158-199-X*, Pub. by Charta) Dist Art Pubs.
Roda, Bot & Maxwell, Ronald F. Gettysburg Storyboards. LC 97-76411. (Illus.). 176p. 1998. pap. 19.95 (*1-891961-01-2*) Prsn to Prsn.
Roda, E., et al. Workshops in Bile Acid Research: Serum Bile Acids in Health & Disease-Pathophysiology of the Enterohepatic Circulation. 144p. 1983. text 122.00 (*0-85200-749-3*) Kluwer Academic.
Rodabaugh, Barbara J., et al. Developing Consultation & Education Services for Sexual Assault. 1978. pap. 3.00 (*0-89785-565-5*) Am Inst Res.

An Asterisk (*) at the beginning of an entry indicates that the title is appearing for the first time.

R

Rodabaugh, Don. Now, When I Was a Kid. (Illus.). 127p. 1998. pap. 10.95 (*1-890622-40-0*) Leathers Pub.

Rodabaugh, E. C., jt. ed. see Schneider, R. W.

Rodabaugh, Stephen E., ed. Applications of Category Theory to Fuzzy Subsets. (Theory & Decision Library Series B). 412p. (C). 1991. text 175.00 (*0-7923-1511-1*) Kluwer Academic.

Rodack, Jaine. Forgotten Recipes. 190p. 1980. spiral bd. 12.95 (*0-918544-60-2*, Tradery) Wimmer Cos.

Rodack, Madeleine T., tr. see Bandelier, Adolph F.

Rodahl, Kaare. Stress Monitoring for Improved Worker Performance. 176p. 1993. lib. bdg. 75.00 (*0-87371-655-8*, L655) Lewis Pubs.

Rodahl, Kaare, ed. The Physiology of Work. 250p. 1989. 110.00 (*0-85066-478-0*) Taylor & Francis.

Rodahl, Kaare, jt. auth. see Astrand, Per-Olof.

Rodak. Diagnostic Hematology. 1995. 380.00 (*0-7216-4736-7*) Harcourt.

Rodak, Bernadette F. Diagnostic Hematology. LC 94-11097. (Illus.). 608p. 1995. text 62.95 (*0-7216-4727-8*, W B Saunders Co) Harcrt Hlth Sci Grp.

Rodak, Bernadette F., jt. auth. see Carr, Jacqueline H.

Rodak, Frederick. Homeowners Guide to Wildfires: In the Urban Interface. 84p. 1991. pap. 6.95 (*0-9630493-0-5*) Wildfire Tech.

Rodale, Ardath. Climbing Toward the Light: A Journey of Growth, Understanding & Love. LC 89-32896. (Illus.). 240p. 1989. 17.95 (*0-87857-834-X*, 05-406-0) Rodale Pr Inc.

— Gifts of the Spirit: True Stories to Renew Your Soul. (Illus.). 96p. 38.85 (*0-87596-513-X*) Rodale Pr Inc.

Rodale, Ardath H., jt. auth. see Rodale Press Staff.

Rodale Center for Executive Development Staff. Secrets of Executive Success: How Anyone Can Handle the Human Side of Work & Grow Their Career. LC 91-19377. 416p. 1991. 35.95 (*0-87857-973-7*, 18-320-0) Rodale Pr Inc.

Rodale Center for Women's Health Staff. The Healthy Woman. Feinstein, Alice, ed. LC 93-32831. (Illus.). 304p. (Orig.). 1994. pap. 14.95 (*0-87596-197-5*) Rodale Pr Inc.

Rodale Food Center Staff, jt. auth. see Claessens, Sharon S.

***Rodale, J. I.** Encyclopedia of Organic Gardening. (Illus.). 1152p. 2000. text 25.00 (*0-87596-841-4*) Rodale Pr Inc.

— How to Grow Vegetables & Fruits by the Organic Method. (Illus.). 928p. 2000. text 25.00 (*0-87596-842-2*) Rodale Pr Inc.

Rodale, J. I., et al, revs. The Synonym Finder. rev. ed. LC 86-5599. 1361p. 1986. reprint ed. mass mkt. 15.95 (*0-446-37029-0*, Pub. by Warner Bks) Little.

Rodale, Maria. Maria Rodale's Organic Gardening: Your Seasonal Companion to Creating a Beautiful & Delicious Garden. LC 98-8913. (Illus.). 352p. 1998. text 35.00 (*0-87596-799-X*) Rodale Pr Inc.

***Rodale, Maria.** Maria Rodale's Organic Gardening Companion. (Illus.). 96p. 2000. pap. 19.95 (*0-87596-835-X*) Rodale Pr Inc.

Rodale Press Editors. Cut Your Spending in Half, Without Settling for Less! How to Pay the Lowest Price for Everything. (Illus.). 480p. 1994. 27.95 (*0-87596-188-6*) Rodale Pr Inc.

— Cut Your Spending in Half (Without Settling for Less!) How to Pay the Lowest Price for Everything. 480p. 1995. pap. 14.95 (*0-87596-313-7*) Rodale Pr Inc.

— Foolproof Planting. 1994. 9.98 (*1-56731-040-0*, MJF Bks) Fine Comms.

— Prevention's Guide to High-Speed Healing. 1995. reprint ed. 12.98 (*1-56731-072-9*, MJF Bks) Fine Comms.

Rodale Press Editors, ed. see Hupping, Carol.

Rodale Press Garden Books Editors, jt. auth. see Cox, Jeff.

Rodale Press Inc., Editors. Rodale's Illustrated Encyclopedia of Gardening & Landscaping Techniques. (Illus.). 432p. 1995. pap. 17.95 (*0-87596-693-4*) Rodale Pr Inc.

Rodale Press Staff. Amish. (Classic American Quilt Collection Ser.). (Illus.). 128p. 1997. pap. text 14.95 (*0-87596-971-2*) Rodale Pr Inc.

— Log Cabin. (Classic American Quilt Collection Ser.). (Illus.). 138p. 1997. pap. text 14.95 (*0-87596-972-0*) Rodale Pr Inc.

— Quilting Made Easy. (Classic American Quilt Collection Ser.). (Illus.). 122p. 1997. pap. text 14.95 (*0-87596-973-9*) Rodale Pr Inc.

Rodale Press Staff & Rodale, Ardath H. Gifts of the Spirit: True Stories to Renew Your Soul. LC 97-6590. (Illus.). 96p. 1997. text 12.95 (*0-87596-487-7*) Rodale Pr Inc.

Rodale Quilt Book Editors. Fantastic Finishes. (Successful Quilting Library). 128p. 1999. text 19.95 (*0-87596-821-X*) Rodale Pr Inc.

Rodale's Home Improvement Books Staff & Burton, Kenneth S. Adding On: How to Design & Built the Perfect Addition for Your Home. (Illus.). 384p. 1995. 29.95 (*0-87596-605-5*) Rodale Pr Inc.

Rodan. Singapore Changes Guard. Date not set. text. write for info. (*0-582-87610-9*, Pub. by Addison-Wesley) Longman.

Rodan, Christian. Horn Madness. 52p. (Orig.). 1996. pap. 9.00 (*0-9653758-2-X*) Ammo.

Rodan, Garry. Political Oppositions in Industrialising Asia. LC 96-3329. (New Rich in Asia Ser.). 360p. (C). 1996. pap. 27.99 (*0-415-14865-0*) Routledge.

— Political Oppositions in Industrialising Asia. 2nd ed. LC 96-3329. (New Rich in Asia Ser.). 360p. (C). 1996. 90.00 (*0-415-14864-2*) Routledge.

Rodan, Garry, ed. Singapore Changes Guard. LC 93-16580. 272p. 1993. text 49.95 (*0-312-09687-9*) St Martin.

Rodan, Garry, et al, eds. The Political Economy of Southeast-Asia: An Introduction. LC HC441.P647 1997. (Illus.). 314p. 1998. pap. text 19.95 (*0-19-553736-X*) OUP.

Rodanas, Kristina. Dragonfly's Tale. LC 90-28758. (Illus.). 32p. (J). (ps-3). 1995. pap. 6.95 (*0-395-72076-1*, Clarion Bks) HM.

— Dragonfly's Tale. 1992. 12.15 (*0-606-07446-5*, Pub. by Turtleback) Demco.

— Follow the Stars: A Native American Woodlands Tale. LC 95-7103. (Illus.). (J). (gr. k-3). 1998. lib. bdg. 15.95 (*0-7614-5029-7*) Marshall Cavendish.

Rodanas, Kristina. The Birds of Summer: An Ojibwa Tale. LC 95-7103. (J). 1996. write for info. (*0-316-75333-5*) Little.

Rodanas, Kristina, retold by. Dragonfly's Tale. LC 90-28758. (Illus.). 32p. (J). (ps-3). 1992. 16.00 (*0-395-57003-4*, Clarion Bks) HM.

Rodaniche-Taylor, Brittannia. Hu Am Ay! Who Am I? LC 98-90663. 1999. pap. 12.95 (*0-533-12871-4*) Vantage.

Rodano, Philip J. Me-ow: A Book of Pur-rific Cat Cartoons. LC 90-90370. (Illus.). 144p. (Orig.). 1990. pap. text 8.95 (*0-9627648-1-7*) Top Cat.

Rodari, Florian. A Weekend with Matisse. Knight, Joan, tr. from FRE. LC 93-41671. 64p. (J). 1994. 19.95 (*0-8478-1792-X*, Pub. by Rizzoli Intl) St Martin.

— A Weekend with Picasso. LC 91-12427. (Weekend with...Ser.). (Illus.). 64p. 1993. 19.95 (*0-8478-1437-8*, Pub. by Rizzoli Intl) St Martin.

— A Weekend with Picasso. LC 91-12427. (Illus.). 64p. 1996. pap. 9.95 (*0-8478-1920-5*, Pub. by Rizzoli Intl) St Martin.

Rodari, Gianni. The Grammar of Fantasy: An Introduction to the Art of Inventing Stories. Zipes, Jack D., tr. from ITA.Tr. of Grammatica Della Fantasia. 168p. 1996. pap. 13.95 (*0-915924-51-X*); text 25.95 (*0-915924-50-1*) Tchrs & Writers Coll.

Rodarmor, William, tr. see Belloc, Denis.

Rodarmor, William, tr. see Collard, Cyril.

Rodarmor, William, tr. see Lehmann, Christian.

Rodarmor, William, tr. see Modiano, Patrick.

Rodarmor, William, tr. see Moitessier, Bernard.

Rodarmor, William, tr. see Place, Francois.

Rodarte, jt. auth. see Verde.

Rodarte, J. M., et al. Stresses in the Webs of Helical Gears. (Technical Papers: Vol. P109.41). 33p. 1983. pap. text 30.00 (*1-55589-076-8*) AGMA.

Rodasta, Joanne C. Take a Moment & Create Your Life! A Guide to the Life-Creating Process. LC 96-92601. (Illus.). 144p. (Orig.). 1997. pap. 9.95 (*0-9652628-0-4*, Pub. by Spiritsmith) New Leaf Dist.

Rodasto, Mario. The Spelling Bee. LC 97-61047. (Aesop's Fables Running Start Ser.). (Illus.). 32p. (J). (gr. 2-4). 1997. pap. 4.95 (*1-890570-23-0*) Huckleberry CT.

Rodbell, K. P., et al, eds. Polycrystalline Metal & Magnetic Thin Films Vol. 562: Materials Research Society Symposium Proceedings. LC 99-49143. 348p. 1999. text 69.00 (*1-55899-469-6*) Materials Res.

Rodberg, C. V., jt. auth. see May, Vicki.

Rodbertus, J. Karl. Overproduction & Crises. Franklin, Julia, tr. LC 69-18027. (Reprints of Economic Classics Ser.). 140p. 1969. reprint ed. 29.50 (*0-678-00497-8*) Kelley.

Rodburg, Maxine. Law of Return. 1999. pap. text 15.95 (*0-88748-313-5*) Carnegie-Mellon.

Rodby, John, contrib. by. Solos for Jazz Piano. (All That Jazz Ser.). 64p. (Orig.). 1988. pap. 9.95 (*0-8258-0398-5*, ATJ305) Fischer Inc NY.

Rodby, Judith. Appropriating Literacy: Writing & Reading English As a Second Language. LC 92-18835. 151p. (C). 1992. pap. text 21.50 (*0-86709-308-0*, 0308, Pub. by Boynton Cook Pubs) Heinemann.

— Writing by Choice: Intermediate Composition for Students of ESL. (Illus.). 144p. (C). 1987. pap. text 12.00 (*0-13-970328-4*) P-H.

Rodcay, Gayle K., ed. Geo Directory 1997. Orig. Title: GIS World Sourcebook. (Orig.). 1996. pap. 149.95 (*1-899762-08-6*) GIS World Bks.

— GIS World Sourcebook 1996. (Illus.). 772p. 1995. pap. 149.95 (*1-882610-18-0*) GIS World Bks.

Rodchue, Soawalak, jt. auth. see Moore, John.

Rodd, Cyril S. The Book of Job. LC 90-33941. (Narrative Commentaries Ser.). 160p. (Orig.). (C). 1990. pap. 13.00 (*0-334-02473-0*) TPI PA.

— Foundation Documents of the Faith. 192p. (C). 1996. pap. 24.95 (*0-567-29138-3*, Pub. by T & T Clark) Bks Intl VA.

Rodd, Cyril S., ed. New Occasions Teach New Duties? Christian Ethics for Today. 240p. 1996. pap. 29.95 (*0-567-29300-9*, Pub. by T & T Clark) Bks Intl VA.

— The Pastor's Opportunities. 256p. (Orig.). 1989. pap. 29.95 (*0-567-29167-7*, Pub. by T & T Clark) Bks Intl VA.

— The Pastor's Problems. 240p. 1993. pap. 27.95 (*0-567-29117-0*, Pub. by T & T Clark) Bks Intl VA.

Rodd, E. J., jt. ed. see Walton, C. W.

Rodd, Jillian. Leadership in Early Childhood: The Pathway to Professionalism. 208p. 1994. pap. 2.00 (*0-335-19303-X*) OpUniv Pr.

— Leadership in Early Childhood: The Pathway to Professionalism. LC 93-39282. (Early Childhood Education Ser.). 200p. 1994. pap. text 18.95 (*0-8077-3353-9*) Tchrs Coll.

— Leadership in Early Childhood: The Pathway to Professionalism. 2nd ed. 224p. 1998. pap. 29.95 (*1-86448-566-3*, Pub. by Allen & Unwin Pty) Paul & Co Pubs.

— Leadership in Early Childhood: The Pathway to Professionalism. 2nd ed. 224p. 1998. pap. write for info. (*0-335-20281-0*) Taylor & Francis.

— Leadership in Early Childhood: The Pathway to Professionalism. 2nd ed. 224p. 1998. pap. text 18.95 (*0-8077-3776-3*) Tchrs Coll.

— Understanding Young Children's Behavior: A Guide for Early Childhood Professionals. LC 96-34336. (Early Childhood Education Ser.). 208p. (Orig.). 1996. pap. text 19.95 (*0-8077-3595-7*) Tchrs Coll.

— Understanding Young Children's Behaviour: A Guide for Early Childhood Professionals. 208p. 1997. pap. 24.95 (*1-86448-163-3*, Pub. by Allen & Unwin Pty) Paul & Co Pubs.

Rodd, John. Repairing & Restoring Antique Furniture. rev. ed. (Illus.). 224p. pap. 19.95 (*0-7153-0684-7*, Pub. by D & C Pub) Sterling.

— Repairing & Restoring Antique Furniture. rev. ed. (Illus.). 224p. 1995. 27.95 (*0-7153-0304-X*, Pub. by D & C Pub) Sterling.

Rodd, Judith S. A Guide to Coopers Rock State Forest. (Illus.). 80p. (Orig.). 1994. pap. 7.95 (*0-9630920-2-2*) South Wind.

Rodd, Laurel R. Nichiren: Selected Writings. LC 79-17054. (Asian Studies at Hawaii: No. 26). 201p. reprint ed. pap. 62.40 (*0-608-13710-3*, 202044400018) Bks Demand.

Rodd, Laurel R. & Henkenius, Mary C. Kokinshu: A Collection of Poems Ancient & Modern. 1996. pap. 19.95 (*0-88727-249-5*) Cheng & Tsui.

Rodd, M. G., jt. auth. see Kopetz, H.

Rodd, M. G., ed. see IFAC Workshop on Distributed Computer Control Syst.

Rodd, Michael G., jt. auth. see Motus, Leo.

Rodd, Michael G., jt. ed. see Verbruggen, Henk B.

Rodd, Mike G. & Lalive D'Epinay, Th., eds. Distributed Computer Control Systems, 1988: Proceedings of the 8th IFAC Workshop, Vitznau, Switzerland, 13-15 September, 1988. (IFAC Publication Ser.: No. 84). (Illus.). 145p. 1989. 82.25 (*0-08-036938-3*, Pergamon Pr) Elsevier.

Rodd, Mike G., jt. ed. see Knuth, Elod.

Rodd, Stewart, tr. Prophecies on World Events by Nostradamus. 4th ed. (Illus.). (Orig.). 1991. pap. 8.95 (*0-87140-220-3*, Pub. by Liveright) Norton.

Rodda, Annabel. Women & the Environment. (Women & World Development Ser.). (Illus.). 192p. (C). 1991. text 49.95 (*0-86232-984-1*, Pub. by Zed Books) St Martin.

— Women & the Environment. 2nd ed. (Women & World Development Ser.). (Illus.). 192p. (C). 1991. text 22.50 (*0-86232-985-X*, Pub. by St Martin) St Martin.

Rodda, Dorothy. Church & Synagogue Library Resources. 5th ed. LC 75-1178. 24p. 1992. pap. 6.25 (*0-915324-33-4*) CSLA.

Rodda, Emily. The Best Kept Secret. 112p. (J). (gr. 5). 1991. reprint ed. pap. 2.95 (*0-380-75870-9*, Avon Bks) Morrow Avon.

— Finders Keepers. LC 90-47850. (Illus.). (J). (gr. 5 up). 1991. 12.95 (*0-688-10516-5*, Grenwillow Bks) HarpC Child Bks.

— Finders Keepers. large type ed. (Illus.). 1993. 49.50 (*0-614-09824-6*, L-34104-00) Am Printing Hse.

— The Pigs Are Flying! Orig. Title: Pigs Might Fly. (Illus.). 144p. (J). (gr. 2 up). 1989. reprint ed. pap. 2.95 (*0-380-70555-9*, Avon Bks) Morrow Avon.

— Power & Glory. LC 95-1842. (Illus.). 32p. (J). (gr. k-4). 1996. 15.00 (*0-688-14214-1*, Grenwillow Bks) HarpC Child Bks.

— Yay! LC 96-46251. (Illus.). 40p. (J). (gr. k-3). 1997. 15.00 (*0-688-15255-4*, Grenwillow Bks) HarpC Child Bks.

Rodda, Gordon H. The Mating Behavior of Iguana. LC 92-2499. (Smithsonian Contributions to Zoology Ser.: No. 534). (Illus.). 44p. reprint ed. pap. 30.00 (*0-7837-3877-3*, 204371900010) Bks Demand.

— Problem Snake Management: Habu & Brown Treesnake Examples. LC 98-15664. (Illus.). 520p. 1998. 47.50 (*0-8014-3507-2*, Comstock Pub) Cornell U Pr.

***Rodda, Jeanette.** Go Ye & Study the Beehive: The Making of a Western Working Class. LC 99-42072. (Studies in the History of American Labor). 1999. write for info. (*0-8153-2653-X*) Garland.

Rodda, Jeanette & Smith, Nancy. Experience Jerome. rev. ed. Caillou, Aliza, ed. (Illus.). 68p. 1995. pap. text 6.95 (*0-9628329-7-9*) Thorne Enterprises.

Rodda, John C., ed. Facets of Hydrology. LC 75-26568. 384p. reprint ed. pap. 119.10 (*0-608-10834-0*, 201967000013) Bks Demand.

Rodda, Michael & Grove, Carl. Language, Cognition & Deafness. (Zillman-Bryant: Communication Ser.). 456p. 1987. text 79.95 (*0-89859-871-5*) L Erlbaum Assocs.

Roddan, Brooks. The Light of the Light. 10p. 1987. pap. 12.00 (*0-944034-00-4*) Blue Earth.

Rodden, Clement J., ed. see AEC Technical Information Center Staff.

***Rodden, John.** The Literary Interview: Rhetoric, Invention, Performance. 2000. text 70.00 (*0-8032-3939-4*) U of Nebr Pr.

Rodden, John, ed. Lionel Trilling & the Critics: Opposing Selves. LC 98-53491. 407p. 1999. pap. text 29.95 (*0-8032-8974-X*) U of Nebr Pr.

***Rodden, John, ed.** Lionel Trilling & the Critics: Opposing Selves. LC 98-53491. 407p. 1999. text 70.00 (*0-8032-3922-X*) U of Nebr Pr.

Rodden, John, ed. Understanding Animal Farm: A Student Casebook to Issues, Sources & Historical Documents. LC 98-55338. (Literature in Context Ser.). 256p. 1999. 39.95 (*0-313-30201-4*) Greenwood.

Rodden, John, ed. & tr. see Allende, Isabel.

Rodden, John G. Repainting the Little Red Schoolhouse: A History of Eastern German Education, 1945-1995. LC 98-30620. 480p. 2000. text 75.00 (*0-19-511244-X*) OUP.

Rodden, Lois M. Astro Data, No. IV. 1997. pap. 38.00 (*0-86690-355-0*, 3045-014) Am Fed Astrologers.

— Astro Data Two. rev. ed. 1993. pap. 32.00 (*0-917086-23-6*) Am Fed Astrologers.

— Astro-Data V: Profiles in Crime. 256p. 1992. pap. text 36.00 (*0-9633716-0-6*) Data News Pr.

— Mercury Method of Chart Comparison. 228p. 1973. 19.00 (*0-86690-150-7*, R1413-014) Am Fed Astrologers.

— Modern Transits. LC 78-56415. 200p. 1978. 19.95 (*0-86690-151-5*, R1414-014) Am Fed Astrologers.

— Money, How to Find It with Astrology. Rodden, Lynn, ed. (Illus.). 275p. 1994. pap. text 20.00 (*0-9633716-1-4*) Data News Pr.

— Money, How to Find It with Astrology. 2nd ed. (Illus.). 278p. 1994. pap. 20.00 (*0-9633716-2-2*) Data News Pr.

— Profiles of Women: Astro-Data. 5th enl. rev. ed. (Astro-Data Ser.: Vol. 1). 416p. 1996. pap. 46.00 (*0-9633716-3-0*) Data News Pr.

Rodden, Lynn, ed. see Rodden, Lois M.

Rodden, Mary. Her Eyes Were Blue. 24p. 1999. pap. 7.00 (*0-8059-4622-5*) Dorrance.

Rodden, William & Johnson, Erwin. MSC - Nastran Aerolastic Analysis User's Guide. 1994. pap. text 75.00 (*1-58524-006-0*) MacNeal-Schwendler.

Roddenberry, Gene. The Q Chronicles, Vol. 1. LC 99-212213. (Star Trek: The Next Generation Ser.: Vol. 1). 752p. 1998. pap. 18.00 (*0-671-03446-4*) PB.

— Star Trek. 1990. mass mkt. 5.99 (*0-671-72300-6*) PB.

— Star Trek-the Motion Picture. 1980. 9.95 (*0-686-60888-7*) S&S Trade.

Roddenberry, Gene & Friedman, Michael J. The God Thing. Stern, Dave, ed. (Star Trek: The Next Generation Ser.). 1992. 20.00 (*0-671-78070-0*) PB.

Roddenberry, Gene & Parker. Becoming Human: The Seven of Nine Scripts. LC 99-176670. (Star Trek Ser.: Vol. 1). 1998. pap. 16.00 (*0-671-03447-2*) PB.

Roddenberry, Gene & Sackett, Susan. Star Trek: The First Twenty-Five Years. 256p. 1991. 45.00 (*0-671-73233-1*) PB.

Roddenberry, Gene, jt. auth. see Blish, James.

Roddenberry, Gene, jt. auth. see Whitfield, Stephen E.

Roddenbery, Seaborn A. I Swear by Apollo: A Black Surgeon in the Deep South. 186p. 20.00 (*0-9640075-0-9*) Grandy Pr.

Rodder, Mark, et al, eds. Microelectronic Device Technology, Vol. 3212. LC 98-122056. 406p. 1997. 89.00 (*0-8194-2644-X*) SPIE.

Roddey, G. J., jt. auth. see Gemayel, A. H.

Roddick, B. The Thirteenth Juror at the Lawrencia Bembenek Murder Trial. 1982. pap. 4.95 (*0-937816-23-X*) Tech Data.

Roddick, Bill & Korotko, Robin. Bembenek: After the Verdict. (Illus.). 240p. (Orig.). 1991. pap. 9.95 (*0-9629136-0-X*) Composition Hse.

Roddick, J. A., ed. Circum-Pacific Plutonic Terranes. LC 83-1557. (Geological Society of America, Memoir Ser.: No. 159). (Illus.). 322p. reprint ed. pap. 99.90 (*0-8357-3830-2*, 203655400004) Bks Demand.

***Roddick, J. F., ed.** Database Systems '99: Proceedings of the 10th Australasian Database Conference (ADC'99) 235p. 1999. pap. 69.95 (*981-4021-55-5*) Spr-Verlag.

Roddick, Nick. The Festival Business. (Distributed for the British Film Institute Ser.). 192p. 1996. 44.00 (*0-85170-475-1*) Ind U Pr.

Roddie, Ian C. & Wallce, William F. Multiple Choice Questions in Human Physiology. 5th ed. 200p. 1997. pap. text 26.50 (*0-340-66234-4*, Pub. by E A) OUP.

***Roddie, Shen.** Not Now, Mrs. Wolf. LC 99-49410. (Illus.). 32p. (J). (ps-3). 2000. 5.95 (*0-7894-5613-3*, D K Ink) DK Pub Inc.

— Not Now, Mrs. Wolf. (Illus.). 32p. (J). (ps-3). 2000. 9.95 (*0-7894-6355-5*) DK Pub Inc.

Roddie, Shen. The Terrible Itch. (Illus.). 24p. (J). (ps-1). 1993. boxed set 13.00 (*0-671-79169-9*) S&S Bks Yung.

— Toes Are to Tickle. LC 96-31428. (Illus.). 24p. (J). (ps-k). 1997. 13.95 (*1-883672-49-X*) Tricycle Pr.

— Too Close Friends. LC 96-48566. (Illus.). 32p. (J). 1998. 14.99 (*0-8037-2188-9*, Dial Yng Read) Peng Put Young Read.

Roddie, Shen & Healey, Tim. Adventure on Treasure Island. Reader's Digest Editors, ed. (Playmobil Sticker Bks.: Vol. 2). (Illus.). 16p. (J). (gr. k-3). 1998. pap. 8.99 (*1-57584-237-8*, Pub. by Rdrs Digest) Random.

Roddier, Francois, ed. Adaptive Optics in Astronomy. (Illus.). 375p. (C). 1999. text 80.00 (*0-521-55375-X*) Cambridge U Pr.

Roddis, Ingrid & Roddis, Miles. Sudan: Major World Nations. LC 99-11831. (Illus.). 144p. 1999. 19.95 (*0-7910-5398-9*) Chelsea Hse.

Roddis, Louis H. A Short History of Nautical Medicine. LC 75-23757. reprint ed. 39.50 (*0-404-13363-0*) AMS Pr.

Roddis, Miles, jt. auth. see Roddis, Ingrid.

Roddis, W. M., jt. ed. see Easterling, W. Samuel.

Roddon, Guy. Pastel Painting Techniques. (Illus.). 144p. 1991. pap. 22.99 (*0-89134-396-2*, 30306, North Lght Bks) F & W Pubns Inc.

Roddy, Chris. Conceptual Physics. (C). 1998. text. write for info. (*0-201-84525-3*) Addison-Wesley.

Roddy, Dennis J. Satellite Communications. 2nd ed. LC 95-22077. (Illus.). 516p. 1995. 69.00 (*0-07-053370-9*) McGraw.

Roddy, Dennis J., jt. auth. see Coolen, John.

Roddy, Edward G. Mills, Mansions, & Mergers: The Life of William M. Wood. 2nd ed. LC 82-81081. (Illus.). 148p. 1997. reprint ed. pap. text 15.00 (*0-937474-04-5*) Am Textile Hist.

Roddy, Jan P., ed. Let My People Go: Cairo, Illinois, 1967-1973. LC 96-7578. (Illus.). 124p. (C). 1996. 49.95 (*0-8093-2085-1*); pap. 19.95 (*0-8093-2086-X*) S Ill U Pr.

Roddy, Kevin P. RICO in Business & Commercial Litigation. 1991. text 190.00 (*0-07-017898-4*) McGraw.

— RICO in Business & Commercial Litigation. 1840p. 1991. ring bd. 160.00 (*0-07-017989-1*) Shepards.

***Roddy, Lauren S.** My Scriptural Rosary. (Illus.). 48p. (J). (gr. 2-5). 1999. 3.95 (*0-8198-4797-6*) Pauline Bks.

An Asterisk (*) at the beginning of an entry indicates that the title is appearing for the first time.

Roddy, Lee. An American Adventure, Bks. 6-9. (American Adventure Ser.). (J). 1994. pap., boxed set 23.99 (*1-55661-792-5*, 252792) Bethany Hse.
— An American Adventure, Vols. 1-5. (American Adventure Ser.). (J). 1994. pap., boxed set 29.99 (*1-55661-791-7*, 252791) Bethany Hse.
— Bear Cub Disaster. (D.J. Dillon Adventure Ser.). 132p. (J). 1996. pap. 4.99 (*1-56476-503-2*, 6-3503, Victor Bks) Chariot Victor.
— Burden of Honor. LC 99-6625. (Between Two Flags Ser.: No. 3). 144p. (YA). (gr. 6-9). 1999. pap. 5.99 (*0-7642-2027-6*) Bethany Hse.
— Case of the Dangerous Cruise. (Ladd Family Adventure Ser.: Vol. 11). (J). (gr. 3-7). 1995. pap. 5.99 (*1-56179-349-3*) Focus Family.
— Cinnabar. LC 94-21915. (Giants on the Hill Ser.: Vol. 2). 304p. 1995. pap. 12.99 (*0-8499-3832-5*) Word Pub.
— Cry of Courage. LC 98-226129. (Between Two Flags Ser.: 1). 176p. (YA). (gr. 6-9). 1998. pap. 5.99 (*0-7642-2025-X*, 212025) Bethany Hse.
— Cry of Courage. large type ed. LC 99-22370. 206p. (gr. 6-9). 1999. pap. text 21.95 (*0-7838-8611-X*, G K Hall & Co) Mac Lib Ref.
— Danger on Thunder Mountain. (American Adventure Ser.: Bk. 3). 176p. (Orig.). (J). (gr. 3 up). 1989. pap. 5.99 (*1-55661-028-9*) Bethany Hse.
— The Dangerous Canoe Race. (Ladd Family Adventure Ser.: No. 4). (Orig.). (J). (gr. 3-7). 1990. pap. 5.99 (*0-929608-62-3*) Focus Family.
— Days of Deception. (Pinkerton Lady Chronicles Ser.: 1). 320p. 1998. write for info. (*1-56476-686-1*, Victor Bks) Chariot Victor.
— The Desperate Search. LC 88-63476. (American Adventure Ser.: Vol. 2). 176p. (J). (gr. 4-7). 1989. pap. 5.99 (*1-55661-027-0*) Bethany Hse.
— Dooger, the Grasshopper Hound. (D.J. Dillon Adventure Ser.: No. 3). (Illus.). 144p. (J). (gr. 3-7). 1985. pap. 5.99 (*0-88207-497-0*, 6-2497, Victor Bks) Chariot Victor.
— Escape down the Raging Rapids. (D.J. Dillon Adventure Ser.: No. 10). 132p. (J). (gr. 3-7). 1988. pap. 5.99 (*0-89693-477-2*, 6-1477, Victor Bks) Chariot Victor.
— Eye of the Hurricane. LC 94-11781. (Ladd Family Adventure Ser.: Vol. 9). 170p. (J). (gr. 3-7). 1994. pap. 5.99 (*1-56179-220-9*) Focus Family.
— The Flaming Trap. (American Adventure Ser.: Vol. 5). 176p. (Orig.). (J). (gr. 3-8). 1990. pap. 5.99 (*1-55661-095-5*) Bethany Hse.
— The Ghost Dog of Stoney Ridge. (D.J. Dillon Adventure Ser.: No. 4). 144p. (J). (gr. 3-7). 1985. pap. 5.99 (*0-88207-498-9*, 6-2498, Victor Bks) Chariot Victor.
— Giants on the Hill. LC 94-21915. (Giants on the Hill Ser.: Vol. 1). 1994. pap. 10.99 (*0-8499-3492-3*) Word Pub.
— The Gold Train Bandits. (American Adventure Ser.: Vol. 8). 176p. (Orig.). (J). (gr. 3-8). 1992. pap. 5.99 (*1-55661-211-7*) Bethany Hse.
— The Hair-Pulling Bear Dog. (D.J. Dillon Adventure Ser.: No. 1). 144p. (J). (gr. 3-7). 1985. pap. 5.99 (*0-88207-499-7*, 6-2499, Victor Bks) Chariot Victor.
— The Hair-Pulling Bear Dog. rev. ed. (D.J. Dillon Adventure Ser.: Vol. 1). 132p. (J). (gr. 4-7). 1996. pap. 4.99 (*1-56476-502-4*, 6-3502, Victor Bks) Chariot Victor.
— High Country Ambush. (American Adventure Ser.: Vol. 9). 176p. (Orig.). (J). (gr. 3-8). 1992. pap. 5.99 (*1-55661-287-7*) Bethany Hse.
— Hunted in the Alaskan Wilderness. (Ladd Family Adventures Ser.: Vol. 13). (Orig.). (J). (gr. 3-7). 1996. pap. 5.99 (*1-56179-445-7*) Focus Family.
— The Legend of Fire. (Ladd Family Adventure Ser.: Vol. 2). 148p. (J). (gr. 3-6). 1989. reprint ed. pap. 5.99 (*0-929608-17-8*) Focus Family.
— The Legend of the White Raccoon. (D. J. Dillon Ser.: No. 6). 144p. (J). (gr. 3-7). 1986. pap. 5.99 (*0-89693-500-0*, 6-2500, Victor Bks) Chariot Victor.
— Legend of White Raccoon. rev. ed. (D.J. Dillon Adventure Ser.). 132p. (J). 1996. pap. 5.99 (*1-56476-507-5*, 6-3507, Victor Bks) Chariot Victor.
— The Mad Dog of Lobo Mountain. rev. ed. (D.J. Dillon Adventure Ser.). 132p. (J). 1996. pap. 5.99 (*1-56476-506-7*, 6-3506, Victor Bks) Chariot Victor.
— The Mystery of the Black Hole Mine. (D.J. Dillon Adventure Ser.). 132p. (J). 1996. pap. 5.99 (*1-56476-508-3*, 6-3508, Victor Bks) Chariot Victor.
— Mystery of the Island Jungle. (Ladd Family Adventure Ser.: Vol. 3). 160p. (Orig.). (J). (gr. 3-7). 1989. pap. 5.99 (*0-929608-19-4*) Focus Family.
— Mystery of the Phantom Gold. (American Adventure Ser.: Bk. 7). 176p. (Orig.). (J). (gr. 3-8). 1991. pap. 5.99 (*1-55661-210-9*) Bethany Hse.
— Mystery of the Wild Surfer. (Ladd Family Adventure Ser.: Vol. 6). 160p. (Orig.). (J). (gr. 3-7). 1990. pap. 5.99 (*0-929608-64-X*) Focus Family.
— Night of the Vanishing Lights. LC 94-15779. (Ladd Family Adventure Ser.: No. 10). (J). (gr. 3-7). 1994. pap. 5.99 (*1-56179-256-X*) Focus Family.
— The Overland Escape. LC 88-63471. (American Adventure Ser.: No. 1). 176p. (J). (gr. 3-8). 1989. pap. 5.99 (*1-55661-026-2*) Bethany Hse.
— Panic in the Wild Waters. LC 95-10951. (Ladd Family Adventure Ser.: No. 12). (J). (gr. 3-7). 1995. pap. 5.99 (*1-56179-392-2*) Focus Family.
***Roddy, Lee.** Risking the Dream. (Between Two Flags Ser.: Vol. 6). (Illus.). 144p. (J). (gr. 6-9). 2000. pap. 5.99 (*0-7642-2030-6*) Bethany Hse.
Roddy, Lee. Road to Freedom, 4. LC 99-6626. (Between Two Flags Ser.). 144p. 1999. pap. text 5.99 (*0-7642-2028-4*) Bethany Hse.
— Robert E. Lee: Gallant Christian Soldier. (Sower Ser.). (Illus.). 169p. (YA). (gr. 5-9). 1977. pap. 7.99 (*0-915134-40-3*) Mott Media.
— The Secret of the Howling Cave. (American Adventure Ser.: Vol. 4). 192p. (Orig.). (J). (gr. 4-10). 1990. pap. 5.99 (*1-55661-094-7*) Bethany Hse.
Roddy, Lee. Secret of the Shark Pit. (Ladd Family Adventure Ser.: Vol. 1). 136p. (Orig.). (J). (gr. 3-7). 1989. pap. 5.99 (*0-929608-14-3*) Focus Family.
Roddy, Lee. Secret of the Sunken Sub. (Ladd Family Adventure Ser.: Vol. 5). 160p. (Orig.). (J). (gr. 3-7). 1990. pap. 5.99 (*0-929608-63-1*) Focus Family.
— Shiloh's Choice. (Giants of the Hill Ser.: No. 3). 288p. 1996. pap. 10.99 (*0-8499-3833-3*) Word Pub.
— Stranded on Terror Island, No. 14. LC 97-170102. (Ladd Family Adventure Ser.). (J). (gr. 3-7). 1996. pap. 6.00 (*1-56179-482-1*) Focus Family.
— Terror at Forbidden Falls. LC 93-3379. (Ladd Family Adventure Ser.: Vol. 8). (J). (gr. 3-7). 1993. pap. 5.99 (*1-56179-137-7*) Focus Family.
— Terror in the Sky. (American Adventure Ser.: Vol. 6). 176p. (Orig.). (J). (gr. 3-8). 1991. pap. 5.99 (*1-55661-096-3*) Bethany Hse.
— Tomorrow's Promise. (Pinkerton Lady Chronicles Ser.: 3). 360p. 2000. pap. 10.99 (*1-56476-688-8*, Victor Bks) Chariot Victor.
— Tracked by the Wolf Pack. LC 97-10869. (Ladd Family Adventure Ser.: Bk. 15). (J). (gr. 3-7). 1997. pap. 6.00 (*1-56179-548-8*) Focus Family.
***Roddy, Lee.** Uprising at Dawn. LC 99-51012. (Between Two Flags Ser.: Vol. 5). (Illus.). 160p. (J). (gr. 4-7). 2000. pap. 5.99 (*0-7642-2029-2*) Bethany Hse.
Roddy, Lee. Where Bugles Call. LC 98-226142. (Between Two Flags Ser.: Vol. 2). 176p. (YA). (gr. 6-9). 1998. pap. 5.99 (*0-7642-2026-8*, 212026) Bethany Hse.
— Yesterday's Shadows. LC 97-35531. (Pinkerton Lady Chronicles: 2). 320p. 1999. 10.99 (*1-56476-635-7*, Victor Bks); 10.99 (*1-56476-687-X*, Victor Bks) Chariot Victor.
Roddy, Michael. Beginning English Day by Day. 224p. 1991. pap. text 16.00 (*0-87879-907-9*) Acad Therapy.
— English Day by Day. Kratoville, Betty Lou, ed. LC 88-27428. (Illus.). 304p. (Orig.). 1989. pap. text 18.00 (*0-87879-668-1*) Acad Therapy.
Roddy, Miryam S., ed. see Brody, Marjorie.
Roddy, Miryam Strassberg, ed. see Brody, Marjorie.
Roddy, Peter. The International Tin Trade. (International Trade Ser.). (Illus.). 192p. 1995. 170.00 (*1-85573-043-X*, Pub. by Woodhead Pubng) Am Educ Systs.
Roddy, Ruth M. Kids' Stuff. 64p. (J). (gr. 1-3). 1993. pap. 9.95 (*0-940669-23-4*, D-30) Dramaline Pubns.
— Monologues for Kids. 64p. (Orig.). (J). (gr. 1-3). 1987. pap. 8.95 (*0-940669-02-1*, D-7) Dramaline Pubns.
— More Monologues for Kids. 64p. (Orig.). (J). (gr. 1-3). 1992. pap. 8.95 (*0-940669-18-8*, D-8) Dramaline Pubns.
— Scenes for Kids. 64p. (Orig.). (J). (gr. 2-6). 1990. pap. 8.95 (*0-940669-14-5*, D-9) Dramaline Pubns.
***Roddy, Ruth Mae.** Minute Monologues for Kids. 2000. pap. write for info. (*0-940669-45-5*, Pub. by Dramaline Pubns) Distributors.
Roddy, Stephen, et al. Literati Identity & Its Fictional Representations in Late Imperial China. LC 97-40032. 1998. write for info. (*0-8047-3131-4*) Stanford U Pr.
Roddy, Vernon. The Lost Town of Bledsoesborough, Tennessee: Its Beginning, Its End: Two Essays in the Record of Tennessee's Upper Cumberland of Old. 1984. pap. 10.00 (*0-318-03885-4*) Upper Country.
— Whatever Happened to Epperson Springs? 1974. pap. 10.00 (*0-686-40797-0*) Upper Country.
Roddy, Vernon & Reddy, Joan C. On the Early Story of Red Boiling Springs, Tennessee, with Selected Supporting Materials. (Illus.). 438p. 1991. 28.00 (*0-614-29710-9*) Upper Country.
Rode, A., jt. ed. see Shephard, R. J.
Rode, Andris, jt. auth. see Shephard, Roy J.
Rode-Breymann, Susanne, ed. see Mahler-Werfel, Alma.
Rode, Heinz, jt. auth. see Herwig, Dieter.
Rode, Pierre. Twenty-Four Caprices: Studies - Violin. 56p. 1986. pap. 8.95 (*0-7935-5133-1*) H Leonard.
Rode, Reinhard. Deutsche Auenpolitik. (Politologische Studienbucher Ser.). (GER.). 224p. 1996. text 54.00 (*90-5708-001-X*); pap. text 27.00 (*90-5708-002-8*) Gordon & Breach.
Rodean, Howard C. Nuclear-Explosion Seismology. LC 73-170333. (AEC Critical Review Ser.). 168p. 1971. pap. 12.00 (*0-87079-288-1*, TID-25572); fiche 9.00 (*0-87079-289-X*, TID-25572) DOE.
Rodean, Howard C., ed. Stochastic Lagrangian Models of Turbulent Diffusion: Meteorological Monograph (MM48) (Meteorological Monograph: Vol. 26). (Illus.). 84p. (C). 1996. 55.00 (*1-878220-23-3*) Am Meteorological.
Rodebough, Paul, jt. auth. see Gentry, Martha.
Rodecap, Vera E. The Country Schoolteacher: A Kansas Legacy. 141p. (Orig.). 1993. pap. text 12.00 (*0-9639944-0-9*) ThreeRs Pubg.
Rodecap, Vera E. & Hamm, W. Howard. Trail Dust: Sketches on the Trail. rev. ed. (Illus.). 84p. 1995. pap. 4.95 (*0-9639944-1-7*) ThreeRs Pubg.
Rodechko, James P. Patrick Ford & His Search for America: A Case Study of Irish-American Journalism, 1870-1913. LC 76-6362. (Irish Americans Ser.). 1976. 29.95 (*0-405-09354-3*) Ayer.
***Rodeck, C. H. & Whittle, M., eds.** Fetal Medicine: Basic Science & Clinical Practice. (Illus.). 640p. 1999. text. write for info. (*0-443-05357-X*, W B Saunders Co) Harcrt Hlth Sci Grp.
Rodeck, C. H., jt. ed. see Evans, Mark I.
Rodecker, Stephen B. & Quon-Warner, Maryanna. Las Ciencias Fisicas: Metodos, Investigaciones, Retos y Actividades - M.I.R.A. Appel, Sergio, tr. 342p. (YA). (gr. 7 up). 1993. student ed. 39.95 (*0-9638008-1-7*) Spectrum CA.
— Laboratory Experiments & Activities in Physical Science. 342p. (YA). (gr. 7 up). 1993. student ed. 39.95 (*0-9638008-0-9*) Spectrum CA.
Roded. Women, in Islam & the Middle East. 288p. 1998. pap. 25.00 (*1-86064-309-4*, Pub. by I B T); text 59.50 (*1-86064-308-6*, Pub. by I B T) St Martin.
Roded, Ruth. Women in Islamic Biographical Collections from Ibn Sa'd to Who's Who. 175p. 1996. 34.00 (*0-614-21402-5*, 1328) Kazi Pubns.
— Women in Islamic Biographical Collections from Ibn Sa'd to Who's Who. LC 93-28276. 158p. 1993. lib. bdg. 37.00 (*1-55587-442-8*) L Rienner.
Rodee, Marian. Weaving of the Southwest. LC 86-63764. (Illus.). 248p. 1987. 39.95 (*0-88740-095-7*); pap. 29.95 (*0-88740-091-4*) Schiffer.
Rodee, Marian & Ostler, James. Zuni Pottery. LC 87-60505. (Illus.). 92p. 1987. pap. 9.95 (*0-88740-100-7*) Schiffer.
Rodee, Marian E. One Hundred Years of Navajo Rugs. LC 94-48682. Orig. Title: Old Navajo Rugs. (Illus.). 187p. 1995. pap. 29.95 (*0-8263-1576-3*) U of NM Pr.
Rodefer, Stephen. Emergency Measures. 1987. per. 7.50 (*0-935724-24-9*) Figures.
***Rodefer, Stephen.** Mon Canard. 128p. 2000. pap. 12.50 (*1-930589-03-4*, Pub. by Figures) SPD-Small Pr Dist.
Rodefer, Stephen. One or Two Love Poems from the White World. 1976. pap. 2.50 (*0-685-79190-4*) Duende.
— Passing Duration: Prose Poems. (Burning Deck Poetry Ser.). 80p. 1991. pap. 8.00 (*0-930901-76-2*) Burning Deck.
— Passing Duration: Prose Poems. limited ed. (Burning Deck Poetry Ser.). 80p. 1991. pap. 15.00 (*0-930901-77-0*) Burning Deck.
Rodegast, Pat & Stanton, Judith. Emmanuel's Book. (New Age Ser.). 288p. 1987. pap. 13.95 (*0-553-34387-4*) Bantam.
— Emmanuel's Book II: The Choice for Love. LC 94-144226. 256p. 1997. pap. 13.95 (*0-553-34750-0*) Bantam.
Rodegast, Pat & Stanton, Judith, eds. What Is an Angel Doing Here? LC 94-16006. (Emmanuel's Bks.: 3). 272p. 1997. pap. 13.95 (*0-553-37412-5*) Bantam.
Rodegast, Roland, jt. auth. see Reardon, Ruth.
Rodeghier, Mark. UFO Reports Involving Vehicle Interference: A Catalogue & Data Analysis. 156p. (C). 1981. pap. 8.00 (*0-929343-55-7*) J A Hynek Ctr UFO.
Rodeghier, Mark, jt. auth. see Nachmias, Chava.
Rodehaver, Myles W., et al. The Sociology of the School. LC 80-26021. 262p. (C). 1981. reprint ed. lib. bdg. 65.00 (*0-313-22897-3*, ROSSC, Greenwood Pr) Greenwood.
Rodeheaver, Homer A. Hymnal Handbook for Standard Hymns & Gospel Songs. LC 72-1686. reprint ed. 31.50 (*0-404-09913-0*) AMS Pr.
— Singing Black. LC 72-1681. reprint ed. 31.50 (*0-404-08330-7*) AMS Pr.
Rodeheaver, NimFa, jt. auth. see Guillermo, Art.
Rodeheaver, Steve. Snapshots of the Kingdom. LC 97-47388. 120p. 1998. pap. 8.99 (*0-8341-1706-1*) Beacon Hill.
***Rodeheffer, Jane Kelley, et al.** Core Texts in Conversation. LC 00-23480. 224p. 2000. pap. 27.50 (*0-7618-1679-8*) U Pr of Amer.
Rodeike, Peter, jt. auth. see Prien, Jochen.
Rodekohr, Mark E. & Northup, Mary E. Privatization & the Globalization of Energy Markets. (Illus.). 108p. (C). 1997. reprint ed. pap. text 30.00 (*0-7881-4742-0*) DIANE Pub.
Rodekohr, Mark E., jt. auth. see Kilgore, W. Calvin.
Rodel, Mark-Oliver. Amphibien der Westafrikanischen Savanne. (GER., Illus.). 282p. (Orig.). 1996. pap. 39.95 (*3-930612-06-2*, Pub. by Edition Chimaira) Bibliomania.
Rodell, Chris, jt. auth. see Zullo, Allan.
Rodell, Fred. Nine Men: A Political History of the Supreme Court from 1790 to 1955. xii, 338p. 1988. reprint ed. 45.00 (*0-8377-2541-0*, Rothman) W S Hein.
— Woe unto You, Lawyers. 2nd ed. 184p. 1987. reprint ed. 35.00 (*0-8377-2536-4*, Rothman) W S Hein.
Rodell, Mark. Abandoned Lines & Broken Ties. Ayres, D. R., ed. (Railroad Fiction Ser.: Vol. 3). (Illus.). 262p. (Orig.). 1997. pap. 8.95 (*0-943857-08-2*) D R Ayres.
Rodell, Susanna. Dear Fred. LC 94-19926. (Illus.). 32p. (J). (ps-2). 1995. 14.95 (*0-395-71544-X*) Ticknor & Flds Bks Yng Read.
Rodellar, Jose, jt. auth. see Holnicki-Szulc, Jan.
Rodemann, Patricia. Patterns in Interior Environments: Perception, Psychology, & Practice. LC 98-33560. 272p. 1999. 49.95 (*0-471-24162-8*) Wiley.
Rodemich, Christine, jt. auth. see Paquette, Mary.
Roden, Albert C. Van, see Van Roden, Albert C.
Roden, Anne Van, see Van Roden, Anne.
Roden, Barbara, jt. ed. see Roden, Christopher.
Roden, Barbara, ed. see Sanders, Dave & Gibson, Brian.
Roden, Barbara, ed. see Wakefield, H. Russell.
Roden, Barbara, ed. see Wakefield, Herbert Russell.
Roden, Bob, ed. see Health for Life Staff.
Roden, Caldwell Van, see Van Roden, Caldwell.
***Roden, Christopher & Roden, Barbara, eds.** The Blue Carbuncle. (Case Files of Sherlock Holmes Ser.: Vol. 4). 202p. 1999. pap. 21.50 (*1-899562-65-6*, Calabash Pr) Ash-Tree.
— The Blue Carbuncle. (Case Files of Sherlock Holmes Ser.: Vol. 4). (Illus.). 202p. 1999. 31.50 (*1-899562-64-8*, Calabash Pr) Ash-Tree.
— The Case Files of Sherlock Holmes: The Dying Detective. (Chronicles of Sherlock Holmes Ser.: Vol. 3). (Illus.). 153p. 1998. 30.00 (*1-899562-53-2*, Calabash Pr) Ash-Tree.
— The Case Files of Sherlock Holmes: The Dying Detective. (The Chronicles of Sherlock Holmes Ser.: Vol. 3). (Illus.). 153p. 1998. pap. 21.00 (*1-899562-54-0*, Calabash Pr) Ash-Tree.
— The Speckled Band. (Case Files of Sherlock Holmes Ser.: Vol. 2). (Illus.). 188p. 1999. 30.00 (*1-899562-24-9*, Calabash Pr); pap. 21.00 (*1-899562-25-7*, Calabash Pr) Ash-Tree.
Roden, Christopher, ed. see Doyle, Arthur Conan.
Roden, Christopher, ed. see Symons, Julian.
Roden, Christopher, ed. & intro. see Doyle, Arthur Conan.
Roden, Claudia. The Book of Jewish Food: An Odyssey from Samarkand to New York. 1996. 35.00 (*0-394-53258-9*) Knopf.
— A Book of Middle Eastern Food. (Illus.). 1974. pap. 16.00 (*0-394-71948-4*) Knopf.
— Invitation to Mediterranean Cooking: 150 Vegetarian & Seafood Recipes. LC 97-10536. (Illus.). 160p. 1997. 30.00 (*0-8478-2020-3*, Pub. by Rizzoli Intl) St Martin.
***Roden, Claudia.** New Book of Middle Eastern Food. (Illus.). 560p. 2000. 35.00 (*0-375-40506-2*) Knopf.
Roden, Donald T. Schooldays in Imperial Japan: A Study in the Culture of a Student Elite. LC 79-64477. (Illus.). 314p. reprint ed. pap. 97.40 (*0-7837-4842-6*, 204448900003) Bks Demand.
Roden, Joanne Van, see Van Roden, Joanne.
Roden, Joanne Van, see Shipley, Shirley & Van Roden, Joanne.
Roden, Joanne Van, see Van Roden, Joanne.
Roden, Joanne Van, see Shipley, Shirley & Van Roden, Joanne.
Roden, Joanne Van, see Van Roden, Joanne.
Roden, Joanne Van, see Dutery, Polly & Van Roden, Joanne.
Roden, Katie. Farming. (Then & Now Ser.). (Illus.). 32p. (YA). (gr. 4 up). 1996. lib. bdg. 21.90 (*0-7613-0493-2*, Copper Beech Bks) Millbrook Pr.
— Ghosts. LC 97-9951. (Illus.). 40p. (J). (gr. 4-6). 1997. lib. bdg. 22.40 (*0-7613-0606-4*, Copper Beech Bks) Millbrook Pr.
— The Mummy. (In the Footsteps of...Ser.). (Illus.). 40p. (J). (gr. 4-6). 1996. lib. bdg. 21.90 (*0-7613-0451-7*, Copper Beech Bks) Millbrook Pr.
— The Mummy. LC 95-39829. (In the Footsteps Of--Ser.). 1996. 12.15 (*0-606-09462-8*, Pub. by Turtleback) Demco.
— Plague. (Illus.). 40p. (J). (gr. 4-6). 1996. pap. 6.95 (*0-7613-0516-5*, Copper Beech Bks); lib. bdg. 23.90 (*0-7613-0541-6*, Copper Beech Bks) Millbrook Pr.
— Solving International Crime. (Crimebusters Ser.). (Illus.). 32p. (J). (gr. 4-6). 1996. lib. bdg. 20.90 (*0-7613-0528-9*, Copper Beech Bks) Millbrook Pr.
Roden, Lincoln, III. Golf's Golden Age, 1945-1954. 115p. (Orig.). 1995. pap. 12.95 (*0-9655136-0-2*) ReedDrabick.
***Roden, Marie-Louise, ed.** Ab Aquilone: Nordic Studies in Honour & Memory of Leonard E. Boyle, O. P. (Skrifter Utgivna av Riksarkivet 14 Ser.). (ENG, FRE & GER., Illus.). 272p. 1999. 62.50 (*91-7042-161-7*, Pub. by Paul Astrom) Coronet Bks.
Roden, Marie-Louise, ed. Politics & Culture in the Age of Christina. LC 99-184327. (Suecoromana Ser.: No. IV). (Illus.). 129p. 1997. 59.50 (*91-7042-156-0*) Coronet Bks.
***Roden, Martin S.** Analog & Digital Communication Systems. 4th ed. (Illus.). 574p. (C). 2000. 50.00 (*0-9646969-6-7*) Discover CA.
Roden, Martin S. Micro-Cap II: Student Manual & Software. (C). 1989. pap. text 24.95 (*0-685-18622-9*); 5.25 hd 37.45 (*0-201-50542-8*) Benjamin-Cummings.
Roden, Martin S. & Carpenter, Gordon L. Electronic Design: From Concept to Reality. (Illus.). 1002p. (C). 1997. text 59.95 (*0-9646969-1-6*) Discover CA.
Roden, Michael. Jesus & Ourselves: An Alternative Understanding of Christianity. LC 96-77328. 144p. (Orig.). 1996. pap. 12.95 (*0-9652996-0-0*) Infinite Passion.
— Songs of the Morning: Meditations for Healing & Self-Knowledge. LC 96-79639. 112p. (Orig.). 1997. pap. 11.95 (*0-9652996-1-9*) Infinite Passion.
Roden, Robert B. Journey to Wholeness: How to Create Lasting Change & Discover True Happiness. LC 95-60753. 288p. 1995. 23.95 (*0-9646217-3-8*) WillowBrk Pub.
Roden, Steve, jt. auth. see Labelle, Brandon.
Rodenas, Adriana M. Gender & Nationalism in Colonial Cuba: The Travels of Santa Cruz y Montalvo, Condesa de Merlin. LC 97-21193. (Illus.). 312p. 1998. 34.95 (*0-8265-1299-2*) Vanderbilt U Pr.
Rodenbach, Georges. Bruges-La-Morte. Mosley, Philip, tr. LC 86-51023. (FRE.). 78p. 1986. pap. 14.95 (*0-905075-23-4*, Pub. by Wilfion Bks) Dufour.
— Bruges-La-Morte. Hale, Terry, ed. & tr. by. from FRE. (Illus.). 90p. 1993. reprint ed. pap. 12.99 (*0-947757-58-9*, Pub. by Atlas Pr) Serpents Tail.
***Rodenbach, Georges.** Le Voile et le Mirage. (FRE.). 1999. pap. 24.95 (*0-85989-641-2*) Univ Exeter Pr.
Rodenbaugh, Marcia. Marci Books: Dragon Who Chewed Purple Bubble Gum, Papsee's Pup, Calling All Detectives, Woody & Wendy Woodpecker, 4 bks. 2nd ed. (Illus.). 56p. 1983. pap. text 1.00 (*1-57543-047-9*) Mar Co Prods.
Rodenbaugh, William B. Beighley, 1737-1934: Acorns from Colonial Oaks, Vol. I. (Illus.). 86p. 1996. reprint ed. pap. 17.00 (*0-8328-5338-0*); reprint ed. lib. bdg. 27.00 (*0-8328-5337-2*) Higginson Bk Co.
***Rodenbeck, Adolph J.** The Anatomy of the Law: A Logical Presentation of the Parts of the Body of the Law. xi, 292p. 2000. reprint ed. 92.00 (*1-56169-607-2*) Gaunt.

R

Rodenbeck, Adolph J. Anatomy of the Law: A Logical Presentation of the Parts of the Body of the Law. xi, 292p. 1992. reprint ed. 42.50 (0-8377-2546-1, Rothman) W S Hein.

Rodenbeck, Max. Cairo: City Victorious. LC 98-14214. 320p. 2000. pap. 14.00 (0-679-76727-4) Vin Bks.

— Cairo: The City Victorious. LC 98-14214. (Illus.). 300p. (YA). 1999. 27.50 (0-679-44651-6) Random.

Rodenberg, Howard, jt. auth. see Martin, Terence.

Rodenberger, Lou H. Jane Gilmore Rushing. LC 95-75725. (Western Writers Ser.: No. 118). (Illus.). 49p. (C). 1995. pap. 4.95 (0-88430-117-6) Boise St U W Writ Ser.

Rodenberger, Lou H., jt. ed. see Grider, Sylvia A.

Rodenborg, L. Epilithische Vegetation in Einem Alten Waldgebiet auf Mittel-Oeland, Schweden. (Bibliotheca Lichenologica Ser.: No. 8). (GER., Illus.). 1977. pap. text 32.00 (3-7682-1151-7) Lubrecht & Cramer.

Rodenborn, Billie J. Changing Image, Vol. 1. 165p. 1999. pap. 10.95 (0-9669909-0-0) D L Rodenborn.

Rodenbough, Theo F. Photographic History of the Civil War, Vol. II. (Illus.). 750p. 1987. 14.98 (1-55521-199-2) Bk Sales Inc.

— Photographic History of the Civil War, Vol. 3. 750p. 1987. 15.98 (1-55521-203-4) Bk Sales Inc.

— Photographic History of the Civil War, Vol. IV. (Illus.). 750p. 1987. 14.98 (1-55521-201-8) Bk Sales Inc.

— Photographic History of the Civil War: Forts & Artillery - The Navies, Vol. 3. 322p. 1987. 14.98 (1-55521-200-X) Bk Sales Inc.

— Photographic History of the Civil War: The Armies & Leaders - Poetry & Eloquence, Vol. 5. (Illus.). 750p. 1987. 14.98 (1-55521-202-6) Bk Sales Inc.

— Photographic History of the Civil War: The Opening Battles - Two Years of Grim War. (Illus.). 750p. 1987. 14.98 (1-55521-174-7) Bk Sales Inc.

***Rodenbough, Theophilus F.** From Everglade to Canyon with the Second United States Cavalry: An Authentic Account of Service in Florida, Mexico, Virginia & the Indian Country: Including the Personal Recollections of Prominent Officers: With an Appendix Containing Orders, Reports & Correspondence, Military Records... 1836-1875. LC 99-55163. (Illus.). 576p. 2000. 19.95 (0-8061-3228-0) U of Okla Pr.

Rodenburg, Eric, et al. Environmental Indicators for Global Cooperation. 46p. 1995. pap. 22.00 (1-884122-12-4, 72212) World Bank.

Rodenburg, J. M. & Institute of Physics (Great Britain) Staff. Electron Microscopy & Analysis, 1997: Proceedings of the Institute of Physics Electron Microscopy & Analysis Group Conference, Cavendish Laboratory, University of Cambridge, 2-5 September, 1997. LC 97-48374. (Conference Ser.). 1997. pap. 315.00 (0-7503-0441-3) IOP Pub.

Rodenburg, Janet. In the Shadow of Migration: Rural Women & Their Households in North Tapanuli, Indonesia. LC 97-223724. (Verhandelingen Ser.: No. 174). (Illus.). 241p. 1997. pap. 37.00 (90-6718-108-0, Pub. by KITLV Pr) Cellar.

***Rodenburg, Patsy.** The Actor & His Body. 320p. 1998. pap. 16.95 (0-413-70020-8) Methn.

— The Actor Speaks. 320p. 2000. text 26.95 (0-312-23343-4) St Martin.

Rodenburg, Patsy. The Need for Words. LC 93-7959. 45.00 (0-685-65135-5) Routledge.

— The Need for Words: Voice & the Text. 256p. (gr. 13). 1993. pap. 17.99 (0-87830-051-1, Thtre Arts Bks) Routledge.

— The Right to Speak: Working with the Voice. LC 93-17448. 320p. (gr. 13). 1993. pap. 18.99 (0-87830-055-4) Routledge.

Rodengen, Jeffery L. & Stephenson, Larry W. State of the Heart: The Practical Guide to Your Heart & Heart Surgery, (Illus.). 287p. 2000. 39.95 (0-945903-26-X) Write Stuff Syndicate.

Rodengen, Jeffrey L. Boston Scientific Story. 1999. 39.95 (0-945903-50-2) Write Stuff Syndicate.

— Evinrude, Johnson & the Legend of OMC. (Illus.). 144p. 1992. 39.95 (0-945903-10-3) Write Stuff Syndicate.

— Iron Fist: The Lives of Carl Kiekhaefer. 640p. 1992. 24.95 (0-945903-04-9) Write Stuff Syndicate.

— Legend of American Standard. 1999. 39.95 (0-945903-48-0) Write Stuff Syndicate.

— The Legend of AMP. Nitken, Karen, ed. LC 96-61251. (Illus.). 1998. 39.95 (0-945903-33-2) Write Stuff Syndicate.

— The Legend of Applied Materials. Nitkin, Karen, ed. LC 96-62226. (Illus.). 160p. 1997. 39.95 (0-945903-14-6) Write Stuff Syndicate.

— The Legend of Briggs & Stratton. Nitkin, Karen, ed. LC 95-60793. (Illus.). 176p. 1995. 39.95 (0-945903-11-1) Write Stuff Syndicate.

— The Legend of Cessna. Nitken, Karen, ed. LC 97-60423. (Illus.). 1997. 39.95 (0-945903-30-8) Write Stuff Syndicate.

— The Legend of Chris-Craft. (Illus.). 304p. 1988. 49.95 (0-945903-02-2) Write Stuff Syndicate.

— The Legend of Chris-Craft, Vol. 3. 3rd rev. ed. LC 93-60544. (Illus.). 268p. 1998. 49.95 (0-945903-20-0) Write Stuff Syndicate.

— The Legend of Dr. Pepper - 7-Up. Nitkin, Karen, ed. LC 95-60796. (Illus.). 142p. 1995. 39.95 (0-945903-49-9) Write Stuff Syndicate.

— Legend of Federal-Mogul, 1. 1999. 39.95 (0-945903-44-8) Write Stuff Syndicate.

— Legend of Fleetwood. 1997. 39.95 (0-945903-47-2) Write Stuff.

— The Legend of Goodyear: The First 100 Years. Lieber, Alex, ed. LC 96-61249. (Illus.). 208p. 1997. 39.95 (0-945903-35-9) Write Stuff Syndicate.

— The Legend of Halliburton. LC 95-62227. (Illus.). 208p. 1997. 39.95 (0-945903-16-2) Write Stuff Syndicate.

— The Legend of Honeywell. Nitkin, Karen, ed. (Illus.). 240p. 1995. 39.95 (0-945903-25-1) Write Stuff Syndicate.

— Legend of IBP, 1. 1999. 39.95 (0-945903-52-9) Write Stuff Syndicate.

— The Legend of Ingersoll-Rand. Nitkin, Karen, ed. LC 95-60794. (Illus.). 208p. 1995. 39.95 (0-945903-08-1) Write Stuff Syndicate.

— Legend of Inter-Tel. 1999. 39.95 (0-945903-31-6) Write Stuff Syndicate.

— Legend of Litton Industries, 1. 1999. 39.95 (0-945903-51-0) Write Stuff Syndicate.

— The Legend of Mercury, 1. LC 98-61061. (Illus.). 207p. 1999. 39.95 (0-945903-23-5) Write Stuff Syndicate.

— The Legend of Nucor. Nitken, Karen, ed. LC 96-61248. (Illus.). 144p. 1997. 39.95 (0-945903-36-7) Write Stuff Syndicate.

— Legend of Pfizer, 1. 1999. 39.95 (0-945903-37-5) Write Stuff Syndicate.

— The Legend of Rowan. LC 97-62154, (Illus.). 183p. 1998. 39.95 (0-945903-45-6) Write Stuff Syndicate.

— The Legend of Stanley. Nitkin, Karen, ed. LC 95-60795. (Illus.). 192p. 1996. 39.95 (0-945903-13-8) Write Stuff Syndicate.

— Legend of Tenet Healthcare, 1. 1999. 39.95 (0-945903-54-5) Write Stuff Syndicate.

— Legend of Trinity Industries, Inc., 1. 1999. 39.95 (0-945903-53-7) Write Stuff Syndicate.

— Legend of VF Corporation. LC 96-61246. 1998. 39.95 (0-945903-38-3) Write Stuff Syndicate.

— Legend of Worthington Industries, 1. 1999. 39.95 (0-945903-55-3) Write Stuff Syndicate.

— The Legend of York. Nitkin, Karen, ed. LC 96-60604. (Illus.). 208p. 1997. 39.95 (0-945903-17-0) Write Stuff Syndicate.

— The MicroAge Way. LC 96-60604. 1997. 39.95 (0-945903-12-X) Write Stuff Syndicate.

***Rodengen, Jeffrey L.** New Horizons: The Story of Ashland Inc. LC 97-62155. xi, 223 p. 1999. 39.95 (0-945903-42-1) Write Stuff Syndicate.

Rodengen, Jeffrey L. Serving the Silent Service: The Legend of Electric Boat. LC 94-60763. (Illus.). 144p. 1994. 39.95 (0-945903-24-3) Write Stuff Syndicate.

Rodengen, Jeffrey L., jt. auth. see Stephenson, Larry W.

Rodengen, Jeffrey L., ed. see Aronow, Michael.

Rodenger, Jeffrey L. The Spirit of AMD: The Legend of Advanced Micro Devices, Vol. 1. LC 96-60605. (Illus.). 160p. 1998. 39.95 (0-945903-21-9) Write Stuff Syndicate.

***Rodenhauser, Paul.** Mental Health Care Administration: A Guide for Practitioners. LC 99-50531. (Illus.). 280p. (C). 2000. text 49.50 (0-472-11116-7, 11116) U of Mich Pr.

Rodenhauser, Paul, ed. see Reichard, Birge D. & Siewers, Christiane M.

Rodenhouse, Mary P. HEP Higher Education Directory, 1999. 15th ed. Torregrosa, Constance H., ed. 704p. 1998. pap. 57.00 (0-914927-24-8) Higher Ed Pubns.

Rodenhouse, Mary P. Jesus, the Way, Truth & Life. 1996. pap. 10.95 (0-89870-338-7) Ignatius Pr.

***Rodenhouse, Mary Pat & Torregrosa, Constance Healy, eds.** Higher Education Directory, 2000. LC 83-641119. 812p. 2000. pap. 60.00 (0-914927-29-9) Higher Ed Pubns.

Rodenstein, Judith. Dietetic Career Recruitment Study. 32p. 1990. spiral bd. 16.50 (0-88091-075-5, 0405) Am Dietetic Assn.

— Microcomputers in Vocational Education: Programs & Practices. (Illus.). 224p. 1986. pap. text 25.00 (0-13-580507-4) P-H.

Rodenwalt, Gerhart. The Acropolis. 2nd ed. LC 58-6859. (Illus.). 167p. reprint ed. pap. 51.80 (0-8357-5082-5, 201625800002) Bks Demand.

***Roder, Joseph.** Veterinary Toxicology: The Practical Veterinarian. (Illus.). 352p. 2000. pap. text 45.00 (0-7506-7240-4) Buttrwrth-Heinemann.

***Roder-Thiede, Maike.** Chinchillas. LC 98-52819. (Complete Pet Owner's Manual Ser.). (Illus.). 104p. 1999. pap. 6.95 (0-7641-0934-0) Barron.

Roder, Wolf. Human Adjustment to Kainji Reservoir in Nigeria: An Assessment of the Economic & Environmental Consequences of a Major Man-Made Lake in Africa. 206p. (Orig.). (C). 1994. pap. text 29.50 (0-8191-9334-8); lib. bdg. 52.50 (0-8191-9333-X) U Pr of Amer.

Rodereda, Merce. The Time of the Doves. Rosenthal, David H., tr. from CAT. LC 85-80976. 208p. 1986. reprint ed. pap. 12.95 (0-915308-75-4) Graywolf.

Roderer, Phyllis. Human Resource Management in Associations. Sabo, Sandra R., ed. LC 94-21905. (Finance & Administration Section Ser.). vi, 221p. 1994. pap. 35.95 (0-88034-083-5) Am Soc Assn Execs.

Roderick, jt. auth. see Bell.

Roderick, Alan, ed. Gwent Anthology. 351p. 1988. 44.95 (0-8464-4869-6) Beekman Pubs.

Roderick, Arthur, jt. ed. see Davies, Euros.

Roderick, Colin A. Banjo Paterson: Poet by Accident. LC 93-164864. 263 p. 1993. write for info. (1-86373-292-6) Allen & Unwn AT.

Roderick, Don, ed. see Lawson, L. & Hardy, H.

Roderick, G. W., jt. auth. see Stephens, M. D.

Roderick, Gary, jt. auth. see Sims, Charles.

Roderick, Gordon W., jt. ed. see Stephens, Michael D.

Roderick, Hilliard. Acid Rain & Friendly Neighbors: The Policy Dispute Between Canada & the United States. rev. ed. Schmandt, Jurgen, ed. LC 88-25605. (Duke Press Policy Studies). (Illus.). 340p. (C). 1989. text 49.95 (0-8223-0870-3) Duke.

Roderick, Hilliard & Magnusson, Ulla. Avoiding Inadvertent War: Crisis Management. (Tom Slick World Peace Ser.). 175p. 1983. pap. 5.00 (0-89940-005-1) LBJ Sch Pub Aff.

Roderick, Jack. Crude Dreams: A Personal History of Oil & Politics in Alaska. Graydon, Don, ed. LC 97-227979. (Illus.). 416p. (Orig.). 1997. pap. 24.95 (0-945397-60-7) Epicenter Pr.

Roderick, James, jt. auth. see Begich, Nick.

Roderick, John. Covering China: The Story of an American Reporter from Revolutionary Days to the Deng Era. (Illus.). 230p. 1993. 39.95 (1-879176-18-1); pap. 19.95 (1-879176-17-3) Imprint Pubns.

Roderick, Kyle, jt. auth. see Maggio, Carole.

Roderick, Lee. Leading the Charge: Orrin Hatch & 20 Years of America. LC 94-2048. 447p. 1994. 22.95 (1-882723-09-0) Gold Leaf Pr.

Roderick, Libby. When I Hear Music. (Illus.). 118p. (Orig.). 1994. pap. write for info. (0-9641114-1-1) Turtle Islnd.

Roderick, Melissa. The Path to Dropping Out: Evidence for Intervention. LC 92-42905. 240p. 1993. 55.00 (0-86569-206-8, T206, Auburn Hse) Greenwood.

Roderick, Pamela H. Wall Street Work: How to Find a Great Job in the Securities Industry. 1999. 30.00 (0-938609-38-6) Graduate Group.

***Roderick, Timothy.** Apprentice to Power: A Wiccan Odyssey to Spiritual Awakening. 2000. pap. 18.95 (1-58091-077-7) Crossing Pr.

Roderick, Timothy. Dark Moon Mysteries: Wisdom, Power & Magick of the Shadow World. LC 96-13525. (Illus.). 224p. (Orig.). 1999. pap. 14.95 (1-56718-345-X) Llewellyn Pubns.

— The Once Unknown Familiar: Shamanic Paths to Unleash Your Animal Powers. LC 94-5748. (Illus.). 240p. 1994. pap., wbk. ed. 10.00 (0-87542-439-2) Llewellyn Pubns.

Roderick, Wanda W. Legal Studies to Wit: Basic Legal Terminology & Transcription. 2nd ed. 1984. write for info. (0-538-11360-X, K36) S-W Pub.

Roderman. Vocabulary Exercises: Analyzing Word Parts. 1994. pap. 2.50 (0-8092-3580-3) NTC Contemp Pub Co.

— Vocabulary Exercises: Getting the Most from Your Dictionary. 1994. pap. 2.50 (0-8092-3581-1) NTC Contemp Pub Co.

— Vocabulary Exercises: Understanding Language. 1994. pap. 2.50 (0-8092-3587-0) NTC Contemp Pub Co.

— Vocabulary Exercises: Using a Dictionary. 1994. pap. 2.50 (0-8092-3585-4) NTC Contemp Pub Co.

Roderman, Winifred H., jt. auth. see Echaore-McDavid, Susan.

Rodero, Cristina G. Espana Oculta: Public Celebrations in Spain, 1974-1989. (ENG & SPA., Illus.). 140p. 1995. pap. 45.00 (1-56098-530-5) Smithsonian.

Rodero, Paz & Escriva, Vivi. The Storyteller (El Cuentista) LC 98-5892. (Tales in Two Languages (Cuentos en Dos Idiomas) Ser.). (ENG & SPA.). (J). 1998. 16.95 (1-56492-249-9) Laredo.

Roderos, Paula. The Random House Book of Horses & Horsemanship. (J). 1997. pap. 0.18 (0-679-88726-1, Pub. by Random Bks Yng Read) Random.

Roderus, Frank. Duster. LC 85-14759. (Chaparral Bks.). (Illus.). 266p. (J). (gr. 6 up). 1987. reprint ed. pap. 10.95 (0-87565-095-3) Tex Christian.

— Hayseed. 208p. 1998. mass mkt. 4.50 (0-8439-4432-3, Leisure Bks) Dorchester Pub Co.

***Roderus, Frank.** Jason Evers: His Own Story. 192p. 1999. mass mkt. 3.99 (0-8439-4573-7, Pub. by Dorchester Pub Co) CMG.

— Left to Die. 2000. mass mkt. 5.99 (0-425-17637-1) Berkley Pub.

Roderus, Frank. Mustang War. large type ed. (Sagebrush Large Print Westerns Ser.). 292p. 1995. lib. bdg. 17.95 (1-57490-011-0) T T Beeler.

— Old Marsden. 272p. 1999. mass mkt. 4.50 (0-8439-4506-0) Dorchester Pub Co.

— Potter's Fields. large type ed. LC 97-34314. (Wheeler Large Print Book Ser.). 1997. pap. 22.95 (1-56895-492-1) Wheeler Pub.

— Stillwater Smith. 192p. 1997. reprint ed. mass mkt. 3.99 (0-8439-4306-8, Leisure Bks) Dorchester Pub Co.

***Roderus, Frank.** Tropper Donovan. 256p. 2000. mass mkt. 4.50 (0-8439-4731-4, Leisure Bks) Dorchester Pub Co.

Roderus, Frank, jt. auth. see Brady, Steve.

Rodes. Manual of Medicine. (SPA.). 1995. 73.00 (84-458-0093-0, Little Brwn Med Div) Lppncott W & W.

Rodes, Barbara, jt. auth. see Irwin, Frances H.

Rodes, Barbara K. & Odell, Rice, compiled by. A Dictionary of Environmental Quotations. LC 97-17903. 344p. 1997. reprint ed. pap. text 19.95 (0-8018-5738-4) Johns Hopkins.

Rodes, Daniel. I Shall Not Die: The Biblical Truth about Healing. LC 97-222087. 126p. 1996. pap. 7.99 (1-884369-46-4, EBED Pubns) McDougal Pubng.

Rodes, Daniel D. Seven Keys to Victory: Restoring the Power of Biblical Praise. 182p. (Orig.). 1998. pap. 9.99 (1-884369-71-5) McDougal Pubng.

Rodes, David S., ed. see Shadwell, Thomas.

Rodes, David S., ed. see Southerne, Thomas.

Rodes, Marian E. & Ostler, James. Fetish Carvers of Zuni. rev. ed. LC 90-63002. (Illus.). 112p. 1995. pap. 18.95 (0-912535-10-5) Max Mus.

Rodes, Robert E., Jr. Law & Modernization in the Church of England: Charles II to the Welfare State. LC 91-50567. (Study of the Legal History of Establishment in England Ser.: Vol. 3). (C). 1991. text 40.50 (0-268-01293-8) U of Notre Dame Pr.

Rodes, Robert E. Lay Authority & Reformation in the English Church. LC 82-7038. 319p. 1982. text 34.50 (0-268-01265-2) U of Notre Dame Pr.

— Pilgrim Law. LC 97-37190. 224p. 1998. pap. 18.00 (0-268-03822-8) U of Notre Dame Pr.

Rodes, Robert E., jt. auth. see Pospesel, Howard.

Rodewald, Fred A., ed. see Hays, John Q.

Rodewald, G., jt. auth. see Willner, A. E.

Rodewald, Janet D. Reviewing German Grammar: A Self-Instructional Reference Book for Elementary German Grammar. LC 84-21884. 364p. (Orig.). 1985. pap. text 38.00 (0-8191-4366-9) U Pr of Amer.

Rodewald-Rudescu, Ludwig. Das Schilfrohr: Phragmites Communis Trinius. (Binnengewasser Ser.: Band 27). (GER., Illus.). ix, 302p. 1974. 58.00 (3-510-40038-0, Pub. by E Schweizerbartsche) Balogh.

Rodewalt, Vance. Rodewalt: With Weapons Drawn. (Illus.). 128p. (Orig.). 1994. pap. 16.95 (1-55059-092-8) Temeron Bks.

Rodey, Dickason, Sloan, Akin & Robb Staff. New Mexico Environmental Law Handbook. 4th ed. 443p. 1996. pap. text 95.00 (0-86587-530-8) Gov Insts.

Rodey, Glenn. HLA Beyond Tears. 190p. 1991. pap. text 24.95 (0-9631020-0-1) De Novo TX.

Rodge, Mary K. Where the Creosote Blooms. LC 98-14193. (Chisholm Trail Ser.: Vol. 19). 176p. 1999. pap. 14.95 (0-87565-193-3) Tex Christian.

Rodger, Alan. Owners & Neighbours in Roman Law. (C). 1972. text 12.00 (0-19-825309-5) OUP.

Rodger, Alison & Norden, Bengt. Circular Dichroism & Linear Dichroism. (Oxford Chemistry Masters Ser.). (Illus.). 160p. (C). 1997. text 60.00 (0-19-855897-X) OUP.

Rodger, Alison & Rodger, P. Mark. Molecular Geometry. (Illus.). 208p. (C). 1995. pap. text 34.95 (0-7506-2295-4, Prgamon Press) Buttrwrth-Heinemann.

Rodger, Angus, jt. auth. see Merkin, Robert.

Rodger, C. A., jt. auth. see Lindner, Charles C.

Rodger, Eleanor J. Commitment to Renewal: Baltimore County Public Library Long Range Plan, 1989-1993. (Illus.). 55p. 1988. pap. 20.00 (0-937076-04-X) Baltimore Co Pub Lib.

— Repositioning for the Future: Baltimore County Public Library Long Range Plan 1994-1999. (Illus.). 32p. 1994. 20.00 (0-937076-05-8) Baltimore Co Pub Lib.

Rodger, Eleanor J., jt. auth. see D'Elia, George.

Rodger, Elizabeth. Boo to You, Too. LC 92-40023. (J). 1993. write for info. (0-671-86765-2) S&S Bks Yung.

— Boo to You, Too. LC 92-40023. (Illus.). 32p. (J). (ps up). 1993. pap. 2.95 (0-671-86766-0) S&S Bks Yung.

— Caterpillar to Butterfly Pop-Up Book. LC 95-69164. (Illus.). 8p. (J). (ps-k). 1996. pap. 4.95 (0-590-54345-8, Cartwheel) Scholastic Inc.

— A Christmas Story for You. (Illus.). 24p. (Orig.). (J). (ps-3). 1996. pap. 3.95 (0-8167-4115-8, Whistlstop) Troll Communs.

— Christmas Without a Tree. LC 94-44399. (Illus.). 32p. (J). 1995. pap. 3.25 (0-689-80157-2) Aladdin.

— Don't Rock the Ark. (Illus.). 1997. pap. 4.95 (0-8167-4199-9) Troll Communs.

— Firefighters to the Rescue. LC 99-184719. (Illus.). 1997. pap. 4.95 (0-8167-4198-0) Troll Communs.

— Pop-Up Caterpillar to Butterfly. (J). (ps-1). 1996. 4.95 (0-614-15771-4, Cartwheel) Scholastic Inc.

— Pop-Up Tadpole to Frog. (J). (ps-1). 1996. 4.95 (0-614-15772-2, Cartwheel) Scholastic Inc.

— Tadpole to Frog Pop-Up. (Illus.). 8p. (J). (ps-k). 1996. pap. 4.95 (0-590-54346-6, Cartwheel) Scholastic Inc.

***Rodger, George.** Humanity & Inhumanity: The Photographic Journey of George Rodger. 320p. 1999. pap. 29.95 (0-7148-3901-9) Phaidon Pr.

Rodger, George. Village of the Nubas. (Contemporary Artists Ser.). 1999. 19.95 (0-7148-3840-3) Phaidon Press.

Rodger, Iain, jt. auth. see Evans, Michael.

Rodger, Ian, et al, eds. Leukotrienes: New Concepts & Targets for Therapy. 160p. 1998. 85.00 (0-7923-8738-4) Kluwer Academic.

Rodger, Ian W., et al, eds. Asthma: Basic Mechanisms & Clinical Management. 2nd ed. (Illus.). 782p. 1992. text 184.00 (0-12-079026-2) Acad Pr.

***Rodger, John J.** From a Welfare State to a Welfare Society: The Changing Context of Social Policy in a Postmodern Era. LC 99-54953. 2000. text 65.00 (0-312-23122-9) St Martin.

Rodger, N. A. The Admiralty. 216p. (C). 1988. 120.00 (0-900963-94-8, Pub. by T Dalton) St Mut.

— Articles of War: The Statutes Which Governed Our Fighting Navies 1661-1749 & 1866. 62p. 1987. 40.00 (0-85937-275-8, Pub. by K Mason Pubns Ltd) St Mut.

— The Safeguard of the Sea: A Naval History of Britain, 660-1649. 692p. 1999. pap. 17.95 (0-393-31960-1) Norton.

— The Wooden World: An Anatomy of the Georgian Navy. (Illus.). 456p. 1996. pap. 14.95 (0-393-31469-3, Norton Paperbks) Norton.

Rodger, N. A., ed. Naval Power in the 20th Century. 318p. 1996. 47.95 (1-55750-616-7) Naval Inst Pr.

Rodger, N. A., jt. auth. see Raven, G. J.

Rodger, N. A. M. The Safeguard of the Sea: A Naval History of Britain, 660-1649. LC 97-52403. (Illus.). 691p. 1998. 39.95 (0-393-04579-X) Norton.

***Rodger, N. A. M.** Naval Records for Genealogists. 230p. 1999. pap. 24.95 (1-873162-58-8, Pub. by PRO Pubns) Midpt Trade.

Rodger, P. Mark, jt. auth. see Rodger, Alison.

Rodger, Richard. A Consolidated Bibliography of Urban History, 2 vols., Set. LC 96-5203. 700p. 1996. 166.95 (1-85928-113-3, Pub. by Scolar Pr) Ashgate Pub Co.

— Housing in Urban Britain, 1780-1914: Class, Capitalism & Construction. (New Studies in Economic & Social History: No. 8). 114p. (C). 1995. text 34.95 (0-521-55267-2); pap. text 10.95 (0-521-55786-0) Cambridge U Pr.

— Research in Urban History: A Classified Survey of Doctoral & Masters' Theses. 281p. 1994. 86.95 (1-85928-082-X, Pub. by Scolar Pr) Ashgate Pub Co.

— Urban History Yearbook, 1989. 280p. 1989. 42.00 (0-7185-6089-2) St Martin.

An Asterisk (*) at the beginning of an entry indicates that the title is appearing for the first time.

Rodger, Richard, ed. European Urban History: Prospect & Retrospect. 224p. 1993. text 54.00 (*0-7185-1432-7*, Pub. by Leicester U Pr) Cassell & Continuum.

— Scottish Housing: Policy & Politics, 1885-1985. 250p. 1990. text 45.00 (*0-7185-1278-2*) St Martin.

— Scottish Housing in the Twentieth Century. 264p. 1993. pap. 20.00 (*0-7185-1493-9*, Pub. by Leicester U Pr) Cassell & Continuum.

— Urban History Yearbook, 1988. 280p. 1989. 39.00 (*0-7185-6088-4*) St Martin.

— Urban History Yearbook, 1990. (Illus.). 300p. 1990. 39.00 (*0-7185-6090-6*) St Martin.

— Urban History Yearbook, 1991. (Illus.). 300p. 1992. text 65.00 (*0-7185-6091-4*) St Martin.

Rodger, Richard, jt. ed. see Morris, R. J.

***Rodger, Rosemary.** Planning an Appropriate Curriculum for the under Fives. 1999. pap. 26.95 (*1-85346-550-X*) David Fulton.

Rodger, Rosemary, jt. auth. see Abbott, Lesley.

Rodgers. Essentials of Diagnostic Microbiology. (Medical Lab Technician Ser.). 1998. 49.95 (*0-8273-7391-0*) Delmar.

— Essentials of Diagnostic Microbiology. (Medical Lab Technician Ser.). (C). 1998. wbk. ed. 24.95 (*0-8273-7390-2*) Delmar.

— Flower Drum Song. (Vocal Score Ser.). 172p. 1981. per. 45.00 (*0-88188-018-3*, 00312141) H Leonard.

***Rodgers.** Foundations of Nursing Knowled. 2002. pap. text. write for info. (*0-7216-8010-0*, W B Saunders Co) Harcrt Hlth Sci Grp.

— IBM Way. 1987. 8.95 (*0-06-337043-3*) HarpC.

Rodgers. Introduction & Coordination of Solid. 1993. student ed. 17.19 (*0-07-053389-X*) McGraw.

— Life of Robert Watts. 1991. pap. 2.50 (*1-871676-15-0*, Pub. by Christian Focus) Spring Arbor Dist.

***Rodgers.** My Fav Things. 2000. lib. bdg. 15.89 (*0-06-029233-4*) HarpC.

— Untitled on Physiology of Sex. Date not set. pap. text. write for info. (*0-7167-3744-2*) W H Freeman.

Rodgers, ed. Palladii. (LAT.). 1975. 53.50 (*3-322-00214-4*, T1573, Pub. by B G Teubner) U of Mich Pr.

***Rodgers & Hammerstein, Oscar, II.** Rodgers & Hammerstein's Cinderella. 56p. 1999. pap. 10.95 (*0-7935-9125-2*) H Leonard.

Rodgers & Hammerstein, Oscar, II. You'll Never Walk Alone: From Carousel. 4p. 1987. 3.95 (*0-7935-0736-7*, 01120241) H Leonard.

***Rodgers & Hart.** Jumbo Vocal Selections. 32p. 1998. pap. 8.95 (*0-7935-9070-1*) H Leonard.

Rodgers, Alan, jt. auth. see Diaz, Gisele.

Rodgers, Allan & Halas, Monica. Massachusetts Unemployment Advocacy Guide, 1997 Edition. rev. ed. LC 96-79771. 108p. 1996. pap. text 5.00 (*1-57589-048-8*, 97-15.11-BK) Mass CLE.

Rodgers, Anne Brown, ed. see Nass, Terri.

Rodgers, Audrey T. Denise Levertov: The Poetry of Engagement. LC 92-53065. (Illus.). 240p. (C). 1993. 37.50 (*0-8386-3494-X*) Fairleigh Dickinson.

Rodgers, Barbara. Bible Activities in a Snap: Bible Stories Come to Life. 64p. (J). (ps-3). 1998. pap. 9.95 (*1-885358-42-3*, RB36811) Rainbow CA.

— Bible Activities in a Snap: Holidays. 64p. (J). (ps-3). 1999. pap. 9.95 (*1-885358-44-X*, RB36813) Rainbow CA.

— Bible Activities in a Snap: Living by God's Word. (Illus.). 64p. (J). (ps-3). 1998. pap. 9.95 (*1-885358-43-1*) Rainbow CA.

— Bible Activities in a Snap: Sharing God's Love. (Illus.). 64p. (J). (gr. 3-8). 1998. pap. 9.95 (*1-885358-45-8*, RB36814) Rainbow CA.

Rodgers, Barbara S., jt. auth. see Nixon, C. E.

Rodgers, Beth L. & Knafl, Kathleen A. Concept Development in Nursing: Foundations, Techniques, & Applications. LC 99-31082. (Illus.). 405p. 2000. pap. text. write for info. (*0-7216-8243-X*, W B Saunders Co) Harcrt Hlth Sci Grp.

Rodgers, Beth L. & Knafl, Kathleen A., eds. Concept Development in Nursing: Foundations, Techniques, & Applications. (Illus.). 270p. 1993. pap. text 43.00 (*0-7216-3674-8*, W B Saunders Co) Harcrt Hlth Sci Grp.

Rodgers, Beverly & Rodgers, Tom. How to Find Mr. or Ms. Right: A Practical Guide to Finding a Soul Mate. LC 99-17938. 160p. 1999. per. 19.95 (*0-89390-451-1*) Resource Pubns.

— Soul-Healing Love: Ten Practical, Easy-to-Learn Techniques for Couples in Crisis. LC 98-15104. 208p. 1998. pap. 19.95 (*0-89390-434-1*) Resource Pubns.

Rodgers, Bill. Bill Rodgers' Lifetime Running Plan: Definitive Programs for Runners of All Ages & Levels. 240p. 1998. pap. 13.00 (*0-06-273499-7*) HarpC.

***Rodgers, Bill & Douglas, Scott.** Bill Rodgers' Lifetime Running Plan: Definitive Program for Runners of All Ages & Levels. (Illus.). 254p. 2000. text 24.00 (*0-7881-9115-2*) DIANE Pub.

Rodgers, Bill & Douglas, Scott. Complete Idiot's Guide to Jogging & Running. LC 98-84950. (Complete Idiot's Guide Ser.). 352p. 1998. pap. text 17.95 (*0-02-862386-X*) Macmillan Gen Ref.

Rodgers, Bill & Welch, Priscilla. Bill Rodgers & Priscilla Welch on Master's Running & Racing. (Illus.). 192p. 1995. pap. 12.95 (*0-87596-330-7*, 12-751-1) Rodale Pr Inc.

Rodgers, Bradley A. Guardian of the Great Lakes: The U. S. Paddle Frigate Michigan. LC 95-48841. 248p. (C). 1996. pap. 19.95 (*0-472-06607-2*, 06607) U of Mich Pr.

— Guardian of the Great Lakes: The U. S. Paddle Frigate Michigan. LC 95-48841. (Illus.). 248p. (C). 1996. text 42.50 (*0-472-09607-9*, 09607) U of Mich Pr.

Rodgers, Caroline, jt. auth. see Thurman, Jean.

Rodgers, Carrie. My Husband, Jimmie Rodgers. 2nd ed. LC 95-68521. (Illus.). 222p. 1995. reprint ed. pap. 14.95 (*0-915608-16-2*) Country Music Found.

Rodgers, Charles. Scottish Monuments & Tombstones, Vol. 1. xvi, 534p. 1997. reprint ed. pap. 36.50 (*0-7884-0684-1*, R527) Heritage Bk.

— Scottish Monuments & Tombstones, Vol. 2. xi, 439p. 1997. reprint ed. pap. 31.50 (*0-7884-0685-X*, R528) Heritage Bk.

Rodgers, Charles J. Coin-collecting in Northern India. LC 98-902740. vi, 135p. 1997. write for info. (*81-206-1238-8*) Asian Educ Servs.

Rodgers, Christopher P. & Margrave-Jones, Clive V. Agricultural Law. 1991. pap. 100.00 (*0-406-11269-X*, UK, MICHIE) LEXIS Pub.

Rodgers, Christopher P., jt. ed. see Howarth, William.

Rodgers, Crull. Sugars & Sweeteners: Trends & Developments Processed Foods & Beverages. 197p. 1998. 3150.00 (*1-56965-124-8*, GA-102) BCC.

Rodgers, Daniel T. Atlantic Crossings: Social Politics in a Progressive Age. LC 98-3188. 1998. 35.00 (*0-674-05131-9*) Belknap Pr.

***Rodgers, Daniel T.** Atlantic Crossings: Social Politics in a Progressive Age. 2000. pap. text 18.95 (*0-674-00201-6*) HUP.

Rodgers, Daniel T. Contested Truths: Keywords in American Politics since Independence. 288p. 1998. pap. text 15.95 (*0-674-16711-2*) HUP.

— The Work Ethic in Industrial America: 1850-1920. LC 77-81737. 316p. 1979. pap. text 17.50 (*0-226-72352-6*) U Ch Pr.

— The Work Ethic in Industrial America: 1850-1920. LC 77-81737. 1992. lib. bdg. 26.00 (*0-226-72351-8*) U Ch Pr.

Rodgers, David. Rossetti. (Color Library). (Illus.). 128p. 1996. pap. 14.95 (*0-7148-3341-X*, Pub. by Phaidon Press) Phaidon Pr.

Rodgers, Dirk. John a Lasco in England Vol. 168, Vol. 1. LC 93-41633. (American University Studies: No. VII). XI, 205p. (C). 1995. text 42.95 (*0-8204-2340-8*) P Lang Pubng.

Rodgers, Don. Moontan. 72p. 1996. pap. 14.95 (*1-85411-154-X*, Pub. by Seren Bks) Dufour.

Rodgers, Drew. Business Communications: International Case Studies in English. 176p. (C). 1995. pap. text 17.95 (*0-521-65751-2*) Cambridge U Pr.

— Business Communications: International Case Studies in English: Instructor's Manual. 45p. (C). 1995. pap., teacher ed. 6.00 (*0-521-65750-4*) Cambridge U Pr.

— English for International Negotiations: A Cross-Cultural Case Study Approach. 176p. (C). 1997. pap. text 17.95 (*0-521-65749-0*) Cambridge U Pr.

— English for International Negotiations: A Cross-Cultural Case Study Approach: Instructor's Manual. 40p. (C). 1997. pap., teacher ed. 6.00 (*0-521-65748-2*) Cambridge U Pr.

Rodgers, Eamonn, ed. Encyclopedia of Contemporary Spanish Culture. LC 98-42158. (Encyclopedias of Contemporary Culture Ser.). 624p. 1999. 140.00 (*0-415-13187-1*) Routledge.

Rodgers, Edith C. Discussion of Holidays in the Latter Middle Ages. LC 41-3851. (Columbia University. Studies in the Social Sciences: No. 474). reprint ed. 20.00 (*0-404-51474-X*) AMS Pr.

Rodgers, Elizabeth. Ollie Goes to School. (Illus.). 32p. (J). (ps-2). 1992. pap. 2.50 (*0-590-44785-8*, Cartwheel) Scholastic Inc.

Rodgers, Eugene. Beyond the Barrier: The Story of Byrd's First Expedition to Antarctica. LC 89-28450. (Bluejacket Bks.). (Illus.). 400p. 1997. pap. 16.95 (*1-55750-713-9*) Naval Inst Pr.

— Flying High: The Story of Boeing & the Rise of the Jetliner Industry. LC 96-244453. 512p. 1996. 27.50 (*0-87113-655-4*, Atlntc Mnthly) Grove-Atltic.

Rodgers-Farmer, Antoinette Y., jt. ed. see Potocky, Miriam.

Rodgers, Frank. I Can't Get to Sleep. LC 90-19607. (Illus.). 32p. (J). (ps-1). 1993. pap. 7.95 (*0-671-79848-0*) S&S Bks Yung.

Rodgers, Frank. Pirate & the Pig. (Illus.). 32p. (J). pap. 9.95 (*0-14-055561-7*, Pub. by Pnguin Bks Ltd) Trafalgar.

Rodgers, Frank. Who's Afraid of the Ghost Train? (Illus.). 32p. (J). (ps-1). 1989. 12.95 (*0-15-200642-7*, Gulliver Bks) Harcourt.

Rodgers, G., ed. The Poverty Agenda & the ILO: Issues For Research & Action. (New Approaches to Poverty Analysis & Policy Ser.: Vol. I). 202p. 1995. pap. 24.75 (*92-9014-536-6*) Intl Labour Office.

Rodgers, G. & Van der Hoeven, R., eds. The Poverty Agenda: Trends & Policy Options. (New Approaches to Poverty Analysis & Policy: No.III). 205p. (C). 1995. pap. 27.00 (*92-9014-569-2*) Intl Labour Office.

Rodgers, Gerry, ed. Urban Poverty & the Labour Market: Access to Jobs & Incomes in Asian & Latin American Cities. vi, 257p. (Orig.). 1989. 42.75 (*92-2-106499-9*); pap. 31.50 (*92-2-106500-6*) Intl Labour Office.

Rodgers, Gerry, et al, eds. The Institutional Approach to Labour & Development. LC 95-44532. (EADI Book Ser.: No. 17). 236p. (C). 1996. pap. 26.50 (*0-7146-4242-8*, Pub. by F Cass Pubs) Intl Spec Bk.

— Social Exclusion: Rhetoric, Reality, Responses: A Contribution to the World Summit for Social Development. LC 96-113405. xii, 311p. 1995. pap. 36.00 (*92-9014-537-4*) Intl Labour Office.

Rodgers, Gerry & Rodgers, Janine, eds. Precarious Jobs in Labour Market Regulation: The Growth of Atypical Employment in Western Europe. x, 301p. (Orig.). 1989. pap. 22.50 (*92-9014-453-X*); pap. 31.50 (*92-9014-452-1*) Intl Labour Office.

Rodgers, Gerry & Standing, Guy, eds. Child Work, Poverty & Underdevelopment: Issues for Research in Low-Income Countries. (WEP Study). xii, 310p. (Orig.). 1981. 31.50 (*92-2-102812-7*); pap. 22.50 (*92-2-102813-5*) Intl Labour Office.

Rodgers, Gerry, jt. ed. see Deshpande, L. K.

Rodgers, Glen E. Introduction to Coordination, Solid State, & Descriptive Inorganic Chemistry. LC 93-15952. (C). 1994. text 69.74 (*0-07-053384-9*) McGraw.

Rodgers, H. J. Twenty-Three Years under a Skylight: or Life & Experiences of a Photographer. LC 72-9233. (Literature of Photography Ser.). (Illus.). 1973. reprint ed. 21.95 (*0-405-04938-2*) Ayer.

***Rodgers, Hael.** Oh, What a Beautiful Morning. 32p. (J). (ps-3). 2000. 24.95 (*0-06-027925-7*) HarpC Child Bks.

Rodgers, Harold R., et al, eds. Arlington Dictionary of Electronics. (Illus.). 1971. 25.00 (*0-8464-0146-0*) Beekman Pubs.

Rodgers, Harrell & Weither, Gregory R., eds. Rural vs. Urban Poverty. (Orig.). 1988. pap. 15.00 (*0-944285-05-8*) Pol Studies.

***Rodgers, Harrell R., Jr.** American Poverty in a New Era of Reform. LC 99-86079. 255p. 2000. pap. text 22.95 (*0-7656-0626-7*) M E Sharpe.

— American Poverty in a New Era of Reform. LC 99-86079. (Illus.). 255p. 2000. text 58.95 (*0-7656-0625-9*) M E Sharpe.

— Beyond Welfare: New Approaches to the Problem of Poverty in America. LC 87-28876. 184p. (gr. 13). 1988. pap. text 42.95 (*0-87332-461-7*) M E Sharpe.

— Cost of Human Neglect: America's Welfare Failure. LC 82-10390. 236p. (gr. 13). 1982. pap. text 35.95 (*0-87332-238-X*) M E Sharpe.

Rodgers, Harrell R. The Cost of Human Neglect: America's Welfare Failure. LC 82-10390. (Illus.). 236p. reprint ed. pap. 73.20 (*0-7837-9992-6*, 206071900006) Bks Demand.

Rodgers, Harrell R., Jr. Poor Women, Poor Children: American Poverty in the 1990's. 3rd ed. LC 89-24372. 216p. (C). (gr. 13). 1996. text 64.95 (*1-56324-607-4*); pap. text 28.95 (*1-56324-608-2*) M E Sharpe.

— Poor Women, Poor Families: The Economic Plight of America's Female-Headed Households. 2nd ed. LC 95-41481. 204p. (C). (gr. 13). 1990. text 66.95 (*0-87332-594-X*) M E Sharpe.

Rodgers, Harrell R., Jr. Poor Women, Poor Families: The Economic Plight of America's Female-Headed Households. 2nd rev. ed. LC 89-24372. 204p. (C). (gr. 13). 1990. pap. text 34.95 (*0-87332-595-8*) M E Sharpe.

Rodgers, Harrell R., Jr., ed. Beyond Welfare: New Approaches to the Problem of Poverty in America. LC 87-28876. 183p. 1988. reprint ed. pap. 56.80 (*0-7837-9971-3*, 206069800006) Bks Demand.

Rodgers, Harrell R., Jr. & Weiher, Gregory R., eds. Rural Poverty: Special Causes & Policy Reforms, 12. LC 88-35817. (Studies in Social Welfare Policies & Programs: No. 12). 190p. 1989. 49.95 (*0-313-26630-1*, RRR/, Greenwood Pr) Greenwood.

Rodgers, J. Buddy & LeFever, Chuck. Poems for the Manly-Man: A State of Mind. rev. ed. (Illus.). 64p. 1997. reprint ed. pap. 9.95 (*0-9657732-0-5*) Protocol Grp.

Rodgers, Jack. Navigator's Log of a Tour in Bomber Command. (C). 1989. 35.00 (*0-86303-254-0*) St Mut.

— Selected Options for Expanding Health Insurance Coverage. (Illus.). 79p. (Orig.). (C). 1994. pap. text 30.00 (*0-7881-0418-7*) DIANE Pub.

Rodgers, James A., Jr., et al, eds. Rare & Endangered Biota of Florida Vol. V: Birds. (Illus.). 736p. 1997. 65.00 (*0-8130-1448-4*); pap. 29.95 (*0-8130-1449-2*) U Press Fla.

Rodgers, James B. An Archaeological Investigation of Buckeye Hills East, Maricopa County, Arizona. (Anthropological Research Papers: No. 10). (Illus.). vii, 116p. 1976. 10.00 (*0-685-19295-4*) AZ Univ ARP.

— Archaeological Investigations along the Granite Reef Aqueduct, Cave Creek Archaeological District, Arizona. (Anthropological Research Papers: No. 12). (Illus.). ix, 185p. 1977. pap. 15.00 (*0-685-19296-2*) AZ Univ ARP.

Rodgers, James B., jt. auth. see Henderson, T. Kathleen.

Rodgers, James T., jt. auth. see Rodgers-Rose, LaFrancis.

Rodgers, James W. A Winnie-the-Pooh Christmas Tail: Christmas Musical. 1994. pap. 5.95 (*0-87129-225-4*, W03) Dramatic Pub.

Rodgers, James W., adapted by. It's a Wonderful Life - Musical. 114p. Date not set. pap. 5.95 (*0-87129-963-1*, I02) Dramatic Pub.

Rodgers, James W. & Rodgers, Wanda C. Play Director's Survival Kit. 286p. 1997. pap. 29.50 (*0-87628-565-5*) Ctr Appl Res.

— Play Director's Survival Kit: A Complete Step-by-Step Guide to Producing Theater in Any School or Community Setting. LC 94-43944. (Illus.). 286p. 1995. pap. text 29.95 (*0-87628-862-X*) Ctr Appl Res.

Rodgers, Janine, jt. ed. see Rodgers, Gerry.

Rodgers, Jeff, ed. Acoustic Guitar Artist Songbook: 1997 Edition. 100p. 1997. pap. text 10.00 (*1-890490-02-4*) String Letter.

— Acoustic Guitar Artist Songbook, 1997 Edition. 100p. 1997. pap. text 29.95 (*1-890490-03-2*) String Letter.

Rodgers, Jeffrey P., ed. Acoustic Blues Guitar Essentials. LC 99-10966. (Acoustic Guitar Magazine's Private Lessons Ser.). 96p. 1999. pap. 19.95 (*1-890490-10-5*) String Letter.

— Acoustic Guitar Magazine's Private Lessons: 24 In-Depth Lessons. 100p. 1998. pap. 24.95 (*1-890490-04-0*) String Letter.

***Rodgers, Jeffrey P., ed.** Alternate Tunings Guitar Collection: CD Songbook. 64p. 2000. pap. 16.95 (*1-890490-27-X*) String Letter.

Rodgers, Jeffrey P., ed. Fingerstyle Guitar Essentials. LC 98-37042. (Acoustic Guitar Magazine's Private Lessons Ser.). 88p. 1998. pap. 19.95 (*1-890490-06-7*) String Letter.

***Rodgers, Jeffrey P., ed.** Habits of the Heart: CD Songbook. 80p. 1999. pap. 16.95 (*1-890490-16-4*) String Letter.

— Performing Acoustic Music. LC 00-23689. (Acoustic Guitar Guides Ser.). (Illus.). 104p. 2000. pap. 19.95 (*1-890490-22-9*) String Letter.

— Solo Fingerstyle Guitar Basics. 64p. 2000. pap. 14.95 (*1-890490-32-6*) String Letter.

— Songwriting & the Guitar. 96p. 2000. pap. 14.95 (*1-890490-28-8*) String Letter.

— What Goes Around: CD Songbook. 72p. 1999. pap. 16.95 (*1-890490-12-1*) String Letter.

Rodgers, Jeffrey P., ed. see James, Steve.

Rodgers, Jimmie. Jimmie Rodgers Memorial Folios, 2 vols., 1. 1979. pap. 12.95 (*0-89898-661-3*, A0053OPX) Wrner Bros.

— Jimmie Rodgers Memorial Folios, 2 vols., 2. 1979. pap. 12.95 (*0-686-09064-0*, A0054OPX) Wrner Bros.

Rodgers, Joann. Drugs & Pain. (Encyclopedia of Psychoactive Drugs Ser.: No. 2). (Illus.). 128p. (YA). (gr. 7 up). 1987. lib. bdg. 19.95 (*1-55546-212-X*) Chelsea Hse.

Rodgers, Joann E. & Adams, William C. Media Guide for Academics. 2nd ed. Ferring, Mike, ed. LC 94-61228. (Illus.). 72p. 1994. pap. 10.00 (*0-910755-02-7*) Foun Am Comm.

Rodgers, Joel, jt. auth. see Teixeira, Ruy.

Rodgers, John. Liturgy & Communication. (C). 1988. 45.00 (*0-85439-113-4*, Pub. by St Paul Pubns) St Mut.

Rodgers, John, jt. ed. see Schaer, Jean-Paul.

Rodgers, John H. Five Great Men: The Men of Rushmore & Dwight D. Eisenhower. (Illus.). 89p. 1998. pap. 12.00 (*0-9667280-0-9*) J H Rodgers.

Rodgers, Joni. Crazy for Trying. 1999. pap. 13.00 (*1-878448-92-7*) MacMurray & Beck.

— Sugar Land. LC 99-11176. 352p. 1999. pap. 12.00 (*1-883523-32-X*, Pub. by Spinsters Ink) SPD-Small Pr Dist.

Rodgers, Joseph J., Jr., tr. see Gounard, Jean-Francois.

Rodgers, Judith. Winston Churchill. (World Leaders Past & Present Ser.). (Illus.). 120p. (YA). (gr. 5 up). 1987. lib. bdg. 19.95 (*0-87754-563-4*) Chelsea Hse.

Rodgers, Julie B., jt. auth. see Boyko, Carrie J.

Rodgers, June S. Silver Linings: Triumph of the Challenger 7. LC 95-36078. (Illus.). 128p. 1995. 15.00 (*1-57312-034-0*) Smyth & Helwys.

Rodgers, June S., jt. auth. see Makuch, Jack.

Rodgers, Kathleen E., jt. auth. see DiZerega, Gere S.

Rodgers, Lawrence R. Canaan Bound: The African-American Great Migration Novel. LC 96-25270. 256p. 1997. pap. text 14.95 (*0-252-06605-7*) U of Ill Pr.

***Rodgers, Linda.** The Harvest of Great Poetry. 1999. pap. write for info. (*1-58235-139-2*) Watermrk Pr.

Rodgers, Linda H. Telling It Like It Is. 1998. pap. write for info. (*1-57553-964-0*) Watermrk Pr.

***Rodgers, Lori M., ed.** The P. U. R. Guide: Principles of Public Utilities Operations & Management. (Illus.). 560p. 1999. pap. 350.00i (*0-910325-76-6*) Public Util.

Rodgers, M. A., jt. auth. see Farhataziz.

Rodgers, M. E. Family Law: Cases & Materials. (Blackstone's LLB Ser.). 474p. 1998. pap. 42.00 (*1-85431-746-6*) Gaunt.

— Family Law: Learning Text. (Blackstone's LLB Ser.). 316p. 1998. pap. 42.00 (*1-85431-741-5*) Gaunt.

Rodgers, M. J. The Adventuress. (American Romance Ser.). 1994. per. 3.50 (*0-373-16520-X*, 1-16520-8) Harlequin Bks.

— Baby vs. the Bar. LC 95-22128. 251p. 1995. per. 3.50 (*0-373-22342-0*, 1-22342-9) Harlequin Bks.

— Beauty vs. the Beast. LC 96-437. (Intrigue Ser.). 251p. 1995. per. 3.50 (*0-373-22335-8*, 1-22335-3) Harlequin Bks.

— Bones of Contention. (Intrigue Ser.: No. 176). 1991. per. 2.79 (*0-373-22176-2*, 1-22176-1) Harlequin Bks.

— The Dream Wedding. (Intrigue Ser.: No. 445). 1997. per. 3.75 (*0-373-22445-1*, 1-22445-0) Harlequin Bks.

— Fire Magic. (American Romance Ser.). 1993. per. 3.50 (*0-373-16492-0*, 1-16492-0) Harlequin Bks.

— Love vs. Illusion. (Intrigue Ser.). 1996. per. 3.75 (*0-373-22375-7*, 1-22375-9) Harlequin Bks.

— Overruled by Love (Delta Justice) (Delta Justice Ser.). 1998. per. 4.50 (*0-373-82567-6*, 1-82567-8) Harlequin Bks.

— Risky Business. (Intrigue Ser.: No. 185). 1992. per. 2.89 (*0-373-22185-1*, 1-22185-2) Harlequin Bks.

— Santa Claus Is Coming. (Intrigue Ser.). 1993. per. 2.99 (*0-373-22254-8*, 1-22254-6) Harlequin Bks.

— To Die For. (Intrigue Ser.). 1993. per. 2.89 (*0-373-22214-9*, 1-22214-0) Harlequin Bks.

— To Die For. (Men at Work Ser.: Vol. 43). 1998. mass mkt. 4.50 (*0-373-81055-5*, 1-81055-5) Harlequin Bks.

— To Have vs. to Hold. (Intrigue Ser.). 1996. per. 3.75 (*0-373-22392-7*, 1-22392-4) Harlequin Bks.

— Who Is Jane Williams? LC 97-10542. (Intrigue Ser.). 250p. 1994. per. 2.99 (*0-373-22290-4*, 1-22290-0) Harlequin Bks.

Rodgers, Margaret. Locating Alexandra. LC 95-234501. (Illus.). 175p. 1995. pap. 20.00 (*1-55022-248-1*, Pub. by ECW) Genl Dist Srvs.

Rodgers, Margaret, ed. see Anglican Consultative Council Staff.

Rodgers, Marie E. The Harlem Renaissance: An Annotated Reference Guide for Student Research. LC 97-46660. (Illus.). 30p. 1998. student ed. 28.00 (*1-56308-580-1*) Libs Unl.

Rodgers, Mark. Guardian of the Gods: An Inside Look at the Dangerous Business of Music. (Illus.). 272p. 1999. 22.95 (*0-9671288-0-3*) Monkey Boy.

Rodgers, Mark E. Tracings the Civil War Veteran Pension System in the State of Virginia: Entitlement or Privilege. LC 98-4902. (Studies in American History: Vol. 24). 624p. 1999. text 129.95 (*0-7734-8198-2*) E Mellen.

***Rodgers, Marle E.** Multicultural Information Quests: Instant Research Lessons, Grades 5-8. LC 99-39119. 250p. 2000. pap. 29.50 (*1-56308-686-7*) Libs Unl.

Rodgers, Mary. Billion for Boris. (J). 1974. 9.05 (*0-606-00671-0*, Pub. by Turtleback) Demco.

— A Billion for Boris. LC 74-3586. (Trophy Bk.). 192p. (J). (gr. 5 up). 1976. reprint ed. pap. 3.95 (*0-06-440075-1*, HarpTrophy) HarpC Child Bks.

— ESP TV. LC 74-3586. 224p. (YA). (gr. 5 up). 1999. 4.95 (*0-06-440838-8*) HarpC Child Bks.

— Freaky Friday. LC 74-183158. 144p. (J). (gr. 4-7). 1972. 15.95 (*0-06-025048-8*) HarpC Child Bks.

— Freaky Friday. LC 74-183158. 144p. (YA). (gr. 4-7). 1972. lib. bdg. 15.89 (*0-06-025049-6*) HarpC Child Bks.

Rodgers, Mary. Freaky Friday. 145p. (J). (gr. 4-6). pap. 4.95 (*0-8072-1479-5*); pap. 4.95 (*0-8072-1390-X*) Listening Lib.

— Freaky Friday. (J). 1972. 10.05 (*0-606-04374-8*, Pub. by Turtleback) Demco.

Rodgers, Mary. Freaky Friday. LC 74-183158. (Trophy Bk.). (Illus.). 144p. (J). (gr. 5-9). 1972. reprint ed. pap. 4.95 (*0-06-440046-8*, HarpTrophy) HarpC Child Bks.

— Freaky Friday - Viernes Embrujado. McShane, Barbara & Alfaya, Javier, trs. (SPA.). 118p. (J). (gr. 5-8). 1987. pap. 5.95 (*84-204-3640-2*) Santillana.

— Summer Switch. LC 79-2690. (Charlotte Zolotow Bk.). 192p. (J). (gr. 5 up). 1982. 14.95 (*0-06-025058-5*); lib. bdg. 12.89 (*0-06-025059-3*) HarpC Child Bks.

— Summer Switch. LC 72-2690. (Trophy Bk.). (Illus.). 208p. (J). (gr. 5 up). 1982. pap. 4.95 (*0-06-440140-5*, HarpTrophy) HarpC Child Bks.

Rodgers, Mary. Summer Switch. 224p. (J). (gr. 4-6). pap. 4.95 (*0-8072-1550-3*) Listening Lib.

Rodgers, Mary. Un Viernes Embrujado. 1987. 11.05 (*0-606-10525-5*, Pub. by Turtleback) Demco.

Rodgers, Mary Augusta. Country Roads of Kentucky. 2nd ed. (Country Roads of... Ser.). 176p. pap. 12.95 (*1-56626-096-5*, 60965) NTC Contemp Pub Co.

Rodgers, Mary C. Catholic Marriage Poems, 1962-1979. rev. ed. (Illus.). 102p. 1998. pap. 10.00 (*0-89848-376-X*) Open Univ Am.

— Catholic Open University Poems, 1962-2000. (Illus.). 250p. 2000. pap. 20.00 (*0-89848-383-2*) Open Univ Am.

— Catholic Teacher Poems, 1945-1995. rev. ed. (Illus.). 262p. 1998. pap. 20.00 (*0-89848-378-6*) Open Univ Am.

— Catholic Widow with Children Poems, 1979-1993. rev. ed. (Illus.). 85p. 1998. pap. 10.00 (*0-89848-377-8*) Open Univ Am.

— Catholic Widow with Children Poems 1979-1993. LC 94-48866. 84p. 1995. pap. 14.95 (*0-7734-2756-2*, Mellen Poetry Pr) E Mellen.

— Convent Poems, 1943-1961. LC 92-32473. 76p. 1992. pap. 12.95 (*0-7734-0037-0*) E Mellen.

— Convent Poems, 1943-1961. rev. ed. (Illus.). 75p. 1998. pap. 10.00 (*0-89848-375-1*) Open Univ Am.

— First Access List to the Mary Columbro Rodgers Literary Trust (By Year) LC 95-109599. 60p. 1994. pap. text 10.00 (*0-89848-299-2*) Open Univ Am.

— Open University of America Founder, Mary Columbro Rodgers: Short Bio-Bibliography for Researchers. 220p. 1999. pap. 30.00 (*0-89848-381-6*) Open Univ Am.

— Open University of America the First Thirty-Five Years, 1965-2000: Memoir of the Founder. (Illus.). 350p. 2000. 35.00 (*0-89848-385-9*); pap. 29.00 (*0-89848-386-7*) Open Univ Am.

— Second Access List to the Mary Columbro Rodgers Literary Trust, by Alphabet. 60p. 1995. pap. text 10.00 (*0-89848-315-8*) Open Univ Am.

— Third Access List to the Mary Columbro Rodgers Literary Trust (By Subject) LC 98-66513. 60p. 1999. pap. 10.00 (*0-89848-379-4*) Open Univ Am.

Rodgers, Mary M. & Hoff, Mary K. Our Endangered Planet: Oceans. (Illus.). 72p. (J). (gr. 4 up). 1991. lib. bdg. 22.60 (*0-8225-2505-4*, Lerner Publctns) Lerner Pub.

Rodgers, Mary M., jt. auth. see Hoff, Mary K.

Rodgers, Mary M., jt. auth. see Winckler, Suzanne.

Rodgers, Mary M., jt. auth. see Yount, Lisa.

Rodgers, Megan, ed. Actor's Training Guide. 80p. 2000. pap. 6.00 (*1-56850-043-2*) Chicago Plays.

Rodgers, Mikkie. Homegrown . . . Back in the Day. 265p. 1997. reprint ed. pap. 14.95 (*0-9663541-1-7*) Creat Novels.

Rodgers, Nancy. Learning to Reason: An Introduction to Logic, Sets & Relations. 384p. 2000. 74.95 (*0-471-37122-X*) Wiley.

Rodgers, Nigel, ed. see Man, John, et al.

Rodgers, O. D. God's Plan Included Lupus. LC 98-85906. 152p. 1998. text 18.95 (*1-56167-443-5*) Noble House.

Rodgers, Patricia H. A Symphony of Color: Stained Glass at First Church. (Illus.). 63p. (Orig.). 1990. pap. write for info. (*0-9626196-0-4*) United Ch Cambridge.

Rodgers, Peter. Croatian-English-Croatian Prayer Book. 150p. 1986. pap. 12.00 (*0-614-08448-2*) Ragusan Pr.

— Knowing Jesus. rev. ed. 44p. (Orig.). 1990. pap. 1.95 (*0-88028-110-3*, 1076) Forward Movement.

Rodgers, R. E. The Incarnation of the Antithesis. 105p. (C). 1989. pap. text 40.00 (*1-872795-91-9*, Pub. by Pentland Pr) St Mut.

Rodgers, Raboo. Magnum Fault. 192p. (J). (gr. 5 up). 1984. 11.95 (*0-685-07882-5*, 5-95260) HM.

Rodgers, Richard. Do Re Mi: Sing-a-Song Storybooks. (J). (ps-3). 1994. 9.95 (*0-7935-3196-9*) H Leonard.

— Musical Stages: An Autobiography. (Illus.). 379p. 1995. reprint ed. pap. 14.95 (*0-306-80634-7*) Da Capo.

Rodgers, Richard. My Favorite Things. 32p. pap. 5.95 (*0-06-443627-6*) HarpC Child Bks.

— My Favorite Things. LC 99-63086. 32p. (J). 2000. 15.95 (*0-06-028710-1*) HarpC Child Bks.

Rodgers, Richard. Pipe Dream. (Vocal Score Ser.). 232p. 1981. per. 45.00 (*0-88188-045-0*, 00312321) H Leonard.

— Victory at Sea: Symphonic Scenario Intermediate. 24p. 1981. pap. 3.95 (*0-7935-4728-8*, 00312750) H Leonard.

Rodgers, Richard & Hammerstein, Oscar, II. Carousel: IMP Custom Print & Domestic. 56p. 1993. pap. 8.95 (*0-7935-2963-8*, 01121007) H Leonard.

— Carousel: Souvenir Edition. 64p. 1994. per. 15.95 (*0-7935-3688-X*, 00312513) H Leonard.

— Cinderella - Vocal Selections: Vocal Selections from the Show. rev. ed. (Illus.). 48p. 1981. pap. 8.95 (*0-88188-069-8*, HL 00312091) H Leonard.

— Climb Ev'ry Mountain: From the Sound of Music. (Piano-Vocal-Guitar Ser.). 4p. 1981. 3.95 (*0-7935-0607-7*, 00303393); spiral bd. 16.95 (*0-7935-3772-X*, 00312100) H Leonard.

— Edelweiss: From the Sound of Music. 6p. 1985. 3.95 (*0-7935-0606-9*, 00303525) H Leonard.

— Edelweiss from The Sound of Music. 4p. 1981. pap. 3.95 (*0-7935-0968-8*, 00300526) H Leonard.

— Honey Bun: From South Pacific. 6p. 1981. 3.95 (*0-7935-0816-9*, 00303932) H Leonard.

— I Enjoy Being a Girl: From Flower Drum Song. (Piano-Vocal-Guitar Ser.). 8p. 1981. 3.95 (*0-7935-0385-X*, 00304009) H Leonard.

— My Favorite Things: From the Sound of Music. (Piano-Vocal-Guitar Ser.). 6p. 1981. 3.95 (*0-7935-1149-6*, 00304530) H Leonard.

— Oklahoma! 72p. 1981. pap. 5.95 (*0-7935-3342-2*, 00301805) H Leonard.

— Rodgers & Hammerstein. 64p. 1989. pap. 9.95 (*0-7935-2115-7*, 00240825) H Leonard.

— Rodgers & Hammerstein: The Piano Duet Book for One Piano, Four Hands. 56p. 1981. pap. 7.95 (*0-7935-0498-8*, 00312691) H Leonard.

— Rodgers & Hammerstein Easy Piano Duets. 64p. 1991. pap. 6.95 (*0-7935-0560-7*, 00290327) H Leonard.

— Rodgers & Hammerstein Favorites. 48p. 1991. pap. 7.95 (*0-7935-0608-5*, 00290326) H Leonard.

— Rodgers & Hammerstein Styling of Dick Hyman: Easy Piano Solos. 64p. 1993. pap. 10.95 (*0-7935-1106-2*, 00290352) H Leonard.

— Selections from the Sound of Music. 16p. 1981. pap. 5.95 (*0-7935-0887-8*, 00301932) H Leonard.

— So Long, Farewell: From the Sound of Music. (Piano-Vocal-Guitar Ser.). 8p. 1981. 3.95 (*0-7935-0821-5*, 00305099) H Leonard.

— The Sound of Music: Big Note Piano. 64p. 1982. pap. 6.95 (*0-7935-1150-X*, 00302211) H Leonard.

— The Sound of Music: Piano Selection. 20p. 1981. pap. 5.95 (*0-7935-2562-4*, 00312713) H Leonard.

— The Sound of Music: Souvenir Folio. 76p. 1981. otabind 9.95 (*0-88188-218-6*, 00312394) H Leonard.

— The Sound of Music: Upper Intermediate for One Piano, Four Hands. 24p. 1981. pap. 6.95 (*0-7935-1152-6*, 00312714) H Leonard.

— The Sound of Music Selections: Beginners. 16p. 1981. pap. 5.95 (*0-7935-0967-X*, 00301933) H Leonard.

— The Sound of Music Xylotone Book. 1993. pap. 4.95 (*0-7935-2881-X*) H Leonard.

— South Pacific Selections: Piano. 16p. 1981. pap. 5.95 (*0-7935-5185-4*, 00301934) H Leonard.

— Younger Than Springtime: From South Pacific. 6p. 1981. 3.95 (*0-7935-0735-9*, 00305823) H Leonard.

Rodgers, Richard & Hammserstein, Oscar. The Sound of Music. 48p. 1982. pap. 7.95 (*0-7935-0758-8*, 00312715) H Leonard.

Rodgers, Richard, et al. Do Re Mi (Sing-a-Song Storybook Ser.). (Illus.). 24p. (J). 1994. 9.95 (*0-685-74740-9*) H Leonard.

Rodgers, Richard, jt. auth. see Head.

Rodgers, Richard K. Marketing Legal Services: Developing & Growing Client Relationships for the 1990s. 212p. 1993. student ed., spiral bd. write for info. (*0-9641994-0-8*) K Rodgers Grp.

Rodgers, Rick. Christmas 101. LC 99-31151. 192p. 1999. pap. 15.00 (*0-7679-0399-4*) Bantam.

— 50 Best Stuffings & Dressings. LC 97-40477. (Illus.). 112p. (Orig.). 1997. pap. 10.00 (*0-7679-0044-8*) Broadway BDD.

— Fondue: Great Food To Dip, Dunk, Savor, And Swirl. LC 97-38058. 112p. 1998. 15.00 (*0-688-15866-8*, Wm Morrow) Morrow Avon.

— Fried & True: Crispy & Delicious Dishes from Appetizers to Desserts. LC 98-13202. (Illus.). 144p. 1999. pap. 16.95 (*0-8118-1606-0*) Chronicle Bks.

***Rodgers, Rick.** Kaffee Haus. 2001. 35.00 (*0-609-60453-8*, Pub. by Crown Pub Group) Random House.

Rodgers, Rick. Mister Pasta's Healthy Cookbook: More Than 150 Delicious, Low-Fat Pastas, Pasta Sauces... LC 94-6664. 260p. 1994. 15.95 (*0-688-13077-1*, Wm Morrow) Morrow Avon.

— Mr. Pasta's Healthy Pasta Cookbook: More Than 150 Delicious, Low-Fat Pastas, Pasta Sauces, & Pasta Meals! 272p. 1996. reprint ed. pap. 12.00 (*0-688-14953-7*, Wm Morrow) Morrow Avon.

— On Rice: 60 Fast & Easy Toppings That Make the Meal. LC 96-7069. (Illus.). 144p. 1997. pap. 16.95 (*0-8118-1352-5*) Chronicle Bks.

— Simply Shrimp: Over 100 Recipes for Everybody's Favorite Seafood. LC 97-44798. 168p. 1998. pap. 16.95 (*0-8118-1967-1*) Chronicle Bks.

— The Slow Cooker Ready & Waiting Cookbook: 160 Sumptuous Meals That Cook Themselves. 256p. 1998. pap. 12.00 (*0-688-15803-X*, Wm Morrow) Morrow Avon.

— Thanksgiving 101: Celebrate America's Favorite Holiday with America's Thanksgiving Expert. LC 98-6290. 192p. 1998. pap. 15.00 (*0-7679-0136-3*) Broadway BDD.

***Rodgers, Rick & Ward, Arlene.** Pressure Cooking for Everyone. LC 99-53959. 2001. pap. 19.95 (*0-8118-2525-6*) Chronicle Bks.

Rodgers, Rick, jt. auth. see Kerr, W. Park.

Rodgers-Rose, Lafrancis. The Black Woman. LC 79-28712. (Focus Editions Ser.: Vol. 21). (Illus.). 316p. 1980. pap. 26.00 (*0-8039-1312-5*) Sage.

Rodgers-Rose, LaFrancis, ed. Violence Against Black Women Vol. 1: A Sociocultural Perspective. unabridged ed. 348p. (Orig.). 1996. pap. text 18.95 (*0-934185-02-6*) Traces Inst.

Rodgers-Rose, LaFrancis & Rodgers, James T. Resolving Conflict in Black Male-Female Relationships. LC 85-51272. 70p. (Orig.). 1985. pap. 10.95 (*0-934185-00-X*) Traces Inst.

Rodgers-Rose, LaFrancis, jt. ed. see Aldridge, Delores P.

Rodgers-Rose, LaFrancis, jt. ed. see Lawson, Erma J.

***Rodgers, S. J.** Missouri Palace. large type ed. 256p. 1999. pap. 18.99 (*0-7089-5500-2*, Linford) Ulverscroft.

Rodgers, Sanda, jt. ed. see Andrew, Caroline.

Rodgers, Sandy. Needlework Tips for the Novice & Expert. LC 95-90755. 115p. 1995. pap. text 27.95 (*0-9649081-6-6*) Yarn Cellar.

— Silk & Metal Threads on Canvas. expanded ed. LC 96-61312. 94p. 1996. pap. text 27.95 (*0-9649081-7-4*) Yarn Cellar.

Rodgers, Sandy, jt. auth. see Castelnuovo, Sheri.

Rodgers, Sarah S. The Ties of the Past: The Gettysburg Diaries of Salome Myers Stewart 1854-1922. (Illus.). 300p. (Orig.). 1996. pap. text 14.95 (*0-939631-91-1*) Thomas Publications.

Rodgers, Silvia. Red Saint, Pink Daughter. 292p. 1998. pap. 19.95 (*1-85754-325-4*, Pub. by Carcanet Pr) Paul & Co Pubs.

— Red Saint, Pink Daughter: A Communist Childhood in Berlin & London LC 96-183616. x, 282 p. 1996. write for info. (*0-233-98973-0*, Pub. by Andre Deutsch) Trafalgar.

Rodgers, Slats, jt. auth. see Stilwell, Hart.

Rodgers, Stephen, jt. auth. see Bleile, Henry R.

Rodgers, Susan. Power & Gold: Jewelry from Indonesia, Malaysia, & the Philippines from the Collection of the Barbier-Mueller Museum, Geneva. (Illus.). 369p. 1988. 85.00 (*3-7913-0859-9*, Pub. by Prestel) te Neues.

Rodgers, Susan, ed. Telling Lives, Telling Histories: Autobiography & Historical Imagination in Modern Indonesia. LC 94-30282. 1995. 23.00 (*0-520-08547-7*, Pub. by U CA Pr); pap. text 60.00 (*0-520-08546-9*, Pub. by U CA Pr) Cal Prin Full Svc.

Rodgers, Terry. The Library Paraprofessional: Notes from the Underground. LC 96-26371. 367p. 1997. lib. bdg. 48.50 (*0-7864-0222-9*) McFarland & Co.

Rodgers, Theodore S., jt. auth. see Richards, Jack C.

Rodgers, Tom, jt. auth. see Rodgers, Beverly.

Rodgers, Tom, jt. ed. see Berlekamp, Elwyn R.

Rodgers, Ulka. Oracle: A Database Developer's Guide. 2nd ed. 400p. (C). 1998. pap. text 49.99 (*0-13-841420-3*) P-H.

Rodgers, Vimala. Change Your Handwriting, Change Your Life. LC 93-6843. 144p. (Orig.). 1995. pap. 11.95 (*0-89087-693-2*) Celestial Arts.

— Your Handwriting Can Change Your Life: Handwriting as a Tool for Personal Growth. LC 99-46322. 176p. 2000. per. 11.00 (*0-684-86541-6*, Fireside) S&S Trade Pap.

Rodgers, W. A., jt. auth. see Holmwood, K. M.

Rodgers, W. R. & Longley, Michael. Poems. 108p. 1993. pap. 16.95 (*1-85235-106-3*) Dufour.

Rodgers, Wanda C., jt. auth. see Rodgers, James W.

Rodgers, Waymond. Throughput Modeling: Financial Information Used by Decision Makers. Epstein, Marc J., ed. LC 97-45684. (Studies in Managerial & Financial Accounting: Vol. 6). 1997. 78.50 (*0-7623-0340-9*) Jai Pr.

Rodgers, William, jt. auth. see Hoste, William.

Rodgers, William, jt. ed. see Cherry, Robert.

Rodgers, William H., Jr. Environmental Law: Air & Water, 2 vols. LC 86-5578. 1222p. 1987. reprint ed. text. write for info. (*0-314-98410-0*) West Pub.

— Environmental Law Vol. 3: Pesticides & Toxic Substances. 662p. 1989. reprint ed. text. write for info. (*0-314-43778-9*) West Pub.

— Environmental Law Vol. 4: Hazardous Waste & Substance. 702p. (C). 1991. pap. text. write for info. (*0-314-90896-X*) West Pub.

Rodgers, William H. Environmental Law Handbook. 2nd ed. 959p. Date not set. pap. text 10.00 (*0-314-06360-9*) West Pub.

Rodgers, William H., Jr. Environmental Law, 1996 Pocket Part. (Handbook Ser.). 200p. 1996. write for info. (*0-314-09682-5*) West Pub.

— Environmental Law, 1997 Pocket Part. 2nd ed. (Hornbook Ser.). 325p. 1997. text. write for info. (*0-314-22589-7*) West Pub.

Rodgers, William H. Hornbook on Environmental Law. 2nd ed. LC 94-11577. (Paralegal). 1158p. (C). 1998. text 41.00 (*0-314-03576-1*) West Pub.

Rodgers, William L. Greek & Roman Naval Warfare. LC 79-121795. (Illus.). 555p. 1964. reprint ed. 37.50 (*0-87021-226-5*) Naval Inst Pr.

Rodgerson, Thomas E. Spirituality, Stress & You. LC 94-31705. (Illumination Bks.). 80p. 1994. pap. 5.95 (*0-8091-3514-0*) Paulist Pr.

Rodgerson, Thomas E., jt. auth. see Wicks, Robert J.

Rodgon, Maris M. Single-Word Usage, Cognitive Development, & the Beginnings of Combinatorial Speech: A Study of Ten English-Speaking Children. LC 75-7211. 173p. reprint ed. pap. 49.40 (*0-608-12493-1*, 2024520) Bks Demand.

Rodhe, Henning & Herrera, R., eds. Acidification in Tropical Countries: (SCOPE 36) LC 88-5667. 424p. 1988. 530.00 (*0-471-91870-9*) Wiley.

Rodhe, W., et al, eds. Lake Metabolism & Management: Papers Emanating from the Limnological Jubilee Symposium of Uppsala University, 1477-1977. (Advances in Limnology Ser.: Vol. 13). (GER., Illus.). iv, 349p. (Orig.). 1979. 76.00 (*3-510-47011-7*, Pub. by E Schweizerbartsche) Balogh.

Rodi, jt. auth. see Swokowski.

Rodi, Frithjof, ed. see Dilthey, Wilhelm.

Rodi, Robert. The Bird Cage. 1996. pap. 10.95 (*0-452-27668-3*, Plume) Dutton Plume.

— Closet Case: A Novel. LC 93-47343. 336p. 1994. pap. 12.95 (*0-452-27211-4*, Plume) Dutton Plume.

— Drag Queen. 272p. 1996. pap. 12.95 (*0-452-27344-7*, Plume) Dutton Plume.

— Fag Hag. LC 91-20293. 304p. 1993. pap. 12.95 (*0-452-26940-7*, Plume) Dutton Plume.

— Kept Boy. 1997. pap. 12.95 (*0-452-27345-5*, Plume) Dutton Plume.

Rodi, W., et al, eds. Numerical Simulation of Unsteady Flows, Transition to Turbulence. (Illus.). 528p. (C). 1992. text 74.95 (*0-521-41618-3*) Cambridge U Pr.

Rodi, Wolfgang. Turbulence Models & Their Application in Hydraulics: A-State-of-the-Art Review. rev. ed. (IAHR Monograph Ser.). (Illus.). 120p. (C). 1995. 45.00 (*90-5410-150-4*, Pub. by A A Balkema) Ashgate Pub Co.

Rodi, Wolfgang & Bergeles, G., eds. Engineering Turbulence Modelling & Experiments 3: Proceedings of the Third International Symposium on Engineering Turbulence Modelling & Measurements, Crete, Greece, May 27-29, 1996. LC 96-12450. (Series in Thermal & Fluid Sciences). 932p. 1996. text 386.00 (*0-444-82463-4*) Elsevier.

Rodican, Andrew J. Get into the PA School of Your Choice. LC 97-29065. 125p. (C). 1998. pap. 41.95 (*0-8385-3132-6*, A-3132-6, Apple Lange Med) McGraw.

Rodichok, Lawrence D., jt. auth. see Russell, Garfield B.

Rodicio, Jose, ed. see Zanchetti, Albert.

Rodick, A., tr. see Fedoryuk, M. V.

Rodick, Burleigh C. Appomattox: The Last Campaign. 220p. 1988. reprint ed. 25.00 (*0-942211-58-8*) Olde Soldier Bks.

Rodieck, Jorma. The Little Bitty Snake. Burnett, Yumiko M., tr. LC 82-60393.Tr. of Le Tout P'tit Serpent. (ENG & JPN., Illus.). 24p. (J). (ps-4). 1983. pap. 4.95 (*0-940880-07-5*) Open Hand.

— The Little Bitty Snake. Confreras, Moyra, tr. LC 82-60393.Tr. of Le Tout P'tit Serpent. (ENG & SPA., Illus.). 24p. (J). (ps-4). 1983. pap. 4.95 (*0-940880-03-2*) Open Hand.

— The Little Bitty Snake. Presse, Michele, tr. LC 82-60393.Tr. of Le Tout P'tit Serpent. (ENG & FRE., Illus.). 24p. (J). (ps-4). 1983. pap. 4.95 (*0-940880-05-9*) Open Hand.

Rodieck, R. W. The First Steps in Seeing. LC 98-3963. (Illus.). 562p. 1998. text 81.95 (*0-87893-757-9*) Sinauer Assocs.

Rodiek, Jon E. & Bolen, Eric G. Wildlife & Habitats in Managed Landscapes. LC 90-41593. (Illus.). 217p. 1991. text 50.00 (*1-55963-053-1*); pap. text 30.00 (*1-55963-052-3*) Island Pr.

Rodier, Ann. What Do You Say to a Man Who Is Dying . . . ? LC 95-67828. 144p. (Orig.). 1995. pap. 13.95 (*1-886036-06-3*) Passages Pbg.

Rodier, David F., jt. ed. see Durfee, Harold A.

Rodier, G., tr. see Aristotle.

Rodig, Oscar R. Organic Chemistry Lab. (C). 1990. pap. text, teacher ed. 34.00 (*0-03-012648-7*) Harcourt Coll Pubs.

— Organic Chemistry Laboratory. 2nd ed. LC 96-68142. (C). 1996. pap. text, lab manual ed. 76.50 (*0-03-011648-1*, Pub. by Harcourt Coll Pubs) Harcourt.

Rodimzeva, C. The Kremlin & Its Treasures. (C). 1990. 575.00 (*0-7855-4489-5*, Pub. by Collets) St Mut.

Rodin, A. E. & Key, Jack. Medicine, Literature & Eponyms: Encyclopedia of Medical Eponymns Derived from Literary Characters. LC 88-542. 370p. 1989. pap. 32.50 (*0-89464-960-4*) Krieger.

— Medicine, Literature & Eponyms: Encyclopedia of Medical Eponyms Derived from Literary Characters. LC 88-542. 370p. (C). 1989. lib. bdg. 44.50 (*0-89464-277-4*) Krieger.

Rodin, A. E. & Key, Jack D. Medical Casebook of Doctor Arthur Conan Doyle: From Practitioner to Sherlock Holmes & Beyond. LC 83-16232. 506p. 1984. 53.50 (*0-89874-592-6*) Krieger.

Rodin, Alvin E., intro. Oslerian Pathology: An Assessment & Annotated Atlas of Museum Specimens. (Illus.). 250p. (C). 1981. 25.00 (*0-87291-144-6*) Coronado Pr.

Rodin, Auguste. Drawings of Rodin. Longstreet, Stephen, ed. (Master Draughtsman Ser.). (Illus.). 1965. pap. 4.95 (*0-87505-184-7*) Borden.

— Rodin. LC 99-201988. (Pegasus Library). 1999. 14.95 (*3-7913-2005-X*, Pub. by Prestel) te Neues.

Rodin, Auguste & Bonnet, Anne-Marie. Auguste Rodin: Erotic Drawings. LC 96-146062. 159p. 1995. write for info. (*0-500-09258-3*) Thames Hudson.

Rodin, Auguste, jt. auth. see Benedek, Nelly S.

Rodin, Cuia & Rodin, Tibor S. King Solomon's Feast: Culinary Delights from the Cuisine of Biblical Israel. Lee, Linda, ed. (Illus.). 175p. (Orig.). 1994. pap. 14.95 (*0-9644036-0-9*) C & T Rodin.

Rodin, Ermila. Sunset on an African Horizon. LC 99-72735. (Illus.). 120p. 1999. pap. text 8.95 (*1-58521-010-2*) Bks Black Chldn.

Rodin, Ervin Y. Computers & Mathematics with Applications: A Memorial Dedicated to Cornelius Lanczos. 1976. pap. 100.00 (*0-08-020521-6*, Pergamon Pr) Elsevier.

An Asterisk (*) at the beginning of an entry indicates that the title is appearing for the first time.

Rodin, Ervin Y. & Avula, Xavier J. Mathematical Modelling in Science & Technology: Proceedings of 6th International Conference, St Louis, MO, August 1987. (Mathematical Modeling Ser.). 1300p. 1989. pap. 315.00 (*0-08-036380-6*, Pergamon Pr) Elsevier.

Rodin, Gary, et al. Depression in the Medically Ill: An Integrated Approach. LC 90-26064. 384p. 1991. text 48.95 (*0-87630-596-6*) Brunner-Mazel.

Rodin, Gary M., ed. see Craven, John.

Rodin, Judith, et al, eds. Self-Directedness: Causes & Effects Throughout the Life Course. 280p. 1990. 59.95 (*0-8058-0562-1*) L Erlbaum Assocs.

Rodin, Judith, jt. ed. see Collins, A.

Rodin, R. Scott. Evil & Theodicy in the Theology of Karl Barth. LC 96-30661. (Issues in Systematic Theology Ser.: Vol. 3). X, 310p. (C). 1997. pap. text 34.95 (*0-8204-3496-5*) P Lang Pubng.

***Rodin, R. Scott.** Stewards in the Kingdom: A Theology of the Abundant Life. LC 99-53609. 2000. pap. 18.99 (*0-8308-1576-7*) InterVarsity.

***Rodin, Robert & Hartman, Curtis.** Free, Perfect & Now: Connecting to the Three Insatiable Customer Demands: A CEO's True Story. (Illus.). 256p. 2000. pap. 13.00 (*0-684-86312-X*, Touchstone) S&S Trade Pap.

Rodin, Robert L. Articles of Faith. LC 98-5521. 288p. 1998. 22.95 (*0-312-18532-4*, Thomas Dunne) St Martin.

— Free, Perfect & Now: Connecting to the Three Insatiable Customer Demands; A CEO's True Story. LC 98-47849. 256p. 1999. 25.00 (*0-684-85022-2*) S&S Trade.

Rodin, S. N. Graphs & Genes. Mirkin, B. G. & Beus, H. L., trs. (Biomathematics Ser.: Vol. II). 197p. 1984. 75.95 (*0-387-12657-0*) Spr-Verlag.

Rodin, S. N., et al. Molecular Evolution. (Biomathematics Ser.: Vol. 24). (Illus.). 445p. 1995. 152.95 (*0-387-57083-7*) Spr-Verlag.

Rodin, Tibor S., jt. auth. see Rodin, Cuia.

Rodin, Y. L. Generalized Analytic Functions on Riemann Surfaces. (Lecture Notes in Mathematics Ser.: Vol. 1288). v, 128p. 1987. 31.95 (*0-387-18572-0*) Spr-Verlag.

— The Riemann Boundary Problem on Riemann Surfaces. (C). 1988. text 140.50 (*90-277-2653-1*) Kluwer Academic.

Rodine, Floyd H. Yalta-Responsibility & Response: January-March 1945. 156p. 1974. pap. 8.50 (*0-87291-049-0*) Coronado Pr.

Rodini, Robert J. Antonfrancesco Grazzini, Poet, Dramatist, & Novelliere, 1503-1584. LC 71-106041. (Illus.). 262p. reprint ed. pap. 81.30 (*0-8357-6780-9*, 203545700095) Bks Demand.

Rodini, Robert J. & Di Maria, Salvatore. Ludovico Ariosto: An Annotated Bibliography of Criticism, 1956-1980. LC 84-2196. 288p. 1985. text 34.95 (*0-8262-0445-7*) U of Mo Pr.

Rodino, L. Linear Partial Differential Operators in Gevrey Spaces. 250p. 1993. text 61.00 (*981-02-0845-6*) World Scientific Pub.

Rodino, L., jt. ed. see Huang, Chen Z.

Rodino, Luigi, jt. auth. see Mascarello, Maria.

Rodinson, M. Cult, Ghetto & State: The Persistance of the Jewish Question. 240p. 1993. text 32.50 (*0-86356-110-1*, Pub. by Saqi) Intl Spec Bk.

Rodinson, Maxime. The Arabs. Goldhammer, Arthur, tr. LC 80-25916. (Illus.). 206p. (C). 1981. pap. text 13.00 (*0-226-72356-9*) U Ch Pr.

— Cult, Ghetto, & State: The Persistence of the Jewish Question. Rothschild, Jon, tr. from FRE. 239p. (Orig.). 1984. pap. 10.95 (*0-685-08870-7*) Evergreen Dist.

— Israel: A Colonial-Settler State? LC 73-78187. 120p. (Orig.). 1973. reprint ed. pap. 11.95 (*0-913460-23-0*) Pathfinder NY.

— Marxism & the Muslim World. Matthews, Jean, tr. LC 81-81695. 349p. reprint ed. pap. 108.20 (*0-7837-3910-9*, 204375800010) Bks Demand.

Rodinson, Maxime. Muhammad. 1996. pap. 17.95 (*0-14-024964-8*, Pub. by Pnguin Bks Ltd) Trafalgar.

***Rodio, Mary.** Me & My Sister. (J). (gr. k-3). 1999. pap. 5.95 (*0-533-13125-1*) Vantage.

Rodionov, Sergei N. Global & Regional Climate Interaction: The Caspian Sea Experience. (Water Science & Technology Library). 256p. (C). 1994. text 127.50 (*0-7923-2784-5*) Kluwer Academic.

Rodionov, Victor. America, America... (RUS., Illus.). 162p. 1998. pap. 10.00 (*0-9643971-6-1*) Isometry.

Rodionova. Russian-English Dictionary of Socio-Economic Terms. (ENG & RUS.). 1987. 75.00 (*0-8288-3974-3*, F39311) Fr & Eur.

Rodionova, Ludmila, jt. auth. see Karr, Nonna.

Rodis-Lewis, Genevieve. Descartes: His Life & Thought. Todd, Jane M., tr. from FRE. LC 97-38681. 264p. 1998. 39.95 (*0-8014-3372-X*, Comstock Pub) Cornell U Pr.

***Rodis-Lewis, Genevieve.** Descartes: His Life & Thought. 1999. pap. text 18.95 (*0-8014-8627-0*) Cornell U Pr.

Roditi, Edouard. Aphorisms: (Or Life with God the Father) 16p. 1991. 5.00 (*0-88031-068-5*) Invisible-Red Hill.

— Choose Your Own World. LC 91-73681. (Illus.). 112p. (Orig.). 1992. 20.00 (*1-878580-40-X*); pap. 7.95 (*1-878580-39-6*) Asylum Arts.

— Oscar Wilde. enl. rev. ed. LC 86-8578. 224p. 1986. pap. 10.95 (*0-8112-0995-4*, NDP633, Pub. by New Directions) Norton.

— Thrice Chosen. LC 81-9946. 135p. (Orig.). (C). 1981. pap. 5.00 (*0-87685-350-5*) Black Sparrow.

Roditi, Edouard, tr. see Bosquet, Alain.

Roditi, Edouard, tr. see Kemal, Yashar.

Roditti, Esther C. Computer Contracts, 4 vols. 1987. ring bd. 790.00 (*0-8205-1508-6*) Bender.

Rodke, Tamie. Bunnies, Bears, & Blooms. (Illus.). 40p. 1997. pap. 9.99 (*1-58050-012-9*, 40-6136) Provo Craft.

— I've Been Framed. (Illus.). 50p. 1998. 9.99 (*1-58050-052-8*) Provo Craft.

— Jolly Christmas Season. (Illus.). 40p. 1998. 9.99 (*1-58050-027-7*, 40-6156) Provo Craft.

Rodker, John. Poems & Adolphe, 1920. LC 96-182524. 280p. 1996. pap. 27.95 (*1-85754-060-3*, Pub. by Carcanet Pr) Paul & Co Pubs.

Rodkey, Geoff. Newtisms: Newt Gingrich on the Issues--From A to Z. 1995. mass mkt. 5.00 (*0-671-53533-1*) PB.

Rodkinson, Michael L. History of Amulets, Charms & Talismans. 1977. lib. bdg. 59.95 (*0-8490-1966-4*) Gordon Pr.

Rodla, Becky. Another Fire. LC 99-167281. 19p. 1997. pap. 7.00 (*0-938566-78-4*) Adastra Pr.

Rodley, Chris. Lynch on Lynch. 304p. 1999. pap. 15.95 (*0-571-19548-2*) Faber & Faber.

Rodley, Chris, ed. Cronenberg on Cronenberg. 1992. pap. 13.60 (*0-394-22270-9*) Beginner.

Rodley, Lyn. Byzantine Art & Architecture: An Introduction. LC 92-33797. (Illus.). 394p. (C). 1996. pap. text 39.95 (*0-521-35724-1*) Cambridge U Pr.

Rodley, Nigel S. The Treatment of Prisoners under International Law. 2nd ed. LC 98-45050. 510p. 1999. text 112.00 (*0-19-826564-6*) OUP.

Rodley, Nigel S. The Treatment of Prisoners under International Law. LC 86-16433. 335p. 1987. pap. 45.00 (*0-19-825563-2*) OUP.

***Rodley, Nigel S.** The Treatment of Prisoners under International Law. 2nd ed. 512p. 2000. pap. text 39.95 (*0-19-826563-8*) OUP.

Rodley, Nigel S., ed. To Loose the Bands of Wickedness: International Intervention in Defense of Human Rights. 287p. 1992. 40.00 (*1-85753-047-0*, Pub. by Brasseys) Brasseys.

Rodli, Agnes. Alone in My Kayak. 280p. (Orig.). 1993. pap. 9.99 (*1-56043-768-5*, Treasure Hse) Destiny Image.

***Rodli, Agnes.** Strait Gate: A Norse Saga - Mission to the Diomede Islands in the 1920's. LC 99-63243. 192p. 1999. pap. 10.99 (*1-57921-198-4*, Pub. by WinePress Pub) BookWorld.

Rodlich, Friedrich H. Von der Bleicherei Zur Textilchemie: Strukturwandlungen der Textilveredlung Seit 1945, Dargestellt Am Beispiel des Westmunsterlandes. (Illus.). 242p. 1998. 39.95 (*3-631-33709-4*) P Lang Pubng.

Rodman. The New Bulic Speaker, 97. (C). 1996. 26.00 (*0-15-505505-4*) Harcourt.

Rodman, Barbara. Love Stories for All Centuries. 96p. 1984. 8.95 (*0-89697-143-0*) Intl Univ Pr.

Rodman, Blake H., jt. ed. see Wolk, Ronald A.

Rodman, Debra, jt. auth. see Hinckley, David.

Rodman, Dennis. Bad As I Wanna Be. 336p. 1997. mass mkt. 6.99 (*0-440-22266-4*) Dell.

Rodman, Dennis & Keown, Tim. Bad As I Wanna Be. (Illus.). 240p. 1996. 22.95 (*0-385-31639-9*) Delacorte.

***Rodman, F. R.** The Spontaneous Gesture: Selected Letters of D. W. Winnicott. 256p. 1999. pap. 30.00 (*1-85575-234-4*, Pub. by H Karnac Bks Ltd) Other Pr LLC.

Rodman, F. Robert, ed. The Spontaneous Gesture: Selected Letters of D. W. Winnicott. LC 86-18483. (Illus.). 256p. 1987. pap. 32.00 (*0-674-83336-8*) HUP.

Rodman, George. The New Public Speaker. (C). 1997. pap. text, teacher ed. 17.75 (*0-15-503159-7*) Harcourt Coll Pubs.

Rodman, George & Adler, Ronald B. The New Public Speaker. LC 95-81786. 496p. (C). 1996. pap. text 46.50 (*0-15-502708-5*, Pub. by Harcourt Coll Pubs) Harcourt.

Rodman, George, jt. auth. see Adler, Ronald B.

Rodman, Gilbert B. Elvis after Elvis: The Posthumous Career of a Living Legend. LC 96-8157. (Illus.). 280p. (C). 1996. 80.00 (*0-415-11002-5*); pap. 17.99 (*0-415-11003-3*) Routledge.

***Rodman, Helen D.** From This Day Forward: Memoirs of an Attache Wife. LC 99-30577. 354p. 1999. 15.95 (*1-883911-33-8*) Brandylane.

Rodman, Hyman & Trost, Jan, eds. The Adolescent Dilemma: International Perspectives on Family Planning - Rights of Minors. LC 86-608. 270p. 1986. 49.95 (*0-275-92080-1*, C2080, Praeger Pubs) Greenwood.

Rodman, Hyman, et al. The Abortion Question. 250p. 1990. pap. text 20.00 (*0-231-05333-9*) Col U Pr.

— The Sexual Rights of Adolescents: Competence, Vulnerability, & Parental Control. LC 83-14440. 183p. 1988. pap. text 18.50 (*0-231-04917-X*) Col U Pr.

Rodman, John S., et al. No More Kidney Stones. LC 95-52786. 240p. 1996. pap. 15.95 (*0-471-12587-3*) Wiley.

Rodman, John S., ed. see Carrithers, Russell L.

Rodman, Kenneth. Sanctity vs. Sovereignty: The United States & the Nationalization of Natural Resource Investments. 448p. 1988. text 69.00 (*0-231-06448-9*) Col U Pr.

Rodman, L., jt. auth. see Lancaster, P.

Rodman, Leiba. An Introduction to Operator Polynomials. (Operator Theory Ser.: No. 38). 394p. 1989. 150.50 (*0-8176-2324-8*) Birkhauser.

Rodman, Margaret & Cooper, Matthew, eds. The Pacification of Melanesia. LC 83-14551. (ASAO Monographs: No. 7). 246p. (C). 1983. reprint ed. lib. bdg. 52.00 (*0-8191-3404-X*) U Pr of Amer.

Rodman, Margaret, jt. ed. see Rensel, Jan.

Rodman, Margaret C., jt. auth. see Cooper, Matthew.

Rodman, Philander, Jr. & Storm, Tom. The Original Bad Boy: Meet Dennis Rodman's Father. (Illus.). 64p. 1997. pap. 11.95 (*1-880047-57-8*) Creative Des.

***Rodman, Randy.** Extreme Investor: Intelligent Information from the Edge. 2000. pap. 17.95 (*1-891984-16-0*, Pub. by Entrepreneur) Natl Bk Netwk.

Rodman, Randy, jt. auth. see Brourman, Sherri.

Rodman, Randy, jt. auth. see Brourman, Sherry.

Rodman, Richard S. 17 Laws of Successful Investing: Ignore Them at Your Own Risk. LC 96-84039. (Illus.). 119p. 1996. 14.95 (*0-9651353-2-2*) Alidan Pr.

Rodman, Richard S. & Konkle, Burton A. Early Relations of Delaware & Pennsylvania. Incl. Delaware: A Grant Yet Not a Grant. LC 79-164622. LC 79-164622. (Select Bibliographies Reprint Ser.). 1977. reprint ed. 15.95 (*0-8369-5905-1*) Ayer.

Rodman, Robert. Computer Speech Technology. LC 98-51804. 439p. 1999. 73.00 (*0-89006-297-8*) Artech Hse.

Rodman, Robert, jt. auth. see Fromkin, Victoria.

Rodman, Robert D., jt. auth. see Klevans, Richard L.

Rodman, Robert M. Commercial Arbitration with Forms. LC 84-15345. (Handbook Ser.). 767p. 1988. reprint ed. text 80.00 (*0-314-86732-5*) West Pub.

— Commercial Arbitration with Forms: 1992 Pocket Parts. 180p. 1992. pap. text. write for info. (*0-318-68976-6*) West Pub.

— Commercial Arbitration with Forms: 1995 Pocket Part. Fever, William, ed. (West's Handbook Ser.). 240p. 1994. write for info. (*0-314-05382-4*) West Pub.

Rodman, Selden. The Brazil Traveler. LC 75-13350. (Illus.). 104p. 1975. pap. 9.95 (*0-8159-5113-2*) Devin.

— Eye of Man. (Illus.). 1955. 15.00 (*0-8159-5403-4*) Devin.

— Genius in the Backlands: The Popular Artists of Brazil. 10.00 (*0-8159-5616-9*) Devin.

— Geniuses & Other Eccentrics: Photographing My Friends. LC 96-78049. (Illus.). 185p. (Orig.). 1997. 22.00 (*0-9645891-1-7*) Green Trees CA.

— The Insiders: Rejection & Rediscovery of Man in the Arts of Our Time. LC 60-15433. (Illus.). 186p. 1960. reprint ed. pap. 57.70 (*0-7837-9878-4*, 206060400006) Bks Demand.

— Tongues of Fallen Angels. LC 73-89485. (Illus.). 288p. 1974. 12.00 (*0-8112-0528-2*, Pub. by New Directions); pap. 3.75 (*0-8112-0529-0*, NDP373, Pub. by New Directions) Norton.

— Where Art Is Joy: Haitian Art--The First Forty Years. 1988. 60.00 (*0-938291-01-7*) R deLatour.

Rodman, Selden, ed. Poetry of Flight. LC 75-76939. (Granger Index Reprint Ser.). 1977. 19.95 (*0-8369-6041-6*) Ayer.

Rodman, Selden & Cleaver, Carole. Spirits of the Night: The Vaudun Gods of Haiti. (Illus.). 144p. (Orig.). 1992. pap. 16.00 (*0-88214-354-9*) Spring Pubns.

Rodman, Selden & Kearns, James. The Heart of Beethoven. LC 76-51291. (Illus.). 157p. 1977. reprint ed. lib. bdg. 49.75 (*0-8371-9441-5*, ROHE, Greenwood Pr) Greenwood.

Rodman, Selden & Thompson, Robert F. Artists in Tune with Their World: Popular Artists of the Americas from the Selden Rodman Collection. Komanecky, Michael, ed. (Illus.). 32p. (Orig.). 1985. pap. 4.50 (*0-89467-037-9*) Yale Art Gallery.

Rodman, Selden, jt. ed. see Bingham, Alfred M.

Rodman, Selden, jt. ed. see Eberhart, Richard.

Rodman, William L. & Counts, Dorothy A., eds. Middlemen & Brokers in Oceania. (ASAO Monographs: No. 9). 318p. (C). 1983. reprint ed. pap. text 23.00 (*0-8191-3468-6*) U Pr of Amer.

Rodmann, Dorothy, et al. Career Transitions for Chemists: Making It Happen. LC 94-38410. (An American Chemical Society Publication). 178p. 1995. pap. 15.95 (*0-8412-3038-2*, Pub. by Am Chemical); text 34.00 (*0-8412-3052-8*, Pub. by Am Chemical) OUP.

Rodmell, Jane. Summer Weekend Cookbook: Recipes, Tips & Entertaining Ideas. (Illus.). 224p. 1997. pap. 24.95 (*0-9696922-2-6*) Firefly Bks Ltd.

***Rodner, Clemencia, et al.** A Checklist of the Birds of Northern South America: An Annotated Checklist of the Species & Subspecies of Ecuador, Colombia, Venezuela, Aruba, Curacao, Bonaire, Trinidad & Tobago, Guyana, Suriname & French Guiana. (Illus.). 136p. 2000. pap. 23.50 (*0-300-08740-3*) Yale U Pr.

Rodner, William S. & Turner, J. M. J. M. W. Turner: Romantic Painter of the Industrial Revolution. LC 97-11127. 210p. 1997. 45.00 (*0-520-20479-4*, Pub. by U CA Pr) Cal Prin Full Svc.

***Rodnesky, Stephen.** A Broken Covenant: The Rape of the American Middle Class. LC HD75. 142p. 2000. pap. 12.95 (*0-9700890-0-7*) BMES.

Rodney, Janet. The Book of Craving. deluxe limited ed. (Illus.). 59p. 1996. 125.00 (*0-9652272-0-0*) Grey Spider.

— Orphydice. 56p. (Orig.). 1986. 17.50 (*0-938535-76-5*); pap. 7.00 (*0-938535-75-7*) Salt-Works Pr.

Rodney, Janet. Incloser: An Essay by Susan Howe. 54p. 1992. 175.00 (*1-878460-01-3*) Weaselsleeves Pr.

Rodney, Janet, ed. see Prechtel, Martin.

Rodney, Patricia. The Caribbean State, Health Care & Women: An Analysis of Barbados & Grenada During the 1979-1983 Period. LC 96-47412. 294p. 1996. 79.95 (*0-86543-516-2*); pap. 21.95 (*0-86543-517-0*) Africa World.

Rodney, Reginald. The Songwriters Song. 148p. 1998. pap. 12.95 (*1-85756-352-2*, Pub. by Janus Pubng) Paul & Co Pubs.

Rodney, Robert M. Mark Twain Overseas. (Time - Place Ser.: No. 5). 350p. 1993. pap. 20.00 (*1-57889-055-1*) Passeggiata.

Rodney, Robert M., ed. Mark Twain International: A Bibliography & Interpretation of His Worldwide Popularity. LC 81-13441. 275p. 1982. lib. bdg. 65.00 (*0-313-23135-4*, RMT/, Greenwood Pr) Greenwood.

Rodney, Thomas. Diary of Captain Thomas Rodney. (American Biography Ser.). 53p. 1991. reprint ed. lib. bdg. 59.00 (*0-7812-8325-6*) Rprt Serv.

— A Journey Through the West: Thomas Rodney's 1803 Journal from Delaware to the Mississippi Territory. Smith, Dwight L. & Swick, Ray, eds. LC 97-8182. (Illus.). 270p. 1997. text 44.95 (*0-8214-1179-9*) Ohio U Pr.

Rodney, Walter. A History of the Guyanese Working People, 1881-1905. 312p. 1981. pap. 16.95 (*0-8018-2447-8*) Johns Hopkins.

— How Europe Underdeveloped Africa. rev. ed. LC 81-6240. 312p. 1982. pap. 12.95 (*0-88258-096-5*) Howard U Pr.

Rodney, William. Kootenai Brown: Canada's Unknown Frontiersman. LC 94-910601. (Illus.). 256p. 1996. pap. 17.95 (*1-895811-31-7*) Heritage Hse.

Rodney, William S., jt. auth. see Rolfs, Claus E.

Rodnick, David. The Fort Belknap Assinboine of Montana: A Study in Culture Change. LC 76-43811. reprint ed. 37.50 (*0-404-15666-5*) AMS Pr.

R

Rodnight, Richard, jt. ed. see Marks, Neville.

Rodning, Charles B. Swaying Grass: Haiku & Senryu. (Scots Plaid Press Haiku Ser.). 160p. 1988. pap. 25.00 (*1-879009-29-3*) Old Barn Entrprs.

Rodning, Charles B. & Rodning, Mary E. Elan Vital: A Chapbook of Oriental Poetry & Sumi-e Painting. LC 88-50166. (Illus.). 78p. 1988. 15.95 (*0-8048-1539-9*) Tuttle Pubng.

Rodning, Mary E., jt. auth. see Rodning, Charles B.

Rodning, Warren. Controlling Public Health Nuisances: A Guide for Community Health Boards (in Minnesota) (Illus.). 84p. (C). 1999. reprint ed. pap. text 30.00 (*0-7881-8002-9*) DIANE Pub.

Rodnitsky, Donna. The Complete Indoor/Outdoor Grill: 175 Delicious Recipes with Variations Based on Where You Cook. LC 97-39139. 336p. 1998. spiral bd. 18.00 (*0-7615-1233-0*) Prima Pub.

Rodnitzky, Conna. Lowfat Grill. 336p. 1998. per. 18.00 (*0-7615-1789-8*) Prima Pub.

Rodnitzky, Donna. Main Course Salads: Creative Salads That Satisfy. LC 99-15219. (Illus.). 255p. 1999. pap. 14.95 (*0-89529-928-3*, Avery) Penguin Putnam.

— 101 Great Lowfat Desserts: No Butter, No Cream, No Kidding! LC 94-33548. 304p. 1995. pap. 12.95 (*1-55958-666-4*) Prima Pub.

***Rodnitzky, Donna Pliner.** Ultimate Juicing: Delicious Recipes for over 125 of the Best Fruit & Vegetable Juice Combinations. (Illus.). 2000. pap. 12.95 (*0-7615-2576-9*) Prima Pub.

— Ultimate Smoothies: Delicious Recipes for over 125 of the Best Smoothies, Freezes & Blasts. (Illus.). 2000. pap. 12.95 (*0-7615-2575-0*) Prima Pub.

Rodnitzky, Jerome L. Minstrels of the Dawn: The Folk-Protest Singer As a Cultural Hero. LC 76-4520. 214p. 1976. text 34.95 (*0-88229-284-6*); pap. text 24.95 (*0-88229-427-X*) Burnham Inc.

Rodnitzky, Jerry & Rodnitzky, Shirley. Jazz-Age Boomtown. LC 96-52031. (Charles & Elizabeth Prothro Texas Photography Ser.: Vol. 5). (Illus.). 160p. (C). 1997. pap. 20.95 (*0-89096-757-1*) Tex A&M Univ Pr.

Rodnitzky, Jerry L. Feminist Phoenix: The Rise & Fall of a Feminist Counterculture, 1960-1995. LC 98-53394. 232p. 1999. 55.00 (*0-275-96575-9*, Praeger Pubs) Greenwood.

Rodnitzky, Shirley, jt. auth. see Rodnitzky, Jerry.

Rodnyi, Piotr A. Physical Process in Inorganic Scintillators. LC 96-29773. 240p. 1997. boxed set 149.95 (*0-8493-3788-7*) CRC Pr.

Rodo, C., et al. AP Examination in Spanish. LC 98-67396. (SPA.). 400p. 1999. pap. text 28.95 incl. audio (*0-87891-699-7*) Res & Educ.

Rodo, Jose E. Ariel. Peden, Margaret Sayers, tr. LC 87-19202. 156p. 1988. pap. 9.95 (*0-292-70396-1*) U of Tex Pr.

— Ariel: Estudio Critico de Leopaldo Alas (Clarin) (Nueva Austral Ser.: Vol. 216). (SPA.). 1991. pap. text 24.95 (*84-239-7216-X*) Elliots Bks.

— The Motives of Proteus. 1973. lib. bdg. 250.00 (*0-87968-384-8*) Gordon Pr.

Rodolff, Rebecca, ed. see Cutburth, Ronald W.

Rodolfo, Benavides. Diccionario De Suenos. (SPA.). 385p. 1997. pap. text 19.98 (*968-13-2365-3*) Libros Fronteras.

— Dramaticas Profecias De La Gran Piramide. (SPA., Illus.). 413p. 1997. pap. text 23.98 (*968-13-1011-X*) Edit Diana.

Rodolfo, Kelvin S., ed. see Lisitzin, Alexander P.

Rodolph, Stormy. Quest for Courage. (Indian Culture Ser.). (Illus.). 102p. (Orig.). (J). (gr. 4-12). 1984. pap. 6.95 (*0-89992-092-6*) Coun India Ed.

— Quest for Courage. 2nd ed. (Council for Indian Education Ser.). (Illus.). 112p. (Orig.). (J). (gr. 4-7). 1993. pap. 8.95 (*1-879373-57-2*) Roberts Rinehart.

Rodolphe de la Chavanne Dareste. La Science du Droit en Grece: Platon, Aristote, Theophraste. LC 75-13259. (History of Ideas in Ancient Greece Ser.). (FRE.). 1976. reprint ed. 23.95 (*0-405-07301-1*) Ayer.

Rodon, Francesc, jt. auth. see Vila-Grau, Joan.

Rodono, Marcello, jt. ed. see Byrne, Patrick B.

Rodoreda, Merce. My Christina & Other Stories. Rosenthal, David H., tr. from CAT. LC 84-81626. (Short Fiction Ser.). 133p. 1984. pap. 11.00 (*0-915308-65-7*) Graywolf.

Rodorf, E. Hugh, jt. ed. see Hodges, Richard E.

Rodot, ed. Renewable Energies in Europe. 210p. 1994. pap. text 508.00 (*3-7186-5618-3*, Harwood Acad Pubs) Gordon & Breach.

Rodowick, D. N. Crisis of Political Modernism: Criticism & Ideology in Contemporary Film Criticism. LC 94-25112. 1994. pap. 16.95 (*0-520-08771-2*, Pub. by U CA Pr) Cal Prin Full Svc.

— The Crisis of Political Modernism: Criticism & Ideology in Contemporary Film Theory. 320p. 1988. text 29.95 (*0-252-01533-9*) U of Ill Pr.

— Gilles Deleuze's Time-Machine. LC 96-38132. 258p. 1997. pap. text 16.95 (*0-8223-1970-5*) Duke.

Rodowick, David N. Gilles Deleuze's Time-Machine. LC 96-38132. 320p. 1997. lib. bdg. 49.95 (*0-8223-1962-4*) Duke.

Rodowksy, Colby. Lucy Peale. large type ed. 216p. 1993. reprint ed. lib. bdg. 15.95 (*1-56054-611-5*) Thorndike Pr.

Rodowsky, Colby. Dog Days. 144p. (J). (gr. 4-7). 1993. pap. 4.50 (*0-374-41818-7*) FS&G.
— Dog Days. (J). 1993. 9.60 (*0-606-05237-2*, Pub. by Turtleback) Demco.
— Gathering Room. 1995. 11.05 (*0-606-09311-7*, Pub. by Turtleback) Demco.
— H, My Name Is Henley. LC 82-12164. 184p. (YA). (gr. 5 up). 1982. 14.00 (*0-374-32831-5*) FS&G.
— Hannah in Between. LC 93-35478. 160p. (YA). (gr. 7 up). 1994. 15.00 (*0-374-32837-4*) FS&G.
— Hannah in Between. 160p. (J). (gr. 3-7). 1996. pap. 3.95 (*0-8167-3740-1*, Troll Medallion) Troll Communs.
Rodowsky, Colby. Hannah in Between. (J). 1994. 9.05 (*0-606-08769-9*, Pub. by Turtleback) Demco.
— Jason Rat a Tat. LC 99-54085. 2001. text. write for info. (*0-374-33671-7*) FS&G.
Rodowsky, Colby. Keeping Time. LC 83-14122. 137p. (J). (gr. 4-7). 1983. 11.95 (*0-374-34061-7*) FS&G.
— Lucy Peale. 208p. (YA). 1992. 15.00 (*0-374-36381-1*) FS&G.
— Lucy Peale. (Aerial Fiction Ser.). 176p. (YA). (gr. 7 up). 1994. pap. text 3.95 (*0-374-44659-8*, Sunburst Bks) FS&G.
— Not My Dog. (Illus.). 80p. (J). (gr. 2-5). 1999. 15.00 (*0-374-35531-2*) FS&G.
— Remembering Mog. LC 95-30616. 144p. (J). (gr. 7 up). 1996. 15.00 (*0-374-34663-1*) FS&G.
— Remembering Mog. LC 95-30616. 144p. (YA). (gr. 7-12). 1998. mass mkt. 3.99 (*0-380-72922-9*, Avon Bks) Morrow Avon.
— Remembering Mog. 1998. 9.09 (*0-606-13736-X*, Pub. by Turtleback) Demco.
***Rodowsky, Colby.** Spindrift. LC 99-36263. (Illus.). 144p. (YA). (gr. 5-9). 2000. 15.00 (*0-374-37155-5*) FS&G.
Rodowsky, Colby. Sydney, Herself. 192p. (YA). (gr. 7 up). 1993. pap. 4.50 (*0-374-47390-0*, Sunburst Bks) FS&G.
— Sydney, Herself. 1993. 9.60 (*0-606-06044-8*, Pub. by Turtleback) Demco.
— Sydney, Invincible. LC 94-22440. 160p. (YA). (gr. 7 up). 1995. 14.00 (*0-374-37365-5*) FS&G.
Rodowsky, Colby. The Turnabout Shop. LC 97-33229. 144p. (J). (gr. 4-7). 1998. 16.00 (*0-374-37889-4*) FS&G.
***Rodowsky, Colby.** The Turnabout Shop. LC 97-33229. (Illus.). 144p. (J). (gr. 3-7). 2000. pap. 4.95 (*0-380-73192-4*) Morrow Avon.
Rodrick, Gary E., jt. auth. see Otwell, Steven.
Rodrick, Scott. 2000 Employee Stock Ownership Plans: A Practical Guide to Esops & Other Broad Ownership Plans. 1999. pap. text 89.00 (*0-15-606975-X*) Harcourt.
***Rodrick, Scott.** 2000 Employee Stock Ownership Plans: A Practical Guide to Esops & Other Broad Ownership Plans. 1999. pap. text 89.00 (*0-15-606976-8*) Harcourt.
Rodrick, Scott, ed. Incentive Compensation & Employee Ownership. 2nd ed. (Illus.). 186p. 1998. pap. 35.00 (*0-926902-45-8*) NCEO.
— Model Equity Compensation Plans. 1999. ring bd. 75.00 (*0-926902-37-7*) NCEO.
***Rodrick, Scott S.** Leveraged ESOPs & Employee Buyouts: How to Use an Employee Ownership Plan (ESOP) 3rd rev. enl. ed. (Illus.). viii, 272p. 2000. pap. 35.00 (*0-926902-62-8*) NCEO.
***Rodrick, Scott S., ed.** Equity-Based Compensation for Multinational Corporations: Using Stock Options & Other Plans to Reward a Global Workforce. 2nd ed. 152p. 1999. pap. 35.00 (*0-926902-61-X*) NCEO.
— ESOP Valuation. (Illus.). 184p. 1999. pap. 35.00 (*0-926902-58-X*) NCEO.
— Incentive Compensation & Employee Ownership. 3rd ed. (Illus.). 200p. 1999. pap. 35.00 (*0-926902-54-7*) NCEO.
Rodrick, Scott S., ed. Section 401(k) Plans & Employee Ownership. 2nd rev. ed. (Illus.). 120p. 1999. pap. 35.00 (*0-926902-51-2*) NCEO.
***Rodrick, Scott S., ed.** Selling to an ESOP: How to Sell a Closely Held Business to Its Employees & Achieve a Win-Win Outcome. 5th ed. (Illus.). 200p. 1999. pap. 35.00 (*0-926902-60-1*) NCEO.
— Stock Options: Beyond the Basics. 256p. 1999. pap. 35.00 (*0-926902-59-8*) NCEO.
— The Stock Options Book: How You Can Use Broad-Based Employee Stock Option Plans & Related Programs. 3rd ed. 258p. 1999. pap. 35.00 (*0-926902-56-3*) NCEO.
Rodrick, Scott S., ed. see Kardas, Peter A., et al.
Rodrick, Sharon, jt. auth. see Butler, Des.
Rodricks, Dan. Mencken Doesn't Live Here Anymore. (Orig.). 1989. 18.95 (*0-913123-27-7*) Galileo.
Rodricks, Dan & Brown, Carolyn S. Baltimore: Charm City. LC 97-40374. (Urban Tapestry Ser.). (Illus.). 400p. 1997. 44.95 (*1-881096-50-5*) Towery Pub.
Rodricks, J. V., jt. auth. see Tardiff, R. G.
Rodricks, Joseph V. Calculated Risks: The Toxicity & Human Health Hazards of Chemicals in Our Environment. (Illus.). 282p. (C). 1994. pap. text 17.95 (*0-521-42331-7*) Cambridge U Pr.
Rodricks, Joseph V., ed. Mycotoxins & Other Fungal Related Food Problems. LC 76-4547. (Advances in Chemistry Ser.: No. 149). 1976. 49.95 (*0-8412-0222-2*) Am Chemical.
— Mycotoxins & Other Fungal Related Food Problems. LC 76-4547. (Advances in Chemistry Ser.: Vol. 149). 422p. 1976. reprint ed. pap. 130.90 (*0-608-03889-X*, 206433600008) Bks Demand.
Rodricks, Joseph V. & Tardiff, Robert G., eds. Assessment & Management of Chemical Risks. LC 83-25851. (ACS Symposium Ser.: No. 239). 184p. 1984. lib. bdg. 44.95 (*0-8412-0821-2*) Am Chemical.
— Assessment & Management of Chemical Risks. LC 83-25851. (ACS Symposium Ser.: Vol. 239). 191p. 1984. reprint ed. pap. 59.30 (*0-608-03070-8*, 206352300007) Bks Demand.

Rodridge, Ron. Tao Te Ching: About the Way of Nature & Its Powers. LC 91-46362. 176p. (Orig.). 1992. pap. 8.95 (*0-89529-506-7*, Avery) Penguin Putnam.
Rodriggs, Lawrence R. We Remember Pearl Harbor: Honolulu Civilians Recall the War Years, 1941-1945. LC 91-73254. (Illus.). xvii, 425p. 1991. reprint ed. 29.95 (*0-9663739-0-1*) Comns Concepts.
Rodrigo, contrib. by. Guitar Music of Spain No. 3: Volume 3. 1994. 24.95 (*0-7119-3305-7*, AM90242) Omnibus NY.
***Rodrigo, G. Chris.** Technology, Economic Growth & Crises in East Asia. 224p. 1999. 80.00 (*1-85898-477-7*) E Elgar.
Rodrigo, Garcia I., jt. auth. see Pauchet, Victor.
Rodrigo, Jennifer. Malaysia the Beautiful. 1999. 49.95 (*1-85368-744-8*) New5 Holland.
Rodrigo, Juan J. Orthopaedic Surgery: Basic Science & Clinical Science. 770p. 1985. 80.00 (*0-316-75369-6*, Little Brwn Med Div) Lppncott W & W.
Rodrigo, Paul. The Numerology Workbook. 192p. 1996. pap. text, wbk. ed. 22.50 (*0-572-02214-X*, Pub. by W Foulsham) Trans-Atl Phila.
Rodrigo, R. G., et al, eds. Progress in Atmospheric Physics. (C). 1988. text 162.50 (*90-277-2753-8*) Kluwer Academic.
Rodrigo, T. & Ruiz, A. Fundamental Physics - The Top Quark, Heavy Flavor Physics & Symetry Breaking. LC 96-213925. 400p. 1996. text 108.00 (*981-02-2368-4*) World Scientific Pub.
Rodrigo, Victoria Kamhi De, see Kamhi de Rodrigo, Victoria.
Rodrigue, Aron. French Jews, Turkish Jews: The Alliance Israelite Universelle & the Politics of Jewish Schooling in Turkey, 1860-1925. LC 89-46327. (Illus.). 250p. 1990. 29.95 (*0-253-35021-2*) Ind U Pr.
Rodrigue, Aron, ed. Ottoman & Turkish Jewry: Community & Leadership. LC 91-77684. (Turkish Studies: Vol. 12). 292p. (C). 1992. pap. 18.95 (*1-878318-03-9*) IN Univ Turkish.
Rodrigue, Aron, jt. auth. see Benbassa, Esther.
Rodrigue, Aron, jt. ed. see Benbassa, Esther.
Rodrigue, Barry H. Tom Plant: The Making of a Franco-American Entrepreneur, 1859-1941. LC 93-42755. (Studies in Entrepreneurship). 304p. 1994. text 20.00 (*0-8153-0988-0*) Garland.
***Rodrigue, George.** Blue Dog. 2000. 17.95 (*1-58479-012-1*) Stewart Tabori & Chang.
— Blue Dog. (Illus.). (J). 2001. 50.00 (*1-58479-025-3*) Stewart Tabori & Chang.
— Blue Dog Christmas. 2000. 14.95 (*1-58479-020-2*) Stewart Tabori & Chang.
— Blue Dog Man. LC 99-15470. (Illus.). 160p. 1999. 50.00 (*1-55670-976-5*) Stewart Tabori & Chang.
Rodrigue, George. The Cajuns of George Rodrigue. 1976. 35.00 (*0-8487-0443-6*) Claitors.
— Rodrigue Retrospective. 216p. 1999. text 75.00 (*0-670-86948-1*) Viking Penguin.
Rodrigue, James R., et al. Child Health Assessment: A Handbook of Measurement Techniques. LC 99-21430. 256p. (C). 1999. 54.50 (*0-205-19832-5*) Allyn.
Rodrigue, S. Bayou: Cajus Art Short Stories. 1984. 29.95 (*0-87511-936-0*, SBAYOU) Claitors.
Rodrigue, Yves. Nat-Pwe: Burma's Supernatural Subculture. (Illus.). 128p. (C). 1995. pap. 25.00 (*1-870838-11-4*, Pub. by Kiscadale) Weatherhill.
Rodrigues. Computer Writing Book. (EC - HS Communication/English Ser.). 1991. mass mkt. 18.95 (*0-538-60400-X*) S-W Pub.
— English that Works. (C). 1992. pap. text 26.36 (*0-395-53510-7*) HM.
— English That Works. (C). 1991. pap. text 21.96 (*0-395-57379-3*) HM.
— English That Works. (C). 1991. pap. text, teacher ed. 2.76 (*0-395-63090-8*) HM.
***Rodrigues.** Internation Management. 2nd ed. 2000. pap. 89.95 (*0-324-04150-0*) Sth-Wstrn College.
Rodrigues, jt. auth. see Nicolas.
Rodrigues, A. E., ed. Ion Exchange: Science & Technology. (NATO Advanced Science Institutes Series C: Mathematical & Physical Sciences). 1986. text 292.50 (*90-247-3281-6*) Kluwer Academic.
Rodrigues, A. E., et al. Multiphase Chemical Reactors: Design Methods, Vol. II. 1981. text 184.00 (*90-286-2821-5*) Kluwer Academic.
Rodrigues, A. Guimaraes, ed. Operations Research & Management in Fishing. (NATO Advanced Study Institutes Series E, Applied Sciences). (C). 1990. lib. bdg. 201.00 (*0-7923-1051-9*) Kluwer Academic.
Rodrigues-Armas, J. L. & Tejera, E. B. Contribution Al Estudio de los Aphyllophorales (Basidopmycotina) del Monteverde de las Islas Canarias: Tejera, Beltran. (Bibliotheca Mycologica: Vol. 160). (SPA., Illus.). ii, 456p. 1995. 112.00 (*3-443-59062-4*, Pub. by Gebruder Borntraeger) Balogh.
Rodrigues, Aroldo & Levine, Robert, eds. Reflections on 100 Years of Social Psychology. LC 98-53162. 224p. 1999. pap. 60.00 (*0-8133-9086-9*, Pub. by Westview) HarpC.
Rodrigues-Bachiller, Agustin. Town Planning Education. 240p. 1988. text 78.95 (*0-566-05500-7*, Pub. by Avebry) Ashgate Pub Co.
Rodrigues, Carl A. International Management: A Cultural Approach. 600p. (C). 1996. mass mkt. 92.95 (*0-314-06741-8*) West Pub.
***Rodrigues, Dawn & Rodrigues, Raymond J.** The Research Paper & the World Wide Web 2nd ed. LC 99-35189. 188p. 1999. pap. text 22.20 (*0-13-021020-X*) P-H.
Rodrigues, Dawn, jt. auth. see Gebhardt, Richard C.
Rodrigues, Dawn, jt. auth. see Zimmerman, Donald E.

Rodrigues, Eusebio L. Quest for the Human: An Exploration of Saul Bellow's Fiction. LC 80-66707. 380p. 1982. 38.50 (*0-8387-2368-3*) Bucknell U Pr.
***Rodrigues-Filho, Saulo & Mueller, German.** A Holocene Sedimentary Record from Lake Silvana, SE Brazil. LC 99-40868. (Lecture Notes in Earth Sciences Ser.: Vol. 88). (Illus.). xii, 96p. 1999. pap. 46.00 (*3-540-66205-7*) Spr-Verlag.
***Rodrigues, Isabelle.** Streetwise French: Speak & Understand Everyday French. 2000. pap. 14.95 (*0-658-00416-6*) NTC Contemp Pub Co.
Rodrigues, J. F. Mathematical Models for Phase Change Problems. (International Series of Numerical Mathematics: No. 88). 408p. 1989. 137.00 (*0-8176-2309-4*) Birkhauser.
Rodrigues, J. F. & Sequeira, A., eds. Mathematical Topics in Fluid Mechanics. 280p. 1992. 65.95 (*0-582-20954-4*, LM0954, Chap & Hall CRC) CRC Pr.
Rodrigues, John. American Canadian Cruise Ship Employment Manual. 1998. per. 19.95 (*0-9663596-0-7*) Cruise Ship.
Rodrigues, Josefina B. De, see Rodrigues, Louis J.
Rodrigues, Josefina B. De, see Rodrigues, Louis J. & De Rodrigues, Josefina B.
Rodrigues, Josefina Bernet De, see Rodrigues, Louis J. & Bernet De Rodrigues, Josefina.
Rodrigues-Kalson, Patricia, tr. see Morton, Arthur.
Rodrigues, Larry. It's All in Your Hands: Hand Analysis Guidebook to Self-Understanding. 4th rev. ed. Howell, Joan, ed. (Illus.). 405p. (Orig.). 1998. pap. 32.95 (*0-9640866-9-7*) EastWest Inst.
Rodrigues, Livi. Rural Political Protest in Western India. LC 98-907629. (Illus.). 242p. 1998. text 24.95 (*0-19-564304-6*) OUP.
***Rodrigues, Louis J.** Best Practices: DOD Can Help Suppliers Contribute More to Weapon System Programs. (Illus.). 69p. 1999. pap. text 20.00 (*0-7881-8082-7*) DIANE Pub.
— Best Practices: Successful Application to Weapon Acquisitions Requires Changes in DOD[0012]s Environment. Schinasi, Katherine V., ed. (Illus.). 81p. 2000. reprint ed. pap. text 20.00 (*0-7881-8573-X*) DIANE Pub.
Rodrigues, Louis J. Harrap's Glossary of English & Spanish Commercial & Industrial Terms. (ENG & SPA.). 288p. 1990. 35.00 (*0-8288-7966-4*, 133833992) Fr & Eur.
— 1997 Defense Budget: Potential Reductions & Rescissions to DOD's Procurement & RDT&E Programs. (Illus.). 64p. (Orig.). (C). 1996. pap. text 25.00 (*0-7881-3579-1*) DIANE Pub.
Rodrigues, Louis J. & Bernet De Rodrigues, Josefina. Harrap's Spanish Idioms. 896p. 1991. pap. 25.00 (*0-13-377649-2*, Harraps IN) Macmillan Gen Ref.
Rodrigues, Louis J. & De Rodrigues, Josefina B. Harrap's Spanish Idioms. 256p. 1991. pap. 5.00 (*0-13-385022-6*) P-H.
Rodrigues, Louis J., ed. see Murphy, Robert D.
Rodrigues, M. R., jt. auth. see Abbott, Peter.
***Rodrigues, Marcos A.** Invariants for Pattern Recognition & Classification. 250p. 2000. 68.00 (*981-02-4278-6*) World Scientific Pub.
Rodrigues, Natascha. Das Interview in der Spanischen Presse: Formen, Arbetismethoden, Absichten und Moglichkeiten zur Manipulation. (Hispano-Americana Ser.: Bd. 4). (Illus.). 246p. 1996. 44.95 (*3-631-30119-7*) P Lang Pubng.
Rodrigues, Otilio, jt. tr. see Kavanaugh, Kieran.
Rodrigues, P. R., jt. auth. see Loenen, T.
Rodrigues, Paulo J. Computer-Aided Analysis of Nonlinear Microwave Circuits. LC 97-42883. 472p. 1997. 99.00 (*0-89006-690-6*) Artech Hse.
Rodrigues, Raymond J., jt. auth. see Rodrigues, Dawn.
Rodrigues, Tina. Country at Heart, Vol. 3. (Illus.). 70p. 1997. pap. 10.50 (*1-56770-401-8*) S Scheewe Pubns.
— Country at Heart, Vol. 4. 64p. 1997. pap. 10.50 (*1-56770-410-7*) S Scheewe Pubns.
— Country Fun. 1997. pap. 10.50 (*1-56770-383-6*) S Scheewe Pubns.
— Country Fun for Christmas, Vol. 1. (Illus.). 60p. 1996. pap. 10.50 (*1-56770-367-4*) S Scheewe Pubns.
Rodrigues, W. A. & Letelier, P. S., Jr. Gravitation: The Spacetime Structure - Proceedings of the VIII Latin American Symposium on Relativity & Gravitation. 604p. 1994. text 135.00 (*981-02-1601-7*) World Scientific Pub.
Rodrigues, W. A., jt. auth. see Grib, Andrefi A.
Rodriguez. International Management. Date not set. teacher ed. write for info. (*0-314-06978-X*) West Pub.
— Writing Essentials. 2nd ed. 1998. pap. text. write for info. (*0-393-97358-1*) Norton.
Rodriguez, ed. Directory of Simulation Software, 1993. 56p. 1993. pap. 30.00 (*1-56555-015-3*, DSS-93) Soc Computer Sim.
— Directory of Simulation Software, 1995. (Illus.). 56p. (Orig.). 1995. pap. 40.00 (*1-56555-036-6*, DSS-95) Soc Computer Sim.
— 1994 Directory of Simulation Software. 56p. 1994. pap. 40.00 (*1-56555-064-1*, DSS-94) Soc Computer Sim.
Rodriguez & Cruz. Razonamiento Matematico Fundamentos Y Aplicaciones. pap. write for info. (*968-7529-06-7*) Thomson Learn.
Rodriguez, jt. auth. see Droz, Georges A.
Rodriguez, jt. auth. see Sanders.
Rodriguez, A. Images of Sephardi: The Teachers of the Alliance Israelite Universelle, 1860-1939. LC 93-15121. 320p. (C). 1993. 40.00 (*0-295-97281-5*) U of Wash Pr.
Rodriguez, A. R., jt. auth. see Stricker, G.
Rodriguez, Abraham, Jr. The Boy Without a Flag: Tales of the South Bronx. 2nd ed. 120p. 1999. pap. 13.95 (*1-57131-028-2*) Milkweed Ed.

Rodriguez, Abraham. The Buddha Book. 384p. 2002. write for info. (*0-7868-6087-1*) Hyperion.
Rodriguez, Abraham, Jr. Spidertown. LC 98-37727. (SPA.). 336p. 1999. pap. 13.00 (*0-375-70178-8*) Vin Bks.
— Spidertown. 336p. 1994. reprint ed. pap. 11.95 (*0-14-023838-7*, Penguin Bks) Viking Penguin.
Rodriguez, Abraham, Jr. Spidertown: A Novel. LC 92-34088. 336p. (J). 1993. 19.45 (*1-56282-845-2*, Pub. by Hyperion) Time Warner.
Rodriguez Adrados, Francisco. Diccionario Griego-Espanol. 2nd ed. (GRE & SPA.). 320p. 1989. pap. 85.00 (*0-7859-5682-4*, 8400046528) Fr & Eur.
Rodriguez, Agatha A. Catability. (Illus.). 20p. (Orig.). (J). 1990. pap. text 7.95 (*0-933196-04-0*) Bilingue Pubns.
— Paracaidas, Paracaidas. (Children's Storybook Ser.). (SPA., Illus.). 20p. (Orig.). (J). 1992. pap. 5.00 (*0-933196-05-9*) Bilingue Pubns.
***Rodriguez, Albert F.** An Honors Thesis: "An Electronic Spreadsheet: Function & Application" (Illus.). 23p. (YA). (gr. 9-12). 1999. pap. 25.00 (*0-9642829-5-X*) AFR Software.
Rodriguez, Albert F. Touche: Programming Tools for Shaping Solutions. 50p. (Orig.). (C). 1994. pap. text 12.50 (*0-9642829-4-1*) AFR Software.
Rodriguez, Alberto. La Conversacion En el Quijote: Subdialogo, Memoria y Asimetria. LC 94-67394. (SPA.). 141p. (C). 1995. 30.00 (*0-938972-26-X*) Spanish Lit Pubns.
Rodriguez, Aleida. Garden of Exile. LC 98-51440. 96p. 1999. pap. 20.95 (*1-889330-32-9*, Pub. by Sarabande Bks); pap. 12.95 (*1-889330-33-7*, Pub. by Sarabande Bks) Consort Bk Sales.
Rodriguez, Aleida, ed. see Labbe, Armand J.
***Rodriguez, Alejandro.** Como Emprender un Proyecto de Fe Sin Morir en el Intento. (SPA.). 1999. pap. 11.99 (*0-8297-1687-4*) Vida Pubs.
Rodriguez, Alex. Hit a Grand Slam. 1998. 14.95 (*0-87833-997-3*) Taylor Pub.
Rodriguez, Alfonso. La Estructura Mitica del Popol Vuh. LC 84-81886. (SPA.). 108p. (Orig.). 1985. pap. 10.00 (*0-89729-360-6*) Ediciones.
Rodriguez, Alfonso R., et al. Soil Mechanics in Highway Engineering. (Series on Rock & Soil Mechanics: Vol. 16). 900p. 1987. text 100.00 (*0-87849-072-8*, Pub. by Trans T Pub) Enfield Pubs NH.
Rodriguez, Alfred, ed. see Rojas Zorrilla, Francisco D.
Rodriguez, Alfredo. Estas Tierras. (SPA.). 104p. 1987. pap. 12.00 (*0-9615403-1-1*) Dos Pasos Ed.
Rodriguez, Alison W., jt. auth. see Rivers, William L.
Rodriguez, Andres. The Book of the Heart: The Poetics, Letters, & Life of John Keats. 256p. (Orig.). 1993. pap. 16.95 (*0-940262-57-6*, Lindisfarne) Anthroposophic.
***Rodriguez, Andrew.** Introduction to Alcohol & Substance Abuse. (Social Work Ser.). 2001. pap. text. write for info. (*0-534-35781-4*) Brooks-Cole.
***Rodriguez, Angel.** Jewelry in the Bible. 125p. 1999. pap. 5.95 (*1-57847-054-4*) Genl Conf Svnth-day.
Rodriguez, Angel & Black, Carla. The Tandem Book. (Illus.). 154p. (Orig.). 1997. pap. 14.95 (*0-924272-03-1*) Info Net Pub.
Rodriguez, Angel M. Esther: A Theological Approach. LC 94-72881. 175p. (C). 1995. pap. 16.99 (*1-883925-03-7*) Andrews Univ Pr.
Rodriguez, Angelyn. Your Relationship to God: A Four Week Study to Help Teenagers Understand Their Relationship to God. Swyers, Gary, ed. (Bible Basics Ser.). (Illus.). 32p. (YA). (gr. 6-12). 1991. pap. 8.95 (*0-89827-084-7*, BKS00) Wesleyan Pub Hse.
Rodriguez, Antonio, jt. auth. see Kranin.
Rodriguez, Armando R. The Gypsy Wagon. (Creative Ser.: No. 2). 90p. 1974. pap. 15.00 (*0-89551-005-7*) UCLA Chicano Studies.
Rodriguez-Armas, O., et al. Infertility & Contraception: A Textbook for Clinical Practice. LC 98-26809. 250p. 1998. 49.00 (*1-85070-056-7*) Prthnon Pub.
Rodriguez, Art. East Side Dreams. 2nd ed. LC 99-93257. 266p. 1999. pap. 12.95 (*0-9671555-0-9*, Pub. by Dream Hse Pr) Partners-West.
— The Monkey Box. LC 99-93258. 340p. 2000. pap. 12.95 (*0-9671555-1-7*, Pub. by Dream Hse Pr) Partners-West.
Rodriguez-Artalejo, M., jt. ed. see Flum, J.
Rodriguez-Artalejo, M., jt. ed. see Levi, G.
Rodriguez, Artemio, jt. auth. see Herrera, Juan Felipe.
***Rodriguez, Arturo.** Rumba Guaguanco Conversations. 104p. 1999. spiral bd. 19.95 (*0-7866-4693-4*, 98079BCD) Mel Bay.
Rodriguez, Arturo P., et al, eds. Los Documentos Liturgicos: Un Recurso Pastoral. (SPA.). 400p. 1997. pap. 15.00 (*1-56854-089-2*, SLITDC) Liturgy Tr Pubns.
Rodriguez, Arturo P. & Francis, Mark. Primero Dios: Hispanic Liturgical Resource. 160p. 1997. pap. 18.00 (*1-56854-142-2*, CUSTOM) Liturgy Tr Pubns.
Rodriguez-Bachiller, A. A Small, Robust & Updated Computer Program for Lowry Type Models. (C). 1979. 29.00 (*0-7855-3874-7*, Pub. by Oxford Polytechnic) St Mut.
Rodriguez-Bachiller, A., ed. Streamlining Local Government? (C). 1984. 35.00 (*0-7855-3838-0*, Pub. by Oxford Polytechnic) St Mut.
***Rodriguez, Barbara.** Autobiographical Inscriptions: Form, Personhood & the American Woman Writer of Color. LC PS366.A88R63 1999. (The W.E.B. Du Bois Institute Ser.). (Illus.). 240p. 1999. text 45.00 (*0-19-512341-7*) OUP.
Rodriguez Barrientos. Maritime Dictionary English-Spanish - Spanish-English. 2nd ed. (ENG & SPA.). 248p. 1995. 49.95 (*0-7859-9767-9*) Fr & Eur.

Rodriguez-Barrueco, C., ed. Fertilizers & Environment: Proceedings of the International Symposium Held in Salamanca, Spain, 26-29 September 1994. LC 95-35896. (Developments in Plant & Soil Sciences Ser.: Vol. 66). 512p. (C). 1996. text 242.50 (*0-7923-3729-8*) Kluwer Academic.

Rodriguez, Benjamin, jt. auth. see Damiani, Bruno.

Rodriguez, Bertha D., et al. Amigo. (ENG & SPA.). 1995. 93.25 incl. disk (*0-8442-7674-X*, Passprt Bks) NTC Contemp Pub Co.

Rodriguez Beruff, Jorge. Cuba en Crisis. (Caribbean Collection). (SPA.). 248p. 1995. pap. 14.95 (*0-8477-0210-3*) U of PR Pr.

***Rodriguez, Bobbie.** Sarah's Sleepover. LC 99-32058. (Illus.). 32p. (J). (gr. k-4). 2000. 15.99 (*0-670-87750-6*, Viking Child) Peng Put Young Read.

Rodriguez Bravo, Juan L., jt. ed. see Del Mar Martinez Rodriguez, Maria.

Rodriguez, Brenda M. & Garcia, Jill B. Extending the Dialogue on Diversity Issues in Family Support. LC 98-18225. (Culture & Family Support Ser.). 64p. 1998. pap. 7.00 (*1-885429-18-5*) Family Resource.

Rodriguez-Brown, Flora, jt. ed. see Shanahan, Timothy.

Rodriguez, C. Senor, Hazme Llorar.Tr. of Please Make Me Cry!. (SPA.). 256p. 1975. pap. 5.99 (*0-8297-0597-X*) Vida Pubs.

Rodriguez Caceres, Milagros, jt. auth. see Pedraza Jimenez, Felipe B.

Rodriguez, Camille & Perez, Ramon B., eds. Puerto Ricans & Higher Education Policies: Issues of Scholarship, Fiscal Policies & Admissions. 68p. 1994. pap. 10.00 (*1-878483-52-8*) Hunter Coll CEP.

Rodriguez, Camille, ed. see Bonilla, Frank & Campos, Ricardo.

Rodriguez, Camilo. Patrones de Asentamiento de los Agricultores Prehispanicos en "El Limon," Municipio de Chaparral (Tolima) (SPA., Illus.). 108p. 1991. pap. 8.50 (*1-877812-29-3*, BR027) UPLAAP.

Rodriguez-Carbajal, Jesus, ed. Neuroradiology & Head & Neck Imaging. LC 99-19267. 583p. 1998. pap. 80.00 (*0-7817-1447-8*) Lppncott W & W.

Rodriguez, Carlos, jt. auth. see Sams, Robert A.

Rodriguez, Carmen. And a Body to Remember With. 176p. 1998. pap. text 12.95 (*1-55152-044-3*, Pub. by Arsenal Pulp) LPC InBook.

— Guerra Prolongada/Protracted War. (Not a Luxury Poetry Ser.). (ENG & SPA.). 112p. pap. 9.95 (*0-88961-171-8*, Pub. by Womens Pr) LPC InBook.

— Problemas Verbales para Algebra Intermedia. (SPA.). 138p. 1993. pap. write for info. (*0-929441-57-5*) Pubns Puertorriquenas.

Rodriguez, Carmen J., jt. auth. see West-Rodiguez, Helen.

Rodriguez, Caro. The Mystery of Freemasonry Unveiled. unabridged ed. 254p. 1962. reprint ed. pap. 15.00 (*0-945001-27-4*) GSG & Assocs.

Rodriguez, Carol, jt. auth. see Larson, John.

Rodriguez Casona, Alejandro. Flor de Leyendas. (Clasicos Ser.). (SPA.). 122p. 1996. pap. write for info. (*0-929441-88-5*) Pubns Puertorriquenas.

Rodriguez, Castro M. Del Nacionalismo Al Populismo: Cultura y Politica en Puerto Rico. 205p. 1993. pap. 9.50 (*0-929157-25-7*) Ediciones Huracan.

Rodriguez, Clara. Changing Race. text 55.00 (*0-8147-7546-2*); pap. text 19.00 (*0-8147-7547-0*) NYU Pr.

Rodriguez, Clara E. Puerto Rican: Born in the USA. 256p. 1989. 44.95 (*0-04-497041-2*); pap. 14.95 (*0-04-497042-0*) Routledge.

Rodriguez, Clara E., ed. Latino Looks: Images of Latinas & Latinos in the U. S. Media. LC 97-1840. (C). 1997. pap. text 25.00 (*0-8133-2766-0*, Pub. by Westview) HarpC.

Rodriguez, Clara E. & Korrol, Virginia S., eds. Historical Perspectives on Puerto Rican Survival in the United States. 196p. (C). 1998. text 29.95 (*1-55876-117-9*); pap. text 12.95 (*1-55876-118-7*) Wiener Pubs Inc.

Rodriguez, Claudio. El Poeta y Su Obra. 146p. 1994. 10.00 (*84-599-3368-7*) Hispanic Inst.

Rodriguez-Clemente, R. & Paorici, C., eds. Crystalline Materials: Growth & Characterization. 250p. 1992. text 100.00 (*0-87849-543-6*, Pub. by Trans T Pub) Enfield Pubs NH.

Rodriguez-Clemente, R., jt. auth. see Sangwal, K.

Rodriguez, Conchita. The Cash-Credit Connection: The Way to Solve All Your Credit & Financial Problems Plus Make a Fortune. 200p. (Orig.). 1990. 19.95 (*1-879497-02-6*) Natl Crdt Ctr.

Rodriguez-Consuegra, Francisco A. Kurt Godel: Unpublished Philosophical Essays. 226p. 1996. 69.50 (*3-7643-5310-4*) Spr-Verlag.

— The Mathematical Philosophy of Bertrand Russell: Origins & Development. xiv, 236p. 1991. 100.00 (*0-8176-2656-5*) Birkhauser.

Rodriguez-Consuegra, Francisco A., ed. & intro. see Godel, Kurt.

Rodriguez, Consuelo. Cesar Chavez: Mexican-American Labor Leader. (Hispanics of Achievement Ser.). (Illus.). 120p. (YA). (gr. 5 up). 1991. lib. bdg. 19.95 (*0-7910-1232-8*) Chelsea Hse.

— Cesar Chavez: Mexican-American Labor Leader. (Hispanics of Achievement Ser.). (Illus.). 120p. (YA). (gr. 5 up). 1995. pap. 8.95 (*0-7910-1259-X*) Chelsea Hse.

Rodriguez Cuadros, Evangelina, ed. see Calderon de la Barca, Pedro.

Rodriguez, Daniel G., jt. auth. see Shipman, Stephanie L.

Rodriguez, Dave & Rodriguez, Judy. Times Tables the Fun Way Book for Kids Parent's Set: A Picture Method of Learning the Multiplication Facts, Incl. Flash Cards & Student Workbook. 2nd enl. rev. ed. (Illus.). 86p. (J). (gr. 2-8). 1994. spiral bd. 33.85 (*1-883841-40-2*) Cty Creek Pr.

— Times Tables the Fun Way Book for Kids Starter Set: A Picture Method of Learning the Multiplication Facts, Incl. Flash Cards. 2nd enl. rev. ed. (Illus.). 86p. (J). (gr. 2-8). 1994. spiral bd. 25.90 (*1-883841-39-9*) Cty Creek Pr.

Rodriguez, David & Rodriquez, Judy. Times Tables the Fun Way Book for Kids: A Picture Method of Learning the Multiplication Facts. 3rd enl. rev. ed. (Illus.). 88p. (gr. 2-8). 1999. spiral bd. 19.95 (*1-883841-43-7*) Cty Creek Pr.

Rodriguez, David A., ed. see Rodriguez, Lisa M.

Rodriguez, David A., ed. & tr. see Rodriguez, Lisa M.

Rodriguez, Dawn & Tuman, Myron C. Writing Essentials: Pocket Guide. 2nd ed. LC 98-34152. 1998. pap. text. write for info. (*0-393-97336-0*) Norton.

Rodriguez De Castro, Jose. Biblioteca Espanola, 2 vols., Set. (Textos y Estudios Clasicos De las Literaturas Hispanicas Ser.). 1417p. 1977. reprint ed. write for info. (*3-487-06272-0*) G Olms Pubs.

Rodriguez de la Fuen, Felix. Enciclopedia Salvat de la Fauna, Vol. 1. 162p. 1986. 24.95 (*0-7859-6127-5*, 8471378507) Fr & Eur.

— Enciclopedia Salvat de la Fauna, Vol. 2. 162p. 1986. 24.95 (*0-7859-6128-3*, 8471378515) Fr & Eur.

— Enciclopedia Salvat de la Fauna, Vol. 3. 162p. 1986. 24.95 (*0-7859-6129-1*, 8471378523) Fr & Eur.

— Enciclopedia Salvat de la Fauna, Vol. 4. 162p. 1986. 24.95 (*0-7859-6130-5*, 8471378531) Fr & Eur.

— Enciclopedia Salvat de la Fauna, Vol. 5. 162p. 1986. 24.95 (*0-7859-6482-7*) Fr & Eur.

— Enciclopedia Salvat de la Fauna, Vol. 6. 162p. 1986. 24.95 (*0-7859-6131-3*, 8471378558) Fr & Eur.

— Enciclopedia Salvat de la Fauna, Vol. 7. 162p. 1986. 24.95 (*0-7859-6132-1*, 8471378566) Fr & Eur.

— Enciclopedia Salvat de la Fauna, Vol. 8. 162p. 1986. 24.95 (*0-7859-6133-X*) Fr & Eur.

— Enciclopedia Salvat de la Fauna, Vol. 9. 162p. 1986. 24.95 (*0-7859-6134-8*, 8471378582) Fr & Eur.

— Enciclopedia Salvat de la Fauna, Vol. 10. 162p. 1986. 24.95 (*0-7859-6135-6*, 8471378590) Fr & Eur.

— Enciclopedia Salvat de la Fauna, Vol. 11. 162p. 1986. 24.95 (*0-7859-6136-4*, 8471378604) Fr & Eur.

— Enciclopedia Salvat de la Fauna, Vol. 12. 162p. 1986. 24.95 (*0-7859-6137-2*, 8471378612) Fr & Eur.

— Enciclopedia Salvat de la Fauna, Vol. 13. 162p. 1986. 24.95 (*0-7859-6138-0*, 8471378620) Fr & Eur.

— Enciclopedia Salvat de la Fauna, Vol. 14. 162p. 1986. 24.95 (*0-7859-6139-9*, 8471378639) Fr & Eur.

— Enciclopedia Salvat de la Fauna, Vol. 15. 162p. 1986. 24.95 (*0-7859-6140-2*, 8471378647) Fr & Eur.

— Enciclopedia Salvat de la Fauna, Vol. 16. 162p. 1986. 24.95 (*0-7859-6141-0*, 8471378655) Fr & Eur.

— Enciclopedia Salvat de la Fauna, Vol. 17. 162p. 1986. 24.95 (*0-7859-6142-9*, 8471378663) Fr & Eur.

— Enciclopedia Salvat de la Fauna, Vol. 18. 162p. 1986. 24.95 (*0-7859-6143-7*, 8471378671) Fr & Eur.

— Enciclopedia Salvat de la Fauna Iberica y Europea, Vol. 1. 308p. 1984. 69.95 (*0-7859-5944-0*, 8434536463) Fr & Eur.

— Enciclopedia Salvat de la Fauna Iberica y Europea, Vol. 2. 308p. 1984. 69.95 (*0-7859-5945-9*, 8434536471) Fr & Eur.

— Enciclopedia Salvat de la Fauna Iberica y Europea, Vol. 4. 308p. 1984. 69.95 (*0-7859-5946-7*, 8434536498) Fr & Eur.

— Enciclopedia Salvat de la Fauna Iberica y Europea, Vol. 5. 308p. 1984. 69.95 (*0-7859-5947-5*, 8434536501) Fr & Eur.

— Enciclopedia Salvat de la Fauna Iberica y Europea, Vol. 6. 308p. 1984. 69.95 (*0-7859-6467-3*) Fr & Eur.

— Enciclopedia Salvat de la Fauna Iberica y Europea, Vol. 7. 308p. 1984. 69.95 (*0-7859-5948-3*, 8434536528) Fr & Eur.

— Enciclopedia Salvat de la Fauna Iberica y Europea, Vol. 8. 308p. 1984. 69.95 (*0-7859-5949-1*, 8434536536) Fr & Eur.

Rodriguez de la Fuente, Felix. Enciclopedia Salvat de la Fauna: Obra Completa, 16 vols. (SPA.). 2916p. 1986. 450.00 (*0-7859-5121-0*) Fr & Eur.

— Enciclopedia Salvat de la Fauna Iberica y Europea, 8 vols., Set. (SPA.). 2464p. 1975. 395.00 (*0-8288-5873-X*, S50539) Fr & Eur.

Rodriguez del Pino, Salvador. La Novela Chicana Escrita en Espanol: Cinco Autores Comprometidos. LC 81-71730. (SPA.). iv, 159p. 1982. pap. 18.00 (*0-916950-28-X*) Biling Rev-Pr.

Rodriguez del Pino, Salvador, ed. Six Plays in Translation from Mexican Contemporary Theatre: A New Golden Age. LC 98-40428. (Hispanic Literature Ser.: Vol. 42). 364p. 1998. text 99.95 (*0-7734-8274-1*) E Mellen.

Rodriguez, Douglas. Latin Ladles. LC 97-31653. (Illus.). 128p. (Orig.). 1998. pap. text 17.95 (*0-89815-851-6*) Ten Speed Pr.

***Rodriguez, Douglas & DiCataldo, Andrew.** Latin Flavors on the Grill. (Illus.). 224p. 2000. 39.95 (*1-58008-055-3*) Ten Speed Pr.

Rodriguez, Douglas & Harrisson, John. Nuevo Latino: Recipes That Celebrate the New Latin-American Cuisine. (Illus.). 168p. 1995. 29.95 (*0-89815-752-8*) Ten Speed Pr.

Rodriguez, E. M. & Van Wimersma Greidanus, T., eds. The Cerebrospinal Fluid (CSF) & Peptide Hormones. (Frontiers of Hormone Research Ser.: Vol. 9). (Illus.). viii, 220p. 1981. 115.00 (*3-8055-2823-X*) S Karger.

Rodriguez, Edel. Alice in Wonderland. abr. large type ed. (Illus.). 32p. (Orig.). (J). (gr. k up). 1995. pap. 14.95 (*1-886201-01-3*) Nana Banana.

Rodriguez, Edgar E. Fauna Precolombina de Narino. (SPA., Illus.). 122p. 1992. pap. 10.00 (*1-877812-23-4*, BR021) UPLAAP.

***Rodriguez, Eduardo Luis.** The Havana Guide: Modern Architecture, 1925-1965. LC 99-35579. (Illus.). 304p. 2000. pap. 24.95 (*1-56898-210-0*) Princeton Arch.

Rodriguez, Eleanor R. & Bellanca, James. What Is It about Me You Can't Teach? An Instructional Guide for the Urban Educator. LC 96-78752. (Illus.). 208p. (Orig.). 1996. pap. 30.95 (*1-57517-066-3*, 1444) SkyLght.

Rodriguez, Eleanor R., et al. Valuing Diversity in the School System: Facilitator's Guide. (Illus.). 129p. 1996. pap., teacher ed. 159.95 (*1-57517-017-5*, 1367) SkyLght.

— Valuing Diversity in the School System: Participant's Manual. (Illus.). 97p. 1996. ring bd. 24.95 (*1-57517-018-3*, 1423) SkyLght.

Rodriguez, Elizabeth, ed. Engineering Test Principles for Operational Suitability. 181p. 1992. 39.00 (*0-937194-23-9*) A Deepak Pub.

Rodriguez, Elmer, et al. De Perlas: Intermediate Spanish. 192p. 1997. pap., wbk. ed. 37.95 (*0-471-10995-9*, FL12) Wiley.

Rodriguez, Estevan A., et al. Agua Fresca. (SPA., Illus.). 59p. 1980. pap. 3.50 (*0-918358-10-8*) Pajarito Pubns.

Rodriguez, Esther & Kirvatis, Joanna. Selected Experiments in General Chemistry & Qualitative Analysis. 1994. spiral bd. 21.90 (*0-88252-163-2*) Paladin Hse.

Rodriguez, Esther M. College Admission Requirements: A New Role for States. (SHEEO/ECS Monograph Ser.). 1995. 12.00 (*0-614-13548-6*) SHEEO.

Rodriguez, Esther M. Postsecondary Education & the New Workforce. 29p. 1996. pap. 2.25 (*0-16-063598-5*) USGPO.

Rodriguez, Esther M., jt. ed. see Mingle, James R.

Rodriguez, Eugene, Jr. Henry B. Gonzalez: A Political Profile. Cortes, Carlos E., ed. LC 76-1568. (Chicano Heritage Ser.). 1977. 15.95 (*0-405-09522-8*) Ayer.

Rodriguez, Evangelina & Tordera, Antonio. Calderon Y la Obra Corta Dramatica del Siglo XVII. (Monagrafias A Ser.: Vol. XCI). (SPA.). 228p. (Orig.). (C). 1983. pap. 57.00 (*0-7293-0159-1*, Pub. by Tamesis Bks Ltd) Boydell & Brewer.

Rodriguez, F. & Marchetti, N. Italian Commercial Correspondence: Corrispondenza Comerciale Italiana. (ITA.). 272p. 1980. pap. 39.95 (*0-8288-1559-3*, M14183) Fr & Eur.

Rodriguez-Farrisi, Theresa. Diaper Changes: The Complete Diapering Book & Resource Guide. 2nd rev. ed. LC 98-75450. (Illus.). xviii, 175p. (Orig.). 1998. pap. 12.95 (*0-9656955-7-3*) Homekeepers Pub.

***Rodriguez, Felix V. Matos.** Women & Urban Change in San Juan, Puerto Rico, 1820-1868. LC 99-17872. 1999. write for info. (*0-8130-1676-2*) U Press Fla.

Rodriguez, Ferdinand. Principles of Polymer Systems. 3rd ed. (Illus.). 612p. 1989. 66.95 (*0-89116-176-7*) Hemisp Pub.

— Principles of Polymer Systems. 4th ed. 732p. 1996. 85.00 (*1-56032-325-6*) Hemisp Pub.

Rodriguez Forteza, Adela. Manual de Investigacion Intelectual. (UPREX, Manuales Ser.: No. 7). 114p. (C). 1972. pap. 1.50 (*0-8477-0007-0*) U of PR Pr.

Rodriguez, Francisco E. Pancho Montana: Un Viaje Inesperado. (SPA., Illus.). 55p. (Orig.). (J). (gr. 4-6). 1996. pap. 7.95 (*1-887578-45-5*) SpanPr.

Rodriguez-Fraticelli, Carlos. Education & Imperialism: The Puerto Rican Experience in Higher Education, 1898-1986. 51p. 1986. lib. bdg. 5.00 (*1-878483-07-2*) Hunter Coll CEP.

Rodriguez, Fred. Affirming Equity: A Framework for Teachers & Schools. 238p. (C). 1997. pap. text, per. 46.95 (*0-7872-3034-0*) Kendall-Hunt.

***Rodriguez, Fred.** Affirming Equity: A Framework for Teachers & Schools. 3rd ed. 292p. (C). 1999. per. 52.95 (*0-7872-6001-0*, 41600101) Kendall-Hunt.

Rodriguez, G., et al, eds. Environmental Coastal Regions III. (Environmental Studies). 450p. 2000. 222.00 (*1-85312-827-9*, 8279, Pub. by WIT Pr) Computational Mech MA.

***Rodriguez-Garcia, Rosalia, et al, eds.** From Humanitarian Assistance to Human Development. (Illus.). 127p. 1998. pap. text 14.95 (*0-9636369-2-8*) PAHO.

Rodriguez-Garcia, Rosalia, et al. La Conexion Salud-Desarrollo. (ENG & SPA., Illus.). xv, 207p. (Orig.). 1996. pap. text. write for info. (*0-9636369-1-X*) PAHO.

— The Health-Development Link. 164p. 1993. pap. text. write for info. (*0-9636369-0-1*) PAHO.

***Rodriguez-Garcia, Rosalia A., et al.** Microenterprise Development For Better Health Outcomes. Vol. 222. 2001. write for info. (*0-313-31633-3*) Greenwood.

Rodriguez, Gina M. Green Corn Tamales - Tamales de Elote. (ENG & SPA., Illus.). 40p. (J). 1994. 14.95 (*0-938243-00-4*) Hispanic Bk Dist.

Rodriguez, Gloria. Criando A Nuestros Ninos. 320p. 1999. per. 13.00 (*0-684-84126-6*) S&S Trade.

— Raising Nuestros Ninos.Tr. of Our Children. 400p. 1999. per. 13.00 (*0-684-83969-5*) S&S Trade.

***Rodriguez, Gloria & Casado, Silvia.** The Spiritual Experience of Henry de Osso. Roxborough, Judy, ed. Chamorro, Grace, tr. LC 98-61757. 276p. 1999. pap. 7.95 (*0-9638041-4-6*) Soc St Teresa.

Rodriguez, Grace. Beginning: Exploring Genesis. LC 98-90446. 1999. 16.95 (*0-533-12806-4*) Vantage.

Rodriguez, Graciela, et al. Sueno en el Yunque. (Illus.). 36p. (J). 1993. 12.95 (*0-8477-0204-9*) U of PR Pr.

***Rodriguez, Gregory.** The Successful Integration of Immigrants to American Society. 25p. 1999. pap. 10.00 (*0-9645220-2-0*) Nat Immig Forum.

Rodriguez, Helen. Helen of Burma. large type ed. 320p. 1984. 27.99 (*0-7089-1189-7*) Ulverscroft.

Rodriguez Howard, Pauline, jt. auth. see Galindo, Mary Sue.

Rodriguez-Hunter, Suzanne. Ckecklist for a Perfect Honeymoon. 224p. 1996. mass mkt. 7.99 (*0-385-47649-3*, Main St Bks) Doubleday.

— Found Meals of the Lost Generation: Recipes & Anecdotes from 1920s Paris. 265p. 1997. pap. 14.95 (*0-571-19925-9*) Faber & Faber.

Rodriguez-Ibabe, J. M., et al, eds. Microalloying in Steels: Proceedings of the International Conference on Microalloying in Steels, Donostia-San Sebastian, Basque Country, Spain, September 1998. (Materials Science Forum Ser.: Vols. 284-286). (Illus.). 604p. (C). 1998. text 230.00 (*0-87849-816-8*, Pub. by Trans T Pub) Enfield Pubs NH.

Rodriguez, Ileana. House - Garden - Nation: Space, Gender, & Ethnicity in Post-Colonial Latin American Literatures by Women. Carr, Robert, tr. LC 93-42502. (Post-Contemporary Interventions Ser.). 272p. 1994. text 49.95 (*0-8223-1450-9*) Duke.

— House-Garden-Nation: Space, Gender, & Ethnicity in Post-Colonial Latin American Literatures by Women. Carr, Robert, tr. LC 93-42502. (Post-Contemporary Interventions Ser.). 272p. 1994. pap. text 17.95 (*0-8223-1465-7*) Duke.

— Women, Guerrillas, & Love: Understanding War in Central America. LC 96-33834. 232p. (C). 1996. pap. 19.95 (*0-8166-2627-8*); text 49.95 (*0-8166-2626-X*) U of Minn Pr.

Rodriguez, Irene & Clay, Marie M. Arena. 24p. 1995. pap. text 5.00 (*0-435-08855-6*, 08855) Heinemann.

Rodriguez Irlanda, Dalila. Manual de Orientacion al Maestro. (SPA.). 262p. 1990. pap. write for info. (*0-929441-03-6*) Pubns Puertorriquenas.

— Medicion y Evaluacion. (SPA.). 282p. 1991. pap. write for info. (*0-929441-11-7*) Pubns Puertorriquenas.

Rodriguez, Isabel. Sin Tiempo Ni Distancia. LC 90-81212. (Coleccion Cuba y sus Jueces). (SPA., Illus.). 94p. (Orig.). 1990. pap. 9.95 (*0-89729-566-8*) Ediciones.

Rodriguez, Israel. La Estatua de Sal. LC 88-80053. (Coleccion Espejo de Paciencia). (SPA., Illus.). 63p. (Orig.). 1989. pap. 9.95 (*0-89729-474-2*) Ediciones.

— El Hombre y las Metaforas de Dios en la Literatura Hispanoamericana. LC 90-8496. (SPA.). 144p. (Orig.). 1991. pap. 19.95 (*0-89729-585-4*) Ediciones.

— Poemas de Israel. LC 80-51403. (SPA.). 91p. 1980. pap. 12.00 (*0-89295-016-1*) Society Sp & Sp-Am.

Rodriguez-Iturbe, Ignacio & Rinaldo, Andrea. Fractal River Basins: Chance & Self-Organization. LC 97-7735. (Illus.). 563p. (C). 1997. text 100.00 (*0-521-47398-5*) Cambridge U Pr.

Rodriguez-Iturbe, Ignacio, jt. auth. see Bras, Rafael L.

Rodriguez, Ivan, tr. see Wycoff, Cynthia.

Rodriguez, J. Costas, ed. Frontinus - Frontini Index. (Alpha-Omega, Reihe A Ser.: Bd. LI). iii, 804p. 1985. write for info. (*3-487-07708-6*) G Olms Pubs.

Rodriguez, J. G., jt. ed. see Nault, L. R.

Rodriguez, J. R. Promise. 192p. 1999. pap. 12.95 (*1-56279-118-4*) Mercury Hse Inc.

***Rodriguez, Jackie.** Jesus Desea Coronarte: El Proceso Trae la Coronacion y la Coronacion Nos Lleva a su Gloria. (SPA.). 1998. pap. 8.99 (*0-88419-552-X*) Casa Creacion.

Rodriguez, Jaime E. Cruce de Caminos: Poemas Del Barrio Para el Mundo. (SPA., Illus.). 187p. (Orig.). 1995. pap. 9.95 (*1-888109-00-9*) Edit Agenda.

— Down from Colonialism: Mexico's Nineteenth Century Crisis. LC 83-14331. (Popular Ser.: No. 3). 46p. (Orig.). 1983. pap. 10.00 (*0-89551-064-2*, S161) UCLA Chicano Studies.

— The Evolution of the Mexican Political System. LC 92-29839. (Latin American Silhouettes Ser.). (ENG & SPA.). 322p. 1993. 45.00 (*0-8420-2448-4*, SR Bks) Scholarly Res Inc.

Rodriguez, Jaime E., ed. The Independence of Mexico & the Creation of the New Nation. LC 89-2665. 374p. 1989. 32.50 (*0-87903-070-4*) UCLA Lat Am Ctr.

— The Mexican & Mexican American Experience in the 19th Century. LC 88-64099. 136p. 1989. 20.00 (*0-916950-93-X*); pap. 12.00 (*0-916950-94-8*) Biling Rev-Pr.

— Patterns of Contention in Mexican History. LC 91-38845. (Latin American Silhouettes Ser.). (ENG & SPA.). 368p. 1992. lib. bdg. 50.00 (*0-8420-2399-2*) Scholarly Res Inc.

— The Revolutionary Process in Mexico. (Latin American Studies: Vol. 72). 374p. 1990. 34.50 (*0-87903-073-9*) UCLA Lat Am Ctr.

Rodriguez, Jaime E. & Vincent, Kathryn, eds. Common Border, Uncommon Paths: Race, Culture, & National Identity in U. S. - Mexican Relations. LC 97-8951. (Latin American Silhouettes Ser.). (Illus.). 192p. 1997. 45.00 (*0-8420-2673-8*) Scholarly Res Inc.

— Myths, Misdeeds, & Misunderstandings: The Roots of Conflict in U. S. - Mexican Relations. LC 97-1217. (Latin American Silhouettes Ser.). (Illus.). 274p. 1997. 45.00 (*0-8420-2662-2*) Scholarly Res Inc.

Rodriguez, Jaime E., jt. auth. see MacLachlan, Colin M.

Rodriguez, Janel. Gloria Estefan. LC 95-16152. (Contemporary Biographies Ser.). 48p. (J). (gr. 4-7). 1996. pap. 5.95 (*0-8114-9788-7*) Raintree Steck-V.

— Gloria Estefan. LC 95-16152. (Contemporary Biographies Ser.). (Illus.). 48p. (J). (gr. 4-6). 1996. lib. bdg. 24.26 (*0-8172-3982-0*) Raintree Steck-V.

— Gloria Estefan. large type ed. 54p. (J). (gr. 4-8). pap. 13.50 (*0-614-20571-9*, L-86289-00 APHB) Am Printing Hse.

Rodriguez, Jeanette. Our Lady of Guadalupe: Faith & Empowerment among Mexican-American Women. LC 93-31267. (Illus.). 248p. (Orig.). (C). 1994. pap. 15.95 (*0-292-77062-6*); text 35.00 (*0-292-77061-8*) U of Tex Pr.

— Stories We Live: Cuentos Que Vivimos: Hispanic Women's Spirituality, 1996 Madeleva Lecture. (Madeleva Lectures). 64p. 1996. pap. 5.95 (*0-8091-3659-7*, 3659-7) Paulist Pr.

R

An Asterisk (*) at the beginning of an entry indicates that the title is appearing for the first time.

R

***Rodriguez, Jill.** Master AP Spanish Language. 2000. pap. 19.99 (*0-7645-6187-1*, Arco) Macmillan Gen Ref.

Rodriguez, Joaquin P. Reflexiones de un Agricultor. 1978. pap. 10.00 (*0-89729-203-0*) Ediciones.

Rodriguez, Joe. The Oddsplayer. LC 88-10484. 180p. (Orig.). 1989. pap. 9.50 (*0-934770-88-3*) Arte Publico.

***Rodriguez, John.** My Inner Thoughts. LC 98-90946. 1999. pap. 9.95 (*0-533-12999-0*) Vantage.

Rodriguez, Jorge. Politica Militar y Dominacion. LC 88-80499. 270p. 1988. pap. 9.50 (*0-940238-59-4*) Ediciones Huracan.

Rodriguez, Jorge, jt. auth. see Seireg, A. A.

Rodriguez, Jorge A., tr. see Westberg, Granger.

Rodriguez, Jose. Bankruptcy. 28p. pap. 2.75 (*0-685-23159-3*, 41,575B) NCLS Inc.

Rodriguez, Jose A., jt. auth. see Pumari, Antonio N.

Rodriguez, Jose D. & Martell-Otero, Loida I., eds. Teologia de Conjunto: A Collaborative Hispanic-Protestant Theology. LC 97-16944. 1997. pap. 19.95 (*0-664-25665-1*) Westminster John Knox.

Rodriguez, Jose E., jt. auth. see Lehr, Jay H.

Rodriguez, Jose J. Thoughts, Daydreams & Memories. 1998. pap. write for info. (*1-57553-883-0*) Watermrk Pr.

Rodriguez, Joseph. Spanish Harlem. LC 94-35015. (American Scene Ser.: Vol. 3). (Illus.). 1994. pap. 27.50 (*1-881616-24-X*) Dist Art Pubs.

Rodriguez, Joseph, photos by. East Side Stories: Gang Life in East LA. LC 96-21023. (Illus.). 192p. 1998. 39.95 (*1-57687-002-2*, 620311, pwerHse Bks) pwerHse Cultrl.

***Rodriguez, Joseph, photos by.** East Side Stories: Gang Life in East LA. (Illus.). 2000. pap. 24.95 (*1-57687-072-3*, pwerHse Bks) pwerHse Cultrl.

Rodriguez, Joseph A. City Against Suburb: The Culture Wars in an American Metropolis. LC 99-21192. 160p. 1999. 55.00 (*0-275-96406-X*, Praeger Pubs) Greenwood.

Rodriguez, Jovita, jt. auth. see Torres, Vivian.

Rodriguez, Juan. Katherine Sherwood: 1999 Adaline Kent Award. LC 99-71233. (Illus.). 24p. 1999. pap. 5.00 (*0-930495-34-9*) San Fran Art Inst.

***Rodriguez, Juan.** Trivial Obsession: A Life In Questions. (Illus.). 304p. 1999. text. write for info. (*0-7737-3199-7*) Stoddart Publ.

Rodriguez, Juan C. Bay of Pigs & The CIA. 1999. pap. 16.95 (*1-875284-98-2*) Ocean Pr NJ.

Rodriguez, Juan L., et al, eds. Text & Concordance of Biblioteca Nacional Manuscript 9218 Historia del gran Tamerlan. (Spanish Ser.: No. 20). 8p. 1986. 10.00 incl. fiche (*0-942260-62-7*) Hispanic Seminary.

Rodriguez, Judith. Access Mexico: Emerging Market Handbook & Directory. (Emerging Market Access Ser.). (Illus.). 650p. 1992. 239.00 (*1-881765-00-8*) Cambridge Data & Dev.

— New & Selected Poems: The House by Water. (Illus.). 180p. (Orig.). 1989. pap. text 16.95 (*0-7022-2138-4*, Pub. by Univ Queensland Pr) Intl Spec Bk.

Rodriguez, Judith, ed. Jennifer Rankin: Collected Poems. 256p. 1990. pap. 19.95 (*0-7022-2288-7*, Pub. by Univ Queensland Pr) Intl Spec Bk.

Rodriguez, Judy. Addition the Fun Way Book for Kids: A Picture Method of Learning the Addition Facts. LC 95-94946. (Illus.). 92p. (J). (gr. 1-3). 1996. spiral bd. 19.95 (*1-883841-34-8*) Cty Creek Pr.

— Addition the Fun Way Book for Kids Parent Set: A Picture Method of Learning the Addition Facts, Incl. Flash Cards & Student Workbook. (Illus.). 92p. (J). (gr. 1-3). 1996. spiral bd. 33.85 (*1-883841-42-9*) Cty Creek Pr.

— Addition the Fun Way Book for Kids Starter Set: A Picture Method of Learning the Multiplication Facts, Incl. Flash Cards. (Illus.). 92p. (J). (gr. 1-3). 1996. spiral bd. 25.90 (*1-883841-41-0*) Cty Creek Pr.

— Times Tables the Fun Way Activity Book: Warning: Only for Kids Who Want to Have Fun. (Illus.). 98p. (J). (gr. 2-8). 1998. pap. 9.95 (*1-883841-48-8*) Cty Creek Pr.

Rodriguez, Judy, jt. auth. see Carrasquillo, Angela.

Rodriguez, Judy, jt. auth. see Rodriguez, Dave.

Rodriguez-Julia, Edgardo. El Entierro de Cortijo. LC 83-80312. (Nave y el Puerto Ser.). (SPA., Illus.). 96p. 1983. pap. 6.75 (*0-940238-21-7*) Ediciones Huracan.

— Puertorriquenos: Album de la Sagrada Familia Puertorriguena a Partir de 1898. (Biblioteca de Autores de Puerto Rico Ser.). (SPA., Illus.). 176p. (Orig.). 1992. reprint ed. pap. 6.00 (*1-56328-025-6*) Edit Plaza Mayor.

Rodriguez, June. The Weight Loss Workbook: The Essential Companion for Any Weight Loss Program. 144p. 1998. spiral bd. 14.00 (*1-56836-201-3*) Kodansha.

Rodriguez, June N. Quick Escapes from Dallas - Ft. Worth: 30 Weekend Getaways in & Around the Lone Star State. 2nd ed. LC 98-13782. (Quick Escapes Ser.). (Illus.). 240p. 1998. pap. 14.95 (*0-7627-0196-X*) Globe Pequot.

— Texas Off the Beaten Path: A Guide to Unique Places. 3rd ed. LC 99-41723. (Off the Beaten Path Ser.). (Illus.). 320p. 1999. pap. text 13.95 (*0-7627-0534-5*) Globe Pequot.

***Rodriguez, June Naylor.** Quick Escapes - Dallas/Fort Worth: 37 Weekend Getaways in & Around the Lone Star State. 3rd ed. LC 00-25056. (Quick Escapes Ser.). (Illus.). 368p. 2000. pap. 15.95 (*0-7627-0642-2*) Globe Pequot.

Rodriguez, June Naylor. Romantic Days & Nights in Dallas/Fort Worth: Romantic Diversions in & Around the City. LC 99-15496. 256p. 1999. pap. text 15.95 (*0-7627-0411-X*) Globe Pequot.

***Rodriguez, June Naylor.** Southwest. (Recommended Bed & Breakfasts Ser.). (Illus.). 2001. pap. 16.95 (*0-7627-0759-3*) Globe Pequot.

Rodriguez, Junius P. Chronology of World Slavery. LC 99-23170. 580p. (YA). (gr. 9). 1999. lib. bdg. 99.00 (*0-87436-884-7*) ABC-CLIO.

***Rodriguez, Junius P.** The Louisiana Purchase: An Encyclopedia. 2002. lib. bdg. 99.00 (*1-57607-188-X*) ABC-CLIO.

Rodriguez, Junius P., ed. The Historical Encyclopedia of World Slavery, 2 vols., Set. LC 97-42839. (Illus.). 805p. (YA). (gr. 8 up). 1997. lib. bdg. 195.00 (*0-87436-885-5*) ABC-CLIO.

Rodriguez, K. S. Dawson's Creek: The Official Scrapbook. 48p. (gr. 8-12). 1998. per. 8.99 (*0-671-02673-9*) S&S Trade.

— Long Hot Summer. (Dawson's Creek Ser.: No. 1). (YA). (gr. 8 up). 1998. per. 4.99 (*0-671-02474-4*, Archway) PB.

***Rodriguez, K. S.** Major Meltdown. (Dawson's Creek Ser.: No. 4). (YA). (gr. 8 up). 1999. per. 4.99 (*0-671-02477-9*) PB.

Rodriguez, K. S. The Tale of the Horrifying Hockey Team. (Are You Afraid of the Dark? Ser.: No. 23). (YA). (gr. 5-8). 1998. pap. 4.50 (*0-671-02517-1*, Minstrel Bks) PB.

— Will Smith: From Fresh Prince to King of Cool. LC 97-77071. 144p. (J). (gr. 3 up). 1998. mass mkt. 3.99 (*0-06-107319-9*) HarpC Child Bks.

***Rodriguez, K. S., contrib. by.** Ichthyosaurus. LC 99-55474. 32p. (J). 2000. 22.03 (*0-7398-0099-X*) Raintree Steck-V.

— Iguanodon. LC 99-56145. (Prehistoric Creatures Then & Now Ser.). 32p. 2000. 22.03 (*0-7398-0100-7*) Raintree Steck-V.

— Pteranodon. LC 99-54469. (Prehistoric Creatures Then & Now Ser.). 32p. (J). 2000. 22.03 (*0-7398-0101-5*) Raintree Steck-V.

— Stegosaurus. LC 99-55478. (Prehistoric Creatures Then & Now Ser.). 32p. (J). 2000. lib. bdg. 22.03 (*0-7398-0102-3*) Raintree Steck-V.

— Tyrannosaurus Rex. LC 99-53789. 32p. (J). 2000. lib. bdg. 22.03 (*0-7398-0104-X*) Raintree Steck-V.

Rodriguez-Kalson, Patricia, tr. see Morton, Arthur.

Rodriguez-Kalson, Patricia, tr. see Morton, Delma.

Rodriguez-Kalson, Patricia, tr. see Saul, Barbara.

Rodriguez-Kalson, Patricia, tr. see Spencer, Carlleen.

***Rodriguez-Kelly, Margarita.** Women & HIV/AIDS (Las Mujeres y el VIH/SIDA) Issues & Perspectives (Realidades y Perspectivas) (SPA & ENG., Illus.). 300p. 2000. write for info. (*0-9664774-1-3*) Genmark DC.

Rodriguez Lee, Maria L. Juegos Sicologicos en la Narrativa de Mario Vargas Llosa. LC 80-70772. (SPA.). 189p. (Orig.). 1984. pap. 14.95 (*0-89729-279-0*) Ediciones.

Rodriguez-Lee, Maria L. Maria Grever: Poeta y Compositora. 175p. 54.50 (*1-882528-05-0*) Scripta.

Rodriguez-Lee, Maria-L., tr. & intro. see Ponce, Manuel.

***Rodriguez, Leonardo S.** Psychoanalysis with Children: History, Theory & Practice. 280p. 1999. 55.00 (*1-85343-439-6*, Pub. by Free Assoc Bks); pap. 25.00 (*1-85343-440-X*, Pub. by Free Assoc Bks) Intl Spec Bk.

Rodriguez, Levine. Maestros Hispanicos del Siglo Viente. (SPA.). 194p. (C). 1979. pap. text. write for info. (*0-318-69171-X*) Harcourt Coll Pubs.

Rodriguez, Lily O. & Duellman, William E. Guide to the Frogs of the Equitos Region, Amazonian Peru. Trueb, Linda, ed. 80p. (Orig.). (C). 1994. pap. text 19.95 (*0-89338-047-4*) U KS Nat Hist Mus.

Rodriguez, Linda. Goya. (Great Painters Ser.). (Illus.). 176p. 2000. 40.00 (*1-85995-292-5*) Parkstone Pr.

Rodriguez, Linda A., ed. Rank & Privilege: The Military & Society in Latin America. LC 94-14393. (Jaguar Books on Latin America: No. 8). 248p. 1994. 55.00 (*0-8420-2432-8*) Scholarly Res Inc.

***Rodriguez, Lisa M.** Bopo Gets Lost in Space. Rodriguez, David A., ed. & tr. by. LC 99-90424.Tr. of Bopo Se Pierde en el Espacio. (ENG & SPA., Illus.). 32p. (J). (ps-3). 2000. 14.95 (*0-9665575-2-2*) Bopo Biligual.

Rodriguez, Lisa M. Bopo Joins the Circus (BOPO se UNE al CIRCO) Rodriguez, David A., ed. LC 98-96608. (Illus.). 34p. (J). (ps-3). 1998. 14.95 (*0-9665575-0-6*) Bopo Biligual.

Rodriguez-Lopez, M., et al. Blue-Green Algae: Current Research, 4 vols., Vol. 1. 213p. 1974. text 29.50 (*0-8422-7187-2*) Irvington.

Rodriguez, Louis C., Jr. So You Want to Be a Federal Agent. 84p. 1992. 8.95 (*0-9634286-0-8*) Ancur Comms.

Rodriguez, Louis J. Midwestern State University in Photographs. (Illus.). 1995. 25.00 (*0-915323-07-9*) Midwestern St U Pr.

Rodriguez, Louis J. & Fukasawa, Yoshi, eds. The Texas Economy: 21st Century Economic Challenges. LC 96-9266. 278p. 1996. 47.50 (*0-915323-09-5*) Midwestern St U Pr.

Rodriguez, Luis, et al, eds. Power Lines: A Decade of Poetry from Chicago's Guild Complex. 280p. 1999. pap. 14.95 (*1-882688-22-8*, Pub. by Tia Chucha Pr) Northwestern U Pr.

Rodriguez, Luis F. Un Universo en Expansion. (Ciencia para Todos Ser.). (SPA.). pap. 6.99 (*968-16-1891-2*, Pub. by Fondo) Continental Bk.

Rodriguez, Luis J. Always Running: La Vida Loca, Gang Days in L. A. LC 93-44386. 272p. 1994. pap. 11.00 (*0-671-88231-7*) S&S Trade Pap.

— America Is Her Name. LC 96-21345. 32p. (J). (gr. 2-4). 1998. 15.95 (*1-880684-40-3*) Curbstone.

— The Concrete River. LC 90-56217. 125p. (Orig.). 1991. pap. 11.95 (*0-915306-42-5*) Curbstone.

— It Doesn't Have to Be This Way (No Tiene Que Ser Asi) A Barrio Story (Una Historia del Barrio) LC 99-10193. (ENG & SPA., Illus.). 32p. (J). (gr. 1-3). 1999. 15.95 (*0-89239-161-8*) Childrens Book Pr.

— La Llaman America. Villanueva, Tino, tr. LC 96-24508. (SPA., Illus.). 32p. 1998. 15.95 (*1-880684-41-1*) Curbstone.

— Poems Across the Pavement. LC 90-119897. (Illus.). 48p. (Orig.). (C). 1989. pap. 7.95 (*0-9624287-0-1*) Tia Chucha Pr.

— Trochemoche. LC 98-9201. 94p. 1998. pap. 12.95 (*1-880684-50-0*) Curbstone.

— La Vida Loca: El Testimonio de una Pandilla Callejera en Los Angeles.Tr. of Always Running. (SPA.). 288p. 1996. per. 11.00 (*0-684-81551-6*, Fireside) S&S Trade Pap.

Rodriguez-Luis, Julio. The Contemporary Praxis of the Fantastic: Borges & Cortazar. LC 91-23877. (Latin American Studies: Vol. 1). x, 131p. 1991. text 28.00 (*0-8153-0101-4*, 1435) Garland.

Rodriguez-Luis, Julio, ed. Re-Reading Jose Marti (1853-1895) One Hundred Years Later. LC 98-41993. (SUNY Series in Latin American & Iberian Thought & Culture). 200p. 1999. text 49.50 (*0-7914-4239-X*) State U NY Pr.

— Re-Reading Jose Marti (1853-1895) One Hundred Years Later. LC 98-41993. (SUNY Series in Latin American & Iberian Thought & Culture). 158p. (C). 1999. pap. text 16.95 (*0-7914-4240-3*) State U NY Pr.

Rodriguez, Luz I. Entonces. (Biblioteca de Autores de Puerto Rico Ser.). (SPA.). 64p. (Orig.). 1991. pap. text 5.00 (*1-56328-003-5*) Edit Plaza Mayor.

Rodriguez, M. A., jt. ed. see Pesquera, L.

Rodriguez, M. Alma, jt. ed. see Cabanillas, Fernando.

Rodriguez, M. Alma, jt. ed. see Ibort, L. A.

Rodriguez, M. B. Cuentos Alegres. 3rd ed. LC 78-153486. (C). 1972. pap. text 40.00 (*0-03-080276-8*) Harcourt Coll Pubs.

Rodriguez, M. R., tr. see Malgorn, Guy.

Rodriguez, M. Rosanna, jt. auth. see Alexander, G. Rumay.

Rodriguez, M. Rosanna, ed. see Alexander, G. Rumay.

Rodriguez, M. Rosanna, ed. see Crosley, David.

Rodriguez Mahetha, Jose V., et al. Mamiferos de Colombia: Sus Nombres Comunes e Indigenas. (Occasional Papers in Conservation Biology: No. 3). (SPA.). 55p. (Orig.). (C). 1996. pap. text 10.00 (*1-881173-16-X*) Conser Intl.

Rodriguez, Manuel. My True Story. 136p. 1994. pap. 14.95 (*1-56097-141-X*) Fantagraph Bks.

Rodriguez, Manuel G., jt. ed. see Triana, Estrella M.

Rodriguez, Manuel Rivas, see Rivas Rodriguez, Manuel.

Rodriguez, Marcos E., tr. Concrete Repair.Tr. of Reparacion del Concreto. (SPA.). 56p. 1994. pap. 11.95 (*0-924659-66-1*) Hanley.

— Placing, Finishing & Curing Concrete.Tr. of Colocacion, Acabado y Curado del Concreto. (SPA.). 48p. 1994. pap. 11.95 (*0-924659-65-3*, 2120) Hanley.

Rodriguez, Maria, tr. see McBride, Jere J.

***Rodriguez, Maria Pilar.** Vidas Im/propias: Transformaciones del Sujeto, Femenino en la Narrativa Espanola Contemporanea. LC 99-49703. (Studies in Romance Literatures : Vol. 19). (SPA.). 1999. 42.95 (*1-55753-164-1*) Purdue U Pr.

Rodriguez, Mario. Traditional Woodwork: Adding Authentic Details to Your Home. LC 98-24962. (Illus.). 176p. 1998. pap. 19.95 (*1-56158-176-3*, 070303) Taunton.

— William Burke & Francisco de Miranda: The Word & Deed in Spanish America's Emancipation. LC 94-4182. 600p. (C). 1994. lib. bdg. 64.50 (*0-8191-9485-9*) U Pr of Amer.

Rodriguez, Marisol S. Guantanamo, el Ultimo Paso Hacia la Libertad. De Fana, Angel, ed. (SPA., Illus.). 320p. 1997. pap. 19.95 (*1-890829-03-X*) DFana Editions.

Rodriguez-Martin, Conrado, jt. auth. see Aufderheide, Arthur C.

Rodriguez, Marty M., jt. auth. see O'Brien, Matthew J.

Rodriguez, Mary G. Long Story Short. (Poesia Tejana Ser.: Vol. 4). (ENG & SPA.). x, 46p. 1999. pap. 12.00 (*0-930324-45-5*) Wings Pr.

Rodriguez-Matos, Carlos A. Llama de Amor Vivita Jarchas. LC 88-80881. (Arte y Poesia Ser.). (SPA., Illus.). 50p. (Orig.). 1988. pap. 6.00 (*0-685-20049-3*) Ichali.

Rodriguez Matos, Carlos A., jt. auth. see Villanueva-Collado, Alfredo.

Rodriguez, Mattie N. Sodium in Diets, Food & Health: Index of New Information. 160p. Date not set. 47.50 (*0-7883-1880-2*); pap. 44.50 (*0-7883-1881-0*) ABBE Pubs Assn.

***Rodriguez, Max.** Sacred Fire: The QBR 100 Essential Black Books. (Illus.). 231p. 1999. pap. 14.95 (*0-471-34872-4*) Wiley.

***Rodriguez, Max, et al, eds.** Sacred Fire: The QBR 100 Essential Black Books. LC 98-35060. 229p. 1999. 22.95 (*0-471-24376-0*) Wiley.

Rodriguez, Mercedes Mazquiaran de, see Glenn, Kathleen M. & Mazquiaran de Rodriguez, Mercedes, eds.

Rodriguez Monino, Antonio. Diccionario Bibliografico de Liegos Sueltos Poeticos, Siglo XVI. (SPA.). 740p. 1970. 53.95 (*0-8288-6494-2*, S-7006) Fr & Eur.

Rodriguez-Monino, Antonio. Diccionario de Pliegos Sueltos Poeticos.Tr. of Poetry Manuscripts, 16th Century. (SPA.). 735p. 1970. 49.95 (*0-8288-8564-8*) Fr & Eur.

Rodriguez-Monino, Antonio & Marino, Maria B., eds. Catalogo de los Manuscritos Poeticos Castellanos de la Sociedad Hispana de America, 3 vols. (SPA., Illus.). 1966. 50.00 (*0-87535-103-4*); lib. bdg. 60.00 (*0-87535-129-8*) Hispanic Soc.

Rodriguez Monino, Antonio, ed. see Melendez Valdes, Juan.

Rodriguez, N. M., et al, eds. Recent Advances in Catalytic Materials Vol. 497: Materials Research Society Symposium Proceedings. 252p. 1998. text 73.00 (*1-55899-402-5*) Materials Res.

Rodriguez, Narcisco, jt. auth. see Kuhtas, Candace.

Rodriguez, Nice. Throw It to the River. (International Connections Ser.). 156p. pap. 9.95 (*0-88961-187-4*, Pub. by Womens Pr) LPC InBook.

Rodriguez-Nieto, Catherine, tr. Fireflight: Three Latin American Poets. 1976. pap. 2.50 (*0-685-73658-X*) Oyez.

Rodriguez O, Jaime E. The Independence of Spanish America. LC 97-36310. (Latin American Studies: No. 84). 292p. (C). 1998. text 59.95 (*0-521-62298-0*); pap. text 19.95 (*0-521-62673-0*) Cambridge U Pr.

— Mexico in the Age of Democratic Revolutions, 1750-1850. LC 93-33325. 330p. 1994. lib. bdg. 42.00 (*1-55587-476-2*) L Rienner.

Rodriguez O, Jaime E., ed. The Origins of Mexican National Politics, 1808-1847. LC 97-17583. (Latin American Silhouettes Ser.). 144p. 1997. pap. 16.95 (*0-8420-2723-8*, SR Bks) Scholarly Res Inc.

Rodriguez O, Jaime E., tr. see Flores Caballero, Romero R.

Rodriguez, Olga, ed. The Politics of Chicano Liberation. 1977. pap. 15.95 (*0-87348-514-9*); lib. bdg. 40.00 (*0-87348-513-0*) Pathfinder NY.

Rodriguez, Orlando, jt. ed. see Malgady, Robert G.

Rodriguez, Oscar E., tr. see Rusbuldt, Richard E., et al.

Rodriguez, Osvaldo & Neruda, Pablo. La Obra Postuma de Pablo Neruda. LC 95-82060. (SPA.). 128p. (Orig.). 1996. pap. 12.00 (*0-935318-22-4*) Edins Hispamerica.

Rodriguez, Otilio, jt. auth. see Kavanaugh, Kieran.

Rodriguez, Otilio, jt. tr. see Kavanaugh, Kieran.

Rodriguez, P. Pedro. Matrimono y Familia Cristiana. 116p. 1984. pap. 4.95 (*0-915388-20-0*, 171) ACTA Pubns.

Rodriguez, Pamela S., ed. see Blackwell, Donald A.

Rodriguez, Patricia, ed. see Riley, Gay.

Rodriguez, Paul. Breast Cancer: What Every Woman Should Know. (Illus.). 138p. (Orig.). 1988. pap. text 11.45 (*0-9622118-0-X*) Aurora KS.

***Rodriguez, Paul.** Get Slim, Stay Slim Program. (Illus.). 2000. pap. 12.00 (*0-9622118-3-4*) Aurora KS.

***Rodriguez, Paul L. & Klyer, Karen.** The Get Slim Stay Slim Program. 1999. pap. 12.00 (*0-9622118-9-3*) Aurora KS.

Rodriguez, Paulino S. Legado, Poesias y Sonetos. (SPA.). 144p. 1995. lib. bdg. write for info. (*1-888598-01-8*) P S Rodriguez.

— Simplemente Versos y Poesias. 144p. 1995. lib. bdg. write for info. (*1-888598-00-X*) P S Rodriguez.

— Suenos de Cristal. (SPA.). 144p. 1995. lib. bdg. write for info. (*1-888598-02-6*) P S Rodriguez.

Rodriguez, Pedro, tr. see Lewinski, Ronald J.

Rodriguez, Pedro G., jt. auth. see Quigg, Claudia.

Rodriguez Perez, Luis. Diccionario de Dificultades Matematicas Resueltas. (SPA.). 440p. 1984. pap. 55.00 (*0-8288-1900-9*, S60045) Fr & Eur.

Rodriguez-Pose, Andres. Dynamics of Regional Growth in Europe: Social & Political Factors. LC 98-20266. (Oxford Geographical & Environmental Studies Series). (Illus.). 280p. 1999. text 80.00 (*0-19-823383-3*) OUP.

Rodriguez, R., et al, eds. Plant Aging: Basic & Applied Approaches. LC 90-6996. (NATO ASI Ser.: Vol. 186). (Illus.). 462p. (C). 1990. text 162.00 (*0-306-43518-7*, Kluwer Plenum) Kluwer Academic.

Rodriguez, R. L. & Tait, R. C. Recombinant DNA Experiments: An Introduction. 1983. pap. text 29.25 (*0-201-10870-4*) Benjamin-Cummings.

Rodriguez, Rafael, jt. ed. see Zavala, Iris M.

***Rodriguez, Raul M.** The End of Law. xvi, 149p. 2000. pap. 19.95 (*0-9674508-0-2*) Bleak Hse.

Rodriguez-Reinoso, F., et al, eds. Characterization of Porous Solids No. Two: Proceedings of the IUPAC Symposium (COPS II), Alicante, Spain, May 6-9, 1990. (Studies in Surface Science & Catalysis: No. 62). 782p. 1991. 328.00 (*0-444-88569-2*) Elsevier.

Rodriguez, Reymundo & Coleman, Marion T., eds. Mental Health Issues of the Mexican Origin Population in Texas: Proceedings of the Fifth Robert L. Sutherland Seminar. 240p. (Orig.). 1987. pap. 9.45 (*0-943463-00-9*) Hogg Found.

Rodriguez, Ricardo J., jt. auth. see Kolb, Robert.

Rodriguez, Ricardo J., jt. auth. see Kolb, Robert W.

Rodriguez, Richard. Days of Obligation: An Argument with My Mexican Father. 240p. 1993. reprint ed. pap. 12.95 (*0-14-009622-1*, Penguin Bks) Viking Penguin.

— Hunger of Memory: An Autobiography. 208p. 1983. mass mkt. 6.50 (*0-553-27293-4*, Bantam Classics) Bantam.

— Kings Highway. 1999. text 24.95 (*0-670-86582-6*) Viking Penguin.

— Movements. 1999. pap. write for info. (*0-14-025352-1*, Viking) Viking Penguin.

Rodriguez, Richard, jt. auth. see Stubbs, Liz.

Rodriguez, Richardo J., jt. auth. see Kolb, Robert W.

Rodriguez, Rita M., jt. auth. see Riehl, Heinz.

Rodriguez, Robert. Rebel Without a Crew: or How a 23-Year-Old Filmaker with $7,000 Became a Hollywood Player. 1996. pap. 12.95 (*0-452-27187-8*, Plume) Dutton Plume.

Rodriguez, Robert. Mad about Martha: The Fabulous Paper Doll Book. 32p. (Orig.). 1997. pap. 9.95 (*0-8362-2432-9*, Cader Bks) Andrews & McMeel.

Rodriguez, Roberto. Justice: A Question of Race. LC 97-9913. 328p. 1997. 30.00 (*0-927534-69-X*); pap. 19.00 (*0-927534-68-1*) Biling Rev-Pr.

Rodriguez, Roberto, jt. auth. see Gonzales, Patrisia.

Rodriguez, Rod & Stieglitz, Ezra L. Readability Master 2000. 1997. pap. 29.95 incl. disk (*1-57129-031-1*); pap. 29.95 incl. mac ld (*1-57129-038-9*) Brookline Bks.

Rodriguez, Rodolfo, et al, eds. Compendium of Readings in Bilingual Education: Issues & Practices. 334p. 1994. pap. text 29.95 (*1-891074-03-2*) TX Assn Bilingual.

Rodriguez-Roque, Oswaldo. American Furniture at Chipstone. LC 83-40270. (Illus.). 480p. 1984. 50.00 (*0-299-09760-9*) U of Wis Pr.

RODRIGUEZ, ROSAURA. No Hay Mal Que Dure 100 Anos Ni Mujer Que lo Resista. 1997. pap. text 11.98 (*970-05-0756-4*) Grijalbo Edit.

***Rodriguez, Sammy.** Third Day Generation. 224p. 2000. pap. 12.99 (*0-88419-730-1*) Creation House.

Rodriguez Santidrian, Pedro. Diccionario de las Religiones. (SPA.). 472p. 1989. pap. 18.95 (*0-7859-5718-9*, 8420603732) Fr & Eur.

Rodriguez-Saona, Roberto. Colloquial Spanish of Latin America. 1994. audio 19.99 (*0-415-08953-0*) Routledge.

An Asterisk (*) at the beginning of an entry indicates that the title is appearing for the first time.

— Colloquial Spanish of Latin America. LC 93-38248. (Colloquials Ser.). (Illus.). 304p. (gr. 13). 1994. pap. 14.99 (*0-415-08952-2*) Routledge.

— Colloquial Spanish of Latin America, Set. (Colloquials Ser.). 304p. (C). (gr. 13). 1994. pap. 27.99 incl. audio, 5.25 hd (*0-415-08954-9*) Routledge.

Rodriguez-Seda de Laguna, Asela. Shaw en el Mundo Hispanico. LC 79-22415. (Coleccion Mente y Palabra). (SPA.). 142p. 1981. 9.60 (*0-8477-0564-1*); pap. 8.00 (*0-8477-0565-X*) U of PR Pr.

Rodriguez, Sergio G. El Sendero de los Gatos (The Trail of the Cats) (SPA.). 122p. (YA). 1994. pap. 6.99 (*968-16-4228-7*, Pub. by Fondo) Continental Bk.

Rodriguez-Silva, Delfin. Cronologia Martiana: (La Ruta Apostolica de Jose Marti 1853-1895) LC 95-83929. (Coleccion Formacion Martiana). (SPA., Illus.). 359p. (Orig.). 1996. pap. 24.95 (*0-89729-792-X*) Ediciones.

Rodriguez, Sonia, jt. auth. see Quinonez, Gilberto.

Rodriguez Sordo, M. Luisa. El Senor de Alfoz, Level 2. (Leer en Espanol Ser.). (SPA.). (C). 1998. pap. 5.95 (*84-294-4046-1*) Santillana.

Rodriguez, Spain. She: Anthology of Big Bitch. 1993. pap. 14.95 (*0-86719-398-0*) Last Gasp.

Rodriguez, Susan. Art Smart: Ready-to-Use Slides & Activities for Teaching Art History & Appreciation. (Illus.). 288p. (J). (gr. 3-12). 1988. pap. text 79.95 (*0-13-047754-0*, Busn) P-H.

— Culture Smart! LC 99-187317. (Illus.). 320p. 1998. pap. 89.95 (*0-13-145863-9*, Pub. by P-H) S&S Trade.

— The Special Artist's Handbook: Art Activities & Adaptive Aids for Handicapped Children. LC 84-4704. (Illus.). 288p. (Orig.). 1984. pap. 17.95 (*0-13-826355-8*) P-H.

— The Special Artist's Handbook: Art Activities & Adaptive Aids for Handicapped Students. (Illus.). 278p. (J). 1988. pap., teacher ed. 21.50 (*0-86651-476-7*, 11907) Seymour Pubns.

Rodriguez, Susan, ed. see Center for International Legal Studies Staff.

*__Rodriguez, Suzanne & Prell, Bertrand, eds.__ International Judicial Assistance in Civil Matters. LC 99-36509. (International Business Law Practice Ser.). 350p. 1999. text 115.00 (*1-57105-103-1*) Transnatl Pubs.

Rodriguez, Sylvia. Matachines Dance: Ritual Symbolism & Interethnic Relations in the Upper Rio Grande Valley. (Publications of the American Folklore Society). 193p. 1996. 45.00 (*0-8263-1677-8*); pap. 25.00 (*0-8263-1678-6*) U of NM Pr.

Rodriguez, Teresa B. Modalidades Del Caso y Del Proceso Juridico En el Drama Hispanoamericano. LC 89-83954. (SPA.). 141p. (Orig.). 1991. pap. 19.00 (*0-89729-534-X*) Ediciones.

Rodriguez-Turner, Patricia. Illusions on Wings. 1997. pap. write for info. (*1-57553-589-0*) Watermrk Pr.

Rodriguez-Valera. Halophilic Bacteria, Vol. I. 160p. 1987. 95.00 (*0-8493-4367-4*, CRC Reprint) Franklin.

Rodriguez-Valera, Francisco. Halophilic Bacteria, Vol. II. 152p. 1987. 92.00 (*0-8493-4368-2*, CRC Reprint) Franklin.

Rodriguez-Valera, Francisco, ed. General & Applied Aspects of Halophilic Microorganisms. (NATO ASI Ser.: Vol. 201). (Illus.). 414p. (C). text 156.00 (*0-306-43816-X*) Plenum.

Rodriguez-Valera, Fransisco, ed. Halophilic Bacteria, 2 vols., Set. (Bacteriologists Ser.). 1988. 187.00 (*0-8493-4366-6*, QR97, CRC Reprint) Franklin.

Rodriguez-Vergara, Isabel. Haunting Demons: Critical Essays on the Works of Garcia Marquez. LC 98-7774. (Cultural Ser.). 1998. write for info. (*0-8270-3852-6*) OAS.

Rodriguez, Vicente. Vicente Rodriguez - Toccatas for Harpsichord: Thirty Sonatas & a Pastorella, 1744, I. Howell, Almonte, ed. (Recent Researches in Music of the Classic Era Ser.: Vol. RRC22). (Illus.). 102p. 1986. pap. 35.00 (*0-89579-211-7*) A-R Eds.

— Vicente Rodriguez - Toccatas for Harpsichord: Thirty Sonatas & a Pastorella, 1744, II. Howell, Almonte, ed. (Recent Researches in Music of the Classic Era Ser.: Vol. RRC23). (Illus.). xiv, 94p. 1986. pap. 35.00 (*0-89579-212-5*) A-R Eds.

Rodriguez, Victor. Eldorado in East Harlem. LC 92-14985. 156p. 1992. 9.50 (*1-55885-054-6*) Arte Publico.

Rodriguez, Victoria. Women's Participation in Mexican Political Life. LC 98-20771. 304p. 1998. pap. 26.00 (*0-8133-3530-2*, Pub. by Westview) HarpC.

— Women's Participation in Mexican Political Life. LC 98-20771. 304p. 1998. pap. 69.00 (*0-8133-3529-9*, Pub. by Westview) HarpC.

*__Rodriguez, Victoria & Ward, Peter.__ Reaching Across the Border: Intergovernmental Relations Between Texas & Mexico. 254p. 2000. pap. 18.00 (*0-89940-747-1*) LBJ Sch Pub Aff.

Rodriguez, Victoria E. Decentralization in Mexico: From Reforma Municipal to Solidaridad to Nuevo Federalismo. LC 97-20387. 224p. (C). 1997. pap. text 25.00 (*0-8133-2779-2*, Pub. by Westview) HarpC.

Rodriguez, Victoria E. & Ward, Peter M. Political Change in Baja California: Democracy in the Making? (Monographs). 140p. (C). 1994. pap. 13.95 (*1-878367-25-0*, MN-40) UCSD Ctr US-Mex.

Rodriguez, Victoria E. & Ward, Peter M., eds. Opposition Government in Mexico. LC 94-36197. 270p. 1995. pap. 22.50 (*0-8263-1578-X*) U of NM Pr.

Rodriguez, Victoria E., jt. auth. see Ward, Peter.

Rodriguez, Victorino R. The Theology of Peace. LC 88-70763. (Illus.). 62p. (Orig.). (C). 1988. pap. 4.00 (*1-877905-04-6*) Am Soc Defense TFP.

Rodriguez, Victorio, jt. ed. see Bodey, Gerald P.

Rodriguez, Vivian, jt. auth. see Carrasquillo, Angela L.

Rodriguez, W. R. The Shoe Shine Parlor Poems Et Al. 48p. 1984. pap. 6.50 (*0-941160-08-4*) Ghost Pony Pr.

Rodriguez, Walter E. The Modeling of Design Ideas: Graphics & Visualization Techniques for Engineers. 1992. text write for info. (*0-07-079744-7*) McGraw.

— The Modeling of Design Ideas: Graphics & Visualization Techniques for Engineers. (C). 1992. text 40.00 (*0-07-053394-6*) McGraw.

Rodriguez, Wanda C. Consejeria Psicologica. (SPA.). 256p. 1991. pap. write for info. (*0-929441-25-7*) Pubns Puertorriquenas.

Rodriguez, Wanda C., jt. auth. see Bernal, Guillermo.

Rodriguez, Yesenia M. La Narrativa de Salvador Garmendia: Mas Alla de la Razon. LC 97-40309. 108p. 1997. 59.95 (*0-7734-2215-3*) E Mellen.

Rodrik, Dani. Has Globalization Gone Too Far? LC 96-6545. 108p. 1997. pap. 17.95 (*0-88132-241-5*) Inst Intl Eco.

Globalization is exposing social fissures between those with the education, skills & mobility to flourish in an unfettered world market-the apparent "winners" & those without. These apparent "losers" are increasingly anxious about their standards of living & their precarious place in an integrated world economy. The result is severe tension between the market & broad sectors of society, with governments caught in the middle. Compounding the very real problems that need to be addressed by all involved, the kneejerk rhetoric of both sides threatens to crowd out rational debate. From the United States to Europe to Asia, positions are hardening. Author Don Rodrik brings a clear & reasoned voice to these questions. Has Globalization Gone Too Far? takes an unblinking & objective look at the economists for downplaying its dangers. It also makes a unique & perusaive case that the "winners" have as much at stake from the possible consequences of social instability as the "losers." As Rodrik points out "...social disintegration is not a spectator sport those on the sidelines also get splashed with mud from the fields. Ultimately, the deepening of social fissures can harm all." President Clinton has read the book & it provided the conceptual basis for the trade/IMF portions of the State of the Union message in January 1998. *Publisher Paid Annotation.*

— New Global Economy & Developing Countries. LC 98-54766. 10p. 1998. pap. text 13.95 (*1-56517-027-X*) Overseas Dev Council.

Rodrik, Dani, jt. auth. see Collins, Susan M.

Rodrik, Dani, jt. auth. see Diwan, Ishac.

Rodrique, Gary, ed. Parallel Processing for Scientific Computing. LC 88-62233. (Proceedings in Applied Mathematics Ser.: No. 35). xxix, 428p. 1988. pap. 50.50 (*0-89871-228-9*) Soc Indus-Appl Math.

Rodriques, A. & Tondeur, D., eds. Percolation Processes: Theory & Applications. (NATO Advanced Study Institute Ser.: Applied Science, No. 33). 594p. 1981. text 184.00 (*90-286-0579-7*) Kluwer Academic.

*__Rodriques, Jose Carlos.__ Bibliotheca Brasiliense: Catalogo Annotado dos Libros Sobre o Brasil. fac. ed. 680p. 2000. 95.00 (*1-57898-198-0*) Martino Pubng.

Rodriquez. Modeling of Design Ideas. 1992. student ed. 18.75 (*0-07-053393-8*) McGraw.

Rodriquez, Alex. 9 Innings with Cal Ripken Jr. By the People Who Know Him Best. (Illus.). 1998. 19.95 (*1-887432-46-9*) Beckett Pubns.

Rodriquez, Andres. Night Song. 78p. (Orig.). 1994. pap. 7.95 (*1-882688-05-8*) Tia Chucha Pr.

Rodriquez, Anita, et al, eds. Accelerator-Driven Transmutation Technologies & Applications: Proceedings of the International Conference on Accelerator-Driven Transmutation Technologies & Applications Held 1994, Las Vegas, NV. LC 95-78691. (AIP Conference Proceedings Ser.: No. CP 346). (Illus.). 954p. 1995. 175.00 (*1-56396-505-4*) Am Inst Physics.

Rodriquez-Barrientos. Diccionario Maritimo: Ingles - Espanol, Espanol - Ingoles. (ENG & SPA.). 1987. write for info. (*0-7859-3684-X*, 8428315140) Fr & Eur.

Rodriquez-Barrueco, C., jt. auth. see Subbarao, N. S.

Rodriquez-Castellano, Juan. En Busca de Oro Negro. (SPA., Illus.). (C). 1945. 21.95 (*0-8290-2396-8*) Irvington.

Rodriquez, Consuelo. Cesar Chavez. (Hispanos Notables Ser.). (SPA., Illus.). 120p. (YA). (gr. 5 up). 1991. pap. 8.95 (*0-7910-3112-8*) Chelsea Hse.

Rodriquez de Lecea, Teresa, ed. see Giner de Los Rios, Francisco.

Rodriquez de Montalvo, Garci. Amadis de Gaula, I. Avalle-Arce, Juan B., ed. (Nueva Austral Ser.: Vol. 119). (SPA.). 1991. pap. text 42.95 (*84-239-1919-6*) Elliots Bks.

— Amadis de Gaula, II. Avalle-Arce, Juan B., ed. (Nueva Austral Ser.: Vol. 120). (SPA.). 1991. pap. text 42.95 (*84-239-1920-X*) Elliots Bks.

Rodriquez, Elmer, et al. De Perlas: Intermediate Spanish. LC 97-1753. (SPA.). 320p. 1997. pap. 48.95 (*0-471-10997-5*) Wiley.

Rodriquez, Eugenio C. Latinoamerica: Su Civilizacion y Su Cultura. 432p. (C). 1983. mass mkt. 18.50 (*0-8384-3541-6*, Newbury) Heinle & Heinle.

Rodriquez, Jorge L. Civil Engineering Problem Solving Flowcharts. 2nd ed. (Illus.). 160p. 1999. reprint ed. pap. 31.50 (*1-57645-038-4*, 384) Engineering.

Rodriquez, Judith. La Biblia Me Ensena: The Bible Teaches Me. De Fajardo, Vilma, ed. 96p. (J). (ps). 1988. pap. 7.45 (*0-311-11454-7*) Casa Bautista.

Rodriquez, Judy, jt. auth. see Rodriguez, David.

Rodriquez, Judy, tr. see Brinkley, Ginny & Sampson, Sherry.

Rodriquez, K. S. The Backstreet Boys. (Illus.). 128p. (J). (gr. 3-7). 1997. pap. 4.99 (*0-06-107075-0*) HarpC.

Rodriquez, M. J. & Adams, Simon. England, Spain & the Grand Armada, 1585-1604. 324p. (C). 1991. text 78.00 (*0-389-20955-4*) B&N Imports.

Rodriquez, Maria Del Mar Martinez, see Del Mar Martinez Rodriquez, Maria, ed.

Rodriquez, Mario. The Cadiz Experiment in Central America, 1808 to 1826. LC 76-50256. 328p. reprint ed. pap. 101.70 (*0-7837-4844-2*, 204449100003) Bks Demand.

Rodriquez, Otillo, tr. see Kavanaugh, Kieran.

Rodriquez-Peralta, Phyllis W. Jose Santos Chocano. LC 71-99529. (Twayne's World Authors Ser.). 1970. lib. bdg. 17.95 (*0-685-02668-X*) Irvington.

Rodriquez, R. & Costas, M. Lectures on Thermodynamics & Statistical Mechanics: Proceedings of the XXIII Winter Meeting on Statistical Physics. 292p. 1994. text 71.00 (*981-02-1915-6*) World Scientific Pub.

Rodriquez, Richard, et al. Crossing the Frontier: Photographs of the Developing West, 1849 to the Present. LC 96-22072. (Illus.). 180p. 1996. pap. 29.95 (*0-8118-1420-3*) Chronicle Bks.

Rodriquez Salgado, Maria J., jt. auth. see Adams, Simon.

Rodriquez Sellas, Jose R., tr. see Glasser, Ruth.

*__Rodriquez, Stephanie.__ Time to Stop Pretending: A Mother's Story of Domestic Violence, Homelessness, Poverty & Escape. 2nd ed. 192p. 1999. reprint ed. pap. 14.95 (*0-8397-8061-3*, Pub. by Eriksson) IPG Chicago.

Rodriquez, Susan. Art Smart! Ready-to-Use Slides & Activities for Teaching Art History & Appreciation. 12p. (C). 1989. pap. text 29.95 (*0-13-047622-6*) P-H.

*__Rodseth, Asbjorn.__ Open Economy Macroeconomics. (Illus.). 432p. 2000. write for info. (*0-521-78304-6*); pap. write for info. (*0-521-78874-9*) Cambridge U Pr.

Rodseth, T. Models for Multispecies Management. LC 98-16486. (Contributions to Economics Ser.). (Illus.). viii, 246p. 1998. pap. 67.00 (*3-7908-1001-0*) Spr-Verlag.

Rodson, Johan. Alone in the Dark: Official Strategy Guide. LC 94-66258. (Illus.). 224p. 1994. pap. 19.95 (*1-55958-604-4*) Prima Pub.

Rodstein, Harvey E. Pick for Professionals: Advanced Methods & Techniques. 368p. 1990. 34.95 (*0-07-156991-X*) McGraw.

— Pick for Professionals: Advanced Methods & Techniques. (Pick Library). (Illus.). 256p. 1989. 34.95 (*0-8306-0125-2*) McGraw-Hill Prof.

Rodu, Brad. For Smokers Only: How Smokeless Tobacco Can Save Your Life. 2nd ed. (Illus.). 190p. (Orig.). 1998. reprint ed. pap. 14.95 (*0-9666239-0-8*) Sumner Bks CA.

Roduit, Mary A., tr. see Cusson, Gilles.

Rodvold, Keith A., jt. ed. see Piscitelli, Stephen C.

Rodway, Allan E., ed. Godwin & the Age of Transition. LC 76-52953. (English Literature Ser.: No. 33). 1977. lib. bdg. 75.00 (*0-8383-2146-1*) M S G Haskell Hse.

Rodway, Allan E., jt. auth. see De Sola Pinto, Vivian.

Rodway, Howard. Old Path Tarot, Vol. 1. 1990. pap. 20.00 (*0-88079-490-9*, OP78) US Games Syst.

— Old Path Tarot Set: Includes Tarot of the Old Path. 160p. 1990. pap. 39.95 (*0-88079-492-5*, OPT99) US Games Syst.

— Tarot of the Old Path. 1997. pap. text 12.95 (*0-88079-491-7*, BK111) US Games Syst.

Rodway, Howard, jt. auth. see Gainsford, Sylvia.

Rodway, James. In the Guiana Forest: Studies of Nature in Relations to the Struggle for Life. LC 69-18997. (Illus.). 242p. 1970. reprint ed. lib. bdg. 49.50 (*0-8371-1027-0*, ROG&, Greenwood Pr) Greenwood.

Rodway, Juliet. Little Book of Renoir. 1994. 4.98 (*1-55521-985-3*) Bk Sales Inc.

— Little Book of Van Gogh. 1994. 4.98 (*1-55521-986-1*) Bk Sales Inc.

Rodway, Margaret & Wright, Marianne, eds. Sociopsychological Aspects of Sexually Transmitted Diseases. LC 88-638. (Journal of Social Work & Human Sexuality: Vol. 6, No. 2). (Illus.). 162p. 1988. text 49.95 (*0-86656-737-2*) Haworth Pr.

Rodway, Margaret R. Counseling Diverse Client Groups: An International Perspective on Human Social Functioning. LC 89-9297. (Studies in Health & Human Services). 376p. 1989. lib. bdg. 99.95 (*0-88946-139-2*) E Mellen.

Rodway, Margaret R. & Trute, Barry, eds. The Ecological Perspective in Family-Centered Therapy. LC 93-29860. (Studies in Health & Human Services: Vol. 19). 364p. 1993. text 99.95 (*0-7734-9362-X*) E Mellen.

Rodway, Margaret R. & Wingrove, Brian L. Healthy Homosexual. LC 84-90340. 1984. 9.95 (*0-87212-180-1*) Libra.

Rodway, Marie. Wiccan Herbal. 128p. 1997. pap. text 17.95 (*0-572-02340-5*, Pub. by W Foulsham) Trans-Atl Phila.

Rodway, Stella, tr. see Wiesel, Elie.

*__Rodway, Susan & Levene, Simon.__ Medical Negligence: Managing Medical Disputes. 260p. 2000. 98.60 (*1-902558-05-7*, Pub. by Palladian Law) Gaunt.

Rodwell, Dorothy, jt. auth. see American Production & Inventory Control Society St.

Rodwell, J. M., tr. The Koran. 510p. 1995. lib. bdg. 5.50 (*0-460-87438-1*, Everyman's Classic Lib) Tuttle Pubng.

Rodwell, J. S. British Plant Communities Vol. 1: Woodlands & Scrub. (Illus.). 406p. (C). 1998. reprint ed. pap. text 54.95 (*0-521-62721-4*) Cambridge U Pr.

— British Plant Communities Vol. 3: Grasslands & Montane Communities. (Illus.). 550p. (C). 1998. reprint ed. pap. text 54.95 (*0-521-62719-2*) Cambridge U Pr.

— British Plant Communities Vol. 4: Aquatic Communities, Swamps, & Tall-Herb Fens. (Illus.). 296p. (C). 1998. reprint ed. pap. text 54.95 (*0-521-62718-4*) Cambridge U Pr.

Rodwell, J. S., ed. British Plant Communities Vol. 1: Woodlands & Scrub. (Illus.). 400p. (C). 1991. text 160.00 (*0-521-23558-8*) Cambridge U Pr.

— British Plant Communities Vol. 2: Mires & Heaths. (Illus.). 638p. (C). 1992. text 195.00 (*0-521-39165-2*) Cambridge U Pr.

— British Plant Communities Vol. 2: Mires & Heaths. (Illus.). 638p. (C). 1998. pap. text 54.95 (*0-521-62720-6*) Cambridge U Pr.

— British Plant Communities Vol. 3: Grasslands & Montane Communities. (Illus.). 550p. (C). 1993. text 195.00 (*0-521-39166-0*) Cambridge U Pr.

— British Plant Communities Vol. 4: Aquatic Communities, Swamps & Tall-Herb Fens. (Illus.). 295p. (C). 1995. text 115.00 (*0-521-39168-7*) Cambridge U Pr.

*__Rodwell, J. S., ed.__ British Plant Communities Vol. 5: Maritime Communities & Vegetation of Open Habitats. (Illus.). 608p. (C). 2000. 120.00 (*0-521-39167-9*); pap. 54.95 (*0-521-64476-3*) Cambridge U Pr.

Rodwell, Jenny. Acrylic Workbook: Complete Course in Ten Lessons. LC 99-187458. (Illus.). 128p. 1998. 19.95 (*0-7153-0720-7*, Pub. by D & C Pub) Sterling.

*__Rodwell, Jenny.__ Flower Painting. (Illus.). 2000. 14.99 (*0-7858-1245-8*) Bk Sales Inc.

— Painting with Acrylics. 1999. 14.99 (*0-7858-1143-5*) Book Sales.

— Potter's Workshop: 20 Unique Ceramic Projects for the Small Home Studio. (Illus.). 144p. 2000. 27.95 (*0-7153-0928-5*, Pub. by D & C Pub) Sterling.

Rodwell, Jenny. Step by Step Art School: Drawing. 1987. 12.98 (*0-671-08906-4*) S&S Trade.

— Watercolorist's Guide to Mixing Colors. (Illus.). 128p. 1997. 27.99 (*0-89134-797-6*, North Lght Bks) F & W Pubns Inc.

Rodwell, Jenny, jt. auth. see Monahan, Patricia.

Rodwell, John. Participative Training Skills. Taylor, Billie, ed. LC 94-1072. 192p. 1994. 96.95 (*0-566-07444-3*, Pub. by Gower) Ashgate Pub Co.

Rodwell, John & Patterson, Gordon. Creating New Native Woodlands. (Forestry Commission Bulletin Ser.: No. 112). 85p. 1994. pap. 17.00 (*0-11-710320-9*, HM03209, Pub. by Statnry Office) Bernan Associates.

Rodwell, John Medows. The Koran. Ivy Books Staff, Books, ed. (Orig.). 1993. mass mkt. 5.99 (*0-8041-1125-1*) Ivy Books.

Rodwell, Mary K. Social Work Constructivist Research. LC 98-19159. (Social Psychology Reference Ser.). (Illus.). 328p. 1998. 70.00 (*0-8153-2552-5*, SS1134); pap. 34.95 (*0-8153-2567-3*, SS1134) Garland.

Rodwell, Warwick. The Archaeology of Religious Places: Churches & Cemeteries in Britain. rev. ed. LC 89-24964. (Illus.). 208p. (C). 1990. text 38.95 (*0-8122-8244-2*) U of Pa Pr.

— The Origins & Early Development of Witham, Essex. (Illus.). 128p. 1993. pap. 48.00 (*0-946897-50-6*, Pub. by Oxbow Bks) David Brown.

Rodwin, L. & Hollister, R. M. Cities of the Mind: Images & Themes of the City in the Social Sciences. LC 84-1991. (Environment, Development, & Public Policy: Public Policy & Social Services Ser.). (Illus.). 370p. (C). 1984. 65.00 (*0-306-41426-0*, Plenum Trade) Perseus Pubng.

Rodwin, Lloyd. Cities & City Planning. LC 81-13956. (Environment, Development, & Public Policy: Public Policy & Social Services Ser.). 318p. (C). 1981. 49.50 (*0-306-40666-7*, Plenum Trade) Perseus Pubng.

Rodwin, Lloyd, ed. Shelter, Settlement & Development. LC 87-1038. 448p. (C). 1987. text 39.95 (*0-04-711023-6*) Routledge.

*__Rodwin, Lloyd & Sanyal, Bishwapriya, eds.__ The Profession of City Planning: Changes, Images & Challenges, 1950-2000. 416p. 2000. text 49.95 (*0-88285-166-7*) Ctr Urban Pol Res.

Rodwin, Lloyd & Sanyal, Bishwapriya, eds. The Profession of City Planning: Changes, Images & Challenges, 1950-2000. LC 99-33272. 416p. (C). 2000. pap. text 29.95 (*0-88285-165-9*) Ctr Urban Pol Res.

Rodwin, Lloyd & Sazanami, Hidehiko. European Deindustrialization & Regional Economic Transformation. 256p. (C). 1990. text 65.00 (*0-04-445882-7*); pap. text 24.95 (*0-04-445883-5*) Routledge.

Rodwin, Lloyd & Sazanami, Hidehiko, eds. Deindustrialization & Regional Economic Transformation: The Experience of the United States. (Illus.). 288p. 1989. 65.00 (*0-04-445538-0*); pap. 27.95 (*0-04-445539-9*) Routledge.

Rodwin, Lloyd & Schon, Donald A., eds. Rethinking the Development Experience: Essays Provoked by the Work of Albert O. Hirschman. LC 94-12644. 369p. (C). 1994. 44.95 (*0-8157-7552-0*); pap. 19.95 (*0-8157-7551-2*) Brookings.

Rodwin, Marc A. Medicine, Money & Morals: Physicians' Conflicts of Interest. (Illus.). 432p. 1995. pap. 13.95 (*0-19-509647-9*) OUP.

Rodwin, Victor G., et al, eds. Public Hospital Systems in New York & Paris. 320p. (C). 1992. text 50.00 (*0-8147-7422-9*) NYU Pr.

*__Rody, Caroline.__ The Daughter's Return: African-American & Caribbean Women's Fictions of History. 288p. 2000. text 49.95 (*0-19-513888-0*) OUP.

Rody, Martyn. The Breakup of Yugoslavia. (Conflicts Ser.). (Illus.). 48p. (YA). (gr. 6 up). 1994. text, lib. bdg. 13.95 (*0-02-792529-3*, New Dscvry Bks) Silver Burdett Pr.

R

R

Rodzianko, M. The Truth about the Russian Church Abroad. Hilko, Michael P., tr. from RUS. LC 74-29321. (Illus.). 48p. (Orig.). 1975. pap. 1.50 (*0-88465-004-9*) Holy Trinity.

Rodzianko, M. V. Krushenie Imperii. rev. ed. LC 85-52365. (Illus.). 384p. 1986. pap. 16.00 (*0-9616413-0-4*) Multilingual.

Roe. Coaching. (Training Ser.). 1995. pap. text 39.95 (*0-07-999990-5*) McGraw.

— Con Me Hermano.Tr. of With My Brother. (J). 1998. pap. 5.99 (*0-87628-126-9*) Ctr Appl Res.

— Food for Health. Date not set. pap. text. write for info. (*0-582-22479-9*, Pub. by Addison-Wesley) Longman.

— From Mechanism to Organism. 1999. 24.95 (*0-8057-9518-9*, Twyne); per. 14.95 (*0-8057-9519-7*, Twyne) Mac Lib Ref.

— Home & Consumer. Date not set. pap. text. write for info. (*0-582-22477-2*, Pub. by Addison-Wesley) Longman.

— Radical Biology Enlightenment. 1993. pap. text 14.95 (*0-226-72365-8*) U Ch Pr.

— Secondary School Reading Exam, 5 vols. LC 94-76545. (C). Date not set. text 61.96 (*0-395-71900-3*) HM.

— Social Biology Enlightenment. 1993. lib. bdg. 34.95 (*0-226-72363-1*) U Ch Pr.

— Using Visual Basic with Autocad. LC 98-35329. (CAD/CAM Ser.). 432p. 1998. 47.95 (*0-7668-0366-X*) Delmar.

***Roe.** Using Visual Basic with Autocad 2000. 2nd ed. (C). 2000. text 44.95 (*0-7668-2091-2*) Delmar.

Roe. Winning New Business in the Service Sector. 224p. 1999. pap. text 29.95 (*0-7506-4127-4*) Buttrwrth-Heinemann.

Roe, A. D., jt. auth. see Moss, G. P.

Roe, Alan, et al. International Finance Strategies for Developing Countries. LC 92-35776. (EDI Policy Seminar Reports: No. 31). 50p. 1992. pap. 22.00 (*0-8213-2283-4*, 12283) World Bank.

Roe, Alan, jt. auth. see Pyatt, F. Graham.

Roe, Alan R. Instruments of Economic Policy in Africa. 238p. (C). 1992. pap. 29.95 (*0-435-08973-0*, 08074) Heinemann.

Roe, Alf S. The Thirty-Ninth Regiment, Massachusetts Volunteers, 1862-1865. (Illus.). 493p. 1998. reprint ed. lib. bdg. 55.00 (*0-8328-7026-9*) Higginson Bk Co.

— The Twenty-Fourth Regiment Massachusetts Volunteers, 1861-66: New England Guard Regiment. (Illus.). 573p. 1998. reprint ed. lib. bdg. 62.00 (*0-8328-7028-5*) Higginson Bk Co.

Roe, Alfred S. Civil War Infantry, the 10th Regiment, Massachusetts Volunteer Infantry, 1861-1864, a Western Massachusetts Regiment. (Illus.). 535p. 1995. reprint ed. lib. bdg. 57.50 (*0-8328-6528-1*) Higginson Bk Co.

— Civil War Infantry, 5th Regiment, Mass. Volunteers Infantry, in Its Three Tours of Duty, 1861, 1862-3, 1864. (Illus.). 510p. 1995. reprint ed. lib. bdg. 56.00 (*0-8328-4639-2*) Higginson Bk Co.

Roe, Alfred S. Monocacy. Harlowe, Jerry L., ed. Orig. Title: Monocacy: A Sketch of the Battle of Monocacy, Maryland. 64p. 1996. pap. 9.95 (*0-9612670-5-4*) Toomey Pr.

Roe, Alfred S. & Nutt, Chas. Civil War Artillery, 1st Regiment of Heavy Artillery, Mass. Volunteers, (Formerly the 14th Regiment of Infantry), 1861-1865. 507p. 1995. reprint ed. lib. bdg. 55.00 (*0-8328-4640-6*) Higginson Bk Co.

Roe, Andrew G. Using Visual Basic with AutoCAD IML. 2nd rev. abr. ed. 96p. 1999. pap. 19.95 (*0-7668-0367-8*, AutoDesk Pr) Delmar.

Roe, Anne. The Making of a Scientist. LC 73-15059. 244p. 1974. reprint ed. lib. bdg. 65.00 (*0-8371-7151-2*, ROMS, Greenwood Pr) Greenwood.

— The Psychology of Occupations. Stein, Leon, ed. LC 77-70529. (Work Ser.). (Illus.). 1977. reprint ed. lib. bdg. 35.95 (*0-405-10197-X*) Ayer.

Roe, Anne & Simpson, George G. Behavior & Evolution. LC 58-11260. 567p. reprint ed. pap. 175.80 (*0-8357-7105-9*, 200307000018) Bks Demand.

Roe, Anne K. Learning Experience Guide, Nursing. (Nursing Education Ser.). 1989. 15.95 (*0-8273-4348-5*) Delmar.

Roe, Anne K., et al. Learning Experience Guides for Nursing Students: Instructor's Guide. 5th ed. 65p. 1994. 15.95 (*0-8273-6172-6*) Delmar.

— Nursing Communication Skills: Workbook. LC 75-8753. (Wiley Biomedical-Health Publication Ser.). (Illus.). 90p. reprint ed. pap. 30.00 (*0-608-10330-6*, 201258400083) Bks Demand.

Roe, Barbara. Donald Barthelme: A Study of the Short Fiction. (Twayne's Studies in Short Fiction). 200p. (C). 1992. 22.95 (*0-8057-8338-5*) Macmillan.

Roe, Betty D. & Ross, Elinor P. Developing Power in Reading. 5th ed. 432p. 1993. per. 29.95 (*0-8403-7919-6*) Kendall-Hunt.

— Student Teaching & Field Experiences. 4th ed. LC 96-40022. 271p. 1997. pap. text, teacher ed., student ed. 44.00 (*0-13-490780-9*) P-H.

Roe, Betty D., et al. Secondary School Reading Instruction: The Content Areas, 5 vols. 5th ed. 592p. (C). 1994. text 61.96 (*0-395-70868-0*) HM.

— Secondary School Reading Instruction: The Content Areas, 5 vols. 5th ed. (C). 1995. text, teacher ed. 11.96 (*0-395-71663-2*) HM.

— Teaching Through Stories: Yours, Mine & Theirs. LC 97-69083. 256p. (C). 1997. pap. text, teacher ed. 32.90 (*0-926842-71-4*) CG Pubs Inc.

Roe, Betty D., jt. auth. see Burns, Paul C.

Roe, Bonnie C., jt. auth. see Anderson, Peter.

Roe, Bruce A. DNA Isolation & Sequencing. LC 95-48844. (Essential Techniques Ser.). 176p. 1996. pap. 49.95 (*0-471-96324-0*) Wiley.

Roe, Byron P. Particle Physics at the New Millennium. LC 95-44879. 406p. 1996. 59.00 (*0-387-94615-2*) Spr-Verlag.

— Probability & Statistics in Experimental Physics. LC 92-12653. (Illus.). 224p. 1992. write for info. (*3-540-97849-6*) Spr-Verlag.

— Probability & Statistics in Experimental Physics. LC 92-12653. (Illus.). 224p. 1997. 39.95 (*0-387-97849-6*) Spr-Verlag.

Roe, C. F. A Classy Touch of Murder. (Dr. Jean Montrose Mystery Ser.: No. 3). 256p. 1993. mass mkt. 5.99 (*0-451-17713-4*, Sig) NAL.

— A Classy Touch of Murder. 256p. 24.00 (*0-7278-5183-7*) Severn Hse.

— A Fiery Hint of Murder. (Dr. Jean Montrose Mystery Ser.: No. 2). 272p. 1993. reprint ed. mass mkt. 5.50 (*0-451-17606-5*, Sig) NAL.

***Roe, Caroline.** An Antidote for Avarice. (Chronicles of Issac of Girona Ser.: 3). 1999. mass mkt. 5.99 (*0-425-17260-0*, Prime Crime) Berkley Pub.

Roe, Caroline. Cure for a Charlatan. (Chronicles of Issac of Girona Ser.: 2). 1999. pap. 5.99 (*0-425-16734-8*, Prime Crime) Berkley Pub.

— Remedy for Treason. (Chronicles of Issac of Girona Ser.: 1). 260p. 1998. mass mkt. 5.99 (*0-425-16295-8*, Prime Crime) Berkley Pub.

Roe, Charles. North Carolina Wildlife Viewing Guide. Cauble, Chris, ed. LC 91-58883. (Watchable Wildlife Ser.). (Illus.). 96p. (Orig.). 1992. pap. 5.95 (*1-56044-055-4*) Falcon Pub Inc.

Roe, Clifford A., Jr. The Ohio Corporation: Legal Aspects of Organization & Operation. (Corporate Practice Ser.: No. 55). 1989. 95.00 (*1-55871-102-3*) BNA.

***Roe, Clifford A., Jr.** The Ohio Corporation: Legal Aspects of Organization & Operation. 2nd ed. (Corporate Practice Ser.: Vol. 55). 1999. pap. 95.00 (*1-55871-419-7*) BNA.

Roe, Clifford A., Jr. Ohio Corporations. DeLuca, Christopher, ed. LC 98-15102. 670p. 1998. 250.00 (*0-8366-0038-X*) West Group.

Roe, Daphne A. Clinical Nutrition for the Health Scientist. 144p. 1980. 83.00 (*0-8493-5417-X*, QP141, CRC Reprint) Franklin.

— Handbook on Drug & Nutrient Interactions: A Problem-Oriented Reference Guide. 4th ed. LC 89-17781. 150p. 1989. spiral bd. 21.95 (*0-88091-046-1*, 0102) Am Dietetic Assn.

— Handbook on Drug & Nutrient Interactions: A Reference & Study Guide. 5th ed. LC 94-35993. (Illus.). 1994. spiral bd. 29.95 (*0-88091-135-2*) Am Dietetic Assn.

Roe, Daphne A. & Campbell, T. Colin. Drugs & Nutrients: The Interactive Effects. (Drugs & the Pharmaceutical Sciences Ser.: Vol. 21). (Illus.). 624p. 1984. text 255.00 (*0-8247-7054-4*) Dekker.

Roe, David B., et al, eds. Voice Communication Between Humans & Machines. 560p. (C). 1994. text 79.95 (*0-309-04988-1*) Natl Acad Pr.

Roe, Derek A. Prehistory: An Introduction. LC 70-81799. (Illus.). 288p. reprint ed. pap. 89.30 (*0-608-18296-6*, 203154600075) Bks Demand.

Roe, Dilys J. The Welfare of Pet Parrots. 1991. pap. 23.00 (*0-900767-75-8*, Pub. by Univs Fed Animal Welfare) St Mut.

Roe, Earl O., ed. see Sproul, R. C.

Roe, Edward P. Barriers Burned Away. LC 70-129370. reprint ed. 24.50 (*0-404-05378-5*) AMS Pr.

— Barriers Burned Away. LC 71-104552. (Illus.). 480p. (C). 1988. reprint ed. pap. text 4.95 (*0-317-66470-0*); reprint ed. lib. bdg. 11.00 (*0-8398-1762-2*) Irvington.

— Barriers Burned Away. (BCL1-PS American Literature Ser.). 472p. 1992. reprint ed. lib. bdg. 99.00 (*0-7812-6845-1*) Rprt Serv.

— Barriers Burned Away. (Notable American Authors Ser.). 1999. reprint ed. lib. bdg. 125.00 (*0-7812-8809-6*) Rprt Serv.

— Barriers Burned Away. (Illus.). 1971. reprint ed. 9.00 (*0-403-01185-X*) Scholarly.

— A Day of Fate. (Notable American Authors Ser.). 1999. reprint ed. lib. bdg. 125.00 (*0-7812-8816-9*) Rprt Serv.

— Driven Back to Eden. (Notable American Authors Ser.). 1999. reprint ed. lib. bdg. 125.00 (*0-7812-8821-5*) Rprt Serv.

— The Earth Trembled. (Notable American Authors Ser.). 1999. reprint ed. lib. bdg. 125.00 (*0-7812-8823-1*) Rprt Serv.

— A Face Illumined. (Notable American Authors Ser.). 1999. reprint ed. lib. bdg. 125.00 (*0-7812-8815-0*) Rprt Serv.

— Found Yet Lost. (Notable American Authors Ser.). 1999. reprint ed. lib. bdg. 125.00 (*0-7812-8825-8*) Rprt Serv.

— From Jest to Earnest. (Notable American Authors Ser.). 1999. reprint ed. lib. bdg. 125.00 (*0-7812-8812-6*) Rprt Serv.

— He Fell in Love with His Wife. (Notable American Authors Ser.). 1999. reprint ed. lib. bdg. 125.00 (*0-7812-8822-3*) Rprt Serv.

— His Sombre Rivals. (Notable American Authors Ser.). 1999. reprint ed. lib. bdg. 125.00 (*0-7812-8818-5*) Rprt Serv.

— The Home Acre. (Notable American Authors Ser.). 1999. reprint ed. lib. bdg. 125.00 (*0-7812-8831-2*) Rprt Serv.

— The Hornet's Nest. (Notable American Authors Ser.). 1999. reprint ed. lib. bdg. 125.00 (*0-7812-8826-6*) Rprt Serv.

— A Knight of the Nineteenth Century. (Notable American Authors Ser.). 1999. reprint ed. lib. bdg. 125.00 (*0-7812-8814-2*) Rprt Serv.

— A Manual on the Culture of Small Fruits. (Notable American Authors Ser.). 1999. reprint ed. lib. bdg. 125.00 (*0-7812-8828-2*) Rprt Serv.

— Miss Lou. (Notable American Authors Ser.). 1999. reprint ed. lib. bdg. 125.00 (*0-7812-8824-X*) Rprt Serv.

— Nature-Play & Profit in My Garden. (Notable American Authors Ser.). 1999. reprint ed. lib. bdg. 125.00 (*0-7812-8827-4*) Rprt Serv.

— Nature's Serial Story. (Notable American Authors Ser.). 1999. reprint ed. lib. bdg. 125.00 (*0-7812-8830-4*) Rprt Serv.

— Near to Nature's Heart. (Notable American Authors Ser.). 1999. reprint ed. lib. bdg. 125.00 (*0-7812-8813-4*) Rprt Serv.

— Opening a Chestnut Burr. (Notable American Authors Ser.). 1999. reprint ed. lib. bdg. 125.00 (*0-7812-8811-8*) Rprt Serv.

— An Original Belle. (Notable American Authors Ser.). 1999. reprint ed. lib. bdg. 125.00 (*0-7812-8820-7*) Rprt Serv.

— Success with Small Fruits. (Notable American Authors Ser.). 1999. reprint ed. lib. bdg. 125.00 (*0-7812-8829-0*) Rprt Serv.

— What Can She Do. (Notable American Authors Ser.). 1999. reprint ed. lib. bdg. 125.00 (*0-7812-8810-X*) Rprt Serv.

— Without a Home. (Notable American Authors Ser.). 1999. reprint ed. lib. bdg. 125.00 (*0-7812-8817-7*) Rprt Serv.

— A Young Girl's Wooing. (Notable American Authors Ser.). 1999. reprint ed. lib. bdg. 125.00 (*0-7812-8819-3*) Rprt Serv.

Roe, Eileen. Con Mi Hermang/With My Brother. 1994. 11.19 (*0-606-06289-0*, Pub. by Turtleback) Demco.

Roe, Eileen. Con Mi Hermano/With My Brother. (SPA & ENG., Illus.). 32p. (J). 1994. mass mkt. 5.99 (*0-689-71855-1*) Aladdin.

— Con Mi Hermano/With My Brother. LC 90-33983. (Illus.). 32p. (J). (ps-3). 1991. lib. bdg. 14.00 (*0-02-777373-6*, Bradbury S&S) S&S Childrens.

Roe, Elizabeth A. Recollections of Frontier Life. Baxter, Annette K., ed. LC 79-8809. (Signal Lives Ser.). (Illus.). 1980. reprint ed. lib. bdg. 34.95 (*0-405-12855-X*) Ayer.

Roe, Emery. Development of Livestock, Agriculture & Water Supplies in Botswana Before Independence: A Short History & Policy Analysis. (Occasional Paper Ser.: No. 10). 56p. 1980. 6.45 (*0-86731-023-5*) Cornell CIS RDC.

— Except-Africa: Remaking Development, Rethinking Power. LC 98-40494. 192p. 1999. 29.95 (*1-56000-399-5*) Transaction Pubs.

— Taking Complexity Seriously: Policy Analysis, Triangulation & Sustainable Development. LC 97-40994. 152p. 1998. text 108.50 (*0-7923-8058-4*) Kluwer Academic.

Roe, Emery & Fortmann, Louise. Season & Strategy: The Changing Organization of the Rural Water Sector in Botswana. (Special Series on Resource Management: No. 1). 257p. (Orig.). (C). 1982. pap. text 10.00 (*0-86731-082-0*) Cornell CIS RDC.

Roe, Emery M. Narrative Policy Analysis: Theory & Practice. LC 94-7248. (Illus.). 240p. 1994. text 49.95 (*0-8223-1502-5*); pap. text 17.95 (*0-8223-1513-0*) Duke.

Roe, Ernest, jt. auth. see Moses, Ingrid.

***Roe, F. G.** Red River Hunt. 48p. 2000. pap. 7.00 (*1-886560-74-9*) Quintin Pub RI.

Roe, F. J. & Deeny, A. A. Microbiological Standardisation of Laboratory Animals. 116p. 1983. text 57.95 (*0-470-27401-8*) P-H.

Roe, Frances M. Army Letters from an Officer's Wife, 1871-1888. LC 81-7571. (Illus.). xxii, 387p. 1981. pap. 15.95 (*0-8032-8905-7*, Bison Books) U of Nebr Pr.

— Army Letters from an Officer's Wife, 1871-1888. Kohn, Richard H., ed. LC 78-22395. (American Military Experience Ser.). (Illus.). 1980. reprint ed. lib. bdg. 30.95 (*0-405-11871-6*) Ayer.

Roe, Francis. Under the Knife. 1998. mass mkt. 6.50 (*0-451-40702-4*, Onyx) NAL.

Roe, Frank G. The North American Buffalo: Critical Study of the Species in Its Wild State. 2nd ed. LC 79-18945. 1010p. reprint ed. pap. 200.00 (*0-608-12870-8*, 202366300033) Bks Demand.

Roe, Frederick W. Social Philosophy of Carlyle & Ruskin. LC 76-116555. 342p. (C). 1970. reprint ed. 60.00 (*0-87752-095-X*) Gordian.

— The Social Philosophy of Carlyle & Ruskin. (BCL1-PR English Literature Ser.). 335p. 1992. reprint ed. lib. bdg. 89.00 (*0-7812-7493-1*) Rprt Serv.

— Victorian Prose. LC 47-12149. 774p. 1947. reprint ed. pap. 200.00 (*0-608-08457-3*, 205509000008) Bks Demand.

Roe, Frederick W., ed. English Prose: A Series of Related Essays for the Discussion & Practice of the Art of Writing. LC 77-37838. (Essay Index Reprint Ser.). 1977. reprint ed. 27.95 (*0-8369-2621-8*) Ayer.

— Nineteenth Century English Prose: Early Essayists. LC 73-152209. (Essay Index Reprint Ser.). 1977. reprint ed. 31.95 (*0-8369-2331-6*) Ayer.

Roe, Frederick W., ed. & intro. see Ruskin, John.

Roe, Gary. Mormons Against the Mob. 200p. (Orig.). 1996. pap. 12.95 (*1-888106-23-9*) Agreka Bks.

Roe, George, jt. auth. see Afterman, Allan B.

Roe, George M., ed. Our Police: A History of the Cincinnati Police Force, from the Earliest Period Until the Present Day. LC 77-156024. reprint ed. 72.50 (*0-404-09125-3*) AMS Pr.

Roe, Gerald, jt. auth. see Anthony, Rebecca.

Roe, Gerald, jt. auth. see Anthony, Rebecca J.

Roe, H. S. Progress in Oceanography, Vol. 13, Nos. 3-4. (Illus.). 276p. 1984. pap. 83.00 (*0-08-031735-9*, Pergamon Pr) Elsevier.

Roe-Hafer, Ann. The Medical & Health Sciences Word Book. 3rd ed. 448p. 1992. 12.00 (*0-395-60664-0*) HM.

Roe, Harry & Dooley, Ann, trs. Tales of the Elders of Ireland. (Oxford World's Classics Ser.). (Illus.). 304p. 1999. pap. 12.95 (*0-19-283918-7*) OUP.

Roe, Ian, tr. see von Humboldt, Wilhelm.

Roe, Ian F. Franz Grillparzer: A Century of Criticism. (LCGERM Ser.). xx, 172p. (C). 1995. 55.00 (*1-57113-008-X*) Camden Hse.

— An Introduction to the Major Works of Franz Grillparzer, 1791-1872, Austrian Dramatist & Poet. LC 91-20515. (Studies in German Language & Literature: Vol. 7). 320p. 1991. lib. bdg. 99.95 (*0-7734-9725-0*) E Mellen.

Roe, Ian F., et al, eds. The Biedermeier & Beyond: Selected Papers from the Symposium Held at St. Peter's College, Oxford from 19-21 September 1997. LC 98-32073. (British & Irish Studies in German Language & Literature: Vol. 17). 253p. 1999. pap. 42.95 (*3-906761-63-0*, Pub. by P Lang) P Lang Pubng.

Roe, Ian F. & Warren, John, II, eds. The Biedermeier & Beyond Vol. 17: Selected Papers from the Symposium Held at St. Peter's College, Oxford from 19-21 September 1997, No.17. LC 98-32073. (British & Irish Studies in German Language & Literature.). 253p. 1998. pap. 42.95 (*0-8204-4216-X*) P Lang Pubng.

Roe, Ivan. Shelley: The Last Phase. LC 72-97078. (Illus.). 256p. 1973. reprint ed. lib. bdg. 53.50 (*0-8154-0464-6*) Cooper Sq.

Roe, J. Elliptic Operators Topology & Asymptotic Methods. 2nd ed. 216p. 1998. 52.95 (*0-582-32502-1*, LM0682, Chap & Hall CRC) CRC Pr.

Roe, J., jt. auth. see Webster, A.

Roe, Jane, jt. auth. see Woodrow, Philip.

Roe, Jill. A New Leaf. large type ed. LC 97-23512. 310p. 1997. 22.95 (*0-7862-1070-2*) Thorndike Pr.

— A New Leaf. large type ed. (Ulverscroft Large Print Ser.). 368p. 1997. 27.99 (*0-7089-3817-5*) Ulverscroft.

Roe, JoAnn. Alaska Cat. (Illus.). 64p. (J). (gr. k-5). 1990. pap. 6.95 (*0-931551-04-8*); lib. bdg. 11.95 (*0-931551-05-6*) Montevista Pr.

— Fisherman Cat. rev. ed. (Illus.). 64p. (J). (gr. k-5). 1994. reprint ed. pap. 6.95 (*0-931551-09-9*); reprint ed. lib. bdg. 11.95 (*0-931551-02-1*) Montevista Pr.

— Ghost Camps & Boom Towns. (Illus.). 288p. (Orig.). 1995. pap. 14.95 (*0-931551-19-6*) Montevista Pr.

— North Cascades Highway: Washington's Popular & Scenic Pass. LC 97-24305. (Illus.). 192p. 1997. pap. 14.95 (*0-89886-517-4*) Mountaineers.

— Ranald MacDonald: Pacific Rim Adventurer. LC 97-2019. (Illus.). 272p. 1997. 35.00 (*0-87422-147-1*); pap. 18.95 (*0-87422-146-3*) Wash St U Pr.

— Samurai Cat. (Illus.). 64p. 1992. pap. 6.95 (*0-931551-07-2*); lib. bdg. 11.95 (*0-931551-08-0*) Montevista Pr.

— Seattle Uncovered. LC 95-20834. 304p. 1995. pap. 16.95 (*1-55622-394-3*, Seaside Pr) Wordware Pub.

— Stevens Pass: The Story of Railroading & Recreation in the North Cascades. (Illus.). 180p. 1995. pap. 12.95 (*0-89886-371-6*) Mountaineers.

Roe, Joann. Vancouver Uncovered. 1998. pap. text 16.95 (*1-55622-619-5*, Seaside Pr) Wordware Pub.

Roe, JoAnne. The Columbia River: A Historical Travel Guide. LC 91-58486. (Illus.). 256p. (Orig.). 1992. pap. 15.95 (*1-55591-102-1*) Fulcrum Pub.

Roe, John. Coarse Cohomology & Index Theory on Complete Riemannian Manifolds. LC 93-17166. (Memoirs of the American Mathematical Society Ser.: No. 497). 90p. 1993. pap. 29.00 (*0-8218-2559-3*, MEMO/104/497) Am Math.

— Elementary Geometry. LC 92-41660. (Illus.). 316p. 1993. pap. text 41.95 (*0-19-853456-6*) OUP.

— Index Theory, Coarse Geometry, & Topology of Manifolds. LC 96-22058. (Regional Conference Series in Mathematics: Vol. 90). 100p. 1996. pap. 17.00 (*0-8218-0413-8*, CBMS/90) Am Math.

Roe, John, ed. see Shakespeare, William.

Roe, Jon, jt. auth. see McCray, Billy Q.

Roe, Kathleen M., jt. auth. see Minkler, Meredith.

Roe, Kathy L. From Barren to Fulfilled. LC 97-90808. 83p. 1998. pap. 8.95 (*0-533-12484-0*) Vantage.

Roe, Keith E. & Frederick, Richard G. Dictionary of Theoretical Concepts in Biology. LC 80-19889. 380p. 1981. 40.00 (*0-8108-1353-X*) Scarecrow.

Roe, Margie, jt. auth. see Harper, James.

Roe, Mark J. Strong Managers, Weak Owners: The Political Roots of American Corporate Finance. LC 94-12179. 336p. 1994. text 42.50 (*0-691-03683-7*, Pub. by Princeton U Pr) Cal Prin Full Svc.

Roe, Mark J., jt. ed. see Blair, Margaret M.

Roe, Mary A. Total Quality Education - Teaching Techniques for Technical Educators. 32p. (C). 1991. pap. text 5.95 (*0-940017-16-4*) Info Tec OH.

Roe, Mary A., et al. Teaching Factories: A Strategy for World Class Manufacturing Application & Education Networks. 208p. 1993. pap. 16.95 (*1-887406-01-8*) ICTwo Inst.

Roe, Melvin W., ed. Readings in the History of the American Indian. 1971. pap. 9.95 (*0-8422-0134-3*) Irvington.

Roe, Michael. Australia, Britain & Migration: A Study of Desperate Hopes, 1915-1940. (Studies in Australian History). (Illus.). 320p. (C). 1995. text 64.95 (*0-521-46507-9*) Cambridge U Pr.

— Commercialisation in Central & East European Shipping. LC 98-70980. (Plymouth Studies in Contemporary Shipping). 192p. 1998. text 59.95 (*1-84014-170-0*, Pub. by Ashgate Pub) Ashgate Pub Co.

— East European International Road Haulage. 174p. 1992. 82.95 (*1-85628-310-0*, Pub. by Avebry) Ashgate Pub Co.

— Strategic Management in the Maritime Sector: A Case Study of Poland & Germany. LC 98-74931. (Plymouth Studies in Contemporary Shipping). 5p. 1999. 65.95 (*1-84014-892-6*, Pub. by Ashgate Pub) Ashgate Pub Co.

Roe, Michael, ed. Developments in the Baltic Maritime Marketplace. LC 97-74454. (Plymouth Studies in Contemporary Shipping). 140p. 1998. text 59.95 (*1-84014-169-7*, Pub. by Ashgate Pub) Ashgate Pub Co.

An Asterisk (*) at the beginning of an entry indicates that the title is appearing for the first time.

— Shipping in the Baltic Region. LC 96-86731. (Plymouth Studies in Contemporary Shipping). 96p. 1997. text 55.95 (1-85972-501-5, Pub. by Avebry) Ashgate Pub Co.

Roe, Michael, jt. auth. see Ferch, Susanne.

Roe, Michael, jt. auth. see Ledger, Gillian.

Roe, Michael, jt. auth. see Yercan, H. Funda.

Roe, Michael T., jt. auth. see Soutter, Charlotte.

Roe, Nancy, ed. The New Quilt: Quilt National, 1989. LC 88-63933. (Illus.). 96p. 1989. pap. 14.95 (0-88740-157-0) Schiffer.

Roe, Nicholas. John Keats & the Culture of Dissent. LC 96-34554. (Illus.). 336p. 1997. text 75.00 (0-19-818396-8) OUP.

— John Keats & the Culture of Dissent. (Illus.). 336p. 1999. pap. text 24.95 (0-19-818629-0) OUP.

— Wordsworth & Coleridge: The Radical Years. (Oxford English Monographs). (Illus.). 324p. 1990. reprint ed. pap. text 19.95 (0-19-811969-0) OUP.

Roe, Nicholas, ed. John Keats. (Everyman's Poetry Ser.). 116p. 1997. pap. 1.95 (0-460-87808-5, Everyman's Classic Lib) Tuttle Pubng.

— Keats & History. (Illus.). 338p. (C). 1995. text 69.95 (0-521-44245-1) Cambridge U Pr.

Roe, Nicholas, ed. see Keats, John.

***Roe, Patrick C.** The Dragon Strikes: China & the Korean War: June-December 1950. LC 00-28566. (Illus.). 432p. 2000. 34.95 (0-89141-703-6) Presidio Pr.

Roe, Patrick R., tr. see Rossi, Mario.

Roe, Paul F. Choral Music Education. 2nd ed. (Illus.). 355p. (C). 1994. pap. text 30.95 (0-88133-807-9) Waveland Pr.

Roe, Peter, jt. auth. see Braun, Barbara.

Roe, Peter G. The Cosmic Zygote: Cosmology in the Amazon Basin. LC 80-39908. 400p. 1982. reprint ed. pap. 124.00 (0-608-02328-0, 206296900004) Bks Demand.

Roe, R. A., jt. ed. see Koopman-Iwema, A. M.

Roe, R. M., et al, eds. Herbicide Activity: Toxicology, Biochemistry & Molecular Biology. LC 96-79142. 205p. Date not set. 82.00 (90-5199-311-0, 311-0) IOS Press.

Roe, Richard. Bringer of Songs. 54p. (Orig.). 1994. pap. 6.00 (1-878660-13-6) Fireweed WI.

— Burnt Toast. LC 79-87687. (Orig.). pap. 7.95 (0-9602100-2-4) St Wrks Cooperative.

Roe, Richard L., jt. auth. see Arbetman, Lee P.

Roe, Richard L., ed. see Ables, C.

Roe, Richard L., ed. see Biebuyck, Daniel P. & Biech, E.

Roe, Richard L., ed. see Kinlaw, D.

Roe, Richard L., ed. see McLain, L.

Roe, Richard L., ed. see Wills, John C.

***Roe, Robert A.** Values & Work: A Special Issue of the Journal Applied Psychology. 1999. pap. 24.95 (0-86377-994-8) L Erlbaum Assocs.

Roe, Ryong-Joon. Methods of X-ray & Neutron Scattering in Polymer Science. LC 99-37446. (Topics in Polymer Science Ser.). (Illus.). 352p. (C). 2000. text 80.00 (0-19-511321-7) OUP.

Roe, Shirley A. Matter, Life & Generation: Eighteenth Century Embryology & the Haller-Wolff Debate. LC 80-19611. (Illus.). 225p. 1981. text 59.95 (0-521-23540-5) Cambridge U Pr.

Roe, Shirley A. & Cohen, I. Bernard, eds. The Natural Philosophy of Albrecht Von Haller. LC 80-2109. (Development of Science Ser.). (Illus.). 1981. lib. bdg. 44.95 (0-405-13874-1) Ayer.

***Roe, Sue & Sellers, Susan, eds.** The Cambridge Companion to Virginia Woolf. (Cambridge Companions to Literature Ser.). 320p. (C). 2000. 59.95 (0-521-62393-6); pap. 19.95 (0-521-62548-3) Cambridge U Pr.

Roe, Sue, ed. see Woolf, Virginia.

***Roe, Timothy D.** The First Americans. deluxe ed. (Illus.). 54p. 1999. 65.75 (0-9678078-0-8) Native Am Art.

Roeber, A. G. Faithful Magistrates & Republican Lawyers: Creators of Virginia Legal Cultures, 1680-1810. LC 80-19524. (Studies in Legal History). 312p. 1981. reprint ed. pap. 96.80 (0-608-02804-5, 206387100007) Bks Demand.

— Palatines, Liberty & Property: German Lutherans in Colonial British America. LC 92-25647. (Early America Ser.). 448p. 1993. text 52.00 (0-8018-4459-2) Johns Hopkins.

— Palatines, Liberty, & Property: German Lutherans in Colonial British America. (Early America). 448p. 1998. reprint ed. pap. text 18.95 (0-8018-5968-9) Johns Hopkins.

Roeber, Jane A. 1998 Summer Library Program Manual - "Make Waves: Read" (Illus.). 200p. (Orig.). 1997. pap. text 18.00 (1-57337-045-2) WI Dept Pub Instruct.

— 1997 Summer Library Program Manual - "Zap into the Past" (Illus.). 218p. (Orig.). 1997. pap. text 18.00 (1-57337-040-1) WI Dept Pub Instruct.

— 1996 Summer Library Program Manual - "Razzle Dazzle Read" 200p. (C). 1996. pap. text 18.00 (1-57337-027-4) WI Dept Pub Instruct.

***Roeber, Jane A.** 2000 Summer Library Program Manual: Ticket for Tomorrow. (Illus.). 200p. 1999. pap. 18.00 (1-57337-076-2) WI Dept Pub Instruct.

Roeber, Joe. Evolution of Oil Markets: Trading Instruments & Their Role in Oil Price Formation. 1993. pap. text 14.95 (0-905031-68-7, Pub. by Royal Inst Intl Affairs) Brookings.

Roeber, Joe. The Hidden Market. 25.95 (1-56584-631-1, Pub. by New Press NY) Norton.

Roeberg, Shelly, ed. see Muth, Jon.

Roebert, Ed. El Arrepentimiento.Tr. of Repentance. (SPA.). 125p. 1995. 3.50 (1-56063-431-6, 550015) Editorial Unilit.

— Atrevete a Dar Amor. (Serie Realidades - Realities Ser.). (SPA.). 125p. 1995. write for info. (0-614-24410-2) Editorial Unilit.

***Roebert, Ed.** What Christians Should Know about the Glory of God. (What Christians Should Know Ser.). 1999. pap. 5.99 (1-85240-231-8) SOV5.

Roebke, John, jt. auth. see Melchert, Paul A.

Roebling, Karl. The Age of Individuality: America's Kinship with the Brooklyn Bridge. 190p. 1983. 10.95 (0-942910-05-2) Dynapress.

— Great Myths of World War II. LC 85-60763. (Illus.). 288p. 1985. 14.95 (0-942910-11-7) Dynapress.

— Not His Death-His Overcoming of Death. 30p. 1983. pap. 5.00 (0-942910-10-9) Dynapress.

— Pentecostal Origins & Trends: Early & Modern. 3rd rev. ed. LC 85-63631. 112p. 1985. 10.00 (0-942910-12-5) Dynapress.

— Sea Nation. (Illus.). 245p. 1987. 14.95 (0-942910-14-1) Dynapress.

***Roebroeks, Wil & Gamble, Clive, eds.** The Middle Palaeolithic Occupation of Europe. (Illus.). 240p. 1999. 65.00 (90-73368-12-X, Pub. by Leiden Univ Pr) David Brown.

Roebroeks, Wil & Van Kolfschoten, Thijs, eds. The Earliest Occupation of Europe. 329p. 1996. 75.00 (90-73368-06-5) David Brown.

Roebuck, Carl. Economy & Society In the Early Greek World: Collected Essays. Thomas, Carol G., ed. 172p. 1984. pap. 25.00 (0-89005-261-1) Ares.

— Ionian Trade & Colonization. 154p. 1985. reprint ed. pap. 25.00 (0-89005-528-9, ROEO2) Ares.

— The World of Ancient Times. 1984. 18.95 (0-684-13726-7) S&S Trade.

Roebuck, Chris. Effective Communication: The Essential Guide to Thinking & Working Smarter. LC 98-53812. (Self-Development for Success Ser.: Vol. 8). (Illus.). 96p. 1999. pap. 12.95 (0-8144-7020-3) AMACOM.

— Effective Delegation. LC 98-53811. (Self-Development for Success Ser.: Vol. 8). (Illus.). 96p. 1999. pap. 12.95 (0-8144-7019-X) AMACOM.

***Roebuck, Chris.** Effective Leadership. LC 99-37539. (Self-Development for Success Ser.: Vol. 12). 96p. 1999. pap. 12.95 (0-8144-7059-9) AMACOM.

Roebuck, Deborah Britt. Essentials Business Writing & Speaking: Guideline. 88p. (C). 1995. text 17.60 (0-536-59133-4) Pearson Custom.

Roebuck, Derek, ed. The Criminal Law of Hong Kong: A Descriptive Text. 286p. 1996. 69.95 (7-301-02959-4) Austin & Winfield.

— Law Relating to Banking in Hong Kong. 2nd ed. 340p. 1996. pap. 47.50 (962-209-353-1, Pub. by HK Univ Pr) Coronet Bks.

Roebuck, Derek & Wang Le M, eds. A Digest of Hong Kong Contract Law. (Illus.). 301p. 1995. 69.95 (7-301-02887-3) Austin & Winfield.

Roebuck, Derek, et al. Banking Law in Hong Kong - Cases & Materials. xxxviii, 802p. 1995. write for info. (0-409-99700-5, MICHIE) LEXIS Pub.

Roebuck, Derek, jt. auth. see Hoe, Susanna.

Roebuck, John A., Jr. Anthropometric Methods: Designing to Fit the Human Body. LC 93-16975. 200p. 1995. pap. 20.00 (0-945289-01-4) Human Factors.

Roebuck, John A. & Kroemer, K. H. Engineering Anthropometry Methods. LC 74-34272. (Wiley Series in Human Factors). 477p. reprint ed. pap. 147.90 (0-7837-0006-7, 201584900097) Bks Demand.

Roebuck, Johnnie J. Celebrate the Temporary. LC 91-67362. (Illus.). xii, 124p. (Orig.). 1992. pap. 9.95 (0-934955-23-9) Watercress Pr.

Roebuck, Julian B. & Hickson, Mark L., III. The Southern Redneck: A Phenomenological Class Study. LC 82-9831. 210p. 1982. 38.50 (0-275-90886-0, C0886, Praeger Pubs) Greenwood.

Roebuck, Julian B. & Murty, Komanduri S. Historically Black Colleges & Universities: Their Place in American Higher Education. LC 93-2858. 240p. 1993. 59.95 (0-275-94267-8, C4267, Praeger Pubs) Greenwood.

— The Southern Subculture of Drinking & Driving: A Generalized Deviance Model for the Southern White Male. McShane, Marilyn D. & Williams, Frank P., III, eds. LC 95-53726. (Current Issues in Criminal Justice Ser.: Vol. 17). (Illus.). 248p. 1996. text 40.00 (0-8153-2376-X, SS1107) Garland.

Roebuck, Kenneth C. Gun-Dog Training Pointing Dogs. LC 83-4948. 192p. 1983. 16.95 (0-8117-0714-8) Stackpole.

— Gun-Dog Training Spaniels & Retrievers. LC 82-5667. (Illus.). 192p. 1982. 18.95 (0-8117-0778-4) Stackpole.

Roebuck, Nigel. Chasing the Title: Fifty Years of Formula 1. (Illus.). 224p. 1999. 35.95 (1-85960-604-0, 129066AE, Pub. by Haynes Manuals) Motorbooks Intl.

Roebuck, P., jt. ed. see O'Brien, G.

Roebuck, R. Cornelius Nepos: Three Lives, Alcibiades-Dion-Atticus. (ENG & LAT., Illus.). 138p. 1987. reprint ed. pap. 13.00 (0-86516-207-7) Bolchazy-Carducci.

Roebuck, R., ed. Nepos: 3 Lives (Alcibiades, Dion, Atticus) (Bristol Latin Texts Ser.). (LAT.). 140p. 1993. pap. 18.95 (0-86292-284-4, Pub. by Brist Class Pr) Focus Pub-R Pullins.

Roebuck, Regina. Reading & Recall in L1 & L2: A Sociocultural Approach. LC 98-28085. (Contemporary Studies in Second Language Learning). 1999. 73.25 (1-56750-411-6); pap. 39.50 (1-56750-412-4) Ablx Pub.

Roebuck, Valerie J. Circle of Stars: An Introduction to Indian Astrology. 1992. pap. 15.95 (1-85230-303-4, Pub. by Element MA) Penguin Putnam.

— Improving Business Communication Skills. 2nd ed. LC 97-9739. 270p. 1997. pap. text 56.00 (0-13-235243-5) P-H.

Roeburt, John. The Hollow Man. large type ed. (Linford Mystery Large Print Ser.). 1995. pap. 16.99 (0-7089-7807-X, Linford) Ulverscroft.

Roeck, A. De, see De Roeck, A., ed.

Roeck, Alan L. Twenty-Four Hours a Day. large type ed. 400p. 1980. pap. 7.95 (0-89486-108-5) Hazelden.

— Twenty-Four Hours a Day for Everyone. LC 78-52007. 383p. (Orig.). 1977. pap. 6.95 (0-89486-040-2) Hazelden.

***Roeckelein, Jon E.** The Concept of Time in Psychology: A Resource Book & Annotated Bibliography. LC 99-54454. 352p. 2000. lib. bdg. 79.50 (0-313-31100-5, Greenwood Pr) Greenwood.

Roeckelein, Jon E. Dictionary of Theories, Laws & Concepts in Psychology. LC 97-43941. 584p. 1998. lib. bdg. 115.00 (0-313-30460-2, Greenwood Pr) Greenwood.

Roecker, Ann. A Women's Workshop on Time Management. 96p. 1988. pap. 4.95 (0-310-37931-8, 11736P) Zondervan.

Roecker, W. A. Fresh One! Standup Fishing: Saltwater Methods, Tackle & Techniques. (Standup Ser.). (Illus.). 264p. (Orig.). 1990. pap. 14.95 (0-9645319-0-9) Oceanic Prod.

Roecklein, John C. & Leung, PingSun, eds. A Profile of Economic Plants. 608p. 1987. 89.95 (0-88738-167-7) Transaction Pubs.

Roed, Tom, ed. Best of Schultz: Big Note. 48p. (Orig.). 1992. pap. 7.95 (0-7692-0136-9, F3258P3X) Wrner Bros.

— Dave's Diary: A Collection of Dave Brubeck Piano Solos. 56p. (Orig.). (YA). 1995. pap. text 12.95 (0-89724-613-6, P1085P9X) Wrner Bros.

— Floyd Cramer: Just Me & My Piano. 60p. 1990. pap. text 14.95 (0-89898-631-1, P0877P9X) Wrner Bros.

— Tom Petty: Wildflowers. 104p. (Orig.). (YA). 1995. pap. text 19.95 (0-89724-702-7, PG9507); pap. text 16.95 (0-89724-703-5, PF9508) Wrner Bros.

— World's Greatest Fakebook: Bb Instruments. 728p. (Orig.). 1994. pap. 39.95 (0-89898-916-7, F3288FBX) Wrner Bros.

— World's Greatest Fakebook: Eb Instruments. 728p. (Orig.). 1994. pap. 39.95 (0-89898-917-5, F3289FBX) Wrner Bros.

Roed, Tom, ed. see Garson, Mike.

Roed, Tom, ed. see Petty, Tom.

Roeda, Daniel. Amigos y Enemigos de Jesucristo-bL-Alumno. (SPA.). 1993. pap. 1.25 (1-55955-154-2) CRC Wrld Lit.

— Amigos y Enemigos de Jesucristo-C-Alumno. (SPA.). 1993. pap. 1.25 (1-55955-150-X) CRC Wrld Lit.

— Amigos y Enemigos de Jesucristo-Db-Alumno. (SPA.). 1993. pap. 1.25 (1-55955-152-6) CRC Wrld Lit.

— Nacimiento de Jesucristo: Promesas y Profecias bL-Alumno. (SPA.). 1991. pap. 1.00 (1-55955-134-8) CRC Wrld Lit.

— Nacimiento de Jesucristo: Promesas y Profecias C-Alumno. (SPA.). 1991. pap. 1.00 (1-55955-130-5) CRC Wrld Lit.

— Nacimiento de Jesucristo: Promesas y Profecias Db-Alumno. (SPA.). 1991. pap. 1.00 (1-55955-132-1) CRC Wrld Lit.

Roeda, Jack. Decisions. 2nd ed. (Illus.). 80p. (YA). (gr. 9-12). 1992. pap., teacher ed. 10.75 (1-56212-000-X, 1240-4940); text, student ed. 8.50 (0-930265-96-3, 1240-4920) CRC Pubns.

Roedder, Edwin. Fluid Inclusions. (Reviews in Mineralogy Ser.: Vol. 12). 644p. 1984. per. 32.00 (0-939950-16-2) Mineralogical Soc.

Roede, Ann. The Ghost of Brannock Hall. Reccenda, Ann B., ed. (Illus.). 268p. (Orig.). (J). (gr. 5-9). 1994. pap. 4.95 (0-9638237-0-1) Playgrnd Bks.

Roedel, Phil M. & Ripley, William E. Common Marine Fishes & California Sharks & Rays. LC 87-51660. (Illus.). 248p. reprint ed. write for info. (0-9610602-6-3) Teaparty Bks.

Roedell, Wendy C., et al. Gifted Young Children. LC 80-10707. (Perspectives on Gifted & Talented Education Ser.). 128p. (Orig.). 1980. reprint ed. pap. 39.70 (0-608-00541-X, 206142000008) Bks Demand.

Roeder. Communities of Enterprise. (C). 1997. pap. text. write for info. (0-15-501572-9) Harcourt Coll Pubs.

— Communities of Enterprise, Vol. 1. (C). 1997. pap. text. write for info. (0-15-501571-0) Harcourt Coll Pubs.

— Communities of Enterprise, Vol. C. (C). 1997. pap. text. write for info. (0-15-501575-3) Harcourt Coll Pubs.

— Communities of Enterprise, Vol. A. (C). 1997. pap. text. write for info. (0-15-501573-7) Harcourt Coll Pubs.

— Communities of Enterprise, Vol. B. (C). 1997. pap. text. write for info. (0-15-501574-5) Harcourt Coll Pubs.

— Communities of Enterprise: A World History. (C). 1997. text. write for info. (0-15-501570-2) Harcourt Coll Pubs.

***Roeder, Catherine A., et al.** How to Deal with CPA Financial Issues. 1999. pap. 99.00 (0-7646-0722-7) Prctnrs Pub Co.

Roeder, Charles W., ed. Composite & Mixed Construction: Proceedings of a U. S.-Japan Joint Seminar. 352p. 1985. 33.00 (0-87262-476-5) Am Soc Civil Eng.

Roeder, David C. & Roeder, Linda L. Counselor's Manual. (Illus.). xviii, 87p. 1997. teacher ed. 25.00 (0-9658882-1-5) Paraklesis Minist.

— The Intimate Marriage. unabridged ed. (Illus.). xii, 87p. 1997. pap., wbk. ed. 20.00 (0-9658882-0-7) Paraklesis Minist.

— Two Shall Become One . . . Mt. 19:5: A Marriage Workbook. unabridged ed. (Illus.). xi, 86p. 1997. wbk. ed. 20.00 (0-9658882-2-3) Paraklesis Minist.

Roeder, Dietrich H. Rocky Mountains: Der Geologische Aufbau des Kanadischen Felsengebirges. (Beitraege Zur Regionalen Geologie der Erde. Ser.: Vol. 5). (Illus.). xii, 318p. 1967. 84.00 (3-443-11005-3, Pub. by Gebruder Borntraeger) Balogh.

Roeder, Dietrich H., et al, eds. Joint Interpretation of Geophysical & Geological Data Applied to Lithospheric Studies. (C). 1991. text 155.50 (0-7923-1306-2) Kluwer Academic.

Roeder, Dorothy. Crystal Co-Creators. 288p. 1994. pap. 14.95 (0-929385-40-3) Light Tech Pubng.

— The Next Dimension Is Love. 148p. (Orig.). 1993. pap. 11.95 (0-929385-50-0) Light Tech Pubng.

— Reach for Us: Your Cosmic Teachers & Friends. 204p. 1995. reprint ed. pap. 14.95 (0-929385-69-1) Light Tech Pubng.

Roeder, Edward, ed. PACs Americana: The Directory of Political Action Committees & Their Interests. 2nd ed. 1986. 250.00 (0-942236-01-7) Sunshine Serv.

Roeder, George H., Jr. The Censored War: American Visual Experience During World War II. LC 92-31859. 189p. (C). 1993. 40.00 (0-300-05723-7) Yale U Pr.

Roeder, George H. Censored War: American Visual Experience During World War II. 1995. pap. 20.00 (0-300-06291-5) Yale U Pr.

Roeder, Kenneth D. Insect Physiology. 1100p. 1985. pap. 175.00 (0-7855-0368-4, Pub. by Intl Bks & Periodicals) St Mut.

— Nerve Cells & Insect Behavior. LC 98-136606. (Illus.). 256p. 1998. pap. text 16.95 (0-674-60801-1) HUP.

— Nerve Cells & Insect Behavior. rev. ed. LC 67-27092. (Books in Biology: No. 4). 91p. 1967. 17.00 (0-674-60800-3) HUP.

Roeder, Linda L., jt. auth. see Roeder, David C.

Roeder, Michael T. A History of the Concerto. LC 92-41967. (Illus.). 480p. 1994. 39.95 (0-931340-61-6, Amadeus Pr) Timber.

Roeder, Peter M., et al, eds. Pluralism & Education: Current World Trends in Policy, Law, & Administration. LC 95-42849. 345p. (Orig.). 1995. pap. 21.95 (0-87772-366-4) UCB IGS.

Roeder, Rick. A Quizzical Look at the Rock Era. McLean, Diane, ed. (Illus.). 136p. (Orig.). 1987. pap. 9.95 (0-9619648-0-4) Big Bop Bks.

Roederer, Charlotte. Little Red Riding Hood. (Little Puppet Theaters Ser.). 1998. 19.95 (1-57178-075-0) Coun Oak Bks.

Roederer, Charlotte. Goldilocks & the Three Bears: A Classic Fairy Tale. LC 97-23046. (Little Pebbles Ser.). 32p. (J). (ps-1). 1999. 6.95 (0-7892-0420-7, Abbeville Kids) Abbeville Pr.

Roederer, J. G. Progress in Solar-Terrestrial Physics. 1983. text 296.00 (90-277-1559-9) Kluwer Academic.

Roederer, Juan G. Introduction to the Physics & Psychophysics of Music. 2nd ed. (Heidelberg Science Library). (Illus.). 202p. 1975. reprint ed. pap. 21.00 (3-540-90116-7) Spr-Verlag.

— The Physics & Psychophysics of Music. 3rd ed. (Illus.). 219p. 1994. 29.95 (0-387-94366-8) Spr-Verlag.

— The Physics & Psychophysics of Music: An Introduction. 3rd ed. LC 94-16447. (Illus.). 219p. 1994. 64.95 (0-387-94298-X) Spr-Verlag.

Roederer, Scott, jt. auth. see Hafele, Rick.

Roediger. Psychology. 4th ed. 1991. mass mkt., student ed. 19.75 (0-314-94270-X) Wadsworth Pub.

— Shades of Pale. 1997. 25.00 (0-02-926885-0) Free Pr.

Roediger, jt. auth. see Kantowitz.

Roediger, Dave & Rosemont, Franklin, eds. Haymarket Scrapbook: A Centennial Anthology. LC 86-80843. (Illus.). 256p. 1986. 35.00 (0-88286-147-6); pap. 18.95 (0-88286-122-0) C H Kerr.

Roediger, Dave, ed. see Abrams, Irving.

Roediger, Dave, ed. & intro. see Thompson, Fred.

Roediger, David R. Black on White. 1999. pap. 14.00 (0-8052-1114-4) Schocken.

— Towards the Abolition of Whiteness: Essays on Race, Politics, & Working Class History. LC 93-49387. (Haymarket Ser.). 200p. (C). 1994. pap. 18.00 (0-86091-658-8, Pub. by Verso) Norton.

— The Wages of Whiteness: Race & the Making of the American Working Class. 2nd ed. (Haymarket Ser.). 224p. 2000. pap. 19.00 (1-85984-240-2, Pub. by Verso) Norton.

Roediger, David R. & Foner, Philip S. Our Own Time: A History of American Labor & the Working Day, 23. LC 87-29543. (Contributions in Labor Studies: No. 23). 392p. 1989. 65.00 (0-313-26062-1, ROO/, Greenwood Pr) Greenwood.

Roediger, David R., ed. see Hall, Covington.

Roediger, H. L., III & Craik, F. I., eds. Varieties of Memory & Consciousness: Essays in Honour of Endel Tulving. 464p. 1989. 89.95 (0-89859-935-0) L Erlbaum Assocs.

— Varieties of Memory & Consciousness: Essays in Honour of Endel Tulving. 464p. 1989. pap. 45.00 (0-8058-0546-X) L Erlbaum Assocs.

Roediger, Henry L. Psychology. 4th ed. Date not set. pap. text, teacher ed. write for info. (0-314-09383-4) West Pub.

— Psychology. 4th ed. 1996. mass mkt., student ed. 15.75 (0-314-08964-0) West Pub.

— Psychology: Reader. 1996. mass mkt. 25.95 (0-314-09382-6) West Pub.

Roediger, Henry L., III, et al. Psychology. 4th ed. LC 95-43775. 750p. (C). 1997. pap. 83.95 (0-314-06160-6) Thomson Learn.

Roediger, Virginia M. Ceremonial Costumes of the Pueblo Indians: Their Evolution, Fabrication, & Significance in the Prayer Drama. (Illus.). 268p. 1991. 60.00 (0-520-07630-3, Pub. by U CA Pr); pap. 32.50 (0-520-07631-1, Pub. by U CA Pr) Cal Prin Full Svc.

Roegdke, Soren & Busse, Kay. Crockett: The True Story of a Cowboy. LC 92-91045. 300p. (Orig.). 1993. pap. 20.00 (0-9629242-1-0) WKB Enterp.

R

— Sadie: The True Story of a Western Lady. LC 94-90087. (True Story Ser.). 268p. (Orig.). 1994. pap. 20.00 (*0-9629242-2-9*) WKB Enterp.
— Silk: An Expose of Commercial Fishing. LC 94-61842. 364p. (Orig.). (C). 1995. pap. 20.00 (*0-9629242-3-7*) WKB Enterp.
Roeges, Noel P. G. A Guide to the Complete Interpretation of Inferred Spectral of Organic Structures. LC 94-2445. 356p. 1994. 195.00 (*0-471-93998-6*) Wiley.
Roegiers, Jean-Claude, ed. Rock Mechanics As a Multidisciplinary Science: Proceedings of the 32nd U. S. Symposium on Rock Mechanics, Norman, Oklahoma, 10-12 July 1991. (Illus.). 1236p. (C). 1991. text 175.00 (*90-6191-194-X*, Pub. by A A Balkema) Ashgate Pub Co.
***Roegiers, Patrick.** Herb Ritts. LC 00-100981. (Illus.). 184p. 2000. 45.00 (*0-500-97489-6*, Pub. by Thames Hudson) Norton.
Roeglin, Kris & Fullerton, Linda. Munchies, Meals & Mayhem! Simple Recipes & Fun Projects for Kids. (Illus.). 110p. (J). (ps-6). 1996. pap. 12.95 (*0-9655480-2-3*) Wooden Spoon Pub.
Roeher, H. D., jt. ed. see Clark, O.
Roehklepartain, Jolene. Ideas for Parents Newsletter Master Set. (Illus.). 1995. 95.00 (*1-57482-354-X*) Search Inst.
Roehl-Anderson, Janice M. & Bragg, Steven M. The Controller's Function: The Work of the Managerial Accountant. 112p. 1996. pap. text, teacher ed. 14.00 (*0-471-14593-9*) Wiley.
***Roehl-Anderson, Janice M. & Bragg, Steven M.** The Controller's Function: The Work of the Managerial Accountant. 2nd ed. 466p. 2000. pap. 59.95 (*0-471-38307-4*) Wiley.
Roehl-Anderson, Janice M. & Bragg, Steven M. The Controller's Function: The Work of the Managerial Accountant (College Edition) LC 95-30644. 488p. 1996. pap. 59.95 (*0-471-14592-0*) Wiley.
Roehl, Bernie & Couch, Justin. Late Night VRML 2.0 with Java. LC 98-160275. 710p. 1997. 44.99 (*1-56276-504-3*, Ziff-Davis Pr) Que.
Roehl, Evelyn. Whole Food Facts: The Complete Reference Guide. LC 96-3961. (Illus.). 192p. 1996. pap. 19.95 (*0-89281-635-X*, Heal Arts VT) Inner Tradit.
Roehl, H., ed. Inscriptiones Graecae Antiquissimae: Praeter Atticas in Attica Repertas. (Illus.). 193p. 1977. reprint ed. 30.00 (*0-89005-221-2*) Ares.
Roehl, Harvey N. A Carousel of Limericks. LC 85-22538. (Illus.). 80p. (Orig.). (J). (gr. 4-8). 1986. pap. 7.95 (*0-911572-47-3*, Vestal Pr) Madison Bks UPA.
— Cornell & Ithaca in Early Postcards. LC 86-18937. (Illus.). 112p. (Orig.). 1986. pap. 11.95 (*0-911572-59-7*, Vestal Pr) Madison Bks UPA.
Roehl, Harvey N., jt. auth. see Palmer, Richard F.
Roehl, Harvey N., ed. see Leverett, Willard M.
Roehl, Jan, jt. ed. see Mazerolle, Lorraine Green.
Roehl, P. O. & Choquette, P. W. Carbonate Petroleum Reservoir. (Casebooks in Earth Sciences Ser.). (Illus.). 480p. 1985. 175.00 (*0-387-96012-0*) Spr-Verlag.
Roehl, Thomas W., jt. ed. see Hanson, Kermit.
Roehl, Tim. Christmas Hearts: Images of Immanuel Through the Eyes of Those Who Saw Him First. (Illus.). 112p. 1998. 14.99 (*1-57748-377-4*) Barbour Pub.
***Roehl, Tim.** Christmas Hearts: Twelve Stories of the first Christmas. 2000. pap. text 9.99 (*1-57748-849-0*) Barbour Pub.
— Surprised by Grace: Twelve Stories of Lives Changed. (Illus.). 150p. 2000. pap. 9.99 (*1-57748-841-5*, Promise Pr) Barbour Pub.
Roehler, Ernst. Fischereischutz, Fischverwertung, Fischereirecht und-Organisation. (Handbuch der Binnenfischerei Mitteleuropas Ser.: Lieferung 4). (GER., Illus.). v, 74p. 1937. 15.00 (*3-510-41036-X*, Pub. by E Schweizerbartsche) Balogh.
Roehler, Laura R., jt. auth. see Duffy, Gerald G.
***Roehlkepartain, Eugene C.** Building Assets in Congregations: A Practical Guide for Helping Youth Grow up Healthy. 176p. 1998. pap. 18.95 (*1-57482-113-X*) Search Inst.
— Kids Have a Lot to Give: How Congregations Can Nurture the Habits of Giving & Serving for the Common Good. 36p. 1999. pap. 8.95 (*1-57482-169-5*) Search Inst.
Roehlkepartain, Eugene C. The Teaching Church: Moving Christian Education to Center Stage. LC 92-41987. 208p. (Orig.). 1993. pap. 13.95 (*0-687-41083-5*) Abingdon.
— Youth Development in Congregations: An Exploration of the Potential & Barriers. 96p. (Orig.). 1995. pap. 14.95 (*1-57482-123-7*) Search Inst.
Roehlkepartain, Eugene C. & Benson, Peter L. Beyond Leaf Raking: Service: Learning & Youth Ministry. LC 93-28845. (Essentials for Christian Youth Ser.). 122p. (Orig.). 1993. pap. 13.95 (*0-687-21328-2*) Abingdon.
Roehlkepartain, Eugene C. & Blyth, Dale A. Healthy Communities, Healthy Youth: How Communities Contribute to Positive Youth Development. 76p. 1993. pap. 10.00 (*1-57482-318-3*) Search Inst.
Roehlkepartain, Eugene C. & Draayer, Donald. Learning & Living: How Asset-Building for Youth Can Unify a School's Mission. (Everyone's an Asset-Builder Ser.). 16p. 1998. pap. 3.95 (*1-57482-331-0*) Search Inst.
Roehlkepartain, Eugene C., jt. auth. see Benson, Peter L.
Roehlkepartain, Eugene C., jt. auth. see Feldmeyer, Dean.
Roehlkepartain, Eugene C., jt. auth. see Seefeldt, Glenn A.
Roehlkepartain, Jolene L. Building Assets Together: One Hundred Thirty-Five Group Activities for Helping Youth Succeed. 128p. 1997. pap. 21.95 (*1-57482-333-7*) Search Inst.
— Creating Intergenerational Community: 75 Ideas for Building Relationships Between Youth & Adults. 20p. 1996. pap. 4.95 (*1-57482-356-6*) Search Inst.
— Fidget Busters: 101 Quick Attention-Getters for Children's Ministry. (Illus.). 96p. 1992. pap. 14.99 (*1-55945-058-4*) Group Pub.
***Roehlkepartain, Jolene L.** Prescription for a Healthy Church. 2000. pap. 17.99 (*0-7644-2215-4*) Group Pub.
— Taking Asset Building Personally: An Action & Reflection Workbook. 84p. 1999. pap. 12.95 (*1-57482-397-3*) Search Inst.
— Teaching Kids to Care & Share: 300+ Mission & Service Ideas for Children. LC 99-55636. (Illus.). 96p. 2000. pap. 13.00 (*0-687-08428-8*) Abingdon.
Roehlkepartain, Jolene L. Wiggle Tamers: 101 Ideas for Keeping Kids Focused. Parolini, Stephen, ed. 96p. 1995. pap. 14.99 (*1-55945-615-9*) Group Pub.
Roehlkepartain, Jolene L., ed. Children's Ministry That Works! The Basics & Beyond. (Illus.). 228p. 1991. pap. 15.99 (*0-931529-69-7*, Group Bks) Group Pub.
Roehlkepartain, Jolene L. & Leffert, Nancy. A Leader's Guide to What Young Children Need to Succeed: Working Together to Build Assets from Birth to Age 11. 96p. 2000. pap. 14.95 (*1-57542-071-6*) Free Spirit Pub.
— What Young Children Need to Succeed: Working Together to Build Assets from Birth to Age 11. LC 99-37224. (Illus.). 300p. 1999. pap. 9.95 (*1-57542-070-8*) Free Spirit Pub.
Roehm, Carolyne. Carolyne Roehm's Fall Notebook. (Illus.). 144p. 1999. 25.00 (*0-06-019412-X*) HarpC.
***Roehm, Carolyne.** Carolyne Roehm's Seasonal Notebooks: Boxed Set. (Illus.). 144p. 2000. 100.00 (*0-06-018428-0*, HarpCollins) HarperTrade.
— Carolyne Roehm's Spring Notebook. (Illus.). 192p. 2000. 25.00 (*0-06-019453-7*) HarpC.
Roehm, Carolyne. Carolyne Roehm's Summer Notebook. LC 99-219516. (Illus.). 144p. 1999. 23.00 (*0-06-019387-5*) HarpC.
***Roehm, Carolyne.** Carolyne Roehm's Winter Notebook. 144p. 1999. 25.00 (*0-06-019452-9*) HarpC.
Roehm, Carolyne. A Passion for Flowers. LC 98-104832. (Illus.). 288p. 1997. 60.00 (*0-06-757513-7*) HarpC.
Roehm, Klaus-Jurgen. Polyphonie und Improvisation: Zur Offenen Form in Gunter Grass' Die Rattin. LC 91-31480. (Studies in Modern German Literature: Vol. 47). (GER.). 185p. (C). 1992. text 36.95 (*0-8204-1693-2*) P Lang Pubng.
Roehm, Marjorie C. The Letters of George Catlin & His Family: A Chronicle of the American West. LC 66-13090. (Illus.). 485p. reprint ed. pap. 150.40 (*0-608-17987-6*, 202906100058) Bks Demand.
Roehm, Michelle, ed. Boys Know It All: Wise Thoughts & Wacky Ideas from Guys Like You. LC 98-7590. (Kids Books by Kids: No. 5). (Illus.). 168p. (J). (gr. 1-9). 1998. pap. 8.95 (*1-885223-87-0*) Beyond Words Pub.
— Girls Know Best: Advice for Girls from Girls on Just about Everything. LC 97-19942. 160p. (J). (gr. 5-9). 1997. pap. 8.95 (*1-885223-63-3*) Beyond Words Pub.
***Roehm, Michelle, ed.** Girls Know Best: Advice for Girls on Just about Everything. 160p. 1999. 6.98 (*1-56731-313-2*, MJF Bks) Fine Comms.
Roehm, Michelle, ed. Girls Know Best 2: Tips on Life & Fun Stuff to Do. LC 98-7591. (Girl Power Ser.: No. 3). (Illus.). 152p. (YA). (gr. 5-8). 1998. pap. 8.95 (*1-885223-84-6*) Beyond Words Pub.
Roehm, Michelle, ed. see Acker, Loren E., et al.
Roehm, Michelle, ed. see Burke-Weiner, Kimberly.
Roehm, Michelle, ed. see White Deer of Autumn Staff.
Roehman, Frank L., jt. ed. see Wilson, Frank P.
Roehmann, Franz L., ed. Music & Child Development. (Illus.). 442p. (Orig.). 1990. pap. 25.00 (*0-918812-58-5*, ST011) MMB Music.
Roehme, Carolyne. At Home with Carolyne Roehm. 2000. 55.01 (*0-06-019357-3*) HarpC.
Roehmer, Harriet. Brother Anansi & the Cattle Ranch: El Hermano Anansi Y El Rancho De Ganado Read Along Set. Olivarez, Anna, ed. (ENG & SPA.). (YA). (ps-7). 1989. 25.95 incl. audio (*0-89239-063-8*) Childrens Book Pr.
Roehner, Bertrand M. Theory of Markets: Trade & Space-Time Patterns of Price Fluctuations: A Study in Analytical Economics. LC 95-5873. (Advances in Spatial & Network Economics Ser.). 1995. 125.00 (*3-540-58815-9*) Spr-Verlag.
***Roehr, Mary.** Craft Sewing for Fun & Profit. LC 99-57534. 2000. pap. 19.99 (*0-7615-2043-0*) Prima Pub.
Roehr, Mary A. Altering Men's Ready-to-Wear. (Illus.). 150p. (Orig.). (C). 1987. pap. text 17.95 (*0-9619229-1-5*) M Roehr Bks Vid.
— Altering Women's Ready-to-Wear. (Illus.). 190p. (Orig.). (C). 1987. pap. 19.95 (*0-9619229-0-7*) M Roehr Bks Vid.
— Sew Hilarious. (Illus.). 64p. (Orig.). 1995. pap. 9.95 (*0-9619229-4-X*) M Roehr Bks Vid.
— Sewing As a Home Business. (Illus.). 135p. (Orig.). (C). 1987. reprint ed. pap. 14.95 (*0-9619229-2-3*) M Roehr Bks Vid.
— Speed Tailoring. (Illus.). 45p. (C). 1992. reprint ed. pap. 14.95 (*0-9619229-3-1*) M Roehr Bks Vid.
Roehr, Sabine. A Primer on German Enlightenment: With a Translation of Karl Leonhard Reinhold's the Fundamental Concepts & Principles of Ethics. LC 94-44811. 304p. 1995. text 39.95 (*0-8262-0997-1*) U of Mo Pr.
Roehrborn, Claus G. Benign Prostatic Hyperplasia (BPH) A Guide for Men. Webster, G. D., ed. (Men's Health Ser.). (Illus.). 24p. (Orig.). 1996. pap. 2.95 (*1-885274-28-9*) Health InfoNet Inc.
Roehrborn, Claus G., tr. see Schild, Hans H., et al, eds.
Roehrenbeck, Carol A., et al. Complying with the ADA: Law Library Services & Facilities. LC 97-16119. (Law Library Information Reports: Vol. 20). (Illus.). 254p. 1997. pap. text 50.00 (*0-87802-109-4*) Glanville.
Roehrich-Rubio, Esther, tr. see Crebbin, June.
Roehrich-Rubio, Esther, tr. see Gilman, Phoebe.
Roehrich-Rubio, Esther, tr. see Waddell, Martin.
Roehrick, Kaye L., ed. Brevet's North Dakota Historical Markers & Sites. LC 74-79978. (Historical Markers-Sites Ser.). (Illus.). 176p. 1975. 12.95 (*0-88498-024-3*) Brevet Pr.
Roehrig, Catherine H., tr. see Teynard, Felix.
Roehrig, Catherine H. Fun with Hieroglyphs: From the Metropolitan Museum of Art. LC 91-169201. (Illus.). (J). (gr. 7 up). 1990. 22.50 (*0-670-83576-5*, Viking Child) Peng Put Young Read.
Roehrig, Michael F. Foreign Joint Ventures in Contemporary China. LC 94-11018. 1994. text 55.00 (*0-312-12131-8*) St Martin.
Roehrkasse, Lucille, jt. auth. see Kramin, Norma.
Roehrman, Hendrik. The Way of Life. LC 70-144677. Orig. Title: Marlow & Shakespeare. reprint ed. 21.50 (*0-404-05386-6*) AMS Pr.
Roehrs, Mark D., jt. auth. see Renzi, William A.
Roehrs, Susanne, jt. auth. see Metzger, Sue McFarland.
Roekard, Karen. The Santa Cruz Haggadah: A Passover Haggadah, Coloring Book & Journal for the Evolving Consciousness. 1992. student ed. 5.95 (*0-9628913-8-X*) Hineni Concisus.
— The Santa Cruz Haggadah Kids Passover Fun Book. (Illus.). 56p. (Orig.). (J). (ps-10). 1994. pap. 4.95 (*0-9628913-0-4*) Hineni Concisus.
— The Santa Cruz Haggadah Leader's Edition: A Passover Haggadah, Coloring Book & Journal for the Evolving Consciousness. 1992. 13.95 (*0-9628913-4-7*) Hineni Concisus.
Roelandt, Jos R. The Practice of M-Mode & Two-Dimensional Echocardiagraphy. 1983. text 191.50 (*90-247-2745-6*) Kluwer Academic.
Roelandt, Jos R., ed. Color Doppler Flow Imaging. (Developments in Cardiovascular Medicine Ser.). 1986. lib. bdg. 184.00 (*0-89838-806-6*) Kluwer Academic.
— Digital Techniques in Echocardiography. (Developments in Cardiovascular Medicine Ser.). 1987. text 184.00 (*0-89838-861-9*) Kluwer Academic.
Roelandt, Jos R., et al, eds. Intravascular Ultrasound. LC 93-1382. (Developments in Cardiovascular Medicine Ser.). 184p. (C). 1993. text 89.00 (*0-7923-2301-7*) Kluwer Academic.
Roelandt, Jos R. & Hugenholtz, P. G. Long-Term Ambulatory Electrocardiography. 1982. text 126.50 (*90-247-2664-6*) Kluwer Academic.
Roelandt, Jos R. & Meltzer, Richard S. Contrast Echocardiography. 1982. text 226.00 (*90-247-2531-3*) Kluwer Academic.
Roelandt, Jos R. & Pandian, Natesa G., eds. Multiplane Transesophageal Echocardiography. 257p. 1995. text 115.00 (*0-443-07950-1*) Church.
Roelandt, Jos R., jt. ed. see Bom, N.
Roelandt, Joseph R. Practical Echocardiology. LC 77-1619. (Ultrasound in Biomedicine Ser.: No. 1). (Illus.). 330p. reprint ed. pap. 102.30 (*0-8357-4554-6*, 203745300008) Bks Demand.
Roelant, C. A Comparative Study of Luminol & Lucigenin in the Mediation of Chemiluminescence Produced by Stimulated Human Polymorphonuclear Neutrophils & Neutroplasts. No. 13. 169p. (Orig.). 1989. pap. 32.50 (*90-6186-323-6*, Pub. by Leuven Univ) Coronet Bks.
Roelants, G. E., jt. ed. see Loor, F.
Roelcke, Thorsten. Dramatische Kommunikation: Modell und Reflexion bei Duerrenmatt, Handke, Weiss. (Quellen und Forschungen zur Sprach und Kulturgeschichte der Germanischen Voelker: No. 231). (GER.). xii, 313p. (C). 1994. lib. bdg. 113.85 (*3-11-014646-0*, 98-94) De Gruyter.
— Periodisierung der Deutschen Sprachgeschichte: Analysen & Tabellen. (Studia Linguistica Germanica: Vol. 40). (GER.). xi, 494p. 1995. lib. bdg. 169.25 (*3-11-015075-1*) De Gruyter.
— Sprachtypologie des Deutschen. 248p. 1997. text 19.90 (*3-11-015276-2*) De Gruyter.
Roelen, Jerry. Rock Art Tarot. LC 95-61761. 1997. pap. text 9.95 (*0-88079-194-2*, BK32) US Games Syst.
— Rock Art Tarot Deck & Book Set. 208p. 1997. pap. 26.00 (*0-88079-195-0*, RKS99) US Games Syst.
Roeliff Jansen Historical Society Staff. The Mill on the Roeliff Jansen Kill: Two Hundred Fifty Years of American Industrial History. Faber, Harold, ed. LC 93-79570. (Illus.). 144p. 1993. pap. 15.00 (*0-9628523-9-2*) Blk Dome Pr.
Roelker, Nancy L. One King, One Faith: The Parlement of Paris & the Religious Reformations of the Sixteenth Century. LC 94-40396. (Centennial Bk.). 532p. (C). 1996. text 68.00 (*0-520-08626-0*, Pub. by U CA Pr) Cal Prin Full Svc.
— Queen of Navarre, Jeanne D'Albret, 1528-1572. LC 68-54024. (Illus.). 515p. 1968. 42.50 (*0-674-74150-1*) Belknap Pr.
Roell, Craig H. The Piano in America, 1890-1940. LC 88-14326. (Illus.). 416p. 1989. reprint ed. pap. 129.00 (*0-608-03181-X*, 206363400007) Bks Demand.
— Remember Goliad! A History of la Bahia. LC 94-25973. (Fred Rider Cotten Popular History Ser.: No. 9). (Illus.). 108p. 1994. pap. 7.95 (*0-87611-141-X*) Tex St Hist Assn.
Roell, Craig H., jt. auth. see Gould, Lewis L.
Roelli, H. J. Das Behinderte Kind. Anderhalden, A., ed. (Paediatrische Fortbildungskurse fuer die Praxis Ser.: Vol. 56). (Illus.). vi, 110p. 1982. pap. 46.25 (*3-8055-3493-0*) S Karger.
***Roelof J. Stroeker, et al.** Discovering Mathematics with Maple: An Interactive Exploration for Mathematicians, Engineers & Econometricians LC 99-26202. 1999. write for info. (*0-8176-6091-7*) Birkhauser.
Roelofs, Faith M. Adventures Around Kilauea: Kilauea Volcano. (Exploring the Islands: Island of Hawai'i Ser.). 1994. pap. write for info. (*1-882163-30-3*) Moanalua Grdns Fnd.
— Aiea Loop Trail & Keaiwa Heiau. (Exploring Oahu: Field Site Guides for Teachers Ser.). 24p. 1992. pap. write for info. (*1-882163-02-8*) Moanalua Grdns Fnd.
— Aiea Loop Trail & Keaiwa Heiau: Field Site Guide for Teachers. (Exploring the Islands Ser.). 1992. teacher ed. write for info. (*1-882163-38-9*) Moanalua Grdns Fnd.
— Central & East Molokai Field Site Guide for Teachers. (Exploring the Islands Ser.). 1994. teacher ed. write for info. (*1-882163-27-3*) Moanalua Grdns Fnd.
— Exploring Hawaii: Field Site Guides for Teachers, Set. 1993. teacher ed. write for info. (*1-882163-07-9*) Moanalua Grdns Fnd.
— Exploring Kauai: Field Site Guides for Teachers, 3 vols., Set. 1993. teacher ed. write for info. (*1-882163-05-2*) Moanalua Grdns Fnd.
— Exploring Maui: Field Site Guides for Teachers, Set. 1993. teacher ed. write for info. (*0-318-69543-X*) Moanalua Grdns Fnd.
— Exploring Molokai: Field Site Guides for Teachers, 2 vols., Set. (Exploring the Islands Ser.). 1994. teacher ed. write for info. (*1-882163-24-9*) Moanalua Grdns Fnd.
— Exploring the Islands: Island of Hawai'i, 4 vols., Set. 1994. pap. write for info. (*1-882163-44-3*) Moanalua Grdns Fnd.
— Exploring the Islands: Island of Kaua'i, 3 vols., Set. 1994. pap. write for info. (*1-882163-42-7*) Moanalua Grdns Fnd.
— Exploring the Islands: Island of O'ahu, 4 vols., Set. 1994. pap. write for info. (*1-882163-41-9*) Moanalua Grdns Fnd.
— Exploring the Islands: Islands of Maui & Moloka'i, 4 vols., Set. 1994. pap. write for info. (*1-882163-43-5*) Moanalua Grdns Fnd.
— Hamakua to Waipio Field Site Guide for Teachers. (Exploring the Islands Ser.). 1994. teacher ed. write for info. (*1-882163-35-4*) Moanalua Grdns Fnd.
— Hauula Loop Trail. (Exploring Oahu: Field Site Guides for Teachers Ser.). 20p. 1992. pap. write for info. (*1-882163-03-6*) Moanalua Grdns Fnd.
— Hauula Loop Trail Field Site Guide for Teachers. (Exploring the Islands Ser.). 1992. teacher ed. write for info. (*1-882163-39-7*) Moanalua Grdns Fnd.
— High & Wild: Waikamoi & Halemau'u Trail. (Exploring the Islands: Islands of Maui & Moloka'i Ser.). 24p. 1993. pap. write for info. (*1-882163-15-X*) Moanalua Grdns Fnd.
— Investigating the South Coast: Punalu'u to Manuka. (Exploring the Islands: Island of Hawai'i Ser.). 1994. pap. write for info. (*1-882163-32-X*) Moanalua Grdns Fnd.
— Kilauea Volcano Field Site Guide for Teachers. (Exploring the Islands Ser.). 1994. teacher ed. write for info. (*1-882163-34-6*) Moanalua Grdns Fnd.
— Koolaupoko Field Site Guide for Teachers. (Exploring the Islands Ser.). 1992. teacher ed. write for info. (*1-882163-37-0*) Moanalua Grdns Fnd.
— Makawehi Dunes & Sinkhole. (Exploring Kauai: Field Site Guides for Teachers Ser.). 1993. pap. write for info. (*1-882163-11-7*) Moanalua Grdns Fnd.
— Makewehi Dunes & Sinkhole Field Site Guide for Teachers. (Exploring the Islands Ser.). 1993. teacher ed. write for info. (*1-882163-22-2*) Moanalua Grdns Fnd.
— On the Wild Side: West Moloka'i. (Exploring the Islands: Islands of Maui & Moloka'i Ser.). 28p. 1994. pap. write for info. (*1-882163-26-5*) Moanalua Grdns Fnd.
— Place of Power: Central & East Moloka'i. (Exploring the Islands: Islands of Maui & Moloka'i Ser.). 36p. 1994. pap. write for info. (*1-882163-25-7*) Moanalua Grdns Fnd.
— Punaluu to Manuka Field Site Guide for Teachers. (Exploring the Islands Ser.). 1994. teacher ed. write for info. (*1-882163-36-2*) Moanalua Grdns Fnd.
— Saddle Road Field Site Guide for Teachers. (Exploring the Islands Ser.). 1994. teacher ed. write for info. (*1-882163-33-8*) Moanalua Grdns Fnd.
— Saddle Sojourn: Saddle Road, Big Island. (Exploring the Islands: Island of Hawai'i Ser.). 1994. pap. write for info. (*1-882163-29-X*) Moanalua Grdns Fnd.
— Up the Coast & into the Past: Hamakua to Waipio. (Exploring the Islands: Island of Hawai'i Ser.). 1994. pap. write for info. (*1-882163-31-1*) Moanalua Grdns Fnd.
— Waianae Coast & Kuaokala Ridge Trail. (Exploring Oahu: Field Site Guides for Teachers Ser.). 24p. 1992. pap. write for info. (*1-882163-04-4*) Moanalua Grdns Fnd.
— Waianae Coast & Kuaokala Trail Field Site Guide for Teachers. (Exploring the Islands Ser.). 1992. teacher ed. write for info. (*1-882163-40-0*) Moanalua Grdns Fnd.
— Waihe'e Trail & Haleki'i Field: Site Guide for Teachers. (Exploring the Islands Ser.). 36p. 1993. pap. write for info. (*1-882163-16-8*) Moanalua Grdns Fnd.
— Waihee Trail & Halekii Field Site Guide for Teachers. 1993. teacher ed. write for info. (*1-882163-18-4*) Moanalua Grdns Fnd.
— Waikamoi & Halemauu Trail: Field Site Guide for Teachers. (Exploring the Islands Ser.). 1993. teacher ed. write for info. (*1-882163-17-6*) Moanalua Grdns Fnd.
— Wailua Basin & Heiau Complex. (Exploring Kauai: Field Site Guides for Teachers Ser.). 1993. pap. write for info. (*1-882163-10-9*) Moanalua Grdns Fnd.
— Wailua Basin & Heiau Complex Field Site Guide for Teachers. (Exploring the Islands Ser.). 1994. teacher ed. write for info. (*1-882163-21-4*) Moanalua Grdns Fnd.
— Waimea Canyon & Kaluapuhi Trail Field Site Guide for Teachers. (Exploring the Islands Ser.). 1994. teacher ed. write for info. (*1-882163-23-0*) Moanalua Grdns Fnd.

An Asterisk (*) at the beginning of an entry indicates that the title is appearing for the first time.

An Asterisk (*) at the beginning of an entry indicates that the title is appearing for the first time.

*Roes, C. B., et al. Statistical Process Control in Industry: Implimentation & Assurance of SPC. LC 98-53216. 24p. 1999. 138.12 (0-7923-5570-9) Kluwer Academic.

Roes, Mimi. The Do Nothing Way to Health & Beauty. (Illus.). 128p. 1979. pap. 4.95 (0-89780-000-1) NAR Pubns.

— Poems for Young Children. (Illus.). (J). (ps-6). 1979. pap. 1.95 (0-89780-003-6) NAR Pubns.

Roes, Mon. Inherited Memories: Biogenetic Evolution of Intellect. rev. ed. 148p. (C). 1992. 18.00 (0-9618960-6-X) M M Fain.

— El Mejor: And Other Stories. 151p. (Orig.). (C). 1988. pap. 1.95 (0-9618960-1-9) M M Fain.

— The Orgy Room: And Other Stories. 118p. (C). 1988. pap. 1.95 (0-9618960-2-7) M M Fain.

— Sex Preferences. 2nd rev. ed. 190p. (C). 1990. 14.00 (0-9618960-5-1) M M Fain.

— Sex Preferences: Origins & Influences. 126p. (Orig.). (C). 1988. pap. 8.95 (0-9618960-0-0) M M Fain.

— Sitting on a Wall: Selected Writings of Mon Roes. 194p. 1993. 18.00 (0-685-67895-4) M M Fain.

Roes, Nicholas A. America's Lowest Cost Colleges. 256p. (Orig.). 1985. 12.95 (0-88191-026-0) Freundlich.

— Helping Children Watch TV. (Illus.). 52p. 1977. text 6.95 (0-89780-031-1); pap. text 4.95 (0-89780-030-3) NAR Pubns.

— Helping Children Watch TV: A Practical Handbook with More Than 100 TV-Related Learning Activities. rev. ed. 108p. 1992. pap. 9.95 (0-89780-013-3) NAR Pubns.

Roes, Nicholas A. & DuBacher, Monique E. Pick-Your-Own Farms: A Comprehensive Guide to Over 3,000 Farms Where You Can "Pick-Your-Own" Fruits & Vegetables. 242p. (Orig.). 1990. pap. 24.95 (0-89780-011-7) NAR Pubns.

Roes, Nick. Gambling for Fun. 100p. 1988. pap. 9.95 (0-89780-009-5) NAR Pubns.

Roesch, Josef, jt. ed. see Lanzer, Peter.

Roesch, Joseph E., tr. see Chapuis, Alfred.

Roesch, R., et al, eds. Psychology & the Law: The State of the Discipline. LC 98-45167. (Perspectives in Law & Psychology Ser.: No. 10). (Illus.). 434p. (C). 1999. write for info. (0-306-45949-3, Kluwer Plenum) Kluwer Academic.

— Psychology & the Law: The State of the Discipline. LC 98-45167. (Perspectives in Law & Psychology Ser.: No. 10). (Illus.). xviii, 459p. (C). 1999. pap. write for info. (0-306-45950-7, Plenum Trade) Perseus Pubng.

Roesch, Robert C., jt. auth. see Engelmann, Curtis H.

Roesch, Roberta. The Encyclopedia of Depression. 270p. (C). 1991. 45.00 (0-8160-1936-3) Facts on File.

— Smart Talk: The Art of Savvy Business Conversation. LC 89-45455. 256p. 1989. pap. 14.95 (0-8144-7713-5) AMACOM.

— Time Management for Busy People. 272p. 1998. pap. 16.95 (0-07-053406-3) McGraw.

— The Working Woman's Guide to Managing Time: Take Charge of Your Job & Your Life While Taking Care of Yourself. LC 95-37227. 288p. (C). 1996. pap. 14.95 (0-13-097429-3) P-H.

— You Can Make It Without a College Degree. 1986. 8.95 (0-13-976812-2) S&S Trade.

Roesch, Roberta, jt. auth. see Schlenger, Sunny.

Roesch, Ronald & Golding, Stephen L. Competency to Stand Trial. LC 80-12456. 282p. 1981. text 29.95 (0-252-00825-1) U of Ill Pr.

Roesch, T. & Classen, M. Gastroenterologic Endosonography. (Illus.). 120p. 1992. text 129.00 (0-86577-454-4) Thieme Med Pubs.

Roesch Wagner, Sally. She Who Holds the Sky: Matilda Joslyn Gage. (Illus.). 77p. (Orig.). 1998. pap. 12.95 (1-880589-31-1) Sky Carrier Pr.

— A Time of Protest: Suffragists Challenge the Republic. 2nd ed. (Illus.). 157p. (Orig.). 1998. reprint ed. pap. 12.00 (1-880589-25-7) Sky Carrier Pr.

Roesch Wagner, Sally, ed. see Gage, Matilda Joslyn.

Roesdahl, Else. Vikings. LC 99-178674. 352p. 1999. pap. 15.95 (0-14-025282-7, Penguin Classics) Viking Penguin.

Roesdahl, Else, ed. see Jorgensen, Jorgen H.

Roese, John J. Switched LAN's: Implementation, Operation, Maintenance. LC 98-14473. (Computer Communications Ser.). 352p. 1998. pap. 45.00 (0-07-053413-6) McGraw.

— Switched Local Area Networks. LC 97-34128. (ITCP-US Computer Science Ser.). 350p. 1997. pap. 44.99 incl. cd-rom (1-85032-896-X) ITCP.

Roese, John J. & Gorsky, John Paul. DHCP: Managing IP Networks with Dynamic Host Configuration Protocol. 416p. 1999. pap. text 55.00 (0-07-135426-3) McGraw.

Roese, Neal J. & Olson, James M., eds. What Might Have Been: The Social Psychology of Counterfactual Thinking. 416p. 1995. text 89.95 (0-8058-1613-5); pap. text 45.00 (0-8058-1614-3) L Erlbaum Assocs.

Roesel, Catherine E. Immunology: A Self-Instructional Approach. 1978. pap. text 26.95 (0-07-053411-X) McGraw.

Roesel, Charles L., jt. auth. see Atkinson, Donald A.

Roesel, Martin. Uebersetzung Als Vollendung der Auslegung: Studien Zur Genesis-Septuaginta. (Beiheft zur Zeitschrift fuer die Alttestamentliche Wissenschaft Ser.: Bd. 223). (GER.). viii, 290p. (C). 1994. lib. bdg. 106.15 (3-11-014234-1, 8-94) De Gruyter.

Roeseler, Karl. The Adventures of Gesso Martin. 111p. (Orig.). 1994. pap. 8.95 (0-9639192-1-0) Trip St Pr.

— Last Decade. LC 99-19469. 20p. 1999. pap. 7.00 (0-942996-37-2, Pub. by Post Apollo Pr) SPD-Small Pr Dist.

Roeseler, Karl, ed. see Mathews, Harry, et al.

*Roeser, H. J., et al, eds. The Radio Galaxy Messier 87: Proceedings of a Workshop Held at Schloss Ringberg, Germany, September 15-19, 1997. LC 99-42742. (Lecture Notes in Physics Ser.: Vol. 530). (Illus.). xiii, 342p. 1999. 86.00 (3-540-66209-X) Spr-Verlag.

Roeser, Robert W., ed. Schooling & Mental Health: Issues, Research, & Future Directions. A Special Issue of Educational Psychologist. 90p. 1998. pap. write for info. (0-8058-9808-5) L Erlbaum Assocs.

*Roeser, Ross J. Audiology Diagnosis. LC 99-52571. (Illus.). 560p. 2000. 55.00 (0-86577-857-4) Thieme Med Pubs.

Roeser, Ross J., ed. Audiology Desk Reference: A Guide to the Practice of Audiology. (Illus.). 400p. 1996. pap. 45.00 (0-86577-574-5) Thieme Med Pubs.

Roeser, Ross J., et al, eds. Speech Pathology Desk Reference. LC 97-22115. (Illus.). 448p. 1997. pap. 45.00 (0-86577-696-2) Thieme Med Pubs.

Roeser, Ross J. & Downs, Marion P., eds. Auditory Disorders in School Children: Identification & Remediation. 3rd ed. (Illus.). 400p. 1995. text 45.00 (0-86577-550-8) Thieme Med Pubs.

*Roeser, Ross J., et al. Audiology: Diagnosis. LC 99-52571. (Illus.). 2000. write for info. incl. trans. (3-13-116431-X) Thieme Med Pubs.

Roeser, Ross J., et al. Speech-Language Pathology Desk Reference. LC 97-22115. 1998. write for info. (3-13-110541-0) Thieme Med Pubs.

Roeser, Steve, jt. auth. see Jancik, Wayne.

Roesgaard, Marie H. Moving Mountains: Japanese Education Reform. LC 98-189528. (Acta Jutlandica 73:1 Ser.: Vol. 71). (Illus.). 265p. 1998. pap. 24.95 (87-7288-477-0, Pub. by Aarhus Univ Pr) David Brown.

Roeske, Nancy A. Examination of the Personality. LC 72-8914. 176p. reprint ed. pap. 54.60 (0-608-30667-3, 205544100022) Bks Demand.

Roeske, Paulette. Divine Attention: Poems. LC 94-38208. 80p. (C). 1995. 11.95 (0-8071-1950-4). pap. 9.95 (0-8071-1951-2) La State U Pr.

Roesky, Herbert W. & Mockel, Klaus. Chemical Curiosities: Spectacular Experiments & Inspired Quotes. LC 96-31295. (Illus.). 340p. 1996. 54.95 (3-527-29414-7, Wiley-VCH) Wiley.

Roesler, A., jt. ed. see Pilger, A.

Roesler, Artur, jt. ed. see Pilger, Andreas.

Roesler, Bob. The Fair Grounds Big Shots & Long Shots. LC 98-235185. 208p. 1998. per. 19.95 (0-930892-52-6) A Hardy & Assocs.

Roesler, Dietmar. Sprachbruecke: Handbuch Fuer Den Unterricht. (GER.). 119p. (C). 1994. pap. text 21.75 (3-12-557230-4, Pub. by Klett Edition) Intl Bk Import.

Roesler, Dietmar, et al. Business - Auf Deutsch: Kopiervorlagen. (C). 1993. audio 42.25 (3-12-675222-5, Pub. by Klett Edition) Intl Bk Import.

— Kleine Deutsche Partikellehre: Ein Lehr-Und Uebungsbuch fuer Deutsch als Fremdsprache: Lehr-Und Uebungsbuch. (GER.). 171p. (C). 1973. pap. text 23.75 (3-12-554630-3, Pub. by Klett Edition) Intl Bk Import.

— Kleine Deutsche Partikellehre: Ein Lehr-Und Uebungsbuch fuer Deutsch als Fremdsprache: Lehr-Und Uebungsbuch. (GER.). (C). 1983. audio 36.00 (3-12-554640-0, Pub. by Klett Edition) Intl Bk Import.

— Sprachbruecke: Lehrbuch. (GER.). 251p. (C). 1987. pap. text 25.25 (3-12-557100-6, Pub. by Klett Edition) Intl Bk Import.

Roesler, H., ed. see Medical Cyclotron Users Conference Staff.

Roesler, John B. How to Find the Best Lawyers - & Save over 50 Percent on Legal Fees! (Orig.). 1996. pap. 14.95 (0-9650419-0-5) Blagden Roesler.

— How to Find the Best Lawyers...& Save over 50 Percent on Legal Fees. LC 96-75023. 200p. (Orig.). 1996. pap. 14.95 (1-57282-012-8) Message NM.

Roesler, Theodore W., jt. auth. see Lamphear, F. Charles.

Roesliep, Raymond. Rabbit in the Moon: Haiku. LC 83-6445. (Illus.). 128p. 1983. 30.00 (0-934184-15-1); pap. 20.00 (0-934184-16-X) Alembic Pr.

Roesling, Ralph. Roesling Nakamura Architects: Objective in Practice. 1999. pap. 40.00 (88-7838-041-5) L'Arca IT.

Roesner, Edward H., jt. ed. see Wolf, Eugene K.

Roesner, Larry A., ed. Effects of Watershed Development & Management on Aquatic Ecosystems: Proceedings of an Engineering Foundation Conference. LC 97-11470. 608p. 1997. 46.00 (0-7844-0232-9) Am Soc Civil Eng.

Roesner, Larry A., et al, eds. Design of Urban Runoff Quality Controls. 502p. 1989. 47.00 (0-87262-695-4) Am Soc Civil Eng.

Roesner, Larry A., jt. ed. see Urbonas, Ben.

Roess, Anne C. Public Utilities: An Annotated Guide to Information Sources. LC 91-22954. 406p. 1991. 50.00 (0-8108-2443-4) Scarecrow.

Roess, Roger P., et al. Traffic Engineering. 2nd ed. LC 97-32531. 714p. 1997. 105.00 (0-13-461336-8) P-H.

Roessel, David, ed. see Hughes, Langston.

Roessel, Monty. Kinaalda: A Navajo Girl Grows Up. (Illus.). (J). (gr. 3-6). 1993. pap. 6.95 (0-8225-9641-5, Lerner Publctns) Lerner Pub.

— Songs from the Loom: A Navajo Girl Learns to Weave. LC 94-48765. (We Are Still Here Ser.). (Illus.). (J). (gr. 4-6). 1995. lib. bdg. 21.27 (0-8225-2657-3, Lerner Publctns) Lerner Pub.

— Songs from the Loom: A Navajo Girl Learns to Weave. (Illus.). (J). 1995. pap. 6.95 (0-8225-9712-8) Lerner Pub.

Roessel, Monty, photos by. Kinaalda: A Navajo Girl Grows Up. LC 92-35204. (We are Still Here Ser.). (Illus.). 48p. (J). (gr. 3-6). 1993. lib. bdg. 21.27 (0-8225-2655-7, Lerner Publctns) Lerner Pub.

Roessel, Robert A. Navajo Education, 1948-78, Its Progress & Its Problems. 340p. 1979. 10.00 (0-912586-38-9) Rough Rock Pr.

Roessel, Ruth. Navajo Stories of the Long Walk Period. LC 73-78328. 272p. 1973. pap. 15.00 (0-912586-16-8) Dine College Pr.

*Roesset, Jose M., ed. Analysis, Design, Construction & Testing of Deep Foundations: Proceedings of the OTRC '99 Conference. LC 99-12876. 336p. 1999. 45.00 (0-7844-0422-4) Am Soc Civil Eng.

Roesset, Jose M., ed. Dynamics of Structures. 892p. 1987. 84.00 (0-87262-615-6) Am Soc Civil Eng.

Roessing, H. Two Thousand Two Hundred Eighty-Six Traditional Stencil Designs. (Illus.). 128p. 1991. reprint ed. pap. 8.95 (0-486-26845-4) Dover.

Roessing-Hager, Monika, ed. Wortindex zu Georg Buechner, Dichtungen und Uebersetzungen. (Deutsche Wortindices Ser.: No. 1). (C). 1970. 132.30 (3-11-006448-0) De Gruyter.

Roessing-Hager, Monika & Soerensen, Niels, eds. Wortindex zu Gottfried Keller, die Leute von Seldwyla, 2 Pts. (Deutsche Wortindices Ser.: No. 2). (C). 1971. 280.75 (3-11-006441-3) De Gruyter.

Roessingh, Martijn A. Ethnonationalism & Political Systems in Europe: A State of Tension. LC 97-144258. (Orig.). 1997. pap. 49.50 (90-5356-217-6, Pub. by Amsterdam U Pr) U of Mich Pr.

Roessler, A. C. A. C. Roessler's Standard Historical Souvenir Airmail Catalog. Mellone, Michael A., ed. (Illus.). 1978. pap. 4.50 (0-89794-007-5) FDC Pub.

Roessler, Carl. Coral Kingdoms. (Illus.). 244p. 1990. 39.95 (0-8109-0774-7); pap. 19.98 (0-8109-8095-9) Abrams.

— Lonely Planet Diving & Snorkeling Guide to Australia: Coral Sea & Great Barrier Reef. (Diving & Snorkeling Guides Ser.). 96p. 1991. pap. 14.95 (1-55992-044-0, Pisces Books) Lonely Planet.

— Lonely Planet Diving & Snorkeling Guide to Cayman Islands: Grand Cayman, Little Cayman & Cayman Brac. 2nd ed. (Pisces Diving & Snorkeling Guides Ser.). 96p. 1993. pap. 14.95 (1-55992-042-4, Pisces Books) Lonely Planet.

— Lonely Planet Great Reefs of the World. (Diving & Snorkeling Guides Ser.). (Illus.). 128p. 1992. pap. 19.95 (1-55992-058-0, 2058, Pisces Books) Lonely Planet.

Roessler, Carol A. Politicians Say the Dumbest Things. (Illus.). 228p. 1999. per. 11.95 (0-9668446-0-2) Wright Strategies.

Roessler, Dietrich. Grundriss der Praktischen Theologie. 2nd enl. ed. (GER.). xvii, 660p. 1993. lib. bdg. 60.00 (3-11-013534-5) De Gruyter.

Roessler, Edward B., jt. auth. see Amerine, Maynard A.

Roessler, Marcia J., jt. ed. see Wurster, Georgia B.

Roessler, Mark. The Last Magician in Blue Haven. LC 94-75954. (Illus.). 52p. (Orig.). (J). (gr. 4-8). 1994. pap. 10.00 (0-9638293-0-0) Hundelrut Studio.

Roessler, Martin. Schleiermacher's Program der Philosophischen Theologie. (Schleiermacher-Archiv Ser.: Bd. 14). (GER.). 247p. (C). 1994. lib. bdg. 121.55 (3-11-014171-X) De Gruyter.

Roessler, Richard & Rubin, Stanford E. Case Management & Rehabilitation Counseling: Procedures & Techniques. 3rd ed. LC 97-35024. 1998. write for info. (0-89079-741-2) PRO-ED.

Roessler, Richard, jt. auth. see Rubin, Stanford E.

Roessler, Richard T. & Brolin, Donn E. Life Centered Career Education: Competency Units for Occupational Guidance & Preparation. LC 92-18255. 670p. 1992. ring bd. 300.00 (0-86586-226-5, P369) Coun Exc Child.

Roessler, Richard T. & Rubin, Stanford E. Case Management & Rehabilitation Counseling: Procedures & Techniques. 2nd ed. LC 91-26385. 227p. 1992. pap. text 28.00 (0-89079-519-3, 3657) PRO-ED.

Roessler, Richard T., jt. auth. see Marr, John N.

Roessler, Richard T., jt. auth. see Rubin, Stanford E.

Roessler, Robert & Decker, Norman. Emotional Disorders in Physically Ill Patients. LC 85-15120. (Illus.). 269p. 1986. 35.95 (0-89885-254-4, Kluwer Acad Hman Sci) Kluwer Academic.

Roessler, Robert & Greenfield, Norman S., eds. Physiological Correlates of Psychological Disorder: Proceedings of an Interdisciplinary Research Conference Sponsored by the Wisconsin Psychiatric Institute & the Dept. of Psychiatry of the University of Wisconsin Medical Center, August 29-31, 1961. LC 62-15990. 294p. reprint ed. pap. 91.20 (0-608-14474-6, 202114500021) Bks Demand.

Roessler, Rudolf. Woerterbuch des Steuerrechts. (GER.). 1971. 75.00 (0-8288-6491-8, M-6934) Fr & Eur.

Roesslin, Eucharius. On Minerals & Mineral Products. (Ars Medica Ser.: Section IV, Vol. 1). (C). 1978. 300.00 (3-11-006907-5) De Gruyter.

Roessner, A., jt. ed. see Vollmer, E.

Roessner, David, ed. Innovation Policy. (Orig.). 1984. pap. 15.00 (0-918592-66-6) Pol Studies.

Roessner, J. David, et al. The Impact of Office Automation on Clerical Employment, 1985-2000: Forcasting Techniques & Plausible Futures in Banking & Insurance. LC 85-6523. (Illus.). 297p. 1985. 75.00 (0-89930-119-3, ROU/, Quorum Bks) Greenwood.

*Roessner, Jane. A Decent Place to Live: From Columbia Point to Harbor Point - A Community History. LC 99-86659. (Illus.). 320p. 2000. text 55.00 (1-55553-437-6); pap. text 24.95 (1-55553-436-8) NE U Pr.

*Roessner, Michaela. The Stars Compel. LC 99-36368. 430p. 1999. 25.95 (0-312-85755-1, Pub. by Tor Bks) St Martin.

— Stars Compel. 480p. 2000. mass mkt. 6.99 (0-8125-5015-3) Tor Bks.

Roessner, Michaela. The Stars Dispose. 1999. mass mkt. 6.99 (0-8125-5014-5, Pub. by Tor Bks) St Martin.

— Vanishing Point. 1994. pap. 4.99 (0-8125-1672-9, Pub. by Tor Bks) St Martin.

Roest, Aryan I. A Key-Guide to Mammal Skulls & Lower Jaws. (Illus.). 39p. (Orig.). (C). 1986. pap. 5.95 (0-916422-71-2) Mad River.

Roest, F. C., jt. auth. see Crul, R. C.

Roest, Jaijer M. Catalog der Reichhalltigen Sammlungen Hebraischer und Judischer Bucher und Handschriften, Kupferstiche, Portrats Etc. (GER.). viii, 429p. 1990. reprint ed. write for info. incl. 3.5 hd (3-487-09292-1) G Olms Pubs.

Roest, Mark, jt. auth. see Flynn, Rebecca.

Roest, Michele. Animal Tracks Activity Guide. (Illus.). 176p. (Orig.). (J). (gr. 4-6). 1995. pap. write for info. (0-945051-59-X) Natl Wildlife.

Roet, Brian. The Confidence to Be Yourself: How to Boost Your Self-Esteem. 1999. pap. 14.95 (0-7499-1926-4, Pub. by Piatkus Bks) London Brdge.

— Personal Therapy: How to Change Your Life for the Better. (Illus.). 130p. 1997. pap. 17.95 (0-09-181305-0) Trafalgar.

Roeta, Perry J. The Person in the Social Order. LC B 0828.5.R64. 390p. reprint ed. pap. 120.90 (0-608-30610-X, 202116200021) Bks Demand.

Roetger, Doris. Weather Watch. (J). (gr. k-3). 1991. pap. 8.99 (0-86653-969-7) Fearon Teacher Aids.

Roethel. Logic, Sets & Numbers. 2nd ed. (Math). 1976. 23.25 (0-534-00491-1) Brooks-Cole.

Roethel, David A., ed. Professional Directory, 1987. rev. ed. 225p. 1987. pap. 50.00 (0-939293-01-3) Amer Inst Chem.

Roethel, Hans K. & Benjamin, Jean K. Kandinsky Vol. I: Catalogue Raisonne of the Oil Paintings, 1900-1915. LC 81-69483. (Illus.). 480p. 1982. text 295.00 (0-8014-1478-4) Cornell U Pr.

Roether, Barbara, ed. see McBrien, Richard P.

Roether, Darlene. Hairwrapping Techniques: Creative Jewelry for Hair. (Illus.). 96p. 1995. pap. 9.95 (0-9644178-0-4) Roaring Forties.

Roethke, Theodore. The Collected Poems of Theodore Roethke. LC 65-23785. 288p. 1974. reprint ed. pap. 14.95 (0-385-08601-6, Anchor NY) Doubleday.

Roethlisberger. Elusive Phenomena. 1978. 29.95 (0-07-103283-5) McGraw.

Roethlisberger-Bianco, Marcel. Cavalier Pietro Tempesta & His Time. LC 78-101052. (Illus.). 313p. 75.00 (0-87413-105-7) U Delaware Pr.

Roethlisberger, Fritz J. Management & Morale. LC 41-4302. 317p. reprint ed. pap. 98.30 (0-608-10747-6, 200158700079) Bks Demand.

Roethlisberger, Fritz J. & Dickson, William J. Management & the Worker: An Account of a Research Program Conducted by the Western Electric Co, Hawthorne Works, Chicago. 639p. 1939. 52.50 (0-674-54676-8) HUP.

Roethlisberger, Marcel. Bartholomeus Breenbergh: The Paintings. (Illus.). 332p. 1980. 246.15 (3-11-001837-3) De Gruyter.

Roethlisberger, Marcel, ed. see Gelee, Glaude Lorrain.

*Roets, Lois F. Famous People. 3rd rev. ed. 48p. (YA). (gr. 3-8). 1999. pap. text 11.00 (0-911943-66-8) Leadership Pub.

Roets, Lois F. Giving Children Roots & Wings: How to Survive & Thrive As Parents of High-Ability Children. 2nd ed. 1999. pap. 12.00 (0-911943-64-1) Leadership Pub.

— How to Survive & Thrive as Educator of Gifted & Talented. 4th ed. 96p. 1999. 12.00 (0-911943-63-3) Leadership Pub.

— In-Service Manual for Gifted & Talented. 4th ed. 64p. 1999. pap. text, teacher ed. 35.00 (0-911943-62-5) Leadership Pub.

— Incomplete Plays. 4th ed. 62p. (J). (gr. 5-12). 1995. pap., teacher ed. 11.00 (0-911943-46-3) Leadership Pub.

— Jumbo Reading Yearbook: Grade 1. (Jumbo Reading Ser.). 96p. (gr. 1). 1979. 18.00 (0-8209-0012-5, JRY 1) ESP.

— Leadership: A Skills Training Program, Ages 8-18. 112p. 1997. pap. 20.00 (0-911943-52-8) Leadership Pub.

*Roets, Lois F. Leadership for Ages 4-8: Identification & Talent Development. 2nd rev. ed. 2000. teacher ed. 22.00 (0-911943-70-6) Leadership Pub.

Roets, Lois F. Modifying Standard Curriculum for High-Ability Learners. 6th ed. LC 97-150523. 96p. 1997. pap. 18.00 (0-911943-50-1) Leadership Pub.

— Philosophy & Philosophers. 50p. (J). (gr. 5-12). 1994. pap., teacher ed. 10.00 (0-911943-37-4) Leadership Pub.

— Public Speaking, Grades 2-12. rev. ed. 44p. (J). (gr. k-12). 1989. pap., teacher ed. 9.00 (0-911943-17-X) Leadership Pub.

— Readers' Theater Vol. 1: General Interest. 106p. (Orig.). (YA). (gr. 5-12). 1992. pap. text 16.00 (0-911943-29-3) Leadership Pub.

— Readers' Theater Vol. 2: Famous People. 108p. (Orig.). (YA). (gr. 5-12). 1992. pap. text 16.00 (0-911943-30-7) Leadership Pub.

— Readers' Theater Vol. 3: Entrepeneurs, Vol. 3. 2nd ed. 100p. (Orig.). (YA). (gr. 4-12). 1995. pap. text 16.00 (0-911943-43-9) Leadership Pub.

— Serving High School Gifted & Talented - 100+ Suggestions. 2nd ed. 64p. 1998. pap. text 20.00 (0-911943-57-9) Leadership Pub.

*Roets, Lois F. Standard & Gifted Education: Issues of Mutual Concern. 2nd rev. ed. 96p. 2000. pap. text 24.00 (0-911943-71-4) Leadership Pub.

— Standards & Benchmarks for Education of Gifted & Talented High-Ability Students, K-12. 5th rev. ed. 64p. 2000. pap. 39.00 (0-911943-72-2) Leadership Pub.

Roets, Lois F. Student Projects: Ideas & Plans. 288p. (J). (gr. 3 up). 1994. pap. text 30.00 (0-911943-39-0) Leadership Pub.

— Survey & Public Opinion Research: Grades Five to Twelve. 2nd ed. 120p. (J). (gr. 3 up). 1988. 16.00 (0-911943-14-5) Leadership Pub.

An Asterisk (*) at the beginning of an entry indicates that the title is appearing for the first time.

R

***Roets, Lois F.** When Bright Students Won't Do Their Assignments. 2nd ed. 1998. pap. 15.00 (0-911943-60-9) Leadership Pub.
— Writing Fiction. 56p. (YA). (gr. 3-12). 2000. pap. 12.00 (0-911943-69-2) Leadership Pub.
Roets, Lois S. Understanding Success & Failure. 36p. (YA). (gr. 5 up). 1997. 10.00 (0-911943-51-X) Leadership Pub.
Roets, Perry J. The Economic Ideas of Bernard W. Dempsey, S.J. LC 90-63708. 1991. 15.00 (0-87462-995-0) Marquette.
— Pillars of Catholic Social Teaching: A Brief Social Catechism. LC 98-13910. 136p. 1999. pap. 25.50 (1-57309-228-2, Cath Scholar Pr) Intl Scholars.
Roets, Philip G. Books of the Bible. 155p. (Orig.). (C). 1992. pap. text 20.00 (0-911943-34-X) Leadership Pub.
— Greek & Latin Prefixes & Word Parts. 3rd rev. expanded ed. 54p. (YA). (gr. 5-12). 1998. pap. text 16.00 (0-911943-58-7) Leadership Pub.
Roett, Riordan. Brazil: Politics in a Patrimonial Society. 5th ed. LC 99-21593. 264p. 1999. 65.00 (0-275-95899-X, Praeger Pubs); pap. 24.95 (0-275-95900-7, Praeger Pubs) Greenwood.
— Brazil in the Seventies. LC 76-54880. (AEI Studies: No. 132). 126p. reprint ed. pap. 39.10 (0-8357-4437-X, 203727100008) Bks Demand.
— The Challenge of Institutional Reform in Mexico. LC 95-3465. 216p. 1995. lib. bdg. 40.00 (1-55587-545-9) L Rienner.
— The Mexican Peso Crisis: Program on U. S.-Mexico Relations, the Paul H. Nitze School of Advanced International Studies, Johns Hopkins University. LC 96-8605. 1996. 13.95 (1-55587-667-6) L Rienner.
— The Politics of Foreign Aid in the Brazilian Northeast. LC 73-166403. 214p. 1972. reprint ed. pap. 66.40 (0-7837-9886-5, 206061200006) Bks Demand.
Roett, Riordan, compiled by. La Crisis del Peso Mexicano (The Mexican Peso Crisis) Perspectivas Internacionales (International Perspectives) (SPA.). 195p. 1996. pap. 9.99 (968-16-5064-6, Pub. by Fondo) Continental Bk.
Roett, Riordan, ed. Mercosur: Regional Integration, World Markets. LC 98-37779. 140p. 1998. lib. bdg. 25.00 (1-55587-837-7) L Rienner.
***Roett, Riordan, ed.** Mercosur: Regional Integration, World Markets. LC 98-37779. 140p. 1998. pap. 13.95 (1-55587-838-5) L Rienner.
Roett, Riordan, ed. Mexico's Private Sector: Recent History, Future Challenges. LC 98-25921. 252p. 1998. lib. bdg. 49.95 (1-55587-713-3) L Rienner.
Roett, Riordan, jt. auth. see Purcell, Susan K.
Roetteis, W. C., jt. auth. see Measell, James.
Roetter, Randy K. Guidelines for Being a Minor League Baseball Trainer. LC 97-69593. 43p. 1997. 6.99 (0-944183-23-9) PRC Pub.
Roettgen, Steffi. Anton Raphael Mengs: And His British Patrons. 1993. 50.00 (0-302-00623-0, Pub. by Zwemmer Bks) Intl Spec Bk.
— Italian Frescoes: The Flowering of the Renaissance, 1470-1510. (Illus.). 464p. 1997. 135.00 (0-7892-0221-2) Abbeville Pr.
Roettgen, Steffi & Stockman, Russell. Italian Frescoes: The Early Renaissance. LC 96-8196. (Illus.). 452p. 1996. 135.00 (0-7892-0139-9) Abbeville Pr.
Roettger, Doris. Bugs & Other Insects. 1991. 8.99 (0-86653-992-1) Fearon Teacher Aids.
— The Environment. 1993. pap. 8.99 (0-86653-939-5) Fearon Teacher Aids.
— Geography. (It's a Student's World Ser.). 72p. (J). (gr. 4-6). 1996. 8.99 (1-56417-868-4, FE7868) Fearon Teacher Aids.
— Growing up Healthy. (J). (gr. k-3). 1991. pap. 8.99 (0-86653-970-0) Fearon Teacher Aids.
— It's a Child's World Set, 5 bks., Set. (J). (gr. k-3). 42.99 (1-56417-745-9, FE0025) Fearon Teacher Aids.
— Many Cultures. (It's a Student's World Ser.). 64p. (J). (gr. 4-6). 1996. 8.99 (0-86653-867-4, FE3867) Fearon Teacher Aids.
— Our Ecosystem. 1993. pap. 8.99 (0-86653-936-0) Fearon Teacher Aids.
— Pollution, Recycling, Trash, & Litter. 1991. 8.99 (0-86653-981-6) Fearon Teacher Aids.
— Seeds & Plants. 1991. 8.99 (0-86653-982-4) Fearon Teacher Aids.
Roettger, Gerhard. Hellas, Kurzlehrgang Griechisch. (GER.). 132p. 1978. 13.80 (3-296-70501-5, Pub. by Weidmann) Lubrecht & Cramer.
Roettger, Gregory, tr. see Gruen, Anselm & Scharper, Philip J.
Roettger, Gregory J., jt. auth. see Gruen, Anselm.
Roettger, Gregory J., tr. see Colombas, Garcia M.
Roettger, Gregory J., tr. see Gruen, Anselm.
Roettger, Gregory J., tr. see Gruen, Anselm & Dufner, Meinrad.
Roettger, Gregory J., tr. see Ruppert, Fidelis & Gruen, Anselm.
Roettgers, Kurt. Kritik und Praxis: Zur Geschichte des Kritikbegriffs Von Kant bis Marx. LC 73-93165. (Quellen und Studien zur Philosophie: Vol. 8). x, 302p. (C). 1974. 115.40 (3-11-004604-0) De Gruyter.
Roettges, Heinz. Nietzsche und die Dialektik der Aufklaerung. (Monographien und Texte zur Nietzscge-Forschung Ser.: Vol. 2). (C). 1972. 130.80 (3-11-004018-2) De Gruyter.
Roetz, Heiner. Confucian Ethics of the Axial Age: A Reconstruction under the Aspect of the Breakthrough Toward Postconventional Thinking. LC 92-39938. (SUNY Series in Chinese Philosophy & Culture). 373p. (C). 1993. text 22.50 (0-7914-1649-6) State U NY Pr.
***Roetzel, Bernhard.** Gentlemen Style. (Illus.). 360p. 1999. 19.95 (3-8290-2029-5) Konemann.
Roetzel, Calvin. Paul: The Man & the Myth. 1999. pap. 22.00 (0-8006-3173-0, Fortress Pr) Augsburg Fortress.
Roetzel, Calvin J. The Letters of Paul: Conversations in Context. 3rd ed. LC 74-21901. 240p. 1991. pap. 22.95 (0-664-25201-X) Westminster John Knox.
— The Letters of Paul: Conversations in Context. 4th ed. LC 98-37903. 248p. 1998. pap. 20.00 (0-664-25782-8) Westminster John Knox.
— Paul: The Man & the Myth. LC 98-25446. (Studies on Personalities of the New Testament). 245p. 1998. text 34.95 (1-57003-264-5) U of SC Pr.
— The World That Shaped the New Testament. LC 85-12492. 180p. 1985. pap. 19.95 (0-8042-0455-1) Westminster John Knox.
Roetzel, W., et al, eds. Design & Operation of Heat Exchangers: Proceedings of the EUROTHERM Seminar No. 18 Hamburg, February 27 - March 1, 1991. (EUROTHERM Seminar Ser.: No. 18). (Illus.). 432p. 1992. 126.95 (0-387-53771-6) Spr-Verlag.
Roetzel, Wilfred & Xuan, Yimin. Dynamic Behaviour of Heat Exchangers. LC 97-81196. (Developments in Heat Transfer Ser.: Vol. 3). 400p. 1998. 192.00 (1-85312-506-7, 5067, Pub. by WIT Pr) Computational Mech MA.
Roetzheim, William. PC Magazine Programming Windows with Borland C++ (Illus.). 464p. (Orig.). 1992. pap. 39.95 incl. disk (1-56276-040-8, Ziff-Davis Pr) Que.
— Programming Windows with Borland C++ 4.0. LC 95-125997. (Programming Ser.). (Illus.). 496p. (Orig.). 1995. pap. 39.95 incl. disk (1-56276-269-9, Ziff-Davis Pr) Que.
— Software Development for Government Standards. 2nd ed. (C). 2001. text 24.00 (0-13-461690-1) P-H.
Roetzheim, William H, & Beasley, Reyna. Software Project Cost & Schedule Estimating: Best Practices. LC 97-29163. 208p. (C). 1997. text 47.00 incl. disk (0-13-682089-1) P-H.
Roetzler, Jochen. Zur Petrogenese Im Saechsischen Granulitgebirge. (Geotektonische Forschungen Ser.: Vol. 77). (GER.). 167p. 1992. 82.00 (3-510-50043-1, Pub. by E Schweizerbartsche) Balogh.
Roever, Dave & Crump, Karen C. Nobody's Ever Cried for Me . . . 157p. 1992. pap. 15.00 (0-9648148-1-1) Roever Commun.
Roever, David & Koch, Kathy. Scarred. (Illus.). 200p. 1995. pap. 15.00 (0-9648148-0-3) Roever Commun.
Roever, Joan M. Snake Secrets. LC 78-4318. (Illus.). (J). (gr. 5 up). 1979. lib. bdg. 11.85 (0-8027-6333-2) Walker & Co.
Roever, W. P. De, see De Roever, W. P.
Roey, Guy Van, see Van Roey, Guy.
***Roey, Stephen.** Fall Staff in Postsecondary Institutions, 1995. 196p. 1998. pap. 16.00 (0-16-049469-9) USGPO.
Rof Carballo, Juan. Entre el Silencio y la Palabra. (Nueva Austral Ser.: Vol. 147). (SPA.). 1991. pap. text 24.95 (84-239-1947-1) Elliots Bks.
— Violencia y Ternura. (Nueva Austral Ser.: Vol. 19). (SPA.). 1991. pap. text 24.95 (84-239-1819-X) Elliots Bks.
Rofail, Ash & Martin, Tony. Building N-Tier Applications with COM & Visual Basic. LC 98-55320. 560p. 1999. pap. 49.99 incl. cd-rom (0-471-29549-3) Wiley.
***Rofail, Ash & Shohoud, Yasser.** Mastering Com & Com+ 4th ed. 720p. 1999. pap. 39.99 (0-7821-2384-8) Sybex.
Rofail, Samir S. & Yeo, Kiat Seng. Low-Voltage Low-Power Digital BiCMOS Circuits: Circuit Design, Comparative Study & Sensitivity. LC 99-11804. 384p. (C). 1999. 75.00 (0-13-011380-8) P-H.
Rofe, Alexander. The Book of Balaam: A Study in Methods of Criticism & the History of Biblical Literature & Religion. (Jerusalem Biblical Studies: Vol. 1). (HEB.). 77p. 1979. pap. text 6.50 (0-685-49416-0, Pub. by Simor Ltd) Eisenbrauns.
***Rofe, Alexander.** Introduction to the Composition of the Pentateuch. (Biblical Seminar Ser.: No. 58). 152p. 1999. pap. 19.95 (1-85075-992-8, Pub. by Sheffield Acad) CUP Services.
Rofe, Alexander. Introduction to the Prophetic Literature. Seeligmann, Judith H., tr. from HEB. (Biblical Seminar Ser.: Vol. 49). 118p. 1997. pap. 17.95 (1-85075-805-0, Pub. by Sheffield Acad) CUP Services.
— Magic Spells & Formulas: The Prophetical Stories: The Narratives about the Prophets in the Hebrew Bible, Their Literary Types & History. 218p. 1988. text 20.00 (965-223-685-3, Pub. by Magnes Pr) Eisenbrauns.
Rofe, Husein. The Path of Subud. 1972. 250.00 (0-8490-0805-0) Gordon Pr.
— The Path of Subud. 2nd ed. 162p. 1988. reprint ed. pap. text 8.95 (0-945126-03-4) Undiscovd Worlds Pr.
Rofe, Yacov. Repression & Fear: New Approaches to Resolve the Crisis in Psychopathology. 500p. 1989. 78.95 (0-89116-056-6) Hemisp Pub.
Rofel, Lisa. Other Modernities: Gendered Yearnings in China After Socialism. LC 98-38034. 321p. 1998. 40.00 (0-520-21078-6, Pub. by U CA Pr); pap. 16.95 (0-520-21079-4, Pub. by U CA Pr) Cal Prin Full Svc.
***Rofer, Cheryl K. & Kaasik, T.** Turning a Problem into a Resource - Remediation & Waste Management at the Sillam. 288p. 2000. pap. 64.00 (0-7923-6187-3) Kluwer Academic.
***Rofer, Cheryl K. & Kaasik, Tdonis.** Turning a Problem into a Resource: Remediation & Waste Management at the Sillamhae Site, Estonia. LC 00-21728. (Nato Science Ser.). 2000. write for info. (0-7923-6186-5) Kluwer Academic.
Rofes, Eric. Dry Bones Breathe: Gay Men Creating Post-AIDS Identities & Cultures. LC 98-9555. 352p. (C). 1998. 49.95 (0-7890-0470-4, Harrington Park); pap. 24.95 (1-56023-934-4, Harrington Park) Haworth Pr.
— Reviving the Tribe: Regenerating Gay Men's Sexuality & Culture in the Ongoing Epidemic. LC 95-35017. 318p. 1995. 39.95 (1-56024-987-0); pap. 14.95 (1-56023-876-3) Haworth Pr.
Rofes, Eric E. I Thought People Like That Killed Themselves: Lesbians, Gay Men & Suicide. LC 82-9301. 176p. pap. 7.95 (0-912516-69-0) Grey Fox.
Rofes, Eric E. The Kids' Book about Death & Dying. 132p. (J). 1996. pap. write for info. (0-316-75447-1) Little.
Rofes, Eric E., jt. auth. see Miles, Sara.
Roff, Derek A. Evolutionary Quantitative Genetics. LC 96-47079. 448p. 1997. pap. write for info. (0-412-12971-X) Kluwer Academic.
Roff, Jason T. ADO: The Definitive Guide. Petrusha, Ron, ed. (Illus.). 450p. 1999. pap. 27.95 (1-56592-415-0) OReilly & Assocs.
— DAO Object Model: The Definitive Reference. Petrusha, Ronald, ed. (Illus.). 435p. 2000. pap. 34.95 incl. cd-rom (1-56592-435-5) OReilly & Assocs.
Roff, Renee, compiled by. Directory of American Book Workers. LC 80-52837. 1981. 19.95 (0-935164-05-7) Prairie Bk Ctr.
***Roff, Sandra, et al.** From the Free Academy to CUNY: Illustrating Public Higher Education in New York City, 1847-1997. (Illus.). 154p. 2000. 27.50 (0-8232-2019-2, Pub. by Fordham); pap. 19.95 (0-8232-2020-6) Fordham.
Roff, Sue R. Hotspots: The Legacy of Hiroshima & Nagasaki. LC 95-15514. 1995. pap. 24.95 (0-304-33438-3) Continuum.
— Overreaching in Paradise: United States Policy in Palau since 1945. LC 90-3608. (Illus.). xii, 244p. (Orig.). (C). 1991. pap. 27.50 (0-938737-22-8) Denali Press.
— Timor's Anschluss: Indonesian & Australian Policy in East Timor, 1974-76. (Illus.). 142p. 1992. lib. bdg. 69.95 (0-7734-9500-2) E Mellen.
Roff, Sue R., ed. see Eleanor Roosevelt Institute Staff.
Roff, William R. The Origins of Malay Nationalism. (Illus.). 352p. 1995. pap. 29.95 (967-65-3059-X) OUP.
— The Wandering Thoughts of a Dying Man: The Life & Times of Haji Abdul Majid bin Zainuddin. (Oxford in Asia Historical Memoirs Ser.). 1978. 19.95 (0-19-580349-3) OUP.
***Roffe, David.** Domesday: The Inquest & the Book. LC 99-56324. 260p. 2000. text 45.00 (0-19-820847-2) OUP.
Roffe, Mercedes. La Cuestion del Genero en Grisel y Mirabella de Juan de Flores. (SPA.). 228p. (Orig.). 1996. pap. 16.00 (0-936388-77-3) Juan de la Cuesta.
***Roffe, Mercedes.** Definiciones Mayas. (Poesia Ser.: Vol. 2). (SPA.). 24p. 1999. pap. 4.00 (0-9673260-1-X) Pen Pr.
Roffe, Mercedes, tr. see De Beer, Hans.
***Roffe, Pedro, et al.** International Technology Transfer: The Origins & Aftermath of the United Nations Negotiations on Draft Code of Conduct. LC 00-39112. 2000. write for info. (90-411-9792-3) Kluwer Law Intl.
Roffe, Reina, ed. see Borges, Jorge Luis.
Roffel, Brian & Chin, Patrick. Computer Control in the Process Industries. (Illus.). 257p. (C). 1987. text 153.00 (0-87371-122-X, TS156, CRC Reprint) Franklin.
***Roffer, Robin Fisher.** Make a Name for Yourself. LC 00-36040. 2000. write for info. (0-7679-0492-3) Broadway BDD.
— Make a Name for Yourself: Eight Steps for Creating an Unforgettable Personal Brand of Success. 272p. 2000. 23.95 (0-7679-0491-5) Broadway BDD.
Roffey, C. Photogeneration of Reactive Species for U. V. Curing. LC 96-49972. 1002p. 1997. 425.00 (0-471-94177-8) Wiley.
Roffey, C. G. Photopolymerization of Surface Coatings. LC 81-12916. (Wiley-Interscience Publications). 371p. reprint ed. pap. 115.10 (0-7837-1880-2, 204208100001) Bks Demand.
Roffey, Leane E., jt. auth. see Weinland, Linda S.
Roffey, Maureen. The Grand Old Duke of York. (J). 1993. 12.15 (0-606-08754-0, Pub. by Turtleback) Demco.
— I Spy at the Zoo. LC 88-19360. (Illus.). 32p. (J). (ps-2). 1989. reprint ed. mass mkt. 3.95 (0-689-71227-8) Aladdin.
Roffey, Maureen. Aladdin: A Foldout Playbook. 10p. (J). (ps). 1997. 12.95 (0-316-85342-9) Little.
— If I Were Bigger. (Duplo Playbks.). 14p. (J). (ps up). 1995. bds. 7.50 (0-316-72387-8) Little.
***Roffey, Maureen.** Noisy Farm Friends. (Squeak & Rattle Ser.). (J). (ps). 2001. write for info. (1-57584-724-8, Pub. by Rdrs Digest) S&S Trade.
Roffey, Maureen. Rocket to the Moon: A Foldout Playbook. 10p. (J). (ps). 1997. 12.95 (0-316-85341-0) Little.
Roffey, Maureen & Lodge, Bernard. Door to Door: A Split Page Picture Book. (Illus.). 32p. (J). (ps-3). 1996. pap. 6.95 (1-879085-64-X, Whispering Coyote) Charlesbridge Pub.
— The Grand Old Duke of York. (Illus.). 32p. (J). (ps-2). 1996. pap. 6.95 (1-879085-62-3, Whispering Coyote) Charlesbridge Pub.
Roffey, Sue. Special Needs in the Early Years: Collaboration, Communication & Coordination. Vol. 1. 1999. pap. 27.95 (1-85346-604-2) David Fulton.
Roffey, Sue & O'Reirdan, Terry. Infant Classroom Behavior: Needs, Perspectives & Strategies. LC 97-202557. 112p. 1997. pap. 24.95 (1-85346-446-5, Pub. by David Fulton) Taylor & Francis.
Roffler, Roger W. Write - Right to Happiness. 1998. pap. 8.95 (0-533-12751-3) Vantage.
***Roffman, Arlyn J.** Meeting the Challenges of Learning Disabilities in Adulthood. LC 99-86790. 2000. 25.95 (1-55766-430-7) P H Brookes.
***Roffman, Deborah.** Sex & Sensibility. 288p. 2001. text 24.00 (0-7382-0293-2) Perseus Pubng.
Roffman, Harold. Maintenance Management. 187p. 1997. ring bd. 44.50 (0-929442-05-9, 2210pp) Prof Prnting & Pub.
Roffman, Harold, jt. auth. see Stipanuk, David M.
***Roffman, Howard.** Jagged Youth. 2000. 39.95 (3-86187-163-7) B Gmunder.
Roffman, Howard. Postcard Book #13, Best Of Tales, 13. 1999. pap. text 8.95 (3-86187-138-6) B Gmunder.
— Tales. 1997. 39.95 (3-86187-104-1) LPC InBook.
— Three. (Illus.). 1998. pap. text 7.95 (3-86187-116-5) B Gmunder.
— Understanding the Cold War. LC 75-5251. 198p. (C). 1976. 29.50 (0-8386-1740-9) Fairleigh Dickinson.
Roffman, Marvin B. & Schwager, Michael J. Fire Your Broker: Straight Talk on Managing Your Money from the Financial Analyst Who Defied Donald Trump. (Illus.). 224p. 1993. 18.95 (1-55972-207-X, Birch Ln Pr) Carol Pub Group.
— Take Charge of Your Financial Future: Straight Talk on Managing Your Money from the Financial Analyst Who Defied Donald Trump. 272p. 1996. pap. 12.95 (0-8065-1718-2, Citadel Pr) Carol Pub Group.
Roffman, Peter & Purdy, Jim. The Hollywood Social Problem Film: Madness, Despair, & Politics from the Depression to the Fifties. LC 80-8100. 384p. reprint ed. pap. 119.10 (0-8357-3961-9, 205605300044) Bks Demand.
Roffman, Rosaly, jt. ed. see Walker, Sue B.
Roffmann, Harold, jt. auth. see Stipanuk, David M.
Rog, Debra A., jt. ed. see Bickman, Leonard.
Rog, Debra J., et al. The Family Unification Program: Final Evaluation Report. LC 97-49126. 56p. 1998. pap. 9.95 (0-87868-726-2, 7262, CWLA Pr) Child Welfare.
Rog, Debra J., jt. auth. see Bickman, Leonard.
Rog, Debra J., jt. ed. see Bickman, Leonard.
Rog, James A., jt. ed. see Baker, William J.
Rogacheva, Nellya N. Theory of Piezoelectric Plates & Shells. 272p. 1994. boxed set 187.95 (0-8493-4459-X) CRC Pr.
Rogahn, Cinda B. Achievement Through Attitude. 65p. 1988. student ed. 15.00 (0-9616898-1-1) Phoenix Pr FL.
***Rogak, Lawrence.** Rogak's New York Insurance & Negligence Digest. 1999. write for info. (1-58012-047-4) James Pub Santa Ana.
Rogak, Lisa. The Complete Country Business Guide: Everything You Need to Know to Become a Rural Entrepreneur. LC 98-96672. (Illus.). 224p. 1998. pap. 24.95 (0-9652502-1-0) Williams Hill.
— Escape to a Small Town! Create a New Life & Fulfill Your Dreams in a Place Where You Can Breathe. 192p. 1999. pap. 14.95 (0-9652502-2-9) Williams Hill.
— Managing Your Time. LC 99-12221. (Smart Guides Ser.). 192p. 1999. pap. 10.95 (0-471-31886-8) Wiley.
— New England Farm Vacations. LC 93-37245. (Illus.). 128p. (Orig.). 1994. pap. 9.95 (1-56626-044-2, Cntry Rds Pr) NTC Contemp Pub Co.
— Smart Guide to Starting a Small Business. LC 99-12219. (Smart Guides Ser.). 192p. 1999. pap. 10.95 (0-471-31885-X) Wiley.
— Steroids: Dangerous Game. (Coping with Modern Issues Ser.). 64p. (J). (gr. 4 up). 1992. lib. bdg. 19.95 (0-8225-0048-5, Lerner Publctns) Lerner Pub.
Rogak, Lisa, jt. auth. see Ramsay, Gregg.
Rogak, Lisa A. Get Started in Your Own Antiques & Collectibles Business: Everything You Need to Know How to Make Money. 1999. pap. 15.95 (0-9652502-7-X) Williams Hill.
— Latin for Pigs. 1999. pap. 6.95 (0-452-27540-7, Plume) Dutton Plume.
— Pretzel Logic: A Novel. 256p. 1999. pap. 15.00 (0-9652502-4-5) Williams Hill.
— The Quotable Cat. 144p. 1992. 11.00 (0-8092-3941-8, 394180, Contemporary Bks) NTC Contemp Pub Co.
— Time Out from Work: Using Sabbaticals to Enhance Your Life While Keeping Your Career on Track. 209p. 1998. pap. text 15.00 (0-7881-5635-7) DIANE Pub.
Rogak, Lisa A., ed. The Cat on My Shoulder. 192p. 1994. pap. 10.00 (0-380-72337-9, Avon Bks) Morrow Avon.
Rogak, Lisa A. & Bangs, David H., Jr. One Hundred Best Retirement Businesses. 393p. 1994. pap. 15.95 (0-936894-54-7) Dearborn.
Rogal, Owen & Pugh, Wesly. The Headache Rx: A Doctor's Proven Guide to Lasting Headache Relief. 256p. 1996. text 24.95 (0-13-156936-8) P-H.
Rogal, Samuel J. A Biographical Dictionary of 18th Century Methodism Vol. III: I-L. LC 97-3381. 348p. 1997. text 99.95 (0-7734-8682-8) E Mellen.
— A Biographical Dictionary of 18th-Century Methodism. 494p. 1998. 109.95 (0-7734-8688-7) E Mellen.
— A Biographical Dictionary of 18th Century Methodism, Vol. 2. LC 97-3381. (Illus.). 552p. 1997. text 119.95 (0-7734-8680-1) E Mellen.
***Rogal, Samuel J.** A Biographical Dictionary of 18th Century Methodism, Vol. VIII, T-V. LC 97-3381. 444p. 1999. text 109.95 (0-7734-8024-2) E Mellen.
— A Biographical Dictionary of 18th Century Methodism, Vol. IX, W, LC 97-3381. 524p. 1999. text 109.95 (0-7734-8026-9) E Mellen.
Rogal, Samuel J. A Biographical Dictionary of 18th Century Methodism: P-Q, Vol. V. LC 97-3381. 400p. 1998. text 99.95 (0-7734-8686-0) E Mellen.
— A Biographical Dictionary of 18th Century Methodism Vol. I: A-D, Vol. II. LC 97-3381. 484p. 1997. text 109.95 (0-7734-8678-X) E Mellen.
— A Biographical Dictionary of 18th Century Methodism Vol. IV: M-O. LC 97-3381. 500p. 1998. text 109.95 (0-7734-8684-4) E Mellen.
— A Biographical Dictionary of 18th Century Methodism Vol. 7: Smo-Sym. LC 97-3381. 227p. 1998. 109.95 (0-7734-8022-6) E Mellen.
***Rogal, Samuel J.** A Biographical Dictionary of 18th Century Methodism Vol. 10: X-Z. LC 97-3381. 313p. 1999. 109.95 (0-7734-8028-5) E Mellen.

R

Rogal, Samuel J. A Chronological Outline of American Literature, 8. LC 86-33472. (Bibliographies & Indexes in American Literature Ser.: No. 8). 460p. 1987. lib. bdg. 79.95 (0-313-25471-0, RCE/, Greenwood Pr) Greenwood.

— A Chronological Outline of British Literature. LC 79-8577. 341p. 1980. lib. bdg. 42.95 (0-313-21477-8, ROB/, Greenwood Pr) Greenwood.

— A Companion to the Characters in the Fiction & Drama of W. Somerset Maugham. LC 95-26448. 488p. 1996. lib. bdg. 79.50 (0-313-29917-X, Greenwood Pr) Greenwood.

— The Educational & Evangelical Missions of Mary Emilie Holmes (1850-1906) "Not to Seem, but to Be" LC 94-12361. (Studies in Women & Religion: Vol. 33). (Illus.). 113p. 1994. text 59.95 (0-7734-9095-7) E Mellen.

— For Whom the Dinner Bell Tolls: The Role & Function of Food & Drink in the Prose of Ernest Hemingway. (Illus.). 316p. 1997. 69.95 (1-57309-107-3); pap. 34.95 (1-57309-106-5) Intl Scholars.

— A General Introduction to Hymnody & Congregational Song. LC 91-16693. (American Theological Library Association Monograph). 336p. 1991. 50.00 (0-8108-2416-7) Scarecrow.

— An Index to the Biblical References, Parallels, & Allusions in the Poetry & Prose of John Milton. LC 93-48814. (Biblical Press Ser.: Vol. 22). 356p. 1994. 99.95 (0-7734-2390-7, Mellen Biblical Pr) E Mellen.

— John Wesley in Ireland, 1747-1789, 2 pts., Pt. 1. LC 92-47035. (Studies in the History of Missions: Vol. 9). (Illus.). 418p. 1993. text 109.95 (0-7734-9243-7) E Mellen.

— John Wesley in Ireland, 1747-1789, Pt. 2. LC 92-47035. (Studies in the History of Missions: Vol. 9). (Illus.). 420p. 1993. text 109.95 (0-7734-9245-3) E Mellen.

— John Wesley in Wales, 1739-1790: Lions & Lambs. LC 93-30969. (Studies in the History of Missions: Vol. 11). 452p. 1993. text 109.95 (0-7734-9397-2) E Mellen.

— John Wesley's London: A Guidebook. LC 87-22038. (Texts & Studies in Religion: Vol. 34). (Illus.). 480p. 1988. lib. bdg. 109.95 (0-88946-823-0) E Mellen.

— John Wesley's Mission to Scotland. LC 87-31371. (Studies in the History of Missions: Vol. 2). (Illus.). 1988. lib. bdg. 109.95 (0-88946-070-1) E Mellen.

— Sing Glory & Hallelujah! Historical & Biographical Guide to Gospel Hymns Nos. 1 to 6 Complete, 49. LC 95-32893. (Music Reference Collection: Vol. 49). 256p. 1996. lib. bdg. 82.95 (0-313-29690-1, Greenwood Pr) Greenwood.

— A William Somerset Maugham Encyclopedia. LC 96-35025. 400p. 1997. lib. bdg. 82.95 (0-313-29916-1, Greenwood Pr) Greenwood.

Rogal, Samuel J., compiled by. The Children's Jubilee: A Bibliographical Survey of Hymnals for Infants, Youth & Sunday Schools Published in Britain & America, 1655-1900. LC 83-1661. (Illus.). 91p. 1983. lib. bdg. 42.95 (0-313-23880-4, RCJ/) Greenwood.

— The Education of the British Literati: A Guide to Their Schools, Colleges, & Universities. LC 92-21163. 432p. 1993. text 109.95 (0-7734-9232-1) E Mellen.

— Guide to the Hymns & Tunes of American Methodism, 7. LC 85-27114. (Music Reference Collection: No. 7). 337p. 1986. lib. bdg. 59.95 (0-313-25123-1, RGH/, Greenwood Pr) Greenwood.

— Medicine in Great Britain from the Restoration to the Nineteenth Century, 1660-1800: An Annotated Bibliography, 8. LC 91-39004. (Bibliographies & Indexes in Medical Studies: No. 8). 272p. 1992. lib. bdg. 75.00 (0-313-28115-7, RMH, Greenwood Pr) Greenwood.

Rogal, Samuel J., ed. Agriculture in Britain & America, 1660-1820: An Annotated Bibliography of the Eighteenth-Century Literature, Vol. 33. LC 94-12323. (Bibliographies & Indexes in World History Ser.: No. 33). 280p. 1994. lib. bdg. 75.00 (0-313-29352-X, Greenwood Pr) Greenwood.

Rogal, Samuel J., ed. Calendar of Literary Facts: A Daily Guide to Noteworthy Events in World Literature from 1450 Through 1988. 877p. 1990. 70.00 (0-8103-2943-3) Gale.

Rogal, Stan. The Imaginary Museum. 76p. 1993. pap. 12.00 (1-55022-200-7, Pub. by ECW) Genl Dist Srvs.

***Rogal, Stan.** The Long Drive Home. 177p. (Orig.). 1999. pap. write for info. (1-895837-56-1) Insomniac.

Rogal, Stan. Restless. LC 98-175180. 224p. 1998. pap. text 13.99 (1-895837-19-7) Insomniac.

— What Passes for Love: Short Stories. LC 96-153014. 144p. pap. 12.99 (1-895837-34-0) Insomniac.

Rogala, Jozef. A Collector's Guide to Books on Japan in English: An Annotated List of over 2500 Titles with Subject Index. 288p. 1999. text 55.00 (1-873410-90-5, Pub. by Japan Library); pap. text 24.95 (1-873410-91-3, Pub. by Japan Library) UH Pr.

Rogalewski, Tadeusz. Founder of the Marians: Fr. Stanislaus Papczynski. write for info. (0-944203-28-0) Marian Pr.

— Theological Foundations of the Christian Life in the Teaching of the Founder & the Renovator of the Congregation of Marians. 1999. pap. write for info. (0-944203-35-3) Marian Pr.

Rogalin, Elizabeth, ed. see Bacchus, Noel C.

Rogalla & Harremoes, O. Biofilm Reactors. (Water Science & Technology Ser.). 548p. 1994. pap. 280.25 (0-08-042544-5, Pergamon Pr) Elsevier.

Rogalla, H. & Blank, D. H. Applied Superconductivity, 1997: Proceedings of Eucas 1997, the 3rd European Conference on Applied Superconductivity, Held in The Netherlands, 30 June-3 July, 1997. LC 97-48267. (Institute of Physics Conference Ser.). 1997. write for info. (0-7503-0487-1) Institute of Personal Magnetism.

Rogalla, Hanna & Rogalla, Willy. German for Academic Purposes: A Reading Course. (GER.). 110p. 1985. 17.50 (3-468-49880-2) Langenscheidt.

— Grammar Handbook for Reading German Texts. 208p. 1985. pap. 23.50 (3-468-49881-0) Langenscheidt.

***Rogalla, P., et al, eds.** Virtual Endoscopy & Related 3D Techniques. (Medical Radiology Ser.). (Illus.). 200p. 2000. 112.00 (3-540-65157-8) Spr-Verlag.

Rogalla, Willy, jt. auth. see Rogalla, Hanna.

***Rogalski, A.** Infrared Detectors. 795p. 1999. text 250.00 (90-5699-203-1) Gordon & Breach.

Rogalski, Antoni. New Ternary Alloy Systems for Infrared Detectors. LC 94-10019. 1994. 91.00 (0-8194-1583-9, PM14/HC); pap. 76.00 (0-8194-1582-0) SPIE.

Rogalski, Antoni, ed. Selected Papers on Semiconductor Infrared Detectors. LC 92-31686. (Milestone Ser.: Vol. MS 66). 1993. pap. 45.00 (0-8194-1064-0) SPIE.

— Selected Papers on Semiconductor Infrared Detectors. LC 92-31686. (Milestone Ser.: Vol. MS 66/HC). 1993. 55.00 (0-8194-1063-2) SPIE.

Rogalski, Antoni, et al, eds. Solid State Crystals in Optoelectronics & Semiconductor Technology, Vol. 3179. LC 98-120039. 334p. 1997. 80.00 (0-8194-2605-9) SPIE.

***Rogalski, Antoni & Rutkowski, Jaroslaw, eds.** Epilayers & Heterostructures in Optoelectronics & Semiconductor Technology. 362p. 1999. pap. text 84.00 (0-8194-3199-0) SPIE.

Rogalski, Antoni, et al. Infrared Photon Detectors. LC 94-48051. 1995. 80.00 (0-8194-1798-X, PM20) SPIE.

***Rogalski, Antoni, et al.** Narrow-Gap Semiconductor Photodiodes. LC 00-26570. (Press Monographs). (Illus.). 2000. write for info. (0-8194-3619-4) SPIE.

***Rogalski, M. S. & Palmer, S. B.** Quantum Physics. 488p. 1999. text 70.00 (90-5699-184-1, G & B Science); pap. text 35.00 (90-5699-185-X, G & B Science) Gordon & Breach.

Rogalski, M. S., jt. auth. see Palmer, Stuart B.

***Rogalski, Mircea S. & Palmer, Stuart B.** Solid State Physics. 488p. 2000. pap. 42.00 (90-5699-273-2, G & B Science); text 80.00 (90-5699-272-4, G & B Science) Gordon & Breach.

Rogalski, Richard J., jt. auth. see Logue, Dennis E.

***Rogalsky, Dave.** Playiing God: Rebellion & Grace in 1 & 2 Kings. (Good Ground Ser.: No. 2, Pt. 6). 46p. 2000. pap. 5.95 (0-87303-365-5) Faith & Life.

Rogalsky, David, jt. auth. see Snyder, Eleanor.

Rogalsky, Yakov, jt. auth. see Clorfene, Chaim.

Rogaly, Ben. Sonar Bangla? Agricultural Growth & Agrarian Change in West Bengal & Bangladesh. LC 98-50749. 1999. 59.95 (0-7619-9307-X) Sage.

***Rogaly, Ben & Roche, Chris.** Learning from North-South Links in Microfinance. 1998. pap. 11.95 (0-85598-408-2, Pub. by Oxfam Pub) Stylus Pub VA.

Rogaly, Ben, jt. auth. see Johnson, Susan.

Rogan, Barbara. Heartbeat Away. 304p. 1995. per. 5.99 (0-671-89087-5) PB.

***Rogan, Barbara.** Rowing in Eden. 1998. mass mkt. 6.99 (0-425-16458-6) Berkley Pub.

— Suspicion. 448p. 2000. 6.99 (0-7434-0057-7) PB.

Rogan, Barbara. Suspicion. LC 98-31034. 304p. 1999. 24.00 (0-684-81415-3) Scribner.

***Rogan, Barbara.** Suspicion. large type ed. LC 00-24172. 2000. pap. 22.95 (1-56895-874-9) Wheeler Pub.

Rogan, Clare I., jt. auth. see Cohn, Marjorie B.

Rogan, Eugene, jt. ed. see Bowman, Alan K.

***Rogan, Eugene L.** Frontiers of the State in the Late Ottoman Empire: Transjordan, 1850-1921. LC 99-11032. (Cambridge Middle East Studies: No. 12). (Illus.). 291p. (C). 2000. 64.95 (0-521-66312-1) Cambridge U Pr.

Rogan, Helen, jt. auth. see Gingold, Alfred.

Rogan, John. The Biggest Snowball Ever. 2nd ed. LC 95-67984. (Illus.). 32p. (J). (ps-2). 1999. pap. 3.99 (0-7636-0485-2) Candlewick Pr.

***Rogan, John, ed.** Bristol Cathedral: History & Architecture. (Illus.). 176p. 2000. pap. 24.99 (0-7524-1482-8, Pub. by Tempus Pubng) Arcadia Publng.

Rogan, Johnny. The Complete Guide to the Music of Crosby, Stills, Nash & Young. (Illus.). 191p. 1998. pap. 8.95 (0-7119-6309-6, OP47876) Omnibus NY.

— Complete Guide to the Music of the Kinks. (Illus.). 192p. 1998. pap. 8.95 (0-7119-6314-2, OP47877) Omnibus NY.

— Crosby, Stills, Nash & Young: Visual Documentary. (Illus.). 160p. (Orig.). pap. 24.95 (0-7119-4982-4, OP 47776, Pub. by Omnibus Press) Omnibus NY.

— Morrissey & Marr: The Severed Alliance. (Illus.). 392p. pap. 17.95 (0-7119-3000-7, OP46804) Omnibus NY.

— Neil Young. (Illus.). 176p. (Orig.). 1996. pap. 8.95 (0-7119-5399-6, OP47807) Omnibus NY.

— The Smiths. (Illus.). 120p. (Orig.). (C). 1995. pap. 8.95 (0-7119-4900-X, OP 47768) Omnibus NY.

Rogan, M. T., ed. Analytical Parasitology. (Illus.). 250p. 1997. ring bd. 99.50 (3-540-58919-8) Spr-Verlag.

Rogan, Patricia M., jt. auth. see Murphy, Stephen T.

Rogan, Randall G., et al. Dynamic Processes of Crisis Negotiation: Theory, Research, & Practice. LC 96-26877. 192p. 1997. 62.95 (0-275-95224-X) Greenwood.

Rogan, Tom, et al. Beyond the Wall: Adventures in the North of Arthur's Britain. Shirley, Sam, ed. (Pendragon Roleplaying Ser.). (Illus.). 128p. (Orig.). 1995. pap. 19.95 (1-56882-026-7, 2717) Chaosium.

Rogasa, M., et al. Coding Microbiological Data for Computers. (Microbiology Ser.). (Illus.). 310p. 1986. 68.00 (0-387-96417-7) Spr-Verlag.

Rogasky, Barbara. The Golem: A Version. LC 94-13040. (Illus.). 128p. (YA). (gr. 7-12). 1996. 18.95 (0-8234-0964-3) Holiday.

***Rogasky, Barbara, ed.** Winter Poems, Vol. 1. (Illus.). 40p. (gr. 2-6). 1999. mass mkt. 5.95 (0-590-42873-X) Scholastic Inc.

Rogat, Steven E. Healing Thoughts, Therapeutic Shamanism: A Bridge Between Metaphysics & Psychotherapy. LC 97-65381. (Illus.). 160p. (Orig.). 1997. pap. 11.95 (0-9672206-0-2) Creat Thought.

Rogawski, Jonathan D. Automorphic Representations of Unitary Groups in Three Variables. (Annals of Mathematics Studies: No. 123). 288p. 1990. pap. text 35.00 (0-691-08587-0, Pub. by Princeton U Pr) Cal Prin Full Svc.

Rogawski, Jonathan D., ed. see Lubotzky, Alexander.

Rogawski, Michael A. & Barker, Jeffrey L., eds. Neurotransmitter Actions in the Vertebrate Nervous System. 536p. 1985. 125.00 (0-306-41991-2, Plenum Trade) Perseus Pubng.

Rogel, Anne M. Songs of Nature. (Illus.). 109p. (Orig.). 1995. pap. 10.00 (0-9645205-0-8) Dandelion Drms.

Rogel, Carole. The Breakup of Yugoslavia & the War in Bosnia. LC 97-33145. (Greenwood Press Guides to Historic Events of the Twentieth Century Ser.). 224p. 1998. 39.95 (0-313-29918-8, Greenwood Pr) Greenwood.

Rogel, Carole, jt. auth. see Plut-Pregelj, Leopoldina.

Rogen, Arthur. Street Smart Salesman; Making Opportunities Happen. LC 91-19025. (Illus.). 224p. (Orig.). pap. 9.95 (0-89529-487-7, Avery) Penguin Putnam.

Roger. Epileptic Sydromes in Infancy. 432p. 92.00 (0-86196-320-2, Pub. by J Libbey Med) Bks Intl VA.

Roger, Francis, ed. see Babalawo, Ifagbemi R. & Babalawo, Francis R.

Roger, A. & Hartley, D. Curriculum & Assessment in Scotland. 126p. 1989. pap. 26.00 (0-7073-0596-9, Pub. by Mercat Pr Bks) St Mut.

Roger, A., jt. auth. see Haatley, J. S.

Roger, Alan. Bonsai. rev. ed. (Wisley Handbooks Ser.). (Illus.). 64p. (Orig.). 1990. pap. 6.95 (0-304-32001-3, Pub. by Cassell) Sterling.

***Roger, C. Martinez, et al, eds.** Globular Clusters. LC 99-32417. (Cambridge Contemporary Astrophysics Ser.). (Illus.). 400p. (C). 1999. 69.95 (0-521-77058-0) Cambridge U Pr.

Roger, Derek, jt. ed. see Bull, Peter.

Roger, F. H., et al, eds. Medical Informatics Europe, 1984: Proceedings. (Lecture Notes in Medical Informatics Ser.: Vol. 24). xxvii, 778p. 1984. 81.95 (0-387-13374-7) Spr-Verlag.

Roger-France, F. & Santucci, G., eds. Perspectives of Information Processing in Medical Application: Strategic Issues, Requirements & Options for the European Community. (Health Systems Research Ser.). 320p. 1991. 71.95 (0-387-53856-9) Spr-Verlag.

Roger-France, F., et al. Case-Based Telematic Systems: Towards Equity in Health Care. LC 94-77522. (Studies in Health Technology & Informatics: Vol. 14). 207p. (gr. 12). 1994. 93.00 (90-5199-182-7) IOS Press.

Roger, Gertrude M. Lady Rancher. (Illus.). 182p. 1979. pap. 12.95 (0-88839-099-8) Hancock House.

***Roger, J.** Epileptic Syndromes in Infancy, Childhood & Adolescence. 3rd ed. 99p. 2001. 99.00 (0-86196-611-2, Pub. by John Libby) Buttrwrth-Heinemann.

Roger, J. Identity in Adolescence: The Balance Between Self & Other. (Adolescence & Society Ser.). 200p. 1989. 47.50 (0-415-01087-X, A3362); pap. 15.95 (0-415-01088-8, A3366) Routledge.

Roger, J., et al, eds. Epileptic Syndromes in Infancy, Childhood & Adolescence. (Current Problems in Epilepsy Ser.: Vol. 2). 1985. 60.00 (0-86196-045-9, Pub. by J Libbey Med) Bks Intl VA.

Roger, Jacques. Buffon: A Life in Natural Hisotry. Bonnefoi, Sarah L., tr. LC 96-37948. (Cornell History of Science Ser.). (Illus.). 512p. 1997. text 49.95 (0-8014-2918-8) Cornell U Pr.

Roger, John. Blessings of Light. 1981. pap. 5.00 (0-88238-949-1) Law Arts.

— Blessings of Light. 94p. 1981. pap. 5.00 (0-914829-02-5, 949-1) Mandeville LA.

***Roger, John.** Divine Essence: Barakas. 2000. pap. 10.00 (1-893020-04-5) Mandeville LA.

— Forgiveness: The Key to the Kingdom. 2000. pap. 12.50 (0-914829-62-9) Mandeville LA.

Roger, John. Loving Each Day. 1989. 10.00 (0-914829-26-2) Mandeville LA.

— Psychic Protection. LC 99-167071. 1998. mass mkt. 6.95 (0-914829-69-6) Mandeville LA.

***Roger, John.** Relationships: Love, Marriage & Spirit. 2000. 20.00 (1-893020-05-3) Mandeville LA.

— Sex, Spirit & You. 2000. pap. 10.00 (1-893020-03-7) Mandeville LA.

Roger, John. The Spiritual Promise. rev. ed. 60p. 1989. lib. bdg. 7.00 (0-914829-22-X) Mandeville LA.

Roger, Marc. Financial Freedom Starting Today. 92p. 1998. pap. 8.95 (1-57502-995-2, PO2715) Morris Pubng.

Roger-Marx, Claude. Vuillard: Interiors. (Rhythm & Color Two Ser.). (FRE.). 76p. 1948. pap. write for info. (0-7859-5250-0) Fr & Eur.

— Vuillard, His Life & Work. LC 75-41229. reprint ed. 34.00 (0-404-14718-6) AMS Pr.

— Vuillard's Graphic Work: A Catalogue Raisonne. (Illus.). 192p. 1990. 150.00 (1-55660-123-9) A Wofsy Fine Arts.

Roger, Maurice. L' Enseignement des Lettres Classiques d'Ausone a Alcuin. (FRE.). xvi, 459p. 1968. reprint ed. write for info. (0-318-71277-6) G Olms Pubs.

— L' Enseignement des Lettres Classiques d'Ausone A Alcuin. (FRE.). xvi, 459p. 1968. reprint ed. write for info. (0-318-71404-3) G Olms Pubs.

Roger of Taize, jt. auth. see Mother Teresa of Calcutta.

Roger of Wendover. Flowers of History, 2 vols. Giles, J. A., tr. LC 68-55556. (Bohn's Antiquarian Library). reprint ed. 95.00 (0-404-50070-6) AMS Pr.

Roger, Patron Lujan. Magia de un Regalo Excepcional. (SPA.). 1997. pap. text 19.98 (968-409-984-3) Edamex.

— Un Nuevo Regalo. (SPA.). 1997. pap. text 14.98 (968-409-918-5) Edamex.

— Un Nuevo Regalo Excepcional. (SPA.). 1997. pap. text 18.98 (968-409-762-X) Edamex.

— Por Favor Vive Plenamente. (SPA.). (gr. 7 up). 1997. pap. text 4.99 (968-409-894-4) Edamex.

Roger, Patron Lujuan. Un Regalo Excepcional, 3. 1997. pap. text 18.98 (968-409-833-2) Edit Diana.

Roger, Pierre A. Impact of Pesticides on Farmer Health & the Rice Environment. Pingali, Prabhu L., ed. LC 94-45040. (Natural Resources Managment & Policy Ser.). 688p. (C). 1995. text 205.50 (0-7923-9521-2) Kluwer Academic.

Roger, R. S. & Dewdney, P. E., eds. Regions of Recent Star Formation. 1982. text 199.50 (90-277-1383-9) Kluwer Academic.

Roger, R. S. & Landecker, T. L., eds. The Interaction of Supernova Remnants with the Interstellar Medium: Colloquium One Hundred One of the International Astronomical Union. 552p. 1988. text 95.00 (0-521-35062-X) Cambridge U Pr.

Roger, Robert. A Concise Account of North America. (Notable American Authors Ser.). 1999. reprint ed. lib. bdg. 125.00 (0-7812-8832-0) Rprt Serv.

— Journals. (Notable American Authors Ser.). 1999. reprint ed. lib. bdg. 125.00 (0-7812-8833-9) Rprt Serv.

— Ponteach: Or The Savanges of America. (Notable American Authors Ser.). 1999. reprint ed. lib. bdg. 125.00 (0-7812-8834-7) Rprt Serv.

Roger, Sherry A. You Are What You Ate. rev. ed. 303p. 1995. pap. 12.95 (0-9618821-8-2) Prestige NY.

Roger, Sue. El Ocio. (Breviarios Ser.). (SPA.). pap. 6.99 (968-16-3944-8, Pub. by Fondo) Continental Bk.

***Roger, Vernon.** Roger's Cajun Cookbook: Naturally Right. 2000. spiral bd. write for info. (0-935545-23-9) Land & Land.

Rogers. Administrative Law & Procedure. (Paralegal Ser.). (C). 2002. pap. 41.75 (0-7668-1833-0) Delmar.

— Adolescence Psychology. (Psychology Ser.). 1972. pap. 5.25 (0-8185-0030-1) Brooks-Cole.

***Rogers.** After the Spirit. 2000. 52.00 (0-8133-6701-8, Pub. by Westview) HarpC.

Rogers. AIDS Clinical Pharmacology. 1989. pap. text 31.00 (0-443-03971-2, W B Saunders Co) Harcrt Hlth Sci Grp.

— College Business Mathematics. LC 99-31666. 868p. 1999. 69.33 incl. cd-rom (0-13-080769-9) P-H.

— Complete Avengers. 1998. pap. 143.70 (0-312-19031-X) St Martin.

***Rogers.** Complete Guide to TOEFL. 3rd ed. 2000. 10.00 (0-8384-1232-7) Heinle & Heinle.

Rogers. The Heritage of World Civilizations, Vol. 2. 3rd ed. 1994. pap. text, student ed. 24.80 (0-02-403126-7, Macmillan Coll) P-H.

— Humans & the Life Sciences. 3rd ed. (C). 1993. pap. text, lab manual ed. 12.74 (0-07-053550-7) McGraw.

— Legal Foundations of Post. Date not set. 22.95 (0-465-03903-0); pap. write for info. (0-465-03904-9) Basic.

— Retailing. 3rd ed. (C). 1999. text 68.00 (0-03-009602-2, Pub. by Harcourt Coll Pubs) Harcourt.

— Romance, Vol. 1. 1998. 5.99 (0-312-96611-3, Pub. by Tor Bks) St Martin.

— Secrecy & Power in British State: A History of British Official Secrets Act, 1911-1989. LC 96-53336. 1997. 49.95 (0-7453-1093-1, Pub. by Pluto GBR) Stylus Pub VA.

— Secrecy & Power in British State: A History of the Official Secrets Act. 1997. pap. 16.95 (0-7453-1092-3, Pub. by Pluto GBR) Stylus Pub VA.

***Rogers.** Untitled Romance. 1999. mass mkt. write for info. (0-312-96895-7) St Martin.

— What Can You See. (J). 2000. pap. 8.95 (0-552-54588-0, Pub. by Transworld Publishers Ltd) Trafalgar.

***Rogers & HADG Staff.** Guide for Interventional Radiology Coding. 2000. pap. 89.00 (0-8342-1723-6) Aspen Pub.

Rogers & Klofas, John. A Freshman Year Reader. (Freshman Orientation Ser.). 1909. mass mkt. 19.95 (0-534-21480-0) Wadsworth Pub.

Rogers, et al. Communication Workbook. 156p. (C). 1998. per. 17.95 (0-7872-5295-6, 41529501) Kendall-Hunt.

Rogers, jt. auth. see Andersen.

Rogers, jt. auth. see Luschei, Glenna.

Rogers, jt. auth. see MacDonald.

Rogers, jt. auth. see Palmanteer.

***Rogers, Ben.** A. J. Ayer: A Life. 2000. 30.00 (0-8021-1673-6, Grove) Grove-Atltic.

Rogers & Manson Staff. One Hundred Turn-of-the-Century Brick Bungalows with Floor Plans. LC 94-6540. (Illus.). 128p. 1994. reprint ed. pap. 8.95 (0-486-28119-1) Dover.

Rogers, A. Southwell Minster after the Civil Wars. 1974. pap. 21.00 (0-902031-32-5, Pub. by Continuing Education Pr) St Mut.

Rogers, A. Southwell Minster after the Civil Wars. (C). 1974. text 40.00 (0-7855-3205-6, Pub. by Univ Nottingham) St Mut.

— The Spirit & the Form. 159p. (C). 1976. text 60.00 (0-7855-3198-X, Pub. by Univ Nottingham) St Mut.

— The Spirit & the Form Essays in Adult Education in Honour of Professor Harold Wiltshire. (C). 1976. 39.00 (0-902031-38-4, Pub. by Univ Nottingham) St Mut.

— Teaching Adults. 2nd ed. LC 96-10731. 224p. 1996. pap. 26.95 (0-335-19623-3) OpUniv Pr.

Rogers, A. & Howe, P. Supermanifolds: Theory & Applications. 300p. 1998. text 53.00 (981-02-1228-3) World Scientific Pub.

Rogers, A., tr. see Beveridge, Henry.

Rogers, A. C., jt. auth. see Cohen, Leon J.

Rogers, A. G., ed. see Eden, Frederick M.

Rogers, A. M., et al. Earthquake Hazards in the Pacific Northwest: An Overview. (Illus.). 74p. (Orig.). (C). 1994. pap. text 50.00 (0-7881-0437-3) DIANE Pub.

An Asterisk (*) at the beginning of an entry indicates that the title is appearing for the first time.

Rogers, A. P., jt. auth. see Biggs, A. K.

Rogers, A. T., ed. Heat & Mass Transfer in Severe Reactor Accidents. 300p. 1996. 107.50 (*1-56700-059-2*) Begell Hse.

Rogers, A. W. Textbook of Anatomy. (Illus.). 779p. (Orig.). 1992. pap. text 55.95 (*0-443-02672-6*) Church.

Rogers, Adam, ed. Taking Action: An Environmental Guide for You & Your Community. 248p. pap. 14.95 (*92-807-1568-2*) UN.

Rogers-Adkinson, Diana L. & Griffith, Penny L. Communication Disorders & Children with Psychiatric & Behavioral Disorders. LC 98-23248. (School-Age Children Ser.). (Illus.). 420p. 1998. pap. 49.95 (*1-56593-746-5*, 1454) Thomson Learn.

Rogers, Adrian. Believe in Miracles but Trust in Jesus. 201p. 1999. reprint ed. pap. 12.99 (*1-58134-076-1*) Crossway Bks.

— A Family Christmas Treasury. LC 97-21561. (Illus.). 144p. (J). 1997. 14.99 (*0-89107-970-X*) Crossway Bks.

***Rogers, Adrian.** God's Hidden Treasures: Biblical Wisdom for the Seasons of Life. LC 99-22150. 1999. 14.99 (*0-8423-3319-3*) Tyndale Hse.

Rogers, Adrian. The Lord Is My Shepherd: Reflections on God's Loving Care. LC 98-51509. (Illus.). 111p. 1999. 14.99 (*1-58134-048-6*) Crossway Bks.

***Rogers, Adrian.** Love Worth Finding: King James Version, 100. 1999. pap. 8.75 (*5-553-91952-5*, Goodnews); pap. text 8.75 (*5-553-91960-6*, Goodnews) Black Bayou.

Rogers, Adrian. The Power of His Presence. LC 94-24968. 192p. 1995. 14.99 (*0-89107-841-X*) Crossway Bks.

— Ten Secrets for a Successful Family: A Perfect 10 for Homes That Win. 1998. pap. 10.99 (*1-58134-033-8*) Crossway Bks.

***Rogers, Adrian.** What Every Christian Ought to Know Facilitator Guide: Essential Truths for Growing Your Faith. Rogers, Steve, ed. 48p. 2000. pap. 6.95 (*0-9701958-3-4*) Growing Your Faith.

— What Every Christian Ought to Know Workbook: Essential Truths for Growing Your Faith. Rogers, Steve, ed. 72p. 2000. pap., wbk. ed. 8.95 (*0-9701958-2-6*) Growing Your Faith.

Rogers, Adrian & Perry, John. The Incredible Power of Kingdom Authority. 17.99 (*0-8054-1676-5*) Broadman.

Rogers, Alan. Adults Learning for Development. 256p. 1992. pap. text 31.95 (*0-304-32420-5*) Continuum.

***Rogers, Alan.** Alto, Mas Alto. 2000. mass mkt. 2.95 (*1-58728-961-X*) Two Can Pub.

Rogers, Alan. Approaches to Local History. 2nd ed. LC 76-54265. 283p. reprint ed. pap. 87.80 (*0-8357-5695-5*, 202525300043) Bks Demand.

***Rogers, Alan.** Blue Tortoise. (Little Giants Ser.). (Illus.). (J). (ps-k). 2000. pap. 2.95 (*1-58728-158-9*) Two Can Pub.

— Blue Tortoise. rev. ed. (Little Giants Ser.). (Illus.). (J). (ps-k). 2000. 4.95 (*1-58728-150-3*) Two Can Pub.

Rogers, Alan. Bright & Breezy. LC 98-60730. (Little Giants Ser.). (Illus.). 16p. (YA). (ps). 1999. pap. 2.95 (*0-7166-4417-7*) World Bk.

***Rogers, Alan.** Bright & Breezy. rev. ed. (Little Giants Ser.). (Illus.). (J). (ps-k). 2000. 4.95 (*1-58728-151-1*) Two Can Pub.

— En Camino. 2000. mass mkt. 2.95 (*1-58728-960-1*) Two Can Pub.

— En Forma de Barco. 2000. mass mkt. 2.95 (*1-58728-962-8*) Two Can Pub.

— Green Bear. (Little Giants Ser.). (Illus.). (J). (ps-k). 2000. pap. 2.95 (*1-58728-159-7*) Two Can Pub.

— Green Bear. rev. ed. (Little Giants Ser.). (Illus.). (J). (ps-k). 2000. 4.95 (*1-58728-152-X*) Two Can Pub.

— Red Rhino. (Little Giants Ser.). (Illus.). (J). (ps-k). 2000. pap. 2.95 (*1-58728-161-9*) Two Can Pub.

— Red Rhino. rev. ed. (Little Giants Ser.). (Illus.). (J). (ps-k). 2000. 4.95 (*1-58728-154-6*) Two Can Pub.

— Sol y Lluvia. 2000. mass mkt. 2.95 (*1-58728-963-6*) Two Can Pub.

— Yellow Hippo. (Little Giants Ser.). (Illus.). (J). (ps-k). 2000. pap. 2.95 (*1-58728-160-0*) Two Can Pub.

— Yellow Hippo. rev. ed. (Little Giants Ser.). (Illus.). (J). (ps-k). 2000. 4.95 (*1-58728-157-0*) Two Can Pub.

Rogers, Alan, jt. auth. see Rogers, Joyce.

Rogers, Albert, et al. Liability of Lawyers & Indemnity Insurance for the Legal Profession. Frikkee, Karin C., ed. LC 95-43581. 1995. 109.00 (*90-411-0876-9*) Kluwer Law Intl.

Rogers, Alexander. Shah-Namah of Fardusi. (C). 1995. 14.00 (*81-86142-84-3*, Pub. by Low Price) S Asia.

Rogers, Alice. Dance Bands & Big Bands. (Illus.). 190p. 1986. pap. 19.95 (*0-932117-01-5*) Osborne Enterps.

Rogers, Alisdair. The Illustrated World Atlas. (Illus.). 80p. (J). (gr. 3-7). 1998. pap. 14.95 (*0-86505-911-X*); lib. bdg. 29.95 (*0-86505-897-0*) Crabtree Pub Co.

Rogers, Alisdair, et al, eds. The Urban Context: Ethnicity, Social Networks & Situational Analysis. LC 94-25313. (Explorations in Anthropology Ser.). (Illus.). 320p. 1995. 49.50 (*0-85496-317-0*, Pub. by Berg Pubs); pap. 19.50 (*1-85973-072-8*, Pub. by Berg Pubs) NYU Pr.

Rogers, Alisdair, jt. ed. see Keith, Michael.

Rogers, Alisdair, jt. ed. see Vertovec, Steven.

Rogers, Allan, et al. Peonies. LC 94-48535. (Illus.). 384p. 1995. 34.95 (*0-88192-317-6*) Timber.

Rogers, Alvin L., jt. auth. see Beneke, Everette S.

***Rogers, Amy.** All Chalked Up. (Powerpuff Girls Ser.: No. 2). (Illus.). 64p. (J). (gr. 1-4). 2000. mass mkt. 3.99 (*0-439-16020-0*) Scholastic Inc.

— Power Professor. (Powerpuff Girls Ser.: No. 1). (Illus.). 64p. (J). (gr. 1-4). 2000. mass mkt. 3.99 (*0-439-16019-7*) Scholastic Inc.

Rogers, Amy. Red Pepper Fudge & Blue Ribbon Biscuits: Favorite Recipes & Stories from North Carolina State Fair Winners. (Illus.). 157p. 1995. pap. 13.95 (*1-878086-43-X*, Pub. by Down Home NC) Blair.

***Rogers, Amy, et al, eds.** Novello: Ten Years of Great American Writing. 300p. 2000. pap. 16.95 (*1-878086-87-1*, Pub. by Down Home NC) Blair.

Rogers, Amy T., jt. auth. see Rogers, John R.

Rogers, Andrei. Multiregional Demography: Principles, Methods & Extensions. 248p. 1995. 110.00 (*0-471-95892-1*) Wiley.

Rogers, Andrei & Willekens, Frans. Migration & Settlement. (C). 1980. text 33.00 (*0-8133-0103-3*) Westview.

— Molecular Astrophysics: Migration & Settlement. 1985. lib. bdg. 162.50 (*90-277-2119-X*) Kluwer Academic.

Rogers, Andrei, et al. Elderly Migration & Population Redistribution: A Comparative Perspective. Frey, William H., ed. LC 92-24769. 204p. 1993. text 125.00 (*0-471-94766-0*) Wiley.

Rogers, Andrew D., III. Bernhard Eduard Fernow: A Story of North American Forestry. 2nd ed. 623p. 1991. reprint ed. 21.95 (*0-89030-047-X*) Forest Hist Soc.

Rogers, Andy W., ed. Cells & Tissues. 1983. pap. text 52.00 (*0-12-593120-4*) Acad Pr.

Rogers, Ann. Lewis & Clark in Missouri. 1994. 14.95 (*0-941088-01-4*) Meredco.

Rogers, Ann, jt. auth. see Rogers, Minor.

Rogers, Anne. Demanding Patients? Analysing the Use of Primary Care. (State of Health Ser.). 1998. 99.00 (*0-335-20091-5*) Taylor & Francis.

— Demanding Patients? Analyzing the Use of Primary Care. LC 98-4299. (State of Health Ser.). 1998. pap. 29.95 (*0-335-20090-7*) OpUniv Pr.

Rogers, Anne & Elliott, Heather. Primary Care: Understanding Health Need & Demand. LC 97-14955. (National Primary Care Research & Development Centre Ser.). 1997. write for info. (*1-85775-237-6*, Radcliffe Med Pr) Scovill Paterson.

Rogers, Anne, jt. auth. see Pilgrim, David.

Rogers, Anne M. & Hubbard, Susan. Kalamazoo Valley Consortium Education for Employment Case Study Report. (Cross Case Report & Case Studies). 50p. 1995. text, teacher ed. 20.00 (*0-614-24548-6*) Natl Inst Work.

— Metro Tech Vocational Institute of Phoenix Case Study Report. (Cross Case Report & Case Studies). 50p. 1995. text, teacher ed. 20.00 (*0-614-24546-X*); pap. text, teacher ed. 10.00 (*0-614-24547-8*) Natl Inst Work.

— Rothsay, Minnesota School Based Enterprises Case Study Report. (Cross Case Report & Case Studies). 50p. 1995. text, teacher ed. 20.00 (*0-614-24534-6*); pap. text, teacher ed. 10.00 (*0-614-24535-4*) Natl Inst Work.

Rogers, Anne M. & Menzel, Scott. Baltimore Commonwealth Case Study Report. (Cross Case Report & Case Studies). 50p. 1995. text, teacher ed. 20.00 (*0-614-24528-1*); pap. text, teacher ed. 10.00 (*0-614-24529-X*) Natl Inst Work.

— Central Valley High School Scope Case Study Report. (Cross Case Report & Case Studies). 50p. 1995. text, teacher ed. 20.00 (*0-614-24553-2*); pap. text, teacher ed. 10.00 (*0-614-24554-0*) Natl Inst Work.

— Pasadena Graphic Arts Academy Case Study Report. (Cross Case Report & Case Studies). 50p. 1995. text, teacher ed. 20.00 (*0-614-24542-7*); pap. text, teacher ed. 10.00 (*0-614-24543-5*) Natl Inst Work.

Rogers, Anne M., et al. Learning from Experience: A Cross Case Comparison of School to Work Transition Reform Initiatives. (Cross Case Report & Case Studies). 110p. 1995. text, teacher ed. 20.00 (*0-614-24526-5*); pap. text, teacher ed. 10.00 (*0-614-24527-3*) Natl Inst Work.

Rogers, Anne M., jt. auth. see Horne, Richard.

Rogers, Anne M., jt. auth. see Hubbard, Susan.

Rogers, Anne M., jt. auth. see Weinbaum, Alexandra.

Rogers, Annie, jt. ed. see Shibles, Loana.

Rogers, Annie G. A Shining Affliction: A Story of Harm & Healing in Psychotherapy. LC 94-45171. 336p. 1996. pap. 13.95 (*0-14-024012-8*, Penguin Bks) Viking Penguin.

Rogers, Annie G., et al, eds. Women, Girls, & Psychotherapy: Reframing Resistance. LC 91-20845. (Women & Therapy Ser.). 243p. 1991. lib. bdg. 39.95 (*1-56024-196-9*); lib. bdg. 14.95 (*1-56023-012-6*, Harrington Park) Haworth Pr.

***Rogers, Anthony.** Battle over Malta: Aircraft Losses & Crash Sites, 1940-1942. (Illus.). 224p. 2000. pap. 16.95 (*0-7509-2392-X*) Sutton Publng.

***Rogers, April R.** Mother & Child: Reflections of Our First Year Together. 144p. 1999. 17.95 (*0-9643763-7-7*, Pub. by U-Talk Pubns) Partners Pubs Grp.

Rogers, April R. My Teen Years. (YA). (gr. 6-12). 1993. spiral bd. 12.95 (*0-9643763-1-8*) U-Talk Pubns.

— My Teen Years Memory Journal. (YA). (gr. 6-12). 1995. spiral bd. 12.95 (*0-9643763-2-6*) U-Talk Pubns.

— A Teen Yearbook: My Life in My Own Words. 3rd rev. ed. (My Teen Years Ser.). Orig. Title: My Teen Years Memory Journal. (Illus.). 64p. (YA). (gr. 7-12). 1999. 19.95 (*0-9643763-5-0*) U-Talk Pubns.

Rogers, Arthur & Durand de Bousingen, Denis. Bioethics in Europe. LC 95-209684. (European Issues Ser.). 366p. (Orig.). 1995. pap. 25.00 (*92-871-2566-X*, Pub. by Council of Europe) Manhattan Pub Co.

Rogers, Arthur K. Morals in Review. LC 72-126697. reprint ed. 34.50 (*0-404-05379-3*) AMS Pr.

Rogers, Austin F. & Staples, Lloyd. Introduction to the Study of Minerals. 3rd ed. LC 75-41235. reprint ed. 47.50 (*0-404-14699-6*) AMS Pr.

***Rogers, Avain M.** Y2K Family Survival Guide. LC 99-30663. (Illus.). 200p. 1999. pap. 14.95 (*1-55853-718-X*) Rutledge Hill Pr.

Rogers, B. G., jt. auth. see Jong, I. C.

Rogers, Barb. Costuming Made Easy: How to Make Theatrical Costumes from Cast-off Clothing. LC 98-49796. (Illus.). 128p. 1999. pap. 19.95 (*1-56608-048-7*) Meriwether Pub.

Rogers, Barbara. The Domestication of Women: Discrimination in Developing Societies. 200p. (C). 1981. pap. 25.99 (*0-415-04010-8*) Routledge.

Rogers, Barbara & Rogers, Stillman. Massachusetts: Off the Beaten Path: A Guide to Unique Places. 3rd ed. LC 99-18078. (Off the Beaten Path Ser.). 224p. 1999. pap. 12.95 (*0-7627-0398-9*) Globe Pequot.

— Rhode Island Guide. (Illus.). 320p. 1998. pap. 17.95 (*1-55591-300-8*) Fulcrum Pub.

Rogers, Barbara, jt. auth. see Rogers, Lura.

Rogers, Barbara, jt. ed. see Ball, Caroline.

Rogers, Barbara R. AOW New York & New England States. (Illus.). 512p. 1996. 14.95 (*0-02-860932-8*) Macmillan.

— The Domestication of Women: Discrimination in Developing Societies. 1981. pap. 15.95 (*0-422-77630-0*, NO.6529, Pub. by Tavistock) Routldge.

— Drying Flowers. 128p. 1994. pap. 9.95 (*1-56799-025-8*, Friedman-Fairfax) M Friedman Pub Grp Inc.

— Giant Pandas. 128p. 1994. pap. 11.95 (*1-56799-070-3*, Friedman-Fairfax) M Friedman Pub Grp Inc.

— God Rescues His People Activity Book. 72p. (Orig.). (J). (ps-1). 1983. pap., student ed. 3.99 (*0-8361-3338-2*) Herald Pr.

— God's Chosen King Activity Book. 88p. (Orig.). (J). (ps-1). 1984. pap. 3.99 (*0-8361-3370-6*) Herald Pr.

— Making Wreaths. 128p. 1994. pap. 9.95 (*1-56799-026-6*, Friedman-Fairfax) M Friedman Pub Grp Inc.

— White Wealth & Black Poverty: American Investments in Southern Africa, 2. LC 75-35353. (Studies in Human Rights: No. 2). 331p. 1976. 55.00 (*0-8371-8277-8*, RWW/, Greenwood Pr) Greenwood.

Rogers, Barbara R. & Rogers, Stillman. Natural Wonders of Vermont. (Natural Wonders of... Ser.). (Illus.). 180p. (Orig.). 1996. pap. 12.95 (*1-56626-145-7*, 61457, Cntry Rds Pr) NTC Contemp Pub Co.

Rogers, Barbara R. & Scholz, Bernard W., trs. from LAT. Carolingian Chronicles: Royal Frankish Annals & Nithard's Histories. 248p. 1970. pap. text 15.95 (*0-472-06186-0*, 06186, Ann Arbor Bks) U of Mich Pr.

Rogers, Barbara R., jt. auth. see Rogers, Stillman D.

Rogers, Barbara Radcliffe. New England Snow Country: 701 Ways to Enjoy Winter Whether You Ski or Not. 1999. pap. 14.95 (*0-9652502-6-1*) Williams Hill.

***Rogers, Barbara Radcliffe.** Toronto. (Cities of the World Ser.). (Illus.). (J). 2000. write for info. (*0-516-22034-9*) Childrens.

***Rogers, Barbara Radcliffe & Rogers, Stillman.** The Adventure Guide to the Chesapeake Bay - Including Maryland & Washington DC. (Adventure Guides Ser.). (Illus.). 400p. 2000. pap. 17.95 (*1-55650-889-1*) Hunter NJ.

— Canada LC 99-37400. (Enchantment of the World Ser.). 2000. 33.00 (*0-516-21076-9*) Childrens.

— New Hampshire: Off the Beaten Path. 4th ed. LC 99-88412. (Off the Beaten Path Ser.). (Illus.). 176p. 2000. pap. 12.95 (*0-7627-0626-0*) Globe Pequot.

— Signpost Guide: Portugal. 2000. pap. 22.95 (*0-7627-0689-9*) Globe Pequot.

Rogers, Bernard. Art of Orchestration: Principles of Tone Color in Modern Scoring. LC 73-97353. 198p. 1970. reprint ed. lib. bdg. 49.75 (*0-8371-2969-9*, ROAO, Greenwood Pr) Greenwood.

***Rogers, Bernard.** Pascal: Great Philosophers. LC 99-22484. 1999. pap. 6.00 (*0-415-92398-0*) Routledge.

***Rogers, Bertha.** Beowulf. LC 00-130426. 136p. 2000. pap. 20.00 (*0-913559-59-8*) Birch Brook Pr.

Rogers, Bertha. For the Girl Buried in the Peat Bog: Illuminated Poems & Pictures. (Six Swans Artists Editions Ser.). (Illus.). 40p. (Orig.). 1998. pap. 15.00 (*1-893389-00-6*) Six Swans.

— The Fourth Beast: Illuminated Poems & Pictures. (Six Swans Artists Editions Ser.). (Illus.). 32p. (Orig.). 1999. pap. 15.00 (*1-893389-01-4*) Six Swans.

— Out of the Catskills & Just Beyond: Literary & Visual Works by Catskills Writers & Artists. (Illus.). 384p. (Orig.). 1997. pap. 24.95 (*0-9646844-6-2*) Bright Hill.

— Sleeper, You Wake: Poems. Schultz, Patricia, ed. LC 91-29832. (Poetry Ser.: Vol. 17). (Illus.). 84p. 1991. pap. 14.95 (*0-7734-9669-6*) E Mellen.

— While the Old Man Died. (Six Swans Artists Editions Ser.). (Illus.). 48p. (Orig.). 1999. pap. 15.00 (*1-893389-03-0*) Six Swans.

Rogers, Bertha, ed. Speaking the Words Anthology. 48p. 1994. pap. 5.00 (*0-9646844-0-3*) Bright Hill.

— The Word Thursdays Anthology, Vol. II, Pt. 2. LC 99-21998. 300p. 1998. pap. text 17.50 (*0-9646844-9-7*) Bright Hill.

— The Word Thursdays Anthology of Poetry & Fiction. 198p. 1995. pap. 12.95 (*0-9646844-1-1*) Bright Hill.

Rogers, Bertha, ed. Iroquois Voices, Iroquois Visions: A Celebration of Contemporary S. Nations Arts. (Illus.). 130p. (Orig.). 1996. pap. 12.00 (*0-9646844-3-8*) Bright Hill.

Rogers, Bertha & Jolliff, William, eds. No Title. (Poetry Chapbook Ser.: Vol. 2). 26p. (Orig.). 1998. mass mkt. 6.00 (*0-9646844-8-9*) Bright Hill.

Rogers, Bertha, ed. see Bernard, Pam.

Rogers, Bertha, ed. see Blevins-Church, Adrian.

Rogers, Bertha, ed. see Harris, Lisa.

Rogers, Bertha, ed. see O'Melveny, Regina.

Rogers, Bessie R. Householder. Householders of America: Genealogy of Johannes Hausshalter, Early Inhabitant of Maryland & Pennsylvania, with Families from Pennsylvania & Elsewhere of Householder, Housholder & Haushalter. 2nd ed. 151p. 1997. reprint ed. pap. 24.50 (*0-8328-9217-3*); reprint ed. lib. bdg. 34.50 (*0-8328-9216-5*) Higginson Bk Co.

Rogers, Beth. Creating Product Strategies. LC 95-34298. (Marketing for Managers Ser.). 168p. 1996. pap. 14.95 (*0-415-13256-8*) Thomson Learn.

— Seize the Future for Your Business: Using Imagination to Power Growth. LC 99-208037. (ITBP PROFESSIONAL). 224p. 1998. pap. 19.99 (*1-86152-203-7*) Thomson Learn.

Rogers, Betsy. The Healing Heart. LC 98-97004. 192p. 1999. lib. bdg. 18.95 (*0-8034-9347-9*, Avalon Bks) Bouregy.

Rogers, Betty. Will Rogers. LC 79-4743. (Illus.). 312p. 1982. pap. 15.95 (*0-8061-1600-5*) U of Okla Pr.

***Rogers, Betty C. & Hokanson, Clifford M.** Mathematics for Agriculture. 2nd ed. xiv, 317p. 2000. 43.75 (*0-8134-3174-3*) Interstate.

— Mathematics for Agriculture: Answer Key. 2nd ed. 2000. 1.00 (*0-8134-3196-4*) Interstate.

Rogers, Betty P., et al. In the Company of Their Peers: A Geriatric Peer Counselor Training Manual. (Illus.). 415p. (Orig.). 1993. 19.95 (*0-9632698-2-8*) Veda Vangarde.

Rogers, Bettye. Paul Wylie from Cowboy to Cowboy Artist. 96p. 1998. pap. 25.00 (*0-9664491-0-X*) B Rogers.

— Prairie Dog Town. (Smithsonian Wild Heritage Collection). 1993. 10.15 (*0-606-08035-X*, Pub. by Turtleback) Demco.

Rogers, Bill. Behavior Recovery. 15.95 (*0-86431-155-9*, Pub. by Aust Council Educ Res); pap. 15.95 (*0-86431-154-0*, Pub. by Aust Council Educ Res) Stylus Pub VA.

Rogers, Bill. You Know the Fair Rule. (C). 1990. pap. 60.00 (*0-86431-068-4*, Pub. by Aust Council Educ Res) St Mut.

— "You Know the Fair Rule" & More: Strategies for Making the Hard Job of Discipline & Behavior Management in School Easier. 2nd ed. 368p. 1998. pap. 27.50 (*0-86431-254-7*, Pub. by Aust Council Educ Res) Stylus Pub VA.

Rogers, Bob & Dunn, Ralph. Non-Fiction Poems & by the Blood: A Chapbook Duet. (Illus.). 40p. 1985. pap. 5.00 (*0-929170-07-5*) Paper Plant.

Rogers, Bonnie. Occupational Health Nursing: Concepts & Practice. LC 93-48841. (Illus.). 543p. 1994. text 60.00 (*0-7216-7588-3*, W B Saunders Co) Harcrt Hlth Sci Grp.

Rogers, Brian D., jt. ed. see Lint, Gregory A.

Rogers, Brian J., jt. auth. see Howard, Ian P.

Rogers, Brian T., jt. auth. see Arvedson, Joan C.

Rogers, Bruce. The Centaur Types. LC 95-40156. (Illus.). 90p. 1996. pap. 16.95 (*1-55753-076-9*) Purdue U Pr.

— Complete Guide to the TOEFL. 2nd ed. (College ESL Ser.). (YA). 1997. pap. text 27.95 incl. audio (*0-8384-6795-4*) Heinle & Heinle.

— Complete Guide to TOEFL. (J). 1993. audio 42.95 (*0-8384-4133-5*) Heinle & Heinle.

— Complete Guide to TOEFL. (J). 1997. 27.95 (*0-8384-6671-0*) Heinle & Heinle.

— The Complete Guide to Toefl. (J). 1993. text 30.95 incl. audio (*0-8384-4226-9*) Heinle & Heinle.

— Complete Guide to TOEFL - Answer Key. 2nd ed. (College Esl Ser.). (YA). 1997. mass mkt. 10.95 (*0-8384-6790-3*) Heinle & Heinle.

— Complete Guide to TOEFL - Tests. 2nd ed. LC 96-29654. (College Esl Ser). 350p. (YA). 1997. mass mkt. 32.95 (*0-8384-6789-X*) Heinle & Heinle.

— Heinle & Heinle's Complete Guide to the TOEIC Test. (Illus.). 240p. 1996. pap. 28.95 incl. audio (*0-8384-6660-5*) Heinle & Heinle.

Rogers, Bruce. Paragraphs on Printing. LC 79-50699. (Illus.). 198p. 1980. reprint ed. pap. 6.95 (*0-486-23817-2*) Dover.

Rogers, Bruce. PI: A Hodge-Podge of the Letters, Papers, & Addresses Written During the Last Sixty Years. LC 79-167407. (Essay Index Reprint Ser.). 1977. reprint ed. 20.95 (*0-8369-2669-2*) Ayer.

***Rogers, Bruce.** TOEFL Practice Tests 2001. 4th ed. 318p. 2000. pap. 16.95 (*0-7689-0528-1*); pap. text 29.95 incl. audio (*0-7689-0416-1*) Petersons.

— TOEFL Success 2001. 5th ed. 580p. 2000. pap. 29.95 incl. audio (*0-7689-0415-3*); pap. 16.95 (*0-7689-0527-3*) Petersons.

Rogers, Bruce, ed. see Kaneda, Fujihiko.

Rogers, Bruce, jt. ed. see Kaneda, Fujihiko.

Rogers, Bruce H. Tales & Declarations. (Dog River Review Poetry Ser.: No. 9). 32p. (Orig.). (YA). 1991. pap. 4.00 (*0-916155-13-7*) Trout Creek.

***Rogers, Bruce Holland.** Flaming Arrows. large type ed. LC 00-105560. 2000. pap. 20.00 (*0-9671912-2-X*) I F D Pubg.

— Flaming Arrows. large type ed. LC 00-105560. (Illus.). 2000. 45.00 (*0-9671912-3-8*) I F D Pubg.

Rogers, Buck. Packet Made Easy. (Illus.). 72p. 1992. pap. 9.95 (*1-891237-15-2*, MFJ-32) MFJ Ent.

— Packetradio Operators Handbook. (Illus.). 121p. (Orig.). 1992. pap. 12.95 (*1-891237-09-8*, MFJ-3036) MFJ Ent.

Rogers, C. A. Hausdorff Measures. 2nd rev. ed. LC 98-7167. (Mathematical Library). 226p. (C). 1998. pap. text 29.95 (*0-521-62491-6*) Cambridge U Pr.

Rogers, C. A., et al, eds. Analytic Sets. LC 80-40647. (London Mathematical Society Symposia Ser.). 1981. text 180.00 (*0-12-593150-6*) Acad Pr.

Rogers, C. A. & Rogers, R. C. Recent Advances in Adaptive & Sensory Materials & Their Applications. LC 92-80289. 850p. 1992. text 89.95 (*0-87762-947-1*) Technomic.

Rogers, C. Clark. The Guest Log. (Illus.). 98p. (Orig.). 1988. pap. 15.95 (*1-878797-07-7*) Weems & Plath.

Rogers, C. D., et al, eds. Lime Stabilisation: Proceedings of the Seminar Held at Loughborough University Civil & Building Engineering Department on September 25, 1996. LC 97-109139. 192p. 1996. 48.00 (*0-7277-2563-7*) Am Soc Civil Eng.

Rogers, C. E., ed. see American Chemical Society Symposium on Permselecti.

Rogers, C. Leland, jt. auth. see Snyder, John A.

R

Rogers, C. M. Linaceae. LC 84-14891. (North American Flora Ser.: No. 2, Pt. 12). (Illus.). 58p. 1984. 10.75 (*0-89327-260-4*) NY Botanical.

Rogers, C. Paul, jt. auth. see Andersen, William R.

Rogers, C. Paul, 3rd, jt. auth. see Roberts, Robin.

Rogers, Campbell, jt. ed. see Simon, Daniel I.

Rogers, Carl Ransom. Measuring Personality Adjustment in Children 9 to 13 Years of Age. LC 76-177202. (Columbia University. Teachers College. Contributions to Education Ser.: No. 458). reprint ed. 37.50 (*0-404-55458-X*) AMS Pr.

— On Becoming a Person: A Therapist's View of Psychotherapy. 416p. 1995. pap. 16.00 (*0-395-75531-X*) HM.

— The Therapeutic Relationship & Its Impact. LC 76-14790. 625p. 1976. reprint ed. lib. bdg. 62.50 (*0-8371-8358-8*, ROTR, Greenwood Pr) Greenwood.

— Therapist's View of Personal Goals. LC 60-11607. (Orig.). 1960. pap. 4.00 (*0-87574-108-8*) Pendle Hill.

— A Way of Being. LC 96-109887. 416p. 1995. pap. 15.00 (*0-395-75530-1*) HM.

Rogers, Carl Ransom & Freiberg, H. Jerome. Freedom to Learn. 3rd rev. ed. LC 93-34791. (Illus.). 352p. (C). 1994. pap. text 41.00 (*0-02-403121-6*, Macmillan Coll) P-H.

Rogers, Carl Ransom & Skinner, B. F. A Dialogue on the Control of Human Behavior. unabridged ed. Gladstein, Gerald, ed. 30p. pap. 49.50 incl. audio (*0-88432-028-6*, S29244) Audio-Forum.

Rogers, Carla S. How to Get into the Right Dental School. LC 98-28071. 176p. 1998. pap. 14.95 (*0-8442-6454-7*, 64547) NTC Contemp Pub Co.

— How to Get into the Right Medical School. LC 96-325. (Illus.). 192p. (Orig.). 1996. pap. 14.95 (*0-8442-4161-X*, 4161X, VGM Career) NTC Contemp Pub Co.

— How to Get into the Right Nursing Program. LC 97-51235. (Illus.). 160p. 1998. pap. 14.95 (*0-8442-4192-X*, 4192X, VGM Career) NTC Contemp Pub Co.

Rogers, Carleton. I Remember: Memories from My Ministry. LC 94-79190. (Illus.). 134p. 1994. pap. 15.00 (*0-916445-41-0*) Crossroads Comm.

Rogers, Carol, et al, compiled by. Directory of European Anthropologists in North America. 1987. 6.00 (*0-913167-20-7*) Am Anthro Assn.

Rogers, Carol, jt. auth. see Crown, Cate.

Rogers, Carol A. Just Picture This: My Own Photo Album. (Illus.). 10p. (J). 1993. vinyl bd. 24.95 (*0-9635899-0-3*) New Vision VA.

Rogers, Carol Felsinger, jt. auth. see Calter, Paul.

Rogers, Carol L., jt. ed. see Friedman, Sharon M.

Rogers, Carole G. Poverty, Chastity & Change: Lives of Contemporary American Nuns. (Illus.). 256p. 1996. per. 28.95 (*0-8057-9136-1*, Twyne) Mac Lib Ref.

Rogers, Cathy, ed. Malibu's Cooking Again. (Illus.). 126p. (Orig.). 1995. pap. 19.95 (*0-9644695-0-2*) Image Maker Pub.

Rogers, Charles. Book of Robert Burns, 3 vols. LC 78-144470. reprint ed. 155.00 (*0-404-08530-X*) AMS Pr.

— Colt: Genealogical Memoirs of the Families of Colt & Coutts. 59p. 1992. reprint ed. pap. 12.00 (*0-8328-2647-2*) Higginson Bk Co.

— Eleven Ninety-Nine. 304p. (Orig.). 1988. mass mkt. 3.95 (*0-373-97089-7*) Harlequin Bks.

— Knox: Genealogical Memoirs of John Knox, & of the Family of Knox. (Illus.). 184p. 1994. reprint ed. pap. 28.00 (*0-8328-4028-9*); reprint ed. lib. bdg. 38.00 (*0-8328-4027-0*) Higginson Bk Co.

Rogers, Charles B. Art Observations. (Illus.). 64p. 1980. pap. 5.95 (*0-686-64396-8*) Rogers Hse Mus.

— Country Neighbor. (Illus.). (Orig.). 1977. pap. 1.49 (*0-685-77026-5*) Rogers Hse Mus.

Rogers, Charles E. & Irvine, Jerry. Model Rocket Computer Programs: Malewicki Closed-Form Altitude, Coefficient of Drag & Center of Pressure. 1983. 39.95 (*0-912468-12-2*) CA Rocketry.

— Near-Orbital Rocket: Multi-Stage Capable Altitude Prediction, Drag, Center of Pressure, Plotting Ogive Nose Cones, Trajectory, Reentry. 60p. 1983. 99.95 (*0-912468-14-9*) CA Rocketry.

— Sub & Supersonic Experimental Rocket Computer Programs: Fourth Order Range-Kutta, Altitude Prediction, Drag , Center of Pressure. 50p. 1983. 49.95 (*0-912468-13-0*) CA Rocketry.

Rogers, Chester B., jt. auth. see Renstrom, Peter G.

Rogers, Chris. Bitch Factor. 336p. 1998. mass mkt. 5.99 (*0-553-58001-9*) Bantam.

***Rogers, Chris.** Chill Factor. LC 99-46455. 320p. 2000. 23.95 (*0-553-10661-9*) Bantam.

Rogers, Chris. Haynes Honda G L-1100 Goldwing Owners Workshop Manual, No. 669: 1979 Thru 1981. 180p. 1982. pap. 16.95 (*0-85696-669-X*) Haynes Manuals.

— Haynes Honda XL-XR 80, 100, 125, 185 & 200 Owners' Workshop Manual, No. M566: 1978-1987. 23.95 (*1-85010-347-X*) Haynes Manuals.

***Rogers, Chris.** Rage Factor. 400p. 2000. mass mkt. 5.99 (*0-553-58070-1*) Bantam.

Rogers, Chris, jt. auth. see Clew, Jeff.

Rogers, Chris, jt. auth. see Darlington, Mansur.

Rogers, Christopher P. Rodgers: Agricultural Law. 2nd ed. 1997. pap. write for info. (*0-406-00221-5*, RAL2, MICHIE) LEXIS Pub.

Rogers, Chuck, jt. auth. see Irvine, Jerry.

Rogers, Cindy. Create Your Desires... Affirmations for Daily Living. 48p. 1997. spiral bd. 5.95 (*0-9664435-0-0*) Insghtful Soltns.

Rogers, Cindy, jt. auth. see Dardis, Sharon.

Rogers, Clark D. & Vidic, Brian A. Community Information Service Management Guidelines. rev. ed. (Illus.). 200p. (Orig.). 1995. pap. 79.95 (*0-9648192-3-6*) InfoWorks Partner.

Rogers Clausen, Ruth, jt. auth. see Courtier, Jane.

Rogers, Cleon L., 3rd & Rogers, Cleon L., Jr. The New Linguistic & Exegetical Key to the Greek New Testament. LC 97-45109. 896p. 1998. 39.99 (*0-310-20175-6*) Zondervan.

Rogers, Cleon L., Jr., jt. auth. see Rogers, Cleon L., 3rd.

Rogers, Clifford J., ed. Military Revolution Debate: Readings on the Military Transformation of Early Mondern Europe. (History & Warfare Ser.). (C). 1995. pap. 34.00 (*0-8133-2054-2*, Pub. by Westview) HarpC.

***Rogers, Clifford J., ed.** The Wars of Edward III: Sources & Interpretations. LC 99-37411. (Warfare in History Ser.). (Illus.). 320p. 2000. 72.00 (*0-85115-646-0*) Boydell & Brewer.

Rogers, Clinton, ed. see Rogers, Jean D.

Rogers, Colin D. The Family Tree Detective: A Manual for Analysing & Solving Genealogical Problems in England & Wales, 1538 to the Present Day. 3rd ed. LC 97-10564. 180p. 1998. pap. 15.95 (*0-7190-5213-0*, Pub. by Manchester Univ Pr) St Martin.

— The Surname Detective: Investigating Surname Distribution in England, 1086-Present Day. LC 94-24441. 1995. text 69.95 (*0-7190-4047-7*, Pub. by Manchester Univ Pr); text 24.95 (*0-7190-4048-5*, Pub. by Manchester Univ Pr) St Martin.

— Tracing Your English Ancestors: A Manual for Analysing & Solving Genealogical Problems in England & Wales, 1538 to the Present Day. 196p. 1989. text 39.95 (*0-7190-3172-9*) Manchester Univ Pr.

Rogers, Colin D., jt. auth. see Gibson, J. S. W.

Rogers, Constance, jt. auth. see Rogers, David J.

Rogers, Cornish R., jt. ed. see Jeter, Joseph R., Jr.

Rogers, Cosby S. & Sawyers, Janet K. Play in the Lives of Children. LC 87-62314. 135p. 1988. pap. 6.00 (*0-935989-09-9*, NAEYC #301) Natl Assn Child Ed.

Rogers, Cosby S., jt. auth. see Sawyers, Janet K.

Rogers, Craig A. Smart Materials, Structures & Mathematical Issues: Selected Papers from the U. S. Army Research Office Workshop, Smart Materials, Structures & Mathematical Issues, September 1988. LC 89-85344. 244p. 1989. pap. 59.95 (*0-87762-582-0*) Technomic.

Rogers, Craig A., et al, eds. 6th International Conference on Adaptive Structures Technology: Proceedings, November 13-15, 1995, Key West, Florida, U. S. A. 552p. 1996. 49.95 (*1-56676-427-0*) Technomic.

Rogers, Craig A. & Wallace, Gordon G. Proceedings of the Second International Conference on Intelligent Materials. (Illus.). 1409p. 1994. 319.95 (*1-56676-171-9*) Technomic.

Rogers, Curt, jt. auth. see Vanston, Lawrence K.

Rogers, Cynthia S. Chocolate Companion. LC 93-74032. (Traditional Country Life Recipe Ser.). (Illus.). 96p. (Orig.). 1994. pap. 9.95 (*1-883283-02-7*) Brick Tower.

Rogers, D. The Anesthesia Handbook. 1993. 27.95 (*0-8016-7997-4*) Mosby Inc.

Rogers, D., ed. Gabriel Tellez: El Condenado por Desconfiado. LC 73-7964. 172p. (C). 1974. 26.00 (*0-08-017247-4*, Pergamon Pr); pap. 15.50 (*0-08-017248-2*, Pergamon Pr) Elsevier.

Rogers, D. E. White Lie. 167p. 1999. pap. 13.95 (*0-7414-0025-1*) Buy Books.

Rogers, D. F., et al, eds. Airway Mucus: Basic Mechanisms & Clinical Perspectives. LC 97-8040. (Respiratory Pharmacology & Pharmacotherapy Ser.). 370p. 1997. 175.00 (*3-7643-5691-X*) Spr-Verlag.

Rogers, D. F. & Earnshaw, P. A., eds. State of the Art in Computer Graphics: Visualization & Modeling. (Illus.). 368p. 1991. 130.00 (*0-387-97560-8*) Spr-Verlag.

Rogers, D. F. & Earnshaw, Rae A., eds. Computer Graphics Techniques: Theory & Practice. (Illus.). v, 542p. 1990. 130.95 (*0-387-97237-4*) Spr-Verlag.

— Techniques for Computer Graphics. (Illus.). 590p. 1987. 118.00 (*0-387-96492-4*) Spr-Verlag.

Rogers, D. F. & Lethem, M. I. Airway Mucus Basic Mechanisms & Clinical Perspectives. LC 97-8040. (Respiratory Pharmacology & Pharmacotherapy Ser.). 1997. write for info. (*0-8176-5691-X*) Birkhauser.

Rogers, D. M., jt. auth. see Allison, A. F.

Rogers, D. W. Computational Chemistry Using the PC. 2nd ed. 240p. 1994. 89.95 (*0-471-18599-X*, Wiley-VCH) Wiley.

Rogers, D. W. Computational Chemistry Using the PC. 2nd ed. LC 94-35434. (Illus.). xiv, 247p. 1995. 65.00 incl. disk (*1-56081-672-4*, Wiley-VCH) Wiley.

Rogers, Dale E. Angel Unaware. 64p. 1991. reprint ed. lib. bdg. 10.95 (*0-89966-811-9*) Buccaneer Bks.

— God in the Hard Times. large type ed. (Large Print Inspirational Ser.). 1985. pap. 8.95 (*0-8027-2516-3*) Walker & Co.

***Rogers, Dale Evans.** Life Is a Blessing. 2000. 9.99 (*0-88486-282-8*, Inspirational Pr) Arrowood Pr.

Rogers, Dale Evans & Carlson, Carole C. Our Values: Stories & Wisdom. (Illus.). 160p. 1999. mass mkt. 5.99 (*0-8007-8671-8*, Spire) Revell.

Rogers, Dale Evans & Rohrer, Norman B. Dale Evans Rogers: Rainbow on a Hard Trail. LC 99-22391. (Illus.). 141p. 1999. 15.99 (*0-8007-1769-4*) Revell.

Rogers, Dale Evans, see Evans Rogers, Dale.

***Rogers, Dale S. & Tibben-Lembke, Ronald S.** Going Backwards: Reverse Logistics Trends & Practices. (Illus.). xv, 280p. 1999. pap. 20.00 (*0-9674619-0-1*) Reverse Logistics.

Rogers, Damian, ed. see Fahey, John.

Rogers, Daniel. Earthquakes. LC 98-28895. (Geography Starts Here Ser.). (J). 1999. 15.98 (*0-8172-5546-X*) Raintree Steck-V.

— Volcanoes. LC 98-28894. (Geography Starts Here Ser.). (J). 1999. 15.98 (*0-8172-5547-8*) Raintree Steck-V.

Rogers, Daniel E. Politics after Hitler: The Western Allies & the German Party System. (C). 1995. text 45.00 (*0-8147-7461-X*) NYU Pr.

Rogers, Daniel L. & Page, Mary D. The Traveler Ken Page & the Fallen Angel: An Adventure Story. (Traveler Ser.). 196p. (Orig.). 1995. pap. text 11.95 (*0-9649703-0-9*) Clr Light Arts.

Rogers, Daniel T. Environmental Geology of Metropolitan Detroit. (Illus.). xi, 152p. (Orig.). 1996. pap. 50.00 (*0-9653542-0-2*) Clayton Environ.

Rogers, Dave. Comp Avengers. 1989. pap. 14.95 (*0-312-03187-4*) St Martin.

— The ITV Encyclopedia of Adventure. 800p. 1988. 75.00 (*1-85283-205-3*, Pub. by Boxtree); pap. 40.00 (*0-7855-2136-4*, Pub. by Boxtree) St Mut.

— The ITV Encyclopedia of Adventure. 593p. (C). 1990. 125.00 (*1-85283-217-7*, Pub. by Boxtree) St Mut.

***Rogers, David.** The Big Four British Banks: Organization, Strategy & the Future. LC 99-40680. 240p. 1999. text 65.00 (*0-312-22869-4*) St Martin.

Rogers, David. Big Rock at Candy's Mountain. 112p. (YA). (gr. 7 up). 1970. pap. 5.00 (*0-87129-842-2*, B18) Dramatic Pub.

— The Bodleian Library & Its Treasures, 1320-1700. (Illus.). 176p. 1995. 50.00 (*0-85628-128-X*, 128-X) A Schwartz & Co.

— Boys & Ghouls Together. 102p. 1965. pap. 5.50 (*0-87129-698-5*, B30) Dramatic Pub.

— Foundations of Psychology: Some Personal Views. LC 84-13374. 256p. 1984. 59.95 (*0-275-91253-1*, C1253, Praeger Pubs) Greenwood.

— Get Witch Quick. 99p. (YA). (gr. 10 up). 1966. pap. 5.25 (*0-87129-922-4*, G15) Dramatic Pub.

— Here & Now. 1973. 5.25 (*0-87129-538-5*, H16) Dramatic Pub.

— It Happens Every Summer. 89p. (C). 1963. pap. 5.25 (*0-87129-539-3*, I29) Dramatic Pub.

— May the Farce Be with You. 96p. 1978. pap. 5.25 (*0-87129-614-4*, M43) Dramatic Pub.

— Monarch Notes on O'Neill's Plays. (Orig.). (C). 3.95 (*0-671-00627-4*, Arco) Macmillan Gen Ref.

— Never Mind What Happened, How Did It End? 104p. 1976. pap. 5.25 (*0-87129-103-7*, N11) Dramatic Pub.

***Rogers, David.** Politics, Prayer & Parliament. LC 99-48976. 2000. pap. 21.95 (*0-304-70633-7*) Continuum.

Rogers, David. Soft Soap. 1982. 5.25 (*0-87129-529-6*, S65) Dramatic Pub.

— Stories by an Atheist. 267p. (Orig.). 1991. pap. 5.95 (*0-9618064-1-9*) D Rogers NY.

— Sunday Morning. LC 86-90807. 95p. (Orig.). 1986. pap. 6.95 (*0-9618064-0-0*) D Rogers NY.

Rogers, David, adapted by. The Sting. 1985. pap. 5.95 (*0-87129-280-7*, S69) Dramatic Pub.

Rogers, David, ed. The Best of Broadway: A Revue. 126p. (C). 1961. pap. 5.95 (*0-87129-937-2*, B04) Dramatic Pub.

— The First & the Third. 157p. (Orig.). 1997. pap. 9.95 (*1-889534-09-9*) Jay St Pubs.

Rogers, David & Chung, Norman H. One Hundred Ten Livingston Street Revisited: Decentralization in Action. LC 83-3937. 264p. (C). 1984. pap. text 18.50 (*0-8147-7392-3*) NYU Pr.

Rogers, David & Fielding, Henry. Tom Jones, 1-Act. 48p. 1964. pap. 3.95 (*0-87129-763-9*, T54) Dramatic Pub.

Rogers, David & Keyes, Daniel. Flowers for Algernon: One Act. 1969. pap. 3.95 (*0-87129-387-0*, F28) Dramatic Pub.

Rogers, David & Scoppettone, Sandra. The Late Great Me. 127p. (YA). 1977. pap. 5.50 (*0-87129-700-0*, L38) Dramatic Pub.

Rogers, David, et al. Twelve Dancing Princesses - Musical. 1976. 5.95 (*0-87129-516-4*, T04) Dramatic Pub.

Rogers, David, jt. auth. see Keyes, Daniel.

Rogers, David, jt. ed. see Hawley, Willis D.

Rogers, David B. Prehistoric Man of the Santa Barbara Coast. fac. ed. (Santa Barbara Museum of Natural History Ser.). (Illus.). 547p. (C). 1929. reprint ed. pap. text 56.25 (*1-55567-802-5*) Coyote Press.

Rogers, David B. Prehistoric Man of the Santa Barbara Coast. LC 76-43812. reprint ed. 74.50 (*0-404-15667-3*) AMS Pr.

Rogers, David E., ed. see Ryan, Will G.

***Rogers, David F.** An Introduction to Nurbs: With Historical Perspective. LC 00-39119. (Illus.). 2001. pap. write for info. (*1-55860-669-6*) Morgan Kaufmann.

Rogers, David F. Laminar Flow Analysis. (Illus.). 436p. (C). 1992. text 130.00 (*0-521-41152-1*) Cambridge U Pr.

— Procedural Elements for Computer Graphics. (C). 1985. text 54.50 (*0-07-053534-5*) McGraw.

— Procedural Elements for Computer Graphics. 2nd ed. LC 97-13301. 752p. 1999. 64.06 (*0-07-053548-5*) McGraw.

Rogers, David F. & Adams, J. Alan. Mathematical Elements for Computer Graphics. 2nd ed. 512p. (C). 1989. pap. 54.69 (*0-07-053530-2*) McGraw.

Rogers, David F. & Earnshaw, Rae A., eds. State-of-the-Art in Computer Graphics: Aspects of Visualization. LC 93-33016. 1993. 219.00 (*0-387-94164-9*) Spr-Verlag.

Rogers, David F., ed. see Bechtolsheim, Stephen V.

Rogers, David F., ed. see Scheaffer, Richard L., et al.

Rogers, David J. Waging Business Warfare. 448p. 1988. mass mkt. 4.95 (*0-8217-2510-6*, Zebra Kensgtn) Kensgtn Pub Corp.

Rogers, David J. & Rogers, Constance. Woody Ornamentals for Deep South Gardens. (Illus.). 325p. 1991. 34.95 (*0-8130-1011-X*) U Press Fla.

Rogers, David L. & Whetten, David A. Interorganizational Coordination: Theory, Research, & Implementation. LC 82-142. 214p. 1982. reprint ed. pap. 66.40 (*0-608-00177-5*, 206095900006) Bks Demand.

Rogers, David S., jt. ed. see Davies, R. L.

Rogers, Dawn, jt. ed. see McFadden, E.

Rogers, Debi, jt. auth. see Rogers, Mike.

Rogers, Deborah D. Ann Radcliffe: A Bio-Bibliography, 4. LC 95-41982. (Bio-Bibliographies in World Literature Ser.: No. 4). 224p. 1996. lib. bdg. 57.95 (*0-313-28379-6*, Greenwood Pr) Greenwood.

— Bookseller As Rogue: John Almon & the Politics of Eighteenth-Century Publishing. (American University Studies: English Language & Literature: Ser. IV, Vol. 28). XVIII, 153p. 1986. text 28.50 (*0-8204-0221-4*) P Lang Pubng.

Rogers, Deborah D., ed. The Critical Response to Ann Radcliffe, 7. LC 93-28048. (Critical Responses in Arts & Letters Ser.: No. 7). 320p. 1993. lib. bdg. 65.00 (*0-313-28031-2*, Greenwood Pr) Greenwood.

Rogers, Delores J. The American Empirical Movement in Theology. LC 89-77291. (American University Studies: Theology & Religion: Ser. VII, Vol. 70). VIII, 248p. (C). 1990. text 47.50 (*0-8204-1218-X*) P Lang Pubng.

Rogers, Denis. Second Harvest. Davis, Owen, Sr., ed. LC 81-84333. 196p. (Orig.). 1981. 12.95 (*0-935400-07-9*); pap. 7.95 (*0-935400-08-7*) News & Observer.

Rogers, Denise, compiled by. Selected Bibliography of Books & Articles on Censorship (1950-1983) LC 83-204879. (Washington University Law Library Bibliography Ser.: No. 4). vi, 22p. (Orig.). 1983. pap. text 8.00 (*0-317-00753-X*) Wash U Law Lib.

Rogers, Dennis. Crossroads. LC 84-61699. 206p. 1985. 12.95 (*0-935400-10-9*); 7.95 (*0-935400-11-7*) News & Observer.

— It's Bad News When the Bartender Cries. Munger, Guy, ed. LC 88-62088. (Illus.). 208p. 1988. 12.95 (*0-935400-14-1*) News & Observer.

— Site Guides: Costa Rica & Panama: A Guide to the Best Birding Locations. (Illus.). 183p. (Orig.). 1996. pap. 19.95 (*0-9637765-6-8*) Cinclus Pubns.

— Site Guides: Venezuela: A Guide to the Best Birding Locations. 54p. 1993. spiral bd. 14.50 (*0-9637765-0-9*) Cinclus Pubns.

Rogers, Diane L. The Economic Effects of Comprehensive Tax Reform. (Illus.). 78p. (C). 1998. pap. text 25.00 (*0-7881-4630-0*) DIANE Pub.

Rogers, Diane L., jt. auth. see Fullerton, Don.

Rogers, Dick, jt. auth. see Gallagher, Lyn.

Rogers, Dilwyn J., ed. A Bibliography of African Ecology: A Geographically & Topically Classified List of Books & Articles, 6. LC 78-19935. (Special Bibliographic Ser.: No. 6). 499p. 1979. lib. bdg. 115.00 (*0-313-20552-3*, RAE/, Greenwood Pr) Greenwood.

Rogers, Don, jt. auth. see Sloboda, John A.

Rogers, Don, jt. ed. see Branthwaite, Alan.

Rogers, Donald B., ed. Urban Church Education. LC 89-4024. 213p. 1989. pap. 21.95 (*0-89135-070-5*) Religious Educ.

Rogers, Donald B., jt. auth. see Coe, James M.

Rogers, Donald W., ed. Voting & the Spirit of American Democracy: Essays on the History of Voting & Voting Rights in America. 136p. 1992. text 17.50 (*0-252-01918-0*); pap. text 10.95 (*0-252-06247-7*) U of Ill Pr.

Rogers, Donna C., jt. auth. see Mayer, Susan B.

Rogers, Donna W. Faces in the Crowd. 72p. 1998. pap. 12.50 (*0-9668052-0-8*) GoForth Enters.

Rogers, Dorothy. How to Market Your College Degree. (Illus.). 168p. 1993. pap. 12.95 (*0-8442-4163-6*, 41636, VGM Career) NTC Contemp Pub Co.

***Rogers, Dorothy & Bettinson, Craig.** Market Your College Degree. (Here's How Ser.). 168p. 1999. pap. 14.95 (*0-8442-2623-8*) NTC Contemp Pub Co.

Rogers, Douglas G., ed. Many Marriages by Sherwood Anderson. LC 78-2353. 316p. 1978. 31.00 (*0-8108-1122-7*) Scarecrow.

Rogers, E. Earle, ed. see Goodspeed, M. Hill.

Rogers, E. T. & Owens, D. H. Stability Analysis for Linear Repetitive Processes. (Lecture Notes in Control & Information Sciences: Vol. 175). (Illus.). 201p. 1992. 63.95 (*0-387-55264-2*) Spr-Verlag.

Rogers, E. W. Answers to Bible Problems. 1996. 15.99 (*0-946351-00-7*, Pub. by John Ritchie) Loizeaux.

Rogers, Earl, jt. ed. see Morrow, John H., Jr.

Rogers, Earl M. & Rogers, Susan H. The American Farm Crisis: An Annotated Bibliography. LC 89-31667. 162p. 1989. text 10.00 (*0-8240-7243-X*) Garland.

Rogers, Edgar. A Handy Guide to Jewish Coins. LC 77-77252. (Illus.). 1990. reprint ed. lib. bdg. 35.00 (*0-915262-14-2*) S J Durst.

Rogers, Edith R. The Perilous Hunt: Symbols in Hispanic & European Balladry. LC 79-4010. (Studies in Romance Languages: No. 22). 187p. reprint ed. pap. 58.00 (*0-7837-5787-5*, 204545300006) Bks Demand.

***Rogers, Edmund.** Circle of Loyalty. LC 99-91802. 2000. 25.00 (*0-7388-1266-8*); pap. 18.00 (*0-7388-1267-6*) Xlibris Corp.

Rogers, Edward. An Essay on Some General Principles of Political Economy. LC 74-11496. (Reprints of Economic Classics Ser.). viii, 72p. 1976. reprint ed. 25.00 (*0-678-01247-4*) Kelley.

Rogers, Elizabeth & Stoval, Iris. Beginning Chemistry: A Workbook to Use in the Laboratory. 7th ed. 1997. spiral bd. 10.80 (*0-87563-499-0*) Stipes.

Rogers, Elizabeth A., jt. auth. see Piotrowski, Christine M.

Rogers, Elizabeth B., et al. Rebuilding Central Park: A Management & Restoration Plan. (Illus.). 176p. 1987. 40.00 (*0-262-18127-4*) MIT Pr.

Rogers, Elizabeth F. Peter Lombard & the Sacramental System. 250p. 1976. reprint ed. lib. bdg. 19.50 (*0-915172-22-4*) Richwood Pub.

Rogers, Elizabeth F., ed. The Archives of British History & Culture, Vols. I-II: Letters of Sir John Hackett, 1526-1534. LC 70-105970. 419p. 1974. 15.00 (*0-87012-089-1*) West Va U Pr.

An Asterisk (*) at the beginning of an entry indicates that the title is appearing for the first time.

— Letters of Sir John Hackett, 2 vols. LC 70-105570. (Archives of British History & Culture Ser). 419p. 1971. 15.00 (*0-937058-05-X*) West Va U Pr.

Rogers, Elizabeth F., ed. see More, Thomas.

Rogers, Elizabeth S. & Rogers, Timothy J., eds. In Retrospect: Essays on Latin American Literature (In Memory of Willis Knapp Jones) LC 86-61056. 195p. 1987. 20.00 (*0-938972-10-3*) Spanish Lit Pubns.

Rogers, Ellen. The Lone Wolf. (Stolen Moments Ser.). 1993. pap. 1.99 (*0-373-83287-7*, 1-83287-2) Harlequin Bks.

Rogers, Elwin. Labyrinths of Speculation. LC 97-92733. (Illus.). 68p. 1997. pap. write for info. (*1-57579-096-3*) Pine Hill Pr.

Rogers, Emma, ed. Life & Letters of William Barton Rogers, 2 vols., Set. (Illus.). 874p. 1995. reprint ed. lib. bdg. 97.50 (*0-8328-4502-7*) Higginson Bk Co.

Rogers, Emma, jt. auth. see Rogers, Paul.

Rogers, Eric M. Astronomy for the Inquiring Mind: The Growth & Use of Theory in Science. LC 81-47286. (Illus.). 173p. reprint ed. pap. 53.70 (*0-8357-2921-4*, 203916100011) Bks Demand.

***Rogers, Ernest E.** Connecticut's Naval Office at New London During the War of the American Revolution. (Illus.). 276p. 1999. reprint ed. pap. 31.00 (*0-7884-1239-6*, R522) Heritage Bk.

Rogers, Eugene. Sexuality & the Christian Body: The Way of the Body into the Triune God. LC 98-33149. 300p. 1999. 59.95 (*0-631-21069-5*); pap. 26.95 (*0-631-21070-9*) Blackwell Pubs.

Rogers, Eugene F., Jr. Thomas Aquinas & Karl Barth: Sacred Doctrine & the Natural Knowledge of God. LC 94-42830. (Revisions Ser.: Vol. 13). (C). 1996. text 34.95 (*0-268-01889-8*) U of Notre Dame Pr.

— Thomas Aquinas & Karl Barth: Sacred Doctrine & the Natural Knowledge of God. LC 94-42830. (Revisions: A Series of Books on Ethics: No. 13). 266p. 1999. pap. 24.00 (*0-268-04208-X*) U of Notre Dame Pr.

Rogers, Evan. A Funny Old Quist: Memories of a Gamekeeper. 288p. 1986. pap. 14.95 (*0-907871-61-5*) Hippocrene Bks.

Rogers, Evelyn. Betrayal. 400p. 1997. mass mkt. 5.99 (*0-8439-4262-2*, Leisure Bks) Dorchester Pub Co.

— Crown of Glory. (Texas Empires Ser.). 400p. 1998. mass mkt. 5.99 (*0-8439-4403-X*, Leisure Bks) Dorchester Pub Co.

— The Forever Bride. 368p. (Orig.). 1997. mass mkt. 5.50 (*0-8439-4177-4*) Dorchester Pub Co.

***Rogers, Evelyn.** Golden Man. 400p. 1999. mass mkt. 5.99 (*0-505-52295-0*, Love Spell) Dorchester Pub Co.

Rogers, Evelyn. Hot Temper. 400p. (Orig.). 1997. mass mkt. 5.99 (*0-8439-4329-7*, Leisure Bks) Dorchester Pub Co.

— Lone Star, 1. (Texas Empires Ser.). 400p. 1999. mass mkt. 5.99 (*0-8439-4533-8*) Dorchester Pub Co.

***Rogers, Evelyn.** Longhorn. (Texas Empires Ser.). 400p. 2000. mass mkt. 5.99 (*0-8439-4679-2*, Leisure Bks) Dorchester Pub Co.

— Second Opinion. 400p. 1999. mass mkt. 5.99 (*0-505-52332-9*, Pub. by Dorchester Pub Co) CMG.

Rogers, Evelyn. Sweet Vidalia Onions/Blue Ribbon Recipes. 122p. 1995. pap. 8.95 (*0-9614318-3-0*) Rogers Cookbooks.

***Rogers, Evelyn.** Wicked. 448p. (Orig.). 2000. pap. 5.50 (*0-505-52359-0*, Love Spell) Dorchester Pub Co.

Rogers, Evelyn C. Sweet Vidalia Onions: Blue Ribbon Recipes/Fried Onion Blossoms. 2nd rev. ed. Butler, Helen, ed. LC 86-90484. Orig. Title: Sweet Vidalia Onions Blue Ribbon Recipes. (Illus.). 120p. 1999. pap. write for info. (*0-9614318-4-9*, 9.19128786224) Rogers Cookbooks.

Rogers, Everett, et al, eds. Media Revolution in America & Western Europe. LC 84-21680. (Communication & Information Science Ser.). 352p. 1985. text 78.50 (*0-89391-258-1*) Ablx Pub.

Rogers, Everett M. Diffusion of Innovations. 4th ed. 1995. 49.95 (*0-02-874074-2*); pap. 32.95 (*0-02-926671-8*) Free Pr.

— The High Technology of Silicon Valley. (Urban Studies: No. 4). (Illus.). 35p. (Orig.). 1985. pap. 5.00 (*0-913749-02-8*) U MD Urban Stud.

— A History of Communication: A Bibliographic Approach. 550p. 1994. 35.00 (*0-02-926735-8*) Free Pr.

— History of Communication Study. 1997. pap. 18.95 (*0-684-84001-4*) S&S Trade.

Rogers, Everett M. & Steinfatt, Thomas M. Intercultural Communication. LC 99-192680. (Illus.). 292p. (C). 1998. pap. text 21.95 (*1-57766-032-3*) Waveland Pr.

Rogers, Everett M., jt. auth. see Gibson, David V.

Rogers, Everett M., jt. auth. see Singhal, Arvind.

Rogers, Everett M., jt. ed. see Backer, Thomas E.

Rogers, Everett M., ed. see Schramm, Wilbur L.

Rogers, Everette M., jt. auth. see Dearing, James W.

***Rogers, Fairman.** Manual on Coaching. 5th ed. 5p. 2000. reprint ed. 60.00 (*1-880499-09-6*) Carriage Museum.

Rogers, Floyd. Hangman's Gulch. large type ed. (Linford Western Library). 1991. pap. 16.99 (*0-7089-7124-5*) Ulverscroft.

Rogers, Forest. Pedal Steel Guitar Licks for Guitar. 1995. pap. text 15.95 incl. audio compact disk (*1-57424-019-6*) Centerstream Pub.

Rogers, Forrest J. & Dewitt, Hugh E., eds. Strongly Coupled Plasma Physics. (NATO ASI Series B, Physics: Vol. 154). (Illus.). 610p. 1987. 135.00 (*0-306-42581-5*, Plenum Trade) Perseus Pubng.

Rogers, Francis. Some Famous Singers of the 19th Century. Farkas, Andrew, ed. LC 76-29963. (Opera Biographies Ser.). (Illus.). 1977. reprint ed. lib. bdg. 18.95 (*0-405-09703-4*) Ayer.

Rogers, Francis M. Atlantic Islanders of the Azores & Madeiras. LC 78-72837. (Illus.). 1979. 17.50 (*0-8158-0373-7*) Chris Mass.

— The Quest for Eastern Christians: Travels & Rumor in the Age of Discovery. LC 62-18138. 233p. reprint ed. pap. 72.30 (*0-608-18670-8*, 205590100039) Bks Demand.

Rogers, Francis M. & Haberly, David T. Brazil, Portugal, & Other Portuguese-Speaking Lands: A List of Books Primarily in English. LC 68-7564. (Texts from the Romance Languages Ser.: No. 4). 75p. (C). 1968. pap. 1.95 (*0-674-08050-5*) HUP.

Rogers, Frank C. The Great Saltmine & Hifwip Direct Phonics Reading Program. 50p. 1987. ring bd. 10.00 (*0-9616691-0-1*) Parents As Tchrs.

Rogers, Franklin R. Occidental Ideographs: Image, Sequence, & Literary History. LC 89-45972. 288p. 1991. 39.50 (*0-8387-5179-2*) Bucknell U Pr.

— Painting & Poetry: Forms, Mataphor & the Language of Literature. LC 83-46175. (Illus.). 248p. 1986. 42.50 (*0-8387-5077-X*) Bucknell U Pr.

Rogers, Franklin R., ed. see Twain, Mark, pseud.

Rogers, Fred. Extraordinary Friends. LC 99-17615. (Let's Talk about It Ser.). (Illus.). 32p. (J). (ps-3). 2000. 15.99 (*0-399-23146-3*, G P Putnam) Peng Put Young Read.

***Rogers, Fred.** Extraordinary Friends. LC 99-17615. (Illus.). 32p. (J). (ps-3). 2000. pap. 6.99 (*0-698-11861-8*) Putnam Pub Group.

Rogers, Fred. Friends with Special Needs. LC 97-32970. (Let's Talk about It Ser.). (Illus.). (J). 1999. pap. 7.95 (*0-399-23147-1*) Putnam Pub Group.

***Rogers, Fred.** The Giving Box. 2000. 12.95 (*0-7624-0825-1*) Running Pr.

Rogers, Fred. Going to the Hospital. (Illus.). 32p. (J). (ps-1). 1997. pap. 5.99 (*0-698-11574-0*, PapStar) Peng Put Young Read.

— Going to the Potty. (Illus.). 32p. (J). (ps-1). 1997. pap. 5.99 (*0-698-11575-9*, PapStar) Peng Put Young Read.

— Let's Talk About: Stepfamilies. LC 96-34176. (Let's Talk about It Ser.). (Illus.). 32p. 1997. 15.95 (*0-399-23144-7*, G P Putnam) Peng Put Young Read.

— Let's Talk About: Stepfamilies. LC HQ759.92.R64 1997. (Let's Talk about It Ser.). (Illus.). 32p. (J). 1997. pap. 7.95 (*0-399-23145-5*, G P Putnam) Peng Put Young Read.

— Let's Talk about It: Adoption. LC 92-15607. (Mister Rogers' Neighborhood Ser.). (Illus.). 32p. (J). (ps-1). 1998. pap. 6.99 (*0-698-11625-9*, PapStar) Peng Put Young Read.

— Let's Talk about It: Divorce. LC 94-2312. (Illus.). 32p. (J). (ps-3). 1996. 15.95 (*0-399-22449-1*, G P Putnam) Peng Put Young Read.

— Let's Talk about It: Divorce. (Mister Rogers' Neighborhood Ser.). (Illus.). 32p. (J). (ps-3). 1998. pap. 6.99 (*0-698-11670-4*, PapStar) Peng Put Young Read.

— Making Friends. (Illus.). 32p. (J). (ps-1). 1996. pap. 6.99 (*0-698-11409-4*, PapStar) Peng Put Young Read.

— The New Baby. LC 84-26210. (Illus.). 32p. (J). (ps-3). 1996. pap. 5.99 (*0-698-11366-7*, PapStar) Peng Put Young Read.

***Rogers, Fred.** Special Friends. (Let's Talk about It Ser.). (Illus.). (J). 2000. 12.44 (*0-606-18417-1*) Turtleback.

— Stepfamilies: Let's Talk About it. pap. 5.95 (*0-698-11665-8*) Putnam Pub Group.

Rogers, Fred. When a Pet Dies. (First Experience Bks.). (Illus.). 32p. (J). (ps-3). 1998. pap. 5.99 (*0-698-11666-6*, PapStar) Peng Put Young Read.

Rogers, Fred & Head, Barry. Mister Rogers Talks with Parents. 320p. 1993. pap. 7.95 (*0-7935-2642-6*, 00815004) H Leonard.

Rogers, Fred B. Montgomery & the Portsmouth. LC 90-20215. (Portsmouth Marine Society Ser.: Vol. 17). (Illus.). 176p. 1990. reprint ed. 25.00 (*0-915819-16-3*, 17) Portsmouth Marine Soc.

Rogers, G. A., ed. Locke's Philosophy: Content & Context. 272p. 1994. 55.00 (*0-19-824076-7*) OUP.

— Locke's Philosophy: Content & Context. 270p. 1997. reprint ed. pap. text 24.00 (*0-19-823684-0*) OUP.

Rogers, G. A., ed. Leviathan: Contemporary Responses to the Political Theory of Thomas Hobbes. (Key Issues Ser.). 317p. 1995. 72.00 (*1-85506-407-3*); pap. 24.00 (*1-85506-406-5*) Bks Intl VA.

Rogers, G. A., et al, eds. The Cambridge Platonists in Philosophical Context Politics, Metaphysics & Religion. LC 97-10318. 1997. text 167.00 (*0-7923-4530-4*) Kluwer Academic.

Rogers, G. A., intro. Henry More: Major Philosophical Works, Set, Vols. 1-9. (Cambridge Platonists Ser.). 3880p. 1996. 1100.00 (*1-85506-427-8*) Bks Intl VA.

Rogers, G. A. & Ryan, Alan, eds. Perspectives on Thomas Hobbes. (Mind Association Occasional Ser.). 218p. 1991. pap. text 27.00 (*0-19-823914-9*) OUP.

Rogers, G. A. & Tomaselli, Sylvana, eds. The Philosophical Canon in the Seventeenth & Eighteenth Centuries: Essays in Honor of John W. Yolton. LC 96-16388. 240p. (C). 1996. 65.00 (*1-878822-64-0*) Univ Rochester Pr.

Rogers, G. A., ed. see Locke, John.

Rogers, G. Aaron. The Messianic Jewish Book of Why. LC 97-49086. 110p. (Orig.). 1996. pap. 9.95 (*0-89036-631-4*) Liahona Pub Trust.

— The Messianic Jewish Book of Why?, Vol. 1. 126p. 1997. pap. 9.95 (*1-890828-00-9*, 00-9, Pub. by Camden Ct) Origin Bk Sales.

— The Messianic Jewish Book of Why?, Vol. 2. LC 97-49086. 160p. 1997. pap. 9.95 (*1-890828-05-X*, 05-X, Pub. by Camden Ct) Origin Bk Sales.

Rogers, G. F. Engineering Thermodynamics. 4th ed. 736p. (C). 1996. pap. text 59.95 (*0-582-04566-5*) Addison-Wesley.

Rogers, G. F. & Mayhew, Y. R. Thermodynamic & Transport Properties of Fluids: SI Units. 5th ed. 30p. 1995. pap. 16.95 (*0-631-19703-6*) Blackwell Pubs.

Rogers, G. G. Colloquial Nepali. (C). 1991. reprint ed. 16.00 (*81-206-0634-5*, Pub. by Asian Educ Servs) S Asia.

Rogers, G. K. Gleasonia, Henriquezia & Platycarpum. LC 84-19080. (Flora Neotropica Monographs: No. 39). (Illus.). 135p. 1984. 25.00 (*0-89327-257-4*) NY Botanical.

Rogers, G. S., jt. auth. see Nguyen, H. T.

Rogers, Gaj. Early Responses to Hobbes, 6 vols. 1699p. (C). 1997. text, boxed set 745.00 (*0-415-14760-3*) Routledge.

Rogers-Gallagher, Kim. Astrology for the Light Side of the Brain. 224p. (Orig.). 1995. pap. 12.95 (*0-935127-35-6*) ACS Pubns.

— Astrology for the Light Side of the Future. 320p. 1998. pap. 14.95 (*0-935127-45-3*) ACS Pubns.

Rogers-Gardner, Barbara. Jung & Shakespeare: Hamlet, Othello, & the Tempest. LC 91-27361. (Chiron Monographs: Vol.7). 128p. (Orig.). 1992. pap. 17.95 (*0-933029-55-1*) Chiron Pubns.

Rogers, Garry F. Then & Now: A Photographic History of Vegetation Change in the Central Great Basin Desert. LC 82-4825. (Illus.). 164p. (Orig.). reprint ed. pap. 50.90 (*0-7837-6865-6*, 204669500003) Bks Demand.

Rogers, Garry F., et al. Bibliography of Repeat Photography for Evaluating Landscape Change. LC 84-23437. (Illus.). 215p. reprint ed. pap. 66.70 (*0-7837-6867-2*, 204669700003) Bks Demand.

Rogers, Gay A. American Silver Thimbles. LC 88-82066. (Illus.). 224p. 1989. 47.95 (*1-869812-03-4*) Needlewrk Unltd.

— An Illustrated History of Needlework Tools. (Illus.). 243p. 1989. reprint ed. 45.00 (*0-9622310-0-2*) Needlewrk Unltd.

***Rogers, Gayle.** Gladyce with a C. LC 99-74580. 368p. 2000. 25.95 (*1-57197-194-7*) Pentland Pr.

***Rogers, George & Holder, Ayanda.** The Grasses of Barbados (Poaceae) (Illus.). 77p. 1999. pap. text. write for info. (*1-889878-03-0*) Botanical Res.

Rogers, George C., Jr. Charleston in the Age of the Pinckneys. LC 68-31371. (Illus.). xvi, 202p. 1980. pap. 10.95 (*0-87249-297-4*) U of SC Pr.

— Generations of Lawyers: A History of the South Carolina Bar (1690-1990) (Illus.). 367p. 1992. write for info. (*0-945036-01-9*) SC Bar Found.

— The History of Georgetown County, South Carolina. (Illus.). xviii, 566p. 1995. reprint ed. 37.50 (*0-87152-443-0*) Reprint.

— A Social Portrait of the South at the Turn of the Eighteenth Century. 14p. 1988. reprint ed. pap. 4.00 (*0-944026-03-6*) Am Antiquarian.

Rogers, George C., Jr. & Taylor, C. James. A South Carolina Chronology, 1497-1992. 2nd ed. LC 93-27306. 188p. (C). 1994. pap. text 12.95 (*0-87249-971-5*) U of SC Pr.

Rogers, George C., ed. see Laurens, Henry.

Rogers, George E., jt. auth. see Anderson, Judy C.

Rogers, George L. Mac & Zach from Hackensack. (Illus.). 32p. (J). (gr. k-6). 1992. pap. 4.95 (*0-938399-06-3*); lib. bdg. 12.95 (*0-938399-07-1*) Acorn Pub MN.

Rogers, George L., ed. see Franklin, Benjamin.

Rogers, George W. Alaska in Transition: The Southeast Region. LC 59-14895. 398p. reprint ed. pap. 123.40 (*0-8357-5293-3*, 205211000034) Bks Demand.

— Change in Alaska: People, Petroleum & Politics. (ENG.). 213p. 1970. pap. text 8.00 (*1-57833-013-0*) Todd Commns.

Rogers, George W. Change in Alaska: People, Petroleum & Politics. LC 75-11734. 213p. 1970. 7.95 (*0-912006-40-4*) U of Alaska Pr.

Rogers, Gerald S. Matrix Derivatives. LC 80-24248. (Lecture Notes in Statistics Ser.). 221p. reprint ed. pap. 68.60 (*0-7837-3548-0*, 204338500009) Bks Demand.

Rogers, Gerhild B. Das Romanwerk von Ingeborg Drewitz. (Studies in Modern German Literature: Vol. 26). 256p. (C). 1989. text 37.00 (*0-8204-0715-1*) P Lang Pubng.

Rogers Gessert, Kate. The Beautiful Food Garden: Creative Landscaping with Vegetables, Herbs, Fruits & Flowers. Burns, Deborah, ed. LC 86-46162. (Illus.). 272p. 1987. pap. 12.95 (*0-88266-461-1*, Garden Way Pub) Storey Bks.

Rogers, Ginger. Ginger: My Story. large type ed. LC 92-15294. (General Ser.). 608p. 1992. pap. 16.95 (*0-8161-5437-6*, G K Hall Lrg Type) Mac Lib Ref.

Rogers, Glenn. The San Antonio Spurs Basketball Team. LC 96-46527. (Great Sports Teams Ser.). (Illus.). 48p. (YA). (gr. 4-10). 1997. lib. bdg. 18.95 (*0-89490-797-2*) Enslow Pubs.

Rogers, Glenn. The San Antonio Spurs Basketball Team. LC 96-46527. (Great Sports Teams Ser.). (Illus.). 48p. (YA). (gr. 4-10). 1997. pap. 9.95 (*0-7660-1753-2*) Enslow Pubs.

Rogers, Glenn C. Patterns & Themes. 4th ed. LC 99-16860. 1999. pap. 21.95 (*0-534-26190-6*) Wadsworth Pub.

Rogers, Glenn C., jt. auth. see Rogers, Judy R.

Rogers, Glenn T. Medical Dictionary. 2nd ed. (ENG & SPA.). 1997. pap. text. write for info. (*0-07-053580-9*); pap. text. write for info. (*0-07-055680-6*) McGraw.

Rogers, Glenn T., ed. English-Spanish/Spanish-English Medical Dictionary. 2nd ed. LC 96-50377. (ENG & SPA.). 272p. 1997. pap. text 19.95 (*0-07-053680-5*) McGraw-Hill HPD.

Rogers, Gloree. Love: or A Reasonable Facsimile. 2nd ed. 160p. (Orig.). 1989. pap. 10.00 (*0-932112-27-7*) Carolina Wren.

Rogers, Godfrey, tr. see Lepetit, Bernard.

Rogers, Godfrey, tr. see Rioux, Jean-Pierre.

Rogers, Gordon, ed. see Wright, Peter.

Rogers, Greg. Impact. 250p. (Orig.). 1997. 19.95 (*0-89036-575-X*); pap. 9.95 (*0-89036-639-X*) Liahona Pub Trust.

Rogers, Gregg, ed. see Alpiar, Hal.

Rogers, Gregg, ed. see Costain, Lynne R. & Moawad, Karen.

Rogers, Gregg, ed. see Fish, Raymond M., et al.

Rogers, Gregg, ed. see Goyette, Richert E.

Rogers, Gregg, ed. see Isler, Charlotte.

Rogers, Gregg, ed. see Lorenzini, Jean A. & Lorenzini-Ley, Laura.

Rogers, Gregg, ed. see Perez-Sabido, Jesus.

Rogers, Gregg, ed. see Prather, Stephen E., et al.

Rogers, Gregory. Apostolic Succession. 42p. 1996. pap. 2.95 (*0-9622713-7-3*, APS) Conciliar Pr.

Rogers, Gregory F. Framework-Based Software Development. LC 96-39678. 400p. (C). 1997. pap. 59.00 (*0-13-533365-2*) P-H.

Rogers, Guy, jt. auth. see Rogers, Nell.

Rogers, Guy, jt. ed. see Lefkowitz, Mary R.

Rogers, H. Reaching for the Crescent Moon. 8.50 (*1-85792-123-2*, Pub. by Christian Focus) Spring Arbor Dist.

Rogers, H., ed. see Howe, John.

Rogers, H. C. A History of Artillery. 1977. pap. 4.95 (*0-8065-0597-4*, Citadel Pr) Carol Pub Group.

***Rogers, H. C. B.** The Confederates & Federals at War. 2000. pap. 18.95 (*1-58097-031-1*, 970031) Combined Pub.

Rogers, H. Kendall. Before the Revisionist Controversy: Kautsky, Bernstein, & the Meaning of Marxism, 1895-1898. LC 92-29718. (Modern European History Ser.). (Illus.). 496p. 1992. text 35.00 (*0-8153-0674-1*) Garland.

***Rogers, Hal.** Ambulances. LC 99-26590. (Illus.). 24p. (J). 1999. lib. bdg. 19.93 (*1-56766-655-8*) Childs World.

— Cherry Pickers. LC 99-26591. (Illus.). 24p. (J). 1999. lib. bdg. 19.93 (*1-56766-650-7*) Childs World.

— Combines. LC 99-89472. 2000. lib. bdg. write for info. (*1-56766-754-6*) Childs World.

Rogers, Hal. Cranes. LC 99-20857. (Illus.). 24p. 1999. lib. bdg. 19.93 (*1-56766-651-5*) Childs World.

— Earthmovers. LC 99-20859. (Illus.). 24p. 1999. lib. bdg. 19.93 (*1-56766-652-3*) Childs World.

— Generals. LC 92-9478. (Football Heroes Ser.). 48p. (J). (gr. 3-8). 1992. lib. bdg. 15.95 (*0-86593-154-2*) Rourke Corp.

— Graders. LC 99-20858. (Illus.). 24p. 1999. lib. bdg. 19.93 (*1-56766-653-1*) Childs World.

***Rogers, Hal.** Milking Machines: By Hal Rogers. LC 99-89470. 2000. lib. bdg. write for info. (*1-56766-753-8*) Childs World.

— Plows. LC 99-89469. 2000. lib. bdg. write for info. (*1-56766-755-4*) Childs World.

— Rescue Helicopters. LC 99-20856. (Illus.). 24p. (J). 1999. lib. bdg. 19.93 (*1-56766-657-4*) Childs World.

Rogers, Hal. Skiing. LC 93-23410. (Pro-Am Sports Ser.). 48p. (J). (gr. 3-8). 1993. lib. bdg. 17.95 (*0-86593-348-0*) Rourke Corp.

***Rogers, Hal.** Snowplows. LC 00-23085. (Illus.). (YA). 2000. lib. bdg. write for info. (*1-56766-756-2*) Childs World.

— Tow Trucks. LC 99-28597. (Illus.). 24p. (J). 1999. lib. bdg. 19.93 (*1-56766-658-2*) Childs World.

— Tractors. LC 99-89468. 2000. lib. bdg. write for info. (*1-56766-752-X*) Childs World.

Rogers, Hal, jt. auth. see Reinhardt, Ed.

Rogers, Harrell R., Jr. & Nagel, Stuart S., eds. Public Policy & Social Institutions: A Multi-Volume Treatise. LC 84-9680. (Public Policy Studies: Vol. 1). 375p. 1984. 73.25 (*0-89232-377-9*) Jai Pr.

Rogers, Hartley. Multivariable Calculus with Vectors. LC 98-3635. 789p. 1998. 89.33 (*0-13-605643-1*) P-H.

— Problems Book: Engineering Drawing & Graphic Technology. 13th ed. (Illus.). 256p. (C). 1986. pap., wbk. ed. 40.00 (*0-07-053491-8*) McGraw.

Rogers, Hartley, Jr. Theory of Recursive Functions & Effective Computability. 504p. (Orig.). 1987. pap. text 27.00 (*0-262-68052-1*) MIT Pr.

Rogers, Heather, et al. Experience RPG IV CD-ROM Tutorial. (IBM Centre for Advanced Studies Ser.). 320p. (gr. 10 up). 1998. pap. 39.95 (*1-889671-22-3*) Advice Pr.

Rogers, Heather, jt. auth. see Nicol, Andrew.

***Rogers, Hedda.** Poems in the Afternoon. 56p. 2000. pap. write for info. (*0-7541-0952-6*, Pub. by Minerva Pr) Unity Dist.

Rogers, Helen P. Alternatives. 600p. (C). 1992. pap. 19.95 (*0-915915-26-X*) Wellington Pubns.

— The American Deficit-Fulfillment of a Prophecy? "America Will Spend Herself Out of Existence?" (Lenin 1917) LC 85-52235. 244p. 1988. 17.95 (*0-915915-07-3*) Wellington Pubns.

— The Deficit: Twelve Steps to Ease the Crisis. LC 87-51350. 465p. 1988. 17.95 (*0-915915-06-5*) Wellington Pubns.

— The Election Process: A Grass Roots Call for Reform. LC 87-51351. 280p. 1988. 12.95 (*0-915915-05-7*) Wellington Pubns.

— Everyone's Guide to Financial Planning. LC 83-51159. (Winn-When If Not Now Ser.). (Illus.). 325p. 1984. 12.95 (*0-915915-00-6*) Wellington Pubns.

— Social Security: An Idea Whose Time Has Passed. 2nd ed. LC 85-51900. (Illus.). 150p. 1986. pap. 6.95 (*0-915915-04-9*) Wellington Pubns.

— Taking a Stand on Civil Rights. LC 91-66842. 80p. (Orig.). 1991. pap. 6.95 (*0-915915-19-7*) Wellington Pubns.

— Taking a Stand on Education. LC 91-67469. 80p. (Orig.). 1991. pap. text 6.95 (*0-915915-11-1*) Wellington Pubns.

— Taking a Stand on Health Care. LC 91-75100. 64p. (Orig.). 1991. pap. 6.95 (*0-915915-08-1*) Wellington Pubns.

— Taking a Stand on Housing. LC 91-75106. 64p. (Orig.). 1991. pap. 6.95 (*0-915915-15-4*) Wellington Pubns.

— Taking a Stand on Our National Debt. LC 91-66841. 128p. (Orig.). 1991. pap. 6.95 (*0-915915-10-3*) Wellington Pubns.

R

— Taking a Stand on Poverty. LC 91-67468. 96p. (Orig.). 1991. pap. 6.95 (*0-915915-17-0*) Wellington Pubns.
— Taking a Stand on Regulation. LC 91-75101. 96p. (Orig.). 1991. pap. 6.95 (*0-915915-13-8*) Wellington Pubns.
— Taking a Stand on Taxes. LC 91-65692. 90p. (Orig.). 1991. pap. 6.95 (*0-915915-16-2*) Wellington Pubns.
— Taking a Stand on the Environment. LC 91-67467. 90p. (Orig.). 1991. pap. 6.95 (*0-915915-12-X*) Wellington Pubns.
— Taking a Stand on U. S. Competitiveness. LC 91-67462. 128p. (Orig.). 1991. pap. 6.95 (*0-915915-14-6*) Wellington Pubns.
Rogers, Helga, jt. auth. see Rogers, J. A.
***Rogers, Henry.** The Sounds of Language: An Introduction to Phonetics. LC 99-89810. (Learning about Language Ser.). 2000. pap. write for info. (*0-582-38182-7*) Longman.
Rogers, Henry C. Rogers' Rules for Success: Tips That Will Take You to the Top by One of America's Foremost Public Relations Experts. 304p. 1986. pap. 8.95 (*0-312-68830-X*) St Martin.
***Rogers, Henry J.** Silent War: Ministering to Those Trapped in Deception of Pornography. LC 99-69241. 240p. 2000. pap. 11.99 (*0-89221-491-0*) New Leaf.
Rogers, Henry W. The Law of Expert Testimony. 2nd enl. ed. xlvii, 542p. 1991. reprint ed. 47.50 (*0-8377-2544-5*, Rothman) W S Hein.
***Rogers, Hiram.** Exploring the Black Hills & Badlands: A Guide for Hikers, Cross-Country Skiers & Mountain Bikers. LC 98-56035. 208p. (Orig.). 1999. pap. 17.00 (*1-55566-240-4*) Johnson Bks.
Rogers, Horatio. Hadden's Journal & Orderly Books. LC 72-8761. (American Revolutionary Ser.). (Illus.). 704p. 1979. reprint ed. lib. bdg. 97.50 (*0-8398-1772-X*) Irvington.
Rogers, Howard, ed. China: 5,000 Years. (Guggenheim Museum Publication Ser.). (Illus.). 496p. 1998. 85.00 (*0-8109-6908-4*) Abrams.
Rogers, Howard & Lee, Sherman E. Masterworks of Ming & Qing Painting from the Forbidden City: A Color Catalogue of Paintings from the Palace Museum in Bejing, China. (Illus.). 224p. (Orig.). 1989. 70.00 (*0-9621061-2-7*); pap. 65.00 (*0-9621061-1-9*) Intl Arts Coun.
Rogers, Howard E. Yes Means No. 1950. pap. 5.25 (*0-8222-1286-2*) Dramatists Play.
Rogers, Howard J., ed. Congress of Arts & Science. LC 73-14177. (Perspectives in Social Inquiry Ser.). 342p. 1974. reprint ed. 24.95 (*0-405-05520-X*) Ayer.
Rogers, Hoyt. Poetics of Inconstancy: Etienne Durand & the End of Renaissance Verse. LC 98-4924. (North Carolina Studies in the Romance Languages & Literatures: Vol. 256). 1998. pap. 29.95 (*0-8078-9260-2*) U of NC Pr.
Rogers, Hugh F. Engineering Drawing & Graphic Technology. (C). 1993. pap., wbk. ed. 33.75 (*0-07-053541-8*) McGraw.
— Workbook in Graphics. (C). 1991. pap., wbk. ed. 20.63 (*0-07-053536-1*) McGraw.
Rogers, Ian T., jt. ed. see Oliver, J. David.
Rogers, Ingrid. Glimpses of China. fac. ed. LC 88-39447. (Illus.). 159p. (Orig.). 1994. pap. 49.30 (*0-7837-7349-8*, 204730200007) Bks Demand.
— Swords into Plowshares: A Collection of Plays about Peace & Social Justice. LC 82-24492. 281p. 1983. reprint ed. pap. 87.20 (*0-608-02168-7*, 206283700004) Bks Demand.
Rogers, J. Presbyterian Creeds: A Guide to the Book of Confessions. 1991. pap. 17.95 (*0-664-25496-9*) Westminster John Knox.
— World's Great Men of Color, Vol. I. (Illus.). 448p. 1996. per. 15.00 (*0-684-81581-8*) S&S Trade Pap.
— World's Great Men of Color, Vol. II. (Illus.). 592p. 1996. per. 15.00 (*0-684-81582-6*, Touchstone) S&S Trade Pap.
Rogers, J., jt. auth. see Smith, Norman D.
Rogers, J. A. Africa's Gift to America. rev. ed. LC 98-140653. (Illus.). 272p. 1962. 18.95 (*0-9602294-6-9*) H M Rogers.
— As Nature Leads. LC 89-61275. 1987. reprint ed. pap. text 14.95 (*0-933121-15-6*) Black Classic.
— Five Negro Presidents. 19p. 1965. pap. 2.25 (*0-9602294-8-5*) H M Rogers.
— From "Superman to Man" 19.95 (*0-8488-1462-2*) Amereon Ltd.
— From "Superman to Man" rev. ed. 132p. 1941. reprint ed. 12.95 (*0-9602294-4-2*) H M Rogers.
— Ku Klux Spirit. 36p. 1980. reprint ed. pap. 3.00 (*0-933121-06-7*) Black Classic.
— Nature Knows No Color Line. 242p. 1952. reprint ed. 13.95 (*0-9602294-5-0*) H M Rogers.
— The Real Facts about Ethiopia. (Illus.). 34p. 1982. reprint ed. pap. 3.00 (*0-933121-07-5*) Black Classic.
— Sex & Race, 3 vols. (Illus.). 1074p. 1994. 44.85 (*0-9602294-3-4*) H M Rogers.
— Sex & Race Vol. I: The Old World. (Illus.). 411p. 1940. reprint ed. 14.95 (*0-9602294-0-X*) H M Rogers.
— Sex & Race Vol. II: The New World. (Illus.). 304p. 1942. reprint ed. 14.95 (*0-9602294-1-8*) H M Rogers.
— Sex & Race Vol. III: Why White & Black Do Mate. (Illus.). 359p. 1944. reprint ed. 14.95 (*0-9602294-2-6*) H M Rogers.
— Your History. LC 89-61277. (Illus.). 100p. 1983. reprint ed. pap. 11.95 (*0-933121-04-0*, BC-10) Black Classic.
Rogers, J. A. & Rogers, Helga. One Hundred Amazing Facts about the Negro. rev. ed. (Illus.). (Orig.). 1995. reprint ed. pap. 4.95 (*0-9602294-7-7*) H M Rogers.
Rogers, J. Arthur. Cove Hopping South to Panama: Cruising a Pleasure Boat from Southern California to the San Blas Islands. (Illus.). 254p. 1996. pap. 20.00 (*0-9633412-1-9*) J A Rogers.
— Cove Hopping South to the Virgin Islands: Cruising a Pleasure Boat from South Florida to the U. S. Virgin Islands. (Illus.). 254p. 1996. pap. 20.00 (*0-9633412-2-7*) J A Rogers.
— How to Build a Mango: An Inexpensive & Easy-to-Build Sailing Dinghy. (Illus.). 78p. 1995. pap. 12.00 (*0-9633412-7-8*) J A Rogers.
— Sailing Haiti Single Handed: Sailing the North, East & South Coasts of Haiti. (Illus.). 92p. 1995. pap. 8.00 (*0-9633412-8-6*, 184) J A Rogers.
— Tropical American Cruising: Hundreds of Practical Ideas on Preparing for a Pleasure Boat Cruise to the Tropics. (Illus.). 250p. (Orig.). 1996. pap. 18.00 (*0-9633412-9-4*, 187) J A Rogers.
Rogers, J. D. & Wilson, S. M. Ethnohistory & Archaeology: Approaches to Postcontact Change in the Americas. (Interdisciplinary Contributions to Archaeology Ser.). (Illus.). 254p. (C). 1993. 42.50 (*0-306-44176-4*, Plenum Trade) Perseus Pubng.
Rogers, J. Daniel, et al, eds. Contributions to Spiro Archeology: Mound Excavations & Regional Perspectives. (Studies in Oklahoma's Past: Vol. 16). (Illus.). 285p. (C). 1989. pap. text 11.00 (*1-881346-09-9*) Univ OK Archeol.
Rogers, J. Daniel & Smith, Bruce D., eds. Mississippian Communities & Households. LC 94-44049. (Illus.). 320p. 1995. pap. text 29.95 (*0-8173-0768-0*) U of Ala Pr.
Rogers, J. M. Empire of the Sultans: Ottoman Art from the Collection of Nasser D. Khalili. LC 96-175018. (Illus.). 288p. 1996. 90.00 (*1-898592-04-7*, Pub. by Art Bks Intl) Partners Pubs Grp.
— Uses of Anachrohism on Cultural Methodological Diversity in Islamic Art. (C). 1994. 8.50 (*0-7286-0225-3*, Pub. by Sch Orient & African Stud) S Asia.
Rogers, J. M., tr. Topkapi Architecture. 215p. 1996. 150.00 (*0-614-21593-5*, 1240) Kazi Pubns.
Rogers, J. M. & Art Services International Staff. Empire of the Sultans: Ottoman Art from the Collection of Nasser D. Khalili. LC 99-28966. 2000. pap. 39.95 (*0-88397-132-1*) Art Srvc Intl.
Rogers, J. Philip. Through a Glass Darkly: The Impact of Cognitive Psychological Factors on Crisis Decision-Making. (Ridgeway International Security Studies). 320p. (C). 1999. pap. 62.00 (*0-8133-8592-X*) Westview.
Rogers, J. S. James Rogers of New London, Connecticut, & His Descendants. (Illus.). 514p. 1989. reprint ed. pap. 77.00 (*0-8328-1027-4*); reprint ed. lib. bdg. 85.00 (*0-8328-1026-6*) Higginson Bk Co.
Rogers, J. T. Fission Product & Transport Processes in Reactor Accidents. LC 95-25192. xii, 870p. 1990. 198.00 (*0-89116-876-1*) Hemisp Pub.
Rogers, J. W. & Millan, W. H. Coil Slitting. LC 73-7903. 127p. 1967. reprint ed. pap. 59.00 (*0-08-017696-8*, Pub. by Pergamon Repr) Franklin.
Rogers, Jack. Claiming the Center: Churches & Conflicting Worldviews. LC 95-30148. 256p. (Orig.). 1995. pap. 19.95 (*0-664-25613-9*) Westminster John Knox.
— Reading the Bible & the Confessions: The Presbyterian Way. LC 99-24404. 96p. 1999. pap. 10.95 (*0-664-50046-3*) Geneva Press.
***Rogers, Jack B. & McKim, Donald K.** The Authority & Interpretation of the Bible: An Historical Approach. 562p. 1999. pap. 40.00 (*1-57910-213-1*) Wipf & Stock.
***Rogers, Jack B., et al.** Introduction to Philosophy: A Case Method Approach. 254p. 1998. pap. 23.00 (*1-57910-139-9*) Wipf & Stock.
Rogers, Jack D., jt. auth. see Ju, Yu-Ming.
***Rogers, Jackie Krasas.** Temps: The Many Faces of the Changing Workplace. LC 99-88451. 208p. 2000. 39.95 (*0-8014-3638-9*); pap. 15.95 (*0-8014-8662-9*) Cornell U Pr.
Rogers, Jacqueline. Best Friends Sleep Over. LC 92-56895. 32p. (J). (ps-1). 1993. 14.95 (*0-590-44793-9*) Scholastic Inc.
***Rogers, Jacqueline.** Best Friends Sleep Over. (Illus.). 32p. (YA). (ps-4). 2000. pap. text 5.99 (*0-439-19994-8*) Scholastic Inc.
Rogers, Jacqueline. Monster Soup & Other Spooky Poems. (J). 1992. 10.15 (*0-606-07883-5*, Pub. by Turtleback) Demco.
— Tiptoe into Kindergarten. LC 98-45430. (Illus.). 32p. (J). (ps-1). 1999. 10.95 (*0-590-46653-4*, Pub. by Scholastic Inc) Penguin Putnam.
— You Can Stop Smoking. 288p. 1990. mass mkt. 5.50 (*0-671-70295-5*) PB.
— You Can Stop Smoking. Rubenstein, Julie, ed. 1995. mass mkt. 6.99 (*0-671-52303-1*) PB.
Rogers, Jacqueline. Weird Pet Poems. LC 96-30302. 40p. (J). (ps up). 1997. per. 16.00 (*0-689-80734-1*) S&S Childrens.
Rogers, Jacqueline, jt. auth. see Van Leeuwen, Jean.
Rogers, Jacqueline, tr. see Dumas, Alexandre.
Rogers, Jacqueline A. Open Minded Heart: Pathway to an Open Hearted Mind. 100p. (Orig.). 1995. pap. 9.00 (*0-9633540-5-1*) ARC Pub.
Rogers, Jacqueline L., jt. auth. see Cassini, Kathleen K.
Rogers, Jacqueline M. Aspects of the Female Novel. LC 91-6859. 200p. (C). 1991. text 30.00 (*0-89341-663-0*); pap. text 17.50 (*0-89341-664-9*) Hollowbrook.
Rogers, James. A Descriptive Approach to Language - Theoretic Complexity. (Studies in Logic, Language & Information: Vol. 13). 220p. (C). 1999. text 59.95 (*1-57586-137-2*); pap. text 22.95 (*1-57586-136-4*) CSLI.
— The Dictionary of Cliches. 384p. 1987. mass mkt. 5.99 (*0-345-33814-6*) Ballantine Pub Grp.
— The Dictionary of Cliches. 320p. 1992. reprint ed. 8.99 (*0-517-06020-5*) Random.
***Rogers, James.** The Nature of True Grace. LC 98-167701. 1998. write for info. (*0-939241-31-5*) Faith Print.
Rogers, James. Savage Life. LC 94-68597. 262p. 1998. pap. 12.99 (*1-85242-384-6*, Pub. by Serpents Tail) Consort Bk Sales.
Rogers, James & Warda, Mark. How to Win in Small Claims Court in New York. LC 97-37047. (Legal Survival Guides Ser.). 160p. 1997. pap. 14.95 (*1-57071-187-9*) Sourcebks.
Rogers, James A., jt. auth. see Dorland, Wayne E.
Rogers, James H. Capitalism in Crisis. 1938. 59.50 (*0-686-83499-2*) Elliots Bks.
***Rogers, James L. & Warda, Mark.** How to Make a New York Will. 2nd ed. LC 98-54391. (Legal Survival Guides Ser.). 112p. 1999. pap. 12.95 (*1-57248-095-5*, Sphinx Pubng) Sourcebks.
Rogers, James N., ed. see Shumacker, Harris B.
Rogers, James R. A Uniform Approach to Rate & Ratio Problems. (Hi Map Ser.: No. 15). (Illus.). 60p. pap. text 11.99 (*0-614-05311-0*, HM 5615) COMAP Inc.
Rogers, James S. The Early History of the Law of Bills & Notes: A Study of the Origins of Anglo-American Commerical Law. (Cambridge Studies in English Legal History). 293p. (C). 1995. text 59.95 (*0-521-44212-5*) Cambridge U Pr.
Rogers, James S., ed. Anatomy of a Personal Injury Lawsuit. 3rd ed. (Illus.). 556p. 1991. boxed set 80.00 (*0-941916-61-8*) Alta Pr.
Rogers, James T. The Antislavery Movement. LC 93-40960. (Social Reform Movements Ser.). 128p. (J). 1994. 19.95 (*0-8160-2907-5*) Facts on File.
— The Secret War: Espionage in World War II. (World Espionage Ser.). (Illus.). 128p. (YA). (gr. 7-10). 1991. lib. bdg. 16.95 (*0-8160-2395-6*) Facts on File.
— Woodrow Wilson: Visionary for Peace. LC 96-3454. (Makers of America Ser.). (Illus.). 112p. (YA). (gr. 7-12). 1997. 19.95 (*0-8160-3396-X*) Facts on File.
***Rogers, Jane.** Island. 2000. 25.95 (*1-58567-076-6*, Pub. by Overlook Pr) Penguin Putnam.
Rogers, Jane. Mr. Wroe's Virgins. LC 99-10232. 288p. 1999. text 24.95 (*0-87951-702-6*, Pub. by Overlook Pr) Penguin Putnam.
***Rogers, Jane.** Mr. Wroe's Virgins: A Novel. 288p. 2000. pap. 13.00 (*0-618-06613-6*, Mariner Bks) HM.
Rogers, Jane. Promised Lands. LC 96-29265. 388p. 1997. 24.95 (*0-87951-753-0*, Pub. by Overlook Pr) Penguin Putnam.
— Promised Lands. 376p. 1998. pap. 14.95 (*0-87951-866-9*, Pub. by Overlook Pr) Penguin Putnam.
Rogers, Janet E., ed. Visions: QuiltArt. LC 96-28178. (Illus.). 88p. (Orig.). 1996. pap. 21.95 (*1-57120-021-5*, 10145) C & T Pub.
Rogers, Janice, jt. auth. see Cunningham, Loren.
Rogers, Janice L., ed. see Dittman, Richard & Schmieg, Glenn.
Rogers, Janice Steiner, jt. auth. see Soud, Treesa E.
Rogers, Jean. King Island Christmas. 32p. 1998. mass mkt. 4.95 (*0-688-16449-8*, Wm Morrow) Morrow Avon.
— Left Field Bear. LC 95-81527. (Illus.). 32p. (Orig.). (J). (gr. k-3). 1996. pap. 6.95 (*0-9641998-2-3*) Lapcat Pubns.
Rogers, Jean. Runaway Mittens. LC 99-69043. (Illus.). 22p. (J). pap. 10.00 (*1-57833-108-0*) Todd Commns.
Rogers, Jean, ed. Prevention's Cooking for Good Health: Easy Recipes for Low-Fat Living. (Illus.). 384p. 1994. 27.95 (*0-87596-210-6*) Rodale Pr Inc.
— Prevention's Low-Fat Italian Favorites. LC 95-24995. (Illus.). 320p. 1996. pap. 15.95 (*0-87596-306-4*) Rodale Pr Inc.
Rogers, Jean, ed. Prevention's Quick & Healthy Low-Fat Cooking: Featuring All-American Food. LC 94-39507. (Illus.). 320p. 1995. pap. 15.95 (*0-87596-237-8*) Rodale Pr Inc.
Rogers, Jean, ed. Prevention's Quick & Healthy Low-Fat Cooking: Featuring All-American Food. LC 94-39507. (Illus.). 320p. 1995. text 25.95 (*0-87596-235-1*) Rodale Pr Inc.
— Prevention's Quick & Healthy Low-Fat Cooking: Featuring Healthy Cuisines from the Mediterranean. LC 93-35544. (Illus.). 320p. 1994. pap. 15.95 (*0-87596-193-2*) Rodale Pr Inc.
— Prevention's Quick & Healthy Low-Fat Cooking: Featuring Healthy Cuisines from the Mediterranean. LC 93-35544. (Illus.). 320p. 1994. text 25.95 (*0-87596-192-4*) Rodale Pr Inc.
— Prevention's Quick & Healthy Low-Fat Cooking: Featuring Pasta & Other Italian Favorites. LC 95-24994. (Illus.). 320p. 1996. text 25.95 (*0-87596-305-6*) Rodale Pr Inc.
— Prevention's Quick & Healthy Low-Fat Cooking: From Entertaining to Everyday. 272p. 1993. 25.95 (*0-87596-174-6*) Rodale Pr Inc.
— Prevention's Quick & Healthy Low-Fat Cooking: From Entertaining to Everyday. (Illus.). 272p. 1993. pap. 15.95 (*0-87596-175-4*) Rodale Pr Inc.
Rogers, Jean B. A Prolog Primer. LC 85-22846. 214p. (C). 1986. pap. text 23.75 (*0-201-06467-7*) Addison-Wesley.
— A Turbo Prolog Primer. LC 86-28707. (Illus.). 240p. (C). 1987. pap. text 23.75 (*0-201-12198-0*) Addison-Wesley.
Rogers, Jean D. Beyond the Dreaming Moon: And Other Poems. Rogers, Clinton, ed. 80p. 1998. pap. 12.95 (*1-882063-44-9*, Heritage Hse) Cottage Pr MA.
— The Hour of Enchantment: Selected Early Poems. Rogers, Clinton, ed. 94p. (Orig.). 1996. pap. 11.95 (*1-882063-36-8*, Heritage Hse) Cottage Pr MA.
Rogers, Jeff. Business Planning for Growing Companies: The Experts' Guide to Business Survival & Prosperity. 2nd rev. ed. (Illus.). 180p. 1996. wbk. ed. 49.00 (*0-923680-04-7*, 4201) Amer ComVision Inc.
— Business Planning for Healthcare Organizations: The Experts' Guide to Creating & Maintaining a Competitive Advantage. (Illus.). 180p. (C). 1996. 49.00 (*0-923680-00-4*) Amer ComVision Inc.
— Managed Care Strategies: A Strategy Guide for Healthcare Organizations. (Illus.). 186p. 1996. wbk. ed. 49.00 (*0-923680-08-X*, 4203) Amer ComVision Inc.
— Valor at Polebrook: Last Flight of Ten Horsepower. LC 98-71188. (Illus.). 144p. 1998. pap. 30.00 (*0-9652491-5-8*) Ken Cook.
Rogers, Jeffrey. The Dead Sea Scrolls & Christianity. 120p. 1998. pap. 15.95 (*0-687-01609-6*) Abingdon.
Rogers, Jeffrey S. A Grammar for Biblical Hebrew Handbook. rev. ed. 128p. (Orig.). 1996. pap. 19.95 (*0-687-01155-8*) Abingdon.
Rogers, Jeffrey S. & Hamilton, Jeffries M. A Grammar for Biblical Hebrew: Handbook. LC 96-33026. 1997. student ed. 11.95 (*0-687-05370-6*) Abingdon.
Rogers, Jeffrey S., jt. auth. see Hamilton, Jeffries M.
Rogers, Jennifer. Adults Learning. 256p. 1977. pap. 16.00 (*0-335-00044-4*) OpUniv Pr.
— Jigsaws. 87p. 1990. pap. 5.60 (*0-87129-016-2*, J19) Dramatic Pub.
Rogers, Jenny. Adults Learning. 3rd ed. 256p. 1989. pap. 28.95 (*0-335-09215-2*) OpUniv Pr.
— Caring for People. 192p. 1990. pap. 28.95 (*0-335-09429-5*) OpUniv Pr.
— Effective Interviews: The Essential Guide to Thinking & Working Smarter. LC 98-53809. (Self-Development for Success Ser.: Vol. 8). (Illus.). 95p. 1999. pap. 12.95 (*0-8144-7021-1*) AMACOM.
***Rogers, Jenny.** Influencing People. LC 99-37536. (Self-Development for Success Ser.: Vol. 12). 96p. 1999. pap. 12.95 (*0-8144-7056-4*) AMACOM.
Rogers, Jerry. The Art of Knitting. (Illus.). 240p. 1991. pap. 29.95 (*0-207-17026-6*) HarpC.
Rogers, Jerry, ed. Global Risk Assessments: Issues, Concepts & Applications, Bk. 1. (Illus.). 176p. 1983. pap. 29.95 (*0-914325-00-0*) Global Risk.
— Global Risk Assessments: Issues, Concepts & Applications, Bk. 2. (Illus.). 240p. 1986. pap. 32.50 (*0-914325-01-9*) Global Risk.
— Global Risk Assessments: Issues, Concepts & Applications, Bk. 3. 239p. 1988. pap. 32.50 (*0-914325-02-7*) Global Risk.
Rogers, Jerry, ed. see Suzman, Cedric L. & Srivastava, Mahendra.
Rogers, Jerry R., et al. Civil Engineering History: Engineers Make History: Proceedings of the First National Symposium on Civil Engineering History. LC 96-44710. 208p. 1996. 28.00 (*0-7844-0209-4*) Am Soc Civil Eng.
— Engineering History & Heritage: Proceedings of the Second National Congress on Civil Engineering History & Heritage. LC 98-38924. 184p. 1998. 32.00 (*0-7844-0394-5*) Am Soc Civil Eng.
Rogers, Jerry S. & Bullock, William P., Jr., eds. Revenue Enhancement for Water & Wastewater Systems: Proceedings of the Session. LC 94-34443. 40p. 1994. 17.00 (*0-7844-0030-X*) Am Soc Civil Eng.
Rogers, Jim. In Care of the Conductor. 270p. 1994. pap. 5.95 (*0-929292-76-6*) Hannibal Bks.
— Investment Biker: Around the World with Jim Rogers. 1995. pap. 12.95 (*1-55850-529-6*) Adams Media.
— Planes, Pilots & Gofer Tales of Lynchburg, Virginia's Old Preston Glenn Airport. LC 98-134005. (Illus.). 160p. 1997. pap. 15.95 (*1-883912-05-9*) Hamiltons.
— Romans 6. (Lost City: Poetic Broadside Ser.: Vol. 1). Date not set. pap. 2.00 (*1-892494-13-2*) Repossessed Head.
Rogers, Jimmie N. The Country Music Message: Revisited. LC 88-17176. 288p. 1988. pap. 16.00 (*1-55728-052-5*) U of Ark Pr.
Rogers, Jimmy. Jimmy Rogers School of Fishing. (Illus.). 85p. 1997. pap. 9.95 (*0-937866-57-1*) Atlantic Pub Co.
Rogers, Joel & Streeck, Wolfgang, eds. Work Councils: Consultation, Representation, & Cooperation in Industrial Relations. LC 95-13423. (NBER Comparative Labor Markets Ser.). 436p. 1995. 55.00 (*0-226-72376-3*) U Ch Pr.
Rogers, Joel, jt. auth. see Cohen, Joshua.
Rogers, Joel, jt. auth. see Ferguson, Thomas.
Rogers, Joel, jt. auth. see Freeman, Richard B.
Rogers, Joel, jt. auth. see Luria, Daniel D.
Rogers, Joel, ed. see Schor, Juliet.
Rogers, Joel, tr. see Solem, Karen.
Rogers, Joel A. Selected Writings of Joel Augustus Rogers. Kiongozi, Kinya, ed. 100p. (Orig.). 1989. write for info. (*0-939841-04-5*); pap. write for info. (*0-939841-03-7*) Pyramid MD.
Rogers, Joel E. Divide & Conquer: Post War U. S. Labor Policy. Date not set. 22.00 (*0-465-01695-2*, Pub. by Basic); pap. write for info. (*0-465-01697-9*) Basic.
Rogers, Joel Townsley. The Red Right Hand. 192p. 1997. mass mkt. 4.95 (*0-7867-0446-2*) Carroll & Graf.
***Rogers, Joel W.** Hidden Coast: Coastal Adventures from Alaska to Mexico. 2nd ed. LC 99-86651. (Illus.). 2000. pap. 14.95 (*1-55868-533-2*) Gr Arts Ctr Pub.
Rogers, Joel W. Watertrail: The Hidden Path Through Puget Sound. LC 97-46783. (Illus.). 128p. 1998. pap. 21.95 (*1-57061-095-9*) Sasquatch Bks.
Rogers, Joey. Object-Oriented Neural Networks in C++ LC 96-28409. (Illus.). 310p. 1996. pap. text 29.95 (*0-12-593115-8*) Acad Pr.
Rogers, John. John Rogers & the Rogers Groups, (1829-1904) LC 88-50731. (Illus.). (Orig.). (C). 1990. pap. text. write for info. (*0-939958-03-1*) New Canaan.
— Locke's Enlightenment: Aspects of the Origin, Nature & Impact of His Philosophy. Ecole, Jean & Theis, Robert, eds. (Studien und Texte zur Geschichte der Europaischen Ideen: No. 1, Vol. 3). 208p. 1998. write for info. (*3-487-10529-2*) G Olms Pubs.
— The Matter of Revolution: Science, Poetry, & Politics in the Age of Milton. 288p. 1996. 45.00 (*0-8014-3238-3*) Cornell U Pr.

An Asterisk (*) at the beginning of an entry indicates that the title is appearing for the first time.

— The Matter of Revolution: Science, Poetry, & Politics in the Age of Milton. 280p. 1998. pap. text 16.95 (*0-8014-8525-8*) Cornell U Pr.

— Red World & White: Memories of a Chippewa Boyhood. LC 96-19036. (Civilization of the American Indian Ser.: Vol. 126). 176p. 1996. pap. 11.95 (*0-8061-2891-7*) U of Okla Pr.

Rogers, John, ed. Medical Ethics, Human Choices: A Christian Perspective. LC 87-29747. 176p. (Orig.). 1988. pap. 12.99 (*0-8361-3460-5*) Herald Pr.

Rogers, John A. The Elephant on the Tracks & Other Stories. LC 92-61744. 66p. 1992. pap. 8.00 (*1-882265-01-7*) Maine Writers.

Rogers, John B., Jr. In Him Is Life: How Christ Meets Our Deepest Needs. LC 93-24245. 96p. 1994. pap. 9.99 (*0-8066-2652-6*, 9-2652, Augsburg) Augsburg Fortress.

Rogers, John C., III, jt. auth. see Robinson, David G.

Rogers, John C., III, ed. see Conference of the Academy of Marketing Science.

Rogers, John E. & Whitman, William B., eds. Microbial Production & Consumption of Greenhouse Gases: Methane, Nitrogen Oxides, & Halomethanes. (Illus.). 308p. 1991. text 64.00 (*1-55581-035-7*) ASM Pr.

— Microbial Production & Consumption of Greenhouse Gases: Methane, Nitrogen Oxides, & Halomethanes. LC 91-15621. 308p. reprint ed. pap. 95.50 (*0-608-08632-0*, 206915500003) Bks Demand.

Rogers, John G. Origins of Sea Terms. (American Maritime Library: Vol. 11). xv, 220p. 1984. 20.00 (*0-913372-31-5*) Mystic Seaport.

Rogers, John H. The Giant Planet Jupiter. (Practical Astronomy Handbooks Ser.: 6). (Illus.). 428p. (C). 1995. text 99.95 (*0-521-41008-8*) Cambridge U Pr.

Rogers, John H., ed. British Short Fiction Writers, 1915-1945. (Dictionary of Literary Biography Ser.: Vol. 162). 400p. 1996. text 155.00 (*0-8103-9357-3*) Gale.

Rogers, John J. A History of the Earth. (Illus.). 326p. (C). 1993. text 125.00 (*0-521-39480-5*) Cambridge U Pr.

Rogers, John J. & Feiss, P. Geoffrey. People & the Earth: Basic Issues in the Sustainability of Resources & Environment. LC 97-25901. (Illus.). 360p. (C). 1998. text 80.00 (*0-521-56028-4*); pap. text 32.95 (*0-521-56872-2*) Cambridge U Pr.

Rogers, John L., jt. auth. see Rogers, Linda K.

Rogers, John M. International Law & United States Law. LC 99-28894. 254p. 1999. text 70.95 (*1-84014-060-7*) Ashgate Pub Co.

Rogers, John N. PC Write for Students. 2nd ed. LC 90-42093. 64p. (Orig.). 1991. pap. 5.00 (*0-914061-19-4*) Orchises Pr.

Rogers, John N., III. Superintendent's Handbook for Golf Course Maintenance & Construction. (Advances in Turfgrass Science Ser.). 1999. 75.00 (*0-87371-972-7*, L972) Lewis Pubs.

Rogers, John P. Allison. New Jersey-New York Families: Allison, Davenport, Shawger (Shauger), Wendel (Wandle) (Illus.). 108p. 1997. reprint ed. pap. 17.50 (*0-8328-7249-0*); reprint ed. lib. bdg. 27.50 (*0-8328-7248-2*) Higginson Bk Co.

Rogers, John R. Free Land, Inalienable Rights of Man. LC 00-5557. 52p. 1987. reprint ed. pap. 5.00 (*0-942153-17-0*) Entropy Conserv.

Rogers, John R. & Rogers, Amy T. Charlotte: Its Historic Neighborhoods. LC 97-133980. (Images of America Ser.). 1999. pap. 16.99 (*0-7524-0515-2*) Arcadia Publng.

Rogers, Joseph. Candle & Darkness: Current Research in Alzheimer's Disease. LC 98-9280. (Illus.). 166p. 1998. pap. 13.95 (*1-56625-095-1*) Bonus Books.

Rogers, Joseph M., ed. see Beissel, James D., Sr.

Rogers, Joseph P. Realm of Haden: A Space-Age Fantasy. 183p. 1995. pap. 8.95 (*0-9642331-0-X*) Rogers Pubng.

Rogers, Joseph W. U. S. National Bibliography & the Copyright Law: An Historical Study. LC 60-15545. 119p. reprint ed. pap. 36.90 (*0-608-11354-9*, 205096300074) Bks Demand.

Rogers, Joseph W. & Mays, G. Larry. Juvenile Delinquency & Juvenile Justice. LC 86-32389. 1987. text 37.50 (*0-471-81915-8*) P-H.

***Rogers, Josephine.** Dental Health, Beautiful Teeth Activities Book. (Illus.). 32p. (J). (gr. k-6). 2000. pap. 7.00 (*0-9679975-0-X*) J H Rogers.

Rogers, Joyce. The Second Best Bed: Shakespeare's Will in a New Light, 48. LC 92-33763. (Contributions to the Study of World Literature Ser.: No. 48). 160p. 1993. 49.95 (*0-313-28831-3*, GM8831, Greenwood Pr) Greenwood.

Rogers, Joyce & Rogers, Alan. Let's Eat Out in Montgomery County. 4th ed. Siegel, A. & Siegel, Joyce, eds. 256p. 1997. pap. 11.95 (*1-883720-02-8*) A Siegel Assocs.

Rogers, Judi. Fun with Kids in the Kitchen Cookbook. LC 96-166711. 96p. (YA). 1996. 12.99 (*0-8280-1071-4*) Review & Herald.

Rogers, Judith & Matsumura, Molleen. Mother to Be: A Guide to Pregnancy & Birth for Women with Disabilities. 424p. 1991. pap. 39.95 (*0-939957-30-2*) Demos Medical.

Rogers, Judy. Why Can't I See God. 1991. pap. 9.99 (*0-00-531007-5*) HarperColl Religious.

Rogers, Judy R. & Rogers, Glenn C. Patterns & Themes: A Basic English Reader. xi, 228p. (C). 1985. mass mkt. write for info. (*0-534-03348-2*) Wadsworth Pub.

— Patterns & Themes: A Basic English Reader. 2nd ed. 267p. (C). 1988. mass mkt. write for info. (*0-534-08832-5*) Wadsworth Pub.

— Patterns & Themes: A Basic English Reader. 3rd ed. 240p. (C). 1992. pap. 24.50 (*0-534-17988-6*) Wadsworth Pub.

Rogers, Judy S., ed. see Liebhardt, Paul W.

Rogers, Juliette. Holiday Cookies. 72p. 1991. 15.00 (*0-385-25335-4*) Doubleday.

Rogers, June W. The Dream on Royal Street: Musical. 101p. (YA). (gr. 7 up). 1981. pap. 5.95 (*0-87129-133-9*, D02) Dramatic Pub.

— The Golden Goose. (J). 1973. pap. 5.25 (*0-87129-709-4*, G25) Dramatic Pub.

— Heidi. (J). 1969. pap. 5.50 (*0-87129-200-9*, H14) Dramatic Pub.

— A Little Princess. 1978. pap. 3.75 (*0-87129-197-5*, L40) Dramatic Pub.

— The Magic Flute. 1976. pap. 5.25 (*0-87129-078-2*, M10) Dramatic Pub.

— The Nutcracker. 1975. 3.75 (*0-87129-543-1*, N22) Dramatic Pub.

— Playing the Palace - Musical. 77p. 1989. pap. 5.95 (*0-87129-680-2*, P63) Dramatic Pub.

— Snow White & the 7 Dwarfs of the Black Forest. 1969. 5.25 (*0-87129-440-0*, S42) Dramatic Pub.

— The Truth about Cinderella - Musical. 1974. 5.60 (*0-87129-235-1*, T03) Dramatic Pub.

Rogers, Justus H. Colusa County (California) (Illus.). 473p. 1993. reprint ed. lib. bdg. 49.50 (*0-8328-3524-2*) Higginson Bk Co.

Rogers, Kalen. Marilyn Manson: The Unauthorized Biography. 78p. 1997. pap. 19.95 (*0-8256-1643-3*, OP48034) Omnibus NY.

— No Doubt: The Story Of. LC 97-162236. (Illus.). 48p. 1997. pap. 12.95 (*0-8256-1383-3*) Omnibus NY.

— The Story of Alanis Morissette. LC 96-181119. (Illus.). 48p. 1996. pap. 11.95 (*0-8256-1548-8*, OP47847) Omnibus NY.

— The Story of Green Day: Omnibus Press Presents the Story Of... LC 95-193621. (Illus.). 56p. (Orig.). pap. 11.95 (*0-8256-1504-6*, OP 47781) Omnibus NY.

— Tori Amos, All These Years: The Authorized Biography. 2nd rev. ed. (Illus.). 132p. (Orig.). (C). pap. 19.95 (*0-8256-1448-1*, OP 47756) Omnibus NY.

***Rogers, Karen.** Lo Mejor Que Hago. Alvarado, Ana M., tr. (Think-Kids Book Collection).Tr. of What I Do Best!. (SPA., Illus.). 16p. (J). 2000. pap. 2.95 (*1-58237-052-4*) Creat Think.

Rogers, Karen. What I Do Best! LC 98-71336. (Think-Kids Book Collection). (Illus.). 16p. (J). (gr. 1-4). 1998. pap. 2.95 (*1-58237-001-X*) Creat Think.

Rogers, Karen B., jt. ed. see Friedman, Reva C.

Rogers, Karen M. The Club. LC 98-71346. (Think-Kids Book Collection). (Illus.). 16p. (J). (gr. 1-4). 1998. pap. 2.95 (*1-58237-005-2*) Creat Think.

***Rogers, Karen M.** El Club de Piensa-Tu. Alvarado, Ana M., tr. (Think-Kids Book Collection).Tr. of Club. (SPA., Illus.). 16p. (J). 2000. pap. 2.95 (*1-58237-042-7*) Creat Think.

— Como Hay Rayas! Alvarado, Ana M., tr. (Think-Kids Book Collection).Tr. of Yipes! Stripes!. (SPA.). 16p. (J). 2000. pap. 2.95 (*1-58237-043-5*) Creat Think.

— Como Pienso Patrones! Alvarado, Ana M., tr. (Think-Kids Book Collection).Tr. of Patterns in My Head. (SPA., Illus.). 16p. (J). 2000. pap. 2.95 (*1-58237-054-0*) Creat Think.

Rogers, Karen M. Good Thinking! LC 98-71330. (Think-Kids Book Collection). (Illus.). 16p. (J). (gr. 1-4). 1998. pap. 2.95 (*1-58237-015-X*) Creat Think.

— Hand over Hand. LC 98-71335. (Think-Kids Book Collection). (Illus.). 16p. (J). (gr. 1-4). 1998. pap. 2.95 (*1-58237-007-9*) Creat Think.

— Let's Find Out. LC 98-71342. (Think-Kids Book Collection). (Illus.). 16p. (J). (gr. 1-4). 1998. pap. 2.95 (*1-58237-003-6*) Creat Think.

***Rogers, Karen M.** Mano Sobre Mano. Alvarado, Ana M., tr. (Think-Kids Book Collection).Tr. of Hand over Hand. (SPA., Illus.). 16p. (J). 2000. pap. 2.95 (*1-58237-053-2*) Creat Think.

Rogers, Karen M. Max & Me. LC 98-71338. (Think-Kids Book Collection). (Illus.). 16p. (J). (gr. 1-4). 1998. pap. 2.95 (*1-58237-013-3*) Creat Think.

***Rogers, Karen M.** Mingo y Yo. Alvarado, Ana M., tr. (Think-Kids Book Collection).Tr. of Max & Me. (SPA., Illus.). 16p. (J). (gr. 1-4). 2000. pap. 2.95 (*1-58237-050-8*) Creat Think.

Rogers, Karen M. Patterns in My Head. LC 98-71334. (Think-Kids Book Collection). (Illus.). 16p. (J). (gr. 1-4). 1998. pap. 2.95 (*1-58237-019-2*) Creat Think.

***Rogers, Karen M.** Puedo Intentario? Alvarado, Ana M., tr. (Think-Kids Book Collection).Tr. of Can I Try?. (SPA., Illus.). 16p. (J). (gr. 1-4). 2000. pap. 2.95 (*1-58237-039-7*) Creat Think.

— Que Buena Idea! Alvarado, Ana M., tr. (Think-Kids Book Collection).Tr. of Good Thinking. (SPA., Illus.). 16p. (J). (gr. 1-4). 2000. pap. 2.95 (*1-58237-058-3*) Creat Think.

— Quien Puedo Aer? Alvarado, Ana M., tr. (Think-Kids Book Collection).Tr. of Who Can I Be?. (SPA., Illus.). 16p. (J). (gr. 1-4). 2000. pap. 2.95 (*1-58237-051-6*) Creat Think.

— Vamos a Descubrir. Alvarado, Ana M., tr. (Think-Kids Book Collection).Tr. of Let's Find Out. (SPA., Illus.). 16p. (J). 2000. pap. 2.95 (*1-58237-046-X*) Creat Think.

Rogers, Karen M. Who Can I Be? LC 98-71337. (Think-Kids Book Collection). (Illus.). 16p. (J). (gr. 1-4). 1998. pap. 2.95 (*1-58237-004-4*) Creat Think.

— Yipes! Stripes! LC 98-71345. (Think-Kids Book Collection). (Illus.). 16p. (J). (gr. 1-4). 1998. pap. 2.95 (*1-58237-002-8*) Creat Think.

Rogers, Karen M. & Rucker, Neima. Can I Try? LC 98-71349. (Think-Kids Book Collection). (Illus.). 16p. (J). (gr. 1-4). 1998. pap. 2.95 (*1-58237-016-8*) Creat Think.

Rogers, Kasey & Wood, Mark. The Official Bewitched Cookbook. LC 97-112125. 256p. 1995. pap. 15.95 (*1-57566-095-4*, Knsington) Kensgtn Pub Corp.

Rogers, Katharine M. The Cat & the Human Imagination: Feline Images from Bast to Garfield. LC 97-39175. 232p. (C). 1998. 29.95 (*0-472-10826-3*, 10826) U of Mich Pr.

***Rogers, Katharine M.** The Cat & the Human Imagination: Feline Images from Bast to Garfield. (Illus.). 232p. 2000. pap. 17.95 (*0-472-08750-9*, 08750) U of Mich Pr.

Rogers, Katharine M., ed. The Meridian Anthology of Restoration & Eighteenth-Century Plays by Women. 560p. (Orig.). 1998. pap. text 16.00 (*0-7881-5784-1*) DIANE Pub.

Rogers, Katherin A. The Anselmian Approach to God & Creation. LC 97-2068. (Studies in the History of Philosophy: Vol. 44). 272p. 1997. text 89.95 (*0-7734-8668-2*) E Mellen.

— The Neoplatonic Metaphysics & Epistemology of Anselm of Canterbury. LC 97-13027. (Studies in the History of Philosophy: No. 45). 280p. 1997. text 89.95 (*0-7734-8622-4*) E Mellen.

Rogers, Katherine. A Dinosaur Dynasty: The Sternberg Fossil Hunters. LC 99-33184. 302p. 1999. reprint ed. pap. 14.00 (*0-87842-404-0*) Mountain Pr.

Rogers, Kathleen A. Writing to Explain. (J). (gr. 3-6). 1987. pap. 8.99 (*0-8224-7537-5*) Fearon Teacher Aids.

— Writing to Inform. (J). (gr. 3-6). 1987. pap. 8.99 (*0-8224-7536-7*) Fearon Teacher Aids.

— Writing to Persuade. (J). (gr. 3-6). 1987. pap. 8.99 (*0-8224-7538-3*) Fearon Teacher Aids.

Rogers, Kathryn S. U. S. Coal Goes Abroad: A Social Action Perspective in Interorganizational Networks. LC 85-12467. 272p. 1985. 55.00 (*0-275-90036-3*, C0036, Praeger Pubs) Greenwood.

Rogers, Kathy. Animals: An Integrated Unit. (Primary Thematic Units Ser.). (Illus.). 96p. (Orig.). 1993. pap. 12.95 (*0-944459-75-7*) ECS Lrn Systs.

— Bears Everywhere: An Integrated Unit. (Primary Thematic Units Ser.). (Illus.). 96p. (Orig.). 1993. pap. 12.95 (*0-944459-78-1*) ECS Lrn Systs.

— Color & Learn Mexico. (Illus.). 32p. 1999. pap., wbk. ed. 3.99 (*1-56472-205-8*) Edupress Inc.

— Dinosaurs: An Integrated Unit. (Primary Thematic Units Ser.). (Illus.). 96p. (Orig.). 1993. pap. 12.95 (*0-944459-79-X*) ECS Lrn Systs.

— Fairy Tales: An Integrated Unit. (Primary Thematic Units Ser.). (Illus.). 96p. (Orig.). 1994. pap. 12.95 (*0-944459-80-3*) ECS Lrn Systs.

— Fall Harvest: An Integrated Unit. (Primary Thematic Units Ser.). (Illus.). 80p. (Orig.). 1993. pap. 12.95 (*0-944459-73-0*) ECS Lrn Systs.

— Folktales: An Integrated Unit. (Primary Thematic Units Ser.). (Illus.). 96p. (Orig.). 1994. pap. 12.95 (*0-944459-81-1*) ECS Lrn Systs.

— Love & Friendship: An Integrated Unit. (Primary Thematic Units Ser.). (Illus.). 96p. (Orig.). 1994. pap. 12.95 (*0-944459-88-9*) ECS Lrn Systs.

— Maps & Globes: An Integrated Unit. (Primary Thematic Units Ser.). (Illus.). 96p. (Orig.). 1993. pap. 12.95 (*0-944459-76-5*) ECS Lrn Systs.

— Native Americans: An Integrated Unit. (Primary Thematic Units Ser.). (Illus.). 80p. (Orig.). 1993. pap. 12.95 (*0-944459-74-9*) ECS Lrn Systs.

— Oceans & Sea Life: An Integrated Unit. (Primary Thematic Units Ser.). (Illus.). 96p. (Orig.). 1993. pap. 12.95 (*0-944459-82-X*) ECS Lrn Systs.

— Plants: An Integrated Unit. (Primary Thematic Units Ser.). (Illus.). 96p. (Orig.). 1994. pap. 12.95 (*0-944459-83-8*) ECS Lrn Systs.

— Sports: An Integrated Unit. (Primary Thematic Units Ser.). (Illus.). 96p. (Orig.). 1993. pap. 12.95 (*0-944459-84-6*) ECS Lrn Systs.

— Stars & Planets: An Integrated Unit. (Primary Thematic Units Ser.). (Illus.). 96p. (Orig.). 1993. pap. 12.95 (*0-944459-85-4*) ECS Lrn Systs.

— Toys: An Integrated Unit. (Primary Thematic Units Ser.). (Illus.). 96p. (Orig.). 1993. pap. 12.95 (*0-944459-86-2*) ECS Lrn Systs.

— Ugh! Bugs! An Integrated Unit. (Primary Thematic Units Ser.). (Illus.). 96p. (Orig.). 1994. pap. 12.95 (*0-944459-87-0*) ECS Lrn Systs.

— Weather: An Integrated Unit. (Primary Thematic Units Ser.). (Illus.). 96p. (Orig.). 1993. pap. 12.95 (*0-944459-77-3*) ECS Lrn Systs.

Rogers, Kathy, ed. Color & Learn - Deserts. (Color & Learn Science Coloring Bks.). (Illus.). 32p. 1999. pap., teacher ed., wbk. ed. 3.99 (*1-56472-216-3*) Edupress Inc.

— Color & Learn - Dinosaurs. (Color & Learn Science Coloring Bks.). (Illus.). 32p. 1999. pap., teacher ed., wbk. ed. 3.99 (*1-56472-224-4*) Edupress Inc.

— Color & Learn - Insects. (Color & Learn Science Coloring Bks.). (Illus.). 32p. 1999. pap., teacher ed., wbk. ed. 3.99 (*1-56472-213-9*) Edupress Inc.

— Color & Learn - Landforms. (Color & Learn Science Coloring Bks.). (Illus.). 32p. 1999. pap., teacher ed., wbk. ed. 3.99 (*1-56472-217-1*) Edupress Inc.

— Color & Learn - Ocean Life. (Color & Learn Science Coloring Bks.). (Illus.). 32p. 1999. pap., teacher ed., wbk. ed. 3.99 (*1-56472-214-7*) Edupress Inc.

— Color & Learn - Plants. (Color & Learn Science Coloring Bks.). (Illus.). 32p. 1999. pap., teacher ed., wbk. ed. 3.99 (*1-56472-215-5*) Edupress Inc.

— Color & Learn - Rain Forest. (Color & Learn Science Coloring Bks.). (Illus.). 32p. 1999. pap., teacher ed., wbk. ed. 3.99 (*1-56472-218-X*) Edupress Inc.

— Color & Learn - Reptiles. (Color & Learn Science Coloring Bks.). (Illus.). 32p. 1999. pap., teacher ed., wbk. ed. 3.99 (*1-56472-223-6*) Edupress Inc.

— Color & Learn - Rocks & Minerals. (Color & Learn Science Coloring Bks.). (Illus.). 32p. 1999. pap., teacher ed., wbk. ed. 3.99 (*1-56472-219-8*) Edupress Inc.

— Color & Learn - Solar System. (Color & Learn Science Coloring Bks.). (Illus.). 32p. 1999. pap., teacher ed., wbk. ed. 3.99 (*1-56472-222-8*) Edupress Inc.

— Color & Learn - Space Exploration. (Color & Learn Science Coloring Bks.). (Illus.). 32p. 1999. pap., teacher ed., wbk. ed. 3.99 (*1-56472-220-1*) Edupress Inc.

— Color & Learn - Weather. (Color & Learn Science Coloring Bks.). (Illus.). 32p. 1999. pap., teacher ed., wbk. ed. 3.99 (*1-56472-221-X*) Edupress Inc.

— Color & Learn Africa. (Illus.). 32p. 1999. pap., wbk. ed. 3.99 (*1-56472-208-2*) Edupress Inc.

— Color & Learn Ancient Egypt. (Illus.). 32p. 1999. pap., wbk. ed. 3.99 (*1-56472-200-7*) Edupress Inc.

— Color & Learn Ancient Greece. (Illus.). 32p. 1999. pap., wbk. ed. 3.99 (*1-56472-209-0*) Edupress Inc.

— Color & Learn Ancient Rome. (Illus.). 32p. 1999. pap., wbk. ed. 3.99 (*1-56472-210-4*) Edupress Inc.

— Color & Learn Australia. (Illus.). 32p. 1999. pap., wbk. ed. 3.99 (*1-56472-203-1*) Edupress Inc.

— Color & Learn China. (Illus.). 32p. 1999. pap., wbk. ed. 3.99 (*1-56472-207-4*) Edupress Inc.

— Color & Learn Colonial America. (Illus.). 32p. (YA). 1999. pap. 3.99 (*1-56472-204-X*) Edupress Inc.

— Color & Learn Inca, Aztec, Maya. (Illus.). 32p. 1999. pap., wbk. ed. 3.99 (*1-56472-211-2*) Edupress Inc.

— Color & Learn Japan. (Illus.). 32p. 1999. pap., wbk. ed. 3.99 (*1-56472-206-6*) Edupress Inc.

— Color & Learn Native America. (Illus.). 32p. 1999. pap., wbk. ed. 3.99 (*1-56472-202-3*) Edupress Inc.

Rogers, Kathy, jt. auth. see Keller, Mary Jo.

Rogers, Kathy, jt. auth. see Milliken, Linda.

Rogers, Kathy, jt. auth. see Warner, Penny.

Rogers, Kathy, ed. see Adams, Elizabeth.

Rogers, Kathy, ed. see Button, Beth.

Rogers, Kathy, ed. see Campbell, Joanie, et al.

Rogers, Kathy, ed. see Chasin, Rachel.

Rogers, Kathy, ed. see Hamilton, Robyn.

Rogers, Kathy, ed. see Hudson, Dave.

Rogers, Kathy, ed. see Hudson, David.

Rogers, Kathy, ed. see Keller, Mary J.

Rogers, Kathy, ed. see Keller, Mary Jo.

Rogers, Kathy, ed. see Milliken, Linda.

Rogers, Kathy, ed. see Ryan, Concetta D.

Rogers, Kathy, ed. see Ryan, Constance Doti.

Rogers, Kathy, ed. see Shaw, Nancy.

Rogers, Kathy, ed. see Sterling, Mary Ellen.

Rogers, Kathy, ed. see Stout, Charlene.

Rogers, Kathy, ed. see Sussman, Ellen.

Rogers, Katrina. Toward a Postpositivist World: Hermeneutics for Understanding International Relations, Environment, & Other Important Issues of the Twenty-First Century. LC 94-10288. (San Francisco State University Series in Philosophy: Vol. 3). XXX, 185p. (C). 1996. text 47.95 (*0-8204-2486-2*) P Lang Pubng.

Rogers, Kelly. Self-interest: Anthology of Philosophical Perspectives from Antiquity to the Present. LC 96-48798. 296p. (C). 1997. 75.00 (*0-415-91251-2*); pap. 24.99 (*0-415-91252-0*) Routledge.

Rogers, Ken. Everton Greats. 176p. (C). 1989. pap. text 30.00 (*0-85976-274-2*, Pub. by J Donald) St Mut.

***Rogers, Ken E.** The Magnificent Mesquite. LC 99-50890. (Corrie Herring Hooks Ser.: Vol. 46). (Illus.). 200p. 2000. 24.95 (*0-292-77105-3*) U of Tex Pr.

***Rogers, Kenny & Junkermann, Kelly.** The Toy Shoppe Presents. (Illus.). 32p. (J). (gr. 2-7). 2000. 16.95 (*1-886110-94-8*, Pub. by Addax Pubng) Midpt Trade.

***Rogers, Kenny & Schlitz, Don.** Kenny Rogers Presents "The Greatest" (Illus.). 32p. (J). (gr. 2-7). 1999. 16.95 incl. audio compact disk (*1-886110-91-3*, Pub. by Addax Pubng) Midpt Trade.

Rogers, Kerry, jt. auth. see Timmons, Dayle M.

Rogers, Kim, jt. ed. see Mulchandani, Ashok.

Rogers, Kim L. Righteous Lives: Narratives of the New Orleans Civil Rights Movement. (Illus.). 254p. (C). 1992. text 45.00 (*0-8147-7431-8*) NYU Pr.

— Righteous Lives: Narratives of the New Orleans Civil Rights Movement. (Illus.). 254p. (C). 1995. pap. text 18.50 (*0-8147-7456-3*) NYU Pr.

***Rogers, Kim L., et al.** Trauma & Life Stories: International Perspectives. LC 99-28901. 1999. text. write for info. (*0-415-20688-X*) Routledge.

Rogers, Kim L., jt. ed. see McMahan, Eva M.

Rogers, Kim R., et al, eds. Biosensor & Chemical Sensor Technology: Process Monitoring & Control. LC 95-39897. (ACS Symposium Ser.: No. 613). (Illus.). 200p. 1995. text 59.00 (*0-8412-3330-6*, Pub. by Am Chemical) OUP.

Rogers, Kirsteen, ed. The Usborne Complete Book of the Microscope. (Complete Bks.). (Illus.). 96p. (YA). (gr. 3 up). 1999. pap. 14.95 (*0-7460-3106-8*, Usborne); lib. bdg. 22.95 (*1-58086-162-8*, Usborne) EDC.

Rogers, Krista F., ed. see Fritz, E. Mae.

Rogers, L. C. & Talay, D., eds. Numerical Methods in Finance. 336p. 1997. text 57.95 (*0-521-57354-8*) Cambridge U Pr.

***Rogers, L. C. G. & Williams, D.** Diffusions, Markov Processes & Martingales: Ito Calculus. (Cambridge Mathematical Library Ser.). 490p. (C). 2000. pap. Price not set. (*0-521-77593-0*) Cambridge U Pr.

— Diffusions, Markov Processes & Martingales Vol. 1: Foundations. 2nd ed. (Cambridge Mathematical Library Ser.). (Illus.). 406p. (C). 2000. pap. 37.95 (*0-521-77594-9*) Cambridge U Pr.

Rogers, L. E., ed. Methods in Plant Biochemistry Vol. 5: Amino Acids, Proteins & Nucleic Acids. 368p. 1991. text 104.00 (*0-12-461015-3*) Acad Pr.

Rogers, L. Edna, jt. ed. see Conville, Richard L.

R

Rogers, L. J. The Development of Brain & Behaviour in the Chicken. LC 97-179019. 288p. 1996. text 100.00 (0-85198-924-1) OUP.

***Rogers, L. Ken.** Post Traumatic Stress Disorder: A Police Officers Report. LC 99-75954. 272p. 2000. pap. 14.95 (1-882792-83-1) Proctor Pubns.

Rogers, L. W. Dreams & Premonitions. 144p. 1993. pap. 12.00 (0-89540-225-4, SB-225) Sun Pub.

— Dreams & Premonitions (1923) 144p. 1998. reprint ed. pap. 11.95 (0-7661-0339-0) Kessinger Pub.

— Elementary Theosophy (1929) 200p. 1998. reprint ed. pap. 17.95 (0-7661-0137-1) Kessinger Pub.

— The Ghosts in Shakespeare. LC 72-3658. (Studies in Shakespeare: No. 24). 1972. reprint ed. lib. bdg. 75.00 (0-8383-1567-4) M S G Haskell Hse.

— The Ghosts in Shakespeare: A Study of the Occultism in the Shakespeare Plays. 185p. 1995. reprint ed. pap. 17.95 (1-56459-497-1) Kessinger Pub.

— The Occultism in the Shakespeare Plays. 50p. 1993. reprint ed. pap. 6.00 (1-56459-401-7) Kessinger Pub.

— Reincarnation & Other Lectures (1925) 138p. 1998. reprint ed. pap. 17.95 (0-7661-0323-4) Kessinger Pub.

Rogers-Lafferty, Sarah. Encore: The Contemporary Arts Center's Fiftieth Anniversary. Krause, Carolyn, ed. (Illus.). 72p. 1989. pap. 25.00 (0-917562-54-2) Contemp Arts.

Rogers-Lafferty, Sarah, jt. auth. see Grundberg, Andy.

Rogers, Larry. Boatowner's Legal & Financial Advisor. (Illus.). 256p. 1993. pap. text 19.95 (0-87742-341-5) Intl Marine.

Rogers, Laura. A Collection of Fashion Drawings, 1901. (Illus.). 165p. 1983. pap. text 24.95 (0-914921-00-2) Graphic Ent.

Rogers, Laurette. The California Freshwater Shrimp Project. (Illus.). 40p. (Orig.). 1996. pap., teacher ed. 5.00 (0-930588-84-3) Heyday Bks.

Rogers, Laurine, jt. auth. see Rogers, Richard A.

Rogers, Lawrence, tr. see Agawa, Hiroyuki.

Rogers, Leah L., jt. auth. see Dowla, Farid U.

Rogers, Lee. All These Splendid Sins. (Orig.). 1979. mass mkt. 2.50 (0-89083-480-6, Zebra Kensgtn) Kensgtn Pub Corp.

Rogers, Lee F. Radiology of Skeletal Trauma, 2 vols. 2nd ed. LC 92-9204. (Illus.). 1619p. 1992. text 400.00 (0-443-08550-1) Church.

— Radiology of Skeletal Trauma, Vol. 1. LC 82-4181. (Illus.). 467p. reprint ed. pap. 144.80 (0-8357-6563-6, 203593600001) Bks Demand.

— Radiology of Skeletal Trauma, Vol. 2. LC 82-4181. (Illus.). 519p. reprint ed. pap. 160.90 (0-8357-6564-4, 203593600002) Bks Demand.

Rogers, Len. The Barclays Guide to Marketing for the Small Business. (Barclays Small Business Ser.). (Illus.). 180p. 1990. pap. text 31.95 (0-631-17247-5) Blackwell Pubs.

Rogers, Leon. Basic Construction Management: The Superintendent's Job. 3rd rev. ed. LC 95-12274. (Illus.). 96p. 1995. pap. 27.50 (0-86718-406-X) Home Builder.

***Rogers, Leon.** Basic Construction Management: The Superintendent's Job. 4th ed. LC 98-45915. 1998. 35.00 (0-86718-452-3) Home Builder.

Rogers, Leon & Weidman, Brent. Your Business Plan: How to Create It, How to Use It. Lamberton, Sharon, ed. LC 93-37571. (Illus.). 128p. (Orig.). 1993. pap. 22.00 (0-86718-390-X) Home Builder.

Rogers, Leonard C., et al. Clinical Outcomes in Home Health Care: A Guide to Performance Measurement & Oryx Implementation. LC 98-24895. 352p. 1998. ring bd. 159.00 (0-8342-0979-9, S477) Aspen Pub.

***Rogers, Lesley.** Sexing the Brain. (Maps of the Mind Ser.). 2001. 24.95 (0-231-12010-9) Col U Pr.

Rogers, Lesley J. Minds of Their Own: Thinking & Awareness in Animals. 212p. 1998. pap. 19.00 (0-8133-9065-6, Pub. by Westview) HarpC.

***Rogers, Lesley J. & Kaplan, Gisela T.** Songs, Roars, Rituals: Communication in Birds, Mammals & Other Animals. LC 00-25602. (Illus.). 224p. 2000. 29.95 (0-674-00058-7) HUP.

Rogers, Lesley J., jt. auth. see Kaplan, Gisela.

Rogers, Lilian, tr. see McCarthy, Rockne M., et al.

***Rogers, Lilith.** Persimmons: And Other Lesbian Erotica. (Illus.). 84p. 1999. pap. 11.95 (0-9671715-0-4) Earthy Mama.

Rogers, Lillian, ed. see Johnson, Veronica.

Rogers, Linda. Country Doughcraft Designs: 55 Step-by-Step Projects. LC 97-3329. 1997. 14.95 (0-89577-966-8, Pub. by RD Assn) Penguin Putnam.

— Country Doughcraft for Your Home. LC 98-85200. (Illus.). 128p. 1998. pap. 19.95 (0-8230-0964-5) Watsn-Guptill.

— 55 Celebration Doughcraft Designs. (Illus.). 128p. 1996. 24.95 (0-7153-0389-9, Pub. by D & C Pub) Sterling.

— 55 Celebration Doughcraft Designs. 1999. pap. text 14.95 (0-7153-0802-5) D & C Pub.

— 55 Country Doughcraft Designs. (Illus.). 128p. 1995. 24.95 (0-7153-0168-3, Pub. by D & C Pub) Sterling.

— The Magic Flute. 36p. 1992. pap. write for info. (0-88984-129-2) Porcup Quill.

— Ultimate Woman: Release Your Shining Spirit - Discover the Secrets of Total Concept Dress. unabridged ed. (Illus.). 224p. 1998. pap. 18.95 (0-9662246-0-4) DavLor Pubg.

— Wish I Were: Felt Pathways of the Self. (Illus.). 235p. 1998. pap. text 23.95 (1-891859-24-2) Atwood Pub LLC.

— Woman at Mile Zero. 1990. pap. 9.95 (0-88982-101-1, Pub. by Oolichan Bks) Genl Dist Srvs.

Rogers, Linda, jt. auth. see Rogers, Neal.

***Rogers, Linda J. & Swadener, Beth Blue.** Semiotics & Disability: Interrogating Categories of Difference. (C). 2001. pap. text 22.95 (0-7914-4906-8) State U NY Pr.

— Semiotics & Disability: Interrogating Categories of Difference. (C). 2001. text 68.50 (0-7914-4905-X) State U NY Pr.

Rogers, Linda K. & Rogers, John L. Geographic Literacy Through Children's Literature. LC 97-12081. (Illus.). 200p. 1997. lib. bdg. 22.00 (1-56308-439-2) Teacher Ideas Pr.

Rogers, Linda T. How to Start a Leadership Class. Rough, Jackie, ed. 64p. (Orig.). 1990. pap. 10.00 (0-88210-245-1, 6209004) Natl Assn Student.

Rogers, Lindsay. The Postal Powers of Congress: A Study in Constitutional Expansion. LC 78-63956. (Johns Hopkins University. Studies in the Social Sciences. Thirtieth Ser. 1912: 2). reprint ed. 37.50 (0-404-61204-0) AMS Pr.

— Tatting Collage, 1. LC 99-203163. (Illus.). 86p. 1999. pap. 9.95 (1-86108-020-4, Pub. by Guild Master) Sterling.

Rogers, Lisa W. Texas Sampler Workbook. 1998. pap. text 8.95 (0-89672-409-3) Tex Tech Univ Pr.

Rogers, Lisa W., ed. A Texas Sampler: Historical Recollections. LC 98-24589. (Illus.). 160p. (J). (gr. 4-7). 1998. pap. 14.95 (0-89672-393-3) Tex Tech Univ Pr.

***Rogers, Lisa Waller.** Angel of the Alamo. (Illus.). 48p. (J). (gr. 3-8). 2000. 18.95 (0-87443-125-5, 125-5); pap. 8.95 (0-87443-126-3, 126-3) Benson.

Rogers, Liz, jt. auth. see Hill, Harold.

Rogers, Lori. Feminine Nation: Performance, Gender & Resistance in the Works of John McGahern & Neil Jordan. LC 97-41212. 168p. (C). 1997. 49.00 (0-7618-0950-3); pap. 27.50 (0-7618-0951-1) U Pr of Amer.

Rogers, Lori, jt. auth. see Thornock, Chriscilla M.

Rogers, Louis. First Thanksgiving. (Illus.). (J). (ps-2). 1991. lib. bdg. 7.95 (0-8136-5206-5) Modern Curr.

Rogers, Louis, ed. see Al-Jerrahi, Muzaffer O.

Rogers, Louisa. Book of Forms: For Everyday Living. 3rd ed. LC 96-68780. (Illus.). 80p. 1997. pap. 11.95 (0-8442-0816-7, 08167) NTC Contemp Pub Co.

— Book of Forms for Everyday Living. 2nd ed. 88p. 1995. pap. 10.95 (0-8442-5327-8, Natl Textbk Co) NTC Contemp Pub Co.

Rogers, Louise. Rancho Santa Fe Coloring Book. LC 97-24463. (Illus.). 40p. (Orig.). (J). (gr. k-6). 1997. pap. 3.00 (0-938711-48-2) Tecolote Pubns.

***Rogers, Lura.** Switzerland. LC 99-56158. (Enchantment of the World Ser.). (Illus.). (J). 2001. write for info. (0-516-21080-7) Childrens.

Rogers, Lura & Rogers, Barbara. The Dominican Republic. LC 98-37087. (Enchantment of the World Ser.). 144p. (YA). (gr. 5-9). 1999. write for info. (0-516-21125-0) Childrens.

Rogers, Lynn. Great American Bear. (Illus.). 1990. 39.00 (1-55971-079-9, NorthWord Pr) Creat Pub Intl.

Rogers, Lynn, jt. auth. see Henry, Mari L.

Rogers, Lynne. Working in Show Business: Behind-the-Scenes Careers in Theater, Film & Television. LC 97-39335. (Illus.). 400p. 1997. pap. 18.95 (0-8230-8842-1, Back Stage Bks) Watsn-Guptill.

Rogers, Lynne, jt. auth. see Henry, Mari Lyn.

Rogers, M. Count with Teddy One Two Three. (Learn with Teddy Ser.). 32p. (J). 1995. 4.98 (1-85854-149-2) Brimax Bks.

— Dear God. (My First Prayers Ser.). (Illus.). 12p. (J). (ps). 1995. bds. 2.98 (0-86112-218-6) Brimax Bks.

— God Bless. (My First Prayers Ser.). (Illus.). 12p. (J). (ps). 1995. bds. 2.98 (0-86112-195-3) Brimax Bks.

— God Made. (My First Prayers Ser.). (Illus.). 12p. (J). (ps). 1994. bds. 2.98 (0-86112-219-4) Brimax Bks.

— Learn with Teddy ABC. (Learn with Teddy Ser.). 32p. (J). 1995. 4.98 (1-85854-150-6) Brimax Bks.

— Teddy & the Duckling. (Read to Me Ser.). 10p. (J). 1995. bds. 3.98 (1-85854-244-8) Brimax Bks.

— Teddy & the Frog. (Read to Me Ser.). 10p. (J). 1995. bds. 3.98 (1-85854-247-2) Brimax Bks.

— Teddy & the Mice. (Read to Me Ser.). 10p. (J). 1995. bds. 3.98 (1-85854-246-4) Brimax Bks.

— Teddy & the Puppy. (Read to Me Ser.). 10p. (J). 1995. bds. 3.98 (1-85854-245-6) Brimax Bks.

— Thank You God. (My First Prayers Ser.). (Illus.). 12p. (J). (ps). 1995. bds. 2.98 (0-86112-196-1) Brimax Bks.

Rogers, M. J. One Tough Texan. (Intrigue Ser.: No. 423). 1997. per. 3.75 (0-373-22423-0, 1-22423-7) Harlequin Bks.

Rogers, Maggie, ed. see Terninko, John.

Rogers, Malcolm. Elizabeth II: Portraits of Sixty Years. (Illus.). 112p. 1986. pap. 11.95 (0-904017-74-5, Pub. by Natl Port Gall) Antique Collect.

— Master Drawings: From the National Portrait Gallery. (Illus.). 224p. 1993. 49.50 (1-85514-134-5) Antique Collect.

— Museums & Galleries of London. 3rd rev. ed. (Blue Guide Ser.). (Illus.). 408p. 1991. pap. 22.95 (0-393-30774-3) Norton.

Rogers, Malcolm & Wohlauer, Gilian. Treasures of the Museum of Fine Arts, Boston. LC 96-13377. (Tiny Folio Ser.). (Illus.). 320p. 1996. pap. 11.95 (0-7892-0146-1) Abbeville Pr.

Rogers, Malcolm & Wohlauer, Gilian, intros. Treasures of the Museum of Fine Arts, Boston. (Illus.). 320p. 1998. 11.95 (0-7892-0506-8) Abbeville Pr.

Rogers, Malcolm, ed. see Piper, David.

***Rogers, Mara R.** Best 50 Brownies & Blondies. 80p. 2000. pap. 5.95 (1-55867-255-9, Best Fifty Ckbks) Bristol Pub Ent CA.

Rogers, Mara R. Creative Garnishing: Beautiful Ways to Enhance Meals. LC 94-7777. (Illus.). 128p. 1994. pap. 11.95 (1-56799-100-9, Friedman-Fairfax) M Friedman Pub Grp Inc.

— Instant Ethnic Cook: An Herb & Spice Blend Cookbook. LC 93-78928. 1993. 19.95 (0-9627403-4-9) Lake Isle Pr.

— Onions: A Celebration of the Onion Through Recipes, Lore, & History. 1995. 16.00 (0-201-62680-2) Addison-Wesley.

— Onions: A Celebration of the Onion Through Recipes, Lore, & History. (Illus.). 193p. 1998. text 16.00 (0-7881-5621-7) DIANE Pub.

Rogers, Marc. Saving Seeds: The Gardner's Guide to Growing & Storing Vegetable & Flower Seeds. Watson, Ben, ed. LC 90-50353. (Illus.). 176p. 1991. pap. 12.95 (0-88266-634-7) Storey Bks.

Rogers, Margaret. Make-Up Types & Styles. 128p. 1995. pap. text 24.50 (0-572-02142-9, Pub. by W Foulsham) Trans-Atl Phila.

Rogers, Margaret, jt. auth. see Makiya, Hind.

Rogers, Margaret, jt. ed. see Anderman, Gunilla.

Rogers, Marge. Once upon a Rhyme. (Illus.). 100p. (C). 1997. pap. text. write for info. (1-886352-14-3) Natl Poets Assn.

Rogers, Maria M., compiled by. In Other Words: Oral Histories of the Colorado Frontier. (Illus.). 204p. 1995. 24.95 (1-55591-218-4) Fulcrum Pub.

Rogers, Marion. Caribbean ABC. (Illus.). 26p. (Orig.). (J). (ps-1). 1992. reprint ed. pap. 3.50 (0-935357-02-5) CRIC Prod.

Rogers, Marion, ed. see Miller, Daniel W.

Rogers, Mark, jt. auth. see Jackson, R. Eugene.

Rogers, Mark C. Textbook of Pediatric Intensive Care, Vol. 2. 2nd ed. (Illus.). 1792p. 1992. text 195.00 (0-683-07319-2) Lppncott W & W.

Rogers, Mark C. & Helfaer, Mark A. Handbook of Pediatric Intensive Care. 2nd ed. (Illus.). 873p. 1994. 59.00 (0-683-07326-5) Lppncott W & W.

Rogers, Mark C. & Helfaer, Mark A., eds. Case Studies in Pediatric Intensive Care. LC 93-12263. (Illus.). 362p. 1993. 49.00 (0-683-07323-0) Lppncott W & W.

— Handbook of Pediatric Intensive Care. 3rd ed. LC 98-23780. 994p. 1998. pap. 49.00 (0-683-30571-9) Lppncott W & W.

Rogers, Mark C. & Nichols, David G., eds. Textbook of Pediatric Intensive Care. 3rd ed. LC 96-14624. (Illus.). 1832p. 1996. 179.00 (0-683-18034-7) Lppncott W & W.

Rogers, Mark C., ed. see Year Book of Critical Care Medicine Staff.

Rogers, Mark E. Samurai Cat Goes to Hell. LC 98-5555. 320p. 1998. pap. 13.95 (0-312-86642-9) St Martin.

— Samurai Cat Goes to the Movies. 288p. 1994. pap. 10.95 (0-312-85744-6, Pub. by Tor Bks) St Martin.

Rogers, Marliss. Weekly Prayer Services for Parish Meetings, Year B: Lectionary Based on Year B. LC 94-60153. 120p. (Orig.). 1996. pap. 12.95 (0-89622-693-X) Twenty-Third.

Rogers, Marliss, ed. Weekly Prayer Services for Parish Meetings, Cycle C. LC 94-60153. 120p. (Orig.). 1994. pap. 12.95 (0-89622-599-2) Twenty-Third.

— Weekly Prayer Services for Parish Meetings, Year A. LC 94-60153. 118p. (Orig.). 1995. pap. 12.95 (0-89622-646-8) Twenty-Third.

Rogers, Marliss, jt. auth. see Rademacher, William J.

Rogers, Martha, jt. auth. see Peppers, Don.

Rogers, Martin. Opting Out: Choice & the Future of Schools. 200p. (C). 1992. pap. 18.50 (0-85315-769-3, Pub. by Lawrence & Wishart) NYU Pr.

***Rogers, Martin, et al.** Electre & Decision Support. LC 99-44531. 1999. write for info. (0-7923-8647-7) Kluwer Academic.

Rogers, Mary. Baby Birds: Big. (Foundations Ser.). 33p. (J). (ps). 1992. pap. text 4.50 (1-56843-053-1) EMG Networks.

— Baby Birds: Big Book. (Foundations Ser.). 33p. (J). (ps-k). 1992. pap. text 23.00 (1-56843-003-5) EMG Networks.

— Big Brother. (Foundations Ser.). 19p. (J). (gr. k). 1992. pap. text 23.00 (1-56843-010-8); pap. text 4.50 (1-56843-060-4) EMG Networks.

— Daniel's First Bus Ride. (Foundations Ser.). 30p. (J). (gr. k). 1992. pap. text 4.50 (1-56843-058-2) EMG Networks.

— Daniel's First Bus Ride: Big Book. (Foundations Ser.). 30p. (J). (gr. k). 1992. pap. text 23.00 (1-56843-008-6) EMG Networks.

— The Ducks. (Foundations Ser.). 28p. (J). (ps). 1992. pap. text 23.00 (1-56843-000-0); pap. text 4.50 (1-56843-050-7) EMG Networks.

— Funny Names. (Foundations Ser.). 35p. (J). (gr. 1). 1992. pap. text 4.50 (1-56843-066-3) EMG Networks.

— Funny Names: Big Book. (Foundations Ser.). 35p. (J). (gr. 1). 1992. pap. text 23.00 (1-56843-016-7) EMG Networks.

— I Want to Play. (Foundations Ser.). 26p. (J). (gr. 1). 1992. pap. text 4.50 (1-56843-070-1) EMG Networks.

— I Want to Play: Big Book. (Foundations Ser.). 26p. (J). (gr. 1). 1992. pap. text 23.00 (1-56843-020-5) EMG Networks.

— Moving. (Foundations Ser.). 32p. (J). (ps). 1992. pap. text 23.00 (1-56843-001-9); pap. text 4.50 (1-56843-051-5) EMG Networks.

— New Puppy: Big Book. (Foundations Ser.). 35p. (J). (gr. k). 1992. pap. text 23.00 (1-56843-012-4); pap. text 4.50 (1-56843-062-0) EMG Networks.

— Too Little. (Foundations Ser.). 30p. (J). (ps). 1992. pap. text 4.50 (1-56843-052-3) EMG Networks.

— Too Little: Big Book. (Foundations Ser.). 30p. (J). (ps). 1992. pap. text 23.00 (1-56843-002-7) EMG Networks.

— The Torn Jacket. (Foundations Ser.). 30p. (J). (gr. 1). 1992. pap. text 4.50 (1-56843-068-X) EMG Networks.

— The Torn Jacket: Big Book. (Foundations Ser.). 30p. (J). (gr. 1). 1992. pap. text 23.00 (1-56843-018-3) EMG Networks.

— The Twins' First Bike. (Foundations Ser.). 34p. (J). (gr. 1). 1992. pap. text 4.50 (1-56843-069-8) EMG Networks.

— The Twins' First Bike: Big Book. (Foundations Ser.). 34p. (J). (gr. 1). 1992. pap. text 23.00 (1-56843-019-1) EMG Networks.

***Rogers, Mary, ed.** Fashioning Identities in Renaissance Art. (Illus.). 248p. 2000. text 78.95 (0-7546-0021-1, Pub. by Ashgate Pub) Ashgate Pub Co.

Rogers, Mary & Rosario, Bernada D. New Glasses. (Foundations Ser.). 28p. (J). (gr. 1). 1992. pap. text 4.50 (1-56843-071-X) EMG Networks.

— New Glasses: Big Book. (Foundations Ser.). 28p. (J). (gr. 1). 1992. pap. text 23.00 (1-56843-021-3) EMG Networks.

Rogers, Mary, jt. ed. see Ames-Lewis, Francis.

Rogers, Mary, tr. see Shanta, N.

Rogers, Mary A., ed. see Laborde, Errol.

***Rogers, Mary Beth.** Barbara Jordan: American Hero. (Illus.). 432p. 2000. pap. 14.95 (0-553-38066-4) Bantam.

Rogers, Mary Beth. Cold Anger: A Story of Faith & Power Politics. LC 90-35619. (Illus.). 226p. (Orig.). 1990. pap. 14.95 (0-929398-13-0) UNTX Pr.

Rogers, Mary Beth, jt. auth. see Terrell, Tracy D.

Rogers, Mary E. Domestic Life in Palestine. 390p. 1988. pap. 19.95 (0-7103-0290-8) Routledge.

***Rogers, Mary F.** Barbie Culture LC 98-61735. (Core Culture Icons Ser.). 171p. 1999. write for info. (0-7619-5888-6) Sage.

Rogers, Mary F. Contemporary Feminist Theory: A Text Reader. LC 97-40213. 512p. 1997. pap. 34.38 (0-07-054002-0) McGraw.

— Multicultural Experiences, Multicultural Theorizing. Ritzer, George, ed. LC 95-25248. 438p. (C). 1995. pap. 38.75 (0-07-053560-4) McGraw.

— Novels, Novelists, & Readers: Toward a Phenomenological Sociology of Literature. LC 90-9890. (SUNY Series in the Sociology of Culture). 332p. (C). 1991. pap. text 21.95 (0-7914-0603-2) State U NY Pr.

Rogers, Mary F., jt. auth. see Chase, Susan E.

Rogers, Mary S., jt. auth. see Palardy, Michael J.

Rogers, Marylyle. Chanting the Storm. Tolley, Carolyn, ed. (Illus.). 320p. (Orig.). 1994. mass mkt. 5.50 (0-671-87185-4) PB.

— Dark Whispers. Tolley, Carolyn, ed. 368p. (Orig.). 1992. mass mkt. 4.99 (0-671-70952-6) PB.

— The Eagle's Song. Tolley, Carolyn, ed. 368p. (Orig.). 1992. mass mkt. 4.99 (0-671-74561-1, Pocket Star Bks) PB.

— Happily Ever After. 1996. mass mkt. 5.99 (0-312-96046-8) St Martin.

— Hidden Hearts. 1989. mass mkt. 5.50 (0-671-65880-8) PB.

— The Keepsake. Tolley, Carolyn, ed. 336p. (Orig.). 1993. mass mkt. 5.50 (0-671-74562-X, Pocket Star Bks) PB.

— Long Ago & Far Away, Vol. 1. 1997. mass mkt. 5.99 (0-312-96314-9) St Martin.

— Once upon a Time. 1996. mass mkt. 5.99 (0-312-95758-0, Pub. by Tor Bks) St Martin.

— Proud Hearts. Tolley, Carolyn, ed. 352p. (Orig.). 1990. mass mkt. 5.50 (0-671-70235-1) PB.

— Twilight Secrets. Tolley, Carolyn, ed. 336p. (Orig.). 1994. mass mkt. 5.50 (0-671-87186-2, Pocket Star Bks) PB.

Rogers, May. The Waverley Dictionary. 1972. 75.00 (0-8490-1279-1) Gordon Pr.

Rogers, Meyric R. American Interior Design: The Traditions & Development of Domestic Design from Colonial Times to the Present. LC 75-22838. (America in Two Centuries Ser.). (Illus.). 1976. reprint ed. 34.95 (0-405-07709-2) Ayer.

Rogers, Meyric R., et al. Four American Painters: George Caleb Bingham, Winslow Homer, Thomas Eakins, Albert P. Ryder. LC 72-86438. (Museum of Modern Art Publications in Reprint). (Illus.). 1969. reprint ed. 20.95 (0-405-01547-X) Ayer.

Rogers, Michael. Public Sector Accounting. 318p. (C). 1999. pap. 64.50 (0-7487-1908-3, Pub. by S Thornes Pubs) Trans-Atl Phila.

Rogers, Michael & Losack, Marcus. Glendalough: A Celtic Pilgrimage. LC 97-21290. (Illus.). 144p. (Orig.). 1997. pap. 11.95 (0-8192-1694-1) Morehouse Pub.

Rogers, Michael A. The Secrets to Buying Diamonds. (Illus.). 114p. 1999. pap. 14.95 (0-9670148-0-8) Dakota.

Rogers, Michael C., et al. College Korean. 380p. 1991. pap. 34.95 (0-520-06994-3, Pub. by U CA Pr) Cal Prin Full Svc.

Rogers, Michael J. From Sherborne to a See: The Life of Bishop David Coutts. 205p. (C). 1989. 100.00 (0-7223-2364-6, Pub. by A H S Ltd) St Mut.

Rogers, Michael R. Teaching Approaches in Music Theory: An Overview of Pedagogical Philosophies. LC 83-10167. 236p. 1984. 31.95 (0-8093-1147-X) S Ill U Pr.

***Rogers, Michael Roger.** God Has No Secrets. 258p. 1999. 12.00 (0-9700244-0-1) Wars Over.

Rogers, Michelle. Bartow County, Georgia. LC 97-149469. (Images of America Ser.). (Illus.). 128p. 1999. pap. 16.99 (0-7524-0528-4) Arcadia Publng.

Rogers, Mike & Rogers, Debi. The Kingdom Agenda: Experiencing God in Your Workplace. (Everyday Discipleship Ser.). 96p. 1997. pap. text 7.95 (0-7673-3408-6, LifeWay Press) LifeWay Christian.

— Mi Experiencia Con Dios en el Trabajo. Orig. Title: The Kingdom Agenda. (SPA.). 160p. 1998. pap. text 9.50 (0-311-11200-5, Edit Mundo) Casa Bautista.

Rogers, Mikki. Home Grown Back in the Day. 265p. 1997. 24.95 (0-9663541-0-9) Creat Novels.

— $236.52 Every 2 Weeks . . . In Corporate America. 345p. 1998. pap. 17.95 (0-9663541-2-5) Creat Novels.

Rogers, Millard B., jt. auth. see Moseley, Spencer.

Rogers, Minor & Rogers, Ann. Rennyo: The Second Founder of Shin Buddhism. LC 91-43551. (Nanzan Studies in Asian Religions: Vol. 3). (Illus.). 456p. (C). 1992. pap. text 30.00 (0-89581-930-9) Asian Humanities.

An Asterisk (*) at the beginning of an entry indicates that the title is appearing for the first time.

R

Rogers, Murphy P. A State's Supervision of Its Elementary Schools. LC 73-177204. (Columbia University. Teachers College. Contributions to Education Ser.: No. 679). reprint ed. 37.50 (*0-404-55679-5*) AMS Pr.
Rogers, N. Bruce, ed. see Swedenborg, Emanuel.
Rogers, N. Bruce, tr. see Swedenborg, Emanuel.
Rogers, Nancy H. & McEwen, Craig A. Mediation: Law, Policy & Practice. 2nd ed. LC 94-39341. 1994. 120.00 (*0-614-32213-8*) West Group.
Rogers, Naomi. An Alternative Path: The Making & Remaking of Hahnemann Medical College & Hospital. LC 97-43595. (Illus.). 360p. (C). 1998. text 50.00 (*0-8135-2535-7*); pap. text 20.00 (*0-8135-2536-5*) Rutgers U Pr.
— Dirt & Disease: Polio Before FDR. LC 91-32642. (Health & Medicine in American Society Ser.). (Illus.). 276p. (C). 1992. text 45.00 (*0-8135-1785-0*); pap. text 17.95 (*0-8135-1786-9*) Rutgers U Pr.
Rogers, Natalie. The Creative Connection. LC 93-83958. 262p. 1993. pap. 29.95 (*0-8314-0080-3*) Sci & Behavior.
— Emerging Woman: A Decade of Midlife Transitions. LC 79-92627. 1980. 9.95 (*0-9605634-0-7*) Personal Press.
Rogers, Natalie H. The New Talkpower: A "Pain Clinic" for Public Speaking. LC 98-28266. (Illus.). 300p. 1998. 24.95 (*1-892123-03-7*) Capital VA.
***Rogers, Natalie H.** New Talkpower: The Mind-Body Way to Speak Like a Pro. 2000. pap. 15.95 (*1-892123-24-X*) Capital VA.
Rogers, Nathalie B. Fictions du Scandale: Corps Feminin et Realisme Romanesque Au Dix Neuvieme Siecle. (FRE.). 1998. 36.95 (*1-55753-123-4*) Purdue U Pr.
Rogers, Neal & Rogers, Linda. Saltwater Fly-Fishing Magic. (Illus.). 144p. 1993. 45.00 (*1-55821-253-1*) Lyons Pr.
Rogers, Nell & Rogers, Guy. The Medical Mischief, You Say! Degerminating the Germ Theory. 1996. reprint ed. spiral bd. 8.50 (*0-7873-0735-1*) Hlth Research.
Rogers, Neville. Keats, Shelley & Rome. LC 75-22076. (English Literature Ser.: No. 33). 1975. lib. bdg. 75.00 (*0-8383-2080-5*) M S G Haskell Hse.
Rogers, Nicholas. Crowds, Culture & Politics in Georgian Britain. LC 98-13096. 304p. 1998. text 75.00 (*0-19-820172-9*) OUP.
— Valley of the Stour from Western Green to Harwich. unabridged ed. (Illus.). 144p. 1999. pap. 20.00 (*0-86025-444-5*, Pub. by I Henry Pubns) Empire Pub Srvs.
— Whigs & Cities: Popular Politics in the Age of Walpole & Pitt. 450p. 1990. text 95.00 (*0-19-821785-4*) OUP.
Rogers, Nicholas, jt. auth. see Hay, Douglas.
Rogers, Nicholas, jt. ed. see Lovejoy, Paul E.
***Rogers, Nicola & Immigration Law Practitioners' Association Staff.** A Practitioners' Guide to the EC-Turkey Association Agreement. LC 99-48000. 256p. 1999. 111.00 (*90-411-1281-2*) Kluwer Law Intl.
Rogers, P. L. & Fleet, Graham H., eds. Biotechnology & the Food Industry. 320p. 1989. text 92.00 (*2-88124-354-1*) Gordon & Breach.
Rogers, P. P. & Lapuente, F. A. Diccionario de Seudonimos Literarios Espanoles, Con Algunas Iniciales. (SPA.). 610p. 1993. 69.50 (*84-249-1352-3*) Elliots Bks.
Rogers, P. Thomas. The Medical Student's Guide to Top Board Scores. (Illus.). 236p. (Orig.). (C). 1994. pap. text 24.95 (*0-9632231-0-0*) Innovat Pub & Graph.
Rogers, Pamela & Baldwin, Steve, compiled by. Controlled or Reduced Smoking: An Annotated Bibliography, 11. LC 99-22095. (Bibliographies & Indexes in Psychology Ser.: No. 11). 168p. 1999. lib. bdg. 65.00 (*0-313-30988-4*, GR0988, Greenwood Pr) Greenwood.
Rogers, Pat. The Economy of the Arts in the 18th Century. 224p. 1989. 39.00 (*0-7185-1281-2*) St Martin.
— Essays on Pope. LC 92-29785. 273p. (C). 1993. text 64.95 (*0-521-41869-0*) Cambridge U Pr.
— Johnson & Boswell: The Transit of Caledonia. (Illus.). 256p. 1995. text 60.00 (*0-19-818259-7*) OUP.
— The Samuel Johnson Encyclopedia. LC 95-33072. 520p. 1996. lib. bdg. 89.50 (*0-313-29411-9*, Greenwood Pr) Greenwood.
— The Text of Great Britain: Theme & Design in Defoe's "Tour" LC 97-727. 248p. (C). 1998. 40.50 (*0-87413-617-2*) U Delaware Pr.
Rogers, Pat, ed. An Outline of English Literature. 2nd ed. LC 98-17245. (Illus.). 528p. 1998. pap. 15.95 (*0-19-288078-0*) OUP.
— The Oxford Illustrated History of English Literature. (Illus.). 544p. 1990. reprint ed. pap. 24.95 (*0-19-282728-6*) OUP.
Rogers, Pat, intro. Persuasion. 318p. 1994. 3.95 (*0-460-87529-9*, Everyman's Classic Lib) Tuttle Pubng.
Rogers, Pat & Kaiser, Gabriele, eds. Equity in Mathematics Education: Influences of Feminism & Culture. LC 94-43477. 1995. 85.00 (*0-7507-0400-4*, Falmer Pr) Taylor & Francis.
— Equity in Mathematics Education: Influences of Feminism & Culture. LC 94-43477. 278p. 1995. pap. 27.95 (*0-7507-0401-2*, Falmer Pr) Taylor & Francis.
Rogers, Pat, ed. see Johnson, Samuel & Boswell, James.
Rogers, Pat, ed. see Pope, Alexander.
Rogers, Pat, ed. see Swift, Jonathan.
Rogers, Pat, ed. & intro. see Swift, Jonathan.
Rogers, Patricia, jt. auth. see Owen, John M.
Rogers, Patricia, jt. auth. see Rogers, Steve.
Rogers, Patricia N., ed. JTEC Program Summary. (Program Summaries Ser.). xvi, 99p. 1991. pap. write for info. (*1-883712-18-1*, JTEC) Intl Tech Res.
Rogers, Patricia S., jt. auth. see Rogers, Steve.
Rogers, Patrick, tr. see Martini, Carlo C.
Rogers, Patrick F. Target Zone. (Omega Ser.). 1993. per. 3.50 (*0-373-63209-6*, 1-63209-0) Harlequin Bks.
— War God. 1990. mass mkt. 4.50 (*1-55817-436-2*, Pinncle Kensgtn) Kensgtn Pub Corp.
— War Machine. (Omega Ser.). 1993. per. 3.50 (*0-373-63207-X*, 1-63207-4) Harlequin Bks.
— Zero Hour. (Omega Ser.). 1993. mass mkt. 3.50 (*0-373-63208-8*, 1-63208-2) Harlequin Bks.
Rogers, Pattiann. The Dream of the Marsh Wren: Writing As Reciprocal Creation. LC 98-50946. (Credo Ser.: Vol. 2). 160p. 1999. 20.00 (*1-57131-228-5*); pap. 12.00 (*1-57131-225-0*) Milkweed Ed.
— Eating Bread & Honey. LC 96-46697. 120p. (Orig.). 1997. pap. 13.95 (*1-57131-406-7*) Milkweed Ed.
— Firekeeper: New & Selected Poems. LC 94-10655. (Illus.). 262p. (Orig.). 1994. pap. 12.95 (*1-57131-400-8*) Milkweed Ed.
— Splitting & Binding. LC 88-28065. (Wesleyan Poetry Ser.). 61p. 1989. pap. 12.95 (*0-8195-1173-0*, Wesleyan Univ Pr) U Pr of New Eng.
Rogers, Pattiann, jt. auth. see Curry, David P.
Rogers, Paul. Nearly but Not Quite. (J). 1997. 19.95 (*0-370-32423-4*, Pub. by Random) Trafalgar.
Rogers, Paul. The Shapes Game. LC 89-19957. (Illus.). 32p. (J). (ps-2). 1995. 12.95 (*0-8050-1280-X*, Bks Young Read) H Holt & Co.
— What Can You See? LC 97-32716. (Illus.). 32p. (J). (ps-2). 1998. 15.95 (*0-385-32603-3*) Doubleday.
Rogers, Paul, text. Subject of Painting: A Selection by Paul Rogers of 9 Contemporary Painters Working in France. (Illus.). 1982. pap. 20.00 (*0-905836-32-4*, Pub. by Museum Modern Art) St Mut.
Rogers, Paul & Prater, John. Nearly but Not Quite. (Illus.). 32p. (J). (ps-1). 1998. 19.95 (*0-370-32432-3*, Pub. by Bodley Head) Trafalgar.
Rogers, Paul & Rogers, Emma. Bat Boy. (Illus.). 96p. (J). (gr. 5-8). 1993. pap. 6.95 (*0-460-88153-1*, Pub. by J M Dent & Sons) Trafalgar.
— Our House. LC 92-53015. (Illus.). 40p. (J). (ps up). 1993. 14.95 (*1-56402-134-3*) Candlewick Pr.
Rogers, Paul, jt. auth. see Dando, Malcolm.
Rogers, Paul, jt. auth. see Landais-Stamp, Paul.
Rogers, Paul, jt. auth. see Randle, Michael.
Rogers, Paul P. The Bitter Years: MacArthur & Sutherland. LC 90-36984. 376p. 1990. 75.00 (*0-275-92919-1*, C2919, Praeger Pubs) Greenwood.
— Insurance in the Soviet Union. LC 86-9437. 222p. 1986. 67.95 (*0-275-92255-3*, C2255, Praeger Pubs) Greenwood.
— MacArthur & Sutherland: The Good Years. LC 89-27560. 408p. 1990. 75.00 (*0-275-92918-3*, C2918, Praeger Pubs) Greenwood.
Rogers, Paul P., compiled by. The Spanish Civil War: An Exhibit. (Illus.). 1978. pap. 8.00 (*0-87959-083-1*) U of Tex H Ransom Ctr.
Rogers, Paul P., et al. Insurance in Socialist East Europe. LC 87-29248. 204p. 1988. 59.95 (*0-275-92903-5*, C2903, Praeger Pubs) Greenwood.
Rogers, Paul T. Forget-Me-Not. (Picture Puffin Ser.). (Illus.). 32p. (J). (ps). 1986. pap. 3.50 (*0-685-43615-2*, PuffinBks) Peng Put Young Read.
— Saul's Book. 1983. 15.95 (*0-916366-16-2*, Pub. by Pushcart Pr) Norton.
— Saul's Book. 1996. reprint ed. mass mkt. 6.95 (*1-56333-462-3*, Hard Candy) Masquerade.
Rogers, Paul T. & Coleman, Harry. Medical Care in Down Syndrome: A Preventive Medicine Approach. No. 8. (Pediatric Habilitation Ser.: Vol. 8). (Illus.). 360p. 1992. text 75.00 (*0-8247-8684-X*) Dekker.
Rogers, Pauline B. Art of Visual Effects: Interviews on the Tools of the Trade. LC 99-23410. 352p. 1999. pap. 32.95 (*0-240-80375-2*, Focal) Buttrwrth-Heinemann.
— Contemporary Cinematographers on Their Art. LC 97-40152. 240p. 1998. pap. 19.95 (*0-240-80309-4*, Focal) Buttrwrth-Heinemann.
***Rogers, Pauline B.** More Contemporary Cinematographers on Their Art. 224p. 2000. pap. 19.95 (*0-240-80368-X*, Focal) Buttrwrth-Heinemann.
***Rogers, Peggy O.** Heart to Heart... World's Apart. (Illus.). 170p. 1999. pap. 7.99 (*0-9676501-0-0*, Pub. by P A Rogers) Granite Pub.
Rogers, Penelope R., jt. auth. see Essa, Eva.
Rogers, Perry M. Aspects of Western Civilization: Problems & Sources in History. 4th ed. LC 99-26935. 519p. 1999. pap. text 32.00 (*0-13-083202-2*) P-H.
Rogers, Perry M., ed. Aspects of Western Civilization, Vol. 1. 3rd ed. 592p. (C). 1996. pap. text 35.00 (*0-13-341588-0*) P-H.
Rogers, Peter. America's Water: Federal Roles & Responsibilities. (Twentieth Century Fund Bk.). (Illus.). 297p. 1996. reprint ed. pap. text 17.00 (*0-262-68090-4*) MIT Pr.
— From Paul with Love. 32p. (J). 1996. 15.99 (*1-56476-572-5*, 6-3572, Victor Bks) Chariot Victor.
— A Painter's Quest: Art As a Way of Revelation. (Orig.). 1994. pap. 17.95 (*1-879041-22-7*) Sigo Pr.
Rogers, Peter & Bacon, Michael, eds. Costs Law Reports. 330p. 1997. pap. 231.00 (*1-85811-134-X*, Pub. by CLT Prof) Gaunt.
Rogers, Peter & Llamas, M. Ramon. Wetlands: A Multidisciplinary Approach. Date not set. 59.95 (*1-56670-153-8*) CRC Pr.
Rogers, Peter & Lydon, Peter, eds. Water in the Arab World: Perspectives & Prognoses. LC 94-37287. 1994. write for info. (*0-674-94789-4*) HUP.
— Water in the Arab World: Perspectives & Prognoses. (Illus.). 300p. 1995. pap. text 25.00 (*0-674-94780-0*, ROGWAT) HUP.
Rogers, Peter, et al. Measuring Environmental Quality in Asia. 386p. 1998. pap. 15.00 (*971-561-104-4*, Pub. by Asian Devel Bank) Paul & Co Pubs.
Rogers, Peter, jt. auth. see McKay, Mathew.
Rogers, Peter, jt. auth. see Willett, Ed.
Rogers, Peter S. Proust: Speculative Scripture: The Reader of His Own Self. Olds, Marshall C., ed. (STCL Monographs: No. 2). 200p. (Orig.). 1992. pap. 4.40 (*0-9624892-1-2*) Studies Twentieth.
Rogers, Peter S., tr. see Finkielkraut, Alain.
Rogers, Peter T. The Medical Student's Guide to Top Board Scores. 2nd ed. LC 95-34056. 146p. 1995. pap. text 15.95 (*0-316-75436-6*, Little Brwn Med Div) Lppncott W & W.
Rogers, Peter T. & Ruiz-Rogers, Olga. Quick Medical Spanish. 2nd ed. LC 96-31450. 183p. (C). 1997. pap. text 24.95 incl. audio (*0-8385-8258-3*, A8258-4, Apple Lange Med) McGraw.
Rogers, Phil. Ash Glazes. 2nd ed. (Illus.). 144p. 1992. reprint ed. text 39.95 (*1-889250-12-0*) Gentle Br.
— Throwing Pots. (Illus.). 128p. (Orig.). 1995. pap. 22.95 (*1-889250-04-X*) Gentle Br.
Rogers, Phila. California Tales: From the Mountains to the Sea. (Illus.). 92p. 1999. boxed set 36.95 incl. audio (*1-893366-00-6*); boxed set 36.95 (*1-893366-01-4*) Sola Pub.
Rogers, Philip, et al. Coal: Carriage by Sea. (Illus.). 250p. 1991. 120.00 (*1-85044-391-2*) LLP.
Rogers, Phillip A., jt. auth. see Craig, John R.
Rogers, R. Colossians. 1989. pap. 22.00 (*0-86217-032-X*, Pub. by Veritas Pubns) St Mut.
— Latin Siege Warfare in the Twelfth Century. (Oxford Historicals Monographs). (Illus.). 304p. 1997. pap. text 21.00 (*0-19-820689-5*) OUP.
Rogers, R. C., jt. auth. see Rogers, C. A.
Rogers, R. J., jt. auth. see Australian Bureau of Statistics Staff.
Rogers, R. Mark. Handbook of Key Economic Indicators. 288p. 1994. text 50.00 (*0-7863-0193-7*, Irwn Prfssnl) McGraw-Hill Prof.
— The Handbook of Key Economic Indicators. 2nd ed. LC 97-51903. 300p. 1998. 55.00 (*0-07-054045-4*) McGraw-Hill Prof.
Rogers, R. R. Short Course in Cloud Physics. 3rd ed. LC 88-22709. 304p. 2000. pap. text 49.95 (*0-7506-3215-1*) Buttrwrth-Heinemann.
Rogers, R. Vashon, Jr. Drinks, Drinkers & Drinking: or The Law & History of Intoxicating Liquors. iv, 241p. 1985. reprint ed. 37.00 (*0-8377-1043-X*, Rothman) W S Hein.
— Law & Medical Men. xiii, 214p. 1981. reprint ed. 38.00 (*0-8377-1032-4*, Rothman) W S Hein.
— Law of the Road: Or Wrongs & Rights of a Traveller. LC 97-1952. (Legal Recreations Ser.: Vol. IV). viii, 275p. 1997. reprint ed. 41.00 (*0-8377-2580-1*, Rothman) W S Hein.
Rogers, Rachel Watkins & Chan, Susan D., eds. Zoo & Aquarium Professionals: The History of AAZK. (Illus.). 206p. 1992. pap. 10.00 (*1-929672-04-7*) Am Assn Zoo Keep.
Rogers, Ralph B. Splendid Torch. LC 93-39006. (Illus.). 1993. 25.00 (*0-914659-66-9*) Phoenix Pub.
Rogers, Raymond A. Nature & the Crisis of Modernity. 187p. 1995. pap. 19.99 (*1-55164-014-7*, Pub. by Black Rose) Consort Bk Sales.
— The Oceans Are Emptying: Fish Wars & Sustainability. LC 95-79350. 176p. 1995. 48.99 (*1-55164-031-7*, Pub. by Black Rose); pap. 19.99 (*1-55164-030-9*, Pub. by Black Rose) Consort Bk Sales.
— Solving History: The Challenge of Environmental Activism. 275p. 1997. pap. text 24.99 (*1-55164-112-7*, Pub. by Black Rose) Consort Bk Sales.
— Solving History: The Challenge of Environmental Activism. 275p. 1998. 53.99 (*1-55164-113-5*, Pub. by Black Rose) Consort Bk Sales.
Rogers, Renee & Scardellato, Gabriele P., compiled by. A Bibliography of Canada's Peoples, 1980-1989. 275p. 1996. 25.00 (*0-919045-71-5*) U of Toronto Pr.
— A Bibliography of Canada's Peoples, 1980-1989, 2 vols., Vol. 1. 524p. 1995. 32.00 (*0-919045-69-3*) U of Toronto Pr.
Rogers, Rex & Rogers, Wendy. Stories of Childhood: Shifting Agendas of Child Concern. 228p. 1992. text 65.00 (*0-8020-2974-4*) U of Toronto Pr.
Rogers, Rex M. Seducing America: Is Gambling a Good Bet? LC 96-50062. 176p. (Orig.). 1997. pap. 10.99 (*0-8010-5759-0*) Baker Bks.
Rogers, Rex S. Stories of Childhood: Shifting Agendas of Child Concern. LC 93-136336. 228p. 1994. pap. text 19.95 (*0-8020-6944-4*) U of Toronto Pr.
Rogers, Rex S., ed. Sex Education, Rationale & Reaction. LC 73-89764. 295p. reprint ed. pap. 84.10 (*0-608-12492-3*, 2024519) Bks Demand.
Rogers, Richard. Architecture: A Modern View. LC 90-71314. (Walter Neurath Memorial Lectures). (Illus.). 64p. 1991. 14.95 (*0-500-55022-0*, Pub. by Thames Hudson) Norton.
— Architecture: A Modern View. LC 90-71314. (Walter Neurath Memorial Lectures). (Illus.). 64p. 1992. pap. 9.95 (*0-500-27651-X*, Pub. by Thames Hudson) Norton.
— Cities for a Small Planet. 196p. 1998. pap. text 18.00 (*0-8133-3553-1*, Pub. by Westview) HarpC.
***Rogers, Richard.** Dome. 2000. pap. 15.95 (*1-86154-148-1*) Booth-Clibborn.
Rogers, Richard. Judges. 1983. 69.99 (*0-85151-377-8*) Banner of Truth.
— Temping: The Insider's Guide. 1996. 14.95 (*0-02-861060-1*) Macmillan.
Rogers, Richard, ed. Clinical Assessment of Malingering & Deception. 2nd ed. LC 96-43033. 5250p. 1997. lib. bdg. 50.00 (*1-57230-173-2*) Guilford Pubns.
***Rogers, Richard & Shuman, Daniel W.** Conducting Insanity Evaluations. 2nd ed. 342p. 2000. lib. bdg. 40.00 (*1-57230-521-5*, C0521) Guilford Pubns.
Rogers, Richard & Sparacino, Frank. Roosevelt & the Magic Box. (Illus.). 24p. (J). 1994. lib. bdg. 11.95 (*0-9642564-9-5*) Bookbuddy.
Rogers, Richard, et al. Adventure on Thunder Island. LC 95-83842. (Illus.). 32p. (J). (gr. k-3). 1996. lib. bdg. 11.95 (*0-9642564-8-7*) Bookbuddy.
Rogers, Richard, jt. auth. see Marland, Michael.
Rogers, Richard, jt. ed. see Barton, John.
Rogers, Richard A. & Rogers, Laurine. The Outrageous Atlas: A Guide to North America's Strangest Places. (Illus.). 160p. 1993. pap. 9.95 (*0-8065-1445-0*, Citadel Pr) Carol Pub Group.
***Rogers, Richard B., ed.** Trustee Responsibilities Pt. II: Enhancing Staff Understanding. 72p. 2000. pap. 12.00 (*1-888310-90-1*) A A Knoll Pubs.
Rogers, Richard B., jt. ed. see Schneider, Edward L.
Rogers, Richard G., et al. Living & Dying in the U. S. A. Behavioral, Health, & Social Differentials of Adult Mortality. LC 99-61537. (Illus.). 368p. 1999. 69.95 (*0-12-593130-1*) Acad Pr.
Rogers, Richard M. Looking for Love On-Line. 1997. 12.95 (*0-614-19925-5*) Macmillan.
Rogers, Richard T., jt. ed. see Royer, Jeffrey S.
***Rogers, Richard W., text.** Shipwrecks of Hawaii: A Maritime History of the Big Island. (Shipwrecks of the Sandwich Islands: Vol. 1). (Illus.). 296p. (Orig.). 1999. pap. 24.04 (*0-9673467-0-3*, Pub. by Pilialoha) Booklines Hawaii.
***Rogers, Rick.** Surveying the Living Religions: A Student Workbook. 124p. (C). 1999. spiral bd. 17.95 (*0-7872-5965-9*, 41596501) Kendall-Hunt.
— Theophilus of Antioch: The Life & Thought of a Second-Century Bishop. 224p. 2000. 55.00 (*0-7391-0132-3*) Lxngtn Bks.
Rogers-Ripoll, Doris B. Childhood's Fires & Rivers. LC 97-17836. 60p. 1997. pap. 14.95 (*0-7734-2834-8*, Mellen Poetry Pr) E Mellen.
***Rogers, Rita S. & Garnett, N.** From One World to Another. large type ed. (Illus.). 304p. 1999. 31.99 (*0-7089-9062-2*) Ulverscroft.
Rogers, Rita S., jt. auth. see Mack, John E.
Rogers, Robert. Journals of Major Robert Rogers. Hough, Franklin B., ed. (New Jersey in the French & Indian Wars Ser.: Vol. 3). 278p. 1997. 21.95 (*1-58057-021-6*, JMRR003B) Digital Antiq.
— Rogers' Reminiscences of the French War & Memoir of General Stark. LC 88-80441. (Illus.). 343p. (Orig.). 1988. pap. 20.00 (*0-9620261-3-1*) Freedom Historical.
— Self & Other: Object Relations in Psychoanalysis & Literature. (Psychoanalytic Crosscurrents Ser.). 228p. (C). 1991. text 45.00 (*0-8147-7418-0*) NYU Pr.
— Self & Other: Object Relations in Psychoanalysis & Literature. (Psychoanalytic Crosscurrents Ser.). 228p. (C). 1993. pap. text 18.50 (*0-8147-7443-1*) NYU Pr.
Rogers, Robert C. Old Dorset. LC 76-140338. (Short Story Index Reprint Ser.). 1977. 17.95 (*0-8369-3730-9*) Ayer.
Rogers, Robert C., jt. auth. see Renardy, Michael.
Rogers, Robert F. Destiny's Landfall: A History of Guam. LC 94-25845. (Illus.). 416p. (C). 1995. pap. text 25.00 (*0-8248-1678-1*) UH Pr.
Rogers, Robert L. & Copp, Tara. The Daily Texan: The First Hundred Years. LC 99-13404. 1999. 29.95 (*1-57168-302-X*, Eakin Pr) Sunbelt Media.
Rogers, Robert M. Our 125th Regiment Illinois Volunteer Infantry: Attention Batallion! (Illus.). 226p. 1999. reprint ed. lib. bdg. 35.00 (*0-8328-9813-9*) Higginson Bk Co.
Rogers, Robert S. Studies in the Reign of Tiberius. LC 77-152601. 181p. 1972. reprint ed. lib. bdg. 52.50 (*0-8371-6036-7*, RORT, Greenwood Pr) Greenwood.
Rogers, Robert S. & Chamberlain, V. B., eds. National Account Marketing Handbook. LC 80-25435. 299p. reprint ed. pap. 92.70 (*0-608-15005-3*, 205608900047) Bks Demand.
Rogers, Robert T. Love Will Live & Other Selected Poems. Ware, Claude, ed. & frwd. by. (Illus.). 80p. 1995. pap. 8.00 (*0-9640995-1-9*) Mitram Bks.
Rogers, Robert W. A History of Ancient Persia. LC 70-168502. (Select Bibliographies Reprint Ser.). 1977. reprint ed. 42.95 (*0-8369-5942-6*) Ayer.
— A History of Babylonia & Assyria, 2 vols, Set. LC 76-165806. (Select Bibliographies Reprint Ser.). 1977. reprint ed. 60.95 (*0-8369-5961-2*) Ayer.
Rogers, Robert W., ed. Cuneiform Parallels to the Old Testament. 1977. lib. bdg. 250.00 (*0-8490-1695-9*) Gordon Pr.
Rogers, Robert W., ed. see Warns, E. Fredy & Boulette, Jack.
***Rogers, Roberta S.** Is That You, Lord? Practical Methods for Learning Spiritual Discernment. LC 99-59680. 224p. 2000. pap. 12.99 (*0-8007-9275-0*) Chosen Bks.
Rogers, Robin D. & Eiteman, Mark A., eds. Aqueous Biphasic Separations: Biomolecules to Metal Ions, Vol. 1. (Illus.). 200p. (C). 1995. text 85.00 (*0-306-45019-4*, Kluwer Plenum) Kluwer Academic.
Rogers, Robin D. & Zaworotko, Michael J., eds. Crystal Engineering. (Translations of the American Crystallographic Association Ser.: Vol. 30). (Illus.). 178p. (C). 1997. pap. text 25.00 (*0-937140-43-0*) Am Crystallographic.
Rogers, Rolf E., ed. Implementation of Total Quality Management: A Comprehensive Training Program. LC 95-35018. (Illus.). 117p. (C). 1996. 39.95 (*1-56024-996-X*, Intl Busn Pr) Haworth Pr.
— Implementation of Total Quality Management: A Comprehensive Training Program. LC 95-35018. 117p. (C). 1997. pap. 14.95 (*0-7890-0209-4*, Intl Busn Pr) Haworth Pr.
Rogers, Ronald C., jt. auth. see Doeleman, David.
Rogers, Ronald L. & McMillan, C. Scott. The Healing Bond: Treating Addictions in Groups. (C). 1989. pap. 13.95 (*0-393-70088-7*) Norton.
Rogers, Ronald L. & McMillan, Chandler S. Freeing Someone You Love from Alcohol & Other Drugs. 1992. pap. 14.95 (*0-399-51727-8*, Perigee Bks) Berkley Pub.

Rogers, Rosemary. All I Desire. LC 98-93300. 384p. 1999. mass mkt. 6.99 (*0-380-80025-X*, Avon Bks) Morrow Avon.
— Bound by Desire. 416p. 1988. mass mkt. 6.50 (*0-380-75451-7*, Avon Bks) Morrow Avon.
— The Crowd Pleasers. 528p. 1980. mass mkt. 6.50 (*0-380-75622-6*, Avon Bks) Morrow Avon.
— Dangerous Man. LC 96-96437. 384p. 1996. mass mkt. 6.99 (*0-380-78604-4*, Avon Bks) Morrow Avon.
— Dark Fires Bk. 2: Steve & Ginny. (Steve & Ginny Ser.: Bk. 1). 608p. 1976. reprint ed. mass mkt. 6.99 (*0-380-00425-9*, Avon Bks) Morrow Avon.
***Rogers, Rosemary.** In Your Arms. 384p. 1999. mass mkt. 6.99 (*0-380-80026-8*, Avon Bks) Morrow Avon.
Rogers, Rosemary. The Insiders. 1979. mass mkt. 6.50 (*0-380-40576-8*, Avon Bks) Morrow Avon.
— Lost Love, Last Love. (Steve & Ginny Ser.: Bk. 3). 384p. 1980. reprint ed. mass mkt. 5.99 (*0-380-75515-7*, Avon Bks) Morrow Avon.
— Love Play. 384p. 1982. mass mkt. 6.50 (*0-380-81190-1*, Avon Bks) Morrow Avon.
— Midnight Lady. LC 97-93179. 390p. 1997. mass mkt. 6.99 (*0-380-78605-2*, Avon Bks) Morrow Avon.
***Rogers, Rosemary.** Savage Desire. 2000. mass mkt. 7.50 (*1-55166-621-9*, Mira Bks) Harlequin Bks.
Rogers, Rosemary. Surrender to Love. LC 82-90286. 624p. 1982. mass mkt. 6.50 (*0-380-80630-4*, Avon Bks) Morrow Avon.
— Sweet Savage Love. (Steve & Ginny Ser.: Bk. 1). 640p. 1976. mass mkt. 5.99 (*0-380-00815-7*, Avon Bks) Morrow Avon.
— Tea Planter's Bride. 416p. 1995. mass mkt. 6.99 (*0-380-76477-6*, Avon Bks) Morrow Avon.
— The Wanton. 336p. 1985. mass mkt. 6.50 (*0-380-86165-8*, Avon Bks) Morrow Avon.
— Wicked Loving Lies. 672p. 1983. mass mkt. 6.99 (*0-380-00776-2*, Avon Bks) Morrow Avon.
— Wildest Heart. 608p. 1976. mass mkt. 6.99 (*0-380-00137-3*, Avon Bks) Morrow Avon.
Rogers, Rosemary & Stasi, Linda. Boomer Babes: A Woman's Guide to the New Middle Ages. LC 97-38274. 256p. 1998. pap. 12.95 (*0-312-18061-6*) St Martin.
Rogers, Rosemary, jt. auth. see Kelly, Sean.
Rogers, Roxanne S. The Successful Job Search: A Step-by-Step Guide for a Successful Job Search in the 1990's. 320p. 1993. 29.95 (*1-884274-00-5*) Rogers Res.
Rogers, Roy. Happy Trails: Our Life Story. (Illus.). 256p. 1995. pap. 12.00 (*0-684-80436-0*, Fireside) S&S Trade Pap.
Rogers, Ruth & Gray, Rose. Roger & Gray Italian Cookbook. 1996. 40.00 (*0-676-51948-2*) Random.
— The Rogers & Gray Italian Country Cookbook. 317p. 1996. 40.00 (*0-679-45001-7*) Fodors Travel.
Rogers, Ruth, jt. auth. see Gray, Rose.
Rogers, S. Sources of Operating Grants. 455p. 1998. pap. 102.00 (*1-56925-103-7*) Capitol VA.
Rogers, S., et al. Coal Liquefaction & Gas Conversion: Contractor's Review Conference: Proceedings (1995), 2 vols. (Illus.). 2224p. (Orig.). (C). 1995. pap. text 95.00 (*0-7881-2130-8*) DIANE Pub.
Rogers, Sally. Breathless Surge of Words. Spurr, Anna M., ed. LC 91-90407. (Illus.). 80p. (Orig.). 1991. pap. 12.95 (*0-9629738-0-7*) Sentimntl Sal.
— Earthsong. LC 97-44608. (Illus.). 32p. (J). 1998. 16.99 (*0-525-45873-5*) NAL.
Rogers, Sally J., et al, eds. Hospitals & the Uninsured Poor: Measuring & Paying for Uncompensated Care. 192p. 1985. 30.00 (*0-934459-00-2*) United Hosp Fund.
Rogers, Sandra B. Anatomy Charts for Reflexology. Issel, Christine, ed. (Illus.). 21p. 1994. student ed. write for info. (*0-9638862-0-7*) B J Scott.
— Anatomy Charts for Reflexology: Student Edition. Issel, Christine, ed. (Illus.). 55p. 1994. student ed. write for info. (*0-9638862-1-5*) B J Scott.
— Anatomy Charts for Reflexology: Teacher's Edition. Issel, Christine, ed. (Illus.). 56p. 1994. teacher ed. write for info. (*0-9638862-2-3*) B J Scott.
Rogers, Sandra H. Lessons from the Light: Insights from a Journey to the Other Side. 112p. 1995. mass mkt. 4.99 (*0-446-60277-9*, Pub. by Warner Bks) Little.
Rogers, Sarah B. Ezra Hardman, M. A. of Wayback College. LC 78-163046. (Short Story Index Reprint Ser.). 1977. reprint ed. 19.95 (*0-8369-3960-3*) Ayer.
Rogers, Sarah J. The Body & the Object: Ann Hamilton, 1984-1996. (Illus.). 89p. 1996. pap. 45.00 incl. cd-rom (*1-881390-13-6*) OSU Wexner Ctr.
— Lisbon/Matzko: 2 Views. (Illus.). 48p. 1995. pap. 10.00 (*1-881390-11-X*) OSU Wexner Ctr.
Rogers, Sarah J., et al. Carmel Buckley: Tools for the Imagination. (Illus.). 32p. 1994. pap. 10.95 (*1-881390-06-3*) OSU Wexner Ctr.
— Soft 2.1: The Imperial Message. (Illus.). 64p. 1994. pap. 15.00 (*1-881390-07-1*) OSU Wexner Ctr.
***Rogers, Seth & Iba, Wayne, eds.** Adaptive User Interfaces: Papers from the AAAI Spring Symposium. (Technical Reports: Vol. SS-00-01). (Illus.). 154p. 2000. spiral bd. 25.00 (*1-57735-107-X*) AAAI Pr.
Rogers, Sharon & Person, Ruth J. Recruiting Academic Library Director: A Companion to the Search Committee Handbook. 1991. pap. 19.00 (*0-8389-7484-8*) Assn Coll & Res Libs.
Rogers, Shawn B. Novell's Groupwise 5 User's Handbook. LC 96-78235. (Illus.). 300p. 1996. pap. 24.99 (*0-7645-4509-4*) IDG Bks.
Rogers, Shawn B. Novell's Groupwise 5 Administrator's Guide. LC 97-70944. 736p. 1997. pap. 44.99 incl. cd-rom (*0-7645-4521-3*) IDG Bks.
Rogers, Shawn B. & McTague, Richard H. Novell's GroupWise 5.5 User's Handbook. LC HF5548.4.N68R636. 288p. 1998. 24.99 (*0-7645-4552-3*) IDG Bks.
— Novell's GroupWise "X" Administrator's Guide. 750p. 1999. pap. 44.99 incl. cd-rom (*0-7645-4556-6*) IDG Bks.
Rogers, Sheena. Cross Stitch on Color. (Illus.). 128p. 1996. pap. 17.95 (*0-946819-85-8*, Pub. by Guild Master) Sterling.
Rogers, Sheena J., jt. ed. see Epstein, William.
Rogers, Sherbrooke. Grandfather Webster's Strange Will. 90p. (J). (gr. 6-7). 1995. pap. 9.99 (*0-88092-066-1*) Royal Fireworks.
Rogers, Sheri Everts & Danielson, Kathy Everts. Teacher Portfolios: Literacy Artifacts & Themes. LC 96-28883. 1996. pap. text 27.50 (*0-435-08881-5*) Heinemann.
Rogers, Sherry. Chemical Sensitivity. 48p. 1995. pap. 3.95 (*0-87983-634-2*, 36342K, Keats Publng) NTC Contemp Pub Co.
Rogers, Sherry A. The Cure Is in the Kitchen. 368p. 1991. pap. 14.95 (*0-9618821-3-1*) Prestige NY.
— Depression: Cured at Last! 718p. 1997. 24.95 (*1-887202-00-5*); pap. 19.95 (*1-887202-01-3*) Prestige NY.
— The E. I. Syndrome: Environmental Illness. rev. ed. 1995. pap. 17.95 (*0-9618821-7-4*) Prestige NY.
***Rogers, Sherry A.** No More Heartburn. 2000. pap. 15.00 (*1-57566-510-7*) Kensgtn Pub Corp.
Rogers, Sherry A. The Scientific Basis for Selected Environmental Medicine Techniques. LC 94-69079. 130p. 1994. reprint ed. pap. 17.95 (*0-9618821-6-6*) Prestige NY.
— Tired or Toxic. 438p. 1990. pap. 17.95 (*0-9618821-2-3*) Prestige NY.
— Wellness Against All Odds. LC 94-65045. 384p. 1994. reprint ed. pap. 17.95 (*0-9618821-5-8*) Prestige NY.
— You Are What You Ate. 225p. (Orig.). (C). 1988. pap. 9.95 (*0-9618821-1-5*) Prestige NY.
Rogers, Sherry A. & Gallinger, Shirley. Macro Mellow. (Orig.). 1992. pap. 12.95 (*0-9618821-4-X*) Prestige NY.
Rogers, Shirle, jt. auth. see Russ, Diane.
Rogers, Shirley. Conveniently His. (Desire Ser.). 2000. per. 3.75 (*0-373-76266-6*, 1-76266-5) Silhouette.
— Cowboys, Babies & Shotgun Vows: Women to Watch. (Desire Ser.: No. 1176). 1998. per. 3.75 (*0-373-76176-7*, 1-76176-6) Harlequin Bks.
***Rogers, Shirley.** Solo Amistad. (Deseo Ser.).Tr. of Only Friendship. (SPA.). 2000. mass mkt. 3.50 (*0-373-35348-0*, 1-35348-1) Harlequin Bks.
Rogers Smith, Jean Dawson, see Dawson Rogers Smith, Jean.
***Rogers, Spence.** Teaching Tips: 105 Ways to Increase Motivation & Learning. Renard, Lisa, ed. LC 99-74442. (Illus.). 183p. 1999. spiral bd. 19.95 (*1-889852-13-9*) Peak Lrning Systs.
Rogers, Spence & Graham, Shari. The High Performance Toolbox: Succeeding with Performance Tasks, Projects & Assessments. 3rd rev. ed. LC 98-67970. (Illus.). 387p. 1997. pap. 29.95 (*1-889852-07-4*) Peak Lrning Systs.
Rogers, Spence, et al. Motivation & Learning: A Teachers Guide to Building Excitement for Learning & Igniting the Drive for Quality. LC 96-72327. (Illus.). 286p. 1997. pap. 24.95 (*1-889852-30-9*) Peak Lrning Systs.
Rogers, Spencer L. The Colors of Mankind: The Range & Role of Human Pigmentation. (Illus.). 68p. (C). 1990. text 23.95 (*0-398-05643-9*) C C Thomas.
— The Human Skull: Its Mechanics, Measurements & Variations. (Illus.). 118p. (C). 1984. 27.95 (*0-398-04955-6*) C C Thomas.
— Personal Identification from Human Remains. (Illus.). 94p. 1987. 35.95 (*0-398-05307-3*) C C Thomas.
— The Shaman: His Symbols & His Healing Power. (Illus.). 224p. 1982. pap. 27.95 (*0-398-06406-7*) C C Thomas.
— The Shaman: His Symbols & His Healing Power. (Illus.). 224p. (C). 1982. 40.95 (*0-398-04594-1*) C C Thomas.
— The Testimony of Teeth: Forensic Aspects of Human Dentition. (Illus.). 126p. (C). 1988. text 37.95 (*0-398-05450-9*) C C Thomas.
Rogers, Spencer L. & Graham, Sharif. The High Performance Toolbox: Succeeding with Performance Tasks, Projects, & Assessments. LC 96-72328. xxii, 384 p. 1997. write for info. (*1-889852-03-1*) Peak Lrning Systs.
***Rogers, Sterling.** Hunkered Down. (Illus.). 280p. 2000. pap. 14.95 (*0-9657929-0-X*) JONA Bks.
Rogers, Steve. Model Boat Building Made Simple. LC 91-67007. (Illus.). 64p. 1992. pap. 12.95 (*0-88740-388-3*) Schiffer.
***Rogers, Steve & Rogers, Patricia.** Building a Model Working Boat. (Illus.). 64p. 2000. pap. 14.95 (*0-7643-1070-4*) Schiffer.
Rogers, Steve & Rogers, Patricia S. Model Boat Building: The Lobster Boat. LC 94-66369. (Illus.). 64p. (Orig.). 1994. pap. 12.95 (*0-88740-642-4*) Schiffer.
Rogers, Steve & Staby-Rogers, Patricia. Model Boat Building: The Skipjack. (Illus.). 64p. (YA). (gr. 10-13). 1996. pap. 14.95 (*0-88740-937-7*) Schiffer.
— Model Boat Building: The Spritsail Skiff. LC 93-85082. (Illus.). 64p. 1992. pap. 12.95 (*0-88740-534-7*) Schiffer.
Rogers, Steve, ed. see Rogers, Adrian.
Rogers, Steven. Cops & God: I Am with You Always. 76p. 1998. pap. 7.95 (*1-57502-726-7*, PO2032) Morris Pubng.
***Rogers, Steven.** Making Big Money! Marketing Your Own Web Site Business. (Illus.). 56p. 1998. spiral bd. (*0-9677963-0-X*) S R Rogers Enter.
Rogers, Steven K., ed. Applications & Science of Artificial Neural Networks III. LC 97-175317. 89p. 1997. pap. 124.00 (*0-8194-2492-7*) SPIE.
Rogers, Steven K., et al, eds. Applications & Science of Computational Intelligence, Vol. 3390. LC 98-213335. 690p. 1998. 116.00 (*0-8194-2839-6*) SPIE.
Rogers, Steven K. & Kabrisky, Matthew. An Introduction to Biological & Artificial Neural Networks for Pattern Recognition. 220p. 1991. 15.00 (*0-8194-0534-5*, VOL. TT04) SPIE.
Rogers, Steven L. Community Policing: A Guide for Police Officers & Citizens. LC 98-29880. 96p. 1998. pap. 10.95 (*1-889031-18-6*) Looseleaf Law.
— Tears: From a Father's Eyes. 126p. (Orig.). 1996. pap. 6.95 (*1-57502-099-8*) Morris Pubng.
***Rogers, Stillman.** Montreal LC 99-33908. (Cities of the World Ser.). (J). 2000. 26.00 (*0-516-21637-6*) Childrens.
Rogers, Stillman, jt. auth. see Rogers, Barbara.
Rogers, Stillman, jt. auth. see Rogers, Barbara R.
Rogers, Stillman, jt. auth. see Rogers, Barbara Radcliffe.
Rogers, Stillman, ed. see Shaw, Lisa.
***Rogers, Stillman D. & Rogers, Barbara R.** Country Towns of Vermont: Charming Small Towns & Villages to Explore. LC 98-39742. (Country Towns of... Ser.). (Illus.). 160p. 1999. pap. 12.95 (*1-56626-195-3*, 61953, Cntry Rds Pr) NTC Contemp Pub Co.
Rogers, Sue, jt. ed. see Ruthven, Beverly.
Rogers, Susan, jt. auth. see Abadi, Mauricio.
Rogers, Susan C. Shaping Modern Times in Rural France: The Transformation & Reproduction of an Aveygronnais Community. (Illus.). 235p. 1991. text 49.50 (*0-691-09458-6*, Pub. by Princeton U Pr); pap. text 17.95 (*0-691-02858-3*, Pub. by Princeton U Pr) Cal Prin Full Svc.
Rogers, Susan F. Close Calls. 288p. 1997. pap. 12.95 (*0-312-16802-0*) St Martin.
Rogers, Susan F., ed. Alaska Passages: 20 Voices from above the 54th Parallel. LC 96-19611. 256p. 1996. pap. 15.95 (*1-57061-046-0*) Sasquatch Bks.
— Another Wilderness: Notes from the New Outdoorwoman. LC 97-198249. (Adventura Bks.). 320p. 1997. pap. 16.00 (*1-878067-30-3*) Seal Pr WA.
— Homestretch: Chasing the American Dyke Dream. LC 98-14274. 200p. 1998. pap. 14.95 (*1-57344-036-1*) Cleis Pr.
— Solo: On Her Own Adventure. LC 96-6947. 288p. (Orig.). 1996. pap. 12.95 (*1-878067-74-5*) Seal Pr WA.
— Sportsdykes: Stories from on & off the Field. LC 95-5497. 1995. pap. 8.95 (*0-312-13187-9*) St Martin.
Rogers, Susan F., ed. Two in the Wild: Tales of Adventure from Friends, Mothers & Daughters. LC 99-20934. (Vintage Departures Ser.). 256p. 1999. pap. 13.00 (*0-375-70201-6*) Vin Bks.
Rogers, Susan Fox, ed. Women on the Verge: Lesbian Tales of Power & Play. LC 99-22066. 288p. 1999. pap. 13.95 (*0-312-20971-1*) St Martin.
Rogers, Susan H., jt. auth. see Rogers, Earl M.
Rogers, Susan H., tr. see Rascovsky, Arnaldo.
Rogers, T. Georgian Poetry, Nineteen Eleven to Nineteen Twenty-Two: The Critical Heritage. (Critical Heritage Ser.). 1977. 69.50 (*0-7100-8278-9*, Routledge Thoemms) Routledge.
Rogers, T. & Clifford, D. Choosing the Right IT Consultant. (Financial Times Management Briefings Ser.). 1997. pap. 94.50 (*0-273-63212-4*, Pub. by F T P-H) Trans-Atl Phila.
Rogers, T. & Clifford, D. How to Choose & Use IT Consultants. 1996. pap. 129.00 (*1-85953-057-5*, Pub. by Tech Comm) St Mut.
Rogers, T., tr. see Buddhaghosa.
Rogers, T. D., jt. auth. see Clapinson, Mary.
Rogers, T. D., jt. auth. see Wakeling, B. F.
Rogers, T. K. Forchess: The Ultimate Social Game. 64p. 1992. pap. 4.95 (*0-9632959-0-X*) Smallbook Assocs.
Rogers, T. N. Too Far from Home & Other Stories. LC 87-25514. 128p. (Orig.). 1988. pap. 12.95 (*0-8262-0671-9*) U of Mo Pr.
Rogers, Ted. Fit & Fast Foods. 164p. 1994. pap., ring bd. 12.00 (*0-9647006-0-3*) Fit Forty Plus.
Rogers, Terence A. Elementary Human Physiology. LC 61-11245. (Illus.). 429p. reprint ed. 133.00 (*0-8357-9880-1*, 201610100004) Bks Demand.
Rogers, Teresa, jt. auth. see Shulman, Jeffrey.
Rogers, Terri. Top Secrets. Breese, Martin, ed. (Illus.). 128p. 1998. 40.00 (*0-947533-22-2*, Pub. by Breese Bks) Firebird Dist.
Rogers, Theresa & Soter, Anna O., eds. Reading Across Cultures: Teaching Literature in a Diverse Society. LC 96-32594. (Language & Literacy Ser.: Vol. 28). 256p. (C). 1996. text 45.00 (*0-8077-3552-3*); pap. text 21.95 (*0-8077-3551-5*) Tchrs Coll.
Rogers, Theresa F., jt. auth. see Friedman, Natalie.
Rogers, Theresa F., jt. auth. see Friedman, Nathalie.
Rogers, Thomas. Confessions of a Child of the Century by Samuel Heather. LC 72-189740. 1972. 25.00 (*0-671-21266-4*) Ultramarine Pub.
— Men in Families. (Godly Man Bible Study). 96p. 1997. pap. text 5.50 (*0-570-09690-1*, 20-3029) Concordia.
Rogers, Thomas E., jt. auth. see Reid, Robert L.
***Rogers, Thomas F.** A Call to Russia: Glimpses of Missionary Life. (BYU Studies). (Illus.). xvi, 192p. 1999. pap. 11.95 (*0-8425-2461-4*) Brigham.
Rogers, Thomas F. Huebener. 50p. (Orig.). 1992. pap. 4.00 (*1-57514-135-3*, 1109) Encore Perform Pub.
— Myth & Symbol in Soviet Fiction: Images of the Savior Hero, Great Mother, "Anima," & Child in Selected Novels & Films. LC 91-46783. (Illus.). 348p. 1992. lib. bdg. 99.95 (*0-7734-9849-4*) E Mellen.
— Superfluous Men & the Post-Stalin Thaw: The Alienated Hero in Soviet Prose During the Decade 1953-1963. 1972. text 87.70 (*90-279-2118-0*) Mouton.
Rogers, Thomas G. Stepping Inside the Story: Sermons for Pentecost, Last Third - First Lesson. LC 94-1001. (Orig.). 1994. pap. 10.50 (*0-7880-0045-4*) CSS OH.
Rogers, Thomas J., jt. auth. see Gilman, Steven C.
***Rogers, Timothy.** The Quality Analects of Mr. Funny Guy. 168p. 1999. pap. 10.00 (*0-9672452-0-6*) Entropy Enter.
Rogers, Timothy, ed. Georgian Poetry, 1911-22. (Critical Heritage Ser.). 452p. (C). 1997. 140.00 (*0-415-15938-5*) Routledge.
***Rogers, Timothy & Graham, Fiona.** Responding to Stress. (Essentials Ser.). 71p. 2000. pap. 9.95 (*1-85703-512-7*, Pub. by How To Bks) Midpt Trade.
Rogers, Timothy J., ed. Autobiography at the Trigger by Etelvina Astrada. LC 82-60922.Tr. of Autobiografia con gatillo. 128p. 1984. 13.00 (*0-938972-04-9*) Spanish Lit Pubns.
Rogers, Timothy J., intro. Death on the Run. LC 86-62497.Tr. of Muerte Arrebatada. 99p. 1987. 13.00 (*0-938972-11-1*) Spanish Lit Pubns.
Rogers, Timothy J., jt. ed. see Rogers, Elizabeth S.
Rogers, Timothy L. Aboard the Euterpe: A Historical Novel about the Tall Ship "Euterpe" large type ed. (Illus.). (Orig.). (J). (gr. 4-9). 1996. mass mkt. 10.95 (*0-9630182-1-3*) T L Rogers.
***Rogers, Timothy L.** The Chilkoot: Trail to Yukon Gold: Historic Trail, Yesterday & Today, Used to Reach Klondike. unabridged ed. 96p. 1999. pap. 12.95 (*0-9630182-5-6*) T L Rogers.
Rogers, Timothy L. Growing up in View of America: A Life of an American. 290p. 1997. pap. 14.95 (*0-9630182-2-1*) T L Rogers.
— Health Is an Inside Job. unabridged ed. 48p. 1999. pap. 5.95 (*0-9630182-4-8*) T L Rogers.
— The Power of Goalsetting. 96p. (Orig.). 1991. pap. 7.95 (*0-9630182-0-5*) T L Rogers.
— Tale of Roeg. LC 99-60659. 320p. 1999. pap. 17.95 (*1-56167-497-4*, Five Star Spec Ed) Am Literary Pr.
***Rogers, Tom.** Because God Has Called: Devotions for Church Workers. LC 99-34452. 176p. 1999. 11.00 (*0-570-05392-7*) Concordia.
Rogers, Tom. Life in the Fishbowl: Building up Church Workers. 160p. 1996. 10.99 (*0-570-04871-0*, 12-3360) Concordia.
— The Soviet Withdrawal from Afghanistan: Analysis & Chronology. LC 92-24260. 256p. 1992. lib. bdg. 65.00 (*0-313-27907-1*, RSE, Greenwood Pr) Greenwood.
— Understanding PCM. 2nd ed. (ABC Pocket Guide for the Field Ser.). (Illus.). 52p. (C). 1986. pap. text 7.95 (*1-56016-028-4*) ABC TeleTraining.
Rogers, Tony. Someone Else's War: Mercenaries from 1960 to the Present. 256p. 1998. 28.95 incl. 5.25 hd (*0-00-472077-6*) Collins SF.
Rogers, Truett. West Virginia Baptist History: The Convention Years, 1865-1965. 1994. 21.95 (*0-929915-12-7*) Headline Bks.
Rogers, Truitt, tr. see Pellecchia, Michael.
Rogers, Trumbull. Editorial Freelancing: A Practical Guide. LC 94-7451. 200p. 1995. pap. 14.95 (*0-9639260-1-2*) Aletheia.
Rogers, Vickie L. Applying Inpatient Coding Skills under Prospective Payment. rev. ed. 198p. 1998. pap. text 56.00 (*1-58426-015-7*, AC200398) Am Hlth Info.
Rogers, Virgil M., jt. auth. see Marks, John H.
Rogers, W. Planning & the Heritage. 1997. 57.95 (*0-419-15100-1*, E & FN Spon) Routledge.
Rogers, W. G. Wise Men Fish Here: The Story of Frances Steloff & the Gotham Book Mart. 288p. 1994. reprint ed. pap. 14.95 (*1-879923-08-4*) Booksellers Pub.
Rogers, W. Lane. Crimes & Misdeeds: Headlines from Arizona's Past. LC 95-11110. (Illus.). 160p. (Orig.). 1995. pap. 9.95 (*0-87358-631-X*) Northland AZ.
Rogers, W. Lane, ed. see Gray, John P.
Rogers, Walter. The Professional Practice of Landscape Architecture: A Complete Guide to Starting & Running Your Own Firm. 448p. 1996. 75.00 (*0-471-28680-X*, VNR) Wiley.
Rogers, Walter. The Professional Practice of Landscape Architecture: A Complete Guide to Starting & Running Your Own Firm. LC 96-24289. (Landscape Architecture Ser.). (Illus.). 422p. 1996. text 59.95 (*0-442-01964-5*, VNR) Wiley.
Rogers, Walter T. A Manual of Bibliography. 1977. lib. bdg. 75.00 (*0-8490-2204-5*) Gordon Pr.
Rogers, Warren S. My Own Los Angeles, 1894 to 1982. (Los Angeles Miscellany Ser.: No. 13). (Illus.). 53p. 1982. 15.00 (*0-87093-313-2*) Dawsons.
Rogers, Wendy, jt. auth. see Rogers, Rex.
Rogers, Wendy A., et al, eds. Aging & Skilled Performance: Advances in Theory & Applications. LC 96-17205. 272p. 1996. text 59.95 (*0-8058-1909-6*); pap. text 29.95 (*0-8058-1910-X*) L Erlbaum Assocs.
Rogers, Wendy A., jt. ed. see Fisk, Arthur D.
Rogers, Wendy A., ed. see Human Factors & Ergonomics Society Staff.
Rogers, Will. Autobiography of Will Rogers. Day, Donald, ed. LC 76-6592. reprint ed. 39.50 (*0-404-15293-7*) AMS Pr.
— The Papers of Will Rogers. Wertheim, Arthur F. & Bair, Barbara, eds. LC 94-24165. (Illus.). 640p. 1996. 45.00 (*0-8061-2745-7*) U of Okla Pr.
— Will Rogers at the Ziegfeld Follies. Wertheim, Arthur F., ed. LC 92-54137. (Illus.). 288p. 1992. 24.95 (*0-8061-2357-5*) U of Okla Pr.
Rogers, Will & Day, Donald. The Autobiography of Will Rogers. LC 98-30710. 1998. write for info. (*1-56000-526-2*) Transaction Pubs.
Rogers, Will, et al. Storm Center: The USS Vincennes & Iran Air Flight 655. LC 92-9202. (Illus.). 264p. 1992. 24.95 (*1-55750-727-9*) Naval Inst Pr.
Rogers, William. Creating Positive Behavior - in the Classroom. 83p. (Orig.). 1995. pap. text, teacher ed. 18.95 (*1-890732-00-1*) Behavior Research.
— Humpty Dumpty Was Pushed: The Psychology of "Fabricated" Reality. 232p. 1999. pap. 10.00 (*1-890732-02-8*) Behavior Research.

An Asterisk (*) at the beginning of an entry indicates that the title is appearing for the first time.

— Kids in Chaos: What Every Parent & Teacher Must Know. 63p. (Orig.). 1996. pap. text, teacher ed., wbk. ed. 18.95 (*1-890732-01-X*) Behavior Research.

— Recovered Memory & Other Assaults upon the Mysteries of Consciousness: Hypnosis, Psychotherapy, Fraud & the Mass Media. LC 95-15794. 152p. 1995. lib. bdg. 30.00 (*0-7864-0109-5*) McFarland & Co.

Rogers, William A. Managing Teacher Stress. (Illus.). 129p. (Orig.). 1996. pap. 57.50 (*0-273-62215-3*, Pub. by Pitman Pub) Trans-Atl Phila.

— The Shepherd & His Sheep. 1983. pap. 6.99 (*1-56632-011-9*) Revival Lit.

Rogers, William B. Being a Christian Educator: Discovering Your Identity, Heritage, & Vision. LC 96-38533. (FaithGrowth Ser.: Vol. 1). (Illus.). 112p. 1996. pap. text 13.00 (*1-57312-092-8*) Smyth & Helwys.

— Outcast Red: The P-47 in the South Pacific. 320p. (Orig.). 1987. pap. 9.95 (*0-89896-260-9*) Larksdale.

— We Are All Together Now: Fredrick Douglass, William Lloyd Garrison, & the Prophetic Tradition. 9501st ed. LC 94-24749. (Studies in African American History & Culture). 182p. 1995. text 44.00 (*0-8153-1868-5*) Garland.

Rogers, William B., ed. see Abernathy, Alta & Harris, Barbara.

***Rogers, William Curran, Sr.** Black Ash & White Clay. LC 99-96667. 2000. 19.95 (*0-533-13321-1*) Vantage.

Rogers, William E. How to Cut Workers' Comp Costs: 115 Proven Ways. 276p. 1991. ring bd. 125.00 (*0-9635070-0-1*) Cntry Rd Pubns.

— Interpreting Interpretation: Textual Hermeneutics as an Ascetic Discipline. 256p. 1993. 40.00 (*0-271-01059-2*); pap. text 18.95 (*0-271-01061-4*) Pa St U Pr.

— The Three Genres & the Interpretation of Lyric. LC 82-12293. 288p. reprint ed. pap. 89.30 (*0-7837-1936-1*, 204215100001) Bks Demand.

Rogers, William E., jt. auth. see Sharma, Man M.

Rogers, William F., Jr. Dorothy Maynor & the Harlem School of the Arts: The Diva & the Dream. LC 93-32243. (Illus.). 308p. 1993. 99.95 (*0-7734-9377-8*) E Mellen.

Rogers, William P. & Kirkham, Robert M. Contributions to Colorado Siesmicity & Tectonics: A 1986 Update. (Special Publications: No. 28). (Illus.). 301p. (Orig.). 1986. pap. 15.00 (*1-884216-43-9*) Colo Geol Survey.

Rogers, William P. & Practising Law Institute. Securities Offerings 1998. LC 98-194879. (Corporate Law & Practice Course Handbook Ser.). 592 p. 1998. write for info. (*0-87224-432-6*) PLI.

Rogers, William P., et al. Guidelines & Criteria for Identification & Land-Use Controls of Geologic Hazard & Mineral Resource Areas. (Special Publications: No. 6). (Illus.). 146p. (Orig.). 1974. pap. 6.00 (*1-884216-35-8*) Colo Geol Survey.

Rogers, William P., jt. auth. see Kirkham, Robert M.

Rogers, William W. Confederate Home Front: Montgomery During the Civil War. LC 98-58028. 1999. 29.95 (*0-8173-0962-4*) U of Ala Pr.

— Outposts on the Gulf: Saint George Island & Apalachicola from Early Exploration to World War II. LC 85-17802. (Illus.). 312p. 1987. 34.95 (*0-8130-0832-8*) U Press Fla.

— Thomas County, 1865-1900. LC 72-93329. xiv, 486p. 1973. write for info. (*0-87307-063-1*) FL State U Pr.

Rogers, William W. & Brown, Canter, Jr. Florida's Clerks of the Circuit Court, Their History & Experiences. (Illus.). Date not set. write for info. (*1-889574-00-7*) Sentry Press.

Rogers, William W. & Clark, Erica R. The Croom Family & Goodwood Plantation: Land, Litigation, & Southern Lives. LC 98-40767. (Illus.). 304p. 1999. 35.00 (*0-8203-2069-2*) U of Ga Pr.

Rogers, William W. & Willis, Lee. At the Water's Edge: A Pictorial & Narrative History of Apalachicola & Franklin County. LC 97-13711. 1997. write for info. (*1-57864-001-6*) Donning Co.

Rogers, William W., et al. Alabama: The History of a Deep South State. LC 93-27240. (Illus.). 768p. 1994. pap. 29.95 (*0-8173-0714-1*); text 49.95 (*0-8173-0712-5*) U of Ala Pr.

Rogers, William W., jt. auth. see Ward, Robert D.

Rogers, William W., jt. ed. see Ward, Robert D.

***Rogers, Wilson.** Modern Manners for Little Monsters. LC 97-62145. (Illus.). 16p. (J). (ps-3). 1998. 9.98 (*0-7651-9068-0*) Smithmark.

Rogers, Yvonne, et al, eds. Models in the Mind: Perspective, Theory & Application. (Computers & People Ser.). (Illus.). 330p. 1992. text 79.95 (*0-12-592970-6*) Acad Pr.

Rogerson, Barnaby. Cadogan Guide to Tunisia. 2nd ed. (Cadogan Guides Ser.). 1998. pap. text 17.95 (*1-86011-059-2*, Pub. by Cadgn Bks) Macmillan.

— Essential Istanbul. 2nd ed. (Essential Travel Guides Ser.). (Illus.). 128p. 1996. pap. 7.95 (*0-8442-8898-5*, Passprt Bks) NTC Contemp Pub Co.

— Essential Morocco. LC 93-5573. (Essential Travel Guides Ser.). (Illus.). 128p. 1995. pap. text 7.95 (*0-8442-8956-6*, Passprt Bks) NTC Contemp Pub Co.

— Essential Scotland. 2nd ed. LC 96-70464. (Illus.). 128p. 1997. pap. 7.95 (*0-8442-4809-6*) NTC Contemp Pub Co.

— Morocco. 3rd ed. (Cadogan Country Guides Ser.). (Illus.). 576p. 1997. pap. text 19.95 (*1-86011-043-6*, Pub. by Cadgn Bks) Macmillan.

***Rogerson, Barnaby.** Morocco: Marrakesh, Fez, Rabat. (City Guides Ser.). (Illus.). 2000. pap. 17.95 (*1-86011-973-5*) Cadgn Bks.

Rogerson, Barnaby. Traveller's History of North Africa. LC 98-29666. (Traveller's History Ser.). (Illus.). 304p. 1998. pap. text 14.95 (*1-56656-252-X*) Interlink Pub.

***Rogerson, Barnaby.** A Traveller's History of North Africa. 2nd ed. 408p. 1999. pap. 15.95 (*1-56656-351-8*) Interlink Pr.

Rogerson, Barnaby & Baring, R. Essential Istanbul. LC 93-85614. (Essential Travel Guides Ser.). (Illus.). 128p. 1994. pap. 7.95 (*0-8442-8916-7*, Passprt Bks) NTC Contemp Pub Co.

Rogerson, C. M. Managing Urban Growth in the Developing World. text 59.95 (*0-470-22111-9*); pap. text 24.95 (*0-470-22112-7*) Wiley.

Rogerson, Carole, jt. auth. see Swinton, Katherine.

Rogerson, Dale. Inside COM. LC 96-45094. 416p. 1997. pap. text 34.99 incl. cd-rom (*1-57231-349-8*) Microsoft.

Rogerson, Fred. Weird Is the Night. 50p. 1973. pap. 3.50 (*0-87129-114-2*, W14) Dramatic Pub.

Rogerson, Holly D., et al. Words for Students of English: A Vocabulary Series for ESL. LC 88-159613. (Pitt Series in English As a Second Language). (Illus.). 200p. (C). 1992. pap. text 15.00 incl. audio (*0-472-00241-4*, 00241) U of Mich Pr.

— Words for Students of English: A Vocabulary Series for ESL, Vol. 3. LC 88-159613. (Pitt Series in English As a Second Language). (Illus.). 232p. (C). 1992. pap. text 15.00 incl. audio (*0-472-00243-0*, 00243) U of Mich Pr.

— Words for Students of English: A Vocabulary Series for ESL, Vol. 4. LC 88-159613. (Pitt Series in English As a Second Language). (Illus.). 214p. (C). 1992. pap. text 15.00 incl. audio (*0-472-00244-9*, 00244) U of Mich Pr.

— Words for Students of English: A Vocabulary Series for ESL, Vol. 5. LC 88-159613. (Pitt Series in English As a Second Language). (Illus.). 272p. (C). 1992. audio 15.00 (*0-472-00245-7*, 00245) U of Mich Pr.

— Words for Students of English: A Vocabulary Series for ESL, Vol. 6. LC 88-159613. (Pitt Series in English As a Second Language). (Illus.). 316p. (C). 1992. audio 15.00 (*0-472-00246-5*, 00246) U of Mich Pr.

***Rogerson, J. W.** Introduction to the Bible. 1999. pap. 12.95 (*0-14-025261-4*) Viking Penguin.

Rogerson, John. The Atlas of the Bible. (Cultural Atlas Ser.). (Illus.). 240p. 1985. 45.00 (*0-8160-1207-5*) Facts on File.

— The History of Christian Theology: The Study & Use of the Bible, Vol. 2. fac. ed. Avis, Paul, ed. LC 87-47429. 427p. 1988. reprint ed. pap. 132.40 (*0-7837-7943-7*, 204769900002) Bks Demand.

***Rogerson, John, et al, contrib. by.** Rethinking Contexts, Rereading Texts: Contributions from the Social Sciences to Biblical Interpretation. (Journal for the Study of the Old Testament Supplement Ser.: No. 299). 281p. 2000. 82.00 (*1-84127-058-X*, Pub. by Sheffield Acad) CUP Services.

Rogerson, John & Rooney, Margaret. European Director's Guide to Quality Management. 176p. 1996. 55.00 (*0-412-72640-8*) Chapman & Hall.

Rogerson, John, et al. Beginning Old Testament Study. 176p. 1998. pap. 15.99 (*0-8272-0227-X*) Chalice Pr.

Rogerson, John W. Anthropology & the Old Testament. (Biblical Seminar Ser.: No. 1). 128p. 1984. pap. 17.95 (*0-905774-82-5*, Pub. by Sheffield Acad) CUP Services.

— The Bible & Criticism in Victorian Britain: Profiles of F. D. Maurice & William Robertson Smith. (JSOT Supplement Ser.: Vol. 201). 188p. 1995. 57.50 (*1-85075-553-1*, Pub. by Sheffield Acad) CUP Services.

Rogerson, John W. The Chronicle of the Old Testament Kings: The Reign-by-Reign Record of the Rulers of Ancient Israel. LC 98-61829. (Illus.). 208p. 1999. 34.95 (*0-500-05095-3*, Pub. by Thames Hudson) Norton.

— Genesis 1-11. (Old Testament Guides Ser.). 89p. 1991. pap. 12.50 (*1-85075-274-5*, Pub. by Sheffield Acad) CUP Services.

— Myth in Old Testament Interpretation. LC 73-78234. (Beiheft zur Zeitschrift fuer die Alttestamentliche Wissenschaft Ser.). (C). 1974. 76.95 (*3-11-004220-7*) De Gruyter.

Rogerson, John W. Old Testament Criticism in the Nineteenth Century. 320p. 1984. 85.00 (*0-281-04094-X*, Pub. by Society Prom Christ Know) Intl Pubs Mktg.

Rogerson, John W. The Pentateuch: A Sheffield Reader. (Biblical Seminar Ser.: No. 39). 371p. 1996. pap. 19.95 (*1-85075-785-2*, Pub. by Sheffield Acad) CUP Services.

— W. M. L. de Wette, Founder of Modern Biblical Criticism: An Intellectual Biography. (JSOT Supplement Ser.: No. 126). 313p. (C). 1992. 85.00 (*1-85075-330-X*, Pub. by Sheffield Acad) CUP Services.

Rogerson, John W., ed. Industrial Mission in a Changing World: Papers from the Jubilee Conference of the Sheffield Industrial Mission. (SAP Title Ser.). 195p. 1996. 58.00 (*1-85075-620-1*, Pub. by Sheffield Acad); pap. 23.00 (*1-85075-791-7*, Pub. by Sheffield Acad) CUP Services.

Rogerson, John W. & Davies, Margaret, eds. The Bible in Ethics: The Second Sheffield Colloquium. LC 96-114834. (JSOT Supplement Ser.: No. 207). 379p. 1996. 85.00 (*1-85075-573-6*, Pub. by Sheffield Acad) CUP Services.

Rogerson, Kenneth F. Introduction to Ethical Theory. 416p. (C). 1991. pap. text 50.00 (*0-03-023094-2*, Pub. by Harcourt Coll Pubs) Harcourt.

Rogerson, Margaret, jt. ed. see Johnston, Alexandra F.

Rogerson, Paul, jt. auth. see Turnbull, Michael.

Rogerson, Peter, jt. ed. see Fotheringham, A. Stewart.

Rogerson, Peter A., jt. auth. see Plane, David A.

Rogerson, R. G., et al, eds. Class, Consumption & Quality of Life. (Progress in Planning Ser.: Vol. 45). 70p. 1996. pap. text 100.75 (*0-08-042882-7*, Pergamon Pr) Elsevier.

Rogerson, Sidney. Propaganda in the Next War. LC 72-4678. (International Propaganda & Communications Ser.). 188p. 1972. reprint ed. 17.95 (*0-405-04762-2*) Ayer.

— Twelve Days. 172p. 1988. 65.00 (*0-947893-10-5*, Pub. by Gliddon Bks) St Mut.

Roget. Roget's II Desk Thesaurus. 528p. 1995. 9.00 (*0-395-74447-4*) HM.

Roget, ed. Concise Rogets Intnl The. 5th ed. (C). 1997. pap. 15.73 (*0-673-99706-5*) Addison-Wesley.

***Roget, Audrey.** After Life. 1999. 19.95 (*0-9675028-2-9*); pap. 12.95 (*0-9675028-1-0*) Beacon Light Bks.

Roget, John L., ed. see Roget, Peter M.

Roget, Paul. The New Roget's Thesaurus in Dictionary Form: Student Edition. 1990. mass mkt., student ed. 5.99 (*0-425-12361-8*) Berkley Pub.

Roget, Peter M. Roget's New American Thesaurus. 1999. pap. write for info. (*0-451-18025-9*, Sig) NAL.

— Roget's II: The New Thesaurus. 1984. 11.09 (*0-606-02619-3*, Pub. by Turtleback) Demco.

— Thesaurus of English Words & Phrases. rev. ed. Roget, John L. & Roget, Samuel R., eds. 42.50 (*0-87559-049-7*) Shalom.

Roget, Peter M. & Day, A. Colin. Roget's International Thesaurus of the Bible Index. LC 92-53896. 944p. 1992. 35.00 (*0-06-061773-X*, Pub. by Harper SF) HarpC.

Roget, Samuel R., ed. see Roget, Peter M.

Rogg, Bernd, jt. ed. see Peters, Norbert.

Rogg, Carla S. Atlanta Area School Directory Your Complete Guide to Greater Atlanta Area Public & Private Education. 7th ed. 1998. pap. 14.95 (*1-887203-06-0*) Care Solutions.

Rogg, Carla S. & Rogg, Oskar H. Georgia Mental Health Sourcebook: A Resource Guide for Consumers & Professionals. 177p. (Orig.). 1994. pap. 19.95 (*0-9631939-6-1*); spiral bd. 24.95 (*0-9631939-8-8*) Care Solutions.

— Georgia Senior Resource Guide: A Guide for Older Adults, Caregivers & Eldercare Professionals. 258p. (Orig.). 1995. pap. 19.95 (*0-9631939-9-6*) Care Solutions.

— Houston Eldercare Directory: A Resource Guide for Older Adults, Caregivers, & Eldercare Professionals. (Orig.). 1992. pap. 24.95 (*0-9631939-1-0*) Care Solutions.

— North Carolina Eldercare Sourcebook: A Resource Guide for Older Adults & Caregivers. (Orig.). 1995. spiral bd. 24.95 (*0-9631939-4-5*) Care Solutions.

— North Carolina Senior Resource Guide: A Resource Guide for Older Adults, Caregivers & Eldercare Professional. 277p. (Orig.). 1995. pap. 19.95 (*0-9631939-7-X*) Care Solutions.

— North Texas Eldercare Sourcebook: A Resource Guide for Older Adults & Caregivers & Eldercare Professionals. 186p. (Orig.). 1995. pap. 14.95 (*0-9631939-3-7*) Care Solutions.

Rogg, Carla S., et al. The Boarding School Guide: The Indispensable Guide on Leading Schools Throughout the U. S. (Orig.). 1996. pap. 19.95 (*1-887203-02-8*) Care Solutions.

Rogg, Fay F. & Borsi, Emilia. El Arte de Escribir. 256p. (C). 1994. pap. 27.50 (*0-07-053543-4*) McGraw.

Rogg, Oskar. The Atlanta Area School Directory: Your Complete Guide to Greater Atlanta Area Public & Private Education. 5th ed. 271p. 1996. pap. text 11.95 (*1-887203-03-6*) Care Solutions.

Rogg, Oskar H., jt. auth. see Rogg, Carla S.

Roggan, Andre, jt. ed. see Muller, Gerhard J.

Rogge, A. E., et al. Raising Arizona's Dams: Daily Life, Danger, & Discrimination in the Dam Construction Camps of Central Arizona, 1890s-1940s. LC 94-21368. (Illus.). 212p. 1995. lib. bdg. 48.00 (*0-8165-1491-7*) U of Ariz Pr.

— Raising Arizona's Dams: Daily Life, Danger, & Discrimination in the Dam Construction Camps of Central Arizona, 1890s-1940s. LC 94-21368. (Illus.). 212p. 1995. pap. 23.95 (*0-8165-1492-5*, 20016) U of Ariz Pr.

Rogge, A. E., jt. auth. see Brown, Patricia E.

Rogge, Benjamin A. Can Capitalism Survive? LC 78-17378. 1979. 12.00 (*0-913966-46-0*) Liberty Fund.

Rogge, Benjamin A., ed. see Smith, Adam.

Rogge, Constance, ed. see Achad, Frater.

***Rogge, Iris.** Die schone weibliche Gestalt im dramatischen Werk Goethes: Ubernahme und Umgestaltung des antiken Schonheitsideals. 2000. 52.95 (*3-631-35924-1*) P Lang Pubng.

Rogge, John R. Too Many, Too Long: Sudan's Twenty-Year Refugee Dilemma. LC 85-2058. (Illus.). 214p. (C). 1985. 56.50 (*0-8476-7412-6*, R7412) Rowman.

Rogge, Robert H. The Book---Alzheimer's Disease: Caregiver's Home Management. LC 95-70766. 308p. 1996. pap. 24.00 (*1-57087-182-5*) Prof Pr NC.

— The Rat's Tale: Alzheimer's Mystery Story. LC 97-93263. 193p. (Orig.). 1997. pap. 18.95 (*0-9657319-0-1*) Longleaf Pr NC.

— Surviving Alzheimer's: Caregiver's Home Management of Alzheimer's Disease. 2nd rev. ed. (Illus.). 73p. 1997. pap. 9.95 (*0-9657319-1-X*) Longleaf Pr NC.

***Rogge-Wiest, Gudrun.** Wahrnehmung Und Perspektivik in Ausgewahlten Romanen Virginia Woolfs. IX, 268p. 1998. 48.95 (*3-631-34251-9*) P Lang Pubng.

Roggeman, Willem M. Vanishing Emptiness. LC 88-8259. 108p. 1989. pap. 16.95 (*0-948259-51-5*) Dufour.

***Roggemann, Michael C. & Bissonnette, Luc R., eds.** Propagation & Imaging Through the Atmosphere III. 1999. pap. text 72.00 (*0-8194-3249-0*) SPIE.

Roggemann, Michael C. & Welsh, Byron. Imaging Through Turbulence. LC 95-45367. 336p. 1996. boxed set 119.95 (*0-8493-3787-9*) CRC Pr.

Roggemans, Paul, ed. Handbook for Visual Meteor Observations. 2nd ed. (Illus.). 192p. 1989. student ed. 18.95 (*0-933346-57-3*) Sky Pub.

Roggenkamp, Edward K. American Roughshooting: The Practice & Pleasure of Sport Hunting. LC 95-34344. (Illus.). 256p. 1996. 25.95 (*0-87605-427-0*) Howell Bks.

Roggenkamp, Klaus W. & Taylor, Martin J. Group Rings & Class Groups. LC 92-10083. (DMV Seminar Ser.: Bd. 18). 216p. 1994. 56.50 (*0-8176-2734-0*, Pub. by Birkhauser) Princeton Arch.

Roggenkamp, Klaus W., jt. ed. see Reiner, Irving.

Roggenthen, Eileen S. Teenage Violence: A Deadly Trend. 111p. 1992. pap. 6.95 (*1-57515-015-8*) PPI Pubng.

Rogger, Hans. Russia in the Age of Modernization & Revolution, 1881-1917. LC 83-714. (History of Russia Ser.). 323p. (Orig.). (C). 1983. pap. 44.00 (*0-582-48912-1*, 73395) Longman.

Rogger, Hans J. National Consciousness in Eighteenth-Century Russia. LC 60-8450. (Russian Research Center Studies: No. 38). 327p. 1960. 29.95 (*0-674-60150-5*) HUP.

Roggeri, Henri. Tropical Freshwater Wetlands: A Guide to Current Knowledge & Sustainable Management. (Developments in Hydrobiology Ser.: Vol. 112). 1995. text 147.00 (*0-7923-3785-9*) Kluwer Academic.

Roggli, Linda S. Durham, Doorway to Discovery: City Business Profiles. Turner, James E., ed. (Illus.). 192p. 1995. 39.00 (*1-885352-19-0*) Community Comm.

— Durham, Doorway to Discovery: City Business Profiles. (Illus.). 1995. pap. text. write for info. (*1-885352-22-0*) Community Comm.

Roggli, Victor L., et al. Pathology of Asbestos-Associated Diseases. LC 92-13417. 432p. 1992. text 169.00 (*0-316-75423-4*, Little Brwn Med Div) Lppncott W & W.

Roggow. Buyer Agency. 80p. (C). 1997. pap. text 8.20 (*0-13-780156-4*) P-H.

Roggow, Linda & Owens, Carolyn. Pregnant & Single: Help for the Tough Choices. LC 98-21074. 152p. (YA). 1998. pap. 9.99 (*0-8361-9092-0*) Herald Pr.

Roggow, Paul A., et al. The Home Rehabilitation Program Guide. rev. ed. LC 89-43335. (Illus.). 184p. 1993. pap. 29.00 (*1-55642-231-8*) SLACK Inc.

Roghair, Gene H., tr. The Epic of Palnadu: A Study & Translation of Palnati Virula Katha, a Telegu Oral Tradition from Andhra Pradesh, India. (Illus.). 1983. 59.00 (*0-19-815456-9*) OUP.

Roghair, Gene H., jt. tr. see Rao, Velcheru N.

Rogich, Daniel M. Becoming Uncreated: The Journey to Human Authenticity. LC 96-79926. 251p. (Orig.). 1997. pap. 14.95 (*1-880971-28-3*) Light&Life Pub Co MN.

— St. Gregory Palamas: Treatise on the Spiritual Life. 105p. (Orig.). 1994. pap. 12.95 (*1-880971-05-4*) Light&Life Pub Co MN.

— Sebian Patericon Vol. 1: Saints of the Serbian Orthodox Church. Herman, Abbot, ed. LC 94-65911. (Illus.). 331p. (Orig.). 1994. pap. 15.00 (*0-938635-75-1*) St Herman Pr.

Rogier, J. Y. & Stanford-Smith, B., eds. Advances in Information Technologies: The Business Challenge. 100p. Date not set. write for info. (*90-5199-385-4*) IOS Press.

Rogier, June & Wolfe, MaryLou, prefs. Nursery & Seed Catalogs: A Directory of Collections. 87p. (Orig.). 1989. pap. write for info. (*0-9621791-2-4*) CBHL Inc.

Rogier, Philippe & Wagner, Lavern J. Philippe Rogier: Eleven Motets. (Recent Researches in Music of the Renaissance Ser.: Vol. RRR2). (Illus.). 111p. 1966. pap. 35.00 (*0-89579-003-3*) A-R Eds.

Rogiers, Vera, et al, eds. Human Cells in In-Vitro Pharmaco-Toxicology: Present Status Within Europe. (Illus.). 328p. 1994. 55.00 (*90-5487-041-9*) Paul & Co Pubs.

Rogilds, Flemming. In the Land of the Elephant Bird: Voices of South Africa. 165p. 1994. 61.95 (*1-85628-892-7*, Pub. by Avebry) Ashgate Pub Co.

Rogin, Leo. Meaning & Validity of Economic Theory. LC 78-134129. (Essay Index Reprint Ser.). 1977. 42.95 (*0-8369-2126-7*) Ayer.

Rogin, Michael. Blackface, White Noise: Jewish Immigrants in the Hollywood Melting Pot. 1998. pap. text 17.95 (*0-520-21380-7*, Pub. by U CA Pr) Cal Prin Full Svc.

— Independence Day. LC 98-206640. (Modern Classics Ser.). (Illus.). 96p. 1998. pap. 10.95 (*0-85170-662-2*) Ind U Pr.

Rogin, Michael, jt. ed. see Post, Robert.

Rogin, Michael P. Blackface, White Noise: Jewish Immigrants in the Hollywood Melting Pot. LC 95-44109. (Illus.). 336p. (C). 1996. 40.00 (*0-520-20407-7*, Pub. by U CA Pr) Cal Prin Full Svc.

— Fathers & Children: Andrew Jackson & the Subjugation of the American Indian. 419p. (C). 1995. pap. 24.95 (*0-88738-886-8*) Transaction Pubs.

— Ronald Reagan the Movie, & Other Episodes in Political Demonology. 480p. (C). 1987. pap. 17.95 (*0-520-06469-0*, Pub. by U CA Pr) Cal Prin Full Svc.

— Subversive Genealogy: The Politics & Art of Herman Melville. 370p. 1985. pap. 21.95 (*0-520-05178-5*, Pub. by U CA Pr) Cal Prin Full Svc.

Rogin, Michael P. & Shover, John L. Political Change in California: Critical Elections & Social Movements, 1890-1966, 5. LC 72-95506. (Contributions in American History Ser.: No. 5). 231p. 1970. 55.00 (*0-8371-2346-1*, ROP/, Greenwood Pr) Greenwood.

Rogin, Michael P., jt. auth. see Post, Robert.

Rogin, Neal, ed. see Emery, Stewart.

Roginets, I. I., jt. auth. see Plotnikov, N. I.

Roginski, Henrietta. Penrod, the Dancing Emperor Penguin. unabridged ed. LC 96-92654. (Illus.). 24p. (J). (ps-6). 1996. pap. 20.95 incl. VHS (*0-9652248-1-3*, 1) H Roginski.

— Penrod, the Dancing Emperor Penguin. unabridged ed. LC 96-92654. (Illus.). 24p. (J). (ps-6). 1996. pap. 10.95 (*0-9652248-0-5*, 1) H Roginski.

Roginski, Jim, ed. see Brown, Muriel & Foudray, Rita S.

Roginski, Jim, ed. see Cooper, Kay.

Roginski, Jim, ed. see Sharkey, Paulette B.

Roginsky, Rachel J., jt. auth. see Raleigh, Lori E.

Roginsky, Rachel J., jt. ed. see Raleigh, Lori E.

Rogister, John. Louis the XV & the "Parlement" of Paris, 1737-1755. (Illus.). 314p. (C). 1995. text 69.95 (*0-521-40395-2*) Cambridge U Pr.

R

Rogl, P. & Schuster, J. C., eds. Phase Diagrams of Ternary Boron Nitride & Silicon Nitride Systems. 289p. 1992. 252.00 (*0-87170-445-5*, 57743G) ASM.

***Rogland, Robert.** Pinocchio's Quest. (Illus.). 192p. (J). (gr. 4-6). 2000. 2.95 (*1-930367-40-6*, CLP 29650); pap. 8.95 (*1-930367-39-2*, CLP 29650) Christian Liberty.

Rogland, Robert. Romans: A Study Manual. 1988. pap., student ed. 6.99 (*0-87552-403-6*) P & R Pubng.

Rogler, Ingrid. Small Folk Quilters. Watts, Pamela M., ed. LC 89-60974. (Illus.). 66p. (Orig.). (J). (gr. 3-10). 1989. pap. 9.95 (*0-9622565-0-1*) Chitra Pubns.

Rogler, Lloyd H., jt. auth. see Farber, Anne.

Roglieri, John L. Dante & Music. 67.95 (*1-85928-255-5*) Ashgate Pub Co.

Rogne, Carol. Control & Power in Relationships. 68p. 1991. pap. text 4.95 (*1-881565-01-7*) Discov Counsel.

— Dealing with Anger. 51p. 1991. pap. text 4.95 (*1-881565-02-5*) Discov Counsel.

— Understanding & Enhancing Self-Esteem. 527p. 1991. pap. text 8.95 (*1-881565-00-9*) Discov Counsel.

Rognebakke, Myrtle, jt. auth. see Driessle, Hannelore.

Rognehaugh, Richard. The Health Information Technology Dictionary. LC 98-46547. 240p. 1999. pap. 19.95 (*0-8342-1277-3*, 12773) Aspen Pub.

— Managed Health Care Dictionary. 2nd ed. LC 98-3103. 240p. 1998. 19.95 (*0-8342-1144-0*, 11440) Aspen Pub.

***Rogner, Bud.** Filming of "Runaway Bride" in Historic Berlin, Maryland. (Illus.). viii, 78p. 1999. pap. text 19.90 (*0-935045-09-0*) D-OR Pr.

Rogner, E. A. Living in Arcadia: Ocean Pines, Maryland. (Illus.). 80p. (Orig.). 1990. pap. text 9.95 (*0-935045-07-4*) D-OR Pr.

— The Pentagon: "A National Institution": Its History, Its Functions, Its People. rev. ed. LC 85-72559. (Illus.). 1986. pap. text 3.50 (*0-935045-05-8*) D-OR Pr.

— The Pentagon: "A National Showplace"; What to See & Where to See It. (Illus.). 48p. (Orig.). pap. text 4.95 (*0-935045-06-6*) D-OR Pr.

— The Pentagon: Facts about the Building (Monograph) rev. ed. 1986. pap. text 0.95 (*0-935045-04-X*) D-OR Pr.

— The Pentagon: Flags Displayed in the Building. LC 85-72558. (Illus.). 36p. (Orig.). 1985. pap. 3.50 (*0-935045-03-1*) D-OR Pr.

— The Pentagon: Flags Displayed in the Flag Corridor (Monograph) (Orig.). pap. 0.95 (*0-935045-02-3*) D-OR Pr.

Rogner, H. H. & Khan, A. Economics, Modelling, Planning & Management of Energy. 628p. (C). 1989. text 130.00 (*9971-5-0949-0*) World Scientific Pub.

Rogner, Manfred. Lizards, 2 vols. Hackworth, John, tr. Incl. Vol. 2. Lizards 2. LC 95-31852. (Illus.). 318p. 1997. 54.50 (*0-89464-968-X*); Vol. 1. LC 95-31852. (Illus.). 328p. 1997. 59.50 (*0-89464-939-6*); LC 95-31852. 97.50 (*0-89464-972-8*) Krieger.

Rognes, Knut. Blowflies (Diptera, Calliphoridae) of Fennoscandia & Denmark. LC 90-40545. (Fauna Entomologica Scandinavica Ser.: No. 24). (Illus.). 272p. 1990. lib. bdg. 110.50 (*90-04-09304-4*) Brill Academic Pubs.

Rogness, Alvin N. My Personal Prayer Book. LC 88-28625. (Illus.). 64p. 1988. kivar 8.99 (*0-8066-2358-6*, 10-4599, Augsburg) Augsburg Fortress.

— When Things Go Wrong: A Book of Comfort. LC 98-48282. (Comfort Ser.). 48p. 1999. pap. 4.99 (*0-8066-3841-9*, 9-3841, Augsburg) Augsburg Fortress.

— When You Are Afraid: A Book of Comfort. LC 98-48283. (Comfort Ser.). 48p. 1999. pap. 4.99 (*0-8066-3842-7*, 9-3842, Augsburg) Augsburg Fortress.

— When You Are Suffering: A Book of Comfort. LC 98-48281. (Comfort Ser.). 48p. 1999. pap. 4.99 (*0-8066-3839-7*, 9-3839, Augsburg) Augsburg Fortress.

— When You Have Doubts: A Book of Comfort. LC 98-49366. (Comfort Ser.). 48p. 1999. pap. 4.99 (*0-8066-3840-0*, 9-3840, Augsburg) Augsburg Fortress.

Rogness, Andrew. Crossing Boundary Waters: A Spiritual Journey in Canoe Country. 1994. pap. 11.99 (*0-8066-2730-1*, 9-2730, Augsburg) Augsburg Fortress.

Rogness, Michael. Preaching to a TV Generation: Preaching for an Electronic Age. LC 93-47208. 1994. pap. 11.50 (*1-55673-838-2*) CSS OH.

Rognli, O. A., et al, eds. Breeding Fodder Crops for Marginal Conditions: Proceedings of the 18th Eucarpia Fodder Crops Section Meeting, Loen, Norway, 25-28 August 1993. LC 94-21242. (Developments in Plant Breeding Ser.: Vol. 2). 300p. (C). 1994. text 178.50 (*0-7923-2948-1*) Kluwer Academic.

Rognum, Torleiv, ed. Sudden Infant Death Syndrome: Journal: Pediatrician. 300p. 1995. 37.00 (*82-00-22419-8*) Scandnvan Univ Pr.

Rogo, D. Scott. Leaving the Body. 204p. 1983. per. 10.00 (*0-671-76394-6*) S&S Trade Pap.

— Life after Death: The Case for Survival of Bodily Death. 144p. 1987. pap. 9.95 (*0-85030-504-7*, Pub. by Aqrn Pr) HarpC.

— Methods & Models for Education in Parapsychology. LC 73-75209. (Parapsychological Monographs: No. 14). 1973. pap. 5.00 (*0-912328-22-3*) Parapsych Foun.

— Mind over Matter. 1988. 7.95 (*0-85030-485-7*, Pub. by Aqrn Pr) HarpC.

— Miracles: A Parascientific Exploration of Wondrous Phenomena. (Illus.). 384p. 1991. pap. 14.00 (*1-85538-055-2*, Pub. by Aqrn Pr) Harper SF.

— New Techniques of Inner Healing. 248p. (Orig.). 1994. pap. 12.95 (*1-56924-930-X*) Marlowe & Co.

— On the Track of the Poltergeist. 1985. 16.95 (*0-13-634445-3*) P-H.

— The Poltergeist Experience. 1990. 12.95 (*0-85030-887-9*, Pub. by Aqrn Pr) Harper SF.

— Psychic Breakthroughs Today. (Illus.). 240p. (Orig.). 1988. pap. 12.95 (*0-85030-570-5*, Pub. by Aqrn Pr) HarpC.

Rogo, Thomas Paul. The Surfrider: A Midwestern Odyssey. (Illus.). 80p. (J). (gr. 3 up). 1999. 19.95 (*1-57306-082-8*) Bess Pr.

***Rogo, Thomas Paul.** The Surfrider: A Midwestern Odyssey. (Illus.). 80p. (J). (gr. 3 up). 1999. pap. 14.95 (*1-57306-110-7*) Bess Pr.

***Rogoff.** Terra Infirma: Geography's Visual Culture. LC 99-52594. 192p. 2000. pap. 21.95 (*0-415-09616-2*) Routledge.

— Terra Infirma: Geography's Visual Culture. LC 99-52594. (Illus.). 192p. (C). (gr. 13). 2000. 75.00 (*0-415-09615-4*) Routledge.

Rogoff, Abraham M. Formative Years of the Jewish Labor Movement in the United States: (1890-1900) LC 78-21163. 1979. reprint ed. lib. bdg. 65.00 (*0-313-20881-6*, ROFJ, Greenwood Pr) Greenwood.

Rogoff, Barbara. Apprenticeship in Thinking: Cognitive Development in Social Context. (Illus.). 272p. (C). 1991. reprint ed. pap. text 24.95 (*0-19-507003-8*) OUP.

Rogoff, Barbara, ed. Artistic Development. (Human Development Ser.: Vol. 40, No. 3, 1997). 68p. 1997. pap. 21.75 (*3-8055-6555-0*) S Karger.

— Reflecting on a History of Developmental Research. (Journal: No. 40). (Illus.). 68p. 1992. pap. 21.75 (*3-8055-6517-8*) S Karger.

Rogoff, Barbara & Lave, Jean, eds. Everyday Cognition: Its Development in Social Context. (Illus.). 320p. 1984. 44.00 (*0-674-27030-4*) HUP.

Rogoff, Barbara, et al. Guided Participation in Cultural Activity by Toddlers & Caregivers. (Monographs of the Society for Research on Child Development). 300p. 1993. pap. text 15.00 (*0-226-72391-7*) U Ch Pr.

Rogoff, Charles, et al, eds. Guidelines for Public Sector Hazardous Materials Training. 600p. (C). 1998. pap. text 65.00 (*0-7881-7355-3*) DIANE Pub.

***Rogoff, Gordon.** Vanishing Acts: Theater since the Sixties. 320p. 2000. 37.50 (*0-300-08248-7*); pap. 17.95 (*0-300-08777-2*) Yale U Pr.

Rogoff, Herbert, ed. see DISTEFANO, DOMENIC.

Rogoff, Herbert, ed. see Schlemm, Betty L.

Rogoff, Herbert, ed. see Van Wyk, Helen.

Rogoff, Irit, ed. The Divided Heritage: Themes & Problems in German Modernism. (Illus.). 406p. (C). 1991. text 80.00 (*0-521-34553-7*) Cambridge U Pr.

Rogoff, Irit, jt. ed. see Sherman, Daniel J.

Rogoff, Jay. The Cutoff. 64p. (Orig.). 1995. pap. 10.00 (*0-915380-31-5*) Word Works.

— First Hand. (Premier Ser.: Vol. 3). (Illus.). 24p. (Orig.). 1997. pap. 5.00 (*0-9654421-4-4*) Mica Press.

Rogoff, K., jt. ed. see Grossman, G. M.

Rogoff, Kenneth, jt. auth. see Obstfeld, Maurice.

Rogoff, Kenneth S., jt. auth. see Grossman, Gene M.

***Rogoff, Leonard.** Homelands: Southern-Jewish Identity in Durham & Chapel Hill, North Carolina. 2000. 39.95 (*0-8173-1055-X*) U of Ala Pr.

Rogoff, Leonard. Office Guide to Business Letters, Memos & Reports. 2nd ed. LC 94-25593. 256p. 1994. per. 5.95 (*0-671-89664-4*, Arc) IDG Bks.

Rogoff, Marc J. & Williams, John F. Approaches to Implementing Solid Waste Recycling Facilities. LC 94-3865. (Illus.). 216p. 1994. 109.00 (*0-8155-1352-6*) Noyes.

Rogoff, Mark J. How to Implement Waste-to-Energy Projects. LC 87-12211. (Illus.). 202p. 1988. 45.00 (*0-8155-1132-9*) Noyes.

Rogoff, Natalie. Recent Trends in Occupational Mobility. Coser, Lewis A. & Powell, Walter W., eds. LC 79-7016. (Perennial Works in Sociology). (Illus.). 1979. reprint ed. lib. bdg. 18.95 (*0-405-12115-6*) Ayer.

Rogols-Siegel, Linda, tr. see Lewald, Fanny.

Rogolsky, Janet, ed. see Thompson, Alan.

Rogondino, Michael. Computer Color, Ten Thousand Computer-generated Process Colors. 108p. 1990. pap. 24.95 (*0-87701-739-5*) Chronicle Bks.

— Computer Type: A Designer's Guide to Computer-Generated Type. (Illus.). 464p. (Orig.). (C). 1998. pap. text 30.00 (*0-7881-5363-3*) DIANE Pub.

***Rogondino, Michael & Rogondino, Pat.** Process Color Manual: 24,000 CMYK Combinations for Design, Prepress, & Printing. rev. expanded ed. (Illus.). 256p. 2000. spiral bd. 35.00 (*0-8118-2757-7*) Chronicle Bks.

Rogondino, Pat, jt. auth. see Rogondino, Michael.

Rogosheske, Walter, jt. auth. see Houts, Marshall.

Rogosin, Donn. Invisible Men: Life in Baseball's Negro Leagues. Turner, Philip, ed. (Kodansha Globe Trade Paperback Ser.). (Illus.). 320p. 1995. pap. 14.00 (*1-56836-085-1*, Kodansha Globe) Kodansha.

Rogosin, Sergei V., jt. auth. see Mityushev, Vladimir V.

Rogove, Susan T. Pyrex by Corning: A Supplement & 1997-98 Price Guide. (Illus.). 32p. 1996. pap. 9.95 (*1-57080-029-4*, 4105) Antique Pubns.

Rogove, Susan T. & Steinhauer, Marcia B. Pyrex by Corning: A Collector's Guide. (Illus.). 140p. 1993. pap. 24.95 (*0-915410-94-X*, 4044) Antique Pubns.

Rogovin. 1001 Activities for Children. LC 97-50527. 208p. 1999. 6.99 (*0-517-20283-2*) Random Hse Value.

Rogovin, Anne. Let Me Do It! rev. ed. LC 90-30226. 160p. 1990. pap. 5.48 (*0-687-21376-2*) Abingdon.

— 1001 Wonderful Wonders: Activities for All Children. 208p. (Orig.). 1992. pap. 12.95 (*0-687-29193-3*) Abingdon.

Rogovin, Janice. A Sense of Place - Tu Barrio: Jamaica Plain People & Where They Live - La Gente de Jamaica Plain y Donde Ellos Viven. Rivas, Yolanda, tr. (ENG & SPA., Illus.). 48p. (Orig.). 1981. pap. text 10.00 (*0-9621783-1-4*) Stonybrook Pr.

Rogovin, Milton, photos by. The Bonds Between Us: A Celebration of Mothers, Fathers, & Children. (Illus.). 96p. 1999. pap. 20.00 (*1-893996-02-6*, Pub. by White Pine) Consort Bk Sales.

Rogovin, Milton & Frisch, Michael, photos by. Portraits in Steel. LC 92-56776. (Illus.). 288p. 1993. pap. text 29.95 (*0-8014-8102-3*) Cornell U Pr.

Rogovin, Paula. Classroom Interviews: A World of Learning. LC 98-10079. (Teacher to Teacher Ser.). 153p. 1998. pap. text 20.00 (*0-325-00047-6*) Heinemann.

Rogovin, Sarah, jt. ed. see Grady, John.

***Rogovin, Sheila, et al.** Couple Fits: How to Live with the Person You Love. LC 99-46782. 288p. 2000. pap. 13.95 (*0-399-52573-4*, Perigee Bks) Berkley Pub.

Rogovin, Vadim Z. 1937: Stalin's Year of Terror, Vol. 4. Choate, Frederick S., tr. from RUS. LC 97-50514. (Illus.). 550p. 1998. pap. 29.95 (*0-929087-77-1*) Mehring Bks.

— Two Lectures; Stalin's Great Terror: Origins & Consequences: Leon Trotsky & the Fate of Marxism in the U. S. S. R. (Illus.). 46p. (Orig.). 1996. pap. 9.95 (*1-875639-13-6*, Pub. by Mehring Bks); pap. 9.95 (*0-929087-83-6*) Mehring Bks.

***Rogovoy, Seth.** The Essential Klezmer: A Music Lover's Guide to Jewish Roots & Soul Music, from the Old World to the Jazz Age to the Downtown Avant Garde. LC 00-20837. 320p. 2000. pap. 19.95 (*1-56512-244-5*, 72244) Algonquin Bks.

Rogow, Arnold A. Fatal Friendship: Alexander Hamilton & Aaron Burr. (Illus.). 336p. 1998. 27.50 (*0-8090-4753-5*) Hill & Wang.

***Rogow, Arnold A.** A Fatal Friendship: Alexander Hamilton & Aaron Burr. (Illus.). 368p. 1999. pap. 14.00 (*0-8090-1621-4*) Hill & Wang.

Rogow, Arnold A., ed. Politics, Personality & Social Science in the Twentieth Century: Essays in Honor of Harold D. Lasswell. LC 76-75812. 466p. 1969. lib. bdg. 40.00 (*0-226-72399-2*) U Ch Pr.

Rogow, Arnold A. & Shore, Peter. The Labour Government & British Industry, 1945-1951. LC 73-22508. 196p. (C). 1974. reprint ed. lib. bdg. 79.50 (*0-8371-6374-9*, ROLG, Greenwood Pr) Greenwood.

Rogow, Arnold A., jt. auth. see Burks, Ardath W.

Rogow, Debbie & Grasmuck, Sherri. Get Real Comics. (Illus.). 24p. (Orig.). (J). (gr. 4-8). 1996. mass mkt. 1.95 (*1-891103-00-8*) Tides Ctr.

— Get Real Comics, No. 2. (Illus.). 24p. (Orig.). (J). (gr. 4-8). 1997. mass mkt. 1.95 (*1-891103-01-6*) Tides Ctr.

— Get Real Comics, Vol. 3. (Illus.). 24p. (Orig.). (J). (gr. 4-8). 1998. mass mkt. 1.95 (*1-891103-02-4*) Tides Ctr.

***Rogow, Roberta.** Problem of the Evil Editor: A Charles Dodgson/Arthur Conan Doyle Mystery. 288p. 2000. 23.95 (*0-312-20903-7*) St Martin.

Rogow, Roberta. Problem of the Spiteful Spiritualist. LC 99-21750. (Charles Dodgson/Arthur Conan Doyle Myste Ser.). 272p. 1999. text 23.95 (*0-312-20570-8*) St Martin.

Rogow, Sally M. Helping the Visually Impaired Child with Developmental Problems: Effective Practice in Home, School & Community. LC 88-2222. (Special Education Ser.). 216p. (C). 1988. pap. text 18.95 (*0-8077-2902-7*) Tchrs Coll.

Rogow, Sally M. & Hass, Julia L. Shared Moments: Learning Games for Disabled Children. 64p. 1993. pap. 8.95 (*0-936389-33-8*) Tudor Pubs.

Rogow, Zack. Preview of the Dream. 64p. (Orig.). 1985. pap. 6.00 (*0-940584-10-7*) Gull Bks.

Rogow, Zack, tr. see Breton, Andre.

Rogowitz, B. E., ed. Human Vision, Visual Processing, & Digital Display III. 1992. 20.00 (*0-8194-0820-4*, 1666) SPIE.

***Rogowitz, Bernice E., et al, eds.** Human Vision & Electronic Imaging IV. 628p. 1999. pap. text 111.00 (*0-8194-3115-X*) SPIE.

Rogowitz, Bernice E. & Pappas, Thrasyvoulos N., eds. Human Vision & Electronic Imaging II, Vol. 3016. LC 98-114631. 536p. 1997. 99.00 (*0-8194-2427-7*) SPIE.

— Human Vision & Electronic Imaging III. LC 98-227304. (Proceedings of SPIE Ser.: Vol. 3299). 638p. 1998. 107.00 (*0-8194-2739-X*) SPIE.

Rogowski, Christian. Distinguished Outsider: Robert Musil & His Critics. (LCGERM Ser.). x, 230p. 1994. 60.00 (*1-879751-52-6*) Camden Hse.

— Implied Dramaturgy: Robert Musil & the Crisis of Modern Drama. (Studies in Austrian Literature, Culture, & Thought). 313p. 1993. 37.50 (*0-929497-59-7*) Ariadne CA.

Rogowski, Gary. Router Joinery. LC 97-6238. (Illus.). 192p. 1997. 24.95 (*1-56158-174-7*, 070299) Taunton.

Rogowski, Jeannette A. Private Versus Public Sector Insurance Coverage for Drug Abuse. LC 93-12592. 1993. pap. text 13.00 (*0-8330-1345-9*, MR-166-DPRC) Rand Corp.

Rogowski, Jeannette A. & Harrison, Ellen R. Treatment Costs for Very Low Birthweight Infants: The California Medicaid Experience. 66p. (Orig.). 1995. pap. text 13.00 (*0-8330-2345-4*, MR-451-AHCPR) Rand Corp.

Rogowski, Jeannette A., jt. auth. see Carter, Grace M.

Rogowski, Ralf, ed. Civil Law. LC 95-8007. (International Library of Essays in Law & Legal Theory: No. 10). 500p. (C). 1996. lib. bdg. 150.00 (*0-8147-7465-2*) NYU Pr.

Rogowski, Ralf, jt. ed. see Wilson, Geoffrey.

Rogowski, Ronald. Commerce & Coalitions: How Trade Affects Domestic Political Alignments. (Illus.). 224p. (C). 1989. text 39.50 (*0-691-07812-2*); pap. text 16.95 (*0-691-02330-1*, Pub. by Princeton U Pr) Cal Prin Full Svc.

— How Economies of Scale Trade Affects Domestic Politics. (New Ser.: Vol. 13). 27p. 1997. pap. 15.00 (*0-86682-129-5*) Ctr Intl Relations.

— Rational Legitimacy: A Theory of Political Support. LC 74-2975. (Illus.). 324p. 1974. reprint ed. pap. 100.50 (*0-7837-9434-7*, 206017600004) Bks Demand.

Rogowski, Ronald, ed. Comparative Politics & the International Political Economy, 2 vols., Set. LC 94-22995. (Library of International Political Economy: Vol. 8). 992p. 1995. 350.00 (*1-85278-654-X*) E Elgar.

Rogowski, Ronald, jt. ed. see Tiryakian, Edward A.

Rogoyska, Jane. Gustave Klimt: Austrian Painter. (Reveries Ser.). 120p. 1999. 14.95 (*1-85995-476-6*) Parkstone Pr.

— Socialist Realism. (Schools & Movements Ser.). (Illus.). 208p. 2000. 55.00 (*1-85995-409-X*) Parkstone Pr.

Rogozhin, Nikolai, jt. auth. see Jansson, Maija.

***Rogozinski, Jan.** Brief History of the Caribbean: From the Arawak & Carib to the Present. 2000. pap. 16.00 (*0-452-28193-8*) Penguin Books.

Rogozinski, Jan. A Brief History of the Caribbean: From the Arawak & the Carib to the Present. LC 94-15039. (Illus.). 336p. 1994. pap. 15.95 (*0-452-01134-5*, Mer) NAL.

— A Brief History of the Caribbean: From the Arawak & the Carib to the Present. rev. ed. LC 98-51304. (Illus.). 432p. 1999. 35.00 (*0-8160-3811-2*) Facts on File.

***Rogozinski, Jan.** Honor among Thieves: Captain Kidd, Henry Every & the Pirate Republic Libertalia. (Illus.). 256p. 2000. 24.95 (*0-8117-1529-9*) Stackpole.

Rogozinski, Jan. Pirates! Brigands, Buccaneers, & Privateers in Fact, Fiction & Legend. LC 94-12717. 432p. 1995. 50.00 (*0-8160-2761-7*) Facts on File.

— Pirates! Brigands, Buccaneers, & Privateers in Fact, Fiction, & Legend - An A-Z Encyclopedia. LC 96-11351. (Illus.). 416p. 1996. pap. 19.95 (*0-306-80722-X*) Da Capo.

— Power, Caste & Law: Social Conflict in Fourteenth-Century Montpellier. LC 78-70247. (Medieval Academy Bks.: No. 91). 1982. 30.00 (*0-910956-72-3*) Medieval Acad.

— Smokeless Tobacco in the Western World. 194p. 1990. 25.00 (*0-8159-6856-6*) Devin.

— Smokeless Tobacco in the Western World, 1550-1950. LC 90-6899. 208p. 1990. 55.00 (*0-275-93600-7*, C3600, Praeger Pubs) Greenwood.

Rogozinski, Jan & Reindeau, Roger. A Brief History of Canada. LC 99-23494. (Illus.). 336p. 1999. 29.95 (*0-8160-3157-6*, Checkmark) Facts on File.

Rogozkin, Victor A. Metabolism of Anabolic-Androgenic Steroids. (Illus.). 168p. 1991. lib. bdg. 225.00 (*0-8493-6415-9*, QP) CRC Pr.

Rogozkin, Victor A. & Maughan, Ron J., eds. Current Research in Sports Sciences: An International Perspective. (Illus.). 356p. (C). 1996. text 114.00 (*0-306-45319-3*, Kluwer Plenum) Kluwer Academic.

Rogrigues, Lawrence. The Awesome Power of JAVA BEANS. LC 98-17352. 576p. 1998. pap. 44.95 (*1-884777-56-2*) Manning Pubns.

Rogriquez, K. S. The Dolphins of Coral Cove. LC 94-70052. (Little Mermaid Novels Ser.: No. 11). (Illus.). 80p. (J). (gr. 1-4). 1994. pap. 3.50 (*0-7868-4001-3*, Pub. by Disney Pr) Time Warner.

Rogue, E. Dictionnaire Pratique Cybersante (Internet) (FRE.). 1998. 95.00 (*0-320-00386-8*) Fr & Eur.

***Roguemore, Patt & Carlton, Jane.** Standing on the Blood. 130p. 1999. 17.95 (*0-9676817-0-7*) P Roguemore.

Roguet, A. M. Homilies for the Celebration of Baptism. Du Charme, Jerome, tr. from FRE. LC 76-53546. 58p. 1977. pap. 2.95 (*0-8199-0655-7*, Frncscn Herld) Franciscan Pr.

— Homilies for the Celebration of Marriage. Du Charme, Jerome, tr. from FRE. LC 76-53538. 111p. 1977. pap. 5.95 (*0-8199-0656-5*, Frncscn Herld) Franciscan Pr.

— Saint Joseph Weekday Missal: Advent to Pentecost, Vol. 1. 1306p. 1975. vinyl bd. 15.75 (*0-89942-920-3*, 920/09) Catholic Bk Pub.

— Saint Joseph Weekday Missal Vol. 2: Pentecost to Advent. 1306p. 1975. vinyl bd. 15.75 (*0-89942-921-1*, 921/09) Catholic Bk Pub.

Rogulic-Newsome, Lisa. Theme for a Day. 128p. (J). (gr. 1-6). 1990. 10.99 (*0-86653-545-4*, GA1154) Good Apple.

— Theme of the Week. 208p. 1991. 13.99 (*0-86653-602-7*, GA1321) Good Apple.

Rogus, Joseph F., jt. auth. see Ristau, Karen M.

Rogus, Timothy J. J'Ecris, Tu Ecris. (FRE.). 104p. (C). 1992. pap. 8.40 (*0-8442-1313-6*, VF1313-6) NTC Contemp Pub Co.

Roguski. Academic Mini-Lectures. (J). 1991. audio 29.95 (*0-8384-3383-9*) Heinle & Heinle.

Rogut, Lynn. Reshaping Inpatient Care: Efficiency & Quality in New York City Hospitals. LC 96-45277. (Papers). 44p. 1996. 12.00 (*1-881277-29-1*) United Hosp Fund.

Rogut, Lynn & Hudson, Avery. Meeting Patient's Needs: Quality Care in a Changing Environment. (Papers). 1995. pap. 12.00 (*1-881277-27-5*) United Hosp Fund.

Rogut, Lynn & United Hospital Fund of New York Staff. Beyond the Clinic: Redefining Hospital Ambulatory Care. LC 97-15726. (Paper Ser.). 1997. write for info. (*1-881277-34-8*) United Hosp Fund.

Roh, Franz & Tschichold, Jan, eds. Foto-Auge, Oeil et Photo, Photo-Eye. LC 72-9234. (Literature of Photography Ser.). 1977. reprint ed. 18.95 (*0-405-04939-0*) Ayer.

Roh, Mark. Clinical Atlas of Surgical Oncology. (Illus.). 600p. 2001. text 125.00 (*1-57626-014-3*) Quality Med Pub.

***Rohan.** Cloud Castles. 2000. 22.00 (*0-380-97239-5*) Morrow Avon.

Rohan, Karen, ed. see Garrett, Laurie.

Rohan, Karen M., ed. And Justice for All: The Universal Declaration of Human Rights at 50. LC 98-73867. (Headline Ser.: Vol. 318). 128p. 1998. pap. text 10.95 (*0-87124-187-0*) Foreign Policy.

Rohan, Karen M., ed. see Foreign Policy Association Staff & Lewinski, Marcel.

Rohan, Karen M., jt. ed. see Foreign Policy Association Staff.

An Asterisk (*) at the beginning of an entry indicates that the title is appearing for the first time.

Rohan, Karen M., ed. see Kristof, Nicholas D. & WuDunn, Sheryl.

Rohan, Karen M., ed. see Lewinski, Marcel.

Rohan, Michael S. Chase the Morning. 352p. 1992. mass mkt. 4.99 (*0-380-70871-X*, Avon Bks) Morrow Avon.

— Cloud Castles. (Spiral Ser.). 336p. 1995. reprint ed. mass mkt. 5.50 (*0-380-77554-9*, Avon Bks) Morrow Avon.

— The Gates of Noon. 320p. 1994. mass mkt. 4.99 (*0-380-71718-2*, Avon Bks) Morrow Avon.

— Ww #1: Anvil of Ice Vol. I. (Winter of the World Ser.). 368p. 1989. mass mkt. 4.99 (*0-380-70547-8*, Avon Bks) Morrow Avon.

— Ww #2: Forge in the Forest, Vol. II. (Winter of the World Ser.). 416p. 1989. mass mkt. 4.99 (*0-380-70548-6*, Avon Bks) Morrow Avon.

— Ww #3: Hammer of the Sun. (Winter of the Sun Ser.). 512p. 1990. mass mkt. 4.99 (*0-380-70549-4*, Avon Bks) Morrow Avon.

Rohan, Patrick J. Home Owner Associations & Planned Unit Developments: Law & Forms, 5 vols. (Real Estate Transactions Ser.). 1977. ring bd. 720.00 (*0-8205-1327-X*) Bender.

— New York Civil Practice: EPTL, 7 vols. 1969. ring bd. 1260.00 (*0-8205-1806-9*) Bender.

— Real Estate Brokerage: Law & Practice, 2 vols. (Real Estate Transactions Ser.). 1985. 175.00 (*0-8205-1486-1*) Bender.

— Real Estate Financing: Text, Forms, Tax Analysis, 8 vols. (Real Estate Transactions Ser.). 1973. ring bd. 1530.00 (*0-8205-1592-2*) Bender.

— Zoning & Land Use Controls, 10 vols., Set. 1978. ring bd. 1400.00 (*0-8205-1845-X*) Bender.

Rohan, Patrick J. & Donovan, Caroline. Current Leasing Law & Techniques: Forms, 4 vols., Updates available. (Real Estate Transactions Ser.). 1982. ring bd. 870.00 (*0-8205-1401-2*) Bender.

Rohan, Patrick J. & Reskin, Melvin A. Condemnation Procedures & Techniques-Forms, 6 vols. (Real Estate Transactions Ser.). 1969. ring bd. 1060.00 (*0-8205-1243-5*) Bender.

— Cooperative Housing: Law & Practice-Forms, 6 vols. (Real Estate Transactions Ser.). 1967. ring bd. 860.00 (*0-8205-1239-7*) Bender.

Rohan, Patrick J., jt. auth. see Powell, Richard R.

Rohan, Rebecca. Got a Minute? 101 Marketing Tips for Writers. 136p. (Orig.). 1990. pap. 8.95 (*0-942980-12-3*) CNW.

Rohan, Rebecca F. Building Better Web Pages. LC 98-3862. (Illus.). 288p. (C). 1998. pap. 34.95 (*0-12-593185-9*) Morgan Kaufmann.

Rohani, M. K. The Accents of God: Sections from the World's Sacred Scriptures. (Illus.). 96p. 1994. pap. 12.95 (*1-85168-023-3*, Pub. by Onewrld Pubns) Penguin Putnam.

— Contemplating Life's Great Questions: Selections from the Writings of Baha'u'llah, with Commentary. 96p. 1990. pap. 7.95 (*1-85168-024-1*, Pub. by Onewrld Pubns) Penguin Putnam.

Rohatgi, P. K. & Khan, P. A., eds. Processing, Properties & Applications of Cast Metal Matrix Composites. (Illus.). 200p. 1996. 68.00 (*0-87339-344-9*, 3449) Minerals Metals.

Rohatgi, P. K., ed. see ASM International Staff.

Rohatgi, Pauline, et al, eds. Bombay to Mumbai: Changing Perspectives. LC 97-900351. (C). 1997. 98.00 (*81-85026-37-8*, Pub. by Marg Publns) Art Media Resources.

Rohatgi, Pauline & Godrej, Pheroza, eds. Under the Indian Sun: British Landscape Artists. LC 95-901566. (C). 1995. 105.00 (*81-85026-29-7*, Pub. by Marg Publns) Art Media Resources.

Rohatgi, Pradeep, ed. Solidification of Metal Matrix Composites: Proceedings of a Conference Jointly Sponsored by TMS Solidification Committee & TMS-ASM Composites Committee at Indianapolis, 1989. LC 90-62372. 229p. 1990. reprint ed. pap. 71.00 (*0-608-00779-X*, 206157700010) Bks Demand.

Rohatgi, Pradeep K., ed. Microstructure Formation During Solidification of Metal Matrix Composites. LC 93-79590. (Illus.). 171p. 1993. pap. 53.10 (*0-608-04881-X*, 206557300004) Bks Demand.

Rohatgi, U. S. Preliminary Phenomena Identification & Ranking Tables (PIRT) for SBWR Start-up Stability. 92p. 1997. pap. 8.50 (*0-16-062819-9*) USGPO.

— Ramona-4B, Computer Code with Three Dimensional Neutron Kinetics For BWR & SBWR System Transients: Models & Correlations. 449p. 1998. per. 35.00 (*0-16-062897-0*) USGPO.

— Ramona-4B, Computer Code with Three Dimensional Neutron Kinetics for BWR & SBWR System Transient: User's Manual. 355p. 1998. per. 28.00 (*0-16-062898-9*) USGPO.

Rohatgi, U. S., et al, eds. Fluid Machinery - 1995. LC 90-55406. (1995 ASME/JSME Fluids Engineering Conference Ser.: FED-Vol. 222). 196p. 1995. 96.00 (*0-7918-1477-7*, G00972) ASME.

— Gas-Liquid Flows - 1995. LC 93-71646. (1995 ASME/JSME Fluids Engineering Conference Ser.: FED-Vol. 225). 212p. 1995. 104.00 (*0-7918-1480-7*, G00975) ASME.

— Gas-Liquid Flows, 1993. LC 93-71646. (FED Ser.: Vol. 165). 223p. 1993. pap. 45.00 (*0-7918-0973-0*, H00805) ASME.

Rohatgi, U. S. & Ogut, A., eds. Fluid Machinery, 1994. LC 90-55406. (Fluid Engineering Division Conference Ser.: Vol. 195). 1994. pap. 22.50 (*0-7918-1379-7*) ASME.

Rohatgi, U. S. & Sharma, Madhav P., eds. Multiphase Flow in Wells & Pipelines. (FED Ser.: Vol. 144). 180p. 1992. 50.00 (*0-7918-1129-8*, G00773) ASME.

Rohatgi, U. S., jt. ed. see Zakem, S. B.

Rohatgi, Vijay K. An Introduction to Probability Theory & Mathematical Statistics. LC 75-14378. (Series in Probability & Mathematical Statistics). 704p. 1976. 189.95 (*0-471-73135-8*) Wiley.

***Rohatgi, Vijay K. & Saleh, A. K.** An Introduction to Probability & Statistics. 2nd ed. 704p. 2000. 94.95 (*0-471-34846-5*) Wiley.

Rohatyn, Dennis. The Reluctant Naturalist: A Study of G.E. Moore's Principia Ethica. 150p. (Orig.). (C). 1987. lib. bdg. 40.50 (*0-8191-5767-8*) U Pr of Amer.

Rohatyn, Dennis A. Naturalism & Deontology. LC 73-92240. (Studies in Philosophy: No. 27). 128p. (Orig.). 1975. pap. text 29.25 (*90-279-3233-6*) Mouton.

— Two Dogmas of Philosophy & Other Essays in the Philosophy of Philosophy. LC 75-63. 199p. (C). 1976. 29.50 (*0-8386-1673-9*) Fairleigh Dickinson.

Rohatynskyj, Marta A., jt. auth. see Jaarsma, Sjoerd R.

Rohd, Michael. Theatre for Community, Conflict & Dialogue: The Hope Is Vital Training Manual. LC 98-6132. 176p. 1998. pap. 16.95 (*0-325-00002-6*) Heinemann.

Rohde, Barbara. In the Simple Morning Light: A Meditation Manual. LC 93-40866. 1994. pap. 7.00 (*1-55896-275-1*, Skinner Hse Bks) Unitarian Univ.

***Rohde, Betty.** Celebrations: So Fat, Low Fat, No Fat: More Than 150 Recipes for Special Occasions. 192p. 1999. per. 12.00 (*0-684-84687-X*) S&S Trade.

Rohde, Betty. Italian So Fat, Low Fat, No Fat. LC 96-45247. 1997. pap. 12.00 (*0-684-82920-7*, Fireside) S&S Trade Pap.

— Mexican So Fat, Low Fat, No Fat. LC 97-29292. 1998. pap. 12.00 (*0-684-83525-8*) S&S Trade.

— More So Fat, Low Fat, No Fat: Recipes for Family & Friends that Cut the Fat but Not the Flavor! 256p. 1996. per. 12.00 (*0-684-81574-5*, Fireside) S&S Trade Pap.

— So Fat, Low Fat, No Fat. 94p. 1993. 9.00 (*0-9637239-0-1*) Be Ro Pub.

— So Fat, Low Fat, No Fat. 256p. 1995. pap. 12.00 (*0-671-89813-2*, Fireside) S&S Trade Pap.

— So Fat, Low Fat, No Fat Desserts. LC 98-26413. 224p. 1998. pap. 12.00 (*0-684-83526-6*, Fireside) S&S Trade Pap.

Rohde, Carl C., jt. auth. see Platteel, Andre.

Rohde, Chris. On Track in Math: Decimals. 95p. 1998. pap. text 13.49 (*1-891559-06-0*) R & R.

— On Track in Math: Whole Numbers. 103p. 1998. pap. text 13.49 (*1-891559-05-2*) R & R.

Rohde, David. End Game: The Betrayal & Fall of Srebrenica: Europe's Worst Massacre Since the Holocaust. LC 96-51729. 400p. 1997. 24.00 (*0-374-25342-0*) FS&G.

— Endgame: The Betrayal & Fall of Srebrenica, Europe's Worst Massacre since World War II. LC 98-26127. 480p. 1998. pap. 18.00 (*0-8133-3533-7*, Pub. by Westview) HarpC.

Rohde, David W. Parties & Leaders in the PostReform House. LC 90-22984. (American Politics & Political Economy Ser.). (Illus.). 244p. 1991. pap. text 14.95 (*0-226-72407-7*) U Ch Pr.

— Parties & Leaders in the PostReform House. LC 90-22984. (American Politics & Political Economy Ser.). (Illus.). 244p. 1991. lib. bdg. 45.00 (*0-226-72406-9*) U Ch Pr.

Rohde, David W., jt. ed. see Fiorina, Morris P.

Rohde, Dennis. The Wild Game Cookbook. LC 96-8354. (Illus.). 176p. 1996. spiral bd. 14.95 (*0-87358-641-7*) Northland AZ.

Rohde, Eleanor S. Garden-Craft in the Bible, & Other Essays. LC 67-26775. (Essay Index Reprint Ser.). 1977. 23.95 (*0-8369-0829-5*) Ayer.

— Garden of Herbs. LC 75-81736. 1969. reprint ed. pap. 8.95 (*0-486-22308-6*) Dover.

— The Old English Herbals. 1989. pap. 8.95 (*0-486-26193-X*) Dover.

— Rose Recipes from Olden Times. (Illus.). 95p. 1973. reprint ed. pap. 3.95 (*0-486-22957-2*) Dover.

— The Scented Garden. 1974. reprint ed. 46.00 (*1-55888-222-7*) Omnigraphics Inc.

— Shakespeare's Wild Flowers. LC 76-153350. reprint ed. 32.50 (*0-404-05385-8*) AMS Pr.

Rohde, Elliot S. Producing Corrugated Containers Profitably. LC 94-7893. (Illus.). 256p. 1995. reprint ed. 81.00 (*0-9616302-7-2*) Jelmar Pub.

Rohde, Erwin. Der Griechische Roman und Seine Vorlaufer. (GER.). xxxi, 636p. 1964. reprint ed. write for info. (*0-318-70495-1*) G Olms Pubs.

— Der Griechische Roman und Seine Vorlaufer. (GER.). xxxi, 636p. 1974. reprint ed. write for info. (*3-487-05401-9*) G Olms Pubs.

— Kleine Schriften, 2 vols. (GER.). xxxi, 917p. 1969. reprint ed. write for info. (*0-318-70496-X*); reprint ed. write for info. (*0-318-70497-8*); reprint ed. write for info. (*0-318-70498-6*); reprint ed. write for info. (*0-318-71009-9*); reprint ed. write for info. (*0-318-71010-2*) G Olms Pubs.

— Kleine Schriften, 2 vols., Set. xxxi, 917p. 1969. reprint ed. write for info. (*0-318-71008-0*) G Olms Pubs.

— Psyche: The Cult of Souls & Belief in Immortality Among the Greeks. LC 75-37911. (Select Bibliographies Reprint Ser.). 1980. reprint ed. 57.95 (*0-8369-6749-6*) Ayer.

— Psyche, the Cult of Souls & Belief in Immortality among Ancient Greeks. xvi, 626p. 1987. reprint ed. pap. 35.00 (*0-89005-477-0*) Ares.

Rohde, Fred C., et al. Freshwater Fishes of the Carolinas, Virginia, Maryland, & Delaware. LC 93-32535. (Illus.). 228p. (C). 1994. 45.00 (*0-8078-2130-6*) U of NC Pr.

— Freshwater Fishes of the Carolinas, Virginia, Maryland, & Delaware. LC 93-32535. (Illus.). 228p. 1996. pap. 22.50 (*0-8078-4579-5*) U of NC Pr.

Rohde, Gisela, jt. auth. see Rohde, Jerry.

Rohde, Grace. Just One More Word: Vocabulary One. 90p. 1998. pap. text 8.95 (*1-891559-00-1*) R & R.

— Just One More Word: Vocabulary Two. 90p. 1998. pap. text 8.95 (*1-891559-01-X*) R & R.

— Learning with Wordsearch. 67p. 1998. pap. text 7.95 (*1-891559-02-8*) R & R.

— Riding with Grammar: Capitalization. 94p. 1998. pap. text. write for info. (*1-891559-04-4*) R & R.

Rohde, Grave. Riding with Grammar: Punctuation. 99p. 1998. pap. text. write for info. (*1-891559-03-6*) R & R.

***Rohde, Holger.** Verteilte Komponentensysteme: Einsatzmoglichkeiten Zur Computergestutzten Unternehmensuergreifenden Koordination. (Illus.). XX, 239p. 1999. 48.95 (*3-631-34749-9*) P Lang Pubng.

Rohde, Ilse. Heinrich Vogeler und die Arbeitsschule Barkenhoff: Ein Beitrag zur Historiographie der Reformpadagogik. (Europaische Hochschulschriften, Reihe 11: Bd. 720). (GER., Illus.). 286p. 1997. 54.95 (*3-631-32070-1*) P Lang Pubng.

Rohde, Jerry & Rohde, Gisela. Humboldt Redwoods State Park: A Complete Guide. LC 92-60250. (Illus.). 301p. (Orig.). 1992. pap. 15.95 (*0-936810-25-4*) M & M.

— Mount Rainier National Park: Tales, Trails, & Auto Tours. LC 96-75512. (Illus.). 320p. (Orig.). 1996. pap. 17.95 (*0-9640261-1-2*) MtnHome Bks.

— Redwood National & State Parks: Tales, Trails, & Auto Tours. LC 94-75098. (Illus.). 320p. 1994. pap. 15.95 (*0-9640261-0-4*) MtnHome Bks.

Rohde, Jerry, jt. auth. see Bennion, Lowell.

Rohde, Jon E., et al, eds. Reaching Health for All. (Illus.). 540p. 1993. pap. text 19.95 (*0-19-563236-2*) OUP.

***Rohde, Katherine M.** In Pictures Lake Mead: The Continuing Story. LC 99-60057. (Illus.). 48p. 1999. pap. 7.95 (*0-88714-146-3*) KC Pubns.

— In Pictures Lake Mead: The Continuing Story. Hosford, Helga, tr. from ENG. LC 99-60057. (GER., Illus.). 48p. 1999. pap. 8.95 (*0-88714-827-1*) KC Pubns.

— In Pictures Lake Mead: The Continuing Story. Petzinger, Saori, tr. from ENG. LC 99-60057. (JPN., Illus.). 48p. 1999. pap. 8.95 (*0-88714-828-X*) KC Pubns.

— In Pictures Lake Mead: The Continuing Story. Le Bras, Yvon, tr. from ENG. LC 99-60057. (FRE., Illus.). 48p. 1999. pap. 8.95 (*0-88714-829-8*) KC Pubns.

Rohde, Klaus. Ecology of Marine Parasites. LC 81-12934. (Australian Ecology Ser.). (Illus.). 245p. (C). 1982. pap. text 24.95 (*0-7022-1670-4*) Intl Spec Bk.

— Ecology of Marine Parasites. 2nd ed. (Illus.). 304p. 1993. pap. text 47.50 (*0-85198-845-8*) OUP.

***Rohde, Michael.** Gambit Guide to the Bogo-Indian. 1998. pap. text 19.95 (*1-901983-04-8*) Gambit.

Rohde, Michael. Great Evans Gambit Debate. 1996. pap. 15.95 (*0-938650-75-0*) Thinkers Pr.

***Rohde, Roland.** Die Politische Okonomie Des East Asian Miracle: Ursachen Fur Erfolg und Miaerfolg Einer Protektionistischen Wirtschaftspolitik Am Beispiel Taiwans und der Philippinen. (GER., Illus.). xxi, 419p. 1999. 67.95 (*3-631-34423-6*) P Lang Pubng.

Rohde, S. M., ed. see American Society of Mechanical Engineers Staff.

Rohde, S. M., ed. see Design Engineering Conference (1979: Chicago, IL).

Rohde, S. M., ed. see Fluid Film Bearing Committee of the Lubrication Di.

***Rohde, Ulrich L.** Communications Receivers: DSP, Software Radios & Design. 3rd ed. (Telecommunications Ser.). (Illus.). 700p. 2000. 75.00 (*0-07-136121-9*) McGraw-Hill Prof.

Rohde, Ulrich L. RF & Microwave Digital Frequency Synthesizers: Theory & Design. LC 96-2841. 656p. 1997. 118.95 (*0-471-52019-5*) Wiley.

***Rohde, Ulrich L. & Newkirk, David P.** RF/Microwave Circuit Design for Wireless Applications. LC 99-39546. 1312p. 2000. text 125.00 (*0-471-29818-2*) Wiley.

Rohde, Ulrich L., et al. Communications Receivers: Principles & Design. 2nd ed. (Illus.). 669p. 1996. 69.95 (*0-07-053608-2*) McGraw.

Rohden, Peter R., jt. auth. see Bayle, Francis.

***Rohder, Regis.** Padre to the Papagos: Father Bonaventura Oblasser. (Illus.). 73p. 1999. reprint ed. pap. text 14.00 (*0-7881-6180-6*) DIANE Pub.

Rohdie, Sam. Antonioni. (Illus.). 224p. 1990. 49.95 (*0-85170-273-2*, Pub. by British Film Inst); pap. 19.95 (*0-85170-274-0*, Pub. by British Film Inst) Ind U Pr.

— The Passion of Pier Pablo Pasolini. 224p. 1995. 35.00 (*0-85170-517-0*, Pub. by British Film Inst); pap. 15.95 (*0-85170-518-9*, Pub. by British Film Inst) Ind U Pr.

— The Passion of Pier Paolo Pasolini. LC 95-38575. (Perspectives Ser.). 230p. 1995. 35.00 (*0-253-32951-5*) Ind U Pr.

— The Passion of Pier Paolo Pasolini. LC 95-38575. (Perspectives Ser.). 1996. pap. 15.95 (*0-253-21010-0*) Ind U Pr.

— Rocco & His Brothers. (BFI Film Classics Ser.). (Illus.). 80p. 1993. pap. 10.95 (*0-85170-340-2*, Pub. by British Film Inst) Ind U Pr.

Rohds, Richard, jt. auth. see Mackie, Thomas T.

Rohe, Deborah, jt. auth. see Breighner, Kathryn.

Rohe, John F. A Bicentennial Malthusian Essay: Conservation Population & the Indifference to Limits. LC 97-66724. (Illus.). 192p. 1997. 18.95 (*1-890394-00-9*) Rhodes & Easton.

Rohe, John F. Michigan Construction Liens. 500p. 95.00 (*0-327-12337-0*) LEXIS Pub.

Rohe, John F. Michigan Construction Liens. 500p. 1995. 95.00 (*1-55834-235-4*, 66615, MICHIE) LEXIS Pub.

— Michigan Construction Liens: 1998 Cumulative Supplement. 1998. suppl. ed. 29.50 (*0-327-00186-0*, 66616-11) LEXIS Pub.

***Rohe, John F.** Michigan Construction Liens, 1999 Cumulative Supplement: Pocketpart. 71p. 1999. write for info. (*0-327-01393-1*, 6661612) LEXIS Pub.

Rohe, Matthias. Untersuchungen Zur Phylogenese Linearer Genetischer Elemente: Extrachromosomale DNA des Ascomyceten Morchella Conica. (Bibliotheca Mycologica: Vol. 146). (GER., Illus.). 118p. 1992. 36.00 (*3-443-59047-0*, Pub. by Gebruder Borntraeger) Balogh.

Rohe, Terry & Cohen, Sally. Good Old-Fashioned Maine Cookery: From Red Flannel Hash to Maine Lobster Stew - Here Is a Collection of 125 Traditional Down East Recipes. LC 93-33001. 256p. 1994. spiral bd. 14.95 (*1-55958-430-0*) Prima Pub.

Rohe, William M. & Gates, Lauren B. Planning with Neighborhoods. LC 84-17221. (Urban & Regional Policy & Development Studies). xi, 238p. (C). 1985. pap. text 22.50 (*0-8078-4133-1*) U of NC Pr.

Roheim, Geza. Eternal Ones of the Dream: Myth & Ritual, Dreams & Fantasies-Their Role in the Lives of Primitive Man. 1970. reprint ed. pap. 24.95 (*0-8236-8044-4*, 021760) Intl Univs Pr.

— The Eternal Ones of the Dream, a Psychoanalytic Interpretation of Australian Myth & Ritual. LC BF1078.R6. 290p. reprint ed. pap. 89.90 (*0-608-11341-7*, 201042500070) Bks Demand.

— Fire in the Dragon & Other Psychoanalytic Essays on Folklore. 224p. 1992. text 49.50 (*0-691-09471-3*, Pub. by Princeton U Pr); pap. text 15.95 (*0-691-02868-0*, Pub. by Princeton U Pr) Cal Prin Full Svc.

— Gates of the Dream. 1969. reprint ed. pap. 24.95 (*0-8236-8060-6*, 22110) Intl Univs Pr.

— The Gates of the Dream. LC 53-10679. 564p. reprint ed. pap. 174.90 (*0-608-11337-9*, 201042800070) Bks Demand.

— Hungarian & Vogul Mythology. LC 84-45522. (American Ethnological Society Monographs: No. 23). 1988. reprint ed. 20.00 (*0-404-62922-9*) AMS Pr.

— Psychoanalysis & Anthropology. 496p. 1968. reprint ed. pap. 24.95 (*0-8236-8234-X*, 25120) Intl Univs Pr.

— War, Crime & the Covenant. Branham, V. C., ed. LC 46-5116. (Journal of Clinical Psychopathology Monograph Ser.: No. 1). 166p. reprint ed. pap. 51.50 (*0-608-30819-6*, 201070500070) Bks Demand.

Rohen, Harold. The Tennessee Locator. 387p. (Orig.). 1992. pap. 19.95 (*0-9634593-0-9*) Budro.

Rohen, Johannes W., et al. Color Atlas of Anatomy: A Photographic Study of the Human Body. 3rd ed. LC 92-49387. (Illus.). 494p. 1993. 64.95 (*0-89640-228-2*) Igaku-Shoin.

— Color Atlas of Anatomy: A Photographic Study of the Human Body. 4th ed. LC 97-42744. (Illus.). 486p. 1998. 62.00 (*0-683-30492-5*) Lppncott W & W.

Rohen, Johannes W., jt. auth. see Lutjen-Drecoll, Elke.

Rohen, Johannes W., jt. auth. see Yokochi, Chihiro.

Roher, H. D., jt. ed. see Goretzki, P. E.

Roher, Josef. Essen. (GER., Illus.). 33p. (Orig.). (YA). (gr. 7 up). 1995. pap. text 22.00 (*0-939990-93-8*) Intl Linguistics.

Roherty, James M. State Security in South Africa: Civil-Military Relations under P. W. Botha. LC 91-14446. 240p. (C). (gr. 13). 1992. text 74.95 (*0-87332-877-9*) M E Sharpe.

Rohfritsch, Odette, jt. ed. see Shorthouse, Joseph D.

***Rohi, Rajinder K.** Semitic & Sikh Monotheism: A Comparative Study. LC 99-933154. xi, 187p. 1999. write for info. (*81-7380-550-4*, Pub. by Pubn Bureau) S Asia.

***Rohl, Brenda.** The Circulation of Metal in the Bronze Age: The Results of Lead Isotope Analysis LC 98-232978. (Occasional Papers). 234p. 1998. write for info. (*0-86159-102-X*, Pub. by British Mus Pr) U of Pa Pr.

Rohl, David. Pharaohs & Kings. 1997. pap. 24.00 (*0-609-80130-9*) Random Hse Value.

Rohl, Ernst. Deutsch-Deutsch: Ein Satirisches Woerterbuch. (GER.). 103p. 1991. 29.95 (*0-7859-8322-8*, 3359004957) Fr & Eur.

Rohl, J. S. Programming in Algol. LC 79-555612. 112 p. 1970. write for info. (*0-7190-0443-8*) Manchester Univ Pr.

Rohl, John C. From Bismarck to Hitler: The Problem of Continuity in German History. LC 72-181319. (Problems & Perspectives in History Ser.). 207p. reprint ed. pap. 64.20 (*0-8357-2532-4*, 205714500013) Bks Demand.

— The Kaiser & His Court: Wilhelm II & the Government of Germany. Cole, Terence F., tr. 287p. (C). 1995. text 59.95 (*0-521-40223-9*) Cambridge U Pr.

— Young Wilhelm: The Kaiser's Early Life, 1859-1888. Gaines, Jeremy & Wallach, Rebecca, trs. LC 98-12909. (Illus.). 1006p. (C). 1999. text 74.95 (*0-521-49752-3*) Cambridge U Pr.

Rohl, John C. & Cole, Terence F. The Kaiser & His Court: Wilhelm II & the Government of Germany. 284p. 1996. pap. text 19.95 (*0-521-56504-9*) Cambridge U Pr.

Rohl, Klaus F. & Machura, Stefan, eds. Procedural Justice. LC 97-469. (Onati International Series in Law & Society). (Illus.). 256p. 1997. pap. 32.95 (*1-85521-921-2*, Pub. by Ashgate Pub) Ashgate Pub Co.

— Procedural Justice. LC 97-469. (Onati International Series in Law & Society). (Illus.). 256p. 1997. 82.95 (*1-85521-919-0*, Pub. by Dartmth Pub) Ashgate Pub Co.

Rohl, Wolfgang G. Die Rezeption des Johannesevangeliums in Christlich-Gnostischen Schriften Aus Nag Hammadi. (Europaische Hochschulschriften Ser.: Reihe 23, Bd. 428). (GER.). 232p. 1991. 45.80 (*3-631-43860-5*) P Lang Pubng.

Rohlck, Theresa N., jt. auth. see Madden, Carolyn G.

Rohleder, Bernhard. Vom Giftmulltourismus Zum Binnenmarkt Fur Abfall: Internationale Politik zur Steuerung der Problematik Gefahrlicher Abfalle in der EG: Entstehung, Stand, Wirkung, Restriktionen. (GER., Illus.). 294p. 1997. 54.95 (*3-631-32055-8*) P Lang Pubng.

R

An Asterisk (*) at the beginning of an entry indicates that the title is appearing for the first time.

R

Rohlen, Thomas P. For Harmony & Strength: Japanese White-Collar Organization in Anthropological Perspective. LC 73-91668. (Center for Japanese Studies, UC Berkeley: No. 9). 1974. pap. 15.95 (*0-520-03849-5*, Pub. by U CA Pr) Cal Prin Full Svc.

— Japan's High Schools. (Center for Japanese Studies, UC Berkeley: No. 21). (Illus.). 360p. 1983. pap. 16.95 (*0-520-04863-6*, Pub. by U CA Pr) Cal Prin Full Svc.

Rohlen, Thomas P. & Bjork, Christopher. Education & Training in Japan. LC 97-23340. 1160p. (C). 1998. 535.00 (*0-415-16842-2*) Routledge.

Rohlen, Thomas P. & LeTendre, Gerald K., eds. Teaching & Learning in Japan. (Illus.). 405p. (C). 1996. text 52.95 (*0-521-49587-3*) Cambridge U Pr.

***Rohlen, Thomas P. & LeTendre, Gerald K., eds.** Teaching & Learning in Japan. (Illus.). 405p. (C). 1999. pap. text 18.95 (*0-521-65115-8*) Cambridge U Pr.

Rohlen, Thomas P., jt. ed. see Okimoto, Daniel I.

Rohler, Lloyd. Ralph Waldo Emerson: Preacher & Lecturer, 21. LC 95-2105. (Great American Orators Ser.: Vol. 21). 216p. 1995. lib. bdg. 59.95 (*0-313-26328-0*, Greenwood Pr) Greenwood.

Rohler, Lloyd & Cook, Roger, eds. Great Speeches for Criticism & Analysis. 3rd rev. ed. LC 98-162556. 300p. 1997. pap. text 22.00 (*1-889388-00-9*) Alistair Pr IN.

Rohler, Lloyd E. & Cook, Roger. Great Speeches for Criticism & Analysis. 2nd ed. ix, 358 p. (C). 1992. pap. text 18.95 (*0-9616489-4-5*) Alistair Pr IN.

Rohlf, Daniel. The Endangered Species Act: Protection & Implementation. 207p. (Orig.). (C). 1989. pap. 12.00 (*0-942007-33-6*) Stanford Enviro.

Rohlf, F. James & Sokal, Robert R. Introduction to Biostatistics. 2nd ed. LC 86-31838. (Biology-Statistics Ser.). (Illus.). 363p. (C). 1987. pap. text 59.95 (*0-7167-1805-7*) W H Freeman.

— Statistical Tables. 2nd ed. LC 81-2576. (Illus.). 219p. (C). 1981. pap. text 13.60 (*0-7167-1258-X*) W H Freeman.

Rohlf, F. James, jt. auth. see Sokal, Robert R.

Rohlf, James W. Modern Physics from A to Z. 664p. 1994. text 93.95 (*0-471-57270-5*) Wiley.

Rohlf, W. D. Introduction to Economic Reasoning: Instructor's Manual. 4th ed. 480p. 1998. 24.00 (*0-201-38066-8*) Addison-Wesley.

Rohlf, William D., Jr. Introduction to Economic Reasoning. (Illus.). 510p. (C). 1989. text 41.95 (*0-201-15743-8*) Addison-Wesley.

Rohlf, William D. Introduction to Economic Reasoning. 3rd ed. (C). 1995. pap. text. write for info. (*0-201-88315-5*) Addison-Wesley.

— Introduction to Economic Reasoning. 4th ed. LC 98-15488. 592p. (C). 1998. pap. text 72.00 (*0-201-18558-X*) Addison-Wesley.

Rohlf, William D., Jr. Introduction to Economic Reasoning: Test Bank & Transparency. 3rd ed. 368p. 1995. 24.00 incl. trans. (*0-201-47600-2*) Addison-Wesley.

Rohlfing, Helmut, jt. auth. see Unte, Wolfhart.

Rohlfs, Anna K. The Forsaken Inn: A Novel. LC 78-164575. (American Fiction Reprint Ser.). 1977. reprint ed. 29.95 (*0-8369-7052-7*) Ayer.

Rohlfs, Gerhard. From Vulgar Latin to Old French: An Introduction to the Study of the Old French Language. Almazan, Vincent & McCarthy, Lillian, trs. from GER. LC 71-98131. 291p. reprint ed. pap. 90.30 (*0-7837-3685-1*, 204355900009) Bks Demand.

Rohlfs, Gerhard, jt. ed. see Rohlfs, Heinrich.

Rohlfs, Heinrich & Rohlfs, Gerhard, eds. Deutsches Archiv: Fur Geschichte der Medicin und Medicinische Geographie. xxvii, 3896p. 1971. reprint ed. write for info. (*3-487-04127-8*) G Olms Pubs.

***Rohlfs, Henry D.** Without Shark Cartilage & Better Than Chicken Soup. 130p. 1999. pap. write for info. (*0-7392-0381-9*, PO3601) Morris Pubng.

Rohlfs, K. Tools of Radio Astronomy. (Astronomy & Astrophysics Library). (Illus.). xii, 319p. 1986. 79.00 (*0-387-16188-0*) Spr-Verlag.

— Tools of Radio Astronomy: Study Edition. 2nd ed. Harwit, Martin D. et al, eds. (Astronomy & Astrophysics Library). (Illus.). xv, 319p. 1990. reprint ed. pap. 45.00 (*0-387-52744-3*) Spr-Verlag.

***Rohlfs, K. & Wilson, T.** Tools of Radio Astronomy. 3rd rev. enl. ed. Appenzeller, I. et al, eds. LC 99-37540. (Astronomy & Astrophysics Library). (Illus.). xvi, 430p. 1999. 76.00 (*3-540-66016-X*) Spr-Verlag.

Rohlfs, K. & Wilson, T. L. Tools of Radio Astronomy. 2nd enl. rev. ed. LC 96-5678. (Astronomy & Astrophysics Library). (Illus.). 464p. 1996. 69.50 (*3-540-60981-4*) Spr-Verlag.

Rohlich, Gerard A. & Howe, Richard S. Environmental Regulation & the Chemical Industry. LC 82-83536. 122p. 1982. pap. 8.00 (*0-89940-806-0*) LBJ Sch Pub Aff.

— The Toxic Substances Control Act: Overview & Evaluation. (Policy Research Project Reports: Vol. 50). 247p. (C). 1982. pap. 7.50 (*0-89940-650-5*) LBJ Sch Pub Aff.

Rohlich, Thomas H. A Tale of Eleventh Century Japan: Hamamatsu Chunagon Monogatari. LC 82-61380. (Princeton Library of Asian Translations). 261p. 1983. reprint ed. pap. 81.00 (*0-608-03358-8*, 206407000008) Bks Demand.

Rohling, Augustus. Louise Lateau: Her Stigmas & Ecstasy. 55p. 1994. reprint ed. spiral bd. 14.00 (*0-7873-1288-6*) Hlth Research.

Rohling, Claudia, jt. auth. see Murphy Payne, Lauren.

Rohling, Claudia, jt. auth. see Payne, Lauren M.

Rohling, Dan. Funeral Information: The Consumer Guide. large type ed. LC 96-79305. 65p. 1991. pap. 19.95 (*0-9678672-0-7*) W A Pubng.

Rohlman, Jeff, jt. auth. see Beecham, John J.

Rohlmeier, Charles. Drafting: Metric. LC 79-55761. 320p. reprint ed. pap. 99.20 (*0-608-11856-7*, 202320200032) Bks Demand.

Rohloff, Christoph, jt. auth. see Pfetsch, Frank R.

Rohloff, Florence H. Flight from Benghazi. LC 95-91045. 1997. 19.95 (*0-533-11856-5*) Vantage.

Rohls, Jan. Reformed Confessions: Theology from Zurich to Barmen. Hoffmeyer, John, tr. from GER. LC 97-38079. (Columbia Series in Reformed Theology). 328p. 1998. 35.00 (*0-664-22078-9*) Westminster John Knox.

Rohlsen, Beatrix. The Art of Taste: A Gourmet Guide to Vegeterian Cooking. (Illus.). 141p. 1994. pap. 19.95 (*0-9643302-0-2*) Gourmet Creat.

Rohm & Haas Co. Staff, et al, eds. Artificial Intelligence Applications in Chemistry. LC 86-3315. (ACS Symposium Ser.: No. 306). (Illus.). 394p. 1986. 65.95 (*0-8412-0966-9*) Am Chemical.

Rohm, Frederic W. No Braver Man: The Story of Fritz Rohm, Buglar, 16th PA, Cavalry. LC 97-40047. 180p. 1998. pap. 19.95 (*1-887901-18-3*) Sergeant Kirk.

Rohm, K. H., jt. auth. see Koolman, J.

***Rohm, Robert.** Sponsor with Style. 1999. pap. 14.95 (*0-9641080-4-6*) Prsnality Insights.

***Rohm, Robert A.** Descubra su Verdadera Personalidad. (SPA.). 200p. 1998. pap. 11.95 (*0-9641080-5-4*) JayMar Servs.

Rohm, Robert A. Positive Personality Profiles: Discover Personality Insights to Understand Yourself & Others. 4th ed. Carey, Chris & Enis, Nancy, eds. (Illus.). 200p. 1994. reprint ed. pap. 11.95 (*0-9641080-0-3*) Prsnality Insights.

— Tales Out of School: Why 200 Teachers Say "My Students Are My Best Teachers" 2nd rev. ed. 305p. 1995. pap. 11.95 (*0-9641080-2-X*) Prsnality Insights.

— Who Do You Think You Are . . . Anyway? How Your Unique Personality Style Acts, Interacts, & Reacts with Others. Carey, E. Chris, ed. (Illus.). 325p. 1997. pap. 14.95 (*0-9641080-3-8*) Prsnality Insights.

***Rohm, Wendy Goldman.** El Informe Microsoft. (SPA.). 1999. 24.95 (*84-239-7782-X*) Espasa Calpe.

Rohm, Wendy Goldman. The Microsoft File: The Secret Case Against Bill Gates. LC 98-4450. 1998. 25.95 (*0-8129-2716-8*, Times Bks) Crown Pub Group.

Rohman, Jane M. The Dogs' Guide to New York City with Jack, the City Dog: With over 200 Wonderful Walks, Outings, Activities, Getaways & Places You Never Thought You Could Take Your Pooch. (Illus.). 200p. (Orig.). 1994. pap. 14.95 (*0-9641824-0-8*) Richmond Pr.

Rohmann, Chris. A World of Ideas: A Dictionary of Important Theories, Concepts, Beliefs & Thinkers. LC 98-39543. 1999. 24.95 (*0-345-39059-8*) Ballantine Pub Grp.

Rohmann, Eric. The Cinder-Eyed Cats. LC 97-6763. (Illus.). 40p. (J). 1997. lib. bdg. 18.99 (*0-517-70897-3*, Pub. by Crown Bks Yng Read) Random.

— The Cinder-Eyed Cats. LC 97-6763 (Illus.). 40p. (J). (ps-3). 1997. 17.00 (*0-517-70896-5*, Crown) Crown Pub Group.

— Time Flies. LC 93-28200. (Illus.). 32p. (J). (ps-4). 1994. lib. bdg. 17.99 (*0-517-59599-0*, Pub. by Crown Bks Yng Read) Random.

Rohmann, Eric. Time Flies. 1997. 13.19 (*0-606-12827-1*, Pub. by Turtleback) Demco.

Rohmann, Eric. Time Flies. (J). (ps-4). 1997. reprint ed. 7.99 (*0-614-29248-4*) Knopf Bks Yng Read.

— Times Flies. (Illus.). 32p. 1997. pap. 6.99 (*0-517-88555-7*) Crown Pub Group.

Rohmann, Steven O. & Lilienthal, Nancy. Tracing a River's Toxic Pollution: A Case Study of the Hudson, 2 vols., Vol. 1. LC 85-60234. 218p. 1985. write for info. (*0-918780-30-6*) INFORM NY.

— Tracing a River's Toxic Pollution: A Case Study of the Hudson, 2 vols., Vol. 2. LC 85-60234. 162p. 1987. pap. 20.00 (*0-918780-40-3*) INFORM NY.

Rohmer, Elizabeth S. Master of Villa ny. 322p. Date not set. 24.95 (*0-8488-2383-4*) Amereon Ltd.

***Rohmer, Harriet.** Honoring Our Ancestors. 1999. 21.27 (*0-516-21697-X*) Capstone Pr.

Rohmer, Harriet. Invisible Hunters: A Legend from the Miskito Indians of Nicaragua. (Stories from Central America Ser.). (J). 1987. 12.15 (*0-606-05378-6*, Pub. by Turtleback) Demco.

— Uncle Nacho's Hat (El Sombrero del Tio Macho) (ENG & SPA.). (J). 1989. 12.15 (*0-606-05678-5*, Pub. by Turtleback) Demco.

***Rohmer, Harriet, ed.** Honoring Our Ancestors: Stories & Pictures by Fourteen Artists. LC 98-38686. (Illus.). 32p. (J). (gr. 3-7). 1999. 15.95 (*0-89239-158-8*) Childrens Book Pr.

Rohmer, Harriet, ed. Just Like Me: Stories & Self-Portrait by Fourteen Artists. LC 97-4467. (Illus.). 32p. (J). (gr. 2-6). 1997. 15.95 (*0-89239-149-9*) Childrens Book Pr.

Rohmer, Harriet, ed. Just Like Me: Stories & Self-Portraits by Fourteen Artists. (Illus.). (J). (gr. 2-4). 1997. 21.20 (*0-516-20938-8*) Childrens.

Rohmer, Harriet & Anchondo, Mary. How We Came to the Fifth World (Como Vinimos al Quinto Mundo) LC 76-7240. (ENG & SPA., Illus.). 24p. (YA). (gr. 1 up). 1988. 14.95 (*0-89239-024-7*) Childrens Book Pr.

Rohmer, Harriet & Guerrero Rea, Jesus. Atariba & Niguayona (Atariba y Niquoyona) rev. ed. LC 76-17495. (ENG & SPA., Illus.). 24p. (YA). (ps-3). 1998. 15.95 (*0-89239-026-3*) Childrens Book Pr.

Rohmer, Harriet & Wilson, Dorminster. Mother Scorpion Country (La Tierra de la Madre Escorpion) LC 86-32649. (ENG & SPA., Illus.) 32p. (YA). (gr. 4-7). 1987. 14.95 (*0-89239-032-8*) Childrens Book Pr.

Rohmer, Harriet, jt. auth. see De Sauza, James.

Rohmer, Harriet, jt. auth. see Gomez, Cruz.

Rohmer, Harriet, ed. see Garza, Carmen L.

Rohmer, Harriet, ed. see Gomez, Cruz.

Rohmer, John J., jt. auth. see Meck, Charles R.

Rohmer, Richard. Death by Deficit: A 2001 Novel. 224p. 1996. 26.95 (*0-7737-2902-X*) Stoddart Publ.

— E. P. Taylor. 332p. 1978. mass mkt. 5.95 (*0-88780-113-7*, Pub. by Formac Publ Co) Formac Dist Ltd.

***Rohmer, Richard.** Golden Phoenix: The Biography of Peter Munk. LC 98-110600. (Illus.). 360p. 1999. 30.00 (*1-55013-912-6*) Key Porter.

Rohmer, Richard. Patton's Gap: An Account of the Battle of Normandy, 1944. 2nd rev. ed. (Illus.). 264p. 1998. 23.95 (*0-7737-3118-0*) Stoddart Publ.

Rohmer, Sax, pseud. Bimbashi Baruk of Egypt. 1970. 8.50 (*0-685-26777-6*) Bookfinger.

— The Bride of Fu Manchu. 1976. reprint ed. lib. bdg. 21.95 (*0-89190-801-3*, Rivercity Pr) Amereon Ltd.

— Daughter of Fu Manchu. lib. bdg. 22.95 (*0-8488-2112-2*) Amereon Ltd.

— The Day the World Ended. 1976. reprint ed. lib. bdg. 24.95 (*0-89190-804-8*, Rivercity Pr) Amereon Ltd.

— Dream Detective. 18.95 (*0-89190-810-2*) Amereon Ltd.

— Drums of Fu Manchu. 20.95 (*0-8488-0619-0*) Amereon Ltd.

Rohmer, Sax, pseud. The Emperor of America. 1976. reprint ed. lib. bdg. 24.95 (*0-89190-805-6*) Amereon Ltd.

Rohmer, Sax, pseud. Exploits of Captain O'Hagan. 1968. 6.00 (*0-685-22715-4*) Bookfinger.

— The Fu Manchu Omnibus, Vol. 1. 650p. 1996. pap. 14.95 (*0-7490-0271-9*) Allison & Busby.

— The Fu Manchu Omnibus, Vol. II. LC 98-226518. 656p. 1997. pap. text 14.95 (*0-7490-0222-0*) Allison & Busby.

***Rohmer, Sax, pseud.** The Fu Manchu Omnibus, Vol. 4. 1999. pap. 18.95 (*0-7490-0328-6*) Allison & Busby.

Rohmer, Sax, pseud. The Golden Scorpion. 1976. reprint ed. lib. bdg. 24.95 (*0-89190-806-4*, Rivercity Pr) Amereon Ltd.

— The Hand of Fu Manchu. Date not set. reprint ed. lib. bdg. 20.95 (*0-89190-802-1*, Am Repr) Amereon Ltd.

— Hangover House. 22.95 (*0-89190-807-2*) Amereon Ltd.

— The Insidious Dr. Fu Manchu. 1976. lib. bdg. 13.95 (*0-89968-143-3*, Lghtyr Pr) Buccaneer Bks.

— The Insidious Dr. Fu Manchu. LC 97-15050. (Dover Classic Mystery Ser.). (Illus.). 224p. 1997. pap. 2.00 (*0-486-29898-1*) Dover.

— The Mask of Fu Manchu. LC 84-23983. 362 p. 1985. write for info. (*0-89621-588-1*) Chivers N Amer.

— The Mask of Fu Manchu. 1976. reprint ed. lib. bdg. 21.95 (*0-89190-803-X*, Rivercity Pr) Amereon Ltd.

— The Moon Is Red. 1976. 12.50 (*0-685-80029-6*) Bookfinger.

— Orchard of Tears. 1969. 8.50 (*0-685-22716-2*) Bookfinger.

— The Return of Dr. Fu-Manchu. 20.95 (*0-89190-828-5*) Amereon Ltd.

— The Return of Dr. Fu-Manchu. 1976. lib. bdg. 13.95 (*0-89968-141-7*, Lghtyr Pr) Buccaneer Bks.

— The Romance of Sorcery. 1976. reprint ed. lib. bdg. 24.95 (*0-89190-808-0*, Rivercity Pr) Amereon Ltd.

— Salute to Bazarada & Other Stories. 311p. 1972. 12.50 (*0-685-26828-4*) Bookfinger.

— Sand & Satin. 1978. 8.50 (*0-685-90566-7*) Bookfinger.

— Seven Sins. 1972. 8.50 (*0-685-33437-6*) Bookfinger.

— Sinister Madonna. (Sumuru Ser.). 1977. reprint ed. 8.50 (*0-685-88226-8*) Bookfinger.

— Sins of Severac Bablon. 1967. 10.00 (*0-685-22714-6*) Bookfinger.

— Sins of Sumuru. 1977. reprint ed. 8.50 (*0-685-88227-6*) Bookfinger.

Rohmer, Sax, pseud. Slaves of Sumuru. (Sumuru Ser.). 1979. 8.50 (*0-686-65266-5*) Bookfinger.

Rohmer, Sax, pseud. Tales of Chinatown. LC 75-178459. (Short Story Index Reprint Ser.). 1977. reprint ed. 22.95 (*0-8369-4060-1*) Ayer.

— Tales of East & West. 1976. 8.50 (*0-685-79490-3*) Bookfinger.

— Tales of Secret Egypt. 1976. reprint ed. lib. bdg. 24.95 (*0-89190-809-9*) Amereon Ltd.

— Trail of Fu Manchu. 25.95 (*0-8488-0317-5*) Amereon Ltd.

— Trail of Fu Manchu. 1985. pap. 3.50 (*0-8217-1619-0*) Kensgtn Pub Corp.

— Virgin in Flames. 1978. 8.50 (*0-685-90567-5*) Bookfinger.

— Wulfheim. 1972. 12.50 (*0-685-33438-4*) Bookfinger.

— The Yellow Claw. 14.95 (*0-8488-1463-0*) Amereon Ltd.

— The Yellow Claw. 1976. lib. bdg. 13.95 (*0-89968-142-5*, Lghtyr Pr) Buccaneer Bks.

Rohmetra, Neelu. Human Resource Development in Commercial Banks in India. LC 98-70983. (Illus.). 214p. 1998. text 59.95 (*1-85972-564-3*, Pub. by Ashgate Pub) Ashgate Pub Co.

Rohn, Charles L. Analytical Polymer Rheology: Structure - Processing - Property Relationships. 320p. (C). 1995. 130.00 (*1-56990-149-X*) Hanser-Gardner.

Rohn, E. The Pentecostal Bible Study Course: Study Guide. 512p. (Orig.). 1978. pap. 24.99 (*0-912315-43-1*) Word Aflame.

Rohn, E. James. Leading An Inspired Life. LC 97-224950. 460p. 1996. 34.95 (*1-55525-459-4*) Nightingale-Conant.

Rohn, Jim. Seven Strategies for Wealth & Happiness. 160p. 1988. pap. 9.95 (*0-914629-73-5*) Prima Pub.

Rohn, Jim. 7 Strategies for Wealth & Happiness: Power Ideas from America's Foremost Business Philosopher. 176p. 1996. pap., per. 12.00 (*0-7615-0616-0*) Prima Pub.

Rohn, Jim. The Treasury of Quotes. 120p. 1996. 20.00 (*1-55874-394-4*) Health Comm.

Rohn, John. Seven Strategies for Wealth & Happiness: Power Ideas from America's Foremost Business Philosopher. 168p. (Orig.). 1987. 13.95 (*0-914629-02-6*) Prima Pub.

Rohn, Matthew. Visual Dynamics in Jackson Pollock's Abstractions. LC 86-30746. (Studies in the Fine Arts - Art Theory: No. 14). 190p. reprint ed. pap. 58.90 (*0-8357-1790-9*, 207066200015) Bks Demand.

Rohn, Peter H. World Treaty Index, 5 vols. 2nd ed. LC 97-80197. 1997. reprint ed. 550.00 (*1-57588-396-1*, 311340) W S Hein.

— World Treaty Index, 5 vols., 2. 2nd ed. LC 83-3872. 4271p. 1983. lib. bdg. 210.00 (*0-87436-160-5*) ABC-CLIO.

— World Treaty Index, 5 vols., 3. 2nd ed. LC 83-3872. 4271p. 1983. lib. bdg. 210.00 (*0-87436-161-3*) ABC-CLIO.

— World Treaty Index, 5 vols., 4. 2nd ed. LC 83-3872. 4271p. 1983. lib. bdg. 210.00 (*0-87436-162-1*) ABC-CLIO.

— World Treaty Index, 5 vols., 5. 2nd ed. LC 83-3872. 4271p. 1983. lib. bdg. 210.00 (*0-87436-163-X*) ABC-CLIO.

Rohne. Total Auto Body Repair. 2nd ed. 1983. 51.71 (*0-02-682110-9*) Macmillan.

Rohner, Eric. My Night at Maud's. LC 92-32891. (Films in Print Ser.: Vol. 19). (Illus.). 220p. (C). 1993. text 40.00 (*0-8135-1939-X*); pap. text 17.00 (*0-8135-1940-3*) Rutgers U Pr.

***Rohner, John R.** Art Treasures from African Runners. LC 99-39539. (Illus.). 232p. 1999. 59.95 (*0-87081-549-0*) Univ Pr Colo.

Rohner, Kurt. Marketing in the Cyber Age: Paradigms, Perspectives & Implementation. LC 98-3083. 240p. 1998. pap. 74.95 (*0-471-97023-9*) Wiley.

Rohner, Linda K., ed. A Dictionary for Lupus Patients. 60p. 1993. pap. text 9.95 (*0-9638245-0-3*) Mtn Gem Pubng.

Rohner, Peter. Automation with Programmable Logic Controllers. 200p. 1996. pap. 54.95 (*0-86840-215-X*, Pub. by New South Wales Univ Pr) Intl Spec Bk.

***Rohner, Ralph J., et al.** Rohner & Miller on Truth in Lending. LC 99-87485. 2000. write for info. (*1-57073-697-9*) Amer Bar Assn.

Rohner, Ronald P. Handbook for the Study of Parental Acceptance & Rejection. rev. ed. 181p. 1990. pap. text 20.00 (*1-881628-00-0*) Rohner Res.

— The Warmth Dimension. LC 85-19623. 248p. (C). 1986. text 48.00 (*0-8039-2353-8*) Rohner Res.

Rohner, Ronald P. & Bettauer, Evelyn C. The Kwakiutl: Indians of British Columbia. (Illus.). 111p. (C). 1986. reprint ed. pap. text 10.50 (*0-88133-225-9*) Waveland Pr.

Rohner, Ronald P. & Chaki-Sircar, Manjusri. Women & Children in a Bengali Village. LC 87-25463. (Illus.). 231p. 1988. text 35.00 (*0-87451-431-2*) Rohner Res.

***Rohner, Ronald Preston.** They Love Me, They Love Me Not: A Worldwide Study of the Effects of Parental Acceptance Rejection. 1999. write for info. (*0-87536-332-6*) HRAFP.

Rohnke. Back Pocket Adventure. 112p. 1998. pap. text 4.50 (*0-536-01761-1*) Pearson Custom.

Rohnke & Grout. Back Pocket. LC 99-192943. 112p. (C). 1998. pap. text 8.50 (*0-536-01419-1*) Pearson Custom.

Rohnke, Karl. Fun Stuff, Vol. III. 128p. 1998. per. 15.95 (*0-7872-4665-4*) Kendall-Hunt.

***Rohnke, Karl.** Fun Stuff, Vol. IV. 128p. 2000. per. 18.95 (*0-7872-7133-0*) Kendall-Hunt.

Rohnke, Karl. On-the-Edge Games for Youth Ministry. Simpson, Amy, ed. LC 98-15310. (Illus.). 112p. (YA). 1998. per. 14.99 (*0-7644-2058-5*, Vital Ministry) Group Pub.

— Quicksilver. 1997. pap. text 23.50 (*0-7872-1610-0*) Kendall-Hunt.

Rohnke, Karl, et al. The Complete Ropes Course Manual. 2nd ed. LC 97-205176. 208p. 1997. per. 28.50 (*0-7872-2831-1*) Kendall-Hunt.

Rohnke, Karl, jt. auth. see Priest, Simon.

Rohnke, Karl E. Forget Me Knots. 80p. (C). 1994. spiral bd. 10.00 (*0-8403-7138-1*) Kendall-Hunt.

— Forget Me Knots: All the Knots You Need to Know to Run a Ropes Course. (Illus.). 75p. (Orig.). 1991. pap. 10.00 (*0-934387-10-9*) Project Advent.

— Funn Stuff. LC 97-131137. 128p. 1995. pap. 15.95 (*0-7872-1633-X*) Kendall-Hunt.

— Funn Stuff, Vol. 2. 108p. 1996. pap. text 15.95 (*0-7872-2316-6*) Kendall-Hunt.

— Silver Bullets: A Guide to Initiative Problems, Adventure Games & Trust Activities. 192p. 1984. per. 20.00 (*0-8403-5682-X*) Kendall-Hunt.

— Slightly Skewed Vignettes: Confessions of an Incorrigible Kid. 144p. 1992. pap. text 9.95 (*0-8403-7852-1*) Kendall-Hunt.

Rohnke, Karl E., jt. auth. see Butler.

Rohnstock, Katrin, ed. Stiefschwestern: Was Ost-Frauen und West-Fruen voneinander Denken. (GER.). 192p. 1994. pap. 13.50 (*3-596-12221-X*, Pub. by Fischer Tasch) Intl Bk Import.

Rohonyi, K. & Marot, M. Walking Around Budapest: Budapest Corvina, 1988. (Illus.). 156p. (C). 1988. pap. 70.00 (*0-569-08215-3*, Pub. by Collets) St Mut.

Rohou, ed. see Ryer.

Rohr, Bettina. Das Komische Bei Shakespeare: Eine Analyse Komischer Strukturen in "As You Like It" Sowie "A Midsummer Night's Dream", "Twelfth Night" und "Much Ado about Nothing" (Europaische Hochschulschriften, Reihe 14: No. 337). X, 224p. 1997. 44.95 (*3-631-32207-0*) P Lang Pubng.

Rohr, Charles J. The Governor of Maryland, a Constitutional Study. LC 78-64147. (Johns Hopkins University. Studies in the Social Sciences. Thirtieth Ser. 1912: No. 3). reprint ed. 21.00 (*0-404-61258-X*) AMS Pr.

Rohr-Dietschi, Ursula. Zur Genese des Selbstbewusstseins: Eine Studie ueber den Beitrag des phaenomenologischen Denkens zur Frage der Entwicklung des Selbstbewusstseins. LC 72-81567. (Phaenomenologisch-Psychologische Forschungen Ser.: Vol. 14). 197p. (C). 1975. 79.25 (*3-11-004048-4*) De Gruyter.

An Asterisk (*) at the beginning of an entry indicates that the title is appearing for the first time.

Rohr, Ellen. How Much Should I Charge? Pricing Basics for Making & Doing What You Love. LC 99-60691. (MAXROHR Business Basics Ser.). (Illus.). 99p. 1999. pap. 19.99 (*0-9665719-1-6*) Maxrohr.

— Where Did the Money Go? Super Easy Accounting Basics for the Business Owner Who Hates Numbers! 2nd ed. LC 98-83070. (MAXROHR Business Basics Ser.: No. 1). (Illus.). 95p. 1999. pap. 19.95 (*0-9665719-2-4*) Maxrohr.

Rohr, Erwin K. Meditations. (Illus.). 260p. 1989. 13.95 (*0-931660-07-6*) R Oman Pub.

Rohr, Gerhard. Fremdsprachen-Unterricht in Theorie und Praxis: ErschlieBen Aus Dem Kontext: Lehren, Lernen, Trainieren. (GER.). 112p. 1996. 20.00 (*3-468-49448-3*) Langenscheidt.

***Rohr, J.** Bioorganic Chemistry: Deoxysugars, Polyketides & Related Classes, Synthesis, Biosynthesis, Enzymes. LC 00-20460. (Desktop Editions in Chemistry Ser.: 188). x, 195p. 2000. pap. 42.95 (*3-540-66971-X*) Spr-Verlag.

Rohr, J., ed. Bioorganic Chemistry: Deoxysugars, Polyketides & Related Classes: Synthesis, Biosynthesis, Enzymes. (Topics in Current Chemistry: Vol. 188). (Illus.). 232p. 1997. 157.00 (*3-540-62488-0*) Spr-Verlag.

Rohr, J. A. Ethics for Bureaucrats: An Essay on Law & Values. 2nd expanded rev. ed. (Public Administration & Public Policy Ser.: Vol. 36). (Illus.). 352p. 1988. text 69.75 (*0-8247-8032-9*) Dekker.

Rohr, Janelle, ed. Eastern Europe: Opposing Viewpoints. LC 90-44330. (Opposing Viewpoints Ser.). (Illus.). 288p. (YA). (gr. 10 up). 1990. pap. text 16.20 (*0-89908-455-9*) Greenhaven.

Rohr, John A. Founding Republics in France & America: A Study in Constitutional Governance. LC 95-31166. (Studies in Government & Public Policy). 392p. (C). 1995. 45.00 (*0-7006-0733-1*); pap. 19.95 (*0-7006-0734-X*) U Pr of KS.

— Public Service, Ethics, & Constitutional Practice. LC 98-28445. (Studies in Government & Public Policy). 208p. 1999. 29.95 (*0-7006-0925-3*) U Pr of KS.

— Public Service, Ethics & Constitutional Practice. LC 98-28445. (Studies in Government & Public Policy). 208p. 1999. pap. 15.95 (*0-7006-0926-1*) U Pr of KS.

— To Run a Constitution: The Legitimacy of the Administrative State. LC 85-28867. xvi, 272p. 1986. 35.00 (*0-7006-0291-7*); pap. 14.95 (*0-7006-0301-8*) U Pr of KS.

Rohr, Martina, jt. auth. see Herde, Dieter.

Rohr, Michael E. Adolescent Runaway Behavior: Who Runs & Why. LC 96-49246. (Children of Poverty Ser.). 99p. 1997. text 36.00 (*0-8153-2292-5*) Garland.

Rohr, Moritz Von, see Von Rohr, Moritz.

Rohr, Neal, jt. auth. see Grant, Zoilita.

Rohr, Rene R. Sundials: History, Theory, & Practice. unabridged ed. Godin, Gabriel, tr. LC 95-45661. (Illus.). 176p. 1996. reprint ed. pap. text 11.95 (*0-486-29139-1*) Dover.

Rohr, Richard. Enneagram II: Advancing Spiritual Discernment. LC 94-41710. 168p. 1995. 17.95 (*0-8245-1451-3*) Crossroad NY.

— Enneagram II: Advancing Spiritual Discernment. 208p. 1998. pap. 14.95 (*0-8245-1766-0*, Crsrd) Crossroad NY.

— Everything Belongs: The Gift of Contemplative Prayer. LC 98-40822. 456p. 1999. 14.95 (*0-8245-1652-4*) Crossroad NY.

— The Good News According to Luke: Spiritual Reflections. LC 97-753. 180p. 1997. 19.95 (*0-8245-1490-4*) Crossroad NY.

— Job & the Mystery of Suffering. 192p. pap. 14.95 (*0-8245-1734-2*, Pub. by Crossroad NY) Natl Bk Netwk.

— Near Occasions of Grace. LC 92-33193. 125p. (Orig.). 1993. pap. 12.00 (*0-88344-852-1*) Orbis Bks.

— Quest for the Grail. 192p. 1997. pap. 14.95 (*0-8245-1654-0*) Crossroad NY.

— Radical Grace: Daily Meditations by Richard Rohr. Feister, John B., ed. 410p. 1995. pap. 13.95 (*0-86716-257-0*) St Anthony Mess Pr.

— Simplicity: The Art of Living. 180p. 1992. pap. 11.95 (*0-8245-1251-0*, Pub. by Crossroad NY) Natl Bk Netwk.

Rohr, Richard & Ebert, Andreas. Discovering the Enneagram: An Ancient Tool a New Spiritual Journey. 256p. 1992. pap. 14.95 (*0-8245-1185-9*, Pub. by Crossroad NY) Natl Bk Netwk.

Rohr, Richard & Feister, John B. Jesus' Plan for a New World: The Sermon on the Mount. 190p. 1996. pap. text 9.95 (*0-86716-203-1*) St Anthony Mess Pr.

Rohr, Richard & Martos, Joseph. The Great Themes of Scripture: New Testament. (Great Themes of Scripture Ser.). 179p. (Orig.). 1988. pap. 7.95 (*0-86716-098-5*) St Anthony Mess Pr.

— The Great Themes of Scripture: Old Testament. (Great Themes of Scripture Ser.). 131p. (Orig.). 1987. pap. 7.95 (*0-86716-085-3*) St Anthony Mess Pr.

— Why Be Catholic? Understanding Our Experience & Tradition. 146p. (Orig.). 1989. pap. 6.95 (*0-86716-101-9*) St Anthony Mess Pr.

— The Wild Man's Journey: Reflections on Male Spirituality. rev. ed. LC 98-113784. (Fifty-Two Weekends Ser.). 264p. 1996. pap. 10.95 (*0-86716-279-1*, B2791) St Anthony Mess Pr.

Rohr, Richard, et al. Experiencing the Enneagram. LC 92-26317. 228p. (Orig.). 1992. pap. 16.95 (*0-8245-1201-4*, Pub. by Crossroad NY) Natl Bk Netwk.

— Grace in Action. 160p. (Orig.). 1994. pap. 12.95 (*0-8245-1379-7*) Crossroad NY.

Rohr-Rouendal, Petra. Talking AIDS, a Guide for Community Work. 110p. (Orig.). 1989. pap. 9.95 (*0-333-49781-3*) Scholium Intl.

Rohr, Rudolf von, see Von Rohr, Rudolf.

***Rohr, Walter.** An Introduction to Small-Scale Thermochemistry. 72p. (YA). (gr. 9-12). 1999. pap. text 29.95 (*1-877991-56-2*) Flinn Scientific.

Rohrbach, Fred, jt. auth. see Graetz, Rick.

Rohrbach, Jim. Business Success Skills: Everything You Always Wanted to Know about Success, but Didn't Know Who to Ask, Because They Probably Didn't Know Either... (Illus.). 132p. (Orig.). 1994. pap. 20.00 (*0-9627754-1-X*) J M Rohrbach.

— The Social Skills Playbook: Why Be Shy? LC 90-91986. 96p. (Orig.). 1990. pap. 15.00 (*0-9627754-0-1*) J M Rohrbach.

Rohrbach, Lewis B. Hoffelbauer Genealogy, 1660-1989. LC 93-85401. 640p. 1993. 59.50 (*0-929539-12-5*, 1112) Picton Pr.

Rohrbach, Lewis B., ed. The Records of the Church of Christ in Buxton, Maine, 1763-1817. rev. ed. LC 88-63778. 104p. 1989. reprint ed. 20.00 (*0-929539-02-8*, 1102) Picton Pr.

Rohrbach, Lewis B., frwd. Swiss Surnames: A Complete Register. 3 vols. LC 41-18702. 1995. 149.50 (*0-89725-206-3*, 1630) Picton Pr.

Rohrbach, Lewis B., intro. Boston Taxpayers in Eighteen Twenty-One. rev. ed. LC 88-90540. 256p. 1988. reprint ed. 35.00 (*0-929539-01-X*, 1101) Picton Pr.

***Rohrbach, Lewis Bunker, ed.** Salzburger Expulsion Lists. 800p. 1999. 69.95 (*0-89725-385-X*) Picton Pr.

Rohrbach, Mike & Rydberg, Denny. Run to Win: Devotions & Chapel Talks for Athletes, Coaches & Sports Fans. 142p. (Orig.). (YA). (gr. 6 up). 1993. pap. 8.95 (*1-887002-05-7*) Cross Trng.

Rohrbach, Peter T. Conversation with Christ. LC 82-50586. 171p. 1994. reprint ed. pap. 10.00 (*0-89555-180-2*) TAN Bks Pubs.

— The Largest Event: A Library of Congress Resource Guide for the Study of World War II. LC 93-16487. 137p. 1993. pap. 15.00 (*0-8444-0782-8*) Lib Congress.

Rohrbach, Peter T. Largest Event: A Library of Congress Resource Guide for the Study of World War 2. 151p. 1994. pap. text 16.00 (*0-16-043133-6*, Library of Cong) USGPO.

Rohrbach, Peter T. & Newman, Lowell S. American Issue: The U. S. Postage Stamp, 1842-1869. LC 83-27146. (Illus.). 232p. 1985. 34.95 (*0-87474-816-X*, ROAI) Smithsonian.

Rohrbach, Roger P., jt. auth. see Christianson, Leslie L.

Rohrbacher, jt. auth. see Burfeindt-Moral, H.

Rohrbacher, Bernhard W. Morphology-Driven Syntax: A Theory of V to I Raising & Pro- Drop. LC 99-19817. (Linguistik Aktuell/Linguistics Today Ser.: Vol. 15). viii, 296p. 1999. 75.00 (*1-55619-234-7*) J Benjamins Pubng Co.

Rohrbacher, Charles. Book of the Elect. 128p. 1988. 49.95 (*0-8146-1435-3*) Liturgical Pr.

Rohrbacher, George. Zen Ranching & the Farming Game: A Story of a Family & the Land They Loved & Fought For. LC 96-78618. 224p. 1997. pap. 14.95 (*1-885221-50-9*) BookPartners.

Rohrbacher, Richard W., jt. auth. see Westwood, Phoebe L.

Rohrback. Introduction of Chemometrics. 1993. write for info. (*0-8493-7323-9*) CRC Pr.

Rohrback, John, et al. A Passion for Birds: Eliot Porter's Photography. LC 97-29177. (Illus.). 64p. 1997. pap. 19.95 (*0-88360-089-7*) Amon Carter.

Rohrback, Lew, ed. Index to Place Names in Soldiers, Sailors, & Patriots of the Revolutionary War - Vermont. 32p. 1993. pap. 7.50 (*0-89725-132-6*, 1445) Picton Pr.

Rohrback, Peter-Thomas, tr. see De Saint-Marie, Francois, ed.

Rohrbaugh, Eugene. Scalar Interpretation in Deontic Speech Acts. rev. ed. LC 97-11818. (Outstanding Dissertations in Linguistics Ser.). (Illus.). 182p. 1997. text 51.00 (*0-8153-2885-0*) Garland.

Rohrbaugh, John W., et al, eds. Event-Related Brain Potentials: Basic Issues & Applications. (Illus.). 402p. 1990. text 95.00 (*0-19-504891-1*) OUP.

Rohrbaugh, Richard L., ed. The Social Sciences & New Testament Interpretation. 240p. (C). 1996. 19.95 (*1-56563-239-7*) Hendrickson MA.

Rohrbaugh, Richard L., jt. auth. see Malina, Bruce J.

Rohrberger, Mary, jt. auth. see Iftekharuddin, Farhat.

Rohrborn, Claus, tr. see Soekeland, Jurgen.

Rohrbough, F. W. Rohrbough Family. (Illus.). 130p. 1993. reprint ed. pap. 26.00 (*0-8328-3743-1*); reprint ed. lib. bdg. 36.00 (*0-8328-3742-3*) Higginson Bk Co.

Rohrbough, Linda. Start Your Own Computer Repair Business. 1995. pap., pap. text 32.95 incl. disk (*0-07-911901-8*) McGraw.

— Upgrade Your Own PC. 2nd ed. LC TK7887.R64 1998. 480p. 1998. pap. 29.99 (*0-7645-3215-4*, MIS Pr) IDG Bks.

***Rohrbough, Malcolm J.** Aspen: The History of a Silver Mining Town, 1879-1893. (Illus.). 363p. 2000. pap. 24.95 (*0-87081-592-X*) U of Okla Pr.

Rohrbough, Malcolm J. Days of Gold: The California Gold Rush & the American Nation. LC 96-34836. (Illus.). 569p. 1997. 40.00 (*0-520-20622-3*, Pub. by U CA Pr) Cal Prin Full Svc.

— Days of Gold: The California Gold Rush & the American Nation. (Illus.). 569p. 1998. pap. 16.95 (*0-520-21659-8*, Pub. by U CA Pr) Cal Prin Full Svc.

— The Trans-Appalachian Frontier: People, Societies, & Institutions, 1775-1850. 403p. (C). 1989. 25.25 (*0-534-12336-8*) Wadsworth Pub.

Rohrer, Alyce. The True Believers. LC 85-18521. 1987. 22.95 (*0-87949-253-8*) Ashley Bks.

Rohrer, Ann & Flamholtz, Cathy J. The Tibetan Mastiff Book: Legendary Guardian of the Himalayas. LC 89-3377. (Illus.). 160p. 1989. 16.95 (*0-940269-02-3*) OTR Pubns.

Rohrer, C., jt. ed. see Reyle, Uwe.

Rohrer, Doug. More Thought Provokers. (YA). (gr. 9-12). 1994. 9.95 (*1-55953-070-7*) Key Curr Pr.

— Thought Provokers. 57p. (YA). (gr. 9-12). 1993. pap. 9.95 (*1-55953-065-0*) Key Curr Pr.

Rohrer, Eva, jt. auth. see Puttner, Herta.

Rohrer, James E. Planning for Community-Oriented Health Systems. 168p. (Orig.). 1996. pap. 32.00 (*0-87553-230-6*) Am Pub Health.

— Quality Assurance in Long-Term Care: Managing the Process. (Learning the Continuum: AUPHA Modules for Management Education Ser.). (Illus.). 48p. (Orig.). (C). 1989. pap. text 20.00 (*0-910591-21-0*) AUPHA Pr.

Rohrer, James R. Keepers of the Covenant: Frontier Missions & the Decline of Congregationalism, 1774-1818. (Religion in America Ser.). 224p. 1995. text 49.95 (*0-19-509166-3*) OUP.

Rohrer, John N. & Sherif, Muzafer, eds. Social Psychology at the Crossroads: Conference on Social Psychology, University of Oklahoma, 1950. LC 73-111822. (Essay Index Reprint Ser.). 1977. 28.95 (*0-8369-1600-X*) Ayer.

Rohrer, Josef, ed. see Hildebrand, Sigrid S. & Hildebrand, Eckart.

Rohrer, Josef, ed. see Winitz, Harris.

Rohrer, Josef, tr. see Winitz, Harris.

Rohrer, Judith C. & Cooper-Hewitt Museum. The Catalan Spirit: Gaud I & His Contemporaries. LC 87-70113. 1988. write for info. (*0-910503-54-0*) Cooper-Hewitt Museum.

Rohrer, Julie A. His Eternal Servant. (Illus.). 29p. (C). 1995. 25.00 (*0-9641149-3-3*) Main Graphics.

***Rohrer, Martha.** Our Baby's Book. (Illus.). 32p. 1999. pap. 5.25 (*0-7399-0250-4*, 2124) Rod & Staff.

— Poetry Pointers. 48p. (YA). (gr. 7). 1989. pap. 2.15 (*0-7399-0243-1*, 2435) Rod & Staff.

Rohrer, Martha. Treasure Beyond Meaasure Pattern Book. 66p. 1997. pap. 3.90 (*0-7399-0228-8*, 2449) Rod & Staff.

Rohrer, Matthew. Hummock in the Malookas: Poems. 74p. 1996. pap. 11.00 (*0-393-31548-7*) Norton.

Rohrer, Norman. Indomitable Mr. O. (CEF History Ser.). 150p. 1970. pap. 6.99 (*1-55976-124-5*) CEF Press.

Rohrer, Norman B., jt. auth. see Engstrom, Ted W.

Rohrer, Norman B., jt. auth. see Rogers, Dale Evans.

Rohrer, P. Project Management Software & Systems. 1989. text. write for info. (*0-442-27707-5*, VNR) Wiley.

Rohrer, R. System Theory. write for info. (*0-318-51860-0*) Entropy Ltd.

Rohrer, Richard L., jt. auth. see Greenwood, L. Larry.

Rohrer, Ronald A., jt. auth. see Reed, Michael L.

Rohrer, Wayne & Douglas, Louis H. Agrarian Transition in America: Dualism & Change. LC 68-15586. 1969. 32.50 (*0-672-60806-5*) Irvington.

Rohret, Cheryl, jt. auth. see Keefer, Derl.

Rohrhirsch, Ferdinand. Wissenschaftstheorie und Qumran: Zum Problem der Geltungsbegrundung von Aussagen in der Biblischen Archaologie, Aufgezeigt in den Ausgrabungen von Chirbet Qumran und En Feschcha. (Novum Testamentum et Orbis Antiquus Ser.: Vol. 32). (GER.). 408p. 1996. text 68.75 (*3-7278-1076-9*, Pub. by Presses Univ Fribourg) Eisenbrauns.

Rohrich, Lutz. Folktales & Reality. Tokofsky, Peter, tr. from GER. LC 90-26381. (Folklore Studies in Translation). 324p. 1991. 19.95 (*0-253-35028-X*) Ind U Pr.

***Rohrich, Rod J., ed.** Dallas Rhinoplasty Symposium. 2000. text 100.00 (*1-57626-129-8*) Quality Med Pub.

Rohrich, Rod J., et al. Secondary Rhinoplasty & Nasal Reconstruction. Grotting, James C., ed. (Illus.). 160p. 1995. text 125.00 (*0-942219-80-5*) Quality Med Pub.

— Ultrasound-Assisted Liposuction. LC 98-24569. (Illus.). 412p. 1998. 225.00 (*1-57626-081-X*, QMP) Quality Med Pub.

Rohricht, Jo A., jt. auth. see Nelson, James B.

Rohrick, Lisa. Any Road - Any Cost. LC 99-164647. 1998. pap. 8.99 (*0-87509-798-7*) Chr Pubns.

Rohrick, Lisa M. Both Feet on God's Path: The Story of Julie Fehr. (Junior Jaffray Collection of Missionary Stories: Bk. 16). (Illus.). (J). 1996. pap. 3.99 (*0-87509-673-5*) Chr Pubns.

— Both Feet on God's Path Bk. 16: The Story of Julie Fehr. LC 96-83899. Vol. 16. (Illus.). xiii, 221p. 1996. pap. 9.99 (*0-87509-672-7*) Chr Pubns.

***Rohrig, Bernhard, et al.** KDE Guide. 400p. 1999. 29.99 (*0-7357-0915-7*) New Riders Pub.

Rohrig, Carl-W. Rohrig Tarot. 72p. 1995. 25.00 (*1-885394-08-X*) Bluestar Communs.

Rohrig, Carl W. The Rohrig-Tarot Book. (Orig.). 1997. pap. text 15.95 (*1-57281-071-8*, BK171) US Games Syst.

Rohrig, Carl W. & Marzano-Fritz, Francesca. The Rohrig-Tarot Book. Fine, Howard, tr. from GER. LC 96-30801. (Illus.). 160p. (Orig.). 1997. pap. 15.95 (*1-885394-18-7*, 94187) Bluestar Communs.

Rohrig, E. & Ulrich, B. Temperate Deciduous Forests. (Ecosystems of the World Ser.: Vol. 7). 636p. 1991. 329.75 (*0-444-88599-4*) Elsevier.

Rohrig, Ernst & Bartsch, Norbert. Der Wald Als Vegetationsform und Seine Bedeutung Fuer Den Menschen (Forest Vegetation & Its Meaning for Man) 6th rev. ed. (Waldbau Auf Okologischer Grundlage (Forest Cultivation & Its Ecological Basis) Ser.: Vol. 1). (Illus.). 350p. 1992. 64.00 (*3-8263-2567-2*, Pub. by Blckwell Wissenschafts) Balogh.

Rohrig, Ernst & Gussone, Hans A. Baumartenwahl, Bestandesbegruendung und Bestandespflege (Tree Species Choice, Establishment & Cultivation) 6th rev. ed. (Waldbau Auf Okologischer Grundlage (Forest Cultivation & Its Ecological Basis) Ser.: Vol. 2). (Illus.). 1990. 58.00 (*3-8263-2566-4*, Pub. by Blckwell Wissenschafts) Balogh.

Rohrl, Boris. Wilhelm Leibl - Briefe. (GER., Illus.). x, 372p. 1996. write for info. (*3-487-10164-5*) G Olms Pubs.

Rohrl, H. & Pumplun, D. Convexity Theory. (Pure & Applied Mathematics Ser.). Date not set. write for info. (*0-8247-9331-5*) Dekker.

Rohrlich, Beulah F. A Handbook for Visitors to the U. S. A. (Illus.). 114p. (Orig.). 1986. pap. 7.50 (*971-10-0214-0*, Pub. by New Day Pub) Cellar.

Rohrlich, Chester. Law & Practice in Corporate Control. LC 34-1197. (Business Enterprises Reprint Ser.). vii, 268p. 1982. reprint ed. lib. bdg. 65.00 (*0-89941-184-3*, 302360) W S Hein.

Rohrlich, Chester & Bender's Editors. Organizing Corporate & Other Business Enterprises. 5th ed. 1975. ring bd. 240.00 (*0-8205-1595-7*) Bender.

Rohrlich, Fritz. Classical Charged Particles. 2nd ed. (C). 1994. pap. 43.00 (*0-201-48300-9*) Addison-Wesley.

— Classical Charged Particles. 2nd ed. (Classics Ser.). 336p. (C). 1990. reprint ed. 45.00 (*0-201-51501-6*) Addison-Wesley.

— From Paradox to Reality: Basic Concepts of the Physical World. (Illus.). 240p. (C). 1989. pap. text 31.95 (*0-521-37605-X*) Cambridge U Pr.

Rohrlich, Fritz, jt. auth. see Jauch, J. M.

Rohrlich-Leavitt, Ruby, ed. Women Cross-Culturally: Change & Challenge. (World Anthropology Ser.). (Illus.). xiv, 670p. 1975. 58.50 (*90-279-7649-X*) Mouton.

Rohrlich, Ruby. Resisting the Holocaust. 256p. 1998. 65.00 (*1-85973-211-9*, Pub. by Berg Pubs); pap. 19.50 (*1-85973-216-X*) Berg Pubs.

Rohrlich, Ruby R. The Puerto Ricans: Culture Change & Language Deviance. LC 73-90914. (Viking Fund Publications in Anthropology: No. 51). 278p. 1974. pap. 86.20 (*0-608-05653-7*, 206610700006) Bks Demand.

Rohrman, Larry G. Fit to Be Tied: How to Be Married & Happy. (Illus.). (Orig.). 1990. pap. 6.00 (*0-9628956-0-1*) Carousel AL.

Rohrmann, Bernd, jt. auth. see Renn, Ortwin.

Rohrs. Linear Control Systems. 1993. student ed. 20.62 (*0-07-041526-9*) McGraw.

Rohrs, Charles E. Linear Control Systems. 672p. (C). 1992. 82.19 (*0-07-041525-0*) McGraw.

Rohrs, Hermann & Lenhart, Volker, eds. Progressive Education Across the Continents: A Handbook. 446p. 1995. 69.95 (*3-631-48917-X*) P Lang Pubng.

Rohrs, Richard C., jt. auth. see Darcy, R.

Rohrschneider, Robert. Learning Democracy: Democratic & Economic Values in Unified Germany. LC 98-54769. (Comparative Politics Ser.). (Illus.). 326p. 1999. text 72.00 (*0-19-829517-0*) OUP.

Rohs, Timothy H., jt. auth. see Britton, Ann H.

Rohse, Mitch. Land Use Planning in Oregon: A No-Nonsense Handbook in Plain English. LC 86-12457. (Illus.). 296p. 1987. text 29.95 (*0-87071-349-3*) Oreg St U Pr.

Rohsenow, John, jt. auth. see Binyong, Yin.

Rohsenow, John S. A Chinese-English Dictionary of Enigmatic Folk Similes (Xiehouyu) LC 90-25213. 324p. 1991. 57.50 (*0-8165-1031-8*) U of Ariz Pr.

Rohsenow, Warren M., et al, eds. Handbook of Heat Transfer. 3rd ed. LC 97-51381. (Illus.). 1600p. 1997. 140.00 (*0-07-053555-8*) McGraw-Hill Prof.

Roht-Arriaza, Naomi. Impunity & Human Rights in International Law & Practice. 416p. 1995. text 85.00 (*0-19-508136-6*) OUP.

Rohter, Ira. A Green Hawaii: Sourcebook for Development Alternatives. LC 92-82826. (Illus.). 480p. (Orig.). 1992. 25.95 (*1-878751-12-3*); pap. 16.95 (*1-878751-13-1*) Na Kane O Ka Malo.

Rohwedder, W. J. & Alm, Andy. Using Computers in Environmental Education: Interactive Multimedia & On-Line Learning. (EEToolbox-Workshop Resource Manual Ser.). 72p. 1994. teacher ed. 8.00 (*1-884782-11-6*) Natl Consort EET.

Rohwer, Claude D. & Schaber, Gordon D. CONTRACTS IN A NUTSHELL 4E. 4th ed. LC 97-21701. (Paralegal). 477p. (C). 1997. pap. text 22.95 (*0-314-21201-9*) West Pub.

Rohwer, Claude D., jt. auth. see Schaber, Gordon D.

Rohwer, Gotz, jt. auth. see Blossfeld, Hans-Peter.

Rohwer, Jens G. Lauraceae: Nectandra. (Flora Neotropica Monographs: No. 60). (Illus.). 333p. 1993. pap. text 43.50 (*0-89327-373-2*) NY Botanical.

Rohwer, Jens R. Die Frucht und Samenstrukturen der Oleaceae: Eine Vergleichend-Anatomische Untersuchung. (Bibliotheca Botanica: Vol. 148). (GER., Illus.). vi, 178p. 1996. 111.00 (*3-510-48019-8*, Pub. by E Schweizerbartsche) Balogh.

Rohwer, Jim. Asia Rising: Why America Will Prosper As Asia's Economies Boom. 382p. 1998. text 25.00 (*0-7881-5477-X*) DIANE Pub.

***Rohwer, Jim.** Re-Made in America: How Asia Is Rebuilding Its Economies American-Style. 320p. 2000. 27.50 (*0-8129-3251-X*, Times Business) Crown Pub Group.

Rohwer, Jurgen. Allied Submarine Attacks of World War II: European Theatre of Operations, 1939-1945. LC 96-71810. 288p. 1997. 39.95 (*1-55750-038-X*) Naval Inst Pr.

— Axis Submarine Successes of World War Two: German, Italian & Japanese Submarine Successes in World War II. LC 98-67929. 1999. 49.95 (*1-55750-029-0*) Naval Inst Pr.

Rohwer, Jurgen & Hummelchen, Gerhard. Chronology of the War at Sea, 1939-1945: The Naval History of World War Two. rev. expanded ed. 416p. 1992. 65.00 (*1-55750-105-X*) Naval Inst Pr.

***Rohwer, Jurgen & Monakov, Mikhail.** Stalin's Ocean-Going Fleet: Soviet Naval Strategy & Shipbuilding Programs 1935-1953. (Illus.). 256p. 2000. 59.50 (*0-7146-4895-7*); pap. 27.50 (*0-7146-4448-X*) F Cass Pubs.

Rohwer, Lee O. What Is God Like? (Illus.). 64p. (Orig.). (J). (gr. k-4). 1986. pap. 5.95 (*0-9617788-0-6*) Damon Pub.

R

An Asterisk (*) at the beginning of an entry indicates that the title is appearing for the first time.

— What Is God Like? 2nd rev. ed. (Illus.). 68p. (Orig.). (YA). (gr. 8 up). 1989. reprint ed. pap. 7.95 (*0-9617788-1-4*) Damon Pub.

Rohwer, Sievert. Specific Distinctness & Adaptive Differences in Southwestern Meadowlarks. (Occasional Papers: No. 44). 14p. 1976. pap. 1.00 (*0-317-04634-9*) U KS Nat Hist Mus.

Rohy, David A. & Sharpless, Jananne. California Energy Commission: 1996 Electricity Report. (Illus.). 130p. (C). 1998. pap. text 25.00 (*0-7881-2759-4*) DIANE Pub.

***Rohy, Valerie.** Impossible Women: Lesbian Figures & American Literature. LC 99-87706. 2000. pap. 16.95 (*0-8014-8638-6*) Cornell U Pr.

Rohy, Valerie, ed. see Ammons, Elizabeth.

Rohy, Valerie, jt. ed. see Ammons, Elizabeth.

Roi, Denyse Du, see Du Roi, Denyse.

Roi, Michael L. Alternative to Appeasement: Sir Robert Vansittart & Alliance Diplomacy, 1934-1937. LC 97-5865. (Praeger Studies in Diplomacy & Strategic Thought). 216p. 1997. 59.95 (*0-275-95909-0*, Praeger Pubs) Greenwood.

Ro'i, Yaacov. From Encroachment to Involvement: A Documented Study of Soviet Policy in the Middle East 1945-1973. 616p. 1974. boxed set 49.95 (*0-87855-158-1*) Transaction Pubs.

***Roi, Yaacov.** Islam in the Soviet Union. LC 99-41848. 2000. pap. write for info. (*0-231-11955-0*) Col U Pr.

Ro'i, Yaacov. Soviet Decision Making in Practice: The U. S. S. R. & Israel, 1947-1954. LC 79-64857. 540p. 1980. 44.95 (*0-87855-267-7*) Transaction Pubs.

— The Struggle for Soviet Jewish Emigration, 1948-1967. (Cambridge Russian, Soviet & Post-Soviet Studies: No. 75). (Illus.). 478p. (C). 1991. text 69.95 (*0-521-39084-2*) Cambridge U Pr.

Roi, Yaacov, ed. Jews & Jewish Life in Russia & the Soviet Union. LC 94-33683. (Cummings Center Ser.). 448p. 1995. 57.50 (*0-7146-4619-9*, Pub. by F Cass Pubs) Intl Spec Bk.

Ro'i, Yaacov, ed. Jews & Jewish Life in Russia & the Soviet Union. LC 94-33683. (Cummings Center Ser.). 1995. pap. 27.50 (*0-7146-4149-9*, Pub. by F Cass Pubs) Intl Spec Bk.

— The Muslim Eurasia: Conflicting Legacies. 1995. pap. 24.50 (*0-7146-4142-1*, Pub. by F Cass Pubs) Intl Spec Bk.

— The Muslim Eurasia: Conflicting Legacies. LC 94-40028. (Cummings Center Ser.). 330p. 1995. 52.50 (*0-7146-4615-6*, Pub. by F Cass Pubs) Intl Spec Bk.

Ro'i, Yaacov & Beker, Avi, eds. Jewish Culture & Identity in the Soviet Union. 480p. (C). 1992. pap. text 21.00 (*0-8147-7432-6*) NYU Pr.

Roiblat, Herbert L., et al. From Animals to Animates 2: Proceedings of the 2nd International Conference on Simulation of Adaptive Behavior. LC 93-12410. (Bradford Series in Complex Adaptive Systems). (Illus.). 536p. 1993. pap. text 63.00 (*0-262-63149-0*, Bradford Bks) MIT Pr.

Roicek, M., jt. ed. see Hawking, Stephen W.

Roider, Karl A. Austria's Eastern Question, 1700-1970. LC 81-48141. 271p. reprint ed. pap. 84.10 (*0-8357-4195-8*, 203697300006) Bks Demand.

— Baron Thugut & Austria's Response to the French Revolution. LC 87-2240. (Illus.). 436p. 1987. reprint ed. pap. 135.20 (*0-608-07123-4*, 206734900009) Bks Demand.

— The Reluctant Ally: Austria's Policy in the Austro-Turkish War, 1737-1739. LC 72-79336. 206p. 1972. pap. 63.90 (*0-7837-8521-6*, 204933000011) Bks Demand.

Roidon Co. Staff. Yo-Leven. (United States Ser.). (Illus.). 108p. (Orig.). 1990. pap. 7.00 (*1-879374-00-5*) Roidon.

Roig. Tonal Harmony. 2001. wbk. ed. 17.00 (*0-07-303998-5*) McGraw.

Roig de Lluis, Luis, tr. see Plato.

Roig, Joan. New Bridges. (Illus.). 192p. 1996. pap. text 60.00 (*84-252-1681-8*) Watsn-Guptill.

Roig, Jose G., tr. see Oberlander, June R.

Roig, Pedro. La Guerra de Marti. LC 84-81165. (Coleccion Cuba y sus Jueces). (SPA., Illus.). 257p. (Orig.). 1984. pap. 9.95 (*0-89729-353-3*) Ediciones.

Roijackers, R., et al, eds. Eutrophication Research. 252p. 1998. pap. 159.00 (*0-08-043381-2*, Pergamon Pr) Elsevier.

Roinard, P. M., et al. La Poesie Symboliste. LC 77-11482. reprint ed. 40.00 (*0-404-16343-2*) AMS Pr.

Roine, Eva. Psychodrama: Group Psychotherapy As Experimental Theater. LC 98-137745. 224p. 1997. pap. 28.95 (*1-85302-494-5*, Pub. by Jessica Kingsley) Taylor & Francis.

Roiphe, Anne. 1185 Park Avenue: A Memoir. LC 98-51939. (Illus.). 272p. 1999. 25.00 (*0-684-85731-6*) Free Pr.

***Roiphe, Anne.** 1185 Park Avenue: A Memoir. 272p. 2000. per. 13.00 (*0-684-85732-4*) S&S Trade.

— For Rabbit, with Love & Squalor: An American Read. 256p. 2000. 22.50 (*0-7432-0505-7*) Free Pr.

Roiphe, Anne. Fruitful: Living the Contradictions: A Memoir of Modern Motherhood. 1997. pap. 12.95 (*0-14-026672-0*) Viking Penguin.

— Lovingkindness. 256p. 1989. mass mkt. 5.99 (*0-446-35274-8*, Pub. by Warner Bks) Little.

— Lovingkindness. LC 97-25388. 272p. 1997. mass mkt. 11.99 (*0-446-67388-9*, Pub. by Warner Bks) Little.

— The Pursuit of Happiness. 579p. 1992. mass mkt. 5.99 (*0-446-36334-0*, Pub. by Warner Bks) Little.

Roiphe, Anne R. If You Knew Me. 224p. 1995. mass mkt. 11.99 (*0-446-67071-5*, Pub. by Warner Bks) Little.

— If You Knew Me. large type ed. LC 93-34586. 291p. 1994. lib. bdg. 21.95 (*0-7862-0077-4*) Thorndike Pr.

Roiphe, Herman & Galenson, Eleanor. Infantile Origins of Sexual Identity. LC 81-14290. 301p. 1981. 47.50 (*0-8236-2368-8*) Intl Univs Pr.

Roiphe, Katie. Last Night in Paradise. LC 97-12006. 1997. pap. 12.00 (*0-375-70053-4*) Vin Bks.

— Morning After: Sex, Fear, & Feminism, Vol. 1. 200p. 1994. pap. 8.95 (*0-316-75432-3*) Little.

Roisman, Hanna M. Nothing Is As It Seems: The Tragedy of the Implicit in Euripides' "Hippolytus" LC 98-36863. (Greek Studies). 304p. 1998. 68.00 (*0-8476-9092-X*); pap. 24.95 (*0-8476-9093-8*) Rowman.

Roisman, Hannah M., jt. auth. see Ahl, Frederick.

Roisman, Joseph. Alexander the Great. (Problems in European Civilization Ser.). 250p. (C). 1995. pap. text 18.36 (*0-669-34501-6*) HM Trade Div.

Roisum, David R. The Mechanics of Rollers. LC 95-52109. 1996. 90.00 (*0-89852-313-3*, 0101R255) TAPPI.

— The Mechanics of Web Handling. LC 98-7173. 1998. 90.00 (*0-89852-346-X*) TAPPI.

***Roitberg, Yakov.** Boundary Value Problems in the Spaces of Distributions. LC 99-50107. (Mathematics & Its Applications Series). 1999. write for info. (*0-7923-6025-7*) Kluwer Academic.

Roitberg, Yakov. Elliptic Boundary Value Problems in the Spaces of Distributions. LC 96-36623. (Mathematics & Its Applications Ser.: Vol. 384). 415p. (C). 1996. text 247.00 (*0-7923-4303-4*) Kluwer Academic.

Roitblat, Herbert L., et al, eds. Animal Cognition. (Comparative Cognition & Neuroscience Ser.). 696p. 1984. pap. text 99.95 (*0-89859-334-4*) L Erlbaum Assocs.

— Language & Communication: Comparative Perspectives. (Comparative Cognition & Neuroscience Ser.). 520p. 1993. pap. 39.95 (*0-8058-0947-3*); text 110.00 (*0-8058-0946-5*) L Erlbaum Assocs.

Roitblat, Herbert L. & Meyer, Jean-Arcady, eds. Comparative Approaches to Cognitive Science. (Illus.). 550p. 1995. 62.50 (*0-262-18166-5*) MIT Pr.

Roiter, A. V., jt. auth. see Gabriel, P.

Roiter, Howard, jt. auth. see Kohn, Nahum.

Roith, Derek Le, see Le Roith, Derek, ed.

Roith, Derek Le, see Draznin, Boris & Le Roith, Derek, eds.

Roith, Estelle. The Riddle of Freud: Jewish Influences on His Theory of Female Sexuality. 250p. (C). 1987. lib. bdg. 55.00 (*0-422-61380-0*, Pub. by Tavistock) Routldge.

— The Riddle of Freud: Jewish Influences on His Theory of Female Sexuality. 250p. (C). 1987. pap. text 29.99 (*0-422-61760-1*, Pub. by Tavistock) Routldge.

Roithinger, Franz X., jt. auth. see Lesh, Michael D.

Roitman, Janet, tr. see Geschiere, Peter.

Roitman, Jeffrey L. ACSM's Resource Manual for Guidelines for Exercise Testing & Prescription. 3rd ed. 715p. text 64.95 (*0-683-30790-8*) Lppncott W & W.

Roitman, Joel M. The Immigrants, the Progressives, & the Schools: Americanization & the Impact of the New Immigration upon Public Education in the United States, 1890-1920. 376p. 1996. 45.00 (*0-936128-48-8*) De Young Pr.

Roitman, Judith. Introduction to Modern Set Theory. LC 89-33698. 176p. 1990. 99.95 (*0-471-63519-7*) Wiley.

***Roitman, Judith.** Slippage. 50p. 1999. pap. 7.00 (*0-937013-97-8*, Pub. by Potes Poets) SPD-Small Pr Dist.

Roitt. Immunology. 4th ed. 1995. 52.00 (*0-7234-2586-8*) Wolfe Pubng AZ.

Roitt, Ivan. Immunology. 5th ed. 1997. 45.00 (*0-7234-2918-9*, Pub. by Wolfe Pub) Mosby Inc.

Roitt, Ivan, jt. auth. see Rabson, Arthur.

Roitt, Ivan M. Roitt's Essential Immunology. 9th ed. LC 97-7044. (Illus.). 476p. 1997. pap. 48.95 (*0-86542-729-1*) Blackwell Sci.

Roitt, Ivan M., jt. ed. see Delves, Peter J.

Roitt, Ivan M., jt. ed. see Delves, Peter J.

Roizen, Judith & Jepson, Mark. Degrees for Jobs: Employer Expectations of Higher Education. 225p. 1985. pap. write for info. (*0-335-15617-7*) OpUniv Pr.

— Degrees for Jobs: Employer Expectations of Higher Education. LC 85-15343. 224p. 1985. pap. 38.00 (*1-85059-005-2*) OpUniv Pr.

Roizen, Michael F. Anesthesia for Vascular Surgery. (Illus.). 518p. 1989. text 115.00 (*0-443-08567-6*) Church.

***Roizen, Michael F.** Real Age: Are You as Young as You Can Be? LC 98-42766. 352p. 1999. 25.95 (*0-06-019134-1*, Cliff Street) HarperTrade.

— Real Age: Are You as Young as You Can Be? 1999. audio 18.95 (*0-694-52242-2*, Pub. by HarperTrade) HarpC.

Roizen, Michael F. RealAge: Are You as Young as You Can Be? 352p. 2000. pap. 15.00 (*0-06-093075-6*, Cliff Street) HarperTrade.

***Roizen, Michael F.** RealAge: Are You as Young as You Can Be? large type ed. LC 99-51973. (Large Print Book Ser.). 1999. write for info. (*1-56895-790-4*, Wheeler) Wheeler Pub.

Roizen, Michael F. & Fleisher, Lee A. Essence of Anesthesia Practice. Reines, Lew, ed. (Illus.). 620p. 1996. pap. text 55.00 (*0-7216-5972-1*, W B Saunders Co) Harcrt Hlth Sci Grp.

Roizin, Leon, et al, eds. Neurotoxicology, Vol. 1, 1977. LC 77-4632. (Illus.). 686p. 1977. reprint ed. pap. 200.00 (*0-608-00631-9*, 206121900001) Bks Demand.

Roizman, Bernard, ed. The Herpesviruses, Vol. 1. LC 82-15034. (Viruses Ser.). (Illus.). 460p. (C). 1982. 132.00 (*0-306-40922-4*, Kluwer Plenum) Kluwer Academic.

— The Herpesviruses, Vol. 2. LC 82-15034. (Viruses Ser.). (Illus.). 458p. (C). 1983. text 132.00 (*0-306-41083-4*, Kluwer Plenum) Kluwer Academic.

— The Herpesviruses, Vol. 3. LC 82-15034. (Viruses Ser.). (Illus.). 432p. (C). 1985. text 132.00 (*0-306-41778-2*, Kluwer Plenum) Kluwer Academic.

— Infectious Diseases in an Age of Change: The Impact of Human Ecology & Behavior on Disease Transmission. 272p. (Orig.). (C). 1995. text 44.95 (*0-309-05136-3*) Natl Acad Pr.

Roizman, Bernard, et al, eds. The Human Herpes Viruses: Biology, Pathogenesis, & Treatment. LC 93-21719. 448p. 1993. text 103.00 (*0-7817-0024-8*) Lppncott W & W.

Roizman, Bernard & Lopez, Carlos, eds. The Herpesviruses: Immunobiology & Prophylaxis of Human Herpesvirus Infections, Vol. 4. LC 82-15034. (Viruses Ser.). (Illus.). 458p. (C). 1985. text 132.00 (*0-306-41793-6*, Kluwer Plenum) Kluwer Academic.

Roizman, Bernard, jt. ed. see Lopez, Carlos.

Roja, Harry, jt. auth. see Blackwell, Kenneth.

Roja, Tormenta. Red Storm Rising. 1998. pap. 10.95 (*84-01-49521-0*) Lectorum Pubns.

Rojahn, Jurgen, jt. ed. see Van der Linden, Marcel.

Rojahn, Matthias. Ami Pro 2.0 Einfuhrung und Leitfaden. (GER.). (C). 1991. text. write for info. (*0-201-56572-2*) Addison-Wesley.

— Ventura. (C). 1991. text. write for info. (*0-201-55925-0*) Addison-Wesley.

— Word Fur Windows Einstieg und Leitfaden. (GER.). (C). 1990. text. write for info. (*0-201-55923-4*) Addison-Wesley.

Rojak, Lisa. The Everything One-Pot Cookbook. LC 99-33168. (Everything Cookbook Ser.). (Illus.). 304p. 1999. pap. 12.95 (*1-58062-186-4*) Adams Media.

Rojanasakul, Yongyut, jt. ed. see Wu-Pong, Susanna.

Rojankovsky, Feodor. Award Puzzles: Frog Went a-Courting. (Caldecott Collection). (J). 1991. 6.95 (*0-938971-69-7*) JTG Nashville.

— Tall Book of Nursery Tales. LC 44-3881. (Tall Bks.). (Illus.). 120p. (J). (ps-3). 1944. 9.95 (*0-06-025065-8*) HarpC Child Bks.

Rojankovsky, Feodor. Wild Animals. LC 97-228181. 24 p. 1960. write for info. (*0-307-90960-3*, Whitman Coin) St Martin.

Rojankovsky, Feodor & Langstaff, John M. Frog Went A-Courtin' LC 55-5237. (Illus.). 32p. (J). (ps-3). 1955. 14.95 (*0-15-230214-X*, Harcourt Child Bks) Harcourt.

— Frog Went A-Courtin' LC 91-17693. (Illus.). 32p. (C). (ps-3). 1972. pap. 7.00 (*0-15-633900-5*, Voyager Bks) Harcourt.

— Over in the Meadow. LC 57-8587. (Illus.). 32p. (J). (ps-3). 1957. 16.00 (*0-15-258854-X*, Harcourt Child Bks) Harcourt.

— Over in the Meadow. LC 57-8587. (Illus.). 32p. (J). (ps-3). 1973. reprint ed. pap. 7.00 (*0-15-670500-1*, Voyager Bks) Harcourt.

Rojansky, Vladimir. Electromagnetic Fields & Waves. LC 79-52648. 464p. 1980. pap. text 12.95 (*0-486-63834-0*) Dover.

Rojany, Lisa. Hands-On Book of Big Machines. 14p. (J). (gr. k-3). 1992. 11.95 (*0-316-41904-4*) Little.

— I Love You Because... Love, Barbie. (Illus.). 10p. (YA). 1999. 14.95 (*0-307-33201-2*) Gldn Bks Pub Co.

— The Magic Feather: A Jamaican Legend. (Legends of the World Ser.). 1995. 9.15 (*0-606-07819-3*, Pub. by Turtleback) Demco.

— The Story of Hanukkah: A Lift-the-Flap Rebus Book. (Illus.). 16p. (J). (ps-3). 1993. 12.95 (*1-56282-420-1*, Pub. by Hyprn Child) Little.

Rojany, Lisa, ed. The Magic Feather: A Jamaican Legend. LC 95-9982. (Legends of the World Ser.). (Illus.). 32p. (J). (gr. 2-6). 1997. lib. bdg. 18.60 (*0-8167-3751-7*) Troll Communs.

— The Magic Feather: A Jamaican Legend. LC 95-9982. (Illus.). 32p. (J). (gr. 2-6). 1998. pap. 4.95 (*0-8167-3752-5*) Troll Communs.

Rojas. La Celestina. unabridged ed. (SPA.). pap. 7.95 (*84-410-0002-6*, Pub. by Bookking Intl) Distribks Inc.

Rojas, Atenedor, ed. Belleza Natural. deluxe ed. (SPA., Illus.). 176p. 1999. pap. 5.95 (*0-939193-48-5*) Edit Concepts.

— Un Botiquin de Salud en su Cocina. deluxe ed. (SPA., Illus.). 328p. 1998. pap. 5.95 (*0-939193-44-2*) Edit Concepts.

— Las Mejores Curas y Remedios Naturales. deluxe ed. (SPA., Illus.). 322p. 1996. pap. 5.95 (*0-939193-42-6*) Edit Concepts.

— Remedios Caseros para Proteger su Salud. deluxe ed. (SPA., Illus.). 192p. 1999. pap. 5.95 (*0-939193-32-9*) Edit Concepts.

Rojas, Beatriz. Breve Historia de Aguascalientes (Consise History of Aguascalientes) (Breves Historias de los Estados de Mexico Ser.). (SPA.). 1994. pap. 13.99 (*968-16-4540-5*, Pub. by Fondo) Continental Bk.

Rojas, Carlos. The Garden of Janus. Lee, Cecilia C., tr. from SPA. LC 96-5290. 224p. 1996. 35.00 (*0-8386-3672-1*) Fairleigh Dickinson.

— The Garden of the Hesperides. Glad, Diana, tr. from SPA. LC 98-35809. 232p. 1999. 36.00 (*0-8386-3794-9*) Fairleigh Dickinson.

— Salvador Dali: or The Art of Spitting on Your Mother's Portrait. Amell, Alma, tr. from SPA. 208p. (C). 1993. 35.00 (*0-271-00842-3*) Pa St U Pr.

— Yo, Goya. 1998. pap. 14.95 (*84-320-4534-9*) Planeta.

Rojas, Carmen, compiled by. How to Read the Bible Everyday: A Guide for Catholics. 48p. (Orig.). 1988. pap. text 3.99 (*0-89283-399-8*, Charis) Servant.

Rojas, De, see De Rojas.

Rojas, Don. The NAACP & the New Black Agenda. 1997. write for info. (*0-8129-2687-0*, Times Bks) Crown Pub Group.

Rojas, Don, ed. One People, One Destiny: The Caribbean & Central America Today. LC 88-62937. 115p. (Orig.). 1988. pap. 11.95 (*0-87348-535-1*); lib. bdg. 35.00 (*0-87348-536-X*) Pathfinder NY.

Rojas, Duque De, see De Rojas, Duque.

Rojas, Edgar, ed. see Cunningham, Scott.

Rojas, Edgar, ed. see Paulus, Stefan.

Rojas, Edgar, ed. & tr. see Buckland, Raymond.

Rojas, Edgar, ed. & tr. see Malbrough, Ray T.

***Rojas, Eduardo.** Old Cities, New Assets: Preserving Latin America's Urban Heritage. 2000. pap. text 26.95 (*1-886938-62-8*) IADB.

Rojas, Eduardo & Daughters, Robert, eds. La Ciudad en el Siglo XXI. (SPA.). 368p. 1998. pap. text 12.50 (*1-886938-42-3*) IADB.

Rojas, Emilio. Little Friend. (Illus.). 125p. 1992. pap. 16.95 (*1-85230-281-X*, Pub. by Element MA) Penguin Putnam.

Rojas, Enrique. El Laberinto de la Afectividad. (Nueva Austral Ser.: Vol. 11). (SPA.). 1991. pap. text 24.95 (*84-239-1811-4*) Elliots Bks.

Rojas, Fernando De. Celestina. Mabbe, James, tr. from SPA. 112p. 1992. pap. 7.95 (*0-936839-01-5*) Applause Theatre Bk Pubs.

— La Celestina. (SPA.). pap. 9.95 (*84-206-1200-6*, Pub. by Alianza Editorial) Continental Bk.

— La Celestina. (SPA.). 224p. 1996. pap. text 4.00 (*1-56328-114-7*) Edit Plaza Mayor.

***Rojas, Fernando De.** La Celestina. (SPA.). 1999. 13.00 (*84-481-0626-1*, McGrw-H College) McGrw-H Hghr Educ.

Rojas, Fernando De. La Celestina. (Clasicos Ser.). (SPA.). 317p. 1997. pap. write for info. (*0-929441-95-8*) Pubns Puertorriquenas.

— La Celestina. 2nd ed. Lacarra, Maria E., ed. (Spanish Ser.: No. 109). lxvi, 189p. 1995. 30.00 (*1-56954-037-3*) Hispanic Seminary.

— Celestina: A Play in Twenty-One Acts, Attributed to Fernando de Rojas. Singleton, Mack H., tr. from SPA. LC 58-13446. 318p. reprint ed. pap. 98.60 (*0-7837-4385-8*, 204412500012) Bks Demand.

— Celestina or the Tragicke-Comedy of Calisto & Melibea. Mabbe, James, tr. LC 01-19039. (Tudor Translations, First Ser.: No. 6). reprint ed. 57.50 (*0-404-51853-2*) AMS Pr.

— Celestine or the Tragick-Comedie of Calisto & Melibea. LaCalle, Guadalupe M., ed. Mabbe, James, tr. (Series B: Textos, XIV). (Illus.). 268p. (Orig.). (C). 1972. pap. 51.00 (*0-900411-56-2*, Pub. by Tamesis Bks Ltd) Boydell & Brewer.

Rojas, Fernando De, adapted by. La Celestina, Level 6. (Leer en Espanol Ser.). (SPA.). (C). 1998. pap. 6.95 (*84-294-4331-2*) Santillana.

Rojas, Francisco. Lola Casanova. (SPA.). pap. 7.99 (*968-16-1559-X*, Pub. by Fondo) Continental Bk.

Rojas, Gonzalo. Schizotext & Other Poems: Esquizotexto y Otros Poemas. Quackenbush, Howard & Cluff, Russel, eds. (ENG & SPA.). XII, 135p. (C). 1988. text 34.00 (*0-8204-0561-2*) P Lang Pubng.

Rojas, Hector. Origami Animals. LC 91-18266. (Illus.). 160p. (YA). (gr. 7 up). 1993. pap. 14.95 (*0-8069-8649-2*) Sterling.

Rojas, John, Jr Chula Vista - The Early Years Vol. 6: Historic Churches of Chula Vista. Bowers, Carol, ed. (Illus.). 80p. (Orig.). 1997. pap. 9.95 (*0-938711-45-8*) Tecolote Pubns.

— Chula Vista's Trees. 260p. (Orig.). 1996. pap. 20.00 (*0-938711-37-7*) Tecolote Pubns.

Rojas, John, Jr., intro. Chula Vista: The Early Years, Vol. 1. 80p. (Orig.). 1992. pap. 7.95 (*0-938711-14-8*) Tecolote Pubns.

Rojas, John, Jr., et al. Chula Vista: The Early Years, Vol. 3. (Illus.). 72p. (Orig.). 1994. pap. 7.95 (*0-938711-24-5*) Tecolote Pubns.

Rojas, John, Jr., ed. see Chula Vista Historical Society Staff.

Rojas, John I. Gente Pequenita.Tr. of Little People. (SPA.). 64p. (J). (gr. 4-6). 1994. 14.99 (*958-07-0312-4*, Pub. by Santillana) T R Bks.

— Ninos Desobedientes.Tr. of Disobedient Children. (SPA.). 92p. (J). (gr. 4-6). 1994. 14.99 (*958-07-0313-2*, Pub. by Santillana) T R Bks.

Rojas, Jorge N. Gramatica Esencial, 2 vols. 2nd ed. (C). 1994. pap. text 40.36 (*0-395-67406-9*) HM.

Rojas, Jorge N. & Curry, Richard A. Gramatica Esencial: Repaso y Practica: Answer Key, 2 vols. 2nd ed. (SPA.). (C). 1995. pap. text 11.96 (*0-395-71641-1*) HM.

— Rojas Gramatica Esencial+Answe, 2 vols. 2nd ed. (SPA.). (C). 1994. text 40.36 (*0-395-71640-3*) HM.

Rojas, Juan. Diccionario. Popular De la Biblia.Tr. of Popular Bible Dictionary. (SPA., Illus.). 253p. 1971. write for info. (*0-614-27030-8*) Editorial Unilit.

— Diccionario Popular de la Biblia.Tr. of Popular Bible Dictionary. (SPA., Illus.). 1992. 9.99 (*1-56063-191-0*, 497693); pap. 5.99 (*0-685-74928-2*, 497692) Editorial Unilit.

— Diccionario Popular de la Biblia - Popular Dictionary of the Bible. (SPA., Illus.). 253p. 1971. write for info. (*0-614-24361-0*) Editorial Unilit.

Rojas, Juan, tr. see Graham, Billy.

Rojas, L., ed. see Dewey, Melvil.

Rojas-Lombardi, Felipe. Art of S American Co. LC 90-56395. 528p. 1991. 35.00 (*0-06-016425-5*) HarperTrade.

— Game Cookery. LC 72-12215. (Illus.). 1973. 3.95 (*0-915180-16-2*) Harrowood Bks.

Rojas, M. Para Vivir en Paz.Tr. of To Live in Peace. (SPA.). 52p. 22.29 (*0-7899-0222-2*, 496255) Editorial Unilit.

***Rojas, Marcos Luis.** Antidotos De La Nostalgia. LC 99-166044. (SPA.). 1999. pap. 21.95 (*84-239-7776-5*) Espasa Calpe.

Rojas, Maria P., jt. auth. see Pascal, Nanette R.

Rojas, Mary H. Lady in Waiting: Poems in English & Spanish. Lombeida, Ernesto, tr. from SPA. LC 93-87093. (Illus.). 88p. (Orig.). 1994. pap. 8.95 (*0-9634090-1-8*) Spillway Pubns.

An Asterisk (*) at the beginning of an entry indicates that the title is appearing for the first time.

Rojas, Nelson. Redaccion Comercial Estructurada. 2nd ed. 200p. 1982. text 15.36 (*0-07-053566-3*) McGraw.

Rojas Osorio, Carlos. Foucault y el Pensamiento Contemporaneo. (SPA.). 352p. 1995. pap. 11.95 (*0-8477-0219-7*) U of PR Pr.

Rojas, R. Condor Herido.Tr. of Condor Rojas Story. (SPA.). 112p. 1997. pap. 4.99 (*0-8297-1833-8*) Vida Pubs.

— Neural Nets: A Systematic Introduction. 504p. 1996. pap. 35.95 (*3-540-60505-3*) Spr-Verlag.

Rojas, Rafael. Isla Sin Fin: Contribucion a la Critica Del Nacionalismo Cubano. (Coleccion Cuba y sus Jueces). 240p. (Orig.). 1998. pap. 19.95 (*0-89729-886-1*) Ediciones.

***Rojas, Raul & Hashagen, Ulf, eds.** The First Computers: History & Architectures. LC 99-44811. (History of Computing Ser.). (Illus.). 432p. 2000. 35.00 (*0-262-18197-5*) MIT Pr.

Rojas, Raul, jt. auth. see Zimmerman, Marc.

Rojas, Sonia R. & Rehbein, Edna A. Critical Approaches to Isabel Allende's Novels. LC 91-11499. (American University Studies: Latin American Literature: Ser. XXII, Vol. 14). 201p. (C). 1992. text 35.95 (*0-8204-1495-6*) P Lang Pubng.

Rojas-Suarez, Liliana, ed. Como Lograr Sistemas Financieros Solidos y Seguros en America Latina. (SPA.). 268p. 1998. pap. text 21.95 (*1-886938-40-7*) IADB.

— Safe & Sound Financial Systems: What Works for Latin America? LC 97-77121. (Inter-American Development Bank Ser.). 236p. 1998. pap. text 21.95 (*1-886938-20-2*) IADB.

Rojas-Suarez, Liliana & Weisbrod, Steven R. Financial Fragilities in Latin America: The 1980s & 1990s. (Occasional Papers: Vol. 132). 1995. 15.00 (*1-55775-502-7*) Intl Monetary.

Rojas-Suarez, Liliana, jt. auth. see Mathieson, Donald J.

Rojas-Suarez, Liliana, jt. ed. see Hausmann, Ricardo.

Rojas, Tony H. TDR vs Gravimetric: A Comparison of Soil Moisture Determination Methods. LC QC0981.8. (University of Michigan Reports: No. 030613-1-T). 15p. reprint ed. pap. 30.00 (*0-7837-6780-3*, 204661000003) Bks Demand.

Rojas-Trempe & Vallejo, Catharina. Poetica de Escritoras Hispanoamericanas al Alba del Proximo Milenio. LC 97-80049. (Coleccion Polymita). (SPA.). 248p. 1998. pap. 16.00 (*0-89729-850-0*, 850-0) Ediciones.

Rojas Zorrilla, Francisco D. Progne y Filomena de Francisco de Rojas Zorrilla: Edicion, Introduccion y Notas de Dr. Alfred Rodriguez y Saul Roll-Velez. Rodriguez, Alfred & Roll-Velez, Saul, eds. LC 93-2531. (Iberica Ser.: No. 8). 147p. (C). 1994. text 38.95 (*0-8204-2080-8*) P Lang Pubng.

Rojcewicz, Rebekah, tr. see Cavalletti, Sofia.

Rojcewicz, Richard, ed. & tr. see Husserl, Edmund.

Rojcewicz, Richard, tr. see Heidegger, Martin.

Rojcewicz, Richard, tr. see Husserl, Edmund.

Rojeck, Chris. Decentring Leisure. (Theory, Culture & Society Ser.). 240p. 1995. text 69.95 (*0-8039-8812-5*); pap. text 26.95 (*0-8039-8813-3*) Sage.

***Rojecki, Andrew.** Silencing the Opposition: Antinuclear Movements & the Media in the Cold War. LC 99-6180. 200p. 1999. 37.50 (*0-252-02510-5*) U of Ill Pr.

Rojecki, Andrew. Silencing the Opposition: Antinuclear Movements & the Media in the Cold War. LC 99-6180. (History of Communication Ser.). 200p. 1999. pap. 16.95 (*0-252-06824-6*) U of Ill Pr.

Rojecki, Andrew, jt. auth. see Entman, Robert M.

Rojek. Leisure & Culture. LC 99-15308. 2000. text 65.00 (*0-312-22591-1*) St Martin.

Rojek, Chris. Capitalism & Leisure Theory. LC 85-2869. 224p. (Orig.). 1985. 45.00 (*0-422-79060-5*, 9558, Pub. by Tavistock); pap. 14.95 (*0-422-79070-2*, 9559, Pub. by Tavistock) Routldge.

— Ways of Escape: Modern Transformation in Leisure & Travel. LC 93-33328. (Postmodern Social Futures Ser.). 250p. (C). 1994. lib. bdg. 47.50 (*0-8476-7898-9*) Rowman.

Rojek, Chris, ed. Leisure for Leisure: Critical Essays. 256p. 1989. text 32.50 (*0-415-90065-4*) Routledge.

Rojek, Chris & Turner, Bryan S., eds. Forget Baudrillard? LC 93-14835. (Illus.). 224p. (C). 1993. pap. 22.99 (*0-415-05989-5*) Routledge.

Rojek, Chris, et al. Forget Lyotard? LC 97-46826. (Studies in Social & Political Thought). 176p. (C). 1998. 75.00 (*0-415-11724-0*) Routledge.

Rojek, Chris, jt. ed. see Cashmore, Ellis.

Rojek, Chris, jt. ed. see Dunning, Eric.

Rojek, Dean G., jt. auth. see Jensen, Gary F.

Rojek, Dean G., jt. ed. see Jensen, Gary F.

Rojer, Olga E. Exile in Argentina, 1933-1945: A Historical & Literary Introduction. (American University Studies: Ser. XXII, Vol. 3). XXII, 250p. (C). 1990. text 55.80 (*0-8204-0785-2*) P Lang Pubng.

***Rojey, A., ed.** Gas Cycling: A New Approach. 147p. 1999. 55.00 (*2-7108-0759-9*) Edits Technip.

Rojey, Alexandre & Jaffret, Claude, eds. Natural Gas: Production Processing, Transport. 420p. 1995. pap. 425.00 (*2-7108-0693-2*, Pub. by Edits Technip) Enfield Pubs NH.

Rojiani, Kamal B. Programming in C for Engineers. 500p. (C). 1995. text 74.00 (*0-13-726498-4*) P-H.

Rojkind, Marcos, ed. Connective Tissue in Health & Disease. 224p. 1989. lib. bdg. 35.00 (*0-8493-4161-2*, RC924) CRC Pr.

Rojkind, Marcos, jt. ed. see Perez-Tamayo, Ruy.

Rojo, Alba C. De, see De Rojo, Alba C., ed.

Rojo, Alfonso L. Diccionario Enciclopedico de Anatomia de Peces: Ingles-Espanol. (ENG & SPA.). write for info. (*0-318-56672-9*, S-36994) Fr & Eur.

— Diccionario Enciclopedico de Anatomia de Peces, Ingles-Espanol. (SPA.). 564p. 1988. write for info. (*0-7859-6226-3*) Fr & Eur.

— Dictionary of Evolutionary Fish Osteology. LC 96-20332. (Illus.). 280p. 1991. lib. bdg. 84.95 (*0-8493-4214-7*, QL639) CRC Pr.

Rojo, Andrea. Arc-en-Ciel: French for Elementary Students. (FRE.). (J). (gr. 1-5). Date not set. pap. text. write for info. (*0-9671053-2-3*, 0210) Language Adventure.

***Rojo, Andrea S.** Arcoiris: Spanish for Elementary Students. (SPA., Illus.). 64p. (Orig.). (J). (gr. 1-5). 1999. pap. text. write for info. (*0-9671053-0-7*, 0101) Language Adventure.

Rojo, Antonio B. Las Estatuas Sepultadas y Otros Relatos. Echevarria, Roberto G., ed. (SPA.). 233p. 1984. pap. 11.00 (*0-910061-20-3*, 1112) Ediciones Norte.

— The Magic Dog: And Other Stories. Janney, Frank, ed. 261p. 1990. 26.00 (*0-685-46973-5*); pap. 14.00 (*0-685-46974-3*) Ediciones Norte.

Rojo, Grinor. Diran Que Esta en la Gloria (Mistral) 525p. 1997. pap. 23.99 (*956-7083-68-1*) Fondo CA.

Rojo, Grinor & Hassett, John J. Chile: Dictatorship & the Struggle for Democracy. LC 88-82164. 112p. 1988. 12.00 (*0-935318-14-3*) Edins Hispamerica.

Rojo, Grinor & Steele, Cynthia. Ritos de Iniciacion: Tres Nouvelas Cortas de Hispanoamerica, 001. LC 85-80939. (SPA.). 224p. (C). 1985. text 31.96 (*0-395-38125-8*) HM.

Rojo, J. P. Pterocarpus (Leguminosae-Papilionaceae) Revised for the World. 1971. 36.00 (*3-7682-0726-9*) Lubrecht & Cramer.

***Rojo, Jerry.** An Acting Method Using the Psychophysical Experience of Workshop Games-Exercises. LC 00-24657. (Studies in Theatre Arts: 11). 228p. 2000. 89.95 (*0-7734-7750-0*) E Mellen.

***Rojos, Edgar, ed.** Almanaque Astrologico 1999 - 1999 Astrological Almanac. (SPA., Illus.). 36p. 1998. pap. 9.95 (*1-56718-947-4*) Llewellyn Pubns.

Rojot, J., jt. auth. see Despax, M.

***Rojstaczer, Stuart.** Gone for Good: Tales of University Life after the Golden Age. LC 98-45609. 208p. 1999. 22.00 (*0-19-512682-3*) OUP.

Rojtman, Betty. Black Fire on White Fire: An Essay on Jewish Hermeneutics: From Midrash to Kabbalah. Rendall, Steven, tr. LC 97-3010. (Contraversions Ser.). (ENG & FRE.). 205p. 1998. 45.00 (*0-520-20320-8*, Pub. by U CA Pr); pap. 17.95 (*0-520-20321-6*, Pub. by U CA Pr) Cal Prin Full Svc.

Roka, Alex. Wishes at the Bottom of the Well. LC 90-84625. 216p. 1991. 30.00 (*0-9627936-0-4*) Bk Elan.

Rokach, A., jt. auth. see Weitz, R.

Rokach, Abraham J. Schaum's Outline of Structural Steel Design. (Schaum's Outline Ser.). 210p. (C). 1991. pap. 15.95 (*0-07-053563-9*) McGraw.

Rokach, Allen, ed. Focus on Travel: Creating Memorable Photographs of Journeys to New Places. LC 92-27282. (Illus.). 288p. 1993. 19.98 (*1-55859-371-3*) Abbeville Pr.

Rokach, Allen & Millman, Anne. The Field Guide to Photographing Birds. (Center for Nature Photography Ser.). (Illus.). 128p. 1995. pap. 16.95 (*0-8174-3873-4*, Amphoto) Watsn-Guptill.

— The Field Guide to Photographing Flowers. LC 94-36839. (Center for Nature Photography Ser.). (Illus.). 128p. 1995. pap. 16.95 (*0-8174-3870-X*, Amphoto) Watsn-Guptill.

— The Field Guide to Photographing Gardens. LC 97-46887. (Center for Nature Photography Ser.). 128p. 1998. pap. 16.95 (*0-8174-3876-9*, Amphoto) Watsn-Guptill.

— The Field Guide to Photographing Landscapes. LC 94-36840. (Illus.). 128p. 1995. pap. text 16.95 (*0-8174-3871-8*, Amphoto) Watsn-Guptill.

— The Field Guide to Photographing the Seasons. LC 97-46886. (Center for Nature Photography Ser.). 128p. 1998. 16.95 (*0-8174-3875-0*, Amphoto) Watsn-Guptill.

— The Field Guide to Photographing Trees. LC 95-12035. (Center for Nature Photography Ser.): (Illus.). 128p. 1995. pap. 16.95 (*0-8174-3872-6*, Amphoto) Watsn-Guptill.

— Focus on Flowers: Discovering & Photographing Beauty in Gardens & Wild Places. (Illus.). 228p. 1990. 39.95 (*1-55859-066-8*) Abbeville Pr.

Rokach, Livia. Israel's Sacred Terrorism. unabridged ed. 63p. 1980. reprint ed. pap. 9.00 (*0-945001-26-6*) GSG & Assocs.

Rokach, Livia. Israel's Sacred Terrorism: A Study Based on Moshe Sharett's "Personal Diary" & Other Documents. 3rd rev. ed. LC 85-19946. (Information Papers: No. 23). 90p. 1985. pap. 5.95 (*0-937694-70-3*) Assn Arab-Amer U Grads.

Rokas. Hellenic Insurance Law. 1993. pap. text 56.00 (*90-6544-735-0*) Kluwer Academic.

Rokeach, Barrie. KODAK Guide to Aerial Photography. LC 96-68466. (Illus.). 164p. (Orig.). (C). 1996. pap. 29.95 (*0-87985-766-8*, O-27, Kodak) Saunders Photo.

Rokeach, Milton. Understanding Human Values: Individual & Societal. LC 78-24753. (Illus.). 1979. 35.00 (*0-02-926760-9*) Free Pr.

Rokeah, D. The Yemenite Tradition of the Targum of Lamentations: Critical Text & Analysis of the Variant Readings. 232p. (C). 1982. text 15.00 (*90-04-06560-1*, Pub. by Magnes Pr) Eisenbrauns.

***Rokem, Freddie.** Performing History: Theatrical Representations of the Past in Contemporary Theatre. (Studies in Theatre History & Culture). (Illus.). 264p. 2000. text 42.95 (*0-87745-737-9*) U of Iowa Pr.

Rokem, Freddie. Theatrical Space in Ibsen, Chekhov & Strindberg: Public Forms of Privacy. Brockett, Oscar G., ed. LC 85-16415. (Theater & Dramatic Studies: No. 32). (Illus.). 119p. reprint ed. 36.90 (*0-8357-1707-0*, 207044100089) Bks Demand.

***Roker, Al.** Don't Make Me Stop This Car! Adventures in Fatherhood. LC 00-28467. (Illus.). 256p. 2000. 23.50 (*0-684-86893-8*, Scb1) S&S Trade.

Roker, Debi, jt. auth. see Coleman, John.

Rokhlin, V. A., jt. auth. see Fuks, D. B.

Rokitansky, Friederike Von, see Von Rokitansky, Friederike.

Rokkan, Elizabeth, tr. see Borgen, Johan.

Rokkan, Elizabeth, tr. see Gaarder, Jostein.

Rokkan, Elizabeth, tr. see Sandel, Cora, pseud.

Rokkan, Elizabeth, tr. see Vesaas, Tarjei.

Rokkan, Stein. State Formation, Nation-Building, & Mass Politics in Europe. Kuhnle, Stein et al, eds. LC 95-24645. (Comparative Politics Ser.). (Illus.). 440p. 1999. text 70.00 (*0-19-828032-7*) OUP.

Rokkan, Stein, ed. Comparative Research Across Cultures & Nations. 1968. text 50.00 (*3-10-800123-X*) Mouton.

Rokkan, Stein, et al. Comparative Survey Analysis. (Confluence Ser: Vol. 12). 1969. text 32.35 (*90-279-6246-4*) Mouton.

Rokkan, Stein, jt. ed. see Eisenstadt, Shmuel N.

***Rokke, Ervin & Solomon, Richard H., eds.** Managing Communications: Lessons from Intervention in Africa. 63p. 2000. reprint ed. pap. text 20.00 (*0-7881-8672-8*) DIANE Pub.

Rokke, Ervin J., ed. see Head, Richard G.

Rokke, Kathi R., jt. auth. see Dowell, Andrea C.

Rokkum, Arne. Goddesses, Priestesses & Sisters: Mind, Gender & Power in the Monarchic Tradition of the Ryvleyus. 281p. (C). 1998. text 43.00 (*82-00-12842-3*) Scandnvan Univ Pr.

Roklina, Natalie, ed. Flights into the Past & Present: Polyoty v Proshloe i Nastoiashchee - a Russian Reader. (Illus.). 158p. (Orig.). (C). 1995. pap. text 14.95 (*0-89357-259-4*) Slavica.

Rokne, J., et al. New Computer Methods for Global Optimization. 200p. 1988. text 52.95 (*0-470-21208-X*) P-H.

Rokne, J., jt. auth. see Ratschek, Helmut H.

Rokne, J., tr. see Robert, F.

Rokop, Frank J., jt. auth. see Brandon, Jeffrey L.

Rokosz, Francis M. Procedures for Structuring & Scheduling Sports Tournaments: Elimination, Consolation, Placement, & Round Robin Design. 2nd ed. (Illus.). 300p. (C). 1993. pap., spiral bd. 54.95 (*0-398-05829-6*) C C Thomas.

***Rokosz, Francis M.** Procedures for Structuring & Scheduling Sports Tournaments: Elimination, Consolation, Placement & Round-Robin Design. 3rd ed. LC 99-56507. (Illus.). 2000. spiral bd. write for info. (*0-398-07050-4*) C C Thomas.

Rokosz, Francis M. & Taylor, Howard H. Administrative Procedures for Conducting Recreational Sports Tournaments: From Archery to Wrestling. 2nd ed. LC 93-33148. (Illus.). 418p. (C). 1994. pap., spiral bd. 75.95 (*0-398-05895-4*) C C Thomas.

Rokseth, Yvonne. La Musique d'Orgue au XVe Siecle et au Debut du XVIe. (GER.). xviii, 418p. 1996. reprint ed. 150.00 (*3-487-10036-3*) G Olms Pubs.

Rokumoto, Kahei, ed. Sociological Theories of Law. LC 93-27760. (International Library of Essays in Law & Legal Theory: Vol. 12). xxi, 466 p. (C). 1994. lib. bdg. 150.00 (*0-8147-7425-3*) NYU Pr.

***Rol, Pascal O., et al, eds.** Ophthalmic Technologies IX. 48p. 1999. pap. text 103.00 (*0-8194-3061-7*) SPIE.

Rol, Pascal O., et al, eds. Ophthalmic Technologies VIII, Vol. 3246. 324p. 1998. 89.00 (*0-8194-2685-7*) SPIE.

Rol, Pascal O. & Joos, Karen M., eds. Ophthalmic Technologies VII, Vol. 2971. 226p. 1997. 80.00 (*0-8194-2382-3*) SPIE.

Rola, Fatima & Buster, Dave, eds. Formwork for Contractor's Exams: Sample Questions & Solutions Based on Tables in ACI's Formwork for Concrete (Hurd) 66p. 1985. pap. 7.50 (*0-935715-09-6*, 1586) Construct Bkstore.

Rola-Pleszczynski, Marek, ed. Immunopharmacology of Lymphocytes. (Handbook of Immunopharmacology Ser.). (Illus.). 304p. (C). 1994. text 59.95 (*0-12-593390-8*) Acad Pr.

Rola, Stanislas K. De, see De Rola, Stanislas K.

Rola, Stanislas Klossowski De, see Klossowski de Rola, Stanislas.

Rolak, Loren A. Neurology Secrets: Questions You Will be Asked on Rounds, in the Clinic & on Oral Exams. 2nd ed. LC 98-21152. 1998. write for info. (*1-56053-251-3*) Hanley & Belfus.

Roland. Chanson de Roland. Calin, William C., ed. LC 67-29335. (Medieval French Literature Ser.). (FRE.). (C). 1968. pap. text 12.95 (*0-89197-071-1*) Irvington.

— Communicative American English: Building Fluency & Cultural Understanding Through Functional Conversations & Activities. 192p. 1992. pap., student ed. 18.30 (*0-8442-0720-9*) NTC Contemp Pub Co.

Roland, Alan. Cultural Pluralism & Psychoanalysis: The Asian & North American Experience. LC 96-30239. 228p. (C). 1996. 75.00 (*0-415-91478-7*) Routledge.

— Cultural Pluralism & Psychoanalysis: The Asian & North American Experience. LC 96-30239. 228p. (C). 1996. pap. 20.99 (*0-415-91479-5*) Routledge.

Roland, Alan & Harris, Barbara, eds. Career & Motherhood: Struggles for a New Identity. LC 78-8026. 212p. 1979. 35.95 (*0-87705-372-3*, Kluwer Acad Hman Sci) Kluwer Academic.

Roland, Alex. Underwater Warfare in the Age of Soil. LC 77-74436. (Illus.). 254p. reprint ed. pap. 78.80 (*0-8357-6698-5*, 205687800094) Bks Demand.

Roland, Berta & Waide, Linda. Chicago Review Press NCLEX-PN. rev. ed. LC 98-20596. 252p. 1998. pap. 17.95 (*1-55652-329-7*) Chicago Review.

— Chicago Review Press NCLEX-RN. rev. ed. LC 98-29573. 1998. pap. 17.95 (*1-55652-328-9*) Chicago Review.

Roland, Berta C., jt. auth. see Waide, Linda L.

***Roland, Charles G. & Bernier, Jacques.** Secondary Sources in the History of Canadian Medicine Vol. 2: A Bibliography/Bibliographie de l'Histoire de la Medicine. LC 99-932186. (FRE.). 264p. (C). 2000. text 55.00 (*0-88920-344-X*) Wilfrid Laurier.

Roland, Charles G., jt. auth. see Golden, Richard L.

***Roland, Charles P.** Albert Sidney Johnston: Soldier of Three Republics. rev. ed. (Illus.). 400p. 2000. reprint ed. pap. 19.00 (*0-8131-9000-2*) U Pr of Ky.

Roland, Charles P. An American Iliad: The Story of the Civil War. 272p. (C). 1991. pap. 30.31 (*0-07-053594-9*) McGraw.

— An American Iliad: The Story of the Civil War. LC 90-38392. (Illus.). 304p. 1991. text 32.00 (*0-8131-1737-2*) U Pr of Ky.

— Confederacy. LC 60-12573. (Chicago History of American Civilization Ser.). (Illus.). 232p. 1962. pap. text 23.00 (*0-226-72451-4*, CHAC18) U Ch Pr.

— The Improbable Era: The South Since World War II. rev. ed. LC 76-46033. (Illus.). 240p. 1976. pap. 17.00 (*0-8131-0139-5*) U Pr of Ky.

— Louisiana Sugar Plantations During the Civil War. LC 97-24368. (Illus.). 160p. 1997. pap. text 11.95 (*0-8071-2221-1*) La State U Pr.

— Reflections on Lee: A Historian's Assessment. LC 95-3685. (Illus.). 128p. 1995. 16.95 (*0-8117-0719-9*) Stackpole.

***Roland, Charles Pierce.** Albert Sidney Johnston: Jefferson Davis's Greatest General. LC 99-56314. (Civil War Campaigns & Commanders Ser.). (Illus.). 2000. pap. 12.95 (*1-893114-20-1*) McWhiney Found.

— Albert Sidney Johnston, Soldier of Three Republics. LC 99-89855. 2000. pap. write for info. (*0-8131-0990-6*) U Pr of Ky.

Roland, Christopher, et al. Corporate Experiential Learning. 256p. 1995. per., boxed set 50.00 (*0-7872-0308-4*) Kendall-Hunt.

Roland, Christopher P. Children's Responsibilities & Safety Measures: Children's Education, Motivational & Safety Book. Bey, Malik R., ed. (Illus.). 20p. (Orig.). (J). (gr. k-5). 1997. pap. 3.99 (*1-890301-00-0*) M Bey.

Roland, Christopher P., Jr. The Two Brothers That Aren't the Same. Bey, Malik R., ed. (Illus.). (Orig.). (J). (gr. k-4). 1997. pap. 1.99 (*0-9656137-8-X*) M Bey.

Roland, Daisy & Goodridge, Sandi, eds. North Carolina UFOs: E. T. Tales from the Tar Heel State. 94p. 1998. pap. 10.00 (*0-9649370-3-4*) Shadowbox.

Roland, David. The Confident Performer. LC 98-20118. 98p. 1998. pap. 15.95 (*0-325-00092-1*) Heinemann.

Roland, David, ed. see DeBlij, Harm J.

Roland de la Platiere, Jeanne M. Appeal to Impartial Posterity, 1795. LC 90-36680. (Revolution & Romanticism Ser.). 364p. 1990. reprint ed. 55.00 (*1-85477-054-3*) Continuum.

Roland de la Platiere, Marie J. An Appeal to Impartial Posterity, 2 vols., Set. LC 74-37718. reprint ed. 125.00 (*0-404-56826-2*) AMS Pr.

Roland De La Platiere, Marie J. The Private Memoirs of Madame Roland. 2nd ed. LC 78-37719. (Women of Letters Ser.). (Illus.). reprint ed. 47.50 (*0-404-56829-7*) AMS Pr.

Roland, Dewitt. Who's Boss of the Church? Mayes, Eric A., Jr., ed. & photos by by. (Illus.). 30p. 1997. pap. 3.99 (*1-890025-05-4*) B E A M Oklhma City.

Roland, Donna. Grandfather's Stories. (Illus.). (Orig.). (J). (gr. k-3). 1993. 12.00 (*0-685-73481-1*); VHS 32.00 (*0-685-73482-X*) Open My World.

— Grandfather's Stories. (Illus.). (Orig.). (J). (gr. k-3). 1995. audio 5.95 (*0-685-73483-8*) Open My World.

— Grandfather's Stories. (Illus.). 28p. (Orig.). (J). (gr. k-3). 1997. pap. 5.95 (*0-941996-00-X*) Open My World.

— Grandfather's Stories from Cambodia. (J). (gr. k-3). 1984. pap. 5.95 (*0-941996-05-0*) Open My World.

— Grandfather's Stories from Germany. (J). (gr. k). 1984. teacher ed. 6.50 (*0-941996-15-8*) Open My World.

— Grandfather's Stories from Germany. (J). (gr. k-3). 1984. pap. 5.95 (*0-941996-03-4*) Open My World.

— Grandfather's Stories from Mexico. (J). (gr. k-3). 1986. teacher ed. 6.50 (*0-941996-16-6*); pap. 5.95 (*0-941996-09-3*) Open My World.

— More of Grandfather's Stories. (Grandfather's Stories Ser.). (Illus.). 25p. (Orig.). (J). (gr. k-3). 1995. teacher ed. 6.50 (*0-941996-13-1*) Open My World.

— More of Grandfather's Stories. (Grandfather's Stories Ser.). (Illus.). 25p. (Orig.). (J). (gr. k-3). 1997. pap. 5.95 (*0-941996-02-6*) Open My World.

— More of Grandfather's Stories from Cambodia. (J). (gr. k-3). 1984. teacher ed. 6.50 (*0-941996-14-X*); pap. 5.95 (*0-941996-06-9*) Open My World.

— More of Grandfather's Stories from Germany. (J). (gr. k-3). 1984. pap. 5.95 (*0-941996-04-2*) Open My World.

— More of Grandfather's Stories from Mexico. (J). (gr. k-3). 1986. pap. 5.95 (*0-941996-10-7*) Open My World.

— More of Grandfather's Stories from the Philippines. (J). (gr. k-3). 1985. teacher ed. 6.50 (*0-941996-17-4*); pap. 5.95 (*0-941996-08-5*) Open My World.

— More of Grandfather's Stories from Vietnam. (J). (gr. k-3). 1985. pap. 5.95 (*0-941996-12-3*) Open My World.

Roland, George, jt. auth. see Reed, Otis L.

***Roland, Gerard.** Transition & Economics: Politics, Markets & Firms. LC 00-28246. (Illus.). 745p. 2000. 45.00 (*0-262-18203-3*) MIT Pr.

Roland, Harold E. & Moriarity, Brian. Systems Safety Engineering Man. 2nd ed. LC 90-12109. 384p. 1990. 150.00 (*0-471-61816-0*) Wiley.

R

R

Roland, Harold E. & Moriarty, Brian. System Safety Engineering & Management. (Wiley Interscience Ser.). 368p. 1983. 34.95 (*0-317-01156-1*, 1-09695-4) DeLeuw-Cather Co.

Roland, Helen E. California Endangered Species Act: Overview of Issues in the Reform Debate. 159p. 1996. pap. write for info. (*1-58703-047-0*, CRB-96-003) CA St Libry.

— Residential Common Interest Developments: An Overview. 65p. 1998. pap. write for info. (*1-58703-084-5*, CRB-98-006) CA St Libry.

Roland, Henri. Dictionnaire des Expressions Juridiques. (FRE.). 440p. 1983. pap. 36.95 (*0-7859-8116-0*, 2859341102) Fr & Eur.

***Roland, Hubert.** Die Deutsche Literarische "kriegskolonie" in Belgien, 1914-1918. xvii, 343p. 1999. 48.95 (*3-906761-71-1*) P Lang Pubng.

Roland, Hubert, jt. auth. see Leonardy, Ernst.

Roland, Jacques, et al, eds. Extragalactic Radio Sources: From Beams to Jets. (Illus.). 388p. (C). 1992. text 80.00 (*0-521-41602-7*) Cambridge U Pr.

Roland, Joan G. The Jewish Communities of India: Identity in a Colonial Era. 2nd ed. LC 98-12272. 370p. 1998. pap. text 29.95 (*0-7658-0439-5*) Transaction Pubs.

— Jews in British India: Identity in a Colonial Era. LC 88-40113. (Tauber Institute for the Study of European Jewry Ser.: Vol. 9). 368p. 1989. reprint ed. pap. 114.10 (*0-608-03013-9*, 206346300006) Bks Demand.

Roland, John. Human Biology Activities Kit: Ready-to-Use Lessons & Worksheets for General Science & Health. 352p. 1993. pap. text 27.95 (*0-87628-121-8*) Ctr Appl Res.

Roland, L., jt. auth. see Blum, Werner.

Roland, La Chanson de, see La Chanson de Roland.

Roland, Lillian D. Manipulating Language: How to Move Students Successfully from Composition to Literary Analysis. 284p. (C). 1997. per. 47.95 (*0-7872-3477-X*) Kendall-Hunt.

Roland, Lillian D. Women in Robbe-Grillet: A Study in Thematics & Diegetics. LC 91-43247. (American University Studies: Romance Languages & Literature: Ser. II, Vol. 177). IX, 302p. (C). 1993. text 59.95 (*0-8204-1643-6*) P Lang Pubng.

Roland-Manuel, Claude. Histoire de la Musique, 2 vols. (FRE.). 2260p. 1973. 145.00 (*0-7859-4542-3*) Fr & Eur.

— Histoire de la Musique, 2 vols., 1. (Historique Ser.). 69.95 (*0-686-56457-X*) Fr & Eur.

— Histoire de la Musique, 2 vols., 2. (Historique Ser.). 65.50 (*0-686-56458-8*) Fr & Eur.

— Histoire de la Musique, Vol. 2. (Historique Ser.). 1894p. 65.50 (*0-686-56459-6*) Fr & Eur.

— Histoire de la Musique, Vol. 2: Du XVIIIe Siecle a Nos Jours. (FRE.). 1896p. 1975. lib. bdg. 145.00 (*0-7859-3773-0*, 2070104044) Fr & Eur.

Roland, Marie-Jeanne P. Memoirs of Madame Roland: A Heroine of French Revolution. Shuckburgh, E. S., tr. from FRE. (Illus.). 264p. 1992. pap. 12.95 (*1-55921-015-X*) Moyer Bell.

Roland, Martin & Coulter, Angela, eds. Hospital Referrals. LC 92-19067. (Oxford General Practice Ser.: No. 22). (Illus.). 234p. 1993. pap. text 35.00 (*0-19-262174-2*) OUP.

Roland, Montie. The Businessman's Guide to OSHA. 256p. 1996. pap. 29.95 (*0-9651486-0-2*) SBC Safety.

Roland, Nelson, jt. auth. see D'Hondt, Jacques.

***Roland, Paul.** Angels. (Guides Ser.). 144p. 2000. pap. 6.95 (*0-7499-2020-3*, Pub. by Piatkus Bks) London Brdge.

— How to Meditate: An Illustrated Guide to Calming the Mind & Relaxing the Body. (Illus.). 128p. 2000. pap. 16.95 (*1-56975-227-3*) Ulysses Pr.

— Kabbalah. (Guides Ser.). 144p. 2000. pap. 6.95 (*0-7499-1957-4*, Pub. by Piatkus Bks) London Brdge.

— New Age Living: A Guide to Principles, Practices & Beliefs. 2000. 29.95 (*0-600-59768-7*, Pub. by Hamlyn Publishing Group Ltd) Sterling.

Roland, Paul. Revelations: Wisdom of the Ages. LC 95-61354. (Illus.). 160p. (Orig.). 1995. pap. 17.95 (*1-56975-047-5*) Ulysses Pr.

***Roland, Paul.** Teach Yourself Rock & Pop. 192p. 2000. pap. 9.95 (*0-8442-2869-9*, Teach Yrslf) NTC Contemp Pub Co.

Roland, Paul. Yakovlev Yak-22 (Bb-22) (World War II Monograph Ser.: No. 16). (Illus.). 20p. 1998. 15.00 (*1-57638-148-X*, M16-H); pap. 5.00 (*1-57638-147-1*, M16-S) Merriam Pr.

***Roland, Paul, ed.** Jazz Singers: The Great Song Stylists in Their Own Words. (Illus.). 160p. 2000. pap. 24.95 (*0-8230-8342-X*, Billboard Bks) Watsn-Guptill.

Roland, Pere E. Brain Activation. (Series in Neuroscience). 600p. 1993. 164.95 (*0-471-50867-5*) Wiley.

— Brain Activation. 600p. 1997. pap. 69.95 (*0-471-18441-1*) Wiley.

Roland, Peter, jt. auth. see Meyerhoff, William L.

Roland, Peter S. Tympanoplasty: Repair of the Tympanic Membrane. LC 99-14321. (Self-Instructional Package Ser.). (Illus.). 89p. 1999. 25.00 (*1-56772-071-4*, 5506340) AAO-HNS.

Roland, Peter S. & Marple, Bradley F. Diagnosis & Management of Acoustic Neuroma. LC 98-14985. (Self-Instructional Package Ser.). (Illus.). 108p. 1998. pap. text 25.00 (*1-56772-060-9*, 5506320) AAO-HNS.

Roland, Regina & Sandberg, Jane L. A Hat for All Seasons: Fall & Winter. (ECS Activity Book for Language Arts Ser.). (Illus.). 128p. (Orig.). 1994. pap. 15.95 (*0-944459-96-X*) ECS Lrn Systs.

— A Hat for All Seasons: Spring & Summer. (ECS Activity Book Ser.). (Illus.). 96p. 1994. pap. 14.95 (*1-57022-002-6*) ECS Lrn Systs.

Roland, Regina E., jt. auth. see Sandberg, Jane L.

Roland, Richard G. Pilgrim in Rome. LC 94-92066. (Illus.). 80p. 1994. per. 18.75 (*0-9640694-0-7*) R G Roland.

Roland, Susan. France, the Crossroads of Europe. 2nd ed. LC 96-53373. (Discovering Our Heritage Ser.). (J). 1998. lib. bdg. write for info. (*0-382-39863-7*, Dillon Silver Burdett) Silver Burdett Pr.

Roland, Timothy. Come Down Now, Flying Cow! LC 96-42560. (J). 1997. lib. bdg. 11.99 (*0-679-98110-1*, Pub. by Random Bks Yng Read) Random.

Rolandelli, Rolando H., jt. auth. see Rombeau, John L.

Rolandi, L., jt. auth. see Blum, Werner.

Rolando, Akika, tr. see Lukas, Larry.

***Rolando, Jorge A.** Manual de MS FrontPage 2000 en Espanol - Spanish con CD-ROM: Diseno, Publicacion y Mantenimiento de Sitios Web. (Manuales para PC Users Ser.). (SPA., Illus.). 255p. 1999. pap. 19.90 incl. cd-rom (*987-526-017-7*, Pub. by MP Ediciones) Am Wholesale.

Rolater, Fred S. Japanese Americans. (American Voices Ser.). 112p. (J). 1991. lib. bdg. 18.95 (*0-86593-138-0*) Rourke Corp.

Rolbein, Seth. About Face: Cleanup, Conflict & New Directions on Cape Cod. Kahn, Hamilton, ed. (Illus.). 160p. 1998. pap. 12.00 (*0-9645260-1-8*) APCC.

— The Enemy Within: The Struggle to Clean up Cape Cod's Military SuperFund Site. 177p. (Orig.). 1995. pap. 12.00 (*0-9645260-0-X*) APCC.

Rolbin, Ann. Basic Russian Vocabulary: A Handy Reference of Everyday Words Arranged by Topic. LC 98-22737. (RUS., Illus.). 224p. 1998. pap. 14.06 (*0-8442-4297-7*, 42977, Passprt Bks) NTC Contemp Pub Co.

— First Reader in Russian. (BBC Phrase Books for Teenagers). (RUS., Illus.). 64p. 1994. pap. 9.94 (*0-8442-4281-0*, 42810, Passprt Bks) NTC Contemp Pub Co.

— First Reader in Russian: Beginning. (RUS., Illus.). 64p. (C). Date not set. pap., teacher ed. 5.60 (*0-8442-4282-9*, X4282-9) NTC Contemp Pub Co.

Rolcik, Karen A. How to Probate an Estate in Texas. 2nd ed. LC 98-39684. (Legal Survival Guides Ser.). 128p. 1998. pap. 19.95 (*1-57071-418-5*) Sourcebks.

— Living Trusts & Simple Ways to Avoid Probate. 2nd ed. LC 97-45084. (Legal Survival Guides Ser.). 176p. 1998. pap. 19.95 (*1-57071-336-7*) Sourcebks.

Rolcik, Karen A. & Haman, Edward A. How to File for Divorce in Texas. 2nd ed. LC 97-42874. (Legal Survival Guides Ser.). 146p. 1998. pap. 19.95 (*1-57071-330-8*) Sourcebks.

Rolcik, Karen A. & Warda, Mark. How to Make a Texas Will. 2nd ed. LC 98-8581. (Legal Survival Guides Ser.). 96p. 1998. pap. 12.95 (*1-57071-417-7*) Sourcebks.

***Rolcik, Karen Ann & Warda, Mark.** How to Form a Corporation in Texas: With Forms. 2nd ed. LC 00-29704. (Legal Survival Guides Ser.). 208p. 2000. pap. 19.95 (*1-57248-114-5*, Sphinx Pubng) Sourcebks.

Rold, Cindy. Real Life Guide to Buying Your First Home: How to Find, Negotiate & Finance Your New Home! (Real Life Ser.). 1998. pap. 16.95 (*1-890586-07-2*) Pipeline Pr.

Rold, Cynthia L. Real Life Guide to Graduate & Professional School: How to Choose, Apply for & Finance Your Advanced Degree! Foster, Kerry & Poole, Laura, eds. (Real Life Guide Ser.). 300p. 1998. pap. 27.95 (*1-890586-05-6*) Pipeline Pr.

Rold, Jim. First Degree Love: A Novel of Euthanasia. 208p. (Orig.). 1992. pap. 9.95 (*0-89407-106-8*) Strawberry Hill.

Roldan, Arturo A., jt. ed. see Vermeulen, Han.

Roldan, Aurora H., ed. Gifted & Talented Children, Youth & Adults: Their Social Perspectives & Culture. 563p. 1985. pap. 15.00 (*0-89824-047-6*) Trillium Pr.

Roldan, Marggi, ed. College Facts Chart. 39th rev. ed. 92p. 1994. pap. 5.00 (*0-9614726-6-9*) Natl Beta Club.

— College Facts Chart. 41st rev. ed. 92p. 1996. pap. 7.00 (*0-9614726-8-5*) Natl Beta Club.

— College Facts Chart, 1996-1997. 40th rev. ed. 92p. 1996. pap. 7.00 (*0-9614726-7-7*) Natl Beta Club.

Roldan, Martha, jt. auth. see Beneria, Lourdes.

Roldan-Ventura, Diana. God Comes at 11:59:59. 2000. pap. 7.00 (*0-8059-4801-5*) Dorrance.

Roldban, Jorge, et al. The Financing Requirements of Nature & Heritage Tourism in the Caribbean. LC 96-149711. 56 p. 1993. write for info. (*0-8270-3523-3*) OAS.

Rolde, Neil. The Baxters of Maine: Downeast Visionaries. LC 97-29670. (Illus.). 386p. 1997. 24.95 (*0-88448-190-5*); pap. 14.95 (*0-88448-191-3*) Tilbury Hse.

— An Illustrated History of Maine. LC 95-61976. (Illus.). 207p. 1995. 55.00 (*0-913764-26-4*) Maine St Mus.

— Maine: A Narrative History. (Illus.). 368p. (Orig.). 1990. pap. 19.95 (*0-88448-069-0*) Tilbury Hse.

Role of Karl Marx in the Development of Contempora. Marx & Contemporary Scientific Thought: Proceedings. (Publications of the International Social Science Council: No. 13). 1970. 69.25 (*90-279-6276-6*) Mouton.

Role, Reague, jt. auth. see Jr. League of Raleigh Staff.

***Roleder, George.** Flights of Bird Fancy. LC 99-93670. 2000. pap. 8.95 (*0-533-13117-0*) Vantage.

Rolef, Susan H. & Shim. Political Dictionaries of the Arab World & State of Israel, 2 vols. 1988. 90.00 (*0-02-916423-0*) S&S Trade.

***Roleff, Tamara L.** The Atom Bomb. LC 99-34739. (Turning Points in World History Ser.). 288p. 2000. 17.45 (*0-7377-0215-X*); pap. 13.96 (*0-7377-0214-1*) Greenhaven.

Roleff, Tamara L. Business Ethics. (At Issue Ser.). 112p. 1996. lib. bdg. 18.70 (*1-56510-385-8*) Greenhaven.

— Business Ethics. (At Issue Ser.). 112p. (J). (gr. 5-12). 1996. pap. 11.20 (*1-56510-384-X*) Greenhaven.

***Roleff, Tamara L.** Civil Liberties: Opposing Viewpoints. LC 98-11808. (Opposing Viewpoints Ser.). 208p. 1999. pap. 17.45 (*1-56510-936-8*) Greenhaven.

— Civil Liberties: Opposing Viewpoints. LC 98-11808. (Opposing Viewpoints Ser.). (Illus.). 208p. (YA). (gr. 9 up). 1999. lib. bdg. 27.45 (*1-56510-937-6*) Greenhaven.

— Crime & Criminals. LC 99-29108. (Opposing Viewpoints Ser.). 312p. (gr. 9-12). 2000. pap. 17.45 (*0-7377-0120-X*) Greenhaven.

— Crime & Criminals. LC 99-29108. (Opposing Viewpoints Ser.). 192p. (YA). (gr. 9-12). 2000. lib. bdg. 27.45 (*0-7377-0121-8*) Greenhaven.

— Domestic Violence. LC 99-47825. (Opposing Viewpoints Ser.). 360p. (YA). 2000. 17.45 (*0-7377-0346-6*) Greenhaven.

— Domestic Violence: Opposing Viewpoints. LC 99-47825. (Opposing Viewpoints Ser.). 360p. (YA). 2000. pap. 13.96 (*0-7377-0345-8*) Greenhaven.

Roleff, Tamara L. Gay Rights. LC 96-36298. (Current Controversies Ser.). (J). (gr. 5-12). 1997. pap. 16.20 (*1-56510-531-1*); lib. bdg. 26.20 (*1-56510-532-X*) Greenhaven.

***Roleff, Tamara L.** Guns & Crime. LC 99-37174. (At Issue Ser.). 128p. (J). (gr. 9-12). 2000. pap. 13.70 (*0-7377-0152-8*); lib. bdg. 21.20 (*0-7377-0153-6*) Greenhaven.

— Hate Crimes. LC 00-37205. 2000. pap. write for info. (*0-7377-0454-3*) Greenhaven.

Roleff, Tamara L. The Homeless: Opposing Viewpoints. (Opposing Viewpoints Ser.). (Illus.). 240p. 1996. pap. text 16.20 (*1-56510-360-2*) Greenhaven.

Roleff, Tamara L. The Homeless: Opposing Viewpoints. (Opposing Viewpoints Ser.). (Illus.). 240p. (J). (gr. 5-12). 1996. lib. bdg. 26.20 (*1-56510-361-0*) Greenhaven.

Roleff, Tamara L. The Legal System: Opposing Viewpoints. 1996. pap. 16.20 (*1-56510-404-8*); lib. bdg. 26.20 (*1-56510-405-6*) Greenhaven.

***Roleff, Tamara L.** Pollution: Opposing Viewpoints. LC 99-17677. (Opposing Viewpoints Ser.). 192p. (YA). (gr. 9-12). 2000. lib. bdg. 27.45 (*0-7377-0135-8*) Greenhaven.

Roleff, Tamara L. The Rights of Animals. LC 98-45934. (Current Controversies Ser.). 320p. 1999. pap. 17.45 (*0-7377-0068-8*); lib. bdg. 27.45 (*0-7377-0069-6*) Greenhaven.

***Roleff, Tamara L.** Sex. LC 00-34128. (Teen Decisions Ser.). 2001. pap. write for info. (*0-7377-0494-2*) Greenhaven.

— Teen Suicide. (At Issues Ser.). 128p. (YA). 2000. 13.70 (*1-56510-691-1*); pap. 10.96 (*1-56510-690-3*) Greenhaven.

— Teen Suicide: Opposing Viewpoints. LC 99-55610. 2000. 21.81 (*0-7377-0327-X*) Greenhaven.

— Teen Suicide: Opposing Viewpoints. LC 99-55610. (At Issue Ser.). 2000. pap. 18.96 (*0-7377-0328-8*) Greenhaven.

Roleff, Tamara L., ed. Abortion: Opposing Viewpoints. LC 96-17342. (Opposing Viewpoints Ser.). (Illus.). 1996. lib. bdg. 26.20 (*1-56510-506-0*) Greenhaven.

— Abortion: Opposing Viewpoints. LC 96-17342. (Opposing Viewpoints Ser.). (Illus.). 1996. pap. 16.20 (*1-56510-505-2*) Greenhaven.

— Biomedical Ethics: Opposing Viewpoints. LC 97-51374. (Opposing Viewpoints Ser.). (YA). (gr. 5-12). 1998. pap. 16.20 (*1-56510-792-6*); lib. bdg. 26.20 (*1-56510-793-4*) Greenhaven.

— Gay Marriage. LC 97-26614. (At Issue Ser.). (YA). (gr. 5 up). 1997. pap. 13.96 (*1-56510-692-X*); lib. bdg. 20.96 (*1-56510-693-8*) Greenhaven.

— Gun Control: Opposing Viewpoints. LC 96-48029. (Opposing Viewpoints Ser.). (Illus.). (YA). (gr. 5-12). 1997. pap. 16.20 (*1-56510-662-8*); lib. bdg. 26.20 (*1-56510-663-6*) Greenhaven.

— Immigration: Opposing Viewpoints. LC 98-5034. (Opposing Viewpoints Ser.). (YA). (gr. 5-12). 1998. lib. bdg. 26.20 (*1-56510-799-3*) Greenhaven.

***Roleff, Tamara L., ed.** Immigration: Opposing Viewpoints. LC 98-5034. (Opposing Viewpoints Ser.). 218p. (YA). (gr. 5-12). 1998. pap. 16.20 (*1-56510-798-5*) Greenhaven.

— Native American Rights. LC 97-37078. (Current Controversies Ser.). 208p. (J). (gr. 5-12). 1997. pap. 16.20 (*1-56510-684-9*); lib. bdg. 26.20 (*1-56510-685-7*) Greenhaven.

Roleff, Tamara L., ed. Police Brutality. LC 98-26633. (Current Controversies Ser.). 226p. (YA). (gr. 9-12). 1998. lib. bdg. 27.45 (*0-7377-0013-0*) Greenhaven.

***Roleff, Tamara L., ed.** Police Brutality. LC 98-26633. (Current Controversies Ser.). 170p. (YA). (gr. 9-12). 1998. pap. 17.45 (*0-7377-0012-2*) Greenhaven.

— Pollution: Opposing Viewpoints. LC 99-17677. (Opposing Viewpoints Ser.). 312p. (YA). (gr. 9-12). 2000. pap. 17.45 (*0-7377-0134-X*) Greenhaven.

Roleff, Tamara L., ed. Sex Education. LC 98-35008. (At Issue Ser.). 96p. (YA). (gr. 9-12). 1998. lib. bdg. 21.20 (*0-7377-0009-2*) Greenhaven.

***Roleff, Tamara L., ed.** Sex Education. LC 98-35008. (At Issue Ser.). 96p. (YA). (gr. 9-12). 1998. pap. 12.45 (*0-7377-0008-4*) Greenhaven.

Roleff, Tamara L., ed. Suicide: Opposing Viewpoints. LC 97-6697. (Opposing Viewpoints Ser.). (Illus.). (J). (gr. 5-12). 1997. lib. bdg. 26.20 (*1-56510-665-2*) Greenhaven.

Roleff, Tamara L., ed. Suicide: Opposing Viewpoints. LC 97-6697. (Opposing Viewpoints Ser.). (Illus.). 192p. (ps up). 1997. pap. 16.20 (*1-56510-664-4*) Greenhaven.

— War. LC 98-32019. (Opposing Viewpoints Ser.). 312p. (YA). (gr. 7-12). 1999. pap. 17.45 (*0-7377-0060-2*) Greenhaven.

— War: Opposing Viewpoints. LC 98-32019. (Opposing Viewpoints Ser.). 312p. 1999. lib. bdg. 27.45 (*0-7377-0061-0*) Greenhaven.

Roleff, Tamara L., et al, eds. Global Warming: Opposing Viewpoints. LC 96-25705. (Opposing Viewpoints Ser.). (Illus.). 16.20p. (J). (gr. 5-12). 1997. pap. 13.96 (*1-56510-511-7*); lib. bdg. 26.20 (*1-56510-512-5*) Greenhaven.

***Roleff, Tamara L., et al, eds.** Hate Groups: Opposing Viewpoints. LC 98-36586. (Opposing Viewpoints Ser.). (Illus.). (YA). (gr. 9-12). 1998. pap. 16.20 (*1-56510-942-2*); lib. bdg. 26.20 (*1-56510-943-0*) Greenhaven.

— Tobacco & Smoking: Opposing Viewpoints. LC 97-51730. (Opposing Viewpoints Ser.). (J). (gr. 5-12). 1998. lib. bdg. 26.20 (*1-56510-803-5*) Greenhaven.

***Roleff, Tamara L., et al, eds.** Tobacco & Smoking: Opposing Viewpoints. LC 97-51730. (Opposing Viewpoints Ser.). (YA). (gr. 5-12). 1998. pap. 16.20 (*1-56510-802-7*) Greenhaven.

Roleff, Tamara L. & Cozic, Charles P., eds. AIDS: Opposing Viewpoints. LC 97-28424. (Opposing Viewpoints Ser.). (Illus.). (J). (gr. 5-12). 1997. pap. 16.20 (*1-56510-666-0*) Greenhaven.

Roleff, Tamara L. & Cozic, Charles P., eds. AIDS: Opposing Viewpoints. LC 97-28424. (Opposing Viewpoints Ser.). (Illus.). (J). (gr. 5-12). 1997. lib. bdg. 26.20 (*1-56510-667-9*) Greenhaven.

***Roleff, Tamara L. & Egendorf, Laura K.** Mental Illness. LC 99-55632. (Opposing Viewpoints Ser.). 360p. (YA). 2000. 17.45 (*0-7377-0348-2*) Greenhaven.

— Mental Illness. LC 99-55632. (Opposing Viewpoints Ser.). 360p. (YA). 2000. pap. 13.96 (*0-7377-0347-4*) Greenhaven.

Roleff, Tamara L. & Williams, Mary E., eds. Marriage & Divorce. LC 97-4941. (Current Controversies Ser.). (J). (gr. 5-12). 1997. pap. 16.20 (*1-56510-567-2*); lib. bdg. 26.20 (*1-56510-568-0*) Greenhaven.

Roleff, Tamara L., jt. ed. see Williams, Mary E.

Rolek, Loren A. & Harati, Yadollah. Neuro-Immunology for the Clinician. LC 96-50466. 440p. 1997. text 97.00 (*0-7506-9616-8*) Buttrwrth-Heinemann.

Rolek, Michiko J. Mental Fitness: Basic Workouts for Mind, Body & Souls. 1996. pap. text 14.95 (*0-8348-0373-9*) Weatherhill.

Rolen, Mats, ed. see Svedin, Uno, et al.

***Rolens, Sharon.** Worthy's Town. 304p. 2000. 22.95 (*1-882593-35-9*) Bridge Wrks.

Roles, Patricia. Facing Teenage Pregnancy: A Handbook for the Pregnant Teen. 1990. 14.95 (*0-87868-368-2*) Child Welfare.

Roles, Patricia E. Saying Goodbye to a Baby Vol. 1: The Birthparent's Guide to Loss & Grief in Adoption, Vol. 1. 1989. pap. 12.95 (*0-87868-387-9*) Child Welfare.

— Saying Goodbye to a Baby Vol. 2: A Counselor's Guide to Birthparent Loss & Grief in Adoption, Vol. 2. 34p. 1989. pap. 10.95 (*0-87868-393-3*) Child Welfare.

***Rolett, Barry Vladimir.** Hanamiai: Prehistoric Colonization & Cultural Change in the Marquesa. (YUPA Ser.: Vol. 81). (Illus.). 277p. (C). 1998. pap. 25.00 (*0-913516-18-X*) Yale U Anthro.

Rolett, Karin. Organizing Community Resources in Sexuality Counseling & Family Planning for the Retarded: A Community Workers' Manual. 1976. pap. 3.00 (*0-89055-118-9*) Carolina Pop Ctr.

***Roletto, Martha.** Calculost? A Guide to Surviving First Semester Calculus. (Illus.). iii, 143p. 2000. spiral bd. write for info. (*0-615-11536-5*) Roletto Math.

Rolewicz, Stefan. Functional Analysis & Control Theory: Linear Systems. (C). 1987. text 326.50 (*90-277-2186-6*) Kluwer Academic.

— Metric Linear Spaces. 1985. text 269.50 (*90-277-1480-0*) Kluwer Academic.

Rolewicz, Stefan, jt. auth. see Pallaschke, Diethard.

Roley, Paul, ed. & comment see Egger, Bruce E. & Otts, Lee M.

Rolf. Finite Mathematics. 4th ed. 186p. 1998. pap. 20.00 (*0-03-022072-6*) SCP.

— Graphing Calculator Manual to Accompany Finite Mathematics. 4th ed. 176p. 1998. 15.00 (*0-03-020947-1*) SCP.

— Instructor's Manual to Accompany Finite Mathematics. 4th ed. 452p. 1998. 20.00 (*0-03-022069-6*) SCP.

— Inventory of World Topographic Mapping: Eastern Europe, Asia, Oceania & Antartica, Vol. 3. LC 89-7760. 466p. 1993. 342.50 (*1-85861-034-6*) Elsevier.

— Student Solutions Manual to Accompany Finite Mathematics. 4th ed. 208p. 1998. 13.00 (*0-03-022073-4*) SCP.

Rolf, Eckard. Die Funktionen der Gebrauchstextsorten. (Grundlagen der Kommunikation & Kognition (Foundations of Communication & Cognition) Ser.). (GER.). xii, 339p. (C). 1993. lib. bdg. 120.00 (*3-11-012551-X*) De Gruyter.

Rolf, F. James & Sokal, Robert R. Statistical Tables. 3rd ed. LC 94-11121. 208p. (C). 1994. pap. text 22.95 (*0-7167-2412-X*) W H Freeman.

Rolf, Gerald. The Event. 350p. 1997. pap. 12.95 (*0-9661836-0-6*) G Rolf.

— The Event. 350p. Date not set. pap. 12.95 (*1-887150-13-7*) Millennia Bks.

Rolf, Gustavsen & Streeck, Renate. Training Therapy: Prophylaxis & Rehabilitation. 2nd rev. ed. Gilliar, Wolfgang G., tr. from GER. & adapted by by. LC 92-48359. (Flexibook Ser.). (Illus.). 240p. 1993. pap. text 28.00 (*0-86577-483-8*) Thieme Med Pubs.

Rolf, Howard. Finite Mathematics. 4th ed. 672p. (C). 1998. text 85.50 (*0-03-021314-2*, Pub. by SCP) Harcourt.

Rolf, Howard L. & Williams, Gareth. Explorations in Finite Mathematics. 3rd ed. 68p. (C). 1994. text, spiral bd. 15.00 incl. 3.5 hd (*0-697-24113-0*, WCB McGr Hill) McGrw-H Hghr Educ.

— Finite Mathematics. 624p. (C). 1989. text 15.63 (*0-697-07423-4*, WCB McGr Hill) McGrw-H Hghr Educ.

An Asterisk (*) at the beginning of an entry indicates that the title is appearing for the first time.

— Finite Mathematics. 2nd ed. 720p. (C). 1991. text 55.00 (*0-697-08577-5*, WCB McGr Hill) McGrw-H Hghr Educ.

— Finite Mathematics. 3rd ed. 672p. (C). 1993. text 58.13 (*0-697-16171-4*, WCB McGr Hill) McGrw-H Hghr Educ.

— Finite Mathematics. 3rd ed. 672p. (C). 1993. text, teacher ed. 19.38 (*0-697-16173-0*, WCB McGr Hill) McGrw-H Hghr Educ.

Rolf, Ida P. Rolfing: Reestablishing the Natural Alignment & Structural Integration of the Human Body for Vitality & Well-Being. (Illus.). 304p. 1989. pap. 24.95 (*0-89281-335-0*, Heal Arts VT) Inner Tradit.

— Rolfing: The Integration of Human Structures. LC 76-52192. (Illus.). 1977. 27.50 (*0-930422-10-4*) Dennis-Landman.

— Rolfing & Physical Reality. 224p. 1990. pap. 14.95 (*0-89281-380-6*) Inner Tradit.

— What in the World Is Rolfing? 1975. pap. 4.00 (*0-930422-05-8*) Dennis-Landman.

Rolf, Jon, et al, eds. Risk & Protective Factors in the Development of Psychopathology. (Illus.). 570p. (C). 1990. text 74.95 (*0-521-35099-9*) Cambridge U Pr.

— Risk & Protective Factors in the Development of Psychopathology. (Illus.). 570p. (C). 1993. pap. text 27.95 (*0-521-43972-8*) Cambridge U Pr.

Rolf, Robert T. & Gillespie, John K., eds. Alternative Japanese Drama: Ten Plays. LC 92-5185. (Illus.). 520p. 1992. pap. 15.00 (*0-8248-1379-0*) UH Pr.

Rolf, Shane De, see De Rolf, Shane.

Rolfe. The Sacred Vessel. 189p. 1978. 8.50 (*0-85435-324-0*, Pub. by C W Daniel) Natl Bk Netwk.

Rolfe, Bari. Actions Speak Louder: A Workbook for Actors. LC 92-80826. (Illus.). 68p. (YA). (gr. 9-12). 1992. pap., wbk. ed. 10.00 (*0-932456-07-3*) Personabks.

— Behind the Mask. LC 77-76975. (Illus.). 66p. 1977. pap. 8.00 (*0-932456-01-4*) Personabks.

— Commedia Dell'Arte: A Scene Study Book. LC 77-73190. (Illus.). 100p. (YA). (gr. 9-12). 1977. pap. 10.00 (*0-932456-00-6*) Personabks.

— Farces, Italian Style. LC 78-60783. (Illus.). 68p. (YA). (gr. 9-12). 1978. pap. 10.00 (*0-932456-02-2*) Personabks.

— The History & Mystery of Mime: Learning by Doing - A Syllabus. LC 91-65678. (Illus.). 116p. (YA). (gr. 9-12). 1991. pap. 12.00 (*0-932456-06-5*) Personabks.

— Movement for Period Plays. LC 85-73125. (Illus.). 160p. 1985. pap. 12.00 (*0-932456-04-9*) Personabks.

— Ruses of Rusante. (FRE & ITA., Illus.). 64p. 1998. pap. 10.00 (*0-932456-05-7*) Personabks.

Rolfe, Bari, ed. Mimes on Miming: An Anthology of Writings on the Art of Mime. (Illus.). 256p. (C). 1980. 15.95 (*0-915572-32-X*); pap. 8.95 (*0-915572-31-1*) Panjandrum.

Rolfe, Christopher, jt. ed. see Parrinder, Patrick.

Rolfe, Edwin. Collected Poems. 352p. 1997. pap. text 20.95 (*0-252-06640-5*) U of Ill Pr.

— Lincoln Battalion. LC 74-651. (World History Ser.: No. 48). 1974. lib. bdg. 75.00 (*0-8383-1762-6*) M S G Haskell Hse.

— Trees Became Torches: Selected Poems. Nelson, Cary & Hendricks, Jefferson, eds. LC 94-6722. (American Poetry Recovery Ser.). write for info. (*0-252-02131-2*) U of Ill Pr.

— Trees Became Torches: Selected Poems. Nelson, Cary & Hendricks, Jefferson, eds. LC 94-6722. (American Poetry Recovery Ser.). 168p. 1995. 13.95 (*0-252-06417-8*) U of Ill Pr.

Rolfe, Eugene. Encounter with Jung. 1989. 24.95 (*0-938434-26-8*); pap. 13.95 (*0-938434-27-6*) Sigo Pr.

— Intelligent Agnostics Introduction to Christianity. 2nd ed. LC 90-40142. Date not set. 32.50 (*0-938434-90-X*); pap. 17.95 (*0-938434-89-6*) Sigo Pr.

Rolfe, Eugene, tr. see Meier, Carl A.

Rolfe, F. W., jt. auth. see Rolfe, R. T.

Rolfe, Frederick C. The Desire & Pursuit of the Whole: A Romance of Modern Venice. LC 77-10836. 299p. 1977. reprint ed. lib. bdg. 35.00 (*0-8371-9808-9*, RODP, Greenwood Pr) Greenwood.

Rolfe, Frederick C. & Woolf, Cecil. Nicholas Crabbe: or The One & the Many, a Romance. LC 77-11680. 1977. reprint ed. lib. bdg. 65.00 (*0-8371-9816-X*, RONC, Greenwood Pr) Greenwood.

Rolfe, Frederick W. The Desire & Pursuit of the Whole: A Romance of Modern Venice. LC 78-21374. (Gay Experience Ser.). reprint ed. 25.50 (*0-404-61536-8*) AMS Pr.

— In His Own Image. LC 70-157795. (Short Story Index Reprint Ser.). 1977. reprint ed. 26.95 (*0-8369-3907-7*) Ayer.

Rolfe, Frederick W., et al. Hubert's Arthur: Being Certain Curious Documents Found Among the Literary Remains of Mr. N. C., Here Produced by Prospero & Caliban. Reginald, R. & Melville, Douglas, eds. LC 77-92409. (Lost Race & Adult Fantasy Ser.). 1978. reprint ed. lib. bdg. 40.95 (*0-405-11005-7*) Ayer.

Rolfe, G. L., jt. auth. see Holland, I. I.

Rolfe, Gary. Closing the Theory-Practice Gap: A New Paradigm for Nursing. LC 96-15969. 224p. 2000. pap. text 40.00 (*0-7506-2616-X*) Buttrwrth-Heinemann.

— Expanding Nursing Knowledge: Understanding & Reseaching Your Own Practice. LC 97-36320. (Illus.). 224p. 1998. pap. text 35.00 (*0-7506-3013-2*) Buttrwrth-Heinemann.

Rolfe, J. C., tr. Lives of the Caesars, 2 vols., 1. (Loeb Classical Library: No. 31, 38). 532p. 1914. 18.95 (*0-674-99035-8*) HUP.

— War with Catiline, War with Jugurtha, Etc. (Loeb Classical Library: No. 116). 562p. 18.95 (*0-674-99128-1*) HUP.

Rolfe, J. C., tr. see Cornelius Nepos.

Rolfe, J. M. & Staples, K. J., eds. Flight Simulation. (Cambridge Aerospace Ser.). 296p. 1988. pap. text 44.95 (*0-521-35751-9*) Cambridge U Pr.

Rolfe, Jack W. The 10 A's of Spiritual Therapy. Passic, Jon T. & Edwards, John W., eds. (Illus.). 1998. pap. write for info. (*1-890984-52-3*) Rolfe Lrdrship.

Rolfe, Jock W. & Knight, Gladys. Many Different Roads: A Common Path. (YA). (gr. 8-12). 1998. pap. write for info. (*1-890984-51-5*) Rolfe Lrdrship.

Rolfe, John. Curveballs Strikes Again: More Wacky Facts to Bat Around. (J). 1991. pap. write for info. (*0-316-75458-7*) Little.

— Head-to-Head Baseball: Ken Griffey, Junior & Frank Thomas. Siede, Margaret, ed. (Illus.). 144p. (Orig.). (J). (gr. 5). 1996. pap. 4.99 incl. Beta (*1-886749-10-8*) SI For Kids.

— Wayne Gretsky. (J). 1992. pap. write for info. (*0-316-75463-3*) Little.

***Rolfe, John & Troob, Peter.** Monkey Business: Swinging Through the Wall Street Jungle. LC 99-39604. 288p. 2000. 24.95 (*0-446-52556-1*, Pub. by Warner Bks) Little.

Rolfe, John, ed. see Collie, Ashley.

Rolfe, John, ed. see Schwarz, Alan.

Rolfe, John C. Suetonius. LC 99-217169. (Loeb Classical Library). 507p. 1998. 18.95 (*0-674-99570-8*) HUP.

Rolfe, John C., ed. see Horace.

Rolfe, John C., tr. see Gentili, Alberico.

Rolfe, Julia R. Portrait of a Lady: Sargent & Lady Agnew. (Illus.). 96p. 1997. pap. 19.95 (*0-903598-71-X*, Pub. by Natl Galleries) Antique Collect.

Rolfe, Linda & Harlow, Mary. Let's Look at Dance! Using Professional Dance on Video. LC 97-204498. 80p. 1997. pap. 24.95 (*1-85346-430-9*, Pub. by David Fulton) Taylor & Francis.

Rolfe, Lionel. Fat Man on the Left: Four Decades in the Underground. LC 99-172054. (Illus.). 184p. 1998. pap. 14.95 (*1-879395-01-0*) CA Classics Bks.

— In Search of Literary L. A. (Illus.). 208p. (Orig.). 1991. pap. 11.95 (*1-879395-00-2*) CA Classics Bks.

— Last Train North. 1987. pap. 6.95 (*0-915572-95-8*) Panjandrum.

Rolfe, Lionel & Lennon, Nigey. The Heal Yourself Home Handbook of Unusual Remedies. LC 82-14274. 205p. 1982. pap. 4.95 (*0-13-384677-6*, Parker Publishing Co) P-H.

— Nature's 12 Magic Healers. LC 97-31475. 144p. 1997. pap. 12.95 (*0-87983-800-0*, 38000K, Keats Publng) NTC Contemp Pub Co.

Rolfe, Lionel M. The Menuhins: A Family Odyssey. LC 78-13051. 256p. 1978. 15.95 (*0-915572-22-2*) Panjandrum.

Rolfe, Lisa K. & Wehner, Paul. Making the Physician Network Work: Leadership, Design & Incentives. LC 95-11325. 116p. 1995. pap. 56.50 (*1-55648-142-X*, 164101) AHPI.

Rolfe, Lyle. Greater Aurora & the Fox Valley: Valley with a Vision. (Illus.). 150p. 1998. 34.95 (*1-890291-07-2*) Platinum Pubng.

Rolfe, Margaret. Go Wild with Quilts: Fourteen North American Birds & Animals. Reikes, Ursula G. & Weiland, Barbara, eds. LC 93-9765. (Illus.). 80p. (Orig.). 1993. pap. 19.95 (*1-56477-019-2*, B155) Martingale & Co.

— Go Wild with Quilts - Again! 10 New Bird & Animal Designs. LC 95-35894. 92p. 1995. pap. 21.95 (*1-56477-126-1*, B244) Martingale & Co.

— Patchwork Quilts to Make for Children. LC 91-21702. (Illus.). 160p. (Orig.). 1991. pap. 14.95 (*0-8069-8498-8*) Sterling.

— A Quilter's Ark: More Than 50 Designs for Foundation Piecing. Lowe, Melissa, ed. LC 97-23693. (Illus.). 96p. 1997. pap. 21.95 (*1-56477-197-0*, B311) Martingale & Co.

Rolfe, Margaret, jt. auth. see Hooworth, Judy.

Rolfe, Maro O. Old Tioga & Ninety Years of Existence: A Descriptive, Statistical & Chronological History of Tioga County from Its Earliest Settlement to (1877) (Illus.). 116p. 1997. reprint ed. pap. 15.00 (*0-8328-6455-2*) Higginson Bk Co.

Rolfe, Mel. Hell on Earth. (Illus.). 224p. 1999. 29.95 (*1-902304-29-2*, Pub. by Grub St) Seven Hills Bk.

— To Hell & Back: Further Experiences of Bomber Command's War. (Illus.). 192p. 1997. 29.95 (*1-898697-70-1*, Pub. by Grub St) Seven Hills Bk.

Rolfe, Mona. Initiation by the Nile. 140p. (Orig.). pap. 20.95 (*0-8464-4241-8*) Beekman Pubs.

— Initiation by the Nile. 185p. (Orig.). 1976. pap. 13.95 (*0-85435-093-4*, Pub. by C W Daniel) Natl Bk Netwk.

— The Sacred Vessel. 140p. pap. 12.95 (*0-8464-4286-8*) Beekman Pubs.

— The Spiral of Life. 176p. (Orig.). pap. 12.50 (*0-8464-4291-4*) Beekman Pubs.

— The Spiral of Life. 189p. (Orig.). 1992. pap. 12.50 (*0-85435-432-8*, Pub. by C W Daniel) Natl Bk Netwk.

Rolfe, R. A. Orchidaceae in Flora of Tropical Africa. 595p. (C). 1984. 50.00 (*0-7855-3283-8*, Pub. by Scientific) St Mut.

Rolfe, R. A. & Hurst, C. C. The Orchid Stud Book: Enumeration of Hybrid Orchids of Artificial Origin: With Historical Introduction. (Illus.). 327p. 1986. reprint ed. text 50.00 (*81-211-0003-8*) Lubrecht & Cramer.

Rolfe, R. T. & Rolfe, F. W. The Romance of the Fungus World: An Account of Fungus Life in Its Numerous Guises, Both Real & Legendary. LC 74-81401. (Illus.). 352p. 1974. reprint ed. pap. 6.95 (*0-486-23105-4*) Dover.

Rolfe, Randall C. You Can Postpone Anything but Love: Expanding Our Potential As Parents. 1990. pap. 9.95 (*0-446-39058-5*) Warner Bks.

Rolfe, Randy. The Seven Secrets of Successful Parents. 336p. 1998. pap. 14.95 (*0-8092-2954-4*, 295440, Contemporary Bks) NTC Contemp Pub Co.

Rolfe, Rial D. & Finegold, Sydney M., eds. Clostridium Difficile. (Its Role in Intestinal Disease Ser.). 384p. 1988. text 146.00 (*0-12-593410-6*) Acad Pr.

Rolfe, Stanley T., jt. auth. see Barsom, John M.

Rolfe, Stanley T., jt. ed. see Barsom, John M.

Rolfe, William J. Life of William Shakespeare. LC 70-174961. reprint ed. 57.50 (*0-404-05387-4*) AMS Pr.

— Shakespeare the Boy. 251p. 1982. reprint ed. 24.95 (*0-87928-111-1*) Corner Hse.

— Shakespeare the Boy. LC 78-128411. (Studies in Shakespeare: No. 24). 1970. reprint ed. lib. bdg. 75.00 (*0-8383-1103-2*) M S G Haskell Hse.

Rolfes, Ellen, ed. Why Didn't I Think of That? 96p. 1979. spiral bd. 5.95 (*1-882232-15-1*) Kitchen Collect.

Rolfes, Ellen, ed. see Southeast Out Press Writers Assoc. Staff.

Rolfes, Harold L., jt. auth. see Basu, Sam N.

Rolfes, Sharon R. & Debruyne. Lifespan Nutrition with InfoTrac. 2nd ed. (Health Sciences Ser.). 1997. 49.25 (*0-534-53836-3*) Wadsworth Pub.

Rolfes, Sharon R., et al. Lifespan Nutrition: Conception Through Aging. Marshall, ed. 528p. (C). 1990. mass mkt. 43.50 (*0-314-66811-X*) West Pub.

— Lifespan Nutrition: Conception Through Life. 2nd ed. (C). 1997. text 53.95 (*0-534-53739-1*) Wadsworth Pub.

Rolfes, Sharon R., jt. auth. see Whitney, Eleanor N.

Rolfes, Sharon Rady & DeBruyne, Linda. Life Span Nutrition. 2nd ed. LC 97-36769. (Health Sciences). 540p. 1997. 49.25 (*0-534-53834-7*) Brooks-Cole.

Rolfo, Luigi. James Alberione: Apostle for Our Times. LC 87-1102. 442p. 1987. pap. 19.95 (*0-8189-0518-2*) Alba.

Rolfs, A. PCR: Clinical Diagnostics & Research. 2nd ed. 300p. 1997. pap. text 68.00 (*3-540-59432-9*) Spr-Verlag.

Rolfs, A., et al, eds. PCR: Clinical Diagnostics & Research. (Laboratory Ser.). (Illus.). 280p. 1992. 59.00 (*0-387-55440-8*) Spr-Verlag.

Rolfs, Arndt, et al, eds. Methods in DNA Amplification. LC 94-43082. (Illus.). 262p. (C). 1994. text 95.00 (*0-306-44908-0*, Kluwer Plenum) Kluwer Academic.

Rolfs, Claus E. & Rodney, William S. Cauldrons in the Cosmos: Nuclear Astrophysics. (Theoretical Astrophysics Ser.). (Illus.). xviii, 562p. 1994. lib. bdg. 74.95 (*0-226-72456-5*) U Ch Pr.

— Cauldrons in the Cosmos: Nuclear Astrophysics. (Theoretical Astrophysics Ser.). (Illus.). xviii, 562p. 1996. pap. text 42.00 (*0-226-72457-3*) U Ch Pr.

Rolfs, Daniel. Beginner's Italian Reader. 64p. 1990. pap. 7.95 (*0-8442-8030-5*) NTC Contemp Pub Co.

Rolfs, Donald, jt. auth. see Foreman, Dale M.

Rolfs, Judith. Love Always, Mom: How a Family Fights Cancer. 130p. (Orig.). 1997. pap. 11.95 (*1-57502-365-2*, PO1170) Morris Pubng.

— A Woman's Guide to Keeping Promises: 52 Ways to Choose Happiness & Fulfillment. LC 96-16867. 176p. 1996. pap. 10.99 (*0-8254-3627-3*) Kregel.

Rolfs, Judith, jt. auth. see Rolfs, Wayne.

Rolfs, Richard W. The Sorcerer's Apprentice: The Life of Franz von Papen. LC 95-43733. (Illus.). 484p. (Orig.). (C). 1994. pap. text 42.00 (*0-7618-0163-4*); lib. bdg. 58.00 (*0-7618-0162-6*) U Pr of Amer.

Rolfs, Wayne & Rolfs, Judith. 52 Ways to Keep Your Promises: As a Man, As a Husband, As a Father. 152p. 1996. pap. 10.99 (*0-8254-3626-5*) Kregel.

Rolfsen, Dale. Knot Theory & Manifolds. (Lecture Notes in Mathematics Ser.: Vol. 1144). v, 163p. 1985. 34.95 (*0-387-15680-1*) Spr-Verlag.

— Knots & Links. LC 76-15514. (Mathematics Lectures: No. 7). (Illus.). 439p. 1976. pap. text 40.00 (*0-914098-16-0*) Publish or Perish.

Rolfsmeyer, Janet L. & Triggs, Tracy. Gardening for Nature: A Teacher's Guide to Hands-On Activities for Wildlife Gardening. (Illus.). 53p. 1993. pap. 5.95 (*1-884549-17-9*) VA Mus Natl Hist.

Rolfson, H., tr. see Van Ruusbroec, Jan.

***Rolheiser-Bennett, Noreen Carol, et al.** The Portfolio Organizer: Succeeding with Portfolios in Your Classroom. LC 00-8817. 2000. write for info. (*0-87120-374-X*) ASCD.

Rolheiser, Ronald. Against an Infinite Horizon. 192p. 1996. pap. text 14.95 (*0-8245-1586-2*) Crossroad NY.

— Forgotten among the Lilies: Learning to Live Beyond Our Own Obsessions. 284p. 1991. pap. 15.95 (*0-340-53624-1*, Pub. by Hodder & Stought Ltd) Lubrecht & Cramer.

— The Holy Longing: The Search for a Christian Spirituality. LC 98-46109. 272p. 1999. 21.95 (*0-385-49418-1*) Doubleday.

***Rolheiser, Ronald.** The Shattered Lantern: Rediscovering a Felt Presence of God. 2001. pap. 14.95 (*0-8245-1884-5*) Crossroad NY.

Rolheiser, Ronald, et al. A Fresh Approach to St. John of the Cross: Growth Through Pain & Sexuality. 160p. 1996. pap. 39.95 (*0-85439-450-8*, Pub. by St Paul Pubns) St Mut.

***Roli, Ghigo.** Tuscany 360. LC 99-44106. 2000. 75.00 (*0-375-50410-9*) Random.

***Rolider, Amos & Axelrod, Saul.** How to Teach Self-Control Through Trigger Analysis. LC 99-45963. (How to Manage Behavior Ser.). 2000. pap. write for info. (*0-89079-771-4*) PRO-ED.

Rolim, J., et al, eds. Parallel & Distributed Processing. LC 99-25670. (Lecture Notes in Computer Science Ser.: Vol. 1586). xvii, 1443p. 1999. pap. 129.00 (*3-540-65831-9*) Spr-Verlag.

***Rolim, Josbe D. P., ed.** Parallel & Distributed Processing: Proceedings of the LPDPS 2000 Workshops, Cancun, Mexico, May 1-5, 2000. LC 00-38821. (Lecture Notes in Computer Science Ser.: Vol. 1800). 2000. pap. 110.00 (*3-540-67442-X*) Spr-Verlag.

Rolim, Jose D. P., ed. Randomization & Approximation Techniques in Computer Science: Proceedings, International Workshop Random '97, Bologna, Italy, July 11-12, 1997, Vol. 126. LC 97-27556. (Lecture Notes in Computer Science Ser.: Vol. 1269). viii, 227p. 1997. pap. 44.00 (*3-540-63248-4*) Spr-Verlag.

Rolim, Jose D. P., et al, eds. Parallel & Distributed Processing: 10th International IPPS/SPDP'98 Workshops, Held in Conjunction with the 12th International Parallel Processing Symposium on Parallel & 9th Symposium on Parallel & Distributed Processing, Orlando, Florida, U. S. A., March 30-April 3, 1998, Vol. 138. LC 98-18273. (Lecture Notes in Computer Science: Vol. 1388). xvii, 1168p. 1998. pap. 109.00 (*3-540-64359-1*) Spr-Verlag.

Rolim, Jose D. P., jt. ed. see Ferreira, Afonso A.

Rolim, Jose D. P., jt. ed. see Ferreira, Alfonso.

Rolim, Jose D. P., jt. ed. see Jansen, Klaus.

Rolin, Dominique. The Garden of Delights. Nagem, Monique F., tr. LC 97-11705. (Belgian Francophone Library: No. 10). 145p. 1998. 39.95 (*0-8204-3819-7*) P Lang Pubng.

Rolin, Dominique, jt. auth. see Gage, Jennifer C.

Roling, B. V., jt. ed. see Cassese, Antonio.

***Roling, Niels & Wagemakers, Annemarie Elisabeth, eds.** Facilitating Sustainable Agriculture: Participatory Learning & Adaptive Management in Times of Environmental Uncertainty. (Illus.). 344p. (C). 2000. pap. text Price not set. (*0-521-79481-1*) Cambridge U Pr.

Rolingson, Martha A. Toltec Mounds & Plum Bayou Culture: Mound D Excavations. LC 98-36995. (Arkansas Archeological Survey Research Ser.: No.54). (Illus.). 142p. (C). 1998. pap. 25.00 (*1-56349-085-4*) AR Archaeol.

Rolingson, Martha A., jt. auth. see Schambach, Frank F.

Rolingson, Martha A., jt. auth. see Sherrod, P. Clay.

Rolingson, Martha A., ed. see McCartney, Nancy G., et al.

Rolison, Debra R., jt. auth. see Pons, Stanley.

Rolka, Gail M. 100 Women Who Shaped World History. (One Hundred Ser.). (Illus.). 112p. (Orig.). 1994. pap. 7.95 (*0-912517-06-9*) Bluewood Bks.

Rolke, Karl-Hermann. Die Bildhaften Vergleiche in Den Fragmenten der Stoiker von Zenon Bis Panaitios. (Spudasmata Ser.: Bd. 32). (GER.). vii, 531p. 1975. write for info. incl. 3.5 hd (*3-487-05595-3*) Lubrecht & Cramer.

Roll, Bob. Bobke: A Ride on the Wild Side of Cycling. LC 97-215286. (Illus.). 144p. 1995. pap. 16.95 (*1-884737-12-9*) VeloPress.

Roll, Charles. Colonel Dick Thompson, the Persistent Whig. 315p. 1948. 10.00 (*1-885323-11-5*) IN Hist Bureau.

Roll, Christine, ed. Recht und Reich im Zeitalter der Reformation: Festschrift fur Horst Rabe unter Mitarbeit von Bettina Braun und Heide Stratenwerth 2, Uberarbeitete Auflage. 2nd ed. (GER., Illus.). XIX, 528p. 1997. 95.95 (*3-631-31136-2*) P Lang Pubng.

***Roll, Claudia M.** A Home for Nathan. LC 99-65973. (Illus.). 48p. (J). (ps-2). 1999. pap. 6.95 (*0-9674058-0-7*) W Snyder.

Roll, Eric & British Association for the Advancement of Science Staff. The Mixed Economy: Proceedings of Section F (economics) of The British Association for The Advancement of Science, Salford, 1980. LC 82-174648. 233 p. 1982. write for info. (*0-333-31540-5*) Macmillan.

Roll, Eric L. An Early Experiment in Industrial Organization: Being a History of the Firm of Boulton & Watt 1775-1804. LC 68-56059. (Reprints of Economic Classics Ser.). (Illus.). xvi, 310p. 1968. reprint ed. 45.00 (*0-678-05193-3*) Kelley.

Roll, F., jt. auth. see Rapatz, F.

Roll, Hans U., tr. see Dietrich, Gunter.

Roll-Hansen, Nils, jt. auth. see Broberg, Gunnar.

***Roll, Israel & Tal, Oren, eds.** Apollonia-Arsuf: Final Report of the Excavations. (Monograph Series of the Sonia & Marco Nadler Institute of Archaeology: Vol. 16). xv, 299p. 1999. text 60.00 (*965-266-012-4*, Pub. by Inst Archaeology) Eisenbrauns.

***Roll, Lance.** It's Not Just Camp Food Anymore. 80p. 1999. pap. 9.99 (*0-9676661-1-2*) Calvary Dist.

Roll, Serafima, ed. Contextualizing Transition: Interviews with Contemporary Russian Writers & Critics. LC 96-53921. (Middlebury Studies in Russian Language & Literature). (Illus.). X, 182p. 1998. 43.95 (*0-8204-3779-4*) P Lang Pubng.

Roll, Steve. Holy Burnout: Turning Brokenness into Blessing, Through the Power of God's Restoring Love. 232p. (Orig.). 1996. pap. 10.99 (*1-56322-060-1*, 060-1) Hensley Pub.

Roll, Susanne, tr. see Dietrich, Gunter.

Roll-Velez, Saul, ed. see Rojas Zorrilla, Francisco D.

Roll, William G. Theory & Experiment in Psychical Research. LC 75-7398. (Perspectives in Psychical Research Ser.). (Illus.). 1975. 42.95 (*0-405-07047-0*) Ayer.

Roll, William G., ed. see Parapsychological Association Staff.

Rolla, G., jt. auth. see Embery, G.

Rolla, Gregory M. Your Inner Music: Creative Analysis & Music Memory. LC 93-25463. 144p. (Orig.). 1993. pap. 3.95 (*0-933029-74-8*) Chiron Pubns.

***Rolland, Alain, ed.** Advanced Gene Delivery: From Concepts to Pharmaceutical Products. (Drug Targeting & Delivery Ser.). 414p. 1999. text 125.00 (*90-5702-438-1*, Harwood Acad Pubs) Gordon & Breach.

R

Rolland, Alain, ed. Pharmaceutical Particulate Carriers: Therapeutic Applications. (Drugs & the Pharmaceutical Sciences Ser.: Vol. 61). (Illus.). 448p. 1993. text 215.00 (0-8247-9016-2) Dekker.

***Rolland, Bruce & Rolland, Cindi.** Hey Mom... Do You Think God Drinks Coffee? 142p. 1999. pap. 12.95 (0-9644644-0-3) DC Publ.

***Rolland, Bruce L.** Cassandra's Return. 174p. 1999. pap. 12.95 (0-9644644-3-8) DC Publ.

Rolland, C., et al, eds. Advanced Information Systems Engineering: Proceedings of the 5th International Conference, CAISE '93, Paris, France, June 8-11, 1993. (Lecture Notes in Computer Science Ser.: Vol. 685). v, 648p. 1993. 93.95 (0-387-56777-1) Spr-Verlag.

Rolland, Cindi, jt. auth. see Rolland, Bruce.

Rolland, Eugene. Faune Populaire de la France: Noms Vulgaires, Dictons, Proverbes, Legendes, Etc. (FRE.). 72p. 1967. 795.00 (0-7859-5314-0) Fr & Eur.

— Flore Populaire de la France: Historie Naturelle des Plantes dans leurs Rapports avec la Linguistique. (FRE.). 2948p. 1968. 695.00 (0-7859-5315-9) Fr & Eur.

Rolland, F. D. The Essence of Databases. LC 97-2835. (Essence of Computing Ser.). 240p. (C). 1997. pap. text 19.95 (0-13-727827-6) P-H.

Rolland, Fred. Relational Database Management with Oracle. 2nd ed. (C). 1992. pap. text 36.95 (0-201-56520-X) Addison-Wesley.

Rolland, Gerard, jt. auth. see Dupuy, Yves.

Rolland, Jim, ed. Sing Out Your Praise, Vol. 2. 160p. 1993. pap., ring bd. 8.95 (0-937779-26-1) Greenlawn Pr.

Rolland, John. Seven Sages, in Scottish Metre. Laing, David, ed. LC 74-144429. (Bannatyne Club, Edinburgh. Publications: No. 57). xxvii, 334 p. 1973. reprint ed. 57.50 (0-404-52767-1) AMS Pr.

Rolland, Michael. Descent into Madness: An Inmate's Experience of the New Mexico State Prison Riot. LC 97-71307. 153p. (C). 1997. pap. 23.95 (0-87084-748-1) Anderson Pub Co.

Rolland, Paul, ed. see Szigeti, Joseph.

Rolland, Romain. Un Beau Visage a Tous Sens: Avec: Choix de Lettres de R. Rolland (1886-1944) (FRE.). 400p. 1967. pap. 15.95 (0-7859-5439-2) Fr & Eur.

— Beethoven. LC 76-95077. (Select Bibliographies Reprint Ser.). 1977. 29.95 (0-8369-5077-1) Ayer.

— Beethoven. Hull, A. Eaglefield, ed. Hull, B. Constanace, tr. 244p. 1990. reprint ed. lib. bdg. 69.00 (0-7812-9046-5) Rprt Serv.

— Beethoven: Les Grandes Epoques Creatices. (FRE.). 1520p. 1992. reprint ed. 115.00 (0-7859-5440-6) Fr & Eur.

— Choix de Lettres a Malwida Von Meysenburg. (FRE.). 336p. 1948. pap. 9.95 (0-7859-5443-0) Fr & Eur.

— Le Cloitre de la Rue D'Ulm: Avec: Journal de Romain Rolland a l'Ecole Normal (1886-1899) (FRE.). 416p. 1952. pap. 9.95 (0-7859-5444-9) Fr & Eur.

Rolland, Romain. Colas Breugnon. (FRE.). 280p. 1988. 28.95 (0-686-55241-5); pap. 10.95 (0-7859-5445-7) Fr & Eur.

Rolland, Romain. De la Decadence de la Peinture Italienne au 16e Siecle. (FRE., Illus.). 169p. 1957. pap. 9.95 (0-7859-5446-5) Fr & Eur.

— D'une Rive a l'Autre: Herman Hess et Romain Rolland, Correspondance et Fragments du Journal. (FRE., Illus.). 192p. 1972. pap. 9.95 (0-7859-5448-1) Fr & Eur.

Rolland, Romain. Empedocle d'Agrigente. (FRE., Illus.). 136p. 1931. pap. 19.95 (0-7859-5449-X) Fr & Eur.

Rolland, Romain. Fraulein Elsa. Wolff, Elsa, ed. (FRE.). 328p. 1964. pap. 9.95 (0-7859-5450-3) Fr & Eur.

— Goethe & Beethoven. LC 67-13338. (Illus.). 254p. 1972. reprint ed. 24.95 (0-405-08896-5, Pub. by Blom Pubns) Ayer.

— Haendel. (FRE., Illus.). 320p. 1975. pap. 18.95 (0-7859-1449-8, 2226001255) Fr & Eur.

— Handel. LC 75-151597. (Illus.). reprint ed. 34.50 (0-404-05388-2) AMS Pr.

— Handel. 210p. 1990. reprint ed. lib. bdg. 69.00 (0-7812-9066-X) Rprt Serv.

— I Will Not Rest. 1977. text 18.95 (0-8369-8190-1, 8328) Ayer.

— Inde Journal Nineteen Fifteen to Nineteen Forty-Three. (FRE.). 628p. 1960. pap. 36.95 (0-7859-5451-1) Fr & Eur.

— Je Commence a Devenir Dangereux. (FRE.). 1973. pap. 14.95 (0-7859-5452-X) Fr & Eur.

— Jean-Christophe, 3 vols. 1962. 4.50 (0-685-73292-4) Fr & Eur.

— Jean-Christophe. (FRE.). 1656p. 1978. 115.00 (0-7859-5283-7) Fr & Eur.

— Le Jeu de l'Amour et de la Mort. (FRE.). 192p. 1955. pap. 9.95 (0-7859-5453-8) Fr & Eur.

— Les Leonides. (FRE.). 252p. 1928. pap. 8.95 (0-7859-5565-8) Fr & Eur.

— Life of Ramakrishna. 310p. 1928. 4.95 (81-85301-44-1, Pub. by Advaita Ashrama) Vedanta Pr.

— Life of Vivekananda: Universal Gospel. 382p. pap. 5.95 (81-85301-00-X) Vedanta Pr.

— Liluli. (FRE.). 218p. 1926. pap. 10.95 (0-7859-5454-6) Fr & Eur.

— Mahatma Gandhi. Groth, Catherine, tr. from FRE. 132p. (C). 1994. 10.00 (0-934676-81-X) Greenlf Bks.

— Memoires, Souvenirs de Jeunesse, Complements, Fragments du Journal. (FRE.). 336p. 1956. pap. 18.95 (0-686-55260-1) Fr & Eur.

— Musical Tour Through the Land of the Past. Miall, Bernard, tr. LC 67-30229. (Essay Index Reprint Ser.). 1977. 19.95 (0-8369-0830-9) Ayer.

— Musicians of To-Day. Blaiklock, M., tr. LC 72-86777. (Essay Index Reprint Ser.). 1977. 21.95 (0-8369-1188-1) Ayer.

— Les Origines du Theatre Lyrique Moderne. 332p. 1971. 85.00 (0-7859-5566-6) Fr & Eur.

— Peguy, 2 vols. (FRE.). 696p. 1973. pap. 16.95 (0-7859-5456-2) Fr & Eur.

— Pierre et Luce. (FRE.). 160p. 1959. pap. 15.95 (0-7859-5457-0) Fr & Eur.

— Printemps Romain: Avec: Choix de Lettres de Romain Rolland a sa Mere (1889-1890) (FRE.). 360p. 1954. pap. 8.95 (0-7859-5459-7) Fr & Eur.

— Recueil de Chansons Populaires, 6 tomes. 85.00 (0-685-36691-X) Fr & Eur.

— Retour Au Palais Farnese: Avec: Choix de Lettres de Romain Rolland a sa Mere (1890-1891) (FRE., Illus.). 368p. 1956. pap. 8.95 (0-7859-5461-9) Fr & Eur.

— Robespierre. (FRE.). 318p. 1939. pap. 15.95 (0-7859-5463-5) Fr & Eur.

— Romain Rolland et le Mouvement Florentin de la Voce. (FRE., Illus.). 400p. 1966. pap. 14.95 (0-7859-5464-3) Fr & Eur.

— Salut et Fraternite: Avec: Alain et R. Rolland. (FRE.). 184p. 1969. pap. 8.95 (0-7859-5465-1) Fr & Eur.

— Selected Letters of Romain Rolland. Dore, Francis & Prevost, Marie-Laure, eds. (Illus.). 168p. 1990. 16.95 (0-19-562551-X) OUP.

— Some Musicians of Former Days. LC 68-8490. (Essay Index Reprint Ser.). 1977. 23.95 (0-8369-0831-7) Ayer.

— Some Musicians of Former Days. LC 76-177517. 374p. 1972. 26.95 (0-405-08897-3, Pub. by Blom Pubns) Ayer.

— Textes Politiques, Sociaux & Philosophiques Choisis. Albertini, Jean, ed. (FRE.). 1973. pap. 13.95 (0-7859-5466-X) Fr & Eur.

— Les Tragedies de la Foi. (FRE.). 296p. 1970. pap. 11.95 (0-7859-5467-8) Fr & Eur.

— Le Triomphe de la Raison. (FRE.). 88p. 1971. pap. 8.95 (0-7859-5468-6) Fr & Eur.

— La Vie de Ramakrishna. (FRE.). 320p. 1978. pap. 36.95 (0-7859-5469-4) Fr & Eur.

— La Vie de Vivekananda. (FRE.). 352p. 1978. pap. 36.95 (0-7859-5470-8) Fr & Eur.

— Voyage Musical aux Pays du Passe. (FRE., Illus.). 271p. 1976. pap. 49.95 (0-7859-5471-6) Fr & Eur.

Rolland, Romain & Bertolini Guerrieri-Gonzaga. Chere Sofia: Choix de Lettres de Romain Rolland a Sofia Bertolini Guerrieri-Gonzaga (1901-1908), 2 vols. (Illus.). 387p. 1959. 6.95 (0-685-73254-1) Fr & Eur.

Rolland, Romain & Bloch, Jean-Richard. Deux Hommes Se Rencontrent. (FRE.). 384p. 1964. pap. 10.95 (0-7859-5447-3) Fr & Eur.

Rolland, Romain & Peguy, Charles. Une Amitie Francaise: Avec: Correspondance entre Charles Peguy et Romain Rolland. (FRE.). 360p. 1955. pap. 8.95 (0-7859-5438-4) Fr & Eur.

— Pour l'Honneur de l'Esprit: Correspondance, 1898-1914. (FRE., Illus.). 352p. 1973. pap. 12.95 (0-7859-5458-9) Fr & Eur.

Rolland, Romain & Seche, Alphonse. Ces Jours Lointains: Avec: Alphonse Sechee et Romain Rolland, Lettres et autres Ecrits. (FRE.). 176p. 1962. pap. 8.95 (0-7859-5441-4) Fr & Eur.

Rolland, Romain & Strauss, Richard. Richard Strauss et Romain Rolland. (FRE., Illus.). 248p. 1951. pap. 8.95 (0-7859-5462-7) Fr & Eur.

Rolland, Romain & Suares, Andre. Cette Ame Ardente: Avec: Choix de Lettres d'Andre Suares a Romain Rolland (1887-1891) (FRE.). 408p. 1954. pap. 8.95 (0-7859-5442-2) Fr & Eur.

Rolland, Romain & Tagore, Rabindranath. Rabindranath Tagore et Romain Rolland: Lettres et Autres Ecrits. (FRE., Illus.). 208p. 1961. pap. 8.95 (0-7859-5460-0) Fr & Eur.

Rolland, Romain, et al. French Thought in the Eighteenth Century. LC 70-152172. (Essay Index Reprint Ser.). 1977. reprint ed. 29.95 (0-8369-2316-2) Ayer.

Rolland, Rosalind M., et al, eds. Chemically Induced Alterations in Functional Development & Reproduction of Fishes: Proceedings from a Session at the Wingspread Conference Center, 21-23 July 1995, Racine, Wisconsin. LC 97-28652. (Technical Publications Ser.). (Illus.). 1997. 60.00 (1-880611-19-8, SETAC Pr) SETAC.

Rolland, Solange C., jt. auth. see Graham, Gwethalyn.

Rolland, Thomas, jt. auth. see McLean, Mick.

Rolland, Will. Tasmanian Tiger: The Elusive Thylacine. 1998. pap. 6.95 (0-86417-866-2, Pub. by Kangaroo Pr) Seven Hills Bk.

Rollant. Mosby's ABCs of Test Taking for Nurses: Anchor Your Anxiety, Build Your Basic. LC 99-10465. (Illus.). 240p. (C). (gr. 13). 1999. pap. text 21.95 (0-8151-3858-X, 31669) Mosby Inc.

Rollant, Paulette D. Mental Health Nursing. (Review Ser.). (Illus.). 416p. (C). (gr. 13). 1996. write for info. (0-8151-7247-8, 24860) Mosby Inc.

— Pediatric Nursing. LC 95-36764. (Mosby's Review Ser.). (Illus.). 432p. (C). (gr. 13). 1995. pap. text 24.95 incl. 3.5 hd (0-8151-7248-6, 24861) Mosby Inc.

Rollant, Paulette D. & Ennis, Deborah A. Medical-Surgical Nursing. LC 95-24828. (Mosby's Review Ser.). (Illus.). 544p. (C). (gr. 13). 1995. pap. text 24.95 incl. disk, 3.5 hd (0-8151-7249-4, 24862) Mosby Inc.

Rollant, Paulette D. & Hill, Karen. Nursing Pharmacology. LC 95-36828. (Mosby's Review Ser.). (Illus.). 400p. (C). (gr. 13). 1995. pap. text 24.95 incl. 3.5 hd (0-8151-7245-1, 24858) Mosby Inc.

Rollant, Paulette D. & Piotrowski, Karen A. Maternity - Women's Health Nursing. (Mosby's Review Ser.). (Illus.). 560p. (C). (gr. 13). 1995. pap. text 24.95 incl. 3.5 hd (0-8151-7246-X, 24859) Mosby Inc.

Rollant, Paulette D., jt. auth. see Multi-Resources Incorporation.

***Rollason, David, ed.** Symeon of Durham: Libellus de Exordio Atque Procursu Istius Hoc Est Dunhelmensis. (Oxford Medieval Texts Ser.). 540p. 2000. text 90.00 (0-19-820207-5) OUP.

Rollason, David, et al, eds. Anglo-Norman Durham, 1093-1193. 536p. 1998. pap. 55.00 (0-85115-654-1, Boydell Pr) Boydell & Brewer.

Rollberg, P., jt. auth. see Moser, Charles A.

Rollberg, Peter, ed. Modern Encyclopedia Russia & Soviet Literatures, Vol. 9. 1989. 40.00 (0-87569-038-6) Academic Intl.

Rolle, Andrew. Henry Mayo Newhall & His Times: A California Legacy. LC 91-38697. (Illus.). 178p. 1991. 29.95 (0-87328-136-5) Huntington Lib.

— The Italian Americans: Troubled Roots. LC 84-40282. 240p. 1984. reprint ed. pap. 12.95 (0-8061-1907-1) U of Okla Pr.

— John Charles Fremont: Character As Destiny. LC 91-50305. (Illus.). 432p. 1991. 29.95 (0-8061-2380-X) U of Okla Pr.

— John Charles Fremont: Character as Destiny. 1999. pap. text 15.95 (0-8061-3135-7) U of Okla Pr.

— The Lost Cause: The Confederate Exodus to Mexico. LC 65-11228. (Illus.). 272p. 1992. pap. 14.95 (0-8061-1961-6) U of Okla Pr.

***Rolle, Andrew.** Westward the Immigrants: Italian Adventurers & Colonists in an Expanding America. LC 99-41007. 424p. 1999. pap. 24.95 (0-87081-529-6) Univ Pr Colo.

***Rolle, Andrew & Gaines, John S.** The Golden State: California History & Government. 4th ed. LC 99-53735. (Illus.). 300p. 2000. 24.95 (0-88295-954-9) Harlan Davidson.

— Study Guide to the Golden State: California History & Government. 4th ed. (Illus.). 45p. 2000. pap. text, student ed. Price not set. (0-88295-989-1) Harlan Davidson.

Rolle, Andrew F. An American in California: The Biography of William Heath Davis 1822-1909. LC 56-10064. (Illus.). 155p. 1981. reprint ed. pap. 9.95 (0-87328-120-9) Huntington Lib.

— California: A History. 5th ed. LC 97-21438. 1998. 42.95 (0-88295-943-3) Harlan Davidson.

— Los Angeles. 2nd ed. Hundley, Norris, Jr. & Schutz, John A., eds. (Golden State Ser.). (Illus.). 240p. 1995. pap. 12.00 (0-929651-01-4) MTL.

— Los Angeles: From Pueblo to City Future. Hundley, Norris, Jr. & Schutz, John A., eds. (Physical Education). (Illus.). 128p. 1981. pap. 8.75 (0-87835-119-1) Thomson Learn.

Rolle, Andrw F. California: A History. 5th ed. LC 97-21438. (Illus.). 371p. (C). 1997. pap. text 31.95 (0-88295-938-7) Harlan Davidson.

Rolle, Denys. The Humble Petition of Denys Rolle, Esq., Setting Forth the Hardships, Inconveniences, & Grievances Which Have Attended Him in His Attempts to Make a Settlement in East Florida, Humbly Praying Such Relief as in their Lordships Wisdom Shall Seem Meet. Sturgill, Claude C., ed. LC 77-5133. (Floridiana Facsimile & Reprint Ser.). 137p. 1977. reprint ed. 17.95 (0-8130-0417-9) U Press Fla.

Rolle, Gunter. Lexikon Computerwissen Von A-Z: German-English, English-German. 124p. 1990. 19.95 (0-7859-8441-0, 3572033500) Fr & Eur.

***Rolle, Kurt C.** Heat & Mass Transfer. LC 99-46326. (Illus.). 598p. 1999. 77.00 (0-13-919309-X) P-H.

Rolle, Kurt C. Thermodynamics & Heat Power. 4th ed. (Illus.). 864p. (C). 1993. teacher ed. write for info. incl. disk (0-318-69909-5) Macmillan.

— Thermodynamics & Heat Power. 5th ed. LC 98-19111. 711p. (C). 1998. 105.00 (0-13-095561-2) P-H.

Rolle, L. Warren. Helping Hands: From Misconception to Reality about Black Men & Sexual Promiscuity. LC 97-90259. xii, 130p. 1997. 17.95 (0-533-12335-6) Vantage.

Rolle, Lutz J., jt. auth. see Gutknecht, Christoph.

Rolle, Renate. Totenkult der Skythen. (Vorgeschichtliche Forschungen Ser.). (Illus.). (C). 1979. 307.70 (3-11-006620-3) De Gruyter.

Rolle, Richard. English Prose Treatises. Perry, G. G., ed. (EETS, OS Ser.: No. 20). 1972. reprint ed. 30.00 (0-527-00021-3) Periodicals Srv.

— English Writings. 180p. 1931. reprint ed. 49.00 (0-403-04052-3) Somerset Pub.

— English Writings of Richard Rolle: Hermit of Hampole. LC 74-161958. 180p. 1931. reprint ed. 29.00 (0-403-01328-3) Scholarly.

— Richard Rolle: Prose & Verse. Ogilvie-Thomson, Sarah, ed. (OS 293 Ser.: No. 293). (Illus.). 370p. 1989. 39.95 (0-19-722295-1) OUP.

— Some Minor Works of Richard Rolle, with the Privity of the Passion by S. Bonaventura. (BCL1-PR English Literature Ser.). 225p. 1992. reprint ed. lib. bdg. 79.00 (0-7812-7191-6) Rprt Serv.

Rolle, Richard, ed. see Harvey, Ralph & Misyn, R.

Rolle Richard of Hampole. The Pricke of Conscience (Stimulus Conscientiae) A Northumbrian Poem. LC 74-178551. reprint ed. 42.50 (0-404-56666-9) AMS Pr.

Rolle, Sojourner K. Common Ancestry. 48p. 1999. pap. 6.00 (1-890887-06-4) Mille Grazie.

Rolle-Whatley, R., ed. see Parham, Vanessa R.

Rolle-Whatley, Renee, ed. see Stevens, Chambers.

Rolle-Whatley, Renee M. Baby Products Basics: The Busy Person's Guide to Baby Products on a Budget. LC 90-92125. (Illus.). 128p. (Orig.). 1991. pap. 8.95 (0-9627756-0-6) Sandcastle Pub.

Rolle-Whatley, Renee M., ed. see Jones, Richard O.

Rolle-Whatley, Renee M., ed. see Wunder, Matthew R.

Rollenhagen, Gabriel. Nucleus Emblematum Selectissimorum. (GER.). 45p. 1985. reprint ed. write for info. (3-487-07505-9) G Olms Pubs.

Roller, jt. ed. see Thomas, J. R.

Roller, Dirk. Religionsunterricht als Zeichenbildung: Studien Zu Semiosen in Schule und Stadtischem Kontext. (Religion in der Offentlichkeit Ser.: Bd. 3). (GER., Illus.). 158p. 1998. 31.95 (3-631-33109-6) P Lang Pubng.

Roller, Alyse F. The Literary Imagination of Ultra-Orthodox Jewish Women: An Assessment of a Writing Community. LC 99-25985. (Illus.). 198p. 1999. lib. bdg. 29.95 (0-7864-0721-2) McFarland & Co.

Roller, Becky. Grandma's Postcards. 1992. pap. text 6.95 (0-913515-85-X, Starrhill Press) Black Belt Communs.

Roller, Bill. The Promise of Group Therapy: How to Build a Vigorous Training & Organizational Base for Group Therapy in Managed Behavioral Healthcare. LC 96-48494. 252p. 1997. 34.95 (0-7879-0842-8) Jossey-Bass.

Roller, Bill & Nelson, Vivian. The Art of Co-Therapy: How Therapists Work Together. LC 90-44744. 256p. 1991. lib. bdg. 40.00 (0-89862-557-2) Guilford Pubns.

Roller, Bill, ed. see Roller, Twila J.

Roller, Cathy M. So What's a Tutor to Do? LC 98-14427. 199p. 1998. pap. 24.95 (0-87207-191-X, 191) Intl Reading.

— Variability Not Disability: Struggling Readers in a Workshop Classroom. LC 95-46674. 1996. pap. 21.95 (0-87207-142-1) Intl Reading.

Roller, Cathy M., jt. auth. see Jackson, Nancy E.

Roller, D., et al. CAD Systems Development: Tools & Methods. LC 97-7338. 1997. write for info. (3-540-62535-6) Spr-Verlag.

Roller, D., jt. ed. see Bruderlin, B.

Roller, David. How to Make Big Money in Multi-Level Marketing. 204p. (C). 1989. pap. text 14.95 (0-13-417866-1, Busn) P-H.

Roller, Dick. Indiana Glass Factories Notes. (Illus.). 140p. (Orig.). 1994. pap. 26.00 (0-915627-00-0) Acorn Pr IL.

Roller, Duane. Early Travellers in Eastern Boiotia. (McGill University Monographs in Classical Archaeology & History: Vol. 8). 221p. 1988. 57.00 (90-5063-006-5, Pub. by Gieben) J Benjamins Pubng Co.

Roller, Duane. Fundamental Physics: Mechanics, Waves & Thermodynamics, Vol. 1. (Illus.). 818p. 1981. text 40.00 (0-8162-7284-0) Holden-Day.

— Tanagran Studies No. I: Sources & Documents on Tanagra in Boiotia. (McGill University Monographs in Classical Archaeology & History: Vol. 9.1). 185p. 1989. 50.00 (90-5063-030-8, Pub. by Gieben) J Benjamins Pubng Co.

— Tanagran Studies No. II: The Prosopography of Tanagra in Boiotia. (McGill University Monographs in Classical Archaeology & History: Vol. 9.2). 132p. 1989. 47.00 (90-5063-031-6, Pub. by Gieben) J Benjamins Pubng Co.

Roller, Duane & Blum, Ronald. Fundamental Physics, 2 vols. Incl. Vol. 2. Electricity, Magnetism & Light. LC 81-81011. (Illus.). 790p. 1981. Vol. 2. Electricity, Magnetism & Light. LC 81-81011. (Illus.). 790p. 1981. 40.00 (0-8162-7285-9); LC 81-81011. (Illus.). 1981. write for info. (0-318-53448-7) Holden-Day.

Roller, Duane E. The Early Development of the Concepts of Temperature & Heat: The Rise & Decline of the Caloric Theory. LC 50-8653. (Harvard Case Histories in Experimental Science Ser.: Case 3). 110p. reprint ed. pap. 34.10 (0-608-10282-2, 201160700079) Bks Demand.

Roller, Duane W. The Building Program of Herod the Great. LC 96-54003. 351p. 1998. 50.00 (0-520-20934-6, Pub. by U CA Pr) Cal Prin Full Svc.

Roller, Elisa, jt. auth. see Kennedy, J. Ray.

Roller, Gerhard, jt. auth. see Von Wilmowsky, Peter.

Roller, Judi M. The Politics of the Feminist Novel. LC 85-12718. (Contributions in Women's Studies: No. 63). 206p. 1986. pap. 12.95 (0-313-25445-1, RPNPB) Greenwood.

— The Politics of the Feminist Novel, 63. LC 85-12718. (Contributions in Women's Studies: No. 63). 206p. 1986. 49.95 (0-313-24663-7, RPN) Greenwood.

Roller, Leonard H. The Profits of Persuasion: Speaking Effectively for Your Company. (Illus.). 224p. 1988. 18.95 (0-914598-24-4) Intl Resources.

Roller, Lynn E. Gordon Special Studies Vol. I: The Nonverbal Graffiti, Dipinti & Stamps. Kohler, Ellen L., ed. (University Museum Monographs: No. 63). (Illus.). xxii, 103p. 1987. text 45.00 (0-934718-70-9) U Museum Pubns.

— In Search of God the Mother: The Cult of Anatolian Cybele. LC 98-20627. 431p. 1999. 60.00 (0-520-21024-7, Pub. by U CA Pr) Cal Prin Full Svc.

Roller, Lynn E., tr. see Schleiner, Louise.

Roller, Martin, jt. ed. see Niblo, Graham.

Roller, Pat. Grand Friends, Young Friends - Leader's Guide. Watkins, Virginia, ed. LC 98-31555. 24p. 1999. pap. 9.50 (1-57895-069-4, Bridge Res) Curriculm Presbytrn KY.

Roller, Patricia Kay. Grand Friends, Young Friends: Participant's Book. Watkins, Virginia, ed. LC 98-45131. 32p. (J). (gr. 5-7). 1999. 5.95 (1-57895-068-6, Bridge Res) Curriculm Presbytrn KY.

Roller, Rebecca T. Guess What, Gram! (Illus.). (J). (ps-3). 1996. 6.95 (0-913515-91-4, Elliott Clark) Black Belt Communs.

Roller, Sibel & Jones, Sylvia A., eds. Handbook of Fat Replacers. 336p. 1996. boxed set 149.95 (0-8493-2512-9) CRC Pr.

Roller, Toni. Indian Pottery by Toni Roller of Santa Clara Pueblo: A Guide. LC 97-16532. (Illus.). 64p. (Orig.). 1997. pap. 12.95 (0-86534-263-6) Sunstone Pr.

Roller, Twila J. Methodism in Their Madness. Roller, Bill, ed. (Illus.). 152p. (Orig.). (C). 1993. pap. text 6.95 (1-880047-04-7) Creative Des.

Roller, William L., jt. auth. see Shashkan, Donald A.

Rolleri-Freire, Liliana, tr. see Link, Edward P.

An Asterisk (*) at the beginning of an entry indicates that the title is appearing for the first time.

Rolleston, F. S., jt. auth. see Halperin, M. L.

Rolleston, James. Narratives of Ecstasy: Romantic Temporality in Modern German Poetry. LC 87-2020. 244p. 1987. 34.95 (*0-8143-1841-X*) Wayne St U Pr.

— Rilke in Transition: An Exploration of His Earliest Poetry. LC 73-99839. (Yale Germanic Studies: 4). 256p. reprint ed. pap. 79.40 (*0-608-14255-7*, 202203500024) Bks Demand.

Rolleston, James, tr. see Witte, Bernd.

Rolleston, T. W. Celtic Mythology: History Legends & Dietics. 6th ed. (Illus.). 460p. 1997. reprint ed. pap. 18.95 (*0-87877-241-3*) Newcastle Pub.

— Celtic Myths & Legends. (Illus.). 512p. 1998. pap. 9.95 (*0-486-26507-2*) Dover.

Rollet. Coline Serreau. LC 99-165151. (Illus.). 166p. 1998. 79.95 (*0-7190-5087-1*, Pub. by Manchester Univ Pr); pap. 22.95 (*0-7190-5088-X*, Pub. by Manchester Univ Pr) St Martin.

Rollet, B., et al. Stratification of Tropical Forests As Seen in Leaf Structure, Pt. 2. (Tasks for Vegetation Science Ser.). (C). 1990. text 285.00 (*0-7923-0397-0*) Kluwer Academic.

Rollet, Brigitte, jt. auth. see Coleman, James A.

Rollet, Jean. Les Maitres de la Lumiere. (FRE., Illus.). 301p. 1980. lib. bdg. 75.00 (*2-04-010496-8*) Hacker.

Rollett, A. D., ed. see Minerals, Metals & Materials Society Staff.

Rollett, A. P., jt. auth. see Cundy, H. M.

Rollett, R., et al. Fertilizers & Soil Amendments. 1981. text 54.20 (*0-13-314336-8*) P-H.

Rolley, Claude. Greek Bronzes. LC 85-51623. (Illus.). 300p. 1986. lib. bdg. 95.00 (*0-85667-300-5*, Pub. by P Wilson) Scala Books.

Rolley, Katrina & Aish, Caroline. Fashions in Photographs, 1900-1920. 144p. (C). 1992. text 85.00 (*0-7134-6119-5*) B&N Imports.

Rollfinke, Dieter & Rollfinke, Jacqueline. The Call of Human Nature: The Role of Scatology in Modern German Literature. LC 86-1490. (Illus.). 256p. 1986. lib. bdg. 30.00 (*0-87023-536-2*) U of Mass Pr.

Rollfinke, Jacqueline, jt. auth. see Rollfinke, Dieter.

Rolliet, D. G. Your Name & Colors: Blueprints to Your Chemistry--The Rolliet Letter-Color Theory. (Illus.). (Orig.). 1988. pap. text. write for info. (*0-318-64366-9*) Spectra Pubns Hse.

— Your Name & Colors: Secret Keys to Your Beauty, Personality & Success, the Rolliett Letter-Color Theory. Reanult, Michael & Wolf, Jeannie, eds. LC 89-91991. (Illus.). 192p. (Orig.). (YA). 1990. pap. 12.95 (*0-9621693-0-7*) Spectra Pubns Hse.

Rollig, Aaron E. Jurisprudence & Medical Mistakes: Index & Bibliography. LC 88-47579. 150p. 1988. 47.50 (*0-88164-718-7*); pap. 44.50 (*0-88164-719-5*) ABBE Pubs Assn.

Rollig, Wolfgang, ed. see Brunner, Hellmut.

Rollin, A., ed. see Bille-de Mot, Eleonore.

Rollin, A. L. & Rigo, J. M., eds. Geomembranes: Identification & Performance Testing. 352p. 1991. 88.95 (*0-442-31272-5*) Chapman & Hall.

Rollin, B. E. The Teaching of Responsibility. 1983. 20.00 (*0-7855-1115-6*) St Mut.

Rollin, Bernard. The Experimental Animal in Biomedical Research, I. 464p. 1990. boxed set 294.95 (*0-8493-4981-8*, HV4915) CRC Pr.

— An Introduction to Veterinary Medical Ethics: Theory & Cases. LC 99-24729. (Illus.). 430p. 1999. pap. 39.95 (*0-8138-1659-9*) Iowa St U Pr.

— The Unheeded Cry: Animal Consciousness, Animal Pain & Science. LC 98-3110. 344p. 1998. pap. 22.95 (*0-8138-2576-8*) Iowa St U Pr.

— The Unheeded Cry: Animal Consciousness, Animal Pain & Science. rev. ed. LC 98-3110. 344p. 1998. text 54.95 (*0-8138-2575-X*) Iowa St U Pr.

Rollin, Bernard E. Animal Rights & Human Morality. rev. ed. LC 92-21979. 248p. (C). 1992. pap. 18.95 (*0-87975-789-2*) Prometheus Bks.

— The Experimental Animal in Biomedical Research, Vol. II. 560p. 1995. boxed set 239.95 (*0-8493-4982-6*) CRC Pr.

— Farm Animal Welfare: Social, Bioethical & Research Issues. LC 95-21992. (Illus.). 208p. 1995. text 19.95 (*0-8138-2563-6*) Iowa St U Pr.

— The Frankenstein Syndrome. (Cambridge Studies in Philosophy & Public Policy). (Illus.). 255p. (C). 1995. pap. text 23.95 (*0-521-47807-3*) Cambridge U Pr.

— The Frankenstein Syndrome: Ethical & Social Issues in the Genetic Engineering of Animals. (Cambridge Studies in Philosophy & Public Policy). (Illus.). 255p. (C). 1995. text 64.95 (*0-521-47230-X*) Cambridge U Pr.

***Rollin, Betty.** First, You Cry. LC 00-38243. 224p. 2000. pap. 13.00 (*0-06-095630-5*, Quil) HarperTrade.

Rollin, Betty. Last Wish. LC 98-19185. 272p. 1998. pap. text 12.00 (*1-891620-01-0*, Pub. by PublicAffairs NY) HarpC.

— Last Wish. 240p. 1986. pap. 8.95 (*0-446-37032-0*) Warner Bks.

Rollin, C. E. 52 Maneras de Elevar Tu Autoestima. 1997. pap. text 7.99 (*0-88113-433-3*) Caribe Betania.

***Rollin, Catherine.** Bean Bag Dog. 1999. pap. 2.50 (*0-7390-0300-3*, 18534) Alfred Pub.

— Carol of the Bells, Piano Duet. 8p. 1999. pap. 2.95 (*0-7390-0371-2*, 18976) Alfred Pub.

— Christmas Impressions: Eight Favorite Christmas Carols Arranged for Intermediate Pianists, Bk. 2. 24p. 1993. pap. 5.95 (*0-7390-0361-5*, 6682) Alfred Pub.

— Concerto Romantique. 48p. 1999. pap. 9.95 (*0-7390-0523-5*, 18075) Alfred Pub.

— Jazz Cat. (Alfred's Signature Ser.). 4p. 1989. pap. 2.50 (*0-7390-0812-9*, 3639) Alfred Pub.

— The Kangaroo That Almost Flew. 4p. 1998. pap. 2.50 (*0-7390-0729-7*, 18179) Alfred Pub.

— Lyric Moments, Bk. 1. 24p. 1995. pap. 5.95 (*0-7390-0367-4*, 14663) Alfred Pub.

— My Ducks Love to Quack. 4p. 1998. pap. 2.50 (*0-7390-0731-9*, 18176) Alfred Pub.

— Prelude in F Major. 4p. Date not set. pap. 2.50 (*0-7390-0725-4*, 19707) Alfred Pub.

— Preludes for Piano, Bk. 1. 16p. 1989. pap. 5.50 (*0-7390-0898-6*, 3609) Alfred Pub.

— Sounds of Spain, Bk. 1. 24p. 1999. pap. 5.95 (*0-7390-0354-2*, 17601) Alfred Pub.

— Sounds of Spain, Bk. 2. 24p. 1999. pap. 5.95 (*0-7390-0355-0*, 17602) Alfred Pub.

— Spotlight on Christmas. 24p. 1998. pap. 5.95 (*0-7390-0579-0*, 18761) Alfred Pub.

— Summer's Nocturne. 4p. 1993. pap. 2.50 (*0-7390-0732-7*, 5466) Alfred Pub.

— Sunlight Waltz. 4ap. 1997. pap. 2.50 (*0-7390-0825-0*, 18134) Alfred Pub.

— We Wish You a Jazzy Christmas: 6 Seasonal Duets in Jazz Style for Early Intermediate Pianists. 32p. 1996. pap. 6.50 (*0-7390-0559-6*, 16882) Alfred Pub.

Rollin, Frank A. Life & Public Services of Martin R. Delany, Sub-Assistant Commissioner, Bureau Relief of Refugees, Freedmen & of Abandoned Lands, & Late Major 104th U. S. Colored Troops. LC 77-92236. (American Negro: His History & Literature. Series 3). 1970. reprint ed. 19.95 (*0-405-01934-3*) Ayer.

Rollin, Frank A., jt. auth. see Brown, Josephine.

Rollin, Libby. Age Plus Wisdom: The Art of Thriving in a Retirement Community. 276p. 1995. 23.00 (*1-885420-07-2*) Peradam Pr.

Rollin, Lucy. Twentieth-Century Teen Culture by the Decades: A Reference Guide. LC 98-51892. (Illus.). 416p. 1999. 59.95 (*0-313-30223-5*) Greenwood.

Rollin, Lucy, ed. The Antic Art: Enhancing Children's Literary Experiences Through Film & Video. (Illus.). 243p. 1994. pap. text 14.50 (*0-917846-27-3*, 95552) Highsmith Pr.

***Rollin, Lucy & West, Mark I.** Psychoanalytic Responses to Children's Literature. LC 98-54256. 190p. 1999. lib. bdg. 34.50 (*0-7864-0674-7*) McFarland & Co.

Rollin, Lucy, ed. see Twain, Mark, pseud.

Rollin, Roger, ed. The Americanization of the Global Village: Essays in Comparative Popular Culture. LC 89-83393. (Illus.). 154p. (C). 1990. 26.95 (*0-87972-469-2*); pap. 13.95 (*0-87972-470-6*) Bowling Green Univ Popular Press.

Rollin, Roger B. Robert Herrick. (Twayne's English Authors Ser.: No. 34). 180p. 1992. 32.00 (*0-8057-7012-7*, Twyne) Mac Lib Ref.

Rollin, Roger B., ed. see Robert Herrick Memorial Conference, University of.

Rollin, Sue & Streetly, Jane. Blue Guide Jordan. 2nd ed. (Blue Guide Ser.). (Illus.). 256p. 1998. pap. 21.95 (*0-393-31872-9*, Norton Paperbks) Norton.

***Rollin, Walter J.** Counseling Individuals with Communication Disorders: Psychodynamic & Family Aspects. 2nd ed. LC 99-461973. 272p. 2000. 45.00 (*0-7506-7178-5*) Buttrwrth-Heinemann.

Rolling, Danny & London, Sondra. The Making of a Serial Killer: The Real Story of the Gainsville Student Murders in the Killer's Own Words. LC 98-134716. (Illus.). 250p. (Orig.). 1996. pap. 12.95 (*0-922915-40-7*) Feral Hse.

Rolling Stone Editors. Cobain. 1994. 146.70 (*0-316-88407-3*) Little.

— Cobain. 144p. 1997. pap. 16.95 (*0-316-88015-9*) Little.

— Crazy, Sexy, Cool. 1996. 29.95 (*0-614-20392-9*) Little.

— Garcia. (Illus.). 238p. (gr. 8). 1996. 29.95 (*0-316-75449-8*) Little.

— Garcia. 240p. 1999. pap. 20.00 (*0-316-75445-5*) Little.

— Garcia. 1999. write for info. (*0-316-75416-1*) Little.

***Rolling Stone Editors.** HotHouse. 128p. 2000. 30.00 (*0-06-039367-X*, ReganBks) HarperTrade.

Rolling Stone Editors. Neil Young - The Rolling Stone Files: The Ultimate Compendium of Interviews, Articles, Facts, & Opinions from the Files of "Rolling Stone" LC 94-11012. 320p. (J). 1994. pap. 12.45 (*0-7868-8043-0*, Pub. by Hyperion) Time Warner.

— REM: The "Rolling Stone" Files: The Ultimate Compendium of Interviews, Articles, Facts & Opinions from the Files of "Rolling Stone" 208p. (J). 1995. pap. 12.45 (*0-7868-8054-6*, Pub. by Hyperion) Time Warner.

— Rolling Stone Interviews, 1967-1980. 1989. pap. 15.95 (*0-312-03486-5*) St Martin.

— Rolling Stone Rock Almanac. 1987. pap. 19.95 (*0-02-604490-0*) Macmillan.

— U2 - The Rolling Stone Files: The Ultimate Compendium of Interviews, Articles, Facts & Opinions from the Files of "Rolling Stone" 256p. (J). 1994. pap. 12.45 (*0-7868-8001-5*, Pub. by Hyperion) Time Warner.

Rolling Stone Editors, ed. The Rolling Stone Environmental Reader. LC 92-5175. 268p. (Orig.). 1992. pap. 17.95 (*1-55963-166-X*) Island Pr.

***Rolling Stone Editors, ed.** The Seventies: A Tumultuous Decade Reconsidered. (Illus.). 288p. 2000. pap. 19.95 (*0-316-81547-0*) Little.

Rolling Stone Editors, jt. auth. see Wenner, Jann S.

Rolling Stone Magazine Editors. Rolling Stone Images of Rock & Roll. (Illus.). 256p. 1997. pap. 24.95 (*0-316-75679-2*) Little.

Rolling Stones Editors. Rolling Stone Images of Rock & Roll. 256p. (gr. 8). 1995. 50.00 (*0-316-75468-4*) Little.

Rolling Thunder staff. Rolling Thunder Speaks, Vol. 1. LC 99-12791. (Illus.). 266p. 1999. pap. 14.95 (*1-57416-026-5*) Clear Light.

Rollings, Alane. In Your Own Sweet Time. LC 88-5746. (Wesleyan Poetry Ser.). 72p. 1989. pap. 12.95 (*0-8195-1157-9*, Wesleyan Univ Pr) U Pr of New Eng.

— The Logic of Opposites. LC 98-5806. 96p. 1998. text 35.00 (*0-8101-5081-6*); pap. text 14.95 (*0-8101-5082-4*, TriQuart) Northwestern U Pr.

— Struggle to Adore. 105p. 1994. pap. 12.95 (*0-934257-97-3*) Story Line.

Rollings, Andrew. Game Architecture & Design Gold Book. LC 99-45764. 1999. pap. text 49.99 (*1-57610-425-7*) Coriolis Grp.

Rollings, Charles. Stalag Luft III: The Full Story. 1000p. (C). 1992. 125.00 (*0-946771-58-8*, Pub. by Spellmnt Pubs) St Mut.

Rollings, Dale. Exit Laughing: What Every Business Owner Must Know Before Thinking of Selling. 1999. pap. 29.95 (*1-58374-002-3*) Chicago Spectrum.

Rollings, Gwen C. Seasons of a Women: A Book of Poetry. (Illus.). 65p. Date not set. pap. 9.95 (*0-9668650-0-6*) Maximilian Pr.

Rollings, Kim, ed. Compositions of Note Vol. 1: Dallas Symphony Chorus, Orchestra & Staff Cookbook. Facchiano, J. A., tr. (Illus.). 345p. (Orig.). 1996. pap. 20.00 (*0-9651339-0-7*) Dallas Symphony.

Rollings, Laurie M. Mother Goose Rhymes-Versos Infantiles-Vers D'Enfance. 64p. 1988. 19.95 incl. audio (*0-945206-00-3*) Matterplay.

Rollings, Marian P. & Rollings, Raymond S. Geotechnical Materials in Construction. LC 95-20882. 523p. 1995. 64.95 (*0-07-053665-1*) McGraw.

Rollings, Raymond S., jt. auth. see Rollings, Marian P.

Rollings, Willard H. The Osage: An Ethnohistorical Study of Hegemony on the Prairie-Plains. (Illus.). 336p. 1995. pap. 17.95 (*0-8262-1006-6*) U of Mo Pr.

***Rollino, John.** Laboratory Notes for Introductory Physics 750: 205-206. 56p. (C). 1998. pap. text 23.95 (*0-7872-0719-5*) Kendall-Hunt.

***Rollins.** Managing Children's Psychosocial Needs. 2000. 49.00 (*0-8342-1677-9*) Aspen Pub.

Rollins, Alden M. The Rollins Family in New Hampshire Provincial Deeds, 1655-1771. LC 98-109571. vi, 204p. 1997. pap. 19.00 (*0-7884-0673-6*, R544) Heritage Bk.

— Vermont Warnings Out, 1779-1817, Vol. 2. LC 96-68448. 608p. 1997. 49.50 (*0-89725-266-7*, 1749) Picton Pr.

Rollins, Alden M., tr. Vermont Warnings Out, 1779-1817, Vol. 1. 448p. 1995. 39.50 (*0-89725-234-9*, 1619) Picton Pr.

Rollins, Arline M., jt. auth. see Gouke, Mary N.

Rollins, Barrett J. Chemokines & Cancer. LC 98-48424. (Contemporary Cancer Research Ser.). (Illus.). 336p. 1999. 125.00 (*0-89603-562-X*) Humana.

Rollins, Boyd C., jt. ed. see Barber, Brian K.

Rollins, C. E. 52 Maneras de Alentar a Otros. (Fifty-Two Maneras de... Ser.). (SPA.). 150p. 1996. pap. 7.99 (*0-88113-429-5*) Caribe Betania.

***Rollins, Cal E.** Male Rain: Selected Poems. LC 99-462195. 64p. 2000. pap. 14.95 (*1-890688-05-3*) Kalimat.

— No Roosters in This Blue City: Selected Poems. LC 99-16675. 1999. 9.95 (*1-890688-24-X*) Kalimat.

Rollins, Carole. The Ecology Book Vol. I: Introduction. (Illus.). 22p. (J). (gr. k-3). 1996. pap. text 7.95 (*1-889862-02-9*) ECF.

— The Ecology Book Vol. II: Exploring. unabridged ed. (Illus.). 27p. (J). (gr. k-3). 1996. pap. text 7.95 (*1-889862-03-7*) ECF.

— Me & My Friends. (Illus.). 36p. (J). (gr. k-3). 1996. 14.95 (*1-889862-00-2*); pap. 9.95 (*1-889862-01-0*) ECF.

Rollins, Catherine E. Building Self-Esteem & Confidence in Yourself & Your Child. 1994. 7.98 (*0-88365-857-7*) Galahad Bks.

— Fifty-Two Ways to Get Along with Your College Roommate. LC 94-4726. 1994. pap. 7.99 (*0-8407-9261-1*) Nelson.

Rollins, Charlemae H., ed. Christmas Gif' An Anthology of Christmas Poems, Songs, & Stories, Written by & about African Americans. LC 92-18976. (Illus.). 128p. (J). 1993. 14.00 (*0-688-11667-1*, Wm Morrow) Morrow Avon.

— Christmas Gif' An Anthology of Christmas Poems, Songs, & Stories, Written by & about Black People. LC 92-18976. (Illus.). 128p. (J). 1993. lib. bdg. 13.93 (*0-688-11668-X*, Wm Morrow) Morrow Avon.

Rollins, Doug. John Metcalf & His Works. (Canadian Author Studies). 57p. (C). 1985. pap. 9.95 (*0-920802-73-7*, Pub. by ECW) Genl Dist Srvs.

Rollins, George W. The Struggle of the Cattleman, Sheepman & Settler for Control of Lands in Wyoming, 1867-1910. Bruchey, Stuart, ed. LC 78-56671. (Management of Public Lands in the U. S. Ser.). (Illus.). 1979. lib. bdg. 35.95 (*0-405-11353-6*) Ayer.

Rollins, Harold. Geology Lecture Notes. 72p. 1993. spiral bd. 10.95 (*0-8403-8884-5*) Kendall-Hunt.

Rollins, Henry. Black Coffee Blues. 2nd ed. LC 98-113419. 120p. 1997. pap. 11.00 (*1-880985-55-1*) Two Thirteen Sixty-one.

— Do I Come Here Often? Pt. 2: Black Coffee Blues. (Illus.). 189p. 1998. pap. 12.00 (*1-880985-61-6*) Two Thirteen Sixty-one.

— Eye Scream. 219p. (Orig.). 1996. pap. 15.00 (*1-880985-32-2*) Two Thirteen Sixty-one.

— The First Five. 536p. 1997. pap. 20.00 (*1-880985-51-9*) Two Thirteen Sixty-one.

— Get in the Van: On the Road with Black Flag. 2nd ed. (Illus.). 256p. 1995. reprint ed. pap. 20.00 (*1-880985-24-1*) Two Thirteen Sixty-one.

— The Portable Henry Rollins. 1998. write for info. (*0-679-45965-0*) Villard Books.

— The Portable Henry Rollins. LC 97-2931. 400p. 1998. pap. 19.95 (*0-375-75000-2*) Villard Books.

— See a Grown Man Cry/Now Watch Him Die. 352p. 1997. pap. 17.00 (*1-880985-37-3*) Two Thirteen Sixty-one.

— Smile, You're Traveling Pt. 3: Black Coffee Blues. 190p. 2000. pap. 15.00 (*1-880985-69-1*) Two Thirteen Sixty-one.

— Solipsist. LC 98-215544. 160p. 1998. pap. text 11.00 (*1-880985-59-4*) Two Thirteen Sixty-one.

— Won't Sleep, Won't Shut Up: Henry Rollins Live, 1. (Illus.). 180p. 2000. pap. 17.00 (*1-880985-66-7*) Two Thirteen Sixty-one.

Rollins, Henry, ed. The Best of 2.13.61 Publications. 339p. 1998. pap. 17.00 (*1-880985-62-4*) Two Thirteen Sixty-one.

Rollins, Hyder. Contribution to the History of English Commonwealth Drama. (Studies in Drama: No. 39). (C). 1970. reprint ed. pap. 39.95 (*0-8383-0065-0*) M S G Haskell Hse.

— Troilus-Cressida Story from Chaucer to Shakespeare. LC 76-100782. (English Literature Ser.: No. 33). (C). 1970. reprint ed. lib. bdg. 59.00 (*0-8383-0338-2*) M S G Haskell Hse.

Rollins, Hyder & Baker, Herschel, eds. The Renaissance in England: Non-Dramatic Prose & Verse of the Sixteenth Century. 1014p. (C). 1992. reprint ed. pap. text 39.95 (*0-88133-673-4*) Waveland Pr.

Rollins, Hyder E. The Keats Circle: Letters & Papers, & More Letters & Poems of the Keats Circle, 2 vols., 1. 2nd ed. LC 65-13632. (Illus.). 492p. 1965. reprint ed. pap. 152.60 (*0-7837-4890-6*, 205905800001) Bks Demand.

— The Keats Circle: Letters & Papers, & More Letters & Poems of the Keats Circle, 2 vols., 2. LC 65-13632. (Illus.). 661p. 1965. reprint ed. pap. 200.00 (*0-7837-4891-4*, 205905800002) Bks Demand.

Rollins, Hyder E., et al. Pack of Autolycus or Strange & Terrible News of Ghosts: Broadside Ballads of the Years 1624-1693. LC 27-4308. (Illus.). 287p. 1969. 17.50 (*0-674-65125-1*) HUP.

— Phoenix Nest, 1593. LC 31-4893. (Illus.). 285p. 1959. 16.50 (*0-674-66610-0*) HUP.

Rollins, Hyder E., ed. see Keats, John.

Rollins, Hyder E., ed. see Pepys, Samuel.

Rollins, Hyder E., ed. see Robinson, Clement.

Rollins, Hyder E., ed. see Shakespeare, William.

Rollins, Hyder E., ed. see Tottel, Richard.

Rollins, Hyder Edward, ed. see Keats, John.

Rollins, Jack, jt. auth. see Nelson, Steve.

***Rollins, James.** Excavation. 432p. 2000. mass mkt. 6.99 (*0-380-81093-X*) Morrow Avon.

Rollins, James. Subterranean. LC 98-93549. 416p. 1999. mass mkt. 6.99 (*0-380-79264-8*, Avon Bks) Morrow Avon.

Rollins, Joan H. Womens Minds, Womens Bodies. 546p. 1996. pap. text 57.00 (*0-13-720343-8*) P-H.

Rollins, John P., ed. Compressed Air & Gas Handbook. 5th ed. 384p. 1988. reprint ed. text 145.00 (*0-13-162611-6*) P-H.

Rollins, Judith. All Is Never Said: The Narrative of Odette Harper Hines. (Illus.). 320p. (C). 1995. pap. 19.95 (*1-56639-308-6*); lib. bdg. 49.95 (*1-56639-307-8*) Temple U Pr.

— Between Women: Domestics & Their Employers. LC 85-8022. (Labor & Social Change Ser.). 256p. 1987. pap. 19.95 (*0-87722-491-9*) Temple U Pr.

Rollins, Judy A., jt. ed. see Broome, Marion E.

***Rollins, Korea.** Black Queen. 32p. 2000. pap. 4.95 (*1-56167-518-0*) Am Literary Pr.

Rollins, Kyle M., ed. In-Situ Deep Soil Improvement: Proceedings of Sessions Sponsored by the Geotechnical Engineering Division of the American Society of Civil Engineers in Conjunction with the ASCE National Convention in Atlanta, Georgia, October 9-13, 1994. LC 94-34442. (Geotechnical Special Publications: Vol. 45). 160p. 1994. 22.00 (*0-7844-0058-X*) Am Soc Civil Eng.

Rollins, Kyle M., jt. auth. see Adan, Scott M.

Rollins, Kyle M., jt. ed. see Owens, Russell L.

Rollins, L. A. Lucifer's Lexicon. 144p. (Orig.). 1987. pap. text 8.95 (*0-915179-43-1*) Loompanics.

Rollins, Leighton & Corrigan, Daniel. Disasters of War. LC 80-69430. (Illus.). 48p. 1981. pap. 4.00 (*0-932274-15-3*) Cadmus Eds.

Rollins, Leslie E., ed. see Association of Theatrical Artists & Craftspeople S.

Rollins, Marilyn. Lifestyle Changes: 12 Step Recovery Nutrition & Diet Guide. LC 91-24619. 128p. (Orig.). pap. 7.95 (*0-934125-23-6*) Hazelden.

Rollins, Marion J. The God of the Old Testament in Relation to War. LC 72-176551. (Columbia University. Teachers College. Contributions to Education Ser.: No. 263). reprint ed. 37.50 (*0-404-55263-3*) AMS Pr.

Rollins, Mark, jt. ed. see Campbell, Mary B.

Rollins, Mary R. Patients, Pain & Politics: Nursing Home Inspector's Shocking True Story & Expert Advice for You & Your Family. Davis, Barbara, ed. 248p. (Orig.). 1994. pap. 11.95 (*1-884348-20-3*) N Century Pubng.

Rollins, Nancy. Child Psychiatry in the Soviet Union: Preliminary Observations. LC 72-76560. (Illus.). 315p. 1972. 41.50 (*0-674-11475-2*) HUP.

***Rollins, Pamela L.** Straight & Narrow. Reeck, Karen Ann L., ed. LC 99-69865. 69p. (YA). (gr. 5-8). 2000. pap. 15.00 (*0-9678627-0-1*) C W R Pubng.

Rollins, Patrick J., ed. U. S. S. R. Legislative Documents Series, 2 vols. in 1, Ea. 1993. 180.00 (*0-87569-166-8*) Academic Intl.

Rollins, Peter, jt. ed. see Rollins, Susan.

Rollins, Peter C. Will Rogers: A Bio-Bibliography. LC 83-10696. (Popular Culture Bio-Bibliographies Ser.). 282p. 1984. lib. bdg. 42.95 (*0-313-22633-4*, RWR/, Greenwood Pr) Greenwood.

Rollins, Peter C. & O'Connor, John E., eds. Hollywood's Indian: The Portrayal of the Native American in Film. (Illus.). 240p. 1999. reprint ed. pap. 18.00 (*0-8131-0952-3*) U Pr of Ky.

— Hollywood's World War I: Motion Picture Images. LC 97-26062. (Illus.). 220p. 1997. pap. 19.95 (*0-87972-756-X*) Bowling Green Univ Popular Press.

R

Rollins, Philip A. The Cowboy: An Unconventional History of Civilization on the Old-Time Cattle Range. LC 96-39162. (Illus.). 462p. 1997. pap. 19.95 (*0-8061-2936-0*) U of Okla Pr.

***Rollins, Philip A.** The Cowboy: His Character, Equipment & His Part in the Development of the West. 2nd unabridged ed. 370p. 1999. reprint ed. pap. 18.95 (*0-87928-120-0*) Corner Hse.

Rollins, Philip A., ed. see Stuart, Robert.

***Rollins, R.** Like Breathing. 258p. 1998. pap. 14.00 (*1-892096-33-1*) Ishai Creat.

Rollins, Reed C. The Cruciferae of Continental North America: Systematics of the Mustard Family from the Arctic to Panama. LC 92-35018. (Illus.). 1000p. (C). 1993. 129.50 (*0-8047-2064-9*) Stanford U Pr.

Rollins, Reed C. & Shaw, Elizabeth A. Genus Lesquerella (Cruciferae) in North America. LC 72-87777. (Illus.). 300p. 1973. 40.50 (*0-674-34775-7*) HUP.

***Rollins, Ric.** Breathe Again. 300p. 1999. pap. 16.00 (*1-892096-31-5*) Ishai Creat.

Rollins, Richard. Black Southerners in Gray: Essays on African-Americans in Confederate Armies. 2nd ed. (Illus.). 210p. 1997. reprint ed. pap. 16.95 (*0-9638993-9-2*, Pub. by Rank & File) Stackpole.

— The Damned Red Flags of Rebellion: The Confederate Battle Flag at Gettysburg. (Illus.). 302p. 1997. 38.95 (*0-9638993-3-3*) Rank & File.

— The Damned Red Flags of Rebellion: The Confederate Battle Flags at Gettysburg. LC 96-67594. (Illus.). 262p. 1999. pap. text 19.95 (*1-888967-04-8*, Pub. by Rank & File) Stackpole.

Rollins, Richard, ed. Pickett's Charge: Eyewitness Accounts. xxxi, 376p. 1994. 35.00 (*0-9638993-1-7*); pap. 18.00 (*0-9638993-0-9*) Rank & File.

— The Returned Battle Flags. 1995. pap. 25.00 (*0-9638993-4-1*) Rank & File.

Rollins, Richard & Shultz, David. Guide to Pennsylvania Troops at Gettysburg. 2nd ed. LC 99-192231. (Orig.). 1998. pap. 17.95 (*1-888967-02-1*) Rank & File.

Rollins, Ronald G. Sean O'Casey's Drama: Verisimilitude & Vision. LC 77-14462. (Illus.). 150p. 1979. pap. 46.50 (*0-7837-8401-5*, 205921200009) Bks Demand.

Rollins, Scott. Borderlines: Selected Poems & Fictions, 1972-1992. LC 94-79583. (Essential Poets Ser.: No. 66). 150p. (C). 1997. pap. 13.00 (*1-55071-009-5*) Guernica Editions.

Rollins, Scott, tr. see Barkan, Stanley H., ed.

Rollins, Scott, tr. see Bernlef, J.

Rollins, Scott, tr. see De Winter, Leon.

***Rollins, Susan.** New Shoes, Red Shoes. LC 99-48058. (Illus.). 32p. (J). (ps-1). 2000. 15.95 (*0-531-30268-7*) Orchard Bks Watts.

Rollins, Susan & Rollins, Peter, eds. Gender in Popular Culture: Images of Men & Women in Literature, Visual Media, Material Culture. (Illus.). 234p. (Orig.). (C). 1995. pap. 16.50 (*0-9641755-0-9*) Ridgemont Pr.

Rollins, Thomas & Roberts, Darryl. Work Culture, Organizational Performance & Business Success. LC 98-4933. 272p. 1998. 59.95 (*1-56720-122-9*, Quorum Bks) Greenwood.

Rollins, Tim, et al. Tim Rollins & K. O. S. The Red Badge of Courage. Margolis, Nancy H., ed. (Illus.). 1994. 8.00 (*0-9611560-4-X*) SEC Contemp Art.

Rollins, Wayne. Soul & Psyche: The Bible in Psychological Perspective. LC 99-39508. 1999. pap. 22.00 (*0-8006-2716-4*, Fortress Pr) Augsburg Fortress.

Rollins, William, Jr. The Shadow Before. LC 74-22808. reprint ed. 45.00 (*0-404-58464-0*) AMS Pr.

Rollins, William H. A Greener Vision of Home: Cultural Politics & Environmental Reform in the German Heimatschutz Movement, 1904-1918. LC 97-4705. (Social History, Popular Culture, & Politics in Germany). 344p. (C). 1997. text 57.50 (*0-472-10809-3*, 10809) U of Mich Pr.

Rollins, Wilma E., jt. auth. see Ranucci, Ernest R.

Rollins, Yuriko U., jt. auth. see Young, John.

***Rollinson, David & Joseph, Sam.** Microbial Pathogenesis: Lecture Supplements. 166p. (C). 1999. per. 29.95 (*0-7872-6500-4*, 41650001) Kendall-Hunt.

Rollinson, David & Simpson, Andrew J., eds. The Biology of Schistosomes: From Genes to Latrines. 472p. 1988. text 136.00 (*0-12-593692-3*) Acad Pr.

Rollinson, Hugh R. Using Geochemical Data: Evaluation, Presentation, Interpretation. (Longman Geochemistry Ser.). (C). 1990. pap. text 67.95 (*0-582-06701-4*) Longman.

Rollinson, Mark. Popular Legal Delusions. viii, 169p. 1992. 22.95 (*0-9614303-6-2*) Summertown.

Rollinson, Mark, jt. auth. see Harvey, Carolyn.

Rollinson, Neil. A Spillage of Mercury. 64p. 1997. pap. 14.95 (*0-224-04008-1*, Pub. by Jonathan Cape) Trafalgar.

Rollinson, Philip & Geckle, Richard. GuideTo Classical Rhetoric. LC 98-31617. 209p. 1998. 29.95 (*1-893009-01-7*); pap. 15.95 (*1-893009-00-9*) Summertown.

Rollinson, Philip & Ross, Mark E. The Children's Catechism: A New, Modern Version. 26p. (Orig.). 1988. pap. text 1.95 (*0-9614303-2-X*) Summertown.

Rollinson, Philip, jt. auth. see Kelly, Douglas.

Rollinson, Philip, jt. ed. see Ball, John H., III.

Rollinson, Philip, jt. ed. see Howard-Hill, T. H.

Rollinson, Philip, jt. ed. see Howard-Hill, Trevor.

Rollinson, Philip, jt. ed. see Williams, George W.

Rollinson, Philip, tr. see Viperano, Giovanni A.

***Rollison, David & Blackwell, Jennifer, eds.** Exploring Parasite Genomes. (Parasitology Ser.: No. 118). 86p. (C). 2000. 39.95 (*0-521-77574-4*) Cambridge U Pr.

Rollison, Jeffrey, jt. auth. see Tatem, Jill M.

***Rollmann, Hans, et al.** The Quest for Unity, Peace & Purity in Thomas Campbell's Declaration & Address: Text & Studies. LC 00-32947. (ATLA Monographs). 2000. pap. write for info. (*0-8108-3843-5*) Scarecrow.

Rollnick, Stephen. Behavior Guide. 11th ed. (C). Date not set. pap. text 19.00 (*0-443-05850-4*) Church.

Rollnick, Stephen, jt. auth. see Miller, William R.

***Rollo, David.** Glamorous Sorcery: Magic & Literacy in the High Middle Ages. LC 00-9010. (Medieval Cultures Ser.). 2000. pap. write for info. (*0-8166-3547-1*) U of Minn Pr.

Rollo, David. Historical Fabrication, Ethnic Fable & French Romance in Twelfth-Century England. LC 97-75360. (Edward C. Armstrong Monographs on Medieval Literature: Vol. 9). 334p. 1998. pap. 34.50 (*0-917058-91-7*) French Forum.

Rollo, Duncan J., jt. auth. see Gehle, Quentin L.

Rollo, E. M., ed. see Flemming, John.

Rollo, J. M. The New Eastern Europe: Western Responses. LC 90-34197. (Chatham House Papers). 148p. 1990. pap. 14.95 (*0-87609-085-4*) Coun Foreign.

***Rollo, Joe.** Contemporary Melbourne Architecture. 192p. 1999. pap. 35.00 (*0-86840-546-9*, Pub. by New South Wales Univ Pr) Intl Spec Bk.

Rollo, May. Discovery of Being. 192p. 1994. pap. 11.95 (*0-393-31240-2*) Norton.

Rollo, Naomi J. Goldy Lark: A Novel. LC 91-48138. 224p. (Orig.). 1992. pap. 10.95 (*1-56474-018-8*) Fithian Pr.

Rollo, Ned. Man, I Need a Job! Finding Employment with a Criminal History. 2nd ed. (Information Ser.). 76p. (Orig.). 1993. pap. 5.95 (*1-878436-15-5*) OPEN TX.

— Necesito Empleo! La Busqueda de Empleo con Historial Penal. (Information Ser.). (SPA.). 75p. (Orig.). 1993. pap. 5.95 (*1-878436-13-9*) OPEN TX.

— Ninety-Nine Days & Get Up: A Pre- & Post-Release Survival Manual for Inmates & Their Loved Ones. 2nd ed. (Information Ser.). 29p. (Orig.). 1988. pap. 3.95 (*1-878436-04-X*) OPEN TX.

Rollo, Ned & Adams, Louis W. A Map Through the Maze: A Guide to Surviving the Criminal Justice System with Advice for Families of Offenders. (Illus.). 119p. (Orig.). 1993. pap. 8.95 (*1-878436-14-7*) OPEN TX.

Rollo, Vera F. The American Flag. LC 89-42930. (Illus.). 64p. (J). 1989. 12.95 (*0-917882-28-8*); pap. 5.95 (*0-917882-31-8*) MD Hist Pr.

— Aviation Insurance. LC 86-62107. 438p. 1987. lib. bdg. 14.50 (*0-917882-22-9*) MD Hist Pr.

— Aviation Programs in the Postsecondary Schools of the United States: 1950 & 1985. 240p. 1990. 50.00 (*0-614-01410-7*); pap. 40.00 (*0-614-01411-5*) MD Hist Pr.

— Burt Rutan: Reinventing the Airplane. LC 91-52844. (Illus.). 300p. 1991. 24.50 (*0-917882-33-4*) MD Hist Pr.

— Maryland Today: A Geography. 3rd ed. LC 99-33419. 188p. (J). (gr. 4). 1999. 22.50 (*0-917882-49-0*) MD Hist Pr.

— The Presidents & Their Pets. LC 93-86023. 120p. 1993. 19.50 (*0-917882-29-6*) MD Hist Pr.

— The Presidents & Their Pets. LC 93-86023. (Illus.). 120p. 1993. pap. 14.25 (*0-917882-36-9*) MD Hist Pr.

— The Proprietorship of Maryland: A Documented Account. LC 87-43200. 550p. 1988. 49.75 (*0-917882-26-1*) MD Hist Pr.

— Your Maryland: A History. rev. ed. 414p. 1993. 22.50 (*0-917882-35-0*) MD Hist Pr.

Rollock, Barbara. Black Authors & Illustrators of Children's Books: A Biographical Dictionary. 2nd ed. LC 91-37402. (Illus.). 252p. 1992. text 40.00 (*0-8240-7078-X*, H01316) Garland.

Rollon, Analiza Palenzuela. Anaerobic Digestion of Fish Processing Wastewater with Special Emphasis on Hydrolysis of Suspended Solids. (IHE Thesis Ser.: 19). (Illus.). 130p. 1999. pap. text 40.00 (*90-5410-417-1*, Pub. by A A Balkema) Ashgate Pub Co.

Rollon, R. N. Spatial Variation & Seasonality in Growth & Reproduction of Enhalus Acoroides (L. F.) Royle Populations in the Coastal Waters off Cape Bolinao, NW Philippines. (IHE Thesis Ser.: Vol. 14). (Illus.). 135p. (C). 1998. text 40.00 (*90-5410-412-0*, Pub. by A A Balkema) Ashgate Pub Co.

Rollot, Jean-Claude. English-French, French-English Lexicon of Management Terms: Lexique Anglais-Francais-Anglais des Termes de Gestion. (ENG & FRE.). 1987. 15.95 (*0-8288-0085-5*, F127520) Fr & Eur.

Rolls, jt. auth. see Williston.

***Rolls, Albert.** The Theory of the King's Two Bodies in the Age of Shakespeare. LC 00-32436. (Studies in Renaissance Literature: Vol. 19). 336p. 2000. 99.95 (*0-7734-7692-X*) E Mellen.

***Rolls, Barbara & Barnett, Robert.** Volumetrics: Feel Full on Fewer Calories. Friedland, Susan, ed. LC 99-53243. (Illus.). 336p. 2000. 24.00 (*0-06-019483-9*) HarpC.

***Rolls, Brian A. & Walker, Ann F.** Infant Nutrition: Issues in Nutrition & Toxicology. 2nd ed. 228p. 1999. 115.00 (*0-8342-1359-1*) Aspen Pub.

Rolls, Charles J. The Names & Titles of Jesus Christ, 5 vols. Incl. Vol. 2. World's Greatest Name: (H-K) rev. ed. LC 84-15416. 183p. 1985. pap. 8.99 (*0-87213-732-5*); Vol. 3. Time's Noblest Name: (L-O) rev. ed. LC 84-14825. 192p. 1985. pap. 8.99 (*0-87213-733-3*); Vol. 4. Name above Every Name: (P-S) rev. ed. LC 85-6927. 255p. 1985. pap. 8.99 (*0-87213-734-1*); Vol. 5. His Glorious Name: (T-Z) 2nd ed. LC 85-6926. 267p. 1986. reprint ed. pap. 43.99 (*0-87213-735-X*); 43.99 (*0-87213-736-8*) Loizeaux.

Rolls, David, jt. auth. see Bland, Will.

Rolls, Edmund. Brain & Emotion. LC 98-43140. (Illus.). 386p. 1998. text 59.95 (*0-19-852464-1*) OUP.

***Rolls, Edmund T.** The Brain & Emotion. (Illus.). 386p. 2000. pap. text 39.95 (*0-19-852463-3*) OUP.

Rolls, Edmund T. & Treves, Alessandro. Neural Networks & Brain Function. LC 97-41669. (Illus.). 432p. 1997. text 115.00 (*0-19-852433-1*); pap. text 52.50 (*0-19-852432-3*) OUP.

Rolls, Eric C. Celebration of the Senses. LC 99-204723. 1998. 24.95 (*0-7022-3047-2*, Pub. by Univ Queensland Pr) Intl Spec Bk.

— Citizens: Flowers & the Wide Sea, Continuing the Epic Story of China's Centuries-Old Relationship with Australia. 631p. 1998. pap. 49.95 (*0-7022-3042-1*, Pub. by Univ Queensland Pr) Intl Spec Bk.

— From Forest to Sea: Australia's Changing Environment. 176p. 1994. pap. 16.95 (*0-7022-2576-2*, Pub. by Univ Queensland Pr) Intl Spec Bk.

— River. LC 75-323923. 75p. 1974. write for info. (*0-207-12667-4*) Angus & Roberts.

— Sojourners: The Epic Story of China's Centuries-Old Relationship with Australia. (Orig.). 1992. 49.95 (*0-7022-2478-2*, Pub. by Univ Queensland Pr) Intl Spec Bk.

— They All Ran Wild: The Animals & Plants That Plague Australia abr. ed. LC 85-225861. (Illus.). xvi, 546 p. 1984. write for info. (*0-207-14510-5*) Angus & Roberts.

Rolls, Mark G., jt. ed. see McInnes, Colin J.

Rollwagen, J. R. Anthropological Filmmaking: Anthropological Perspectives on the Production of Film & Video for General Public Audiences. xvi, 396p. 1988. pap. text 69.00 (*3-7186-0478-7*) Gordon & Breach.

Rollwagen, Jack R., intro. Anthropological Film & Video in the Nineteen Nineties. LC 93-79690. (Case Studies in Documentary Filmmaking). (Illus.). 450p. (Orig.). (C). 1993. pap. text 30.00 (*0-9635206-1-X*) Institute NY.

Rollyson, Carl. The Literary Legacy of Rebecca West. LC 97-33532. 266p. 1997. pap. 54.95 (*1-57309-181-2*) Intl Scholars.

— The Literary Legacy of Rebecca West. LC 97-33532. 266p. 1998. 74.95 (*1-57309-182-0*) Intl Scholars.

— Martha Gellhorn: Her Life & Times. 1999. text. write for info. (*0-312-04348-1*) St Martin.

***Rollyson, Carl.** Notable American Novelists. LC 99-34407. 2000. write for info. (*0-89356-162-2*); write for info. (*0-89356-163-0*); write for info. (*0-89356-164-9*) Salem Pr.

Rollyson, Carl. Pablo Picasso. LC 92-44757. (Arts Ser.). 112p. (YA). 1993. lib. bdg. 25.27 (*0-86625-488-9*) Rourke Pubns.

— Teenage Refugees from Eastern Europe Speak Out. (In Their Own Voices Ser.). (Illus.). 64p. (YA). (gr. 7-12). 1997. lib. bdg. 16.95 (*0-8239-2437-8*, D2437-8) Rosen Group.

— Uses of the Past in the Novels of William Faulkner. LC 98-15060. 240p. 1998. 74.95 (*1-57309-279-7*) Intl Scholars.

— Uses of the Past in the Novels of William Faulkner. LC 98-15060. 240p. 1998. pap. 54.95 (*1-57309-278-9*) Intl Scholars.

***Rollyson, Carl, ed.** Critical Survey of Long Fiction. 8 vols. 2nd rev. ed. (Illus.). 4500p. 2000. lib. bdg. 475.00 (*0-89356-882-1*) Salem Pr.

***Rollyson, Carl & Paddock, Lisa.** Susan Sontag: The Making of an Icon. 448p. 2000. 29.95 (*0-393-04928-0*) Norton.

Rollyson, Carl E. Marilyn Monroe: A Life of the Actress. LC 86-11322. (Studies in Cinema: No. 39). (Illus.). 269p. reprint ed. pap. 83.40 (*0-8357-1771-2*, 207052000097) Bks Demand.

Rollyson, Carl E., Jr. Marilyn Monroe: A Life of the Actress. (Illus.). 269p. 1993. reprint ed. pap. 14.95 (*0-306-80542-1*) Da Capo.

Rollyson, Carl E. Uses of the Past in the Novels of William Faulkner. LC 84-2745. (Studies in Modern Literature: No. 37). 234p. reprint ed. pap. 72.60 (*0-8357-1554-X*, 207059800004) Bks Demand.

***Rollyson, Carl E. & Paddock, Lisa.** Herman Melville A to Z: The Essential Reference to His Life & Work. LC 00-35338. (Illus.). 352p. 2001. 50.00 (*0-8160-3851-1*); pap. 17.95 (*0-8160-4160-1*, Checkmark) Facts on File.

Rolnick, Philip A. Analogical Possibilities: How Words Refer to God. LC 92-46630. (American Academy of Religion Academy Ser.: No. 81). 328p. 1993. 29.95 (*1-55540-824-9*, 010181); pap. 19.95 (*1-55540-825-7*, 010181) OUP.

Rolnick, Philip A., ed. see Greensboro College Staff.

Rolnick, William B. The Fundamental Particles & Their Interactions. LC 93-31895. (Illus.). 446p. (C). 1993. 86.00 (*0-201-57838-7*) Addison-Wesley.

Rolnick, William B., ed. see American Institute of Physics.

Rolnicki, Kenneth. Managing Channels of Distribution: The Marketing Executive's Complete Guide. LC 97-31322. 288p. 1996. 59.95 (*0-8144-0335-2*) AMACOM.

Rolo. Royalty Only: Do Not Use. 1999. write for info. (*0-316-75455-2*) Little.

Rolo, Charles J., ed. Psychiatry in American Life. LC 76-156711. (Essay Index Reprint Ser.). 1977. reprint ed. 20.95 (*0-8369-2424-X*) Ayer.

Rolo, Charles J. & Klein, Robert J. Gaining on the Market: Your Complete Guide to Investment Strategy. rev. ed. LC 87-29758. 1988. 18.95 (*0-316-75456-0*) Little.

Rolof, Marcia C. Tie the Moon to Your Car: My Cancer, My Way. 1994. 10.95 (*0-533-10890-X*) Vantage.

Roloff, A. & Bartels, A. Gartenflora (Garden Flora) Band 1: Gehoelze (Woody Plants) (GER., Illus.). 694p. 1996. 66.00 (*3-8001-3479-9*, Pub. by Eugen Ulmer) Balogh.

Roloff, Hans-Gert, ed. Georg Wickram - Samtliche Werke: Band XIII: Ovids Metamorphosen, 2 vols., Vol. 1. (Ausgaben Deutscher Literatur des XV bis XVIII Jahrhunderts Ser.). iv, 490p. (C). 1990. lib. bdg. 298.50 (*3-11-012121-2*) De Gruyter.

— Georg Wickram - Samtliche Werke: Band XIII: Ovids Metamorphosen, 2 vols., Vol. 2. (Ausgaben Deutscher Literatur des XV bis XVIII Jahrhunderts Ser.). iv, 405p. (C). 1990. lib. bdg. 247.70 (*3-11-012644-3*) De Gruyter.

***Roloff, Hans-Gert, ed.** Munich 1900 Site de la Modernite Munchen 1900 Als Ort der Moderne. (Jahrbuch fur International Germanistik Ser.: Bd. 47). (Illus.). 289p. 1998. 61.95 (*3-906760-79-0*, Pub. by P Lang) P Lang Pubng.

Roloff, Hans-Gert, ed. Thomas, Naogeorg, Werke Vol. 1: Tragoedia Nova Pammachius, Mit der Deutschen Uebersetzung des Johann Tyrolff. (Ausgaben Deutscher Literatur des XV bis XVIII Jahrhunderts Ser.). (C). 1974. 426.95 (*3-11-004074-3*) De Gruyter.

Roloff, Hans-Gert, et al, eds. Gottsched, Johann Christoph: Ausgewaehlte Werke, 2 pts., Vol. 8. Incl. Pt. 1. (C). 1978. 170.75 (*3-11-007467-2*); (C). write for info. (*0-318-51619-5*) De Gruyter.

Roloff, Hans-Gert & Traub, Andreas. Die Geistlichen Spiele des Sterzinger Spielarchivs Bd. 3: Rabers Passion (1514) - Haller Passion - Fragment Einer Passion - Grundonnerstagsspiel - Ludus Pascalis (1520) - Planctus Beate Mariae Virginis - Ludus de Nativitate Domini (1511) (Mittlere Deutsche Literatur in Neu- und Nachdrucken Ser.: Bd. 16). (GER., Illus.). 445p. 1996. 133.95 (*3-906755-27-4*, Pub. by P Lang) P Lang Pubng.

— Die Geistlichen Spiele des Sterzinger Spielarchivs Bd. 4: Palmsonntagsspiel (2 Fassungen) - In Cena Domini - Ludus de Ascensione Domini - Penthecostes (1522) (Mittlere Deutsche Literatur in Neu- und Nachdrucken Ser.: Bd. 17). (GER., Illus.). 383p. 1991. 144.80 (*3-261-03736-9*) P Lang Pubng.

— Die Geistlichen Spiele des Sterzinger Spielarchivsv Vd. 2: Sterzinger Passionen: Passion I (1486) - Passion II (1496) (Mittlere Deutsche Literatur in Neu- und Nachdrucken Ser.: Bd. 15). (GER.). 376p. 1988. 158.80 (*3-261-03676-1*) P Lang Pubng.

Roloff, Hans-Gert, et al. Die Geistlichen Spiele des Sterzinger Spielarchivs Bd. 6,1 & 6,2: Kommentar zu den Spieltexten & Kommentar zur Edition der Melodien. (Mittlere Deutsche Literatur in Neu- und Nachdrucken Ser.: Bd. 19). (GER., Illus.). 183p. 1996. 81.95 (*3-906756-90-4*, Pub. by P Lang) P Lang Pubng.

Roloff, Hans-Gert, ed. see Brant, Sebastian.

Roloff, Hans-Gert, ed. see Czepko, Daniel.

Roloff, Hans-Gert, ed. see Grotzinger, Vera.

Roloff, Hans-Gert, ed. see Weise, Christian.

Roloff, Jurgen. Revelation. 208p. 1993. 38.00 (*0-8006-9650-6*, 1-9650, Fortress Pr) Augsburg Fortress.

Roloff, M. Val, ed. Human Risk Assessment: The Roles of Animal Selection & Extrapolation, Proceedings of the Symposium, St. Louis, Missouri, 1985. 280p. 1987. 132.00 (*0-85066-368-7*) Taylor & Francis.

Roloff, Matt. Against Tall Odds: Being a David in a Goliath World. LC 99-32270. 250p. 1999. 19.99 (*1-57673-583-4*) Multnomah Pubs.

Roloff, Michael, tr. see Hesse, Hermann.

Roloff, Michael, tr. see Schindel, Robert.

Roloff, Michael, tr. see Skwara, Erich W.

Roloff, Michael, tr. see Winkler, Josef.

Roloff, Michael, tr. see Zauner, Friedrich C.

Roloff, Michael, tr. & afterword by see Handke, Peter.

Roloff, Michael E. Interpersonal Communication: The Social Exchange Approach. LC 81-4451. (CommText Ser.: Vol. 6). (Illus.). 149p. (C). 1981. 42.00 (*0-8039-1604-3*); pap. 18.95 (*0-8039-1605-1*) Sage.

— Interpersonal Communication: The Social Exchange Approach. LC 81-4451. (Sage Commtext Ser.: No. 6). 151p. reprint ed. pap. 46.90 (*0-7837-1130-1*, 204166000022) Bks Demand.

Roloff, Michael E. & Berger, Charles R., eds. Social Cognition & Communication. LC 82-10715. 328p. reprint ed. pap. 101.70 (*0-8357-4850-2*, 203778100009) Bks Demand.

Roloff, Michael E. & Miller, Gerald R., eds. Interpersonal Processes: New Directions in Communication. LC 87-9639. (Sage Annual Reviews of Communications Research Ser.: Vol. 14). 302p. 1987. reprint ed. pap. 93.70 (*0-608-02985-8*, 205962500006) Bks Demand.

— Interpersonal Processes: New Directions in Communication Research. (Annual Reviews of Communication Research Ser.: Vol. 14). 304p. 1987. text 58.00 (*0-8039-2654-5*); pap. text 26.00 (*0-8039-2655-3*) Sage.

— Persuasion: New Directions in Theory & Research. LC 79-21202. (Sage Annual Reviews of Communication Research Ser.: No. 8). 311p. 1980. reprint ed. pap. 96.50 (*0-608-01447-8*, 205949100001) Bks Demand.

Roloff, Michael E. & Paulson, Gaylen D., eds. Communication Yearbook, 21. 511p. 1998. 85.00 (*0-7619-1428-5*) Sage.

***Roloff, Michael E. & Paulson, Gaylen D., eds.** Communication Yearbook 23. LC 76-45943. 456p. 2000. 95.00 (*0-7619-2112-5*) Sage.

— Communication Yearbook 22. LC 76-45943. 504p. 1999. 89.95 (*0-7619-1935-X*) Sage.

Roloff, Michael E., jt. auth. see Putnam, Linda L.

Roloff, Roger R. Gathered from the Wild: Poems of a Wanderer. (Illus.). 84p. 1998. pap. 12.00 (*0-9665367-0-3*) Rhodora Pr.

Roloff, Tricia A. Navigating Through a Strange Land: A Book for Brain Tumor Patients & Their Families. LC 94-25863. (Illus.). 248p. 1995. pap. 16.95 (*0-9641214-1-7*) Indigo Pr AR.

Rolofson, Kristine. Baby Blues. 1994. per. 2.99 (*0-373-25594-2*, 1-25594-2) Harlequin Bks.

***Rolofson, Kristine.** Billy & the Kid: (Bachelors & Babies) (Temptation Ser.: No. 765). 2000. per. 3.99 (*0-373-25865-8*, 1-25865-6, Harlequin) Harlequin Bks.

— Blame it on Cowboys: Boots & Beauties. (Temptation Ser.: Bk. 802). 2000. mass mkt. 3.99 (*0-373-25902-6*, 1-25902-7) Harlequin Bks.

— Boots & Booties: The Last Man in Montana, The Only Man in Wyoming, The Next Man in Texas. 2000. per. 6.99 (*0-373-20171-0*, 1-20171-4) Harlequin Bks.

An Asterisk (*) at the beginning of an entry indicates that the title is appearing for the first time.

Rolofson, Kristine. Bound for Bliss. (Family Continuity Program Ser.: No. 20). 1999. per. 4.50 (*0-373-82168-9*, 1-82168-5) Harlequin Bks.
— The Bride Rode West. 1997. per. 3.50 (*0-373-25753-8*, 1-25753-4) Harlequin Bks.
— The Cowboy. LC 96-3653. (Temptation Ser.). 217p. 1996. per. 3.25 (*0-373-25669-8*, 1-25669-2) Harlequin Bks.
— I'll Be Seeing You: Lovers & Legends. (Temptation Ser.). 1993. per. 2.99 (*0-373-25569-1*, 1-25569-4) Harlequin Bks.
— Jessie's Lawman. LC 96-629. (Temptation Ser.). 219p. 1995. per. 3.25 (*0-373-25648-5*, 1-25648-6) Harlequin Bks.
— Jessie's Lawman. (Promo Ser.). 1999. per. 4.50 (*0-373-21985-7*, 1-21985-6) Harlequin Bks.
— The Last Man in Montana. 1997. per. 3.50 (*0-373-25717-1*, 1-25717-9) Silhouette.
— Madeleine's Cowboy. (Temptation Ser.). 1994. per. 2.99 (*0-373-25578-0*, 1-25578-5) Harlequin Bks.
— Madeleine's Cowboy. (Bestselling Authors Ser.). 1998. mass mkt. 1.99 (*0-373-83360-1*, 1-83360-7) Harlequin Bks.
— Make-Believe Honeymoon. LC 95-22322. 219p. 1995. mass mkt. 3.25 (*0-373-25660-4*, 1-25660-1) Harlequin Bks.
— The Next Man in Texas: Boots & Booties. 1997. per. 3.50 (*0-373-25725-2*, 1-25725-2) Harlequin Bks.
— On Ne Se Marie Qu'une Fois. (Rouge Passion Ser.). 1999. mass mkt. 3.50 (*0-373-37513-1*, 1-37513-8) Harlequin Bks.
— The Only Man in Wyoming. (Temptation Ser.). 1997. per. 3.50 (*0-373-25721-X*, 1-25721-1) Harlequin Bks.
— Pillow Talk (Matching Moms) 1997. per. 3.50 (*0-373-44027-8*, 1-44027-0) Harlequin Bks.
***Rolofson, Kristine.** Plain Jane's Man. 2000. mass mkt. 4.50 (*0-373-82210-3*, 1-82210-5) Harlequin Bks.
Rolofson, Kristine. The Right Man in Montana: Boots & Booties. (Temptation Ser.: No. 712). 1998. per. 3.75 (*0-373-25812-7*, 1-25812-8) Harlequin Bks.
— The Texan Takes a Wife. (Temptation Ser.). 1996. per. 3.50 (*0-373-25704-X*, 1-25704-7) Harlequin Bks.
— The Texan Takes a Wife. 256p. 1999. per. 4.50 (*0-373-83420-9*, 1-83420-9) Harlequin Bks.
— A Touch of Texas. (Hometown Reunion Ser.). 256p. 1997. per. 4.50 (*0-373-82555-2*, 1-82555-3) Harlequin Bks.
— The Wrong Man in Wyoming: Boots & Booties. (Temptation Ser.: Vol. 692). 1998. per. 3.75 (*0-373-25792-9*, 1-25792-2) Harlequin Bks.
Rolofson, Kristine, et al. Millennium Baby: Baby, It's Cold Outside; One-Night Stand Baby; Baby Jane Doe. (Promo Ser.). 2000. per. 5.99 (*0-373-83418-7*, 1-83418-3) Harlequin Bks.
Rolph, Daniel N. To Shoot, Burn & Hang: Folk History from a Kentucky Mountain Family & Community. LC 93-48781. (Illus.). 171p. (C). 1994. 26.00 (*0-87049-844-4*) U of Tenn Pr.
Rolph, Earl R. The Theory of Fiscal Economics. LC 54-10435. (Publications of the Bureau of Business & Economic Research, University of California, California Library Reprint Ser.). (Illus.). 324p. reprint ed. pap. 100.50 (*0-608-18503-5*, 203151100075) Bks Demand.
Rolph, Elizabeth S. & Moller, Erik. Evaluating Agency Alternative Dispute Resolution Programs: A User's Guide to Data Collection & Use. LC 95-3897. 104p. 1995. pap. text 13.00 (*0-8330-1630-X*, MR-534-ACUS/ICJ) Rand Corp.
Rolph, Elizabeth S., et al. Escaping the Courthouse: Private Alternative Dispute Resolution in Los Angeles. LC 94-24074. 121p. (Orig.). 1995. pap. text 15.00 (*0-8330-1611-3*, MR-472-JRHD/ICJ) Rand Corp.
Rolph, J. Automobile Accident Compensation: Vol. 1, Who Pays How Much How Soon. Vol. I. 33p. 1985. pap. 4.00 (*0-8330-0622-3*, R-3050-ICJ) Rand Corp.
Rolph, J., jt. ed. see Morton, S.
Rolph, Mic, jt. auth. see Balkwill, Fran.
Rolshoven, Jurgen & Tietz, Manfred, eds. Pedro Calderon de la Barca: Konkordanz Zu Calderon, Pt. II: Konkordanz Zu denn Comedias y Dramas. write for info. (*0-318-71994-0*) G Olms Pubs.
Rolski. Stochastic Processes in Non-Life Insurance. LC 98-44624. 680p. 1999. 125.00 (*0-471-95925-1*) Wiley.
Rolski, T. Stationary Random Processes Associated with Point Processses. (Lecture Notes in Statistics Ser.: Vol. 5). 152p. 1981. 50.95 (*0-387-90575-8*) Spr-Verlag.
Rolstad, Bent. Natural Immunity to Normal Hemopoietic Cells. 256p. 1993. lib. bdg. 189.00 (*0-8493-4837-4*, QR185) CRC Pr.
Rolstad, Bent, jt. ed. see Fossum, S.
Rolstadas, A., ed. Computer-Aided Production Management. (IFIP State-of-the-Art Reports). (Illus.). 415p. 1988. 122.95 (*0-387-18748-0*) Spr-Verlag.
***Rolstadjas, A. & Andersen, Bjorn.** Enterprise Modeling: Improving Global Industrial Competitiveness. LC 00-31341. (International Series in Engineering & Computer Science). 2000. write for info. (*0-7923-7874-1*) Kluwer Academic.
Rolston. Biology Ethics & Origins Of Life. (Philosophy). (C). 1995. 43.95 (*0-534-54261-1*) Wadsworth Pub.
Rolston, Adam, jt. auth. see Crimp, Douglas.
Rolston, Bill. Drawing Support: Murals in the North of Ireland. (Illus.). 60p. (Orig.). 1996. pap. 19.95 (*0-9514229-3-6*, Pub. by Beyond the Pale) Irish Bks Media.
— Drawing Support Vol. 2: Murals of War & Peace. (Illus.). 60p. (Orig.). 1995. pap. 19.95 (*0-9514229-7-9*, Pub. by Beyond the Pale) Irish Bks Media.
— Politics & Painting: Murals & Conflict in Northern Ireland. LC 89-45981. (Illus.). 1991. 60.00 (*0-8386-3386-2*) Fairleigh Dickinson.
— Turning the Page Without Closing the Book: The Right to Truth in the Irish Conflict. LC 97-132638. 48p. 1996. pap. 6.95 (*1-900900-00-9*, Pub. by Beyond the Pale) Irish Bks Media.
— War & Words: The Northern Ireland Media Reader. Miller, David, ed. LC 97-107744. 300p. (Orig.). 1996. pap. 25.95 (*1-900960-00-1*, Pub. by Beyond the Pale) Irish Bks Media.
Rolston, Bill & Eggert, Anna, eds. Abortion in the New Europe: A Comparative Handbook. LC 93-44510. 344p. 1994. lib. bdg. 79.50 (*0-313-28723-6*, Greenwood Pr) Greenwood.
Rolston, David L. Traditional Chinese Fiction & Fiction Commentary: Reading & Writing Between the Lines. LC 96-12369. 1997. write for info. (*0-8047-2720-1*) Stanford U Pr.
Rolston, Dennis E., et al, eds. Agricultural Ecosystem Effects on Trace Gases & Global Climate Change. LC 92-45593. (ASA Special Publications: No. 55). 206p. 1993. 30.00 (*0-89118-113-X*) Am Soc Agron.
Rolston, Holmes, III. Conserving Natural Value. 1994. pap. 23.50 (*0-231-07901-X*) Col U Pr.
— Environmental Ethics: Duties to & Values in the Natural World. (Ethics & Action Ser.). 408p. 1987. 49.95 (*0-87722-501-X*) Temple U Pr.
— Environmental Ethics: Duties to & Values in the Natural World. LC 87-6499. (Ethics & Action Ser.). 408p. 1989. pap. 22.95 (*0-87722-628-8*) Temple U Pr.
— Genes, Genesis & God: Values & Their Origins in Natural & Human History. LC 98-20715. (Illus.). 432p. (C). 1999. text 59.95 (*0-521-64108-X*) Cambridge U Pr.
— Genes, Genesis & God: Values & Their Origins in Natural & Human History. LC 98-20715. (Studies in Philosophy & Biology). (Illus.). 432p. (C). 1999. pap. text 18.95 (*0-521-64674-X*) Cambridge U Pr.
— Philosophy Gone Wild: Essays in Environmental Ethics. 2nd ed. LC 86-60106. 269p. (C). 1989. pap. 19.95 (*0-87975-556-3*) Prometheus Bks.
Rolston, Joyce N. & Stanton, Anne G. Historical Maps of Louisiana: An Annotated Bibliography. LC 98-54843. (Fred B. Kniffen Cultural Resources Laboratory Monographs: No. 3). 1999. pap. 25.00 (*0-938909-02-9*) Geosci Pubns LSU.
Rolston, Ken. Fires of Dis. 1992. 12.95 (*0-7869-0100-4*, Pub. by TSR Inc) Random.
Rolston, Les. Lost Soul: The Confederate Soldier in New England. LC 99-25079. 312p. 1998. pap. 12.95 (*0-916489-88-4*) Ancestry.
Rolt. Victorian Engineering. pap. 17.95 (*0-14-016745-5*, Pub. by Pnguin Bks Ltd) Trafalgar.
Rolt, C. E. Dionysius the Areopagite. 225p. 1992. reprint ed. pap. 19.95 (*0-922802-97-1*) Kessinger Pub.
Rolt, L. T. C. From Sea to Sea. 200p. 1995. pap. 125.00 (*2-910185-02-8*, Pub. by Laurie Norie & Wilson Ltd) St Mut.
— Landscape with Canals: The Second Part of His Autobiography. (Illus.). 192p. 1994. pap. 15.95 (*0-86299-141-2*, Pub. by Sutton Pub Ltd) Intl Pubs Mktg.
— Landscape with Figures: The Final Part of His Autobiography. (Illus.). 256p. 1994. pap. 15.95 (*0-7509-0593-X*, Pub. by Sutton Pub Ltd) Intl Pubs Mktg.
— Landscape with Machines: The First Part of His Autobiography. (Illus.). 240p. 1994. pap. 15.95 (*0-86299-140-4*, Pub. by Sutton Pub Ltd) Intl Pubs Mktg.
— The Making of a Railway. (Illus.). 160p. 1997. pap. 22.95 (*0-7509-1354-1*, Pub. by Sutton Pub Ltd) Intl Pubs Mktg.
— Railway Adventure. (Illus.). 192p. 1992. 26.95 (*0-86299-367-9*, Pub. by Sutton Pub Ltd) Intl Pubs Mktg.
— Railway Adventure. LC 98-159101. (Illus.). 208p. 1998. pap. 24.95 (*0-7509-1578-1*, Pub. by Sutton Pub Ltd) Intl Pubs Mktg.
— Red for Danger: The Classic History of British Railway Disasters. LC 99-193466. 1999. pap. text 24.00 (*0-7509-2047-5*) A Sutton.
— Sleep No More: Railway, Canal & Other Stories of the Supernatural. LC 97-156508. (Pocket Classics Ser.). 144p. 1996. pap. 8.95 (*0-7509-1157-3*, Pub. by Sutton Pub Ltd) Intl Pubs Mktg.
Rolt, L. T. C. Thomas Telford. pap. 15.95 (*0-14-008125-9*, Pub. by Pnguin Bks Ltd) Trafalgar.
Rolt, Lionel T. George & Robert Stephenson: The Railway Revolution. LC 77-22800. (Illus.). 356p. 1977. reprint ed. lib. bdg. 38.50 (*0-8371-9747-3*, RORR, Greenwood Pr) Greenwood.
Rolt, Richard. The Lives of the Principal Reformers: Both Englishmen & Foreigners. (Illus.). 202p. 1997. reprint ed. 39.95 (*1-882542-17-7*) Fndtns NC.
Rolt, Sonia. Canal People: The Photographs of Robert Longden. (Illus.). 160p. 1998. pap. 24.95 (*0-7509-1776-8*, Pub. by Sutton Pub Ltd) Intl Pubs Mktg.
— Canal People: The Photographs of Robert Longden of Coventry. LC 97-130392. (Illus.). 160p. 1996. 35.95 (*0-7509-1048-8*, Pub. by Sutton Pub Ltd) Intl Pubs Mktg.
Rolt, Sonia, jt. auth. see Rolt, Tom.
Rolt, Tom & Rolt, Sonia. Hold on a Minute. 188p. (C). 1989. 65.00 (*0-947712-14-3*, Pub. by S A Baldwin) St Mut.
Rolt-Wheeler, F. Mystic Gleams from the Holy Grail. 1972. 59.95 (*0-8490-0694-5*) Gordon Pr.
Rolte, J., tr. Palatinate-a Full Declaration of the Faith & Ceremonies Professed in the Dominions of Prince Fredericke, 5. Prince Elector Palatine. LC 79-84129. (English Experience Ser.: No. 947). 208p. 1979. reprint ed. lib. bdg. 20.00 (*90-221-0947-X*) Walter J Johnson.
Rolte, John & Gramling, Scott. Grant Hill. rev. ed. Sielk, Margaret, ed. (Sports Illustrated for Kids Bks.). 112p. (J). (gr. 4-6). Date not set. pap. 3.99 (*1-886749-59-0*) SI For Kids.
Rolte, John & Ross, Dalton. Ken Griffey, Jr. (Sports Illustrated for Kids Bks.). 112p. (J). (gr. 4-6). 1999. pap. 3.99 (*1-886749-58-2*) SI For Kids.
Roltgen, Ingrid, jt. auth. see Muller-Lux, William.
Roluti, Michael J., ed. Waterpower, '85, 3 vols. (Conference Proceedings Ser.). 2280p. 1986. 17.00 (*0-87262-536-2*) Am Soc Civil Eng.
Rolvaag, Ole Edvart. The Boat of Longing. Solum, Nora O., tr. from NOR. LC 84-29466. xv, 304p. 1985. reprint ed. pap. 10.95 (*0-87351-184-0*, Borealis Book) Minn Hist.
— The Boat of Longing, a Novel. Solum, Nora O., tr. LC 73-11844. 304p. 1974. reprint ed. lib. bdg. 65.00 (*0-8371-7069-9*, ROBL, Greenwood Pr) Greenwood.
***Rolvaag, Ole Edvart.** Concerning Our Heritage. Lovoll, Odd Sverre, ed. Zempel, Solveig, tr. from NOR. LC 98-212411. (Travel & Description Ser.: Vol. 12). Orig. Title: Omkring Faedrearven. 219p. 1998. 20.00 (*0-87732-087-X*) Norwegian-Am Hist Assn.
Rolvaag, Ole Edvart. Giants in the Earth: A Saga of the Prairie. 560p. 1999. pap. 13.00 (*0-06-093193-0*) HarpC.
— Giants in the Earth: A Saga of the Prairie. LC 65-6531. 480p. 1991. mass mkt. 8.00 (*0-06-083047-6*, Perennial) HarperTrade.
Rolvaag, Ole Edvart. Giants in the Earth: A Saga of the Prairie. 1955. 13.10 (*0-606-00702-4*, Pub. by Turtleback) Demco.
Rolvaag, Ole Edvart. Peder Victorious: A Tale of the Pioneers 20 Years Later. Solum, Nora O., tr. from NOR. LC 81-16402. xx, 325p. 1982. reprint ed. pap. 13.95 (*0-8032-8906-5*, Bison Books) U of Nebr Pr.
— Their Fathers' God. Ager, Trygve M., tr. LC 82-17636. viii. 338p. 1983. reprint ed. pap. 13.95 (*0-8032-8911-1*, Bison Books) U of Nebr Pr.
Rolwing, Richard J. Israel's Original Sin: A Catholic Confession. 516p. 1994. pap. 54.95 (*1-883255-61-9*) Intl Scholars.
— Israel's Original Sin: A Catholic Confession. 516p. 1995. 74.95 (*1-883255-60-0*) Intl Scholars.
Rom. Environmental & Occupational Medicine. 3rd ed. LC 97-42366. 1920p. 1998. 195.00 (*0-316-75578-8*) Lppncott W & W.
Rom, jt. auth. see Hung.
Rom, Elena, jt. auth. see Koester, Soia.
Rom, Mark C. Public Spirit in the Thrift Tragedy. LC 95-48261. (Policy & Institutional Studies). 325p. (C). 1996. pap. 22.95 (*0-8229-5600-4*); text 49.95 (*0-8229-3943-6*) U of Pittsburgh Pr.
Rom, Mark C., jt. auth. see Peterson, Paul E.
Rom, R. & Sidi, M. Multiple Access Protocols: Performance & Analysis. Gerla, M. et al, eds. (Telecommunications Networks & Computer Systems Ser.). (Illus.). viii, 177p. 1990 60.95 (*0-387-97253-6*) Spr-Verlag.
Rom, William N., Jr. Canoe Country Wilderness: Canoe Trails & Tales from the BWCA, Quetico & Beyond. (Illus.). 224p. (Orig.). 1995. reprint ed. pap. 12.95 (*0-89658-065-2*) Voyageur Pr.
Rom, William N. Environmental & Occupational Medicine. 2nd limited ed. 1520p. 1992. text 227.00 (*0-316-75567-2*) Lppncott W & W.
Rom, William N. & Garay, Stuart M., eds. Tuberculosis. LC 95-10766. 1002p. 1995. text 196.00 (*0-316-75574-5*, Little Brwn Med Div) Lppncott W & W.
Roma, Thomas. Come Sunday: Photographs by Thomas Roma. LC 95-82057. (Illus.). 128p. 1996. 35.00 (*0-8109-6157-1*, Pub. by Abrams) Time Warner.
— Thomas Roma: Higher Ground. (Illus.). 96p. 1999. 45.00 (*1-891024-00-0*, 910161) Dist Art Pubs.
Roma, Thomas, photos by. Sunset Park. LC 98-18926. (Photographers at Work Ser.). (Illus.). 60p. 1998. pap. 16.95 (*1-56098-643-3*) Smithsonian.
Roma, Thomas, jt. photos by see Harris, Alex.
Roma, Tom J. Tom Jerome Roma's 1997 Weekly Astrological Forecasts & Guide. Ball, John D., ed. (Illus.). 124p. 1996. spiral bd. 14.50 (*0-9650599-1-X*) Amass Pubng.
— Tom Jerome Roma's 1996 Weekly Astrological Forecasts. unabridged ed. Ball, John D., ed. 124p. 1995. spiral bd. 12.95 (*0-9650599-0-1*) Amass Pubng.
Roma, Tom J. & Farnell, Kim. Tom Jerome Roma's Weekly Astrological Forecasts & Guide for 1999: The Practitioner's Datebook. Ball, John D., ed. 222p. 1998. spiral bd. 16.95 (*0-9650599-7-9*) Amass Pubng.
***Roma, Tom Jerome.** Tom Jerome Roma's Weekly Astrological Forecasts & Guide for 2000: The Practitioner's Datebook. 226p. 1999. spiral bd. 18.95 (*0-9650599-9-5*, Pub. by Amass Pubng) DeVorss.
Roma, Tomas. Found in Brooklyn. LC 96-22860. (Illus.). 96p. 1996. 35.00 (*0-393-03953-6*); pap. 18.95 (*0-393-31430-8*) Norton.
***Romac International Staff, creator.** PeopleSoft Financials: A Beginner's Guide. 512p. 1999. 39.99 (*0-7821-2394-5*) Sybex.
Romadanov, Alexander. Ozhivi Pokoinika (To Wake the Dead) Roman (A Novel) LC 90-86134. (RUS., Illus.). 240p. (Orig.). 1991. pap. text 15.00 (*0-911971-63-7*) Effect Pub.
Romagna, Gene M. More Money Is No Mystery: 3 Key Questions to Grow Your Business. (Illus.). 120p. 1997. pap. 14.95 (*0-9664389-0-6*) Learn Group.
Romagnani, S., jt. ed. see Coffman, R. L.
Romagnani, Sergio, ed. Th1 & Th2 Cells in Health & Disease. (Chemical Immunology Ser.: Vol. 63, 1996). (Illus.). xii, 222p. 1996. 224.50 (*3-8055-6241-1*) S Karger.
Romagnano, Lew. Wrestling with Change: The Dilemmas of Teaching Real Mathematics. LC 93-38257. (Illus.). 191p. (J). 1994. pap. text 21.50 (*0-435-08342-2*, 08342) Heinemann.
Romagnesi, Henri. Les Fondements de la Taxonomie des Rhodophylles et Leur Classification. (Nova Hedwigia Beiheft Ser.: No. 59). (Illus.). 1979. pap. text 15.00 (*3-7682-1191-6*) Lubrecht & Cramer.
— Petit Atlas des Champignons, 2 vols., Vols. 1 & 2. (Illus.). 1964. 50.00 (*0-934454-91-4*) Lubrecht & Cramer.
— Les Russules d'Europe et d'Afrique du Nord: Essai sur la Valeur Taxinomique et Specifique des Caracteres Morphologiques et Microchimiques des Spores et des Revetements. (Illus.). 1094p. 1996. reprint ed. 250.00 (*3-904144-01-4*, 000387, Pub. by Gantner Verlag) Lubrecht & Cramer.
— Les Russules d'Europe et d'Afrique du Nord: With English Translation of the Keys by R. W. G. Dennis. (Illus.). 1030p. 1985. reprint ed. lib. bdg. 150.00 (*3-7682-1316-1*) Lubrecht & Cramer.
Romagnesi, Henri & Gilles, G. Les Rhodophylles des Forets Cotieres du Gabon et de la Cote d'Ivoire. (Nova Hedwigia Beiheft Ser.: No. 59). (Illus.). 1979. lib. bdg. 150.00 (*3-7682-5459-3*) Lubrecht & Cramer.
Romagnesi, Henri, jt. auth. see Kuhner, R.
Romagnoli, G. Franco & Romagnoli, Margaret O. Romagnolis' Italian Fish Cookery: A Large Embrace & A Light Touch. LC 93-21633. 1995. 25.00 (*0-8050-2526-X*) H Holt & Co.
Romagnoli, G. Franco, jt. auth. see Romagnoli, Margaret.
Romagnoli, Jose A. Data Processing & Reconciliation for Chemical Process Operations. (Process Systems Engineering Ser.). 290p. 1999. 79.95 (*0-12-594460-8*) Acad Pr.
Romagnoli, Margaret. Romagnolis' Italian Fish Cookbook. 89p. 1995. pap. 15.95 (*0-8050-2538-3*) H Holt & Co.
Romagnoli, Margaret & Romagnoli, G. Franco. The New Romagnolis' Table: Classic & Contemporary Italian Family Recipes Designed for Today's Faster Pace & Lighter Palate. LC 87-22871. (Illus.). 320p. 1988. pap. 15.95 (*0-87113-214-1*, Atlntc Mnthly) Grove-Atltic.
— Zuppa! A Seventeen-Region Tour of the Soups of Italy, with 144 Inviting Recipes. 288p. 1995. 25.00 (*0-8050-3833-7*) H Holt & Co.
— Zuppa! Italian Soups. 1995. pap. 13.50 (*0-8050-3834-5*) H Holt & Co.
Romagnoli, Margaret O., jt. auth. see Romagnoli, G. Franco.
Romagnoli, Maureen. 1998 Year-Round Fun Places for Families. 1998. ring bd. 8.98 (*1-891486-03-9*) Romagnoli.
Romain, A. German-English Dictionary of Legal & Commercial Terms. (ENG & GER.). 1994. 162.50 (*0-7859-9427-0*) Fr & Eur.
Romain, Alfred. Dictionary of German & English Legal & Economic Terminology: Woerterbuch der Rechtssprache und Wirtschaftssprache, Vol. 1. 4th ed. (ENG & GER.). 854p. 1989. 225.00 (*0-8288-0393-5*, M 7101) Fr & Eur.
— Dictionary of German & English Legal & Economic Terminology: Woerterbuch der Rechtssprache und Wirtschaftssprache, Vol. 2. 2nd ed. (ENG & GER.). 882p. 1985. 225.00 (*0-8288-0394-3*, M7100) Fr & Eur.
— German-English Dictionary of Legal & Commercial Terms. 3rd ed. (ENG & GER.). 939p. 1994. 125.00 (*0-7859-8762-2*) Fr & Eur.
— German-English Dictionary of Legal & Commercial Terms. 3rd rev. ed. (ENG & GER.). 939p. 1994. 162.50 (*3-406-35836-5*, Pub. by CH Beck Verlag) IBD Ltd.
Romain, Dianne. Thinking Things Through: Critical Thinking for Decisions You Can Live With. LC 96-8152. (Illus.). 376p. (C). 1996. pap. text 42.95 (*1-55934-175-0*, 1175) Mayfield Pub.
— Thinking Things Through Instructor's Manual: Critical Thinking for Decisions You Can Live With. 185p. (C). 1996. pap. text. write for info. (*1-55934-176-9*, 1176) Mayfield Pub.
Romain, Effie & Hawkey, Sue. Herbal Remedies in Pots. 96p. 1996. 16.95 (*0-7894-0431-1*) DK Pub Inc.
Romain, Elizabeth, ed. Popular Variations in Latin-American Dancing. 1984. lib. bdg. 79.95 (*0-87700-514-1*) Revisionist Pr.
Romain, Jonathan. Renewing the Vision: Rabbis Speak Out on Modern Jewish Issues. 1997. pap. 23.00 (*0-334-02657-1*) TPI PA.
Romain, Jonathan A., jt. auth. see Harpur, Jaes.
***Romain, Joseph.** Jesse "The Body" Ventura. (Champion Sports Biography Ser.). (Illus.). 96p. 2000. pap. 8.95 (*1-894020-73-1*) Warwick Publ.
Romain, Joseph. The Mystery of the Wagner Whacker. (Warwick Young Adult Sports Ser.). 208p. (Orig.). (YA). (gr. 5 up). 1997. pap. 8.95 (*1-895629-94-2*) Warwick Publ.
***Romain, Joseph.** Tiger Woods. (Champion Sports Biography Ser.). (Illus.). 96p. 2000. pap. 8.95 (*1-894020-75-8*) Warwick Publ.
Romain, Joseph. Two Minutes for Roughing. 84p. (J). (gr. 3-8). 1995. pap. 8.95 (*1-55028-458-4*); bds. 16.95 (*1-55028-459-2*) Formac Dist Ltd.
***Romain, Joseph.** Venus & Serena Williams. (Champion Sports Biography Ser.). (Illus.). 2000. pap. 8.95 (*1-894020-72-3*) Warwick Publ.
— Wayne Gretzky. (Champion Sports Biography Ser.). (Illus.). 96p. 2000. pap. 8.95 (*1-894020-74-X*) Warwick Publ.
***Romain, Joseph, ed.** Mia Hamm. (Champion Sports Biography Ser.). (Illus.). 96p. 2000. pap. 8.95 (*1-894020-76-6*) Warwick Publ.
Romain, Joseph, jt. auth. see Rondina, Catherine.
***Romain, Lothar.** Peter Basseler. (ENG & GER., Illus.). 200p. 2001. 89.00 (*3-932565-00-2*) Edition A Menges.

R

— Rainer Fetting: Self Portraits, 1973-1998. (Illus.). 2000. 55.00 (*3-87584-886-1*) Nicol.

Romain, Michael, ed. A Profile of Jonathan Miller. (Illus.). 251p. (C). 1991. pap. 22.95 (*0-521-40953-5*); text 69.95 (*0-521-40137-2*) Cambridge U Pr.

Romain, R. & Crabtree, J. A Day with Biff. (C). 1995. 199.60 incl. mac hd (*0-201-48975-9*) Addison-Wesley.

Romain, Ron, et al. A Day with Biff. LC 96-114442. (Illus.). 96p. 1995. pap. 24.95 incl. disk (*0-201-88368-6*) Peachpit Pr.

Romain, Simon. How to Live Safely in a Dangerous World: The Essential, Practical Guide. (Illus.). 121p. 1995. pap. 8.95 (*0-86051-723-3*, Robson-Parkwest) Parkwest Pubns.

Romain, Trevor. The Big Cheese. (Illus.). 32p. (Orig.). (J). (ps-3). 1992. pap. 5.25 (*1-880092-00-X*) Bright Bks TX.

— The Boy Who Swallowed a Rainbow. (Illus.). 32p. (J). (ps-5). 1993. 13.95 (*1-880092-05-0*) Bright Bks TX.

— Bullies Are a Pain in the Brain. LC 97-11677. (Illus.). 112p. (J). (gr. 3-7). 1997. pap. text 9.95 (*1-57542-023-6*) Free Spirit Pub.

— Cliques, Phonies, & Other Baloney. LC 98-36248. (Illus.). 136p. (J). (gr. 2-7). 1998. pap. 9.95 (*1-57542-045-7*) Free Spirit Pub.

— Err . . . Excuse Me! Mind Leaving Your Bad Mood Outside? (Illus.). 32p. (J). (ps-6). 1997. 14.95 (*0-9660995-0-8*) Any Baby Can.

Romain, Trevor. How to Do Homework Without Throwing Up. Verdick, Elizabeth, ed. LC 96-47405. (Illus.). 72p. (J). (gr. 2-7). 1997. pap. 8.95 (*1-57542-011-2*) Free Spirit Pub.

Romain, Trevor. The Keeper of the Dreams. (Illus.). 32p. (J). (ps-5). 1992. 13.50 (*1-880092-03-4*) Bright Bks TX.

— The Little People's Guide to the Big World, Vol. 1. (Illus.). 48p. (J). (ps-5). 1993. 13.95 (*1-880092-04-2*) Bright Bks TX.

— The Little People's Guide to the Big World, Vol. 2. LC 94-71144. (Illus.). 32p. (J). (ps-5). 1994. 13.95 (*1-880092-16-6*) Bright Bks TX.

— The Other Side of the Invisible Fence. Willerman, Benne, ed. LC 94-72241. 96p. (J). (gr. 3-11). 1994. pap. 7.95 (*1-880092-17-4*) Bright Bks TX.

— The Silent Voice. 32p. (J). (gr. k-5). 1994. 13.95 (*1-880092-23-9*) Bright Bks TX.

— Under the Big Sky. (Illus.). 64p. (YA). (gr. 5-12). 1994. 13.95 (*1-880092-13-1*) Bright Bks TX.

***Romain, Trevor.** Under the Big Sky. LC 00-32033. (Illus.). (J). 2001. lib. bdg. write for info. (*0-06-029495-7*) HarpC.

Romain, Trevor. What on Earth Do You Do When Someone Dies? LC 98-47611. (Illus.). 72p. (J). (gr. k-5). 1999. pap. 7.95 (*1-57542-055-4*) Free Spirit Pub.

Romain, Trevor, jt. auth. see Verdick, Elizabeth.

Romaine, Barbara, tr. see Taher, Bahaa.

Romaine-Davis, Ada. Advanced Practice Nurses: Education, Roles, Trends. LC 97-1397. 1997. write for info. (*0-07-637037-2*) McGraw.

— John Gibbon & His Heart-Lung Machine. LC 91-40290. (Illus.). 278p. (C). 1992. text 39.95 (*0-8122-3073-6*) U of Pa Pr.

Romaine-Davis, Ada, ed. see Boondas, Jennifer, et al.

Romaine, Debbie, jt. auth. see Wikoff, Johanina.

***Romaine, Deborah S.** Health Care. LC 99-36999. (Overview Ser.). (Illus.). 128p. (YA). (gr. 6-9). 2000. lib. bdg. 23.70 (*1-56006-488-9*) Lucent Bks.

Romaine, Deborah S. Roe vs. Wade: Abortion & the Supreme Court. LC 98-2540. (Famous Trials Ser.). 112p. (YA). (gr. 7 up). 1998. lib. bdg. 22.45 (*1-56006-274-6*) Lucent Bks.

***Romaine, Deborah S. & DeWitt, Dawn E.** The Complete Idiot's Guide to Back Pain. (Complete Idiot's Guides (Lifestyle) Ser.). (Illus.). 344p. 1999. pap. 16.95 (*0-02-863115-3*, Pub. by Macmillan Gen Ref) S&S Trade.

***Romaine, Deborah S. & Marks, Jennifer B.** Syndrome X: Managing Insulin Resistance. 2000. write for info. (*0-380-81444-7*, Torch) HarpC.

Romaine, L. E. Second. 41p. 1996. pap. 3.50 (*0-936728-64-7*) Word for Today.

Romaine, Lawrence B. A Guide to American Trade Catalogs, 1744-1900. LC 75-22839. (America in Two Centuries Ser.). 1976. reprint ed. 37.95 (*0-405-07710-6*) Ayer.

— A Guide to American Trade Catalogs, 1744-1900, Vol. 900. 422p. 1990. pap. 12.95 (*0-486-26475-0*) Dover.

***Romaine, Lawrence B.** A Guide to American Trade Catalogues, 1744-1900. 422p. 1999. reprint ed. 65.00 (*1-57898-188-3*) Martino Pubng.

Romaine, Suzanne. Bilingualism. 2nd ed. LC 94-9462. (Language in Society Ser.: Vol. 13). 416p. 1994. pap. 29.95 (*0-631-19539-4*) Blackwell Pubs.

— Communicating Gender. LC 98-17562. 416p. 1999. 89.95 (*0-8058-2925-3*); pap. 45.00 (*0-8058-2926-1*) L Erlbaum Assocs.

— Language, Education, & Development: Urban & Rural Tok Pisin in Papua New Guinea. (Oxford Studies in Language Contact). (Illus.). 410p. 1992. text 105.00 (*0-19-823966-1*) OUP.

— Language in Society: An Introduction to Sociolinguistics. (Illus.). 250p. 1994. pap. text 11.95 (*0-19-875134-6*) OUP.

***Romaine, Suzanne.** Language in Society: An Introduction to Sociolinguistics. 2nd ed. (Illus.). 290p. 2000. pap. 14.95 (*0-19-873192-2*) OUP.

Romaine, Suzanne. Pidgin & Creole Languages. (Linguistics Library). (Illus.). 376p. (C). 1989. pap. text 26.04 (*0-582-29647-1*, 71828) Longman.

— Pidgin & Creole Languages: Longman Linguistics Library. (Linguistics Library). (Illus.). 376p. (C). 1988. pap. text 39.95 (*0-582-01474-3*, 71828) Longman.

Romaine, Suzanne, ed. The Cambridge History of the English Language, 1776-1997, Vol. 4. (Illus.). 810p. (C). 1999. text 125.00 (*0-521-26477-4*) Cambridge U Pr.

Romaine, Suzanne, jt. auth. see Nettle, Daniel.

Romaine, Suzanne, jt. ed. see Rickford, John R.

Romains, Jules, pseud. Amities et Rencontres. (FRE.). 231p. 1970. pap. 17.95 (*0-7859-1412-9*, 2080604899) Fr & Eur.

— Le Besoin de Voir Clair. (FRE.). 256p. 1958. pap. 10.95 (*0-7859-1394-7*, 2080505890) Fr & Eur.

— Body's Rapture. (Black & Gold Library). 1937. 7.95 (*0-87140-855-4*, Pub. by Liveright) Norton.

— Boen Ou la Possession des Biens. (FRE.). 160p. 1959. pap. 10.95 (*0-7859-1311-4*, 2070255247) Fr & Eur.

— Choix de Poemes. (FRE.). 286p. 1948. pap. 10.95 (*0-7859-1309-2*, 2070255220) Fr & Eur.

— Les Copains. (FRE.). 1982. pap. 10.95 (*0-7859-3987-3*) Fr & Eur.

— Les Copains. (Folio Ser.: No. 182). (FRE.). 160p. 1972. pap. 6.95 (*2-07-036182-9*) Schoenhof.

— Le Couple France-Allemagne. (FRE.). 140p. 1965. pap. 10.95 (*0-7859-1597-4*, 208050794X) Fr & Eur.

— Cromedeyre le Vieil. (FRE.). 172p. 1926. pap. 11.95 (*0-7859-1392-0*, 2080505903) Fr & Eur.

— Le Dieu des Corps. (FRE.). 244p. 1928. pap. 10.95 (*0-7859-1306-8*, 2070255123) Fr & Eur.

— Donogoo Tonga: Avec: Le Bourg Regenere. (FRE.). 246p. 1920. pap. 18.95 (*0-7859-1308-4*, 2070255190) Fr & Eur.

— Examen de Conscience des Francais. (FRE.). 168p. 1954. pap. 10.95 (*0-7859-1395-5*, 2080505904) Fr & Eur.

— Le Fils de Jerphanion. (FRE.). 320p. 1956. pap. 10.95 (*0-7859-1396-3*, 2080505912) Fr & Eur.

— Un Grand Honnete Homme. 268p. 4.95 (*0-686-55309-8*) Fr & Eur.

— Les Hauts et les Bas de la Liberte. (FRE.). 272p. 1960. pap. 10.95 (*0-7859-1397-1*, 2080505920) Fr & Eur.

— L' Homme Blanc. (FRE.). 144p. 1953. pap. 10.95 (*0-7859-1398-X*, 2080505939) Fr & Eur.

— Hommes, Medecins, Machines. (FRE.). 256p. 1959. pap. 10.95 (*0-7859-1399-8*, 2080505947) Fr & Eur.

— Jean le Maufranc. (FRE.). 176p. 1959. pap. 10.95 (*0-7859-1310-6*, 2070255239) Fr & Eur.

— Knock. (FRE.). (C). 1924. pap. 7.95 (*0-8442-1825-1*, VF1825-1) NTC Contemp Pub Co.

— Knock. (Folio Ser.: No. 60). (FRE.). 1972. pap. 5.25 (*2-07-036060-1*) Schoenhof.

— Knock ou le Triomphe de la Medecine. (FRE.). 1972. pap. 10.95 (*0-7859-2857-X*, 2070360601) Fr & Eur.

— Lettre Ouverte Contre une Vaste Conspiration. (FRE.). 176p. 1965. pap. 10.95 (*0-7859-5472-4*) Fr & Eur.

— Lettres a un Ami, 1. (FRE.). 238p. 1964. pap. 4.95 (*0-686-55316-0*, 2080506137) Fr & Eur.

— Lettres a un Ami, 2. (FRE.). 238p. 1964. pap. 10.95 (*0-7859-1400-5*) Fr & Eur.

Romains, Jules, pseud. Lucienne. (Folio Ser.: No. 1671). (FRE.). 280p. 1922. 14.95 (*2-07-037671-0*) Schoenhof.

— Lucienne - Le Dieu des Corps Quand le Navire: Psyche I, II, III. (FRE.). 1985. pap. 18.95 (*0-7859-4228-9*) Fr & Eur.

Romains, Jules, pseud. Marc Aurele. (FRE.). 252p. 1968. pap. 16.95 (*0-7859-1411-0*, 2080603620) Fr & Eur.

— Le Mariage de M. le Trouhadec. (FRE.). 160p. 1959. pap. 10.95 (*0-7859-1313-0*, 2070255271) Fr & Eur.

— Memoires de Madame Chauverel, 2 vols. (FRE.). 304p. 1959. pap. 10.95 (*0-7859-1640-7*, 2080505955) Fr & Eur.

— Memoires de Madame Chauverel, 2 vols., Set. (FRE.). 304p. 1959. pap. 10.95 (*0-7859-1642-3*, 2080505963) Fr & Eur.

— Mission a Rome. (FRE., Illus.). 356p. 1958. pap. 14.95 (*0-7859-1402-1*, 2080506161) Fr & Eur.

— Monsieur le Trouhadec Saisi par la Debauche. (FRE.). 160p. 1975. pap. 10.95 (*0-7859-1371-8*, 2070366510) Fr & Eur.

— Mort de Quelqu'un. (Folio Ser.: No. 1882). (FRE.). 160p. 1970. pap. 6.95 (*2-07-037882-9*) Schoenhof.

— Le Moulin et l'Hospice. (FRE.). 240p. 1950. pap. 10.95 (*0-7859-1596-6*, 208050617X) Fr & Eur.

— Musse ou l'Ecole de l'Hypocrisie. (FRE.). 144p. 1959. pap. 10.95 (*0-7859-1312-2*, 2070255255) Fr & Eur.

— Odes et Prieres. (FRE.). 176p. 1923. pap. 10.95 (*0-7859-1304-1*, 2070255026) Fr & Eur.

— Paul Landowski: Le Main et l'Esprit. 308p. 39.50 (*0-686-55328-4*) Fr & Eur.

— Pieces en un Acte: Avec: La Scintillante, Amedes et les Messieurs en rang. (FRE.). 176p. 1930. pap. 10.95 (*0-7859-1307-6*, 2070255166) Fr & Eur.

— Portraits d'Inconnue. (FRE.). 240p. 1962. pap. 10.95 (*0-7859-1620-2*, 208050620X) Fr & Eur.

— Pour Raison Garder, 3 vols., 1. (FRE.). 272p. 1967. pap. 10.95 (*0-7859-1408-0*, 2080507486) Fr & Eur.

— Pour Raison Garder, 3 vols., 2. (FRE.). 272p. 1967. pap. 13.95 (*0-7859-1409-9*, 2080602098) Fr & Eur.

— Pour Raison Garder, 3 vols., 3. (FRE.). 272p. 1967. pap. 13.95 (*0-7859-1410-2*, 2080602101) Fr & Eur.

Romains, Jules, pseud. Recherche d'une Eglise. (FRE.). 192p. 1962. pap. 10.95 (*0-7859-1403-X*, 2080506226) Fr & Eur.

Romains, Jules, pseud. Saints de Notre Calendrier. (FRE.). 256p. 1952. pap. 10.95 (*0-7859-1404-8*, 2080506234) Fr & Eur.

— Seven Mysteries of Europe. Bree, Germaine, tr. from FRE. LC 78-152210. (Essay Index Reprint Ser.). 1977. reprint ed. 20.95 (*0-8369-2294-8*) Ayer.

— Situation de la Terre. (FRE.). 244p. 1958. pap. 10.95 (*0-7859-1405-6*, 2080506242) Fr & Eur.

— Verdun. (FRE.). 376p. 1964. pap. 17.95 (*0-7859-1598-2*, 208060211X) Fr & Eur.

***Romains, Jules, pseud.** Verdun. (Lost Treasures Ser.). 500p. 2000. pap. 17.95 (*1-85375-358-0*, Pub. by Prion) Trafalgar.

Romains, Jules, pseud. Le Vin Blanc de la Villette. (FRE.). 224p. 1923. pap. 10.95 (*0-7859-1305-X*, 2070255034) Fr & Eur.

— Violations de Frontieres. (FRE.). 288p. 1951. pap. 10.95 (*0-7859-1406-4*, 2080506277) Fr & Eur.

Romaji Kai, Hyojun. All-Romanized English-Japanese Dictionary. 9th ed. (ENG & JPN.). 732p. 1980. pap. 14.95 (*0-8288-1611-5*, M9548) Fr & Eur.

Romalis, Shelly. Pistol Packin' Mama: Aunt Molly Jackson & the Politics of Folksong. LC 98-19726. (Music in American Life Ser.). 264p. 1998. pap. 18.95 (*0-252-06728-2*); text 39.95 (*0-252-02421-4*) U of Ill Pr.

Romalov, Nancy T., jt. ed. see Dyer, Carolyn S.

Roman. Speed Racer. 1998. mass mkt. 6.99 (*0-671-01199-5*) S&S Trade.

***Roman & Finch.** Family Financial Management Simulation. 6th ed. 1998. 27.95 (*0-538-67501-2*) Thomson Learn.

Roman, jt. auth. see Kranc, Benjamin A.

Roman, Bobbi. Walking in Grandma's Garden. LC 98-96901. (Illus.). 32p. (Orig.). (J). (ps-6). 1999. pap. 16.95 (*0-9668846-0-4*) Stargazer WI.

Roman, Adele B., jt. ed. see Wetherington, Cora L.

Roman, Agnes, jt. auth. see Lasker, Bruno.

Roman, Alex. Low-Fat Back Packing. 2nd ed. McCall, Yvonne, ed. LC 97-66525. (Illus.). 40p. (Orig.). (YA). 1997. reprint ed. pap. text 15.95 (*1-887003-41-X*) Dancng Jester.

Roman, Alfred. The Military Operations of General Beauregard: In the War Between the States, 1861 to 1865, 2 vols. (Illus.). 1994. reprint ed. pap. 17.95 (*0-306-80551-0*) Da Capo.

— The Military Operations of General Beauregard Vol. 1: In the War Between the States, 1861 to 1865, 2 vols. (Illus.). 614p. 1994. reprint ed. write for info. (*0-306-80546-4*) Da Capo.

— The Military Operations of General Beauregard Vol. 2: In the War Between the States, 1861 to 1865, 2 vols. (Illus.). 715p. 1994. reprint ed. 17.95 (*0-306-80547-2*) Da Capo.

Roman and Little Field Inc, jt. auth. see Besterman, Theodore.

***Roman, Annette.** Fresh Pulp: Dispatches from the Japanese Popular Culture Front (1997-1999) 120p. 1999. pap. text 19.95 (*1-56931-371-7*) Viz Commns Inc.

Roman, Beverly. The Insiders' Guide to Relocation. (Insiders' Guide Travel Ser.). (Illus.). 192p. 1996. pap. 14.95 (*1-57380-001-5*, The Insiders Guide) Falcon Pub Inc.

***Roman, Beverly D.** Footsteps Around the World: Relocation Tips for Teens. Bickel, Dalene R., ed. (Illus.). 88p. 1999. pap. 13.95 (*1-888891-19-X*) BR Anchor.

— Home Away from Home: Turning Your International Assignment into a Lifetime Enhancement. Bickel, Dalene R., ed. (Illus.). 110p. 1999. pap. 14.95 (*1-888891-18-1*) BR Anchor.

— Let's Make a Move! A Creative Visualization Activity Book for Children. rev. ed. Bickel, Dalene, ed. (Illus.). 32p. (J). (gr. k-7). 1999. pap. 7.45 (*1-888891-04-1*) BR Anchor.

Roman, Beverly D. Let's Move Overseas: The International Edition of Let's Make a Move! Bickel, Dalene, ed. (Illus.). 32p. (J). (gr. 2-6). 1999. pap., mass mkt. 8.45 (*1-888891-16-5*) BR Anchor.

***Roman, Beverly D.** Relocating 101: Making the Most of Your Move. Bickel, Dalene R., ed. (Illus.). 110p. 1999. pap. 14.95 (*1-888891-20-3*) BR Anchor.

Roman, Camille. Elizabeth Bishop & the Cold War. text. write for info. (*0-312-23078-8*) St Martin.

Roman, Camille, et al, eds. The Women & Language Debate: A Sourcebook. LC 93-7642. 500p. (C). 1993. text 48.00 (*0-8135-2011-8*); pap. text 18.00 (*0-8135-2012-6*) Rutgers U Pr.

Roman, Camille P., jt. auth. see Brandler, Sondra.

Roman, Carlos, ed. see Editorial America, S. A. Staff.

Roman, Catherine. Bang for a Buck: A True Story from the Dark Side. 24.95 (*0-921051-27-1*) Somerville Hse.

***Roman Catholic Liturgy Committee.** In Sure & Certain Hope. 208p. 1999. 21.50 (*0-225-66870-X*, Pub. by G Chapman) Cassell & Continuum.

Roman, Charles V. American Civilization & the Negro. LC 74-37316. (Black Heritage Library Collection). 1977. reprint ed. 39.95 (*0-8369-8953-8*) Ayer.

— Meharry Medical College. LC 71-38019. (Black Heritage Library Collection). 1977. reprint ed. 26.95 (*0-8369-8986-4*) Ayer.

***Roman, Constantin.** Continental Drift: Colliding Continents, Converging Cultures. LC 99-49926. 244p. 2000. 40.00 (*0-7503-0686-6*) IOP Pub.

Roman Corp. Staff, ed. see Roman, Dan.

Roman, Cynthia E. Canaletto to Constable: Paintings of Town & Country from the Yale Center for British Art. LC 97-6220. (Illus.). 120p. 1998. pap. 19.95 (*0-930606-85-X*) Yale Ctr Brit Art.

Roman, D. Project Management. 240p. 1985. 42.25 (*0-444-00966-3*) P-H.

Roman, D. M. Fried Calamari. unabridged ed. 126p. 1998. pap. 11.95 (*1-892896-28-1*) Buy Books.

Roman, Daisy, jt. auth. see Roman, John.

Roman-D'Amat, Jean-Claude, jt. auth. see Prevost, Michel.

Roman-D'Amat, Jean-Claude, jt. auth. see Prevot, Floriane.

Roman, Dan. D A N: A Man Without Youth. LC 87-50276. 416p. 1987. write for info. (*0-9618449-0-6*) Teneco Corp.

— The Satanic Conspiracy: A Man Without Youth & A Dead Man Alive, Pts. 1 & 2 Roman Corp. Staff, ed. LC 90-91755. 612p. 1990. write for info. (*0-9627447-0-0*) Roman Corp.

Roman, Daniel. Asi Era Cuba. LC 94-61122. (Coleccion Caniqui). (SPA.). 160p. (Orig.). 1994. pap. 16.00 (*0-89729-760-1*) Ediciones.

— Los Seis Grandes Errores de Marti. LC 93-70879. (Coleccion Cuba y sus Jueces). (SPA.). 181p. (Orig.). 1993. pap. 18.00 (*0-89729-679-6*) Ediciones.

Roman, David. Acts of Intervention, Performance, Gay Culture & AIDS, Unnatural Acts: Theorizing the Performative. LC 97-35808. (Unnatural Acts Ser.). (Illus.). 376p. 1998. 39.95 (*0-253-33370-9*); pap. 19.95 (*0-253-21168-9*) Ind U Pr.

Roman, David, jt. ed. see Hughes, Holly.

Roman de Bera, P. Diccionario Castellano-Vasco. 4th ed. (BAQ & SPA.). 524p. 1975. 39.95 (*0-8288-5804-7*, S50440) Fr & Eur.

***Roman, Ed.** Mastering Enterprise JavaBeans & the Java 2 Platform, Enterprise Edition: Proven Methods for Building Enterprise Applications. LC 99-49590. 752p. 1999. pap. 49.99 incl. cd-rom (*0-471-33229-1*) Wiley.

***Roman, Emilio Fernandez.** The Fisherman's Guide to Tackle: Essential Hints, Tactics & Techniques. (Illus.). 160p. 2000. pap. 24.95 (*1-84037-056-4*, Pub. by Swan Hill Pr) Voyageur Pr.

Roman, Eric. Hungary & the Victor Powers, 1945-1950. 275p. 1996. text 55.00 (*0-312-15891-2*) St Martin.

***Roman, Eric.** The Stalin Years in Hungary. LC 99-12200. 449p. 1999. text 109.95 (*0-7734-8163-X*) E Mellen.

Roman, Ernan. Integrated Direct Marketing: Techniques & Strategies for Success. 2nd ed. Knudsen, Anne, ed. LC 94-17508. (International Business Culture Ser.). (Illus.). 128p. 1995. 45.00 (*0-8442-3349-8*, NTC Business Bks) NTC Contemp Pub Co.

Roman, Eva. Art of Dictation. (Illus.). 135p. 1971. pap. 11.95 (*0-8464-1077-X*) Beekman Pubs.

Roman, G. Martin. How to Maximize Your Job Security: By Knowing Your Employment Rights. 165p. 1992. pap. text 19.95 (*0-9635073-0-3*) Employ Rights.

Roman, Gail H. & Marquardt, Virginia H., eds. The Avant-Garde Frontier: Russia Meets the West, 1910-1930. LC 92-11323. (Illus.). 320p. 1992. 49.95 (*0-8130-1157-4*) U Press Fla.

Roman, George & Smith, Michael. Celebrity Love Rhythms: Biorhythm Compatibilities of 101 Celebrity Couples. 300p. 1998. pap. 19.95 (*0-9660897-0-7*) G & M Pub.

Roman, Hebby. Betrayed. 320p. 1996. pap. 4.99 (*0-7860-0226-3*) Kensgtn Pub Corp.

— Betrayed. 320p. 1997. mass mkt. 4.99 (*0-8217-5788-1*, Zebra Kensgtn) Kensgtn Pub Corp.

***Roman, Hebby.** Border Heat/Pasion en la Frontera. (Encanto Ser.). 384p. 2000. pap. text 5.99 (*0-7860-1058-4*, Pinncle Kensgtn) Kensgtn Pub Corp.

Roman, Hebby. Love Me Only. 384p. 1999. mass mkt. 4.99 (*0-8217-6206-0*) Kensgtn Pub Corp.

— Midnight Promise. 352p. 1998. mass mkt. 4.99 (*0-8217-6003-3*, Zebra Kensgtn) Kensgtn Pub Corp.

— Summer Dreams. (Encanto Ser.). 1999. mass mkt. 5.99 (*0-7860-0667-6*) Kensgtn Pub Corp.

Roman, Herschel L., et al, eds. Annual Review of Genetics, Vol. 1. LC 67-29891. (Illus.). 1967. text 40.00 (*0-8243-1201-5*) Annual Reviews.

— Annual Review of Genetics, Vol. 2. LC 67-29891. (Illus.). 1968. text 40.00 (*0-8243-1202-3*) Annual Reviews.

— Annual Review of Genetics, Vol. 3. LC 67-29891. (Illus.). 1969. text 40.00 (*0-8243-1203-1*) Annual Reviews.

— Annual Review of Genetics, Vol. 4. LC 67-29891. (Illus.). 1970. 40.00 (*0-8243-1204-X*) Annual Reviews.

— Annual Review of Genetics, Vol. 5. LC 67-29891. (Illus.). 1971. text 40.00 (*0-8243-1205-8*) Annual Reviews.

— Annual Review of Genetics, Vol. 6. LC 67-29891. (Illus.). 1972. text 40.00 (*0-8243-1206-6*) Annual Reviews.

— Annual Review of Genetics, Vol. 7. LC 67-29891. (Illus.). 1973. text 40.00 (*0-8243-1207-4*) Annual Reviews.

— Annual Review of Genetics, Vol. 8. LC 67-29891. (Illus.). 1974. text 40.00 (*0-8243-1208-2*) Annual Reviews.

— Annual Review of Genetics, Vol. 9. LC 67-29891. (Illus.). 1975. text 40.00 (*0-8243-1209-0*) Annual Reviews.

— Annual Review of Genetics, Vol. 10. LC 67-29891. (Illus.). 1976. text 40.00 (*0-8243-1210-4*) Annual Reviews.

— Annual Review of Genetics, Vol. 11. LC 67-29891. (Illus.). 1977. text 40.00 (*0-8243-1211-2*) Annual Reviews.

— Annual Review of Genetics, Vol. 12. LC 67-29891. (Illus.). 1978. text 40.00 (*0-8243-1212-0*) Annual Reviews.

— Annual Review of Genetics, Vol. 15. LC 67-29891. (Illus.). 1981. text 40.00 (*0-8243-1215-5*) Annual Reviews.

— Annual Review of Genetics, Vol. 16. LC 67-29891. (Illus.). 1982. text 40.00 (*0-8243-1216-3*) Annual Reviews.

— Annual Review of Genetics, Vol. 17. LC 67-29891. (Illus.). 1983. text 40.00 (*0-8243-1217-1*) Annual Reviews.

— Annual Review of Genetics, Vol. 18. LC 67-29891. (Illus.). 1984. text 40.00 (*0-8243-1218-X*) Annual Reviews.

Roman, I., jt. auth. see Baum, H.

***Roman, Inc. Staff.** Holiday Traditions: A Collection of Stories, Traditions & Folklore. (Illus.). 32p. 1999. 12.50 (*0-937739-34-0*) Roman IL.

***Roman, J. R.** Let's Motivate Our People! 1999. pap. text 8.99 (*0-8297-2170-3*) Vida Pubs.

— Los Retos del Lider en el Siglo XXI. 1998. 6.99 (*0-8297-1581-9*) Vida Pubs.

An Asterisk (*) at the beginning of an entry indicates that the title is appearing for the first time.

***Roman, Jaime Rene & Ruff, Susan A.** California Administrative Hearing Practice, 5/99 Update. 2nd ed. Johnson, Elizabeth M., ed. LC 97-68156. 302p. 1999. ring bd. 52.00 (*0-7626-0310-0*, CP-32672) Cont Ed Bar-CA.

— California Administrative Hearing Practice, 6/98 Update. 2nd ed. Tindel, Kay E., ed. LC 97-68156. 399p. 1998. ring bd. 50.00 (*0-7626-0237-6*, CP-32671) Cont Ed Bar-CA.

Roman, James. Love, Light & a Dream: Television's Past, Present & Future. LC 95-47213. 320p. 1998. pap. 24.95 (*0-275-96437-X*, Praeger Pubs) Greenwood.

Roman, Joe. The Complete Guide to Installing the 44 Split Defense. (Illus.). 256p. 1999. pap. 16.95 (*1-57167-373-3*) Coaches Choice.

***Roman, John.** On Trial. 1999. pap. 18.95 (*1-58374-006-6*) Chicago Spectrum.

Roman, John & Roman, Daisy. Cliches by Kids. (As Kids See It Ser.: Vol. 1). 114p. (Orig.). 1995. pap. write for info. (*1-888273-00-3*) Inmark Assocs.

Roman, John C. Family Financial Management Simulation. 5th ed. (HM - Consumer Education Ser.). 1989. 20.95 (*0-538-60098-5*) S-W Pub.

Roman, Jose M. Enciclopedia de la Cocina: Encyclopedia of Cooking, 3 vols. 6th ed. (SPA.). 824p. 1986. pap. 325.00 (*0-7859-5074-5*) Fr & Eur.

Roman, Joseph. Octavio Paz: Mexican Poet & Critic. LC 92-47051. (Hispanics of Achievement Ser.). (Illus.). 120p. (YA). (gr. 5 up). 1994. lib. bdg. 19.95 (*0-7910-1249-2*) Chelsea Hse.

— Pablo Neruda: Chilean Poet & Diplomat. (Hispanics of Achievement Ser.). (Illus.). 120p. (YA). (gr. 5 up). 1992. lib. bdg. 19.95 (*0-7910-1248-4*) Chelsea Hse.

Roman, Kenneth. Writing That Works. 160p. 1995. mass mkt. 4.99 (*0-06-109381-5*, Harp PBks) HarpC.

***Roman, Kenneth.** Writing That Works: How to Write Effective E-Mails, Letters, Resumes, Presentations, Plans, Reportsand Other Business Communications. 3rd ed. 160p. 2000. pap. 13.00 (*0-06-095643-7*) HarpC.

Roman, Kenneth & Maas, Jane. How to Advertise. 2nd ed. LC 97-23112. (Illus.). 208p. 1997. pap. 14.95 (*0-312-17108-0*) St Martin.

— The New How to Advertise. expanded rev. ed. (Illus.). 192p. 1992. 22.95 (*0-685-52426-4*) St Martin.

Roman, Klara G. Handwriting: A Key to Personality. (Illus.). 383p. 1952. reprint ed. pap. 12.95 (*0-929732-02-2*) GRAPHEX.

Roman-Lagunas, Jorge. The Chlean Novel: A Critical Study of Secondary Sources & a Bibliography. annot. ed. LC 94-4566. 578p. 1995. 94.00 (*0-8108-2868-5*) Scarecrow.

Roman-Lagunas, Jorge, ed. La Literatura Centroamericana: Visiones y Revisiones. LC 94-5647. (SPA.). 364p. 1994. text 99.95 (*0-7734-9082-5*) E Mellen.

Roman-Lagunas, Jorge, jt. ed. see Promis, Jose.

Roman, Laurie Beth. Who's Looking for Whom in Native American Ancestry. 224p. 1999. pap. 22.00 (*0-7884-1111-X*, D826) Heritage Bk.

Roman, Lawrence. Under the Yum Yum Tree. 1961. pap. 5.25 (*0-8222-1195-5*) Dramatists Play.

Roman, Leslie & Eyre, Linda, eds. Dangerous Territories: Struggles for Difference & Equality in Education. LC 97-16909. 288p. (C). 1997. pap. 18.99 (*0-415-91596-1*) Routledge.

— Dangerous Territories: Struggles for Difference & Equality in Education. LC 97-16909. 288p. (C). 1997. 70.00 (*0-415-91595-3*) Routledge.

Roman, Leslie G., et al, eds. Becoming Feminine: The Politics of Popular Culture. 230p. 1988. pap. 27.00 (*1-85000-329-7*, Falmer Pr) Taylor & Francis.

Roman, Leslie G., jt. ed. see Dworkin, Dennis L.

Roman, Lewis. Principate. 1973. 20.00 (*0-88866-574-1*) Edgar Kent.

***Roman, Lisa.** Institutions in Transition: Vietnamese State Bank Reform. LC 98-33293. 7p. 1998. 120.00 (*0-7923-8384-2*) Kluwer Academic.

Roman Lord, Jill. Snuggles with God: Big Hugs for Little Hearts. (Illus.). 160p. (J). (ps-6). 1999. 5.99 (*1-56292-548-2*) Honor Bks OK.

Roman, Lydia Velez, see Velez Roman, Lydia.

Roman, Madeline. Estado y Criminalidad en Puerto Rico. (SPA.). 164p. 1993. pap. write for info. (*0-929441-50-8*) Pubns Puertorriquenas.

Roman, Manuel. Growth & Stagnation of the Spanish Economy: The Long Wave: 1954-1993. 208p. 1997. text 65.95 (*1-85972-337-3*, Pub. by Avebry) Ashgate Pub Co.

Roman, Margaret. Sarah Orne Jewett: Reconstructing Gender. LC 90-20598. 264p. 1992. text 34.95 (*0-8173-0533-5*) U of Ala Pr.

Roman, Michael, ed. see Splaver, Bernard.

Roman, Michael, ed. see Splaver, Bernard R.

***Roman, Mike A., II.** Bernie Sudzenegger's Beer Drinkers Guide to Physical Fitness. (Illus.). 84p. 1999. pap. 5.95 (*0-9674585-0-1*) Liquid Magik.

Roman, Murray. Telephone Marketing Techniques. LC 78-32000. (AMA Management Briefing Ser.). 34p. reprint ed. pap. 30.00 (*0-608-30178-7*, 205156500089) Bks Demand.

Roman, Nat. Why Can't We Say Goodbye? 516p. 1981. pap. 21.95 (*0-686-32931-7*) Roman Enter.

Roman, O. V., jt. ed. see Arunachalam, V. S.

Roman, P., jt. auth. see Macdonald, S.

Roman, Paul M. Alcohol: The Development of Sociological Perspectives on Use & Abuse. 401p. 1991. 27.95 (*0-911290-23-0*) Rutgers Ctr Alcohol.

— Some Modern Mathematics for Physicists & Other Outsiders Vol. 2: Introduction to Algebra, Topology, & Functional Analysis. LC 75-101. 1975. 151.00 (*0-08-018134-1*, Pub. by Pergamon Repr) Franklin.

Roman, Paul M., ed. Alcohol Problem Intervention in the Workplace: Employee Assistance Programs & Strategic Alternatives. LC 89-27239. 432p. 1990. 89.50 (*0-89930-459-1*, RAD/, Quorum Bks) Greenwood.

Roman, Paul M., jt. auth. see Blum, Terry C.

Roman, Paul M., jt. auth. see Trice, Harrison M.

Roman, Peter. People's Power: Cuba's Experience with Representative Government. LC 98-55919. (Latin American Perspectives Ser.). 296p. 1999. text 60.00 (*0-8133-3586-8*, Pub. by Westview) HarpC.

Roman, Peter J. Eisenhower & the Missile Gap. (Studies in Security Affairs). (Illus.). 280p. 1996. text 37.50 (*0-8014-2797-5*) Cornell U Pr.

Roman, Radu Anton & Lungu, Radu. Bucharest. (Great Cities Ser.). (Illus.). 96p. 1999. 20.00 (*1-85995-597-5*) Parkstone Pr.

Roman, Robert. Survival 21: Futurology for the 21st Century. 17.50 (*0-912314-00-1*) Academy Santa Clara.

Roman, Sanaya. Living with Joy: Keys to Personal Power & Spiritual Transformation. Ratner, Elaine, ed. LC 86-80207. (Earth Life Ser.: Bk. I). 216p. (Orig.). 1986. pap. 12.95 (*0-915811-03-0*) H J Kramer Inc.

— Personal Power Through Awareness: A Guidebook for Sensitive People. Ratner, Elaine, ed. (Earth Life Ser.: Bk. II). 216p. 1986. pap. 12.95 (*0-915811-04-9*) H J Kramer Inc.

— Soul Love: Awakening Your Heart Centers. LC 97-19845. (Soul Life Ser.: Bk. 1). (Illus.). 252p. (Orig.). 1997. pap. 12.95 (*0-915811-77-4*) H J Kramer Inc.

— Spiritual Growth: Being Your Higher Self. Ratner, Elaine, ed. LC 88-81721. (Earth Life Ser.: Bk. III). 252p. 1989. pap. 12.95 (*0-915811-12-X*) H J Kramer Inc.

Roman, Sanaya & Packer, Duane. Creating Money: Keys to Abundance. Ratner, Elaine, ed. (Life Mastery Ser.). 288p. 1988. pap. 12.95 (*0-915811-09-X*) H J Kramer Inc.

— Opening to Channel: How to Connect with Your Guide. Armstrong, Gregory, ed. (Birth into Light Ser.). 252p. (Orig.). 1987. pap. 12.95 (*0-915811-05-7*) H J Kramer Inc.

Roman, Santa I. Quien Era Ella? (Romance Real Ser.). (SPA.). 192p. 1981. pap. 1.50 (*0-88025-005-4*) Roca Pub.

Roman, Stephan. The Development of Islamic Library Collections in Western Europe & North America. 272p. 1990. text 130.00 (*0-7201-2065-9*) Continuum.

Roman, Steven. Access Database Design & Programming. 2nd ed. Petrusha, Ron, ed. (Illus.). 300p. 1999. pap. 32.95 (*1-56592-626-9*) OReilly & Assocs.

— Advanced Linear Algebra. LC 92-11860. (Graduate Texts in Mathematics Ser.: Vol. 135). (Illus.). xii, 363p. 1995. 59.95 (*0-387-97837-2*) Spr-Verlag.

***Roman, Steven.** Applications of Exponents & Logarithms. 4th ed. 49p. (C). 1999. pap. text. write for info. (*1-878015-22-2*) Innov Textbooks.

Roman, Steven. Basic Algebra. (Illus.). 126p. (Orig.). (C). 1992. pap. text. write for info. (*1-878015-10-9*) Innov Textbooks.

***Roman, Steven.** Codes & Coding. 3rd ed. (Illus.). 68p. (C). 1998. pap. text. write for info. (*1-878015-21-4*) Innov Textbooks.

Roman, Steven. College Algebra. 526p. (C). 1988. pap. text, teacher ed. 28.00 (*0-15-507891-7*) SCP.

— College Algebra: A Student Study Manual. 526p. (C). 1987. pap. text, student ed. 24.50 (*0-15-507892-5*) SCP.

— College Algebra & Trigonometry. 702p. (C). 1987. text 82.50 (*0-15-507911-5*) SCP.

— College Algebra & Trigonometry. 702p. (C). 1987. teacher ed. write for info. (*0-15-507914-X*) SCP.

— College Algebra & Trigonometry: Student Solutions Manual. 702p. (C). 1987. pap. text, student ed. 24.50 (*0-15-507913-1*) SCP.

— Concepts of Object-Oriented Programming with Visual BASIC. LC 96-43296. (Illus.). 188p. 1997. pap. 29.95 (*0-387-94889-9*) Spr-Verlag.

***Roman, Steven.** Counting & Probability. 3rd ed. (Illus.). 102p. (C). 1999. pap. text. write for info. (*1-878015-18-4*) Innov Textbooks.

— Cryptology. 3rd ed. (Illus.). 42p. (C). 1999. pap. text. write for info. (*1-878015-16-8*) Innov Textbooks.

— Developing Visual Basic Add-Ins: The VB IDE Extensibility Model. Petrusha, Ron, ed. (Illus.). 171p. 1998. pap. 27.95 (*1-56592-527-0*) OReilly & Assocs.

Roman, Steven. Field Theory. LC 94-36400. (Graduate Texts in Mathematics Ser.: Vol. 158). 1994. 59.00 (*0-387-94407-9*); 32.95 (*0-387-94408-7*) Spr-Verlag.

***Roman, Steven.** Graph Theory. 3rd ed. (Illus.). 95p. (C). 1999. pap. text. write for info. (*1-878015-24-9*) Innov Textbooks.

Roman, Steven. An Introduction to Coding & Information Theory. LC 96-11738. (Undergraduate Texts in Mathematics Ser.). 1996. write for info. (*0-614-14030-7*) Spr-Verlag.

— An Introduction to Discrete Mathematics. 2nd ed. 469p. (C). 1988. text 86.50 (*0-15-541730-4*) SCP.

— An Introduction to Discrete Mathematics. 2nd ed. 469p. (C). 1989. pap. text 34.00 (*0-15-541732-0*); suppl. ed. write for info. (*0-318-64380-4*) SCP.

— An Introduction to Linear Algebra with Applications. 2nd ed. 504p. (C). 1988. teacher ed. write for info. (*0-15-542737-7*); text 87.50 (*0-15-542736-9*) SCP.

***Roman, Steven.** Logic. 3rd ed. (Illus.). 54p. (C). 1999. pap. text. write for info. (*1-878015-19-2*) Innov Textbooks.

— The Mathematics of Finance. 2nd ed. (Illus.). 66p. (C). 1999. pap. text. write for info. (*1-878015-23-0*) Innov Textbooks.

— The Mathematics of Social Science. 3rd ed. (Illus.). 93p. (C). 1999. pap. text. write for info. (*1-878015-20-6*) Innov Textbooks.

— Modern Geometry. 2nd ed. (Illus.). 51p. (C). 1999. pap. text. write for info. (*1-878015-25-7*) Innov Textbooks.

Roman, Steven. Precalculus. 672p. (C). 1987. text 81.00 (*0-15-571052-4*); teacher ed. write for info. (*0-15-571055-9*) SCP.

— Precalculus: A Student Study Manual. 672p. (C). 1987. text, student ed. 24.50 (*0-15-571054-0*) SCP.

— Supplement to Accompany Discrete Mathematics. 2nd ed. (C). 1989. text 91.00 (*0-15-541733-9*) SCP.

— Systems of Linear Equations. (Illus.). 84p. (Orig.). (C). 1992. pap. text. write for info. (*1-878015-11-7*) Innov Textbooks.

***Roman, Steven.** Topics in Mathematics. 2nd ed. (Illus.). 52p. (C). 1999. pap. text. write for info. (*1-878015-26-5*) Innov Textbooks.

— Win32 API Programming with Visual Basic. Petrusha, Ron, ed. (Illus.). 250p. 1999. pap. 34.95 incl. cd-rom (*1-56592-631-5*) OReilly & Assocs.

Roman, Steven. Writing Excel Macros. Petrusha, Ronald, ed. (Illus.). 256p. 1999. pap. 29.95 (*1-56592-587-4*) OReilly & Assocs.

***Roman, Steven.** Writing Word Macros. 2nd ed. Petrusha, Ronald, ed. (Illus.). 410p. 1999. pap. 29.95 (*1-56592-725-7*) OReilly & Assocs.

— X-Men - Red Skull. (Chaos Engine Ser.: Bk. 3). 2000. 14.00 (*0-7434-0723-7*, Pub. by ibooks) S&S Trade.

Roman, Steven, ed. Understanding Personal Computer Hardware: Everything You Need to Know to Be an Informed PC User/Byer/Upgrader. LC 98-17536. (Illus.). 400p. 1998. pap. 39.95 (*0-387-98531-X*) Spr-Verlag.

***Roman, Steven & Timmons, Stan.** X-Men - Magneto. (Chaos Engine Ser.: Bk. 2). 2000. pap. 14.00 (*0-7434-0023-2*, Pub. by ibooks) S&S Trade.

Roman, Steven, et al. Coding & Information Theory. Ewing, J. H. et al, eds. (Graduate Texts in Mathematics Ser.: Vol. 134). (Illus.). 496p. 1992. 59.95 (*0-387-97812-7*) Spr-Verlag.

***Roman, Steven A. & Timmons, Stan.** The Chaos Engine. (X-Men/Doctor Doom Ser.: Bk. 1). 2000. per. 14.95 (*0-7434-0019-4*, Pub. by ibooks) S&S Trade.

Roman, Trish F., ed. Voices under One Sky: Contemporary Native Literature. LC 94-12477. 224p. 1994. pap. 12.95 (*0-89594-720-X*) Crossing Pr.

***Roman-Velazquez, Patria.** The Making of Latin London: Salsa Music, Place & Identity. LC 99-72849. 167p. 1999. 61.95 (*1-84014-881-0*, Pub. by Ashgate Pub) Ashgate Pub Co.

Roman, Zoltan. Gustav Mahler & Hungary. (Studies in Central & Eastern European Music). (Illus.). 1991. lib. bdg. 64.00 (*0-9605560-9-5*) Pendragon NY.

— Gustav Mahler & Hungary. (Studies in Central & Eastern European Music: No. 5). 255p. 1991. 126.00 (*963-05-5609-X*) Pendragon NY.

— Gustav Mahler's American Years 1907-1911. LC 88-38639. (Illus.). 530p. 1989. lib. bdg. 62.00 (*0-918728-73-8*) Pendragon NY.

Romana-Cruz, Neni S. Why the Pina Has a Hundred Eyes & Other Classic Philippine Folk Tales about Fruits. (Illus.). (J). (gr. 3-7). 1995. 11.95 (*971-630-026-3*, Pub. by Tahanan Pacific) Paperworks.

Romana, M., ed. Rock Mechanics & Power Plants: Proceedings of the ISRM Symposium, 12-16 September, 1988, 2 vols. 900p. (C). 1988. text 188.00 (*90-6191-827-8*, Pub. by A A Balkema) Ashgate Pub Co.

Romanach, Julio, Jr. Bustamante Code/Codigo Bustamante. LC 97-109605. (ENG & SPA.). 209p. (Orig.). 1996. pap. text 29.95 (*0-9633610-2-3*) Lawrence LA.

— Dictionary of Legal Terms - Spanish-English - English-Spanish: Diccionario de Terminos Juridicos - Espanol-Ingles - Ingles-Espanol. (ENG & SPA.). 216p. 1992. pap. text 34.50 (*0-9633610-0-7*) Lawrence LA.

— Mexican Law of Sales, a Primer. LC 97-209977. 208p. (C). 1997. pap. text 34.50 (*0-9633610-3-1*) Lawrence LA.

— Teach Yourself... Legal Spanish: Bilingual Guide to the Legal Terminology & Laws of Latin America & Spain. LC 99-184940. 357p. 1999. pap. text 38.95 (*0-9633610-4-X*) Lawrence LA.

Romanach, Julio, Jr., tr. from SPA. Civil Code of Spain. 521p. 1994. pap. text 65.00 (*0-9633610-1-5*) Lawrence LA.

Romanack, Mark. Advanced Walleye Strategies. LC 92-62042. (Complete Angler's Library). 250p. 1993. write for info. (*0-914697-52-8*) N Amer Outdoor Grp.

***Romanack, Mark.** Catch More Walleyes. LC 99-67651. (Illus.). 256p. 2000. pap. 19.95 (*0-87341-826-3*) Krause Pubns.

Romanack, Mark. Five Roads to Walleye: Tips & Techniques for Walleye Anglers. 1998. pap. text 14.95 (*0-9663017-0-6*) Outdoor Commns.

— Trolling Top to Bottom: Tactics for Bass, Walleye, Salmon, Trout & More. 1998. pap. text 18.95 (*0-9663017-1-4*) Outdoor Commns.

Romanaska, Anna B., jt. auth. see Smith, Jonathan D.

***Romance Club Staff, ed.** Romance Companion. 200p. 2000. pap. 19.99 (*1-58365-749-5*, Timeless Treasures) BT Pub.

Romance Club Staff, ed. see Soard, Lori.

Romance, Joseph, jt. auth. see Lowi, Theodore J.

Romanch, Pedro, tr. see Shepard, Martin.

Romanchek, Robert A., jt. auth. see Sugar, David M.

Romanchik, Brenda. A Birthmother's Book of Memories. 60p. 1994. 19.95 (*0-9641035-2-4*) R-Squared Pr.

***Romanchik, Brenda.** Birthparent Grief. unabridged ed. (Open Adoption Pocket Guide Book Ser.). 18p. 1999. pap. 5.95 (*0-9641035-6-7*) R-Squared Pr.

— Birthparents in Open Adoptions: Finding Our Place. unabridged ed. (Open Adoption Pocket Guide Book Ser.). 18p. 1999. pap. 5.95 (*0-9641035-9-1*) R-Squared Pr.

— What Is Open Adoption? unabridged ed. (Open Adoption Pocket Guide Book Ser.). 18p. 1999. pap. 5.95 (*0-9641035-4-0*) R-Squared Pr.

— Your Rights & Responsibilities: A Guide for Expectant Parents Considering Adoption. unabridged ed. (Open Adoption Pocket Guide Book Ser.). 21p. 1999. pap. 5.95 (*0-9641035-0-8*, OAPGB1) R-Squared Pr.

Romanczyk, Raymond G. & Lockshin, Stephanie. How to Create a Curriculum for Autistic & Other Handicapped Children. (Teaching the Autistic Ser.). 46p. 1981. pap. text 8.00 (*0-89079-057-4*, 1038) PRO-ED.

Romand, Didier & Schurr, Gerald. Le Dictionnaire du Marche de l'Art.Tr. of Dictionary of the Art Market. (FRE.). 416p. 1978. pap. 95.00 (*0-8288-5193-X*, M6490) Fr & Eur.

Romand, Raymond, jt. auth. see Ehret, Gunter.

Romane, F., et al, eds. Quercus Ilex L. Ecosystems: Function, Dynamics, & Management. LC 92-13699. (Advances in Vegetation Science Ser.: Vol. 13). 384p. (C). 1992. text 426.00 (*0-7923-1764-5*) Kluwer Academic.

Romane, M. Vance. Wellness Journey. LC 97-186828. (Illus.). 164p. 1997. pap. 15.00 (*1-896880-02-9*) MVP Ltd.

Romanek. Skills That Work: Communication Skills 2, Bk. 2. 1991. pap., wbk. ed. 11.93 (*0-8092-4121-8*) NTC Contemp Pub Co.

Romanek, Betty. GED Preparation for the High School Equivalency Examination Literature & the Arts: New GED Test. 1987. pap. 9.93 (*0-8092-5040-3*) NTC Contemp Pub Co.

Romanek, Elizabeth. Foundations: Social Studies. LC 92-36112. 1993. pap. 11.26 (*0-8092-3831-4*) NTC Contemp Pub Co.

— GED Literature & the Arts. LC 93-43846. 336p. 1994. pap. 11.93 (*0-8092-3779-2*) NTC Contemp Pub Co.

Romanek, Elizabeth, ed. GED Literature & Arts. 1987. pap., wbk. ed. 8.46 (*0-8092-4714-3*) NTC Contemp Pub Co.

— Pre-GED Writing & Language Skills Exercises. 1992. pap., wbk. ed. 7.65 (*0-8092-3884-5*) NTC Contemp Pub Co.

Romanek, Mark, photos by. Mark Romanek: Music Video Stills. (Illus.). 200p. 2000. 50.00 (*1-892041-08-1*, Tondo Bks) Arena Editions.

Romanell, Patrick. Croce Versus Gentile: A Dialogue on Contemporary Italian Philosophy. LC 78-63709. (Studies in Fascism: Ideology & Practice). (Illus.). 80p. reprint ed. 20.00 (*0-404-16979-1*) AMS Pr.

— John Locke & Medicine. LC 84-42846. (Illus.). 225p. 1984. 37.95 (*0-87975-250-5*) Prometheus Bks.

— A Letter Concerning Toleration: Locke. 64p. (C). 1955. pap. text 3.80 (*0-02-403400-2*, Macmillan Coll) P-H.

— Making of the Mexican Mind: A Study in Recent Mexican Thought. LC 76-86778. (Essay Index Reprint Ser.). 1977. 18.95 (*0-8369-1189-X*) Ayer.

Romanell, Patrick, tr. see Croce, Benedetto.

Romanelli, Dorothy H., ed. see Romanelli, Nicholas.

Romanelli, Elaine, jt. ed. see Shoonhoven, Claudia Bird.

Romanelli, Giandomenico. Portrait of Venice. Shugaar, Antony, tr. from ITA. LC 97-65575. (Illus.). 324p. 1997. 95.00 (*0-8478-2035-1*, Pub. by Rizzoli Intl) St Martin.

Romanelli, Giandomenico, ed. Venice: Art & Architecture, 2 Vols. (Illus.). 912p. 1997. boxed set 99.95 (*3-89508-593-6*, 520351) Konemann.

Romanelli, Nicholas. Una Vita: A Grandfather's Story. Romanelli, Dorothy H., ed. (Illus.). 185p. (Orig.). 1981. pap. 6.50 (*0-9606104-0-5*) Port Pr.

Romanelli, Raffaele. How Did They Become Voters? The History of Franchise in Modern European Representation. LC 98-20004. (FRE.). 1998. 108.00 (*90-411-1012-7*) Kluwer Law Intl.

Romanelli, Samuel A. Travail in an Arab Land. LC 88-3931. (Judaic Studies). (Illus.). 238p. 1989. reprint ed. pap. 73.80 (*0-608-01679-9*, 206233500002) Bks Demand.

Romanelli, Serena. Gogo e l'Aquilone Bianco.Tr. of Little Bobo Saves the Day. (ITA., Illus.). (J). (gr. k-3). pap. 15.95 (*88-8203-065-2*, Pub. by North-South Bks NYC) Chronicle Bks.

— Kleiner Dodo, Lass den Drachen Fliegen!Tr. of Little Bobo Saves the Day. (GER., Illus.). (J). (gr. k-3). pap. 15.95 (*3-314-00825-2*, Pub. by North-South Bks NYC) Chronicle Bks.

Romanelli, Serena. Little Bobo. LC 95-20321. (Illus.). 32p. (J). (gr. k-3). 1995. 15.95 (*1-55858-490-0*, Pub. by North-South Bks NYC) Chronicle Bks.

— Little Bobo. LC 95-20321. (Illus.). 32p. (J). (gr. k-3). 1999. pap. 6.95 (*0-7358-1097-4*, Pub. by North-South Bks NYC) Chronicle Bks.

Romanelli, Serena. Monki et el Grand Oiseau Blanc. (FRE., Illus.). (J). (gr. k-3). pap. 15.95 (*3-314-21087-6*, Pub. by North-South Bks NYC) Chronicle Bks.

Romanelli, Serena. El Pequeno Coco. Lamas, Blanca Rosa, tr. LC 98-37181. (Illus.). 32p. (J). (gr. k-3). 1999. 15.95 (*0-7358-1121-0*, Pub. by North-South Bks NYC) Chronicle Bks.

— El Pequeno Coco. Lamas, Blanca Rosas, tr. LC 98-37181. (Illus.). 32p. (J). (gr. k-3). 1999. pap. 6.95 (*0-7358-1122-9*, Pub. by North-South Bks NYC) Chronicle Bks.

Romanenghi de Powell, Elsie R., tr. see Fletcher, William M.

Romanenko, Vitaliy, jt. auth. see Rosenfeld, Dina.

Romanes, Charles S. Call: The Calls of Norfold & Suffolk, Their Paston Connections & Descendants. (Illus.). 103p. 1997. reprint ed. pap. 16.50 (*0-8328-7819-7*); reprint ed. lib. bdg. 26.50 (*0-8328-7818-9*) Higginson Bk Co.

Romanes, G. J. Cunningham's Manual of Practical Anatomy Vol. 1: Upper & Lower Limbs, 3 vols., Vol. 1. 15th ed. (Illus.). 272p. (C). 1986. pap. text 27.50 (*0-19-263138-1*) OUP.

— Cunningham's Manual of Practical Anatomy Vol. 2: Thorax & Abdomen, Vol. 2. 15th ed. (Illus.). 304p. (C). 1986. pap. text 27.50 (*0-19-263139-X*) OUP.

— Cunningham's Textbook of Anatomy. 12th ed. (Illus.). 1,090p. (C). 1981. text 79.50 (*0-19-263134-9*) OUP.

Romanes, George J. Cunningham's Manual of Practical Anatomy Vol. 3: Head & Neck & Brain, Vol. 3. 15th ed. (Illus.). 352p. 1986. pap. text 27.50 (*0-19-263140-3*) OUP.

— An Examination of Weismannism. reprint ed. 49.50 (*0-404-19358-7*) AMS Pr.

— Mental Evolution in Animals: With a Posthumous Essay on Instinct by Charles Darwin. LC 71-96472. reprint ed. 55.00 (*0-404-05389-0*) AMS Pr.

Romanes, George J. Mental Evolution in Man. 466p. 100.00 (*1-85506-677-7*) Thoemmes Pr.

Romanes, George J. Mental Evolution in Man: Origin of Human Faculty. LC 74-21426. (Classics in Child Development Ser.). 466p. 1975. reprint ed. lib. bdg. 38.95 (*0-405-06475-6*) Ayer.

Romani, Cinzia. Tainted Goddesses: Female Film Stars of the Third Reich. Teal, D., ed. Connolly, Bob, tr. from ITA. (Illus.). 182p. 1992. pap. 19.95 (*0-9627613-1-1*) Sarpedon.

Romani, Gian Luca, jt. ed. see Erne, S. N.

Romaniello, Kerry D. Out of the Earth: A Heritage Farm Coast Cookbook. McCabe, Marsha & Thomas, Joseph D., eds. (Illus.). 176p. 1999. 39.95 (*0-932027-40-7*) Spinner Pubns.

Romanillos, Jose L. Antonio De Torres, Guitar Maker: His Life & Work. rev. ed. Miccinello, Angela, ed. (Illus.). 300p. 1997. pap. 52.50 (*0-933224-93-1*, ST425); text 75.00 (*0-933224-92-3*, ST006) Bold Strummer Ltd.

Romanini, C., jt. auth. see Tranquilli, A. L.

Romanini, Judith & Daly, John, eds. Critical Care Nursing: Australian Perspectives. (Illus.). 1115p. 1994. text 84.00 (*0-7295-1245-2*) Bailliere Tindall.

Romanini, Maria. Assisi: The Frescoes in the Basilica of Saint Francis. LC 97-76300. (Illus.). 160p. 1998. 35.00 (*0-8478-2111-0*, Pub. by Rizzoli Intl) St Martin.

Romaniouk, Mikhass. Belorussian National Dress: Belaruskae Narodnae Adzenne. (BEL, ENG, FRE, GER & RUS.). 1981. 143.00 (*0-7855-1578-X*) St Mut.

Romanish, Bruce. Empowering Teachers: Restructuring Schools for the 21st Century. 162p. (C). 1992. pap. text 22.50 (*0-8191-8423-3*); lib. bdg. 44.50 (*0-8191-8422-5*) U Pr of Amer.

Romaniuk. Who's Wealthy in America, 1995, Vol. 1. 95th ed. 1994. write for info. (*0-930807-55-3*) Fund Raising.

— Who's Wealthy in America, 1995?, Vol. 2. 95th ed. 1994. write for info. (*0-930807-56-1*) Fund Raising.

Romaniuk, Anatole. Fertility in Canada: From Baby-Boom to Baby-Bust LC 85-134081. (Current Demographic Analysis Ser.). 156 p. 1984. write for info. (*0-660-11330-9*, Pub. by Can7 Govern Pub) Intl Spec Bk.

Romaniuk, Bohdan R. America's New Foundations, 1997. 11th ed. 1288p. 1996. 180.00 (*1-56995-001-6*) Taft Group.

— America's New Foundations 1996, Vol. 1. 96th ed. 1995. 170.00 (*1-56995-000-8*) Taft Group.

— Corporate & Foundation Grants, 1997, 2 vol., 1. 1996. write for info. (*1-56995-029-6*) Taft Group.

— Corporate & Foundation Grants, 1997, 2 vol., 2. 1996. write for info. (*1-56995-030-X*) Taft Group.

— Corporate & Foundation Grants, 1997, 2 vol., Set. 1996. 195.00 (*1-56995-028-8*) Taft Group.

— Corporate Giving Directory, 1995. 95th ed. 1994. 395.00 (*1-56995-002-4*) Taft Group.

— Corporate Giving Directory, 1996. 96th ed. 1995. 395.00 (*1-56995-003-2*) Taft Group.

— Corporate Giving Directory, 1997. 1996. 410.00 (*1-56995-004-0*) Taft Group.

— Corporate Giving Yellow Pages, 1997. 97th ed. 340p. 1996. 99.00 (*1-56995-007-5*) Taft Group.

— Corporate Giving Yellow Pages, 1995, Vol. 1. 95th ed. 1994. 88.00 (*1-56995-005-9*) Taft Group.

— Corporate Giving Yellow Pages, 1996. 96th ed. 1995. 95.00 (*1-56995-006-7*) Taft Group.

— Foundation Reporter, 1997. 28th ed. 1969p. 1996. 390.00 (*1-56995-056-3*) Taft Group.

— Foundation Reporter 1996. 96th ed. 1995. 375.00 (*1-56995-055-5*) Taft Group.

— FR Guide to Human Service 1995. 95th ed. 1994. 120.00 (*1-56995-017-2*) Taft Group.

— Fund Raiser's Guide to Human Service Funding, 1997. 8th ed. 1469p. 1996. 130.00 (*1-56995-019-9*) Taft Group.

— Fundraiser's Guide to Human Resources, 1996. 96th ed. 1995. 125.00 (*1-56995-018-0*) Taft Group.

Romaniuk, Bohdan R., ed. America's New Foundations, 1993. 93rd ed. 1041p. 1992. 145.00 (*1-879784-38-6*, 600364) Taft Group.

— Corporate & Foundation Grants, 1992, 2 vols. 92nd ed. 2901p. 1992. 150.00 (*1-879784-56-4*, 600349) Taft Group.

— Corporate & Foundation Grants, 1993, 2 vols. 94th ed. 1993. 155.00 (*0-930807-64-2*, 600484) Taft Group.

— Foundation Reporter, 1992: Comprehensive Profiles & Giving Analyses of America's Major Private Foundations. 92nd ed. 1083p. 1991. 327.00 (*1-879784-15-7*, 600225) Taft Group.

— Foundation Reporter, 1993. 93rd ed. 1180p. 1992. 335.00 (*1-879784-40-8*, 600345) Taft Group.

— Who's Wealthy in America, 1995? A Prospect List & Directory of Nearly 100,000 Affluent Americans, 2 vols. 95th ed. 2300p. 1994. 415.00 (*0-930807-54-5*) Taft Group.

Romaniuk, Bohdan R. & Deangelis, eds. Foundation Reporter 1995: Comprehensive Profiles & Giving Analysis of America's Major Private Foundations. 95th ed. 1994. pap. 365.00 (*0-930807-79-0*) Taft Group.

Romaniuk, Bohdan R. & DeAngelis, James, eds. Corporate & Foundation Grants, 1995: A Comprehensive Listening of Nearly 95,000 Recent Grants to Nonprofit Organizations in the U. S., 2 Vol., Vol. 2. 95th ed. 3916p. 1994. 195.00 (*0-930807-67-7*) Taft Group.

Romaniuk, Bohdan R., jt. ed. see Elnicki, Susan.

Romaniuk, Roman B. Roman's Notes on DNA. rev. ed. Tanner, Rosemary, ed. (Illus.). 76p. pap. 12.95 (*1-895579-93-7*, Pub. by Trifolium Inc) ACCESS Pubs Network.

Romaniuk, Ryszard S., jt. ed. see Dorosz, Jan.

Romankiw, L. T., et al, eds. Proceedings of the International Symposium on Electrochemical Technology Applications in Electronics, 2nd. LC 93-70065. (Proceedings Ser.: Vol. 93-20). 560p. 1993. 54.00 (*1-56677-062-9*) Electrochem Soc.

Romankiw, L. T. & Herman, D. A., Jr., eds. Magnetic Materials, Processes & Devices: 4th International Symposium. LC 95-61591. (Proceedings Ser.: Vol. 95-18). (Illus.). 802p. 1996. 92.00 (*1-56677-113-7*) Electrochem Soc.

— Proceedings of the International Symposium on Magnetic Materials, Processe & Devices, 3rd. LC 93-72865. (Proceedings Ser.: Vol. 94-06). 312p. 1994. 48.00 (*1-56677-036-X*) Electrochem Soc.

— Second International Symposium on Magnetic Materials, Processes & Devices. LC 92-71336. (Proceedings Ser.: Vol. 92-10). 464p. 1992. 60.00 (*1-56677-010-6*) Electrochem Soc.

Romann, Michael & Weingrod, Alex. Living Together Separately: Arabs & Jews in Contemporary Jerusalem. LC 90-9073. (Princeton Studies on the Near East). 272p. 1991. reprint ed. pap. 84.40 (*0-608-02572-0*, 206321700004) Bks Demand.

Romano. Printing & Workflow. 288p. 1998. pap. text 39.99 (*0-13-020837-X*) P-H.

— Prof Prepress Printing & Publisher. LC 98-50144. 656p. 1999. 59.99 (*0-13-099744-7*) P-H.

Romano, jt. auth. see McMahon.

Romano, jt. auth. see McMahon, Romano.

Romano, A. Thermomechanics of Phase Transition in Classical Field Theory. (Advances in Mathematics for Applied Sciences Ser.). 272p. 1993. text 48.00 (*981-02-1398-0*) World Scientific Pub.

Romano, Alba C. Irony in Juvenal. (Altertumswissenschaftliche Texte und Studien: Bd. 7). viii, 366p. 1979. write for info. (*3-487-06892-3*) G Olms Pubs.

Romano, Anne T. Taking Charge: Crisis Intervention in Criminal Justice, 25. LC 89-37995. (Contributions in Criminology & Penology Ser.: No. 25). 208p. 1990. 55.00 (*0-313-26890-8*, RTA/, Greenwood Pr) Greenwood.

Romano, Anne T., jt. auth. see Martin, John M.

Romano, Antonio. The Charism of the Founder. 160p. 1993. 29.00 (*0-85439-453-2*, Pub. by St Paul Pubns) St Mut.

Romano, Bernardo. Lexikon der Italienische Wirtschaftsfachbegriffe: German-Italian. (GER & ITA.). 312p. 1991. 29.95 (*0-7859-7053-3*) Fr & Eur.

Romano, Branko E. Bone Appetit: The World's Finest Dog Biscuit Recipe Cookbook. LC 97-51401. 96p. 1997. pap. 16.00 (*1-890613-01-0*) West Coast Media.

— Chicken Toons. LC 82-83844. 1982. pap. 1.95 (*0-89229-010-2*) TQS Pubns.

***Romano, Cesare.** The Peaceful Settlement of International Environmental Disputes: A Pragmatic Approach. LC 00-42083. (International Environmental Law & Policy Ser.). 2000. write for info. (*90-411-9808-3*) Kluwer Law Intl.

Romano, Clare, jt. auth. see Ross, John.

Romano, David G. Athletics & Mathematics in Archaic Corinth: An Early Design of the Greek Stadion. LC 92-75705. (Memoirs Ser.: Vol. 206). (Illus.). 117p. (C). 1993. pap. 20.00 (*0-87169-206-6*, M206-PAP) Am Philos.

Romano, David Gilman & Romano, Irene Bald. Catalogue of the Classical Collection of the Glencairn Museum. (Illus.). 300p. 1999. write for info. (*0-9669494-0-4*); pap. write for info. (*0-9669494-1-2*) Glencairn.

Romano, Dennis. Housecraft & Statecraft: Domestic Service in Renaissance Venice, 1400-1600. LC 95-53743. (Illus.). 360p. 1996. text 45.00 (*0-8018-5288-9*) Johns Hopkins.

— Patricians & Popolani: The Social Foundations of the Venetian Renaissance State. LC 87-2826. 220p. 1988. text 38.50 (*0-8018-3513-5*) Johns Hopkins.

Romano, Dennis, jt. auth. see Martin, John.

Romano, Donato, jt. auth. see Bishop, Richard C.

Romano, Dora R. De, see De Romano, Dora R.

Romano, Dugan. Intercultural Marriage: Promises & Pitfalls. 2nd ed. LC 97-14597. 244p. 1997. pap. 18.95 (*1-877864-51-X*) Intercult Pr.

Romano, Elizabeth, ed. see Alimonti, Joan M.

Romano, Emily. Pear Blossoms Drift. 20p. 1981. pap. 2.00 (*0-913719-51-X*, High Coo Pr) Brooks Books.

Romano, Eugene L. A Way of Desert Spirituality: The Plan of Life of the Hermits of Bethlehem. 2nd rev. ed. LC 98-19439. (Illus.). 160p. 1998. pap. 8.95 (*0-8189-0821-1*) Alba.

Romano, Eugene L., ed. In the Silence of Solitude: Contemporary Witnesses of the Desert. LC 95-42971. 128p. 1995. pap. 7.50 (*0-8189-0754-1*) Alba.

***Romano, Frank.** Acrobat Pdf & Workflow Indetail. 400p. 2000. pap. 39.99 (*0-13-088948-2*) P-H.

Romano, Frank. Delmar's Dictionary of Digital Printing & Publishing. LC 97-4453. (Illus.). 704p. (C). 1997. mass mkt. 41.95 (*0-8273-7990-0*) Delmar.

— Digital Media: Publishing Technologies for the 21st Century. 256p. 1996. pap. 27.95 (*0-941845-18-4*) Micro Pub Pr.

Romano, Frank. Pocket Guide to Digital Prepress. LC 95-20087. 352p. (C). 1995. pap. 17.95 (*0-8273-7198-5*) Delmar.

Romano, Frank. The TypEncyclopedia: A User's Guide to Better Typography. 224p. 1984. pap. 34.95 (*0-8352-1925-9*) Bowker.

Romano, Frank & Knaflewska, Magda, eds. QUI's QuarkXPress Tips & Tools. 2nd ed. LC 96-194110. (Illus.). 176p. 1995. pap. 27.95 (*0-941845-16-8*) Micro Pub Pr.

Romano, Frank & Romano, Richard. The GATF Encyclopedia of Graphic Communications. LC 97-74138. (Illus.). 1000p. (C). 1998. text 250.00 (*0-88362-190-8*, 1306) GATFPress.

Romano, Frank, et al. PDF Printing & Publishing: The Next Revolution after Gutenberg. (Illus.). 208p. (Orig.). 1997. pap. 27.95 (*0-941845-22-2*) Micro Pub Pr.

Romano, Frank, jt. auth. see Adams, Richard M.

***Romano, Frank J.** Designer's Guide to Digital & Variable Data Printing. (Illus.). 120p. (C). 2000. pap. text 35.00 (*0-88362-301-3*) GATFPress.

Romano, Frank J. Encyclopedia of Graphic Communications. LC 98-8329. 992p. 1998. 99.99 (*0-13-096422-0*) P-H.

— Machine Writing & Typesetting. (Illus.). 146p. 1986. lib. bdg. 24.95 (*0-938853-00-7*) GAMA Comns.

Romano, Frank J. & Broudy, David. In-Design In-Depth. 449p. (C). 1999. pap. text 39.99 (*0-13-016521-2*) P-H.

Romano, Frank J. & Erickson, Bill. Professional Digital Photography. LC 99-18428. (Illus.). 336p. 1999. 49.99 (*0-13-099745-5*) P-H.

Romano, Frank J. & Oresick, Peter. A Short History of Printing. (Illus.). 180p. 2000. pap. text 25.00 (*0-88362-218-1*) GATFPress.

Romano, Frank J. & Romano, Richard. The GATF Encyclopedia of Graphic Communications. deluxe ed. LC 97-74138. (Illus.). 1000p. (C). 1998. lthr. 500.00 (*0-88362-215-7*, 1306L) GATFPress.

***Romano, Frank J. & Romano, Richard M.** Yearbook 2000: The GATF Encyclopedia of Graphic Communications Yearbook. 100p. (C). 2000. pap. text 35.00 (*0-88362-300-5*) GATFPress.

Romano, Frank J., jt. auth. see Adams, Richard M., II.

Romano, Frank J., jt. auth. see Fenton, Howard M.

Romano, Frank J., jt. auth. see Lumma, Eike.

Romano, Giuseppe. Opus Dei: Who? How? Why? Lane, Edmund C., tr. from ITA. LC 95-23355. 214p. (Orig.). 1995. pap. 9.95 (*0-8189-0739-8*) Alba.

Romano, Guardimi. Living the Drama of Faith: What Faith Is & Where It Leads You. rev. ed. LC 98-23177. Orig. Title: The Life of Faith. 158p. 1998. pap. 11.95 (*0-918477-77-8*) Sophia Inst Pr.

Romano, Hermimia H., tr. see Perez, Jose A. & Mejias, Antonio I.

Romano, Irene B. Gordion Special Studies Vol. II: The Terracotta Figurines & Related Vessels. (University Museum Monographs: No. 86). (Illus.). xxviii, 90p. 1995. 40.00 (*0-924171-29-4*) U Museum Pubns.

Romano, Irene Bald, jt. auth. see Romano, David Gilman.

Romano, J. F., et al. The Luxor Museum of Ancient Egyptian Art Catalog. (American Research Center in Egypt, Catalogs Ser.: Vol. 1). (Illus.). xv, 219p. 1979. 32.50 (*0-913696-30-7*, Pub. by Amer Res Ctr Egypt) Eisenbrauns.

Romano, Jaime, ed. see De Romano, Dora R.

Romano, James F. Daily Life of the Ancient Egyptians. LC 89-85823. (Illus.). 56p. (Orig.). 1990. pap. text 7.95 (*0-911239-18-9*) Carnegie Mus.

— Death, Burial & Afterlife in Ancient Egypt. LC 89-85822. (Illus.). 48p. (Orig.). (C). 1990. pap. text 7.95 (*0-911239-19-7*) Carnegie Mus.

Romano, James V., ed. Poetica de la Poblacion Marginal: Sensibilidades Determinantes. (Literature & Human Rights Ser.: No. 2). (SPA.). 488p. (Orig.). 1988. pap. 14.95 (*0-910235-20-1*) Prisma Bks.

Romano, Joe. It All Comes Together Right Here. 28p. 1993. 12.95 (*0-614-00506-X*) Non-Toxic Music.

Romano, John. Circumstantial Evidence: 1989 Cumulative Supplement. 1989. write for info. (*0-930273-70-2*, 66652-10, MICHIE) LEXIS Pub.

— Muscle Meals: A Cookbook to Build Muscle & Lose Fat. Richmond, Jessica, ed. LC 97-71088. (Illus.). 224p. 1997. 19.95 (*1-889462-01-2*) Advanced Research Pr.

Romano, John F. & McHale, Michael J. Strategic Use of Circumstantial Evidence. 2nd ed. 773p. 1991. 80.00 (*0-87473-774-5*, 66653-10, MICHIE) LEXIS Pub.

Romano, Joseph P., jt. auth. see Siegel.

Romano, Karen J., jt. auth. see Martin, Raquel.

Romano, Lalla. The Penumbra. Williams, Sian, tr. 1999. pap. 12.95 (*0-7043-8071-4*) Interlink Pub.

Romano-Lax, Andromeda. Walking Southeast Alaska: 40 Walks & Easy Hikes for Inside Passage Travelers. LC 97-897. (Illus.). 192p. (Orig.). 1997. pap. 13.95 (*0-89997-208-X*) Wilderness Pr.

Romano-Lax, Andromeda, jt. auth. see Wilderness Press Staff.

Romano, Lila E. Italian Fairy Tales. (Illus.). 134p. 1999. 16.95 (*0-7818-0702-6*) Hippocrene Bks.

Romano, Locus G., jt. auth. see Georgrady, Nicholas P.

Romano, Louis A. Manual & Industrial Education at Girard College, 1831-1965: An Era in American Educational Experimentation. Cordasco, Francesco, ed. LC 80-1075. (American Ethnic Groups Ser.). 1981. lib. bdg. 47.95 (*0-405-13450-9*) Ayer.

Romano, Louis G., ed. Focus on a Middle School Belief System. (Illus.). 1979. pap. text 3.00 (*0-918449-01-4*) MI Middle Educ.

Romano, Louis G., et al, eds. Focus on Successful Characteristics of a Middle School. rev. ed. 12p. 1985. pap. text 2.50 (*0-918449-04-9*) MI Middle Educ.

Romano, Louis G. & Georgiady, Nicholas P. Building an Effective Middle School. 318p. (C). 1993. text. write for info. (*0-697-15179-4*) Brown & Benchmark.

— The Middle School Distinction. LC 97-69144. (Fastback Ser.: No. 418). 44p. 1997. pap. 3.00 (*0-87367-618-1*, FB#418) Phi Delta Kappa.

Romano, Louis G., jt. auth. see Georgiady, Nicholas P.

Romano, Louis G., jt. auth. see Georgisky, Nicholas P.

Romano, Louis G., jt. auth. see Hamachek, Alice L.

Romano, Louis G., ed. see Bouth, Anita J.

Romano, Louis G., ed. see Costar, James W.

Romano, Louis G., ed. see Gilliland, Katherine.

Romano, Louis G., ed. see Kaminski, Lorraine B. & Dornbos, Karen L.

Romano, Louis G., ed. see Maksimowicz, Michelle.

Romano, Louis G., ed. see Marlow, Jean, et al.

Romano, Louis G., ed. see McEwin, C. Kenneth.

Romano, Louis G., ed. see Mowen, Carol & Mowen, Gregg.

Romano, Louis G., ed. see Muldrew, Jessie.

Romano, Louis G., ed. see Powell, William F.

Romano, Louis G., ed. see Scullen, Thomas.

Romano, M. E., tr. see Zoja, Luigi.

Romano, Marc, tr. see Messadie, Gerald.

Romano, Mary A. Beatrice Webb (1858-1943) - The Socialist with a Sociological Imagination. LC 98-27079. (Studies in Sociology Ser.: Vol. 17). 152p. 1998. lib. bdg. 69.95 (*0-7734-8312-8*) E Mellen.

Romano, Mary Jo, et al, eds. Massachusetts Paralegal Practice Manual. LC 96-77822. 750p. 1997. ring bd. 125.00 (*1-57589-022-4*, 97-22.06-BK) Mass CLE.

Romano, Melora. Meow, What Now? (Illus.). 12p. (J). (gr. k-2). 1998. pap. 3.75 (*1-880612-78-X*) Seedling Pubns.

***Romano, Mike.** Murder in Palm Springs. 190p. 2000. pap. Price not set. (*0-88100-116-3*) Natl Writ Pr.

Romano, Nicholas. Chemistry. 5th ed. Garnsey, Wayne, ed. (Science Ser.). (Illus.). 320p. 1998. pap. text 7.95 (*0-935487-41-7*) N & N Pub Co.

Romano, Octavio I. Geriatric Fu. LC 89-20500. 256p. 1990. pap. 11.95 (*0-89229-018-8*) TQS Pubns.

Romano, Osservatore, tr. see O'Byrne, Seamus, ed.

Romano, Patrick L. & Barth, Claire, eds. Activity-Based Management in Action. LC 94-210418. (Illus.). 160p. 1994. pap. 40.00 (*0-86641-227-1*, 94289) Inst Mgmt Account.

Romano, Paul & Stone, Ria. The American Worker. ix, 70p. 1972. reprint ed. pap. 3.00 (*0-935590-01-3*) Bewick Edns.

***Romano, Rafi, ed.** Lingual Orthodontics. 211p. 1998. boxed set 169.00 incl. cd-rom (*1-55009-040-2*) DEKR.

Romano, Ray. Everything & a Kite. 208p. 1999. mass mkt. 6.50 (*0-553-58037-X*) Bantam.

— Everything & a Kite. large type ed. LC 98-55246. 1999. 26.95 (*0-7862-1831-2*) Thorndike Pr.

Romano, Richard, jt. auth. see Romano, Frank.

Romano, Richard, jt. auth. see Romano, Frank J.

Romano, Richard M., jt. auth. see Romano, Frank J.

Romano, Rita. Dining in the Raw. 224p. 1997. 19.95 (*1-57566-192-6*, Knsington) Kensgtn Pub Corp.

Romano, Robert. Overkill. 246p. 1997. pap. 9.95 (*1-57502-627-9*, P01785) Morris Pubng.

Romano, Robert M. & Practising Law Institute Staff. Coping with Broker-dealer Regulation & Enforcement. LC 98-193376. (Corporate Law & Practice Course Handbook Ser.). 336p. 1998. 129.00 (*0-87224-428-8*) PLI.

Romano, Robert R., ed. Optical Remote Sensing for Environmental & Process Monitoring, Vol. 2883. 721p. 1996. 80.00 (*0-8194-2281-9*) SPIE.

Romano, Roberta. The Genius of American Corporate Law. LC 93-18917. 50p. (Orig.). 1993. pap. 9.75 (*0-8447-3836-0*) Am Enterprise.

Romano, Roberta, ed. Foundations of Corporate Law. LC 92-34550. (Interdisciplinary Readers in Law Ser.). (Illus.). 352p. (C). 1993. pap. text 26.95 (*0-19-507413-0*) OUP.

Romano, Rose. The Wop Factor. write for info. (*1-883112-05-2*) Malafemmina.

Romano, Sergio, ed. An Outline of European History: From 1789 to 1989. Gunzberg, Lynn, tr. from ITA. LC 98-27407.Tr. of Disegno Della Storia D'Europa pal 1789 al 1989. 192p. (C). 1998. 39.95 (*1-57181-076-5*) Berghahn Bks.

Romano, Stephen, et al. The Beyond: A Nightmare Beyond Imagination. (Graphic Novel Ser.: Vol. 1). (Illus.). 125p. 1998. pap. 20.00 (*0-9667514-0-X*) Blackest Heart.

***Romano, Tom.** Blending Genre, Altering Style: Writing Multigenre Papers. 208p. 2000. pap. text 18.50 (*0-86709-478-8*, Pub. by Boynton Cook Pubs) Heinemann.

Romano, Tom. Clearing the Way: Working with Teenage Writers. LC 86-29558. 191p. (C). 1987. pap. text 22.00 (*0-435-08439-9*, 08439) Heinemann.

— Writing with Passion: Life Stories, Multiple Genres. LC 95-8647. 238p. 1995. pap. text 22.50 (*0-86709-362-5*, 0362, Pub. by Boynton Cook Pubs) Heinemann.

Romano, V., ed. Advances in Phenylketonuria Research. (Journal: Developmental Brain Dysfunction: Vol. 6, Nos. 1-3, 1993). (Illus.). 192p. 1993. pap. 85.25 (*3-8055-5759-0*) S Karger.

Romanoff, Alan, ed. Birthdays of the Rich & Famous Bk. 1: Entertainers: The Birthdays of More Than 12,000 People from All Part of the Entertainment World. LC 95-68813. 144p. 1995. pap. 10.95 (*1-887320-00-8*) Darco Pr OH.

— Birthdays of the Rich & Famous Bk. 3: Popular Music: The Birthdays of More Than 12,000 People in Rock-Pop-Soul-Country & Other Popular Music Forms. 144p. (Orig.). 1997. pap. 10.95 (*1-887320-02-4*) Darco Pr OH.

An Asterisk (*) at the beginning of an entry indicates that the title is appearing for the first time.

— Who Was That Klingon? A Detailed Cast Guide to the Star Trek Television Series & Movies. LC 97-77162. 128p. Date not set. pap. 9.95 (*1-887320-03-2*) Darco Pr OH.

Romanoff, Alexis L. The Avian Embryo: Structural & Functional Development. LC 59-7975. 1323p. reprint ed. pap. 200.00 (*0-8357-5932-6*, 205197000019) Bks Demand.

Romanoff, Lena. Your People, My People: Finding Acceptance & Fulfillment As a Jew by Choice. 2nd rev. ed. LC 90-34693. 280p. 1999. pap. 16.95 (*1-893382-00-1*) Identity Plus.

Romanoff, Marjorie. Language & Study Skills for Learners of English. 144p. (C). 1991. pap. text 23.20 (*0-13-847229-7*, 640306) P-H.

Romanoff, Steve. The Steve Romanoff Songbook: Songs Written for Schooner Fare. 160p. 1993. spiral bd. 24.95 (*0-9638602-0-8*) Outer Green Recs.

Romanofsky, Peter, ed. Social Service Organizations, 2 vols., 2. LC 77-84754. (Encyclopedia of American Institutions Ser.: No. 2). 1978. lib. bdg. 150.00 (*0-8371-9829-1*, RSS/) Greenwood.

— Social Service Organizations, 2 vols., Vol. 1. LC 77-84754. (Encyclopedia of American Institutions Ser.: No. 2). 1978. lib. bdg. 95.00 (*0-8371-9902-6*, RSS/1) Greenwood.

— Social Service Organizations, 2 vols., Vol. 2. LC 77-84754. (Encyclopedia of American Institutions Ser.: No. 2). 1978. lib. bdg. 95.00 (*0-8371-9903-4*, RSS/2) Greenwood.

Romanofsky, Peter, jt. ed. see Fisher, Robert M.

***Romanos, Michael, ed.** Spatial Transformations: Turning Points in the Evolution of Cities. (Illus.). xiii, 271p. (C). 2000. pap. 20.00 (*0-9675582-1-2*) Univ of Cin Schl Plan.

Romanov, et al. Azure Cities. LC 72-3284. (Short Story Index Reprint Ser.). 1977. reprint ed. 23.95 (*0-8369-4143-8*) Ayer.

Romanov, A. C. & Wedel, E. Romanov's Russian-English, English-Russian Dictionary. 3rd ed. (ENG & RUS.). 509p. 1992. 29.95 (*0-7859-1083-2*, 5850540113) Fr & Eur.

Romanov, A. S. Russian-English Dictionary. (RUS & ENG.). 1990. mass mkt. 5.99 (*0-671-70924-0*) PB.

***Romanov, Albert.** Atlas of Antarctic Sea Ice & Icebergs. Tunik, Alfred, ed. (Illus.). 176p. 1999. pap. 495.00 (*0-9644311-8-1*) Backbone Pubng.

Romanov, Andrey. Mystery of Masochism: Art of Sex. Romanova, Irina, ed. 112p. 1998. pap. write for info. (*1-57502-002-5*, P01945) Morris Pubng.

Romanov, Ilia P. Atlas of Ice & Snow of the Arctic Basin & Siberian Shelf Seas. Tunik, Alfred, ed. (Illus.). 278p. 1995. 695.00 (*0-9644311-3-0*) Backbone Pubng.

Romanov, Jane F., jt. ed. see Anderson, Owen.

Romanov, Panteleimon S. Without Cherry Blossom. Graham, Stephen, ed. Zarine, Leonide, tr. LC 78-142275. (Short Story Index Reprint Ser.). 1977. 17.95 (*0-8369-3759-7*) Ayer.

Romanov, V. G. Inverse Problems of Mathematical Physics. Yuzina, L. Ya, tr. from RUS. 248p. 1986. lib. bdg. 170.00 (*90-6764-056-5*, Pub. by VSP) Coronet Bks.

Romanov, V. G. & Kabanikhin, S. I. Inverse Problems for Maxwell's Equations. (Inverse & Ill-Posed Problems Ser.). 257p. 1994. 155.00 (*90-6764-172-3*, Pub. by VSP) Coronet Bks.

Romanova, Irina, ed. see Romanov, Andrey.

Romanova, M., tr. see Bisnovatyi-Kogan, G. S.

Romanova, Natalia. Once There Was a Tree. 1989. 11.19 (*0-606-05056-6*, Pub. by Turtleback) Demco.

Romanova, Natalie. Once There Was a Tree. 1992. pap. 5.99 (*0-14-054677-4*) NAL.

Romanovskaya, L., et al. The Beginner's Guide to OOP Using C Plus Plus. Dodson, Julian, ed. 550p. 1994. pap. 29.95 (*1-874416-27-3*) Wrox Pr Inc.

Romanovsky, jt. auth. see Kutateladze, S. S.

Romanovsky, M. Y., jt. ed. see Korobkin, V. V.

Romanow & Soderlund. Media Canada: Introductory Analysis. 1992. pap. text. write for info. (*0-7730-5187-2*) Addison-Wes.

***Romanow, Walter I., et al, eds.** Television Advertising in Canadian Elections: The Attack Mode, 1993. LC 99-930634. (Illus.). 252p. 1999. pap. 29.95 (*0-88920-323-7*) Wilfrid Laurier.

Romanowich, Barbara, jt. auth. see Kemnitz, Thomas M.

Romanowicz, Barbara A., jt. ed. see Mitchell, Brian J.

Romanowicz, Bartlomiej F. Methodology for the Modeling & Simulation of Microsystems. LC 98-41309. (Microsystems Ser.). 136p. 1998. 98.00 (*0-7923-8306-0*) Kluwer Academic.

Romanowski, Nick. Aquatic & Wetland Plants: A Field Guide for Non-Tropical Australia. (Illus.). 118p. 1998. pap. 29.95 (*0-86840-632-5*, Pub. by New South Wales Univ Pr) Intl Spec Bk.

— Planting Wetlands & Dams: A Practical Guide to Wetland Design, Construction & Propagation. LC 99-165249. (Illus.). 80p. 1998. pap. 22.95 (*0-86840-608-2*, Pub. by New South Wales Univ Pr) Intl Spec Bk.

***Romanowski, Nick.** Water Garden Plants & Animals: The Complete Guide for All Australia. (Illus.). 120p. 2000. 34.50 (*0-86840-418-7*, Pub. by NSW U Pr) Intl Spec Bk.

Romanowski, Patricia, et al, eds. The New Rolling Stone Encyclopedia of Rock & Roll. 1120p. pap. 25.00 (*0-7866-2588-0*, MB96454) Mel Bay.

Romanowski, Patricia, jt. auth. see Funicello, Annette.

Romanowski, Patricia, jt. auth. see Greggains, Joanie.

Romanowski, Patricia, jt. auth. see Martin, Joel.

Romanowski, Patricia, jt. auth. see Neuman, M. Gary.

Romanowski, Patricia, jt. auth. see Osmond, Donny.

Romanowski, Patricia, jt. auth. see Pendergrass, Teddy.

Romanowski, Patty, jt. auth. see Osmond, Donny.

Romanowski, Perry, jt. ed. see Schueller, Randy.

Romanowski, Sylvie & Bilezikian, Monique A., eds. Homage to Paul Benichou. LC 94-67074. 340p. 1994. lib. bdg. 44.95 (*0-917786-98-X*) Summa Pubns.

Romanowski, William D. Pop Culture Wars: Religion & the Role of Entertainment in American Life. LC 96-16490. 380p. (Orig.). 1996. pap. 19.99 (*0-8308-1988-6*, 1988) InterVarsity.

Romans, Bernard & Holland Braund, Kathryn E. A Concise Natural History of East & West Florida. LC 99-6088. 1999. 44.95 (*0-8173-0876-8*) U of Ala Pr.

***Romans, John R., et al.** The Meat We Eat. 14th ed. (Illus.). xvi, 1200p. 2001. 93.25 (*0-8134-3175-1*) Interstate.

Romans, Lois E. Introduction to Computed Tomography. LC 94-43673. (Illus.). 224p. 1995. pap. 25.00 (*0-683-07353-2*) Lppncott W & W.

— Review Questions & Explanations in Computed Tomography. LC 96-1773. 300p. 1996. pap. 24.95 (*0-683-07330-3*) Lppncott W & W.

Romans, Sarah. Women's Mental Health: A New Zealand Perspective. LC 99-193547. 280p. 1998. pap. 39.95 (*1-877133-49-3*, Pub. by Univ Otago Pr) Intl Spec Bk.

Romanski, Kate D. & McKinney, Beth C., eds. The English Cocker Spaniel Handbook. 3rd ed. (Illus.). 152p. 1989. pap. 10.00 (*0-9613761-4-7*) Eng Cocker Spaniel.

Romanski, Kate D., jt. auth. see McKinney, Beth C.

***Romanski, Phyllis.** Mastering Solaris 8 with CD-ROM. (Mastering Ser.). 800p. 2000. pap. 49.99 incl. cd-rom (*0-7821-2816-5*) Sybex.

Romantowski, Jane, jt. auth. see Lipson, Greta B.

Romantz, David & Vinson, Kathy. Legal Analysis: The Fundamental Skill. LC 98-26063. 160p. 1998. pap. 15.00 (*0-89089-905-3*) Carolina Acad Pr.

Romanucci-Ross, Lola. Conflict, Violence, & Morality in a Mexican Village. (Illus.). xii, 222p. 1993. pap. text 10.95 (*0-226-72465-4*) U Ch Pr.

— Conflict, Violence, & Morality in a Mexican Village. (Illus.). xii, 222p. 1993. lib. bdg. 30.00 (*0-226-72464-6*) U Ch Pr.

Romanucci-Ross, Lola & DeVos, George, eds. Ethnic Identity: Creation, Conflict & Accommodation. 3rd ed. LC 95-32537. 400p. 1995. 69.00 (*0-7619-9110-7*); pap. 25.95 (*0-7619-9111-5*) AltaMira Pr.

Romanucci-Ross, Lola, jt. auth. see De Vos, George.

Romanucci-Ross, Lola E. Mead's Other Manus: Phenomenology of the Encounter. (Illus.). 256p. 1985. 34.95 (*0-89789-064-7*, H064, Bergin & Garvey) Greenwood.

— One Hundred Towers: An Italian Odyssey of Cultural Survival. LC 90-1123. 240p. 1991. 59.95 (*0-89789-250-X*, H250, Bergin & Garvey) Greenwood.

Romanucci-Ross, Lola E., et al, eds. The Anthropology of Medicine: From Culture to Method. 3rd ed. LC 96-53993. 416p. 1997. pap. 30.95 (*0-89789-516-9*, Bergin & Garvey) Greenwood.

Romanucci-Ross, Lola E. & Moerman, Daniel R., eds. The Anthropology of Medicine: From Culture to Method. 3rd ed. LC 96-53993. 416p. 1997. 79.50 (*0-89789-490-1*, Bergin & Garvey) Greenwood.

Romanucci-Ross, Lola E., jt. auth. see Moerman, Daniel R.

***Romanuk, Paul.** Hockey Superstars 1999-2000: Today's Hottest Names in the Game! (Illus.). 48p. (J). (gr. 1-5). 1999. pap. 4.99 (*1-55209-399-9*) Firefly Bks Ltd.

Romanus, Peter, ed. Lyonel Feininger: Die Halle-Bilder. (GER., Illus.). 120p. 1991. 64.00 (*3-7913-1155-7*, Pub. by Prestel) te Neues.

Romany, Celina, jt. auth. see Fernandez, Demetrio.

Romanyshyn, Robert. Soul in Grief: Love, Death & Transformation. LC 99-29798. 200p. 1999. pap. 14.95 (*1-55643-315-8*) North Atlantic.

— Technology As Symptom & Dream. (Illus.). 320p. 1989. 45.00 (*0-415-00786-0*, A3877) Routledge.

— Technology As Symptom & Dream. (Illus.). 304p. (C). 1989. pap. 27.99 (*0-415-00787-9*, A3881) Routledge.

Romao, J. C. & Freire, F. Electroweak Physics & the Early Universe: Proceedings of a NATO ARW Held in Sintra, Portugal, Lisbon, March 23-25, 1994. (NATO ASI Ser.: Vol. 338). (Illus.). 420p. (C). 1995. text 162.00 (*0-306-44909-9*) Plenum.

Romao, J. C. & Valle, J. W. Neutrinos in Supersymmetry. 300p. 1997. 78.00 (*981-02-3275-6*) World Scientific Pub.

Romary, Thomas G. Topics of Mathematics Simplified: Factoring Polynomials. 2nd ed. Wetherington, Judy, ed. 30p. 1999. pap. 6.88 (*0-07-235150-0*) McGraw.

— Topics of Mathematics Simplified: Simplex Method. Wetherington, Judy, ed. (College Custom Ser.). 30p. 1997. pap. 7.19 (*0-07-054042-X*) McGraw.

***Romas, John A.** Practical Stress Management: A Comprehensive Workbook for Managing Change & Promoting Health. 2nd ed. LC 99-35928. 304p. 1999. pap. text 34.00 incl. cd-rom, audio compact disk (*0-205-31132-6*) P-H.

Romas, Nicholas A. & Vaughan, E. Darracott, eds. Alternate Methods in the Treatment of Benign Prostatic Hyperlasia. LC 92-48354. 1993. write for info. (*3-540-56389-X*); 109.00 (*0-387-56389-X*) Spr-Verlag.

Romashkevitch, P. A., ed. Polnij Russkij Orthograficheskij Slovar'Tr. of Complete Russian Orthographic Dictionary. 264p. reprint ed. pap. 10.00 (*0-317-29290-0*) Holy Trinity.

Romashko, Sandra. Poisonous & Hazardous Marine Life: Animals That Bite, Sting, Cut, or Are Poisonous or Dangerous to Eat. (Illus.). 64p. 1998. pap. 4.95 (*0-89317-045-3*) Windward Pub.

Romashko, Sandra, ed. see Eashton, Ray, Jr. & Ashton, Patricia S.

Romashko, Sandra D. The Complete Collector's Guide to Shells & Shelling. 2nd ed. LC 81-51067. (Illus.). 112p. (Orig.). 1994. pap. 9.95 (*0-89317-032-1*) Windward Pub.

— Handbook of Saltwater Fishes. LC 91-65377. (Illus.). 64p. (Orig.). 1992. pap. 3.95 (*0-89317-040-2*) Windward Pub.

— Shark: Lord of the Sea. 6th ed. LC 76-150452. (Illus.). 64p. 1991. pap. 4.95 (*0-89317-001-1*) Windward Pub.

— The Shell Book: A Complete Guide to Collecting & Identifying. 6th ed. LC 76-360976. (Illus.). 64p. 1992. pap. 5.95 (*0-89317-000-3*) Windward Pub.

— Wild Ducks & Geese of North America. LC 77-81167. (Illus.). 1978. pap. 3.95 (*0-89317-018-6*) Windward Pub.

Romashko, Sandra D., ed. see Ashton, Ray E., Jr. & Ashton, Patricia S.

Romashko, Sandra D., ed. see Erwin, Wilma C.

Romashko, Sandra D., ed. see Stachowicz, Jim.

Romasic, Roman. Corporation Law: Principles, Policy & Process. 2nd ed. 1072p. 1992. pap. 87.00 (*0-409-30671-1*, Austral, MICHIE) LEXIS Pub.

Romatowski, Michael & King, L. Neil. The Super Power Golfer: Exercise Secrets for Dramatically Improving Your Golf Game. (Illus.). 160p. 1998. pap. 14.95 (*1-889337-00-5*) Pierpoint-Martin.

Romatowski, Michael & Underwood, David. Weekend Warrior: Becoming an Athlete (Again) (Illus.). 160p. 2000. pap. 19.95 (*1-889337-01-3*) Pierpoint-Martin.

Romb, Anselm W. Kolbe Reader. (Orig.). 1987. pap. 10.95 (*0-913382-35-3*, 101-35) Marytown Pr.

— Man of Peace - Casimir Michael Cypher: His Meaning in Life Was Found in Death. (Illus.). 67p. (Orig.). 1985. pap. 3.75 (*0-913382-17-5*, 105-42) Marytown Pr.

— Maximilian Kolbe: Authentic Franciscan. (Illus.). 192p. (Orig.). 1990. pap. 7.95 (*0-913382-56-6*, 101-37) Marytown Pr.

— Total Consecration to Mary, Spouse of the Holy Spirit. 64p. 1982. pap. 2.00 (*0-913382-13-2*, 105-37) Marytown Pr.

— Walk with the Lord - Advent - Christmas: Sharing the Silence, Sharing the Life. LC 90-44397. 182p. (Orig.). 1990. pap. 6.95 (*0-8198-8245-3*) Pauline Bks.

Romb, Anselm W., ed. & pref. see McHugh, Joan C.

Romba, John J. Controlling Your Dog Away from You. LC 84-71305. (Illus.). 112p. 1984. pap. 9.95 (*0-915359-00-6*) Abmor Pub.

Rombach, H. D., et al, eds. Experimental Software Engineering Issues - Critical Assessment & Future Directions: Proceedings of an International Workshop, Dagstuhl Castle, Germany, September 14-18, 1992. (Lecture Notes in Computer Science Ser.: Vol. 706). xviii, 261p. 1993. pap. write for info. (*3-540-57092-6*) Spr-Verlag.

— Experimental Software Engineering Issues - Critical Assessment & Future Directions: Proceedings of the International Workshop Held at Dagstuhl Castle, Germany, September 14-18, 1992. (Lecture Notes in Computer Science Ser.: Vol. 706). xviii, 261p. 1993. 44.95 (*0-387-57092-6*) Spr-Verlag.

Rombakis, Efthemia, ed. see Crawford, Bill.

***Rombauer, Irma.** Joy of Cooking. (Illus.). 2000. 4.95 (*0-7624-0841-3*) Running Pr.

Rombauer, Irma. The Joy of Cooking, 2 vols., Set. 1991. mass mkt. 11.98 (*0-451-92511-4*, Sig) NAL.

— The Joy of Cooking: A Compilation of Reliable Recipes with a Casual Culinary Chat. LC 98-4832. 395p. 1998. 24.50 (*0-684-83358-1*) Scribner.

— The Joy of Cooking Vol. 1: Main Course Dishes, Vol. 1. 688p. 1998. mass mkt. 7.99 (*0-451-19514-0*, Sig) NAL.

— The Joy of Cooking Vol. 2: Appetizers, Desserts & Baked Goods, Vol. 2. 688p. 1998. mass mkt. 7.50 (*0-451-19515-9*, Sig) NAL.

— Joy of Cooking Multimedia. 1998. 49.95 (*0-671-31708-3*) ScrB.

Rombauer, Irma & Becker, Marion R. The Joy of Cooking. 930p. 1985. 25.50 (*0-02-604570-2*) Macmillan.

— The Joy of Cooking. rev. ed. LC 75-10772. (Illus.). 930p. 1975. write for info. (*0-672-52385-X*) Macmillan.

— Joy of Cooking. rev. ed. LC 75-10772. (Illus.). 930p. 1975. 16.95 (*0-672-51831-7*) Macmillan.

— The Joy of Cooking, 2 vols., 2. 1974. mass mkt. 5.99 (*0-451-16825-9*, AE1711, Sig) NAL.

— The Joy of Cooking: The All-Purpose Cookbook. rev. expanded ed. (Illus.). 915p. 1997. pap. 16.95 (*0-452-27923-2*) NAL.

— The Joy of Cooking: The All-Purpose Cookbook. 2nd rev. ed. (Illus.). 915p. 1997. pap. 14.95 (*0-452-27915-1*, Plume) Dutton Plume.

Rombauer, Irma, et al. Joy of Cooking. LC 97-36451. (Illus.). 1152p. 1997. 29.50 (*0-684-81870-1*, Scbl) S&S Trade.

— The Joy of Cooking Christmas Cookies. (Illus.). 128p. 1996. 18.95 (*0-684-83357-3*) Scribner.

***Rombauer, Irma R., et al.** The Miniature Edition Joy of Cooking Keepsake. (Illus.). 2000. 9.95 (*0-7624-0842-1*) Running Press Min.

Rombauer, Marjorie D. Legal Problem Solving: Analysis, Research & Writing, Teacher's Manual & 1991-92 Problem Supplement. 5th ed. (American Casebook Ser.). 69p. (C). 1992. reprint ed. pap. text. write for info. (*0-314-00076-3*) West Pub.

Rombauer, Marjorie D., jt. auth. see Squires, Lynn B.

Rombeau, John L. Atlas of Nutritional Support Techniques. 1989. 51.00 (*0-316-75575-3*, Little Brwn Med Div) Lppncot W & W.

Rombeau, John L. & Caldwell, Michael D. Clinical Nutrition: Parenteral Nutrition. 2nd ed. (Illus.). 912p. 1993. text 130.00 (*0-7216-3600-4*, W B Saunders Co) Harcrt Hlth Sci Grp.

Rombeau, John L. & Rolandelli, Rolando H. Clinical Nutrition: Enteral & Tube Feeding. 3rd ed. Kersey, Ray, ed. (Illus.). 670p. 1996. text 99.00 (*0-7216-2155-4*, W B Saunders Co) Harcrt Hlth Sci Grp.

Rombeau, John L. & Rolandelli, Rolando H. Clinical Nutrition: Parenteral Nutrition. 2nd ed. (Illus.). 670p. Date not set. text. write for info. (*0-7216-8120-4*, W B Saunders Co) Harcrt Hlth Sci Grp.

Rombeau, John L. & Takala, J. Gut Dysfunction in Critically Ill Patients, No. 26. LC 96-27697. (Update in Intensive Care & Emergency Medicine). 420p. 1996. 139.50 (*3-540-61127-4*) Spr-Verlag.

Romberg, Alan, et al. The United States & Japan in Asia. Twomey, Christopher & Stankeiwicz, Michael, eds. (IGCC Policy Papers: No. 10). 50p. (Orig.). 1994. pap. 3.50 (*0-934637-25-3*) U of CA Inst Global.

Romberg, Alan D. Same Bed, Different Dreams: America & Japan - Societies in Transition. LC 90-1523. 152p. 1990. reprint ed. pap. 47.20 (*0-608-02005-2*, 206266100003) Bks Demand.

***Romberg, Jan.** ICC Guide to Incoterms 2000: Understanding & Practical Use. 1999. pap. text 54.95 (*92-842-1269-3*) ICC Pub.

Romberg, Jenean. Let's Discover Crayon. (Arts & Crafts Discovery Units Ser.). (Illus.). 64p. 1994. reprint ed. pap. text 9.95 (*0-87628-523-X*) Ctr Appl Res.

— Let's Discover Mobiles. (Arts & Crafts Discovery Units Ser.). (Illus.). 64p. 1994. reprint ed. pap. text 9.95 (*0-87628-524-8*) Ctr Appl Res.

— Let's Discover Paper. (Arts & Crafts Discovery Units Ser.). (Illus.). 64p. 1994. reprint ed. pap. text 9.95 (*0-87628-525-6*) Ctr Appl Res.

— Let's Discover Puppets. (Arts & Crafts Discovery Units Ser.). (Illus.). 64p. 1994. reprint ed. pap. text 9.95 (*0-87628-528-0*) Ctr Appl Res.

— Let's Discover Tempera. (Arts & Crafts Discovery Units Ser.). (Illus.). 64p. 1994. reprint ed. pap. text 9.95 (*0-87628-529-9*) Ctr Appl Res.

— Let's Discover Tissue. (Arts & Crafts Discovery Units Ser.). (Illus.). 64p. 1994. reprint ed. pap. text 9.95 (*0-87628-530-2*) Ctr Appl Res.

— Let's Discover Weaving. (Arts & Crafts Discovery Units Ser.). (Illus.). 64p. 1994. pap. text 9.95 (*0-87628-532-9*) Ctr Appl Res.

Romberg, Jenean & Rutz, Miriam. Art Today & Every Day: Classroom Activities for the Elementary School Year. (Illus.). 272p. (C). 1982. pap. text 28.95 (*0-13-049049-0*) P-H.

Romberg, Nina. Shadow Walkers. 304p. 1993. mass mkt. 4.50 (*1-55817-696-9*, Pinncle Kensgtn) Kensgtn Pub Corp.

Romberg, T. M., et al. Signal Processing for Industrial Diagnostics. LC 96-5957. (Series in Measurement Science & Technology). 336p. 1996. 159.95 (*0-471-96166-3*) Wiley.

Romberg, Thomas & Webb, Norman L. Reforming Mathematics Education in America's Cities: The Urban Mathematics Collaborative Project. (Ways of Knowing in Science Ser.). 256p. (C). 1994. text 46.00 (*0-8077-3383-0*) Tchrs Coll.

Romberg, Thomas, jt. auth. see Webb, Norman L.

Romberg, Thomas A. Toward Effective Schooling: The IGE Experience. LC 85-3156. (Illus.). 246p. (Orig.). 1985. pap. text 22.50 (*0-8191-4581-5*); lib. bdg. 48.00 (*0-8191-4580-7*) U Pr of Amer.

Romberg, Thomas A., ed. Mathematics Assessment & Evaluation: Imperatives for Mathematics Educators. LC 91-11157. (SUNY Series, Reform in Mathematics Education). 369p. (C). 1992. pap. text 23.95 (*0-7914-0900-7*) State U NY Pr.

— Reform in School Mathematics & Authentic Assessment. (SUNY Series, Reform in Mathematics Education). 291p. (C). 1995. text 59.50 (*0-7914-2161-9*); pap. text 19.95 (*0-7914-2162-7*) State U NY Pr.

Romberg, Thomas A., et al, eds. Integrating Research on the Graphical Representation of Functions. (Studies in Mathematical Thinking & Learning). 368p. 1993. text 79.95 (*0-8058-1134-6*) L Erlbaum Assocs.

Romberg, Thomas A., jt. ed. see Fennama, Elizabeth.

Romberg, Thomas A., jt. ed. see Fennema, Elizabeth.

Romberger, J. A. Plant Structure: Function & Development - A Treatise on Anatomy & Vegetative Development, With Special Reference to Woody Plants. LC 93-20242. 1993. 219.00 (*0-387-56305-9*) Spr-Verlag.

Romberger, John A. Virology in Agriculture. LC 76-42139. (Beltsville Symposia in Agricultural Research Ser.: No. 1). 320p. 1977. text 41.00 (*0-916672-14-X*) Rowman.

Rombke, Jorg & Moltmann, Johann F., eds. Applied Ecotoxicology. 304p. 1995. lib. bdg. 75.00 (*1-56670-070-1*, L1070) Lewis Pubs.

Rombold, Judith. B&Bs of Kansas: A Comprehensive Guide to Bed & Breakfasts in Kansas. 176p. (Orig.). 1996. pap. 14.95 (*0-9649065-1-1*) Parkwood Pr.

Rombold, Judy, ed. see VanSoyoc, Mary C.

Rombos, Theodora. The Iconography of Attic Late Geometric II Pottery. (Studies in Mediterranean Archaeology & Literature: No. 68). (Illus.). 650p. (Orig.). 1988. pap. 97.50 (*91-86098-77-2*, Pub. by P Astroms) Coronet Bks.

Rombouts, A. Guidebook to Pecten Shells: Recent Pectinidae & Propeamussiidae of the World. Coomans, H. E. et al, eds. (Illus.). 184p. 1991. 57.00 (*90-73348-07-2*, Pub. by Backhuys Pubs) Balogh.

***Rome & Zlotnik.** Social Policy. 2002. pap. 29.00 (*0-534-54199-2*) Thomson Learn.

Rome, Benjamin T., ed. see Steiner, Ruth.

Rome, David, ed. see Trungpa, Chogyam.

Rome, Denise De, see De Rome, Denise.

Rome, Donald L., et al. Business Workouts Manual. 2nd ed. (Bankruptcy Law Ser.). 736p. 1992. 149.00 (*0-7913-1014-0*) Warren Gorham & Lamont.

Rome, Dorothy, ed. see Parr, Judith D.

Rome, Edwin P. & Roberts, William H. Corporate & Commercial Free Speech: First Amendment Protection of Expression in Business. LC 84-26496. 269p. 1985. 65.00 (*0-89930-041-3*, RCR/, Quorum Bks) Greenwood.

R

R

Rome, Marcus. Abreactions. 144p. (Orig.). 1989. pap. 15.00 (*0-913559-13-X*) Birch Brook Pr.
— Abreactions. deluxe limited ed. 144p. (Orig.). 1989. 30.00 (*0-913559-12-1*) Birch Brook Pr.
***Rome, Marcus.** Repercussions. LC 99-73049. (Illus.). 136p. 2000. pap. 19.00 (*0-913559-55-5*) Birch Brook Pr.
Rome, Margaret. Chateau of Flowers. large type ed. 1990. 27.99 (*0-7089-2340-2*) Ulverscroft.
— The Girl at Eagle's Mount. large type ed. 288p. 1992. 27.99 (*0-7089-2595-2*) Ulverscroft.
Rome, Sandra M. The Outing: An Original Chintzland Prenatal Storybook. LC 98-96653. (Illus.). iii, 18p. (J). 1998. pap. write for info. (*0-9668895-0-9*) Chintzland.
Romei, Francesca. Leonardo da Vinci: Artist, Inventor & Scientist of the Renaissance. (Masters of Art Ser.). (Illus.). 64p. (J). (gr. 5). 1994. lib. bdg. 22.50 (*0-87226-313-4*, 63134B, P Bedrick Books) NTC Contemp Pub Co.
— The Story of Sculpture: From Prehistory to the Present. LC 95-7006. (Masters of Art Ser.). (Illus.). 64p. (J). (gr. 5). 1995. lib. bdg. 22.50 (*0-87226-316-9*, 63169B, P Bedrick Books) NTC Contemp Pub Co.
***Romei, Francesca, et al.** Leonardo da Vinci: Artist, Inventor & Scientist of the Renaissance. 2nd ed. LC 00-39745. (Masters of Art Ser.). (Illus.). (YA). 2000. write for info. (*0-87226-640-0*, P Bedrick Books) NTC Contemp Pub Co.
Romeijn, A. Stress & Strain Concentration Factors of Welded Multiplanar Tubular Joints. 170p. 1994. pap. 57.50 (*90-407-1057-0*, Pub. by Delft U Pr) Coronet Bks.
Romeis, James C., et al, eds. Applying Health Services Research to Long Term Care. LC 95-41301. (Illus.). 232p. 1996. 42.95 (*0-8261-9140-1*) Springer Pub.
Romeis, James C. & Coe, Rodney, eds. Quality & Cost-Containment in Care of the Elderly: Health Services Research Perspectives. LC 90-10439. 248p. 1990. 42.95 (*0-8261-7170-2*) Springer Pub.
Romeiser, John B. Andre Malraux: A Reference Guide, 1940-1990. LC 93-46322. (Reference Publications in Literature). 384p. 1994. 60.00 (*0-8161-9071-2*, G K Hall & Co) Mac Lib Ref.
— Critical Reception of Andre Malraux's l'Espoir in the French Press: December 1937-June 1940. LC 79-19837. (Romance Monographs: No. 37). 176p. 1980. 24.00 (*84-499-3368-4*) Romance.
Romen, A. S. Self-Suggestion & Its Influence on the Human Organism. Lewis, A. J. & Forsky, Valentina, trs. LC 80-28703. Orig. Title: Samovnushenie I Ego Vliianie Na Organizm Cheloveka. (Illus.). 235p. reprint ed. pap. 72.90 (*0-608-18132-3*, 203278600081) Bks Demand.
Romenesko, James. Death Log. LC 82-90083. (Orig.). 1982. pap. 9.95 (*0-942724-00-3*) Police Beat Pr.
Romeny, Bart M., ed. Geometry-Driven Diffusion in Computer Vision. (Computational Imaging & Vision Ser.). 472p. (C). 1994. text 208.00 (*0-7923-3087-0*) Kluwer Academic.
Romeo, Catherine, jt. auth. see Panuthos, Claudia.
***Romeo, Darby.** Did You Come? The Best of a Decade of Ben Is Dead. 2000. pap. 15.00 (*1-888277-23-8*) Incommcdo San Diego.
Romeo, Felicia F. Understanding Anorexia Nervosa. 116p. (C). 1986. 30.95 (*0-398-05191-7*) C C Thomas.
Romeo, Jean B., jt. auth. see Wolf, Jack S.
***Romeo, Joe & Barnett, LaQuela.** Road Trip Survival Kit. (Illus.). 24p. (J). (ps-2). 1999. spiral bd. 9.99 (*1-929140-00-2*) Music Inc.
***Romeo, John T.** Phytochemicals in Human Health Protection, Nutrition & Plant Defense. LC 99-37365. (Recent Advances in Phytochemistry Ser.). (C). 1999. text. write for info. (*0-306-46203-6*, Kluwer Plenum) Kluwer Academic.
Romeo, John T., ed. Phytochemical Signals & Plant-Microbe Interactions: Proceedings of a Joint Meeting of the Phytochemical Society of North America & the Phytochemical Society of Europe Held in Noordwijkerhout, the Netherlands, April 20-23, 1997. LC 98-19421. (Recent Advances in Phytochemistry Ser.). (Illus.). 264p. 1998. 95.00 (*0-306-45917-5*, Kluwer Plenum) Kluwer Academic.
Romeo, John T., et al, eds. Phytochemical Diversity & Redundancy in Ecological Interactions: Proceedings of the 35th Annual Meeting of the Phytochemical Society of North America Held in Sault St. Marie, Ontario, Canada, August 12-16, 1995. LC 96-47605. (Recent Advances in Phytochemistry Ser.: Vol. 30). (Illus.). 327p. (C). 1996. text 107.00 (*0-306-45500-5*, Kluwer Plenum) Kluwer Academic.
Romeo, John T., jt. ed. see Johns, Timothy.
Romeo, Leticia B., ed. see American Institute of Certified Public Accountants.
Romeo, Luigi. Ecce Homo! A Lexicon of Man. xv, 163p. 1979. 46.00 (*90-272-2006-9*) J Benjamins Pubng Co.
Romeo-Mark, Althea. Palaver: West Indian Poems. 1978. pap. 1.50 (*0-917402-10-3*) Downtown Poets.
Romeo, Sharon L., tr. see Lesourne, Jacques.
Romeo, Thomas J. The Marfan Syndrome: Physical Activity Guidelines for Physical Educators, Coaches & Physicians. 77p. pap. 15.00 (*0-918335-08-6*) Natl Marfan Foun.
— The Marfan Syndrome: Physical Activity Guidelines for Physical Educators, Coaches & Physicians. 78p. 1992. pap. 15.00 (*0-918335-06-X*) Natl Marfan Foun.
Romer. Advanced Macroeconomics. 2nd ed. 2000. 37.00 (*0-07-231855-4*) McGraw.
Romer, Alfred S. Osteology of the Reptiles. LC 97-5401. (Illus.). 800p. Date not set. reprint ed. 96.50 (*0-89464-985-X*) Krieger.
— Vertebrate Paleontology. 3rd ed. LC 66-13886. (Illus.). 1992. lib. bdg. 45.00 (*0-226-72488-3*) U Ch Pr.
Romer, Alfred S. & Price, Llewellyn I. Review of the Pelycosauria: Geological Society of American Special Papers, Vol. 28. Gould, Stephen Jay, ed. LC 79-8346. (History of Paleontology Ser.). (Illus.). 1980. reprint ed. lib. bdg. 55.95 (*0-405-12740-5*) Ayer.
Romer, Alfred S., et al. Bibliography of Fossil Vertebrates, Exclusive of North America, 1509-1927. LC 63-1118. (Geological Society of America, Memoir Ser.: No. 87, Vol. 2). 779p. reprint ed. pap. 200.00 (*0-8357-7183-0*, 203179200077) Bks Demand.
Romer, C. J., jt. ed. see Manciaux, M.
Romer, Christina & Romer, David. Reducing Inflation: Motivation & Strategy. LC 96-44811. (National Bureau of Economic Research Project Reports). 1997. 58.00 (*0-226-72484-0*) U Ch Pr.
Romer, Cornelia E. & Gagos, Traianos, eds. P. Michigan Koenen: Michigan Texts Published in Honor of Ludwig Koenen. (Studia Amstelodamensia ad Epigraphicam, Ius Antiquum et Papyrologicam Pertinentia: Vol. XXXVI). (ENG & GER., Illus.). 440p. 1996. lib. bdg. 227.00 (*90-5063-127-4*, Pub. by Gieben) J Benjamins Pubng Co.
Romer, David. Advanced Macroeconomics. LC 95-37228. (Advanced Series in Economics Ser.). 432p. (C). 1995. 47.19 (*0-07-053667-8*) McGraw.
Romer, David, jt. auth. see Romer, Christina.
Romer, David, jt. ed. see Mankiw, N. Gregory.
Romer, David Lo, see Lo Romer, David.
Romer, Elizabeth. The Tuscan Year: Life & Food in an Italian Valley. LC 88-37226. 182p. 1989. pap. 13.00 (*0-86547-387-0*) N Point Pr.
Romer, Elizabeth, jt. auth. see Romer, John.
Romer, F. E. & Mela, Pomponius. Pomponius Mela's Description of the World. LC 97-40709. (Illus.). 184p. (C). 1998. pap. text 21.95 (*0-472-08452-6*, 08452) U of Mich Pr.
Romer, George, jt. ed. see Nelson, Mike.
Romer, Hartmann, jt. auth. see Honerkamp, Josef.
Romer, Joe. Hydroponic Crop Production. (Illus.). 142p. 1997. 24.95 (*0-86417-527-2*, Pub. by Kangaroo Pr); pap. 20.95 (*0-86417-833-6*, Pub. by Kangaroo Pr) Seven Hills Bk.
***Romer, Joe.** Hydroponic Crop Production. 142p. 2000. per. 15.00 (*0-684-87211-0*) S&S Trade.
Romer, John. The Seven Wonders of the World. 1995. 30.00 (*0-8050-4122-2*) H Holt & Co.
— Testament: The Bible & History. (Illus.). 368p. 1995. pap. 18.95 (*0-8050-2692-4*) H Holt & Co.
— Valley of the Kings. (Illus.). 288p. 1995. pap. 19.95 (*0-8050-3027-1*) H Holt & Co.
Romer, John & Romer, Elizabeth. The Rape of Tutankhamun. (Illus.). 160p. 1993. 44.50 (*1-85479-169-9*, Pub. by M OMara) Trans-Atl Phila.
Romer, Jorgen & Antonsen, Lasse. Jorgen Romer: The Subtle Gesture. (Illus.). 20p. 1998. 10.00 (*0-9666437-1-2*) U of MA Art Gallery.
Romer, Lyle T., ed. see Haring, Norris G.
Romer, Paul M. Changing Tastes: How Evolution & Experience Shape Economic Behaviour. (Oscar Morgenstern Memorial Lectures). (Illus.). 140p. (C). 1997. text 24.95 (*0-521-56347-X*) Cambridge U Pr.
Romer, Robert H. Energy Facts & Figures. LC 84-16278. 72p. (Orig.). 1985. pap. 8.95 (*0-931691-17-6*) Spring St Pr.
Romer, Roy, jt. frwd. see Underwood, Cecil H.
***Romer, T. E., ed.** European Society for Pediatric Endocrinology (ESPE) 38th Annual Meeting, Warsaw, August 1999: Abstracts. (Hormone Research Ser.: Vol. 51, Suppl. 2). (Illus.). viii, 154p. 1999. pap. 45.25 (*3-8055-6959-9*) S Karger.
Romer Taylor, Wanda, tr. see Lepage, Robert.
Romer, Theodore. Fight to Live - Live to Fight. 180p. (Orig.). 1989. pap. text 4.95 (*0-9616898-3-8*, TX 2-779-127) Phoenix Pr FL.
Romer, Therese, tr. see Dion, Leon.
***Romer, W. H.** Die Sumerologie: Einfuhrung in die Forschung und Bibliographie in Auswahl. 2nd ed. (Alter Orient und Altes Testament Ser.: Vol. 262). xii, 250p. 1999. text 70.00 (*3-927120-72-3*, Pub. by Ugarit-Verlag) Eisenbrauns.
Romer, Willem H. Das Sumerische Kurzepos Bilgames und Akka Vol. 1: Versuch einer Neubearbeitung. (Alter Orient und Altes Testament: Vol. 209/1). (GER.). 123p. 1980. text 14.50 (*3-7887-0638-4*) NeukirchenerV.
Romera, Luis. Pensar el Ser, No. 20, Vol. 447. v, 352p. 1994. 53.95 (*3-906753-28-X*) P Lang Pubng.
Romeralo, Antonio S. La Realidad Invisible (Nineteen Seventeen-Nineteen Twenty, Nineteen Twenty-Four) Jimenez, Juan Ramon, ed. (Textos B Ser.: Vol. XXI). (SPA.). 383p. (C). 1983. 63.00 (*0-7293-0070-6*, Pub. by Tamesis Bks Ltd) Boydell & Brewer.
Romerdahl, Nancy S., jt. auth. see Gehrke, Nathalie J.
Romeril, John. Love Suicides. 1997. pap. 14.95 (*0-86819-515-4*, Pub. by Currency Pr) Accents Pubns.
Romero. World Music Survey. 2001. 79.95 (*0-07-054014-4*) McGraw.
Romero, Brest J. La Pintura del Siglo XX. (Breviarios Ser.). (SPA.). pap. 11.99 (*968-16-0149-1*, Pub. by Fondo) Continental Bk.
Romero, C. Gilbert. Hispanic Devotional Piety: Tracing the Biblical Roots. LC 91-18620. (Faith & Cultures Ser.). 150p. reprint ed. pap. 46.50 (*0-608-20191-X*, 207145000012) Bks Demand.
Romero, Carlos. Handbook of Critical Issues in Goal Programming. 136p. 1991. text 86.50 (*0-08-040661-0*, Pergamon Pr) Elsevier.
Romero, Carlos & Rehman, T. Multiple Criteria Analysis for Agricultural Designs. (Developments in Agricultural Economics Ser.: No. 5). 258p. 1989. 148.25 (*0-444-87408-9*) Elsevier.
Romero, Carlos, jt. auth. see Ballestero, Enrique.
Romero, Christie. Warman's Jewelry. 2nd ed. LC 94-25278. (Illus.). 320p. 1998. pap. 22.95 (*0-87069-768-4*, WJEW2) Krause Pubns.
Romero, Christina, jt. auth. see Kumanduri, Ramanujachary.
Romero, Danny. Calle 10. LC 96-24414. 160p. (Orig.). 1996. pap. 12.95 (*1-56279-090-0*) Mercury Hse Inc.
Romero, Dave, ed. see Genibrel, Jean L.
***Romero, Denzil.** Belated Declaration of Love to Seraphine Louis: A Bilingual, Critical Edition of Denzil Romero's Short Stories; Edited & Translated by Stephen J. Clark. Clark, Stephen John, tr. LC 00-41768. 144p. 2000. pap. 26.50 (*0-7618-1756-5*) U Pr of Amer.
Romero, Edna. A Bug C. (Illus.). 48p. (J). (ps-3). 1993. pap. 10.95 (*1-880812-07-X*) S Ink WA.
Romero, Emilio. Las Ratas Suben a la Ciudad. Verde Doncella O el Marido para Despues. (Nueva Austral Ser.: Vol. 76). (SPA.). 1991. pap. text 24.95 (*84-239-1876-9*) Elliots Bks.
Romero, Enrique, jt. auth. see Avenell, Donne.
Romero, Enrique M. Church of Immaculate Conception: Berino, New Mexico, U. S. A. Land of Enchantment. (Illus.). 68p. 1996. 24.95 (*0-944551-11-4*) Sundance Pr TX.
Romero, Enrique M., jt. ed. see Cassaro, Michael A.
Romero, Federico. The United States & the European Trade Union Movement, 1944-1951. Fergusson, Harvey, II, tr. LC 92-27645. xvi, 292p. (C). 1993. 55.00 (*0-8078-2065-2*) U of NC Pr.
Romero, Francisco. Life Chemistry Reports: Proceedings of the International Meeting on Antioxidants, Inflammation, Cardiovascular & Ophthalmic Diseases. (Life Chemistry Reports: Vol. 12). 104p. 1994. pap. text 215.00 (*3-7186-5639-6*) Gordon & Breach.
Romero, Fred E. Chicano Workers: Their Utilization & Development. (Monographs: No. 8). (Illus.). 160p. (Orig.). 1979. pap. 10.00 (*0-89551-011-1*) UCLA Chicano Studies.
Romero, Gabriela De, see De Romero, Meilij & De Romero, Gabriela.
Romero Garcia, Luz V. El Aldeanismo en la Poesia de Luis Pales Matos. (UPREX, Estudios Literarios Ser.: No. 42). 119p. (C). 1976. pap. 1.50 (*0-8477-0042-9*) U of PR Pr.
Romero Gualda, Maria V. Vocabulario de Cine y Television en Espana. (SPA.). 400p. 1976. pap. 29.95 (*0-8288-5763-6*, S50002) Fr & Eur.
Romero Gutierrez, Astrid. Cuentos De Angeles Para Ninos. (SPA., Illus.). 151p. (ps-3). 1997. pap. text 7.98 (*970-643-065-2*) Selector.
Romero, Hector H. Nuevas Perspectivas Sobre La Generacion Del 27: Ensayos Literaries. LC 81-69021. (SPA.). 169p. (Orig.). 1983. pap. 14.95 (*0-89729-299-5*) Ediciones.
Romero, Hector R. La Evolucion Literaria De Juan Goytisolo. LC 78-74702. (SPA.). 162p. 1979. pap. 10.00 (*0-89729-222-7*) Ediciones.
Romero, Javiedes, tr. see Suzanne, Jamie.
Romero, Javier. Instante e Intensidad. (UPREX, Poesia Ser.: No. 56). (SPA.). 64p. 1978. pap. text 1.50 (*0-8477-0056-9*) U of PR Pr.
Romero, Javier, jt. auth. see Acosta, Jorge R.
Romero, Joan A., ed. see Plaskow, Judith.
Romero, John. Daikatana: John Romero's Official Strategies & Secrets. 192p. 1999. pap. 19.99 (*0-7821-2206-X*) Sybex.
— How to Beat Stress. 1992. pap. 9.95 (*0-9630158-4-2*) Baker-Hill.
— Secrets of Casino Marketing: How Casinos Find Gamblers & Keep Them Coming Back. 2nd ed. Romero, Robin, ed. LC 98-93193. (Casino Marketing Ser.: No. 2). 268p. 1998. 49.95 (*0-9642414-1-2*) Amer Eagle Arts.
Romero, John S. Casino Marketing. Quiroga, Robin M., ed. LC 94-78077. 288p. 1994. 49.95 (*0-9642414-0-4*) Amer Eagle Arts.
Romero, Jose L. A History of Argentine Political Thought. McGann, Thomas F., tr. xvii, 270p. 1963. 35.00 (*0-8047-0108-3*) Stanford U Pr.
— A History of Argentine Political Thought. LC JL2011.R613. 294p. reprint ed. pap. 91.20 (*0-7837-3948-6*, 204377700011) Bks Demand.
— Latin America: Its Cities & Ideas. LC 98-53038. 1999. write for info. (*0-8270-3539-X*) OAS.
Romero, Jose M. Breve Historia de Colima (Concise History of Colima) (Breves Historias de los Estados de Mexico Ser.). (SPA.). 1994. pap. 13.99 (*968-16-4538-3*, Pub. by Fondo) Continental Bk.
Romero, Jose R. Notes of a Villager: A Mexican Poet's Youth & Revolution. Mitchell, John & de Aguilar, Ruth M., trs. from SPA. LC 88-4042. 222p. 1988. 15.95 (*0-917635-04-3*); pap. 9.95 (*0-917635-05-1*) Plover Pr.
Romero, Leo. Agua Negra. 4th ed. Boyer, Dale, ed. LC 81-68459. (Ahsahta Press Modern & Contemporary Poets of the West Ser.). (SPA.). 55p. 1981. pap. 6.95 (*0-916272-17-6*) Ahsahta Pr.
— Celso. LC 84-72302. 96p. (C). 1985. pap. 7.00 (*0-934770-36-0*) Arte Publico.
— Going Home Away Indian. Boyer, Dale K., ed. LC 89-80859. (Ahsahta Press Modern & Contemporary Poets of the West Ser.). 110p. (Orig.). 1990. pap. 6.95 (*0-916272-41-9*) Ahsahta Pr.
— Rita & Los Angeles. LC 95-1032. 144p. (Orig.). 1994. pap. 13.00 (*0-927534-44-4*) Biling Rev-Pr.
Romero, Levi. In the Gathering of Silence. 48p. (Orig.). 1996. pap. 7.95 (*0-931122-84-8*) West End.
Romero, Lora. Home Fronts: Domesticity & Its Critics in the Antebellum United States. LC 97-7611. (New Americanists Ser.). 168p. 1997. text 49.95 (*0-8223-2030-4*); pap. text 15.95 (*0-8223-2042-8*) Duke.
Romero, Luis. Cuerda Tensa. 2nd ed. LC 79-66063. 62p. 1979. pap. 12.00 (*0-89295-011-0*) Society Sp & Sp-Am.
Romero, Luis A. Breve Historia Contemporanea de Argentina. (Histories of Latin American Nations Ser.). (SPA.). 455p. 1994. pap. 12.99 (*968-16-4357-7*, Pub. by Fondo) Continental Bk.
Romero, M., jt. ed. see Rincon, Jesus M.
Romero, Mario. Catholic Pocket Evangelist: Biblical Outlines for Scripturally-Based Discussions of the Roman Ca. 1999. pap. text 2.95 (*1-57918-057-4*) Queenship Pub.
— Unabridged Christianity: Biblical Answers to Common Questions about the Roman Catholic Faith. 380p. 1999. pap. text 12.95 (*1-57918-056-6*) Queenship Pub.
Romero, Maritza. Ellen Ochoa: The First Hispanic Woman Astronaut. LC 97-11546. (Great Hispanics of Our Time Ser.). (Illus.). 24p. (J). (gr. k-4). 1997. lib. bdg. 15.93 (*0-8239-5087-5*, PowerKids) Rosen Group.
— Henry Cisneros: A Man of the People. LC 97-7431. (Great Hispanics of Our Time Ser.). 24p. (J). (gr. k-4). 1997. lib. bdg. 15.93 (*0-8239-5082-4*, PowerKids) Rosen Group.
Romero, Maritza. Jaime Escalante: Inspiring Educator. LC 97-11603. (Great Hispanics of Our Time Ser.). (Illus.). 24p. (J). (gr. k-4). 1997. lib. bdg. 15.93 (*0-8239-5085-9*, PowerKids) Rosen Group.
Romero, Maritza. Joan Baez: Folk Singer. LC 97-7432. (Great Hispanics of Our Time Ser.). (J). (gr. k-4). 1997. lib. bdg. 15.93 (*0-8239-5084-0*, PowerKids) Rosen Group.
— Roberto Clemente: Baseball Hall of Famer. LC 97-4231. (Great Hispanics of Our Time Ser.). (J). (gr. k-4). 1997. lib. bdg. 15.93 (*0-8239-5083-2*, PowerKids) Rosen Group.
— Selena Perez: Queen of Tejano Music. LC 97-6730. (Great Hispanics of Our Time Ser.). (Illus.). 24p. (J). (gr. k-4). 1997. lib. bdg. 15.93 (*0-8239-5086-7*, PowerKids) Rosen Group.
Romero, Mary. Maid in the U. S. A. (Perspectives on Gender Ser.). 256p. (C). (gr. 13). 1992. 70.00 (*0-415-90611-3*, A7362); pap. 19.99 (*0-415-90612-1*, A7366) Routledge.
***Romero, Mary.** Women's Untold Stories: Breaking Silence, Talking Back, Voicing Complexity. 1999. pap. 19.99 (*0-415-92207-0*) Routledge.
Romero, Mary, et al, eds. Challenging Fronteras: Structuring Latina & Latino Lives in the U. S. LC 96-34287. 336p. 1997. pap. 25.99 (*0-415-91608-9*) Routledge.
— Challenging Fronteras: Structuring Latina & Latino Lives in the U. S. LC 96-34287. 336p. (C). 1997. 75.00 (*0-415-91607-0*) Routledge.
***Romero, Mary & Stewart, Abigail J., eds.** Women's Untold Stories: Breaking Silence Talking Back Voicing Complexity. 272p. (C). 1999. text 75.00 (*0-415-92206-2*) Routledge.
Romero, Mary, jt. ed. see Higginbotham, Elizabeth.
Romero, Meilij De, see De Romero, Meilij.
Romero, Melissa. Long Way Home. (Illus.). 200p. (YA). 2000. pap. 11.00 (*1-883573-15-7*) Pride & Imprints.
Romero-Oak, Judy. The Secret Place. 97p. 1994. pap. 14.95 (*0-9644174-0-5*) Writing Designs.
Romero, Orlando. Nambe-Year One. LC 76-13385. 1976. pap. 5.95 (*0-89229-003-X*) TQS Pubns.
Romero, Oscar. The Violence of Love. 2nd rev. ed. Plough Publishing House Staff, ed. Brockman, James R., tr. & compiled by by. LC 97-51460. 234p. 2000. pap. 14.00 (*0-87486-951-X*) Plough.
— Voice of the Voiceless: The Four Pastoral Letters & Other Statements. Walsh, Michael J., tr. from SPA. LC 84-14722. 208p. (Orig.). 1985. pap. 18.00 (*0-88344-525-5*) Orbis Bks.
Romero, Patricia. Profiles in Diversity: Women in the New South Africa. LC 98-20674. 235p. 1994. pap. 24.95 (*0-87013-447-7*) Mich St U Pr.
Romero, Patricia W. Lamu: History, Society, & Family in an East African Port City. LC 96-45647. (Illus.). 360p. (C). 1997. text 44.95 (*1-55876-106-3*) Wiener Pubs Inc.
— Lamu: History, Society, & Family in an East African Port City. LC 96-45647. (Illus.). 360p. (C). 1997. pap. text 18.95 (*1-55876-107-1*) Wiener Pubs Inc.
Romero, Patricia W., ed. Life Histories of African Women. LC 87-1441. (C). 1987. pap. 15.95 (*0-948660-05-8*, Pub. by Ashfield Pr) Humanities.
Romero, Patricia W., intro. Women's Voices on Africa. LC 91-36228. (Topics in World History Ser.). (Illus.). 298p. (C). 1992. text 39.95 (*1-55876-047-4*); pap. text 14.95 (*1-55876-048-2*) Wiener Pubs Inc.
Romero, Patricia W., ed. see Taylor, Susie K.
Romero, Pepe. The Journey of the Guitar: A Portrait of Pepe Romero. Price, Robin, ed. (Illus.). 36p. 1998. write for info. (*0-924433-07-8*) R Price.
Romero, Regina. Flora's Kitchen: Recipes from a New Mexico Family. (Illus.). 128p. 1998. 10.95 (*1-887896-10-4*, Rio Nuevo) Treas Chest Bks.
Romero, Roberto, et al. Prenatal Diagnosis of Congenital Anomalies. (Illus.). 466p. (C). 1997. pap. text 135.00 (*0-8385-7921-3*, A7921-8, Apple Lange Med) McGraw.
Romero, Robin, ed. see Romero, John.
***Romero Salvadbo, Francisco J.** Spain: Between War & Revolution. LC 99-10069. 1999. text. write for info. (*0-415-21293-6*) Routledge.
Romero Salvado, Francisco J. Twentieth Century Spain: Politics & Society in Spain, 1898-1998. LC 98-17662. 240p. 1999. pap. 19.95 (*0-312-21629-7*); text 59.95 (*0-312-21626-2*) St Martin.
Romero-Sierra, C. Neuroanatomy: A Conceptual Approach. LC 85-28060. (Illus.). 463p. (Orig.). reprint ed. pap. 143.60 (*0-7837-1609-5*, 204190100024) Bks Demand.
Romero, Sophia G. Always Hiding: A Novel. LC 97-16192. 224p. 1998. 22.50 (*0-688-15632-0*, Wm Morrow) Morrow Avon.

An Asterisk (*) at the beginning of an entry indicates that the title is appearing for the first time.

Romero Stevens, Jan. Twelve Lizards Leaping: A New Twelve Days of Christmas. LC 99-17614. (Illus.). 176p. (J). (ps-3). 1999. lib. bdg. 21.95 (*0-87358-744-8*, Rising Moon Bks) Northland AZ.

Romero, Vicki L. & Henry, Judith B. CFO's Expectations for Patient Financial Services. 50p. 1992. 20.00 (*0-930228-87-1*) Hlthcare Fin Mgmt.

Romero, William J. The Illustrated Guide for Modeling HMS Warrior (74), 1781: Basic Hull Construction. unabridged ed. LC 98-67182. (Illus.). 372p. 1998. spiral bd. 80.00 (*0-9657205-1-9*) Pier Bks & Dupont.

— The Illustrated Guide for Modelling the Royal Yacht FUBBS 1724. unabridged ed. LC 97-65241. (Illus.). 671p. 1997. spiral bd. 95.00 (*0-9657205-0-0*) Pier Bks & Dupont.

Romerstein, Herbert. The World Peace Council & Soviet Active Measures. 1983. pap. 5.00 (*0-935067-01-9*) Nathan Hale Inst.

***Romerstein, Herbert & Breindel, Eric.** The Verona Secrets: Exposing America's Cold War Traitors. 2000. 27.95 (*0-89526-275-4*) Regnery Pub.

Romerstein, Herbert, jt. auth. see Breindel, Eric.

Romesburg, Don, ed. Young, Gay & Proud! 4th ed. (Illus.). 120p. (YA). (gr. 7-12). 1995. pap. 5.95 (*1-55583-279-2*) Alyson Pubns.

Romesburg, H. Charles. Cluster Analysis for Researchers. LC 89-24453. 350p. (C). 1990. reprint ed. lib. bdg. 48.50 (*0-89464-426-2*) Krieger.

Rometsch, Dietrich & Wessels, Wolfgang, eds. The European Union & Member States: Towards Institutional Fusion? (European Policy Research Unit Studies: Vol. 2). 352p. 1996. text 79.95 (*0-7190-4809-5*) Manchester Univ Pr.

Romeu, Emma. Gregorio y El Mar. 1998. pap. text 9.95 (*968-19-0316-1*) Libros Fronteras.

Romeu, Jose A. Panorama del Periodismo Puertorriqueno. (UPREX, Communicacion Ser.: No. 67). 225p. 1985. pap. 6.00 (*0-8477-0067-4*) U of PR Pr.

***Romeu, Rafael.** Understanding Direct Access Trading: Making the Move from Your Online Broker to Direct Access Trading. (Direct Access Trader Ser.). 2001. 24.95 (*0-07-136250-9*) McGraw.

Romeu, Xavier. Breu Diccionari Ideologic Catala. (CAT.). 270p. 1977. pap. 19.95 (*0-8288-5291-X*, S50236) Fr & Eur.

Romey, Bill. Confluent Education in Science. LC 75-36718. (Illus.). 121p. (C). 1976. pap. text 5.00 (*0-915492-01-6*) Ash Lad Pr.

— Consciousness & Creativity: Transcending Science, Humanities, & the Arts. LC 75-5095. (Illus.). 278p. (C). 1975. pap. 10.00 (*0-915492-00-8*) Ash Lad Pr.

Romey, Linda. Esperanzas: An Easy Spanish Reader. (SPA., Illus.). 56p. 1998. pap. 3.00 (*1-890890-03-0*) Benetvision.

Romey, William D. Plus Ca Change... For the Love of France. LC 96-85369. (Illus.). 352p. (Orig.). 1996. pap. 19.95 (*0-915492-04-0*) Ash Lad Pr.

Romey, William D. & Hibert, Mary L. Teaching the Gifted & Talented in the Science Classroom. 2nd ed. 64p. 1988. pap. 8.95 (*0-8106-0748-4*) NEA.

Romeyn, Mary. Nutrition & HIV: A New Model for Treatment. 353p. 1998. pap. text 19.00 (*0-7881-5711-6*) DIANE Pub.

— Nutrition & HIV: A New Model for Treatment. rev. ed. LC 97-41330. 384p. 1998. mass mkt. 19.95 (*0-7879-3964-1*) Jossey-Bass.

Romhany, Paul, jt. auth. see Ring, Ken.

Romich. Guide to Veterinary Medical Terminology. LC 99-45427. (Agriculture Ser.). 323p. (C). 1999. mass mkt. 36.95 (*0-7668-0751-7*) Delmar.

Romicki, R., jt. auth. see Meshcherskii, I.

Romig, A. D., et al, eds. Structure-Property Relationships for Metal-Metal Interfaces Vol. 229: Materials Research Society Symposium Proceedings. 357p. 1991. text 30.00 (*1-55899-123-9*) Materials Res.

Romig, A. D., Jr., ed. see Metallurgical Society of AIME Staff.

Romig, Anne L., jt. auth. see Romig, Ronald E.

***Romig, Dennis A.** Breakthrough Teamwork: Outstanding Results Using Structured Teamwork. Olson, Kathy, ed. LC 99-74493. (Illus.). 303p. 1999. reprint ed. pap. 16.00 (*0-9672350-0-6*) Perf Res Pr.

Romig, Ella M. & Movius, Phyllis D. When the Geese Come: The Journals of a Moravian Missionary Ella Mae Ervin Romig 1898-1905, Southwest Alaska. LC 96-51588. 1997. pap. 20.00 (*0-912006-89-7*) U of Alaska Pr.

Romig, Emily. Pioneer Woman in Alaska. (American Autobiography Ser.). 140p. 1995. reprint ed. lib. bdg. 69.00 (*0-7812-8628-X*) Rprt Serv.

Romig, Harry G., jt. auth. see Dodge, Harold F.

Romig, Jack, jt. auth. see Bennett, Carolyn.

Romig, Nancy B. Scrips & Scraps: Scrapbook Abstracts Venango County & Surrounding Counties. 318p. 1995. per. 24.95 (*1-55856-191-9*, 349) Closson Pr.

Romig, Ralph. Sacred Refuge. LC 80-14984. 1987. pap. 13.95 (*0-87949-189-2*) Ashley Bks.

Romig, Ronald E. & Romig, Anne L. Stewardship Concepts & Practices. LC 92-24180. (Studies in Restoration History). 35p. 1992. pap. 5.00 (*0-8309-0622-3*) Herald Pub Hse.

Romig, Walter. Michigan Place Names. LC 86-15858. (Great Lakes Bks.). 676p. 1986. reprint ed. pap. 21.95 (*0-8143-1838-X*) Wayne St U Pr.

Romig, Walter, ed. Book of Catholic Authors, Fourth Series: Informal Self-Portraits of Famous Modern Catholic Writers. LC 70-179740. (Biography Index Reprint Ser.). 1977. reprint ed. 30.95 (*0-8369-8108-1*) Ayer.

Romijn, Elizabeth & Seely, Contee. Live Action English. 3rd ed. (Live Action Ser.). (Illus.). 96p. 1997. pap. text 9.95 (*0-929724-16-X*, 16-x) Command Performance.

Romijn, Elizabeth, jt. auth. see Seely.

Romijn, Elizabeth, jt. auth. see Seely, Contee.

Romijn, Elizabeth K. Puppies or Poppies? ESL Bingo. (Illus.). viii, 184p. 1998. pap. 19.95 (*0-929724-42-9*) Command Performance.

Romijn, Henny. Acquisition of Technological Capability in Small Firms in Developing Countries. LC 98-21907. 392p. 1998. text 79.95 (*0-312-21773-0*) St Martin.

Romilly, Hugh H. From My Verandah in New Guinea: Sketches & Traditions. 1977. text 18.95 (*0-8369-9233-4*, 9087) Ayer.

Romilly, Jacqueline De, see De Romilly, Jacqueline.

Romina, Francesca. Mangia, Little Italy! Secrets from a Sicilian Family Kitchen. LC 97-34027. 320p. 1997. pap. text 18.95 (*0-8118-1533-1*) Chronicle Bks.

Romine, A. Russell, jt. auth. see Evans, Lynn D.

Romine, A. Russell, jt. auth. see Smith, Kelly L.

Romine, A. Russell, jt. auth. see Wilson, Thomas P.

Romine, Andrea & Butcher, Betty. Christmas in the Forest: Three Plays. LC 97-72343. (Illus.). 42p. (Orig.). (J). (gr. k-2). 1997. pap. text 15.00 incl. audio (*0-9630310-2-3*) Will Hall.

Romine, Charlie. Where Duty Calls: Growing up in the Marine Corps. 1997. 21.95 (*1-887269-23-1*); pap. text 12.95 (*1-887269-31-2*) J Culler & Sons.

— Where Duty Calls: Growing up in the Marine Corps. LC 99-31094. 103p. 1999. pap. text 12.95 (*1-55571-499-4*) PSI Resch.

Romine, Gregory S. Classical Physics: Concepts & Applications. 896p. (C). 2000. 73.33 (*0-13-532466-1*, Macmillan Coll) P-H.

Romine, Jack S. & Ehrlich, Henry. Quick Vocabulary Power: A Self-Teaching Guide. 2nd rev. ed. LC 95-30999. (Self-Teaching Guides Ser.). 256p. 1995. pap. 16.95 (*0-471-05008-3*) Wiley.

Romine, Jack S., et al. College Business English. 3rd ed. (Illus.). 400p. 1981. pap. text 25.07 (*0-13-141960-9*) P-H.

Romine, Jim, jt. auth. see Shah, Rawn.

Romine, Linda. City Smart: Memphis. 2nd ed. (Illus.). 216p. 1999. pap. 13.95 (*1-56261-504-1*, City Smart) Avalon Travel.

Romine, Scott. Narrative Forms of Southern Community. LC 99-14905. (Southern Literary Studies). 248p. 1999. text 49.95 (*0-8071-2401-X*); pap. text 24.95 (*0-8071-2527-X*) La State U Pr.

Romines, Ann. Constructing the Little House: Gender, Culture, & Laura Ingalls Wilder. LC 97-14675. (Illus.). 304p. 1997. 55.00 (*1-55849-121-X*); pap. 18.95 (*1-55849-122-8*) U of Mass Pr.

— The Home Plot: Women, Writing, & Domestic Ritual. LC 91-34053. 336p. (C). 1992. pap. text 19.95 (*0-87023-794-2*) U of Mass Pr.

***Romines, Ann.** Willa Cather's Southern Connections: New Essays on Cather & the South. LC 00-25943. 256p. 2000. pap. 18.50 (*0-8139-1960-6*) U Pr of Va.

***Romines, Ann, ed.** Willa Cather's Southern Connections: New Essays on Cather & the South. LC 00-25943. 256p. 2000. 59.50 (*0-8139-1957-6*) U Pr of Va.

Romines, Ken. A Principal's Story: Two-Year Effort to Turn Around Edison Elementary School in San Francisco. Beggs, Marjorie, ed. LC 96-70005. 112p. 1997. pap. 12.95 (*0-936434-98-8*) SF Study Ctr.

Rominger, James M., jt. auth. see Mayes, Vernon O.

Romiszowski, A. J. Designing Instructional Systems. 424p. 1988. pap. 39.95 (*0-85038-787-6*, Pub. by Kogan Pg) Stylus Pub VA.

Romiszowski, A. J. Designing Instructional Systems: Decision-Making in Course Planning & Curriculum Design. 418p. 1984. 34.95 (*0-89397-181-2*) Nichols Pub.

— Developing Auto-Instructional Materials. 464p. (Orig.). 1987. pap. 39.95 (*1-85091-281-5*, Pub. by Kogan Pg) Stylus Pub VA.

Romiszowski, A. J. Developing Auto-Instructional Materials. 460p. (Orig.). 1987. pap. 37.95 (*0-89397-269-X*) Nichols Pub.

Romiszowski, A. J., et al. Strategic Human Resource Management. 172p. 1990. 44.00 (*90-265-1092-6*) Swets.

Romiszowski, Alexander J. Computer Mediated Communication: A Selected Bibliography. LC 91-43966. 55p. (Orig.). 1992. pap. 24.95 (*0-87778-243-1*) Educ Tech Pubns.

Romiszowski, Alexander J. & Gratch, Bonnie. Telecommunications & Teleconferencing in Education & Training: A Selected Bibliography. LC 95-6110. (Educational Technology Selected Bibliography Ser.: Vol. 13). 63p. 1995. pap. 24.95 (*0-87778-281-4*) Educ Tech Pubns.

Romiszowski, Alexander J., jt. ed. see Dills, Charles R.

Romita, John S., et al. The Power of Iron Man. (Illus.). 160p. 1984. pap. 15.95 (*0-87135-599-X*) Marvel Entrprs.

— Spider-Man vs. Green Goblin. (Illus.). 176p. 1995. pap. 15.95 (*0-7851-0139-X*) Marvel Entrprs.

— X-Men: From the Ashes. (Illus.). 226p. 1990. pap. 19.95 (*0-87135-615-5*) Marvel Entrprs.

Romjue, John L. American Army Doctrine for the Post-Cold War. (Illus.). 160p. 1998. pap. text 35.00 (*0-7881-2958-9*) DIANE Pub.

Romke, Adam & Novak, Derry, eds. The Communist States in the Era of Detente. 360p. 1991. pap. 12.95 (*0-88962-095-4*) Mosaic.

Romkey, Michael. I, Vampire. 368p. (Orig.). 1990. mass mkt. 5.99 (*0-449-14638-3*, GM) Fawcett.

— Vampire Hunter. 1999. mass mkt. 5.99 (*0-449-00200-4*, GM) Fawcett.

— The Vampire Papers. 1994. mass mkt. 5.99 (*0-449-14804-1*) Fawcett.

— The Vampire Princess. 1996. mass mkt. 5.99 (*0-449-14937-4*) Fawcett.

— The Vampire Virus. 1998. mass mkt. 5.99 (*0-449-00261-6*, GM) Fawcett.

Romkowska, S. English-Polish Dictionary of Abbreviations in Electronics. 150p. (C). 1988. 65.00 (*0-7855-6682-1*, Pub. by Collets) St Mut.

Romm. Strategies in Reading: Level A, Level A. 1984. pap. text 17.00 (*0-15-337118-8*); pap. text, teacher ed. 24.00 (*0-15-312124-2*) Holt R&W.

— Strategies in Reading: Level B, Level B. 1984. pap. text 17.00 (*0-15-337119-6*); pap. text, teacher ed. 24.00 (*0-15-337125-0*) Holt R&W.

— Strategies in Reading: Level C, Level C. 1984. pap. text 17.00 (*0-15-337120-X*); pap. text, teacher ed. 24.00 (*0-15-337126-9*) Holt R&W.

***Romm, Aviva.** Naturally Healthy Babies & Children: A Commonsense Guide to Herbal Remedies. 352p. 2000. pap. 16.95 (*1-58017-285-7*) Storey Bks.

***Romm, Aviva J.** ADHA Alternatives: A Natural Approach to Treating Attention Deficit Hyperactivity Disorder. (Medicinal Herb Guide Ser.). (Illus.). 128p. 2000. pap. 12.95 (*1-58017-248-2*) Storey Bks.

Romm, Aviva J. Natural Healing for Babies & Children. (Illus.). 256p. (Orig.). 1996. pap. text 16.95 (*0-89594-786-2*) Crossing Pr.

— The Natural Pregnancy Book: Herbs, Nutrition, & Other Holistic Choices. LC 97-11514. (Illus.). 304p. 1997. pap. 19.95 (*0-89594-819-2*) Crossing Pr.

— Pocket Guide to Midwifery Care. LC 98-10584. (Crossing Press Pocket Ser.). (Illus.). 112p. 1998. pap. 6.95 (*0-89594-855-9*) Crossing Pr.

Romm, Celia T. Doing Business on the Internet: Opportunities & Pitfalls. LC 99-25194. 300p. 1999. 69.95 (*1-85233-030-9*) Spr-Verlag.

— Virtual Politicking: Playing Politics in Electionically Linked Organizations. LC 98-28943. (Hampton Press Communication Ser.). 256p. 1998. text 49.50 (*1-57273-202-4*); pap. text 21.95 (*1-57273-203-2*) Hampton Pr NJ.

Romm, Celia T. & Sudweeks, Fay. Doing Business Electronically: A Global Perspective of Electronic Commerce. LC 98-9920. (Computer Supported Cooperative Work Ser.). 1998. pap. 59.95 (*3-540-76159-4*) Spr-Verlag.

Romm, Diane. The Jewish Guide to the Internet. LC 95-46114. 225p. 1996. pap. 25.00 (*1-56821-914-8*) Aronson.

Romm, J. Leonard. The Swastika on the Synagogue Door. 2nd ed. LC 93-46454. (Lazarus Family Mystery Ser.). (Illus.). 168p. (Orig.). (J). (gr. 6-9). 1994. reprint ed. pap. 6.95 (*1-881283-05-4*) Alef Design.

Romm, James S. The Edges of the Earth in Ancient Thought: Geography, Exploration, & Fiction. 256p. 1992. text 39.50 (*0-691-06933-6*, Pub. by Princeton U Pr) Cal Prin Full Svc.

— Edges of the Earth in Ancient Thought: Geography, Exploration, & Fiction. 247p. 1992. pap. text 14.95 (*0-691-03788-4*, Pub. by Princeton U Pr) Cal Prin Full Svc.

— Herodotus. LC 98-10983. (Hermes Bks.). 176p. 1998. 30.00 (*0-300-07229-5*); 15.00 (*0-300-07230-9*) Yale U Pr.

Romm, Joseph J. Cool Companies: How the Best Businesses Boost Profits & Productivity by Cutting Greenhouse-Gas Emissions. LC 99-18911. 277p. 1999. 24.95 (*1-55963-709-9*, Shearwater Bks) Island Pr.

— Lean & Clean Management: How to Boost Profits & Productivity by Reducing Pollution. 224p. 1994. 23.00 (*1-56836-037-1*) Kodansha.

Romm, N. R., jt. auth. see Flood, R. L.

Romm, Norma R., jt. auth. see Flood, Robert L.

Romm, Sharon. The Unwelcome Intruder: Freud's Struggle with Cancer. LC 83-13649. (Illus.). 164p. 1983. 55.00 (*0-275-91409-7*, C1409, Praeger Pubs) Greenwood.

Romme, Jac, jt. ed. see Hoekstra, Sjoerd.

Rommel. Simplicity Wins. 1995. 27.95 (*0-07-103617-2*) McGraw.

Rommel, Carol A. Integrating Beginning Math & Literature. (Illus.). 80p. (Orig.). (J). (gr. k-3). 1991. pap. text 9.95 (*0-86530-215-4*, IP 192-9) Incentive Pubns.

Rommel, Erwin. Attacks. rev. ed. Allen, Lee, ed. Driscoll, J. R., tr. LC 79-52022.Tr. of Infantrie Greift an. (GER., Illus.). 1979. pap. 16.50 (*0-9602736-0-3*) Athena Pr.

— Infantry Attacks. (Illus.). 288p. 1995. pap. 17.95 (*1-85367-199-1*, Pub. by Greenhill Bks) Stackpole.

— Problems for Platoon & Company. Hanesalo, Bruce A., ed. Koob, Cyril, tr. from GER. (Illus.). 74p. 1994. vinyl bd. 20.00 (*1-886848-01-7*) Mil-Info.

Rommel, Gunter, et al. Simplicity Wins: How Germany's Mid-Sized Industrial Companies Succeed. LC 94-34599. 240p. 1995. 27.95 (*0-87584-504-5*) Harvard Busn.

Rommel, Herbert. Zum Begriff des Bosen Bei Augustinus und Kant: Der Wandel von der Ontologischen Zur Autonomen Perspektive. (Europaische Hochschulschriften Ser.: Reihe 20, Bd. 521). (GER.). 335p. 1996. 57.95 (*3-631-30888-4*) P Lang Pubng.

Rommel, Sentiel A., jt. ed. see Reynolds, John E., III.

Rommelaere, J., jt. ed. see Faisst, S.

Rommele, Andrea, ed. see Karasimeonov, Georgi.

Rommell, Otto, ed. see Nestroy, Johann N.

Rommelman, Nancy, jt. auth. see Johnson, Hillary.

Rommelmann, Nancy. Everything You Pretend to Know about Food & Are Afraid Someone Will Ask. LC 97-36246. 256p. 1998. pap. 10.95 (*0-14-026373-X*) Penguin Putnam.

Rommen, Edward & Corwin, Gary, eds. Missiology & the Social Sciences: Contributions, Cautions, & Conclusions. LC 96-34634. (Evangelical Missiological Society Ser.). 1996. 8.95 (*0-87808-378-2*) William Carey Lib.

Rommen, Edward & Netland, Harold, eds. Christianity & the Religions: A Biblical Theology of World Religions. LC 95-36773. (World Evangelical Fellowship Ser.: Vol. 2). (Illus.). 280p. (Orig.). 1995. pap. text 9.95 (*0-87808-376-6*, WCL376-6) William Carey Lib.

Rommen, Edward, jt. auth. see Hesselgrave, David J.

Rommen, Heinrich A. The Natural Law. Mayer, J. P., ed. LC 78-67382. (European Political Thought Ser.). 1980. reprint ed. lib. bdg. 23.95 (*0-405-11732-9*) Ayer.

— The Natural Law: A Study in Legal & Social History & Philosophy. Hanley, Thomas R., tr. from GER. LC 97-26334.Tr. of Ewige Wiederkehr des Naturrechts. 1998. 15.00 (*0-86597-160-9*); pap. 8.50 (*0-86597-161-7*) Liberty Fund.

— Die Staatslehre des Franz Suarez, S. J. Mayer, J. P., ed. LC 78-67381. (European Political Thought Ser.). (GER.). 1980. reprint ed. lib. bdg. 30.95 (*0-405-11731-0*) Ayer.

— State in Catholic Thought: A Treatise in Political Philosophy. LC 74-91770. 747p. 1970. reprint ed. lib. bdg. 38.50 (*0-8371-2437-9*, ROCT, Greenwood Pr) Greenwood.

***Rommer, Barbara.** Blessing in Disguise: Another Side of the Near-Death Experience. LC 99-89967. 264p. 2000. pap. 12.95 (*1-56718-585-1*) Llewellyn Pubns.

***Rommerskirchen, Barbara.** Constructing Reality: Constructivism & Narration in John Fowles's The Magus. LC 99-89216. (Aachen British & American Studies: Vol. 13). 126p. (C). 1999. pap. text 26.95 (*0-8204-4375-1*) P Lang Pubng.

— Constructing Reality: Constructivism & Narration in John Fowles's the Magus. (Aachen British & American Studies). 126p. 1999. pap. 26.95 (*3-631-35385-5*) P Lang Pubng.

Rommetveit, Ragnar. On Message Structure: A Framework for the Study of Language & Communication. LC 74-174. 151p. reprint ed. pap. 46.90 (*0-608-14620-X*, 202428400035) Bks Demand.

Romness. Business of Living. (OX - Home Economics Ser.). 1986. pap., wbk. ed. 13.95 (*0-538-32011-7*) S-W Pub.

Romney & Steinbart, Paul J. Accounting Information Systems. 8th ed. (C). 2000. ring bd. write for info. (*0-13-086350-5*) P-H.

Romney, et al. Casebook in Accounting Information Systems. 2nd ed. 1997. pap. 15.95 (*0-87393-731-7*) Dame Pubns.

Romney, A. Kimball, jt. auth. see Weller, Susan C.

Romney, Brad, jt. auth. see Romney, Keith B.

Romney, David M., ed. Improving the Quality of Life: Recommendations for People with & Without Disabilities. 1994. text 102.00 (*0-7923-3234-2*) Kluwer Academic.

Romney, David M. & Bynner, John M. The Structure of Personal Characteristics. LC 92-18845. 160p. 1992. 49.95 (*0-275-93995-2*, C3995, Praeger Pubs) Greenwood.

Romney, Ed. Fixing up Nice Old Radios. 186p. 1990. pap. text 35.00 (*88-699-6563-5*) Hillcrst Pub.

Romney, Edward H. Basic Training in Camera Repair Tape Learning Program. 2nd rev. ed. 132p. 1998. 99.00 incl. audio (*1-886996-69-5*) Hillcrst Pub.

— Compur & Copal Leaf Shutter Repair. rev. ed. 223p. Date not set. pap. 39.00 (*1-886996-66-0*) Hillcrst Pub.

— Contax Camera Repair. 44p. 1992. pap. text 29.00 (*1-886996-65-2*) Hillcrst Pub.

— Ed Romney & His Cameras. 52p. 1995. pap. 9.00 (*1-886996-57-1*) Hillcrst Pub.

— Ed Romney & His Cameras: A Brief Autobiography. 2nd rev. ed. 1998. pap. 9.00 (*1-886996-68-7*) Hillcrst Pub.

— Ed Romney's Graphic Repair for Graphic Cameras. 35p. 1989. pap. text 20.00 (*1-886996-58-X*) Hillcrst Pub.

— Ed Romney's Rolleiflex RolleiCord Camera Repair: Repair & User's Guide. 36p. 1978. pap. 29.00 (*1-886996-61-X*) Hillcrst Pub.

— Home Repair & Restoration of Antique Cameras. 33p. 1976. pap. text 19.00 (*1-886996-62-8*) Hillcrst Pub.

— Leica Camera Repair. 64p. 1985. pap. text 29.00 (*1-886996-56-3*) Hillcrst Pub.

— Living Well on Practically Nothing. (Illus.). 160p. 1992. pap. 21.95 (*0-87364-694-0*) Paladin Pr.

— Revised Basic Training in Camera Repair: 1998 Edition. 2nd rev. ed. (Illus.). 132p. 1998. pap. text 35.00 (*1-886996-67-9*) Hillcrst Pub.

— Romney Dealer Text: How to Make Money Buying & Selling Old Cameras. 2nd ed. 87p. 1998. pap. text 24.00 (*1-886996-70-9*) Hillcrst Pub.

— Stereo Realist Camera Repair Manual: Repair & User's Manual. 26p. 1992. pap. text 18.00 (*1-886996-64-4*) Hillcrst Pub.

Romney, Eldon C. World's Stupidest I. Q. Test. (Illus.). 64p. (Orig.). (C). 1992. pap. 4.95 (*0-9632451-0-4*) Creat Diversions.

Romney, G. Ott. Off the Job Living. Date not set. write for info. (*0-8434-0439-6*, Pub. by McGrath NH) Ayer.

Romney, George. Drawings of Romney. Longstreet, Stephen, ed. (Master Draughtsman Ser.). 1970. 10.95 (*0-87505-032-8*); pap. 4.95 (*0-87505-185-5*) Borden.

Romney, George, jt. auth. see Cross, David.

Romney, Jonathan. Celluloid Jukebox: Popular Music & the Movies since the 50s. LC 95-224068. (Illus.). 192p. 1995. 45.00 (*0-85170-506-5*, Pub. by British Film Inst) Ind U Pr.

— Short Orders: Film Writings. LC 97-66229. 224p. 1998. pap. text 16.00 (*1-85242-512-1*) Serpents Tail.

Romney, Jonathan & Wootton, Adrian, eds. Celluloid Jukebox: Popular Music & the Movies since the 50s. LC 95-224068. (Illus.). 192p. 1995. pap. 19.95 (*0-85170-507-3*, Pub. by British Film Inst) Ind U Pr.

Romney, Keith B. & Romney, Brad. Condominium Development Guide. 2nd ed. 1000p. 1990. boxed set 98.00 (*0-88262-908-5*) Warren Gorham & Lamont.

R

— Condominium Development Guide, No. 1. 2nd ed. 1000p. 1990. suppl. ed. 59.50 (*0-7913-0699-2*) Warren Gorham & Lamont.

*__Romney, Marshall B.__ Accounting Information Systems. 8th ed. LC 99-32593. 796p. (C). 1999. 94.00 (*0-201-35721-6*, Prentice Hall) P-H.

Romney, Marshall B. Accounting Information Systems WSS: Accounting Information Systems. 7th ed. (C). 1997. pap. text. write for info. (*0-201-55281-7*) Addison-Wesley.

— Accounting Information Systems, WSS Version. 7th ed. 880p. (C). 1997. pap. text. write for info. (*0-201-58899-4*) Addison-Wesley.

Romney, Marshall B., jt. auth. see Cushing, Barry E.

Romney, Marshall D., jt. auth. see Cushing, Barry E.

Romney, Mary. The Devil Take You, Sweetest. large type ed. 336p. 1987. 27.99 (*0-7089-1669-4*) Ulverscroft.

— The Long Vacation. large type ed. 304p. 1987. 27.99 (*0-7089-1715-1*) Ulverscroft.

— Love Lies Waiting. large type ed. (General Ser.). 432p. 1993. 27.99 (*0-7089-2867-6*) Ulverscroft.

Romney, Paul. Mr. Attorney: The Attorney General for Ontario in Court, Cabinet & Legislature, 1791-1899. 456p. 1986. text 47.50 (*0-8020-3431-4*) U of Toronto Pr.

Romney, Paul, ed. see Wise, S. F.

*__Romney, Rodney.__ Wilderness Spirituality: Finding Your Way in an Unsettled World. 304p. 1999. text 24.95 (*1-86204-623-9*, Pub. by Element MA) Penguin Putnam.

— Wilderness Spirituality: Finding Your Way in an Unsettled World. 2001. pap. 15.99 (*1-86204-737-5*) Element MA.

Romney, Valerie A. Strategic Planning & Needs Assessment for Schools & Communities. 96p. (Orig.). 1996. pap. 14.95 (*0-930388-14-3*) Comm Collaborators.

Romney, Valerie A., jt. auth. see Decker, Larry E.

*__Romo.__ Aesthetic Facial Plastic Surgery. (Illus.). 320p. 2000. 179.00 (*0-86577-807-8*) Thieme Med Pubs.

Romo, Alberto. Marianela: Classic Spanish Literature. (C). 1987. pap. text 14.80 (*0-13-556069-1*) P-H.

Romo, Alberto, jt. auth. see Rice, R. Hugh.

Romo, Alberto, tr. see Bach, Mary.

Romo, Alberto, tr. see Baker, Betty L.

Romo, Alberto, tr. see Beveridge, Donna.

Romo, Alberto, tr. see Blanchard, Patricia & Suhr, Joanne.

Romo, Alberto, tr. see Blanchard, Pat & Suhr, Joanne.

Romo, Alberto, tr. see Boland, Janice.

Romo, Alberto, tr. see Boss, Kittie.

Romo, Alberto, tr. see Cogan, Karen.

Romo, Alberto, tr. see Cox, Rhonda.

Romo, Alberto, tr. see Ecton, Ann.

Romo, Alberto, tr. see Fleagle, Gail S.

Romo, Alberto, tr. see Hardin, Suzanne.

Romo, Alberto, tr. see Helmso, Candy G.

Romo, Alberto, tr. see Jackson, Marjorie.

Romo, Alberto, tr. see Latta, Rich.

Romo, Alberto, tr. see Livesey, Claire.

Romo, Alberto, tr. see Mace, Ann.

Romo, Alberto, tr. see Marzollo, Jean.

Romo, Alberto, tr. see Moeller, Kathleen H.

Romo, Alberto, tr. see Podoshen, Lois.

Romo, Alberto, tr. see San Souci, Robert D.

Romo, Alberto, tr. see Sawyer, Walter.

Romo, Alberto, tr. see Schaefer, Lola.

Romo, Alberto, tr. see Shahan, Sherry.

Romo, Alberto, tr. see Slaughter, Robert.

Romo, Alfonso. Quimica, Universo, Tierra y Vida. (Ciencia para Todos Ser.). (SPA.). pap. 6.99 (*968-16-2705-9*, Pub. by Fondo) Continental Bk.

Romo-Carmona, Mariana. Living at Night. LC 97-26929. 300p. (Orig.). 1997. pap. 10.95 (*1-883523-22-2*) Spinsters Ink.

— Speaking Like an Immigrant: A Collection. LC 98-75487. 156p. 1999. pap. 12.00 (*0-9619450-3-6*) LLHP.

Romo, Harriet D. Latinos & Blacks in the Cities: Policies for the 1990's. (Symposia Ser.). 236p. 1990. pap. 10.50 (*0-89940-423-5*) LBJ Sch Pub Aff.

Romo, Harriet D. & Falbo, Toni. Latino High School Graduation: Defying the Odds. LC 95-16645. (Hogg Foundation Ser.). (Illus.). (C). 1996. pap. 17.95 (*0-292-72495-0*); text 37.50 (*0-292-72494-2*) U of Tex Pr.

Romo, Harriett D. Reaching Out: Best Practices for Educating Mexican-Origin Children & Youth. LC 99-22126. 1999. pap. 24.00 (*1-880785-22-6*) ERIC-CRESS.

Romo, Harriett D., jt. auth. see McLemore, S. Dale.

*__Romo, Ito.__ El Puente - The Bridge. LC 00-8197. 2000. 18.95 (*0-8263-2252-2*) U of NM Pr.

Romo, Jesus, jt. auth. see Sanchez, Guadalupe L.

Romo, Miguel P., jt. ed. see Resendiz, Daniel.

Romo, Ricardo. East Los Angeles: History of a Barrio. LC 82-10891. 232p. 1983. pap. 13.95 (*0-292-72041-6*) U of Tex Pr.

Romo, Ricardo & Paredes, Raymund, eds. New Directions in Chicano Scholarship. rev. ed. (Monographs in Chicano Studies). 279p. (C). 1977. reprint ed. pap. 18.95 (*0-930929-00-4*) U CA Ctr Chicano Stud.

Romo, Richard & Brinson, Boone. Easy Visuals for English Language Teachers: How to Make & Use Them. 152p. 1995. pap. 18.30 (*0-8442-0797-7*) NTC Contemp Pub Co.

Romo, Terecita & Ybarra-Frausto, Tomas. Carmen Lomas Garza: Lo Real Maravilloso.Tr. of Carmen Lomas Garza: The Marvelous/The Real. 23p. 1987. 8.50 (*0-614-24045-X*) Mexican Museum.

Romo, Terezita & Mesa-Bains, Amalia. Patssi Valdez: A Precarious Comfort. Ptak, Elizabeth, ed. (Illus.). 104p. 1999. pap. 24.95 (*1-880508-07-9*) Mexican Museum.

*__Romoff, Adam.__ Estrogen: How & Why It Can Save Your Life. 2001. reprint ed. pap. write for info. (*0-312-97712-3*) St Martin.

Romoff, Adam & Yalof, Ina. Estrogen: How & Why It Can Save Your Life. LC 98-31174. 144p. 1999. text 16.00 (*1-58238-012-0*, Golden Adult) St Martin.

Romond, Edwin. Home Fire. 72p. 1992. pap. 8.00 (*1-879462-01-X*) Belle Mead Pr.

Romond, Marguerite P., ed. see Pfeiffer, Philip A.

Romoser, George K., jt. ed. see Wallach, H. G.

Romoser, William & Stoffolano, John G., Jr. The Science of Entomology. 3rd ed. 552p. (C). 1993. text 63.00 (*0-697-03349-X*, WCB McGr Hill) McGrw-H Hghr Educ.

Romoser, William & Stoffolano, John G. The Science of Entomology. 4th ed. LC 96-86438. 720p. (C). 1997. text. write for info. (*0-697-22848-7*, WCB McGr Hill) McGrw-H Hghr Educ.

*__Romp, Billy & Urbanska, Wanda.__ Christmas on Jane Street: A True Story. LC 98-34905. (Illus.). 128p. 1998. 12.95 (*0-688-16442-0*, Wm Morrow) Morrow Avon.

Romp, Graham. Game Theory: Introduction & Applications. LC 97-475. (Illus.). 294p. 1997. pap. text 24.95 (*0-19-877502-4*) OUP.

Rompaey, Luc Van, see Van Rompaey, Luc.

Rompert, Ann. Rabbit Loses His Tail. LC 96-21513. (Illus.). 32p. (J). 1997. 14.95 (*0-395-82281-5*) HM.

Rompf, Kraft, jt. auth. see Diyanni, Robert.

Rompf, Kraft, jt. auth. see DiYanni, Robert.

Rompf, Shirley J., jt. auth. see Mackie, Benita.

Rompkey, Ronald. Grenfell of Labrador: A Biography. 448p. 1991. text 35.00 (*0-8020-5919-8*) U of Toronto Pr.

Rompkey, Ronald, ed. Expeditions of Honour: The Journal of John Salusbury in Halifax, Nova Scotia, 1749-1753. LC 79-13797. (Illus.). 224p. 1982. 32.50 (*0-87413-169-3*) U Delaware Pr.

— Labrador Odyssey: The Journal & Photographs of Eliot Curwen on the Second Voyage of Wilfred Grenfell, 1893. pap. 27.95 (*0-7735-1870-3*) McG-Queens Univ Pr.

— Labrador Odyssey: The Journal & Photographs of Eliot Curwen on the Second Voyage of Wilfred Grenfell, 1893. LC 96-194042. (Illus.). 208p. 1996. 49.95 (*0-7735-1366-3*, Pub. by McG-Queens Univ Pr) CUP Services.

Romportle, Milan. Studies in Phonetics. (Janua Linguarum, Ser. Major: No. 61). 217p. (C). 1973. text 46.15 (*90-279-2667-0*) Mouton.

Rompp, Georg. Husserls Phanomenologie der Intersubjektivitat: Und Ihre Bdedutung Fur eine Theorie Intersubjektiver Objektivitat und die Konzeption Einer Phanomenologischen Philosophie. 248p. (C). 1992. lib. bdg. 175.00 (*0-7923-1361-5*, Pub. by Kluwer Academic) Kluwer Academic.

Rompuy, Paul Van, see Friedrich, Peter & Van Rompuy, Paul, eds.

Romrell, Lynn J., et al. Sectional Anatomy of the Head & Neck with Correlative Radiology. LC 92-49088. (Illus.). 230p. 1994. text 125.00 (*0-8121-1673-9*) Lppncott W & W.

Romsics, Ignac. Istvan Bethlen: A Great Conservative Statesman of Hungary, 1874-1946. (Atlantic Studies on Society in Change). 491p. 1996. 56.00 (*0-88033-321-9*, 424, Pub. by East Eur Monographs) Col U Pr.

Romsics, Ignac, ed. Twentieth Century Hungary & the Great Powers. (Atlantic Studies on Society in Change). 391p. 1995. 39.00 (*0-88033-314-6*, 417, Pub. by East Eur Monographs) Col U Pr.

— Wartime America Plans for a New Hungary: Developments from the U. S. Department of State, 1942-44. (Atlantic Studies on Society & Change: No. 77). 316p. (C). 1993. text 50.00 (*0-88033-251-4*, 354, Pub. by East Eur Monographs) Col U Pr.

Romsics, Ignac & Kiraly, Bela K., eds. Geopolitics in the Danube Region: Hungarian Reconciliation Efforts, 1848-1998. LC 98-43974. 413p. (C). 1998. 49.95 (*963-9116-29-7*); pap. 21.95 (*963-9116-28-9*) Ctrl Europ Univ.

Romski, Mary A., jt. auth. see Adamson, Lauren.

Romstad, Eirik, et al, eds. Controlling Mineral Emissions in European Agriculture: Economics, Policies & the Environment. LC 97-13543. (A CAB International Publication). 304p. 1997. text 90.00 (*0-85199-182-3*) OUP.

Romstedt. Building Academic Fluency. (J). 1992. mass mkt. 26.95 (*0-8384-3412-6*) Heinle & Heinle.

— Building Academic Fluency. (J). 1992. mass mkt., teacher ed. 7.95 (*0-8384-3988-8*) Heinle & Heinle.

Romtvedt, David. Certainty. LC 96-200741. 96p. (Orig.). 1996. pap. 12.00 (*1-877727-59-8*) White Pine.

— Crossing Wyoming. 263p. 1992. pap. 12.00 (*1-877727-23-7*) White Pine.

— A Flower Whose Name I Do Not Know. LC 92-8819. (National Poetry Ser.). 80p. (Orig.). 1992. pap. 10.00 (*1-55659-046-6*) Copper Canyon.

— Letters from Mexico. (Illus.). 55p. (Orig.). 1988. pap. 50.00 (*0-937459-04-6*) Kutenai Pr.

— Moon. LC 82-22812. (Illus.). 1984. 195.00 (*0-931460-14-X*) Bieler.

— Windmill: Essays from Four Mile Ranch. LC 96-29729. (Literature Ser.). (Illus.). 264p. 1997. pap. 14.95 (*1-878610-62-7*) Red Crane Bks.

Romtvedt, David, jt. ed. see Iberlin, Dollie.

Romulea, M. P. De Vos, see De Vos Romulea, M. P.

Romulo, Beth D. Forty Years: A Third World Soldier at the UN. LC 87-2370. (Studies in Freedom: No. 3). (Illus.). 239p. 1987. pap. 14.95 (*0-275-92729-6*, B2729, Praeger Pubs) Greenwood.

— Forty Years: A Third World Soldier at the UN, 3. LC 85-30200. (Studies in Freedom: No. 3). (Illus.). 240p. 1986. 55.00 (*0-313-25358-7*, RFY/, Greenwood Pr) Greenwood.

Romulo, Carlos P. Crusade in Asia: Philippine Victory. LC 73-5206. 309p. 1973. reprint ed. lib. bdg. 35.00 (*0-8371-6865-1*, ROCA, Greenwood Pr) Greenwood.

— I See the Philippines Rise. LC 79-163491. reprint ed. 27.50 (*0-404-09038-9*) AMS Pr.

Romund, Camilla. Ecotourism Development Manual. LC 97-80341. 143p. 1997. write for info. (*0-9656227-0-3*) Words Out.

Romvary, F., jt. auth. see Hars, E.

Romvary, Susan. Zsuzsa Not Zsazsa: Balance with a Smile. (Illus.). 140p. pap. 11.95 (*0-9695180-4-8*) Sh1oreline.

Romweber, Marilyn. Favorites from the Little Mushroom: Elegant & Easy Recipes from Marilyn Romweber. LC 87-21049. 376p. 1987. pap. 13.95 (*0-87833-594-3*) Taylor Pub.

*__Ron, A.__ Year at St. Gargoyle's. 1999. pap. text 8.95 (*1-85311-315-8*) Canterbury Press Norwich.

Ron, Aviva, et al. Health Insurance in Developing Countries: The Social Security Approach. x, 231p. (Orig.). 1993. pap. 27.00 (*92-2-106475-1*) Intl Labour Office.

Ron, E. Z. & Rottem, S., eds. Microbial Surface Components & Toxins in Relation to Pathogenesis. (FEMS Symposium Ser.: No. 51). (Illus.). 210p. (C). 1991. text 107.00 (*0-306-43908-5*, Kluwer Plenum) Kluwer Academic.

Ron Hubbard, L. Dianetics: The Modern Science of Mental Health. (SPA.). pap. 19.95 incl. VHS (*1-57318-001-7*) Bridge Pubns Inc.

Ron, Maria A. & David, Anthony S., eds. Disorders of Brain & Mind. (Illus.). 386p. (C). 1998. text 90.00 (*0-521-47306-3*) Cambridge U Pr.

*__Ron, Maria A. & David, Anthony S., eds.__ Disorders of the Brain & Mind. (Illus.). 388p. 1999. pap. 44.95 (*0-521-77851-4*) Cambridge U Pr.

*__Ron, Marz & Robinson, James.__ Wildstorm Rising: (D. C. Comics Graphic Novel) 1999. mass mkt. 19.95 (*1-56389-588-9*, Pub. by Warner Bks) Little.

Ron, Yacov, jt. ed. see Sigal, Leonard H.

Rona, Bengisu. Getting by in Turkish: A Quick Beginner's Course in Spoken Turkish for Tourists & Businesspeople. rev. ed. LC 96-254. (Barron's Educational Ser.). 1996. pap. 18.95 incl. audio (*0-8120-8454-3*) Barron.

— Turkish in Three Months. LC 98-31744. (Hugo Ser.). (TUR & ENG.). 1999. 29.95 incl. audio (*0-7894-4219-1*, D K Ink); pap. text 14.95 (*0-7894-4218-3*) DK Pub Inc.

Rona, Donna C. Environmental Permits: A Time-Saving Guide. (Illus.). 320p. (gr. 13). 1988. text 60.95 (*0-442-27838-1*) Chapman & Hall.

Rona, G., ed. see Schibsbye, Knud & Kossmann, H.

Rona, Jeff. MIDI - The In's, Out's & Thru's. 96p. (Orig.). 1987. pap. 12.95 (*0-88188-560-6*, 00183495) H Leonard.

— The MIDI Companion. (Illus.). 96p. 1994. per. 14.95 (*0-7935-3077-6*, HL00183500) H Leonard.

*__Rona, Jeff.__ The Reel World: Scoring for Pictures. (Illus.). 240p. 2000. pap. 24.95 (*0-87930-591-6*) Miller Freeman.

Rona, Jeff. Synchronization: From Reel to Reel - A Complete Guide for the Synchronization of Audio, Film & Video. (Illus.). 120p. (Orig.). 1990. per. 16.95 (*0-88188-905-9*, 00239235) H Leonard.

Rona, Peter A., et al, eds. Hydrothermal Processes at Seafloor Spreading Centers. LC 83-17747. (NATO Conference Series IV, Marine Sciences: Vol. 12). 810p. 1983. 145.00 (*0-306-41482-1*, Plenum Trade) Perseus Pubng.

Rona, Roberto J. & Chinn, Susan. National Study of Health & Growth. LC 99-14033. (Illus.). 144p. 1999. text 98.50 (*0-19-262919-0*) OUP.

Rona-Tas, A. An Introduction to Turkology. (Studio Uralo-Altaica (SUA) Ser.: No. 33). 170p. 1993. pap. 76.00 (*0-685-68160-2*) J Benjamins Pubng Co.

Rona-Tas, A., ed. Studies in Chuvash Etymology I. (Studia Oralo-Altaica Ser.: No. 17). 240p. 1982. 48.00 (*0-686-36268-3*) J Benjamins Pubng Co.

Rona-Tas, Akos. The Great Surprise of the Small Transformation: The Demise of Communism & the Rise of the Private Sector in Hungary. LC 96-54238. 312p. (C). 1997. text 52.50 (*0-472-10795-X*, 10795) U of Mich Pr.

Rona-Tas, Andras. Hungarians & Europe in the Early Middle Ages: An Introduction to Early Hungarian History. (Illus.). 500p. 1999. 64.95 (*963-9116-48-3*) Ctrl Europ Univ.

— Language & History: Contributions to Comparative Altaistics. (Studia Uralo-Altaica Ser.: No. 25). iv, 270p. (C). 1986. pap. 78.00 (*0-317-60113-X*) J Benjamins Pubng Co.

Rona, Thomas P. Our Changing Geopolitical Premises. LC 81-16192. 364p. reprint ed. pap. 112.90 (*0-608-13016-8*, 202415900035) Bks Demand.

Rona, Zoltan P. Child Illness & the Allergy Connection: A Nutritional Approach to Overcoming & Preventing Childhood Illness. 272p. 1996. pap., per. 14.00 (*0-7615-0611-X*) Prima Pub.

Rona, Zoltan P. The Colostrum Option: All the Natural Anti-Aging Growth Hormones & Immune Enhancer's Provided by Mother Nature! Handing, Trina, ed. Kasmylo, Nicholas J., tr. (Illus.). 100p. 1998. pap. 9.95 (*0-9663879-0-2*) Life Link UT.

— The Joy of Health: A Doctor's Guide to Nutrition & Alternative Medicine. 2nd ed. LC 92-34054. (Illus.). 280p. 1999. pap. 12.95 (*0-87542-684-0*) Llewellyn Pubns.

Rona, Zoltan P. & Martin, Jeanne M. Return to the Joy of Health: Natural Medicine & Alternative Treatments for All Your Health Complaints. LC 95-910586. 425p. 1995. pap. 19.95 (*0-920470-62-9*) Alive Bks.

Ronai, Andras Z., jt. ed. see Szekeley, Jozsef I.

Ronai, Andras Z., jt. ed. see Szekely, Jozsef I.

Ronai, Carol R., et al. Everyday Sexism in the Third Millennium. LC 96-34631. 264p. (C). 1997. 70.00 (*0-415-91550-3*); pap. 18.99 (*0-415-91551-1*) Routledge.

Ronald, Ann. Earthtones: A Nevada Album. LC 94-45450. (Illus.). 136p. 1995. 39.95 (*0-87417-270-5*) U of Nev Pr.

— Functions of Setting in the Novel: From Mrs. Radcliffe to Charles Dickens. Varma, Devendra P., ed. LC 79-8475. (Gothic Studies & Dissertations). 1980. lib. bdg. 31.95 (*0-405-12659-X*) Ayer.

— The New West of Edward Abbey. LC 87-32074. 271p. 1988. pap. 84.10 (*0-608-01265-3*, 206201400001) Bks Demand.

*__Ronald, Ann.__ The New West of Edward Abbey. 2nd ed. 300p. 2000. pap. 18.95 (*0-87417-357-4*) U of Nev Pr.

Ronald, Ann. Zane Grey. LC 75-7010. (Western Writers Ser.: No. 17). (Illus.). 46p. (Orig.). 1975. pap. 4.95 (*0-88430-016-1*) Boise St U W Writ Ser.

Ronald, Ann, ed. Words for the Wild: The Sierra Club Trailside Reader. LC 86-22097. (Totebook Ser.). 384p. (Orig.). 1987. pap. 14.00 (*0-87156-709-1*, Pub. by Sierra) Random.

Ronald, Barnett. The Limits of Competence: Knowledge, Higher Education & Society. LC 94-22170. 160p. 1994. pap. 34.95 (*0-335-19341-2*) OpUniv Pr.

Ronald, Belluomini. Thirteenth Labor. LC 85-70532. (Living Poets' Library). 1985. pap. 5.00 (*0-934218-32-3*) Dragons Teeth.

Ronald, Bruce. Dracula, Baby - Musical Comedy. 104p. 1970. pap. 5.95 (*0-87129-626-8*, D01) Dramatic Pub.

Ronald, Bruce, jt. auth. see Ronald, Virginia.

*__Ronald, Charles.__ Some Survived: A True Story of the Desert War Against Rommel. LC 98-88884. 312p. 1999. pap. 16.95 (*1-56167-507-5*) Am Literary Pr.

Ronald, Jack, ed. see Casey, Tom.

Ronald, K. The Mediterranean Monk Seal. (UNEP Technical Ser.). 1979. pap. 10.00 (*0-08-025684-8*, Pergamon Pr) Elsevier.

Ronald, K., ed. see International Conference on the Mediterranean Monk.

Ronald, Kate & Roskelly, Hephzibah, eds. Farther Along: Transforming Dichotomies in Rhetoric & Composition. 208p. (C). 1989. pap. text 23.00 (*0-86709-249-1*, 0249, Pub. by Boynton Cook Pubs) Heinemann.

Ronald, Kate, jt. auth. see Roskelly, Hephzibah.

*__Ronald McDonald House Staff.__ From the Heart of Our House. 1998. 18.95 (*0-9663648-0-5*) R McDonald.

Ronald McDonald House Staff, ed. see Mott Hospital Staff.

Ronald, Nick & Roberts, David. Grand Illusions: Paint Effects & Instant Decoration for Furniture, Fabric, Walls & Floors. LC 96-60772. (Illus.). 144p. 1997. 29.95 (*1-57076-071-3*, Trafalgar Sq Pub) Trafalgar.

*__Ronald, Nick & Roberts, David.__ Grand Illusions New Country. (Illus.). 2000. 29.95 (*1-57076-158-2*, Trafalgar Sq Pub) Trafalgar.

Ronald, Nick & Roberts, David. Grand Illusions New Decorating: Techniques, Ideas & Inspiration for Creating a Fresh Look. LC 98-84278. (Illus.). 144p. 1998. 29.95 (*1-57076-122-1*, Trafalgar Sq Pub) Trafalgar.

Ronald, Robert. Last Train to Freedom. LC 97-92659. (Illus.). 184p. 1997. lib. bdg. 18.95 (*0-9660677-0-3*) R Ronald.

Ronald, Virginia & Ronald, Bruce. The Lands Between the Miamis: A Bicentennial Celebration of the Dayton Area, Vol. 2. Kaye, Alexander, ed. (Bicentennial Bookshelf Ser.). (Illus.). 438p. 1996. 34.95 (*0-913428-77-9*) Landfall Pr.

Ronalds, Francis, compiled by. Catalogue of Books & Papers Relating to Electricity, Magnetism... 591p. 1994. reprint ed. 85.00 (*1-888262-62-1*) Martino Pubng.

Ronalds, J. A., jt. auth. see Henry, R. J.

Ronall, Ruth, jt. ed. see Feder, Bud.

*__Ronan, Anne M.__ Muffles in New York. (Illus.). 32p. (J). (ps-4). 1999. pap. 8.00 (*1-930248-00-8*) Polka Dot Pr.

Ronan, Charles E. Francisco Javier Clavigero, S. J. (1731-1787) Fogure of the Mexican Enlightenment. 1978. pap. 26.00 (*0-8294-8340-3*) Loyola Pr.

— Francisco Javier Clavigero, S. J. (1731-1787): Figure of the Mexican Enlightment: His Life & Work. 1977. pap. 26.00 (*88-7041-340-3*) Jesuit Hist.

Ronan, Christine. Apache. (Ancient & Living Cultures Ser.). 1998. pap. 9.95 (*0-673-36399-6*, GoodYrBooks) Addson-Wesley Educ.

— North Africa: Morocco. 1997. pap. text 9.95 (*0-673-36358-9*) Addson-Wesley Educ.

— South India. 1997. pap. text 9.95 (*0-673-36359-7*) Addson-Wesley Educ.

— Ukraine. Dempsey, Roberta, ed. (Ancient & Living Cultures Ser.). (Illus.). 24p. 1998. pap. 9.95 (*0-673-36400-3*, GoodYrBooks) Addson-Wesley Educ.

Ronan, Christine, jt. auth. see Bartok, Mira.

Ronan, Colin A. The Natural History of the Universe. 200p. 1991. 45.00 (*0-385-25327-3*) Doubleday.

— Science: Its History & Development among the World's Cultures. LC 82-12176. 543p. reprint ed. pap. 168.40 (*0-7837-2675-9*, 204304600006) Bks Demand.

— Science Explained: The World of Science in Everyday Life. 128p. 1993. 50.00 (*0-385-25443-1*) Doubleday.

— Shorter Science & Civilisation in China, Vol. 1. LC 77-82513. (Illus.). 337p. 1980. pap. text 30.95 (*0-521-29286-7*) Cambridge U Pr.

— Shorter Science & Civilisation in China, Vol. 2. LC 77-82513. (Illus.). 480p. 1985. pap. text 33.95 (*0-521-31536-0*) Cambridge U Pr.

— The Shorter Science & Civilisation in China, Vol. 5. (Illus.). 380p. (C). 1995. pap. text 35.95 (*0-521-46773-X*, Vol. 5) Cambridge U Pr.

— The Shorter Science & Civilisation in China Vol. 4: An Abridgement of Joseph Needham's Original Text of Volume IV. 350p. 1994. text 85.00 (*0-521-32995-7*); pap. text 35.95 (*0-521-33873-5*) Cambridge U Pr.

An Asterisk (*) at the beginning of an entry indicates that the title is appearing for the first time.

R

— The Shorter Science & Civilisation in China Vol. 5, Vol. 5. (Illus.). 380p. (C). 1995. text 85.00 (0-521-46214-2) Cambridge U Pr.
— The Skywatchers Handbook. 1989. pap. 16.00 (0-517-57326-1, Crown) Crown Pub Group.
— The Universe Explained: The Earth-Dweller's Guide to the Mysteries of Space. 1996. pap. 22.50 (0-614-20832-7, Owl) H Holt & Co.
Ronan, Colin A., ed. Science Explained: The World of Science in Everyday Life. LC 93-15439. (Reference Bks.). (Illus.). 89p. 1995. 35.00 (0-8050-2551-0, Bks Young Read) H Holt & Co.
— Science Explained: The World of Science in Everyday Life. 1995. pap. 19.95 (0-614-15514-2, Owl) H Holt & Co.
— The Universe Explained: The Earth-Dweller's Guide to the Mysteries of Space. LC 94-16294. 89p. 1995. 35.00 (0-8050-3488-9) H Holt & Co.
Ronan, David T. Practical VCR Repair. LC 94-20858. 592p. 1994. pap. 69.95 (0-8273-6583-7) Delmar.
Ronan, John. The Catching Self. (Chapbook Ser.: No. 3). 40p. (Orig.). 1996. pap. 8.95 (0-9649463-2-7) Folly Cove.
***Ronan, John.** The Cunable Corpse. (Chapbooks Ser.). 40p. (Orig.). 1999. pap. 8.95 (1-891701-00-2) Folly Cove.
Ronan, John & Ayers, Shirley. Terrorism: First Response, Leaders Guide. Massingham, Gordon, ed. (Orig.). 1997. pap. 20.00 (0-945790-12-0) Detrick Lawrence.
Ronan, Richard. Narratives from America. LC 81-67639. 139p. 1982. 12.00 (0-937872-04-0); pap. 6.00 (0-937872-05-9) Dragon Gate.
— A Radiance Like Wind or Water. LC 83-72376. 73p. 1984. 14.00 (0-937872-14-8); pap. 6.00 (0-937872-15-6) Dragon Gate.
Ronan, S. Orphic Fragments. 150p. (C). 1988. text 95.00 (0-948366-22-2, Pub. by Chthonios Bks) St Mut.
Ronan, Sean G. Irish Writing on Lafcadio Hearn & Japan: Writer, Journalist & Teacher. 1998. write for info. (1-901903-05-2, Pub. by Global Oriental) Midpt Trade.
Ronart, Nandy. Lexikon der Arabischen Welt. (GER.). 295.00 (3-7608-0138-2, M-7277); 295.00 (0-8288-7969-9, M7277) Fr & Eur.
Ronaszeki, A. Hemodynamic Consequences of the Timing of Atrial Contraction During Complete Atrioventricular Block. No. 15. 134p. (Orig.). pap. 32.50 (90-6186-344-9, Pub. by Leuven Univ) Coronet Bks.
Ronay, Camille. Around the South!!! Vol. 3: Fairs Festivals & Special Event Directory. rev. unabridged ed. Ronay, W. R., ed. 88p. 1998. pap. 16.95 (1-56736-071-8) A Step Ahead.
***Ronay, Camille.** Around the South!!! Vol. 3: Fairs, Festivals & Special Events Directory. 2nd rev. ed. Ronay, W. R., ed. 96p. 1999. pap. 16.95 (1-56736-072-6) A Step Ahead.
— Around the South!!! Vol. 4, No. 1: Fairs, Festivals & Special Events Directory. Ronay, W. R., ed. 92p. 2000. pap. 16.95 (1-56736-076-9) A Step Ahead.
Ronay, Camille. The Ronay Guide Vol. 8: Arts & Crafts Shows in Virginia. rev. unabridged ed. Ronay, W. R., ed. 48p. 1998. pap. 10.95 (1-56736-070-X) A Step Ahead.
— The Ronay Guide Vol. 12: Arts & Crafts Shows in the Carolinas. rev. ed. Ronay, W. R., ed. 60p. 1998. pap. 10.95 (1-56736-069-6) A Step Ahead.
— The Ronay Guide Vol. 13: Arts & Crafts Shows in Georgia. rev. unabridged ed. Ronay, W. R., ed. 60p. 1998. pap. 10.95 (1-56736-068-8) A Step Ahead.
***Ronay, Camille.** The Ronay Guide 2000 Vol. 9, No. 1: Arts & Crafts Shows in Virginia. Ronay, W. R., ed. 44p. 1999. pap. 10.95 (1-56736-075-0) A Step Ahead.
— The Ronay Guide 2000 Vol. 13, No. 1: Arts & Crafts Shows in the Carolinas. Ronay, W. R., ed. 56p. 1999. pap. 10.95 (1-56736-074-2) A Step Ahead.
— The Ronay Guide 2000 Vol. 14, No. 1: Arts & Crafts Shows in Georgia. Ronay, W. R., ed. 56p. 1999. pap. 10.95 (1-56736-073-4) A Step Ahead.
Ronay, Egon. The Egon Ronay Visitor's Handbook to the U. K. & Ireland, 1997-98. (Illus.). 360p. (Orig.). 1997. pap. 14.95 (1-898718-80-6, Pub. by Ringpr Bks) Seven Hills Bk.
***Ronay, Gabriel.** The Lost King of England: The East European Adventures of Edward the Exile. (Illus.). 222p. 2000. pap. 24.95 (0-85115-785-8) Boydell & Brewer.
Ronay, Gerard. The Gerard Ronay Chocolate Kit. (Illus.). 64p. (Orig.). 1997. pap. 33.50 (0-7522-0554-4, Pub. by Boxtree) Trans-Atl Phila.
Ronay, W. R., ed. see Ronay, Camille.
Ronayne, Diane, ed. see Sarriugarte, Tracy D. & Ward, Peggy R.
Ronayne, Edmond. Blue Lodge. 18.95 (0-685-38430-6) Wehman.
— Blue Lodge & Chapter. 1947. pap. 20.00 (0-911164-02-2) Powner.
— Chapter Degrees. pap. 13.00 (0-911164-05-7) Powner.
— Chapter Masonry: Being the Opening, Closing, Secret Work & Lectures of the Mark Master, Past Master, Most Excellent Master & Royal Arch Degrees. 320p. 1996. reprint ed. pap. 24.95 (1-56459-746-6) Kessinger Pub.
— Freemasonry Handbook. 16.95 (0-685-21949-6) Wehman.
— Handbook of Freemasonry. pap. 13.00 (0-911164-11-1) Powner.
— Masters Carpet. 15.95 (0-685-41897-9) Wehman.
— The Master's Carpet or Masonry & Baal-Worship Identical (1887) 280p. 1998. reprint ed. pap. 24.95 (0-7661-0195-9) Kessinger Pub.
— Ranayne's Handbook of Freemasonry. enl. rev. ed. 1996. reprint ed. spiral bd. 27.50 (0-7873-0736-X) Hlth Research.
— Ronayne's Hand-Book of Freemasonry: With Appendix, Revised, Enlarged, Complete (1917) 282p. 1996. reprint ed. pap. 19.95 (1-56459-745-8) Kessinger Pub.
Ronayne, John. ISDN: From Concept to Application. 2nd ed. 280p. 1997. pap. text 39.95 (0-387-91505-2) Spr-Verlag.
Ronayne, John, jt. auth. see Langley, Graham.
Ronberg, Gert. A Way with Words: The Language of English Renaissance Literature. 192p. 2000. text 16.95 (0-340-49307-0, A6109, Pub. by E A) Routldge.
Ronca, Italo, ed. & tr. see William of Conches.
Roncaglia, Alessandro. Petty, the Origins of Political Economy. Cherubini, Isabella, tr. LC 84-23549. 128p. 1985. reprint ed. pap. 39.70 (0-7837-9939-X, 206066600006) Bks Demand.
***Roncaglia, Alessandro.** Piero Sraffa: His Life, Thought & Cultural Heritage. LC 00-28075. 2000. write for info. (0-415-23480-8) Routledge.
Roncaglia, Alessandro. Sraffa & the Theory of Prices. Kregel, J. A., tr. from ITA. LC 77-7241. 196p. reprint ed. pap. 60.80 (0-608-18148-X, 203283500081) Bks Demand.
Roncaglia, Alessandro, et al, eds. The Economics of Joan Robinson. LC 95-19891. 384p. (C). 1996. 90.00 (0-415-13616-4) Routledge.
Roncali, ed. Senecae Philosophi: Apocolocyntosis. (LAT.). 1990. 22.95 (3-322-00670-0, T1795, Pub. by B G Teubner) U of Mich Pr.
Roncali, Emerito M., ed. Artritis: Osteoporosis y Otras Enfermedades. deluxe ed. (SPA., Illus.). 1999. pap. 5.95 (0-939193-34-5) Edit Concepts.
— Corazon, Siempre Saludable. deluxe ed. (SPA., Illus.). 1998. pap. 5.95 (0-939193-40-X) Edit Concepts.
— Cuando el Corazon se Enferma, Vol. 2. deluxe ed. (SPA., Illus.). 192p. 1998. pap. 5.95 (0-939193-41-8) Edit Concepts.
— Diabetes: El Enemigo Que Acecha en Silencia. deluxe ed. (SPA., Illus.). 192p. 1999. pap. 5.95 (0-939193-33-7) Edit Concepts.
— Todo Sobre el Cancer. deluxe ed. (SPA., Illus.). 224p. 1998. pap. 5.95 (0-939193-39-6) Edit Concepts.
Roncalli, Angelo G. Days of Devotion. 320p. 1998. pap. 11.95 (0-14-025807-8) Penguin Putnam.
Roncalli, Angelo G., see John XXIII, pseud.
Roncalli, Francesco. Vatican City. (Illus.). 126p. 1989. pap. 25.00 (88-86921-07-1) Treasures Inc.
Roncarelli, R. Computer Animation Dictionary. 1989. 42.95 (0-387-97022-3, 2937) Spr-Verlag.
Ronce, David. California Hazardous Waste Directory, 1991-1992. 482p. 1991. pap. text 199.00 (1-880720-00-0) In Media Res.
***Roncevic, Thomas.** An Introduction to HTML for Win 95-98 & NT Computers. (Illus.). 100p. 1999. wbk. ed. 19.95 (0-9671262-0-7) Univ Control Sys.
Ronch, Judah L., et al, eds. The Counseling Sourcebook: A Practical Reference on Contemporary Issues. 536p. (Orig.). 1993. pap. 24.95 (0-8245-1241-3) Crossroad NY.
Ronchetti, Elvezio, jt. auth. see Field, Christopher A.
Ronchetti, Elvezio, jt. auth. see Krishnakumar, Jayalakshmi.
Ronchetti, Elvezio, ed. see Morgenthaler, Stephan & Franscini, Stefano.
Ronchi, C., ed. see European Institute for Transuranium Elements Staff.
Ronchi, Elettra. Xenotransplantation: International Policy Issues. (Proceedings Ser.). 116p. 1999. pap. 27.00 (92-64-17030-8, 93 1999 03 1 P) Org for Econ.
Ronchi, Elettra, ed. Gene Delivery Systems: A State-of-the-Art Review. 448p. (Orig.). 1996. pap. 59.00 (92-64-14887-6, 93-96-04-1, Pub. by Org for Econ) OECD.
Ronchi, Vasco. Optics: The Science of Vision. (Illus.). ix, 360p. 1991. reprint ed. pap. 11.95 (0-486-66846-0) Dover.
Ronci, Marcio. The Quest for Monetary Stability. Langoni, Carlos G. & Ferrer, James, Jr., eds. LC 97-139042. 248p. (Orig.). 1996. pap. text 7.50 (0-9654065-0-4) Inst of Brazilian.
Ronciere, Delort de la, see De La Ronciere, Delort.
Ronck, Ron, jt. auth. see Buffet, Guy.
***Ronck, Ronn.** Battleship Missouri. (Illus.). 72p. 1999. 14.95 (1-56647-253-9); pap. 10.95 (1-56647-252-0) Mutual Pub HI.
Ronck, Ronn. The Hawaiian Lei: A Tradition of Aloha. (Illus.). 54p. 1997. 12.95 (1-56647-194-X) Mutual Pub HI.
— The Hawaiian Lei Book: A Tradition of Aloha. (Illus.). 64p. 1997. pap. 9.95 (1-56647-169-9) Mutual Pub HI.
***Ronck, Ronn.** Pocket Guide to the Hawaiian Lei: A Tradition of Aloha. (Illus.). 80p. 1999. pap. 8.95 (1-56647-181-8) Mutual Pub HI.
Ronck, Ronn, ed. Firsts & Almost Firsts in Hawai'i. LC 95-24713. (Illus.). 288p. (Orig.). 1995. pap. 15.95 (0-8248-1282-4, Kolowalu Bk) UH Pr.
— Kauai: A Many Splendored Island. (Illus.). 160p. 1985. boxed set 25.95 (0-935180-18-4) Mutual Pub HI.
***Ronco, C., et al, eds.** Automated Peritoneal Dialysis. LC 99-40841. (Contributions to Nephrology Ser.: Vol. 129). (Illus.). x, 274p. 1999. 198.25 (3-8055-6934-3) S Karger.
***Ronco, C. & La Greca, G., eds.** Vitamin E-Bounded Membrane: A Further Step in Dialysis Optimization. LC 99-40842. (Contributions to Nephrology Ser.: Vol. 127). (Illus.). x, 278p. 1999. 198.25 (3-8055-6906-8) S Karger.
Ronco, C., jt. ed. see Bellomo, R.
Ronco, C., jt. ed. see Lameire, N.
Ronco, Claudio, et al, eds. Circulation in Native & Artificial Kidneys: 3rd Annual Symposium on Applied Physiology of the Peripheral Circulation, Barcelona, September 1996. (Reprint of Blood Purification Ser.: Vol. 15, Nos. 4-6, 1997). (Illus.). iv, 172p. 1997. 78.25 (3-8055-6599-2) S Karger.
Ronco, Claudio & Bellomo, Rinaldo, eds. Critical Care Nephrology. LC 97-17215. 1264p. 1997. 525.00 (0-7923-4610-6) Kluwer Academic.
Ronco, Claudio V., ed. Polymethylmethacrylate: A Flexible Membrane for a Tailored Dialysis. LC 98-42558. (Contributions to Nephrology Ser.: Vol. 125). (Illus.). viii, 246p. 1998. 198.25 (3-8055-6760-X) S Karger.
Ronco, Neil. Elevator Symphonies: A Novel. LC 99-18375. 1999. 22.50 (0-936389-66-4) Tudor Pubs.
Ronco, W. & Peattie, Lisa. Making Work: Self-Created Jobs in Participatory Organizations. LC 83-9527. (Environment, Development, & Public Policy: Public Policy & Social Services Ser.). (Illus.). 224p. 1983. 49.50 (0-306-41230-6, Plenum Trade) Perseus Pubng.
Ronco, William C. Project Partnering Manual for Design & Construction. LC 95-46348. (Construction Engineering Ser.). 312p. 1995. 59.95 (0-07-053669-4) McGraw.
Rond, Mark de, jt. ed. see Faulkner, David.
Ronda, Bruce A. Elizabeth Palmer Peabody: A Reformer on Her Own Terms. LC 98-33902. 1999. 45.00 (0-674-24695-0) HUP.
Ronda, C., et al, eds. Luminescent Materials VI. LC 98-218280. (Proceedings Ser.: Vol. 97-29). 1998. 73.00 (1-56677-182-X) Electrochem Soc.
Ronda, James P. Astoria & Empire. LC 89-38464. (Illus.). xiv, 400p. 1990. pap. 12.95 (0-8032-8942-1, Bison Books) U of Nebr Pr.
— The Exploration of North America. Phillips, Carla R. & Weber, David J., eds. (Essays on the Columbian Encounter Ser.). 60p. (Orig.). (C). 1992. pap. 7.00 (0-87229-067-0) Am Hist Assn.
— Lewis & Clark among the Indians. LC 84-3544. (Illus.). xvii, 310p. 1984. pap. 15.00 (0-8032-8929-4, Bison Books) U of Nebr Pr.
Ronda, James P., ed. Revealing America: Image & Imagination in the Exploration of North America. 278p. (C). 1996. pap. text 25.96 (0-669-35175-X) HM Trade Div.
— Voyages of Discovery: Essays on the Lewis & Clark Expedition. LC 98-11224. (Illus.). 368p. 1998. 45.00 (0-917298-44-6); pap. 19.95 (0-917298-45-4) MT Hist Soc.
Ronda, James P., ed. see Eliot, John.
Ronda, James P., ed. see Missouri Historical Society Staff.
***Rondal, J., ed.** Coupled Instabilities in Metal Structures: Theoretical & Design Aspects. (CISM International Centre for Mechanical Sciences Ser.: No. 379). (Illus.). viii, 372p. 1998. pap. 79.95 (3-211-82917-2) Spr-Verlag.
Rondal, J., et al, eds. Coupled Instabilities in Metal Structures - Cims'96. LC 97-103411. 596p. 1996. 99.00 (1-85094-033-1) World Scientific Pub.
Rondal, J. A. & Edwards, Susan. Language in Mental Retardation. LC 97-118479. xi, 310p. 1997. write for info. (1-86156-004-4) Whurr Pub.
Rondal, Jean A. Adult-Child Interaction & the Promise of Language Acquisition. 236p. 1985. 59.95 (0-275-90157-2, C0157, Praeger Pubs) Greenwood.
— Down's Syndrome: A Review of Current Knowledge. 1998. pap. text 65.00 (1-86156-062-1) Whurr Pub.
— Exceptional Language Development in Down Syndrome: Implications for the Cognition-Language Relationship. (Cambridge Monographs & Texts in Applied Psycholinguistics). (Illus.). 367p. (C). 1995. pap. text 27.95 (0-521-36966-5) Cambridge U Pr.
— Exceptional Language Development in Down Syndrome: Implications for the Cognition-Language Relationship. (Cambridge Monographs & Texts in Applied Psycholinguistics). (Illus.). 367p. (C). 1995. text 69.95 (0-521-36167-2) Cambridge U Pr.
— Language in Mental Retardation. 322p. (Orig.). 1996. pap. 45.00 (1-56593-812-7, 1590) Singular Publishing.
Rondal, Jean A., et al, eds. Down's Syndrome: Psychological, Psychobiological, & Socio-Educational Perspectives. (Illus.). 264p. (Orig.). (C). 1996. pap. text 45.00 (1-56593-740-6, 1444) Thomson Learn.
Rondanelli, E. G. Amphizoic Amoebae: Human Pathology. (Infectious Diseases Color Atlas Monographs: No. 1). 276p. 1988. text 32.00 (1-57235-028-8) Piccin Nuova.
Rondanelli, E. G. Ampizoic Amoebae: Human Pathology. (Illus.). 276p. 1988. text 36.00 (88-299-0563-1, Pub. by Piccin Nuova) Gordon & Breach.
— Blood Transfusion & Infectious Diseases. (Illus.). 322p. 1989. text 50.00 (88-299-0777-4, Pub. by Piccin Nuova) Gordon & Breach.
Rondanelli, E. G. Blood Transfusions & Infectious Diseases. (Infectious Diseases Color Atlas Monographs: No. 2). 322p. 1989. text 45.00 (1-57235-029-6) Piccin Nuova.
Rondanelli, E. G. Human Pathogenic Protozoa: Atlas of Electron-Microscopy. 356p. 1987. text 71.00 (88-299-0228-4, Pub. by Piccin Nuova) Gordon & Breach.
Rondanelli, E. G., et al. Human Pathogenic Protozoa: Atlas of Electron-Microscopy. 356p. 1987. text 64.00 (1-57235-027-X) Piccin Nuova.
— Pathology of Erythroblastic Mitosis in Occupational Benzenic Erythropathy & Erythremia. (Bibliotheca Haematologica Ser.: No. 35). (Illus.). 1969. pap. 66.25 (3-8055-0139-0) S Karger.
Rondanelli, R. Clinical Pharmacology of Drug Interactions. 864p. 1988. text 50.00 (1-57235-032-6) Piccin Nuova.
Rondanelli, R. Clinical Pharmacology of Drug Interactions. 864p. 1988. text 55.00 (88-299-0650-6, Pub. by Piccin Nuova) Gordon & Breach.
Rondberg, Cindy. The CA Advisor Training Manual. (Illus.). 120p. 1998. lib. bdg. 50.00 (0-9647168-5-2) Chiropractic Jrnl.
Rondberg, Terry A. Chiropractic First: The Fastest Growing Healthcare Choice Before Drugs or Surgery. LC 95-92465. (Illus.). 160p. 1996. pap. 12.95 (0-9647168-2-8) Chiropractic Jrnl.
— Under the Influence of Modern Medicine. 156p. 1998. lib. bdg. 12.95 (0-9647168-3-6) Chiropractic Jrnl.
Rondberg, Terry A. & Feuling, Timothy. Chiropractic: Compassion & Expectation. 160p. 1999. pap. 12.95 (0-9647168-6-0) Chiropractic Jrnl.
Ronde, S. M., ed. Fluid Film Lubrication: A Century of Progress. 217p. 1983. pap. text 44.00 (0-317-03526-6, I00162) ASME.
Rondeau, Edmond P., et al. Facility Management. LC 94-48240. (Real Estate Practice Library). 648p. 1995. 90.00 (0-471-03806-7) Wiley.
Rondeau, S. Space Robotics. LC 99-88494. 191p. 1999. pap. 73.00 (0-08-043050-3) Elsevier.
Rondeel, H. E., et al, eds. Geology of Gas & Oil in the Netherlands: Selection of Papers Prepared on the Occasion of the 1993 International Conference of the American Association of Petroleum Geologists in the Hague. 304p. (C). 1996. text 161.50 (0-7923-3749-2) Kluwer Academic.
***Rondell.** Clinical Data Management. LC 99-31926. 366p. 2000. 120.00 (0-471-98329-2) Wiley.
Rondia, D., et al, eds. Mobile Source Emissions Included Polycyclic Organic Species. 1983. text 184.00 (90-277-1633-1) Kluwer Academic.
Rondina, Catherine & Romain, Joseph. Ladies Day: A Woman's Guide to Pro Baseball. (Illus.). 160p. (Orig.). 1997. pap. 12.95 (1-895629-80-2) Warwick Publ.
***Rondina, Christopher.** Vampire Hunter's Guide to New England. (Illus.). 128p. (C). 2000. pap. 12.95 (1-58066-055-X, Covered Brdge Pr) Douglas Charles Ltd.
Rondina, Christopher. Vampire Legends of Rhode Island. (Illus.). 96p. (Orig.). 1997. pap. 9.95 (0-924771-91-7, Covered Brdge Pr) Douglas Charles Ltd.
Rondina, Marisa. Vocabulary of Family Violence. (Terminology Bulletin Ser.: No. 222). (FRE.). 209p. (Orig.). 1994. pap. 19.95 (0-660-59106-5, Pub. by Canadian Govt Pub) Accents Pubns.
Rondinelli, Robert D. & Katz, Richard T. Impairment Rating & Disability Evaluation. Lampert, Richard, ed. LC 99-26872. (Illus.). 225p. 1999. text. write for info. (0-7216-7772-X, W B Saunders Co) Harcrt Hlth Sci Grp.
Rondinelli, Dennis A. Development Projects As Policy Experiments: An Adaptive Approach to Development Administration. LC 83-8117. (Development & Underdevelopment Ser.). 180p. 1983. pap. 10.95 (0-416-73640-8, NO. 3914) Routledge.
— Development Projects As Policy Experiments: An Adaptive Approach to Development Administration. 2nd ed. LC 92-17773. (Development & Underdevelopment Ser.). (Illus.). 192p. (C). (gr. 13). 1993. 80.00 (0-415-06622-0, A9845) Routledge.
— Secondary Cities in Developing Countries: Policies for Diffusing Urbanization. LC 82-23165. (Sage Library of Social Research: No. 145). 288p. reprint ed. pap. 89.30 (0-8357-4851-0, 203778200009) Bks Demand.
Rondinelli, Dennis A., ed. Expanding Sino-American Business & Trade: China's Economic Transition. LC 94-8543. 288p. 1994. 59.95 (0-89930-932-1, Quorum Bks) Greenwood.
— Privatization & Economic Reform in Central Europe: The Changing Business Climate. LC 93-27714. 304p. 1994. 67.95 (0-89930-851-1, Quorum Bks) Greenwood.
Rondinelli, Dennis A. & Litvak, Jennie I., eds. Market Reform in Vietnam: Building Institutions for Development. LC 98-44555. 216p. 1999. 59.95 (1-56720-288-8, Quorum Bks) Greenwood.
Rondinelli, Dennis A., et al. Planning Education Reforms in Developing Countries: The Contingency Approach. LC 89-36234. 225p. (C). 1990. text 45.95 (0-8223-0966-1); pap. text 19.95 (0-8223-0974-2) Duke.
Rondinelli, Dennis A., jt. auth. see Montgomery, John D.
Rondinelli, Dennis A., jt. ed. see Cheema, G. Shabbir.
***Rondinelli, Michael Lauren.** The Encyclopedia of Double Bass Drumming. 84p. 2000. spiral bd. 12.95 (0-634-01467-6) H Leonard.
Rondinone, et al. The Advancing Writer, Bk. I. 420p. (C). 1997. pap. text 57.00 (0-06-500301-2) Addson-Wesley Educ.
Rondinone, P. J. The Digital Hood. LC 98-5377. 226p. 1998. pap. 16.00 (0-312-18686-X, Picador USA) St Martin.
— The Digital Hood. 240p. 1999. pap. 10.00 (0-312-20402-7, Picador USA) St Martin.
Rondogiannis, Panos, jt. ed. see Gergatsoulis, Manolis.
Rondon, Javier. The Absent-Minded Toad. Corbett, Kathryn, tr. from SPA. LC 94-14407. (Illus.). 32p. (J). (ps-1). 1994. 9.95 (0-916291-53-7) Kane-Miller Bk.
***Rondoni, Davide.** Communion & Liberation: A Movement in the Church. 200p. 2000. pap. 15.95 (0-7735-2031-7, Pub. by McG-Queens Univ Pr) CUP Services.
***RONDOT, BERTRAND.** Pioneering French Porcelain at the Saint-Cloud Manufacture, CA 1690-1766. LC 99-24633. (Illus.). 368p. 1999. 75.00 (0-300-08107-3) Yale U Pr.
Rondot, Jean. La Compagnie Francaise Des Petroles: Du Franc-or Au Petrole-Franc. Wilkins, Mira, ed. LC 76-29773. (European Business Ser.).Tr. of French Petroleum Company: from the Gold Franc to the Petroleum Franc. (FRE.). 1977. reprint ed. lib. bdg. 19.95 (0-405-09785-9) Ayer.
Rondstadt, Linda, et al. Tucson. (Illus.). 2000. 49.95 (1-881096-77-7) Towery Pub.
Rondthaler, Edward & Lias, Edward. Dictionary of Simplified American Spelling: An Alternative Spelling for English. 312p. 1986. 25.00 (1-890319-03-1) Am Literacy Coun.
Rondthaler, Katharine B. Tell Me a Story. (Illus.). 64p. (J). (ps-5). 1992. reprint ed. pap. 4.00 (1-878422-06-5) Moravian Ch in Amer.
Ronell, Avital. Crack Wars: Literature, Addiction, Mania. LC 81-18917. (Texts & Contexts Ser.: Vol. 2). 187p. 1992. pap. 53.30 (0-608-04825-9, 2065482) Bks Demand.

An Asterisk (*) at the beginning of an entry indicates that the title is appearing for the first time.

R

— Dictations: On Haunted Writing. LC 93-8475. xxix, 205p. 1993. pap. 15.00 (0-8032-8945-6, Bison Books) U of Nebr Pr.
— Finitude's Score: Essays for the End of the Millennium. LC 93-11942. (Texts & Contexts Ser.). (Illus.). xv, 370p. 1998. pap. text 20.00 (0-8032-8949-9) U of Nebr Pr.
— The Telephone Book: Technology, Schizophrenia, Electric Speech. LC 88-27960. (Illus.). xviii, 466p. 1989. text 60.00 (0-8032-3876-2); pap. text 35.00 (0-8032-8938-3, Bison Books) U of Nebr Pr.
*Ronell, Avital, et al. 13 Alumni Artists. (Illus.). 80p. 2000. pap. 14.95 (1-928825-01-X) Middlebury Coll Mus.
Ronell, Avital, tr. see Derrida, Jacques.
Ronen, Avraham. Stones & Bones! How Archaeologists Trace Human Origins. LC 93-2480. (Buried Worlds Ser.). (YA). (gr. 6 up). 1993. lib. bdg. 23.93 (0-8225-3207-7, Lerner Publctns) Lerner Pub.
Ronen, Dov. The Challenge of Ethnic Conflict, Democracy & Self-Determination in Central Europe. LC 97-16418. 192p. 1997. 52.50 (0-7146-4752-7, Pub. by F Cass Pubs); pap. 19.50 (0-7146-4308-4, Pub. by F Cass Pubs) Intl Spec Bk.
Ronen, Ela & Baefour, Bernice. Migraine Headache: Prevention & Treatment by Phytotherapy, Herbal Medicine. 68p. (Orig.). 1993. pap. 15.95 (0-9638677-0-9) E M D Ent.
Ronen, Joshua, ed. Accounting & Financial Globalization. LC 90-26406. 184p. 1991. 57.95 (0-89930-618-7, RAF/, Quorum Bks) Greenwood.
Ronen, Joshua, et al, eds. Off-Balance Sheet Activities. LC 90-8909. 192p. 1990. 55.00 (0-89930-613-6, ROD/, Quorum Bks) Greenwood.
Ronen, Joshua & Sorter, George H. Relevant Financial Statements: Original Anthology. Brief, Richard P., ed. LC 77-87318. (Development of Contemporary Accounting Thought Ser.). 1978. lib. bdg. 30.95 (0-405-10930-X) Ayer.
Ronen, Omry. The Fallacy of the Silver Age in Twentieth-Century Russian Literature. 114p. 1997. text 26.00 (90-5702-549-3, Harwood Acad Pubs) Gordon & Breach.
— The Fallacy of the Silver Age in Twentieth-Century Russian Literature. 114p. 1997. pap. text 12.00 (90-5702-550-7, Harwood Acad Pubs) Gordon & Breach.
Ronen, Ruth. Possible Worlds in Literary Theory. (Literature, Culture, Theory Ser.: No. 7). 256p. (C). 1994. text 64.95 (0-521-45017-9); pap. text 19.95 (0-521-45648-7) Cambridge U Pr.
Ronen, Simcha. Comparative & Multinational Management. LC 85-17971. (International Business Ser.). 656p. (C). 1986. text 89.95 (0-471-86875-2) Wiley.
Ronen, Tammie. Cognitive Developmental Therapy with Children. LC 97-9107. 1997. pap. text 35.50 (0-471-97007-7) Wiley.
Ronen, Yigal. Handbook on Nuclear Reactors Calculations, Vol. 2. 536p. 1987. boxed set 359.00 (0-8493-2926-4) CRC Pr.
— Handbook on Nuclear Reactors Calculations, Vol. 3. 480p. 1987. boxed set 359.00 (0-8493-2927-2) CRC Pr.
— High Converting Water Reactors. 272p. 1989. lib. bdg. 195.00 (0-8493-6081-1, TK9203) CRC Pr.
— Uncertainty Analysis. 272p. 1988. 166.00 (0-8493-6714-X, Q375, CRC Reprint) Franklin.
Ronen, Yigal, ed. Handbook of Nuclear Reactors Calculations, 3 vols., Set. 1986. 885.00 (0-8493-2924-8, TK9153) CRC Pr.
— Handbook of Nuclear Reactors Calculations, Vol. I. 448p. 1986. 268.00 (0-8493-2925-6, TK9153, CRC Reprint) Franklin.
— Handbook of Nuclear Reactors Calculations, Vol. I: Introduction. 448p. 1986. write for info. (0-318-60779-4) CRC Pr.
— Handbook of Nuclear Reactors Calculations, Vol. II. 1986. write for info. (0-318-60777-8) CRC Pr.
— Handbook of Nuclear Reactors Calculations, Vol. III: Ctrl Rods & Burnable Absorber Calculatns. 492p. 1986. write for info. (0-318-60778-6) CRC Pr.
Ronet, Jorge & Carriles, Lazaro G. Diptico Cubano: La Mueca de la Paloma Negra Desertores del Paraiso. (Biblioteca Cubana Contemporanea Ser.). (SPA.). 126p. (Orig.). 1988. pap. 12.00 (84-359-0539-X, Pub. by Editorial Playor) Ediciones.
Ronet, Jorge & Hernandez-Alende, Andres. Guaguasi-Los Simbolos del Delirio. (Biblioteca Cubana Contemporanea Ser.). (SPA., Illus.). 325p. (Orig.). 1986. pap. 9.95 (84-359-0452-0, Pub. by Editorial Playor) Ediciones.
Roney, Alex. Appointing Commercial Agents in Europe: The Essential Facts. LC 96-28879. xxxiii, 367 p. 1999. pap. text 46.50 (0-471-96438-7) Wiley.
— EC-EU Fact Book: A Complete Question & Answer Guide. 5th ed. LC 98-193351. 1998. pap. text 29.95 (0-7494-2430-3) Kogan Page Ltd.
*Roney, Alex. EC/EU Fact Book: A Complete Question & Answer Guide. 6th ed. 288p. 2000. pap. 29.95 (0-7494-3192-X) Kogan Page Ltd.
— Untitled Memoir Diabetes. 2000. pap. 13.00 (0-8050-5645-9) St Martin.
Roney, Alex & Cooper, Cary L. Professionals on Workplace Stress: The Essential Facts. LC 97-23239. (Essential Facts Ser.). 1997. pap. text 46.50 (0-471-97651-2) Wiley.
Roney, Bob, et al. Guide to Yosemite High Sierra Trails. (Illus.). 1981. pap. 2.50 (0-939666-34-0) Yosemite Assn.
Roney, C. W. Assessing the Business Environment: Guidelines for Strategists. LC 99-13716. 288p. 1999. 65.00 (1-56720-235-7, Quorum Bks) Greenwood.
*Roney, Carley. The Knot Guide to Wedding Vows & Traditions: Readings, Rituals, Music, Dances, Speeches & Toasts. LC 00-30471. (Illus.). 224p. 2000. 15.00 (0-7679-0248-3) Broadway BDD.
Roney, Carley. The Knot Ultimate Wedding Planner. 224p. 1999. pap. 15.00 (0-7679-0247-5) Bantam.
Roney, Carly & Knot Editors. The Knot's Complete Guide to Weddings in the Real World: The Ultimate Source of Ideas, Advice, & Relief for the Bride & Groom & Those Who Love Them. LC 98-11805. (Illus.). 416p. 1998. pap. 18.00 (0-7679-0246-7) Broadway BDD.
Roney, Deborah W., jt. auth. see Krzyzanowski, Jerzy R.
Roney-Dougal, Serena. Where Science Magic Meet: Quantum Physics & Parapsychology: the Reunion of Intellect Intuition. rev. ed. 272p. 1993. pap. 19.95 (1-85230-446-4, Pub. by Element MA) Penguin Putnam.
Roney, Frank. Frank Roney: Irish Rebel & California Labor Leader. LC 74-22758. (Labor Movement in Fiction & Non-Fiction Ser.). reprint ed. 45.00 (0-404-58511-6) AMS Pr.
— Frank Roney: Irish Rebel & California Labor Leader: An Autobiography. (American Biography Ser.). 573p. 1991. reprint ed. lib. bdg. 99.00 (0-7812-8326-4) Rprt Serv.
— Irish Rebel & California Labor Leader: An Autobiography. Cross, Ira B., ed. LC 76-6363. (Irish Americans Ser.). (Illus.). 1976. reprint ed. 54.95 (0-405-09355-1) Ayer.
Roney, Jennifer Lynn. Webs of Resistance: Organizational Transformation in a Polish Factory. LC 99-30104. 250p. 1999. 50.00 (0-8153-3390-0) Garland.
Roney, John B. The Inside of History: Jean Henri Merle d'Aubigne & Romantic Historiography. LC 95-504. (Studies in Historiography: No. 3). 232p. 1996. 62.95 (0-313-28807-0, Greenwood Pr) Greenwood.
Roney, John B. & Klauber, Martin I., eds. The Identity of Geneva: The Christian Commonwealth, 1564-1864, 59. LC 97-37494. (Contributions to the Study of World History Ser.: Vol. 59). 248p. 1998. 59.95 (0-313-29868-8, Greenwood Pr) Greenwood.
Roney, Judy R., et al. A Resource List for ESL Practitioners: 1994 Able Curriculum Guide. 5th ed. (Illus.). 48p. (C). 1996. reprint ed. pap. text 20.00 (0-7881-3309-8) DIANE Pub.
Roney, Lisa. Sweet Invisible Body: Reflections on a Life with Diabetes. LC 98-51819. 320p. 1999. 23.95 (0-8050-5625-4, Pub. by H Holt & Co) VHPS.
Roney, Lois. Chaucer's Knight's Tale & Theories of Scholastic Psychology. 376p. (C). 1990. 49.95 (0-8130-1006-3); pap. 19.95 (0-8130-1027-6) U Press Fla.
Roney, Lois, jt. ed. see Wasserman, Julian N.
*Roney, Lynn & Smith, Pat. Wow the Dow! The Complete Guide to Teaching Your Kids How to Invest in the Stock Market. (Illus.). 288p. 2000. pap. 14.00 (0-684-87149-1, Fireside) S&S Trade Pap.
Roney, Michael. Bowling. 32p. (C). 1997. pap. text 10.95 (0-7872-4300-0, 41430001) Kendall-Hunt.
Roney, Michael & Utvich, Michael. Guerrilla Guide to High-Tech Trade Shows: The Underground Resource for Saving You Time, Money... LC 97-160852. 208p. 1995. pap. 12.95 (0-679-76961-7) Random.
*Roney-O'Brien, Susan. Farmwife. Zarucchi, Roy, ed. (William & Kingman Page Poetry Book Award Ser.). (Illus.). 48p. 2000. pap. 11.95 (1-879205-83-1) Nightshade Pr.
*Roney, R. Craig. The Story Performance Handbook. 256p. 2000. pap. write for info. (0-8058-3628-4) L Erlbaum Assocs.
Ronfeldt, David, et al. The Zapatista "Social Netwar" in Mexico. LC 98-30809. (Illus.). 175p. 1999. pap. 15.00 (0-8330-2656-9, MR-994-A) Rand Corp.
Ronfeldt, David, jt. auth. see Arquilla, John.
Ronfeldt, David, jt. auth. see Gonzalez, Edward.
Ronfeldt, David F., jt. ed. see Arquilla, John.
Ronfeldt, Paul & McCallum, R. C., eds. Enterprise Bargaining, Trade Unions & the Workplace. LC 96-136040. 320p. 1995. pap. 49.00 (1-86287-202-3, Pub. by Federation Pr) Gaunt.
Ronfor, Philip A. Rio Grande Southern Album. Lankenau, Walter C., ed. (Illus.). 36p. (Orig.). 1989. pap. 18.00 (1-878343-01-7) E Crist.
Rong, Du, et al, eds. Speaking Chinese about China, No. 2. (Chinese Language Library). (Illus.). 602p. (Orig.). (C). 1987. pap. 18.95 (0-8351-1905-X) China Bks.
Rong, Du, et al. Speaking Chinese about China, No. 1. (Chinese Language Library). (Illus.). 490p. (Orig.). (C). 1985. pap. 18.95 (0-8351-1583-6) China Bks.
Rong, K. & Zhu, S. Computer-Aided Fixture Design. LC 99-14705. (Manufacturing Engineering & Materials Processing Ser.). (Illus.). 496p. 1999. text 175.00 (0-8247-9961-5) Dekker.
*Rong, Situ. Reflecting Stochastic Differential Equations with Jumps & Applications, Vol. 408. LC 99-33103. (C&H/CRC Research Notes in Mathematics Series). 224p. 1999. per. 69.95 (1-58488-125-9, Chap & Hall CRC) CRC Pr.
Rong, Wang. Introduction to Differential Geometry & Topology in Mathematical Physics. 1998. 38.00 (981-02-3559-3) World Scientific Pub.
Rong Yang. P-Prolog: A Parallel Logic Programming Language. (Series in Computer Science: Vol. 9). 152p. (C). 1988. text 49.00 (9971-5-0508-8) World Scientific Pub.
Rongen, G. V. The Church: Its Unity in Confession & History. LC 98-29001. 1998. pap. write for info. (0-921100-90-6) Inherit Pr.
Rongen, G. Van, see Van Rongen, G.
Rongieras. Allez, Viens: Holt French Language. 1996. text, student ed. 56.50 (0-03-096526-8) Holt R&W.
Rongsheng, Chen. Dictionnaire Chinois-Francais de Termes et Expressions Moder. (CHI & FRE.). 1989. 75.00 (0-7859-8706-1, 7800280144) Fr & Eur.
Rongstad, L. James. The Lodge. rev. ed. LC 95-23063. (How to Respond Ser.). 64p. 1995. 3.99 (0-570-04670-X, 12-6003) Concordia.
Rongstad, Richard H. The Glasnost Primer. 45p. 1989. pap. text 7.95 (1-887897-00-3) Vikng-Phoenix.
— Special Report: Guide to Overseas Correspondence Clubs & Services. 108p. 1994. pap. text 25.00 (1-887897-01-1) Vikng-Phoenix.
Rongstad, Richard H., jt. auth. see Cunningham, Ernest G.
Rongxi, Li, tr. & intro. see Numata Center for Buddhist Translation & Research.
Roni. Sensuous Cinema of My Mind. x, 91p. (Orig.). 1996. pap. 16.95 (0-9654292-0-2) Laugh Buddha Pr.
Roniger, Luis. Hierarchy & Trust in Modern Mexico & Brazil. LC 90-37775. 256p. 1990. 65.00 (0-275-93628-7, C3628, Praeger Pubs) Greenwood.
*Roniger, Luis & Herzog, Tamar, eds. The Collective & the Public in Latin America: Cultural Identities & Political Order. 272p. 2000. 65.00 (1-902210-13-1, Pub. by Sussex Acad Pr) Intl Spec Bk.
Roniger, Luis & Sznajder, Mario, eds. Constructing Collective Identities & Shaping Public Spheres: Latin American Paths. LC 97-49241. vi, 280p. 1998. 65.00 (1-898723-77-X, Pub. by Sussex Acad Pr) Intl Spec Bk.
Roniger, Luis, jt. auth. see Sznajder, Mario.
Roniger, Luis, ed. see Gunes-Ayata, Ayse.
Ronin. Malevolent Silence & Poems for Sandy. 88p. 1998. pap. 10.00 (1-57502-909-X, PO2505) Morris Pubng.
Ronin, L. David. Thinking about Divorce? What to Do Before You See a Lawyer. 1999. pap. text 14.95 (1-888960-05-1) Fine Print Pr.
Roningen, Vernon O. Managing Free Trade for Agriculture. LC 93-87573. 200p. 1993. pap. 25.00 (0-9640007-0-9) Natl Ctr Food.
Roninson, I. B. Molecular & Cellular Biology of Multidrug Resistance in Tumor Cells. (Illus.). 424p. (C). 1990. text 120.00 (0-306-43547-0, Kluwer Plenum) Kluwer Academic.
*Ronis, Diane L. Brain-Compatible Mathematics LC 98-61808. 203 p. 1999. write for info. (1-57517-150-3) SkyLght.
Ronis, Willy, photos by. Sundays by the River: Photographs by Will Ronis. LC 98-47592. (Motta Photography Ser.). (Illus.). 60p. 1999. 24.95 (1-56098-887-8) Smithsonian.
Ronish, Martha J., jt. auth. see Burrows, Donald.
*Ronit, Karsten & Schneider, Volker. Private Organisations in Global Politics. LC 00-42469. 2000. write for info. (0-415-20128-4) Routledge.
RonJon Publishing Staff. Experiments in Astronomy. Date not set. text 26.53 (1-56870-284-1) RonJon Pub.
— Experiments in Biology. Date not set. text 27.86 (1-56870-334-1) RonJon Pub.
— Experiments in Chemistry. Date not set. text 25.07 (1-56870-333-3) RonJon Pub.
— Experiments in Marine Aquatics. Date not set. text 17.22 (1-56870-335-X) RonJon Pub.
— Experiments in Physical Science. Date not set. text 57.12 (1-56870-336-8) RonJon Pub.
— Experiments in Physics. Date not set. text 37.19 (1-56870-269-8) RonJon Pub.
— Integrated in Science. Date not set. text 119.63 (1-56870-337-6) RonJon Pub.
*RonJon Publishing Staff. Select Earth Science: Student Edition. 1999. pap. text 36.95 (1-56870-344-9) RonJon Pub.
— Select Earth Science: Teachers Edition. 1999. pap. text, teacher ed. 46.50 (1-56870-345-7) RonJon Pub.
— Select Life Science: Student Edition. 1999. pap. text, student ed. 34.95 (1-56870-346-5) RonJon Pub.
— Select Life Science: Teacher Edition. 1999. pap. text, teacher ed. 46.50 (1-56870-347-3) RonJon Pub.
— Select Physical Science: Student Edition. 1999. pap. text, student ed. 37.95 (1-56870-348-1) RonJon Pub.
— Select Physical Science: Teacher Edition. 1999. pap. text, teacher ed. 46.50 (1-56870-349-X) RonJon Pub.
Ronk, A. T. History of Brethren Missionary Movements. LC 70-184490. 1971. pap. 1.50 (0-934970-02-5) Brethren Church.
— History of the Brethren Church. LC 68-23554. 1968. 5.00 (0-934970-03-3) Brethren Church.
— A Search for Truth. LC 73-82191. 1973. pap. 0.75 (0-934970-04-1) Brethren Church.
Ronk, Martha. Desert Geometries. (Littoral Bks.). 62p. 1993. pap. 9.95 (1-55713-151-1) Sun & Moon CA.
— State of Mind. (New American Poetry Ser.: No. 21). 120p. (Orig.). 1996. pap. 10.95 (1-55713-236-4) Sun & Moon CA.
Ronk, Martha C. Desire in L. A. LC 89-34552. (Contemporary Poetry Ser.). 96p. 1990. pap. 14.95 (0-8203-1176-6) U of Ga Pr.
*Ronk, Martha C. Displeasures of the Table, Vol. 66. 2000. pap. 9.95 (1-892295-44-X) Green Integer.
Ronk, Martha C. Eyetrouble: Poems by Martha Ronk. LC 97-40043. (The Contemporary Poetry Ser.). 1998. pap. 14.95 (0-8203-1992-9) U of Ga Pr.
Ronkainen, Ilkka A., jt. auth. see Czinkota, Michael R.
Ronkin, Bruce, ed. see Hadcock, Peter.
Ronkin, Bruce, ed. see Londeix, Jean-Marie.
Ronkin, L. I. Introduction to the Theory of Entire Functions of Several Variables. Israel Program for Scientific Translations Staff, tr. LC 74-12068. (Translations of Mathematical Monographs: Vol. 44). 273p. 1974. text 80.00 (0-8218-1594-6, MMONO/44) Am Math.
Ronn, Ehud I. & Bliss, Robert R., Jr. A New Method for Valuing Treasury Bond Futures Options. 1992. pap. text 20.00 (0-943205-15-8) RFICFA.
Ronnas, Per, et al, eds. Institutional Adjustment for Economic Growth: Small Scale Industries & Economic Transition in Asia & Africa. LC 97-77531. (Illus.). 250p. 1998. text 63.95 (1-84014-362-2, Pub. by Ashgate Pub) Ashgate Pub Co.
*Ronnas, Per & Ramamurthy, Bhargavi, eds. Entrepreneurship in Vietnam: Transformation & Dynamics in Manufacturing in the First Decade of Reform. 320p. 2000. 45.00 (87-87062-84-4, Pub. by NIAS) Paul & Co Pubs.
Ronnby, Alf. Mobilizing Local Communities. 400p. 1996. 101.95 (1-85972-189-3, Pub. by Avebry) Ashgate Pub Co.
Ronneau, C. & Bitchaeva, O. Biotechnology for Waste Management & Site Restoration: Technological, Educational, Business, Political Aspects. LC 97-29307. (NATO ASI Series, Partnership Sub-Series 2, Environment). 272p. 1997. text 130.50 (0-7923-4769-2) Kluwer Academic.
Ronneberg, Prudence H., ed. see Dornheim, John F.
Ronneberg, Prudence H., ed. see Dornheim, John F.C.
Ronneberg, Rod L. A Little Book of Canons. Renneberg, Prue, ed. (Illus.). 67p. (Orig.). 1997. spiral bd., wbk. ed. 15.00 (1-892573-00-8, 0001) Campanile Pr.
Ronner, Amy D. W. H. Hudson: The Man, the Novelist, the Naturalist. LC 85-48068. (Studies in Modern Literature: No. 16). 1986. 34.50 (0-404-61586-4) AMS Pr.
Ronner, Devon, ed. see Lowe, Paul.
Ronner, John. The Angel Calendar Book: 365 Days Tied to the Angels. LC 99-56440. (Illus.). 192p. (Orig.). 2000. pap. 12.95 (0-932945-44-9) Mamre Pr.
Ronner, John E. Angels of Cokeville: And Other True Stories of Heavenly Intervention. 192p. (Orig.). 1995. pap. 10.95 (0-932945-43-0) Mamre Pr.
— Do You Have a Guardian Angel? & Other Questions Answered about Angels. LC 84-62980. (Illus.). 188p. (Orig.). 1985. pap. 10.95 (0-932945-37-6) Mamre Pr.
— Know Your Angels: The Angel Almanac with Biographies of 100 Prominent Angels in Legend & Folklore - & Much More. (Illus.). 112p. (Orig.). 1993. pap. 10.95 (0-932945-40-6) Mamre Pr.
— Seeing Your Future: A Modern Look at Prophecy & Prediction. (Illus.). 190p. (Orig.). 1990. pap. 10.95 (0-932945-38-4) Mamre Pr.
Ronner, Wanda, jt. auth. see Marsh, Margaret.
Ronnett, Alexander . Romanian Nationalism: The Legionary Movement. Barsan, Uasile C., tr. from RUM. LC 74-3350. 93p. reprint ed. pap. 30.00 (0-8357-9431-8, 201506200092) Bks Demand.
*Ronngren, Diane. Color: A Secret Language Revealed. 2nd rev. ed. 40p. 1999. 4.95 (0-9641339-2-X) E T C Pub.
— Tarot: Secrets of Card Reading. 3rd ed. 44p. 1998. reprint ed. 7.95 (0-9641339-6-2) E T C Pub.
*Ronngren, Diane & Stellhorn, Donna. Money & Prosperity Workbook. (Illus.). 46p. 1999. wbk. ed. 5.95 (1-930038-00-3) E T C Pub.
Ronnholm, Paul F., jt. auth. see Ronnholm, Ursula O.
Ronnholm, Paul F., ed. see Ronnholm, Ursula O.
Ronnholm, Ursala O. Aprende a Leer a Traves de Musica, Juegos y Ritmos. Deliz, Osdila O., ed. (SPA., Illus.). 42p. (J). (gr. k up). 1986. text 20.00 incl. audio (0-941911-01-2) Two Way Bilingual.
Ronnholm, Ursula O. Aprende a Leer a Traves de Musica, Juegos y Ritmos. rev. ed. Rabell, Edda, ed. & tr. by. (SPA., Illus.). 42p. (J). (gr. k-2). 1989. pap. text 20.00 incl. audio (0-941911-07-1) Two Way Bilingual.
— Learning to Read Through Music, Games & Reading. Ronnholm, Paul F., ed. Montero, Miguel, tr. (Illus.). 60p. (Orig.). 1985. pap. text 20.00 (0-941911-00-4); audio. write for info. (0-318-61899-0) Two Way Bilingual.
— Mi Libro de Escritura. (SPA., Illus.). 74p. (J). (gr. k-3). 1986. 4.00 (0-941911-05-5) Two Way Bilingual.
— Mi Libro de Palabras: Oraciones y Cuentos. rev. ed. Rabell, Edda, ed. & tr. by. Montero, Miguel, tr. (SPA., Illus.). 100p. (J). (gr. k-6). 1989. reprint ed. pap. 7.00 (0-941911-08-X) Two Way Bilingual.
— Mi Libro de Palabras, Oraciones y Cuentos. Deliz, Osdila O., ed. (Illus.). 100p. (J). (gr. k-6). pap. text 7.00 (0-941911-02-0) Two Way Bilingual.
— Two Way Bilingual Songs for Elementary School. (Illus.). 41p. (J). (gr. k-12). 1987. 8.00 incl. audio (0-941911-06-3) Two Way Bilingual.
— Writing Through Music. rev. ed. Ronnholm, Paul F., ed. Montero, Miguel, tr. from SPA. (Illus.). 74p. (J). (gr. k-3). 1989. pap. text 4.00 (0-941911-09-8) Two Way Bilingual.
Ronnholm, Ursula O. & Ronnholm, Paul F. My Book of Words, Songs & Sentences. (Illus.). 91p. (J). (gr. k-3). 1986. pap. text 7.00 (0-941911-03-9) Two Way Bilingual.
Ronnie, Art. Counterfeit Hero: Fritz Duquesne, Adventurer & Spy. LC 95-12401. (Illus.). 360p. 1995. 32.50 (1-55750-733-3) Naval Inst Pr.
Ronnie, Mary. Education for Library & Information Science in New Zealand & the Pacific Islands. LC 95-53302. (Education of Library & Information Professionals: No. 1). 224p. 1996. 100.00 (0-7201-2179-5) Continuum.
Ronnie Sellers Production Staff. Tibetan Portrait, 1. 1999. 11.95 (1-56906-166-1) R Sellers Prods.
Ronnie Sellers Productions Staff. Literary Year, 1. 1999. 11.95 (1-56906-150-5) R Sellers Prods.
Ronning, C. Neale. Jose Marti & the Emigre Colony in Key West: Leadership & State Formation. LC 89-38802. 175p. 1990. 45.00 (0-275-93368-7, C3368, Greenwood Pr) Greenwood.
Ronning, C. Neale & Vannucci, Albert P., eds. Ambassadors in Foreign Policy: The Influence of Individuals on U. S. - Latin American Policy. LC 87-2833. 166p. 1987. 55.00 (0-275-92393-2, C2393, Praeger Pubs) Greenwood.
Ronning, Kari, ed. see Cather, Willa.
Ronning, Kari A., ed. see Cather, Willa.
Ronning, R. R., jt. auth. see Glover, J. A.

An Asterisk (*) at the beginning of an entry indicates that the title is appearing for the first time.

R

Ronningen, Thor. Butler's Battlin Blue Bastards: The Story of Men of the 3rd Battalion-395th Infantry in WW II under the Leadership of Lt. Col. McClernand Butler. LC 93-9515. (Illus.). 236p. 1993. pap. 19.95 (*1-55618-132-9*) Brunswick Pub.

***Ronningstam, Elsa.** Disorders of Narcissism: Diagnostic, Clinical & Empirical Implications. LC 99-59531. 2000. pap. write for info. (*0-7657-0259-2*) Aronson.

Ronningstam, Elsa, ed. Disorders of Narcissism: Diagnostic, Clinical, & Empirical Implications. 304p. 1997. text 44.50 (*0-88048-701-1*, 8701) Am Psychiatric.

Ronnow, Robert. Janie Huzzie Bows. LC 83-70121. 64p. (Orig.). 1983. pap. 6.95 (*0-935306-18-8*) Barnwood Pr.

— White Waits. LC 83-71219. 64p. (Orig.). 1984. pap. 6.95 (*0-935306-27-7*) Barnwood Pr.

Ronohardjo, Purnomo, jt. ed. see Daniels, P. W.

Ronowicz, Eddie & Yallop, Colin, eds. English: One Language, Different Cultures. LC 99-11756. 256p. 1999. 69.95 (*0-304-70118-1*); pap. 22.95 (*0-304-70119-X*) Continuum.

Ronsard, Pierre De. Amours. (FRE.). 480p. 1981. pap. 13.95 (*0-7859-4641-1*) Fr & Eur.

— Amours. (Poesie Ser.). (FRE.). 448p. 1974. pap. 13.95 (*2-07-032134-7*) Schoenhof.

— Les Amours: Amours de Cassandre; Amours de Marie. (FRE.). 1974. pap. 17.95 (*0-7859-2777-8*) Fr & Eur.

— Discours: Derniers Vers. Bellenger, Y., ed. (FRE.). 1979. pap. 10.95 (*0-7859-2973-8*) Fr & Eur.

— Oeuvres Completes, Vol. 1. Cerard, Jean, ed. (FRE.). 1184p. 1993. lib. bdg. 110.00 (*0-7859-3787-0*, 2070104850) Fr & Eur.

— Poesies Choisies. Joukovsky, Francois, ed. (FRE., Illus.). 539p. 1989. 45.00 (*0-7859-1271-1*, 2040173234) Fr & Eur.

— Les Quatre Saisons. (Poesie Ser.). (FRE.). 320p. 1985. pap. 11.95 (*2-07-032308-0*) Schoenhof.

— Les Quatre Saisons de Ronsard. (FRE.). 1985. pap. 16.95 (*0-7859-2797-2*) Fr & Eur.

— Le Second Livre des Amours. (FRE.). 227p. 1951. pap. 14.95 (*0-7859-5473-2*) Fr & Eur.

— Sonnets pour Helene. (FRE., Illus.). 228p. 1970. pap. 29.95 (*0-7859-5474-0*) Fr & Eur.

Ronsard, Pierre De & Baillou, Jean. Discours des Miseres de Ce Temps. (FRE.). 290p. 1949. pap. 18.95 (*0-7859-1460-9*, 2251360913) Fr & Eur.

Ronsard, Pierre De, et al. La Fleur des Musiciens de P. de Ronsard. Expert, Henry, ed. (FRE., Illus.). 116p. 1965. reprint ed. pap. 37.50 (*0-8450-1245-2*) Broude.

Ronsard, Pierre De, jt. auth. see De Castro, Jean.

Ronsaville, Donna, ed. see Radke-Yarrow, Marian, et al.

Ronsch, Hermann. Itala und Vulgata. xvi, 526p. 1979. reprint ed. write for info. (*3-487-06728-5*) G Olms Pubs.

Ronsil, Rene. Bibliographie Ornithologique Francaise. (FRE.). 627p. 1994. reprint ed. 85.00 (*1-888262-63-X*) Martino Pubng.

Ronsivalli, Louis J. The Best True Stories I Know, Vol. 1. 2nd rev. ed. LC 96-94093. (Illus.). 175p. 1996. pap. 12.95 (*1-888201-01-0*) Mermakk Publns.

— Fluoridation of Public Water Supplies: (The Motives That Drive the Two Sides of the Issue) LC 98-65964. 164p. 1998. pap. text 8.00 (*1-888201-06-1*) Mermakk Publns.

— The Invisible Wall. LC 96-94560. 255p. (Orig.). 1996. pap. 14.95 (*1-888201-03-7*) Mermakk Publns.

— Mermakk's Behavioral Guide to Success. LC 96-94141. (Illus.). 165p. 1996. pap. 20.00 (*1-888201-02-9*) Mermakk Publns.

— Mermarkk's Stories for Children at Bedtime. LC 96-94907. (Illus.). 140p. (Orig.). (J). 1997. pap. 8.95 (*1-888201-04-5*) Mermakk Publns.

— The Twelfth Commandment. LC 98-65053. 372p. 1998. pap. 15.00 (*1-888201-05-3*) Mermakk Publns.

Ronsivalli, Louis J. & Vieira, Ernest R. Elementary Food Science. 4th ed. 416p. 1996. pap. 49.00 (*0-8342-1657-4*) Aspen Pub.

Ronsley, Joseph. Yeats's Autobiography: Life As Symbolic Pattern. LC 68-15642. 184p. 1968. reprint ed. pap. 57.10 (*0-7837-6088-4*, 205913400007) Bks Demand.

Ronsley, Joseph, ed. Denis Johnston: A Retrospective. (Irish Literary Studies: Vol. # 8). 284p. 1981. 40.00 (*0-86140-078-X*, Pub. by Smyth) Dufour.

Ronsley, Joseph, frwd. The Dramatic Works of Denis Johnston: Radio & Television Plays, Vol. 3. 516p. 1992. 70.00 (*0-86140-080-1*, Pub. by Smyth) Dufour.

Ronsley, Joseph, ed. see Johnston, Denis.

Ronson, Bonnie. The Lessons All Around You. LC 98-67322. 76p. (C). 1998. per. 20.95 (*0-7872-5148-8*, 41514801) Kendall-Hunt.

***Ronson, Bonnie.** The Lessons All Around You. 348p. (C). 1999. pap. text 62.95 (*0-7872-6450-4*, 41645001) Kendall-Hunt.

Ronspus, Daniel. Where Is Easter? 122p. 1999. pap. write for info. (*0-7392-0130-1*, PO3049) Morris Pubng.

Ronstadt, Edward F., ed. see Ronstadt, Federico J.

Ronstadt, Federico J. Borderman: Memoirs of Federico Jose Maria Ronstadt. Ronstadt, Edward F., ed. LC 93-3853. (Illus.). 182p. reprint ed. pap. 56.50 (*0-608-20971-6*, 207184300002) Bks Demand.

Ronstadt, Karen, jt. auth. see Patricca, Nicholas A.

Ronstadt, Robert, et al, eds. Frontiers of Entrepreneurship Research, 1986: Proceedings of the 6th Annual Entrepreneurship Research Conference. 730p. 1986. pap. text 65.00 (*0-910897-07-7*) Babson College.

Ronstadt, Robert C. Art of Case Analysis: A Guide to the Diagnosis of Business Situations. 3rd ed. 1994. pap. 16.95 (*0-685-69348-1*) Lord Pub.

— Entrepreneurial Finance. 49.95 (*0-685-69355-4*) Lord Pub.

— Entrepreneurial Finance: Taking Control of Your Financial Decision Making. 250p. 1988. 49.95 (*0-930204-23-9*) Lord Pub.

— Entrepreneurship: Text, Cases & Notes. 800p. (C). 1985. text 59.95 (*0-930204-11-5*) Lord Pub.

— Small Business Management. (GC - Principles of Management Ser.). 1996. text. write for info. (*0-538-81940-5*) S-W Pub.

— Venture Feasibility Plan. 1988. 49.95 (*0-930204-25-5*) Lord Pub.

Ronstadt, Robert C. & Shuman. Venture Feasibility Planning Guide. 150p. 1988. pap. 49.95 (*0-930204-21-2*) Lord Pub.

Ronstadt, Robert C., et al. Ronstadt's Financials. 250p. 1988. 159.95 (*0-930204-24-7*) Lord Pub.

Ronsvalle, John & Ronsvalle, Sylvia. Behind the Stained Glass Windows: Money Dynamics in the Church. LC 96-1101. 384p. (gr. 12). 1996. 24.99 (*0-8010-9011-3*) Baker Bks.

— Hidden Billions: The Potential of the Church in the U. S. 175p. (Orig.). 1984. pap. 8.00 (*0-914527-18-5*) C-Four Res.

— The Poor Have Faces: Loving Your Neighbor in the Twenty-First Century. LC 92-916. 160p. (gr. 10). 1992. pap. 8.99 (*0-8010-7764-8*) Baker Bks.

Ronsvalle, John, et al. At Ease: Discussing Money & Values in Small Groups. LC 98-73456. x, 110 p. 1998. pap. 12.25 (*1-56699-202-8*, AL193) Alban Inst.

Ronsvalle, John L. & Ronsvalle, Sylvia. The State of Church Giving through 1996. 8th ed. (State of Church Giving Series). 104p. 1998. pap. 16.00 (*0-9639962-8-2*) Empty Tomb.

***Ronsvalle, John L. & Ronsvalle, Sylvia.** The State of Church Giving Through 1997. 9th ed. 112p. 1999. pap. 17.00 (*0-9639962-9-0*) Empty Tomb.

Ronsvalle, Sylvia, jt. auth. see Ronsvalle, John.

Ronsvalle, Sylvia, jt. auth. see Ronsvalle, John L.

***Rontal, Gene.** Sterile Justice. LC 99-65324. 192p. 2000. pap. 11.95 (*1-56315-250-9*, Pub. by SterlingHse) Natl Bk Netwk.

Rontgen, Robert E. The Book of Meissen. rev. ed. (Illus.). 333p. 1996. 95.00 (*0-7643-0170-5*) Schiffer.

— Marks on German, Bohemian & Austrian Porcelain. rev. ed. 640p. 1998. 95.00 (*0-7643-0353-8*) Schiffer.

***Ronthal, Michael.** Neck Complaints. LC 99-37382. (Most Common Complaints Ser.). 152p. 1999. pap. text 25.00 (*0-7506-7156-4*) Buttrwrth-Heinemann.

***Ronto, G. & Tarjan, I.** An Introduction to Biophysics with Medical Orientation. 3rd ed. 448p. 1999. 82.00 (*963-05-7607-4*, Pub. by Akade Kiado) Intl Spec Bk.

Ronto, G., jt. auth. see Tarjan, Imre.

Ronto, Gyorgyi & Tarjan, Imre, eds. An Introduction to Biophysics with Medical Orientation. 2nd enl. rev. ed. LC 94-220531. 442p. 1997. pap. 198.00 (*963-05-6757-1*, Pub. by Akade Kiado) St Mut.

Ronto, M. & Samoilenko, A. M. Numerical-Analytic Methods in the Theory of Boundary Value Problems. 360p. 1999. 58.00 (*981-02-3676-X*) World Scientific Pub.

Ronveaux, A., ed. Heun's Differential Equations. (Illus.). 378p. (C). 1995. text 105.00 (*0-19-859695-2*) OUP.

Rony, A. Kohar. Unveiling Indonesia: Indonesian Holdings in the Library of Congress, Bibliography, 2, Vol. 1-2. 2 Bks. (2167p. 1997. per. 81.00 (*0-16-061803-7*, Library of Cong) USGPO.

Rony, A. Kohar, compiled by. Philippine Holdings in the Library of Congress, 1960-1987: A Bibliography. LC 92-3438. 702p. 1993. 46.00 (*0-8444-0744-5*) Lib Congress.

— Vietnamese Holdings in the Library of Congress: A Bibliography. LC 81-2847. 236p. 1982. suppl. ed. 13.00 (*0-8444-0564-7*, 030-000-00196-6) Lib Congress.

Rony, Ellen & Rony, Peter. The Domain Name Handbook: High Stakes & Strategies in Cyberspace. LC 98-207077. xxvi, 680p. 1998. pap. 39.95 incl. cd-rom (*0-87930-515-0*) C M P Books.

Rony, Fatimah T. The Third Eye: Race, Cinema, & Ethnographic Spectacle. LC 96-13255. 328p. 1996. text 49.95 (*0-8223-1834-2*); pap. text 17.95 (*0-8223-1840-7*) Duke.

Rony, Fatimah T., jt. auth. see Griffin, Farah J.

Rony, Peter, jt. auth. see Rony, Ellen.

Rony, Peter R. Fundamentals of Z-80 Microcomputer Programming Interfacing with Experiments. (Foxware Ser.: Module 11). 300p. 1988. ring bd. write for info. (*0-89704-042-2*) E&L Instru.

Ronyoung, Kim. Clay Walls. LC 86-60589. 304p. 1986. 22.00 (*0-932966-66-7*) Permanent Pr.

— Clay Walls. 3rd ed. 301p. 1996. reprint ed. pap. 16.00 (*1-877946-78-8*) Permanent Pr.

Ronzani, Maggie, jt. auth. see Bloom, Susan.

Ronzheimer, Philip. Trust Me! Trust Me! 1992. pap. 1.59 (*0-87509-498-8*) Chr Pubns.

Ronzio, Camille & Wilkinson, Trina. Microwave Delights. 4th rev. ed. LC 80-65640. (Illus.). 206p. 1980. pap. 7.95 (*0-686-85760-7*) Cam-Tri Prods.

Ronzio, Robert A. The Encyclopedia of Nutrition & Good Health. LC 96-17858. 496p. 1997. 45.00 (*0-8160-2665-3*) Facts on File.

— Encyclopedia of Nutrition & Good Health. 496p. 1997. reprint ed. pap. text 19.95 (*0-8160-3755-8*) Facts on File.

Ronzitti, Natalino, ed. The Law of Naval Warfare. (C). 1988. lib. bdg. 304.50 (*90-247-3652-8*) Kluwer Academic.

— Maritime Terrorism & International Law. (C). 1990. lib. bdg. 92.00 (*0-7923-0734-8*) Kluwer Academic.

Ronzitti, Natalino, jt. ed. see De Guttry, Andrea.

Roo, A. J. De, see De Roo, A. J.

Roo, Annie J. De, see De Roo, Annie J., ed.

Roo, De, see De Roo.

Roo, Gert De, see Miller, Donald & De Roo, Gert, eds.

Roo, Peter De, see De Roo, Peter.

Roob, Alexander. Alchemy & Mysticism: Hermetic Museum. (Illus.). 704p. 1997. pap. 29.99 (*3-8228-8653-X*) Taschen Amer.

Roob, Alexander. Ko-Alquimia & Mistica. 1997. 38.99 (*3-8228-8543-6*) Taschen Amer.

Roobol, M. John, jt. auth. see Smith, Alan L.

Roobol, Norman R. Industrial Painting: Principles & Practices. 2nd ed. LC 96-38488. 352p. 1997. 49.95 (*1-56990-215-1*) Hanser-Gardner.

Roobol, W. Tsereteli: A Democrat in the Russian Revolution. (Studies in Social History: No. 1). 1977. lib. bdg. 148.50 (*90-247-1915-1*) Kluwer Academic.

Roochnik, David. Of Art & Wisdom: Plato's Understanding of Techne. 1996. 45.00 (*0-271-01563-2*) Pa St U Pr.

— Of Art & Wisdom: Plato's Understanding of Techne. 312p. 1998. pap. 18.95 (*0-271-01841-0*) Pa St U Pr.

Roochvarg, Alida, ed. The Alida Roochvarg Collection of Books about Books. (Illus.). 428p. 1981. 45.00 (*0-938768-00-X*) Oak Knoll.

Roocroft, Alan & Zoll, Donald A. Managing Elephants: An Introduction to Their Training & Management. 198p. (Orig.). 1994. pap. text 20.00 (*0-9640073-0-4*) Fever Tree.

***Rood.** Logic & Structured Design for Computer Programmers. 3rd ed. (C). 2000. pap. 45.00 (*0-534-37386-0*) Thomson Learn.

— Wetlands. LC 92-47140. (Nature Study Ser.). 48p. (J). (gr. 2-5). 1999. pap. 7.95 (*0-06-446158-0*) HarpC Child Bks.

Rood, A. Van, see Burgers, H. S.

Rood, Andrew. Managing Object-Oriented Software Projects. 1996. pap. text 41.91 (*0-201-63404-X*) Addison-Wesley.

Rood, Arnold, ed. Edward Gordon Craig, Artist of the Theatre, 1872-1966: A Memorial Exhibition in the Amsterdam Gallery. LC 73-137703. (New York Public Library Publications in Reprint). (Illus.). 1971. reprint ed 11.95 (*0-405-18768-8*) Ayer.

Rood, Beverly, jt. auth. see Pisano, Ronald G.

Rood, Dean. A Practical Guide to the Care, Maintenance, & Troubleshooting of Capillary Gas Chromatographic Systems. 2nd ed. LC 95-226863. (Chromatographic Methods Ser.). 323p. 1995. 60.00 (*3-7785-2319-8*, Pub. by Huethig BRD) U Pr of Amer.

— A Practical Guide to the Care, Maintenance & Troubleshooting of Capillary Gas Chromatographic Systems. 3rd ed. LC 99-192528. 344p. 1999. 115.00 (*3-527-29750-2*) Wiley.

Rood, E. P., ed. Holographic Particle Image Velocimetry. LC 93-71635. (FED Ser.: Vol. 148). 67p. 1993. pap. 25.00 (*0-7918-0956-0*, H00788) ASME.

Rood, E. P. & Katz, J., eds. Free-Surface Turbulence. LC 94-71261. (Fluid Engineering Division Conference Ser.: Vol. 181). 169p. 1994. pap. 37.50 (*0-7918-1364-9*) ASME.

Rood, Harold J. Logic & Structured Design for Computer Programmers. 2nd ed. 304p. (C). 1992. mass mkt. 48.95 (*0-534-92966-4*) PWS Pubs.

Rood, J. J. Van, see Van Rood, J. J., ed.

Rood, John. Sculpture in Wood. LC 50-9725. 191p. reprint ed. pap. 59.30 (*0-608-14632-3*, 205590200039) Bks Demand.

— Sculpture with a Torch. LC 63-13883. (Illus.). 117p. reprint ed. pap. 36.30 (*0-608-15978-6*, 203328600084) Bks Demand.

Rood, Julian, et al, eds. The Clostridia: Molecular Biology & Pathogenesis. LC 96-37807. (Illus.). 480p. 1997. text 129.95 (*0-12-595020-9*) Morgan Kaufmann.

Rood, Justin, ed. see Thomas Rivera Center Staff.

Rood, Karen L., ed. American Literary Almanac: From 1608 to Present: an Original Compendium of Facts & Anecdotes about Literary Life in the United States of America. LC 88-3689. 439p. 1988. reprint ed. pap. 136.10 (*0-608-02807-X*, 206387400007) Bks Demand.

Rood, Karen L., ed. American Writers in Paris, 1920-1939. LC 79-26101. (Dictionary of Literary Biography Ser.: Vol. 4). (Illus.). 448p. 1980. text 155.00 (*0-8103-0916-5*) Gale.

Rood, Karen L., et al, eds. Dictionary of Literary Biography Yearbook, 1980. 80th ed. LC 81-4188. 344p. 1981. text 155.00 (*0-8103-1600-5*) Gale.

Rood, Lois S. Beyond Severe Disability: Models & Strategies for Change. 43p. (Orig.). 1983. pap. 3.15 (*1-55719-006-2*) U NE CPAR.

— Beyond Severe Disability: Nebraska Services Guide. 38p. (Orig.). 1985. pap. 3.15 (*1-55719-013-5*) U NE CPAR.

Rood, Lois S. & Davis, Carole M. Beyond Severe Disability: The Challenge of Private Enterprise. 38p. (Orig.). 1985. pap. 3.15 (*1-55719-015-1*) U NE CPAR.

Rood, Lois S. & Faison, Karen. Beyond Severe Disability: A Functional Bibliography. 32p. (Orig.). 1985. pap. 2.50 (*1-55719-014-3*) U NE CPAR.

Rood, Pauls. Gift of Words: Writing & Literature in the Elementary Classroom. 1992. text 17.95 (*0-201-81536-2*) Addison-Wesley.

Rood, R. T. & Renzini, Alvio, eds. Advances in Stellar Evolution. LC 97-16352. (Cambridge Contemporary Astrophysics Ser.). (Illus.). 356p. (C). 1997. text 74.95 (*0-521-59184-8*) Cambridge U Pr.

Rood, Ronald. Animals Nobody Loves. LC 87-62516. (Illus.). 224p. 1987. pap. text 10.95 (*0-933050-54-2*) New Eng Pr VT.

— Beachcombers All: Exploring the New England Seashore. LC 90-5817. (Illus.). 128p. (Orig.). 1990. pap. 9.95 (*0-933050-80-1*) New Eng Pr VT.

— How Do You Spank a Porcupine? LC 83-62565. (Illus.). 160p. (J). (gr. 7 up). 1983. reprint ed. pap. 10.95 (*0-933050-19-4*) New Eng Pr VT.

— A Land Alive: The World of Nature at One Family's Door. LC 92-61232. (Illus.). 160p. (Orig.). 1992. pap. 9.95 (*0-933050-89-5*) New Eng Pr VT.

Rood, Ronald. Loon in My Bathtub. LC 85-61031. (Illus.). 192p. (Orig.). 1985. reprint ed. pap. 12.95 (*0-933050-28-3*) New Eng Pr VT.

Rood, Ronald. Ron Rood's Vermont: A Nature Guide. LC 88-9856. (Illus.). 224p. (Orig.). 1988. pap. 10.95 (*0-933050-56-9*) New Eng Pr VT.

***Rood, Sally A.** Government Laboratory Technology Transfer: Process & Impact. 382p. 2000. text 78.95 (*0-7546-1065-9*, Pub. by Ashgate Pub) Ashgate Pub Co.

Rood, Stephen C. Computer Hardware Maintenance: An IS-IT Manager's Guide. 160p. 1995. pap. 34.95 (*0-7506-9494-7*, Digital DEC) Buttrwrth-Heinemann.

Rood, T. C. Thucydides: Narrative & Explanation. LC 98-7982. 352p. 1999. text 85.00 (*0-19-815256-6*) OUP.

Rood, W. A. Dominican Republic Investors Handbook: A Guide for Investing in Santo Domingo. 1978. lib. bdg. 69.95 (*0-8490-1389-5*) Gordon Pr.

Rood, Y. Van, see Balner, H. & Van Rood, Y., eds.

Rooda, Rhonda, jt. auth. see Simon, Rita James.

Roodenberg, J. J. Le Mobilier en Pierre de Bouqras: Utilisation de la Pierre dans un Site Neolithique sur le Moyen Euphrate (Syrie) vii, 207p. 1986. pap. text 52.50 (*90-6258-061-0*, Pub. by Netherlands Inst) Eisenbrauns.

Roodenburg, Herman, ed. see Bremmer, Jan.

Roodenburg, Herman, jt. ed. see Bremmer, Jan.

Roodman, David, jt. auth. see Lenssen, Nicholas.

Roodman, David M. Getting the Signals Right: Tax Reform to Protect the Environment & the Economy. LC 97-60022. 70p. 1997. pap. 5.00 (*1-878071-36-X*) Worldwatch Inst.

— The Natural Wealth of Nations: Harnessing the Market for Environmental Protection & Economic Strength. LC 98-228480. 303p. 1998. pap. 13.00 (*0-393-31852-4*) Norton.

— Paying the Piper: Subsidies, Politics, & the Environment. 70p. (Orig.). 1996. pap. 5.00 (*1-878071-35-1*) Worldwatch Inst.

Roodyn, Donald B., ed. see Luzikov, Valentin N.

***Roof.** Contemporary American Religion, 1. LC 99-46712. 1999. 115.00 (*0-02-864926-5*) Mac Lib Ref.

— Contemporary American Religion, 2. LC 99-46712. 1999. 115.00 (*0-02-864927-3*) Mac Lib Ref.

Roof, Christopher, ed. see Montague, Bill.

Roof, Jonathan. Pathways to God: A Study Guide to the Teachings of Sathya Sai Baba. LC 91-61787. 218p. 1991. pap. 12.00 (*0-9629835-0-0*) Leela Pr.

Roof, Judith. Come As You Are: Sexuality & Narrative. LC 96-10159. 248p. 1996. 52.00 (*0-231-10436-7*); pap. 17.50 (*0-231-10437-5*) Col U Pr.

— A Lure of Knowledge: Lesbian Sexuality & Theory. Faderman, Lillian & Gross, Larry, eds. (Gay & Lesbian Ser.). 285p. (C). 1991. text 57.50 (*0-231-07486-7*) Col U Pr.

— A Lure of Knowledge: Lesbian Sexuality & Theory. Faderman, Lillian & Gross, Larry, eds. (Gay & Lesbian Ser.). 285p. (C). 1993. pap. 19.00 (*0-231-07487-5*) Col U Pr.

— Reproductions of Reproduction: Imaging Symbolic Change. LC 95-43749. 232p. (C). 1996. 75.00 (*0-415-91242-3*); pap. 21.99 (*0-415-91243-1*) Routledge.

Roof, Judith & Wiegman, Robyn. Who Can Speak? Authority & Critical Identity. LC 95-4115. 264p. 1995. pap. text 14.95 (*0-252-06487-9*) U of Ill Pr.

Roof, Judith & Wiegman, Robyn, eds. Who Can Speak? Authority & Critical Identity. LC 95-4115. 264p. 1995. text 32.50 (*0-252-02191-6*) U of Ill Pr.

Roof, Judith, jt. ed. see Burkman, Katherine H.

Roof, Judith, jt. ed. see Feldstein, Richard.

Roof, Larry. Professional Visual Basic for Windows CE Programming. LC 99-494990. 450p. 1998. pap. 49.99 (*1-86100-162-2*) Wrox Pr Inc.

— The Revolutionary Guide to Visual Basic 4 Professional. 700p. 1996. pap. 44.95 incl. cd-rom (*1-874416-37-0*) Wrox Pr Inc.

Roof, Wade C., ed. Contemporary American Religion, 2 Vols. LC 99-46712. (Illus.). 861p. 1999. 225.00 (*0-02-864928-1*) Mac Lib Ref.

— World Order & Religion. LC 90-45447. (SUNY Series in Religion, Culture, & Society). 328p. (C). 1991. pap. text 21.95 (*0-7914-0740-3*) State U NY Pr.

Roof, Wade C., jt. ed. see Ammerman, Nancy T.

***Roof, Wade Clark.** Spiritual Marketplace: Baby Boomers & the Remaking of American Religion. LC 99-22825. 360p. 1999. 24.95 (*0-691-01659-3*, Pub. by Princeton U Pr) Cal Prin Full Svc.

Roofer Magazine Editors, jt. auth. see Scharff, Robert.

Roohan, James E. American Catholics & the Social Question, 1865-1900. LC 76-6364. (Irish Americans Ser.). 1976. 41.95 (*0-405-09356-X*) Ayer.

Roohizadegan, Olya. Olya's Story: A Survivor's Dramatic Account of the Persecution of Baha in Revolutionary Iran. 238p. 1994. pap. 12.95 (*1-85168-073-X*, Pub. by Onewrld Pubns) Penguin Putnam.

Rooij, A. C. Van, see Buskes, Gerard & Van Rooij, A. C.

Rooij, A. J., et al. Neural Network Training Using Genetic Algorithms. LC 96-49415. (Series in Machine Perception & Artificial Intelligence). 1996. write for info. (*981-02-2919-4*) World Scientific Pub.

Roojen, Pepin Van, see Van Roojen, Pepin.

Rook, An. Judy's Own Pet Kitten. (Illus.). 26p. (J). 1991. pap. 4.50 (*0-921100-34-5*) Inhtce Pubns.

Rook, Arthur, et al. History of Addenbrooke's Hospital, Cambridge. (Illus.). 535p. (C). 1992. text 69.95 (*0-521-40529-7*) Cambridge U Pr.

***Rook, Deborah.** Distress for Rent. 300p. 1999. 45.00 (*1-85431-981-7*, Pub. by Blackstone Pr) Gaunt.

Rook, Dennis W., ed. see Levy, Sidney J.

Rook, Derek, jt. photos by see Broom, Michael.

Rook, E. C. & Rook, Lizzie J., compiled by. Child's Own Speaker. LC 71-116413. (Granger Index Reprint Ser.). 1977. 16.95 (*0-8369-6154-4*) Ayer.

Rook, E. C. & Rook, Lizzie J., eds. Drills & Marches. LC 75-116414. (Granger Index Reprint Ser.). 1977. 16.95 (*0-8369-6155-2*) Ayer.

— Young Folks' Entertainments: Comprising Many New & Novel Motion Songs, Charades, Pantomimes, Tableaux, Concert Recitations, Drills, etc., for Home - School Entertainment. LC 72-168787. (Granger Index Reprint Ser.). 1977. reprint ed. 17.95 (*0-8369-6307-5*) Ayer.
— Young People's Speaker: Designed for Young People of Twelve Years. LC 70-37019. (Granger Index Reprint Ser.). (YA). (gr. 7 up). 1977. reprint ed. 17.95 (*0-8369-6318-0*) Ayer.
Rook, Fern, jt. auth. see Brockmann, R. John.
Rook, Harry L., jt. ed. see Beard, Michael E.
Rook, Lance W. Federal Income Taxation of Banks & Financial Institutions. 6th ed. 1990. ring bd. 215.00 (*0-685-69566-2*, FITB) Warren Gorham & Lamont.
— Financial Management & Accounting for the Construction Industry, 2 vols. 1988. 180.00 (*0-8205-1153-6*) Bender.
— Tax Planning for the Alternative Minimum Tax. 1989. ring bd. 195.00 (*0-8205-1694-5*) Bender.
Rook, Lizzie J. & Goodfellow, E. J. Tiny Tot's Speaker. LC 73-160907. (Granger Index Reprint Ser.). (YA). (gr. 7 up). 1977. reprint ed. 17.95 (*0-8369-6271-0*) Ayer.
Rook, Lizzie J., jt. compiled by see Rook, E. C.
Rook, Lizzie J., jt. ed. see Rook, E. C.
Rook, P. F. & Carter, P. B. Offences Against the Person. (Criminal Law Library). 400p. 1991. 100.00 (*0-08-039202-4*, K130) Macmillan.
Rook, P. F. & Ward, R. Sexual Offences. (Waterlow Criminal Law Library). 320p. 1990. 72.01 (*0-685-33555-0*) Macmillan.
Rook, Tony. Roman Baths in Britain. (Archaeology Ser.: No. 69). (Illus.). 64p. 1989. pap. 10.50 (*0-7478-0157-6*, Pub. by Shire Pubns) Parkwest Pubns.
Rooke, Constance. Literature & the Modern World. 212p. (C). 1990. pap. 37.40 (*0-536-57833-8*) Pearson Custom.
Rooke, Constance. Writing Home: The Pen Canada Travel Anthology. LC 97-204811. 356p. 1997. pap. text 15.95 (*0-7710-6961-8*) McCland & Stewart.
Rooke, Constance, ed. Writing Away: The PEN Canada Travel Anthology. LC 95-109239. 304p. 1994. pap. 14.95 (*0-7710-6956-1*) McCland & Stewart.
Rooke, D. P., jt. auth. see Aliabadi, M. H.
***Rooke, Deborah W.** Zadok's Heirs: The Role & Development of the High Priesthood in Ancient Israel. (Oxford Theological Monographs). 280p. 2000. text 72.00 (*0-19-826998-6*) OUP.
Rooke, Denis, et al. Energy for the Future. LC 94-74709. (Technology in the Third Millennium Ser.). (Illus.). 240p. (C). 1995. 100.00 (*0-419-20050-9*, E & FN Spon) Routledge.
Rooke, John. An Inquiry into the Principles of National Wealth. LC 68-56573. (Reprints of Economic Classics Ser.). xii, 476p. 1969. reprint ed. 57.50 (*0-678-00566-4*) Kelley.
Rooke, Leon. The Broad Back of the Angel. LC 77-70901. 1977. 15.95 (*0-914590-42-1*); pap. 6.95 (*0-914590-43-X*) Fiction Coll.
— The Happiness of Others. 260p. 1991. pap. write for info. (*0-88984-125-X*) Porcup Quill.
— How I Saved the Province. 1989. pap. text 9.95 (*0-88982-089-9*, Pub. by Oolichan Bks) Genl Dist Srvs.
— Muffins. 24p. 1995. pap. write for info. (*0-88984-167-5*) Porcup Quill.
— Shakespeare's Dog. 176p. 1986. reprint ed. pap. 8.50 (*0-88001-093-2*) HarpC.
Rooke, Patricia T. & Schnell, R. L. Discarding the Asylum: From Child Rescue to the Welfare State in English-Canada (1800-1950) LC 83-10569. (Illus.). 510p. (Orig.). (C). 1983. pap. text 36.00 (*0-8191-3305-1*) U Pr of Amer.
Rooke, Patrick J. The Age of Dickens. LC 70-497201. (Documentary History Ser.). 128p. 1970. write for info. (*0-85340-009-1*) Wayland Pubs.
Rooke, Richard. Crossing the Border: And Other Poems. (Illus.). 48p. 1992. 25.00 (*0-930126-37-8*) Typographeum.
Rooke, Tetz. In My Childhood: A Study of Arabic Autobiography. LC 98-118475. (Stockholm Oriental Ser.: No. 15). 304p. 1997. pap. 52.50 (*91-22-01766-6*, Pub. by Almqvist Wiksell) Coronet Bks.
Rooker, Margaret, ed. see Davis, Carolyn O.
Rooker, Mark F. Biblical Hebrew in Transition: The Language of the Book of Ezekiel. (JSOT Supplement Ser.: No. 90). 222p. 1990. 65.00 (*1-85075-230-3*, Pub. by Sheffield Acad) CUP Services.
Rooker, Mark F. Leviticus-Numbers, Vol. 3. (The New American Commentary Ser.). 2000. 29.99 (*0-8054-0103-2*) Broadman.
***Rookes, Paul & Willson, Jane.** Perception: Theory, Development & Organisation. LC 99-57668. (Modular Psychology Ser.). 176p. (C). 1999. pap. write for info. (*0-415-19094-0*); text. write for info. (*0-415-19093-2*) Routledge.
Rookey, Peter M. The Scriptural Rosary of the Seven Sorrows of Our Blessed Lady (Servite Scriptural Rosary) 24p. 1995. pap. 3.00 (*0-9649001-0-6*) Marys Helpers.
Rookmaaker, H. R. Modern Art & the Death of a Culture. Chang, Robert, tr. (CHI.). 229p. 1985. pap. 8.50 (*1-56582-051-7*) Christ Renew Min.
— Modern Art & the Death of a Culture. LC 94-16587. 256p. 1994. reprint ed. pap. 15.99 (*0-89107-799-5*) Crossway Bks.
Rookmaaker, H. R., Jr. Towards a Romantic Conception of Nature: Coleridge's Poetry up to 1803. LC 84-24633. (Utrecht Publications in General & Comparative Literature Ser.: 20). ix, 214p. 1984. 71.00 (*90-272-2205-3*) J Benjamins Pubng Co.
— Towards a Romantic Conception of Nature: Coleridge's Poetry up to 1803. A Study of History of Ideas. LC 84-24633. (Utrecht Publications in General & Comparative Literature Ser.: 20). ix, 214p. 1984. pap. 37.00 (*90-272-2215-0*) J Benjamins Pubng Co.
Rookmaaker, L. C. Bibliography of the Rhinoceros. 312p. 1983. 112.00 (*90-6191-261-X*, Pub. by A A Balkema) Ashgate Pub Co.
— The Zoological Exploration of Southern Africa, 1650-1790. (Illus.). 392p. (C). 1989. text 165.00 (*90-6191-867-7*, Pub. by A A Balkema) Ashgate Pub Co.
***Rooks.** Paragraph Power: Communicating Ideas Through Paragraphs. 2nd ed. LC 98-31833. 224p. 1998. pap. text 22.00 (*0-13-660754-3*) P-H.
Rooks. Share Your Paragraph. 2nd ed. LC 98-22319. 1998. pap. text. write for info. (*0-13-660796-9*) P-H.
Rooks, Belvie, jt. ed. see Bomani, Asake.
Rooks, Brian, jt. auth. see Mortimer, John.
Rooks, Charles S. Rainbows & Reality: Selected Writings of the Author. Diamond, John C., ed. (Black Church Scholars Ser.: Vol. 1). 158p. (C). 1985. pap. 10.95 (*0-614-08303-6*) Jrnl Interdenom.
Rooks, George M. Can't Stop Talking. 2nd ed. 177p. (J). 1990. mass mkt. 15.00 (*0-8384-2914-9*, Newbury) Heinle & Heinle.
— Let's Start Talking: Conversation for High Beginning & Low Intermediate Students of English. LC 93-41508. 160p. (J). 1994. mass mkt. 15.00 (*0-8384-4825-9*) Heinle & Heinle.
— Non-Stop Discussion Workbook! Problems for Intermediate & Advanced Students of English. 2nd ed. 162p. (Orig.). (C). 1996. mass mkt. 15.00 (*0-8384-2938-6*, Newbury) Heinle & Heinle.
— Paragraph Power: Communicating Ideas Through Paragraphs. (Illus.). 128p. (C). 1989. pap. text 31.40 (*0-13-648585-5*) P-H.
— Share Your Paragraph: The Process Approach to Writing. (Illus.). 144p. (C). 1987. pap. text 25.00 (*0-13-808271-5*) P-H.
Rooks, James, ed. see Roscoe Pound Foundation Staff.
Rooks, James E., jt. auth. see Turley, Windle.
Rooks, James E., Jr., ed. see Roscoe Pound Foundation Staff.
Rooks, John. Love's Courtly Ethic in "The Faerie Queene" From Garden to Wilderness. LC 91-37408. (University of Kansas Humanistic Studies: Vol. 58). XIII, 244p. (C). 1992. text 38.95 (*0-8204-1708-4*) P Lang Pubng.
Rooks, Judith P. Midwifery & Childbirth in America. LC 97-12790. 592p. 1997. text 54.95 (*1-56639-565-8*) Temple U Pr.
— Midwifery & Childbirth in America. 592p. 1999. pap. 34.95 (*1-56639-711-1*) Temple U Pr.
Rooks, Marcus. Toy Steam Accessories. (Illus.). 32p. 1996. pap. 4.75 (*0-7478-0313-7*, Pub. by Shire Pubns) Parkwest Pubns.
Rooks, Noliwe M. Hair Raising: Beauty, Culture, & African American Women. LC 95-51395. (Illus.). 210p. (C). 1996. pap. 15.95 (*0-8135-2312-5*); text 38.00 (*0-8135-2311-7*) Rutgers U Pr.
Rooks, Robert. Spiritual Hand Grenades. (Illus.). 112p. 1997. pap. 10.00 (*0-8059-4166-5*) Dorrance.
Rooks, Robert L. & Jankowski, Connie. Canine Orthopedics. LC 96-49793. (Illus.). 288p. 1997. 27.95 (*0-87605-720-2*) Howell Bks.
Rooksby, Bikky, ed. Fast Forward: Lead Guitar Solos. (Illus.). 60p. 1998. pap. text 14.95 (*0-7119-7064-5*, AM950939) Omnibus NY.
Rooksby, Ricky. Classic Blues Guitar Licks. 64p. 1997. pap. 14.95 incl. cd-rom (*0-7119-4527-6*) Omnibus NY.
***Rooksby, Ricky.** Fast Foward- Rock Guitar Improvisation: Riffs, Chords & Tricks You Can Learn Today. (Illus.). 48p. 2000. pap. text 14.95 (*0-7119-7831-X*, AM953250) Music Sales.
Rooksby, Ricky, ed. Fast Forward: Finger Picking Guitar. (Illus.). 60p. (YA). 1998. pap. text 14.95 incl. audio compact disk (*0-7119-7051-3*, AM951159) Omnibus NY.
Rooksby, Rikki. A Complete Guide to the Music of Fleetwood Mac. (Illus.). 192p. 1998. pap. text 8.95 (*0-7119-6310-X*, OP47886) Omnibus NY.
Rooksby, Rikky. A. C. Swinburne: A Poet's Life. LC 96-29712. (Nineteenth Century Ser.). 336p. 1997. text 52.95 (*1-85928-069-2*, PR5513.R66, Pub. by Scolar Pr) Ashgate Pub Co.
— The Complete Guide to the Music of Madonna. (Illus.). 130p. 1998. pap. 8.95 (*0-7119-6311-8*, OP47885) Omnibus NY.
— Fast Forward: Acoustic Guitar Chords. (Illus.). 60p. 1998. pap. text 14.95 incl. audio compact disk (*0-7119-7065-3*, AM950940) Omnibus NY.
— First Guitar Blues Licks with CD (Audio) (First Guitar Ser.). 31p. 1999. pap. 11.95 (*0-7119-7262-1*, AM953227) Omnibus NY.
— First Guitar Lead Licks. (First Guitar Ser.). (Illus.). 31p. 1999. pap. 11.95 incl. audio compact disk (*0-7119-7261-3*, AM953216) Omnibus NY.
— First Guitar Power Chords. (First Guitar Ser.). (Illus.). 31p. 1999. pap. 11.95 incl. audio compact disk (*0-7119-7263-X*, AM953238) Omnibus NY.
— First Guitar Rhythm Patterns. (First Guitar Ser.). (Illus.). 31p. 1999. pap. 11.95 incl. audio compact disk (*0-7119-7264-8*, AM953249) Omnibus NY.
***Rooksby, Rikky.** How to Write Songs on Guitar: A Guitar-Playing & Songwriting Course. (Illus.). 192p. 2000. pap. 19.95 (*0-87930-611-4*) Miller Freeman.
Rooksby, Rikky. Killer Metal Lead Licks. 64p. 1997. pap. 14.95 incl. cd-rom (*0-7119-4530-6*) Omnibus NY.
— Lead Guitar Licks. 64p. 1997. pap. 14.95 incl. cd-rom (*0-7119-4524-1*) Omnibus NY.
Rooksby, Rikky & Shrimpton, Nicholas, eds. The Whole Music of Passion: New Essays on Swinburne. 300p. 1993. 74.95 (*0-85967-925-X*, Pub. by Scolar Pr) Ashgate Pub Co.
Rooley, Anthony. Performance: Revealing the Orpheus Within. 1993. pap. 13.95 (*1-85230-160-0*, Pub. by Element MA) Penguin Putnam.
Room, Adrian. African Placenames: Origins & Meanings of the Names for over 2000 Natural Features, Towns, Cities, Provinces & Countries. LC 93-40261. 245p. 1994. lib. bdg. 49.95 (*0-89950-943-6*) McFarland & Co.
— An Alphabetical Guide to the Language of Name Studies. LC 96-33729. 136p. 1996. 34.00 (*0-8108-3169-4*) Scarecrow.
***Room, Adrian.** Brewer's Dictionary of Phrase & Fable, 16e. 16th ed. 1326p. 2000. 50.00 (*0-06-019653-X*) HarpC.
Room, Adrian. Cassell Dictionary of Proper Names. LC 94-231872. 640p. 1994. 27.95 (*0-304-34447-8*, Pub. by Cassell) Sterling.
— Cassell Dictionary of Word Histories. 690p. 1999. 37.50 (*0-304-35007-9*) Continuum.
— A Concise Dictionary of Modern Place-Names in Great Britain & Ireland. LC 83-2472. (Oxford Paperback Reference Ser.). 192p. 1986. pap. write for info. (*0-19-281900-3*) OUP.
***Room, Adrian.** A Dictionary of Art Titles: The Origins of the Names & Titles of 3,000 Works of Art. LC 99-56537. 294p. 2000. 55.00 (*0-7864-0770-0*) McFarland & Co.
Room, Adrian. Dictionary of Astronomical Names. 1988. 27.50 (*0-415-01298-8*) Routledge.
***Room, Adrian.** Dictionary of Confusable Words. 250p. 2000. 30.00 (*1-57958-271-0*) Fitzroy Dearborn.
Room, Adrian. Dictionary of Contrasting Pairs. 492p. (C). 1988. text 35.00 (*0-415-00217-6*) Routledge.
***Room, Adrian.** The Dictionary of Foreign Words & Phrases in English. 384p. 1999. 29.95 (*0-304-35008-7*) Continuum.
Room, Adrian. A Dictionary of Irish Place Names. 2nd ed. LC 94-178808. 144p. 1997. reprint ed. pap. 13.95 (*0-86281-460-X*, Pub. by Appletree Pr) Irish Bks Media.
***Room, Adrian.** A Dictionary of Music Titles: The Origins of the Names & Titles of 3,500 Musical Compositions. LC 99-57638. 304p. 2000. 55.00 (*0-7864-0771-9*) McFarland & Co.
Room, Adrian. A Dictionary of Pseudonyms & Their Origins, with Stories of Name Changes. 3rd ed. LC 97-31640. 412p. 1998. lib. bdg. 55.00 (*0-7864-0423-X*) McFarland & Co.
— Dictionary of Trade Name Origins. 1990. 39.95 (*0-7102-0174-5*, Routledge Thoemms) Routledge.
— Dictionary of Trade Name Origins. rev. ed. (Illus.). 220p. 1994. 39.95 (*0-8442-3190-8*, Natl Textbk Co) NTC Contemp Pub Co.
— Dictionary of Translated Names & Titles. 336p. 1986. 57.50 (*0-7100-9953-3*, Routledge Thoemms) Routledge.
— Dictionary of World Place-Names Derived from English Names. (Illus.). 272p. 1989. 35.00 (*0-415-02811-6*) Routledge.
— Dunces, Gourmands & Petticoats: 1,300 Words Whose Meanings Have Changed Through the Ages. (Artful Wordsmith Ser.). (Illus.). 304p. 1998. pap. 12.95 (*0-8442-0921-X*, 0921X) NTC Contemp Pub Co.
— Fascinating Origins of Everyday Words. LC 97-17219. (Artful Wordsmith Ser.). 208p. 1997. pap. 12.95 (*0-8442-0910-4*) NTC Contemp Pub Co.
— Literally Entitled: A Dictionary of the Origins of the Titles of over 1,300 Major Literary Works of the Nineteenth & Twentieth Century. LC 95-38299. 255p. 1996. lib. bdg. 48.50 (*0-7864-0110-9*) McFarland & Co.
— The Naming of Animals: An Appellative Reference to Domestic, Work & Show Animals Real & Fictional. LC 92-56684. 244p. 1993. lib. bdg. 42.50 (*0-89950-795-6*) McFarland & Co.
— NTC Dictionary of Word Origins. (Illus.). 194p. 1994. pap. 12.95 (*0-8442-5179-8*, 51798, Natl Textbk Co) NTC Contemp Pub Co.
— NTC's Classical Dictionary. 252p. 1994. 29.95 (*0-8442-5473-8*, Natl Textbk Co) NTC Contemp Pub Co.
— NTC's Dictionary of Changes in Meaning: A Comprehensive Reference to the Major Changes in Meanings in English Words. (Illus.). 304p. 1994. 29.95 (*0-8442-5136-4*) NTC Contemp Pub Co.
— NTC's Dictionary of Changes in Meaning: A Comprehensive Reference to the Major Changes in Meanings in English Words. (Illus.). 304p. 1995. pap. text 14.95 (*0-8442-5135-6*) NTC Contemp Pub Co.
— NTC's Dictionary of World Origins. (Illus.). 194p. 1993. 19.95 (*0-8442-5137-2*, 51372, Natl Textbk Co) NTC Contemp Pub Co.
— Placenames of Russia & the Former Soviet Union: Origins & Meanings of the Names for over 2000 Natural Features, Towns, Regions & Countries. LC 96-1916. 288p. 1996. lib. bdg. 58.50 (*0-7864-0042-0*) McFarland & Co.
— Placenames of the World: Origins & Meanings of the Names for over 5,000 Natural Features, Countries, Capitals, Territories, Cities & Historic Sites. LC 97-38011. 441p. 1997. lib. bdg. 65.00 (*0-7864-0172-9*) McFarland & Co.
— Trade Name Origins. LC 97-20606. (Artful Wordsmith Ser.). 224p. 1997. pap. 12.95 (*0-8442-0904-X*) NTC Contemp Pub Co.
— Who's Who in Classical Mythology. (Illus.). 352p. 1996. 16.95 (*0-8442-5469-X*, 5469X, Natl Textbk Co) NTC Contemp Pub Co.
Room, Adrian, compiled by. Place-Name Changes, 1900-1991. LC 93-5159. 322p. 1993. 45.00 (*0-8108-2600-3*) Scarecrow.
Room, Adrian, ed. see Evans, Ivor H.
Room, Robin, jt. auth. see Cahalan, Don.
***Rooman, Lily.** Chakras. 1999. pap. 4.95 (*965-494-036-1*) Astrolog Pub.
Roomans, G. M., jt. auth. see Malecki, M.
Roomans, Godfried M. & Forslind, Bo, eds. Cell Structure & Cell Function: A Symposium in Honor of Bjorn Afzelius on His Sixtieth Birthday Stockholm, Dec. 1985. (Illus.). vi, 138p. 1988. pap. text 23.00 (*0-931288-38-X*) Scanning Microscopy.
Roomans, Godfried M., ed. see Murphy, Judith A.
Roome. Mehndi. LC 98-3362. 128p. 1998. pap. 16.95 (*0-312-18743-2*) St Martin.
Roome, D. Faith, Hope & Cyanide. 1973. pap. 3.50 (*0-87129-085-5*, F10) Dramatic Pub.
Roome, Diana R., jt. auth. see Gluckman, Perry.
Roome, Nigel J. Management & Business. LC 94-33847. (Environmental Agenda Ser.). 80p. (C). 1994. pap. 8.95 (*0-7453-0925-9*, Pub. by Pluto GBR) Stylus Pub VA.
Roome, Nigel J., ed. Sustainability Strategies for Industry: The Future of Corporate Practice. LC 98-22500. 208p. 1998. text 55.00 (*1-55963-598-3*); pap. text 30.00 (*1-55963-599-1*) Island Pr.
Roome, William D., jt. auth. see Gehani, Narain.
Roomkin, Myron J., ed. Managers As Employees: An International Comparison of the Changing Character of Managerial Employment. 304p. 1989. text 65.00 (*0-19-504322-7*) OUP.
— Profit Sharing & Gain Sharing. LC 90-8777. (Institute of Management & Labor Relations Ser.: No. 2). (Illus.). 190p. 1990. 35.00 (*0-8108-2335-7*) Scarecrow.
Roomy, David. Inner Journey to Sacred Places. LC 96-69359. 140p. (Orig.). 1997. pap. 13.95 (*1-57197-035-5*) Pentland Pr.
Rooney, A., jt. ed. see Albert, Michelle.
Rooney, Andrew A. And More by Andy Rooney. 256p. 1991. reprint ed. pap. 9.95 (*0-02-010202-X*) Macmillan.
— A Few Minutes with Andy Rooney. 1987. mass mkt. 4.95 (*0-446-34766-3*, Pub. by Warner Bks) Little.
— A Few Minutes with Andy Rooney. (Illus.). 272p. 1991. reprint ed. pap. 9.95 (*0-02-010201-1*) Macmillan.
— Pieces of My Mind. 1985. mass mkt. 4.95 (*0-380-69885-4*, Avon Bks) Morrow Avon.
— Sweet & Sour. large type ed. LC 92-40343. (Basic Ser.). 350p. 1993. reprint ed. lib. bdg. 22.95 (*1-56054-628-X*) Thorndike Pr.
Rooney, Andy. The Most of Andy Rooney. 784p. 1990. 14.98 (*0-88365-765-1*) Galahad Bks.
***Rooney, Andy.** My War. (Illus.). 2000. 20.00 (*1-58648-010-3*) PublicAffairs NY.
Rooney, Andy. Sincerely, Andy Rooney. LC 99-43726. 336p. 1999. 23.00 (*1-891620-34-7*, Pub. by PublicAffairs NY) HarpC.
***Rooney, Andy.** Sincerely, Andy Rooney. large type ed. LC 00-21194. (Americana Series). 435p. 2000. 28.95 (*0-7862-2483-5*) Thorndike Pr.
Rooney, Anne. Hunting in Middle English Literature. 221p. (C). 1993. 75.00 (*0-85991-379-1*) Boydell & Brewer.
Rooney, Charles J., Jr. Dreams & Visions: A Study of American Utopias, 1865-1917, 77. LC 84-8932. (Contributions in American Studies: No. 77). (Illus.). 209p. 1985. 55.00 (*0-313-23727-1*, RUL/, Greenwood Pr) Greenwood.
Rooney, Cynthia J., jt. auth. see Fiorelli, Paul E.
Rooney, D. E. & Czepulkowski, B. H. Human Chromosome Preparation: Essential Techniques. LC 96-38485. 154p. 1997. pap. 49.95 (*0-471-96299-6*) Wiley.
Rooney, D. E. & Czepulkowski, B. H., eds. Human Cytogenetics: A Practical Approach, 2 vols. Vols. I-II. (Illus.). 1992. 60.00 (*0-318-69015-2*); pap. 40.00 (*0-318-69016-0*) OUP.
— Human Cytogenetics: A Practical Approach, 2 vols., II. (Practical Approach Ser.: Vols. I-II). (Illus.). 320p. 1992. 85.00 (*0-19-963290-1*) OUP.
— Human Cytogenetics: Essential Data. LC 94-30736. (Essential Data Ser.). 128p. 1995. pap. 39.95 (*0-471-95076-9*) Wiley.
***Rooney, David.** Military Mavericks: Extraordinary Men of Battle. (Illus.). 2000. 27.95 (*0-304-35316-7*) Continuum.
***Rooney, David A., et al.** Guide to Divorce Taxation, Vol. 1. 1999. 79.00 (*0-7646-0794-4*) Prctnrs Pub Co.
***Rooney, Dawn.** Angkor. 3rd ed. 1999. pap. 19.95 (*962-217-601-1*) Norton.
Rooney, Dawn. Angkor: Temples of Cambodia's Kings. (Illus.). 256p. 1994. pap. 15.95 (*0-8442-9888-3*, Passprt Bks) NTC Contemp Pub Co.
***Rooney, Dawn F.** Angkor. 4th rev. ed. (Illus.). 2000. pap. 19.95 (*962-217-683-6*) China Guides.
Rooney, Dawn F. Folk Pottery in South-East Asia. (Images of Asia Ser.). (Illus.). 88p. 1988. 18.95 (*0-19-588866-9*) OUP.
Rooney, Dawn F., ed. see Khoo, Joo E.
Rooney, Diane, ed. The Hidden Link: Energy & Economic Development. 86p. (Orig.). 1987. pap. 15.00 (*1-55657-003-1*) Pub Tech Inc.
Rooney, E. Gene. Amphorae: Metaphoric Techniques for Understanding, Enhancing, & Improving Your Self-Image. 244p. (Orig.). 1993. student ed. 35.00 (*1-881596-03-6*) L E A D Cnslts.
— Listening with the Mind's Inner Ear: The Value of Metaphors in Forming & Developing Belief Systems & Attitudes. 165p. (Orig.). 1993. student ed. 25.00 (*1-881596-02-8*) L E A D Cnslts.
— Metaphors for Metamorphosis: The Power of Metaphors & Personal Story. 2nd ed. 94p. reprint ed. student ed. 20.00 (*1-881596-04-4*) L E A D Cnslts.
— The Simon Syndrome: A Wholistic Metaphoric Approach to 20th Century Problems of Leaders, Leading & Leadership. 507p. (Orig.). 1995. 45.00 (*1-881596-06-0*) L E A D Cnslts.
— Speaking Heart to Heart: Metaphors & Parables As a Communication Form. 102p. (Orig.). 1993. student ed. 20.00 (*1-881596-01-X*) L E A D Cnslts.
— When the Bough Breaks: Metaphors & Meanings about

An Asterisk (*) at the beginning of an entry indicates that the title is appearing for the first time.

Institutional Problems & Dysfunctional Organizations. (Illus.). 384p. (Orig.). Date not set. student ed. 35.00 (*1-881596-05-2*) L E A D Cnslts.

Rooney, Ellen. Seductive Reasoning: Pluralism as the Problematic of Contemporary Literary Theory. LC 88-47917. 288p. 1989. 39.95 (*0-8014-2192-6*) Cornell U Pr.

Rooney, Frances. Our Lives: Lesbian Personal Writings. 280p. (Orig.). 1991. pap. 14.95 (*0-929005-21-X*, Pub. by Sec Story Pr) LPC InBook.

Rooney Heuer, Ann. Creating the Peaceful Home. LC 99-18464. 1999. text 35.00 (*1-56799-799-6*, Friedman-Fairfax) M Friedman Pub Grp Inc.

***Rooney Heuer, Ann.** Sponge Painting. (Illus.). 2000. pap. 14.95 (*1-86108-134-0*) Guild Master.

Rooney, James. Bossmen: Bill Monroe & Muddy Waters. (Quality Paperbacks Ser.). (Illus.). 163p. 1991. reprint ed. pap. 11.95 (*0-306-80427-1*) Da Capo.

— The Demon Cat. (Short Play Ser.). 1974. pap. 1.00 (*0-912262-34-6*) Proscenium.

— The Lame Horse. (Illus.). 237p. 1984. reprint ed. text 19.95 (*0-914327-04-6*) Breakthrgh NY.

Rooney, James F., jt. auth. see Frederickson, Jon.

Rooney, James R. The Lame Horse. LC 97-39892. 1997. 29.95 (*0-929346-55-6*) R Meerdink Co Ltd.

— Lame Horse - Causes, Symptoms & Treatment. 1975. pap. 15.00 (*0-87980-308-8*) Wilshire.

Rooney, James R. & Robertson, John L. Equine Pathology. LC 96-4630. (Illus.). 368p. 1996. text 119.95 (*0-8138-2334-X*) Iowa St U Pr.

Rooney, James W., ed. see Haas, Wilbur H., et al.

Rooney, Jim. Organizing the South Bronx. LC 93-49671. (SUNY Series, the New Inequalities). 283p. (C). 1994. text 57.50 (*0-7914-2209-7*); pap. text 23.95 (*0-7914-2210-0*) State U NY Pr.

Rooney, Jim, jt. auth. see Von Schmidt, Eric.

Rooney, John. Khabar Gembira: A History of the Catholic Church in East Malaysia & Brunei, 1880-1976. 316p. 1994. pap. 36.00 (*0-86012-122-4*, Pub. by Srch Pr) St Mut.

— Struggling to Be Prophets: The Mill Hill Missionaries in North America, 1871-1985. 188p. 1991. pap. 10.00 (*0-317-04686-1*) Mill Hill Fthrs.

Rooney, John, tr. see Thomas, a Kempis.

Rooney, John F. The Recruiting Game: Toward a New System of Intercollegiate Sports. 2nd rev. ed. LC 86-19152. 254p. reprint ed. pap. 78.80 (*0-7837-6177-5*, 204589900009) Bks Demand.

Rooney, John W., Jr. Revolt in the Netherlands: Brussels, 1830. 250p. (C). 1982. pap. text 17.50 (*0-87291-156-X*) Coronado Pr.

Rooney, John W., Jr., et al. New Perspectives on the Belgian Revolution. 338p. 1994. 35.00 (*0-87291-204-3*); pap. text 17.50 (*0-87291-208-6*) Coronado Pr.

Rooney, Liam & Christini, Ed. Wreck Diving: The Diver's Field Guide to Wreck Exploration Procedures. 31p. 1986. pap. text 5.50 (*0-943717-29-9*) Concept Sys.

Rooney, Liam & Hardy, Jon. Boat Diving: The Diver's Field Guide to Planning & Procedures for Diving from Boats. 27p. 1986. pap. text 5.50 (*0-943717-30-2*) Concept Sys.

Rooney, Lisa, jt. auth. see Bell, Alison.

Rooney, Lucy & Faricy, Robert S. Lord Jesus, Teach Me to Pray: A 7 Week Course in Personal Prayer. 2nd ed. LC 95-68113. 111p. 1994. pap. 5.95 (*1-882972-55-4*) Queenship Pub.

— Medjugorje Journal: Mary Speaks to the World. (Illus.). 200p. (Orig.). 1988. reprint ed. pap. 9.50 (*0-8199-0916-5*, Frncscn Herld) Franciscan Pr.

— Medjugorje Up-Close: Mary Speaks to the World. 105p. 1986. pap. 5.95 (*0-8199-0902-5*, Frncscn Herld) Franciscan Pr.

Rooney, Lucy, jt. auth. see Faricy, Robert.

Rooney, Lucy, jt. auth. see Faricy, Robert S.

Rooney, Lucy, jt. auth. see Faricy, RobertS.

Rooney, Margaret, jt. auth. see Harms, Richard.

Rooney, Margaret, jt. auth. see Rogerson, John.

***Rooney, Marijo T.** Administration Manual for the ChIPS & ChIPS. LC 99-25644. 1999. 24.95 (*0-88048-849-2*) Am Psychiatric.

Rooney, Mickey. The Search for Sonny Skies: A Novel. large type ed. LC 95-2631. 314p. 1995. lib. bdg. 22.95 (*0-7838-1254-X*, G K Hall Lrg Type) Mac Lib Ref.

— The Search for Sunny Skies: A Novel. LC 93-44187. 1994. 19.95 (*1-55972-231-2*, Birch Ln Pr) Carol Pub Group.

Rooney, Miriam T. Lawlessness, Law & Sanction: A Dissertation. (Catholic University of America Philosophical Studies: Vol. XXXIV). 176p. 1982. reprint ed. 34.00 (*0-8377-1036-7*, Rothman) W S Hein.

Rooney, Pat, Jr., jt. auth. see Doty, Betty.

Rooney, Paul. Divine Command Morality. (Avebury Series in Philosophy). 134p. 1997. text 63.95 (*1-85972-505-8*, Pub. by Avebury) Ashgate Pub Co.

Rooney, Rebecca, ed. see Getz, Lowell.

Rooney, Richard, ed. see Paul, Jan.

Rooney, Robert & Lipuma, Anthony. Learn to Be the Master Student: How to Develop Self-Confidence & Effective Study Skills. LC 92-80281. (Illus.). 248p. (Orig.). (YA). (gr. 9-12). 1992. pap. 14.95 (*0-9632530-8-5*) Maydale Pub.

Rooney, Robert C. Equal Opportunity in the United States: A Symposium on Civil Rights. 185p. 1973. pap. 3.00 (*0-89940-400-6*) LBJ Sch Pub Aff.

Rooney, Ronald H. Strategies for Work with Involuntary Clients. (Illus.). 392p. 1992. text 76.00 (*0-231-06768-2*); pap. text 29.00 (*0-231-06769-0*) Col U Pr.

Rooney, Seamus A. Lung Surfactant: Cellular & Molecular Processing. LC 98-9173. (Molecular Biology Intelligence Unit Ser.). 227p. 1998. pap. 99.00 (*1-57059-479-1*) Landes Bioscience.

Rooney, Terrie M. Contemporary Theatre, Film & Television, Vol. 14. 450p. 1995. text 155.00 (*0-8103-9373-3*) Gale.

Rooney, Terrie M., ed. Contemporary Theatre, Film & Television, Vol. 13. 450p. 1995. text 155.00 (*0-8103-5729-1*, 070831) Gale.

Rooney, Thomas. Fine Arts: Humanities. 56p. 1989. pap. 8.95 (*0-8106-0302-0*) NEA.

Rooney, Victor M., jt. auth. see Ismail, Amin R.

Rooney, William. Infidelity. LC 98-29849. 218p. 1998. 24.95 (*0-7890-0621-9*) Haworth Pr.

— Infidelity. 1999. pap. 17.95 (*1-56023-946-8*) Haworth Pr.

Rooney, William. Rooney's Shorts. LC 99-10329. 138p. 2000. pap. 14.95 (*0-7890-0719-3*, Harrington Park) Haworth Pr.

***Rooney, William.** Rooney's Shorts. LC 99-10329. 137p. (C). 2000. 39.95 (*1-56023-954-9*, Harrington Park); pap. 14.95 (*1-56023-150-5*, Harrington Park) Haworth Pr.

Rooney, William J. The Problem of "Poetry & Belief" in Contemporary Criticism. LC 50-2632. 175p. reprint ed. pap. 54.30 (*0-608-18715-1*, 202949400061) Bks Demand.

Roonwal, G. S. The Indian Ocean: Exploitable Mineral & Petroleum Resources. (Illus.). 235p. 1986. 112.95 (*0-387-16881-8*) Spr-Verlag.

Roonwal, M. L. Termite Life & Termite Control in Tropical South Asia. 117p. (C). 1979. 80.00 (*81-85046-02-6*, Pub. by Scientific) St Mut.

Roonwal, Mithan L. & Mohnot, S. M. Primates of South Asia: Ecology, Sociobiology, & Behavior. LC 76-28309. (Illus.). 442p. reprint ed. pap. 137.10 (*0-7837-4184-7*, 205903400012) Bks Demand.

***Roop, Connie.** Diary of David K. Leeper: Rushing for Gold. (In My Own Words Ser.). (Illus.). 2000. 24.21 (*0-7614-1011-2*, Benchmark NY) Marshall Cavendish.

— Diary of Joseph Plumb Martin: A Revolutionary War Soldier. (In My Own Words Ser.). (Illus.). 2000. 24.21 (*0-7614-1014-7*, Benchmark NY) Marshall Cavendish.

Roop, Connie. Goodbye for Today. 1999. pap. 4.99 (*0-14-037703-4*, Viking) Viking Penguin.

***Roop, Connie.** Let's Celebrate Thanksgiving. LC 98-51380. (Illus.). 32p. (J). (gr. 1-3). 1999. 19.90 (*0-7613-0973-X*, Copper Beech Bks) Millbrook Pr.

Roop, Connie. Let's Celebrate Valentine's Day. LC 98-13971. (Illus.). 32p. (J). (gr. k-3). 1999. lib. bdg. 21.90 (*0-7613-0972-1*, Copper Beech Bks) Millbrook Pr.

— My Captivity. 64p. 1999. pap. 4.99 (*0-14-037719-0*, Viking) Viking Penguin.

***Roop, Connie & Roop, Peter.** Benjamin Franklin. LC 00-23183. (In Their Own Words Ser.). (Illus.). (J). 2000. write for info. (*0-439-15806-0*) Scholastic Inc.

— Christopher Columbus. LC 99-88546. (In Their Own Words Ser.). (Illus.). (J). 2000. write for info. (*0-439-15807-9*) Scholastic Inc.

Roop, Connie & Roop, Peter. Let's Celebrate Valentine's Day. LC 98-13971. (Illus.). 32p. (J). (gr. k-3). 1999. pap. 5.95 (*0-7613-0428-2*, Copper Beech Bks) Millbrook Pr.

— Walk on the Wild Side. LC 96-7708. (Illus.). 40p. (J). (gr. 3-6). 1997. lib. bdg. 21.40 (*0-7613-0021-X*) Millbrook Pr.

Roop, Connie & Roop, Peter, eds. Pilgrim Voices: Our First Year in the New World. LC 95-10114. (Illus.). 48p. (J). (gr. 3-7). 1997. 16.95 (*0-8027-8314-7*); pap. 7.95 (*0-8027-7530-6*); lib. bdg. 17.85 (*0-8027-8315-5*) Walker & Co.

***Roop, Connie, et al.** Endurance: Shackleton's Escape from the Ice. LC 00-26557. (Hello Reader! Ser.). 2001. pap. write for info. (*0-439-20640-5*) Scholastic Inc.

— Let's Celebrate Thanksgiving. LC 98-51380. (Books for Halloween & Thanksgiving Ser.). 32p. (J). (gr. k-3). 1999. 5.95 (*0-7613-0429-0*, Copper Beech Bks) Millbrook Pr.

Roop, Connie, jt. auth. see Roop, Peter.

Roop, Connie, ed. see Columbus, Christopher.

Roop, Connie, jt. ed. see Roop, Peter.

Roop, D. Haigh, jt. auth. see Cornyn, William S.

Roop, Edward. Best Deal for New Wheels. 1992. pap. 3.99 (*0-425-13585-3*) Berkley Pub.

— Best Deals for New Wheels. 144p. (Orig.). 1992. mass mkt. 3.99 (*0-425-13473-3*) Berkley Pub.

Roop, Eugene F. Esther. LC 96-34467. (Covenant Bible Studies). 1997. 5.95 (*0-87178-002-X*) Brethren.

— Genesis. LC 87-10969. (Believers Church Bible Commentary Ser.: Vol. 2). 352p. (Orig.). 1987. pap. 21.99 (*0-8361-3443-5*) Herald Pr.

— Heard in Our Land. LC 91-25132. (Illus.). 112p. 1991. reprint ed. pap. 34.80 (*0-608-04180-7*, 206491500011) Bks Demand.

— Let the Rivers Run: Stewardship & the Biblical Story. fac. ed. LC 91-26338. (Library of Christian Stewardship). 120p. (Orig.). 1991. reprint ed. pap. 37.20 (*0-7837-7972-0*, 204772800008) Bks Demand.

Roop, Mike & Wright, Richie. Confined Space & Structural Rescue. 1997. student ed. write for info. (*0-8151-7340-7*) Mosby Inc.

Roop, Mike & Wright, Richie. Industrial & Confined Space Rescue. LC 97-22071. (Illus.). 400p. (gr. 13). 1998. pap. text 35.95 (*0-8151-7383-0*, 27761) Mosby Inc.

Roop, Peter. Ahyoka & the Talking Leaves. (J). 1994. 10.15 (*0-606-06166-5*, Pub. by Turtleback) Demco.

Roop, Peter. The Buffalo Jump. LC 95-39417. (Illus.). 32p. (J). (gr. 1-3). 1996. lib. bdg. 14.95 (*0-87358-616-6*, Rising Moon Bks) Northland AZ.

***Roop, Peter.** An Eye for an Eye: A Story of the Revolutionary War. (Jamestown's American Portraits Ser.). 144p. 2000. pap. 5.95 (*0-8092-0628-5*, 06285E, Jamestwn Pub) NTC Contemp Pub Co.

Roop, Peter. Greece: Peter & Connie Roop. LC 98-12450. (ps-3). 1998. 19.92 (*1-57572-709-9*) Heinemann Lib.

— If You Lived with the Cherokee. LC 98-206156. (Illus.). 80p. (J). (gr. 2-5). 1998. pap. 5.99 (*0-590-95606-X*) Scholastic Inc.

— Keep the Lights Burning, Abbie. (Carolrhoda on My Own Bks.). 1987. 11.15 (*0-606-12385-7*, Pub. by Turtleback) Demco.

***Roop, Peter.** Let's Celebrate Thanksgiving. (Illus.). (J). 1999. 11.40 (*0-606-18293-4*) Turtleback.

Roop, Peter. Little Blaze & the Buffalo Jump. (Indian Culture Ser.). (Illus.). 28p. (Orig.). (J). (gr. 3-8). 1984. pap. 4.95 (*0-89992-089-6*) Coun India Ed.

— Natosi: Strong Medicine. 32p. (J). (gr. 3-8). 1984. pap. 4.95 (*0-89992-090-X*) Coun India Ed.

— Sik-Ki-Mi. (Indian Culture Ser.). 32p. (J). (gr. 3-6). 1984. pap. 4.95 (*0-89992-091-8*) Coun India Ed.

Roop, Peter & Roop, Connie. Ahyoka & the Talking Leaves. LC 91-3036. (Illus.). 48p. (J). (gr. 1 up). 1992. 15.00 (*0-688-10697-8*) Lothrop.

— Ahyoka & the Talking Leaves. Cohn, Amy, ed. LC 91-30366. (Illus.). 64p. (J). (gr. 4-7). 1994. reprint ed. mass mkt. 4.95 (*0-688-13082-8*, Wm Morrow) Morrow Avon.

***Roop, Peter & Roop, Connie.** Brazil. LC 97-37236. (Illus.). 32p. (J). 1998. 19.92 (*1-57572-125-2*) Heinemann Lib.

Roop, Peter & Roop, Connie. Buttons for General Washington. LC 86-6120. (Carolrhoda On My Own Bks.). (Illus.). 48p. (J). (gr. k-3). 1986. pap. 5.95 (*0-87614-476-8*, Carolrhoda); lib. bdg. 18.60 (*0-87614-294-3*, Lerner Publctns) Lerner Pub.

***Roop, Peter & Roop, Connie.** China. LC 97-37921. (Illus.). 32p. (ps-4). 1998. 19.92 (*1-57572-123-6*) Heinemann Lib.

— A City. LC 98-14933. (Walk Around Ser.). 32p. (J). 1999. 21.36 (*1-57572-129-5*) Heinemann Lib.

— A City Album. LC 98-15553. (Long Ago & Today Ser.). (Illus.). 24p. (J). 1999. 19.92 (*1-57572-600-9*) Heinemann Lib.

Roop, Peter & Roop, Connie. Martin Luther King, Jr. LC 97-13732. (Lives & Times Ser.). (J). (gr. 2-4). 1998. 19.92 (*1-57572-560-6*) Heinemann Lib.

***Roop, Peter & Roop, Connie.** Egypt. LC 97-37920. (Illus.). 32p. (gr. 2-4). 1998. 19.92 (*1-57572-122-8*) Heinemann Lib.

— A Farm Album. LC 98-18059. (Long Ago & Today Ser.). (Illus.). 24p. (J). 1999. lib. bdg. 19.92 (*1-57572-601-7*) Heinemann Lib.

Roop, Peter & Roop, Connie. A Farming Town. LC 98-14917. (Walk Around Ser.). (Illus.). 32p. (J). 1998. 21.36 (*1-57572-127-9*) Heinemann Lib.

***Roop, Peter & Roop, Connie.** Girl of the Shining Mountains: Sacagawea's Story. LC 99-24227. 178p. (J). (gr. 3-7). 1999. 14.99 (*0-7868-0492-0*, Pub. by Hypm Child) Time Warner.

— Good Eye for Today: The Diary of a Young Girl at Sea. LC 99-27034. (J). (gr. 4-6). 2000. 16.00 (*0-689-82222-7*) Atheneum Yung Read.

Roop, Peter & Roop, Connie. Grace's Letter to Lincoln. LC 98-11259. (Illus.). 64p. (J). (gr. 3-4). 1998. pap. 3.95 (*0-7868-1296-6*, Pub. by Hyprn Child); lib. bdg. 14.49 (*0-7868-2375-5*, Pub. by Hyprn Child) Little.

***Roop, Peter & Roop, Connie.** A Home Album. LC 98-17900. (Long Ago & Today Ser.). (Illus.). 24p. (J). 1998. lib. bdg. 19.92 (*1-57572-602-5*) Heinemann Lib.

Roop, Peter & Roop, Connie. India. LC 98-12451. (Visit to Ser.). (Illus.). 32p. (J). 1998. 13.95 (*1-57572-710-2*) Heinemann Lib.

***Roop, Peter & Roop, Connie.** Israel. LC 98-12449. (Illus.). 32p. (J). 1998. 19.92 (*1-57572-711-0*) Heinemann Lib.

Roop, Peter & Roop, Connie. Japan. LC 98-12448. (Visit to Ser.). (Illus.). 32 p. (J). 1998. 13.95 (*1-57572-712-9*) Heinemann Lib.

— Keep the Lights Burning, Abbie. LC 84-27446. (Carolrhoda On My Own Bks.). (Illus.). 40p. (J). (gr. k-3). 1985. lib. bdg. 18.60 (*0-87614-275-7*, Carolrhoda) Lerner Pub.

— Keep the Lights Burning, Abbie. LC 84-27446. (Carolrhoda on My Own Bks.). (Illus.). 40p. (J). (ps-3). 1985. pap. 5.95 (*0-87614-454-7*, Lerner Publctns) Lerner Pub.

— Keep the Lights Burning, Abbie. unabridged ed. (Illus.). (J). (gr. 2-4). 1989. 24.95 incl. audio (*0-87499-135-8*); pap. 15.95 incl. audio (*0-87499-134-X*) Live Oak Media.

— Keep the Lights Burning, Abbie, 4 bks., Set. unabridged ed. (Illus.). (J). (gr. 2-4). 1989. pap., teacher ed. 33.95 incl. audio (*0-87499-136-6*) Live Oak Media.

— Let's Celebrate Christmas. LC 97-4268. (Illus.). 32p. (J). (gr. k-3). 1997. lib. bdg. 19.90 (*0-7613-0115-1*) Millbrook Pr.

— Let's Celebrate Halloween. LC 96-36466. (Illus.). 32p. (J). (gr. k-3). 1997. pap. 5.95 (*0-7613-0284-0*); lib. bdg. 19.90 (*0-7613-0113-5*) Millbrook Pr.

***Roop, Peter & Roop, Connie.** Long Ago & Today Series, 4 bks. 24p. 1999. 79.68 (*1-57572-604-1*) Heinemann Lib.

Roop, Peter & Roop, Connie. Off the Map: The Journals of Lewis & Clark. LC 92-18340. (Illus.). 48p. (J). (gr. 3-7). 1993. 14.95 (*0-8027-8207-8*) Walker & Co.

— Sacagawea. LC 99-24227. (Illus.). 144p. (J). (gr. 3-7). 1999. lib. bdg. 15.49 (*0-7868-2422-0*, Pub. by Hyperion) Little.

***Roop, Peter & Roop, Connie.** Sacagawea. (Illus.). 208p. (J). (gr. 3-7). 1999. pap. 5.99 (*0-7868-1323-7*, Pub. by Hyprn Child) Little.

— A School Album. LC 98-17899. (Long Ago & Today Ser.). (Illus.). 24p. (J). 1999. lib. bdg. 19.92 (*1-57572-603-3*) Heinemann Lib.

Roop, Peter & Roop, Connie. Seasons of the Cranes. (Illus.). 32p. (J). (gr. 4-7). 1989. 14.95 (*0-8027-6859-8*); lib. bdg. 15.85 (*0-8027-6860-1*) Walker & Co.

— Stick Out Your Tongue! Jokes about Doctors & Patients. (Make Me Laugh! Joke Bks.). (Illus.). 32p. (J). (gr. 1-4). 1986. pap. 2.95 (*0-8225-9546-X*, Lerner Publctns) Lerner Pub.

***Roop, Peter & Roop, Connie.** A Suburb. LC 98-14934. (Walk Around Ser.). 32p. (J). 1999. 21.36 (*1-57572-130-9*) Heinemann Lib.

Roop, Peter & Roop, Connie. Susan B. Anthony. LC 97-13731. (Lives & Times Ser.). (J). 1998. 21.36 (*1-57572-563-0*) Heinemann Lib.

— A Town. LC 98-14918. (Walk Around Ser.). 1998. write for info. (*1-57572-128-7*) Heinemann Lib.

***Roop, Peter & Roop, Connie.** Up to the Challenge. LC 00-38612. 2001. write for info. (*0-689-83022-X*) Atheneum Yung Read.

— Vietnam. LC 97-37919. (Illus.). 32p. (ps-4). 1998. 19.92 (*1-57572-120-1*) Heinemann Lib.

— Walk Around Series, 4 bks. 32p. 1999. 85.44 (*1-57572-126-0*) Heinemann Lib.

Roop, Peter & Roop, Connie. Westward, Ho, Ho, Ho! (Illus.). 48p. (J). (gr. 3-6). 1996. lib. bdg. 21.90 (*0-7613-0020-1*) Millbrook Pr.

Roop, Peter & Roop, Connie, eds. Capturing Nature: The Writings & Art of John James Audubon. LC 92-15662. (Illus.). 48p. (J). (gr. 5 up). 1993. 16.95 (*0-8027-8204-3*); lib. bdg. 17.85 (*0-8027-8205-1*) Walker & Co.

— Off the Map: The Journals of Lewis & Clark. rev. ed. (Illus.). 48p. (J). (gr. 3-7). 1998. pap. 7.95 (*0-8027-7546-2*); lib. bdg. 15.85 (*0-8027-8208-6*) Walker & Co.

Roop, Peter, et al. Educational Psychology. 2nd ed. LC 95-18552. 560p. 1995. pap. text 75.00 (*0-205-17420-5*) Allyn.

— Let's Celebrate Christmas. LC 97-4268. (Illus.). 32p. (J). (gr. k-3). 1997. pap. 5.95 (*0-7613-0283-2*) Millbrook Pr.

***Roop, Peter, et al.** Whales & Dolphins. LC 99-41766. (Hello Reader! Ser.). (Illus.). (J). 2000. pap. 3.99 (*0-439-09912-9*) Scholastic Inc.

Roop, Peter, jt. auth. see Roop, Connie.

Roop, Peter, ed. see Columbus, Christopher.

Roop, Peter, jt. ed. see Roop, Connie.

Roop, Ray M., jt. ed. see Chau, Kevin.

***Roopenian, Derry & Simpson, Elizabeth.** Minor Histocompatibility Antigens: From the Laboratory to the Clinic. LC 99-31656. (Molecular Biology Intelligence Unit Ser.). 225p. 1999. 99.00 (*1-57059-599-2*) Landes Bioscience.

***Roopnarine, Jaipaul L.** Approaches to Early Childhood Education. 3rd ed. 431p. 1999. pap. 45.00 (*0-13-085254-6*) P-H.

Roopnarine, Jaipaul L., et al, eds. Children's Play in Diverse Cultures. LC 93-12177. (SUNY Series, Children's Play in Society). 234p. (C). 1994. text 64.50 (*0-7914-1753-0*); pap. text 21.95 (*0-7914-1754-9*) State U NY Pr.

— Parent-Child Socialization in Diverse Cultures. (Advances in Applied Developmental Psychology Ser.: Vol. 5). 336p. (C). 1992. text 73.25 (*0-89391-849-0*) Ablx Pub.

Roopnarine, Jaipaul L. & Brown, Janet. Caribbean Families: Diversity among Ethnic Groups. LC 96-50185. (Advances in Applied Developmental Psychology Ser.: Vol. 14). 1997. pap. 39.50 (*1-56750-298-9*); text 73.25 (*1-56750-297-0*) Ablx Pub.

***Roorbach, Bill.** Summers with Juliet. LC 99-40172. 304p. 2000. pap. 20.00 (*0-8142-5052-1*) Ohio St U Pr.

— Writing Life Stories. LC 98-20993. 224p. 1998. 17.99 (*1-884910-36-X*, Story Press) F & W Pubns Inc.

***Roorbach, Bill.** Writing Life Stories. 2000. pap. 14.99 (*1-884910-47-5*, Story Press) F & W Pubns Inc.

Roorbach, O. A. Bibliotheca Americana: Eighteen Fifty-Two to Eighteen Sixty-One, 3 vols. in 1, Vols. 2, 3 & 4. 1990. 30.50 (*0-8446-1389-4*) Peter Smith.

Roorda, Eric. The Dictator Next Door: The Good Neighbor Policy & the Trujillo Regime in the Dominican Republic, 1930-1945. LC 98-12100. (American Encounters/Global Interactions Ser.). 1998. write for info. (*0-8223-2234-X*); pap. 17.95 (*0-8223-2123-8*) Duke.

Roorda, J. & Srivastava, N. K. Trends in Structural Mechanics: Theory, Practice & Education. LC 97-20237. (Solid Mechanics & Its Applications Ser.). 1997. text 197.50 (*0-7923-4603-3*) Kluwer Academic.

Roorda, John G. The Wood Burcher's Illustrated Manual: Level One, Level 1. unabridged ed. LC 97-93410. (Illus.). 102p. 1997. 15.95 (*0-9657953-0-6*, WB-100) Able Two.

Roorda, Randall. Dramas of Solitude: Narratives of Retreat in American Nature Writing. LC 97-16933. (SUNY Series, Literacy, Culture, & Learning Ser.). 283p. (C). 1998. text 65.50 (*0-7914-3677-2*); pap. text 21.95 (*0-7914-3678-0*) State U NY Pr.

***Rooryck, Johan.** Configurations of Sentential Complementation: Perspectives from Romance Languages. LC 99-18881. 1999. text. write for info. (*0-415-18779-6*) Routledge.

Rooryck, Johan & Zaring, Laurie, eds. Phrase Structure & the Lexicon. LC 95-37660. (Studies in Natural Language & Linguistic Theory: Vol. 33). 308p. (C). 1995. text 132.50 (*0-7923-3745-X*) Kluwer Academic.

Roos, Aarand, ed. Estonia: A Nation Unconquered. (Illus.). 96p. (Orig.). 1985. pap. 5.00 (*0-932595-00-6*) Estonian Wrld.

Roos, Albert De, see Van Der Wall, Ernst E. & De Roos, Albert, eds.

Roos, B. O., jt. ed. see European Summer School in Quantum Chemistry Staff.

Roos, B. O., ed. see Third European Summer School in Quantum Chemistry.

Roos, Barbara. Collie Concept. rev. ed. (Illus.). 232p. 1988. 29.95 (*0-931866-36-7*) Alpine Pubns.

An Asterisk (*) at the beginning of an entry indicates that the title is appearing for the first time.

Roos, C. & Terlaky, T. Theory & Algorithms for Linear Optimization: An Interior Point Approach. LC 97-134680. 508p. 1997. 139.95 (*0-471-95676-7*) Wiley.

Roos-Collins, Margit. Flavors of Home: A Guide to Wild Edible Plants of the San Francisco Bay Area. (Illus.). 224p. (Orig.). 1990. pap. 11.95 (*0-930588-46-0*) Heyday Bks.

Roos, Diane F. Yazoo County, Mississippi, 1850 Census & Marriages. 140p. (Orig.). 1990. pap. 20.00 (*1-55613-343-X*) Heritage Bk.

***Roos, Don.** Bounce: A Screenplay. (Illus.). (J). 2000. pap. 10.95 (*0-7868-8589-0*, Pub. by Talk Miramax Bks) Time Warner.

Roos, Frank J., Jr. Bibliography of Early American Architecture: Writings on Architecture Constructed Before 1860 in Eastern & Central U. S. LC 68-24624. (Illus.). 399p. reprint ed. 123.70 (*0-8357-9665-5*, 201498400094) Bks Demand.

Roos, H. G., et al. Numerical Methods for Singularly Perturbed Differential Equations: Convection-Diffusion & Flow Problems. LC 96-1184. (Springer Series in Computational Mathematics: Vol. 24). (Illus.). 368p. 1996. 98.00 (*3-540-60718-8*) Spr-Verlag.

Roos, J. E., ed. Algebra, Algebraic Topology & Their Interactions. (Lecture Notes in Mathematics Ser.: Vol. 1183). xi, 396p. 1986. pap. 53.40 (*0-387-16453-7*) Spr-Verlag.

Roos, J. W., jt. ed. see Hjortso, Martin A.

Roos, Jane M. Early Impressionism & the French State. (Illus.). 307p. (C). 1996. text 80.00 (*0-521-55244-3*) Cambridge U Pr.

***Roos, Jane M., et al.** A Painter's Poet: Stephane Mallarme & His Impressionist Circle. (Illus.). 135p. 1999. pap. 20.00 (*1-885998-17-1*) Hunter College.

***Roos, Jane Mayo.** Early Impressionism & the French State (1866-1874) 320p. 2000. pap. 27.95 (*0-521-77542-6*) Cambridge U Pr.

Roos, Johan. European Casebook on Cooperative Strategies. LC 94-17228. (European Casebook Series on Management). 1994. 32.40 (*0-13-097155-3*) P-H.

***Roos, Johan, et al, eds.** Knowing in Firms: Understanding, Managing & Measuring Knowledge. LC 98-61329. 272p. 1999. 82.00 (*0-7619-6013-9*) Sage.

Roos, Johan, et al. Intellectual Capital: Navigating in the New Business Landscape. LC 97-38912. 208p. 1998. text 45.00 (*0-8147-7512-8*) NYU Pr.

Roos, Johan, jt. auth. see Lissack, Michael.

Roos, Johan De, see Van Den Hout, Theo P. & De Roos, Johan, eds.

Roos, Karen. Meningitis: 100 Maxims. (One Hundred Maxims in Neurology Ser.). (Illus.). 224p. 1996. pap. text 35.00 (*0-340-60879-X*) OUP.

Roos, Karen L., ed. Central Nervous System Infectious Diseases & Therapy. LC 97-7153. (Neurological Disease & Therapy Ser.: Vol. 44). (Illus.). 784p. 1997. text 220.00 (*0-8247-9811-2*) Dekker.

Roos, Kelley. Ghost of a Chance. 200p. 1994. 19.50 (*0-7451-8648-3*, Black Dagger) Chivers N Amer.

Roos, Leslie L., Jr., jt. ed. see Caporaso, James A.

Roos, M. C. Phylogenetic Systematics of the Drynarioideae (Polypodiaceae) (Verhandelingen der Koninklijke Nederlandse Akademie van Wetenschappen, Afd. Natuurkunde Ser.: No. 85). 318p. 1987. pap. text 59.50 (*0-444-85668-4*) Elsevier.

Roos, M. C., jt. auth. see Hennipman, E.

Roos, Matts. Introduction to Cosmology. 2nd ed. LC 97-310. 238p. 1997. 135.00 (*0-471-97229-0*); pap. 69.95 (*0-471-97383-1*) Wiley.

Roos, Murphre. Sonnets & Other Dead Forms. 1980. pap. 3.50 (*0-916696-15-4*) Cross Country.

Roos, Paavo. The Rock Tombs of Caunus, No. 1. (Studies in Mediterranean Archaeology: Vol. XXXIV:1). (Illus:). 144p. 1972. pap. 42.50 (*91-85058-52-1*) P Astroms.

— The Rock Tombs of Caunus, No. 2. (Studies in Mediterranean Archaeology: Vol. XXXIV:2). (Illus.). 75p. 1974. pap. write for info. (*91-85058-53-X*) P Astroms.

— Survey of Rock-Cut Chamber-Tombs in Caria Pt. I: Southeastern Caria & the Lyco-Carian Borderland. (Studies in Mediterranean Archaeology). (Illus.). 132p. (Orig.). 1985. pap. text 156.00 (*0-685-16885-9*) Coronet Bks.

Roos, Patricia A., jt. auth. see Reskin, Barbara F.

Roos, Raymond P., ed. Molecular Neurovirology: Pathogenesis of Viral CNS Infections. LC 91-20851. (Illus.). 625p. 1992. 135.00 (*0-89603-222-1*) Humana.

Roos, Rein A. The Forgotten Pollution. LC 95-48180. 384p. (C). 1996. text 217.50 (*0-7923-3917-7*) Kluwer Academic.

Roos, Rosalie. Travels in America, 1851-1855. Anderson, Carl L., ed. LC 81-187. 170p. 1982. 21.95 (*0-8093-1018-X*) S Ill U Pr.

Roos, Roy E. The History & Development of Portland's Irvington Neighborhood. Craw, R. Andy, ed. & illus. by. 180p. 1997. pap. text 26.95 (*0-9662224-0-7*) R E Roos.

Roos, Stephen. Confessions of a Wayward Preppie. (J). (gr. k-12). 1987. mass mkt. 2.75 (*0-440-91586-4*, LLL BDD) BDD Bks Young Read.

— Cottontail Caper. (Illus.). (J). 1992. 7.95 (*0-385-30722-5*) Doubleday.

— The Fair-Weather Friends. 128p. (J). (gr. 2-9). 1997. reprint ed. pap. 2.95 (*0-8167-1306-5*) Troll Communs.

***Roos, Stephen.** The Gypsies Never Came. LC 99-58951. (Illus.). (J). 2001. write for info. (*0-689-83147-1*) S&S Childrens.

Roos, Stephen. My Favorite Ghost. LC 87-15186. (Illus.). 128p. (J). (gr. 3-7). 1988. lib. bdg. 13.95 (*0-689-31301-2*) Atheneum Yung Read.

— My Favorite Ghost. (J). 1996. pap. 2.95 (*0-8167-1824-5*) Troll Communs.

— Never Trust a Sister over Twelve. LC 92-34406. (J). 1995. 9.09 (*0-606-09679-5*, Pub. by Turtleback) Demco.

— Thirteenth Summer. 112p. (J). (gr. 4-7). 1992. pap. 2.95 (*0-8167-1840-7*) Troll Communs.

— A Young Person's Guide to the Twleve Steps. LC 92-21818. 128p. (YA). (gr. 7 up). 1992. 6.00 (*0-89486-851-9*, 5432A) Hazelden.

Roos, Steve. Double Jeopardy. 1997. pap. 9.95 (*1-57008-305-3*) Bookcraft Inc.

Roos, Willem & Seignette, Jacqueline, eds. Multimedia Deals in the Music Industry. (Reports Presented at the Meeting of the International Association of Entertainment Lawyers MIDEM 1994, Cannes). 169p. 1996. pap. 100.00 (*90-6715-014-2*, Pub. by Maklu Uitgev) Gaunt.

Roos, Wilma & Van Renterghem, Omer. Ecuador in Focus: A Guide to the People, Politics & Culture. LC 97-9942. (In Focus Guides Ser.). (Illus.). 88p. 1997. pap. 12.95 (*1-56656-262-7*) Interlink Pub.

Roos, Yrjo. Phase Transitions in Foods. LC 95-5987. (Food Science & Technology International Ser.). (Illus.). 360p. 1995. text 94.00 (*0-12-595340-2*) Acad Pr.

Roos, Yrjo H., et al. Water Management in the Design & Distribution of Quality Foods: ISOPOW7. LC 99-63163. 620p. 1999. text 189.95 (*1-56676-763-6*) Technomic.

Roosa, Bertha. The HoBERT Bears' Big Surprise!! (Illus.). 88p. 1994. 25.00 (*0-9639391-0-6*) Hobert Ent.

— The HoBERT Bears' New Discoveries!! (Illus.). 90p. (J). 1997. 25.00 (*0-9639391-1-4*) Hobert Ent.

Roosa, Dean M. & Runkel, Sylvan T. Wildflowers & Other Plants of Iowa Wetlands. LC 99-10922. (Illus.). 388p. 1999. pap. 24.95 (*0-8138-2174-6*) Iowa St U Pr.

Roosa, Dean M., jt. auth. see Eilers, Lawrence J.

Roosa, Dean M., jt. auth. see Runkel, Sylvan T.

Roosa, Lois A. Whispers of Comfort: A Devotional. LC 96-69299. 100p. (Orig.). 1998. pap., spiral bd. 8.95 (*0-9653265-0-0*) Sandstone Ent.

Roosa, Mark & Gottlieb, Jane, compiled by. Knowing the Score: Preserving Collections of Music. LC 94-14390. (Music Library Association Index & Bibliography Ser.: No. 23). 92p. 1994. pap. 22.00 (*0-914954-48-2*) Scarecrow.

Roosa, Robert V. The United States & Japan in the International Monetary System, 1946-1985. (Occasional Paper Ser.: No. 21). 75p. 1986. pap. 10.00 (*1-56708-020-0*) Grp of Thirty.

Roosa, Robert V., et al. Countertrade in the World Economy. (Reports). 80p. 1984. pap. 10.00 (*1-56708-067-7*) Grp of Thirty.

— Reserve Currencies in Transition. (Report Ser.). 71p. 1982. pap. 10.00 (*1-56708-058-8*) Grp of Thirty.

Roosa, Ruth A. Russian Industrialists in an Era of Revolution: The Association of Industry & Trade, 1906-1917. Owen, Thomas C., ed. & frwd. by. LC 97-8403. 288p. (C). (gr. 13). 1997. text 78.95 (*0-7656-0154-0*) M E Sharpe.

Roosa, Vernon, jt. auth. see Bronzino, Joseph D.

Roosblad, Judith, jt. ed. see Penninx, Rinus.

Roose, Dirk, jt. ed. see Mittlemann, Hans D.

Roose, Dirk, ed. see Spence, Alstair A.

Roose-Evans, James. Experimental Theatre: From Stanislavsky to Peter Brook. 2nd ed. 224p. (Orig.). (C). 1996. pap. 22.99 (*0-415-00963-4*) Routledge.

— One Foot on the Stage: The Biography of Richard Wilson. (Illus.). 256p. 1997. 40.00 (*0-297-81662-4*, Pub. by Weidenfeld & Nicolson) Trafalgar.

— Passages of the Soul: Rediscovering the Importance of Rituals in Everyday Life. 176p. 1995. pap. 12.95 (*1-85230-708-0*, Pub. by Element MA) Penguin Putnam.

— Passages of the Soul: Rituals for Today. 1994. pap. 19.95 (*1-85230-474-X*, Pub. by Element MA) Penguin Putnam.

Roose, Steven P. & Glick, Robert A., eds. Anxiety as Symptom & Signal. 192p. 1995. text 29.95 (*0-88163-118-3*) Analytic Pr.

Roose, Steven T., jt. ed. see Glick, Robert A.

Roosen, G., et al, eds. Photorefractive Materials: Proceedings of Symposium C of the 1994 E-MRS Spring Conference, Strasbourg, France, 24-27 May, 1994. (European Materials Research Society Symposia Proceedings Ser.: Vol. 48). 300p. 1995. 191.50 (*0-444-82167-8*, North Holland) Elsevier.

Roosen, Rudolf. Die Kirchgemeinde - Sozialsystem in Wandel: Analysen & Anregungen fuer die Reform der Evangelischen Gemeindearbeit. (Arbeiten zur Prkatischen Theologie Ser.: Vol. 9). (GER.). vi, 644p. (C). 1996. lib. bdg. 183.70 (*3-11-015572-9*) De Gruyter.

Roosen-Runge, Edward C. The Process of Spermatogenesis in Animals. LC 76-9169. (Developmental & Cell Biology Ser.: 5). 222p. reprint ed. pap. 63.30 (*0-608-16855-6*, 2027239) Bks Demand.

Roosen, William. Daniel Defoe & Diplomacy. LC 85-40508. (Illus.). 144p. 1986. 32.50 (*0-941664-12-0*) Susquehanna U Pr.

Roosen, William J. The Age of Louis the Fourteenth: The Rise of Modern Diplomacy. 208p. 1976. pap. text 39.25 (*0-87073-581-0*) Transaction Pubs.

Roosens, Eugeen. Creating Ethnicity: The Process of Ethnogenesis. LC 89-10549. 168p. 1989. reprint ed. pap. 52.10 (*0-608-04454-7*, 205966900001) Bks Demand.

Roosens, Eugeen E. Creating Ethnicity: The Process of Ethnogenesis. (Frontiers of Anthropology Ser.). 200p. (C). 1989. text 52.00 (*0-8039-3422-X*); pap. text 25.00 (*0-8039-3423-8*) Sage.

Roosens, Laurent P. History of Photography: A Bibliography of Books, Vol. 2. 192p. 1994. 130.00 (*0-7201-2152-3*) Continuum.

— History of Photography Vol. 3: A Bibliography of Books. 444p. 1996. 130.00 (*0-7201-2310-0*) Continuum.

***Roosens, Laurent P. & Salu, Luc.** History of Photography Vol. 4: A Bibliography of Books. 448p. 1999. 130.00 (*0-7201-2354-2*) Continuum.

Rooses, Max. Art in Flanders. LC 79-100819. (Illus.). reprint ed. 41.50 (*0-404-05397-1*) AMS Pr.

***Roosevelt, Anna.** Scamper: Bunny Who Went to the White House. (Illus.). 72p. (J). (gr. 3-6). 2000. pap. 11.95 (*1-888683-20-1*) Wooster Bk.

Roosevelt, Anna, ed. Amazonian Indians from Prehistory to the Present: Anthropological Perspectives. 420p. 1997. pap. 24.95 (*0-8165-1821-1*) U of Ariz Pr.

Roosevelt, Anna C. Moundbuilders of the Amazon: Geophysical Archaeology on Marajo Island, Brazil. 495p. 1991. text 110.00 (*0-12-595348-8*) Acad Pr.

Roosevelt, Anna Curtenius. The Excavations at Corozal, Venezuela: Stratigraphy & Ceramic Seriation. (YUPA Ser.: Vol. 83). (Illus.). 393p. 1997. pap. 25.00 (*0-913516-17-1*) Yale U Anthro.

Roosevelt, Corinne A. & Roosevelt, Kermit, III. Exploring Nature on Nantucket. LC 93-78238. (Illus.). 112p. (Orig.). 1993. pap. 9.00 (*0-9640372-0-3*) Kerriemuir Pr.

Roosevelt, Eleanor. The Autobiography of Eleanor Roosevelt. (Illus.). 498p. 2000. reprint ed. pap. 16.95 (*0-306-80476-X*, Pub. by Da Capo) HarpC.

— Courage in a Dangerous World: The Political Writings of Eleanor Roosevelt. Black, Allida M., ed. LC 98-33807. 1999. reprint ed. pap. 16.95 (*0-231-11181-9*) Col U Pr.

— Letters, Vols. 5-6. 25.00 (*0-674-52802-6*) HUP.

— This I Remember. LC 74-11884. (Illus.). 387p. 1975. reprint ed. lib. bdg. 85.00 (*0-8371-7702-2*, ROTI, Greenwood Pr) Greenwood.

***Roosevelt, Eleanor.** Universal Declaration of Human Rights. 32p. 2000. 9.95 (*1-55709-455-1*) Applewood.

Roosevelt, Eleanor. You Learn by Living: Eleven Keys for a More Fulfilling Life. LC 83-6838. 220p. 1983. reprint ed. pap. 14.00 (*0-664-24494-7*) Westminster John Knox.

***Roosevelt, Eleanor & Black, Allida M.** Courage in a Dangerous World: The Political Writings of Eleanor Roosevelt. LC 98-33807. 360p. 1999. 29.95 (*0-231-11180-0*) Col U Pr.

Roosevelt, Eleanor & Ideals Publications Editors. Eleanor Roosevelt: Great Americans. LC 97-163943. (Great American Ser.). 80p. 1996. pap. 14.95 (*0-8249-4079-2*) Ideals.

Roosevelt, Eleanor, et al. The Papers of Eleanor Roosevelt, 1933-1945. LC 88-890656. (Research Collections in Women's Studies). 20 p. 1986. write for info. (*0-89093-925-X*) U Pubns Amer.

Roosevelt, Elliott. A First Class Murder. 224p. 1993. reprint ed. mass mkt. 4.99 (*0-380-71238-5*, Avon Bks) Morrow Avon.

— The Hyde Park Murder. 240p. 1986. mass mkt. 4.50 (*0-380-70058-1*, Avon Bks) Morrow Avon.

— Murder & the First Lady. (Eleanor Roosevelt Mystery Ser.). 240p. 1985. mass mkt. 4.99 (*0-380-69937-0*, Avon Bks) Morrow Avon.

— Murder at Hobcaw Barony. (Eleanor Roosevelt Mystery Ser.). 224p. 1987. mass mkt. 4.50 (*0-380-70021-2*, Avon Bks) Morrow Avon.

— Murder at Midnight: An Eleanor Roosevelt Mystery. LC 96-53530. 224p. 1997. 20.95 (*0-312-15596-4*) St Martin.

— Murder at Midnight: An Eleanor Roosevelt Mystery. (Eleanor Roosevelt Mystery Ser.). 240p. 1998. mass mkt. 5.99 (*0-312-96554-0*) St Martin.

— Murder at the Palace. 272p. 1989. mass mkt. 4.99 (*0-380-70405-6*, Avon Bks) Morrow Avon.

***Roosevelt, Elliott.** Murder in Georgetown. LC 99-26719. 230p. 1999. 23.95 (*0-312-24221-2*, Thomas Dunne) St Martin.

— Murder in Georgetown. 240p. 2000. pap. 5.99 (*0-312-97321-7*, Minotaur) St Martin.

— Murder in Georgetown. large type ed. LC 99-56313. (Illus.). 1999. pap. 22.95 (*1-56895-807-2*) Wheeler Pub.

Roosevelt, Elliott. Murder in the Blue Room. 240p. 1992. mass mkt. 4.99 (*0-380-71237-7*, Avon Bks) Morrow Avon.

— Murder in the Blue Room. large type ed. (General Ser.). 377p. 1991. lib. bdg. 21.95 (*0-8161-5100-8*, G K Hall Lrg Type) Mac Lib Ref.

— Murder in the Chateau. 1996. 19.95 (*0-614-96760-0*) St Martin.

— Murder in the Chateau. 1996. mass mkt. 5.99 (*0-312-96050-6*) St Martin.

***Roosevelt, Elliott.** Murder in the Chateau. large type ed. LC 99-38385. 1999. 22.95 (*1-56895-769-6*, Wheeler) Wheeler Pub.

Roosevelt, Elliott. Murder in the East Room. (Eleanor Roosevelt Mystery Ser.). 1995. mass mkt. 4.99 (*0-312-95410-7*) St Martin.

— Murder in the Executive Mansion. LC 98-23159. 256 p. 1998. write for info. (*0-7540-3423-2*) Chivers N Amer.

— Murder in the Executive Mansion. 1996. mass mkt. 5.50 (*0-312-95578-2*, Pub. by Tor Bks) St Martin.

— Murder in the Executive Mansion. large type ed. LC 98-23159. 1998. 19.95 (*0-7838-0284-6*, G K Hall Lrg Type) Mac Lib Ref.

***Roosevelt, Elliott.** Murder in the Lincoln Bedroom. (Eleanor Roosevelt Mysteries Ser.). 224p. 2000. 22.95 (*0-312-26150-0*, Thomas Dunne) St Martin.

Roosevelt, Elliott. Murder in the Map Room: An Eleanor Roosevelt Mystery. (Eleanor Roosevelt Mystery Ser.). 256p. 1998. text 21.95 (*0-312-18168-X*) St Martin.

— Murder in the Map Room: An Eleanor Roosevelt Mystery. LC 97-37243. (Eleanor Roosevelt Mystery Ser.). 256p. 1999. mass mkt. 5.99 (*0-312-96764-0*) St Martin.

— Murder in the Map Room: An Eleanor Roosevelt Mystery. large type ed. LC 98-24431. (Large Print Book Ser.). 1998. 22.95 (*1-56895-619-3*) Wheeler Pub.

— Murder in the Oval Office. 1990. mass mkt. 4.99 (*0-380-70528-1*, Avon Bks) Morrow Avon.

— Murder in the Red Room. (Eleanor Roosevelt Mystery Ser.). 256p. 1994. mass mkt. 4.99 (*0-380-72143-0*, Avon Bks) Morrow Avon.

***Roosevelt, Elliott.** Murder in the Red Room. large type ed. LC 00-39869. 2000. write for info. (*1-56895-901-X*) Wheeler Pub.

Roosevelt, Elliott. Murder in the Rose Garden. (Eleanor Roosevelt Mystery Ser.). 256p. 1991. reprint ed. mass mkt. 4.95 (*0-380-70529-X*, Avon Bks) Morrow Avon.

— Murder in the West Wing: An Eleanor Roosevelt Mystery. (Eleanor Roosevelt Mystery Ser.). 1993. mass mkt. 5.99 (*0-312-95144-2*) St Martin.

— A Royal Murder. large type ed. LC 94-40019. 284 p. 1995. 22.95 (*1-56895-171-X*) Wheeler Pub.

— The White House Pantry Murder. (Eleanor Roosevelt Mystery Ser.). 224p. 1988. mass mkt. 4.50 (*0-380-70404-8*, Avon Bks) Morrow Avon.

Roosevelt, Frank & Belkin, David, eds. Why Market Socialism? Voices from Dissent. LC 94-19803. 412p. (C). (gr. 13). 1994. text 77.95 (*1-56324-465-9*); pap. text 35.95 (*1-56324-466-7*) M E Sharpe.

Roosevelt, Franklin. Wartime Correspondence Between President Roosevelt & Pope Pius XII. LC 74-31356. (American Autobiography Ser.). 127p. 1995. reprint ed. lib. bdg. 69.00 (*0-7812-8629-8*) Rprt Serv.

Roosevelt, Franklin D. America's Entry into World War Two: An Angry President Franklin Roosevelt Asks the Congress to Declare War on Japan. Hubbard, Douglass, ed. (Illus.). 12p. 1995. pap. 2.50 (*0-915266-23-7*) Awani Pr.

— The Complete Presidential Press Conferences of Franklin Delano Roosevelt (1933-1945), 12 annual vols., Set. LC 78-155953. (FDR & the Era of the New Deal Ser.). 7000p. 1973. 495.00 (*0-306-77500-X*) Da Capo.

— The Essential Franklin Delano Roosevelt. Hunt, John G., ed. LC 94-40318. (Library of Freedom). 352p. 1995. 7.99 (*0-517-12289-8*) Random.

— Franklin D. Roosevelt & Foreign Affairs, 3 vols. Nixon, Edgar B., ed. Incl. Vol. 1. January 1933 - Feburary 1934. LC 68-25617. 1969. (*0-674-31816-1*); Vol. 2. March 1934 - August 1935. LC 68-25617. 1969. (*0-674-31818-8*); Vol. 3. September 1935 - January 1937. LC 68-25617. 1969. (*0-674-31819-6*); LC 68-25617. 1969. 100.00 (*0-674-31815-3*) HUP.

— Great Speeches. LC 99-31543. (Thrift Editions Ser.). 128p. (Orig.). 1999. pap. text 1.50 (*0-486-40894-9*) Dover.

— Looking Forward. LC 72-2382. (FDR & the Era of the New Deal Ser.). 284p. 1973. reprint ed. lib. bdg. 35.00 (*0-306-70477-3*) Da Capo.

Roosevelt, Franklin D., Jr. Nothing to Fear. LC 76-128302. (Essay Index Reprint Ser.). 1977. 30.95 (*0-8369-1845-2*) Ayer.

Roosevelt, Franklin D. On Our Way. LC 72-2383. (FDR & the Era of the New Deal Ser.). 216p. 1973. reprint ed. lib. bdg. 39.50 (*0-306-70476-5*) Da Capo.

— Wartime Correspondence Between President Roosevelt & Pope Pius XII. (FDR & the Era of the New Deal Ser.). 1975. reprint ed. lib. bdg. 22.50 (*0-306-70709-8*) Da Capo.

Roosevelt, Franklin D., et al. American Visions of Europe: Franklin D. Roosevelt, George F. Kennan & Dean G. Acheson. 389p. 1996. pap. 17.95 (*0-521-56628-2*) Cambridge U Pr.

Roosevelt, Grace G. Reading Rousseau in the Nuclear Age. 288p. 1990. 44.95 (*0-87722-679-2*) Temple U Pr.

Roosevelt, Hilborne L. Hilborne L. Roosevelt Organs. (Illus.). 1978. reprint ed. pap. 30.00 (*0-913746-12-6*) Organ Lit.

Roosevelt, James, ed. Liberal Papers. LC 79-111861. (Essay Index Reprint Ser.). 1977. 26.95 (*0-8369-1716-2*) Ayer.

Roosevelt, Kermit, III, jt. auth. see Roosevelt, Corinne A.

Roosevelt, Kermit, jt. auth. see Roosevelt, Theodore.

Roosevelt, Nicholas. Philippines: A Treasure & a Problem. LC 71-100510. reprint ed. 39.50 (*0-404-00618-3*) AMS Pr.

Roosevelt, Priscilla. Life on the Russian Country Estate: A Social & Cultural History. LC 94-42337. (Illus.). 384p. 1995. 55.00 (*0-300-05595-1*) Yale U Pr.

— Life on the Russian Country Estate: A Social & Cultural History. (Illus.). 384p. 1997. pap. 25.00 (*0-300-07262-7*) Yale U Pr.

Roosevelt, R. B., ed. see Halpine, Charles G.

Roosevelt, Rita K., jt. auth. see Laird, Nick L.

Roosevelt, Robert B. Superior Fishing: The Striped Bass, Trout, & Black Bass of the Northern States. LC 84-29451. xxiii, 310p. 1985. reprint ed. pap. 8.95 (*0-87351-176-X*, Borealis Book) Minn Hist.

Roosevelt, Ruth & Lofas, Jeannette. Living in Step. (Paperbacks Ser.). 1977. reprint ed. mass mkt. 10.95 (*0-07-053596-5*) McGraw.

Roosevelt, Ruth B. Exceptional Trading: The Mind Game. 288p. 1999. 39.95 (*0-934380-54-6*) Traders Pr.

Roosevelt, Theodore. African Game Trails. 5th ed. (Peter Capstick Library). (Illus.). 620p. 1988. text 24.95 (*0-312-02151-8*) St Martin.

— American Bears: Selections from the Writings of Theodore Roosevelt. LC 82-71701. (Illus.). 206p. reprint ed. pap. 63.90 (*0-7837-5167-2*, 204489600004) Bks Demand.

— American Bears: Selections from the Writings of Theodore Roosevelt. 3rd ed. Schullery, Paul D., ed. (Illus.). 208p. 1997. pap. 14.95 (*1-57098-122-1*) Roberts Rinehart.

— American Ideals & Other Essays, Social & Political. LC 70-106519. reprint ed. 34.50 (*0-404-05398-X*) AMS Pr.

— American Ideals & Other Essays, Social & Political. 1971. reprint ed. 15.00 (*0-403-00195-1*) Scholarly.

— Autobiography of Theodore Roosevelt. (Quality Paperbacks Ser.). 628p. 1985. reprint ed. pap. 16.95 (*0-306-80232-5*) Da Capo.

— Colonial Policies of the United States. LC 71-111705. (American Imperialism: Viewpoints of United States Foreign Policy, 1898-1941 Ser.). 1977. reprint ed. 19.95 (*0-405-02048-1*) Ayer.

— The Essential Theodore Roosevelt. 352p. 1994. 7.99 (*0-517-11848-3*) Random Hse Value.

Roosevelt, Theodore. Frontier Types & In Cowboy Land. (Illus.). 44p. 1997. pap. 4.95 (*0-86541-041-0*) Filter.

Roosevelt, Theodore. Gouverneur Morris. Morse, John T., Jr., ed. LC 76-128972. (American Statesmen Ser.: No. 8). reprint ed. 45.00 (*0-404-50858-8*) AMS Pr.

— Gouverneur Morris. LC 68-24996. (American Biography Ser.: No. 32). 1969. reprint ed. lib. bdg. 75.00 (*0-8383-0274-2*) M S G Haskell Hse.

— Gouverneur Morris. (BCL1 - U. S. History Ser.). 341p. 1992. reprint ed. lib. bdg. 89.00 (*0-7812-6128-7*) Rprt Serv.

— Gouverneur Morris. LC 70-108532. 1971. reprint ed. 20.00 (*0-403-00313-X*) Scholarly.

— Hunting Trips. 1998. audio 15.00 (*0-676-54507-6*) SRA McGraw.

— Hunting Trips of a Ranchman: Sketches of Sport on the Northern Cattle Plains; & The Wilderness Hunter: an Account of the Big Game of the United States & Its Chase with Horse, Hound, & Rifle. LC 96-19364. 1996. 22.00 (*0-679-60234-8*) Modern Lib NY.

— Hunting Trips of a Ranchman & the Wilderness Hunter. 795p. 1998. pap. 16.95 (*0-375-75152-1*) Modern Lib NY.

— Maxims. LC 79-104554. reprint ed. lib. bdg. 20.00 (*0-8398-1764-9*) Irvington.

— The Naval War of 1812. Carr, Caleb, ed. LC 98-48973. (Modern Library War Ser.). 560p. 1999. pap. 15.95 (*0-375-75419-9*) Modern Lib NY.

— The Naval War of 1812. LC 68-24994. (American History & Americana Ser.: No. 47). 1969. reprint ed. lib. bdg. 75.00 (*0-8383-0235-1*) M S G Haskell Hse.

— The Naval War of 1812, or, the History of the United States Navy During the Last War with Great Britain: To Which is Appended an Acount of the Battle of New Orleans. LC 98-54660. (Illus.). 512p. 1999. reprint ed. mass mkt. 16.95 (*0-306-80910-9*, Pub. by Da Capo) HarpC.

— The Naval War of 1812: or The History of the United States Navy. 1988. reprint ed. lib. bdg. 59.00 (*0-7812-0174-8*) Rprt Serv.

— The Naval War of 1812: or The History of the United States Navy. LC 74-108533. (Illus.). 1971. reprint ed. 49.00 (*0-403-00312-1*) Scholarly.

— Outdoor Pastimes of an American Hunter. LC 70-25762. (American Environmental Studies). 1971. reprint ed. 31.95 (*0-405-02687-0*) Ayer.

— Outdoor Pastimes of an American Hunter. LC 90-9884. (Classics of American Sport Ser.). (Illus.). 480p. 1990. reprint ed. pap. 18.95 (*0-8117-3033-6*) Stackpole.

— Ranch Life & the Hunting Trail. LC 76-125761. (American Environmental Studies). 1971. reprint ed. 18.95 (*0-405-02688-9*) Ayer.

— Ranch Life & the Hunting-Trail. LC 82-20091. (Illus.). x, 210p. 1983. reprint ed. pap. 16.95 (*0-8032-8913-8*, Bison Books) U of Nebr Pr.

— Ranch Life in the Far West. (Illus.). 1978. reprint ed. pap. 7.95 (*0-89646-034-7*) Vistabooks.

— Realizable Ideals. LC 77-90676. (Essay Index Reprint Ser.). 1977. 19.95 (*0-8369-1233-0*) Ayer.

***Roosevelt, Theodore.** Rough Riders. Carr, Caleb, ed. LC 99-25584. (Modern Library War Ser.). 1999. pap. 12.95 (*0-375-75476-8*) Modern Lib NY.

Roosevelt, Theodore. The Rough Riders. LC 98-36314. (Illus.). xxi, 316p. 1998. pap. 12.95 (*0-8032-8973-1*, Bison Books) U of Nebr Pr.

— The Rough Riders. (Quality Paperbacks Ser.). (Illus.). 296p. 1990. reprint ed. pap. 13.95 (*0-306-80405-0*) Da Capo.

— Selections from the Correspondence of Theodore Roosevelt & Henry Cabot Lodge, 1884-1918. (American Biography Ser.). 72p. 1991. reprint ed. lib. bdg. 59.00 (*0-7812-8327-2*) Rprt Serv.

— Selections from the Correspondence of Theodore Roosevelt & Henry Cabot Lodge, 1884-1918, 2 vols., Set. (History - United States Ser.). 1992. reprint ed. lib. bdg. 150.00 (*0-7812-6221-6*) Rprt Serv.

— Social Justice & Popular Rule: Essays, Addresses, & Public Statements of the Progressive Movement, 1910-1916. LC 73-19173. (Politics & People Ser.). (Illus.). 604p. 1974. reprint ed. 44.95 (*0-405-05909-4*) Ayer.

— The Strenuous Life. 30p. 1991. 9.95 (*1-55709-142-0*) Applewood.

— The Strenuous Life: Essays & Addresses. 1902. reprint ed. 39.00 (*0-403-00311-3*) Scholarly.

— Theodore Roosevelt's America: American Naturalists Ser. Wiley, Farida A., ed. (Selections from the Writings of the Oyster Bay Naturalist). (Illus.). 1955. 18.95 (*0-8159-6714-4*) Devin.

— Thomas H. Benton. Morse, John T., Jr., ed. LC 79-128972. (American Statesmen Ser.: No. 23). reprint ed. 45.00 (*0-404-50873-1*) AMS Pr.

— Thomas Hart Benton. LC 68-24995. (American Biography Ser.: No. 32). 1969. reprint ed. lib. bdg. 75.00 (*0-8383-0275-0*) M S G Haskell Hse.

***Roosevelt, Theodore.** Through the Brazilian Wilderness. 2000. reprint ed. pap. 19.95 (*0-8154-1095-6*, Pub. by Cooper Sq) Natl Bk Netwk.

Roosevelt, Theodore. The Wilderness Hunter: An Account of the Big Game of the United States & its Chase with Horse Hound & Rifle. 279p. reprint ed. write for info. (*0-8290-1955-3*) Irvington.

— The Winning of the West. Wish, Harvey, ed. & intro. by. 1990. 16.00 (*0-8446-2827-1*) Peter Smith.

— The Winning of the West, 4 vols. 1992. reprint ed. 295.00 (*0-403-04339-5*) Somerset Pub.

— The Winning of the West Vol. 1: From the Alleghanies to the Mississippi, 1769-1776. LC 94-46645. (Illus.). 353p. 1995. pap. 19.95 (*0-8032-8954-5*, Bison Books) U of Nebr Pr.

Roosevelt, Theodore. The Winning of the West Vol. 3: The Founding of the Trans-Alleghany Commonwealths, 1784-1790. LC 94-46645. (Illus.). xx, 339p. 1995. pap. 19.95 (*0-8032-8956-1*, Bison Books) U of Nebr Pr.

Roosevelt, Theodore. The Winning of the West Vol. 4: Louisiana & the Northwest, 1791-1807. LC 94-46645. (Illus.). xx, 363p. 1995. pap. 19.95 (*0-8032-8957-X*, Bison Books) U of Nebr Pr.

— The Writings of Theodore Roosevelt. Harbaugh, William H., ed. LC 66-14828. 407p. 1967. 39.50 (*0-8290-0221-9*) Irvington.

Roosevelt, Theodore, ed. Desk Drawer Anthology. LC 72-99032. (Granger Index Reprint Ser.). 1977. 24.95 (*0-8369-6107-2*) Ayer.

Roosevelt, Theodore & Bak, Richard. Rough Riders. LC 97-14743. (Illus.). 256p. 1997. 29.95 (*0-87833-982-5*) Taylor Pub.

***Roosevelt, Theodore & Bak, Richard.** The Rough Riders. expanded ed. (Illus.). 2000. reprint ed. pap. 18.95 (*0-87833-194-8*) Taylor Pub.

***Roosevelt, Theodore & Lodge, Henry Cabot.** Hero Tales: How Common Lives Reveal the Uncommon Genius of America. LC 99-89505. 288p. (J). (gr. 4-8). 2000. pap. 8.95 (*1-58182-063-1*, Cumberland Hearthside) Cumberland Hse.

Roosevelt, Theodore & Roosevelt, Kermit. East of the Sun & West of the Moon. 1988. 25.00 (*0-935632-70-0*) Wolfe Pub Co.

Roosevelt, Theodore, et al. Elk Hunting Tales: An Anthology of Historic Outdoor Adventures from the Pages of BUGLE Magazine. Schelvan, Lance, ed. LC 90-62302. (Rocky Mountain Elk Foundation Conservation Library: Vol. 1). (Illus.). 210p. (C). 1990. 14.95 (*0-9627248-1-5*); write for info. (*0-9627248-2-3*); write for info. (*0-9627248-0-7*) Rocky Mntn Elk.

Roosevelt, Theodore, jt. ed. see Grinnell, George B.

***Roosta, Seyed H.** Parallel Processing & Parallel Algorithms: Theory & Computation. LC 99-13243. 550p. 1999. 69.95 (*0-387-98716-9*) Spr-Verlag.

***Roosz, A., et al, eds.** Solidification & Gravity 2000. (Materials Science Forum Ser.: Vols. 329-330). (Illus.). 538p. 2000. text 162.00 (*0-87849-852-4*, Pub. by Trans T Pub) Enfield Pubs NH.

Roosz, A. & Rettenmayr, M., eds. Solidification & Gravity. (Materials Science Ser.: 215-216). (Illus.). 544p. 1996. text 195.00 (*0-87849-728-5*, Pub. by Trans T Pub) Enfield Pubs NH.

Root, jt. auth. see Grohe.

Root, A. I. Encyclopedia of Bee Culture: An Encyclopedia Pertaining to Scientific & Practical Culture of Bees. 30th ed. 717p. 1985. pap. 175.00 (*0-7855-2721-4*, Pub. by Intl Bks & Periodicals) St Mut.

Root, Barrett. April, Bubbles, Chocolate. LC 92-17100. 48p. (J). (ps-2). 1994. pap. 14.00 (*0-671-75911-6*) S&S Bks Yung.

Root, Barry, ed. see Ray, M. L.

***Root, Benjamin.** Understanding Panic & Other Anxiety Disorders. (Understanding Health & Sickness Ser.). 140p. 2000. pap. 12.00 (*1-57806-245-4*); text 28.00 (*1-57806-244-6*) U Pr of Miss.

Root, Benjamin M., ed. & illus. see Radabaugh, Joseph.

Root-Bernstein, Michele. Boulevard Theater & Revolution in Eighteenth- Century Paris. LC 84-2545. (Theater & Dramatic Studies: No. 22). (Illus.). 340p. reprint ed. pap. 105.40 (*0-8357-1551-5*, 207057300001) Bks Demand.

Root Bernstein, Michele, jt. auth. see Bernstein, Robert.

Root-Bernstein, Michele, jt. auth. see Root-Bernstein, Robert.

***Root-Bernstein, Robert & Root-Bernstein, Michele.** Sparks of Genius: The Thirteen Thinking Tools of the World's Most Creative People. LC 99-48005. (Illus.). 400p. 2000. 24.00 (*0-395-90771-3*) HM.

Root-Bernstein, Robert Scott. Discovering. LC 88-35768. (Illus.). 520p. 1989. text 46.50 (*0-674-21175-8*) HUP.

— Discovering: Inventing & Solving Problems at the Frontiers of Scientific Knowledge. 520p. (C). 1991. pap. text 17.95 (*0-674-21176-6*) HUP.

— Discovering: Inventing & Solving Problems at the Frontiers of Scientific Knowledge. LC 97-44819. 515p. 1997. reprint ed. lib. bdg. 37.95 (*0-7351-0007-1*) Replica Bks.

Root, Betty. Dictionary. LC 91-26178. (Picture Pockets Ser.). (Illus.). 96p. (J). (gr. 1-5). 1992. pap. 13.00 (*0-671-76002-5*) S&S Bks Yung.

— Help Your Child Learn to Read. (Parents' Guides Ser.). 1989. pap. 6.95 (*0-7460-0224-6*, Usborne) EDC.

— Help Your Child Learn to Read. (Parents' Guides Ser.). 48p. 1999. lib. bdg. 14.95 (*0-88110-366-7*) EDC.

— My First Dictionary. LC 93-20145. (Illus.). 96p. (J). (gr. k-4). 1993. 17.95 (*1-56458-277-9*) DK Pub Inc.

Root, Betty & Langley, Jonathan. My First Dictionary. (Illus.). (J). text 23.95 (*0-590-74595-6*) Scholastic Inc.

Root, Betty & Schindler, Nina. Duden: Mein Erstes Lexikon A-Z. (GER.). 104p. (J). 1996. 26.50 (*3-411-05451-4*); 26.50 (*3-411-05452-2*) Langenscheidt.

Root, Christine, jt. auth. see Dumicich, John.

Root, Christine B., jt. auth. see Blanchard, Karen.

Root, Christine B., jt. auth. see Blanchard, Karen L.

Root, Darrell K., jt. auth. see Basarab, David J., Sr.

Root, Deane L. American Popular Stage Music, 1860-1880. LC 81-1512. (Studies in Musicology: No. 44). (Illus.). 294p. reprint ed. pap. 91.20 (*0-8357-1509-4*, 207029300065) Bks Demand.

Root, Deborah. Cannibal Culture: Art, Appropriation & the Commodification of Difference. (Illus.). 242p. (C). 1996. pap. 26.00 (*0-8133-2089-5*, Pub. by Westview) HarpC.

Root, Don. Moon Handbooks: Idaho. 3rd ed. (Illus.). 610p. 1997. pap. 18.95 (*1-56691-088-9*, Moon Handbks) Avalon Travel.

Root, Edward. Philip Hooker. 242p. 1993. reprint ed. lib. bdg. 79.00 (*0-7812-5305-5*) Rprt Serv.

Root, Eileen. Hawaiian Names - English Names. 163p. (Orig.). 1988. pap. 9.95 (*0-916630-62-5*) Pr Pacifica.

***Root, Eldon, ed.** A Star for Benny Peeples. LC 99-41304. (Illus.). 383 p. 1999. pap. 9.95 (*1-929117-01-9*) BlueOak.

Root, Elihu. Addresses on Government & Citizenship. LC 70-86779. (Essay Index Reprint Ser.). 1977. 29.95 (*0-8369-1190-3*) Ayer.

— Addresses on International Subjects. LC 74-86780. (Essay Index Reprint Ser.). 1977. 26.95 (*0-8369-1191-1*) Ayer.

— Addresses on International Subjects. Bacon, Robert & Scott, James B., eds. LC 97-74791. ix, 463p. 1997. reprint ed. 142.50 (*1-56169-328-6*) Gaunt.

— The Citizen's Part in Government & Experiments in Government & the Essentials of the Constitution, 2 vols. LC 73-19174. (Politics & People Ser.). 220p. 1974. reprint ed. 19.95 (*0-405-05895-0*) Ayer.

— Men & Policies: Addresses. Bacon, Robert & Scott, J. B., eds. LC 68-22942. (Essay Index Reprint Ser.). 1977. reprint ed. 23.95 (*0-8369-0832-5*) Ayer.

— Military & Colonial Policy of the United States. LC 70-121030. reprint ed. 47.50 (*0-404-05399-8*) AMS Pr.

— North Atlantic Coast Fisheries Arbitration at the Hague: Argument on Behalf of the United States. (Illus.). cix, 445p. 1982. reprint ed. 49.95 (*0-8377-1035-9*, Rothman) W S Hein.

***Root, Elihu & Carnegie Endowment for International Peace Staff.** The Effect of Democracy on International Law: Opening Address by Elihu Root As President of the American Society of International Law at the 11th Annual Meeting of the Society in Washington, April 26, 1917. LC 99-47543. 1999. write for info. (*1-57588-605-7*) W S Hein.

Root, Elizabeth. Hawaiian Quilting. 48p. 1989. pap. 3.95 (*0-486-25948-X*) Dover.

Root, Elizabeth, ed. see Pioneer Museum Staff.

Root, Esther S. Over Periscope Pond: Letters from Two American Girls in Paris, October 1916-January 1918. (American Biography Ser.). 295p. 1991. reprint ed. lib. bdg. 69.00 (*0-7812-8328-0*) Rprt Serv.

***Root, Evelyn E.** How to Learn the Alphabet the Pictured Sound Symbol Way: Speak & Spell with Alphabet Letters. LC 98-93350. (Illus.). 50p. (J). (ps-3). 2000. 15.95 (*0-9654548-4-3*) Donalyn Bks.

Root, Evelyn E. How to Read, Speak, Write & Spell English: The Pictured Sound Symbol Way. LC 96-86349. (Illus.). 288p. 1999. 49.95 (*0-9654548-3-5*) Donalyn Bks.

Root, Frank A. & Connelly, William E. The Overland Stage to California: Personal Reminiscences & Authentic History of the Great Overland Stage Line & Pony Express. (Illus.). xvii, 630p. 1989. reprint ed. lib. bdg. 64.00 (*0-8328-1428-8*) Higginson Bk Co.

Root, Franklin R. Entry Strategies for International Markets. expanded rev. ed. LC 98-24872. (Business & Management Ser.). 272p. 1998. reprint ed. pap. 25.95 (*0-7879-4571-4*) Jossey-Bass.

— International Strategic Management: Challenges & Opportunities. (International Business & Trade Ser.). 240p. 1992. pap. 41.95 (*0-8448-1666-3*) Taylor & Francis.

— International Trade & Investment. 5th ed. (Thomson Executive Press). (C). 1983. pap. 43.00 (*0-538-08610-6*, H61) S-W Pub.

— International Trade & Investment. 6th ed. (SWC-Economics). 704p. (C). 1990. pap. 42.00 (*0-538-08620-3*, H62) S-W Pub.

Root, G. A., jt. auth. see Cone, W. W.

Root, George F. George F. Root: The Haymakers. Martin, Dennis R., ed. (Recent Researches in American Music Ser.: No. RRAM9-10). (Illus.). 205, xviiip. 1989. pap. 65.00 (*0-89579-192-7*) A-R Eds.

— The Story of a Musical Life. LC 71-174964. reprint ed. 31.50 (*0-404-07205-4*) AMS Pr.

— The Story of a Musical Life: An Autobiography. LC 70-126072. (Music Ser.). 1970. reprint ed. lib. bdg. 35.00 (*0-306-70031-X*) Da Capo.

— The Story of a Musical Life: An Autobiography. (American Biography Ser.). 256p. 1991. reprint ed. lib. bdg. 69.00 (*0-7812-8329-9*) Rprt Serv.

Root, George L. The Ancient Arabic Order of the Nobles of the Mystic Shrine. 88p. 1997. reprint ed. pap. 14.95 (*0-7661-0060-X*) Kessinger Pub.

Root, Gineke. Innovative Beaded Jewelry Techniques. 56p. 1994. pap. 14.00 (*0-916896-60-9*) Lacis Pubns.

Root, H. E., ed. see Hume, David.

Root, Hal & Koenig, Steve. The Small Business Start-Up Guide: A Surefire Blueprint to Successfully Launch Your Own Business. 2nd rev. ed. LC 97-49212. (Illus.). 224p. 1997. pap. 12.95 (*1-57071-221-2*) Sourcebks.

Root, Hilton. Small Countries, Big Lessons: Governance & the Rise of East Asia. (Illus.). 268p. 1997. text 19.95 (*0-19-590026-X*) OUP.

Root, Hilton L. The Fountain of Privilege: Political Foundations of Economic Markets in Old Regime France & England. LC 93-5066. (California Series on Social Choice & Political Economy: Vol. 26). 1994. 50.00 (*0-520-08415-2*, Pub. by U CA Pr) Cal Prin Full Svc.

— Has China Lost Its Way? Getting Stuck in Transition. LC 95-12510 (Essays in Public Policy Ser.: No. 62). 1995. pap. 5.00 (*0-8179-5672-7*) Hoover Inst Pr.

— India, Asia's Next Tiger? LC 97-32967. (Essays in Public Policy Ser.: No. 82). 1997. pap. 5.00 (*0-8179-5872-X*) Hoover Inst Pr.

— Peasants & King in Burgundy: Agrarian Foundations of French Absolutism. (California Series on Social Choice & Political Economy: Vol. 9). (C). 1992. pap. 15.95 (*0-520-08097-1*, Pub. by U CA Pr) Cal Prin Full Svc.

Root, Hilton L., jt. auth. see Bueno de Mesquita, Bruce.

Root, Hilton L., jt. auth. see Campos, Jose E.

Root, J. P. Root Genealogical Records, 1600-1870, Comprising the History of the Root & Roots Family in America. 533p. 1989. reprint ed. pap. 80.00 (*0-8328-1031-2*); reprint ed. lib. bdg. 88.00 (*0-8328-1030-4*) Higginson Bk Co.

Root, Jack B., Sr. & Mortensen, Douglas L. The 7 Secrets of Financial Success. rev. ed. LC 98-152045. xxi, 437p. 1998. 28.95 (*0-07-054049-7*) McGraw-Hill Prof.

Root, Jane, jt. auth. see Colvin, Ruth J.

Root, Jane H., jt. ed. see Colvin, Ruth J.

Root, Janet. Open the Box: About Television. (Comedia Bks.). 128p. (C). 1988. pap. text 16.99 (*0-906890-78-0*, Pub. by Comedia) Routldge.

Root, Jason. Parables That Jesus Told. LC 98-4428. (Illus.). 40p. (J). (ps-1). 1999. pap. 10.95 incl. audio (*0-689-82536-6*, Rabbit Ears) Litle Simon.

Root, Jerry. Space to Speke: The Confessional Subject in Medieval Literature. LC 96-44618. (American University Studies: Vol. 225, No. II). (Illus.). 271p. (C). 1997. text 46.95 (*0-8204-3711-5*) P Lang Pubng.

Root, Jerry, ed. see Lewis, C. S.

Root, John W. & Krohn, Kenneth A., eds. Short-Lived Radionuclides in Chemistry & Biology. LC 81-19148. (Advances in Chemistry Ser.: No. 197). 1982. 80.95 (*0-8412-0603-1*) Am Chemical.

— Short-Lived Radionuclides in Chemistry & Biology. LC 81-19148. (Advances in Chemistry Ser.: Vol. 197). 562p. 1981. reprint ed. pap. 174.30 (*0-608-03502-5*, 206422100008) Bks Demand.

Root, Judith. Weaving the Sheets. LC 87-73141. 1988. pap. 11.95 (*0-88748-070-5*) Carnegie-Mellon.

***Root, K., et al.** The What Investment A-Z Guide to the Stock Exchange. 210p. 1998. 27.95 (*0-7134-8377-6*) B T B.

Root, Kathleen B. & Byers, Edward E. Medical Typing Practice. 2nd ed. 1967. text 50.32 (*0-07-053585-X*) McGraw.

Root, Kimberly B. Billy Beg & His Bull: An Irish Tale. LC 93-7730. 32p. (J). (gr. k-3). 1994. lib. bdg. 15.95 (*0-8234-1100-1*) Holiday.

— Boots & His Brothers: A Tale from Norway. LC 90-23659. 32p. (J). (ps-3). 1992. lib. bdg. 14.95 (*0-8234-0886-8*) Holiday.

— Gulliver in Lilliput. LC 94-15037. 32p. (J). (gr. k-3). 1995. lib. bdg. 16.95 (*0-8234-1147-8*) Holiday.

— Gulliver in Lilliput. (J). (gr. k-3). 1995. reprint ed. pap. text 6.95 (*0-8234-1303-9*) Holiday.

Root, Kimberly B., jt. auth. see Wolff, Patricia Rae.

Root, L. Bad Back Exercises. 1979. mass mkt. 5.95 (*0-446-97008-5*, Pub. by Warner Bks) Little.

Root, Lawrence, jt. auth. see LaFever, Malcolm.

Root, Leon. No More Aching Back: Dr. Root's New, Fifteen-Minute-a-Day Program for a Healthy Back. 240p. 1991. mass mkt. 5.99 (*0-451-17091-1*, Sig) NAL.

Root, Lindy, jt. auth. see Sherman, Richard.

Root, Loren F. Microwave Robust: Ssri RF. LC 92-26383. (Six Sigma Research Institute Ser.). 1992. pap. 16.95 (*0-201-63428-7*) Addison-Wesley.

Root, Margaret C. & Garrison, Mark B. Persepolis Seal Studies: An Introduction with Provisional Concordances of Seal Numbers & Associated Documents on Fortification Tablets I-2087. (Achaemenid History Ser.: No. 9). (Illus.). 142p. 1996. text 40.00 (*90-6258-409-8*, Pub. by Netherlands Inst) Eisenbrauns.

Root, Maria P. Racially Mixed People in America: Within, Between & Beyond Race. (Illus.). 400p. 1992. 62.00 (*0-8039-4101-3*); pap. 28.00 (*0-8039-4102-1*) Sage.

Root, Maria P., ed. Filipino Americans: Transforming Identity. LC 97-4591. 314p. 1997. 58.00 (*0-7619-0578-2*); pap. 26.95 (*0-7619-0579-0*) Sage.

— The Multiracial Experience: Racial Borders As the New Frontier. (Illus.). 498p. 1995. 62.00 (*0-8039-7058-7*); pap. 28.00 (*0-8039-7059-5*) Sage.

Root, Maria P., jt. ed. see Brown, Laura S.

***Root, Maria P. P.** Love's Revolution: Racial Intermarriage. (Illus.). 264p. 2001. 69.50 (*1-56639-825-8*); pap. 22.95 (*1-56639-826-6*) Temple U Pr.

Root, Marilyn & Avila, Carolina. Sabor! A Guide to Tropical Fruits & Vegetables & Central American Foods. (Illus.). 224p. 1997. pap. 15.95 (*0-9673054-0-3*) Sabor.

Root, Marilyn. Women at the Wheel: 42 Stories of Freedom, Fanbelts & the Lure of the Open Road. LC 99-12636. (Illus.). 176p. 1999. pap. 12.95 (*1-57071-443-6*) Sourcebks.

***Root, Martha L.** Tahirih the Pure. 3rd rev. ed. LC 99-56978. (Illus.). 156p. 2000. reprint ed. pap. 21.95 (*1-890688-04-5*, Pub. by Kalimat) Pubs Services.

Root, Michael. DirectX Complete. LC 98-53499. 635p. 1999. pap. text 54.99 incl. cd-rom (*0-07-913780-6*) McGraw.

— Philosophy of Social Science: The Methods, Ideals & Politics of Social Inquiry. 272p. 1993. pap. 26.95 (*0-631-19042-2*) Blackwell Pubs.

Root, Michael & Saarinen, Risto, eds. Baptism & the Unity of the Church. LC 97-44687. 213p. 1998. pap. 20.00 (*0-8028-4462-6*) Eerdmans.

Root, Michael, jt. auth. see Fackre, Gabriel.

Root, Mike. Life's Cobwebs: Breaking Free from the Entrapments of the World. LC 96-1632. 1996. pap. 9.99 (*0-89900-760-0*) College Pr Pub.

— Unbroken Bread: Healing Worship Wounds. LC 97-11028. 270p. (Orig.). (C). 1997. pap. 8.99 (*0-89900-779-1*) College Pr Pub.

Root, Monica, jt. auth. see NCSL Legislative Management Staff.

An Asterisk (*) at the beginning of an entry indicates that the title is appearing for the first time.

R

Root, Phyllis. All for the Newborn Baby. LC 98-17231. (J). 1900. write for info. (*0-7636-0735-5*) Candlewick Pr.
***Root, Phyllis.** All for the Newborn Baby. (Illus.). 40p. (J). (gr. 1-5). 2000. 12.99 (*0-7636-0093-8*) Candlewick Pr.
Root, Phyllis. Aunt Nancy & Cousin Lazybones. LC 97-51157. (Illus.). 32p. (J). (gr. k-3). 1998. 16.99 (*1-56402-425-3*) Candlewick Press.
— Aunt Nancy & Old Man Trouble. LC 95-23732. (Illus.). 32p. (J). (gr. k-3). 1996. 16.99 (*1-56402-347-8*) Candlewick Pr.
— Aunt Nancy & Old Man Trouble. LC 95-23732. (Illus.). 32p. (J). (gr. k-3). 1998. pap. 6.99 (*0-7636-0650-2*) Candlewick Pr.
— Contrary Bear. LC 95-31644. (Illus.). 32p. (J). (ps-1). 1996. 13.95 (*0-06-025085-2*) HarpC Child Bks.
***Root, Phyllis.** Grandmother Winter. LC 98-50515. (Illus.). 32p. (J). (gr. k-3). 1999. 15.00 (*0-395-88399-7*) HM.
— Here Comes Tabby Cat. (Illus.). (J). 2000. pap. 4.99 (*0-7636-0772-X*) Candlewick Pr.
— Hey, Tabby Cat! (Illus.). 8p. (J). (ps-2). 2000. pap. 4.99 (*0-7636-0800-9*) Candlewick Pr.
Root, Phyllis. The Hungry Monster. LC 96-6225. (Illus.). 24p. (J). (ps up). 1997. 9.99 (*0-7636-0060-1*) Candlewick Pr.
— Hungry Monster. LC 96-6225. (Illus.). 24p. (J). (ps-1). 1998. pap. 3.29 (*0-7636-0380-5*) Candlewick Pr.
***Root, Phyllis.** Kiss the Cow. LC 00-20926. (Illus.). 32p. (J). (ps-3). 2000. 15.99 (*0-7636-0298-1*) Candlewick Pr.
— Meow Monday. LC 99-47078. (Illus.). 24p. (J). (ps up). 2000. pap. 3.29 (*0-7636-0831-9*) Candlewick Pr.
Root, Phyllis. Moon Tiger. LC 85-7572. (Illus.). 32p. (J). (ps-2). 1995. 14.95 (*0-8050-0896-9*, Bks Young Read); pap. 4.95 (*0-8050-0803-9*, Bks Young Read) H Holt & Co.
— Mrs. Potter's Pig. LC 95-38194. (Illus.). 32p. (J). (ps-2). 1997. reprint ed. pap. 5.99 (*0-7636-0160-8*) Candlewick Pr.
— The Old Red Rocking Chair. (Illus.). 32p. (J). (ps-3). 1992. 14.45 (*1-55970-063-7*, Pub. by Arcade Pub Inc) Time Warner.
— One Duck Stuck. LC 97-34103. (Illus.). 40p. (J). (ps-k). 1998. 15.99 (*0-7636-0334-1*) Candlewick Pr.
— One Windy Wednesday. LC 96-4237. (Illus.). 24p. (J). (ps-k). 1996. 9.99 (*0-7636-0054-7*) Candlewick Pr.
— One Windy Wednesday. LC 96-4237. (Giggle Club Ser.). (Illus.). 24p. (J). (ps-1). 1997. reprint ed. pap. 3.29 (*0-7636-0278-7*) Candlewick Pr.
— Rosie's Fiddle. LC 93-37430. (Illus.). 32p. (J). (ps up). 1997. 16.00 (*0-688-12852-1*); lib. bdg. 15.93 (*0-688-12853-X*) Lothrop.
Root, Phyllis. Sam Who Was Swallowed by a Shark. LC 93-2884. 1996. 11.19 (*0-606-10297-3*, Pub. by Turtleback) Demco.
Root, Phyllis. Sam Who Was Swallowed by a Shark. LC 93-2884. (Illus.). 32p. (J). (ps-2). 1996. reprint ed. pap. 5.99 (*1-56402-955-7*) Candlewick Pr.
— Soup for Supper. LC 85-45273. (Illus.). 32p. (J). (ps-2). 1986. 13.95 (*0-06-025070-4*) HarpC Child Bks.
— Turnover Tuesday. LC 97-18456. (Illus.). 24p. (J). (ps-1). 1998. 10.99 (*0-7636-0447-X*); pap. 10.99 (*0-7636-0455-0*) Candlewick Press.
***Root, Phyllis.** What Baby Wants. (Illus.). 18p. 1998. pap. 12.98 (*1-58048-027-6*) Sandvik Pub.
Root, Phyllis & Barton, Jill. What Baby Wants. LC 97-40424. (Illus.). 40p. (J). (ps-3). 1998. 15.99 (*0-7636-0207-8*) Candlewick Pr.
***Root, Phyllis & Craig, Helen.** Foggy Friday. LC 99-47079. (Illus.). 24p. (J). (ps up). 2000. pap. 3.29 (*0-7636-0833-5*) Candlewick Pr.
***Root, Phyllis & McEwen, Katharine.** Here Comes Tabby Cat. LC 99-48494. (Illus.). 48p. (J). (ps-2). 2000. 10.95 (*0-7636-1038-0*) Candlewick Pr.
— Hey, Tabby Cat! LC 99-48493. (Illus.). 48p. (J). (ps-2). 2000. 10.99 (*0-7636-1039-9*) Candlewick Pr.
Root, Richard K. Immunization. LC 88-34220. (Contemporary Issues in Infectious Diseases Ser.: No. 8). (Illus.). 288p. 1989. reprint ed. pap. 89.30 (*0-7837-9753-2*, 206048100005) Bks Demand.
***Root, Richard K., et al, eds.** Clinical Infectious Diseases. (Practical Approach Ser.). (Illus.). 1040p. 2000. pap. text 98.50 (*0-19-514349-3*) OUP.
Root, Richard K., et al, eds. Clinical Infectious Diseases: A Practical Approach. (Illus.). 1040p. 1998. text 149.50 (*0-19-508103-X*) OUP.
Root, Richard K. & Sande, Merle A. Viral Infections. (Contemporary Issues in Infectious Diseases Ser.: Vol. 10). (Illus.). 218p. 1992. text 89.00 (*0-443-08859-4*) Church.
Root, Richard K. & Sande, Merle A., eds. New Dimensions in Antimicrobial Therapy. fac. ed. LC 83-23135. (Contemporary Issues in Infectious Diseases Ser.: No. 1). (Illus.). 360p. 1984. reprint ed. pap. 111.60 (*0-7837-7872-4*, 204762900007) Bks Demand.
— Septic Shock. (Contemporary Issues in Infectious Diseases Ser.: Vol. 4). (Illus.). 281p. 1985. text 54.95 (*0-443-08397-5*) Church.
Root, Richard K., jt. ed. see Sande, Merle A.
Root, Robert. Critical Essays on E. B. White. (Critical Essays on American Literature Ser.). 224p. 1994. 49.00 (*0-8161-7321-4*, Twyne) Mac Lib Ref.
— Time by Moments Steals Away: The 1848 Journal of Ruth Douglass. 1998. 24.95 (*0-8143-2813-X*, Great Lks Bks) Wayne St U Pr.
Root, Robert K. Classical Mythology in Shakespeare. LC 65-24996. 134p. 1965. reprint ed. 50.00 (*0-87752-096-8*) Gordian.
— Classical Mythology in Shakespeare. (BCL1-PR English Literature Ser.). 134p. 1992. reprint ed. lib. bdg. 69.00 (*0-7812-7306-4*) Rprt Serv.
— The Poetical Career of Alexander Pope. 1990. 16.50 (*0-8446-1392-4*) Peter Smith.
— The Poetry of Chaucer: A Guide to Its Study & Appreciation. rev. ed. 1990. 16.50 (*0-8446-1391-6*) Peter Smith.
Root, Robert L., Jr. E. B. White: The Emergence of an Essayist. LC 98-48375. 256p. 1999. text 29.95 (*0-87745-667-4*) U of Iowa Pr.
— The Rhetorics of Popular Culture: Advertising, Advocacy & Entertainment, 16. LC 86-14974. (Contributions to the Study of Popular Culture Ser.: No. 16). 189p. 1987. 49.95 (*0-313-24403-0*, Greenwood Pr) Greenwood.
Root, Robert L. Wordsmithery. 2nd ed. LC 97-29543. 157p. 1997. pap. text 25.00 (*0-205-27024-7*) P-H.
Root, Robert L., Jr. Working at Writing: Columnists & Critics Composing. LC 90-38873. 264p. (C). 1991. 26.95 (*0-8093-1686-2*) S Ill U Pr.
Root, Robert L. & Steinberg, Michael. Fourth Genre: Contemporary Writers of/on Creative Nonfiction. 205th ed. LC 98-23267. 472p. (C). 1998. pap. text 38.00 (*0-205-27595-8*) Allyn.
Root, Robert L., Jr., ed. see National Council of Teachers of English Staff.
Root, Steven. Beyond Coso: Internal Control to Enhance Corporate Governance. LC 97-51810. 352p. 1998. 74.95 (*0-471-17809-8*) Wiley.
Root, Steven J., jt. auth. see Willson, James D.
Root, Susan, jt. ed. see Wellish, Pam.
Root Taucher, Mary, tr. see Barron's Educational Editors.
Root, Taylor, ed. Reversing the Flow: A Practical Guide to Greater Bay Area Corporate Giving Programs. 4th rev. ed. 120p. 1998. pap. 60.00 (*1-890759-04-X*) Chardon Pr.
Root, Terry. Atlas of Wintering North American Birds: An Analysis of Christmas Bird Count Data. LC 88-8591. (Illus.). 336p. 1989. pap. text 42.00 (*0-226-72540-5*) U Ch Pr.
— Atlas of Wintering North American Birds: An Analysis of Christmas Bird Count Data. LC 88-8591. (Illus.). 336p. 1996. lib. bdg. 72.00 (*0-226-72539-1*) U Ch Pr.
Root, W. & Pavlicek, Richard. Modern Bridge Conventions. 1995. pap. 16.00 (*0-517-88429-1*) Random.
Root, Waverley & De Rochemont, Richard. Eating in Am. LC 76-16145. 488p. 1981. reprint ed. pap. 9.95 (*0-912946-88-1*, Ecco Press) HarperTrade.
Root, Waverly. Food of France. 1992. pap. 15.00 (*0-679-73897-5*) Vin Bks.
— Food of Italy. 1992. pap. 17.00 (*0-679-73896-7*) Vin Bks.
Root, Waverly & De Rochemont, Richard. Eating in America: A History. 488p. 1981. pap. 9.95 (*0-88001-399-0*) HarpC.
Root, Wayne A. The Joy of Failure: How to Fail Your Way to the Top. LC 96-45824. (Illus.). 262p. (Orig.). 1996. pap. 16.95 (*1-56530-206-0*) Summit TX.
Root, Wayne A. & Cross, Wilbur. Betting to Win on Sports. 1989. pap. 8.95 (*0-685-28265-1*) Bantam.
Root, Wells. Writing the Script: A Practical Guide for Films & Television. LC 79-1927. 228p. 1995. pap. 11.95 (*0-8050-0237-5*, Owl) H Holt & Co.
— Writing the Script: A Practical Guide for Films & Television. 1980. pap. 6.95 (*0-03-044221-4*) Holt R&W.
Root, William A. & Liebman, John R. United States Export Controls. 3rd ed. 914p. 1991. ring bd. 116.00 (*0-13-109281-2*) Aspen Law.
— United States Export Controls. 3rd ed. ring bd. 165.00 (*1-56706-166-4*, 29813) Panel Pubs.
***Root, William A. & Liebman, John R.** United States Export Controls. 4th ed. LC 00-42155. 2000. write for info. (*0-7355-1547-6*) Panel Pubs.
Root, William L., jt. auth. see Davenport, Wilbur B.
Root, William P. Trace Elements from a Recurring Kingdom. LC 94-71360. 1994. 25.00 (*1-881090-12-4*); pap. 15.00 (*1-881090-11-6*) Confluence Pr.
Root, William P., et al. The Tribute of His Peers: Elegies for Robinson Jeffers. 85p. (Orig.). 1989. pap. write for info. (*0-9622774-0-1*) Tor Hse Pr.
Root, William S. The ABC's of Bridge. LC 98-8096. 304p. 1998. pap. 14.00 (*0-609-80162-7*, Crown) Crown Pub Group.
— Common Sense Bidding. 1995. pap. 15.00 (*0-517-88430-5*) Random.
— How to Defend a Bridge. 1995. pap. 16.00 (*0-517-88393-7*) Crown.
— How to Play a Bridge Hand. 1994. pap. 16.00 (*0-517-88159-4*) Crown Pub Group.
Root, Winfred T. Relations of Pennsylvania with the British Government, 1696-1765. LC 71-99249. reprint ed. 51.50 (*0-404-00608-6*) AMS Pr.
— The Relations of Pennsylvania with the British Government, 1696-1765. (BCL1 - United States Local History Ser.). 422p. 1991. reprint ed. lib. bdg. 99.00 (*0-7812-6278-X*) Rprt Serv.
Rootes. Social Change & Political Transformation: A New Europe? 224p. 1994. 75.00 (*1-85728-147-0*, Pub. by UCL Pr Ltd); pap. 27.50 (*1-85728-148-9*, Pub. by UCL Pr Ltd) Taylor & Francis.
Rootes, Chris, jt. ed. see Richardson, Dick.
Rootes, Christopher, ed. Environmental Movements: Local, National & Global. LC 99-21228. 328p. 1999. 49.50 (*0-7146-5008-0*, Pub. by F Cass Pubs); pap. 24.50 (*0-7146-8066-4*, Pub. by F Cass Pubs) Intl Spec Bk.
Rootes, David. The Arctic. (J). 1996. lib. bdg. 22.60 (*0-8225-2776-6*) Lerner Pub.
Rootes, Nina, tr. see Apollinaire, Guillaume.
Rootes, Nina, tr. see Cendrars, Blaise.
Rootes, Nina, tr. see Lacarriere, Jacques.
Rooth, Anna B. The Cinderella Cycle. Dorson, Richard M., ed. LC 80-748. (Folklore of the World Ser.). 1981. reprint ed. lib. bdg. 29.95 (*0-405-13322-7*) Ayer.
Rooth, Anne R. & White, James P. The Ninth Car. 1978. 8.95 (*0-399-12284-2*) Putnam Pub Group.
Rooth, Anne Reed. Southern Exposure. 384p. 1999. mass mkt. 6.50 (*0-06-101364-1*) HarpC.
Rooth, G., jt. auth. see Huch, R.
Rooth, Tim. British Protectionism & the International Economy: Overseas Commercial Policy in the 1930s. (Illus.). 373p. (C). 1993. text 69.95 (*0-521-41608-6*) Cambridge U Pr.
Rootham, Helen, tr. see Rimbaud, Jean N.
Rootland, Nancy. Anne's World, Maud's World: The Sacred Sites of L. M. Montgomery. LC 97-106026. (Illus.). 96p. 1998. 19.95 (*1-55109-142-9*) Nimbus Publ.
Rootman, I. & Hughes, P. Drug-Abuse Reporting Systems. (WHO Offset Publications: No. 55). 98p. 1980. 10.00 (*92-4-170055-6*) World Health.
Rootman, I. & Moser, J. Guidelines for Investigating Alcohol Problems & Developing Appropriate Responses. (WHO Offset Publications: No. 81). 120p. 1984. 12.00 (*92-4-170081-5*) World Health.
Rootman, I., jt. auth. see Raeburn, John.
Rootman, Jack, et al. Orbital Surgery: A Conceptual Approach. (Illus.). 416p. 1995. text 225.00 (*0-7817-0254-2*) Lppncott W & W.
Roots, Betty I., jt. ed. see Vernadakis, Antonia.
Roots, Charles R. The Sandwich Generation: Adult Children Caring for Aging Parents. LC 97-40761. (Studies on the Elderly in America). 150p. 1998. text 42.00 (*0-8153-3004-9*) Garland.
***Roots, David, et al.** Rocks & Fossils. (Nature Company Guides Ser.). (Illus.). 288p. 2000. pap. write for info. (*0-7370-0078-3*) Time-Life Educ.
Roots, Guy, et al, eds. Ryde on Rating & the Council Tax. 1995. ring bd. write for info. (*0-406-00634-2*, RRCTSET, MICHIE) LEXIS Pub.
Roots, Ivan. The Great Rebellion, 1642-1660. LC 96-116754. 1997. pap. text 26.95 (*0-7509-0921-8*, Pub. by Sutton Pub Ltd) Intl Pubs Mktg.
Roots, Ivan, ed. Conflicts in Tudor & Stuart England. LC 68-97374. (Selections from History Today Ser.: No. 5). (Illus.). 1969. pap. 9.95 (*0-05-001536-2*) Dufour.
— "Into Another Mould" Aspects of the Interregnum. rev. ed. 144p. 1998. pap. text 21.95 (*0-85989-417-7*) Univ Exeter Pr.
Roots, Leon. Oh My Aching Back. 1966. write for info. (*0-679-50384-6*) Random.
Roots, Schuylkill. Salem Evangelical Lutheran Church, Killinger, Upper Paxton Township, Dauphin County, PA, 1770-1859. 57p. 1996. per. 6.00 (*1-55856-215-X*, 061) Closson Pr.
Rooum, Donald. What Is Anarchism? An Introduction. (Illus.). 74p. (Orig.). 1992. pap. 4.50 (*0-900384-66-2*) Left Bank.
— Wildcat: ABC of Bosses. (Illus.). 48p. (Orig.). 1991. pap. 5.00 (*0-900384-60-3*) Left Bank.
— Wildcat: Anarchist Comics. rev. ed. (Illus.). 47p. 1987. pap. 5.00 (*0-900384-30-1*) Left Bank.
— Wildcat Strikes Again. (Illus.). 48p. (Orig.). 1989. pap. 5.00 (*0-900384-47-6*) Left Bank.
Roovelli, Riccardo, jt. ed. see Angeloni, Ignazio.
Roover, Dick De, see De Roover, Dick.
Roovers, J., ed. Branched Polymers II. (Advances in Polymer Science Ser.: Vol. 143). x, 271p. 1999. 189.00 (*3-540-65005-9*) Spr-Verlag.
Roovers, J. & Charleux, B., eds. Branched Polymers I. (Advances in Polymer Science Ser.: Vol. 142). (Illus.). x, 242p. 1999. 189.00 (*3-540-64923-9*) Spr-Verlag.
Rooy, Cynthis. Man in Uniform. 1997. mass mkt. 1.78 (*0-8217-5776-8*) Kensgtn Pub Corp.
Rooy, Elwin L., ed. see Minerals, Metals & Materials Society Staff.
Rooy, H. F. van, see van Rooy, H. F.
Rooy, J. M. van Medenbach de, see Van der Maesen, L. J.
Rooy, R. Van, see Van Rooy, R.
Rooyackers, Paul. 101 Dance Games for Children: Fun & Creativity with Movement. LC 95-13201. (Smart Fun Bks.). (Illus.). 160p. 1996. pap. 11.95 (*0-89793-171-8*); spiral bd. 14.95 (*0-89793-172-6*) Hunter Hse.
— 101 Drama Games for Children: Fun & Learning with Acting & Make-Believe. LC 97-20957. (Smart Fun Bks.). (Illus.). 160p. 1996. spiral bd. 14.95 (*0-89793-212-9*) Hunter Hse.
Rooyackers, Paul. 101 Drama Games for Children: Fun & Learning with Acting & Make-Believe. LC 97-20957. (Smart Fun Ser.). (Illus.). 160p. (J). (ps-6). 1998. pap. 11.95 (*0-89793-211-0*) Hunter Hse.
Rooyen, Johann Van, see Van Rooyen, Johann.
Rooyen, Margaretha W. Van, see Van Rheede-Van Oudtshoorn, Karen & Van Rooyen, Margaretha W.
Rooyen, Van, see Van Rooyen.
***Roozeboom, F., et al, eds.** Advances in Rapid Thermal Processing. 452p. 1999. 74.00 (*1-56677-232-X*, PV 99-10) Electrochem Soc.
Roozeboom, Fred, ed. Advances in Rapid Thermal & Integrated Processing: Proceedings of the NATO Advanced Study Institute Acquafredda di Maratea, Italy, July 3-4, 1995. (NATO ASI Ser.: Series E, Vol. 318). 580p. (C). 1996. text 291.00 (*0-7923-4011-6*) Kluwer Academic.
Roozen, David A., jt. auth. see Hadaway, C. Kirk.
Roozenburg, N. F. & Eekels, J. Product Design: Fundamentals & Methods. 422p. 1995. pap. 85.00 (*0-471-95465-9*) Wiley.
***Ropa, John.** The Non Product Consolidation Operation: A Novel. LC 00-190637. 187p. 2000. 25.00 (*0-7388-1880-1*); pap. 18.00 (*0-7388-1881-X*) Xlibris Corp.
Ropars, C., et al, eds. Red Blood Cells As Carriers for Drugs: Potential Therapeutic Applications. (Illus.). 272p. 1987. 120.00 (*0-08-036137-4*, Pergamon Pr) Elsevier.
Roparz, Hemon. Dictionnaire Francais-Breton. (BRE & FRE.). 42p. 1984. pap. 14.95 (*0-7859-4890-2*) Fr & Eur.
— Dictionnaire Historique du Breton: Geriadur Istorel ar Brezhoneg. (FRE.). 1975. reprint ed. 695.00 (*0-8288-9534-1*) Fr & Eur.
Rope, Frederick T. Opinion Conflict & School Support. LC 70-177206. (Columbia University. Teachers College. Contributions to Education Ser.: No. 838). viii, 164 p. 1972. reprint ed. 37.50 (*0-404-55838-0*) AMS Pr.
Ropeid, Andreas, jt. ed. see Riddervold, Astri.
Ropeka, W. International Order & Economic Integration. Trinks, G. E. et al, trs. from GER. 276p. 1960. lib. bdg. 154.50 (*90-277-0100-8*) Kluwer Academic.
Ropelewski & Ryan. Study Guide to Accompany Clinical Drug Therapy. 5th ed. 256p. 1997. pap. text 17.00 (*0-397-55373-0*) Lppncott W & W.
Roper. Business Law & Contracts for Paralegals. (C). 1999. mass mkt. 44.00 (*0-7668-0749-5*) Delmar.
— Elements of Nursing. 4th ed. 1996. pap. text 37.95 (*0-443-05201-8*, W B Saunders Co) Harcrt Hlth Sci Grp.
— Practical Law Office Mgmt- Study Guide. (Paralegal). (C). 1994. student ed. 14.25 (*0-314-04851-0*) Delmar.
— Tis Pity She's a Whore. LC 96-34810. 1997. pap. 9.95 (*0-7190-4359-X*) St Martin.
— Using Computers in the Law Office. 3rd ed. LC 99-58163. (Paralegal Ser.). (C). 1999. pap. 59.95 (*0-7668-0454-2*) Thomson Learn.
Roper, A. Woman to Woman. (C). 1990. 45.00 (*0-946211-23-X*) St Mut.
Roper, Alan. Arnold's Poetic Landscapes. LC 70-86097. 280p. reprint ed. pap. 86.80 (*0-8357-5751-X*, 202074900018) Bks Demand.
Roper, Alan & Vinton, Dearing A., eds. The Works of John Dryden Vol. XVIII: Prose: The History of the League, 1684. 1975. 80.00 (*0-520-02131-2*, Pub. by U CA Pr) Cal Prin Full Svc.
— The Works of John Dryden Vol. XIX: Prose: The Life of St. Francis Xavier. 1979. 80.00 (*0-520-02132-0*, Pub. by U CA Pr) Cal Prin Full Svc.
Roper, Allen G. Ancient Eugenics. 1982. reprint ed. 16.00 (*0-941694-05-4*) Cliveden Pr.
Roper, Beryl C. Seekers after Truth. 90p. (YA). (gr. 9-11). 1998. pap. write for info. (*1-885812-04-3*) Aquamarine.
— Trementina Revisited. 82p. 1994. 24.95 (*1-885812-00-0*) Aquamarine.
Roper, Beryl C., ed. see Blake, Alice A.
Roper, Brent D. Computers & the Law: Concepts & Applications. Hannan, ed. 481p. (C). 1992. pap. text 52.00 (*0-314-93374-3*) West Pub.
— Practical Law Office Mgmt. LC 94-19945. (Paralegal). 520p. (C). 1994. mass mkt. 36.50 (*0-314-04305-5*) West Pub.
— Using Computers in the Law Office. 2nd ed. LC 95-39259. (Paralegal). 500p. (C). 1996. mass mkt. 59.95 (*0-314-06519-9*) West Pub.
Roper, Brent S., jt. compiled by see Chalfant, H. Paul.
Roper, Brian & Rudd, Chris, eds. State & Economy in New Zealand. (Oxford Readings in New Zealand Politics Ser.: No. 2). (Illus.). 292p. 1993. pap. text 45.00 (*0-19-558273-X*) OUP.
Roper, Brian, jt. ed. see Rudd, Chris.
Roper, C. A. Risk Management for Security Professionals. LC 99-11119. 354p. 1999. write for info. (*0-7506-7113-0*) Buttrwrth-Heinemann.
Roper, C. A. & Phillips, Bill. The Complete Book of Locks & Locksmithing. 3rd ed. (Illus.). 360p. 1991. pap. 19.95 (*0-8306-3522-X*) McGraw-Hill Prof.
Roper, Carl A. Physical Security & the Inspection Process. LC 96-43147. 290p. 1996. 56.95 (*0-7506-9712-1*) Buttrwrth-Heinemann.
Roper Center for Public Opinion Research Staff. America at the Polls, 1996. Ladd, Everett C., ed. (Occasional Papers & Monographs: No. 3). (Illus.). 200p. (C). 1997. pap. 29.95 (*1-887415-02-5*) RCPOR.
Roper Center for Public Opinion Research Staff & Ladd, Everett C. America at the Polls, 1994. (Occasional Papers & Monographs Ser.: No. 2). (Illus.). 170p. (Orig.). (C). 1995. pap. text 19.95 (*1-887415-01-7*) RCPOR.
***Roper, Charles N.** High Bottom Drunk: A Novel... And the Truth about Addiction & Recovery. xii, 465p. 2000. pap. 18.95 (*0-9677529-0-6*) Small Change Pub.
Roper, Charles S. & Park, Andy, eds. Managing the Living Forest. (Illus.). 450p. 1999. pap. 160.00 (*0-11-710343-8*, Pub. by Statnry Office) Balogh.
***Roper, Christopher.** Foundations for Continuing Legal Education. 228p. 1999. pap. 46.50 (*0-909136-69-6*, Pub. by Ctr For Legal Educ) Gaunt.
Roper, D., et al, eds. Shakespeare in the New Europe. LC 95-234897. 35.00 (*1-85075-474-8*, Pub. by Sheffield Acad) CUP Services.
Roper, Daniel C. Fifty Years of Public Life. (History - United States Ser.). 422p. 1993. reprint ed. lib. bdg. 99.00 (*0-7812-4923-6*) Rprt Serv.
— Fifty Years of Public Life. (American Autobiography Ser.). 422p. 1995. reprint ed. lib. bdg. 99.00 (*0-7812-8630-1*) Rprt Serv.
Roper, David. A Burden Shared: Encouragement for Leaders. LC 91-11617. 192p. 1991. pap. 11.99 (*0-929239-40-7*) Discovery Hse Pubs.
— Elijah: A Man Like Us. LC 97-46005. 256p. 1998. pap. 10.99 (*1-57293-031-4*) Discovery Hse Pubs.
***Roper, David.** Growing Slowly Wise: Building a Faith That Works. 2000. pap. text 9.95 (*1-57293-064-0*) Discovery Hse Pubs.
Roper, David. In Quietness & Confidence. LC 98-43635. 160p. 1999. 12.99 (*1-57293-043-8*) Discovery Hse Pubs.
— A Man to Match the Mountain: Overcoming the Obstacles of Life. LC 96-33524. 288p. (Orig.). 1996. pap. 10.99 (*1-57293-013-6*) Discovery Hse Pubs.
— Precious Memories: Girl/Boy. 1987. pap. 2.75 (*0-89137-443-4*) Quality Pubns.
— Psalm 23: The Song of a Passionate Heart. LC 94-9196. 168p. 1996. 12.99 (*1-57293-012-8*) Discovery Hse Pubs.
— Psalm 23. 168p. 1996. pap. 5.99 (*0-929239-86-5*, Pub. by Discovery Hse Pubs) Barbour Pub.

An Asterisk (*) at the beginning of an entry indicates that the title is appearing for the first time.

— The Strength of a Man: Encouragement for Today. LC 89-1180. 160p. 1989. pap. 9.99 (*0-929239-07-5*) Discovery Hse Pubs.

Roper, David, ed. see Martin, Norman R.

Roper, David L. Getting Serious about Love. 219p. 1992. pap. 8.95 (*0-945441-11-8*) Res Pubns AR.

— Practical Christianity: Studies in the Book of James. 148p. 1987. pap. 6.99 (*0-89225-291-X*, G5291X) Gospel Advocate.

Roper, Derek. Reviewing Before the Edinburgh, 1788-1802. LC 77-2446. (Illus.). 1978. 40.00 (*0-87413-128-6*) U Delaware Pr.

Roper, Derek, ed. see Bronte, Emily Jane.

Roper, Donna C. The Airport Site: A Multicomponent Site in the Sangamon River Drainage. (Research Series: Papers in Anthropology: No. 4). (Illus.). 32p. 1978. pap. 2.00 (*0-89792-074-0*) Ill St Museum.

— The Distribution of Middle Woodland Sites Within the Environment of the Lower Sangamon River, Illinois. (Reports of Investigations: No. 30). (Illus.). 22p. 1974. pap. 1.00 (*0-89792-054-6*) Ill St Museum.

Roper, E. The Ropers of Sterling & Rutland. (Illus.). 473p. 1989. reprint ed. pap. 71.00 (*0-8328-1033-9*); reprint ed. lib. bdg. 79.00 (*0-8328-1032-0*) Higginson Bk Co.

Roper, Ed M. Guidelines for Health & Safety in Metal Finishing. 80p. 1991. 95.00 (*0-904477-06-1*, Pub. by FMJ Intl) St Mut.

Roper-Evans, Emma, tr. see Hankiss, Agnes.

Roper, Faith A., ed. see Roper, Ida J.

Roper, Fred W. Alfred William Pollard: A Selection of His Essays. LC 76-25547. (Great Bibliographers Ser.: No. 2). 252p. 1976. 18.50 (*0-8108-0958-3*, Pub. by Scarecrow) Oak Knoll.

Roper, Gail. Who Done It? LC 94-11889. 48p. (J). 1996. pap. 3.99 (*0-7814-0079-1*, Chariot Bks) Chariot Victor.

Roper, Gayle. The Adventures of Scooter & Jake: Bear Scare. (Adventures of Scooter & Jake Ser.). (Illus.). 48p. (Orig.). (J). (gr. 3-6). 1996. pap. 3.99 (*0-7814-0080-5*) Chariot Victor.

— The Case of the Missing Melody. LC 92-39317. (East Edge Mysteries Ser.). (Illus.). 128p. (J). 1993. pap. 4.99 (*1-55513-702-4*, Chariot Bks) Chariot Victor.

— Cat Burglars? (Adventures of Scooter & Jake Ser.). (Illus.). 48p. (Orig.). (J). (gr. 1-3). 1995. pap. 3.99 (*0-7814-0077-5*, Chariot Bks) Chariot Victor.

***Roper, Gayle.** Caught in a Bind. LC 99-88547. (Amherst Mystery Ser.). 2000. pap. 9.99 (*0-310-21850-0*) Zondervan.

Roper, Gayle. Caught in the Act? LC 98-23125. (Amhearst Mystery Ser.: 2). 272p. 1998. pap. 9.99 (*0-310-21909-4*) Zondervan.

***Roper, Gayle.** Caught in the Middle. LC 99-87868. (Christian Fiction Ser.). 216p. 2000. 23.95 (*0-7862-2439-8*) Thorndike Pr.

Roper, Gayle. Caught in the Middle. LC 96-50279. (Amhearst Mystery Ser.: Vol. 1). 256p. 1997. pap. 9.99 (*0-310-20995-1*) Zondervan.

— Caught in the Middle. (Amhearst Mystery Ser.: 1). 1997. pap. 9.99 (*0-614-27305-6*) Zondervan.

***Roper, Gayle.** The Decision. LC 99-39372. 352p. 1999. pap. 6.99 (*1-57673-406-4*) Multnomah Pubs.

Roper, Gayle. The Document, Vol. 2. LC 98-30771. 1998. pap. 9.99 (*1-57673-295-9*, Palisades OR) Multnomah Pubs.

— Enough. LC 97-17218. 202p. 1997. pap. 10.99 (*1-57673-185-5*, Palisades OR) Multnomah Pubs.

— Here, Boy! (Adventures of Scooter & Jake Ser.). (Illus.). 48p. (Orig.). (J). (gr. 1-3). 1995. pap. 3.99 (*0-7814-0078-3*, Chariot Bks) Chariot Victor.

— The Key. LC 97-37109. 250p. 1998. pap. 9.99 (*1-57673-223-1*, Palisades OR) Multnomah Pubs.

— The Mystery of the Poison Pen. LC 94-6755. 128p. (J). 1994. write for info. (*0-7814-1507-1*, Chariot Bks) Chariot Victor.

— A Race to the Finish. LC 90-21160. (Sports Stories for Boys Ser.). 128p. (J). (gr. 3-7). 1991. pap. 4.99 (*1-55513-816-0*, 38166, Chariot Bks) Chariot Victor.

— Whoo Done It? (Adventures of Scooter & Jake Ser.). (Illus.). 48p. (Orig.). (J). (gr. 3-6). 1996. pap. 3.99 (*0-614-11766-6*) Chariot Victor.

Roper, Gayle G. Balancing Your Emotions: For Women Who Want Consistency under Stress. LC 92-30983. 144p. 1992. pap. 7.99 (*0-87788-075-1*, H Shaw Pubs) Waterbrook Pr.

***Roper, Gayle G.** Caught in the Act. LC 00-41712. 2000. write for info. (*0-7862-2776-1*) Five Star.

Roper, Geoffrey. World Survey of Islamic Manuscripts Vol. 2: Iraq-Russian Federation. 724p. 1993. 156.00 (*1-873992-02-5*, Pub. by Al-Furqan Islamic) Brill Academic Pubs.

Roper, Geoffrey, ed. World Survey of Islamic Manuscripts, Vol. 1. xviii, 570p. 1992. 156.00 (*1-873992-01-7*) Brill Academic Pubs.

Roper, Gordon, ed. see Hawthorne, Nathaniel.

Roper-Hall, Michael J., ed. Microsurgery of the Anterior & Posterior Segments for the Eye. (Developments in Ophthalmology Ser.: Vol. 5). (Illus.). vi, 134p. 1982. pap. 78.50 (*3-8055-2711-X*) S Karger.

Roper-Hall, Michael J., et al, eds. Advances in Ophthalmology, Vol. 26. 1972. 116.75 (*3-8055-1354-2*) S Karger.

— Advances in Ophthalmology, Vol. 35. (GER., Illus.). 1978. 115.00 (*3-8055-2657-1*) S Karger.

— Advances in Ophthalmology, Vol. 39. (Illus.). 1979. 163.50 (*3-8055-3030-7*) S Karger.

Roper-hall, Michael J., et al, eds. Advances in Ophthalmology, Vol. 40. (Illus.). 1979. 136.75 (*3-8055-3031-5*) S Karger.

— Commemorative Volume in Honour of Prof. Streiff. (Advances in Ophthalmology Ser.: Vol. 36). (FRE & GER., Illus.). 1978. 163.50 (*3-8055-2828-0*) S Karger.

Roper-Hall, Michael J., jt. auth. see Eagling, Elizabeth.

***Roper-Hall, Micheal J.** Records of the War Office & Related Departments, 1660-1964. 2nd rev. ed. LC 99-219597. (PRO Handbks.: No. 29). (Illus.). 386p. 1999. pap. text 39.95 (*1-873162-45-6*, Pub. by PRO Pubns) Midpt Trade.

Roper, Harlin J. In the Beginning God: Genesis - Exodus 18. (Through the Bible Studies: No. 1Y). 64p. (YA). (gr. 7-12). 1988. student ed. 4.98 (*0-86606-362-5*, 1Y) Treasure Pub.

— In the Beginning God: Genesis - Exodus 18. (Through the Bible Studies: No. 1J). (Illus.). 64p. (J). (gr. 4-6). 1989. student ed. 4.98 (*0-86606-374-9*, 1J) Treasure Pub.

— In the Beginning God: Genesis - Exodus 18. (Through the Bible Studies: No. 1). 64p. 1989. student ed. 4.98 (*0-86606-350-1*, 1) Treasure Pub.

Roper, Hazel A., jt. auth. see Burt, Steven E.

Roper, Hazel Ann, jt. auth. see Burt, Steven E.

Roper, Hugh T., ed. & abr. see Macaulay, Thomas Babington.

Roper, Ida J. Joyful Journeys: A Book of Poetry. Roper, Faith A., ed. 62p. 1999. pap. write for info. (*0-7392-0184-0*, PO3151) Morris Pubng.

Roper, Ingrid. Moneymakers: Good Cents for Girls. LC 98-21076. (American Girl Library Ser.). (Illus.). 110p. (J). (gr. 3-7). 1998. pap. text 7.95 (*1-56247-668-8*) Pleasant Co.

Roper, Ingrid. Yo-Yos. (J). 15.95 (*0-688-14663-5*, Wm Morrow); lib. bdg. 15.89 (*0-688-14664-3*, Wm Morrow) Morrow Avon.

Roper, James E. The Founding of Memphis, 1818-1820. (Illus.). 100p. 1970. 17.00 (*0-937130-07-9*) Burkes Bk Store.

Roper, Janet, jt. auth. see McDougall, Nancy.

***Roper, Janice M. & Shapira, Jill.** Ethnography in Nursing Research. LC 99-50407. (Methods in Nursing Research Ser.: Vol. 1). 150p. 2000. 49.95 (*0-7619-0873-0*) Sage.

Roper, John, ed. The Future of the British Defense Policy. (Joint Studies in Public Policy). 200p. 1985. text 67.95 (*0-566-00922-6*) Ashgate Pub Co.

Roper, John, et al. Keeping the Peace in the Post-Cold War Era: Strengthening Multilateral Peacekeeping. LC 93-30079. (Triangle Papers: Vol. 43). 101p. (C). 1993. pap. 12.00 (*0-930503-70-8*) Trilateral Comm.

Roper, John H. C. Vann Woodward, Southerner. LC 86-25020. 398p. 1987. 35.00 (*0-8203-0933-8*) U of Ga Pr.

— U. B. Phillips: A Southern Mind. LC 84-682. vi, 204p. 1984. 16.95 (*0-86554-112-4*, MUP-H103) Mercer Univ Pr.

Roper, John H., ed. see Green, Paul.

Roper, John Herbert. C. Vann Woodward: A Southern Historian & His Critics. LC 96-21759. 1997. 50.00 (*0-8203-1876-0*); pap. 25.00 (*0-8203-1877-9*) U of Ga Pr.

Roper, Jon. Democracy & Its Critics: Anglo-American Democratic Thought in the Nineteenth Century. LC 88-17659. 240p. (C). 1989. pap. text 22.95 (*0-04-445130-X*) Routledge.

Roper, Jon, jt. auth. see Melling, Phil.

Roper, Jon, jt. ed. see Melling, Phil.

Roper, Katherine A. Bands of Love. (Illus.). 214p. 1997. pap. 7.99 (*1-57502-585-X*, PO1676) Morris Pubng.

Roper, Kenneth N., jt. auth. see Gatehouse, Anthony L.

Roper, Lila, ed. see Ethier, Roger.

Roper, Lyndal. The Holy Household: Women & Morals in Reformation Augsburg. (Oxford Studies in Social History). (Illus.). 306p. 1991. reprint ed. pap. text 35.00 (*0-19-820280-6*) OUP.

— Oedipus & the Devil: Witchcraft, Sexuality, & Religion in Early Modern Europe. LC 93-5903. 256p. (C). (gr. 13). 1994. pap. 24.99 (*0-415-10581-1*) Routledge.

Roper, Mac, jt. auth. see Parrington, Norman.

Roper, Nancy. The Elements of Nursing. 3rd ed. (Illus.). 376p. 1990. pap. text 45.00 (*0-443-03950-X*) Church.

— New American Pocket Medical Dictionary. 2nd ed. 372p. 1988. pap. 17.00 (*0-684-19031-1*, Scribners Ref) Mac Lib Ref.

— Principles of Nursing in Process Context. 4th ed. (Illus.). 336p. (Orig.). 1988. text 30.00 (*0-443-03576-8*) Church.

Roper, Nancy, ed. Gray's Pocket Medical Dictionary. 2nd rev. ed. 1995. pap. text 16.00 (*0-443-07683-9*) Church.

— New American Pocket Medical Dictionary. 2nd ed. (Illus.). 368p. 1988. pap. text 12.95 (*0-443-08581-1*) Church.

Roper, Paul, jt. auth. see Connon, Heather.

Roper, Peter. Badminton: The Skills of the Game. (Illus.). 128p. 1995. pap. 19.95 (*1-85223-887-9*, Pub. by Crolwood) Trafalgar.

Roper, R. G., ed. Interim Results of the Middle Atmosphere Program: A Selection of Invited Papers from the Symposium Jointly Sponsored by the IAGA & IAMAP at the XVIII General Assembly of the IUGG, Hamburg, Federal Republic of Germany, August 1985. 112p. 1985. pap. 36.00 (*0-08-032594-7*, Pergamon Pr) Elsevier.

Roper, Rudiger. Anschauung und Begriff von Proportionsbeziehungen. (Illus.). 302p. 1997. 57.95 (*3-631-31681-X*) P Lang Pubng.

Roper, Sandi, ed. see Mohr, Jeanne M.

Roper, Stephen D., jt. ed. see Simon, Sidney A.

Roper, Steve. Camp 4: Recollections of a Yosemite Rockclimber. (Illus.). 256p. 1998. pap. 16.95 (*0-89886-587-5*) Mountaineers.

— Climber's Guide to the High Sierra. rev. ed. LC 75-45108. (Totebook Ser.). (Illus.). 384p. 1982. pap. 14.00 (*0-87156-147-6*, Pub. by Sierra) Random.

— The Sierra High Route: Traversing Timberline Country. 2nd rev. ed. LC 96-49269. (Illus.). 224p. (Orig.). 1997. pap. 16.95 (*0-89886-506-9*) Mountaineers.

Roper, Steve & Steck, Allen. Fifty Classic Climbs of North America. (Illus.). 336p. 1996. pap. 25.00 (*0-87156-884-5*, Pub. by Sierra) Random.

— Fifty Classic Climbs of North America. LC 79-1300. (Sierra Club Guides Ser.). (Illus.). 336p. 1982. reprint ed. pap. 20.00 (*0-87156-292-8*, Pub. by Sierra) Random.

Roper, Steve, jt. ed. see Steck, Allen.

***Roper, Steven D.** Romania Vol. 8: The Unfinished Revolution. 150p. 2000. pap. 19.95 (*90-5823-028-7*, Harwood Acad Pubs) Gordon & Breach.

— Romania Vol.8: The Unfinished Revolution. 150p. 2000. 33.00 (*90-5823-027-9*, Harwood Acad Pubs) Gordon & Breach.

Roper, Trey. Japanese-English Idioms. LC 94-60129. vi, 500 p. (C). 1994. pap. text 30.00 (*0-9640744-3-5*) US-Asia Res.

Roper, Walter F., jt. auth. see McHenry, Roy C.

Roper-Wickstrom, C. Kristina. A Study of High Altitude Obsidian Distribution in the Southern Sierra Nevada, California. 178p. (C). 1992. pap. text 19.38 (*1-55567-112-8*) Coyote Press.

Roper, William. Life of Sir Thomas More. (Illus.). 125p. 1983. pap. 9.95 (*0-87243-118-5*) Templegate.

— Life of Sir Thomas More. write for info. Yale U Pr.

— Sequoyah & His Miracle. 32p. (J). (gr. 5-12). 1972. pap. 4.95 (*0-89992-056-X*) Coun India Ed.

Ropers-Huilman, Becky. Feminist Teaching in Theory & Practice: Situating Power & Knowledge in Poststructural Classrooms. LC 97-35310. (Critical Issues in Curriculum Ser.). 1998. 44.00 (*0-8077-3694-5*); pap. 21.95 (*0-8077-3693-7*) Tchrs Coll.

Ropers, R. H. Persistent Poverty: The American Dream Turned Nightmare. LC 91-14. (Illus.). 268p. (C). 1991. 23.95 (*0-306-43764-3*, Plen Insight) Perseus Pubng.

Ropers, Richard H. The Invisible Homeless: A New Urban Ecology. (Illus.). 224p. (C). 1988. 32.95 (*0-89885-406-7*, Kluwer Acad Hman Sci) Kluwer Academic.

— Toward a Kinder & Gentler America: Ending Poverty & Homelessness & Fulfilling the American Dream. (Distinguished Faculty Lecture Ser.). 29p. 1989. pap. text 6.95 (*0-935615-08-3*) S Utah U Pr.

***Ropert, Jon, ed.** American Civil War, 3 vols. 1500p. (C). (gr. 13). 1999. text 375.00 (*1-873403-12-7*) Routledge.

Ropert, M., jt. auth. see Brown, R.

Ropert, M., jt. auth. see Pavey, N. L.

Ropes, Hannah A. Six Months in Kansas, by a Lady. LC 76-38020. (Black Heritage Library Collection). 1977. reprint ed. 23.95 (*0-8369-8987-2*) Ayer.

Ropes, James H. St. James: Critical & Exegetical Commentary. LC 16-6543. (International Critical Commentary Ser.). 336p. 1997. 39.95 (*0-567-05035-1*, Pub. by T & T Clark) Bks Intl VA.

Ropes, Linda. Just a Little off the Top. large type unabridged ed. Davenport, May, ed. LC 97-67645. 44p. (YA). (gr. 7-12). 1998. pap. text 6.95 (*0-943864-89-5*) Davenport.

Ropes, Linda B. Health Care Crisis in America. LC 92-31474. (Contemporary World Issues Ser.). 1991. lib. bdg. 39.50 (*0-87436-616-X*) ABC-CLIO.

Ropes, M. E. Honesty the Best Policy: And Other Stories. 3rd rev. ed. LC 96-97152. (Illus.). 92p. 1997. reprint ed. pap. 5.95 (*0-9658838-0-9*) Yng Advent Pilgrims.

Ropes, Marian W. Systemic Lupus Erythematosus. LC 75-31988. 183p. reprint ed. pap. 56.80 (*0-7837-6089-2*, 205913500007) Bks Demand.

***Ropes, Mary.** Mary Jones & Her Bible. (Children's Victorian Classics Ser.). 1999. pap. 6.99 (*0-88270-789-2*) Bridge-Logos.

Ropka, Gerald W. The Evolving Residential Patterns of the Mexican, Puerto Rican, & Cuban Population in the City of Chicago. Cortes, Carlos E., ed. LC 79-6222. (Hispanics in the United States Ser.). (Illus.). 1981. lib. bdg. 23.95 (*0-405-13169-0*) Ayer.

Ropka, Mary & Williams, Ann. Handbook of HIV Nursing. LC 98-13527. (Nursing Ser.). 806p. 1998. pap. 40.00 (*0-7637-0544-6*) Jones & Bartlett.

Ropke, Ian M. Historical Dictionary of Osaka & Kyoto. Woronoff, Jon, ed. LC 98-43671. (Historical Dictionaries of Cities Ser.: No. 10). 312p. 1999. 59.50 (*0-8108-3622-X*) Scarecrow.

Ropke, Wilhelm. Economics of the Free Society. 288p. 1994. pap. 13.95 (*0-910884-28-5*) Libertarian Press.

— A Humane Economy: The Social Framework of the Free Market. 3rd ed. LC 98-73066. 312p. 1998. reprint ed. 24.95 (*1-882926-24-2*) ISI Books.

— International Economic Disintegration. LC 78-11239. (Studies in International Economics: No. 4). xii, 283p. 1978. reprint ed. lib. bdg. 39.50 (*0-87991-853-5*) Porcupine Pr.

Ropohl, G. Wie die Technik Zur Vernunft Kommt: Reason & Technolgy. (Technik Interdisziplinar Ser.). 192p. 1998. pap. text 16.00 (*90-5708-036-2*) Gordon & Breach.

— Wied die Technik Zur Vernunft Kommt: Reason & Technology. (Technik Interdisziplinar Ser.). 192p. 1998. text 30.00 (*90-5708-035-4*) Gordon & Breach.

Ropp, Harry L. Is Mormonism Christian? A Look at the Teachings of the Mormon Religion. rev. ed. LC 95-30456. Orig. Title: Are the Mormon Scriptures Reliable?. 1995. pap. 8.99 (*0-89900-742-2*) College Pr Pub.

Ropp, Paul S. Banished Immortal: Searching for Shuangqing, China's Peasant Woman Poet. (Illus.). 304p. (C). text 42.50 (*0-472-11195-7*) U of Mich Pr.

Ropp, Paul S., ed. The Heritage of China: Contemporary Perspectives on Chinese Civilization. 1990. 75.00 (*0-520-06440-2*, Pub. by U CA Pr); pap. 22.50 (*0-520-06441-0*, Pub. by U CA Pr) Cal Prin Full Svc.

Ropp, R. C. The Chemistry of Artificial Lighting Devices: Lamps, Phosphors, & Cathode Ray Tubes. LC 93-33113. (Studies in Inorganic Chemistry: No. 17). 682p. 1993. 399.50 (*0-444-81709-3*) Elsevier.

— Inorganic Polymeric Glasses. LC 92-14445. (Studies in Inorganic Chemistry: Vol. 15). 322p. 1992. 268.75 (*0-444-89500-0*) Elsevier.

— Luminescence & the Solid State. (Studies in Inorganic Chemistry: Vol. 12). xvi, 454p. 1991. 250.75 (*0-444-88940-X*) Elsevier.

Ropp, Robert S. Man Against Aging. Kastenbaum, Robert J., ed. LC 78-22216. (Aging & Old Age Ser.). 1979. reprint ed. lib. bdg. 28.95 (*0-405-11829-5*) Ayer.

Ropp, Steve. One on One: Making the Most of Your Mentoring Relationship. Janzen, Susan E., ed. LC 93-71182. 90p. (Orig.). 1993. pap., spiral bd. 15.95 (*0-87303-206-3*) Faith & Life.

— Some Body! (Fast Lane Bible Studies). 44p. (YA). (gr. 7-9). 1998. pap. 9.95 (*0-87303-333-7*) Faith & Life.

— A Speck in the Universe: The Bible on Self-Esteem & Peer Pressure. (Generation Why: Vol. 2:4). 40p. (YA). (gr. 9-12). 1996. pap. 14.95 (*0-87303-268-3*) Faith & Life.

Ropp, Steve C. Panamanian Politics: From Guarded Nation to National Guard. LC 81-17831. (Politics in Latin America, A Hoover Institution Ser.). 151p. 1982. 33.95 (*0-275-91817-3*, C1817, Praeger Pubs) Greenwood.

Ropp, Theodore. The Development of a Modern Navy: French Naval Policy 1871-1904. Roberts, Stephen S., ed. (Illus.). 439p. 1987. 45.00 (*0-87021-141-2*) Naval Inst Pr.

— History & War. LC 84-80149. 90p. 1984. pap. 7.50 (*0-916587-00-2*) Hamburg Pr.

— War in the Modern World. LC 60-5274. 416p. reprint ed. pap. 129.00 (*0-608-10684-4*, 201025000068); reprint ed. pap. 118.60 (*0-608-30585-5*, 2010250); reprint ed. pap. 118.60 (*0-608-30304-6*, 2010250) Bks Demand.

— War in the Modern World. LC 81-6448. 400p. 1981. reprint ed. lib. bdg. 89.50 (*0-313-22844-2*, ROWM, Greenwood Pr) Greenwood.

***Ropp, Theodore.** War in the Modern World. rev. ed. LC 99-87565. 2000. 18.95 (*0-8018-6445-3*) Johns Hopkins.

Roppatte, Vincent & Cohen, Sherry S. Big City Look: How to Achieve That Metropolitan Chic. LC TT507.R67 1998. (Illus.). 224p. 1998. 30.00 (*0-06-017589-3*, Cliff Street) HarperTrade.

Roppel, Patricia. Alaska's Salmon Hatcheries, 1891-1959. LC 82-600591. (Alaska Historical Commission Studies in History: No. 20). (Illus.). 299p. 1982. 18.00 (*0-943712-09-2*) Alaska Hist.

— Fortunes from the Earth: An History of the Base & Industrial Minerals of Southeast Alaska. (Illus.). 152p. 1991. pap. 18.95 (*0-89745-136-8*) Sunflower U Pr.

Roppel, Patricia. Land of Mists: Revillagigedo & Gravina Islands, Misty Fiords National Monument, Alaska. 3rd ed. 60p. pap. text 35.00 (*1-57833-111-0*) Todd Commns.

— Where Can I Buy One of These? A History of Ketchikan, Alaska's Business Community. 60p. pap. text 15.00 (*1-57833-110-2*) Todd Commns.

Roppelt, Donna & Mowl, Mary. Tomorrow, We're Taking a Test. 1982. pap. 1.95 (*0-932666-16-7*) T J Pubs.

Ropper, Allan H., ed. Neurological & Neurosurgical Intensive Care. 3rd ed. LC 92-49216. 528p. 1992. text 109.00 (*0-88167-981-X*) Lppncott W & W.

Ropper, Benard R. Biology of Dust & Allergens: Index of New Information & Research Reference Book. 150p. 1996. 47.50 (*0-7883-1200-6*); pap. 44.50 (*0-7883-1201-4*) ABBE Pubs Assn.

Ropzhkovskaya, Tamara, tr. see Godunov, S. K.

Roque, Ana. Luz y Sombra. 200p. 1991. pap. 8.50 (*0-8477-3648-2*) U of PR Pr.

Roque, Guillaume De La, see De La Roque, Guillaume.

Roque, Juan P. Deserter: An Inside Look Book at the Cuban Military by a Defector Ace Pilot. 110p. 1995. pap. text 16.00 (*1-884619-06-1*) Endowment CAS.

Roque, Oswaldo R. Directions in American Painting, 1875-1925: Works from the Collection of Dr. & Mrs. John J. McDonough. LC 82-6473. (Illus.). 112p. (Orig.). 1982. pap. text 12.95 (*0-88039-003-4*) Mus Art Carnegie.

Roque, Raquel R. Las Mejozes Recetas de la Cocina Cubana. (SPA.). 176p. 1987. pap. 4.95 (*0-941010-02-3*) Downtown Bk.

Roque, Raquel Rbade, see Rbade Roque, Raquel.

Roquebert, Anne. Degas. (Grandes Monografias). (SPA., Illus.). 200p. 1993. 200.00 (*84-343-0538-0*) Elliots Bks.

Roquebrune, J. Synopsis '96: Specialist Cardiological Investigations. Date not set. write for info. (*0-397-58732-5*) Lppncott W & W.

Roquefeuil, Camille de. Voyage Around the World, 1816-1819. 143p. 1983. 19.95 (*0-87770-258-6*) Ye Galleon.

Roquelaure, Ann N., pseud. Beauty's Punishment. (Sleeping Beauty Ser.: No. 2). 1999. pap. 12.95 (*0-452-28143-1*) NAL.

— Beauty's Punishment. (Sleeping Beauty Ser.: No. 2). 1999. pap. 5.99 (*0-451-17697-9*, Sig) NAL.

— Beauty's Release. (Sleeping Beauty Ser.: No. 3). 1999. pap. 12.95 (*0-452-28145-8*) NAL.

— Beauty's Release. (Sleeping Beauty Ser.: No. 3). 1999. pap. 5.99 (*0-451-17696-0*, Sig) NAL.

— The Claiming of Sleeping Beauty. (Sleeping Beauty Ser.: No. 1). 1999. pap. 12.95 (*0-452-28142-3*) NAL.

— The Claiming of Sleeping Beauty. (Sleeping Beauty Ser.: No. 1). 1999. pap. 5.99 (*0-451-17698-7*, Sig) NAL.

— Sleeping Beauty Trilogy. (Sleeping Beauty Ser.). 1999. pap. text 38.85 (*0-452-15661-0*) NAL.

Roquemore, Cliff, ed. see Roquemore, Erma.

Roquemore, Erma. How to Develop a Goal Mind: Using Left & Right Brain Functions to Achieve Your Goals. Roquemore, Cliff, ed. (Illus.). 119p. 1995. pap. 11.95 (*1-882518-70-5*) Contrast Pubng.

***Roquemore, Erma.** Sex Goals: How Men Penetrate & Women Embrace Goal Achievement. 136p. 2000. pap. 12.95 (*1-882518-00-4*) Contrast Pubng.

R

— 24Kt. Goal: Ten Steps to Personal & Professional Success. Michaels, Joe, ed. 144p. 1998. pap. 12.95 (*1-882518-79-9*) Contrast Pubng.

Roquemore, Erma. 24Kt. Goal: Ten Steps to Personal & Professional Success. Michael, Joi, ed. LC 98-92327. 128p. 1999. pap. 12.95 (*1-882518-99-3*) Contrast Pubng.

— 24kt. Goal: Using Left & Ten Steps to Personal & Professional Success. 2nd rev. ed. Tronslin, Andrea, ed. 128p. 1995. pap. 11.95 (*1-882518-19-5*) Contrast Pubng.

Roquemore, Glenn, ed. The Seismic Risk in the San Diego Region: Special Focus on the Rose Canyon Fault Systems: Workshop Proceedings. (Illus.). 129p. (C). 1997. reprint ed. pap. text 45.00 (*0-7881-4262-3*) DIANE Pub.

Roquemore, Joseph. History Goes to the Movies: A Viewer's Guide to the Best (And Some of the Worst) Historical Films Ever Made. 384p. 1997. 25.00 (*0-393-04615-X*); pap. 15.00 (*0-393-31711-0*) Norton.

***Roquemore, Joseph.** History Goes to the Movies: A Viewer's Guide to the Best (& Some of the Worst) Historical Films Ever Made. LC 99-29079. 400p. 1999. pap. 16.95 (*0-385-49678-8*, Anchor NY) Doubleday.

Roquemore, Libby L., jt. auth. see Bridges, Francis J.

Roques, H., ed. Chemical Water Treatment: Principles & Practice. 620p. 1996. 198.00 (*0-471-18563-9*, Wiley-VCH) Wiley.

Roques, Henri. Chemical Water Treatment: Principles & Practice. Altmann, Scott, tr. from FRE. LC 95-25805. 620p. 1996. 165.00 (*1-56081-518-3*, Wiley-VCH) Wiley.

— The "Confessions" of Kurt Gerstein. Percival, Ronald, tr. from FRE. Orig. Title: Les 'Confessions' de Kurt Gerstein. 325p. (Orig.). 1989. pap. 7.50 (*0-939484-27-7*, 0687, Inst Hist Rev) Legion Survival.

Roques, Marlo, ed. Le Roman de Renart, 6 tomes. 75.00 (*0-685-34018-X*) Fr & Eur.

Roques, Marlo, jt. auth. see Chretien de Troyes.

Roques, Marlo, jt. ed. see Mujumdar, Arun S.

Roquette, P., jt. auth. see Prestel, A.

Roquette, Peter, ed. see Hasse, Helmut.

Rorabacher, David B. & Endicott, John F. Mechanistic Aspects of Inorganic Reactions. LC 82-13817. (ACS Symposium Ser.: Vol. 198). 496p. 1982. reprint ed. pap. 153.80 (*0-608-03121-6*, 206357400007) Bks Demand.

Rorabacher, David B. & Endicott, John F., eds. Mechanistic Aspects of Inorganic Reactions. LC 82-13817. (ACS Symposium Ser.: No. 198). 480p. 1982. 60.95 (*0-8412-0734-8*) Am Chemical.

Rorabaugh. DSP Primer. 1998. 75.00 (*0-07-134206-0*) McGraw.

Rorabaugh, Britt. Mechanical Devices for the Electronics Experimenter. LC 94-36306. 1995. 29.95 (*0-07-053546-9*); pap. 19.95 (*0-07-053547-7*) McGraw-Hill Prof.

— Signal Processing Design Techniques. (Illus.). 304p. 1986. 32.50 (*0-8306-0457-X*, NO. 2657) McGraw-Hill Prof.

Rorabaugh, C. Britton. Circuit Design & Analysis: Featuring C Routines. 256p. 1992. pap. 34.95 (*0-8306-4275-7*, 4308) McGraw-Hill Prof.

— Digital Filter Designer's Handbook: With C++ Algorithms. 2nd ed. LC 97-6189. (Illus.). 700p. 1998. 69.50 incl. cd-rom (*0-07-053806-9*) McGraw.

— DSP Primer. LC 98-36445. 1998. 79.95 (*0-07-054004-7*) McGraw.

— Error Coding Cookbook: Practical C Routines & Recipes for Error Detection & Correction. LC 95-22892. (Illus.). 251p. 1996. 55.00 (*0-07-911720-1*) McGraw.

Rorabaugh, W. J. The Alcoholic Republic: An American Tradition. (Illus.). 318p. 1981. pap. text 15.95 (*0-19-502990-9*) OUP.

— Berkeley at War: The Nineteen Sixties. (Illus.). 336p. 1990. pap. text 14.95 (*0-19-506667-7*) OUP.

— The Craft Apprentice: From Franklin to the Machine Age in America. (Illus.). 288p. 1988. pap. text 22.00 (*0-19-505189-0*) OUP.

Rorabaugh, William J. & Critchlow, Donald T. America! A Concise History. 626p. 1993. 32.50 (*0-534-13614-1*) Wadsworth Pub.

Roraff, Susan & Camacho, Laura. Culture Shock! Chile. LC 97-74479. (Culture Shock! Ser.). 1998. pap. 12.95 (*1-55868-402-6*) Gr Arts Ctr Pub.

***Rorby, Ginny.** Dolphin Sky. 1998. 11.09 (*0-606-13338-0*, Pub. by Turtleback) Demco.

Rord, Elinor R. & Durante, Sheila R. As We Teach & Learn Module 3: Recognizing Our Catholic Identity: Religion Curriculum Articulation, 10 modules. Ristau, Karen & Haney, Regina, eds. 68p. 1997. pap. 64.00 (*1-55833-154-9*) Natl Cath Educ.

Rorden, Judith W. Discharge Planning Handbook. (Illus.). 384p. 1990. pap. text 39.00 (*0-7216-2845-1*, W B Saunders Co) Harcrt Hlth Sci Grp.

Rorech, Gregory J. Ground Water Treatment Equipment Design Handbook. (Geraghty & Miller Environmental Science & Engineering Ser.). Date not set. 69.95 (*0-87371-974-3*) Lewis Pubs.

Rorem, C. Rufus. Accounting Method. LC 82-48382. (Accounting in Transition Ser.). 613p. 1982. text 15.00 (*0-8240-5327-3*) Garland.

Rorem, Ned. Knowing When to Stop. (Illus.). 512p. 1994. 30.00 (*0-671-72872-5*) S&S Trade.

***Rorem, Ned.** The Later Diaries, 1961-1972. (Illus.). 456p. 2000. pap. 20.00 (*0-306-80964-8*) Da Capo.

— Lies: A Diary, 1986-1999. 2000. 30.00 (*1-58243-057-8*, Pub. by Counterpt DC) HarpC.

Rorem, Ned. The Paris Diary & the New York Diary, 1951-1961. LC 97-46200. (Illus.). 431p. 1998. reprint ed. pap. 16.95 (*0-306-80838-2*) Da Capo.

— Settling the Score: Essays on Music. 352p. 1988. 27.95 (*0-15-180895-3*) Harcourt.

Rorem, Ned, jt. auth. see Bowles, Paul.

Rorem, Paul. Biblical & Liturgical Symbols within the Pseudo-Dionysian Synthesis. xii, 177p. pap. text 22.29 (*0-88844-071-5*) Brill Academic Pubs.

— Pseudo-Dionysius: A Commentary on the Texts & an Introduction to Their Influence. LC 92-15353. 288p. (C). 1993. text 65.00 (*0-19-507664-8*) OUP.

Rorem, Paul & Lamoreaux, John C. John of Scythopolis & the Dionysian Corpus: Annotating the Areopagite. (Oxford Early Christian Studies). 304p. 1998. text 75.00 (*0-19-826970-6*) OUP.

Rorer, David. American Inter-State Law. Mayer, Levy, ed. lvii, 400p. 1983. reprint ed. 48.00 (*0-8377-1038-3*, Rothman) W S Hein.

Rorie, David, jt. ed. see Simpkins, John E.

Rorie, Joy D. Time Has No Echo. 48p. 1998. pap. 5.00 (*1-890644-15-3*) Union Cnty.

Rorimer, Katherine S. Leave It to Me. LC 97-91250. 1998. 16.95 (*0-533-12606-1*) Vantage.

Roripaugh, Lee Ann. Beyond Heart Mountain. LC 98-47428. 80p. 1999. pap. 14.95 (*0-14-058920-1*) Viking Penguin.

Roripaugh, Robert. Learn to Love the Haze. LC 95-44856. 1996. pap. 9.95 (*0-931271-35-5*) Hi Plains Pr.

Rorison, I. H., et al, eds. Frontiers of Comparative Plant Ecology. 317p. (Orig.). 1987. pap. text 62.00 (*0-12-595960-5*) Acad Pr.

Rorison, I. H. & Hunt, Roderick, eds. Amenity Grassland: An Ecological Perspective. LC 79-40823. (Illus.). 275p. reprint ed. pap. 85.30 (*0-8357-5345-X*, 203038400069) Bks Demand.

***Roriz, Aydano.** Diamonds are Forgiving. 1999. pap. 9.95 (*1-892668-12-2*) Prospect Pr.

Rorke, Lucy B. Pathology of Perinatal Brain Injury. LC 81-40674. (Illus.). 168p. 1982. reprint ed. pap. 52.10 (*0-608-00635-1*, 206122300007) Bks Demand.

Rorlich, Azade-Ayse. The Volga Tatars: A Profile in National Resilience. (Publication Ser.: No. 339). 288p. (C). 1986. pap. 19.95 (*0-8179-8392-9*); text 31.95 (*0-8179-8391-0*) Hoover Inst Pr.

Rorres, Chris, jt. auth. see Anton, Howard.

Rorrison, Hugh. Erwin Piscator: Political on the Stage in the Weimar Republic. (Theatre in Focus Ser.). 120p. 1987. pap. write for info. (*0-85964-166-X*) Chadwyck-Healey.

Rorrison, Hugh, tr. see Fontane, Theodor.

Rorro, Thomas A. Assessing Risk on Wall Street. LC 83-51720. 224p. 1984. 19.95 (*0-89709-134-5*) Liberty Pub.

Rorschach, Hermann. Psychodiagnostics: A Diagnostic Test Based on Perception. 10th ed. 228p. 1998. pap. text 54.00 (*3-456-83024-6*) Hogrefe & Huber Pubs.

Rorschach, Kimerly. Blake to Beardsley: The Artist As Illustrator. (Illus.). 55p. 1988. pap. 12.50 (*0-939084-24-4*) R Mus & Lib.

— Drawings by Jean-Baptiste Le Prince for the Voyage en Siberie. (Illus.). 36p. 1986. pap. 15.00 (*0-939084-20-1*) R Mus & Lib.

— Eighteenth-Century French Book Illustration: Drawings by Fragonard & Gravelot from the Rosenbach Museum & Library. (Illus.). 40p. 1985. pap. 5.00 (*0-939084-17-1*) R Mus & Lib.

Rorty, Amelia O., jt. ed. see McLaughlin, Brian P.

Rorty, Amelie. Essays on Descartes' Meditations. (Major Thinkers Ser.: No. 4). 1986. pap. 19.95 (*0-520-05509-8*, Pub. by U CA Pr) Cal Prin Full Svc.

— Philosophers on Education. LC 98-4865. 496p. 1998. pap. 35.00 (*0-415-19131-9*) Routledge.

— Philosophers on Education. LC 98-4865. 496p. (C). 1998. 99.99 (*0-415-19130-0*) Routledge.

Rorty, Amelie O. Essays on Aristotle's Ethics. LC 78-62858. (Major Thinkers Ser.: No. 2). 446p. reprint ed. pap. 138.30 (*0-608-17936-1*, 202906200058) Bks Demand.

Rorty, Amelie O., ed. Essays on Aristotle's Ethics. LC 78-62858. (Major Thinkers Ser.: No. 2). 1980. pap. 19.95 (*0-520-04041-4*, Pub. by U CA Pr) Cal Prin Full Svc.

— Essays on Aristotle's Poetics. 480p. 1992. pap. text 19.95 (*0-691-01498-1*, Pub. by Princeton U Pr) Cal Prin Full Svc.

— Essays on Aristotle's Rhetoric. LC 95-14304. (Philosophical Traditions Ser.: Vol. 6). 466p. 1996. pap. 22.50 (*0-520-20228-7*, Pub. by U CA Pr) Cal Prin Full Svc.

— Explaining Emotions. LC 78-62859. (Topics in Philosophy Ser.: Vol. V). 1980. pap. 19.95 (*0-520-03921-1*, Pub. by U CA Pr) Cal Prin Full Svc.

— The Identities of Persons. LC 75-13156. (Topics in Philosophy Ser.: Vol. III). 1976. pap. 18.95 (*0-520-03309-4*, Pub. by U CA Pr) Cal Prin Full Svc.

Rorty, Amelie O., jt. ed. see Nussbaum, Martha C.

Rorty, James. McCarthy & the Communists. LC 78-138179. 163p. 1972. reprint ed. lib. bdg. 69.50 (*0-8371-5636-X*, ROCO, Greenwood Pr) Greenwood.

— Our Master's Voice: Advertising. LC 75-39272. (Getting & Spending: The Consumer's Dilemma Ser.). 1976. reprint ed. 33.95 (*0-405-08044-1*) Ayer.

Rorty, James & Norman, N. Philip. Tomorrow's Food. enl. rev. ed. LC 56-8132. 309p. reprint ed. pap. 95.80 (*0-608-13470-8*, 202271200029) Bks Demand.

Rorty, James & Norman, Philip. Tomorrow's Food. 9.95 (*0-8159-6906-6*) Devin.

***Rorty, Richard.** Philosophy & Social Hope. 320p. 2000. pap. 13.95 (*0-14-026288-1*) Viking Penguin.

Rorty, Richard McKay. Achieving Our Country: Leftist Thought in Twentieth-Century America. LC 97-43210. (William E. Massey, Sr. Lectures in the History of American Civilization). 144p. 1999. 19.50 (*0-674-00311-X*) HUP.

— Achieving Our Country: Leftist Thought in Twentieth-Century America. LC 97-43210. (History of American Civilization Ser.). 159p. 1999. pap. 12.95 (*0-674-00312-8*) HUP.

— Against Bosses, Against Oligarchies: A Conversation with Richard Rorty. Nystrom, Derek & Puckett, Kent, eds. LC 98-66694. (Prickly Pear Pamphlets Ser.: Vol. 11). 64p. 1998. pap. text 5.00 (*1-891754-10-6*) Prickly Pear Pmphlts NA.

— The Barber of Kasbeam: Nabokov on Cruelty. (Chapbooks in Literature Ser.). 32p. 1988. pap. text 5.00 (*0-9614940-6-9*) Bennington Coll.

— Consequences of Pragmatism: Essays 1972-1980. LC 82-2597. 239p. (C). 1982. pap. 17.95 (*0-8166-1064-9*) U of Minn Pr.

— Contingency, Irony, & Solidarity. 224p. (C). 1989. pap. 19.95 (*0-521-36781-6*) Cambridge U Pr.

— Essays on Heidegger & Others Vol. 2: Philosophical Papers. 212p. (C). 1991. text 59.95 (*0-521-35370-X*); pap. text 20.95 (*0-521-35878-7*) Cambridge U Pr.

— Objectivity, Relativism, & Truth Vol. 1: Philosophical Papers, 2 vols. (Illus.). 236p. (C). 1990. pap. text 20.95 (*0-521-35877-9*) Cambridge U Pr.

— Philosophy & the Mirror of Nature. LC 79-84013. 401p. 1979. pap. text 17.95 (*0-691-02016-7*, Pub. by Princeton U Pr) Cal Prin Full Svc.

— Truth & Progress Vol. 3: Philosophical Papers. 364p. (C). 1998. pap. 18.95 (*0-521-55686-4*) Cambridge U Pr.

— Truths & Progress Vol. 3: Philosophical Papers. LC 97-37618. 368p. (C). 1998. text 59.95 (*0-521-55347-4*) Cambridge U Pr.

Rorty, Richard McKay, ed. The Linguistic Turn: Essays in Philosophic Method. 416p. 1992. pap. text 19.95 (*0-226-72569-3*) U Ch Pr.

— The Linguistic Turn: Recent Essays in Philosophic Method. viii, 402p. 1997. pap. text 19.95 (*0-226-72568-5*, Midway Reprint) U Ch Pr.

Rorty, Richard McKay, et al, eds. Philosophy in History: Essays in the Historiography of Philosophy. (Ideas in Context Ser.). 414p. 1984. pap. text 21.95 (*0-521-27330-7*) Cambridge U Pr.

Rorvig, Mark, jt. ed. see Schwarte, Candy.

Rorvik, David M., jt. auth. see Shettles, Landrum B.

Ros, Amanda M. Thine in Storm & Calm: An Amanda McKittrick Ros Reader. LC 88-7510. 166p. 1989. pap. 12.95 (*0-85640-408-X*, Pub. by Blackstaff Pr) Dufour.

***Ros, Enrique.** La Adventura Africana de Fidel Castro. LC 99-65287. (Coleccion Cuba y Sus Jueces). (Illus.). 300p. 1999. pap. 29.95 (*0-89729-908-6*) Ediciones.

Ros, Enrique. Anos Criticos: Del Camino de la Accion Al Camino del Entendimiento. LC 96-86701. (Coleccion Cuba y sus Jueces). (SPA., Illus.). 314p. (Orig.). 1996. pap. 25.00 (*0-89729-814-4*) Ediciones.

— Cubanos Combatiente: Peleando en Distingos Frentes. LC 98-84604. (Coleccion Cuba y sus Jueces). (SPA., Illus.). 364p. 1998. pap. 29.95 (*0-89729-868-3*) Ediciones.

— Playa Giron: La Verdadera Historia. 3rd ed. LC 94-71749. (Coleccion Cuba y sus Jueces). (SPA., Illus.). 314p. (Orig.). 1998. pap. 25.00 (*0-89729-738-5*) Ediciones.

Ros, Enrique & Beato, Virgilio I. De Giron a la Crisis de los Cohetes: La Segunda Derrota. LC 95-60655. (SPA., Illus.). 313p. (Orig.). 1995. pap. 25.00 (*0-89729-773-3*) Ediciones.

Ros, Frank. The Lost Secrets of Ayurvedic Acupuncture: An Ayurvedic Guide to Acupuncture. LC 93-80314. 206p. (Orig.). 1994. pap. 15.95 (*0-914955-12-8*) Lotus Pr.

Ros, Jaime. Development Theory & the Economics of Growth. (Development & Inequality in the Market Economy Ser.). (Illus.). 408p. (C). text 59.50 (*0-472-11141-8*, 11141) U of Mich Pr.

Ros, Jaime, jt. ed. see Bouzas, Roberto.

Ros-Lehtinen, Ileana, ed. Crisis in Liberia: Hearing Before the Committee on International Relations, U. S. House of Representatives. 47p. 1998. pap. text 20.00 (*0-7881-7108-9*) DIANE Pub.

— A Current Assessment of the Peace Process in Angola: Hearing Before the Subcommittee on Africa, House of Representatives. 57p. 1998. pap. text 20.00 (*0-7881-7109-7*) DIANE Pub.

— The Current Human Rights Situation in Africa: Hearing Before the Committee on International Relations, U. S. House of Representatives. (Illus.). 74p. 1998. pap. text 25.00 (*0-7881-7026-0*) DIANE Pub.

Ros, M., jt. ed. see Ghosh, M. M.

Ros, Martin. Night of Fire: The Black Napoleon & the Battle for Haiti. Ford, Karen, tr. from DUT. (Illus.). 256p. 1994. 27.50 (*0-9627613-8-9*); pap. 14.95 (*0-9627613-7-0*) Sarpedon.

Ros, Martin. Night of Fire: The Black Napoleon & the Battle for Haiti. 256p. 1997. 68.00 (*1-873376-35-9*, Pub. by Spellmnt Pubs); 40.00 (*1-873376-36-7*, Pub. by Spellmnt Pubs) St Mut.

Ros, Martin R., jt. auth. see Altschul, Jeffrey H.

Ros, Milenko. Respirometry of Activated Sludge. LC 93-60579. 155p. 1993. text 84.95 (*1-56676-029-1*) Technomic.

Ros, Pablo R. Radiologia Abdominal: Organos Accesorios Aparato Digestivo Tomo II. Stoopen, Miguel E. & Fujikami, Kenji Kimura, eds. 1998. 80.00 (*0-7817-1894-5*) Lppncott W & W.

Ros, Pablo R. & Lee, Sylvester. CT & MRI of the Abdomen & Pelvis: A Teaching File. LC 97-1121. 340p. 1997. 89.00 (*0-683-18218-8*) Lppncott W & W.

***Ros, R. G.** Programmes & Services of Training & Promotion Centres for Adolescents. (SPA.). 86p. 1999. write for info. (*92-806-3516-6*) U N I C E.

Ros, Roser. El Zapatero y el Demonio. Batiste, Enric, tr.Tr. of Shoemaker & the Devil. (SPA., Illus.). (J). (gr. k-3). 1997. 14.95 (*84-246-4720-3*, Pub. by SM Ediciones) IBD Ltd.

Ros, Saphan, tr. The Two Brothers. LC 94-14516. (Illus.). 32p. (J). (gr. k up). 1995. 15.00 (*0-688-12550-6*) Lothrop.

Ros-Tonen, M., et al. Commercial & Sustainable Extraction of Non-Timber Forest Products. (Tropenbos Technical Ser.). (Illus.). 32p. 1995. 17.00 (*90-5113-028-7*, Pub. by Backhuys Pubs) Balogh.

***Rosa.** Language of Accountancy. (C). 1999. pap. text. write for info. (*0-03-025236-9*) Harcourt.

Rosa. Language of Accountancy. 528p. (C). 1999. text 29.50 (*0-03-025252-0*) Harcourt Coll Pubs.

— The Writer's Pocket Handbook. LC 99-14333. 221p. (C). 1999. spiral bd. 15.00 (*0-205-28536-8*, Macmillan Coll) P-H.

Rosa & Eschholz. Models for Writers Developmental Exercises & ESL Workbook. 6th ed. pap. text, wbk. ed. 26.95 (*0-312-17953-7*) St Martin.

Rosa, Albert J., jt. auth. see Thomas, Roland E.

Rosa, Alex, jt. auth. see Colbourn, Charles J.

Rosa, Alfred F. Models for Writers: Short Essays for Composition. 6th ed. 1999. pap. text 10.00 (*0-312-17960-X*) St Martin.

— Models for Writing. 5th ed. 1994. pap. text, teacher ed. 21.50 (*0-312-10122-8*) St Martin.

— Salem, Transcendentalism & Hawthorne. LC 77-89784. 108p. 1978. 28.50 (*0-8386-2159-7*) Fairleigh Dickinson.

Rosa, Alfred F., ed. The Old Century & the New. LC 76-2853. 287p. 1978. 38.50 (*0-8386-1954-1*) Fairleigh Dickinson.

Rosa, Alfred F. & Eschholz, Paul A. Controversies: Arguments for College Writers. (C). 1991. pap., teacher ed. write for info. (*0-02-403612-9*, U5914-9) Allyn.

— Outlooks & Insights: A Reader for College Writers. 4th ed. 656p. (C). 1994. pap. 38.95 (*0-312-10110-4*) St Martin.

— Themes for Writers. 6th ed. 544p. 1994. pap. 33.95 (*0-312-09204-0*) St Martin.

— The Writer's Brief Handbook. 3rd ed. LC 97-48700. 382p. (C). 1998. spiral bd. 33.00 (*0-205-28512-0*) Allyn.

Rosa, Alfred F., et al. Controversies: Contemporary Arguments for College Writers. 639p. (C). 1990. pap. 42.00 (*0-02-403611-0*, Macmillan Coll) P-H.

Rosa, Alfred F., jt. contrib. by see Eschholz, Paul A.

Rosa, Alfred F., jt. ed. see Eschholz, Paul A.

Rosa, Casanova S. Mama Provi & the Pot of Rice. LC 95-44677. (Illus.). 32p. (J). (gr. k-3). 1997. 16.00 (*0-689-31932-0*) Atheneum Yung Read.

Rosa, Elva, ed. see Stamper, Melvin.

Rosa, Frank. Legionnaires' Disease: Prevention & Control. LC 92-45807. 1993. 29.95 (*0-912524-79-0*) Busn News.

— Water Treatment Specification Manual. LC 92-45808. 1993. 29.95 (*0-912524-80-4*) Busn News.

Rosa, James & Villani, Kathleen. Integrated Accounting: Using Simply Accounting for Windows Version 3.0. (C). 1997. text, teacher ed. 11.96 (*0-395-81119-8*) HM.

— Integrated Accounting: Using Simply Accounting for Windows Version 3.0. LC 97-72538. 320p. (C). 1998. pap. text. write for info. (*0-395-81118-X*) HM.

Rosa, Jean J., ed. World Crisis in Social Security. 245p. (Orig.). 1982. pap. text 24.95 (*0-917616-44-8*) Transaction Pubs.

Rosa, Jean-Jacques. France: 1950-1985. 24p. 1987. pap. 9.95 (*0-917616-97-9*) ICS Pr.

Rosa, Jean-Jacques, ed. The Economics of Trade Unions: New Directions. 1984. lib. bdg. 148.50 (*0-89838-147-9*) Kluwer Academic.

Rosa, Jose & Altman, Nathaniel. Power Spots. 96p. 1988. pap. 8.95 (*0-85030-474-1*, Pub. by Aqrn Pr) Harper SF.

Rosa, Jose A. Antologia De La Superacion Personal. (SPA.). 1997. pap. text 19.98 (*968-13-2410-2*) Libros Fronteras.

***Rosa, Joseph.** Albert Frey, Architect. rev. ed. LC 99-23419. (Illus.). 160p. 1999. pap. 35.00 (*1-56898-205-4*) Princeton Arch.

Rosa, Joseph. A Constructed View: The Architectural Photography of Julius Shulman. (Illus.). 224p. 1999. pap. 29.95 (*0-8478-2207-9*, Pub. by Rizzoli Intl) St Martin.

Rosa, Joseph G. Age of the Gunfighter: Men & Weapons on the Frontier, 1840-1900. LC 95-4992. (Illus.). 192p. 1995. pap. 19.95 (*0-8061-2761-9*) U of Okla Pr.

— Gunfighter: Man or Myth? LC 68-31378. (Illus.). 1979. reprint ed. pap. 14.95 (*0-8061-1561-0*) U of Okla Pr.

— Guns of the American West. 1988. 12.98 (*0-671-10036-X*) S&S Trade.

— They Called Him Wild Bill. 2nd ed. (Illus.). 1979. pap. 21.95 (*0-8061-1538-6*) U of Okla Pr.

— The West of Wild Bill Hickok. LC 81-21945. (Illus.). 202p. 1994. pap. 14.95 (*0-8061-2680-9*) U of Okla Pr.

— Wild Bill Hickok: The Man & His Myth. (Illus.). 304p. 1996. 29.95 (*0-7006-0773-0*) U Pr of KS.

Rosa, Joseph G. & May, Robin. Buffalo Bill & His Wild West: A Pictorial Biography. LC 88-34426. (Illus.). xii, 244p. 1996. pap. 14.95 (*0-7006-0399-9*) U Pr of KS.

Rosa, L. Guerra, jt. ed. see Branco, C. Moura.

Rosa, Loretta De, see De Rosa, Loretta.

Rosa, Luigi De, see Glazier, Ira & De Rosa, Luigi, eds.

Rosa, Michael R., jt. ed. see Walsh, Jeremy R.

Rosa-Nieves. Voz Folklorica de Puerto Rico. 1967. 16.95 (*0-87751-009-1*) E Torres & Sons.

Rosa-Nieves & Melon. Biografias Puertorriquenas. 1970. 18.95 (*0-685-73206-1*) E Torres & Sons.

Rosa-Nieves, Cesario. Romanticism in Puerto Rican Literature. (Puerto Rico Ser.). 1979. lib. bdg. 59.95 (*0-8490-3003-X*) Gordon Pr.

Rosa, Pablo La, see La Rosa, Pablo.

Rosa, Paul. The Complete Idiot Letters: One Man's Hilarious Assault on Corporate America. 150p. 1997. pap. 12.95 (*0-89526-404-8*, Gateway Editions) Regnery Pub.

— Idiot Letters: One Man's Relentless Assault on Corporate America. LC 94-38428. 160p. 1995. pap. 9.95 (*0-385-47508-X*) Doubleday.

An Asterisk (*) at the beginning of an entry indicates that the title is appearing for the first time.

Rosa, Paul M. How Electrons Whirl Our Wheels: Nikola Tesla. 1995. pap. 20.00 (*1-885522-03-7*) Telecommunity Pr.

Rosa, Peter, ed. The Role & Contribution of Small Business Research: Proceedings of the Ninth National Small Firms Policy & Research Conference, 1986. (Illus.). 256p. 1989. text 82.95 (*0-566-07103-7*, Pub. by Avebry) Ashgate Pub Co.

Rosa, Peter, et al, eds. Educating Entrepreneurs in Modernising Economies. LC 95-83571. 216p. (C). 1996. 63.95 (*1-85972-184-2*, Pub. by Avebry) Ashgate Pub Co.

Rosa, Peter De, see De Rosa, Peter.

Rosa, Portada De Rafael, see Agramonte, Roberto D. & De Rafael Rosa, Portada.

Rosa, Portada de Rafael, jt. auth. see Agramonte, Roberto D.

Rosa, Rene Di, see Di Rosa, Rene.

Rosa, Rodrigo R. The Pelcari Project. 72p. 1991. 25.00 (*0-7206-0805-8*, Pub. by P Owen Ltd) Dufour.

— The Pelcari Project - Carcel de Arboles. Bowles, Paul, tr. from SPA. LC 95-83136. (ENG & SPA.). 117p. pap. 11.95 (*0-932274-48-X*) Cadmus Eds.

— The Pelcari Project - Carcel de Arboles. deluxe limited ed. Bowles, Paul, tr. from SPA. LC 95-83136. (ENG & SPA.). 128p. 1997. bds. 35.00 (*0-932274-49-8*) Cadmus Eds.

Rosa, Roger. Plain Language about Shiftwork. 44p. 1997. pap. 5.00 (*0-16-061560-7*) USGPO.

Rosa, Rosa, jt. auth. see Jaffe, Hilda.

Rosa, Sheila De La, see De La Rosa, Sheila.

Rosa, Veronica Di, see Feuer, Janice.

Rosa, Vincent, jt. auth. see Horan, George J.

Rosaaen, Robin. All the King's Things: The Ultimate Elvis Memorabilia Book. (Illus.). 40p. 1993. text 12.95 (*0-912517-04-2*) Bluewood Bks.

Rosadi, Giovanni. The Trial of Jesus. 1977. lib. bdg. 59.95 (*0-8490-2767-5*) Gordon Pr.

Rosado, Anibal C. Filosofia de la Tecnica. 162p. 1992. pap. 8.50 (*0-8477-2832-3*) U of PR Pr.

Rosado, Jose A. & Gomez, C. El Rostro y la Mascara. (SPA.). 208p. 1995. pap. 12.95 (*0-8477-0240-5*) U of PR Pr.

Rosado, Judith H., jt. auth. see Rosado, Robert.

Rosado, Maria. Armando's Great Big Surprise No. 5: Armando's Great Big Surprise. LC 96-68722. (Illus.). 24p. (ps-1). 1996. 3.25 (*0-689-80825-9*) S&S Childrens.

— Blizzards! And Ice Storms. LC 99-31150. (Weather Channel Ser.: No. 5). (Illus.). 64p. (J). (gr. 4-6). 1999. pap. 3.99 (*0-689-82016-X*, Simon Spot) Litle Simon.

— Book 'Em Tommy! (Rugrats Chapter Bks.: No. 8). (Illus.). 64p. (J). (gr. 1-4). 2000. 3.99 (*0-689-83124-2*, Simon Spot) Litle Simon.

***Rosado, Maria.** Family Face-Off. (Wild Thornberrys Chapter Bk.: Vol. 1). Orig. Title: Survival of the Thornberrys!. 64p. (J). (gr. 2-5). 2000. pap. 3.99 (*0-689-83325-3*, Simon Spot) Litle Simon.

***Rosado, Maria, et al.** Wild Thornberry's Trivia Book. Vol. 1. 48p. (J). (gr. 1-4). 2000. pap. 2.99 (*0-689-83278-8*, Simon Spot) Litle Simon.

Rosado, Olga. Donde Termina la Noche. LC 78-74598. (Coleccion Caniqui). (Illus.). 1979. pap. 6.00 (*0-89729-217-0*) Ediciones.

— Dos Decadas (Versos) LC 86-83334. (Coleccion Espejo de Paciencia). (SPA.). 41p. (Orig.). 1987. pap. 5.00 (*0-89729-424-6*) Ediciones.

— Guajiro. LC 89-83448. (Coleccion Espejo de Paciencia). (SPA.). 69p. (Orig.). 1990. pap. 9.00 (*0-89729-526-9*) Ediciones.

— Mas Alla del Recuerdo. LC 96-83697. (Coleccion Caniqui). (SPA.). 85p. (Orig.). 1996. pap. 9.95 (*0-89729-800-4*) Ediciones.

— Pecadora (Seleccion de Poesias) LC 80-68759. (SPA.). 66p. (Orig.). 1984. pap. 5.00 (*0-89729-268-5*) Ediciones.

— Un Rostro Inolvidable. LC 97-80039. (Coleccion Caniqui Ser.). (SPA.). 105p. (Orig.). 1997. pap. 9.95 (*0-89729-837-3*, 837-3) Ediciones.

— Tengo Prisa. (Coleccion Espejo de Paciencia). 1978. pap. 5.00 (*0-89729-197-2*) Ediciones.

***Rosado, Raul.** Hands-On Origami, Vol. 1. (Illus.). 120p. (YA). (gr. 3 up). 1998. 14.95 (*0-9664101-0-6*) Rosado Arts.

Rosado, Robert & Rosado, Judith H. Recipes from La Isla: New & Traditional Puerto Rican Cuisine. LC 95-31564. 368p. 1995. 28.00 (*1-56565-339-4*) Lowell Hse.

— Recipes from La Isla! New & Traditional Puerto Rican Cuisine. 368p. 1996. pap. 18.00 (*1-56565-476-5*) Lowell Hse.

Rosador, Karl T. Von, see Fabian, Bernhard & Von Rosador, Karl T., eds.

Rosaforte, Tim. Heartbreak Hill: Anatomy of a Ryder Cup. (Illus.). 256p. 1996. 23.95 (*0-312-14351-6*) St Martin.

— Heartbreak Hill: Anatomy of a Ryder Cup. LC 97-209038. (Illus.). 288p. 1997. pap. 13.95 (*0-312-16862-4*) St Martin.

— Tiger Woods, Vol. 1. 1997. mass mkt. 5.99 (*0-312-96437-4*) St Martin.

— Tiger Woods: The Making of a Champion. 1996. text 21.95 (*0-312-15672-3*) St Martin.

— Tiger Woods, the Makings of a Champion. (J). 1997. 11.09 (*0-606-13851-X*, Pub. by Turtleback) Demco.

Rosaforte, Tim, et al. PGA Championship Annual 1998. Norwood, Bev, ed. (Illus.). 80p. 1998. write for info. (*1-878843-22-2*) Intl Merc OH.

— PGA Championships Annual, 1997. Norwood, Bev, ed. (Illus.). 96p. 1997. write for info. (*1-878843-21-4*) Intl Merc OH.

***Rosaforte, Tim, et al.** PGA Championships Annual, 1999. Norwood, Bev, ed. (Illus.). 96p. 1999. write for info. (*1-878843-26-5*) Intl Merc OH.

***Rosage, David E.** Beginning Spiritual Direction. 198p. (Orig.). 1999. pap. 21.00 (*1-57910-238-7*) Wipf & Stock.

Rosage, David E. Mary, Star of the New Millennium: Guiding Us to Renewal. LC 96-52394. (Celebrate 2000! Ser.). 200p. (Orig.). 1997. pap. 10.99 (*0-89283-994-5*, Charis) Servant.

— Rekindle Your Love for Jesus. 180p. 1996. pap. 9.99 (*0-89283-932-5*) Servant.

— Speak Lord, Your Servant Is Listening. large type ed. (Large Print Inspirational Ser.). 1987. pap. 9.95 (*0-8027-2568-6*) Walker & Co.

— Speak, Lord, Your Servant Is Listening: A Daily Guide to Scriptural Prayer. rev. ed. 131p. 1987. pap. 6.99 (*0-89283-371-8*) Servant.

Rosai, et al. Tumors of the Thyroid Gland. (AFIP Atlas of Tumor Pathology Ser.: Vol. 5). (Illus.). 343p. 1993. pap. text 58.00 (*1-881041-03-4*) Am Registry Path.

Rosai, Juan. Ackerman's Surgical Pathology. 8th ed. (Illus.). 2896p. (C). (gr. 13). 1995. text 315.00 (*0-8016-7004-7*, 07004) Mosby Inc.

***Rosai, Juan.** Histological Typing of Tumours of the Thymus. 2nd ed. LC 99-36794. (World Health Organization Ser.). (Illus.). 80p. 1999. pap. 70.00 (*3-540-65731-2*) Spr-Verlag.

Rosai, Juan. Manual of Surgical Pathology Gross Room Procedures. (Illus.). 132p. (C). 1981. pap. 29.95 (*0-8166-1027-4*) U of Minn Pr.

Rosair, David & Cottridge, David. Photographic Guide to the Shorebirds of the World. LC 95-2502. (Illus.). 176p. 1995. 29.95 (*0-8160-3309-9*) Facts on File.

Rosak, Theodore. Why Astrology Endures. (Broadside Editions Ser.). 20p. (C). 1986. pap. 3.95 (*0-9609850-9-3*) Rob Briggs.

Rosakis, A. J., jt. ed. see Knauss, W. G.

Rosal, Marcia. Approaches to Art Therapy with Children. 1996. pap. text 23.95 (*1-885762-01-1*) Abbeygate Pr.

Rosal, Oscar. Adios, Papa, Level 1. (Leer en Espanol Ser.). (SPA.). (C). 1998. pap. 5.95 (*84-294-3610-3*) Santillana.

Rosaldo, Michelle Z. & Lamphere, Louise, eds. Woman, Culture, & Society. LC 73-89861. 360p. 1974. pap. 15.95 (*0-8047-0851-7*) Stanford U Pr.

Rosaldo, Renato. Culture & Truth: The Remaking of Social Analysis. LC 93-18158. 288p. 1993. pap. 16.00 (*0-8070-4623-X*) Beacon Pr.

— Ilongot Headhunting, 1883-1974: A Study in Society & History. LC 79-64218. (Illus.). xii, 313p. 1980. 47.50 (*0-8047-1046-5*) Stanford U Pr.

Rosaler, Robert C. Standard Handbook of Plant Engineering. 2nd ed. 1568p. 1991. 125.00 (*0-07-052164-6*) McGraw.

Rosaler, Robert C., ed. HVAC Maintenance & Operations Handbook. LC 97-31235. (Illus.). 1216p. 1997. 64.95 (*0-07-052169-7*) McGraw-Hill Prof.

Rosaler, Robert C., jt. auth. see Grimm, Nils R.

Rosales, Arturo. Pobre Raza! LC 98-58049. 304p. 1999. 45.00 (*0-292-77094-4*); pap. 19.95 (*0-292-77095-2*) U of Tex Pr.

***Rosales, David.** Raising Right-Hearted Kids in a Wrong-Way World. 111p. 1999. pap. 6.99 (*0-9676661-2-0*) Calvary Dist.

Rosales-Dordelly, Carmen L. & Short, Edmund C. Curriculum Professors' Specialized Knowledge. (Illus.). 124p. (Orig.). 1985. pap. text 13.50 (*0-8191-4639-0*) U Pr of Amer.

Rosales, F. Arturo. Chicano! The History of the Mexican American Civil Rights Movement. LC 97-227451. 304p. 1997. pap. 24.95 (*1-55885-201-8*) Arte Publico.

Rosales, F. Arturo & Foster, David W. Hispanics & the Humanities in the Southwest: A Directory of Resources. LC 83-20993. 327p. (C). 1983. pap. 15.00 (*0-87918-055-2*) ASU Lat Am St.

***Rosales, Francisco A.** Testimonio: A Documentary History of the Mexican-American Struggle for Civil Rights. LC 00-24328. (Hispanic Civil Rights Ser.). 308p. 2000. pap. 22.95 (*1-55885-299-9*) Arte Publico.

Rosales, Gerardo P., jt. auth. see Fernandez-Shaw, Carlos M.

Rosales, Guillermo. El Juego de la Viola. LC 93-73441. (Coleccion Caniqui). 96p. 1994. pap. 9.95 (*0-89729-707-5*) Ediciones.

***Rosales, J. C. & Garcia-Sanchez, P. A.** Finitely Generated Commutative Monoids. 185p. 1999. 79.00 (*1-56072-670-9*) Nova Sci Pubs.

***Rosales, Jan Wolfe.** Given in Love, but Not Mine to Keep: Finding Strength in the Loss of a Newborn Child. LC 99-68528. 176p. 2000. pap. 14.95 (*1-893162-15-X*) Erica Hse.

***Rosales, Jesus.** La Narrativa de Alejandro Morales: Encuentro, Historia y Compromiso Social. (Wor(l)ds of Change Ser.: Vol. 39). (SPA.). XIII, 190p. 1999. text 46.95 (*0-8204-3995-9*, 39959) P Lang Pubng.

Rosales, Melodye. The Adventures of Minny: Book One. LC 99-19896. (J). 1998. write for info. (*0-316-75605-9*) Little.

— The Adventures of Minny: Book Three. (J). 2000. write for info. (*0-316-75633-4*) Little.

— Adventures of Minny: Book Two. (J). 1999. write for info. (*0-316-75688-1*) Little.

***Rosales, Melodye.** Leola & the Honeybears. (Illus.). (J). 1999. 95.70 (*0-439-11756-9*) Scholastic Inc.

Rosales, Melodye. 'Twas the Night B'fore Christmas: An African-American Version. LC 95-53236. 32p. (J). (ps-3). 1996. 14.95 (*0-590-73944-1*, Cartwheel) Scholastic Inc.

Rosales, Melodye Benson. Leola & the Honeybears. LC 97-31871. (Illus.). 40p. (J). (ps-3). 1999. 15.95 (*0-590-38358-2*, Pub. by Scholastic Inc) Penguin Putnam.

***Rosales, Rodolfo.** The Illusion of Inclusion: The Untold Political Story of San Antonio. LC 99-42794. 224p. 1999. pap. 14.95 (*0-292-77103-7*) U of Tex Pr.

— The Illusion of Inclusion: The Untold Political Story of San Antonio. 224p. 2000. 30.00 (*0-292-77102-9*) U of Tex Pr.

Rosalia, Antonius De, see De Rosalia, Antonius, ed.

Rosalki, Sydney B., jt. ed. see Moss, Donald W.

***Rosalsky, Mitch.** Encyclopedia of Rhythm & Blues & Doo Wop Vocal Groups. LC 99-32194. (Illus.). 736p. 2000. text 89.50 (*0-8108-3663-7*) Scarecrow.

***Rosamond, Ben.** Theories of European Integration. LC 99-54661. (European Union Ser.). 2000. pap. 22.95 (*0-312-23120-2*); text 65.00 (*0-312-23119-9*) St Martin.

Rosamond, Peggy Jo. Paper Doll Greeting Cards Activity Book. (Illus.). 32p. (J). 1990. pap. 5.95 (*0-87588-327-3*) Hobby Hse.

— Paper Doll Portrait: Antique German Bisque Dolls. (Illus.). 32p. 1990. pap. 5.95 (*0-87588-246-3*) Hobby Hse.

***Rosamond, Sandi.** You Know You Travel Too Much When... 98p. 1999. pap. 8.95 (*0-7392-0332-0*, PO3501) Morris Pubng.

Rosan, Burton, jt. ed. see Mergenhagen, Stephan E.

Rosand, David. The Meaning of the Mark: Leonardo & Titian. (Franklin D. Murphy Lectures: No. 8). 1988. 12.00 (*0-913689-01-7*) Spencer Muse Art.

— Painting in Sixteenth-Century Venice: Titian, Veronese, Tintoretto. rev. ed. LC 96-50388. (Illus.). 352p. (C). 1997. pap. text 24.95 (*0-521-56568-5*) Cambridge U Pr.

Rosand, David, ed. Robert Motherwell on Paper: Drawings, Prints, Collages. LC 96-19574. (Illus.). 208p. 1997. 60.00 (*0-8109-4294-1*, Pub. by Abrams) Time Warner.

Rosand, Ellen. Opera in Seventeenth-Century Venice: The Creation of a Genre. (Illus.). 710p. 1990. 150.00 (*0-520-06808-4*, Pub. by U CA Pr) Cal Prin Full Svc.

Rosander, A. C. Applications of Quality Control to the Service Industry. (Quality & Reliability Ser.: Vol. 5). (Illus.). 432p. 1985. text 75.00 (*0-8247-7466-3*) Dekker.

Rosander, A. C. Deming's Fourteen Points Applied to Services. (Quality & Reliability Ser.: Vol. 25). (Illus.). 168p. 1991. text 65.00 (*0-8247-8517-7*) Dekker.

— The Quest for Quality in Services. (Illus.). 579p. 1989. text 37.50 (*0-527-91644-7*, 916447) Productivity Inc.

— Washington Story: Behind the Scenes in the Federal Government - An Official under Civil Service Describes His Experiences. LC 85-227965. xiii, 546p. 1985. 7.95 (*0-9615168-0-1*) Natl Directions.

Rosander, Arlyn C. Case Studies in Sample Design. LC 76-12283. (Statistics, Textbooks & Monographs: 21). 438p. reprint ed. pap. 135.80 (*0-608-17224-3*, 202783600056) Bks Demand.

Rosander, Eva E. Transforming Female Identities: Women's Organizational Forms in West Africa. LC 98-135616. (Seminar Proceedings Ser.: No. 31). 241p. 1997. pap. 48.50 (*91-7106-403-6*, Pub. by Almqvist Wiksell) Coronet Bks.

— Women in a Borderland: Managing Muslim Identity Where Morocco Meets Spain. (Stockholm Studies in Social Anthropology: No. 26). 313p. (Orig.). 1991. pap. 47.50 (*91-7146-918-4*) Coronet Bks.

Rosander, Eva E. & Westerlund, David, eds. African Islam & Islam in Africa. LC 97-15866. 333p. 1997. text 39.95 (*0-8214-1213-2*); pap. text 19.95 (*0-8214-1214-0*) Ohio U Pr.

Rosander, Eva Evers, see Evers Rosander, Eva.

Rosandich, Ryan G. Fundamentals of Programmable Logic Controllers. LC 96-78405. iv, 106p. 1997. 31.95 (*0-87288-639-5*) Intertec Pub.

Rosanes-Berrett, Marilyn B. Do You Really Need Eyeglasses? enl. ed. (Illus.). 140p. 1990. 20.95 (*0-88268-107-9*) Station Hill Pr.

— Do You Really Need Eyeglasses? enl. ed. (Illus.). 140p. 1990. pap. 10.95 (*0-88268-104-4*) Station Hill Pr.

Rosaniec, Zbigniew, jt. auth. see Baltba Calleja, Francisco J.

Rosanik, Ralph. Hawk Safari: The Search for a Rare Bird. 200p. 1993. pap. 12.95 (*0-9637153-0-5*) C & D Mktg.

— Hawk Safari: The Search for a Rare Bird. 12.95 (*0-614-13190-1*, 21-50211) EAA Aviation.

Rosano, Aureleo. The Rosano Sculptures. LC 83-90393. (Illus.). 120p. 1984. 38.00 (*0-914817-00-0*) Rose Pubns AZ.

Rosano, Dick. Wine Heritage: The Story of Italian-American Vintners. Pinney, Tom, ed. (Illus.). 256p. 1999. 29.95 (*1-891267-13-2*) Wine Appreciation.

Rosano, Henri L. Microemulsion Systems. (Surfactant Science Ser.: Vol. 24). (Illus.). 440p. 1987. text 245.00 (*0-8247-7439-6*) Dekker.

Rosanoff, Nancy. Intuition Workout: A Practical Guide to Discovering & Developing Your Inner Knowing. rev. ed. LC 91-76. (Illus.). 176p. 1991. reprint ed. pap. 12.95 (*0-944031-14-5*) Aslan Pub.

Rosanoff, Nancy, jt. auth. see Alpha Development Group Staff.

Rosanske, Thomas W., jt. ed. see Riley, Christopher M.

Rosansky, Victor, jt. auth. see Labovitz, George.

***Rosanvallon, Pierre.** The New Social Question: Rethinking the Welfare State. Harshav, Barbara, tr. from FRE. LC 99-37483. (New French Thought Ser.). 139p. 2000. 22.95 (*0-691-01640-2*, Pub. by Princeton U Pr) Cal Prin Full Svc.

Rosario. El Espanol de America. (SPA.). 1970. 12.95 (*0-685-73205-3*) E Torres & Sons.

Rosario, Ahumada. Juguemos a Leer. 1997. pap. text 19.98 (*968-24-5633-9*) Trillas Edit.

***Rosario-Andujar, Julio A.** Felisberto Hernandez y el Pensamiento Filosofico. (Wor(l)ds of Change Ser.: Vol. 43). XIV, 142p. 1999. text 40.95 (*0-8204-4197-X*, 4197X) P Lang Pubng.

Rosario, Benjamin, jt. auth. see Martinez, Felix J.

Rosario, Bernada D., jt. auth. see Rogers, Mary.

Rosario-Braid, Florangel. Communication Strategies for Productivity Improvement. rev. ed. 300p. 1983. text 24.75 (*92-833-1053-5*) Productivity Inc.

***Rosario, I. J. M.** Power, Politics & Portraits: Art & Propaganda in the Fourteenth-Century Court of Charles IV of Bohemia. (Illus.). 288p. 2000. 75.00 (*0-85115-787-4*) Boydell & Brewer.

Rosario, Idalia. Idalia's Project ABC-Proyecto ABC: An Urban Alphabet Book in English & Spanish. LC 80-21013. (Illus.). (J). (ps-2). 1995. pap. 5.95 (*0-8050-0296-0*, Bks Young Read) H Holt & Co.

Rosario, Idalia. Idalia's Project ABC (Proyecto ABC) An Urban Alphabet Book in English & Spanish. (ENG & SPA.). (J). 1981. 11.15 (*0-606-02180-9*, Pub. by Turtleback) Demco.

Rosario, Jose C. The Development of the Puerto Rican Jibaro & His Present Attitude Towards Society. LC 74-14248. (Puerto Rican Experience Ser.). (Illus.). 124p. 1975. reprint ed. 11.95 (*0-405-06234-6*) Ayer.

Rosario, Nahum. Atrevete a Cambiar. (SPA.). 45p. (Orig.). 1995. pap. 5.00 (*0-9634761-6-5*) Maran Revival.

— Confrontando a Satana's. (SPA.). (Orig.). 1993. pap. text. write for info. (*0-9634761-3-0*) Maran Revival.

— La Escalera del Exito. (SPA.). 64p. 1992. pap. 5.50 (*0-9634761-0-6*) Maran Revival.

— Las Riquezas de Su Gracia. (SPA.). 151p. (Orig.). 1994. pap. 8.00 (*0-9634761-4-9*) Maran Revival.

— Los Secretos de la Uncion. 120p. (Orig.). 1993. pap. 7.00 (*0-9634761-1-4*) Maran Revival.

— The Secrets of the Anointing. Toledo, Efren, tr. from SPA. 112p. (Orig.). 1994. pap. 7.00 (*0-9634761-5-7*) Maran Revival.

***Rosario, Patty Jill W., et al.** FTCE Mathematics High School. (C). 2000. per. 50.00 (*1-58197-073-0*) XAM.

Rosario, Ric, jt. auth. see Klein, Ron.

Rosario, Ruben D. Diccionario de Terminos Aerauticos. (ENG & SPA.). 125.00 (*0-685-42438-3*, S-37343) Fr & Eur.

Rosario-Sievert, Heather. Honor My Father. LC 94-24145. 1995. write for info. (*0-7734-2736-8*, Irwn McGrw-H) McGrw-H Hghr Educ.

Rosario, Vernon, 2nd, jt. ed. see Bennett, Paula.

Rosario, Vernon A., II. The Erotic Imagination: French Histories of Perversity. LC 96-29552. (Ideologies of Desire Ser.). (Illus.). 256p. 1997. 35.00 (*0-19-510483-8*) OUP.

Rosario, Vernon A. Science & Homosexualities. LC 96-9673. 288p. (C). 1996. pap. 19.99 (*0-415-91502-3*) Routledge.

— Science & Homosexualities. LC 96-9673. 288p. (C). 1997. 70.00 (*0-415-91501-5*) Routledge.

Rosario, Vernon A., 2nd, jt. ed. see Bennett, Paula.

Rosas, Allan, ed. International Human Rights Norms in Domestic Law: Finnish & Polish Perspectives. 300p. (Orig.). 1990. pap. 118.00 (*951-640-509-6*) Coronet Bks.

Rosas, Allan & Antola, Esko, eds. A Citizens' Europe: In Search of a New Order. 272p. (C). 1995. 69.95 (*0-8039-7560-0*); pap. 21.95 (*0-8039-7561-9*) Sage.

Rosas, Allan & Helgesen, Jan, eds. The Strength of Diversity: Human Rights & Pluralist Democracy. LC 92-32721. (International Studies in Human Rights: Vol. 25). 1992. lib. bdg. 98.00 (*0-7923-1987-7*) Kluwer Academic.

Rosas, Carlos. Misa de Tepeyac. (SPA.). write for info. (*0-614-04900-8*) Mex Am Cult.

Rosas, Guido. El Grandioso Juego de Aprender a Divertirse (The Great Game of Learning How to Have Fun) (SPA.). 112p. 1998. pap. 7.95 (*970-9095-00-5*) Mango Digital.

Rosas, Marian D. Deposition of an Awakening Experience. (Illus.). 104p. 1998. pap. 10.00 (*0-8059-4360-9*) Dorrance.

***Rosas, Marie.** Simple Words in Thoughts & Poems. 2000. write for info. (*1-58235-450-2*) Watermrk Pr.

Rosas, Ramon De, see De Rosas, Ramon.

Rosas, Yolanda, ed. see Rossetti, Ana.

Rosasco, Gregory J., ed. Workshop on Federal Programs Involving Supercritical Water Oxidation: Proceedings. 303p. (Orig.). (C). 1993. pap. text 65.00 (*0-7881-0042-4*) DIANE Pub.

***Rosati.** The Politics of U. S. Foreign Policy. 2nd ed. LC 98-71719. (C). 1998. pap. text 49.00 (*0-03-018063-5*, Pub. by Harcourt Coll Pubs) Harcourt.

Rosati, Flavio Joseph. Fingers of the Black Hand. 312p. Date not set. mass mkt. 4.99 (*1-896329-46-2*) Picasso Publ.

Rosati, Gabriel. Latin American Trumpet Music. 120p. 1996. spiral bd. 15.00 incl. audio compact disk (*0-7866-0726-2*, 95601BCD) Mel Bay.

Rosati, Jeral A. The Politics of United States Foreign Policy. 560p. (C). 1993. pap. text 46.00 (*0-03-047024-2*) Harcourt Coll Pubs.

Rosati, Jerel A. Reading in the Politics of United States Foreign Policy. LC 97-71705. 192p. (C). 1997. pap. text 34.00 (*0-15-505364-7*, Pub. by Harcourt Coll Pubs) Harcourt.

Rosati, Kitty G. Heal Your Heart: The New Rice Diet Program for Reversing Heart Disease Through Nutrition, Exercise & Spiritual Renewal. LC 96-42087. 384p. 1996. pap. 17.95 (*0-471-15702-3*) Wiley.

Rosati, L. A., ed. Buildings & the Geometry of Diagrams. (Lecture Notes in Mathematics Ser.: Vol. 1181). vii, 277p. 1986. 38.95 (*0-387-16466-9*) Spr-Verlag.

Rosati, Mark. Human Biology for Allied Health - Exam (156) 1996. pap. text 23.81 (*1-56870-238-8*) RonJon Pub.

— Human Biology for Allied Health - Lab (156) 1996. pap. text 15.16 (*1-56870-239-6*) RonJon Pub.

Rosati, S., jt. ed. see Fantoni, S.

R

Rosato, Angelo A. Encyclopedia of the Modern Elongated: Encyclopedia on Elongated Coins. LC 90-83073. (Illus.). 1760p. 1990. 129.95 (0-9626996-2-4) Angros Pubs.
— Rerolls - Restrikes: Supplement. (Encyclopedia of the Modern Elongated Ser.). (Illus.). 40p. 1992. pap. text 25.00 (0-9626996-3-2) Angros Pubs.
— Supplement to the Encyclopedia of the Modern Elongated. LC 98-93218. 320p. 1998. pap. 59.95 (0-9626996-4-0) Angros Pubs.
Rosato, Beth, jt. auth. see Eddington, John.
Rosato, D. V. & Grove, C. S., Jr. Filament Winding: Its Development, Manufacture, Applications, & Design. LC 64-14998. (Polymer Engineering & Technology Ser.). 371p. reprint ed. pap. 115.10 (0-608-13856-8, 205598900042) Bks Demand.
Rosato, Dominick V. Designing with Reinforced Composites: Technology, Performance, Economics. LC 96-44405. 401p. 1997. 148.00 (1-56990-211-9) Hanser-Gardner.
— Rosato's Plastics Encyclopedia & Dictionary. 884p. 1992. 98.00 (1-56990-088-4) Hanser-Gardner.
***Rosato, Dominick V., et al.** Injection Molding Handbook. 3rd ed. LC 99-49946. 2000. write for info. (0-7923-8619-1) Kluwer Academic.
Rosato, Dominick V., jt. auth. see Rosato, Donald V.
Rosato, Donald V. Plastics Processing Data Handbook. (Illus.). 392p. 1989. mass mkt. 67.95 (0-412-73920-8, Chap & Hall NY) Chapman & Hall.
Rosato, Donald V. & Rosato, Dominick V. Blow Molding Handbook. 1010p. 1989. 197.50 (1-56990-089-2) Hanser-Gardner.
***Rosato, Donald V., et al.** Concise Encyclopedia of Plastics. LC 99-29441. 1999. write for info. (0-7923-8496-2) Kluwer Academic.
Rosato, Donald V., et al. Designing with Plastics & Composites: A Handbook. LC 90-46378. (Illus.). 928p. (gr. 13). 1991. text 126.95 (0-442-00133-9) Chapman & Hall.
Rosato, Frank D. Jogging & Walking for Health & Wellness. 3rd ed. (Health Sciences Ser.). (Illus.). 160p. (C). 1999. pap. text 16.95 (0-89582-295-4) Wadsworth Pub.
Rosato, Maria. Let's Play Games. (Stickers 'n' Shapes Ser.). (Illus.). 24p. (J). (gr. k-3). 1997. per. 3.99 (0-689-81303-1) S&S Childrens.
Rosato, Peter C., jt. auth. see Poulenez, Donovan.
Rosato, Philip. The Spirit As Lord. 240p. 1981. 44.95 (0-567-09305-0, Pub. by T & T Clark) Bks Intl VA.
Rosauer, Elmer A. Instruments for Materials Analysis. LC 80-28235. (Illus.). 210p. 1981. reprint ed. pap. 65.10 (0-608-00078-7, 206084100006) Bks Demand.
Rosauer, Janet. Life after Grief. (Illus.). 120p. 1998. pap. 9.95 (1-890676-25-X) Beavers Pond.
Rosaw, Jerome M. & Lotto, Jill C. People, Partnership, & Profits Pt. 2: The New Labor-Management Agenda. (Strategic Partners for High Performance Ser.). 138p. 1994. pap. text, per. 95.00 (0-89361-051-8) Work in Amer.
Rosazza, John P., ed. Microbial Transformations of Bioactive Compounds, Vol. II. 200p. 1982. 114.00 (0-8493-6066-8, QR88, CRC Reprint) Franklin.
Rosbach-Chandler, Ruth. Attention Training & Heeling: What Other Books Didn't Tell You. LC 95-67088. 64p. 1995. pap. text 9.95 (0-9645303-0-9) Olympic Press.
***Rosbe, Judith.** Marion. (Images of America Ser.). (Illus.). 128p. 2000. pap. 18.99 (0-7385-0419-X) Arcadia Publng.
Rosberg, Barbara, jt. auth. see Rosberg, Gary.
Rosberg, Carl G., jt. auth. see Apter, David E.
Rosberg, G. Escoja Amar de Nuevo.Tr. of Choosing to Love Again. (SPA.). 12.99 (1-56063-876-1, 498398) Editorial Unilit.
Rosberg, Gary. Dr. Rosberg's Do-It-Yourself Relationship Mender. 443p. 1999. mass mkt. 6.99 (1-56179-760-X) Focus Family.
Rosberg, Gary. Guard Your Heart: Protection from the Attacks Every Man Faces. 254p. 1997. pap. text 12.99 (1-57673-172-3) Multnomah Pubs.
***Rosberg, Gary & Rosberg, Barbara.** Building Your Mate's Self-Esteem. Group Publishing Staff, ed. (Homebuilders Couples Ser.). (Illus.). 142p. 2000. spiral bd. 10.99 (0-7644-2235-9) Group Pub.
— The Five Love Needs of Men & Women. LC 00-27107. 2000. pap. write for info. (0-8423-4239-7) Tyndale Hse.
Rosberg, Rose. Breathe in, Breathe Out. 56p. (Orig.). 1992. pap. 7.50 (1-880286-09-2) Singular Speech Pr.
Rosberger, Paul. The Theory of Total Consonance. LC 71-92560. (Illus.). 108p. 1975. 16.50 (0-8386-7570-0) Fairleigh Dickinson.
Rosbert, C. Joseph. Flying Tiger Joe's Adventure Story Cookbook. 343p. 1985. 18.95 (0-9616536-0-4) Giant Poplar Pr.
Rosboro, William. Sensitive Stories: Poems. 78p. 1999. pap. 7.00 (0-7392-0252-9, PO3307) Morris Pubng.
Rosborough, E. H. Tying & Fishing the Fuzzy Nymphs. 4th rev. ed. LC 88-2190. (Illus.). 192p. 1988. 21.95 (0-8117-1818-2) Stackpole.
Rosbotham, Lyle. Extinction Event. (Illus.). 96p. (Orig.). 1988. pap., wbk. ed. 12.00 (0-917796-04-7) Press Four Fifty One.
— High School Students. (Illus.). 120p. 1983. pap. 12.00 (0-917796-03-9) Press Four Fifty One.
Rosbottom, Betty. American Favorites: All-American Cooking for a New Generation. (Illus.). 399p. 1999. pap. 18.00 (0-395-97171-3) HM.
— American Favorites: Streamlined & Updated Renditions of the Recipes We Love. Martin, Rux, ed. (Illus.). 384p. 1996. 29.95 (1-57630-016-1, Chapters Bks) HM.
***Rosbottom, Betty.** Weekend with Friends: Recipes. LC 99-43382. (Williams-Sonoma Lifestyles Ser.). (Illus.). 112p. 2000. 14.95 (0-7370-2031-8) Time-Life.
Rosbrow-Reich, Susan, jt. auth. see Raymond, Laurie W.
Rosburg, Helen A. Call of the Trumpet. 320p. 1998. mass mkt. 4.99 (0-8439-4385-8, Leisure Bks) Dorchester Pub Co.
Rosch, Barry C. Luftwaffe Codes, Markings & Units, 1939-1945. LC 95-67631. (Illus.). 368p. 1995. 59.95 (0-88740-796-X) Schiffer.
Rosch, Eleanor & Lloyd, Barbara B., eds. Cognition & Categorization. LC 78-6570. 336p. reprint ed. pap. 104.20 (0-8357-3404-8, 203966100013) Bks Demand.
Rosch, J. Thomas. Manual of Federal Trade Commission Practice. 2nd ed. (Corporate Practice Series Portfolio: No. 21). 1989. ring bd. 92.00 (1-55871-144-9) BNA.
Rosch, Leah, ed. The Recipes of the Five Brothers. (Illus.). 42p. 1997. text 10.00 (0-9655889-0-4) Van den Bergh.
Rosch, Paul J., jt. auth. see Lawrence, Ronald.
***Rosch, T., et al.** Longitudinal Endosonography: Atlas & Manual for Use in the Upper Gastrointestinal Tract LC 99-36126. 1999. write for info. (3-540-65586-7) Spr-Verlag.
Rosch, Winn L. Using & Upgrading PCs. LC 97-81179. 1998. pap. text 29.99 (0-7897-1607-0) Que.
— The Winn L. Rosch Hardware Bible. LC 96-67965. 1248p. 1997. 65.00 (0-672-30954-8) Sams.
— The Winn L. Rosch's Printer Bible. 89p. 1995. pap. 34.95 incl. cd-rom (1-55828-436-2, MIS Pr) IDG Bks.
— The Winn Rosch Hardware Bible. 1989. pap. 29.95 (0-13-160979-3) Brady Pub.
— Winn Rosch Troubleshooter's Bible. 1990. pap. 29.95 (0-13-962655-7) P-H.
Roschar, Frans M., jt. auth. see Mokken, Robert J.
Rosche, Christine. The Insurance Reimbursement Manual: For America's Bodyworkers, Bodytherapists & Message Professionals. 5th ed. LC 99-176439. 262 p. 1997. write for info. (0-9646428-1-6) Bodytherapy Busn Inst.
Rosche, Larry, ed. A Field Book of Birds of the Cleveland Region. 2nd ed. (Illus.). 44p. 1988. pap. 3.50 (1-878600-05-2) Cleve Mus Nat Hist.
Roschelle, Anne R. No More Kin: Exploring Race, Class, & Gender in Family Networks. LC 97-4677. (Understanding Families Ser.: Vol. 8). 272p. 1997. 45.00 (0-7619-0158-2); pap. 21.95 (0-7619-0159-0) Sage.
Roschelle, Marlene, jt. auth. see Klubnik, Joan P.
Roschenthaler, Ute. Ejagham. LC 96-12298. (Heritage Library of African Peoples: Set 3). (Illus.). 64p. (J). (gr. 7-12). 1996. lib. bdg. 16.95 (0-8239-1993-5) Rosen Group.
Roscher, Marina & Fishman, Charles, eds. Catlives: Sarah Kirsch's Katzenleben. 177p. 1990. 24.95 (0-89672-232-5); pap. 12.95 (0-89672-231-7) Tex Tech Univ Pr.
Roscher, Richard R. Auditing: Integration of the AICPA Professional Standards & CPA Examination. 272p. (C). 1995. text 15.75 (0-256-19730-X, Irwn McGrw-H) McGrw-H Hghr Educ.
Roscher, Wilhelm H. Ausfuhrliches Lexikon der Griechischen und Romischen Mythologie, 10 vols. (GER.). 1992. reprint ed. write for info. (3-487-00915-3) G Olms Pubs.
— Omphalos, Vol. I. (Abhandlungen der Kgl. Sachsischen Gesellschaft der Wissenschaften. Philologisch-Historische Klasse, 29 Ser.: Bd., Nr. 9). (GER.). 142p. 1974. reprint ed. write for info. (3-487-05279-2) G Olms Pubs.
Roscher, Wilhelm H., jt. auth. see Hillman, James.
Roscher, William. Principles of Political Economy. LC 72-38255. (Evolution of Capitalism Ser.). 964p. 1972. reprint ed. 65.95 (0-405-04136-5) Ayer.
Roschke, Carl A. State Capitalism Won't Buy Real Growth. (Issue Papers: No. 6-87). 8p. 1987. pap. text 8.00 (1-57655-020-6) Independ Inst.
— What Excellence at What Price? How to Get Colorado Higher Education off the Spending Treadmill. 18p. 1989. pap. text 8.00 (1-57655-122-9) Independ Inst.
Roschlau, Walter H., jt. ed. see Kalant, Harold.
Roschwalb, Suzanne A. & Stack, Richard A. Litigation Public Relations: Courting Public Opinion. LC 95-6541. xix, 240p. 1995. pap. 45.00 (0-8377-1048-0, Rothman) W S Hein.
Rosciglione, Salvatore. Possible e l'Improbarile: Italian Novel.Tr. of Possible & the Improbable. (ITA.). 167p. 1988. pap. 10.00 (0-89304-657-4) Cross-Cultrl NY.
Rosciszewski, Jan. Ionizing Fronts in Plasma Propulsion & Power Generation Systems. LC 70-131402. 191p. 1969. 19.00 (0-403-04532-0) Scholarly.
Roscoe, A. Theory & Practice of Concurrency. 512p. 1997. pap. 72.00 (0-13-674409-5) P-H.
Roscoe, Adrian & Msika, Hangson. Quiet Chameleon: Modern Poetry from Central Africa. (New Perspectives on African Literature Ser.: No. 2). 216p. 1991. lib. bdg. 85.00 (0-905450-52-3, Pub. by H Zell Pubs) Seven Hills Bk.
Roscoe, Andrew, et al. Cellular Market Trends, 1988-2000. LC 89-133756. iv, 241p. 1989. write for info. (0-934960-53-4) Phillips Business.
Roscoe, David, tr. see Meier, Carl A.
Roscoe, Edward S. Growth of English Law: Being Studies in the Evolution of Law & Procedure in England. viii, 260p. 1980. reprint ed. 39.50 (0-8377-1029-4, Rothman) W S Hein.
Roscoe, Fred. From Humboldt to Kodiak, 1886-1895: Recollections of a Frontier Childhood & the Founding of the First American School & the Baptist Mission of Kodiak, Alaska. Roscoe, Stanley N., ed. (Alaska History Ser.: 40). (Illus.). 232p. (Orig.). 1992. pap. 14.95 (0-919642-40-3) Limestone Pr.
Roscoe, George B. Here's the Dirt. LC 84-50310. (Illus.). 140p. 1984. 13.95 (0-932673-01-5) Sense Pubns.
Roscoe, Gerald. Triple Gem: An Introduction to Buddhism. LC 94-916181. 198p. 1998. pap. text 12.95 (974-7047-27-6) U of Wash Pr.
Roscoe, Gerald & Larkin, David. Westward: The Epic Crossing of the American Landscape. LC 95-21909. (Illus.). 240p. 1995. 60.00 (1-885254-09-1, Pub. by Monacelli Pr) Penguin Putnam.
— Westward: The Epic Crossing of the American Landscape, 4 vols., Set. LC 95-21909. (Illus.). 240p. 1995. 240.00 (1-885254-19-9) Monacelli Pr.
Roscoe, Henry. Lives of Eminent British Lawyers. 428p. 1982. reprint ed. 46.50 (0-8377-1037-5, Rothman) W S Hein.
Roscoe, Jennifer, ed. see Smith, Joyce M. & Ippolito, Joseph.
Roscoe, John. Logica Post-Moderna. LC 93-37303. (Revisioning Philosophy Ser.: Vol. 16). 1994. write for info. (0-8204-2352-1) P Lang Pubng.
— Northern Bantu. (Illus.). 305p. 1966. reprint ed. 45.00 (0-7146-1713-X, BHA-01713, Pub. by F Cass Pubs) Intl Spec Bk.
***Roscoe, Lewis.** Planning the Campus: Process, Organization & Recommendations. LC 00-191052. (Illus.). 2000. pap. 29.95 (0-9700916-0-5) L & A Pubns.
Roscoe, Lorraine, jt. auth. see Denenberg, Dennis.
Roscoe, Mike, ed. see Anderson, Dave.
Roscoe Moss Company Staff. Handbook of Ground Water Development. LC 89-30002. 512p. 1990. 180.00 (0-471-85611-8) Wiley.
Roscoe, Patric. Love Is Starving for Itself. 240p. Date not set. pap. 16.50 (1-55128-015-9, Pub. by Mercury Bk) LPC InBook.
Roscoe, Patrick. Beneath the Western Slopes. 190p. (Orig.). 1987. pap. 14.95 (0-88784-502-9, Pub. by Hse of Anansi Pr) Genl Dist Srvs.
— The Lost Oasis. 324p. (Orig.). 1995. pap. 14.95 (0-7710-7579-0) McCland & Stewart.
Roscoe, Paul, jt. ed. see Lutkehaus, Nancy.
Roscoe Pound-American Trial Lawyers Assn. Staff, jt. auth. see Colley, Michael F.
Roscoe Pound-American Trial Lawyers Foundation Sta. Church, State & Politics: Final Report of the 1981 Chief Justice Earl Warren Conference on Advocacy in the United States. LC 81-85556. (Annual Chief Earl Warren Conference on Advocacy in the U. S. Ser.). 147p. 1982. pap. 25.00 (0-933067-03-8) Roscoe Pound Inst.
— Dispute Resolution Devices in a Democratic Society: Final report of the 1985 Chief Justice Earl Warren Conference on Advocacy in the United States. 152p. 1985. pap. 25.00 (0-941916-41-3) Roscoe Pound Inst.
***Roscoe Pound Foundation Staff.** Assaults on the Judiciary: Attacking the Great Bulwark of Public Loberty. Rooks, James E., Jr., ed. (Papers of the Roscoe Pound Foundation). 170p. 1999. pap. 40.00 (0-933067-20-8) Roscoe Pound Inst.
Roscoe Pound Foundation Staff. The Courts: Separation of Powers. LC 83-61923. (Annual Chief Earl Warren Conference on Advocacy in the U.S. Ser.). 141p. 1983. pap. 25.00 (0-933067-05-4) Roscoe Pound Inst.
— The Courts: The Pendulum of Federalism. LC 79-92328. (Annual Chief Justice Earl Warren Conference on Advocacy in the U.S. Ser.). 166p. 1979. pap. 25.00 (0-933067-01-1) Roscoe Pound Inst.
— Ethics & Government. LC 82-62513. (Annual Chief Earl Warren Conference on Advocacy in the U.S. Ser.). 158p. 1982. pap. 25.00 (0-933067-04-6) Roscoe Pound Inst.
— Justice Denied: Underfunding of the Courts: Report of a Roundtable Discussion. Wolfson, Barbara, ed. 26p. 1994. pap. 20.00 (0-933067-15-1) Roscoe Pound Inst.
— The Penalty of Death. LC 80-54626. (Annual Chief Earl Warren Conference on Advocacy in the U.S. Ser.). 121p. 1980. pap. 25.00 (0-933067-02-X) Roscoe Pound Inst.
— Possible State Court Responses to the ALI's Proposed Restatement of Products Liability: Report of the 1996 Forum for State Court Judges. Rooks, James, ed. 75p. 1997. pap. 35.00 (0-933067-18-6) Roscoe Pound Inst.
— Preserving Access to Justice: The Impact on State Courts of the "Proposed Long Range Plan for Federal Courts" Rooks, James & Wolfson, Barbara, eds. (Papers of the Roscoe Pound Foundation). 82p. (Orig.). (C). 1996. pap. 35.00 (0-933067-17-8) Roscoe Pound Inst.
— Preserving the Independence of the Judiciary: Report of the 1993 Forum for State Court Judges. Wolfson, Barbara, ed. LC 94-67264. 67p. 1994. pap. 35.00 (0-933067-16-X) Roscoe Pound Inst.
— Protecting Individual Rights: The Role of State Constitutionalism: Report of the 1992 Forum for State Court Judges. Wolfson, Barbara, ed. 82p. 1993. pap. 35.00 (0-933067-14-3) Roscoe Pound Inst.
Roscoe Pound Foundation Staff. Scientific Evidence in the Courts: Concepts & Controversies. Rooks, James, ed. (Papers of the Roscoe Pound Foundation). 140p. 1997. pap. 35.00 (0-933067-19-4) Roscoe Pound Inst.
Roscoe, S. & Brimmell, R. A. James Lumsden & Son of Glasgow. 134p. 1981. 28.00 (0-900002-04-2, Pub. by Priv Lib Assn) Oak Knoll.
Roscoe, Stanley N. Aviation Psychology. LC 79-27539. (Illus.). 318p. 1982. reprint ed. pap. 29.95 (0-8138-1927-X) Iowa St U Pr.
Roscoe, Stanley N., jt. auth. see O'Hare, David.
Roscoe, Stanley N., ed. see Roscoe, Fred.
Roscoe, Theodore. United States Destroyer Operations in World War II. LC 53-4273. (Illus.). 581p. 1953. 47.50 (0-87021-726-7) Naval Inst Pr.
— United States Submarine Operations in World War II. LC 50-5198. (Illus.). 577p. 1949. 47.50 (0-87021-731-3) Naval Inst Pr.
— The Wonderful Lips of Thibong Linh. (Illus.). 1981. 15.00 (0-937986-36-4) D M Grant.
Roscoe, Theodore & Were, Mary W., eds. Poems by Contemporary Women. LC 79-51967. (Granger Poetry Library). 1980. reprint ed. 20.00 (0-89609-195-3) Roth Pub Inc.
Roscoe, Thomas, ed. see Roscoe, William.
Roscoe, W. Zuni Man-Women. LC 90-21397. (Illus.). 328p. 1992. pap. 15.95 (0-8263-1370-1) U of NM Pr.
Roscoe, Will. Changing Ones. (Illus.). 334p. 1999. pap. 16.95 (0-312-22479-6) St Martin.
— Changing Ones: Third & Fourth Genders in Native North America. LC 97-41762. (Illus.). 336p. 1998. text 24.95 (0-312-17539-6) St Martin.
Roscoe, Will, ed. Queer Spirits: A Gay Men's Myth Book. 368p. 1996. pap. 15.00 (0-8070-7939-1) Beacon Pr.
Roscoe, Will & Murray, Stephen O., eds. Boy-Wives & Female-Husbands: Studies in African Homosexualities. LC 98-21464. 336p. 1998. text 29.95 (0-312-21216-X) St Martin.
Roscoe, Will, ed. see Hay, Harry.
Roscoe, Will, jt. ed. see Murray, Stephen O.
Roscoe, William. Life & Pontificate of Pope Leo the Tenth, 2 vols. 6th rev. ed. Roscoe, Thomas, ed. LC 75-174965. reprint ed. 125.00 (0-404-05430-7) AMS Pr.
Roscoe, William E. History of Schoharie County, N. Y. 1713-1882 with Illustrations & Biographical Sketches of Some of Its Prominent Men & Pioneers. (Illus.). 502p. (Orig.). 1994. pap. text 58.00 (0-7884-0060-6) Heritage Bk.
— History of Schoharie County, New York. (Illus.). 470p. 1994. reprint ed. lib. bdg. 49.50 (0-8328-4353-9) Higginson Bk Co.
— History of Schoharie County, with Illustrations & Biographical Sketches of Some of Its Prominent Men & Pioneers. (Illus.). 498p. 1997. reprint ed. lib. bdg. 52.00 (0-8328-6235-5) Higginson Bk Co.
Roscoe, Wilma J., ed. Accreditation of Historically & Predominantly Black Colleges & Universities. LC 88-39408. (Illus.). 68p. (Orig.). (C). 1989. lib. bdg. 25.00 (0-8191-7288-X) U Pr of Amer.
Roscow, Gregory, ed. see Bliss, Arthur.
Rosdahl, Caroline. Basic Nursing. 6th ed. 304p. 1995. pap. text, student ed. 18.95 (0-397-55137-1) Lppncott W & W.
Rosdahl, Caroline B. Textbook of Basic Nursing. 6th ed. LC 94-30640. 1,616p. 1995. text 49.95 (0-397-55109-6) Lppncott W & W.
Rosdahl, Caroline B., jt. auth. see Earnest, Vicki V.
Rosdahl, Kurt, tr. see Jackins, Harvey.
Rosden, George E. & Rosden, Peter E. The Law of Advertising, 4 vols. 1973. ring bd. 1030.00 (0-8205-1357-1) Bender.
Rosden, Peter E., jt. auth. see Rosden, George E.
Rosdhal, Robert. My Family Secrets. (Illus.). 272p. 1998. pap. write for info. (1-57579-108-0) Pine Hill Pr.
Rosdolsky, Roman. The Making of Marx's Capital, Vol. 1. 452p. (C). 1992. pap. 22.95 (0-86104-915-2, Pub. by Pluto GBR) Stylus Pub VA.
— The Making of Marx's "Capital", Vol. 2. (C). pap. 22.95 (0-86104-305-7, Pub. by Pluto GBR) Stylus Pub VA.
Rose. The American Profile. 1986. 7.16 (0-07-545019-4) McGraw.
— Brain Injury & After: Towards Improved Outcome. 1996. pap. 42.00 (0-471-96288-0) Wiley.
— Heathcliff in Outer Space. 1987. pap. 1.95 (0-8167-1264-6) Troll Communs.
— Hippies. 1999. pap. write for info. (0-14-012270-2, Viking) Viking Penguin.
— In-Service Training Manual. LC 99-24986. 416p. 1999. 163.95 (0-7668-0516-6) Delmar.
***Rose.** Innocents. 2000. pap. 15.95 (1-85702-845-7, Pub. by Fourth Estate) Trafalgar.
Rose. Money & Capital Markets. 7th ed. LC 99-27993. 864p. 1999. 88.44 (0-07-231002-2) McGraw.
***Rose.** Politics in England: Change & Persistance. 6th ed. (C). 1999. pap. text Price not set. (0-321-00523-6) Addison-Wesley.
Rose. Secondary Products of Metabolism. 1979. text 104.00 (0-12-596553-2) Acad Pr.
— The Short History of Neurology. LC 99-10462. 282p. 1999. pap. text 50.00 (0-7506-4165-7) Buttrwrth-Heinemann.
— Social Stratification U S Post. 48p. 2000. pap. 18.95 (1-56584-550-1) Norton.
Rose. Understanding Sociology. (Rose-Glazer-Sociology). 1990. text. write for info. (0-13-823253-9) P-H.
Rose. Understanding the U. K. Date not set. pap. text. write for info. (0-582-29591-2, Pub. by Addison-Wesley) Longman.
Rose, contrib. by. Rose's Story: Rose, A Survivor of Our Social Services. LC 91-33602. 128p. 1991. pap. 13.95 (0-87304-244-1) Manticore Pubs.
Rose, ed. Wheels of Progress? Motor Transport, Pollution & the Environment. x, 160p. 1973. text 128.00 (0-677-15425-9) Gordon & Breach.
Rose & Myers, eds. Clinical Decision Making (Proceedings) 95p. 1989. pap. 21.00 (0-912452-71-4, P-68) Am Phys Therapy Assn.
Rose & O'Rourke. Hippies. 1999. text 24.95 (0-670-82854-8) Viking Penguin.
***Rose & Rose, Kathi.** Living or Dying by the Sword. 1999. pap. text 9.95 (0-9666819-3-2) Winners Success Netwrk.
***Rose, et al.** Literacy in Perspective. 2000. pap. text 46.95 (0-312-25042-8) St Martin.
Rose, jt. auth. see Drier.
Rose, jt. auth. see Waterhouse.
Rose, ed. see Gomez, Antonio-Enriquez.
Rose, ed. see International Association of Agricultural Librarians Staff.
Rose, A. G. The Pathology of Heart Valve Replacement. 1987. text 229.00 (0-85200-984-4) Kluwer Academic.
Rose, A. H. Advances in Microbial Physiology. 1985. text 99.00 (0-12-031723-0) Acad Pr.
— Insects of Eastern Spruces, Fir, & Hemlock. 2nd rev. ed. (Illus.). 159p. (Orig.). 1994. pap. 51.95 (0-660-15112-X, Pub. by Canadian Govt Pub) Accents Pubns.

An Asterisk (*) at the beginning of an entry indicates that the title is appearing for the first time.

Rose, A. H., ed. Advances in Microbial Physiology, Vol. 33. (Illus.). 424p. 1992. text 104.00 (*0-12-027733-6*) Acad Pr.
— Advances in Microbial Physiology, Vol. 34. (Illus.). 356p. 1993. text 99.00 (*0-12-027734-4*) Acad Pr.
— Advances in Microbial Physiology, Vol. 35. (Illus.). 352p. 1993. text 104.00 (*0-12-027735-2*) Acad Pr.
— Economic Microbiology: Fermented Foods, Vol. 7. (Economic Microbiology Ser.). 1982. text 104.00 (*0-12-596557-5*) Acad Pr.
— Economic Microbiology: Microbial Biodeterioration, Vol. 6. 516p. 1981. text 104.00 (*0-12-596556-7*) Acad Pr.
Rose, A. H., et al, eds. Advances in Microbial Physiology, Vol. 24. (Serial Publication Ser.). 1983. text 99.00 (*0-12-027724-7*) Acad Pr.
— Advances in Microbial Physiology, Vol. 25. (Serial Publication Ser.). 1985. text 99.00 (*0-12-027725-5*) Acad Pr.
— The Yeasts Vol. 6: Yeast Genetics. 2nd ed. (Illus.). 708p. 1995. text 105.00 (*0-12-596416-1*) Acad Pr.
Rose, A. H. & Harrison, J. S. The Yeasts: Edited Treatise, Vol. 1. 2nd ed. 391p. 1987. text 104.00 (*0-12-596411-0*) Acad Pr.
Rose, A. H. & Harrison, J. S., eds. The Yeasts, Vol. 5. 2nd ed. (Illus.). 660p. 1993. text 104.00 (*0-12-596415-3*) Acad Pr.
— The Yeasts Vol. 3: Metabolism & Physiology of Yeasts. 2nd ed. 635p. 1989. text 104.00 (*0-12-596413-7*) Acad Pr.
— The Yeasts Vol. 4: Yeast Organelles. 2nd ed. (Serial Publication Ser.). 765p. 1991. text 104.00 (*0-12-596414-5*) Acad Pr.
Rose, A. H. & Morris, Gareth, eds. Advances in Microbial Physiology, Vol. 20. LC 67-19850. (Serial Publication Ser.). 1980. text 187.00 (*0-12-027720-4*) Acad Pr.
— Advances in Microbial Physiology, Vol. 21. LC 67-19850. (Serial Publication Ser.). 1981. text 99.00 (*0-12-027721-2*) Acad Pr.
Rose, A. H. & Morris, J. Gareth, eds. Advances in Microbial Physiology, Vol. 22. (Serial Publication Ser.). 1981. text 104.00 (*0-12-027722-0*) Acad Pr.
— Advances in Microbial Physiology, Vol. 23. (Serial Publication Ser.). 268p. 1982. text 104.00 (*0-12-027723-9*) Acad Pr.
Rose, A. H. & Tempest, David W., eds. Advances in Microbial Physiology. (Serial Publication Ser.: Vol. 30). 276p. 1990. text 99.00 (*0-12-027730-1*) Acad Pr.
— Advances in Microbial Physiology, Vol. 27. (Serial Publication Ser.). 368p. 1986. text 99.00 (*0-12-027727-1*) Acad Pr.
— Advances in Microbial Physiology, Vol. 28. (Serial Publication Ser.). 268p. 1987. text 99.00 (*0-12-027728-X*) Acad Pr.
— Advances in Microbial Physiology, Vol. 29. (Serial Publication Ser.). 365p. 1988. text 99.00 (*0-12-027729-8*) Acad Pr.
— Advances in Microbial Physiology, Vol. 31. 311p. 1990. text 99.00 (*0-12-027731-X*) Acad Pr.
— Advances in Microbial Physiology, Vol. 32. (Illus.). 257p. 1991. text 99.00 (*0-12-027732-8*) Acad Pr.
Rose, A. H. & Wilkinson, J. F., eds. Advances in Microbial Physiology, 18. (Serial Publication Ser.). 1979. text 187.00 (*0-12-027718-2*) Acad Pr.
— Advances in Microbial Physiology, 19. (Serial Publication Ser.). 1979. text 170.00 (*0-12-027719-0*) Acad Pr.
Rose, A. James. Inquiring Children & Their Teachers. (Catherine Molony Memorial Lectures). 1987. pap. text 5.00 (*0-918374-26-X*) City Coll Wk.
Rose, Aaron. Dysfunctional: One Messed up Version of Skating. (Illus.). 208p. 1999. pap. 29.95 (*1-58423-002-9*) Gingko Press.
Rose-Ackerman, Susan. Controlling Environmental Policy: The Limits of Public Law in Germany & the United States. LC 94-40558. 1995. 32.50 (*0-300-06065-3*) Yale U Pr.
— Corruption: A Study in Political Economy. 1978. text 39.95 (*0-12-596350-5*) Acad Pr.
— Corruption & Government: Causes, Consequences & Reform. LC 98-43631. (Illus.). 272p. 1999. 49.95 (*0-521-63293-5*) Cambridge U Pr.
— Corruption & Government: Causes, Consequences & Reform. LC 98-43631. (Illus.). 266p. 1999. pap. 18.95 (*0-521-65912-4*) Cambridge U Pr.
Rose-Ackerman, Susan, jt. auth. see James, Estelle.
Rose, Adam & Kolk, David, eds. Forecasting Natural Gas Demand in a Changing World. (Contemporary Studies in Economic & Financial Analysis: Vol. 60). 152p. 1987. 78.50 (*0-89232-838-X*) Jai Pr.
Rose, Adam, et al. Natural Resource Policy & Income Distribution. LC 87-2788. (Illus.). 158p. reprint ed. pap. 49.00 (*0-608-06134-4*, 206646700008) Bks Demand.
Rose, Adam Z. & Stevens, Benjamin H. Transboundary Income & Expenditure Flows in Regional Input-output Models. (Discussion Papers: No. 133). 32p. (C). 1989. pap. 10.00 (*1-55869-138-3*) Regional Sci Res Inst.
Rose, Adrian, ed. see Dolmetsch, Rudolph.
Rose, Agatha. Hide & Seek in the Yellow House. 1995. 10.19 (*0-606-07645-X*, Pub. by Turtleback) Demco.
Rose, Aidan & Lawton, Alan. Public Services Management. 448p. 1998. pap. 54.50 (*0-273-62524-1*, Pub. by Pitman Pub) Trans-Atl Phila.
Rose, Al. Born in New Orleans: Notables of Two Centuries. (Illus.). 1983. 20.00 (*0-916620-68-9*) Portals Pr.
— Storyville, New Orleans: Being an Authentic, Illustrated Account of the Notorious Red Light District. 240p. 1978. pap. 19.95 (*0-8173-4403-9*) U of Ala Pr.
Rose, Alan. Miami Beach Deco. (Illus.). 24p. 1997. pap. 16.95 (*0-312-14679-5*) St Martin.
***Rose, Alan.** Miami Beach Deco: The World at Your Feet. (Illus.). 15p. 2000. pap. text 17.00 (*0-7881-6988-2*) DIANE Pub.
Rose, Alan. Route 66 Souvenirs. (Illus.). 54p. 1998. pap. 17.95 (*0-312-18755-6*) St Martin.
— Surrealism & Communism: The Early Years. LC 91-2231. (American University Studies: History: Ser. IX, Vols. 96). XV, 343p. (C). 1991. text 49.95 (*0-8204-1384-4*) P Lang Pubng.
Rose, Albert. Electron Phonon Interactions: A Novel Semiclassical Approach. 192p. 1989. text 46.00 (*9971-5-0635-1*) World Scientific Pub.
— Governing Metropolitan Toronto: A Social & Political Analysis, 1953-1971. LC 72-157821. (Lane Studies in Regional Government). 227p. reprint ed. pap. 70.40 (*0-608-18277-X*, 203151200075) Bks Demand.
Rose, Alexander G., III & Savoye, Jeffrey A. Such Friends As These. 1986. pap. 5.00 (*0-910556-24-5*) Enoch Pratt.
Rose, Alison. How I Got to Be a Single Woman. 1999. write for info. (*0-316-03661-7*) Little.
Rose, Allen J., jt. auth. see Gilman, Leonard.
Rose, Andrea. 100 Quick Fashion Tips. Michelle, Amber, ed. 26p. 1998. pap. 9.00 (*1-890469-04-1*) A R Prod.
— The Pre-Raphaelites. (Color Library). (Illus.). 128p. (C). 1994. pap. 14.95 (*0-7148-2907-2*, Pub. by Phaidon Press) Phaidon Pr.
— Secrets of a Fashion Designer: How to Be Your Own Fashion Consultant. Michelle, Amber, ed. (Illus.). 107p. 1998. pap. 18.00 (*1-890469-09-2*) A R Prod.
— 24 Hours of Accessorizing. Michelle, Amber, ed. 17p. 1998. pap. 9.00 (*1-890469-03-3*) A R Prod.
Rose, Andrea, pref. The Germ: Literary Magazine of the Pre-Raphaelites. (Illus.). 194p. 1995. 19.95 (*1-85444-023-3*, 0233, Pub. by Ashmolean Mus) A Schwartz & Co.
— The Germ: Literary Magazine of the Pre-Raphaelites. (Illus.). 194p. 1995. pap. 15.95 (*1-85444-024-1*, 0241, Pub. by Ashmolean Mus) A Schwartz & Co.
Rose, Andy, jt. ed. see Balka, Christie.
Rose, Angie & Weiss, Lynn. Self Esteem: Giving Children from Birth to Six the Freedom to Grow. rev. ed. LC 83-81434. 170p. (Orig.). 1984. pap. 17.95 (*0-89334-046-4*) Humanics Ltd.
— Self Esteem Activities: Giving Children from Birth to Six the Freedom to Grow. LC 83-81434. (Illus.). 192p. (Orig.). 1995. lib. bdg. 27.95 (*0-89334-238-6*, 2246X09) Humanics Ltd.
Rose, Anna. Cookin' n' Kin. unabridged ed. 102p. 1996. spiral bd. 7.95 (*0-9653084-1-3*) Mtn Hse Pub.
Rose, Anne C. Victorian America & the Civil War. (Illus.). 320p. (C). 1992. text 59.95 (*0-521-41081-9*) Cambridge U Pr.
— Victorian America & the Civil War. (Illus.). 320p. (C). 1994. pap. text 17.95 (*0-521-47883-9*) Cambridge U Pr.
— Voices of the Marketplace: American Thought & Culture, 1830-1860. (American Thought & Culture Ser.). (Illus.). 272p. 1994. 33.00 (*0-8057-9065-9*, Twyne) Mac Lib Ref.
Rose, Anne K. Double Vision: Twelve Stories. LC 97-20029. 111p. 1997. pap. 24.95 (*1-887841-11-3*, 61405, Psychosocial) Intl Univs Pr.
Rose, Anthony H. Chemical Microbiology. 2nd ed. LC 68-28664. 324p. reprint ed. pap. 100.50 (*0-608-16519-0*, 202628800049) Bks Demand.
Rose, Arnold M. Assuring Freedom to the Free: A Century of Emancipation in the U. S. A. LC 63-14634. 311p. reprint ed. pap. 96.50 (*0-7837-3789-0*, 204360900010) Bks Demand.
— The Institutions of Advanced Societies. LC 57-11006. 703p. reprint ed. pap. 200.00 (*0-608-14674-9*, 205590300039) Bks Demand.
— Libel & Academic Freedom: A Lawsuit Against Political Extremists. LC 68-19743. 299p. reprint ed. pap. 92.70 (*0-608-14155-0*, 205590500039) Bks Demand.
— Migrants in Europe: Problems of Acceptance & Adjustment. LC 76-76162. 206p. reprint ed. pap. 63.90 (*0-608-15979-4*, 203328700084) Bks Demand.
Rose, Arnold M., ed. Aging in Minnesota: A Report of the Minnesota Planning Committee for the White House Conference on Aging, Governor's Citizens Council on Aging. LC 63-13884. 334p. reprint ed. pap. 103.60 (*0-8357-5260-7*, 205590400039) Bks Demand.
Rose, Arthur, jt. auth. see Rose, Terry.
Rose, Arthur P. Illustrated History of Lyon County. (Illus.). 616p. 1997. reprint ed. lib. bdg. 64.50 (*0-8328-6804-3*) Higginson Bk Co.
— Illustrated History of the Counties Rock & Pipestone. (Illus.). 802p. 1997. reprint ed. lib. bdg. 84.00 (*0-8328-6813-2*) Higginson Bk Co.
Rose, Arthur W., et al. Geochemistry in Mineral Exploration. 2nd ed. (Illus.). 652p. 1996. reprint ed. 80.00 (*0-9650968-0-7*) A W Rose.
Rose, Augustus. How to Work Copper for Fun & Profit. unabridged ed. (Illus.). 125p. 1993. pap. 14.95 (*1-57002-077-9*) Univ Publng Hse.
Rose, Augustus F. & Cirino, Antonio. Jewelry Making & Design. (Illus.). 306p. 1949. pap. 8.95 (*0-486-21750-7*) Dover.
Rose, Barbara. American Painting: The Twentieth Century, Vol. II. LC 85-43548. (Illus.). 180p. 1991. pap. 25.00 (*0-8478-0716-9*, Pub. by Rizzoli Intl) St Martin.
— Beverly Pepper: Three Site Specific Sculptures. (Land Marks Ser.). 1998. pap. text 24.95 (*1-888931-14-0*) Watsn-Guptill.
Rose, Barbara. Cleanliness Is Godliness: Complete Instructions for the "Lighten-Up Program", a 2 Week Intestinal Cleanse. unabridged ed. 167p. 1991. pap. 12.00 (*0-9678598-0-8*) Let There Be Lgt.
Rose, Barbara. Ellsworth Kelly: Curves - Rectangles. Bell, Suzanne, ed. 32p. 1989. pap. 20.00 (*0-924008-04-0*) Blum Helman.
— Joseph Stella: Flora. Eaton, Timothy A., ed. (Illus.). 80p. 1997. 34.95 (*0-9655819-4-2*, 2000) Eaton Fine Art.
— Lucas Samaras: Gold. LC 98-88819. (Illus.). 64p. 1998. pap. write for info. (*1-878283-81-2*) PaceWildenstein.
— Magdalena Abakanowicz. LC 93-26843. (Illus.). 224p. 1994. 49.50 (*0-8109-1947-8*, Pub. by Abrams) Time Warner.
— Ronald Davis: Dodecagons, 1968-69. (Illus.). 32p. (Orig.). 1989. pap. 15.00 (*0-924008-03-2*) Blum Helman.
— Tsuda Umeko & Women's Education in Japan. (Illus.). 224p. 1992. 35.00 (*0-300-05177-8*) Yale U Pr.
Rose, Barbara, ed. Art As Art: The Selected Writings of Ad Reinhardt. (Illus.). 253p. 1991. reprint ed. pap. 15.95 (*0-520-07670-2*, Pub. by U CA Pr) Cal Prin Full Svc.
Rose, Barbara, et al. Arshile Gorky & the Genesis of Abstraction: Drawings from the Early 1930s. LC 94-78407. (Illus.). 112p. (Orig.). 1994. pap. 30.00 (*1-886055-00-9*) S Mazoh.
Rose, Barbara, ed. see Namuth, Hans.
Rose, Barry. The Family Health Guide to Homeopathy. LC 93-3586. (Illus.). 310p. 1995. pap. 34.95 (*0-89087-695-9*) Celestial Arts.
Rose, Barry & Scott-Moncrieff, Christina. Homeopathy for Women: A Comprehensive, Easy-to-Use Guide for Women of All Ages. (Illus.). 176p. 1999. pap. 19.95 (*1-55209-303-4*) Firefly Bks Ltd.
Rose, Ben L. The History of Hebron Presbyterian Church: Manakin-Sabot, Virginia. (Illus.). 128p. 1993. 19.95 (*1-881576-12-4*) Providence Hse.
— T. U. L. I. P. The Five Disputed Points of Calvinism. 2nd ed. LC 96-32985. 64p. 1996. pap. 9.95 (*1-57736-021-4*) Providence Hse.
Rose, Bernice. Bonnard/Rothko: Color & Light. LC 97-65346. (Illus.). 72p. (Orig.). 1997. pap. write for info. (*1-878283-69-3*) PaceWildenstein.
— Brice Marden: Drawings. LC 95-71792. (Illus.). 32p. (Orig.). 1995. pap. write for info. (*1-878283-57-X*) PaceWildenstein.
— Henry Moore: A Sculptor's Drawings. (Illus.). 70p. (Orig.). 1993. pap. write for info. (*1-878283-39-1*) PaceWildenstein.
— Robert Rauschenberg: Anagrams. LC 96-70256. (Illus.). 80p. (Orig.). 1996. pap. write for info. (*1-878283-65-0*) PaceWildenstein.
— Robert Rauschenberg: Arcadian Retreats. LC 97-206988. (Illus.). 40p. 1997. pap. write for info. (*1-878283-71-5*) PaceWildenstein.
Rose, Bernice, contrib. by. Picasso & Drawing. (Illus.). 120p. (Orig.). 1995. pap. write for info. (*1-878283-50-2*) PaceWildenstein.
***Rose, Bernice & Glimcher, Arne.** Saul Steinberg: Drawing into Being. (Illus.). 84p. 1999. pap. write for info. (*1-878283-89-8*) PaceWildenstein.
Rose, Beth. Appendix to "The Rice Economy of Asia" Rice Statistics by Country: Tables & Notes. 398p. 1985. pap. text 19.95 (*0-915707-22-5*, Pub. by Resources Future) Johns Hopkins.
Rose, Betty B., jt. auth. see Dole, Jim W.
Rose, Beverly. Mis' Luci. 2nd rev. ed. LC 96-79733. (Rosebrier Collection: Vol. 1). (Illus.). 46p. (J). (ps-2). 1997. 17.50 (*0-9655612-2-4*) Laurel Pub SC.
Rose, Bill. Life under a Rock. LC 96-14244. 65p. (Orig.). 1996. pap. 15.00 (*1-883302-07-2*) Trning Res.
Rose, Bill, jt. auth. see Moffitt, Merra L.
Rose, Billy. Wine, Women & Words. (American Autobiography Ser.). 295p. 1995. reprint ed. lib. bdg. 79.00 (*0-7812-8631-X*) Rprt Serv.
Rose, Blandina, ed. see Kline, John L.
Rose, Bob. RCA/GE Television. LC 98-67777. (HWS Servicans Ser.). 1999. pap. text 34.95 (*0-7906-1171-6*) Prompt Publns.
Rose, Bob. Zenith Televisions. (SAMS Servicing Ser.). 34.95 (*0-7906-1216-X*, 61216) Prompt Publns.
Rose, Brian, jt. auth. see Matsuoka, Mikihiro.
Rose, Brian A. Jekyll & Hyde Adapted: Dramatizations of Cultural Anxiety, 66. LC 95-24765. (Contributions in Drama & Theatre Studies: No. 66). 192p. 1996. 57.95 (*0-313-29721-5*, Greenwood Pr) Greenwood.
Rose, Brian G. Directing for Television: Conversations with American TV Directors. LC 98-39159. 232p. 1998. text 32.50 (*0-8108-3591-6*) Scarecrow.
— An Examination of Narrative Structure in Four Films of Frank Capra. Jowett, Garth S., ed. LC 79-6683. (Dissertations on Film, 1980 Ser.). 1980. lib. bdg. 18.95 (*0-405-12915-7*) Ayer.
— Televising the Performing Arts: Interviews with Merrill Brockway, Kirk Browning, & Roger Englander, 29. LC 92-10677. (Contributions to the Study of Music & Dance Ser.: No. 29). 216p. 1992. 52.95 (*0-313-28617-5*, RTR/, Greenwood Pr) Greenwood.
— Television & the Performing Arts: A Handbook & Reference Guide to American Cultural Programming. LC 85-14555. 291p. 1986. lib. bdg. 59.95 (*0-313-24159-7*, RTV/, Greenwood Pr) Greenwood.
Rose, Brian G. & Alley, Robert S., eds. TV Genres: A Handbook & Reference Guide. LC 84-22460. 453p. 1985. lib. bdg. 75.00 (*0-313-23724-7*, RHG/, Greenwood Pr) Greenwood.
Rose, Brinda, et al, eds. Interventions: Feminist Dialogues on Third World Women's Literature & Film. LC 96-26295. 296p. 1996. text 60.00 (*0-8153-2129-5*) Garland.
***Rose, Bryce.** A Time for All Seasons. 64p. 2000. pap. 6.95 (*1-56167-600-4*) Am Literary Pr.
Rose, Bud, et al. Clinical Physiology of Acid-Base & Electrolyte Disorders. 5th ed. (Illus.). 960p. 1999. pap. write for info. (*0-07-134682-1*) McGraw-Hill HPD.
Rose, Burton D. Clinical Physiology of Acid-Base & Electrolyte Disorders. 4th ed. (Illus.). 915p. 1993. pap. text 42.00 (*0-07-053663-5*) McGraw-Hill HPD.
— Manual of Complete Neph ISE. 1988. 15.95 (*0-316-75635-0*, Little Brwn Med Div) Lppncott W & W.
— Pathophysiology of Renal Disease. 2nd ed. (Illus.). 623p. 1987. pap. text 39.00 (*0-07-053629-5*) McGraw-Hill HPD.
Rose, Burton D. & Black, Robert. Manual of Clinical Problems in Nephrology. 375p. 1988. 31.95 (*0-316-75637-7*, Little Brwn Med Div) Lppncott W & W.
Rose, Burton D. & Rennke, Helmut G. Renal Pathophysiology. LC 93-13959. (Illus.). 352p. 1994. 27.00 (*0-683-07354-0*) Lppncott W & W.
Rose, C. L. & De Torres, A. R. Storage of Natural History Collections: Ideas & Practical Solutions. LC 95-223. 360p. (C). 1992. spiral bd. 36.00 (*0-9635476-0-7*) Soc Preser NHC.
Rose, Calvin W., jt. ed. see Ghadiri, Hossein.
Rose, Candi & Thomas, Dirk. Net.Sex: A Discreet Guide to the Adult Side of the Internet. (Illus.). 243p. (Orig.). 1994. pap. 19.99 (*0-672-30702-2*) Sams.
Rose, Carl. Teach Yourself Digital Photography in 14 Days. 1998. 39.99 (*1-56205-912-2*, New Riders Sftwre) MCP SW Interactive.
***Rose, Carla.** Sams Teach Yourself Adobe Photoshop X in 24 Hours. (Teach Yourself... in 24 Hours Ser.). (Illus.). 450p. 2000. pap. text 19.99 (*0-672-31955-1*) Sams.
Rose, Carla. Sams Teach Yourself Photoshop 5.0 in 24 Hours. LC 98-84022. (Teach Yourself Ser.). 1998. pap. 19.99 (*0-672-31301-4*) Sams.
***Rose, Carla.** Teach Yourself Adobe Photoshop X in 24 Hours. (Teach Yourself Ser.). (Illus.). 400p. 1999. 19.99 (*0-672-31723-0*) Sams.
Rose, Carla. Teach Yourself Digital Photography in 14 Days. (Teach Yourself Ser.). 382p. 1997. 39.99 (*1-56830-405-6*) Hayden.
Rose, Carla, jt. auth. see Hayden Development Staff.
***Rose, Carol.** Giants, Monsters, & Dragons: An Encyclopedia of Folklore, Legend, & Myth. 2000. lib. bdg. 65.00 (*0-87436-988-6*) ABC-CLIO.
Rose, Carol. Spirits, Fairies, Gnomes, & Goblins: An Encyclopedia of the Little People. LC 96-8460. 370p. 1996. lib. bdg. 75.00 (*0-87436-811-1*) ABC-CLIO.
— Spirits, Fairies, Leprechauns, & Goblins: An Encyclopedia. (Illus.). 368p. 1998. pap. 15.95 (*0-393-31792-7*) Norton.
***Rose, Carol.** Wild Woman. (Bouquet Ser.: Vol. 64). 2000. mass mkt. 3.99 (*0-8217-6687-2*, Zebra Kensgtn) Kensgtn Pub Corp.
Rose, Carol, ed. see Miller, Arthur, et al.
Rose, Carol J. Tarot Comparisons: 78 Packs of 78 Cards. (Illus.). 350p. 1999. 69.00 (*1-878490-73-7*) Rosehips Prodns.
Rose, Carol Jean. The Full Four: Indigo Hymns to Inner Seasons. 135p. (C). 1990. 29.00 (*1-878490-60-5*) Rosehips Prodns.
— Singing in My Chains: Violet Formalist Verse. 148p. 1996. 29.00 (*1-878490-66-4*) Rosehips Prodns.
— Step Mother: A Chocolate Epistolary Novel. LC 89-92530. 300p. (C). 1990. 39.00 (*1-878490-58-3*) Rosehips Prodns.
— The Tarot Gypsy Tales: Definitive Resource on the Cards. LC 89-92413. (Illus.). 300p. (C). 1990. 59.00 (*1-878490-50-8*) Rosehips Prodns.
— The Tarot Gypsy Trips: Emerald Secrets of a Road Scholar. 1995. 49.00 (*1-878490-64-8*); lib. bdg. 59.00 (*1-878490-65-6*) Rosehips Prodns.
Rose, Caroline. Interpreting History in Sino-Japanese Relations: A Case Study in Political Decision Making. LC 98-235187. (Nissan Institute/Routledge Japanese Studies Ser.). 272p. (C). (gr. 13). 1998. 85.00 (*0-415-17296-9*, D6183) Routledge.
Rose, Caroline, jt. auth. see Erlande-Brandenburg, Alain.
Rose, Carolyn L., et al, eds. Storage of Natural History Collections: A Preventive Conservation Approach, Vol. 1. LC 95-223. 1995. 36.00 (*0-9635476-1-5*) Soc Preser NHC.
Rose, Catherine & Rose, Neil. Amare. MacIntyre, Tom, tr. ix, 152p. 1999. pap. 14.95 (*0-9668797-5-9*) Flaming Rose Pr.
Rose, Cecy. Profound Writings, East & West. 242p. 1988. 14.00 (*1-878683-05-5*) TAT Found.
Rose, Charles, jt. auth. see Thomas, Dick.
Rose, Charles B. Dynastic Commemoration & Imperial Portraiture in the Julio-Claudian Period. LC 96-5232. (Cambridge Studies in Classical Art & Iconography). (Illus.). 332p. (C). 1997. text 85.00 (*0-521-45382-8*) Cambridge U Pr.
Rose, Charles C. & Valentine, G. Edward, eds. Food Industry Environmental Conference Proceedings, 1990. (Illus.). 600p. (C). 1990. 60.00 (*0-9624647-3-2*) GA Tech Rsch Inst.
— Food Industry Environmental Conference Proceedings, 1992. (Illus.). 600p. (C). 1992. 60.00 (*0-9624647-6-7*) GA Tech Rsch Inst.
Rose, Charles M. & Gregath, Ann C. Gathering the Roses. (Illus.). xiv, 457p. 1998. reprint ed. lib. bdg. 50.00 (*0-944619-10-X*) Gregath Pub Co.
Rose, Christiana. Healing Wonders. LC 84-11547. 80p. (Orig.). 1984. pap. 5.95 (*0-87961-145-6*) Naturegraph.
Rose, Christine. Ancestors & Descendants of Robert Rose of Wethersfield & Branford, Connecticut, Who Came on the Ship "Francis" in 1634 from Ipswich, England. LC 83-62117. (Illus.). xvi, 512p. 1983. write for info. (*0-929626-02-8*) Rose Family Assn.
— Ancestors & Descendants of the Brothers Rev. Robert Rose & Rev. Charles Rose of Colonial Virginia & Wester Alves, Morayshire, Scotland: With Information on Their Brothers Patrick, James, Hugh, George & Alexander. LC 84-62409. (Illus.). xvi, 318p. 1985. write for info. (*0-929626-01-X*) Rose Family Assn.
— Nicknames: Past & Present. 29p. 1991. pap. 4.50 (*0-929626-04-4*) Rose Family Assn.

R

— Rose War Files Vol. I: Abstracts of Rose Land Bounty Records. 210p. 1987. pap. 13.50 (*0-929626-00-1*) Rose Family Assn.

— Santa Clara County, California Declarations of Intention, Bk. A, B, & C. iv, 76p. 1990. per. 9.75 (*0-929626-03-6*) Rose Family Assn.

Rose, Christine & Ingalls, Kay G. Complete Idiot's Guide to Genealogy. LC 97-73157. 352p. 1997. 17.95 (*0-02-861947-1*) Macmillan Gen Ref.

Rose, Christine, jt. auth. see Stothard, Charley.

Rose, Christine M. The Middle English Translation of Trevet's Les Cronicles. Edwards, Anthony, ed. (Garland Medieval Texts Ser.). 500p. Date not set. text 75.00 (*0-8153-1424-8*) Garland.

Rose, Clare & Nyre, G. F., eds. Agents of Academic Change: The Pandora's Box. (Journal Ser.: Vol. 6, No. 1, 1980). 1980. pap. 16.75 (*3-8055-0554-X*) S Karger.

***Rose, Claudia.** Rebecca's Legacy: A Guide for Turning Challenges into Blessings. (Illus.). 2000. pap. write for info. (*0-9676857-1-0*) Mentoring Rose.

— Rebecca's Legacy: Embracing Ancestors As Your Mentors. 232p. 2000. pap. 16.95 (*0-9676857-0-2*, Pub. by Mentoring Rose) ACCESS Pubs Network.

Rose, Clifford F., ed. Methodological Problems of Clinical Trials in Dementia. (Journal: Neuroepidemiology: Vol. 9, No. 4, 1990). (Illus.). 60p. 1990. pap. 39.25 (*3-8055-5239-4*) S Karger.

— Modern Approaches to the Dementias Pt. I: Etiology & Pathophysiology. (Interdisciplinary Topics in Gerontology Ser.: Vol. 19). (Illus.). x, 230p. 1985. 155.00 (*3-8055-3980-0*) S Karger.

Rose, Clifford F. & Fields, William S., eds. Neuro Oncology. (Progress in Experimental Tumor Research Ser.: Vol. 29). (Illus.). xiv, 274p. 1985. 200.00 (*3-8055-4054-X*) S Karger.

Rose, Clive & Blaker, Peter. Perception & Reality: An Opinion Poll on Defence & Disarmament Commentaries. (C). 1990. 45.00 (*0-907967-72-8*, Pub. by Inst Euro Def & Strat) St Mut.

Rose, Colin. Master It Faster. pap. 19.95 (*0-905553-62-4*) Acclrtd Learn.

— Master It Faster: How to Learn Faster, Make Good Decisions & Think Creatively. 192p. 2000. pap. 19.95 (*1-85835-806-X*, Indust Soc) Stylus Pub VA.

Rose, Colin & Nicholl, Malcolm J. Accelerated Learning for the 21st Century: The Six-Step Plan to Unlock Your Master-Mind. 416p. 1998. pap. 12.95 (*0-440-50779-0*, Delta Trade) Dell.

Rose, Colin & Rose, Diana. Accelerated Learning. (Illus.). 240p. (Orig.). (C). 1985. pap. text 11.95 (*0-905553-12-8*, Pub. by Accel Lrn Sys) McClelland & Stewart.

Rose, Colliston R. Fundamental Approaches in Mastering the Sciences: A Practical Guide for Science Students. LC 89-81166. (Illus.). 350p. (Orig.). (C). 1988. pap. text 24.95 (*0-935132-10-4*) C H Fairfax.

Rose, Constance H. Alonso Nunez de Reinoso. LC 77-99324. 309p. 1975. 35.00 (*0-8386-7612-X*) Fairleigh Dickinson.

Rose, Cordelia B. Courierspeak: A Phrase Book for Couriers of Museum Objects. LC 92-33621. (Illus.). 160p. (Orig.). 1993. pap. text 15.95 (*1-56098-195-4*) Smithsonian.

Rose, Cornelia B., Jr. National Policy for Radio Broadcasting. LC 71-161172. (History of Broadcasting: Radio to Television Ser.). 1977. reprint ed. 26.95 (*0-405-03580-2*) Ayer.

Rose, Courtice G., jt. ed. see Rittenhouse, Jonathan.

Rose, Craig. England in the 1690s. LC 98-39045. (History of Early Modern England Ser.). 352p. 1999. 69.95 (*0-631-17545-8*); pap. 34.95 (*0-631-20936-0*) Blackwell Pubs.

***Rose, Crystal.** The Turning Point. 260p. 1999. pap. 12.95 (*1-892944-03-0*, Crystal Rose Pub) Endeavor Bks.

Rose, Cynthia. Lottie Deno: Gambling Queen of Hearts. LC 93-5335. (Illus.). 116p. 1993. 22.95 (*0-940666-33-2*); pap. 12.95 (*0-940666-38-3*) Clear Light.

Rose, Cynthia & Champagne, Duane, eds. Native North American Alamanac, 2 vols. LC 96-150840. 341p. (J). 1994. text 67.00 (*0-8103-9820-6*, UXL) Gale.

Rose, D. Intro Data Analysis. 2nd ed. LC 96-4035. 272p. 1996. pap. 35.95 (*0-335-19617-9*) OpUniv Pr.

Rose, D. A Popular History of Greece: From the Earliest Period to the Roman Empire. Dulcken, H. W., ed. 30.00 (*0-8196-2866-2*) Biblo.

Rose, D. J., ed. Nuclear-Electric Power in the Asia-Pacific Region: Proceedings of the Workshop Held in Honolulu, Hawaii, 23-28 January 1983. 265p. 1985. pap. 61.00 (*0-08-031654-9*, Pergamon Pr) Elsevier.

Rose, Dan. Black American Street Life: South Philadelphia, 1969-1971. LC 87-17830. (Conduct & Communication Ser.). (Illus.). 288p. (C). 1987. text 46.95 (*0-8122-8071-7*); pap. text 18.50 (*0-8122-1245-2*) U of Pa Pr.

— Living the Ethnographic Life. (Qualitative Research Methods Ser.: Vol. 23). 64p. (C). 1990. text 24.00 (*0-8039-3998-1*); pap. text 10.50 (*0-8039-3999-X*) Sage.

— Patterns of American Culture: Ethnography & Estrangement. LC 89-33964. (Contemporary Ethnography Ser.). (Illus.). 138p. (C). 1989. pap. text 14.95 (*0-8122-1285-1*) U of Pa Pr.

***Rose, Daniel A.** Hiding Places: A Father & His Sons Retrace Their Family's Escape from the Holocaust. 384p. 2000. 25.00 (*0-684-85478-3*) S&S Trade.

Rose, Daniel E. A Symbolic & Connectionist Approach to Legal Information Retrieval. 328p. 1994. text 59.95 (*0-8058-1388-8*) L Erlbaum Assocs.

Rose, Danis. The Textual Diaries of James Joyce. LC 95-202441. 198p. 1995. 39.95 (*1-874675-58-9*) Dufour.

Rose, Danis, jt. auth. see McCarthy, Jack.

Rose, Danis, ed. see Joyce, James.

Rose, Darlene D. Evidence Not Seen: A Woman's Miraculous Faith in the Jungles of World War II. LC 86-43018. 256p. 1990. reprint ed. pap. 14.00 (*0-06-067020-7*, Pub. by Harper SF) HarpC.

Rose, Darrell D. Digital Circuit Logic & Design Through Experimentation. (Illus.). 256p. (C). 1982. pap. text 12.50 (*0-911908-13-7*) Tech Ed Pr.

Rose, David. Home, School & Faith: Towards an Understanding of Religious Diversity. 128p. 1992. pap. 23.00 (*1-85346-179-2*, Pub. by David Fulton) Taylor & Francis.

— In the Name of the Law: The Collapse of Criminal Justice. 356p. 1996. 40.00 (*0-224-03744-7*, Pub. by Jonathan Cape) Trafalgar.

— Off the Record: The Life & Times of a Black Watch Officer. (Illus.). 272p. 1997. 34.95 (*1-873376-76-6*, Pub. by Spellmnt Pubs) St Mut.

— Passover. 1999. pap. text 6.95 (*0-8172-3885-9*) Raintree Steck-V.

Rose, David & Dobson, Vernon G., eds. Models of the Visual Cortex. LC 84-29143. (Illus.). 608p. 1985. reprint ed. pap. 188.50 (*0-7837-8873-8*, 204958400001) Bks Demand.

***Rose, David & Douglas, Edward M.** Regions of the Heart: The Triumph & Tragedy of Alison Hargreaves. LC 00-28072. (Illus.). 304p. 2000. 25.00 (*0-7922-7696-5*) Natl Geog.

Rose, David & Gregson, Richard. Beneath the Mountains. large type ed. (Illus.). 416p. 1988. 27.99 (*0-7089-1886-7*) Ulverscroft.

Rose, David, et al. Hanukkah. (World of Holidays Ser.). (Illus.). 32p. (J). (gr. 2-5). 1998. pap. 7.95 (*0-8172-8105-3*) Raintree Steck-V.

Rose, David, jt. auth. see Meyer, Anne.

Rose, David, jt. ed. see Radford, John.

Rose, David J. Learning about Energy. LC 85-28218. (Modern Perspectives in Energy Ser.). (Illus.). 528p. (C). 1986. 132.00 (*0-306-42124-0*, Plenum Trade) Perseus Pubng.

Rose, David P. Endocrinology of Cancer, 3 vols., Vol. 1. 160p. 1979. 91.00 (*0-8493-5337-8*, RC271, CRC Reprint) Franklin.

— Endocrinology of Cancer, 3 vols., Vol. 2. 160p. 1979. 98.00 (*0-8493-5338-6*, CRC Reprint) Franklin.

— Endocrinology of Cancer, 3 vols., Vol. 3. 208p. 1982. 119.00 (*0-8493-5339-4*, RC271, CRC Reprint) Franklin.

Rose, David S. Loving God: Journey to a More Mature Faith. (Illus.). 70p. (Orig.). 1990. pap. text 9.50 (*0-9627687-0-7*) Proctors Hall Pr.

Rose, David W. & Rose, Gill. Passover. LC 96-42306. (World of Holidays Ser.). (Illus.). 32p. (J). 1997. lib. bdg. 22.83 (*0-8172-4607-X*) Raintree Steck-V.

Rose, Deborah L. The People Who Hugged the Trees: An Environmental Folk Tale. (Illus.). 32p. 1990. lib. bdg. 13.95 (*0-911797-80-7*) Roberts Rinehart.

— The People Who Hugged the Trees: An Environmental Folk Tale. LC 90-62832. (Illus.). 32p. (J). (gr. 4-8). 1994. pap. 6.95 (*1-879373-50-5*) Roberts Rinehart.

— The Rose Horse. LC 94-19629. (Illus.). 80p. (J). (gr. 3-7). 1995. 16.00 (*0-15-200068-2*, Harcourt Child Bks) Harcourt.

***Rose, Deborah Lee.** Into the A, B, Sea: An Ocean Alphabet Book. LC 99-50034. (Illus.). 40p. (J). (ps-3). 2000. 15.95 (*0-439-09696-0*) Scholastic Inc.

***Rose, Deborah Lee & Jenkins, Steve.** Into the A, B, Sea. LC 99-50034. (Illus.). (J). 2000. write for info. (*0-439-09697-9*) Scholastic Inc.

Rose, Debra A., ed. see International Symposium on the Trade of Bear Parts.

Rose, Debra J. A Multilevel Approach to the Study of Motor Control & Learning. LC 96-24476. 331p. 1996. text 59.00 (*0-02-403621-8*) Allyn.

— A Multilevel Approach to the Study of Motor Control & Learning. (C). 1997. teacher ed., boxed set. write for info. (*0-02-403623-4*, U5916-4, Macmillan Coll) P-H.

***Rose, Delbert R.** Vital Holiness: A Theology of Christian Experience. 4th rev. ed. 264p. 2000. pap. 13.99 (*0-88019-402-2*) Schmul Pub Co.

Rose, Delfina. Star Song Oracle: The Original Lemurian Devination Amulets. LC 98-160479. 104p. 1997. boxed set 29.95 (*1-57174-067-8*) Hampton Roads Pub Co.

Rose, Dennis. Lewis: Australian Bankruptcy Law. 10th ed. 1994. write for info. (*0-455-21236-8*, Pub. by LawBk Co); pap. write for info. (*0-455-21237-6*, Pub. by LawBk Co) Gaunt.

Rose, Diana, jt. auth. see Rose, Colin.

Rose, Diana, ed. see Bate, Michele & Miller, Arthur.

Rose, Diana, ed. see Gateva, Evelyna.

Rose, Diana, ed. see Gatti-Doyle, Gigi & Doyle, Terry.

Rose, Diana, ed. see Kattan-Ibarra, Juan & Stockton, Dennis.

Rose, Diana, ed. see Labiosa-Cassone, Libyan.

Rose, Diana, ed. see Margulies, Nancy.

Rose, Diana, ed. see Schlotmann, Lisa, et al.

Rose, Dilys. Our Lady of the Pickpockets. 1995. pap. 6.99 (*0-7493-2118-0*) Buttrwrth-Heinemann.

Rose, Dom Bede, tr. see Garrigou-Lagrange, Reginald.

Rose, Donald, ed. see Swedenborg, Emanuel.

Rose, Donald K. The Vacation-Condo Game. LC 84-60563. (Illus.). 126p. 1984. pap. 11.95 (*0-88100-042-6*) Natl Writ Pr.

Rose, Donna, ed. see Krigger, John T.

Rose, Donna L., ed. see Magnin, John D.

Rose, Dorothy. Haunted House. (Illus.). 32p. (J). (ps-k). 1985. pap. 2.50 (*0-671-52539-5*) S&S Trade.

Rose, Dorothy, ed. see Harvey, William J., III.

Rose, Dorothy J., ed. see Harvey, William J., III.

Rose, Doug. Fly Fishing the Olympic Peninsula. (Illus.). 96p. 1997. pap. 12.95 (*1-57188-099-2*) F Amato Pubns.

Rose, Douglas, ed. The Emergence of David Duke & the Politics of Race. LC 92-5331. (Tulane Studies in Political Science: No. 19). (Illus.). 270p. (C). 1992. text 29.95 (*0-8078-2043-1*); pap. text 19.95 (*0-8078-4381-4*) U of NC Pr.

Rose, E. J. The Southern Railway, 1923-47: Steam on the Portsmouth Direct Line. LC 97-130664. (Illus.). 144p. 1996. 30.95 (*0-7509-1195-6*, Pub. by Sutton Pub Ltd) Intl Pubs Mktg.

***Rose, Ed.** 50 Ways to Teach Your Learner: Activities & Interventions for Building High-Performance Teams. LC 98-40206. 1999. pap. 39.95 (*0-7879-4504-8*) Jossey-Bass.

Rose, Ed. Mr. Ed Rose' Industrial Relations. (C). 1997. pap. text. write for info. (*0-201-34299-5*) Addison-Wesley.

— Presenting & Training with Magic: 50 Simple Magic Tricks You Can Use to Energize Any Audience. LC 97-41426. (Illus.). 184p. 1997. pap. 24.95 (*0-07-054040-3*) McGraw.

— Presenting & Training with Magic: 50 Simple Magic Tricks You Can Use to Energize Any Audience. LC 97-41426. (Illus.). 288p. 1997. 34.95 (*0-07-054041-1*) McGraw.

***Rose, Ed & Buckley, Steve.** Self-Directed Work Teams: A Trainer's Role in the Transition. LC 99-73475. 195p. 1999. pap. 32.95 (*1-56286-129-8*) Am Soc Train & Devel.

***Rose, Eddie.** You Still Here? (Illus.). 95p. 2000. pap. 9.00 (*0-8059-4893-7*) Dorrance.

Rose, Edward J. Henry George. (Twayne's United States Authors Ser.). 1968. lib. bdg. 20.95 (*0-8290-1700-3*) Irvington.

Rose, Edwin. Planetary Music: Understanding Astrological Rhythms. (Illus.). 445p. 1998. pap. 19.95 (*0-9661522-0-4*) Guiding Star.

Rose, Elaine, jt. ed. see Edward, Joyce.

Rose, Elaine O., jt. auth. see Irvin, Judith L.

***Rose, Elizabeth.** Eden's Garden. 2000. pap. 8.95 (*1-58571-018-0*, Pub. by Genesis Press) BookWorld.

— Kyros' Secret. Basile, Teresa, ed. LC 00-105336. 216p. 2000. pap. 12.95 (*1-930076-03-7*, New Leaf Books) WigWam Pubng Co.

Rose, Elizabeth. A Mother's Job: The History of Day Care, 1890-1960. (Illus.). 296p. 1999. text 45.00 (*0-19-511112-5*) OUP.

Rose, Ellen & Strand, Jessica. Intimate Gatherings: Great Food for Good Friends. LC 97-34150. 132p. 1998. 18.95 (*0-8118-1575-7*) Chronicle Bks.

Rose, Ellen C. The Novels of Margaret Drabble: Equivocal Figures. (Illus.). 141p. 1980. 44.00 (*0-389-20006-9*, N6783) B&N Imports.

Rose, Ellen C., jt. auth. see Kaplan, Carey.

Rose, Ellen C., jt. auth. see Mayberry, Maralee.

Rose, Ellen C., jt. ed. see Kaplan, Carey.

Rose, Elliot. Cases of Conscience: Alternatives Open to Recusants & Puritans under Elizabeth I & James I. LC 74-76947. 274p. reprint ed. pap. 78.10 (*0-608-16868-8*, 2027243) Bks Demand.

— A Razor for a Goat: A Discussion of Certain Problems in the History of Witchcraft & Diabolism. 265p. 1989. pap. 15.95 (*0-8020-6768-9*) U of Toronto Pr.

Rose, Elliott H. Aesthetic Facial Restoration. LC 97-29602. 400p. 1998. text 205.00 (*0-316-75646-6*, Little Brwn Med Div) Lppncott W & W.

Rose, Emilie P. Reaching for the Light: A Guide for Ritual Abuse Survivors & Their Therapists. LC 95-52521. 264p. (Orig.). 1996. pap. 14.95 (*0-8298-1079-X*) Pilgrim OH.

Rose, Emma. Ballet Magic: A Pop-up Book. (Illus.). 12p. (J). (ps-1). 1996. 12.95 (*0-590-26242-4*, Cartwheel) Scholastic Inc.

— Pumpkin Faces: A Glowing Book You Can Read in the Dark. (Illus.). 24p. (J). (ps). 1997. 6.95 (*0-590-13454-X*) Scholastic Inc.

Rose, Emma, tr. see Morazzoni, Marta.

Rose, Enid. Gordon Craig & the Theatre. LC 72-6840. (Studies in Drama: No. 39). (Illus.). 260p. 1972. reprint ed. lib. bdg. 75.00 (*0-8383-1641-7*) M S G Haskell Hse.

Rose, Eric. Management of End-Stage Heart Disease. LC 98-15838. 304p. 1998. text 125.00 (*0-316-75697-0*) Lppncott W & W.

***Rose, Eric.** Second Opinion: The Columbia-Presbyterian Guide to Surgery. LC 99-89285. (Illus.). 336p. 2000. text 27.95 (*0-312-20584-8*) St Martin.

Rose, Eugene. Nihilism: The Root of the Revolution of the Modern Age. 104p. 1994. pap. 5.95 (*0-938635-15-8*) St Herman Pr.

Rose, Evelyn. The New Complete International Jewish Cookbook. 736p. 1996. pap. 14.98 (*0-88365-955-7*) Galahad Bks.

— The New Complete International Jewish Cookbook. 700p. 1998. pap. 24.95 (*1-86105-143-3*, Pub. by Robson Bks) Parkwest Pubns.

Rose, Evelyn & Leon, Sula. Weekend Cook: 100 Sensational Recipes for the Cook in a Hurry. (Illus.). 1998. pap. 14.95 (*0-7499-1535-8*, Pub. by Piatkus Bks) London Brdge.

Rose, Evelyn & Rose, Judi. The First-Time Cookbook. LC 83-61273. 207p. 1984. 9.95 (*0-86051-184-7*, Pub. by Robson Bks) Parkwest Pubns.

— Mother & Daughter Jewish Cooking: Two Generations Of Jewish Women Share Traditional And Contemporary Recipes. LC 99-38247. (Illus.). 304p. 2000. 26.00 (*0-688-16451-X*, Wm Morrow) Morrow Avon.

Rose, F., ed. Contract & Tort Statutes. (C). 1991. 75.00 (*1-85431-181-6*, Pub. by Blackstone Pr) Gaunt.

Rose, F. Clifford. Advances in Headache Research. (Current Problems in Neurology Ser.: Vol. 4). 288p. 1987. 74.95 (*0-86196-097-1*, Pub. by J Libbey Med) Bks Intl VA.

— James Parkinson: His Life & Times by A. D. Morris. 308p. 1989. 87.50 (*0-8176-3401-0*) Birkhauser.

— Parkinson's Disease. (Current Problems in Neurology Ser.: Vol. 6). 224p. 1987. 74.95 (*0-86196-110-2*, Pub. by J Libbey Med) Bks Intl VA.

— Towards Migraine 2000. LC 96-38504. (Developments in Neurology Ser.: 12). (Illus.). 328p. 1996. 218.50 (*0-444-82494-4*) Elsevier.

Rose, F. Clifford, ed. Advances in Migraine Research & Therapy. LC 82-47507. (Illus.). 248p. 1982. reprint ed. pap. 76.90 (*0-608-00643-2*, 206123100007) Bks Demand.

— Advances in Stroke Therapy. LC 82-47508. (Illus.). 348p. 1982. reprint ed. pap. 107.90 (*0-608-00642-4*, 206123000007) Bks Demand.

— Clinical Trials in Multiple Sclerosis. (Journal: Neuroepidemiology: Vol. 6, No. 1-2, 1987). (Illus.). 92p. 1987. pap. 59.25 (*3-8055-4577-0*) S Karger.

— The Control of the Hypothalamo-Pituitary-Adrenocortical Axis. 470p. 1989. 65.00 (*0-8236-1070-5*) Intl Univs Pr.

— Interdisciplinary Topics in Gerontology, Set, Vols. 19 & 20. (Illus.). xx, 432p. 1985. 292.25 (*3-8055-3982-7*) S Karger.

— The Management of Headache. LC 86-42503. 192p. 1988. reprint ed. pap. 59.60 (*0-608-03442-8*, 206414300008) Bks Demand.

— Modern Approaches to the Dementias Pt. II: Clinical & Therapeutic Aspects. (Interdisciplinary Topics in Gerontology Ser.: Vol. 20). (Illus.). x, 202p. 1985. 137.50 (*3-8055-3981-9*) S Karger.

— Progress in Aphasiology. fac. ed. LC 84-15979. (Advances in Neurology Ser.: No. 42). (Illus.). 382p. pap. 118.50 (*0-7837-7269-6*, 204703600005) Bks Demand.

— Recent Advances in Tropical Neurology. LC 95-49192. (Developments in Neurology Ser.: No. 10). 438p. 1995. 278.50 (*0-444-82272-0*) Elsevier.

Rose, F. Clifford, et al, eds. Aphasia. 578p. 1990. pap. 87.75 (*1-56593-578-0*, 0061) Singular Publishing.

Rose, F. Clifford & Jones Staff. MS: Immunological, Diagnostic & Therapeutic Aspects. (Current Problems in Neurology Ser.: Vol. 3). 272p. 1987. 74.95 (*0-86196-109-9*, Pub. by J Libbey Med) Bks Intl VA.

Rose, F. D. New Foundations for Insurance Law: Current Legal Problems. (C). 1987. 210.00 (*0-7855-4071-7*, Pub. by Witherby & Co) St Mut.

Rose, F. D., ed. Blackstone's Statues on Commercial & Consumer Law, 1997/8. 6th rev. ed. 492p. 1997. pap. 32.00 (*1-85431-659-1*, Pub. by Blackstone Pr) Gaunt.

***Rose, F. D., ed.** Blackstone's Statutes on Commercial & Consumer Law 1999-2000. 8th ed. 555p. 1999. pap. 29.00 (*1-85431-924-8*, 18422, Pub. by Blackstone Pr) Gaunt.

Rose, F. D., ed. Blackstone's Statutes on Contract, Tort & Restitution, 1997-98. 8th ed. 456p. 1997. pap. 26.00 (*1-85431-660-5*, Pub. by Blackstone Pr) Gaunt.

***Rose, F. D., ed.** Blackstone's Statutes on Contract, Tort & Restitution 1999-2000. 10th ed. 507p. 1999. pap. 23.50 (*1-85431-926-4*, 18429, Pub. by Blackstone Pr) Gaunt.

Rose, F. D., ed. New Foundations for Insurance Law. (Current Legal Problems Ser.). xvii, 106p. 1987. pap. 48.00 (*0-420-47780-2*) W S Hein.

Rose, F. D. & Johnson, D. A. Recovery from Brain Damage: Reflections & Directions. (Advances in Experimental Medicine & Biology Ser.: Vol. 325). (Illus.). 224p. (C). 1993. text 102.00 (*0-306-44344-9*, Kluwer Plenum) Kluwer Academic.

Rose, F. David & Johnson, David A., eds. Brain Injury & After: Towards Improved Outcome. LC 96-34970. 216p. 1996. 167.00 (*0-471-95276-1*) Wiley.

Rose, F. M. Chopmarks. 54p. 1987. pap. 10.00 (*1-889172-13-8*) Numismatic Intl.

Rose, Ferrell. Guises of Modesty: Marie von Ebner-Eschenbach's Female Artists. (GERM Ser.). viii, 214p. 1994. 55.00 (*1-879751-69-0*) Camden Hse.

Rose, Frances L. Wildflowers of the Llano Estacado. 1990. 12.95 (*0-9617102-0-9*) Rose-Strandtmann.

Rose, Francesca, ed. see Cartwright, Derrick R.

Rose, Francesca, ed. see Mayer, Stephanie.

Rose, Francis. International Commercial & Maritime Arbitration. (C). 1988. 150.00 (*0-7855-4123-3*, Pub. by Witherby & Co) St Mut.

— Lloyd's Maritime & Commercial Law Quarterly Index, 1974-1994. 1995. 180.00 (*1-85044-804-3*) LLP.

Rose, Francis, ed. The Failure of Contracts: Contract, Restitutionary & Proprietary Consequences. LC 98-136314. 320p. 1997. pap. 70.00 (*1-901362-04-3*, Pub. by Hart Pub) Northwestern U Pr.

— Restitution & Banking Law. 208p. 1999. 74.00 (*0-9526499-1-8*, Pub. by Hart Pub) Northwestern U Pr.

— Restitution & the Conflict of Laws. LC 96-176562. 272p. 1995. pap. 48.00 (*0-9526499-0-X*, 15144, Pub. by Mansfield) Gaunt.

Rose, Francis D. Blackstone's Statutes on Commercial & Consumer Law. 5th ed. 474p. 1996. pap. 32.00 (*1-85431-557-9*, Pub. by Blackstone Pr) Gaunt.

— Blackstone's Statutes on Commercial Law. 2nd ed. 1992. pap. 34.00 (*1-85431-247-2*, Pub. by Blackstone Pr) Gaunt.

— Blackstone's Statutes on Contract, Tort & Restitution. 5th ed. 332p. 1996. pap. 18.00 (*1-85431-429-7*, Pub. by Blackstone Pr) Gaunt.

— Blackstone's Statutes on Contract, Tort & Restitution, 1994-1995. 5th ed. 309p. 1994. pap. 22.00 (*1-85431-385-1*, Pub. by Blackstone Pr) Gaunt.

— Blackstone's Statutes on Contract, Tort & Restitution, 1996-97. 7th ed. 412p. 1996. pap. 24.00 (*1-85431-558-7*, Pub. by Blackstone Pr) Gaunt.

— Rose: Restitution. 1997. write for info. (*0-406-01453-1*, RR1, MICHIE) LEXIS Pub.

Rose, Frank. The Agency: William Morris & the Hidden History of Show Business. (Illus.). 532p. Date not set. 30.00 (*0-614-32365-7*, HarpBusn) HarpInfo.

— The Economics, Concept & Design of Information

Intermediaries: A Theoretic Approach. LC 98-44822. (Information Age Economy Ser.). 266p. 1999. pap. 63.00 (*3-7908-1168-8*) Spr-Verlag.

— Employment Law. (C). 1987. 125.00 (*0-901812-45-5*); pap. 89.00 (*0-901812-46-3*) St Mut.

Rose, Frank. In Heart of the Mind. 1985. mass mkt. 6.95 (*0-394-74103-X*) Random.

Rose, Frank. West of Eden: The End of Innocence at Apple Computer. LC 88-40302. 288p. 1990. 19.95 (*0-685-23144-5*); pap. 8.95 (*0-685-23145-3*) Viking Penguin.

Rose, Frank & Maginel, Robert. The Joy of Spiritual Growth: Real Encounters. LC 99-34380. 160p. 1999. pap. 13.95 (*0-87785-384-3*, Chrysalis Books) Swedenborg.

***Rose, Fred.** Coalitions Across the Class Divide: Lessons from the Labor, Peace, & Environmental Movements. LC 99-41669. 272p. 2000. 45.00 (*0-8014-3605-2*) Cornell U Pr.

Rose, Fred. Coalitions Across the Class Divide: Lessons from the Labor, Peace & Environmental Movements. LC 99-41669. 272p. 2000. pap. 17.95 (*0-8014-8636-X*) Cornell U Pr.

Rose, G. A. & Blackburn, H. Cardiovascular Survey Methods. (Monographs: No. 56). (ENG, FRE, RUS & SPA.). 178p. 1982. pap. text 22.00 (*92-4-140056-0*, 1140056) World Health.

Rose, Gary L. The American Presidency under Siege. LC 96-48608. (SUNY Series on the Presidency). 231p. (C). 1997. text 56.50 (*0-7914-3337-4*); pap. text 19.95 (*0-7914-3338-2*) State U NY Pr.

— Connecticut Politics at the Crossroads. LC 92-16636. 122p. (Orig.). (C). 1992. lib. bdg. 44.50 (*0-8191-8755-0*) U Pr of Amer.

— Connecticut Politics at the Crossroads. LC 92-16636. 122p. (Orig.). (C). 1992. pap. text 21.50 (*0-8191-8756-9*) U Pr of Amer.

Rose, Gary L., ed. Controversial Issues in Presidential Selection. 2nd ed. LC 93-5713. (SUNY Series on the Presidency: Contemporary Issues). 358p. (C). 1994. text 49.50 (*0-7914-1935-5*); pap. text 16.95 (*0-7914-1936-3*) State U NY Pr.

Rose, Gene. Magic Yosemite Winters: A Century of Winter Sports. Frohlich, Robert & Lippert, Laurel H., eds. LC 99-72749. (Illus.). 160p. 1999. 40.00 (*1-893057-00-3*) Coldstream Pr.

Rose, Geoffrey. The Strategy of Preventive Medicine. (Illus.). 150p. 1994. reprint ed. pap. text 32.50 (*0-19-262486-5*) OUP.

Rose, Geoffrey, ed. see Coggin, D.

Rose, Gerald. Grumps. (Illus.). 32p. (J). (gr. k-2). 1993. 17.95 (*0-370-31575-8*, Pub. by Bodley Head) Trafalgar.

Rose, Gerald L. Management Decision Making. (C). 1987. text 22.00 (*0-316-75638-5*) Little.

Rose, Geraldine & Wilcox, Cassandra. Sun Signs for New Millen. LC 98-24816. 432p. 1998. pap. 14.00 (*0-380-78942-6*, Avon Bks) Morrow Avon.

Rose, Gilbert J. Necessary Illusion - Art As "Witness" Resonance & Attunement to Forms & Feelings. 148p. 1996. 27.50 (*0-8236-3510-4*) Intl Univs Pr.

— The Power of Form: A Psychoanalytic Approach to Aesthetic Form. 2nd ed. 288p. (C). 1992. reprint ed. pap. 24.95 (*0-8236-8188-2*) Intl Univs Pr.

— Trauma & Mastery in Life & Art: With an Original New Docudrama. LC 96-23726. 1996. pap. 24.95 (*0-8236-8319-2*) Intl Univs Pr.

Rose, Gilbert J. & Farge, Andrew. The Power of Form. LC 79-53592. (Psychological Issues Monographs: No. 49, Vol. 13, No. 1). (Illus.). 252p. 1980. 35.00 (*0-8236-4171-6*) Intl Univs Pr.

Rose, Gilbert P. Plato: Crito. 2nd ed. 1983. pap. text 6.00 (*0-929524-24-1*) Bryn Mawr Commentaries.

— Plato Apology. (Greek Commentaries Ser.). 104p. (Orig.). (C). 1989. pap. text 7.00 (*0-929524-56-X*) Bryn Mawr Commentaries.

— Plato's Republic, Bk. 1. (Greek Commentaries Ser.). 91p. (Orig.). (C). 1983. pap. text 6.00 (*0-929524-31-4*) Bryn Mawr Commentaries.

— Plato's Symposium. 2nd ed. (Greek Commentaries Ser.). 158p. (C). 1985. pap. text 8.00 (*0-929524-32-2*) Bryn Mawr Commentaries.

— Sophocles Oedipus at Colonus. (Greek Commentaries Ser.). 132p. (Orig.). (C). 1988. pap. text 7.00 (*0-929524-34-9*) Bryn Mawr Commentaries.

Rose, Gill, jt. auth. see Rose, David W.

Rose, Gillian. The Broken Middle: Out of Our Ancient History. 336p. 1992. pap. text 29.95 (*0-631-18221-7*) Blackwell Pubs.

— Feminism & Geography: The Limits of Geographical Knowledge. LC 93-10411. 206p. 1993. pap. 17.95 (*0-8166-2418-6*); text 44.95 (*0-8166-2417-8*) U of Minn Pr.

— Hegel: Contra Sociology. 260p. (C). 1995. pap. 25.00 (*0-485-12036-4*, Pub. by Athlone Pr) Humanities.

— Judaism & Modernity: Philosophical Essays. 256p. 1993. pap. 27.95 (*0-631-18971-8*) Blackwell Pubs.

— Love's Work. 1997. pap. 2.99 (*0-8052-1078-4*) Schocken.

— Love's Work: A Reckoning with Life. 160p. 1996. 20.00 (*0-8052-4135-3*) Schocken.

— Melancholy Science: An Introduction to the Thought of Theodor W. Adorno. 212p. 1979. text 60.50 (*0-231-04584-0*) Col U Pr.

— Mourning Becomes the Law: Philosophy & Representation. 170p. (C). 1996. text 54.95 (*0-521-57045-X*); pap. text 17.95 (*0-521-57849-3*) Cambridge U Pr.

Rose, Gillian, jt. ed. see Blunt, Alison.

Rose, Gloria. The Color Purple Notes. (Cliffs Notes Ser.). 80p. (Orig.). (C). 1986. pap. text 4.95 (*0-8220-0308-2*, Cliff) IDG Bks.

— Enjoying Good Health. 320p. (Orig.). 1987. 12.50 (*0-944785-00-X*) Herm Barr Pub.

— Low-Fat Cooking for Good Health: 200+ Delicious Quick & Easy Recipes. LC 93-617. 384p. 1993. pap. 13.95 (*0-89529-577-6*, Avery) Penguin Putnam.

— Low-Fat Cooking for Good Health: 200+ Delicious Quick & Easy Recipes Without Added Fat, Sugar or Salt. (Illus.). 384p. 1996. pap. 14.95 (*0-89529-686-1*, Avery) Penguin Putnam.

Rose Goldman, Molly, see Wyse, Lois & Goldman, Molly Rose.

Rose, Gordon & Marshall, Tony F. Counselling & School Social Work: An Experimental Study. LC 74-2449. 355p. reprint ed. pap. 110.10 (*0-608-10820-0*, 201652400004) Bks Demand.

***Rose, Greg.** GURPS Special Ops. 1999. 19.95 (*1-55634-366-3*, Pub. by S Jackson Games) BookWorld.

— GURPS Special Ops: Counterterrorism, Hostage Rescue, & Behind-the-Lines Action. 2nd ed. Punch, Sean, ed. pap. 19.95 (*1-55634-157-1*) S Jackson Games.

Rose, Greg, ed. The 6th USENIX Security Symposium Proceedings. 222p. 1996. pap. 35.00 (*1-880446-79-0*) USENIX Assn.

***Rose-Grippa, Kathleen & Gorney-Moreno, Mary Jo.** Study Guide & Computerized Learning Resources T-A Nursing Research: Methods, Critical Appraisal & Utilization. 4th ed. 240p. 1998. student ed. write for info. (*0-8151-2810-X*) Mosby Inc.

Rose, Gustav. Humboldt's Travels in Siberia, 1837-1842: The Gemstones by Gustav Rose. Sinkankas, George M., ed. Sinkankas, John, tr. from GER. LC 94-76637. 80p. 1994. 25.00 (*0-945005-17-2*) Geoscience Pr.

Rose, H., et al. Emerson's Essays Notes. LC 75-315891. (Cliffs Notes Ser.). 80p. (C). 1975. pap. text, student ed. 4.95 (*0-8220-0429-1*) IDG Bks.

Rose, H. E. A Course in Number Theory. 2nd ed. 416p. (C). 1995. text 92.95 (*0-19-853479-5*) OUP.

— A Course in Number Theory. 2nd ed. (Illus.). 414p. (C). 1995. pap. text 45.00 (*0-19-852376-9*) OUP.

Rose, H. J. A Handbook of Greek Literature: From Homer to the Age of Lucian. 5th ed. 463p. 1996. reprint ed. pap. text 22.00 (*0-86516-321-9*) Bolchazy-Carducci.

— Handbook of Greek Mythology. 6th ed. 376p. (C). 1958. pap. 25.99 (*0-415-04601-7*) Routledge.

— A Handbook of Latin Literature. 550p. reprint ed. 25.00 (*0-8196-0356-2*) Biblo.

Rose, H. J., tr. see Plutarch.

Rose-Hall, Lynn, jt. auth. see Hall, Burt.

Rose, Harold. The Changing World of Finance & Its Problems. 57p. (Orig.). 1993. pap. text 9.00 (*0-89068-116-3*, NPA 264) Natl Planning.

— The Question of Saving. 53p. (Orig.). 1991. pap. text 8.00 (*0-89068-106-6*, BNAC 38(NPA249)) Natl Planning.

Rose, Harold M. & McClain, Paula D. Race, Place, & Risk: Black Homicide in Urban America. LC 89-48538. (SUNY Series in Afro-American Studies). 297p. (C). 1990. pap. text 23.95 (*0-7914-0394-7*) State U NY Pr.

Rose, Harriet W. Something's Wrong with My Child: A Valuable Resource to Help Parents & Professionals to Better Understand Themselves in Dealing with the Emotionally Charged Subject of Children with Disabilities. 2nd ed. LC 98-26329. 234p. 1998. text 46.95 (*0-398-06898-4*); pap. text 33.95 (*0-398-06899-2*) C C Thomas.

Rose, Harvey, jt. ed. see Campbell, David R.

Rose, Helen. Just Make Them Beautiful. LC 76-4764. (Illus.). 1982. 17.50 (*0-930422-09-0*) Dennis-Landman.

Rose, Helen W. Quick & Easy Strip Quilting. (Illus.). 80p. 1989. pap. 5.95 (*0-486-26018-6*) Dover.

— Quilting with Strips & Strings: Full with Complete Instructions for Making 12 Patchwork Quiltblocks. (Quilting Ser.). (Illus.). 48p. (Orig.). 1983. pap. 4.95 (*0-486-24357-5*) Dover.

Rose, Henrietta. Tom - A Gift in Disguise. (Illus.). 112p. (Orig.). 1998. pap. 10.95 (*1-899171-22-3*, Pub. by Findhorn Pr) Words Distrib.

Rose, Henry. Henrik Ibsen: Poet, Mystic & Moralist. LC 72-1323. (Studies in Scandinavian Life & Literature: No. 18). 1972. reprint ed. lib. bdg. 75.00 (*0-8383-1428-7*) M S G Haskell Hse.

— Nonmodular Lattice Varieties. LC 83-22449. (Memoirs Ser.: No. 47/292). 76p. 1984. pap. 16.00 (*0-8218-2292-6*, MEMO/47/292) Am Math.

— On Maeterlinck. LC 73-21891. (Studies in French Literature: No. 45). 1974. lib. bdg. 75.00 (*0-8383-1829-0*) M S G Haskell Hse.

Rose, Henry, jt. auth. see Jipsen, Peter.

Rose, Herbert J. A Handbook of Latin Literature: From the Earliest Times to the Death of St. Augustine. LC 95-43375. 591p. 1996. reprint ed. pap. 22.00 (*0-86516-317-0*) Bolchazy-Carducci.

— Primitive Culture in Italy. LC 73-168503. (Select Bibliographies Reprint Ser.). 1977. reprint ed. 27.95 (*0-8369-5948-5*) Ayer.

Rose, Herbert J., ed. see Plutarch.

Rose, Hieromonk S., tr. see Pomazansky, Michael.

Rose, Hieromonk S., tr. see Saint Theophan the Recluse.

Rose, Hilary. Love, Power, & Knowledge: Towards a Feminist Transformation of the Sciences. LC 94-1883. 352p. 1994. 45.00 (*0-253-35046-8*); pap. 19.95 (*0-253-20907-2*) Ind U Pr.

***Rose, Hilary & Rose, Steven, eds.** Alas, Poor Darwin: Arguments Against Evolutionary Psychology. 400p. 2000. 25.00 (*0-609-60513-5*) Harmony Bks.

Rose, Hilary, jt. ed. see Nowotny, Helga.

Rose, Horace A., ed. see Brown, John P.

Rose, Howard. The Marrano. LC 92-60817. 256p. 1992. 20.00 (*1-878352-08-3*); pap. 10.00 (*1-878352-09-1*) R Saroff Pub.

— Oak Street Beach. 120p. 1990. 16.00 (*1-878352-06-7*); pap. 9.00 (*1-878352-07-5*) R Saroff Pub.

— The Pooles of Pismo Bay. 430p. 1990. 20.00 (*1-878352-04-0*); pap. 10.00 (*1-878352-05-9*) R Saroff Pub.

— Twelve Ravens. 405p. 1990. reprint ed. 20.00 (*1-878352-02-4*); reprint ed. pap. 10.00 (*1-878352-03-2*) R Saroff Pub.

— Unexpected Eloquence: The Art in American Folk Art. (Illus.). 160p. 1990. 25.00 (*1-878352-00-8*); pap. 15.00 (*1-878352-01-6*) R Saroff Pub.

Rose, Howard A. No Bull Diet: A Lifetime Beyond Dieting. 1992. pap. 10.00 (*0-9631828-0-3*) Hart Mktg.

Rose-Hulman, jt. auth. see Grimaldi, Ralph P.

Rose, I. A. Conservatism & Foreign Policy During the Lloyd George Coalition, 1918-1922. LC 98-7955. xxix, 289 p. 1999. 26.50 (*0-7146-4486-2*) F Cass Pubs.

— Conservative Foreign Policy During the Lloyd George Coalition, 1918-1922. LC 98-7955. 320p. 1999. 59.50 (*0-7146-4868-X*, Pub. by F Cass Pubs) Intl Spec Bk.

Rose, I. Nelson. Blackjack & the Law. 1999. pap. 24.95 (*0-910575-08-8*) RGE Publishing.

Rose, Ian, jt. auth. see Tupper, Stephen.

Rose, Ingrid & Quiroz, Roderick S., eds. The Lithographs of Prentiss Taylor: A Catalogue Raisonne. (Illus.). xii, 133p. 1996. 49.95 (*0-8232-1672-1*) Fordham.

Rose-Innes, A. Vocabulary of Common Japanese Words. (JPN.). 1945. 8.95 (*0-88710-123-2*) Yale Far Eastern Pubns.

Rose-Innes, A. C. & Rhoderick, E. H. Introduction to Superconductivity. 2nd ed. 288p. 1978. pap. text 59.95 (*0-08-021652-8*, Prgamon Press) Buttrwrth-Heinemann.

— Introduction to Superconductivity. 2nd ed. 1978. text 92.00 (*0-08-021651-X*, Pergamon Pr) Elsevier.

Rose-Innes, Arthur. Beginners' Dictionary of Chinese-Japanese Characters & Compounds. (CHI & JPN.). 509p. 1977. reprint ed. pap. 11.95 (*0-486-23467-3*) Dover.

Rose, Irene B., jt. auth. see Conger, Flora S.

Rose, J. Progress of Cybernetics, Vol. 2. xvi, 438p. 1970. 314.00 (*0-685-47155-1*) Gordon & Breach.

Rose, J., ed. Acid Rain: Current Situation & Remedies. LC 94-1936. (Environmental Topics Ser.: Vol. 4, No. 1945-5294). 272p. 1994. text 116.00 (*2-88124-850-0*) Gordon & Breach.

— Environmental Concepts, Policies & Strategies, Vol. 2. (Environmental Topics Ser.). vii, 244p. 1991. text 125.00 (*2-88124-737-7*) Gordon & Breach.

— Environmental Health: Impact of Pollutants, Vol. 1. (Environmental Topics Ser.). ix, 456p. 1990. text 165.00 (*2-88124-738-5*) Gordon & Breach.

— Environmental Toxicology: Current Developments. (Environmental Topics Ser.: Vol. 7). (Illus.). 414p. 1998. text 115.00 (*90-5699-140-X*, ECU121) Gordon & Breach.

— Human Stress & the Environment: Health Aspects, Vol.5. LC 94-2603. (Environmental Topics Ser.: Vol. 5). 240p. 1994. text 179.00 (*2-88124-851-9*) Gordon & Breach.

***Rose, J., ed.** Population Problems: Topical Issues. Vol. 8. 176p. 1999. text 55.00 (*90-5699-230-9*) Gordon & Breach.

Rose, J., ed. Technological Injury: The Effect of Technological Advances on Environment Life & Society. 244p. 1969. pap. 63.00 (*0-677-13645-5*) Gordon & Breach.

— Water & the Environment. (Environmental Topics Ser.). ix, 458p. 1991. text 178.00 (*2-88124-747-4*) Gordon & Breach.

Rose, J. & Schluchter, C., eds. Quaternary Type Sections: Imagination or Reality?: Proceedings of the INQUA-Subcommission on European Quaternary Stratigraphy Symposium, Zurich, 14-15 October 1985. 216p. 1989. 110.00 (*90-6191-734-4*, Pub. by A A Balkema) Ashgate Pub Co.

Rose, J., et al. Shades of Darkness. (Rolemaster Standard System Ser.). (Illus.). 128p. 1998. pap. 16.00 (*1-55806-338-2*, 5702) Iron Crown Ent Inc.

Rose, J., jt. ed. see Menzies, J.

Rose, J. C., jt. auth. see Woollard, G. P.

Rose, J. H. Select Despatches from the British Foreign Office Archives. (Camden Third Ser.). 54.00 (*0-86193-007-X*) David Brown.

Rose, J. L. Durative & Aoristic Tenses in Thucydides. (LD Ser.: No. 35). 1942. pap. 25.00 (*0-527-00781-1*) Periodicals Srv.

Rose, J. N., jt. auth. see Britton, Nathaniel L.

Rose, J. R. Fun with Pup! Activity Book. LC 96-232456. (Illus.). 64p. (gr. 1-4). 1997. pap. 4.95 (*1-56554-230-4*) Pelican.

***Rose, J. R.** More Fun with Pup! Activity Book. (Illus.). 64p. (J). (gr. k-3). 1998. pap. text 4.95 (*1-56554-368-8*) Pelican.

Rose, J. R., ed. see Gattefosse, Rene-Maurice.

Rose, Jack & Phil, M. Square Feet: The Autobiography of Jack Rose. 160p. 1993. pap. 59.00 (*0-85406-565-2*, Pub. by R-I-C-S Bks) St Mut.

Rose, Jack H. Christianity & Education: A Manifesto. LC 86-90551. 302p. (Orig.). 1986. pap. 34.95 (*0-9617430-0-X*) J H Rose.

Rose, Jacqueline. The Haunting of Sylvia Plath. (Convergences Ser.). 312p. (C). 1992. text 24.95 (*0-674-38225-0*) HUP.

— Haunting of Sylvia Plath. 288p. 1993. pap. text 18.50 (*0-674-38226-9*) HUP.

— States of Fantasy. (Clarendon Lectures in English Ser.). 198p. 1998. reprint ed. pap. text 19.95 (*0-19-818327-5*) OUP.

— Why War? Psychoanalysis, Politics & the Return to Melanie Klein. Schweizer, Harold, ed. (Bucknell Lectures in Literary Theory). 144p. 1993. pap. 19.95 (*0-631-18924-6*) Blackwell Pubs.

Rose, Jacqueline, jt. ed. see Mitchell, Juliet.

Rose, Jacqueline, ed. see Sachs, Wulf.

Rose, James B. A Guide to American Christian Education for the Home & School: The Principle Approach. LC 85-82560. (Illus.). 550p. 1987. lib. bdg. 38.00 (*0-9616201-1-0*) Am Christ Hist.

Rose, James M. New York Vehicle & Traffic Law. LC 92-70344. 1984. 120.00 (*0-318-01917-5*) West Group.

— New York Vehicle & Traffic Law. LC 84-80365. 1993. suppl. ed. 45.00 (*0-317-03245-3*) West Group.

Rose, James M. & Brown, Barbara W. Tapestry. (Illus.). 163p. (Orig.). 1979. pap. 4.95 (*0-9607744-2-4*) New London County.

Rose, Jane, ed. see Davis, Rebecca H.

Rose, Jane A. Rebecca Harding Davis. (Twayne's United States Authors Ser.). 216p. 1993. 32.00 (*0-8057-3958-0*, Twyne) Mac Lib Ref.

***Rose, Jay.** Producing Great Sound for Digital Video. LC 99-43323. (Illus.). 349p. 1999. pap. 39.95 incl. cd-rom, audio compact disk (*0-87930-597-5*, Pub. by Miller Freeman) Publishers Group.

Rose, Jeanne. Aroma-Color-Plant-Sound Correlations for Healing: A Practical Reference Table. (Illus.). 1990. student ed. 15.00 (*0-9620838-7-9*, J R Herb Pubns) Herb Studies.

— The Aromatherapy Book: Applications & Inhalations. (Jeanne Rose Herbal Library). (Illus.). 395p. (Orig.). 1992. pap. 18.95 (*1-55643-073-6*) North Atlantic.

— Good Night, My Love. (Shadows Ser.). 1996. per. 3.50 (*0-373-27064-X*, 1-27064-4) Silhouette.

— Guide to Essential Oils: Over Two Hundred Twenty-Five EO Listed. (Illus.). 90p. (Orig.). (C). 1994. spiral bd. 30.00 (*1-879687-02-X*) Herb Studies.

— Heart of Dreams. (Shadows Ser.). 1995. mass mkt. 3.50 (*0-373-27055-0*, 1-27055-2) Silhouette.

— The Herbal Body Book Pt. II: Herbs & Aromatherapy for Healthy Skin & Hair. Earle, Susan, ed. (Jeanne Rose Earth Medicine Ser.). (Illus.). 55p. (Orig.). 1994. pap., per. 4.95 (*1-879687-04-6*) Herb Studies.

— Herbs & Aromatherapy for the Reproductive System. LC 94-19980. 128p. (Orig.). (C). 1994. pap. 7.95 (*1-883319-17-X*) Frog Ltd CA.

— Herbs & Things: Jeanne Rose's Herbal. (Illus.). 1972. pap. 12.95 (*0-399-50944-5*, Perigee Bks) Berkley Pub.

— Herbs for the Reproductive System, with Charts: Herbs for Men & Women, for Health, for Reproduction, Menstrual Regularity & Abortives. (Illus.). 1988. student ed. 7.95 (*0-9620838-9-5*, J R Herb Pubns) Herb Studies.

— A History of Herbs & Herbalism: A Chronology from 10,000 BC to the Present. (Illus.). 52p. 1988. student ed. 25.00 (*0-9620838-6-0*, J R Herb Pubns) Herb Studies.

— Jeanne Rose's Herbal Body Book. (Illus.). 400p. 1976. pap. 12.00 (*0-399-50790-6*, Perigee Bks) Berkley Pub.

***Rose, Jeanne.** Jeanne Rose's Herbal Body Book: Natural Beauty & Health for Men & Women. rev. ed. (Illus.). 400p. 1999. pap. 16.95 (*1-58394-004-9*) Frog Ltd CA.

Rose, Jeanne. Jeanne Rose's Herbal Guide to Food: Eating Healthy the Herbal Way. 250p. (Orig.). 1989. 25.00 (*1-55643-063-9*); pap. 14.95 (*1-55643-056-6*) North Atlantic.

— Jeanne Rose's Herbal Studies Course: A Complete Home Study Herb Course, 3 vols., Set. (Herbal Studies). (Illus.). 1200p. 1988. ring bd. 375.00 (*0-9620838-1-X*, J R Herb Pubns) Herb Studies.

— Jeanne Rose's Herbal Studies Course Pt. I: The Seasonal Herbal. (Herbal Studies). (Illus.). 350p. 1988. 125.00 (*0-9620838-2-8*, J R Herb Pubns) Herb Studies.

— Jeanne Rose's Herbal Studies Course Pt. II: The Medicinal Herbal. (Herbal Studies). (Illus.). 1200p. 1988. 125.00 (*0-9620838-4-4*, J R Herb Pubns) Herb Studies.

— Jeanne Rose's Herbal Studies Course Pt. III: The Reference Herbal. (Herbal Studies). (Illus.). 1200p. 1988. 125.00 (*0-9620838-3-6*, J R Herb Pubns) Herb Studies.

— Jeanne Rose's Kitchen Cosmetics: Using Herbs, Fruit & Flowers for Natural Bodycare. 3rd ed. 128p. 1991. pap. 11.95 (*1-55643-101-5*) North Atlantic.

— Jeanne Rose's Modern Herbal. (Illus.). 224p. 1987. pap. 11.00 (*0-399-51394-9*, Perigee Bks) Berkley Pub.

— Kitchen Cosmetics: Using Herbs, Fruits & Eatables in Natural Cosmetics. 2nd rev. ed. (Illus.). 131p. (YA). (gr. 8 up). 1988. pap. 12.95 (*0-9620838-0-1*) Herb Studies.

— Kitchen Cosmetics: Using Plants & Herbs in Cosmetics. LC 77-17077. 128p. 1978. 12.95 (*0-915572-25-7*); pap. 6.95 (*0-915572-24-9*) Panjandrum.

— Love on the Run. (Silhouette Romance Ser.). 1994. per. 2.75 (*0-373-19027-1*, 1-19027-1) Harlequin Bks.

***Rose, Jeanne.** 375 Essential Oils & Hydrosols. LC 98-48682. (Illus.). 200p. 1999. pap. 14.95 (*1-883319-89-7*) Frog Ltd CA.

Rose, Jeanne & Earle, Susan, eds. Women of Aromatherapy: Complete Aromatherapy by the People Who Made It So. (Illus.). 310p. (Orig.). 1996. pap. 17.95 (*1-879687-06-2*) Herb Studies.

— The World of Aromatherapy. LC 95-48253. (Illus.). 350p. 1996. pap. 18.95 (*1-883319-49-8*) Frog Ltd CA.

Rose, Jed, jt. auth. see Shipley, Robert H.

Rose, Jeffrey S. Medicine & the Information Age. LC 97-77013. (Illus.). xx, 278p. 1998. 50.00 (*0-924674-57-1*) Am Coll Phys Execs.

Rose, Jennifer. The Old Direction of Heaven: Poems. LC 99-53745. 64p. 2000. pap. 15.00 (*0-943549-23-X*) Truman St Univ.

Rose, Jennifer, ed. see Fleming, Red.

Rose, Jennifer S., et al, eds. Multivariate Applications in Substance Use Research. LC 99-28611. (Multivariate Applications Ser.). 450p. 1999. write for info. (*0-8058-2942-3*); pap. write for info. (*0-8058-2943-1*) L Erlbaum Assocs.

***Rose, Jenny C.** The Image of Zoroaster: The Persian Mage Through European Eyes. LC 00-25284. (Persian Studies). 2000. write for info. (*0-933273-45-2*) Bibliotheca Persica.

Rose, Jenny C. Large Motor Play. Bittinger, Gayle, ed. (101 Tips for Toddler Teachers Ser.). (Illus.). 24p. (Orig.). 1997. pap. 3.95 (*1-57029-155-1*, 4016) Totline Pubns.

Rose, Jerome C., ed. see Limp, Fredrick, et al.

Rose, Jerome C., ed. see Owsley, Douglas W., et al.

Rose, Jerome G. Landlords & Tenants. LC 72-82194. 288p. 1976. text 39.95 (*0-87855-042-9*); pap. text 24.95 (*0-87855-538-2*) Transaction Pubns.

Rose, Jerome G., ed. The Transfer of Development Rights: A New Technique of Land Use Regulation. 356p. 1975. boxed set 29.95 (*0-87855-119-0*) Transaction Pubs.

Rose, Joan B. & Smith, Huw V. Giardia & Cryptosporidium Handbook: A Practical Guide. Date not set. 79.95 (*0-87371-220-X*) Lewis Pubs.

Rose, Joanna. Little Miss Strange. LC 98-11366. 384p. 1998. pap. 12.00 (*0-684-84741-8*) S&S Trade.

— Little Miss Strange: A Novel. LC 96-46817. 384p. 1997. 20.95 (*1-56512-154-6*, 72154) Algonquin Bks.

Rose, Joe. Pedi-Wheel First Responder: Pediatric Emergency Pocket Reference. (Illus.). 2p. 1997. 9.95 (*0-9658618-1-3*) EMS Advan.

Rose, Joel. The Big Book of Thugs: Tough-As-Nails True Tales of the World's Baddest Mobs, Gangs, & Ne'er Do Wells! (Factoid Books Big Book Ser.). 192p. 1996. 14.95 (*1-56389-285-5*, Pub. by DC Comics) Time Warner.

— Kill Kill Faster Faster. 224p. 1998. pap. 11.95 (*0-14-027329-8*) Viking Penguin.

— Kill the Poor. LC 88-15417. (Atlantic Monthly Press Fiction Ser.). 312p. 1988. pap. 8.95 (*0-87113-260-5*, Atlntc Mnthly) Grove-Atltic.

***Rose, Joel.** New York Sawed in Half: An Urban Historical. (Illus.). 2001. 19.95 (*1-58234-098-6*) Bloomsbury Pubg.

Rose, Joel & Texier, Catherine, eds. Love Is Strange: Stories of Postmodern Romance. LC 92-15411. 288p. 1993. pap. 12.95 (*0-393-30965-7*) Norton.

Rose, John & Hankin, Linda. Running Your Own Photographic Business. 2nd ed. 145p. (Orig.). 1992. pap. 27.95 (*0-8464-1378-7*) Beekman Pubs.

Rose, John & Pillider, Sarah. Breeding the Competition Horse. 2nd ed. LC 93-27092. 1993. 26.95 (*0-632-03727-X*) Blackwell Sci.

Rose, John, jt. auth. see Steinhorst, Lori.

Rose, John H. Armenians in Jerusalem: Memories of Life in Palestine. (Illus.). 320p. (C). 1993. text 45.00 (*1-85043-596-0*) I B T.

— The Mediterranean in the Ancient World. 1970. reprint ed. lib. bdg. 59.50 (*0-8371-1933-2*, ROME, Greenwood Pr) Greenwood.

— Nationality in Modern History. 1977. 13.95 (*0-8369-6989-8*, 7866) Ayer.

— William Pitt & the Great War. LC 71-110862. (Illus.). 596p. 1971. reprint ed. lib. bdg. 75.00 (*0-8371-4533-3*, ROWP, Greenwood Pr) Greenwood.

Rose, John H., et al. Germany in the Nineteenth Century: Five Lectures. LC 67-30189. (Manchester University Publications Historical Series No. 13, Essay Index Reprint Ser.). 1977. 18.95 (*0-8369-0471-0*) Ayer.

Rose, John R. Beyond Reason. 432p. 1993. pap. 19.95 (*1-881170-03-9*) Rose Pub OR.

— Cartoons That Fit the Bill: An Editorial Cartoon Book about Washington & Beyond. LC 96-17501. (Illus.). 160p. 1996. pap. 8.95 (*1-56554-215-0*) Pelican.

— The Donkey Hide. 261p. (Orig.). (J). 1993. pap. 10.00 (*1-881170-04-7*) Rose Pub OR.

— Keys to Success. 128p. (YA). 1992. pap. write for info. (*1-881170-00-4*) Rose Pub OR.

— Manual for Legal Investigators. rev. ed. LC 96-158224. 319p. (C). 1995. 50.00 (*1-881170-05-5*) Rose Pub OR.

— The Old Roper. 224p. 1992. pap. write for info. (*1-881170-01-2*) Rose Pub OR.

— Ten Thousand Dollars Per Month as a Private Investigator. 264p. (Orig.). 1992. pap. 29.95 (*1-881170-02-0*) Rose Pub OR.

Rose, John S. A Course of Group Theory. LC 76-22984. 320p. reprint ed. pap. 91.20 (*0-608-15608-6*, 2031721) Bks Demand.

— A Course on Group Theory. unabridged ed. LC 94-20435. 310p. 1994. reprint ed. pap. text 8.95 (*0-486-68194-7*) Dover.

Rose, Jon. Classic U. S. Imperforate Stamps. (Illus.). 100p. (Orig.). 1990. pap. 14.95 (*0-940403-29-3*) Linns Stamp News.

— United States Postage Stamps of 1869. (Linn's Handbook Ser.: No. 5). (Illus.). 200p. (Orig.). 1996. pap. 14.95 (*0-940403-66-8*) Linns Stamp News.

***Rose, Jonathan, ed.** The Holocaust & the Book: Destruction & Preservation. (Studies in Print Culture & the History of the Book). (Illus.). 432p. 2000. 39.95 (*1-55849-253-4*) U of Mass Pr.

Rose, Jonathan & Anderson, Patricia. British Literary Publishing Houses, 1881-1965 / LC 91-31918. (Dictionary of Literary Biography Ser.). 420p. 1991. text 155.00 (*0-8103-4592-7*) Gale.

***Rose, Jonathan, et al.** Emanuel Swedenborg: Essays for the New Century Edition on His Life, Work & Impact. (New Century Edition of the Works of Emanuel Swedenborg). 225p. 2000. 49.00 (*0-87785-473-4*) Swedenborg.

Rose, Jonathan, et al. Innocents: How Justice Failed Stefan Kiszko & Lesley Molseed. (Illus.). 1997. 35.00 (*1-85702-402-8*) Fourth Estate.

***Rose, Jonathan, et al.** Scribe of Heaven: Swedenborg's Life, Work & Impact. 225p. 2000. pap. 12.00 (*0-87785-472-6*) Swedenborg.

Rose, Jonathan, jt. auth. see Anderson, Patricia.

Rose, Jonathan, tr. see Swedenborg, Emanuel.

***Rose, Jonathan W.** Making "pictures in Our Heads" Government Advertising in Canada. LC 99-46404. (Praeger Series in Political Communication). 272p. 2000. write for info. (*0-275-96842-1*, Praeger Pubs) Greenwood.

Rose, Joseph. Pedi-Wheel: Pediatric Emergency Pocket Reference. (Illus.). 2p. 1995. 9.95 (*0-9658618-0-5*) EMS Advan.

Rose, Joseph L. Ultrasonic Waves in Solid Media. LC 98-45447. (Illus.). 384p. 1999. write for info. (*0-521-64043-1*) Cambridge U Pr.

Rose, Joshua. Modern Machine Shop Practice of 1887, 2 vols. (Illus.). 1000p. 1998. reprint ed. pap. text 200.00 (*0-87556-844-0*) Saifer.

— The Pattern Maker's Assistant: Embracing Lathe Work, Branch Work, Core Work, Sweep Work & Practical Gear Construction, & Preparation & Use of Tools. 6th ed. (Illus.). 248p. 1995. reprint ed. pap. 19.95 (*1-879335-59-X*) Astragal Pr.

Rose, Judi, jt. auth. see Rose, Evelyn.

Rose, Judy S. Dragon's Awry. 16p. 1995. pap. 3.95 (*0-9649940-0-3*) J Rose.

Rose, Julie, tr. see Ranciere, Jacques.

Rose, Julie, tr. see Thomas, Chantal.

Rose, Julie, tr. see Virilio, Paul.

Rose, Julio L. & Afrika, Llaila O. Heru-tage Ra-staured, Pt. I. (Illus.). 120p. 1996. pap. 12.00 (*0-9658331-0-0*) Starlight Communs.

— Heru-tage Ra-staured, Pt. II. (Illus.). 120p. 1996. pap. 12.00 (*0-9658331-1-9*) Starlight Communs.

Rose, June. Suzanne Valadon: The Mistress of Montmartre. LC 98-47609. 304p. 1999. text 27.95 (*0-312-19921-X*) St Martin.

Rose, K., jt. auth. see Geuskens, Bibiche.

Rose, K. D., jt. ed. see Bown, T. M.

Rose, Kalima. Where Women Are Leaders: The SEWA Movement in India. (Illus.). 288p. (C). 1993. text 25.00 (*1-85649-084-X*, Pub. by Zed Books) St Martin.

Rose, Karen. That First Bite: Journal of a Compulsive Overeater. 1990. pap. 8.95 (*0-88282-070-2*) New Horizon NJ.

Rose, Karol, jt. auth. see Adolf, Barbara.

Rose, Kathi, jt. auth. see Rose.

Rose, Kathy, ed. & illus. see Sanders, Pete A., Jr.

Rose, Katie. A Case for Romance. 384p. 1999. mass mkt. 5.99 (*0-553-57772-7*) Bantam.

***Rose, Katie.** Courting Trouble. 336p. 2000. mass mkt. 5.99 (*0-553-58139-2*) Bantam.

Rose, Katie. A Hint of Mischief. 400p. 1998. mass mkt. 5.50 (*0-553-57771-9*, Fanfare) Bantam.

Rose, Kenneth D. American Women & the Repeal of Prohibition. (American Social Experience Ser.). (Illus.). 230p. (C). 1995. text 47.50 (*0-8147-7464-4*) NYU Pr.

— American Women & the Repeal of Prohibition. (American Social Experience Ser.). 1997. pap. text 17.50 (*0-8147-7466-0*) NYU Pr.

Rose, Kenneth D., et al. Sport Medicine: Physiology. LC 73-11032. (Sport Medicine Ser.: Vol. 4). 202p. 1974. text 32.00 (*0-8422-7139-2*) Irvington.

Rose, Kenneth J. Quick Scientific Terminology: A Self-Teaching Guide. LC 88-725. 267p. 1988. pap. 16.95 (*0-471-85763-7*) Wiley.

Rose, Kenneth T. Knowing the Real: John Hick on the Cognitivity of Religions & Religious Pluralism. LC 94-23673. (Toronto Studies in Religion: Vol. 20). X, 185p. (C). 1997. 44.95 (*0-8204-2636-9*) P Lang Pubng.

Rose, Kenneth W., et al. Survey of Sources at the Rockefeller Archive Center for the Study of African-American History & Race Relations. Sherman, Lois, ed. 120p. (Orig.). (C). pap. write for info. (*1-884354-01-7*) IN Univ Ctr.

***Rose, Kents.** Involuntary Exile. LC 99-64377. 1999. 25.00 (*0-7388-0458-4*); pap. 18.00 (*0-7388-0459-2*) Xlibris Corp.

Rose, Kieran. Diverse Communities. 64p. 1994. pap. 8.95 (*0-902561-73-1*, Pub. by Cork Univ) Stylus Pub VA.

Rose, Kurt. The Islands of the Sulu Sea: A True Adventure. LC 93-61096. (Illus.). 1993. pap. 15.95 (*0-9637586-1-6*) Glencannon Pr.

Rose, L. Diario de Mama.Tr. of Mom's Diary. (SPA.). 1996. pap. 9.99 (*0-8297-0461-2*) Vida Pubs.

Rose, L. J., Jr. L. J. Rose of Sunnyslope, 1827-1899: California Pioneer, Fruit Grower, Winemaker, Horse Breeder. (Illus.). 236p. 1993. 19.95 (*0-87328-144-6*) Huntington Lib.

Rose, L. M. Distillation Design in Practice. (Computer Aided Chemical Engineering Ser.: No. 1). 308p. 1985. pap. 94.50 (*0-444-42481-4*) Elsevier.

Rose, L. M., jt. auth. see Wells, G. L.

Rose, Lance. Netlaw. 1997. pap. text 24.99 (*0-07-882358-7*) McGraw.

— Netlaw: Your Rights in the Online World. Cuthbertson, Joanne, ed. (Internet Ser.). 432p. 1995. pap. text 19.95 (*0-07-882077-4*) Osborne-McGraw.

Rose, Larry. Show Me the Way to Go Home. LC 94-61038. 150p. (Orig.). 1995. pap. 10.95 (*0-943873-08-8*) Elder Bks.

***Rose, Laura.** Easy Reading: Finding Joy & Meaning in Words. LC 00-33401. 2000. write for info. (*1-56976-119-1*) Zephyr Pr AZ.

Rose, Laura. Life Isn't Weighed on the Bathroom Scales. 185p. 1994. 18.95 (*0-9653369-0-5*) Rose Prods.

***Rose, Laura.** The Tender Deception. large type ed. 336p. 1999. pap. 18.99 (*0-7089-5489-8*, Linford) Ulverscroft.

Rose, Laurel L. Disputes in Common Property Regimes (CPRs) (LTC Paper Ser.: Vol. 154). iv, 55p. (C). 1996. pap. 7.00 (*0-934519-72-2*, LTC154) U of Wis Land.

— The Politics of Harmony: Land Dispute Strategies in Swaziland. (African Studies: No. 69). (Illus.). 254p. (C). 1992. text 74.95 (*0-521-39296-9*) Cambridge U Pr.

Rose, Lauren. The Human Handbook: Lessons from the Heart. LC 98-88288. 325p. 1998. 25.00 (*0-7388-0137-2*) Xlibris Corp.

Rose, Laurence. The Human Handbook. LC 98-88288. 325p. 1998. pap. 15.00 (*0-7388-0138-0*) Xlibris Corp.

Rose, Laurence M. Fitzgerald v. Nita & Western R. R. 212p. 1994. pap. 22.95 (*1-55681-447-X*) Natl Inst Trial Ad.

Rose, Lavera. Grandchildren of the Lakota. LC 98-5307. (World's Children Ser.). 40p. (J). (gr. 3-6). 1998. 21.27 (*1-57505-279-2*, Carolrhoda) Lerner Pub.

Rose, Leo E. & Gonsalves, Eric, eds. Toward a New World Order: Adjusting India-U. S. Relations. LC 92-70529. (Research Papers & Policy: No. 38). 1992. pap. 15.00 (*1-55729-032-6*) IEAS.

Rose, Leo E. & Husain, Noor A., eds. U. S.-Pakistan Relations. LC 85-80563. (Research Papers & Policy: No. 13). 245p. 1985. pap. 17.00 (*0-912966-78-5*) IEAS.

Rose, Leo E. & Matinuddin, Kamal, eds. Beyond Afghanistan: The Emerging U. S. - Pakistan Relations. LC 89-81688. (Research Papers & Policy). 336p. (Orig.). (C). 1990. pap. 20.00 (*1-55729-017-2*) IEAS.

Rose, Leo E. & Scholz, John T. Nepal: Profile of a Himalayan Kingdom. LC 79-17857. (Nations of Contemporary Asia Ser.). (Illus.). 156p. 1980. text 32.00 (*0-89158-651-2*) Westview.

Rose, Leo E., jt. auth. see Sisson, Richard.

Rose, Leo E., jt. ed. see Husain, Noor A.

Rose, Leonie M., jt. auth. see Johnson, Nancy J.

Rose, Linda. Hands: The Total Guide to Beauty, Health, Language & Lore. LC 84-22665. (Illus.). 188p. 1985. pap. 9.95 (*0-87951-991-6*, Pub. by Overlook Pr) Penguin Putnam.

***Rose, Linda J.** Your Mind: The Owner's Manual. 1999. pap. text 12.95 (*1-895383-09-9*) Babajls.

Rose, Linda M. Mortgaging a Home Vol. 1: Simple Guide to Financing a Home in Basic Terms - What to Do...What Not to Do...& Why. Di Ianni, Marisa, ed. 200p. (Orig.). 1994. pap. 14.95 (*1-885878-00-1*) Essent Finan.

Rose, Lionel. Massacre of the Innocents: Infanticide in Britain, 1800-1939. (Illus.). 215p. (C). 1986. 45.00 (*0-7102-0339-X*, Routledge Thoemms) Routledge.

— Rogues & Vagabonds: The Vagrant Underworld in Britain 1815-1985. 272p. (C). 1988. lib. bdg. 65.00 (*0-415-00275-3*) Routledge.

— Rogues & Vagabonds: Vagrant Underworld in Britain. LC 87-33767. (Illus.). 264p. reprint ed. pap. 81.90 (*0-608-20376-9*, 207162900002) Bks Demand.

Rose, Lisle A. The Cold War Comes to Main Street: America in 1950. LC 98-24677. 416p. 1999. 39.95 (*0-7006-0928-8*) U Pr of KS.

— The Roots of Tragedy: The United States & the Struggle for Asia, 1945-1953, 48. LC 75-35354. (Contributions in American History Ser.: No. 48). 262p. 1976. 55.00 (*0-8371-8592-0*, RRT/, Greenwood Pr) Greenwood.

— The Ship That Held the Line: The U. S. S. Hornet & the First Year of the Pacific War. LC 95-8683. (Illus.). 328p. 1995. 34.95 (*1-55750-729-5*) Naval Inst Pr.

— Survey of American Economic Fiction. (BCL1-PS American Literature Ser.). 22p. 1993. reprint ed. lib. bdg. 59.00 (*0-7812-6593-2*) Rprt Serv.

Rose, Loretta. Daycare: What Can a Mother Do. 16p. 1994. pap., per. 6.00 (*0-8059-3653-X*) Dorrance.

Rose, Louis. The Freudian Calling: Early Viennese Psychoanalysis & the Pursuit of Cultural Science. LC 97-37080. (Kritik). 232p. 1998. pap. 24.95 (*0-8143-2622-6*) Wayne St U Pr.

***Rose, Louis F., et al.** Periodontal Medicine. 352p. 1999. boxed set 89.95 incl. cd-rom (*1-55009-120-4*) DEKR.

Rose, Louis J. How to Investigate Your Friends & Enemies. rev. ed. Byrne, Robert & Fiquette, Lawrence, eds. LC 81-68851. (Illus.). 137p. 1983. pap. 7.95 (*0-9606846-1-1*) Albion Pr.

Rose, Louis J. & Malone, Roy. Make the Jerk Pay: Tracking down a Deadbeat Dad/And Getting Child Support. Lindecke, Fred W., ed. LC 98-93329. (Illus.). xiv, 188p. 1999. pap. 14.95 (*0-9606846-3-8*) Albion Pr.

Rose, Lucy A. Sharing the Word: Preaching in the Roundtable Church. 176p. (Orig.). 1997. pap. 19.95 (*0-664-25658-9*) Westminster John Knox.

Rose, Lucy A., jt. auth. see Ormond, J. Will.

Rose, Lucy A., jt. compiled by see Childers, Jana L.

Rose, Lucy A., jt. ed. see Childers, Jana L.

Rose, Lucy Atkinson, see Atkinson Rose, Lucy.

Rose, Lynn E. Sun, Moon & Sothis: Calenders & Calender Reforms in Ancient Egypt. (Osiris Ser.: Vol. II). 350p. 1999. 38.00 (*0-917994-15-9*) Kronos Pr.

Rose, Lynn E., et al. Velikovsky & Establishment Science. Greenberg, L. M., ed. LC 77-93288. (Illus.). 1977. pap. 12.00 (*0-917994-04-3*) Kronos Pr.

Rose, M. The Highest Form of Killing. LC 91-31889. 240p. (YA). (gr. 9 up). 1992. 16.95 (*0-15-234270-2*, Harcourt Child Bks) Harcourt.

Rose, M., compiled by. The Care & Use of Animals for Scientific Purposes. 69p. 1991. pap. 100.00 (*0-646-05678-6*, Pub. by Univs Fed Animal Welfare) St Mut.

Rose, M., ed. Heidelberg Congress on Taxing Consumption: Proceedings of the International Congress on Taxing Consumption, Heidelberg, June 28-30, 1989. (Illus.). xvii, 541p. 1990. 142.95 (*0-387-52728-1*) Spr-Verlag.

Rose, M. A., jt. auth. see Jaswon, M. A.

Rose, M. E. Elementary Theory of Angular Momentum. LC 94-41223. (Illus.). 256p. 1995. pap. text 7.95 (*0-486-68480-6*) Dover.

Rose, M. Gaddis, tr. see Villiers de l'Isle-Adam, Philippe A.

***Rose, M. J.** In Fidelity. 2001. pap. 12.95 (*0-7434-0645-1*, PB Trade Paper) PB.

— Lip Service. LC 99-35880. 304p. 1999. 18.00 (*0-671-04131-2*, PB Hardcover) PB.

— Lip Service. 320p. 2000. reprint ed. per. 12.95 (*0-671-04132-0*) PB.

***Rose, M. J. & Adair-Hoy, Angela.** How to Publish & Promote Online. 2001. pap. write for info. (*0-312-27191-3*, St Martin Griffin) St Martin.

Rose, Mabelle A., jt. compiled by see Simmons, Joseph T.

Rose, Mac. Teacher Tips. (Illus.). 1997. pap., teacher ed. 23.75 (*1-56234-158-8*) Educ Ctr.

***Rose, Malcolm.** The Alibi: The Perfect Murder... large type ed. (Illus.). (J). 2000. pap. write for info. (*0-7540-6099-3*) Chivers N Amer.

Rose, Malcolm. Concrete Evidence. 208p. (gr. 7-9). 1995. mass mkt. 3.50 (*0-590-20358-4*) Scholastic Inc.

— Concrete Evidence. (Point Crime Ser.). 1995. 8.60 (*0-606-07388-4*, Pub. by Turtleback) Demco.

— Formula for Murder. 208p. (YA). (gr. 7-9). 1994. pap. 3.50 (*0-590-48320-X*) Scholastic Inc.

— The Highest Form of Killing. LC 91-31889. 240p. (YA). (gr. 9 up). 1995. pap. 5.00 (*0-15-200373-8*) Harcourt.

— The Highest Form of Killing. 1995. 10.10 (*0-606-07647-6*, Pub. by Turtleback) Demco.

***Rose, Malcolm.** The Smoking Gun. large type ed. (Illus.). (J). 1998. pap. 16.95 (*0-7540-6009-8*, Galaxy Child Lrg Print) Chivers N Amer.

Rose, Malcolm E. Mass Spectrometry, Vol. 6. 1990. 142.00 (*0-85186-308-6*) CRC Pr.

— Mass Spectrometry, Vol. 7. 1989. 175.00 (*0-85186-318-3*) CRC Pr.

— Mass Spectrometry, Vol. 8. 1989. 208.00 (*0-85186-328-0*) CRC Pr.

— Mass Spectrometry, Vol. 10. 1989. 252.00 (*0-85186-348-5*) CRC Pr.

Rose, Malcolm E., ed. Mass Spectrometry, Vol. 9. (Specialist Periodical Reports). (Illus.). 502p. 1987. text 171.00 (*0-85186-338-8*, Pub. by Royal Soc Chem) Spr-Verlag.

Rose, Malcolm E., jt. auth. see Johnstone, Robert A.

Rose, Marc, ed. see Peachment, Corinne.

Rose, Marc R., et al. Save Your Sight! Natural Ways to Prevent & Reverse Macular Degeneration & Other Eye Diseases. LC 97-41030. 320p. 1998. mass mkt. 13.99 (*0-446-67402-8*, Pub. by Warner Bks) Little.

***Rose, Marc R., et al.** A Woman's Guide to Male Menopause: Real Solutions for Helping Him Maintain Vitality & Virility. 304p. 2000. pap. 17.95 (*0-658-00143-4*, 001434, Keats Publng) NTC Contemp Pub Co.

Rose, Marcia. Hospital. 1999. pap. text 11.95 (*84-08-02323-3*) Planeta.

— Nurses. 1997. mass mkt. 6.99 (*0-345-39001-6*) Ballantine Pub Grp.

— Time to Heal. 1998. mass mkt. 6.99 (*0-345-40226-X*) Ballantine Pub Grp.

Rose, Margaret, ed. see Robinson, Ronald.

Rose, Marilyn G. Katharine Tynan. LC 71-126276. (Irish Writers Ser.). 97p. 1975. 8.50 (*0-8387-7770-8*); pap. 1.95 (*0-8387-7771-6*) Bucknell U Pr.

Rose, Marilyn G., ed. Translation Spectrum: Essays in Theory & Practice. LC 80-20302. 172p. (C). 1980. pap. text 14.95 (*0-87395-437-8*) State U NY Pr.

Rose, Marilyn G., tr. see De L'Isle-Adam, Villers.

Rose, Marilyn G., tr. see Sainte-Beuve, Charles-Augustin.

Rose, Marilyn P. On the Move: A Study of Migration & Ethnic Persistence among Mennonites from East Freeman, South Dakota. LC 87-45793. (Immigrant Communities & Ethnic Minorities in the U. S. & Canada Ser.: No. 28). 1988. 45.00 (*0-404-19438-9*, F659) AMS Pr.

Rose, Marilyn S. My First Horse. 53p. (Orig.). (J). (gr. 3-4). 1991. pap. 9.95 (*0-9632117-0-6*) AMI & Arabian Mktg.

Rose, Marilynn J., tr. see Hamburger, Kate.

Rose, Mark. Alien Encounters: Anatomy of Science Fiction. LC 81-683. 220p. 1981. pap. text 13.50 (*0-674-01566-5*) HUP.

— Authors & Owners: The Invention of Copyright. LC 92-43010. 192p. (Orig.). 1993. text 34.95 (*0-674-05308-7*) HUP.

— Authors & Owners: The Invention of Copyright. 192p. (Orig.). (C). 1995. pap. text 17.00 (*0-674-05309-5*) HUP.

— Heroic Love: Studies in Sidney & Spenser. LC 68-29182. 168p. 1985. reprint ed. pap. 52.10 (*0-7837-2322-9*, 205741000004) Bks Demand.

— Shakespearean Design. LC 72-88129. (Illus.). 204p. reprint ed. pap. 63.30 (*0-7837-4185-5*, 205903500012) Bks Demand.

— Spenser's Art: A Companion to Book One of "The Faerie Queene" LC 74-21229. 160p. (C). 1975. 19.00 (*0-674-83193-4*) HUP.

Rose, Mark, ed. Shakespeare's Early Tragedies: A Collection of Critical Essays. LC 94-11740. (New Century Views Ser.). 265p. (C). 1994. pap. text 12.95 (*0-13-035544-5*) P-H.

Rose, Mark, ed. see Shakespeare, William.

Rose, Mark D., et al. Methods in Yeast Genetics: A Laboratory Course Manual. (Illus.). 200p. (C). 1990. text 20.00 (*0-87969-354-1*) Cold Spring Harbor.

Rose, Mark H. Cities of Light & Heat: Domesticating Gas & Electricity in Urban America. LC 94-16202. (Illus.). 256p. 1995. 38.50 (*0-271-01349-4*) Pa St U Pr.

— Interstate: Express Highway Politics, 1939-1989. LC 90-12343. 208p. 1990. reprint ed. pap. text 18.95 (*0-87049-671-9*) U of Tenn Pr.

— Interstate: Express Highway Politics, 1941-1956. LC 78-14940. 1979. 25.00 (*0-7006-0186-4*) U Pr of KS.

Rose, Mark H., jt. ed. see Daniels, George H.

Rose, Mark V. The Actor & His Double: Mime & Movement for the Theatre of Cruelty. LC 85-73269. 80p. 1986. pap. 8.95 (*0-9616087-0-6*) ATRI Pr.

Rose, Marlene L. & Yacoub, Magdi H., eds. Immunology of Heart & Lung Transplantation. (Illus.). 324p. 1993. text 125.00 (*0-340-56016-9*, Pub. by E A) OUP.

An Asterisk (*) at the beginning of an entry indicates that the title is appearing for the first time.

Rose, Marshall T. Internet Messaging: From the Desktop to the Enterprise. LC 98-19174. 352p. 1998. pap. text 44.95 (*0-13-978610-4*) P-H.
— The Simple Book: An Introduction to Networking Management. 2nd rev. ed. LC 96-7192. (Series in Innovative Technology). 336p. (C). 1996. 68.00 (*0-13-451659-1*) P-H.
Rose, Marshall T. & McCloghrie, Keith. How to Manage Your Network Using SNMP: The Networking Management Practicum. LC 94-5350. 576p. 1994. pap. 73.00 (*0-13-141517-4*) P-H.
Rose, Marshall T., jt. auth. see Lynch, Daniel C.
Rose, Martial. Stories in Stone: The Medieval Roof Carvings of Norwich Cathedral. LC 96-61180. (Illus.). 194p. (Orig.). 1997. pap. 19.95 (*0-500-27937-3*, Pub. by Thames Hudson) Norton.
***Rose, Martin.** Rien de Nouveau: Nouvelles Approches du Livre de Qoheleth. (Orbis Biblicus et Orientalis Ser.: No. 168). (FRE.). 629p. 1999. text 98.00 (*3-7278-1255-9*, Pub. by Ed Univ Fri) Eisenbrauns.
Rose, Martin R., et al. The Past Climate of Arroyo Hondo, New Mexico, Reconstructed from Tree Rings. LC 80-21834. (Arroyo Hondo Archaeological Ser.: Vol. 4). (Illus.). 114p. 1981. pap. 14.95 (*0-933452-05-5*) Schol Am Res.
Rose, Martin R., jt. auth. see Altschul, Jeffrey H.
Rose, Mary. The Gift of Touch: Comfort Touch: Massage for the Elderly & the Chronically & Terminally Ill. 60p. (Orig.). 1996. pap. 10.00 (*0-9655182-0-5*) Hospice of Bldr Cty.
Rose, Mary. The Horsemaster's Notebook. (Illus.). 255p. 1997. pap. 34.95 (*1-872082-92-0*) Half Halt Pr.
— 10 Easy Writing Lessons That Get Kids Ready for Standardized Tests. 1999. pap. 14.95 (*0-439-05010-3*) Scholastic Inc.
Rose, Mary, jt. auth. see Sussman, Lane.
Rose, Mary, jt. auth. see Wood, Erskine.
Rose, Mary, ed. see Dring, Harry.
Rose, Mary, jt. ed. see Jones, Geoffrey.
Rose, Mary B. The Expense of Spirit: Love & Sexuality in English Renaissance Drama. LC 88-47742. 272p. 1991. reprint ed. pap. text 14.95 (*0-8014-9695-0*) Cornell U Pr.
***Rose, Mary B.** Firms, Networks & Business Values: The British & American Cotton Industries Since 1750. (Cambridge Studies in Modern Economic History: Vol. 8). (Illus.). 336p. (C). 2001. text Price not set. (*0-521-78255-4*) Cambridge U Pr.
Rose, Mary B. Women in the Middle Ages & the Renaissance: Literary & Historical Perspectives. LC 85-22153. 272p. (Orig.). 1986. pap. 19.95 (*0-8156-2352-6*) Syracuse U Pr.
Rose, Mary B., ed. Explorations in Renaissance Drama. (Renaissance Drama Ser.: Vol. XXVI). 200p. 1997. 59.95 (*0-8101-1521-2*) Northwestern U Pr.
— Family Business. LC 95-11877. (International Library of Critical Writings in Business History: Vol. 13). 736p. 1995. 310.00 (*1-85898-049-6*) E Elgar.
— International Competition & Strategic Response in Textile Industries since 1870. 165p. 1991. text 42.50 (*0-7146-3412-3*, Pub. by F Cass Pubs) Intl Spec Bk.
— Renaissance Drama, Vol. 27. (Drama & Performance Studies). 250p. 1998. text 59.95 (*0-8101-1645-6*) Northwestern U Pr.
— Renaissance Drama: Disorder & Drama. (New Ser.: No. XXI). 260p. 1991. 59.95 (*0-8101-0684-1*) Northwestern U Pr.
— Renaissance Drama: Dramatic Intertextuality & Theatrical Conditions. (New Ser.: No. XXII). (Illus.). 275p. 1993. 59.95 (*0-8101-0685-X*) Northwestern U Pr.
— Renaissance Drama: Essays on Renaissance Dramatic Traditions. (New Ser.: Vol. XX). 238p. 1990. 59.95 (*0-8101-0681-7*) Northwestern U Pr.
— Renaissance Drama: Essays on Texts of Renaissance Plays. (New Ser.: Vol. XIX). 270p. 1989. 49.95 (*0-8101-0680-9*) Northwestern U Pr.
— Renaissance Drama: Renaissance Drama & the Law, No. XXIV. (New Ser.). 270p. 1995. 59.95 (*0-8101-1195-0*) Northwestern U Pr.
— Renaissance Drama: Renaissance Drama in an Age of Colonization. (New Ser.: Vol. XXIII). 210p. 1994. 59.95 (*0-8101-0686-8*) Northwestern U Pr.
Rose, Mary B., jt. ed. see Casson, Mark.
Rose, Mary B., jt. ed. see Kirby, Maurice W.
***Rose, Mary Beth.** The Two Gentlemen of Verona. (Shakespeare Ser.). 224p. 2000. pap. 5.95 (*0-14-071461-8*) Penguin Putnam.
Rose, Mary E., ed. see Tyrrell, Albert E.
Rose, Mary Kathleen. Bereavement - Dealing with Grief & Loss. 32p. (Orig.). 1996. pap. 5.00 (*0-9636234-3-5*) Wild Rose CO.
— The Children's Tarot: The Road Is a River. (Illus.). 52p. (Orig.). (J). (gr. k-6). 1993. pap. 18.95 incl. audio (*0-9636234-0-0*) Wild Rose CO.
***Rose, Matthew F.** John Witherspoon: An American Leader. LC 99-64992. (Illus.). 82p. 1999. pap. 13.00 (*1-55872-005-7*) Fam Res Council.
Rose, Mavis. Indonesia Free Vol. 67: A Biography of Mohammad Hatta. (Modern Indonesia Project Ser.). 252p. 1987. pap. 10.50 (*0-87763-033-X*) Cornell Mod Indo.
Rose, Melvyn. Healing Hurt Minds: The Peper Harow Experience. LC 89-10415. 234p. reprint ed. pap. 72.60 (*0-608-20377-7*, 207163000002) Bks Demand.
— Transforming Hate to Love: An Outcome Study of the Peper Harow Adolescent Treatment Process. LC 96-46581. 168p. (C). 1997. 80.00 (*0-415-13831-0*); pap. 24.99 (*0-415-13832-9*) Routledge.
Rose, Michael. For the Record: 160 Years of Aboriginal Print Journalism. LC 96-202200. (Illus.). 256p. 1997. pap. text 24.95 (*1-86448-058-0*, Pub. by Allen & Unwin Pty) Paul & Co Pubs.
— German Shopping & Restaurant Guide U. S. A. (Deutscher Einkaufs und Restaurant Fuhrer U. S. A.) (ENG & GER., Illus.). 208p. 1998. pap. 14.95 (*0-9655517-1-7*) Palm Coast.
— German Shopping & Restaurant Guide U. S. A. 1997: Deutscher Einkaufs - und Restaurant Fuhrer U. S. A. 1997. (ENG & GER., Illus.). 128p. (Orig.). 1996. pap. 14.95 (*0-9655517-0-9*) Palm Coast.
— Images of Music. (GER, FRE & ENG., Illus.). 320p. 1997. 29.95 (*3-89508-216-3*, 810068) Konemann.
Rose, Michael, jt. auth. see Atlanta History Center Staff.
Rose, Michael, jt. ed. see Amis, John.
Rose, Michael D. The Law of Federal Income Taxation, 1994: Pocket Part. 3rd ed. (Hornbook Ser.). 150p. (C). 1994. pap. text. write for info. (*0-314-04332-2*) West Pub.
— Selected Federal Taxation, Statutes & Regulations. 13th ed. 1776p. (C). 1997. pap. text 29.95 (*0-314-21224-8*) West Pub.
— Selected Federal Taxation, Statutes & Regulations: 1996 Edition. 1664p. (C). 1995. pap. text 25.00 (*0-314-06723-X*) West Pub.
— Selected Federal Taxation Statutes & Regulations: 1997 Edition. 12th ed. 908p. (C). 1996. pap. text. write for info. (*0-314-09751-1*) West Pub.
Rose, Michael D. & Chommie, John C. Federal Income Taxation. 3rd ed. (Hornbook Ser.). 923p. (C). 1992. reprint ed. text 38.00 (*0-314-64224-2*) West Pub.
***Rose, Michael E.** Joe Karson - Beyond Zombie. LC 00-90488. (Illus.). 209p. 2000. 35.00 (*0-9678925-0-3*) M Rose Magic.
Rose, Michael R. Darwin's Spectre: Evolutionary Biology in the Modern World. LC 98-11494. 227p. 1998. 27.95 (*0-691-01217-2*, Pub. by Princeton U Pr) Cal Prin Full Svc.
***Rose, Michael R.** Darwin's Spectre: Evolutionary Biology in the Modern World. LC 98-11494. 233p. 2000. pap. text 16.95 (*0-691-05008-2*) Princeton U Pr.
Rose, Michael R. Evolutionary Biology of Aging. (Illus.). 240p. 1994. reprint ed. pap. text 29.95 (*0-19-509530-8*) OUP.
— Quantitative Ecological Theory: An Introduction to Basic Models. LC 87-4106. (Illus.). 215p. reprint ed. pap. 66.70 (*0-608-06135-2*, 206646800008) Bks Demand.
Rose, Michael R. & Finch, Caleb E., eds. Genetics & Evolution of Aging. LC 94-16569. (Contemporary Issues in Genetics & Evolution Ser.: Vol. 3). 312p. (C). 1994. text 213.00 (*0-7923-2902-3*) Kluwer Academic.
Rose, Michael R. & Lauder, George V., eds. Adaptation. (Illus.). 511p. (C). 1996. pap. text 41.00 (*0-12-596421-8*) Acad Pr.
— Adaptation: Natural Selection in Evolution. LC 96-33932. (Illus.). 511p. (C). 1996. text 34.95 (*0-12-596420-X*) Acad Pr.
Rose, Michael T. Prayer for Relief: The Constitutional Infirmities of the Military Academies' Conduct, Honor & Ethics Systems. vii, 194p. 1973. pap. 17.50 (*0-8377-1025-1*, Rothman) W S Hein.
Rose, Mike. Lives on the Boundary: A Moving Account of the Struggles & Achievements of America's Educational Underclass. LC 89-38513. 256p. (C). 1998. pap. text 12.95 (*0-14-012403-9*) Addson-Wesley Educ.
— Lives on the Boundary: The Struggles & Achievements of America's Underprepared. 288p. 1989. 29.95 (*0-02-926821-4*) Free Pr.
— Possible Lives: The Promise of Public Education. 1996. pap. 13.95 (*0-614-20717-7*) Viking Penguin.
— Possible Lives: The Promise of Public Education in America. 464p. (C). 1996. pap. 13.95 (*0-14-023617-1*) Viking Penguin.
Rose, Mike, ed. When a Writer Can't Write: Studies in Writer's Block & Other Composing-Process Problems. LC 84-19304. (Perspectives in Writing Research Ser.). 288p. 1985. reprint ed. pap. 89.30 (*0-608-07587-6*, 205990200010) Bks Demand.
Rose, Mike, et al. How to Save Your Child or Baby: When Every Second Counts. (C). 1987. 19.95 (*0-685-28882-X*) Pacific Stat.
Rose, Mike, jt. auth. see Kiniry, Malcolm.
Rose, Minnie B., ed. Little Black Book of Home Care Cues. LC 96-31652. (Illus.). 144p. (Orig.). 1996. ring bd. 21.95 (*0-87434-880-3*) Springhouse Corp.
Rose, Miriam. Baker's Dozen No. 12: The Baker Family Circus. 172p. (J). (gr. 6-8). 1994. pap. 9.95 (*1-56871-062-3*) Targum Pr.
Rose, Mitchell, jt. illus. see Young, Ruth.
Rose, Mondra, ed. see Vogel, Thomas A.
Rose, N., jt. ed. see Potter, M.
Rose, N. A. Gentile Zionists: Study in Anglo-Zionist Diplomacy, 1929-1939. 246p. 1973. 49.50 (*0-7146-2940-5*, Pub. by F Cass Pubs) Intl Spec Bk.
Rose, N. R., ed. see International Convocation on Immunology Staff.
Rose, Nanci H., jt. auth. see Warren, Bill.
***Rose, Nancy, et al.** Growing Shrubs & Small Trees in Cold Climates. LC 00-31513. (Contemporary Gardener Ser.). (Illus.). 2001. write for info. (*0-8092-2491-7*, Contemporary Bks) NTC Contemp Pub Co.
Rose, Nancy E. Put to Work: Relief Programs in the Great Depression. (Illus.). 144p. 26.00 (*0-85345-870-7*, Pub. by Monthly Rev) NYU Pr.
— Put to Work: Relief Programs in the Great Depression. LC 93-26617. (J). (ps-12). 1993. pap. 13.00 (*0-85345-871-5*, Pub. by Monthly Rev) NYU Pr.
— Workfare or Fair Work: Women, Welfare & Government Work Programs. LC 95-8589. 320p. (C). 1995. text 52.00 (*0-8135-2232-3*); pap. text 19.95 (*0-8135-2233-1*) Rutgers U Pr.
Rose, Neil, jt. auth. see Rose, Catherine.
Rose, Nicholas D. Essential Psychiatry. 2nd ed. LC 93-34958. (Essentials Ser.). 336p. 1994. 39.95 (*0-632-03737-7*, Pub. by Blckwll Scitfc UK) Blackwell Sci.
***Rose, Nikolas.** Governing the Soul: The Shaping of the Private Self. 2nd ed. 320p. 1999. 55.00 (*1-85343-443-4*, Pub. by Free Assoc Bks); pap. 25.00 (*1-85343-444-2*, Pub. by Free Assoc Bks) Intl Spec Bk.
Rose, Nikolas. Inventing Our Selves: Psychology, Power & Personhood. LC 95-42608. (Studies in the History of Psychology). 230p. (C). 1996. text 54.95 (*0-521-43414-9*) Cambridge U Pr.
— Inventing Our Selves: Psychology, Power & Personhood. (Cambridge Studies in the History of Psychology). 232p. (C). 1999. pap. text 18.95 (*0-521-64607-3*) Cambridge U Pr.
— Powers of Freedom: Reframing Political Thought. LC 98-40306. 320p. (C). 1999. text 59.95 (*0-521-65075-5*); pap. text 22.95 (*0-521-65905-1*) Cambridge U Pr.
***Rose, Nikolas, ed.** The Self - A Reader. 388p. 1999. 55.00 (*1-85343-441-8*, Pub. by Free Assoc Bks); pap. 25.00 (*1-85343-442-6*, Pub. by Free Assoc Bks) Intl Spec Bk.
Rose, Noel R., et al, eds. Immune Mediated Heart Disease. LC 92-49773. 1992. write for info. (*0-387-55614-1*) Spr-Verlag.
— International Convocation on Immunology. 1969. 104.50 (*3-8055-0888-3*) S Karger.
— Manual of Clinical Laboratory Immunology. 5th rev. ed. LC 96-49032. (Illus.). 1282p. 1997. 125.00 (*1-55581-118-3*) ASM Pr.
Rose, Noel R. & MacKay, Ian R., eds. The Autoimmune Diseases. 3rd ed. LC 98-84368. (Illus.). 895p. (C). 1998. boxed set 139.95 (*0-12-596923-6*) Acad Pr.
— The Autoimmune Diseases Two. (Illus.). 444p. 1992. text 105.00 (*0-12-596922-8*) Acad Pr.
Rose, Noel R. & Siegel, Benjamin V., eds. The Reticuloendothelial System Vol. 4: A Comprehensive Treatise: Immunopathology. LC 79-25933. 464p. 1983. 105.00 (*0-306-40979-8*, Plenum Trade) Perseus Pubng.
Rose, Noel R., ed. see American Society for Microbiology Staff, et al.
Rose, Norman. Churchill: The Unruly Giant. LC 95-4125. 450p. 1995. 25.50 (*0-02-874009-2*) Free Pr.
— DHEA & No Fat Cooking Vol. 1: The Miracle Hormone. (Illus.). 168p. (Orig.). 1996. pap. 14.95 (*0-9631847-6-8*) N Rose Co.
— Lewis Namier & Zionism. 192p. 1980. text 29.95 (*0-19-822621-7*) OUP.
— No Fat Fudge: Forever Changing the Way America Makes Fudge. LC 94-233795. 100p. (Orig.). 1994. 19.95 (*0-9631847-5-X*) N Rose Co.
Rose, Norman, ed. From Palmerston to Balfour: Collected Essays of Mayir Verete. 248p. 1992. text 45.00 (*0-7146-3441-7*, Pub. by F Cass Pubs) Intl Spec Bk.
Rose, Norton, ed. see Briggs, Adrian.
***Rose, Odessa.** Water in a Broken Glass. LC 00-35206. 1999. write for info. (*0-9647635-7-5*) La Caille-Nous.
Rose, Oma L. Lobdell Genealogy & Family History a Sequel. LC 95-72999. (Illus.). 736p. 1996. write for info. (*0-89725-253-5*, 1723, Penobscot Pr) Picton Pr.
Rose, Osiamder. A World of Words Works: A Portrait of Meaning, Vol. I. unabridged ed. Wegeng, Lana, ed. (Illus.). 85p. 1998. pap. 8.95 (*1-892651-02-5*) Columbia Pubns.
***Rose, Osiander.** A World of Words Works. 70p. 1998. pap. 8.95 (*1-892651-08-4*) Columbia Pacific U Pr.
Rose, Osiander. A World of Words Works: A Close look at Us, Vol. III. unabridged ed. (Illus.). 55p. 1998. pap. 8.95 (*1-892651-12-2*) Columbia Pubns.
Rose, P. & Schacht, R. M. An Analysis of the Navajo Nation Labor Market: Job Development for American Indians with Disabilities. 94p. 1994. pap. text. write for info. (*1-888557-21-4*, 100028) No Ariz Univ.
***Rose, P. K.** Founding Fathers of American Intelligence. 29p. 1999. pap. 4.25 (*0-16-058877-4*) USGPO.
Rose, P. M. & Alamdari, F. Low Temperature Air Cooling Design Considerations. 1992. 60.00 (*0-86022-326-4*, Pub. by Build Servs Info Assn) St Mut.
Rose, P. M., jt. auth. see Dodd, J. M.
Rose, P. R. & Lidz, B. Diagnostic Foraminiferal Assemblages of Shallow-Water Modern Environments: South Florida & the Bahamas, No. VI. (Sedimenta Ser.: Vol. VI). 55p. 1977. 9.00 (*0-932981-05-4*) Univ Miami CSL.
Rose, Patti E. In Search of Serenity: A Black Family's Struggle with the Threat of AIDS. LC 92-60058. 200p. (Orig.). 1993. pap. 10.95 (*0-88378-069-0*) Third World.
Rose, Paul A., jt. auth. see Dreier, William A.
Rose, Paul A., jt. auth. see Miller, Leslie A.
Rose, Paul L. German Question-Jewish Question: Revolutionary Antisemitism in Germany from Kant to Wagner. 411p. (C). 1991. pap., pap. text 19.95 (*0-691-00890-6*, Pub. by Princeton U Pr) Cal Prin Full Svc.
— Wagner: Race & Revolution. 1996. pap. text 16.00 (*0-300-06745-3*) Yale U Pr.
Rose, Paul L. & Druks, Herbert, eds. The Hecht Archive, University of Haifa. LC 89-16915. (Archives of the Holocaust Ser.: Vol. 12). 520p. 1990. reprint ed. text 143.00 (*0-8240-5494-6*) Garland.
Rose, Paul Lawrence. Heisenberg & the Nazi Atomic Bomb Project. LC 97-18143. 391p. 1998. 35.00 (*0-520-21077-8*, Pub. by U CA Pr) Cal Prin Full Svc.
Rose, Pauline, tr. see Grekov, Boris.
Rose, Peter. George Tinworth. (Illus.). 192p. 1982. 125.00 (*0-9609320-0-3*, Pub. by R Dennis) Antique Collect.
— How the Troubles Came to Northern Ireland LC 99-25772. 1999. text 69.95 (*0-312-22434-6*) St Martin.
Rose, Peter & Anderson, John. The Insiders' Guide to Boise & Sun Valley. 2nd ed. (Insiders' Guide Travel Ser.). (Illus.). 328p. 1999. pap. 15.95 (*1-57380-134-8*, The Insiders Guide) Falcon Pub Inc.
Rose, Peter, jt. auth. see Anderson, John G.
Rose, Peter, jt. auth. see Oakley, Robin.
***Rose, Peter G.** Foods of the Hudson. 2000. pap. 16.95 (*1-58567-095-2*, Pub. by Overlook Pr) Penguin Putnam.
Rose, Peter G. Foods of the Hudson: A Seasonal Sampling of the Region's Bounty. LC 92-35040. 272p. 1993. 22.95 (*0-87951-489-2*, Pub. by Overlook Pr) Penguin Putnam.
— The Sensible Cook: Dutch Foodways in the Old & the New World. LC 89-33457. (Illus.). 160p. 1989. 34.95 (*0-8156-0241-3*) Syracuse U Pr.
Rose, Peter G., ed. The Sensible Cook: Dutch Foodways in the Old & the New World. (Illus.). 162p. 1998. pap. 19.95 (*0-8156-0503-X*) Syracuse U Pr.
Rose, Peter I. Group Status in America. (Task Force on the Eighties Ser.). 30p. 1981. pap. 2.50 (*0-87495-039-2*) Am Jewish Comm.
— Mainstream & Margins: Jews, Blacks, & Other Americans. LC 83-4693. 241p. 1983. 39.95 (*0-87855-473-4*) Transaction Pubs.
— Strangers in Their Midst: Small-Town Jews & Their Neighbors. 1977. lib. bdg. 12.95 (*0-915172-32-1*) Richwood Pub.
— Tempest-Tost: Race, Immigration & the Dilemmas of Diversity. LC 96-38822. 272p. 1997. 30.00 (*0-19-510070-0*) OUP.
— They & We: Racial & Ethnic Relations in the United States. 4th ed. (C). 1990. text 21.00 (*0-07-053640-6*) McGraw.
— They & We: Racial & Ethnic Relations in the United States. 5th ed. LC 96-24404. 1996. write for info. (*0-07-053971-5*) McGraw.
— They & We: Racial & Ethnic Relations in the United States. 5th ed. LC 96-24404. 284p. (C). 1996. pap. 25.94 (*0-07-053970-7*) McGraw.
Rose, Peter I. & Kahn, Roger. Pete Rose: My Story. 288p. 1989. text 18.95 (*0-02-560611-5*) Macmillan.
Rose, Peter I., et al. Sociology: Understanding Society. (gr. 11-12). 1978. text 24.88 (*0-13-821322-4*) P-H.
Rose, Peter Q. The Gardener's Guide to Growing Ivies. LC 96-19065. (Gardener's Guide Ser.). (Illus.). 160p. 1996. 29.95 (*0-88192-364-8*) Timber.
Rose, Peter R., ed. Guiding Your Career As a Professional Geologist. iv, 78p. 1994. pap. 5.00 (*0-89181-818-9*, 432) AAPG.
Rose, Peter S. Banking Across State Lines: Public & Private Consequences. LC 96-46085. 192p. 1997. 59.95 (*1-56720-007-9*, Quorum Bks) Greenwood.
— The Changing Structure of American Banking: Competition, Concentration, & Performance. LC 86-18843. (Columbia Studies in Business, Government & Society). 392p. 1987. text 81.00 (*0-231-05980-9*) Col U Pr.
— Commercial Bank Management. 3rd ed. LC 95-23214. 832p. (C). 1995. text 71.75 (*0-256-14476-1*, Irwn Prfssnl) McGraw-Hill Prof.
— Commercial Bank Management. 4th ed. LC 98-16998. (Irwin Series in Finance). 840p. 1998. 88.44 (*0-256-15211-X*) McGraw.
— The Interstate Banking Revolution: Benefits, Risks, & Tradeoffs for Bankers & Consumers. LC 89-10476. 244p. 1989. 62.95 (*0-89930-438-9*, REC/, Greenwood Pr) Greenwood.
— Japanese Banking & Investment in the United States: An Assessment of Their Impact upon U. S. Markets & Institutions. LC 91-2275. 224p. 1991. 62.95 (*0-89930-622-5*, RJB, Quorum Bks) Greenwood.
— Money & Capital Markets. 5th ed. LC 93-30804. (Series in Finance). 864p. (C). 1993. text 71.75 (*0-256-12199-0*, Irwn McGrw-H) McGrw-H Hghr Educ.
— Money & Capital Markets. 5th ed. (C). 1996. text 72.58 (*0-256-18570-0*, Irwn McGrw-H) McGrw-H Hghr Educ.
— Money & Capital Markets. 6th ed. LC 96-8515. 800p. (C). 1996. text 71.75 (*0-256-15239-X*, Irwn McGrw-H) McGrw-H Hghr Educ.
***Rose, Peter S.** Money & Capital Markets: Financial Institutions & Instruments in a Global Marketplace. 7th ed. LC 99-27993. (Illus.). 2000. write for info. (*0-07-116980-6*, Irwn Prfssnl) McGraw-Hill Prof.
Rose, Peter S. Money & Capital Markets: The Financial System in an Increasingly Global Economy. 4th ed. 380p. (C). 1991. text 66.95 (*0-256-08300-2*, Irwn McGrw-H) McGrw-H Hghr Educ.
— Readings on Financial Institutions & Markets: 1995-1996 Edition. 8th ed. 304p. (C). 1995. text 22.85 (*0-256-14530-X*, Irwn McGrw-H) McGrw-H Hghr Educ.
Rose, Peter W. Sons of the Gods, Children of Earth: Ideology & Literary Form in Ancient Greece. LC 91-31562. 432p. 1992. 49.95 (*0-8014-2425-9*); pap. text 18.95 (*0-8014-9983-6*) Cornell U Pr.
Rose, Peter W. & Lucassen, Anneke. Practical Genetics for Primary Care. LC 99-35034. (Oxford General Practice Ser.: 45). (Illus.). 384p. 1999. pap. text 65.00 (*0-19-262931-X*) OUP.
***Rose, Phil.** Which One's Pink? (Illus.). 2000. pap. 9.95 (*1-896522-17-3*) CN06.
Rose, Philip M. The Italians in America. LC 74-17946. (Italian American Experience Ser.). (Illus.). 168p. 1975. reprint ed. 15.95 (*0-405-06416-0*) Ayer.
Rose, Phyllis. The Norton Book of Womens' Lives. 832p. 1995. pap. 18.95 (*0-393-31290-9*, Norton Paperbks) Norton.
— Parallel Lives: Five Victorian Marriages. LC 84-40026. 336p. 1984. pap. 12.00 (*0-394-72580-8*) Vin Bks.
— Woman of Letters: A Life of Virginia Woolf. (Illus.). 320p. 1987. pap. 8.95 (*0-15-698190-4*, Harvest Bks) Harcourt.

R

— The Year of Reading Proust: A Memoir in Real Time. LC 97-17700. 268p. 1997. 22.50 (*0-684-83984-9*) S&S Trade.

***Rose, Phyllis.** Year of Reading Proust: A Memoir in Real Time. LC 99-45920. 272p. 1999. pap. text 15.00 (*1-58243-055-1*, Pub. by Counterpt DC) HarpC.

Rose, Phyllis, ed. The Norton Book of Women's Lives. LC 92-40015. 1993. 30.00 (*0-393-03532-8*) Norton.

Rose Publishing Staff. Creation & Evolution Pamphlet. (Illus.). 20p. pap. 3.95 (*1-890947-01-6*, 409X, Pub. by Rose Publshg) Riverside-World.

— The Trinity Pamphlet: Trinity. (Illus.). 20p. pap. 3.95 (*1-890947-02-4*, 410X, Pub. by Rose Publshg) Riverside-World.

Rose, R., et al. The Banks & Their Competitors. (C). 1989. 40.00 (*0-85297-057-9*, Pub. by Chartered Bank) St Mut.

Rose, R. B. Tribes & Amazons: Men & Women of Revolutionary France, 1789-1871. Hill, Diana, ed. (Illus.). 383p. 1998. 24.95 (*1-876492-00-7*) Macleay Pr.

Rose, R. S. Beyond the Pale of Pity: Key Episodes of Elite Violence in Brazil to 1930. LC 98-15185. (Illus.). 336p. 1998. 75.00 (*1-57292-123-4*); pap. 55.00 (*1-57292-122-6*) Austin & Winfield.

***Rose, R. S.** One of the Forgotten Things: Getulio Vargas & Brazilian Social Control, 1930-1954. LC 99-88457. (Contributions in Latin American Studies: Vol. 15). 272p. 2000. 59.95 (*0-313-31358-X*, GM1358, Greenwood Pr) Greenwood.

Rose Ramirez, Michael. Live from Cedar Hills!, 4. (Chana! Ser.). (J). 1998. 9.09 (*0-606-13263-5*, Pub. by Turtleback) Demco.

Rose, Randall T., jt. auth. see Freeman, Paul B.

Rose, Ray. Bulldust & Ballads: Stories in Verse. (Illus.). 137p. 1996. pap. 19.95 (*1-875902-07-4*, Pub. by Central Queensland) Accents Pubns.

Rose, Redland. Greenlings. LC 98-140111. (Pseudonymous Ser.). 192p. 1998. 21.00 (*0-915090-19-8*) Firefall.

Rose, Reginald. Dear Friends. 1968. pap. 5.25 (*0-8222-0287-5*) Dramatists Play.

Rose, Reginald. The Death & Life of Larry Benson. 61p. 1988. pap. 5.50 (*0-87129-843-0*, 012) Dramatic Pub.

Rose, Reginald. Dino. 71p. 1956. pap. 5.50 (*0-87129-656-X*, D16) Dramatic Pub.

— The Remarkable Incident at Carson Corners. 71p. 1955. pap. 5.50 (*0-87129-704-3*, R13) Dramatic Pub.

— Thunder on Sycamore Street. 1986. pap. 5.00 (*0-87129-325-0*, T27) Dramatic Pub.

— Twelve Angry Men. rev. ed. 1983. 5.95 (*0-87129-327-7*, T42) Dramatic Pub.

— Twelve Angry Men: A Screen Adaptation, Directed by Sidney Lumet. Garrett, George P. et al, eds. LC 71-135273. (Film Scripts Ser.). 1989. reprint ed. pap. text 19.95 (*0-89197-970-0*) Irvington.

— Twelve Angry Women. rev. ed. 1983. 5.95 (*0-87129-401-X*, T43) Dramatic Pub.

Rose, Reuben J. & Hodgson, David R. Manual of Equine Practice. LC 92-21745. (Illus.). 544p. 1992. pap. text 72.00 (*0-7216-3739-6*, W B Saunders Co) Harcrt Hlth Sci Grp.

— Manual of Equine Practice. 2nd ed. Donley, Stephanie, ed. LC 98-28631. 750p. 1999. text. write for info. (*0-7216-8665-6*, W B Saunders Co) Harcrt Hlth Sci Grp.

Rose, Reuben J., jt. auth. see Hodgson, David R.

Rose, Richard. The Albigen Papers. rev. ed. LC 75-2784. 240p. 1978. reprint ed. pap. 10.00 (*1-878683-00-4*) TAT Found.

— The Albigen Papers. 3rd rev. ed. LC 75-2784. 240p. 1978. reprint ed. 14.00 (*1-878683-07-1*) TAT Found.

— AppleWorks User's Handbook. 288p. 1986. pap. 15.95 (*0-938862-78-2*) Weber Systems.

— Carillon: Poems, Essays & Philosophy of Richard Rose. (Illus.). 147p. (Orig.). 1982. pap. 8.00 (*1-878683-03-9*) TAT Found.

— The Direct-Mind Experience. (Illus.). 316p. (Orig.). 1985. pap. 10.00 (*1-878683-01-2*) TAT Found.

— The Direct-Mind Experience. LC 85-211272. (Illus.). 316p. (Orig.). 1985. 14.00 (*1-878683-08-X*) TAT Found.

— Do Parties Make a Difference? 2nd ed. LC 84-9560. (Chatham House Series on Change in American Politics). 238p. reprint ed. pap. 73.80 (*0-8357-3452-8*, 203971300013) Bks Demand.

— Energy Transmutation, Between-Ness & Transmission. 2nd rev. ed. 68p. 1985. reprint ed. pap. 7.00 (*1-878683-02-0*) TAT Found.

***Rose, Richard.** International Encyclopedia of Elections. LC 99-56836. 500p. 2000. 195.00 (*1-56802-415-0*) CQ Pr.

Rose, Richard. Lesson-Drawing in Public Policy: A Guide to Learning Across Time & Space. LC 92-36205. 192p. (C). 1993. pap. text 21.95 (*0-934540-32-2*, Chatham House Pub) Seven Bridges.

— Ministers & Ministries: A Functional Analysis. LC 86-23739. (Illus.). 296p. 1987. text 65.00 (*0-19-827486-6*) OUP.

— Northern Ireland: Time of Choice. LC 76-10080. (Foreign Affairs Study Ser.: No. 33). (Illus.). 185p. reprint ed. pap. 57.40 (*0-8357-4515-5*, 203737300008) Bks Demand.

— Northern Ireland Loyalty Study, 1968. LC 75-32210. 1975. write for info. (*0-89138-116-3*) ICPSR.

— Ordinary People in Public Policy: A Behavioural Analysis. 208p. (C). 1989. text 45.00 (*0-8039-8135-X*); pap. text 17.95 (*0-8039-8136-8*) Sage.

— Politics in England: Change & Persistence (Scott Foresman/Little Brown Series in Political Science) 5th ed. (C). 1989. text 38.44 (*0-673-39892-7*) Addson-Wesley Educ.

— The Postmodern President: George Bush Meets the World. 2nd ed. LC 91-12614. 408p. (C). 1991. pap. text 24.95 (*0-934540-94-2*, Chatham House Pub) Seven Bridges.

— Psychology of the Observer. (Illus.). 92p. 1979. pap. 7.00 (*1-878683-06-3*) TAT Found.

— The Territorial Dimension in Government: Understanding the United Kingdom. LC 82-9680. 240p. reprint ed. pap. 74.40 (*0-8357-4827-8*, 203776400009) Bks Demand.

— Understanding Big Government: The Programme Approach. LC 83-51198. iii, 261p. 1984. 39.95 (*0-8039-9778-7*); pap. 16.95 (*0-8039-9779-5*) Sage.

— What Europe. 530p. (C). 1997. pap. text 56.00 (*0-673-98087-1*) Addson-Wesley Educ.

Rose, Richard & Davies, Phillip L. Inheritance in Public Policy: Change Without Choice in Britain. LC 93-49088. 256p. 1994. 35.00 (*0-300-05877-2*) Yale U Pr.

Rose, Richard & McAllister, Ian. The Loyalties of Voters: A Lifetime Learning Model. 256p. (C). 1990. text 45.00 (*0-8039-8274-7*); pap. text 19.95 (*0-8039-8275-5*) Sage.

— United Kingdom Facts. LC 85-672794. x, 168p. 1982. write for info. (*0-333-25341-8*) Macmillan.

— Voters Begin to Choose: From Closed-Class to Open Elections in Britain. 192p. (Orig.). 1986. text 45.00 (*0-8039-9743-4*); pap. text 17.50 (*0-8039-9744-2*) Sage.

Rose, Richard, et al. Democracy & Its Alternatives: Understanding Post-Communist Societies. LC 98-20989. 272p. 1998. 49.00 (*0-8018-6037-7*); pap. 16.95 (*0-8018-6038-5*) Johns Hopkins.

Rose, Richard, jt. ed. see Gwyn, William B.

Rose, Richard C. & Garrett, Echo M. How to Make a Buck & Still Be a Decent Human Being: A Week in the Life of Dataflex. LC 92-52611. 288p. 1992. 20.00 (*0-88730-584-9*, HarpBusn) HarpInfo.

Rose, Robert, compiled by. Beef, Pork & Lamb: Robert Rose's Favorites. (Illus.). 96p. (Orig.). 1999. pap. 7.95 (*0-7788-0007-5*, Pub. by R Rose Inc) Firefly Bks Ltd.

— Casseroles & Stir-Fries: Robert Rose's Favorite. (Illus.). 96p. (Orig.). 1999. pap. 7.95 (*0-7788-0009-1*, Pub. by R Rose Inc) Firefly Bks Ltd.

***Rose, Robert, compiled by.** Favorite Light Cooking. (Illus.). 96p. 1999. pap. 7.95 (*0-7788-0016-4*) Firefly Bks Ltd.

Rose, Robert, compiled by. Meals in Minutes: Robert Rose's Favorites. (Illus.). 96p. (Orig.). 1999. pap. 7.95 (*0-7788-0008-3*, Pub. by R Rose Inc) Firefly Bks Ltd.

— The Robert Rose Book of Classic Desserts. (Illus.). 192p. (Orig.). 1997. pap. 17.95 (*1-896503-11-X*, Pub. by R Rose Inc) Firefly Bks Ltd.

— The Robert Rose Book of Classic Pasta. (Illus.). 192p. (Orig.). 1997. pap. 17.95 (*1-896503-03-9*, Pub. by R Rose Inc) Firefly Bks Ltd.

— Robert Rose's Favorite Chicken. (Illus.). 96p. 1998. pap. 7.95 (*1-896503-53-5*, Pub. by R Rose Inc) Firefly Bks Ltd.

— Robert Rose's Favorite Cookies, Cakes & Pies. (Illus.). 96p. 1998. pap. 7.95 (*1-896503-71-3*, Pub. by R Rose Inc) Firefly Bks Ltd.

***Rose, Robert, compiled by.** Robert Rose's Favorite Cooking for Kids. (Illus.). 96p. (J). 1999. pap. 7.95 (*0-7788-0015-6*, Pub. by R Rose Inc) Firefly Bks Ltd.

Rose, Robert, compiled by. Robert Rose's Favorite Light Desserts. (Illus.). 96p. 1998. pap. 7.95 (*1-896503-72-1*, Pub. by R Rose Inc) Firefly Bks Ltd.

— Robert Rose's Favorite Meatless Meals. (Illus.). 96p. 1998. pap. 7.95 (*1-896503-67-5*, Pub. by R Rose Inc) Firefly Bks Ltd.

— Robert Rose's Favorite Pasta. (Illus.). 96p. 1998. pap. 7.95 (*1-896503-74-8*, Pub. by R Rose Inc) Firefly Bks Ltd.

— Robert Rose's Favorite Snacks, Salads & Appetizers. (Illus.). 96p. 1998. pap. 7.95 (*1-896503-51-9*, Pub. by R Rose Inc) Firefly Bks Ltd.

— Robert Rose's Favorite Soups & Stews. (Illus.). 96p. 1998. pap. 7.95 (*1-896503-69-1*, Pub. by R Rose Inc) Firefly Bks Ltd.

Rose, Robert & Tilton, Buck. Sex in the Outdoors: A Humorous Approach to Recreation. LC 93-27919. (Illus.). 96p. (Orig.). 1993. pap. 6.95 (*0-934802-86-6*) Globe Pequot.

Rose, Robert, jt. auth. see Bryan, W. S.

Rose, Robert, jt. auth. see Bryan, William S.

Rose, Robert C. The Lonely Eagles. (Illus.). 1976. 20.00 (*0-917612-00-0*) Aviation.

Rose, Robert G. Practical Issues in Employment Testing. LC 93-27798. 156p. 1993. pap. 27.00 (*0-911907-09-2*) Psych Assess.

— Psychological Consultation to Business. LC 94-8302. 195p. 1994. pap. 25.00 (*0-911907-15-7*) Psych Assess.

Rose, Robert M. & Barrett, James E., eds. Alcoholism: Origins & Outcome. LC 87-45365. (American Psychopathological Association Ser.). 314p. 1988. reprint ed. pap. 97.40 (*0-608-04721-X*, 206544200004) Bks Demand.

Rose, Robert M., jt. auth. see Chernyak, Yuri B.

Rose, Robert M., ed. see American Psychopathological Association Staff.

Rose, Robin, et al, eds. Target Seedling Symposium: Proceedings, Combined Meeting of the 1990 Western Forest Nursery Association. (Illus.). 286p. (C). 1998. reprint ed. pap. text 40.00 (*0-7881-7263-8*) DIANE Pub.

Rose, Robin, et al. Propagation of Pacific Northwest Native Plants. LC 97-41008. (Illus.). 256p. 1998. pap. 21.95 (*0-87071-428-7*) Oreg St U Pr.

Rose, Roger G. Reconciling the Past: Two Basketry Ka'ai & the Legendary Liloa & Lonoikamakahiki. (Bishop Museum Bulletin in Anthropology Ser.: No. 5). 1992. pap. 12.95 (*0-930897-76-5*) Bishop Mus.

Rose, Roger G., jt. ed. see Dark, Philip J.

Rose, Ron. Diario de Papa.Tr. of Dad's Diary. (SPA.). 1996. pap. 9.99 (*0-8297-0462-0*) Vida Pubs.

***Rose, Ron, et al.** Hugs for Those in Love: Stories, Sayings, & Scriptures to Encourage & Inspire. (Hugs Ser.). 128p. 2000. 10.99 (*1-58229-097-0*) Howard Pub LA.

Rose, Ronald. Joys of Words. 1996. pap. text 16.95 (*0-86417-686-9*, Pub. by Kangaroo Pr) Seven Hills Bk.

Rose, Ronald E. English Dial Clocks. 2nd ed. (Illus.). 256p. 1988. 69.50 (*1-85149-062-0*) Antique Collect.

Rose, Rose K. Women in the Biological Sciences: A Biobibliographic Sourcebook. Grinstein, Louise S. & Biermann, Carol A., eds. LC 96-43783. 640p. 1997. lib. bdg. 99.50 (*0-313-29180-2*, Greenwood Pr) Greenwood.

***Rose, Ruth.** Norfolk, Virginia. (Black America Ser.). 128p. (YA). 2000. pap. 18.99 (*0-7385-0564-1*) Arcadia Publng.

Rose, Ruth P., jt. auth. see Netherton, Nan.

Rose, S. Gastrointestinal & Hepatobiliary Pathophysiology. (Pathophysiology Ser.). (C). 1997. pap. 24.95 (*1-889325-01-5*) Fence Crk Pubng.

— Lifelines, Vol. 1. 1999. text 25.00 (*0-8050-3538-9*) St Martin.

Rose, S. J., ed. Laser Interaction with Matter: Proceedings of the 23rd European Conference, St. John's College, Oxford, 19-23 Sept. 1994. LC 95-17284. (Institute of Physics Conference Ser.: No. 140). (Illus.). 492p. 1995. 273.00 (*0-7503-0193-7*) IOP Pub.

Rose, S. P. Principles of Poultry Science. LC 96-48884. (CAB International Publication). 145p. 1997. pap. text 25.00 (*0-85199-122-X*) OUP.

Rose, Sally. El Nino! And La Nina. LC 99-31149. (Weather Channel Ser.: No. 6). (Illus.). 63p. (J). (gr. 4-6). 1999. 3.99 (*0-689-82015-1*, Simon Spot) Litle Simon.

***Rose, Sally.** Tornadoes! LC 98-33458. (Weather Channel Ser.: Vol. 4). (Illus.). 64p. (J). (gr. 2-5). 1999. pap. 3.99 (*0-689-82022-4*, 076714003996) S&S Childrens.

Rose, Saul. Britain & South-East Asia. LC 62-18415. (Britain in the World Today Ser.: No. 2). 208p. reprint ed. pap. 64.50 (*0-8357-7407-4*, 200524900051) Bks Demand.

Rose, Scarlett. Baskets Celtic Style. LC 97-32176. 1997. pap. 19.95 (*0-89145-891-3*, 4830, Am Quilters Soc) Collector Bks.

— Celtic Style Floral Applique: Designs Using Interlaced Scrollwork. LC 94-46521. (Illus.). 128p. 1998. 14.95 (*0-89145-841-7*, No. 3926) Collector Bks.

Rose, Seraphim. The Future of Russia & the End of the World. 12p. (Orig.). 1985. pap. 1.00 (*0-912927-16-X*, X016) St John Kronstadt.

— God's Revelation to the Human Heart. (Illus.). 46p. (Orig.). 1997. reprint ed. pap. 5.00 (*0-938635-03-4*) St Herman Pr.

— Little Russian Philokalia Vol. I: St. Seraphim of Sarov. LC 90-64253. (Illus.). 158p. 1990. reprint ed. pap. 10.00 (*0-938635-30-1*) St Herman Pr.

— Little Russian Philokalia Vol. II: Abbot Nazarius of Valaam. (Illus.). 143p. 1983. reprint ed. pap. 10.00 (*0-938635-31-X*) St Herman Pr.

— Orthodoxy & the Religion of the Future. 272p. 1996. pap. 10.00 (*1-887904-00-X*) St Herman Pr.

— The Place of Blessed Augustine in the Orthodox Church. (Illus.). 143p. 1997. pap. 10.00 (*0-938635-12-3*) St Herman Pr.

— The Soul after Death: Contemporary "After-Death" Experiences in the Light of the Orthodox Teaching on the Afterlife. LC 93-85175. 296p. 1998. reprint ed. pap. 9.95 (*0-938635-14-X*) St Herman Pr.

Rose, Seraphim & Herman, Abbot. Blessed John the Wonderworker. 3rd ed. St. Herman of Alaska Brotherhood Staff, ed. LC 86-90658. (Illus.). 480p. 1998. reprint ed. pap. 19.00 (*0-938635-01-8*) St Herman Pr.

Rose, Seraphim & Podmoshensky, Herman, eds. Northern Thebaid: Monastic Saints of the Russian North. 3rd ed. LC 75-18031. (RUS., Illus.). 308p. 1995. pap. 17.00 (*0-938635-37-9*) St Herman Pr.

Rose, Seraphim, tr. see St. Theophan the Recluse.

Rose, Seraphim, tr. see Taushev, Averky.

Rose, Seraphim, tr. & intro. see Andrew of New Diveyevo.

Rose, Seraphim, tr. & intro. see Maximovitch, John.

Rose, Seraphim, tr. & intro. see Platon, Schema-Monk.

Rose, Seraphim, tr. & intro. see St. Symeon the New Theologian.

Rose, Sharon, ed. CDs, Super Glue & Salsa Vol. 6: How Everyday Products Are Made, 2 vols. Incl. Vol. 1. Automobile to Lawn Mower., 2 LC 94-35243. (J). 1994. (*0-8103-9792-7*, UXL); Vol. 2. Light Bulb to Zipper., 2 LC 94-35243. (J). 1994. (*0-8103-9793-5*, UXL); LC 94-35243. 320p. 1994. Set text 49.00 (*0-8103-9791-9*, UXL) Gale.

Rose, Sharon & Stevens, Cris, eds. Bisexual Horizons: Politics, Histories & Lives. 288p. (C). 1996. pap. 18.50 (*0-85315-831-2*, Pub. by Lawrence & Wishart) NYU Pr.

Rose, Sharon, ed. see Edwards, Lynne.

Rose, Sharon, ed. see Martin, Nancy J.

Rose, Sharon, jt. ed. see Nagel, Rob.

Rose, Sharon, ed. see Swain, Gabrielle.

Rose, Sheldon D. Group Therapy with Troubled Youth: A Cognitive Behavioral Interactive Approach. LC 97-33797. 512p. 1998. 36.00 (*0-7619-0927-3*); pap. 16.99 (*0-7619-0928-1*) Sage.

— Treating Children in Groups: A Behavioral Approach. LC 78-189609. (Jossey-Bass Behavioral Science Ser.). 239p. reprint ed. pap. 74.10 (*0-8357-6890-2*, 203794200009) Bks Demand.

Rose, Sheldon D. & Edleson, Jeffrey L. Working with Children & Adolescents in Groups: A Multimethod Approach. LC 86-20181. (Social & Behavioral Science Ser.). 404p. 1987. text 39.95 (*1-55542-009-5*) Jossey-Bass.

Rose, Sheldon D. & Feldman, Ronald A., eds. Research in Social Group Work. LC 86-29526. (Social Work with Groups Ser.: Vol. 9, No. 3). 124p. 1987. text 4.95 (*0-86656-645-7*) Haworth Pr.

Rose, Sheldon D., jt. ed. see Brower, Aaron M.

Rose, Shirley. Let's Discover the Bible, Vol. 1. (Illus.). 64p. (J). (gr. k-2). pap. 4.75 (*0-87441-538-1*) Behrman.

Rose, Shirley K. & Weiser, Irwin H. The Writing Program Administer As Researcher: Inquiry in Reflection & Action. LC 99-28749. 1999. 24.00 (*0-86709-464-8*, Pub. by Boynton Cook Pubs) Heinemann.

Rose, Silver. Women Who Joke Too Much. LC 95-8210. 192p. (Orig.). 1995. pap. 9.00 (*0-399-52154-2*, Perigee Bks) Berkley Pub.

Rose, Sonia O. Limited Livelihoods: Gender & Class in Nineteenth-Century England. (Studies on the History of Society & Culture: No. 13). (Illus.). 320p. 1991. 50.00 (*0-520-07478-5*, Pub. by U CA Pr); pap. 16.95 (*0-520-07479-3*, Pub. by U CA Pr) Cal Prin Full Svc.

Rose, Sonya O., jt. ed. see Frader, Laura L.

Rose, Stephen & Fasenfest, David. Family Incomes in the Nineteen Eighty's. (Working Papers: No. 103). 1988. 10.00 (*0-944826-28-8*) Economic Policy Inst.

Rose, Stephen, jt. auth. see Bluestone, Barry.

Rose, Stephen C., et al. Design Engineering Aspects of Waterflooding. 108p. 1989. 49.00 (*1-55563-016-2*, EORMONO011) Soc Petrol Engineers.

Rose, Stephen J. Social Stratification in the United States: The American Profile Poster. LC 92-18940. 48p. 1992. pap. 14.95 (*1-56584-021-6*, Pub. by New Press NY) Norton.

Rose, Stephen M. The Betrayal of the Poor: The Transformation of Community Action. LC 76-178829. 199p. 1972. pap. text 17.95 (*0-87073-285-4*) Schenkman Bks Inc.

Rose, Steve. Leap of Faith: God Must Be a Packer Fan. (Illus.). 192p. (Orig.). 1996. pap. 12.99 (*0-939995-21-2*) Angel Pr WI.

— Leap of Faith: God Must Be a Packer Fan. (Illus.). 192p. (Orig.). 1996. 25.00 (*0-939995-23-9*) Angel Pr WI.

— Leap of Faith 2: God Loves Packer Fans. LC 97-37794. (Illus.). 224p. 1997. 27.50 (*1-879483-46-7*) Prairie Oak Pr.

— Leap of Faith 2: God Loves Packer Fans. LC 97-37794. Vol. 2. (Illus.). 224p. 1997. pap. 14.95 (*1-879483-47-5*) Prairie Oak Pr.

— Packer Hall of Faith. (Leap of Faith Ser.). 1998. pap. text 14.95 (*0-9666819-0-8*) Winners Success Netwrk.

***Rose, Steve.** Seven Steps from Your Dreams to Your Destiny; Making Your Dreamgoals Happen, 1. 1999. pap. text 16.95 (*0-9666819-1-6*) Winners Success Netwrk.

Rose, Steven. Lifelines: Biology Beyond Determinism. LC 97-29738. (Illus.). 352p. 1997. 30.00 (*0-19-512035-3*) OUP.

***Rose, Steven.** The Making of Memory. 2000. pap. 14.95 (*0-553-40748-1*, Pub. by Transworld Publishers Ltd) Trafalgar.

Rose, Steven. Molecules & Minds: Biology & the Social Order. 160p. 1991. pap. 79.95 (*0-471-93259-0*, Wiley-Liss) Wiley.

— Molecules & Minds: Essays on Biology & the Social Order. 160p. 1991. 260.00 (*0-471-93260-4*, Wiley-Liss) Wiley.

Rose, Steven & Lichtenfels, Alexander. Brainbox. Balkwill, Fran, ed. (Making Sense of Science Ser.). (Illus.). 32p. (J). 1997. pap. 12.00 (*1-85578-096-8*, Pub. by Portland Pr Ltd) Ashgate Pub Co.

Rose, Steven, jt. ed. see Rose, Hilary.

Rose, Steven P. From Brains to Consciousness? Essays on the New Science of the Mind. LC 98-24383. 1999. 29.95 (*0-691-00469-2*, Pub. by Princeton U Pr) Cal Prin Full Svc.

Rose, Steven R. Group Work with Children & Adolescents: Prevention & Intervention in School & Community Systems. LC 98-9035. (Sourcebooks for the Human Services). 200p. 1998. 36.00 (*0-7619-0160-4*); pap. 16.99 (*0-7619-0161-2*) Sage.

Rose, Steven R., jt. auth. see Fatout, Marian F.

Rose, Stewart. Ignatius Loyola & the Early Jesuits. LC 83-45596. reprint ed. 52.00 (*0-404-19889-9*) AMS Pr.

Rose, Stuart R. International Travel Health Guide. 7th ed. 1996. pap. 17.95 (*0-923947-07-8*) Travel Med.

— International Travel Health Guide. 8th ed. 1998. pap. text 19.95 (*0-923947-16-7*) Travel Med.

— International Travel Health Guide. 9th ed. 19.95 (*0-923947-24-8*) Travel Med.

— International Travel Health Guide. 10th ed. 480p. 1999. pap. 19.95 (*0-923947-15-9*) Travel Med.

— International Travel Health Guide, 1995. 6th ed. (Illus.). 454p. 1995. pap. 17.95 (*0-923947-05-1*) Travel Med.

— 1995 International Travel Health Guide. 1994. pap. text 17.95 (*0-923947-06-X*) Travel Med.

Rose, Stuart W. Mandeville: A Guide for the Marketing of Professional Services. 379p. 1995. lthr. 89.00 (*1-887133-00-3*) Prof Dev Res.

Rose, Susan. Me & Effie. 47p. Date not set. pap. 8.95 (*1-879934-09-4*) St Andrews NC.

Rose, Susan D. Keeping Them Out of the Hands of Satan: Evangelical Schooling in America. (Critical Social Thought Ser.). 228p. (C). 1990. pap. 18.99 (*0-415-90299-1*) Routledge.

— Keeping Them Out of the Hands of Satan: Evangelical Schooling in America. (Critical Social Thought Ser.). 224p. 1990. text 35.00 (*0-415-90004-2*) Routledge.

Rose, Susan E. Celestial Inspirations: Channeled Affirmations & Prayers by the "Nameless Ones", St. Therese, Archangel Michael, St. Germain, & Thalius. 48p. 1995. pap. write for info. (*0-9644840-0-5*) Celestial Insp.

Rose, Susanna Van, see Van Rose, Susanna.

Rose, Suzanna & Larwood, Laurie, eds. Women's Careers: Pathways & Pitfalls. LC 88-2344. 234p. 1988. 59.95 (*0-275-92724-5*, C2724, Praeger Pubs) Greenwood.

Rose, T. K. & Newman, W. A. The Metallurgy of Gold. 49.95 (*0-931913-05-5*) Met-Chem Rsch.

Rose, T. L., et al, eds. Proceedings of the Symposium on Water Purification by Photocatalytic, Photoelectrochemical, & Electrochemical Processes. LC 94-70851. (Proceedings Ser.: Vol. 94-19). 384p. 1994. 48.00 (*1-56677-076-9*) Electrochem Soc.

An Asterisk (*) at the beginning of an entry indicates that the title is appearing for the first time.

Rose, Tania. Aspects of Political Censorship, 1914-1918. 104p. 1995. pap. 17.95 (*0-85958-632-4*, Pub. by Univ of Hull Pr) Paul & Co Pubs.

Rose, Tania, jt. auth. see Price, M. Philips.

Rose, Tania, jt. auth. see Price, Philips M.

Rose, Tania, ed. see Price, Morgan P.

Rose, Tania, ed. see Price, Morgan Phillips.

***Rose, Tara, et al.** Essentials of Rorschach Assessment. 256p. 2000. pap. 29.95 (*0-471-33146-5*) Wiley.

Rose, Ted. Discovering Drawing. LC 93-74646. (Illus.). 256p. 1995. 31.70 (*0-87192-281-9*) Davis Mass.

— Discovering Drawing. LC 93-74645. (Illus.). (YA). (gr. 9-12). 1995. text, teacher ed. 39.50 (*0-87192-282-7*) Davis Mass.

***Rose, Ted.** In the Traces: Railroad Paintings of Ted Rose. LC 00-26972. (Railroads Past & Present Ser.). (Illus.). 2000. 49.95 (*0-253-33769-0*) Ind U Pr.

Rose, Terry & Rose, Arthur. The Return of Sherlock Holmes: A Play by J. E. Harold: Acting Edition. 122p. 1997. 10.00 (*0-86025-281-7*, Pub. by I Henry Pubns) Empire Pub Srvs.

Rose, Thomas. Winter Book. limited ed. (Winter Bks.: No. 8). (Illus.). 48p. 1995. 300.00 (*1-879832-10-0*) MN Ctr Book Arts.

— Winter Book. limited ed. (Winter Book Ser.: Vol. 8). (Illus.). 48p. 1995. 900.00 (*1-879832-12-7*); pap. 90.00 (*1-879832-11-9*) MN Ctr Book Arts.

Rose, Thomas, jt. auth. see Ansello, Edward F.

Rose, Thomasine. Verbivocovisual. (Illus.). 72p. (C). 1982. 12.95 (*0-9606540-3-8*) Classic Nonfic.

***Rose, Timothy.** The Interactivity Kit: Exploring the Fine Art of Mobiles. (Illus.). 48p. (J). (gr. 7). 2000. 17.95 (*0-8118-2563-9*) Chronicle Bks.

Rose, Toby, jt. ed. see Payant, Katherine B.

Rose, Tom. Economics: Principles & Policy from a Christian Perspective. rev. ed. 124p. 1992. pap., teacher ed. 8.95 (*0-9612198-6-6*) A E P.

— Economics: Principles & Policy from a Christian Perspective. 2nd ed. LC 85-72235. (Illus.). 380p. (C). 1996. text 22.95 (*0-9612198-5-8*) A E P.

— Economics: The American Economy from a Christian Perspective. LC 85-72866. 132p. 1985. pap., teacher ed. 8.95 (*0-9612198-1-5*) A E P.

— Economics: The American Economy from a Christian Perspective. LC 83-72165. (Illus.). 388p. (C). 1985. 22.95 (*0-9612198-0-7*) A E P.

— Free Enterprise Economics. 2nd ed. LC 88-70057. 20p. (C). 1992. pap. 2.00 (*0-9612198-7-4*) A E P.

— Freeing the Whales: How the Media Created the World's Greatest Non-Event. Black, Hillel, ed. (Illus.). 252p. 1989. 16.95 (*1-55972-011-5*, Birch Ln Pr) Carol Pub Group.

— How to Succeed in Business. LC 74-33827. (Illus.). 88p. (C). 1975. 4.95 (*0-9612198-2-3*); pap. 1.95 (*0-9612198-3-1*) A E P.

— Reclaiming the American Dream by Reconstructing the American Republic. LC 96-84287. 44p. (Orig.). (C). 1996. pap. 6.95 (*0-9612198-8-2*) A E P.

— When the Union Organizer Knocks. (Illus.). 150p. (C). 1972. pap. 6.95 (*0-9612198-4-X*) A E P.

Rose, Tony, ed. see Fornay, Alfred.

Rose, Tony, ed. see Harris-Johnson, Debrah.

Rose, Tony, ed. see Howard, Florence.

Rose Township Historical Society Staff. Rose Township, 1837-1987. Trimmer, Betty, ed. LC 86-63912. (Illus.). 141p. 1987. 15.00 (*0-9617648-0-5*) Rose Twsp Hist Soc.

Rose, Tricia, jt. ed. see Ross, Andrew.

Rose-Troup, Frances. The Massachusetts Bay Company & Its Predecessors. LC 98-157379. 176p. 1998. reprint ed. pap. 18.50 (*0-7884-0867-4*, R574) Heritage Bk.

— The Massachusetts Bay Company & Its Predecessors. LC 73-15804. xi, 176p. 1973. reprint ed. 35.00 (*0-678-00871-X*) Kelley.

Rose, Tui. Dinosaur Dust: Natures Own Bugicide Plus Other Home Uses. Love, Karen, ed. LC 97-179612. (Illus.). 200p. (Orig.). 1997. pap. 9.95 (*1-885735-44-8*) Crown Jewel.

— How to Make a Flea Itch: 501 Less Toxic Petcare Ways for Happy Cats & Dogs. Love, Karen et al, eds. (Illus.). 280p. 1997. pap. write for info. (*1-885735-14-6*) Crown Jewel.

— How to Make a House Hum: 2001 Easy Ways to Take Care of Your Home More Naturally. Love, Karen, ed. (Illus.). 336p. (Orig.). 1997. pap. write for info. (*1-885735-29-4*) Crown Jewel.

— How to Make a Snail Sneeze: 501 Less Toxic Greenthumbs-Up Gardening Successes. Roberts, Jackie et al, eds. LC 97-170830. (Illus.). 176p. (Orig.). 1997. per. write for info. (*1-885735-05-7*) Crown Jewel.

— Money Is Honey: 501 Dollar-Wise Ways to Save Thousands & Prevent Big Losses. Roberts, Jackie & Love, Karen, eds. (Illus.). 272p. 1997. pap. 9.95 (*1-885735-13-8*) Crown Jewel.

Rose-Turner, Clarinda. Ruminations: Poetry, Images & Memories. (Illus.). 30p. (Orig.). 1989. pap. 4.00 (*0-924120-02-9*) Intl Oil Work.

Rose, V. M. The Anti-Representational Response: Gertrude Stein's Lucy Church Amiably. 232p. (Orig.). 1985. pap. text 33.00 (*91-554-1751-5*) Coronet Bks.

Rose, Valentin. Aristoteles Pseudepigraphus. 728p. 1971. reprint ed. write for info. (*0-318-71011-0*) G Olms Pubs.

Rose, Valentin & Schillmann, Fritz. Verzeichnis der Lateinischen Handschriften der Koniglichen Bibliothek Zu Berlin, 5 vols. in 3. l, 2035p. 1976. reprint ed. write for info. (*3-487-06038-8*) G Olms Pubs.

***Rose, Valerie.** Cappuccino in the Winter. 300p. 1999. mass mkt. 6.50 (*1-929613-08-3*) Avid MI.

Rose, Vernon E., jt. ed. see Perkins, Jimmy L.

***Rose, Walter.** Good Neighbours: Recollections of an English Village & Its People. large type unabridged ed. 1999. 25.95 (*0-7531-5092-1*, 150921, Pub. by ISIS Lrg Prnt) ISIS Pub.

Rose, Walter. The Village Carpenter. LC 88-3. (Illus.). 146p. (YA). (gr. 10 up). 1988. reprint ed. pap. 9.95 (*0-941533-18-2*, NAB) I R Dee.

Rose, Wendy. Aboriginal Tattooing in California. (Archaeological Research Facility, Department of Anthropology, UC Berkeley Ser.). (Illus.). 82p. (C). 1979. reprint ed. pap. text 9.38 (*1-55567-600-6*) Coyote Press.

— Bone Dance: New & Selected Poems, 1965-1993. LC 93-21117. (Sun Tracks Ser.: Vol. 27). 108p. (Orig.). (C). 1994. pap. 11.95 (*0-8165-1428-3*); lib. bdg. 21.95 (*0-8165-1412-7*) U of Ariz Pr.

— The Halfbreed Chronicles & Other Poems. (Illus.). 72p. (Orig.). (C). 1985. pap. 8.95 (*0-931122-39-2*) West End.

— Lost Copper. LC 80-81849. 1992. pap. 10.00 (*0-939046-35-0*) Malki Mus Pr.

— Now Poof She Is Gone. LC 94-29772. 104p. (Orig.). 1994. pap. 8.95 (*1-56341-048-6*); lib. bdg. 18.95 (*1-56341-049-4*) Firebrand Bks.

— What Happened When the Hopi Hit New York? (Chapbook Ser.). (Illus.). 56p. (Orig.). (J). 1982. pap. 3.50 (*0-936556-08-0*) Contact Two.

Rose, Will. The Vanishing Village. 350p. 1970. 5.50 (*0-9600350-0-1*) Catskill Art.

Rose, Willi, jt. auth. see McMahan, Dean.

Rose, William. U. S. Unilateral Arms Control Initiatives: When Do They Work?, 82. LC 88-17774. (Contributions in Military Studies Ser.: No. 82). 209p. 1988. 55.00 (*0-313-25787-6*, RUR/, Greenwood Pr) Greenwood.

Rose, William & Isaacs, Jacob, eds. Contemporary Movements in European Literature. (Essay Index Reprint Ser.). 1977. 20.95 (*0-8369-0833-3*) Ayer.

Rose, William, jt. auth. see Garett, Kenneth.

Rose, William, ed. see Rilke, Rainer Maria.

Rose, William, tr. see Bejar-Rivera, Hector.

Rose, William G. Cleveland: The Making of a City (1950) 1950th ed. LC 90-4853. (Black Squirrel Bks.: No. 1). (Illus.). 1286p. 1990. 75.00 (*0-87338-428-8*) Kent St U Pr.

Rose, William J. The Polish Memoirs of William John Rose. Stone, Daniel, ed. LC 74-79986. 274p. 1975. reprint ed. pap. 85.00 (*0-608-08211-2*, 202367300033) Bks Demand.

Rose, William K. Advanced Stellar Astrophysics. (Illus.). 494p. (C). 1998. text 80.00 (*0-521-58188-5*); pap. text 35.95 (*0-521-58833-2*) Cambridge U Pr.

Rose, William M. Pleading Without Tears: A Guide to Legal Drafting. 2nd ed. 316p. (C). 1992. pap. 32.00 (*1-85431-216-2*, Pub. by Blackstone Pr) Gaunt.

— Pleadings Without Tears: A Guide to Legal Drafting. 4th ed. 353p. 1997. pap. 34.00 (*1-85431-639-7*, Pub. by Blackstone Pr) Gaunt.

***Rose, William R.** Pleadings Without Tears: A Guide to Legal Drafting under the Civil Procedure Rules. 5th ed. 1999. pap. 31.00 (*1-85431-890-X*, Pub. by Blackstone Pr) Gaunt.

Rose, Willie L. Rehearsal for Reconstruction: The Port Royal Experiment. LC 98-3851. 1999. pap. 16.95 (*0-8203-2061-7*) U of Ga Pr.

— Rehearsal for Reconstruction: The Port Royal Experiment. 456p. 1976. reprint ed. pap. text 16.95 (*0-19-519882-4*) OUP.

Rose, Willie L., ed. A Documentary History of Slavery in North America. LC 99-25537. 560p. 1999. reprint ed. pap. 25.00 (*0-8203-2065-X*) U of Ga Pr.

***Rose, Wolter H.** Zemah & Zerubbabel: Messianic Expectations in the Early Postexilic Period. (Journal for the Study of the Old Testament Supplement Ser.: No. 304). 326p. 2000. 85.00 (*1-84127-074-1*, Pub. by Sheffield Acad) CUP Services.

Rose, Yvonne, et al. Is Modeling for You? The Handbook & Guide for the Young Aspiring Black Model. LC 97-93317. (Illus.). 272p. (Orig.). 1997. pap. 14.95 (*0-9655064-0-1*) Amber Books.

Rose, Yvonne, ed. see Hughes, Dorothy Pitman.

***Rosean, Lexa.** Easy Enchantments. LC 99-16444. 240p. 1999. text 14.95 (*0-312-24296-4*) St Martin.

— Supermarket Sorceress: Spells, Charms, & Enchantments That You Can Make from Supermarket Ingredients. LC 96-148551. 131p. 1996. mass mkt. 8.99 (*0-312-95768-8*) St Martin.

Rosean, Lexa. The Supermarket Sorceress' Sexy Hexes, Vol. 1. LC BF1572.S4R67 1997. 1997. mass mkt. 8.99 (*0-312-96328-9*) St Martin.

— The Supermarket Sorceress's Enchanted Evenings. 144p. 1998. mass mkt. 9.99 (*0-312-96673-3*) St Martin.

Roseau, M. Vibrations in Mechanical Systems. (Illus.). 530p. 1987. 129.00 (*0-387-17950-X*) Spr-Verlag.

Rosebault, Charles J. When Dana Was the Sun. LC 77-103657. (Select Bibliographies Reprint Ser.). 1977. 30.95 (*0-8369-5157-3*) Ayer.

— When Dana Was the Sun: A Story of Personal Journalism. 1970. reprint ed. lib. bdg. 75.00 (*0-8371-4009-9*, RODS, Greenwood Pr) Greenwood.

Rosebaum, Robert A., ed. see Neumann, Inge S.

Rosebberg, Janet, ed. see Landis, Carney & Bolles, M. Marjorie.

Roseberry, C. R. Flashback: A Fresh Look at Albany's Past. Dumbleton, Susanne, ed. (Illus.). 208p. (Orig.). 1986. 10.00 (*0-9605460-5-7*); pap. 7.50 (*0-9605460-4-9*) Wash Park.

— Glenn Curtiss: Pioneer of Flight. (Illus.). 526p. (Orig.). 1991. reprint ed. pap. 18.95 (*0-8156-0264-2*) Syracuse U Pr.

Roseberry, Eric. Shostakovich. (Illustrated Lives of the Great Composers Ser.). (Illus.). 192p. 1996. 17.95 (*0-7119-0258-5*, OP 42449) Omnibus NY.

Roseberry, John. Self-Development Through Self-Defense: A Course in Personal Security. (Illus.). 58p. (Orig.). 1994. pap., student ed. 19.95 (*0-9639936-0-7*) J Samuel Pubng.

Roseberry, John L. & Klimstra, Willard D. Population Ecology of the Bobwhite. LC 83-2481. (Illus.). 282p. 1984. 31.95 (*0-8093-1116-X*) S Ill U Pr.

***Roseberry-McKibbin, Celeste & Hegde, M. N.** An Advanced Review of Speech-language Pathology: Freparation for NESPA & Comprehensive Examination. LC 99-24479. 1999. write for info. (*0-89079-821-4*) PRO-ED.

***Roseberry-McKibbin, Celeste & Hegde, M. N.** Preventing school dropouts: Comprehensive Preparation for Students & Practitioners. 2nd ed. LC 99-24479. 1999. write for info. (*0-89079-824-9*) PRO-ED.

Roseberry, Robert & Weinstock, Rachel. Reading Etc. An Integrated Skills Text. 304p. (C). 1991. pap. text 34.00 (*0-13-763467-6*, 640806) P-H.

Roseberry, Robert L., jt. auth. see Chimombo, Moira.

Roseberry, William. Anthropologies & Histories: Essays in Culture, History, & Political Economy. LC 89-30378. 255p. (C). 1989. text 38.00 (*0-8135-1445-2*); pap. text 17.00 (*0-8135-1446-0*) Rutgers U Pr.

Roseberry, William, et al, eds. Coffee, Society, & Power in Latin America. LC 94-14193. (Johns Hopkins Studies in Atlantic History & Culture Ser.). 304p. 1995. text 49.55 (*0-8018-4884-9*) Johns Hopkins.

Rosebery, Ann S. & Warren, Beth. Boats, Balloons & Classroom Video: Science Teaching as Inquiry. LC 97-47087. 1998. pap. 21.00 incl. VHS (*0-325-00033-6*) Heinemann.

— Boats, Balloons & Classroom Video: Science Teaching as Inquiry. LC 99-26130. 1999. pap. text 23.00 (*0-325-00001-8*) Heinemann.

Rosebery, Ann S., jt. ed. see Warren, Beth.

Rosebery, Archibald P. Miscellanies: Literary & Historical, 2 vols. LC 71-152211. (Essay Index Reprint Ser.). 1977. reprint ed. 47.95 (*0-8369-2253-0*) Ayer.

— Pitt. LC 78-106521. reprint ed. 34.00 (*0-404-05405-6*) AMS Pr.

— Pitt. LC 68-25264. (English Biography Ser.: No. 31). 1969. reprint ed. lib. bdg. 75.00 (*0-8383-0236-X*) M S G Haskell Hse.

Rosebery, Glenita. Against Great Odds: Love Found a Way. (Orig.). 1995. pap. 10.00 (*0-7880-0609-6*, Fairway Pr) CSS OH.

Roseblade, James E., jt. ed. see Gruenberg, Karl W.

Roseblade, James E., ed. see Hall, Philip.

Roseblum, Richard. Stars & Stripes & Soldiers. 32p. (J). (ps-3). 1993. pap. 3.95 (*0-590-45222-3*) Scholastic Inc.

Roseboom & Weisenburger Staff. A History of Ohio. pap. 14.99 (*0-318-42416-9*) Ohio Hist Soc.

Roseboom, Catharine, et al. Roseboom, 1630-1897, Brief History of the Ancestors & Descendants of John Roseboom (1739-1805) & Jess Johnson (1745-1832) (Illus.). 140p. 1997. reprint ed. pap. 21.00 (*0-8328-9499-0*); reprint ed. lib. bdg. 31.00 (*0-8328-9498-2*) Higginson Bk Co.

Roseboom, Eugene H. History of Ohio. 1993. reprint ed. lib. bdg. 89.00 (*0-7812-5398-5*) Rprt Serv.

Roseboom, Eugene Holloway. History of Presidential Elections. 1985. 17.95 (*0-02-604890-6*) Macmillan.

Roseboom, Johannes, jt. ed. see Pardey, Philip G.

Roseboro, Viola. Players & Vagabonds. LC 70-101291. (Short Story Index Reprint Ser.). 1977. 21.95 (*0-8369-3228-5*) Ayer.

Roseborough, Margaret M. Outline of Middle English Grammar. LC 70-109833. 112p. 1970. reprint ed. lib. bdg. 35.00 (*0-8371-4324-1*, ROMI, Greenwood Pr) Greenwood.

Rosebrock, Ellen F. Counting-House Days in South Street: New York's Early Brick Seaport Buildings. (Illus.). (Orig.). 1975. pap. 2.50 (*0-913344-18-4*) South St Sea Mus.

— Farewell to Old England, New York in Revolution. LC 75-3941. (Illus.). 64p. (Orig.). 1976. pap. 1.95 (*0-913344-21-4*) South St Sea Mus.

— Walking Around in South Street: Discoveries in New York's Old Shipping District. (Illus.). (Orig.). 1974. pap. 3.95 (*0-913344-17-6*) South St Sea Mus.

***Rosebrook, Don.** American Level Patents Illustrated & Explained. (Illus.). 251p. 2000. pap. 24.95 (*1-879335-92-1*) Astragal Pr.

— American Levels & Their Makers Vol. I: New England. (Illus.). 3.8p. 1999. 65.00 (*1-879335-90-5*) Astragal Pr.

Rosebrough, Robert F. Climbing Colorado's San Juan Mountains. LC 98-49960. (Guide Ser.). (Illus.). 258p. 1999. pap 14.95 (*1-56044-870-9*) Falcon Pub Inc.

Rosebury, Brian. Tolkein: A Critical Assessment. LC 91-33345. 176p. 1992. text 49.95 (*0-312-07583-9*) St Martin.

Rosebury, Fred. Handbook of Electron Tube & Vacuum Techniques. LC 92-46418. (AVS Classics of Vacuum Science & Technology Ser.). 1993. write for info. (*1-56396-121-0*) Am Inst Physics.

— Symbols: Myth, Magic, Fact, & Fancy. LC 74-22888. (Illus.). 411p. 1974. reprint ed. pap. 127.50 (*0-608-08412-3*, AU0035800078) Bks Demand.

***Rosebush, Beatrice.** What Would I Do if I Met a Moose? (Illus.). 24p. 1999. pap. 8.00 (*0-9678193-0-X*) Ebeemee Pubs.

Rosebush, Judson. Computer-Generated Animation. 1991. text. write for info. (*0-442-20526-0*, VNR) Wiley.

— Electronic Publishing on CD-ROM. LC 96-211729. 412p. 1996. pap. 26.95 (*1-56592-209-3*) Thomson Learn.

Rosebush, Judson, jt. auth. see Kerlow, Isaac V.

Rosebush, Waldo E. American Firearms & the Changing Frontier. 1962. pap. 4.50 (*0-910524-01-7*) Eastern Wash.

Roseby, jt. auth. see Johnston.

Roseby, Vivienne, jt. auth. see Johnston, Janet.

Rosecan, Jeffrey S., jt. ed. see Spitz, Henry I.

***Rosecrance.** Rise of the Virtual State. 260p. 2000. pap. 15.00 (*0-465-07142-2*, Pub. by Basic) HarpC.

Rosecrance, Richard. Cooperation in a World Without Enemies: Solving the Public Goods Problem in International Relations. (New Ser.: No. 2). 54p. 1992. pap. 15.00 (*0-86682-092-2*) Ctr Intl Relations.

***Rosecrance, Richard.** The International Political Implications of the Euro. (New Ser.: Vol. 23). 13p. 1999. pap. 15.00 (*0-86682-109-0*) Ctr Intl Relations.

Rosecrance, Richard. The Rise of the Virtual State: Wealth & Power in the Coming Century. LC 99-46146. 256p. 1999. 26.00 (*0-465-07141-4*, Pub. by Basic) HarpC.

Rosecrance, Richard & Stein, Arthur A., eds. The Domestic Bases of Grand Strategy. LC 93-15396. (Cornell Studies in Security Affairs). 256p. 1993. text 39.95 (*0-8014-2880-7*); pap. text 15.95 (*0-8014-8116-3*) Cornell U Pr.

Rosecrance, Richard N. Action & Reaction in World Politics: International Systems in Perspective. LC 77-2329. 314p. 1977. reprint ed. lib. bdg. 35.00 (*0-8371-9548-9*, ROAR, Greenwood Pr) Greenwood.

Rosecrance, Richard N., jt. ed. see Brown, Michael E.

Rosedale, Herbert L., jt. ed. see Giambalvo, Carol.

Rosee, Severine, tr. see Schnapper, Dominique.

Roseen, Jane. InfoMaker 5: A Guide to Developing Client/Server Applications. LC 97-1554. (Client/Server Computing Ser.). (Illus.). 416p. 1997. pap. 44.95 (*0-07-053999-5*) McGraw.

Roseen, Sven, tr. see Schwarze, William N., et al.

Rosefeld, Stuart. Vocational Education & Economic Growth: Connections & Conundrums. 22p. 1986. 3.00 (*0-318-22232-9*, OC 112) Ctr Educ Trng Employ.

Rosefeldt, Paul. The Absent Father in Modern Drama. 2nd ed. (American University Studies III: Vol. 54). 162p. (C). 1996. pap. text 24.95 (*0-8204-3709-3*) P Lang Pubng.

Rosefielde, Steven. False Science: Underestimating the Soviet Arms Buildup. 2nd rev. ed. 452p. 1987. 49.95 (*0-88738-088-3*) Transaction Pubs.

Rosefielde, Steven, ed. Efficiency & Russia's Recovery Potential to the Year 2000 & Beyond. LC 98-20664. 362p. 1998. text 72.95 (*1-84014-411-4*, HC340.12.Z9I524, Pub. by Ashgate Pub) Ashgate Pub Co.

— World Communism at the Crossroads: Military Ascendancy, Political Economy & Human Welfare. 1980. lib. bdg. 73.50 (*0-89838-041-3*) Kluwer Academic.

***Rosefsky.** Personal Finance. 7th ed. 751p. (C). 1998. text. write for info. (*0-471-33064-7*) Wiley.

— Personal Finance. 7th ed. 1999. text 63.00 (*0-471-37375-3*) Wiley.

— Personal Finance: Study Guide. 7th ed. 162p. 1998. pap., student ed. 33.95 (*0-471-29954-5*) Wiley.

Rosefsky. Personal Finance Telecourse Study System Set. 6th ed. 354p. 1995. pap. text 22.00 (*0-471-13143-1*) Wiley.

Rosefsky, Robert S. Personal Finance. 7th ed. LC 98-5649. 736p. 1998. text 95.95 (*0-471-23822-8*) Wiley.

— Personal Finance Telecourse Viewers Guide: Textbook & Study Guide. 6th ed. 1152p. 1996. pap. 113.85 (*0-471-16909-9*) Wiley.

Rosegg, Peter, jt. auth. see McCutcheon, Susan.

Rosegger, Gerhard. The Economics of Production & Innovation. 3rd ed. LC 96-111503. 313p. 1995. pap. text 56.95 (*0-7506-2433-7*) Buttrwrth-Heinemann.

— The Economics of Production & Innovation: An Industrial Perspective. (Illus.). 1980. pap. text 17.00 (*0-08-024046-1*, Pergamon Pr) Elsevier.

Rosegrant, Mark A., ed. see Agcaoili-Sombilla, Mercedita.

***Rosegrant, Mark W. & Hazell, Peter B. R.** Transforming the Rural Economy in Asia: The Unfinished Revolution. (A Study of Rural Asia: Vol. 1). 496p. 2000. pap. 35.00 (*0-19-592448-7*); text 65.00 (*0-19-592447-9*) OUP.

Rosegrant, Mark W., jt. auth. see Mendoza, Meyra S.

Rosegrant, Teresa, jt. auth. see Bredekamp, Sue.

Rosegrant, Teresa, jt. ed. see Bredekamp, Sue.

Rosehope, Cara. The Forever Garden: Creating an Easy-Care Garden. (Illus.). 224p. (Orig.). 1997. pap. 19.95 (*1-875657-70-3*, Pub. by Hyland Hse) Seven Hills Bk.

Rosei, Peter. From Here to There. Thorpe, Kathleen E., tr. & afterword by by. (Studies in Austrian Literature, Culture, & Thought. Translation Ser.). 94p. 1991. pap. 10.50 (*0-929497-43-0*) Ariadne CA.

— Try Your Luck. Thorpe, Kathleen E., tr. from GER. & afterword by by. LC 93-25580. (Studies in Austrian Literature, Culture, & Thought. Translation Ser.).Tr. of Schnelle Gluck. 1994. pap. 10.50 (*0-929497-76-7*) Ariadne CA.

Roseire, Gabrielle. Fortune Telling & Character Reading. 1996. reprint ed. spiral bd. 16.50 (*0-7873-0737-8*) Hlth Research.

Rosekrans, Spreck, jt. auth. see Rasmussen, Steven.

Rosekraus, Spreck, jt. auth. see Rasmussen, Steven.

Rosel, Hartmut N. Israel in Kanaan: Zum Problem der Entsehung Israels. (Beitrage zur Erforschung des Alten Testaments & Antiken Judentums Ser.: Bd. 11). (GER.). 150p. 1992. 36.80 (*3-631-43456-1*) P Lang Pubng.

***Rosel, Hartmut N.** Von Josua Bis Jojachin: Untersuchungen Zu Den Deuteronomistischen Geschichtsbuchern des Alten Testaments. 144p. 1999. 65.00 (*90-04-11352-5*) Brill Academic Pubs.

Rosel, Manfred. Das Ist ein Weites Feld: Wahrheit und Weisheit Einer Fontaneschen Sentenz Mit Einem Vorwort von Helmuth Nurnberger. (GER.). 152p. 1997. 35.95 (*3-631-31954-1*) P Lang Pubng.

Roselaar, Cees S., jt. auth. see Engelmoer, Meinte.

An Asterisk (*) at the beginning of an entry indicates that the title is appearing for the first time.

R

Roseland, Mark. Toward Sustainable Communities: Resources for Citizens & Their Governments. LC 99-182084. (Illus.). 256p. 1997. pap. 19.95 (*0-86571-374-X*) New Soc Pubs.

Roseland, Mark, ed. Eco-City Dimensions: Healthy Communities, Healthy Planet. LC 97-199979. (Illus.). 224p. (Orig.). 1996. pap. 16.95 (*0-86571-353-7*) New Soc Pubs.

Roseler, Robert O., ed. see Von Le Fort, Gertrud F.

Roseliep, Raymond. Love Makes the Air Light. (Orig.). 1965. pap. 1.95 (*0-393-04243-X*) Norton.

Rosell, Steven A. Renewing Governance: Governing By Learning In The Information Age. LC 99-234314. (Illus.). 328p. 1999. pap. text 27.95 (*0-19-541425-X*) OUP.

Rosell, Fred E., Jr. Planet Earth's Secrets Unveiled. (Orig.). 1996. pap. 27.00 (*0-9653323-0-6*) Mstr Prods.

Rosell, Garth, ed. see Barton, William E.

Rosell, Garth M. & Dupuis, Richard A., eds. The Memoirs of Charles G. Finney: The Complete Restored Text. 736p. 1997. pap. 22.99 (*0-310-21925-6*) Zondervan.

Rosell, Garth M., ed. see Moody, Dwight Lyman.

Rosell, Rosendo. Mas Cuentos Picantes de Rosendo Rosell. LC 79-5001. (Coleccion Caniqui). (Illus.). 138p. 1980. pap. 9.95 (*0-89729-219-7*) Ediciones.

— Vida y Milagros de la Farandula de Cuba, Tomo IV. LC 91-72527. (Coleccion Cuba Sus Jueces Ser.). (SPA., Illus.). 430p. 1997. pap. 25.00 (*0-89729-820-9*) Ediciones.

— Vida y Milagros de la Farandula de Cuba, Vol. III. LC 91-72527. (Coleccion Cuba y sus Jueces). (SPA., Illus.). 468p. 1994. pap. 20.00 (*0-89729-754-7*) Ediciones.

— Vida y Milagros de la Farandula de Cuba, Vol. V. (SPA.). Date not set. pap. write for info. (*0-89729-841-1*) Ediciones.

Rosell, Steven A., et al. Governing in an Information Society. 167p. 1992. pap. text 14.95 (*0-88645-147-7*, Pub. by Inst Res Pub) Ashgate Pub Co.

Roselle, Daniel. A Parent's Guide to the Social Studies. 16p. 1974. pap. 1.25 (*0-87986-053-7*, 491-15274) Nat Coun Soc Studies.

— Vignettes from the Little World of Mainton Mall. LC 97-92481. 250p. 1997. 15.00 (*0-9660461-0-2*) D Roselle.

Roselle, Daniel, ed. Voices of Social Education, Nineteen Thirty-Seven to Nineteen Eighty-Seven. 528p. (C). 1987. 34.95 (*0-02-922380-6*) Free Pr.

Roselle, Laura, jt. auth. see Mickiewicz, Ellen Propper.

Roselle, Laurie P. Litigation Techniques for Legal Assistants: Becoming a More Effective Member of the Litigation Team. 476p. 1991. 70.00 (*0-685-69462-3*); VHS 195.00 (*0-685-69463-1*) PLI.

Roselle, William C., jt. auth. see Gabriel, Michael R.

Rosellini, ed. Iuli Valeri. (LAT.). 1993. 59.50 (*3-8154-1369-9*, T1369, Pub. by B G Teubner) U of Mich Pr.

Rosellini, Eleanor F. The Puzzle in the Portrait. LC 99-71651. (Illus.). 115p. (gr. 3-6). 1999. 16.95 (*1-57860-026-X*) Guild Pr IN.

Rosellini, Gayle. Co-Alcoholics: The Partner Paradox. rev. ed. 1999. pap. 0.50 (*0-89230-199-6*) Do It Now.

— Drinking, Drugs & Driving. rev. ed. 2000. pap. 0.50 (*0-89230-149-X*) Do It Now.

— Of Course, You're Angry. 1986. pap. 5.95 (*0-86683-576-8*) Harper SF.

— Sex & Recovery: A Woman's Guide. rev. ed. 1999. pap. 0.50 (*0-89230-150-3*) Do It Now.

— Stinking Thinking. 24p. (Orig.). 1985. pap. 2.00 (*0-89486-326-5*, 5451B) Hazelden.

— Stools & Bottles. 160p. 10.00 (*0-89486-027-5*, 1040A) Hazelden.

***Rosello, Luis R., ed.** Research & Technology Development of Telematic Systems for Flexible & Distance Learning. (Illus.). 136p. (C). 1999. reprint ed. pap. text 25.00 (*0-7881-8177-7*) DIANE Pub.

Rosello, Mireille. Declining the Stereotype: Ethnicity & Representation in French Cultures. LC 97-31507. (Contemporary French Culture & Society Ser.). (Illus.). 224p. 1998. text 50.00 (*0-87451-834-2*) U Pr of New Eng.

***Rosello, Mireille.** Declining the Stereotype: Ethnicity & Representation in French Cultures. LC 97-31507. (Contemporary French Culture & Society Ser.). (Illus.). 224p. 1998. pap. 25.00 (*0-87451-835-0*) U Pr of New Eng.

Rosello, Mireille. Infiltrating Culture. LC 95-33690. (Illus.). 256p. 1996. text 69.95 (*0-7190-4875-3*) Manchester Univ Pr.

— Practices of Hybridity. 96p. 1996. pap. 22.50 (*0-7486-0638-6*, Pub. by Edinburgh U Pr) Col U Pr.

***Roseman, Barbara.** Notes from the Closet. 2000. pap. 9.95 (*1-56167-564-4*) Am Lit Soc.

Roseman, Christina H. Pytheas of Massalia: On the Ocean. (Illus.). 190p. (Orig.). 1994. pap. 15.00 (*0-89005-545-9*) Ares.

Roseman, Curtis C. Changing Migration Patterns Within the United States. Natoli, Salvatore J., ed. LC 76-57033. (Resource Papers for College Geography). (Illus.). 1977. pap. text 15.00 (*0-89291-123-9*) Assn Am Geographers.

Roseman, Curtis C., et al, eds. EthniCity: Geographic Perspectives on Ethnic Change in Modern Cities. 342p. (C). 1996. text 67.50 (*0-8476-8032-0*); pap. text 26.95 (*0-8476-8033-9*) Rowman.

Roseman, Dennis. Introduction to Topology. LC 99-26005. 400p. (C). 1999. 82.67 (*0-13-863879-9*, Macmillan Coll) P-H.

Roseman, Dennis M. Elementary Topology. 192p. 1998. text. write for info. (*0-697-14964-1*, WCB McGr Hill) McGrw-H Hghr Educ.

Roseman, Donald P., ed. The MarAd Systematic Series of Full-Form Ship Models. 421p. 1987. 50.00 (*0-614-06722-7*) Soc Naval Arch.

Roseman, Ed. Edly's Music Theory for Practical People. rev. ed. (Illus.). vi, 146p. 1996. pap. 25.00 (*0-9661616-9-6*) Mus EdVents.

Roseman, Edward. Managing Employee Turnover: A Positive Approach. LC 80-69690. 272p. reprint ed. pap. 84.40 (*0-608-15007-X*, 205608800047) Bks Demand.

***Roseman, Edward B.** Edly Paints the Ivories Blue: A Blues-Based, Improvisation-Friendly Alternative Piano Method & Supplement. 2nd rev. ed. (Illus.). 46p. 1999. pap. 12.00 (*0-9661616-8-8*) Mus EdVents.

— Edly's Music Theory for Practical People. 2nd rev. ed. (Illus.). 1999. pap. 25.00 (*0-9661616-0-2*) Mus EdVents.

Roseman, Herbert C., ed. see Tucker, Benjamin.

Roseman, Janet L. The Way of the Woman Writer. LC 94-22764. 156p. (Orig.). 1994. lib. bdg. 39.95 (*1-56024-905-6*) Haworth Pr.

— The Way of the Woman Writer. LC 94-22764. (Illus.). 120p. (Orig.). 1994. pap. 12.95 (*1-56023-860-7*) Haworth Pr.

Roseman, Janet L. & Silver, Stephen J. Beach Blanket Babylon: A Hats-Off Tribute to San Francisco's Most Extraordinary Musical Revue. LC 96-42337. 1997. pap. 14.95 (*0-8118-1699-0*) Chronicle Bks.

Roseman, Kenneth. The Melting Pot: An Adventure in New York. (Do-It-Yourself Jewish Adventure Ser.). (Illus.). 144p. (Orig.). (J). (gr. 4-6). 1984. pap. 7.95 (*0-8074-0269-9*, 146065) UAHC.

— Until the Messiah Comes. LC 99-26328. (Do-It-Yourself Jewish Adventure Ser.). 128p. (J). (gr. 5-8). 1999. pap. 7.95 (*0-8074-0706-2*, 140073) UAHC.

Roseman, Kenneth D. All in My Jewish Family. (Illus.). 32p. (J). (gr. k-3). 1984. pap., student ed. 5.00 (*0-8074-0266-4*, 103800) UAHC.

— The Cardinal's Snuffbox. (Do-It-Yourself Jewish Adventure Ser.). (Illus.). 128p. (J). (gr. 4-6). 1982. pap. text 7.95 (*0-8074-0059-9*, 140060) UAHC.

— Escape from the Holocaust. (Do-It-Yourself Jewish Adventure Ser.). 192p. (J). (gr. 4-6). 1985. pap. 7.95 (*0-8074-0307-5*, 140070) UAHC.

— The Other Side of the Hudson: A Jewish Immigrant Adventure. (Do-It-Yourself Jewish Adventure Ser.). (J). (gr. 4-6). 1993. pap. 7.95 (*0-8074-0506-X*, 140061) UAHC.

— The Tenth of Av. (Do-It-Yourself Jewish Adventure Ser.). 96p. (Orig.). (J). (gr. 4-6). 1988. pap. text 7.95 (*0-8074-0359-8*, 123928) UAHC.

Roseman, Kenneth D., et al. Gates of Prayer for Young People: Youth & Family Services. LC 94-5003. (Illus.). 228p. 1997. 15.00 (*0-88123-045-6*) Central Conf.

Roseman, Marina. Healing Sounds from the Malaysian Rainforest: Temiar Music & Medicine. LC 90-11253. (Comparative Studies of Health Systems & Medical Care: Vol. 28). (Illus.). 278p. 1991. pap. 16.95 (*0-520-08281-8*, Pub. by U CA Pr) Cal Prin Full Svc.

Roseman, Marina, jt. ed. see Laderman, Carol.

Roseman, Mark. The Past in Hiding. pap. (*0-8050-6325-0*) H Holt & Co.

— A Past in Hiding: Memory & Survival in Nazi Germany. (Illus.). 416p. 2001. text 27.50 (*0-8050-6326-9*) H Holt & Co.

Roseman, Mark. Recasting the Ruhr, 1945-1958: Manpower, Economic Recovery & Labour Relations. (Illus.). 370p. 1992. 30.00 (*0-85496-606-4*) Berg Pubs.

Roseman, Mark, ed. Generations in Conflict: Youth Revolt & Generation Formation in Germany 1770-1968. 328p. (C). 1995. text 64.95 (*0-521-44183-8*) Cambridge U Pr.

Roseman, Mark, jt. ed. see Diekhans, Mark.

Roseman, Mark E., et al. You the Jury: A Recovered Memory Case. LC 96-48102. 288p. 1997. 27.95 (*0-929765-54-0*) Seven Locks Pr.

Roseman, Mindy, jt. auth. see Gesensway, Deborah.

Roseman, Pearl, ed. see Women's League, AdatAriEl Staff.

Roseman, Stanley. Stanley Roseman & the Dance: Drawings from the Paris Opera. (Illus.). 256p. 1996. 75.00 (*0-9652950-0-1*) R Davis NY.

Roseman, Theodore J. & Mansdorf, S. Z. Controlled Released Delivery Systems. (Illus.). 424p. 1983. text 175.00 (*0-8247-1728-7*) Dekker.

***Roseman, Tova.** Notecards. (Tova's Garden Ser.). (Illus.). 4p. 1999. mass mkt. 2.50 (*0-943674-03-4*) Roseman Publng.

Roseman, Tova. Perennials for Intermountain & High Desert Gardening. LC 99-176299. (Tova's Garden Ser.: No. 1). (Illus.). 104p. 1998. pap. 14.95 (*0-943674-01-8*) Roseman Publng.

Roseman, Tova, ed. & photos by see Klump, Gene.

Roseman, V. S. Model Railroading's Guide to the Railway Express. 100p. 1992. pap. 12.95 (*0-9612692-5-1*) Rocky Mntn Pub Co.

Rosemann, Philipp W. Omneagens Agit Sibi Simili: A "Repetition" of Scholastic Metaphysics. LC 98-126078. (Louvain Philosophical Studies: No. 12). (Illus.). 368p. 1998. pap. 67.50 (*90-6186-777-0*, Pub. by Leuven Univ) Coronet Bks.

***Rosemann, Philipp W.** Scholastic Episteme: Understanding Medieval Thought with Foucault. LC 99-23062. (New in the Middle Ages Ser.). 263p. 1999. text 49.95 (*0-312-21713-7*) St Martin.

Rosemary. One Day at a Time in Phobics Victorious. LC 94-71004. 1995. pap. 9.95 (*0-8158-0500-4*) Chris Mass.

Rosemary, Kristine. The War Against Gravity. 192p. 1993. pap. 10.95 (*0-930773-24-1*); lib. bdg. 20.95 (*0-930773-20-9*) Black Heron Pr.

Rosemberg, Alan, ed. see Nicholson, Graeme.

***Rosemblatt, Karin Alejandra.** Gendered Compromises: Political Cultures & the State in Chile, 1920-1950. (Illus.). 416p. 2000. pap. 19.95 (*0-8078-4881-6*); lib. bdg. 59.95 (*0-8078-2567-0*) U of NC Pr.

Rosembloom, Paul S., et al, eds. The Soar Papers: Research on Integrated Intelligence, 2 vols. LC 91-48463. (Artificial Intelligence Ser.). (Illus.). 1482p. (C). 1993. pap. text 72.00 (*0-262-68071-8*) MIT Pr.

Rosemergy, Jim. Closer Walk with God. 1997. reprint ed. pap. 12.95 (*1-889051-21-7*, Awakening) Acrpls Bks CO.

— A Daily Guide to Spiritual Living. LC 90-71582. 505p. 1991. pap. 6.48 (*0-87159-028-X*) Unity Bks.

***Rosemergy, Jim.** Even Mystics Have Bills to Pay. 210p. 2000. pap. 12.95 (*0-87159-262-2*, Unity Hse) Unity Bks.

Rosemergy, Jim. Una Guia Diaria para la Vida Espiritual. LC 97-13415. (SPA.). 501p. 1998. pap. 18.95 (*0-87159-212-6*) Unity Bks.

— The Quest for Meaning: Living a Life of Purpose. LC 98-18423. (Continuing Quest Ser.: Vol. 1). 134p. 1998. pap. 9.95 (*0-87159-222-3*) Unity Bks.

— A Recent Revelation. LC 81-50146. 139p. 1981. 3.98 (*0-87159-002-6*) Unity Bks.

— The Transcendent Life: Understanding the Nature of True Power. LC 98-20155. 135p. 1998. pap. 13.95 (*1-889051-25-X*) Acrpls Bks CO.

Rosemire, Adeline. Christmas Shortcuts. Rosemire, Mike, ed. LC 98-27370. (Illus.). 64p. 1998. pap. 9.95 (*0-9640044-1-0*) Meridian Calif.

— How to Find the Shoes You Want: From Designer Shoes to Running Shoes, & Much More! LC 99-70406. 136p. 1999. pap. text 12.95 (*0-9640044-7-X*) Meridian Calif.

— The Other Mid-Life Crisis: Everything You Need to Know about Wills, Hospitals, Life-&-Death Decisions, & Final Matters (but Were Never Taught) LC 94-22698. 98p. (Orig.). 1994. pap. 14.95 (*0-9640044-0-2*) Meridian Calif.

— The 2-Ingredient Cookbook. LC 95-37458. 110p. (Orig.). 1996. pap. 9.95 (*0-9640044-8-8*) Meridian Calif.

— The Two-Ingredient Cookbook: The Easy Way to Make Delicious Meals Fast. 1996. pap. text 9.95 (*0-07-053996-0*) McGraw.

Rosemire, Mike, ed. see Rosemire, Adeline.

Rosemond, Irene, ed. Reflections: An Oral History of Detroit. LC 92-90956. 106p. (YA). (gr. 12 up). 1992. pap. 10.00 (*0-940713-08-X*) Broadside Pr.

Rosemond, John. John Rosemond's Daily Guide to Parenting. 1994. spiral bd. 9.00 (*1-882835-44-1*) STA-Kris.

— Poised for Success. Cox, Mary & Fettig, Pam, eds. (Illus.). 24p. 1997. mass mkt., wbk. ed. 24.95 incl. audio (*0-9663173-0-0*) MC Mktging.

***Rosemond, John.** Teen-Proofing: A Revolutionary Approach to Fostering Responsible Decision Making in Your Teenager. 2000. pap. 10.95 (*0-7407-1021-4*) Andrews & McMeel.

Rosemond, John. Teen-Proofing: Six Simple Steps to Raising a Responsible Teenager. LC 98-27069. 224p. 1998. 19.95 (*0-8362-2765-4*) Andrews & McMeel.

Rosemond, John K. Because I Said So! A Collection of 366 Insightful & Thought-Provoking Reflections on Parenting & Family Life. LC 96-14992. 384p. (Orig.). 1996. pap. 14.95 (*0-8362-0499-9*) Andrews & McMeel.

— Ending the Homework Hassle: Understanding, Preventing, & Solving School Performance Problems. 172p. (Orig.). 1990. pap. 8.95 (*0-8362-2807-3*) Andrews & McMeel.

— A Family of Value: Six-Point Plan for Raising Happy, Healthy Children. 320p. 1995. pap. 8.95 (*0-8362-0505-7*) Andrews & McMeel.

— John Rosemond's Six-Point Plan for Raising Happy Healthy Children. 204p. (Orig.). 1989. pap. 8.95 (*0-8362-2806-5*) Andrews & McMeel.

— Making the "Terrible" Twos Terrific! 194p. 1993. pap. 8.95 (*0-8362-2811-1*) Andrews & McMeel.

— Parent Power! A Common-Sense Approach to Parenting in the '90s & Beyond. 358p. (Orig.). 1991. pap. 9.95 (*0-8362-2808-1*) Andrews & McMeel.

***Rosemond, John K.** Raising a Non-Violent Child. LC 00-30502. 2000. 19.95 (*0-7407-0671-3*) Andrews & McMeel.

Rosemond, John K. To Spank or Not to Spank: A Parent's Handbook. LC 94-30050. (Illus.). 128p. 1994. pap. 8.95 (*0-8362-2813-8*) Andrews & McMeel.

Rosemont, Franklin. The Apple of the Automatic Zebra's Eye. 2nd ed. (Surrealist Research & Development Monographs). (Illus.). 1971. pap. 9.00 (*0-941194-03-5*) Black Swan Pr.

— Arsenal, No. 4: Surrealist Subversion. (Illus.). 224p. (Orig.). 1989. pap. 17.00 (*0-941194-27-2*); lib. bdg. 27.50 (*0-941194-28-0*) Black Swan Pr.

— Lamps Hurled at the Stunning Algebra of Ants. (Illus.). 72p. (Orig.). 1990. pap. 12.00 (*0-941194-22-1*) Black Swan Pr.

— The Morning of a Machine Gun: Including Surrealist Documents, 1966-68. (Illus.). 1968. pap. 12.00 (*0-941194-00-0*) Black Swan Pr.

— The One Hundredth Anniversary of Hysteria: Catalog of 1978 International Surrealist Exhibition. (Illus.). 24p. 1978. pap. 8.00 (*0-941194-11-6*) Black Swan Pr.

— Penelope. (Illus.). 62p. 1998. pap. 9.00 (*0-941194-42-6*) C H Kerr.

Rosemont, Franklin, ed. Marvelous Freedom: Vigilance of Desire. (Catalog of the 1976 World Surrealist Exhibition Ser.). (Illus.). 1976. pap. 15.00 (*0-941194-09-4*) Black Swan Pr.

— Surrealism: Revolution Against Whiteness. (Race Traitor Ser.). (Illus.). 144p. 1998. pap. 5.00 (*0-88286-239-1*) C H Kerr.

Rosemont, Franklin, intro. You Have No Country! Workers' Struggle Against War. 80p. pap. 4.95 (*0-88286-058-5*) C H Kerr.

Rosemont, Franklin & Garon, Paul. The Forecast Is Hot: Collective Statements of the Surrealist Movement in the U. S. 380p. 1997. 35.00 (*0-941194-41-8*); pap. text 14.95 (*0-941194-67-1*) Black Swan Pr.

Rosemont, Franklin, ed. see Bellamy, Edward.

Rosemont, Franklin, ed. see Breton, Andre.

Rosemont, Franklin, ed. see Brundage, Slim.

Rosemont, Franklin, jt. ed. see Roediger, Dave.

Rosemont, Franklin, ed. see Slim, T-Bone.

Rosemont, Franklin, ed. & intro. see Duncan, Isadora.

Rosemont, Henry, Jr. A Chinese Mirror: Moral Reflections on Political Economy & Society. LC 91-29013. 140p. (C). 1991. 27.95 (*0-8126-9161-X*); pap. 10.95 (*0-8126-9162-8*) Open Court.

— Chinese Texts & Philosophical Contexts: Essays Dedicated to Angus C. Graham. LC 90-41104. 352p. (C). 1991. 54.95 (*0-8126-9121-0*); pap. 24.95 (*0-8126-9122-9*) Open Court.

Rosemont, Henry, Jr., jt. ed. see Feinberg, Walter.

Rosemont, Henry, Jr., ed. see Leibniz, Gottfried Wilhelm.

Rosemont, Henry, Jr., ed. see Workshop on Classical Chinese Thought Staff.

Rosemont, Henry, jt. tr. see Ames, Roger.

Rosemont, Jane. Saving Faces: Photographic Portraits & Musings. (Illus.). v, 75p. (Orig.). 1996. pap. 18.95 (*0-9654500-7-4*) Wom-in-the-Moon.

***Rosemont, Penelope.** Surrealist Experiences: 1001 Dawns, 221 Midnights. LC 99-73761. (Illus.). 220p. 1999. (*0-941194-44-2*); pap. 12.00 (*0-941194-43-4*, Pub. by Black Swan Pr) SPD-Small Pr Dist.

Rosemont, Penelope, ed. Surrealist Women: An International Anthology. LC 97-35357. (Surrealist Revolution Ser.). (Illus.). 592p. 1998. 50.00 (*0-292-77087-1*); pap. 24.95 (*0-292-77088-X*) U of Tex Pr.

Rosemont, Penelope & Baj, Enrico. Beware of the Ice. LC 97-48645. (Illus.). 64p. 1992. pap. 12.00 (*0-941194-29-9*) Black Swan Pr.

Rosemont, Penelope, ed. see Maclane, Mary.

Rosemoor, Patricia. After the Dark: Seven Sins. (Intrigue Ser.: No. 451). 1998. per. 3.75 (*0-373-22451-6*, 1-22451-8) Harlequin Bks.

— Ambushed. (Intrigue). 1988. mass mkt. 2.25 (*0-373-22095-2*) Harlequin Bks.

— Before the Fall. 1997. per. 3.75 (*0-373-22439-7*, 1-22439-3) Harlequin Bks.

— Cowboy Justice. (Intrigue Ser.). 1999. mass mkt. 3.99 (*0-373-22530-X*, 1-22530-9) Harlequin Bks.

— Crimson Holiday. (Intrigue). 1988. mass mkt. 2.25 (*0-373-22081-2*) Harlequin Bks.

— Crimson Nightmare. (Intrigue Ser.). 1994. per. 2.99 (*0-373-22291-2*, 1-22291-8) Harlequin Bks.

— Dangerous Illusions. (Intrigue). 1986. mass mkt. 2.25 (*0-373-22055-3*) Harlequin Bks.

— Dead Heat. (Intrigue Ser.). 1993. per. 2.99 (*0-373-22243-2*, 1-22243-9) Harlequin Bks.

— Death Spiral. (Intrigue). 1977. mass mkt. 2.25 (*0-373-22074-X*) Harlequin Bks.

— The Desperado (Timeless Love) LC 95-22382. 251p. 1995. per. 3.50 (*0-373-22346-3*) Harlequin Bks.

— Double Images. (Intrigue). 1986. mass mkt. 2.25 (*0-373-22038-3*) Harlequin Bks.

— Drop Dead Gorgeous: (Dangerous Man) LC 95-8355. (Intrigue Ser.). 248p. 1995. per. 3.50 (*0-373-22317-X*, 1-22317-1) Harlequin Bks.

— Haunted. (Intrigue Ser.). 1993. per. 2.99 (*0-373-22250-5*, 1-22250-4) Harlequin Bks.

***Rosemoor, Patricia.** Heart of a Lawman. (Intrigue Ser.: Vol. 559). 2000. per. 4.25 (*0-373-22559-8*) Harlequin Bks.

Rosemoor, Patricia. The Kiss of Death. (Intrigue Ser.). 1992. per. 2.89 (*0-373-22199-1*, 1-22199-3) Harlequin Bks.

***Rosemoor, Patricia.** The Lone Wolf's Child: Sons of Silver Springs. 2000. per. 4.25 (*0-373-22563-6*) Harlequin Bks.

Rosemoor, Patricia. A Lover Awaits: Seven Sins. 1998. per. 3.99 (*0-373-22499-0*, 1-22499-7, Mira Bks) Harlequin Bks.

— Lucky Devil (Dangerous Men) (Intrigue Ser.). 1996. per. 3.75 (*0-373-22361-7*, 1-22361-9) Harlequin Bks.

— Never Cry Wolf. (Intrigue Ser.: Vol. 483). 1998. per. 3.99 (*0-373-22483-4*, 1-22483-1) Harlequin Bks.

— No Holds Barred. (Intrigue Ser.: No. 165). 1991. per. 2.75 (*0-373-22165-7*) Harlequin Bks.

— Pushed to the Limit. (Intrigue Ser.: No. 161). 1991. per. 2.75 (*0-373-22161-4*) Harlequin Bks.

— See Me in Your Dreams. (Intrigue Ser.). 1996. per. 3.75 (*0-373-22382-X*, 1-22382-5) Harlequin Bks.

— Squaring Accounts. (Intrigue Ser.: No. 163). 1991. pap. 2.75 (*0-373-22163-0*) Harlequin Bks.

— Tell Me No Lies. (Intrigue Ser.). 1996. per. 3.75 (*0-373-22386-2*, 1-22386-6) Harlequin Bks.

— Torch Job. (Intrigue Ser.). 1993. per. 2.89 (*0-373-22219-X*, 1-22219-9) Harlequin Bks.

— Touch Me in the Dark. (Intrigue Ser.). 1996. per. 3.75 (*0-373-22390-0*, 1-22390-8) Harlequin Bks.

Rosemount Data Research Staff. Deskbook Encyclopedia of Public Employment Law. LC 90-81822. xv, 310p. 1990. write for info. (*0-939675-19-6*) Data Res MN.

— Handicapped Students & Special Education. 6th ed. LC 89-16875. 1989. 67.50 (*0-939675-15-3*) Data Res MN.

***Rosen.** Allyn & Bacon. 4th ed. LC 99-39238. 852p. 1999. 39.00 (*0-205-29856-7*, Longwood Div) Allyn.

Rosen. Assembling, Upgrading, & Repairing PCS. (Electronic Technology Ser.). 1997. pap. 46.95 (*0-8273-7324-4*, VNR) Wiley.

— Bruno Bauer & Karl Marx. (Studies in Social History: No. 2). 1977. lib. bdg. 148.50 (*90-247-1948-8*) Kluwer Academic.

— Case Studies in Immunology. 1998. pap. text 23.00 (*0-443-05725-7*, W B Saunders Co) Harcrt Hlth Sci Grp.

— Discrete Math Applications. 4th ed. LC 98-44231. 824p. 1998. 81.88 (*0-07-289905-0*) McGraw.

An Asterisk (*) at the beginning of an entry indicates that the title is appearing for the first time.

— Introduction to Greek Political Theory. (C). 1999. write for info. (0-415-01396-8) Routledge.

— Introduction to Photography. 3rd ed. (Mass Communication Ser.). 1989. mass mkt., teacher ed. write for info. (0-534-13441-6) Wadsworth Pub.

— Public Finance. 6th ed. 2001. 67.51 (0-07-237405-5) McGraw.

— Species of Aphytis of the World (Hymenoptera: Aphelinidae) (Entomologica Ser.: No. 17). 1979. text 426.00 (90-6193-127-4) Kluwer Academic.

Rosen, ed. Herodoti Vol. I: Libri I-IV. (GRE.). 1987. 115.00 (3-322-00359-0, T1403, Pub. by B G Teubner) U of Mich Pr.

— Herodoti Vol. II: Libri V-IX. (GRE.). 1997. 135.00 (3-8154-1404-0, T1404, Pub. by B G Teubner) U of Mich Pr.

Rosen & Dornan. Multiple Voices, Multiple Texts: Reading in the Secondary Content Areas. LC 97-27064. (Orig.). (C). 1997. pap. text 35.00 (0-86709-417-6, 0417, Pub. by Boynton Cook Pubs) Heinemann.

Rosen & Oberman. Tumors of the Mammary Gland. (AFIP Atlas of Tumor Pathology Ser.: Vol. 7). (Illus.). 390p. 1993. pap. text 59.00 (1-881041-07-7) Am Registry Path.

Rosen & Sternbach, George L. Atlas of Emergency Procedures. (Illus.). 800p. (C). (gr. 13). 1999. text 125.00 (0-8151-7402-0, 23605) Mosby Inc.

Rosen, jt. auth. see Harris.

Rosen, Sibyl & Nielsen, Cliff. Speed of Light. LC 98-40546. 160p. (J). (gr. 4-6). 1999. 16.00 (0-689-82437-8) Atheneum Yung Read.

Rosen, Aaron. Taps for Space. LC 80-52194. 83p. (Orig.). 1980. pap. 12.95 (0-935296-16-6, Pub. by Sheep Meadow) U Pr of New Eng.

— Traces. LC 91-13792. 101p. 1991. pap. 12.95 (1-878818-10-4, Pub. by Sheep Meadow) U Pr of New Eng.

Rosen, Abraham, et al, eds. Kaminits-Podolsk & Its Environs: A Memorial Book of the Jewish Community. Sohn, Bonnie Schooler, tr. from HEB. LC 98-43423. 248p. 1999. text 35.00 (0-9668021-0-1) Avotaynu Found.

Rosen, Al. Business Rescue: How to Fix a Company That's Losing Money. 1989. pap. 11.95 (0-9620675-0-4) Busn Univ Pr.

— True Mint. LC 94-77496. (Illus.). 304p. 1994. pap. 14.95 (0-87341-327-X, MI01) Krause Pubns.

Rosen, Alan & Garr, Doug. Mr. Mint's Insider's Guide to Investing in Baseball Cards & Collectibles. 1991. mass mkt. 8.99 (0-446-39252-9, Pub. by Warner Bks) Little.

Rosen, Alan C., ed. see Wiesel, Elie.

Rosen, Albert P. Health Hints for Hikers. LC 94-31690. (Illus.). 131p. 1994. pap. 5.95 (1-880775-02-6) NY-NJ Trail Confer.

Rosen, Alexander. How to Find, Hire, Train & Manage Salespeople. (Illus.). 83p. (Orig.). 1990. pap., student ed. 19.95 (0-9620675-1-2) Busn Univ Pr.

Rosen, Allen D. Kant's Theory of Justice. 240p. 1993. text 39.95 (0-8014-2757-6) Cornell U Pr.

— Kant's Theory of Justice. 256p. 1996. pap. text 15.95 (0-8014-8038-8) Cornell U Pr.

Rosen, Amy. Generation Eats: Great Recipes for a Fast Forward Culture. (Illus.). 208p. (Orig.). 1997. pap. 19.95 (1-895629-91-8) Warwick Publ.

Rosen, Andrew. Rise up, Women! The Militant Campaign of the Women's Social & Political Union, 1903-1914. (Modern Revivals in History Ser.). 340p. 1993. 63.95 (0-7512-0173-1, Pub. by Gregg Revivals) Ashgate Pub Co.

***Rosen, Anita.** The E-Commerce Question & Answer Book: A Survival Guide for Business Managers. LC 99-40100. 224p. 1999. pap. 19.95 (0-8144-0525-8) AMACOM.

Rosen, Ann. Better Shape Up. (Illus.). 32p. 1984. pap. 6.00 (0-318-35556-6) Visual Studies.

— Sexual Satisfaction: Achieving Sexual Ecstasy Through Higher Consciousness. 1995. pap. 16.95 (0-935016-31-7) Zinn Pub Grp.

Rosen, Arlene M. Cities of Clay: The Geoarcheology of Tells. LC 85-11215. (Prehistoric Archeology & Ecology Ser.). (Illus.). 188p. 1999. pap. text 11.00 (0-226-72627-4) U Ch Pr.

Rosen, Arnold. Quick Reference Guide to PageMaker 4.0: IBM Version. 80p. (C). 1992. text 10.15 (0-697-14661-8) Bus & Educ Tech.

Rosen, Arnold & Dolan, James. Quick Reference Guide to Harvard Graphics. 96p. (C). 1992. text 10.87 (0-697-20026-4, Irwn McGrw-H) McGrw-H Hghr Educ.

— Quick Reference Guide to Lotus 1-2-3 for Windows. 80p. (C). 1993. text 10.15 (0-697-20025-6, Irwn McGrw-H) McGrw-H Hghr Educ.

— Quick Reference Guide to PageMaker 5.0, Windows Version. 112p. (C). 1994. text 11.23 (0-697-22531-3) Bus & Educ Tech.

— Quick Reference Guide to Windows. 96p. 1994. spiral bd. write for info. (0-697-22284-5) Bus & Educ Tech.

— Quick Reference Guide to WordPerfect for Windows. 80p. (C). 1992. text 10.15 (0-697-20029-9) Brown & Benchmark.

— Quick Reference Guide to WordPerfect 6.0. 128p. (C). 1994. text 8.70 (0-697-24278-1) Bus & Educ Tech.

Rosen, Arnold, et al. Administrative Procedures for the Electronic Office. 2nd ed. LC 84-13141. 519p. 1985. text 38.95 (0-471-80854-7); pap. text 15.95 (0-471-81879-8) P-H.

Rosen, Arthur R., jt. auth. see Comeau, Paul R.

Rosen, Arye & Rosen, Harel D., eds. New Frontiers in Medical Device Technology. LC 94-26892. (Series in Microwave & Optical Engineering). 364p. 1995. 112.00 (0-471-59189-0) Wiley.

Rosen, Arye & Zutavern, Fred J., eds. High-Power Optically Activated Solid-State Switches. (Optoelectronics Library). 500p. 1993. text 29.00 (0-89006-507-1) Artech Hse.

Rosen, Avi. Steps to Success. 176p. 1995. pap. text 19.95 (0-7872-1624-0) Kendall-Hunt.

Rosen, Barbara. Arriaga, the Forgotten Genius: The Short Life of a Basque Composer. LC 88-19219. (Basque Studies Program Occasional Papers: No. 3). (Illus.). 78p. 1989. 12.00 (1-877802-01-8) UNV Reno Basque.

Rosen, Barbara, ed. Witchcraft in England, 1558-1618. LC 91-18279. (Illus.). 424p. 1991. reprint ed. pap. 19.95 (0-87023-753-5) U of Mass Pr.

Rosen, Barbara, ed. see Shakespeare, William, et al.

***Rosen, Barrie.** The Unofficial Classic Star Trek Internet Guide. 40p. 1999. pap. 10.00 (1-883573-46-7, Lightning Rod) Pride & Imprints.

— The Unofficial Sailor Moon Internet Guide. 40p. 1999. pap. 10.00 (1-883573-40-8, Lightning Rod) Pride & Imprints.

Rosen, Barry. The Dog That Didn't Give Up. (Illus.). 32p. (J). (gr. 1-7). 1995. pap. 5.95 (0-614-07270-0) B R Pub Co TN.

— Marriage 101: Back to the Basics. (Marriage & Family Romance SelfHelp Ser.). 98p. 1993. pap. 4.25 (0-9625593-1-8) B R Pub Co TN.

— 250 Ways to Be Romantic: The King of Romance. 189p. 1990. pap. 9.95 (0-9625593-0-X) B R Pub Co TN.

Rosen, Barry A., ed. Iran since the Revolution: Internal Dynamics, Regional Conflict, & the Superpowers. (Brooklyn College Studies in Society in Change: No. 47). 200p. 1985. 20.00 (0-88033-075-9) Brooklyn Coll Pr.

Rosen, Barry P., ed. Bacterial Transport. LC 78-16191. (Microbiology Ser.: No. 4). 700p. reprint ed. pap. 200.00 (0-7837-3383-6, 204334100008) Bks Demand.

***Rosen, Bernard.** The Centrality of Normative Ethical Theory. LC 98-28435. (Studies in Theoretical & Applied Ethics: Vol. 2). XII, 228p. (C). 1999. text 51.95 (0-8204-4100-7) P Lang Pubng.

Rosen, Bernard. Ethical Theory: Strategies & Concepts. LC 92-15891. xiv, 306p. (C). 1993. pap. text (1-55934-088-6, 1088) Mayfield Pub.

— Ethics Companion. 144p. (C). 1989. pap. text 20.00 (0-13-291691-6) P-H.

— Holding Government Bureaucracies Accountable. 3rd ed. LC 97-33702. 248p. 1998. 65.00 (0-275-95372-6, Praeger Pubs); pap. 22.95 (0-275-95373-4, Praeger Pubs) Greenwood.

Rosen, Bernard & Caplan, Arthur L. Ethics in the Undergraduate Curriculum. LC 80-12351. (Teaching of Ethics Ser.). 67p. 1980. pap. 4.00 (0-916558-13-4) Hastings Ctr.

Rosen, Bernard C. Winners & Losers of the Information Revolution: Psychosocial Change & Its Discontents. LC 98-15652. 336p. 1998. 49.95 (0-275-96277-6, Praeger Pubs) Greenwood.

— Women, Work & Achievement: The Endless Revolution. LC 88-7802. 256p. 1992. pap. text 18.95 (0-333-48869-5) St Martin.

Rosen, Betty. And None of It Was Nonsense: The Power of Storytelling in the School. LC 87-35272. 176p. (C). 1988. pap. text 19.50 (0-435-08464-X, 08464) Heinemann.

— How to Set & Achieve Goals. 1981. pap. 5.95 (0-917386-47-7) Exec Ent Pubns.

Rosen, Brenda, jt. ed. see Nicholson, Shirley.

Rosen, C., et al, eds. Piezoelectricy. LC 90-24044. (Illus.). 552p. (C). 1992. 125.00 (0-88318-647-0) Spr-Verlag.

Rosen, C., jt. auth. see Wilkes, A.

Rosen, Carol. Plays of Impasse: Contemporary Drama Set in Confining Institutions. LC 82-61381. 357p. 1983. reprint ed. pap. 110.70 (0-608-02887-8, 206395100007) Bks Demand.

Rosen, Carol J., jt. ed. see Estaville, Lawrence E.

Rosen, Carole. The Goossens: A Musical Century. 546p. 1994. text 45.00 (1-55553-210-1) NE U Pr.

Rosen, Ceil & Rosen, Moishe. Christ in the Passover. (C). pap. 6.99 (0-8024-1392-7, 110) Moody.

Rosen, Ceil, jt. auth. see Rosen, Moishe.

Rosen, Charles. Arnold Schoenberg. 136p. (Orig.). (C). 1996. reprint ed. pap. text 10.95 (0-226-72643-6) U Ch Pr.

— Classical Style: Haydn, Mozart, Beethoven. 2nd ed. LC 96-27335. 496p. 1997. 35.00 (0-393-04020-8) Norton.

— Classical Style: Haydn, Mozart, Beethoven. 2nd expanded ed. LC 96-27335. (Illus.). 512p. 1998. pap. 18.95 (0-393-31712-9) Norton.

***Rosen, Charles.** Critical Entertainments: Music Old & New. LC 99-88602. 384p. 2000. pap. text 29.95 (0-674-17730-4) HUP.

Rosen, Charles. The Frontiers of Meaning: Three Informal Lectures on Music. LC 93-39614. 112p. 1994. 21.00 (0-8090-7254-8) Hill & Wang.

— The Romantic Generation. LC 94-46239. (Illus.). 736p. 1995. 39.95 (0-674-77933-9, ROSROM) HUP.

— The Romantic Generation. 744p. 1998. pap. 18.95 (0-674-77934-7) HUP.

— Romantic Poets, Critics, & Other Madmen. LC 98-14316. 288p. 1998. 27.95 (0-674-77951-7) HUP.

***Rosen, Charles.** Romantic Poets, Critics & Other Madmen. 2000. pap. 15.95 (0-674-00202-4) HUP.

Rosen, Charles. Sonata Forms. 2nd rev. ed. (Illus.). 352p. 1988. reprint ed. pap. 17.95 (0-393-30219-9) Norton.

Rosen, Charley. Barney Polan's Game: A Novel. LC 97-24273. 320p. 1997. 23.95 (1-888363-56-8) Seven Stories.

— Barney Polan's Game: A Novel of the 1951 College Basketball Scandals. LC 98-40772. 264p. 1999. pap. 13.00 (0-15-600688-X, Harvest Bks) Harcourt.

— The Cockroach Basketball League: A Novel. LC 98-34454. 240p. 1998. pap. 13.95 (1-888363-78-9) Seven Stories.

***Rosen, Charley.** The House of Moses All-Stars. LC 97-43482. 480p. 1998. pap. 13.00 (0-15-600570-0) Harcourt.

Rosen, Charley. The House of Moses All-Stars. LC 96-30235. 496p. 1996. 24.95 (1-888363-33-9) Seven Stories.

— Scandals of '51: How the Gamblers Almost Killed College Basketball. LC 99-11325. (Illus.). 272p. 1999. pap. text 14.95 (1-888363-91-6, Pub. by Seven Stories) Publishers Group.

Rosen, Charlotte. Culture Shock! Sweden. LC 96-77212. (Culture Shock Ser.). 1996. pap. 12.95 (1-55868-299-6) Gr Arts Ctr Pub.

Rosen, Cheryl B., ed. see Rudrananda, Swami, pseud.

Rosen, Christine. The Limits of Power: Great Fires & the Process of City Growth in America. 418p. 1986. text 89.95 (0-521-30319-2) Cambridge U Pr.

Rosen, Clifford J. The Aging Skeleton: Aspects of Human Bone Involution. LC 98-89311. (Illus.). 632p. 1999. 125.00 (0-12-098655-8) Acad Pr.

Rosen, Clifford J., ed. Osteoporosis: Diagnostic & Therapeutic Principles. (Current Clinical Practice Ser.). 312p. 1996. 99.50 (0-89603-374-0) Humana.

Rosen, Corey & Ludwig, Ron. Model ESOP. rev. ed. 78p. 1999. pap. 75.00 (0-926902-05-9) NCEO.

Rosen, Corey & Young, Karen M., eds. Understanding Employee Ownership. 248p. (Orig.). 1991. text 39.95 (0-87546-171-9, ILR Press); pap. text 17.95 (0-87546-172-7, ILR Press) Cornell U Pr.

***Rosen, Courtney.** How to Do Everything: Just About. 2000. 24.50 (0-7432-1110-3) S&S Trade.

Rosen, Craig. Billboard Book of Number One Albums. (Illus.). 448p. 1996. pap. text 21.95 (0-8230-7586-9) Watsn-Guptill.

— R. E. M. Inside Out: The Stories Behind Every Song. 1997. pap. text 21.95 (1-56025-177-8, Thunders Mouth) Avalon NY.

Rosen, Cynthia, jt. auth. see Kane, Raven.

Rosen, D. Armored Scale Insects, Vols. A & B: Their Biology, Natural Enemies & Control, 2 vols., Vol. A. (World Crop Pests Ser.: Vol. 4). 386p. 1990. 244.50 (0-444-42854-2) Elsevier.

— Armored Scale Insects, Vols. A & B: Their Biology, Natural Enemies & Control, 2 vols., Vol. B. (World Crop Pests Ser.: Vol. 4). 688p. 1991. 294.00 (0-444-42902-6) Elsevier.

Rosen, D. H. & Luebbert, M. C., eds. The Evolution of the Psyche. LC 98-24561. (Human Evolution, Behavior & Intelligence Ser.). 248p. 1999. 59.95 (0-275-96312-8, Praeger Pubs) Greenwood.

Rosen, Daniel. Behind the Open Door: Foreign Enterprises in the Chinese Marketplace. LC 98-29814. 1999. pap. 25.00 (0-88132-263-6) Inst Intl Eco.

This study describes the experiences of foreign-invested firms in the mainland Chinese economy & projects the implications of those experiences for the foreign commercial policies of the industrial countries, including the United States. It draws on extensive interviews with expatriate managers & other professionals currently at work in China. Dan Rosen analyzes developments at each phase of running a business in China & then derives a set of conclusions, including that the World Trade Organization cannot hope to solve all the commercial concerns of China's trading partners. Whereas recent books on Chinese marketplace conditions focus on a single firm or issue, or lack a discussion of policy conclusions (because they are prepared for a commercial audience), this study is distinguished by the breadth of industry interviews & its concern for policy implications. Rosen offers a rare attempt to deduce the policy implications of current experiences of foreign firms in China, presenting conclusions that go beyond those found in today's usual policy debate. Behind the Open Door is a must for China specialists & should be read by anyone with general or business interests in China or the Asia-Pacific region. The report will be an ideal text for MBA programs that focus on region & political science & Asian studies courses on China. ***Publisher Paid Annotation.***

Rosen, Daniel B., jt. auth. see Langellier, John P.

Rosen, David. Advances in the Study of Aphytis: Hymenoptera: Aphelinidae. LC 93-172995. xiii, 362 p. 1994. write for info. (0-946707-47-2) Intercept UK.

— The Changing Fictions of Masculinity. LC 92-35300. (Illus.). 216p. 1993. text 34.95 (0-252-02004-9); pap. text 14.95 (0-252-06309-0) U of Ill Pr.

— Henry's Tower. LC 84-61581. (Illus.). 36p. (J). (gr. k-5). 1984. 10.95 (0-930905-01-6); pap. 4.95 (0-930905-00-8) Platypus Bks.

— The Role of Hyperparasitism in Biological Control: A Symposium. LC 81-65779. (Illus.). 52p. 1981. pap. 3.00 (0-931876-47-8, 4103) ANR Pubns CA.

— Verdi: Requiem. (Cambridge Music Handbks.). 125p. (C). 1995. pap. text 13.95 (0-521-39767-7) Cambridge U Pr.

Rosen, David, jt. auth. see DeBach, Paul.

Rosen, David, jt. auth. see Rosen, Harry.

Rosen, David, ed. see Reagle, Merl.

Rosen, David, ed. see Universi Tah Ha-Ivrit Bi-Yerushalayim Staff.

Rosen, David, ed. see Verdi, Giuseppe.

Rosen, David H. The Tao of Jung: The Way of Integrity. LC 96-10240. (Illus.). xxiii, 197p. 1997. pap. 12.95 (0-14-019502-5) Viking Penguin.

— Transforming Depression: Healing the Soul Through Creativity. (Illus.). 304p. 1996. pap. 15.95 (0-14-019537-8, Penguin Bks) Viking Penguin.

Rosen, David H. & Reiser, Stanley J. Medicine As a Human Experience. 192p. 1984. 55.00 (0-8391-2037-0, 12037) Aspen Pub.

Rosen, David H., ed. & frwd. see Beebe, John.

Rosen, David P. Public Capital: Revitalizing America's Communities. 150p. 1987. 14.95 (0-89788-102-8) CPA Washington.

Rosen, David S., jt. auth. see Helen Keller International Vitamin A Technical Ass.

Rosen, Deborah A. Courts & Commerce: Gender, Law, & the Market Economy in Colonial New York. LC 97-10411. (Historical Perspectives on Business Enterprise Ser.). 312p. 1997. text 47.50 (0-8142-0736-7); pap. text 18.95 (0-8142-0737-5) Ohio St U Pr.

Rosen, Deborah C. & Sataloff, Robert T. The Psychology of Voice Disorders. LC 96-50038. (Illus.). 302p. (Orig.). 1997. pap. 76.95 (1-56593-839-9, 1638) Thomson Learn.

Rosen, Dennis. Mathematics Recovered for the Natural & Medical Sciences. (Illus.). 224p. (C). (gr. 13). 1992. ring bd. 49.95 (0-412-41040-0, A6503, Chap & Hall CRC) CRC Pr.

Rosen, Diana. The Book of Green Tea. LC 98-19863. 1998. pap. 16.95 (1-58017-090-0) Storey Bks.

— Chai: The Spice Tea of India. LC 99-18361. 1999. pap. 16.95 (1-58017-166-4) Storey Bks.

— Coffee Lover's Companion. LC 96-37638. (Illus.). 208p. 1996. 16.95 (1-55972-368-8, Birch Ln Pr) Carol Pub Group.

***Rosen, Diana.** Green Tea for Good Health. LC 00-38790. (Country Wisdom Bulletin Ser.). 2000. pap. write for info. (1-58017-302-0) Storey Bks.

Rosen, Diana. Ice Cream Lover's Companion: The Ultimate Connoisseur's Guide to Buying, Making & Enjoying Ice Cream. LC 98-7556. (Illus.). 208p. 1998. 15.95 (1-55972-468-4, Birch Ln Pr) Carol Pub Group.

— Steeped in Tea: Creative Ideas, Activities, & Recipes for Tea Lovers. LC 98-47384. (Illus.). 1999. pap. 16.95 (1-58017-093-5, Storey Pub) Storey Bks.

***Rosen, Diana.** Taking Time for Tea: Fifteen Tea Parties to Soothe the Soul & Celebrate the Spirit. LC 00-25545. (Illus.). 80p. 2000. 16.95 (1-58017-245-8) Storey Bks.

Rosen, Diana, jt. auth. see Wemischner, Robert.

Rosen, Diana, ed. see Pratt, James N.

Rosen, Dorothy & Rosen, Sidney. Death & Blintzes. LC 98-2815. 180p. 1998. reprint ed. pap. 10.95 (0-89733-450-7) Academy Chi Pubs.

***Rosen, Dorothy & Rosen, Sidney.** Death & Strudel. LC 99-51854. 225p. 1999. 22.00 (0-89733-478-7) Academy Chi Pubs.

Rosen, Dorothy, jt. auth. see Rosen, Sidney.

Rosen, Dorothy S. A Fire in Her Bones: The Story of Mary Lyon. LC 94-1978. 96p. (J). (gr. 4-7). 1994. lib. bdg. 22.60 (0-87614-840-2, Carolrhoda) Lerner Pub.

Rosen, E. M., jt. auth. see Goldberg, I. D.

Rosen, E. M., jt. ed. see Goldberg, I. D.

Rosen, Edward. Copernicus & His Successors. LC 95-20560. 1995. 55.00 (1-85285-071-X) Hambledon Press.

— Copernicus & the Scientific Revolution. LC 83-9380. (Anvil Ser.). 220p. (Orig.). 1984. pap. text 13.50 (0-89874-573-X) Krieger.

— Three Imperial Mathematicians. 367p. 1986. lib. bdg. 25.00 (0-89835-242-8) Abaris Bks.

Rosen, Edward, tr. see Kepler, Johann.

Rosen, Elana Y. Changing the World Through Media Education. LC 97-44906. (Illus.). 160p. 1998. pap. text 17.95 (1-55591-971-5) Fulcrum Pub.

Rosen, Eliot J. Experiencing the Soul: Before Birth, During Life, After Death. LC 97-51709. 320p. 1998. pap. text 13.95 (1-56170-461-X) Hay House.

Rosen, Ellen D. Improving Public Productivity: Concepts & Practice. (Illus.). 288p. 1993. 52.00 (0-8039-4572-8); pap. 24.00 (0-8039-4573-6) Sage.

Rosen, Ellen F., jt. auth. see Harcum, E. Rae.

Rosen, Ellen I. Bitter Choices: Blue Collar Women In & Out of Work. LC 87-5867. (Women in Culture & Society Ser.). (Illus.). 230p. (C). 1990. pap. text 15.95 (0-226-72645-2) U Ch Pr.

— Bitter Choices: Blue Collar Women In & Out of Work. LC 87-5867. (Women in Culture & Society Ser.). (Illus.). 230p. (C). 1998. 32.50 (0-226-72644-4) U Ch Pr.

Rosen, Elliott J. Families Facing Death: A Guide for Healthcare Profesionals & Volunteers. rev. ed. LC 97-42590. 224p. 1998. pap. text 24.95 (0-7879-4050-X) Jossey-Bass.

***Rosen, Emanuel.** The Anatomy of Buzz: How to Create Word-of-Mouth Marketing. LC 00-31453. 304p. 2000. 24.95 (0-385-49667-2, Currency) Doubleday.

Rosen, Emanuel & Rosen, William. Ophthalmology. LC 97-157872. (Medico-Legal Practitioner Ser.). 304p. 1997. 80.00 (1-85941-211-4, Pub. by Cavendish Pubng) Gaunt.

***Rosen, Emanuel, et al.** Refractive Surgery & Optometric Practice. (Illus.). 256p. 2000. text 90.00 (0-7506-3959-8) Buttrwrth-Heinemann.

R

Rosen, Esther K. A Comparison of the Intellectual & Educational Status of Neurotic & Normal Children in Public Schools. LC 78-177208. (Columbia University. Teachers College. Contributions to Education Ser.: No. 188). reprint ed. 37.50 (*0-404-55188-2*) AMS Pr.

Rosen, Evan & Manning Publications Staff. Personal Videoconferencing. (Illus.). 416p. 1996. pap. text 39.50 (*0-13-268327-X*) P-H.

***Rosen, Evelyn Bodek.** The Philadelphia Fels, 1880-1920: A Social Portrait. LC 99-31740. (Illus.). 232p. 2000. 28.00 (*0-8386-3823-6*) Fairleigh Dickinson.

Rosen, F., ed. see Bentham, Jeremy.

***Rosen, Fred.** Deacon of Death. 2000. mass mkt. 6.50 (*0-7860-1094-0*, Pinncle Kensgtn) Kensgtn Pub Corp.

Rosen, Fred. Gang Mom. 256p. 1998. mass mkt. 6.50 (*0-312-96810-8*) St Martin.

— How to Travel: A Guidebook for Persons with a Disability. LC 97-66325. (Illus.). 120p. (Orig.). 1997. pap. 9.95 (*1-888725-05-2*) Sci & Human Pr.

— How to Travel: A Guidebook for Persons with a Disability. large type ed. LC 98-87109. (Illus.). 120p. (Orig.). 1998. pap. 19.95 (*1-888725-17-6*) Sci & Human Pr.

— Lobster Boy. LC 95-182794. (Illus.). 331p. 1995. mass mkt. 4.99 (*0-7860-0133-X*, Pinncle Kensgtn) Kensgtn Pub Corp.

Rosen, Fred & McFadyen, Deidre, eds. Free Trade & Economic Restructuring in Latin America: A NACLA Reader. 288p. 1995. 30.00 (*0-85345-952-5*, CL9525, Pub. by Monthly Rev); pap. 16.00 (*0-85345-953-3*, PB9533, Pub. by Monthly Rev) NYU Pr.

Rosen, Fred, jt. auth. see Proctor, Dorothy.

Rosen, Fred S. & Geha, Raif. Case Studies in Immunology: A Clinical Companion. LC 96-12776. (Illus.). 134p. 1996. pap. text 24.95 (*0-8153-2174-0*) Garland.

Rosen, Fred S. & Geha, Raif S. Case Studies in Immunobiology: A Clinical Companion. 2nd ed. LC 98-46006. 214p. 1999. pap. 29.95 (*0-8153-3363-3*) Garland.

Rosen, Fred S. & Seligmann, Maxime, eds. Immunodeficiencies. LC 92-48452. 765p. 1993. text 334.00 (*3-7186-5343-5*); pap. text 131.00 (*3-7186-5344-3*) Gordon & Breach.

Rosen, Frederic, ed. & tr. see Muhammad Ibn Musa, Al K.

Rosen, Frederick S. Jeremy Bentham & Representative Democracy: A Study of the Constitutional Code. 262p. 1983. text 65.00 (*0-19-822656-X*) OUP.

Rosen, Frederick S., ed. see Gentham, Jeremy.

Rosen, Gary. American Compact: James Madison & the Problem of Founding. LC 98-55508. (American Political Thought Ser.). 318p. 1999. 29.95 (*0-7006-0960-1*) U Pr of KS.

Rosen, Gary & Pietra, Charles. Inside Softdesk Civil, 7. 448p. (C). 1996. pap. 52.95 (*1-56690-109-X*) Thomson Learn.

Rosen, George. Contrasting Styles of Industrial Reform: China & India in the 1980s. LC 91-31762. 182p. 1992. 29.95 (*0-226-72646-0*) U Ch Pr.

— Economic Development in Asia. 304p. 1996. text 77.95 (*1-85972-248-2*, Pub. by Avebry) Ashgate Pub Co.

— A History of Public Health. LC 93-9821. 535p. 1993. reprint ed. pap. text 19.95 (*0-8018-4645-5*) Johns Hopkins.

— Madness in Society: Chapters in the Historical Sociology of Mental Illness. LC 68-13112. 348p. 1998. pap. text 14.95 (*0-226-72642-8*, P913) U Ch Pr.

— Preventive Medicine in the United States, 1900-1975. Trends & Interpretations. LC 75-35978. (Illus.). 128p. 1976. pap. text 6.95 (*0-685-63141-9*, Sci Hist); lib. bdg. 15.00 (*0-88202-103-6*, Sci Hist) Watson Pub Intl.

— The Specialization of Medicine with Particular Reference to Ophthalmology. LC 79-180586. (Medicine & Society in America Ser.). 106p. 1972. reprint ed. 13.95 (*0-405-03966-2*) Ayer.

— Western Economists & Eastern Societies: Agents of Change in South Asia, 1950-1970. LC 84-4370. (Johns Hopkins Studies in Development). 293p. 1985. reprint ed. pap. 90.90 (*0-608-06136-0*, 206646900008) Bks Demand.

Rosen, George, jt. auth. see Bullough, Bonnie.

Rosen, George S., ed. Four Treatises. Temkin, C. Lillian et al, trs. LC 96-30930. 256p. 1996. reprint ed. pap. text 15.95 (*0-8018-5523-3*) Johns Hopkins.

Rosen, Gerald. Growing up Bronx. LC 84-1193. 190p. 1984. 18.95 (*0-938190-37-7*); pap. 7.95 (*0-938190-36-9*) North Atlantic.

— Mahatma Gandhi in a Cadillac. LC 95-18529. 275p. (Orig.). 1995. 21.95 (*1-883319-35-8*) Frog Ltd CA.

— Mahatma Gandhi in a Cadillac. LC 95-18529. 275p. (Orig.). 1995. pap. 12.95 (*1-883319-36-6*) North Atlantic.

Rosen, Gerald H. A New Science of Stock Market Investing: How to Predict Stock Price Movements. 224p. 1989. 18.95 (*0-88730-393-5*, HarpBusn) HarpInfo.

Rosen, Gerald M. Free Radicals: Biology & Detection by Spin Trapping. LC 98-38929. (Illus.). 496p. 1999. text 110.00 (*0-19-509505-7*) OUP.

Rosen, Gideon, jt. auth. see Burgess, John P.

Rosen, Gladys. Jewish Life in America: Historical Perspectives. 17.50 (*0-87068-346-2*) Ktav.

Rosen, Gladys, jt. auth. see Reisman, Bernard.

Rosen, Gladys, jt. ed. see Bayme, Steven.

Rosen, Gladys L., ed. Jewish Life in America: Historical Perspectives. LC 78-16560. 198p. 1978. pap. 6.95 (*0-686-74514-0*) Am Jewish Comm.

Rosen Group Staff, ed. Border Crossings: Emigration & Exile. (Icarus World Issues Ser.). (Illus.). (YA). (gr. 7-12). 1992. pap. 8.95 (*0-8239-1365-1*); lib. bdg. 16.95 (*0-8239-1364-3*) Rosen Group.

— Career Discovery Encyclopedia: An A-Z Source for Career Exploration, 6 vols. (Illus.). (J). (gr. 4-8). 1997. lib. bdg. 119.95 (*0-8239-2650-8*, D1150-0) Rosen Group.

— East - West: The Landscape Within. (Icarus World Issues Ser.). (Illus.). (YA). (gr. 7-12). 1992. lib. bdg. 16.95 (*0-8239-1375-9*) Rosen Group.

— Encyclopedia of Careers & Vocational Guidance, 4 vols., Set. 10th ed. (Illus.). (YA). (gr. 7-12). 1996. 149.95 (*0-8239-2532-3*, D2532-3) Rosen Group.

— Guide to Apprenticeship Programs: For Non-College Bound Youth, Apprenticeship Programs Offer an Opportunity to Bridge the Gap Between School & Work, 2 vols., Set. (Illus.). 850p. (YA). (gr. 7-12). 1996. 89.95 (*0-8239-2156-5*, D2156-5) Rosen Group.

Rosen Group Staff & Reybold, Laura. Everything You Need to Know about the Dangers of Tattooing & Body Piercing. (Need to Know Library). (Illus.). 64p. (YA). 1998. lib. bdg. 16.95 (*0-8239-2742-3*) Rosen Group.

Rosen, H., jt. ed. see Keating, D.

Rosen, Haiim B. A Textbook of Israeli Hebrew: With an Introduction to the Classical Language. 2nd ed. LC 62-9116. 424p. 1976. pap. text 27.50 (*0-226-72603-7*, P689) U Ch Pr.

Rosen, Harel D., jt. ed. see Rosen, Arye.

Rosen, Harold. Old High German Preposition Compounds in Relation to Their Latin Originals. (LD Ser.: No. 16). 1934. pap. 25.00 (*0-527-00762-5*) Periodicals Srv.

Rosen, Harold J. Architectural Materials for Construction. LC 95-45663. 320p. 1995. 59.95 (*0-07-053741-0*) McGraw.

— Construction Specifications Writing: Principles & Procedures. 4th ed. LC 98-14374. (Illus.). 352p. 1998. 79.00 (*0-471-19032-2*) Wiley.

Rosen, Harry & Rosen, David. But Not Next Door. 1962. 12.95 (*0-8392-1007-8*) Astor-Honor.

Rosen, Harry R. The Complete Guide for Building Your New Jewish Community Center. Wundohl, Frank F., ed. LC 83-80776. (Illus.). 217p. 1983. text 225.00 (*0-914820-11-7*) JWB.

Rosen, Harvey. Apple Garnishing: (Packaged with Tools) (Illus.). 1989. 24.99 (*0-9612572-8-8*, 4436); boxed set 17.99 (*0-9612572-7-X*, 4437) Int Culinary.

— Como Crear Decoracionas Culinaris. (Illus.). 1995. boxed set 17.99 (*0-939763-05-2*, 4440) Int Culinary.

— Como Crear Decoracionas Culinaris: (Packaged with Tools) (Illus.). 1995. boxed set 24.99 (*0-939763-08-7*, 4441) Int Culinary.

— Culinary Carving & Plate Decorating. (Illus.). 1997. boxed set 39.99 (*0-939763-07-9*, 4479) Int Culinary.

— Garnishing for the Beginner: (Packaged with Tools) (Illus.). 1996. boxed set 12.99 (*0-939763-06-0*, 4400) Int Culinary.

— How to Garnish. (Illus.). 1996. boxed set 17.99 (*0-939763-09-5*, 4433) Int Culinary.

— How to Garnish: (Packaged with Tools) (Illus.). 1996. boxed set 24.99 (*0-939763-10-9*, 4431) Int Culinary.

— Melon Garnishing: Packaged with Tools. (Illus.). 192p. 1985. boxed set 29.99 (*0-939763-12-5*, 4435) Int Culinary.

— Public Finance. 4th ed. 1994. write for info. (*0-318-72960-1*, Irwn McGrw-H) McGrw-H Hghr Educ.

— Public Finance. 4th ed. 623p. (C). 1994. text 69.75 (*0-256-16019-8*, Irwn McGrw-H) McGrw-H Hghr Educ.

— Public Finance, International. 3rd ed. (C). 1991. text, student ed. 32.50 (*0-256-11393-9*, Irwn McGrw-H) McGrw-H Hghr Educ.

Rosen, Harvey M. Aesthetic Perspectives in Jaw Surgery. LC 97-26331. (Illus.). 184p. 1998. text 175.00 (*0-387-98304-X*) Spr-Verlag.

Rosen, Harvey S. The Fiscal Behavior of State & Local Governments: Selected Papers of Harvey S. Rosen. LC 97-25023. (Studies in Fiscal Federalism & State-Local Finance). 368p. 1997. 95.00 (*1-85898-654-0*) E Elgar.

— Fiscal Federalism: Quantitative Studies. (National Bureau of Economic Research Project Report Ser.). (Illus.). x, 272p. 1988. lib. bdg. 48.00 (*0-226-72619-3*) U Ch Pr.

— Public Finance. 5th ed. LC 98-13616. 1998. 85.93 (*0-256-17329-X*, Irwn Prfssnl) McGraw-Hill Prof.

Rosen, Harvey S., ed. Studies in State & Local Public Finance. (National Bureau of Economic Research Project Report Ser.). x, 248p. 1986. lib. bdg. 40.00 (*0-226-72621-5*) U Ch Pr.

Rosen, Harvey S. & Brown, Eleanor. Public Finance: "Readings, Issues, & Problems" 4th ed. 296p. (C). 1995. text 25.00 (*0-256-16174-7*, Irwn McGrw-H) McGrw-H Hghr Educ.

Rosen, Harvey S., jt. auth. see Katz, Michael.

Rosen, Harvey S., jt. auth. see Katz, Michael L.

Rosen, Harvey S., jt. auth. see Quandt, Richard E.

Rosen, Howard. Leasing Law in the European Union (EU) 2nd ed. 250p. 1994. pap. 170.00 (*1-85564-208-5*, Pub. by Euromoney) Am Educ Systs.

Rosen, Howard & Greenwood, John, prefs. The Flood Control Challenge: Past, Present, & Future Proceedings of a National Symposium in Commemoration of the 50th Anniversary of the 1936 Flood Control Act, September 1986, New Orleans. (Illus.). 160p. (C). 1988. text 20.00 (*1-882102-00-2*, TC423, F58) Pub Works Hist Soc.

Rosen, Howard & Keating, Ann D., eds. Water & the City: The Next Century. (Illus.). 300p. (C). 1990. 25.00 (*1-882102-01-0*) Pub Works Hist Soc.

Rosen, Howard & Mendes, Joel, eds. One Hundred Years of Public Works Equipment: An Illustrated History. (Illus.). 96p. 1986. pap. text 10.00 (*1-882102-03-7*) Pub Works Hist Soc.

Rosen, Howard, jt. auth. see Armstrong, Ellis L.

Rosen, Howard, jt. auth. see Clawson, Patrick L.

Rosen, Hugh. The Development of Sociomoral Knowledge: A Cognitive Structural Approach. LC 80-20. 208p. 1980. pap. text 23.00 (*0-231-04999-4*) Col U Pr.

— Piagetian Dimensions of Clinical Relevance. LC 85-2608. 320p. 1985. text 64.50 (*0-231-06076-9*) Col U Pr.

Rosen, Hugh & Kuehlwein, Kevin T., eds. Constructing Realities: Meaning-Making Perspectives for Psychotherapists. LC 95-37811. (Psychology Ser.). 560p. 1996. 43.95 (*0-7879-0195-4*) Jossey-Bass.

Rosen, Hugh, jt. auth. see Kuehlwein, Kevin T.

Rosen, Hugo. Clinical Psychopharmacology for the Busy Practitioner. 2nd rev. ed. Wills, Susan E., ed. LC 93-76875. (Illus.). 362p. 1993. lib. bdg. 39.00 (*1-883122-01-5*) Pearce Pub.

Rosen, Hy & Slocum, Peter. From Rocky to Pataki: Character & Caricatures in New York Politics. LC 98-24245. (Illus.). 1998. 26.95 (*0-8156-0543-9*) Syracuse U Pr.

Rosen, Isaac. Manny. unabridged ed. LC 96-42294. 1996. 20.00 (*1-880909-52-9*) Baskerville.

Rosen, Ismond. Sexual Deviation. 3rd ed. 496p. 1996. pap. text 36.00 (*0-19-262924-7*) OUP.

Rosen, Ismond, ed. Sexual Deviation. 3rd ed. (Illus.). 508p. (C). 1996. text 125.00 (*0-19-262516-0*) OUP.

Rosen, J. Symmetry in Science: An Introduction to the General Theory. 213p. 1996. pap. 29.95 (*0-387-94836-8*) Spr-Verlag.

Rosen, J., jt. auth. see Essinger, James.

Rosen, J. B., et al. Topics in Parallel Computing in Mathematical Programming. Du Dingzhu, ed. (Applied Discrete Mathematics & Theoretical Computer Science Ser.: Vol. 2). 124p. 1993. 32.95 (*1-880132-11-7*) Sci Pr NY.

Rosen, J. C. & McReynolds, Paul. Advances in Psychological Assessment, Vol. 8. (Illus.). 282p. (C). 1992. 65.00 (*0-306-44251-5*, Plenum Trade) Perseus Pubng.

Rosen, Jamie H. & Westerdahl, John. Nice Job! The Guide to Cool, Odd, Risky & Gruesome Ways to Make a Living. LC 98-56096. 224p. 1999. pap. 14.95 (*1-58008-033-2*) Ten Speed Pr.

Rosen, Jan. Swedish Software Law: As Related Primarily to EC Directives. (Skriftserien Ser.: No. 46). 118p. 1995. lib. bdg. 52.50 (*91-7598-096-7*) Coronet Bks.

Rosen, Jay. What Are Journalists For? LC 99-29891. 352p. 1999. 29.95 (*0-300-07823-4*) Yale U Pr.

Rosen, Jay & Taylor, Paul, eds. The New News vs. the Old News: Press & Politics in the 1990s. LC 92-32299. (Perspectives on the News Ser.). (Orig.). 1992. pap. 9.95 (*0-87078-344-0*) Century Foundation.

Rosen, Jay, jt. auth. see Marcus, Michael B.

***Rosen, Jeffrey.** The Unwanted Gaze: The Destruction of Privacy in America. LC 99-56498. 288p. 2000. 24.95 (*0-679-44546-3*) Random.

***Rosen, Jeremy.** Exploding Myths That Jews Believe. LC 99-57348. 2000. write for info. (*0-7657-6135-1*) Aronson.

Rosen, Jo A. Marketing Made Easy for the Small Accounting Firm. LC 95-31172. 244p. 1997. pap. 19.95 (*0-471-17411-4*) Wiley.

Rosen, Jo-Anne, ed. see Fixel, Lawrence.

Rosen, Joan M. Guessing: Reading As Prediction. (Illus.). 198p. 1986. pap. text 11.95 (*0-9616224-0-7*) Innovative Lrn.

— TPR Student Kit Stories. (Illus.). 80p. 1997. pap. 10.95 (*1-56018-420-5*) Sky Oaks Prodns.

Rosen, Joe. The Capricious Cosmos: Universe Beyond Law. 192p. 1992. text 19.95 (*0-02-604931-7*) Macmillan.

— Symmetry Discovered: Concepts & Applications in Nature & Science. enl. ed. LC 98-9334. (Illus.). 160p. 1997. reprint ed. pap. text 6.95 (*0-486-29433-1*) Dover.

Rosen, Jonathan. Eve's Apple. LC 98-13714. 320p. 1998. pap. 12.95 (*0-452-27998-4*, Plume) Dutton Plume.

***Rosen, Jonathan.** The Talmud & the Internet: A Journey Between Worlds. LC 99-85987. 112p. 2000. 16.00 (*0-374-27238-7*) FS&G.

Rosen, Joseph. The Handbook of Investment Technology: A State-of-the-Art Guide to Selection, Implementation, & Utilization. LC 96-8790. 408p. 1996. text 70.00 (*0-7863-0996-2*, Irwn Prfssnl) McGraw-Hill Prof.

— Symmetry in Science: An Introduction to the General Theory. LC 94-30622. (Illus.). 213p. 1995. 52.95 (*0-387-94375-7*) Spr-Verlag.

Rosen, Joseph D., et al, eds. Sulfur in Pesticide Action & Metabolism. LC 81-7916. (ACS Symposium Ser.: No. 158). 1981. 38.95 (*0-8412-0635-X*) Am Chemical.

— Sulfur in Pesticide Action & Metabolism: Based on a Symposium. LC 81-7916. (ACS Symposium Ser.: Vol. 158). 203p. 1981. reprint ed. pap. 63.00 (*0-608-03039-2*, 206349200007) Bks Demand.

Rosen, Judith. Grazyna Bacewicz: Her Life & Works. Wilk, Wanda, ed. LC 84-80101. (Polish Music History Ser.: No. 2). (Illus.). 70p. (Orig.). 1984. pap. 10.00 (*0-916545-02-4*, ML 410 B05 R7) Friends of Pol Mus.

Rosen, Karen. Twenty-Five Years of the Peachtree Road Race. LC 93-81144. (Illus.). 144p. 1994. 25.00 (*1-56352-127-X*) Longstreet.

Rosen, Karen, jt. auth. see Rosen, Mel.

Rosen, Kay. XY Equals Z. (Illus.). 40p. 1992. pap. text 20.00 (*1-881138-02-X*) Tallgrass Pr.

***Rosen, Kenneth.** Discrete Math: Solutions Guide. 4th ed. (C). 1998. pap., student ed. 26.56 (*0-07-289906-9*) McGrw-H Hghr Educ.

Rosen, Kenneth. Elementary Number Theory. 4th ed. LC 99-35685. 544p. (C). 2000. 92.00 (*0-201-87073-8*) Addison-Wesley.

— Longfellow Square. Burke, Elizabeth, ed. (Illus.). 64p. (Orig.). 1992. pap. 11.95 (*1-878112-00-7*) Ascensius Pr.

Rosen, Kenneth, ed. see Mollin, Richard A.

Rosen, Kenneth H. The Best UNIX Tips Ever. 752p. 1993. pap. 29.95 (*0-07-881924-5*) Osborne-McGraw.

— Discrete Mathematics & Its Applications. 3rd ed. LC 95-942. (C). 1995. text 60.00 (*0-07-053965-0*) McGraw.

— Discrete Mathematics & Its Applications. 3rd ed. (C). 1995. pap. text, student ed. 28.75 (*0-07-053966-9*) McGraw.

— Elementary Number Theory & Its Applications. 1984. write for info. (*0-201-06561-4*) Addison-Wesley.

— Elementary Number Theory & Its Applications. 3rd ed. (Mathematics Ser.). (Illus.). 544p. (C). 1992. text 91.00 (*0-201-57889-1*) Addison-Wesley.

— Exploring Discrete Mathematics with Maple. 4th ed. LC 96-219979. 400p. (C). 1996. pap. 24.69 (*0-07-054128-0*) McGraw.

— Standard Reference of Discrete Math. 1999. boxed set 36.95 (*0-8493-0140-8*) CRC Pr.

Rosen, Kenneth H., ed. Hemingway Repossessed. LC 93-16260. 208p. 1994. 55.00 (*0-275-94546-4*, C4546, Praeger Pubs) Greenwood.

— Voices of the Rainbow: Contemporary Poetry by Native Americans. 256p. 1993. pap. 11.45 (*1-55970-224-9*, Pub. by Arcade Pub Inc) Time Warner.

Rosen, Kenneth H., intro. The Man to Send Rain Clouds: Contemporary Stories by American Indians. 192p. 1992. reprint ed. pap. 12.95 (*0-14-017317-X*, Penguin Bks) Viking Penguin.

***Rosen, Kenneth H. & Host, Doug.** UNIX: The Complete Reference. 1999. 39.99 (*0-07-211892-X*) McGraw.

Rosen, Kenneth H., et al. UNIX System V Release 4: An Introduction. 1228p. 1989. text 34.95 (*0-07-881552-5*) Osborne-McGraw.

— UNIX System V Release 4: An Introduction. 2nd ed. LC 96-216553. 1175p. 1996. pap. 39.95 (*0-07-882130-4*) McGraw.

Rosen, Kenneth H., jt. auth. see Michaels, John G.

Rosen, Larry D. & Weil, Michelle M. The Mental Health Technology Bible. LC 96-42475. 256p. 1997. pap. 55.00 incl. cd-rom (*0-471-17618-4*) Wiley.

Rosen, Larry D., jt. auth. see Weil, Michelle M.

Rosen, Larry S., et al. Values-Based Teaching Skills: Introduction & Implementation. rev. ed. 180p. 1995. pap. 25.95 (*1-885435-02-9*) Twin Lights.

Rosen, Laura. Manhattan Shores: An Expedition Around Manhattan Island. LC 98-60187. (Illus.). 160p. 1998. 35.00 (*0-500-54221-X*, Pub. by Thames Hudson) Norton.

Rosen, Laura E. & Amador, Xavier F. When Someone You Love Is Depressed. 1996. 23.00 (*0-02-874131-5*) Free Pr.

— When Someone You Love Is Depressed. 256p. 1997. per. 12.00 (*0-684-83407-3*, Fireside) S&S Trade Pap.

Rosen, Laurie, ed. see di Stefano, Ted.

Rosen, Lawrence. American Indians & the Law. LC 77-80868. 230p. 1978. reprint ed. 44.95 (*0-87855-266-9*) Transaction Pubs.

— The Anthropology of Justice: Law As Culture in Islamic Society. (Lewis Henry Morgan Lectures). (Illus.). 118p. (C). 1989. pap. text 18.95 (*0-521-36740-9*) Cambridge U Pr.

— Bargaining for Reality: The Construction of Social Relations in a Muslim Community. LC 84-2501. (Illus.). 224p. 1984. pap. 16.95 (*0-226-72611-8*) U Ch Pr.

— Bargaining for Reality: The Construction of Social Relations in a Muslim Community. LC 84-2501. (Illus.). 264p. 1994. lib. bdg. 20.00 (*0-226-72609-6*) U Ch Pr.

***Rosen, Lawrence.** The Justice of Islam: Comparative Perspectives on Islamic Law & Society. LC 99-49281. (Oxford Socio-Legal Studies). 350p. 2000. 80.00 (*0-19-829884-6*); 29.95 (*0-19-829885-4*) OUP.

Rosen, Lawrence, ed. Other Intentions: Cultural Contexts & the Attribution of Inner States. LC 94-27115. (Advanced Seminar Ser.). 264p. 1995. pap. 24.95 (*0-933452-89-6*) Schol Am Res.

Rosen, Lawrence & Harris, Jennifer. Other Intentions: Cultural Contexts & the Attribution of Inner States. Ziegfeld, Richard, ed. LC 94-27115. (Advanced Seminar Ser.). 264p. 1995. text 55.00 (*0-933452-88-8*) Schol Am Res.

Rosen, Leonard J. Decisions: A Writer's Handbook. LC 97-34469. 400p. 1997. spiral bd. 33.00 (*0-205-20020-6*) Allyn.

— Discovery & Commitment: A Guide for College Writers. LC 94-39162. 696p. 1994. 50.00 (*0-205-14249-4*) Allyn.

— Discovery & Commitment: A Guide for College Writers. 616p. (C). 1994. text, teacher ed. write for info. (*0-205-16637-7*, H6637-6) Allyn.

— Discovery & Commitment: A Guide for College Writers. abr. ed. LC 94-39163. 616p. 1994. pap. text 48.00 (*0-205-17126-5*) Allyn.

— Discovery & Commitment: A Guide for College Writers: Examination Copy. 784p. (C). 1994. text. write for info. (*0-205-16636-9*, H6636-8) Allyn.

— Elementary Number Theory. 480p. 1988. teacher ed. 40.95 (*0-318-35471-3*) Addison-Wesley.

Rosen, Leonard J. & Behrens, Laurence. The Allyn & Bacon Handbook: CLAST Study Guide. 2nd ed. (C). 1994. text, student ed. write for info. (*0-205-16315-7*, H6315-9) Allyn.

Rosen, Leora N. & Etlin, Michelle. The Hostage Child: Sex Abuse Allegations in Custody Disputes. LC 95-47113. 225p. 1996. 29.95 (*0-253-33045-9*) Ind U Pr.

Rosen, Lillian. Just Like Everybody Else. LC 81-47534. 155p. (YA). (gr. 7 up). 1981. 12.95 (*0-15-241652-8*, Harcourt Child Bks) Harcourt.

Rosen, Linda, jt. auth. see Reynolds, Monica.

Rosen, Lon M., jt. auth. see Feldman, J.

Rosen, Louis. School Discipline: Best Practices for School Administrators. LC 96-51307. (Illus.). 120p. 1997. 59.95 (*0-8039-6572-9*) Corwin Pr.

— School Discipline: Best Practices for School Administrators. LC 96-51307. (Illus.). 120p. 1997. pap. 24.95 (*0-8039-6573-7*) Corwin Pr.

An Asterisk (*) at the beginning of an entry indicates that the title is appearing for the first time.

— The South Side: The Racial Transformation of an American Neighborhood. LC 98-13267. 192p. 1998. 25.00 (*1-56663-190-4*) I R Dee.

— The South Side: The Racial Transformation of an American Neighborhood. LC 98-13267. 192p. 1999. pap. 14.95 (*1-56663-274-9*, Pub. by I R Dee) Natl Bk Netwk.

Rosen, Louis & Glasser, Robert, eds. Climate Change & Energy Policy. 564p. 1992. pap. 69.95 (*1-56396-017-6*) Spr-Verlag.

Rosen, Lucy. High Performance Through Communicating Information, 10 vols. (Learning-a-Living Library). (Illus.). 64p. (YA). (gr. 7-12). 1996. lib. bdg. 16.95 (*0-8239-2201-4*) Rosen Group.

***Rosen, Lynn.** My Pregnancy Journal: A Guided Journal. (Guided Journals). (Illus.). 128p. 2000. 11.99 (*0-88088-219-0*) Peter Pauper.

Rosen, M. Mathscore. Date not set. pap. text. write for info. (*0-582-18393-6*, Pub. by Addison-Wesley) Longman.

Rosen, Maggie. The Complete Idiot's Travel Guide to England. 528p. 2000. pap. 16.95 (*0-02-863695-3*) Macmillan.

Rosen, Marc. Let's Talk! 425p. (Orig.). 1992. pap. 14.95 (*0-9629821-0-5*) Baron Pied.

Rosen, Marcia. How the Animals Got Their Colors: Animal Myths from Around the World. LC 91-30113. (Illus.). 48p. (J). (ps-5). 1992. 14.95 (*0-15-236783-7*, Harcourt Child Bks) Harcourt.

***Rosen, Marcia.** The Woman's Business Therapist: Eliminate the Mindblocks & Roadblocks to Success. 244p. 2000. 23.50 (*1-886284-55-5*, Pub. by Chandler Hse) Natl Bk Netwk.

Rosen, Marcia & Hunt, Gerry. The Cheers Bartending Guide. 192p. 1986. pap. 3.95 (*0-380-70189-8*, Avon Bks) Morrow Avon.

Rosen, Marcia & Lisk, Eunice A. Test Your Fitness I. Q. (Illus.). 96p. 1986. pap. 6.95 (*0-13-906868-6*) P-H.

Rosen, Marcia, jt. auth. see Ireland, K.

Rosen, Margery D., et al. Childhood Revealed: Art Expressing Pain, Discovery & Hope. Koplewicz, Harold S. & Goodman, Robin F., eds. LC 99-17415. (Illus.). 160p. 1999. 35.00 (*0-8109-4101-5*, Pub. by Abrams) Time Warner.

Rosen, Margery D., jt. auth. see Greer, Jane.

Rosen, Margery D., ed. see Ladies' Home Journal Editors.

Rosen, Marion. Don't Speak to Strangers. 1993. mass mkt. 4.99 (*0-312-95000-4*) St Martin.

Rosen, Marion & Brenner, Susan. Rosen Method of Movement. LC 91-35742. 97p. (Orig.). 1991. pap. 12.95 (*1-55643-117-1*) North Atlantic.

Rosen, Mark. Thank You for Being Such a Pain. 1999. pap. 14.00 (*0-609-80414-6*) Random Hse Value.

***Rosen, Mark Allen.** Spider Matrix. LC 98-90995. 240p. 1999. 10.95 (*0-533-13021-2*) Vantage.

Rosen, Mark J. & Beck, James M., eds. Human Immunodeficiency Virus & the Lung. LC 98-7847. (Lung Biology in Health & Disease Ser.). (Illus.). 584p. 1998. text 195.00 (*0-8247-9883-X*) Dekker.

Rosen, Marvin. Treating Children in Out-of-Home Placements. LC 97-45116. 216p. 1998. lib. bdg. 39.95 (*0-7890-0163-2*, Hawrth Medical) Haworth Pr.

Rosen, Marvin J. Introduction to Photography: A Self-Directing Approach. 3rd ed. 495p. (C). 1989. mass mkt. 28.25 (*0-534-13440-8*) Wadsworth Pub.

Rosen, Marvin J. & DeVries, David L. Introduction to Photography. 4th ed. 494p. (C). 1993. 44.25 (*0-534-17850-2*) Wadsworth Pub.

Rosen, Mel. Random House Club Crosswords, Vol. 2. 2nd ed. Vol. 2. 176p. 1997. pap. 13.00 (*0-8129-2892-X*, Times Bks) Crown Pub Group.

***Rosen, Mel.** Random House Club Crosswords, Vol. 5. 176p. 2000. pap. 13.00 (*0-8129-3290-0*, Times Bks) Crown Pub Group.

Rosen, Mel. Random House Editor's Choice, Vol. 3. 1999. pap. 9.50 (*0-8129-3123-8*, Times Bks) Crown Pub Group.

***Rosen, Mel.** Random House Editors' Choice Crossword Puzzle, Vol. 4. Vol. 4. 64p. 2000. pap. 9.95 (*0-8129-3371-0*, Times Bks) Crown Pub Group.

Rosen, Mel. Random House Editors Choice Crosswords. 64p. 1997. pap. 9.95 (*0-8129-2895-4*, Times Bks) Crown Pub Group.

— Random House Editor's Choice Crosswords, Vol. 2. 2nd ed. 1998. pap. 9.00 (*0-8129-2975-6*, Times Bks) Crown Pub Group.

— Sports Illustrated Tracking - Running. 1988. pap. 9.95 (*1-56800-040-5*, Pub. by Sports Illus Bks) Natl Bk Netwk.

***Rosen, Mel.** Ultimate Crosswords Omnibus. 1999. 9.98 (*0-7624-0663-1*) Running Pr.

Rosen, Mel, ed. The Ultimate Crosswords Omnibus, Vol. 2. (Illus.). 1998. 9.98 (*0-7624-0389-6*, Courage) Running Pr.

Rosen, Mel & Newman, Stanley. Random House Club Crosswords, Vol. 4. 1999. pap. 13.00 (*0-8129-3124-6*, Times Bks) Crown Pub Group.

Rosen, Mel & Newman, Stanley, eds. Random House Club Crosswords: Sunday-Size Puzzles from America's Exclusive Clubs, Vol. 1. Vol. 1. 176p. 1996. pap. 12.50 (*0-8129-2638-2*, Times Bks) Crown Pub Group.

Rosen, Mel & Rosen, Karen. Sports Illustrated Track: Championship Running. LC 93-28169. (Illus.). 1993. pap. 12.95 (*1-56800-008-1*, Pub. by Sports Illus Bks) Natl Bk Netwk.

Rosen, Mel, et al. Practical Coaching Techniques, 10 bks., Set. 1981. 39.95 (*0-932741-95-9*) Championship Bks & Vid Prodns.

Rosen, Menahem. Problems of the Hegelian Dialectic: Dialectic Reconstructed as a Logic of Human Reality. 282p. 1992. lib. bdg. 152.50 (*0-7923-2047-6*, Pub. by Kluwer Academic) Kluwer Academic.

Rosen, Meyer R. A Novel Synergy of Auriculotherapy, Kinesiology & Temporomandibular Dysfunction (TMD) Treatment Protocols for the Quantitative Characterization & Treatment Of: Hyperacusis - a Pain-Causing Ultra-Sensitivity to Normal Sounds. LC 94-77159. 112p. 1994. pap. 60.00 (*0-9641617-0-2*) Interact Cnslting.

— Quantitative Auriculotherapy. LC 94-76974. 52p. 1994. pap. 35.00 (*0-9641617-1-0*) Interact Cnslting.

Rosen, Meyer R., jt. auth. see Braun, David B.

***Rosen, Michael.** Avalanche. (Illus.). 32p. (YA). (gr. k up). 2000. pap. 5.99 (*0-7636-1262-6*) Candlewick Pr.

Rosen, Michael. Classic Poetry: An Illustrated Collection. LC 98-18282. (Illus.). 160p. (YA). (gr. 4 up). 1998. 21.99 (*1-56402-890-9*) Candlewick Pr.

— The Company of Cats. 304p. 1996. 9.98 (*0-88365-965-4*) Galahad Bks.

— Company of Dogs. 336p. 1996. 9.99 (*0-88365-966-2*) Galahad Bks.

***Rosen, Michael.** Dogs I Have Scratched. 2000. 26.00 (*0-06-019656-4*); pap. 14.00 (*0-06-095650-X*) HarpC.

Rosen, Michael. The James Thurber Book of American Humor, Vol. 2. Date not set. 13.00 (*0-06-095322-5*) HarpC.

— Michael Rosen's ABC. (Illus.). 64p. (J). (ps-1). 1996. 16.95 (*0-7613-0127-5*); lib. bdg. 24.90 (*1-56294-138-0*) Millbrook Pr.

— Mind Your Own Business. LC 74-9969. (Illus.). 96p. (J). (gr. 3 up). 1974. 26.95 (*0-87599-209-9*) S G Phillips.

— Mission Ziffoid. LC 98-33760. (Illus.). (J). (ps-k). 1999. pap. text 3.29 (*0-7636-0806-8*) Candlewick Pr.

— Mission Ziffoid. LC 98-33760. (Illus.). 24p. (YA). (ps up). 1999. text 10.99 (*0-7636-0805-X*) Candlewick Pr.

— Night, Night, Knight: Level Three, Blue. LC 98-88075. (Reading Together Ser.). (Illus.). 32p. (J). 1999. pap. write for info. (*0-7636-0856-4*) Candlewick Pr.

— On Voluntary Servitude: False Consciousness & the Theory of Ideology. LC 95-51510. 304p. (C). 1996. 95.00 (*0-674-63779-8*) HUP.

— Rover. (J). 1999. 14.95 (*0-385-32677-7*) BDD Bks Young Read.

— The Skin of Your Back: Sexy - Jewish - Punchy - Funny - Political. 64p. 1997. pap. 11.95 (*0-907123-66-X*, Pub. by Five Leaves) AK Pr Dist.

Rosen, Michael. South & North, East & West: The Oxfam Book of Children's Stories. 1994. 18.19 (*0-606-06755-8*, Pub. by Turtleback) Demco.

Rosen, Michael. This Is Our House. LC 95-36137. (Illus.). 32p. (J). (ps-1). 1996. 15.99 (*1-56402-870-4*) Candlewick Pr.

— This Is Our House. LC 95-36137. (Illus.). 32p. (J). (ps-1). 1998. pap. 5.99 (*0-7636-0290-6*) Candlewick Pr.

***Rosen, Michael.** This is Our House. (J). 1998. 11.19 (*0-606-13845-5*, Pub. by Turtleback) Demco.

Rosen, Michael. Walking the Bridge of Your Nose. LC 95-3007. (Illus.). 64p. (J). (gr. 2-5). 1995. 16.95 (*1-85697-596-7*) LKC.

— Walking the Bridge of Your Nose. (Illus.). 64p. (YA). (gr. k-12). 1999. pap. 8.95 (*0-7534-5186-7*) LKC.

— We're Going on a Bear Hunt. LC 92-8836. (Illus.). 32p. (J). (ps-4). 1992. 5.95 (*0-689-71653-2*) Aladdin.

— We're Going on a Bear Hunt. (Illus.). (J). 1997. write for info. (*0-614-29303-0*) Litle Simon.

— We're Going on a Bear Hunt. (Classic Board Bks.). (Illus.). 34p. (J). (ps-k). 1997. bds. 7.99 (*0-689-81581-6*) Litle Simon.

— We're Going on a Bear Hunt. LC 88-13338. (Illus.). 40p. (J). (ps-3). 1989. 17.00 (*0-689-50476-4*) McElderry Bks.

Rosen, Michael. You Wait Till I'm Older Than You. (Illus.). 128p. (J). pap. 7.95 (*0-14-038014-0*, Pub. by Pnguin Bks Ltd) Trafalgar.

— Zoo at Night. (Illus.). 12p. (J). (ps-k). 1996. bds. 10.95 (*1-896580-00-9*, Pub. by T1rad Bks) Tricycle Pr.

Rosen, Michael, ed. Poems for the Very Young. LC 92-45574. (Illus.). 80p. (J). (ps-3). 1993. 17.95 (*1-85697-908-3*, Kingfisher) LKC.

— South & North, East & West: The Oxfam Book of Children's Stories. LC 91-58749. (Illus.). 96p. (J). (ps up). 1992. 19.95 (*1-56402-117-3*) Candlewick Pr.

— South & North, East & West: The Oxfam Book of Children's Stories. LC 91-58749. (Illus.). 96p. (J). (ps-6). 1994. pap. 12.99 (*1-56402-396-6*) Candlewick Pr.

— South & North, East & West: The Oxfam Book of Children's Stories. (Illus.). 96p. 1992. 12.99 (*0-7445-2193-9*, Pub. by Oxfam Pub) Stylus Pub VA.

— South & North, East & West: The Oxfam Book of Children's Stories. (Illus.). 96p. 1995. pap. 7.95 (*0-7445-4366-5*, Pub. by Oxfam Pub) Stylus Pub VA.

Rosen, Michael, et al, eds. Handbook of Percutaneous Central Venous Catheterisation. 2nd ed. (Illus.). 264p. 1992. text 48.00 (*0-7020-1539-3*, Pub. by W B Saunders) Saunders.

Rosen, Michael, selected by. The Kingfisher Book of Children's Poetry. LC 92-26444. (Illus.). 256p. (J). (gr. 3-9). 1993. 18.95 (*1-85697-910-5*, Kingfisher); pap. 14.95 (*1-85697-909-1*, Kingfisher) LKC.

Rosen, Michael & McGough, Roger. You Tell Me. 1984. pap. 7.95 (*0-14-031286-2*, Pub. by Pnguin Bks Ltd) Trafalgar.

***Rosen, Michael, et al.** Integrating CORBA & COM Applications. LC 98-24818. 352p. 1998. pap. 39.99 (*0-471-19827-7*) Wiley.

Rosen, Michael, jt. ed. see Wolff, Jonathan.

Rosen, Michael, jt. ed. see Zaza, Antonio.

Rosen, Michael A. Lust & Romance: Rated X Fine Art Photographs LC 98-91662. 63 p. 1998. write for info. (*0-86719-460-X*) Last Gasp.

— Sexual Art: Photographs That Test the Limits. (Illus.). 64p. (Orig.). 1994. pap. 30.00 (*0-936705-03-5*) Shaynew Pr.

— Sexual Magic: The S-M Photographs. (Illus.). 72p. (Orig.). 1986. pap. 30.00 (*0-936705-69-8*) Shaynew Pr.

— Sexual Portraits: Photographs of Radical Sexuality. (Illus.). 64p. (Orig.). 1990. pap. 30.00 (*0-936705-88-4*) Shaynew Pr.

***Rosen, Michael F.** Songbird Story. (Illus.). (J). 1999. pap. text 7.99 (*0-7112-1251-1*) F Lincoln.

Rosen, Michael J. All Eyes on the Pond. LC 93-11743. (Illus.). 32p. (J). (ps-2). 1994. 14.45 (*1-56282-475-9*, Pub. by Hyprn Child) Time Warner.

— All Eyes on the Pond. LC 93-11743. 1995. 10.15 (*0-606-08685-4*, Pub. by Turtleback) Demco.

— Avalanche. LC 98-14050. (Illus.). 32p. (J). (gr. k-3). 1998. 15.99 (*0-7636-0589-1*) Candlewick Press.

***Rosen, Michael J.** The Blessing of the Animals. LC 99-34323. (Illus.). 96p. (J). (gr. 3-7). 2000. 15.00 (*0-374-30838-1*) FS&G.

Rosen, Michael J. Bonesy & Isabel. LC 93-7892. (Illus.). 32p. (J). (ps-7). 1995. 15.00 (*0-15-209813-5*) Harcourt.

***Rosen, Michael J.** Chanukah Lights Everywhere. LC 00-8269. (Illus.). (J). 2001. write for info. (*0-15-201810-7*) Harcourt.

Rosen, Michael J. The Dog Who Walked with God. LC 97-27710. (Illus.). 40p. (J). (gr. 1 up). 1998. 16.99 (*0-7636-0470-4*) Candlewick Pr.

— Down at the Doctor's: The Sick Book. (Illus.). 24p. (J). (gr. k-4). 1991. 10.95 (*0-13-218942-9*) Litle Simon.

— Down to Earth. LC 97-11658. (Illus.). 64p. (J). (gr. 4-6). 1998. 18.00 (*0-15-201341-5*) Harcourt.

— Elijah's Angel. LC 91-37552. (Illus.). 32p. (J). 1992. 16.00 (*0-15-225394-7*, Harcourt Child Bks) Harcourt.

— Elijah's Angel. LC 91-37552. (Illus.). 32p. (J). 1997. reprint ed. pap. 6.00 (*0-15-201558-2*, Harcourt Child Bks) Harcourt.

— Elijah's Angel: A Story for Chanukah & Christmas. (J). 1997. 11.20 (*0-606-12276-1*, Pub. by Turtleback) Demco.

— Fishing with Dad. LC 95-43892. (Illus.). 32p. (J). 1996. 14.95 (*1-885183-38-0*) Artisan.

— The Greatest Table: A Banquet to Fight Against Hunger. LC 94-1611. (Illus.). 18p. 1994. 18.95 (*0-15-200028-3*) Harcourt.

— The Heart Is Big Enough: Five Stories. LC 96-22785. (Illus.). 208p. (J). 1997. 16.00 (*0-15-201402-0*) Harcourt.

— The Heart Is Big Enough: Five Stories. (Illus.). (J). (gr. 4). 1997. 16.00 (*0-614-28816-9*) Harcourt.

Rosen, Michael J. Home: A Collaboration of Thirty Distinguished Authors & Illustrators of Children's Books. 1992. 11.15 (*0-606-09427-X*, Pub. by Turtleback) Demco.

Rosen, Michael J. Kids' Best Dog Book & Field Guide to Neighborhood Dogs. (Illus.). 128p. (J). (gr. 4-7). 1993. pap. 12.95 (*1-56305-317-9*, 3317) Workman Pub.

— The Kids' Book of Fishing & Tackle Box. LC 90-50949. (Illus.). 96p. (Orig.). (YA). (gr. 3 up). 1991. pap. 12.95 (*0-89480-866-4*, 1866) Workman Pub.

— Little Rabbit Foo Foo. LC 90-9598. (Illus.). 32p. (J). (ps-1) 1993. pap. 5.99 (*0-671-79604-6*) Litle Simon.

— Little Rabbit Foo Foo. LC 90-9598. (Illus.). 32p. (J). (ps-1). 1990. pap. 15.00 (*0-671-70968-2*) S&S Bks Yung.

— The Lullaby & Goodnight Sleepkit: The Gift of Sweet Dreams & Family Memories, Mini Edition. (Illus.). 32p. (J). (ps-3). 1992. 14.95 incl. audio (*1-880444-02-X*) Times to Treas.

— A School for Pompey Walker. LC 94-6240. (Illus.). 48p. (J). (gr. 2-7). 1995. 16.00 (*0-15-200114-X*, Harcourt Child Bks) Harcourt.

— Telling Things: Poems. LC 96-28800. 112p. 1997. 22.00 (*0-15-100240-1*); pap. write for info. (*0-15-600482-8*) Harcourt.

— A Thanksgiving Wish. LC 97-42208. (Illus.). 32p. (YA). (ps-3). 1998. 16.95 (*0-590-25563-0*, Pub. by Scholastic Inc) Penguin Putnam.

— Traveling in Notions: The Story of Gordon Penn. LC 96-25391. 1996. pap. 9.95 (*1-57003-157-6*); text 15.95 (*1-57003-156-8*) U of SC Pr.

***Rosen, Michael J.** 21st Century Dog: A Visionary Compendium. LC 00-30113. (Illus.). 2000. pap. 19.95 (*1-58479-041-5*) Stewart Tabori & Chang.

Rosen, Michael J. Winter Stripes. LC 96-23862. (Illus.). (J). 1997. 11.95 (*0-15-201535-3*) Harcourt.

***Rosen, Michael J.** With a Dog Like That, a Kid Like Me-- LC 98-53362. (Illus.). 32p. (J). (ps-3). 2000. 15.99 (*0-8037-2059-9*, Dial Yng Read) Peng Put Young Read.

Rosen, Michael J., ed. Dog People: Writers & Artists on Canine Companionship. LC 95-23914. (Illus.). 160p. 1995. 25.00 (*1-885183-17-8*) Artisan.

— Home: A Collaboration of Thirty Authors & Illustrators of Children's Books to Aid the Homeless. LC 91-29125. (Trophy Picture Bk.). (Illus.). 32p. (J). (ps-3). 1996. pap. 6.95 (*0-06-443470-2*, HarpTrophy) HarpC Child Bks.

— Horse People: Writers & Artists on the Horses They Love. LC 97-45059. (Illus.). 160p. 1998. 30.00 (*1-885183-93-3*, 85093) Artisan.

— Mirth of a Nation: The Best Contemporary Humor. LC 99-44293. 656p. 2000. pap. 15.00 (*0-06-095321-7*, Perennial) HarperTrade.

— My Bug. LC 99-32504. (Illus.). 160p. 1999. 19.95 (*1-57965-135-6*, 85135) Artisan.

— Purr... Children's Book Illustrators Brag About Their Cats. LC 95-17622. (Illus.). 42p. (J). (gr. 2 up). 1996. 18.00 (*0-15-200837-3*) Harcourt.

— Speak! Children's Book Illustrators Brag about Their Dogs. LC 92-30325. (Illus.). 48p. (J). (ps-3). 1993. 16.95 (*0-15-277848-9*) Harcourt.

***Rosen, Michael J., ed.** Food Fight: Poets Join the Fight Against Hunger with Poems to Favorite Foods. 45p. (YA). (gr. 6-7). 2000. text 17.00 (*0-7881-9112-8*) DIANE Pub.

Rosen, Michael J. Food Fight: Poets Join the Fight Against Hunger with Poems about Their Favorite Food. LC 95-37919. 56p. (J). 1996. 17.00 (*0-15-201065-3*) Harcourt.

Rosen, Michael J. & DiSalvo-Ryan, DyAnne. Our Eight Nights of Hanukkah. LC 99-11001. 32p. (J). 2000. 16.95 (*0-8234-1476-0*) Holiday.

Rosen, Michael J., et al. The Lullaby & Goodnight Sleepkit: The Gift of Sweet Dreams & Family Memories. LC 91-67933. (Illus.). 32p. (J). (ps-3). 1992. pap. 14.95 (*1-880444-01-1*) Times to Treas.

— The Lullaby & Goodnight Sleepkit: The Gift of Sweet Dreams & Family Memories, Set. LC 91-67933. (Illus.). 32p. (J). (ps-3). 1992. teacher ed., boxed set 28.95 incl. audio (*1-880444-00-3*) Times to Treas.

Rosen, Michael J., jt. auth. see Ireland, K.

Rosen, Michael J., ed. see Thurber, James.

Rosen, Michael R., ed. Paleoclimate & Basin Evolution of Playa Systems. LC 93-50091. (Special Papers: No. 289). 1994. pap. 33.75 (*0-8137-2289-6*) Geol Soc.

Rosen, Michael R. & Hoffman, Brian F., eds. Cardiac Therapy. 1983. text 290.50 (*0-89838-564-4*) Kluwer Academic.

Rosen, Michael R. & Palti, Yoram, eds. Lethal Arrhythmias Resulting from Myocardial Ischemia & Infarction: Proceedings of Second Rappaport Symposium Haifa, Israel, March 13-16, 1988. (Developments in Cardiovascular Medicine Ser.). (C). 1988. text 170.00 (*0-89838-401-X*) Kluwer Academic.

Rosen, Milt, ed. see Berle, Milton.

Rosen, Milton. Surfactants & Interfacial Phenomena. 2nd ed. LC 88-5404. 448p. 1989. 120.00 (*0-471-83651-6*) Wiley.

Rosen, Milton J. Structure-Performance Relationships in Surfactants. LC 84-6384. (ACS Symposium Ser.: No. 253). 356p. 1984. lib. bdg. 60.95 (*0-8412-0839-5*) Am Chemical.

Rosen, Milton J., ed. Structure-Performance Relationships in Surfactants. LC 84-6384. (ACS Symposium Ser.: No. 253). (Illus.). 368p. 1984. reprint ed. pap. 114.10 (*0-608-03131-3*, 206358400007) Bks Demand.

— Surfactants in Emerging Technology. (Surfactant Science Ser.: Vol. 26). (Illus.). 216p. 1987. text 157.00 (*0-8247-7801-4*) Dekker.

***Rosen, Milton J. & Dahanayake, Manilal.** Industrial Utilization of Surfactants: Principles & Practice. 2000. text. write for info. (*1-893997-11-1*) Am Oil Chemists.

Rosen, Milton J. & Goldsmith, Henry A. Systematic Analysis of Surface-Active Agents. 2nd ed. LC 78-173678. (Chemical Analysis Ser.: Vol. 12). 617p. reprint ed. pap. 191.30 (*0-608-13355-8*, 205577200037) Bks Demand.

Rosen, Moishe. The Universe Is Broken: Who on Earth Can Fix It? LC 91-67710. (Illus.). 52p. 1991. pap. 3.00 (*0-9616148-8-9*) Purple Pomegranate.

— Y'shua. 128p. mass mkt. 4.99 (*0-8024-9842-6*, 332) Moody.

Rosen, Moishe & Rosen, Ceil. Witnessing to Jews: Practical Ways to Relate the Love of Jesus. 212p. 1998. pap. 10.00 (*1-881022-35-8*, BK065) Purple Pomegranate.

***Rosen, Moishe & Rosen, Ceil.** Witnessing to Jews Seminar. 218p. 1999. pap. 40.00 incl. vdisk (*1-881022-42-0*) Purple Pomegranate.

Rosen, Moishe, jt. auth. see Rosen, Ceil.

***Rosen, Monica.** Gender Difference in Patterns of Knowledge. LC 98-215481. (Goteborg Studies in Educational Sciences: No. 124). (Illus.). 187p. 1998. pap. 52.50 (*91-7346-333-7*, Pub. by Almqvist Wiksell) Coronet Bks.

Rosen, Mortimer G., jt. auth. see Hale, Ralph W.

Rosen, Myriam, tr. see Mazier, Jacques, et al.

Rosen, Myrna & Loon, Lesley. South African Gourmet Food & Wine: Traditional South African Food & More . . . (Illus.). 256p. 1997. pap. 28.00 (*0-8059-4187-8*) Dorrance.

Rosen, Nancy, jt. auth. see Drucker, Mindy.

Rosen, Ned. Teamwork & the Bottom Line: Groups Make a Difference. 240p. 1989. 49.95 (*0-8058-0459-5*) L Erlbaum Assocs.

— Teamwork & the Bottom Line: Groups Make a Difference. (Series in Applied Psychology). 240p. 1989. pap. text 27.50 (*0-8058-0461-7*) L Erlbaum Assocs.

Rosen, Nina G. Javier: A Young Man Arrives in the U. S. LC 93-45483. 224p. (C). 1994. pap. text 19.13 (*0-13-512120-5*) P-H.

Rosen, Norma. Accidents of Influence: Writing As a Woman & a Jew in America. LC 91-29320. (SUNY Series in Modern Jewish Literature & Culture). 210p. (C). 1992. pap. text 19.95 (*0-7914-1092-7*) State U NY Pr.

— At the Center: A Novel. LC 96-24253. (Library of Modern Jewish Literature). 340p. 1996. reprint ed. pap. 17.95 (*0-8156-0428-9*, ROACP) Syracuse U Pr.

— Biblical Women Unbound: New Tales. LC 96-11502. 224p. 1996. 14.95 (*0-8276-0580-3*) JPS Phila.

— John & Anzia: An American Romance. LC 96-43755. (Library of Modern Jewish Literature). 192p. 1997. pap. 16.95 (*0-8156-0451-3*) Syracuse U Pr.

— Touching Evil. LC 89-38145. 278p. (C). 1990. reprint ed. 34.95 (*0-8143-2298-0*); reprint ed. pap. 14.95 (*0-8143-2299-9*) Wayne St U Pr.

Rosen, Ora M. & Krebs, Edwin G., eds. Protein Phosphorylation, 2 bks. LC 81-10184. (Cold Spring Harbor Conferences on Cell Proliferation Ser.: Vol. 8). 1421p. (C). 1981. 177.00 (*0-87969-140-9*) Cold Spring Harbor.

Rosen, Paul & Brother, Marvin. Accounting Applications for Spreadsheets. 104p. 1988. 19.50 (*0-936862-37-8*, AC/SP); teacher ed. 10.00 (*0-936862-40-8*, AS-TM); trans. 175.00 (*0-936862-42-4*, AS-TOR); disk 7.50 (*0-936862-71-8*, SAD-1, SAD-3) DDC Pub.

Rosen, Paul M., jt. auth. see Walsh, Barent W.

R

Rosen, Paul P. Breast Pathology: Diagnosis by Needle Core Biopsy. LC 98-31090. 1998. text. write for info. (*0-397-58790-2*) Lppncott W & W.

— Pathology Annual, 1993, Vol. 28, Pt. 2. Fechner, Robert E., ed. 272p. (C). 1993. pap. text 95.00 (*0-8385-7722-9*, A7722-0, Apple Lange Med) McGraw.

— Pathology of the Breast. LC 96-6385. 928p. 1996. text 288.00 (*0-397-51694-0*) Lppncott W & W.

Rosen, Paul P. & Fechner, Robert E. Pathology Annual, 1990, Vol. 25, Pt. 1. (Illus.). 416p. (C). 1989. pap. text 95.00 (*0-8385-7714-8*, A7714-7, Apple Lange Med) McGraw.

— Pathology Annual, 1990, Vol. 25, Pt. 2. (Illus.). 400p. (C). 1990. pap. text 95.00 (*0-8385-7814-4*, A7814-5, Apple Lange Med) McGraw.

— Pathology Annual, 1995, Vol. 30, Pt 2. (Illus.). 208p. (C). 1995. pap. text 95.00 (*0-8385-8109-9*, A8109-9, Apple Lange Med) McGraw.

— Pathology Annual, 1994, Vol. 29, Pt. 1. (Illus.). 320p. (C). 1994. pap. text 95.00 (*0-8385-7723-7*, A7723-8, Apple Lange Med) McGraw.

— Pathology Annual, 1994, Vol. 29, Pt. 2. (C). 1994. pap. text 95.00 (*0-8385-7700-8*, A7700-6, Apple Lange Med) McGraw.

— Pathology Annual, 1993, Vol. 28, Pt. 1. (Illus.). 304p. (C). 1992. pap. text 95.00 (*0-8385-7721-0*, A7721-2, Apple Lange Med) McGraw.

Rosen, Paul P. & Fechner, Robert E., eds. Pathology Annual, 1988, Vol. 23, Pt. 1. (Illus.). 352p. (C). 1988. pap. text 95.00 (*0-8385-7781-4*, A7781-6, Apple Lange Med) McGraw.

— Pathology Annual, 1988, Vol. 23, Pt. 2. (Illus.). 416p. (C). 1992. pap. text 95.00 (*0-8385-7789-X*, A7789-9, Apple Lange Med) McGraw.

— Pathology Annual, 1989, Vol. 24, Pt. 1. 400p. (C). 1989. pap. text 95.00 (*0-8385-7733-4*, A7733-7, Apple Lange Med) McGraw.

— Pathology Annual, 1989, Vol. 24, Pt. 1. 2nd ed. 352p. (C). 1989. pap. text 95.00 (*0-8385-7713-X*, A7713-9, Apple Lange Med) McGraw.

— Pathology Annual, 1991, Vol. 26, Pt. 2. (Illus.). 304p. (C). 1992. pap. text 95.00 (*0-8385-7717-2*, A7717-0, Apple Lange Med) McGraw.

— Pathology Annual, 1992, Vol. 27, Pt. 2. (Illus.). 320p. (C). 1992. pap. text 95.00 (*0-8385-7720-2*, A7720-4, Apple Lange Med) McGraw.

Rosen, Paul P., jt. auth. see Fechner, Robert E.

Rosen, Paul P., jt. ed. see Fechner, Robert E.

***Rosen, Peter.** Emergency Medicine. 4th ed. (Illus.). (C). 1998. text. write for info. incl. cd-rom (*0-323-00461-X*) Mosby Inc.

Rosen, Peter. The Luminous Life: How to Shine Like the Sun. Iozzi, Carol, ed. 420p. (Orig.). 1994. pap. 20.00 (*1-878682-01-6*) Roaring Lion Pub.

Rosen, Peter, et al. Diagnostic Radiology in Emergency Medicine. (Illus.). 704p. (C). (gr. 13). 1991. text 145.00 (*0-8016-6267-2*, 06267) Mosby Inc.

— Diagnostic Radiology in Emergency Medicine. (SPA.). 674p. (C). (gr. 13). 1994. text 110.00 (*84-8086-047-2*) Mosby Inc.

— The 5 Minute Emergency Medicine Consult. LC 99-22602. 1024p. 1998. 69.95 (*0-683-30177-2*) Lppncott W & W.

Rosen, Peter, jt. auth. see Barkin, Roger M.

Rosen, Philip. Narrative, Apparatus, Ideology: A Film Theory Reader. LC 86-2619. 560p. 1986. pap. text 26.00 (*0-231-05881-0*) Col U Pr.

Rosen, Philip E. & Epstein, Eric Joseph. Dictionary of the Holocaust: Biography, Geography, & Terminology. LC 97-8779. 440p. 1997. lib. bdg. 55.00 (*0-313-30355-X*, Greenwood Pr) Greenwood.

Rosen, Philip T. The Modern Stentors: Radio Broadcasters & the Federal Government, 1920-1934, 31. LC 79-8952. (Contributions in Economics & Economic History Ser.: No. 31). (Illus.). 267p. 1980. 65.00 (*0-313-21231-7*, RMS/, Greenwood Pr) Greenwood.

Rosen, Philip T., ed. International Handbook of Broadcasting Systems. LC 87-29986. 326p. 1988. lib. bdg. 85.00 (*0-313-24348-4*, ROH/, Greenwood Pr) Greenwood.

Rosen, Philip T., jt. ed. see Mellencamp, Patricia.

Rosen, R. K., jt. auth. see Granet, Roger.

Rosen, Ralph. Old Comedy & the Iambographic Tradition. LC 88-33324. (American Philological Association, American Classical Studies). 103p. 1988. pap. 12.95 (*1-55540-305-0*, 40 04 19) OUP.

Rosen, Ralph M. & Farrell, Joseph, eds. Nomodeiktes: Greek Studies in Honor of Martin Oswald. (Illus.). 752p. (C). 1994. text 67.00 (*0-472-10297-4*, 10297) U of Mich Pr.

Rosen, Randy, et al. Making Their Mark: Women Artists Move into the Mainstream, 1970-85. Brawer, Catherine, ed. (Illus.). 300p. 1991. pap. 35.00 (*1-55859-161-3*) Abbeville Pr.

Rosen, Raymond C. & Beck, J. Gayle. Patterns of Sexual Arousal: Psychophysiological Processes & Clinical Applications. LC 87-19726. 404p. 1988. lib. bdg. 49.95 (*0-89862-712-5*) Guilford Pubns.

Rosen, Raymond C. & Leiblum, Sandra R. Case Studies in Sex Therapy. LC 94-49590. 400p. 1995. lib. bdg. 47.00 (*0-89862-848-2*, C2848) Guilford Pubns.

Rosen, Raymond C. & Leiblum, Sandra R., eds. Erectile Disorders: Assessment & Treatment. LC 91-38062. 378p. 1992. lib. bdg. 44.00 (*0-89862-792-3*) Guilford Pubns.

Rosen, Raymond C., jt. ed. see Leiblum, Sandra R.

Rosen, Rebecca Jo. Reflections: 19th Century Gravestones. LC 97-74719. (Illus.). 164p. (Orig.). 1997. pap. 19.95 (*0-9660234-0-4*) R Jo Rosen.

Rosen, Richard. World of Hurt. LC 94-11253. 264p. 1994. 20.95 (*0-8027-3251-8*) Walker & Co.

***Rosen, Richard A.** Settlement Agreements in Commercial Disputes: Negotiating, Drafting & Enforcement. LC 00-32298. 2000. write for info. (*0-7355-1478-X*) Panel Pubs.

***Rosen, Robert.** Essays on Life Itself. LC 99-24034. (Complexity in Ecological Systems Ser.). 416p. 1999. 55.00 (*0-231-10510-X*); pap. 25.00 (*0-231-10511-8*) Col U Pr.

Rosen, Robert. Leading People. 1997. pap. 13.95 (*0-14-024272-4*) Viking Penguin.

— Life Itself. (Illus.). 320p. 1991. text 55.50 (*0-231-07564-2*) Col U Pr.

***Rosen, Robert.** Nowhere Man: The Final Days of John Lennon. 212p. 2000. 22.50 (*1-887128-46-8*) Soft Skull Pr.

Rosen, Robert, ed. Foundations of Mathematical Biology, 3 vols. Incl. Vol. 1. Subcellular Systems. 1972. 57.50 (*0-12-597201-6*); Vol. 2. Cellular Systems. 1972. 65.00 (*0-12-597202-4*); Vol. 3. 1973. 74.50 (*0-12-597203-2*); 198.50 (*0-685-00055-9*) Acad Pr.

Rosen, Robert, et al. Global Literacies: Lessons on Business Leadership & National Cultures. 320p. 2000. 26.50 (*0-684-85902-5*) S&S Trade.

Rosen, Robert C. John Dos Passos: Politics & the Writer. LC 81-1928. 207p. reprint ed. pap. 64.20 (*0-7837-6178-3*, 204590000009) Bks Demand.

Rosen, Robert C., et al, eds. International Securities Regulation. 5 vols., Set. LC 86-12602. 1987. ring bd. 800.00 (*0-379-20825-3*) Oceana.

— International Securities Regulation: Stock Exchanges of the World: Selected Rules & Regulations. 1992. ring bd. 325.00 (*0-379-20827-X*) Oceana.

Rosen, Robert C., jt. auth. see Annas, Pamela J.

Rosen, Robert H. & Berger, Lisa. The Healthy Company: Eight Strategies to Develop People, Productivity & Profits. LC 92-29602. 304p. 1992. pap. 16.95 (*0-87477-708-9*, Tarcher Putnam) Putnam Pub Group.

Rosen, Robert L., jt. ed. see Bone, Roger C.

Rosen, Robert N. Confederate Charleston: An Illustrated History of the City & the People During the Civil War. LC 94-13751. 224p. 1994. 39.95 (*0-87249-991-X*) U of SC Pr.

***Rosen, Robert N.** The Jewish Confederates. LC 00-9492. (Illus.). 536p. 2000. 39.95 (*1-57003-363-3*) U of SC Pr.

Rosen, Robert N. A Short History of Charleston. rev. ed. Howe, M. Rita & Cole, Tom, eds. (Illus.). 176p. 1992. 19.95 (*0-9635154-1-1*); pap. 13.95 (*0-9635154-0-3*) Peninsula SC.

Rosen, Rochelle K., ed. see Chazotte, Cynthia, et al.

Rosen, Rochelle S. College in California: The Inside Track 1995: Comprehensive Guide for Students, Parents, & Educators. 3rd ed. 592p. (YA). (gr. 9-12). 1994. pap., per. 24.95 (*1-880403-13-7*) Baywood.

— College in California, the Inside Track: The Comprehensive & Practical Guide for Students, Parents, & Educators. LC 92-96890. (Illus.). 576p. (Orig.). 1992. pap. 24.95 (*1-880403-11-0*) Baywood.

— College in California, the Inside Track, 1994 Edition: The Comprehensive & Practical Guide for Students, Parents, & Educators. LC 93-72476. (Illus.). 592p. (YA). (gr. 8 up). 1993. pap. 24.95 (*1-880403-12-9*) Baywood.

Rosen, Roger. Georgia: A Sovereign Country of the Caucasus. 2nd ed. LC 00-270314. (Odyssey Passport Ser.). (Illus.). 350p. 1999. pap. 19.95 (*962-217-502-3*) Odyssey Press.

— The Georgian Republic. (Soviet Guides Ser.). (Illus.). 272p. 1993. pap. 15.95 (*0-8442-9677-5*, Passprt Bks) NTC Contemp Pub Co.

— Georgian Republic. 2nd ed. (Illus.). 272p. 1995. pap. text 15.95 (*0-8442-9679-1*) NTC Contemp Pub Co.

— The Livelong Day: Working in the World. McSharry, Patra, ed. (Icarus World Issues Ser.). (Illus.). (YA). (gr. 7-12). 1992. lib. bdg. 16.95 (*0-8239-1361-9*) Rosen Group.

Rosen, Roger & McSharry, Patra, eds. Coming of Age: The Art of Growing Up. LC 94-27347. (Icarus World Issues Ser.). (Illus.). (YA). (gr. 7-12). 1994. lib. bdg. 16.95 (*0-8239-1805-X*) Rosen Group.

— East - West: The Landscape Within. (Icarus World Issues Ser.). (Illus.). (YA). (gr. 7-12). 1992. pap. 8.95 (*0-8239-1376-7*) Rosen Group.

— The Livelong Day: Working in the World. (Icarus World Issues Ser.). (Illus.). (YA). (gr. 7-12). 1992. pap. 8.95 (*0-8239-1362-7*) Rosen Group.

— Planet Earth: Egotists & Ecosystems. (World Issues Ser.: Vol. 4). (Illus.). 176p. (YA). (gr. 7-12). 1991. pap. 8.95 (*0-8239-1335-X*); lib. bdg. 16.95 (*0-8239-1334-1*) Rosen Group.

— Street Gangs: Gaining Turf, Losing Ground. LC 91-22204. (Icarus World Issues Ser.: Vol. 3). (Illus.). (YA). (gr. 7-12). 1991. lib. bdg. 16.95 (*0-8239-1332-5*) Rosen Group.

Rosen, Roger & Sevastiades, Patra M., eds. Celebration: Visions & Voices of the African Diaspora. LC 93-47413. (Icarus World Issues Ser.). (Illus.). (gr. 7-12). 1994. pap. 8.95 (*0-8239-1809-2*) Rosen Group.

— Celebration: Visions & Voices of the African Diaspora. LC 93-47413. (Icarus World Issues Ser.). (Illus.). (YA). (gr. 7-12). 1994. lib. bdg. 16.95 (*0-8239-1808-4*) Rosen Group.

— A Circle of Women: Stories of the Sisterhood. LC 94-15049. (Icarus World Issues Ser.). (Illus.). (YA). (gr. 7-12). 1994. pap. 8.95 (*0-8239-1812-2*); lib. bdg. 16.95 (*0-8239-1811-4*) Rosen Group.

— Coming of Age: The Art of Growing Up. LC 94-27347. (Icarus World Issues Ser.). (Illus.). (YA). (gr. 7-12). 1994. pap. 8.95 (*0-8239-1806-8*) Rosen Group.

— End of Empire: Fifteen New Works from the Fifteen Republics of the Former Soviet Union. LC 94-29833. (Icarus World Issues Ser.). (Illus.). (gr. 7-12). 1995. pap. 8.95 (*0-8239-1803-3*) Rosen Group.

Rosen, Roger & Sevstiades, Patra M., eds. End of Empire: Fifteen New Works from the Fifteen Republics of the Former Soviet Union. LC 94-29833. (Icarus World Issues Ser.). (Illus.). (YA). (gr. 7-12). 1995. lib. bdg. 16.95 (*0-8239-1802-5*) Rosen Group.

Rosen, Roger, ed. see Beit-Hallahmi, Benjamin.

Rosen, Roger, ed. see Buckalew, Walker.

Rosen, Roger, ed. see Cooney, Judith.

Rosen, Roger, ed. see Dumond, Michael.

Rosen, Roger, ed. see Macdonald, Robert.

Rosen, Roger, ed. see Mahoney, Ellen V.

Rosen, Roger, ed. see McClaskey, Marilyn H.

Rosen, Roger, jt. ed. see McSharry, Patra.

Rosen, Roger, ed. see Rue, Nancy N.

Rosen, Roger, ed. see Webb, Margot.

Rosen, Romy. Spunk. (Orig.). 1997. mass mkt. 6.95 (*1-56333-492-5*, Rhinoceros) Masquerade.

Rosen, Ronald. Strategic Management: An Introduction. (Illus.). 197p. (Orig.). 1995. pap. 44.50 (*0-273-61250-6*, Pub. by Pitman Pub) Trans-Atl Phila.

***Rosen, Rosanne.** Complete Idiot's Guide to Handling a Breakup. (Complete Idiot's Guides (Lifestyle) Ser.). (Illus.). 284p. 1999. pap. 16.95 (*0-02-862928-0*) Macmillan Gen Ref.

Rosen, Rosanne. The Living Together Trap: Everything Women & Men Should Know. LC 92-63124. 176p. 1993. pap. 13.95 (*0-88282-075-3*) New Horizon NJ.

Rosen, Roseanne. Marriage Secrets: How to Have a Lifetime Love Affair. LC 93-9442. 1993. 17.95 (*1-55972-166-9*, Birch Ln Pr) Carol Pub Group.

Rosen, Roslyn, intro. Business & Industry. (Female Firsts in Their Field Ser.). (Illus.). 64p. (YA). (gr. 3 up). 1999. 16.95 (*0-7910-5142-0*, Chelsea Juniors) Chelsea Hse.

— Entertainment & Performing Arts. LC 98-47614. (Female Firsts in Their Field Ser.). (Illus.). 64p. (YA). (gr. 3 up). 1999. 16.95 (*0-7910-5145-5*) Chelsea Hse.

— Literature. LC 98-44004. (Female Firsts in Their Field Ser.). (Illus.). 64p. (YA). (gr. 4-7). 1999. 16.95 (*0-7910-5146-3*) Chelsea Hse.

— Science & Medicine. (Female Firsts in Their Field Ser.). (Illus.). 64p. (YA). (gr. 3 up). 1999. 16.95 (*0-7910-5143-9*) Chelsea Hse.

— Sports & Athletics. (Female Firsts in Their Field Ser.). (Illus.). 64p. (YA). (gr. 3 up). 1999. 16.95 (*0-7910-5144-7*) Chelsea Hse.

Rosen, Rudiger Von, see Walter, Norbert & Von Rosen, Rudiger, eds.

***Rosen, Ruth.** The World Split Open: How the Modern Women's Movement Changed America. LC 99-54439. (Illus.). 420p. 2000. 34.95 (*0-670-81462-8*, Viking) Viking Penguin.

Rosen, Ruth, ed. Jewish Doctors Meet the Great Physician. 2nd rev. ed. 349p. 1998. pap. 7.00 (*1-881022-34-X*, BK069) Purple Pomegranate.

Rosen, Ruth, ed. see Brickner, David.

Rosen, Ruth, ed. see Wertheim, Janie-Sue & Shapiro, Kathy.

Rosen, Ruth C. The Lost Sisterhood: Prostitution in America, 1900-1918. LC 81-23678. 272p. (C). 1983. pap. 15.95 (*0-8018-2665-9*) Johns Hopkins.

Rosen, Ruth C., ed. Testimonies of Jews Who Believe in Jesus: If Jesus Is the Messiah at All, Then He Is the Messiah for All. rev. ed. LC 92-3656. Orig. Title: Jesus for Jews. 349p. 1992. pap. 7.00 (*1-881022-00-5*) Purple Pomegranate.

Rosen, Ruth C. & Lee, Mary P. Coping with Money. (Coping Ser.). (YA). (gr. 7-12). 1988. lib. bdg. 17.95 (*0-8239-0783-X*) Rosen Group.

Rosen, Ruth C., ed. see Ayer, Eleanor H.

Rosen, Ruth C., ed. see Beyer, Kay.

Rosen, Ruth C., ed. see Black, Beryl.

Rosen, Ruth C., ed. see Buckalew, M. Walter.

Rosen, Ruth C., ed. see Carter, Sharon & Monnig, Judith.

Rosen, Ruth C., ed. see Clayton, Lawrence.

Rosen, Ruth C., ed. see Clayton, Lawrence & Carter, Sharon.

Rosen, Ruth C., ed. see Clayton, Lawrence & Morrison, Jaydene.

Rosen, Ruth C., ed. see Cohen, Shari & Cohen, Payl.

Rosen, Ruth C., ed. see Collins, Robert F.

Rosen, Ruth C., ed. see Connors, Patricia & Perucci, Dorianne.

Rosen, Ruth C., ed. see Cristall, Barbara.

Rosen, Ruth C., ed. see Feller, Robyn M.

Rosen, Ruth C., ed. see Field, Shelly.

Rosen, Ruth C., ed. see Gartner, Bob.

Rosen, Ruth C., ed. see Gooden, Kimberly W.

Rosen, Ruth C., ed. see Grosshandler, Janet.

Rosen, Ruth C., ed. see Grosshandler-Smith, Janet.

Rosen, Ruth C., ed. see Hopkins, Margaret & Hopkins, Del.

Rosen, Ruth C., ed. see Hurwitz, Sue & Hurwitz, Ann R.

Rosen, Ruth C., ed. see Hurwitz, Sue & Hurwitz, Jane.

Rosen, Ruth C., ed. see Johnson, Barbara L.

Rosen, Ruth C., ed. see Johnson, Linda C.

Rosen, Ruth C., ed. see Kane, June K.

Rosen, Ruth C., ed. see Kurland, Morton L.

Rosen, Ruth C., ed. see Lobus, Catherine O.

Rosen, Ruth C., ed. see McFarland, Rhoda.

Rosen, Ruth C., ed. see McGlothin, Bruce.

Rosen, Ruth C., ed. see Milios, Rita.

Rosen, Ruth C., ed. see Miller, Deborah.

Rosen, Ruth C., ed. see Miller, Maryann.

Rosen, Ruth C., ed. see Moe, Barbara.

Rosen, Ruth C., ed. see Nelson, Cordner.

Rosen, Ruth C., ed. see Peck, Rodney G.

Rosen, Ruth C., ed. see Pinzer, Maimie.

Rosen, Ruth C., ed. see Raab, Robert A.

Rosen, Ruth C., ed. see Ratto, Linda L.

Rosen, Ruth C., ed. see Rawls, Bea O. & Johnson, Gwen.

Rosen, Ruth C., ed. see Reynolds, Moira D.

Rosen, Ruth C., ed. see Schaver, Donald D.

Rosen, Ruth C., ed. see Schleifer, Jay.

Rosen, Ruth C., ed. see Shuker-Haines, Frances.

Rosen, Ruth C., ed. see Simpson, Carolyn.

Rosen, Ruth C., ed. see Simpson, Carolyn & Simpson, Dwain.

Rosen, Ruth C., ed. see Smith, Judie.

Rosen, Ruth C., ed. see Smith, Sandra L.

Rosen, Ruth C., ed. see Spencer, Jean W.

Rosen, Ruth C., ed. see St. Pierre, Stephanie.

Rosen, Ruth C., ed. see Taylor, Barbara.

Rosen, Ruth C., ed. see Webb, Margot.

Rosen, Ruth C., ed. see White, Carl P.

Rosen, Ruth C., ed. see Wilkinson, Beth.

Rosen, Ruth C., ed. see Woods, Samuel G. & Diskavich, Laura.

Rosen, Ruth C., ed. see Zeldis, Yona.

Rosen, S. P., jt. ed. see Ginocchio, J. N.

Rosen, Samuel R. A Judge Judges Mushrooms. (Illus.). 92p. 1988. pap. 8.00 (*0-913617-01-6*) Lubrecht & Cramer.

Rosen, Sara. My Lost World: A Survivor's Tale. (Library of Holocaust Testimonies). 320p. 1993. pap. text 19.50 (*0-85303-254-8*, Pub. by M Vallentine & Co) Intl Spec Bk.

Rosen, Saul. Lectures on the Measurement & Evaluation of the Performance of Computing Systems. (CBMS-NSF Regional Conference Ser.: No. 23). 320p. 1976. reprint ed. pap. text 26.00 (*0-89871-020-0*) Soc Indus-Appl Math.

Rosen-Sawyer, Fran. I Wish I Had Known. (Orig.). 1990. pap. 13.00 (*0-944909-02-7*) Fivefold Path.

Rosen, Selina. Fright Eater. (Host Ser.). 176p. (Orig.). 1998. spiral bd. 6.00 (*1-893687-01-5*) Yard Dog.

— The Host. 164p. 1997. spiral bd. 6.00 (*1-893687-00-7*) Yard Dog.

— Queen of Denial. 380p. 1999. pap. 12.00 (*1-892065-06-1*) Meisha Merlin.

Rosen, Selma. Children's Clothing: Designing, Selecting Fabrics, Patternmaking, Sewing. LC 82-83319. (Illus.). 157p. 1983. pap. 40.00 (*0-87005-430-9*) Fairchild.

Rosen, Sherwin, ed. Implicit Contract Theory. LC 93-39146. (International Library of Critical Writings in Economics: No. 35). 496p. 1994. 230.00 (*1-85278-748-1*) E Elgar.

— Studies in Labor Markets. LC 81-7488. (National Bureau of Economic Research Ser.: Universities-Nat'l Conference Series No. 31). (Illus.). 406p. (C). 1981. lib. bdg. 56.50 (*0-226-72628-2*) U Ch Pr.

Rosen, Sherwin, jt. auth. see Nadiri, M. Ishaq.

Rosen, Shirley. Truman of St. Helens: The Man & His Mountain. 6th ed. (Illus.). 163p. reprint ed. pap. 12.95 (*0-9623297-1-1*) Rosebud Pub.

Rosen, Sidney. Can You Catch a Falling Star? LC 94-38478. (Question of Science Bks.). (Illus.). 40p. (J). 1995. lib. bdg. 19.93 (*0-87614-882-8*, Carolrhoda) Lerner Pub.

— Can You Find a Planet? (Question of Science Book). 40p. (J). (gr. k-3). 1991. lib. bdg. 19.93 (*0-87614-683-3*, Carolrhoda) Lerner Pub.

— Can You Hitch a Ride on a Comet? (Question of Science Book). (Illus.). (J). (gr. k-3). 1993. lib. bdg. 19.93 (*0-87614-773-2*) Lerner Pub.

— How Far Is a Star? (Question of Science Book). (Illus.). 40p. (J). (gr. k-3). 1991. lib. bdg. 19.95 (*0-87614-684-1*, Carolrhoda) Lerner Pub.

— My Voice Will Go with You. 1991. pap. 13.95 (*0-393-30135-4*) Norton.

— Where Does the Moon Go? (Question of Science Book). (Illus.). 40p. (J). (gr. k-3). 1992. lib. bdg. 14.95 (*0-87614-685-X*, Carolrhoda) Lerner Pub.

— Where's the Big Dipper. LC 94-39379. (Illus.). 40p. (J). (gr. 2-4). 1995. 14.95 (*0-87614-883-6*, Carolrhoda) Lerner Pub.

Rosen, Sidney & Rosen, Dorothy. The Baghdad Mission. LC 93-36965. (Adventures in Time Ser.). (J). (gr. 4-7). 1994. lib. bdg. 21.27 (*0-87614-828-3*, Carolrhoda) Lerner Pub.

— The Magician's Apprentice. LC 93-10781. (J). (gr. 4-7). 1993. lib. bdg. 19.95 (*0-87614-809-7*, Carolrhoda) Lerner Pub.

Rosen, Sidney, jt. auth. see Rosen, Dorothy.

Rosen, Sidney M., et al. Toward a Gang Solution: The Redirectional Method. (Illus.). 88p. 1996. pap. 13.95 (*1-878848-43-7*, 187) Natl Res Ctr.

Rosen, Sonia, et al. By the Sweat & Toil of Children: The Use of Child Labor in U. S. Manufactured & Mined Imports. 185p. 1997. pap. text 30.00 (*0-7881-4577-0*) DIANE Pub.

Rosen, Sonia, jt. ed. see Jaffe, Maureen.

Rosen, Sonia A., et al. The Apparel Industry & Codes of Conduct: A Solution to the International Child Labor Problems. (Illus.). 242p. 1997. pap. text 40.00 (*0-7881-4576-2*) DIANE Pub.

Rosen, Stanley. The Ancients & the Moderns: Rethinking Modernity. 246p. (C). 1991. reprint ed. pap. 16.00 (*0-300-05030-5*) Yale U Pr.

***Rosen, Stanley.** The Examined Life. LC 99-59064. 2000. 35.00 (*0-375-40501-1*) Random Ref & Info.

— G. W. F. Hegel: An Introduction to the Science of Wisdom. (Carthage Reprints Ser.). 324p. 2000. reprint ed. pap. 25.00 (*1-890318-48-5*, Pub. by St Augustines Pr) U Ch Pr.

Rosen, Stanley. Hermeneutics As Politics. (Odeon Ser.). 224p. 1990. reprint ed. pap. text 21.00 (*0-19-506161-6*) OUP.

***Rosen, Stanley.** The Limits of Analysis. unabridged ed. LC 99-48139. 296p. 2000. reprint ed. pap. 28.00 (*1-890318-36-1*, Pub. by St Augustines Pr) Chicago Distribution Ctr.

An Asterisk (*) at the beginning of an entry indicates that the title is appearing for the first time.

Rosen, Stanley. The Mask of Enlightenment: Nietzsche's Zarathustra. (Modern European Philosophy Ser.). 286p. (C). 1995. text 59.95 (*0-521-49546-6*); pap. text 21.95 (*0-521-49889-9*) Cambridge U Pr.
— Metaphysics in Ordinary Language. LC 98-26477. 304p. 1999. 30.00 (*0-300-07478-6*) Yale U Pr.
— Nihilism: A Philosophical Essay. LC 70-81428. 261p. reprint ed. pap. 81.00 (*0-8357-8250-6*, 203387700087) Bks Demand.
***Rosen, Stanley.** Nihilism: A Philosophical Essay. unabridged ed. LC 99-48134. 272p. 2000. reprint ed. pap. 25.00 (*1-890318-45-0*, Pub. by St Augustines Pr) Chicago Distribution Ctr.
Rosen, Stanley. Plato's Sophist: The Drama of Original & Image. LC 99-13195. 352p. 1999. pap. 29.00 (*1-890318-63-9*) St Augustines Pr.
— Plato's Statesman: The Web of Politics. LC 94-44016. 197p. 1995. 30.00 (*0-300-06264-8*) Yale U Pr.
— Plato's Statesman: The Web of Politics. 208p. 1997. pap. text 16.00 (*0-300-07281-3*) Yale U Pr.
— Plato's Symposium. 2nd ed. LC 99-21495. 428p. 1999. reprint ed. pap. 32.00 (*1-890318-64-7*) St Augustines Pr.
— The Quarrel Between Philosophy & Poetry: Studies in Ancient Thought. 256p. 1988. text 29.95 (*0-415-00184-6*) Routledge.
— The Quarrel Between Philosophy & Poetry: Studies in Ancient Thought. 256p. (C). 1993. pap. 19.99 (*0-415-90745-4*, B0257) Routledge.
— The Question of Being: A Reversal of Heidegger. LC 92-34934. 368p. (C). 1993. 40.00 (*0-300-05356-8*) Yale U Pr.
— Question of Being: A Reversal of Heidegger. 1995. pap. 18.00 (*0-300-06315-6*) Yale U Pr.
Rosen, Stanley, jt. ed. see Burns, John P.
Rosen, Stanley L. D. C. Circuits. LC 80-12328. (Avionics Technician Training Course Ser.). 158p. (Orig.). 1980. pap. text 15.50 (*0-89100-121-2*, JS312635) Jeppesen Sanderson.
Rosen, Stephen & Paul, Celia. Career Renewal: Tools for Scientists & Technical Professionals. LC 97-29068. (Illus.). 352p. 1997. pap. text 24.95 (*0-12-597060-9*) Morgan Kaufmann.
Rosen, Stephen L. Fundamental Principles of Polymeric Materials. 2nd ed. LC 92-10973. (SPE Monographs). 448p. 1993. 69.95 (*0-471-57525-9*) Wiley.
Rosen, Stephen P. Societies & Military Power: India & Its Armies. LC 96-11014. (Studies in Security Affairs). 296p. 1996. text 39.95 (*0-8014-3210-3*) Cornell U Pr.
— Winning the Next War: Innovation & the Modern Military. (Cornell Studies in Security Affairs). 288p. 1994. pap. text 15.95 (*0-8014-8196-1*) Cornell U Pr.
Rosen, Steve. Alpha Hand ABC Shorthand: Notetaking & Secretarial. (Alpha Hand Ser.). 172p. 1989. 18.00 (*0-936862-02-5*, AH-1); student ed. 8.00 (*0-936862-09-2*, AHWB); audio 7.50 (*0-936862-33-5*, 98) DDC Pub.
— Alpha Hand Dictionary. (Alpha Hand Ser.). 63p. 1980. 5.00 (*0-936862-08-4*, AHD) DDC Pub.
Rosen, Steven. Diet for Transcendence: Vegetarianism & the World Religions. rev. ed. Greene, Joshua, ed. LC 97-16123. Orig. Title: Food for the Spirit. (Illus.). 144p. 1997. reprint ed. pap. 11.95 (*1-887089-05-5*) Torchlght Pub.
— India's Spiritual Renaissance: The Life & Times of Lord Chaitanya. (Illus.). 250p. (Orig.). 1988. pap. 12.95 (*0-9619763-0-6*) Folk Bks.
— Passage from India: The Life & Times of His Divine Grace A. C. Bhaktivedanti Swami Prabhupada. A Summary Study of Satsvarupa Dasa Goswami's Srila Prabhupada Lilamrta. (C). 1992. 14.00 (*81-215-0558-5*, Pub. by M Manoharial) Coronet Bks.
Rosen, Steven, et al, eds. Innovations in Urologic Oncology. LC 91-67426. 144p. 1991. 29.95 (*0-944496-25-3*) Precept Pr.
Rosen, Steven A. Lithics after the Stone Age: A Handbook of Stone Tools from the Levant. LC 96-51250. (Illus.). 184p. 1997. 69.00 (*0-7619-9123-9*); pap. 27.95 (*0-7619-9124-7*) AltaMira Pr.
Rosen, Steven J. The Proliferation of Land-Based Technologies: Implications for Local Military Balances. (CISA Working Papers: No. 12). 35p. (Orig.). 1978. pap. 15.00 (*0-86682-011-6*) Ctr Intl Relations.
— The Reincarnation Controversy: Uncovering the Truth in the World Religions. LC 97-18655. 144p. 1997. pap. 11.95 (*1-887089-11-X*) Torchlght Pub.
— Samuel Beckett & the Pessimistic Tradition. LC 76-2506. 262p. 1976. reprint ed. pap. 81.30 (*0-7837-5662-3*, 205908800005) Bks Demand.
— Vaisnavi: Women & the Worship of Krishna. LC 97-902526. 1997. 27.00 (*81-208-1437-1*, Pub. by Motilal Bnarsidass) S Asia.
— Vaisnavi: Women & the Worship of Krishna. LC 97-902526. (C). 1997. pap. 17.50 (*81-208-1438-X*, Pub. by Motilal Bnarsidass) S Asia.
— What a Fifth Arab-Israeli War Might Look Like: An Exercise in Crisis Forecasting. (CISA Working Papers: No. 8). 46p. (Orig.). 1977. pap. 15.00 (*0-86682-007-8*) Ctr Intl Relations.
Rosen, Steven J., ed. Vaisnavism: Contemporary Scholars Discuss the Gaudiya Tradition. LC 92-71546. 1992. pap. write for info. (*0-9619763-6-5*) Folk Bks.
Rosen, Steven M. Science, Paradox, & the Moebius Principle: The Evolution of a "Transcultural" Approach to Wholeness. LC 93-3091. (SUNY Series in Science, Technology, & Society). 317p. (C). 1994. pap. text 21.95 (*0-7914-1770-0*) State U NY Pr.
— Science, Paradox, & the Moebius Principle: The Evolution of a "Transcultural" Approach to Wholeness. LC 93-3091. (SUNY Series in Science, Technology, & Society). 317p. (C). 1994. text 64.50 (*0-7914-1769-7*) State U NY Pr.
Rosen, Steven T. & Kuzel, Timothy M., eds. Immunoconjugate Therapy of Hematologic Malignancies. LC 93-15382. (Cancer Treatment & Research Ser.: Vol. 68). 224p. (C). 1993. text 191.00 (*0-7923-2270-3*) Kluwer Academic.
Rosen, Steven T., ed. see Abrams.
Rosen, Steven W., intro. A Catalog of the Ceramics Collection of the Nora Eccles Harrison Museum of Art. (Illus.). 72p. (Orig.). 1993. pap. write for info. (*1-882710-00-2*) USU N E H Mus.
Rosen, Steven W., et al. Henry Moore: The Reclining Figure. LC 84-71383. (Illus.). 148p. (Orig.). 1984. pap. 17.50 (*0-918881-12-9*) Columbus Mus Art.
Rosen, Stuart & Howell, Peter. Signals & Systems for Speech & Hearing. 332p. (C). 1991. pap. text 44.95 (*0-12-597231-8*) Acad Pr.
Rosen, Stuart D., et al. Self-Assessment Color Review of Cardiology. 192p. 1997. pap. text 27.00 (*0-316-75813-2*) Lppncott W & W.
Rosen, Sylvia. Dreaming the Poem. 1994. pap. 9.95 (*0-9622847-8-5*) Red Wind Bks.
Rosen, Teresa. The OTA Children's Coloring Book. (Illus.). 24p. (J). (ps-8). 1989. pap. 3.95 (*0-944227-04-X*) Prac Psych Pr.
Rosen, Theodore, et al. Nurse's Atlas of Dermatology. 203p. 1983. 25.50 (*0-316-75705-5*, Little Brwn Med Div) Lppncott W & W.
Rosen, Thomas. The Slavonic Translation of the Apocryphal Infancy Gospel of Thomas. (Acta Universitatis Upsaliensis Ser.: Vol. 39). 173p. 1997. pap. 44.50 (*91-554-3964-0*, Pub. by Almqvist Wiksell) Coronet Bks.
Rosen, Valentina S. German Indologists: Biographies of Scholars in Indian Studies Writing German - with a Summary of Indology German Speaking Countries. 1990. 22.50 (*81-85054-97-5*, Pub. by Manohar) S Asia.
Rosen, Vicki. The Cellular & Molecular Basis of Bone Formation & Repair. Thies, R. Scott, ed. (Molecular Biology Intelligence Unit Ser.). 161p. 1995. 79.00 (*1-57059-289-6*) Landes Bioscience.
***Rosen, Walter, et al.** Welcome to Junior's! Remembering Brooklyn with Recipes & Memories from Its Favorite Restaurant. LC 98-38877. (Illus.). 320p. 1999. 25.00 (*0-688-15900-1*, Wm Morrow) Morrow Avon.
Rosen, Walter K., jt. auth. see Tellalian, Chuck D.
Rosen, Wendy. Crafting As a Business. LC 99-179460. (Illus.). 256p. 1998. pap. 24.95 (*0-8069-8553-4*) Sterling.
Rosen, William. Shakespeare & the Craft of Tragedy. LC 60-8002. 245p. 1960. reprint ed. pap. 76.00 (*0-7837-4127-8*, 205795000011) Bks Demand.
Rosen, William, jt. auth. see Drooyan, Irving.
Rosen, William, jt. auth. see Rosen, Emanuel.
Rosen, William, ed. see Shakespeare, William, et al.
Rosen, Wilma G., jt. ed. see Mayeux, Richard.
Rosenak, Chuck. Saint Makers: Contemporary Santeras & Santeros. LC 98-24958. 1998. pap. 14.95 Northland AZ.
Rosenak, Chuck & Rosenak, Jan. Contemporary American Folk Art: A Collector's Guide. (Illus.). 320p. 1996. pap. 29.95 (*1-55859-897-9*) Abbeville Pr.
— Museum of American Folk Art Encyclopedia of Twentieth-Century American Folk Art & Artists. (Illus.). 416p. 1991. 75.00 (*1-55859-041-2*) Abbeville Pr.
— Navajo Folk Art: The People Speak. rev. ed. (Illus.). 176p. 1994. pap. 14.95 (*0-87358-693-X*) Northland AZ.
— The Saint Makers: Contemporary Santeras y Santeros. (Illus.). 160p. 1998. pap. 14.95 (*0-87358-718-9*) Northland AZ.
Rosenak, Jan, jt. auth. see Rosenak, Chuck.
Rosenak, Michael. Roads to the Palace: Jewish Texts & Teaching. LC 95-17226. (Faith & Culture in Contemporary Education Ser.). 288p. (C). 1995. 45.00 (*1-57181-058-7*) Berghahn Bks.
— Roads to the Palace: Jewish Texts & Teaching. LC 95-17226. 304p. 1998. pap. 18.50 (*1-57181-137-0*) Berghahn Bks.
Rosenau. Successful Project Management. 3rd ed. (Business Technology Ser.). 1998. text 59.95 (*0-442-02684-6*, VNR) Wiley.
Rosenau, Douglas E. A Celebration of Sex: A Guide to Enjoying God's Gift of Married Sexual Pleasure. 368p. 1996. pap. 14.99 (*0-7852-7366-2*) Nelson.
Rosenau, Hartmut. Allversoehnung: Ein Transzendentaltheologischer Grundlegungsversuch. (Theologische Bibliothek Toepelmann Ser.: No. 57). (GER.). x, 544p. 1993. lib. bdg. 163.10 (*3-11-013738-0*) De Gruyter.
Rosenau, Helen. The Ideal City: And Its Architectural Evolution in Europe. 3rd ed. (Illus.). 210p. 1983. 49.50 (*0-416-32850-4*, NO.3768) Routledge.
Rosenau, James N. Along the Domestic-Foreign Frontier: Exploring Governance in a Turbulent World. (Studies in International Relations: Vol. 53). 488p. (C). 1997. text 64.95 (*0-521-58283-0*); pap. text 24.95 (*0-521-58764-6*) Cambridge U Pr.
— National Leadership & Foreign Policy: A Case Study in the Mobilization of Public Support. LC 63-7160. 427p. reprint ed. pap. 132.40 (*0-608-17851-9*, 203263700080) Bks Demand.
— Turbulence in World Politics: A Theory of Change & Continuity. (Illus.). 459p. (Orig.). 1990. pap. text 19.95 (*0-691-02308-5*, Pub. by Princeton U Pr) Cal Prin Full Svc.
— The United Nations in a Turbulent World. LC 91-45522. (International Peace Academy Occasional Paper Ser.). 88p. 1992. pap. text 8.95 (*1-55587-330-8*) L Rienner.
Rosenau, James N. & Czempiel, Ernst-Otto, eds. Governance Without Government: Order & Change in World Politics. (Studies in International Relations: No. 20). (Illus.). 323p. (C). 1992. pap. text 22.95 (*0-521-40578-5*) Cambridge U Pr.
Rosenau, James N. & Durfee, Mary. Thinking Theory Thoroughly: Coherent Approaches to an Incoherent World. LC 95-1095. 218p. (C). 1995. pap. 23.00 (*0-8133-2595-1*, Pub. by Westview) HarpC.
— Thinking Theory Thoroughly: Coherent Approaches to an Incoherent World. 2nd ed. LC 99-51431. 256p. 1999. pap. 22.00 (*0-8133-6676-3*) Westview.
Rosenau, Milton, Jr. Faster New Product Development: Getting the Right Product to Market Quickly. LC 89-81027. 432p. 1990. 55.00 (*0-8144-5942-0*) AMACOM.
Rosenau, Milton D., Jr. The PDMA Handbook of Product Development. LC 96-33743. 656p. 1996. 99.00 (*0-471-14189-5*) Wiley.
Rosenau, Milton D. Successful Product Development: Speeding from Opportunity to Profit. LC 99-30972. 168p. 1999. 39.95 (*0-471-31532-X*) Wiley.
***Rosenau, Milton D.** Successful Project Management: A Step-by-Step Approach with Practical Examples. 3rd ed. LC 98-17751. 368p. 1998. 64.95 (*0-471-29304-0*) Wiley.
Rosenau, Milton D. & Moran, John J. Managing the Development of New Products: Achieving Speed & Quality Simultaneously Through Multifunctional Teamwork. 272p. 1993. 69.95 (*0-471-29183-8*, VNR) Wiley.
Rosenau, Milton D., Jr., jt. auth. see Lewin, Marsha D.
Rosenau, Pauline M. Post-Modernism & the Social Sciences: Insights, Inroads, & Intrusions. 220p. 1992. text 45.00 (*0-691-08619-2*, Pub. by Princeton U Pr); pap. text 15.95 (*0-691-02347-6*, Pub. by Princeton U Pr) Cal Prin Full Svc.
Rosenau, Pauline V., ed. Health Care Reform in the Nineties. LC 94-6009. 268p. (C). 1994. text 54.00 (*0-8039-5729-7*); pap. text 24.50 (*0-8039-5730-0*) Sage.
***Rosenau, Pauline Vaillancourt, ed.** Public-Private Policy Partnerships. LC 99-89689. (Illus.). 225p. 2000. 45.00 (*0-262-18198-3*); pap. 19.95 (*0-262-68114-5*) MIT Pr.
Rosenau, William. Jewish Ceremonial Institutions & Customs. 3rd rev. ed. LC 89-71334. 190p. 1992. reprint ed. lib. bdg. 45.00 (*1-55888-912-4*) Omnigraphics Inc.
Rosenau, William, jt. auth. see Flanagan, Linda H.
Rosenauer. Texas Real Estate Contracts. LC 99-35207. (Illus.). 340p. (C). 1999. pap. text 27.20 (*0-13-081133-5*) P-H.
Rosenauer, Johnnie, et al. Farm & Ranch Marketing. LC 97-2371. 228p. (C). 1997. 43.00 (*0-13-485590-6*) P-H.
Rosenauer, Johnnie L., et al. Prepare for the Texas Real Estate Exam. 6th ed. LC 97-21407. 232p. (C). 1997. pap. text 20.40 (*0-13-636416-0*) P-H.
Rosenauer, Libby. The Aware Person Series. pap. write for info. (*1-881762-05-X*) Aware Pr.
— One Hundred Fifty-One Ways to Raise Your Self-Esteem: A Book of Activities That Will Enhance Your Life. (Aware Person Ser.). 96p. (Orig.). 1993. pap. 9.95 (*1-881762-00-9*) Aware Pr.
— You Are More Prosperous Than You Think: A Book of Activities That Will Enhance Your Life. (Aware Person Ser.). 96p. 1993. pap. 9.95 (*1-881762-01-7*) Aware Pr.
Rosenaur, Johnnie. Effective Real Estate Sales & Marketing. 2nd ed. (Illus.). 258p. 1987. pap. 25.95 (*0-88462-599-0*, 1562-0202, Real Estate Ed) Dearborn.
Rosenbach, A. S. An American Jewish Bibliography: Being a List of Books & Phamphlets by Jews or Relating to Them Printed in the United States from the Establishment of the Press in the Colonies Until 1850. LC 98-23090. (Illus.). xi, 486p. 1998. reprint ed. 85.00 (*0-9631902-9-6*) Canonymous.
— Early American Children's Books. (Illus.). 413p. 1995. reprint ed. 75.00 (*1-888262-29-X*) Martino Pubng.
Rosenbach, Abraham S. An American Jewish Bibliography: Being a List of Books & Pamphlets by Jews, or Relating to Them, Printed in the United States from the Establishment of the Press in the Colonies until 1850. LC Z 6366.R81. (American Jewish Historical Society Publications: No. 30). (Illus.). 509p. reprint ed. pap. 157.80 (*0-8357-5376-X*, 201781600008) Bks Demand.
— Book Hunter's Holiday: Adventures with Books & Manuscripts. LC 68-29242. (Essay Index Reprint Ser.). 1977. reprint ed. 23.95 (*0-8369-0834-1*) Ayer.
— The Unpublished Memoirs. (American Biography Ser.). 151p. 1991. reprint ed. lib. bdg. 59.00 (*0-7812-8330-2*) Rprt Serv.
Rosenbach, Detlev. Alexej von Jawlensky's Life & Graphic Work. (GER., Illus.). 176p. 1985. 120.00 (*0-915346-96-6*) A Wofsy Fine Arts.
— Bargheer's Graphic Work. (Illus.). 200p. 1974. 120.00 (*0-915346-97-4*) A Wofsy Fine Arts.
— Bremer's Graphic Work. (Illus.). 230p. 1974. 120.00 (*0-915346-98-2*) A Wofsy Fine Arts.
— Heinrich Zille's Graphic Work. (Illus.). 228p. 1984. 165.00 (*0-915346-95-8*) A Wofsy Fine Arts.
Rosenbach, Joseph B. College Algebra with Trigonometry. LC 73-79572. 512p. reprint ed. pap. 158.80 (*0-608-30033-0*, 205510300008) Bks Demand.
Rosenbach, Kevin P. Pharmacology: MedCharts, Tables & Summaries for Review. LC 92-49118. 1993. pap. 14.95 (*1-882531-00-0*) ILOC.
Rosenbach, Margo L. The Use of Physicians' Services by Low-Income Children. LC 92-48901. (Children of Poverty Ser.). 200p. 1993. text 15.00 (*0-8153-1113-3*) Garland.
Rosenbach, O., et al. Studienhefte zur Angewandten Geophysik. xii, 275p. 1977. 35.00 (*3-443-24001-1*, Pub. by Gebruder Borntraeger) Balogh.
Rosenbach, O., ed. see Kappelmeyer, O. & Haenel, Ralph.
Rosenbach, William E. Military Leadership: In Pursuit of Excellence. 3rd ed. Taylor, Robert L., ed. (C). 1996. pap. text 25.00 (*0-8133-3024-6*, Pub. by Westview) HarpC.
Rosenbach, William E. & Taylor, Robert L. Leadership: Challenges for Today's Manager. 220p. 1989. 29.95 (*0-89397-317-3*) Nichols Pub.
Rosenbach, William E. & Taylor, Robert L., eds. Contemporary Issues in Leadership. 4th ed. LC 98-13677. 272p. 1998. pap. 28.00 (*0-8133-9995-5*, Pub. by Westview) HarpC.
***Rosenbalm, D.R.** The Way of the Natural Horseman: Handbook & Guide to Becoming "Connected" ix, 63p. 2000. mass mkt. 9.95 (*0-9700474-0-1*, DR1) Savahorse.
***Rosenband, Leonard N.** Papermaking in Eighteenth-Century France: Management, Labor & Revolution at the Montgolfier Mill, 1761-1805. LC 99-86391. 240p. 2000. 39.95 (*0-8018-6392-9*) Johns Hopkins.
Rosenband, Leonard N., jt. ed. see Safley, Thomas Max.
Rosenbauer, Tom. Casting Illusions: The World of Fly-Fishing. 2nd abr. rev. ed. LC 97-228383. (Illus.). 176p. 1997. 45.00 (*1-890674-02-8*) Lickle Pubng.
— Flyfishing. (Illus.). 80p. 1996. text 18.95 (*0-7893-0071-0*) St Martin.
— The Orvis Fly-Fishing Guide. (Illus.). 272p. 1988. 32.95 (*0-941130-91-6*); pap. 17.95 (*0-941130-92-4*) Lyons Pr.
***Rosenbauer, Tom.** Orvis Guide to Prospecting for Trout. (Illus.). 2000. pap. 19.95 (*1-58574-090-X*) Lyons Pr.
— The Orvis Guide to Reading Trout Streams. LC 99-29589. 1999. 17.95 (*1-55821-933-1*) Lyons Pr.
— Orvis Pocket Guide to Dry-Fly Fishing. (Illus.). 2001. 16.95 (*1-58574-158-2*) Lyons Pr.
— Orvis Pocket Guide to Nymphing Techniques. (Illus.). 2000. 16.95 (*1-58574-077-2*) Lyons Pr.
— Orvis Pocket Guide to Stillwater Fly-Fishing Techniques. (Illus.). 2000. 16.95 (*1-58574-078-0*) Lyons Pr.
— Orvis Streamside Guide to Approach & Presentation. (Orvis Streamside Guides Ser.). (Illus.). 2000. 16.95 (*1-55821-985-4*) Lyons Pr.
— Orvis Streamside Guide to Leaders, Lines & Tippets. LC 99-45681. (Orvis Streamside Guides Ser.). 2000. 16.95 (*1-55821-984-6*) Lyons Pr.
— Orvis Streamside Guide to Trout Foods & Their Imitations. (Orvis Streamside Guides Ser.). (Illus.). 2000. 16.95 (*1-55821-986-2*) Lyons Pr.
Rosenbauer, Tom. Reading Trout Streams: An Orvis Guide. (Illus.). 160p. 1988. 17.95 (*0-941130-77-0*); pap. 17.95 (*0-941130-78-9*) Lyons Pr.
Rosenbauer, Wolfgang. Better Vision Naturally. LC 98-19655. (Illus.). 96p. 1998. 10.95 (*0-8069-9981-0*) Sterling.
Rosenbaum. Aspects Bloomsbury: Studies in Modern English Literary & Intellectual History. LC 97-41112. 272p. 1998. text 45.00 (*0-312-21305-0*) St Martin.
— From Soapbox to Soundbite, 1945 to Present. LC 96-35408. 192p. 1997. text 59.95 (*0-312-16566-8*) St Martin.
Rosenbaum. Is the Holocaust Unique? Perspective on Comparative Genocide. pap. 20.00 (*0-8133-3686-4*) Westview.
Rosenbaum, jt. auth. see Volpe, Erminio Peter.
Rosenbaum, Alan S. Coercion & Autonomy: Philosophical Foundations, Issues & Practices, 31. LC 86-7578. (Contributions in Philosophy Ser.: No. 31). 208p. 1986. 49.95 (*0-313-22819-1*, RHA/, Greenwood Pr) Greenwood.
— Prosecuting Nazi War Criminals. 144p. 1999. reprint ed. pap. text 17.00 (*0-7881-6753-7*) DIANE Pub.
Rosenbaum, Alan S., ed. Constitutionalism: The Philosophical Dimension, 46. LC 88-5634. (Contributions in Legal Studies: No. 46). 288p. 1988. 65.00 (*0-313-25671-3*, RCU/, Greenwood Pr) Greenwood.
— The Philosophy of Human Rights: International Perspectives, 15. LC 79-6191. (Contributions in Philosophy Ser.: No. 15). 272p. 1980. 49.95 (*0-313-20985-5*, RHR/, Greenwood Pr) Greenwood.
Rosenbaum, Alan S., ed. Is the Holocaust Unique? Perspectives on Comparative Genocide. LC 96-33949. (C). 1997. pap. text 21.00 (*0-8133-2642-7*, Pub. by Westview) HarpC.
Rosenbaum, Allan, ed. Employment Training Policy. 204p. (Orig.). 1987. pap. 15.00 (*0-918592-92-5*) Pol Studies.
Rosenbaum, Allen. In Celebration: Works of Art from the Collections of Alumni & Friends of the Art Museum Princeton University. Guthrie, Jill, ed. LC 96-80813. (Illus.). 386p. (Orig.). 1997. per. 35.00 (*0-943012-22-8*) Prince U Art.
Rosenbaum, Alvin. The Complete Home Office. 224p. 1999. pap. 16.95 (*0-14-023516-7*) Viking Penguin.
— Usonia: Frank Lloyd Wright's Design for America. LC 93-7612. (Illus.). 216p. 1995. 29.95 (*0-471-14430-4*) Wiley.
— Works in Progress. LC 94-7912. (Illus.). 208p. 1994. 45.00 (*0-87654-069-8*) Pomegranate Calif.
***Rosenbaum, Art.** Art of the Mountain Banjo. 96p. (Orig.). 1998. pap. 22.95 (*0-7866-3378-6*, 96711BCD) Mel Bay.
Rosenbaum, Art. Art of the Mountain Banjo. 84p. (Orig.). 1988. reprint ed. pap. text 11.95 (*0-931759-24-2*) Centerstream Pub.
— Old Time Mountain Banjo. (Illus.). 88p. 1968. pap. 15.95 (*0-8256-0116-9*, OK62034, Oak) Music Sales.
— Shout Because You're Free: The African-American Ring Shout Tradition in Coastal Georgia. (Illus.). 216p. 1998. 24.95 (*0-8203-1934-1*) U of Ga Pr.
Rosenbaum, Art, intro. Slave Songs of the Georgia Sea Islands. LC 91-22948. (Brown Thrasher Bks.). (Illus.). 312p. 1992. reprint ed. 24.95 (*0-8203-1397-1*) U of Ga Pr.
Rosenbaum, Arthur L. Revolution & Social Change. 1996. text 24.50 (*0-89158-888-4*) Westview.
— Revolution & Social Change. (C). 1996. pap. text 12.00 (*0-89158-889-2*) Westview.
***Rosenbaum, Arthur L. & Lee, Chae-Jin.** The Cold War--Reassessments. Keck Center for International & Strategic Studies Staff, ed. LC 00-21011. (Monographs). 2000. write for info. (*0-930607-22-8*) Keck Ctr.

R

An Asterisk (*) at the beginning of an entry indicates that the title is appearing for the first time.

Rosenbaum, Arthur L. & Santiago, Alvina P. Clinical Strabismus Management. Lambert, Richard, ed. LC 98-48475. (Illus.). 575p. (C). 1999. text 185.00 (*0-7216-7673-1*, W B Saunders Co) Harcrt Hlth Sci Grp.

Rosenbaum, Barbara. Index of English Literary Manuscripts, 1800-1900, Vol. IV, Pt. 2: Hardy-Lamb. (Illus.). 768p. 1990. text 560.00 (*0-7201-1660-0*) Continuum.

Rosenbaum, Barbara & Pearson, Richard. Index of English Literary Manuscripts, 1800-1900, Vol. IV, Pt. 3: Landor-Patmore. (Index of English Literary Manuscripts). (Illus.). 860p. 1994. 540.00 (*0-7201-2153-1*) Continuum.

Rosenbaum, Barbara, jt. auth. see White, P.

Rosenbaum, Barbara A., jt. auth. see Kuglin, Fred A.

Rosenbaum, Ben. Legs the Caterpillar. Inter Continental Publishers Staff, ed. Orig. Title: The Insect Brigade. (Illus.). 32p. (J). (gr. k-3). 1995. 19.95 incl. audio (*0-9650244-0-7*, 125) Inter Contntl Pubs.

— Legs the Caterpillar. Inter Continental Publishers Staff, ed. Orig. Title: The Insect Brigade. (Illus.). 32p. (J). (ps-3). 1995. pap. 9.95 (*0-9650244-4-X*, 125) Inter Contntl Pubs.

— Legs the Caterpillar. abr. large type ed. Inter Continental Publishers Staff, ed. Orig. Title: The Insect Brigade. (Illus.). 32p. (J). (ps-3). 1995. pap. 9.95 (*0-9650244-3-1*, 125) Inter Contntl Pubs.

— Legs the Caterpillar. abr. large type ed. Inter Continental Publishers Staff, ed. Orig. Title: The Insect Brigade. (Illus.). 32p. (J). (ps-3). 1995. 14.95 (*0-9650244-2-3*, 125); lib. bdg. 14.95 incl. audio (*0-9650244-1-5*, 125) Inter Contntl Pubs.

Rosenbaum, Brenda. With Our Heads Bowed: The Dynamics of Gender in a Maya Community. LC 92-76220. (IMS Studies on Culture & Society: No. 5). (Illus.). 239p. (Orig.). (C). 1992. pap. 18.00 (*0-942041-14-3*) Univ Albany IFMS.

Rosenbaum, C. Peter. Italian for Educated Guessers: Shortcuts to the Language. (Illus.). 254p. (Orig.). 1984. pap. 12.00 (*0-9614045-1-5*) Forza Pr.

Rosenbaum, Cindy, et al. For the Love of Animals. unabridged ed. (Illus.). 24p. (J). (ps-4). 1992. pap. text 3.95 incl. audio (*1-881567-00-1*) Happy Kids Prods.

Rosenbaum, Claire M. A Gem of a College: History of Westhampton College, 1914-1989. Lancaster, Ann & Beville, Don, eds. (Illus.). 156p. 1989. text 19.95 (*0-685-29350-5*) Westhampton College.

Rosenbaum, Dave. If They Don't Win It's a Shame: The Year the Marlins Bought the World Series. LC 97-75702. (Illus.). 320p. 1998. 23.95 (*0-9653846-8-3*) McGregor Pub.

Rosenbaum, David. Goyim. 1998. 24.00 (*0-89296-660-2*) Mysterious Pr.

— Miami Ice: Winning the NHL Rat Race with the Florida Panthers. LC 96-78068. (Illus.). 252p. (Orig.). 1997. pap. 18.95 (*0-9653846-6-7*) McGregor Pub.

— Zaddik. LC 92-50695. 448p. 1993. 19.95 (*0-89296-540-1*) Mysterious Pr.

Rosenbaum, David A. Human Motor Control. 411p. (C). 1990. text 49.95 (*0-12-597300-4*) Acad Pr.

Rosenbaum, David A. & Collyer, Charles E., eds. Timing of Behavior: Neural, Psychological, & Computational Perspectives. LC 97-37189. (Illus.). 396p. 1998. 42.50 (*0-262-18188-6*, Bradford Bks) MIT Pr.

Rosenbaum, David G. Patents, Trademarks & Copyrights: Practical Strategies for Protecting Your Ideas & Inventions. 1993. pap. 9.95 (*0-9630356-6-5*) Makai.

Rosenbaum, David I., ed. Market Dominance: How Firms Gain, Hold, or Lose It & the Impact on Economic Performance. LC 97-27004. 280p. 1998. 69.50 (*0-275-95604-0*, Praeger Pubs) Greenwood.

Rosenbaum, Deborah & Dresser, Michelle. Interpharm International Clinical Research Coordinator Handbook: GCP Tools & Techniques. LC 96-27948. (Practical Clinical Trials Ser.: Vol. 1). 309p. 1996. ring bd. 145.00 (*1-57491-022-1*) Interpharm.

Rosenbaum, Deborah & Smith, Fred O. Clinical Research Monitor Handbook: GCP Tools & Techniques. (Practical Clinical Trials Ser.: Vol. 3). (Illus.). 428p. 1997. 145.00 (*1-57491-048-5*) Interpharm.

— Physician Investigator Handbook: GCP Tools & Techniques. LC 96-48071. (Practical Clinical Trials Ser.: Vol. 2). (Illus.). 300p. 1997. 145.00 (*1-57491-040-X*) Interpharm.

Rosenbaum, Dennis P. Drugs & the Community: Involving Community Residents in Combatting the Sale of Illegal Drugs. Davis, Robert C. et al, eds. LC 93-33880. (Illus.). 328p. 1993. pap. 44.95 (*0-398-06086-X*) C C Thomas.

Rosenbaum, Dennis P., ed. Community Crime Prevention: Does It Work? LC 85-26057. (Sage Criminal Justice System Annuals Ser.: No. 22). 318p. 1986. reprint ed. pap. 98.60 (*0-608-01114-2*, 205941800001) Bks Demand.

Rosenbaum, Dennis P. & Lurigio, Arthur J. The Prevention of Crime: Social & Situational Strategies. LC 98-14883. (Criminal Justice Ser.). (C). 1998. 35.95 (*0-534-50760-3*) Wadsworth Pub.

Rosenbaum, Dennis P., et al. Community Responses to Drug Abuse: A Program Evaluation. (Illus.). 52p. (Orig.). (C). 1994. pap. text 25.00 (*0-7881-1435-2*) DIANE Pub.

— Taking a Bite Out of Crime: The Impact of the National Citizens' Crime Prevention Media Campaign. 176p. 1996. 45.00 (*0-8039-5988-5*) Sage.

Rosenbaum, Dennis P., ed. see Bayley, David H., et al.

Rosenbaum, Dora, jt. auth. see McGreevy, Mary.

***Rosenbaum, Eckehard F., et al.** Privatization, Corporate Governance & the Emergence of Markets. LC 99-47836. (Studies in Economic Transition Ser.). 2000. text 79.95 (*0-312-23034-6*) St Martin.

Rosenbaum, Eduard & Sherman, A. J. M. M. Warburg & Company, 1798-1938: Merchant Bankers of Hamburg. LC 79-511. (Illus.). 190p. 1979. 39.95 (*0-8419-0477-4*) Holmes & Meier.

Rosenbaum, Elisabeth, ed. see Erasmus, Desiderius.

Rosenbaum, Eliza. Friends Afloat. LC 92-39029. (Publish-a-Book Contest Ser.). (Illus.). 24p. (J). (gr. 1-6). 1992. lib. bdg. 22.83 (*0-8114-3584-9*) Raintree Steck-V.

Rosenbaum, Elizabeth. A Catalogue of Cyrenaican Portrait Sculpture. 160p. 1979. 26.00 (*0-7855-7148-5*) St Mut.

Rosenbaum, Ernest H. You Can Prevent Cancer. Mahoney, Sheila & Wiltsek, Nancy, eds. (Illus.). 29p. 1984. pap. 2.50 (*0-933161-00-X*) Better H Prog.

Rosenbaum, Ernest H. & Rosenbaum, Isadora R. Inner Fire: Your Will to Live: Stories of Courage, Hope, & Determination. (Illus.). 224p. 1999. pap. 14.95 (*1-889762-12-1*) Plexus.

Rosenbaum, Ernest H., et al. Lifestyle & Cancer Prevention. Mahoney, Sheila & Wiltsek, Nancy, eds. (Illus.). 49p. 1985. pap. 2.50 (*0-933161-05-0*) Better H Prog.

— Tobacco, Alcohol & Cancer Prevention. Mahoney, Sheila & Wiltsek, Nancy, eds. (Illus.). 29p. 1984. pap. 2.50 (*0-933161-02-6*) Better H Prog.

Rosenbaum, Ernest H., jt. auth. see Wheat, Mary E.

Rosenbaum, Fred. Architects of Reform: Congregation & Community Leadership, Emanu-El of San Francisco, 1849-1980. LC 80-54032. 241p. 1980. 19.95 (*0-943376-14-9*); pap. 9.95 (*0-943376-13-0*) Magnes Mus.

Rosenbaum, Ginny. Corporate Takeover Defenses, 1998. 1995p. 1998. 395.00 (*1-879775-59-X*) IRRC Inc DC.

Rosenbaum, H. Jon & Tyler, William G., eds. Contemporary Brazil: Issues in Economic & Political Development. LC 73-180851. (Special Studies in International Economics & Development). 1972. 67.50 (*0-275-28289-9*) Irvington.

Rosenbaum, Hans-Udo, jt. ed. see Aland, Kurt.

Rosenbaum, Harold D. Pearls in Diagnostic Radiology. LC 80-19014. 296p. reprint ed. pap. 91.80 (*0-7837-3148-5*, 204283700006) Bks Demand.

Rosenbaum, Herbert D. & Bartelme, Elizabeth, eds. Franklin D. Roosevelt: The Man, the Myth, the Era, 1882-1945, 189. LC 87-8456. (Contributions in Political Science Ser.: No. 189). 426p. 1987. 75.00 (*0-313-25949-6*, RRS/, Greenwood Pr) Greenwood.

Rosenbaum, Herbert D. & Ugrinsky, Alexej, eds. Jimmy Carter: Foreign Policy & Post-Presidential Years, 328. LC 93-9320. (Contributions in Political Science Ser.: No. 328). 528p. 1993. 85.00 (*0-313-28844-5*, GM8844, Greenwood Pr) Greenwood.

— The Presidency & Domestic Policies of Jimmy Carter, 327. LC 93-9321. (Contributions in Political Science Ser.: No. 327). 876p. 1993. 110.00 (*0-313-28845-3*, GM8845, Greenwood Pr) Greenwood.

Rosenbaum, Howard, jt. auth. see Champelli, Lisa.

Rosenbaum, Irving. Fixin' City Hall: Entrepreneurial Solutions for a Municipal Makeover. (Illus.). 128p. (Orig.). (C). 1994. pap. 25.00 (*0-9647971-0-0*) U Pr Ft Lauderdale.

Rosenbaum, Irving J. Holocaust & Halakhah. (Library of Jewish Law & Ethics: Vol. II). 16.95 (*0-87068-296-2*) Ktav.

Rosenbaum, Isadora R., jt. auth. see Rosenbaum, Ernest H.

Rosenbaum, J. F. & Pollack, Mark H. Panic Disorder & Its Treatment. LC 98-4110. (Medical Psychiatry Ser.). (Illus.). 376p. 1998. text 99.75 (*0-8247-0216-6*) Dekker.

Rosenbaum, J. F., jt. ed. see Fava, Mathilde.

Rosenbaum, J. F., jt. ed. see Jonsson, B.

Rosenbaum, James E., jt. auth. see Rubinowitz, Leonard S.

Rosenbaum, Jean & Prine, Mary. Opportunites in Fitness Careers. (Illus.). 146p. 1988. 13.95 (*0-8442-6151-3*, VGM Career) NTC Contemp Pub Co.

— Opportunites in Fitness Careers. (Illus.). 146p. 1991. pap. 10.95 (*0-8442-6152-1*, VGM Career) NTC Contemp Pub Co.

— Opportunities in Fitness Careers. LC 90-50731. (Opportunities in...Ser.). 160p. (YA). (gr. 7 up). 1992. 14.95 (*0-8442-8185-9*, VGM Career) NTC Contemp Pub Co.

— Opportunities in Fitness Careers. LC 90-50731. (Opportunities in...Ser.). 160p. (YA). (gr. 7 up). 1994. pap. 11.95 (*0-8442-8186-7*, VGM Career) NTC Contemp Pub Co.

Rosenbaum, Jean & Rosenbaum, Veryl. Living with Teenagers. LC 79-3711. 192p. (C). 1982. pap. 7.95 (*0-8128-6144-2*, Scrbrough Hse) Madison Bks UPA.

Rosenbaum, Jean, jt. auth. see Rosenbaum, Veryl.

Rosenbaum, Jerold F. Issues in the Management of Depression: The Importance of Antidepressant Pharmacokinetics for the Primary Care Physician. Fellner, Chris, ed. (Series of Slide Lecture Programs: Vol. 3). (Orig.). 1997. pap. write for info. (*1-57130-024-4*) Medicine Grp USA.

Rosenbaum, Joel & Gallo, Tom. The Broadway Limited. LC 88-32103. (Illus.). 96p. (C). 1988. pap. 18.00 (*0-9621541-0-5*) Railpace Co.

***Rosenbaum, Jonathan.** Dead Man. 2000. pap. 12.95 (*0-85170-806-4*, Pub. by British Film Inst) Ind U Pr.

Rosenbaum, Jonathan. Film: The Front Line 1983. (Illus.). 238p. (Orig.). 1983. pap. 10.95 (*0-912869-03-8*) Arden Pr.

— Greed. (Illus.). 64p. (C). 1993. pap. 10.95 (*0-85170-358-5*, Pub. by British Film Inst) Ind U Pr.

***Rosenbaum, Jonathan.** Movie Wars: How Hollywood & the Media Conspire to Limit What Films We Can See. 256p. 2000. 24.00 (*1-55652-406-4*, Pub. by A Cappella Bks) IPG Chicago.

Rosenbaum, Jonathan. Movies as Politics. LC 96-9916. 350p. 1997. pap. 18.95 (*0-520-20615-0*, Pub. by U CA Pr) Cal Prin Full Svc.

— Moving Places: A Life at the Movies. LC 94-28364. (Orig.). 1995. reprint ed. pap. text 18.95 (*0-520-08907-3*, Pub. by U CA Pr) Cal Prin Full Svc.

— Placing Movies: The Practice of Film Criticism. LC 93-42954. 1995. 50.00 (*0-520-08632-5*, Pub. by U CA Pr); pap. 18.95 (*0-520-08633-3*, Pub. by U CA Pr) Cal Prin Full Svc.

Rosenbaum, Jonathan, jt. auth. see Dalin, David G.

Rosenbaum, Jonathan, jt. auth. see Hoberman, J.

Rosenbaum, Jonathan, ed. see Welles, Orson & Bogdanovich, Peter.

Rosenbaum, Jonathan, tr. see Bazin, Andre.

Rosenbaum, Judith, jt. auth. see Lubet, Steven.

Rosenbaum, Kurt. Community of Fate: German-Soviet Diplomatic Relations, 1922-1928. LC 65-18573. 335p. 1965. reprint ed. pap. 103.90 (*0-608-06947-7*, 206715500009) Bks Demand.

Rosenbaum, Larry. You Shall Be My Witnesses: How to Reach Your City for Christ. LC 86-90426. 144p. (Orig.). 1986. pap. 5.00 (*0-938573-00-4*) SOS Minist Pr.

Rosenbaum, Lilian. Biofeedback Frontiers: Self-Regulation of Stress Reactivity. LC 86-82030. (Stress in Modern Society Ser.: No. 15). 1988. 32.50 (*0-404-63266-1*) AMS Pr.

Rosenbaum, M. & Elizari, M., eds. Frontiers of Cardiac Electrophysiology. 1983. text 475.50 (*90-247-2663-8*) Kluwer Academic.

Rosenbaum, M., jt. auth. see Silbermann, A. M.

Rosenbaum, M. G., tr. see Pliskin, Zelig.

Rosenbaum, Marcus D. & Dinges, John, eds. Sound Reporting: National Public Radio's Guide to Radio Journalism & Production. 180p. 1993. pap. text 38.95 (*0-8403-7202-7*) Kendall-Hunt.

Rosenbaum, Marcus D., ed. see Apte, Helen J.

Rosenbaum, Marsha. Safety First: A Reality-Based Approach to Teens, Drugs & Drug Education. 22p. pap. write for info. (*1-930517-01-7*) Lindesmith Ctr.

Rosenbaum, Marsha, jt. auth. see Beck, Jerome.

Rosenbaum, Marsha, jt. auth. see Murphy, Sheigla.

Rosenbaum, Martin. Children & the Environment. 90p. 1994. pap. 22.00 (*1-874579-01-6*, Pub. by Natl Childrens Bur) Paul & Co Pubs.

Rosenbaum, Mary H. & Rosenbaum, Stanley. Celebrating Our Differences: Living Two Faiths in One Marriage. LC 94-8447. 238p. 1999. reprint ed. pap. 15.95 (*1-57249-163-9*, Ragged Edge) White Mane Pub.

Rosenbaum, Maurice, tr. see Mehnert, Klaus.

Rosenbaum, Maury. The Business Traveler's Guide to Good Health on the Road. Neumann, Karl, ed. 224p. 1993. pap. 12.95 (*0-471-34665-9*) Wiley.

Rosenbaum, Maury, jt. ed. see Neumann, Karl.

Rosenbaum, Max, ed. Complaint Behavior: Beyond Obedience to Authority. 254p. 1983. 35.95 (*0-89885-115-7*, Kluwer Acad Hman Sci) Kluwer Academic.

— Handbook of Short-Term Therapy Groups. LC 96-35207. (Master Works). 448p. 1996. pap. 65.00 (*0-7657-0045-X*) Aronson.

Rosenbaum, Max, jt. ed. see Rabin, H. M.

Rosenbaum, Michael. Street Fighting Tactics from Karate-Do. 96p. (Orig.). 1985. pap. 5.95 (*0-89826-015-9*) Natl Paperback.

— Word-Order Variation in Isaiah 40-55. xii, 259p. 1997. pap. text 70.00 (*90-232-3262-3*, Pub. by Van Gorcum) Eisenbrauns.

Rosenbaum, Michael, jt. auth. see Lee, William H.

Rosenbaum, Michael, jt. auth. see Susser, Murray.

Rosenbaum, Michael E. & Bosco, Dominick. Super Fitness Beyond Vitamins. 1989. pap. 4.95 (*0-318-40124-X*, Sig) NAL.

Rosenbaum, Myron G. Understanding Arthritis. LC 73-9498. (Illus.). 112p. 1975. 10.00 (*0-87527-121-9*) Green.

Rosenbaum, Nelson M. Citizen Involvement in Land Use Governance: Issues & Methods. (Illus.). 82p. (Orig.). 1976. pap. text 11.50 (*0-87766-140-5*) Urban Inst.

Rosenbaum, O. Dictionary Computer English: German/English/German. (ENG & GER.). 231p. 1995. 49.95 (*0-320-00550-X*) Fr & Eur.

— Lexicon of Internet-Speak, English to German. (ENG & GER.). 280p. 1996. 49.95 (*0-320-00502-X*) Fr & Eur.

Rosenbaum, Paul R. Observational Studies. LC 95-2178. (Springer Series in Statistics). (Illus.). 230p. 1995. 54.95 (*0-387-94482-6*) Spr-Verlag.

Rosenbaum, Peter A., jt. auth. see Volpe, E. Peter.

Rosenbaum, Philip. Friendly Schoolwork Helpers: Learning Colors. (Illus.). 48p. (Orig.). (J). (ps-k). 1995. pap., wbk. ed. 2.89 (*0-943263-66-2*, TF-2510) Teachers Friend Pubns.

Rosenbaum, Phillip. Friendly Schoolwork Helpers: Alike & Different. (Illus.). 48p. (Orig.). (J). (ps-k). 1995. pap., wbk. ed. 2.89 (*0-943263-64-6*, TF-2508) Teachers Friend Pubns.

— Friendly Schoolwork Helpers: Alphabet Dot-to-Dot. (Illus.). 48p. (Orig.). (J). (ps-k). 1995. pap., wbk. ed. 2.89 (*0-943263-59-X*, TF-2503) Teachers Friend Pubns.

— Friendly Schoolwork Helpers: Alphabet Practice. (Illus.). 48p. (Orig.). (J). (ps-k). 1995. pap., wbk. ed. 2.89 (*0-943263-58-1*, TF-2502) Teachers Friend Pubns.

— Friendly Schoolwork Helpers: Beginning Alphabet. (Illus.). 48p. (J). (ps-k). 1995. pap., wbk. ed. 2.89 (*0-943263-57-3*, TF-2501) Teachers Friend Pubns.

— Friendly Schoolwork Helpers: Beginning Sounds. (Illus.). 48p. (Orig.). (J). (ps-k). 1995. pap., wbk. ed. 2.89 (*0-943263-67-0*, TF-2511) Teachers Friend Pubns.

— Friendly Schoolwork Helpers: Beginning Writing. (Illus.). 48p. (Orig.). (J). (ps-k). 1995. pap., wbk. ed. 2.89 (*0-943263-63-8*, TF-2507) Teachers Friend Pubns.

— Friendly Schoolwork Helpers: Counting Dot-to-Dot. (Illus.). 48p. (Orig.). (J). (ps-k). 1995. pap., wbk. ed. 2.89 (*0-943263-62-X*, TF-2506) Teachers Friend Pubns.

— Friendly Schoolwork Helpers: Counting 1-20. (Illus.). 48p. (Orig.). (J). (ps-k). 1995. pap., wbk. ed. 2.89 (*0-943263-60-3*, TF-2504) Teachers Friend Pubns.

— Friendly Schoolwork Helpers: Kindergarten Practice. (Illus.). 48p. (Orig.). (J). (ps-k). 1995. pap., wbk. ed. 2.89 (*0-943263-68-9*, TF-2512) Teachers Friend Pubns.

— Friendly Schoolwork Helpers: Number Practice 1-20. (Illus.). 48p. (Orig.). (J). (ps-k). 1995. pap., wbk. ed. 2.89 (*0-943263-61-1*, TF-2505) Teachers Friend Pubns.

— Friendly Schoolwork Helpers: Shapes & Patterns. (Illus.). 48p. (Orig.). (J). (ps-k). 1995. pap., wbk. ed. 2.89 (*0-943263-65-4*, TF-2509) Teachers Friend Pubns.

Rosenbaum, Phillip, ed. Practice! & Learn! Alphabet Fun! (Illus.). 144p. (J). (ps-1). 1997. pap., teacher ed., wbk. ed. 10.95 (*1-57882-016-2*, TF-4003) Teachers Friend Pubns.

— Practice! & Learn! Colors, Numbers & Shapes. (Illus.). 144p. (J). (ps-1). 1997. pap., teacher ed., wbk. ed. 10.95 (*1-57882-014-6*, TF-4001) Teachers Friend Pubns.

— Practice! & Learn! Learning to Trace & Write. (Illus.). 144p. (J). (ps-1). 1997. pap., teacher ed., wbk. ed. 10.95 (*1-57882-017-0*, TF-4004) Teachers Friend Pubns.

— Practice! & Learn! Numbers & Counting 1-20. (Illus.). 144p. (J). (ps-1). 1997. pap., teacher ed., wbk. ed. 10.95 (*1-57882-015-4*, TF-4002) Teachers Friend Pubns.

Rosenbaum, Ray. Falcons Bk. 1: Wings of War. LC 92-29016. 416p. (Orig.). 1995. pap. 9.95 (*0-89141-559-9*) Presidio Pr.

Rosenbaum, Ray, jt. auth. see Brennan, T. C.

Rosenbaum, Richard B. & Ochoa, Jose L. Carpal Tunnel Syndrome & Other Disorders of the Median Nerve. 358p. 1992. text 105.00 (*0-7506-9229-4*) Buttrwrth-Heinemann.

Rosenbaum, Richard R., et al. Clinical Neurology in Rheumatic Diseases. LC 96-28925. 436p. 1996. pap. text 97.00 (*0-7506-9613-3*) Buttrwrth-Heinemann.

Rosenbaum, Robert. Aviators. (American Profiles Ser.). (Illus.). 128p. (YA). (gr. 6-12). 1992. lib. bdg. 19.95 (*0-8160-2539-8*) Facts on File.

***Rosenbaum, Robert.** Aviators: American Profiles. (Illus.). 122p. (YA). (gr. 7-9). 2000. reprint ed. text 17.00 (*0-7881-6932-7*) DIANE Pub.

— Zen & the Heart of Psychotherapy. LC 98-22924. 320p. 1998. 49.95 (*0-87630-891-4*) Brunner-Mazel.

***Rosenbaum, Robert.** Zen & the Heart of Psychotherapy, 1. 1999. pap. text 18.95 (*1-58391-040-9*) Brunner-Mazel.

Rosenbaum, Robert A. The Public Issues Handbook: A Guide for the Concerned Citizen. LC 82-15812. (Illus.). 409p. 1983. lib. bdg. 75.00 (*0-313-23504-X*, RPI/, Greenwood Pr) Greenwood.

Rosenbaum, Robert D. & Parker, L. Stevenson. State Takeover Statutes & Poison Pills, 2 vols. 2006p. 1989. ring bd. 185.00 (*0-13-808882-9*) Aspen Law.

Rosenbaum, Robert J. History of Mexican Americans in Texas. (Texas History Ser.). (Illus.). 38p. 1981. pap. text 9.95 (*0-89641-042-0*) American Pr.

Rosenbaum, Robert J. Mexicano Resistance in the Southwest. LC 98-3839. (Illus.). 264p. 1998. reprint ed. pap. 14.95 (*0-87074-429-1*) SMU Press.

Rosenbaum, Robert J., ed. People in Texas. (Illus.). 192p. (C). 1982. pap. text 16.95 (*0-89641-102-8*) American Pr.

— Readings in Texas History. (Illus.). 216p. (C). 1982. pap. text 17.95 (*0-89641-136-2*) American Pr.

Rosenbaum, Ron. Explaining Hitler. write for info. (*0-06-099602-1*) HarpC.

— Explaining Hitler. LC 97-34468. 444p. 1998. 30.00 (*0-679-43151-9*) Random.

— Explaining Hitler. 1999. text 25.00 (*0-670-82158-6*) Viking Penguin.

— Explaining Hitler: The Search for the Origins of His Evil. LC 99-25965. 496p. 1999. pap. 16.00 (*0-06-095339-X*) HarpC.

***Rosenbaum, Ron.** The Secret Parts of Fortune: Three Decades of Intense Investigations & Edgy Enthusiasms. LC 99-89067. 576p. 2000. 29.95 (*0-375-50338-2*) Random.

Rosenbaum, S. E. A Voyage to America Ninety Years Ago: The Diary of a Bohemian Jew on His Voyage from Hamburg to New York in 1847. Kisch, Guido et al, eds. Kravetz, Nathan, tr. LC 93-2898. (Studies in Judaica & the Holocaust: No. 3). 120p. 1995. reprint ed. pap. 17.00 (*0-89370-471-7*) Millefleurs.

Rosenbaum, S. P. Edwardian Bloomsbury: The Early Literary History of the Bloomsbury Group, Vol. 2. 559p. 1994. text 39.95 (*0-312-23909-2*) St Martin.

— Victorian Bloomsbury: The Early Literary History of the Bloomsbury Group, Vol. 1. 298p. 1987. text 29.95 (*0-312-84051-9*) St Martin.

Rosenbaum, S. P., ed. The Bloomsbury Group: A Collection of Memoirs, Commentary & Criticism. 1975. pap. 21.95 (*0-8020-6268-7*) U of Toronto Pr.

— English Literature & British Philosophy. LC 71-157147. (Patterns of Literary Criticism Ser.). 1993. pap. text 3.25 (*0-226-72657-6*, PLC10) U Ch Pr.

— English Literature & British Philosophy. LC 71-157147. (Patterns of Literary Criticism Ser.). 1994. lib. bdg. 20.00 (*0-226-72656-8*) U Ch Pr.

Rosenbaum, S. P., ed. see James, Henry.

Rosenbaum, Samuel. Rule-Making Authority in the English Supreme Court. xiv, 321p. 1993. reprint ed. 42.00 (*0-8377-2547-X*, Rothman) W S Hein.

Rosenbaum, Sara, et al. An Evaluation of Contracts Between Managed Care Organizations & Community Mental Health & Substance Abuse Treatment & Prevention Agencies & Between State Medicaid Agencies & Managed Care Organizations. (Illus.). 117p. 1998. pap. text 40.00 (*0-7881-3900-2*) DIANE Pub.

An Asterisk (*) at the beginning of an entry indicates that the title is appearing for the first time.

Rosenbaum, Sonia. Quantitative Methods & Statistics: A Guide to Social Research. LC 79-12570. 171p. 1979. reprint ed. pap. 53.10 (*0-608-01465-6*, 205950900001) Bks Demand.

Rosenbaum, Stanford P., ed. see Dickinson, Emily.

Rosenbaum, Stanley, jt. auth. see Rosenbaum, Mary H.

Rosenbaum, Stanley N. Amos of Israel: A New Interpretation. LC 89-39065. xii, 129p. (C). 1990. text 25.00 (*0-86554-355-0*, MUP/H296) Mercer Univ Pr.

Rosenbaum, Stuart, jt. ed. see Baird, Robert.

Rosenbaum, Stuart E., jt. auth. see Baird, Robert M.

Rosenbaum, Stuart E., jt. ed. see Baird, Robert M.

Rosenbaum, Thane. Elijah Visible. 224p. 1996. text 21.95 (*0-312-14325-7*) St Martin.

— Elijah Visible: Stories. LC 98-53792. 1999. pap. 12.95 (*0-312-19865-5*) St Martin.

— Second Hand Smoke. LC 98-43787. 320p. 1999. text 24.95 (*0-312-19954-6*) St Martin.

***Rosenbaum, Thane.** Second Hand Smoke: Novel. 320p. 2000. pap. 13.95 (*0-312-25418-0*) St Martin.

Rosenbaum, Ute, jt. auth. see Beutelspacher, Albrecht.

Rosenbaum, Veryl & Rosenbaum, Jean. Stepparenting. LC 77-22070. 160p. 1977. 12.95 (*0-88316-530-9*) Chandler & Sharp.

Rosenbaum, Veryl, jt. auth. see Rosenbaum, Jean.

Rosenbaum, Virginia K. Corporate Takeover Defenses - 90. 2nd ed. 1551p. 1990. 50.00 (*0-931035-52-X*) IRRC Inc DC.

— Corporate Takeover Defenses, 1993. 1530p. 1993. 95.00 (*1-879775-09-3*) IRRC Inc DC.

Rosenbaum, Virginia K., compiled by. Corporate Takeover Defenses, 1995. 1533p. (Orig.). 1995. pap. 195.00 (*1-879775-29-8*) IRRC Inc DC.

Rosenbaum, Walter A. Environmental Politics & Policy. 3rd ed. LC 94-34158. 372p. (YA). (gr. 11). 1995. pap. text 26.95 (*0-87187-848-8*) Congr Quarterly.

— Environmental Politics & Policy. 4th ed. LC 98-8614. 384p. 1998. 31.95 (*1-56802-335-9*) Congr Quarterly.

Rosenbek, John C., et al. Aphasia: A Clinical Approach. LC 90-52763. 311p. (C). 1989. pap. text 38.00 (*0-89079-270-4*, 1781) PRO-ED.

Rosenberg. Clinician's Guide to Alternative Medicine. 7p. 1999. write for info. (*0-7506-9639-7*) Buttrwrth-Heinemann.

— Companion Chemical Thermodynamics. pap. text. write for info. (*0-471-37220-X*) Wiley.

— Foundations of Behavioral Research. (C). 1993. pap. text, teacher ed. 35.00 (*0-03-055559-0*) Harcourt Coll Pubs.

— Fundamentals of Obstetric & Gynecological Radiology. 1999. pap. text. write for info. (*0-7216-5157-7*, W B Saunders Co) Harcrt Hlth Sci Grp.

— Harper's Grammar of French. (FRE.). (C). 1991. text 44.95 (*0-8384-3746-X*) Heinle & Heinle.

— Investigating Child Death. Date not set. 45.00 (*0-02-927085-5*) Jossey-Bass.

***Rosenberg.** KTHW: SILVER STON(HC), Vol. 2. 2000. 22.00 (*0-380-97266-2*) HarpC.

Rosenberg. Louise Erdrich & Michael Dorris. 1998. 22.95 (*0-8057-4573-4*, Twyne) Mac Lib Ref.

— The New Adventures of Mother Goose: Gemstones Christmas. (Illus.). 32p. (J). (ps-k). 1999. 9.95 (*0-689-82438-6*) S&S Trade.

***Rosenberg.** Pain Management. (C). 1999. text 120.00 (*0-7020-2285-3*, Pub. by Harcourt Coll Pubs) Harcourt.

Rosenberg. The Priest's Secret. 1996. 20.00 (*1-883402-53-0*) S&S Trade.

— Readings/Lessons Harper's Grammar French. (College French Ser.). (FRE.). (C). 1991. mass mkt. 30.95 (*0-8384-3747-8*) Heinle & Heinle.

— Vulture. rev. ed. 404p. 2000. 29.95 (*0-471-36189-5*) Wiley.

Rosenberg, ed. I'm American Voices. 1997. pap. text 5.66 (*0-06-365932-8*) P-H.

Rosenberg & Swinney. Dragon's Lair Jewlery Business Project 4. 5th ed. (BB - Record Keeping I Ser.). 1985. pap. 6.95 (*0-538-11294-8*) S-W Pub.

— George's Market Business Project 6. 5th ed. (BB - Record Keeping I Ser.). 1985. pap. 6.95 (*0-538-11296-4*) S-W Pub.

Rosenberg & Wolfe. Critical Thinking for Reading & Writing. 386p. 1998. pap. text 30.00 (*0-536-01855-3*) Pearson Custom.

Rosenberg, et al. Cancer: Principles & Practice of Oncology, 2 vols. 5th ed. DeVita, Vincent T. & Hellman, Samuel, eds. (Illus.). 3456p. 1996. 255.00 (*0-397-51574-X*) Lppncott W & W.

Rosenberg, jt. auth. see Evans.

Rosenberg, Aaron, jt. auth. see Brucato, Phil.

Rosenberg, A. Nicolas Gueudeville & His Work 1652-1725. 1982. lib. bdg. 177.50 (*90-247-2533-X*) Kluwer Academic.

Rosenberg, A. J. Mishnah Kodashim Vol. 3A: Arachin. Danziger, Y. & Adelman, Y., eds. (Artscroll Mishanh Ser.). 1991. 22.99 (*0-89906-312-8*) Mesorah Pubns.

Rosenberg, A. J., ed. Chronicles I & II: Hebrew Text, English Translation & Commentary Digest. 2nd rev. ed. LC 93-8763. 2001. reprint ed. 16.95 (*1-871055-85-7*) Soncino Pr.

— Ezekiel: Hebrew Text, English Translation & Commentary Digest. LC 93-5029. (ENG & HEB.). 2001. reprint ed. 16.95 (*1-871055-95-4*) Soncino Pr.

Rosenberg, A. J., tr. Book of Chronicles I - Hebrew Text & Commentary with English Translation: Hebrew Text, English Translation & Commentary Digest. (Books of the Prophets & Holy Writings). 1992. 20.95 (*0-910818-97-5*) Judaica Pr.

— The Book of Esther - Hebrew Text & Commentary with English Translation: Hebrew Text, English Translation & Commentary Digest. (Book of the Prophets & Holy Writings Ser.). 52p. 1992. pap. 8.95 (*1-880582-00-7*) Judaica Pr.

— Book of Exodus. (Books of the Bible: Vol. 2). (Illus.). 660p. 1996. 24.95 (*1-880582-16-3*) Judaica Pr.

— The Book of Exodus, Vol. 1. LC 95-47076. (Books of the Bible). (ENG & HEB.). 704p. 1996. 24.95 (*1-880582-15-5*) Judaica Pr.

— Book of Ezekiel - Hebrew Text & Commentary with English Translation Vol. 1, Chaps. 1-25: Hebrew Text, English Translation & Commentary Digest. (Books of the Prophets & Holy Writings). 1991. 20.95 (*0-910818-87-8*) Judaica Pr.

— Book of Ezekiel - Hebrew Text & Commentary with English Translation Vol. 2, Chaps. 26-48: Hebrew Text, English Translation & Commentary Digest. (Books of the Prophets & Holy Writings Ser.). 469p. 1991. 18.95 (*0-910818-86-X*) Judaica Pr.

— The Book of Genesis: A New Translation, with Hebrew Text & Commentary Digest, 3. LC 93-4128. 534p. 1994. 22.50 (*1-880582-10-4*) Judaica Pr.

— The Book of Genesis: A New Translation with Hebrew Text & Commentary Digest, Vol. 2. LC 93-15795. 1994. 22.50 (*1-880582-09-0*) Judaica Pr.

— Book of Genesis Vol. 1: A New Translation with Hebrew Text & Commentary Digest, Vol. 1. LC 93-1547. 1993. 22.50 (*1-880582-08-2*) Judaica Pr.

— Book of Isaiah: Hebrew Text & Commentary with English Translation, Vol. 1. (Books of the Prophets & Holy Writings). (HEB.). 520p. 1982. 20.95 (*0-910818-50-9*) Judaica Pr.

— Book of Isaiah: Hebrew Text & Commentary with English Translation, Vol. 2. (Books of the Prophets & Holy Writings). (HEB.). 616p. 1983. 20.95 (*0-910818-52-5*) Judaica Pr.

— Book of Jeremiah: Hebrew Text & Commentary with English Translation, Vol. 1. (Books of the Prophets & Holy Writings). 480p. 1985. 20.95 (*0-910818-59-2*) Judaica Pr.

— Book of Jeremiah Vol. 2: Hebrew Text & Commentary with English Translation. (Books of the Prophets & Holy Writings). (HEB.). 468p. 1985. 20.95 (*0-910818-60-6*) Judaica Pr.

— Book of Job - Hebrew Text & Commentary with English Translation: Hebrew Text, English Translation & Commentary Digest. (Books of the Prophets & Holy Writings). (HEB.). 512p. 1989. 20.95 (*0-910818-80-0*) Judaica Pr.

— Book of Joshua - Hebrew Text & Commentary with English Translation: Hebrew Text, English Translation & Commentary Digest. (Books of the Prophets & Holy Writings). 368p. 1984. 20.95 (*0-910818-08-8*) Judaica Pr.

— Book of Judges-Hebrew Text & Commentary with English Translation: Hebrew Text, English Translation & Commentary Digest. (Books of the Prophets & Holy Writings). (HEB.). 400p. 1979. 20.95 (*0-910818-17-7*) Judaica Pr.

— Book of Kings: Hebrew Text & Commentary with English Translation, Vol. 1. (Books of the Prophets & Holy Writings). (HEB.). 520p. 1980. 20.95 (*0-910818-30-4*) Judaica Pr.

— Book of Kings: Hebrew Text & Commentary with English Translation, Vol. 2. (Books of the Prophets & Holy Writings). (HEB.). 448p. 1980. 20.95 (*0-910818-31-2*) Judaica Pr.

— The Book of Proverbs - Hebrew Text & Commentary with English Translation: Hebrew Text, English Translation & Commentary Digest. (Books of the Prophets & Holy Writings). 1993. 18.95 (*0-910818-79-7*) Judaica Pr.

— Book of Samuel 1 Vol. 1: Hebrew Text & Commentary with English Translation. (Books of the Prophets & Holy Writings). (HEB.). 512p. 1981. 20.95 (*0-910818-07-X*) Judaica Pr.

— Book of Samuel 2: Hebrew Text & Commentary with English Translation. (Books of the Prophets & Holy Writings). (HEB.). 450p. 1982. 20.95 (*0-910818-11-8*) Judaica Pr.

— Book of Twelve Prophets: Hebrew Text & Commentary with English Translation. (Books of the Prophets & Holy Writings: Vol. 1). 480p. 1986. 20.95 (*0-910818-70-3*) Judaica Pr.

— Book of Twelve Prophets: Hebrew Text & Commentary with English Translation. (Books of the Prophets & Holy Writings: Vol. 2). 536p. 1988. 20.95 (*0-910818-78-9*) Judaica Pr.

— Chronicles II - Hebrew Text & Commentary with English Translation: Hebrew Text, English Translation & Commentary Digest. 1992. 20.95 (*0-910818-98-3*) Judaica Pr.

— Daniel, Ezra, & Nehemiah - Hebrew Text & Commentary with English Translation: Hebrew Text, English Translation & Commentary Digest. (Books of the Prophets & Holy Writings). 1992. 20.95 (*0-910818-94-0*) Judaica Pr.

— The Five Megilloth-Hebrew Text & Commentary with English Translation Vol. 1: Esther, The Song of Songs, Ruth. LC 92-13500. (Books of the Prophets & Holy Writings). 1992. 20.95 (*1-880582-01-5*) Judaica Pr.

— Five Megilloth-Hebrew Text & Commentary with English Translation Vol. 2: Lamentations, Ecclesiastes. LC 92-13500. (Books of the Prophets & Holy Writings). 1992. 20.95 (*1-880582-02-3*) Judaica Pr.

— Psalms: Hebrew Text & Commentary with English Translation, Vol. 1 (Chaps. 1-41) LC 59-10454.Tr. of Sefer Tehillim. 352p. 1990. 20.95 (*0-910818-84-3*) Judaica Pr.

— Psalms: Hebrew Text & Commentary with English Translation, Vol. 2 (Chaps. 42-89)Tr. of Sefer Tehillim. 432p. 1990. 20.95 (*0-910818-85-1*) Judaica Pr.

— Psalms: Hebrew Text & Commentary with English Translation, Vol. 3 (Chaps. 90-150) LC 59-10454. (Books of the Prophets & Holy Writings).Tr. of Sefer Tehillim. 432p. 1990. 20.95 (*0-910818-86-X*) Judaica Pr.

Rosenberg, A. Y. Mishnah-Moed: Shabbos. Danziger, Y. & Gold, A., eds. (ArtScroll Mishnah Ser.). (Illus.). 396p. 1982. 22.95 (*0-89906-250-4*) Mesorah Pubns.

— Mishnah-Nashim: Kesubos. Arem, T. Z., ed. (ArtScroll Mishnah Ser.). (Illus.). 258p. 1984. 22.99 (*0-89906-277-6*) Mesorah Pubns.

— Mishnah-Nezikin: Bava Kamma. Arem, T. Z., ed. (ArtScroll Mishnah Ser.). 240p. 1986. 22.99 (*0-89906-289-X*) Mesorah Pubns.

— Mishnah-Nezikin: Bava Metzia. Arem, T. Z., ed. (ArtScroll Mishnah Ser.). (Illus.). 264p. 22.99 (*0-89906-291-1*) Mesorah Pubns.

— Mishnah-Nezikin: Makkos/Shevos. Finkel, G., ed. (ArtScroll Mishnah Ser.). (Illus.). 310p. 1987. 22.99 (*0-89906-297-0*) Mesorah Pubns.

Rosenberg, Aaron G., ed. see Galante, Jorge O.

Rosenberg, Abraham, ed. Biology of the Sialic Acids. (Illus.). 394p. (C). 1995. text 110.00 (*0-306-44974-9*, Kluwer Plenum) Kluwer Academic.

Rosenberg, Alan, et al, eds. Contemporary Portrayals of Auschwitz: Philosophical Challenges. LC 99-53621. 345p. 2000. 69.95 (*1-57392-733-3*, Humanity Bks) Prometheus Bks.

Rosenberg, Alan & Myers, Gerald, eds. Echoes from the Holocaust: Philosophical Reflections on a Dark Time. 472p. 1990. pap. 24.95 (*0-87722-686-5*) Temple U Pr.

Rosenberg, Alan & Myers, Gerald E., eds. Echoes from the Holocaust: Philosophical Reflections on a Dark Time. LC 87-18109. 453p. (C). 1988. 49.95 (*0-87722-539-7*) Temple U Pr.

Rosenberg, Alan, jt. ed. see Marcus, Paul.

Rosenberg, Alan, jt. ed. see Milchman, Alan.

Rosenberg, Albert & Armstrong, Cindy. The American Gladiators: Taft Versus Remus. LC 95-80892. 265p. 1995. 18.75 (*0-9648784-0-2*) Aimwell Pr.

Rosenberg, Alex, jt. ed. see Jacob, Bill.

***Rosenberg, Alexander.** Darwinism in Philosophy, Social Science & Policy. (Cambridge Studies in Philosophy & Biology). (Illus.). 288p. 2000. 59.95 (*0-521-66297-4*); pap. 19.95 (*0-521-66407-1*) Cambridge U Pr.

Rosenberg, Alexander. Economics: Mathematical Politics or Science of Diminishing Returns? (Science & Its Conceptual Foundations Ser.). xvii, 284p. 1994. pap. text 14.95 (*0-226-72724-6*) U Ch Pr.

— Economics - Mathematical Politics or Science of Diminishing Returns? (Science & Its Conceptual Foundations Ser.). (Illus.). 283p. 1992. lib. bdg. 36.00 (*0-226-72723-8*) U Ch Pr.

— Instrumental Biology, or the Disunity of Science. (Science & Its Conceptual Foundations Ser.). 204p. 1994. pap. text 15.95 (*0-226-72726-2*) U Ch Pr.

— Instrumental Biology, or the Disunity of Science. (Science & Its Conceptual Foundations Ser.). 204p. 1994. lib. bdg. 38.00 (*0-226-72725-4*) U Ch Pr.

***Rosenberg, Alexander.** Philosophy of Science: A Contemporary Introduction. LC 00-26960. (Contemporary Introductions to Philosophy Ser.). 2001. pap. write for info. (*0-415-15281-X*) Routledge.

Rosenberg, Alexander. Philosophy of Social Science. 2nd ed. Daniels, Norman & Lehrer, Keith, eds. LC 95-14102. (Dimensions of Philosophy Ser.). 256p. (C). 1995. pap. text 27.00 (*0-8133-2660-5*, Pub. by Westview) HarpC.

— Sociobiology & the Preemption of Social Science. LC 80-8091. 240p. 1981. text 38.00 (*0-8018-2423-0*) Johns Hopkins.

Rosenberg, Alexander L. Noncommutative Algebraic Geometry & Representations of Quantized Algebras. (Mathematics & Its Applications Ser.). 328p. (C). 1995. text 155.00 (*0-7923-3575-9*) Kluwer Academic.

Rosenberg, Alfred. Kampf Um die Macht: Aufsatze Von 1921-1932, Herausgegeben Von Thilo Von Trotha. LC 77-180426. reprint ed. 54.00 (*0-404-56160-8*) AMS Pr.

— The Myth of the Twentieth Century. Orig. Title: Der Mythos des 20. Jahrhunderts. 1984. lib. bdg. 250.00 (*0-87700-605-9*) Revisionist Pr.

— Der Mythus des 20 Jahrhunderts. LC 78-63710. (Studies in Fascism: Ideology & Practice). reprint ed. 64.50 (*0-404-16983-X*) AMS Pr.

— Nietzsche. 1975. lib. bdg. 250.00 (*0-8490-0732-1*) Gordon Pr.

Rosenberg, Allison A., et al, eds. American Psychologist Special Issue Vol. 46, No. 11: Homelessness. 156p. 1991. pap. 16.00 (*1-55798-161-2*) Am Psychol.

Rosenberg, Amy, jt. auth. see Slesin, Louis.

Rosenberg, Amye. Bitsy Bear's Christmas. (Stickers & Shapes Ser.). (Illus.). 24p. (J). (ps-1). 1998. pap 4.99 (*0-689-81808-4*) Litle Simon.

— Even an Easter Bunny Needs Treats. (Stickers 'n' Shapes Ser.). 24p. (J). (ps-1). 1997. 3.99 (*0-689-81252-3*) S&S Childrens.

— Everyone Loves a Picnic. (Stickers 'n' Shapes Ser.). (J). 1997. 3.99 (*0-689-81253-1*) S&S Childrens.

— Good Job, Jelly Bean! (Sticker Bks.). (Illus.). 24p. (J). (ps-1). 1992. per. 3.99 (*0-671-75512-9*) Litle Simon.

— Jelly Bean's Picnic. (Stickers & Shapes Ser.). (Illus.). (J). (ps-1). 1997. 3.99 (*0-614-29110-0*) Litle Simon.

— Jewels for Josephine. (Illus.). 28p. (J). (ps-2). 1993. 12.95 (*0-448-40457-5*, G & D) Peng Put Young Read.

— Kitt's Special Christmas. (Stickers & Shapes Ser.). (Illus.). 24p. (J). (ps-1). 1998. pap. 4.99 (*0-689-81809-2*) Litle Simon.

— The Magical Gemstones Christmas. (Illus.). 16p. (J). (ps-2). 1999. pap. 9.99 (*0-689-82439-4*) Litle Simon.

— Melly's Magic Dreidel. (Stickers & Shapes Ser.). (Illus.). 24p. (J). (ps-1). 1998. pap. 4.99 (*0-689-81810-6*) Litle Simon.

— Melly's Menorah. (Illus.). 24p. (J). (ps-1). 1991. per. 3.99 (*0-671-74495-X*) Litle Simon.

— Mitzvot. (Illus.). 30p. (J). (gr. 1-5). pap. text 4.95 (*0-87441-387-7*) Behrman.

— Sam the Detective's Reading Readiness Book. (Illus.). 63p. (J). (ps). 1995. pap. text 5.95 (*0-87441-362-1*) Behrman.

— Surf Otters: Trick or Treat. LC 96-130027. (Illus.). 28p. (J). 1995. pap. 2.95 (*0-689-80379-6*) Litle Simon.

— Surf Otters: Very Merry Christmas. LC 96-130315. (Illus.). 28p. (J). 1995. pap. 2.95 (*0-689-80380-X*) Litle Simon.

— Teeny Weenie's Halloween Night. (Stickers & Shapes Ser.). (Illus.). 24p. (J). (ps-1). 1998. pap. 4.99 (*0-689-81811-4*) Litle Simon.

— Ten Treats for Ginger. (Sticker Bks.). (Illus.). 24p. (J). (ps-3). 1992. mass mkt. 2.95 (*0-671-75511-0*) Litle Simon.

— Tzedakah. (Jewish Awareness Ser.). (Illus.). (J). (gr. k-1). 1979. pap. text 4.95 (*0-87441-279-X*) Behrman.

Rosenberg, Amye. Nursery Rhymes. (Happytime Ser.). 24p. (J). (ps-1). 1987. pap. 1.25 (*0-7214-9550-8*, S871-6, Ladybrd) Penguin Putnam.

— The Pudgy Peek-a-Boo Book. (Pudgy Board Bks.). 18p. (J). (ps). 1983. bds. 3.95 (*0-448-10205-6*, G & D) Peng Put Young Read.

Rosenberg, Amye & Mason, Patrice G. Sam the Detective & the Alef Bet Mystery. Rossel, Seymour, ed. (Illus.). 64p. (Orig.). (J). (gr. 1-3). 1980. pap. text 5.50 (*0-87441-328-1*) Behrman.

Rosenberg, Amye & Newman, Shirley. A Child's Introduction to the Early Prophets, No. 1. LC 75-14052. (Illus.). 128p. (J). (gr. 3-4). 1975. pap., wbk. ed. 3.95 (*0-87441-268-4*) Behrman.

Rosenberg, Andrew. Differential Diagnosis Soft Tissue Tumors. (Illus.). 128p. 1998. write for info. (*0-89640-323-8*) Igaku-Shoin.

— The PACU Manual. 300.p. 1998. text 49.00 (*0-397-58791-0*) Lppncott W & W.

Rosenberg, Andrew D., jt. auth. see Bernstein, Ralph L.

Rosenberg, Andrew E. Case Records of the Massachusetts General Hospital. 1995. vdisk 700.00 (*1-56815-028-8*) Mosby Inc.

Rosenberg, Angelica & Rosenberg, Jeanette L. Secrets to Running a Successful Business: How to Have Fun Getting More Business. 120p. 1994. student ed. 19.95 (*0-9639304-0-0*) JLR Pub.

***Rosenberg, Anne.** Nigeria the Culture. (Lands, Peoples & Cultures Ser.). (Illus.). 32p. (YA). (gr. 4-9). 2000. pap. 7.95 (*0-86505-329-4*); lib. bdg. 20.60 (*0-86505-249-2*) Crabtree Pub Co.

— Nigeria the Land. (Lands, Peoples & Cultures Ser.). (Illus.). 32p. (YA). (gr. 4-9). 2000. pap. 7.95 (*0-86505-327-8*); lib. bdg. 20.60 (*0-86505-247-6*) Crabtree Pub Co.

— Nigeria the People. (Lands, Peoples & Cultures Ser.). (Illus.). 32p. (YA). (gr. 4-9). 2000. pap. 7.95 (*0-86505-328-6*); lib. bdg. 20.60 (*0-86505-248-4*) Crabtree Pub Co.

Rosenberg, Arnold J., jt. ed. see Utterback, Ann S.

***Rosenberg, Arnold S.** Jewish Liturgy as a Spiritual System: A Prayer by Prayer Explanation of the Nature & Meaning of Jewish Worship. 312p. 2000. pap. 30.00 (*0-7657-6134-3*) Aronson.

Rosenberg, Art, jt. auth. see Anderson, Paul.

Rosenberg, Arthur. Untersuchungen zur Romischen Zenturienverfassung. LC 75-7337. (Roman History Ser.). (GER.). 1975. reprint ed. 13.95 (*0-405-07058-6*) Ayer.

Rosenberg, Arthur & Hizer, David V. The Resume Handbook: How to Write Outstanding Resume & Cover Letters for Every Situation. 3rd ed. 176p. 1996. pap. 7.95 (*1-55850-616-0*) Adams Media.

Rosenberg, Arthur D. Career Busters: 22 Things People Do to Mess up Their Careers & How to Avoid Them. 1996. text 19.95 (*0-07-053990-1*) McGraw.

— Manipulative Memos: The Art of Control Through the Medium of the Memo. 148p. 1994. 18.95 (*0-89815-614-9*) Ten Speed Pr.

Rosenberg, Aubrey. Tyssot de Patot & His Work (1655-1738) (International Archives of the History of Ideas Ser.: No. 47). 243p. 1972. lib. bdg. 106.00 (*90-247-1199-1*) Kluwer Academic.

Rosenberg, Aura & Tillman, Lynne, photos by. Head Shots. (Illus.). 96p. pap. 24.95 (*1-881616-56-8*) Dist Art Pubs.

Rosenberg, Avrohom Y. Mishnah-Kodashim Vol. 2A: Chullin. Danzigger, H., ed. (ArtScroll Mishnah Ser.). (Illus.). 286p. 1989. 22.99 (*0-89906-305-5*) Mesorah Pubns.

— The Mishnah-Seder Moed Vol. 4: Tranis-Megillah-Moed Katan-Chaggigah. (ArtScroll Mishnah Ser.). 352p. 1979. 22.99 (*0-89906-258-X*) Mesorah Pubns.

Rosenberg, Barbara S., et al. How to Succeed with Chicken Without Even Frying. LC 84-90615. (Illus.). (Orig.). 1984. pap. 8.95 (*0-9613733-7-7*) Marlance Bks.

Rosenberg, Barry. Kornshell Programming Tutorial. (Illus.). 348p. 1991. pap. text. write for info. (*0-318-68379-2*) Addison-Wesley.

— Kornshell Programming Tutorial. 2nd ed. LC 98-29949. 480p. (C). 1998. pap. text 44.95 (*0-201-31018-X*) Addison-Wesley.

— Kornshell Script Programming. 352p. (C). 1991. pap. text 44.95 (*0-201-56324-X*) Addison-Wesley.

Rosenberg, Barry, jt. auth. see Hart, Johnson M.

Rosenberg, Barry A. Assembled. 1990. per. 12.00 (*0-932706-17-7*) WSU Art Gallrs.

Rosenberg, Barry A. & Nathanson, Carol. Words & Numbers: An Exhibition Organized by the Museum of Contemporary Art at Wright State University Curated by Barry A. Rosenberg with Assistance by Teresa Schalnat. Wukeson, Ron, ed. 72p. (Orig.). 1991. pap. 15.00 (*0-932706-18-5*) WSU Art Gallrs.

Rosenberg, Barry A., ed. see University Art Galleries, Wright State University.

R

R

Rosenberg, Bernard & Fliegel, Norris. The Vanguard Artist: Portrait & Self-Portrait. Coser, Lewis A. & Powell, Walter W., eds. LC 79-7017. (Perennial Works in Sociology). 1980. reprint ed. lib. bdg. 24.95 (0-405-12116-4) Ayer.

— The Vanguard Artist: Portrait & Self-Portrait. 366p. (C). 1990. reprint ed. pap. 14.95 (0-941533-97-2, NAB) I R Dee.

Rosenberg, Bernard & Goldstein, Ernest. Creators & Disturbers: Reminiscences by Jewish Intellectuals of New York. LC 82-4281. 432p. 1982. text 57.50 (0-231-04712-6) Col U Pr.

Rosenberg, Bernard & Harburg, Ernest. The Broadway Musical: A Collaboration in Hits & Flops. (Illus.). 350p. (C). 1992. text 45.00 (0-8147-7433-4) NYU Pr.

Rosenberg, Bernard & Rosenberg, Deena. The Music Makers. LC 78-15564. 1979. text 64.50 (0-231-03953-0) Col U Pr.

Rosenberg, Bernard, jt. ed. see Coser, Lewis A.

Rosenberg, Beth C. Virginia Woolf & Samuel Johnson: Common Readers. LC 94-27520. 176p. 1995. text 45.00 (0-312-10741-2) St Martin.

Rosenberg, Beth C. & Dubino, Jeanne. Virginia Woolf & the Essay. LC 97-21442. 320p. 1997. text 45.00 (0-312-17233-8) St Martin.

Rosenberg, Betsy, tr. see Grossman, David.

Rosenberg, Betsy, tr. see Kenaz, Yehoshua.

Rosenberg, Blanca. To Tell At Last: Survival under False Identity, 1941-45. 206p. (C). 1995. 14.95 (0-252-06520-4) U of Ill Pr.

Rosenberg, Brian. Little Dorrit's Shadows: Character & Contradiction in Dickens. 200p. (C). 1995. text 35.95 (0-8262-1058-9) U of Mo Pr.

— Mary Lee Settle's Beulah Quintet: The Price of Freedom. LC 85-23683. (Southern Literary Studies). 203p. 1991. 30.00 (0-8071-1674-2) La State U Pr.

Rosenberg, Bruce. Can These Bones Live? The Art of the American Folk Preacher. rev. ed. LC 87-5895. 328p. 1988. pap. text 14.95 (0-252-01416-2) U of Ill Pr.

— Folklore & Literature: Rival Siblings. LC 90-40630. 296p. 1991. text 34.95 (0-87049-681-6) U of Tenn Pr.

Rosenberg, Bruce A. The Code of the West. LC 81-47014. (Illus.). 223p. 1982. reprint ed. pap. 69.20 (0-7837-1760-1, 205729700024) Bks Demand.

— Folksongs of Virginia: A Checklist of the WPA Holdings at Alderman Library, University of Virginia. LC 75-88185. 167p. reprint ed. pap. 51.80 (0-608-16125-X, 201720900004) Bks Demand.

— The Neutral Ground: The Andre Affair & the Background of Cooper's The Spy, 42. LC 94-16127. (Contributions to the Study of Popular Culture Ser.: No. 42). 168p. 1994. 52.95 (0-313-29319-8, Greenwood Pr) Greenwood.

Rosenberg, Bruce A. & Brown, Mary E., eds. Encyclopedia of Folklore & Literature. LC 98-19904. 766p. (YA). 1998. lib. bdg. 99.50 (1-57607-003-4, AD-FLKLTC) ABC-CLIO.

Rosenberg, Bruce A. & Stewart, Ann H. Ian Fleming. (English Authors Ser.). 168p. 1989. 22.95 (0-8057-6977-3, TEAS 466) Macmillan.

Rosenberg, Bruce A., jt. auth. see Cawelti, John G.

Rosenberg, Carroll-Smith, jt. auth. see Rosenberg, Charles E.

Rosenberg, Carroll-Smith, jt. ed. see Rosenberg, Charles E.

Rosenberg, Charles E. The Care of Strangers: The Rise of America's Hospital System. LC 94-36036. (Illus.). 448p. 1995. pap. text 16.95 (0-8018-5082-7) Johns Hopkins.

— Cholera Years: The United States in 1832, 1849, & 1866. LC 62-18121. 1997. pap. text 8.00 (0-226-72679-7, P320) U Ch Pr.

— The Cholera Years: The United States in 1832, 1849, & 1866. LC 62-18121. (Illus.). x, 276p. (C). 1987. pap. text 12.00 (0-226-72677-0) U Ch Pr.

— Explaining Epidemics: And Other Studies in the History of Medicine. 367p. (C). 1992. text 64.95 (0-521-39340-X); pap. text 18.95 (0-521-39569-0) Cambridge U Pr.

— No Other Gods: On Science & American Social Thought. expanded rev. ed. LC 96-51657. 352p. 1997. text 48.50 (0-8018-5608-6); pap. text 16.95 (0-8018-5598-5) Johns Hopkins.

— No Other Gods: On Science & American Social Thought. LC 75-36942. 288p. reprint ed. pap. 89.30 (0-8357-7882-7, 203630000002) Bks Demand.

— Trial of the Assassin Guiteau: Psychiatry & the Law in the Gilded Age. LC 68-16713. 1976. pap. 14.95 (0-226-72717-3, P682) U Ch Pr.

— The Trial of the Assassin Guiteau: Psychiatry & the Law in the Gilded Age. xviii, 290p. 1995. pap. text 17.50 (0-226-72718-1, Midway Reprint) U Ch Pr.

Rosenberg, Charles E., ed. Caring for the Working Man: The Rise & Fall of the Dispensary. (Medical Care in the United States Ser.). 250p. 1989. reprint ed. text 20.00 (0-8240-8341-5) Garland.

— Healing & History: Essays for George Rosen. 1979. lib. bdg. 27.00 (0-88202-180-X) Watson Pub Intl.

— Medical Care in the United States: The Debate Before 1940, 14 vol. 433.00 (0-8153-0321-1) Garland.

— Medicine & Society in America, 47 bks., Set. 1972. 1073.00 (0-405-03930-1) Ayer.

— On the Administrative Frontier of Medicine: The First Ten Years of the American Hospital Association, 1899-1908. (Medical Care in the United States Ser.). 440p. 1989. text 25.00 (0-8240-8330-X) Garland.

— The Origins of Specialization in American Medicine: An Anthology of Sources. (Medical Care in the United States Ser.: Vol. 13). 200p. 1989. reprint ed. lib. bdg. 15.00 (0-8240-8342-3) Garland.

Rosenberg, Charles E. & Golden, Janet, eds. Framing Disease: Studies in Cultural History. LC 91-19164. (Health & Medicine in American Society Ser.). 450p. (C). 1992. text 48.00 (0-8135-1756-7); pap. text 17.00 (0-8135-1757-5) Rutgers U Pr.

Rosenberg, Charles E. & Rosenberg, Carroll-Smith. Fertility Controlled: The British Argument for Family Limitation. LC 73-20644. (Sex, Marriage & Society Ser.). 137p. 1974. reprint ed. 17.95 (0-405-05799-7) Ayer.

— The Male-Midwife & the Female Doctor. LC 73-20642. (Sex, Marriage & Society Ser.). (Illus.). 224p. 1979. reprint ed. 28.95 (0-405-05810-1) Ayer.

Rosenberg, Charles E. & Rosenberg, Carroll-Smith, eds. Sexual Indulgence & Denial. LC 73-20650. (Sex, Marriage & Society Ser.). 188p. 1974. reprint ed. 19.95 (0-405-05818-7) Ayer.

Rosenberg, Charles E. & Smith-Rosenberg, Carroll, eds. Sex, Marriage & Society, 35 bks. 1974. 832.00 (0-405-05790-3) Ayer.

Rosenberg, Charles E., jt. auth. see Golden, Janet.

Rosenberg, Charles E., jt. auth. see Numbers, Ronald L.

Rosenberg, Charles E., jt. ed. see Numbers, Ronald L.

Rosenberg, Charles M. The Este Monuments & Urban Development in Renaissance Ferrara. LC 96-31668. (SPA., Illus.). 347p. (C). 1997. text 75.00 (0-521-56139-6) Cambridge U Pr.

Rosenberg, Claude. Wealthy & Wise: How You & America Can Get the Most of Your Giving. 224p. (gr. 8). 1994. 25.95 (0-316-75741-1) Little.

Rosenberg, Claude N., Jr. Investing with the Best: What to Look for, What to Look for in Your Search for a Superior Investment Manager. 2nd ed. LC 93-7865. 256p. 1993. 29.95 (0-471-55827-3) Wiley.

Rosenberg, Claude N. Stock Market Primer. rev. ed. 1991. mass mkt. 14.99 (0-446-38718-5, Pub. by Warner Bks) Little.

***Rosenberg, Claude N., Jr.** Stock Market Primer. rev. ed. 2001. pap. write for info. (0-446-67638-1) Warner Bks.

Rosenberg, Craig H., jt. auth. see Peddie, Sandra.

Rosenberg, Craig H., jt. auth. see Peddle, Sandra.

Rosenberg, D. J., jt. auth. see Cushman, W. H.

Rosenberg, D. N. Oaten Reeds & Trumpets: Pastoral & Epic in Virgil, Spenser, & Milton. LC 80-17974. 288p. 1981. 38.50 (0-8387-5002-8) Bucknell U Pr.

Rosenberg, Dale, ed. see Charest-Papagno, Noella.

Rosenberg, Dan, ed. see Carlock, Marty.

Rosenberg, Dan, ed. see Jamison, Cheryl A. & Jamison, Bill.

Rosenberg, Dan, ed. see Jarratt, Claudia J.

Rosenberg, Dan, ed. see Kelleher, James B.

Rosenberg, Dan, ed. see Lieberman, Adrienne B.

Rosenberg, Dan, ed. see Naylor, Honey.

Rosenberg, Dan, ed. see Ziedrich, Linda.

Rosenberg, Daniel, jt. ed. see Foner, Phillip S.

Rosenberg, Danny, jt. auth. see DeSensi, Joy T.

Rosenberg, David. Blues of the Sky: Interpreted from the Original Hebrew Book of Psalms. LC 76-991. 53p. 1976. 15.00 (0-89366-241-0) Ultramarine Pub.

— The Book of David: A New Story of the Spiritual Warrior & Leader Who Shaped Our Inner Consciousness. 288p. 1998. pap. 12.00 (0-609-80225-9) Harmony Bks.

***Rosenberg, David.** Dreams of Being Eaten Alive: The Literary Core of the Kabbalah. LC 99-41901. 192p. 2000. 22.00 (0-609-60306-X, REL040000) Harmony Bks.

Rosenberg, David. Genesis As It Is Written: Contemporary Writers on Our First Stories. LC 96-22427. 1996. pap. 12.00 (0-06-066736-2) Harper SF.

***Rosenberg, David.** Handbook of Solomon's Wisdom. 2001. 24.00 (0-609-60305-1, Pub. by Crown Pub Group) Random House.

Rosenberg, David. The Hidden Holmes: His Theory of Torts in History. 288p. (C). 1995. 50.95 (0-674-39002-4) HUP.

— Job Speaks. 101p. 1980. reprint ed. 9.95 (0-934450-09-9) Unmuzzled Ox.

— Lightworks: Interpreted from the Original Hebrew Book of Isaiah. LC 78-3356. 78p. 1978. 15.00 (0-89366-249-6) Ultramarine Pub.

— The Lost Book of Paradise: Adam & Eve in the Garden of Eden. 192p. (J). 1995. pap. 12.45 (0-7868-8073-2, Pub. by Hyperion) Time Warner.

— The Official Baby License Exam. LC 97-156042. (Illus.). 72p. (Orig.). 1996. pap. 9.95 (0-9646603-0-X) Hse of Toast.

Rosenberg, David, ed. Communion: Contemporary Writers Reveal the Bible in Their Lives. 560p. 1997. pap. 14.95 (0-385-47484-9, Anchor NY) Doubleday.

— Congregation: Contemporary Writers Read the Jewish Bible. 1987. 29.95 (0-15-146350-6) Harcourt.

— Congregation: Contemporary Writers Read the Jewish Bible. 1989. pap. 14.95 (0-15-622040-7, Harvest Bks) Harcourt.

Rosenberg, David, et al, eds. Textbook of Pharmacotherapy for Child & Adolescent Psychiatric Disorders. LC 94-6401. 576p. 1994. text 67.95 (0-87630-740-3) Brunner-Mazel.

Rosenberg, David, et al. Pocket Guide for the Textbook of Pharmacotherapy for Child & Adolescent Psychiatric Disorders. LC 97-33193. 192p. 1997. pap. 24.95 (0-87630-871-X) Brunner-Mazel.

Rosenberg, David, tr. see Bloom, Harold.

Rosenberg, David A. & Rosenberg, Jean G. Landless Peasants & Rural Poverty in Selected Asian Countries. (Special Series on Landlessness & Near-Landlessness: No. 2). 108p. (Orig.). (C). 1978. pap. text 7.95 (0-86731-069-3) Cornell CIS RDC.

Rosenberg, David A., jt. auth. see Rosenberg, Jean G.

Rosenberg, David M., jt. ed. see Resh, Vincent H.

***Rosenberg, DeAnne.** A Manager's Guide to Hiring the Best Person for Every Job. LC 99-51372. 300p. 2000. pap. 18.95 (0-471-38074-1) Wiley.

Rosenberg, Deena. Fascinating Rhythm: The Collaboration of George & Ira Gershwin. LC 91-41926. (Illus.). 560p. 1997. reprint ed. pap. 22.95 (0-472-08469-0, 08469) U of Mich Pr.

Rosenberg, Deena, jt. auth. see Rosenberg, Bernard.

***Rosenberg, Donald K.** Open Source: The Unauthorized White Papers. 250p. 2000. pap. text 19.99 (0-7645-4660-0) IDG Bks.

Rosenberg, Donna. Folklore, Myths, & Legends: A World Perspective. 304p. 1996. 26.95 (0-8442-5763-X); pap. write for info. (0-8442-5784-2) NTC Contemp Pub Co.

— Folklore, Myths, & Legends: A World Perspective. 1998. pap., teacher ed. 16.93 (0-8442-5785-0) NTC Contemp Pub Co.

— Mythology & You. 304p. 1992. pap., student ed. 22.53 (0-8442-5561-0) NTC Contemp Pub Co.

— World Literature. 896p. 1992. 38.12 (0-8442-5480-0) NTC Contemp Pub Co.

— World Literature. 896p. 1995. pap. 35.63 (0-8442-5482-7, 54827, Natl Textbk Co) NTC Contemp Pub Co.

— World Mythology. 544p. 1993. pap. 23.95 (0-8442-5548-3, Natl Textbk Co) NTC Contemp Pub Co.

— World Mythology. 2nd ed. LC 93-85887. 592p. 1994. 38.12 (0-8442-5765-6); pap. 33.86 (0-8442-5766-4) NTC Contemp Pub Co.

— World Mythology. 2nd ed. (Illus.). 584p. 1995. pap. 19.95 (0-8442-5767-2, 57672, Natl Textbk Co) NTC Contemp Pub Co.

— World Mythology: An Anthology of the Great Myths & Epics. 2nd ed. 1994. 25.05 (0-606-01467-5, Pub. by Turtleback) Demco.

***Rosenberg, Donna.** World Mythology: An Anthology of the Great Myths & Epics. 3rd ed. LC 98-45342. 1998. 39.95 (0-8442-5965-9); pap. 38.69 (0-8442-5966-7) NTC Contemp Pub Co.

Rosenberg, Donna, ed. Folklore, Myths, & Legends: A World Perspective. 592p. 1996. pap. 26.95 (0-8442-5780-X, 5780X) NTC Contemp Pub Co.

— World Literature: An Anthology of Great Short Stories, Drama, & Poetry. 1998. teacher ed. 16.93 (0-8442-5481-9) NTC Contemp Pub Co.

Rosenberg, Donna & Baker, Sorelle. Mythology & You. (Illus.). 304p. 1993. pap. 19.95 (0-8442-5594-7, 55947, Natl Textbk Co) NTC Contemp Pub Co.

Rosenberg, Dorothy, jt. ed. see Lukens, Nancy.

Rosenberg, Dorothy B., jt. auth. see Camurati, Mireya.

Rosenberg, Duska & Hutchinson, Chris. Design Issues in CSCW. LC 94-13514. (Computer Supported Cooperative Work Ser.). 1994. 71.95 (0-387-19810-5) Spr-Verlag.

Rosenberg, Duska, jt. auth. see Devlin, Keith J.

Rosenberg, E. Meat & Dairy. 1991. 18.99 (0-89906-898-7); pap. 15.99 (0-89906-899-5) Mesorah Pubns.

Rosenberg, Edgar, ed. see Dickens, Charles.

Rosenberg, Edna L. von Gonten. Von Rosenberg Family of Texas Cookbook. LC 99-208572. 297p. 1993. 16.95 (1-57168-914-1, Nortex Pr) Sunbelt Media.

Rosenberg, Ehud. The Laws of Cooking on Sabbath & Festivals. 76p. 1986. 8.95 (1-58330-094-5) Feldheim.

Rosenberg, Eileen P. Principles of Law Office Management: Concepts & Applications. Hannan, ed. LC 93-9794. (Paralegal). 510p. (C). 1993. text 43.25 (0-314-01359-8) West Pub.

Rosenberg, Eileen Popkoski. Principles of Law Office Managment. (Paralegal Ser.). (C). 1993. 15.25 (0-314-02910-9) Thomson Learn.

***Rosenberg, Elinor B.** The Adoption Life Cycle: The Children & Their Families Through the Years. 209p. 2000. 28.00 (0-7881-9348-1) DIANE Pub.

Rosenberg, Elinor B. The Adoption Life Cycle: The Children & Their Families Through the Years. LC 92-9031. 250p. 1992. 27.95 (0-02-927055-3) Free Pr.

Rosenberg, Ellen. Get a Clue! What's Really Going on with Pre-Teens & How Parents Can Help. LC 99-20602. 320p. 1999. pap. 15.00 (0-8050-5895-8) H Holt & Co.

— Growing up Feeling Good. rev. ed. LC 95-5617. 624p. (YA). (gr. 4 up). 1996. pap. 13.99 (0-14-037718-2, PuffinBks) Peng Put Young Read.

Rosenberg, Ellen M. The Southern Baptists: A Subculture in Transition. LC 88-31610. (Illus.). 256p. reprint ed. pap. 79.40 (0-608-07781-X, 206786900010) Bks Demand.

Rosenberg, Elliot. But Were They Good for the Jews? Over 150 Historical Figures Viewed from a Jewish Perspective. 320p. 1997. 22.50 (1-55972-436-6, Birch Ln Pr) Carol Pub Group.

Rosenberg, Emily. Spreading the American Dream: American Economic & Cultural Expansion 1890-1945. (American Century Ser.). 264p. 1982. pap. 12.00 (0-8090-0146-2) Hill & Wang.

Rosenberg, Emily S. Financial Missionaries to the World: The Politics & Culture of Dollar Diplomacy, 1900-1930. LC 99-22995. 352p. 1999. 45.00 (0-674-00059-5) HUP.

Rosenberg, Emily S., jt. auth. see Rosenberg, Norman L.

Rosenberg, Erika, jt. auth. see Schindler, Emilie W.

Rosenberg, Erika L., jt. ed. see Ekman, Paul.

Rosenberg, Eugene, ed. Microbial Ecology & Infectious Disease. LC 98-30758. 340p. 1998. 79.95 (1-55581-148-5) ASM Pr.

— Microorganisms to Combat Pollution. LC 93-3223. 288p. (C). 1993. text 233.00 (0-7923-2226-6) Kluwer Academic.

— Myxobacteria: Development & Cell Interactions. (Molecular Biology Ser.). (Illus.). 325p. 1984. 159.00 (0-387-90962-1) Spr-Verlag.

Rosenberg, Eugene & Cohen, Irun. Microbial Biology. 433p. (C). 1983. text 75.00 (0-03-085658-2, Pub. by SCP) Harcourt.

Rosenberg, Eugene, jt. ed. see Cohen, Yehuda.

Rosenberg, G. D. & Runcorn, S. K., eds. Growth Rhythms & the History of the Earth's Rotation. LC 74-18096. 575p. reprint ed. pap. 178.30 (0-608-14247-6, 202400800035) Bks Demand.

Rosenberg, Gail S., jt. auth. see McCarthy, Maureen E.

Rosenberg, Gary & Clarke, Sylvia S., eds. Social Workers in Health Care Management: The Move to Leadership. LC 87-15026. (Social Work in Health Care Ser.: Vol. 12, No. 3). 159p. 1987. 39.95 (0-86656-672-4) Haworth Pr.

— Social Workers in Health Care Management: The Move to Leadership. LC 87-15026. (Social Work in Health Care Ser.: Vol. 12, No. 3). 159p. 1988. pap. text 14.95 (0-86656-815-8) Haworth Pr.

Rosenberg, Gary & Rehr, Helen, eds. Advancing Social Work Practice in the Health Care Field: Emerging Issues & New Perspectives. LC 82-9249. (Social Work in Health Care Ser.: Vol. 8, No. 3). 162p. 1983. text 49.95 (0-917724-91-7); pap. text 19.95 (0-86656-232-X) Haworth Pr.

Rosenberg, Gary & Weissman, Andrew, eds. Social Work in Ambulatory Care: New Implications for Health & Social Services. (Social Work in Health Care Ser.). (Illus.). 108p. 1994. lib. bdg. 19.95 (1-56024-697-9) Haworth Pr.

— Social Work Leadership in Healthcare: Directors' Perspectives. LC 95-23135. 116p. 1995. 34.95 (1-56024-764-9) Haworth Pr.

Rosenberg, Gary, jt. ed. see Lurie, Abraham.

Rosenberg, Gary, jt. ed. see Rehr, Helen.

***Rosenberg, George.** M. 2nd ed. (New Voices in American Fiction Ser.). 95p. 2000. reprint ed. pap. 12.95 (1-883938-72-4) Dry Bones Pr.

Rosenberg, George, jt. auth. see Broadbent, Bill.

Rosenberg, George S. The Worker Grows Old. LC 78-110628. (Jossey-Bass Behavioral Science Ser.). 222p. reprint ed. pap. 68.90 (0-608-30426-3, 201391900088) Bks Demand.

Rosenberg, Gerald N. The Hollow Hope: Can Courts Bring about Social Change? LC 90-22391. (American Politics & Political Economy Ser.). (Illus.). xii, 437p. (C). 1993. pap. text 16.95 (0-226-72703-3) U Ch Pr.

— The Hollow Hope: Can Courts Bring about Social Change? LC 90-22391. (Illus.). 438p. 1997. 35.95 (0-226-72702-5) U Ch Pr.

Rosenberg, Graciella, tr. see Dragon, Osvaldo.

Rosenberg, H. M. The Solid State: An Introduction to the Physics of Crystals for Students of Physics, Materials Science, & Engineering. 3rd ed. (Oxford Physics Ser.: No. 9). (Illus.). 324p. (C). 1988. pap. text 27.95 (0-19-851870-6) OUP.

Rosenberg, H. S., ed. Transplantation & Developmental Biology of the Liver. (Perspectives in Pediatric Pathology Ser.: Vol. 14). xii, 220p. 1991. 240.00 (3-8055-5156-8) S Karger.

Rosenberg, H. S., et al, eds. Pediatric Molecular Pathology: Quantitation & Applications. (Perspectives in Pediatric Pathology Ser.: Vol. 16). (Illus.). xii, 170p. 1992. 182.75 (3-8055-5496-6) S Karger.

Rosenberg, H. S. & Bernstein, J., eds. Cardiovascular Diseases. (Perspectives in Pediatric Pathology Ser.: Vol. 12). (Illus.). x, 162p. 1988. 172.25 (3-8055-4716-1) S Karger.

— Central Nervous System Diseases. (Perspectives in Pediatric Pathology Ser.: Vol. 10). viii, 264p. 1987. 229.75 (3-8055-4403-0) S Karger.

— Neoplasia in Infancy & Childhood. (Perspectives in Pediatric Pathology Ser.: Vol. 9). viii, 248p. 1986. 191.50 (3-8055-4373-5) S Karger.

— Respiratory & Alimentary Tract Disease. (Perspectives in Pediatric Pathology Ser.: Vol. 11). (Illus.). x, 218p. 1987. 191.50 (3-8055-4435-9) S Karger.

Rosenberg, Harold. Abstract Expressionism - A Tribute to Harold Rosenberg: Paintings & Drawings from Chicago Collections. LC 79-67698. (Illus.). 48p. (Orig.). 1979. pap. 4.00 (0-935573-06-2) D & A Smart Museum.

— The Act & the Actor: Making the Self. 238p. (C). 1992. pap. 7.95 (0-226-72675-4) U Ch Pr.

— Act & the Actor: Making the Self. LC 82-25100. (Phoenix Bk.). (Illus.). 224p. reprint ed. pap. 69.50 (0-608-09514-1, 205431500005) Bks Demand.

— The Anxious Object. 272p. (C). 1998. pap. 19.95 (0-226-72682-7) U Ch Pr.

— Arshile Gorky: The Man, the Time, the Idea. LC 62-11237. (Illus.). 144p. 1981. reprint ed. pap. 13.95 (0-935296-20-4, Pub. by Sheep Meadow) U Pr of New Eng.

— Art & Other Serious Matters. 312p. 1986. pap. 11.95 (0-226-72695-9) U Ch Pr.

— Art & Other Serious Matters. 312p. 1992. 25.00 (0-226-72694-0) U Ch Pr.

— Art on the Edge: Creators & Situations. LC 82-24807. (Illus.). xiv, 318p. (C). 1983. pap. 17.95 (0-226-72674-6) U Ch Pr.

— Artwork & Packages. LC 82-13406. (Illus.). 232p. (C). 1994. pap. 7.95 (0-226-72683-5) U Ch Pr.

— Artworks & Packages. LC 82-13406. (Illus.). 238p. reprint ed. pap. 73.80 (0-608-09515-X, 205431600005) Bks Demand.

— The De-Definition of Art. LC 83-1101. (Illus.). 256p. (C). 1983. pap. 17.95 (0-226-72673-8) U Ch Pr.

— Discovering the Present: Three Decades in Art, Culture & Politics. LC 72-92852. xii, 348p. 1999. pap. 13.95 (0-226-72681-9) U Ch Pr.

— The Tradition of the New. LC 72-134130. (Essay Index Reprint Ser.). 1977. 21.95 (0-8369-2127-5) Ayer.

— The Tradition of the New. LC 82-13509. 286p. (C). 1982. pap. 10.95 (0-226-72684-3) U Ch Pr.

— The Tradition of the New. LC 82-13509. 288p. reprint ed. pap. 89.30 (0-608-09035-2, 206967000005) Bks Demand.

— The Tradition of the New. 286p. 1994. reprint ed. pap. 14.95 (*0-306-80596-0*) Da Capo.

Rosenberg, Harold, jt. auth. see Neuse, Eberhard W.

Rosenberg, Harold S. Nutrition & Stress. Passwater, Richard A. & Mindell, Earl R., eds. (Good Health Guide Ser.). 32p. (Orig.). 1983. pap. 3.95 (*0-87983-298-3*, 32983K, Keats Publng) NTC Contemp Pub Co.

Rosenberg, Harriet G. A Negotiated World: 3 Centuries of Change in a French Alpine Community. (Illus.). 256p. 1988. text 35.00 (*0-8020-2640-0*) U of Toronto Pr.

Rosenberg, Harris. A Handbook on School Fundraising. 384p. 1997. 65.00 (*0-7494-2265-3*, Kogan Pg Educ) Stylus Pub VA.

***Rosenberg, Harry M.** Quality of Deaths by Race & Hispanic Origin: A Summary of Current Research, 1999. 17p. 1999. pap. 2.25 (*0-16-050138-5*) USGPO.

***Rosenberg, Harry M. & National Center for Health Statistics Staff.** Quality of Death Rates by Race & Hispanic-Origin. LC 99-41288. (Vital & Health Statistics Ser.). 1999. pap. write for info. (*0-8406-0559-5*) Natl Ctr Health Stats.

Rosenberg, Harvey. Joey's Cabbage Patch. 32p. (J). (gr. k-3). 1991. write for info. (*0-9629587-0-0*) Go Jolly Pubns.

Rosenberg, Harvey S. & Bolande, Robert P., eds. Perspectives in Pediatric Pathology, Vol. 3. LC 72-88828. 377p. reprint ed. pap. 107.50 (*0-608-11596-7*, 2022730) Bks Demand.

— Perspectives in Pediatric Pathology, Vol. 4. LC 72-88828. 533p. pap. 165.30 (*0-608-15509-8*, 202974000064) Bks Demand.

Rosenberg, Helane S. & Epstein, Yakov M. Getting Pregnant When You Thought You Couldn't. 400p. (Orig.). 1993. mass mkt. 13.99 (*0-446-39388-6*, Pub. by Warner Bks) Little.

Rosenberg, Helane S. & Prendergast, Christine. Theatre for Young People: A Sense of Occasion. 366p. (C). 1983. pap. text 51.50 (*0-03-039911-4*, Pub. by Harcourt Coll Pubs) Harcourt.

Rosenberg, Helen, ed. see Kalb, Ira S.

Rosenberg, Helena H. How to Get Married after 35. LC 97-36024. 288p. 1998. 22.00 (*0-06-017493-5*) HarpC.

***Rosenberg, Helena H.** How to Get Married after 35. 1998. audio 12.00 (*0-694-51943-X*, CPN10140) HarperAudio.

— How to Get Married After 35: A Game Plan for Love. 288p. 1999. pap. 12.95 (*0-06-093033-0*, Perennial) HarperTrade.

***Rosenberg, Helena Hacker.** How to Get Married after 35: A Game Plan for Love. 262p. 2000. reprint ed. text 22.00 (*0-7881-6871-1*) DIANE Pub.

Rosenberg, Hilary. A Traitor to His Class: Robert A. G. Monks & the Battle to Change Corporate America. LC 98-34982. 378p. 1998. 29.95 (*0-471-17448-3*) Wiley.

— The Vulture Investors: A Searing Expose of the Winners & Losers of the Great American Bankruptcy Feeding Frenzy. LC 91-58511. 288p. 1992. 22.00 (*0-88730-555-5*, HarpBusn) HarpInfo.

Rosenberg, Hilary. The Vulture Investors: The Winners & Losers of the Great American Bankruptcy Feeding Frenzy. LC 91-58511. 416p. 1993. pap. 12.00 (*0-88730-648-9*, HarpBusn) HarpInfo.

Rosenberg, Howard G. How to Succeed Without a Career Path: Jobs for People with No Corporate Ladder. LC 94-457. 1995. pap. 13.95 (*1-57023-003-X*) Impact VA.

Rosenberg, Howard R., et al. Labor Management Laws in California Agriculture. 2nd ed. LC 90-85383. x, 179p. 1995. pap. 20.00 (*1-879906-29-5*, 21404) ANR Pubns CA.

Rosenberg, I. Protein Analysis & Purification. 560p. 1996. 120.00 (*0-8176-3717-6*) Birkhauser.

— Protein Analysis & Purification: Benchtop Techniques. 434p. 1996. pap. 59.95 (*0-8176-3665-X*) Birkhauser.

Rosenberg, I. J. Comeback! The Inside Story, in Words & Pictures of the 1991 Atlanta Braves' Race for Baseball Glory. 192p. 1991. 29.95 (*0-9631594-0-2*) AJ & the AC.

— Encore! Inside Story of the Atlanta Braves' Second Consecutive National League Championship. LC 92-84003. (Illus.). 231p. 1992. 29.95 (*1-56352-062-1*) Longstreet.

Rosenberg, Irwin H., ed. Nutritional Assessment of Elderly Populations: Measure & Function: Proceedings of the 13th Annual Bristol-Myers Squibb/Mead Johnson Symposium on Nutrition Research, Held in Boston on Oct. 11-13, 1993, No. 13. LC 94-26017. (Bristol-Meyers Squibb-Mead Johnson Nutrition Symposia Ser.: Vol. 13). 336p. 1995. 65.00 (*0-7817-0232-1*) Random.

Rosenberg, Irwin H., et al, eds. Nutritional Assessment of Elderly Populations: Measure & Function. LC 94-26017. (Bristol-Myer Squibb/Mead Johnson Nutrition Symposia Ser.: No. 13). (Illus.). 335p. 1995. reprint ed. pap. 103.90 (*0-608-05802-5*, 205976700007) Bks Demand.

Rosenberg, Ivo G., ed. Algebras & Orders: Proceedings of the NATO Advanced Study Institute & Seminaire De Mathematiques Superieures, Montreal, Canada, July 29-August 9, 1991. (NATO Advanced Science Institutes Series C: Mathematical & Physical Sciences). 572p. (C). 1993. text 325.00 (*0-7923-2143-X*) Kluwer Academic.

Rosenberg, J. & Schochet, C. The Kunneth Theorem & the Universal Coefficient Theorem for Equivariant K-Theory & KK-Theory. LC 86-10959. (Memoirs of the AMS Ser.: No. 62/348). 95p. 1986. pap. 18.00 (*0-8218-2349-3*, MEMO/62/348) Am Math.

Rosenberg, J., et al. Multi-Media Document Translation: ODA & the EXPRES Project. (Illus.). 824p. 1990. 96.95 (*0-387-97397-4*) Spr-Verlag.

Rosenberg, J. F. Linguistic Representation. LC 74-26886. (Philosophical Studies: No. 1). 166p. 1974. lib. bdg. 70.50 (*90-277-0533-X*) Kluwer Academic.

— Linguistic Representation. LC 74-26886. (Philosophical Studies: No. 1). 166p. 1978. pap. text 39.50 (*90-277-0946-7*) Kluwer Academic.

Rosenberg, Jack, et al. Body Self & Soul: Sustaining Integration. LC 85-2293. (Illus.). 352p. 1985. lib. bdg. 29.95 (*0-89334-196-7*, 196-7) Humanics Ltd.

Rosenberg, Jakob. Great Draughtsmen from Pisanello to Picasso. LC 59-7661. 436p. reprint ed. pap. 135.20 (*0-7837-2323-7*, 205741100004) Bks Demand.

— Rembrandt: Life & Work. 3rd ed. LC 68-18911. (Paidon Paperback, Ph54). xi, 386 p. 1968. write for info. (*0-7148-1338-9*) Phaidon Pr.

Rosenberg, Jakob & Slive, Seymour. Dutch Painting, 1600-1800. rev. ed. LC 95-14215. (Pelican History of Art Ser.). (Illus.). 392p. 1995. 70.00 (*0-300-06418-7*) Yale U Pr.

Rosenberg, Jakob, et al. Dutch Art & Architecture: 1600-1800. 3rd ed. (Pelican History of Art Ser.). (Illus.). 502p. (C). 1987. reprint ed. pap. 26.50 (*0-300-05312-6*) Yale U Pr.

Rosenberg, James, jt. auth. see Bennett, William H.

Rosenberg, James L. The Death & Life of Sneaky Fitch: A Farcical Tragedy in Three Acts. 47p. 1987. reprint ed. pap. 5.25 (*0-8222-0289-1*) Dramatists Play.

— Mel Says to Give You His Best. 1975. pap. 3.25 (*0-8222-0746-X*) Dramatists Play.

Rosenberg, Jan. Women's Reflections: The Feminist Film Movement. Kirkpatrick, Diane, ed. LC 83-1271. (Studies in Cinema: No. 22). 154p. reprint ed. 43.70 (*0-8357-1400-4*, 2070759) Bks Demand.

Rosenberg, Jane. Dance Me a Story. LC 84-51701. (Illus.). 128p. 1993. pap. 16.95 (*0-500-27739-7*, Pub. by Thames Hudson) Norton.

— Sing Me a Story: The Metropolitan Opera's Book of Opera Stories for Children. LC 88-51929. (Illus.). 160p. (J). 1996. pap. 15.95 (*0-500-27873-3*, Pub. by Thames Hudson) Norton.

Rosenberg, Jane A. Nation's Great Library: Herbert Putnam & the Library of Congress. LC 92-37287. 256p. (C). 1993. text 39.95 (*0-252-02001-4*) U of Ill Pr.

Rosenberg, Janet, ed. see Anderson, Roy N.

Rosenberg, Janet, ed. see Axford, Wendy A. & McMurtrie, Douglas C.

Rosenberg, Janet, ed. see Barton, George E.

Rosenberg, Janet, ed. see Berkowitz, Edward D.

Rosenberg, Janet, ed. see Carling, Finn & Haecker, Theodor.

Rosenberg, Janet, ed. see Charity Organisation Society Staff.

Rosenberg, Janet, ed. see Eisenson, Jon, et al.

Rosenberg, Janet, ed. see Giralestone, Gathrone R.

Rosenberg, Janet, ed. see Graham, Earl C. & Mullen, Marjorie.

Rosenberg, Janet, ed. see Hathaway, Katharine B.

Rosenberg, Janet, ed. see Hinshaw, David.

Rosenberg, Janet, ed. see Hoyer, Louis & Hay, Charles K.

Rosenberg, Janet, ed. see Hunt, Agnes.

Rosenberg, Janet, ed. see Kenny, Elizabeth & Ostenso, Martha.

Rosenberg, Janet, ed. see Kessler, Henry H.

Rosenberg, Janet, ed. see Leavitt, Moses A.

Rosenberg, Janet, ed. see Macdonald, Mary E.

Rosenberg, Janet, ed. see Mallinson, Vernon.

Rosenberg, Janet, ed. see Mawson, Thomas.

Rosenberg, Janet, ed. see McMurtrie, Douglas C.

Rosenberg, Janet, ed. see Obermann, C. Esco.

Rosenberg, Janet, ed. see Orr, H. Winnett.

Rosenberg, Janet, jt. ed. see Phillips, William R.

Rosenberg, Janet, ed. see Sullivan, Oscar M. & Snortum, Kenneth O.

Rosenberg, Janet, ed. see Tracy, Susan R.

Rosenberg, Janet, ed. see Watson, Frederick.

Rosenberg, Janet, ed. see Wright, Beatrice A.

Rosenberg, Janet, ed. see Wright, Henry C.

Rosenberg, Janet, ed. see Wurtz, Hans.

Rosenberg, Janet, ed. see Ziegler, Carlos R.

Rosenberg, Jay F. Beyond Formalism: Naming & Necessity for Human Beings. LC 93-12691. 256p. 1994. 69.95 (*1-56639-118-0*) Temple U Pr.

— The Practice of Philosophy: A Handbook for Beginners. 3rd ed. LC 95-12865. 133p. 1995. pap. text 23.60 (*0-13-230848-7*) P-H.

— Thinking Clearly about Death. 2nd rev. ed. LC 98-28462. 256p. (C). 1998. pap. 16.95 (*0-87220-426-X*); lib. bdg. 34.95 (*0-87220-427-8*) Hackett Pub.

Rosenberg, Jean G. & Rosenberg, David A. Landless Peasants & Rural Poverty in Indonesia & the Philippines. (Special Series on Landlessness & Near-Landlessness: No. 3). 133p. (Orig.). (C). 1980. pap. text 8.65 (*0-86731-070-7*) Cornell CIS RDC.

Rosenberg, Jean G., jt. auth. see Rosenberg, David A.

Rosenberg, Jeanette L., jt. auth. see Rosenberg, Angelica.

Rosenberg, Jeffrey, jt. auth. see Horn, Wade.

Rosenberg, Jerome L. College Chemistry. 1999. pap. text 8.95 (*0-07-052714-8*) McGraw-Hill Pubng.

Rosenberg, Jerome L. & Epstein, Lawrence M. Schaum's Outline of College Chemistry. 8th ed. LC 96-46610. (Illus.). 384p. (C). 1996. pap. 15.95 (*0-07-053709-7*) McGraw.

Rosenberg, Jerry M. Business Dictionary of Computers. 3rd ed. LC 93-15268. (Business Dictionary Ser.). 416p. 1993. pap. 14.95 (*0-471-58574-2*) Wiley.

— Dictionary of Administration & Finance - English & Spanish. 2nd ed. (ENG & SPA.). 652p. 1991. 195.00 (*0-7859-5222-5*) Fr & Eur.

— The Dictionary of Banking. 3rd ed. (Business Dictionary Ser.). 384p. 1992. pap. 19.95 (*0-471-57436-8*) Wiley.

— Dictionary of Business & Management. 3rd ed. LC 92-7977. (Business Dictionary Ser.). 384p. 1992. pap. 14.95 (*0-471-54536-8*) Wiley.

— Dictionary of International Trade. (Business Dictionary Ser.). 314p. 1993. pap. 14.95 (*0-471-59731-7*) Wiley.

Rosenberg, Jerry M. Dictionary of International Trade. (Business Dictionary Ser.). 314p. 1993. 79.95 (*0-471-59732-5*) Wiley.

Rosenberg, Jerry M. Dictionary of Investing. 2nd ed. LC 92-6357. (Business Dictionary Ser.). 384p. 1992. 79.95 (*0-471-57433-3*); pap. 19.95 (*0-471-57434-1*) Wiley.

— Dictionary of Marketing & Advertising. LC 94-25576. 384p. 1995. 79.95 (*0-471-02503-8*) Wiley.

— Dictionary of Retailing & Merchandizing. LC 95-17899. (Wiley Small Business Editions). 261p. 1995. 27.95 (*0-471-11023-X*) Wiley.

— Encyclopedia of the Middle East Peace Process & the Middle East North Africa Economic Community: Jerry M. Rosenber. LC 97-39512. 1997. 143.50 (*0-7623-0350-6*) Jai Pr.

— Encyclopedia of the North American Free Trade Agreement, the New American Community, & Latin-American Trade. LC 94-16984. 576p. 1994. lib. bdg. 85.00 (*0-313-29069-5*, Greenwood Pr) Greenwood.

— The New American Community: A Response to the European & Asian Economic Challenge. LC 91-35038. 200p. 1992. 57.95 (*0-275-94206-6*, C4206, Praeger Pubs) Greenwood.

Rosenberg, Jerry M., ed. McGraw-Hill Dictionary of Business Acronyms, Initials & Abbreviations. 336p. 1992. 29.95 (*0-07-053734-8*) McGraw.

***Rosenberg, Jerry Martin.** Arafat's Palestinian State & IPTA: The Best Hope for Lasting Peace in the Middle East. LC 99-47018. 1999. write for info. (*0-7623-0609-2*) Jai Pr.

Rosenberg, Joe. El Bully. (Bilingual Childrens Theatre Ser.). (ENG & SPA.). 33p. (Orig.). (J). (gr. k-8). 1996. pap. text 3.00 (*1-57514-161-2*, 3031) Encore Perform Pub.

— El Gato Sin Amigos: The Cat Who Had No Friends. (Multicultural Theatre Ser.). 14p. (Orig.). (J). (gr. k-6). 1993. pap. 2.50 (*1-57514-102-7*, 3016) Encore Perform Pub.

— La Rana Juana (Jeanie the Frog) (Bilingual Plays for Children Ser.). (Orig.). (J). (gr. k-6). 1996. pap. 2.50 (*1-57514-162-0*, 3045) Encore Perform Pub.

Rosenberg, Joe, ed. Aplauso! Hispanic Children's Theater. LC 94-36005. 278p. (J). (ps-11). 1995. pap. 10.00 (*1-55885-127-5*, Pinata Bks) Arte Publico.

Rosenberg, Joe, tr. see Dragon, Osvaldo.

***Rosenberg, Joel.** The Fire Duke. 2000. 22.00 (*0-380-97252-2*) Morrow Avon.

Rosenberg, Joel. Hour of the Octopus. 272p. (Orig.). 1994. mass mkt. 4.99 (*0-441-16975-9*) Ace Bks.

***Rosenberg, Joel.** Keepers of the Hidden Ways: The Crimson Sky, Bk. 3. 352p. 1998. mass mkt. 5.99 (*0-380-78932-9*, Eos) Morrow Avon.

Rosenberg, Joel. Keepers of the Hidden Ways Bk. 1: The Fire Duke. 1996. pap. 5.99 (*0-614-98029-1*, Avon Bks) Morrow Avon.

— Keepers of the Hidden Ways, Book One: The Fire Duke. (Keepers of the Hidden Ways Ser.: Bk. 1). 368p. 1996. mass mkt. 5.99 (*0-380-72207-0*, Avon Bks) Morrow Avon.

— King & Kin: Political Allegory in the Hebrew Bible. LC 85-45160. (Indiana Studies in Biblical Literature). (Illus.). 270p. 1986. 31.95 (*0-253-14624-0*) Ind U Pr.

— Not Exactly the Three Musketeers. LC 98-43785. (Guardians of the Flame Ser.). 320p. 2000. 23.95 (*0-312-85782-9*, Pub. by Tor Bks) St Martin.

***Rosenberg, Joel.** Not Exactly the Three Musketeers. 384p. 2000. mass mkt. 6.99 (*0-8125-5046-3*, Pub. by Tor Bks) St Martin.

— Not Quite Scaramouche. 2001. text 23.95 (*0-312-86897-9*) St Martin.

Rosenberg, Joel, mem. Keepers of the Hidden Ways, Book Two: The Silver Stone. LC 96-24232. (Keepers of the Hidden Ways Ser.: Bk. 2). 352p. 1998. mass mkt. 5.99 (*0-380-72208-9*, Eos) Morrow Avon.

Rosenberg, Joel, tr. see Green, Arthur, ed.

Rosenberg, Joel, tr. see Teutsch, David, ed.

Rosenberg, John, jt. auth. see Glossbrenner, Alfred.

Rosenberg, John D. Carlyle & the Burden of History. LC 85-8407. (Illus.). 276p. 1986. 37.95 (*0-674-09754-8*) HUP.

— The Darkening Glass. LC 86-17148. 274p. 1986. pap. text 22.00 (*0-231-06387-3*) Col U Pr.

— The Fall of Camelot. LC 73-77992. viii, 182 p. (C). 1973. 16.95 (*0-674-29175-1*) HUP.

Rosenberg, John D., ed. see Ruskin, John.

Rosenberg, John M. First in Peace: George Washington, the Constitution & the Presidency. LC 98-18631. (Illus.). 256p. (J). (gr. 7 up). 1998. lib. bdg. 22.40 (*0-7613-0422-3*, Copper Beech Bks) Millbrook Pr.

Rosenberg, John R. The Circular Pilgrimage: An Anatomy of Confessional Autobiography in Spain. LC 92-17656. (University of Kansas Humanistic Studies: Vol. 59). XVI, 204p. (C). 1994. text 41.95 (*0-8204-1952-4*) P Lang Pubng.

Rosenberg, John S., jt. auth. see Healy, Robert G.

Rosenberg, Jonathan. Algebraic K-Theory & Its Applications. LC 94-8077. (Graduate Texts in Mathematics Ser.: Vol. 147). (Illus.). 408p. 1995. 54.95 (*0-387-94248-3*) Spr-Verlag.

— How Debuggers Work: Algorithms, Data Structures, & Architecture. LC 96-9195. 272p. 1996. pap. 44.99 (*0-471-14966-7*) Wiley.

Rosenberg, Jonathan, et al, eds. Novikov Conjectures, Index Theorems & Rigidity, Vol. 1. (London Mathematical Society Lecture Note Ser.: No. 226). (Illus.). 382p. (C). 1996. pap. text 47.95 (*0-521-49796-5*) Cambridge U Pr.

— Novikov Conjectures, Index Theorems & Rigidity, Vol. 2. (London Mathematical Society Lecture Note Ser.: No. 227). (Illus.). 374p. (C). 1996. pap. text 47.95 (*0-521-49795-7*) Cambridge U Pr.

Rosenberg, Joseph. German: How to Speak & Write It. (Illus.). 384p. 1962. pap. 8.95 (*0-486-20271-2*) Dover.

Rosenberg, Joshua D., jt. auth. see Lathrope, Daniel J.

Rosenberg, Judith P. A Question of Balance: Artists & Writers on Motherhood. LC 95-7216. 288p. 1995. 25.00 (*0-918949-54-8*); pap. 14.00 (*0-918949-53-X*) Rosenberg.

Rosenberg, Judy. Kick It 5 Day Stop Smoking Plan, 6 audio cassettes. 40p. 1999. 79.95 incl. audio (*0-9671313-0-8*) Habit Breakers.

— Rosie's Bakery All-Butter, Fresh Cream, Sugar-Packed, No-Holds-Barred Baking Book. rev. ed. LC 91-50380. (Illus.). 256p. (Orig.). 1996. pap. 13.95 (*0-7611-0633-2*, 10633) Workman Pub.

— Rosie's Bakery Chocolate-Packed, Jam-Filled, Butter-Rich No-Holds-Barred Cookie Book. LC 96-43823. (Illus.). 272p. 1996. 22.95 (*0-7611-0625-1*, 10625); pap. 12.95 (*1-56305-506-6*, 3506) Workman Pub.

Rosenberg, Justin. The Empire of Civil Society: A Critique of the Realist Theory of International Relations. LC 93-47997. 256p. (C). 1994. pap. 19.00 (*0-86091-607-3*, Pub. by Verso) Norton.

Rosenberg, Karen, jt. ed. see Groza, Victor F.

Rosenberg, Ken & Daly, Helen. Foundations of Psychological Research: A Basic Question. LC 92-70921. (Illus.). 420p. (C). 1993. pap. text 62.00 (*0-03-055558-2*, Pub. by Harcourt Coll Pubs) Harcourt.

Rosenberg, Kenneth A. Wilderness Preservation: A Reference Handbook. LC 94-19336. (Contemporary World Issues Ser.). 292p. 1994. lib. bdg. 45.00 (*0-87436-731-X*) ABC-CLIO.

Rosenberg, Kenneth M. Statistics for the Behavioral Sciences. 496p. (C). 1990. write for info. (*0-318-66913-7*) Brown & Benchmark.

— Statistics for the Behavioral Sciences. 496p. (C). 1990. text, student ed. 23.75 (*0-697-11257-8*) Brown & Benchmark.

Rosenberg, Kenneth V., et al. Birds of the Lower Colorado River Valley. LC 90-11120. (Illus.). 416p. 1990. 48.50 (*0-8165-1174-8*) U of Ariz Pr.

Rosenberg, Kenyon C. A Basic Classical & Operatic Recordings Collection for Libraries. LC 87-12747. 269p. 1987. 47.50 (*0-8108-2041-2*) Scarecrow.

— A Basic Classical & Operatic Recordings Collection on Compact Discs for Libraries: A Buying Guide. LC 90-8317. 395p. 1990. 41.50 (*0-8108-2322-5*) Scarecrow.

Rosenberg, Kris. Talk to Me: Opening up Your Silent Man. 192p. 1995. mass mkt. 5.50 (*0-380-72470-7*, Avon Bks) Morrow Avon.

Rosenberg, L. M., ed. see Kessler, Milton.

Rosenberg, Larry. The Berry Book, Vol. 37. 64p. 1995. pap., per. 3.95 (*0-942320-48-4*) Am Cooking.

***Rosenberg, Larry.** Breath by Breath: The Liberating Practice of Insight Meditation. LC 97-29041. 1998. 22.00 (*1-57062-335-X*, Pub. by Shambhala Pubns) Random.

Rosenberg, Larry. Breath by Breath: The Liberating Practice of Insight Meditation. 1999. pap. 14.95 (*1-57062-350-3*, Pub. by Shambhala Pubns) Random.

***Rosenberg, Larry & Guy, David.** Living in the Light of Death: On the Art of Being Truly Alive. LC 99-58716. 192p. 2000. 22.95 (*1-57062-425-9*, Pub. by Shambhala Pubns) Random.

Rosenberg, Larry J. & Assael, Henry, eds. The Roots of Marketing Strategy: An Original Anthology. LC 78-289. (Century of Marketing Ser.). 1979. lib. bdg. 47.95 (*0-405-11189-4*) Ayer.

Rosenberg, Laurie. Jewish Synagogue. (Illus.). 32p. 1998. 16.95 (*0-7136-4338-2*) Adlard Coles.

***Rosenberg, Laurie.** Jewish Synagogue. (Keystones Ser.). (Illus.). 32p. (J). (gr. 2-6). 2000. reprint ed. pap. write for info. (*0-7136-5343-4*, Pub. by A & C Blk) Midpt Trade.

Rosenberg, Lawrence M. Muffins & Cupcakes. Levine, Marian, ed. (Collector's Ser.: Vol. 18). 64p. (Orig.). 1986. pap., per. 3.95 (*0-942320-13-1*) Am Cooking.

Rosenberg, Lawrence M., jt. auth. see Duguid, William P.

Rosenberg, Lenore. How to Eat Out in the U. S. A. & U. K. (JPN., Illus.). Date not set. pap. 6.95 (*88-7301-109-8*, Pub. by Gremese Intl); pap. 6.95 (*88-7301-108-X*, Pub. by Gremese Intl); pap. 6.95 (*88-7301-106-3*, Pub. by Gremese Intl); pap. 6.95 (*88-7301-105-5*, Pub. by Gremese Intl); pap. 6.95 (*88-7301-107-1*, Pub. by Gremese Intl) Natl Bk Netwk.

Rosenberg, Leon E., jt. auth. see Bondy, Philip K.

Rosenberg, Liz. Adelaide & the Night Train. LC 88-39948. (Charlotte Zolotow Bk.). (Illus.). 32p. (J). (ps-2). 1989. 13.95 (*0-06-025102-6*) HarpC Child Bks.

— A Big & Little Alphabet. LC 96-53305. (Illus.). 32p. (J). (ps-k). 1997. 15.95 (*0-531-30050-1*); lib. bdg. 16.99 (*0-531-33050-8*) Orchard Bks Watts.

— The Carousel. LC 94-47323. (Illus.). 32p. (J). (ps-3). 1995. 16.00 (*0-15-200853-5*, Harcourt Child Bks) Harcourt.

— The Carousel. LC 94-47323. (Illus.). 32p. (J). (gr. k-3). 1998. pap. 6.00 (*0-15-201887-5*) Harcourt.

— The Carousel. LC 94-7332. (Illus.). (J). (ps-3). 1995. 15.95 (*0-399-22704-0*, Philomel) Peng Put Young Read.

— Carousel. 1998. 11.20 (*0-606-13244-9*, Pub. by Turtleback) Demco.

— Children of Paradise. LC 92-62426. (Poetry Ser.). 80p. (C). 1993. pap. 10.95 (*0-8229-5502-4*); text 19.95 (*0-8229-3750-6*) U of Pittsburgh Pr.

— The Fire Music. LC 85-40856. (Pitt Poetry Ser.). 71p. reprint ed. pap. 30.00 (*0-608-10637-2*, 207125900009) Bks Demand.

— Heart & Soul. LC 95-23569. 224p. (YA). (gr. 7 up). 1996. pap. 5.00 (*0-15-201270-2*) Harcourt.

— Heart & Soul. LC 95-23569. 224p. (YA). (gr. 7 up). 1996. 11.00 (*0-15-200942-6*) Harcourt.

R

R

— I Did It Anyway. LC 97-2045. (Illus.). (J). Date not set. write for info. (0-15-201675-9) Harcourt.

*Rosenberg, Liz. Light-Gathering Poems: Poems of Hope & Healing. LC 99-49231. 128p. (YA). 2000. pap. text 16.95 (0-8050-6223-8) St Martin.

Rosenberg, Liz. Monster Mama. LC 91-46825. (Illus.). 32p. (J). (ps-3). 1993. 15.95 (0-399-21989-7, Philomel) Peng Put Young Read.

Rosenberg, Liz. Monster Mama. LC 91-46825. (J). 1997. 11.15 (0-606-11633-8, Pub. by Turtleback) Demco.

— On Christmas Eve. LC 99-462310. (Illus.). (J). 2000. write for info. (0-7894-2620-X) DK Pub Inc.

— Roots & Flowers. 2001. text 17.95 (0-8050-6433-8) H Holt & Co.

Rosenberg, Liz. The Silence in the Mountains. LC 97-35016. (Illus.). 32p. (J). (gr. k-4). 1998. 15.95 (0-531-30084-6) Orchard Bks Watts.

— The Silence in the Mountains. LC 97-35016. (Illus.). 32p. (J). (gr. k-4). 1999. lib. bdg. 16.99 (0-531-33084-2) Orchard Bks Watts.

*Rosenberg, Liz. We Wanted You. LC 98-47255. (J). 1999. write for info. (0-7894-2600-5) DK Pub Inc.

Rosenberg, Liz. Window, Mirror, Moon. LC 89-26971. (Charlotte Zolotow Bk.). (Illus.). 32p. (J). (ps-3). 1990. 12.95 (0-06-025075-5) HarpC Child Bks.

Rosenberg, Liz, ed. Earth-Shattering Poems. LC 97-16097. (YA). (gr. 7 up). 1995. 15.95 (0-8050-4821-9) H Holt & Co.

— The Invisible Ladder: A Young Readers' Anthology of Contemporary Poetry. (Illus.). 144p. (YA). (gr. 7 up). 1995. 16.95 (0-8050-3836-1, B Martin BYR) H Holt & Co.

*Rosenberg, Liz & Yardley, Joanna. Eli's Night-Light. LC 00-39149. (Illus.). (J). 2001. write for info. (0-531-33316-7) Orchard Bks Watts.

Rosenberg, Louis. Canada's Jews: A Social & Economic Study of Jews in Canada in the 1930s. (McGill-Queen's Studies in Ethnic History). (Illus.). 448p. 1993. pap. 32.95 (0-7735-1109-1, Pub. by McG-Queens Univ Pr) CUP Services.

— Canada's Jews: A Social & Economic Study of Jews in Canada in the 1930s. (McGill-Queen's Studies in Ethnic History). (Illus.). 448p. 1993. 75.00 (0-7735-0997-6, Pub. by McG-Queens Univ Pr) CUP Services.

Rosenberg, Love, ed. see Caine, Dona & Caine, Michael.

Rosenberg, M. B. English-Russian Dictionary of Refrigerating & Cryogenic Engineering. (ENG & RUS.). 467p. 1978. 75.00 (0-8288-5237-5, M9063) Fr & Eur.

Rosenberg, M. E., tr. see Kovalevsky, A. L.

Rosenberg, Madge. The Best Bread Machine Cookbook Ever. LC 92-52548. 224p. 1992. 17.95 (0-06-016927-3) HarperTrade.

Rosenberg, Madge. The Best Low-Fat, No-Sugar Bread Machine Cookbook Ever. LC 95-7034. 224p. 1995. 16.95 (0-06-017174-X) HarpC.

Rosenberg, Magda & Rossman, Isadore. Sixty-Plus & Fit Again: Exercises for Older Men & Women. LC 76-49130. (Illus.). 156p. 1977. 12.95 (0-87131-224-7) M Evans.

Rosenberg, Marc. Dingo. 76p. (C). 1992. pap. 17.95 (0-86819-317-8, Pub. by Currency Pr) Accents Pubns.

Rosenberg, Marc L., ed. Violence in America: A Public Health Approach. (Illus.). 216p. 1991. text 37.50 (0-19-506437-2) OUP.

Rosenberg, Marc L. & Nadolny, Paul R. CPA Firm Administration Handbook. LC 94-46311. 338p. 1995. 135.00 (0-471-58548-3) Wiley.

Rosenberg, Marie B. & Bergstrom, Len V., eds. Women & Society: A Critical Review of the Literature with a Selected Annotated Bibliography. LC 73-77874. 360p. reprint ed. pap. 111.60 (0-608-11367-0, 202194800026) Bks Demand.

Rosenberg, Marilyn R. Circumambience Can Be. 18p. 1985. pap. 100.00 (0-913615-09-9) Marilyn R Rosenberg.

— Coming Around. 14p. 1985. pap. 100.00 (0-913615-10-2) Marilyn R Rosenberg.

— One Way. 4p. 1977. pap. 8.00 (0-317-14975-X) Marilyn R Rosenberg.

— Philip One. 55p. 1980. pap. 8.00 (0-913615-01-3) Marilyn R Rosenberg.

— Philip II. 70p. 1980. pap. 8.00 (0-913615-02-1) Marilyn R Rosenberg.

— Query, Quest, & Quasi: What Is It Supposed to Be? (Illus.). 20p. 1997. pap. 8.00 (0-913615-15-3) Marilyn R Rosenberg.

— Spall Spirula. limited unabridged ed. (Illus.). 37p. (Orig.). 1994. pap. 12.00 (0-614-13815-9) Marilyn R Rosenberg.

— Unit of Measure. 18p. 1977. pap. 8.00 (0-913615-04-8) Marilyn R Rosenberg.

— Wheelwork. 14p. 1986. pap. 100.00 (0-913615-11-0) Marilyn R Rosenberg.

Rosenberg, Marion Lignana, tr. see Merlo, Claudio.

Rosenberg, Marjorie Von, see Von Rosenberg, Marjorie.

Rosenberg, Mark, jt. auth. see Tardanico, Richard.

Rosenberg, Mark B., ed. The Changing Hemispheric Trade Environment: Opportunities & Obstacles. LC 91-32431. (Orig.). (C). 1991. pap. text 11.95 (1-879862-01-8) FL Intl U Latin.

Rosenberg, Mark B., et al, eds. Americas: An Anthology. (Illus.). 400p. (C). 1992. pap. text 24.95 (0-19-507792-X) OUP.

Rosenberg, Mark B. & Hiskey, Jonathan. Florida-Mexico: Strategies & Recommendations for an Expanding Market. 91p. 1992. 35.00 (1-879862-02-6) FL Intl U Latin.

Rosenberg, Marshall B. Nonviolent Communications: A Language of Compassion. LC 98-67231. (Illus.). 212p. 1999. pap. 17.95 (1-892005-02-6, BK033, Pub. by PuddleDancer) IPG Chicago.

Rosenberg, Martin. Opportunities in Accounting Careers. (Opportunities in . . . Ser.). (Illus.). 160p. pap. 11.95 (0-8442-4636-0, 46360, Natl Textbk Co) NTC Contemp Pub Co.

— Opportunities in Accounting Careers. (Illus.). 160p. 1993. pap. 10.95 (0-8442-8578-1, VGM Career) NTC Contemp Pub Co.

— Opportunities in Accounting Careers. (Illus.). 160p. 1994. 13.95 (0-8442-8577-3, VGM Career) NTC Contemp Pub Co.

— Opportunities in Accounting Careers. (Opportunities in...Ser.). 160p. 1996. 14.95 (0-8442-4635-2, 46352, Natl Textbk Co) NTC Contemp Pub Co.

— Raphael & France: The Artist As Paradigm & Symbol. (Illus.). 265p. (C). 1995. 55.00 (0-271-01300-1) Pa St U Pr.

Rosenberg, Martin & Moore, Gordon P., eds. The Pharmacology of Monoclonal Antibodies. LC 93-44948. (Handbook of Experimental Pharmacology Ser.: Vol. 113). (Illus.). 460p. 1994. 379.95 (0-387-57123-X) Spr-Verlag.

Rosenberg, Marvin. The Adventures of a Shakespeare Scholar: To Discover Shakespeare's Art. LC 96-6222. 368p. 1997. 52.50 (0-87413-598-2) U Delaware Pr.

— The Masks of Hamlet. LC 92-22566. 992p. (C). 1993. 69.50 (0-87413-480-3) U Delaware Pr.

— The Masks of King Lear. LC 74-115492. 440p. 1993. reprint ed. 30.00 (0-87413-482-X); reprint ed. pap. 15.00 (0-87413-485-4) U Delaware Pr.

— The Masks of Macbeth. LC 76-14295. 816p. 1993. reprint ed. 30.00 (0-87413-483-8); reprint ed. pap. 15.00 (0-87413-486-2) U Delaware Pr.

— The Masks of Othello: The Search for the Identity of Othello, Iago, & Desdemona by Three Centuries of Actors & Critics. LC 61-7521. 328p. 1993. reprint ed. 30.00 (0-87413-481-1); reprint ed. pap. 15.00 (0-87413-484-6) U Delaware Pr.

— Shakespearean Illuminations: Essays in Honor of Marvin Rosenberg. Halio, Jay L. & Richmond, Hugh M., eds. LC 98-13769. (Illus.). 376p. 1998. 57.50 (0-87413-657-1) U Delaware Pr.

Rosenberg, Marvin M., et al. Periodontal & Prosthetic Management for Advanced Cases. (Illus.). 375p. 1988. text 182.00 (0-86715-162-5, 1625) Quint Pub Co.

*Rosenberg, Mary. Assessing Basic Skills for Primary Students. 80p. 2000. pap. 9.95 (1-57690-651-5) Tchr Create Mat.

— Brain Teasers & Squeezers. 80p. 2000. pap. 9.95 (1-57690-653-1) Tchr Create Mat.

— Daily Skills Practice. Taggart, Leasha, ed. (Illus.). 240p. (J). (gr. 1-2). 1999. pap., teacher ed. 16.95 (1-57690-514-4, TCM2514) Tchr Create Mat.

— A Guide for Using the Mitten in the Classroom. (Illus.). 48p. 2000. pap., teacher ed. 7.95 (1-57690-627-2, TCM 2627) Tchr Create Mat.

— How to Add & Subtract: Grade 1. (Illus.). 48p. 2000. pap., teacher ed. 7.95 (1-57690-942-5, TCM 2942) Tchr Create Mat.

— How to Add & Subtract: Grade 2. 48p. 2000. pap., teacher ed. 7.95 (1-57690-943-3, TCM 2943) Tchr Create Mat.

— How to Add & Subtract: Grade 3. (Illus.). 48p. 2000. pap., teacher ed. 7.95 (1-57690-944-1, TCM 2944) Tchr Create Mat.

— How to Calculate Measurements: Grades 1-3. (Illus.). 48p. 2000. pap., teacher ed. 7.95 (1-57690-952-2, TCM 2952) Tchr Create Mat.

— How to Multiply Grades 2-3: Primary. 48p. 2000. pap. 7.95 (1-57690-945-X) Tchr Create Mat.

— How to Work with Fractions: Grades 2-3. (Illus.). 48p. 2000. pap., teacher ed. 7.95 (1-57690-954-9, TCM 2954) Tchr Create Mat.

— Learning Sight Words Is Easy! (Illus.). 96p. (J). 2000. pap. 10.95 (0-439-14113-3) Scholastic Inc.

— Writing Skills for Primary Students. (Illus.). 80p. 2000. pap., teacher ed. 9.95 (1-57690-652-3, TCM 2652) Tchr Create Mat.

Rosenberg, Mary, jt. auth. see Winnick, Sheila.

Rosenberg, Matthew T. The Handy Geography Answer Book. LC 98-36290. (Illus.). 400p. 1998. pap. 19.95 (1-57859-062-0) Visible Ink Pr.

Rosenberg, Maurice & Dreyfuss, Hans S. Elements of Civil Procedure: Cases & Materials, 1996 Supplement. 5th ed. (University Casebook Ser.). 165p. 1996. pap. text, suppl. ed. write for info. (1-56662-430-4) Foundation Pr.

Rosenberg, Maurice & Hay, Peter. Conflict of Laws, 1994: Cases & Materials. 9th ed. 47p. 1994. pap. text 4.95 (1-56662-171-2) Foundation Pr.

Rosenberg, Maurice, et al. Conflict of Laws, Cases & Materials. 10th ed. LC 96-577. (University Casebook Ser.). 1012p. (C). 1996. text. write for info. (1-56662-333-2) Foundation Pr.

— Elements of Civil Procedure: Cases & Materials On. 5th ed. (University Casebook Ser.). 1155p. 1990. text 43.75 (0-88277-797-1) Foundation Pr.

— Elements of Civil Procedure: Cases & Materials, Teachers Manual For. 5th ed. (University Casebook Ser.). 137p. 1990. pap. text. write for info. (0-88277-842-0) Foundation Pr.

— Elements of Civil Procedure: Cases & Materials, 1994 Supplement. 5th ed. (University Casebook Ser.). 110p. 1994. pap. text 6.95 (1-56662-186-0) Foundation Pr.

— Elements of Civil Procedure: Cases & Materials, 1997 Supplement. 5th ed. (University Casebook Ser.). 750p. 1997. pap. text. write for info. (1-56662-551-3) Foundation Pr.

Rosenberg, Max. The Building of Perry's Fleet on Lake Erie: 1812-1813. LC 50-9593. 72p. (Orig.). 1988. pap. 6.95 (0-911124-49-7) Pa Hist & Mus.

Rosenberg, Maxine B. Being Adopted. LC 83-17522. (Illus.). 48p. (J). (gr. 1-4). 1984. 16.00 (0-688-02672-9) Lothrop.

— Hiding to Survive: Fourteen Jewish Children & the Gentiles Who Rescued Them from the Holocaust. LC 93-28328. 176p. (J). (gr. 4 up). 1994. 16.00 (0-395-65014-3, Clarion Bks) HM.

— Hiding to Survive: Stories of Jewish Children Rescued from the Holocaust. LC 93-28328. 176p. 1998. pap. 8.95 (0-395-90020-4, Clarion Bks) HM.

— Hiding to Survive: Stories of Jewish Children Rescued from the Holocaust. 1998. 14.05 (0-606-13481-6, Pub. by Turtleback) Demco.

— Living with a Single Parent. LC 92-3883. (Illus.). 128p. (J). (gr. 4 up). 1992. text 14.95 (0-02-777915-7, Bradbury S&S) S&S Childrens.

— Mommy's in the Hospital Having a Baby. LC 96-12442. (Illus.). 32p. (J). (ps-1). 1997. 15.00 (0-395-71813-9, Clarion Bks) HM.

Rosenberg, Mel, jt. ed. see Doyle, Ronald J.

Rosenberg, Michael. The Flexible Thinker: A Guide to Creative Wealth. (Illus.). 153p. 1999. pap. 16.95 (0-9662511-0-5) Orange You Glad.

Rosenberg, Michael R. Currency Forecasting: A Guide to Fundamental & Technical Models of Exchange Rate Determination. 376p. 1996. 60.00 (1-55738-918-7, Irwn Prfssnl) McGraw-Hill Prof.

Rosenberg, Michael S. & Wilson, Rich. Education Student & Behavioral Disorder. 2nd ed. 464p. 1996. 74.00 (0-205-26467-0) Allyn.

Rosenberg, Michael S., et al. Educating Students with Behavior Disorders. 2nd ed. (C). 1997. pap., teacher ed. write for info. (0-205-26468-9, T6468-7) Allyn.

*Rosenberg, Michael S., et al. Metaluin 2.0 (User's Manual) Statistical Software for Meta-Analysis. rev. ed. (C). 1999. pap. text 25.00 (0-87893-760-9) Sinauer Assocs.

Rosenberg, Michael S., et al. Student Teacher to Master Teacher: A Guide for Preservice & Beginning Teachers of Students with Mild to Moderate Disabilities. 2nd ed. LC 97-13532. 411p. (C). 1997. spiral bd. 52.00 (0-13-632514-9, Merrill Coll) P-H.

— Student Teacher to Master Teacher: A Handbook for Preservice & Beginning Teachers of Students with Mild & Moderate Handicaps. 352p. (C). 1990. pap. text 32.20 (0-02-403650-1, Macmillan Coll) P-H.

Rosenberg, Milton J., ed. Beyond Conflict & Containment: Critical Studies of Military & Foreign Policy. LC 79-189565. 250p. 1972. 34.95 (0-87855-038-0); pap. text 19.95 (0-87855-534-X) Transaction Pubs.

Rosenberg, Milton J., et al. Attitude Organization & Change: An Analysis of Consistency among Attitude Components, Volume 3. LC 80-14704. (Yale Studies in Attitude & Communication: Vol. 3). (Illus.). 239p. 1980. reprint ed. lib. bdg. 65.00 (0-313-22435-8, ROAT) Greenwood.

Rosenberg, Mindy S., jt. ed. see Rossman, B. B.

Rosenberg, Monda. Quickies: 1000 Recipes, Ten Quick Ways with Everyday Foods. LC 98-225434. (Chatelaine Food Express Ser.). (Illus.). 224p. 1998. pap. 19.95 (0-7710-7592-8) McCland & Stewart.

*Rosenberg, Monda. Quickies Chicken: Delicious Ideas from Bakes to Wraps. (Chatelaine Food Express Ser.). (Illus.). 144p. 2000. pap. 16.95 (0-7710-7595-2) McCland & Stewart.

Rosenberg, Monda. Quickies 2: Veggies & More. (Chatelaine Food Express Ser.). 1998. pap. text 16.95 (0-7710-7593-6) McCland & Stewart.

— Sizzlers: Fast Ideas for Year-Round Grilling, over 200 Recipes. (Chatelaine Food Express Ser.). (Illus.). 144p. 1998. pap. 15.95 (0-7710-2007-4) McCland & Stewart.

*Rosenberg, Monda. Starters: Great Beginnings from Appetizers to Soups. (Chatelaine Food Express Ser.: Vol. 5). (Illus.). 144p. 1999. pap. 16.95 (0-7710-7594-4) McCland & Stewart.

Rosenberg, Monda. Sweeties: Fast & Easy Delectable Desserts. (Illus.). 144p. 1998. pap. 15.95 (0-7710-2012-0) McCland & Stewart.

Rosenberg, Morris. Conceiving the Self. LC 86-7431. 336p. 1986. reprint ed. text 42.00 (0-89874-961-1) Krieger.

— Occupations & Values. Zuckerman, Harriet & Merton, Robert K., eds. LC 79-9020. (Dissertations on Sociology Ser.). 1980. reprint ed. lib. bdg. 18.95 (0-405-12989-0) Ayer.

*Rosenberg, Morris. Society & the Adolescent Self-Image. rev. ed. 347p. 1999. reprint ed. pap. text 25.00 (0-7881-6399-X) DIANE Pub.

Rosenberg, Morris & Kaplan, Howard B., eds. Social Psychology of the Self-Concept. (Illus.). 576p. (C). 1982. text 32.50 (0-88295-214-5); pap. text 22.50 (0-88295-215-3) Harlan Davidson.

Rosenberg, Morris & Turner, Ralph H., eds. Social Psychology: Sociological Perspectives. 798p. (C). 1990. pap. 29.95 (0-88738-854-X) Transaction Pubs.

Rosenberg, Morris, jt. ed. see Greenley, James R.

Rosenberg, Morris D. Vacation with Love: "A Monumental Mexican Mix-Up" (Illus.). vi, 159p. 1999. pap. 14.99 (0-9669787-1-4, 30) Premio Pr.

*Rosenberg, Nancy Taylor. Abuse of Power. 1999. pap. 287.40 (0-525-94319-6, Dutt) Dutton Plume.

Rosenberg, Nancy Taylor. Abuse of Power. 1997. mass mkt. 6.99 (0-451-18006-2, Sig) NAL.

Rosenberg, Nancy Taylor. Abuse of Power. 1997. mass mkt. 251.64 (0-451-98437-4, Sig) NAL.

Rosenberg, Nancy Taylor. Abuse of Power. large type ed. LC 97-1515. 554p. 1997. 27.95 (0-7838-8093-6, G K Hall Lrg Type) Mac Lib Ref.

*Rosenberg, Nancy Taylor. Buried Evidence. 368p. 2000. 24.95 (0-7868-6619-5, Pub. by Disney Pr) Time Warner.

— Buried Evidence. 2001. mass mkt. write for info. (0-7868-8983-7) Disney Pr.

Rosenberg, Nancy Taylor. California Angel. large type ed. LC 95-15713. 1995. 25.95 (1-56895-214-7) Wheeler Pub.

— California Angel. rev. ed. 1996. mass mkt. 6.99 (0-451-19177-3, Sig) NAL.

— First Offense. 448p. 1995. mass mkt. 6.99 (0-451-18432-7, Sig) NAL.

— First Offense. large type ed. LC 94-35474. 1994. 25.95 (1-56895-155-8) Wheeler Pub.

— Interest of Justice. 448p. 1994. mass mkt. 7.50 (0-451-18021-6, Sig) NAL.

— Interest of Justice. large type ed. LC 93-40896. 1993. 25.95 (1-56895-047-0) Wheeler Pub.

— Mitigating Circumstances. 448p. 1993. mass mkt. 6.99 (0-451-17672-3, Sig) NAL.

— Trial by Fire. 1996. mass mkt. 6.99 (0-451-18005-4, Sig) NAL.

— Trial by Fire. large type ed. LC 96-2290. (Large Print Bks.). 1996. 26.95 (1-56895-305-4) Wheeler Pub.

Rosenberg-Naparsteck, Ruth & Curtis, Edward P. Runnin' Crazy: A Portrait of the Genesee River. LC 96-38421. 1997. write for info. (0-89865-978-7) Donning Co.

Rosenberg, Nathan. The Emergence of Economic Ideas: Essays in the History of Economics. LC 94-21289. (Economists of the Twentieth Century Ser.). 208p. 1994. 90.00 (1-85898-047-X) E Elgar.

— Exploring the Black Box: Technology, Economics & History. (Illus.). 284p. (C). 1994. text 59.95 (0-521-45270-8); pap. text 19.95 (0-521-45955-9) Cambridge U Pr.

— Inside the Black Box: Technology & Economics. LC 82-4563. 304p. 1983. pap. text 25.95 (0-521-27367-6) Cambridge U Pr.

— Perspectives on Technology. LC 84-23495. 360p. 1985. reprint ed. pap. 111.60 (0-7837-9948-9, 206067500006) Bks Demand.

*Rosenberg, Nathan. Schumpeter & the Endogeneity of Technology: Some American Perspectives. LC 99-46088. (Graz Schumpeter Lectures). 2000. 85.00 (0-415-22652-X) Routledge.

— Technology & American Economic Growth. LC 76-52621. 214p. (C). (gr. 13). 1977. reprint ed. pap. text 31.95 (0-87332-104-9) M E Sharpe.

Rosenberg, Nathan, et al, eds. Technology & the Wealth of Nations. 464p. (C). 1992. 52.50 (0-8047-2082-7); pap. 17.95 (0-8047-2083-5) Stanford U Pr.

Rosenberg, Nathan & Birdzell, L. E., Jr. How the West Grew Rich: The Economic Transformation of the Industrial World. LC 85-47551. 368p. 1987. pap. 20.00 (0-465-03109-9, Pub. by Basic) HarpC.

Rosenberg, Nathan, jt. auth. see Mowery, David C.

Rosenberg, Neil V. Bluegrass: A History. LC 93-3590. 464p. (C). 1993. 19.95 (0-252-06304-X) U of Ill Pr.

Rosenberg, Neil V., ed. Transforming Tradition: Folk Music Revivals Examined. LC 92-26727. (Music in American Life, Folklore & Society Ser.). 336p. (C). 1993. text 29.95 (0-252-01982-2) U of Ill Pr.

Rosenberg, Neil V., jt. auth. see Fleischhauer, Carl.

Rosenberg, Norman. Handbook of Carotid Artery Surgery: Facts & Figures. 328p. 1989. lib. bdg. 175.00 (0-8493-2957-4, RD598) CRC Pr.

— Handbook of Carotid Artery Surgery: Facts & Figures. 2nd ed. LC 93-29684. 368p. 1994. reprint ed. boxed set 179.00 (0-8493-3252-4, RD598) CRC Pr.

Rosenberg, Norman J., ed. Drought in the Great Plains: Research on Impacts & Strategies. LC 80-51532. 1980. 30.00 (0-918334-34-9) WRP.

— Towards an Integrated Impact Assessment of Climate Change: The Mink Study. LC 93-26849. 172p. (C). 1993. text 107.00 (0-7923-2448-X) Kluwer Academic.

Rosenberg, Norman J., et al, eds. Greenhouse Warming: Abatement & Adaptation. LC 89-8483. 182p. 1989. pap. 18.95 (0-915707-50-0) Resources Future.

*Rosenberg, Norman J., et al. Carbon Sequestration in Soils: Science, Monitoring & Beyond. LC 99-35376. 210p. 1999. 34.95 (1-57477-084-5) Battelle.

Rosenberg, Norman J., et al. Microclimate: The Biological Environment. 2nd ed. LC 83-7031. 528p. 1983. 140.00 (0-471-06066-6) Wiley.

Rosenberg, Norman J., jt. ed. see Frederick, Kenneth D.

Rosenberg, Norman L. Protecting the Best Men: An Interpretive History of the Law of Libel. LC 85-1174. (Studies in Legal History). xi, 369p. (C). 1990. reprint ed. pap. text 22.50 (0-8078-4290-7) U of NC Pr.

Rosenberg, Norman L. & Rosenberg, Emily S. In Our Times: America Since World War II. 6th ed. LC 98-29563. 330p. (C). 1998. pap. text 38.40 (0-13-911082-8) P-H.

Rosenberg, P., ed. Topical French. 10p. 1979. pap. 14.95 (0-8288-4838-6, M9205) Fr & Eur.

Rosenberg, Paul. The Alternative Energy Handbook. LC 92-30937. 259p. 1992. 259.00 (0-88173-140-4) Fairmont Pr.

— Audel Guide to the Nineteen Ninety-Six National Electric Code. 608p. 1996. 25.00 (0-02-861062-8) Macmillan.

— Audel Questions & Answers for Elective Exams. 12th ed. 288p. 1996. 20.00 (0-02-861061-X) Macmillan.

— Data Communications PAL: The Basic Pocket Reference Guide for the Data Communications Industry. LC 98-68625. (Illus.). 350p. 1999. pap. 20.00 (0-9652171-1-6, 100) Pal Pubns.

— Electrical Pal: The Basic Pocket Reference Guide for the Electrical Industry. (Illus.). 350p. 1996. pap. 20.00 (0-9652171-0-8) Pal Pubns.

— Electricians Pocket Manual. LC 96-79619. 384p. 1996. per. 14.95 (0-02-036425-3, Aude IN) IDG Bks.

*Rosenberg, Paul. HVAC PAL: The Pocket Reference Guide for the Climate Control Industry. (Illus.). 350p. 1999. pap. 20.00 (0-9652171-2-4, 101) Pal Pubns.

Rosenberg, Paul. The Illustrated Energy Dictionary. LC 95-38783. 1995. write for info. (*0-88173-179-X*) Fairmont Pr.

— Introduction to the National Electrical Code. 39p. 1993. teacher ed. 13.50 (*0-8273-5306-5*) Delmar.

***Rosenberg, Paul.** Wiring Diagram Pal: The Pocket Reference Guide for Electrical, Data Com & HVAC Wiring. (Wiring Diagram Pal Ser.: No. 4). (Illus.). 350p. 2000. pap. 20.00i (*0-9652171-3-2*) Pal Pubns.

Rosenberg, Paul, rev. Questions & Answers for Electrician's Examinations. 11th ed. LC 92-33277. 1993. write for info. (*0-02-604962-7*) Macmillan.

Rosenberg, Paul & Fairmont Press Staff. The Illustrated Energy Dictionary. (C). 2000. 58.00 (*0-13-100348-8*) P-H.

Rosenberg, Paul, jt. auth. see Hayes, Jim.

Rosenberg, Peter D. Patent Law Basics. LC 92-15593. (IP Ser.). 1992. ring bd. 125.00 (*0-87632-897-4*) West Group.

— Patent Law Fundamentals, 3 vols. 2nd ed. LC 80-10710. (IP Ser.). (C). 1980. ring bd. 425.00 (*0-87632-098-1*) West Group.

Rosenberg, Philip. The House of Lords. Date not set. 26.00 (*0-06-019415-4*) HarpC.

— House of Lords. 2002. mass mkt. 6.99 (*0-06-109861-2*) HarpC.

Rosenberg, Phillip. The Seventh Hero: Thomas Carlyle & the Theory of Radical Activism. LC 73-87659. 288p. 1974. 25.95 (*0-674-80260-8*) HUP.

***Rosenberg, Pierre.** Chardin. (Illus.). 192p. 2000. 65.00 (*3-7913-2339-3*) Prestel Pub NY.

— Chardin. (Illus.). 360p. 2000. 65.00 (*0-300-08348-3*) Yale U Pr.

— From Drawing to Painting: Poussin, Watteau, David & Ingres. LC 99-88620. (Bollingen Ser.). 2000. 65.00 (*0-691-00918-X*, Pub. by Princeton U Pr) Cal Prin Full Svc.

Rosenberg, Pierre & Prat, Louis-Antoine. Antoine Watteau 1684-1721: Catalogue Raisonne des Dessins. (FRE., Illus.). 1516p. 1996. 960.00 (*88-7813-703-0*, Pub. by Art Bks Intl) Partners Pubs Grp.

— Nicolas Poussin, 1594-1665: Catalogue Raisonne des Dessins. (FRE., Illus.). 1218p. 1994. 800.00 (*88-355-0258-6*, Pub. by Art Bks Intl) Partners Pubs Grp.

Rosenberg, Pierre & Stewart, Marion C. French Paintings 1500-1825: The Fine Museums of San Francisco. (Illus.). 376p. 1987. pap. 19.95 (*0-88401-055-4*, ND544.F56) Fine Arts Mus.

Rosenberg, Pierre, jt. auth. see Prigent, Helene.

Rosenberg, R. Robert. Business Mathematics, Exercises, Problems, & Tests. 7th rev. ed. 1970. text 16.12 (*0-07-053772-0*) McGraw.

Rosenberg, R. Robert & Karnopp, Dean C. Introduction to Physical Systems Dynamics. 512p. (C). 1983. text 79.50 (*0-07-053905-7*) McGraw.

Rosenberg, R. Robert & Sexton, J. E. Business Math on the Job: Practice Set. 1969. text 12.96 (*0-07-053770-4*) McGraw.

Rosenberg, R. Robert, et al. Business Mathematics. 9th rev. ed. LC 80-18533. 576p. (gr. 9-12). 1982. text 24.88 (*0-07-053726-7*) McGraw.

— Consumer Math & You: Activity Guide. (Illus.). 1979. text 24.56 (*0-07-053641-4*) McGraw.

— Understanding Business & Consumer Law. 6th ed. (Illus.). (YA). (gr. 11-12). 1979. text 25.12 (*0-07-053631-7*) McGraw.

Rosenberg, R. Robert, jt. auth. see Alvey, G. C.

Rosenberg, R. Robert, jt. auth. see Bonnice, Joseph G.

Rosenberg, R. Robert, jt. auth. see Brown, Gordon W.

Rosenberg, Ralph G., jt. auth. see Millet, Gary W.

Rosenberg, Ray F. One World & Our Knowledge of It: The Problematic of Realism in Post-Kantian Perspective. (Philosophical Studies: No. 23). 225p. 1980. text 106.00 (*90-277-1136-4*, D Reidel) Kluwer Academic.

Rosenberg, Richard. Competence in Mathematics, Bk. I. (Mathematics Ser.). 96p. 1981. student ed. 4.95 (*0-9602800-4-9*) Comp Pr.

— Competence in Mathematics, Bk. II. (Mathematics Ser.). 90p. 1981. student ed. 4.95 (*0-9602800-5-7*) Comp Pr.

Rosenberg, Richard S. The Social Impact of Computers. 2nd ed. LC 97-8076. (Illus.). 522p. 1997. pap. text 39.95 (*0-12-597131-1*) Morgan Kaufmann.

Rosenberg, Rita. Mushrooms: Over 100 Tantalizing International Recipes. LC 94-37128. (Illus.). 192p. 1995. reprint ed. pap. 12.95 (*1-55561-071-4*) Fisher Bks.

Rosenberg, Robert. An Accidental Murder. LC 98-46783. 288p. 1999. 22.00 (*0-684-85032-X*) Scribner.

— Bill Cosby: The Changing Black Image. (YA). 1992. pap. 5.70 (*0-395-63615-9*) HM.

— Bill Cosby: The Changing Black Image. (New Directions Ser.). (Illus.). 96p. (YA). (gr. 7 up). 1991. pap. 5.95 (*1-56294-828-8*) Millbrook Pr.

— Crimes of the City. (Missing Mysteries Ser.: Vol. 3). 1997. mass mkt. 7.95 (*1-890208-03-5*) Poisoned Pen.

— The Cutting Room: An Avram Cohen Mystery. 320p. 1993. 20.00 (*0-671-74344-9*) S&S Trade.

***Rosenberg, Robert.** House of Guilt, Vol. 25. (Missing Mysteries Ser.: Vol. 25). 2000. pap. 14.95 (*1-890208-41-8*) Poisoned Pen.

Rosenberg, Robert, et al, eds. In Situ Patterning - Selective Area Deposition & Etching Vol. 158: Material Research Society Symposium Proceedings. (Symposium Proceedings Ser.). 496p. 1990. text 17.50 (*1-55899-046-1*) Materials Res.

— Interfaces Between Polymers, Metals, & Ceramics Vol. 153: Materials Research Society Symposium Proceedings. 426p. 1989. text 17.50 (*1-55899-026-7*) Materials Res.

Rosenberg, Robert, et al, eds. Materials Reliability in Microelectronics VI. (MRS Symposium Proceedings Ser.: Vol. 428). 583p. 1996. 76.00 (*1-55899-331-2*, 428) Materials Res.

Rosenberg, Robert & Hand, August. Electric Motor Repair. 3rd ed. 752p. (C). 1987. text 97.50 (*0-03-059584-3*, Pub. by SCP) Harcourt.

Rosenberg, Robert, ed. see Betser, Muki.

Rosenberg, Robert A., et al, eds. The Papers of Thomas A. Edison Vol. 2: From Workshop to Laboratory, June 1873-March 1876. LC 88-9017. (Illus.). 776p. 1991. text 75.00 (*0-8018-3101-6*) Johns Hopkins.

Rosenberg, Robert J. Bankruptcy Developments for Workout Officers & Lenders Counsel. 758p. 1990. pap. text 17.50 (*0-685-49896-4*, A4-4348) PLI.

— Doing Business with Troubled Companies, 1991. 732p. 1991. pap. text 17.50 (*0-685-49892-1*, A4-4340) PLI.

Rosenberg, Robert J., et al. Collier Lending Institutions & the Bankruptcy Code. 1986. 230.00 (*0-8205-1119-6*); write for info. (*0-8205-2025-X*) Bender.

Rosenberg, Robert M. & Klotz, Irving M. Chemical Thermodynamics: Basic Theory & Methods. 6th ed. LC 99-39541. 560p. 2000. text 89.95 (*0-471-33107-4*) Wiley.

Rosenberg, Robert M., jt. auth. see Klotz, Irving M.

Rosenberg, Roberta. The Language of Power Vol. 19: Women & Literature, 1945 to the Present. (Writing about Women Ser.). XIII, 273p. (C). 1996. pap. text 29.95 (*0-8204-2799-3*) P Lang Pubng.

Rosenberg, Robin & Stein, Steve, eds. Advancing the Miami-Process: Civil Society & the Summit of the Americas. 11th ed. 1995. pap. 29.95 (*0-935501-99-1*, Pub. by U Miami N-S Ctr) L Rienner.

Rosenberg, Robin, jt. ed. see Munoz, Heraldo.

Rosenberg, Robin L. Spain & Central America: Democracy & Foreign Policy, 288. LC 91-824. (Contributions in Political Science Ser.: No. 288). 288p. 1992. 59.95 (*0-313-27885-7*, RSJ, Greenwood Pr) Greenwood.

Rosenberg, Robin L., jt. auth. see Fineberg, Richard E.

Rosenberg, Robin S., jt. auth. see Kosslyn, Stephen M.

Rosenberg, Roger N., ed. Atlas of Clinical Neurology. LC 97-6024. 500p. 1997. text 143.50 (*0-7506-9922-1*) Buttrwrth-Heinemann.

— Comprehensive Neurology. LC 90-9172. (Illus.). 936p. 1991. reprint ed. pap. 200.00 (*0-608-07245-1*, 206747000009) Bks Demand.

Rosenberg, Roger N. & Pleasure, David E., eds. Comprehensive Neurology. 2nd ed. LC 97-40569. 948p. 1998. 245.00 (*0-471-16958-7*, Wiley-Liss) Wiley.

Rosenberg, Roger N., et al. The Molecular & Genetic Basis of Neurological Disease. 2nd ed. LC 96-47652. 1430p. 1996. text 368.00 (*0-7506-9668-0*) Buttrwrth-Heinemann.

— The Molecular & Genetic Basis of Neurological Disease. 2nd ed. Fenichel, Gerald M., ed. 328p. 1998. pap. text 47.50 (*0-7506-7043-6*) Buttrwrth-Heinemann.

Rosenberg, Ron. Breaking Out of the Change Trap: A Practical Guide to Organizational Change. Buland, Roberta J., ed. LC 98-93253. (Illus.). 168p. 1998. pap. 14.95 (*1-887980-01-6*) Banbury Pr.

Rosenberg, Ronald H. The Environment, Property & the Law. Finkelman, Paul, ed. (Controversies in Constitutional Law Ser.). 350p. 1998. text 75.00 (*0-8153-2697-1*); text 75.00 (*0-8153-2698-X*) Garland.

Rosenberg, Ronald H., jt. auth. see Schoenbaum, Thomas J.

Rosenberg, Ronald L. & Finkelman, Paul, eds. The Environment, Property & the Law: Federal & State Case Decisions & Journal Articles, 3 vols. LC 97-39264. (Controversies in Constitutional Law Ser.: Vol. 3). 1224p. 1998. reprint ed. text 225.00 (*0-8153-2696-3*) Garland.

Rosenberg, Rosalind. Beyond Separate Spheres: Intellectual Roots of Modern Feminism. LC 81-15967. (Illus.). 1983. pap. 18.00 (*0-300-03092-4*, Y-464) Yale U Pr.

— Divided Lives: American Women in the Twentieth Century. Foner, Eric, ed. (American Century Ser.). 288p. 1992. pap. 12.00 (*0-374-52347-9*) FS&G.

Rosenberg, Roy A. The Concise Guide to Judaism: History, Practice, Faith. 160p. 1994. pap. 12.95 (*0-452-01136-1*, Mer) NAL.

— Everything You Need to Know about America's Jews & Their History. LC 97-226311. 288p. 1997. pap. 13.95 (*0-452-27628-4*, Plume) Dutton Plume.

— Everything You Need to Know about Jewish-American History. 1997. pap. write for info. (*0-452-27912-7*, Plume) Dutton Plume.

— The Veneration of Divine Justice: The Dead Sea Scrolls & Christianity, 40. LC 95-5266. (Contributions to the Study of Religion Ser.: Vol. 40). 160p. 1995. 49.95 (*0-313-29655-3*, Greenwood Pr) Greenwood.

Rosenberg, Rutger, jt. ed. see Barrett, Gary W.

Rosenberg, Ruth. Everything About America. 320p. 1999. pap. 12.95 (*0-452-27901-1*, Plume) Dutton Plume.

Rosenberg, S. The Laplacian on a Riemannian Manifold. (London Mathematical Society Student Texts Ser.: No. 31). (Illus.). 182p. (C). 1997. text 59.95 (*0-521-46300-9*); pap. text 21.95 (*0-521-46831-0*) Cambridge U Pr.

Rosenberg, S. The State & the Labor Market. LC 89-33437. (Studies & Work & Industry). (Illus.). 276p. (C). 1989. 49.50 (*0-306-43170-X*, Plenum Trade) Perseus Pubng.

Rosenberg, S., jt. ed. see Calatchi, R.

Rosenberg, Samuel. Naked Is the Best Disguise: The Death & Revolution of Sherlock Holmes. 22.95 (*0-89190-169-8*) Amereon Ltd.

Rosenberg, Samuel N. Modern French CE: The Neuter Pronoun in Adjectival Predication. (Janua Linguarum, Ser. Practica: No. 116). 1970. pap. text 90.80 (*90-279-0747-1*) Mouton.

Rosenberg, Samuel N., et al, eds. Songs of the Troubadours & Trouveres: An Anthology of Poems & Melodies. LC 97-14045. (Illus.). 392p. 1997. text 94.00 incl. audio compact disk (*0-8153-1341-1*, H1740) Garland.

Rosenberg, Samuel N. & Danon, Samuel. Ami & Amile. LC 96-47708. 168p. (Orig.). (C). 1996. pap. 21.95 (*0-472-06647-1*, 06647) U of Mich Pr.

Rosenberg, Samuel N. & Danon, Samuel, trs. Ami & Amile. LC 96-47708. 168p. (Orig.). 1996. text 44.50 (*0-472-09647-8*, 09647) U of Mich Pr.

Rosenberg, Samuel N. & Tischler, Hans. The Monophonic Songs in the ROMAN de FAUVEL. LC 90-751897. (Illus.). x, 171p. 1991. text 60.00 (*0-8032-3898-3*) U of Nebr Pr.

Rosenberg, Seth, jt. auth. see Silverstein, Herbert.

Rosenberg, Seymour, ed. 1996 Consular Posts Handbook. 50p. 1996. 35.00 (*1-878677-96-9*, 52.60) Amer Immi Law Assn.

Rosenberg, Shawn, et al. Political Reasoning & Cognition: A Piagetian View. LC 88-16225. 192p. (C). 1988. text 45.95 (*0-8223-0856-8*) Duke.

Rosenberg, Sheldon, ed. Advances in Applied Psycholinguistics, Vols. 1. (Cambridge Monographs & Texts in Applied Psycholinguistics). (Illus.). 318p. 1987. pap. text 29.95 (*0-521-31732-0*) Cambridge U Pr.

— Advances in Applied Psycholinguistics, Vols. 1 & 2. (Cambridge Monographs & Texts in Applied Psycholinguistics). (Illus.). 656p. 1987. text 95.00 (*0-521-30027-4*) Cambridge U Pr.

— Handbook of Applied Psycholinguistics: Major Thrusts of Research & Theory. LC 81-9891. (Illus.). 608p. 1982. text 120.00 (*0-89859-173-2*) L Erlbaum Assocs.

Rosenberg, Sheldon & Abbeduto, Leonard. Language & Communication in Mental Retardation: Development, Processes, & Intervention. (Topics in Applied Psycholinguistics Ser.). 272p. 1993. text 59.95 (*0-8058-0302-5*) L Erlbaum Assocs.

Rosenberg, Shelley. Adoption & the Jewish Family. LC 98-20879. 256p. 1998. pap. 19.95 (*0-8276-0653-2*) JPS Phila.

Rosenberg, Shirley S., ed. see Henderson, Michael.

Rosenberg, Sidney. Any Dog Named Papageno Rosenberg Must Be a Little Bit of All Right! LC 77-79785. (Illus.). 1977. 5.95 (*0-88435-008-8*) Chateau Pub.

Rosenberg, Stanley, jt. auth. see Farrell, Michael P.

Rosenberg, Stanley D. & Bergen, Bernard J. The Cold Fire: Alienation & the Myth of Culture. LC 76-3918. 224p. reprint ed. pap. 69.50 (*0-608-14767-2*, 202563700045) Bks Demand.

Rosenberg, Stephen. Last Minute Estate Planning: It's Never Too Late to Plan for the Future. LC 98-46523. (Last Minute Ser.). 160p. 1998. pap. 9.99 (*1-56414-393-7*) Career Pr Inc.

— Last Minute Retirement Planning: It's Never Too Late to Plan for the Future. LC 98-34860. (Last Minute Ser.). 160p. 1998. pap. 9.99 (*1-56414-376-7*) Career Pr Inc.

***Rosenberg, Stephen Gabriel.** The Haphtara. 2000. write for info. (*0-7657-6145-9*) Aronson.

Rosenberg, Stephen J. & Dougherty, Karla. The Pocket Idiot's Guide to First Aid. LC 97-73179. (Pocket Idiot's Guides Ser.). (Illus.). 192p. 1997. pap. 9.95 (*0-02-862015-1*) Macmillan Gen Ref.

Rosenberg, Stephen J., jt. auth. see Dougherty, Karla.

Rosenberg, Stephen M. Keep Uncle Sam (And Cousin George) from Devouring Your Estate. LC 91-75531. 330p. (Orig.). 1992. pap. text 19.95 (*1-880380-11-0*) Capital Pub GA.

— Keep Uncle Sam (And Cousin George) from Devouring Your Estate - Physician's Edition. LC 91-75532. (Orig.). 1991. pap. 19.95 (*1-880380-10-2*) Capital Pub GA.

Rosenberg, Stephen M. & Peterson, Ann Z. Every Woman's Guide to Financial Security. 382p. 1994. pap. 16.95 (*1-880380-14-5*) Capital Pub GA.

— Every Woman's Guide to Financial Security. (Smart Woman's Guides Ser.). 271p. 1996. lib. bdg. 26.95 (*0-7910-4449-1*) Chelsea Hse.

— Every Woman's Guide to Financial Security. 2nd rev. ed. LC 96-37860. 352p. 1997. pap. 16.99 (*1-56414-279-5*) Career Pr Inc.

Rosenberg, Stephen N. The Johnson & Johnson First Aid Book. 176p. (Orig.). 1985. mass mkt. 16.95 (*0-446-38252-3*, Pub. by Warner Bks) Little.

***Rosenberg, Steve.** Diving & Snorkeling Monterey Peninsula & Northern California. 3rd ed. (Illus.). 128p. 2000. pap. 15.95 (*0-86442-775-1*) Lonely Planet.

Rosenberg, Steve. Diving Cozumel. rev. ed. LC 92-26488. (Illus.). 114p. (Orig.). 1999. pap. 18.95 (*0-9623389-7-4*) Aqua Quest.

— Diving Hawaii. rev. ed. LC 90-82635. (Illus.). 128p. (Orig.). 2000. pap. 18.95 (*0-9623389-1-5*) Aqua Quest.

— Lonely Planet Diving & Snorkeling Guide to Northern California & the Monterey Peninsula. 2nd ed. (Diving & Snorkeling Guides Ser.). 96p. 1992. pap. 14.95 (*1-55992-052-1*, Pisces Books) Lonely Planet.

Rosenberg, Steve & Ratterree, John. Pisces Guide to Shooting Underwater Video. 256p. 1991. pap. 15.95 (*1-55992-041-6*, Pisces Books) Lonely Planet.

Rosenberg, Steve & Stoddard, Blaine. Diving Bahamas. (Illus.). 128p. 2000. pap. 18.95 (*1-881652-13-0*, Pub. by Aqua Quest) Natl Bk Netwk.

Rosenberg, Steven & Barry, John M. The Transformed Cell: Unlocking the Mysteries of Cancer. viii, 376p. 1993. reprint ed. pap. 12.50 (*0-380-72115-5*, Avon Bks) Morrow Avon.

Rosenberg, Steven A. Principles & Practice of Biologic Therapy of Cancer. 3rd ed. 1056p. text 145.00 (*0-7817-2272-1*) Lppncott W & W.

***Rosenberg, Steven A. & Barry, John M.** The Transformed Cell: Unlocking the Mysteries of Cancer. 353p. 2000. 26.00 (*0-7881-9396-1*) DIANE Pub.

Rosenberg, Steven A., jt. ed. see Whipple, Terry L.

Rosenberg, Steven M. I Hope the Hell I Win! Turning Hope into Reality: How Winners Win. LC 97-68876. 144p. 1997. 15.95 (*1-887750-69-X*) Rutledge Bks.

Rosenberg, Stuart E. Secrets of the Jews. 220p. 1994. pap. 18.95 (*0-88962-548-4*) Mosaic.

Rosenberg, Stuart G., jt. ed. see Duke, James C.

Rosenberg, Sue E., intro. West Wind Review. 216p. (C). 1994. write for info. (*0-9630694-3-8*) So Oregon.

Rosenberg, Suzanna, jt. auth. see Bloch, Talia.

Rosenberg, Terry, jt. auth. see Stanyer, Peter.

Rosenberg, Terry J. Residence, Employment, & Mobility of Puerto Ricans in New York City. LC 73-87828. (University of Chicago, Department of Geography, Research Paper Ser.: No. 151). 244p. 1974. reprint ed. pap. 75.70 (*0-608-02279-9*, 206292000004) Bks Demand.

— Updated Poverty Tables for New York City with March 1994 Current Population Survey Estimates. 28p. 1995. 5.00 (*0-88156-170-3*) Comm Serv Soc NY.

***Rosenberg, Thomas.** Phantom on His Wheel. 2000. 24.50 (*0-88739-278-4*) Creat Arts Bk.

Rosenberg, Thomas. Phantom on His Wheel. LC 98-83261. 256p. 2000. pap. 14.95 (*0-88739-253-9*) Creat Arts Bk.

Rosenberg, Tina. Children of Cain: Violence & the Violent in Latin America. 400p. 1992. reprint ed. pap. 14.95 (*0-14-017254-8*, Penguin Bks) Viking Penguin.

— The Haunted Land: Facing Europe's Ghosts after Communism. 1996. pap. 13.00 (*0-679-74499-1*) Vin Bks.

Rosenberg, Victor & Whitney, Gretchen, eds. The Transfer of Scholarly Scientific & Technical Information Between North & South America: Proceedings of a Conference. LC 86-15625. (Illus.). 739p. 1986. 62.50 (*0-8108-1935-X*) Scarecrow.

Rosenberg, William, ed. Social & Cultural History of the Soviet Union: The Lenin & Stalin Years. LC 91-44186. (Articles on Russian & Soviet History, 1500-1991 Ser.: Vol. 6). 536p. 1992. text 25.00 (*0-8153-0563-X*) Garland.

Rosenberg, William & Bittar, E. Edward, eds. Problem Solving in Medicine, Vol. 1. Date not set. 128.50 (*0-7623-0397-2*) Jai Pr.

Rosenberg, William G., ed. Bolshevik Visions: First Phase of the Cultural Revolution in Soviet Russia, Pt. 1: The Culture of a New Society: Ethics, Gender & the Family, Law & Problems of Tradition. 2nd rev. ed. LC 90-10958. 292p. 1990. pap. text 18.95 (*0-472-06424-X*, 06424) U of Mich Pr.

— Bolshevik Visions: First Phase of the Cultural Revolution in Soviet Russia, Pt. 2: Creating Soviet Cultural Forms: Art, Architecture, Music, Film & the New Tasks of Education. 2nd rev. ed. LC 90-10958. 332p. 1990. text 49.50 (*0-472-09425-4*, 09425); pap. text 18.95 (*0-472-06425-8*, 06425) U of Mich Pr.

Rosenberg, William G. & Siegelbaum, Lewis H., eds. Social Dimensions of Soviet Industrialization. LC 92-19627. (Indiana-Michigan Series in Russian & East European Studies). 320p. 1993. 39.95 (*0-253-34993-1*); pap. 15.95 (*0-253-20772-X*) Ind U Pr.

Rosenberg, William G. & Young, Marilyn B. Transforming Russia & China: Revolutionary Struggle in the Twentieth Century. 416p. 1982. pap. text 23.95 (*0-19-502966-6*) OUP.

Rosenberg, William G., jt. auth. see Koenker, Diane P.

***Rosenberger.** Workbook for Synonyms,Homonyms & Antonyms. 1999. 39.00 (*0-7616-0200-3*) Commun Skill.

Rosenberger, F. Fundamentals of Crystal Growth I: Macroscopic Equilibrium & Transport Concepts. 2nd ed. (Solid-State Sciences Ser.: Vol. 5). (Illus.). 530p. 1981. 82.95 (*0-387-09023-1*) Spr-Verlag.

Rosenberger, Francis C. One Season Here: Poems, 1943-1946. LC 76-150451. 87p. reprint ed. pap. 30.00 (*0-7837-4345-9*, 204405500012) Bks Demand.

— Virginia Reader: A Treasury of Writings. lib. bdg. 33.95 (*0-8488-2108-4*) Amereon Ltd.

Rosenberger, Francis C., ed. Washington & the Poet. LC 77-81771. 87p. reprint ed. pap. 30.00 (*0-608-15289-7*, 202960100061) Bks Demand.

Rosenberger, Gerhard, jt. auth. see Fine, Benjamin.

Rosenberger, Homer T. Adventures & Philosophy of a Pennsylvania Dutchman: An Autobiography in a Broad Setting. LC 79-165295. (Illus.). 665p. 1971. lib. bdg. 15.00 (*0-917264-03-7*) Rose Hill.

— The Enigma: How Shall History Be Written? LC 78-68731. (Illus.). 453p. 1980. lib. bdg. 12.00 (*0-917264-02-9*) Rose Hill.

— Grassroots Philosophy for the Modern Mind. LC 75-32703. (Horizons of the Humanities Ser.: Vol. 2). 255p. 1976. lib. bdg. 9.00 (*0-917264-00-2*) Rose Hill.

— Letters from Africa. LC 65-16638. 209p. 1965. pap. 3.50 (*0-917264-04-5*) Rose Hill.

— Man & Modern Society: Philosophical Essays. LC 72-85861. (Horizons of the Humanities Ser.: Vol. 1). 272p. 1972. lib. bdg. 8.00 (*0-917264-05-3*) Rose Hill.

— Vignettes of Philosophy: Thirty-Five Vital Subjects. LC 77-71070. (Horizons of the Humanities Ser.: Vol. 3). 258p. 1977. lib. bdg. 9.00 (*0-917264-01-0*) Rose Hill.

Rosenberger, Homer T. & Shriver, Harry C. The Philadelphia & Erie Railroad: Its Place in American Economic History. LC 74-75110. (Illus.). 748p. 1975. lib. bdg. 22.50 (*0-914932-02-0*) Rose Hill.

Rosenberger, Jeremy. Sams Teach Yourself CORBA in 14 Days. 480p. 1998. 29.99 (*0-672-31208-5*) Sams.

Rosenberger, Jesse L. Pennsylvania Germans. 1993. reprint ed. lib. bdg. 89.00 (*0-7812-5825-1*) Rprt Serv.

Rosenberger, Leif R. America's Drug War Debacle. 120p. 1996. 39.95 (*1-85972-120-6*, Pub. by Avebry) Ashgate Pub Co.

Rosenberger, Lisa. Integrated Programs of Incentives & Controls for Farmland Preservation in Three Metropolitan Areas. (Discussion Papers: No. 121). 1980. pap. 10.00 (*1-55869-059-X*) Regional Sci Res Inst.

R

An Asterisk (*) at the beginning of an entry indicates that the title is appearing for the first time.

Rosenberger, Lisa & Coughlin, Robert E. Planning for Vegetation in Urbanizing Areas. (Discussion Papers: No. 115). 1979. pap. 10.00 (*1-55869-096-4*) Regional Sci Res Inst.

Rosenberger, Mark. The Plus 1090 Game: 52 High Impact Leverage Points for Enhancing Sales, Customer Loyalty & Teamwork. (Illus.). 160p. 1997. 19.95 (*0-9656567-0-5*) WOW Pubng.

Rosenberger, Mary S. Harmless As Doves: Witnessing for Peace in Vietnam. LC 88-39526. 192p. 1988. reprint ed. pap. 59.60 (*0-608-02169-5*, 206283800004) Bks Demand.

— The Lord's Prayer. (Covenant Bible Studies). 48p. 1989. pap. 4.95 (*0-87178-541-2*, 8412) Brethren.

Rosenberger, Michael. Team Leadership: School Boards at Work. LC 96-62020. 185p. 1998. pap. text 34.95 (*1-56676-526-9*) Scarecrow.

Rosenberger, Noah B. The Place of the Elementary Calculus in the Senior High School Mathematics. LC 71-177209. (Columbia University. Teachers College. Contributions to Education Ser.: No. 117). reprint ed. 37.50 (*0-404-55117-3*) AMS Pr.

Rosenberger, Richard F. & Kaufmann, Charles. The Longrifles of Western Pennsylvania: Allegheny & Westmoreland Counties. LC 92-12625. (Illus.). 192p. (C). 1993. text 60.00 (*0-8229-3727-1*) U of Pittsburgh Pr.

***Rosenberger, Sharon.** Building Vocabulary, 3 vols. Evans, Marilyn, ed. (Big Books & Charts: Vol. 1). (Illus.). 88p. (J). (gr. 1-2). 1999. pap., teacher ed. 14.95 (*1-55799-679-2*, 647) Evan-Moor Edu Pubs.

— Building Vocabulary, 3 vols. Evans, Marilyn, ed. (Big Books & Charts: Vol. 2). (Illus.). 88p. (J). (gr. 3-4). 1999. pap., teacher ed. 14.95 (*1-55799-680-6*, 648) Evan-Moor Edu Pubs.

— Building Vocabulary, 3 vols. Evans, Marilyn, ed. (Big Books & Charts: Vol. 3). (Illus.). 88p. (J). (gr. 5-6). 1999. pap., teacher ed. 14.95 (*1-55799-681-4*, 649) Evan-Moor Edu Pubs.

Rosenberger, William F., jt. ed. see Flournoy, Nancy.

Rosenberry, C. R. The Challenging Skies: The Colorful Story of Aviation's Most Exciting Years, 1919-1939. Gilbert, James B., ed. LC 79-7294. (Flight: Its First Seventy-Five Years Ser.). (Illus.). 1980. reprint ed. lib. bdg. 80.95 (*0-405-12201-2*) Ayer.

Rosenberry, Katharine & Treese, Clifford J. Community Association Insurance: A Guide for Condominiums, Cooperatives & Planned Communities. rev. ed. (GAP Reports: Vol. 4). (C). 1994. pap. 17.50 (*0-944715-27-3*) CAI.

Rosenberry, Katharine N., jt. auth. see Sproul, Curtis C.

Rosenberry, Naomi. Carmi of Judea. (Illus.). 152p. (YA). (gr. 7-10). 1997. 8.55 (*0-7399-0128-1*, 2153) Rod & Staff.

Rosenberry, Sara & Hartman, Chester, eds. Housing Issues of the Nineties. LC 88-15560. 407p. 1989. 75.00 (*0-275-92362-2*, C2362, Praeger Pubs) Greenwood.

Rosenberry, Vera. Run - Jump - Whiz - Splash. LC 98-14060. (Illus.). 32p. (J). 1998. 15.95 (*0-8234-1378-0*) Holiday.

***Rosenberry, Vera.** Vera Runs Away. LC 99-33611. (Illus.). 32p. (J). (ps-2). 2000. 16.00 (*0-8050-6267-X*) H Holt & Co.

Rosenberry, Vera. Vera's First Day of School. LC 98-43347. 32p. (J). (gr. k-2). 1999. 15.95 (*0-8050-5936-9*) H Holt & Co.

— When Vera Was Sick. LC 97-50442. (J). (ps-2). 1998. 15.95 (*0-8050-5405-7*) H Holt & Co.

***Rosenberry, Vera.** Who Is in the Garden? LC 99-37166. 2001. write for info. (*0-8234-1529-5*) Holiday.

Rosenberry, Ward & Teague, Jim. Distributing Applications Across DCE & Windows NT. 302p. 1993. pap. 24.95 (*1-56592-047-3*) Thomson Learn.

Rosenberry, Ward, et al. Understanding DCE. (Computer Science). (Illus.). 266p. (Orig.). 1992. pap. 24.95 (*1-56592-005-8*) Thomson Learn.

***Rosenbladt, Rod.** Christ Alone. LC 99-36910. (Today's Issues Ser.). 48p. 2000. pap. 4.99 (*1-58134-115-6*) Crossway Bks.

Rosenblat, Rebecca. An Eastern Seduction. 226p. mass mkt. 4.99 (*1-55197-519-X*) Picasso Publ.

— Smooth As Silk. 192p. mass mkt. 4.99 (*1-55197-517-3*) Picasso Publ.

Rosenblat, Roger. Coming Apart. 1998. pap. write for info. (*0-316-75913-9*) Little.

***Rosenblatt.** Museums & Cultural Facilities: Building Type Basics. 304p. 2000. write for info. (*0-471-34915-1*) Wiley.

Rosenblatt, et al. Law & the American Health Care System: 1998 Supplement. 1998. 12.95 (*1-56662-605-6*) Foundation Pr.

Rosenblatt, jt. ed. see London.

Rosenblatt, Aaron & Waldfogel, Diana, eds. Handbook of Clinical Social Work. LC 82-49042. (Jossey-Bass Social & Behavioral Science Ser.). 1211p. reprint ed. pap. 200.00 (*0-8357-4920-7*, 203785000009) Bks Demand.

Rosenblatt, Allan & Thickstrun, James. Modern Psychoanalytic Concepts in a General Psychology Pts. 1 & 2: Including General Concepts & Principles & Motivation. LC 77-14712. (Psychological Issues Monographs: Nos. 42 & 43). 348p. 1978. text 52.50 (*0-8236-3430-2*) Intl Univs Pr.

Rosenblatt, Arthur S. Please Hang Up. 18p. 1984. pap. 3.50 (*0-87129-107-X*, P58) Dramatic Pub.

Rosenblatt, Arthur S., ed. see Shakespeare, William.

Rosenblatt, Bill. Learning the Korn Shell. Loukides, Mike, ed. (Computer Science). (Illus.). 363p. 1993. pap. 29.95 (*1-56592-054-6*) Thomson Learn.

Rosenblatt, Bill, jt. auth. see Newham, Cameron.

Rosenblatt, Daniel. The Gestalt Therapy Primer. 153p. (C). 1944. pap. 10.00 (*0-9647037-1-8*) Yurisha Pr.

— Opening Doors: What Happens in Gestalt Therapy. Date not set. pap. 20.00 (*0-939266-33-4*) Gestalt Journal.

Rosenblatt, David J. An Inventory to the Kingsley A. Taft Collection. 103p. 1973. 1.50 (*0-318-03222-8*) Ohio Hist Soc.

Rosenblatt, Elihu, ed. Criminal Injustice: Confronting the Prison Crisis. LC 96-32716. (Illus.). 374p. 1996. 40.00 (*0-89608-540-6*); pap. 18.00 (*0-89608-539-2*) South End Pr.

Rosenblatt, Emil & Rosenblatt, Ruth, eds. Hard Marching Every Day: The Civil War Letters of Private Wilbur Fisk, 1861-1865. LC 91-46739. (Modern War Studies). 400p. 1994. pap. 15.95 (*0-7006-0681-5*) U Pr of KS.

— Hard Marching Every Day: The Civil War Letters of Private Wilbur Fisk, 1861-1865. LC 91-46739. (Modern War Studies). 400p. 1992. reprint ed. 27.50 (*0-7006-0529-0*) U Pr of KS.

Rosenblatt, F. F., jt. auth. see Slosson, Preston W.

Rosenblatt, Frank F. Chartist Movement in Its Social & Economic Aspects. 248p. 1967. reprint ed. 32.50 (*0-7146-1103-4*, BHA-01103, Pub. by F Cass Pubs) Intl Spec Bk.

Rosenblatt, G. M. & Worrell, W. L., eds. Progress in Solid State Chemistry, Vol. 13. (Illus.). 376p. 1982. 140.00 (*0-08-029712-9*, Pergamon Pr) Elsevier.

— Progress in Solid State Chemistry, Vol. 14. (Illus.). 302p. 1983. 130.00 (*0-08-030998-4*, Pergamon Pr) Elsevier.

— Progress in Solid State Chemistry, Vol. 15. (Illus.). 374p. 1985. 145.00 (*0-08-033664-7*, E115, E125, C140, Pub. by PPL) Elsevier.

Rosenblatt, Helena. Rousseau & Geneva: From the First Discourse to the Social Contract, 1749-1762. LC 96-36780. (Ideas in Context Ser.: No. 46). 316p. 1997. text 59.95 (*0-521-57004-2*) Cambridge U Pr.

Rosenblatt, J., tr. see Sirjaev, A. N.

Rosenblatt, Jack & Friedman, M. Harold. Direct & Alternating Current Machinery. 2nd ed. 568p. (C). 1990. text 70.60 (*0-675-20160-8*, Merrill Coll) P-H.

Rosenblatt, Jason P. Torah & Law in Paradise Lost. LC 93-37043. 288p. 1994. text 39.50 (*0-691-03340-4*, Pub. by Princeton U Pr) Cal Prin Full Svc.

Rosenblatt, Jason P. & Sitterson, Joseph C., Jr., eds. Not in Heaven: Coherence & Complexity in Biblical Narrative. LC 91-6317. (Indiana Studies in Biblical Literature). (Illus.). 272p. 1991. 41.95 (*0-253-35036-0*); pap. 6.95 (*0-253-20678-2*, MB-678) Ind U Pr.

Rosenblatt, Jay S., et al, eds. Advances in the Study of Behavior Vol. 25: Parental Care: Evolution, Mechanisms, & Adaptive Significance. LC 97-167761. (Illus.). 715p. (C). 1996. text 99.00 (*0-12-004525-7*) Acad Pr.

Rosenblatt, Jeanette, jt. auth. see Schoenfield, Mark.

Rosenblatt, Jeremy. International Adoption. 236p. 1995. pap. 64.00 (*0-421-52770-6*, Pub. by Sweet & Maxwll) Gaunt.

***Rosenblatt, Jeremy.** International Conventions Affecting Children. LC 00-33065. 2000. write for info. (*90-411-1386-X*) Kluwer Law Intl.

Rosenblatt, Jeremy & Lewis, Ian. Children & Immigration. v, 386p. 1997. pap. 72.00 (*1-85941-197-5*, Pub. by Cavendish Pubng) Gaunt.

Rosenblatt, Joe. Beds & Consenting Dreamers. 88p. 1994. pap. text 11.95 (*0-88982-125-9*, Pub. by Oolichan Bks) Genl Dist Srvs.

— Brides of the Stream. 1988. text 8.95 (*0-88982-048-1*, Pub. by Oolichan Bks) Genl Dist Srvs.

Rosenblatt, Judah. Mathematical Analysis for Modeling. LC 98-40054. (Mathematical Modelling Ser.). 880p. 1998. boxed set 74.95 (*0-8493-8337-4*) CRC Pr.

Rosenblatt, Judith, ed. Serbs in the United States & Canada: A Comprehensive Bibliography. 2nd enl. rev. ed. LC 92-71568. (Ethnic Bibliography Ser.: No. 1). x, 193p. 20.00 (*0-932833-12-8*) Immig His Res.

Rosenblatt, Judith, ed. see Moses, John G. & Nassar, Eugene P.

Rosenblatt, Jules. Key Punch. 1969. student ed. write for info. (*0-672-96027-3*); student ed. write for info. (*0-672-96029-X*) Macmillan.

Rosenblatt, Julia C. & Schmidt, Frederic H. Sonnen. Dining with Sherlock Holmes: A Baker Street Cookbook. 2nd ed. LC 76-11610. (Illus.). xiv, 287p. 1990. pap. 18.95 (*0-8232-1271-8*) Fordham.

Rosenblatt, Julius, et al. The Common Agricultural Policy of the European Community: Principles & Consequences. (Occasional Papers: No. 62). 70p. 1988. pap. 7.50 (*1-55775-036-X*) Intl Monetary.

Rosenblatt, Kathleen F. Rene Daumal: The Life & Work of a Mystic Guide. rev. ed. LC 98-41577. (Suny Series, Western Esoteric Traditions Ser.). (Illus.). 252p. (C). 1999. pap. text 21.95 (*0-7914-3634-9*) State U NY Pr.

— Rene Daumal: The Life & Work of a Mystic Guide. rev. ed. LC 98-41577. (Series in Western Esoteric Traditions). (Illus.). 176p. (C). 1999. text 65.50 (*0-7914-3633-0*) State U NY Pr.

Rosenblatt, Kenneth, jt. auth. see Laudon, Kenneth C.

Rosenblatt, Kenneth S. High-Technology Crime: Investigating Cases Involving Computers. LC 95-78740. 601p. 1995. pap. text 69.95 incl. disk (*0-9648171-0-1*) KSK Pubns.

Rosenblatt, L., tr. see Sirjaev, A. N.

Rosenblatt, L., tr. see Walter, Wolfgang.

Rosenblatt, Lily. Fire Diary. Grant, Christy, ed. LC 93-45917. (Albert Whitman Concept Bks.). (Illus.). 32p. (J). (gr. 2-5). 1994. lib. bdg. 14.95 (*0-8075-2439-5*) A Whitman.

Rosenblatt, Louise M. L' Idee de l'Art pour l'Art dans la Litterature Anglaise Pendant la Periode Victorienne. LC 75-148289. reprint ed. 45.00 (*0-404-08896-1*) AMS Pr.

— Literature As Exploration. 5th ed. LC 95-38208. xx, 321p. 1995. pap. 12.50 (*0-87352-568-X*, T301P); lib. bdg. 28.00 (*0-87352-567-1*, T301C) Modern Lang.

— The Reader, the Text, the Poem: The Transactional Theory of the Literary Work. LC 94-1302. 210p. (C). 1994. pap. 16.95 (*0-8093-1805-9*) S Ill U Pr.

Rosenblatt, Lynn. Monarch Magic! Butterfly Activities & Nature Discoveries. LC 98-34421. (Good Times Ser.: Vol. 2). (Illus.). 96p. (J). (ps-7). 1998. pap. 12.95 (*1-885593-23-6*) Williamson Pub Co.

Rosenblatt, M., ed. Errett Bishop: Reflections on Him & His Research. LC 85-152. (Contemporary Mathematics Ser.: Vol. 39). 91p. 1985. pap. 24.00 (*0-8218-5040-7*, CONM/39) Am Math.

Rosenblatt, Marie-Eloise. Paul the Accused: His Portrait in Acts of the Apostles. LC 94-16103. (Zacchaeus Studies, New Testament). 136p. (Orig.). 1995. pap. 8.95 (*0-8146-5750-8*, M Glazier) Liturgical Pr.

***Rosenblatt, Murray.** Gaussian & Non-Gaussian Linear Time Series & Random Fields. Bickel, P. et al, eds. LC 99-42811. (Series in Statistics). 256p. 1999. 69.95 (*0-387-98917-X*) Spr-Verlag.

Rosenblatt, Murray. Markov Processes: Structure & Asymptotic Behavior. LC 70-161441. (Grundlehren der Mathematischen Wissenschaften Ser.: Vol. 184). 1971. 75.00 (*0-387-05480-4*) Spr-Verlag.

— Random Processes. LC 74-10956. (Graduate Texts in Mathematics Ser.: Vol. 17). (Illus.). 225p. 1974. 49.00 (*0-387-90085-3*) Spr-Verlag.

— Stationary Sequences & Random Fields. 288p. 1985. 52.00 (*0-8176-3264-6*) Birkhauser.

— Stochastic Curve Estimation. (NSF-CBMS Regional Conference Series in Probability & Statistics: Vol. 3). (Illus.). 93p. (C). 1991. pap. 25.00 (*0-940600-22-6*) Inst Math.

Rosenblatt, Murray, ed. Studies in Probability Theory. LC 78-71935. (MAA Studies in Mathematics: Vol. 18). 268p. 1978. text 5.00 (*0-88385-118-0*, MAS-18) Math Assn.

Rosenblatt, Murray, jt. auth. see Grenander, Ulf.

Rosenblatt, Naomi. Rainforest for Beginners. (Illus.). 96p. (Orig.). 1992. pap. 7.95 (*0-86316-005-0*) Writers & Readers.

Rosenblatt, Naomi H. & Horwitz, Joshua. Wrestling with Angels: What Genesis Teaches Us about Our Spiritual Identity, Sexuality, & Personal Relationships. 416p. 1996. pap. 13.95 (*0-385-31333-0*, Delta Trade) Dell.

Rosenblatt, Nate. Encyclopedia of Money Making Sales Letters. 372p. 1992. pap. 19.95 (*0-929543-08-4*) Round Lake Pub.

Rosenblatt, Nate, jt. auth. see Barton, Judi.

Rosenblatt, Paul. A Constant Lover. 175p. 1990. 17.50 (*0-922820-11-2*) Watermark Pr.

— John Woolman. (Great American Thinkers Ser.). 1969. lib. bdg. 17.95 (*0-89197-813-5*) Irvington.

— The Sun in Capricorn. 185p. 1989. 18.50 (*0-922820-00-7*) Watermark Pr.

Rosenblatt, Paul, jt. auth. see McFadden, Dennis.

Rosenblatt, Paul C. Bitter, Bitter Tears: Nineteenth-Century Diarists & Twentieth-Century Brief Theories. LC 83-3485. 217p. 1983. reprint ed. pap. 67.30 (*0-7837-2924-3*, 205753000006) Bks Demand.

— Farming Is in Our Blood: Farm Families in Economic Crisis. LC 89-26967. 197p. 1990. reprint ed. pap. 61.10 (*0-608-06852-7*, 206705800009) Bks Demand.

***Rosenblatt, Paul C.** Help Your Marriage Survive the Death of a Child. 200p. 2000. 49.50 (*1-56639-804-5*); pap. 18.95 (*1-56639-805-3*) Temple U Pr.

Rosenblatt, Paul C. Metaphors of Family Systems Theory: Toward New Constructions. LC 93-19476. (Perspectives on Marriage & the Family Ser.). 239p. 1993. lib. bdg. 39.95 (*0-89862-321-9*) Guilford Pubns.

— Metaphors of Family Systems Theory: Toward New Constructions. LC 93-19476. (Perspectives on Marriage & the Family Ser.). 239p. 1997. pap. text 22.00 (*1-57230-172-4*, 0172) Guilford Pubns.

Rosenblatt, Paul C., et al. The Family in Business. LC 84-83033. (Joint Publication in the Jossey-Bass Management Series & the Jossey-Bass Social & Behavioral Science Ser.). 345p. 1985. reprint ed. pap. 107.00 (*0-608-06464-5*, AU0049300009) Bks Demand.

Rosenblatt, Rand E., et al. Law & the American Health Care System. LC 97-200705. (University Casebook Ser.). 1355p. 1997. text 42.00 (*1-56662-481-9*) Foundation Pr.

— Law & the American Health Care System. (University Casebook Ser.). 1346p. 1997. pap. text, teacher ed., suppl. ed. write for info. (*1-56662-572-6*) Foundation Pr.

Rosenblatt, Rich. Michael Irvin. LC 96-52618. (Football Legends Ser.). (Illus.). 64p. (J). (gr. 3 up). 1997. lib. bdg. 15.95 (*0-7910-4397-5*) Chelsea Hse.

Rosenblatt, Richard. Troy Aikman. LC 95-18223. (Football Legends Ser.). (Illus.). 64p. (J). (gr. 3 up). 1996. lib. bdg. 15.95 (*0-7910-2457-1*) Chelsea Hse.

Rosenblatt, Richard, jt. auth. see Kellner, Jenny.

Rosenblatt, Richard H., jt. auth. see Matsui, Tetsuo.

Rosenblatt, Roger. Black Fiction. LC 74-81387. 272p. 1974. 32.00 (*0-674-07620-6*); pap. 14.00 (*0-674-07622-2*) HUP.

***Rosenblatt, Roger.** Rules for Aging: Do Less, Live Longer, Attain Perfection. (Illus.). 160p. 2000. 18.00 (*0-15-100659-8*) Harcourt.

Rosenblatt, Roger, et al, eds. Consuming Desires: Consumption, Culture & the Pursuit of Happiness. LC 99-21667. 300p. 1999. 24.95 (*1-55963-535-5*, Shearwater Bks) Island Pr.

Rosenblatt, Ruth, jt. ed. see Rosenblatt, Emil.

Rosenblatt, Samuel, tr. Saadia Gaon: Book of Beliefs & Opinions. LC 90-133833. Vol. 1. 498p. 1989. pap. 27.50 (*0-300-04490-9*) Yale U Pr.

Rosenblatt, Samuel, tr. see Abraham Ben Moses Ben Maimon.

***Rosenblatt, Sarah.** On the Waterbed They Sank to Their Own Levels. LC 99-74770. (Poetry Ser.). (Illus.). 88p. 2000. pap. 12.95 (*0-88748-331-3*, Pub. by Carnegie-Mellon) CUP Services.

Rosenblatt, Stanley M. Murder of Mercy: Euthanasia on Trial. LC 92-25910. (Illus.). 352p. (C). 1992. 28.95 (*0-87975-772-8*) Prometheus Bks.

— Trial Lawyer. LC 84-73. 416p. 1984. 19.95 (*0-8184-0360-8*); pap. 9.95 (*0-8184-0361-6*) Carol Pub Group.

Rosenblatt, Suzanne. Shorelines. (Open Meeting Bks.). (Illus.). 64p. 1991. pap. 15.00 (*0-87924-072-5*) Membrane Pr.

Rosenbli. In the Beginning. 1985. 31.50 (*0-534-02846-2*) Sage.

Rosenblit, Daniel. Broken by the Light: Judgment Day Experience. (Orig.). 1995. pap. write for info. (*0-9656468-0-7*) D Rosenblit.

— Transformed by the Light: A Judgement Day Experience. Orig. Title: Broken by the Light. 92p. 1998. pap., per. 4.95 (*0-9656468-1-5*) D Rosenblit.

Rosenblith, Judy F. In the Beginning: Development from Conception to Age Two. 2nd ed. (Illus.). 600p. (C). 1992. 55.00 (*0-8039-4690-2*) Sage.

Rosenbloom. Get Well Quick! Jokes & Riddles. (Illus.). pap. 3.95 (*0-8069-5754-9*) Sterling.

Rosenbloom. Gigantic Joke Book: Oversize Version. 1998. pap. 14.95 (*0-8069-4804-3*) Sterling.

— Marketing Channels. 5th ed. (C). 1995. pap. text, teacher ed. 49.75 (*0-03-010493-9*) Harcourt Coll Pubs.

— Marketing Channels. 6th ed. LC 97-78266. (C). 1998. text 91.50 (*0-03-024482-X*, Pub. by Harcourt Coll Pubs); text, teacher ed. 66.50 (*0-03-024786-1*) Harcourt Coll Pubs.

Rosenbloom, et al. Personnel Management in Government: Politics & Process. 4th ed. (Public Administration & Public Policy Ser.: Vol. 44). (Illus.). 576p. 1991. text 59.75 (*0-8247-8590-8*) Dekker.

Rosenbloom, Alfred J. & Morgan, Meredith W., eds. Vision & Aging. 2nd ed. (Illus.). 463p. 1993. text 84.00 (*0-7506-9311-8*) Buttrwrth-Heinemann.

Rosenbloom, Arlan, jt. ed. see Shiverick, Kathleen T.

Rosenbloom, Arthur H., jt. auth. see Bendaniel, David J.

Rosenbloom, Bert. Marketing Channels: A Management View. 5th ed. LC 94-70288. 774p. (C). 1994. text 91.00 (*0-03-097736-3*) Dryden Pr.

Rosenbloom, Bert, intro. Direct Selling Channels. LC 92-40395. (Journal of Marketing Channels: Vol. 2, No. 2). (Illus.). 124p. 1993. pap. text 14.95 (*1-56024-446-1*); lib. bdg. 39.95 (*1-56024-445-3*) Haworth Pr.

— Wholesale Distribution Channels: New Insights & Perspectives. LC 93-44293. (Journal of Marketing Channels). (Illus.). 167p. 1994. pap. text 14.95 (*1-56024-618-9*); lib. bdg. 39.95 (*1-56024-617-0*) Haworth Pr.

***Rosenbloom, Christine & American Dietetic Association Staff.** Sports Nutrition. 3rd ed. LC 99-52142. 1999. pap. write for info. (*0-88091-176-X*) Am Dietetic Assn.

Rosenbloom, David, ed. Public Personnel Policy in a Political Environment: A Symposium. (Orig.). 1982. pap. 15.00 (*0-918592-59-5*) Pol Studies.

Rosenbloom, David & Morgan, Meredith W. Principles & Practice of Pediatric Optometry. (Illus.). 496p. 1990. text 73.00 (*0-397-50917-0*) Lppncott W & W.

Rosenbloom, David, et al. Clinical Trials in the Rheumatic Diseases: A Selected Critical Review. LC 84-9911. 386p. 1985. 89.50 (*0-275-91323-6*, C1323, Praeger Pubs) Greenwood.

Rosenbloom, David, jt. ed. see Ingraham, Patricia W.

***Rosenbloom, David H.** Building a Legislative-Centered Public Administration: Congress & the Administrative State, 1946-1999. LC 00-8739. 2000. 34.95 (*0-8173-1048-7*) U of Ala Pr.

Rosenbloom, David H., et al, eds. Centenary Issues of the Pendleton Act of 1883: The Problematic Legacy of Civil Service Reform. LC 82-10041. (Annals of Public Administration Ser.: No. 3). 149p. reprint ed. pap. 46.20 (*0-7837-3357-7*, 204331500008) Bks Demand.

— Contemporary Public Administration. LC 93-47904. (C). 1993. pap. text. write for info. (*0-07-053939-1*) Prntice Hall Bks.

Rosenbloom, David H. & Goldman, Deborah D. Public Administration: Understanding Management, Politics, & Law in the Public Sector. 2nd ed. (Illus.). 576p. (C). 1989. text. write for info. (*0-318-62942-9*) Random.

— Public Administration: Understanding Management, Politics & Law in the Public Sector. 4th ed. LC 96-53404. 600p. (C). 1997. 63.44 (*0-07-053972-3*) McGraw.

Rosenbloom, David H. & O'Leary, Rosemary, eds. Public Administration & Law. 2nd ed. LC 96-31378. (Public Administration & Public Policy Ser.: Vol. 61). (Illus.). 368p. 1996. text 150.00 (*0-8247-9769-8*) Dekker.

Rosenbloom, David H. & Schwartz, Richard D., eds. Handbook of Regulation & Administrative Law. (Public Administration & Public Policy Ser.: Vol. 54). (Illus.). 600p. 1994. text 189.00 (*0-8247-9167-3*) Dekker.

Rosenbloom, David H., jt. ed. see Ingraham, Patricia W.

Rosenbloom, David H., jt. ed. see Nivola, Pietro S.

Rosenbloom, Deborah & Aspen Health Law Center Staff. Employee Benefits: A Guide for Health Care Professionals. LC 98-9617. (Health Law Center Current Issues Ser.). 1998. pap. write for info. (*0-8342-1124-6*) Aspen Pub.

Rosenbloom, Deborah, jt. auth. see Isaacson, Judith.

Rosenbloom, Dena & Williams, Mary Beth. Life after Trauma: A Workbook for Healing. LC 99-203928. 352p. 1999. pap. text 18.95 (*1-57230-239-9*) Guilford Pubns.

Rosenbloom, Gerry & Hallman, Victor G. Employee Benefit Planning. 3rd ed. 496p. (C). 1990. text 66.00 (*0-13-275496-7*) P-H.

R

Rosenbloom, Jerry S. Automobile Liability Claims: Insurance Company Philosophies & Practices. (C). 1968. 9.50 (*0-256-00677-6*, Irwn McGrw-H) McGrw-H Hghr Educ.

— The Handbook of Employee Benefits: Design, Funding & Administration. 2nd ed. 1988. 85.00 (*1-55623-068-0*, Irwn Prfssnl) McGraw-Hill Prof.

— The Handbook of Employee Benefits: Design, Funding, & Administration. 4th ed. LC 96-20203. 1120p. 2001. text 95.00 (*0-7863-0473-1*, Irwn Prfssnl) McGraw-Hill Prof.

— Handbook of Employee Benefits: Design, Funding, & Administration. 4th ed. (C). 1996. text 97.50 (*0-7863-0471-5*, Irwn Prfssnl) McGraw-Hill Prof.

— Handbook of Employee Benefits Vol. 2: Designing, Funding & Administration. 3rd ed. 1992. text 117.95 (*1-55623-944-0*, Irwn Prfssnl) McGraw-Hill Prof.

Rosenbloom, Jerry S., jt. auth. see Hallman, G. Victor.

Rosenbloom, Joseph. Biggest Riddle Book in the World. rev. ed. LC 76-1165. (Illus.). 256p. (J). (gr. 4-7). 1983. pap. 6.95 (*0-8069-8884-3*) Sterling.

Rosenbloom, Joseph. Deputy Dan & the Bank Robbers. LC 84-159969. (Step into Reading Ser.: A Step 3 Book). (Illus.). 48p. (J). (ps-3). 1985. pap. 3.99 (*0-394-87045-X*, Pub. by Random Bks Yng Read) Random.

Rosenbloom, Joseph. Deputy Dan & the Bank Robbers. (Step into Reading Ser.: A Step 3 Book). (J). (gr. 2-3). 1985. 9.19 (*0-606-12250-8*, Pub. by Turtleback) Demco.

Rosenbloom, Joseph. Deputy Dan Gets His Man. LC 85-1686. (Step into Reading Ser.: A Step 3 Book). (Illus.). 48p. (J). (ps-3). 1985. pap. 3.99 (*0-394-87250-9*, Pub. by Random Bks Yng Read) Random.

Rosenbloom, Joseph. Deputy Dan Gets His Man. (Step into Reading Ser.: A Step 3 Book). (J). (gr. 2-3). 1985. 9.19 (*0-606-06119-3*, Pub. by Turtleback) Demco.

Rosenbloom, Joseph. Doctor Knock-Knock's Official Knock-Knock Dictionary. LC 76-19796. (Illus.). 128p. (J). (gr. 3 up). 1980. pap. 4.95 (*0-8069-8936-X*) Sterling.

— Doctor Knock-Knock's Official Knock-Knock Dictionary. (J). 1976. 10.05 (*0-606-04202-4*, Pub. by Turtleback) Demco.

— Funny Insults & Snappy Put-Downs. LC 82-50547. (Illus.). 128p. (J). (gr. 4 up). 1982. pap. 4.95 (*0-8069-7644-6*) Sterling.

— Gigantic Joke Book. LC 77-93310. (Illus.). 256p. (J). (gr. 4-6). 1981. pap. 6.95 (*0-8069-7514-8*) Sterling.

— Giggles, Gags & Groaners. LC 86-30052. (Illus.). 128p. (J). (gr. 2-8). 1987. pap. 4.95 (*0-8069-6536-3*) Sterling.

— Great Book of Riddles & Jokes. 1999. pap. text 4.95 (*0-8069-9834-2*) Sterling.

— The Little Giant Book of Jokes. LC 96-28373. (Illus.). 352p. (J). 1996. 6.95 (*0-8069-6101-5*) Sterling.

— The Little Giant Book of Riddles. (Illus.). 352p. (J). 1996. pap. 6.95 (*0-8069-6100-7*) Sterling.

— Nutty Knock Knocks! LC 85-27626. (Illus.). 128p. (J). (gr. 4-7). 1986. pap. 4.95 (*0-8069-6304-2*) Sterling.

Rosenbloom, Joseph. Nutty Knock Knocks! (J). 1986. 10.05 (*0-606-04286-5*, Pub. by Turtleback) Demco.

Rosenbloom, Joseph. Perfect Put-Downs & Instant Insults. LC 88-11710. (Illus.). 128p. (J). (gr. 2-8). 1989. pap. 4.95 (*0-8069-6940-7*) Sterling.

— Six Hundred Ninety-Six Silly School Jokes & Riddles. (Illus.). 128p. (J). (gr. 2 up). 1986. pap. 4.95 (*0-8069-6392-1*) Sterling.

— Spooky Riddles & Jokes. LC 87-17972. (Illus.). 128p. (J). (gr. 4 up). 1988. pap. 4.95 (*0-8069-6736-6*) Sterling.

— Sports Riddles. LC 81-7232. (Illus.). 64p. (J). (gr. 6 up). 1982. 8.95 (*0-15-277994-9*, Harcourt Child Bks) Harcourt.

— World's Toughest Tongue Twisters. LC 86-5983. (Illus.). 128p. (J). (gr. 2-8). 1987. pap. 4.95 (*0-8069-6596-7*) Sterling.

— The Zaniest Riddle Book in the World. LC 83-18102. (Illus.). 128p. (J). (gr. 3 up). 1985. pap. 4.95 (*0-8069-6252-6*) Sterling.

Rosenbloom, Joseph R. Conversion to Judaism: From the Biblical Period to the Present. LC 78-9409. 192p. reprint ed. pap. 59.60 (*0-7837-2999-5*, 204294200006) Bks Demand.

Rosenbloom, Lewis, jt. auth. see Sullivan, Peter B.

Rosenbloom, Paul S., et al, eds. The Soar Papers: Research on Integrated Intelligence, 2 vols. (Artificial Intelligence Ser.). (Illus.). 1300p. (C). 1993. 135.00 (*0-262-18152-5*) MIT Pr.

***Rosenbloom, Rachel.** Giving My Body to Science. (Hugh MacLennan Poetry Ser.). 160p. 1999. pap. 12.95 (*0-7735-1904-1*) McG-Queens Univ Pr.

Rosenbloom, Rachel. Unspoken Rules: Sexual Orientation & Women's Human Rights. LC 96-199926. (Sexual Politics Ser.). (Illus.). 272p. 1996. 69.95 (*0-304-33763-3*) Continuum.

Rosenbloom, Rachel, ed. Secreto a Voces: Orientacion Sexual y los Derechos Humanos de las Mujeres. (SPA.). 274p. (C). 1997. pap. 15.00 (*1-884955-03-7*) Intl Gay & Lesbian.

Rosenbloom, Richard S. & Burgelman, Robert A., eds. Research on Technological Innovation, Management & Policy, Vol. 1. 149p. 1983. 78.50 (*0-89232-273-X*) Jai Pr.

— Research on Technological Innovation, Management & Policy, Vol. 2. 224p. 1985. 73.25 (*0-89232-426-0*) Jai Pr.

— Research on Technological Innovation, Management & Policy, Vol. 3. 262p. 1987. 73.25 (*0-89232-688-3*) Jai Pr.

— Research on Technological Innovation, Management & Policy, Vol. 5. 197p. 1994. 73.25 (*1-55938-083-7*) Jai Pr.

— Research on Technological Innovation, Management & Policy, Vol. 6. 1997. 73.25 (*1-55938-984-2*) Jai Pr.

— Research on Technological Innovation, Management & Policy, Vol. 7. Date not set. 73.25 (*0-7623-0369-7*) Jai Pr.

— Research on Technological Innovation, Management & Policy: Tech, Competition, & Organization Theory, Vol. 4. 296p. 1989. 78.50 (*0-89232-798-7*) Jai Pr.

Rosenbloom, Richard S. & Marris, Robin, eds. Social Innovation in the City: New Enterprises for Community Development, A Collection of Working Papers. LC 69-72560. (Studies in Technology & Society). 212p. 1969. pap. 4.00 (*0-674-81350-2*) HUP.

Rosenbloom, Richard S. & Spencer, William J., eds. Engines of Innovation: U. S. Industrial Research at the End of an Era. LC 95-43852. 288p. (C). 1996. 34.95 (*0-87584-675-0*) Harvard Busn.

Rosenbloom, Richard S. & Wolek, Francis W. Technology & Information Transfer: A Survey of Practice in Industrial Organizations. LC 70-119550. 190p. reprint ed. pap. 58.90 (*0-608-11498-7*, 200222500012) Bks Demand.

Rosenblum, A., ed. Relativity, Supersymmetry, & Strings. LC 87-21294. (Illus.). 136p. 1990. 65.00 (*0-306-42680-3*, Plenum Trade) Perseus Pubng.

Rosenblum, Andrew, jt. ed. see Magura, Stephen.

Rosenblum, Art. The Natural Birth Control Book. 6th rev. ed. (Illus.). 168p. 1984. reprint ed. pap. 6.00 (*0-916726-03-7*, 84-70295) Aquarian Res.

Rosenblum, Barbara, jt. auth. see Butler, Sandra.

Rosenblum-Cale, Karen. Thinking Skills: Teaching Social Studies. 48p. 1987. pap. 7.95 (*0-8106-0205-9*) NEA.

Rosenblum-Cale, Karen, jt. ed. see Gruenwald, Oskar.

***Rosenblum, Constance.** Gold Digger: The Outrageous Life & Times of Peggy Hopkins Joyce. LC 99-47455. (Illus.). 288p. 2000. 26.00 (*0-8050-5089-2*, Metropol Bks) H Holt & Co.

Rosenblum, Daniel. A Time to Hear, a Time to Help: Listening to People with Cancer. 250p. 1993. text 27.95 (*0-02-927105-3*) Free Pr.

Rosenblum, Dolores. Christina Rossetti: The Poetry of Endurance. LC 85-30739. (Ad Feminam Ser.). 264p. 1987. text 31.95 (*0-8093-1269-7*) S Ill U Pr.

Rosenblum, I. Y. & Heyner, Susan, eds. Growth Factors in Mammalian Development. 240p. 1989. lib. bdg. 206.00 (*0-8493-4540-5*, QP552) CRC Pr.

Rosenblum, Illith, jt. auth. see Esh, Tina.

Rosenblum, J. Reb Yaakov. 1993. 20.99 (*0-89906-413-2*); pap. 17.99 (*0-89906-415-9*) Mesorah Pubns.

Rosenblum, James B. & Zarin, Ira, eds. Medical Litigation Alert. 1990. ring bd. 250.00 (*0-9626905-0-3*) Med Litigation.

***Rosenblum, Joe & Kohn, David.** Defy the Darkness: A Tale of Courage in the Shadow of Mengele. LC 00-27734. 320p. 2000. 25.00 (*0-275-96862-6*, C6862, Praeger Trade) Greenwood.

Rosenblum, Jonathan D. Copper Crucible: How the Arizona Miners' Strike of 1983 Recast Labor-Management Relations. 2nd ed. LC 98-11699. 280p. 1998. pap. text 17.95 (*0-8014-8554-1*, ILR Press) Cornell U Pr.

— Copper Crucible: How the Arizona Miners' Strike of 1983 Recast Labor-Management Relations in America. LC 94-27852. 264p. 1994. text 42.50 (*0-87546-331-2*, ILR Press); pap. text 16.95 (*0-87546-332-0*, ILR Press) Cornell U Pr.

Rosenblum, Joseph. A Bibliographic History of the Book: An Annotated Guide to the Literature. annot. ed. LC 95-5327. (History of the Bk.: No. 3). 439p. 1995. 58.00 (*0-8108-3009-4*) Scarecrow.

— Land Banking. Linger, Juyne, ed. 8p. (Orig.). 1978. pap. 8.00 (*0-317-04908-9*) Natl Coun Econ Dev.

***Rosenblum, Joseph.** Practice to Deceive: The Amazing Stories of Literary Forgery's Most Notorious Practices. LC 99-48636. (Illus.). 370p. 2000. 39.95 (*1-58456-010-X*) Oak Knoll.

Rosenblum, Joseph. Shakespeare. (Magill Bibliographies Ser.). 307p. 1992. 42.00 (*0-8108-2802-2*) Scarecrow.

— Urban Industrial Parks. Bell, Stephanie, ed. 8p. (Orig.). 1978. pap. 8.00 (*0-317-05496-1*) Natl Coun Econ Dev.

Rosenblum, Joseph, tr. from FRE. Prince of Forgers. LC 98-14515. (Illus.). 200p. 1998. 39.95 (*1-884718-51-5*, 50317) Oak Knoll.

Rosenblum, Joseph, jt. auth. see Greg, W. W.

Rosenblum, Joseph, ed. see Salem Press Editors.

Rosenblum, Karen & Travis, Toni-Michelle. Meaning of Difference: American Constructions of Race, Sex & Gender, Social Class & Sexual Orientation. 2nd ed. LC 99-34828. 480p. 1999. pap. 38.13 (*0-07-229602-X*) McGraw.

Rosenblum, Karen E. & Travis, Toni-Michelle C. The Meaning of Difference: American Constructions of Race, Sex, & Gender, Social Class, & Sexual Orientation. LC 95-36974. (C). 1995. pap. text 29.74 (*0-07-053962-6*) McGraw.

Rosenblum, Karen E., jt. auth. see Haines, David W.

Rosenblum, L. Penny, jt. auth. see Corn, Anne L.

Rosenblum, Larry, et al, eds. IEEE Virtual Reality '99: Proceedings IEEE Virtual Reality International Symposium (1999: Houston, TX) 299p. 1999. pap. 120.00 (*0-7695-0093-5*) IEEE Comp Soc.

Rosenblum, Leonard A. & Coe, Christopher L. Handbook of Squirrel Monkey Research. LC 84-24859. (Illus.). 524p. (C). 1985. text 150.00 (*0-306-41754-5*, Kluwer Plenum) Kluwer Academic.

Rosenblum, Leonard A., et al. Scientific Visualization: Advances & Challenges. (Illus.). 532p. 1994. text 53.00 (*0-12-227742-2*) Acad Pr.

Rosenblum, Leonard A., jt. ed. see Lewis, Michael.

Rosenblum, Leonard A., ed. see Moltz, Howard.

Rosenblum-Lowden, Renee. You Have to Go to School . . . You're the Teacher! 200 Tips to Make Your Job Easier & More Fun!!! LC 96-51288. 136p. 1997. 45.95 (*0-8039-6555-9*); pap. 19.95 (*0-8039-6556-7*) Corwin Pr.

— You Have to Go to School . . . You're the Teacher! 200 Tips to Make Your Job Easier & More Fun. 136p. 1997. 41.95 (*2-8106-6555-9*); pap. 17.95 (*2-8106-6556-7*) NEA.

***Rosenblum-Lowden, Renee.** You Have to Go to School... You're the Teacher! 250 Classroom Management Strategies to Make Your Job Easier & More Fun. 2nd ed. LC 00-9207. (Illus.). 2000. pap. write for info. (*0-7619-7682-5*) Corwin Pr.

Rosenblum, M. L. & Wilson, C. B., eds. Brain Tumor Biology. (Progress in Experimental Tumor Research Ser.: Vol. 27). (Illus.). xvi, 260p. 1984. 136.75 (*3-8055-3698-4*) S Karger.

— Brain Tumor Therapy. (Progress in Experimental Tumor Research Ser.: Vol. 28). (Illus.). xvi, 288p. 1984. 136.75 (*3-8055-3699-2*) S Karger.

Rosenblum, Martin J. Divisions-One. 5.00 (*0-686-15300-6*) Great Raven Pr.

— The Holy Ranger: Harley-Davidson Poems. LC 89-83936. 75p. (Orig.). 1989. pap. 14.95 (*0-89018-053-9*) Lion Pub-Roar Rec.

— The Holy Ranger: Harley-Davidson Poems. deluxe limited ed. LC 89-83936. 75p. (Orig.). 1989. pap. 29.95 (*0-89018-054-7*) Lion Pub-Roar Rec.

— Home. 2nd deluxe limited ed. LC 74-171995. 50p. (Orig.). (C). 1989. reprint ed. pap. 10.00 (*0-89018-056-3*) Lion Pub-Roar Rec.

— Home. 2nd ed. LC 74-171995. 50p. (Orig.). (C). 1989. reprint ed. pap. 5.00 (*0-89018-055-5*) Lion Pub-Roar Rec.

— Protractive Verse. 1976. pap. 0.50 (*0-89018-001-6*) Cats Pajamas.

— The Werewolf Sequence (A Poem in 100 Sequences) 150p. (Orig.). 1974. pap. 50.00 (*0-87924-029-6*) Membrane Pr.

Rosenblum, Martin J., ed. Brewing: Twenty Milwaukee Poets. LC 72-89435. 1972. pap. 6.00 (*0-89018-007-5*) Pentagram.

Rosenblum, Marvin & Rovnyak, James. Hardy Classes & Operator Theory. LC 96-42333. 176p. 1997. reprint ed. pap. text 9.95 (*0-486-69536-0*) Dover.

— Topics in Hardy Classes & Univalent Functions. LC 94-23454. (Baser Lehrb Ucher). 1994. write for info. (*3-7643-5111-X*) Birkhauser.

— Topics in Hardy Classes & Univalent Functions. LC 94-23454. (Baser Lehrb Ucher). xii, 250p. 1994. 49.50 (*0-8176-5111-X*) Birkhauser.

Rosenblum, Mary. Synthesis & Other Virtual Realities. LC 95-43950. (Illus.). 280p. 1996. 22.95 (*0-87054-170-6*, Arkham Hse) Arkham.

Rosenblum, Mendel. The Design & Implementation of a Log-Structured File System. (International Series in Engineering & Computer Science). 144p. (C). 1994. text 107.50 (*0-7923-9541-7*) Kluwer Academic.

Rosenblum, Morris, jt. auth. see Nurnberg, Maxwell.

***Rosenblum, Mort.** A Goose in Toulouse & Other Culinary Adventures in France. (Illus.). 320p. 2000. 25.00 (*0-7868-6465-6*, Pub. by Hyperion) Time Warner.

Rosenblum, Mort. Olives: The Life & Lore of a Noble Fruit. (Illus.). 250p. 1996. 25.00 (*0-86547-503-2*) N Point Pr.

— Olives: The Life & Lore of a Noble Fruit. (Illus.). 336p. 1998. pap. 15.00 (*0-86547-526-1*) N Point Pr.

— The Secret Life of the Seine. LC 93-42107. 1994. 21.00 (*0-201-62461-3*) Addison-Wesley.

— The Secret Life of the Seine. 304p. 1995. pap. 14.00 (*0-201-48941-4*) Addison-Wesley.

— Who Stole the News ? Why We Can't Keep up with What Happens. LC 93-15559. 298p. 1995. pap. 14.95 (*0-471-12032-4*) Wiley.

Rosenblum, Nancy L. Another Liberalism: Romanticism & the Reconstruction of Liberal Thought. LC 87-365. 240p. 1987. 43.00 (*0-674-03765-0*) HUP.

— Bentham's Theory of the Modern State. LC 77-17034. (Harvard Political Studies). 188p. 1978. reprint ed. pap. 58.30 (*0-7837-2324-5*, 205741200004) Bks Demand.

— Membership & Morals: The Personal Uses of Pluralism in America. LC 97-27937. 425p. 1998. text 29.95 (*0-691-01689-5*, Pub. by Princeton U Pr) Cal Prin Full Svc.

***Rosenblum, Nancy L.** Membership & Morals: The Personal Uses of Pluralism in America. 2000. pap. text 18.95 (*0-691-05023-6*, Pub. by Princeton U Pr) Cal Prin Full Svc.

— Obligations of Citizenship & Demands of Faith: Religious Accomodation in Pluralist Democracies. LC 99-48917. 2000. pap. text 19.95 (*0-691-00708-X*, Pub. by Princeton U Pr) Cal Prin Full Svc.

— Obligations of Citizenship & Demands of Faith: Religious Accomodation in Pluralist Democracies. LC 99-48917. (Illus.). 400p. 2000. text 70.00 (*0-691-00707-1*, Pub. by Princeton U Pr) Cal Prin Full Svc.

Rosenblum, Nancy L., ed. Liberalism & the Moral Life. 312p. (C). 1989. pap. 18.50 (*0-674-53021-7*) HUP.

— Liberalism & the Moral Life. LC 89-30983. 312p. 1989. 46.50 (*0-674-53020-9*) HUP.

Rosenblum, Nancy L., ed. see Thoreau, Henry David.

***Rosenblum, Naomi.** Documenting a Myth: The South as Seen by Three Women Photographers: Chansonetta Stanley Emmons. (Illus.). 19p. 1999. 19.95 (*0-295-97767-1*) U of Wash Pr.

Rosenblum, Naomi. A History of Women Photographers. LC 94-6713. (Illus.). 356p. 1994. 60.00 (*1-55859-761-1*) Abbeville Pr.

***Rosenblum, Naomi.** A History of Women Photographers. 2nd expanded rev. ed. LC 00-36249. (Illus.). 400p. 2000. 65.00 (*0-7892-0658-7*) Abbeville Pr.

Rosenblum, Naomi. A World History of Photography. 3rd rev. ed. LC 96-36153. (Illus.). 696p. 1997. 65.00 (*0-7892-0028-7*); pap. 40.00 (*0-7892-0329-4*) Abbeville Pr.

Rosenblum, Naomi & Heinemann, Larry, eds. Changing Chicago: A Photodocumentary. LC 88-38929. (Visions of Illinois Ser.). (Illus.). 208p. 1989. 29.95 (*0-252-06083-0*) U of Ill Pr.

Rosenblum, Peter M., et al. A Practical Guide to Massachusetts Limited Liability Companies. LC 96-77819. 566p. 1996. ring bd. 125.00 (*1-57589-043-7*, 97-04.36-BK) Mass CLE.

Rosenblum, R. Transformation in Late Eighteenth Century Art. 344p. 1967. pap. text 21.95 (*0-691-00302-5*, Pub. by Princeton U Pr) Cal Prin Full Svc.

Rosenblum, Ralph & Karen, Robert. When the Shooting Stops... The Cutting Begins: A Film Editor's Story. (Illus.). 304p. 1988. pap. 12.95 (*0-306-80272-4*) Da Capo.

Rosenblum, Richard. Brooklyn Dodger Days. LC 90-36691. (Illus.). 32p. (J). (gr. 1-5). 1991. text, lib. bdg. 13.95 (*0-689-31512-0*) Atheneum Yung Read.

— Journey to the Golden Land. LC 91-44941. (Illus.). 32p. (J). (gr. k-4). 1992. 9.95 (*0-8276-0405-X*) JPS Phila.

Rosenblum, Robert. Cubism & the 20th Century. (Illus.). 348p. 1976. 34.95 (*0-8109-0767-4*, Pub. by Abrams) Time Warner.

— Cubism & Twentieth Century Art. 1976. 20.95 (*0-685-03819-X*) P-H.

— The Dog in Art: From Rococo to Post-Modernism. (Illus.). 119p. 1995. reprint ed. 29.95 (*0-8109-1143-4*, Pub. by Abrams) Time Warner.

— On Modern American Art: Selected Essays. LC 99-22015. 384p. 1999. 39.95 (*0-8109-3683-6*, Pub. by Abrams) Time Warner.

— Paintings in the Musee d'Orsay. LC 89-11338. (Illus.). 686p. 1989. 65.00 (*1-55670-099-7*) Stewart Tabori & Chang.

— The Romantic Child: From Runge to Sendak. (Walter Neurath Memorial Lecture). (Illus.). 1989. 12.95 (*0-500-55020-4*, Pub. by Thames Hudson) Norton.

Rosenblum, Robert, text. Diane Burko, Paintings: Luci Ed Ombra di Bellagio. 32p. 1994. pap. 20.00 (*1-879173-19-0*) Locks Gallery.

Rosenblum, Robert & Bantens, Robert J. Eugene Carriere: The Symbol of Creation. Wasilik, Jeanne M., ed. (Illus.). 132p. 1990. 40.00 (*1-878607-08-1*) Kent Gallery.

Rosenblum, Robert & Ingres, Jean A. Ingres. (Masters of Art Ser.). (Illus.). 128p. 1990. 24.95 (*0-8109-3451-5*, Pub. by Abrams) Time Warner.

Rosenblum, Robert & Janson, H. W. Nineteenth-Century Art. LC 83-3882. (Illus.). 528p. 1984. 65.00 (*0-8109-1362-3*, Pub. by Abrams) Time Warner.

— Nineteenth Century Art (Abrams Book) (Illus.). 528p. (C). 1983. text 73.33 (*0-13-622621-3*) P-H.

***Rosenblum, Robert & Powers, Kimiko.** Willem de Kooning - Mostly Women: Paintings & Drawings from the John & Kimiko Powers Collection. Monk, Robert, ed. (Illus.). 100p. 2000. write for info. (*1-880154-37-4*) Gagosian Gallery.

Rosenblum, Robert & Testori, Giovanni, trs. Igor Mitoraaj: Sculptures & Drawings, 1990. (Illus.). 74p. 1990. 25.00 (*0-935037-24-1*) G Peters Gallery.

Rosenblum, Robert, et al. Jeff Koons: Celebration. (Illus.). 144p. 1996. 75.00 (*0-8109-6893-2*, Pub. by Abrams) Time Warner.

— The Landscape in Twentieth-Century American Art: Selections from the Metropolitan Museum of Art. (Illus.). 174p. 1991. pap. 25.00 (*0-917418-93-X*) Am Fed Arts.

— Messers Macdermott & Macgough: Paintings, Photographs & Time Experiments, 1950. LC 98-229857. 203 p. 1997. 39.95 (*90-74377-64-5*) Stichting Kunst.

***Rosenblum, Robert, et al.** 1900: Art at the Crossroads. LC 99-69361. (Illus.). 448p. 2000. 75.00 (*0-8109-4303-4*, Pub. by Abrams) Time Warner.

Rosenblum, Robert, et al. The Romantic Spirit in German Art, 1790-1990. LC 94-60293. (Illus.). 400p. 1994. 75.00 (*0-500-23693-3*, Pub. by Thames Hudson) Norton.

Rosenblum, Robert, jt. auth. see Freemont, Vincent.

Rosenblum, Robert, jt. auth. see Ratcliff, Carter.

Rosenblum, Robert, jt. text see Kertess, Klauss.

Rosenblum, S. & Louis, K. S. Stability & Change: Innovation in an Educational Context. LC 80-28291. (Environment, Development, & Public Policy Ser.). 370p. 1981. 55.00 (*0-306-40665-9*, Plenum Trade) Perseus Pubng.

Rosenblum, Sandra P. Performance Practices in Classic Piano Music: Their Principles & Applications. LC 87-45437. (Music: Scholarship & Applications Ser.). 544p. 1988. 52.50 (*0-253-34314-3*, MB-680) Ind U Pr.

— Performance Practices in Classic Piano Music: Their Principles & Applications. LC 87-45437. (Music: Scholarship & Applications Ser.). 544p. 1991. pap. 23.95 (*0-253-20680-4*) Ind U Pr.

Rosenblum, Sheila, ed. Leadership Skills for Jewish Educators: A Casebook. LC 93-37122. 1994. 35.00 (*0-87441-555-1*) Behrman.

Rosenblum, Simon, jt. ed. see Joseph, Paul.

Rosenblum, Victor G., jt. auth. see Zemans, Frances K.

Rosenblum, Walter. Walter Rosenblum. (Illus.). 224p. 1991. 76.00 (*0-89381-472-5*) Aperture.

Rosenblum, Walter, intro. America & Lewis Hine. (Illus.). 144p. 1997. pap. 12.95 (*0-89381-016-9*) Aperture.

Rosenblum, William M. & Benjamin, William J., eds. Selected Papers on Optometry. LC 92-29543. (Milestone Ser.: Vol. MS 62). 1992. pap. 45.00 (*0-8194-1050-0*) SPIE.

Rosenblum, Yonoson. Rabbi Yissocher Frand: In Print. 18.99 (*0-89906-630-5*, FIPH); pap. 15.99 (*0-89906-631-3*, FIPP) Mesorah Pubns.

Rosenblum, Yonoson, jt. auth. see Birnbaum, M.

Rosenbluth. Rolf & Edgar. (J). 1998. 11.95 (*0-671-75272-3*) S&S Bks Yung.

Rosenbluth, Frances M., jt. auth. see Ramseyer, J. Mark.

R

Rosenbluth, Gideon. Concentration in Canadian Manufacturing Industries. (General Ser.: No. 61). 168p. 1957. reprint ed. 43.70 (*0-87014-060-4*) Natl Bur Econ Res.

Rosenbluth, Gideon & Thorburn, H. G. Canadian Anti-Combines Administration, 1952-1960. LC 64-982. 114p. reprint ed. pap. 35.40 (*0-8357-7992-0*, 202653500050) Bks Demand.

Rosenbluth, Gideon, jt. ed. see Allen, Robert A.

Rosenbluth, Hal F. Good Company: Caring As Fiercely As You Compete. LC 98-11995. 272p. 1998. 25.00 (*0-201-33982-X*) Addison-Wesley.

Rosenbluth, Hal F. 2nd-Customer Always. 1994. pap. 12.95 (*0-688-13246-4*, Quil) HarperTrade.

***Rosenbluth, Hal F. & Peters, Diane M.** Care to Compete? Secrets from America's Best Companies on How to Manage with People & Profits--in Mind, 1. 224p. 1999. pap. text 15.00 (*0-7382-0135-9*, Pub. by Perseus Pubng) HarpC.

Rosenbluth, Marshall N. New Ideas in Tokamak Confinement. (Research Trends in Physics Ser.). (Illus.). 496p. 1994. boxed set 99.00 (*1-56396-131-8*) Spr-Verlag.

Rosenbluth, Michael & Yalom, Irvin D. Treating Difficult Personality Disorders. LC 96-8761. (Jossey-Bass Library of Current Clinical Technique). 219p. 1996. pap. 26.95 (*0-7879-0315-9*) Jossey-Bass.

Rosenbluth, Michael, jt. ed. see Silver, Daniel.

Rosenbluth, Roz. Nettie's Spaghetti. (Illus.). 12p. (J). (ps-2). 1999. pap. 3.75 (*1-880612-88-7*) Seedling Pubns.

Rosenbluth, Vera. Keeping Family Stories Alive: Discovering & Recording the Stories & Reflections of a Lifetime. 2nd rev. ed. LC 97-10683. (Illus.). 256p. 1997. pap. 19.95 (*0-88179-149-0*) Hartley & Marks.

Rosenbluth, Vera & McDiarmid, Susan. Classic Scrapbooking: The Art & Craft of Creating a Book of Memories. LC 98-40792. (Illus.). 256p. 1998. pap. 19.95 (*0-88179-163-6*) Hartley & Marks.

Rosenbrock, Howard. Machines with a Purpose. (Illus.). 234p. 1990. text 55.00 (*0-19-856346-9*) OUP.

Rosenbrock, Howard, ed. Designing Human-Centered Technology. (Artificial Intelligence & Society Ser.). (Illus.). 225p. 1990. pap. 71.00 (*0-387-19567-X*, 3414) Spr-Verlag.

***Rosenbrock, Rolf & Wright, Michael T.** Partnership & Pragmatism: Germany's Response to Aids Prevention & Care. LC 00-31133. 2000. pap. write for info. (*0-415-24106-5*) Routledge.

Rosenburg. UNIX Tools. 1996. write for info. (*0-201-41854-1*) Addison-Wesley.

***Rosenburg, Vivan.** Lonely Love. LC 00-190570. 475p. 2000. 25.00 (*0-7388-1717-1*); pap. 18.00 (*0-7388-1718-X*) Xlibris Corp.

Rosenburg, Arthur D. Career Busters: 22 Things People Do to Mess up Their careers & How to Avoid Them. LC 96-37269. 256p. 1996. pap. 10.95 (*0-07-053991-X*) McGraw.

***Rosenburg, Doug.** Use Case Driven Object Modeling with UML: A Practical Approach. LC 99-12043. 192p. 1999. pap. 31.95 (*0-201-43289-7*) Addison-Wesley.

Rosenburg, John. First in War: George Washington in the American Revolution. LC 97-34012. (Illus.). 256p. (YA). (gr. 5 up). 1998. lib. bdg. 24.40 (*0-7613-0311-1*) Millbrook Pr.

Rosenburg, John M. William Parker: Rebel Without Rights. (Illus.). 144p. (J). (gr. 5-8). 1996. lib. bdg. 21.90 (*1-56294-139-9*) Millbrook Pr.

— Young George Washington: The Making of a Hero. LC 96-21665. (Illus.). 176p. (J). (gr. 4-6). 1997. lib. bdg. 22.40 (*0-7613-0043-0*) Millbrook Pr.

Rosenburg, Kristi S., jt. auth. see Falk, John H.

Rosenburg, Louis, jt. auth. see Grigsby, William G.

***Rosenburg, Marc J.** E-Learning: Strategies for Delivering Knowledge in the Digital Age. (Illus.). 300p. 2000. 29.95 (*0-07-136268-1*) McGraw.

Rosenburg, Nathan & Frischtak, Claudio, eds. International Technology Transfer: Concepts, Measures, & Comparisons. LC 85-6276. 364p. 1985. 75.00 (*0-275-90221-8*, C0221, Praeger Pubs) Greenwood.

Rosenburg, Pierre. Chardin: New Thoughts. LC 83-50337. (Franklin D. Murphy Lectures: No. 1). (Illus.). 1983. 12.00 (*0-913689-11-4*) Spencer Muse Art.

Rosenburg, R. B. Living Monuments: Confederate Soldiers' Homes in the New South. LC 93-12465. (Illus.). xvi, 240p. (C). 1993. 45.00 (*0-8078-2109-8*) U of NC Pr.

Rosenburgh, V. A. Malayan Fern Allies: Handbook to the Determination of the Fern Allies of the Malayan Island. 261p. (C). 1985. text 175.00 (*0-89771-649-3*, Pub. by Intl Bk Distr) St Mut.

— Malayan Fern Allies: Handbook to the Determination of the Fern Allies of the Malayan Islands. 261p. (C). 1985. reprint ed. 175.00 (*81-7089-033-0*, Pub. by Intl Bk Distr) St Mut.

Rosenbusch, Gerd, et al. Radiology in Medical Diagnostics: Evolution of X-Ray Applications 1895-1995. 570p. 1995. 110.00 (*0-86542-899-9*) Blackwell Sci.

Rosenbusch, Gerd, jt. auth. see Reeders, Jacques W.

Rosenbusch, Harry F. Die Petrographisch Wichtigen Mineralien und die Methoden Ihrer Untersuchung, Zwei Teile, Teil 1. (Mikroskopische Physiographie der Mineralien und Gesteine Ser.: Band I). (Illus.). xxiv, 847p. 73.00 (*3-510-99070-6*, Pub. by E Schweizerbartsche) Balogh.

— Die Petrographisch Wichtigen Mineralien und die Methoden Ihrer Untersuchung, Zwei Teile, Teil 2. (Mikroskopische Physiographie der Mineralien und Gesteine Ser.: Band I). (Illus.). xv, 814p. 86.00 (*3-510-99071-4*, Pub. by E Schweizerbartsche) Balogh.

Rosenbush, Amanita, ed. see Dunn, Gloria.

Rosenbush, Ellen, jt. ed. see Lapham, Lewis H.

Rosenbush, Ellen, ed. see Lyons, Gene & Harpers Magazine Staff.

Rosenbush, Steven. Telecom Business Opportunities: The Entrepreneur's Guide to Making Money in the Telecommunications Revolution. LC 97-73916. 316p. (Orig.). 1997. pap. 24.95 (*1-890154-04-0*) Aegis Pub Grp.

Rosencher, E., et al. Intersubband Transitions in Quantum Wells. LC 92-10016. (NATO ASI Ser.: Vol. 288). (Illus.). 360p. (C). 1992. text 115.00 (*0-306-44204-3*, Kluwer Plenum) Kluwer Academic.

Rosencher, Emmanuel, jt. ed. see Nissim, Yves I.

Rosencrans, Bobbie. The Last Secret: Daughters Sexually Abused by Mothers. Bear, Euan, ed. LC 98-234806. 261p. 1997. pap. 20.00 (*1-884444-36-9*) Safer Soc.

Rosencrans, Gladys. The Spelling Book: Teaching Children How to Spell, Not What to Spell. LC 98-27308. 1998. pap. 23.95 (*0-87207-192-8*) Intl Reading.

Rosencrantz, Barbara G., ed. From Consumption to Tuberculosis: A Documentary History. LC 93-23171. (Disease, Epidemics & Medicine Ser.: Vol. 1). 648p. 1994. text 109.00 (*0-8153-0608-3*, SS808) Garland.

Rosencranz, Armin, jt. auth. see Divan, Shyam.

Rosencwaig, Allan. Photoacoustics & Photoacoustic Spectroscopy. 320p. 1990. 69.50 (*0-89464-450-5*) Krieger.

Rosendahl, Carl O. Trees & Shrubs of the Upper Midwest. LC 55-8489. (Illus.). 419p. reprint ed. pap. 129.90 (*0-608-15980-8*, 203328800084) Bks Demand.

Rosendahl, Mona. Conflict & Compliance: Class Consciousness among Swedish Workers. 214p. (Orig.). 1985. pap. text 54.00 (*91-85284-24-6*) Coronet Bks.

— Inside the Revolution: Everyday Life in Socialist Cuba. LC 97-16517. (Anthropology of Contemporary Issues Ser.). (Illus.). 208p. 1996. text 37.50 (*0-8014-3381-9*); pap. text 14.95 (*0-8014-8412-X*) Cornell U Pr.

Rosendahl, Mona, ed. The Current Situation in Cuba: Challenges & Alternatives. (Institute of Latin American Studies). (ENG & SPA., Illus.). 168p. 1997. pap. 79.50 (*91-85894-17-6*, Pub. by Almqvist Wiksell) Coronet Bks.

Rosendahl, Peter J. More han Ola og han Per. Haugen, Einar & Buckley, Joan N., eds. LC 87-30208. (Bur Oak Bk.). (Illus.). 195p. (Orig.). 1988. pap. 25.95 (*0-87745-192-3*) U of Iowa Pr.

***Rosendal, G. Kristin.** The Convention on Biological Diversity & Developing Countries. 336p. 2000. 159.00 (*0-7923-6375-2*) Kluwer Academic.

Rosendale, D. M. & Orme, T. Validation of Pharmaceutical Process Equipment. (Illus.). Date not set. text. write for info. (*0-8247-9887-2*) Dekker.

***Rosendale, Laura G.** Rethinking Basic Writing: Exploring Identity, Politics & Community in Interaction. LC 99-54100. 1999. write for info. (*0-8058-3416-8*) L Erlbaum Assocs.

Rosendall, Heidi J. A Phonological Study of the Gwari Lects. LC 92-81460. (Language Data, African Ser.: No. 24). x, 128p. 1992. pap. 10.00 (*0-88312-186-7*) S I L Intl.

Rosendorfer, Herbert. The Architect of Ruins. Mitchell, Mike, tr. from GER. (European Classics). 384p. 1992. pap. 14.95 (*0-7818-0001-3*, Pub. by Dedalus) Hippocrene Bks.

— The Architect of Ruins. 2nd ed. Mitchell, Mike, tr. from GER. (Dedalus European Fiction Classics Ser.). 368p. 1999. reprint ed. pap. 14.95 (*0-946626-91-X*) Subterranean Co.

— Letters Back to Ancient China. Mitchell, Mike, tr. from GER. (Europe 1997 Ser.). 274p. 1998. pap. 15.99 (*1-873982-97-6*, Pub. by Dedalus) Subterranean Co.

— Stephanie: A Previous Existence. Mitchell, Mike, tr. from GER. (Dedalus Europe 1992-97 Ser.). 153p. (Orig.). 1997. pap. 11.99 (*1-873982-17-8*, Pub. by Dedalus) Subterranean Co.

Rosendorfer, Theo, jt. auth. see Grigorevich, Viktor.

Rosendorff. Essential Cardiology. LC 99-89412. (C). Date not set. pap. text. write for info. (*0-7216-8144-1*, W B Saunders Co) Harcrt Hlth Sci Grp.

Rosendorff, Clive. Clinical Cardiovascular & Pulmonary Physiology. LC 83-13848. 382p. 1983. reprint ed. pap. 118.50 (*0-608-00433-2*, 206114800007) Bks Demand.

Rosene, Linda R. Civil War in the American Workplace. LC 96-137712. (Illus.). 206p. (Orig.). 1995. pap. 12.95 (*1-887868-00-3*) Target Systs.

Rosene, Marcella. Pasta & Co. by Request: Coveted Recipes from Seattle's Leading Take-Out Foodshop. LC 91-5108. 264p. (Orig.). 1991. 13.95 (*0-912365-49-8*) Sasquatch Bks.

— Pasta & Co. Encore: More Famous Foods from Seattle's Leading Take-Out Foodshop. LC 96-29751. 240p. (Orig.). 1997. pap. 16.95 (*1-57061-109-2*) Sasquatch Bks.

Rosene, Marcella, ed. see Pasta & Co. Staff.

Roseneil, Sasha. Common Women, Uncommon Practices: The Queer Feminism of Greenham. LC 99-29093. (Lesbian & Gay Studies). 256p. 1999. 69.95 (*0-304-33553-3*); pap. 17.95 (*0-304-33554-1*) Continuum.

— Disarming Patriarchy: Feminism & Political Action at Greenham. LC 94-40164. 192p. 1995. 112.95 (*0-335-19058-8*); pap. 31.95 (*0-335-19057-X*) OpUniv Pr.

Roseneil, Sasha & Seymour. Practicing Identities. LC 99-18649. 257p. 1999. text 65.00 (*0-312-22227-0*) St Martin.

Rosener, Judy B. America's Competitive Secret: Utilizing Women as a Management Strategy. (Illus.). 256p. 1995. 27.50 (*0-19-508079-3*) OUP.

— America's Competitive Secret: Women Managers. (Illus.). 256p. 1997. reprint ed. pap. 15.95 (*0-19-511914-2*) OUP.

Rosener, Judy B., jt. auth. see Loden, Marilyn.

Rosener, Maureen, ed. see Pillsbury Company.

Rosener, Werner. Peasants in the Middle Ages. Stutzer, Alexander, tr. from GER. & frwd. by. (Illus.). 352p. (Orig.). (C). 1993. pap. text 21.95 (*0-252-06289-2*) U of Ill Pr.

Rosenfarb, Chava. Bociany. LC 98-54858. 432p. 1999. 29.95 (*0-8156-0576-5*) Syracuse U Pr.

— Of Lodz & Love. LC 98-52709. 362p. 1999. 29.95 (*0-8156-0577-3*) Syracuse U Pr.

Rosenfeld. Digital Picture, 2 vols. 2nd ed. 1982. 168.00 (*0-12-597303-9*) Acad Pr.

— Four Centuries of Clinical Chemistry. 580p. 1999. text 145.00 (*90-5699-645-2*) Gordon & Breach.

— Pocket Guide to Organic Chemistry. (C). 1999. pap. text 13.50 (*0-15-601654-0*) Harcourt Coll Pubs.

Rosenfeld, et al. Vision Geometry. LC 91-2408. (Contemporary Mathematics Ser.). 237p. 1991. pap. 90.00 (*0-8218-5125-X*, CONM/119) Am Math.

Rosenfeld, jt. auth. see Christy.

Rosenfeld, jt. auth. see Cox.

Rosenfeld, jt. auth. see Messner.

Rosenfeld, A. A., jt. auth. see Shapiro, E. G.

Rosenfeld, Abraham, tr. Selichot for the Whole Year. (ENG & HEB.). 832p. 1956. 21.95 (*0-910818-10-X*) Judaica Pr.

Rosenfeld, Alla, ed. Defining Russian Graphic Arts: From Diaghilev to Stalin, 1898-1934. LC 98-26046. (Illus.). 256p. (C). 1999. 55.00 (*0-8135-2604-3*) Rutgers U Pr.

Rosenfeld, Alla & Dodge, Norton, eds. Nonconformist Art: The Soviet Experience, 1956-1986. LC 95-60469. (Illus.). 360p. 1995. 60.00 (*0-500-23709-3*, Pub. by Thames Hudson) Norton.

***Rosenfeld, Alvin.** The Over-scheduled. 2000. pap. write for info. (*0-312-26339-2*, St Martin Griffin) St Martin.

Rosenfeld, Alvin & Wasserman, Saul. Healing the Heart: A Therapeutic Approach to Disturbed Children in Group Care. 96p. 1990. pap. 15.95 (*0-87868-391-7*) Child Welfare.

***Rosenfeld, Alvin & Wise, Nicole.** Hyper-Parenting: Are You Hurting Your Child by Trying Too Hard? LC 99-56670. 272p. 2000. text 22.95 (*0-312-20315-2*) St Martin.

Rosenfeld, Alvin H. The Americanization of the Holocaust. LC 97-100444. (David W. Belin Lectures in American Jewish Affairs). 56p. 1996. pap. 2.00 (*1-881759-04-0*) J&S Frankel Ctr.

— A Double Dying: Reflections on Holocaust Literature. LC 79-3006. 222p. 1980. pap. 68.90 (*0-608-05041-5*, 205970200004) Bks Demand.

— Thinking about the Holocaust: After Half a Century. LC 97-3086. (Jewish Literature & Culture Ser.). 1997. 39.95 (*0-253-33331-8*); pap. 14.95 (*0-253-21137-9*) Ind U Pr.

Rosenfeld, Alvin H. & Greenberg, Irving, eds. Confronting the Holocaust: The Impact of Elie Wiesel. LC 78-15821. 255p. reprint ed. pap. 79.10 (*0-608-13216-0*, 205605400044) Bks Demand.

Rosenfeld, Alvin H., ed. see Wheelwright, John.

Rosenfeld, Andree, jt. ed. see Bahn, Paul.

***Rosenfeld, Arthur.** A Cure for Gravity. 382p. 2000. text 23.95 (*0-312-87455-3*) St Martin.

Rosenfeld, Arthur. Dark Money. 256p. (Orig.). 1992. mass mkt. 4.99 (*0-380-76486-5*, Avon Bks) Morrow Avon.

— Dark Tracks. 224p. (Orig.). 1992. mass mkt. 4.99 (*0-380-76487-3*, Avon Bks) Morrow Avon.

Rosenfeld, Arthur H., ed. see American Institute of Physics Staff.

Rosenfeld, Arthur H., jt. ed. see De Almeida, Anibal T.

Rosenfeld, Azriel, ed. Multiresolution Image Processing & Analysis. (Information Sciences Ser.: Vol. 12). (Illus.). 400p. 1984. 74.95 (*0-387-13006-3*) Spr-Verlag.

Rosenfeld, Azriel & Kak, Avinash C. Digital Picture Processing, 1. 2nd ed. LC 81-17611. (Computer Science & Applied Mathematics Ser.). 1982. text 84.00 (*0-12-597301-2*) Acad Pr.

— Digital Picture Processing, 2. 2nd ed. LC 81-17611. (Computer Science & Applied Mathematics Ser.). 1982. text 84.00 (*0-12-597302-0*) Acad Pr.

Rosenfeld, Azriel, et al. Advances in Fuzzy Theory & Technology, Vol. I. abr. ed. (FT&T Ser.). (Illus.). 331p. (C). 1993. 69.00 (*1-880404-07-9*) P P Wang.

Rosenfeld, Azriel, jt. ed. see Kong, T. Yung.

Rosenfeld, Azriel, jt. ed. see Simon, J. C.

Rosenfeld, B. A. The History of Non-Euclidean Geometry. (Studies in the History of Mathematics & Physical Sciences: Vol. 12). (Illus.). 488p. 1988. 89.00 (*0-387-96458-4*) Spr-Verlag.

Rosenfeld, B. A., jt. auth. see Akivis, M. A.

Rosenfeld, Boris. Geometry of Lie Groups. LC 96-40243. (Mathematics & Its Applications Ser.). 1997. lib. bdg. 195.00 (*0-7923-4390-5*) Kluwer Academic.

Rosenfeld, Charles, ed. The Uterine Circulation. LC 89-16219. (Reproductive & Perinatal Medicine Ser.: No. X). 1989. 102.50 (*0-916859-30-4*) Perinatology.

Rosenfeld, Charles, jt. ed. see Kalvoda, Jan.

Rosenfeld, D. L., ed. see Stillerman, Marci.

Rosenfeld, D. L., ed. see Waysman, Dvora.

Rosenfeld, D. L., ed. see Wolcowitz, Pia.

Rosenfeld, Daniel, ed. European Painting & Sculpture in the Museum of Art, Rhode Island School of Design, Circa 1770-1937. LC 91-61492. (Illus.). 288p. (Orig.). 1991. pap. text 30.00 (*0-911517-55-3*) Mus of Art RI.

Rosenfeld, David. Psychoanalysis & Groups: History & Dialectics. 212p. 1989. reprint ed. pap. text 15.00 (*0-946439-48-6*, Pub. by H Karnac Bks Ltd) Other Pr LLC.

— The Psychotic: Aspects of the Personality. 336p. 1991. pap. text 37.50 (*0-946439-96-6*, Pub. by H Karnac Bks Ltd) Other Pr LLC.

Rosenfeld, Dee. The Office Worker's Game of up from Under. (Illus.). 85p. 1999. pap. 8.95 (*0-9669335-1-6*, 001) MDR Pr.

— The Office Worker's Game of Up from Under. LC 99-93026. 1999. pap. 8.95 (*0-9669335-0-8*) MDR Pr.

Rosenfeld, Dina. All About Us. (Illus.). 32p. (J). (ps-k). 1989. 8.95 (*0-922613-02-8*) Hachai Pubng.

— All About Us. (Illus.). 32p. (J). (ps-1). 1989. pap. 6.95 (*0-922613-03-6*) Hachai Pubng.

— A Chanukah Story for Night Number Three. Pape, David S., ed. (Illus.). 32p. (J). (ps-1). 1989. 9.95 (*0-922613-16-8*); pap. 7.95 (*0-922613-17-6*) Hachai Pubng.

— Dovid the Little Shepherd. LC 94-77373. (Little Greats Ser.). (Illus.). 32p. (J). (ps-1). 1996. 9.95 (*0-922613-67-2*) Hachai Pubng.

— Kind Little Rivka. LC 94-102067. (Little Greats Ser.). (Illus.). 32p. (J). (ps-1). 1991. 9.95 (*0-922613-44-3*); pap. 6.95 (*0-922613-45-1*) Hachai Pubng.

— Kind Little Rivka. Englin, A., tr. from ENG. (Little Greats Ser.). (RUS., Illus.). 32p. (J). (ps-1). 1993. 9.95 (*0-922613-29-X*) Hachai Pubng.

— Labels for Laibel. (Illus.). 32p. (J). (ps-1). 1990. 9.95 (*0-922613-35-4*) Hachai Pubng.

— A Little Boy Named Avram. (Little Greats Ser.). (Illus.). 32p. (J). (ps-1). 1989. 9.95 (*0-922613-08-7*); pap. 6.95 (*0-922613-09-5*) Hachai Pubng.

— A Little Girl Named Miriam. (Little Greats Ser.). (Illus.). (J). (ps-1). Date not set. 9.95 (*0-922613-79-6*) Hachai Pubng.

— On the Ball. LC 97-75102. (Yossi & Laibel Ser.). (Illus.). (J). 1998. 9.95 (*0-922613-83-4*) Hachai Pubng.

— Peanut Butter & Jelly for Shabbos. LC 95-75435. (Illus.). 32p. (J). (ps-1). 1995. 9.95 (*0-922613-69-9*) Hachai Pubng.

— Tiny Treasures: The Wonderful World of a Jewish Child. (Illus.). 26p. (J). 1988. reprint ed. 12.00 (*0-8266-0365-3*, Merkos LInyonei Chinuch) Kehot Pubn Soc.

— Why the Moon Only Glows. (Illus.). 32p. (J). (ps-1). 1992. 8.95 (*0-922613-00-1*); pap. 6.95 (*0-922613-01-X*) Hachai Pubng.

— Yossi & Laibel Hot on the Trail. LC 94-103747. (Illus.). 32p. (J). (ps-1). 1991. 9.95 (*0-922613-47-8*); pap. 6.95 (*0-922613-48-6*) Hachai Pubng.

Rosenfeld, Dina & Romanenko, Vitaliy. The Very Best Book. LC 94-80242. (Illus.). 32p. (J). (ps-k). 1997. 11.95 (*0-922613-76-1*) Hachai Pubng.

Rosenfeld, Dina, ed. see Emerman, Ellen.

Rosenfeld, Dina, ed. see Grossblatt, Ruby.

Rosenfeld, Dina, ed. see Jacobs, Chana R.

Rosenfeld, Dina, ed. see Pertzig, Faigy.

Rosenfeld, Dina, ed. see Sandman, Rochel.

Rosenfeld, Dina, ed. see Sharfstein, Chana.

Rosenfeld, Dina, ed. see Wieder, Joy N.

Rosenfeld, Dina H. A Tree Full of Mitzvos. (Illus.). 48p. (J). 1985. reprint ed. 12.00 (*0-8266-0363-7*, Merkos LInyonei Chinuch) Kehot Pubn Soc.

— The Very Best Place for a Penny. (Illus.). 32p. (J). 1984. reprint ed. 12.00 (*0-8266-0362-9*, Merkos LInyonei Chinuch) Kehot Pubn Soc.

Rosenfeld, Douglas E., jt. auth. see Coleman, Francis T.

Rosenfeld, Edward, jt. auth. see Wysong, Joe.

Rosenfeld, Edward, jt. ed. see Anderson, James A.

Rosenfeld, Erwin & Geller, Harriet. Global Studies, Vol. I. 2nd ed. 656p. 1993. 32.95 (*0-8120-6197-7*); pap. 23.95 (*0-8120-4771-0*) Barron.

Rosenfeld, Eugene, jt. auth. see Prouty, Chris.

Rosenfeld, F. H. & Bojnicic, J. Adel von Galizien, Lodomerien U. der Bukowina. (GER & POL.). 275p. 1990. reprint ed. 195.00 (*0-317-03845-1*) Szwede Slavic.

Rosenfeld, Gary C. & Loose-Mitchell, David S. Pharmacology. 3rd ed. LC 97-25644. (Board Review Ser.). (Illus.). 370p. 1997. pap. 22.95 (*0-683-18050-9*) Lppncott W & W.

***Rosenfeld, Gavriel David.** Munich & Memory: Architecture, Monuments & the Legacy of the Third Reich. LC 99-43091. (Weimar & Now Ser.: Vol. 22). (Illus.). 450p. 2000. 45.00 (*0-520-21910-4*, Pub. by U CA Pr) Cal Prin Full Svc.

Rosenfeld, Georglyn, jt. auth. see Johnson, Laurene.

Rosenfeld, Gerry. Shut Those Thick Lips! A Study of Slum School Failure. 120p. (C). 1983. reprint ed. pap. text 10.50 (*0-88133-022-1*) Waveland Pr.

Rosenfeld, Harvey. Diary of a Dirty Little War: The Spanish-American War of 1898. LC 99-27610. 224p. 2000. 57.95 (*0-275-96673-9*) Greenwood.

— Ironman: Cap Ripken Story. 1996. mass mkt. 5.99 (*0-312-95781-5*, Pub. by Tor Bks) St Martin.

— Raoul Wallenberg: Angel of Rescue. rev. ed. (Illus.). 290p. 1995. pap. 19.95 (*0-8419-1359-5*) Holmes & Meier.

Rosenfeld, Harvey & Zborowski, Eli, eds. A Legacy Recorded: Martyrdom & Resistance. 368p. 1994. lib. bdg. 25.00 (*0-9619503-0-7*) Martyrdom & Resist Found.

Rosenfeld, Herbert. Impasse & Interpretation: Therapeutic & Anti-therapeutic Factors in the Psyco-analytic Treatment of Psychotic, Boderline, & Neutrotic Patients. Tuckett, David, ed. (New Library of Psychoanalysis). 250p. 1987. lib. bdg. 37.50 (*0-422-61010-0*, Pub. by Tavistock) Routldge.

Rosenfeld, Hy. Money Isn't Everything--It's Nothing. LC 93-7299. 149p. (Orig.). 1994. pap. 9.95 (*0-9638145-3-2*) Carillon Hse.

Rosenfeld, Isaac. Passage from Home. LC 87-40105. (Masterworks of Modern Jewish Writings). 300p. 1988. reprint ed. pap. 9.95 (*0-910129-75-4*) Wiener Pubs Inc.

— Preserving the Hunger: An Isaac Rosenfeld Reader. Schechner, Mark, ed. & intro. by. LC 87-27929. 464p. reprint ed. pap. 143.90 (*0-608-10600-3*, 2071221) Bks Demand.

Rosenfeld, Isadore. Am I Sick? Is It Serious? What Your Symptoms Really Mean. 1989. 18.95 (*0-318-41500-3*) S&S Trade.

— The Best Treatment. 448p. 1992. mass mkt. 6.99 (*0-553-29879-8*) Bantam.

An Asterisk (*) at the beginning of an entry indicates that the title is appearing for the first time.

— The Best Treatment. large type ed. LC 92-32815. (General Ser.). 600p. 1993. 24.95 (*0-8161-5657-3*, G K Hall Lrg Type) Mac Lib Ref.
— Distress Signals. 1989. 18.95 (*0-318-37668-7*) S&S Trade.
— Dr. Rosenfeld's Guide to Alternative Medicine: What Works, What Doesn't - And What's Right for You. 384p. 1997. pap. 13.95 (*0-449-00074-5*) Fawcett.
— Dr. Rosenfeld's Guide to Alternative Medicine: What Works, What Doesn't - And What's Right for You. 342p. 1999. reprint ed. text 26.00 (*0-7881-6290-X*) DIANE Pub.
— Doctor, What Should I Eat? Nutrition Prescriptions for Ailments in Which Diet Can Really Make a Difference. 448p. 1996. mass mkt. 13.99 (*0-446-67261-0*, Pub. by Warner Bks) Little.
***Rosenfeld, Isadore.** Doctor What Should I Eat? Nutritional Prescriptions for Ailments in Which Diet Can Really Make a Difference. 528p. 2000. reprint ed. mass mkt. 7.99 (*0-446-60922-6*) Warner Bks.
— Live Now, Age Later: Proven Ways to Slow down the Clock. 480p. 2000. mass mkt. 7.99 (*0-446-60910-2*, Warner Vision) Warner Bks.
— Live Now, Age Later: Proven Ways to Slow down the Clock. 400p. 2000. pap. 13.95 (*0-446-67602-0*) Warner Bks.
— Live Now, Age Later: Proven Ways to Slow down the Clock, Vol. 1. large type ed. LC 99-37437. 1999. 28.95 (*0-7838-8741-8*, G K Hall Lrg Type) Mac Lib Ref.
Rosenfeld, Isadore. Live Now, Age Later: Proven Ways to Turn Back the Clock. LC 98-50859. 384p. 1999. 24.00 (*0-446-52060-8*, Pub. by Warner Bks) Little.
— Symptoms. 512p. 1994. mass mkt. 6.99 (*0-553-56813-2*) Bantam.
Rosenfeld, Israel. Gemarah l'Mas'Chilim: Talmud for Beginners. (HEB.). 1997. pap., wbk. ed. 7.00 (*0-914131-23-0*, A200) Torah Umesorah.
— Targilon for Sefer Bamidbar, Vol. 1. (HEB.). 1997. pap., wbk. ed. 6.25 (*0-914131-64-8*, A180) Torah Umesorah.
— Targilon for Sefer Bamidbar, Vol. 2. (HEB.). 1997. pap., wbk. ed. 6.00 (*0-914131-65-6*, A181) Torah Umesorah.
— Targilon for Sefer Shmos, Pt. II. (HEB.). 1997. pap. 7.50 (*1-878895-22-2*, A156) Torah Umesorah.
— Targilon for Sefer Vayikrah. (HEB., Illus.). 1997. pap., wbk. ed. 7.00 (*0-914131-92-3*, A160) Torah Umesorah.
Rosenfeld, J. Eye of the Storm: Inside the World's Deadliest Hurricanes, Tornadoes & Blizzards. LC QC944.R68 1999. (Illus.). 345p. (C). 1999. 26.95 (*0-306-46014-9*, Kluwer Plenum) Kluwer Academic.
Rosenfeld, J. L. & Morton, J. Long-Term Energy Storage in Solar Systems. (C). 1984. 140.00 (*0-7855-4195-0*, Pub. by Interntl Solar Energy Soc) St Mut.
— Long-Term Energy Storage in Solars Systems (C35) 77p. (C). 1984. 165.00 (*0-685-30221-0*, Pub. by Interntl Solar Energy Soc) St Mut.
Rosenfeld, Jean E. The Island Broken in Two Halves: Land & Renewal Movements among the Maori of New Zealand. LC 98-23951. (Hermeneutics, Studies in the History of Religions). 620p. 1999. 49.50 (*0-271-01852-6*) Pa St U Pr.
Rosenfeld, Jeffrey P. Legacy of Aging: Inheritance & Disinheritance in Social Perspective. LC 78-24209. (Modern Sociology Ser.). (Illus.). 152p. 1979. text 73.25 (*0-89391-011-2*) Ablx Pub.
Rosenfeld, Jo A. Yeah, You Rite! An Adventure in Comedy & Courage. (Illus.). 240p. (Orig.). 1995. pap. 11.95 (*0-9647266-0-2*) Medica-Spera.
Rosenfeld, Jo A., et al, eds. Women's Health in Primary Care. LC 96-13729. (Illus.). 921p. 1997. 59.95 (*0-683-07366-4*) Lppncott W & W.
Rosenfeld, Joan. Flute Music. 52p. 1987. pap. 4.95 (*0-912159-00-6*) Center Pr CA.
Rosenfeld, Joann, jt. auth. see Thiedke, Carolyn.
***Rosenfeld, Jona M. & Tardieu, Bruno.** Artisans of Democracy: How Ordinary People, Families in Extreme Poverty, & Social Institutions Became Allies to Overcome Social Exclusion. LC 00-23496. 2000. write for info. (*0-7618-1666-6*) U Pr of Amer.
Rosenfeld, Joseph. The Next Step: Etiology & Treatment of Addiction. LC 95-16788. 1995. 15.95 (*0-938475-06-1*) Lighthouse Inst.
Rosenfeld, Joseph G., jt. auth. see Blanco, Ralph F.
Rosenfeld, Linda & Prupas, Marilynne. Left Alive: After a Suicide Death in the Family. 120p. 1984. text 31.95 (*0-398-04953-X*); pap. text 20.95 (*0-398-06650-7*) C C Thomas.
***Rosenfeld, Lois G.** The Garden Tourist 2001, Northeast: A Guide to Gardens, Garden Tours, Shows & Special Events. vi, 106p. 2000. pap. 12.95 (*0-9702505-1-7*) Garden Tourist.
— The Garden Tourist 2001, Midwest: A Guide to Gardens, Garden Tours, Shows & Special Events. vi, 106p. 2000. pap. 12.95 (*0-9702505-0-9*) Garden Tourist.
— The Garden Tourist 2001, Southeast: A Guide to Gardens, Garden Tours, Shows & Special Events. vi 106p. 2000. pap. 12.95 (*0-9702505-2-5*) Garden Tourist.
— The Garden Tourist 2001, Southwest & Rockies: A Guide to Gardens, Garden Tours, Shows & Special Events. vi, 106p. 2000. pap. 12.95 (*0-9702505-3-3*) Garden Tourist.
— The Garden Tourist 2001, West: A Guide to Gardens, Garden Tours, Shows & Special Events. vi, 106p. 2000. pap. 12.95 (*0-9702505-4-1*) Garden Tourist.
Rosenfeld, Lois G., ed. The Garden Tourist, 1999: A Guide to Gardens, Garden Tours, Shows & Special Events. 8th ed. 240p. 1998. pap. 18.90 (*0-9639082-7-8*) Garden Tourist.
***Rosenfeld, Louis.** Four Centuries of Clinical Chemistry. 592p. 1999. 85.00 (*90-5699-646-0*) Gordon & Breach.
Rosenfeld, Louis. Thomas Hodgkin: Morbid Anatomist & Social Activist. LC 92-28528. (Illus.). 356p. 1992. 24.95 (*0-8191-8633-3*) Madison Bks UPA.
Rosenfeld, Louis & Morville, Peter. Information Architecture for the World Wide Web: Designing Large-Scale Web Sites. Mui, Linda, ed. LC 98-149802. (Illus.). 224p. 1998. reprint ed. pap. 27.95 (*1-56592-282-4*) OReilly & Assocs.
Rosenfeld, Louis B., et al. The Internet Compendium: Guides to Resources by Subject, 3 vols. LC 94-36685. 1994. 190.00 (*1-55570-188-4*) Neal-Schuman.
***Rosenfeld, Lucinda.** What She Saw In Roger Mancuso, Gunter Hopstock, Jason Barry Gold, Spitty Clark, Jack Geezo, Humphrey Fung, Claude Duvet, Bruce Bledstone, Kevin McFeeley, Arnold Allen, Pablo Miles, Anonymous 1-4, Nobody 5-8, Neil Schmertz, Bo Pierce: A Novel. LC 00-29066. 304p. 2000. 23.95 (*0-375-50375-7*) Random.
***Rosenfeld, Lucy D.** Amazing Space: Architect Designed Houses under $300,000. LC 98-29628. (Illus.). 160p. 1998. 39.95 (*0-7643-0642-1*) Schiffer.
— Yesterday's Structures, Today's Homes: Adapting Yesterday's Buildings into Today's Living Spaces. LC 99-41801. 176p. 1999. 39.95 (*0-7643-1014-3*) Schiffer.
Rosenfeld, Lucy D., jt. auth. see Harrison, Marina.
Rosenfeld, Mark, jt. ed. see Parr, Joy.
Rosenfeld, Mark S. Wellness & Lifestyle Renewal: A Manual for Personal Change. (Orig.). 1993. pap. text 28.00 (*0-910317-92-5*) Am Occup Therapy.
Rosenfeld, Max, ed. & tr. see Albert, Nachum.
Rosenfeld, Max, ed. & tr. see Alpert, Nachum.
Rosenfeld, Max, tr. see Blinkin, Meir.
Rosenfeld, Max, tr. see Smolar, Hersh.
***Rosenfeld, Michael & Harrisburg, Halley K.** Michael Rosenfeld Gallery: The First Decade. (Illus.). 96p. 2000. 25.00 (*1-930416-04-0*) M Rosenfeld.
***Rosenfeld, Michael & Kocher, Gregory B.** The Practice of Speech Language Pathology: A Study of Clinical Activities & Knowledge Areas for the Certified SLP. 2000. 30.00 (*1-58041-065-0*) Am Speech Lang Hearing.
Rosenfeld, Michel. Affirmative Action & Justice: A Philosophical & Constitutional Inquiry. 384p. (C). 1991. 45.00 (*0-300-04781-9*) Yale U Pr.
— Affirmative Action & Justice: A Philosophical & Constitutional Inquiry. LC 90-37995. 384p. (C). 1993. reprint ed. pap. 20.00 (*0-300-05508-0*) Yale U Pr.
— Just Interpretations: Law Between Ethics & Politics. LC 97-8384. (Philosophy, Social Theory, & the Rule of Law Ser.). 312p. 1998. 45.00 (*0-520-21097-2*, Pub. by U CA Pr) Cal Prin Full Svc.
Rosenfeld, Michel, ed. Constitutionalism, Identity, Difference & Legitimacy: Theoretical Perspectives. LC 94-15777. 448p. 1994. text 54.95 (*0-8223-1505-X*); pap. text 21.95 (*0-8223-1516-5*) Duke.
Rosenfeld, Michel & Arato, Andrew. Habermas on Law & Democracy: Critical Exchanges. LC 97-26887. (Philosophy, Social Theory & the Rule of Law Ser.). 400p. 1998. 55.00 (*0-520-20466-2*, Pub. by U CA Pr) Cal Prin Full Svc.
Rosenfeld, Mordecai. A Backhanded View of the Law: Irreverent Essays on Justice. LC 91-27013. 1992. 24.95 (*0-918024-90-0*) Ox Bow.
Rosenfeld, Morris. Songs from the Ghetto. LC 76-104556. 123p. reprint ed. lib. bdg. 22.00 (*0-8398-1766-5*) Irvington.
Rosenfeld, Nancy. Unfinished Journey: Two People, Two Worlds - from Tyranny to Freedom. LC 93-17961. 294p. (Orig.). (C). 1993. pap. text 18.95 (*0-8191-9196-5*); lib. bdg. 47.50 (*0-8191-9195-7*) U Pr of Amer.
***Rosenfeld, Nancy & Bolen, Dianna W.** Just As Much a Woman: Your Personal Guide to Hysterectomy & Beyond. LC 99-15124. (Illus.). 264p. 1999. 22.00 (*0-7615-1820-7*) Prima Pub.
***Rosenfeld, Natania.** Outsiders Together: Virginia & Leonard Woolf. LC 99-53742. 2000. 37.50 (*0-691-05884-9*, Pub. by Princeton U Pr) Cal Prin Full Svc.
Rosenfeld, Paul. By Way of Art: Criticisms of Music, Literature, Painting, Sculpture & the Dance. LC 67-30230. (Essay Index Reprint Ser.). 1977. 20.95 (*0-8369-0835-X*) Ayer.
— Men Seen: Twenty-Four Modern Authors. LC 67-26776. (Essay Index Reprint Ser.). 1977. 24.95 (*0-8369-0836-8*) Ayer.
— Musical Chronicle, 1917-1923. LC 77-175877. 17.00 (*0-685-26463-7*) Ayer.
— Musical Portraits: Interpretations of Twenty Modern Composers. LC 68-29243. (Essay Index Reprint Ser.). 1977. 20.95 (*0-8369-0837-6*) Ayer.
Rosenfeld, Paul, et al, eds. Improving Organizational Surveys: New Directions, Methods, & Applications. (Focus Editions Ser.: Vol. 158). (Illus.). 280p. (C). 1993. text 59.95 (*0-8039-5193-0*); pap. text 26.00 (*0-8039-5194-9*) Sage.
Rosenfeld, Paul, jt. ed. see Giacalone, Richard A.
Rosenfeld, Paul, jt. ed. see Giacalone, Robert A.
Rosenfeld, Paul, jt. ed. see Thomas, Patricia J.
Rosenfeld, R., jt. auth. see Everly, G. S., Jr.
Rosenfeld, Rachel. Farm Women: Work, Farm, & Family in the United States. LC 85-13945. (Institute for Research in Social Science Monograph Ser.). 368p. 1985. pap. 114.10 (*0-608-05220-5*, 206575700001) Bks Demand.
Rosenfeld, Richard, jt. auth. see DK Publishing Staff.
Rosenfeld, Richard, jt. auth. see Messner, Steven F.
***Rosenfeld, Richard M. & Bluestone, Charles D.** Evidence-Based Otitis Media. (Evidence-Based Ser.). 420p. 1999. boxed set 89.95 incl. cd-rom (*1-55009-083-6*) DEKR.
Rosenfeld, Richard N. American Aurora. 988p. 1998. pap. 19.95 (*0-312-19437-4*) St Martin.
— American Aurora: A Democratic-Republican Returns: The Suppressed History of Our Nation's Beginnings & the Heroic Newspaper That Tried to Report It. LC 96-30680. (Illus.). 988p. 1997. text 39.95 (*0-312-15052-0*) St Martin.
Rosenfeld, Robert, et al. Understanding Statistics. 3rd ed. (Illus.). 368p. (C). 1983. text 80.75 (*0-07-045863-4*) McGraw.
Rosenfeld, Robert, jt. auth. see Christy, Dennis T.
Rosenfeld, Robert, jt. auth. see Naiman, Arnold.
Rosenfeld, Ron G. & Roberts, Charles, eds. The IGF System: Molecular Biology, Physiology & Clinical Applications. LC 98-55264. (Contemporary Endocrinology Ser.: Vol. 17). (Illus.). 800p. 1999. 175.00 (*0-89603-692-8*) Humana.
Rosenfeld, Ron G., et al. Turner Syndrome. 647p. 1989. text 225.00 (*0-8247-8108-2*) Dekker.
Rosenfeld, Ron G., jt. ed. see Hintz, Raymond L.
Rosenfeld, Ruth. Beyond These Shores: Poems & Diary of a Jewish Girl Who Escaped from Nazi Germany. Dorsett, Thomas, tr. (Illus.). 80p. (Orig.). 1996. pap. 9.95 (*0-944806-09-0*) Icarus Press.
Rosenfeld Saltiel, Jennifer, jt. auth. see Sarlin, Janeen A.
Rosenfeld, Sara R., ed. see Dabney, Colleen.
Rosenfeld, Sheila D. & White, Susan A. Nuclear Medicine Technology Review. LC 76-57458. (Illus.). 264p. reprint ed. pap. 81.90 (*0-8357-7601-8*, 205692300096) Bks Demand.
Rosenfeld, Sidney, tr. see Amery, Jean.
Rosenfeld, Sidney, tr. see Richarz, Monika, ed.
Rosenfeld, Stella P., tr. see Amery, Jean.
Rosenfeld, Stella P., tr. see Richarz, Monika, ed.
Rosenfeld, Stephanie, jt. auth. see Bello, Walden.
Rosenfeld, Steven. Making History in Vermont: The Election of a Socialist to Congress. LC 91-34055. 500p. (C). 1992. text 35.00 (*0-89341-698-3*); pap. text 17.50 (*0-89341-699-1*) Hollowbrook.
Rosenfeld, Stuart. Basic Skills for Organic Chemistry: A Toolkit. 288p. 1998. pap. 15.00 (*0-7637-0741-4*) Jones & Bartlett.
— Learning.Now: Skills for the Information Economy. 250p. 2000. pap. 33.00 (*0-87117-325-5*) Comm Coll Pr Am Assn Comm Coll.
— Over Achievers: Business Clusters That Work: Prospects for Regional Development. 52p. (Orig.). 1996. pap. 7.00 (*0-9636927-3-9*) Reg Tech Strat.
Rosenfeld, Stuart, et al. Community Colleges, Coalitions, & Competitiveness: Associating with Industry. 58p. (Orig.). (C). 1996. pap. 12.00 (*0-9636927-4-7*) Reg Tech Strat.
Rosenfeld, Stuart, jt. auth. see Bhushan, Nalini.
Rosenfeld, Stuart, jt. auth. see Bosworth, Brian.
Rosenfeld, Stuart A. Advancing Opportunity in Advanced Manufacturing. 145p. 1995. 15.00 (*0-9636927-1-2*) Reg Tech Strat.
— Competitive Manufacturing: New Strategies for Regional Development. LC 91-39699. 418p. (C). 1992. 19.95 (*0-88285-137-3*) Ctr Urban Pol Res.
— Exports, Competitiveness, & Synergy in Appalachian Industry Clusters. (Illus.). 235p. (C). 1998. pap. text 40.00 (*0-7881-7435-5*) DIANE Pub.
— New Technologies & New Skills: Two Year Colleges at the Vanguard of Modernization. 159p. (Orig.). (C). 1995. 20.00 (*0-9636927-2-0*) Reg Tech Strat.
Rosenfeld, Sydney, jt. auth. see Lloyd, David.
Rosenfeld, Tzvi A., ed. see Nachman of Breslov.
Rosenfeld, U., jt. ed. see Miller, H.
Rosenfeld, Ulrich. Kleines Fachworterbuch. (Sammlung Geologischer Fuehrer Ser.: Band 46). (GER., Illus.). vii, 1975p. 1966. 17.00 (*3-443-39048-X*, Pub. by Gebruder Borntraeger) Balogh.
Rosenfeld, V. Kleines Fachwoerterbuch Geologie. (GER.). 97p. 1966. 39.95 (*0-7859-6724-0*, M-7500) Fr & Eur.
Rosenfeld, Zvi A., ed. see Nachman of Breslov.
Rosenfelder, Lewis. Advanced IBM BASIC Faster & Better, Vol. I. (IBM Information Ser.). (Illus.). 396p. (Orig.). 1985. pap. 19.95 (*0-932679-01-3*); disk 29.95 (*0-685-43124-X*) Blue Cat.
— BASIC Disk I-O Faster & Better & Other Mysteries. 432p. 1984. 29.95 (*0-936200-09-X*) Blue Cat.
— BASIC Faster & Better & Other Mysteries. (TRS-80 Information Ser.: Vol. 4). (Illus.). 290p. (Orig.). 1981. pap. text 29.95 (*0-936200-03-0*) Blue Cat.
— IBM BASIC Faster & Better. Evans, Carl M. & Trapp, Charles, eds. (IBM PC Information Ser.: Vol. 1). (Illus.). 392p. 1984. pap. text 19.95 (*0-936200-52-9*) Blue Cat.
Rosenfelder, Ruth, jt. auth. see Setoguchi, Yoshio.
***Rosenfeldt, Niels E., et al.** Mechanisms of Power in the Soviet Union. LC 99-53109. 2000. text 69.95 (*0-312-23089-3*) St Martin.
Rosenfels, Paul. Freud & the Scientific Method. LC 80-118217. (Ninth Street Center Monographs). (Orig.). 1980. pap. 3.95 (*0-932961-06-1*) Ninth St Ctr.
— Homosexuality: The Psychology of the Creative Process. LC 86-23698. 1989. reprint ed. pap. 9.95 (*0-932961-08-8*) Ninth St Ctr.
— Letters to Dean. LC 87-402040. (Ninth Street Center Monographs). (Orig.). 1981. pap. 3.95 (*0-932961-07-X*) Ninth St Ctr.
— Love & Power: The Psychology of Interpersonal Creativity. LC 66-25081. 1966. 12.95 (*0-87212-909-0*) Libra.
— The Nature of Civilization: A Psychological Analysis. LC 86-143005. (Ninth Street Center Monographs). (Orig.). 1977. pap. 3.95 (*0-932961-03-7*) Ninth St Ctr.
— The Nature of Psychological Maturity. LC 86-143042. (Ninth Street Center Monographs). (Orig.). 1978. pap. 3.95 (*0-932961-04-5*) Ninth St Ctr.
— Psychic Exhaustion & the Growth Process: An Appendix to Homosexuality: The Psychology of the Creative Process. LC 86-142957. (Ninth Street Center Monographs). (Orig.). 1976. pap. 3.95 (*0-932961-02-9*) Ninth St Ctr.
— Psychoanalysis & Civilization. LC 62-18668. 1963. 10.95 (*0-87212-016-3*) Libra.
— The Relationship of Adaptation & Fun & Pleasure to Psychological Growth: An Appendix to Homosexuality: The Psychology of the Creative Process. LC 86-142926. (Ninth Street Center Monographs). (Orig.). 1975. pap. 3.95 (*0-932961-01-0*) Ninth St Ctr.
— A Renegade Psychiatrist's Story: An Introduction to the Science of Human Nature. LC 86-142970. (Ninth Street Center Monographs). (Orig.). 1979. pap. 3.95 (*0-932961-05-3*) Ninth St Ctr.
— Subjectivity & Objectivity: Further Aspects of Psychological Growth (An Appendix to Homosexuality: The Psychology of the Creative Process) LC 86-143018. (Ninth Street Center Monographs). (Orig.). 1974. pap. 3.95 (*0-932961-00-2*) Ninth St Ctr.
Rosenfelt, D., jt. ed. see Newton, Judith L.
Rosenfelt, Deborah, jt. ed. see Hoffman, Leonore.
Rosenfelt, Deborah S., ed. Internationalizing the Curriculum. (Womens Studies Quarterly Ser.: Vol. 98, Nos. 3 & 4). 224p. 1998. pap. 18.00 (*1-55861-210-6*) Feminist Pr.
Rosenfelt, Deborah S., ed. see Olsen, Tillie.
Rosenfield, A., et al, eds. Family Planning. (F. I. G. O. Manual of Human Reproduction Ser.: Vol. 2). (Illus.). 237p. 1989. text 35.00 (*1-85070-193-8*) Prthnon Pub.
— Reproductive Health: Global Issues. (F. I. G. O. Manual of Human Reproduction Ser.: Vol. 3). (Illus.). 224p. 1990. text 35.00 (*1-85070-194-6*) Prthnon Pub.
— Reproductive Physiology. (F. I. G. O. Manual of Human Reproduction Ser.: Vol. 1). (Illus.). 114p. 1989. text 35.00 (*1-85070-192-X*) Prthnon Pub.
Rosenfield, A. & Fathalla, Mahmoud F., eds. The F. I. G. O. Manual of Human Reproduction, 3 vols., Set, Vols. 1-3. (Illus.). 1989. text 90.00 (*1-85070-190-3*) Prthnon Pub.
Rosenfield, A. R., et al, eds. What Does the Charpy Test Really Tell Us? Proceedings of a Symposium Held at the Annual Meeting of the American Institute of Mining, Metallurgical & Petroleum Engineers, 1978. LC 78-10109. 240p. reprint ed. pap. 74.40 (*0-608-12400-1*, 205214500041) Bks Demand.
Rosenfield, Aaron & Mann, Roger, eds. Dispersal of Living Organisms into Aquatic Ecosystems. 1992. 35.00 (*0-943676-56-8*) MD Sea Grant Col.
Rosenfield, Allan, ed. see Institute of Medicine Staff.
Rosenfield, Claire. Paradise of Snakes: An Archetypal Analysis of Conrad's Political Novels. LC 67-25522. 1994. lib. bdg. 12.50 (*0-226-72754-8*) U Ch Pr.
Rosenfield, Geraldine. The Heroes of Masada. (Illus.). 38p. (J). (gr. 6-10). pap. 1.50 (*0-8381-0733-8*, 10-732) USCJE.
Rosenfield, Geraldine, jt. ed. see Ettenberg, Sylvia C.
Rosenfield, Israel. La Conscience: Une Biologie du Moi. exp. ed. 1991. write for info. (*0-318-68136-6*) Knopf.
— A Critique of Artificial Intelligence: The Enchanted Loom. 400p. 1990. 60.00 (*0-685-47601-4*) OUP.
***Rosenfield, Israel.** Freud's Megalomania: A Novel. LC 00-20401. 160p. 2000. 21.95 (*0-393-04898-5*) Norton.
Rosenfield, Israel, et al. DNA for Beginners. 1983. 14.95 (*0-86316-022-0*); pap. 9.95 (*0-86316-023-9*) Writers & Readers.
Rosenfield, James R. Bank Marketer's Self-Assessment Guide: A Financial Services Marketing Guide to Help You Improve Your Customer Service, Marketing & Profitability. 200p. 1995. 50.00 (*1-55738-779-6*, Irwn Prfssnl) McGraw-Hill Prof.
Rosenfield, John, ed. see Kageyama, Haruki.
Rosenfield, John, ed. see Okudaira, Hideo.
Rosenfield, John, tr. see Noma, Seiroku.
Rosenfield, John M. Dynastic Arts of the Kushans. (C). 1993. 110.00 (*81-215-0579-8*, Pub. by M Manoharial) Coronet Bks.
Rosenfield, John M. & Cranston, Fumiko E. Extraordinary Persons: Works by Eccentric, Nonconformist Japanese Artists of the Early Modern Era (1580-1868) in the Collection of Kimiko & John Powers, 3 vols. Richards, Naomi Noble, ed. LC 98-43293. (Illus.). 936p. 1998. boxed set 175.00 (*1-891771-00-0*, Pub. by Harvard Art Mus) Art Media Resources.
Rosenfield, John M. & Ten Grotenhuis, Elizabeth. Journey of the Three Jewels: Japanese Buddhist Paintings from Western Collections. LC 79-15072. (Illus.). 1979. 19.95 (*0-87848-054-4*) Asia Soc.
Rosenfield, John M., jt. auth. see Shimizu, Yoshiaki.
Rosenfield, Judith F., jt. auth. see Mulpeter, Virginia A.
Rosenfield, Kenneth. Automobile Dealerships: A Tax, Accounting & Financial Guide. 352p. 1998. text 105.00 (*0-471-16451-8*) Wiley.
Rosenfield, Lawrence W. Aristotle & Information Theory: A Comparison of the Influence of Causal Assumptions on Two Theories of Communication. (Janua Linguarum, Ser. Major: No. 35). 1971. text 81.55 (*90-279-1849-X*) Mouton.
Rosenfield, Leonara C., tr. see Koyre, Alexandre.
Rosenfield, Mark & Gilmartin, Bernard. Myopia & Nearwork. LC 98-10422. 232p. 1998. text 65.00 (*0-7506-3784-6*) Buttrwrth-Heinemann.
Rosenfield, Maxine. Counselling by Telephone. LC 96-70928. 160p. 1997. 45.00 (*0-8039-7998-3*); pap. 18.95 (*0-8039-7999-1*) Sage.
Rosenfield, Nancy S. The Radiology of Childhood Leukemia & Its Therapy. (Illus.). 128p. (C). 1981. pap. text 22.50 (*0-87527-173-1*) Green.
Rosenfield Noun, Louise, et al. An Uncommon Vision: The Des Moines Art Center. (Illus.). 334p. 1999. 60.00 (*1-879003-20-1*) Edmundson.
Rosenfield, Patricia L. The Management of Schistosomiasis. (Resources for the Future Ser.). 148p. 1979. pap. text 11.00 (*0-8018-2328-5*) Johns Hopkins.

R

R

Rosenfield, Paul. Accounting & Auditing for Employee Benefit Plans, No. 2254. 2nd ed. 624p. 1987. boxed set 152.00 (0-88712-793-2) Warren Gorham & Lamont.

— Accounting & Auditing for Employee Benefit Plans, No. 2254. annuals 2nd ed. 624p. 1991. suppl. ed. 68.00 (0-7913-1038-8) Warren Gorham & Lamont.

Rosenfield, Randall A., jt. auth. see McGee, Timothy J.

Rosenfield, Rick, jt. auth. see Flax, Larry.

Rosenfield, S. A. Instructional Consultation. 304p. 1987. 36.00 (0-8058-0014-X) L Erlbaum Assocs.

Rosenfield, Sybil. The Richmond Theatre, Yorkshire: A History of the Georgian Theatre, One of Only Four Remaining 18th Century English Playhouses. (C). 1989. 34.00 (0-900657-91-X, Pub. by W Sessions) St Mut.

Rosenfield, Sylvia A. & Gravois, Todd A. Instructional Consultation Teams: Collaborating for Change. LC 95-33486. (School Practitioner Ser.). 218p. 1996. lib. bdg. 32.00 (1-57230-013-2, 0013) Guilford Pubns.

Rosengard, Jay K. Property Tax Reform in Developing Countries. LC 97-38894. 232p. 1998. lib. bdg. 104.50 (0-7923-8095-9) Kluwer Academic.

Rosengard, Jay K., jt. auth. see Patten, Richard H.

Rosengard, Peter, jt. auth. see Wilmut, Roger.

Rosengart. Writing & Desktop Publishing on the Computer. 80p. (J). (gr. 5-8). 1996. pap., wbk. ed. 9.95 (1-55734-924-X) Tchr Create Mat.

Rosengart, Axel, jt. ed. see Kessler, Christof M.

Rosengart, Linda E. & Williams, Robert P. How to Get Financial Justice in a Breakup with Your Spouse or Live-In. 50p. 1995. pap. write for info. (0-9646113-0-9) RPW Pubns.

Rosengart, Terry. Clarisworks for Terrified Teachers. LC 97-177700. (Terrified Teachers Ser.). 304p. 1997. pap. 19.95 (1-57690-186-6) Tchr Create Mat.

— Clarisworks for Terrified Teachers. (Terrified Teachers Ser.). 304p. (J). (gr. 3-5). 1997. pap. 19.95 (1-57690-185-8) Tchr Create Mat.

— Clarisworks Simple Projects (Challenging) 80p. (J). (gr. 5-8). 1998. pap. 9.95 (1-57690-417-2) Tchr Create Mat.

— Clarisworks Simple Projects (Intermediate) 80p. (J). (gr. 3-5). 1998. pap. 9.95 (1-57690-416-4) Tchr Create Mat.

***Rosengart, Terry.** Inspiration for Terrified Teachers with CD-ROM. 304p. 2000. pap. 24.95 incl. cd-rom (1-57690-166-1) Tchr Create Mat.

Rosengart, Terry. Writing & Desktop Publishing on the Computer (Intermediate) (Illus.). 80p. (J). 1996. teacher ed. 9.95 (1-55734-923-1, TCM923) Tchr Create Mat.

Rosengarten, jt. auth. see New.

***Rosengarten, Arthur.** Tarot & Psychology: Spectrums of Possibility. LC 99-44720. 2000. 29.95 (1-55778-785-9); pap. 17.95 (1-55778-784-0) Paragon Hse.

Rosengarten, Dale. Row upon Row: Sea Grass Baskets of the South Carolina Lowcountry. (Illus.). 64p. (Orig.). 1986. pap. 10.00 (0-938983-02-4) McKissick.

Rosengarten, David. The Dean & DeLuca Cookbook. LC 97-172787. 1996. 39.95 (0-679-43463-1) Random.

— Taste: One Palate's Journey Through the World's Greatest Dishes. LC 98-16414. 384p. 1998. 45.00 (0-375-50011-1); pap. 29.95 (0-375-75265-X) Random.

Rosengarten, David, et al. The Dean & DeLuca Cookbook. 1996. 35.00 (0-614-12642-8) Random.

— The Dean & DeLuca Cookbook. LC 97-172787. (Illus.). 563p. 1996. pap. 25.95 (0-679-77003-8) Random.

Rosengarten, Frank, ed. see Gramsci, Antonio.

Rosengarten, Frederic, Jr. Wilson Popenoe: Agricultural Explorer, Educator, & Friend of Latin America. 182p. 1993. text 23.00 (0-935868-53-4) Allen Pr.

Rosengarten, Herbert & Flick, Jane, eds. The Broadview Reader. 3rd rev. ed. 719p. 1998. pap. write for info. (1-55111-114-4) Broadview Pr.

Rosengarten, Herbert & Goldrick-Jones, Amanda, eds. The Broadview Anthology of Poetry. 996p. 1994. pap. 19.95 (1-55111-006-7) Broadview Pr.

Rosengarten, Herbert, ed. see Bronte, Anne.

Rosengarten, Herbert, ed. see Bronte, Charlotte.

Rosengarten, Isreal J. Survival: The Story of a Sixteen-Year-Old Jewish Boy. LC 99-25979. 256p. 1999. 29.95 (0-8156-0580-3) Syracuse U Pr.

Rosengarten, J. G. French Colonists & Exiles in the United States. 234p. 1989. reprint ed. pap. 16.50 (1-55613-247-6) Heritage Bk.

***Rosengarten, Lucille.** Social Work in Geriatric Home Health Care: The Blending of Traditional Practice with Cooperative Strategies. LC 99-29261. 124p. 1999. pap. text 24.95 (0-7890-0747-9); lib. bdg. 39.95 (0-7890-0746-0) Haworth Pr.

Rosengarten, Richard. Divine Design & the Incursions of Evil in the Novels of Henry Fie. text. write for info. (0-312-23245-4) St Martin.

Rosengarten, Ruth, jt. auth. see Holloway, Memory.

Rosengarten, Theodore. All God's Dangers: The Life of Nate Shaw. LC 83-19828. 608p. 1989. pap. 17.00 (0-679-72761-2) Vin Bks.

Rosengaus, Joseph. Soviet Steam Generator Technology (Fossil Fuel & Nuclear Power Plants) Tamberg, Andreas, ed. (Illus.). (Orig.). 1987. pap. text 75.00 (1-55831-042-8) Delphic Associates.

Rosenglick, et al. West's Business & Personal Law: Activity Workbook. 1994. student ed. 20.75 (0-314-02413-1) West Pub.

Rosengram, Judson, tr. see Radzinsky, Edvard.

Rosengrant, Judson, tr. see Olesha, IUrii Karlovich.

Rosengrant, Sandra F. Focus on Russian: An Interactive Approach to Communication. 2nd ed. 384p. 1996. pap. text 36.00 (0-471-15757-0) Wiley.

Rosengrant, Sandra F. & Lifschitz, Elena D. Focus on Russian: An Interactive Approach to Communication. 2nd ed. LC 95-35097. 384p. 1996. pap. 53.95 (0-471-10998-3) Wiley.

— The Golden Age: Readings in Russian Literature of the Nineteenth Century. 3rd ed. LC 95-36522. 384p. 1995. pap. 34.95 (0-471-30940-0) Wiley.

Rosengren, Karl E., et al, eds. Media Gratifications Research: Current Perspectives. LC 85-2308. (Illus.). 311p. 1985. reprint ed. pap. 96.50 (0-608-01176-2, 205947400001) Bks Demand.

Rosengren, Karl E. & Windahl, Sven. Media Matter: TV Use in Childhood & Adolescence. Dervin, Brenda, ed. LC 88-38458. (Communication & Information Science Ser.). 304p. (C). 1989. pap. 39.50 (0-89391-570-X); text 73.25 (0-89391-499-1) Ablx Pub.

***Rosengren, Karl S., et al, eds.** Imagining the Impossible: Magical, Scientific & Religious Thinking in Children. LC 99-87643. (Illus.). 480p. (C). 2000. 64.95 (0-521-59322-0); pap. 24.95 (0-521-66587-6) Cambridge U Pr.

Rosenhaft, Eve & Lee, W. R., eds. State, Social Policy & Social Change in Germany, 1880-1994. rev. ed. 320p. 1997. 55.00 (1-85973-197-X, Pub. by Berg Pubs) NYU Pr.

Rosenhagen, Gustav, jt. auth. see Deutschen Akademie der Wissenschaften Staff.

***Rosenhainer, Ernst.** Forward, March! Memoirs of a German Officer. Hanse, Ilse R., ed. LC 99-16699. 208p. 2000. 24.95 (1-57249-158-2, WM Books) White Mane Pub.

Rosenham, David. Abnormality-Trans. (C). 1998. pap. write for info. (0-393-97240-2) Norton.

Rosenhan, David. Abnormal Psychology. 3rd ed. (C). 1996. text. write for info. (0-393-96996-7) Norton.

Rosenhan, David. Abnormal Psychology. 4th ed. (C). text. write for info. (0-393-97417-0) Norton.

Rosenhan, David. Abnormality. LC 97-24504. 500p. (C). 1997. pap. text 59.95 (0-393-97085-X) Norton.

Rosenhan, David L. & Seligman, Martin E. Abnormal Psychology. 3rd ed. LC 94-27953. (C). 1995. text. write for info. (0-393-96644-5) Norton.

Rosenhan, David L. & Seligman, Martin G. Abnormal Psychology. 3rd ed. LC 94-27953. (C). 1995. pap. text, teacher ed. write for info. (0-393-96659-3) Norton.

Rosenhan, David L., et al. Abnormal Psychology. 3rd ed. LC 94-41703. (C). 1995. pap. text, student ed. 18.00 (0-393-96658-5) Norton.

Rosenhaum, Stephanie, jt. auth. see Lees, John.

Rosenhaus, Drew & Yaeger, Don. A Shark Never Sleeps: Wheeling & Dealing with the NFL's Most Ruthless Agent. 320p. 1997. 24.00 (0-671-01525-7, PB Hardcover) PB.

— A Shark Never Sleeps: Wheeling & Dealing with the NFL's Most Ruthless Agent. (Illus.). 256p. 1998. pap. 14.00 (0-671-01526-5, Pocket Books) PB.

Rosenhead. Rational Analysis for a Problematic World. 1999. pap. text 46.50 (0-471-92286-2) Wiley.

Rosenhead, L., ed. Laminar Boundary Layers: An Account of the Development, Structure & Stability of Laminar Boundary Layers in Incompressible Fluids, Together with a Description of the Associated Experimental Techniques. (Illus.). 708p. 1988. reprint ed. pap. 18.95 (0-486-65646-2) Dover.

Rosenhead, L., tr. see Prandtl, Ludwig & Tietjens, O. G.

Rosenheck, K. & Lelkes, P. I. Stimulus Secretion Coupling in Chromaffin Cells, 2 vols., Set. LC 87-6378. 1987. 214.00 (0-8493-6534-1, CRC Reprint) Franklin.

— Stimulus-Secretion Coupling in Chromaffin Cells, Vol. 2. LC 87-6378. 1987. 100.00 (0-8493-6537-6, CRC Reprint) Franklin.

Rosenheck, K., jt. auth. see Lelke.

Rosenheim, Edward W. Swift & the Satirist's Art. LC 63-11400. (Midway Reprint Ser.). (Illus.). 254p. reprint ed. pap. 78.80 (0-608-09516-8, 205431700005) Bks Demand.

***Rosenheim, Edward W.** What Happens in Literature. LC 00-26895. 182p. 2000. pap. text 15.00 (0-226-72795-5) U Ch Pr.

Rosenheim, Edward W. What Happens in Literature: A Guide to Poetry, Drama & Fiction. LC 60-15458. 172p. reprint ed. pap. 53.40 (0-608-09517-6, 205431800005) Bks Demand.

***Rosenheim, James M.** The Emergence of a Ruling Order: English Landed Society, 1650-1750. LC 97-32454. (Studies in Modern History). 304p. (C). 1998. pap. 29.40 (0-582-08741-4) Longman.

— Emergence Ruling Order. LC 97-32454. (Studies in Modern History). (C). 1998. 65.63 (0-582-08742-2) Longman.

Rosenheim, James M. The Townshends of Raynham: Nobility in Transition in Restoration & Early Hanoverian England. LC 89-31140. (Illus.). 288p. reprint ed. pap. 89.30 (0-608-09093-X, 206972700005) Bks Demand.

***Rosenheim, Jeff L.** Unclassified-A Walker Evans Anthology: Selections from the Archive at the Metropolitan Museum. (Illus.). 2000. 39.95 (3-908247-21-7) Scalo Pubs.

Rosenheim, Jeff L. Walker Evans & Jane Ninas in New Orleans, 1935-1936. LC 90-86149. (Illus.). 24p. 1991. pap. 10.00 (0-917860-31-4) Historic New Orleans.

Rosenheim, Margaret K., ed. Pursuing Justice for the Child. LC 75-43238. (Studies in Crime & Justice). (Illus.). 1978. pap. text 6.50 (0-226-72788-2) U Ch Pr.

— Pursuing Justice for the Child. LC 75-43238. (Studies in Crime & Justice). (Illus.). 1992. lib. bdg. 22.50 (0-226-72789-0) U Ch Pr.

Rosenheim, Margaret K. & Testa, Mark T., eds. Early Parenthood & Coming of Age in the 1990s. LC 91-40325. 280p. (C). 1992. text 45.00 (0-8135-1815-6); pap. text 17.95 (0-8135-1816-4) Rutgers U Pr.

Rosenheim, Shawn. The Cryptographic Imagination: Secret Writing from Edgar Poe to the Internet. LC 96-24761. (Parallax). (Illus.). 312p. 1997. text 47.50 (0-8018-5331-1); pap. text 16.95 (0-8018-5332-X) Johns Hopkins.

Rosenheim, Shawn & Rachman, Stephen, eds. The American Face of Edgar Allen Poe. LC 95-10302. 408p. 1995. pap. text 19.95 (0-8018-5025-8) Johns Hopkins.

Rosenheim, Neil B., jt. ed. see Rader, Janet S.

Rosenholm, J. B., et al, eds. Trends in Colloid & Interface Science XI. (Progress in Colloid & Polymer Science Ser.: No. 105). 320p. 1997. 124.00 (3-7985-1086-5, Pub. by D Steinkopff) Spr-Verlag.

Rosenholtz, Stephen. Monkey Moves. unabridged ed. LC 93-93549. (J). (ps-3). 1993. pap. 14.95 incl. audio (0-9630979-2-X) Rosewd Pubns.

— Move Like the Animals. unabridged ed. LC 91-66970. (Illus.). 32p. (J). (ps-3). 1992. 19.95 incl. audio (0-9630979-1-1); pap. 19.95 incl. audio (0-9630979-0-3) Rosewd Pubns.

Rosenholtz, Susan J. Teachers' Workplace: The Organizational Context of Schooling. (Research on Teaching Ser.). 256p. (C). 1991. pap. text 19.95 (0-8077-3149-8) Tchrs Coll.

Rosenhouse, G. Active Noise Control, 2 vols. Incl. Active Noise Control: Fundamentals for Acoustic Design. 300p. 2000. text 224.00 (1-56252-297-3, 3730); Active Noise Control Vol. 2: Technologies & Design Concepts in Active Noise & Vibration Control. 300p. 2000. 125.00 (1-85312-568-7, 5687, Pub. by WIT Pr); 1999. Set text 212.00 (1-85312-608-X, 608X) Computational Mech MA.

***Rosenhouse, G.** Active Noise Control Vol. 1: Fundamentals for Acoustic Design. 615p. 2000. 279.00 (1-85312-373-0, Pub. by WIT Pr) Computational Mech MA.

Rosenhouse, J., et al, eds. Future & Communication: The Role of Scientific & Technical Communication & Translation in Technology Development & Transfer. LC 96-39415. 302p. 1997. 69.95 (1-57309-071-9); pap. 49.95 (1-57309-070-0) Intl Scholars.

Rosenhouse, Nathan & Williams, Bruce H. House Smart: A Step by Step Guide to Making the Best Deal in Buying or Selling a Home. LC 96-92028. (Illus.). 278p. (Orig.). 1995. pap. 19.95 (0-9651955-0-3) Radio Merch.

Roseningrave, Thomas. Eight Suits of Lessons for the Harpsichord or Spinnet in Most of the Keys. fac. ed. (Monuments of Music & Music Literature in Facsimile, I Ser.: Vol. 27). 1967. lib. bdg. 45.00 (0-8450-2027-7) Broude.

Rosenius, Carl O. The Believer Free from the Law. Hult, Adolf, tr. from SWE. 72p. 1996. pap. 4.95 (1-58572-002-X) Ambasdor Pubns.

— A Faithful Guide to Peace with God. Laache, N. J., ed. Rygh, George T., tr. from SWE. 394p. 1990. reprint ed. pap. 4.95 (1-58572-009-7) Ambasdor Pubns.

— Romans: A Devotional Commentary. Dahlgren, J. Elmer & Peterson, Royal F., trs. from SWE. LC 99-63661. (AFLC Heritage Ser.: Vol. 1). Orig. Title: Romarebrev. 288p. 1999. 15.00 (1-58572-000-3) Ambasdor Pubns.

***Rosenius, Carl Olof.** Rosenius' Devotions: Strength for the Helpless, Lessons for All. Lea, A. P., tr. (AFLC Heritage Ser.: Vol. 2). 2000. write for info. (1-58572-043-7) Ambasdor Pubns.

Rosenkrans, A. Rosenkrans: Family in Europe & America. (Illus.). 333p. 1990. reprint ed. pap. 52.50 (0-8328-1621-3); reprint ed. lib. bdg. 60.50 (0-8328-1620-5) Higginson Bk Co.

Rosenkrantz & Gutmann, Barbara S., eds. Philanthropic Foundations & Resources for Health: An Anthology of Sources. (Medical Care in the United States Ser.: Vol. 14). 200p. 1990. text 15.00 (0-8240-8343-1) Garland.

Rosenkrantz, Barbara G. Public Health & the State: Changing Views in Massachusetts, 1842-1936. LC 70-172321. (Illus.). 271p. 1972. 35.95 (0-674-72235-3) HUP.

— Public Health & the State: Changing Views in Massachusetts, 1842-1936. LC 70-172321. (Illus.). 271p. 1972. pap. 17.95 (0-674-72236-1) HUP.

Rosenkrantz, Barbara G., ed. Animalcular & Cryptogamic Theories on the Origins of Fevers: An Original Anthology. LC 76-40658. (Public Health in America Ser.). 1977. reprint ed. 23.95 (0-405-09839-1) Ayer.

— Carrier State: An Original Anthology. LC 76-40660. (Public Health in America Ser.). (Illus.). 1977. reprint ed. 18.95 (0-405-09870-7) Ayer.

— Clean Water & the Health of the Cities: An Original Anthology. LC 76-40661. (Public Health in America Ser.). (Illus.). 1977. reprint ed. lib. bdg. 23.95 (0-405-09871-5) Ayer.

— First American Medical Association Reports on Public Hygiene in American Cities: An Original Anthology. LC 76-40663. (Public Health in America Ser.). 1977. reprint ed. lib. bdg. 21.95 (0-405-09872-3) Ayer.

— Health in the Southern United States: An Original Anthology. LC 76-40667. (Public Health in America Ser.). (Illus.). 1977. reprint ed. lib. bdg. 29.95 (0-405-09875-8) Ayer.

— Health in the Twentieth Century: An Original Anthology. LC 76-40666. (Public Health in America Ser.). 1977. reprint ed. lib. bdg. 39.95 (0-405-09874-X) Ayer.

— Public Health in America, 46 bks. (Public Health in America Ser.). 1977. reprint ed. lib. bdg. 1242.50 (0-405-09804-9) Ayer.

— Selections from Public Health in Reports & Papers: American Public Health Association (1873-1883) LC 76-4065. (Public Health in America Ser.). 1977. reprint ed. lib. bdg. 34.95 (0-405-09838-3) Ayer.

— Selections from Public Health Reports & Papers Presented at the Meetings of the American Public Health Association (1884-1907) An Original Anthology. LC 76-40657. (Public Health in America Ser.). 1977. reprint ed. lib. bdg. 21.95 (0-405-09883-9) Ayer.

— Selections from the Health-Education Series: An Original Anthology. LC 76-40664. (Public Health in America Ser.). 1977. reprint ed. lib. bdg. 17.95 (0-405-09873-1) Ayer.

— Selections from the Journal of the Massachusetts Association of Boards of Health, 1891-1904: An Original Anthology. LC 76-40669. (Public Health in America Ser.). 1977. lib. bdg. 41.95 (0-405-09878-2) Ayer.

— Sewering the Cities: An Original Anthology. LC 76-40352. (Public Health in America Ser.). (Illus.). 1977. reprint ed. lib. bdg. 23.95 (0-405-09879-0) Ayer.

— Smallpox in Colonial America: An Original Anthology. LC 76-40353. (Public Health in America Ser.). (Illus.). 1977. reprint ed. lib. bdg. 23.95 (0-405-09880-4) Ayer.

— Yellow Fever Studies: An Original Anthology. LC 76-40355. (Public Health in America Ser.). 1977. reprint ed. lib. bdg. 26.95 (0-405-09882-0) Ayer.

Rosenkrantz, Barbara G., ed. see Ackerknecht, Erwin H.

Rosenkrantz, Barbara G., ed. see Boston Medical Commission.

Rosenkrantz, Barbara G., ed. see Bowditch, Henry I.

Rosenkrantz, Barbara G., ed. see Buck, Albert H.

Rosenkrantz, Barbara G., ed. see Budd, William.

Rosenkrantz, Barbara G., ed. see Chapin, Charles V.

Rosenkrantz, Barbara G., ed. see Davis, Michael M., Jr. & Warner, Andrew R.

Rosenkrantz, Barbara G., ed. see Dublin, Louis I. & Lotka, Alfred J.

Rosenkrantz, Barbara G., ed. see Dunglison, Robley.

Rosenkrantz, Barbara G., ed. see Emerson, Haven.

Rosenkrantz, Barbara G., ed. see Emerson, Haven & Luginbuhl, Martha.

Rosenkrantz, Barbara G., ed. see Fish, Hamilton.

Rosenkrantz, Barbara G., ed. see Frost, Wade H.

Rosenkrantz, Barbara G., ed. see Gardner, Mary S.

Rosenkrantz, Barbara G., ed. see Greenwood, Major.

Rosenkrantz, Barbara G., ed. see Hartley, Robert M.

Rosenkrantz, Barbara G., ed. see Hill, Hibbert W.

Rosenkrantz, Barbara G., ed. see Knopf, S. Adolphus.

Rosenkrantz, Barbara G., ed. see MacNutt, J. Scott.

Rosenkrantz, Barbara G., ed. see National Quarantine & Sanitary Convention Staff.

Rosenkrantz, Barbara G., ed. see Richards, Ellen H.

Rosenkrantz, Barbara G., ed. see Richardson, Joseph G.

Rosenkrantz, Barbara G., ed. see Royal College of Physicians of London Staff & Greenwood, Major.

Rosenkrantz, Barbara G., ed. see Rumsey, Henry W.

Rosenkrantz, Barbara G., ed. see Shryock, Richard H.

Rosenkrantz, Barbara G., ed. see Simon, John.

Rosenkrantz, Barbara G., ed. see Sternberg, George M.

Rosenkrantz, Barbara G., ed. see Straus, Lina G.

Rosenkrantz, Barbara G., ed. see Wanklyn, J. Alfred & Chapman, Ernest T.

Rosenkrantz, Barbara G., ed. see Whipple, George C.

Rosenkrantz, Gary S. Haecceity: An Ontological Essay. LC 93-27789. (Philosophical Studies in Philosophy). 266p. (C). 1993. lib. bdg. 164.50 (0-7923-2438-2, Pub. by Kluwer Academic) Kluwer Academic.

Rosenkrantz, Gary S., jt. auth. see Hoffman, Joshua.

Rosenkrantz, Linda. Beyond Jennifer & Jason. 2nd rev. ed. 1994. pap. 65.70 (0-312-10740-4) St Martin.

— Disney Names. (J). 13.99 (0-7868-3104-9, Pub. by Disney Pr) Little.

— The Last Word on First Names. 1997. mass mkt. 5.99 (0-312-96106-5) St Martin.

— The Last Word on First Names: The Definite Guide to the Best & Worst in Baby Names. 4th ed. 1995. pap. 9.95 (0-312-11748-5) St Martin.

Rosenkrantz, Linda & Satran, Pamela R. Beyond Charles & Diana: An Anglophile's Guide to Baby Naming. 128p. (Orig.). 1992. pap. 8.95 (0-312-06902-2) St Martin.

— Beyond Jennifer & Jason. 2nd rev. ed. 320p. 1994. pap. 11.95 (0-312-10426-X) St Martin.

— Beyond Sarah & Sam: An Enlightened Guide to Jewish Baby Naming. 128p. (Orig.). 1992. pap. 8.95 (0-312-06904-9) St Martin.

— Beyond Shannon & Sean: An Enlightened Guide to Irish Baby Naming. 128p. 1992. pap. 8.95 (0-312-06905-7) St Martin.

Rosenkrantz, Linda & Satran, Pamela Redmond. Beyond Jennifer & Jason. 1995. mass mkt. 5.99 (0-312-95444-1) St Martin.

***Rosenkrantz, Linda & Satran, Pamela Redmond.** Beyond Jennifer & Jason, Madison & Montana: What to Name Your Baby Now. 400p. 2000. mass mkt. 5.99 (0-312-97462-0, St Martins Paperbacks) St Martin.

Rosenkrantz, Linda & Satran, Pamela Redmond. Beyond Jennifer & Jason, Madison & Montana: What to Name Your Baby Now. 2nd ed. LC 99-22073. 368p. 1999. pap. 12.95 (0-312-19970-8, St Martins Paperbacks) St Martin.

Rosenkrantz, Roger D. Foundations & Applications of Inductive Probability. xiv, 326p. (Orig.). (C). 1981. pap. text 20.00 (0-917930-03-7); lib. bdg. 36.00 (0-917930-23-1) Ridgeview.

— Inference, Method & Decision. (Synthese Library: No. 115). 277p. 1977. pap. text 51.50 (90-277-0818-5, D Reidel); lib. bdg. 88.00 (90-277-0817-7, D Reidel) Kluwer Academic.

Rosenkrantz, Timme, jt. auth. see Smith, Stuff.

Rosenkrantz, Walther. Introduction to Probability & Statistics for Scientists & Engineers. LC 96-50182. 576p. (C). 1997. 80.94 (0-07-053988-X) McGraw.

An Asterisk (*) at the beginning of an entry indicates that the title is appearing for the first time.

Rosenkranz, Bernhard. Vergleichende Untersuchungen der Altanatolischen Sprachen. (Trends in Linguistics, State-of-the-Art Reports: No. 8). 1978. pap. 66.15 (*90-279-7696-1*) Mouton.
Rosenkranz, E. Joshua. Voter Choice '96: A 50-State Report Card on Choice in the Presidential Elections. LC 96-86145. (Illus.). 200p. (Orig.). 1996. pap. text 25.00 (*0-9654063-0-X*) Brennan Ctr.
Rosenkranz, E. Joshua, contrib. by. Buckley Stops Here: Loosening the Judicial Stranglehold on Campaign Finance Reform. LC 98-5106. xi, 155p. 1998. pap. 11.95 (*0-87078-419-6*) Century Foundation.
Rosenkranz, E. Joshua & Schwartz, Bernard, eds. Reason & Passion: Justice Brennan's Enduring Influence. LC 96-43133. 320p. (C). 1997. 30.00 (*0-393-04110-7*) Norton.
Rosenkranz, E. Joshua & Winger, Richard. What Choice Do We Have? How States Manipulate Ballot Rules to Restrict Voter Choice. 1997. write for info. (*0-9654063-2-6*) Brennan Ctr.
***Rosenkranz, E. Joshua, et al.** If Buckley Fell: Designing a First Amendment That Reinforces Democracy. LC 99-41195. .p. 1999. 11.95 (*0-87078-439-0*) Century Foundation.
Rosenkranz, Gary S., jt. auth. see Hoffman, Joshua.
Rosenkranz, George. Eywtka Trump Leads. 1988. pap. 7.95 (*0-910791-49-X*) Devyn Pr.
Rosenkranz, John & Levenson, Edie. Been There, Done That, in Our RV: Mileage & Memories. (Illus.). 224p. (Orig.). 1997. pap. 12.95 (*0-614-29569-6*) That Reminds Me.
Rosenkranz, John, jt. auth. see Levenson, Edie.
Rosenkranz, Karl. Hegel's Naturphilosophie und die Bearbeitung Derselben Durch Den Italienischen Philosophen Augusto Vera. (GER.). 1979. reprint ed. write for info. (*3-487-06878-8*) G Olms Pubs.
— Studien. (GER.). 1975. reprint ed. write for info. (*3-487-05686-0*) G Olms Pubs.
Rosenkranz, Keith. Vipers in the Storm: Diary of a Gulf War Fighter Pilot. 325p. 1999. 24.95 (*0-07-134670-8*) McGraw.
Rosenkranz, Linda. My Life As a List: 207 Things about My Bronx Childhood. LC 98-27681. (Illus.). 89p. 1999. 15.00 (*0-609-60367-1*) Crown Pub Group.
Rosenkranz, Shirley A., ed. Beyond the Doors. LC 88-72070. (Illus.). 240p. (YA). (gr. 5-12). 1988. pap. 5.95 (*0-9620953-3-8*) A Class Act.
Rosenlicht, Maxwell. Introduction to Analysis. 254p. 1986. reprint ed. pap. text 8.95 (*0-486-65038-3*) Dover.
***Rosenlund, Barbara F.** Shadow Across the Land. LC 99-96195. 130p. (YA). (gr. 6-12). 2000. pap. 8.95 (*0-9679354-0-7*) Coastline Pubs.
Rosenlund, Sigurd J. The Chemical Laboratory - It's Design & Operation: A Practical Guide for Planners of Industrial, Medical, or Educational Facilities. LC 86-31183. (Illus.). 158p. 1987. 89.00 (*0-8155-1110-8*) Noyes.
Rosenman, Ellen B. The Invisible Presence: Virginia Woolf & the Mother-Daughter Relationship. LC 85-23683. (Illus.). xiii, 181p. 1986. text 27.50 (*0-8071-1290-9*) La State U Pr.
— A Room of One's Own: Women Writers & the Politics of Creativity. (Twayne's Masterwork Studies: No. 151). 124p. 1994. 29.00 (*0-8057-8374-1*, Twyne); pap. 18.00 (*0-8057-8594-9*, Twyne) Mac Lib Ref.
Rosenman, Helen, tr. & retold by see Dumont d'Urville, Jules-Sebastien-Cesar.
Rosenman, Jane, ed. see Barrett, Andrea.
Rosenman, Jane, ed. see Bennett, James G.
Rosenman, Jane, ed. see Berkey, Brian F.
Rosenman, Jane, ed. see Carkeet, David.
Rosenman, Jane, ed. see Castaneda, Carlos.
Rosenman, Jane, ed. see DeFerrari, Gabriella.
Rosenman, Jane, ed. see Fried, Stephen.
Rosenman, Jane, ed. see Goddard, Robert.
Rosenman, Jane, ed. see Gold, Ivan.
Rosenman, Jane, ed. see Goodman, Eric.
Rosenman, Jane, ed. see Griffith, Patricia B.
Rosenman, Jane, ed. see Harrison, Jim.
Rosenman, Jane, ed. see Helprin, Mark.
Rosenman, Jane, ed. see Houston, Pam.
Rosenman, Jane, ed. see Hynes, James.
Rosenman, Jane, ed. see Johnson, Fenton.
Rosenman, Jane, ed. see Johnson, Joyce.
Rosenman, Jane, ed. see Johnson, Thomas.
Rosenman, Jane, ed. see Kay, Terry.
Rosenman, Jane, ed. see Klavan, Andrew.
Rosenman, Jane, ed. see Lederer, Richard.
Rosenman, Jane, ed. see Lipman, Elinor.
Rosenman, Jane, ed. see Lombreglia, Ralph.
Rosenman, Jane, ed. see Lott, Bret.
Rosenman, Jane, ed. see Malone, Michael.
Rosenman, Jane, ed. see McCauley, Stephen.
Rosenman, Jane, ed. see McMillan, Terry.
Rosenman, Jane, ed. see Meriwether, Louise.
Rosenman, Jane, ed. see Minot, Susan.
Rosenman, Jane, ed. see Narayan, Kirin.
Rosenman, Jane, jt. ed. see O'Brien, Peggy.
Rosenman, Jane, ed. see Pelletier, Cathie.
Rosenman, Jane, ed. see Phillips, Jayne Anne.
Rosenman, Jane, ed. see Ransmayr, Christopher.
Rosenman, Jane, ed. see Robin, Robert.
Rosenman, Jane, ed. see Stark, Stephen.
Rosenman, Jane, ed. see Steinke, Darcey.
Rosenman, Jane, ed. see Strempek-Shea, Suzanne.
Rosenman, Jane, ed. see Upman, Elinor.
Rosenman, Jane, ed. see Walker, Walter.
Rosenman, Jane, ed. see Ward, Robert.
Rosenman, Jane, ed. see Watson, Larry.
Rosenman, Jane, ed. see Wickersham, Joan.
Rosenman, Jane, ed. see Yoshimoto, Banana.
Rosenman, John B. The Best Laugh Last. LC 81-12990. 218p. 1983. reprint ed. pap. 6.95 (*0-914232-62-2*) McPherson & Co.
Rosenman, Ray H., jt. ed. see Byrne, D. G.
Rosenman, Samuel I. Working with Roosevelt. LC 75-168391. (FDR & the Era of the New Deal Ser.). (Illus.). 1972. reprint ed. lib. bdg. 55.00 (*0-306-70328-9*) Da Capo.
Rosenmann, E., jt. ed. see Cohen, A. M.
Rosenmeier, Henrik, tr. see Kierkegaard, Soren.
Rosenmeier, Rosamond. Anne Bradstreet Revisited. (Twayne's United States Authors Ser.: No. 580). 200p. (C). 1991. 22.95 (*0-8057-7625-7*, Twyne) Mac Lib Ref.
— Lines Out. LC 89-14855. 72p. 1989. pap. 9.95 (*0-914086-88-X*) Alice James Bks.
Rosenmeir, Henrik, tr. see Friis-Johansen, K.
Rosenmeyer, Patricia A. The Poetics of Imitation: Anacreon & the Anacreontic Tradition. (Illus.). 297p. (C). 1992. text 69.95 (*0-521-41044-4*) Cambridge U Pr.
Rosenmeyer, Thomas G. Deina Ta Polla: A Classicist's Checklist of Twenty Literary-Critical Positions. (Arethusa Monographs: No. 12). vii, 74p. (C). 1988. pap. 10.00 (*0-930881-09-5*) Dept Classics.
— Masks of Tragedy, Essays on Six Greek Dramas. LC 78-150417. 261p. (C). 1971. reprint ed. 50.00 (*0-87752-140-9*) Gordian.
— Senecan Drama & Stoic Cosmology. 1989. 48.00 (*0-520-06445-3*, Pub. by U CA Pr) Cal Prin Full Svc.
Rosenmeyer, Thomas G., et al. Meters of Greek & Latin Poetry. LC 62-21264. (C). 1973. reprint ed. pap. text 9.95 (*0-8290-1666-X*) Irvington.
***Rosenmhuller, Joachim.** Game Theory: Stochastics, Information, Strategies & Cooperation. LC 99-51948. (Theory & Decision Library). 1999. write for info. (*0-7923-8673-6*) Kluwer Academic.
Rosenn, Keith S. Law & Inflation. LC 81-51139. 491p. reprint ed. pap. 152.30 (*0-7837-3004-7*, 204293700006) Bks Demand.
Rosenn, Keith S. & Downes, Richard. Corruption & Political Reform in Brazil: The Impact of Collor's Impeachment. LC 98-49839. 184p. 1999. 43.00 (*1-57454-065-3*, Pub. by U Miami N-S Ctr) L Rienner.
Rosenn, Keith S., jt. ed. see Dolinger, Jacob.
Rosenne. World Court. 1997. pap. text, student ed. 20.00 (*90-411-0609-X*) Kluwer Law Intl.
Rosenne, Shabtai. Breach of Treaty. (Hersch Lauterpacht Memorial Lectures: Vol. 1). 154p. 1993. text 59.95 (*0-521-46326-2*) Cambridge U Pr..
— Breach of Treaty. 154p. (C). 1985. 50.00 (*0-906496-36-5*, Pub. by Grotius Pubns Ltd) St Mut.
— An International Law Miscellany. LC 92-34736. 1993. lib. bdg. 314.00 (*0-7923-1742-4*) Kluwer Academic.
— Intervention in the International Court of Justice. LC 92-42957. (Nova et Vetera Iuris Gentium Series, Modern International Law: No. 16). 228p. (C). 1993. lib. bdg. 111.00 (*0-7923-2109-X*) Kluwer Academic.
— The Law & Practice of the International Court. LC 85-2997. 1985. lib. bdg. 304.50 (*90-247-2986-6*) Kluwer Academic.
— The Law & Practice of the International Court, 1920-1996. LC 97-37679. 2068p. 1997. lib. bdg. 617.00 (*90-411-0264-7*, Pub. by M Nijhoff) Kluwer Academic.
— Reflections on International Arbitration & Litigation in the International Court of Justice. (Forum Internationale Ser.: No. 9). 1987. 24.00 (*90-6544-351-7*) Kluwer Law Intl.
— The World Court: What It Is & How It Works. (C). 1989. lib. bdg. 139.50 (*90-247-3772-9*) Kluwer Academic.
— The World Court: What It Is & How It Works. 5th rev. ed. LC 94-15816. (Legal Aspects of International Organizations Ser.: Vol. 16). 1995. lib. bdg. 118.00 (*0-7923-2861-2*) Kluwer Academic.
Rosenne, Shabtai, ed. Documents on the International Court of Justice - Documents Relatifs a la Cour International de Justice: First Bilingual Edition - Premiere Edition Bilinque. (C). 1991. lib. bdg. 328.50 (*0-7923-0912-X*) Kluwer Academic.
— The International Law Commission's Draft Articles on State Responsibility, Pt. 1, Articles 1-35. 392p. 1991. lib. bdg. 173.50 (*0-7923-1179-5*) Kluwer Academic.
Rosenne, Shabtai & Sohn, Louis B., eds. United Nations Convention on the Law of the Sea. 2nd ed. (C). 1989. lib. bdg. 225.50 (*90-247-3719-2*) Kluwer Academic.
Rosenoer, Jonathan. Cyberlaw: The Law of the Internet. LC 96-25479. 362p. 1997. 34.95 (*0-387-94832-5*) Spr-Verlag.
***Rosenoer, Jonathan & Armstrong, Douglas.** Clickable Corporation: Successful Strategies for Capturing the Internet Advantage. LC 99-17594. 176p. 1999. 25.50 (*0-684-85553-4*) Free Pr.
Rosenoer, V. & Rothschild, M. A., eds. Controversies in Clinical Care. LC 80-21593. (Illus.). 312p. 1981. text 40.00 (*0-88331-125-9*) R B Luce.
Rosenof, Theodore. Economics in the Long Run: New Deal Theorists & Their Legacies, 1933-1993. LC 96-24647. 240p. (C). (gr. 13). 1997. 37.50 (*0-8078-2315-5*) U of NC Pr.
***Rosenow, Beverly Pavlik, ed.** The Journal of the Washington State Constitutional Convention, 1889 with Analytical Index. LC 99-61655. 946p. 1999. reprint ed. 250.00 (*1-57588-504-2*, 322900) W S Hein.
Rosenow, Diane. Meeker County Cemeteries Vol. 2: Acton, Darwin, Dassel, Forest City, Forest Prairie, Kingston, Manannah, North Kingston, Swede Grove & Union Grove Townships. LC 93-31365. 140p. (Orig.). 1993. pap. 15.00 (*0-915709-11-2*) Pk Geneal Bk.
— Meeker County Minnesota Cemeteries Vol. 1: Cedar Mills, Collinwood, Cosmos, Danielson, Ellsworth, Greenleaf & Litchfield Townships. LC 93-31365. 132p. (Orig.). 1993. pap. 15.00 (*0-915709-10-4*) Pk Geneal Bk.
Rosenow, Diane, jt. auth. see Pendergast, T. H.
Rosenquist, Glenn C. & Bergsma, Daniel, eds. Morphogenesis & Malinformation of the Cardiovascular System. LC 78-14527. (Alan R. Liss Ser.: Vol. 14, No. 7). 1978. 64.00 (*0-685-03292-2*) March of Dimes.
Rosenquist, Valerie. The Iron Ore Eaters: A Portrait of the Mining Community of Moriah, New York. LC 90-3588. (European Immigrants & American Society Ser.). 260p. 1990. reprint ed. text 20.00 (*0-8240-7430-0*) Garland.
Rosenqvist. Cardiac Pacing: New Advances. 1998. text 95.00 (*0-7020-2215-2*) Bailliere Tindall.
Rosenqvist, Jan O. The Hagiographic Dossier of St. Eugenios of Trebizond in Codex Athous Dionysiou 154: A Critical Edition with Introduction, Translation, Commentary & Indexes. (Studia Byzantina Upsaliensia Ser.: No. 5). 560p. (Orig.). 1996. pap. 92.50 (*91-554-3787-7*) Coronet Bks.
Rosenqvist, Jan O., jt. ed. see Ryden, Lennart.
Rosenqvist, Terkel. Principles of Extractive Metallurgy. (Illus.). 528p. (C). 1991. reprint ed. text 129.00 (*1-878907-13-1*) TechBooks.
Rosenrholtz, Heidi K., jt. auth. see Howkins, Nan L.
Rosenroth, Knorr Von, see Von Rosenroth, Knorr.
Rosenschein, Jeffrey S. & Zlotkin, Gilad. Rules of Encounter: Designing Convention for Automated Negotiation among Computers. LC 94-16589. (Artificial Intelligence Ser.). (Illus.). 253p. 1994. 39.50 (*0-262-18159-2*) MIT Pr.
Rosenschein, Stanley J., jt. ed. see Agre, Philip E.
Rosensfit, Gail. MaxNotes - Beowulf. (MaxNotes Ser.). 128p. 1999. pap. text 3.95 (*0-87891-998-8*) Res & Educ.
Rosenshein & Rock. Surgery in the Retroperitoneal Space. 1989. 125.00 (*0-397-50949-9*) Lppncott W & W.
Rosenshein, Joseph & Bennett, Gordon D., eds. Groundwater Hydraulics. (Water Resources Monograph Ser.: Vol. 9). (Illus.). 407p. (Orig.). 1983. 18.00 (*0-87590-310-X*) Am Geophysical.
Rosenshontz. Family Vacation. (Rosenshontz Ser.). (J). (ps-6). 1993. pap. 8.98 incl. audio (*1-879496-60-7*) Lightyear Entrtnmnt.
— It's the Truth. (Rosenshontz Ser.). (J). (ps-6). 1993. pap. 8.98 incl. audio (*1-879496-54-2*) Lightyear Entrtnmnt.
— Share It. (Rosenshontz Ser.). (J). (ps-6). 1993. pap. 8.98 incl. audio (*1-879496-57-7*) Lightyear Entrtnmnt.
— Teddy Bears' Jamboree. (J). (ps-k). 1994. pap. 12.95 incl. VHS (*1-879496-41-0*) Lightyear Entrtnmnt.
Rosenshontz, et al. Teddy Bear's Picnic. (J). (ps-k). 1993. pap. 12.95 incl. VHS (*1-879496-40-2*, 54010-3) Lightyear Entrtnmnt.
Rosenshontz. Tickles You! (Rosenshontz Ser.). (J). (ps-6). 1993. pap. 8.98 incl. audio (*1-879496-35-6*) Lightyear Entrtnmnt.
— Uh-Oh! (Rosenshontz Ser.). (J). (ps-6). 1993. pap. 8.98 incl. audio (*1-879496-38-0*) Lightyear Entrtnmnt.
Rosensohn, William L. The Phenomenology of Charles S. Pierce: From the Doctrine of Categories to Phaneroscopy. ix, 109p. 1974. pap. 24.00 (*90-6032-024-7*, Pub. by B R Gruner) Humanities.
***Rosenstand, Nina.** The Moral of the Story: An Introduciton to Ethics. 3rd ed. LC 99-17115. xi, 564p. 1999. pap. text 44.95 (*0-7674-0595-1*, 0595-1) Mayfield Pub.
Rosenstein, Alan H. Stress. Chesney, Margaret A. & Wiltsek, Nancy, eds. (Illus.). 23p. 1986. pap. 2.50 (*0-933161-06-9*) Better H Prog.
***Rosenstein, Beryl J.** Manual Pediatra Practico. 3rd ed. (C). 1998. text 24.49 (*84-8174-344-5*) Mosby Inc.
Rosenstein, Beryl J. & Seidel, Henry M. Primary Care of the Newborn. 2nd ed. (Illus.). 664p. (C). (gr. 13). 1996. pap. text 32.95 (*0-8151-8681-9*, 28972) Mosby Inc.
Rosenstein, Beryl J., jt. auth. see Fossarelli.
Rosenstein, Carolyn, jt. auth. see Light, Ivan H.
Rosenstein, Eliezer, jt. ed. see Lafferty, William M.
Rosenstein, Emilio S. Diccionario de Especialidades Odontolgicas. (SPA.). 360p. 1989. 85.00 (*0-7859-3446-4*) Fr & Eur.
— Specialized Pharmaceuticals Dictionary: Diccionario de Especialidades Farmaceuticas. 28th ed. (SPA.). 1350p. 1982. 49.95 (*0-8288-1877-0*, S39848) Fr & Eur.
Rosenstein, G. Z., ed. Income & Choice in Biological Control Systems: A Framework for Understanding the Function & Dysfunction of the Brain. 176p. (C). 1991. text 49.95 (*0-8058-0072-7*) L Erlbaum Assocs.
Rosenstein, Ira. Left on the Field to Die Pt. 1: Timothy Richardson. LC 84-242659. 27p. (Orig.). 1980. pap. 3.00 (*0-9605438-0-5*) Starlight Pr.
— Left on the Field to Die Pt. 2: Yehudi Weismann. LC 84-242659. 42p. (Orig.). 1982. pap. 4.00 (*0-9605438-1-3*) Starlight Pr.
— Left on the Field to Die Pt. 3: Peter Koslov. LC 84-242659. 30p. (Orig.). 1984. pap. 3.00 (*0-9605438-2-1*) Starlight Pr.
— Twenty-Two Sonnets. LC 87-102639. 44p. (Orig.). 1986. pap. 4.00 (*0-9605438-3-X*) Starlight Pr.
Rosenstein, Ira, ed. Starlight Poets One. 32p. (Orig.). 1990. pap. 4.00 (*0-9605438-4-8*) Starlight Pr.
— Starlight Poets Two: Sonnets. 40p. (Orig.). 1992. pap. 5.00 (*0-9605438-5-6*) Starlight Pr.
Rosenstein, Joseph G., et al. Discrete Mathematics in the Schools. LC 97-23277. (DIMACS Series in Discrete Mathemetics & Theoretical Computer Science). 452p. 1997. text 30.00 (*0-8218-0448-0*) Am Math.
Rosenstein, Julius, ed. see Crawford, Craig, et al.
Rosenstein, Lucy L. The Devotional Poetry of Svami Haridas: A Study of Early Braj Bhasa Verse. (Groningen Oriental Studies: Vol. XII). xvii, 416p. 1998. pap. 92.00 (*90-6980-102-7*, Pub. by Egbert Forsten) Hodlder & Stoughton.
Rosenstein, Mark. In Praise of Apples: A Harvest of History, Horticulture, & Recipes. Rich, Chris, ed. LC 96-22156. (Illus.). 176p. 1996. 34.95 (*1-887374-04-3*) Lark Books.
— In Praise of Apples: A Harvest of History, Horticulture & Recipes. Rich, Chris, ed. LC 96-22156. (Illus.). 176p. 1999. pap. 19.95 (*1-57990-124-7*, Pub. by Lark Books) Random.
Rosenstein, Marvin, jt. ed. see Kereiakes, James G.
Rosenstein, Mordechai, jt. auth. see Lebovits, Yehudah.
Rosenstein, Nathan S. Imperatores Victi: Military Defeat & Aristocratic Competition in the Middle & Late Republic. LC 89-20653. 208p. 1990. 45.00 (*0-520-06939-0*, Pub. by U CA Pr) Cal Prin Full Svc.
Rosenstein, Nathan S., jt. auth. see Raaflaub, Kurt A.
Rosenstein, Neil. Rabbi Elijah (1720-1797), the Gaon of Vilna & His Cousinhood LC 98-160281. xvi, 437 p. 1997. write for info. (*0-9610578-5-8*) Computer Ctr Jewish Geog.
— The Unbroken Chain. (C). 1990. 79.95 (*0-9610578-4-X*) CIS Comm.
Rosenstein, Neil & Bernstein, Charles B. From King David to Baron David: The Genealogical Connections Between Baron Guy de Rothschild & Baroness Alix de Rothschild. LC 89-81367. (Illus.). 78p. (Orig.). 1990. write for info. (*0-9610578-3-1*); pap. 7.00 (*0-685-33278-0*) Computer Ctr Jewish Geog.
Rosenstein, Sheldon, jt. auth. see Kernahan, Desmond A.
Rosenstein, Sophie, et al. Modern Acting: A Manual. 1936. 5.00 (*0-573-69017-0*) French.
Rosenstiehl, Agnes. Livre de la Langue Francaise. (Gallimard - Decouverte Cadet Ser.: No. 24). (FRE., Illus.). 93p. (J). (gr. 4-9). 1985. 16.95 (*2-07-039524-3*) Schoenhof.
Rosenstiel, Helene Von, see Von Rosenstiel, Helene.
Rosenstiel, Leonie. The Life & Works of Lili Boulanger. LC 75-18244. 408p. (C). 1978. 42.50 (*0-8386-1796-4*) Fairleigh Dickinson.
— Nadia Boulanger: A Life in Music. 440p. 1998. pap. 15.95 (*0-393-31713-7*) Norton.
Rosenstiel, Leonie, jt. auth. see Orrmont, Arthur.
Rosenstiel, Leonie, jt. ed. see Orrmont, Arthur.
Rosenstiel, Stephen, et al. Contemporary Fixed Prosthodontics. 3rd ed. (Illus.). 706p. (C). (gr. 13). 2000. text 69.95 (*0-8151-5559-X*, 30603) Mosby Inc.
Rosenstiel, Stephen F., et al. Contemporary Fixed Prosthodontics. 2nd ed. LC 93-40196. (Illus.). 688p. (C). (gr. 13). 1994. text 74.00 (*0-8016-6528-0*, 06528) Mosby Inc.
Rosenstiel, Tom. The Beat Goes On: President Clinton's First Year with the Media. LC 94-25761. 59p. 1994. 9.95 (*0-87078-369-6*) Century Foundation.
— Strange Bedfellows: How Television & the Presidential Candidates Changed American Politics, 1992. (Illus.). 384p. (J). 1994. pap. 14.45 (*0-7868-8022-8*, Pub. by Hyperion) Time Warner.
Rosenstock, Adele. Etruria. (Illus.). 64p. (Orig.). 1994. pap. write for info. (*0-9641829-0-4*) A Rosenstock.
Rosenstock Arts Staff. American Art in Colorado Collections. (Documents of Colorado Art Ser.). (Illus.). 30p. (Orig.). 1983. pap. 24.95 (*0-938075-47-0*) Ocean View Bks.
Rosenstock, Gabriel. Beginner's Irish. (Beginner's Language Ser.). (IRI.). 200p. 2000. pap. 14.95 (*0-7818-0784-0*) Hippocrene Bks.
— Portrait of the Artist As an Abominable Snowman. LC 89-82064. (ENG & IRI.). 112p. 1990. pap. 18.95 (*0-948259-56-6*, Pub. by Forest Bks) Dufour.
***Rosenstock, Gabriel.** Portrait of the Artist as an Abominable Snowman. 108p. 2000. pap. 10.00 (*1-58345-124-2*) Domhan Bks.
Rosenstock, Gabriel, ed. Irish Love Poems, Quotations, & Triads. LC 98-37957. 153p. 1998. 11.95 (*0-7818-0644-5*) Hippocrene Bks.
Rosenstock, Gabriel, tr. see Breathnach, Padraic.
Rosenstock, Gabriel, tr. see Conaola, Dara O.
Rosenstock, Harvey A. & Rosenstock, Judith D. Tu Estadia en el Hospital . . . Va a Ser Muy Buena.Tr. of Your Hospital Stay...It'll Be Okay. (SPA., Illus.). 36p. (Orig.). (J). (ps-5). 1988. pap. 4.95 (*0-9622172-2-0*) D Miller Fndtn.
— Your Hospital Stay...It'll Be Okay. (Illus.). 36p. (Orig.). (J). (ps-5). 1988. pap. 4.95 (*0-9622172-1-2*) D Miller Fndtn.
Rosenstock, Harvey A., et al. Journey Through Divorce: Five Stages Toward Recovery. 128p. 1988. 28.95 (*0-89885-403-2*, Kluwer Acad Hman Sci) Kluwer Academic.
***Rosenstock-Huessay, Eugen.** Velikie Revoliutsii: Avtobiografiia Zapadnogo Cheloveka. Vitaly, Makhlin, tr. from ENG. LC 99-49962.Tr. of Out of Revolution: Autobiography of Western Man. (RUS., Illus.). 704p. 1999. pap. 25.00 (*1-55779-120-1*) Hermitage Pubs.
Rosenstock-Huessy, Eugen. American Social History - 1959. (Eugen Rosenstock-Huessy Lectures: Vol. 19). 622p. 1997. pap. 255.00 incl. audio (*0-912148-38-1*) Argo Bks.
— Christian Future. 248p. 1997. pap. 19.00 (*0-912148-10-1*) Argo Bks.
— Circulation of Thought - 1954. (Eugen Rosenstock-Huessy Lectures: Vol. 9). 570p. 1997. pap. 203.00 incl. audio (*0-912148-28-4*) Argo Bks.
— Circulation of Thought - 1956. (Eugen Rosenstock-Huessy Lectures: Vol. 15). 21p. 1997. pap. 10.00 incl. audio (*0-912148-34-9*) Argo Bks.
— Circulation of Thought - 1949. (Eugen Rosenstock-Huessy Lectures: Vol. 1). 114p. 1997. pap. 42.00 incl. audio (*0-912148-20-9*) Argo Bks.
— Comparative Religion - 1954. (Eugen Rosenstock-Huessy Lectures: Vol. 8). 638p. 1997. pap. 210.00 incl. audio (*0-912148-27-6*) Argo Bks.

R

— Cross of Reality, 1953, Vol. 5. (Eugen Rosenstock-Huessy Lectures: Vol. 28). 520p. 1997. pap. 184.00 incl. audio (*0-912148-24-1*) Argo Bks.

— Cross of Reality, 1965, Vol. 28. (Eugen Rosenstock-Huessy Lectures). 10p. 1997. pap. 10.00 incl. audio (*0-614-05402-8*); pap. 10.00 (*0-912148-47-0*); audio 5.00 (*0-614-05401-X*) Argo Bks.

— Cruciform Character, 1967, Vol. 31. (Eugen Rosenstock-Huessy Lectures: Vol. 26). 65p. 1997. pap. 30.00 incl. audio (*0-912148-50-0*) Argo Bks.

— Economy of Times - 1965, Vol. 26. (Eugen Rosenstock-Huessy Lectures). 79p. 1997. pap. 34.00 incl. audio (*0-614-05398-6*); pap. 34.00 (*0-912148-45-4*); audio 25.00 (*0-614-05397-8*) Argo Bks.

— Fashions of Atheism - 1968. (Eugen Rosenstock-Huessy Lectures: Vol. 33). 20p. 1997. pap. 10.00 incl. audio (*0-912148-52-7*) Argo Bks.

— Four Disangelists - 1954. (Eugen Rosenstock-Huessy Lectures: Vol. 10). 23p. 1997. pap. 17.00 incl. audio (*0-912148-29-2*) Argo Bks.

— Grammatical Method - 1962. (Eugen Rosenstock-Huessy Lectures: Vol. 24). 51p. 1997. pap. 23.00 incl. audio (*0-912148-43-8*) Argo Bks.

— Greek Philosophy - 1956. (Eugen Rosenstock-Huessy Lectures: Vol. 16). 664p. 1997. pap. 207.00 incl. audio (*0-912148-35-7*) Argo Bks.

— Hinge of Generations - 1953. (Eugen Rosenstock-Huessy Lectures: Vol. 6). 201p. 1997. pap. 87.00 incl. audio (*0-912148-25-X*) Argo Bks.

— Historiography - 1959. (Eugen Rosenstock-Huessy Lectures: Vol. 20). 581p. 1997. pap. 195.00 incl. audio (*0-912148-39-X*) Argo Bks.

— History Must Be Told - 1955. (Eugen Rosenstock-Huessy Lectures: Vol. 13). 14p. 1997. pap. 10.00 incl. audio (*0-912148-32-2*) Argo Bks.

— History Must Be Told - 1954, Vol. 11. (Eugen Rosenstock-Huessy Lectures: Vol. 14). 14p. 1997. pap. 10.00 incl. audio (*0-912148-30-6*) Argo Bks.

— I Am an Impure Thinker. LC 77-103630. 206p. 1970. 19.00 (*0-912148-03-9*) Argo Bks.

— Liberal Arts College - 1960. (Eugen Rosenstock-Huessy Lectures: Vol. 22). 26p. 1997. pap. 15.00 incl. audio (*0-912148-41-1*) Argo Bks.

— Life Lines: Quotations from the Work of Eugen Rosenstock-Huessy. Gardner, Clinton C., ed. LC 88-19392. 1988. pap. 8.00 (*0-912148-16-0*) Argo Bks.

— Lingo of Linguistics, 1966. (Eugen Rosenstock-Huessy Lectures: Vol. 29). 63p. 1997. pap. 23.00 incl. audio (*0-912148-48-9*) Argo Bks.

— Make Bold to Be Ashamed. (Eugen Rosenstock-Huessy Lectures: Vol. 7). 37p. 1997. pap. 18.00 incl. audio (*0-912148-26-8*) Argo Bks.

— Man Must Teach - 1959. (Eugen Rosenstock-Huessy Lectures: Vol. 21). 20p. 1997. pap. 10.00 incl. audio (*0-912148-40-3*) Argo Bks.

— Multiformity of Man. 1973. pap. 7.00 (*0-912148-06-3*) Argo Bks.

— Origin of Speech. LC 81-20527. 1981. pap. 15.00 (*0-912148-13-6*) Argo Bks.

— Out of Revolution: Autobiography of Western Man. LC 93-24321. 820p. 1993. 39.95 (*0-85496-400-2*) Argo Bks.

— Out of Revolution: Autobiography of Western Man. rev. ed. LC 70-103631. (Illus.). 795p. 1993. pap. 24.95 (*0-912148-05-5*) Argo Bks.

— Peace Corps, 1966. (Eugen Rosenstock-Huessy Lectures: Vol. 30). 40p. 1997. pap. 21.00 incl. audio (*0-912148-49-7*) Argo Bks.

— Planetary Service. Huessy, Mark & Von Moltke, Freya, trs. from GER. LC 78-68422. 1978. pap. 13.00 (*0-912148-09-8*) Argo Bks.

— Potential Teachers - 1952. (Eugen Rosenstock-Huessy Lectures: Vol. 4). 34p. 1997. pap. 15.00 incl. audio (*0-912148-23-3*) Argo Bks.

— Practical Knowledge of the Soul. Gardner, Clinton C., ed. Huessy, Mark & Von Moltke, Freya, trs. 66p. 1988. pap. 6.00 (*0-912148-00-4*) Argo Bks.

— Rosenstock-Huessy Papers, Vol. 1. 1981. pap. 25.00 (*0-912148-15-2*) Argo Bks.

— St. Augustine - 1962. (Eugen Rosenstock-Huessy Lectures: Vol. 25). 149p. 1997. pap. 57.00 incl. audio (*0-912148-44-6*) Argo Bks.

— Speech & Reality. LC 72-103629. 1970. 22.00 (*0-912148-01-2*); pap. 18.00 (*0-912148-02-0*) Argo Bks.

— Talk with Franciscans - 1965. (Eugen Rosenstock-Huessy Lectures: Vol. 27). 36p. 1997. pap. 15.00 incl. audio (*0-912148-46-2*) Argo Bks.

— Universal History - 1955. (Eugen Rosenstock-Huessy Lectures: Vol. 14). 91p. 1997. pap. 30.00 incl. audio (*0-912148-33-0*) Argo Bks.

— Universal History - 1954. (Eugen Rosenstock-Huessy Lectures: Vol. 12). 540p. 1997. pap. 192.00 incl. audio (*0-912148-31-4*) Argo Bks.

— Universal History - 1951. (Eugen Rosenstock-Huessy Lectures: Vol. 3). 22p. 1997. pap. 10.00 incl. audio (*0-912148-22-5*) Argo Bks.

— Universal History - 1957. (Eugen Rosenstock-Huessy Lectures: Vol. 18). 595p. 1997. pap. 210.00 incl. audio (*0-912148-37-3*) Argo Bks.

— Universal History - 1956. (Eugen Rosenstock-Huessy Lectures: Vol. 17). 218p. 1997. pap. 87.00 incl. audio (*0-912148-36-5*) Argo Bks.

— Universal History - 1949. (Eugen Rosenstock-Huessy Lectures: Vol. 2). 141p. 1997. pap. 53.00 incl. audio (*0-912148-21-7*) Argo Bks.

— Universal History - 1967, Vol. 32. (Eugen Rosenstock-Huessy Lectures: 32). 396p. 1997. pap. 143.00 incl. audio (*0-912148-51-9*) Argo Bks.

— The University - 1968. (Eugen Rosenstock-Huessy Lectures: Vol. 34). 8p. 1997. pap. 10.00 incl. audio (*0-912148-53-5*) Argo Bks.

— What Future Professions - 1960. (Eugen Rosenstock-Huessy Lectures: Vol. 23). 93p. 1997. pap. 34.00 incl. audio (*0-912148-42-X*) Argo Bks.

Rosenstock-Huessy, Eugen & Battles, Ford L. Magna Carta Latina: The Privilege of Singing, Articulating & Reading a Language & Keeping It Alive. 2nd ed. LC 75-23378. (Pittsburgh Reprint Ser.: No. 1). 296p. 1997. reprint ed. pap. text 19.00 (*0-915138-07-7*) Argo Bks.

Rosenstock, Jerome. The Law of Chemical & Pharmaceutical Invention: Patent & Nonpatent Protection. 901p. ring bd. 155.00 (*0-316-75788-8*, 57888) Aspen Law.

— The Law of Chemical & Pharmaceutical Invention: Patent & Nonpatent Protection. LC 98-31958. 1998. ring bd. 175.00 (*0-7355-0264-1*) Panel Pubs.

— Patent Interference Practice Handbook. LC 98-21054. 1998. ring bd. 160.00 (*0-7355-0114-9*) Panel Pubs.

Rosenstock, Judith D., jt. auth. see Rosenstock, Harvey A.

Rosenstock, Laura. Christopher Wilmarth. (Illus.). 48p. (Orig.). 1989. pap. 9.95 (*0-87070-644-6*, 0-8109-6084-2) Mus of Modern Art.

— Christopher Wilmarth. (Illus.). 48p. 1990. pap. 9.95 (*0-8109-6084-2*, Pub. by Abrams) Time Warner.

***Rosenstock, Linda, frwd.** Identifying High-Risk Small Business Industries: The Basis for Preventing Occupational Injury, Illness & Fatality. (Illus.). 153p. 2000. pap. text 30.00 (*0-7567-0044-2*) DIANE Pub.

Rosenstock, Linda & Cullen, Mark R. Clinical Occupational Medicine. (Illus.). 305p. 1986. text 38.00 (*0-7216-1145-1*, W B Saunders Co) Harcrt Hlth Sci Grp.

— Textbook of Clinical Occupational & Environmental Medicine. LC 93-8640. (Illus.). 944p. 1994. text 145.00 (*0-7216-3482-6*, W B Saunders Co) Harcrt Hlth Sci Grp.

Rosenstock, Linda, jt. ed. see Joseph, Stephen C.

***Rosenstock, Linda Reichlin.** Starry Skies. (Peel & Sparkle Bks.). (Illus.). 16p. (YA). (gr. 1 up). 2000. 14.99 (*1-58476-014-1*) Innovative Kids.

Rosenstock, Morton. Louis Marshall: Defender of Jewish Rights. LC 65-19608. 335p. reprint ed. pap. 103.90 (*0-7837-3680-0*, 204355400009) Bks Demand.

Rosenstock, R., ed. see Maillard, Jean.

Rosenstock, Raymond H., ed. see Maillard, Jean.

Rosenstock, Richard. Rosenstock's Section 1983 Civil Rights Digest. 1997. pap. write for info. (*1-58012-016-4*) James Pub Santa Ana.

— Rosenstock's Section 1983 Civil Rights Digest. 2nd ed. 1998. pap. write for info. (*1-58012-029-6*) James Pub Santa Ana.

***Rosenstock, Richard.** Rosenstock's Section 1983 Civil Rights Digest. 3rd ed. 1999. pap. write for info. (*1-58012-056-3*) James Pub Santa Ana.

***Rosenstock, Ron, photos by.** The Light of Ireland. 2000th ed. (Illus.). 64p. 2000. 45.00 (*0-615-11218-8*) Silver Strand.

Rosenstock, S. S. Habitat Relationships of Breeding Birds in Northern Arizona Ponderosa Pine & Pine-Oak Forests. (Arizona Game & Fish Department Technical Report: No. 23). (Illus.). 53p. (Orig.). 1996. pap. 5.00 (*0-917563-30-1*) AZ Game & Fish.

Rosenstock, S. X. United Artists. Howard, Richard, ed. LC 95-53351. (James Dickey Contemporary Poetry Ser.). 70p. 1996. pap. 9.95 (*1-57003-131-2*); text 15.95 (*1-57003-130-4*) U of SC Pr.

Rosenstone, Robert A. Mirror in the Shrine: American Encounters with Meiji Japan. LC 87-31053. (Illus.). 336p. 1988. text 39.00 (*0-674-57641-1*) HUP.

— Mirror in the Shrine: American Encounters with Meiji Japan. 336p. 1991. pap. 18.00 (*0-674-57642-X*, ROSMIX) HUP.

— Revisioning History: Film & the Construction of the Past. 232p. 1995. pap. text 16.95 (*0-691-02534-7*, Pub. by Princeton U Pr) Cal Prin Full Svc.

— Romantic Revolutionary: A Biography of John Reed. 464p. 1990. pap. text 12.95 (*0-674-77938-X*) HUP.

— Visions of the Past: The Challenge of Film to Our Idea of History. LC 95-6720. 288p. (C). 1995. text 38.50 (*0-674-94097-0*); pap. text 18.50 (*0-674-94098-9*) HUP.

Rosenstone, Steven J. Third Parties in America: Citizen Response to Major Party Failure. 2nd expanded rev. ed. LC 96-510. 306p. 1984. pap. text 16.95 (*0-691-02613-0*, Pub. by Princeton U Pr) Cal Prin Full Svc.

Rosenstone, Steven J., et al, contrib. by. American National Election Study, 1994 Vol. I: Post-Election Survey, 3 vols., Set. 2nd ed. LC 95-82255. (American National Election Studies). 352p. (Orig.). 1996. pap. write for info. (*0-89138-853-2*) ICPSR.

— American National Election Study, 1994 Vol. II: Post-Election Survey, 3 vols., Set. 2nd ed. LC 95-82255. (American National Election Studies). 600p. (Orig.). 1996. pap. write for info. (*0-89138-854-0*) ICPSR.

— American National Election Study, 1994 Vol. III: Post-Election Survey, 3 vols., Set. 2nd ed. LC 95-82255. (American National Election Studies). 672p. (Orig.). 1996. pap. write for info. (*0-89138-855-9*) ICPSR.

Rosenstone, Steven J. & Hansen, John M. Mobilization, Participation & Democracy in America. LC 92-34552. (New Topics in Politics Ser.). (Illus.). 333p. (Orig.). (C). 1993. pap. text 28.00 (*0-02-403660-9*, Macmillan Coll) P-H.

Rosenstone, Steven J., et al. Third Parties in America. LC 83-43091. 266p. 1984. pap. 16.95 (*0-691-02225-9*, Pub. by Princeton U Pr) Cal Prin Full Svc.

— Third Parties in America: Citizen Response to Major Party Failure. 2nd expanded rev. ed. LC 96-510. (Illus.). 325p. 1996. reprint ed. pap. 100.80 (*0-608-07176-5*, 206740100009) Bks Demand.

Rosenstone, Steven J., jt. auth. see Wolfinger, Raymond E.

Rosenstrach, Jerry, et al. Get Ready-Get Set-Go-Go-Go! A Marketing Primer for Home Health Care Professionals. Borgstadt, Nancy, ed. (Orig.). 1997. pap. 39.95 (*0-9658572-0-4*) Vis Nurse Amer.

Rosenstreich, Susan L., ed. Encounters with Quebec: Emerging Perspectives on Quebecois Narrative Fiction. 181p. 1998. pap. 17.00 (*1-883058-58-9*) Global Pubns.

Rosensweig, Jeffery. Winning the Global Game. LC 98-17194. 272p. 1998. 29.50 (*0-684-84919-4*) S&S Trade.

Rosensweig, Linda. New Vegetarian Cuisine: Two Hundred & Fifty Satisfying Recipes for Superior Health. Prevention Magazine Food Editors, ed. LC 93-17792. 376p. 1993. 26.95 (*0-87596-168-1*) Rodale Pr Inc.

— New Vegetarian Cuisine: Two Hundred & Fifty Satisfying Recipes for Superior Health. LC 93-17792. (Illus.). 376p. 1996. pap. 14.95 (*0-87596-314-5*) Rodale Pr Inc.

***Rosensweig, Linda.** Vegetarian & More! Versatile Vegetarian Recipes with Optional Meat Add-Ins. LC 99-89916. 2000. 22.50 (*1-57954-112-7*) Rodale Pr Inc.

Rosensweig, R. E. Ferrohydrodynamics. unabridged ed. LC 97-26734. (Illus.). 350p. 1998. reprint ed. pap. 11.95 (*0-486-67834-2*) Dover.

Rosensweig, Roy. The Park & the People. 1995. pap. 19.95 (*0-8050-3242-8*) H Holt & Co.

Rosentahl, A., et al. Deutsch-Finnisches Schulworterbuch. (FIN & GER.). 673p. 1976. 39.95 (*0-8288-5577-3*, M9637) Fr & Eur.

Rosental, I. L., jt. auth. see Nikitin, Yu P.

Rosenthal. California Here I Come. 48p. 1998. spiral bd. 7.81 (*0-07-292778-X*) McGraw.

— Critical Care. 1993. 145.00 (*0-316-75738-1*, Little Brwn Med Div) Lppncott W & W.

— Critical Care Medicine: Medical. 1993. 39.00 (*0-316-75735-7*) Little.

— Microbiology & Immunology Review. 2000. text. write for info. (*0-323-00840-2*) Harcrt Hlth Sci Grp.

— Rebecca's Dream. 48p. 1998. spiral bd. 7.81 (*0-07-292777-1*) McGraw.

— A Very Good Year. 48p. 1998. spiral bd. 7.81 (*0-07-292780-1*) McGraw.

— Wide Eyed & Legless. 1995. pap. text. write for info. (*0-582-24950-3*, Pub. by Addison-Wesley) Longman.

Rosenthal, jt. auth. see Shaw.

***Rosenthal, A. M.** Thirty-Eight Witnesses. LC 98-34317. 134p. 1999. pap. 12.95 (*0-520-21527-3*, Pub. by U CA Pr) Cal Prin Full Svc.

Rosenthal, Abby. Ardor's Hut. 64p. (Orig.). 1990. 25.00 (*0-934184-22-4*); pap. 15.00 (*0-934184-21-6*) Alembic Pr.

Rosenthal, Abigail L. Conversions: A Philosophical Memoir. LC 93-44719. 240p. (C). 1995. pap. 22.95 (*1-56639-220-9*); text 69.95 (*1-56639-219-5*) Temple U Pr.

Rosenthal, Alan. The Decline of Representative Democracy: Process, Participation, & Power in State Legislatures. LC 97-38196. 369p. (YA). (gr. 11). 1997. pap. 24.95 (*0-87187-974-3*); text 34.95 (*0-87187-975-1*) Congr Quarterly.

— Drawing the Line: Legislative Ethics in the States (A Twentieth Century Fund Book) LC 95-51513. xiv, 270p. 1996. text 45.00 (*0-8032-3919-X*) U of Nebr Pr.

— Governors & Legislatures: Contending Powers. 223p. 1990. 23.95 (*0-87187-545-4*) Congr Quarterly.

— Impurely Academic. LC 79-65226. 88p. 1979. pap. text 19.95 (*0-87855-745-8*) Transaction Pubs.

***Rosenthal, Alan.** Jerusalem, Take One! Memoirs of a Jewish Filmmaker. LC 99-43223. 2000. pap. 24.95 (*0-8093-2312-5*); pap. 24.95 (*0-8093-2311-7*) S Ill U Pr.

Rosenthal, Alan. Legislative Performance in the States: Explorations of Committee Behavior. LC 73-10576. 1974. 14.95 (*0-02-927300-5*) Free Pr.

— Objectif France. annot. ed. (College French Ser.). (C). 1993. mass mkt., teacher ed. 58.95 (*0-8384-3738-9*) Heinle & Heinle.

— The Third House: Lobbyists & Lobbying in the States. LC 92-28705. 242p. 1992. 34.95 (*0-87187-671-X*); pap. 20.95 (*0-87187-672-8*) Congr Quarterly.

— Writing, Directing, & Producing Documentary Films & Videos. rev. ed. LC 95-17159. (C). 1996. pap. 19.95 (*0-8093-2014-2*) S Ill U Pr.

— Writing, Directing, & Producing Documentary Films & Videos. 2nd rev. ed. LC 95-17159. 320p. (C). 1996. 39.95 (*0-8093-2013-4*) S Ill U Pr.

— Writing Docudrama: Dramatizing Reality for Film & TV. 224p. 1994. pap. 29.95 (*0-240-80195-4*, Focal) Buttrwrth-Heinemann.

Rosenthal, Alan, ed. New Challenges to Documentary. 1987. pap. 27.50 (*0-520-05724-4*, Pub. by U CA Pr) Cal Prin Full Svc.

— Why Docudrama? Fact Fiction on Film & TV. LC 97-52387. 480p. 1999. 60.00 (*0-8093-2186-6*) S Ill U Pr.

Rosenthal, Alan & Fuhrman, Susan. Legislative Education Leadership in the States. 118p. 1981. pap. 8.00 (*0-318-03014-4*); lib. bdg. 14.00 (*0-318-03013-6*) Inst Educ Lead.

Rosenthal, Alan & Katz, Illana. Show Me Where It Hurts! Chiropractic Care. (J). (gr. k-6). 1993. pap. 9.95 (*1-882388-10-0*) Real Life Strybks.

Rosenthal, Alan, jt. ed. see Fuhrman, Susan.

Rosenthal, Alan, jt. ed. see Huwa, Randy.

Rosenthal, Alan D., jt. auth. see Katz, Illana.

Rosenthal, Albert H. The Social Programs in Sweden: A Search for Security in a Free Society. LC 67-27098. 213p. reprint ed. pap. 66.10 (*0-608-14154-2*, 205590600039) Bks Demand.

Rosenthal, Albert J., jt. auth. see Henkin, Louis.

***Rosenthal, Albi & Gray, Jaqueline.** Obiter Scripta: Essays, Lectures, Articles, Interviews & Reviews on Music & Other Subjects. LC 00-32948. (FRE, GER, ITA & ENG.). 2000. write for info. (*0-8108-3861-3*) Scarecrow.

Rosenthal, Allen, ed. Why Docudrama? LC 97-52387. 480p. 1999. pap. 29.95 (*0-8093-2187-4*) S Ill U Pr.

Rosenthal, Allen M. Your Mind, the Magician. LC 90-82481. (Illus.). 143p. (Orig.). 1991. pap. 10.95 (*0-87516-619-9*) DeVorss.

Rosenthal, Amy K. The Book of Eleven: An Itemized Collection of Brain Lint. LC 98-14068. 144p. 1998. 9.95 (*0-8362-6775-3*) Andrews & McMeel.

Rosenthal, Amy Krouse. Same Phrase Describes My Marriage & My Breasts: Before the Kids, They Used to Be Such a Cute Couple. LC 99-24165. 144p. 1999. 10.95 (*0-7407-0050-2*) Andrews & McMeel.

***Rosenthal, Amy Krouse.** Spoken Gems: A Journal for Recording the Funny, Odd & Poignant Things Your Child Says. 2000. 10.95 (*0-7407-0571-7*) Andrews & McMeel.

Rosenthal, Andrew J. Food Texture: Perception & Measurement. LC 98-45264. 450p. 1999. 79.00 (*0-8342-1238-2*) Aspen Pub.

Rosenthal, Barbara. Soul & Psyche. (Illus.). 148p. 1998. pap. 15.00 (*0-89822-121-8*) Visual Studies.

Rosenthal, Bernard. City of Nature: Journeys to Nature in the Age of American Romanticism. LC 78-68879. 280p. 1980. 38.50 (*0-87413-147-2*) U Delaware Pr.

— Salem Story: Reading the Witch Trials of 1692. (Studies in American Literature & Culture: No. 73). 302p. (C). 1995. pap. text 18.95 (*0-521-55820-4*) Cambridge U Pr.

Rosenthal, Bernard, ed. see Parkman, Francis.

Rosenthal, Bernice G., ed. Nietzsche & Soviet Culture: Ally & Adversary. LC 93-29255. (Cambridge Studies in Russian Literature). (Illus.). 439p. (C). 1994. text 69.95 (*0-521-45281-3*) Cambridge U Pr.

— Nietzsche in Russia. LC 86-12290. (Illus.). 441p. 1986. reprint ed. pap. 136.80 (*0-608-07153-6*, 206737800009) Bks Demand.

— The Occult in Russian & Soviet Culture. LC 96-37566. (Illus.). 480p. 1996. pap. 24.95 (*0-8014-8331-X*); text 59.95 (*0-8014-3258-8*) Cornell U Pr.

Rosenthal, Bernice M., jt. auth. see Rosenthal, Jon K.

Rosenthal, Bert. Anfernee Hardaway: Star Guard. LC 98-19533. (Sports Reports Ser.). (Illus.). 104p. (YA). (gr. 4-10). 1999. lib. bdg. 20.95 (*0-7660-1234-4*) Enslow Pubs.

Rosenthal, Beth E. Meltdown! Diet & Cookbook: Burn Fat 24 Hours a Day, Even While You Sleep. Bradley, Margaret, ed. LC 94-90295. (Illus.). 134p. (Orig.). 1994. pap. text 15.00 (*1-885676-01-8*) Meltdown Intl.

***Rosenthal, Beth E., ed.** Medical Quality Management 2000 Edition. (Illus.). 576p. 1999. pap. 325.00 (*1-57987-119-4*) Faulkner & Gray.

Rosenthal, Beth E., jt. auth. see Naxon, Jan L.

Rosenthal, Beth E., ed. see Watts, David L.

Rosenthal, Bianca. Pathways to Paul Celan Vol. 73: A History of Critical Responses as a Chorus of Discordant Voices. LC 94-23691. (Studies in Modern German Literature). VII, 239p. (C). 1996. text 49.95 (*0-8204-2695-4*) P Lang Pubng.

Rosenthal, Bob. Rude Awakenings. LC 81-21943. 1981. pap. 3.50 (*0-916328-16-3*) Yellow Pr.

Rosenthal, Bob, ed. see Ginsberg, Allen.

Rosenthal, Bruce P., ed. see Cole, Roy.

Rosenthal, Bruce P., jt. ed. see Cole, Roy G.

Rosenthal, C. J. & Rotman, M., eds. Clinical Applications of Continuous Infusion Chemotherapy & Concomitant Radiation Therapy. LC 86-4890. 262p. 1986. 75.00 (*0-306-42260-3*, Plenum Trade) Perseus Pubng.

Rosenthal, C. Julian, ed. Neoplastic Diseases. LC 91-62100. 891p. 1991. 129.00 (*0-944496-24-5*) Precept Pr.

Rosenthal, C. Julian & Rotman, Marvin. Infusion Chemotherapy--Irradiation Interactions: Principles & Applications to Organ Salvage & Prevention of Secondprimary Neoplasms. LC 97-43316. 468p. 1997. 245.00 (*0-444-82608-4*) Elsevier.

Rosenthal, C. P. Elena of the Stars. 192p. 1996. pap. 10.95 (*0-312-14592-6*) St Martin.

Rosenthal, Carolyn J. & Hendricks, Jon, eds. The Remainder of Their Days: Domestic Policy & Older Families in the United States & Canada. LC 92-44317. 248p. 1993. text 44.00 (*0-8153-0483-8*, SS795) Garland.

Rosenthal, Charles L. The Art World at Your Fingertips: For Artists, Students, Art Dealers & Their Patrons & Essential for Those Interested in the Visual Arts. (Illus.). 100p. 1991. pap. 8.95 (*0-9629041-0-4*); pap., spiral bd. 8.95 (*0-9629041-2-0*); text 17.50 (*0-9629041-1-2*) J-C Ranch Pr.

Rosenthal, Cindy Simon. When Women Lead: Integrative Leadership in State Legislatures. LC 97-53246. (Illus.). 256p. 1998. pap. 18.95 (*0-19-511541-4*); text 49.95 (*0-19-511540-6*) OUP.

Rosenthal, Clifford N., jt. ed. see Engel, Barbara A.

Rosenthal, Curt, tr. see Simmel, Georg.

Rosenthal, Daniel I., ed. see Chew, Felix S. M., et al.

Rosenthal, David, et al. X Window System: The Complete Reference to XLib, X Protocol, ICCM, XLFD, X Version 11, Release 5. 3rd rev. ed. (Illus.). 1000p. 1992. pap. 59.95 (*1-55558-088-2*, EY-J802E-DP, Digital DEC) Buttrwrth-Heinemann.

Rosenthal, David, ed. see McFarlane, Evelyn.

Rosenthal, David, tr. see Catala, Victor.

Rosenthal, David A. An Inquiry Driven Vision System Based on Visual & Conceptual Hierarchies. LC 81-7616. (Computer Science: Artificial Intelligence Ser.: No. 7). (Illus.). 210p. 1981. reprint ed. pap. 65.10 (*0-608-17728-8*, 207004900063) Bks Demand.

Rosenthal, David F. & Okuno, Hirishi G., eds. Readings in Computational Auditory Scene Analysis: Proceedings of the IJCAI-95 Workshop. LC 97-5936. 408p. 1997. pap. 25.00 (*0-8058-2284-4*) L Erlbaum Assocs.

Rosenthal, David F. & Okuno, Hiroshi G., eds. Readings in Computational Auditory Scene Analysis: Proceedings of the IJCAI-95 Workshop. LC 97-5936. 408p. 1997. text 50.00 (*0-8058-2283-6*) L Erlbaum Assocs.

An Asterisk (*) at the beginning of an entry indicates that the title is appearing for the first time.

Rosenthal, David H. Hard Bop: Jazz & Black Music 1955-1965. 224p. 1993. reprint ed. pap. 10.95 (*0-19-508556-6*) OUP.
— The Journey: Poems. LC 92-20333. 1992. 9.95 (*0-89255-181-X*) Persea Bks.
— Loves of the Poets: Poems. 86p. 1989. 17.95 (*0-89255-139-9*); pap. 9.95 (*0-89255-132-1*) Persea Bks.
— Postwar Catalan Poetry. LC 89-43048. (Illus.). 128p. 1991. 29.50 (*0-8387-5178-4*) Bucknell U Pr.
Rosenthal, David H., ed. Modern Catalan Poetry. 93p. 1979. pap. 6.00 (*0-89823-000-4*) New Rivers Pr.
Rosenthal, David H., tr. Four Postwar Catalan Poets. LC 78-67773. (Cross-Cultural Review Chapbook Ser.: No. 1). (CAT & ENG., Illus.). 1978. 15.00 (*0-89304-600-0*, CCC14); pap. 5.00 (*0-89304-601-9*) Cross-Cultrl NY.
Rosenthal, David H., tr. When I Sleep, Then I See Clearly: Selected Poems of J. V. Foix. (Illus.). 1988. pap. 12.95 (*0-89255-130-5*) Persea Bks.
Rosenthal, David H., ed. see Azevedo, Aluisio.
Rosenthal, David H., tr. see Martorell, Joanot & De Galba, Marti J.
Rosenthal, David H., tr. see Rodereda, Merce.
Rosenthal, David H., tr. see Rodoreda, Merce.
Rosenthal, David H., tr. & intro. see Estelles, Vicent A.
Rosenthal, David K. The Complete Guide to Racetrack Betting. 160p. (Orig.). 1986. pap. 9.95 (*0-89709-144-2*) Liberty Pub.
***Rosenthal, David M., ed.** Materialism & the Mind-Body Problem. 296p. (C). 2000. lib. bdg. 34.95 (*0-87220-479-0*) Hackett Pub.
— Materialism & the Mind-Body Problem. 2nd ed. 296p. (C). 2000. pap. 10.95 (*0-87220-478-2*) Hackett Pub.
Rosenthal, David M., ed. The Nature of Mind. 656p. (C). 1991. pap. text 36.95 (*0-19-504671-4*) OUP.
Rosenthal, David M., ed. Materialism & the Mind-Body Problem. LC 87-23794. 249p. (C). 1987. reprint ed. pap. text 8.95 (*0-87220-023-X*); reprint ed. lib. bdg. 29.95 (*0-87220-024-8*) Hackett Pub.
Rosenthal, David W., jt. auth. see Brown, Lew G.
Rosenthal, Debra J., jt. ed. see Reynolds, David S.
***Rosenthal, Don & Rosenthal, Martha.** Intimacy: The Noble Adventure. 225p. 2000. pap. 16.95 (*1-898256-77-2*, Pub. by Collins Press) Dufour.
Rosenthal, Donald A. La Grande Maniere: Religious & Historical Painting in France, 1700-1800. (Illus.). 200p. 1987. pap. 24.95 (*0-295-96475-8*) U of Wash Pr.
Rosenthal, Donald B. The Limited Elite: Politics & Government in Two Indian Cities. LC 70-121818. 1994. lib. bdg. 22.50 (*0-226-72810-2*) U Ch Pr.
— Urban Housing & Neighborhood Revitalization: Turning a Federal Program into Local Projects, 208. LC 87-32259. (Contributions in Political Science Ser.: No. 208). 238p. 1988. 59.95 (*0-313-26148-2*, RND/, Greenwood Pr) Greenwood.
Rosenthal, Donna. Passport Israel: Your Pocket Guide to Israeli Business, Customs, & Etiquette. Szerlip, Barbara, ed. LC 96-28183. (Passport to the World Ser.). (Illus.). 96p. (Orig.). 1996. pap. 6.95 (*1-885073-22-4*) Wrld Trade Pr.
Rosenthal, Donna M., jt. ed. see Nadel, Lynn.
Rosenthal, Doreen A., jt. auth. see Moore, Susan M.
Rosenthal, Dorothy B. Environmental Case Studies: Central Region, Vol. 2. 64p. (C). 1996. pap. 15.95 (*0-471-14262-X*, BG42) Wiley.
— Environmental Case Studies: Northeastern Region, Vol. 1. 72p. (C). 1996. pap. 18.95 (*0-471-14258-1*, BG42) Wiley.
— Environmental Case Studies: Southeast Region, Vol. 3. LC 96-138978. 72p. (C). 1996. pap. 15.95 (*0-471-14259-X*, BG42) Wiley.
— Environmental Case Studies: Western Region, Vol. 4. 63p. (C). 1996. pap. 18.95 (*0-471-14257-3*, BG42) Wiley.
— Environmental Science Activities. LC 95-158020. 236p. 1994. pap. 18.95 (*0-471-07626-0*) Wiley.
Rosenthal, Dorothy L. Cytology of the Central Nervous System. (Monographs in Clinical Cytology Ser.: Vol. 8). (Illus.). x, 206p. 1984. 85.25 (*3-8055-3808-1*) S Karger.
— Cytopathology of Pulmonary Disease. (Monographs in Clinical Cytology Ser.: Vol. 11). (Illus.). x, 238p. 1988. 116.75 (*3-8055-4740-4*) S Karger.
Rosenthal, Douglas E. Lawyer & Client: Who's in Charge? LC 73-83891. 230p. 1974. 29.95 (*0-87154-725-2*) Russell Sage.
Rosenthal, Douglas E., jt. ed. see Green, Carl J.
Rosenthal, Earl E. The Palace of Charles V in Granada. LC 85-3366. (Illus.). 401p. 1985. reprint ed. pap. 124.40 (*0-608-07164-1*, 206738900009) Bks Demand.
Rosenthal, Ed. Closet Cultivator. (Illus.). 115p. 1999. pap. 19.95 (*0-932551-21-1*, Pub. by Quick Am Pub) Publishers Group.
***Rosenthal, Ed.** Easy Marijuana Gardening. (Illus.). 64p. 2000. pap. 14.95 (*0-932551-37-8*, Pub. by Quick Am Pub) Publishers Group.
Rosenthal, Ed. Marijuana Beer. (Illus.). 53p. 1996. pap. 14.95 (*0-932551-22-X*) Quick Am Pub.
— Marijuana Grower's Handbook: The Indoor High Yield Guide. 3rd ed. (Illus.). 282p. 1998. pap. text 19.95 (*0-932551-25-4*) Quick Am Pub.
— Marijuana Grower's Handbook: The Indoor High Yield Guide. 3rd rev. ed. (Illus.). 282p. 1998. spiral bd. 23.95 (*0-932551-26-2*) Quick Am Pub.
— Marijuana Growing Tips. (Illus.). 128p. 1986. reprint ed. pap. 12.95 (*0-932551-05-X*) Quick Am Pub.
— Marijuana Growing Tips. 2nd ed. (Illus.). 111p. 1999. pap. 12.95 (*0-932551-31-9*) Quick Am Pub.
— Marijuana Question? Ask Ed: The Encyclopedia of Marijuana. (Illus.). 284p. 1987. reprint ed. pap. 19.95 (*0-932551-01-7*) Quick Am Pub.
— Why Marijuana Should Be Legal. LC 96-16079. (Illus.). 128p. 1996. pap. 9.95 (*1-56025-110-7*, Thunders Mouth) Avalon NY.
***Rosenthal, Ed & Logan, William.** Don't Get Busted. (Ask Ed Ser.: Vol. 1). 192p. 2000. pap. 14.95 (*0-932551-36-X*, Pub. by Quick Am Pub) Publishers Group.
Rosenthal, Ed, et al. Marijuana Medical Handbook: A Guide to Therapeutic Use. 270p. 1996. pap. 16.95 (*0-932551-16-5*) Quick Am Pub.
Rosenthal, Ed, ed. see Gold, David.
Rosenthal, Ed, ed. see Gold, D. & Green, Bud.
Rosenthal, Elizabeth. Where to Go When You're Hurting: A Healing Resource Guide. 216p. 1998. pap. 19.95 (*0-9660472-0-6*) EMPR.
Rosenthal, Eric. Civilians at Risk: Military & Police Abuses in the Mexican Countryside. (North America Project Special Reports). 37p. 1993. pap. 5.00 (*0-911646-58-2*) World Policy.
Rosenthal, Erik. The Calculus of Murder. large type ed. 416p. 1988. 27.99 (*0-7089-1887-5*) Ulverscroft.
***Rosenthal, Erwin.** Judaism, Philosophy, Culture: Selected Studies by E. I. J. Rosenthal. 288p. 2000. 80.00 (*0-7007-1243-7*, Pub. by Curzon Pr Ltd) Paul & Co Pubs.
Rosenthal, Erwin I. Political Thought in Medieval Islam: An Introductory Outline. LC 85-21909. 324p. 1985. reprint ed. lib. bdg. 55.50 (*0-313-25094-4*, ROPTH, Greenwood Pr) Greenwood.
Rosenthal, Erwin I. & Katz, Steven, eds. Saadya Studies: In Commemoration of the One Thousandth Anniversary of the Death of R. Saadya Gaon. LC 79-7170. (Jewish Philosophy, Mysticism & History of Ideas Ser.). 1980. reprint ed. lib. bdg. 28.95 (*0-405-12284-5*) Ayer.
Rosenthal, Evelyn. Woman Aging & Ageism. 1990. pap. 14.95 (*0-918393-73-6*, Harrington Park) Haworth Pr.
— Women, Aging & Ageism. LC 90-4644. (Journal of Women & Aging: Vol. 2, No. 2). 161p. 1994. text 39.95 (*0-86656-984-7*) Haworth Pr.
Rosenthal, F., jt. auth. see Brann, M.
Rosenthal, Frank. The Jews of Des Moines: The First Century. (Illus.). 213p. 1998. reprint ed. lib. bdg. 32.50 (*0-8328-7095-1*) Higginson Bk Co.
Rosenthal, Franz. Ahmad B, at-Tayyib as-Sarahsi. (American Oriental Ser.: Vol. 26). 1943. pap. 5.00 (*0-940490-26-9*) Am Orient Soc.
— The Classical Heritage in Islam. 310p. 1996. pap. 18.95 (*0-614-21214-6*, 136) Kazi Pubns.
— The Classical Heritage in Islam. (Illus.). 320p. (C). 1994. pap. 27.99 (*0-415-07693-5*) Routledge.
— Greek Philosophy in the Arab World: A Collection of Essays. 300p. 1990. text 101.95 (*0-86078-271-9*, Pub. by Variorum) Ashgate Pub Co.
— Muslim Intellectual & Social History: A Collection of Essays. (Collected Studies: No. CS309). 336p. 1990. text 115.95 (*0-86078-257-3*, Pub. by Variorum) Ashgate Pub Co.
— Science & Medicine in Islam. 250p. 1996. 79.95 (*0-614-21608-7*, 1111) Kazi Pubns.
— Science & Medicine in Islam: A Collection of Essays. (Collected Studies: No. 330). 250p. 1991. text 106.95 (*0-86078-282-4*, Pub. by Variorum) Ashgate Pub Co.
Rosenthal, Franz, ed. The History of al-Tabari Vol. 38: The Return of the Caliphate to Baghdad: The Caliphate of al-Multadid al-Muktafi & al-Mugtadir, A.D. 892-915 - A.H. 279-302. LC 83-18115. (SUNY Series in Near Eastern Studies). 239p. (C). 1985. text 57.50 (*0-87395-876-4*) State U NY Pr.
— The History of al-Tabari Vol. 38: The Return of the Caliphate to Baghdad: The Caliphate of al-Multadid al-Muktafi & al-Mugtadir, A.D. 892-915 - A.H. 279-302. LC 83-18115. (SUNY Series in Near Eastern Studies). 239p. 1990. pap. text 22.95 (*0-7914-0626-1*) State U NY Pr.
Rosenthal, Franz, tr. The History of al-Tabari Vol. 1: General Introduction & from the Creation to the Flood. LC 87-33532. (SUNY Series in Near Eastern Studies). 413p. (C). 1989. pap. text 27.95 (*0-88706-563-5*) State U NY Pr.
— The History of al-Tabari Vol. 1: General Introduction & from the Creation to the Flood. LC 87-33532. (SUNY Series in Near Eastern Studies). 413p. (C). 1989. text 64.50 (*0-88706-562-7*) State U NY Pr.
Rosenthal, Franz, tr. see Al-Tabari.
Rosenthal, Franz, tr. see Khaldun, Ibn.
Rosenthal, Gabriele. The Holocaust in Three Generations: Families of Victims & Perpetrators of the Nazi Regime. LC 97-12151. 308p. 1998. 55.00 (*0-304-33991-1*) Continuum.
Rosenthal, Gary. Soccer: The Game & How to Play It. rev. ed. LC 72-129116. (Illus.). 256p. (J). (gr. 3-9). 1978. lib. bdg. 14.95 (*0-87460-258-0*) Lion Bks.
— Soccer Skills & Drills. (Illus.). 224p. (gr. 7 up). 1984. pap. 14.00 (*0-684-18217-3*) S&S Trade.
***Rosenthal, Gary.** The You That Is Everywhere. LC 98-67533. 91p. (Orig.). 1999. pap. 12.95 (*0-9665726-0-2*) Point Bonita Bks.
Rosenthal, Gerald A. & Berenbaum, May R., eds. Herbivores Vol. 1: Their Interactions with Secondary Plant Metabolites: The Chemical Participants. 2nd ed. (Illus.). 468p. 1991. text 104.00 (*0-12-597183-4*) Acad Pr.
— Herbivores Vol. 2: Their Interactions with Secondary Plant Metabolites: Ecological & Evolutionary Processes. 2nd ed. (Illus.). 493p. 1992. text 104.00 (*0-12-597184-2*) Acad Pr.
Rosenthal, Gerald A., jt. ed. see Lubec, Gert.
Rosenthal, Gert. Erhaltung und Regeneration Von Feuchtwiesen: Vegetationsoekologische Untersuchungen Auf Dauerflaechen. (Dissertationes Botanicae Ser.: Band 182). (GER., Illus.). viii, 286p. 1992. pap. 71.00 (*3-443-64094-X*, Pub. by Gebruder Borntraeger) Balogh.
Rosenthal, Gertrude. From El Greco to Pollock: Early & Late Works by European & American Artists. LC 68-58201. (Illus.). 1968. pap. 12.00 (*0-912298-05-7*) Baltimore Mus.
Rosenthal, Gertrude, ed. Italian Paintings, XIV-XVIIIth Centuries from the Collection of the Baltimore Museum of Art. LC 80-66714. 1981. pap. 19.98 (*0-912298-51-0*) Baltimore Mus.
Rosenthal, Gilbert S. Contemporary Judaism: Patterns of Survival. 2nd ed. 423p. 1986. 43.95 (*0-89885-260-9*, Kluwer Acad Hman Sci) Kluwer Academic.
— The Many Faces of Judaism: Orthodox, Conservative, Reconstructionist, & Reform. Rossel, Seymour, ed. LC 78-25898. (YA). (gr. 9-10). 1979. pap. 7.95 (*0-87441-311-7*) Behrman.
Rosenthal, Gilbert S., ed. Maimonides: His Wisdom for Our Time. large type ed. (Large Print Jewish Classics Ser.). 120p. 1991. pap. 9.95 (*0-8027-2646-1*) Walker & Co.
Rosenthal, Glenda & Zupnick, Elliot, eds. Contemporary Western Europe: Problems & Responses. LC 84-6835. 512p. 1984. 55.00 (*0-275-91255-8*, C1255, Praeger Pubs) Greenwood.
Rosenthal, Glenda G., jt. ed. see Redmond, John.
Rosenthal, Gloria, jt. auth. see Salamon, Michael J.
Rosenthal, Gottfried E. Literatur der Technologie. (Documenta Technica Ser.: No. 11). 420p. 1972. reprint ed. write for info. (*3-487-04206-1*) G Olms Pubs.
Rosenthal, Gustavus De, see De Rosenthal, Gustavus.
Rosenthal, H. P. Projections onto Translation-Invariant Subspaces of Lp(G) LC 52-42839. (Memoirs Ser.: No. 1/63). 84p. 1966. pap. 16.00 (*0-8218-1263-7*, MEMO/1/63) Am Math.
Rosenthal, H. P., jt. ed. see Odell, E.
Rosenthal, Harald & Wilson, J. Scott. Bibliography on Ozone, Its Biological Effects & Technical Applications. 249p. (Orig.). (C). 1993. pap. text 80.00 (*0-7881-0110-2*) DIANE Pub.
Rosenthal, Harold D. Great Singers of Today. Farkas, Andrew, ed. LC 76-29964. (Opera Biographies Ser.). (Illus.). 1977. reprint ed. lib. bdg. 21.95 (*0-405-09704-2*) Ayer.
Rosenthal, Harold D., ed. Opera, 5 vols., Set. (Music Reprint Ser.). (Illus.). 1980. reprint ed. lib. bdg. 350.00 (*0-306-79583-3*) Da Capo.
Rosenthal, Harold D. & Warrack, John. Dictionnaire de l'Opera. (FRE.). 420p. 1974. pap. 59.95 (*0-8288-6014-9*, M416) Fr & Eur.
Rosenthal, Harry K. German & Pole National Conflict & Modern Myth. LC 76-2402. 185p. 1978. reprint ed. pap. 57.40 (*0-8357-0330-4*, 201552900001) Bks Demand.
***Rosenthal, Herb.** The Lighter Side of Tennis. LC 99-71607. (Illus.). 72p. 1999. pap. 12.95 (*0-87212-267-0*) Libra.
Rosenthal, Howard. Before You See Your First Client: 55 Things Counselors & Human Service Providers Need to Know. LC 99-166422. 176p. 1998. pap. 15.95 (*1-55691-134-3*) Learning Pubns.
Rosenthal, Howard, jt. auth. see Alesina, Alberto.
Rosenthal, Howard, jt. auth. see Poole, Keith T.
Rosenthal, I. Electromagnetic Radiations in Food Science. Yaron, Bruno et al, eds. LC 92-19937. (Advanced Series in Agricultural Sciences: Vol. 19). (Illus.). 184p. 1992. 123.95 (*0-387-54833-5*) Spr-Verlag.
Rosenthal, Ionel. Milk & Dairy Products: Properties & Processing. (Illus.). 218p. 1991. 125.00 (*3-527-27989-X*, Wiley-VCH) Wiley.
Rosenthal, Ionel, jt. ed. see Ben-Hur, Ehud.
Rosenthal, J., ed. Arterial Hypertension: Pathogenisis, Diagnosis, & Therapy. Telger, Terry C., tr. from GER. (Illus.). 576p. 1982. 248.00 (*0-387-90611-8*) Spr-Verlag.
— Focus on Angiotensin-Converting Enzyme Inhibition. (Journal: Clinical Physiology & Biochemistry: Vol. 8, Suppl. 1, 1990). (Illus.). iv, 52p. 1990. pap. 17.50 (*3-8055-5258-0*) S Karger.
— Focus on Beta-Adrenergic Blockade: Journal: Clinical Physiology & Biochemistry, Supplement 2, 1990, Vol. 8. (Illus.). iv, 56p. 1991. pap. 18.50 (*3-8055-5329-3*) S Karger.
Rosenthal, J., et al, eds. The Biochemistry of Hypertension. (Journal: Clinical Physiology & Biochemistry: Vol. 6, No. 3-4, 1988). (Illus.). 124p. 1988. pap. 58.50 (*3-8055-4849-4*) S Karger.
Rosenthal, J. & Franz, H. E., eds. Medical & Surgical Aspects of Renovascular Hypertension. (Contributions to Nephrology Ser.: Vol. 3). (Illus.). 200p. 1976. 29.75 (*3-8055-2341-6*) S Karger.
Rosenthal, J. & Stumpe, K. O., eds. Angiotensin-Converting-Enzym-Hemmer Bei Hypertonie, Teil 1 - Angiotensin Converting Inhibitors in Treatment of Hypertension, Pt. I: Schwerpunkt auf Cilazapril - Emphasis on Cilazapril. (Journal: Cardiology: Vol. 82, Suppl. 1, 1993). (Illus.). iv, 80p. 1993. pap. 35.00 (*3-8055-5764-7*) S Karger.
— Angiotensin-Konversionsenzyme-Hemmer Bei Hypertonie, Teil 2 (Angiotensin Converting Inhibitors in Treatment of Hypertension, Pt. 2) Schwerpunkt auf Cilazapril (Emphasis on Cilazapril) (Journal: Cardiology: Vol. 82, Suppl. 2, 1993). (Illus.). iv, 84p. 1993. pap. 35.00 (*3-8055-5772-8*) S Karger.
Rosenthal, J. & Van Zwieten, Pieter A., eds. Serotonin & Serotonin Antagonists: Journal: Clinical Physiology & Biochemistry, Vol. 8, Suppl. 3. (Illus.). iv, 128p. 1991. pap. 40.00 (*3-8055-5456-7*) S Karger.
Rosenthal, J. William. Spectacles & Other Vision Aids: A History & Guide to Collecting. LC 95-16408. 550p. 1996. 148.00 (*0-930405-71-4*, NP31395) Norman SF.
Rosenthal, Jacques, compiled by. Bibliotheca Magica et Pneumatica: Occult Sciences - Folklore. (GER.). 730p. 1996. reprint ed. 85.00 (*1-888262-31-1*) Martino Pubng.
Rosenthal, James & Ocampo, Juan. Securitization of Credit: Inside the New Technology of Finance. 288p. 1988. 110.00 (*0-471-61368-1*) Wiley.
Rosenthal, James, ed. see Currie, Nicola.
Rosenthal, James A. & Groze, Victor K. Special-Needs Adoption: A Study of Intact Families. LC 91-30278. 264p. 1992. 55.00 (*0-275-93790-9*, C3790, Praeger Pubs) Greenwood.
Rosenthal, James M., ed. see Anglican Consultative Council Staff.
Rosenthal, Jean, jt. auth. see Lindenberger, Jan.
Rosenthal, Jean-Laurent. The Fruits of Revolution: Property Rights, Litigation & French Agriculture, 1700-1860. (Political Economy of Institutions & Decisions Ser.). (Illus.). 232p. (C). 1992. text 64.95 (*0-521-39220-9*) Cambridge U Pr.
***Rosenthal, Jeffrey S.** A First Look at Rigorous Probability Theory. 192p. 2000. 42.00 (*981-02-4303-0*); pap. 24.00 (*981-02-4322-7*) World Scientific Pub.
Rosenthal, Jesse & Soroka, Mort. Managed Vision Benefits. 2nd ed. LC 98-70020. 198p. 1998. pap. 40.00 (*0-89154-524-7*) Intl Found Employ.
Rosenthal, Jim, jt. auth. see Haney, Lee.
Rosenthal, Jim, jt. auth. see Mazzone, Leo.
Rosenthal, Jim, jt. auth. see Tom, Kiana.
Rosenthal, Joanna, jt. ed. see Longinotto, Kim.
Rosenthal, Joe, et al, eds. The Trainee's Companion to General Practice. LC 93-3406. 320p. 1993. text 39.95 (*0-443-04703-0*) Church.
Rosenthal, Joel H. Righteous Realists: Political Realism, Responsible Power, & American Culture in the Nuclear Age. LC 90-48592. (Political Traditions in Foreign Policy Ser.). 184p. 1991. text 27.50 (*0-8071-1649-1*) La State U Pr.
Rosenthal, Joel H., ed. Moral Education. 82p. (Orig.). 1992. pap. write for info. (*0-87641-119-7*) Carnegie Ethics & Intl Affairs.
— Moral Education, Vol. 4. 131p. (Orig.). 1995. pap. write for info. (*0-87641-143-X*) Carnegie Ethics & Intl Affairs.
— Moral Education, Vol. 5. 89p. (Orig.). 1995. pap. write for info. (*0-87641-144-8*) Carnegie Ethics & Intl Affairs.
Rosenthal, Joel H., ed. & pref. see Carnegie Council on Ethics & International Affairs Staff.
Rosenthal, Joel Thomas. Anglo-Saxon History: An Annotated Bibliography: 450-1066. LC 84-45279. (Studies in the Middle Ages: No. 7). vii, 178p. 1985. 39.50 (*0-404-61437-X*) AMS Pr.
— Late Medieval England, 1377-1485: A Bibliography of Historical Scholarship, 1975-1989. LC 94-6595. 1994. boxed set 45.00 (*1-879288-16-8*) Medieval Inst.
— Old Age in Late Medieval England. LC 96-14736. (Middle Ages Ser.). 288p. 1996. text 39.95 (*0-8122-3355-7*) U of Pa Pr.
— Patriarchy & Families of Privilege in 15th-Century England. LC 91-17228. (Middle Ages Ser.). (Illus.). 304p. (C). 1991. text 39.95 (*0-8122-3072-8*) U of Pa Pr.
— The Purchase of Paradise: Gift Giving & the Aristocracy, 1307-1485. LC 72-194728. (Studies in Social History). xiv, 169 p. 1972. write for info. (*0-7100-7262-7*, Routledge Thoemms) Routledge.
Rosenthal, Joel Thomas, jt. auth. see Carin, Martha.
Rosenthal, John. The Myth of Dialectics: Reinterpreting the Marx-Hegel Relation. LC 97-8402. 276p. 1998. text 65.00 (*0-312-17600-7*) St Martin.
Rosenthal, John, photos by. Regarding Manhattan. LC 98-61120. (Illus.). 96p. 1998. 75.00 (*0-9665798-0-1*) Safe Harbor Bks.
***Rosenthal, John, photos by.** Regarding Manhattan. 96p. 1999. reprint ed. pap. 29.95 (*0-9665798-1-X*) Safe Harbor Bks.
Rosenthal, Jon K. Antique Map Price Record & Handbook for 1993, Vol. 11. LC 83-139904. (Illus.). viii, 344p. 1993. lib. bdg. 40.00 (*0-9638100-0-6*) Kimmel Pubns.
— Antique Map Price Record & Handbook for 1994, Vol. 12. LC 94-640696. (Illus.). viii, 360p. 1994. lib. bdg. 40.00 (*0-9638100-1-4*) Kimmel Pubns.
— Antique Map Price Record & Handbook for 1995. LC 94-640696. (Annual Ser.: Vol. 13). (Illus.). 376p. 1995. lib. bdg. 40.00 (*0-9638100-2-2*) Kimmel Pubns.
— Antique Map Price Record & Handbook, 1996, Vol. 14. annuals (Illus.). viii, 360p. 1996. lib. bdg. 42.00 (*0-9638100-3-0*) Kimmel Pubns.
Rosenthal, Jon K. & Rosenthal, Bernice M. Antique Map Price Record & Handbook for 1997-98. LC 94-640696. (Antique Map Price Record & Handbook Ser.: Vol. 15). (Illus.). viii, 408p. 1998. lib. bdg. 46.00 (*0-9638100-4-9*) Kimmel Pubns.
Rosenthal, Joshua, jt. ed. see Grifo, Francesca.
Rosenthal, Joyce, jt. auth. see Beyea, Jan.
Rosenthal, Judah M., intro. Meyer Waxman Jubilee Volume. (ENG & HEB.). 427p. (C). 1967. 30.00 (*0-935982-07-8*, JMR-01) Spertus Coll.
— Perspectives in Jewish Learning, Vol. III. LC 65-27991. 56p. (Orig.). (C). 1967. pap. 3.95 (*0-935982-36-1*, PJL-03) Spertus Coll.
Rosenthal, Judith W. Teaching Science to Language Minority Students: Theory & Practice. LC 95-6554. (Bilingual Education & Bilingualism Ser.: Vol. 3). 1995. 69.00 (*1-85359-273-0*, Pub. by Multilingual Matters); pap. 26.95 (*1-85359-272-2*, Pub. by Multilingual Matters) Taylor & Francis.
Rosenthal, Judy. Possession, Ecstasy, & Law in Ewe Voodoo. LC 98-9396. 320p. 1998. pap. 18.50 (*0-8139-1805-7*); text 52.50 (*0-8139-1804-9*) U Pr of Va.
Rosenthal, Karen, jt. ed. see Brown, Susan A.
***Rosenthal, Karin.** Karin Rosenthal: Twenty Years of Photographs. (Illus.). 2000. pap. 19.95 (*1-889097-41-1*) Hard Pr MA.
Rosenthal, Karl T. Interview with Mrs. Karl (Trudie) Rosenthal: Concentration Camp Survivor Given 1976 to Rabbi Martin M. Wietz Transcribed by A. D. Warshauer, M. D. September 1979. 45p. (Orig.). 1993. pap. 15.00 (*0-9630383-2-X*) Pambrit.

R

An Asterisk (*) at the beginning of an entry indicates that the title is appearing for the first time.

R

Rosenthal, Ken S. Dean Smith: A Tribute. (Illus.). 200p. 1999. 22.95 (*1-58261-003-7*, Pub. by Sprts Pubng) Partners-West.

Rosenthal, Ken S. & Tan, James S. Mosby's USMLE Step 1 Reviews: Microbiology & Immunology. LC 95-52095. (Ace the Boards Ser.). (Illus.). 344p. (C). (gr. 13). 1996. pap. text 30.00 incl. 3.5 hd (*0-8151-7349-0*, 27042) Mosby Inc.

Rosenthal, Kenneth S. Ace Micro Immunology. (Illus.). 344p. 1996. pap. text 30.00 incl. disk (*0-8151-8670-3*, 28951) Mosby Inc.

Rosenthal, Kimmo I. Quantales & Applications. 1990. pap. 43.00 (*0-582-06423-6*, Pub. by Addison-Wesley) Longman.

— Quantales & Their Applications. LC 90-30122. (Pitman Research Notes in Mathematics Ser.: No. 234). 182p. 1990. pap. 56.50 (*0-608-05238-8*, 206577500001) Bks Demand.

— Theory of Quantaloids. (Pitman Research Notes in Mathematics Ser.). 1996. lib. bdg. 47.95 (*0-582-29440-1*) Longman.

***Rosenthal, Laura.** Something Inside Me. 1999. pap. write for info. (*1-58235-384-0*) Watermrk Pr.

Rosenthal, Laura, jt. ed. see Codrescu, Andrei.

Rosenthal, Laura J. Playwrights & Plagiarists in Early Modern England: Gender, Authorship, Literary Property. LC 96-22233. 256p. 1996. text 39.95 (*0-8014-3252-9*) Cornell U Pr.

Rosenthal, Lawrence. Exploring Careers in Accounting. rev. ed. (Careers Ser.). (Illus.). 148p. (YA). (gr. 7-12). 1993. lib. bdg. 16.95 (*0-8239-1501-8*) Rosen Group.

— Exploring Careers in Accounting. rev. ed. (Careers in Depth Ser.). (Illus.). 148p. (YA). (gr. 7-12). 1994. 9.95 (*0-8239-1721-5*) Rosen Group.

***Rosenthal, Lee H.** Federal Civil Procedure & Evidence During Trial, 5th Circuit. LC 97-72229. (Lawyers Cooperative Federal Practice Guide Ser.). 1998. write for info. (*0-7620-0169-0*) West Group.

Rosenthal, Leslie. Resolving Resistance in Group Psychotherapy. LC 85-19940. 230p. 1994. reprint ed. pap. 35.00 (*1-56821-193-7*) Aronson.

Rosenthal, Liliana H., tr. see Biller, Geraldine P., et al.

***Rosenthal, Lisa.** A Dog's Best Friend: An Activity Book for Kids & Their Dogs. LC 99-12455. (Illus.). 181p. (J). (gr. 4-7). 1999. pap. 12.95 (*1-55652-362-9*) Chicago Review.

Rosenthal, Lisa & Rowland, Susan. Academic Reading & Study Skills for International Students. (Illus.). 256p. (C). 1986. pap. text 32.20 (*0-13-000563-0*) P-H.

Rosenthal, Lucy, ed. Great American Love Stories. 1988. 24.95 (*0-316-75734-9*) Little.

Rosenthal, Lucy & Fadiman, Clifton, eds. The World Treasury of Love Stories. 578p. 1999. reprint ed. text 30.00 (*0-7881-6142-3*) DIANE Pub.

Rosenthal, Ludwig. How Was It Possible? 83p. 1971. 6.00 (*0-943376-02-5*) Magnes Mus.

Rosenthal, Lynne M. Rumer Godden. 1996. 32.00 (*0-8057-7930-2*, Hall Reference) Macmillan.

***Rosenthal, M.** The Fertility Sourcebook. 3rd ed. (Illus.). 288p. 2000. pap. 17.95 (*0-7373-0380-8*, 03808W, Pub. by Lowell Hse) NTC Contemp Pub Co.

Rosenthal, M., et al, eds. Rehabilitation of the Adult & Child with Traumatic Brain Injury. 3rd ed. LC 98-37319. (Illus.). 620p. (C). 1999. text 89.00 (*0-8036-0391-6*) Davis Co.

Rosenthal, M., jt. auth. see O'Grady, J.

Rosenthal, M. L. Our Life in Poetry: Selected Essays & Reviews. 550p. 1990. 47.50 (*0-89255-149-6*) Persea Bks.

— Running to Paradise: Yeat's Poetic Art. LC 96-52763. (Illus.). 384p. 1997. reprint ed. pap. 21.00 (*0-19-511391-8*) OUP.

— She. (American Poets Continuum Ser.: No. 2). 38p. 1977. pap. 7.00 (*0-918526-06-X*) BOA Edns.

Rosenthal, M. L., ed. see Williams, William Carlos.

Rosenthal, M. L., ed. & frwd. see Yeats, William Butler.

Rosenthal, M. Sara. Breast Sourcebook: Everything You Need to Know about Cancer Detection, Treatment, & Prevention. 2nd ed. LC 99-54494. 352p. 1999. pap. 18.95 (*0-7373-0249-6*, 02496W) NTC Contemp Pub Co.

— The Breast Sourcebook: Everything You Need to Know about Cancer Detection, Treatment, & Prevention. 2nd ed. 352p. 1997. reprint ed. pap. 16.00 (*1-56565-819-1*, Anodyne) Lowell Hse.

— The Breast Sourcebook: Everything You Need to Know about Cancer, Prevention, Treatment, & Politics. LC 96-43007. (Illus.). 352p. 1996. 30.00 (*1-56565-470-6*) Lowell Hse.

— The Breastfeeding Sourcebook. 2nd rev. ed. (Illus.). 336p. 1998. pap. 18.00 (*0-7373-0019-1*, 00191W) NTC Contemp Pub Co.

***Rosenthal, M. Sara.** Breastfeeding Sourcebook. 3rd rev. ed. (Illus.). 2000. pap. 17.95 (*0-7373-0509-6*) Lowell Hse.

Rosenthal, M. Sara. The Breastfeeding Sourcebook: Everything You Need to Know. 320p. 1995. 25.00 (*1-56565-342-4*) Lowell Hse.

— The Breastfeeding Sourcebook: Everything You Need to Know. 320p. 1996. pap. 16.00 (*1-56565-478-1*) Lowell Hse.

— The Fertility Sourcebook. 272p. 1995. 25.00 (*1-56565-213-4*) Lowell Hse.

— The Fertility Sourcebook. 2nd ed. LC 97-51589. 336p. 1998. pap. 17.00 (*1-56565-866-3*) Lowell Hse.

— The Fertility Sourcebook: Everything You Need to Know. 272p. 1996. pap. 16.00 (*1-56565-455-2*) Lowell Hse.

***Rosenthal, M. Sara.** 50 Ways to Prevent Colon Cancer. LC 00-35216. 160p. 2000. pap. 14.95 (*0-7373-0459-6*, 04596W, Pub. by Lowell Hse) NTC Contemp Pub Co.

— 50 Ways Women Can Prevent Heart Disease. 2000. pap. 14.95 (*0-7373-0502-9*, Pub. by Lowell Hse) NTC Contemp Pub Co.

Rosenthal, M. Sara. The Gastrointestinal Sourcebook. abr. ed. LC 99-461916. (Illus.). 272p. 1999. pap. 16.95 (*0-7373-0081-7*) NTC Contemp Pub Co.

— The Gynecological Sourcebook. 480p. Date not set. 15.00 (*1-56565-634-2*) NTC Contemp Pub Co.

— The Gynecological Sourcebook. 4th rev. ed. LC 99-14428. (Illus.). 448p. 1999. pap. 21.95 (*0-7373-0086-8*) NTC Contemp Pub Co.

— Gynecological Sourcebook: Everything You Need to Know. 480p. 1995. pap. 17.00 (*1-56565-331-9*) Lowell Hse.

— The Gynecological Sourcebook: Everything You Need to Know. 300p. 1994. 25.00 (*1-56565-123-5*) Lowell Hse.

— The Pregnancy Sourcebook. 2nd rev. ed. 288p. 1997. pap. 15.00 (*1-56565-804-3*, Anodyne) Lowell Hse.

— Pregnancy Sourcebook. 3rd ed. (Illus.). 336p. 1999. pap. 17.95 (*0-7373-0105-8*, 01058W) NTC Contemp Pub Co.

— The Pregnancy Sourcebook: Everything You Need to Know. 288p. 1995. pap. 16.00 (*1-56565-345-9*) Lowell Hse.

— The Thyroid Sourcebook: Everything You Need to Know. 272p. 1996. pap. 16.00 (*1-56565-482-X*) Lowell Hse.

***Rosenthal, M. Sara.** The Thyroid Sourcebook: Everything You Need to Know. 3rd ed. (Illus.). 288p. 1998. pap. 16.00 (*0-7373-0014-0*, 00140W) NTC Contemp Pub Co.

Rosenthal, M. Sara. The Type 2 Diabetic Woman. LC 99-13013. 384p. 1999. pap. 17.95 (*0-7373-0078-7*, 00787W) NTC Contemp Pub Co.

***Rosenthal, M. Sara.** Women & Depression. 336p. 2000. pap. 16.95 (*0-7373-0325-5*, 03255W, Pub. by Lowell Hse) NTC Contemp Pub Co.

— Women of the 60s Turning 50: A Wellness Guide. 256p. 2000. pap. 22.95 (*0-13-026814-3*) P-H.

Rosenthal, Macha L. Poetry & the Common Life. 148p. 1987. reprint ed. pap. 8.95 (*0-89255-118-6*) Persea Bks.

— The Poet's Art. 1989. pap. 7.95 (*0-393-30584-8*) Norton.

Rosenthal, Macha L., ed. Poetry in English: An Anthology. (Illus.). 1234p. 1987. pap. text 41.95 (*0-19-520539-1*) OUP.

Rosenthal, Macha L., ed. see Yeats, William Butler.

Rosenthal, Manuel & Thomson, Virgil. Satie, Ravel, Poulenc. 86p. (Orig.). 1987. pap. 5.95 (*0-937815-09-8*) Hanuman Bks.

Rosenthal, Margaret F. The Honest Courtesan: Veronica Franco, Citizen & Writer in Sixteenth-Century Venice. LC 92-14540. (Women in Culture & Society Ser.). 432p. (C). 1992. pap. text 20.00 (*0-226-72812-9*) U Ch Pr.

— The Honest Courtesan: Veronica Franco, Citizen & Writer in Sixteenth-Century Venice. LC 92-14540. (Women in Culture & Society Ser.). 432p. (C). 1998. lib. bdg. 55.00 (*0-226-72811-0*) U Ch Pr.

Rosenthal, Marilyn, ed. see Graham, Carolyn.

Rosenthal, Marilyn S. Amelia Earhart: A Photo-Illustrated Biography. LC 98-46103. (Read & Discover Photo-Illustrated Biographies Ser.). (Illus.). 1999. 14.00 (*0-7368-0203-7*, Bridgestone Bks) Capstone Pr.

— The Magic Boxes: Children & Black English. LC PE3102.N42R6. (CAL-ERIC - CLL Series on Languages & Linguistics: No. 43). 79p. reprint ed. pap. 30.00 (*0-8357-3360-2*, 203959800013) Bks Demand.

Rosenthal, Marilyn S. & Freeman, Daniel B. Longman Photo Dictionary: Beginning & Intermediate. 91p. (C). 1989. pap. text 14.70 (*0-8013-0004-5*, 75670) Longman.

Rosenthal, Marilyn S. & Ioudine, P. Petit Dictionnaire Philosophique. (FRE.). 638p. 1977. pap. 29.95 (*0-8288-5507-2*, M6446) Fr & Eur.

Rosenthal, Marilyn S., et al. Longman Photo Dictionary: Intermediate. (Illus.). 1989. pap. text, student ed. 12.13 (*0-8013-0056-8*, 75720) Longman.

Rosenthal, Marilynn. The Incompetent Doctor: Behind Closed Doors. (State of Health Ser.). 160p. 1994. 114.95 (*0-335-19110-X*); pap. 31.95 (*0-335-19109-6*) OpUniv Pr.

Rosenthal, Marilynn M. Dealing with Medical Malpractice: The British & Swedish Experience. LC 87-27245. xviii, 270p. (C). 1988. text 53.00 (*0-8223-0830-4*) Duke.

Rosenthal, Marilynn M. & Heirich, Max, eds. Health Policy: Understanding Our Choices from National Reform to Market Forces. LC 97-14374. 352p. (C). 1998. pap. 79.00 (*0-8133-9023-0*, Pub. by Westview) HarpC.

Rosenthal, Mark. Anselm Kiefer. LC 87-29007. (Illus.). 216p. (Orig.). 1987. pap. 35.00 (*0-87633-071-5*) Phila Mus Art.

— Jasper Johns: Work since 1974. LC 88-50233. (Illus.). 112p. 1988. pap. 20.00 (*0-87633-074-X*) Phila Mus Art.

— Juan Gris. LC 83-6060. (Illus.). 192p. 1983. pap. 35.00 (*0-89659-401-7*) Abbeville Pr.

— Philadelphia Collects: Art since 1940. (Illus.). 128p. 1986. 59.95 (*0-8122-7955-7*) U of Pa Pr.

— The Robert & Jane Meyerhoff Collection, 1958 to 1995. LC 95-47555. 1996. pap. 39.95 (*0-89468-221-0*) Natl Gallery Art.

Rosenthal, Mark, contrib. by. Richard Serra: Drawings & Etchings from Iceland. (Illus.). 90p. 1992. 19.95 (*1-880146-03-7*) M Marks.

Rosenthal, Mark & Marshall, Richard. Jonathan Borofsky. LC 84-9615. (Illus.). 202p. 1984. pap. 24.95 (*0-87633-059-6*) Phila Mus Art.

Rosenthal, Mark & Percy, Ann. Philadelphia Collects: Art since 1940. LC 86-22490. (Illus.). 128p. 1986. pap. 20.00 (*0-87633-066-9*) Phila Mus Art.

Rosenthal, Mark, et al. Anselm Kiefer. (Illus.). 216p. (Orig.). 1988. pap. 55.00 (*3-7913-0847-5*, Pub. by Prestel) te Neues.

— Donald Lipski: Who's Afraid of Red, White & Blue? Marincola, Paula & Zeigerman, Gerry, eds. 150p. (Orig.). 1991. pap. 10.00 (*0-9619760-2-0*) Fabric Workshop Inc.

— Franz Marc. (Illus.). 160p. 1989. 55.00 (*3-7913-1024-0*, Pub. by Prestel) te Neues.

Rosenthal, Mark, jt. contrib. by see Baptista, Lynne H.

Rosenthal, Mark, jt. ed. see Bowles, Norma.

Rosenthal, Martha, jt. auth. see Rosenthal, Don.

Rosenthal, Martin R. CPCS Training Manual. LC 89-64082. 200p. 1989. pap. text 50.00 (*0-944490-19-0*) Mass CLE.

— CPCS Training Manual for Criminal Defense, 1993 Supplement. LC 89-64082. (Orig.). 1993. pap. text 17.50 (*0-944490-58-1*) Mass CLE.

Rosenthal, Marvin, jt. auth. see Howard, Kevin.

Rosenthal, Marvin J. Pre-Wrath Rapture of the Church. 320p. 1990. pap. 15.99 (*0-8407-3160-4*) Nelson.

Rosenthal, Maureen R. Cookin' on Special: Recipe Reminder System. 97p. (Orig.). 1993. pap. text 6.95 (*0-9634217-1-9*) MorFor Pubns.

Rosenthal, Mel, photos by. In the South Bronx of America. LC 96-25736. (Illus.). 128p. Date not set. 39.95 (*0-915306-96-4*) Curbstone.

Rosenthal, Michael. The Art of Thomas Gainsborough: "A Little Business for the Eye" LC 99-20882. (Illus.). 312p. 2000. 60.00 (*0-300-08137-5*) Yale U Pr.

***Rosenthal, Michael.** Biography of Nicholas Murray Butler. 2000. text. write for info. (*0-374-29994-3*) FS&G.

Rosenthal, Michael. Centennial. 1986. pap. 9.95 (*0-918223-86-5*) Pindar Pr.

— Constable. LC 86-50221. (World of Art Ser.). (Illus.). 168p. 1987. pap. 14.95 (*0-500-20211-7*, Pub. by Thames Hudson) Norton.

Rosenthal, Michael. Constable: The Painter & His Landscape. LC 82-48908. (Illus.). 264p. 1983. 35.00 (*0-300-03014-2*) Yale U Pr.

Rosenthal, Michael. Constable: The Painter & His Landscape. LC 82-48908. (Illus.). 264p. 1986. pap. 35.00 (*0-300-03753-8*) Yale U Pr.

— Official CBS Viewers Guide to the 1992 Winter Olympics. 1991. pap. 3.95 (*0-918223-90-3*) Pindar Pr.

— Official NBC Viewers Guide to the 1992 Summer Olympics. 1992. pap. 14.95 (*0-918223-92-X*) Pindar Pr.

— Prospects for the Nation: Recent Essays in British Landscape, 1750-1880, Vol. 4. LC 97-60730. (Studies in British Art: Vol. 4). 335p. 1997. 50.00 (*0-300-06383-0*) Yale U Pr.

— Virginia Woolf. 270p. 1987. pap. text 20.00 (*0-231-04849-1*, King's Crown Paperbacks) Col U Pr.

Rosenthal, Milton, tr. see Vian, Boris.

Rosenthal, Miriam & Reeves, Marjorie. The French Revolution. (Then & There Ser.). (Illus.). 106p. (Orig.). (gr. 7-12). 1965. pap. text 8.76 (*0-582-20403-8*, 70739) Longman.

Rosenthal, Miriam B. & Smith, D. H., eds. Psychosomatic Obstetrics & Gynecology. (Advances in Psychosomatic Medicine Ser.: Vol. 12). (Illus.). vi, 190p. 1985. 71.50 (*3-8055-3967-3*) S Karger.

Rosenthal, Miriam K. An Ecological Approach to the Study of Child Care: Family Day Care in Israel. 184p. 1994. text 36.00 (*0-8058-1163-X*) L Erlbaum Assocs.

Rosenthal, Morris. Build Your Own PC. 150p. 1998. pap. 24.99 (*0-07-134628-7*) McGraw.

***Rosenthal, Morris.** Build Your Own PC. 2nd ed. (Illus.). 2000. pap. 24.99 (*0-07-212467-9*) Osborne-McGraw.

Rosenthal, Morris. Hand-Me-Down PC: Breathing New Life into Your Pentium, 486, 386 & 286 PC. LC 97-31095. (Illus.). 307p. 1997. pap. 21.95 (*0-07-053523-X*) McGraw.

Rosenthal, Morris, jt. auth. see Dailey, Franklyn E., Jr.

Rosenthal, N. St. John's Wort: The Miracle Cure for Depression. 352p. 1999. mass mkt. 5.99 (*0-06-098439-2*) HarpC.

Rosenthal, Nadine. Speaking of Reading. LC 95-5102. 232p. 1997. pap. 14.95 (*0-435-08118-7*, 08118) Heinemann.

— Teach Someone to Read: A Step-by-Step Guide for Literacy Tutors. 204p. 1987. spiral bd. 17.55 (*0-8224-5834-9*) Fearon Teacher Aids.

Rosenthal, Nadine, compiled by. Speaking of Reading. LC 95-5102. 213p. 1995. 23.95 (*0-435-08119-5*, 08119) Heinemann.

Rosenthal, Nadio, jt. ed. see Harvey, Richard P.

Rosenthal, Nan. Anselm Kiefer: Works on Paper in the Metropolitan Museum of Art. LC 98-44486. (Illus.). 135p. 1999. 45.00 (*0-8109-6531-3*, Pub. by Abrams) Time Warner.

— Anselm Kiefer: Works on Paper in the Metropolitan Museum of Art. LC 98-44486. 135p. 1998. 45.00 (*0-87099-886-2*); pap. write for info. (*0-87099-887-0*) Abrams.

Rosenthal, Nancy. Robert Mangold: Recent Zone Paintings. LC 99-201771. 37p. 1999. write for info. (*1-878283-85-5*) PaceWildenstein.

Rosenthal, Neal H. & Pfleeger, Janet. Employment Outlook, 1994-2005: Job Quality & Other Aspects of Projected Employment Growth. (Illus.). 76p. (C). 1996. reprint ed. pap. text 30.00 (*0-7881-3715-8*) DIANE Pub.

Rosenthal, Neal H. & Pilot, Michael. National Occupational Projections for Voc. Ed. Planning. 26p. 1983. 3.25 (*0-318-22159-4*, IN252) Ctr Educ Trng Employ.

***Rosenthal, Norman.** St. John's Wort: The Herbal Way to Feeling Good. 235p. 2000. text 24.00 (*0-7881-9143-8*) DIANE Pub.

— St. John's Wort: The Herbal Way to Feeling Good. 328p. 2000. reprint ed. pap. 6.00 (*0-7881-9368-6*) DIANE Pub.

— St.John's Wort: The Miracle Cure for Depression, Set. abr. ed. 1998. audio 18.00 (*0-694-51958-6*, 396095) HarperAudio.

***Rosenthal, Norman, et al.** Apocalypse. (Illus.). 288p. 2000. 55.00 (*0-8109-6632-8*, Pub. by Abrams) Time Warner.

Rosenthal, Norman, et al. Sensation: Young British Artists from the Saatchi Collection. LC 97-61608. (Illus.). 224p. 1998. pap. 29.95 (*0-500-28042-8*, Pub. by Thames Hudson) Norton.

Rosenthal, Norman, jt. auth. see Eccher, Danilo.

Rosenthal, Norman, ed. see Joachimides, Christos.

Rosenthal, Norman E. St. John's-Wort: The Miracle Cure for Depression. LC 98-21686. 256p. 1998. 24.00 (*0-06-018382-9*) HarpC.

— St. John's Wort Clip Strip: The Herbal Way to Feeling Good. 1999. mass mkt. 47.92 (*0-06-098444-9*) Harper SF.

— Winter Blues: Seasonal Affective Disorder - What It Is & How to Overcome It. rev. ed. (Illus.). 355p. 1998. pap. 15.95 (*1-57230-395-6*) Guilford Pubns.

Rosenthal, Norman E. & Blehar, Mary C., eds. Seasonal Affective Disorders & Phototherapy. LC 88-24402. 386p. 1989. lib. bdg. 60.00 (*0-89862-741-9*) Guilford Pubns.

Rosenthal, Odeda. Not Strictly Kosher: Pioneer Jews of New Zealand (1831-1901) (Illus.). 208p. (Orig.). 1988. 35.00 (*0-910425-07-8*) Starchand Pr.

Rosenthal, P., jt. auth. see Radjavi, H.

Rosenthal, P. A., et al, eds. In Situ Process Diagnostics & Intelligent Materials Processing Vol. 502: Materials Research Society Symposium Proceedings. LC 98-26892. 290p. 1998. text 75.00 (*1-55899-407-6*) Materials Res.

Rosenthal, Paul. Yo, Aesop! LC 96-22419. (Illus.). 51p. (J). 1998. mass mkt. 16.00 (*0-689-80100-9*) S&S Bks Yung.

***Rosenthal, Peggy.** The Poets' Jesus: Representations at the End of the Millennium. LC 99-23029. 184p. 2000. 29.95 (*0-19-513114-2*) OUP.

Rosenthal, Peggy & Dardess, George. Every Cliche in the Book. LC 87-36032. (Illus.). Date not set. pap. write for info. (*0-688-07956-3*, Quil) HarperTrade.

***Rosenthal, Phil.** The Green Grass Grew All Around: Beginning Level. Bruce, Dix, tr. 40p. 1998. pap. 7.95 (*0-7866-3072-8*, 96706) Mel Bay.

— Turkey in the Straw: Beginning Level. 32p. 1997. pap. 7.95 (*0-7866-3053-1*, 96701) Mel Bay.

— Turkey in the Straw: Bluegrass Songs for Children. 32p. (J). 1997. pap. 22.95 incl. audio compact disk (*0-7866-3364-6*, 96701CDP); pap. 17.95 incl. audio (*0-7866-3368-9*, 96701P) Mel Bay.

Rosenthal, Rachel. Tatti Wattles: A Love Story. (Illus.). 64p. 1997. 20.00 (*0-9646426-9-7*, 620242) Smart Art Pr.

Rosenthal, Raul J., et al, eds. The Pathophysiology of Pneumoperitoneum. LC 97-20208. (Illus.). x, 174p. 1997. write for info. (*3-540-63015-5*) Spr-Verlag.

Rosenthal, Raul J., jt. ed. see Phillips, Edward H.

Rosenthal, Ray. Astanga Yoga, an Aerobic Yoga System, Taught by K. Paltabhi Jois. 1988. 39.95 incl. VHS (*0-685-23252-2*) Hart Prodns.

Rosenthal, Ray, jt. auth. see Jois, Paltabhi.

Rosenthal, Raymond, tr. from ITA. Gabriele D'Annunzio: Nocturne & Five Tales of Love & Death. LC 88-60729. 1988. 29.95 (*0-910395-40-3*); pap. 13.00 (*0-910395-41-1*) Marlboro Pr.

— The Vatican Frescoes of Michelangelo, 2 vols. limited ed. LC 80-66646. (Illus.). 528p. 1980. bond lthr. 8500.00 (*0-89659-158-1*) Abbeville Pr.

Rosenthal, Raymond, tr. see Alvera, Pierluigi & Spada, Marco, eds.

Rosenthal, Raymond, tr. see Aretino, Pietro.

Rosenthal, Raymond, tr. see Brelich, Mario.

Rosenthal, Raymond, tr. see Crotti, Renato.

Rosenthal, Raymond, tr. see Ferrucci, Franco.

Rosenthal, Raymond, tr. see Giorello, Giulio.

Rosenthal, Raymond, tr. see Gramsci, Antonio.

Rosenthal, Raymond, tr. see Levi, Primo.

Rosenthal, Raymond, tr. see Verga, Giovanni.

Rosenthal, Raymond F. & Gordon, James S. The Healing Partnership. 92p. (Orig.). 1984. pap. text 4.95 (*0-931211-01-8*) Aurora Assocs.

— New Directions in Medicine: A Directory of Learning Opportunities. 1984. pap. 15.95 (*0-931211-00-X*) Aurora Assocs.

Rosenthal, Richard. K-9 Cops. LC 99-195835. 1997. per. 6.50 (*0-671-00023-3*) PB.

***Rosenthal, Richard.** Rookie Cop: Deep Undercover in the Jewish Defense League. 250p. 2000. pap. 14.95 (*0-9654578-8-5*, Pub. by Leapfrog Pr) Consort Bk Sales.

Rosenthal, Richard. Sky Cops. Tobias, Eric, ed. 384p. (Orig.). 1994. mass mkt. 5.50 (*0-671-79516-3*) PB.

Rosenthal, Richard J. Reef Animals of the Pacific Northeast. (Illus.). 160p. (C). 1995. pap. 51.00 (*0-907151-54-X*, Pub. by IMMEL Pubng) St Mut.

Rosenthal, Rob. Homeless in Paradise: A Map of the Terrain. LC 93-17275. 352p. 1993. 69.95 (*1-56639-129-6*) Temple U Pr.

Rosenthal, Robert. Judgement Studies: Design, Analysis & Meta-Analysis. (Illus.). 272p. 1987. text 64.95 (*0-521-33191-9*) Cambridge U Pr.

— Meta-Analytic Procedures for Social Research. rev. ed. (Applied Social Research Methods Ser.: Vol. 6). (Illus.). 148p. 1991. text 42.00 (*0-8039-4245-1*); pap. text 18.95 (*0-8039-4246-X*) Sage.

— Pygmalion in the Classroom. 1996. 39.50 (*0-8290-3153-7*) Irvington.

Rosenthal, Robert & Jacobson, Lenore. Pygmalion in the Classroom: Teacher Expectation & Pupils' Intellectual Development. enl. ed. 265p. 1989. text 39.50 (*0-8290-1768-2*); pap. text 14.95 (*0-8290-1265-6*) Irvington.

Rosenthal, Robert & Rosnow, Ralph L. Essentials of Behavioral Research: Methods & Data Analysis. 2nd ed. (Psychology Ser.). 736p. (C). 1991. 94.69 (*0-07-053929-4*) McGraw.

***Rosenthal, Robert, et al.** Contrasts & Effect Sizes in Behavioral Research: A Correlational Approach. LC 99-24199. (Illus.). 240p. (C). 1999. 59.95 (*0-521-65258-8*); pap. 21.95 (*0-521-65980-9*) Cambridge U Pr.

Rosenthal, Robert, et al. PONS (Profile of Nonverbal Sensitivity) Test Manual. (Illus.). 1979. pap. text 19.95 (*0-89197-647-7*) Ardent Media.

An Asterisk (*) at the beginning of an entry indicates that the title is appearing for the first time.

— Sensitivity to Nonverbal Communication: The PONS Test. LC 78-17322. (Illus.). 432p. 1979. reprint ed. pap. 134.00 (*0-7837-1618-4*, 204191100024) Bks Demand.

Rosenthal, Robert, jt. auth. see Rosnow, Ralph L.

Rosenthal, Ronnie A., et al, eds. Principles & Practice of Geriatric Surgery. (Illus.). 848p. 2000. 195.00 (*0-387-98393-7*) Spr-Verlag.

Rosenthal, Rose. Not All Soldiers Wore Pants: Witty World War II WAC Tells All. 239p. 1994. pap. 14.00 (*0-9636931-0-7*) Ryzell Bks.

Rosenthal, Rose, ed. see Thomas, Ida M.

Rosenthal, Rudolf H. Solingen: History of a City: From Its Beginnings to the End of the 17th Century. 2nd ed. Zerbe, Richard S., tr. from GER. LC 98-85565.Tr. of Solingen, Geschichte Einer Stadt: Von den Anfangen Biszum Ausgang des 17 Jahrhunderts. (Illus.). 352p. 1998. 59.50 (*0-89725-345-0*, 1870, Penobscot Pr) Picton Pr.

Rosenthal, Sandra B. Charles Peirce's Pragmatic Pluralism. LC 93-46977. (SUNY Series in Philosophy). 177p. (C). 1994. pap. text 18.95 (*0-7914-2158-9*) State U NY Pr.

— Charles Peirce's Pragmatic Pluralism. LC 93-46977. (SUNY Series in Philosophy). 177p. (C). 1994. text 57.50 (*0-7914-2157-0*) State U NY Pr.

— The Pragmatic a Priori: A Study on the Epistemology of C. E. Lewis. LC 75-41707. 104p. 1975. 10.00 (*0-87527-142-1*) Green.

— Speculative Pragmatism. 214p. 1990. pap. 19.95 (*0-8126-9109-1*) Open Court.

— Speculative Pragmatism. LC 85-31813. 224p. 1986. lib. bdg. 30.00 (*0-87023-526-5*) U of Mass Pr.

— Time, Continuity & Indeterminacy: A Pragmatic Engagement with Contemporary Perspectives. LC 99-15654. (C). 2000. text 59.50 (*0-7914-4493-7*); pap. text 19.95 (*0-7914-4494-5*) State U NY Pr.

Rosenthal, Sandra B. & Bourgeois, Patrick L. Mead & Merleau-Ponty: Toward a Common Vision. LC 90-20226. 231p. (C). 1991. text 64.50 (*0-7914-0789-6*); pap. text 21.95 (*0-7914-0790-X*) State U NY Pr.

— Pragmatism & Phenomenology: A Philosophic Encounter. viii, 199p. (Orig.). 1980. pap. write for info. (*90-6032-179-0*) B R Gruner.

***Rosenthal, Sandra B. & Buchholz, Rogene A.** Rethinking Business Ethics: A Pragmatic Approach. LC 98-48333. (Ruffin Series in Business Ethics). 224p. 1999. text 39.95 (*0-19-511736-0*) OUP.

Rosenthal, Sandra B., et al. Classical American Pragmatism: Its Contemporary Vitality. LC 98-25461. 272p. 1999. 42.50 (*0-252-02454-0*); pap. 16.95 (*0-252-06760-6*) U of Ill Pr.

Rosenthal, Sandra B., jt. auth. see Bourgeois, Patrick L.

Rosenthal, Sandra B., jt. auth. see Buchholz, Rogene A.

***Rosenthal, Saul.** Sex over 40. rev. ed. (Illus.). 320p. 2000. reprint ed. pap. 13.95 (*1-58542-054-9*, Tarcher Putnam) Putnam Pub Group.

Rosenthal, Saul. A Sociology of Chiropractic. LC 86-8532. (Studies in Health & Human Services: Vol. 6). 1986. lib. bdg. 89.95 (*0-88946-130-9*) E Mellen.

***Rosenthal, Saul H.** The New Sex over 40. LC 99-56740. 1999. 24.95 (*1-56895-802-1*) Wheeler Pub.

Rosenthal, Saul H. Sex over Forty. 288p. 1989. pap. 11.95 (*0-87477-495-0*, Tarcher Putnam) Putnam Pub Group.

Rosenthal, Saul M. The New Sex over 40. LC 99-16285. 288p. 1999. 23.95 (*0-87477-998-7*, Tarcher Putnam) Putnam Pub Group.

Rosenthal-Schneider, Ilse. Reality & Scientific Truth: Discussions with Einstein, von Laue, & Planck. LC 80-13950. (Illus.). 149p. reprint ed. pap. 46.20 (*0-608-16057-1*, 203318700084) Bks Demand.

Rosenthal, Simcha. A Joyful Mother of Children. 127p. 1982. 13.95 (*0-87306-978-1*); pap. 10.95 (*0-87306-979-X*) Feldheim.

Rosenthal, Sol R. Challenge: The Joy of Life. (Illus.). 1995. write for info. (*0-9635392-1-3*) Sci-Tech Commun.

Rosenthal, Stephany & Ebone, Jane. Confessions of a Clever Cook. (Illus.). 234p. (Orig.). 1993. spiral bd. 14.95 (*0-9638405-0-9*) Clever Cooks.

Rosenthal, Stephen R. Effective Produce Design & Development: How to Cut Lead Time & Increase Customer Satisfaction. (APICS Ser.). 270p. 1992. 47.50 (*1-55623-603-4*, Irwn Prfssnl) McGraw-Hill Prof.

Rosenthal, Stephen R., jt. auth. see Salzman, Harold.

Rosenthal, Steve, jt. auth. see Crosbie, Michael J.

Rosenthal, Steven T. The Politics of Dependency: Urban Reform in Istanbul, 3. LC 79-7588. (Contributions in Comparative Colonial Studies: No. 3). (Illus.). 220p. 1980. 69.50 (*0-313-20927-8*, RPO/, Greenwood Pr) Greenwood.

Rosenthal, Susan R. & Sheppard, Justine J. Dysphagia & the Child with Developmental Disabilities: Medical, Clinical & Family Interventions. (Illus.). 432p. (Orig.). (C). 1994. pap. text 91.95 (*1-56593-089-4*, 0394) Thomson Learn.

Rosenthal, Sylvia, jt. auth. see Hovis, Gene.

Rosenthal, T. & Silverberg, D., eds. Hypertension in the Community. (Bibliotheca Cardiologica Ser.: No. 42). (Illus.). x, 178p. 1987. 148.00 (*3-8055-4521-5*) S Karger.

Rosenthal, T. G. The Art of Jack B. Yeats. (Illus.). 305p. 1994. 75.00 (*0-233-98849-1*, Pub. by Andre Deutsch) Trafalgar.

— The Art of Jack B. Yeats. (Illus.). 288p. 1996. reprint ed. pap. 29.95 (*0-233-98952-8*, Pub. by Andre Deutsch) Trafalgar.

Rosenthal, Ted. How Could I Not Be Among You? LC 73-80922. (Illus.). 80p. 1987. reprint ed. pap. 8.95 (*0-89255-117-8*) Persea Bks.

Rosenthal-Urey, Ina, intro. Regional Impacts of U. S. - Mexican Relations. (Monographs: No. 16). 152p. (Orig.). (C). 1986. pap. 12.50 (*0-935391-67-3*, MN-16) UCSD Ctr US-Mex.

Rosenthal, Uriel, ed. Crisis Management & Decision Making: Simulation Oriented Scenarios. 168p. (C). 1991. lib. bdg. 102.00 (*0-7923-1177-9*) Kluwer Academic.

Rosenthal, Uriel, et al, eds. Coping with Crises: The Management of Disasters, Riots & Terrorism. (Illus.). 498p. 1989. pap. 60.95 (*0-398-06408-3*) C C Thomas.

— Coping with Crises: The Management of Disasters, Riots & Terrorism. (Illus.). 498p. (C). 1989. text 91.95 (*0-398-05597-1*) C C Thomas.

Rosenthal, Uriel & Hart, Paul T., eds. Flood Response & Crisis Management in Western Europe: A Comparative Analysis. LC 97-43394. (Illus.). 250p. 1998. 64.95 (*3-540-63641-2*) Spr-Verlag.

Rosenthal, Yaffa. Mitzvos We Can Do. (ArtScroll Youth Ser.). (Illus.). 32p. (J). (gr. 1-8). 1982. 13.99 (*0-89906-775-1*); pap. 9.99 (*0-89906-776-X*) Mesorah Pubns.

— Thank You Hashem. (ArtScroll Youth Ser.). (Illus.). 32p. (J). (gr. 1-8). 1983. 13.99 (*0-89906-777-8*); pap. 9.99 (*0-89906-778-6*) Mesorah Pubns.

Rosenthale, M. E., ed. Suprofen. (Journal: Pharmacology: Vol. 27, Suppl. 1). (Illus.). viii, 96p. 1983. pap. 33.25 (*3-8055-3789-1*) S Karger.

Rosenthall, Gary. Soccer - The Game & How to Play It. 1981. pap. 7.00 (*0-87980-310-X*) Wilshire.

Rosenthall, Leonard. The Application of Radioiodinated Rose Bengal & Colloidal Radiogold in the Detection of Hepatobiliary Disease. LC 68-59353. (Illus.). 88p. 1969. 9.50 (*0-87527-068-9*) Green.

Rosenthall, Samuel & Horn, Laurence. Vowel/Glide Alternation in a Theory of Constraint Interaction. LC 97-12241. (Outstanding Dissertations in Linguistics Ser.). 304p. 1997. text 70.00 (*0-8153-2884-2*) Garland.

Rosenthiel, Agnes. Mimi Makes a Splash. Stryker, Sandy, ed. LC 91-11286. (Mimi Ser.). (Illus.). 48p. (Orig.). (J). (ps-4). 1991. pap. 6.95 (*0-911655-51-4*) Advocacy Pr.

Rosenthiel, Agnes & Rosenthiel, Angnes. Mimi Takes Charge. Paine, Penelope C., ed. & tr. by. Stryker, Sandy, ed. LC 91-11285. (Mimi Ser.). (Illus.). 48p. (Orig.). (J). (ps-4). 1991. pap. 6.95 (*0-911655-50-6*) Advocacy Pr.

Rosenthiel, Angnes, jt. auth. see Rosenthiel, Agnes.

Rosentraub, Mark S. Major League Losers: The Real Cost of Sports & Who's Paying for It. LC 96-26446. (Illus.). 528p. 1997. 30.00 (*0-465-08317-X*, Pub. by Basic) HarpC.

***Rosentraub, Mark S.** Major League Losers: The Real Cost of Sports & Who's Paying for It. rev. ed. 496p. 1999. pap. 16.00 (*0-465-07143-0*) HarpC.

Rosentraub, Mark S., ed. Urban Policy Problems: Federal Policy & Institutional Change. LC 86-596. 270p. 1986. 55.00 (*0-275-92120-4*, C2120, Praeger Pubs) Greenwood.

Rosentraub, Mark S., jt. ed. see Warren, Robert.

Rosentswieg, Gerry. Los Angeles Graphic Design. 262p. 1993. 49.95 (*0-942604-33-4*) Madison Square.

— The New Typographic Logo. LC 96-76801. (Illus.). 176p. 1996. 37.50 (*0-942604-55-5*) Madison Square.

— Newest Logo from California. 1998. pap. text 35.00 (*0-8230-6601-0*) Watsn-Guptill.

— San Francisco Graphic Design. (Illus.). 262p. 1993. 49.95 (*0-942604-29-6*) Madison Square.

— Type Faces. LC 95-79530. (Illus.). 224p. 1996. 37.50 (*0-942604-46-6*) Madison Square.

Rosentswieg, Gerry, ed. The New Artistic Logo. (Illus.). 212p. 1994. 37.50 (*0-942604-34-2*) Madison Square.

Rosentswieg, Gerry & Hunt, Wayne. Design & Planning Environmental Graphics. (Illus.). 264p. 1995. 55.00 (*0-942604-35-0*) Madison Square.

Rosenus, Alan. Devil Stories: Modern Man in Search of a Resort. LC 78-64543. (Illus.). 1979. 18.95 (*0-913522-07-4*); pap. 12.95 (*0-913522-08-2*) Urion Pr CA.

— Devil Stories: Modern Man in Search of a Resort. limited ed. LC 78-64543. (Illus.). 1979. 40.00 (*0-913522-09-0*) Urion Pr CA.

— General Vallejo & the Advent of the Americans. LC 99-27932. 312p. 1999. pap. 16.95 (*1-890771-21-X*) Heyday Bks.

Rosenus, Alan, ed. see Miller, Joaquin.

Rosenwaike, Ira. Population History of New York City. LC 75-39829. (New York State Bks.). (Illus.). 274p. 1972. 29.95 (*0-8156-2155-8*) Syracuse U Pr.

Rosenwaike, Ira, ed. Mortality of Hispanic Populations: Mexicans, Puerto Ricans, & Cubans in the United States & in the Home Country, 6. LC 91-2. (Studies in Population & Urban Demography: No. 6). 240p. 1991. 59.95 (*0-313-27500-9*, RMY, Greenwood Pr) Greenwood.

Rosenwaike, Ira & Logue, Barbara. The Extreme Aged in America: A Portrait of an Expanding Population, 3. LC 85-8014. (Contributions to the Study of Aging Ser.: No. 3). (Illus.). 253p. 1985. 55.00 (*0-313-24857-5*, REA/, Greenwood Pr) Greenwood.

Rosenwaks, S., ed. Gas Flow & Chemical Lasers: Proceedings of the International Symposium, Jerusalem, 6th, September 8-12, 1986. (Physics Ser.: Vol. 15). (Illus.). 545p. 1987. 93.95 (*0-387-17481-8*) Spr-Verlag.

Rosenwald, George C. & Ochberg, Richard L., eds. Storied Lives: The Cultural Politics of Self-Understanding. LC 91-38345. 336p. (C). 1992. 45.00 (*0-300-05455-6*) Yale U Pr.

Rosenwald, George C., jt. ed. see Riegel, Klaus F.

Rosenwald, Lawrence. Emerson & the Art of the Diary. 176p. 1988. text 65.00 (*0-19-505333-8*) OUP.

Rosenwald, Lawrence, tr. see Gonnaud, Maurice.

Rosenwasse. Endovascular Surgery. 1999. text. write for info. (*0-7216-7313-9*, W B Saunders Co) Harcrt Hlth Sci Grp.

— Writing Analytically. (C). 1996. pap. text, teacher ed. 26.75 (*0-15-504210-6*) Harcourt.

— Writing Analytically. 2nd ed. (C). 1999. pap. text. write for info. (*0-15-508070-9*) Harcourt Coll Pubs.

***Rosenwasser, E. N. & Lampe, B. P.** Computer Controlled Systems: Analysis & Design with Process-Orientated Models. (Communications & Control Engineering Ser.). xviii, 490p. 2000. pap. 110.00 (*1-85233-307-3*) Spr-Verlag.

Rosenwasser, Edward. Directory of College Alumni Groups: Networking - Local & International Business Sales, Grants & Information for Students. Komer, Barbara E., ed. 304p. (Orig.). 1993. pap. 19.95 (*0-932495-06-0*) Student Coll.

— How to Obtain Maximum College Financial Aid: Helps Students Maximize Their Financial Aid Awards. 3rd ed. 250p. 1993. pap. 17.95 (*0-932495-07-9*) Student Coll.

— How to Obtain Maximum College Financial Aid: Little Known Grants for College Students. 4th ed. 214p. (YA). (gr. 11-12). 1994. pap. 12.95 (*0-932495-08-7*) Student Coll.

Rosenwasser, Edward H. How & Where to Get Good Paying, Career Oriented, College Jobs. 48p. (Orig.). 1985. pap. 7.50 (*0-932495-01-X*) Student Coll.

Rosenwasser, Harvey M. Malpractice & Contact Lenses. 2nd ed. (Illus.). 136p. 1991. text 42.00 (*0-7506-9192-1*) Buttrwrth-Heinemann.

— Malpractice & Contact Lenses: A Guide to Limiting Liability in Contact Lens Practice. 96p. (Orig.). (C). 1988. pap. 15.00 (*0-9620349-0-8*) Gillman-Marcuse.

Rosenwasser, Lanny J. 1997 Year Book of Allergy & Clinical Immunology. 4th ed. (Illus.). 520p. (C). (gr. 13). 1997. text 74.95 (*0-8151-7278-8*, 23107) Mosby Inc.

— Year Book of Allergy & Clinical Immunology, 1998. 5th ed. (Illus.). 408p. (C). (gr. 13). 1998. text 74.95 (*0-8151-7279-6*, 23108) Mosby Inc.

Rosenwasser, Penny. Voices from a Promised Land: Palestinian & Israeli Peace Activists Speak Their Hearts. LC 91-55411. (Illus.). 270p. (Orig.). 1992. pap. 12.95 (*0-915306-57-3*) Curbstone.

Rosenwasser, Penny, ed. Visionary Voices: Women on Power: Conversations with Shaman, Activists, Teachers, Artists & Healers. LC 92-5113. 232p. (Orig.). 1992. pap. 9.95 (*1-879960-20-6*) Aunt Lute Bks.

Rosenwasser, Rena. Desert Flats. (Illus.). 1979. 5.75 (*0-932716-06-7*) Kelsey St Pr.

— Elephants & Angels. LC 84-14413. (Illus.). 48p. 1985. 8.00 (*0-932716-19-9*) Kelsey St Pr.

— Isle. LC 91-43512. (Illus.). 56p. (C). 1992. pap. text 12.95 (*0-932716-28-8*) Kelsey St Pr.

— Isle. limited ed. Dienstfrey, Pat, ed. (Illus.). 56p. 1992. 45.00 (*0-932716-29-6*) Kelsey St Pr.

Rosenwasser, Rena & Delos, Kate. Simulacra. LC 86-18836. (Illus.). 48p. (Orig.). 1986. pap. text 23.00 (*0-932716-21-0*) Kelsey St Pr.

Rosenwasser, Rena, jt. auth. see LaPalma, Marina.

Rosenwasser, Rena, ed. see Berssenbrugge, Mei-Mei & Tuttle, Richard.

Rosenwasser, Rena, ed. see Dienstfrey, Patricia.

Rosenwasser, Rena, ed. see Einzig, Barbara.

Rosenwasser, Rena, ed. see Kitrilakis, Thalia.

Rosenwasser, Rena, ed. see Robinson, Elizabeth.

Rosenwasser, Rena, ed. see Waldrop, Rosmarie & MacDonald, Jennifer.

Rosenwasser, Robert H., et al, eds. Cerebral Ischemia: Clinical Implications & Therapeutics. (Illus.). 179p. (C). 1994. lib. bdg. 145.00 (*1-56072-137-5*) Nova Sci Pubs.

***Rosenwasser, Yefim & Kiiusupov, Rafagel Midkhatovich.** Sensitivity of Automatic Control Systems. LC 99-44791. (Controls Ser.). 436p. 1999. boxed set 89.95 (*0-8493-2293-6*) CRC Pr.

Rosenweig, David J. Spend Less, Sell More: 13 Simple Steps You Can Take Right Now to Grow Your Business. 240p. 1994. per. 21.95 (*1-55738-819-9*, Irwn Prfssnl) McGraw-Hill Prof.

Rosenweig, Marjorie, et al. From the Source: A Guide for Implementing Perinatal Addiction Prevention & Treatment Programs. (Illus.). 196p. (C). 1998. pap. text 35.00 (*0-7881-4876-1*) DIANE Pub.

Rosenwein, Barbara H. Debating the Middle Ages: Issues & Readings. LC 97-32706. 448p. 1998. pap. 34.95 (*1-57718-008-9*) Blackwell Pubs.

— Debating the Middle Ages: Issues & Readings. Little, Lester K., ed. LC 97-32706. 448p. 1998. 64.95 (*1-57718-007-0*) Blackwell Pubs.

— Negotiating Space: Power Restraint, & Privileges of Immunity in Early Medieval Europe. LC 98-31501. 328p. 1999. 55.00 (*0-8014-3523-4*); pap. 18.95 (*0-8014-8521-5*) Cornell U Pr.

— To Be the Neighbor of Saint Peter: The Social Meaning of Cluny's Property, 909-1049. LC 88-47912. 264p. 1989. text 42.50 (*0-8014-2206-X*) Cornell U Pr.

***Rosenwein, Barbara H., ed.** Anger's Past: The Social Uses of an Emotion in the Middle Ages. LC 97-39493. (Illus.). 272p. 1998. text 42.50 (*0-8014-3266-9*); pap. text 16.95 (*0-8014-8343-3*) Cornell U Pr.

Rosenwein, Barbara H., jt. ed. see Hunt.

Rosenwein, Barbara H., jt. auth. see Hunt, Lynn.

Rosenwein, Robert, jt. auth. see Barner-Barry, Carol.

Rosenzweig, jt. auth. see Austad.

Rosenzweig, A., ed. Southeastern Sangre de Cristo Mountains. (Guidebook Ser.: No. 7). (Illus.). 151p. 1956. reprint ed. pap. 20.00 (*1-58546-037-0*) NMex Geol Soc.

Rosenzweig, Cynthia, et al, eds. Climate Change & Agriculture: Analysis of Potential International Impacts. LC 95-14069. (ASA Special Publications: No. 59). 382p. 1995. pap. 34.00 (*0-89118-126-1*) Am Soc Agron.

Rosenzweig, Cynthia & Hillel, Daniel. Climate Change & the Global Harvest: Potential Impacts of the Greenhouse Effect on Agriculture. LC 97-27058. (Illus.). 336p. 1998. text 65.00 (*0-19-508889-1*) OUP.

Rosenzweig, Daphne L. Contemporary Japanese Ceramics. 1988. pap. 5.00 (*0-9619219-1-9*) Polk Mus Art.

Rosenzweig, F. Briefe und Tagebucher Bd. 1, 1900-1918, Bd. 2, 1918-1929: Herausgegeben Von R. Rosenzweig und E. Rosenzweig-Scheinmann unter Mitwirkung Von B. Casper, 2 vols., Set. 1355p. 1987. lib. bdg. 377.50 (*90-247-1769-8*) Kluwer Academic.

— Sprachdenken im Ubersetzen: Band-Arbeitspapiere zur Verdeutschung der Schrift, Vol. 4. 396p. 1984. lib. bdg. 186.00 (*90-247-2854-1*) Kluwer Academic.

Rosenzweig, Franz. God, Man, & the World: Lectures & Essays. Galli, Barbara E., ed. & tr. by. from GER. LC 98-27105. (Library of Jewish Philosophy). 1998. pap. 17.95 (*0-8156-2789-0*) Syracuse U Pr.

***Rosenzweig, Franz.** Ninety-two Poems & Hymns of Yehuda Halevi. Cohen, Richard A., ed. Kovach, Thomas et al, trs. LC 00-2655. 384p. (C). 2000. pap. text 25.95 (*0-7914-4390-6*) State U NY Pr.

— Ninety-two Poems & Hymns of Yehuda Halevi. Cohen, Richard A., ed. Kovach, Thomas et al, trs. LC 00-2655. 384p. (C). 2000. text 75.50 (*0-7914-4389-2*) State U NY Pr.

Rosenzweig, Franz. The Star of Redemption. Hallo, William W., tr. from GER. LC 84-40833. 464p. (C). 1985. reprint ed. pap. text 19.50 (*0-268-01718-2*) U of Notre Dame Pr.

***Rosenzweig, Franz.** Understanding the Sick & the Healthy: A View of World, Man & God: A View of World, Man, & God. LC 98-45818. 1999. pap. 14.95 (*0-674-92119-4*) HUP.

Rosenzweig, Franz & Galli, Barbara E. God, Man, & the World: Lectures & Essays. LC 98-27105. (Library of Jewish Philosophy). 1998. 39.95 (*0-8156-2788-2*) Syracuse U Pr.

Rosenzweig, Franz & Rosenzweig, Rafael. Sprachdenken im Ubersetzen. 286p. 1984. lib. bdg. 143.50 (*90-247-2695-6*, Pub. by M Nijhoff) Kluwer Academic.

Rosenzweig, Franz, et al. Franz Rosenzweig's "The New Thinking" LC 98-22126. (Library of Jewish Philosophy). 1998. 39.95 (*0-8156-2783-1*); pap. 17.95 (*0-8156-2784-X*) Syracuse U Pr.

***Rosenzweig, Franz, et al.** Philosophical & Theological Writings. LC 00-32028. 2000. write for info. (*0-87220-472-3*) Hackett Pub.

***Rosenzweig, Gary.** Advanced Lingo for Games. 485p. 2000. pap. 45.00 (*0-7897-2331-X*) Que.

— Using Macromedia Director X. 1999. pap. text 39.99 (*0-7897-1957-6*) Que.

Rosenzweig, Geri & Bixby, Robert. Half the Story. 41p. 1997. pap. 6.00 (*1-882983-34-3*) March Street Pr.

Rosenzweig, Ilene. The I Hate Madonna Handbook. LC 93-44463. 1994. 83.70 (*0-312-10480-4*) St Martin.

Rosenzweig, Ilene, jt. auth. see Rowley, Cynthia.

Rosenzweig, James, jt. auth. see Kast, Fremont.

Rosenzweig, Linda W. The Anchor of My Life: Middle-Class American Mothers & Daughters, 1880-1920. LC 92-44560. (History of Emotions Ser.). 293p. (C). 1993. text 50.00 (*0-8147-7438-5*) NYU Pr.

— The Anchor of My Life: Middle-Class American Mothers & Daughters, 1880-1920. LC 92-44560. (History of Emotions Ser.). 293p. (C). 1994. pap. text 19.50 (*0-8147-7455-5*) NYU Pr.

— Another Self: Middle Class American Women & Their Friends in the Twentieth Century. LC 99-6215. 1999. text 35.00 (*0-8147-7486-5*) NYU Pr.

Rosenzweig, Luc & Cohen, Bernard. Waldheim. Bacon, Josephine, tr. from FRE.Tr. of Le/Mystere Waldheim. (Illus.). 224p. 1987. 17.95 (*1-55774-010-0*) Lambda Pubs.

Rosenzweig, M. L., jt. ed. see Patil, G. P.

Rosenzweig, M. R. & Stark, O., eds. Handbook of Population & Family Economics, 2 vols. Incl. Vol. IA. LC 98-201816. 630p. 1997. 110.00 (*0-444-82645-9*, North Holland); Vol. IB. LC 98-201816. 672p. 1997. 110.00 (*0-444-82646-7*, North Holland); LC 98-201816. (Handbooks in Economics Ser.: Vol. 14). 1997. 155.00 (*0-444-89647-3*, North Holland) Elsevier.

Rosenzweig, Mark, tr. see Kott, Jan.

Rosenzweig, Mark R., ed. Annual Review of Psychology, Vol. 26. LC 50-13143. (Illus.). 1975. text 40.00 (*0-8243-0226-5*) Annual Reviews.

— Annual Review of Psychology, Vol. 27. LC 50-13143. (Illus.). 1976. text 40.00 (*0-8243-0227-3*) Annual Reviews.

— Annual Review of Psychology, Vol. 28. LC 50-13143. (Illus.). 1977. text 40.00 (*0-8243-0228-1*) Annual Reviews.

— Annual Review of Psychology, Vol. 29. LC 50-13143. (Illus.). 1978. text 40.00 (*0-8243-0229-X*) Annual Reviews.

— Annual Review of Psychology, Vol. 30. LC 50-13143. (Illus.). 1979. text 40.00 (*0-8243-0230-3*) Annual Reviews.

— Annual Review of Psychology, Vol. 33. LC 50-13143. (Illus.). 1982. text 40.00 (*0-8243-0233-8*) Annual Reviews.

— Annual Review of Psychology, Vol. 34. LC 50-13143. (Illus.). 1983. text 40.00 (*0-8243-0234-6*) Annual Reviews.

— Annual Review of Psychology, Vol. 36. LC 50-13143. (Illus.). 1985. text 40.00 (*0-8243-0236-2*) Annual Reviews.

— Annual Review of Psychology, Vol. 37. LC 50-13143. (Illus.). 1986. text 40.00 (*0-8243-0237-0*) Annual Reviews.

— Annual Review of Psychology, Vol. 39. LC 50-13143. (Illus.). 1988. text 40.00 (*0-8243-0239-7*) Annual Reviews.

— Annual Review of Psychology, Vol. 40. LC 50-13143. (Illus.). 1989. text 40.00 (*0-8243-0240-0*) Annual Reviews.

R

An Asterisk (*) at the beginning of an entry indicates that the title is appearing for the first time.

R

— Annual Review of Psychology, Vol. 41. LC 50-13143. 1990. text 40.00 (*0-8243-0241-9*) Annual Reviews.

— Annual Review of Psychology, Vol. 42. LC 50-13143. 1991. text 40.00 (*0-8243-0242-7*) Annual Reviews.

— Annual Review of Psychology, Vol. 43. 1992. text 43.00 (*0-8243-0243-5*) Annual Reviews.

— International Psychological Science: Progress, Problems, & Prospects. 306p. 1992. pap. text 14.95 (*1-55798-168-X*) Am Psychol.

Rosenzweig, Mark R., et al, eds. Annual Review of Psychology, Vol. 35. LC 50-13143. (Illus.). 1984. text 40.00 (*0-8243-0235-4*) Annual Reviews.

Rosenzweig, Mark R., et al. Biological Psychology: An Introduction to Behavioral, Cognitive, & Clinical Neuroscience. 2nd ed. (Illus.). 561p. (C). 1998. text 76.95 incl. cd-rom (*0-87893-791-9*) Sinauer Assocs.

Rosenzweig, Mark R., jt. auth. see Jasso, Guillermina.

Rosenzweig, Mark R., jt. auth. see Renner, M. J.

Rosenzweig, Mark R., jt. ed. see Binswanger, Hans P.

Rosenzweig, Michael L. Species Diversity in Space & Time. (Illus.). 458p. (C). 1995. text 80.00 (*0-521-49618-7*); pap. text 31.95 (*0-521-49952-6*) Cambridge U Pr.

Rosenzweig, N., jt. ed. see Narkis, M.

Rosenzweig, Norman. Community Mental Health Programs in England: An American View. LC 74-13365. 282p. reprint ed. pap. 87.50 (*0-608-16560-3*, 202766400055) Bks Demand.

Rosenzweig, Norman & Griscon, Hilda, eds. Psychopharmacology & Psychotherapy: Synthesis or Antithesis? LC 78-4088. 256p. 1978. 35.95 (*0-87705-354-5*, Kluwer Acad Hman Sci) Kluwer Academic.

Rosenzweig, P. M. Married & Alone: The Way Back. (Illus.). 282p. (C). 1992. 24.50 (*0-306-44125-X*, Plen Insight) Perseus Pubng.

Rosenzweig, Philip M., jt. auth. see Riccomini, Donald R.

Rosenzweig, Phyllis. Dogs. 23p. (Orig.). 1996. pap. 5.00 (*0-9619097-7-3*) Edge Bks.

***Rosenzweig, Phyllis.** Reasonable Accommodation. 52p. 1998. 18.00 (*0-937013-73-0*, Pub. by Potes Poets) SPD-Small Pr Dist.

Rosenzweig, Rafael, jt. auth. see Rosenzweig, Franz.

Rosenzweig, Rafael N. The Economic Consequences of Zionism. LC 89-17405. viii, 260p. (Orig.). 1989. pap. 79.00 (*90-04-09147-5*) Brill Academic Pubs.

Rosenzweig, Robert M. The Political University: Policy, Politics, & Presidential Leadership in the American Research University. LC 97-25109. 200p. 1998. text 31.95 (*0-8018-5721-X*) Johns Hopkins.

Rosenzweig, Robert M. & Turlington, Barbara. The Research Universities & Their Patrons. LC 81-19685. 200p. 1982. pap. 13.95 (*0-520-04735-4*, Pub. by U CA Pr) Cal Prin Full Svc.

Rosenzweig, Rosie. A Jewish Mother in Shangri-La. 192p. Date not set. pap. 13.95 (*1-57062-459-3*) Shambhala Pubns.

Rosenzweig, Rosie. A Jewish Mother in Shangri-La. LC 97-42455. 176p. 1998. 18.00 (*1-57062-353-8*, Pub. by Shambhala Pubns) Random.

Rosenzweig, Rosie, ed. The Jewish Guide to Boston & New England. 260p. 1995. 19.95 (*0-9645367-0-6*) Jewish Adv.

Rosenzweig, Roy. Eight Hours for What We Will: Workers & Leisure in an Industrial City, 1870-1920. (Interdisciplinary Perspectives on Modern History Ser.). (Illus.). 310p. 1985. pap. text 18.95 (*0-521-31397-X*) Cambridge U Pr.

***Rosenzweig, Roy.** Presence of the Past: Popular Uses of History in American Life. 2000. pap. text 18.50 (*0-231-11149-5*) Col U Pr.

Rosenzweig, Roy, et al, eds. Government & the Arts in Thirties America: A Guide to Oral Histories & Other Research Materials. (Illus.). 344p. (Orig.). 1986. 57.00 (*0-8026-0002-6*); pap. 39.00 (*0-8026-0003-4*) Univ Pub Assocs.

Rosenzweig, Roy & Blackmar, Elizabeth. The Park & the People: A History of Central Park. LC 92-7062. (Illus.). 600p. 1992. text 45.00 (*0-8014-2516-6*) Cornell U Pr.

— The Park & the People: A History of Central Park. (Illus.). 640p. 1998. pap. text 22.50 (*0-8014-9751-5*) Cornell U Pr.

Rosenzweig, Roy & Thelen, David P. The Presence of the Past: Popular Uses of History in American Life. LC 97-47535. 320p. 1998. 27.50 (*0-231-11148-7*) Col U Pr.

Rosenzweig, Roy, jt. ed. see Leon, Warren.

***Rosenzweig, Saul.** Freud, Jung & Hall the King-Maker: The Expedition to America, 1909. 477p. 2000. reprint ed. text 27.00 (*0-7881-6864-9*) DIANE Pub.

Rosenzweig, Saul. Freud, Jung & Hall the Kingmaker: The Historic Expedition to America (1909) (Illus.). 400p. 1992. 27.50 (*0-88937-110-5*) Hogrefe & Huber Pubs.

***Rosenzweig, Saul.** The Historic Expedition to America (1909) Freud, Jung & Hall the King-Maker. 477p. 2000. reprint ed. pap. 17.00 (*0-7881-9424-0*) DIANE Pub.

***Rosenzweig, Stan.** Smart Marketing: What Big Companies Practice & Small Enterprises Must Learn. 160p. 2000. pap. 29.95 (*1-58652-002-4*) Emery.

— Smart Selling: How to Turn Ordinary Selling into Extraordinary Income. (Illus.). 160p. 1999. 29.95 (*1-58652-000-8*) Emery.

— Smart Telemarketing: How You Can Turn Ordinary Telemarketing into Extraordinary Income. (Illus.). 64p. 1999. pap. 9.00 (*1-58652-001-6*) Emery.

Roser, Bill, et al, eds. The Tale of the Frog Prince. (J). 1979. pap. 3.75 (*0-87129-199-1*, T48) Dramatic Pub.

***Roser, Birgit.** Mythenbehandlung und Kompositionstechnik in Christa Wolfs Medea. Stimmen. 2000. 26.95 (*3-631-35480-0*) P Lang Pubng.

Roser, Hermann-Josef & Meisenheimer, Klaus. Jets in Extragalactic Radio Sources: Proceedings of a Workshop Held at Ringberg Castle, Tegernsee, FRG, September 22-28, 1991. LC 93-29538. (Lecture Notes in Physics Ser.: Vol. 421). 1993. 80.95 (*0-387-57164-7*) Spr-Verlag.

Roser, Hermann-Josef, jt. ed. see Meisenheimer, Klaus.

Roser, Hugh N. Sales Engineering. LC HF5415.. (Instructional Resource Package Ser.). 140p. 1983. reprint ed. pap., student ed. 43.40 (*0-608-01352-8*, 206209200002) Bks Demand.

Roser, Mark. The Cleansing of the Heavens. LC 99-192930. 1998. pap. 11.99 (*1-56043-311-6*, Treasure Hse) Destiny Image.

Roser, Martin. Karyologische, Systematische und Chrologische Untersuchungen an der Gattung Helictotrichon Besser Ex Schultes & Schultes (Poaceae) Im Westlichen Mittelmeergebiet. (Dissertationes Botanicae Ser.: Band 145). (GER., Illus.). 252p. 1989. pap. 53.00 (*3-443-64056-7*, Pub. by Gebruder Borntraeger) Balogh.

Roser, Nancy L. & Frith, Margaret, eds. Children's Choices: Teaching with Books Children Like. LC 83-10697. 128p. reprint ed. pap. 39.70 (*0-7837-1235-9*, 204137200020) Bks Demand.

Roser, Nancy L. & Martinez, Miriam, eds. Book Talk & Beyond: Children & Teachers Respond to Literature. 320p. 1995. pap. 24.95 (*0-87207-129-4*) Intl Reading.

Roser, Susan E. Mayflower Births & Deaths: From the Files of George Ernest Bowman, at the Massachusetts Society of Mayflower Descendants, 2 vols., Set. 1075p. 1997. reprint ed. pap. 75.00 (*0-8063-1340-4*, 4999) Genealog Pub.

— Mayflower Deeds & Probates: From the Files of George Ernest Bowman, at the Massachusetts Society of Mayflower Descendants. LC 94-77222. 660p. 1994. pap. 44.95 (*0-8063-1423-0*, 4994) Genealog Pub.

— Mayflower Increasings. 2nd ed. LC 95-76482. 170p. 1996. reprint ed. pap. 20.00 (*0-8063-1479-6*) Genealog Pub.

***Roser, T. & Zhang, S. Y., eds.** Workshop on Instabilities of High Intensity, Hadron Beams in Rings, Vol. 496. LC 99-68238. (Conference Proceedings Ser.: Vol. 496). (Illus.). 412p. 1999. 100.00 (*1-56396-910-6*) Am Inst Physics.

Rosernwasser, David & Stephen, Jill. Writing Analytically. LC 96-75317. 272p. (C). 1996. pap. text 24.00 (*0-15-501889-2*, Pub. by Harcourt Coll Pubs) Harcourt.

Roses, A. D., et al, eds. Apolipoprotein E & Alzheimer's Disease. (Illus.). 216p. 1996. 75.00 (*3-540-60798-6*) Spr-Verlag.

***Roses, D. F.** Breast Cancer - Patient Volume. (Illus.). 200p. 1998. pap. write for info. (*0-443-05582-3*) Church.

— Breast Cancer - Physician & Patient Volumes, 2 bks. 1998. write for info. (*0-443-05613-7*) Church.

Roses, Daniel F. Breast Cancer: Physician's Volume. LC 98-12904. 688p. (C). 1999. text 79.60 (*0-443-05581-5*) Church.

Roses, Daniel F., et al. Diagnosis & Management of Cutaneous Malignant Melanoma. (Major Problems in Clinical Surgery Ser.: Vol. 27). (Illus.). 336p. 1983. text 142.00 (*0-7216-7706-1*, W B Saunders Co) Harcrt Hlth Sci Grp.

Roses, Lorraine E. Harlem Renaissance & Beyond: Literary Biographies of 100 Black Women Writers, 1900-1945. (Illus.). 448p. 1997. 18.95 (*0-674-37255-7*) HUP.

— Voices of the Storyteller: Cuba's Lino Novas Calvo, 14. LC 85-27148. (Contributions to the Study of World Literature Ser.: No. 14). 170p. 1986. 49.95 (*0-313-25077-4*, RVS, Greenwood Pr) Greenwood.

Roses, Lorraine E. & Randolph, Ruth E. Harlem Renaissance & Beyond: Literary Biographies of One Hundred Black Women Writers, 1900-1945. (Illus.). 536p. 1989. 50.00 (*0-8161-8926-9*, Hall Reference) Macmillan.

Roses, Lorraine E. & Randolph, Ruth E., eds. Harlem's Glory: Black Women Writing, 1900-1950. LC 96-12342. (Illus.). 544p. 1996. 29.95 (*0-674-37269-7*); 17.95 (*0-674-37270-0*) HUP.

Roseta, Steve, jt. auth. see Dobler, Joe.

Rosetree, Rose. Aura Reading Through All Your Senses: Celestial Perception Made Practical. LC 96-60564. 272p. (Orig.). 1996. pap. 14.95 (*0-9651145-3-8*) Womens Intuition.

— Empowered by Empathy: 50 Ways to Fly in Spirit. (Illus.). 1999. pap. write for info. (*0-9651145-8-9*) Womens Intuition.

— The Power of Face Reading: For Sales, Self-Esteem, & Better Relationships. LC 99-165374. (Illus.). 382p. 1998. pap. 18.95 (*0-9651145-2-X*) Womens Intuition.

Rosett, Arthur. Contract Law & Its Application. 4th ed. (University Casebook Ser.). 1049p. 1991. reprint ed. text 37.75 (*0-88277-633-9*) Foundation Pr.

— Contract Law & Its Application. 5th ed. LC 94-9882. (University Casebook Ser.). 1071p. 1994. text 46.00 (*1-56662-151-8*) Foundation Pr.

— Contract Law & Its Application: Teacher's Manual. 4th ed. (University Casebook Ser.). 191p. 1990. pap. text. write for info. (*0-88277-847-1*) Foundation Pr.

Rosett, Arthur & Burnham, Scott J. Contract Law & Its Application. 5th ed. (University Casebook Ser.). 192p. 1996. pap. text, teacher ed. write for info. (*1-56662-212-3*) Foundation Pr.

Rosett, Henry L. & Weiner, Lyn. Alcohol & the Fetus: A Clinical Perspective. LC 84-919. (Illus.). 220p. 1984. text 37.50 (*0-19-503458-9*) OUP.

Rosett, Richard N., ed. The Role of Health Insurance in the Health Services Sector: A Conference of the Universities-National Bureau Committee for Economic Research. LC 76-8856. (Universities-National Bureau Conference Ser.: 27). 562p. reprint ed. pap. 174.30 (*0-608-15022-3*, 205215800045) Bks Demand.

Rosett, Richard N., jt. auth. see Universities-National Bureau Staff.

Rosetta, Dick, jt. auth. see Miller, Phil.

Rosetta, L. & Mascie-Taylor, C. G., eds. Variability in Human Fertility. (Studies in Biological Anthropology: Vol. 19). (Illus.). 235p. (C). 1996. text 57.95 (*0-521-49569-5*) Cambridge U Pr.

Rosetta, M. T. Compositional Translation. LC 94-20091. (International Series in Engineering & Computer Science, VLSI, Computer Architecture, & Digital Screen Processing: Vol. 273). 496p. (C). 1994. text 153.00 (*0-7923-9462-3*) Kluwer Academic.

Rosette, Jack. Improving Tamper-Evident Packaging: Problems, Tests, & Solutions. LC 91-67903. 152p. 1992. text 84.95 (*0-87762-906-4*) Technomic.

Rosetti, Alexander. Etudes Linguistiques. (Janua Linguarum, Series Major: No. 95). 1973. 110.75 (*90-279-2596-8*) Mouton.

Rosetti, Antonio. Antonio Rosetti: Five Wind Partitas: Music for the Oettingen-Wallerstein Court. Murray, Sterling E., ed. (Recent Researches in Music of the Classic Era Ser.: Vol. RRC30-31). xxiii, 169p. 1989. pap. 60.00 (*0-89579-232-X*) A-R Eds.

Rosetti, Rosalie, jt. auth. see Geiman, Diane.

Rosetti, Rosalie, ed. see American Correctional Association Staff.

Rosetti, Stefano. Stefano Rosetti: Madrigals for Three to Eight Voices. Skei, Allen B., ed. (Recent Researches in Music of the Renaissance Ser.: Vol. RRR66-67). (Illus.). xviii, 208p. 1985. pap. 70.00 (*0-89579-149-8*, RRR66-67) A-R Eds.

Rosetti, William M., ed. see Blake, William.

Rosevear, Francis & McMartin, Barbara. Colvin in the Adirondacks: A Chronology Hudex. 150p. 1992. 22.00 (*0-932052-98-3*) North Country.

Rosevear, Sylvia. Handbook of Obstetric Management. LC 95-21394. 192p. 1996. pap. 29.95 (*0-632-03555-2*) Blackwell Sci.

Roseveare. The British Treasury (From 1066) (Illus.). 1969. lib. bdg. 25.00 (*0-932106-37-4*) S J Durst.

Roseveare, Henry. FINCL REVLTN 1660 1750. (C). 1995. pap. 15.93 (*0-582-35449-8*) Addison-Wesley.

Roseveare, Henry. Markets & Merchants of the Late Seventeenth Century: The Marescoe-David Letters, 1668-1680. (Records of Social & Economic History, New Series British Academy: No. XII). (Illus.). 700p. 1992. reprint ed. pap. text 85.00 (*0-19-726106-X*) OUP.

Rosevold, Doreen, ed. see Bjerke, Luther.

***Rosewall, Ellen.** Sparkle Island: Stories of Life, Love & Walloon Lake. Johnson, Amy, ed. (Illus.). 192p. 2000. pap. 12.95 (*0-9701107-0-7*) Raven Tree Pr.

***Rosewater, Amy.** Jim Thome: Lefty Launcher. (Illus.). 96p. (J). 2000. pap. 4.95 (*1-58261-251-X*) Sports Pub.

Rosewater, Frank. Ninety-Six: A Romance of Utopia. LC 72-154460. (Utopian Literature Ser.). 1976. reprint ed. 23.95 (*0-405-03542-X*) Ayer.

Rosewater, Lynne B. & Walker, Lenore E. A Handbook of Feminist Therapy: Women's Issues in Psychotherapy. 384p. 1985. 44.95 (*0-8261-4970-7*) Springer Pub.

Rosewater, Victor. Special Assessments: A Study in Municipal Finance. LC 68-56686. (Columbia University. Studies in the Social Sciences: No. 7). reprint ed. 29.50 (*0-404-51007-8*) AMS Pr.

Rosewell, Pamela. The Five Silent Years of Corrie Ten Boom. large type ed. (Large Print Inspirational Ser.). 1987. pap. 12.95 (*0-8027-2577-5*) Walker & Co.

Rosewitz, Dawn. The Flying Frog Circus. LC 97-47241. (Mona & Friends in the Land of Ican Ser.). (Illus.). (J). 1998. pap. 7.95 (*0-932991-61-0*, Different Bks) Place in the Woods.

Rosga, Karen S. Jewel Cave: The Story Behind the Scenery. Hosford, Helga, tr. (GER., Illus.). 48p. 1998. pap. 8.95 (*0-88714-825-5*) KC Pubns.

— Jewel Cave: The Story Behind the Scenery. LC 98-65028. (Illus.). 48p. 1998. pap. 7.95 (*0-88714-139-0*) KC Pubns.

Rosgen, Dave. Applied River Morphology. (Illus.). 350p. 1996. text 89.95 (*0-9653289-0-2*) Wildlnd Hydrology.

Rosgen, Dave & Billings, Gene. Finding Birds in Connecticut: A Habitat-Based Guide to 450 Sites. LC 96-68691. (Illus.). 640p. (Orig.). 1996. pap. 25.00 (*0-9652708-0-7*) G Billings.

Rosgen, David L. & Silvey, Hilton L. Field Guide to Stream Classification. (C). 1998. text 45.00 (*0-9653289-1-0*) Wildlnd Hydrology.

Roshal, A., jt. auth. see Karpov, Anatoly.

Roshan & Apurvananda, Swami. Sri Aurobindo in Baroda. 182p. 1993. pap. 9.50 (*81-7058-318-7*, Pub. by SAA) E-W Cultural Ctr.

Roshan, Sorosh, ed. The Elimination of Violence Against Women & Children. 80p. 1998. pap. 10.00 (*0-9667667-0-9*) Intl Health Awareness.

Roshberg, Robert. Game of Thieves. 1980. 19.95 (*0-405-13687-0*) Ayer.

Roshchin, Mikhail. First Love. 140p. 1991. 19.95 (*0-7145-2932-X*) M Boyars Pubs.

Roshchina, Valentina D., jt. auth. see Roshchina, Victoria V.

Roshchina, Victoria V. & Roshchina, Valentina D. The Excretory Function of Higher Plants. LC 93-4993. 1993. 237.95 (*0-387-56544-2*) Spr-Verlag.

Roshco, Bernard. Newsmaking. LC 75-5076. x, 160p. 1979. pap. text 3.95 (*0-226-72815-3*) U Ch Pr.

— Newsmaking. LC 75-5076. x, 160p. 1995. lib. bdg. 14.50 (*0-226-72814-5*) U Ch Pr.

Roshefsky, Eve F. & Hessel, Carolyn S. How to Promote a Jewish Book. rev. ed. 15p. 1994. pap. text 10.00 (*1-885838-01-8*) Jwsh Bk Council.

Rosheim, David L. Galaxy Magazine: The Dark & the Light Years. (Illus.). 361p. 1986. 18.00 (*0-911682-28-7*) Advent.

— Old Iowegian Legends. (Illus.). 196p. (Orig.). 1991. pap. 12.95 (*0-9602996-2-9*) Andromeda.

— Old Iowegian Sagas. (Illus.). 181p. (Orig.). 1989. pap. 12.95 (*0-9602996-1-0*) Andromeda.

— The Other Minneapolis. (Illus.). (Orig.). pap. 6.50 (*0-9602996-0-2*) Andromeda.

— Particles of Light: Jackson County & Its Authors. 214p. (Orig.). 1995. pap. 20.00 (*0-9602996-3-7*) Andromeda.

Rosheim, Mark E. Robot Evolution: The Development of Anthrobotics. 423p. 1994. 99.00 (*0-471-02622-0*) Wiley.

Roshelle, Ariel. The Voices of Angels, Vol. I. (Illus.). 32p. (Orig.). 1995. pap. write for info. (*0-9644530-1-0*) AR-L Pubns.

Roshelle, Ariel, ed. see Roshelle, Danille.

Roshelle, Danille. The Shepherd & His Shepherdess Are Leading Their Sheep to the Ark, Vol. I. Roshelle, Ariel, ed. 340p. (Orig.). 1995. pap. 21.00 (*0-9644530-0-2*) AR-L Pubns.

Roshi, Kosho U. Wholehearted Way: A Translation of Eibei Dogen's Bendowa. 1997. pap. text 14.95 (*0-8048-3105-X*) Tuttle Pubng.

Roshi, Shibayama Z., et al, eds. The Book of the Zen Grove: Phrases for Zen Practice. 2nd expanded rev. ed. Lewis, Zenrin R., tr. from JPN. LC 96-60319. (Illus.). 160p. 1996. 27.95 (*0-9651499-2-7*); pap. 16.90 (*0-9651499-3-5*) Zen Sangha.

Roshi, Shodo H. Morning Dewdrops of the Mind: Teachings of a Contemporary Zen Master. Storandt, Daichi-Priscilla, tr. LC 93-8465. 90p. (Orig.). 1993. pap. 9.95 (*1-883319-10-2*) Frog Ltd CA.

Roshier, Bob. Controlling Crime: The Classical Perspective in Criminology. 160p. 1989. 45.00 (*0-335-15874-9*); pap. 14.99 (*0-335-15873-0*) OpUniv Pr.

Rosholt, Malcolm. Days of the Ching Pao. rev. ed. LC 78-52589. (Illus.). 192p. 1986. 34.95 (*0-910417-07-5*) Rosholt Hse.

— Our County, Our Story: Portage County. (Illus.). 600p. 1999. reprint ed. lib. bdg. 62.50 (*0-8328-9792-2*) Higginson Bk Co.

— The Press Corps of Old Shanghai. (Illus.). 36p. (Orig.). 1994. pap. write for info. (*0-910417-10-5*) Rosholt Hse.

— Trains of Wisconsin. 176p. 1992. text 29.95 (*0-9635065-0-1*) Nat Railrd Mus.

Rosholt, Malcolm & Rosholt, Margaret. The Child of Two Mothers. LC 83-63177. (Illus.). 108p. (J). (gr. 4 up). 1983. lib. bdg. 9.95 (*0-910417-03-2*) Rosholt Hse.

Rosholt, Malcom. Indian Lands. (Illus.). 352p. 1996. pap. text 17.50 (*0-87341-084-X*) Krause Pubns.

Rosholt, Malcom, tr. see Nelson, Clifford A., ed.

Rosholt, Margaret, jt. auth. see Rosholt, Malcolm.

Roshton, M. Legal Secretary's Concise Dictionary. 1974. 8.00 (*0-87511-099-1*) Claitors.

***Roshwald, Aviel.** Ethnic Nationalism & the Unraveling of Empires: Central Europe, Russia & the Middle East, 1914-1923. LC 00-42475. 2001. pap. write for info. (*0-415-24229-0*) Routledge.

Roshwald, Aviel & Stites, Richard, eds. European Culture in the Great War: The Arts, Entertainment & Propaganda, 1914-1918. LC 98-27978. (Studies in the Social & Cultural History of Modern Warfare: No. 6). (Illus.). 400p. (C). 1999. text 64.95 (*0-521-57015-8*) Cambridge U Pr.

***Roshwald, Mordecai.** Liberty: Its Meaning & Scope, 77. LC 99-54455. (Contributions in Philosophy Ser.). 216p. 2000. 65.00 (*0-313-31275-3*, Greenwood Pr) Greenwood.

Roshwald, Mordecai. The Transient & the Absolute, 70. LC 98-44217. (Contributions in Philosophy Ser.: Vol. 70). 208p. 1999. 59.95 (*0-313-30936-1*) Greenwood.

Rosi, Eugene, jt. auth. see Nemerowicz, Gloria.

Rosi, Mauro, jt. ed. see Freundt, Armin.

Rosic, George S., jt. auth. see Klein, Carl R.

Rosich, Katherine J., jt. auth. see Curran, Barbara A.

Rosich, Katherine J., jt. auth. see Levine, Felice J.

Rosicky, J., jt. auth. see Adamek, Jiri.

Rosicruciae. Evolution of Immortality. 1996. reprint ed. spiral bd. 14.50 (*0-7873-0738-6*) Hlth Research.

Rosicrucian Fellowship Staff. Children, Aquarian Age Stories For..., 7 vols., Set, Vols. 1-7. 2nd ed. (Illus.). (J). 1989. pap. text 28.00 (*0-911274-94-4*) Rosicrucian.

— Children, Sunday School Lessons For..., 6 vols., Set, Vols. 1-6. 1985. pap. text 16.00 (*0-911274-63-4*) Rosicrucian.

— Ephemerides 1900-2000 Midnight. (Illus.). (Orig.). 1990. pap. text 37.75 (*0-911274-05-7*) Rosicrucian.

— Ephemerides, 2000-2100: (Noon) - 2000-2100. 1992. pap. 40.50 (*0-911274-24-3*) Rosicrucian.

— Ephemeris, 1980-1989: Ten Year (Noon) 1978. reprint ed. pap. text 19.00 (*0-911274-75-8*) Rosicrucian.

— Ephemeris, 1880-1889: Ten Year (Noon) 1918. pap. text 15.50 (*0-911274-40-5*) Rosicrucian.

— Ephemeris, 1890-1899: Ten Year (Noon) 1918. pap. text 15.50 (*0-911274-41-3*) Rosicrucian.

— Ephemeris, 1900-1909: Ten Year (Noon) 1918. pap. text 15.50 (*0-911274-42-1*) Rosicrucian.

— Ephemeris, 1910-1919: Ten Year (Noon) 1918. pap. text 15.50 (*0-911274-43-X*) Rosicrucian.

— Ephemeris, 1920-1929: Ten Year (Noon) 1918. pap. text 15.50 (*0-911274-44-8*) Rosicrucian.

— Ephemeris, 1930-1939: Ten Year (Noon) 1918. pap. text 15.50 (*0-911274-45-6*) Rosicrucian.

— Ephemeris, 1940-1949: Ten Year (Noon) 1989. reprint ed. pap. text 15.50 (*0-911274-46-4*) Rosicrucian.

— Ephemeris, 1950-1959: Ten Year (Noon) 1949. reprint ed. pap. text 15.50 (*0-911274-47-2*) Rosicrucian.

— Ephemeris, 1960-1969: Ten Year (Noon) 1959. reprint ed. pap. text 15.50 (*0-911274-48-0*) Rosicrucian.

— Ephemeris, 1970-1979: Ten Year (Noon) 1969. reprint ed. pap. text 15.50 (*0-911274-49-9*) Rosicrucian.

— Ephemeris, 1990-1999: Ten Year (Noon) 1988. reprint ed. pap. text 19.00 (*0-911274-76-6*) Rosicrucian.

— Ephmeris, 1950-2000 (Midnight) (Illus.). 1993. pap. text 23.00 (*0-88112-029-4*) Rosicrucian.

An Asterisk (*) at the beginning of an entry indicates that the title is appearing for the first time.

R

An Asterisk (*) at the beginning of an entry indicates that the title is appearing for the first time.

Roskoski, Robert, Jr. Slide Set for Biochemistry. (Text & Review (STAR) Ser.). (Illus.). 24p. 1996. ring bd. 625.00 incl. sl. (0-7216-6527-6, W B Saunders Co) Harcrt Hlth Sci Grp.

Roskoski, Robert & Herbert, Jack D. Biochemistry Review. LC 95-41655. (Illus.). 252p. 1996. pap. text 20.95 (0-7216-5175-5, W B Saunders Co) Harcrt Hlth Sci Grp.

Roslaniec, Julia. Black Surgeon. LC 97-91056. 1999. pap. 13.95 (0-533-12552-9) Vantage.

***Roslanowski, Andrzej & Shelah, Saharon.** Norms on Possibilities: Forcing with Trees & Creatures. LC 99-27220. (Memoirs of the American Mathematical Society Ser.). 1999. write for info. (0-8218-1180-0) Am Math.

Roslavets, H. Museum of Western & Oriental Art: Kiev. (Illus.). 192p. (C). 1985. text 70.00 (0-7855-5849-7, Pub. by Collets) St Mut.

Roslavleva, Natalia. Era of the Russian Ballet. LC 79-11509. (Series in Dance). 1979. reprint ed. 37.50 (0-306-79536-1) Da Capo.

Rosler. Gansebraten und Andere Geschichten: Level A. text 7.95 (0-88436-109-8) EMC-Paradigm.

***Rosler, Axel.** Die Deutschen Universitatsklinika Im Spannungsfeld Ihrer Rahmenedingungen: Eine Standortestimmung Im Hinblick Auf die Wirtschaftlichkeit Im Internationalen Vergleich. (Illus.). XIV, 485p. 1999. 79.95 (3-631-34589-5) P Lang Pubng.

Rosler, Martha. If You Lived Here . . . The City in Art, Theory & Social Activism. Wallis, Brian, ed. (Discussions in Contemporary Culture Ser.: Vol. 6). (Illus.). 312p. 1991. pap. 16.95 (1-56584-498-X, Pub. by New Press NY) Norton.

— In the Place of the Public: Observations of a Frequent Flyer. (Illus.). 168p. 1999. pap. 45.00 (3-89322-880-2, Pub. by Edition Cantz) Dist Art Pubs.

— Service: A Trilogy on Colonization. 36p. 1978. pap. 5.00 (0-89439-007-4) Printed Matter.

***Rosler, Michael & Wendl, Tobias, eds.** Frontiers & Borderlands: Anthropological Perspectives. (Illus.). xii, 239p. 1999. pap. 37.95 (3-631-35013-9) P Lang Pubng.

— Frontiers & Borderlands: Anthropological Perspectives. LC 99-47425. 239p. (C). 1999. pap. text 37.95 (0-8204-4344-1) P Lang Pubng.

Rosler, Roland. Biologie Im Horizont der Philosophie: Der Entwurf Einer Europaischen <<Bioethik>>-Konvention. 285p. 1997. 31.95 (3-631-30870-1) P Lang Pubng.

Rosloniec, Stanislaw. Algorithms for Computer Aided Design of Linear Microwave Circuits. (Microwave Library). 256p. 1990. disk 36.00 (0-89006-873-9) Artech Hse.

Roslyakov, G. S., jt. auth. see Pirumov, U. G.

Rosman. From Catholic to Protestant: Religion & the People in Tudor England. LC 97-108998. 112p. (C). 1996. pap. 11.95 (1-85728-433-X, Pub. by UCL Pr Ltd) Taylor & Francis.

— The Tapestry of Culture. 7th ed. 2000. 29.74 (0-07-232154-7) McGraw.

Rosman, jt. auth. see Rubel.

Rosman, Abraham & Rubel, Paula. Feasting with Mine Enemy: Rank & Exchange among Northwest Coast Societies. (Illus.). 221p. 1986. reprint ed. pap. text 12.50 (0-88133-221-6) Waveland Pr.

Rosman, Abraham & Rubel, Paula G. The Tapestry of Culture: An Introduction to Cultural Anthropology. 6th ed. LC 97-25978. 368p. (C). 1997. pap. 40.00 (0-07-054000-4) McGraw.

Rosman, Abraham, jt. auth. see Rubel, Paula G.

Rosman, Bernice L., jt. ed. see Fishman, H. Charles.

Rosman, Doreen. Evangelicals & Culture. (Modern Revivals in History Ser.). 262p. 1993. 58.95 (0-7512-0056-5, Pub. by Gregg Revivals) Ashgate Pub Co.

Rosman, Lowell R. How to Form a Lasting Love Relationship! The Comprehensive Parental Guide to Causes & Treatment. 1986. pap. text 6.95 (0-936320-24-9) Compact Books.

Rosman, M. S. The Lords' Jews: Magnate-Jewish Relations in the Polish-Lithuanian Commonwealth During the 18th Century. (Harvard Ukrainian Research Institute Monograph). (Illus.). 260p. (C). 1990. reprint ed. text 32.95 (0-916458-18-0) Harvard Ukrainian.

— The Lords' Jews: Magnate-Jewish Relations in the Polish-Lithuanian Commonwealth During the 18th Century. (Harvard Ukrainian Research Institute Monograph). (Illus.). 260p. (C). 1992. reprint ed. pap. text 18.00 (0-916458-47-4) Harvard Ukrainian.

Rosman, Moshe. Founder of Hasidism: A Quest for the Historical Ba'al Shem Tov. LC 95-35641. (Contraversions: Critical Studies in Jewish Literature, Culture, & Society: Vol. 5). (Illus.). 316p. (C). 1996. 48.00 (0-520-20191-4, Pub. by U CA Pr) Cal Prin Full Svc.

Rosman, Steven M. The Bird of Paradise & Other Sabbath Stories. (Illus.). (Orig.). 1994. pap. 8.95 (0-8074-0529-9, 123725) UAHC.

— Jewish Healing Wisdom. LC 97-10003. 144p. 1997. 25.00 (0-7657-9956-1) Aronson.

— Jewish Parenting Wisdom. LC 97-4335. 176p. 1997. 25.00 (0-7657-5969-1) Aronson.

— Sidrah Stories: A Torah Companion. 120p. (J). (gr. 4-6). pap., teacher ed., wbk. ed. 8.95 (0-8074-0429-2, 121723) UAHC.

— The Twenty-Two Gates to the Garden. LC 93-35944. 224p. (J). 1994. pap. 24.95 (1-56821-124-4) Aronson.

Rosman, Steven M., jt. auth. see Schram, Peninnah.

Rosmarin, Leonard. Saint-Evremond: Artiste de l'Euphorie. LC 86-63080. (FRE.). 112p. 1987. 18.95 (0-917786-52-1) Summa Pubns.

***Rosnau, Wendy.** Long Hot Summer. (Intimate Moments Ser.: Vol. 996). 2000. per. 4.50 (0-373-07996-6) Silhouette.

Rosnay, Joel De, see De Rosnay, Joel.

Rosneck, Karen, tr. see Khvoshchinskaya, Nadezhda.

Rosner. Fundamentals of Biostatistics. 3rd ed. (Statistics Ser.). 1989. student ed. 13.50 (0-534-91974-X) Brooks-Cole.

— Fundamentals of Biostatistics 5th ed. (Statistics Ser.). 2000. pap. text, student ed. write for info. (0-534-37120-5) Brooks-Cole.

Rosner, B., jt. ed. see Kalish, R.

Rosner, B. S. & Pickering, J. B. Vowel Perception & Production. LC 93-47078. (Psychology Ser.: No. 23). (Illus.). 444p. (C). 1994. text 120.00 (0-19-852138-3) OUP.

Rosner, Bernard. Fundamentals Of Biostatistics. 3rd ed. (Statistics). 655p. (C). 1989. pap. 51.50 (0-534-91973-1) Wadsworth Pub.

— Fundamentals of Biostatistics. 4th ed. 682p. 1994. pap. 81.95 (0-534-20940-8) Wadsworth Pub.

— Fundamentals of Biostatistics. 4th ed. (Statistics Ser.). 1995. pap., student ed. 25.95 (0-534-20941-6) Wadsworth Pub.

***Rosner, Bob.** Boss's Complete Survival Guide: Everything You Need to Know about Getting Through. (Illus.). 2000. pap. 16.95 (0-07-136273-8) McGraw.

— Working Wounded: Advice That Adds Insight to Injury. LC 97-27159. 272p. 1998. 16.00 (0-446-52289-9, Pub. by Warner Bks) Little.

— Working Wounded: Advice That Adds Insight to Injury. 352p. 1999. pap. 12.99 (0-446-67469-9) Warner Bks.

***Rosner, Bob.** Working Wounded: Advice That Adds Insight to Injury. 304p. 2000. mass mkt. 7.99 (0-446-60866-1) Warner Bks.

Rosner, Brian S. Paul, Scripture & Ethics: A Study of 1 Corinthians 5-7. (Biblical Studies Library Ser.). 264p. 1999. pap. 23.99 (0-8010-2212-6) Baker Bks.

***Rosner, Daniel E.** Transport Processes in Chemically Reacting Flow Systems. 2000. pap. 22.95 (0-486-41182-6) Dover.

Rosner, David. Deadly Dust: Silicosis & the Politics of Occupational Disease in Twentieth-Century America. 248p. 1991. pap. text 16.95 (0-691-03771-X, Pub. by Princeton U Pr) Cal Prin Full Svc.

— A Once Charitable Enterprise: Hospitals & Health Care in Brooklyn & New York, 1855-1915. LC 81-21725. (Interdisciplinary Perspectives on Modern History Ser.). 288p. 1982. text 59.95 (0-521-24217-7) Cambridge U Pr.

— A Once Charitable Enterprise: Hospitals & Health Care in Brooklyn & New York, 1855-1915. LC 81-21725. (Illus.). 248p. 1986. pap. text 16.95 (0-691-02835-4, Pub. by Princeton U Pr) Cal Prin Full Svc.

Rosner, David, ed. Hives of Sickness: Public Health & Epidemics in New York City. LC 94-29784. (Illus.). 230p. (C). 1995. text 35.00 (0-8135-2158-0) Rutgers U Pr.

Rosner, David & Markowitz, Gerald. Deadly Dust: Silicosis & the Politics of Occupational Disease in Twentieth-Century America. (Illus.). 219p. 1991. text 39.50 (0-691-04758-8, Pub. by Princeton U Pr) Cal Prin Full Svc.

Rosner, David, jt. auth. see Markowitz, Gerald.

Rosner, David, jt. auth. see Markowitz, Gerald E.

Rosner, David, jt. ed. see Markowitz, Gerald E.

Rosner, Erhard. Medizingeschichte Japans. LC 89-30046. (Handbuch der Orientalistik Ser.: Vol. 5/3/5). (GER.). vi, 135p. (Orig.). 1989. pap. 128.00 (90-04-08815-6) Brill Academic Pubs.

Rosner, Fred. Encyclopedia of Medicine in the Bible & the Talmud. LC 99-20306. i, 392p. 2000. 30.00 (0-7657-6102-5) Aronson.

— Medical Encyclopedia of Moses Maimonides. LC 97-41034. 288p. 1998. 50.00 (0-7657-5997-7) Aronson.

— The Medical Legacy of Moses Maimonides. LC 97-16874. xii, 308p. 1997. 29.50 (0-88125-573-4) Ktav.

— Medicine in the Mishneh Torah of Maimonides. LC 96-29569. 344p. 1997. pap. 35.00 (0-7657-5979-9) Aronson.

— Modern Medicine & Jewish Ethics. LC 86-2910. (C). 1986. text 29.50 (0-88125-407-X) Ktav.

— Pioneers in Jewish Medical Ethics. LC 97-12965. 280p. 1997. 40.00 (0-7657-9968-5) Aronson.

— Sex Ethics in the Writings of Moses Maimonides. LC 94-19613. 144p. 1994. pap. 25.00 (1-56821-323-9) Aronson.

Rosner, Fred, ed. Medicine & Jewish Law, Vol. I. LC 89-49410. 216p. 1993. pap. 25.00 (1-56821-028-0) Aronson.

— Medicine & Jewish Law, Vol. II. LC 89-49410. 184p. 1993. pap. 25.00 (0-87668-574-2) Aronson.

Rosner, Fred, ed. from HEB. The Existence & Unity of God: Three Treatises Attributed to Moses Maimonides. LC 90-15. 264p. 1990. 40.00 (0-87668-805-9) Aronson.

Rosner, Fred, tr. from HEB. Maimonides' Commentary on Mishnah Sanhedrin. LC 81-51800. 224p. 1981. 17.00 (0-87203-099-7) Hermon.

— Moses Maimonides' Treatise on Resurrection. LC 96-42496. 138p. 1997. pap. 30.00 (0-7657-5954-3) Aronson.

Rosner, Fred, tr. Maimonides' Introduction to His Commentary on the Mishnah. LC 94-14644. 256p. 1995. 35.00 (1-56821-241-0) Aronson.

— Six Treatises Attributed to Maimonides. LC 89-18590. 280p. 1991. 40.00 (0-87668-804-0) Aronson.

Rosner, Fred & Bleich. Jewish Bioethics. 39.50 (0-88125-640-4) Ktav.

Rosner, Fred & Kottek, Samuel S., eds. Moses Maimonides: Physician, Scientist, & Philosopher. LC 92-41882. 304p. 1993. pap. 30.00 (0-87668-470-3) Aronson.

Rosner, Fred & Tendler, Moshe. Practical Medical Halachah. 3rd ed. LC 97-28714. 192p. 1997. pap. 40.00 (0-7657-9990-1) Aronson.

Rosner, Fred, et al. Jewish Bioethics. LC 99-23509. 1999. pap. 24.95 (0-88125-662-5) Ktav.

Rosner, Fred, ed. & tr. see Preuss, Julius.

Rosner, Hilda, tr. see Hesse, Hermann.

Rosner, Jane, ed. Christopher Marlowe's Doctor Faustus. (Barron's Book Notes Ser.). 1985. pap. 2.50 (0-8120-3510-0) Barron.

Rosner, Jeremy D. The New Tug-of-War: Congress, the Executive Branch, & National Security. LC 95-17583. 117p. 1995. pap. 10.95 (0-87003-062-0) Carnegie Endow.

Rosner, Jerome. Helping Children Overcome Learning Difficulties: A Step-by-Step Guide for Parents & Teachers. 2nd rev. ed. (Illus.). 408p. 1993. pap. 18.95 (0-8027-7396-6) Walker & Co.

— Test of Auditory Analysis Skills (TAAS) 1988. teacher ed. 14.00 (0-87879-630-4) Acad Therapy.

— Test of Visual Analysis Skills (TVAS) 1988. teacher ed. 15.00 (0-685-53819-2) Acad Therapy.

— Test of Visual Analysis Skills (TVAS) 1989. teacher ed. 6.00 (0-87879-678-9) Acad Therapy.

Rosner, Jerome & Rosner, Joy. Pediatric Optometry. 2nd ed. (Illus.). 538p. 1990. text 65.00 (0-409-90063-X) Buttrwrth-Heinemann.

— Vision Therapy in a Primary Care Practice. (Illus.). 256p. 1988. text 70.00 (0-87873-077-X) Buttrwrth-Heinemann.

***Rosner, Jonathan L. & Winstein, Bruce.** Kaon Physics. LC 00-41166. 2001. write for info. (0-226-90228-5) U Ch Pr.

Rosner, Joy, jt. auth. see Rosner, Jerome.

***Rosner, Kira.** The Power of Being Human. LC 00-91144. xii, 164p. 2000. pap. 15.00 (0-9679978-0-1, Pub. by Coherent Bks) Anthroposophic.

Rosner, Lisa. Medical Edge of Improv: Students & Apprentices at Edinburgh University. 1991. text 68.00 (0-7486-0245-3, Pub. by Edinburgh U Pr) Col U Pr.

— The Most Beautiful Man in Existence: The Scandalous Life of Alexander Lesassier. LC 98-48567. (Illus.). 304p. 1999. 29.95 (0-8122-3486-3) U of Pa Pr.

— Quick Success: Windows 3.1. LC 94-33239. 1994. write for info. (0-534-21403-7) Course Tech.

***Rosner, Lisa & Theibault, John.** A Short History of Europe, 1600 - 1815: Search for a Reasonable World. (Illus.). 320p. 2000. pap. 25.95 (0-7656-0328-4) M E Sharpe.

— A Short History of Europe, 1600-1815: Search for a Reasonable World. (Illus.). 320p. 2000. text 66.95 (0-7656-0327-6) M E Sharpe.

Rosner, Louis J. & Ross, Shelley. Multiple Sclerosis. 256p. 1992. per. 11.00 (0-671-77809-9, Fireside) S&S Trade Pap.

Rosner, Marc A. Science Fair Success Using the Internet. LC 98-25945. (Science Fair Success Ser.). 112p. (YA). (gr. 6 up). 1999. lib. bdg. 20.95 (0-7660-1172-0) Enslow Pubs.

Rosner, Marc A., jt. auth. see Scientific American Staff.

Rosner, Martic C. Hormones & Hyacinths. LC 79-82087. 1980. 5.95 (0-87212-126-7) Libra.

Rosner, Martin C. Coracle & Other Poems. LC 75-146469. 1971. 3.95 (0-87212-001-5) Libra.

Rosner, Martin M., jt. ed. see Catania, Patrick.

Rosner, Mary, et al. History, Reflection, & Narrative: The Professionalization of Composition, 1963-1983. LC 98-12960. (Perspectives on Writing Ser.). Date not set. 73.25 (1-56750-397-7); pap. 39.50 (1-56750-398-5) Ablx Pub.

Rosner, Menachem, et al. The Second Generation: Continuity & Change in the Kibbutz. 2. LC 90-3905. (Kibbutz Study Ser.: No. 2). 480p. 1990. 75.00 (0-313-27287-5, RSG/, Greenwood Pr) Greenwood.

Rosner, Menachem, jt. ed. see Oldenquist, Andrew G.

Rosner, Michael & Johnson, Roderick, eds. Computational Linguistics & Formal Semantics. (Studies in Natural Language Processing). 341p. (C). 1992. text 80.00 (0-521-41959-X); pap. text 29.95 (0-521-42988-9) Cambridge U Pr.

Rosner, Mina. I Am a Witness. (Illus.). 112p. (YA). (gr. 3 up). pap. write for info. (0-920534-92-9) Hyperion Pr.

Rosner, Neal. On the Road to Freedom: A Pilgrimage in India. 282p. (Orig.). 1987. 13.00 (0-9615875-4-7) M A Ctr.

Rosner, R. Geriatric Psychiatry & the Law. (Critical Issues in American Psychiatry & the Law Ser.: Vol. 3). (Illus.). 386p. (C). 1987. 90.00 (0-306-42522-X, Plenum Trade) Perseus Pubng.

Rosner, R. & Harmon, R. B. Correctional Psychiatry. LC 88-657025. (Critical Issues in American Psychiatry & the Law Ser.: Vol. 6). (Illus.). 320p. (C). 1989. 80.00 (0-306-43070-3, Plenum Trade) Perseus Pubng.

— Criminal Court Consultation. (Critical Issues in American Psychiatry & the Law Ser.: Vol. 5). (Illus.). 344p. (C). 1989. 80.00 (0-306-43061-4, Plenum Trade) Perseus Pubng.

Rosner, R. & Schwartz, H. I. Juvenile Psychiatry & the Law. LC 88-657025. (Critical Issues in American Psychiatry & the Law Ser.: Vol. 4). (Illus.). 452p. (C). 1989. 90.00 (0-306-42958-6, Plenum Trade) Perseus Pubng.

Rosner, R. & Weinstock, R. Ethical Practice in Psychiatry & the Law. LC 88-657025. (Critical Issues in American Psychiatry & the Law Ser.: Vol. 7). (Illus.). 366p. (C). 1990. 95.00 (0-306-43476-8, Plenum Trade) Perseus Pubng.

Rosner, Richard, ed. Critical Issues in American Psychiatry & the Law, Vol. 2. LC 81-9059. 324p. 1985. 80.00 (0-306-41954-8, Plenum Trade) Perseus Pubng.

— Principles & Practice of Forensic Psychiatry. LC 93-20238. (An Arnold Publication). (Illus.). 656p. 1999. text 145.00 (0-442-01118-0) OUP.

Rosner, Rita. The Relationship Between Emotional Expression, Treatment, & Outcome in Psychotherapy: An Empirical Study. LC 96-41164. (European University Studies: Series 6, Vol. 565). (Illus.). 138p. 1996. pap. text 35.95 (0-8204-2983-X) P Lang Pubng.

— The Relationship Between Emotional Expression, Treatment & Outcome in Psychotherapy: An Empirical Study. (European University Studies, Series 6: Vol. 565). (Illus.). 138p. 1996. pap. 35.95 (3-631-49870-5) P Lang Pubng.

Rosner, Roy D. Packet Switching. 2nd ed. 1989. text. write for info. (0-442-31803-0, VNR) Wiley.

— Packet Switching: Tomorrow's Communications Today. (Illus.). 371p. 1982. text 79.95 (0-534-97965-3, VNR) Wiley.

Rosner, Ruth. I Hate My Best Friend. LC 96-11478. (Illus.). 64p. (J). (gr. 2-4). 1997. lib. bdg. 14.49 (0-7868-2079-9, Pub. by Hyprn Child) Little.

— I Hate My Best Friend. LC 96-11478. (Illus.). 64p. (J). (gr. 2-4). 1997. pap. 3.95 (0-7868-1169-2, Pub. by Hyprn Ppbks) Little.

— Nattie Witch. LC 89-2135. (Illus.). 32p. (J). (ps-3). 1989. 11.95 (0-06-025098-4) HarpC Child Bks.

— Rhinos Don't Climb! LC 83-47708. (Illus.). 32p. (J). (ps-3). 1984. 12.95 (0-06-025068-2) HarpC Child Bks.

Rosner, Stanley & Abt, Lawrence E., eds. Essays in Creativity. LC 89-2472. 220p. (C). 1989. reprint ed. lib. bdg. 26.50 (0-89464-384-3) Krieger.

Rosner, Ulrike. Zur Quartaeren Landschaftsentwicklung in den Trockengebieten Syriens. (Relief, Boden, Palaeoklima Ser.: Band 10). (GER., Illus.), xiv, 340p. 1995. pap. 93.00 (3-443-09010-9, Pub. by Gebruder Borntraeger) Balogh.

Rosner, Victoria, intro. The Columbia Guide to New York, 1989-1990. (Illus.). 128p. (Orig.). 1989. pap. 9.95 (0-9611970-1-3) Inside NY.

Rosney, C., jt. auth. see Craig, A.

Rosney, Cliff, jt. auth. see Craig, Annabel.

***Rosnov, Mitchell.** Black Magic. 139p. 2000. pap. 18.00 (0-7388-2164-0) Xlibris Corp.

Rosnow. Writing Papers in Psychology. 5th ed. (Psychology Ser.). 2000. pap. text 17.95 (0-534-52975-5) Wadsworth Pub.

Rosnow, Mimi, jt. auth. see Rosnow, Ralph.

Rosnow, Mimi, jt. auth. see Rosnow, Ralph L.

Rosnow, Ralph & Rosnow, Mimi. Writing Papers in Psychology. 4th ed. LC 97-3844. (Psychology Ser.). 143p. 1997. mass mkt. 17.95 (0-534-34826-2) Brooks-Cole.

Rosnow, Ralph L. People Studying People: Artifacts & Ethics in Behavior Research. LC 96-48978. 176p. 1997. pap. 16.95 (0-7167-3071-5); text 26.95 (0-7167-3070-7) W H Freeman.

Rosnow, Ralph L. & Georgoudi, Marianthi, eds. Contextualism & Understanding in Behavioral Science: Implications for Research & Theory. 392p. 1986. 75.00 (0-275-92121-2, C2121, Praeger Pubs) Greenwood.

Rosnow, Ralph L. & Rosenthal, Robert. Beginning Behavioral Research: A Conceptual Primer. 3rd ed. LC 98-20614. 475p. 1998. 78.00 (0-13-791542-X) P-H.

Rosnow, Ralph L. & Rosnow, Mimi. Writing Papers In Psychology. 2nd ed. (Psychology). 105p. (C). 1991. pap. 18.25 (0-534-16986-4) Brooks-Cole.

— Writing Papers in Psychology: A Student Guide. 68p. (C). 1986. mass mkt. 10.50 (0-534-06780-8) Brooks-Cole.

— Writing Papers in Psychology: A Student Guide. 3rd ed. LC 94-9163. 122p. 1995. pap. 13.95 (0-534-24378-9) Brooks-Cole.

Rosnow, Ralph L., jt. auth. see Rosenthal, Robert.

Rosnowski, T., ed. Moving Sources in Thermoelasticity. 1989. text 49.95 (0-470-21409-0) P-H.

***Roso, Calvin.** The Great Gatsby Study Guide. 78p. (YA). (gr. 9-12). 1998. student ed., ring bd. 14.99 (1-58609-167-0) Progeny Pr WI.

— The Old Man & the Sea: Study Guide. (YA). 2000. pap. 14.99 (1-58609-172-7) Progeny Pr WI.

— Roll of Thunder, Hear My Cry Study Guide. 60p. (YA). (gr. 6-8). 1999. student ed., ring bd. 12.99 (1-58609-152-2) Progeny Pr WI.

— Where the Red Fern Grows Study Guide. 56p. (J). (gr. 5-7). 1998. student ed., ring bd. 12.99 (1-58609-151-4) Progeny Pr WI.

Rosof, Adrienne B. & Felch, William C., eds. Continuing Medical Education: A Primer. 2nd ed. LC 91-24229. 256p. 1992. 65.00 (0-275-94009-8, C4009, Praeger Pubs); pap. 18.95 (0-275-94010-1, B4010, Praeger Pubs) Greenwood.

Rosof, Barbara D. Worst Loss. LC 94-9255. 1995. 25.00 (0-8050-3240-1); pap. 14.95 (0-8050-3241-X) H Holt & Co.

Rosof, Patricia J., et al, eds. Black History. LC 83-87. (Trends in History Ser.: Vol. 3, No. 1). 99p. 1983. text 39.95 (0-86656-135-8) Haworth Pr.

— Ethnic & Immigration Groups: The United States, Canada, & England. LC 82-23323. (Trends in History Ser.: Vol. 2, No. 4). 126p. 1983. text 3.95 (0-917724-46-1) Haworth Pr.

— The Middle East & North Africa: Medieval & Modern History. LC 82-11931. (Trends in History Ser.: Vol. 2, No. 3). 134p. 1983. text 39.95 (0-917724-45-3) Haworth Pr.

— The Military & Society: Reviews of Recent Research. LC 81-20073. (Trends in History Ser.: Vol. 2, No. 2). 120p. (C). 1982. text 39.95 (0-917724-44-5) Haworth Pr.

— Urban History: Reviews of Recent Research. LC 80-27903. (Trends in History Ser.: Vol. 2, No. 1). 97p. 1981. text 39.95 (0-917724-26-7) Haworth Pr.

Rosof, Patricia J. & Zeisel, William, eds. Family History. LC 84-22520. (Trends in History Ser.: Vol. 3, Nos. 3-4). 171p. 1985. text 39.95 (0-86656-136-6) Haworth Pr.

Rosof, Patricia J., jt. ed. see Zeisel, William.

R

Rosoff, Arnold J. & Bergwall, David F., eds. Teaching Health Law: A Guide on Health Law for Health Services Administration. 1986. pap. text 12.95 (*0-910591-01-6*) AUPHA Pr.

Rosoff, Barbara, tr. see Cornell, Donald.

Rosoff, Betty & Tobach, Ethel, eds. Challenging Racism & Sexism: Alternatives to Genetic Determinism. LC 94-18179. (Genes & Gender Ser.: Vol. 7). 350p. (C). 1994. 35.00 (*1-55861-089-8*); pap. 14.95 (*1-55861-090-1*) Feminist Pr.

Rosoff, Betty, jt. ed. see Tobach, Ethel.

Rosoff, David. Safed, the Mystical City. 1991. 18.95 (*0-87306-566-2*) Feldheim.

Rosoff, Ilene, ed. WomanSource Catalog & Review: Tools for Connecting the Community for Women. 1997. pap. 22.95 (*0-89087-831-5*) Celestial Arts.

Rosoff, Iris, ed. see Greene, Jacqueline D.

Rosoff, M., ed. Controlled Release of Drugs: Polymers & Aggregate Systems. 315p. 1989. 139.00 (*0-471-18704-6*, Wiley-VCH) Wiley.

Rosoff, Morton, ed. Controlled Release of Drugs: Polymers & Aggregate Systems. LC 88-19177. 315p. 1989. lib. bdg. 80.00 (*0-89573-321-8*, Wiley-VCH) Wiley.

— Vesicles, No. 2. LC 96-15201. (Surfactant Science Ser.: Vol. 62). (Illus.). 768p. 1996. text 225.00 (*0-8247-9603-9*) Dekker.

Rosoff, Myrna, jt. auth. see Pelzmann, Joy.

Rosoff, Stephen M. & Pontell, Henry N. Profit Without Honor. LC 97-12923. 448p. (C). 1997. pap. text 19.95 (*0-13-669664-3*) P-H.

Rosoff, Stephen M. & Pontell, Henry N. Profit Without Honor: White Collar Crime & the Looting of America. LC 97-12923. 436p. 1997. 28.60 (*0-13-103722-6*) P-H.

Rosofsky, Iris. Miriam. LC 87-45859. (Charlotte Zolotow Bk.). 192p. (YA). (gr. 7 up). 1988. 11.95 (*0-06-024853-X*) HarpC Child Bks.

— My Aunt Ruth. LC 90-4940. (Charlotte Zolotow Bk.). 224p. (YA). (gr. 7 up). 1991. 13.95 (*0-06-025087-9*) HarpC Child Bks.

Rosolack, Stephen, jt. auth. see Haberlen, John.

Rosoli, Gianfusto, ed. Guide to the Archives, Vol. 5. 84p. 1985. 9.95 (*0-913256-85-4*) CMS.

Rosolowsky, Diane. West Germany's Foreign Policy: The Impact of the Social Democrats & the Greens, 192. LC 87-12017. (Contributions in Political Science Ser.: No. 192). 165p. 1987. 49.95 (*0-313-25672-1*, RWG/, Greenwood Pr) Greenwood.

Roson, Roberto & Small, Kenneth A. Environment & Transport in Economic Modelling Vol. 10: Economics, Energy & Environment. LC 97-46745. (Economics, Energy, & Environment Ser.). 240p. 1998. 108.00 (*0-7923-4913-X*) Kluwer Academic.

Rosone, Geraldine A., jt. auth. see DeGaetano, Jean G.

***Rosove, Michael H.** Let Heroes Speak: Antarctic Explorers, 1772-1922. LC 99-56907. (Illus.). 320p. 2000. 34.95 (*1-55750-967-0*) Naval Inst Pr.

Rosovesky, Mory, tr. see Soffer, Arnon.

Rosovsky, Henry. University: An Owner's Manual. 1991. pap. 14.95 (*0-393-30783-2*) Norton.

Rosovsky, Henry, ed. Discord in the Pacific: Challenges to the Japanese-American Alliance. LC 72-93017. 1972. pap. 3.00 (*0-910416-16-8*) Am Assembly.

Rosovsky, Henry, et al, eds. Favorites of Fortune: Technology, Growth & Economic Development since the Industrial Revolution. 558p. (C). 1991. text 58.50 (*0-674-29520-X*) HUP.

Rosovsky, Henry, jt. auth. see Ohkawa, Kazushi.

Rosovsky, Henry, jt. ed. see Kumon, Shumpei.

Rosovsky, Henry, jt. ed. see Patrick, Hugh.

Rosovsky, Nitza. Jerusalemwalks. rev. ed. (Illus.). 272p. 1995. pap. 14.95 (*0-8050-1553-1*, Owl) H Holt & Co.

Rosovsky, Nitza, ed. City of the Great King: Jerusalem from David to the Present. LC 95-20941. (Illus.). 576p. 1996. 39.95 (*0-674-13190-8*) HUP.

Rosovsky, Nitza, jt. auth. see Gavin, Carney.

Rosovsky, Nitza, jt. auth. see Howe, Kathleen S.

Rosow, C. E., ed. Butorphanol Tartrate: Research Advances in Multiple Clinical Settings. (Journal: Acute Care: Vol. 12, Suppl. 1, 1986). (Illus.). iv, 80p. 1988. pap. 26.25 (*3-8055-4752-8*) S Karger.

Rosow, Jerome M., ed. The Global Marketplace. LC 88-16279. 237p. reprint ed. pap. 73.50 (*0-7837-1580-3*, 204187200024) Bks Demand.

— Teamwork: Joint Labor-Management Programs in America. 199p. 1986. 27.50 (*0-08-032799-0*) Work in Amer.

— Views from the Top: Establishing the Foundation for the Future of Business. LC 84-10127. 224p. 1985. reprint ed. pap. 69.50 (*0-7837-9913-6*, 206063900006) Bks Demand.

— The Worker & the Job: Coping with Change. LC 74-765. (American Assembly Guides Ser.). 224p. 1974. 6.95 (*0-317-00261-9*) Am Assembly.

Rosow, Jerome M. & Casner-Lotto, Jill. The Participative Leader: From Autocracy to Empowerment. (New Roles for Managers Ser.: Pt. V). 131p. 1993. 95.00 (*0-89361-044-5*) Work in Amer.

Rosow, Jerome M. & Hickey, John V. How Change Agents Transform the Enterprise. (Startegic Partners for High Performance Ser.: Vol. III). 101p. (Orig.). 1995. pap. 95.00 (*0-89361-052-6*) Work in Amer.

— The Partnership Paradigm for Competitive Advantage, Pt. 1. (Strategic Partners for High Performance Ser.). 115p. 1994. 95.00 (*0-89361-050-X*) Work in Amer.

Rosow, Jerome M. & Zager, Robert. Employee Involvement & the Supervisor's Job. (New Roles for Managers Ser.: Pt. I). 101p. 1989. pap. 95.00 (*0-89361-042-9*) Work in Amer.

— The Future of Older Workers in America: New Options for an Extended Working Life. 135p. 1980. pap. 11.00 (*0-89361-018-6*) Work in Amer.

— Improving Health-Care Management in the Workplace. 162p. 1985. 19.25 (*0-08-032797-4*) Work in Amer.

— Job Strategies for Urban Youth: Complete Study. 102p. 1979. pap. 8.75 (*0-89361-005-4*) Work in Amer.

— Job Strategies for Urban Youth: Executive Summary. 18p. 1979. pap. 4.35 (*0-89361-004-6*) Work in Amer.

— Linking Training Strategy to Corporate Strategy. Casner-Lotto, Jill, ed. (Training for New Technology Ser.: Part I). 76p. 1985. 95.00 (*0-89361-058-5*) Work in Amer.

— Management Involvement for High Commitment. Casner-Lotto, Jill, ed. (New Roles for Managers Ser.: Pt. II). 97p. 1989. pap. 95.00 (*0-89361-046-1*) Work in Amer.

— The Manager As Trainer, Coach & Leader. (New Roles for Managers Ser.: Pt. III). 94p. 1990. pap. 95.00 (*0-89361-045-3*) Work in Amer.

— Meeting the Challenge of Change: Basic Skills for a Competitive Workforce. (Job-Linked Literacy: Innovative Strategies at Work Ser.: Pt. II). 99p. 1992. pap. 95.00 (*0-89361-048-8*) Work in Amer.

— Moving Ahead: Basic Skills for Career Advancement. Casner-Lotto, Jill, ed. (Job-Linked Literacy: Innovative Strategies at Work Ser.: Pt. III). 97p. 1993. 95.00 (*0-89361-047-X*) Work in Amer.

— New Work Schedules for a Changing Society: Complete Study. 128p. 1981. pap. 12.00 (*0-89361-025-9*) Work in Amer.

— New Work Schedules for a Changing Society: Executive Summary. 55p. 1981. pap. 5.50 (*0-89361-026-7*) Work in Amer.

— Productivity Through Work Innovations: Complete Study. 161p. 1982. 18.25 (*0-08-029545-2*) Work in Amer.

— Productivity Through Work Innovations: Executive Summary. 48p. 1982. pap. 7.75 (*0-08-029546-0*) Work in Amer.

— Toward a New Social Contract: Employment Security for Managers & Professionals. Casner-Lotto, Jill, ed. (New Roles for Managers Ser.: Pt. IV). 75p. 1991. pap. 95.00 (*0-89361-043-7*) Work in Amer.

— Vestibule Training: Basic Skills for New Hires, Pt. I. Casner-Lotto, Jill, ed. 97p. 1991. pap. 95.00 (*0-89361-049-6*) Work in Amer.

Rosow, Jerome M., et al. Allies in Educational Reform: How Teachers, Unions, & Administrators Can Join Forces for Better Schools. LC 88-46095. (Education-Higher Education Ser.). 392p. 36.95 (*1-55542-158-X*) Work in Amer.

— The Continuous Learning Employment Security Connection. (Training for New Technology Ser.: Part IV). 83p. 1987. 95.00 (*0-89361-055-0*) Work in Amer.

— Cost-Effective Design & Delivery. Casner-Lotto, Jill, ed. (Training for New Technology Ser.: Part III). 118p. 1986. 95.00 (*0-89361-056-9*) Work in Amer.

— Lean, Not Mean: Restoring Organizational Trust in a Climate of Downsizing. (Strategic Partners for High Performance Ser.: Vol. IV). 97p. (Orig.). 1996. pap. 95.00 (*0-89361-053-4*) Work in Amer.

— Partners in Learning: Manufacturers & Users. Casner-Lotto, Jill, ed. (Training for New Technology Ser.: Part V). 87p. 1987. 95.00 (*0-89361-054-2*) Work in Amer.

— Toward Continuous Learning. rev. ed. Casner-Lotto, Jill, ed. (Training for New Technology Ser.: Part II). 87p. 1991. pap. 95.00 (*0-89361-057-7*) Work in Amer.

— Training--The Competitive Edge: Introducing New Technology into the Workplace. LC 88-42797. (Management Ser.). 269p. 33.95 (*1-55542-109-1*) Work in Amer.

Rosow, Jerome M., jt. ed. see Kerr, Clark.

Rosow, La-Vergne. In Forsaken Hands: How Theory Empowers Literacy Learners. LC 94-43727. 325p. 1995. 24.95 (*0-435-08117-9*, 08116) Heinemann.

— Into Forsaken Hands: How Theory Empowers Literacy Learners. LC 94-43727. 326p. 1995. 24.95 (*0-435-08116-0*) Heinemann.

— Light'n Lively Reads for ESL, Adult, & Teen Readers: A Thematic Bibliography. LC 96-7084. 300p. 1996. lib. bdg. 40.00 (*1-56308-365-5*) Libs Unl.

Rosow, Michael P., jt. ed. see Zager, Robert.

Rosow, Stephen J., et al, eds. The Global Economy As Political Space. LC 93-33348. (Critical Perspectives on World Politics Ser.). 256p. 1994. lib. bdg. 47.00 (*1-55587-462-2*) L Rienner.

Rosow, Stephen J., jt. auth. see Opello, Walter C., Jr.

Rosowski, John J. & Eiber, Albrecht, eds. Biomechanics of Hearing. (Audiology & Neuro-Otology Ser.: Vol. 4, Nos. 3-4 (1999)). (Illus.). 90p. 1999. pap. 34.00 (*3-8055-6847-9*) S Karger.

Rosowski, Susan, contrib. by. Birthing a Nation: Gender, Creativity, & the Significance of the West in American Literature. LC 99-14233. 1999. text 50.00 (*0-8032-3935-1*) U of Nebr Pr.

Rosowski, Susan J. Approaches to Teaching Cather's My Antonia. LC 88-31154. (Approaches to Teaching World Literature Ser.: No. 22). xii, 194p. 1989. pap. 18.00 (*0-87352-520-5*, AP22P); lib. bdg. 37.50 (*0-87352-519-1*, AP22C) Modern Lang.

— The Voyage Perilous: Willa Cather's Romanticism. LC 86-4341. (Illus.). 302p. 1986. reprint ed. pap. 93.70 (*0-608-05996-X*, 206632400008) Bks Demand.

Rosowski, Susan J., ed. Cather Studies, Vol. 1. (Cather Studies). (Illus.). xii, 189p. 1990. text 45.00 (*0-8032-3895-9*) U of Nebr Pr.

— Cather Studies, Vol. 2. 185p. 1993. text 45.00 (*0-8032-3910-6*) U of Nebr Pr.

— Cather Studies, Vol. 3. (Cather Studies). (Illus.). vii, 303p. 1996. text 45.00 (*0-8032-3920-3*) U of Nebr Pr.

— Cather Studies Vol. 4: Willa Cather's Canadian & Old World Connections. 256p. 1999. pap. text 25.00 (*0-8032-6398-8*) U of Nebr Pr.

Rosowski, Susan J., ed. see Cather, Willa.

Rosowsky, Andre, ed. Advances in Cancer Chemotherapy, Vol. 1: 1979. LC 79-643464. (Illus.). 309p. reprint ed. pap. 95.80 (*0-7837-0796-7*, 204111000001) Bks Demand.

Rosowsky, Erlene, et al, eds. Personality Disorders in Older Adults: Emerging Issues in Diagnosis & Treatment. LC 98-49371. (Personality & Clinical Psychology Ser.). 328p. 1999. 39.95 (*0-8058-2683-1*) L Erlbaum Assocs.

Ross. Advanced Business Finance. 1998. 21.50 (*0-07-229769-7*) McGraw.

— Aesthetic Impulse. 1984. 22.10 (*0-08-031304-3*, Pergamon Pr); pap. 12.00 (*0-08-031305-1*, Pergamon Pr) Elsevier.

— American National Government: Institutions, Policy & Participation. 4th ed. 1996. pap. 30.63 (*1-56134-409-5*, Dshkn McG-Hill) McGrw-H Hghr Educ.

— Annotated Solutions Manual for Precalculus: Algebra & Trigonometry. annot. ed. (Mathematics Ser.). 1991. mass mkt., student ed. 15.75 (*0-534-14552-3*) Brooks-Cole.

— Application Software. 3rd ed. (DF - Computer Applications Ser.). (C). 1990. pap. text 37.50 (*0-314-57476-X*) West Pub.

— Canadian Fundamentals of Corporate Finance. 1993. student ed. 19.16 (*0-256-10587-1*) McGraw.

— Christmas Fun. (Illus.). 32p. (J). pap. 1.00 (*0-486-40250-9*) Dover.

Ross. Coming Alive Beware of the King. (Illus.). (J). write for info. (*0-237-51636-5*) EVN1 UK.

— Coming Alive Beware of the King. (Illus.). (J). 1996. pap. write for info. (*0-237-51637-3*) EVN1 UK.

Ross. Corporate Finance. LC 94-79192. 1995. 47.96 (*0-256-15491-0*) McGraw.

— Corporate Finance: Student Problem Manual. 4th ed. 1996. student ed. 89.00 (*0-256-22760-8*) McGraw.

— Cpsm Sel Solut T/a Ess Fin. 2nd ed. 1998. pap. text 8.00 (*0-07-230123-6*) McGraw.

— Digital Design & Synthesis with VHDL. (Design Automation Ser.). (Illus.). 300p. (C). 1994. text 59.95 (*0-9627488-3-8*) Automata Pub.

— Easter Fun. (Illus.). (J). pap. 1.00 (*0-486-29957-0*) Dover.

Ross. Electricity & Magnetism. pap. text 18.00 (*0-471-37442-3*, Wiley Heyden) Wiley.

Ross. Elementary Statistics. 1996. text, teacher ed. 74.68 (*0-07-053933-2*) McGraw.

— Essential Corporate Finance: Student Problem Manual. 1996. student ed. 62.74 (*0-256-22797-7*) McGraw.

— The Essentials of Lotus 1-2-3 Release 2.3. (DF - Computer Applications Ser.). 1992. mass mkt. 9.75 (*0-314-00764-4*) West Pub.

— Essentials of Lotus 1-2-3 Release 2.2. (DF - Computer Applications Ser.). 1991. 9.75 (*0-314-84892-4*) West Pub.

— Essentials of Lotus 1-2-3 Release 2.4. 5th ed. (DF - Computer Applications Ser.). 1993. mass mkt. 9.75 (*0-314-02228-7*) West Pub.

— Essentials of Microsoft Excel 5.0. LC 95-139642. (DF - Computer Applications Ser.). 1995. mass mkt. 13.95 (*0-314-04634-8*) West Pub.

— Fundamentals of Corporate Finance. 5th ed. 1999. 69.25 (*0-07-366128-7*) McGraw.

***Ross.** Here but Not Here. 2001. pap. text 14.00 (*1-58243-110-8*, Pub. by Counterpt DC) HarpC.

Ross. Here Dwell Tygers. 1993. lib. bdg. 34.95 (*0-226-72805-6*) U Ch Pr.

***Ross.** Home-Spun Fun: Family Home Evenings 2. 1999. pap. 9.95 (*1-57734-448-0*, 01113860) Covenant Comms.

Ross. Introduction to Physical Geography & Map Reading. 1988. pap. text. write for info. (*0-582-32243-X*, Pub. by Addison-Wesley) Longman.

— Introduction to Probability & Statistics. 2nd ed. 608p. 1999. 83.95 (*0-12-598472-3*) Acad Pr.

— Introduction to Probability Models. 6th ed. 297p. 1997. 2.00 (*0-12-598471-5*) Acad Pr.

— Introduction to Statistics. 2nd ed. (Illus.). 400p. (C). 1989. pap. text 42.00 (*0-536-57704-8*) Pearson Custom.

— Longman Coordinated Geography Text. Date not set. pap. text. write for info. (*0-582-06299-3*, Pub. by Addison-Wesley) Longman.

***Ross.** Make Yourself a Monster: Aliens. LC 98-50751. 1999. 22.90 (*0-7613-1556-X*) Millbrook Pr.

Ross. Mazes. (Illus.). 32p. (J). pap. 1.00 (*0-486-29565-6*) Dover.

***Ross.** My Fun-tastic Personal Progress Journal Beehive, No. 1. 1999. pap. 8.95 (*1-57734-440-5*, 01113879) Covenant Comms.

— The New Sweatshops. (Illus.). (C). text. write for info. (*0-472-10941-3*) U of Mich Pr.

Ross. Physical Geology. (Earth Science Ser.). 2002. pap., lab manual ed. 29.00 (*0-534-55666-3*) Wadsworth Pub.

— Practical Tv/video Systems Repair. LC 99-46635. (C). 1999. pap. text 54.95 (*0-8273-8547-1*) Delmar.

— Present Theology & Participatory. 1996. pap. 3.90 (*0-86153-177-9*) St Mut.

Ross. Primary Partners: Ages 8 to 11 (New Testament) pap., teacher ed. 9.95 (*1-57734-344-1*, 01113658) Covenant Comms.

— Primary Partners Sharing Time: I Will Make & Keep My Baptismal Covenant. 1999. pap. 9.95 (*1-57734-515-0*, 01114158) Covenant Comms.

— Primary Partners Singing Fun: I Will Make & Keep My Baptismal Covenant. 1999. pap. 9.95 (*1-57734-551-7*, 01114433) Covenant Comms.

— Prosperity: A Woman's Guide to Achieving Spiritual, Financial & Emotional Strength. 208p. 2000. 7.98 (*1-56731-389-2*, MJF Bks) Fine Comms.

Ross. Psychology of Tourism. 212p. 1999. pap. text 34.95 (*0-7506-3459-6*) Buttrwrth-Heinemann.

— Ross Board Books, 2 vols. (J). 1995. bds. 24.00 (*0-15-201274-5*) Harcourt.

— Settlement. Date not set. pap. text. write for info. (*0-582-02425-0*, Pub. by Addison-Wesley) Longman.

***Ross.** Social Work Management & Practice: Systems Principles. 2nd ed. LC 99-41626. 1999. pap. 29.95 (*1-85302-388-4*) Jessica Kingsley.

Ross. Supervision of State Aids. Date not set. text. write for info. (*0-7185-1324-X*) St Martin.

— Supervision of State Aids & Public Undertakings under EEC Law. 1995. 79.95 (*1-85567-298-7*) St Martin.

— Understanding & Using Lotus Release 2.2. 2nd ed. (DF - Computer Applications Ser.). 1990. 27.25 (*0-314-70104-4*) West Pub.

— Vegetables. 1999. pap. write for info. (*0-14-046864-1*) Viking Penguin.

— West's Essentials of Lotus 1-2-3 for Windows Release 4. LC 95-139403. (DF - Computer Applications Ser.). 1994. mass mkt. 9.50 (*0-314-01353-9*) West Pub.

— West's Essentials of Microsoft Excel for Windows 95. 2nd ed. (DF - Computer Applications Ser.). 1996. mass mkt. 12.95 (*0-314-07237-3*) West Pub.

— West's Essentials of Microsoft Windows 95. (DF - Computer Applications Ser.). 1996. mass mkt. 11.95 (*0-314-04638-0*) West Pub.

***Ross.** Writing Journalism. 2000. 26.00 (*1-58243-109-4*, Pub. by Counterpt DC) HarpC.

Ross. You Be the Judge. 216p. 1997. pap. write for info. (*0-471-64199-5*) Wiley.

Ross, ed. From the Source. 2nd ed. (C). 1997. text 29.06 (*0-321-01458-8*) Addson-Wesley Educ.

— Treatment of the Hospitalized Borderline Patient. (Psychoanalytic Inquiry Ser.: Vol. 9, No. 4). 1989. 20.00 (*0-88163-956-7*) Analytic Pr.

***Ross & Guymon-King.** My Fun-tastic Personal Progress Journal Beehive, No. 2. 1999. pap. 8.95 (*1-57734-441-3*, 01113887) Covenant Comms.

— Primary Partners: Ages 8 to 11 (Book of Mormon) 1999. pap. 9.95 (*1-57734-519-3*, 01114484) Covenant Comms.

Ross & Jacob. Elements of College English. 312p. 1998. pap. text 27.50 (*0-536-01661-5*) Pearson Custom.

Ross & Kardulias. From the Source: Readings in World Civilization. (C). 1998. pap. text. write for info. (*0-201-38792-1*) Addison-Wesley.

Ross & Lowenstein. Perspectives on Multiple Personality Disorder. (Psychoanalytic Inquiry Book Ser.: Vol. 12, No. 1). 1992. 20.00 (*0-88163-948-6*) Analytic Pr.

Ross & Mahlck. Planning the Quality of Education. 192p. 1990. text 36.50 (*0-08-041026-X*, Pergamon Pr) Elsevier.

***Ross & Malloy.** Biomedical Ethics for Health Care. 192p. 1999. pap. text 19.95 (*1-55077-090-X*) Thompson Educ.

Ross & Wright. Discrete Mathematics. 4th ed. LC 98-56065. 690p. 1999. 92.00 (*0-13-096141-8*) P-H.

Ross, et al. Bombay Leather, Incorporated a Business Simulation. 5th ed. (BE - Accounting Advanced Ser.). 1992. 19.95 (*0-538-61034-4*) S-W Pub.

***Ross, et al.** Century 21: Accounting Advanced Course. 7th ed. 1998. pap. 54.95 (*0-538-67746-5*) Thomson Learn.

Ross, et al. Diversity of Life. 1996. teacher ed. 10.93 (*0-697-29326-2*, WCB McGr Hill) McGrw-H Hghr Educ.

***Ross, et al.** Fundamentals of Accounting. 7th ed. (C). 1998. pap. 45.95 (*0-538-71873-0*) Thomson Learn.

— Introductory Course-Century 21 Accounting: 1st Year-General Journal Approach. 7th ed. (Accounting - First Year). 1998. pap. 43.95 (*0-538-68735-5*) Sth-Wstrn College.

Ross, et al. Literature Lover's Book of Lists: Serious Trivia for the Bibliophile. LC 98-25544. (Illus.). 380p. 1998. text 25.00 (*0-7352-0017-3*) PH Pr.

— Trans. - Diversity of Life. 1996. 107.18 (*0-697-29327-0*, WCB McGr Hill) McGrw-H Hghr Educ.

***Ross, et al.** Transparencies. 7th ed. 1998. 365.00 (*0-538-67684-1*) Thomson Learn.

Ross, jt. auth. see Burke, Edmund.

Ross, jt. auth. see Jackson.

Ross, jt. auth. see Kennett.

Ross, jt. auth. see Knapp.

Ross, jt. auth. see Swanson.

Ross, Douglas C. Antitrust & Health Care: New Approaches & Challenges. LC 98-86056. vii, 399 p. 1998. write for info. (*1-57073-531-X*) Amer Bar Assn.

***Ross, Julia.** Diet Cure. 416p. 2000. pap. 12.95 (*0-14-028652-7*, Penguin Bks) Viking Penguin.

Ross, Julia. The Diet Cure: The 8-Step Program to Rebalance Your Body Chemistry & End Food Cravings, Weight Problems & Mood Swings - Now. LC 99-19180. 380p. 1999. 23.95 (*0-670-88593-2*) Viking Penguin.

Ross, A., jt. auth. see Ball, J. C.

Ross, A. A. Marine Gear Drives. (Technical Papers: Vol. P65). (Illus.). 8p. 1921. pap. text 30.00 (*1-55589-403-8*) AGMA.

— My Experience with Gear Tooth Forms. (Technical Papers: Vol. P207). (Illus.). 18p. 1940. pap. text 30.00 (*1-55589-451-8*) AGMA.

***Ross, A. C.** Crazy Horse & the Real Reason for the Battle of the Little Big Horn. 2000. pap. 10.00 (*0-9621977-8-5*) Wiconi Waste.

Ross, A. C. Ehanamani: Walks Among. rev. ed. (Illus.). 226p. (Orig.). 1993. pap. 12.00 (*0-9621977-1-8*) Wiconi Waste.

— Keeper of the Female Medicine Bundle: Biography of Wihopa. LC 98-220808. 200p. 1998. pap. 14.95 (*0-9621977-7-7*) Wiconi Waste.

— Mitakuye Oyasin: We Are All Related. LC 97-161684. (Illus.). 215p. (Orig.). 1989. pap. 12.00 (*0-9621977-0-X*) Wiconi Waste.

Ross, A. C., tr. see Bachelard, Gaston.

Ross, Aileen D. The Hindu Family in Its Urban Setting. LC 62-2801. 339p. reprint ed. pap. 105.10 (*0-608-10753-0*, 201438800089) Bks Demand.

Ross, Ain C., ed. see James, Henry.

Ross, Al, jt. auth. see Lambert, John.

Ross, Alan. Brief History of Golf. 1998. pap. text 6.95 (*1-887655-85-9*) Walnut Gr Pr.

— Echoes from the Ball Park. 1998. pap. 6.95 (*1-887655-86-7*) Walnut Gr Pr.

— Golf a la Cart: A Credible Source of Golfing Feats Facts & Fun from the Fairways to the Fantasti. 1998. pap. 6.95 (*1-887655-98-0*) Walnut Grove Pubs.

— Hooked on Hockey. 1998. pap. 6.95 (*1-887655-87-5*) Walnut Gr Pr.

***Ross, Alan.** Lure of the Lighthouse. 1999. pap. 6.95 incl. 5.25 hd (*1-58334-045-9*) Walnut Gr Pr.

— Reflections on Blue Water. (Illus.). 224p. 2000. 26.00 (*1-86046-691-5*) Harvill Press.

— Seminole Wisdom. 160p. 2000. pap. 6.95 (*1-58334-096-3*, Pub. by Walnut Gr Pr) Midpt Trade.

Ross, Alan. Spiritualism & Beyond: A Guide for Life in the World to Come. Jones, Alese, ed. LC 88-70801. (Illus.). 161p. (Orig.). 1988. pap. 6.95 (*0-9617038-4-9*) A Ross Pubns.

***Ross, Alan.** Wildcat Wisdom: The Story of Kentucky Basketball--Through the Voices of the Players, Coaches, Fans & Media. 160p. 1999. pap. 6.95 (*1-58334-037-8*) Walnut Gr Pr.

Ross, Alan. Winter Sea, Vol. 3. 1998. 24.00 (*1-86046-431-9*) Harvill Press.

***Ross, Alan.** Wisdom Between-the-Hedges. 160p. 2000. pap. 6.95 (*1-58334-094-7*, Pub. by Walnut Gr Pr) Midpt Trade.

— Wisdom from the Swamp. 160p. 2000. pap. 6.95 (*1-58334-095-5*, Pub. by Walnut Gr Pr) Midpt Trade.

Ross, Alan, ed. see Atkinson, Barbara F. & Silverman, Jan F.

Ross, Alan, ed. see McCarthy, Edward F. & Frassica, Frank J.

Ross, Alan D., jt. auth. see Gibbs, Harlan.

Ross, Alan Duncan, jt. auth. see Gibbs, Harlan.

Ross, Alan O. Child Behavior Therapy. LC 87-3517. 444p. (C). 1987. reprint ed. lib. bdg. 46.50 (*0-89464-229-4*) Krieger.

— The Sense of Self: Research & Theory. LC 91-868. 208p. (C). 1992. text 32.95 (*0-8261-7430-2*) Springer Pub.

Ross, Alan S., jt. ed. see Dickins, Bruce.

Ross, Albert, jt. auth. see Thomas, Roland.

Ross, Alec & Plant, David. Writing Police Reports: A Practical Guide. LC 76-55879. 1977. pap. 5.95 (*0-916070-03-4*, MTI Film & Video) Coronet.

Ross, Alex, ed. see Waid, Mark.

Ross, Alexander. Adventures of the First Settlers on the Oregon Or Columbia River, 1810-1813. LC 85-24550. 319p. 1986. reprint ed. pap. 98.90 (*0-608-01401-X*, 206216400002) Bks Demand.

***Ross, Alexander.** Adventures of the First Settlers on the Oregon or Columbia Rivers, 1810-1813. (Northwest Reprints Ser.). 320p. 2000. pap. 16.95 (*0-87071-528-3*) Oreg St U Pr.

Ross, Alexander M. The Imprint of the Picturesque on Nineteenth-Century British Fiction. 228p. (C). 1986. text 35.00 (*0-88920-191-9*) W Laurier U Pr.

— Recollections & Experiences of an Abolitionist from 1865-1885. (American Biography Ser.). 224p. 1991. reprint ed. lib. bdg. 69.00 (*0-7812-8331-0*) Rprt Serv.

— William Henry Bartlett: Artist, Author, & Traveller (Containing a Reprint of Dr. William Beattie's Brief Memoir of the Late William Henry Bartlett. LC 72-97783. (Illus.). 176p. reprint ed. pap. 54.60 (*0-608-11311-5*, 202051800018) Bks Demand.

Ross, Alfred J. & Practising Law Institute. International Joint Ventures 1998. LC 98-150188. (Commercial Law & Practice Course Handbook Ser.). 312p. 1998. write for info. (*0-87224-424-5*) PLI.

Ross, Alice & Ross, Kent. The Copper Lady. LC 95-7628. (On My Own Bks.). (Illus.). (J). 1995. lib. bdg. 18.60 (*0-87614-934-4*, Carolrhoda) Lerner Pub.

Ross, Alice, et al. Whistle Punk. LC 93-14187. (Chaparral Books for Young Readers). 142p. (J). (gr. 5-8). 1994. pap. 9.95 (*0-87565-123-2*) Tex Christian.

Ross, Alice, jt. auth. see Ross, Kent.

***Ross, Alice E.** The Fourth Joyful Mystery: The Presentation. (Illus.). 1999. 7.00 (*1-929486-02-2*) SonRises Bk Pubg.

— Michael Meets a Special Friend: A Play about Angels. (Illus.). (J). 1999. write for info. (*1-929486-05-7*) SonRises Bk Pubg.

— The Story of a Famous Statue: The Infant of Prague. (Illus.). 1999. 7.95 (*1-929486-03-0*) SonRises Bk Pubg.

— The Third Joyful Mystery. (Illus.). 1998. 7.00 (*1-929486-00-6*) SonRises Bk Pubg.

Ross, Alison. The Language of Humour. LC 97-24610. (Intertext Ser.). 128p. (C). 1998. pap. 14.99 (*0-415-16912-7*) Routledge.

Ross, Alison. Daytime Baby: Baby Books. 8p. (J). (ps). 1992. text 3.50 (*0-7214-1515-6*, S9212-4, Ladybrd) Penguin Putnam.

— Hello Baby: Baby Books. 8p. (J). (ps). 1992. text 3.50 (*0-7214-1497-4*, S9212-3, Ladybrd) Penguin Putnam.

— Noisy Baby: Baby Books. 8p. (J). (ps). 1992. text 3.50 (*0-7214-1496-6*, S9212-1, Ladybrd) Penguin Putnam.

— Playtime Baby: Baby Books. 8p. (J). (ps). 1992. text 3.50 (*0-7214-1514-8*, S9212-2, Ladybrd) Penguin Putnam.

Ross, Allan, Jr. Administrative Manual, Vol. III. 134p. 1990. 25.00 (*0-915355-79-5*) Am Assn Blood.

Ross, Allan & Helgesen, Jan, eds. Human Rights in a Changing East-West Perspective. 1991. text 69.00 (*0-86187-131-6*, Pub. by P P Pubs) Cassell & Continuum.

Ross, Allan, jt. auth. see Helliwell, Timothy R.

Ross, Allan, ed. see Aminoff, Michael J.

Ross, Allan, ed. see Atlee, John L.

Ross, Allan, ed. see Benzon, Honorio, et al.

Ross, Allan, ed. see Brown, David L.

Ross, Allan, ed. see Dyck, Peter J. & Thomas, P. K.

Ross, Allan, ed. see Finucane, Brendan T.

Ross, Allan, ed. see Hagberg, Cain A.

Ross, Allan, ed. see Kaplan, Joel A.

Ross, Allan, ed. see Kern, William, et al.

Ross, Allan, ed. see Luders, Hans O. & Noachtar, Soheyl.

Ross, Allan, ed. see Miller, Ronald D.

Ross, Allan, ed. see Posnick, Jeffrey C.

Ross, Allan, ed. see Waldman, Steven D.

Ross, Allen P. Creation & Blessing: A Guide to the Study & Exposition of Genesis. LC 88-6173. 744p. (gr. 12). 1997. pap. 34.99 (*0-8010-2107-3*) Baker Bks.

***Ross, Allison J.** Careers in Desktop Publishing. LC 00-8570. 2000. write for info. (*0-8239-3295-8*, PowerKids) Rosen Group.

— Everything You Need to Know about Anemia. LC 00-24825. (Need to Know Library). 2000. lib. bdg. 17.95 (*0-8239-3218-4*) Rosen Group.

***Ross, Allison J. & Harrison, Scott.** Choosing a Career in Carpentry. LC 00-9128. (World of Work Ser.). 2000. lib. bdg. write for info. (*0-8239-3294-X*) Rosen Group.

Ross, Andrea. About the Ant. (Chester Earth Ant Ser.). 20p. (J). (gr. k-3). 1995. 7.95 (*1-887683-01-1*) Strybook Pr.

— All about Turtles. unabridged ed. Davenport, May, ed. LC 89-92455. (Read & Color Tales Ser.). 24p. (J). (ps-3). 1990. pap. 6.95 incl. audio (*0-943864-59-3*) Davenport.

***Ross, Andrea.** Big Surprise Day. (Illus.). 25p. (J). 2000. pap. 9.95 (*1-887683-09-7*) Strybook Pr.

Ross, Andrea. Chester Earth Ant (Alphabets & Numbers/Insects) (Chester Earth Ant Ser.). (Illus.). 26p. (J). (gr. k-3). 1999. pap. 9.95 (*1-887683-35-6*) Strybook Pr.

— Chester Earth Ant & His Hundred Dreams. LC 94-93845. (Chester Earth Ant Ser.). (Illus.). 24p. (J). (gr. k-3). 1995. 9.95 (*1-887683-02-X*) Strybook Pr.

***Ross, Andrea.** Chester Earth Ant in School. (Chester Earth Ant Ser.). (Illus.). 26p. (J). (gr. k-3). 1999. pap. 1.95 (*1-887683-20-8*) Strybook Pr.

Ross, Andrea. Chester Earth Ant in "Spiced Ant Guardian of the World" (Illus.). 30p. (J). (gr. k-3). 1997. pap. 5.95 (*1-887683-23-2*) Strybook Pr.

— Chester Earth Ant Makes the Right Choice. (Chester Earth Ant Ser.). (Illus.). 25p. (Orig.). (J). (gr. k-3). 1996. pap. 7.95 (*1-887683-14-3*) Strybook Pr.

— Chester Earth Ant Meets a Friend. (Chester Earth Ant Ser.). (Illus.). 30p. (Orig.). (J). (gr. k-3). 1996. pap. 7.95 (*1-887683-03-8*) Strybook Pr.

— Chester Earth Ant Meets Timmy. (Illus.). 23p. (J). (gr. k-3). 1996. 7.95 (*1-887683-12-7*) Strybook Pr.

— Chester Earth Ant Visits Margaret. (Chester Earth Ant Ser.). (Illus.). 22p. (J). (gr. k-3). 1996. pap. 5.95 (*1-887683-15-1*) Strybook Pr.

***Ross, Andrea.** Chester Goes to the Moon. (Chester Earth Ant Ser.). (Illus.). 25p. (J). (gr. k-3). 1999. pap. 7.95 (*1-887683-08-9*) Strybook Pr.

Ross, Andrea. Chester's Drawing Book. LC 95-92005. (Chester Earth Ant Ser.). (Illus.). 30p. (Orig.). (J). (gr. k-3). 1996. pap. 7.95 (*1-887683-07-0*) Strybook Pr.

— Littlest Ballerina. (Illus.). 23p. (J). (gr. k-3). 1996. 7.95 (*1-887683-13-5*) Strybook Pr.

***Ross, Andrea.** Nutmeg & the Mutu. (Illus.). 60p. (J). (gr. 3-5). 2000. lib. bdg. 9.95 (*1-887683-29-1*) Strybook Pr.

— To Touch the Sun. large type ed. Davenport, May, ed. LC 99-75015. 195p. (YA). (gr. 9-12). 2000. pap. text 15.95 (*0-943864-99-2*) Davenport.

Ross, Andrea, ed. Selected Figural Works, Vol. 1. (Illus.). 32p. 1989. pap. text. write for info. (*0-318-66432-1*) A Ross Gallery.

***Ross, Andrea.** Chester Goes to the City. (Chester Earth Ant Ser.). 25p. (J). (gr. k-3). 1999. pap. 7.97 (*1-887683-04-6*) Strybook Pr.

— Storybook Castle with Chester. (Chester Earth Ant Ser.). 25p. (J). (gr. k-3). 1999. pap. 6.95 (*1-887683-05-4*) Strybook Pr.

Ross, Andrea F. Let the Lions Roar! The Evolution of Brookfield Zoo. Howes, Christopher, ed. LC 97-66395. (Illus.). 276p. 1997. 40.00 (*0-913934-24-0*) Chicago Zoo.

Ross, Andrew. Amber. LC 98-40382. 1999. 12.95 (*0-674-01729-3*) HUP.

***Ross, Andrew.** Celebration Chronicles: Life, Liberty & the Pursuit of Property Value in Disney's New Town. (Illus.). 352p. 2000. pap. 15.00 (*0-345-41752-6*, Ballantine) Ballantine Pub Grp.

Ross, Andrew. The Celebration Chronicles: Life, Liberty & the Pursuit of Property Values in Disney's New Town. LC 99-26403. 352p. 1999. 25.95 (*0-345-41751-8*) Ballantine Pub Grp.

— Chicago Gangster Theory of Life: Nature's Debt to Society. 288p. 1995. pap. 20.00 (*0-86091-654-5*, Pub. by Verso) Norton.

— John Philip, 1775-1851: Missions, Race & Politics in South Africa. 258p. 1986. text 30.00 (*0-08-032457-6*, Pub. by Aberdeen U Pr) Macmillan.

— No Respect: Intellectuals & Popular Culture. 288p. 1989. 32.50 (*0-415-90036-0*, A1574) Routledge.

— No Respect: Intellectuals & Popular Culture. 288p. 1989. pap. 20.99 (*0-415-90037-9*, A1578) Routledge.

— No Sweat: Fashion, Free Trade & the Rights of Garment Workers. LC 97-31601. (C). 1997. 65.00 (*1-85984-866-4*, Pub. by Verso) Norton.

— No Sweat: Fashion, Free Trade & the Rights of Workers. LC 97-31601. (Illus.). 313p. 1997. pap. 20.00 (*1-85984-172-4*, Pub. by Verso) Norton.

— Real Love: In Pursuit of Cultural Justice. LC 97-45241. 256p. 1998. text 55.00 (*0-8147-7504-7*); pap. text 18.00 (*0-8147-7505-5*) NYU Pr.

— Strange Weather: Culture, Science & Technology in the Age of Limits. LC 91-22782. 240p. (C). 1991. pap. 20.00 (*0-86091-567-0*, A6401, Pub. by Verso) Norton.

Ross, Andrew, ed. Science Wars. LC 96-22506. 352p. 1996. pap. 17.95 (*0-8223-1871-7*); text 49.95 (*0-8223-1881-4*) Duke.

— Universal Abandon? The Politics of Postmodernism. LC 88-10134. (Cultural Politics Ser.). xviii, 300p. (Orig.). 1989. pap. 18.95 (*0-8166-1680-9*) U of Minn Pr.

Ross, Andrew & Rose, Tricia, eds. Microphone Fiends: Youth Music & Youth Culture. LC 93-44005. 288p. (C). (gr. 13). 1994. 80.00 (*0-415-90907-4*); pap. 20.99 (*0-415-90908-2*) Routledge.

Ross, Andrew, jt. auth. see Penley, Constance.

Ross, Andrew, ed. see Cadell, Ava.

Ross, Andrew C. Blantyre Mission & the Making of Modern Malawi. 216p. 1996. pap. 44.95 (*99908-16-02-6*, U Pr W Africa) Intl Scholars.

— A Vision Betrayed: The Jesuits in Japan & China, 1542-1742. LC 94-10623. (Illus.). 234p. reprint ed. pap. 72.60 (*0-608-20193-6*, 207145200012) Bks Demand.

Ross, Andrew L., ed. The Political Economy of Defense: Issues & Perspectives, 112. LC 90-25280. (Contributions in Military Studies Ser.: No. 112). 240p. 1991. 62.95 (*0-313-26462-7*, RPD/, Greenwood Pr) Greenwood.

Ross, Andrew S., ed. see Cadell, Ava.

***Ross, Angus.** The Bradford Business. 336p. 1999. 20.99 (*1-85389-975-5*) Ulverscroft.

Ross, Angus. Doom Indigo. large type ed. (Lythway Ser.). . 256p. 1990. 20.95 (*0-7451-1169-6*, G K Hall Lrg Type) Mac Lib Ref.

— The Last One. large type ed. 248p. 1993. 15.95 (*0-7451-1666-3*, G K Hall Lrg Type) Mac Lib Ref.

— The Leipzig Manuscript. large type ed. (Lythway Ser.). 256p. 1991. 21.95 (*0-7451-1277-3*, G K Hall Lrg Type) Mac Lib Ref.

Ross, Angus, ed. Selections from the Tatler & the Spectator. 1988. pap. 13.95 (*0-14-043298-1*, Penguin Classics) Viking Penguin.

Ross, Angus, et al, eds. Jonathan Swift. (Oxford Authors Ser.). 758p. 1984. pap. text 24.95 (*0-19-281337-4*) OUP.

Ross, Angus, jt. ed. see Bellamy, Richard.

Ross, Angus, jt. ed. see Heap, Shaun H.

Ross, Angus, ed. see Smollett, Tobias George.

Ross, Angus, ed. see Swift, Jonathan.

Ross, Angus, ed. & intro. see Defoe, Daniel.

Ross, Angus, ed. & intro. see Richardson, Samuel.

Ross, Ann. Curiosity Shop: A Drop of Water. 21p. 1998. text 39.95 (*1-878631-47-0*) S Kovalik.

— Curiosity Shop: I've Got a Secret. 20p. 1998. text 39.95 (*1-878631-49-7*) S Kovalik.

Ross, Ann & Olsen, Karen D. The Way We Were . . . The Way We Can Be: A Vision for the Middle School. 3rd rev. ed. Little, Kristen, ed. (Illus.). 292p. 1995. pap. 27.50 (*1-878631-24-1*) S Kovalik.

Ross, Ann, jt. auth. see Trautwein, Jannie.

***Ross, Ann B.** Miss Julia Speaks Her Mind. large type ed. LC 99-46320. 1999. 26.95 (*0-7862-2255-7*) Thorndike Pr.

— Miss Julia Speaks Her Mind: A Novel. LC 98-52489. 288p. 1999. 23.00 (*0-688-16788-8*, Wm Morrow) Morrow Avon.

— Miss Julia Speaks Her Mind: A Novel. 288p. 2000. pap. 13.00 (*0-688-17775-1*) Morrow Avon.

Ross, Anna. Be My Friend. LC 89-24389. (Sesame Street Toddler Bks.). (Illus.). 24p. (J). (ps). 1991. 5.99 (*0-394-85496-9*, Pub. by Random Bks Yng Read) Random.

— Elmo's Big Lift-&-Look Book. (Illus.). 12p. (J). (ps). 1994. 11.99 (*0-679-84468-6*, Pub. by Random Bks Yng Read) Random.

— Elmo's Lift-&-Peek Around the Corner Book. LC 95-68447. (Illus.). (J). 1996. 11.99 (*0-679-87188-8*) Random.

— Elmo's Little Playhouse. LC 91-68111. (Sesame Street Chunky Shape Bks.). (Illus.). 22p. (J). (ps). 1993. 3.99 (*0-679-83270-X*, Pub. by Random Bks Yng Read) Random.

— Grover's Ten Terrific Ways to Help Our Wonderful World. LC 91-11095. (Sesame Street Picturebacks Ser.). (Illus.). 32p. (Orig.). (J). (ps-3). 1992. pap. 3.25 (*0-679-81384-5*, Pub. by Random Bks Yng Read) Random.

— I Have to Go. LC 89-34542. (Sesame Street Toddler Bks.). (Illus.). 24p. (J). (ps). 1990. 5.99 (*0-394-86051-9*, Pub. by Random Bks Yng Read) Random.

— Knock, Knock, Who's There? A Sesame Street Book. (Chunky Flap Bks. Ser.). (Illus.). 22p. (J). (ps). 1994. 3.99 (*0-679-85304-9*, Pub. by Random Bks Yng Read) Random.

— Little Elmo's Book of Colors. LC 91-23979. (Sesame Street Toddler Bks.). (Illus.). 24p. (J). (ps). 1992. 5.99 (*0-679-82238-0*, Pub. by Random Bks Yng Read) Random.

— Little Ernie's ABC's. LC 91-27823. (Sesame Street Toddler Bks.). (Illus.). 24p. (J). (ps). 1992. 5.99 (*0-679-82240-2*, Pub. by Random Bks Yng Read) Random.

— Meet the Sesame Street Babies. LC 92-60973. (Board Bks.). 7p. (J). (ps). 1993. 4.99 (*0-679-83486-9*, Pub. by Random Bks Yng Read) Random.

— Not the Monster. (Sesame Street Baby Board Bks.). (Illus.). 12p. (J). (ps). 1994. 4.99 (*0-679-84739-1*, Pub. by Random Bks Yng Read) Random.

— Open Sesame. LC 91-67671. (Lift-&-Peek-A-Board Bks.). (Illus.). 14p. (J). (ps). 1992. 4.99 (*0-679-83063-4*, Pub. by Random Bks Yng Read) Random.

— Peekaboo, Puppy! LC 93-85494. (My Puppy Loves Me Bk.). (J). (ps). 1994. 3.99 (*0-679-85700-1*, Pub. by Random Bks Yng Read) Random.

— Rock-a-Bye Babies. (Sesame Street Baby Board Bks.). (Illus.). 12p. (J). (ps). 1994. 4.99 (*0-679-84740-5*, Pub. by Random Bks Yng Read) Random.

— Rubber Duckies Don't Say Quack! (Sesame Street Baby Board Bks.). (Illus.). 12p. (J). (ps). 1994. 4.99 (*0-679-84741-3*, Pub. by Random Bks Yng Read) Random.

— Say Bye-Bye. LC 90-52915. (Sesame Street Toddler Bks.). (Illus.). 24p. (J). (ps). 1992. 5.99 (*0-394-85485-3*, Pub. by Random Bks Yng Read) Random.

— Say Good Night. LC 90-52914. (Sesame Street Toddler Bks.). (Illus.). 24p. (J). (ps). 1992. 5.99 (*0-394-85491-8*, Pub. by Random Bks Yng Read) Random.

— Say the Magic Word, Please. LC 89-34544. (Sesame Street Toddler Bks.). (Illus.). 24p. (J). (ps). 1990. 5.99 (*0-394-85857-3*, Pub. by Random Bks Yng Read) Random.

— Sesame Street Whose Knees Are These? LC 93-83725. (J). (ps). 1994. 4.99 (*0-679-84742-1*, Pub. by Random Bks Yng Read) Random.

— Where, Oh, Where? A Sesame Street Book. (Chunky Flap Bks. Ser.). (Illus.). 22p. (J). (ps). 1994. 3.99 (*0-679-85303-0*, Pub. by Random Bks Yng Read) Random.

— Whose Knees Are These? (Illus.). 12p. (J). (ps). 1994. write for info. (*0-318-72490-1*) Random Bks Yng Read.

Ross, Anna, jt. auth. see Sesame Street Staff.

Ross, Anna, ed. see Elz, Ron.

***Ross, Anne.** Druids. (History & Archaeology Ser.). (Illus.). 208p. 1999. 32.50 (*0-7524-1433-X*, Pub. by Tempus Pubng) Arcadia Publng.

Ross, Anne. Druids, Gods & Heroes from Celtic Mythology. LC 93-31615. (World Mythology Ser.). (Illus.). 128p. (YA). 1994. pap. 14.95 (*0-87226-919-1*, P Bedrick Books); lib. bdg. 24.95 (*0-87226-918-3*, P Bedrick Books) NTC Contemp Pub Co.

— Pagan Celtic Britain. 1996. pap. text 17.95 (*0-89733-435-3*) Academy Chi Pubs.

— Pagan Celts. (Illus.). 250p. 1998. pap. 26.95 (*0-8464-4923-4*) Beekman Pubs.

Ross, Anne. The Pagan Celts. (Illus.). 224p. pap. 17.95 (*1-871083-61-3*, Pub. by J Jones Pub) Dufour.

Ross, Annette L. & Disney, Jean A. The Art of Making Good Cookies. 256p. 1987. reprint ed. pap. 4.95 (*0-486-25315-5*) Dover.

Ross, Annie. Moving Image. large type ed. 416p. 1996. 27.99 (*0-7089-3523-0*) Ulverscroft.

***Ross, Annie.** Shot in the Dark. large type ed. 1999. 31.99 (*0-7089-4089-7*) Ulverscroft.

Ross, Anthony C. Economic Stabilization for Developing Countries. 288p. 1991. text 90.00 (*1-85278-314-1*); pap. text 35.00 (*1-85278-452-0*) E Elgar.

Ross, Arnold, jt. ed. see Newman, William A.

Ross, Austin. Ambulatory Care Management. 2nd ed. 432p. 1991. text 44.00 (*0-8273-4613-1*) Delmar.

— Cornerstones of Leadership for Health Services Executives. LC 91-35345. 220p. 1992. text 30.80 (*0-910701-58-X*, 0818) Health Admin Pr.

Ross, Austin & Richardson, Mary, eds. Ambulatory Health Care: Case Studies for the Health Services Executive. LC 96-12939. 352p. (Orig.). 1996. pap. 46.00 (*1-56793-044-1*) Health Admin Pr.

Ross, Austin, et al. Ambulatory Care: Organization & Management. LC 83-16709. (Health Services Ser.: No. 1-456). 453p. 1989. text 41.95 (*0-8273-4349-3*) Delmar.

— Ambulatory Care Management. 3rd ed. LC 96-47935. (Health Services Administration Ser.). 400p. (C). 1997. mass mkt. 76.95 (*0-8273-7664-2*) Delmar.

Ross, B. D. SWAT Patrol: Pledge Paddling on Fraternity Row. 84p. 1994. pap. 11.95 (*0-9645291-8-1*) A D Thompson.

Ross, Barbara. The Chef's Table. 208p. 1991. pap. 19.95 (*0-04-442221-0*, Pub. by Allen & Unwin Pty) Paul & Co Pubs.

— The Illustrated Guide to Sheltie Grooming. (Illus.). 160p. 1993. pap. 24.95 (*0-931866-60-X*) Alpine Pubns.

Ross, Barbara, jt. auth. see Ross, Lindsay.

Ross, Barbara A., jt. auth. see Baron, Howard C.

Ross, Barbara T. American Drawings in the Art Museum, Princeton University: 130 Selected Examples. LC 76-27117. (Illus.). 144p. 1977. text 45.00 (*0-691-03921-6*, Pub. by Princeton U Pr) Cal Prin Full Svc.

Ross, Barry. Hands on Guide to Oscilloscopes. 1994. 21.95 (*0-07-053954-5*) McGraw.

— A Violinist's Guide for Exquisite Intonation. 1988. 13.75 (*0-89917-520-1*) Am String Tchrs.

Ross, Barry, jt. auth. see Ross, Garry.

Ross, Barry, jt. auth. see Tarr, Bill.

Ross, Becki. The House That Jill Built: A Lesbian Nation in Formation. (Illus.). 384p. 1995. text 50.00 (*0-8020-0460-1*); pap. text 19.95 (*0-8020-7479-0*) U of Toronto Pr.

Ross, Bernard H., ed. Urban Management: A Guide to Information Sources. LC 78-10310. (Urban Studies Information Guide Ser.: Vol. 8). 304p. 1979. 68.00 (*0-8103-1430-4*) Gale.

Ross, Bernard H. & Levine, Myron A. Urban Politics: Power in Metropolitan America. 5th rev. ed. LC 95-69692. 539p. (C). 1995. pap. text 40.00 (*0-87581-397-6*, UP5) F E Peacock Pubs.

Ross, Bernard H., et al. How Washington Works: The Executive's Guide to Government. 3rd rev. ed. LC 95-82366. 150p. 1996. pap. 12.95 (*0-913878-55-3*) T Horton & Dghts.

Ross, Bertram. Methods of Summation. ix, 127p. (C). 1987. write for info. (*0-936285-08-7*, JPY7000, Pub. by Descartes); teacher ed. write for info. (*0-318-64056-2*, JPY4000, Pub. by Descartes) NACE Intl.

Ross, Bertram, jt. auth. see Miller, Kenneth.

Ross, Beth, jt. auth. see Ross, John.

Ross, Bette. How to Teach Students to Be Fluent Writers: Intermediate. 1997. pap. text 9.95 (*1-57690-005-3*) Tchr Create Mat.

Ross, Betty. Washington D. C. Museums: Museums, Historic Houses, Art Galleries & Other Special Places. 3rd ed. LC 91-39333. (Illus.). 328p. 1992. pap. 14.95 (*0-939009-85-4*, EPM) Howell Pr VA.

Ross, Beverlee. Annabelle. (Historical Ser.). 1993. per. 3.99 (*0-373-28778-X*, 1-28778-8) Harlequin Bks.

Ross, Beverly B. & Durgin, Jean B. Junior Broadway: How to Produce Musicals with Children 9 to 13. 2nd ed. LC 97-47309. (Illus.). 223p. (Orig.). 1998. pap. 29.95 (*0-7864-0341-1*) McFarland & Co.

Ross, Bianca, jt. ed. see Poppe, Erich.

Ross, Bill. Hey! That's Not What the Bible Says! LC 98-51088. (Illus.). 80p. (YA). (gr. k up). 1999. 9.99 (*0-8499-5922-5*) Tommy Nelson.

— Straight from the Bear's Mouth: The Story of Photosynthesis. LC 95-60387. (Illus.). 32p. (J). (gr. 5-9). 1995. 16.00 (*0-689-31726-3*) Atheneum Yung Read.

Ross, Bill. Crazy Christmas Characters. 12p. (Orig.). (J). (ps-2). 1991. pap. 3.50 (*0-8249-8522-2*, Ideals Child) Hambleton-Hill.

— Easter Bunnyheads. 14p. (Orig.). (J). (ps-2). 1992. pap. 3.50 (*0-8249-8541-9*, Ideals Child) Hambleton-Hill.

— Easter Eggheads. 14p. (Orig.). (J). (ps-2). 1992. pap. 2.95 (*0-8249-8540-0*, Ideals Child) Hambleton-Hill.

— Funny Bunnyheads. 14p. (J). (ps-2). 1995. pap. 3.50 (*1-57102-030-6*, Ideals Child) Hambleton-Hill.

— Scrambled Eggheads. 14p. (J). (ps-2). 1995. pap. 3.50 (*1-57102-031-4*, Ideals Child) Hambleton-Hill.

— Silly Christmas Scenes. 14p. (J). (ps-2). 1991. pap. 3.50 (*0-8249-8523-0*, Ideals Child) Hambleton-Hill.

Ross, Bill, jt. auth. see Roberts, Wess.

Ross, Bill D. Iwo Jima: Legacy of Valor. LC 85-40665. (Illus.). 416p. 1986. pap. 15.00 (*0-394-74288-5*) Vin Bks.

Ross, Bob. Funny Business: The Art of Using Humor Constructively. Moore, Jack, ed. & illus. by. 200p. 1998. pap. 16.95 (*0-9623819-1-8*) Arrowhead Pub.

— Laugh, Lead & Profit: Building Productive Workplaces with Humor. 125p. (Orig.) (YA). 1989. pap. write for info. (*0-318-65545-4*) Arrowhead Pub.

Ross, Bob, jt. auth. see MacKichan, Margaret A.

Ross, Bob L. Acts Two: Thirty-Eight. 1976. mass mkt. 3.00 (*1-56186-503-6*) Pilgrim Pubns.

— Baptism & the Restoration Movement. 1979. pap. 2.00 (*1-56186-507-9*) Pilgrim Pubns.

— Campbellism Its History & Heresies. 1962. mass mkt. 6.00 (*1-56186-502-8*) Pilgrim Pubns.

— Campbellites, Cow-Bells, Rosary Beeds, & Snake-Handling (on Instrumental Music) 1994. pap. 5.00 (*1-56186-522-2*) Pilgrim Pubns.

— Hardshellism (Primitive Baptists) Its History & Heresies. 1994. pap. 7.00 (*1-56186-500-1*) Pilgrim Pubns.

— Killing Effects of Calvinism: Hyper-Calvinistic "Hardshellism" Refuted. 1980. pap. 2.00 (*1-56186-506-0*) Pilgrim Pubns.

— Little Horn of the Book of Daniel. 1983. mass mkt. 3.00 (*1-56186-511-7*) Pilgrim Pubns.

— Not One Stone. 1993. pap. 6.00 (*1-56186-521-4*) Pilgrim Pubns.

— Old Landmarkism & the Baptists. 1979. mass mkt. 4.00 (*1-56186-504-4*) Pilgrim Pubns.

— Pictorial Biography of C. H. Spurgeon. 1974. pap. 7.00 (*1-56186-205-3*) Pilgrim Pubns.

— The Restoration Movement. 1981. mass mkt. 3.00 (*1-56186-509-5*) Pilgrim Pubns.

— Salvation by Grace Through Faith in Contrast to the Restorationist Doctrine. 1979. pap. 2.00 (*1-56186-508-7*) Pilgrim Pubns.

— The Trinity & Eternal Sonship of Christ: A Defense Against "Oneness Pentecostal" Attacks on Historic Christianity. 1993. pap. 12.00 (*1-56186-517-6*) Pilgrim Pubns.

Ross, Bob L., jt. auth. see Spurgeon, Charles H.

Ross, Bonnie, ed. see Vermont Institute of Natural Science Staff.

Ross, Brian H., jt. auth. see Medin, Douglas L.

Ross, Bruce. Haiku Moment: An Anthology of Contemporary North American Haiku. 368p. 1993. pap. 16.95 (*0-8048-1820-7*) Tuttle Pubng.

***Ross, Bruce.** If Not Higher: Lectures on the Poetics of Spiritual Presence & Absence. LC 98-20812. (Studies in Modern Poetry: Vol. 10). (Illus.). viii, 225p. (C). 1999. text 48.95 (*0-8204-4124-4*, 41244) P Lang Pubng.

Ross, Bruce, ed. Journey to the Interior: American Versions of Haibun. LC 98-10476. 221p. 1998. pap. 21.95 (*0-8048-3159-9*) Tuttle Pubng.

Ross, Bruce, ed. see Grainger, Percy.

Ross, Bruce, jt. ed. see Kacian, Jim.

Ross, Bruce M. Recovering the Personal Past: The Conceptual Background of Autobiographical Memory. 256p. 1992. text 40.00 (*0-19-506894-7*) OUP.

Ross, C. & Valentine, Ed, eds. Food Industry Environmental Conference Proceedings, 1991. (Illus.). 500p. (C). 1991. 60.00 (*0-9624647-5-9*) GA Tech Rsch Inst.

Ross, C. Randolph. Common Sense Christianity. LC 88-61552. 266p. 1989. 19.95 (*0-929368-00-2*) Occam Pubs.

Ross, C. T. Advanced Applied Stress Analysis: Theory & Application. (Mechanical Engineering Ser.). 1987. text 54.95 (*0-470-20874-0*) P-H.

— Applied Stress Analysis. LC 86-24182. (Mechanical Engineering Ser.). 322p. 1987. text 59.95 (*0-470-20767-1*) P-H.

— Computational Methods in Structural & Continuum Mechanics. LC 81-20272. 1982. text 67.95 (*0-470-27329-1*) P-H.

— Finite Element Programs for Structural Vibrations. (Illus.). x, 187p. 1991. 151.95 incl. 3.5 hd (*0-387-19693-5*) Spr-Verlag.

— Pressure Vessels under External Pressure: Statics & Dynamics. 250p. 1990. mass mkt. 153.95 (*1-85166-433-5*) Elsevier.

***Ross, C. T. F.** Advanced APplied Finite Element Methods. LC 99-206597. 450p. 1999. 49.95 (*1-898563-51-9*, Pub. by Horwood Pub) Paul & Co Pubs.

— Mechanics of Solids. 480p. 2000. pap. 49.95 (*1-898563-67-5*, Pub. by Horwood Pub) Paul & Co Pubs.

Ross, Cal. Counseling the Gifted: Developing the Whole Child. 1990. pap. 6.00 (*0-89824-710-1*) Trillium Pr.

Ross, Calvert G., et al. War - A Trilogy. 174p. 1993. pap. 6.95 (*1-56794-052-8*, C-2330) Star Bible.

Ross, Calvin. The Aliens of Summer. 321p. (Orig.). 1995. pap. 9.95 (*0-9642658-9-3*) Small Wonder.

— The Frugal Youth Cybrarian: Bargain Computing for Kids. LC 96-45724. 336p. 1996. 28.00 (*0-8389-0694-X*) ALA.

— Whiz Kid Starter Kit: Plugging Your Child into the 21st Century. 127p. (Orig.). 1995. pap. 7.95 (*0-9642658-8-5*) Small Wonder.

— Your Hormoneous Life: Learn the Secrets of Progesterone. (Illus.). 180p. (Orig.). 1996. pap. 12.95 (*1-57901-013-X*) Intl Promotions.

Ross, Cameron. Local Government in the Soviet Union: Problems of Implementation & Control. LC 86-29861. 240p. 1987. text 45.00 (*0-312-00545-8*) St Martin.

Ross, Cameron, jt. auth. see Bowker, Mike.

Ross, Candace, jt. auth. see Ross, Thomas D.

Ross, Carey F., et al. Replicating History: Guide to the Plaster Casts on View at the Michael C. Carlos Museum & in Michael C. Carlos Hall, Emory University. 27p. 1994. pap. 4.50 (*0-9638169-5-0*) M C Carlos Mus.

Ross, Carl, ed. see Appalachian Studies Staff.

Ross, Carl T. Dynamics of Mechanical Systems. LC 98-106840. 260p. 1997. pap. 29.95 (*1-898563-34-9*, Pub. by Horwood Pub) Paul & Co Pubs.

— Finite Element Methods in Structural Mechanics. LC 85-6180. (Mechanical Engineering Ser.). 319p. 1985. text 74.95 (*0-470-20207-6*); pap. text 38.95 (*0-470-20208-4*) P-H.

— Finite Element Programs for Axisymmetric Problems in Engineering. (Mechanical Engineering Ser.: I-476). 297p. 1984. text 97.95 (*0-470-20035-9*) P-H.

— Finite Element Programs in Structural Engineering & Continuum Mechanics. 650p. 1996. 89.00 (*1-898563-28-4*, Pub. by Horwood Pub) Paul & Co Pubs.

— Finite Element Techniques in Structural Mechanics. LC 97-155183. 224p. 1996. pap. 29.95 (*1-898563-25-X*, Pub. by Horwood Pub) Paul & Co Pubs.

Ross, Carol. By the Way of The Cross. LC 95-71144. (Illus.). 468p. 1995. per. write for info. (*0-9648448-1-8*) CMJ Marian Pubs.

— By Way of His Word. LC 97-67803. 1996. 13.75 (*0-9648448-4-2*) CMJ Marian Pubs.

— By Way of Rome. (Illus.). 1996. write for info. (*0-9648448-0-X*) CMJ Marian Pubs.

— Something to Draw On: Activities & Interventions Using an Art Therapy Approach. 150p. 1996. 24.95 (*1-85302-363-9*, Pub. by Jessica Kingsley) Taylor & Francis.

Ross, Carol & Ryan, Amanda. Can I Stay in Today, Miss? 80p. 1990. pap. 15.00 (*0-948080-42-6*, Trentham Bks) Stylus Pub VA.

Ross, Carol, jt. auth. see Askew, Sue.

Ross, Caroline, jt. ed. see MacLarnon, Ann.

Ross, Carolyn. Writing Nature. 1995. pap. text, teacher ed. 5.00 (*0-312-10392-1*); pap. text, teacher ed. 23.00 (*0-312-10811-7*) St Martin.

— Writing Nature: An Ecological Reader for Writers. 672p. 1995. pap. text 38.95 (*0-312-10391-3*) St Martin.

Ross, Catherine. Cognitive Challenge Cards. 1976. pap. 14.00 (*0-87879-188-4*) Acad Therapy.

Ross, Catherine & Dewdney, Patricia. Communicating Professionally: A How-To-Do-It Manual for Library Applications. 2nd ed. LC 98-20556. (How-to-Do-It Manual Ser.). 323p. 1998. pap. 55.00 (*1-55570-340-2*) Neal-Schuman.

Ross, Catherine E., jt. auth. see Mirowsky, John.

Ross, Catherine H., jt. auth. see Ross, John D.

Ross, Catherine L., jt. auth. see Boston, Thomas D.

Ross, Catherine S. Alice Munro: A Double Life. (Illus.). 97p. (Orig.). 1993. pap. 9.95 (*1-55022-153-1*, Pub. by ECW) LPC InBook.

— Alice Munro: A Double Life. large type ed. (Illus.). 133p. (Orig.). 1997. pap. 15.95 (*1-55022-236-8*, Pub. by ECW) Genl Dist Srvs.

Ross, Catherine S. Circles: Shapes in Math, Science & Nature. (Illus.). 80p. (J). 1996. pap. 12.95 (*1-55074-064-4*) Kids Can Pr.

Ross, Catherine S. Squares: Shapes in Math, Science & Nature. unabridged ed. (Shapes in Math, Science & Nature Ser.). (Illus.). 64p. (J). (gr. 4-9). 1997. pap. 12.95 (*1-55074-273-6*, Pub. by Kids Can Pr) Genl Dist Srvs.

— Triangles. unabridged ed. (Shapes in Math, Science & Nature Ser.). (Illus.). 64p. (J). (gr. 4-9). 1994. pap. 12.95 (*1-55074-194-2*, Pub. by Kids Can Pr) Genl Dist Srvs.

Ross, Catrien. Supernatural & Mysterious Japan. (Illus.). 168p. 1995. pap. text 8.95 (*4-900737-37-2*, Pub. by Yen Bks) Tuttle Pubng.

Ross, Cecil. Friends of the Ezekiens: A Science Fiction Novel. 279p. 1998. pap. 12.95 (*0-9649888-2-8*) RIE.

— Logical Physics on the Uncertainty Principle Is a Cop-Out: A Comprehensive Theory of Atomic Structure & Behavior from Physics to Astronomy. LC 97-65061. 217p. 1997. pap. 23.50 (*0-9649888-1-X*) RIE.

Ross, Charles. The Best of Your Personal Finance: Money Management Tips from the Nationally Syndicated Radio Program & Newspaper Column. 164p. (Orig.). 1991. pap. text 12.95 (*0-9629100-0-7*) FMS Pub.

— The Custom of the Castle: From Malory to Macbeth. LC 96-32809. (Illus.). 215p. (C). 1996. 38.00 (*0-520-20430-1*, Pub. by U CA Pr) Cal Prin Full Svc.

— Edward IV. LC 97-61404. (English Monarchs Ser.). (Illus.). 500p. 1998. 40.00 (*0-300-07371-2*); pap. 18.00 (*0-300-07372-0*) Yale U Pr.

— God's Plan for Your Financial Success. 228p. 1998. pap. 10.99 (*0-7852-7052-3*) Nelson.

— The Inner Sanctuary. 247p. 1992. pap. 8.50 (*0-85151-042-6*) Banner of Truth.

— Your Commonsense Guide to Personal Financial Planning: Learn How to Budget, Protect & Save Your Money. 1997. mass mkt. 6.50 (*0-7852-7222-4*) Nelson.

Ross, Charles A., ed. Crocodiles & Alligators. (Illus.). 240p. 1989. 35.00 (*0-8160-2174-0*) Facts on File.

— Paleogeographic Provinces & Provinciality. LC 74-193154. (Society of Economic Paleontologists & Mineralogists, Special Publication Ser.: No. 21). 243p. reprint ed. pap. 75.40 (*0-608-12951-8*, 202474300038) Bks Demand.

Ross, Charles C., ed. Seventh International Symposium on Agricultural & Food Processing Wastes. LC 95-77218. (Illus.). 636p. (Orig.). 1995. pap. 51.00 (*0-929355-66-0*, P0795) Am Soc Ag Eng.

Ross, Charles C. & Drake, Thomas J., III. The Handbook of Biogas Utilization. 2nd ed. (Illus.). 230p. (C). 1997. pap. text 50.00 (*0-7881-3892-8*) DIANE Pub.

Ross, Charles C., jt. ed. see Valentine, G. Edward.

***Ross, Charles D.** Trial by Fire: Science, Technology & the Civil War. LC 99-42228. (Illus.). 228p. 2000. 24.95 (*1-57249-185-X*) White Mane Pub.

Ross, Charles K. Outside the Lines: African-Americans & the Integration of the National Football League. LC 99-6581. 2000. text 35.00 (*0-8147-7495-4*) NYU Pr.

Ross, Charles L. Richard III. LC 81-43381. (English Monarchs Ser.: No. 6). (Illus.). 263p. 1982. pap. 15.95 (*0-520-05075-4*, Pub. by U CA Pr) Cal Prin Full Svc.

— The Wars of the Roses: A Concise History. LC 85-52289. (Illus.). 190p. 1986. pap. 15.95 (*0-500-27407-X*, Pub. by Thames Hudson) Norton.

— Women in Love: A Novel of Mythic Realism. (Twayne's Masterworks Ser.: No. 65). 152p. 1991. 23.95 (*0-8057-8057-2*); pap. 18.00 (*0-8057-8106-4*) Macmillan.

Ross, Charles L. & Jackson, Dennis, eds. Editing D. H. Lawrence: New Versions of a Modern Author. LC 95-10370. (Editorial Theory & Literary Criticism Ser.). 272p. 1996. text 52.50 (*0-472-10612-0*, 10612) U of Mich Pr.

Ross, Charles L., jt. auth. see Cain, William.

Ross, Charles S., jt. ed. see Cavallo, Jo Ann.

Ross, Charles S., tr. & intro. see Boiardo, Matteo M.

Ross, Cheri B. & Sorensen, Jane B. Pet Loss & Human Emotion: Guiding Clients Through Grief. LC 97-38965. 164p. 1998. pap. 19.95 (*1-56032-652-2*) Hemisp Pub.

***Ross, Christopher.** Spain, 1812-1996. 256p. 2000. pap. text 19.95 (*0-340-74113-9*, Pub. by E A) OUP.

— Spain, 1812-1996. (Modern History for Modern Languages). 256p. 2000. text 65.00 (*0-340-74112-0*) E A.

Ross, Christopher. The Urban System & Networks of Corporate Control, Vol. 11. (Contemporary Studies in Sociology). 170p. 1992. 78.50 (*1-55938-474-3*) Jai Pr.

Ross, Christopher J. Contemporary Spain Handbook. LC 96-54868. (Illus.). 256p. 1997. pap. text 19.95 (*0-340-65227-6*) OUP.

— Contemporary Spain Handbook. LC 96-54868. (Illus.). 256p. (C). 1997. text 65.00 (*0-340-65228-4*) OUP.

Ross, Christopher S., ed. see Neville, Peter & O'Farrell, Valerie.

Ross, Christopher W., ed. Patterns of Global Terrorism, 1997. (Illus.). 85p. (C). 1998. pap. text 25.00 (*0-7881-7558-0*) DIANE Pub.

Ross, Cindy. Journey on the Crest: Walking 2,600 Miles from Mexico to Canada. LC 87-28160. (Illus.). 320p. (Orig.). 1987. pap. 14.95 (*0-89886-146-2*) Mountaineers.

***Ross, Cindy.** A Women's Journey. Orig. Title: A Women's Journey on the Appalachian Trail. (Illus.). 128p. 1998. reprint ed. pap. 9.95 (*0-917953-42-8*) Appalachian Trail.

Ross, Cindy & Gladfelter, Todd. A Hiker's Companion: Twelve Thousand Miles of Trail-Tested Wisdom. LC 92-46568. (Illus.). 224p. (Orig.). 1993. pap. 12.95 (*0-89886-353-8*) Mountaineers.

— Kids in the Wild: A Family Guide to Outdoor Recreation. LC 95-37429. (Illus.). 224p. 1995. pap. 12.95 (*0-89886-447-X*) Mountaineers.

***Ross, Clarissa.** Beware the Kindly Stranger. large type ed. LC 99-86161. (G. K. Hall Romance Ser.). 2000. 27.95 (*0-7838-8980-1*, G K Hall Lrg Type) Mac Lib Ref.

Ross, Clarissa. Denver's Lady. 1985. mass mkt. 3.95 (*0-445-20118-5*, Pub. by Warner Bks) Little.

***Ross, Clarissa.** Gemini in Darkness. large type ed. (Candlelight Romance Ser.). 2000. 20.95 (*0-7862-2448-7*) Thorndike Pr.

Ross, Clarissa. Let Your Heart Answer. large type ed. 1994. 27.99 (*0-7089-3210-X*) Ulverscroft.

— A Scandalous Affair. large type ed. 304p. 1995. 27.99 (*0-7089-3248-7*) Ulverscroft.

***Ross, Clarissa.** Secret of the Pale Lover. LC 00-35359. 2000. write for info. (*0-7862-2636-6*) Five Star.

Ross, Clark, jt. auth. see Hess, Peter.

Ross, Clark G., jt. auth. see Hess, Peter N.

Ross, Clay C. Differential Equations: An Introduction with Mathematica. LC 94-36401. (Textbooks in Mathematical Sciences Ser.: Vol. 1). 1995. text 44.95 (*0-387-94301-3*) Spr-Verlag.

— The Relation Between Grade School Record & High School Achievement: A Study of the Diagnostic Value of Individual Record Cards. LC 70-177211. (Columbia University. Teachers College. Contributions to Education Ser.: No. 166). reprint ed. 37.50 (*0-404-55166-1*) AMS Pr.

Ross, Cleo B. Poems in the Tree of Life. LC 96-92482. (Illus.). 80p. 1996. spiral bd. 32.95 (*0-9653709-0-9*) Ginga Pr.

— Poems in the Tree of Life, Act II. 43p. 1997. spiral bd. 21.95 (*0-9653709-1-7*) Ginga Pr.

***Ross, Cleo B.** Rending of the Veil. LC 99-97795. 93p. 2000. spiral bd. 21.00 (*0-9653709-2-5*) Ginga Pr.

Ross, Cleon W., jt. auth. see Salisbury, Frank B.

Ross, Clifford & Wilkin, Karen. The World of Edward Gorey. LC 95-47900. (Illus.). 192p. 1996. 29.95 (*0-8109-3988-6*, Pub. by Abrams) Time Warner.

Ross, Clifton. Fables for an Open Field. 1995. pap. 3.95 (*0-915117-07-X*) Freedom Voices Pubns.

— William Everson: The Light the Shadow Casts. 120p. 1996. pap. 14.95 (*0-915117-05-3*) Freedom Voices Pubns.

Ross, Clifton, ed. & tr. see Zapatista National Liberation Army Staff.

Ross, Clifton, tr. & intro. see Cardenal, Ernesto.

Ross, Clyde. Valdez Creek Mining District Alaska. 56p. reprint ed. pap. 10.00 (*0-8466-0107-9*, S107) Shoreys Bkstore.

Ross, Colin. Adenocarcinoma & Other Poems. (C). 1989. 65.00 (*0-907839-38-X*, Pub. by Brynmill Pr Ltd) St Mut.

Ross, Colin A. Dissociative Identity Disorder: Diagnosis, Clinical Features & Treatment of Multiple Personality. 2nd ed. LC 96-23334. 464p. 1996. 69.50 (*0-471-13265-9*) Wiley.

— Multiple Personality Disorder: Diagnosis, Clinical Features & Treatment. LC 89-14608. 400p. 1989. 90.00 (*0-471-61515-3*) Wiley.

— The Osiris Complex: Case Studies in Multiple Personality Disorder. LC 93-95100. 296p. (C). 1994. pap. 17.95 (*0-8020-7358-1*); text 50.00 (*0-8020-2858-6*) U of Toronto Pr.

Ross, Conrad M. Customer Service Manager's Guide. (C). 1991. 119.50 (*0-13-194275-1*, Macmillan Coll) P-H.

***Ross, Corey.** Constructing Socialism at the Grass-Roots: The Transformation of East Germany, 1945-1965. LC 99-49746. 2000. text 65.00 (*0-312-23041-9*) St Martin.

Ross, Corinne. Christmas in Italy. (Christmas in...Ser.). (Illus.). 80p. 1995. 12.95 (*0-8442-8071-2*, 80712, Passprt Bks) NTC Contemp Pub Co.

***Ross, Cory Paul.** Complete Idiot's Guide to Healing Back Pain for Canadians. 368p. 2000. pap. 25.95 (*0-13-086727-6*, Prentice Hall) P-H.

Ross, Courtney. Listen Up. 1990. mass mkt. write for info. (*0-446-11411-1*, Pub. by Warner Bks) Little.

— Listen Up: The Lives of Quincy Jones. 1990. pap., mass mkt. 39.95 incl. cd-rom (*0-446-39286-3*, Pub. by Warner Bks); mass mkt. 34.95 (*0-446-39233-2*, Pub. by Warner Bks) Little.

Ross, Courtney, et al. Love, Lawyers & Lies. 200p. 1991. per. write for info. (*0-8187-0147-1*) Harlo Press.

Ross-Craig, Stella. Drawings of British Plants, 8 vols., Set. Incl. Vol. 1. 1980. 32.50 (*0-7135-1137-0*); Vol. 2. 1980. 32.50 (*0-7135-1138-9*); Vol. 3. 1980. 32.50 (*0-7135-1139-7*); Vol. 4. 1980. 32.50 Vol. 5. 1980. 32.50 (*0-7135-1141-9*); Vol. 6. 1980. 32.50 (*0-7135-1142-7*); Vol. 7. 1980. 32.50 (*0-7135-1143-5*); Vol. 8. 1980. 32.50 (Illus.). 1980. 256.25 (*0-7135-1110-9*) Lubrecht & Cramer.

Ross, Cynthia. D'Aulaires Book of Greek Myths: A Literature Unit. (Literature Units Ser.). (Illus.). 48p. 1993. student ed. 7.95 (*1-55734-423-X*) Tchr Create Mat.

— Loving Endlessly Bk. XI: Living Learning Loving. (Illus.). 16p. 1999. pap. 4.00 (*0-945768-16-8*) A-Town Pub Co.

— Medieval Times: A Thematic Unit. (Thematic Units Ser.). (Illus.). 80p. (J). (gr. 5-8). 1992. student ed. 9.95 (*1-55734-291-1*) Tchr Create Mat.

Ross, Cynthia M. & Strangl, Karen M. The Music Teacher's Book of Lists. LC 94-2407. 256p. (C). 1994. spiral bd. 29.95 (*0-13-093832-7*, Parker Publishing Co) P-H.

Ross, D. International Treasury Management. 3rd ed. 287p. 1997. 170.00 (*1-85564-536-X*, Pub. by Euromoney) Am Educ Systs.

— Mechanics of Underwater Noise. LC 76-18731. 1976. 179.00 (*0-08-021182-8*, Pub. by Pergamon Repr) Franklin.

— The U. K. Taxation of Modern Financial Instruments & Transactions. 64p. 1989. text 80.00 (*0-304-31831-0*) Continuum.

Ross, D. A., jt. auth. see Forshaw, J. R.

Ross, D. B. & Guder, W. G., eds. Biochemical Aspects of Renal Function: Proceedings of a Symposium Held in Honour of Professor Sir Hans Krebs FRS, at Merton College, Oxford, 16-19 September 1979. (Illus.). 340p. 1980. pap. 67.00 (*0-08-025517-5*, Pergamon Pr) Elsevier.

Ross, D. James. Musick Fyne. 176p. 1996. 68.00 (*1-873644-17-5*, Pub. by Mercat Pr Bks) St Mut.

Ross, D. N., et al. Principles of Cardiac Diagnosis & Treatment: A Surgeon's Guide. 2nd ed. (Illus.). ix, 269p. 1991. 129.00 (*0-387-17494-X*) Spr-Verlag.

Ross, D. W. Introduction to Molecular Medicine. (Illus.). 184p. 1994. pap. 29.50 (*0-387-97724-4*) Spr-Verlag.

— Introduction to Oncogenes & Molecular Cancer Medicine. LC 98-4703. 200p. 1998. pap. 29.95 (*0-387-98392-9*) Spr-Verlag.

— On Drawing & Painting. LC 78-137285. (Illus.). reprint ed. 44.50 (*0-404-05406-4*) AMS Pr.

Ross, Dalton. Top Teams Ever. Sieck, Margaret, ed. 96p. (J). (gr. 1-9). 1999. pap. 3.99 (*1-886749-63-9*) SI For Kids.

***Ross, Dalton.** The Top Teams Ever. rev. ed. Sieck, Margaret, ed. 96p. (J). (gr. 3-8). 2000. pap. 3.99 (*1-930623-06-2*) SI For Kids.

Ross, Dalton, jt. auth. see Rolte, John.

Ross, Dan. Fogbound. large type ed. 1995. 27.99 (*0-7089-3317-3*) Ulverscroft.

***Ross, Dan.** Pro Wrestling's Greatest Wars. (Pro Wrestling Legends Ser.). 2000. 17.95 (*0-7910-5837-9*) Chelsea Hse.

R

R

— Pro Wrestling's Greatest Wars. LC 00-20732. (Pro Wrestling Legends Ser.). (Illus.). 2000. pap. 8.95 (0-7910-5838-7) Chelsea Hse.

— Rock. (Pro Wrestling Legends Ser.). 2000. 17.95 (0-7910-5831-X) Chelsea Hse.

— The Rock: The Story of the Wrestler They Call "The Rock" LC 00-21865. (Pro Wrestling Legends Ser.). (Illus.). 2000. pap. 8.95 (0-7910-5832-8) Chelsea Hse.

Ross, Dan. Steve Austin: Story of the Wrestler They Call "Stone Cold" LC 99-38099. (Illus.). 64p. 1999. 17.95 (0-7910-5403-9) Chelsea Hse.

— Steve Austin: The Story of the Wrestler They Call "Stone Cold" LC 99-38099. (Wrestling Stars Ser.). (Illus.). 64p. (YA). (gr. 3 up). 1999. pap. 9.95 (0-7910-5549-3) Chelsea Hse.

— Story of the Wrestler They Call the Undertaker. LC 99-38098. (Illus.). 64p. 1999. 17.95 (0-7910-5407-1) Chelsea Hse.

— Story of the Wrestler They Call the Undertaker. LC 99-38098. (Wrestling Stars Ser.). (Illus.). 64p. (YA). (gr. 3 up). 1999. pap. 8.95 (0-7910-5553-1) Chelsea Hse.

***Ross, Dana.** Demon of the Darkness. LC 00-23529. 2000. write for info. (0-7862-2507-6) Five Star.

Ross, Dana Fuller. California Glory. large type ed. (General Ser.). 476p. 1992. lib. bdg. 21.95 (0-8161-5310-8, G K Hall Lrg Type) Mac Lib Ref.

— Carolina Courage! large type ed. 400p. 1991. 21.95 (0-8161-5309-4, G K Hall Lrg Type) Mac Lib Ref.

— Hawaii Heritage. large type ed. (General Ser.). 464p. 1992. lib. bdg. 21.95 (0-8161-5421-X, G K Hall Lrg Type) Mac Lib Ref.

— Homecoming. large type ed. 1995. 23.95 (0-7838-1173-X, G K Hall Lrg Type) Mac Lib Ref.

— Honor! Book 1. (Wagons West Ser.: Bk. 1). 400p. (Orig.). 1998. mass mkt. 5.99 (0-553-57764-6) Bantam.

— Justice!, No. 3. 464p. 1999. mass mkt. 6.50 (0-553-57766-2) Bantam.

— New Mexico! large type ed. (General Ser.). 397p. 1990. lib. bdg. 21.95 (0-8161-4771-X, G K Hall Lrg Type) Mac Lib Ref.

— Oklahoma! (Wagons West Ser.: No. 23). 1989. pap. 4.50 (0-685-25336-8) Bantam.

— Oklahoma Pride. large type ed. (General Ser.). 1991. lib. bdg. 20.95 (0-8161-5101-6, G K Hall Lrg Type) Mac Lib Ref.

— Oregon Legacy. large type ed. 482p. 1991. lib. bdg. 21.95 (0-8161-4989-5, G K Hall Lrg Type) Mac Lib Ref.

— Outpost! large type ed. LC 93-8890. (Wagons West Ser.: Vol. 3). 1993. lib. bdg. 23.95 (0-8161-5516-X, G K Hall Lrg Type) Mac Lib Ref.

— Outpost! Wagons West. (Frontier Trilogy Ser.: No. 3). 464p. 1993. mass mkt. 6.50 (0-553-29400-8) Bantam.

— Pacific Destiny. large type ed. LC 94-25460. 507p. 1994. lib. bdg. 23.95 (0-8161-7466-0, G K Hall Lrg Type) Mac Lib Ref.

— Vengeance! Bk. 2: Wagons West Empire Trilogy. (Wagons West Ser.). 384p. 1999. mass mkt. 6.50 (0-553-57765-4) Bantam.

— Wagons West No. 22: New Mexico. 1988. pap. 4.50 (0-318-37676-8) Bantam.

— Westward! large type ed. (General Ser.). 640p. 1992. pap. 16.95 (0-8161-5449-X, G K Hall Lrg Type) Mac Lib Ref.

— Westward!, No. 1. (Wagons West Ser.). 512p. 1992. mass mkt. 6.50 (0-553-29402-4) Bantam.

— Yankee. large type ed. 1993. 21.95 (1-56895-044-6) Wheeler Pub.

— Yankee Rogue. large type ed. LC 94-8217. 1994. 22.95 (1-56895-066-7) Wheeler Pub.

— Yukon Justice. large type ed. LC 92-15296. (General Ser.). 1992. 18.95 (0-8161-5488-0, G K Hall Lrg Type); lib. bdg. 21.95 (0-8161-5487-2, G K Hall Lrg Type) Mac Lib Ref.

Ross, Daniel. UFO's & the Complete Evidence from Space: The Truth about Venus, Mars, & the Moon. (Illus.). 242p. (Orig.). (C). 1987. pap. 9.95 (0-944255-00-0) Pintado Pub.

Ross, Daniel W., ed. The Critical Response to William Styron, 22. LC 95-23564. (Critical Responses in Arts & Letters Ser.: No. 22). 304p. 1995. lib. bdg. 59.95 (0-313-28000-2, Greenwood Pr) Greenwood.

Ross, Daphne. Seascapes of Prince Edward Island. (Island Pathways Ser.). (Illus.). 152p. 1992. spiral bd. 14.95 (0-614-21761-X, Pub. by Gynergy-Ragweed) U of Toronto Pr.

— Seascapes of Prince Edward Island. (Illus.). 92p. 1998. 14.95 (0-921556-26-8, Pub. by Gynergy-Ragweed) U of Toronto Pr.

Ross, Dave. A Book of Friends. LC 98-35266. (Illus.). 40p. (YA). (ps-3). 1999. 12.95 (0-06-028170-7) HarpC Child Bks.

***Ross, Dave.** A Book of Friends. LC 98-35266. (Illus.). 40p. (YA). (ps up). 1999. lib. bdg. 12.89 (0-06-028362-9) HarpC Child Bks.

Ross, Dave. A Book of Friends. LC 98-35266. 40p. (J). 2001. pap. 4.95 (0-06-443525-3) HarpC Child Bks.

— A Book of Hugs. (J). 1980. 6.95 (0-690-04011-3) HarpC Child Bks.

— A Book of Hugs. (J). 1983. 40.45 (0-690-04322-8) HarpC Child Bks.

— A Book of Hugs. LC 98-18659. (Illus.). 40p. (J). (ps-k). 1999. 12.95 (0-06-028147-2) HarpC Child Bks.

***Ross, Dave.** A Book of Hugs. LC 98-18659. (Illus.). 40p. (J). 2000. pap. 5.95 (0-06-443514-8, HarpTrophy) HarpC Child Bks.

Ross, Dave. A Book of Kisses. LC 98-49562. 40p. (J). 2000. pap. 4.95 (0-06-443524-5) HarpC Child Bks.

— A Book of Kisses. LC 98-49562. (Illus.). 40p. (J). (ps-3). 2000. 12.95 (0-06-028169-3) HarpC Child Bks.

— More Hugs! LC 83-46167. (Illus.). 32p. (J). (ps up). 1984. lib. bdg. 11.89 (0-690-04407-0) HarpC Child Bks.

Ross, David. Aristotle. 5th ed. 312p. 1964. pap. 17.95 (0-415-04306-9, NO.2421) Routledge.

— Aristotle. 6th ed. LC 94-43265. 336p. (C). 1995. pap. 22.99 (0-415-12068-3, C0115) Routledge.

— A Book of Kisses. LC 98-49562. 40p. (J). (ps-2). 2000. lib. bdg. 12.89 (0-06-028453-6) HarpC Child Bks.

— Palaces. LC 98-20535. (Great Architecture Ser.). (Illus.). 120p. 1998. 16.98 (1-56799-472-5, MetroBooks) M Friedman Pub Grp Inc.

***Ross, David.** The Pocket Book of Scottish Quotations. 256p. 1999. pap. (1-84158-011-2, Pub. by Birlinn Ltd) Dufour.

Ross, David. Power from the Waves. (Illus.). 224p. 1996. 40.00 (0-19-856511-9) OUP.

***Ross, David.** Quotidiana: The Continuity of the Everyday in 20th Century Art. (Illus.). 2000. pap. 50.00 (88-8158-261-9) Charta.

— Richard Hillary. (Illus.). 2000. 34.95 (1-902304-45-4) Grub St.

— Scottish Curses & Insults. (Orig.). 1999. pap. 7.95 (1-84158-012-0) Birlinn Ltd.

Ross, David. Serpent Shell. 1993. 11.15 (0-606-09842-9, Pub. by Turtleback) Demco.

***Ross, David.** The Xenophobe's Guide to the Scots. (Xenophobe's Guides Ser.). 64p. 1999. pap. 5.95 (1-902825-42-X) Oval Bks.

***Ross, David, ed.** Through Irish Eyes: A Visual Companion to Angela McCourt's Ireland. LC 98-60825. (Illus.). 64p. 1998. 9.98 (0-7651-0887-9) Smithmark.

Ross, David & Smith, Gavin D., eds. Scots-English, English-Scots Practical Dictionary. 256p. 1999. pap. 12.95 (0-7818-0779-4) Hippocrene Bks.

— Welsh English - English Welsh Practical Dictionary. 252p. 1999. pap. 12.95 (0-7818-0781-6) Hippocrene Bks.

Ross, David & Whitney, Bret. Voices of Costa Rican Birds - Caribbean Slope. 1996. pap. 24.95 incl. audio compact disk (0-938027-22-0) Crows Nest Bird.

Ross, David, jt. auth. see Keller, Joe.

Ross, David, jt. auth. see May, Robin.

Ross, David, ed. see Joachim, Harold H.

Ross, David, tr. & intro. see Aristotle.

Ross, David A. Bill Viola. (Illus.). 240p. 1998. 60.00 (2-08-013645-3, Pub. by Flammarion) Abbeville Pr.

***Ross, David A.** The Fisherman's Ocean. LC 00-35785. (Illus.). 288p. 2000. pap. 19.95 (0-8117-2771-8) Stackpole.

— Introduction to Oceanography 3rd ed. (Prentice Hall College Titles Ser.). 1999. 20.00 (0-13-491373-6) P-H.

Ross, David A. The Trouble with Paradise. LC 97-94723. 159p. (Orig.). 1998. pap. 12.00 (0-9661861-0-9) Escape Media.

— Xenos: A Romantic Novel of Travel & Self-Discovery in the Grecian Isles. LC 98-93338. 232p. 1998. pap. 12.95 (0-9661861-1-7) Escape Media.

Ross, David A. & Hyde, Lewis. Bill Viola. LC 97-26976. 1997. write for info. (0-87427-114-2) Whitney Mus.

Ross, David A. & Lewallen, Constance. Terry Fox: Articulations. Longhauser, Elsa, ed. LC 91-62604. (Illus.). 48p. 1992. pap. 25.00 (1-58442-016-2) Galleries at Moore.

Ross, David A., et al. Ilya Kabakov. LC 98-231823. (Contemporary Artists Ser.). (Illus.). 160p. 1998. pap. 29.95 (0-7148-3797-0) Phaidon Pr.

Ross, David A., jt. auth. see Harten, Jurgen.

Ross, David F., et al, eds. Adult Eyewitness Testimony: Current Trends & Developments. LC 93-8004. (Illus.). 448p. (C). 1994. text 64.95 (0-521-43255-3) Cambridge U Pr.

Ross, David H., jt. ed. see Loh, Horace H.

Ross, David O. Virgil's Elements: Physics & Poetry in the Georgics. LC 86-22598. 268p. 1987. reprint ed. pap. 83.10 (0-7837-9435-5, 206017700004) Bks Demand.

Ross, David P. & Usher, Peter J. From the Roots Up: Economic Development As If Community Mattered. LC 85-27972. (Illus.). 174p. (Orig.). 1986. pap. 13.50 (0-942850-04-1) Intermediate Tech.

***Ross, David R.** On the Trail of Robert the Bruce. (On the Trail of... Ser.). (Illus.). 192p. 1999. pap. 14.95 (0-946487-52-9, Pub. by Luath Pr Ltd) Midpt Trade.

— On the Trail of William Wallace. (On the Trail of... Ser.). (Illus.). 192p. 1999. pap. 14.95 (0-946487-47-2, Pub. by Luath Pr Ltd) Midpt Trade.

Ross, David R., et al, eds. Nation in Crisis, 1828-1865. LC 78-101951. (Structure of American History Ser.: Vol. 3). (C). 1970. pap. text 6.95 (0-88295-757-0) Harlan Davidson.

— Progress, War & Reaction, 1900-1933. LC 78-101951. (Structure of American History Ser.: Vol. 5). (C). 1970. pap. text 6.95 (0-88295-759-7) Harlan Davidson.

Ross, David R., et al. The Emergence of Modern America, 1865-1900. LC 78-101951. (Structure of American History Ser.). 256p. (C). 1970. pap. text 6.95 (0-88295-758-9) Harlan Davidson.

— Forging the Nation, 1763-1828, Vol. 2. LC 78-101951. (Structure of American History Ser.). 256p. (C). 1970. pap. text 6.95 (0-88295-756-2) Harlan Davidson.

Ross, David W. Beyond the Stars. 528p. 1991. mass mkt. 5.95 (0-380-71471-X, Avon Bks) Morrow Avon.

— Eye of the Hawk. 512p. 1994. mass mkt. 5.99 (0-380-72232-1, Avon Bks) Morrow Avon.

— Savage Plains. 480p. (Orig.). 1996. mass mkt. 5.99 (0-380-78324-X, Avon Bks) Morrow Avon.

— War Cries. 384p. (Orig.). 1995. mass mkt. 5.99 (0-380-78024-0, Avon Bks) Morrow Avon.

Ross, David W., ed. Physica. (Oxford Classical Texts Ser). 214p. 1951. text 27.00 (0-19-814514-4) OUP.

Ross, Debbie & Caputo, Salvatore. The Insiders' Guide to Phoenix. (Insiders' Guide Travel Ser.). (Illus.). 495p. 1999. pap. 16.95 (1-57380-072-4, The Insiders Guide) Falcon Pub Inc.

Ross, Deborah. The Excellence of Falsehood: Romance, Realism, & Women's Contribution to the Novel. LC 91-22068. 264p. 1991. text 32.00 (0-8131-1764-X) U Pr of Ky.

Ross, Deborah & Spencer, Sara H. Aphasia Rehabilitation: An Auditory & Verbal Task Hierarchy. (Illus.). 272p. 1980. 46.95 (0-398-04031-1) C C Thomas.

— Reading & Writing Task Hierarchy. (Illus.). 350p. (C). 1981. pap., spiral bd. 52.95 (0-398-04642-5) C C Thomas.

Ross, Debra. Federal Equal Opportunity Deskbook, 1996. 1996. pap. 59.00 (0-934753-70-9) LRP Pubns.

— Master Math: Algebra. LC 96-22993. 192p. (Orig.). 1996. pap. 10.99 (1-56414-194-2) Career Pr Inc.

— Master Math: Basic Mathg & Pre-Algebra. LC 96-22992. 192p. 1996. pap. 10.99 (1-56414-214-0) Career Pr Inc.

— Master Math: Calculus, Including Everything from the Derivative & the Integral to Partial Derivatives, Vector Calculus & Differential Equations. LC 98-25769. 352p. 1998. pap. 12.99 (1-56414-337-6) Career Pr Inc.

— Master Math: Pre-Calculus & Geometry. LC 96-22994. 192p. (Orig.). 1996. pap. 10.99 (1-56414-218-3) Career Pr Inc.

Ross, Delmer G. Gold Road to La Paz: An Interpretive Guide to the Bradshaw Trail. (Illus.). 304p. 1992. 22.50 (0-914224-24-7) Tales Mojave Rd.

Ross, Dennis. The Conservation of Strangeness. LC 80-22044. 1980. pap. 9.95 (0-914974-18-1) Holmgangers.

— Incremental or Comprehensive SALT: Is Some SALT Better Than No SALT. (CISA Working Papers: No. 16). 27p. (Orig.). 1979. pap. 15.00 (0-86682-015-9) Ctr Intl Relations.

— Rethinking Soviet Strategic Policy: Inputs & Implications. (CISA Working Papers: No. 5). 46p. (Orig.). 1977. pap. 15.00 (0-86682-004-3) Ctr Intl Relations.

Ross, Dennis W. Introduction to Molecular Medicine. 2nd ed. LC 95-36653. 178p. 1996. 29.00 (0-387-94468-0) Spr-Verlag.

Ross, Derek, et al. International Treasury Management. 1990. 54.95 (0-317-04754-X) NY Inst Finance.

Ross, Dev. The Birthday Ban in Munchkin Land. (We Both Read Ser.). (Illus.). 44p. (J). (gr. 1-2). 1999. 7.99 (1-891327-19-4); pap. 3.99 (1-891327-20-8) Treas Bay Inc.

Ross-Dolen, Mary M. Medical School Companion. LC 96-202427. (Princeton Review Ser.). 1996. pap. 15.00 (0-679-76462-3) Villard Books.

Ross, Don. Flying Models - Rubber CO2 - Electric Micro Radio Control Vol. 2: Tips & Techniques for Beginners to Experts. Markowski, Mike, ed. LC 98-66740. (Illus.). 240p. 1998. pap. 19.95 (0-938716-54-9) Markowski Intl.

— Metaphor, Meaning, & Cognition. LC 93-6956. (American University Studies: Vol. 149). 210p. 1994. 38.95 (0-8204-2151-0) P Lang Pubng.

— Rubber Powered Model Airplanes: Comprehensive Building & Flying Basics Plus Advanced Design-Your-Own Instructions. LC 88-13066. (Illus.). 168p. (Orig.). 1988. pap. 14.95 (0-938716-19-0) Markowski Intl.

***Ross, Don, et al, eds.** Dennett's Philosophy: A Comprehensive Assessment. (Illus.). 448p. (C). 2000. 65.00 (0-262-18200-9, Bradford Bks); pap. 27.95 (0-262-68117-X, Bradford Bks) MIT Pr.

Ross, Donald. Mechanics of Underwater Noise. LC 87-61466. 315p. 1987. reprint ed. 55.95 (0-932146-16-3) Peninsula CA.

— A Public Citizen's Action Manual. 238p. pap. 1.95 (0-686-36537-2) Ctr Responsive Law.

Ross, Donald, jt. auth. see Adams, Stephen.

Ross, Donald, jt. auth. see Bila, Dennis.

Ross, Donald J. Golf Has Never Failed Me: The Lost Commentaries of Legendary Golf Course Architect, Donald J. Ross. (Illus.). 256p. 1996. boxed set 29.95 (1-886947-10-4) Sleepng Bear.

Ross, Donald K. Newspaper Correspondent's Manual. LC PN4781.R67. 40p. reprint ed. pap. 30.00 (0-608-12670-5, 202511000042) Bks Demand.

Ross, Donald K. & Ross, Helen L. 0755: Pearl Harbor Heroes: Heroism of 250 Men & Women 7 December 1941. (Illus.). 158p. 1988. pap. 11.95 (0-930942-15-9) Rokalu Pr.

Ross, Donald K., jt. auth. see Ross, Helen L.

Ross, Donald M., jt. auth. see Ormiston, Hugh.

Ross, Doran H., ed. Visions of Africa: The Jerome L. Joss Collection of African Art at UCLA. (Exhibition Ser.). (Illus.). 164p. 1994. 40.00 (0-930741-33-1) UCLA Fowler Mus.

Ross, Doran H., et al. Wrapped in Pride: Ghanaian Kente & African American Identity. LC 98-41970. (UCLA Fowler Museum of Cultural History Textile Ser.: Vol. 2). (Illus.). 348p. 1998. 70.00 (0-930741-68-4); pap. 39.00 (0-930741-69-2) UCLA Fowler Mus.

Ross, Doran H., jt. auth. see Cameron, Elisabeth L.

Ross, Doran H., jt. auth. see Cameron, Elisabeth L.

Ross, Doran H., ed. see Shoshani, Jesheskel, et al.

Ross, Doran K., ed. Visions of Africa: The Jerome L. Joss Collection of African Art at UCLA. (Exhibition Ser.). (Illus.). 164p. 1994. pap. 24.00 (0-930741-34-X) UCLA Fowler Mus.

Ross, Dorene D., et al. Reflective Teaching for Student Empowerment: Elementary Curriculum & Methods. (Illus.). 376p. (Orig.). (C). 1992. pap. text 69.00 (0-02-403960-8, Macmillan Coll) P-H.

Ross, Dorien. Returning to A. (Illus.). 180p. (Orig.). 1995. pap. 9.95 (0-87286-307-7) City Lights.

— Returning to A. (Illus.). 180p. (Orig.). 1995. 18.95 (0-87286-306-9) City Lights.

Ross, Dorothea M. Childhood Bullying & Teasing: What School Personnel, Other Professionals, & Parents Can Do. 260p. (Orig.). 1996. pap. text 29.95 (1-55620-157-5, 72628) Am Coun Assn.

Ross, Dorothy. G. Stanley Hall: The Psychologist As Prophet. LC 75-165180. 502p. 1998. lib. bdg. 30.00 (0-226-72821-8) U Ch Pr.

— The Origins of American Social Science. (Ideas in Context Ser.: No. 19). 532p. (C). 1990. text 54.95 (0-521-35092-1) Cambridge U Pr.

— The Origins of American Social Science. (Ideas in Context Ser.: No. 19). 533p. (C). 1992. pap. text 20.95 (0-521-42836-X) Cambridge U Pr.

Ross, Dorothy, ed. Modernist Impulses in the Human Sciences, 1870-1930. LC 93-38354. (C). 1994. 60.00 (0-8018-4744-3); pap. 18.95 (0-8018-4745-1) Johns Hopkins.

Ross, Dorothy J. Jenkins Farms: Life on a Family Fruit Farm in Early California. LC 96-85883. (Illus.). vii, 76p. (Orig.). 1996. pap. 12.95 (0-9653769-0-7) Blue Oak Bks.

Ross, Dorothy M. Fundraising for Youth: 349 Wonderful Ways of Raising Funds for Youth Organizations. Zapel, Arthur L., ed. LC 84-61477. (Illus.). 256p. (Orig.). 1985. pap. 9.95 (0-916260-28-3, B184) Meriwether Pub.

Ross, Doug. A Tao of Dialogue: A Manual of Dialogic Communication. 100p. 1998. pap. 10.95 (1-891850-00-8) Med Bear.

Ross, Douglas, jt. auth. see Beneke, Jeff.

Ross, Douglas A. In the Interests of Peace: Canada & Vietnam 1954-1973. 496p. 1984. text 35.00 (0-8020-5632-6) U of Toronto Pr.

— Optoelectronic Devices & Optical Imaging Techniques. (Electrical & Electronic Engineering Ser.). (Illus.). 137p. 1979. pap. text 32.00 (0-333-25335-3) Scholium Intl.

Ross, Drew. Looking into the Eyes of a Killer: A Psychiatrist's Journey Through the Murderer's World. LC 98-13245. (Illus.). 250p. (C). 1998. 26.95 (0-306-45791-1, Plenum Trade) Perseus Pubng.

Ross, Duncan M. History of Banking, 1844-1959, 10 vols., No. II. LC 98-9191. 4000p. 1998. 1150.00 (1-85196-443-6, Pub. by Pickering & Chatto) Ashgate Pub Co.

Ross, Duncan M., jt. ed. see Godley, Andrew.

Ross, E. The Social Revolution in Mexico. 1976. lib. bdg. 59.95 (0-8490-2618-0) Gordon Pr.

Ross, E. Betsy. Life after Suicide: A Ray of Hope for Those Left Behind. LC 97-33703. (Illus.). 322p. (C). 1997. 27.95 (0-306-45630-3, Plen Insight) Perseus Pubng.

Ross, E. C., tr. see Sirhan, Sirhan.

Ross, E. Denison, tr. see Lammens, Henri.

Ross, E. G. Engels Extension. 224p. (Orig.). 1997. pap. 14.95 (0-9633818-6-5) Premiere Edits.

***Ross, E. G.** Project BTB. 2000. pap. 19.95 (1-891519-24-7) Premiere Edits.

Ross, E. M., et al, eds. Clinical Paediatrics. (Illus.). 420p. 1997. write for info. (0-7020-1726-4, Pub. by W B Saunders) Saunders.

Ross, E. M. & Wirtz, K. W., eds. Biological Signal Transduction. (NATO ASI Series H: Cell Biology: Vol. 52). xi, 540p. 1991. 217.95 (0-387-51773-1) Spr-Verlag.

Ross, E. R. An Investigation of Wear on Various Automobile Gear Steels. (Technical Papers: Vol. P8). (Illus.). 22p. 1921. pap. text 30.00 (1-55589-315-5) AGMA.

***Ross, E. Wayne, ed.** The Social Studies Curriculum: Purposes, Problems, & Possibilites. rev. ed. (C). 2001. pap. text. write for info. (0-7914-4962-9) State U NY Pr.

— The Social Studies Curriculum: Purposes, Problems, & Possibilites. rev. ed. (C). 2001. text. write for info. (0-7914-4961-0) State U NY Pr.

Ross, E. Wayne, ed. The Social Studies Curriculum: Purposes, Problems, & Possibilities. LC 96-36305. (SUNY Series in Theory, Research, & Practice). 274p. (C). 1997. pap. text 19.95 (0-7914-3444-3) State U NY Pr.

Ross, E. Wayne, et al, eds. Teacher Personal Theorizing: Connecting Curriculum, Practice, Theory, & Research. LC 91-27209. (SUNY Series, Teacher Preparation & Development). 324p. (C). 1992. pap. text 21.95 (0-7914-1126-5) State U NY Pr.

Ross, E. Wayne, jt. auth. see Hursh, David W.

Ross, Earle. Truths, Half-Truths, & Outright Lies: Tales of the Deep South. Ross, Iris, ed. (Illus.). 230p. (Orig.). 1996. pap. 12.00 (1-57502-144-7) Morris Pubng.

Ross, Earle D. Democracy's College: The Land-Grant Movement in the Formative Stage. LC 74-89226. (American Education: Its Men, Institutions, Ideas. Series 1). 1973. reprint ed. 15.95 (0-405-01463-5) Ayer.

— Liberal Republican Movement. LC 71-137286. reprint ed. 20.00 (0-404-05407-2) AMS Pr.

Ross, Edward. Looking for Friends in All the Right Places. Zahgkuni, Jennifer, ed. LC 98-96489. 264p. (Orig.). 1999. pap. 14.95 (0-9666695-3-3) Baxter Pubg.

Ross, Edward A. Roads to Social Peace. LC 79-117830. (Essay Index Reprint Ser.). 1977. 17.95 (0-8369-1679-4) Ayer.

— Seventy Years of It: An Autobiography. Metzger, Walter P., ed. LC 76-55183. (Academic Profession Ser.). (Illus.). 1977. reprint ed. lib. bdg. 29.95 (0-405-10010-8) Ayer.

— Social Psychology. LC 73-14178. (Perspectives in Social Inquiry Ser.). 394p. 1974. reprint ed. 25.95 (0-405-05521-8) Ayer.

— Social Trend. LC 72-117831. (Essay Index Reprint Ser.). 1977. 20.95 (0-8369-1680-8) Ayer.

— Standing Room Only? Grob, Gerald N., ed. LC 76-46101. (Anti-Movements in America Ser.). 1977. reprint ed. lib. bdg. 31.95 (0-405-09972-X) Ayer.

Ross, Edward D., jt. auth. see Skrine, Francis H.

Ross, Edward Denison, jt. auth. see Skrine, Francis Henry.

An Asterisk (*) at the beginning of an entry indicates that the title is appearing for the first time.

Ross, Edward S. Ants. LC 96-30078. 32p. (J). 1997. lib. bdg. 22.79 (*1-56766-398-2*) Childs World.

— Yellowjackets. LC 92-42934. (Nature Books Ser.). (Illus.). 32p. (J). (gr. 2-6). 1994. lib. bdg. 22.79 (*1-56766-017-7*) Childs World.

Ross, Eileen. The Halloween Showdown. LC 98-12938. (Illus.). 32p. (J). (ps-3). 1998. lib. bdg. 15.95 (*0-8234-1395-0*) Holiday.

— Josh. 93p. (Orig.). (J). (gr. 3-7). 1994. pap. 9.99 (*0-88092-104-8*) Royal Fireworks.

Ross, Eileen, et al. Savage Shadows: Eileen Ross's True Story of Blindness, Rape - & Courage. LC 91-66895. 1992. 21.95 (*0-88282-105-9*) New Horizon NJ.

Ross, Eleanor. School Exercises for Flatwork & Jumping. (Illus.). 95p. 1992. pap. 20.95 (*1-872082-31-9*) Half Halt Pr.

Ross, Eleanora B. After Suicide: A Unique Grief Process. 24p. 1987. pap. 5.95 (*0-940179-02-4*) Lynn Pubns.

Ross, Elinor P. Pathways to Thinking: Strategies for Developing Independent Learners K-8. (Illus.). 256p. (C). 1997. pap. text, teacher ed. 36.95 (*0-926842-68-4*) CG Pubs Inc.

— Pathways to Thinking: Strategies for Developing Independent Learners K-8. expanded ed. LC 97-69047. (Illus.). 316p. (C). 1998. text, teacher ed. 52.95 (*0-926842-69-2*) CG Pubs Inc.

Ross, Elinor P., jt. auth. see Roe, Betty D.

***Ross, Elizabeth.** Cornmeal Country: An American Tradition. 1999. 19.95 (*0-913383-68-6*) McClanahan Pub.

Ross, Elizabeth. Kentucky Keepsakes: Classic Southern Recipes. LC 95-80007. (Illus.). 352p. 1995. 19.95 (*0-913383-38-4*) McClanahan Pub.

Ross, Elizabeth & Sachs, Judith. Healing the Female Heart: A Holistic Approach to Prevention & Recovery from Heart Disease. Rubenstein, Julie, ed. 288p. (Orig.). 1996. per. 12.00 (*0-671-89470-6*, PB Trade Paper) PB.

Ross, Elizabeth, jt. auth. see Patmore, Ruth.

Ross, Ellen M. The Grief of God: Images of the Suffering Jesus in Late Medieval England. LC 96-5502. (Illus.). 240p. 1997. text 49.95 (*0-19-510451-X*) OUP.

— Love & Toil: Motherhood in Outcast London, 1870-1918. LC 92-40849. (Illus.). 336p. 1993. pap. text 22.00 (*0-19-508321-0*) OUP.

Ross, Ellena & Champlin, Allen R., Sr. Ghost Riders in the Sky. Rietveld, Jeffrey & Hartstrom, Noelle, eds. 107p. (Orig.). (YA). (gr. 12). 1993. pap. 7.00 (*0-9628802-1-3*) DeChamp CA.

Ross, Elmer L. Factors in Residence Patterns Among Latin Americans in New Orleans, Louisiana. Cortes, Carlos E., ed. LC 79-6223. (Hispanics in the United States Ser.). (Illus.). 1981. lib. bdg. 29.95 (*0-405-13170-4*) Ayer.

Ross, Eric. Full of Hope & Promise: The Canadas in 1841. (Illus.). 192p. 1991. 55.00 (*0-7735-0855-4*, Pub. by McG-Queens Univ Pr) CUP Services.

Ross, Eric B. Malthus Factor. LC 98-29913. 1998. pap. 25.00 (*1-85649-564-7*) Zed Books.

— Malthus Factor. LC 98-29913. 1998. text 65.00 (*1-85649-563-9*) Zed Books.

Ross, Eric B., jt. auth. see Harris, Marvin.

Ross, Estelle. Martin Luther. LC 83-45673. (Illus.). reprint ed. 37.50 (*0-404-19862-7*) AMS Pr.

Ross, Euan, ed. Paediatric Perspectives on Epilepsy: A Symposium Held at the Grand Hotel, Eastbourne, December 1984, Vol. 198. LC 85-12009. 176p. 1985. 340.00 (*0-471-90817-7*) Wiley.

Ross, Eulalie S. The Spirited Life: Bertha Mahony Miller & Children's Books. LC 73-84132. (Illus.). 274p. 1973. 12.95 (*0-87675-057-9*) Horn Bk.

Ross, Eunice L., jt. auth. see Reed, Thomas J.

Ross, F. Russel & King, Virginia. Multicultural Dance. (Illus.). 174p. (Orig.). 1985. pap. 17.95 (*0-9615280-0-1*); pap. text 14.95 (*0-317-31639-7*) Russel & King.

Ross, Felice, tr. see Durrenmatt, Friedrich & Selz, Peter H.

Ross, Fiona G. The Printed Bengali Character. 288p. (C). 1999. 55.00 (*0-7007-1135-X*, Pub. by Curzon Pr Ltd) UH Pr.

Ross, Fitzgerald & Harwell, Richard B. Cities & Camps of the Confederate States. LC 97-122510. xxii, 262p. 1997. 15.95 (*0-252-06642-1*) U of Ill Pr.

Ross, Fitzroy, jt. ed. see Macgibbon, Lian.

Ross-Flanigan, Nancy. Peyote. LC 96-40105. (Drug Library Ser.). (Illus.). 112p. (YA). (gr. 6 up). 1997. lib. bdg. 20.95 (*0-89490-851-0*) Enslow Pubs.

Ross, Floyd H. Shinto, the Way of Japan. LC 83-12970. (Illus.). 187p. 1983. reprint ed. lib. bdg. 59.95 (*0-313-24240-2*, RSHI, Greenwood Pr) Greenwood.

***Ross, Fran.** Oreo. (Northeastern Library of Black Literature). 224p. 2000. pap. 15.95 (*1-55553-464-3*) NE U Pr.

Ross, Frances. Some Special Times: Selected Poems. (Illus.). 1976. pap. 3.95 (*0-915242-07-9*) Pygmalion Pr.

Ross, Frances A. The Land & People of Canada. rev. ed. LC 64-21547. (Portraits of the Nations Ser.). (Illus.). (J). (gr. 5-9). 1964. lib. bdg. 12.89 (*0-397-31567-8*) HarpC Child Bks.

Ross, Frank, Jr. Oracles, Bones, Stars & the Wheelbarrows: Ancient Chinese Science & Technology. 192p. (YA). (gr. 7-12). 1989. pap. 6.95 (*0-395-54967-1*) HM.

Ross, Franz & Kluepfel, Brian, eds. The Holography MarketPlace. 4th ed. 192p. 1995. pap. 19.95 (*0-89496-059-8*) Ross Bks.

Ross, Franz & Rhody, Alan, eds. Holography Marketplace. 6th ed. 188p. 1997. pap. 19.95 (*0-89496-018-0*) Ross Bks.

Ross, Franz, jt. auth. see Rhody, Alan.

Ross, Franz, jt. ed. see Kluepfel, Brian.

Ross, Franz, jt. ed. see Rhody, Alan.

Ross, Franz, jt. ed. see Yerkes, Elizabeth.

Ross, Fred. Conquering Goliath: Cesar Chavez at the Beginning. 146p. 1992. reprint ed. pap. 15.95 (*0-9625298-0-X*) Wayne St U Pr.

Ross, Fred F. OCR with a Smile! The Most Comprehensive Reference to Operating Any OCR System. French, Judy, ed. LC 98-96352. (Illus.). 205p. 1998. pap. 28.50 (*0-9665904-0-6*, SMILE01) Hse Scan.

Ross, Frederick. Chemistry & Cell Biology for Allied Health Science. 5th ed. 300p. (C). write for info. (*0-7872-1827-8*) Kendall-Hunt.

— Chemistry & Cell Biology for Allied Health Science: An Introduction: Laboratory Manual: An Introduction. 5th ed. 170p. (C). write for info. (*0-7872-4997-1*) Kendall-Hunt.

— Instructor's Manual To Accompany: Chemistry & Cell Biology for Allied Health Science. 5th ed. 82p. (C). 1999. pap. text. write for info. (*0-7872-6314-1*) Kendall-Hunt.

Ross, Frederick, et al. A Glossary of Words Used in Holderness in the East Riding of Yorkshire. (English Dialect Society Publications: No. 16). 1969. reprint ed. pap. 25.00 (*0-8115-0448-4*) Periodicals Srv.

Ross, Frederick A. Slavery Ordained by God. LC 74-83876. (Black Heritage Library Collection). 1977. 17.95 (*0-8369-8647-4*) Ayer.

— Slavery Ordained of God. LC 70-95445. (Studies in Black History & Culture: No. 54). 1970. reprint ed. lib. bdg. 75.00 (*0-8383-1202-0*) M S G Haskell Hse.

Ross, Frederick C., et al. Foundation of Allied Health Sciences. 4th ed. LC 95-79337. 240p. (C). 1996. text. write for info. (*0-697-25151-9*, WCB McGr Hill); text, student ed. 13.12 (*0-697-25153-5*, WCB McGr Hill) McGrw-H Hghr Educ.

— Foundation of the Allied Health Sciences. 4th ed. 144p. (C). 1996. text, lab manual ed. write for info. (*0-697-25154-3*, WCB McGr Hill) McGrw-H Hghr Educ.

Ross, Frederick C., jt. auth. see Enger, Eldon D.

Ross, G., jt. auth. see Fisher, Chris.

Ross, G. J. MLP Manual. 1980. 11.20 (*0-317-52206-X*, Pub. by Rothamsted Stats) Parkwest Pubns.

— Non-Linear Estimation. Brillinger, David R. et al, eds. (Series in Statistics). (Illus.). viii, 189p. 1990. 58.95 (*0-387-97278-1*) Spr-Verlag.

Ross, G. M., jt. ed. see Dorobek, S. L.

Ross, G. MacLeod. The Business of Tanks, 1933 to 1945. 340p. (C). 1989. 75.00 (*0-7855-4648-0*, Pub. by A H S Ltd) St Mut.

— The Business of Tanks, 1933-1945. 340p. (C). 1990. 35.00 (*0-7855-6536-1*, Pub. by A H S Ltd) St Mut.

Ross, G. R., jt. auth. see Descartes, Rene.

Ross, G. W., jt. auth. see Buckingham, W.

Ross, Gaby. Damien the Dragon. 92p. 1990. pap. 6.95 (*1-85371-078-4*, Pub. by Poolbeg Pr) Dufour.

Ross, Garry & Ross, Barry. Lifelines - Training & Conditioning Program. Wright, Barry, ed. (Illus.). 128p. (Orig.). 1989. pap. text 29.95 (*0-931571-04-9*) RP Pubng.

Ross, Gary. John Ward: Entering Nature. (Illus.). 45p. (C). 1993. pap. 10.00 (*0-88920-237-0*) W Laurier U Pr.

***Ross, Gary.** Nature's Guide to Healing. 176p. 2000. pap. 12.95 (*1-893910-06-7*, 904-006, Pub. by Freedom Pr Inc) BookWorld.

— Strengthening Your Immunity with Cat's Claw. 96p. 2000. pap. 4.95 (*1-893910-11-3*, 904-010, Pub. by Freedom Pr Inc) BookWorld.

***Ross, Gary & Steinman, David.** Cure Indigestion, Heartburn, Cholesterol, Triglyceride & Liver Problems with Artichoke Extract. unabridged ed. 48p. 1999. pap. 4.95 (*1-893910-01-6*, Pub. by Freedom Pr Inc) Nutri-Books Corp.

Ross, Gayle. Dat-so-la-lee, Artisan. (Illus.). (J). (gr. 1-4). 1995. pap. 6.35 (*0-8136-5740-7*); lib. bdg. 10.60 (*0-8136-5734-2*) Modern Curr.

Ross, Gayle, reader. How Rabbit Tricked Otter Audio: And Other Cherokee Animal Stories. abr. ed. LC 93-3637. (Stand Alone). 80p. (J). (ps-5). 1992. 11.95 incl. audio (*1-55994-542-7*) HarperAudio.

Ross, Gayle, jt. auth. see Bruchac, Joseph.

Ross, Gayle M. & Nickels, William G. Marketing: Relationships, Quality, Value - Instructor's Manual, Vol. I. 1997. teacher ed. write for info. (*1-57259-315-6*) Worth.

— Marketing: Relationships, Quality, Value - Instructor's Manual, Vol. II. 1997. teacher ed. write for info. (*1-57259-358-X*) Worth.

Ross, George & Martin, Andrew. The Brave New World of European Labor: European Trade Unions at the Millennium. LC 98-42943. 432p. 1999. pap. 25.00 (*1-57181-168-0*) Berghahn Bks.

Ross, George & Martin, Andrew, eds. The Brave New World of European Labor: European Trade Unions at the Millennium. LC 98-42943. 416p. 1999. 75.00 (*1-57181-167-2*) Berghahn Bks.

Ross, George, et al. Unions & Economic Crisis: Britain, West Germany & Sweden. 250p. 1984. text 44.95 (*0-04-331094-X*) Routledge.

Ross, George, jt. auth. see Howorth, Jolyon.

Ross, George, jt. ed. see Hollifield, James F.

Ross, George, jt. ed. see Howorth, Jolyon.

Ross, George E. Centralia: A Pictorial History. (Illinois Pictorial History Ser.). (Illus.). 1992. write for info. (*0-943963-31-1*) G Bradley.

Ross, George E. & Novack, Barbara. Vice-Presidents & Their Wives. 1975. pap. 4.95 (*0-89036-052-9*) Liahona Pub Trust.

***Ross, George L.** The Chicken Dutchman. LC 00-190565. 2000. 25.00 (*0-7388-1830-5*); pap. 18.00 (*0-7388-1831-3*) Xlibris Corp.

Ross, George M. & McWalter, Tony, eds. Kant & His Influence. 392p. 1990. 60.00 (*1-85506-072-8*) Bks Intl VA.

Ross, George R. Treating Adolescent Substance Abuse: Understanding the Fundamental Elements. LC 93-11215. 256p. (C). 1993. 28.00 (*0-205-15255-4*, Longwood Div) Allyn.

Ross, George R., tr. see Aristotle.

***Ross-Gilbertson-Lehman-Hanson, Gilbertson-Lehman-Hanson.** Fundamentals of Accounting. 7th ed. (Accounting Ser.). (C). 1998. text 45.95 (*0-538-71874-9*) Thomson Learn.

— Fundamentals of Accounting: Application Course, Chapters 1-17. 7th ed. (Accounting - First Year). (C). 1998. text 13.00 (*0-538-71877-3*) Thomson Learn.

Ross, Glen. On Coon Mountain: Scenes from a Childhood in the Oklahoma Hills. LC 91-29392. 192p. (C). 1992. 21.95 (*0-8061-2405-9*) U of Okla Pr.

Ross, Glenn, jt. ed. see Roth, Michael D.

Ross, Gloria J., jt. auth. see Giddan, Jane J.

Ross-Gordon, Jovita M. Adults with Learning Disabilities: An Overview for the Adult Educator. 1989. 7.00 (*0-317-03009-4*, IN337) Ctr Educ Trng Employ.

Ross-Gotta, Loretta. Adventually - Waiting for the Messiah. 16p. 1994. pap. text 7.00 (*1-888821-01-9*) Sanctuary.

— Be Not Fearful, Eustochium: You Are Endowed with a Splendid Heritage. 18p. 1995. pap. text 8.00 (*1-888821-07-8*) Sanctuary.

— Blessed Are the Poor: Dramatic Monologues & Readers' Dramas. 20p. 1995. pap. text 8.00 (*1-888821-06-X*) Sanctuary.

— The Feast. 23p. 1995. pap. text 8.00 (*1-888821-04-3*) Sanctuary.

— Is It I, Lord? 16p. 1995. pap. text 7.00 (*1-888821-02-7*) Sanctuary.

***Ross-Gotta, Loretta.** Letters from the Holy Ground: Seeing God Where You Are. 296p. 2000. pap. 16.95 (*1-58051-084-1*) Sheed & Ward WI.

Ross-Gotta, Loretta. Quem Quaeritis? Whom Are You Seeking? 29p. 1995. pap. text 8.00 (*1-888821-03-5*) Sanctuary.

— That They May Be One. 12p. 1995. pap. text 7.00 (*1-888821-05-1*) Sanctuary.

Ross, Graham. Botanica: The Illustrated A-Z of over 10,000 & How to Cultivate Them. (Illus.). 1020p. 1999. 59.95 (*1-56649-175-4*) Welcome Rain.

— The Great Powers & the Decline of the European States System, 1914-1945. 181p. (C). 1989. pap. 36.93 (*0-582-49188-6*, 73517) Longman.

Ross, Graham & Reid, William. Scotland's Forgotten Valour. (Illus.). 100p. pap. 19.95 (*1-899272-00-3*, Pub. by Maclean Pr) Dufour.

Ross, Gwendolyn. A Child's Treasure for a Lifetime. 24p. (J). (gr. 2-6). 1988. pap. 2.95 (*0-88144-134-1*) Christian Pub.

Ross, H. F., jt. ed. see Eggington, S.

Ross, H. John. Integrated Data Processing for Every Office. 1957. pap. 4.00 (*0-911056-03-3*) Office Res.

— Technique of Systems & Procedures. (Illus.). 1948. 19.50 (*0-911056-01-7*) Office Res.

Ross, H. K. Black American Women, No. 3. (Illus.). 160p. (YA). (gr. 6-12). 1999. 14.95 (*0-87460-365-X*) Lion Bks.

Ross, H. K., ed. Great Story Poems: Collection. rev. ed. 160p. (YA). (gr. 5-12). 2000. pap. 12.95 (*0-87460-385-4*) Lion Bks.

Ross, H. L. The Big Red Barn. 12p. (J). 1999. 11.99 (*0-679-87001-6*, Pub. by Random Bks Yng Read) Random.

Ross, H. Laurence. Settled Out of Court: The Social Process of Insurance Claims Adjustment. 2nd ed. LC 80-68523. 285p. 1980. pap. text 27.95 (*0-202-30296-2*); lib. bdg. 48.95 (*0-202-30286-5*) Aldine de Gruyter.

Ross, H. Laurence, ed. Law & Deviance. LC 81-8905. (Sage Annual Reviews of Studies in Deviance: No. 5). (Illus.). 278p. 1981. reprint ed. pap. 86.20 (*0-608-01165-7*, 205946500001) Bks Demand.

Ross, Harley, et al, eds. Liquid Scintillation Counting & Organic Scintillators. 752p. 1991. lib. bdg. 119.00 (*0-87371-246-3*, L246) Lewis Pubs.

Ross, Harold R. & Hill, Bill. Public Speaking: Process & Product. 2nd ed. 240p. 1995. per. 29.95 (*0-8403-8843-8*) Kendall-Hunt.

Ross, Harriet. Great Black Americans in Science. (Illus.). 160p. (J). (gr. 3-9). 2000. lib. bdg. 14.95 (*0-87460-392-7*) Lion Bks.

Ross, Harriet K., compiled by. Heroes & Heroines of Many Lands. 160p. (J). (gr. 3-9). 1999. reprint ed. lib. bdg. 13.95 (*0-87460-214-9*) Lion Bks.

Ross, Harriet K., ed. Great Horror Stories. (Illus.). 160p. (J). (gr. 3-9). 2000. pap. 10.95 (*0-87460-188-6*) Lion Bks.

— Greek Myths: Tales of the Gods, Heroes & Heroines. 160p. (YA). (gr. 6-12). 1999. lib. bdg. 14.95 (*0-87460-383-8*) Lion Bks.

Ross, Harris. Film As Literature, Literature As Film: An Introduction to & Bibliography of Film's Relationship to Literature, 10. LC 87-132. (Bibliographies & Indexes in World Literature Ser.: No. 10). 355p. 1987. lib. bdg. 49.95 (*0-313-24595-9*, RFL/) Greenwood.

Ross, Harvey M. Fighting Depression. 2nd rev. ed. 192p. 1992. pap. 9.95 (*0-87983-582-6*, 35826K, Keats Publng) NTC Contemp Pub Co.

Ross, Harvey M., jt. auth. see Saunders, Jeraldine.

Ross, Heather C. The Art of Arabian Costume: A Saudi Arabian Profile. (Illus.). 188p. 1990. 79.00 (*0-907513-00-X*, Pub. by Arabesque Comm) Empire Pub Srvs.

— The Art of Arabian Costume: A Saudi Arabian Profile. LC 93-26337. (Illus.). 188p. 1993. 79.00 (*0-88734-640-5*) Players Pr.

— The Art of Arabian Costume: A Saudi Arabian Profile. (Illus.). 188p. 1982. 50.00 (*0-7103-0031-X*) Routledge.

— The Art of Bedouin Jewellery: A Saudi Arabian Profile. (Illus.). 133p. 1990. 79.00 (*0-907513-01-8*, Pub. by Arabesque Comm) Empire Pub Srvs.

— The Art of Bedouin Jewelry: A Saudi Arabian Profile. LC 93-35828. 133p. 1994. 79.00 (*0-88734-641-3*) Empire Pub Srvs.

— Bedouin Jewelry in Saudi Arabia. (Illus.). 128p. 1990. 60.00 (*2-88373-002-4*, Pub. by Arabesque Comm) Empire Pub Srvs.

— Bedouin Jewelry in Saudi Arabia. LC 95-32178. 1995. 60.00 (*0-88734-655-3*) Empire Pub Srvs.

Ross, Heather Colyer. Arabian History with Precious Gold in Saudi Arabia. (Illus.). 180p. 1994. 80.00 (*2-88373-003-2*, Pub. by Arabesque Comm) Empire Pub Srvs.

Ross, Heidi A. China Learns English: Language Teaching & Social Change in the People's Republic. LC 93-7876. (Illus.). 320p. 1993. 40.00 (*0-300-05562-5*) Yale U Pr.

Ross, Heidi A., jt. auth. see Liu, Judith.

Ross, Helen, jt. ed. see Alexander, Franz.

Ross, Helen L. Touch of Smile. (Illus.). 1978. pap. 5.00 (*0-933992-01-7*) Coffee Break.

Ross, Helen L. & Ross, Donald K. Washington State Men of Valor: Medal of Honor Action, Biography & Citation of 81 Recipients of Our Nation's Highest Award. 2nd rev. ed. LC 94-68497. (Illus.). 259p. 1994. 22.00 (*0-9620552-1-2*) Rokalu Pr.

Ross, Helen L., jt. auth. see Ross, Donald K.

Ross, Henry D. Free Speech & Talk Radio. LC 95-94778. 144p. (Orig.). 1996. pap. 12.95 (*0-9620231-2-4*) Oleander Pub Hse.

Ross, Herbert, et al. Sleep Disorders: An Alternative Medicine Definitive Guide. 350p. 2000. pap. 14.95 (*1-887299-20-3*) AlternMed Bks.

Ross, Herbert H. Evolution & Classification of the Mountain Caddisflies. LC 56-5681. (Illus.). 221p. reprint ed. 68.60 (*0-8357-9675-2*, 201502500092) Bks Demand.

Ross, Herbert H., et al. A Textbook of Entomology. 704p. (C). 1991. reprint ed. lib. bdg. 77.50 (*0-89464-497-1*) Krieger.

Ross, Howard. Sometimes Something Special: Poetry with 'Heart & Soul' Poetry That Works. 1999. pap. 11.98 (*0-7880-1414-5*, Fairway Pr) CSS OH.

Ross, Howard P. Florida Corporations: Florida Practice Systems Library Selection, 2 vols. LC 79-91141. 1134p. 1992. suppl. ed. 135.00 (*0-317-03206-2*) West Group.

— Florida Corporations: Florida Practice Systems Library Selection, 2 vols., Set. LC 79-91141. 1134p. 1980. ring bd. 230.00 (*0-317-00573-1*) West Group.

Ross, Howard P., et al. Wood Ranch Thermal Anomaly, Iron County, Utah. (Miscellaneous Publication Ser.: Vol. 91-4). (Illus.). 28p. 1991. pap. 5.50 (*1-55791-313-7*, MP-91-4) Utah Geological Survey.

Ross, Hugh. Beyond the Cosmos: The Extra-Dimensionality of God: What Recent Discoveries in Astrophysics Reveal about the Glory & Love of God. LC 98-39375. 1999. 12.00 (*1-57683-112-4*) NavPress.

— Beyond the Cosmos: The Extra-Dimensionality of God/What Recent Discoveries in Astronomy & Physics Reveal about the Nature of God. 240p. 1996. 20.00 (*0-89109-964-6*, 99646) NavPress.

Ross, Hugh. El Creador y el Cosmos. (SPA.). 224p. Date not set. pap. text 11.99 (*0-311-05047-6*, Edit Mundo) Casa Bautista.

Ross, Hugh. Creation & Time: A Biblical & Scientific Perspective on the Creation-Date Controversy. LC 94-4308. 192p. 1994. pap. 12.00 (*0-89109-776-7*) NavPress.

— Creator & the Cosmos: An Astrophysicist Reconciles Science & Scripture. LC 92-64094. 192p. (Orig.). 1993. pap. 12.00 (*0-89109-700-7*) NavPress.

***Ross, Hugh.** The Fingerprint of God. (Illus.). 248p. 2000. pap. 12.99 (*0-88368-627-9*) Whitaker Hse.

Ross, Hugh. The Fingerprint of God. 2nd ed. 248p. 1991. reprint ed. pap. 9.95 (*0-939497-18-2*) Promise Pub.

— The Genesis Question: Scientific Advances & the Accuracy of Genesis. LC 98-23194. 208p. 1998. 20.00 (*1-57683-111-6*) NavPress.

Ross, Hugh McGregor. George Fox Speaks for Himself. 1999. pap. 21.90 (*1-85072-081-9*, Pub. by W Sessions) St Mut.

***Ross, Hugh McGregor, ed.** Jesus Untouched by the Church: His Teachings in the Gospel of Thomas. 1999. pap. 45.00 (*1-85072-213-7*, Pub. by W Sessions) St Mut.

Ross, I. Negotiating Enterprise Agreements in the Federal System. 100p. 1996. pap. write for info. (*0-409-31113-8*, MICHIE) LEXIS Pub.

Ross, Iain, ed. The Gude & Godly Ballatis. 70p. 1986. 30.00 (*0-85411-019-4*, Pub. by Saltire Soc) St Mut.

Ross, Ian. Aging of Cells, Humans, & Societies. LC 93-73882. 240p. (C). 1994. text. write for info. (*0-697-20327-1*, WCB McGr Hill) McGrw-H Hghr Educ.

Ross, Ian C. Umbria: A Tour Through Its History, Landscape, Architecture, Food & Wine. (Illus.). 448p. 1997. pap. 17.95 (*0-14-017597-0*, Pub. by Pnguin Bks Ltd) Trafalgar.

Ross, Ian C., ed. see Kelly, Patrick.

Ross, Ian C., ed. & intro. see James, Henry.

Ross, Ian C., ed. & intro. see Sterne, Laurence.

Ross, Ian K. Aging of Cells, Humans, & Societies. 2nd ed. 1999. pap. text 29.50 (*0-697-28601-0*) McGraw.

Ross, Ian S. The Life of Adam Smith. (Illus.). 524p. 1995. 39.95 (*0-19-828821-2*, Clarendon Pr) OUP.

Ross, Ian S., ed. On the Wealth of Nations: Contemporary Responses to Adam Smith. (Key Issues Ser.: No. 19). 250p. 1998. 72.00 (*1-85506-566-5*); pap. 23.00 (*1-85506-567-3*) Thoemmes Pr.

Ross, Imogen, jt. auth. see Anderson, Kristen.

Ross, Inez. The Adobe Castle: A Southwest Gothic Romance. 160p. 1998. 15.98 (*0-9664337-2-6*) Ashley Hse.

R

An Asterisk (*) at the beginning of an entry indicates that the title is appearing for the first time.

— The Strange Disappearance of Uncle Dudley: A Child's Story of Los Alamos. (Illus.). 40p. (Orig.). (J). (ps-2). 1996. pap. 6.98 (*0-9645703-2-7*) Otowi Crossing Pr.

Ross, Inez A. The Bear & the Castle: The James Oliver Curwood Story. LC 98-92975. (Illus.). 48p. (J). (ps-6). 1998. pap. text 6.98 (*0-9664337-0-X*) Ashley Hse.

Ross, Iris, ed. see Ross, Earle.

Ross, Irwin. The Loneliest Campaign: The Truman Victory of 1948. LC 75-22761. 304p. 1977. reprint ed. lib. bdg. 35.00 (*0-8371-8353-7*, ROLCT, Greenwood Pr) Greenwood.

— Shady Business: Confronting Corporate Corruption. LC 92-29437. 1992. 19.95 (*0-87078-340-8*); pap. 9.95 (*0-87078-341-6*) Century Foundation.

Ross, Isabel. Grace Coolidge & Her Era. LC 62-8017. (Illus.). 370p. (C). 1988. reprint ed. 19.95 (*0-944951-05-8*) C Coolidge Memorial.

— Ladies of the Press: The Story of Women in Journalism by an Insider. LC 74-3972. (Women in America Ser.). (Illus.). 642p. 1974. reprint ed. 46.95 (*0-405-06120-X*) Ayer.

— Margaret Fell: Mother of Quakerism. (C). 1989. pap. 36.00 (*0-900657-83-9*, Pub. by W Sessions) St Mut.

— Silhouette in Diamonds: The Life of Mrs. Potter Palmer. LC 75-1868. (Leisure Class in America Ser.). (Illus.). 1975. reprint ed. 25.95 (*0-405-06934-0*) Ayer.

***Ross, Isabel, ed.** Margaret Fell. 1999. pap. 30.00 (*1-85072-185-8*, Pub. by W Sessions) St Mut.

Ross, Ishbel. Grace Coolidge & Her Era. LC 62-8017. (Illus.). 370p. (C). 1988. reprint ed. pap. 13.95 (*0-944951-04-X*) C Coolidge Memorial.

— Rebel Rose. LC 54-8986. 245p. 1987. pap. 4.95 (*0-89176-026-1*, Mckingbird) R Bemis Pub.

Ross, Ivan A. Medicinal Plants of the World: Chemical Constituents, Traditional & Modern Medicinal Uses. LC 98-34758. (Illus.). 432p. 1998. 99.50 (*0-89603-542-5*) Humana.

Ross, J., jt. auth. see Heusch, G.

Ross, J., jt. ed. see Myneni, R. B.

Ross, J. A. & Erichsen, N. The Story of Lucca. (Mediaeval Towns Ser.: Vol. 7). 1974. reprint ed. pap. 46.00 (*0-8115-0849-8*) Periodicals Srv.

— The Story of Pisa. LC 85-47864. (Mediaeval Towns Ser.: Vol. 3). 1974. reprint ed. pap. 58.00 (*0-8115-0845-5*) Periodicals Srv.

Ross, J. A. & Mauldin, W. Parker, eds. Berelson on Population. (Illus.). 345p. 1988. 44.00 (*0-387-96716-8*) Spr-Verlag.

Ross, J. B., jt. ed. see Lakowicz, Joseph R.

Ross, J. Carlton. Furthur. (Illus.). 288p. 1998. pap. 14.95 (*1-880047-60-8*) J Holmes Inc.

Ross, J. Elliott. Christian Ethics. 250p. 1951. 12.95 (*0-8159-5202-3*) Devin.

Ross, J. H. A Conspectus of the African Acacia Species. (Memoirs of the Botanical Survey of South Africa Ser.: No. 44). (Illus.). 155p. 1979. 15.00 (*0-621-05309-0*, Pub. by Natl Botanical Inst) Balogh.

— Fabaceae, Pt. 2. (Flora of Southern Africa Ser.: Vol. 16). (Illus.). 142p. 1977. 32.00 (*0-621-03832-6*, Pub. by Natl Botanical Inst) Balogh.

— The Flora of Natal. (Memoirs of the Botanical Survey of South Africa Ser.: No. 39). (Illus.). 418p. 1972. 15.00 (*0-621-00327-1*, Pub. by Natl Botanical Inst) Balogh.

Ross, J. J. Some Facts & More About the Self-Styled "Pastor" C. T. Russell. 48p. 1988. reprint ed. pap. 2.95 (*1-883858-40-2*) Witness CA.

Ross, J. L., jt. ed. see Satz, Paul.

Ross, J. M. The Royal New Zealand Air Force. (Official History Ser.: No. 2). (Illus.). 400p. 1993. reprint ed. 49.95 (*0-89839-187-3*) Battery Pr.

Ross, J. Michael. The MotherSong. 32p. 1995. 19.95 (*0-9643748-0-3*) Side Door.

Ross, J. N. The Essence of Power Electronics. LC 96-25452. (Essence of Engineering Ser.). 240p. (C). 1996. pap. text 24.45 (*0-13-525643-7*) P-H.

Ross, Jack, ed. As They Say on the River: A Dictionary of Western Rivers Towing. LC 97-161670. 124p. 1997. pap. 9.95 (*0-9672042-0-8*) Captain J Ross.

Ross, Jack C. An Assembly of Good Fellows: Voluntary Associations in History. LC 75-35355. 328p. 1976. 65.00 (*0-8371-8586-6*, RGF/, Greenwood Pr) Greenwood.

Ross, Jack C. & Wheeler, Raymond H. Black Belonging: A Study of the Social Correlates of Work Relations among Negroes, 7. LC 77-105974. (Contributions in Sociology Ser.: No. 7). 292p. 1971. 65.00 (*0-8371-3298-3*, RBB/, Greenwood Pr) Greenwood.

Ross, Jack L., tr. see Meister, Albert.

Ross, Jacob J. The Virtues of the Family. LC 93-42425. 1994. 27.95 (*0-02-927385-4*) Free Pr.

***Ross, James.** Bleep! A Guide to Popular American Obscenities. 2nd ed. (Orig.). 2000. pap. text 18.95 (*1-879440-33-4*) Optima CA.

— Fragile Branches: Travels Through the Jewish Diaspora. (Illus.). 240p. 2000. 23.95 (*1-57322-165-1*) Putnam Pub Group.

Ross, James. They Don't Dance Much. LC 74-23650. (Lost American Fiction Ser.). 308p. 1975. reprint ed. 16.95 (*0-8093-0714-6*) S Ill U Pr.

Ross, James & Kelson, Michael. Creating Visual C Plus Plus Applications, Incl. disk. (Illus.). 1512p. (Orig.). 1994. 49.99 (*1-56529-806-3*) Que.

Ross, James, et al. Backyard Archaeology at the Willis Allen House, 1857-1945. Rubach, Bonita K., ed. (Illus.). 22p. (Orig.). 1994. pap. 5.95 (*0-913415-08-1*) Am Kestrel Pr.

Ross, James A. How to Buy a Car. 3rd ed. 1993. mass mkt. 4.99 (*0-312-95151-5*) St Martin.

Ross, James B. & McLaughlin, Mary M., eds. Portable Medieval Reader. (Portable Library: No. 46). 704p. 1977. pap. 22.99 (*0-14-015046-3*, Penguin Bks) Viking Penguin.

— Portable Renaissance Reader. (Portable Library: No. 61). 1977. pap. 16.95 (*0-14-015061-7*, Penguin Bks) Viking Penguin.

Ross, James B., ed. see Galbert.

Ross, James D. Cambodia: Justice System & Human Rights Violations. O'Neill, William G. & Posner, Michael J., eds. 74p. (Orig.). 1992. pap. 10.00 (*0-934143-53-6*) Lawyers Comm Human.

Ross, James D., ed. see Gelatt, Timothy.

Ross, James F. Philosophical Theology. 366p. 1982. 49.50 (*0-8290-0335-5*) Irvington.

— Philosophical Theology. LC 68-17707. (C). 1969. write for info. (*0-672-60721-2*, Bobbs) Macmillan.

— Portraying Analogy. LC 81-15463. (Cambridge Studies in Philosophy). (Illus.). 255p. 1982. text 80.00 (*0-521-23805-6*) Cambridge U Pr.

Ross, James F., ed. Inquiries into Medieval Philosophy: A Collection in Honor of Francis P. Clarke, 4. LC 74-105984. (Contributions in Philosophy Ser.: No. 4). 329p. 1971. 57.95 (*0-8371-3311-4*, RMP/, Greenwood Pr) Greenwood.

Ross, James F., tr. Suarez: Disputation Six, on Formal & Universal Unity. LC 64-7799. (Medieval Philosophical Texts in Translation Ser.: No. 23). 1965. pap. 25.00 (*0-87462-215-8*) Marquette.

***Ross, James P., et al.** Crocodiles: Status Survey & Conservation Action Plan 2nd ed. LC 98-194184. vii, 96 p. 1998. write for info. (*2-8317-0441-3*, Pub. by IUCN) Island Pr.

Ross, James R. Caught in a Tornado: A Chinese American Woman Survives the Cultural Revolution. 192p. 1994. text 28.95 (*1-55553-192-X*) NE U Pr.

— Escape to Shanghai: A Jewish Community in China. 280p. 1993. 22.95 (*0-02-927375-7*) Free Pr.

Ross, James W. Social Security Disability Benefits: How to Get Them! How to Keep Them! rev. ed. 104p. 1984. 29.95 (*0-9615202-6-4*); pap. 19.95 (*0-9615202-5-6*) Ross Pub Co.

Ross, Janet. The City That She Loved: A Reflection... LC 93-86933. (Illus.). 147p. (Orig.). 1993. pap. 7.95 (*0-9624229-6-7*) St Thomas Tech.

— Lives of the Early Medici As Told in Their Correspondence. 1977. lib. bdg. 59.95 (*0-8490-2175-8*) Gordon Pr.

Ross, Janet, et al. Words in Action: Abstract Expressionism. LC 76-3403. (Illus.). 1976. pap. 4.95 (*0-614-02729-2*) J S Blanton Mus.

***Ross, Janet Leigh.** The Werewolf? Guevara, Linda L., ed. (Illus.). 36p. (J). (ps-3). 2000. 16.95 (*0-615-11427-X*) All About Kids.

***Ross, Janice.** Moving Lessons: Margaret H'Doubler & the Beginning of Dance in American Education. 2000. 60.00 (*0-299-16930-8*); pap. 24.95 (*0-299-16934-0*) U of Wis Pr.

Ross, Janice, jt. auth. see Steinberg, Stephen C.

Ross, Jason. A World Without Homosexuals. LC 94-66316. (Illus.). 104p. (Orig.). 1994. pap. 10.00 (*0-9641408-1-0*) Road Kill Pr.

Ross, Jean W., ed. Dictionary of Literary Biography Yearbook, 1984. 84th ed. 380p. 1985. text 155.00 (*0-8103-1628-5*) Gale.

Ross, Jeanette. K Ranch. 126p. (Orig.). 1984. 20.00 (*0-938190-42-3*); pap. 7.95 (*0-938190-32-6*) North Atlantic.

Ross, Jeff. Good People, Bad Checks: 30 Hidden Ways Your Checkbook Could Land You in Jail. Wood, Wally, ed. LC 96-60222. (Illus.). 218p. 1996. pap. 12.00 (*0-9651510-0-X*) Walden House.

— The Semantics of Media. LC 96-52724. (Studies in Linguistics & Philosophy). 148p. (C). 1997. text 80.00 (*0-7923-4389-1*) Kluwer Academic.

Ross, Jeff, ed. Nucleic Acid Hybridization: Essential Techniques. LC 97-19726. (Essential Techniques Ser.). 176p. 1998. pap. 49.95 (*0-471-97125-1*) Wiley.

***Ross, Jeffery Ian.** Making News of Police Violence: A Comparative Study of Toronto & New York City. LC 99-54878. 224p. 2000. 64.00 (*0-275-96825-1*, C6825, Praeger Pubs) Greenwood.

Ross, Jeffrey I., ed. Controlling State Crime: An Introduction. LC 94-27125. (Current Issues in Criminal Justice Ser.: Vol. 9). 430p. 1995. text 78.00 (*0-8153-1546-5*, SS933) Garland.

— Cutting the Edge: Current Perspectives in Radical & Critical Criminology. LC 98-11129. 240p. 1998. 59.95 (*0-275-95708-X*, Praeger Pubs) Greenwood.

— Violence in Canada: Sociopolitical Perspectives. (Illus.). 362p. 1996. pap. text 38.00 (*0-19-541058-0*) OUP.

***Ross, Jeffrey Ian.** Controlling State Crime. 2nd ed. LC 00-26701. 450p. 2000. pap. 29.95 (*0-7658-0695-9*) Transaction Pubs.

***Ross, Jeffrey Ian, ed.** Varieties of State Crime & Its Control. 250p. 2000. pap. 25.00 (*1-881798-20-8*, Pub. by Willow Tree NY) Lib Res.

Ross, Jeffrey J., ed. Cataloging Architectural Drawings. (Topical Papers). 96p. 1992. pap. 20.00 (*0-942740-11-4*) Art Libs Soc.

Ross, Jeffrey S. DNA Ploidy & Cell Cycle Analysis in Pathology, Vol. 1. LC 95-38361. (Illus.). 176p. 1996. pap. 55.00 (*0-89640-301-7*) Igaku-Shoin.

Ross, Jeffrey S. MRI of the Spine. 2nd ed. 240p. text 89.00 (*0-7817-2528-3*) Lppncott W & W.

Ross, Jennie-Keith. Old People, New Lives: Community Creation in a Retirement Residence. LC 76-8103. (Illus.). 1995. lib. bdg. 22.00 (*0-226-72825-0*) U Ch Pr.

— Old Peoples, New Lives: Community Creation in a Retirement Residence. LC 76-8103. (Illus.). 240p. 1982. pap. text 10.00 (*0-226-42965-2*) U Ch Pr.

Ross, Jeremy. Acupuncture Point Combinations: The Key to Clinical Success. LC 94-43497. 1995. text 83.00 (*0-443-05006-6*) Church.

— Zang Fu: The Organ Systems of Traditional Chinese Medicine. 2nd ed. (Illus.). 200p. (C). 1989. text 82.00 (*0-443-03482-6*) Church.

Ross, Jerilyn. Triumph over Fear: A Book of Help & Hope for People with Anxiety, Panic Attacks, & Phobias. 320p. 1995. pap. 14.95 (*0-553-37444-3*) Bantam.

***Ross, Jerry.** Permanecerenel Castillo. (SPA., Illus.). 28p. 1999. pap. write for info. (*0-7392-0338-X*) Morris Pubng.

— Stay in the Castle. (Illus.). 28p. 1999. pap. write for info. (*0-7392-0339-8*) Morris Pubng.

— The Teenage Years of Jesus Christ: The Ultimate Pattern for Teenagers Today. 120p. 1999. pap. 7.50 (*0-7392-0440-8*, PO3457) Morris Pubng.

***Ross, Jillian.** Alissa. (Stardust Classics). 1999. boxed set 16.95 (*1-889514-21-7*) Dolls Corp.

Ross, Jillian. Alissa & the Castle Ghost. 2nd ed. LC 97-73129. (Stardust Classics). (Illus.). 113p. (J). (gr. 2-6). 1998. 12.95 (*1-889514-07-1*); pap. 5.95 (*1-889514-08-X*) Dolls Corp.

— Alissa & the Dungeons of Grimrock. LC 98-65893. (Stardust Classics). (Illus.). 106p. (J). (gr. 2-6). 1998. 12.95 (*1-889514-15-2*); pap. 5.95 (*1-889514-16-0*) Dolls Corp.

— Alissa, Princess of Arcadia. 2nd ed. LC 97-73130. (Stardust Classics). (Illus.). 109p. (J). (gr. 2-6). 1997. 12.95 (*1-889514-03-9*); pap. 5.95 (*1-889514-04-7*) Dolls Corp.

— Alissa's Tournament Troubles. LC 99-71563. (Stardust Classics: No. 4). (Illus.). 124p. (J). 1999. 12.95 (*1-889514-31-4*) Dolls Corp.

— Alissa's Tournament Troubles. LC 99-71563. (Stardust Classics: No. 4). (Illus.). 124p. (J). (gr. 2-5). 1999. pap. 5.95 (*1-889514-32-2*) Dolls Corp.

Ross, Jillian & Ford Foundation Staff. Solving the Math Problem. LC 99-13947. 1999. write for info. (*0-916584-52-6*) Ford Found.

Ross, Jim. How You Too Can Become a Flight Attendant! A Step by Step Guide. 104p. (Orig.). 1997. pap. 24.95 (*0-9615202-9-9*) Ross Pub Co.

— Learn Advanced MFC Programming with Visual C++ 9X. 1998. pap. text 52.95 (*1-55622-594-6*) Wordware Pub.

— 1999 Cruise Line Employment Manual. 1999. pap. 19.99 (*0-9670568-0-2*) Cruise Ross.

— Saddle up & R-I-I-D-E. (Illus.). 100p. 1990. pap. 6.95 (*0-9617932-2-8*) J A Ross.

***Ross, Jim.** 2000 Cruise Line Employment Manual. 2nd ed. 88p. 2000. pap. 24.95 (*0-9670568-1-0*) Cruise Ross.

Ross, Jim & Myers, Paul, We Will Never Forget: Eyewitness Accounts of the Oklahoma City Federal Building Bombing. LC 96-18285. 288p. 1996. pap. 15.95 (*1-57168-081-0*, Eakin Pr) Sunbelt Media.

Ross, Jim & Myers, Paul, eds. Dear Oklahoma City, Get Well Soon. LC 95-44819. (Illus.). 48p. (J). (gr. 4-6). 1996. lib. bdg. 17.85 (*0-8027-8437-2*) Walker & Co.

— Dear Oklahoma City, Get Well Soon: America's Children Reach Out to the People of Oklahoma. LC 95-44819. (Illus.). 48p. (J). (gr. 4-6). 1996. 16.95 (*0-8027-8436-4*) Walker & Co.

Ross, Jim, ed. see Cumpton, Lonnie, et al.

Ross, Jim, ed. see Euling, Derrol, et al.

Ross, Jini K. & Kilgore, Thomas, Jr. Servant's Journey: The Life & Work of Thomas Kilgore. LC 98-24178. 256p. 1998. pap. 18.00 (*0-8170-1297-4*) Judson.

Ross, Jini K., ed. see Wright, Jeremiah A.

Ross, Jini K., ed. see Wright, Jeremiah A., Jr.

Ross, Joan. Guarded Moments. (Temptation Ser.: No. 296). 1990. pap. 2.65 (*0-373-25396-6*) Harlequin Bks.

Ross, Joan, jt. auth. see Allen, Layman E.

Ross, Joan, jt. auth. see Higgins, James.

Ross, Joan C. & Langone, Michael D. Cults: What Parents Should Know. 1989. pap. 5.95 (*0-8184-0511-2*, L Stuart) Carol Pub Group.

Ross, JoAnn. Ambushed. 1996. per. 3.50 (*0-373-25713-9*, 1-25713-8) Harlequin Bks.

Ross, Joann. Un Ange Nomme Desir. (Rouge Passion Ser.). 1999. mass mkt. 3.50 (*0-373-37516-6*, 1-37516-1) Harlequin Bks.

— Angel of Desire. (Temptation Ser.). 1994. per. 2.99 (*0-373-25582-9*, 1-25582-7) Harlequin Bks.

— Bait & Switch. 1996. per. 5.50 (*1-55166-172-1*, 1-66172-7, Mira Bks) Harlequin Bks.

Ross, JoAnn. Confessions. LC 96-3535. 401p. 1995. per. 4.99 (*1-55166-092-X*, 1-66092-7, Mira Bks) Harlequin Bks.

— Dark Desires. (Temptation Ser.: No. 382). 1992. per. 2.99 (*0-373-25482-2*, 1-25482-0) Harlequin Bks.

Ross, Joann. Dusk Fire. 249p. 1995. per. 4.99 (*1-55166-022-9*, Mira Bks) Harlequin Bks.

***Ross, JoAnn.** Fair Haven. 432p. 2000. 6.99 (*0-671-78611-3*) PB.

Ross, JoAnn. Far Harbor. 384p. 2000. per. 6.99 (*0-671-02707-7*, Pocket Star Bks) PB.

Ross, Joann. For Richer or Poorer. LC 95-13944. (Temptation Ser.). 218p. 1995. per. 3.25 (*0-373-25641-8*, 1-25641-1) Harlequin Bks.

Ross, JoAnn. Homeplace. 386p. 1999. mass mkt. 6.50 (*0-671-02706-9*) S&S Trade.

Ross, Joann. Hunk of the Month. (Temptation Ser.). 1998. per. 3.75 (*0-373-25783-X*, 0-25783-2) Harlequin Bks.

— I Do, I Do...for Now. (Love & Laughter Ser.). 1996. per. 3.50 (*0-373-44001-4*, 1-44001-5) Silhouette.

— In a Class by Himself. (Western Lovers Ser.). 1995. mass mkt. 3.99 (*0-373-88520-2*, 1-88520-1) Harlequin Bks.

— It Happened One Week. (Yours Truly Ser.). 1996. per. 3.50 (*0-373-52015-8*, 1-52015-4) Silhouette.

— Legacy of Lies. 378p. 1995. per. 4.99 (*1-55166-018-0*, Mira Bks) Harlequin Bks.

— Lovestorm. (Temptation Ser.). 1993. per. 2.99 (*0-373-25571-3*, 1-25571-0) Harlequin Bks.

— Mackenzie's Woman: Bachelor Auction. 1999. mass mkt. 3.75 (*0-373-25817-8*, Harlequin) Harlequin Bks.

— Michael: The Defender. 1997. per. 3.50 (*0-373-25754-6*, 1-25754-2) Harlequin Bks.

— Never a Bride: (Bachelor Arms) LC 95-13564. (Temptation Ser.). 218p. 1995. per. 3.25 (*0-373-25637-X*, 1-25637-9) Harlequin Bks.

— No Regrets. 1997. per. 5.99 (*1-55166-282-5*, 1-66282-4, Mira Bks) Harlequin Bks.

— 1-800-Hero: Hero for the Bride. (Temptation Ser.: Vol. 693). 1998. per. 3.75 (*0-373-25793-7*, 1-25793-0) Harlequin Bks.

— The Outlaw. (Temptation Ser.). 1996. per. 3.50 (*0-373-25685-X*, 1-25685-8) Harlequin Bks.

— Piege pour un Ange Gardien. (Rouge Passion Ser.: Vol 504). (FRE.). 1999. mass mkt. 3.50 (*0-373-37504-2*, 1-37504-7) Harlequin Bks.

— The Prince & the Showgirl. (Men at Work Ser.: Vol. 27). 1998. mass mkt. 4.50 (*0-373-81039-3*, 1-81039-9) Harlequin Bks.

— Private Passions (Secret Fantasies) LC 95-22365. 219p. 1995. per. 3.25 (*0-373-25662-0*) Harlequin Bks.

— The Return of Caine O'Halloran. 1994. per. 2.99 (*0-373-25589-6*) Harlequin Bks.

***Ross, Joann.** The Return of Caine O'Halloran. 2000. mass mkt. 4.50 (*0-373-82245-6*, 1-82245-1) Harlequin Bks.

Ross, Joann. Roarke: The Adventurer. (Temptation Ser.: No. 638). 1997. per. 3.50 (*0-373-25738-4*, 1-25738-5) Harlequin Bks.

— Scandals. (Promo Ser.). 1999. per. 4.50 (*0-373-21958-X*, 1-21958-3) Harlequin Bks.

— Le Serment sur la Plage. (Rouge Passion Ser.: No. 483). (FRE.). 1998. mass mkt. 3.50 (*0-373-37483-6*, 1-37483-4) Harlequin Bks.

— Shayne: The Pretender. 1997. per. 3.50 (*0-373-25746-5*, 1-25746-8) Harlequin Bks.

— Southern Comforts. 1996. per. 5.99 (*1-55166-167-5*, Mira Bks) Harlequin Bks.

— Star-Crossed Lovers. (Temptation Ser.). 1993. mass mkt. 2.99 (*0-373-25532-2*, 1-25532-2) Harlequin Bks.

— Stormy Courtship. LC 96-536. (Mira Bks.). 251p. 1995. per. 4.99 (*1-55166-072-5*, 1-66072-9, Mira Bks) Harlequin Bks.

— Tangled Lives. (Temptation Ser.: No. 345). 1991. per. 2.95 (*0-373-25445-8*) Harlequin Bks.

— Tempting Fate. (Mira Bks.). 1996. per. 5.50 (*1-55166-157-8*, 1-66157-8, Mira Bks) Harlequin Bks.

— Three Grooms & a Wedding. LC 96-618. (Temptation Ser.). 216p. 1995. per. 3.25 (*0-373-25645-0*, 1-25645-2) Harlequin Bks.

— Three Grooms & a Wedding. (Promo Ser.). 1999. per. 4.50 (*0-373-21978-4*, 1-21978-1) Harlequin Bks.

— Un Tournage A Hauts Risques. (Rouge Passion Ser.). 1999. mass mkt. 3.50 (*0-373-37510-7*, 1-37510-4) Harlequin Bks.

— Untamed. (Temptation Ser.). 1996. per. 3.50 (*0-373-25705-8*, 1-25705-4) Harlequin Bks.

— Wanted! 1996. per. 3.50 (*0-373-25709-0*, 1-25709-6) Harlequin Bks.

— A Woman's Heart. 1998. mass mkt. 5.99 (*1-55166-461-5*, Mira Bks) Harlequin Bks.

Ross, Joann & Crowe, Evelyn A. The Bodyguard. LC 95-23273. 634p. 1995. per. 5.50 (*0-373-20117-6*) Harlequin Bks.

Ross, Joann, et al. By Request: Temperature Rising. 1994. mass mkt. 5.50 (*0-373-20099-4*) Harlequin Bks.

— Verdict: Matrimony. 1996. per. 5.99 (*0-373-20127-3*, 1-20127-6) Harlequin Bks.

— Western Loving. 1994. per. 5.50 (*0-373-20097-8*, 1-20097-1) Harlequin Bks.

Ross, Joe. An American Voyage. (New American Poetry Ser.: No. 12). 96p. (Orig.). 1993. pap. 9.95 (*1-55713-070-1*) Sun & Moon CA.

— De-Flections. limited ed. 46p. 1994. 18.00 (*0-937013-52-8*) Potes Poets.

— Equations=Equals. 1999. pap. text 10.95 (*1-55713-393-X*, Pub. by Sun & Moon CA) Consort Bk Sales.

— Guards of the Heart: Four Plays. (Blue Corner Drama Ser.). 112p. (Orig.). 1991. pap. 9.95 (*1-55713-082-5*) Sun & Moon CA.

Ross, Joe, ed. NESFA Hymnal, Vol. 1. 2nd ed. vi, 211p. 1979. pap. 18.00 (*0-915368-69-2*) New Eng SF Assoc.

***Ross, Joel.** Total Quality Management. 3rd ed. (C). 1999. student ed., ring bd. write for info. (*1-57444-275-9*) CRC Pr.

Ross, Joel & Naftali, Lee. Generation E: The Entrepreneurial Guide for Twentysomethings & Other Corporate Rejects. LC 96-54222. 272p. 1997. 11.95 (*0-89815-897-4*) Ten Speed Pr.

Ross, Joel E. Total Quality Management: Text, Cases & Readings. 2nd ed. LC 94-9068. (Illus.). 480p. (C). 1994. per. 44.95 (*1-884015-08-5*) St Lucie Pr.

***Ross, Joel E. & Perry, Susan.** Total Quality Management: Text, Cases & Readings. 3rd ed. LC 99-462632. 568p. 1999. per. 39.95 (*1-57444-266-X*) CRC Pr.

Ross, Joel E., jt. auth. see Murdick, Robert G.

Ross, John. ABCs of Microsoft Internet Explorer 4. 2nd ed. LC 97-68508. 400p. 1997. pap. text 19.99 (*0-7821-2042-3*) Sybex.

— The Annexation of Mexico: From the Aztecs to the IMF. LC 97-29924. 450p. (Orig.). 1997. pap. 19.95 (*1-56751-130-9*); lib. bdg. 39.95 (*1-56751-131-7*) Common Courage.

— Comp Printmaker. rev. ed. 1989. 49.95 (*0-02-927371-4*) Free Pr.

— Dog Talk: Training Your Dog Through a Canine Point of View. 1995. text 15.95 (*0-312-11778-7*) St Martin.

***Ross, John.** Donald Winter: A Failing Marriage - A Novel. LC 99-91885. 2000. 25.00 (*0-7388-1372-9*); pap. 18.00 (*0-7388-1373-7*) Xlibris Corp.

An Asterisk (*) at the beginning of an entry indicates that the title is appearing for the first time.

— HDTV & Video System Repair. 512p. 2000. pap. 31.95 (*0-7668-2354-7*) Delmar.

Ross, John. Lease-Purchase America! Acquiring Real Estate in the '90s & Beyond. LC 92-81393. 192p. 1993. pap. 12.95 (*0-914984-45-4*) Starburst.

— The Manchus: or The Reigning Dynasty of China: Their Rise & Progress. LC 70-38080. (China Ser.). (Illus.). reprint ed. 89.00 (*0-404-56944-7*) AMS Pr.

— Mexico in Focus. (In Focus Ser.). (Illus.). 80p. Date not set. pap. 12.00 (*0-85345-979-7*, Pub. by Lat Am Bur) Monthly Rev.

— Narrative of a Second Voyage in Search of a North-West Passage, & of a Residence in the Arctic Regions During the Years 1829, 1830,1831, 1833, 2 vols., Set. LC 68-55217. 1971. reprint ed. lib. bdg. 75.00 (*0-8371-3860-4*, RONP) Greenwood.

— Narrative of a Second Voyage in Search of a North-West Passage, & of a Residence in the Arctic Regions During the Years 1829, 1830,1831, 1833, 2 vols., Vol. 1. LC 68-55217. 1971. reprint ed. lib. bdg. 55.00 (*0-8371-1332-6*, RONQ) Greenwood.

— Narrative of a Second Voyage in Search of a North-West Passage, & of a Residence in the Arctic Regions During the Years 1829, 1830,1831, 1833, 2 vols., Vol. 2. LC 68-55217. 1971. reprint ed. lib. bdg. 45.00 (*0-8371-1333-4*, RONR) Greenwood.

***Ross, John.** North America's Greatest Bird Hunting Lodges & Preserves: More Than 200 Hotspots in the U. S. & Canada. LC 00-21961. (Illus.). 278p. 2000. pap. 19.95 (*1-57223-279-X*, 279x) Willow Creek Pr.

— North America's Greatest Fishing Lodges: More Than 250 Destinations in the United States, Canada & Central America. 2nd rev. ed. LC 00-26389.Tr. of Aports Afield's guide to North America's Greatest Fishing Lodges. (Illus.). 352p. 2000. pap. 19.95 (*1-57223-297-8*, 2978) Willow Creek Pr.

Ross, John. Poems on Events of the Day, 1582-1607. LC 91-20371. 244p. 1991. 50.00 (*0-8201-1456-1*) Schol Facsimiles.

— Recruiting Officer. 2nd ed. (New Mermaids Ser.). (C). 1991. pap. text. write for info. (*0-393-90065-7*) Norton.

— The RFC to the RAF India, 1919. 122p. (Orig.). 1987. pap. 35.00 (*0-7212-0792-8*, Pub. by Regency Pr GBR) St Mut.

— The Royal Flying Corps-Boy Service, 1917. 192p. (C). 1990. 45.00 (*0-7212-0830-4*, Pub. by Regency Pr GBR) St Mut.

***Ross, John.** TAPI 3.0: Programmer's Guide & Software Developer's Kit. (DV-MPE Software Development Kits Ser.). (Illus.). 2000. pap. text 49.99 incl. cd-rom (*0-7356-0621-8*) Microsoft.

Ross, John. Tonatiuh's People: A Novel of Mexican Cataclysm. LC 98-26237. 288p. 1998. pap. 13.95 (*0-938317-41-5*) Cinco Puntos.

***Ross, John.** Trout Unlimited's Guide to America's 100 Best Trout Streams. LC 99-12303. (Illus.). 353p. 1999. pap. 18.95 (*1-56044-830-X*) Falcon Pub Inc.

Ross, John. Unintended Consequences. 861p. (C). 1996. 28.95 (*1-888118-04-0*) Accurate Pr.

***Ross, John.** The War Against Oblivion: Zapatista Chronicles, 1994-2000. 320p. 2000. pap. 18.95 (*1-56751-174-0*, Pub. by Common Courage); lib. bdg. 29.95 (*1-56751-175-9*, Pub. by Common Courage) Login Brothers Bk Co.

— Windows 98. (I Didn't Know You Could Do That Ser.). (Illus.). 336p. 2000. pap. text 19.99 (*0-7821-2829-7*) Sybex.

Ross, John. World Fly Fishing: Streams of Dreams. 1999. 17.99 (*0-7858-1060-9*) Bk Sales Inc.

Ross, John & McKinney, Barbara. Puppy Preschool: Raising Your Puppy Right-Right from the Start. 3rd ed. LC 95-41346. 224p. 1996. text 22.95 (*0-312-14029-0*) St Martin.

Ross, John & Romano, Clare. The Complete Intaglio Print. LC 74-2697. 1974. pap. text 14.95 (*0-02-927400-1*) Free Pr.

Ross, John & Ross, Beth. Prairie Time: The Leopold Reserve Revisited. LC 97-5268. (Illus.). 240p. 1998. 24.95 (*0-299-15660-5*) U of Wis Pr.

Ross, John, et al. The Complete Printmaker: Techniques - Traditions - Innovations. enl. rev. ed. 352p. 1991. pap. 37.00 (*0-02-927372-2*) Free Pr.

Ross, John, jt. auth. see Borland, Russell.

Ross, John, jt. auth. see Gaudreau, Roger.

Ross, John, jt. ed. see Hand, Q. R.

***Ross, John A.** Howard W. Sams Guide to Satellite TV Technology. 1999. pap. 39.95 (*0-7906-1176-7*) Prompt Publns.

Ross, John A., ed. International Encyclopedia of Population, 2 vols. LC 82-2326. 1982. text 250.00 (*0-02-927430-3*) Free Pr.

Ross, John A., et al, eds. Family Planning & Population: A Compendium of International Statistics. LC 93-93706. 202p. 1993. pap. 25.00 (*0-87834-078-5*) Population Coun.

Ross, John A. & Frankenberg, Elizabeth. Findings from Two Decades of Family Planning Research. LC 93-86577. 108p. 1993. pap. 12.00 (*0-87834-080-7*) Population Coun.

Ross, John A. & Lalond, David E. Principles of Electronic Devices & Circuits: Transparencies. 1994. pap. 69.95 (*0-8273-6421-0*) Delmar.

Ross, John A. & Maynes, Florence J. Teaching Problem-Solving. LC 82-207857. (Informal Ser.: No. 43). (Illus.). 216p. reprint ed. pap. 67.00 (*0-7837-0553-0*, 204089400019) Bks Demand.

Ross, John A., et al. Family Planning & Child Survival Programs: 100 Developing Countries. (Illus.). 258p. (Orig.). 1988. pap. 25.00 (*0-685-21889-9*) CUCFP&FH.

— Management Strategies for Family Planning Programs. LC 89-6029. (Illus.). 71p. (Orig.). 1989. pap. 10.00 (*0-9620952-1-4*) CUCFP&FH.

Ross, John A., jt. auth. see LaLond, David E.

Ross, John A., jt. ed. see Phillips, James F.

Ross, John C., ed. see Shadwell, Thomas.

Ross, John D. Bonnie Jean, a Collection of Papers & Poems Relating to the Wife of Robert Burns. LC 71-144471. reprint ed. 29.50 (*0-404-08526-1*) AMS Pr.

— Burns Almanac. LC 72-144474. reprint ed. 41.50 (*0-404-08534-2*) AMS Pr.

— Burns Handbook. LC 76-144475. reprint ed. 24.50 (*0-404-08535-0*) AMS Pr.

— Early Critical Reviews on Robert Burns. LC 70-144476. reprint ed. 34.50 (*0-404-08536-9*) AMS Pr.

— Robert Burns & His Rhyming Friends. LC 77-144478. reprint ed. 29.50 (*0-404-08538-5*) AMS Pr.

— Round Burns Grave. enl. ed. LC 70-144479. reprint ed. 34.50 (*0-404-08539-3*) AMS Pr.

— Sixty Years of Life & Adventure in the Far East, 2 vols., Set. (Illus.). 1968. reprint ed. 85.00 (*0-7146-2024-6*, Pub. by F Cass Pubs) Intl Spec Bk.

— Story of the Kilmarnock Burns. LC 76-153519. reprint ed. 32.50 (*0-404-08978-X*) AMS Pr.

— Who's Who in Burns. LC 75-144480. reprint ed. 34.50 (*0-404-08547-4*) AMS Pr.

Ross, John D., compiled by. Scottish Poets in America. LC 72-80502. 1972. reprint ed. lib. bdg. 24.95 (*0-405-08899-X*, Pub. by Blom Pubns) Ayer.

Ross, John D. & Ross, Catherine H. Ross Test of Higher Cognitive Process. 1976. 12.00 (*0-685-74188-5*); 8.00 (*0-685-74189-3*); student ed. 25.00 (*0-87879-151-5*); student ed. 20.00 (*0-87879-152-3*); vinyl bd. 70.00 (*0-685-74187-7*) Acad Therapy.

Ross, John E. Sports Afield's Guide to North America's Greatest Fishing Lodges. LC 97-16540. (Illus.). 321p. 1997. pap. 18.95 (*1-57223-105-X*, 105X) Willow Creek Pr.

— Truths to Live By. LC 72-37834. (Essay Index Reprint Ser.). 1977. reprint ed. 21.95 (*0-8369-2622-6*) Ayer.

Ross, John E. & Cassell, Jay. North America's Greatest Big Game Lodges & Outfitters: More Than 250 Hot Spots in the Unites States & Canada. LC 99-31204. (Illus.). 308p. 1999. pap. 19.95 (*1-57223-147-5*, 147X) Willow Creek Pr.

Ross, John F. Linking Europe: Transport Policies & Politics in the European Union. LC 97-21850. 288p. 1998. 59.95 (*0-275-95248-7*, Praeger Pubs) Greenwood.

***Ross, John F.** Living Dangerously: Navigating the Risks of Everyday Life. 208p. 2000. pap. text 14.00 (*0-7382-0321-1*) Perseus Pubng.

Ross, John F. Neutrality & International Sanctions: Sweden, Switzerland & Collective Security. LC 89-32270. 262p. 1989. 59.95 (*0-275-93349-0*, C3349, Praeger Pubs) Greenwood.

— The Polar Bear Strategy: Reflections on Risk in Modern Life. LC HM1101.R67 1999. 288p. 1999. 23.00 (*0-7382-0117-0*, Pub. by Perseus Pubng) HarpC.

— Self-Defense Laws & Violent Crime Rates in the United States. 16p. (C). 1996. pap. text 5.00 (*1-888118-03-2*) Accurate Pr.

Ross, John J. Twentieth Annual Institute on Employment Law. (Litigation & Administrative Practice Ser.). 1018p. 1991. 70.00 (*0-685-59336-3*, H4-5112) PLI.

Ross, John M. Employment/Unemployment & Earnings Statistics in U. S. Documents: A Bibliography of Key Sources. LC 95-46965. 240p. 1996. 45.00 (*0-8108-3099-X*) Scarecrow.

— How to Use the Major Indexes to U. S. Government Publications. 64p. 1989. pap. text 15.00 (*0-8389-0509-9*) ALA.

— What Men Want: Mothers, Fathers, & Manhood. LC 93-46057. 320p. 1994. text 29.95 (*0-674-95080-1*) HUP.

Ross, John R. Salem Electric Against the Odds! (Illus.). 121p. (Orig.). 1991. pap. text 12.95 (*0-945490-02-X*) Carolina Pacific.

Ross, John R., ed. see Borkin, Ann.

Ross, John T. If Saving the Earth. 125p. 1998. 10.00 (*0-9665048-1-X*) Ecodem Pr.

Ross, John W., ed. see Florey, Henry E., Jr.

Ross, Jonathan. Fate Accomplished. large type ed. 384p. 1989. 11.50 (*0-7089-2046-2*) Ulverscroft.

— Murder! Murder! Burning Bright. large type ed. 304p. 1998. pap. 19.99 (*1-85389-904-6*) Ulverscroft.

— None the Worse for a Hanging. large type ed. (Cloak & Dagger Ser.). 320p. 1995. 21.95 (*0-7862-0567-9*) Thorndike Pr.

— This Too, Too Sullied Flesh. LC 98-19075. 299 p. 1998. pap. write for info. (*0-7540-3429-1*) Chivers N Amer.

— This Too, Too Sullied Flesh. large type ed. LC 98-19075. 306p. 1998. write for info. (*0-7838-0290-0*, G K Hall Lrg Type) Mac Lib Ref.

Ross, Josephine. The Relationship Between Depression in Homeless Mothers & Behavioral Problems in Their Preschool Age Children. 40p. 1997. pap. 8.00 (*0-8059-4188-6*) Dorrance.

Ross, Judith W., et al. Health Care Ethics Committees: The Next Generation. LC 93-17509. 198p. 1993. 45.00 (*1-55648-104-7*, 058300) AHPI.

Ross, Judy. Muskoka II. (Illus.). 120p. 1998. 39.95 (*1-55046-237-7*, Pub. by Boston Mills) Genl Dist Srvs.

Ross, Judy, jt. auth. see De Visser, John.

Ross, Judy, jt. auth. see DeVisser, John.

Ross, Juhan. The Radiation Regime & Architecture of Plant Stands. (Tasks for Vegetation Science Ser.: No. 3). 480p. 1981. text 325.00 (*90-6193-607-1*) Kluwer Academic.

***Ross, Julian, ed.** Railway Stations: Planning, Design & Management. LC 00-21016. (Illus.). 350p. 2000. 110.00 (*0-7506-4376-5*) Buttrwrth-Heinemann.

Ross, Julie. What Do I Do Now? LC 97-35513. 256p. 1998. pap. 12.95 (*0-312-18208-2*) St Martin.

Ross, Julie A. Practical Parenting for the 21st Century: The Manual You Wish Had Come with Your Child. LC 92-55103. 160p. (Orig.). 1993. pap. 10.95 (*0-9627226-6-9*) Excalibur Pub.

Ross, June R., ed. Bryozoa: Present & Past. (Illus.). 340p. (Orig.). 1987. pap. 60.00 (*0-930216-02-4*) West Wash Univ.

Ross, June R., jt. auth. see Dick, Mathew H.

Ross, K., ed. International Conference on Harmonic Analysis. LC 97-31839. (Trends in Mathematics Ser.). 432p. 1997. 98.50 (*0-8176-3943-8*) Birkhauser.

Ross, K. A. Elementary Analysis: The Theory of Calculus. Gehring, F. W. & Halmos, P. R., eds. LC 79-24806. (Undergraduate Texts in Mathematics Ser.). (Illus.). 350p. 1980. 26.40 (*3-540-90459-X*) Spr-Verlag.

Ross, K. A., jt. auth. see Hewitt, E.

Ross, K. K. Bert's Little Bedtime Story: A Sesame Street Book. LC 89-64283. (Chunky Tales Ser.). (Illus.). 28p. (J). (ps). 1991. 3.99 (*0-679-80757-8*, Pub. by Random Bks Yng Read) Random.

***Ross, K. K.** The Little Red Car. (Jellybean Bks.). (Illus.). 24p. (J). (ps-k). 1999. lib. bdg. 7.99 (*0-375-90142-6*, Pub. by Random Bks Yng Read) Random.

Ross, K. K. The Little Red Car. (Jellybean Bks.). (Illus.). 24p. (J). (ps-k). 2000. 2.99 (*0-375-80142-1*, Pub. by Random Bks Yng Read) Random.

— Peekaboo, Puppy! A My Puppy Loves Me Book. (Chunky Flap Bks. Ser.). (Illus.). 22p. (J). (ps). 1994. 3.50 (*0-685-71037-8*) Random Bks Yng Read.

Ross, K. W. Multiservice Loss Models for Broadband. LC 94-47039. (Workshops in Computing Ser.). 343p. 1997. 69.00 (*3-540-19918-7*) Spr-Verlag.

Ross, Karen. Black & White Media: Black Images in Popular Film & Television. 200p. (C). 1996. text 58.95 (*0-7456-1126-5*, Pub. by Polity Pr); pap. text 24.95 (*0-7456-1127-3*, Pub. by Polity Pr) Blackwell Pubs.

Ross, Karen K. Holding the Hope: A Parent's Guide to Living with Dystonia. 2nd ed. 1996. reprint ed. pap. write for info. (*0-9659941-2-0*) Natl Spasmodic Dysphonia.

Ross, Karen K. Holding the Hope: A Parent's Guide to Living with Dystonia. 2nd rev. ed. Levitan, Valerie F., ed. 54p. 1996. pap. 10.00 (*0-9659941-0-4*) Natl Spasmodic Dysphonia.

Ross, Kate. A Broken Vessel. 304p. 1995. mass mkt. 6.99 (*0-14-023453-5*, Penguin Bks) Viking Penguin.

— Cut to the Quick. 352p. 1994. pap. 6.99 (*0-14-023394-6*, Penguin Bks) Viking Penguin.

— The Devil in Music. LC 96-48131. 512p. 1998. pap. 6.99 (*0-14-026364-0*) Viking Penguin.

— Songs of the Sea. (Illus.). 60p. 1997. 9.95 (*0-86281-567-3*, Pub. by Appletree Pr) Irish Bks Media.

— Whom the Gods Love. 400p. 1996. pap. 6.99 (*0-14-024767-X*, Penguin Bks) Viking Penguin.

Ross, Katharine. Baby Animals' Party. (J). 1997. 0.05 (*0-679-88360-6*, Pub. by Random Bks Yng Read) Random.

— Bunnies' Ball. LC 92-29930. (Pictureback Ser.). (Illus.). (J). 1994. pap. 3.25 (*0-679-83503-2*, Pub. by Random Bks Yng Read) Random.

— Cozy in the Woods. LC 96-45401. (J). 1997. lib. bdg. 9.99 (*0-679-98538-7*, Pub. by Random Bks Yng Read) Random.

— Cozy in the Woods. LC 96-45401. (Illus.). 32p. 1997. 7.99 (*0-679-88538-2*, Pub. by Random Bks Yng Read) Random.

— Fuzzy Kitten. LC 92-62262. (Fuzzy Chunkies Ser.). (Illus.). 22p. (J). (ps-3). 1993. 3.99 (*0-679-84644-1*, Pub. by Random Bks Yng Read) Random.

— Grover, Grover, Come on Over. LC 90-33947. (Step into Reading Ser.: A Step 1 Book). (Illus.). 32p. (J). (ps-1). 1991. pap. 3.99 (*0-679-81117-6*, Pub. by Random Bks Yng Read) Random.

— The Little Ballerina. LC 92-42093. (J). 1996. pap. 3.25 (*0-679-84915-7*, Pub. by Random Bks Yng Read) Random.

— The Little Pumpkin Book. LC 91-67669. (Chunky Shape Bks.). (Illus.). 22p. (J). (ps). 1992. 3.99 (*0-679-83384-6*, Pub. by Random Bks Yng Read) Random.

***Ross, Katharine.** The Little Pumpkin Book. (Jellybean Bks.). (Illus.). 24p. (J). (ps-k). 1999. 1.99 (*0-375-80106-5*, Pub. by Random Bks Yng Read); lib. bdg. 7.99 (*0-375-90106-X*, Pub. by Random Bks Yng Read) Random.

Ross, Katharine. The Little Quiet Book. LC 88-62101. (Chunky Bks. Ser.). (Illus.). 28p. (J). (ps). 1989. 3.99 (*0-394-82899-2*, Pub. by Random Bks Yng Read) Random.

— Open the Door, Little Dinosaur. LC 92-80950. (Lift-&-Peek-A-Board Bks.). (Illus.). 14p. (J). (ps). 1993. 3.99 (*0-679-83689-6*, Pub. by Random Bks Yng Read) Random.

— Story of the Pilgrims. LC 94-69556. (Illus.). 24p. (J). (ps-1). 1995. pap. 3.25 (*0-679-85292-1*) Random.

***Ross, Katharine.** Sweetie & Petie. (Jellybean Bks.). (Illus.). 24p. (J). (ps-k). 1999. lib. bdg. 7.99 (*0-375-90143-4*, Pub. by Random Bks Yng Read) Random.

Ross, Katharine. Sweetie & Petie. (Jellybean Bks.). (Illus.). 24p. (J). (ps-1). 1999. 2.99 (*0-375-80143-X*, Pub. by Random Bks Yng Read) Random.

— Twinkle, Twinkle, Little Bug. LC 94-48341. (Step into Reading Ser.: A Step 1 Book). (Illus.). 32p. (J). (ps-4). 1996. pap. 3.99 (*0-679-87666-9*) Random.

— Twinkle, Twinkle, Little Bug. LC 94-48341. (Step into Reading Ser.: A Step 1 Book). (Illus.). (J). (ps-3). 1996. lib. bdg. 11.99 (*0-679-97666-3*) Random.

Ross, Katharine. Twinkle, Twinkle, Little Bug. (Step into Reading Ser.: A Step 1 Book). (J). (ps-1). 1996. 9.19 (*0-606-10003-2*, Pub. by Turtleback) Demco.

Ross, Katherine. The Fuzzytail Friends' Great Egg Hunt. LC 87-50812. (Peek-a-Boo Board Bks.). (Illus.). 14p. (J). (ps). 1988. 4.99 (*0-394-89475-8*, Pub. by Random Bks Yng Read) Random.

Ross, Katherine. Story of the Pilgrims. 1995. 8.45 (*0-606-08621-8*, Pub. by Turtleback) Demco.

Ross, Katherine. The Wide-Awake Bunnies. (J). 1999. 1.99 (*0-679-89209-5*, Pub. by Random Bks Yng Read) Random.

Ross, Kathleen. The Baroque Narrative of Carlos de Siguenza y Gongora: A New World Paradise. (Studies in Latin American & Iberian Literature: No. 8). 230p. (C). 1994. text 59.95 (*0-521-45113-2*) Cambridge U Pr.

Ross, Kathleen, jt. ed. see Miller, Yvette E.

Ross, Kathleen, tr. see Dalton, Roque.

Ross, Kathleen, tr. see Vallejo, Cesar.

Ross, Kathleen S. Free to Be Fit: The Ten Minute Morning Fitness Program for Flexibility & Tone. (Illus.). 1998. pap. 39.95 (*1-891875-08-6*, FIT 100) Creat Hlth Wrks.

Ross, Kathryn. Una Amante Esposa (A Devoted Wife) (SPA.). 1999. mass mkt. 3.50 (*0-373-33493-1*, 1-33493-7) Harlequin Bks.

— Bride for a Year: The Big Event! (Presents Ser.: Vol. 1981). 1998. per. 3.75 (*0-373-11981-X*, 1-11981-7) Harlequin Bks.

— Dans les Bras d'Un Ennemi. (Azur Ser.: Vol. 756). (FRE.). 1999. mass mkt. 3.50 (*0-373-34756-1*, 1-34756-6) Harlequin Bks.

— Designed with Love. large type ed. (Magna Large Print Ser.). 278p. 1996. 27.99 (*0-7505-1061-7*, Pub. by Mgna Lrg Print) Ulverscroft.

— Divided by Love. large type ed. 1994. 19.95 (*0-263-13933-6*) Thorndike Pr.

— Etiquete sur un Don Juan. (Azur Ser.: Vol. 703). 1998. mass mkt. 3.50 (*0-373-34703-0*, 1-34703-8) Harlequin Bks.

— Le Femme Trompee. (Azur Ser.). (FRE.). 1994. pap. 3.50 (*0-373-34437-6*, 1-34437-3) Harlequin Bks.

— The Love-Child. (Presents Ser.: No. 1938). 1998. per. 3.75 (*0-373-11938-0*, 1-11938-7) Harlequin Bks.

***Ross, Kathryn.** Matrimonio de Papel.Tr. of Marriage on Paper. (ENG & SPA.). 2000. per. 3.50 (*0-373-33541-5*) Harlequin Bks.

Ross, Kathryn. Un Padre Inesperado (The Unexpected Father) (Bianca Ser.). (SPA.). 1998. per. 3.50 (*0-373-33444-3*, 1-33444-0) Harlequin Bks.

— Playing by the Rules. large type ed. 1996. 11.50 (*0-7505-0855-8*, Pub. by Mgna Lrg Print) Ulverscroft.

— Une Rencontre Providentielle. (Azur Ser.). (FRE.). 1997. pap. 3.50 (*0-373-34657-3*, 1-34657-6) Harlequin Bks.

— Ruthless Contract. large type ed. 288p. 1996. 23.99 (*0-263-14388-0*, Pub. by Mills & Boon) Ulverscroft.

— Ruthless Contract (Wedlocked!) LC 96-2345. 186p. 1996. per. 3.50 (*0-373-11807-4*, 1-11807-4) Harlequin Bks.

— The Unexpected Father. large type ed. (Mills & Boon Large Print Ser.). 288p. 1997. 23.99 (*0-263-15047-X*) Ulverscroft.

***Ross, Kathryn.** The Unexpected Father: Expecting! 1999. per. 3.75 (*0-373-12022-2*, 1-12022-9, Harlequin) Harlequin Bks.

— The Unmarried Father: His Baby. (Presents Ser.). 2000. mass mkt. 3.99 (*0-373-12125-3*, 1-12125-0) Harlequin Bks.

Ross, Kathryn. Whisper of Scandal. (Presents Ser.: No. 1898). 1997. per. 3.50 (*0-373-11898-8*, 1-11898-3) Harlequin Bks.

— Whisper of Scandal. large type ed. 1995. 23.99 (*0-263-14129-2*, Pub. by Mills & Boon) Ulverscroft.

Ross, Kathy. The Best Holiday Crafts Ever! LC 96-14297. (Illus.). 176p. (J). (gr. k-3). 1997. spiral bd. 18.95 (*0-7613-0071-6*) Millbrook Pr.

***Ross, Kathy.** Christmas Decorations Kids Can Make. LC 99-11938. 1999. 23.40 (*0-7613-1565-9*) Millbrook Pr.

Ross, Kathy. Christmas Decorations Kids Can Make. LC 99-11938. (Books for the Holidays Ser.). (Illus.). 64p. (J). (gr. k-3). 1999. pap. 8.95 (*0-7613-1275-7*, Copper Beech Bks) Millbrook Pr.

— Christmas Ornaments Kids Can Make. LC 97-41170. (Illus.). 64p. (J). (ps-6). 1998. 23.40 (*0-7613-0366-9*, Copper Beech Bks); pap. 8.95 (*0-7613-0337-5*, Copper Beech Bks) Millbrook Pr.

— Crafts for Christmas. LC 94-48304. (Holiday Crafts for Kids Ser.). (Illus.). 48p. (J). (gr. k-3). 1995. pap. 6.95 (*1-56294-681-1*); lib. bdg. 21.90 (*1-56294-536-X*) Millbrook Pr.

— Crafts for Christmas. (Holiday Crafts for Kids Ser.). 1995. 12.15 (*0-606-07394-9*, Pub. by Turtleback) Demco.

— Crafts for Easter. (Holiday Crafts for Kids Ser.). (Illus.). 48p. (J). (gr. k-3). 1996. pap. 6.95 (*1-56294-268-9*); lib. bdg. 21.90 (*1-56294-918-7*) Millbrook Pr.

— Crafts for Halloween. LC 93-37249. (Holiday Crafts for Kids Ser.). (Illus.). 48p. (J). (gr. k-3). 1994. pap. 6.95 (*1-56294-741-9*); lib. bdg. 21.90 (*1-56294-411-8*) Millbrook Pr.

— Crafts for Halloween. (Holiday Crafts for Kids Ser.). 1994. 12.15 (*0-606-07395-7*, Pub. by Turtleback) Demco.

— Crafts for Hanukkah. LC 95-25800. (Holiday Crafts for Kids Ser.). (Illus.). 48p. (J). (gr. k-3). 1996. pap. 6.95 (*0-7613-0078-3*); lib. bdg. 21.90 (*1-56294-919-5*) Millbrook Pr.

— Crafts for Kids Who Are Wild about Deserts. LC 97-47093. (Illus.). 48p. (J). (gr. 3-6). 1998. lib. bdg. 22.40 (*0-7613-0954-3*) Millbrook Pr.

— Crafts for Kids Who Are Wild about Dinosaurs. (Crafts for Kids Who Are Wild about Ser.). (Illus.). 48p. (J). (gr. 3-6). 1997. pap. 7.95 (*0-7613-0177-1*); lib. bdg. 22.40 (*0-7613-0053-8*) Millbrook Pr.

— Crafts for Kids Who Are Wild about Insects. LC

R

96-35801. (Crafts for Kids Who Are Wild about Ser.). (Illus.). 48p. (J). (gr. 3-6). 1997. pap. 7.95 (0-7613-0276-X); lib. bdg. 22.40 (0-7613-0116-X) Millbrook Pr.

— Crafts for Kids Who Are Wild about Oceans. (Crafts for Kids Who Are Wild about Ser.). (Illus.). 48p. (J). (gr. 3-6). 1998. pap. 7.95 (0-7613-0331-6); lib. bdg. 22.40 (0-7613-0262-X) Millbrook Pr.

— Crafts for Kids Who Are Wild about Outer Space. (Crafts for Kids Who Are Wild about Ser.). (Illus.). 48p. (J). (gr. 3-6). 1997. pap. 7.95 (0-7613-0176-3); lib. bdg. 22.40 (0-7613-0054-6) Millbrook Pr.

— Crafts for Kids Who Are Wild about Polar Life. LC 98-4580. (Crafts for Kids Who Are Wild about . . . Ser.). (Illus.). (J). 1998. lib. bdg. 22.40 (0-7613-0955-1) Millbrook Pr.

— Crafts for Kids Who Are Wild about Rainforests. LC 96-35802. (Crafts for Kids Who Are Wild about Ser.). (Illus.). 48p. (J). (gr. 3-6). 1997. pap. 7.95 (0-7613-0277-8); lib. bdg. 22.40 (0-7613-0117-8) Millbrook Pr.

— Crafts for Kids Who Are Wild about Reptiles. LC 97-27961. (Crafts for Kids Who Are Wild about Ser.). (Illus.). 48p. (J). (gr. 3-6). 1998. lib. bdg. 22.40 (0-7613-0263-8) Millbrook Pr.

— Crafts for Kids Who Are Wild about Reptiles. LC 97-27961. (Crafts for Kids Who Are Wild about Ser.). (Illus.). 48p. (J). (gr. 3-6). 1998. pap. 7.95 (0-7613-0332-4) Millbrook Pr.

— Crafts for Kids Who Are Wild about the Wild. LC 98-17334. (Illus.). 172p. (J). (gr. 3-6). 1998. 18.95 (0-7613-0440-1) Millbrook Pr.

— Crafts for Kwanzaa. LC 93-36690. (Holiday Crafts for Kids Ser.). (Illus.). 48p. (J). (gr. k-3). 1994. pap. 6.95 (1-56294-740-0); lib. bdg. 21.90 (1-56294-412-6) Millbrook Pr.

— Crafts for Kwanzaa. (Holiday Crafts for Kids Ser.). (J). 1994. 12.15 (0-606-07396-5, Pub. by Turtleback) Demco.

— Crafts for St. Patrick's Day. (Holiday Crafts for Kids Ser.). 48p. (J). (gr. k-3). 1999. pap. 6.95 (0-7613-0447-9, Copper Beech Bks) Millbrook Pr.

— Crafts for St. Patrick's Day. LC 98-8022. (Holiday Crafts for Kids Ser.). (Illus.). 48p. (J). (gr. k-3). 1999. lib. bdg. 21.90 (0-7613-1306-0, Copper Beech Bks) Millbrook Pr.

— Crafts for Thanksgiving. LC 94-48301. (Holiday Crafts for Kids Ser.). (Illus.). 48p. (J). (gr. k-3). 1995. pap. 6.95 (1-56294-682-X); lib. bdg. 21.90 (1-56294-535-1) Millbrook Pr.

— Crafts for Thanksgiving. (Holiday Crafts for Kids Ser.). (J). 1995. 12.15 (0-606-07397-3, Pub. by Turtleback) Demco.

— Crafts for Valentine's Day. LC 94-9834. (Holiday Crafts for Kids Ser.). (Illus.). 48p. (J). (gr. k-3). 1995. lib. bdg. 21.90 (1-56294-489-4) Millbrook Pr.

— Crafts for Valentine's Day. LC 94-9834. (Holiday Crafts for Kids Ser.). (Illus.). 48p. (J). (gr. k-3). 1995. pap. 6.95 (1-56294-887-3) Millbrook Pr.

— Crafts for Valentine's Day. (Holiday Crafts for Kids Ser.). (J). 1995. 12.15 (0-606-07398-1, Pub. by Turtleback) Demco.

***Ross, Kathy.** Crafts from Your Favorite Bible Stories. LC 99-26864. (Christian Crafts Ser.). (Illus.). 64p. (J). (gr. k-3). 2000. 24.90 (0-7613-1619-1) Millbrook Pr.

— Crafts from Your Favorite Children's Songs. LC 00-21228. (Illus.). (J). 2001. lib. bdg. write for info. (0-7613-1912-3) Millbrook Pr.

Ross, Kathy. Crafts from Your Favorite Fairy Tales. LC 96-48517. (Illus.). 64p. (J). (gr. k-3). 1997. lib. bdg. 22.40 (0-7613-0259-X) Millbrook Pr.

— Crafts from Your Favorite Fairy Tales. (Illus.). 48p. (J). 1998. pap. text 8.95 (0-7613-0342-1) Millbrook Pr.

— Crafts to Make in the Fall. LC 97-40184. (Crafts for All Seasons Ser.). (Illus.). 64p. (J). (gr. k). 1998. pap. 8.95 (0-7613-0335-9) Millbrook Pr.

— Crafts to Make in the Fall. LC 97-40184. (Crafts for All Seasons Ser.). (Illus.). 64p. (J). (gr. k-3). 1998. lib. bdg. 23.40 (0-7613-0318-9) Millbrook Pr.

— Crafts to Make in the Spring. LC 97-24644. (Crafts for All Seasons Ser.). (Illus.). 64p. (J). (gr. k-4). 1998. pap. 8.95 (0-7613-0333-2); lib. bdg. 23.40 (0-7613-0316-2) Millbrook Pr.

— Crafts to Make in the Summer. LC 97-25455. (Crafts for All Seasons Ser.). (Illus.). 64p. (J). (gr. k-3). 1999. 23.40 (0-7613-0317-0, Copper Beech Bks) Millbrook Pr.

— Crafts to Make in the Summer. LC 97-25455. (Crafts for All Seasons Ser.). (Illus.). 63p. (J). (gr. k-3). 1999. pap. 8.95 (0-7613-0334-0, Copper Beech Bks) Millbrook Pr.

***Ross, Kathy.** Crafts to Make in the Winter. LC 98-43573. (Crafts for All Seasons Ser.). (Illus.). 64p. (J). (gr. k-3). 1999. pap. 8.95 (0-7613-0336-7, Copper Beech Bks); lib. bdg. 23.40 (0-7613-0319-7, Copper Beech Bks) Millbrook Pr.

Ross, Kathy. Daddy & Me Craft Book. 1999. write for info. (0-7613-1419-9, Copper Beech Bks); pap. write for info. (0-7613-0995-0, Copper Beech Bks) Millbrook Pr.

— Every Day Is Earth Day: A Craft Book. (Holiday Crafts for Kids Ser.). (Illus.). 48p. (J). (gr. k-3). 1995. pap. 5.95 (1-56294-888-1) Millbrook Pr.

— Everyday Is Earth Day: A Craft Book. LC 94-9835. (Holiday Crafts for Kids Ser.). (Illus.). 48p. (J). (gr. k-3). 1995. lib. bdg. 21.90 (1-56294-490-8) Millbrook Pr.

— Gifts to Make for Your Favourite Grownup. LC 95-50294. (Illus.). 64p. (J). (ps-3). 1996. lib. bdg. 24.90 (1-56294-274-3); spiral bd. 12.95 (0-7613-0079-1) Millbrook Pr.

Ross, Kathy. Insects. (Illus.). (J). 1997. 14.40 (0-606-18283-7) Turtleback.

Ross, Kathy. The Jewish Holiday Craft Book. LC 96-31002. (Illus.). 96p. (J). (gr. k-3). 1997. pap. 12.95 (0-7613-0175-5); lib. bdg. 25.90 (0-7613-0055-4) Millbrook Pr.

— Kid's Do-it-Yourself Guide to the Best Birthday Parties. LC 98-27503. (Illus.). 78p. (J). (gr. 2-5). 1999. lib. bdg. 23.90 (0-7613-1410-5, Copper Beech Bks) Millbrook Pr.

— Kid's Do-It-Yourself Guide to the Best Birthday Parties. LC 98-27503. (Illus.). 80p. (J). (gr. 3-6). 1999. pap. 9.95 (0-7613-0989-6, Copper Beech Bks) Millbrook Pr.

— Make Yourself a Monster: Aliens. LC 98-50751. (Books for Halloween & Thanksgiving Ser.). (Illus.). 48p. (J). (gr. k-3). 1999. pap. 6.95 (0-7613-1049-5, Copper Beech Bks) Millbrook Pr.

— Mommy & Me Craft Book. 1999. write for info. (0-7613-1418-0, Copper Beech Bks); pap. write for info. (0-7613-0994-2, Copper Beech Bks) Millbrook Pr.

***Ross, Kathy.** More Christmas Ornaments Kids Can Make. LC 00-20376. (Illus.). (J). 2000. lib. bdg. 8.95 (0-7613-1396-6) Millbrook Pr.

— Oceans. (Illus.). (J). 1998. 14.40 (0-606-18284-5) Turtleback.

— Rainforests. (Illus.). (J). 1997. 14.40 (0-606-18285-3) Turtleback.

***Ross, Kathy & Connelly, Gwen.** Crafts from Your Favorite Bible Stories LC 99-26864. (Christian Crafts Ser.). 2000. 7.95 (0-7613-1295-1) Millbrook Pr.

***Ross, Kathy & Enright, Vicky.** Crafts for All Seasons. LC 99-52760. (Illus.). (YA). 2000. 19.95 (0-7613-1346-X) Millbrook Pr.

***Ross, Kathy & Holm, Sharon Lane.** Crafts for Christian Values. LC 00-21805. 2000. pap. 7.95 (0-7613-1284-6) Millbrook Pr.

Ross, Keith W., jt. auth. see Kurose, James F.

***Ross, Ken.** Environmental Conflict in Alaska. (Illus.). 424p. 2001. 59.95 (0-87081-588-1); pap. 29.95 (0-87081-589-X) Univ Pr Colo.

Ross, Kenneth A. International Conference on Harmonic Analysis. LC 97-31839. (Trends in Mathematics Ser.). 1997. write for info. (3-7643-3943-8) Birkhauser.

Ross, Kenneth A., jt. auth. see Lopez, Jorge M.

Ross, Kenneth G. & Matthews, Robert W., eds. The Social Biology of Wasps. LC 90-44178. (Illus.). 688p. 1991. text 87.50 (0-8014-2035-0); pap. text 39.95 (0-8014-9906-2) Cornell U Pr.

Ross, Kenneth R. Church & Creed in Scotland: The Free Church Case 1900-1904 & Its Origins. LC 92-5153. (Rutherford Studies in Historical Theology). 424p. 1992. reprint ed. lib. bdg. 109.95 (0-7734-1647-1) E Mellen.

— Gospel Ferment in Malawi: Theological Essays. 152p. 1996. pap. 44.95 (0-86922-615-0, U Pr W Africa) Intl Scholars.

Ross, Kenneth R., ed. Christianity in Malawi: A Source Book. 256p. 1996. pap. 49.95 (0-86922-641-X, U Pr W Africa) Intl Scholars.

— Church, University & Theological Education in Malawi: A Model for Third World Theological Education. 84p. 1996. pap. 24.95 (99908-43-00-7, U Pr W Africa) Intl Scholars.

— God People & Power in Malawi: Democratization in Theological Perspective. LC 97-980928. 272p. 1997. pap. 54.95 (99908-16-04-2, U Pr W Africa) Intl Scholars.

Ross, Kenneth R., jt. auth. see Nzunda, Matembo S.

Ross, Kenneth R., ed. see Phiri, Kings M.

Ross, Kent. Copper Lady. (Illus.). 48p. 1996. pap. 5.95 (0-87614-960-3, Carolrhoda) Lerner Pub.

Ross, Kent & Ross, Alice. Cemetery Quilt. LC 94-17617. (Illus.). 32p. (J). (gr. k-3). 1995. 14.95 (0-395-70948-2) HM.

— Jezebel's Spooky Spot. LC 97-32707. (Illus.). (J). (gr. 1-4). 1999. 15.99 (0-525-45448-9, Dutton Child) Peng Put Young Read.

Ross, Kent, jt. auth. see Ross, Alice.

Ross, Kenton E. & Hanson. Four Seasons, Inc. Business Simulation. 5th ed. (BE-Accounting Advanced Ser.). 1992. 19.95 (0-538-61031-X) S-W Pub.

— Galleria, Inc. Business Simulation Narrative. 5th ed. (BE-Accounting Advanced Ser.). 1992. 19.95 (0-538-61030-1) S-W Pub.

Ross, Kenton E. & Swanson. Century 21 Accounting Advanced Course. 4th ed. (BA - Accounting - First Year Ser.). 1987. pap., wbk. ed. 15.95 (0-538-02477-1) S-W Pub.

— Century 21 Accounting Advanced Course. 4th ed. (BE - Accounting Advanced Ser.). 1988. 91.95 (0-538-63240-2); 91.95 (0-538-63241-0) S-W Pub.

— Century 21 Accounting, 1st Year Course. 5th ed. (BA - Accounting - First Year Ser.). 1991. pap. 244.95 (0-538-60602-9) S-W Pub.

— Century 21 Accounting, 1st Year Course - Working Papers. 5th ed. (BA - Accounting - First Year Ser.). 1991. mass mkt., student ed. 23.95 (0-538-60604-5) S-W Pub.

— Century 21 Accounting, 1st Year Course, Chapters 1-19 - Working Papers. 5th ed. (BA - Accounting - First Year Ser.). 1991. mass mkt. 16.95 (0-538-60623-1) S-W Pub.

— Century 21 Accounting, 1st Year Chapter Problems. 6th ed. (BA - Accounting - First Year Ser.). 1994. pap. 4.95 (0-538-62979-7) S-W Pub.

— Century 21 Accounting, 1st Year Objective Tests. 6th ed. (BA - Accounting - First Year Ser.). 1995. pap. 4.95 (0-538-62980-0) S-W Pub.

— Century 21 Accounting, 1st Year. 5th ed. (BA - Accounting - First Year Ser.). 1991. pap. 48.95 (0-538-60600-2) S-W Pub.

— Century 21 Accounting Special Journals, Tests of Demo & Recovery. 5th ed. (BA - Accounting - First Year Ser.). 1992. 27.00 (0-538-61310-6) S-W Pub.

— Century 21 Accounting, 1st year Unit Problem Tests. 6th ed. (BA - Accounting - First Year Ser.). 1994. pap. 4.95 (0-538-62981-9) S-W Pub.

Ross, Kenton E. & Swanson, Robert M. Century 21 Accounting, Advanced Course. 4th ed. (BE - Accounting Advanced Ser.). 1987. pap., wbk. ed. 24.95 (0-538-02471-2) S-W Pub.

— Century 21 Accounting, Advanced Course, Ch. 1-12. 4th ed. (BA - Accounting - First Year Ser.). 1987. pap., student ed. 15.95 (0-538-02476-3) S-W Pub.

— Century 21 Accounting, Emphasizing Special Journals. 4th ed. (BA - Accounting - First Year Ser.). 1986. 3.95 (0-538-02463-1); 4.95 (0-538-02464-X) S-W Pub.

— Century 21 Accounting, 1st Year Course. 4th ed. (BA - Accounting - First Year Ser.). 1987. 96.95 (0-538-63216-X) S-W Pub.

— Century 21 Accounting, 1st Year Course. 6th ed. (BA - Accounting - First Year Ser.). 1994. 166.95 (0-538-63723-4) S-W Pub.

— Century 21 Accounting 1st Year Objectives. 4th ed. (BA - Accounting - First Year Ser.). 1986. 2.95 (0-538-02413-5) S-W Pub.

— Century 21 Accounting 1st Year Problems. 4th ed. (BA - Accounting - First Year Ser.). 1986. 3.95 (0-538-02412-7) S-W Pub.

— Century 21 Accounting, 2nd Year. 4th ed. (BE - Accounting Advanced Ser.). 1987. pap. 48.95 (0-538-02470-4) S-W Pub.

— Demo Recovery Problems: Century 21 Accounting 1st Year. 5th ed. (BA - Accounting - First Year Ser.). 1991. mass mkt., suppl. ed. 12.95 (0-538-61301-7) S-W Pub.

— Fundamentals of Accounting. 5th ed. (BA - Accounting - First Year Ser.). (C). 1991. mass mkt. 32.50 (0-538-70227-3) S-W Pub.

— Fundamentals of Accounting - Adult & Cont Edition. 6th ed. (BA - Accounting - First Year Ser.). (C). 1994. pap. 51.95 (0-538-71193-0) S-W Pub.

— Fundamentals of Accounting - Adult & Continuing Edition. 6th ed. (BE - Accounting Advanced Ser.). (C). 1994. pap. 46.95 (0-538-71197-3) S-W Pub.

— Fundamentals of Accounting - Working Papers & Study Guide. 5th ed. (BA - Accounting - First Year Ser.). (C). 1991. mass mkt. 17.00 (0-538-70228-1) S-W Pub.

— Fundamentals of Accounting - Working Papers & Study Guide. 6th ed. (BA - Accounting - First Year Ser.). (C). 1994. pap. 17.00 (0-538-71196-5) S-W Pub.

— Fundamentals of Accounting Advanced Working Papers & Study Guide. 6th ed. (BE - Accounting Advanced Ser.). (C). 1994. pap. 17.00 (0-538-71200-7) S-W Pub.

— Stellar Attractions: Simplified Pegboard Payroll. 5th ed. (BA - Accounting - First Year Ser.). 1992. 26.95 (0-538-60647-9) S-W Pub.

— Viking Marine, Special Journals, Simulation. 5th ed. (BA - Accounting - First Year Ser.). 1991. pap. 15.95 (0-538-61277-0) S-W Pub.

— Western Rider, Simplified with Narrative: Century 21, First Year. 5th ed. (BA - Accounting - First Year Ser.). 1996. 19.95 (0-538-60637-1) S-W Pub.

Ross, Kenton E., et al. Accounting. 6th ed. (Accounting - First Year). 1994. pap. 15.95 (0-538-63010-8) S-W Pub.

— Century 21 Accounting: Advanced Course. 5th ed. (BE - Accounting Advanced Ser.). 1992. pap. 46.95 (0-538-61025-5) S-W Pub.

— Century 21 Accounting Advanced Course Objectives. 4th ed. (BA - Accounting - First Year Ser.). 1987. 4.95 (0-538-02474-7) S-W Pub.

— Century 21 Accounting, Advanced. 5th ed. (BE - Accounting Advanced Ser.). 1992. 4.95 (0-538-61028-X); 4.95 (0-538-61029-8) S-W Pub.

— Century 21 Accounting Advanced Mac. 5th ed. (BE - Accounting Advanced Ser.). 1993. 96.95 (0-538-63164-3) S-W Pub.

— Century 21 Accounting Advanced Course IBM. 5th ed. (BE - Accounting Advanced Ser.). 1993. 96.95 (0-538-63165-1) S-W Pub.

— Century 21 Accounting Advanced - Working Papers. 5th ed. (BE - Accounting Advanced Ser.). 1992. mass mkt. 19.95 (0-538-61032-8); mass mkt. 19.95 (0-538-61033-6) S-W Pub.

— Century 21 Accounting Advanced Course. 6th ed. (BE - Advanced Accounting Ser.). 1994. pap. 54.95 (0-538-63174-0) S-W Pub.

— Century 21 Accounting Advanced Course. 6th ed. (BE - Accounting Advanced Ser.). 1995. 96.95 (0-538-63207-0); 96.95 (0-538-63209-7) S-W Pub.

— Century 21 Accounting Advanced, Chapters 1-24 - Working Papers. 6th ed. (BE - Accounting Advanced Ser.). 1994. pap., wbk. ed. 17.95 (0-538-63185-6); pap., wbk. ed. 17.25 (0-538-63184-8) S-W Pub.

— Century 21 Accounting Advanced Course - Problem Tests. 6th ed. (BE - Accounting Advanced Ser.). 1995. 4.95 (0-538-63193-7) S-W Pub.

— Century 21 Accounting Advanced Course Objective Test. 6th ed. (BE - Accounting Advanced Ser.). 1995. 4.95 (0-538-63194-5) S-W Pub.

— Century 21 Accounting Advanced Course Galleria Temp. 6th ed. (BE - Accounting Advanced Ser.). 1995. 91.95 (0-538-63204-6) S-W Pub.

— Century 21 Accounting Advanced Course - Four Seasons. 6th ed. (BE - Accounting Advanced Ser.). 1995. 91.95 (0-538-63205-4); 96.95 (0-538-63208-9) S-W Pub.

— Century 21 Accounting Advanced Course - Electronic Auditor. 6th ed. (BE - Accounting Advanced Ser.). 76.95 (0-538-63212-7) S-W Pub.

— Century 21 Accounting Advanced Course - Electronic Auditor. 6th ed. (BE - Accounting Advanced Ser.). 1995. 76.95 (0-538-63213-5) S-W Pub.

— Century 21 Accounting Advanced Course, Ch. 12-24. 6th ed. (BE - Accounting Advanced Ser.). 1994. pap., wbk. ed. 17.95 (0-538-63186-4) S-W Pub.

Ross, kenton E., et al. Century 21 Accounting, Chapters 1-19 - Working Papers. 6th ed. (BA - Accounting - First Year Ser.). 1994. pap. 15.95 (0-538-63009-4) S-W Pub.

Ross, Kenton E., et al. Century 21 Accounting, Chapters 1-26 - Working Papers, Advanced, Ch. 1-26. 5th ed. (BE - Accounting Advanced Ser.). 1992. pap., wbk. ed. 23.95 (0-538-61026-3) S-W Pub.

— Century 21 Accounting, Chapters 11-18 - Working Papers, Mod. 2. 6th ed. (BA - Accounting - First Year Ser.). 1994. mass mkt. 12.95 (0-538-62964-9) S-W Pub.

— Century 21 Accounting, 1st Year Introductory Course Text. 6th ed. (BA - Accounting - First Year Ser.). 1994. pap. 43.95 (0-538-62955-X) S-W Pub.

— Century 21 Accounting, 1st Year Course, Chapters 1-28 - Working Papers. 6th ed. (BA - Accounting - First Year Ser.). 1994. pap., wbk. ed. 19.25 (0-538-62959-2) S-W Pub.

— Century 21 Accounting, 1st Year - Module 1 Chapters 1-10. 6th ed. (BA - Accounting - First Year Ser.). (Illus.). 1994. mass mkt. 31.95 (0-538-62956-8) S-W Pub.

— Century 21 Accounting, 1st Year - Module 2 Textbook C. 6th ed. (BA - Accounting - First Year Ser.). 1994. mass mkt. 31.95 (0-538-62957-6) S-W Pub.

— Century 21 Accounting, 1st Year, Module 3 Textbook C. 6th ed. (AB - Accounting - First Year Ser.). 1994. mass mkt. 31.95 (0-538-62958-4) S-W Pub.

— Century 21 Accounting, 1st Year Dictionary. 6th ed. (BA - Accounting - First Year Ser.). 1994. pap. 3.95 (0-538-62997-5) S-W Pub.

— Century 21 Accounting, 1st Year - Western Rider. 6th ed. (BA - Accounting - First Year Ser.). 1995. 48.95 (0-538-62988-6); 45.95 (0-538-62992-4) S-W Pub.

— Century 21 Accounting, 1st Year - Lotus/Works Temp. 6th ed. (BA - Accounting - First Year Ser.). 1995. 48.95 (0-538-63001-9); 45.95 (0-538-63002-7) S-W Pub.

— Century 21 Accounting, 1st Year Course, Chapters 1-18 - Working Papers. 6th ed. (BA - Accounting - First Year Ser.). 1994. pap. 11.75 (0-538-62960-6) S-W Pub.

— Century 21 Accounting, First Year Course, Chapters 1-28, Ch. 1-28. 6th ed. (BA - Accounting - First Year Ser.). 1994. pap. 54.95 (0-538-62952-5) S-W Pub.

— Century 21 Accounting 1st Year Course, Chapters 19-28 - Working Papers. 6th ed. (BA - Accounting - First Year Ser.). 1995. pap. 11.75 (0-538-62961-4) S-W Pub.

— Century 21 Accounting 1st Year Course, Chapters 1-28 - Working Papers. 6th ed. (BA - Accounting - First Year Ser.). 1994. pap. 24.95 (0-538-63008-6) S-W Pub.

— Century 21 Accounting 1st Year Course, Chapters 19-28 - Working Papers, Mod. 3. 6th ed. (BA - Accounting - First Year Ser.). 1994. mass mkt. 12.95 (0-538-62965-7) S-W Pub.

— Century 21 Accounting, Special Journalistic Approach. 6th ed. (BA - Accounting - First Year Ser.). 1995. 4.95 (0-538-63021-3) S-W Pub.

— Century 21 Accounting, Special Journalistic Approach, 1st Year Course. 6th ed. (BA - Accounting - First Year Ser.). 1994. pap. 54.95 (0-538-63005-1) S-W Pub.

— Century 21, 1st Year - Textbook Temp. 6th ed. (BA - Accounting - First Year Ser.). 1995. 48.95 (0-538-62989-4); 45.95 (0-538-62993-2) S-W Pub.

— Century 21 Accounting 1st Year - Viking Marine. 6th ed. (BA - Accounting - First Year Ser.). 1995. 48.95 (0-538-62987-8); 45.95 (0-538-62991-6) S-W Pub.

— Century 21 Accounting 1st Year Course - Working Papers, Mod. 1. 6th ed. (BA - Accounting - First Year Ser.). 1995. mass mkt. 12.95 (0-538-62963-0) S-W Pub.

— Century 21 Accounting 1st Year Course, Chapters 1-28, Demo/Recycling. 6th ed. (BA - Accounting - First Year Ser.). 1994. pap. 14.95 (0-538-63011-6); pap., wbk. ed. 14.95 (0-538-62962-2) S-W Pub.

— The Courtyard Practice Set, Narrative. 3rd ed. (Accounting - First Year Ser.). 1982. 11.95 (0-538-02313-9) S-W Pub.

— Four Seasons to Mac, Century 21 Accounting Advanced Course. 6th ed. (BE - Accounting Advanced Ser.). 1995. 93.95 (0-538-63199-6) S-W Pub.

— Galleria, Inc. Automated Business Simulation. 5th ed. (Accounting Advanced Ser.). 1992. 18.95 (0-538-61839-6) S-W Pub.

Ross, Kenton E., jt. auth. see Swanson, Robert M.

Ross, Kevin. CB Modification Secrets. (Illus.). 206p. (Orig.). 1996. pap., per. 21.95 (0-939780-25-9) CRB Res.

— Dead Reckonings. 1998. pap. text 12.95 (1-56882-123-9) Chaosium.

Ross, Kevin. The Dreaming Stone: Against the Crawling Chaos. (Call of Cthulhu Roleplaying Ser.). (Illus.). 64p. (C). 1997. pap. 11.95 (1-56882-101-8, 2368) Chaosium.

Ross, Kevin A. Escape from Innsmouth. 2nd ed. (Call of Cthulhu Roleplaying Ser.). (Illus.). 174p. 1997. pap. 22.95 (1-56882-115-8) Chaosium.

Ross, Kimberley L., jt. auth. see Degregorio, Paul S.

Ross-Kinister, Marilyn. Riding: Buying Your First Horse. 124p. 1995. pap. 35.00 (0-85131-625-5, Pub. by J A Allen) St Mut.

***Ross, Kirk B.** The Sky Men: Parachute Rifle Company's Story of the Battle & Jump Across the Rhine. (Illus.). 272p. 2000. 35.00 (0-7643-1172-7) Schiffer.

Ross, Kirsten. Pleasures of the Palettes. 1997. pap. 24.95 (1-885590-22-9) Golden West Pub.

— Pleasures of the Palettes II. (Illus.). 144p. 1998. pap. 24.95 (1-885590-34-2) Golden West Pub.

Ross, Kristin. The Emergence of Social Space: Rimbaud & the Paris Commune. LC 88-4205. (Theory & History of Literature Ser.: Vol. 60). xvi, 170p. 1989. pap. 15.95 (0-8166-1687-6) U of Minn Pr.

— Fast Cars, Clean Bodies: Decolonization & the Reordering of French Culture. LC 94-17815. (Illus.). 273p. 1994. 33.00 (0-262-18161-4) MIT Pr.

— Fast Cars, Clean Bodies: Decolonization & the Reordering of French Culture. (Illus.). 278p. 1996. reprint ed. pap. text 16.50 (0-262-68091-2) MIT Pr.

Ross, Kristin, tr. see Ranciere, Jacques.

An Asterisk (*) at the beginning of an entry indicates that the title is appearing for the first time.

Ross, L. Manning. Businessplan.Com: How to Write a Web-Woven Strategic Business Plan. LC 98-30821. 200p. 1998. pap. 19.95 (*1-55571-455-2*, BPDCP, Oasis Pr) PSI Resch.

Ross, Larry & Wood, Gloria, eds. Sales-Fax Travel Directory: Your Passport to Advertising Decision Makers. rev. ed. 200p. 1996. 950.00 (*0-9649670-1-4*) Ad-Fax Media.

Ross-Larson, Bruce. Edit Yourself: A Manual for Everyone Who Works with Words. LC 96-143484. 128p. 1996. pap. 11.95 (*0-393-31326-3*, Norton Paperbks) Norton.

— Effective Writing: Stunning Sentences, Powerful Paragraphs, & Riveting Reports. LC 99-29996. 384p. 1999. 29.95 (*0-393-04639-7*) Norton.

— Powerful Paragraphs. LC 98-35265. (Effective Writing Ser.). 107p. 1999. pap. 10.00 (*0-393-31794-3*) Norton.

— Riveting Reports. LC 98-30520. (Effective Writing Ser.). 79p. 1999. pap. 10.00 (*0-393-31793-5*) Norton.

— Stunning Sentences. LC 98-35262. (Effective Writing Ser.). 94p. 1999. pap. 10.00 (*0-393-31795-1*) Norton.

Ross, Laura. Hand Puppets: How to Make & Use Them. 192p. 1989. pap. 6.95 (*0-486-26161-1*) Dover.

Ross, Laura, ed. Theatre Profiles Vol. 7: The Illustrated Guide to America's Nonprofit Professional Theatre. 25th ed. (Illus.). 376p. 1986. pap. 18.95 (*0-930452-52-6*) Theatre Comm.

***Ross, Lawrence C., Jr.** The Divine Nine: The History of African-American Fraternities & Sororities in America. 2000. 30.00 (*1-57566-491-7*, Knsington) Kensgtn Pub Corp.

Ross, Lawrence J. On Measure for Measure: An Essay in Criticism of Shakespeare's Drama. LC 96-48852. (Illus.). 184p. 1997. 34.50 (*0-87413-593-1*) U Delaware Pr.

Ross, Lawrence J., ed. see Tourneur, Cyril.

Ross, Lawrence S. Personal Civil War Letters. Morrison, Shelly O., ed. Shelton, Perry W., tr. 130p. 1994. 29.50 (*0-926158-22-8*) W M Morrison.

Ross, Leah. Deadly Silence. 40p. (YA). 1998. pap. 5.00 (*1-57502-777-1*, PO2150) Morris Pubng.

Ross, Lee & Nisbett, Richard E. The Person & the Situation: Essential Contributions of Social Psychology. 192p. (C). 1991. pap. 39.69 (*0-07-053926-X*) McGraw.

— The Person & the Situation: Essential Contributions of Social Psychology. 192p. 1991. 49.95 (*0-87722-851-5*) Temple U Pr.

***Ross, Lee E.** African American Criminologists, 1970-1996: An Annotated Bibliography, Vol. 36. LC 97-52329. (Bibliographies & Indexes in Afro-American & African Studies: Vol. 36). 144p. 1998. lib. bdg. 59.95 (*0-313-30150-6*, Greenwood Pr) Greenwood.

Ross, Lena B., ed. To Speak or Be Silent: The Paradox of Disobedience in the Lives of Women. LC 92-45106. 262p. (Orig.). 1993. pap. 6.95 (*0-933029-68-3*) Chiron Pubns.

Ross, Lena B. & Roy, Manisha, eds. Cast the First Stone: Ethics in Analytic Practice. LC 94-40573. 168p. (Orig.). 1995. pap. 16.95 (*0-933029-89-6*) Chiron Pubns.

Ross, Leon T., jt. auth. see Mimms, Kenneth A.

Ross, Leonard Q. Education of Hyman Kaplan. LC 38-6588. 156p. 1968. reprint ed. pap. 9.00 (*0-15-627811-1*, Harvest Bks) Harcourt.

***Ross, Leone.** Orange Laughter. 240p. 2000. 23.00 (*0-374-22676-8*) FS&G.

Ross, Lesli K. Celebrate! The Complete Jewish Holidays Handbook. LC 94-1940. 376p. 1994. pap. 35.00 (*1-56821-154-6*) Aronson.

Ross, Leslie. Medieval Art: A Topical Dictionary. LC 96-160. 320p. 1996. lib. bdg. 79.50 (*0-313-29329-5*, Greenwood Pr) Greenwood.

— Text, Image, Message: Saints in Medieval Manuscript Illustrations, 3. LC 93-35869. (Contributions to the Study of Art & Architecture Ser.: No. 3). 280p. 1994. 65.00 (*0-313-29046-6*, Greenwood Pr) Greenwood.

Ross, Lester. Environmental Policy in China. LC 87-45587. 252p. 1988. 37.00 (*0-253-31837-8*) Ind U Pr.

Ross, Lester & Silk, Mitchell A. Environmental Law & Policy in the People's Republic of China. LC 86-22503. (Illus.). 465p. 1987. 99.50 (*0-89930-204-1*, SKV/, Quorum Bks) Greenwood.

Ross Lewis, Grace. 1,001 Chemicals in Everyday Products. (Illus.). 344p. 1993. pap. text 26.95 (*0-442-01458-9*, VNR) Wiley.

Ross, Lillian. The Little Old Man & His Dreams. LC 89-34511. (Charlotte Zolotow Bk.). (Illus.). 32p. (J). (gr. k-3). 1990. 14.95 (*0-06-025094-1*) HarpC Child Bks.

— Picture. LC 82-49210. (Cinema Classics Ser.). 264p. 1985. lib. bdg. 16.00 (*0-8240-5775-9*) Garland.

— Picture. LC 96-34440. 1997. 16.50 (*0-679-60254-2*) Modern Lib NY.

***Ross, Lillian.** Portrait of Hemingway. LC 99-26195. 1999. pap. 9.95 (*0-375-75438-5*) Modern Lib NY.

Ross, Lillian B. Blaze Allen. 281p. 1986. pap. 9.95 (*0-88496-241-5*) Coast Pub.

Ross, Lillian H. Buba Leah & Her Paper Children. (Illus.). 32p. (J). (gr. k-3). 1991. 15.95 (*0-8276-0375-4*) JPS Phila.

— Sarah, Also Known As Hannah. LC 93-29601. (Illus.). (J). (gr. 3-6). 1994. lib. bdg. 13.95 (*0-8075-7237-3*) A Whitman.

***Ross, Lillian Hammer.** Daughters of Eve: Strong Women of the Bible. (Illus.). 96p. (J). (gr. 3-7). 2000. 19.99 (*1-902283-82-1*) Barefoot Bks NY.

***Ross, Linda.** Big Book of Phonics Poems: 88 Playful Poems with Easy Lessons That Teach Consonants & Vowels. (Illus.). (J). 2000. pap. 12.95 (*0-439-16032-4*) Scholastic Inc.

Ross, Linda. Nurses' Perceptions of Spiritual Care. LC 97-70635. (Developments in Nursing & Health Care). (Illus.). 224p. (C). 1997. text 69.95 (*1-85972-618-6*, Pub. by Ashgate Pub) Ashgate Pub Co.

Ross, Linda M. Blood & Circulatory Disorders Sourcebook. LC 98-33704. (Health Reference Ser.). 554p. 1998. lib. bdg. 78.00 (*0-7808-0203-9*) Omnigraphics Inc.

Ross, Linda M., ed. Communication Disorders Sourcebook: Basic Information about Deafness & Hearing Loss, Speech, & Language Disorders, Voice Disorders, Balance, & Vestibular Disorders, & Disorders of Smell, Taste, & Touch. (Health Reference Ser.: Vol. 11). 1996. lib. bdg. 78.00 (*0-7808-0077-X*) Omnigraphics Inc.

— Ear, Nose & Throat Disorders Sourcebook. LC 98-29719. (Health Reference Ser.). 576p. 1997. lib. bdg. 78.00 (*0-7808-0206-3*) Omnigraphics Inc.

— Endocrine & Metabolism Diseases & Disorders Sourcebook. LC 98-6657. (Health Reference Ser.). 600p. 1998. lib. bdg. 78.00 (*0-7808-0207-1*) Omnigraphics Inc.

— Gastrointestinal Diseases & Disorders Sourcebook. LC 96-26198. (Health Reference Ser.: Vol. 16). 1996. lib. bdg. 78.00 (*0-7808-0078-8*) Omnigraphics Inc.

— Kidney & Urinary Tract Diseases & Disorders Sourcebook. LC 97-16533. (Health Reference Ser.: Vol. 21). 1997. lib. bdg. 78.00 (*0-7808-0079-6*) Omnigraphics Inc.

— Learning Disabilities Sourcebook. LC 97-52049. (Health Reference Ser.). 579p. 1998. lib. bdg. 78.00 (*0-7808-0210-1*) Omnigraphics Inc.

— Sexually Transmitted Diseases Sourcebook. LC 97-17036. (Health Reference Ser.: Vol. 26). 564p. 1997. 78.00 (*0-7808-0217-9*) Omnigraphics Inc.

***Ross, Lindsay & Ross, Barbara.** Anaesthetic & Sedative Techniques for Aquatic Animals. (Illus.). 174p. 1999. 34.95 (*0-632-05252-X*, Pub. by Blckwell Science) Iowa St U Pr.

— Anaesthetic & Sedative Techniques for Aquatic Animals. 160p. 1999. pap. text 34.95 (*0-8138-2130-4*, Pub. by Blckwell Science) Iowa St U Pr.

Ross, Lisette Lecat. Scent of the Roses. Date not set. pap. 5.95 (*0-8222-1774-0*) Dramatists Play.

Ross, Lissette L. Dark Sun. 1992. pap. 5.25 (*0-8222-0274-3*) Dramatists Play.

Ross, Lloyd. John Curtin: A Biography. 436p. 1996. pap. 24.95 (*0-522-84734-X*, Pub. by Melbourne Univ Pr) Paul & Co Pubs.

Ross, Louise, ed. Jane Austen: Novels, Letters & Memoirs, 19 vols., set. (Collected Works Ser.). 5918p. (C). (gr. 13). 1995. 1900.00 (*0-415-11562-0*, C0483) Routledge.

Ross, Louise G. Jane Austen: Family History, 5 vols., Set. (Illus.). 1566p. (C). (gr. 13 up). 1995. text, boxed set 745.00 (*0-415-13153-7*) Routledge.

Ross, Luana. Inventing the Savage: The Social Construction of Native American Criminality. LC 97-21014. (Illus.). 328p. (C). 1998. 35.00 (*0-292-77085-5*, ROSINV); pap. 17.95 (*0-292-77084-7*, ROSINP) U of Tex Pr.

Ross, Ludwig. Inselreisen. (Klassiker der Archaeologie in Neudrucken Ser.). (GER.). xxxvi, 350p. 1985. reprint ed. write for info. (*3-487-07668-3*) G Olms Pubs.

Ross, Lydia. Cycles: In Universe & Man. rev. ed. Small, W. Emmett & Todd, Helen, eds. (Theosophical Manual Ser.: No. 8). 92p. 1975. reprint ed. pap. 6.00 (*0-913004-19-7*) Point Loma Pub.

Ross, Lydia & Ryan, Charles J. Theosophia: An Introduction. 57p. 1974. pap. 5.00 (*0-913004-13-8*) Point Loma Pub.

Ross, Lynette C. A New Century. LC 99-212495. (Illus.). 32p. 1998. pap. 9.95 (*0-89672-392-5*) Tex Tech Univ Pr.

Ross, Lynn. Introduction to Radiologic Technology. 270p. (C). 1991. text, student ed. 35.00 (*1-880359-02-2*) Par Rad.

Ross, Lynn & Parelli, Robert J. Medical Sonography Clinical Manual. 3rd rev. ed. 210p. (C). 1998. 47.00 (*1-880359-17-0*) Par Rad.

Ross, Lynn C. Career Advancement for Women in the Federal Service: An Annotated Bibliography & Resource Book. LC 93-19100. (Public Affairs & Administration Ser.: Vol. 28). 280p. 1993. text 15.00 (*0-8153-1058-7*, SS867) Garland.

Ross, Lynne M., ed. State Attorneys General: Powers & Responsibilities. LC 89-71288. 471p. 1990. reprint ed. pap. 146.10 (*0-608-00707-2*, 206148000009) Bks Demand.

Ross, Lynne N. Metric Measurement in Food Preparation & Service. LC 78-61488. (Illus.). 73p. 1978. reprint ed. pap. 30.00 (*0-608-00084-1*, 206084700006) Bks Demand.

— Purchasing for Food Service: Self-Instruction. LC 84-81612. (Illus.). 165p. 1985. reprint ed. pap. 51.20 (*0-608-00070-1*, 206083600006) Bks Demand.

— Work Simplification in Food Service: Individualized Instruction. LC 73-171164. 134p. (Orig.). reprint ed. pap. 41.60 (*0-608-12980-1*, 202386500034) Bks Demand.

Ross, Lynne N., jt. auth. see Jernigan, Anna K.

Ross, M. Hotshots - Card Tricks. (Hotshots Ser.). (Illus.). 32p. (Orig.). (J). (gr. 2 up). 1997. pap. 2.95 (*0-7460-2791-5*, Usborne) EDC.

— Hotshots - Stars & Planets. (Hotshots Ser.). (Illus.). 32p. (Orig.). (J). (gr. 2-5). 1997. pap. 2.95 (*0-7460-2795-8*, Usborne) EDC.

Ross, M., ed. Assessment in Arts Education: A Necessary Discipline or a Loss of Happiness? LC 85-297210. (Curriculum Issues in Arts Education Ser.: Vol. 6). 200p. 1986. 105.00 (*0-08-033891-7*, Pub. by Pergamon Repr) Franklin.

Ross, M., et al, eds. Software Quality Management III Vol. 1: Quality Management. 496p. 1995. 190.00 (*1-85312-416-8*) Computational Mech MA.

— Software Quality Management III Vol. 2: Measuring & Maintaining Quality. 464p. 1995. 176.00 (*1-85312-417-6*) Computational Mech MA.

Ross, M., et al, eds. Software Quality Management II, 2 vols., Set. LC 94-70402. (SQM Ser.). 1592p. 1994. text 491.00 (*1-56252-188-8*, 2645) Computational Mech MA.

Ross, M., et al, eds. Software Quality Management II Vol. 1: Managing Quality Systems. 800p. 1994. 273.00 (*1-85312-352-8*) Computational Mech MA.

— Software Quality Management II Vol. 2: Building Quality into Software. 792p. 1994. 270.00 (*1-85312-353-6*) Computational Mech MA.

Ross, M. J. Polar Pioneers: John Ross & James Clark Ross. (Illus.). 464p. 1994. 32.95 (*0-7735-1234-9*, Pub. by McG-Queens Univ Pr) CUP Services.

Ross-MacDonald, Jane. Alternative Weddings. LC 97-6649. 192p. (Orig.). 1997. pap. 12.95 (*0-87833-977-9*) Taylor Pub.

Ross, Malcolm. The Aesthetic Imperative: Relevance & Responsibility in Arts Education. (Curriculum Issues in Arts Education Ser.: Vol. 2). 187p. 1981. 90.00 (*0-08-026766-1*, Pub. by Pergamon Repr) Franklin.

— Tomorrow's Tide. large type ed. 579p. write for info. (*0-7505-1066-8*, Pub. by Mgna Lrg Print) Ulverscroft.

Ross, Malcolm, et al. Assessing Achievement in the Arts. LC 92-31892. 192p. (C). 1993. 123.00 (*0-335-19062-6*); pap. 34.95 (*0-335-19061-8*) OpUniv Pr.

Ross, Malcolm, jt. ed. see Durie, Mark.

Ross, Mandy. Hotshots Creepy Crawlies. (Hotshots Ser.). (Illus.). 32p. (J). (gr. 2 up). 1996. pap. 2.95 (*0-7460-2551-3*, Usborne) EDC.

— Hotshots Joke Book, Vol. 1. (Hotshots Ser.). (Illus.). 32p. (J). (gr. 2-5). 1997. pap. 2.95 (*0-7460-2786-9*, Usborne) EDC.

— Hotshots Seashore. (Hotshots Ser.). (Illus.). 32p. (J). (gr. 2-5). 1996. pap. 2.95 (*0-7460-2555-6*, Usborne) EDC.

— Hotshots Trick Photography. (Hotshots Ser.). (Illus.). 32p. (J). (gr. 2 up). 1996. pap. 2.95 (*0-7460-2784-2*, Usborne) EDC.

Ross, Marc. Quantum Scattering Theory: Selected Papers. LC 63-16622. 313p. reprint ed. pap. 97.10 (*0-608-30602-9*, 205522700011) Bks Demand.

Ross, Marc H. The Culture of Conflict: Interpretations & Interests in Comparative Perspective. LC 92-41994. (Illus.). 164p. (C). 1993. 35.00 (*0-300-05273-1*) Yale U Pr.

— The Management of Conflict: Interpretations & Interests in Comparative Perspective. LC 92-47397. 232p. 1993. 32.50 (*0-300-05398-3*) Yale U Pr.

— Theory & Practice in Ethnic Conflict Management: Theorizing Success & Failure. LC 98-32035. (Ethnic & Inter-Community Conflict Ser.). 1999. text 72.00 (*0-312-22046-4*) St Martin.

Ross, Marc H., jt. ed. see Cobb, Roger W.

Ross, Marc Howard. Management of Conflict: Interpretations & Interests in Comparative Perspective. 1995. pap. 15.00 (*0-300-06517-5*) Yale U Pr.

Ross, Marcus, jt. auth. see Radcliffe, Duane.

Ross, Marcy, et al. How to Tame the Y2K Bug Before It Bites You. 27p. 1999. pap. 4.50 (*0-943973-21-X*) Good Advice Pr.

Ross, Margaret C. Prolonged Echoes Vol. 1: Old Norse Myths in Medieval Northern Society: The Myths. 325p. 1994. 37.00 (*87-7838-008-1*, Pub. by Odense Univ) Intl Spec Bk.

— Prolonged Echoes Vol. 2: Old Norse Myths in Medieval Northern Society: The Reception of Norse Myths in Medieval Island. 222p. 1998. 32.00 (*87-7838-332-3*, Pub. by Odense Univ) Intl Spec Bk.

***Ross, Margaret Clunies, ed.** Old Icelandic Literature & Society. (Cambridge Studies in Medieval Literature: Vol. 42). 340p. 2000. write for info. (*0-521-63112-2*) Cambridge U Pr.

Ross, Margery, ed. Robert Ross, Friend of Friends: Letters to Robert Ross, Art Critic & Writer. LC 79-8074. reprint ed. 34.50 (*0-404-18384-0*) AMS Pr.

Ross, Marilyn. The Amethyst Tears. large type ed. 1995. 27.99 (*0-7089-3297-5*) Ulverscroft.

***Ross, Marilyn.** Don't Look Behind You. large type ed. LC PR9199.3.R5996D66. (Star Romance Ser.). 1999. 24.95 (*0-7862-1810-X*) Thorndike Pr.

Ross, Marilyn. The Haiti Circle. large type ed. (Romance Ser.). 272p. 1994. pap. 16.99 (*0-7089-7543-7*) Ulverscroft.

— National Directory of Newspaper Op-Ed Pages. 158p. 1994. 19.95 (*0-918880-17-3*) Comm Creat.

Ross, Marilyn & Ross, Tom. Big Ideas for Small Service Businesses: How to Successfully Advertise, Publicize, & Maximize Your Business or Professional Practice. 289p. 1994. pap. 15.95 (*0-918880-16-5*) Comm Creat.

— How to Make Big Profits Publishing City & Regional Books: A Guide for Entrepreneurs, Writers, & Publishers. 224p. 1987. pap. 14.95 (*0-918880-12-2*) Comm Creat.

— Jump Start Your Book Sales: A Money-Making Guide for Authors, Independent Publishers & Small Presses. LC 99-11466. (Illus.). 348p. 1999. pap. 19.95 (*0-918880-41-6*, Pub. by Comm Creat) F & W Pubns Inc.

***Ross, Marilyn & Ross, Tom.** Shameless Marketing for Brazen Hussies: 293 Awesome Money-Making Strategies for Savvy Businesswomen. (Illus.). 368p. 2000. pap. 19.95 (*0-918880-44-0*) Comm Creat.

Ross, Marilyn, jt. auth. see Ross, Tom.

Ross, Marilyn, ed. see Alessandra, Tony, et al.

Ross, Marilyn, ed. see Fotiades, John M.

Ross, Marilyn, ed. see Glasser, Selma.

Ross, Marilyn, ed. see Ottosen, Joleen.

Ross, Marilyn, ed. & frwd. see Bone, Bob.

Ross, Marilyn H. & Ross, Tom. Country Bound! Trade Your Business Suit Blues for Blue Jean Dreams. LC 96-38085. 392p. 1997. pap. 19.95 (*0-7931-2358-5*, 1916-1201) Dearborn.

Ross, Marilyn J. Success Factors of Young African-American Males at an Historically Black College. LC 97-37560. 160p. 1998. 55.00 (*0-89789-535-5*, Bergin & Garvey) Greenwood.

Ross, Marion W. Bibliography of Vietnamese Literature in the Wason Collection at Cornell University. LC 74-173511. (Cornell University, Southeast Asia Program, Data Paper Ser.: No. 90). 196p. reprint ed. pap. 60.80 (*0-8357-3679-2*, 203640300003) Bks Demand.

Ross, Maris & Jeans, David S. Adam & Evolution. 256p. 1974. 25.00 (*0-8464-1289-6*) Beekman Pubs.

Ross, Marjory, jt. auth. see Schabacker, Jay.

***Ross, Mark.** Dangerous Beauty: Life & Death in the Wild: True Stories from a Safari Guide. (Illus.). 256p. 2001. 24.95 (*0-7868-6672-1*, Pub. by Talk Miramax Bks) Time Warner.

Ross, Mark. Principles of Aural Rehabilitation. LC 78-183116. (Studies in Communicative Disorders). (C). 1972. pap. write for info. (*0-672-61283-6*, Bobbs) Macmillan.

Ross, Mark, ed. Communication Access for Persons with Hearing Loss: Compliance with the Americans with Disabilities Act. LC 94-2594. (Illus.). 306p. (C). 1994. pap. text 37.50 (*0-912752-35-1*) York Pr.

— Hearing-Impaired Children in the Mainstream. LC 90-71342. (Illus.). 336p. (Orig.). (C). 1990. pap. text 31.50 (*0-912752-22-X*) York Pr.

Ross, Mark, et al. Assessment & Management of Mainstreamed Hearing-Impaired Children: Principles & Practices. LC 90-27495. 415p. (C). 1991. text 41.00 (*0-89079-458-8*, 1969) PRO-ED.

Ross, Mark, jt. auth. see Luterman, David M.

Ross, Mark, jt. auth. see Ross, Raymond S.

Ross, Mark, jt. auth. see Yamada, Thoru.

***Ross, Mark A. & Fine, Brad L.** Mountain Biking Southern California. LC 99-12361. (Illus.). 352p. 1999. pap. 14.95 (*1-56044-807-5*) Falcon Pub Inc.

Ross, Mark D. Let's Talk! A Discussion of Group Dynamics. 208p. (C). 1993. pap. text 29.95 (*0-8403-8237-5*) Kendall-Hunt.

Ross, Mark E., jt. auth. see Rollinson, Philip.

Ross, Martin. The Real Charlotte. Beards, Virginia, ed. LC 85-14248. 326p. 1986. reprint ed. pap. 101.10 (*0-608-02327-2*, 206296800004) Bks Demand.

Ross, Martin, jt. auth. see Somerville, Edith.

Ross, Martin, jt. auth. see Somerville, Edith O.

Ross, Marty. Bulbs. LC 98-66921. (Ortho's All about Ser.). (Illus.). 96p. 1998. pap. 11.95 (*0-89721-425-0*, Ortho Bks) Meredith Bks.

Ross, Marvin C., jt. auth. see Von Erdberg, Joan P.

Ross, Marvin C., ed. & intro. see Catlin, George.

Ross, Mary & Guymon, Jennette. Primary Partners: Achievement Days. (J). (gr. 3-6). 1996. pap. 9.95 (*1-55503-989-8*, 01112406) Covenant Comms.

— Primary Partners: Ages 4 to 7 (CTR B) 1996. pap., teacher ed. 8.95 (*1-57734-034-5*, 01112562) Covenant Comms.

— Primary Partners: Ages 8 to 11 (D & C) (J). (gr. 3-6). 1996. pap. 8.95 (*1-57734-065-5*, 01112759) Covenant Comms.

— Primary Partners: Ages 8 to 11 (Old Testament) (J). (gr. 3-6). 1998. pap. 8.95 (*1-57734-264-X*, 01113291) Covenant Comms.

— Primary Partners Vol. 2: Nursery-Age 3. (J). (ps-3). Date not set. pap. 8.95 (*1-57734-185-6*, 01113208) Covenant Comms.

***Ross, Mary & Guymon-King, Jennette.** Young Women Fun-Tastic! Activities, No. 1. 1999. pap. 9.95 (*1-57734-514-2*, 01114131) Covenant Comms.

— Young Women Fun-Tastic! Activities, No. 3. pap. 9.95 (*1-57734-298-4*, 01113518) Covenant Comms.

Ross, Mary, ed. see Mitchell, Brooks.

Ross, Mary E. Lighten Up: The Art of Low Fat Gourmet Cooking. (Illus.). 304p. 1996. pap. 19.95 (*0-9649771-7-6*, Pub. by Lghten Up Ent) Origin Bk Sales.

Ross, Mary-Ellen. The Best Laid Plans. 263p. 1995. pap. 9.95 (*0-929005-73-2*, Pub. by Sec Story Pr) LPC InBook.

Ross, Mary-Ellen, jt. auth. see Karp, Walter.

Ross, Mary H. Primary Partners: Ages 4 to 7 (CTR A): A-Z Activities to Make Learning Fun! (Illus.). 96p. 1996. pap., teacher ed. 8.95 (*1-55503-905-7*, 01112228) Covenant Comms.

***Ross, Mary H.** Primary Partners: Sharing Time: Faith in the Lord Jesus Christ. LC 99-192544. 123 p. 1998. pap. 2.97 (*1-57734-338-7*, 01113690) Covenant Comms.

Ross, Mary H. & Guymon, Jennette. Primary Partners: Nursery-Age 3: A-Z Activities to Make Learning Fun. (J). (ps-3). 1996. pap. 8.95 (*1-55503-809-3*, 01111914) Covenant Comms.

— Super Scripture Activities: Jesus Is My Friend. (J). 1996. pap. 7.95 (*1-55503-861-1*, 01112104) Covenant Comms.

— Super Scripture Activities: Tell Me the Stories of Jesus. (J). 1996. pap. 7.95 (*1-55503-860-3*, 01112090) Covenant Comms.

***Ross, Mary H. & Guymon-King, Jennette.** File Folder Family Home Evening: Instant Family-Night in a Folder. LC 99-192535. 118p. 1998. pap. 9.95 (*1-57734-297-6*, 01113674) Covenant Comms.

Ross, Mary H. & Guymon-King, Jennette. Home-Spun Fun: Family Home Evenings: Gospel Basic: Lessons & Activities for All Ages with Memorable Thought Treats. LC 98-104499. (Illus.). 130p. 1997. pap. 9.95 (*1-57734-143-0*, 01113097) Covenant Comms.

Ross, Mary Massaron & American Bar Association, Chicago, State and Local Government Law Section. Sword & Shield Revisited: A Practical Approach to Section 1983. LC 97-80528. xvi, 689 p. 1998. write for info. (*1-57073-522-0*) Amer Bar Assn.

R

Ross, Mary S. Frugal Feasts: 101 Quick & Easy Single-Serving Meals from Around the World. 1996. pap. 7.95 (*0-385-25529-2*) Bantam.

Ross, Meg, ed. see Bergrun, Norman R.

***Ross, Mel.** How to Live to 83-Plus Dance-Dance-Dance. (Illus.). v, 32p. 1999. ring bd. 9.95 (*0-9675535-0-4*) M Ross.

Ross, Mel, jt. auth. see Hall, Betty L.

Ross, Melody. The Scrapbooker's Best Friend Vol. 1: Hundreds of Phrases to Make Your Pages Touch the Heart & Tickle the Funnybone. 60p. 1997. spiral bd. 6.95 (*1-892326-01-9*) Chatterbox.

— The Scrapbooker's Best Friend Vol. 2: More Words of Wit, Wimsey & Wisdom. 60p. 1997. spiral bd. 6.95 (*1-892326-02-7*) Chatterbox.

— The Scrapbooker's Best Friend Vol. 3: Quotes & Scriptures. 60p. 1998. spiral bd. 6.95 (*1-892326-03-5*) Chatterbox.

— The Scrapbooker's Book of Alphabets: Thirty-One Easy to Draw Alphabets to Use for Hand Lettering Your Pages & Handmade Projects. 60p. 1998. spiral bd. 7.95 (*1-892326-05-1*) Chatterbox.

— The Scrapbooker's Instant Interviews: Hundreds of Questions to Ask Your Parents & Grandparents, Your Children, Yourself & Everyone Else You Love. 60p. 1998. spiral bd. 6.95 (*1-892326-04-3*) Chatterbox.

Ross, Merrill A., et al. Applied Weed Science. 2nd ed. LC 98-22059. 452p. (C). 1998. 105.00 (*0-13-754003-5*) P-H.

***Ross, Michael.** Get Real, Get Ready, Get Going. LC 99-33492. 192p. (YA). (gr. 7-12). 1999. pap. 8.99 (*0-8007-5712-2*) Revell.

Ross, Michael. Getting Great Guitar Sounds. 2nd ed. 80p. 1998. per. 14.95 (*0-7935-9140-6*) H Leonard.

— Toward Better Teaching: Professional Development in 1993-94. (Illus.). 142p. 1999. pap. text 25.00 (*0-7881-7727-3*) DIANE Pub.

Ross, Michael, ed. Homosexuality, Masculinity, & Femininity. LC 84-19778. (Journal of Homosexuality Ser.: Vol. 9, No. 1). 107p. 1985. pap. text 9.95 (*0-918393-04-3*, Harrington Park) Haworth Pr.

— Pedigrees of Leading Winners, 1960-1980. 198p. 1990. 120.00 (*0-85131-372-8*, Pub. by J A Allen) St Mut.

— Psychopathology & Psychotherapy in Homosexuality. LC 87-29894. (Journal of Homosexuality: Vol. 15, Nos. 1-2). 222p. 1988. text 49.95 (*0-86656-499-3*) Haworth Pr.

Ross, Michael & DeCecco, John P., eds. The Treatment of Homosexuals with Mental Health Disorders. LC 87-30826. (Journal of Homosexuality Ser.: No. 15, No. 1-2). (Illus.). 222p. 1988. pap. 17.95 (*0-918393-47-7*, Harrington Park) Haworth Pr.

***Ross, Michael & Edmondson, Jeff.** Radically Plugged In: High-Voltage Devotionals to Ground Your Faith. LC 97-43856. (Illus.). 136p. (YA). 1998. pap. 9.99 (*0-8341-1707-X*) Beacon Hill.

Ross, Michael, jt. auth. see Johnson, Greg.

Ross, Michael, jt. auth. see Lewis, Lynette.

Ross, Michael, jt. auth. see Myers, Bill.

Ross, Michael, jt. auth. see Pickering, Martin.

Ross, Michael, jt. auth. see Sasso, Mario.

Ross, Michael, jt. auth. see Shellenberger, Susie.

***Ross, Michael A.** BostonWalks' the Jewish Friendship Trail, Guidebook to Jewish Historic Sites of Boston, 1841-1926: Includes 3 Walking Tours of Jewish Boston! (Jewish Friendship Trail Ser.: Vol. 1). (Illus.). 106p. 2000. pap. 18.00 (*0-9700825-0-9*) BostonWalks.

Ross, Michael D., jt. auth. see Doelling, Hellmut H.

Ross, Michael E. Become a Bird & Fly! LC 91-36562. (Illus.). 32p. (J). (gr. k up). 1992. lib. bdg. 21.40 (*1-56294-074-0*) Millbrook Pr.

Ross, Michael E. Bird Watching with Margaret Morse Nice. LC 96-13876. (Illus.). 1996. lib. bdg. 19.93 (*1-57505-002-1*, Carolrhoda) Lerner Pub.

Ross, Michael E. Bug Watching with Charles Henry Turner. LC 96-11972. (Illus.). 48p. (J). 1996. 19.93 (*1-57505-003-X*, Carolrhoda) Lerner Pub.

— Caterpillarology. LC 97-1272. (Backyard Buddies Ser.). (Illus.). (J). 1997. lib. bdg. 19.93 (*1-57505-055-2*, Carolrhoda) Lerner Pub.

— Cricketology. LC 95-4559. (Backyard Buddies Ser.). (Illus.). 48p. (J). (gr. 1-4). 1996. lib. bdg. 19.93 (*0-87614-985-9*, Carolrhoda) Lerner Pub.

— Cycles, Cycles, Cycles. (Illus.). 88p. (J). (gr. 1-3). 1979. pap. 3.95 (*0-939666-01-4*) Yosemite Assn.

— Exploring the Earth with John Wesley Powell. LC 99-19488. (Naturalist's Apprentice Biographies Ser.). (Illus.). 48p. (J). (gr. 3-6). 2000. 19.93 (*1-57505-254-7*, Carolrhoda) Lerner Pub.

— Faces in All Kinds of Places: A Worm's Eye View of Flowers. (Illus.). 50p. 1987. pap. 4.95 (*0-939666-44-8*) Yosemite Assn.

— Flower Watching with Alice Eastwood. LC 96-27576. (Naturalist's Apprentice Ser.). (Illus.). (J). 1997. lib. bdg. 19.93 (*1-57505-005-6*, Carolrhoda) Lerner Pub.

— Happy Camper Handbook: A Guide to Camping for Kids & Their Parents. (Illus.). 64p. (J). (ps-6). 1995. spiral bd. 15.95 (*0-939666-78-2*) Yosemite Assn.

— A Kid's Golden Gate: Guide to Family Adventures in the National Parks at the Golden Gate. LC 96-78729. (Illus.). 64p. (J). (gr. 3-7). 1997. spiral bd. 10.95 (*1-883869-20-X*) Gldn Gate Natl Parks Assoc.

***Ross, Michael E.** Nature Art with Chiura Obata. LC 98-49073. (Naturalist's Apprentice Biographies Ser.). (Illus.). 48p. (J). (gr. 3-6). 2000. 19.93 (*1-57505-378-0*, Carolrhoda) Lerner Pub.

Ross, Michael E. Rolypolyology. LC 94-22327. (Backyard Buddies Ser.). (Illus.). 48p. (J). (gr. 1-4). 1996. lib. bdg. 14.95 (*0-87614-862-3*, Carolrhoda) Lerner Pub.

— Sandbox Scientist: Real Science Activities for Little Kids. LC 95-13508. (Illus.). 144p. (J). (ps-3). 1995. pap. 12.95 (*1-55652-248-7*) Chicago Review.

— Snailology. LC 95-30900. (Illus.). 48p. (J). (gr. 1-4). 1996. lib. bdg. 14.95 (*0-87614-894-1*, Carolrhoda) Lerner Pub.

— What Makes Everything Go? 94p. (J). (gr. k-2). 1979. pap. 3.95 (*0-939666-19-7*) Yosemite Assn.

— Wildlife Watching with Charles Eastman. LC 96-11470. (Naturalist's Apprentice Ser.). (Illus.). (J). (gr. 3-6). 1997. lib. bdg. 14.95 (*1-57505-004-8*, Carolrhoda) Lerner Pub.

— The World of Small: Nature Explorations with a Hand Lens. Medley, Steven P., ed. (Illus.). 64p. (J). (gr. k-6). 1993. spiral bd. 15.95 (*0-939666-62-6*) Yosemite Assn.

— Wormology. LC 94-42435. (Backyard Buddies Ser.). (Illus.). 48p. (J). (gr. 1-4). 1996. lib. bdg. 14.95 (*0-87614-937-9*, Carolrhoda) Lerner Pub.

— Yosemite Fun Book: A Kid's Guide to Yosemite. (Illus.). 48p. (J). (gr. 3-8). 1987. pap. 2.95 (*0-939666-45-6*) Yosemite Assn.

***Ross, Michael Elsohn.** Caterpillarology. (Backyard Buddies Ser.). (Illus.). 48p. (J). (gr. 1-4). 2000. pap. 6.95 (*1-57505-434-5*, First Ave Edns) Lerner Pub.

— Ladybugology. (Backyard Buddies Ser.). (Illus.). 48p. (J). (gr. 1-4). 2000. pap. 6.95 (*1-57505-435-3*, First Ave Edns) Lerner Pub.

— Millipedeology. (Backyard Buddies Ser.). (Illus.). 48p. (J). (gr. 1-4). 2000. pap. 6.95 (*1-57505-436-1*, First Ave Edns) Lerner Pub.

— Snailology. (Backyard Buddies Ser.). (Illus.). 48p. (J). (gr. 1-4). 2000. pap. 6.95 (*1-57505-437-X*, First Ave Edns) Lerner Pub.

— Spiderology. LC 98-51406. (Backyard Buddies Ser.). (Illus.). 48p. (J). (gr. 1-4). 2000. pap. 6.95 (*1-57505-438-8*, First Ave Edns) Lerner Pub.

***Ross, Michael Elsohn.** Children of Northern Ireland. LC 99-50654. (World's Children Ser.). (Illus.). 48p. (J). (gr. 3). 2000. 23.93 (*1-57505-433-7*, Carolrhoda) Lerner Pub.

— Fish Watching with Eugenie Clark. LC 99-19963. (Naturalist's Apprentice Biographies Ser.). (Illus.). 48p. (J). (gr. 3-6). 2000. 19.93 (*1-57505-384-5*, Carolrhoda) Lerner Pub.

Ross, Michael Elsohn. Ladybugology. LC 96-37441. (Illus.). (J). 1997. 19.93 (*1-57505-051-X*, Carolrhoda) Lerner Pub.

***Ross, Michael Elsohn.** Millipedeology. LC 99-35398. (Backyard Buddies Ser.). (Illus.). 48p. (J). (gr. 1-4). 2000. 19.93 (*1-57505-398-5*, Carolrhoda) Lerner Pub.

— Pond Watching with Ann Morgan. LC 99-24953. (Naturalist's Apprentice Biographies Ser.). (Illus.). 48p. (J). (gr. 3-6). 2000. 19.93 (*1-57505-385-3*, Carolrhoda) Lerner Pub.

Ross, Michael Elsohn. Spiderology. LC 98-51406. (Backyard Buddies Ser.). (Illus.). 48p. (J). (gr. 1-4). 2000. 19.93 (*1-57505-387-X*, Carolrhoda) Lerner Pub.

Ross, Michael H., et al. Histology: A Text & Atlas. 2nd ed. (Illus.). 815p. 1989. text 52.00 (*0-683-07368-0*) Lppncott W & W.

Ross, Michael J. California: Its Government & Politics. 5th ed. LC 95-15779. 278p. (C). 1995. pap. text 50.00 (*0-534-23112-8*) Harcourt.

***Ross, Michael J.** California: Its Government & Politics. 6th ed. LC 99-23963. (C). 1999. text 25.00 (*0-15-507874-7*) Harcourt.

Ross, Michael L. Storied Cities: Literary Imaginings of Florence, Venice, & Rome, 51. LC 93-13011. (Contributions to the Study of World Literature Ser.: No. 51). 328p. 1993. 65.00 (*0-313-28717-1*, GM8717, Greenwood Pr) Greenwood.

Ross, Michael R. Fisheries Conservation & Management. LC 95-41533. 374p. 1996. 87.00 (*0-02-403901-2*, Macmillan Coll) P-H.

— Recreational Fisheries of Coastal New England. LC 90-49253. (Illus.). 288p. 1991. pap. 18.95 (*0-87023-743-8*); lib. bdg. 45.00 (*0-87023-742-X*) U of Mass Pr.

Ross, Michael W. HIV - AIDS & Sexuality. LC 95-21375. (Journal of Psychology & Human Sexuality: Vol. 7, Nos. 1 & 2). 222p. 1995. pap. 19.95 (*1-56023-068-1*, Harrington Park) Haworth Pr.

— Psychovenereology: Personality & Lifestyle Factors in Sexually Transmitted Diseases in Homosexual Men, 3. LC 85-25683. (Sexual Medicine Ser.). 258p. 1986. 55.00 (*0-275-92122-0*, C2122, Praeger Pubs) Greenwood.

Ross, Michael W., ed. HIV - AIDS & Sexuality. LC 95-21375. (Journal of Psychology & Human Sexuality: Vol. 7, Nos. 1 & 2). 222p. 1995. 49.95 (*1-56024-730-4*) Haworth Pr.

— Homosexuality & Social Sex Roles. LC 83-12636. (Journal of Homosexuality: Vol. 9, No. 1). 107p. 1983. text 32.95 (*0-86656-235-4*) Haworth Pr.

***Ross, Michael W. & Nilsson, Lena.** Coping with HIV Infection: Psychological & Existential Responses in Gay Men. LC 99-38194. (AIDS Prevention & Mental Health Ser.). 194p. 1999. 75.00 (*0-306-46220-6*, Kluwer Plenum) Kluwer Academic.

***Ross, Michael W., et al.** Sexual Health Concerns: Interviewing & History Taking for Health Practitioners. 2nd ed. (Illus.). 220p. (C). 1999. pap. text 24.95 (*0-8036-0668-0*) Davis Co.

Ross, Mike, jt. auth. see Nowlin, Bill.

Ross, Mildred & Bachner, Susan, eds. Adults with Developmental Disabilities: Current Approaches to Occupational Therapy. 360p. 1998. pap. text 37.00 (*1-56900-084-0*, 1140) Am Occup Therapy.

***Ross, Molly J.** Circumstances. LC 99-91728. 2000. 25.00 (*0-7388-1204-8*); pap. 18.00 (*0-7388-1205-6*) Xlibris Corp.

Ross, Monica L. Clarissa's Closet. (J). (gr. 1-6). 1996. pap. 6.00 (*0-87602-343-X*) Anchorage.

— Montana Molly & the Peppermint Kid: Musical. (J). 1990. 6.00 (*0-87602-285-9*) Anchorage.

— Wilma's Revenge. (J). 1989. 6.00 (*0-87602-288-3*) Anchorage.

Ross, Morton. Sinclair Ross & His Works. (Canadian Author Studies). 42p. (C). 1991. pap. 9.95 (*1-55022-056-X*, Pub. by ECW) Genl Dist Srvs.

Ross, Morton L. An American Critic in Canada: The Literary Memoirs of Morton L. Ross. 1999. pap. 17.95 (*1-896300-44-8*) NeWest Pubs.

Ross, Murray. Stars & Strikes: Unionization of Hollywood. LC 41-24783. reprint ed. 20.00 (*0-404-05408-0*) AMS Pr.

— The Way Must Be Tried: Memoirs of a University Man. 288p. 1992. 29.95 (*0-7737-2571-7*) Genl Dist Srvs.

Ross-Murray, Carmin D., jt. ed. see Murray, Thomas E.

Ross-Murray, Carmin O., jt. ed. see Murray, Thomas E.

Ross, Murray J. Drafting & Negotiating Commercial Leases. 3rd ed. 1989. 100.00 (*0-406-35909-1*, U.K., MICHIE) LEXIS Pub.

Ross, Murray J., ed. see McKibbin, Elizabeth & O'Neil, Dominic.

Ross, Myron H. A Gale of Creative Destruction: The Coming Economic Boom, 1992-2020. LC 89-3556. 184p. 1989. 49.95 (*0-275-93322-9*, C3322, Praeger Pubs) Greenwood.

Ross, Myron H., ed. The Economics of Aging. LC 85-25470. 138p. (C). 1985. text 19.00 (*0-88099-033-3*); pap. text 9.00 (*0-88099-032-5*) W E Upjohn.

Ross, N. M. Nehemiah: Builder for God. (BibleTime Bks.). (J). 1995. 2.99 (*0-906731-11-9*, Pub. by Christian Focus) Spring Arbor Dist.

Ross, N. Phillip, jt. ed. see Cothern, C. Richard.

Ross, Nancy. Cordova's Historic Buildings. LC 83-81337. (Illus.). 20p. 1983. pap. 3.50 (*0-9607358-1-X*) Fathom Pub.

— Westward the Women. LC 76-117832. (Essay Index Reprint Ser.). 1977. 22.95 (*0-8369-1846-0*) Ayer.

Ross, Nancy, jt. ed. see Ross, Steve.

Ross, Nancy P. Matzo Bunny. (Illus.). 20p. (Orig.). (J). (ps-4). 1995. pap. 8.95 (*0-9645964-0-7*) Powerhse Advert.

Ross, Nancy W. Buddhism: A Way of Life & Thought. LC 81-40081. (Illus.). 224p. 1981. pap. 12.00 (*0-394-74754-2*) Vin Bks.

***Ross, Nancy W.** Joan of Arc. LC 98-51932. (Landmark Bks.). 160p. (J). 1999. lib. bdg. 11.99 (*0-375-90232-5*) Random.

— Joan of Arc. LC DC103.5.R67 1999. (Landmark Bks.). 160p. (YA). (gr. 5-8). 1999. pap. 5.99 (*0-375-80232-0*, Pub. by Random Bks Yng Read) Random.

Ross, Nancy W. Westward the Women. 196p. 1996. pap. 7.95 (*0-89174-063-5*) Comstock Edns.

Ross, Nancy W., ed. World of Zen. (Illus.). 1964. pap. 16.00 (*0-394-70301-4*) Vin Bks.

Ross, Neil W., ed. Marina Environment, 1990. (Illus.). 322p. (Orig.). (C). 1990. pap. 65.00 (*0-929803-10-8*) Intl Marina Inst.

— Marina Investment & Appraisal Notebook. (Illus.). 327p. 1995. 75.00 (*0-929803-12-4*) Intl Marina Inst.

— Marina Research, 1989. (Illus.). 344p. (Orig.). (C). 1989. pap. 75.00 (*0-929803-04-3*) Intl Marina Inst.

— Marina Research, 1990. (Illus.). 255p. (Orig.). (C). 1990. pap. 75.00 (*0-929803-05-1*) Intl Marina Inst.

— Marina Research, 1991. (Illus.). 178p. (C). 1991. 75.00 (*0-929803-11-6*) Intl Marina Inst.

Ross, Neil W., intro. Marina Design & Engineering Conference Technical Papers. (Illus.). 305p. (Orig.). (C). 1987. pap. 65.00 (*0-929803-00-0*) Intl Marina Inst.

Ross, Neville, tr. German Draft Penal Code E 1962. (American Series of Foreign Penal Codes: Vol. 11). xiii, 253p. 1966. 20.00 (*0-8377-0031-0*, Rothman) W S Hein.

Ross, Nicholas. Art in Focus: Florence. (Illus.). 128p. 1995. pap. 12.95 (*0-8212-2157-4*, Pub. by Bulfinch Pr) Little.

— Miro. LC 95-35420. (Famous Artists Ser.). (Illus.). 32p. (J). (gr. 5 up). 1995. 11.95 (*0-8120-6535-2*); pap. 6.95 (*0-8120-9427-1*) Barron.

Ross, Nicholas. Miro. (Famous Artists Ser.). 1995. 12.15 (*0-606-08822-9*, Pub. by Turtleback) Demco.

***Ross, Nikki.** Lessons from the Legends of Wall Street: How Warren Buffet, Phil Fisher, Benjamin Graham, T. Rowe Price & John Templeton Can Help You Grow Rich. 2000. 22.00 (*0-7931-3715-2*) Dearborn.

Ross, Nina P. God Will Provide: M.A. Thomas, a Biography. 19.95 (*0-9668796-0-0*); pap. 9.95 (*0-9668796-1-9*) Emmanuel Minst.

— The Norwegian Elkhound. Luther, Luana, ed. LC 93-74007. (Illus.). 320p. 1995. 26.95 (*0-944875-39-4*) Doral Pub.

Ross, Nina P., ed. see Craige, Patricia V.

Ross, Nola M. How to Write the Story of Your Family. (Illus.). 67p. 1991. pap. 8.00 (*1-887144-06-4*) N M Ross.

— Jean Laffite Louisiana Buccaneer. (Illus.). 88p. 1990. pap. 8.00 (*1-887144-05-6*) N M Ross.

— Louisiana's Acadian Homes & Their History. (Illus.). 72p. 1999. lib. bdg. 25.00 (*1-887144-11-0*) N M Ross.

— Mardi Gras in Calcasieu Parrish: A Pictorial History. (Illus.). 111p. 1991. 30.00 (*1-887144-01-3*) N M Ross.

— Pioneers of Calcasieu & Cameron Parish, Vol. III. (Illus.). 102p. 1990. pap. 12.95 (*1-887144-04-8*) N M Ross.

— Pioneers of Calcasieu Parish, Vol. II. (Illus.). 80p. 1988. pap. 12.95 (*1-887144-03-X*) N M Ross.

— Pioneers of Calcasieu Parish: Memories of Early Calcasieu, Vol. I. (Illus.). 72p. 1987. pap. 12.95 (*1-887144-02-1*) N M Ross.

— Southwest Louisiana Veterans Remember Vol. I: A 50th Anniversary Remembrance of World War I. (Illus.). 157p. 1993. 18.00 (*1-887144-00-5*) N M Ross.

— Southwest Louisiana Veterans Remember Vol. II: A 50th Anniversary Remembrance of World War II. (Illus.). 1995. 18.00 (*1-887144-07-2*) N M Ross.

***Ross, Nola Mae.** Airplanes for Breakfast. (Illus.). 98p. 2000. 25.00 (*1-887144-12-9*) N M Ross.

— A Louisiana Blueprint. (Illus.). 126p. 2000. 40.00 (*1-887144-13-7*) N M Ross.

Ross, Nola Mae & Mangum, Harold. If Walls Could Talk! LA Homes, Vol. I. LC 98-181983. 107 p. 1997. 40.00 (*1-887144-09-9*) N M Ross.

Ross, Nola Mae & Mangum, Harold. If Walls Could Talk! LA Homes, Vol. II. (Illus.). 107p. 1997. 40.00 (*1-887144-10-2*) N M Ross.

Ross, Nola W. & Goodson, Susan McFillen. Hurricane Audrey. LC 96-61898. xii, 233 p. 1997. write for info. (*1-887144-08-0*) N M Ross.

Ross, Norm. Dull Moments, Never. 24p. 1993. pap. 3.00 (*1-884226-02-7*) Dark River.

— The Last Caboose. 31p. (Orig.). 1994. pap. 4.95 (*1-884226-03-5*) Dark River.

Ross, Norma Hernandez De, see Hernandez De Ross, Norma.

Ross, Novelene. Toward an American Identity: Selections from the Wichita Art Museum Collection of American Art. Cateforis, David, ed. LC 97-60437. (Illus.). 272p. (Orig.). 1997. pap. 24.95 (*0-939324-51-2*) Wichita Art Mus.

Ross, Novelene G. Body Adornment. (Illus.). 20p. 1986. pap. 3.50 (*0-939324-27-X*) Wichita Art Mus.

— East Meets West in Lawrence, Kansas: An Exhibition of Paintings & Photographs by Martin Cheng, Norman Gee, Pok Chi Lau. (Illus.). 12p. (Orig.). 1992. pap. write for info. (*0-939324-48-2*) Wichita Art Mus.

— Lloyd Foltz (1897-1990) - A Retrospective: An Exhibition of Prints, Drawings & Paintings by Prairie Print Maker Lloyd Foltz. (Illus.). 6p. (Orig.). 1992. pap. write for info. (*0-939324-45-8*) Wichita Art Mus.

— Passing Seasons: Paintings by Robert Sudlow. (Illus.). 24p. (Orig.). 1993. pap. 12.00 (*0-939324-49-0*) Wichita Art Mus.

Ross, Novelene G., et al. Wan Qingli: The Scholar Artist in Modern China. (Illus.). 12p. 1988. pap. 3.00 (*0-939324-34-2*) Wichita Art Mus.

Ross, Novella & Kurth, Paula, eds. Model Entrepreneurship Programs. 283p. 1986. 18.00 (*0-318-23569-2*, SN 53) Ctr Educ Trng Employ.

Ross, Novella, et al. A National Entrepreneurship Education Agenda for Action. 114p. 1984. 9.50 (*0-318-22156-X*, LT66) Ctr Educ Trng Employ.

***Ross, Oakland.** Caledon: The First Forty Years. 120p. 1999. 29.95 (*1-55046-266-0*) Boston Mills.

Ross, Opal. Fields & Pine Trees. 71p. 1977. 9.95 (*0-87770-184-9*) Ye Galleon.

Ross, P. J. Taguchi Techniques for Quality Engineering: Loss Function, Orthogonal Experiments, Parameter & Tolerance Design. 2nd ed. LC 95-15415. 329p. 1995. 54.95 (*0-07-053958-8*) McGraw.

Ross, P. N., jt. ed. see Lipowski, J.

Ross, P. R. & Lloyd, S. D., eds. Thirteenth-Century England I: Proceedings of the Newcastle-Upon-Tyne Conference 1985. 202p. 1986. 75.00 (*0-85115-452-2*) Boydell & Brewer.

Ross, P. Whitcomb, jt. auth. see Ross, Paul W.

Ross, Pamela. Chinook Indians. (Native Peoples Ser.). (J). 1998. 14.00 (*0-516-21354-7*) Childrens.

— The Chinook Indians. LC 98-18424. (Native Peoples Ser.). (J). 1998. 14.00 (*0-7368-0076-X*, Bridgestone Bks) Capstone Pr.

— The Pueblo Indians. LC 98-7244. (Native Peoples Ser.). (J). 1998. 14.00 (*0-7368-0079-4*, Bridgestone Bks) Capstone Pr.

— Pueblo Indians. (Native Peoples Ser.). (J). 1998. 14.00 (*0-516-21357-1*) Childrens.

***Ross, Pat.** A Ceiling of Sky: Special Garden Rooms & the People Who Create Them. LC 99-57162. (Illus.). 208p. 2000. 27.50 (*0-7370-0611-0*) Time-Life Educ.

Ross, Pat. The Circle of Enduring Love: A Celebration of Romance & Affection. LC 98-7798. (Illus.). 144p. 1998. 14.95 (*0-8362-6965-9*) Andrews & McMeel.

***Ross, Pat.** The Country Cupboard: Herbs. LC 99-19990. 1999. text 15.00 (*1-56799-871-2*, Friedman-Fairfax) M Friedman Pub Grp Inc.

Ross, Pat. Country Cupboard: Kitchens. LC 99-18032. 1998. 15.00 (*1-56799-688-4*, Friedman-Fairfax) M Friedman Pub Grp Inc.

— Decorating Your Garden: Inspirational Ideas for Using Objects & Furniture Outdoors. LC 98-3820. (Illus.). 224p. (gr. 11). 1999. 34.95 (*0-7835-5311-0*) Time-Life.

— Flowers: Country Cupboard. 2nd ed. LC 99-13366. 1999. text 15.00 (*1-56799-729-5*) M Friedman Pub Grp Inc.

— Formal Country. LC 88-40639. (Illus.). 240p. 1989. 50.00 (*0-670-82574-3*, Viking Studio) Studio Bks.

***Ross, Pat.** Formal Country. 10th anniversary ed. (Illus.). 240p. 2000. 40.00 (*1-56799-948-4*, Friedman-Fairfax) M Friedman Pub Grp Inc.

Ross, Pat. Hannah's Fancy Notions: A Story of Industrial New England. LC 92-20286. (Once Upon America Ser.). (Illus.). 64p. (J). (gr. 2-6). 1992. pap. 4.99 (*0-14-032389-9*, PuffinBks) Peng Put Young Read.

— Hannah's Fancy Notions: A Story of Industrial New England. (Once upon America Ser.). (J). 1992. 10.19 (*0-606-02662-2*, Pub. by Turtleback) Demco.

— Harvest of Hope. 1999. pap. 8.95 (*0-670-83762-8*) Viking Penguin.

***Ross, Pat.** M & M & the Bad News Babies. (Illus.). (J). 1999. pap. 12.40 (*0-8085-3696-6*) Econo-Clad Bks.

Ross, Pat. M & M & the Bad News Babies. (M & M Ser.). (Illus.). 48p. (J). (ps-3). 1985. pap. 4.99 (*0-14-031851-8*, PuffinBks) Peng Put Young Read.

Ross, Pat. M & M & the Bad News Babies. (Picture Puffin Ser.). (Illus.). (J). 1985. 9.70 (*0-606-01684-8*, Pub. by Turtleback) Demco.

Ross, Pat. M & M & the Haunted House Game. (Puffin Chapters Ser.). (Illus.). 64p. (J). (gr. 2-5). 1997. pap. 3.99 (*0-14-038730-7*, PuffinBks) Peng Put Young Read.

Ross, Pat. M & M & the Haunted House Game. (Young Puffin Ser.). (J). 1990. 10.19 (*0-606-04735-2*, Pub. by Turtleback) Demco.

— M & M & the Mummy Mess. (Illus.). (J). 1999. 8.40 (*0-606-18424-4*) Turtleback.

Ross, Pat. M & M & the Santa Secrets. (Puffin Chapters for Readers on the Move Ser.). 48p. (J). (gr. 2-5). 1998. pap. 3.99 (*0-14-130094-9*, PuffinBks) Peng Put Young Read.

— M & M & the Santa Secrets. (Illus.). (J). (gr. 1-4). reprint ed. pap. 2.95 (*0-317-62234-X*, PuffinBks) Peng Put Young Read.

— Meet M & M. (Puffin Chapters Ser.). (Illus.). 64p. (J). (gr. 2-5). 1997. pap. 3.99 (*0-14-038731-5*, PuffinBks) Peng Put Young Read.

— Meet M & M. (Puffin Chapters Ser.). 1997. 9.19 (*0-606-12766-6*, Pub. by Turtleback) Demco.

— Men Exposed: A Heartless Little Book. LC 99-10530. 64p. 1999. pap. 8.00 (*0-684-85218-7*) S&S Trade.

— Menopause Madness. LC 97-39014. 96p. 1998. per. 8.00 (*0-684-84227-0*, Fireside) S&S Trade Pap.

***Ross, Pat.** Mother & Daughter Reflections. LC 99-55090. 2000. 14.95 (*0-7407-0499-0*) Andrews & McMeel.

Ross, Pat. The Mummy Mess, Vol. 1. (Puffin Chapters Ser.). 1999. pap. 3.99 (*0-14-130654-8*, PuffinBks) Peng Put Young Read.

— Please Come for Dinner: 12 Easy & Elegant Menus for Busy Cooks. LC 97-42911. (Illus.). 84p. (YA). (gr. 11). 1999. 14.95 (*0-7835-5308-0*) Time-Life.

Ross, Pat, ed. Kinship of Women: A Celebration of Enduring Friendship. LC 96-45959. 144p. 1997. 14.95 (*0-8362-2751-4*) Andrews & McMeel.

Ross, Pat O'Connell. National Excellence: A Case for Developing America's Talent. 41p. 1993. pap. 3.25 (*0-16-042928-5*) USGPO.

Ross, Patricia. Goats: A Guide to Management. (Illus.). 112p. 1995. pap. 22.95 (*1-85223-912-3*, Pub. by Crolwood) Trafalgar.

Ross, Patricia & Owens-Kristenson, Jodi. Take Charge of Your Life! LC 95-43173. 383p. 1996. 39.96 (*1-56637-279-8*) Goodheart.

Ross, Patricia T., ed. see Hedgecock, Joseph C.

Ross, Paul W. Using ENABLE: An Introduction to Integrated Software. 448p. 1988. mass mkt. 27.50 (*0-87835-295-3*) Course Tech.

Ross, Paul W., ed. The Handbook of Software for Engineers & Scientists. 1584p. 1995. boxed set 119.95 (*0-8493-2530-7*, 2530) CRC Pr.

Ross, Paul W. & Ross, P. Whitcomb. Using Microsoft Works Effectively: Windows Version. 288p. (C). 1993. text 22.47 (*0-697-17143-4*) Brown & Benchmark.

Ross, Paul W., et al. Understanding Computer Information Systems. Leyh, ed. 204p. (C). 1992. mass mkt. 15.25 (*0-314-93437-5*) West Pub.

Ross, Paula P., tr. see Chekhov, Anton.

Ross, Peter. Advanced Prolog: Techniques & Applications. 250p. (C). 1989. text 37.75 (*0-201-17527-4*) Addison-Wesley.

— History of Long Island from Its Earliest Settlement to the Present Time (1902), 2 vols., Set. (Illus.). 1642p. 1995. reprint ed. lib. bdg. 170.00 (*0-8328-5072-1*) Higginson Bk Co.

Ross, Peter. Italian-English - English-Italian Practical Dictionary. 488p. 1995. pap. 12.95 (*0-7818-0354-3*) Hippocrene Bks.

— New Approaches to Problem Behavior: Practical Guide to Discipline & Behavior Management for Teachers & Parents. 2nd ed. 122p. 1999. pap. 49.95 (*1-884937-55-1*) Manisses Communs.

Ross, Philip. The Government As a Source of Union Power: The Role of Public Policy in Collective Bargaining. LC 65-10155. 334p. reprint ed. 103.60 (*0-608-16600-6*, 202752100055) Bks Demand.

— Talley's Truth. 256p. 1988. pap. 3.50 (*0-8125-8784-7*, Pub. by Tor Bks) St Martin.

— True Lies. 256p. 1994. mass mkt. 3.99 (*0-8125-1376-2*, Pub. by Tor Bks) St Martin.

Ross, Philip, jt. auth. see Migliore, Marilyn.

Ross, Philip, jt. auth. see Myerson, Jeremy.

Ross, Philip J. De-Privatizing Morality. (Avebury Series in Philosophy). 128p. 1994. text 72.95 (*1-85628-659-2*, Pub. by Avebury) Ashgate Pub Co.

Ross, Philip N., jt. auth. see Lipkowski, Jacek.

Ross, Philip N., jt. ed. see Lipkowski, Jacek.

Ross, Philip N., jt. ed. see Lipowski, Jacek.

Ross, Philippe, et al. Water Quality & Toxicity Testing: Appropriate Technology for Transfer to Developing Countries. 320p. 1998. text 99.95 (*1-56032-751-0*); pap. text 42.95 (*1-56032-752-9*) Hemisp Pub.

Ross Pipes & Associates Inc., Staff. The Pocket Proposal Style Manual. 2nd ed. 68p. (Orig.). 1989. pap. 12.95 (*0-923768-02-5*) Tekne Pr.

— The Pocket Proposal Style Manual. 2nd deluxe ed. 68p. (Orig.). 1989. 49.95 (*0-923768-01-7*) Tekne Pr.

Ross, R., ed. Livy, Bk. 5. (Latin Texts Ser.). (LAT.). 112p. 1996. pap. 22.95 (*1-85399-442-1*, Pub. by Brist Class Pr) Focus Pub-R Pullins.

Ross, R. B. Metallic Materials Specification Handbook. 3rd ed. 1980. 120.00 (*0-419-11360-6*, NO. 6339, E & FN Spon) Routledge.

Ross, R. Douglas. MEPC: Obstetrics & Gynecology. 411p. (C). 1997. pap. 21.95 (*0-8385-6328-7*, Apple Lange Med) McGraw.

Ross, R. G., Jr. Cryocoolers: Proceedings of Eighth International Conference on Cryocoolers Held in Vail, Colorado, June 28-30, 1994, Vol. 8. LC 95-8373. (Illus.). 978p. (C). 1995. text 210.00 (*0-306-44913-7*, Kluwer Plenum) Kluwer Academic.

— Cryocoolers No. 9: Proceedings of the 9th International Conference Held in Waterville Valley, New Hampshire, June 25-27, 1996, Vol. 9. LC 97-9269. (Illus.). 986p. (C). 1997. text 234.00 (*0-306-45511-0*, Kluwer Plenum) Kluwer Academic.

Ross, R. J., jt. ed. see Jenkins, R. C.

Ross, R. Lee, et al, eds. Pseudomorphic HEMT Technology & Applications. LC 95-48179. (NATO ASI Series E: Vol. 309). 350p. 1996. text 195.00 (*0-7923-3915-0*) Kluwer Academic.

Ross, R. T. How to Examine the Nervous System. 3rd ed. LC 98-215433. (Illus.). 256p. 1999. pap. 22.00 (*0-8385-3852-5*, Apple Lange Med) McGraw.

— Syncope. (Major Problems in Neurology Ser.: Vol. 18). (Illus.). 176p. 1989. text 73.00 (*0-7020-1326-9*, Pub. by W B Saunders) Saunders.

Ross, R. T., ed. & tr. see Jonesco-Sisesti, N.

Ross, R. W., et al. Aboveground Storage Tanks Vol. 1: A State-of-the-Art Review. (Illus.). 384p. (Orig.). 1991. pap. 25.00 (*1-877914-27-4*) NACE Intl.

Ross, Rachael & Schneider, Robin. From Equality to Diversity: A Business Case for Equal Opportunities. 256p. 1992. 79.50 (*0-273-03370-0*, Pub. by Pitman Pub) Trans-Atl Phila.

Ross, Ralph G., ed. Makers of American Thought: An Introduction to Seven American Writers. LC 74-78993. (Minnesota Library on American Writers). 307p. reprint ed. pap. 95.20 (*0-608-15981-6*, 203328900084) Bks Demand.

Ross, Ralph G., et al, eds. Thomas Hobbes in His Time. LC 74-83134. 160p. reprint ed. pap. 49.60 (*0-608-15952-2*, 203323200084) Bks Demand.

Ross, Ralph G., ed. see Bosanquet, Bernard.

Ross, Ralph G., ed. see Burke, Edmund.

Ross, Ramon R. The Dancing Tree. LC 95-2124. 64p. (J). (gr. 4-8). 1995. 14.00 (*0-689-80072-X*) Atheneum Yung Read.

— Harper & Moon. LC 92-17216. (Illus.). 160p. (YA). (gr. 4 up). 1993. 15.00 (*0-689-31803-0*) Atheneum Yung Read.

Ross, Ramon Royal. Harper & Moon. (J). 1995. 9.09 (*0-606-07623-9*, Pub. by Turtleback) Demco.

Ross, Randal. The Next Seven Great Events of the Future: And What They Mean to You. LC 97-65690. 1997. pap. text 9.99 (*0-88419-457-4*) Creation House.

— Seven Habits of Winning Relationships. (Orig.). 1992. pap. 8.00 (*0-927936-50-X*) Vincom Pubng Co.

Ross, Randall R. & Altmaier, Elizabeth M. Intervention in Occupational Stress: A Handbook of Counselling for Stress at Work. LC 94-65025. 196p. 1994. pap. 24.95 (*0-8039-8673-4*) Sage.

Ross, Randy. The Chocolate Man. 180p. 1999. pap. 14.95 (*0-9662675-0-8*, L001) Larod Pub.

— Government & the Private Sector: Who Should Do What? LC 88-3803. (Illus.). 140p. (C). 1988. text 52.95 (*0-8448-1554-3*, Crane Russak) Taylor & Francis.

Ross, Randy L., jt. auth. see Kakalik, James S.

Ross, Randy L., jt. auth. see Keltner, Brent.

Ross, Raymon R. Storyteller. 3rd ed. LC 96-17345. 1996. pap. text 23.95 (*0-87483-451-1*) August Hse.

Ross, Raymond, jt. ed. see Hendry, Joy.

Ross, Raymond S. The Speechmaking Process. 11th ed. LC 97-16476. 358p. 1997. pap. text 41.00 (*0-205-27304-1*) P-H.

Ross, Raymond S. The Speechmaking Process: Instructor's Manual with Test Bank. 10th ed. 192p. (C). 1997. teacher ed., spiral bd. write for info. (*0-205-27999-6*, T7999-0) Allyn.

— Understanding Persuasion. 4th ed. LC 93-9103. 288p. 1993. pap. text 53.00 (*0-13-501131-0*) P-H.

Ross, Raymond S. & Ross, Mark. Relating & Interacting: An Introduction to Interpersonal Communication. (Illus.). 320p. (C). 1982. pap. text 33.05 (*0-13-771923-X*) P-H.

Ross, Richard. A Day in Part 15: Law & Order in Family Court. LC 96-40292. 160p. 1997. 22.00 (*1-56858-089-4*) FWEW.

— Freshwater Stingrays: A Complete Pet Owner's Manual. LC 99-26857. (Illus.). 104p. 1999. pap. text 6.95 (*0-7641-0897-2*) Barron.

***Ross, Richard.** Handbook of Stock Brokerage Accounting: 2000 Edition. 372p. 2000. 149.00 (*0-9701067-0-X*) Compliance Inter.

Ross, Richard. Museology. (Illus.). 80p. 1989. 65.00 (*0-89381-376-1*) Aperture.

— One Hundred & One Photographs: Selections from the Arthur & Yolanda Steinman Collection. LC 84-71041. (Illus.). (Orig.). 1984. pap. 3.50 (*0-89951-052-3*) Santa Barb Mus Art.

— Reproductive Husbandry of Pythons & Boas. (Illus.). 270p. 1990. 75.00 (*0-9631470-0-5*) Inst Herpeto Res.

***Ross, Richard, photos by.** Gathering Light: Photographs by Richard Ross. (Illus.). 2000. 49.95 (*0-8263-2268-9*) U of NM Pr.

Ross, Richard, photos by. Monet's Garden at Giverny: Postcard. (Illus.). 30p. 1996. pap. 10.95 (*1-55670-480-1*) Stewart Tabori & Chang.

Ross, Richard G., jt. auth. see Ross, Truedie L.

Ross, Robert. Adam Kok's Griquas: A Study in the Development of Stratification in South Africa. LC 75-43368. (African Studies: 21). 208p. reprint ed. pap. 59.30 (*0-8357-5092-2*, 2024526) Bks Demand.

— American National Government: Institutions, Policy, & Participation. 3rd ed. 544p. (C). 1993. text 29.50 (*1-56134-223-8*, Dshkn McG-Hill) McGrw-H Hghr Educ.

— Australia. LC 97-47562. (Travelers' Literary Companions Ser.: Vol. 6). 228p. 1998. pap. 13.95 (*1-883513-05-7*) Whereabouts.

— Carry on Companion: 40th Anniversary Edition. 40th anniversary ed. (Illus.). 216p. 1999. 24.95 (*0-7134-8439-X*) BTB Ent.

— Colonial & Post-Colonial Fiction in English: An Anthology. LC 99-39139. (Reference Library of the Humanities). 480p. 1999. reprint ed. 75.00 (*0-8153-1431-0*) Garland.

— A Concise History of South Africa. LC 98-11691. (Concise Histories Ser.). (Illus.). 225p. (C). 1999. text 49.95 (*0-521-57313-0*) Cambridge U Pr.

***Ross, Robert.** A Concise History of South Africa. LC 98-11691. (Concise Histories Ser.). (Illus.). 225p. (C). 1999. pap. 17.95 (*0-521-57578-8*) Cambridge U Pr.

Ross, Robert. Fatal Volley. LC 94-65013. 1994. pap. text 4.95 (*0-9640357-0-7*) R S Ross.

— Journey Within: A Tale of Astral Travel. Phelps & Associates Staff, ed. LC 98-68623. 242p. 1999. 22.95 (*0-9669588-4-5*) Mach Four.

— Journey Within: An Historical Tale of Astral Travel. Phelps & Associates Staff, ed. 256p. 1999. pap. 14.95 (*0-9669588-3-7*) Mach Four.

***Ross, Robert.** The Love Knot: Ties That Blind Cancer Partners. 2000. pap. 15.00 (*0-7637-1412-7*) Jones & Bartlett.

Ross, Robert. The Monty Python Encyclopedia. LC 99-237219. 1998. pap. text 24.95 (*0-7134-8279-6*, Pub. by B T B) Branford.

— The Monty Python Encyclopedia. 1999. 22.00 (*1-57500-036-9*, Pub. by TV Bks) HarpC.

— Status & Respectability in the Cape Colony, 1750-1870: A Tragedy of Manners. (African Studies Ser.: No. 98). (Illus.). 224p. 1999. write for info. (*0-521-62122-4*) Cambridge U Pr.

Ross, Robert, ed. Colonial & Postcolonial Fiction in English: An Anthology. (Reference Library of the Humanities). 480p. 1999. reprint ed. pap. 24.95 (*0-8153-3320-X*, H1770) Garland.

— International Literature in English: Essays on the Major Writers. LC 90-24468. 784p. 1991. text 100.00 (*0-8240-3437-6*, H1159) Garland.

Ross, Robert A., et al. Wildflowers of the Western Cascades. LC 87-29648. (Illus.). 204p. (Orig.). 1988. pap. 19.95 (*0-88192-078-9*) Timber.

Ross, Robert B. & Catlin, George B. Landmarks of Wayne County & Detroit: With Biographical & Personal Sketches. rev. ed. (Illus.). 1192p. 1997. reprint ed. lib. bdg. 114.50 (*0-8328-6792-6*) Higginson Bk Co.

Ross, Robert E. Beyond the Rope's End. LC 81-83846. (Illus.). 180p. (Orig.). 1982. pap. 12.00 (*0-9607312-0-2*) Priority Proj.

— Even If You've Never Played Before: You Can Play Hymns & Spirituals Using the New Music Notation System for Keyboards! (Illus.). 190p. 1992. write for info. (*0-9630043-3-6*) Keyboard Mus.

— If You Really Want to Learn Piano: A Quicker & Easier Method for Learning to Play Pianos & Electronic Keyboards. rev. ed. LC 91-77293. Orig. Title: For Beginners Only: An Innovative Method for Learning Piano & Electronic Keyboard Playing. (Illus.). 195p. 1992. write for info. (*0-9630043-1-X*) Keyboard Mus.

— A New Music System Especially for Electronic Keyboards: A Quicker & Easier Method for Learning to Play Keyboard Instruments. LC 92-90282. (Illus.). 195p. 1992. write for info. (*0-9630043-2-8*) Keyboard Mus.

Ross, Robert E., ed. The Ross Register of Siberian Industry: A Guide to Resources, Factories, Products, Mines, Banks & Stock Exchanges Throughout Siberia. LC 94-28437. xii, 168p. 1995. 49.00 (*0-88354-125-4*) N Ross.

Ross, Robert G., Sr. Who's Who of the Elite: Members of the Bilderbergs, Council on Foreign Relations, Trilateral Commission. 2nd rev. ed. LC 95-92782. 268p. 1995. pap. 29.95 (*0-9649888-0-1*) RIE.

Ross, Robert H. & Fineberg, Harvey V. Innovators in Physician Education: The Process & Pattern of Reform in North American Medical Schools. (Springer Series on Medical Education: Vol. 19, 1995). (Illus.). 304p. 1996. 46.95 (*0-8261-9200-9*) Springer Pub.

Ross, Robert H., ed. see Tennyson, Alfred Lord.

Ross, Robert J. The Indochina Tangle: China's Vietnam Policy, 1975-1979. (Studies of the East Asian Institute). 392p. 1988. text 69.00 (*0-231-06564-7*) Col U Pr.

— Infinite Syntax. LC 82-24310. (Language & Being Ser.). 344p. 1986. text 73.25 (*0-89391-042-2*) Ablx Pub.

— Racism & Colonialism. 1982. lib. bdg. 152.00 (*90-247-2634-4*) Kluwer Academic.

Ross, Robert J. & Trachte, Kent C. Global Capitalism: The New Leviathan. LC 89-21858. (SUNY Series in Radical, Social & Political Theory). 300p. (C). 1990. text 64.50 (*0-7914-0339-4*); pap. text 21.95 (*0-7914-0340-8*) State U NY Pr.

Ross, Robert L. Australian Literary Criticism, 1945-1988: An Annotated Bibliography. LC 88-31018. 400p. 1989. text 30.00 (*0-8240-1510-X*) Garland.

Ross, Robert M. & Allmon, Warren D., eds. Causes of Evolution: A Paleontological Perspective. (Illus.). 493p. 1990. pap. text 29.95 (*0-226-72824-2*) U Ch Pr.

— Causes of Evolution: A Paleontological Perspective. (Illus.). 368p. 1995. lib. bdg. 78.00 (*0-226-72823-4*) U Ch Pr.

Ross, Robert M., jt. auth. see Jackson, Andrew S.

Ross, Robert N. Experience the Joy of Painting with Bob Ross, Vol. 2. (Joy of Painting with Bob Ross Ser.). (Illus.). 66p. (Orig.). 1984. reprint ed. pap. 14.95 (*0-924639-06-7*) Bob Ross Inc.

— Experience the Joy of Painting with Bob Ross, Vol. 3. (Joy of Painting with Bob Ross Ser.). (Illus.). 74p. (Orig.). 1985. reprint ed. pap. 14.95 (*0-924639-28-8*) Bob Ross Inc.

— Experience the Joy of Painting with Bob Ross, Vol. 4. (Joy of Painting with Bob Ross Ser.). (Illus.). 78p. (Orig.). 1985. reprint ed. pap. 14.95 (*0-924639-33-4*) Bob Ross Inc.

— Experience the Joy of Painting with Bob Ross, Vol. 5. (Illus.). 75p. (Orig.). 1986. reprint ed. pap. 14.95 (*0-924639-29-6*) Bob Ross Inc.

— Experience the Joy of Painting with Bob Ross, Vol. 31. (Illus.). 73p. (Orig.). 1994. pap. 14.95 (*0-924639-38-5*) Bob Ross Inc.

— The Joy of Painting with Bob Ross, Vol. 6. (Illus.). 76p. (Orig.). 1986. reprint ed. pap. 14.95 (*0-924639-03-2*) Bob Ross Inc.

— The Joy of Painting with Bob Ross, Vol. 7. (Illus.). 80p. (Orig.). 1986. reprint ed. pap. 14.95 (*0-924639-08-3*) Bob Ross Inc.

— The Joy of Painting with Bob Ross, Vol. 8. (Illus.). 80p. (Orig.). 1986. pap. 14.95 (*0-924639-23-7*) Bob Ross Inc.

— The Joy of Painting with Bob Ross, Vol. 9. (Illus.). 84p. (Orig.). 1987. reprint ed. pap. 14.95 (*0-924639-27-X*) Bob Ross Inc.

— The Joy of Painting with Bob Ross, Vol. 10. (Illus.). 76p. (Orig.). 1987. pap. 14.95 (*0-924639-21-0*) Bob Ross Inc.

— The Joy of Painting with Bob Ross, Vol. 11. (Illus.). 76p. (Orig.). 1987. pap. 14.95 (*0-924639-12-1*) Bob Ross Inc.

— The Joy of Painting with Bob Ross, Vol. 12. (Illus.). 76p. (Orig.). 1988. reprint ed. pap. 14.95 (*0-924639-04-0*) Bob Ross Inc.

— The Joy of Painting with Bob Ross, Vol. 13. (Illus.). 80p. (Orig.). 1988. pap. 14.95 (*0-924639-10-5*) Bob Ross Inc.

— The Joy of Painting with Bob Ross, Vol. 14. LC 91-204569. (Illus.). 76p. (Orig.). 1989. pap. 14.95 (*0-924639-01-6*) Bob Ross Inc.

— The Joy of Painting with Bob Ross, Vol. 15. (Illus.). 76p. (Orig.). 1989. pap. 14.95 (*0-924639-05-9*) Bob Ross Inc.

— The Joy of Painting with Bob Ross, Vol. 16. (Illus.). 76p. (Orig.). 1989. pap. 14.95 (*0-924639-07-5*) Bob Ross Inc.

— The Joy of Painting with Bob Ross, Vol. 17. (Illus.). 76p. (Orig.). 1990. pap. 14.95 (*0-924639-09-1*) Bob Ross Inc.

— The Joy of Painting with Bob Ross, Vol. 18. (Illus.). 76p. (Orig.). 1990. pap. 14.95 (*0-924639-11-3*) Bob Ross Inc.

— The Joy of Painting with Bob Ross, Vol. 19. (Illus.). 79p. (Orig.). 1990. pap. 14.95 (*0-924639-14-8*) Bob Ross Inc.

— The Joy of Painting with Bob Ross, Vol. 20. (Illus.). 79p. (Orig.). 1990. pap. 14.95 (*0-924639-17-2*) Bob Ross Inc.

— The Joy of Painting with Bob Ross, Vol. 21. (Illus.). 78p. (Orig.). 1990. pap. 14.95 (*0-924639-20-2*) Bob Ross Inc.

— The Joy of Painting with Bob Ross, Vol. 22. (Illus.). 75p. (Orig.). 1991. pap. 14.95 (*0-924639-22-9*) Bob Ross Inc.

— The Joy of Painting with Bob Ross, Vol. 23. (Illus.). 75p. (Orig.). 1991. pap. 14.95 (*0-924639-25-3*) Bob Ross Inc.

— The Joy of Painting with Bob Ross, Vol. 24. (Illus.). 76p. (Orig.). 1991. pap. 14.95 (*0-924639-26-1*) Bob Ross Inc.

— The Joy of Painting with Bob Ross, Vol. 25. (Illus.). 76p. (Orig.). 1992. pap. 14.95 (*0-924639-30-X*) Bob Ross Inc.

— The Joy of Painting with Bob Ross, Vol. 26. (Illus.). 76p. (Orig.). 1993. pap. 14.95 (*0-924639-31-8*) Bob Ross Inc.

— The Joy of Painting with Bob Ross, Vol. 27. (Illus.). 76p. (Orig.). 1993. pap. 14.95 (*0-924639-32-6*) Bob Ross Inc.

— The Joy of Painting with Bob Ross, Vol. 28. LC 91-204569. (Illus.). 72p. (Orig.). 1993. pap. 14.95 (*0-924639-34-2*) Bob Ross Inc.

— The Joy of Painting with Bob Ross, Vol. 29. (Illus.). 76p. (Orig.). 1993. pap. 14.95 (*0-924639-35-0*) Bob Ross Inc.

— The Joy of Painting with Bob Ross, Vol. 30. (Illus.). 76p. (Orig.). 1994. pap. 14.95 (*0-924639-36-9*) Bob Ross Inc.

— Nasalcrom in Clinical Practice. LC 83-81193. (Illus.). 40p. 1983. write for info. (*0-914132-04-0*) Fisons Corp.

— Opticrom Four Percent in Clinical Practice. LC 84-72911. (Illus.). 43p. 1984. write for info. (*0-914132-05-9*) Fisons Corp.

Ross, Robert R. The Non-Existence of God: Linguistic Paradox in Tillich's Thought. LC 78-65486. (Toronto Studies in Theology: Vol. 1). xiv, 216p. 1978. lib. bdg. 89.95 (*0-88946-905-9*) E Mellen.

Ross, Robert R. & Lightfoot, Lynn O. Treatment of the Alcohol-Abusing Offender. 164p. 1985. pap. 21.95 (*0-398-06410-5*) C C Thomas.

— Treatment of the Alcohol-Abusing Offender. 164p. (C). 1985. 33.95 (*0-398-05090-2*) C C Thomas.

Ross, Robert R., jt. auth. see Lobanoff, Val S.

Ross, Robert S. Negotiating Cooperation: The United States & China, 1969-1989. 1995. 39.50 (*0-8047-2453-9*) Stanford U Pr.

— Negotiating Cooperation: The United States & China, 1969-1989. 1997. pap. text 17.95 (*0-8047-2454-7*) Stanford U Pr.

Ross, Robert S., ed. After the Cold War: Domestic Factors & U.S. -China Relations. LC 98-16762. (Studies on Contemporary China). 208p. (gr. 13). 1998. pap. text 25.95 (*0-7656-0292-X*) M E Sharpe.

— After the Cold War Domestic Factors & U.S. -China Relations. LC 98-16762. (Studies on Contemporary China). 208p. (C). (gr. 13). 1998. text 62.95 (*0-7656-0291-1*) M E Sharpe.

— China, the United States, & the Soviet Union: Tripolarity & Policy Making in the Cold War. LC 93-17018. (Studies on Contemporary China). 224p. (C). (gr. 13). 1993. text 79.95 (*1-56324-253-2*, East Gate Bk) M E Sharpe.

Ross, Robert S., ed. China, the United States & the Soviet Union: Tripolarity & Policymaking in the Cold War. LC 93-17018. (Studies on Contemporary China). 224p. (C). (gr. 13). 1993. pap. text 34.95 (*1-56324-254-0*, East Gate Bk) M E Sharpe.

Ross, Robert S., ed. East Asia in Transition: Toward a New Regional Order. LC 94-23743. (Illus.). 388p. (gr. 13). 1995. text 85.95 (*1-56324-560-4*, East Gate Bk); pap. text 26.95 (*1-56324-561-2*, East Gate Bk) M E Sharpe.

An Asterisk (*) at the beginning of an entry indicates that the title is appearing for the first time.

— Perspectives on Local Government. 192p. (C). 1987. pap. 14.95 (*0-89863-119-X*) Star Pub CA.

Ross, Robert S., jt. auth. see Johnston, Alastair I.

Ross, Robert S., jt. auth. see Nathan, Andrew J.

Ross, Robert S., jt. ed. see Johnston, Alastair I.

***Ross, Robert Todd.** The Supercommandos: First Special Service Force Forty Two to Forty Four. (Illus.). 256p. 2000. 59.95 (*0-7643-1171-9*) Schiffer.

Ross, Robert W. So It Was True: The American Protestant Press & the Nazi Persecution of the Jews. 394p. 1998. pap. 30.00 (*1-57910-122-4*) Wipf & Stock.

Ross, Robert W. & Bullington, John J., eds. History of Fayette County Illinois, with Biographical Sketches. (Illus.). 218p. 1998. reprint ed. lib. bdg. 29.50 (*0-8328-7076-5*) Higginson Bk Co.

Ross, Robin D., jt. auth. see Fong, Donald S.

Ross, Robin M., et al, eds. Foundations for Ecological Research West of the Antarctic Peninsula. LC 96-32835. (Antarctic Research Ser.: Vol. 70). 1996. 85.00 (*0-87590-891-8*) Am Geophysical.

Ross, Rockford J., jt. auth. see Starkey, J. Denbigh.

Ross-Rodgers, Martha J. Awakenings. rev. ed. 120p. 1998. pap. 9.95 (*0-9653197-0-9*) Jireh Publishers.

***Ross, Rolanda.** The Christ Inside of a Woman. 20p. 1999. 10.00 (*0-9675858-0-5*) Hezekiah Pubs.

— Recognizing the Spirit of Athaliah. 10p. 2000. pap. 7.00 (*0-9675858-1-3*) Hezekiah Pubs.

Ross, Ron. When I Grow Up . . . I Want to Be an Adult: Christ-Centered Recovery Workbook for Adult Children. rev. ed. LC 90-60660. (Illus.). 197p. (Orig.). 1990. pap., student ed. 12.95 (*0-941405-15-X*) RPI Pubng.

Ross, Ronald D. Your Family Heritage: A Guide to Preserving Family History. LC 88-60501. (Illus.). 140p. 1988. 19.95 (*0-9620144-0-0*) R D Ross.

Ross, Ronald E. Wild Edible Plants of Mother Nature: A Guide to Eating Hardy on Plants Common to 48 States. (Illus.). 92p. (Orig.). 1991. pap. 7.50 (*0-9632601-0-3*) Ronald Ross.

Ross, Ronald G. Bus Rules Appr Client/Se. (C). 1997. 34.95 (*0-201-41971-8*) Addison-Wesley.

— The Business Rule Book: Classifying, Defining & Modeling Rules. 2nd ed. (Illus.). 1997. 79.95 (*0-941049-03-5*) Bus Rule Sol.

— Business Rule Concepts. LC 99-183526. 1998. pap. 39.95 (*0-941049-04-3*) Bus Rule Sol.

— Entity Modeling: Techniques & Application. (Illus.). 218p. 1987. 39.95 (*0-941049-00-0*) Bus Rule Sol.

Ross, Ronald G. & Lam, Gladys S. The Business Rule Solutions Practitioner's Guide for Rule Management. 200p. (C). 1999. 995.00 (*0-941049-05-1*) Bus Rule Sol.

Ross, Ronald G. & Michaels, Wanda I. Resource Life Cycle Analysis: A Business Modeling Technique for IS Planning. (Illus.). 90p. 1992. 39.95 (*0-941049-01-9*) Bus Rule Sol.

Ross, Ronald J. The Failure of Bismarck's Kulturkampf: Catholicism & State Power in Imperial Germany, 1871-1887. LC 96-29995. 219p. 1998. text 66.95 (*0-8132-0894-7*) Cath U Pr.

Ross, Rosa. New Wok Cooking: Easy, Healthy, One-Pot Meals. LC 99-49909. (Illus.). 224p. 2000. 25.00 (*0-609-60418-X*) C Potter.

Ross, Rosemary. Creative Living & Health Workbook: A New & Exciting System for Dealing with the Emotional & Physical Stress of Cancer. 44p. 1989. pap. 8.95 (*0-9647382-1-X*) R Ross.

— Creative Living & Health Workbook: A New & Exciting System for Dealing with the Emotional & Physical Stress of Cancer. 36p. 1994. reprint ed. pap. 8.95 (*0-9647382-2-8*) R Ross.

— I'm Glad I Had Cancer, It Changed My Life: A Guide to Starting & Facilitating Cancer Support Groups. 50p. (Orig.). 1994. pap. 14.95 (*0-9647382-3-6*) R Ross.

Ross-Rovertson, David. Speaking As a Writer. 76p. 1979. 7.75 (*0-9602342-1-7*); pap. 5.95 (*0-9602342-0-9*) Westwind Pr.

Ross, Rupert. Dancing with a Ghost: Exploring Indian Reality. 195p. 1992. pap. 16.95 (*0-409-90648-4*) Buttrwrth-Heinemann.

Ross, Russel, jt. ed. see Numano, Fujio.

Ross, Russell, jt. auth. see Numano, Fujio National Conference on Atheroscleros.

Ross, Russell, jt. ed. see Sato, Gordon H.

Ross-Russell, Noel. Serenade of Fear. 256p. 1995. pap. 12.95 (*1-871871-21-2*) Paul & Co Pubs.

Ross, Russell R. Cambodia: A Country Study. 3rd ed. LC 89-600150. (Area Handbook Ser.). (Illus.). 398p. 1990. per. 23.00 (*0-16-020838-6*, 008-020-01203-3) USGPO.

Ross, Russell R. & Savada, Andrea M. Sri Lanka: A Country Study. 2nd ed. LC 89-600470. (Illus.). 360p. 1990. boxed set 22.00 (*0-16-024055-7*, 008-020-01216-5) USGPO.

Ross, Ruth. Power to Prosper: The Inner Path to Success. 1992. 49.95 incl. audio (*0-9622313-3-9*) Prosper Natural.

Ross, Ruth, jt. auth. see Frances, Allen.

Ross, Ruth, jt. auth. see Weston, David.

Ross, Ruth, ed. see Widiger, Thomas A.

Ross, Ruth I. The Little Book of Irish Family Cooking. 1996. 13.95 (*0-614-19384-2*) St Martin.

— The Little Book of Irish Family Cooking. LC 96-37351. (Illus.). 112p. 1997. text 13.95 (*0-312-15165-9*) St Martin.

— Little Irish Banking Book. (Illus.). 112p. 1996. text 12.95 (*0-312-14005-3*) St Martin.

Ross, S. Bunny Rabbit Mazes. (Illus.). 1997. pap. text 1.00 (*0-486-29825-6*) Dover.

— Nature Hidden Pictures. (J). (ps-3). 1996. pap. 1.00 (*0-486-29363-7*, 253262Q) Dover.

— Soil Processes: A Systematic Approach. (Illus.). 416p. 1989. text 95.00 (*0-415-00205-2*) Routledge.

Ross, S., ed. see Dewdney, A. K.

Ross, S. D. The Scientific Process. 163p. 1971. pap. text 57.00 (*90-247-5026-1*, Pub. by M Nijhoff) Kluwer Academic.

Ross, S. D., jt. ed. see Considine, Douglas M.

Ross, S. John. GURPS Warehouse 23: Things They Don't Want You to Have. Barrett, Sean, ed. (GURPS Ser.). (Illus.). 128p. 1997. pap. 19.95 (*1-55634-328-0*, 6523, Pub. by S Jackson Games) BookWorld.

Ross, S. John & Jackson, Steve, eds. Murphy's Rules. (Illus.). 80p. 1998. pap. 14.95 (*1-55634-363-9*, 9006, Pub. by S Jackson Games) BookWorld.

Ross, S. John, jt. auth. see Thibault, Daniel U.

Ross, S. John, ed. see Scoville, Thomas.

Ross, S. M., ed. Toxic Metals in Soil-Plant Systems. 484p. 1994. 225.00 (*0-471-94279-0*) Wiley.

Ross, Sally. The Acadians of Nova Scotia: Past & Present. (Illus.). 208p. 1998. pap. text 16.95 (*1-55109-012-0*) Nimbus Publ.

Ross, Sally, tr. see Daigle, France.

Ross, Sam. Melov's Legacy. Orig. Title: The Sidewalks Are Free. 308p. 1984. reprint ed. 22.00 (*0-933256-56-6*) Second Chance.

— Melov's Legacy. LC 84-50877. Orig. Title: The Sidewalks Are Free. 308p. 1985. reprint ed. pap. 16.00 (*0-933256-57-4*) Second Chance.

Ross, Sandra B. Pitching In: When Your Elderly Parents Need Help. 190p. 1999. pap. 12.95 (*1-881235-25-4*) Creat Opport.

Ross, Sandra J. The Nicelies at Home. LC 93-70084. (Nicelies Ser.). (Illus.). 76p. (Orig.). (J). (ps-1). 1993. pap. 5.95 (*1-881235-01-7*) Creat Opport.

— The Nicelies Go to School. LC 93-74878. (Nicelies Ser.). (Illus.). 74p. (J). (ps-1). 1994. pap. 5.95 (*1-881235-02-5*) Creat Opport.

— The Nicelies Series, 4 vols. (Illus.). (J). (ps-1). 1994. pap. 19.95 (*1-881235-04-1*) Creat Opport.

— Traveling with the Nicelies. LC 94-94426. (Nicelies Ser.). (Illus.). 64p. (J). (ps-1). 1994. pap. 5.95 (*1-881235-03-3*) Creat Opport.

— Visiting the Nicelies. rev. ed. LC 92-70147. (Nicelies Ser.). (Illus.). 60p. (J). (ps-1). 1994. pap. 5.95 (*1-881235-00-9*) Creat Opport.

Ross, Sandy T. Bairnsangs. (C). 1988. pap. 40.00 (*0-907526-11-X*, Pub. by Alloway Pub) St Mut.

Ross, Sarah. The Ladybird Baby Book. 28p. 1989. pap. 3.95 (*0-7214-5198-5*, S808-1, Ladybrd) Penguin Putnam.

Ross, Sayre, ed. see Berra, "Yogi" (Lawrence).

Ross, Seamus, et al, eds. Computing for Archaeologists. (Illus.). 216p. 1990. pap. 28.50 (*0-947816-18-6*, Pub. by Oxford Univ Comm Arch) David Brown.

Ross, Seth. Internet Now! The Consumer's Guide to Internet Access. (Orig.). 1996. pap. 12.95 (*0-9637025-3-X*) Albion Bks.

— UNIX System Security Tools. LC 99-33666. 512p. 1999. pap. text 39.99 (*0-07-913788-1*) McGraw.

Ross, Sharon. 50 Quick Fix-Ups for Your Home. Johnson, Karen, ed. (Illus.). 96p. (Orig.). 1997. pap. 10.95 (*0-89721-321-1*, 05918, Ortho Bks) Meredith Bks.

— Mastering Fine Decorative Paint Techniques. Robitiz, Kathie, ed. LC 98-89443. (Illus.). 272p. 1999. pap. 24.95 (*1-58011-064-9*) Creative Homeowner.

Ross, Sharon & Boyd, Linda. Graphing Calculator Exercises & Student Experiments for Precalculus Algebra & Trigonometry. 191p. (C). 1992. mass mkt. 18.25 (*0-534-14558-2*) Brooks-Cole.

Ross, Sharon & Sabella, Barbara. Ortho's Patio Plans. LC 97-75855. (Illus.). 96p. 1998. pap. 11.95 (*0-89721-412-9*, Ortho Bks) Meredith Bks.

Ross, Sharon & Toht, Dave. Ortho's 50 Quick Home Improvements. LC 97-76217. (Illus.). 96p. 1998. pap. 11.95 (*0-89721-417-X*, Ortho Bks) Meredith Bks.

Ross, Sharon M. Painting & Wallpapering. rev. ed. Beckstrom, Robert J., ed. LC 94-69599. (Illus.). 96p. 1995. pap. 9.95 (*0-89721-259-2*, 05970B, Ortho Bks) Meredith Bks.

Ross, Shelagh & Scanlon, Eileen. Open Science: Distance Teaching & Open Learning of Science Subjects. 288p. 1995. pap. 29.95 (*1-85396-172-8*, Pub. by P Chapman) Taylor & Francis.

Ross, Sheldon. Explorations in Mathematical Thinking. Smart, Margaret, ed. & illus. by. 64p. (Orig.). (J). (gr. 2-7). 1994. pap. 8.95 (*1-882293-03-7*, A-1695) Activity Resources.

Ross, Sheldon M. Applied Probability Models with Optimization Applications. LC 73-111376. (Holden-Day Series in Management Science). 208p. reprint ed. pap. 64.50 (*0-8357-5685-8*, 205213100039) Bks Demand.

— Applied Probability Models with Optimization Applications. unabridged ed. LC 92-16013. (Illus.). ix, 198p. 1992. reprint ed. pap. text 7.95 (*0-486-67314-6*) Dover.

— A First Course in Probability. 5th ed. LC 97-17297. 472p. 1997. pap. text 88.00 (*0-13-746314-6*) P-H.

— An Introduction to Mathematical Finance: Options & Other Topics. LC 99-25389. (Illus.). 224p. 1999. 39.95 (*0-521-77043-2*) Cambridge U Pr.

— Introduction to Probability & Statistics for Engineers & Scientists. LC 87-10406. 512p. 1987. text 102.95 (*0-471-81752-X*) Wiley.

— An Introduction to Probability Models. 6th ed. LC 96-44003. (Illus.). 669p. 1997. text 59.95 (*0-12-598470-7*) Acad Pr.

***Ross, Sheldon M.** Introduction to Probability Models. 7th ed. LC 99-68566. (Illus.). 650p. (C). 2000. 77.95 (*0-12-598475-8*) Acad Pr.

Ross, Sheldon M. Introductory Statistics: IBM Set. LC 95-19670. (Probability & Statistics Ser.). (C). 1995. 74.06 (*0-07-912244-2*) McGraw.

— Introductory Statistics: MAC Set. LC 95-19670. (Probability & Statistics Ser.). (C). 1995. 74.06 incl. mac hd (*0-07-912245-0*) McGraw.

— Simulation. 2nd ed. LC 96-30669. (Statistical Modeling & Decision Science Ser.). (Illus.). 282p. (C). 1996. text 59.95 (*0-12-598410-3*) Morgan Kaufmann.

— Stochastic Processes. LC 82-8619. (Probability & Mathematical Statistics Ser.). 80p. (C). 1983. pap. text, teacher ed. 20.00 (*0-471-87236-9*) Wiley.

— Stochastic Processes. 2nd ed. LC 95-38012. 528p. 1995. text 99.95 (*0-471-12062-6*) Wiley.

***Ross, Sheldon M.** Topics in Finite & Discrete Mathematics. LC 99-54713. (Illus.). 288p. (C). 2000. text 69.95 (*0-521-77259-1*); pap. text 27.95 (*0-521-77571-X*) Cambridge U Pr.

Ross, Sheldon M., jt. auth. see Derman, Cyrus.

Ross, Shelley, jt. auth. see Rosner, Louis J.

Ross, Shepley L. Differential Equations, Set. 3rd ed. 816p. (C). 1984. text 96.95 (*0-471-03294-8*) Wiley.

— An Introduction to Ordinary Differential Equations. 4th ed. LC 88-21589. 624p. 1989. text 92.95 (*0-471-09881-7*) Wiley.

— An Introduction to Ordinary Differential Equations: Student Solutions Manual. 4th ed. 816p. 1989. pap., student ed. 46.95 (*0-471-63438-7*) Wiley.

Ross, Sherry. Hockey Scouting Report, 1998-1999. (Illus.). 1998. pap. 12.95 (*1-55054-643-0*) Sterling.

***Ross, Sherry.** Hockey Scouting Report 2000: More Than 430 NHL Players. (Illus.). 480p. 1999. pap. text 12.95 (*1-55054-718-6*) DGL.

— Hockey Scouting Report 2001. 2000. pap. 12.95 (*1-55054-794-1*, Pub. by Greystone Bks) Sterling.

Ross, Sherry. Hockey Scouting Report, 1996-1997: Over 420 NHL Players. (Illus.). 480p. 1996. pap. 12.95 (*1-55054-508-6*, Pub. by Greystone Bks) Sterling.

Ross, Sherry Lazarus. The Light of Lucinda. (Illus.). 253p. (J). (gr. 2-6). Date not set. pap. write for info. (*0-615-11146-7*) WellFire Pubns.

— Seeds of the Pomegranate. 53p. 2000. 12.95 (*0-615-11133-5*) WellFire Pubns.

Ross, Sheryl, jt. auth. see Gallo, Birgitta.

Ross, Shirley & Hawke, Mary A. Center Connections. (Illus.). 320p. 1998. pap. 26.95 (*1-57612-049-X*, MM2063) Monday Morning Bks.

Ross, Shirley, et al. Alphabet Connections. (Illus.). 352p. 1993. pap. 24.95 (*1-878279-52-1*) Monday Morning Bks.

***Ross, Shyama.** You Can Heal Breast Cancer Naturally: Potent Holistic Alternatives. 125p. 2000. pap. 18.00 (*0-7388-2166-7*) Xlibris Corp.

Ross, Sidney S. What Is Sex Education All About? A Guide for Parents. LC 78-64612. 1979. pap. 7.95 (*0-9602028-0-3*) Sidney Scott Ross.

Ross, Sinclair. As for Me & My House. 224p. 1996. pap. 7.95 (*0-7710-9997-5*) McCland & Stewart.

— Lamp at Noon & Other Stories. 136p. 1996. pap. text 5.95 (*0-7710-9996-7*) McCland & Stewart.

Ross, Stan. The Joke's on Lawyers. 104p. 1996. pap. 23.95 (*1-86287-240-6*, Pub. by Blackstone Pr) Gaunt.

Ross, Stan & Burgess, Phillip. Income Tax: A Critical Analysis. xxii, 236p. 1991. 60.00 (*0-455-21026-8*, Pub. by LawBk Co); pap. 36.00 (*0-455-21027-6*, Pub. by LawBk Co) Gaunt.

***Ross, Stan D.** Ethics in Law: Lawyers' Responsibility & Accountability in Australia. 2nd ed. LC 98-221470. xxiv, 480 p. 1998. write for info. (*0-409-31340-8*) Buttrwrth-Heinemann.

Ross, Stanley R. Francisco I. Madero: Apostle of Mexican Democracy. LC 79-122591. reprint ed. 34.50 (*0-404-05409-9*) AMS Pr.

Ross, Stanley R., et al, eds. The Motion Picture Guide 1999: The Films of 1998. annuals 1998. 180.00 (*3-598-11415-X*) K G Saur Verlag.

Ross, Stanley R. & Chaffee, Wilber A., eds. Guide to the Hispanic American Historical Review: 1956-1975. LC 58-8501. vii, 432p. 1980. text 49.95 (*0-8223-0429-5*) Duke.

Ross, Stanley R., jt. auth. see Nash, J. R.

Ross, Stanley R., jt. auth. see Nash, Jay R.

Ross, Stanley R., jt. ed. see Erb, Richard D.

Ross, Stanley R., jt. ed. see Glade, William P.

Ross, Stanley R., ed. see Kennedy, Paul P.

Ross, Stanley R., jt. ed. see Nash, Jay R.

Ross, Stanley R., ed. see Ward, Burt.

***Ross, Stanley Ralph.** Gilbert vs. Sullivan. 124p. 2000. pap. 5.95 (*0-87129-991-7*, G05) Dramatic Pub.

Ross, Steart. Spirits & Sorcerers: Myths of Africa, Egypt, & Arabia. LC 97-41200. (Best Tales Ever Told Ser.). (Illus.). 44p. (YA). (gr. 5 up). 1998. 23.90 (*0-7613-0709-5*, Copper Beech Bks) Millbrook Pr.

***Ross, Stella.** Clash of Hearts. large type ed. 248p. 1999. pap. 18.99 (*0-7089-5583-5*, Linford) Ulverscroft.

— A Kiss in Payment. large type ed. LC 98-5511. (Romance Ser.). 186p. 1998. write for info. (*0-7540-3281-7*) Chivers N Amer.

Ross, Stella. A Kiss in Payment. large type ed. LC 98-5511. 208p. 1998. 18.95 (*0-7838-0119-X*, G K Hall Lrg Type) Mac Lib Ref.

— Pain of Betrayal. large type ed. (Linford Romance Library). 272p. 1994. pap. 16.99 (*0-7089-7555-0*) Ulverscroft.

***Ross, Stella.** Sea Spell. large type ed. 240p. 1999. pap. 18.99 (*0-7089-5523-1*, Linford) Ulverscroft.

Ross, Stella. Shadow of the Past. large type ed. (Linford Romance Library). 1989. pap. 16.99 (*0-7089-6793-0*) Ulverscroft.

Ross, Stella. Yesterday's Love. large type ed. 240p. pap. 18.99 (*0-7089-5451-0*) Ulverscroft.

Ross, Stephanie. What Gardens Mean. LC 97-22441. 279p. 1998. 40.00 (*0-226-72822-6*) U Ch Pr.

Ross, Stephanie & Enderle, Judith. What's the Matter, Kelly Beans? LC 95-11337. (Illus.). 112p. (J). (gr. 1-3). 1998. pap. 4.99 (*0-7636-0478-X*) Candlewick Pr.

Ross, Stephen. From Flintlock to Rifle: Infantry Tactics, 1740-1866. 2nd ed. (Illus.). 232p. (C). 1996. text 39.50 (*0-7146-4602-4*, Pub. by F Cass Pubs); pap. text 19.50 (*0-7146-4193-6*, Pub. by F Cass Pubs) Intl Spec Bk.

Ross, Stephen & Polk, Noel. Reading Faulkner: The Sound & the Fury. LC 96-12749. (Illus.). 176p. (C). 1996. text 45.00 (*0-87805-935-0*) U Pr of Miss.

Ross, Stephen A. Corporate Finance: Solutions Manual. 4th ed. (C). 1996. text 10.50 (*0-256-22149-9*, Irwn McGrw-H) McGrw-H Hghr Educ.

— CPS Fundamentals of Corporate Finance, Chapter 5. 2nd ed. 64p. (C). 1995. 4.50 (*0-256-21201-5*, Irwn McGrw-H) McGrw-H Hghr Educ.

***Ross, Stephen A.** Essentials of Corporate 1999. pap. 46.49 (*0-07-235960-9*) McGraw-Hill Pubng.

Ross, Stephen A. Fundamentals of Corporate Finance: Instructor's Guide. 3rd ed. (C). 1996. text 16.00 (*0-256-25204-1*, Irwn McGrw-H) McGrw-H Hghr Educ.

— Fundamentals of Corporate Finance/Financial Calculation. 3rd ed. (C). 1994. text 78.00 (*0-256-17638-8*, Irwn McGrw-H) McGrw-H Hghr Educ.

— Fundamentos de Finanzas Corporativas. 2nd ed. (SPA.). (C). 1996. text 35.50 (*84-8086-250-5*, Irwn McGrw-H) McGrw-H Hghr Educ.

Ross, Stephen A., ed. The Debt Market, 2 vols. (International Library of Critical Writings in Economics). 500p. 2000. 175.00 (*1-85278-987-5*) E Elgar.

Ross, Stephen A. & Westerfield, Randolph W. Corporate Finance: Solutions Manual. 3rd ed. 216p. (C). 1993. text, suppl. ed. 10.50 (*0-256-14379-X*, Irwn McGrw-H) McGrw-H Hghr Educ.

— Essentials of Corporate Finance. 216p. (C). 1996. text, student ed. 22.50 (*0-256-16987-X*, Irwn McGrw-H) McGrw-H Hghr Educ.

— Fundamentals of Corporate Finance. 4th ed. 720p. (C). 1997. text 72.50 (*0-256-25773-6*, Irwn McGrw-H); text 81.25 (*0-256-25774-4*, Irwn McGrw-H) McGrw-H Hghr Educ.

— Fundamentals of Corporate Finance: Irwin/Mc-Graw-Hill Series in Finance, Insurance & Real Estate. 4th ed. LC 97-24835. 1997. pap. 69.25 (*0-256-25772-8*, Irwn Prfssnl) McGraw-Hill Prof.

— Fundamentals of Corporate Finance: Study Guide & Problem Manual. 3rd ed. 296p. (C). 1994. text 25.00 (*0-256-13586-X*, Irwn McGrw-H) McGrw-H Hghr Educ.

— Fundamentals of Corporate Finance: Wall Street Journal Edition. 3rd ed. (C). 1995. text 79.20 (*0-256-18408-9*, Irwn McGrw-H) McGrw-H Hghr Educ.

— Fundamentals of Corporate Finance (Canadian) 2nd ed. LC 95-79287. 928p. (C). 1996. text 48.71 (*0-256-18335-X*, Irwn McGrw-H) McGrw-H Hghr Educ.

Ross, Stephen A. & Westerfield, Randy. Essentials of Corporate Finance: Ready Notes. 416p. (C). 1996. text, suppl. ed. 10.00 (*0-256-21678-9*, Irwn McGrw-H) McGrw-H Hghr Educ.

Ross, Stephen A., et al. Corporate Finance. 4th ed. 928p. (C). 1995. text 73.95 (*0-256-15229-2*, Irwn Prfssnl) McGraw-Hill Prof.

— Corporate Finance. 4th ed. (C). 1995. text 85.20 (*0-256-18458-5*, Irwn McGrw-H) McGrw-H Hghr Educ.

— Corporate Finance. 4th ed. 360p. (C). 1996. text, student ed. 26.88 (*0-256-15230-6*, Irwn McGrw-H) McGrw-H Hghr Educ.

— Corporate Finance. 5th ed. LC 98-21675. (The Irwin/Mcgraw-Hill Series in Finance, Insurance & Real Estate). 1998. write for info. (*0-256-24640-8*, Irwn Prfssnl) McGraw-Hill Prof.

— Corporate Valuation: Tools for Effective Appraisal & Decision Making 01 Ed & Capital Planning: Select Material. 1994. text 76.95 (*0-7863-0396-4*, Irwn Prfssnl) McGraw-Hill Prof.

— CPS - Fundamentals of Corporate Finance Solutions For Selected Problems. 3rd ed. 52p. (C). 1995. text 4.50 (*0-256-19972-8*, Irwn McGrw-H) McGrw-H Hghr Educ.

— Essentials of Corporate Finance. (Irwin Series in Finance). 560p. (C). 1995. text 48.70 (*0-256-16986-1*, Irwn McGrw-H); text 59.95 (*0-256-20017-3*, Irwn McGrw-H) McGrw-H Hghr Educ.

— Essentials of Corporate Finance. 560p. (C). 1996. text 48.70 incl. disk (*0-256-24552-5*, Irwn McGrw-H) McGrw-H Hghr Educ.

— Essentials of Corporate Finance. 2nd ed. LC 98-21049. (Series in Finance, Insurance, & Real Estate). 1998. 59.13 (*0-07-365945-2*) McGraw.

— Essentials of Corporate Finance: With Business Reference Library. (C). 1996. text, pap. text 54.95 incl. cd-rom (*0-256-23120-6*, Irwn McGrw-H) McGrw-H Hghr Educ.

— Fundamentals of Corporate Finance. 3rd ed. LC 94-14328. (Finance Ser.). 816p. (C). 1994. text 71.75 (*0-256-13585-1*, Irwn McGrw-H); text 61.95 (*0-256-17059-2*, Irwn McGrw-H) McGrw-H Hghr Educ.

— Fundamentals of Corporate Finance. 4th ed. LC 97-24835. 1997. write for info. (*0-256-25771-X*, Irwn Prfssnl) McGraw-Hill Prof.

— Fundamentals of Corporate Finance: Chapter Leasing. 3rd ed. 24p. (C). 1994. text 2.95 (*0-256-17061-4*, Irwn McGrw-H) McGrw-H Hghr Educ.

— Fundamentals of Corporate Finance: Chapter Options. 3rd ed. 48p. (C). 1994. text 4.00 (*0-256-17060-6*, Irwn McGrw-H) McGrw-H Hghr Educ.

— Fundamentals of Corporate Finance: Ready Notes. 4th ed. 1997. pap. 11.25 (*0-256-27187-9*) McGraw.

— Fundamentals of Corporate Finance: Wall Street Journal Edition. 3rd ed. 816p. (C). 1994. text 83.00 (*0-256-18407-0*, Irwn McGrw-H) McGrw-H Hghr Educ.

— Fundamentals of Corporate Finance, Alternate Edition. 4th ed. LC 97-24831. 928p. (C). 1997. text 70.00 incl. disk (*0-256-16458-4*, Irwn McGrw-H) McGrw-H Hghr Educ.

— Fundamentals of Corporate Finance CPS: Finance 1

Course Notebook (Georgia Institute of Technology) Edition. 3rd ed. (C). 1994. 15.95 (*0-256-19144-1*, Irwn McGrw-H) McGrw-H Hghr Educ.

— Fundamentals of Corporate Finance Ready Notes. 3rd ed. LC 95-134350. 392p. (C). 1994. text 10.00 (*0-256-13590-8*, Irwn McGrw-H) McGrw-H Hghr Educ.

— Fundamentals of Corporate Finance Wall Street Journal. 3rd ed. (C). 1995. text 85.95 (*0-256-19125-5*, Irwn McGrw-H) McGrw-H Hghr Educ.

Ross, Stephen D. Art & Its Significance: An Anthology of Aesthetic Theory. 3rd ed. LC 93-43609. 692p. (C). 1994. pap. text 23.95 (*0-7914-1852-9*) State U NY Pr.

— The Gift of Beauty: The Good As Art. LC 95-41531. 348p. (C). 1996. text 74.50 (*0-7914-3007-3*); pap. text 24.95 (*0-7914-3008-1*) State U NY Pr.

— The Gift of Kinds: The Good in Abundance, an Ethic of the Earth. LC 99-17962. 352p. (C). 1999. text 73.50 (*0-7914-4253-5*); pap. text 24.95 (*0-7914-4254-3*) State U NY Pr.

— The Gift of Touch: Embodying the Good. LC 98-14289. 448p. (C). 1998. pap. text 26.95 (*0-7914-3874-0*) State U NY Pr.

— The Gift of Touch: Embodying the Good. LC 98-14289. 448p. (C). 1998. text 78.50 (*0-7914-3873-2*) State U NY Pr.

— The Gift of Truth: Gathering the Good. LC 96-38789. 265p. (C). 1997. text 65.50 (*0-7914-3267-X*); pap. text 21.95 (*0-7914-3268-8*) State U NY Pr.

— Inexhaustibility & Human Being: An Essay on Locality. LC 88-82222. x, 331p. 1989. 40.00 (*0-8232-1227-0*) Fordham.

— Injustice & Restitution: The Ordinance of Time. LC 92-42843. 395p. (C). 1993. pap. text 24.95 (*0-7914-1670-4*) State U NY Pr.

— Injustice & Restitution: The Ordinance of Time. LC 92-42843. 395p. (C). 1993. text 74.50 (*0-7914-1669-0*) State U NY Pr.

— The Limits of Language. LC 93-17970. xix, 290p. (C). 1993. 35.00 (*0-8232-1518-0*) Fordham.

— Locality & Practical Judgement: Charity & Sacrifice. LC 93-47206. x, 345p. 1994. 35.00 (*0-8232-1556-3*) Fordham.

— The Nature of Moral Responsibility. LC 72-3399. 271p. reprint ed. pap. 84.10 (*0-7837-3628-2*, 204349400009) Bks Demand.

— Perspective in Whitehead's Metaphysics. LC 82-8332. (SUNY Series in Systematic Philosophy). 295p. (C). 1983. text 59.50 (*0-87395-657-5*); pap. text 19.95 (*0-87395-658-3*) State U NY Pr.

— Philosophical Mysteries. LC 80-26837. (SUNY Series in Systematic Philosophy). 151p. 1981. text 19.50 (*0-87395-524-2*) State U NY Pr.

— Plenishment in the Earth: An Ethic of Inclusion. LC 94-9881. 430p. (C). 1995. text 74.50 (*0-7914-2309-3*); pap. text 24.95 (*0-7914-2310-7*) State U NY Pr.

— The Ring of Representation. LC 91-26923. (SUNY Series in Contemporary Continental Philosophy). 262p. (C). 1992. pap. text 19.95 (*0-7914-1110-9*) State U NY Pr.

— A Theory of Art: Inexhaustibility by Contrast. LC 81-9027. (SUNY Series in Philosophy). 246p. (C). 1982. text 59.50 (*0-87395-554-4*); pap. text 19.95 (*0-87395-555-2*) State U NY Pr.

Ross, Stephen D., ed. Art & Its Significance: An Anthology of Aesthetic Theory. LC 83-9683. (SUNY Series in Philosophy). 574p. (C). 1984. text 16.50 (*0-87395-764-4*) State U NY Pr.

***Ross, Stephen David.** The Gift of Property: Having the Goods. (C). 2001. pap. text 26.95 (*0-7914-4866-5*) State U NY Pr.

— The Gift of Property: Having the Goods. (C). 2001. text 78.50 (*0-7914-4865-7*) State U NY Pr.

Ross, Stephen David. Ideals & Responsibilities. LC 97-202249. (Philosophy Ser.). (C). 1997. 37.95 (*0-534-54262-X*) Wadsworth Pub.

Ross, Stephen F. Principles of Antitrust Law. (University Textbook Ser.). 542p. 1992. text 34.95 (*1-56662-003-1*) Foundation Pr.

Ross, Stephen-Joseph, tr. see Galilea, Segundo.

Ross, Stephen M. Fiction's Inexhaustible Voice: Speech & Writing in Faulkner. LC 88-4720. 304p. 1991. pap. 18.00 (*0-8203-1375-0*) U of Ga Pr.

Ross, Stephen M. & Polk, Noel. Reading Faulkner: The Sound & the Fury. LC 96-12749. (Illus.). 176p. (C). 1996. pap. text 17.50 (*0-87805-936-9*) U Pr of Miss.

***Ross, Stephen T.** Inland Fishes of Mississippi. LC 99-53955. (Illus.). 736p. 2000. 50.00 (*1-57806-246-2*) U Pr of Miss.

Ross, Steve. DOS Windows Secrets. 1994. pap. text 24.80 (*0-929321-18-9*) WEKA Pub.

— Successful Car Buying: How to Come Out a Winner, Whether You Buy New, Buy Used, or Lease. LC 89-35283. (Illus.). 96p. (Orig.). 1990. pap. 9.95 (*0-8117-2246-5*) Stackpole.

Ross, Steve & Ross, Nancy, eds. Keys to Multimedia. (Illus.). 154p. 1996. pap. text 29.95 (*0-929321-38-3*) WEKA Pub.

Ross, Steve W., et al. Endangered, Threatened & Rare Fauna of North Carolina Pt. 2: A Re-evaluation of the Marine & Estuarine Fishes. Potter, Eloise F., ed. (Occasional Papers of the North Carolina Biological Survey). (Illus.). 24p. (Orig.). 1988. pap. text 3.00 (*0-917134-17-6*) NC Natl Sci.

Ross, Steven. American War Plans, 1945-50. rev. ed. LC 95-44735. (Illus.). 208p. (C). 1996. 52.50 (*0-7146-4635-0*, Pub. by F Cass Pubs); pap. 22.50 (*0-7146-4192-8*, Pub. by F Cass Pubs) Intl Spec Bk.

— American War Plans, 1941-1945: The Test of Battle. LC 96-22306. (Illus.). 186p. (C). 1996. 52.50 (*0-7146-4634-2*, Pub. by F Cass Pubs); pap. 24.50 (*0-7146-4194-4*, Pub. by F Cass Pubs) Intl Spec Bk.

— The Caregiver's Mission: A Comprehensive Practical Guide on Caring for Your Elderly Parent, Spouse, or Family Member. LC 93-24305. 160p. 1994. pap. 12.95 (*0-942963-41-5*) Distinctive Pub.

— European Diplomatic History, 1789-1815: France Against Europe. LC 81-8242. 432p. 1981. reprint ed. lib. bdg. 42.50 (*0-89874-369-9*) Krieger.

— From Flintlock to Rifle: Infantry Tactics, 1740-1866. LC 77-74397. (Illus.). 218p. 1979. 29.50 (*0-8386-2051-5*) Fairleigh Dickinson.

— Keys to the Internet. 1994. pap. 24.80 (*0-929321-21-9*) WEKA Pub.

— My Visit to the Nursing Home: A Children's Story of Loving & Sharing Between the Generations. Pabich, Jill, tr. & illus. by. LC 95-24142. 48p. (J). (ps-2). 1995. pap. 5.95 (*0-942963-59-8*) Distinctive Pub.

— A Parent's Guide: When Young Children Visit the Nursing Home. LC 95-23197. (Illus.). 64p. 1995. pap. 9.95 (*0-942963-60-1*) Distinctive Pub.

Ross, Steven & Van Ollefen, William. How to Maximize Your PC. (Illus.). 1050p. 1989. ring bd. 49.95 (*0-929321-03-0*) WEKA Pub.

Ross, Steven C. Essentials of dbase IV. (DF - Computer Applications Ser.). (C). 1991. mass mkt. 9.75 (*0-314-84898-3*) West Pub.

— Essentials of Quattro Program 4. 11th ed. (DF - Computer Applications Ser.). 1993. pap. 11.95 (*0-314-01036-X*) S-W Pub.

— Intermediate DBASE III Plus. (DF - Computer Applications Ser.). (C). 1991. mass mkt. 12.75 (*0-314-84897-5*) West Pub.

Ross, Steven C. Intermediate DBASE IV. (Computer Applications). 1994. pap. 14.00 (*0-314-02869-2*) West Pub.

Ross, Steven C. Intermediate Microsoft Excel 5.0. LC 95-182706. (DF - Computer Applications Ser.). (C). 1994. mass mkt. 12.50 (*0-314-04643-7*) West Pub.

— Intermediate Quattro Pro 4. (DF - Computer Applications Ser.). 1993. mass mkt. 13.50 (*0-314-01037-8*) S-W Pub.

— Introduction to Microsoft Office & Office Manager. (C). 1996. mass mkt. 5.00 (*0-314-05975-X*) West Pub.

— Understanding & Using Application Software, Vol. I. 444p. (C). 1988. mass mkt. 39.75 (*0-314-34739-9*) West Pub.

— Understanding & Using dBase IV. Leyh, ed. 434p. (C). 1990. mass mkt. 28.75 (*0-314-47364-5*) West Pub.

— Understanding & Using dBase IV 2.0. 2nd ed. Leyh, ed. LC 94-8269. (Microcomputing Ser.). 450p. (C). 1994. mass mkt., teacher ed. 25.50 (*0-314-02871-4*) West Pub.

— Understanding & Using dBASE III. (DF - Computer Applications Ser.). (C). 1988. mass mkt. 21.50 (*0-314-39289-0*) West Pub.

— Understanding & Using dBase III Plus. (Microcomputing Ser.). 283p. (C). 1987. mass mkt. 17.00 (*0-314-34744-5*) West Pub.

— Understanding & Using dBASE III Plus. 2nd ed. Leyh, ed. 368p. (C). 1991. pap. text 28.75 (*0-314-81984-3*) West Pub.

— Understanding & Using Lotus 1-2-3. (Illus.). 196p. (Orig.). (C). 1986. pap. text 28.75 (*0-314-96209-3*) West Pub.

— Understanding & Using Lotus 1-2-3: Release 2. (Microcomputing Ser.). 232p. (C). 1987. pap. text 28.75 (*0-314-34741-0*); pap. text, teacher ed. write for info. (*0-314-35880-3*) West Pub.

— Understanding Information Systems. Leyh, ed. LC 93-33048. (Microcomputing Ser.). 224p. (C). 1994. mass mkt. 16.25 (*0-314-02880-3*) West Pub.

— West's Essentials of Microsoft Windows 3. (DF - Computer Applications Ser.). 1993. mass mkt. 9.50 (*0-314-02636-3*) S-W Pub.

— West's Intermediate Microsoft Windows 3. LC 94-153281. (DF - Computer Applications Ser.). 1993. mass mkt. 12.75 (*0-314-02637-1*) S-W Pub.

Ross, Steven C. & Hutson, Stephen V. Understanding & Using Microsoft Excel 5.0. 5th ed. LC 94-5365. (Microcomputing Ser.). 528p. (C). 1995. mass mkt. 36.95 (*0-314-04626-7*) West Pub.

— Understanding & Using Microsoft Excel for Windows 95. 2nd ed. 450p. (C). 1996. mass mkt. 38.95 (*0-314-07239-X*) West Pub.

— Understanding & Using Microsoft Excel 3.0. Leyh, ed. 410p. (C). 1992. spiral bd. 28.75 (*0-314-93406-5*) West Pub.

Ross, Steven C. & Maestas, Ronald W. Understanding & Using Microsoft Windows 3.1. 2nd ed. Leyh, ed. LC 93-8665. 384p. (C). 1994. mass mkt. 26.00 (*0-314-02589-8*) West Pub.

— Understanding & Using Microsoft Windows 4. 450p. 1995. write for info. (*0-314-04659-3*) West Pub.

— Understanding & Using Microsoft Windows 95. 2nd ed. LC 95-45674. (Microcomputing Ser.). 400p. (C). 1996. mass mkt. 35.95 (*0-314-07240-3*) West Pub.

Ross, Steven C. & Reinders, Judy A. Understanding & Using Supercalc 3. (Microcomputing Ser.). 184p. (C). 1987. mass mkt. 25.50 (*0-314-30123-2*) West Pub.

Ross, Steven C., et al. Developing & Using Decision Support Applications. (Microcomputing Ser.). 266p. (C). 1987. mass mkt. 27.25 (*0-314-30124-0*) West Pub.

— Essentials of Application Software, Vol. 1. Leyh, ed. 400p. (C). 1991. pap. text 42.50 (*0-314-81734-4*) West Pub.

— Understanding & Using Application Software, Vol. II. 464p. (C). 1988. pap. text 45.25 (*0-314-34740-2*) West Pub.

— Understanding & Using Application Software, Vol. 5. Leyh, ed. 700p. (C). 1991. mass mkt. 51.00 (*0-314-66779-2*) West Pub.

— Understanding & Using Lotus 1-2-3 for Windows. 4th ed. 544p. (C). 1994. mass mkt., teacher ed. 25.75 (*0-314-01227-3*) West Pub.

Ross, Steven C., jt. auth. see Pusins, Dolores W.

Ross, Steven C., jt. auth. see Reinders, Judy A.

Ross, Steven J. Working Class Hollywood: Silent Film & the Shaping of Class in America. LC 97-8462. 384p. 1998. text 29.95 (*0-691-03234-3*, Pub. by Princeton U Pr) Cal Prin Full Svc.

***Ross, Steven J.** Working-Class Hollywood: Silent Film & the Shaping of Class in America. LC 97-8462. (Illus.). 367p. 2000. pap. text 16.95 (*0-691-02464-2*, Pub. by Princeton U Pr) Cal Prin Full Svc.

***Ross, Steven K.** Roman Edessa: Politics & Culture on Eastern Fringes of the Roman Empire. LC 99-46969. 280p. 2000. 75.00 (*0-415-18787-7*) Routledge.

Ross, Steven M., jt. ed. see Upper, Dennis.

Ross, Steven S., ed. see Council on Economic Priorities Staff, et al.

Ross, Steven T. Historical Dictionary of the Wars of the French Revolution. LC 97-32905. (Historical Dictionaries of War, Revolution, & Civil Unrest Ser.: No. 6). (Illus.). 400p. 1998. 72.00 (*0-8108-3409-X*) Scarecrow.

— U. S. War Plans, 1939-1945. LC 99-58471. 2000. pap. write for info. (*1-57524-059-9*) Krieger.

Ross, Steven T., ed. American War Plans, 1919-1941, 5 vols. rev. ed. LC 92-20669. 1992. 588.00 (*0-8153-0688-1*) Garland.

— Coalition War Plans & Hemispheric Defense Plans, 1940-1941. LC 92-20669. (American War Plans, 1919-1941 Ser.: Vol. 4). 392p. 1992. text 60.00 (*0-8153-0692-X*) Garland.

— Peacetime War Plans, 1919-1935. LC 92-20669. (American War Plans, 1919-1941 Ser.: Vol. 1). 248p. 1992. text 40.00 (*0-8153-0689-X*) Garland.

— Plans for Global War: Rainbow-5 & the Victory Program, 1941. LC 92-20669. (American War Plans, 1919-1941 Ser.: Vol. 5). 328p. 1992. text 50.00 (*0-8153-0693-8*) Garland.

— Plans for War Against the British Empire & Japan: The Red, Orange, & Red-Orange Plans, 1923-1938. LC 92-20669. (American War Plans, 1919-1941 Ser.: Vol. 2). 440p. 1992. text 60.00 (*0-8153-0690-3*) Garland.

Ross, Steven T., intro. Plans to Meet the Axis Threat, 1939-1940, Vol. 3. LC 92-20669. 376p. 1992. text 60.00 (*0-8153-0691-1*) Garland.

Ross, Stewart. And Then... A History of the World in 128 Pages. LC 96-2330. (Illus.). 128p. (J). (gr. 4 up). 1996. pap. 9.95 (*0-7613-0508-4*, Copper Beech Bks); lib. bdg. 27.40 (*0-7613-0531-9*, Copper Beech Bks) Millbrook Pr.

— Arab-Israeli Conflict. LC 95-17097. (Illus.). 80p. (YA). (gr. 7 up). 1995. lib. bdg. 27.11 (*0-8172-4051-9*) Raintree Steck-V.

— Athens Is Saved! The First Marathon. (Illus.). 62p. (J). (gr. 3-5). 1998. 15.95 (*0-237-51747-7*); pap. 8.95 (*0-237-51748-5*) EVN1 UK.

— Bandits & Outlaws. LC 95-13146. (Fact or Fiction Ser.). 1995. 12.15 (*0-606-09249-8*, Pub. by Turtleback) Demco.

— Bandits & Outlaws: The Truth about Outlaws, Highwaymen Smugglers, & Robbers from the Bandit Gangs of Ancient China to the Desperadoes of Today. (Fact or Fiction Ser.). (Illus.). 48p. (YA). (gr. 6 up). 1995. lib. bdg. 24.90 (*1-56294-649-8*, Copper Beech Bks) Millbrook Pr.

— Beasts. LC 97-10018. (Fact or Fiction Ser.). (Illus.). 48p. (YA). (gr. 6 up). 1997. lib. bdg. 24.90 (*0-7613-0547-5*, Copper Beech Bks) Millbrook Pr.

— Causes & Consequences of the Great Depression. LC 97-26532. (Causes & Consequences Ser.). 80p. (J). (gr. 6-10). 1998. 27.11 (*0-8172-4059-4*) Raintree Steck-V.

— Causes & Consequences of World War I. LC 97-27709. (Causes & Consequences Ser.). (J). (gr. 6-10). 1998. 27.11 (*0-8172-4057-8*) Raintree Steck-V.

— Conquerors & Explorers. LC 96-17157. (Fact or Fiction Ser.). (Illus.). 48p. (YA). (gr. 5 up). 1996. pap. 6.95 (*0-7613-0509-2*, Copper Beech Bks); lib. bdg. 24.90 (*0-7613-0532-7*, Copper Beech Bks) Millbrook Pr.

— Conquerors & Explorers. LC 96-17157. (Fact or Fiction Ser.). 1996. 12.15 (*0-606-09250-1*, Pub. by Turtleback) Demco.

— Cowboys. (Fact or Fiction Ser.). (Illus.). 48p. (YA). (gr. 5 up). 1995. pap. 6.95 (*1-56294-636-6*, Copper Beech Bks) Millbrook Pr.

— Cowboys. (Fact or Fiction Ser.). (Illus.). 48p. (YA). (gr. 6 up). 1995. lib. bdg. 24.90 (*1-56294-618-8*, Copper Beech Bks) Millbrook Pr.

— Cowboys. LC 94-43658. (Fact or Fiction Ser.). 1995. 12.15 (*0-606-09251-X*, Pub. by Turtleback) Demco.

***Ross, Stewart.** Crisis in Kosovo. LC 99-89603. (Illus.). 64p. (gr. 4-7). 2000. 27.12 (*0-8172-5540-0*) Raintree Steck-V.

Ross, Stewart. Daily Life. LC 99-18376. (Ancient Greece Ser.). 48p. (J). 1999. 18.95 (*0-87226-599-4*, 65994B, P Bedrick Books) NTC Contemp Pub Co.

— Dragons & Demons: Myths of China, Japan, & India. LC 97-52575. (Best Tales Ever Told Ser.). (Illus.). 44p. (YA). (gr. 5 up). 1998. lib. bdg. 23.90 (*0-7613-0708-7*, Copper Beech Bks) Millbrook Pr.

— Expanding Our Musical Options. 3rd ed. 250p. (C). 1996. per. 29.95 (*0-7872-2890-7*, 41289001) Kendall-Hunt.

***Ross, Stewart.** Find King Alfred! Alfred the Great & the Danes. (Illus.). 62p. (J). (gr. 4-6). 1998. 15.95 (*0-237-51786-8*) EVN1 UK.

Ross, Stewart. Gods & Giants: Myths of Northern Europe. LC 97-19218. (Best Tales Ever Told Ser.). (Illus.). 40p. (J). (gr. 3-4). 1997. 23.90 (*0-7613-0706-0*, Copper Beech Bks) Millbrook Pr.

— Greek Theatre. (Ancient Greece Ser.). 48p. (J). 1999. 18.95 (*0-87226-597-8*, 65978B, P Bedrick Books) NTC Contemp Pub Co.

— Knights. LC 95-39831. (Fact or Fiction Ser.). 1996. 12.15 (*0-606-09252-8*, Pub. by Turtleback) Demco.

— Long Live Mary, Queen of Scots. (Illus.). 62p. (J). (gr. 3-5). 1998. 15.95 (*0-237-51787-6*) EVN1 UK.

— Mark Twain & Huckleberry Finn. LC 98-29892. (Illus.). (gr. 5 up). 1999. 16.99 (*0-670-88181-3*) Viking Penguin.

— Monsters & Magic: Myths of North & South America. LC 97-52739. (Best Tales Ever Told Ser.). (Illus.). 44p. (YA). (gr. 5 up). 1998. lib. bdg. 23.90 (*0-7613-0707-9*, Copper Beech Bks) Millbrook Pr.

— Monsters of the Deep. LC 97-10081. (Fact or Fiction Ser.). (Illus.). 1997. pap. 7.95 (*0-7613-0595-5*, Copper Beech Bks) Millbrook Pr.

— Monsters of the Deep. LC 97-10081. (Fact or Fiction Ser.). (Illus.). 48p. (YA). (gr. 6 up). 1997. lib. bdg. 24.90 (*0-7613-0548-3*, Copper Beech Bks) Millbrook Pr.

— The Original Olympics. (Ancient Greece Ser.). 48p. (J). 1999. 18.95 (*0-87226-596-X*, 6596XB, P Bedrick Books) NTC Contemp Pub Co.

***Ross, Stewart.** The Oxford Children's Book of the 20th Century. LC 98-31233. (Illus.). 48p. (J). 1999. text 18.95 (*0-19-521488-9*) OUP.

Ross, Stewart. Pirates. LC 94-43659. (Fact or Fiction Ser.). 1995. 12.15 (*0-606-09253-6*, Pub. by Turtleback) Demco.

— Pirates: The Story of Buccaneers, Brigands, Corsairs & Their Piracy on the High Seas from the Spanish Main to the China Sea. (Fact or Fiction Ser.). (Illus.). 48p. (YA). (gr. 5 up). 1995. pap. 7.95 (*1-56294-637-4*, Copper Beech Bks) Millbrook Pr.

— Please Help, Miss Nightingale! (Coming Alive Ser.). (Illus.). 62p. (J). (ps-4). 1998. write for info. (*0-237-51749-3*) EVN1 UK.

***Ross, Stewart.** Read about Vikings. LC 99-86046. (Read about Ser.). (Illus.). 32p. (J). (gr. 2-4). 2000. 17.90 (*0-7613-1171-8*, Copper Beech Bks) Millbrook Pr.

Ross, Stewart. Rise of Japan & the Pacific Rim. LC 95-17257. (Causes & Consequences Ser.). (Illus.). 80p. (YA). (gr. 7 up). 1995. lib. bdg. 27.11 (*0-8172-4054-3*) Raintree Steck-V.

— Secret Societies. (Fact or Fiction Ser.). (Illus.). 48p. (YA). (gr. 5 up). 1996. pap. 6.95 (*0-7613-0510-6*, Copper Beech Bks); lib. bdg. 24.90 (*0-7613-0533-5*, Copper Beech Bks) Millbrook Pr.

— Secret Societies. LC 96-24579. (Fact or Fiction Ser.). 1996. 12.15 (*0-606-09254-4*, Pub. by Turtleback) Demco.

Ross, Stewart. Since 1930. (Illus.). (J). 1995. write for info. (*0-237-51583-0*); pap. write for info. (*0-237-51593-8*) EVN1 UK.

Ross, Stewart. Spies & Traitors. LC 95-13147. (Fact or Fiction Ser.). (Illus.). 48p. (YA). (gr. 5 up). 1995. pap. 24.90 (*1-56294-648-X*, Copper Beech Bks) Millbrook Pr.

— Spies & Traitors. LC 95-13147. (Fact or Fiction Ser.). 1995. 12.15 (*0-606-09255-2*, Pub. by Turtleback) Demco.

— Warriors & Witches: Myths of Southern Europe. LC 97-19217. (Best Tales Ever Told Ser.). (Illus.). 44p. (J). (gr. 5 up). 1997. lib. bdg. 23.90 (*0-7613-0705-2*, Copper Beech Bks) Millbrook Pr.

— Witches. LC 95-38885. (Fact or Fiction Ser.). (Illus.). 48p. (YA). (gr. 5 up). 1996. lib. bdg. 24.90 (*0-7613-0452-5*, Copper Beech Bks) Millbrook Pr.

— Witches. LC 95-38885. (Fact or Fiction Ser.). 1996. 12.15 (*0-606-09256-0*, Pub. by Turtleback) Demco.

— World War II. LC 95-7740. (Causes & Consequences Ser.). (Illus.). 80p. (J). 1995. lib. bdg. 27.11 (*0-8172-4050-0*) Raintree Steck-V.

Ross, Stewart & McRae Books Agency Staff. Knights. (Fact or Fiction Ser.). (Illus.). 48p. (YA). (gr. 5 up). 1996. pap. 7.95 (*0-7613-0468-1*, Copper Beech Bks); lib. bdg. 24.90 (*0-7613-0453-3*, Copper Beech Bks) Millbrook Pr.

Ross, Stewart H. The Management of Business-to-Business Advertising: A Working Guide for Small to Mid-Size Companies. LC 85-31726. 175p. 1986. 52.95 (*0-89930-163-0*, RHD/, Quorum Bks) Greenwood.

— Propaganda for War: How the United States Was Conditioned to Fight the Great War of 1914-1918. LC 95-25927. (Illus.). 351p. 1996. lib. bdg. 46.50 (*0-7864-0111-7*) McFarland & Co.

Ross, Stuart. The Inspiration Cha-Cha. 80p. 1996. pap. 12.00 (*1-55022-293-7*, Pub. by ECW) Genl Dist Srvs.

Ross, Stuart, jt. auth. see Freiberg, Arie.

Ross, Sue Imrie & Martins, Helen Elizabeth. This Is My World: The Life of Helen Martins, Creator of the Owl House. LC 98-101921. (Illus.). 1997. write for info. (*0-19-571516-0*) OUP.

Ross, Sueellen. Paint Radiant Realism in Watercolor, Ink & Colored Pencil. LC 99-21136. (Illus.). 128p. 1999. 27.99 (*0-89134-900-6*, 31424, North Lght Bks) F & W Pubns Inc.

Ross, Susan. Comparative Retirement Benefits for General State Employees & Public Safety Personnel. (State Legislative Reports: Vol. 16, No. 5). 14p. 1991. pap. text 15.00 (*1-55516-304-1*, 7302-1605) Natl Conf State Legis.

— Snowflower for Six Viols. (Contemporary Consort Ser.: No. 10). i, 14p. 1990. pap. text 11.00 (*1-56571-005-3*) PRB Prods.

Ross, Susan, ed. & illus. see Welsh, Rose & Grandahl, Shirley.

Ross, Susan A. Extravagant Affections: A Feminist Sacramental Theology. LC 98-25997. 224p. 1998. 24.95 (*0-8264-1083-9*) Continuum.

Ross, Susan A., jt. ed. see Tilley, Maureen A.

Ross, Susan D., et al. The Rights of Women: The Basic ACLU Guide to Women's Rights. rev. ed. 317p. (C). 1993. pap. 9.95 (*0-8093-1633-1*) S Ill U Pr.

— The Rights of Women: The Basic ACLU Guide to Women's Rights. 3rd rev. ed. 336p. (C). 1993. 24.95 (*0-8093-1898-9*) S Ill U Pr.

Ross, Suzanne. Little Rain Forest Activity Book. (Illus.). (J). 1995. pap. 1.00 (*0-486-28569-3*) Dover.

R

An Asterisk (*) at the beginning of an entry indicates that the title is appearing for the first time.

R

Ross, Suzanne. Nature Activity Book. (Little Activity Bks.). (Illus.). (J). 1994. pap. 1.00 (*0-486-28036-5*) Dover.

Ross, Suzanne. Nature Crossword Puzzles. (Little Activity Bks.). (Illus.). (J). 1995. pap. 1.00 (*0-486-28854-4*) Dover.

Ross, Suzanne. Rainy Day Fun. 1999. pap. text 1.00 (*0-486-40557-5*) Dover.

— What's in the Rainforest? One Hundred Six Answers from A to Z. LC 91-72682. (Illus.). 48p. (Orig.). (J). (gr. 1-7). 1991. pap. 5.95 (*0-9629895-0-9*) Enchanted Rain Pr.

Ross-Swain, Deborah. Cognitive-Linguistic Improvement Program CLIP: A Program for Speech-Language Pathologists Treating Neuropathologies of Speech & Language & Learning Disabilities. (Illus.). 264p. (Orig.). (C). 1992. pap. text 49.95 (*1-879105-62-4*, 0276) Thomson Learn.

— Ross Information Processing Assessment (RIPA-2) Examiner's Manual. 2nd ed. 44p. 1996. 49.00 (*0-685-17381-X*, 7641) PRO-ED.

— The Voice Advantage. (Illus.). 50p. (Orig.). (C). 1990. pap. text, student ed. 49.95 (*1-879105-09-8*, 0073) Singular Publishing.

Ross-Swain, Deborah, jt. auth. see Yee, Patricia.

Ross-Swain, Debra & Yee, Patricia. Geriatric Treatment Manual: Practical Tasks & Activities for Stimulating Information Processing Skills. 1998. pap. text 38.00 (*0-89079-733-1*, 8513) PRO-ED.

Ross, Sydney. Nineteenth-Century Attitudes: Men of Science. (C). 1991. text 122.00 (*0-7923-1308-9*) Kluwer Academic.

Ross, Sydney & Morris, Ian. Colloidal Systems & Interfaces. LC 87-30529. 448p. 1988. 145.00 (*0-471-82848-3*) Wiley.

Ross, T. Flash Cards, Bk. 1. 1990. 5.95 (*0-685-32026-X*, P036) Hansen Ed Mus.

— Flash Cards, Bk. 2. 1990. 7.95 (*0-685-32027-8*, P037) Hansen Ed Mus.

Ross, T. J., ed. see Mitchell, Brooks.

Ross, T. R. Henry Gassaway Davis - An Old Fashioned Biography. LC 93-92838. 341p. 1994. 30.00 (*0-87012-514-1*) McClain.
In this book, Professor Ross has provided interesting information about West Virginia Senator Henry Gassaway Davis's private life & friends as well as a careful & impartial study of his public career in business & politics. Henry Gassaway Davis was one of the more prominent & significant secondary political & business leaders of the country a century ago & his contributions continue to enhance our lives today. *Publisher Paid Annotation.*

Ross, Tami & Geil, Patti. The Carbohydrate Counting Cookbook. LC 98-231225. 208p. 1998. pap. 14.95 (*1-56561-146-2*) Wiley.

***Ross, Tami & Geil, Patti.** The Carbohydrate Counting Cookbook. 208p. 1998. pap. 14.95 (*0-471-34671-3*) Wiley.

Ross, Terry & Wright, Richard D. The Divining Mind: A Guide to Dowsing & Self-Awareness. LC 89-17192. (Illus.). 176p. 1990. pap. 10.95 (*0-89281-263-X*, Destiny Bks) Inner Tradit.

Ross, Thomas. A Book of Elisathan Magic: Thomas Hill's Naturall & Artificial Conclusions. 84p. 1974. 16.00 (*3-418-00204-8*) Adlers Foreign Bks.

— Just Stories: How the Law Embodies Racism & Bias. 192p. 1996. 24.00 (*0-8070-4400-8*) Beacon Pr.

— Just Stories: How the Law Embodies Racism & Bias. LC 95-48859. 192p. 1997. pap. 14.00 (*0-8070-4401-6*) Beacon Pr.

Ross, Thomas, jt. ed. see MacGibbon, David.

***Ross, Thomas D. & Ross, Candace.** The Border of the Sky: The Sierrra & Its Moods. LC 99-99585. (Illus.). 96p. 2000. pap. 19.95 (*0-936029-54-4*) Western Bk Journ.

Ross, Thomas E. American Indians in North Carolina: Geographic Interpretations. unabridged ed. LC 98-45814. (Illus.). 242p. 1999. pap. 29.95 (*1-891026-01-1*) Karo Hollow.

— Atlas of Moore County, North Carolina: Portrait of an Eclectic Southern County. LC 96-76290. (Illus.). 112p. (Orig.). 1996. pap. 17.95 (*0-9641628-5-7*) Karo Hollow.

— One Land, Three Peoples: A Geography of Robeson County, North Carolina. LC 94-76044. (Illus.). 130p. (Orig.). 1994. pap. 16.95 (*0-9641628-0-6*) Karo Hollow.

Ross, Thomas E., et al, eds. American Indians: A Cultural Geography. 2nd ed. LC 95-80055. (Illus.). 301p. (C). 1995. text 39.95 (*0-9641628-3-0*) Karo Hollow.

Ross, Thomas W. Good Old Index: The Sherlock Holmes Handbook. LC 96-749. (Illus.). x, 172p. 1997. pap. 29.95 (*1-57113-049-7*) Camden Hse.

Ross, Thomas W. & Brooks, Edward, Jr., eds. English Glosses from British Library MS Additional 37075 (A Fifteenth Century Word-List) LC 84-18877. 250p. 1984. 24.95 (*0-937664-66-9*) Pilgrim Bks OK.

Ross, Thomasina, tr. see Von Humboldt, Alexander.

***Ross, Tim.** Brewster the Rain Makin' Rooster. LC 99-36029. (J). 1999. 14.95 (*1-57168-332-1*, Eakin Pr) Sunbelt Media.

— Brewster, the Rain-Makin' Rooster. (Illus.). (J). (ps-3). 1999. pap. 7.95 (*1-57168-357-7*, Eakin Pr) Sunbelt Media.

Ross, Tim R., jt. auth. see Yacenda, John A.

Ross, Timothy. Fuzzy Logic with Engineering Applications. (C). 1995. 88.25 (*0-07-053917-0*) McGraw.

Ross, Timothy A., jt. ed. see Lau, Joseph S.

Ross, Timothy A., tr. see Chiang, Kuei.

Ross, Timothy L., jt. auth. see Graham-Moore, Brian.

Ross, Todd, ed. see Lybrand, Fred R., Jr.

Ross, Tom. Eggbert, the Slightly Cracked Egg. (Illus.). 32p. (J). (ps-3). 1994. 15.95 (*0-399-22416-5*, G P Putnam) Peng Put Young Read.

— Eggbert, the Slightly Cracked Egg. (Illus.). 32p. (J). (ps-3). 1997. pap. 5.99 (*0-698-11444-2*, PapStar) Peng Put Young Read.

— Eggbert, the Slightly Cracked Egg. 1997. 11.15 (*0-606-11291-X*, Pub. by Turtleback) Demco.

Ross, Tom & Ross, Marilyn. The Complete Guide to Self-Publishing: Everything You Need to Know to Write, Publish, Promote, & Sell Your Own Book. 3rd ed. LC 94-16872. (Illus.). 432p. 1994. pap. 18.99 (*0-89879-646-6*, Wrtrs Digest Bks) F & W Pubns Inc.

— The Force of Us: Living, Loving & Working Together. 224p. 1999. 19.95 (*0-918880-31-9*) Comm Creat.

Ross, Tom, jt. auth. see Ross, Marilyn.

Ross, Tom, jt. auth. see Ross, Marilyn H.

Ross, Tom, frwd. see Bone, Bob.

Ross, Tony. Animales/Pets. (Coleccion LA Princesita/the Little Princess Series). 1996. 7.95 (*84-480-1056-6*) Timur Publishing Inc.

— Bedtime. LC 94-36611. (Little Princess Board Bks.). (Illus.). 14p. (J). (ps). 1995. pap. 6.00 (*0-15-200317-7*, Red Wagon Bks) Harcourt.

— The Boy Who Cried Wolf. 1992. pap. 5.99 (*0-14-054612-X*) NAL.

— The Boy Who Cried Wolf. (J). 1991. 10.19 (*0-606-04619-4*, Pub. by Turtleback) Demco.

— Un Cuento de Hadas (A Fairy Tale) Dominguez, Catalina, tr. (SPA., Illus.). 32p. (J). (gr. 1-3). 1993. 12.99 (*968-16-4115-9*, Pub. by Fondo) Continental Bk.

Ross, Tony. Formas/shapes. (Coleccion LA Princesita/the Little Princess Series). 1996. 7.95 (*84-480-1055-8*) Timur Publishing Inc.

Ross, Tony. Hansel & Gretel. LC 93-31047. (Illus.). 32p. (J). (ps-3). 1994. 13.95 (*0-87951-535-X*, Pub. by Overlook Pr) Penguin Putnam.

— I Want My Dinner. LC 95-18185. (Illus.). 32p. (J). 1996. 12.00 (*0-15-200972-8*) Harcourt.

— I Want My Potty. (SPA., Illus.). 32p. (J). (ps-k). 1996. write for info. (*1-85430-147-0*) MAGI1 UK.

— I Want My Potty. (Illus.). 24p. (J). (ps). 1988. reprint ed. pap. 6.95 (*0-916291-14-6*) Kane-Miller Bk.

— I Want to Be. LC 92-41527. (Illus.). 32p. (J). (ps-1). 1993. 11.95 (*0-916291-46-4*) Kane-Miller Bk.

***Ross, Tony.** L. S. Lowery: A Biography. (Illus.). 432p. 1999. 24.95 (*1-902970-01-2*, Pub. by Lowry Pr) Antique Collect.

— Mister Lowry. (Illus.). 40p. 1999. 11.95 (*1-902970-02-0*, Pub. by Lowry Pr) Antique Collect.

Ross, Tony. Oscar Got the Blame. (J). Date not set. pap. text. write for info. (*0-05-004405-2*) Addison-Wesley.

— Pets. LC 94-36609. (Little Princess Board Bks.). (Illus.). 14p. (J). (ps). 1995. pap. 6.00 (*0-15-200318-5*, Red Wagon Bks) Harcourt.

— Shapes. LC 94-36610. (Little Princess Board Bks.). (Illus.). 14p. (J). (ps). 1995. pap. 6.00 (*0-15-200319-3*, Red Wagon Bks) Harcourt.

***Ross, Tony.** Silly, Silly. (J). 1999. 19.95 (*0-86264-740-1*, Pub. by Andersen Pr) Trafalgar.

Ross, Tony. Stone Soup. 1992. pap. 6.99 (*0-14-054708-8*) NAL.

Ross, Tony. Stone Soup. 1990. 11.19 (*0-606-04813-8*, Pub. by Turtleback) Demco.

Ross, Tony. Super Dooper Jezebel. LC 88-45091. (Illus.). 32p. 1990. pap. 3.95 (*0-374-47342-0*) FS&G.

— This Old Man. 12p. (J). (ps-1). 1990. 9.95 (*0-689-71386-X*) Aladdin.

— El Trapito Feliz (The Happy Rag) Dominguez, Catalina, tr. (SPA.). 24p. (J). (gr. 1-3). 1994. 12.99 (*968-16-4555-3*, Pub. by Fondo) Continental Bk.

***Ross, Tony.** Wash Your Hands! (Illus.). 32p. (J). (ps-3). 2000. 11.95 (*1-929132-00-X*); pap. 6.95 (*1-929132-01-8*) Kane-Miller Bk.

Ross, Tony. Weather. LC 94-36612. (Little Princess Board Bks.). (Illus.). 14p. (J). (ps). 1995. pap. 6.00 (*0-15-200320-7*, Red Wagon Bks) Harcourt.

Ross, Tony. Animals. LC 94-49432. (ENG & FRE.). 26p. (J). (ps-2). 1995. 11.95 (*0-590-55202-3*, Cartwheel) Scholastic Inc.

Ross, Tony. Goldilocks & the Three Bears. 26p. (J). (ps-3). 1992. 13.95 (*0-87951-453-1*, Pub. by Overlook Pr) Penguin Putnam.

Ross, Tony, jt. auth. see Thomson, Pat.

Ross, Tony, jt. illus. see Danziger, Paula.

***Ross, Tracie, ed.** Motor Carrier Safety Regulations: Management Edition. 389p. 2000. pap. 9.95 (*0-940394-83-9*) Labelmaster.

— Motor Carrier Safety Regulations: Management Edition. 389p. 2000. pap. 9.95 (*0-940394-85-5*) Labelmaster.

— Motor Carrier Safety Regulations: Management Edition. rev. ed. 400p. 1999. pap. 7.65 (*0-940394-80-4*) Labelmaster.

Ross, Trevor. Making of the English Literary Canon: From the Middle Ages to the Late Eighteenth Century. 408p. 1998. text 65.00 (*0-7735-1683-2*, Pub. by McG-Queens Univ Pr) CUP Services.

***Ross, Trevor.** The Making of the English Literary Canon: From the Middle Ages to the Late Eighteenth Century. 408p. 2000. pap. 24.95 (*0-7735-2080-5*, Pub. by McG-Queens Univ Pr) CUP Services.

Ross, Trish & Trafford, Jacquie. Easy Beans. 6th ed. (Illus.). 116p. 1996. reprint ed. pap. 10.95 (*0-9698162-0-0*, Pub. by B Bean Pubng) Midpt Trade.

— More Easy Beans. 120p. 1997. pap. 10.95 (*0-9698162-1-9*, Pub. by B Bean Pubng) Midpt Trade.

Ross, Truedie L. & Ross, Richard G. Unclaimed Fortunes: How to Discover Your Share. LC 91-78132. 68p. 1992. pap. 9.95 (*0-9631885-0-X*) Kalia Pubns.

***Ross, Turchaninov & Cox, C. A.** Medical Massage. (Illus.). 413p. 1998. pap. text 50.00 (*0-9675868-0-1*) Aesculapius Bks.

***Ross, Turcheninov.** Therapeutic Massage: A Scientific Approach. (Illus.). 242p. 2000. pap. text 35.00 (*0-9675868-1-X*) Aesculapius Bks.

Ross, Tweed. Planning Educational Facilities for Information Technology. (Illus.). 32p. 1997. pap. text 9.95 (*0-914607-52-9*, 1734) Master Tchr.

Ross, Tweed W., Jr. The Best Way to Destroy a Ship: The Evidence of European Naval Operations in World War II. 219p. (Orig.). 1980. pap. text 35.95 (*0-89126-069-2*) MA-AH Pub.

Ross, Tweed W. & Bailey, Gearld D. Technology-Based Learning: A Handbook for Principals & Technology Leaders. LC 94-12518. (Illus.). 192p. 1995. 29.95 (*0-590-49626-3*) Scholastic Inc.

Ross, Tweed W., Jr. & Bailey, Gerald D. Technology-Based Learning: A Handbook for Principals & Technology Leaders. 2nd rev. ed. LC 96-78481. (Illus.). 172p. 1996. pap. 32.95 (*1-57517-074-4*, 1468) SkyLght.

Ross, Veronica. The Anastasia Connection. 204p. 15.95 (*1-55128-038-8*, Pub. by Mercury Bk) LPC InBook.

— Hannah B. pap. 12.95 (*0-920544-81-9*, Pub. by Mercury Bk) LPC InBook.

— Millicent: A Mystery. 256p. mass mkt. 7.99 (*1-55128-042-6*, Pub. by Mercury Bk) LPC InBook.

Ross, Victor J. Bite the Wall! LC 84-10316. 408p. 1986. 19.95 (*0-88280-108-2*) ETC Pubns.

Ross, Victor J. & Marlowe, John. The Forbidden Apple: Sex in the Schools. LC 84-6152. 112p. 1985. 19.95 (*0-88280-107-4*) ETC Pubns.

Ross, Victoria A., jt. auth. see Flath, Richard.

Ross, W. A. A Little Book of Celtic Proverbs (Irish) (Illus.). 60p. 1996. 9.95 (*0-86281-572-X*, Pub. by Appletree Pr) Irish Bks Media.

— A Little Book of Celtic Verse. (Illus.). 60p. 1996. 9.95 (*0-86281-603-3*, Pub. by Appletree Pr) Irish Bks Media.

— A Little Book of Gaelic Proverbs (Scottish) (Illus.). 60p. 1996. 9.95 (*0-86281-596-7*, Pub. by Appletree Pr) Irish Bks Media.

— A Little Book of Welsh Proverbs. (Illus.). 60p. 1996. 9.95 (*0-86281-624-6*, Pub. by Appletree Pr) Irish Bks Media.

Ross, W. D. The Right & the Good. LC 88-11019. 184p. (C). 1988. reprint ed. pap. 14.95 (*0-87220-058-2*); reprint ed. lib. bdg. 34.95 (*0-87220-059-0*) Hackett Pub.

Ross, W. D., ed. see Theophrast.

Ross, W. David. The Skills of Management. 4th ed. LC 95-35014. 352p. 1996. pap. 28.95 (*0-415-12525-1*) Thomson Learn.

Ross, W. David, ed. Analytica Priora et Posteriora. (Oxford Classical Texts Ser.). 210p. (C). 1981. text 23.00 (*0-19-814562-4*) OUP.

— Ars Rhetorica. (Oxford Classical Texts Ser.). 220p. 1959. text 24.95 (*0-19-814557-8*) OUP.

— De Anima. (Oxford Classical Texts Ser.). 122p. 1956. text 24.95 (*0-19-814508-X*) OUP.

— Fragmenta Selecta. (Oxford Classical Texts Ser.). 170p. 1955. text 27.00 (*0-19-814512-8*) OUP.

— Politica. (Oxford Classical Texts Ser.). 292p. 1957. text 26.00 (*0-19-814515-2*) OUP.

— Topica et Sophistici Elenchi. (Oxford Classical Texts Ser.). 270p. 1958. text 29.95 (*0-19-814516-0*) OUP.

Ross, W. David, ed. see Aristotle.

Ross, W. E. Reunion in Renfrew. large type ed. (Linford Romance Library). 288p. 1992. pap. 16.99 (*0-7089-7190-3*) Ulverscroft.

— This Man I Love. large type ed. (Romance Ser.). 320p. 1995. pap. 16.99 (*0-7089-7665-4*, Linford) Ulverscroft.

Ross, W. Gillies. This Distant & Unsurveyed Country: A Woman's Winter at Baffin Island, 1857-1858. LC 98-214889. (Illus.). 258p. 1997. 34.95 (*0-7735-1674-3*, Pub. by McG-Queens Univ Pr) CUP Services.

Ross, W. Gillies, ed. see Comer, George.

Ross, W. MacLeod. A Guide to the Design & Manufacture of Printed Board Assemblies, Vols. 1 & 2. 744p. 1997. pap. 350.00 (*0-901150-32-0*) St Mut.

Ross, W. McGregor. Kenya from Within: A Short Political History. (Illus.). 486p. 1968. 47.50 (*0-7146-1715-6*, Pub. by F Cass Pubs) Intl Spec Bk.

Ross, W. O., ed. Middle English Sermons from Manuscript Roy, No. 18 B. (EETS, OS Ser.: Vol. 209). 1974. reprint ed. 70.00 (*0-8115-3385-9*) Periodicals Srv.

Ross, W. Ogden. Marketing in Commercial Banks. LC 68-579749. 1968. 19.95 (*0-912164-07-7*) Masterco Pr.

Ross, W. W., jt. auth. see Gustafson, Ralph.

Ross, Walter, jt. auth. see Hitchin, David.

Ross, Walter R. Courage Beyond the Blindfold. 1995. pap. 13.95 (*1-885353-03-0*) Global Press.

Ross, Walter S. How to Quit Smoking Permanently. 1999. pap. write for info. (*0-316-75753-5*) Little.

Ross, Warner A. My Colored Battalion. 17.95 (*0-8488-1142-9*) Amereon Ltd.

Ross, Wilbur L., jt. auth. see Cook, Michael L.

Ross, William. Collection of Pipe Music - Piobaireachd. MacRaonuill, Alasdair, ed. & intro. by. 180p. 1995. pap. 24.00 (*0-614-24063-8*) A MacRaonuill.

Ross, William A. Sex: There's More to It Than You've Been Told. Carlson, Robert, ed. 96p. (Orig.). 1988. pap. 4.95 (*0-9619246-0-8*) Playful Wisdom.

Ross, William A., compiled by. Words from the Masters: A Guide to the God Within. 350p. 1989. pap. 29.95 (*0-9619246-3-2*) Playful Wisdom.

Ross, William A. & Ford, Judy. Lovers' Quarrels: The Other Side of Romance. Carlson, Robert, ed. 96p. (Orig.). 1988. pap. 4.95 (*0-9619246-1-6*) Playful Wisdom.

Ross, William A., jt. auth. see Duff, Jon M.

Ross, William A., jt. auth. see Ford, Judy.

Ross, William D. Plato's Theory of Ideas. LC 75-36510. 250p. 1976. reprint ed. lib. bdg. 69.50 (*0-8371-8635-8*, ROPTI, Greenwood Pr) Greenwood.

Ross, William E. & House, Thomas M. Durham: A Century in Photographs. LC 97-114348. (Images of America Ser.). 1999. pap. 16.99 (*0-7524-0475-X*) Arcadia Publng.

Ross, William G. Forging New Freedoms: Nativism, Education & the Constitution, 1917-1927. LC 93-44308. (Illus.). x, 285p. (C). 1994. text 50.00 (*0-8032-3900-9*) U of Nebr Pr.

— The Honest Hour: The Ethics of Time-Based Billing by Attorneys. LC 95-68698. 296p. (C). 1996. boxed set 35.00 (*0-89089-902-9*) Carolina Acad Pr.

— A Muted Fury: Populists, Progressives, & Labor Unions Confront the Courts, 1890-1937. LC 93-13698. 368p. 1993. text 49.50 (*0-691-03264-5*, Pub. by Princeton U Pr) Cal Prin Full Svc.

Ross, William M. The Ticket to Harmony. 94p. (Orig.). (J). (gr. 4-9). 1993. pap. 5.95 (*1-883787-00-9*) Trolley Car.

— The Ticket to Harmony, Set. 94p. (Orig.). (J). (gr. 4-9). 1993. pap., teacher ed. 7.95 (*1-883787-01-7*) Trolley Car.

Ross, William T., jt. auth. see Cima, Joseph A.

Ross, Williamson H. Sir Walter Raleigh. LC 78-17033. 215p. 1978. reprint ed. lib. bdg. 35.00 (*0-313-20577-9*, ROSI, Greenwood Pr) Greenwood.

Ross-Williamson, Hugh. The Poetry of T. S. Eliot. LC 71-156296. (Studies in T. S. Eliot: No. 11). 1971. reprint ed. lib. bdg. 75.00 (*0-8383-1291-8*) M S G Haskell Hse.

Ross, Wilma. X-15 Rocket Plane. LC 93-1844. (Those Daring Machines Ser.). (Illus.). 48p. (J). (gr. 5-6). 1994. lib. bdg. 13.95 (*0-89686-831-1*, Crstwood Hse) Silver Burdett Pr.

Ross, Wilma S. Fabulous Facts about the 50 States. 1986. 9.09 (*0-606-00986-8*, Pub. by Turtleback) Demco.

Ross, Worley H., et al. Integrated Strategic Change: How OD Builds Competitive Advantage. Payne, Michael, ed. LC 95-22217. (Organized Development Ser.). 158p. (C). 1995. pap. text 40.00 (*0-201-85777-4*) Addison-Wesley.

***Ross, Zoe, ed.** Insight Guide Amsterdam. 2nd rev. ed. (Insight Guides Ser.). (Illus.). 242p. 2000. pap. 22.95 (*1-58573-000-9*, Insight Guides) Langenscheidt.

Rossabi, Morris. Khubilai Khan: His Life & Times. LC 86-25031. (Illus.). 344p. 1988. pap. 18.95 (*0-520-06740-1*, Pub. by U CA Pr) Cal Prin Full Svc.

Rossabi, Morris, ed. China among Equals: The Middle Kingdom & Its Neighbors, 10th-14th Centuries. LC 81-11486. 400p. (C). 1983. pap. 17.95 (*0-520-04562-9*, Pub. by U CA Pr) Cal Prin Full Svc.

Rossano, Anthony. Inside Softimage 3D. LC 98-84639. 1998. 75.00 (*1-56205-885-1*) New Riders Pub.

Rossano, G. S. & Craine, E. R. Near Infrared Photographic Sky Survey: A Field Index. (Astronomy & Astrophysics Ser.: Vol. 8). (Illus.). 208p. 1980. 38.00 (*0-912918-11-X*, 0911) Pachart Pub Hse.

Rossano, Geoffrey L., ed. Creating a Dignified Past: Museums & the Colonial Revival. (Illus.). 129p. (C). 1991. 32.50 (*0-8476-7690-0*) Rowman.

— The Price of Honor: The World War One Letters of Naval Aviator Kenneth Macleish. LC 90-45844. (Illus.). 320p. 1991. 32.95 (*0-87021-584-1*) Naval Inst Pr.

Rossano, Joan, jt. auth. see Schiller, Pam.

Rossant. Fruit. 1999. pap. 30.00 (*0-670-84955-3*) Viking Penguin.

Rossant, Colette. Memories of a Lost Egypt: A Memoir with Recipes. LC 98-31942. 160p. 1999. 21.00 (*0-609-60150-4*, Crown) Crown Pub Group.

— My Mother's House & Sido. 224p. 1995. 14.50 (*0-679-60157-0*) Random.

Rossant, J. & Pedersen, Roger A., eds. Experimental Approaches to Mammalian Embryonic Development. (Illus.). 576p. 1988. pap. text 47.95 (*0-521-36891-X*) Cambridge U Pr.

***Rossant, John.** The Prince. 2000. write for info. (*0-688-16457-9*, Wm Morrow) Morrow Avon.

Rossari, Corinne. Les Operations de Reformulation: Analyse du Processus et des Marques Dans Une Perspective Contrastive Francais - Italien. 2nd ed. (Sciences pour la Communication Ser.: Vol. 40). (FRE.). xii, 220p. 1997. 36.95 (*3-906757-86-2*, Pub. by P Lang) P Lang Pubng.

Rossbach, August & Westphal, Rudolf. Theorie der Musischen Kunste der Hellenen, 3 vols. in 2. cxii, 1783p. 1966. reprint ed. write for info. (*0-318-71012-9*); reprint ed. write for info. (*0-318-71013-7*); reprint ed. write for info. (*0-318-71014-5*); reprint ed. write for info. (*0-318-71015-3*); reprint ed. write for info. (*0-318-71016-1*) G Olms Pubs.

Rossbach, Ed. The Nature of Basketry. rev. ed. LC 85-63576. (Illus.). 192p. 1986. reprint ed. pap. 14.95 (*0-88740-059-0*) Schiffer.

Rossbach, H. John McQueen: The Language of Containment. (Renwick Contemporary American Craft Ser.). (Illus.). 56p. 1992. pap. 14.95 (*0-295-97153-3*) U of Wash Pr.

Rossbach, J. High Energy Accelerators, '92: Proceedings of the Fifteenth International Conference. 1272p. 1993. text 206.00 (*981-02-1152-X*) World Scientific Pub.

Rossbach, Lucille, jt. auth. see Idalia Writing Lab Staff.

Rossbach, M., et al, eds. Specimen Banking: Environmental Monitoring & Modern Analytical Approaches. LC 92-12244. (Illus.). x, 242p. 1992. 153.95 (*0-387-55001-1*) Spr-Verlag.

***Rossbach, Peter.** Java Server & Servlets: Building Portable Web Applications. (Illus.). 352p. 2000. pap. text 44.95 (*0-201-67491-2*) Addison-Wesley.

Rossbach, Sarah. Feng Shui: The Chinese Art of Placement. LC 96-181761. (Illus.). 192p. 1991. pap. 13.95 (*0-14-019353-7*, Arkana) Viking Penguin.

***Rossbach, Sarah.** Feng Shui: The Chinese Art of Placement. (Illus.). 192p. 2000. pap. 13.95 (*0-14-019611-0*) Viking Penguin.

An Asterisk (*) at the beginning of an entry indicates that the title is appearing for the first time.

R

— Interior Design with Feng Shui. expanded ed. (Illus.). 224p. 2000. pap. 15.95 (*0-14-019608-0*, Penguin Bks) Viking Penguin.

Rossbach, Sarah. Living Color: Master Lin Yun's Guide to Feng Shui & the Art of Color. LC 94-10152. (Illus.). 208p. 1994. pap. 18.00 (*1-56836-014-2*) Kodansha.

Rossbach, Sarah & Yun, Lin. Feng Shui Design: From History & Landscape to Modern Gardens & Interiors. LC 98-18275. (Illus.). 192p. 1998. 29.95 (*0-670-88223-2*) Viking Penguin.

***Rossbach, Stefan.** Gnostic Wars: The Cold War in the Context of a History of Western Spirituality. 2000. 75.00 (*0-7486-1024-3*, Pub. by Edinburgh U Pr) Col U Pr.

***Rossbacher, Brigitte.** Illusions of Progress: Christa Wolf & the Critique of Science in GDR Women's Literature. LC 99-37420. (DDR-Studien/East German Studies: Vol. 13). 224p. (C). 2000. text 55.95 (*0-8204-4471-5*) P Lang Pubng.

Rossbacher, Lisa A. & Buchanan, Rex C. Geomedia: A Guide for Geoscientists Who Meet the Press. 45p. 1988. pap. 7.50 (*0-913312-96-7*) Am Geol.

Rossbacher, Nancy. Civil War Collector's Price Guide. 8th ed. (Illus.). 254p. 1997. pap. 27.50 (*0-942365-07-0*) North South Trader.

Rossdale, Peter. Horse's Health from A to Z. LC 98-128717. (Illus.). 472p. 1998. pap. 19.95 (*0-7153-0714-2*, Pub. by D & C Pub) Sterling.

Rossdale, Peter D. The Horse: From Conception to Maturity. 224p. 1990. write for info. (*0-7855-2640-4*, Pub. by J A Allen) St Mut.

— The Horse: From Conception to Maturity. (Illus.). 1984. pap. 25.00 (*0-87556-609-X*) Saifer.

***Rossdale, Peter D.** Horse from Conception to Maturity. 2000. pap. 20.95 (*0-85131-546-1*, Pub. by J A Allen) Trafalgar.

Rosse, Cornelius & Gaddum-Rosse, Penelope. Hollinshead's Textbook of Anatomy. 5th ed. LC 96-8005. 1,054p. 1997. text 52.50 (*0-397-51256-2*) Lppncott W & W.

Rosse, Gerard. The Spirituality of Communion: A New Approach to the Johannine Writings. LC 98-11731. 128p. 1998. pap. 9.95 (*1-56548-116-X*) New City.

***Rosse, John P.** A Whole New Game: Off the Field Changes in Baseball, 1946-1960. LC 99-21308. (Illus.). 263p. 1999. pap. 32.50 (*0-7864-0651-8*) McFarland & Co.

Rosse, Joseph G. & Levin, Robert. High-Impact Hiring: A Comprehensive Guide to Performance-Based Hiring. LC 97-24255. 400p. 1997. 34.95 (*0-7879-0995-5*) Jossey-Bass.

Rosse, R. B. The Love Trauma Syndrome: Free Yourself from the Pain of a Broken Heart. LC RC543.R67 1999. (Illus.). 305p. (C). 1999. 26.95 (*0-306-46006-8*, Pub. by Perseus Pubng) HarpC.

Rosse, Richard B., et al. Concise Guide to Laboratory & Diagnostic Testing in Psychiatry. LC 89-3. (Concise Guides Ser.). 151p. 1989. pap. text 22.95 (*0-88048-333-4*, 8333) Am Psychiatric.

Rosse, Wendell F. Transfusion Support for Patients with Sickle Cell Disease. LC 98-42096. (Orig.). 1998. 79.00 (*1-56395-103-7*) Am Assn Blood.

Rosseau, Jean-Jacques. Emile. Jimack, P. D., ed. 512p. 1993. pap. 6.95 (*0-460-87380-6*, Everyman's Classic Lib) Tuttle Pubng.

Rosseel, Frank R. A Back Number Town: Lewiston, New York. 1984. lib. bdg. 49.95 (*0-88946-025-6*) E Mellen.

***Rosseel, T. M.** Heavy-Section Steel Irradiation Program: Progress Report for April 1997-March 1998. 65p. 2000. pap. 7.00 (*0-16-059223-2*) USGPO.

— Heavy-Section Steel Irradiation Program: Semiannual Progress Report for October 1996-March 1997. 69p. 1998. pap. 6.00 (*0-16-062895-4*) USGPO.

Rossein, Merrick T. Employment Discrimination: Law & Litigation, 2 vols. 1990. ring bd. 220.00 (*0-87632-736-6*) West Group.

Rossel, Greg. Building Small Boats. (Illus.). 288p. 1998. 39.95 (*0-937822-50-7*) WoodenBoat Pubns.

Rossel, Seymour. Bible Legnds. LC 96-8558. (Sefer Ha-Aggadah Ser.: Vol. 1). (Illus.). 90p. (J). (gr. 3-7). 1996. pap. 14.00 (*0-8074-0603-1*, 104031) UAHC.

— A Child's Bible Bk. 1: The Torah & Its Lessons. 96p. 1988. pap., teacher ed. 14.95 (*0-87441-467-9*) Behrman.

— A Child's Bible Bk. 1: The Torah & Its Lessons. (J). (gr. 3 up). 1988. pap., student ed. 9.95 (*0-87441-466-0*) Behrman.

— Child's Bible Bk. 2: Lessons from the Writings & Prophets, Vol. 2. 1989. pap., teacher ed. 14.95 (*0-87441-485-7*) Behrman.

— Child's Bible Bk. 2: Lessons from the Writings & Prophets, Vol. 2. (J). (gr. 4-5). 1989. pap. text 9.95 (*0-87441-487-3*) Behrman.

Rossel, Seymour. The Holocaust: The World & the Jews, 1933-1945. Altshuler, David A., ed. 192p. (YA). (gr. 9-12). 1992. pap. text 8.95 (*0-87441-526-8*) Behrman.

Rossel, Seymour. The Holocaust: The World & the Jews, 1933-1945. 1995. pap., teacher ed. 14.95 (*0-87441-532-2*) Behrman.

— Introduction to Jewish History: From Abraham to the Sages. Kozodoy, Neil, ed. (Illus.). 128p. (J). (gr. 4-5). 1981. pap. text 8.95 (*0-87441-335-4*) Behrman.

— Israel: Covenant People, Covenant Land. (Illus.). 256p. (YA). (gr. 7-9). 1985. pap. 8.95 (*0-8074-0303-2*, 147500) UAHC.

— The Jewish Condition: Essays on Contemporary Judaism Honoring Rabbi Alexander M. Schindler. Hirt-Manheimer, Aron, ed. 93p. 1997. pap. 12.00 (*0-8074-0540-X*, 160006) UAHC.

— Journey Through Jewish History: The Age of Faith & the Age of Freedom, Vol. II. (Illus.). 128p. (J). (gr. 6). 1983. pap. text 8.95 (*0-87441-366-4*) Behrman.

— Lessons from Our Living Past. Harlow, Jules, ed. (J). (gr. 2-3). 1997. reprint ed. pap. 8.95 (*0-87441-085-1*) Behrman.

— Lessons from the Torah: A Child's Bible Gamebook, Bk. 1. 1997. reprint ed. 4.95 (*0-87441-512-8*) Behrman.

— Let Freedom Ring: A History of the Jews in the United States. Strauss, Ruby G., ed. LC 96-132650. (Illus.). 96p. (J). (gr. 5-7). 1995. pap. text 5.95 (*0-87441-582-9*) Behrman.

***Rossel, Seymour.** Managing the Jewish Classroom: How to Transform Yourself into a Master Jewish Teacher. 256p. (C). 1998. pap. 12.95 (*0-933873-96-4*) Torah Aura.

Rossel, Seymour. A Spiritual Journey: The Bar Mitzvah & Bat Mitzvah Handbook. Cutter, William, ed. (Illus.). 64p. pap. 5.95 (*0-87441-551-9*) Behrman.

— Tales of the Sages. (Sefer Ha-Aggadah Ser.: Vol. 2). (Illus.). 96p. (J). (gr. 3-7). 1997. pap. 14.00 (*0-8074-0627-9*, 104033) UAHC.

— A Thousand & One Chickens. LC 95-32230. (Illus.). (J). (gr. 4-6). 1995. pap. 10.00 (*0-8074-0541-8*, 123940) UAHC.

— When a Jew Prays. (Illus.). 192p. (J). (gr. 4-5). pap. 9.50 (*0-87441-093-2*) Behrman.

Rossel, Seymour & Avrami, Malkah L. Introduction to Jewish History: From Abraham to the Sages. Kozodoy, Neil, ed. (Illus.). 128p. (J). (gr. 4-5). 1981. pap., wbk. ed. 4.95 (*0-87441-363-X*) Behrman.

Rossel, Seymour, et al. When a Jew Seeks Wisdom: The Sayings of the Fathers. LC 75-14119. (Jewish Values Ser.). (J). (gr. 7). pap. 9.50 (*0-87441-089-4*) Behrman.

Rossel, Seymour, jt. auth. see Kipper, Lenore C.

Rossel, Seymour, jt. auth. see Sugarman, Morris J.

Rossel, Seymour, ed. see Ben-Aharon, Moshe, et al.

Rossel, Seymour, ed. see Newman, Shirley.

Rossel, Seymour, ed. see Rosenberg, Amye & Mason, Patrice G.

Rossel, Seymour, ed. see Rosenthal, Gilbert S.

Rossel, Seymour, ed. see Singer, Ellen, et al.

Rossel, Sven Hakon. A History of Scandinavian Literature, 1870-1980. Ulmer, Anne C., tr. LC 81-14654. (Nordic Ser.: No. 5). 504p. reprint ed. pap. 156.30 (*0-7837-2923-5*, 205753100006) Bks Demand.

Rossel, Sven Hakon, ed. A History of Danish Literature. LC 91-46729. (History of Scandinavian Literature Ser.: Vol. 1). (Illus.). xvi, 709p. 1992. text 60.00 (*0-8032-3886-X*) U of Nebr Pr.

— Why Not! A Picture Out of Life. Ingalsbe, Lori A., tr. from SWE. & intro. by. 120p. (Orig.). (C). 1994. pap. 9.95 (*1-880755-08-4*) Mermaid Pr.

Rossel, Sven Hakon & Elbrond-Bek, Bo, eds. Christmas in Scandinavia. Colbert, David W., tr. LC 95-26575. 184p. 1996. text 25.00 (*0-8032-3907-6*) U of Nebr Pr.

***Rossel, Sven Hakon & Elbrond-Bek, Bo, eds.** Christmas in Scandinavia. Colbert, David W., tr. LC 95-26575. 184p. 1999. pap. 12.00 (*0-8032-8980-4*) U of Nebr Pr.

Rossel, Sven Hakon, ed. see Bjornvig, Thorkild.

Rossel, Sven Hakon, tr. see Holberg, Ludvig.

Rossel Waugh, Carol-Lynn, ed. see King, Stephen, et al.

***Rosselet, Dale A., et al.** New Jersey WATERS: A Watershed Approach to Teaching the Ecology of Regional Systems. LC 99-56146. (Illus.). 218p. 1999. teacher ed. 30.00 (*0-9624065-3-8*) NJ Audubon Soc.

Rosselet, Joan, jt. auth. see Daix, Pierre.

Rosselini, G. Vip, Pacap & Related Regulatory Peptides. 648p. 1994. text 137.00 (*981-02-1788-9*) World Scientific Pub.

Rossell, Christine H. The Carrot or the Stick for School Desegregation Policy: Magnet Schools or Forced Busing. (Illus.). 272p. 1990. 49.95 (*0-87722-682-2*) Temple U Pr.

— The Carrot or the Stick for School Desegregation Policy: Magnet Schools or Forced Busing. LC 89-37634. 1991. pap. 24.95 (*0-87722-924-4*) Temple U Pr.

Rossell, Christine H. & Baker, Keith. Bilingual Education in Massachusetts: The Emperor Has No Clothes. Ciffolillo, Kathryn, ed. LC 96-278. (Pioneer Paper Ser.: No. 10). 242p. (Orig.). 1996. pap. 15.00 (*0-929930-14-2*) Pioneer Inst.

Rossell, Deac. Living Pictures: The Origins of the Movies. LC 94-27561. (SUNY Series in Cultural Studies in Cinema/Video). (Illus.). 192p. (C). 1998. text 59.50 (*0-7914-3767-1*); pap. text 19.95 (*0-7914-3768-X*) State U NY Pr.

Rossell, Denton. Voice: A Dramatic New Concept. Westman, Delorez, ed. (Illus.). 227p. 1984. 28.50 (*0-913145-00-9*) Clark & Westman-Magnolia.

***Rossell, Joaquin.** Minimalist Interiors. (Illus.). 176p. 2000. pap. write for info. (*0-8230-6636-3*) Watsn-Guptill.

— Waterfront Homes. (Illus.). 176p. 2000. pap. write for info. (*0-8230-6618-5*) Watsn-Guptill.

Rosselli, Carlo. Liberal Socialism. Urbinati, Nadia, ed. McCraig, William, tr. LC 93-42365. 208p. (C). 1994. text 45.00 (*0-691-08650-8*, Pub. by Princeton U Pr); pap. text 14.95 (*0-691-02560-6*, Pub. by Princeton U Pr) Cal Prin Full Svc.

Rosselli, John. The Life of Bellini. LC 95-39270. (Musical Lives Ser.). (Illus.). 194p. (C). 1997. pap. 14.95 (*0-521-46781-0*); text 39.95 (*0-521-46227-4*) Cambridge U Pr.

— The Life of Mozart. LC 97-33013. (Musical Lives Ser.). (Illus.). 184p. (C). 1998. pap. 14.95 (*0-521-58744-1*); text 39.95 (*0-521-58317-9*) Cambridge U Pr.

***Rosselli, John.** The Life of Verdi. LC 99-59952. (Musical Lives Ser.). (Illus.). 220p. (C). 2000. text 49.95 (*0-521-66011-4*); pap. text 17.95 (*0-521-66957-X*) Cambridge U Pr.

Rosselli, John. Lord William Bentinck: The Making of a Liberal Imperialist, 1774-1839. LC 72-95302. 386p. reprint ed. pap. 119.70 (*0-608-18297-4*, 203154700075) Bks Demand.

— Music & Musicians in Nineteenth Century Italy. (Illus.). 176p. 1991. 29.95 (*0-931340-40-3*, Amadeus Pr) Timber.

— Singers of Italian Opera. 288p. 1995. pap. text 19.95 (*0-521-42697-9*) Cambridge U Pr.

***Rosselli, Mark & Wilkie, Tom.** Visions of Heaven: The Mysteries of the Universe Revealed by the Hubble Space Telescope. (Illus.). 210p. 2000. 35.00 (*0-340-71734-3*, Pub. by Hodder & Stought Ltd) Trafalgar.

Rosselli, Mark, jt. auth. see Wilkie, Tom.

Rosselli, Milda, jt. auth. see Sisk, Dorothy.

Rosselli, P. F., jt. auth. see Berg, C. C.

Rossellini, Gayle & Worden, Mark. Of Course You're Angry: A Family guide Dealing with the Emotions of Substance Abuse. LC 96-37533. 120p. pap. 11.95 (*1-56838-141-7*) Hazelden.

Rossellini, Isabella, intro. 10 Years of Dolce & Gabbana. (The Universe of Fashion). (Illus.). 216p. 1996. 67.50 (*0-7892-0277-8*) Abbeville Pr.

Rossellini, Roberto. My Method: Writings & Interviews. 256p. 1995. pap. 12.95 (*0-941419-65-7*) Marsilio Pubs.

— My Method: Writings & Interviews. Cancogni, Annapaola, tr. from ITA. LC 92-82645. (Illus.). 256p. 1995. 24.00 (*0-941419-64-9*) Marsilio Pubs.

— Roberto Rossellini: The War Trilogy. LC 82-49232. (Cinema Classics Ser.). 487p. 1985. lib. bdg. 16.00 (*0-8240-5776-7*) Garland.

Rossello, Elena & De Gorostiza, Fernandez. Technical Guidelines for Field Variety Trials. (Plant Production & Protection Papers: No. 75). 126p. 1993. pap. 17.00 (*92-5-102486-3*, F24863, Pub. by FAO) Bernan Associates.

Rossello, Pedro, jt. frwd. see Clinton, William.

Rosselot, Bernard. Vocabulaire Maritime. (FRE.). 95p. 1980. pap. 19.95 (*0-8288-1581-X*, F136860) Fr & Eur.

Rosselot, Kirsten S., jt. auth. see Allen, David T.

Rosselson, L. Football Crazy. (Illus.). (J). mass mkt. 8.95 (*0-340-72245-2*, Pub. by Hodder & Stought Ltd) Trafalgar.

Rosselson, Leon. Ben's Magic Drum. (Illus.). 64p. (J). pap. 7.95 (*0-14-038969-5*, Pub. by Pnguin Bks Ltd) Trafalgar.

— Swim, Sam, Swim. (Illus.). 64p. (J). (ps-3). 1995. pap. 7.95 (*0-14-036552-4*, Pub. by Pnguin Bks Ltd) Trafalgar.

Rosselson, Leon. Where's My Mom? LC 93-32383. (Illus.). 32p. (J). (ps-k). 1996. pap. 5.99 (*1-56402-835-6*) Candlewick Pr.

— Where's My Mom? LC 93-32383. 1996. 11.09 (*0-606-10061-X*, Pub. by Turtleback) Demco.

Rossem, Cefas Van, see Van Rossem, Cefas.

Rossem, Vincent, text. The Idea of the Functional City: Lectures with Slides by Cornelis Van Eesteren, Berlin 1928. (Illus.). 160p. 1998. text 27.50 (*90-5662-056-8*, 810781, Pub. by NAi Uitgevers) Dist Art Pubs.

Rossen, Howard, et al. Family Law. (Professor Ser.). 233p. 1994. pap. text 15.95 (*1-56542-151-5*) E Pub Corp.

***Rossen, Howard M.** World's Fair Collectibles: Chicago, 1933 & New York, 1939. LC 97-80348. (Illus.). 160p. 1998. pap. 29.95 (*0-7643-0460-7*) Schiffer.

Rossen, Janice. Philip Larkin: His Life's Work. LC 89-51283. 176p. (C). 1990. text 25.95 (*0-87745-271-7*) U of Iowa Pr.

Rossen, Janice, jt. ed. see Wyatt-Brown, Anne M.

Rossen, John, jt. ed. see Rifkin, Jeremy.

Rossen, Robert, et al. Jack London's "The Sea Wolf" A Screenplay. LC 97-26704. 240p. 1998. 19.95 (*0-8093-2179-3*); pap. 45.00 (*0-8093-2176-9*) S Ill U Pr.

Rossen, Susan F., ed. see Boggs, Jean S.

Rossen, Susan F., ed. see Forge, Andrew.

Rosseneu, Maryvonne, ed. Structure & Function of Apolipoproteins. 437p. 1992. lib. bdg. 159.00 (*0-8493-6906-1*, QP99) CRC Pr.

Rosser, Aelred. Guide for Lectors. LC 98-18222. (Basics of Ministry Ser.). 55p. 1998. pap. 5.00 (*1-56854-238-0*) Liturgy Tr Pubns.

Rosser, Aelred R. A Well-Trained Tongue: Formation in the Ministry of Reader. LC 96-8689. 128p. 1996. pap. 9.00 (*1-56854-124-4*, WTTNEW) Liturgy Tr Pubns.

— A Word That Will Rouse Them: Reflections on the Ministry of Reader. LC 95-11671. 93p. (Orig.). 1995. pap. 9.00 (*1-56854-028-0*, ROUSE) Liturgy Tr Pubns.

Rosser, B. R. Gay Catholics down under: The Journeys in Sexuality & Spirituality of Gay Men in Australia & New Zealand. LC 91-47084. 256p. 1992. 55.00 (*0-275-94229-5*, C4229, Praeger Pubs) Greenwood.

— Male Homosexual Behavior & the Effects of AIDS Education: A Study of Behavior & Safer Sex in New Zealand & South Australia. LC 91-4626. 264p. 1991. 69.50 (*0-275-93809-3*, C3809, Praeger Pubs) Greenwood.

Rosser, Bill. Return to Palm Island. LC 95-118607. viii, 147p. 1994. write for info. (*0-85575-244-0*) AIB & TSIS.

— Up Rode the Troopers: The Black Police in Queensland. 1990. pap. 16.95 (*0-7022-2224-0*, Pub. by Univ Queensland Pr) Intl Spec Bk.

***Rosser, Caroline S.** Planning Activities for Child Care: A Curriculum Guide for Early Childhood Education. 2nd ed. LC 97-40259. (Illus.). 504p. 1998. 34.64 (*1-56637-428-6*) Goodheart.

Rosser, David. A Dragon in the House. 235p. (C). 1987. 21.00 (*0-86383-357-8*, Pub. by Gomer Pr) St Mut.

***Rosser, Edward.** Viennese Types: Photographs c. 1910 by Dr. Emil Mayer (1871-1938) LC 99-73187. (Illus.). 76p. 2000. 35.00 (*0-9672975-0-8*, Pub. by Blind River Eds) Dist Art Pubs.

Rosser, Evelyn C. Dancing Naked under Palm Trees. 200p. 1997. pap. 17.50 (*1-890300-00-4*) NIA Pages.

Rosser, Gervase. Medieval Westminster, 1200-1540. (Illus.). 442p. 1989. text 89.00 (*0-19-820156-7*) OUP.

Rosser, Gervase, jt. ed. see Holt, Richard.

Rosser, Gervase, jt. ed. see Slater, T. R.

Rosser, Harry L., jt. auth. see Gutierrez.

Rosser, Harry L., jt. auth. see Gutierrez, John R.

Rosser, J. Allyn. Bright Moves. (Samuel French Morse Poetry Prize Ser.). 88p. 1990. pap. text 11.95 (*1-55553-083-4*) NE U Pr.

Rosser, J. B., ed. see American Mathematical Society Staff.

Rosser, J. Barkley, Jr. From Catastrophe to Chaos: A General Theory of Economic Discontinuities. 416p. (C). 1991. lib. bdg. 139.50 (*0-7923-9157-8*) Kluwer Academic.

Rosser, J. Barkley, Jr. & Rosser, Marina V. Comparative Economics in a Transforming World Economy. LC 95-23362. 544p. (C). 1995. text 69.75 (*0-256-13095-7*, Irwn Prfssnl) McGraw-Hill Prof.

Rosser, James A. The Art of Laparoscopic Suturing. 1995. 59.50 (*1-85775-022-5*, Radcliffe Med Pr) Scovill Paterson.

Rosser, Linda K. Christmas in Oklahoma. (Illus.). 122p. 1982. 14.95 (*0-86546-041-8*) Bobwhite Pubns.

— Memory Album of a Territorial Lady. (Illus.). 72p. 1988. 14.95 (*0-929546-00-8*) Bobwhite Pubns.

— Pioneer Cookery Around Oklahoma. (Illus.). 250p. 1978. reprint ed. pap. 9.95 (*0-929546-01-6*) Bobwhite Pubns.

Rosser, Marina V., jt. auth. see Rosser, J. Barkley, Jr.

Rosser, Mike. Basic Mathematics for Economists. 448p. (C). 1993. pap. 29.99 (*0-415-08425-3*, B0007) Routledge.

Rosser, Phyllis. The SAT Gender Gap: Identifying the Causes. 190p. 1989. pap. 13.00 (*1-877966-00-2*) Ctr Women Policy.

— The SAT Gender Gap: Identifying the Causes. LC 94-115743. 203p. reprint ed. pap. 63.00 (*0-608-08039-X*, 206900400002) Bks Demand.

Rosser, R., ed. Mind-Made Disease: A Clinician's Guide to Recent Research. (Journal of Psychosomatic Research: No. 25). (Illus.). 144p. 1982. pap. 30.00 (*0-08-027957-0*, Pergamon Pr) Elsevier.

Rosser, Rosemary A. Cognitive Development: Psychological & Biological Perspectives. LC 93-18889. 448p. 1993. pap. text 52.00 (*0-205-13965-5*) Allyn.

Rosser, Sue V. Biology & Feminism: A Dynamic Interaction. (Feminist Impact on the Arts & Sciences Ser.). 200p. 1992. pap. 14.95 (*0-8057-9755-6*, Twyne) Mac Lib Ref.

— Biology & Feminism: A Dynamic Interaction. (Feminist Impact on the Arts & Sciences Ser.). 200p. 1993. 26.95 (*0-8057-9770-X*, Twyne) Mac Lib Ref.

— Biology & Feminism: A Dynamic Interaction. 191p. 1999. reprint ed. pap. text 27.00 (*0-7881-6224-1*) DIANE Pub.

— Female-Friendly Science: Applying Women's Studies, Methods & Theories to Attract Students. (Athene Ser.). 176p. (C). 1990. text 13.95 (*0-8077-6241-5*) Tchrs Coll.

— Female Friendly Science: Applying Women's Studies Methods & Theories to Attract Students to Science. (Athene Ser.). 160p. 1990. text 32.50 (*0-08-037469-7*, Pub. by PPI); pap. text 12.95 (*0-08-037470-0*, Pub. by PPI) Elsevier.

— Feminism Within the Science & Health Professions: Overcoming Resistance. (Athene Ser.). 168p. 1988. text 36.50 (*0-08-035558-7*, Pergamon Pr); pap. text 16.95 (*0-08-035557-9*, Pergamon Pr) Elsevier.

— Health: Discipline Analysis. (Women in the Curriculum Ser.: Vol. 7J). (Orig.). 1997. pap. 7.00 (*1-885303-33-5*) Towson St Univ.

— Re-Engineering Female Friendly Science. LC 97-5935. (Athene Ser.). (Illus.). 320p. 1997. text 54.00 (*0-8077-6287-3*); pap. text 24.95 (*0-8077-6286-5*) Tchrs Coll.

— Teaching Health & Science from a Feminist Perspective: A Practical Guide. (Athene Ser.). (Illus.). 200p. 1986. 36.50 (*0-08-033135-1*, Pergamon Pr); pap. 19.95 (*0-08-033997-2*, Pergamon Pr) Elsevier.

— Teaching Science & Health from a Feminist Perspective: A Practical Guide. (Athene Ser.). 256p. (C). 1986. pap. text 19.95 (*0-8077-6223-7*) Tchrs Coll.

— Women's Health - Missing from U. S. Medicine. LC 94-9745. (Race, Gender, & Science Ser.). 224p. 1994. 31.50 (*0-253-34991-5*); pap. 15.95 (*0-253-20924-2*) Ind U Pr.

***Rosser, Sue V., ed.** Building Inclusive Science: Connecting Women's Studies & Women in Science & Engineering. (Women's Studies Quarterly: Vol. 28, Nos. 1 & 2). 256p. 2000. pap. 18.00 (*1-55861-243-2*, Pub. by Feminist Pr) Consort Bk Sales.

Rosser, Sue V., ed. Feminism Within the Science & Health Care Professions: Overcoming Resistance. (Athene Ser.). 178p. (C). 1988. pap. text 17.95 (*0-8077-6208-3*) Tchrs Coll.

— Teaching the Majority: Breaking the Gender Barrier in Science, Mathematics, & Engineering. (Athene Ser.). 272p. (C). 1995. text 50.00 (*0-8077-6277-6*); pap. text 22.95 (*0-8077-6276-8*) Tchrs Coll.

Rosser, W. G. An Introduction to Statistical Physics. LC 81-4139. 382p. 1982. pap. text 33.95 (*0-470-27242-2*) P-H.

— Introductory Special Relativity. 260p. 1992. 95.00 (*0-85066-838-7*, Pub. by Tay Francis Ltd); pap. 45.00 (*0-85066-839-5*, Pub. by Tay Francis Ltd) Taylor & Francis.

Rosser, W. Geraint. Interpretation of Classical Electromagnetism. LC 96-9778. (Fundamental Theories of Physics Ser.). 458p. (C). 1997. lib. bdg. 249.00 (*0-7923-4187-2*) Kluwer Academic.

Rosser, Walter W. & Shafir, M. Sharon. Evidence-Based Family Medicine. (Evidence-Based Ser.). 180p. 1997. boxed set 46.95 incl. cd-rom (*1-55009-053-4*) DEKR.

Rosserkrims, Bonnie. The Redecorated Room. 2001. 30.00 (*0-06-039290-8*, ReganBks) HarperTrade.

Rossert, Helene, tr. see Lotka, Alfred J., ed.

Rosset, Barney, ed. The Blue Moon Erotic Reader. 358p. 2000. pap. 10.95 (*1-56201-119-7*) Blue Moon Bks.

— Evergreen Review Reader, 1957-1966: A Ten Year Anthology. (Northstar-Blue Moon Ser.). 356p. 1993. pap. 15.95 (*1-56201-045-X*) FoxRock.

— Evergreen Review Reader, 1967-1973. LC 98-30041. (Illus.). 544p. 1998. pap. 24.95 (*1-56858-110-6*) FWEW.

— Evergreen Review Reader, 1957-1966. (Illus.). 368p. 1994. pap. 16.45 (*1-55970-273-7*, Pub. by Arcade Pub Inc) Time Warner.

Rosset, Barney, et al, eds. New Olympia Reader, 1957-1966: The Best from the First Ten Years of America's Most Provocative, Most Controversial, Most Important Literary Magazine. (Illus.). 356p. 1993. pap. 15.95 (*1-56201-046-8*) Blue Moon Bks.

Rosset, Lisa. James Baldwin: American Author. (Black American Ser.). (Illus.). 176p. (YA). (gr. 9-12). 1990. mass mkt. 3.95 (*0-87067-564-8*, Pub. by Holloway) All Am Dist Corp.

— James Baldwin: Author. Huggins, Nathan I., ed. (Black Americans of Achievement Ser.). (Illus.). 124p. (YA). (gr. 5 up). 1989. pap. 8.95 (*0-7910-0230-6*) Chelsea Hse.

Rosset, Marc O. Beziehungen Zwischen Vegetation, Bodenwasser, Mikroklima und Energiehaushalt Von Feuchtwiesen Unter Besonderer Beruecksichtigung der Evatransporation. (Dissertationes Botanicae Ser.: Band 159). (GER., Illus.). 244p. 1990. pap. 65.00 (*3-443-64071-0*, Pub. by Gebruder Borntraeger) Balogh.

Rosset, Peter & Benjamin, Medea, eds. The Greening of the Revolution: Cuba's Experiment with Organic Farming. LC 96-181775. 110p. 1995. 11.95 (*1-875284-80-X*) Ocean Pr NJ.

Rosset, Peter, jt. auth. see Mittal, Anuradha.

Rossett, Allison. First Things Fast: A Handbook for Performance Analysis. LC 98-25301. 256p. 1998. 39.95 (*0-7879-4438-6*, Pfffr & Co) Jossey-Bass.

Rossett, Allison. School Technology Planner (STP) Software. (C). 1997. cd-rom 84.00 (*0-205-27027-1*) P-H.

Rossett, Allison. Training Needs Assessment. LC 87-9070. (Illus.). 281p. 1987. 42.95 (*0-87778-195-8*) Educ Tech Pubns.

Rossett, Allison & Gautier-Downes, Jeannette. A Handbook of Job Aids. LC 91-9090. (Illus.). 195p. 1991. 39.95 (*0-88390-290-7*, Pfffr & Co) Jossey-Bass.

Rossett, Arthur, jt. auth. see Dorff, Elliot N.

Rossetter, Laura. Mountain Biking Colorado's Historic Mining Districts. LC 90-85222. (Illus.). 176p. (Orig.). 1991. pap. 10.95 (*1-55591-090-4*) Fulcrum Pub.

***Rossetti.** Communication Intervention. 2nd ed. 2000. pap. 49.95 (*0-7693-0093-6*) Singular Publishing.

— Double Contrast Radiology of the Esophagus. (Illus.). 154p. 1985. text 62.00 (*88-299-0144-X*, Pub. by Piccin Nuova) Gordon & Breach.

Rossetti, Ana. Hubo un Tiempo-There Was a Time: Antologia Selecta de la Obra Poetica de Ana Rossetti-An Anthology Selected from the Poetic Works of Ana Rossetti. Rosas, Yolanda, ed. Rozo-Moorhouse, Teresa, ed. & tr. by. from SPA. McEwan, Angela et al, trs. from SPA. 170p. (Orig.). 1996. pap. 15.95 (*1-886480-16-8*) Edici Latidos.

Rossetti, Ana & Suntree, Susan. Tulips: Ten Poems by Anna Rossetti. Nieman, Nancy D., tr. from SPA. (ENG & SPA., Illus.). 24p. 1990. 7.00 (*1-882623-08-8*) Exiled-Am Pr.

Rossetti, Biagio. Libellus de Rudimentis Musices. fac. ed. (Monuments of Music & Music Literature in Facsimile, II Ser.: Vol. 136). (Illus.). 1968. lib. bdg. 35.00 (*0-8450-2336-5*) Broude.

Rossetti, Christina Georgina. A Choice of Christina Rossetti's Verse. Jennings, Elizabeth, ed. 96p. 1970. pap. 10.95 (*0-571-09018-4*) Faber & Faber.

— Christina Rossetti (1830-1894) Selected Poems. Sisson, C. H., ed. 1985. pap. 7.50 (*0-85635-533-X*, Pub. by Carcanet Pr) Paul & Co Pubs.

— Color. LC 90-25588. (Illus.). 40p. (J). (ps-1). 1992. lib. bdg. 14.89 (*0-06-022650-1*) HarpC Child Bks.

— Complete Poems. 1992. reprint ed. lib. bdg. 37.95 (*0-89968-293-6*, Lghtyr Pr) Buccaneer Bks.

— Complete Poems of Christina Rossetti: A Variorum Edition, Vol. I. Crump, R. W., ed. LC 78-5571. 1979. text 45.00 (*0-8071-0358-6*) La State U Pr.

— Complete Poems of Christina Rossetti: A Variorum Edition, Vol. II. Crump, R. W., ed. LC 78-5571. (Illus.). 525p. 1986. text 70.00 (*0-8071-1246-1*) La State U Pr.

— Complete Poems of Christina Rossetti: A Variorum Edition, Vol. III. Crump, R. W., ed. LC 78-5571. Vol. III. 784p. 1990. text 95.00 (*0-8071-1530-4*) La State U Pr.

— The Family Letters of Christina Georgina Rossetti. (BCL1-PR English Literature Ser.). 242p. 1992. reprint ed. lib. bdg. 79.00 (*0-7812-7624-1*) Rprt Serv.

— Family Letters of Christina Georgina Rossetti, with Some Supplementary Letters & Appendices. Rossetti, William M., ed. LC 68-24915. (English Literature Ser.: No. 33). (Illus.). 1969. reprint ed. lib. bdg. 75.00 (*0-8383-0237-8*) M S G Haskell Hse.

— Goblin Market. Harmon, Peggy, ed. 1987. spiral bd. 16.00 (*0-8222-0452-5*) Dramatists Play.

— Goblin Market: A Tale of Two Sisters. LC 97-13197. 80p. 1997. 14.95 (*0-8118-1649-4*) Chronicle Bks.

— Goblin Market & Other Poems. LC 93-40975. (Thrift Editions Ser.). 80p. (Orig.). 1994. pap. 1.00 (*0-486-28055-1*) Dover.

— The Letters of Christina Rosetti, 1843-1873, Vol. 1. Harrison, Antony H., ed. LC 96-26707. (Victorian Literature & Culture Ser.). 544p. (C). 1997. text 49.50 (*0-8139-1686-0*) U Pr of Va.

— Passion & Devastation. (Illus.). 1999. 19.95 (*1-86019-387-0*) Brockhampton Pr Ltd.

— Poems: Rossetti. LC 93-14362. (Pocket Poets Ser.). 256p. 1993. 0.12 (*0-679-42908-5*) Everymns Lib.

— Poems & Prose. Marsh, Jan, ed. 288p. 1995. lib. bdg. 7.95 (*0-460-87536-1*, Everyman's Classic Lib) Tuttle Pubng.

— Poetical Works. (BCL1-PR English Literature Ser.). 507p. 1992. reprint ed. lib. bdg. 99.00 (*0-7812-7623-3*) Rprt Serv.

— Select Prose of Christina Ross. LC 97-44885. (Illus.). 416p. 1998. text 49.95 (*0-312-15903-X*) St Martin.

— Selected Poems of Christina Rossetti. (Bloomsbury Classic Poetry Ser.). 128p. 1995. text 9.95 (*0-312-13437-1*) St Martin.

— Sing Song: A Nursery Rhyme Book. LC 68-55822. (Illus.). 180p. (J). (gr. 3-7). 1969. reprint ed. pap. 4.95 (*0-486-22107-5*) Dover.

— What Is Pink: A Poem About Colors. LC 99-69946. (Growing Tree Ser.). (Illus.). 14p. (YA). (ps up). 2000. 5.95 (*0-694-01248-3*, HarpFestival) HarpC Child Bks.

— The Works of Christina Rosetti. (Poetry Library). 464p. 1998. pap. 7.95 (*1-85326-429-6*, 4296WW, Pub. by Wrdsworth Edits) NTC Contemp Pub Co.

Rossetti, Christina Georgina & Craik, Dinah M. Maude. Showalter, Elaine, ed. LC 92-38333. (Women's Classics Ser.). 223p. (C). 1993. text 55.00 (*0-8147-7442-3*) NYU Pr.

— Maude. Showalter, Elaine, ed. LC 92-38333. (Women's Classics Ser.). 223p. (C). 1995. pap. text 19.50 (*0-8147-7451-2*) NYU Pr.

Rossetti, Christina Georgina, jt. auth. see Gliori, Debi.

Rossetti, Concetta M. Rainbows of Love. (Illus.). 72p. (Orig.). 1988. pap. 9.99 (*0-925037-03-6*) Great Lks Poetry.

Rossetti, Dante Gabriel. Collected Works, 2 vols., Set. (BCL1-PR English Literature Ser.). 1992. reprint ed. lib. bdg. 150.00 (*0-7812-7626-8*) Rprt Serv.

***Rossetti, Dante Gabriel.** Collected Writings of Dante Gabriel Rossetti. Marsh, Jan, ed. LC 99-47247. 416p. 2000. text 35.00 (*1-56663-280-3*, Pub. by I R Dee) Natl Bk Netwk.

Rossetti, Dante Gabriel. Dante Gabriel Rossetti: His Family Letters, 2 vols. LC 70-130231. reprint ed. 72.50 (*0-404-05434-X*) AMS Pr.

— Dante Gabriel Rossetti: His Family-Letters, 2 vols., Set. (BCL1-PR English Literature Ser.). 1992. reprint ed. lib. bdg. 150.00 (*0-7812-7629-2*) Rprt Serv.

— The House of Life, a Sonnet-Sequence. (BCL1-PR English Literature Ser.). 242p. 1992. reprint ed. lib. bdg. 79.00 (*0-7812-7628-4*) Rprt Serv.

— Poems & Translations, 1850-1870, Together with the Prose Story "Hand & Soul" (BCL1-PR English Literature Ser.). 492p. 1992. reprint ed. lib. bdg. 99.00 (*0-7812-7627-6*) Rprt Serv.

Rossetti, G., et al. Double Contrast Radiology of the Aesophagus. 154p. 1985. text 56.00 (*1-57235-035-0*) Piccin Nuova.

Rossetti, Gabriel C. The Works. (Anglistica & Americana Ser.: No. 135). xxxvii, 684p. 1972. reprint ed. 122.20 (*3-487-04360-2*) G Olms Pubs.

Rossetti, Germana, tr. see McIntyre, Sally.

Rossetti, Guy, ed. see Calderon de la Barca, Pedro.

Rossetti, Louis M. Communication Intervention: Birth to Three. (Illus.). 268p. (C). 1996. pap. text 53.95 (*1-56593-101-7*, 0404) Thomson Learn.

— High-Risk Infants: Identification, Assessment & Intervention. LC 90-9220. 238p. (C). 1986. pap. text 29.00 (*0-89079-367-0*, 1783) PRO-ED.

— Infant-Toddler Assessment: An Interdisciplinary Approach. LC 90-9185. (Illus.). 294p. (C). 1990. pap. text 31.00 (*0-89079-312-3*, 1782) PRO-ED.

— The Rossetti Infant-Toddler Language Scale: A Measure of Communication & Interaction. 165p. 1990. spiral bd. 43.00 (*1-55999-121-6*) LinguiSystems.

— The Rossetti Infant-Toddler Language Scale Kit: A Measure of Communication & Interaction. 165p. (J). (ps). 1990. spiral bd. 69.95 (*1-55999-143-7*) LinguiSystems.

Rossetti, Louis M., ed. Developmental Problems of Drug-Exposed Infants. (Illus.). 80p. (Orig.). (C). 1992. pap. text 24.95 (*1-56593-064-9*, 0370) Singular Publishing.

Rossetti, Louis M. & Kile, Jack E., eds. Early Intervention for Special Populations of Infants & Toddlers. 318p. 1997. 39.95 (*1-56593-798-8*, 1560) Thomson Learn.

Rossetti, Louis Michael. High-Risk Infants: Identification, Assessment & Intervention. LC 86-17139. 1986. write for info. (*0-316-75757-8*) Little.

Rossetti, Maria F. Shadow of Dante: Being an Essay Towards Studying Himself, His World & His Pilgrimage. (Illus.). 310p. 1998. reprint ed. pap. 24.95 (*0-7661-0457-5*) Kessinger Pub.

Rossetti, Michael A. & Sen, Basav. Transportation Receipts & Outlays in the Federal Budget: Fiscal Years 1977-94. (Illus.). 75p. (C). 1998. pap. text 25.00 (*0-7881-7491-6*) DIANE Pub.

Rossetti, Rosemarie, jt. auth. see Powell, Charles C.

Rossetti, Stefano. Stefano Rossetti: Il Libro de Madrigali a Quattro Voci. Skei, Allen B., ed. (Recent Researches in Music of the Renaissance Ser.: Vol. RRR26). (Illus.). xvii, 134p. 1977. pap. 45.00 (*0-89579-088-2*) A-R Eds.

— Stefano Rossetti: Sacrae Cantones. Skei, Allen B., ed. (Recent Researches in Music of the Renaissance Ser.: Vol. RRR15). (Illus.). xiv, 125p. 1973. pap. 45.00 (*0-89579-047-5*) A-R Eds.

Rossetti, Stephen J. Slayer of the Soul: Child Sexual Abuse & the Catholic Church. LC 90-70990. (Illus.). 224p. (Orig.). 1990. pap. 14.95 (*0-89622-452-X*) Twenty-Third.

— A Tragic Grace: The Catholic Church & Child Sexual Abuse. LC 96-22804. 136p. (Orig.). 1996. pap. text 10.95 (*0-8146-2434-0*, Liturg Pr Bks) Liturgical Pr.

Rossetti, William M. American Poems. LC 74-131501. reprint ed. 47.50 (*0-404-05419-6*) AMS Pr.

— Bibliography of the Works of Dante Gabriel Rossetti. LC 71-130242. reprint ed. 24.50 (*0-404-05439-0*) AMS Pr.

— Dante Gabriel Rossetti As Designer & Writer. LC 73-144678. reprint ed. 36.00 (*0-404-05429-3*) AMS Pr.

Rossetti, William M. The Diary of W. M. Rossetti 1870-1873. Bornand, Odette, ed. 1978. 55.00 (*0-19-812458-9*) OUP.

Rossetti, William M. Fine Art, Chiefly Contemporary. LC 73-12670. Orig. Title: Fine Art. reprint ed. 41.50 (*0-404-05417-X*) AMS Pr.

— Letters about Shelley Interchanged by Three Friends-Edward Dowden, Richard Garnett & William Michael Rossetti. LC 77-168058. reprint ed. 24.50 (*0-404-05444-7*) AMS Pr.

— Life of John Keats. LC 75-122695. reprint ed. 29.50 (*0-404-05428-5*) AMS Pr.

— Lives of Famous Poets. LC 77-148292. reprint ed. 42.50 (*0-404-05425-0*) AMS Pr.

— Memoir of Shelley. LC 71-144680. (Shelley Society, Fourth Ser.: No. 2). reprint ed. 39.50 (*0-404-05427-7*) AMS Pr.

— Notes on the Royal Academy Exhibition, 1868. LC 75-144681. reprint ed. 27.50 (*0-404-05418-8*) AMS Pr.

— Rossetti Papers, 1862-1870. LC 76-130238. reprint ed. 32.50 (*0-404-05438-2*) AMS Pr.

— Ruskin: Rossetti: Pre-Raphaelitism, Papers 1854-62. LC 73-127453. reprint ed. 36.00 (*0-404-05437-4*) AMS Pr.

— Some Reminiscences, 2 vols. LC 75-132386. (Illus.). 645p. 1975. reprint ed. 59.50 (*0-404-05440-4*) AMS Pr.

— Swinburne's Poems & Ballads: A Criticism. LC 73-130623. reprint ed. 21.50 (*0-404-05416-1*) AMS Pr.

Rossetti, William M., ed. Humorous Poems. LC 77-139260. reprint ed. 42.50 (*0-404-05426-9*) AMS Pr.

— Preraphaelite Diaries & Letters. LC 70-148293. reprint ed. 52.50 (*0-404-08898-8*) AMS Pr.

Rossetti, William M., ed. see Rossetti, Christina Georgina.

***Rossetti, Yves & Revonsuo, Antti, eds.** Beyond Dissociation: Interaction Between Dissociated Implicit & Explicit Processing. (Advances in Consciousness Research Ser.). 300p. 2000. pap. write for info. (*1-55619-665-2*) J Benjamins Pubng.

Rossetto, L. Major General Orde Charles Wingate & the Development of Long-Range Penetration. 492p. 1982. pap. text 61.95 (*0-89126-107-9*) MA-AH Pub.

Rossetto, Louis, jt. ed. see Plunkett, John.

Rossfeldt, Klaus. Rolls-Royce & Bentley: A History. (Illus.). 304p. 1991. 155.00 (*0-85429-920-3*) Haynes Manuals.

Rossi. Cisco & IP Addressing. 391p. 1999. pap. 55.00 (*0-07-134925-1*) McGraw.

— Clavis Universalis. (C). 2000. 32.00 (*0-226-72826-9*) U Ch Pr.

Rossi. Composition Readers Preview 1994. 1994. pap. text 12.33 (*0-673-55679-4*) Addison-Wesley.

Rossi & Schipper. Case Studies in Preparation for the California Reading Competency Test. 96p. 1998. pap. text, student ed. 11.00 (*0-205-30322-6*) Allyn.

Rossi, et al. Ramba, Bk. 2. (Eros Graphic Novel Ser.: No. 22). 128p. 1996. pap. 14.95 (*1-56097-253-X*) Fantagraph Bks.

Rossi, A. The Rise of Italian Fascism, 1918-1922. 1975. 300.00 (*0-87968-435-6*) Gordon Pr.

***Rossi, Agnes.** Houseguest. 2000. reprint ed. pap. 13.00 (*0-452-28197-0*) Penguin Books.

— The Houseguest: A Novel. large type ed. LC 00-28639. 550p. 2000. 28.95 (*0-7862-2547-5*) Thorndike Pr.

***Rossi, Aldo.** Aldo Rossi: I Quaderni Azzurri. 2304p. 2000. boxed set 600.00 (*0-89236-589-7*) J P Getty Trust.

Rossi, Aldo. The Architecture of the City. Ghirardo, Diane, tr. 252p. 1984. pap. text 19.50 (*0-262-68043-2*) MIT Pr.

— Carlos Jimenez. 96p. Date not set. pap. 29.95 (*84-252-1516-1*) Watsn-Guptill.

Rossi, Aldo. Aldo Rossi: Collector's Edition, 2 vols., Boxed Set. limited ed. 1994. 250.00 (*1-56898-006-X*) Princeton Arch.

Rossi, Aldo & Gravagnuolo, Benedetto. Adolf Loos: Theory & Works. (Illus.). 228p. pap. 39.95 (*0-948835-16-8*) Dist Art Pubs.

Rossi, Alejandro. Lenguaje y Significado (Language & Meaning) (Breviarios Ser.). (SPA.). 157p. 1997. pap. 7.99 (*968-16-4013-6*, Pub. by Fondo) Continental Bk.

Rossi, Alfred. Astonish Us in the Morning: Tyrone Guthrie Remembered. LC 80-11855. (Illus.). 322p. reprint ed. pap. 99.90 (*0-8357-5820-6*, 203317500084) Bks Demand.

Rossi, Alice S. Generational Differences in the Soviet Union. Zuckerman, Harriet & Merton, Robert K., eds. LC 79-9021. (Dissertations on Sociology Ser.). 1980. lib. bdg. 35.95 (*0-405-12990-4*) Ayer.

***Rossi, Alice S.** Sexuality Across the Life Course. (John D. & Catherine T. MacArthur Foundation Series on Mental Health & Development). 1999. pap. text 20.00 (*0-226-72870-6*) U Ch Pr.

Rossi, Alice S., ed. The Feminist Papers: From Adams to de Beauvoir. 716p. 1988. reprint ed. pap. text 18.00 (*1-55553-028-1*) NE U Pr.

— Gender & the Life Course. LC 84-12335. (Illus.). 389p. 1985. pap. text 27.95 (*0-202-30312-8*) Aldine de Gruyter.

— Sexuality Across the Life Course. LC 93-41706. (John D. & Catherine T. MacArthur Foundation Series on Mental Health & Development). 435p. 1994. 34.95 (*0-226-72833-1*) U Ch Pr.

Rossi, Alice S. & Rossi, Peter H. Of Human Bonding: Parent-Child Relations Across the Life-Course. (Social Institutions & Social Change Ser.). 560p. 1990. pap. text 43.95 (*0-202-30361-6*); lib. bdg. 69.95 (*0-202-30360-8*) Aldine de Gruyter.

Rossi, Alice S., ed. see Mill, John Stuart & Mill, Harriet Taylor.

Rossi, Angnes. Fancy. LC 99-36122. (Illus.). 304p. 2000. 23.95 (*0-525-94365-X*) NAL.

Rossi, Arcangelo, jt. ed. see Garola, Claudio.

***Rossi, Azariah B. Moses de & Weinberg, Joanna.** The Light of the Eyes. LC 99-55976. (Judaica Ser.: Vol. 31). (Illus.). 640p. 2000. 75.00 (*0-300-07906-0*) Yale U Pr.

Rossi, Barbara. Barbara Rossi: Selected Works: 1967-1990. (Illus.). 40p. 1991. pap. 20.00 (*0-941548-22-8*) Ren Soc U Chi.

***Rossi, Barbara.** From the Ocean of Painting: India's Popular Painting Traditions A. D. 1589 to the Present. LC 97-15810. (Illus.). 312p. 2000. pap. 29.95 (*0-19-511194-X*) OUP.

Rossi, Barbara. From the Ocean of Painting: India's Popular Paintings, A. D. 1589 to the Present. LC 97-15810. (Illus.). 312p. 1998. 60.00 (*0-19-511193-1*) OUP.

***Rossi, Barbara Ann.** The Masters' Classroom! Apprentice Workbook. (Illus.). 64p. 1999. pap. 13.95 (*0-9673957-1-2*) Lark Enter.

Rossi, Betty & Heggie, Elmo, eds. Going to the Lake. (Illus.). 142p. Date not set. pap. 11.95 (*0-926147-07-2*) Loonfeather.

Rossi, Bruno. Moments in the Life of a Scientist. (Illus.). 194p. (C). 1990. text 54.95 (*0-521-36439-6*) Cambridge U Pr.

Rossi, C. Tempos in Science & Nature: Structures, Relations & Complexity. LC 99-28222. (Annals of the New York Academy of Science Ser.). 1999. write for info. (*1-57331-197-9*) NY Acad Sci.

Rossi, Christine. Heads Up! A Zillion Ways to Survive Negativity in Your Life. LC 97-70102. 208p. 1997. pap. text, per. 16.95 (*0-7872-3533-4*) Kendall-Hunt.

Rossi, Christopher R. Broken Chain of Being: James Brown Scott & the Origins of Modern International Law. LC 98-37870. 1998. write for info. (*90-411-0559-X*) Kluwer Law Intl.

— Equity & International Law: A Legal Realist Approach to the Process of International Decisionmaking. LC 92-46570. (Innovation in International Law Ser.). 309p. (C). 1993. 85.00 (*0-941320-81-2*) Transnatl Pubs.

Rossi, Claudio, ed. Tempos in Science & Nature: Structures, Relations & Complexity. LC 99-28222. 1999. lib. bdg. 60.00 (*1-57331-196-0*) NY Acad Sci.

Rossi, Cristina P. Babel Barbara. Decker, tr. (QRL Poetry Bks.: Vol. XXXI). 545p. 1992. 20.00 (*0-614-06448-1*) Quarterly Rev.

— Evohe: Poemas Eroticas-Erotic Poems. Decker, Diana P., tr. from SPA. LC 93-73117. 128p. (C). 1994. pap. 11.95 (*0-9632363-5-0*) Azul Edits.

— The Ship of Fools. Hughes, Psiche, tr. from SPA. LC 88-61390. (Readers International Ser.). 224p. (Orig.). 1989. pap. 11.95 (*0-930523-54-7*) Readers Intl.

***Rossi, Cristina P., et al.** Solitaire of Love. LC 99-50789. 104p. 2000. 13.95 (*0-8223-2540-3*) Duke.

***Rossi, Cristina Peri.** The Museum of Useless Efforts. Hecht, Tobias, tr. (European Women Writers Ser.). 2001. pap. 15.00 (*0-8032-8764-X*, Bison Books); text 40.00 (*0-8032-3726-X*) U of Nebr Pr.

— Solitaire of Love. Rudder, Robert S., tr. LC 99-50789. 104p. 2000. pap. 13.95 (*0-8223-2503-9*) Duke.

Rossi, Diego. Due Epistole Di Giovanni Conversini Da Ravenna. (Romanistische Texte und Studien: Vol. 3). vi, 64p. 1988. write for info. (*3-487-07965-8*) G Olms Pubs.

— Le Egloghe Viscontee Di Lacopo Allegretti. (Romanistische Texte und Studien: Vol. 1). 55p. 1984. write for info. (*3-487-07566-0*) G Olms Pubs.

— Romanistische Texte und Studien Vol. 1: Le 'Egloghe Viscontee' Di Alligretti. write for info. (*0-318-71469-8*) G Olms Pubs.

— Romanistische Texte und Studien Vol. 3: Due Epistole Di Giovanni Conversini Da Ravenna. write for info. (*0-318-71470-1*) G Olms Pubs.

Rossi, Diego, ed. see Poliziano, Angelo.

Rossi, Doc. Original Jerry Donahue: Guitar Styles of Jerry Donahue. (Illus.). 80p. 1993. pap. 15.95 (*0-7119-2948-3*, AM88360) Music Sales.

Rossi, Donatella. The Philosophical View of the Great Perfection in the Tibetan Bon Religion. LC 99-57690. (ENG & TIB.). 315p. 2000. pap. 21.95 (*1-55939-129-4*) Snow Lion Pubns.

***Rossi, Doug.** Leasing & Marketing for Property Managers. Ambrose, Christine, ed. (Illus.). 420p. 1999. teacher ed., ring bd. 100.00 (*1-928594-12-3*); student ed., ring bd. 100.00 (*1-928594-11-5*) BOMI Inst.

Rossi, E. Bern, ed. Ernaehrung und Stoffwechsel: Die Adipositas im Kindesalter. (Paediatrische Fortbildungskurse fuer die Praxis Ser.: Band 42). (GER., Illus.). 113p. 1975. 30.50 (*3-8055-2158-8*) S Karger.

— Neue Akquisitionen in der Neonatologie: Nouvelles Acquisitions en Neonatologie. (Paediatrische Fortbildungskurse fuer die Praxis Ser.: Vol. 62). (Illus.). x, 660p. 1988. pap. 34.00 (*3-8055-4742-0*) S Karger.

— Perinatologie. (Paediatrische Fortbildungskurse fuer die Praxis Ser.: Band 41). 200p. 1975. 68.75 (*3-8055-2115-4*) S Karger.

— Pulmonale Aspekte der Cystischen Fibrose. (Paediatrische Fortbildungskurse fuer die Praxis Ser.: Vol. 48). (Illus.). 1979. pap. 42.75 (*3-8055-2944-9*) S Karger.

— Solide Maligne Tumoren im Kindesalter. (Paediatrische Fortbildungskurse fuer die Praxis Ser.: Vol. 39). (Illus.). 100p. 1974. 28.75 (*3-8055-1691-6*) S Karger.

Rossi, E. Bern & Wyler, F., eds. Neuere Aspekte der Kinderkardiiology, Set. (Paediatrische Fortbildungskurse fuer die Praxis Ser.: Vol. 47). (FRE & GER., Illus.). 1978. pap. 32.25 (*3-8055-2865-5*) S Karger.

Rossi, E. Bern, ed. see Kinderchirurgisches Symposium Staff.

Rossi, E. Bern, jt. ed. see Oetliker, O.

Rossi, Ennio C., et al. Principles of Transfusion Medicine. (Illus.). 816p. 1990. 115.00 (*0-683-07385-0*) Lppncott W & W.

Rossi, Ennio C., ed. see Simon, Toby L.

Rossi, Ennio C., jt. ed. see Wu, Kenneth K.

Rossi, Enzo. Malta on the Brink: From Western Democracy to Libyan Satellite. (C). 1986. 35.00 (*0-907967-79-5*, Pub. by Inst Euro Def & Strat) St Mut.

An Asterisk (*) at the beginning of an entry indicates that the title is appearing for the first time.

Rossi, Ernest E. & McCrea, Barbara P. The European Political Dictionary. LC 84-24389. (Clio Dictionaries in Political Science Ser.: No. 7). 408p. 1985. pap. text 20.50 (*0-87436-367-5*); lib. bdg. 55.00 (*0-87436-046-3*) ABC-CLIO.

Rossi, Ernest E. & Plano, Jack C., eds. Latin America: A Political Dictionary. LC 92-28946. (Clio Dictionaries in Political Science Ser.). 1992. lib. bdg. 60.00 (*0-87436-608-9*) ABC-CLIO.

— Latin America: A Political Dictionary. LC 92-28946. (Clio Dictionaries in Political Science Ser.). 1992. pap. text 29.95 (*0-87436-698-4*) ABC-CLIO.

Rossi, Ernest L. Dreams & the Growth of Personality: Expanding Awareness in Psychotherapy. 232p. (C). 1972. 109.00 (*0-08-016787-X*, Pub. by Pergamon Repr) Franklin.

— The Psychology of Mind-Body Healing: New Concepts of Therapeutic Hypnosis. 2nd rev. ed. 304p. (C). 1993. 39.00 (*0-393-70168-9*) Norton.

— Western Europe: A Political Dictionary. (Dictionary Ser.). 300p. 1996. 60.00 (*0-87436-754-9*) ABC-CLIO.

Rossi, Ernest L. & Cheek, David B. Mind-Body Therapy: Methods of Ideodynamic Healing in Hypnosis. 544p. 1994. pap. 24.95 (*0-393-31247-X*) Norton.

Rossi, Ernest L. & Nimmons, David. The 20 Minute Break: Using the New Science of Ultradian Rhythms. 210p. 1991. 17.95 (*0-9651985-1-0*) Zeig Tucker.

Rossi, Ernest L., jt. auth. see Erickson, Milton H.

Rossi, Ernest L., ed. see Erickson, Milton H.

Rossi, Ernest L., jt. ed. see Lloyd, David.

Rossi, Ernest Lawrence. Dreams, Consciousness, Spirit: The Quantum Experience of Self-Reflection & Co-Creation. 376p. 2000. pap. 29.95 (*0-9651985-2-9*) Zeig Tucker.

Rossi, Erno. White Death: Blizzard of '77. (Illus.). 356p. pap. 16.95 (*0-920926-03-7*) WNY Wares.

Rossi, F., jt. auth. see Pleyte, E.

Rossi, Faust. Evidence for the Trial Lawyer. 1994. 35.00 (*1-55917-172-3*, 9322); 135.00 incl. audio (*1-55917-171-5*); VHS 495.00 (*0-614-07112-7*) Natl Prac Inst.

— Experts & Hearsay: What Every Trial Lawyer Must Know. 1994. 35.00 (*0-614-06014-1*, 4129) Natl Prac Inst.

Rossi, Francesco, et al. Michelangelo & Raphael in the Vatican. (Illus.). 215p. 1997. 75.00 (*88-86921-05-5*); pap. 55.00 (*88-86921-04-7*) Treasures Inc.

***Rossi, Gabriella.** Italian Vegetarian: Fresh, Tasty Recipes for Healthy Eating. 1999. 11.98 (*1-84038-410-7*) Hermes Hse.

— Pasta & Pizza Prego. 128p. 2000. 14.95 (*0-7548-0081-4*) Anness Pub.

Rossi, Gifford S. An Arabian Adventure: A Dream Achieved. 162p. 1996. 93.50 (*0-7103-0527-3*, Pub. by Kegan Paul Intl) Col U Pr.

Rossi, Giuseppe, et al, eds. Coping with Floods. LC 94-2615. (NATO Advanced Study Institutes Series E, Applied Sciences: Vol. 257). 1994. text 420.50 (*0-7923-2706-3*) Kluwer Academic.

Rossi, Guido A., photos by. Turkey: An Aerial Portrait. LC 93-31352. (Illus.). 192p. 1994. 55.00 (*0-8109-3866-9*, Pub. by Abrams) Time Warner.

***Rossi, Guido Alberto, photos by.** Egypt - Gift of the Nile: An Aerial Portrait. (Illus.). 208p. 2000. 55.00 (*0-8109-3254-7*) Abrams.

Rossi, H. H. Microdosimetry & Its Applications. (Illus.). 352p. 1995. 53.95 (*3-540-58541-9*) Spr-Verlag.

Rossi, H. H., jt. auth. see Hall, E. J.

Rossi, Harald H. Limitation & Assessment in Radiation Protection. LC 84-11041. (Taylor Lectures: No. 8). 1984. pap. 20.00 (*0-913392-69-3*) NCRP Pubns.

Rossi, Harald H., jt. auth. see Zaider, M.

Rossi, Hugh. Landlord & Tenant Act, 1987. 1987. pap. 110.00 (*0-7219-1070-X*, Pub. by Scientific) St Mut.

— Shaw's Guide to the Rent (Agriculture) Act, 1976. (C). 1977. 75.00 (*0-7219-0750-4*, Pub. by Scientific) St Mut.

Rossi, Hugo, ed. Prospects in Mathematics: Invited Talks on the Occasion of the 250th Anniversary of Princeton University. LC 98-36451. 154p. 1998. 29.00 (*0-8218-0975-X*) Am Math.

Rossi, Ino. Community Reconstruction after Earthquake: Dialectical Sociology in Action. LC 93-2856. 208p. 1993. 65.00 (*0-275-94602-9*, C4602, Praeger Pubs) Greenwood.

— From the Sociology of Symbols to the Sociology of Signs: Toward a Dialectical Sociology. LC 83-5261. 359p. reprint ed. pap. 111.30 (*0-8357-6123-1*, 203419200089) Bks Demand.

Rossi, Ino, ed. The Logic of Culture: Advances in Structural Theory & Method. LC 81-29. 304p. 1982. 42.95 (*0-89789-015-9*, Bergin & Garvey) Greenwood.

Rossi, Ino, et al. People in Culture: A Survey of Cultural Anthropology. LC 79-11842. (Praeger Special Studies). 626p. 1979. pap. 22.95 (*0-275-91481-X*, B1481, Praeger Pubs) Greenwood.

— People in Culture: A Survey of Cultural Anthropology. LC 79-11842. (Praeger Special Studies). 626p. 1980. 89.50 (*0-275-90542-X*, C0542, Praeger Pubs) Greenwood.

Rossi, J. P., jt. auth. see Denhiere, G.

Rossi, Jacques. The Gulag Handbook: An Encyclopedia Dictionary of Soviet Penal Institutions. Burnhans, William, tr. 610p. 1989. 29.95 (*1-55778-024-2*) Prof World Peace.

***Rossi, Jasmine.** The Wild Shores of Patagonia: The Valdes Peninsula & Punta Tombo. (Illus.). 224p. 2000. 45.00 (*0-8109-4352-2*, Pub. by Abrams) Time Warner.

Rossi, Jeri C. Angel with a Criminal Kiss. 128p. (Orig.). 1996. pap. 13.95 (*1-871592-45-3*) Creation Books.

Rossi, Jeri Cain. Red Wine Moan: Stories. LC 99-50883. 160p. 2000. pap. 11.95 (*0-916397-62-9*) Manic D Pr.

Rossi, Joanne C., jt. auth. see Schipper, Beth.

Rossi, John. What's Wrong with My Iguana. (Herpetocultural Library). (Illus.). 88p. 1999. pap. 14.00 (*1-882770-48-X*, Pub. by Adv Vivarium) IPG Chicago.

Rossi, John & Rossi, Roxanne. What's Wrong with My Snake? LC 96-15432. (Illus.). 150p. 1996. 14.00 (*1-882770-35-8*) Adv Vivarium.

***Rossi, John J. & Couture, Larry, eds.** Intracellular Ribozyme Applications: Principles & Protocols. 1999. 149.99 (*1-898486-17-4*, Pub. by Horizon Sci) Intl Spec Bk.

***Rossi, John P.** The National Game: Baseball & American Culture. LC 99-53674. (Illus.). 256p. 2000. text 25.00 (*1-56663-287-0*, Pub. by I R Dee) Natl Bk Netwk.

Rossi, John V. Snakes of the United States & Canada, Eastern Area Vol. I: Keeping Them Healthy in Captivity. 224p. (Orig.). 1992. lib. bdg. 54.50 (*0-89464-590-0*) Krieger.

Rossi, John V. & Rossi, Roxanne. Snakes of the United States & Canada: Keeping Them Healthy in Captivity, 2 vols., Set. 566p. 1995. 110.00 (*0-89464-956-6*) Krieger.

***Rossi, John V. & Rossi, Roxanne.** Snakes of the United States & Canada: Natural History & Care in Captivity. LC 99-86782. (C). 2000. text. write for info. (*1-57524-031-9*) Krieger.

Rossi, John V. & Rossi, Roxanne. Snakes of the United States & Canada Vol. II: Keeping Them Healthy in Captivity: Western Area. 2nd ed. LC 91-2199. 342p. 1995. 74.50 (*0-89464-808-X*) Krieger.

Rossi, Joseph S. American Catholics & the Formation of the United Nations. LC 92-37604. (Melville Studies in Church History: Vol. 4). 1993. 64.50 (*0-8191-8548-5*); pap. 37.50 (*0-8191-8980-4*) U Pr of Amer.

Rossi, Joyce. The Gullywasher. LC 95-116544. (Illus.). 32p. (J). (gr. k-3). 1995. lib. bdg. 14.95 (*0-87358-607-7*, Rising Moon Bks) Northland AZ.

***Rossi, Joyce.** The Gullywasher (El Chaparron Torrencial) (ENG & SPA., Illus.). 32p. (J). (gr. k-3). 1998. pap. 7.95 (*0-87358-728-6*, Rising Moon Bks) Northland AZ.

Rossi, Karla, et al. Breaking Bread: A Family History Preserved by Seven Sisters. (Illus.). 463p. 1998. reprint ed. write for info. (*0-9670159-0-1*); reprint ed. write for info. (*0-9670159-1-X*) Seven Sis.

Rossi, Kevin. Lawn Care & Gardening: A Down-to-Earth Guide to the Business. LC 93-74400. (Illus.). 240p. (Orig.). 1994. pap. 21.95 (*0-9639371-9-7*) Acton Circle.

Rossi-Landi, Ferruccio. Between Sign & Non-Sign. Petrilli, Susan, ed. LC 92-24183. (Critical Theory Ser.: No. 10). xxix, 322p. 1992. 89.00 (*1-55619-177-4*) J Benjamins Pubng Co.

— Ideologies of Linguistic Relativity. LC 72-94502. (Approaches to Semiotics Ser.: No. 4). 101p. 1974. pap. text 29.25 (*90-279-2594-1*) Mouton.

— Language As Work & Trade: A Semiotic Homology for Linguistics & Economics. LC 82-4432. 223p. 1983. 55.00 (*0-89789-022-1*, Bergin & Garvey) Greenwood.

— Linguistics & Economics. (Janua Linguarum, Series Major: No. 81). 240p. 1977. pap. text 30.00 (*90-279-3243-3*) Mouton.

— Marxism & Ideology. Griffin, Roger, tr. (Marxist Introductions Ser.). (Illus.). 384p. 1990. text 85.00 (*0-19-876127-9*) OUP.

Rossi, Leandro & Valsecchi, Ambrogio. Diccionario Enciclopedico de Teologia Moral: Encyclopedic Dictionary of Theological Morality. (SPA.). 1488p. 1978. pap. 35.00 (*0-8288-5458-0*, S50078) Fr & Eur.

— Diccionario Enciclopedico de Teologia Moral: Encyclopedic Dictionary of Theological Morality. 3rd ed. (SPA.). 1488p. 1978. 53.95 (*0-8288-5129-8*, S50077) Fr & Eur.

— Diccionario Enciclopedico de Teologia Moral: Suplemento: Encyclopedic Dictionary of Theological Morality, Supplement. (SPA.). 256p. 1978. 49.95 (*0-8288-5130-1*, S50079) Fr & Eur.

Rossi, Lee. Beyond Rescue: New Poems. 72p. (Orig.). 1991. pap. 7.95 (*0-941017-19-2*) Bombshelter Pr.

Rossi, Lee D. The Politics of Fantasy: C. S. Lewis & J. R. R. Tolkien. Scholes, Robert, ed. LC 84-16116. (Studies in Speculative Fiction: No. 10). 153p. 1984. reprint ed. 47.50 (*0-8357-1597-3*, 207043700089) Bks Demand.

Rossi, Lorenza. Who Shall Guard the Guardians Themselves? An Analysis of U. S. Strategy in the Middle East Since 1945. (European University Studies: Vol. 801). 342p. 1998. write for info. (*3-906760-87-1*) P Lang.

— Who Shall Guard the Guardians Themselves? An Analysis of U. S. Strategy in the Middle East since 1945, Vol. 801. LC 98-29060. (European University Studies: No. 3). (Illus.). 342p. 1998. pap. text 49.95 (*0-8204-4210-0*) P Lang Pubng.

Rossi, Louis. Cycling along the Canals of New York: 500 Miles of Bike Riding along the Erie, Champlain, Cayuga-Seneca & Oswego Canals. LC 98-30952. (Illus.). 160p. 1998. pap. 15.95 (*0-941950-35-2*) Vitesse Pr.

***Rossi, Louis D. & Rossi, Thomas.** Cisco Catalyst LAN Switching. LC 99-40272. (Cisco Technical Expert Ser.). 352p. 1999. 55.00 incl. cd-rom (*0-07-134982-0*) McGraw.

Rossi, Louis D., et al. CCIEprep.com Study Guide, Vol. 1. LC 98-51300. (Illus.). 600p. 1998. 89.95 (*1-890911-08-9*, CIEG) Genium Pub.

Rossi, Louis S. Six Years on the West Coast of America, 1856-1862. Wortley, W. Victor, tr. (Illus.). 376p. 1983. 19.95 (*0-87770-293-4*) Ye Galleon.

Rossi, Luca S. Interviews with the Olympic Champions: Clay Target Shooting. Russell, James, ed. & illus. by. 200p. 2001. pap. 34.95 (*0-916367-14-2*, ioc) James Russell.

Rossi, Mario. Acoustics & Electroacoustics. Roe, Patrick R., tr. LC 88-2176. (Illus.). 768p. reprint ed. pap. 200.00 (*0-7837-4620-2*, 204434100002) Bks Demand.

— Roosevelt & the French. LC 93-12973. 224p. 1993. 62.95 (*0-275-94613-4*, C4613, Praeger Pubs) Greenwood.

Rossi, Mark A. The Intruder Bulletins. (Illus.). (Orig.). Date not set. pap. write for info. (*0-614-29882-2*) New Thght Jour Pr.

***Rossi, Mark Antony, et al.** Collages & Bricolages Vol. 13: The Journal of International Writing 2000. Fortis, Marie-Jose, ed. (Illus.). 187p. 2000. pap. 10.00 (*0-9677265-0-6*) Collages & Bricolages.

Rossi, Mary A. Theocritis' "Idyll XVII" A Stylistic Commentary. vii, 249p. 1989. pap. 78.00 (*90-256-0967-8*, Pub. by AM Hakkert) BookLink Distributors.

Rossi, Melissa. Courtney Love: The Queen of Noise. 1996. mass mkt. 5.99 (*0-671-00038-1*) PB.

Rossi, Michael. James Herriot. LC 96-25014. (Critical Companions to Popular Contemporary Writers Ser.). 240p. 1997. 29.95 (*0-313-29449-6*, Greenwood Pr) Greenwood.

Rossi, Michael, jt. auth. see Goldman, Norma.

Rossi, Mitchell S. The Hong Kong Sanction. 384p. 1997. mass mkt. 5.99 (*0-7860-0400-2*, Pinncle Kensgtn) Kensgtn Pub Corp.

Rossi, Nick & Fauntleroy, Talmage. Domenico Cimarosa: His Life & His Operas. 50. LC 98-23934. (Contributions to the Study of Music & Dance: Vol. 50). 240p. 1999. 65.00 (*0-313-30112-3*, Greenwood Pr) Greenwood.

***Rossi, P., et al, eds.** Portal Hypertension: Diagnostic Imaging & Imaging-Guided Therapy. LC 99-55309. (Medical Radiology Ser.). (Illus.). 300p. 2000. 199.00 (*3-540-65797-5*) Spr-Verlag.

Rossi, Paolo. The Dark Abyss of Time: The History of the Earth & the History of Nations from Hooke to Vico. Cochrane, Lydia G., tr. LC 84-8481. 354p. 1987. pap. text 30.00 (*0-226-72832-3*) U Ch Pr.

— The Dark Abyss of Time: The History of the Earth & the History of Nations from Hooke to Vico. Cochrane, Lydia G., tr. LC 84-8481. 352p. 1997. 42.00 (*0-226-72835-8*) U Ch Pr.

Rossi, Patrizio. Roberto Rossellini: A Guide to References & Resources. 1988. 55.00 (*0-8161-7911-5*, Hall Reference) Macmillan.

Rossi, Patrizio & Radcliff-Umstead, Douglas. Italiano Oggi: Italian Review Grammar. LC 71-146362. (ITA.). (C). 1976. reprint ed. pap. text 15.95 (*0-89197-638-8*) Irvington.

Rossi, Paul. Art of the Old West. 1981. 29.98 (*0-88394-045-0*) Promntory Pr.

Rossi, Peggy G. Case Management in Healthcare: A Practical Guide. Eoyang, Tim, ed. LC 98-9757. (Illus.). 416p. (C). 1998. pap. text 39.95 (*0-7216-7175-6*, W B Saunders Co) Harcrt Hlth Sci Grp.

Rossi, Peter. Without Shelter: Homelessness in the 1980s. (Twentieth Century Fund Papers). 1989. 18.95 (*0-87078-235-5*); pap. 8.95 (*0-87078-234-7*) Century Foundation.

Rossi, Peter H. Down & Out in America: The Origins of Homelessness. LC 89-31598. (Illus.). 288p. 1989. 15.95 (*0-226-72828-5*) U Ch Pr.

— Down & Out in America: The Origins of Homelessness. LC 89-31598. (Illus.). 264p. 1991. pap. text 10.95 (*0-226-72829-3*) U Ch Pr.

— Evaluation: A Systematic Approach. 5th ed. (Illus.). 512p. (C). 1993. text 46.00 (*0-8039-4458-6*) Sage.

— Feeding the Poor: Assessing Federal Food Aid. LC 97-24858. 180p. 1998. 29.95 (*0-8447-4010-1*); pap. 14.95 (*0-8447-4011-X*) Am Enterprise.

— Why Families Move. LC 79-25370. 243p. reprint ed. pap. 75.40 (*0-7837-4558-3*, 204408600003) Bks Demand.

Rossi, Peter H., ed. Ghetto Revolts. 2nd ed. LC 72-91469. (Society Bks.). 171p. 1970. reprint ed. 32.95 (*0-87855-067-4*); reprint ed. pap. text 19.95 (*0-87855-564-1*) Transaction Pubs.

— Modelling Stock Market Volatility: Bridging the Gap to Continuous Time. (Illus.). 485p. 1996. text 59.95 (*0-12-598275-5*) Morgan Kaufmann.

Rossi, Peter H. & Berk, Richard A. Just Punishments: Federal Guidelines & Public Views Compared. LC 96-53324. (Social Institutions & Social Change Ser.). 254p. 1997. pap. text 20.95 (*0-202-30573-2*); lib. bdg. 41.95 (*0-202-30572-4*) Aldine de Gruyter.

Rossi, Peter H. & Biddle, Bruce J., eds. The New Media & Education: Their Impact on Society. LC 66-19580. (Monographs in Social Research: No. 12). 1966. 15.00 (*0-202-09005-1*) Natl Opinion Res.

Rossi, Peter H. & Dentler, Robert A. The Politics of Urban Renewal: The Chicago Findings. LC 81-6327. (Illus.). 308p. 1981. reprint ed. lib. bdg. 69.50 (*0-313-22780-2*, ROPR, Greenwood Pr) Greenwood.

Rossi, Peter H. & Lyall, Katharine C. Reforming Public Welfare: A Critique of the Negative Income Tax Experiment. LC 75-41509. 208p. 1976. 29.95 (*0-87154-754-6*) Russell Sage.

Rossi, Peter H., et al. Evaluation: A Systematic Approach. 6th ed. LC 98-40244. 500p. 1998. write for info. (*0-7619-0893-5*) Sage.

— Handbook of Survey Research. (Quantitative Studies in Social Relations). 1985. pap. text 59.95 (*0-12-598227-5*) Acad Pr.

Rossi, Peter H., jt. auth. see Berk, Richard A.

Rossi, Peter H., jt. auth. see Greeley, Andrew M.

Rossi, Peter H., jt. auth. see Rossi, Alice S.

Rossi, Peter H., jt. auth. see Wright, James D.

Rossi, Peter H., jt. ed. see Chen, Huey-tsyh.

Rossi, Peter M. & White, Wayne E., eds. Articles on the Middle East, 1947-1971: A Cumulation of Bibliographies from the Middle East Journal, 4 vols., Set. LC 79-91337. (Cumulated Bibliography Ser.: No. 7). 1980. 180.00 (*0-87650-030-0*) Pierian.

Rossi, Philip. Together Toward Hope: A Journey to Moral Theology. LC 83-1279. 224p. 1983. 26.50 (*0-268-01844-8*) U of Notre Dame Pr.

Rossi, Philip J. & Soukup, Paul A., eds. Mass Media & the Moral Imagination. LC 93-30845. 300p. (Orig.). 1994. pap. 24.95 (*1-55612-622-0*) Sheed & Ward WI.

Rossi, Philip J. & Wreen, Michael, eds. Kant's Philosophy of Religion Reconsidered. LC 90-27310. (Indiana Series in the Philosophy of Religion). 244p. 1991. 26.95 (*0-253-35027-1*) Ind U Pr.

Rossi, Plinio, jt. auth. see Adam, Andy.

Rossi, Plinio, jt. auth. see Pavone, P.

Rossi, Renzo. Living in A Medieval Castle. Paoli, Erika, tr. from ITA. LC 99-10948. (Places of Life Ser.). 1999. 23.50 (*0-382-42237-6*, Dillon Silver Burdett) Silver Burdett Pr.

— Living in A Medieval Monastery. Paoli, Erika, tr. from ITA. LC 99-10944. (The Places of Life Ser.). 1999. 23.00 (*0-382-42238-4*, Dillon Silver Burdett) Silver Burdett Pr.

— Living in A Native American Village. LC 99-18243. (The Places of Life Ser.). 1999. 23.00 (*0-382-42240-6*, Dillon Silver Burdett) Silver Burdett Pr.

— Living in A Roman Villa. LC 99-21163. 1999. 23.00 (*0-382-42239-2*, Dillon Silver Burdett) Silver Burdett Pr.

Rossi, Rita H., jt. ed. see Rossi, Roberto A.

Rossi, Robert. Profiles of Students With Disabilities As Identified In Nels: 88. LC 97-223433. 141p. 1997. pap. 14.00 (*0-16-049099-5*) USGPO.

Rossi, Robert Del, see Del Rossi, Robert.

***Rossi, Robert J.** Education Reform & Students at Risk. LC 97-174274. 133p. 1998. pap. 10.00 (*0-16-048880-X*) USGPO.

Rossi, Robert J. Schools & Students at Risk: Context & Framework for Positive Change. LC 93-44316. 336p. (C). 1994. pap. 23.95 (*0-8077-3325-3*); text 48.00 (*0-8077-3326-1*) Tchrs Coll.

***Rossi, Robert J. & Stringfield, Samuel C.** Education Reform & Students at Risk: Studies of Education Reform. 119p. 1999. pap. text 25.00 (*0-7881-7893-8*) DIANE Pub.

Rossi, Robert J. & Wegman, Raymond F. Critical Materials & Processes in a Changing World: 7th International SAMPE Electronics Conference, Held at the Sheraton Tara Hotel, Parsippany, New Jersey, June 20-23, 1994. LC 95-109258. (International SAMPE Electronics Conference Ser.: No. 7). (Illus.). 727p. 1994. reprint ed. pap. 200.00 (*0-608-00924-5*, 206171700011) Bks Demand.

Rossi, Robert J., et al. Agencies Working Together: A Guide to Coordination & Planning. LC 82-10558. (Sage Human Services Guides Ser.: No. 28). (Illus.). 120p. 1982. reprint ed. pap. 37.20 (*0-608-01086-3*, 205939500001) Bks Demand.

— Using the Talent Profiles in Counseling: A Supplement to the Career Data Book. 1975. pap. 5.25 (*0-89785-516-7*) Am Inst Res.

Rossi, Robert J., jt. auth. see Hawkins, Evelyn F.

Rossi, Robert J., jt. ed. see Gilmartin, Kevin J.

Rossi, Roberto A. & Rossi, Rita H., eds. Aromatic Substitution by the SRN1 Mechanism. LC 82-22829. (ACS Monograph: No. 178). 300p. 1983. text 57.95 (*0-8412-0648-1*, Pub. by Am Chemical) OUP.

***Rossi, Roger.** From the Piano Bench: Memorable Moments with Mobsters, Moguls, Movie Stars & More. LC 00-31322. (Illus.). 2000. pap. 16.95 (*0-944031-87-0*) Aslan Pub.

Rossi, Roxanne, jt. auth. see Rossi, John.

Rossi, Roxanne, jt. auth. see Rossi, John V.

Rossi, Sanna B. Anthony T. Rossi. LC 86-27651. 199p. (Orig.). 1986. pap. 12.99 (*0-8308-4999-8*, 4999) InterVarsity.

Rossi, Sara. Collector's Guide to Paperweights. 1990. 12.98 (*1-55521-541-6*) Bk Sales Inc.

Rossi, Sergio. Modalites d'Institution et de Fonctionnement d'Une Banque Centrale Supranationale: Le Cas de la Banque Centrale Europeenne. (Publications Universitaires Europeennes Ser.: Series 5, Vol. 2013). (FRE., Illus.). xxii, 432p. 1997. 57.95 (*3-906754-85-5*, Pub. by P Lang) P Lang Pubng.

Rossi, T., jt. auth. see Cittadini, E.

Rossi, Thomas, jt. auth. see Rossi, Louis D.

Rossi, V. Paradise by the River. LC 99-172814. 1998. pap. text 11.95 (*0-88922-393-9*, Pub. by Talonbks) Genl Dist Srvs.

Rossi, Vanessa, jt. auth. see Heri, Erwin W.

Rossi, Vinio, tr. see Raboni, Giovanni.

Rossi, William. Profitable Footwear Retailing. 322p. 1988. 43.00 (*0-87005-630-1*) Fairchild.

Rossi, William, ed. see Thoreau, Henry David.

Rossi, William A. The Complete Footwear Dictionary. LC 91-48230. 180p. 1994. lib. bdg. 37.50 (*0-89464-715-6*) Krieger.

— The Sex Life of the Foot & Shoe. LC 90-24686. 272p. 1993. reprint ed. 32.50 (*0-89464-573-0*) Krieger.

***Rossi, William A., ed.** The Complete Footwear Dictionary. 2nd ed. LC 99-88751. (Illus.). 226p. (C). 2000. text 69.50 (*1-57524-114-5*) Krieger.

Rossiaud, Jacques. Medieval Prostitution. Cochrane, Lydia G., tr. from FRE. (Family, Sexuality & Social Relations in Past Times). 272p. 1995. pap. text 28.95 (*0-631-19992-6*) Blackwell Pubs.

Rossides & Maravel. United States Import Trade Law, 2 vols., No. 5. 250p. 1998. ring bd. 100.00 (*0-327-00775-3*, 8269015) LEXIS Pub.

Rossides, Daniel W. American Society: An Introduction to Macrosociology. LC 92-75606. 695p. 1993. text 65.95 (*1-882289-05-6*); pap. text 39.95 (*1-882289-04-8*) Gen Hall.

— Professions & Disciplines. LC 97-12148. 352p. 1997. pap. text 38.60 (*0-13-619982-8*) P-H.

— Social Stratification: The Interplay of Class, Race & Gender. 2nd ed. 524p. (C). 1996. pap. text 60.00 (*0-13-192535-0*) P-H.

R

Rossides, Eugene T. Foreign Unfair Competition: Practice & Procedure. 3rd rev. ed. (Corporate Practice Ser.: No. 28). 1990. ring bd. 95.00 (1-55871-107-4) BNA.

— The Truman Doctrine of Aid to Greece: A Fifty-Year Retrospective. LC 98-19969. 1998. pap. 25.00 (1-889247-02-2) AM Hellenic.

— United States Import Trade Regulation. LC 84-23748. 768p. reprint ed. pap. 200.00 (0-7837-4597-4, 204431600002) Bks Demand.

Rossides, Eugene T., ed. Handbook on U. S. Relations with Greece & Cyprus. 1997. write for info. (0-941882-01-2) Amer Hellenic Inst.

— The United States, Cyprus & the Rule of Law, 1974-1994: Twenty Years of Turkish Aggression & Occupation. LC 96-20080. 320p. 1996. text 40.00 (0-89241-569-X) Caratzas.

Rossides, Eugene T., et al, eds. Doing Business in Greece: A Legal & Practical Reference Service, 2 vols., Vols. I & II. LC 96-24365. 1000p. 1996. ring bd. 250.00 (1-889247-00-6) W S Hein.

***Rossides, Eugene T. & Maravel, Alexandra.** Foreign Unfair Competition: Practice & Procedure. 4th ed. (Corporate Practice Ser.: No. 28). 1999. pap. 95.00 (1-55871-394-8) BNA.

Rossides, Eugene T. & Maravel, Alexandra. U. S. Import Trade Law, 2 vols. 1350p. 1992. spiral bd. 200.00 (0-88063-803-6, 82686-10, MICHIE) LEXIS Pub.

Rossie, Cam & Hylton, Hilary. The Insiders' Guide to Austin. (Insiders' Guide Travel Ser.). (Illus.). 4p. 1998. pap. 15.95 (1-57380-075-9, The Insiders Guide) Falcon Pub Inc.

Rossie, John P. Handbook for Aerospace Education. rev. ed. Duca, Victoria, ed. LC 89-83438. (Illus.). 108p. (Orig.). 1989. reprint ed. pap. 6.00 (0-9620988-0-9) Aerospace EDP.

Rossie, John P., pref. Handbook Two for Aerospace Education: A Guide to Projects & Applications. LC 91-60903. (Illus.). 398p. (Orig.). 1991. pap. text 19.50 (0-911168-80-X) Prakken.

Rossie, Jonathan G., jt. ed. see Gibson, Frederick W.

Rossie, Sandra S., jt. auth. see Armstrong, David L.

Rossie, Sandra S., jt. ed. see Armstrong, David.

Rossier, Bernard. Hermeneutical Principles of Pentecostals. 80p. (Orig.). 1994. pap. text 8.95 (0-930401-72-7) Artex Pub.

— The New Testament Church. 104p. (Orig.). 1990. pap. 8.00 (0-930401-31-X) Artex Pub.

— Prison Epistles: Praise from Prison. 272p. (C). 1987. 6.95 (0-912981-18-0) Hse BonGiovanni.

— Professionalism in Pentecostal Education. 96p. 1992. pap. 7.95 (0-930401-50-6) Artex Pub.

— Proper Pattern for Pentecostal Postsecondary Education. 96p. 1992. pap. text 7.95 (0-930401-53-0) Artex Pub.

Rossier, Francois. L' Intercession Entre les Hommes dans la Bible Hebraique: L'Intercession Entre les Hommes aux Origines de l'Intercession Aupres de Dieu. (Orbis Biblicus et Orientalis Ser.: Vol. 152). (FRE.). 380p. 1996. text 80.00 (3-7278-1101-3, Pub. by Presses Univ Fribourg) Eisenbrauns.

Rossier, H. Meditations on Joshua. 7.25 (0-88172-119-0) Believers Bkshelf.

— Que Pasa Despues de la Muerte? 2nd ed. Bennett, Gordon H., ed. Bautista, Sara, tr. from ENG. (Serie Diamante).Tr. of What Happens After Death?. (SPA., Illus.). 36p. 1982. pap. 0.85 (0-942504-07-0) Overcomer Pr.

— Second Kings. 11.50 (0-88172-182-4) Believers Bkshelf.

Rossier, H. L. Meditations on First Kings. 210p. 8.95 (0-88172-165-4) Believers Bkshelf.

Rossier, Henri L. Meditations on 1st Chronicles.Tr. of First Chronicles. 131p. 1991. 7.95 (0-88172-195-6) Believers Bkshelf.

— Meditations on Ruth & First Samuel, 2. 114p. 1994. 8.95 (0-88172-209-X) Believers Bkshelf.

— Meditations on 2nd Chronicles, 2. 176p. 1993. 8.95 (0-88172-203-0) Believers Bkshelf.

— Meditations on 2nd Samuel, 2, 2. 145p. 1994. 8.95 (0-88172-210-3) Believers Bkshelf.

***Rossier, Robert N.** Dive Like a Pro: 101 Ways to Improve Your Scuba Skills & Safety. LC 98-83116. (Illus.). 104p. 1999. pap. 9.95 (0-941332-75-6, B0995) Best Pub Co.

— Recreational Nitrox Diving. LC 99-68035. (Illus.). 82p. 2000. pap. 9.95 (0-941332-83-7, B1005) Best Pub Co.

Rossignol, F. Beginners Please. mass mkt. 6.95 (0-7472-4926-1, Pub. by Headline Bk Pub) Trafalgar.

— Veronique. 1998. mass mkt. 6.95 (0-7472-5939-9, Pub. by Headline Bk Pub) Trafalgar.

— Willing Girls. mass mkt. 6.95 (0-7472-5429-X, Pub. by Headline Bk Pub) Trafalgar.

Rossignol, Faye. Hotel Nymphomania. pap. 6.95 (0-7472-4887-7, Pub. by Headline Bk Pub) Trafalgar.

Rossignol, J. & Wandsnider, L. Space, Time, & Archaeological Landscapes. (Interdisciplinary Contributions to Archaeology Ser.). (Illus.). 314p. (C). 1992. 54.50 (0-306-44161-6, Plenum Trade) Perseus Pubng.

Rossignol, James E. Le, see Le Rossignol, James E.

Rossignol, Matthew. My Maine Summer. (Illus.). 120p. (Orig.). 1996. pap. 12.95 (0-9646054-8-1) Moosehead Communs.

Rossignol, Rosalyn. Chaucer A to Z: The Essential Reference to His Life & Works. LC 98-51842. (Literary A to Z Ser.). (Illus.). 432p. (YA). 1999. 50.00 (0-8160-3296-3) Facts on File.

***Rossignoli, Marco.** The Complete Pinball Book: Everything You Wanted to Know. LC 99-40286. 256p. 1999. 59.95 (0-7643-1003-8) Schiffer.

***Rossilli, Mariagrazia.** Gender Policies in the European Union. LC 99-15096. 280p. 1999. pap. text 35.95 (0-8204-4508-8) P Lang Pubng.

***Rossing, Barbara R.** The Choice Between Two Cities: Whore, Bride & Empire in the Apocalypse. LC 99-44908. (Harvard Theological Studies). 192p. 1999. pap. 17.00 (1-56338-294-6) TPI PA.

Rossing, John P. Daring to Hope: Sermons for Pentecost First Lesson, Cycle B. LC 93-2759. 1993. pap. 7.95 (1-55673-615-0) CSS OH.

Rossing, Karl-Johan. Letters of Henry Handel Richardson to Nettie Palmer. (Essays & Studies on English Language & Literature: Vol. 14). 1953. pap. 25.00 (0-8115-0212-0) Periodicals Srv.

Rossing, T. D., jt. auth. see Fletcher, N. H.

***Rossing, Thomas D.** Science of Percussion Instruments. (Illus.). 2000. pap. 17.00 (981-02-4159-3) World Scientific Pub.

Rossing, Thomas D. Science of Sound. 2nd ed. 686p. (C). 1990. 80.00 (0-201-15727-6) Addison-Wesley.

— Science of Sound: Musical, Electronic, Environmental. LC 80-12028. (Chemistry Ser.). (Illus.). 512p. 1982. text. write for info. (0-201-06505-3) Addison-Wesley.

Rossing, Thomas D., ed. Environmental Noise Control. 196p. 1979. per. 17.00 (0-917853-75-X, RB-30) Am Assn Physics.

— Musical Acoustics: Selected Reprints. (Reprint Bks.). (Illus.). 227p. (C). 1988. per. 15.00 (0-917853-30-X, RB-51) Am Assn Physics.

Rossing, Thomas D. & Chiaverina, Christopher. Light Science: Physics & the Visual Arts. LC 99-18390. (Undergraduate Texts in Contemporary Physics Ser.). 300p. 1999. 69.00 (0-387-98827-0) Spr-Verlag.

Rossing, Thomas D. & Flechter, N. H. The Physics of Musical Instruments. (Illus.). xvii, 620p. 1991. 69.00 (0-387-96947-0) Spr-Verlag.

Rossing, Thomas D. & Fletcher, Neville H. Principles of Vibration & Sound. LC 94-15494. (Illus.). 250p. 1994. 59.95 (0-387-94304-8) Spr-Verlag.

Rossing, Thomas D., jt. auth. see Fletcher, Neville H.

Rossington, David R., et al, eds. Advances in Materials Characterization. LC 83-4186. (Materials Science Research Ser.: Vol. 15). 692p. 1983. 140.00 (0-306-41347-7, Plenum Trade) Perseus Pubng.

Rossington, Michael, ed. see Shelley, Mary Wollstonecraft.

Rossini, Carlo C. The History of Ethiopia Vol. 1: From Ancient Times to the Medieval Ages. Yuill, Lynn, tr. from ITA. LC 99-23852. 1998. 79.95 (1-56902-090-6) Red Sea Pr.

— The History of Ethiopia Vol. 1: From Ancient Times to the Medieval Ages. Yuill, Lynn, tr. from ITA. LC 99-23852. 1999. pap. 24.95 (1-56902-091-4) Red Sea Pr.

***Rossini, Carlo C.** Principles of the Customary Laws of Eritrea. LC 99-15795. 1999. write for info. (1-56902-111-2) Red Sea Pr.

Rossini, Christine. English As a Legal Language. LC 98-28436. 1998. 103.00 (90-411-9680-3) Kluwer Law Intl.

Rossini, Clare. Winter Morning with Crow. LC 97-15080. (Akron Series in Poetry). 77p. 1997. 24.95 (1-884836-30-5); pap. 12.95 (1-884836-31-3) U Akron Pr.

Rossini, Ellen. 100 Activities: Based on the Catechism of the Catholic Church. 125p. 1996. pap. text 11.95 (0-89870-615-7) Ignatius Pr.

Rossini, Francesco P. & Gay, Nancy G., eds. Atlas of Enteroscopy. LC 98-20746. (Illus.). 200p. 1998. 149.00 (88-470-0025-4) Spr-Verlag.

Rossini, Giaochino. Bianca e Falliero, o Sia Il Consiglio Dei Tre: "Melodramma" in Two Acts by Felice Romani. Dotto, Gabriele, ed. (Critical Edition of the Works of Giaochino Rossini: Vol. 30). lvi, 149p. 1998. lib. bdg. 250.00 (0-226-72855-2) U Ch Pr.

Rossini, Gioacchino. The Barber of Seville. (ENG & ITA.). 88p. 1986. pap. 4.95 (0-7935-2608-6, 50340140) H Leonard.

— The Barber of Seville: Vocal Score.Tr. of Il Barbiere di Siviglia. (ENG & ITA.). 352p. 1986. pap., spiral bd. 24.95 (0-7935-3108-X, 50338220) H Leonard.

— The Barber of Seville in Full Score. 464p. pap. 18.95 (0-486-26019-4) Dover.

***Rossini, Gioacchino.** Five Great Overtures in Full Score. 1999. pap. text 18.95 (0-486-40858-2) Dover.

Rossini, Gioacchino. Italian Girl in Algiers Libretto.Tr. of Italiana In Algeri. (ENG & ITA.). 60p. 1986. pap. 4.95 (0-7935-3394-5, 50340440) H Leonard.

— Italian Girls in Algiers: The Vocal Score. (ENG & ITA.). 376p. 1986. pap. 29.95 (0-7935-3107-1, 50338360) H Leonard.

— Stabat Mater in Full Score. 112p. pap. 9.95 (0-486-28343-7) Dover.

— William Tell & Other Overtures in Full Score. 224p. pap. 12.95 (0-486-28149-3) Dover.

Rossini, Gioachino. Album Francais - Morceaux Reserves: 24 Vocal Pieces (7 Additional Pieces in Appendix) Dalmonte, Rossana, ed. xlii, 466p. 1990. lib. bdg. 120.00 (0-226-72843-9) U Ch Pr.

— Armida: Dramma per Musica in Three Acts by Giovanni Schmidt, 3 vols. Brauner, Charles S. & Brauner, Patricia B., eds. 1395p. 1998. lib. bdg. 250.00 (0-226-72856-0) U Ch Pr.

— The Barber of Seville & Moses. John, Nicholas, ed. Dent, Edward J. et al, trs. from ITA. LC 85-52162. (English National Opera Guide Series: Bilingual Libretto, Articles: No. 36). (Illus.). 160p. (Orig.). (C). 1986. pap. 9.95 (0-7145-4080-3, LIBRETTO, ARTICLES, NO. 36) Riverrun NY.

— Cantata in Onore del Sommo Pontefice Pio IX: Poetry by Giovanni Marchetti. Bucarelli, Mauro, ed. (Critical Edition of the Works of Giaochino Rossini, Sect. II: Vol. 6). xli, 415p. 1997. lib. bdg. 150.00 (0-226-72854-4) U Ch Pr.

— La Cenerentola. John, Nicholas, ed. Jacobs, Arthur, tr. from ITA. (English National Opera Guide Series: Bilingual Libretto, Articles: No. 1). (Illus.). (Orig.). 1980. pap. 9.95 (0-7145-3819-1) Riverrun NY.

— La Donna del Lago: Melo-Dramma in Two Acts, 4 vols. Slim, H. Colin, ed. (Works of Gioachino Rossini Critical Edition Ser.). 1362p. 1992. lib. bdg. 325.00 (0-226-72844-7) U Ch Pr.

— Edipo Coloneo. Tozzi, Lorenzo & Weiss, Piero, eds. Cagli, Bruno et al, trs. from ITA. (Works of Gioachino Rossini Ser.). xxv, 202p. 1986. lib. bdg. 78.00 (0-226-72837-4, 728374) U Ch Pr.

— Ermione: Dramma Per Musica in Two Acts by Andrea Leone Tottola, 3, Set. Bauner, Patricia B. & Gossett, Philip, eds. (Critical Edition of the Works of Gioachino Rossini: Vol. 27, Section I). 965p. 1996. lib. bdg. 225.00 (0-226-72852-8) U Ch Pr.

— La Gazza Ladra, 3 vols., Set. Zedda, Alberto et al, eds. (Works of Gioachino Rossini Ser.). 1418p. 1986. lib. bdg. 300.00 (0-226-72841-2) U Ch Pr.

— Guillaume Tell: Melodramma Tragico in Four Acts by Etienne de Jouy & Hippolyte Bis, 4 vols. Bartlet, M. Elizabeth, ed. (Works of Gioachino Rossini Critical Edition Ser.: Section I: Operas). 2628p. 1994. lib. bdg. 400.00 (0-226-72846-3) U Ch Pr.

— Musique Anodine-Album Italiano: The Critical Edition of the Works of Gioachino Rossini. 1996. lib. bdg. 80.00 (0-226-72853-6) U Ch Pr.

— Le Nozze di Teti, e di Peleo: Azione Coro-Drammatica by Angelo Maria Ricci, Vol. 3. Joerg, Guido J., ed. 451p. 1994. lib. bdg. 75.00 (0-226-72847-1) U Ch Pr.

— L' Occasione fa il Ladro, Ossia il Cambio della Valigia. Ballola, Giovanni C. et al, eds. 168p. 1995. lib. bdg. 135.00 (0-226-72849-8) U Ch Pr.

— Otello, Ossia il Moro di Venezia: Dramma per Musica in Three Acts by Francesco Berio de Salsa, 3 vols. Collins, Michael, ed. (Critical Edition of the Worlds of Gioachino Rossini, Section 1: Operas: Vol. 19). 1130p. 1995. lib. bdg. 195.00 (0-226-72850-1) U Ch Pr.

— Quelques Riens Pour Album. Tartak, Marvin, ed. Cagli, Bruno et al, trs. from ITA. (Works of Gioachino Rossini Ser.). xxii, 346p. 1986. lib. bdg. 78.00 (0-226-72839-0, 728390) U Ch Pr.

— La Scala di Seta: Farsa Comica in One Act, 2 vols., Set. Wiklund, Anders, ed. (Works of Gioachino Rossini Critical Edition Ser.). 600p. 1992. lib. bdg. 198.00 (0-226-72845-5) U Ch Pr.

— Il Signor Bruschino. Fazzanigo, Arrigo, ed. Cagli, Bruno et al, trs. from ITA. (Works of Gioachino Rossini Ser.). xxxv, 504p. 1987. lib. bdg. 216.00 (0-226-72836-6, 728366) U Ch Pr.

— Tancredi, 2 vols. Gossett, Philip, ed. Cagli, Bruno et al, trs. from ITA. (Works of Gioachino Rossini Ser.). 1164p. 1986. lib. bdg. 300.00 (0-226-72838-2, 718382) U Ch Pr.

— Il Turco in Italia: Dramma Buffo in Two Acts. Bent, Margaret, ed. 1374p. 1988. lib. bdg. 300.00 (0-226-72842-0) U Ch Pr.

Rossini, Gioachino, et al. Embellished Opera Arias. Caswell, Austin, ed. (Recent Researches in Music of the 19th & Early 20th Centuries Ser.: Vols. 7 & 8). (Illus.). xxxii, 219p. 1989. pap. 75.00 (0-89579-240-0) A-R Eds.

Rossini, P. M. & Mauguiere, Francois. New Trends & Advanced Techniques in Clinical Neurophysiology. (Supplement to EEG Ser.: Vol. 41). 382p. 1991. 270.50 (0-444-81352-7) Elsevier.

Rossini, Stephane. Egyptian Hieroglyphics: How to Read & Write Them. 96p. 1989. pap. 5.95 (0-486-26013-5) Dover.

Rossini, Stephane, et al. Becoming Osiris: The Ancient Egyptian Death Experience. Graham, Jon, tr. from FRE. LC 98-17679. (Illus.). 128p. 1998. pap. 16.95 (0-89281-652-X, Inner Trad) Inner Tradit.

Rossino, John. Cobb County . . . a Portrait. 95p. (Orig.). 1988. pap. write for info. (0-318-64426-6) CCCC.

Rossinow, Douglas. The Politics of Authenticity. 1999. pap. 18.50 (0-231-11057-X) Col U Pr.

Rossinow, Douglas C. Politics of Authenticity: Liberalism, Christianity, & the New Left in America. LC 97-42950. (Contemporary American History Ser.). 520p. 1998. 34.50 (0-231-11056-1) Col U Pr.

Rossinski, K. I. Dynamics & Thermal Regimes of Rivers. 1986. 18.50 (81-204-0185-9, Pub. by Oxford IBH) S Asia.

Rossinski, K. I., ed. Dynamics & Thermal Regimes of Rivers, Vol. 52. Mishra, R. K., tr. from RUS. 417p. (C). 1987. text 136.00 (90-6191-486-8, Pub. by A A Balkema) Ashgate Pub Co.

Rossipaul. Woerterbuch Englisch Elektronische Windows Version. (ENG & GER.). 1994. 49.95 (0-614-00372-5, 3876865247) Fr & Eur.

— Woerterbuch Englisch Macintosh Version. (ENG & GER.). 1994. 75.00 (0-614-00377-6, 3876867622) Fr & Eur.

— Woerterbuch Franzoesich - Windows Version. (FRE & GER.). 1994. 49.95 (0-614-00373-3, 3876865255) Fr & Eur.

— Woerterbuch Spanische - Windows Version. (GER & SPA.). 1994. 49.95 (0-7859-7230-7, 3876865271) Fr & Eur.

Rossitch, Eugene, jt. auth. see Black, Peter M.

Rossiter. Advertising Promotion Management. 1988. teacher ed. 40.93 (0-07-053908-1) McGraw.

— The Federalist Papers. (C). 1997. pap. text. write for info. (0-321-02608-X) Addson-Wesley Educ.

Rossiter, A. P. Angel with Horns & Other Lectures on Shakespeare. 316p. (C). 1989. pap. text 22.75 (0-582-01499-9, 78287) Longman.

Rossiter, Alan P., ed. Waste Minimization Through Process Design. LC 94-49707. 384p. 1995. 55.00 (0-07-053957-X) McGraw.

Rossiter, Amy. From Private to Public: A Feminist Exploration of Early Mothering. 290p. pap. 12.95 (0-88961-128-9, Pub. by Womens Pr) LPC InBook.

***Rossiter, Andrew & Kawanabe, Hiroya, eds.** Advances in Ecological Research. (Advances in Ecological Research Ser.: Vol. 31). 700p. 2000. 109.95 (0-12-013931-6) Acad Pr.

Rossiter, B. W., ed. see Weisberger, Arnold, et al.

Rossiter, Bryant W., et al, eds. Physical Methods of Chemistry Vol. 7: Determination of Elastic & Mechanical Properties, Vol. 7, Determination of Elastic and Mechanical Pr. 2nd ed. LC 90-13009. 313p. 1991. 189.00 (0-471-53438-2) Wiley.

Rossiter, Bryant W. & Baetzold, Roger C. Physical Methods of Chemistry: Investigations of Surfaces & Interfaces, Vol. 9, Pt. B, Investigations of Surfaces and Inte. 2nd ed. LC 92-24513. 768p. 1993. 379.00 (0-471-54405-1) Wiley.

Rossiter, Bryant W. & Baetzold, Roger C., eds. Physical Methods of Chemistry, 12 vols., Vol. 12. 2nd ed. 7840p. 1993. 2875.00 (0-471-02577-1) Wiley.

— Physical Methods of Chemistry: Investigations of Surfaces & Interfaces, Vol. 9, Pt. A, Investigations of Surfaces and Inte. 2nd ed. LC 91-39605. 528p. 1992. 230.00 (0-471-54406-X) Wiley.

— Physical Methods of Chemistry, 2E, Vol. 8, Determination of Electronic & Optical Properties, Vol. 8, Determination of Electronic and Optical Pr. 2nd ed. LC 92-24323. 544p. 1993. 215.00 (0-471-54407-8) Wiley.

Rossiter, Bryant W. & Hamilton, John F. Physical Methods of Chemistry, 3 vols., Vol. 1. 2nd ed. LC 85-6386. (Techniques of Chemistry Ser.). 834p. 1986. 315.00 (0-471-08034-9) Wiley.

— Physical Methods of Chemistry, 3 vols., Vol. 2. 2nd ed. LC 85-6386. (Techniques of Chemistry Ser.). 928p. 1986. 315.00 (0-471-08027-6) Wiley.

— Physical Methods of Chemistry, 3 vols., Vol. 3, Pt. B, Determination of Chemical Compositi. 2nd ed. (Techniques of Chemistry Ser.). 992p. 1989. 299.00 (0-471-85051-9) Wiley.

Rossiter, Bryant W. & Hamilton, John F., eds. Physical Methods of Chemistry: Determination of Thermodynamic Properties, Vol. 6. 2nd ed. LC 85-6386. 760p. 1992. 375.00 (0-471-57087-7) Wiley.

— Physical Methods of Chemistry Pt. A: Part A: Determination of Chemical Composition & Molecular Structure, Vol. 3, Pt. A, Determination of Chemical Compositi. 2nd ed. 624p. 1987. 299.00 (0-471-85041-1) Wiley.

— Physical Methods of Chemistry Vol. 4: Microscopy, Vol. 4. 2nd ed. LC 90-24799. 560p. 1991. 299.00 (0-471-08026-8) Wiley.

— Physical Methods of Chemistry Vol. 5: Determination of Structural Features of Crystalline & Amorphous Solids, Vol. 5. 2nd ed. LC 85-6386. 618p. 1990. 299.00 (0-471-52509-X) Wiley.

Rossiter, C., et al. Property Law: Cases & Materials. 4th ed. 1988. 109.00 (0-409-49287-6, AT, MICHIE); pap. 94.00 (0-409-49288-4, AT, MICHIE) LEXIS Pub.

***Rossiter, Charles.** Evening Stones. 44p. 1999. pap. 5.00 (1-889289-42-6) Ye Olde Font Shoppe.

Rossiter, Charles, et al. Thirds. LC 85-70935. (Illus.). 64p. (Orig.). 1985. pap. 3.95 (0-9614525-0-1) Distant Pr.

Rossiter, Clare. Galliard's Hay. large type ed. (Ulverscroft Large Print Ser.). 336p. 1997. 27.99 (0-7089-3818-3) Ulverscroft.

— Jacobite Summer. large type ed. 320p. 1996. 27.99 (0-7089-3452-8) Ulverscroft.

— Orphanage Miss. large type ed. (Nightingale Ser.). 1996. pap. 17.95 (0-7838-1623-5, G K Hall Lrg Type) Mac Lib Ref.

— Three Seasons at Askrigg. large type ed. 288p. 1996. 27.99 (0-7089-3508-7) Ulverscroft.

Rossiter, Clinton. The American Presidency. LC 87-2824. 304p. (Orig.). 1987. reprint ed. pap. 15.95 (0-8018-3545-3) Johns Hopkins.

— Conservatism in America. 320p. 1982. pap. 15.00 (0-674-16510-1) HUP.

— Parties & Politics in America. 212p. 1960. pap. text 13.95 (0-8014-9021-9) Cornell U Pr.

— The Supreme Court & the Commander in Chief. Longaker, Richard P., ed. LC 76-12815. 280p. 1976. pap. text 15.95 (0-8014-9161-4) Cornell U Pr.

Rossiter, Clinton & Lare, James, eds. The Essential Lippmann: A Political Philosophy for Liberal Democracy. 576p. 1982. pap. text 18.00 (0-674-26775-3) HUP.

Rossiter, Clinton, ed. see Hamilton, Alexander, et al.

Rossiter, Clinton L. Conservatism in America: The Thankless Persuasion. 2nd rev. ed. LC 80-27937. 306p. 1981. reprint ed. lib. bdg. 35.00 (0-313-22720-9, ROCN, Greenwood Pr) Greenwood.

***Rossiter, David.** Boundary Commissions: Redrawing The Uk's Map of Parliamentary Costituencies. 1999. 69.95 (0-7190-5083-9, Pub. by Manchester Univ Pr) St Martin.

Rossiter, Diane E. & Worth, Richard. A Student's Guide to Success. LC 98-85250. 220 p. 1998. write for info. (1-57163-904-7) Sofsource.

Rossiter, Evelyn, tr. see Boldin, Valery.

Rossiter, Evelyn, tr. see Luria, A. R. & Vygotsky, L. S.

Rossiter, Jill. Human Resources: Mastering Your Small Business. 256p. 1996. pap. 22.95 (1-57410-018-1, 6100-2801) Dearborn.

— Total Quality Management: Mastering Your Small Business. 1996. pap. 22.95 (1-57410-039-4, 61010401) Dearborn.

— Total Quality Management - Mastering Your Small Business: UK & European Edition. 250p. 1998. pap. 80.00 (0-85297-486-8, Pub. by Chartered Bank) St Mut.

Rossiter, John R. Advertising & Promotion Management. (C). 1987. text 78.25 (0-07-053907-3) McGraw.

An Asterisk (*) at the beginning of an entry indicates that the title is appearing for the first time.

Rossiter, John R. & Danaher, Peter J. Advanced Media Planning. LC 98-8744. 1998. 75.00 (*0-7923-8218-8*) Kluwer Academic.

Rossiter, John R. & Percy, Larry. Advertising Communications & Promotion Management. 2nd ed. LC 96-25413. (Illus.). 672p. (C). 1997. 86.25 (*0-07-053943-X*) McGraw.

Rossiter, John R., jt. auth. see Percy, Larry.

Rossiter, Laura. Jelly Belly Princess. (Illus.). 10p. (J). (gr. k-2). 1998. bds. 6.99 (*1-57151-606-9*, Nibble Me Bks) Picture Me Bks.

Rossiter, Louis F., pref. Health Economics & Health Policy in the 1990s: Surprises from the Past, Forecasts for the Future, Vol. 11. (Advances in Health Economics & Health Services Research Ser.). 250p. 1990. 73.25 (*1-55938-137-X*) Jai Pr.

Rossiter, Louis F., jt. ed. see Scheffler, Richard M.

Rossiter, Margaret L. Women in the Resistance. LC 85-16746. (Illus.). 266p. 1985. 59.95 (*0-275-90222-6*, C0222, Praeger Pubs) Greenwood.

Rossiter, Margaret W. Women Scientists in America: Before Affirmative Action, 1940-1972. 624p. 1995. 35.95 (*0-8018-4893-8*) Johns Hopkins.

— Women Scientists in America: Struggles & Strategies to 1940. LC 81-20902. (Illus.). 440p. 1982. reprint ed. pap. text 16.95 (*0-8018-2509-1*) Johns Hopkins.

— Women Scientists in America Vol. 2: Before Affirmative Action, 1940-1972. 624p. 1998. reprint ed. pap. text 17.95 (*0-8018-5711-2*) Johns Hopkins.

Rossiter, Margaret W., jt. ed. see Elliott, Clark A.

Rossiter, Margaret W., jt. ed. see Kohlstedt, Sally G.

***Rossiter-McFarland, Lyn.** The Pirate's Parrot. LC 99-38357. (Illus.). 40p. (J). (gr. k-2). 2000. 14.95 (*1-58246-014-0*) Tricycle Pr.

Rossiter, Nan. Rugby & Rosie. LC 96-14688. (Illus.). 32p. (J). 1997. 14.99 (*0-525-45484-5*) NAL.

Rossiter, Nan P. Way Home. LC 98-54194. 32p. (J). (gr. k-3). 1999. 15.99 (*0-525-45767-4*, Dutton Child) Peng Put Young Read.

Rossiter, Paul L. The Electrical Resistivity of Metals & Alloys. (Solid State Science Ser.). (Illus.). 450p. (C). 1991. pap. text 49.95 (*0-521-40872-5*) Cambridge U Pr.

Rossiter, Phyllis. The Living History of the Ozarks. LC 92-5309. (Illus.). 488p. 1992. pap. 19.95 (*0-88289-801-9*) Pelican.

— Moxie. LC 90-30027. 192p. (J). (gr. 5 up). 1990. text 14.95 (*0-02-777831-2*, Four Winds Pr) S&S Childrens.

— On the Scent of Danger. large type ed. LC 93-30109. 205p. 1993. lib. bdg. 13.95 (*0-7862-0045-6*) Thorndike Pr.

Rossiter, Richard. Best of Boulder Climbs: Rock Climbing Guide. (Illus.). 184p. (Orig.). 1996. reprint ed. pap. 15.00 (*0-934641-26-9*) Falcon Pub Inc.

— Boulder Canyon. (Boulder Climbs Ser.). (Illus.). (Orig.). 1997. pap. write for info. (*1-57540-092-8*) Falcon Pub Inc.

— Classic Rock Climbs Vol. 2: Upper Dream Canyon. (Classic Rock Climbs Ser.). (Illus.). 48p. 1997. pap. 10.95 (*1-57540-030-8*) Falcon Pub Inc.

— The Diamond of Long Peaks. (Classic Rock Climbs Ser.: No. 8). (Illus.). 48p. (Orig.). 1996. pap. 8.95 (*1-57540-026-X*) Falcon Pub Inc.

— The Elorado Canyon. (Boulder Climbs Ser.). (Illus.). (Orig.). 1998. pap. write for info. (*1-57540-093-6*) Falcon Pub Inc.

***Rossiter, Richard.** The Model: Selected Writings of Kenneth Seaforth McKenzie. 2000. pap. 34.95 (*1-876268-34-4*, Pub. by Univ of West Aust Pr) Intl Spec Bk.

Rossiter, Richard. Rock Climbing Boulder Canyon. LC 98-42941. (Illus.). 325p. 1998. pap. 20.00 (*1-56044-750-8*) Falcon Pub Inc.

— Rock Climbing Rocky Mountain National Park: The Crags. (Illus.). 277p. 1996. pap. 20.00 (*0-934641-34-X*) Falcon Pub Inc.

***Rossiter, Richard.** Rock Climbing the Boulder Flatirons. LC 99-38035. (Illus.). 350p. 1999. pap. 20.00 (*1-56044-918-7*) Falcon Pub Inc.

Rossiter, Richard. Teton Classics: Fifty Selected Climbs in Grand Teton National Park. 2nd ed. (Illus.). 126p. (Orig.). 1994. pap. 15.00 (*0-934641-71-4*) Falcon Pub Inc.

Rossiter, Richard H. & MacDonald, Sue. Overcoming Repetitive Motion Injuries the Rossiter Way. LC 98-68749. 256p. 1999. pap. 15.95 (*1-57224-134-9*) New Harbinger.

***Rossiter, Richard T.** Out with a Passion: A United Methodist Pastor's Quest for Authenticity. LC 99-60588. 128p. 1999. pap. 11.95 (*1-886360-07-3*) Alamo Sq Pr.

Rossiter, Sarah. Beyond This Bitter Air: Stories. LC 87-5031. (Illinois Short Fiction Ser.). 144p. 1987. 14.95 (*0-252-01429-4*) U of Ill Pr.

Rossiter, Sean. The Basics: Hockey the NHL Way. (Illus.). 96p. (gr. 4-7). 1996. pap. 10.95 (*1-55054-499-3*, Pub. by Greystone Bks) Sterling.

***Rossiter, Sean.** Dominik Hasek. (Hockey Heroes Ser.). (Illus.). 48p. (YA). (gr. 9-12). 1999. pap. text 6.95 (*1-55054-679-1*, Greystone) DGL.

Rossiter, Sean. Immortal Beaver: The World's Greatest Bush Plane. (Illus.). 192p. 1999. pap. 19.95 (*1-55054-724-0*) DGL.

— Otter & Twin Otter. 208p. 1999. 34.95 (*1-55054-637-6*, Pub. by DGL) Orca Bk Pubs.

Rossiter, Sean & Carlson, Paul. Win with Defense: Hockey the NHL Way. LC 99-193035. (Illus.). 1998. pap. 12.95 (*1-55054-644-9*, Pub. by DGL) Sterling.

Rossiter, Sean, jt. auth. see MacLean, Robert M.

Rossiter, Val. Electromagnetism. LC 81-214054. 180p. reprint ed. pap. 55.80 (*0-608-14924-1*, 202597800048) Bks Demand.

Rossiter, Walter J., Jr. Performance of Tape-bonded Seams of Epdm Membranes: Factors Affecting the Creep-Rupture Response of Tape-bonded & Liquid-Adhesive-Bonded Seams. 55p. 1998. pap. 7.00 (*0-16-056714-9*) USGPO.

Rossiter, Walter J., Jr., ed. Roofing Technology Conference, 9th: Proceedings. 98p. 1989. 28.00 (*0-934809-05-4*) Natl Roofing Cont.

Rossiter, Walter J., jt. ed. see Wallace, J.

Rossiter, Walter J., jt. ed. see Wallace, Thomas J.

Rossiya, Sovetskaya. Folk Russian Costume. 309p. (C). 1989. 250.00 (*0-89771-819-4*, Pub. by Collets) St Mut.

Rosskam, Edwin, photos by. Twelve Million Black Voices. (Classic Reprint Ser.). (Illus.). 160p. 1988. reprint ed. pap. 15.95 (*0-938410-44-X*, Thunders Mouth) Avalon NY.

Rosskopf, Myron F. Children's Mathematical Concepts: Six Piagetian Studies in Mathematics Education. LC 75-12872. (Illus.). 224p. reprint ed. pap. 69.50 (*0-608-30081-0*, 201776700008) Bks Demand.

Rosskopf, W. J., Jr., jt. auth. see Woerpel, R. W.

Rosskopf, Walter J., Jr. & Woerpel, Richard, eds. Diseases of Cage & Aviary Birds. 3rd ed. LC 96-2665. (Illus.). 1088p. 1996. write for info. (*0-683-07382-6*) Lppncott W & W.

Rossl, J., comment. Stifterbuch des Klosters Zwettl "Baerenhaut" fac. limited ed. (Codices Selecti A Ser.: Vol. LXXIII). (GER., Illus.). 394p. 1981. 1130.00 (*3-201-01165-7*, Pub. by Akademische Druck-und) Balogh.

Rossler. Woerterbuch der Deutschen Geschichte, 3 vols. 2nd rev. ed. (GER.). 350.00 (*0-7859-7233-1*, 3907820835) Fr & Eur.

Rossler, Horst, jt. ed. see Hoerder, Dirk.

Rosslerova-Slavikova. Praca S Umeleckym Textom: Metodicka Prirucka Pre Ucitelov 1. Stupna ZS. (SLO.). 256p. 1997. write for info. (*80-08-01434-2*, Pub. by Slov Pegagog Naklad) IBD Ltd.

Rossley, Peter J., jt. auth. see Goudel, Yann.

Rosslyn, Felicity. Alexander Pope: A Literary Life. LC 89-24045. 220p. 1990. text 39.95 (*0-312-04021-0*) St Martin.

Rosslyn, Wendy. Anna Bunina (1774-1829) & the Origins of Women's Poetry in Russia. LC 97-28948. (Studies in Slavic Languages & Literature: Vol. 10). 380p. 1997. 99.95 (*0-7734-8527-9*) E Mellen.

Rossman, A. Y. Mycological Papers No. 157: The Tubeufiaceae & Similar Loculoascomycetes. 71p. (C). 1987. pap. text 31.50 (*0-85198-580-7*) C A B Intl.

Rossman, A. Y., ed. The Phragmosporous Species of Nectria & Related Genera. (Mycological Papers: No. 150). 162p. (C). 1983. pap. 36.00 (*0-00-000078-7*) C A B Intl.

Rossman, Allan J. Workshop Statistics: Discovery with Data. LC 95-16797. (Texbooks in Mathematical Sciences Ser.). (Illus.). 452p. (C). 1996. 28.95 (*0-387-94497-4*) Spr-Verlag.

— Workshop Statistics: Discovery with Data. 2nd ed. 1998. pap. 29.95 (*0-387-98550-6*) Spr-Verlag.

***Rossman, Allan J. & Chance, Beth L.** Workshop Statistics: Discovery with Data. 2nd ed. (Workshop Mathematics Project Ser.). (Illus.). 452p. 2000. pap. 39.95 (*1-930190-03-4*) Key Coll.

Rossman, Allan J. & Chance, Beth L. Workshop Statistics: Discovery with Data & Minitab. LC 97-52162. (Textbooks in Mathematical Sciences Ser.). (Illus.). 512p. 1998. pap. 39.95 (*0-387-98411-9*) Spr-Verlag.

***Rossman, Allan J. & Chance, Beth L.** Workshop Statistics: Discovery with Data & Minitab. 2nd ed. (Workshop Mathematics Project Ser.). (Illus.). 500p. (C). 2000. pap. 39.95 (*1-930190-06-9*) Key Coll.

Rossman, Allan J. & Chance, Beth L. Workshop Statistics: Student Minitab Version. 152p. 1998. pap. 59.95 incl. cd-rom (*0-387-91580-X*) Spr-Verlag.

Rossman, Allan J. & Von Oehsen, Barr. Workshop Statistics: Discovery Through Data & the Graphing Calculator. LC 97-6178. (TIMS - Texts in Mathematical Science Ser.). (Illus.). 460p. 1997. pap. 29.95 (*0-387-94997-6*) Spr-Verlag.

***Rossman, Allan J., et al.** Workshop Statistics: Discovery with Data & Fathom. (Workshop Mathematics Project Ser.). 500p. (C). 2000. pap. 39.95 (*1-930190-07-7*); pap. 44.95 (*1-930190-08-5*) Key Coll.

— Workshop Statistics: Discovery with Data & the Graphing Calculator. 2nd ed. (Workshop Mathematics Project Ser.). 460p. (C). 2000. 44.95 (*1-930190-05-0*) Key Coll.

— Workshop Statistics: Discovery with Data & the Graphing Calculator. 2nd rev. ed. (Workshop Mathematics Project Ser.). 500p. (C). 2000. pap. 39.95 (*1-930190-04-2*) Key Coll.

Rossman, Allan J., jt. auth. see Albert, James.

Rossman, Amy Y., et al, eds. Protocols for an All Taxa Biodiversity Inventory of Fungi in a Costa Rican Conservation Area: Report of the Fungus Twig Workshop 9-19 June 1995. LC 97-44635. (Illus.). xviii, 195p. (Orig.). (C). 1998. 35.00 (*1-887905-05-7*) Pkway Pubs.

Rossman, Amy Y., et al. A Literature Guide for the Identification of Plant Pathogenic Fungi. LC 87-70764. 252p. 1987. 32.00 (*0-89054-080-2*) Am Phytopathol Soc.

Rossman, Amy Y., jt. ed. see Hoagland, K. Elaine.

Rossman, B. B. & Rosenberg, Mindy S., eds. Multiple Victimization of Children: Conceptual, Developmental, Research & Treatment Issues. LC 98-10643. 341p. 1998. 49.95 (*0-7890-0361-9*, Maltreatment & Trauma Pr); pap. 24.95 (*0-7890-0382-1*, Maltreatment & Trauma Pr) Haworth Pr.

Rossman, Charles. Enchanted Rock: Views of a Texas Batholith. limited ed. Stark, David, tr. (Illus.). 96p. 1984. 125.00 (*0-9616212-0-6*); ring bd. 300.00 (*0-9616212-1-4*) Duncan & Gladstone.

Rossman, David. The Heart of a Man: A Collection of Poetry. 164p. 1997. pap. 7.00 (*1-57502-663-5*, PO1882) Morris Pubng.

Rossman, David & Rossman, Donna. Second Chances: Take the Next Step in Love: Another Collection of Poetry. 116p. 1999. pap. 8.10 (*0-7392-0158-1*, PO3105) Morris Pubng.

Rossman, Donna. High Kicks! The Essential Guide to Working As A Dancer. 1999. pap. text 14.95 (*0-7136-5110-5*) A & C Blk.

Rossman, Donna, jt. auth. see Rossman, David.

Rossman, Doreen M. A Light Shone in the Darkness. 256p. 1997. pap. 12.95 (*1-57918-044-2*, 3681) Queenship Pub.

Rossman, Douglas. Where Legends Live: A Pictorial Guide to Cherokee Mythic Places. (Illus.). 48p. 1988. pap. 4.95 (*0-935741-10-0*, Pub. by Cherokee Pubns) Book Pub Co.

Rossman, Douglas & Rossman, Sharon. Valhalla in America: Norse Myths in Wood at Rock Island State Park, Wisconsin. (Illus.). 68p. 1999. 19.95 (*1-890352-06-3*) Jackson Harbor.

Rossman, Douglas A., et al. The Garter Snakes: Evolution & Ecology. LC 95-37746. (Animal Natural History Ser.: Vol. 2). (Illus.). 248p. 1996. 65.00 (*0-8061-2820-8*) U of Okla Pr.

Rossman, Douglas E., jt. auth. see Dundee, Harold A.

Rossman, Gabriel, jt. ed. see Suman, Michael.

***Rossman, George.** Advocacy & the King's English. LC 00-36830. 2000. write for info. (*1-58477-112-7*) Lawbk Exchange.

Rossman, Gretchen B., et al, eds. Change & Effectiveness in Schools: A Cultural Perspective. LC 87-33539. (SUNY Series, Frontiers in Education). 173p. (C). 1988. text 21.50 (*0-88706-725-5*) State U NY Pr.

Rossman, Gretchen B. & Rallis, Sharon F. Learning in the Field: An Introduction to Qualitative Research. LC 97-33901. 1998. 58.00 (*0-7619-0352-6*); pap. 27.95 (*0-7619-0353-4*) Sage.

Rossman, Gretchen B., et al. Dynamic Teachers: Leaders of Change. LC 95-15691. (Illus.). 176p. 1995. 51.95 (*0-8039-6235-5*) Corwin Pr.

Rossman, Gretchen B., jt. auth. see Marshall, Catherine.

Rossman, Gretchen B., jt. auth. see Wilson, Bruce L.

Rossman, Isadore, jt. auth. see Rosenberg, Magda.

Rossman, Isadore, jt. auth. see Smith, Jeanne.

Rossman, J. Robert. Recreation Programming: Designing Leisure Experiences. 2nd ed. (Illus.). 465p. 1994. 44.95 (*0-915611-95-3*) Sagamore Pub.

Rossman, Lewis A., jt. ed. see Arciszewski, Tomasz.

Rossman, M. G. The Molecular Replacement Method, Vol. 13. (International Science Review Ser.). 276p. 1972. text 385.00 (*0-677-13940-3*) Gordon & Breach.

Rossman, Marcela, tr. see Carmona-Agosto, Vivian, ed.

Rossman, Marcela, tr. see Henderson, Celina, ed.

Rossman, Mark H. Negotiating Graduate School: A Guide for Graduate Students. LC 95-3258. 160p. 1995. 42.00 (*0-8039-7114-1*); pap. 19.50 (*0-8039-7115-X*) Sage.

Rossman, Mark H. & Rossman, Maxine E., eds. Applying Adult Development Strategies. LC 85-644750. (New Directions for Adult & Continuing Education Ser.: No. ACE 45). 1990. pap. 22.00 (*1-55542-820-7*) Jossey-Bass.

Rossman, Mark H., et al. Teaching & Learning Basic Skills: A Guide for Adult Basic Education & Developmental Education Programs. LC 83-9118. 188p. reprint ed. pap. 58.30 (*0-7837-3885-4*, 204373300011) Bks Demand.

Rossman, Marlene L. Multicultural Marketing: Selling to a Diverse America. LC 93-41996. 192p. 1994. 22.95 (*0-8144-5071-7*) AMACOM.

— Multicultural Marketing: Selling to a Diverse America. LC 93-41996. 176p. 1996. pap. 16.95 (*0-8144-7921-9*) AMACOM.

— Multicultural Marketing: Selling to a Diverse America. 178p. 1997. reprint ed. text 23.00 (*0-7881-5008-1*) DIANE Pub.

***Rossman, Martin C.** Healing Yourself: A Step-by-Step Program for Better Health Through Imagery. 2nd rev. ed. LC 87-10515. 221p. (Orig.). 1999. pap. 14.95 (*1-929295-01-4*) Awareness Pr.

***Rossman, Martin L.** Guided Imagery for Self-Healing: An Essential Resource for Anyone Seeking Wellness. 2nd ed. (Illus.). 292p. 2000. pap. 14.95 (*0-915811-88-X*, Pub. by H J Kramer Inc) New Wrld Lib.

Rossman, Martin L. Healing Yourself. 1990. pap. 10.00 (*0-671-73029-0*, PB Trade Paper) PB.

Rossman, Maxine E., jt. ed. see Rossman, Mark H.

Rossman, Milton D. & MacGregor, Rob R., eds. Tuberculosis. 352p. 1994. text 69.00 (*0-07-053950-2*) McGraw-Hill HPD.

Rossman, Neil. Consciousness: Separation & Integration. LC 89-48909. 213p. (C). 1991. text 59.50 (*0-7914-0407-2*); pap. text 19.95 (*0-7914-0408-0*) State U NY Pr.

Rossman, Parker. The Emerging Worldwide Electronic University: Information Age Global Higher Education. LC 92-3660. (Studies on the 21st Century). 176p. 1993. pap. 21.95 (*0-275-94776-9*, Praeger Pubs) Greenwood.

— The Emerging Worldwide Electronic University: Information Age Global Higher Education, 57. LC 92-3660. (Contributions to the Study of Education Ser.: No. 57). 184p. 1992. 49.95 (*0-313-27927-6*, REK/, Greenwood Pr) Greenwood.

Rossman, Sharon, jt. auth. see Rossman, Douglas.

Rossman, Thomas D. Rack up a Victory. (Illus.). 182p. (Orig.). 1988. pap. 7.00 (*0-9626414-0-5*) T D Rossman.

Rossman, Toby G., ed. Induced Effects of Genotoxic Agents in Eukaryotic Cells. LC 92-19547. 1992. 85.00 (*1-56032-272-1*) Hemisp Pub.

Rossman, Vladimir. Perspectives of Irony in Medieval French Literature. (De Proprietatibus Litterarum, Ser. Major: No. 35). 198p. (Orig.). 1975. pap. text 60.80 (*90-279-3291-3*) Mouton.

Rossmanith, H. P. Failures & The Law: Structural Failure Product Liability & Technical Insurance. 5th ed. 576p. (C). (gr. 13). 1996. 145.00 (*0-419-22080-1*) Routledge.

Rossmanith, H. P., ed. Damage & Failure of Interfaces: Proceedings of the First International Conference DFI-1, Vienna, Austria, 22-24 September, 1995. (Illus.). 488p. (C). 1998. text 126.00 (*90-5410-899-1*, Pub. by A A Balkema) Ashgate Pub Co.

— Fracture & Damage of Concrete & Rock: Proceedings of the Second International Conference on Fracture & Damage of Concrete & Rock, Vienna, Austria, 9-13 November 1992. LC 93-12576. (Illus.). 696p. (C). 1993. 150.00 (*0-419-18470-8*, E & FN Spon) Routledge.

— Fracture Research in Retrospect: An Anniversary Volume in Honour of G. R. Irwin's 90th Birthday. LC 99-496417. (Illus.). 570p. (C). 1997. text 126.00 (*90-5410-679-4*, Pub. by A A Balkema) Ashgate Pub Co.

— Rock Fracture Mechanics. (CISM International Centre for Mechanical Sciences Ser.: No. 275). 484p. 1983. 72.95 (*0-387-81747-6*) Spr-Verlag.

Rossmanith, H. P., ed. Teaching & Education in Fracture & Fatigue. 376p. (C). (gr. 13). 1996. 115.00 (*0-419-20700-7*) Routledge.

Rossmanith, Hans P., ed. Mechanics of Jointed & Faulted Rock: Proceedings of an International Conference, Vienna, 18-20 April 1990. (Illus.). 1008p. (C). 1990. text 181.00 (*90-6191-155-9*, Pub. by A A Balkema) Ashgate Pub Co.

— Mechanics of Jointed & Faulted Rock: Proceedings of the 2nd International Conference on the Mechanics of Jointed & Faulted Rock, MJFR-2, Vienna, Austria, 10-14 April 1995. (Illus.). 1068p. (C). 1995. text 188.00 (*90-5410-541-0*, Pub. by A A Balkema) Ashgate Pub Co.

— Rock Fragmentation by Blasting: Proceedings, 4th International Symposium, Vienna, Austria, July 1993. (Illus.). 532p. 1993. text 149.00 (*90-5410-316-7*, Pub. by A A Balkema) Ashgate Pub Co.

— Structural Failure: Technical, Legal & Insurance Aspects. (Illus.). 224p. (C). 1995. 110.00 (*0-419-20710-4*, E & FN Spon) Routledge.

Rossmanith, J. P., ed. Mechanics of Jointed & Faulted Rock: Proceedings of the 3rd International Conference, Vienna, 6-9 April, 1998. LC 99-496416. (Illus.). 674p. (C). 1998. text 132.00 (*90-5410-955-6*, Pub. by A A Balkema) Ashgate Pub Co.

Rossmanith, W. G. & Scherbaum, W. A., eds. Neuroendocrinology of Sex Steroids: Basic Knowledge & Clinical Implications. (New Developments in Biosciences Ser.: No. 6). viii, 222p. (Orig.). (C). 1993. pap. text 98.50 (*3-11-013616-3*) De Gruyter.

Rossmanith, W. G., jt. ed. see Scherbaum, W. A.

***Rossmann, J., et al, eds.** The Maz'ya Anniversary Collection, 2 vols. 744p. 1999. 268.00 (*3-7643-6203-0*) Birkhauser.

— The Maz'ya Anniversary Collection Vol. 1: On Maz'yas's Work in Functional Analysis, Partial Differential Equations & Applications. (Operator Theory Ser.: Vol. 109). 376p. 1999. 149.00 (*3-7643-6201-4*) Birkhauser.

— The Maz'ya Anniversary Collection Vol. 2: Rostock Conference on Functional Analysis, Partial Differential Equations & Applications. (Operator Theory Ser.: Vol. 110). 368p. 1999. 149.00 (*3-7643-6202-2*) Birkhauser.

Rossmiller, Richard A. The Flat Tax: Implications for Financing Public Schools. 32p. 1996. 5.00 (*0-87652-226-6*, 021-0587) Am Assn Sch Admin.

— Freshwater Stingrays from South America. (Aqualog Special Ser.: Vol. 13). (Illus.). 64p. 1999. 25.00 (*3-931702-87-1*, Pub. by Verlag ACS) Hollywood.

Rossmo, D. Kim. Geographic Profiling. 376p. 1999. boxed set 69.95 (*0-8493-8129-0*) CRC Pr.

Rossmoore, Harold W. The Microbes, Our Unseen Friends. LC 76-17795. 238p. reprint ed. pap. 73.80 (*0-7837-3643-6*, 204351200009) Bks Demand.

Rossmore, Allan. Airline Operations, an Inside View. (Illus.). 207p. (Orig.). 1996. pap. text 32.95 (*1-889284-21-1*) Kellmark Aeronautics.

— The Highest Level: A Practical Guide to Flight Dispatching & Airline Flight Operations. (Illus.). 233p. (Orig.). 1996. pap. text 31.25 (*1-889284-04-1*) Kellmark Aeronautics.

— The Highest Level, a Practical Guide to Flight Dispatching & Airline Flight Operations. 5th rev. ed. (Illus.). 230p. 1997. pap. text 32.95 (*1-889284-05-X*) Kellmark Aeronautics.

Rossnagel, Stephen, et al, eds. Thin Films, Modelling of Film Deposition for Microelectronic Applications Vol. 22: Advances in Research & Development, Vol. 22. (Illus.). 290p. (C). 1996. text 120.00 (*0-12-533022-7*) Acad Pr.

Rossnagel, Stephen M., et al, eds. Thin Films: Subject & Author Cumulative Index, Volumes 1-24, Vol. 25. (Illus.). 526p. (C). 1998. text 155.00 (*0-12-533025-1*) Acad Pr.

Rossnagel, Stephen M., et al. Handbook of Plasma Processing Technology: Fundamentals, Etching, Deposition, & Surface Interactions. LC 89-22834. (Illus.). 523p. 1990. 109.00 (*0-8155-1220-1*) Noyes.

Rosner, Judith. August. 384p. 1998. pap. 12.00 (*0-395-86006-7*, Mariner Bks) HM.

— August. 1988. mass mkt. 5.95 (*0-446-35667-0*, Pub. by Warner Bks) Little.

— August. 576p. 1989. mass mkt. 6.99 (*0-446-35224-1*) Warner Bks.

— His Little Women. Rubenstein, Julie, ed. 448p. 1991. reprint ed. mass mkt. 5.95 (*0-671-70124-X*) PB.

— Looking for Mr. Goodbar. 1991. mass mkt. 5.95 (*0-671-73575-6*) PB.

— Looking for Mr. Goodbar. 1997. per. 14.00 (*0-671-01901-5*) PB.

— Olivia: or The Weight of the Past. large type ed. LC 94-42583. (Large Print Bks.). 1995. 23.95 (*1-56895-166-3*) Wheeler Pub.

R

R

Rossner, Judith, et al. Hampton Shorts: Fiction Plus from the East End. (Illus.). 288p. 1997. pap., per. 12.00 (*0-9658652-0-7*) Hamptons Lit Pubns.

Rossner, M., et al, eds. Constraints, Language & Computation. (Cognitive Science Ser.). 391p. 1994. text 78.00 (*0-12-597930-4*) Acad Pr.

Rossner, Richard. The Whole Story. (YA). (gr. 9-12). 1988. audio 22.95 (*0-582-01887-0*, 78325) Longman.

— The Whole Story: Short Stories for Pleasure & Language Improvement. (YA). (gr. 9-12). 1988. pap. text 16.93 (*0-582-79109-X*, 78326) Longman.

Rossner, Richard & Bolitho, Rod, eds. Currents of Change in English Language Teaching. (Illus.). 272p. 1990. pap. text 13.95 (*0-19-437010-0*) OUP.

Rosso, Alba, tr. see Noble, Mike.

Rosso-Antonick, Pat, des. Shaker Herbal Fare: " . . . For Remember It Is Christmas. (Illus.). 20p. (Orig.). 1997. pap. 5.00 (*0-9655018-0-9*) Knot Grdn Pr.

Rosso, G. A. & Watkins, Daniel P., eds. Spirits of Fire: English Romantic Writers & Contemporary Historical Methods. LC 89-45548. (Illus.). 296p. 1990. 45.00 (*0-8386-3376-5*) Fairleigh Dickinson.

***Rosso, Gambero.** Gambero Rosso Rome 2000. (Illus.). 2000. pap. text 15.00 (*1-890142-03-4*) Gambero Pr.

Rosso, Gambero. Italian Wines, 1999: A Guide to the World of Italian Wine for Experts & Wine Lovers. Cernilli, Daniele & Petrini, Carlo, eds. 650p. 1999. pap. 24.95 (*1-890142-02-6*) Gambero Pr.

***Rosso, Gambero.** Italian Wines 2000: A Guide to the World of Italian Wine. 696p. 2000. pap. 24.95 (*1-890142-04-2*, Pub. by Gambero Pr) Antique Collect.

Rosso, George A., Jr. Blake's Prophetic Workshop: A Study of the Four Zoas. LC 92-54660. (Illus.). 208p. (C). 1993. 36.50 (*0-8387-5240-3*) Bucknell U Pr.

Rosso, Henry A. Rosso on Fund Raising: Lessons from a Masters Lifetime Experience. LC 96-25320. 185p. 1996. 27.95 (*0-7879-0304-3*) Jossey-Bass.

Rosso, Henry A., et al. Achieving Excellence in Fund Raising: A Comprehensive Guide to Principles, Strategies, & Methods. LC 91-16609. (Nonprofit Sector-Public Administration Ser.). 345p. 1991. text 44.95 (*1-55542-387-6*) Jossey-Bass.

Rosso, Jim. A Guide to Bird Finding in Washington. 182p. 1997. pap. write for info. (*1-57502-454-3*, P01310) Morris Pubng.

Rosso, Joy M. Del, see Del Rosso, Joy M.

Rosso, Julee. Great Good Food. (Illus.). 608p. 1993. 20.00 (*0-517-88122-5*, Crown) Crown Pub Group.

— Great Good Food: Luscious, Lower-Fat Cooking. LC 92-56843. 1993. 29.00 (*0-679-42098-3*); pap. 19.00 (*0-679-74460-6*) Random.

— Less Is More: Simple, Healthful Recipes with Less Fuss. LC 96-31767. 1998. pap. 18.95 (*0-517-88524-7*, Crown) Crown Pub Group.

— Less Is More: Simple, Healthful Recipes with Less Fuss. LC 96-31767. 1999. 30.00 (*0-517-70285-1*) Random Hse Value.

— Menus for Two. (Weekend Menus Ser.: No. 16). 1997. write for info. (*0-517-70705-5*, Crown) Crown Pub Group.

— Week-End Menus. 1997. pap. 10.00 (*0-517-88525-5*, Crown) Crown Pub Group.

Rosso, Julee & Lukins, Sheila. The New Basics Cookbook. LC 88-51581. (Illus.). 864p. 1989. 29.95 (*0-89480-392-1*, 1392) Workman Pub.

Rosso, Julee & Lukins, Sheila. The New Basics Cookbook. LC 88-51581. (Illus.). 849p. 1989. pap. 19.95 (*0-89480-341-7*, 1341) Workman Pub.

Rosso, Julee & Lukins, Sheila. The Silver Palate Cookbook in Large Print. large type ed. LC 93-9108. (Illus.). 650p. 1993. pap. 18.95 (*0-8161-5765-0*, G K Hall Lrg Type) Mac Lib Ref.

— The Silver Palate Cookbook in Large Print. large type ed. LC 93-9108. (Illus.). 650p. 1993. 24.95 (*0-8161-5764-2*, G K Hall Lrg Type) Mac Lib Ref.

Rosso, Julee, et al. The Silver Palate Cookbook. LC 81-43782. (Illus.). 362p. 1982. pap. 14.95 (*0-89480-204-6*, 402) Workman Pub.

— The Silver Palate Cookbook. LC 81-43782. (Illus.). 384p. 1982. 24.95 (*0-89480-203-8*, 316) Workman Pub.

— The Silver Palate Good Times Cookbook. LC 85-5368. (Illus.). 416p. 1985. 22.95 (*0-89480-832-X*, 832); pap. 14.95 (*0-89480-831-1*, 831) Workman Pub.

Rosso-O'Laughlin, Marta, et al. Cuentame: Lecturas Interactivas. Vardy, Katherine L., ed. (SPA., Illus.). 288p. (Orig.). (C). 1990. pap. text 22.00 (*0-03-028759-6*) Harcourt Coll Pubs.

Rosso-O'Laughlin, Marta, jt. auth. see Spinelli, Emily.

Rosso, Pedro. Nutrition Second Metabolism in Pregnancy: Mother & Fetus. (Illus.). 336p. 1990. text 59.95 (*0-19-503928-9*) OUP.

Rosso, R., jt. auth. see Peano, A.

Rosso, Renata & Samek-Lodovici, Vieri. Italian Verbs Skill Builder, Set. (ITA & ENG.). 1999. pap. 29.95 incl. audio (*0-609-60441-4*) Liv Lang.

— Italian Verbs Skill Builder Manual. 1999. pap. 6.95 (*0-609-80427-8*) Liv Lang.

Rosso, Renzo, jt. auth. see Kottegoda, Nathabandu T.

Rossoff, David, tr. see Houminer, Shmuel.

***Rossoff, Dovid.** Where Heaven Touches Earth. large type ed. 650p. 1998. 49.95 (*0-87306-879-3*) Feldheim.

Rossoff, Meg. London Guide. 2nd ed. 312p. 1998. pap. text 14.95 (*1-883323-79-7*) Open Rd Pub.

Rossol, Monona. Artist's Complete Health & Safety Guide. 2nd rev. ed. LC 94-70298. 344p. 1994. pap. 19.95 (*1-880559-18-8*) Allworth Pr.

***Rossol, Monona.** The Health & Safety Guide for Film, TV & Theater. 256p. 2000. pap. 19.95 (*1-58115-071-7*, Pub. by Allworth Pr) Watsn-Guptill.

Rossol, Monona. Stage Fright: Health & Safety in the Theater. LC 85-28080. (Illus.). 128p. 1986. pap. text 12.95 (*0-918875-02-1*) Ctr Occupational Hazards.

— Stage Fright: Health Hazards in Theater. LC 90-85553. (Illus.). 144p. (Orig.). 1991. pap. 16.95 (*0-9607118-3-X*) Allworth Pr.

Rossol, Monona, jt. auth. see Shaw, Susan D.

***Rossoll, Hildegard.** Weltbild und Bildsprache im Werk Irmtraud Morgners: Eine Analyse unter Besonderer Berucksichtigung von "Amanda. Ein Hexenroman" LC 98-53778. (DDR-Studien - East German Studies: Vol. 12). (GER.). 211p. (C). 1999. text 51.00 (*0-8204-3991-6*) P Lang Pubng.

Rossomando, Edward F. High Performance Liquid Chromatography in Enzymatic Analysis: Applications to the Assay of Enzymatic Activity. 2nd ed. LC 97-21334. 451p. 1998. 175.00 (*0-471-10340-3*, Wiley-Interscience) Wiley.

Rossomando, Edward F. & Alexander, Stephen, eds. Morphogenesis: An Analysis of the Development of Biological Form. LC 92-3820. (Illus.). 448p. 1992. text 199.00 (*0-8247-8667-X*) Dekker.

Rosson & Bloom. Therapeutic Gastrointestinal Endoscopy. 1991. write for info. (*0-8151-7399-7*) Mosby Inc.

Rosson, C. Parr, III, et al. North American Free Trade Agreement: Background, Legislative Process, & Provisions for Agricultural Trade. (Illus.). 67p. (Orig.). (C). 1994. pap. text 20.00 (*0-7881-0309-1*) DIANE Pub.

Rosson, James F. Forest Resources of Louisiana, 1991. (Illus.). 71p. 1998. pap. text 30.00 (*0-7881-4347-6*) DIANE Pub.

***Rosson, Joe.** Treasures in Your Attic. 2000. 25.00 (*0-06-019827-3*) HarpC.

Rosson, Kathryn, ed. American Materia Medica Therapeutics & Pharmacognosy. 564p. 1919. reprint ed. text 98.00 (*1-888483-05-9*) Eclectic Med.

— Eclectic Dispensatory of Botanical Therapeutics, Vol. 2. 600p. 1996. text 125.00 (*1-888483-08-3*) Eclectic Med.

— Herb Contraindications & Drug Interactions. 2nd ed. 260p. 1998. reprint ed. pap. 19.95 (*1-888483-07-5*) Eclectic Med.

Rosson, Kathryn, ed. see Brinker, Francis.

Rosson, Philip J. & Reid, Stanley D., eds. Managing Export Entry & Expansion: Concepts & Practice. LC 86-30330. 464p. 1987. 85.00 (*0-275-92361-4*, C2361, Praeger Pubs) Greenwood.

Rossor, M., jt. auth. see Growdon, John H.

Rossos, Andrew. Russia & the Balkans: Inter-Balkan Rivalries & Russian Foreign Policy, 1908-1914. LC 81-142342. 327p. reprint ed. pap. 101.40 (*0-608-16801-7*, 202640500049) Bks Demand.

Rossotti, Hazel. Colour: Why the World Isn't Grey. LC 84-11451. (Illus.). 239p. 1985. pap. text 12.95 (*0-691-02386-7*, Pub. by Princeton U Pr) Cal Prin Full Svc.

— Diverse Atoms: Profiles of the Chemical Elements. (Oxford Chemistry Guides Ser.: No. 3). (Illus.). 602p. (C). 1998. pap. 20.95 (*0-19-855815-5*) OUP.

— The Study of Ionic Equilibria: An Introduction. LC 77-26048. (Illus.). 208p. reprint ed. pap. 64.50 (*0-8357-3555-9*, 203444200090) Bks Demand.

Rossow, Edwin C. Analysis & Behavior of Structures. (Illus.). 735p. (C). 1995. 105.00 (*0-02-403913-6*, Macmillan Coll) P-H.

Rossow, Lawrence & Parkinson, Jerry. The Law of Teacher Evaluation, No. 42. 81p. (C). 1991. pap. 18.00 (*1-56534-031-0*) Ed Law Assn.

***Rossow, Lawrence F. & Parkinson, Jerry.** The Law of Student Expulsions & Suspensions 1999. 2nd rev. ed. 58p. 1999. text 20.00 (*1-56534-071-X*) Ed Law Assn.

Rossow, Lawrence F. & Stefkovich, Jacqueline A. Search & Seizure in the Public Schools. 2nd ed. 70p. (C). 1995. text 20.00 (*1-56534-067-1*) Ed Law Assn.

Rossow, Lawrence F. & Warner, Linda Sue. The Principalship: Dimensions in Instructional Leadership. 2nd ed. LC 98-53521. 300p. 1999. pap. 30.00 (*0-89089-908-8*) Carolina Acad Pr.

Rossow, Randal R. Poems of Inspiration. 1998. pap. write for info. (*1-57553-855-5*) Watermrk Pr.

Rosst, Michael A., jt. auth. see McGannon, A.

Rosstad, Anna. Leonardo da Vinci: The Man & the Mystery. (Illus.). 139p. 1995. 42.00 (*82-560-0972-1*, Pub. by Solum Verlag) Intl Spec Bk.

Rosston, Gregory L. & Waterman, David, eds. Interconnection & the Internet: Selected Papers from the 1996 Telecommunications Policy Research Conference, Vol. 3. LC 97-22934. 330p. 1997. 89.95 (*0-8058-2847-8*) L Erlbaum Assocs.

— Selected Papers from the 1996 Telecommunications Policy Research Conference, Vol. 3. LC 97-22934. 330p. 1997. pap. write for info. (*0-8058-2848-6*) L Erlbaum Assocs.

Rosston, Gregory L., jt. ed. see Brock, Gerald W.

Rossuck, Virginia P. & Cohen, Katherine E. The Best They Can Be: The Wildwood Story. Kruse, Benedict & Kruse, Bettijune, eds. LC 99-71837. (Illus.). 384p. 1999. pap. write for info. (*0-9656553-4-2*) Intl Ctr Ldrship.

***Rossum, Constance & Tarr, Judith.** American Constitutional Law, 2. 5th ed. 1998. pap. text 53.95 (*0-312-18450-6*) St Martin.

Rossum, Ralph A. American Constitutional Law, '95. 1995. pap. text, suppl. ed. 5.00 (*0-312-11719-1*) St Martin.

— The Politics of the Criminal Justice System: An Organizational Analysis. LC 78-18519. (Political Science Ser.: No. 6). (Illus.). 303p. reprint ed. pap. 94.00 (*0-7837-0823-8*, 204113700019) Bks Demand.

— Reverse Discrimination: The Constitutional Debate. LC 80-13777. (Political Science Ser.: No. 10). 240p. reprint ed. pap. 74.40 (*0-8357-3517-6*, 203456400090) Bks Demand.

Rossum, Ralph A. & Tarr, G. Alan. American Constitutional Law. 4th ed. 960p. (C). 1995. pap. text 60.30 (*0-312-10262-3*) St Martin.

***Rossum, Ralph A. & Tarr, G. Alan.** American Constitutional Law, 1. 5th ed. 1998. pap. text 53.95 (*0-312-18451-4*) St Martin.

Rossum, Ralph A. & Tarr, G. Alan. American Constitutional Law, Vol. 1. 4th ed. 512p. (C). 1995. pap. text 53.95 (*0-312-10260-7*) St Martin.

— American Constitutional Law, Vol. 2. 4th ed. 656p. (C). 1995. pap. text 53.95 (*0-312-10261-5*) St Martin.

Rossum-Steenbeek, Monique Van, see Van Rossum-Steenbeek, Monique.

Rossum, W. van, jt. ed. see Hicks, E. E.

***Rosswell, V. E.** At Lunch with the Lord Bk. 2: Tax Haven Trilogy. 320p. 2001. 24.95 (*1-893335-15-1*) Archipelago Pr.

Rosswell, V. E. Into the Deep: The Haven. LC 98-50339. 316p. 1999. 24.95 (*1-893335-04-6*) Archipelago Pr.

Rosswell, V. E. Into the Deep - The Haven Bk. 1: Tax Haven Trilogy. LC 98-50339. 318p. (C). 1999. pap. 18.95 (*1-893335-03-8*) Archipelago Pr.

***Rosswell, V. E.** Into the Deep - The Haven Bk. 1: Tax Haven Trilogy. iv, 312p. 2000. 24.95 (*1-893335-09-7*) Archipelago Pr.

Rosswurm, Mary Ann, ed. Home Care for Older Adults: A Guide for Families & Other Caregivers. LC 98-8674. (Springer Series on Geriatric Nursing). (Illus.). 88p. 1998. 24.95 (*0-8261-1231-5*) Springer Pub.

Rosswurm, Steve, ed. The CIO's Left-Led Unions. LC 91-19467. 330p. (C). 1992. text 45.00 (*0-8135-1769-9*); pap. text 19.00 (*0-8135-1770-2*) Rutgers U Pr.

Rosswurm, Steven. Arms, Country & Class: The Philadelphia Militia & the "Lower Sort" During the American Revolution. 373p. (C). 1990. pap. text 17.95 (*0-8135-1472-X*) Rutgers U Pr.

Rost & Barbour. General Botany. (Biology Ser.). 1998. lab manual ed. 28.25 (*0-534-24952-3*) Wadsworth Pub.

— General Botany. (Biology Ser.). (C). 1998. student ed. 15.75 (*0-534-24932-9*) Wadsworth Pub.

Rost, jt. auth. see Heinig.

Rost, Eleanor. Love Ya: Meditations by Eleanor Rost. iv, 98p. 1998. 14.95 (*0-9662189-0-6*) New Paradigms.

— You: A Source of Strength in Our World. 78p. (Orig.). 1985. pap. 7.95 (*0-87418-007-4*, 142) Coleman Pub.

Rost, F. W. Fluorescence Microscopy, Vol. 1. (Illus.). 267p. (C). 1992. text 110.00 (*0-521-23641-X*) Cambridge U Pr.

— Fluorescence Microscopy, Vol. 2. (Illus.). 473p. (C). 1995. text 180.00 (*0-521-41088-6*) Cambridge U Pr.

— Quantitative Fluorescence Microscopy. (Illus.). 250p. (C). 1991. text 80.00 (*0-521-39422-8*) Cambridge U Pr.

***Rost, F. W. D. & Oldfield, Ronald Jowett.** Photography with a Microscope. 304p. (C). 2000. text 90.00 (*0-521-77096-3*) Cambridge U Pr.

Rost, H. T. Brilliant Stars. 182p. 1979. pap. 9.95 (*0-85398-083-7*) G Ronald Pub.

— The Golden Rule. 1986. 16.75 (*0-85398-226-0*) G Ronald Pub.

***Rost-Holtz, Amy, compiled by.** A Farm Country Christmas: A Treasury of Heartwarming Holiday Memories. LC 99-20116. (Town Square Bks.). (Illus.). 160p. 1999. 29.95 (*0-89658-440-2*) Voyageur Pr.

Rost, J., jt. auth. see Langeheine, R.

Rost, Joseph C. Leadership in the Twenty-First Century. LC 90-40961. 240p. 1991. 47.95 (*0-275-93670-8*, C3670, Praeger Pubs) Greenwood.

— Leadership in the Twenty-First Century. LC 90-40961. 256p. 1993. pap. 19.95 (*0-275-94610-X*, B4610, Praeger Pubs) Greenwood.

Rost, Leo. Jake's Revenge. Gee, Charles G., ed. 153p. reprint ed. pap. 12.95 (*1-889936-09-X*) Skyline Pubs Inc.

Rost, Leonhard. The Succession to the Throne of David. (Historic Texts & Interpreters Ser.: No. 1). 133p. 1982. 46.50 (*0-907459-12-9*, Pub. by Sheffield Acad); pap. 17.95 (*0-907459-13-7*, Pub. by Sheffield Acad) CUP Services.

Rost, Michael. Basics in Listening: Short Task Listen Development. 2nd ed. 1995. pap. text, student ed. 16.73 (*962-00-1029-9*) Addison-Wesley.

— Basics in Speaking. 1997. pap. text, student ed. 16.72 (*962-00-1425-1*) Addison-Wesley.

— Basics in Speaking: Text Book. 1997. pap. text, teacher ed. 14.00 (*962-00-1426-X*) Addison-Wesley.

— Prime Time English, Vol. 1. 1998. pap. text. write for info. (*0-201-49138-9*) Addison-Wesley.

— Prime Time English, Vol. 2. 1998. pap. text. write for info. (*0-201-49139-7*) Addison-Wesley.

— Prime Time English, Vol. 3. 1998. pap. text, student ed. write for info. (*0-201-49140-0*) Addison-Wesley.

— Prime Time English, Vol. 4. 1998. pap. text, student ed. write for info. (*0-201-49141-9*) Addison-Wesley.

— Prime Time English Workbook. 1996. pap. text, wbk. ed. 7.35 (*0-582-25974-6*, Pub. by Addison-Wesley) Longman.

— Strategies in Listening: Tasks Listen Development. 2nd ed. 1995. pap. text, student ed. 16.73 (*962-00-1033-7*) Addison-Wesley.

— Strategies in Speaking. 1997. pap. text, student ed. 16.72 (*962-00-1422-7*) Addison-Wesley.

— Strategies Speaking: Text Book. 1997. pap. text, teacher ed. 14.00 (*962-00-1423-5*) Addison-Wesley.

Rost, Michael A. Listening in Action. 160p. (C). 1991. pap. 24.33 (*0-13-538778-7*) P-H.

— Prime Time English. (YA). 1994. pap. text, teacher ed. 18.95 (*0-582-09224-8*) Longman.

— Real Time English. (YA). 1994. pap. text, teacher ed. 18.95 (*0-582-09223-X*) Longman.

— Strategies in Listening. 80p. 1989. pap. text 15.59 (*0-8013-0520-9*, 78366) Longman.

— Strategies in Listening: Tasks for Listening Development. 80p. 1986. pap. text, teacher ed. 10.95 (*0-8013-0521-7*, 78367) Longman.

Rost, Michael A. & Kumai, Nobuhiro. First Steps in Listening, 2 cass., Set. (Illus.). 52p. 1990. audio 55.00 (*1-85294-002-6*, 78676) Longman.

— First Steps in Listening: Teacher's Edition. (Illus.). 52p. 1990. pap. text, teacher ed. 13.95 (*1-85294-001-8*, 78675) Longman.

Rost, Michael A. & Lance, John. Text Pairallels. (Illus.). 71p. 1984. pap. text 9.71 (*0-940264-24-2*, 78398) Longman.

Rost, Michael A. & Stratton, Robert K. Listening in the Real World: Clues to English Conversation. 144p. 1978. pap. text 14.50 (*0-685-03056-3*, 78390); audio 88.00 (*0-685-03057-1*, 78391) Longman.

Rost, Michael A. & Uruno, M. Basics in Listening: Short Tasks for Listening Development/Tapescript & Answer Key. 71p. 1985. pap. text 10.95 (*0-8013-0518-7*, 78364) Longman.

Rost, Michael A., jt. auth. see Kisslinger, Ellen.

Rost, Pat, et al, eds. Celebrate. (Illus.). 1989. 15.00 (*0-9622333-0-7*) Missouri Bankers.

Rost, Paulus, ed. Die Keilschrifttexte Tiglat-Pilessers III, 2 vols. LC 78-72769. (Ancient Mesopotamian Texts & Studies). reprint ed. 45.00 (*0-404-18223-2*) AMS Pr.

Rost, Randi J. X & Motif Quick Reference Guide. 2nd ed. (X & Motif Ser.). (Illus.). 398p. 1993. pap. 36.95 (*1-55558-118-8*, EY-P953E-DP, Digital DEC) Buttrwrth-Heinemann.

Rost-Roth, Martina, jt. auth. see Dittmar, Norbert.

Rost, Ruth A. Creative Ideas for Catechists. LC 98-104773. (Illus.). 1997. pap. 19.95 (*1-55612-987-4*, LL1987) Sheed & Ward WI.

Rost, Thomas L., et al. General Botany. LC 97-44578. (Biology Ser.). (C). 1998. 49.75 (*0-534-24930-2*) Wadsworth Pub.

Rostad, Lee. Fourteen Cents & Seven Green Apples: The Life & Times of Charles Bair. Tobias, Ronald, ed. (Illus.). 128p. (Orig.). 1992. 25.00 (*0-9633909-2-9*); pap. 9.95 (*0-9633909-1-0*) C M R Museum.

Rostad, Wayne. On the Road Again. (Illus.). 320p. 1997. 24.95 (*0-7710-7582-0*) McCland & Stewart.

— On the Road Again. (Illus.). 352p. 1997. pap. text 19.99 (*0-7710-7583-9*) McCland & Stewart.

Rostagno, Ippolita, tr. see Sereni, Vittorio.

Rostagno, Irene. Searching for Recognition: The Promotion of Latin American Literature in the United States, 72. LC 96-22008. (Contributions to the Study of World Literature Ser.: No. 72). 176p. 1997. 57.95 (*0-313-29869-6*, Greenwood Pr) Greenwood.

Rostaing, Jean-Pierre. Building Policy Coherence: Tools & Tensions. (Public Management Occasional Papers: No. 12). 46p. (Orig.). 1996. pap. 7.00 (*92-64-15335-7*, 42-96-62-1) OECD.

Rostand. Cyrano de Bergerac. (FRE.). (C). 1930. pap. 11.95 (*0-8442-1807-3*, VF1807-3) NTC Contemp Pub Co.

— Rostand: Cyrano de Bergerac. Wooden, C. G., ed. (French Texts Ser.). (FRE.). 298p. 1994. pap. 20.95 (*1-85399-372-7*, Pub. by Brist Class Pr) Focus Pub-R Pullins.

Rostand, Claude. French Music Today. LC 73-4333. (Music Reprint Ser.). 146p. 1973. reprint ed. lib. bdg. 25.00 (*0-306-70578-8*) Da Capo.

Rostand, Edmond. Aiglon. (FRE., Illus.). 434p. 1986. 15.95 (*0-685-74006-4*, 2070377644) Fr & Eur.

— Aiglon. (Folio Ser.: No. 1764). (FRE.). 434p. 1986. pap. 13.95 (*2-07-037764-4*) Schoenhof.

— Chanticleer. Hall, Gertrude, tr. from FRE. (Classic Plays Ser.). 48p. (Orig.). 1996. pap. 4.00 (*1-57514-208-2*, 1118) Encore Perform Pub.

— Cyrano. Bolt, Ranjit, tr. 164p. (Orig.). 1996. pap. 12.95 (*1-899791-00-0*, Pub. by Absolute Classics) Theatre Comm.

— Cyrano de Bergerac. (Classics Illustrated Study Guides Ser.). (Illus.). 1997. mass mkt. 4.99 (*1-57840-030-9*, Pub. by Acclaim Bks) Penguin Putnam.

— Cyrano de Bergerac. 21.95 (*0-8488-0621-2*) Amereon Ltd.

— Cyrano de Bergerac. Burgess, Anthony, tr. from FRE. 192p. 1998. pap. 6.95 (*1-55783-230-7*) Applause Theatre Bk Pubs.

— Cyrano de Bergerac. Via Luis Marti, J. O., tr. (Nueva Austral Ser.: Vol. 206). (SPA.). 1991. pap. text 24.95 (*84-239-7206-2*) Elliots Bks.

— Cyrano de Bergerac. (FRE., Illus.). 216p. 1990. pap. 10.95 (*0-685-74009-9*, 2080705261) Fr & Eur.

Rostand, Edmond. Cyrano de Bergerac. (FRE.). pap. text 6.95 (*2-07-033515-1*) Gallimard Edns.

Rostand, Edmond. Cyrano de Bergerac. 1999. pap. 9.95 (*2-266-08275-2*) Midwest European Pubns.

— Cyrano de Bergerac. (Folio Ser.: No. 1487). (FRE., Illus.). 1962. pap. 10.95 (*2-07-037487-4*) Schoenhof.

— Cyrano de Bergerac. Marowitz, Charles, tr. (Great Translations for Actors Ser.). 224p. 1995. pap. 11.95 (*1-880399-68-7*) Smith & Kraus.

— Cyrano de Bergerac. 301p. 1984. reprint ed. lib. bdg. 25.95 (*0-89968-255-3*, Lghtyr Pr) Buccaneer Bks.

— Cyrano de Bergerac. unabridged ed. (FRE.). pap. 7.95 (*2-87714-126-8*, Pub. by Bookking Intl) Distribks Inc.

— Cyrano de Bergerac: A Heroic Comedy in Five Acts. Hooker, Brian, tr. (Bantam Classics Ser.). 208p. (Orig.). 1950. mass mkt. 4.95 (*0-553-21360-1*, Bantam Classics) Bantam.

— Cyrano de Bergerac: A Heroic Comedy in Five Acts. Blair, Lowell, tr. (Signet Classics Ser.). 240p. (Orig.). 1972. mass mkt. 4.95 (*0-451-52548-5*, Sig Classics) NAL.

***Rostand, Edmond.** Cyrano de Bergerac: A Heroic Comedy in Five Acts. (Illus.). 186p. (Orig.). 1998. pap. 9.95 (*0-19-283643-9*) OUP.

Rostand, Edmond. Cyrano de Bergerac: A Heroic Comedy in Five Acts. (Signet Classics). (Orig.). 1972. 10.05 (*0-606-00514-5*, Pub. by Turtleback) Demco.

An Asterisk (*) at the beginning of an entry indicates that the title is appearing for the first time.

— Cyrano de Bergerac: A New English Version. 181p. 1968. pap. 5.50 (0-87129-640-3, C41) Dramatic Pub.

Rostand, Edmond. Cyrano De Bergerac: Richardson,&Sir Ralph. unabridged ed. Hooker, Brian, tr. LC 66-1509. 1991. audio 17.00 (1-55994-377-7, CDL5 306, Caedmon) HarperAudio.

Rostand, Edmond. Deux Romanciers de Provence: Honore d'Urfe et Emile Zola. (FRE.). 98p. 1921. pap. 36.95 (0-318-51977-1) Fr & Eur.

— The Far Princess. Heard, J., tr. 192p. 1987. reprint ed. lib. bdg. 29.50 (0-86527-359-6) Fertig.

— I Was a Sixth-Grade Zombie. Shefter, Harry, ed. (Ghosts of Fear Street Ser.: No. 30). (J). (gr. 4-7). 1985. pap. 1.50 (0-671-00863-3) PB.

— Les Romanesques. 3.95 (0-686-55337-3) Fr & Eur.

Rostand, Edmond, et al. Cyrano de Bergerac. (Classics Illustrated Ser.). (Illus.). 52p. (YA). pap. 4.95 (1-57209-019-7) Classics Int Ent.

Rostankowski, Cynthia, jt. auth. see Velasquez, Manuel G.

Rostas, Francois, ed. Spectral Line Shapes: Proceedings, Seventh International Congress Aussois, France, June 11-15, 1984. (Illus.). xx, 769p. 1985. 273.10 (3-11-010119-X) De Gruyter.

Rosteck, Mary Kay, jt. auth. see Schmittroth, Linda.

Rosteck, Thomas. See It Now Confronts McCarthyism: Television Documentary & the Politics of Representation. LC 93-4780. (Studies in Rhetoric & Communication). 264p. (C). 1994. text 34.95 (0-8173-0705-2) U of Ala Pr.

Rosteck, Thomas, ed. At the Intersection: Cultural Studies & Rhetorical Studies. LC 98-48304. (Revisioning Rhetoric Ser.). 386p. 1998. pap. text 26.00 (1-57230-399-9); lib. bdg. 50.00 (1-57230-398-0) Guilford Pubns.

Rosten, Leo. Joys of Yiddish. 1991. per. 6.99 (0-671-72813-X) S&S Trade.

— The Joys of Yiddish. 576p. 1999. 12.99 (1-57866-067-X) Galahad Bks.

***Rosten, Leo.** The Joys of Yiddish. 576p. 2000. reprint ed. per. 14.95 (0-7434-0651-6) PB.

Rosten, Leo. Leo Rosten's Carnival of Wit: From Aristotle to Woody Allen. 560p. 1996. pap. 15.95 (0-452-27099-5, Plume) Dutton Plume.

Rosten, Leo, ed. Religions of America. LC 74-11705. 672p. 1975. pap. 17.00 (0-671-21971-5) S&S Trade.

Rosten, Leo C. Hollywood: The Movie Colony, the Movie Makers. LC 74-124036. (Literature of Cinema, Ser. 1). 1975. reprint ed. 30.95 (0-405-01636-0) Ayer.

— Hooray for Yiddish! A Book about English. 368p. 1998. pap. 9.99 (1-57866-026-2) Galahad Bks.

— The Washington Correspondents. LC 73-19175. (Politics & People Ser.). 456p. 1974. reprint ed. 30.95 (0-405-05896-9) Ayer.

Rosten, Norman. Come Slowly, Eden. 1967. pap. 5.25 (0-8222-0228-X) Dramatists Play.

— Selected Poems. LC 79-52399. 171p. 1979. 10.00 (0-8076-0930-7); pap. 4.95 (0-8076-0938-2) Braziller.

Rostenberg, Bill. The Architecture of Imaging. LC 95-17090. 1995. pap. 120.00 (1-55648-140-3, 043183) AHPI.

Rostenberg, Leona. The Library of Robert Hooke: The Scientific Book Trade of Restoration England. (Illus.). 288p. (Orig.). 1989. pap. 18.00 (0-929246-01-2) Modoc Pr.

***Rostenberg, Leona.** New Worlds in Old Books. 1999. 29.95 (1-58574-001-2) Lyons Pr.

Rostenberg, Leona. Old & Rare: Thirty Years in the Book Business. (American Autobiography Ser.). 234p. 1995. reprint ed. lib. bdg. 79.00 (0-7812-8632-8) Rprt Serv.

— Old Books, Rare Friends. large type ed. LC 98-11524. 1998. 25.95 (0-7862-1414-7) Thorndike Pr.

Rostenberg, Leona & Stern, Madeleine B. Between Boards: New Thoughts on Old Books. 240p. 1989. pap. 18.00 (0-929246-02-0) Modoc Pr.

— Connections: Our Selves - Our Books. 238p. (Orig.). 1994. pap. 18.00 (0-929246-06-3) Modoc Pr.

— New Worlds in Old Books. LC 98-56395. (Illus.). 210p. 1999. 29.95 (1-884718-89-2, No. 53940RB) Oak Knoll.

— Old & Rare: Forty Years in the Book Business. rev. ed. (Illus.). 272p. 1988. reprint ed. pap. 18.00 (0-929246-00-4) Modoc Pr.

— Old Books in the Old World: Reminiscences of Book Buying Abroad. (Illus.). 160p. 1996. 22.95 (1-884718-18-3) Oak Knoll.

— Old Books in the Old World: Reminiscences of Book Buying Abroad. deluxe ed. 1996. 45.00 (1-884718-21-3) Oak Knoll.

— Old Books, Rare Friends: Two Literary Sleuths & Their Shared Passion. (Illus.). 288p. 1998. pap. 11.95 (0-385-48515-8) Doubleday.

— Quest Book - Guest Book: A Biblio-Folly. (Illus.). 124p. (Orig.). 1993. pap. 18.00 (0-929246-04-7) Modoc Pr.

Rostenberg, Leona, et al. Bookman's Quintet, Five Catalogues about Books, Bibliography, Printing History, Booksellers, Libraries, Presses, Collectors. (Illus.). 283p. 1980. 25.00 (0-938768-03-4) Oak Knoll.

***Rostenko, Mark M.** Beyond Limits: 21 Days to Personal Transformation. 224p. 2000. pap. write for info. (0-9700416-3-2) Soar Falcon Pr.

Rosters Ltd. Staff & Struthers, S. U. K. Activity Holidays: Over Two Hundred Fifty Ideas Inside. 374p. (C). 1989. pap. text 45.00 (0-948032-93-6, Pub. by Rosters Ltd) St Mut.

Rostgaard, Marianne, jt. ed. see Lorentzen, Anne.

Rosti, Giovanni & European School of Oncology Staff. Dose & Timing: The Pillars of Successful Chemotherapy. LC 98-17786. (Oncology Scientific Updates Ser.). 1998. 103.50 (0-444-82968-7) Elsevier.

Rostig, Dittmar. Bergpredigt und Politik: Zur Struktur und Funktion des Reiches Gottes Bei Leonhard Ragaz. (Europaische Hochschulschriften Ser.: Reihe 23, Bd. 419). (GER.). 288p. 1991. 55.80 (3-631-43577-0) P Lang Pubng.

— Bibliographie Zum Religiosen Sozialismus in der SBZ und der DDR: Berichtszeit, 1945-1985. (GER.). 325p. 1992. 65.80 (3-631-45250-0) P Lang Pubng.

***Rostker, Bernard D. & Harris, Scott A., eds.** Sexual Orientation & U. S. Military Personnel Policy: Options & Assessment. 518p. (C). 1999. reprint ed. pap. text 65.00 (0-7881-8257-9) DIANE Pub.

Rostker, Bernard D., et al. The Defense Officer Personnel Management Act of 1980: A Retrospective Assessment. LC 92-42096. 1993. pap. text 10.00 (0-8330-1287-8, R-4246-FMP) Rand Corp.

Rostkowski, Margaret I. After the Dancing Days. LC 85-45810. 240p. (YA). (gr. 6-9). 1986. 14.00 (0-06-025077-1) HarpC Child Bks.

— After the Dancing Days. LC 85-45810. 224p. (YA). (gr. 7 up). 1986. lib. bdg. 15.89 (0-06-025078-X) HarpC Child Bks.

— After the Dancing Days. LC 85-45810. (Trophy Bk.). 224p. (YA). (gr. 7-12). 1988. pap. 4.95 (0-06-440248-7, HarpTrophy) HarpC Child Bks.

— After the Dancing Days. (J). 1986. 10.05 (0-606-03707-1, Pub. by Turtleback) Demco.

— The Best of Friends. LC 88-33077. 192p. (YA). (gr. 7 up). 1989. 12.95 (0-06-025104-2) HarpC Child Bks.

— Moon Dancer. LC 94-39553. 224p. (YA). (gr. 7 up). 1995. pap. 5.00 (0-15-200194-8, Harcourt Child Bks) Harcourt.

— Moon Dancer. LC 94-39553. (J). 1995. 10.10 (0-606-09627-2, Pub. by Turtleback) Demco.

Rostoker-Gruber, Karen. Remote Controls Are Better Than Women Because: or What Men Would Say If They Could. LC 92-84004. (Illus.). 80p. 1993. pap. 5.95 (1-56352-076-1) Longstreet.

— Telephones Are Better Than Men Because: Or Whatever Women Would Say If They Dared. LC 96-76740. (Illus.). 80p. 1996. pap. 5.95 (1-56352-343-4) Longstreet.

Rostoker, Michael D. Technology Management: Licensing & Protection for Computers in the World Market. 267p. 1993. 29.95 (0-9639750-0-5) Cap Info Assocs.

Rostoker, N., jt. ed. see Reiser, M.

Rostoker, William & Dvorak, Jim. Interpretation of Metallographic Structures. 3rd ed. 282p. 1990. text 81.00 (0-12-598255-0) Acad Pr.

Roston, M., tr. see Rabinovich, Isaiah.

Roston, Murray. Modernist Patterns in Literature & the Visual Arts. LC 98-45373. 1999. text 40.00 (0-8147-7527-6) NYU Pr.

— Renaissance Perspectives in Literature & the Visual Arts. LC 86-18681. (Illus.). 448p. (Orig.). 1987. pap. text 29.95 (0-691-01486-8, Pub. by Princeton U Pr) Cal Prin Full Svc.

— Victorian Contexts: Literature & the Visual Arts. LC 96-33091. (Illus.). 246p. (C). 1996. text 45.00 (0-8147-7485-7) NYU Pr.

Roston, Ruth, ed. Never Like You Plan. (Orig.). 1994. pap. 5.00 (0-927663-23-6) COMPAS.

— A Piece of the Moon Is Missing. (Illus.). 192p. (Orig.). 1985. pap. 7.00 (0-927663-06-6) COMPAS.

Roston, Ruth, jt. ed. see Buchwald, Emilie.

Rostova, Natasha. Black Lace: The Transformation. 1999. mass mkt. 6.95 (0-352-33311-1) London Brdge.

— The Captivation. 1998. mass mkt. 5.95 (0-352-33234-4, Pub. by BLA4) London Brdge.

***Rostova, Natasha.** Naked Truth. 2000. mass mkt. 6.95 (0-352-33497-5) BLA4.

Rostovsky, Demeter B., jt. auth. see Forter, Norman L.

Rostovtsev, Mikhail I. Caravan Cities. LC 75-137287. reprint ed. 37.50 (0-404-05445-5) AMS Pr.

— Dura-Europos & Its Art. LC 75-41237. reprint ed. 34.50 (0-404-14594-9) AMS Pr.

Rostovtzeff, M. A History of the Ancient World, Vol. I: The Orient & Greece. 418p. 1926. pap. 30.00 (0-8196-2162-5) Biblo.

— A History of the Ancient World, Vol. II: Rome. 387p. 1927. pap. 30.00 (0-8196-2163-3) Biblo.

— The Social & Economic History of the Roman Empire. 695p. 1926. pap. 40.00 (0-8196-2164-1) Biblo.

Rostovtzeff, Michael. A Large Estate in Egypt in the Third Century B. C. A Study in Economic History. Finley, Moses, ed. LC 79-5003. (Ancient Economic History Ser.). 1979. reprint ed. lib. bdg. 27.95 (0-405-12392-2) Ayer.

Rostovtzeff, Michael I. Out of the Past of Greece & Rome. LC 63-18047. (Illus.). 1960. 30.00 (0-8196-0126-8) Biblo.

Rostovtzeff, Mikhail I. Greece. 2nd ed. Bickerman, Elias J., ed. Duff, J. D., tr. (Illus.). 352p. 1963. reprint ed. pap. text 23.95 (0-19-500368-3) OUP.

— Rome. Bickerman, Elias J., ed. Duff, J. D., tr. (Illus.). 368p. 1960. reprint ed. pap. text 23.95 (0-19-500224-5) OUP.

— Social & Economic History of the Hellenistic World, 3 vols. (Illus.). 1,824p. 1986. reprint ed. text 198.00 (0-19-814230-7) OUP.

Rostow, Elspeth, jt. auth. see Jordan, Barbara.

Rostow, Eugene V. Breakfast for Bonaparte: United States National Security Interests from the Heights of Abraham to the Nuclear Age. 523p. 1993. per. 27.00 (0-16-035969-4) USGPO.

— The Democratic Character of Judicial Review. (Reprint Series in Political Science). (C). 1993. reprint ed. pap. text 5.00 (0-8290-3723-3, P-247) Irvington.

— The Ideal in Law. LC 77-81733. 1995. 24.00 (0-226-72818-8) U Ch Pr.

— Law, Power, & the Pursuit of Peace. LC 67-10669. (Roscoe Pound Lectureship Ser.: 1966). 153p. reprint ed. pap. 47.50 (0-608-12935-6, 202468800038) Bks Demand.

— The Sovereign Prerogative: The Supreme Court & the Quest for Law. LC 73-17923. 318p. 1974. reprint ed. lib. bdg. 35.00 (0-8371-7276-4, RSOP, Greenwood Pr) Greenwood.

— Toward Managed Peace: The National Security Interests of the United States, 1759 to the Present. LC 92-24550. 352p. (C). 1993. 42.50 (0-300-05700-8) Yale U Pr.

— Toward Managed Peace: The National Security Interests of the United States, 1759 to the Present. 1995. pap. 20.00 (0-300-06316-4) Yale U Pr.

Rostow, Eugene V., et al. Power & Policy in Quest of the Law: Essays in Honor of Eugene Victor Rostow. LC 83-26502. 1985. lib. bdg. 204.00 (90-247-2911-4) Kluwer Academic.

Rostow, Victoria P., et al, eds. Medical Professional Liability & the Delivery of Obstetrical Care: An Interdisciplinary Review, Vol. II. 256p. 1989. text 35.00 (0-309-03986-X) Natl Acad Pr.

Rostow, W. W. The Division of Europe after World War, II 1946. 212p. 1997. reprint ed. pap. text 15.00 (0-7881-5016-2) DIANE Pub.

— Europe after Stalin: Eisenhower's Three Decisions of March 11, 1953. 206p. 1997. reprint ed. pap. text 15.00 (0-7881-5015-4) DIANE Pub.

— The Great Population Spike & After: Reflections on the 21st Century. LC 97-13913. (Illus.). 240p. 1998. 35.00 (0-19-511691-7) OUP.

— Pre-Invasion Bombing Strategy: General Eisenhower's Decision of March 25, 1944. 166p. 1997. reprint ed. pap. text 15.00 (0-7881-5023-5) DIANE Pub.

Rostow, Walt W. British Economy of the Nineteenth Century: Essays. LC 81-13312. 240p. 1982. reprint ed. lib. bdg. 65.00 (0-313-23208-3, ROBR, Greenwood Pr) Greenwood.

— British Trade Fluctuations, 1868-1896. 577p. 1981. 59.95 (0-405-14011-8) Ayer.

— British Trade Fluctuations, 1868-1896: Dissertations in European Economic History II. Bruchey, Stuart, ed. LC 80-2828. (Illus.). 1981. lib. bdg. 49.00 (0-686-73124-7) Ayer.

— Stages of Economic Growth: A Non-Communist Manifesto. 3rd ed. 320p. 1991. pap. text 23.95 (0-521-40928-4) Cambridge U Pr.

— Stages of Economic Growth: A Non-Communist Manifesto. 3rd ed. 320p. 1991. text 80.00 (0-521-40070-8) Cambridge U Pr.

— Theorists of Economic Growth from David Hume to the Present: With a Perspective on the Next Century. (Illus.). 736p. 1992. pap. text 35.00 (0-19-508043-2) OUP.

Rostow, Walt W., jt. auth. see Millikan, Max F.

Rostowski, Jacek. Macroeconomic Instability in Post-Communist Countries. (Illus.). 396p. 1998. text 90.00 (0-19-829048-9) OUP.

Rostowski, Jacek, ed. Banking Reform in Central Europe & the Former Soviet Union. LC 96-100380. (Central European University Press Bks.). (Illus.). 234p. (C). 1995. 51.95 (1-85866-038-6, Pub. by Ctrl Europ Univ) Bks Intl VA.

— Banking Reform in Central Europe & the Former Soviet Union. LC 96-100380. (Central European University Press Bks.). (Illus.). 256p. (C). 1995. pap. 26.95 (1-85866-039-4, Pub. by Ctrl Europ Univ) Bks Intl VA.

***Rostrand, Edmond.** Cyrano de Bergerac. LC 99-87751. 2000. pap. 1.50 (0-486-41119-2) Dover.

***Rostrom, Laura Lee.** My Book of Mormon Activity Book. 32p. (J). (ps-5). 1999. pap. 2.99 (1-55517-425-6) CFI Dist.

— My Book of Mormon Storybook. (Illus.). (J). (ps-6). 1999. 19.95 (1-55517-352-7) CFI Dist.

Rostron. Housing the Physically Disabled. 144p. 1995. pap. 33.95 (1-85742-283-X) Ashgate Pub Co.

Rostron, Andrew & Sewell, David. Microtechnology in Special Education. LC 83-22248. (Illus.). 320p. 1983. reprint ed. pap. 99.20 (0-608-04017-7, 206475300011) Bks Demand.

Rostron, J., ed. Sick Building Syndrome. LC 97-155173. (Illus.). 200p. (C). 1998. pap. 49.99 (0-419-21530-1, E & FN Spon) Routledge.

Rostron, Jack & Fordham, Murray. Adapting Housing for People with Disabilities. 140p. 1996. text 54.95 (1-85742-363-1, Pub. by Arena) Ashgate Pub Co.

— Refurbishing Offices for People with Disabilities: A Design & Assessment Guide for Owners, Occupiers, Developers & Advisers. 128p. 1996. text 54.95 (1-85742-345-3, Pub. by Arena) Ashgate Pub Co.

Rostron, Jack & Nutt, Michael. Dictionary of Housing. LC 97-207202. 200p. 1997. pap. 31.95 (1-85742-370-4, Pub. by Arena) Ashgate Pub Co.

Rostron, Jack, et al. Confronting Prejudice. 200p. (Orig.). 1996. pap. text 31.95 (1-85742-360-7, Pub. by Arena) Ashgate Pub Co.

Rostvig, Maren-Sofie. Configurations: A Topomorphical Approach to Renaissance Poetry. (Illus.). 582p. 1994. 25.00 (82-00-21909-7, Pub. by Scand Univ Pr) IBD Ltd.

Rostworowski, Boguslaw, tr. see Karasek, Krzysztof, et al.

Rostworowski, Buguslaw, tr. see Zbigniew, Herbert.

Rostworowski de Diez Canseco, Maria. History of the Inca Realm. Iceland, Harry B., tr. from SPA. LC 98-15504. (Illus.). 272p. (C). 1998. text 49.95 (0-521-44266-4); pap. text 14.95 (0-521-63759-7) Cambridge U Pr.

Rosty, Pal. A Journey to Mexico, Cuba & the Caribbean in the 1850's. Dell'Oro, Regina, tr. from HUN. LC 98-15741. (Illus.). 486p. 1998. 84.95 (1-57309-202-9) Intl Scholars.

Rosu, Anca. The Metaphysics of Sound in Wallace Stevens. LC 94-43107. 200p. 1995. text 39.95 (0-8173-0797-4) U of Ala Pr.

Rosumek, Peter & Najock, Dietmar. Plinius Maior: Concordantia in C. Plinii Secundi Naturalem Historiam. (GER.). iv, 934p. 1995. write for info. (3-487-10016-9) G Olms Pubs.

— Plinius Maior: Concordantia in C. Plinii Securdi Naturalem Historiam. (GER.). 5036p. 1995. write for info. (3-487-09949-7) G Olms Pubs.

Rosumek, Peter & Najock, Dietmar, eds. Plinius: Konkordanz Zur Naturalis Historia des C. Plinius Secundus, 3 vols. write for info. (0-318-71980-0) G Olms Pubs.

Rosumek, Peter, ed. see Plinius Secundus, C.

Rosumek, Peter, ed. see Secundus, C. Plinius.

Rosumek, Peter, ed. see Secundus, Plinius C.

Rosvall, Bjorn L. The Business Engineer. 364p. 1996. 80.00 (0-86341-312-9, MT905) INSPEC Inc.

Roswal, Glenn M., et al, eds. Including People with Disabilities in Camp Programs: A Resource for Camp Directors. LC 97-19747. (Illus.). 152p. 1998. pap. 31.95 (0-87603-156-4) Am Camping.

Roswell, Florence G., jt. auth. see Chall, Jeanne S.

Roswell Symphony Guild. Savoring the Southwest Again. LC 98-65965. (Illus.). 336p. 1998. 22.50 (0-9612466-1-8) Roswell Symphony Guild.

Roswell Symphony Guild, Board of Directors Staff. Savoring the Southwest. LC 83-62041. (Illus.). 332p. 1994. 18.95 (0-9612466-0-X) Roswell Symphony Guild.

Roswitha. Plays of Roswitha. St. John, Christopher, tr. LC 65-20048. 1972. reprint ed. 22.95 (0-405-08900-7) Ayer.

— Plays of Roswitha. St. John, Christopher, tr. LC 65-20048. 1989. reprint ed. pap. 18.95 (0-88143-106-0) Ayer.

Rosynyaine, J. H. The Xipehuz & the Death of the Earth (Les Xipehuz & la Mort de la Terre), 2 vols. Reginald, R. & Melville, Douglas, eds. LC 77-84283. (Lost Race & Adult Fantasy Ser.). xxii, 183 p. 1978. lib. bdg. 23.95 (0-405-11020-0) Ayer.

Roszak, Theodore. America the Wise: The Longevity Revolution & the True Wealth of Nations. LC 98-21645. 288p. 1998. 25.00 (0-395-85699-X) HM.

— The Cult of Information: A Neo-Luddite Treatise on High Tech, Artificial Intelligence, & the True Art of Thinking. LC 93-37189. 1994. pap. 14.95 (0-520-08584-1, Pub. by U CA Pr) Cal Prin Full Svc.

— Flicker. 592p. 1993. mass mkt. 5.99 (0-553-29792-9) Bantam.

— Fool's Cycle-Full Cycle: Reflections on the Great Trumps of the Tarot. (Broadside Editions Ser.). (Illus.). 36p. (Orig.). (C). 1988. pap. 4.95 (0-931191-07-6) Rob Briggs.

— From Satori to Silicon Valley: San Francisco & the American Counter-Culture. 60p. (Orig.). 1986. pap. 3.95 (0-917583-09-4, Dont Call Frisco) Lexikos.

***Roszak, Theodore.** The Gendered Atom: Reflections on the Sexual Psychology of Science. LC 99-16074. 192p. 1999. 21.95 (1-57324-171-7) Conari Press.

Roszak, Theodore. The Making of a Counter Culture: Reflections on the Technocratic Society & Its Youthful Opposition. LC 94-34092. 310p. (C). 1996. pap. 15.95 (0-520-20122-1, Pub. by U CA Pr) Cal Prin Full Svc.

— The Memoirs of Elizabeth Frankenstein. 448p. 1996. mass mkt. 5.99 (0-553-57637-2) Bantam.

— The Voice of the Earth. (Illus.). 368p. 1993. pap. 13.00 (0-671-86753-9, Touchstone) S&S Trade Pap.

Roszak, Theodore, et al, eds. Ecopsychology: Restoring the Earth, Healing the Mind. LC 94-31179. 1995. pap. 15.00 (0-87156-406-8, Pub. by Sierra) Random.

***Roszel, Renee.** The Billionaire Daddy: (Baby Boom) (Romance Ser.: No. 3589). 2000. per. 3.50 (0-373-03589-6, 1-03589-8, Harlequin) Harlequin Bks.

— The Billionaire Daddy: (Baby Boom) (Larger Print Ser.: No. 435). 2000. per. 3.50 (0-373-15835-1, 1-15835-1, Harlequin) Harlequin Bks.

Roszel, Renee. A Bride for Ransom. (Romance Ser.). 1993. per. 2.89 (0-373-03251-X, 1-03251-5) Harlequin Bks.

— A Bride for Ransom. large type ed. 266p. 1993. reprint ed. pap. 13.95 (1-56054-686-7) Thorndike Pr.

— Brides for Brazen Gulch. (Yours Truly Ser.). 1996. per. 3.50 (0-373-52026-3, 1-52026-1) Silhouette.

***Roszel, Renee.** Coming Home to Wed. (Romance Ser.: Vol. 2603). 2000. per. 3.50 (0-373-03603-5) Harlequin Bks.

— Coming Home to Wed. large type ed. Vol. 449. 2000. mass mkt. 3.50 (0-373-15849-1) Harlequin Bks.

Roszel, Renee. Dare to Kiss a Cowboy. 1994. per. 2.99 (0-373-03317-6, 1-03317-4) Harlequin Bks.

— Getting over Harry. (Romance Ser.). 1997. per. 3.25 (0-373-03448-2, 1-03448-7) Harlequin Bks.

— Getting over Harry. large type ed. 1997. 20.95 (0-263-14920-X) Mac Lib Ref.

— Getting over Harry (Simply the Best) 1997. per. 3.25 (0-373-15694-4) Harlequin Bks.

— Ghost Whispers. LC 97-10531. 219p. 1994. mass mkt. 2.99 (0-373-25612-4, 1-25612-2) Harlequin Bks.

— Gift-Wrapped Baby. (Love & Laughter Ser.: No. 57). 1998. per. 3.50 (0-373-44057-X, 1-44057-7) Harlequin Bks.

— Her Mistletoe Husband. 1998. per. 3.50 (0-373-03528-4, 1-038528-6) Harlequin Bks.

— Her Mistletoe Husband. large type ed. 1998. pap. 3.50 (0-373-15774-6, 1-15774-2) Harlequin Bks.

— Make-Believe Marriage. LC 95-13537. (Romance Ser.). 184p. 1995. per. 2.99 (0-373-03370-2, 1-03370-3) Harlequin Bks.

— Make-Believe Marriage. (Promo Ser.). 1999. per. 4.50 (0-373-21982-2, 1-21982-3) Harlequin Bks.

— Married by Mistake! (Harlequin Romance Ser.: No. 3488). 1998. per. 3.25 (0-373-03488-1, 1-03488-3) Harlequin Bks.

— Married by Mistake! large type ed. 1998. per. 3.25 (0-373-15734-7) Harlequin Bks.

— No More Mr. Nice. (Temptation Ser.). 1993. mass mkt. 2.99 (0-373-25568-3, 1-25568-6) Harlequin Bks.

R

R

— The One-Week Marriage. (Romance Ser.: Bk. 3559). 1999. per. 3.50 (0-373-03559-4, 1-03559-1) Harlequin Bks.
— The One-Week Marriage. large type ed. (Larger Print Ser.: Bk. 405). 1999. per. 3.50 (0-373-15805-X, 1-15805-4) Harlequin Bks.
— Prince of Delights. (Romance Ser.: No. 198). 1992. per. 2.89 (0-373-03198-X, 1-03198-8) Harlequin Bks.
— Prince of Delights. (Family Continuity Program Ser.: No. 38). 1999. mass mkt. 4.50 (0-373-82186-7, 1-82186-7) Harlequin Bks.
— Sex, Lies & Leprechauns. (Temptation Ser.). 1994. per. 2.99 (0-373-25583-7, 1-25583-5) Harlequin Bks.
— There Goes the Bride. (Love & Laughter Ser.). 1998. per. 3.50 (0-373-44043-X, 0-44043-8) Harlequin Bks.
— To Lasso a Lady. LC 95-22568. (Romance Ser.). 187p. 1996. per. 3.25 (0-373-03397-4, 1-03397-6) Harlequin Bks.
— To Marry a Stranger. 1997. per. 3.25 (0-373-15716-9, 1-15716-3); per. 3.25 (0-373-03470-9, 1-03470-1) Harlequin Bks.
— Valentine's Knight. (Men at Work Ser.: Vol. 49). 1998. mass mkt. 4.50 (0-373-81061-X, 1-81061-3) Harlequin Bks.

Roszel, Renee & Collins, Colleen. Bride on the Loose; Married after Breakfast, 2 bks. in 1. (Duets Ser.). 1999. per. 5.99 (0-373-44076-6, 1-44076-7) Harlequin Bks.

Roszel, Renee, jt. auth. see Macomber, Debbie.

Roszell, Calvert. The Near-Death Experience: In the Light of Scientific Research & the Spiritual Science of Rudolf Steiner. LC 91-27842. 96p. 1992. pap. 10.95 (0-88010-360-4) Anthroposophic.

Roszia, Sharon, et al, eds. Creating Kinship. 200p. 1995. pap. text 15.00 (0-939561-27-1); VHS 25.00 (0-939561-26-3) Univ South ME.

Roszia, Sharon K., jt. auth. see Melina, Lois R.

Roszkiewicz, Ron & Straw, Phyllis. The Woodturner's Art. (Illus.). 286p. 1998. text 35.00 (0-7881-5847-3) DIANE Pub.

***Roszkowski.** Business Law: Principles, Cases, & Policy. 1999. pap. text 56.33 (0-201-63591-7) Addison-Wesley.

Roszkowski. S/G Business Law. 4th ed. (C). 1997. pap. text, student ed. 30.00 (0-673-52481-7) Addison-Wesley.

Roszkowski, Leszek, ed. Cosmo-97: Proceedings of the International Workshop on Particle Physics & the Early Universe Lake District, England. 500p. 1998. 86.00 (981-02-3527-5) World Scientific Pub.

Roszkowski, Mark. Baseball Crosswords. 3rd rev. ed. LC 97-2397. (Illus.). 192p. 1997. pap. 12.95 (1-57028-113-0, 81130H) NTC Contemp Pub Co.

Roszkowski, Mark E. Business Law for the CPA Candidate: CPA Problems. 6th ed. 545p. (C). 1996. pap. text 27.80 (0-87563-699-3) Stipes.
— Business Law Principles. 4th ed. LC 95-42092. 1250p. (C). 1997. 110.00 (0-673-52398-5) Addson-Wesley Educ.
— Principles of Business Law. 3rd ed. (C). 1997. pap. text 31.00 (0-673-52219-9) Addson-Wesley Educ.

Roszkowski, Mark E., ed. Business Law: Principles Cases & Policy. alternate ed. (C). 1998. text. write for info. (0-321-01379-4) Addson-Wesley Educ.

Roszkowski, Wojchiech. Landowners in Poland, 1918-1939. 1991. text 46.50 (0-88033-196-8, Pub. by East Eur Monographs) Col U Pr.

Rot, A. The Molecular Biology of Leumocyte Chemotaxis. (Medical Intelligence Unit Ser.). 200p. (C). 1997. 89.95 (0-412-11361-9) Chapman & Hall.

Rota, Anthony. Apart from the Text. LC 99-177769. (Illus.). 234p. 1998. 35.00 (1-884718-52-3, 50319) Oak Knoll.
— Points at Issue: A Bookseller Looks at Bibliography. LC 84-600230. 22p. 1984. 3.95 (0-8444-0471-3) Lib Congress.

Rota, E. Miriandra. The Story of the People. 209p. (Orig.). 1993. pap. 11.95 (0-929385-51-9) Light Tech Pubng.

Rota, G. C., jt. auth. see Hecker, S.

Rota, Gian-Carlo. Indiscrete Thoughts. Palombi, Fabrizio, ed. LC 95-52782. 1996. write for info. (3-7643-3866-0) Birkhauser.
— Indiscrete Thoughts. Palombi, Fabrizio, ed. 280p. 1996. 36.50 (0-8176-3866-0) Birkhauser.

Rota, Gian-Carlo, ed. Studies in Combinatorics. LC 78-60730. (Studies in Mathematics: No. 17). 273p. 1978. 25.00 (0-88385-117-2, MAS-17) Math Assn.

Rota, Gian-Carlo, jt. auth. see Birkhoff, Garrett D.

Rota, Gian-Carlo, jt. auth. see Klain, Daniel A.

Rota, Gian-Carlo, jt. ed. see Gessel, I.

Rota, Gian-Carlo, ed. see Polya, George.

Rota, Gian-Carlo, jt. ed. see Reynolds, Mark.

***Rota, Italo.** New York: Not Only Buildings. (Illus.). 400p. 2000. pap. 22.50 (3-8238-5475-5) te Neues.

Rota, Luciana, jt. auth. see Ballerini, Andrea.

Rota, Luciani, jt. auth. see Martignoni, Steve.

Rota, Maria, tr. see Miravalle, Mark I.

Rotar, Vladimir. Probability Theory. 350p. 1997. text 64.00 (981-02-2213-0) World Scientific Pub.

Rotary Club of Chester, South Carolina Staff. Chiefs. Grant, Tommy & Wilson, Sandy, eds. LC 83-73060. 128p. 1983. 16.95 (0-912081-01-5) Delmar Co.

Rotatori, Anthony F., ed. Advances in Special Education, Vol. 10. 312p. 1997. 78.50 (0-7623-0085-X) Jai Pr.
— Advances in Special Education, Vol. 12. 1999. 78.50 (0-7623-0434-0) Jai Pr.

Rotatori, Anthony F., et al, eds. Advances in Special Education, Vol. 6. 208p. 1987. 78.50 (0-89232-632-8) Jai Pr.
— Advances in Special Education: Basic Constructs & Theoretical Orientation, Vol. 1. 312p. 1980. 78.50 (0-89232-077-X) Jai Pr.
— Advances in Special Education: Basic Constructs & Theoretical Orientation, Vol. 7A. 232p. 1991. 78.50 (1-55938-257-0) Jai Pr.
— Advances in Special Education: Basic Constructs & Theoretical Orientation, Vol. 7B. 216p. 1991. 78.50 (1-55938-258-9) Jai Pr.
— Advances in Special Education: Basic Constructs & Theoretical Orientation, Vol. 9. 272p. 1995. 78.50 (1-55938-691-6) Jai Pr.
— Advances in Special Education: Behavior Mod in Special Education, 2 vols., Set, Vol. 7. 1991. 157.00 (1-55938-256-2) Jai Pr.
— Advances in Special Education: Documenting Program Impact. (Advances in Special Education Ser.: Vol. 4). 312p. 1984. 78.50 (0-89232-291-8) Jai Pr.
— Advances in Special Education: Perspectives on Applications, Vol. 2. 224p. 1983. 78.50 (0-89232-144-X) Jai Pr.
— Advances in Special Education: Perspectives on the Regular Education Initiative & Transitional Programs, Vol. 8. 216p. 1994. 78.50 (1-55938-435-2) Jai Pr.
— Advances in Special Education: Socialization Infu on Exceptionality, Vol. 3. 256p. 1985. 78.50 (0-89232-202-0) Jai Pr.
— Counseling Exceptional Students. 334p. (C). 1986. 45.95 (0-89885-274-9, Kluwer Acad Hman Sci); pap. 21.95 (0-89885-275-7, Kluwer Acad Hman Sci) Kluwer Academic.
— Developmental Problems in Infancy & the Preschool Years. (Advances in Special Education Ser.: Vol. 5). 296p. 1986. 78.50 (0-89232-313-2) Jai Pr.
— Issues, Practices, & Concerns in Special Education. (Advances in Special Education Ser.: Vol. 11). 1998. 78.50 (0-7623-0255-0) Jai Pr.

Rotatori, Anthony F. & Fox, Robert A. Obesity in Children & Youth: Measurement, Characteristics, Causes & Treatment. (Illus.). 188p. 1989. 52.95 (0-398-05594-7) C C Thomas.

Rotatori, Anthony F., et al. Comprehensive Assessment in Special Education: Approaches, Procedures & Concerns. (Illus.). 578p. (C). 1990. text 104.95 (0-398-05645-5) C C Thomas.

Rotatori, Anthony F., jt. ed. see Burkhardt, Sandra A.

Rotbart, Harley A., ed. Human Enterovirus Infections. LC 94-39792. 1994. 79.00 (1-55581-092-6) ASM Pr.

Rotberg, Iris C., et al, eds. Federal Policy Options for Improving the Education of Low-Income Students Vol. II: Commentaries. LC 93-36689. 1994. pap. text 15.00 (0-8330-1457-9, MR-210-LE) Rand Corp.

Rotberg, Robert I. Africa & Its Explorers: Motives, Methods, & Impact. LC 77-134327. (Illus.). 351p. 1970. pap. 17.50 (0-674-00777-8) HUP.
— Christian Missionaries & the Creation of Northern Rhodesia, 1880-1924. LC 65-12993. (Illus.). 264p. reprint ed. pap. 81.90 (0-8357-2924-9, 203916300011) Bks Demand.

***Rotberg, Robert I.** Creating Peace in Sri Lanka: Civil War & Reconciliation. 1999. 26.95 (0-8157-7578-4) Brookings.

Rotberg, Robert I. The Founder: Cecil Rhodes & the Enigma of Power. (Illus.). 854p. 1988. text 45.00 (0-19-504968-3) OUP.

***Rotberg, Robert I.** Peacekeeping & Peace Enforcement in Africa: Methods of Conflict Prevention. 2000. 42.95 (0-8157-7576-8) Brookings.

Rotberg, Robert I. Rise of Nationalism in Central Africa: The Making of Malawi & Zambia, 1873-1964. LC 65-19829. (Center for International Affairs Ser.). (Illus.). 362p. 1965. pap. 16.00 (0-674-77191-5, HP39) HUP.
— Suffer the Future: Policy Choices in Southern Africa. LC 79-25845. (Illus.). 327p. 1980. 37.95 (0-674-85401-2) HUP.

Rotberg, Robert I., ed. Africa in the Nineteen Nineties & Beyond: U. S. Policy Opportunities & Choices. LC 88-6724. (Illus.). 300p. 1988. pap. 16.00 (0-917256-44-1); text 29.00 (0-917256-43-3) Ref Pubns.
— Burma: Prospects for a Democratic Future. LC 98-8987. 292p. 1998. pap. 18.95 (0-8157-7581-4); text 48.95 (0-8157-7582-2) Brookings.
— Haiti Renewed: Political & Economic Prospects. LC 97-4623. 245p. 1997. text 28.95 (0-8157-7586-5) Brookings.

***Rotberg, Robert I., ed.** Health & Disease in Human History: A Journal of Interdisciplinary History Reader. LC 00-35135. (Journal of Interdisciplinary History Readers Ser.). 308p. 2000. pap. 25.00 (0-262-68122-6) MIT Pr.
— Health & Disease in Human History: A Journal of Interdisciplinary History Reader. 308p. (C). 2000. 60.00 (0-262-18207-6) MIT Pr.
— Patterns of Social Capital: Stability & Change in Historical Perspective. (Studies in Interdisciplinary History: Vol. 6). (Illus.). 340p. (C). 2000. text 49.95 (0-521-78086-1); pap. text 18.95 (0-521-78575-8) Cambridge U Pr.
— Social Mobility & Modernization: A Journal of Interdisciplinary History Reader. (Journal of Interdisciplinary History Readers Ser.). 350p. 2000. 60.00 (0-262-18208-4) MIT Pr.
— Social Mobility & Modernization: A Journal of Interdisciplinary History Reader. (Journal of Interdisciplinary History Readers Ser.). 350p. (C). 2000. pap. 25.00 (0-262-68123-4) MIT Pr.

Rotberg, Robert I., ed. War & Peace in Southern Africa. LC 97-45312. 296p. 1997. pap. 18.95 (0-8157-7585-7) Brookings.

Rotberg, Robert I. & Mills, Greg, eds. War & Peace in Southern Africa. LC 97-45312. 296p. 1997. 42.95 (0-8157-7584-9) Brookings.

Rotberg, Robert I. & Rabb, Theodore, eds. Marriage & Fertility: Studies in Interdisciplinary History. LC 80-7816. (Illus.). 384p. 1980. reprint ed. pap. 119.10 (0-7837-9428-2, 206016900004) Bks Demand.

Rotberg, Robert I. & Rabb, Theodore K., eds. Art & History: Images Their Meaning. (Studies in Interdisciplinary History). (Illus.). 314p. 1988. pap. text 20.95 (0-521-33569-8) Cambridge U Pr.
— Art & History: Images Their Meaning. (Studies in Interdisciplinary History). (Illus.). 316p. 1988. text 69.95 (0-521-34018-7) Cambridge U Pr.
— The Origin & Prevention of Major Wars. (Studies in Interdisciplinary History). 360p. (C). 1989. pap. text 21.95 (0-521-37955-5) Cambridge U Pr.

Rotberg, Robert I. & Robb, Theodore K., eds. Population & Economy: From the Traditional to the Modern World. (Studies in Interdisciplinary History). (Illus.). 239p. 1986. pap. text 21.95 (0-521-31055-5) Cambridge U Pr.

***Rotberg, Robert I. & Thompson, Dennis.** Truth vs. Justice: The Morality of Truth Commissions. LC 00-35962. (University Center for Human Values Ser.). 296p. 2000. 55.00 (0-691-05071-6) Princeton U Pr.

***Rotberg, Robert I. & Thompson, Dennis, eds.** Truth vs. Justice: The Morality of Truth Commissions. (University Center for Human Values Ser.). 296p. 2000. 18.95 (0-691-05072-4) Princeton U Pr.

Rotberg, Robert I. & Weiss, Thomas G., eds. From Massacres to Genocide: The Media, Humanitarian Crises, & Policy-Making. LC 95-50159. 203p. 1996. 26.95 (0-8157-7590-3) Brookings.

Rotberg, Robert I., jt. ed. see Chittick, H. Neville.

Rotberg, Robert I., jt. ed. see Kilson, Martin L.

Rotberg, Robert I., jt. ed. see Rabb, Theodore K.

Rotberg, Robert I., ed. see World Peace Foundation Staff.

Rotblat, J. & Konuma, M., eds. Towards a Nuclear Weapon-Free World: Proceedings of the 45th Pugwash Conference, Hiroshima, Japan, 23-29 July 1995. 830p. 1997. 118.00 (981-02-3179-2) World Scientific Pub.

Rotblat, Joseph. Nuclear Weapons: The Road to Zero. LC 98-140971. 344p. (C). 1998. text 79.00 (0-8133-3517-5, Pub. by Westview) HarpC.
— Security, Cooperation & Disarmament: The Unfinished Agenda for the 1990s. (Social Sciences Ser.). 640p. 1998. 86.00 (981-02-3590-9) World Scientific Pub.
— Striving for Peace, Security & Development in the World: Annals of Pugwash, 1991. 296p. 1993. text 55.00 (981-02-1249-6) World Scientific Pub.
— Towards a War-Free World: Annals of Pugwash, 1994. LC 96-114571. 1995. 36.00 (981-02-2492-3) World Scientific Pub.
— World Citizenship. LC 96-50106. 256p. 1997. pap. 21.95 (0-312-17361-X); text 65.00 (0-312-17359-8) St Martin.

***Rotblat, Joseph, ed.** Remember Your Humanity: Proceedings of the 47th Pugwash Conference on Science & World Affairs. 960p. 1999. 96.00 (981-02-4086-4) World Scientific Pub.

Rotblat, Joseph & Holdren, John P., eds. Building Global Security Through Cooperation: Annals of Pugwash 1989. (Illus.). 320p. 1991. text 83.00 (0-387-52813-X) Spr-Verlag.

Rotblat, Joseph, jt. auth. see Hellman, Sven.

Rotblat, Joseph, jt. ed. see Atlmann, J.

Rotch, et al. The Executive's Guide to Management Accounting & Control Systems. 6th ed. LC 96-71822. 1998. 55.95 (0-87393-470-9) Dame Pubns.

Rotch, William, et al. Cases in Management Accounting & Control Systems. 3rd ed. LC 95-5530. 288p. 1995. pap. text 57.00 (0-13-103128-7) P-H.

***Rote, Carey.** Cesar A. Martinez: A Retrospective. 112p. 1999. pap. text 29.95 (0-916677-43-5) M K McNay Art.

Rotella. Golf Between the Ears. 1995. 21.00 (0-671-88999-0) S&S Trade.

Rotella, Alexis. Beards & Wings. 40p. 1985. pap. text 6.00 (0-917951-01-8) White Peony.
— Camembert Comes from the Sea. (Illus.). 40p. 1984. pap. 6.50 (0-917951-00-X) White Peony.

Rotella, Alexis, ed. The Rise & Fall of Sparrows: A Collection of North American Haiku. LC 89-81932. (Orig.). 1990. pap. 8.95 (0-9623497-2-0) Los Hombres.

Rotella, Alexis K. Antiphony of Bells. 20p. 1988. 6.00 (0-917951-02-6) Jade Mtn.
— The Essence of Flowers: Wisdom for the Aquarian Age. (Illus.). 140p. 1991. per. 10.00 (0-917951-11-5) Jade Mtn.
— How Words & Thoughts Affect Your Body: The Book of Affirmations. 94p. 1990. per. 10.00 (0-917951-10-7) Jade Mtn.
— The Lace Curtain. 20p. 1988. pap. 6.00 (0-917951-03-4) Jade Mtn.
— Moonflowers. (Illus.). 20p. (Orig.). 1987. pap. 7.00 (0-916133-05-2) Jade Mtn.
— Musical Chairs: Childhood Haiku. (Illus.). 50p. 1994. pap. text, per. 11.00 (0-917951-26-3) Jade Mtn.

Rotella, Alexis K. & Miller, Florence. Yes: A Dozen Linked Poems. 51p. 1994. pap. 13.00 (0-916133-99-0) Jade Mtn.

Rotella, Alexis K., jt. auth. see Miller, Florence.

Rotella, Bob. The Golf of Your Dreams. LC 97-37655. 224p. 1997. 21.50 (0-684-84285-8) Simon & Schuster.

Rotella, Bob & Cullen, Bob. Golf Is a Game of Confidence. 240p. 1996. 21.50 (0-684-83040-X) Simon & Schuster.
— Life is Not a Game of Perfect: Finding Your Real Talent & Making It Work for You. LC 98-54819. 224p. 1999. 21.50 (0-684-84286-6) S&S Trade.

Rotella, Bob, et al. Case Studies in Sport Psychology. LC 97-9654. (Health Science Ser.). 224p. 1997. pap. 27.50 (0-7637-0355-9) Jones & Bartlett.

Rotella, Carlo. October Cities: The Redevelopment of Urban Literature. LC 97-27980. 384p. 1998. 50.00 (0-520-20763-7, Pub. by U CA Pr); pap. 18.95 (0-520-21144-8, Pub. by U CA Pr) Cal Prin Full Svc.

Rotella, Elyce J. From Home to Office: U. S. Women At Work, 1870-1930. Berkhofer, Robert, ed. LC 80-29154. (Studies in American History & Culture: No. 25). 251p. 1981. reprint ed. pap. 77.90 (0-8357-1163-3, 207011200064) Bks Demand.

Rotella, Guy. Critical Essays on e. e. cummings. (Critical Essays on American Literature Ser.). 352p. (C). 1984. 48.00 (0-8161-8677-4, G K Hall & Co) Mac Lib Ref.
— Reading & Writing Nature: The Poetry of Robert Frost, Wallace Stevens, Marianne Moore, & Elizabeth Bishop. 253p. 1990. text 45.00 (1-55553-086-9) NE U Pr.

Rotella, Guy, ed. see Morse, Samuel F.

Rotella, Guy L. Critical Essays on James Merrill. 1996. 49.00 (0-7838-0031-2, G K Hall & Co) Mac Lib Ref.

Rotella, R. J., jt. ed. see Bunker, Linda K.

Rotella, Robert. Elements of Successful Trading: Developing Your Comprehensive Strategy Through Psychology. (C). 1992. text 37.95 (0-13-204579-6) P-H.

Rotella, Robert & Bunker, Linda. Parenting Your Superstar: How to Help Your Child Balance Achievement & Happiness. (Illus.). 256p. 1998. pap. 14.95 (1-57243-295-0) Triumph Bks.

Rotella, Robert J. Putting Out of Your Mind. 1996. audio 12.00 (0-671-56796-9, 647403) S&S Audio.

Rotella, Robert J. & Coop. Mind Power to Better Golf. unabridged ed. 25p. pap. text 34.50 incl. audio (0-88432-187-8, S01820) Audio-Forum.

Rotella, Robert J. & Cullen, Bob. Golf Is Not a Game of Perfect. 1996. audio 12.00 (0-671-57063-3) S&S Audio.

Rotella, Robert J. & Cullen, Bob. Golf Is Not a Game of Perfect. LC 95-1120. 224p. 1995. 21.50 (0-684-80364-X) S&S Trade.

Rotella, Sebastian. Twilight on the Line: Underworlds & Politics at the Mexican Border. LC 97-11890. 224p. 1998. 25.00 (0-393-04113-1) Norton.

Rotellar, Carlos. Acute Renal Insufficiency Made Ridiculously Simple. (Illus.). 56p. 1996. pap. text 12.95 (0-940780-09-7) MedMaster.

Rotelle, John, ed. see Augustine of Hippo Staff.

Rotelle, John, ed. see Augustine, Saint.

Rotelle, John E. Augustine Day by Day. (Illus.). (Orig.). 1986. vinyl bd. 6.25 (0-89942-170-9, 170-09) Catholic Bk Pub.

***Rotelle, John E.** Book of Augustinian Saints. LC 00-40173. (Augustinian Ser.). 2000. write for info. (1-889542-13-X) Augustinian Pr.

Rotelle, John E. Lord, Let Me Know You: Devotions to Saint Augustine. 72p. 1987. pap. 1.00 (0-941491-04-8) Augustinian Pr.
— Meditations on the Sunday Gospels, Year C. 168p. 1997. pap. 9.95 (1-56548-086-4) New City.
— Woman of Faith: Devotions to Saint Monica. 72p. 1987. pap. 1.00 (0-941491-03-X) Augustinian Pr.

Rotelle, John E., ed. Little Office of the Blessed Virgin Mary. large type rev. ed. 192p. 1988. 9.50 (0-89942-450-3, 450/10) Catholic Bk Pub.
— Meditations on the Sunday Gospels, Year B. (Scriptural Commentaries Ser.). 168p. 1996. pap. 9.95 (1-56548-082-1) New City.
— Take My Advice. rev. ed. 64p. 1987. pap. 1.00 (0-941491-02-1) Augustinian Pr.
— A Word in Season, 4 vols. Barnecut, Edith, tr. (Orig.). 1987. reprint ed. write for info. (0-318-62742-6) Augustinian Pr.
— A Word in Season, 4 vols., Vol. IV. Barnecut, Edith, tr. 304p. (Orig.). 1987. reprint ed. 25.00 (0-941491-45-5) Augustinian Pr.
— A Word in Season: Lectionary for the Divine Office, 4 vols., Vol. I: Advent-Christmas. Barnecut, Edith, tr. 230p. (Orig.). 1987. reprint ed. pap. 12.50 (0-941491-12-9) Augustinian Pr.
— A Word in Season: Lectionary for the Divine Office, 4 vols., Vol. II: Lent. Barnecut, Edith, tr. 230p. (Orig.). 1987. reprint ed. pap. 12.50 (0-941491-13-7) Augustinian Pr.
— A Word in Season: Lectionary for the Divine Office, 4 vols., Vol. III. Barnecut, Edith, tr. 230p. (Orig.). 1987. reprint ed. pap. 12.50 (0-941491-14-5) Augustinian Pr.
— A Word in Season: Lectionary for the Divine Office, 4 vols., Vol. IV. Barnecut, Edith, tr. 304p. (Orig.). 1987. reprint ed. pap. 15.00 (0-941491-15-3) Augustinian Pr.
— A Word in Season: Lectionary of the Divine Office, Vol. V: Ordinary Time, Weeks 1-17. Barnecut, Edith, tr. 264p. 1995. reprint ed. 24.95 (0-941491-82-X); reprint ed. pap. 15.95 (0-941491-81-1) Augustinian Pr.
— A Word in Season: Lectionary of the Divine Office, Vol. VI: Ordinary TIme, Weeks 18-34. Barnecut, Edith, tr. 244p. 1995. reprint ed. 24.95 (0-941491-84-6) Augustinian Pr.
— A Word in Season: Lectionary of the Divine Office, Vol. VI: Ordinary Time, Weeks 18-34. Barnecut, Edith, tr. 244p. 1995. reprint ed. pap. 15.95 (0-941491-83-8) Augustinian Pr.
— A Word in Season: Ordinary Time, Year II, Weeks 1-17. (Word in Season Ser.: No. VII). 316p. 1999. 24.95 (0-941491-86-2, No. AP-5006C) Augustinian Pr.
— A Word in Season: Ordinary Time, Year II, Weeks 1-17, Vol. VII. 316p. 1999. pap. 15.95 (0-941491-85-4, AP-5006P) Augustinian Pr.
— A Word in Season: Ordinary Time, Year II, Weeks 18-34, Vol. VIII. 294p. 1999. 24.95 (0-941491-88-9, AP-5007C); pap. 15.95 (0-941491-87-0, AP-5007P) Augustinian Pr.

Rotelle, John E., ed. Meditations on the Sunday Gospels, Year A. (Scriptural Commentaries Ser.). 168p. 1995. pap. 9.95 (1-56548-032-5) New City.

Rotelle, John E., jt. auth. see Bellini, Pietro.

Rotelle, John E., jt. auth. see Giles.

Rotelle, John E., jt. auth. see Zumkeller, Adolar.

Rotelle, John E., ed. see Alonso, Carlos.

Rotelle, John E., ed. see Augustine, Saint.

An Asterisk (*) at the beginning of an entry indicates that the title is appearing for the first time.

Rotelle, John E., ed. see Back, Siegfried.
Rotelle, John E., ed. see De Orozco, Alonso.
Rotelle, John E., ed. see Hackett, Benedict.
Rotelle, John E., ed. see Hippo, Augustine.
Rotelle, John E., ed. see Hippo, Augustine of.
Rotelle, John E., ed. see Le Proust, Ange.
Rotelle, John E., ed. see Martin, Francis X.
Rotelle, John E., ed. see Pellegrino, Michele.
Rotelle, John E., ed. see Peri, Vittorio.
Rotelle, John E., ed. see Possidius.
Rotelle, John E., ed. see St. Thomas of Villanova.
Rotelle, John E., ed. see Thomas of Villanova.
Rotelle, John E., ed. see Trape, Agostino.
Rotelle, John E., ed. see Van Bavel, T. J.
Rotelle, John E., ed. see Zumkeller, Adolar, et al.
Rotello, Gabriel. Sexual Ecology: AIDS & the Destiny of Gay Men. 336p. 1998. pap. 13.95 (*0-452-27719-1*, Plume) Dutton Plume.
Rotem, A. Managing Systems for Better Health: A Facilitator's Guide. (Western Pacific Education in Action Ser.: No. 2). 204p. 1988. 15.00 (*92-9061-132-4*) World Health.
Rotem, A. & Abbatt, F. Self-Assessment for Teachers of Health Workers: How to Be a Better Teacher. (WHO Offset Publications: No. 68). 59p. 1982. 8.00 (*92-4-170068-8*) World Health.
Rotem, A., jt. auth. see Lawson, James.
Rotem, J. & Kranz, Jacqueline L., eds. Experimental Techniques in Plant Disease. (Illus.). 315p. 1987. 158.95 (*0-387-18128-8*) Spr-Verlag.
Rotem, Joseph. The Genus Alternaria: Biology, Epidemiology & Pathogenicity. LC 93-74153. (Illus.). 326p. 1994. 95.00 (*0-89054-152-3*) Am Phytopathol Soc.
Rotem, Judith. Distant Sisters: The Women I Left Behind. 240p. 1996. 17.50 (*0-8276-0583-8*) JPS Phila.
Rotem, Ornan, jt. auth. see Biderman, Shlomo.
Rotem, Simha. The Past Within Me: Memoirs of a Warsaw Ghetto Fighter. Harshav, Barbara, tr. from HEB. LC 94-17452.Tr. of Uve-Tokhi He-Avar. 192p. 1994. 25.00 (*0-300-05797-0*) Yale U Pr.
Rotemberg, Julio, jt. ed. see Bernanke, Ben S.
Rotemberg, Julio J., jt. ed. see Fischer, Stanley.
Rotenberg, Alexander. Emissaries. (Illus.). 256p. 1987. 17.95 (*0-8065-1062-5*, Citadel Pr) Carol Pub Group.
Rotenberg, David. The Shanghai Murders. LC 98-12828. 320p. 1998. text 24.95 (*0-312-18175-2*, 853565) St Martin.
Rotenberg, K. J., ed. Children's Interpersonal Trust: Sensitivity to Lying, Deception & Promise Violations. (Illus.). viii, 172p. 1991. 49.00 (*0-387-97511-X*) Spr-Verlag.
Rotenberg, Ken J., ed. Disclosure Processes in Children & Adolescents. LC 95-23746. (Cambridge Studies in Social & Emotional Development). (Illus.). 247p. (C). 1995. text 44.95 (*0-521-47098-6*) Cambridge U Pr.
***Rotenberg, Ken J. & Hymel, Shelley, eds.** Loneliness in Childhood & Adolescence. LC 98-45621. (Illus.). 432p. (C). 1999. 59.95 (*0-521-56135-3*) Cambridge U Pr.
Rotenberg, Lisa. Rodeo Pup. (Illus.). 32p. (J). (ps-3). 1998. write for info. (*0-385-25704-X*) Doubleday.
— Rodeo Pup. (Illus.). 32p. (J). (gr. k-4). 1998. 14.95 (*1-55209-245-3*) Firefly Bks Ltd.
— Rodeo Pup. rev. ed. (Illus.). 272p. 1998. write for info. (*0-385-25705-8*) Doubleday.
Rotenberg, M., ed. see Simon, J. D. & Abarbanel, Henry D.
Rotenberg, Marc, jt. ed. see Agre, Philip E.
Rotenberg, Marc, jt. ed. see Agre, Phillip E.
Rotenberg, Marc, jt. ed. see Banisar, David.
***Rotenberg, Mark & Mirsky, Laura.** Rotenberg's Nude Collection. (Illus.). 2000. pap. 39.99 (*3-8228-6413-7*) Taschen Amer.
Rotenberg, Mark Lee. The Rotenberg Collection. 768p. 1999. pap. 29.99 (*3-8228-7194-X*) Taschen Amer.
Rotenberg, Mordechai. Dia-Logo Therapy: Psychonarration & the Pardes. LC 90-44250. 192p. 1991. 59.95 (*0-275-92943-4*, C2943, Praeger Pubs) Greenwood.
— Dialogue with Deviance: The Hasidic Ethic & the Theory of Social Contraction. LC 93-6901. 283p. (C). 1993. reprint ed. pap. 28.50 (*0-8191-8975-8*) U Pr of Amer.
— Re-Biographing & Deviance: Psychotherapeutic Narrativism & the Midrash. LC 87-2451. 256p. 1987. 59.95 (*0-275-92391-6*, C2391, Praeger Pubs) Greenwood.
***Rotenberg, Nancy & Lustbader, Michael.** How to Photograph Close-Ups in Nature. LC 99-11916. (How to Photograph Ser.). (Illus.). 144p. 1999. pap. 19.95 (*0-8117-2457-3*) Stackpole.
Rotenberg, Nancy, jt. auth. see Lustbader, Michael.
Rotenberg, Rena, jt. auth. see Feinberg, Miriam P.
Rotenberg, Robert. Landscape & Power in Vienna. LC 94-42624. (Illus.). 416p. 1995. text 42.50 (*0-8018-4961-6*) Johns Hopkins.
Rotenberg, Robert & McDonogh, Gary. The Cultural Meaning of Urban Space: Contemporary Urban Studies. LC 92-32179. 248p. 1993. 59.95 (*0-89789-319-0*, H319, Bergin & Garvey); pap. 16.95 (*0-89789-320-4*, G320, Bergin & Garvey) Greenwood.
Rotenberg, Shlomo. Am Olam, Vol. 1. 1989. 18.95 (*0-87306-483-6*) Feldheim.
Rotenberg, Shlomo. Am Olam, Vol. 2. 1995. 18.95 (*1-58330-169-0*) Feldheim.
Rotenstreich. On Faith. LC 97-40092. 192p. 1998. lib. bdg. 35.00 (*0-226-72875-7*) U Ch Pr.
Rotenstreich, N. Immediacy & Its Limits: A Study in Martin Buber's Thought. 118p. 1991. text 58.00 (*3-7186-5108-4*, Harwood Acad Pubs) Gordon & Breach.
Rotenstreich, Nathan. Essays in Jewish Philosophy in the Modern Era: With an Introduction by Paul Mendes-Flohr. Munk, Reinier, ed. (Amsterdam Studies in Jewish Thought: Vol. 1). xvi,304p. 1996. lib. bdg. 64.00 (*90-5063-587-3*, Pub. by Gieben) J Benjamins Pubng Co.
— Experience & Its Systematization: Studies in Kant. 2nd enl. ed. 211p. 1972. pap. text 78.50 (*90-247-1306-4*) Kluwer Academic.
— From Substance to Subject: Studies in Hegel. 142p. 1974. pap. text 65.00 (*90-247-1655-1*) Kluwer Academic.
— Order & Might. LC 87-9980. (SUNY Series in Philosophy). 238p. (C). 1988. pap. text 19.95 (*0-88706-630-5*) State U NY Pr.
— Philosophy: The Concept & Its Manifestations. LC 72-77878. 267p. 1972. pap. text 59.50 (*90-277-0284-5*); lib. bdg. 104.50 (*90-277-0236-5*) Kluwer Academic.
— Philosophy, History & Politics. (Melbourne International Philosophy Ser.: No. 1). 166p. 1976. pap. text 82.00 (*90-247-1743-4*) Kluwer Academic.
— Practice & Realization: Studies in Kant's Moral Philosophy. 163p. 1979. lib. bdg. 121.00 (*90-247-2112-1*, Pub. by M Nijhoff) Kluwer Academic.
— Reflection & Action. (Phaenomenologica Ser.: No. 97). 222p. 1984. lib. bdg. 112.00 (*90-247-2969-6*, Pub. by M Nijhoff) Kluwer Academic.
— Reflection & Action. (Phaenomenologica Ser.: No. 97). 222p. 1988. pap. text 49.00 (*90-247-3128-3*, Pub. by M Nijhoff) Kluwer Academic.
— Synthesis & Intentional Objectivity on Kant & Husserl. LC 97-51738. 135p. 1998. lib. bdg. 99.00 (*0-7923-4956-3*) Kluwer Academic.
— Theory & Practice. (Van Leer Jerusalem Foundation Ser.). 248p. 1977. pap. text 99.50 (*90-247-2004-4*, Pub. by M Nijhoff) Kluwer Academic.
— Time & Meaning in History. (Boston Studies in the Philosophy of Science: No. 101). 228p. (C). 1987. text 144.00 (*90-277-2467-9*, D Reidel) Kluwer Academic.
Rotenstreich, Nathan, ed. Essays on Zionism & the Contemporary Jewish Condition. 1981. write for info. (*0-318-53299-9*) Herzl Pr.
Rotenstreich, Nathan & Mendes-Flohr, Paul R. On Faith. LC 97-40092. 192p. 1998. pap. text 15.00 (*0-226-72876-5*) U Ch Pr.
Roter, Debra, jt. ed. see Stewart, Moira A.
Roter, Debra, jt. ed. see Stewart, Moria A.
Roter, Debra L. & Hall, Judith A. Doctors Talking with Patients - Patients Talking with Doctors: Improving Communication in Medical Visits. LC 92-17633. 224p. 1992. 55.00 (*0-86569-048-0*, T048, Auburn Hse) Greenwood.
— Doctors Talking with Patients - Patients Talking with Doctors: Improving Communication in Medical Visits. 2nd ed. LC 92-17633. 224p. 1993. pap. 19.95 (*0-86569-234-3*, Auburn Hse) Greenwood.

Roter, Mike, jt. auth. see Wright, Benjamin.
Rotermund, Heinrich W. Das Gelehrte Hannover Oder Lexikon Von Schriftstellern un Schriftstellerinnen, Gelehrten Geschaftsmannern und Kunstlern die Seit der Reformation in und Auberhalb Den Samtlichen Zum Jetzigen Konigreich Hannover Gehorigen Provinzen Gelebt Haben und Noch Leben, 2 vols. 1983. write for info. incl. fiche (*0-318-71944-4*) G Olms Pubs.
***Rotermund, Manfred K.** The Fog of Peace: Finding the End-State of Hostilities. (Illus.). 65p. 1999. pap. write for info. (*1-58487-009-5*) SSI US Army.
Rotert, Ruth, jt. auth. see Taylor, Alf.
Rotfeld, Adam D., ed. A Co-operative Security Order in & for Europe. (A SIPRI Publication). 400p. 1999. text 65.00 (*0-19-829165-5*) OUP.
— From Helsinki to Lisbon & Beyond: Analysis & Documents of the OSCE, 1973-96. (A SIPRI Publication). 608p. 2000. text 69.00 (*0-19-829181-7*) OUP.
Rotfeld, Adam D. & Stutzle, Walther, eds. Germany & Europe in Transition. (SIPRI Publication). 252p. 1991. text 48.00 (*0-19-829146-9*) OUP.
***Rotfeld, Arthur.** The Art of James Hetfield. 72p. 1999. otabind 17.95 (*1-57560-142-7*, Pub. by Cherry Lane) H Leonard.
Rotgers, Frederick. Rural-urban Integration in Java. 69.95 (*0-7546-1106-X*) Ashgate Pub Co.
Rotgers, Frederick, et al, eds. Treating Substance Abuse: Theory & Technique. (Substance Abuse Ser.). 328p. 1995. lib. bdg. 36.00 (*1-57230-025-6*, 0025) Guilford Pubns.
***Roth.** Adult Motor Speech Disorders Research Guide. 2001. pap. 40.00 (*0-7693-0113-4*, Pub. by Singular Publishing) Thomson Learn.
Roth. American Architecture. 2000. 50.00 (*0-8133-3661-9*); 30.00 (*0-8133-3662-7*) Westview.
— Crime & Punishment: A History of the Criminal Justice Systems. (Criminal Justice Ser.). 2002. pap. 42.00 (*0-534-57798-9*) Thomson Learn.
***Roth.** Digital Systems Design with VHDL & Active-HDL. (Electrical Engineering Ser.). (C). 1999. text 90.00 incl. disk (*0-534-37830-7*) Brooks-Cole.
Roth. Edmund Husserls Ethische Untersuchungen: Dargestellt Anhand Seiner Vorlesungsmanuskripte. (Phaenomenologica Ser.: No. 7). 188p. 1961. lib. bdg. 73.50 (*90-247-0241-0*, Pub. by M Nijhoff) Kluwer Academic.
— English 101. 1998. 27.25 (*0-07-428929-2*) McGraw.
— Fundamentals of Logic Design. 4th ed. (West Engineering Ser.). 1992. pap., teacher ed. 9.50 (*0-534-95473-1*) PWS Pubs.
***Roth.** Fundamentals of Logic Design. 5th ed. (C). 2001. pap. 60.00 (*0-534-37804-8*) Thomson Learn.
Roth. Operations Strategy. 2000. 67.00 (*0-07-230906-7*) McGraw.
— Requiem for Harlem. LC 98-31435. (Mercy of a Rude Stream Ser.: Vol. 4). 304p. 1998. pap. 14.00 (*0-312-20205-9*) St Martin.
— Research Paper. 3rd ed. (Freshman English/Advanced Writing Ser.). 1978. pap. 5.75 (*0-534-00574-8*) Wadsworth Pub.
— The Research Paper. 6th ed. (Freshman English/Advanced Writing Ser.). 1989. pap., teacher ed. write for info. (*0-534-09925-4*) Wadsworth Pub.
— Treatment Resource Manual. 2nd ed. 2000. pap. 52.95 (*0-7693-0018-9*) Singular Publishing.
Roth & Rahdert. Appeals to the Eleventh Circuit Manual, 3 vols. 1984. spiral bd. 180.00 (*0-327-00935-7*, 80147, MICHIE) LEXIS Pub.
— Appeals to the Eleventh Circuit Manual 99-1, 3 vols. 336p. 1999. ring bd. 48.00 (*0-327-01064-9*, 8015224) LEXIS Pub.
Roth & Vaugh. Learning Through Literature: Ecology. (Illus.). 144p. (J). (gr. 3-5). 1996. pap., wbk. ed. 14.95 (*1-55734-475-2*) Tchr Create Mat.
Roth, et al. Organic Chemistry: Chemistry 315. 2nd ed. 76p. (C). 1997. spiral bd., lab manual ed. 17.95 (*0-7872-2721-8*, 41272102) Kendall-Hunt.
Roth, jt. auth. see Bergman.
Roth, jt. auth. see Gold.
Roth, A. Vacuum Sealing Techniques. LC 93-27399. (American Vacuum Society Classics Ser.). (Illus.). 864p. 1994. pap. text 44.95 (*1-56396-259-4*, AIP Pr) Spr-Verlag.
— Vacuum Technology. 3rd enl. ed. 572p. 1990. 139.00 (*0-444-88010-0*, North Holland) Elsevier.
Roth, A. E., jt. ed. see Kagel, J. H.
Roth, Al. Great Lights. (Illus.). 77p. 1992. write for info. (*0-9637380-1-1*) Al Roth.
Roth, Alfred C. Small Gas Engines: Fundamentals, Service, Troubleshooting, Repair, Applications. LC 98-53017. (Illus.). 512p. 2000. 42.64 (*1-56637-574-6*) Goodheart.
Roth, Allen. Sherborne: An Experiment in Transformation. LC 98-39694. 160p. 1998. 75.00 (*1-881408-09-4*); pap. 20.00 (*1-881408-10-8*) Bennett Bks.
Roth, Alvin. Picture Bidding. 317p. 1991. 24.95 (*0-940257-11-4*) Granovetter Bks.
Roth, Alvin E., ed. Game Theoretic Models of Bargaining. (Illus.). 400p. 1985. text 95.00 (*0-521-26757-9*) Cambridge U Pr.
— Laboratory Experiments in Economics: 6 Points of View. 232p. 1987. text 64.95 (*0-521-33392-X*) Cambridge U Pr.
— The Shapley Value: Essays in Honor of Lloyd S. Shapley. (Illus.). 344p. 1988. text 89.95 (*0-521-36177-X*) Cambridge U Pr.
Roth, Alvin E. & Sotomayor, Marilda A. Two-Sided Matching: A Study in Game-Theoretic Modeling & Analysis. (Econometric Society Monographs: No. 18). (Illus.). 279p. (C). 1992. pap. text 23.95 (*0-521-43788-1*) Cambridge U Pr.
Roth, Amy. A Season for Change. 28p. 1990. pap. 3.49 (*0-87227-147-1*, RBP5178) Reg Baptist.
Roth, Andrew. Can Parliament Decide--about Europe, or about Anything? LC 72-184211. 229p. 1971. write for info. (*0-356-03933-1*) Janes Info Group.
— Enoch Powell: Tory Tribune. LC 70-523435. 393p. 1970. write for info. (*0-356-03150-0*) Janes Info Group.
***Roth, Andrew.** Infamous Manhattan: A Colorful Walking History of New York's Most Notorious Crime Sites. (Illus.). 303p. 2000. reprint ed. pap. 15.00 (*0-7881-9243-4*) DIANE Pub.
Roth, Andrew. Infamous Manhattan: A Colorful Walking Tour of New Yorks Most Notorious Crime Sites. (Illus.). 303p. 1995. pap. 14.95 (*0-8065-1701-8*, Citadel Pr) Carol Pub Group.
— Sir Harold Wilson, Yorkshire Walter Mitty. LC 78-307133. 338p. 1977. write for info. (*0-356-08074-9*) Janes Info Group.
Roth, Andrew, jt. auth. see Roth, Jonathan.
***Roth, Ann.** Stranger in a Small Town. (Special Edition Ser.: Bk. 1356). 2000. mass mkt. 4.50 (*0-373-24356-1*, 1-24356-7) Silhouette.
Roth, Ann M. Egyptian Phyles in the Old Kingdom: The Evolution of a System of Social Organization. LC 90-63938. (Studies in Ancient Oriental Civilization: No. 48). (Illus.). xxvi, 243p. 1991. pap. 30.00 (*0-918986-68-0*) Orient Inst.
Roth, Ann M., tr. see Zauzich, Karl-Theodor.
Roth, Anne A. It's Time to Come In! LC 96-29137. (Illus.). (J). 1997. write for info. (*1-56763-243-2*); pap. write for info. (*1-56763-244-0*) Ozark Pub.
— Mikael's Magical Wave. LC 96-32813. (Illus.). (J). 1997. write for info. (*1-56763-239-4*); pap. write for info. (*1-56763-240-8*) Ozark Pub.
— No More Peas, Please! LC 96-32819. (Illus.). (J). 1997. write for info. (*1-56763-241-6*); pap. write for info. (*1-56763-242-4*) Ozark Pub.
Roth, Anthony & Fonagy, Peter. What Works for Whom? A Critical Review of Psychotherapy Research. 484p. 1998. pap. text 27.00 (*1-57230-355-7*, C0355) Guilford Pubns.
Roth, Anthony, et al. What Works for Whom? A Critical Review of Psychotherapy Research. 484p. 1996. lib. bdg. 48.95 (*1-57230-125-2*, 0125) Guilford Pubns.
Roth, Ariel. Origins: Linking Science & Scripture. LC 98-226799. (Illus.). 320p. 1998. 29.99 (*0-8280-1328-4*) Review & Herald.
Roth, Ariel, et al. 3 More by E. S. T. '98. pap. 5.25 (*0-8222-1695-7*) Dramatists Play.
Roth, Arlen. Arlen Roth's Complete Electric Guitar. 160p. 1996. otabind 14.95 (*0-7935-6648-7*) H Leonard.
— Beginning Blues Guitar. LC 75-32888. (Illus.). (Orig.). 1976. pap. 12.95 (*0-8256-2350-2*, AM35189) Music Sales.
— Hot Guitar: Rock Soloing, Blues Power, Rapid-Fire Rockabilly, Slick Turnarounds, Hot Country & Cool Licks. (Illus.). 130p. 1995. pap. 19.95 (*0-87930-276-3*) Miller Freeman.
— Masters of the Telecaster. Stang, Aaron, ed. (Illus.). 188p. (Orig.). (YA). 1996. pap. 34.95 incl. audio compact disk (*0-89724-805-8*, GF9512CD) Wrner Bros.
— Nashville Guitar. (Illus.). 144p. 1997. pap. 19.95 (*0-8256-0172-X*, OK63321, Oak) Music Sales.
— Traditional, Country & Electric Slide Guitar. (Illus.). 128p. 1975. pap. 19.95 (*0-8256-0162-2*, OK62836, Oak) Music Sales.
Roth, Arnold. No Pain, No Strain. (Illus.). 1996. pap. 7.95 (*0-614-20785-1*, St Martin Griffin) St Martin.
— Poor Arnolds Almanac. (Illus.). 112p. 1998. pap. 12.95 (*1-56097-322-6*) Fantagraph Bks.
Roth, Arthur. Eiger: Wall of Death. large type ed. 528p. 1988. 11.50 (*0-7089-1806-9*) Ulverscroft.
***Roth, Arthur.** Eiger: Wall of Death. unabridged deluxe ed. LC 99-68789. (Illus.). 416p. 2000. reprint ed. lib. bdg. 35.00 (*1-885283-19-9*) Advent Library.
Roth, Arthur. Iceberg Hermit. LC 74-7435. 224p. (YA). (gr. 7 up). 1989. pap. 4.50 (*0-590-44112-4*) Scholastic Inc.
Roth, Arthur J. Iceberg Hermit. (Point Ser.). (J). 1974. 9.60 (*0-606-04098-6*, Pub. by Turtleback) Demco.
Roth, Audrey J. The Elements of Basic Writing with Readings. 2nd ed. LC 95-33597. 560p. 1995. pap. text 48.00 (*0-205-18808-7*) Allyn.
— The Elements of Basic Writing with Readings. 2nd annot. ed. (C). 1995. pap. text, teacher ed. write for info. (*0-205-18814-1*, H8814-9) Allyn.
— The Research Paper: Process, Form, & Content. 5th ed. 305p. (C). 1985. pap. write for info. (*0-534-06090-0*) Wadsworth Pub.
— The Research Paper: Process, Form, & Content. 6th ed. 300p. (C). 1988. pap. 15.95 (*0-534-09924-6*) Wadsworth Pub.
— The Research Paper: Process, Form, & Content. 7th ed. 300p. (C). 1994. 18.75 (*0-534-17454-X*) Wadsworth Pub.
— The Research Paper: Process, Form, Content. 8th ed. LC 98-39519. 320p. 1998. pap. 23.95 (*0-534-52380-3*) Wadsworth Pub.
Roth, B., jt. auth. see Bottema, O.
Roth, Barbara J., jt. auth. see McPherron, Shannon P.
Roth, Barry. An Annotated Bibliography of Jane Austen Studies, 1984-94. LC 96-17026. 464p. (C). 1996. 49.95 (*0-8214-1167-5*) Ohio U Pr.
— Associations: The Memory Book. LC 92-70949. (Illus.). 90p. (Orig.). 1993. pap. 6.95 (*1-881140-01-6*) Benidee Prods.
Roth, Bennett E., et al, eds. Difficult Patient in Group: Group Psychotherapy with Borderline & Narcissistic Disorders. (American Group Psychotherapy Association Monographs: No. 6). 350p. 1990. 50.00 (*0-8236-1286-4*) Intl Univs Pr.
Roth, Bettie G. & Schneider, Harriette, eds. Today's Traditional: Jewish Cooking with a Lighter Touch. LC 93-70841. (Illus.). 208p. (Orig.). 1993. pap. 11.95 (*0-9636626-0-0*) Congreg Beth Shalom.
Roth, Beulah, jt. auth. see Roth, Sanford.
Roth, Bob & Doggett, Decker. Official Guide to LGB Trains. LC 98-178884. (Illus.). 193p. 1998. 59.95 (*0-89778-302-6*, 10-7815, Kalmbach Books) Kalmbach.
Roth, Brad. Governmental Illegitimacy in International Law. LC 98-30858. 470p. 1999. text 115.00 (*0-19-826852-1*) OUP.
Roth, Brad R., jt. ed. see Fox, Gregory H.
Roth, Brandi & Van Der Kar-Levinson, Fay. Choosing the Right School for Your Child. 2nd ed. 148p. (Orig.). 1998. pap. 15.00 (*0-9647119-0-7*) Assoc of Ideas.
— Secrets to School Success: Guiding Your Child Through a Joyous Learning Experience. 250p. Date not set. pap. 24.95 (*0-9647119-1-5*) Assoc of Ideas.
Roth, Byron M. Prescription for Failure: Race Relations in the Age of Social Science. LC 93-42745. (Studies in Social Philosophy & Policy: No. 18). 370p. (C). 1994. 49.95 (*1-56000-161-5*); pap. 24.95 (*1-56000-739-7*) Transaction Pubs.

R

Roth, Byron M. & Mullen, John D. Decision Making: Its Logic & Practice. 272p. (C). 1990. lib. bdg. 44.95 (*0-8476-7619-6*) Rowman.

Roth, C. H., Jr., jt. auth. see Matney, Roy M., II.

Roth, Carol. Forget Me Not: A Romance Mystery. v, 230p. 1998. pap. 11.95 (*0-9667555-4-5*) Clouse Pubg.

***Roth, Carol.** In Search of Katherine: The Sequel to "Forget Me Not" 240p. (YA). (gr. 7-12). 2000. pap. 11.95 (*0-9667555-3-7*) Clouse Pubg.

Roth, Carol. Little Bunny's Sleepless Night. LC 98-41047. (Illus.). (J). (ps-2). 1999. 15.95 (*0-7358-1069-9*, Pub. by North-South Bks NYC); lib. bdg. 15.88 (*0-7358-1070-2*, Pub. by North-South Bks NYC) Chronicle Bks.

— Quiet As a Mouse. (Illus.). 32p. (J). (ps-3). 1991. 6.95 (*1-56288-121-3*) Checkerboard.

***Roth, Carol.** Ten Dirty Pigs; Ten Clean Pigs: An Upside-Down, Turn-Around Bathtime Counting Book. LC 99-17367. (Illus.). 32p. (J). (ps-2). 1999. 15.95 (*0-7358-1089-3*, Pub. by North-South Bks NYC); lib. bdg. 15.88 (*0-7358-1090-7*, Pub. by North-South Bks NYC) Chronicle Bks.

Roth, Catharine P., tr. On the Holy Icons. LC 81-18319. 115p. (Orig.). 1981. pap. 8.95 (*0-913836-76-1*) St Vladimirs.

Roth, Catharine P., tr. see St. John Chrysostom.

Roth, Catharine P., tr. & intro. see St. Gregory of Nyssa.

Roth, Catharine P., tr. & intro. see St. John Chrysostom.

Roth, Catherine. The Architectural Heritage of Genesee County, New York. (Illus.). 339p. 1989. per. 15.00 (*0-9624053-1-0*) Lndmrk Soc Genesee.

Roth, Cecil. Dona Gracia of the House of Nasi. LC 77-92984. 232p. 1992. reprint ed. pap. text 19.95 (*0-8276-0411-4*) JPS Phila.

— The Duke of Naxos of the House of Nasi. LC 71-91172. 270p. 1992. reprint ed. pap. text 13.95 (*0-8276-0412-2*) JPS Phila.

— Gleanings: Essays in Jewish History, Letters & Art. 1967. 20.00 (*0-8197-0178-5*) Bloch.

— A History of the Marranos. LC 74-29516. (Modern Jewish Experience Ser.). (Illus.). 1975. reprint ed. 39.95 (*0-405-06742-9*) Ayer.

— A History of the Marranos. (Illus.). xxiv, 424p. 1992. reprint ed. pap. 24.95 (*0-87203-040-7*) Hermon.

— A Life of Menasseh Ben Israel: Rabbi, Printer & Diplomat. LC 74-29518. (Modern Jewish Experience Ser.). (Illus.). 1975. reprint ed. 35.95 (*0-405-06743-7*) Ayer.

— The Sassoon Dynasty. Wilkins, Mira, ed. LC 76-29982. (European Business Ser.). (Illus.). 1977. reprint ed. lib. bdg. 25.95 (*0-405-09747-6*) Ayer.

Roth, Cecil & Wigoder, Geoffrey, eds. Encyclopedia Judaica, 18 vols., Set. 1994. reprint ed. 995.00 incl. 3.5 hd (*965-07-0204-0*) Coronet Bks.

Roth, Cecil, jt. auth. see Wurmbrand, Max.

Roth, Charles. Mind: The Master Power. 3rd rev. ed. LC 97-10435. 210p. 1999. 9.95 (*0-87159-209-6*) Unity Bks.

— More Power to You! LC 82-50122. 158p. 1982. 3.98 (*0-87159-093-X*) Unity Bks.

— Twelve Power Meditation Exercise. LC 89-50837. 89p. 1989. 6.95 (*0-87159-161-8*) Unity Bks.

Roth, Charles, ed. see Cross, Ruth C.

Roth, Charles B. & Alexander, Roy. Secrets of Closing Sales. 6th ed. 400p. (C). 1997. pap. text 16.95 (*0-13-671512-5*) P-H.

Roth, Charles B., jt. auth. see Mayer, Frank H.

Roth, Charles E. The Sky Observer's Guidebook. (Phalarope Bk.). (Illus.). 256p. 1986. 17.95 (*0-13-812793-X*) P-H.

Roth, Charles E., et al. Beyond the Classroom: Exploration of Schoolground & Backyard. Orig. Title: Schoolground Science. 1991. reprint ed. pap. 9.95 (*0-932691-10-2*) MA Audubon Soc.

Roth, Charles E., jt. auth. see Leslie, Clare Walker.

Roth, Charles H. Digital Logic with VHDL. LC 97-24246. (Electrical Engineering Ser.). (C). 1998. mass mkt. 93.95 (*0-534-95099-X*) Wadsworth Pub.

Roth, Charles H., Jr. Fundamentals of Logic Design. 4th ed. (West Engineering Ser.). 770p. (C). 1995. mass mkt. 97.95 (*0-534-95472-3*) PWS Pubs.

Roth, Chaya & Kulb, Steven D. The Multiple Facets of Therapeutic Transactions. LC 96-43562. 1997. 45.00 (*0-8236-3487-6*, BN03487) Intl Univs Pr.

Roth, Chris. The Beetless' Gardening Book: An Organic Gardening Songbook/Guidebook. annot. ed. LC 97-91588. 112p. (Orig.). 1997. pap. 8.95 (*0-9657090-2-7*) Carrotseed.

***Roth, Cliff.** The Low Budget Video Bible: Film School Edition: The Essential Guide to Making Top Notch Student Video. 3rd ed. (Illus.). 524p. (C). 1999. pap. text 27.95 (*0-9635216-5-9*) Desktop Vid.

Roth, Cliff. The Low Budget Video Bible: The Essential Do-It-Yourself Guide to Making Top Notch Video on a Shoestring Budget. 2nd rev. ed. (Illus.). 458p. (Orig.). (C). 1997. pap. 27.95 (*0-9635216-1-6*) Desktop Vid.

Roth, Dana. The Complete Book of Bass Chords. (Complete Book). 256p. 1992. pap. 22.95 (*1-56222-548-0*, 94754) Mel Bay.

— Encyclopedia of Scales & Modes for Electric Bass. 104p. 1992. spiral bd. 11.95 (*1-56222-290-2*, 94695) Mel Bay.

Roth, Daniel. MCAT Essentials. LC 97-16631. (Illus.). 125p. 1997. pap. 14.95 (*0-683-30105-5*) Lppncott W & W.

Roth, Danny. Bridge: Expert Advancer. 1993. pap. 10.95 (*0-00-218530-X*, Pub. by HarpC) Trafalgar.

— Bridge: Expert Club Player. (Illus.). 1993. pap. 10.95 (*0-00-218529-6*, Pub. by HarpC) Trafalgar.

— Bridge: The Expert Improver. (Orig.). 1993. pap. 10.95 (*0-00-218438-9*, Pub. by HarpC) Trafalgar.

Roth, Danny. Hand Reading in Bridge: How to Improve Your Card Play. (Illus.). 128p. 1993. 24.95 (*0-575-05434-4*, Pub. by V Gollancz) Trafalgar.

Roth, Darlene. Greater Atlanta: An Illustrated History of the Region. Parks, Lori, ed. LC 98-73491. (Illus.). 400p. 2000. 49.95 (*1-886483-28-0*) Heritge Media.

Roth, Darlene, jt. auth. see Ambrose, Andy.

Roth, Darlene R. Architecture, Archaeology & Landscapes: Resources for Historic Preservation in Unincorporated Cobb County, Georgia. LC 88-62643. (Illus.). 290p. (Orig.). (C). 1988. student ed. 25.00 (*0-9621120-2-X*); text 25.00 (*0-9621120-0-3*); pap. text 25.00 (*0-9621120-1-1*) CCHPC.

Roth, Dave. Win 32 Perl Programming. LC 98-84226. 575p. 1998. pap. 40.00 (*1-57870-067-1*) Macmillan Tech.

Roth, Dave. Win32 Perl Programming: The Administrator's Handbook. 350p. 40.00 (*1-57870-215-1*) Macmillan Tech.

Roth, David. Sacred Honor. 2000. 6.50 (*0-310-21455-6*) Zondervan.

Roth, David & Warwick, Paul. Study of Comparative Politics. 476p. (C). 1997. 82.00 (*0-06-045626-4*) Addson-Wesley Educ.

Roth, David Lee. Crazy from the Heat. 304p. 1998. mass mkt. 6.99 (*0-7868-8358-8*) Hyperion.

— Crazy from the Heat. (J). 1998. mass mkt. 6.99 (*0-7868-8947-0*, Pub. by Hyperion) Time Warner.

Roth, Dennis M. Rhythm Vision: A Guide to Visual Awareness. LC 90-30610. (Illus.). 128p. (Orig.). 1990. pap. 12.95 (*0-944091-02-4*) Intaglio Pr.

— The Wilderness Movement & the National Forests. 2nd rev. ed. (Illus.). 106p. (C). 1995. pap. 14.95 (*0-944091-05-9*) Intaglio Pr.

Roth, Dick. No, It's Not Hot in Here: A Husband's Guide to Menopause. 174p. 1999. 19.95 (*0-9655067-3-8*, Ant Hill Press) N Star Pubns.

Roth, E., compiled by. Thorium Fuel Cycle. (Bibliographical Ser.: No. 39). 462p. 1972. pap. 60.00 (*92-0-054070-8*, ISP21 39, Pub. by IAEA) Bernan Associates.

Roth, E., et al. Grundlagen und Technik der Infusionstherapie und Klinischen Ernaehrung. (Handbuch der Infusionstherapie und Klinischen Ernaehrung Ser.: Band 2). (GER.). x, 278p. 1985. 108.75 (*3-8055-3746-8*) S Karger.

Roth, E. N., ed. see Chien, S. H. & Hammond, L. L.

Roth, E. N., ed. see Cooper, Peter, et al.

Roth, E. N., ed. see Harris, G. T.

Roth, E. N., ed. see Kaddar, T., et al.

Roth, E. N., ed. see Kanwar, J. S. & Mudahar, Mohinder S.

Roth, E. N., ed. see Martinez, Adolfo, et al.

Roth, E. N., ed. see Mudahar, Mohinder S. & Kapusta, Edwin C.

Roth, E. N., jt. ed. see Schultz, J. J.

Roth, E. N., ed. see Williams, Lewis B.

Roth, Edward S. Functional Gaging. LC 74-118771. (Society of Manufacturing Engineers Manufacturing Data Ser.). 149p. reprint ed. pap. 46.20 (*0-608-16133-0*, 200498400048) Bks Demand.

Roth, Edward S., ed. Gaging: Practical Design & Application. LC 80-53424. 289p. reprint ed. pap. 89.60 (*0-608-13101-6*, 202417000035) Bks Demand.

Roth, Edward S. & Runck, Robert F., eds. Functional Inspection Techniques. LC 67-20359. (American Society of Tool & Manufacturing Engineers Manufacturing Data Ser.). 95p. reprint ed. pap. 30.00 (*0-608-11453-7*, 200498500050) Bks Demand.

***Roth, Eileen.** Organizing for Dummies. 384p. 2000. pap. 19.99 (*0-7645-5300-3*) IDG Bks.

Roth, Eli M. Colesterol Bueno, Colesterol Malo. 1997. pap. text 13.95 (*84-270-2177-1*) Planeta.

Roth, Eli M. & Streicher, Sandra. Good Cholesterol, Bad Cholesterol: What You Need to Know to Reduce Your Risk of Heart Disease. 192p. 1988. reprint ed. 15.95 (*0-914629-85-9*) Prima Pub.

— Good Cholesterol, Bad Cholesterol: What You Need to Know to Reduce Your Risk of Heart Disease. 192p. 1989. reprint ed. pap. 9.95 (*1-55958-025-9*) Prima Pub.

Roth, Eli M., jt. auth. see Streicher-Lankin, Sandra L.

Roth, Etienne & Poty, Bernard, eds. Nuclear Methods of Dating. (C). 1990. text 567.00 (*0-7923-0188-9*) Kluwer Academic.

Roth, Filibert. Forest Regulation. 1925. 12.00 (*0-911586-28-8*) Wahr.

— Forest Valuation. 1926. 12.00 (*0-911586-29-6*) Wahr.

Roth, Froma P. & Worthington, Colleen K. Treatment Resource Manual for Speech-Language Pathology. LC 96-26450. 342p. 1996. pap. 49.95 (*1-56593-636-1*, 1318) Thomson Learn.

Roth, Gabriel. Roads in a Market Economy. LC 98-79273. 292p. 1998. pap. text 39.95 (*1-84014-523-4*, Pub. by Ashgate Pub) Ashgate Pub Co.

Roth, Gabriel & Wynne, George W. Free Enterprise Urban Transportation. (Learning from Abroad Ser.: Vol. 5). 48p. (Orig.). 1982. pap. 10.95 (*0-87855-914-0*) Transaction Pubs.

Roth, Gabrielle. Roads in a Market Economy. 292p. 1996. 91.95 (*0-291-39814-6*, Pub. by Avebury Technical) Ashgate Pub Co.

— Sweat Your Prayers: Movement As Spiritual Practice. LC 97-28991. (Illus.). 240p. 1997. 22.95 (*0-87477-878-6*, Tarcher Putnam) Putnam Pub Group.

— Sweat Your Prayers: Movement As Spiritual Practice. LC 97-28991. (Illus.). 256p. 1998. reprint ed. pap. 12.95 (*0-87477-959-6*, Tarcher Putnam) Putnam Pub Group.

— Les Voies de l'Extase: Enseignement d'une Chamane de la Ville. 1993. 19.95 (*2-920083-73-2*) Edns Roseau.

Roth, Gabrielle & Loudon, John. Maps to Ecstacy: A Healing Journey for the Untamed Spirit. 2nd rev. ed. LC 98-35180. (Illus.). 240p. 1998. pap. 12.95 (*1-57731-045-4*) New Wrld Lib.

Roth, Gary, jt. auth. see Lopes, Ann.

Roth, Geneen. Appetites. 1997. pap. 11.95 (*0-452-27679-9*, Plume); pap. write for info. (*0-452-15529-0*, Plume) Dutton Plume.

— Appetites: On the Search for True Nourishment. 245p. 1998. text 21.00 (*0-7881-5774-4*) DIANE Pub.

— Breaking Free from Compulsive Eating. LC 93-13034. 224p. 1993. reprint ed. pap. 12.95 (*0-452-27084-7*, Plume) Dutton Plume.

— Feeding the Hungry Heart: The Experience of Compulsive Eating. LC 93-13035. 208p. 1993. reprint ed. pap. 12.95 (*0-452-27083-9*, Plume) Dutton Plume.

— When Food Is Love: Exploring the Relationship Between Eating & Intimacy. 224p. 1992. pap. 12.95 (*0-452-26818-4*, Plume) Dutton Plume.

— When You Eat at the Refrigerator, Pull up a Chair: 50 Ways to Be Thin, Gorgeous & Happy When You Feel Anything But. LC 97-38725. (Illus.). 223p. (J). 1998. 15.95 (*0-7868-6395-1*, Pub. by Hyperion) Time Warner.

— When You Eat at the Refrigerator, Pull up a Chair: 50 Ways to Feel Thin, Gorgeous, & Happy (When You Feel Anything But) 256p. 1999. pap. text 9.95 (*0-7868-8508-4*, Pub. by Hyperion) Time Warner.

— Why Weight? A Guide to Ending Compulsive Eating. (Illus.). 224p. 1989. pap. 12.95 (*0-452-26254-2*, Plume) Dutton Plume.

Roth, George. Slaying the Law School Dragon: How to Survive & Thrive in First Year Law School. 2nd ed. LC 90-23358. 192p. 1991. pap. 15.95 (*0-471-54298-9*) Wiley.

Roth, George & Kleiner, Art. Car Launch: The Human Side of Managing Change. LC 99-23938. (Learning History Library). (Illus.). 222p. (C). 1999. 22.95 (*0-19-512946-6*) OUP.

Roth, George, jt. auth. see Kleiner, Art.

Roth, George B., jt. auth. see D'Ambrogio, Kerry J.

Roth, George S., jt. auth. see Adelman, Richard C.

Roth, George S., jt. ed. see Adelman, Richard C.

Roth, Gerhard. The Autobiography of Albert Einstein. Green, Malcolm, tr. from GER. 120p. (Orig.). 1993. pap. 13.99 (*0-947757-47-3*) Serpents Tail.

— The Calm Ocean. Schreckenberger, Helga & Vansant, Jacqueline, trs. LC 92-45048. (Studies in Austrian Literature, Culture, & Thought. Translation Ser.). 238p. 1993. pap. 20.50 (*0-929497-64-3*) Ariadne CA.

***Roth, Gerhard.** The Lake. Winkler, Michael, tr. from GER. & afterword by by. LC 99-23591. (Studies in Austrian Literature, Culture & Thought). 2000. pap. write for info. (*1-57241-084-1*) Ariadne CA.

Roth, Gerhard. The Story of Darkness. Schreckenberger, Helga & Vansant, Jacqueline, trs. from GER. LC 98-46971. (Studies in Austrian Literature, Culture & Thought; Translation Ser.). 115p. 1999. pap. 14.00 (*1-57241-070-1*) Ariadne CA.

***Roth, Gerhard & Wullmann, Mario F., eds.** Brain Evolution & Cognition. 416p. 2000. 99.95 (*0-471-33170-8*) Wiley.

Roth, Glen A. & Lehman, Glenn M. An Instrument of God's Grace: The Story of Sharing Programs/Brotherly Aid. LC 95-82007. xiv, 180p. 1995. write for info. (*1-883294-33-9*) Masthof Pr.

Roth, Glen A., jt. auth. see Schlabach, Sue V.

Roth, Greg, et al, eds. Corn Silage Production, Management, & Feeding. LC 95-1562. 42p. 1995. 5.00 (*0-89118-124-5*) Am Soc Agron.

Roth, Greg & Undersander, Dan, eds. Corn Silage Production, Management & Feeding. (Illus.). 42p. 1999. reprint ed. pap. text 20.00 (*0-7881-7822-9*) DIANE Pub.

Roth, Guenther. The Social Democrats in Imperial Germany: A Study in Working-Class Isolation & National Integration. Coser, Lewis A. & Powell, Walter W., eds. LC 79-7018. (Perennial Works in Sociology). 1980. reprint ed. lib. bdg. 29.95 (*0-405-12117-2*) Ayer.

Roth, Guenther, jt. ed. see Lehmann, Hartmut.

Roth, Guenther, ed. see Weber, Max M.

Roth, Guenther, tr. see Schluchter, Wolfgang.

Roth, Gunter D. Stars & Planets. LC 97-48369. (Illus.). 176p. 1999. pap. 17.95 (*0-8069-9906-3*) Sterling.

Roth, Gunter D., ed. Compendium of Practical Astronomy, 3 vols. rev. ed. Augensen, Harry J. & Heintz, Wulff D., trs. LC 93-27023. (ENG & GER., Illus.). 560p. 1994. 64.95 (*0-387-53596-9*); 54.95 (*0-387-54885-8*); 54.95 (*0-387-54886-6*) Spr-Verlag.

— Compendium of Practical Astronomy, 3 vols., Set. rev. ed. Augensen, Harry J. & Heintz, Wulff D., trs. LC 93-27023. (ENG & GER., Illus.). 1232p. 1994. 139.95 (*0-387-56273-7*) Spr-Verlag.

Roth, H. Chasing the Long Rainbow. 1994. 29.95 (*0-393-90794-5*) Norton.

Roth, H. J. & Kleeman, A. K. Pharmaceutical Chemistry: Drug Synthesis, Vol. 1. 328p. 1988. text 62.95 (*0-470-21037-0*) P-H.

Roth, H. Ling. Oriental Silverwork: Malay & Chinese. (Oxford in Asia Hardback Reprints Ser.). (Illus.). 336p. 1994. 95.00 (*0-19-588605-4*) OUP.

Roth, Hagedorn. Burning Heart. 35.00 (*0-8478-2164-1*, Pub. by Rizzoli Intl) St Martin.

Roth, Hal. Always a Distant Anchorage. LC 97-20178. (Illus.). 348p. 1997. reprint ed. pap. 15.95 (*0-9639566-5-5*, \) Seaworthy WI.

— Chasing the Long Rainbow: The Drama of a Singlehanded Sailing Race Around the World. LC 97-14641. 335p. 1997. reprint ed. pap. 15.95 (*0-9639566-6-3*, \) Seaworthy WI.

— Conversations in a Country Store: Reminiscing on Maryland's Eastern Shore. LC 95-70484. 214p. 1995. reprint ed. pap. 12.95 (*0-9647694-0-9*) Nanticoke Bks.

— The Monster's Handsome Face: Patty Cannon in Fiction & Fact. LC 98-65707. (Illus.). 243p. 1998. boxed set 19.95 (*0-9647694-2-5*) Nanticoke Bks.

— Nei-Yeh. 1999. pap. write for info. (*0-345-38371-0*) Ballantine Pub Grp.

— Two on a Big Ocean. LC 97-15416. 288p. 1997. reprint ed. pap. 15.95 (*0-9639566-4-7*, SW-HROTH1) Seaworthy WI.

— We Followed Odysseus. LC 98-56146. (Illus.). 256p. 1999. 27.95 (*1-892399-03-2*) Seaworthy WI.

— You Can't Never Get to Puckum: Folks & Tales from Delmarva. LC 97-91635. (Illus.). 192p. (Orig.). 1997. pap. 10.95 (*0-9647694-1-7*) Nanticoke Bks.

***Roth, Hal.** You Still Can't Get to Puckum: More Folks & Tales from Delmarva. (Illus.). 256p. 2000. 14.95 (*0-9647694-4-1*, Pub. by Nanticoke Bks) Wash Bk Distrib.

Roth, Hal, ed. & photos by see Townsend, George Alfred.

Roth, Hans-Dieter. Indian Moneylenders at Work. 1984. 18.50 (*0-8364-1106-4*, Pub. by Manohar) S Asia.

Roth, Harald H. & Merz, Unther G., eds. Wildlife Resources: The Economic Use. LC 96-23063. 416p. 1996. 139.50 (*3-540-61357-9*) Spr-Verlag.

***Roth, Harold D.** Original Tao: Inward Training (Nei-Yeh) & the Foundations of Taoist Mysticism. LC 99-20737. (Translations from the Asian Classics). 272p. 1999. 29.50 (*0-231-11564-4*) Col U Pr.

Roth, Harold D. The Textual History of the Huai-nan Tzu. LC 90-85256. (Monographs: No. 46). (CHI., Illus.). xvi, 470p. (Orig.). (C). 1992. pap. 20.00 (*0-924304-06-5*) Assn Asian Studies.

Roth, Harold P., jt. auth. see Morse, Wayne J.

Roth, Harriet. Harriet Roth's Cholesterol Control Cookbook. 1989. 18.95 (*0-317-02813-8*) NAL.

— Harriet Roth's Cholesterol-Control Cookbook. (Illus.). 440p. 1991. reprint ed. pap. 15.95 (*0-452-26612-2*, Plume) Dutton Plume.

— Harriet Roth's Deliciously Healthy Jewish Cooking: 350 New, Low-Fat, Low-Cholestorol, Low-Sodium Recipes for Holidays & Every Day. 400p. 1998. pap. 16.95 (*0-452-27349-8*, Plume) Dutton Plume.

— Harriet Roth's Fat Counter. 2nd rev. ed. (Illus.). 79p. 1999. mass mkt. 3.99 (*0-451-19745-3*, Sig) NAL.

Roth, Harrison. The Irwin Yearbook of Listed Stock Options. 1995. 320p. 1995. 90.00 (*0-7863-0336-0*, Irwn Prfssnl) McGraw-Hill Prof.

— LEAPS - Long-Term Equity Anticipation Securities: What They Are & How to Use Them for Profit & Protection. 360p. 1993. text 55.00 (*1-55623-819-3*, Irwn Prfssnl) McGraw-Hill Prof.

Roth, Henry. Call It Sleep. 448p. 1992. pap. 13.00 (*0-374-52292-8*) FS&G.

— Call It Sleep. large type ed. 655p. 1995. 24.95 (*0-7838-1564-6*, G K Hall Lrg Type) Mac Lib Ref.

— Call It Sleep. limited ed. (Illus.). 482p. 1995. 700.00 (*0-910457-30-1*) Arion Pr.

— Call It Sleep. 1995. reprint ed. lib. bdg. 29.95 (*1-56849-634-6*) Buccaneer Bks.

— A Diving Rock on the Hudson. LC 97-158964. Vol. 2. 432p. 1996. pap. 14.00 (*0-312-14085-1*, Picador USA) St Martin.

— A Diving Rock on the Hudson, 2 vols. 418p. 23.95 (*0-614-32255-3*) St Martin.

— From Bondage. (Mercy of a Rude Stream Ser.: Vol. 3). 416p. 1997. pap. 15.00 (*0-312-15532-8*) St Martin.

— From Bondage, Vol. III. LC 97-158971. (Mercy of a Rude Stream Ser.: Vol. 3). 432p. 1996. text 25.95 (*0-312-14341-9*) St Martin.

— Mercy of a Rude Stream: A Star Shines over Mt. Morris Park. LC 94-45086. Vol. 1. 1994. pap. 13.00 (*0-312-11929-1*) St Martin.

— Requiem for Harlem. LC 97-17824. (Mercy of a Rude Stream Ser.). 304p. 1998. text 24.95 (*0-312-16980-9*) St Martin.

— Violin Virtuosos: From Paganini to the 21st Century. (Illus.). 400p. (Orig.). 1997. pap. 29.95 (*1-879395-15-0*) CA Classics Bks.

— Violin Virtuosos: From Paganini to the 21st Century. (Illus.). 396p. (Orig.). 1997. 44.95 (*1-879395-18-5*) CA Classics Bks.

Roth, Henry H. The Cruz Chronicle: A Novel. (Fiction Ser.). 184p. (C). 1991. reprint ed. pap. 10.95 (*0-8135-1750-8*) Rutgers U Pr.

— In Empty Rooms: Tales of Love. LC 79-50422. (Illus.). 102p. 1980. pap. 15.00 (*0-913204-11-0*) December Pr.

Roth, Henry L. The Natives of Sarawak & British North Borneo, 2 vols., Set. LC 77-87510. reprint ed. 75.00 (*0-404-16780-2*) AMS Pr.

Roth, I. Stratification of a Tropical Forest As Seen in Dispersal Types. (Tasks for Vegetation Science Ser.). 1987. text 316.50 (*90-6193-613-6*) Kluwer Academic.

— Stratification of Tropical Forests As Seen in Leaf Structure. (Tasks for Vegetation Science Ser.). 1984. text 386.50 (*90-6193-946-1*) Kluwer Academic.

Roth, Ilona & Bruce, Vicki. Perception & Representation: Current Issues. 2nd ed. LC 94-41284. 224p. 1995. 32.95 (*0-335-19474-5*) OpUniv Pr.

Roth, Ingrid. Fruits of the Angiosperms. (Handbuch der Pflanzenanatomie Encyclopedia of Plant Anatomy - Traite d' Anatomie Vegetale Ser.: Vol. 10, Pt. 1). (Illus.). xvi, 675p. 1977. 170.00 (*3-443-14010-6*, Pub. by Gebruder Borntraeger) Balogh.

— Leaf Structure: Coastal Vegetation & Mangroves of Venezuela. (Handbuch der Pflanzenanatomie Encyclopedia of Plant Anatomy - Traite d' Anatomie Vegetale Ser.: Vol. 14, Pt. 2). (Illus.). x, 172p. 1992. 80.00 (*3-443-14020-3*, Pub. by Gebruder Borntraeger) Balogh.

— Leaf Structure: Montane Regions of Venezuela. LC 96-105750. (Handbuch der Pflanzenanatomie Encyclopedia of Plant Anatomy - Traite d' Anatomie Vegetale Ser.: Vol. 14, Pt. 3). (Illus.). x, 250p. 1995. 111.00 (*3-443-14022-X*, Pub. by Gebruder Borntraeger) Balogh.

— Leaf Structure of a Venezuelan Cloud Forest, in Relation to the Microclimate. (Handbuch der Pflanzenanatomie

Encyclopedia of Plant Anatomy - Traite d' Anatomie Vegetale Ser.: Vol. 14, Pt. 1). (Illus.). xi, 244p. 1990. 88.00 (*3-443-14018-1*, Pub. by Gebruder Borntraeger) Balogh.

— Microscopic Venation Patterns of Leaves & Their Importance in the Distinction of Tropical Species. LC 96-185014. (Handbuch der Pflanzenanatomie Encyclopedia of Plant Anatomy - Traite d' Anatomie Vegetale Ser.: Vol. 14, Pt. 4). (Illus.). viii, 196p. 1996. 99.00 (*3-443-14023-8*, Pub. by Gebruder Borntraeger) Balogh.

— Structural Patterns of Tropical Barks. (Handbuch der Pflanzenanatomie Encyclopedia of Plant Anatomy - Traite d' Anatomie Vegetale Ser.: Vol. 9, Pt. 3). (Illus.). xvi, 609p. 1981. 170.00 (*3-443-14012-2*, Pub. by Gebruder Borntraeger) Balogh.

Roth, Ingrid & Gimbenez de Bolzbon, Ana-Maria. Argentine Chaco Forests: Dendrology, Tree Structure & Economic Use. LC 98-124447. (Encyclopedia of Plant Anatomy Ser.). 1997. write for info. (*3-443-14025-4*) Gebruder Borntraeger.

Roth, Irene. Cecil Roth, Historian Without Tears: A Memoir. (Illus.). 288p. 1982. 17.50 (*0-87203-103-9*) Hermon.

Roth, J., et al, eds. Polysialic Acid: From Microbes to Men. LC 92-48982. (Advances in Life Sciences Ser.). xxiii, 350p. 1992. 109.50 (*0-8176-2803-7*, Pub. by Birkhauser) Princeton Arch.

Roth, J. D., et al. Propagation of Mammalian Cells in Culture, Vol. I. 1976. text 39.50 (*0-8422-7290-9*) Irvington.

Roth, J. Paul. Mathematical Design: Building Reliable Complex Computer Systems. LC 98-17152. 144p. 1998. 69.95 (*0-7803-3430-2*, PC5706-QOE) Inst Electrical.

Roth, J. Reece. Applications, 2. 1999. 45.00 (*0-7503-0545-2*) IOP Pub.

— Industrial Plasma Engineering. (Illus.). 560p. 1995. 176.00 (*0-7503-0317-4*) IOP Pub.

— Industrial Plasma Engineering. Vol. 1. (Illus.). 560p. 1995. pap. 46.00 (*0-7503-0318-2*) IOP Pub.

— Introduction to Fusion Energy. 600p. 1986. lib. bdg. 57.95 (*0-935005-07-2*) Lincoln-Rembrandt.

Roth, Jack, et al. Thoracic Oncology. 2nd ed. LC 94-26869. (Illus.). 608p. 1995. text 145.00 (*0-7216-4769-3*, W B Saunders Co) Harcrt Hlth Sci Grp.

Roth, Jack A., et al. Lung Cancer. 2nd ed. LC 97-37264. (Illus.). 1998. 110.00 (*0-86542-573-6*) Blackwell Sci.

Roth, James, ed. Virulence Mechanisms. 2nd ed. 500p. 1995. 69.00 (*1-55581-085-3*) ASM Pr.

Roth, James & Institute of Internal Auditors. Research Foundation. Control Model Implementation: Best Practices. LC 97-222262. (Illus.). 1997. write for info. (*0-89413-390-X*) Inst Inter Aud.

Roth, James F., jt. ed. see Forster, Denis.

Roth, James P. COSO Implementation Guide. Campbell, Lee A., ed. (CIP Ser.). 1995. pap., teacher ed. 450.00 (*0-89413-334-9*, A6067); pap., wbk. ed. 15.00 (*0-89413-335-7*, A7011) Inst Inter Aud.

Roth, Jane L., jt. auth. see Ringenberg, Margaret J.

Roth, Jane R., et al. Federal Appellate Procedure - 3rd Circuit: Federal Practice Guide. LC 96-77617. (American Inns of Court Ser.). 1500p. 1996. text. write for info. (*0-7620-0097-X*) West Group.

Roth, Janice L. Charting: The Systematic Approach to Achieving Control. 38p. 1994. pap. 6.95 (*0-9631701-0-4*) R A Rapaport.

Roth, Jay S. All about AIDS. xviii, 300p. (C). 1989. pap. text 49.00 (*3-7186-0488-4*) Gordon & Breach.

— All about Cancer. LC 85-50. (Illus.). 341p. (Orig.). 1985. text 24.95 (*0-397-53068-4*) Lppncott W & W.

— All about Cancer. LC 82-61760. (Illus.). 348p. (Orig.). 1985. reprint ed. pap. 107.90 (*0-608-05877-7*, 205984300007) Bks Demand.

Roth, Jeffrey. The Disturbed Subject: Epistemological & Ethical Implication of Reactivity in Videotape Research. (American University Studies: Psychology: Ser. VIII, Vol. 20). 144p. 1989. text 30.50 (*0-8204-1150-7*) P Lang Pubng.

Roth, Jeffrey A., et al, eds. Taxpayer Compliance, Vol. 1. LC 88-36250. (Law in Social Context Ser.). 414p. 1989. text 49.50 (*0-8122-8182-9*) U of Pa Pr.

— Taxpayer Compliance, Vol. 2. LC 88-36250. (Law in Social Context Ser.). 282p. 1989. text 47.50 (*0-8122-8150-0*) U of Pa Pr.

Roth, Jeffrey A., et al. Compendium of Federal Justice Statistics (1993) (Illus.). 131p. (Orig.). (C). 1997. pap. text 40.00 (*0-7881-3762-X*) DIANE Pub.

Roth, Jeffrey A., ed. see National Research Council, Panel on the Understand.

Roth, Jeffrey A., ed. see National Research Council Staff.

Roth, Jennifer. The Two Princesses: Sleeping Beauty & Beauty & the Beast. abr. large type ed. (Illus.). 32p. (Orig.). (J). (gr. k up). 1995. pap. 14.95 (*1-886201-00-5*) Nana Banana.

Roth, Joachim, jt. ed. see Hofer, Wolfgang O.

Roth, Joan. Jewish Women: A World of Tradition & Changes. Lyons, Harriet, ed. (Illus.). 242p. 1995. 75.00 (*0-942160-12-6*) Jolen Pr.

— Jewish Women: A World of Tradition & Changes. deluxe ed. Lyons, Harriet, ed. (Illus.). 242p. 1995. 75.00 (*0-942160-11-8*) Jolen Pr.

***Roth, Joan.** Jews of Ethiopia: Last Days of an Ancient Community. 2000. 65.00 (*0-942160-03-7*) S Tilatitsky.

Roth, Joan. Shopping Bag Ladies of New York. Walter, Robert, ed. LC 81-85387. (Illus.). 122p. (Orig.). 1982. pap. 10.95 (*0-942160-00-2*) Jolen Pr.

Roth, Joel. The Halakhic Process: A Systemic Analysis. (Moreshet Ser.: No. XIII). 1987. 35.00 (*0-87334-035-3*) Jewish Sem.

***Roth, John.** The Ghost of the Flea of Sodam. unabridged ed. 79p. 2000. pap. 7.00 (*0-9675939-2-1*, 3) Westron Pr.

***Roth, John, et al, eds.** The Holocaust Chronicle: A History in Words & Pictures. LC 99-67861. (Illus.). 765p. 2000. 35.00 (*0-7853-2963-3*) Pubns Intl Ltd.

Roth, John, jt. ed. see Magill, Frank N.

Roth, John, jt. ed. see Rittner, Carol K.

Roth, John E. American Elves: An Encyclopedia of Little People from the Lore of 340 Ethnic Groups of the Western Hemisphere. LC 95-5886. (Illus.). 341p. 1997. lib. bdg. 68.50 (*0-89950-944-4*) McFarland & Co.

Roth, John K. Encyclopedia of Social Issues, 6 vols., Set. LC 96-38361. 1997. 657.07 (*0-7614-0568-2*) Marshall Cavendish.

— Ethics. (Magill Bibliographies Ser.). 169p. 1991. 42.00 (*0-8108-2788-3*) Scarecrow.

— Private Needs, Public Selves: Talk about Religion in America. LC 97-4613. (Public Expressions of Religion in America Ser.). 264p. 1997. 17.95 (*0-252-06651-0*); text 29.95 (*0-252-01933-4*) U of Ill Pr.

***Roth, John K.** World Philosophers & Their Works. LC 99-55143. 2000. write for info. (*0-89356-879-1*); write for info. (*0-89356-880-5*) Salem Pr.

— World Philosophers & Their Works, 3 vols., Set. LC 99-55143. 2000. write for info. (*0-89356-881-3*) Salem Pr.

Roth, John K., ed. American Diversity, American Identity: The Lives & Works of 145 Writers Who Define the American Experience. (Reference Bks.). 736p. 1995. 45.00 (*0-8050-3430-7*) H Holt & Co.

***Roth, John K., ed.** Ethics after the Holocaust: Perspectives, Critiques & Responses. LC 99-10543. 358p. (Orig.). 1999. pap. 18.95 (*1-55778-771-9*) Paragon Hse.

Roth, John K., ed. Inspiring Teaching: Carnegie Professors of the Year Speak. LC 97-118492. 264p. (C). 1996. 35.95 (*1-882982-14-2*) Anker Pub.

— International Encyclopedia of Ethics. 1995. lib. bdg. 175.00 (*1-884964-38-9*) Fitzroy Dearborn.

Roth, John K. & Berenbaum, Michael, eds. Holocaust: Religious & Philosophical Implications. 416p. 1989. pap. 18.95 (*1-55778-212-1*) Paragon Hse.

Roth, John K. & Rubenstein, Richard L. Approaches to Auschwitz: The Holocaust & Its Legacy. LC 86-27749. 420p. 1987. pap. 28.95 (*0-8042-0777-1*) Westminster John Knox.

Roth, John K. & Sontag, Frederick, eds. The Defense of God. (God: The Contemporary Discussion Ser.). 164p. 1991. 24.95 (*0-913757-26-8*); pap. 12.95 (*0-913757-27-6*) Paragon Hse.

Roth, John K., jt. auth. see Rittner, Carol A.

Roth, John K., jt. ed. see Fossum, Robert H.

Roth, John K., jt. ed. see Haynes, Stephen R.

Roth, John K., jt. ed. see Peden, Creighton.

Roth, John K., jt. ed. see Rittner, Carol A.

Roth, John K., jt. ed. see Rittner, Carol.

Roth, John K., ed. see Salem Press Editors.

Roth, John K., ed. & intro. see Royce, Josiah.

Roth, Jonathan. The Logistics of the Roman Army at War (264 B. C.-A. D. 235) LC 98-42368. (Columbia Studies in the Classical Tradition). 1998. 123.50 (*90-04-11271-5*) Brill Academic Pubs.

Roth, Jonathan & Roth, Andrew. Poetic Justice: The Funniest, Meanest Things Ever Said About Lawyers. LC 87-63575. 128p. (Orig.). 1994. pap. 9.95 (*0-87337-072-4*) Nolo com.

Roth, Jordan. Black Belt Karate. (Illus.). 380p. 1992. pap. 24.95 (*0-8048-1851-7*) Tuttle Pubng.

— Black Belt Karate. 22.95 (*0-685-47545-X*) Wehman.

Roth, Joseph. Confession of a Murderer. LC 84-20580. 224p. 1985. 22.50 (*0-87951-989-4*, Pub. by Overlook Pr) Penguin Putnam.

— Confession of a Murderer. LC 84-20580. 224p. 1987. pap. 9.95 (*0-87951-287-3*, Pub. by Overlook Pr) Penguin Putnam.

— The Emperor's Tomb. Hoare, John, tr. from GER. LC 84-5663. 157p. 1987. 22.50 (*0-87951-985-1*, Pub. by Overlook Pr); pap. 12.95 (*0-87951-270-9*, Pub. by Overlook Pr) Penguin Putnam.

— Flight Without End. LeVay, David, tr. LC 76-47077. 144p. 1977. 22.50 (*0-87951-057-9*, Pub. by Overlook Pr) Penguin Putnam.

— Flight Without End. LeVay, David, tr. LC 76-47077. 144p. 1987. pap. 12.95 (*0-87951-279-2*, Pub. by Overlook Pr) Penguin Putnam.

— Flight Without End. LeVay, David, tr. 144p. 1987. 8.95 (*0-317-60441-4*, Penguin Bks) Viking Penguin.

— Hotel Savoy. Hoare, John, tr. from GER. LC 86-125. 192p. 1986. 22.95 (*0-87951-211-3*, Pub. by Overlook Pr) Penguin Putnam.

— Hotel Savoy. 192p. 1988. pap. 13.95 (*0-87951-330-6*, Pub. by Overlook Pr) Penguin Putnam.

— Job: The Story of a Simple Man. Thompson, Dorothy, tr. from GER. LC 81-18901. 252p. 1982. reprint ed. 22.50 (*0-87951-149-4*, Pub. by Overlook Pr) Penguin Putnam.

— Job: The Story of a Simple Man. Thompson, Dorothy, tr. from GER. LC 81-18901. 252p. 1985. reprint ed. pap. 13.95 (*0-87951-202-4*, Pub. by Overlook Pr) Penguin Putnam.

— The Radetzky March. 1996. 18.00 (*0-679-45100-5*) McKay.

— The Radetzky March. Tucker, Eva & Dunlop, Geoffrey, trs. from GER. LC 72-97581. 324p. 1983. 22.50 (*0-87951-198-2*, Pub. by Overlook Pr); pap. 12.95 (*0-87951-189-3*, Pub. by Overlook Pr) Penguin Putnam.

— The Radetzky March. Neugroschel, Joachim, tr. from GER. 352p. 1995. 25.00 (*0-87951-548-1*, Pub. by Overlook Pr); pap. 14.95 (*0-87951-558-9*, Pub. by Overlook Pr) Penguin Putnam.

***Roth, Joseph.** Rebellion. Hofmann, Michael, tr. from GER. LC 99-33996. 160p. 1999. text 21.95 (*0-312-20574-0*) St Martin.

— Rebellion. 2000. pap. 12.00 (*0-312-26383-X*, Picador USA) St Martin.

Roth, Joseph. Right & Left & The Legend of the Holy Drinker. Hofmann, Michael, tr. 320p. 1992. 23.95 (*0-87951-448-5*, Pub. by Overlook Pr) Penguin Putnam.

— Right & Left & the Legend of the Holy Drinker. Hoffman, Michael, tr. 304p. 1993. pap. 13.95 (*0-87951-456-6*, Pub. by Overlook Pr) Penguin Putnam.

— The Silent Prophet. Le Vay, David, tr. 224p. 1990. pap. 11.95 (*0-87951-384-5*, Pub. by Overlook Pr) Penguin Putnam.

— The Spider's Web & Zipper & His Father. Hoare, John, tr. from GER. (ENG.). 224p. 1990. 22.95 (*0-87951-345-4*, Pub. by Overlook Pr) Penguin Putnam.

— The Spider's Web & Zipper & His Father. 224p. 1991. reprint ed. pap. 11.95 (*0-87951-361-6*, Pub. by Overlook Pr) Penguin Putnam.

***Roth, Joseph.** The Tale of the 1002nd Night. 272p. 1999. pap. 14.00 (*0-312-24494-0*, Picador USA) St Martin.

Roth, Joseph. The Tale of the 1002nd Night: A Novel. Hofmann, Michael, tr. LC 98-20032. 272p. 1998. text 23.95 (*0-312-19341-6*) St Martin.

— Tarabas. Katzin, Winifred, tr. from GER. LC 86-31239. 280p. 1987. reprint ed. 18.95 (*0-87951-275-X*, Pub. by Overlook Pr) Penguin Putnam.

— Tarabas: A Guest on Earth. 280p. 1989. pap. 10.95 (*0-87951-299-7*, Pub. by Overlook Pr) Penguin Putnam.

***Roth, Joseph.** Wandering Jews. 144p. 2000. 23.95 (*0-393-04901-9*) Norton.

Roth, Judith P., jt. auth. see Helsel, Sandra K.

Roth, Julee. Get Ready, Get Set, Go! An Advanced Sailing Manual. (Illus.). 193p. (Orig.). (YA). (gr. 7-12). 1993. pap. text 15.95 (*0-9637423-0-2*) JRC Pubns.

Roth, Julian A., jt. auth. see Douglas, Dorothy J.

Roth, Julius A. Health Purifiers & Their Enemies: A Study of the Natural Health Movement in the United States with a Comparison to Its Counterpart in Germany. LC 77-2210. 1977. 15.00 (*0-88202-117-6*); pap. 5.95 (*0-686-67897-4*) Watson Pub Intl.

— Timetables: Structuring the Passage of Time in Hospital Treatment & Other Careers. (Orig.). 1963. pap. 4.95 (*0-672-60851-0*, Bobbs) Macmillan.

Roth, Julius A. & Douglas, Dorothy. No Appointment Necessary: The Hospital Emergency Department in the Medical Services World. 324p. 1983. pap. text 27.50 (*0-8290-1255-9*) Irvington.

Roth, June. How to Cook Like a Jewish Mother. 152p. 1993. 5.98 (*1-55521-899-7*) Bk Sales Inc.

Roth, Jurgen, jt. auth. see Berger, Eric G.

Roth, Jurgen, jt. ed. see Berger, Eric G.

Roth, K., et al, eds. Field-Scale Water & Solute Flux in Soils. (Monte Verita Ser.). 304p. 1991. 86.00 (*0-8176-2510-0*) Birkhauser.

Roth, K., jt. auth. see Halberstam, H.

Roth, K., jt. auth. see Jury, W. A.

Roth, K. Madsen, ed. Hollywood Wits. LC 94-47041. 224p. (Orig.). 1995. pap. 7.50 (*0-380-77765-7*, Avon Bks) Morrow Avon.

Roth, Karen. The Naturalist Intelligence. LC 98-151321. (Illus.). 36p. 1998. pap. 6.95 (*1-57517-078-7*, 1584A) SkyLght.

Roth, Karl S., jt. auth. see Cohn, Robert M.

Roth, Kathleen B. Celine: A Circle of Life. (Illus.). 328p. 1997. pap. write for info. (*1-890184-09-8*) Gothic Pub.

Roth, Kevin. Kevin Roth Songbook. (Illus.). 36p. (J). (gr. k-6). 1995. pap. text 16.95 incl. audio (*0-931759-97-8*) Centerstream Pub.

Roth, Kevin, jt. auth. see Reed, Bella.

Roth, Klaus & Wolf, Gabriele. South Slavic Folk Culture: A Bibliography of Literature in English, German, & French. (ENG, FRE & GER.). 553p. 1994. 29.95 (*0-89357-244-6*) Slavica.

Roth, Kurt & Dwight, Jeffry, eds. Age of Reason: Stories for a New Millennium. (Darkfire Ser.: Vol. 2). 290p. 1999. 75.00 (*0-9669698-2-0*); pap. 14.95 (*0-9669698-1-2*) S F F Net.

Roth, L. O. An Introduction to Agricultural Engineering. 346p. 1994. pap. 49.00 (*0-8342-1308-7*) Aspen Pub.

Roth, Larry. Beating the System: The Next American Revolution. LC 95-94536. (Illus.). 318p. (Orig.). 1995. pap. 17.95 (*0-9625228-3-X*) Living Cheap.

— The Best of "Living Cheap News" LC 96-16029. (Illus.). 256p. 1996. pap. 14.95 (*0-8092-3188-3*, 318830, Contemporary Bks) NTC Contemp Pub Co.

— Living Cheap: The Survival Guide for the 'Nineties. LC 90-91568. (Illus.). 130p. (Orig.). 1990. pap. 14.95 (*0-9625228-1-3*) Living Cheap.

— Living Cheap News: The First Two Years. LC 93-81070. 104p. (Orig.). 1994. pap. 11.95 (*0-9625228-2-1*) Living Cheap.

— Simple Life. LC 98-146179. 272p. 1998. pap. 13.00 (*0-425-16168-4*) Berkley Pub.

Roth, Larry, compiled by. The Best of "Living Cheap News" Practical Advice on Saving Money & Living Well. (Orig.). 1996. pap. 14.95 (*0-614-20828-9*) NTC Contemp Pub Co.

Roth, Larry M. & Rahdert, George K. Appeals to the Eleventh Circuit Manual, 98-2. 300p. 1998. ring bd. write for info. (*0-327-00614-5*, 8015222) LEXIS Pub.

— Appeals to the Eleventh Circuit Manual 98-3, 3 vols. 396p. 1998. write for info. (*0-327-00819-9*, 8015223) LEXIS Pub.

— Appeals to the Eleventh Circuit, 1984-1994, 3 vols., Set. 100p. 1997. ring bd. 180.00 (*0-409-26067-3*, 80147-10, MICHIE) LEXIS Pub.

Roth, Larry M., jt. auth. see Rahdert, George K.

Roth, Laszlo. A Basic Guide to Plastics for Designers, Technicians, & Crafts People. (Illus.). 192p. 1985. 22.95 (*0-13-062373-3*) P-H.

Roth, Laszlo & Wybenga, George. The Packaging Designer's Book of Patterns. (Illus.). 496p. 1991. pap. 46.95 (*0-442-00524-5*, VNR) Wiley.

***Roth, Laszlo & Wybenga, George L.** The Packaging Designer's Book of Patterns. rev. ed. 608p. 2000. pap. 54.95 (*0-471-38504-2*) Wiley.

— Packaging Designer's Book of Patterns. 2nd ed. 496p. 1991. pap. 54.95 (*0-471-28411-4*, VNR) Wiley.

Roth, Laura, ed. see Rinpoche, Khempo K. & Gampopa.

Roth, Laura M. & Inomata, Akira. Fundamental Questions in Quantum Mechanics: Selected Papers from the Fundamental Questions in Quantum Mechanics Symposium, Albany, NY, April 12-14, 1984. x, 33p. 1986. text 277.00 (*2-88124-058-5*) Gordon & Breach.

Roth, Laura M., ed. see Karthar, Khenpo.

Roth, Laurie M. A Critical Examination of the Dual Ladder Approach to Career Advancement. 1982. pap. 12.00 (*0-317-11510-3*) CU Ctr Career Res.

— Managing the Technical Workforce: A Study of Computer Professionals. 1984. pap. 17.50 (*0-317-11514-6*) CU Ctr Career Res.

Roth, Lawrence, jt. auth. see Field, Harry.

Roth, Leland M. Concise Hist of Amern Archit. LC 78-2169. (Icon Editions Ser.). (Illus.). 400p. 1980. pap. 40.00 (*0-06-430086-2*, IN-86, Icon Edns) HarpC.

Roth, Leland M. Understanding Architecture: Its Elements, History & Meaning. 542p. 1994. text. write for info. (*976-8097-65-5*, Harwood Acad Pubs) Gordon & Breach.

— Understanding Architecture: Its Elements, History & Meaning. LC 88-45540. (Illus.). 576p. 1993. pap. 40.00 (*0-06-430158-3*, Perennial) HarperTrade.

Roth, Leland M. Understanding Architecture: Its Elements, History, Meaning. LC 88-45540. (Illus.). 576p. 1993. 45.00 (*0-00-001606-3*, Perennial) HarperTrade.

Roth, Leland M. & Morgan, Bret. Shingle Styles: Innovation & Tradition in American Architecture 1874 to 1984. LC 99-14102. 240p. 1999. 49.50 (*0-8109-4477-4*, Pub. by Abrams) Time Warner.

Roth, Leo. Jim Kelly: Star Quarterback. LC 93-38637. (Sports Reports Ser.). 104p. (J). (gr. 4-10). 1994. lib. bdg. 20.95 (*0-89490-446-9*) Enslow Pubs.

Roth, Leo, jt. ed. see Duwe, Gert.

Roth, Leon. Is There a Jewish Philosophy? Rethinking Fundamentals. LC 98-39901. 192p. 1999. pap. 21.95 (*1-874774-55-2*) Intl Spec Bk.

Roth, Lewis D., ed. see Symposium on Applications of Artificial Intelligen.

Roth, Lloyd J., ed. see International Conference on the Uses of Isotopical.

Roth, Lois, tr. see Sjowall, Maj & Wahloo, Per.

Roth, Loren, jt. auth. see Daley, Dennis.

Roth, Loren H., ed. Clinical Treatment of the Violent Person. LC 86-19543. 270p. 1987. pap. text 25.00 (*0-89862-914-4*) Guilford Pubns.

Roth, Lutz & Rump, Gabriele, eds. Roth Collection of Natural Products Data: Concise Descriptions & Spectra. 511p. 1995. pap. 275.00 (*3-527-28180-0*, Wiley-VCH) Wiley.

Roth, M., et al, eds. Clinical Biochemistry Vol. 1: Principles - Methods - Applications: Mass Spectrometry. (Illus.). xx, 745p. (C). 1989. 253.85 (*3-11-007751-5*) De Gruyter.

Roth, M., jt. ed. see Hansen, Heine H.

Roth, M. Georgene. Unspoken Love. 304p. 1998. pap. 14.95 (*0-9666264-2-7*) BioMed Intl.

Roth, Marcia, jt. ed. see Pollock, Mary.

***Roth, Marie-Louise.** Neue Ansatze Zur Robert-Musil-Forschung: Wiener Kolloquium Zum 20-Jahrigen Bestehen der Internationalen Robert-Musil-Gesellschaft. (Musiliana Ser.). 215p. 1999. 35.95 (*3-906762-74-2*, Pub. by P Lang) P Lang Pubng.

***Roth, Marie-Louise, ed.** Literatur Im Kontext Robert Musil Litterature dans le Contexte de Robert Musil. (Musiliana Ser.: Bd. 6). 366p. 1999. 53.95 (*3-906761-93-2*, Pub. by P Lang) P Lang Pubng.

Roth, Mark, et al. 30 Bicycle Tours in the Finger Lakes Region. 3rd ed. LC 97-43220. (Bicycle Tour Ser.). (Illus.). 212p. 1998. pap. 15.00 (*0-88150-411-4*, Pub. by Countryman) Norton.

Roth, Marlene, jt. auth. see Simmons, Warren.

Roth, Martha. Arousal: Bodies & Pleasure. LC 97-45983. 200p. 1998. 20.00 (*1-57131-220-X*) Milkweed Ed.

— Goodness. 320p. (Orig.). 1996. pap. 10.95 (*1-883523-11-7*) Spinsters Ink.

Roth, Martha, et al, eds. Mother Journeys: Feminists Write about Mothering. LC 94-18338. (Illus.). 352p. (C). 1994. pap. 15.95 (*1-883523-03-6*) Spinsters Ink.

***Roth, Martha T.** The Assyrian Dictionary of the Oriental Institute of the University of Chicago, No. 14R. LC 56-58292. 472p. 1999. write for info. (*1-885923-14-7*) Orient Inst.

Roth, Martha T., et al, eds. The Assyrian Dictionary of the Oriental Institute of the University of Chicago, Vol. 4E. LC 56-58292. (AKK.). xiv, 435p. 1958. reprint ed. text 60.00 (*0-918986-10-9*) Orient Inst.

— The Assyrian Dictionary of the Oriental Institute of the University of Chicago, Vol. 17, Pt. 3S. LC 56-58292. xxxiv, 420p. 1992. text 130.00 (*0-918986-79-6*) Orient Inst.

Roth, Martin. Strictly Murder: A Writer's Guide to Criminal Homicide. LC 98-11877. 208p. 1998. pap. 16.95 (*1-890085-03-0*) Siles Pr.

— The Writer's Complete Crime Reference Book. rev. ed. 304p. 1993. 19.99 (*0-89879-564-8*, Wrtrs Digest Bks) F & W Pubns Inc.

— The Writer's Partner: For Fiction, Television, & Screen. 2nd ed. 346p. (Orig.). 1997. pap. 19.95 (*1-56866-148-7*) Index Pub Grp.

Roth, Martin & Cowie, Valerie, eds. Psychiatry, Genetics & Pathography: A Tribute to Eliot Slater. LC 79-20997. 247p. reprint ed. pap. 76.60 (*0-7837-4917-1*, 204458200004) Bks Demand.

Roth, Martin, jt. auth. see Stevens, John.

R

R

Roth, Martin, ed. see Huppert, Felicia A., et al.

Roth, Marty. Foul & Fair Play: Reading Genre in Classic Detective Fiction. LC 93-30367. 312p. 1994. 45.00 (*0-8203-1622-9*) U of Ga Pr.

Roth, Matthew, jt. auth. see Clouette, Bruce.

Roth, Matthew W. Platt Brothers & Company: Small Business in American Manufacturing. LC 93-11001. (Illus.). 272p. reprint ed. pap. 84.40 (*0-608-09094-8*, 206972800005) Bks Demand.

Roth, Melissa. On the Loose: Big-City Days & Nights of Three Single Women. LC 98-49942. 256p. 1999. 23.00 (*0-688-15801-3*, Wm Morrow) Morrow Avon.

Roth, Michael. The Poetics of Resistance: Heidegger's Line. LC 96-378. (Studies in Phenomenology & Existential Philosophy). (Illus.). 420p. 1996. 75.00 (*0-8101-1317-1*); pap. 29.95 (*0-8101-1318-X*) Northwestern U Pr.

Roth, Michael, ed. Freud: Conflict & Culture. LC 98-12373. (Illus.). 288p. 1998. 26.00 (*0-679-45116-1*) Knopf.

— Freud: Conflict & Culture. 304p. 2000. pap. 14.00 (*0-679-77292-8*) Vin Bks.

— Land Tenure, Land Markets, & Institutional Transformation in Zambia. (Research Papers: No. 124). xi, 267p. 1995. 12.00 (*0-934519-37-4*, RP 124) U of Wis Land.

Roth, Michael, et al. Land Markets, Employment, & Resource Use in the Peri-Urban Green Zones of Maputo, Mozambique: A Case Study of Land Market Rigidities & Institutional Constraints to Economic Growth. (Research Paper Ser.: Vol. 123). (Illus.). xxxi, 122p. (C). 1995. pap. 7.00 (*0-934519-36-6*, RP123) U of Wis Land.

— Land Rights & Intra-Household Employment & Resource Use in the Peri-Urban Area of Banjul, the Gambia. (Research Papers: No. 126). (Illus.). 110p. 1996. 7.00 (*0-934519-39-0*, RP 126) U of Wis Land.

— Tenure Security, Credit Use, & Farm Investment in the Rujumbura Pilot Land Registration Scheme, Rukungiri District, Uganda. (Research Paper Ser.: Vol. 112). iii, 46p. (C). 1993. pap. 4.00 (*0-934519-23-4*, RP112) U of Wis Land.

Roth, Michael, jt. auth. see Barrows, Richard.

Roth, Michael, ed. see Merquior, Jose G.

Roth, Michael, ed. see Post, Robert.

Roth, Michael D. & Galis, Leon, eds. Knowing: Essays in the Analysis of Knowledge. 246p. 1984. reprint ed. pap. text 21.00 (*0-8191-4262-X*) U Pr of Amer.

Roth, Michael D. & Ross, Glenn, eds. Doubting: Contemporary Perspectives on Skepticism. (Philosophical Studies). 225p. (C). 1990. lib. bdg. 118.00 (*0-7923-0576-0*, Pub. by Kluwer Academic) Kluwer Academic.

Roth, Michael G. Protein Expression in Animal Cells. 1994. 53.00 (*0-12-598560-6*) Acad Pr.

Roth, Michael R. & Bruce, John W. Land Tenure, Agrarian Structure, & Comparative Land Use Efficiency in Zimbabwe: Options for Land Tenure Reform & Land Redistribution. (Research Paper Ser.: Vol. 117). (Illus.). xi, 182p. (C). 1994. pap. 12.00 (*0-934519-28-5*, RP117) U of Wis Land.

Roth, Michael S. The Guide to Business Giving in Oregon: A Community Resource. 218p. (Orig.). (C). 1995. pap. text 35.00 (*0-9630866-2-6*) L&C Coll.

— The Ironist's Cage: Memory, Trauma, & the Construction of History. LC 95-5816. 1995. 54.50 (*0-231-10244-5*); pap. 18.50 (*0-231-10245-3*) Col U Pr.

— Knowing & History: Appropriations of Hegel in Twentieth-Century France. LC 87-47870. 272p. 1988. text 39.95 (*0-8014-2136-5*) Cornell U Pr.

— Psycho-Analysis As History: Negation & Freedom in Freud. LC 86-29192. 208p. 1987. 35.00 (*0-8014-1957-3*) Cornell U Pr.

— Psycho-Analysis As History: Negation & Freedom in Freud. 208p. 1995. pap. text 13.95 (*0-8014-8303-4*) Cornell U Pr.

Roth, Michael S., ed. Rediscovering History: Culture, Politics, & the Psyche. LC 93-33732. (Cultural Sitings Ser.). xx, 536p. 1994. 65.00 (*0-8047-2309-5*); pap. 24.95 (*0-8047-2313-3*) Stanford U Pr.

***Roth, Michael S. & Salas, Charles G., eds.** Disturbing Remains: Memory, History, & Crisis in the Twentieth Century. (Illus.). 288p. 2001. 39.95 (*0-89236-538-2*) J P Getty Trust.

Roth, Michael S., jt. ed. see Cohen, Ralph.

Roth, Michael S., jt. ed. see Gourevitch, Victor.

Roth, Michael S., ed. see Lyons, Claire L., et al.

Roth, Milton. Ship Modeling from Stem to Stern. 288p. 1988. pap. 18.95 (*0-07-155060-7*) McGraw.

— Ship Modeling from Stem to Stern. (Illus.). 288p. 1987. pap. 17.95 (*0-8306-2844-4*) McGraw-Hill Prof.

***Roth, Mitchel.** Historical Dictionary of Law Enforcement. LC 00-24646. 424p. 2000. lib. bdg. 97.00 (*0-313-30560-9*, GR0560) Greenwood.

Roth, Mitchel P. Historical Dictionary of War Journalism. LC 96-35024. 496p. 1997. lib. bdg. 89.50 (*0-313-29171-3*, Greenwood Pr) Greenwood.

Roth, Moira, ed. Rachel Rosenthal. LC 97-9332. (PAJ Bks.). (Illus.). 232p. 1997. pap. 19.95 (*0-8018-5629-9*); text 34.95 (*0-8018-5628-0*) Johns Hopkins.

Roth, Moira, intro. Difference Indifference. 184p. 1998. text 22.00 (*90-5701-251-0*, 810591); pap. text 18.00 (*90-5701-331-2*, 810592) Gordon & Breach.

Roth, Moria, jt. auth. see Jones, Kellie.

***Roth, Nancy.** Awake, My Soul! Meditating on Hymns for Year B. LC 99-51885. 1999. pap. write for info. (*0-89869-327-6*) Church Pub Inc.

Roth, Nancy. The Breath of God: An Approach to Prayer. LC 89-29785. 173p. 1990. pap. 9.95 (*0-936384-92-1*) Cowley Pubns.

— A Closer Walk: Meditating on Hymns for Year A. LC 98-38608. 1998. pap. write for info. (*0-89869-303-9*) Church Pub Inc.

— Organic Prayer: Cultivating Your Relationship with God. LC 93-12653. (Illus.). 167p. 1993. pap. 12.95 (*1-56101-077-4*) Cowley Pubns.

Roth, Nancy L. Mediations for Choir Members. LC 98-55964. (Faithful Servants Ser.). 96p. 1999. pap. 6.95 (*0-8192-1779-4*) Morehouse Pub.

— Praying: A Book for Children. (Illus.). 55p. (J). (gr. 3-7). 1991. pap. 8.95 (*0-89869-189-3*) Church Pub Inc.

Roth, Nancy L. & Fuller, Linda K., eds. Women & AIDS: Negotiating Safer Practices, Care, & Representation. LC 97-16980. 330p. 1997. 39.95 (*0-7890-6014-0*); pap. 19.95 (*1-56023-882-8*, Harrington Park) Haworth Pr.

Roth, Nancy L. & Hogan, Katie. Gendered Epidemic: Representations of Women in the Age of AIDS. LC 97-32081. 256p. 1998. pap. 21.99 (*0-415-91785-9*) Routledge.

— Gendered Epidemic: Representations of Women in the Age of AIDS. LC 97-32081. 256p. (C). 1998. 70.00 (*0-415-91784-0*) Routledge.

Roth-Nelson, Stephanie. S. E. E. K. Self-Esteem Enhancement Kit. LC 93-29345. 176p. (Orig.). 1993. pap. 14.95 (*0-942097-49-1*) Ctr Adolescent.

— The S. E. E. K. Journal: A Blank Book with Inspirational Quotations from S. E. E. K. (Self-Esteem Enhancement Kit) 60p. 1997. pap. 4.50 (*0-942097-30-0*) Ctr Adolescent.

Roth-Nelson, Stephanie & Conway, Nancy Jessop. S. E. E. K. Facilitator's Guide: Accompanies the Self-Esteem Enhancement Kit Workbook. 123p. (Orig.). 1994. pap., teacher ed. 29.95 (*0-942097-48-3*) Ctr Adolescent.

Roth-Nelson, Stephanie & Jessop Conway, Nancy. S. E. E. K. Facilitator's Guide: Group Exercises for the Self-Esteem Enhancement Kit (SEEK) Workbook. 2nd ed. 135p. (Orig.). (YA). (gr. 6-12). 1997. pap., teacher ed., wbk. ed. 34.95 (*0-942097-47-5*) Ctr Adolescent.

Roth, Norbert, jt. auth. see Frohn, Arnold.

Roth, Norman. Conversos, Inquisition & the Expulsion of the Jews from Spain. LC 94-23486. 448p. 1995. text 50.00 (*0-299-14230-2*) U of Wis Pr.

— Jews, Visigoths, & Muslims in Medieval Spain: Cooperation & Conflict. LC 94-18401. (Medieval Iberian Peninsula, Texts & Studies: Vol. 10). 1994. 82.00 (*90-04-09971-9*) Brill Academic Pubs.

***Roth, Olaf.** Die Opernlibretti Nach Dramen Gabriele d'Annunzios. 211p. 1998. 37.95 (*3-631-34232-2*) P Lang Pubng.

Roth, Otavio, ed. Children's Declaration of Human Rights. (Illus.). 45p. 1989. 9.95 (*0-685-50854-4*) Amnesty Intl USA.

Roth, Pam, ed. Data Warehousing & Decision Support Vol. 2: The State of the Art, Vol. 2. LC 95-69148. (Management & Technology Ser.). (Illus.). 212p. (Orig.). 1997. pap. 44.95 (*1-57109-010-X*) Spiral Books.

Roth, Pam & Juch, William, eds. Data Warehousing & Decision Support: The State of the Art. LC 95-69148. (Enterprise Computing Ser.). (Illus.). 200p. (Orig.). 1995. pap. 44.95 (*1-57109-005-3*) Spiral Books.

Roth, Patrice T., jt. auth. see Kopstein, Andrea N.

Roth, Patty. Enter at Your Own Risk! 8 Secrets for Parenting Through the Middle School Years. LC 98-53390. 192p. 1999. pap. 10.99 (*0-87788-207-X*, H Shaw Pubs) Waterbrook Pr.

Roth, Paul. Mastering Foreign Exchange & Money Markets: A Step-by-Step Guide to the Products, Applications & Risks. (FT Market Editions Ser.). (Illus.). 320p. (Orig.). 1997. pap. 75.00 (*0-273-62586-1*) F T P-H.

— Seneca Apocolocyntosis. (Latin Commentaries Ser.). 54p. (Orig.). (C). 1988. pap. text 6.00 (*0-929524-51-9*) Bryn Mawr Commentaries.

Roth, Paul A. Meaning & Method in the Social Sciences: A Case for Methodological Pluralism. LC 87-47718. 272p. 1987. text 42.50 (*0-8014-1941-7*); pap. text 15.95 (*0-8014-9605-5*) Cornell U Pr.

Roth, Paul B. Nothing Out There: Poems by Paul B. Roth. LC 96-60530. 80p. 1996. pap. 9.95 (*0-9632547-6-6*) Vida Pub.

Roth, Paul B., jt. auth. see Wiest, Philip W.

Roth, Paula, ed. Alcohol & Drugs Are Women's Issues Vol. 1: A Review of the Issues. LC 90-49988. (Copublished with Women's Action Alliance Ser.). (Illus.). 202p. 1991. 37.50 (*0-8108-2360-8*) Scarecrow.

— Alcohol & Drugs Are Women's Issues Vol. 2: The Model Program Guide, Vol. 2. (Illus.). 155p. 1991. 34.50 (*0-8108-2389-6*) Scarecrow.

Roth, Peter N. C++ Jump Start. ix, 87p. (Orig.). 1995. pap. 14.95 (*0-9655862-2-7*) Engr Objects.

Roth, Philip. American Pastoral. LC 97-35623. 423p. 1998. pap. 14.00 (*0-375-70142-7*) Vin Bks.

— The Anatomy Lesson. 304p. 1996. pap. 12.00 (*0-679-74902-0*) Random.

— The Anatomy Lesson. deluxe limited ed. LC 83-11645. 291p. 1983. text 60.00 (*0-374-10492-1*) FS&G.

— The Breast. LC 93-43498. 1994. pap. 10.00 (*0-679-74901-2*) Vin Bks.

— Conversations with Philip Roth. Searles, George J., ed. LC 91-48004. (Literary Conversations Ser.). 256p. 1992. text 39.50 (*0-87805-557-6*) U Pr of Miss.

— The Counterlife. LC 96-5468. 1996. pap. 12.00 (*0-679-74904-7*) Vin Bks.

— Deception. LC 96-46866. 1997. pap. 12.00 (*0-679-75294-3*) Random.

— The Facts: A Novelist's Autobiography. 328p. 1988. text 17.95 (*0-374-15212-8*) FS&G.

— The Facts: A Novelist's Autobiography. LC 96-28807. 1997. pap. 12.00 (*0-679-74905-5*) Vin Bks.

— The Facts: A Novelist's Autobiography. limited ed. 328p. 1988. text 75.00 (*0-374-15210-1*) FS&G.

— The Ghost Writer. LC 95-6782. 180p. 1995. pap. 11.00 (*0-679-74898-9*) Vin Bks.

— Goodbye, Columbus. (FRE.). 1980. pap. 11.95 (*0-7859-4130-4*) Fr & Eur.

— Goodbye, Columbus. 1995. 15.95 (*0-679-60159-7*) Random.

— Goodbye, Columbus & Five Short Stories. LC 93-1698. 1994. pap. 13.00 (*0-679-74826-1*) Random.

— Goodbye, Columbus & Other Stories. 21.95 (*0-8488-0622-0*) Amereon Ltd.

— The Great American Novel. 1995. pap. 14.00 (*0-679-74906-3*) Vin Bks.

— His Mistress's Voice. deluxe ed. Wheatcroft, John, ed. (Bucknell University Fine Editions). 60p. 1995. boxed set, lthr. 245.00 (*0-916375-21-8*) Press Alley.

***Roth, Philip.** The Human Stain. LC 99-89867. 368p. 2000. 26.00 (*0-618-05945-8*) HM.

— I Married a Communist. LC 98-16797. 326p. 1998. 26.00 (*0-395-93346-3*) HM.

— I Married a Communist. LC 99-18314. 336p. 1999. pap. 13.00 (*0-375-70721-2*) Vin Bks.

— I Married a Communist. limited ed. 1998. 150.00 (*0-395-95106-2*) HM.

Roth, Philip. Laisser Courir, Tome 1. (FRE.). 384p. 1983. pap. 15.95 (*0-7859-4186-X*, 2070374777) Fr & Eur.

— Laisser Courir, Tome II. (FRE.). 1983. pap. 17.95 (*0-7859-4187-8*) Fr & Eur.

— Letting Go. LC 97-6675. 1997. pap. 15.00 (*0-679-76417-8*) Vin Bks.

— My Life As a Man. LC 73-20847. 330p. 1974. write for info. (*0-03-012646-0*) Holt R&W.

— My Life As a Man. LC 75-312299. 6p. (J). 1974. 2.95 (*0-224-00987-7*) Jonathan Cape.

— My Life As a Man. LC 93-15504. 334p. 1994. pap. 12.00 (*0-679-74827-X*) Vin Bks.

— Operation Shylock. 1994. pap. 14.00 (*0-679-75029-0*) Vin Bks.

— Patrimony: A True Story. 1996. pap. 12.00 (*0-679-75293-5*) Vin Bks.

— Portnoy et Son Complexe. (FRE.). 1973. pap. 10.95 (*0-7859-4017-0*) Fr & Eur.

— Portnoy's Complaint. LC 94-16661. 288p. 1994. pap. 13.00 (*0-679-75645-0*) Vin Bks.

— The Prague Orgy. LC 95-24898. 96p. 1996. pap. 10.00 (*0-679-74903-9*) Knopf.

— The Professor of Desire. 1994. pap. 12.00 (*0-679-74900-4*) Vin Bks.

— Quand Elle Etait Gentille. (FRE.). 1985. pap. 19.95 (*0-7859-4233-5*) Fr & Eur.

— Sabbath's Theater. 451p. 1997. 29.99 (*0-7710-7586-3*) McCland & Stewart.

— Sabbath's Theater. 1996. pap. 15.00 (*0-679-77259-6*) McKay.

— Le Sein. (FRE.). 1984. pap. 10.95 (*0-7859-4215-7*) Fr & Eur.

— When She Was Good. LC 94-31360. 1995. pap. 13.00 (*0-679-75925-5*) Vin Bks.

Roth, Philip. Zuckerman Bound. abr. ed. 1988. audio 14.00 (*0-694-50958-2*, SWC 1768) HarperAudio.

Roth, Philip. Zuckerman Unbound. LC 95-6783. 1995. pap. 12.00 (*0-679-74899-7*) Vin Bks.

Roth, Philip, et al. The American West's Acid Rain Test. LC 85-50619. 60p. 1985. pap. text 10.00 (*0-915825-07-4*) World Resources Inst.

Roth, Philip, jt. auth. see Thomas, Dylan.

Roth, Philip A. Masonry in the Formation of Our Government, 1761-1799. 187p. 1996. reprint ed. pap. 17.95 (*1-56459-527-7*) Kessinger Pub.

Roth, Phyllis. Character Poems: A Supplement to the Manual "Job Wheels for Literature Talk Groups" (Illus.). 10p. (J). (gr. 2-6). 1997. spiral bd. 15.00 (*1-892593-02-5*) R & R Creat.

— Genre Poems for Childrens' Literature. (Illus.). 10p. (J). (gr. 2-6). 1998. spiral bd. 15.00 (*1-892593-01-7*) R & R Creat.

— A Literature Talk Play. 10p. 1997. teacher ed., spiral bd. 15.00 (*1-892593-03-3*) R & R Creat.

Roth, Phyllis & Potchka, Robin. Job Wheels for Literature Talk Groups: (Includes Student-Friendly Material to Help Generate Discussions about Book) (Illus.). i, 82p. 1996. teacher ed., spiral bd. 30.00 (*1-892593-00-9*) R & R Creat.

Roth Publishing Editorial Board Staff. Master Index to Poetry. 2nd ed. LC 85-81058. l, 1939p. 1992. 250.00 (*0-89609-309-3*) Roth Pub Inc.

Roth Publishing, Inc. Staff. American Poetry Index, 1984, Vol. 3. 570p. 1987. 52.00 (*0-89609-262-3*) Roth Pub Inc.

— Annual Index to Poetry in Periodicals, 1985. 800p. 1987. 39.99 (*0-89609-263-1*) Roth Pub Inc.

— Poetry Index Annual, 1986. 470p. 1987. 54.99 (*0-89609-264-X*) Roth Pub Inc.

— Poetry Index Annual, 1991. 1992. 54.99 (*0-89609-321-2*) Roth Pub Inc.

— Poetry Index Annual, 1993. 1994. 54.99 (*0-89609-329-8*) Roth Pub Inc.

— Poetry Index Annual, 1992. 1993. 54.99 (*0-89609-324-7*) Roth Pub Inc.

— Roth's Essay Index, Second Cumulative Supplement, Phases VI-X. (Corefiche Ser.). 478p. (Orig.). 1993. pap. text 49.95 (*0-89609-326-3*) Roth Pub Inc.

— Roth's Index to Great American & English Essays. 87p. 1988. pap. text 29.95 (*0-89609-293-3*) Roth Pub Inc.

— Survey of American Poetry Vol. VII: Poetic Renaissance (1913-1919) LC 81-83526. 380p. 1986. 50.00 (*0-89609-219-4*) Roth Pub Inc.

— Survey of American Poetry Vol. VIII: Interval Between World Wars (1920-1939) LC 81-83526. 380p. 1986. 50.00 (*0-89609-220-8*) Roth Pub Inc.

— Survey of American Poetry Vol. IX: World War II & Aftermath (1940-1950) LC 81-83526. 1986. 50.00 (*0-89609-221-6*) Roth Pub Inc.

— Survey of American Poetry Vol. X: Midcentury to 1984. LC 81-83526. 370p. 1986. 50.00 (*0-89609-222-4*) Roth Pub Inc.

— World's Best Poetry Supplement III: Critical Companion. LC 82-84763. 400p. 1986. 60.00 (*0-89609-242-9*) Roth Pub Inc.

— World's Best Poetry Supplement VIII: Cumulative Index. LC 82-84763. 257p. 1993. 60.00 (*0-89609-327-1*) Roth Pub Inc.

Roth Publishing, Inc. Staff, ed. American Poetry Index, Vol. 4. 400p. 1988. 52.00 (*0-89609-268-2*) Roth Pub Inc.

— Annual Index to Poetry in Periodicals, 1984. 540p. 1985. 39.99 (*0-89609-243-7*) Roth Pub Inc.

— Annual Survey of American Poetry, 1985. LC 86-62135. 300p. 1987. 45.00 (*0-89609-266-6*) Roth Pub Inc.

— Annual Survey of American Poetry, 1986. LC 86-62135. 279p. 1987. 45.00 (*0-89609-272-0*) Roth Pub Inc.

— Poetry Index Annual, 1988. 320p. 1989. 54.99 (*0-89609-283-6*, Poetry Index Pr) Roth Pub Inc.

— Poetry Index Annual, 1989. 305p. 1990. 54.99 (*0-89609-296-8*) Roth Pub Inc.

— Poetry Index Annual, 1987. 328p. 1988. 54.99 (*0-89609-269-0*) Roth Pub Inc.

— Poetry Index Annual, 1990. 270p. 1991. 54.99 (*0-89609-311-5*) Roth Pub Inc.

— Roth's American Poetry Annual, 1988. 727p. 1989. 60.00 (*0-89609-285-2*) Roth Pub Inc.

— Roth's American Poetry Annual, 1989. 700p. 1990. 60.00 (*0-89609-295-X*) Roth Pub Inc.

— Roth's American Poetry Annual, 1990. 735p. 1991. 60.00 (*0-89609-302-6*) Roth Pub Inc.

— Roth's Essay Index. LC 88-62954. 494p. 1989. 49.95 (*0-89609-286-0*, Poetry Index Pr) Roth Pub Inc.

— Survey of British Poetry Vol. I: Old English to Renaissance. 442p. 1988. 59.95 (*0-89609-274-7*) Roth Pub Inc.

— Survey of British Poetry Vol. II: Cavalier to Restoration, Vol. 2. 365p. 1989. 59.95 (*0-89609-275-5*) Roth Pub Inc.

— Survey of British Poetry Vol. III: Eighteenth Century. LC 88-60329. 438p. 1991. 59.95 (*0-89609-276-3*) Roth Pub Inc.

— Survey of British Poetry Vol. IV: Nineteenth Century. 400p. 1992. 59.95 (*0-89609-277-1*) Roth Pub Inc.

— The World's Best Poetry, Suppl. IV. LC 82-84763. 370p. 1987. 60.00 (*0-89609-265-8*) Roth Pub Inc.

— World's Best Poetry Supplement V: Twentieth-Century Women Poets. LC 82-84763. 375p. 1987. 60.00 (*0-89609-270-4*) Roth Pub Inc.

— World's Best Poetry Supplement VI: Twentieth Century African & Latin American Verse. LC 82-84763. 400p. 1989. 60.00 (*0-89609-271-2*) Roth Pub Inc.

— World's Best Poetry Supplement VII: Twentieth-Century Asian Verse. LC 82-84763. 350p. 1990. 60.00 (*0-89609-289-5*) Roth Pub Inc.

— World's Best Short Stories, 10 vols. LC 89-60440. 35000p. 1994. 599.50 (*0-89609-301-8*) Roth Pub Inc.

— World's Best Short Stories Vol. 1: Short Story Masters, Vol. I. LC 89-60440. 350p. 1989. 60.00 (*0-89609-303-4*) Roth Pub Inc.

— World's Best Short Stories Vol. 2: Short Story Masters, Vol. II. LC 89-60440. 378p. 1990. 60.00 (*0-89609-304-2*) Roth Pub Inc.

— World's Best Short Stories Vol. 3: Famous Stories. LC 89-60440. 376p. 1990. 60.00 (*0-89609-305-0*) Roth Pub Inc.

— World's Best Short Stories Vol. 4: Fables & Tales. LC 89-60440. 389p. 1991. lib. bdg. 60.00 (*0-89609-306-9*) Roth Pub Inc.

— World's Best Short Stories Vol. 5: Genres, Mystery & Detection. LC 89-60440. 350p. 1991. 60.00 (*0-89609-307-7*) Roth Pub Inc.

— World's Best Short Stories Vol. 6: Genres, Horror & Science Fiction. LC 89-60440. 350p. 1991. 60.00 (*0-89609-312-3*) Roth Pub Inc.

— World's Best Short Stories Vol. 7: Characters. LC 89-60440. 350p. 1992. 60.00 (*0-89609-313-1*) Roth Pub Inc.

— World's Best Short Stories Vol. 8: Places. LC 89-60440. 350p. 1993. 60.00 (*0-89609-314-X*) Roth Pub Inc.

— World's Best Short Stories Vol. 9: Cultures. LC 89-60440. 350p. 1994. 60.00 (*0-89609-315-8*) Roth Pub Inc.

— World's Best Short Stories Vol. 10: Research & Reference: Criticism & Indexes. LC 89-60440. 350p. 1996. 60.00 (*0-89609-316-6*) Roth Pub Inc.

***Roth, R. A.** Toxicology of the Respiratory System, 13 vols. (Comprehensive Toxicology Ser.: Vol. 8). 657p. 1999. 185.50 (*0-08-042973-4*) Elsevier.

Roth, R. S., ed. The Bellman Continuum. 892p. 1987. text 114.00 (*9971-5-0090-6*) World Scientific Pub.

Roth, R. S., et al, eds. Phase Diagrams for Ceramists Vol. IV: Oxides. (Illus.). 330p. 1981. 150.00 (*0-916094-40-5*, PH04) Am Ceramic.

— Phase Diagrams for Ceramists Vol. V: Salts. 404p. 1983. 150.00 (*0-916094-47-2*, PH05) Am Ceramic.

Roth, R. S., jt. auth. see Bellman, Richard Ernest.

Roth, Rachel. Making Women Pay: The Hidden Costs of Fetal Rights. LC 99-44982. 1999. 29.95 (*0-8014-3607-9*) Cornell U Pr.

Roth, Rahdert. Appeals to the Eleventh Circuit Manual 99-2, 3 vols. 366p. 1999. ring bd. write for info. (*0-327-01349-4*, 8015225) LEXIS Pub.

***Roth, Rahdert.** Appeals to the Eleventh Circuit Manual 99-3. 274p. 1999. ring bd. write for info. (*0-327-01705-8*, 8015226) LEXIS Pub.

Roth, Rahdert. Appeals to the Fifth Circuit, Issue 24. 100p. 1999. ring bd. write for info. (*0-327-01353-2*, 8016019) LEXIS Pub.

Roth, Rainer. Lexikon der Arbeits und Soziallere. (GER.). 1976. 65.00 (*0-8288-5729-6*, M7278) Fr & Eur.

An Asterisk (*) at the beginning of an entry indicates that the title is appearing for the first time.

Roth, Randall, ed. The Price of Paradise: Lucky We Live Hawaii? 268p. 1992. pap. 14.95 (*1-56647-016-1*) Mutual Pub HI.

Roth, Randall D. Prayer Powerpoints. LC 95-1640. 192p. 1995. 11.99 (*1-56476-433-8*, 6-3433, Victor Bks) Chariot Victor.

Roth, Randall W., ed. The Price of Paradise, Vol. II. 320p. 1993. pap. 14.95 (*1-56647-042-0*) Mutual Pub HI.

Roth, Randolph A. The Democratic Dilemma: Religion, Reform, & the Social Order in the Connecticut River Valley of Vermont, 1791-1850. 416p. 1987. text 57.95 (*0-521-30183-1*) Cambridge U Pr.

Roth, Ray, ed. Ray's Favorite Recipes. 194p. 1998. spiral bd. 7.95 (*0-9667555-0-2*) Clouse Pubg.

Roth, Richard & Martin, Douglas C. Carving Fish & Pond Life. (Illus.). 224p. 1994. text 39.95 (*0-88740-589-4*) Schiffer.

Roth, Richard & Roth, Susan K. Beauty Is Nowhere. 150p. (C). 1997. 35.00 (*90-5701-231-6*); 18.95 (*90-5701-311-8*) Dist Art Pubs.

Roth, Richard, Sr., jt. ed. see Kunreuther, Howard.

Roth, Richard L., jt. auth. see Braden, Maria.

Roth, Robert. The Natural Law Party. LC 98-23739. 272p. 1998. 23.95 (*0-312-19304-1*, Thomas Dunne) St Martin.

— A Reason to Vote. 320p. 1999. pap. 14.95 (*0-312-24316-2*) St Martin.

— Transcendental Meditation. rev. ed. LC 94-71116. 160p. 1994. pap. 12.95 (*1-55611-403-6*, Don I Fine) Dutton Plume.

Roth, Robert A., ed. The Role of the University in the Preparation of Teachers. LC 99-164247. 269p. 1999. 75.00 (*0-7507-0883-2*, Falmer Pr) Taylor & Francis.

Roth, Robert A., jt. auth. see Gold, Yvonne.

Roth, Robert J. British Empiricism & American Pragmatism: New Directions & Neglected Arguments. LC 93-3064. viii, 205p. 1993. 30.00 (*0-8232-1391-9*); pap. 19.95 (*0-8232-1392-7*) Fordham.

Roth, Robert J., ed. Person & Community: A Philosophical Exploration. LC 73-93143. 187p. reprint ed. pap. 58.00 (*0-7837-0470-4*, 204079300018) Bks Demand.

Roth, Robert J., rev. Radical Pragmatism: An Alternative. 396p. 1998. 35.00 (*0-8232-1851-1*); pap. 18.00 (*0-8232-1852-X*) Fordham.

***Roth, Robert N.** Wond'rous Machine: A Literary Anthology Celebrating the Organ. LC 00-25207. 2000. write for info. (*0-8108-3788-9*) Scarecrow.

Roth, Robert S., et al, eds. Phase Diagrams for Ceramists Vol. VI: Oxides. 550p. 1987. 150.00 (*0-916094-90-1*, PH06) Am Ceramic.

— Phase Diagrams for Ceramists Vol. 11: Oxides. (Phase Equilibria Diagrams Ser.: Vol. XI). (Illus.). 487p. 1995. 150.00 (*0-944904-90-4*, PH11) Am Ceramic.

Roth, Robert S., jt. auth. see Bellman, Richard Ernest.

Roth, Robert S., jt. ed. see McHale, Anna E.

Roth, Robert S., ed. see Whitler, John D.

Roth-Roemer, Sari, et al, eds. The Emerging Role of Counseling Psychology in Health Care. LC 98-7625. 380p. 1998. 45.00 (*0-393-70268-5*) Norton.

Roth, Roger. Fishing for Methuselah. LC 97-49666. (Illus.). 32p. (J). (ps-3). 1998. 14.95 (*0-06-027592-8*) HarpC.

— Sign Painter's Dream. 1995. 12.19 (*0-606-08604-8*, Pub. by Turtleback) Demco.

Roth, Ron. Celebrating God's Healing Love. 121p. 1991. pap. 6.95 (*1-893869-12-1*) Celbrtng Life.

Roth, Ron. I Want to See Jesus. 187p. 1986. pap. 7.95 (*0-318-22779-7*) Celbrtng Life.

***Roth, Ron.** I Want to See Jesus in a New Light: Healing Reflection for People of All Faiths. 2000. pap. 8.95 (*1-56170-677-9*, 5012) Hay House.

— The Miracle-Working Power of Love. 99p. 1986. pap. 5.00 (*1-893869-13-X*) Celbrtng Life.

Roth, Ron. Prayer & the Five Stages of Healing. LC 98-43146. 272p. (C). 1999. text 23.00 (*1-56170-551-9*, 575) Hay House.

***Roth, Ron.** Prayer & the Five Stages of Healing. (SPA., Illus.). 256p. 2001. pap. 13.95 (*1-56170-799-6*) Hay House.

— Praying with Power As Jesus Taught. 92p. 1989. pap. 4.00 (*1-893869-14-8*) Celbrtng Life.

Roth, Ron & Occhiogrosso, Peter. The Healing Path of Prayer: A Modern Mystic's Guide to Spiritual Power. 256p. 1998. pap. 13.00 (*0-609-80226-7*) Harmony Bks.

***Roth, Ron & Occhiogrosso, Peter.** Holy Spirit: The Boundless Energy of God. 160p. 2000. 13.95 (*1-56170-705-8*, 5017) Hay House.

— Holy Spirit for Abundance. 160p. 2001. 13.95 (*1-56170-708-2*, 5019) Hay House.

— Holy Spirit for Healing: Spirituality for the 21st Century. 176p. 2001. 20.00 (*1-56170-706-6*, 5020) Hay House.

— Prayer & the Five Stages of Healing. 272p. 2000. reprint ed. pap. 13.95 (*1-56170-678-7*, 575T) Hay House.

Roth, Ron & Occhuogrosso, Peter. The Healing Path of Prayer: The Moderm Mystic's Guide to Spiritual Power. LC 97-16801. 224p. 1997. 23.00 (*0-517-70843-4*) Crown Pub Group.

Roth, Ronald. Proof: God Exists! (Illus.). iv, 36p. 1998. pap. text 5.95 (*0-9663810-0-9*) Ark of Prose Bks.

Roth, Ronald N., jt. ed. see Paris, Paul M.

Roth, Rosemary A., ed. Perioperative Nursing Core Curriculum: Achieving Competency in Clinical Practice. (Illus.). 392p. 1995. pap. text 41.00 (*0-7216-5197-6*, W B Saunders Co) Harcrt Hlth Sci Grp.

Roth, Roswitha & Borkenstein, H. M., eds. Psychosoziale Aspekte in der Betreuung von Kindern und Jugendlichen mit Diabetes. (Illus.). x, 202p. 1991. 35.00 (*3-8055-5414-1*) S Karger.

Roth, Roy D., et al. Hymn Singing. LC 83-200658. (Worship Ser.). 48 p. 1983. 2.95 (*0-87303-046-X*) Faith & Life.

Roth, Russell. Muddy Glory: America's Indian Wars in the Philippines, 1899 to 1935. LC 80-70230. 1981. reprint ed. pap. 15.00 (*0-8158-0402-4*) Chris Mass.

Roth, Ruth, jt. auth. see Townsend, Carolynn E.

Roth, S., jt. ed. see Plocharski, J.

Roth, S., jt. ed. see Przyluski, Jan.

Roth, S. John. The Blind, the Lame, & the Poor: Character Types in Luke - Acts. (JSNTS Ser.: Vol. 144). 253p. 1997. 75.00 (*1-85075-667-8*, Pub. by Sheffield Acad) CUP Services.

Roth, Sally. Attracting Birds to Your Backyard: 536 Ways to Turn Your Yard & Garden into a Haven for Your Favorite Birds. LC 98-19764. (Illus.). 320p. 1998. text 29.95 (*0-87596-790-6*) Rodale Pr Inc.

***Roth, Sally.** The Backyard Bird Feeder's Bible: The A-to-Z Guide to Feeders, Seed Mixes, Projects & Treats. (Illus.). 384p. 2000. 29.95 (*0-87596-834-1*) Rodale Pr Inc.

Roth, Sally. Natural Landscaping: Working with Nature to Create a Backyard Paradise. LC 96-5912. (Illus.). 256p. 1997. text 29.95 (*0-87596-704-3*) Rodale Pr Inc.

Roth, Samuel. Jews Must Live. 1980. lib. bdg. 69.95 (*0-8490-3204-0*) Gordon Pr.

Roth, Sanford. Atlas of Endocrine Surgical Pathology. 300p. 1996. 135.00 (*0-397-51773-4*) Lppncott W & W.

Roth, Sanford & Roth, Beulah. Italy Fifties. LC 89-27617. (Illus.). 156p. 1990. 24.95 (*0-916515-72-9*) Mercury Hse Inc.

Roth-Scholtz, Friedrich. Bibliotheca Chemica. 238p. 1971. reprint ed. write for info. (*3-487-04117-0*) Lubrecht & Cramer.

— Deutsches Theatrum Chemicum, 3 vols., Set. 1976. reprint ed. write for info. (*3-487-05920-7*) G Olms Pubs.

— Thesaurus Symbolorum Ac Emblematum, I. E. Insignia Bibliopolarum et Typographorum. 184p. reprint ed. write for info. (*0-318-71862-6*) G Olms Pubs.

Roth, Sheldon. Psychotherapy: The Art of Wooing Nature. LC 86-28763. 304p. 1987. 50.00 (*0-87668-945-4*) Aronson.

Roth, Sheldon H. & Miller, Keith W. Molecular & Cellular Mechanisms of Anesthetics. LC 85-28274. (Illus.). 502p. (C). 1986. text 150.00 (*0-306-42128-3*, Kluwer Plenum) Kluwer Academic.

Roth, Shirley P. & Morse, Joyce S., eds. A Life-Span Approach to Nursing Care for Individuals with Developmental Disabilities. 368p. 1994. 49.95 (*1-55766-151-0*, 1510) P H Brookes.

Roth, Sid & Harrell, Irene B. Something for Nothing. LC 75-31396. vii, 133p. 1976. write for info. (*0-88270-145-2*) Bridge-Logos.

Roth, Siegmar. One-Dimensional Metals: Physics & Materials Science. 247p. 1995. 135.00 (*3-527-26875-8*, Wiley-VCH) Wiley.

Roth, Siegmar, jt. ed. see Przyluski, Jan.

Roth-Singer, Lyzz, jt. auth. see Christian, Eleanor.

Roth Smythe, Benjamin. Sir Jason Winters Story: From Deadly Cancer to Perfect Health. rev. ed. 1997. pap. 19.95 (*1-885026-06-4*) Vinton Pubng.

Roth, Sol. Halakhah & Politics: The Jewish Idea of a State. 1988. 19.95 (*0-88125-129-1*) Ktav.

— The Jewish Idea of Culture. LC 96-252. 1996. 23.00 (*0-88125-543-2*) Ktav.

Roth, Stacy F. Past into Present: Trends & Techniques in First-Person Interpretation. LC 97-36874. 280p. 1998. pap. 16.95 (*0-8078-4710-0*) U of NC Pr.

— Past into Present: Trends & Techniques in First-Person Interpretation. LC 97-36874. 1998. 45.00 (*0-8078-2407-0*) U of NC Pr.

Roth, Stanley, ed. see Young, Norman S.

Roth, Stephanie, jt. auth. see Brown, Hariet.

Roth, Stephanie, jt. auth. see Weidlein, Marianne.

Roth, Stephen, ed. Molecular Approaches to Supracellular Phenomena. LC 90-12412. (Developmental Biology Ser.). (Illus.). 242p. (C). 1990. reprint ed. text 45.00 (*0-8122-8251-5*) U of Pa Pr.

Roth, Stephen F., ed. Real World PostScript: Techniques from PostScript. 400p. 1988. pap. 22.95 (*0-201-06663-7*) Addison-Wesley.

Roth, Steve. Daws: Some Descendants of Frank Daws of County Sussex, England, with Information on Associate Kiplinger Family. (Illus.). 89p. 1993. reprint ed. pap. 17.50 (*0-8328-3293-6*); reprint ed. lib. bdg. 27.50 (*0-8328-3294-4*) Higginson Bk Co.

***Roth, Steve.** Genealogy of James & Deborah Reynolds of North Kingstown, R. I., & Descendants, 3 vols., Set. 2263p. 2000. 270.00 (*0-7404-1114-4*); pap. 225.00 (*0-7404-1115-2*) Higginson Bk Co.

Roth, Steve. Roth: The Family of Nicholas Roth, American Settlers from Germany, with Information on Associate Families of Winters, Darnold & Keppler. (Illus.). 197p. 1993. reprint ed. pap. 29.50 (*0-8328-3397-5*); reprint ed. lib. bdg. 39.50 (*0-8328-3396-7*) Higginson Bk Co.

Roth, Steve & Sellers, Don. The QuicKeys 3 Book. LC 94-36390. 352p. (C). 1994. pap. 22.95 (*0-201-40979-8*) Addison-Wesley.

Roth, Sue, jt. auth. see Schaff, Barbara.

Roth, Susan. Cinnamon's Day Out: A Gerbil Adventure. LC 97-24620. (Illus.). 32p. (J). (ps-2). 1998. 15.89 (*0-8037-2323-7*, Dial Yng Read) Peng Put Young Read.

— Marco Polo. 1990. 15.00 (*0-385-44522-9*) Doubleday.

— Moses in the Twentieth Century: A Universal Primer. 1994. 24.95 (*0-9638861-0-X*) S J R Assocs.

Roth, Susan & Batson, Ronald. Naming the Shadows: A New Approach to Individual & Group Psychotherapy for Adult Survivors of Childhood Incest. LC 97-1617. 1997. 29.95 (*0-684-83704-8*) Free Pr.

Roth, Susan A. The Four-Season Landscape: Easy-Care Plants & Plans for Year-Round Color. (Illus.). 352p. 1994. 26.95 (*0-87596-556-3*) Rodale Pr Inc.

— New Complete Guide to Gardening. 2nd ed. Barash, Cathy, ed. LC 97-71339. (Better Homes & Gardens Ser.). (Illus.). 600p. 1997. 34.95 (*0-696-02573-6*, Better Homes) Meredith Bks.

— The Weekend Garden Guide: Work-Saving Ways to a Beautiful Backyard. (Illus.). 368p. 1996. pap. 15.95 (*0-87596-695-0*) Rodale Pr Inc.

***Roth, Susan A. & Schrader, Dennis.** Hot Plants for Cool Climates: Gardening with Tropical Plants in Temperate Zones. LC 99-43589. (Illus.). 240p. 2000. 35.00 (*0-395-96323-0*) HM.

Roth, Susan A., ed. see Buscher, Fred K. & McClure, Susan A.

Roth, Susan K., jt. auth. see Roth, Richard.

Roth, Susan L. The Biggest Frog in Australia. (Illus.). 32p. (J). (ps-3). 2000. pap. 5.99 (*0-689-83314-8*) Aladdin.

— The Biggest Frog in Australia. LC 95-9721. (Illus.). (J). 1996. mass mkt. 15.00 (*0-671-50134-8*) S&S Bks Yung.

— The Biggest Frog in Australia. LC 95-9721. (Illus.). 32p. (J). (ps-3). 1996. per. 15.00 (*0-689-80490-3*) S&S Bks Yung.

— Cinnamon's Day Out: A Gerbil Adventure. LC 97-24620. (Illus.). 32p. (J). (ps-4). 1998. 15.99 (*0-8037-2322-9*, Dial Yng Read) Peng Put Young Read.

— Kanahena: A Cherokee Story. LC 87-43203. 1996. 11.19 (*0-606-09508-X*, Pub. by Turtleback) Demco.

— My Love for You. LC 95-53759. (Illus.). 32p. (J). 1997. 12.99 (*0-8037-2031-9*, Dial Yng Read) Peng Put Young Read.

— My Love for You: Board Book. Serlin, Andra, ed. LC 99-228243. (Illus.). 24p. (J). (ps). 1999. pap. 5.99 (*0-8037-2352-0*, Dial Yng Read) Peng Put Young Read.

— Night-Time Numbers: A Scary Counting Book. 32p. (J). (ps-1). 1999. 15.95 (*1-84148-001-0*) Barefoot Bks NY.

— Princess. LC 92-55042. (Illus.). 32p. (J). (ps-3). 1993. 13.95 (*1-56282-465-1*, Pub. by Hyprn Child) Little.

***Roth, Susan L.** The Story of Light. (Illus.). 14p. (J). (gr. 1-3). 2000. reprint ed. text 20.00 (*0-7881-9063-5*) DIANE Pub.

Roth, Susan L. We'll Ride Elephants Through Brooklyn. LC 89-45613. 32p. (J). (ps-3). 1989. 13.95 (*0-374-38258-1*) FS&G.

Roth, Susan L., jt. illus. see Laufer, Peter.

Roth, Suzanne M. The Reality of Professional Pet Sitting. LC 98-89466. 375p. 1998. text 25.00 (*0-7388-0295-6*); pap. text 15.00 (*0-7388-0296-4*) Xlibris Corp.

Roth, Sydell, jt. auth. see Wax, Edith.

Roth, T., jt. auth. see Cuatrecasas, P.

***Roth, Timothy P.** Ethics, Economics & Freedom: The Failure of Consequentialist Social Welfare Theory. LC 99-76351. 111p. 1999. text 56.95 (*0-7546-1009-8*, Pub. by Ashgate Pub) Ashgate Pub Co.

Roth, Timothy P. Information, Ideology, & Freedom: The Disenfranchised Electorate. LC 94-1573. 138p. (Orig.). 1994. pap. 22.00 (*0-8191-9465-4*); lib. bdg. 47.50 (*0-8191-9464-6*) U Pr of Amer.

— The Present State of Consumer Theory. 2nd ed. LC 89-34175. 220p. (Orig.). (C). 1989. pap. text 22.50 (*0-8191-7506-4*) U Pr of Amer.

— The Present State of Consumer Theory: The Implications for Social Welfare Theory. 3rd ed. LC 97-40090. 236p. (C). 1998. pap. text 31.00 (*0-7618-0944-9*) U Pr of Amer.

Roth, Timothy P., jt. ed. see Bartlett, Bruce.

Roth, Viola, ed. see Kaslow, David.

Roth, Viola, tr. see Dauprat, Louis-Francois.

Roth, Walter. Games, Sports & Amusements. LC 75-35076. (Studies in Play & Games). (Illus.). 1976. reprint ed. 17.95 (*0-405-07926-5*) Ayer.

Roth, Walter & Kraus, Joe. An Accidental Anarchist: How the Killing of a Humble Jewish Immigrant by Chicago's Chief of Police Exposed the Conflict Between Law & Order & Civil Rights in Early 20th Century America. LC 96-52551. (Illus.). 224p. (Orig.). 1997. 26.95 (*0-945213-24-7*); pap. 16.95 (*0-945213-23-9*) Rudi Pub.

Roth, Walter, jt. auth. see Keimel, Klaus.

Roth, Walter E., ed. Additional Studies of the Arts, Crafts & Customs of the Guiana Indians, with Special Reference to Those Southern British Guiana. (Bureau of American Ethnology Bulletins Ser.). 110p. 1995. lib. bdg. 79.00 (*0-7812-4091-3*) Rprt Serv.

Roth, Walton T. & Yalom, Irvin D. Treating Anxiety Disorders. LC 96-28708. (Library of Current Clinical Technique). 302p. 1996. 28.95 (*0-7879-0316-7*) Jossey-Bass.

Roth, Walton T., jt. auth. see Insel, Paul M.

Roth, Wendy & Tompane, Michael. Easy Access to National Parks: The Sierra Club Guide for People with Disabilities. (Illus.). 404p. (Orig.). 1998. pap. text 16.00 (*0-7881-5298-X*) DIANE Pub.

Roth, William. The Evolution of Management Theory: Past, Present, Future. LC 93-92548. 150p. (C). 1994. lib. bdg. 19.95 (*0-9635680-1-9*) Roth & Assocs.

***Roth, William.** Teachers' Guide for Quality Improvement A Systems Approach. 1998. ring bd. write for info. (*1-57444-253-8*) St Lucie Pr.

***Roth, William & Archer, Bill, eds.** General Explanation of Tax Legislation Enacted in 1998: Report of the Joint Committee on Taxation, U. S. Congress. (Illus.). 320p. (C). 2000. reprint ed. pap. text 40.00 (*0-7881-8770-8*) DIANE Pub.

***Roth, William & Heather, Timothy R.** In Our Darkest Hour/Morning Star Over America. (Illus.). 1600p. 1999. 39.00 (*0-9671587-0-2*, bvm22291) Morning Star Lord.

Roth, William, et al. Problem Solving for Results. (Illus.). 208p. (Orig.). 1996. per. 34.95 (*1-57444-018-7*) St Lucie Pr.

Roth, William F. Quality Improvement: A Systems Perspective. LC 98-38861. 288p. 1998. boxed set 49.95 (*1-57444-236-8*) St Lucie Pr.

***Roth, William F.** The Root & Future of Management Theory. LC 99-28913. 1999. 49.95 (*1-57444-243-0*) St Lucie Pr.

Roth, William F., Jr. A Systems Approach to Quality Improvement. LC 91-4204. 208p. 1991. 52.95 (*0-275-94107-8*, C4107, Praeger Pubs) Greenwood.

— Work & Rewards: Redefining Our Work-Life Reality. LC 88-25572. 206p. 1989. 57.95 (*0-275-93166-8*, C3166, Praeger Pubs) Greenwood.

Roth, William J., ed. see Eirinberg, Keith W.

Roth, William U., Jr. Final Report of the Advisory Commission to Study the Consumer Price Index. (Illus.). 67p. (C). 1998. pap. text 20.00 (*0-7881-4933-4*) DIANE Pub.

Roth, William V. Auditing the IRS: The Untold Story of Abuse, Fear & Intimidation by America's Most Secretive. 1998. 25.00 (*0-684-85405-8*) Free Pr.

***Roth, William V., Jr., ed.** IRS Oversight: Congressional Hearings. 303p. (C). 1999. reprint ed. pap. text 45.00 (*0-7881-8255-2*) DIANE Pub.

— IRS Restructuring: Congressional Hearings. 480p. (C). 1999. reprint ed. pap. text 50.00 (*0-7881-8256-0*) DIANE Pub.

— Practices & Proceedings of the Internal Revenue Service: Government Hearings. 357p. (C). 1999. reprint ed. pap. text 45.00 (*0-7881-8239-0*) DIANE Pub.

— Review of Selected Entity Classification & Partnership Tax Issues. 56p. 2000. reprint ed. pap. text 20.00 (*0-7567-0115-5*) DIANE Pub.

***Roth, William V., Jr. & Nixon, William H.** The Power to Destroy: How the IRS Became America's Most Powerful Agency, How Congress Is Taking Control & What You Can Do to Protect Yourself under the New Law. LC 98-52234. 288p. 1999. 23.00 (*0-87113-748-8*, Atlntc Mnthly) Grove-Atltc.

Roth, William V., Jr., jt. ed. see Archer, Bill.

Roth, Wolf-Michael, jt. auth. see Sate.

Roth, Wolff-Michael. Authentic School Science: Knowing & Learning in Open-Inquiry Science Laboratories. LC 94-30832. (Science & Technology Education Library: 1). 320p. 1995. lib. bdg. 106.00 (*0-7923-3088-9*, Pub. by Kluwer Academic) Kluwer Academic.

— Designing Communities. LC 97-27407. (Science & Technology Education Library: No. 3). 313p. 1997. 137.00 (*0-7923-4703-X*); pap. 84.00 (*0-7923-4704-8*) Kluwer Academic.

Roth-Young, Bette. Emma Lazarus: In Her World. 1996. pap. 21.95 (*0-8276-0618-4*) JPS Phila.

Roth, Zvi S., jt. auth. see Zhuang, Hanqi.

Rotha, Charline T. Weida. 204p. 1993. pap. 11.95 (*0-685-69189-6*) Prof Pr NC.

***Rothacker, John P.** The Church: From Babylon to the Promised Land. (Illus.). 256p. 1999. pap. 11.95 (*0-9674869-4-7*) J R Ministries.

Rothafel, Samuel L. & Yates, Raymond F. Broadcasting: Its New Day. LC 70-161153. (History of Broadcasting: Radio to Television Ser.). 1977. reprint ed. 31.95 (*0-405-03571-3*) Ayer.

***Rothamel, Susan Pickering.** The Art of Paper Collage LC 99-39004. 1999. 24.95 (*0-8069-3942-7*) Sterling.

Rothaus. Guide Advan Med&Int Resr. (C). 1997. text 9.75 (*0-673-97258-5*) Addson-Wesley Educ.

Rothaus, Barry, jt. ed. see Scott, Samuel F.

Rothaus, Don. Aardvarks. LC 95-12910. (Nature Books Ser.). (Illus.). 32p. (J). (gr. 2-6). Date not set. lib. bdg. 22.79 (*1-56766-181-5*) Childs World.

— Moray Eels. LC 95-12144. (Nature Books Ser.). (Illus.). 32p. (J). (gr. 2-6). 1995. lib. bdg. 22.79 (*1-56766-187-4*) Childs World.

— Warthogs. LC 95-12143. (Nature Books Ser.). (Illus.). 32p. (J). (gr. 2-6). 1995. lib. bdg. 22.79 (*1-56766-185-8*) Childs World.

Rothaus, James R. Barry Sanders. (Sports Superstars Ser.). (Illus.). 32p. (J). (gr. 2-6). 1991. lib. bdg. 21.36 (*0-89565-737-6*) Childs World.

— Bo Jackson. (Sports Superstars Ser.). (Illus.). 32p. (J). (gr. 2-6). 1991. lib. bdg. 21.36 (*0-89565-731-7*) Childs World.

— David Robinson. (Sports Superstars Ser.). (Illus.). 32p. (J). (gr. 2-6). 1991. lib. bdg. 21.36 (*0-89565-784-8*) Childs World.

— Jose Canseco. (Sports Superstars Ser.). (Illus.). 32p. (J). (gr. 2-6). 1991. lib. bdg. 21.36 (*0-89565-735-X*) Childs World.

— Magic Johnson. (Sports Superstars Ser.). (Illus.). 32p. (J). (gr. 2-6). 1991. lib. bdg. 21.36 (*0-89565-732-5*) Childs World.

— Steffi Graf. (Sports Superstars Ser.). (Illus.). 32p. (J). (gr. 2-6). 1990. lib. bdg. 21.36 (*0-89565-734-1*) Childs World.

— Steve Young. (Sports Superstars Ser.). (Illus.). 32p. (J). (gr. 2-6). 1991. lib. bdg. 21.36 (*0-89565-736-8*) Childs World.

Rothaus, Jim. Baseball Jokes. (Funny Side Up Ser.). (Illus.). 24p. (J). (gr. 1-4). 1996. lib. bdg. 19.93 (*1-56766-268-4*) Childs World.

— Basketball Jokes. LC 95-47110. (Funny Side Up Ser.). (Illus.). 24p. (J). (gr. 1-4). 1996. lib. bdg. 19.93 (*1-56766-269-2*) Childs World.

— Canyons. LC 96-2721. (Biomes of Nature Ser.). (Illus.). 32p. (J). (gr. 2-6). 1996. lib. bdg. 22.79 (*1-56766-322-2*) Childs World.

— Football Jokes. LC 95-50119. (Funny Side Up Ser.). (Illus.). 24p. (J). (gr. 1-4). 1996. lib. bdg. 19.93 (*1-56766-267-6*) Childs World.

— Oceans. LC 96-11468. (Biomes of Nature Ser.). (Illus.). 32p. (J). (gr. 2-6). 1996. lib. bdg. 22.79 (*1-56766-286-2*) Childs World.

— Olympic Jokes. (Funny Side Up Ser.). (Illus.). 24p. (J). (gr. 1-4). 1996. lib. bdg. 19.93 (*1-56766-270-6*) Childs World.

R

Rothaus, Kenneth, jt. auth. see Tyberg, Theodore.

***Rothaus, Richard M.** Corinth, the First City of Greece: An Urban History of Late Antique Cult & Religion. LC 00-26304. (Religions in the Graeco-Roman World Ser.). 220p. 2000. 68.00 (*90-04-10922-6*) Brill Academic Pubs.

Rothausen, Karlheinz & Sonne, Volker. Mainzer Becken. (Sammlung Geologischer Fuehrer Ser.: Band 79). (GER., Illus.). xii, 203p. 1984. spiral bd. 23.00 (*3-443-15043-8*, Pub. by Gebruder Borntraeger) Balogh.

***Rothbard, Murray N.** America's Great Depression. 5th ed. xxix, 368p. 2000. 29.95 (*0-945466-05-6*) Ludwig von Mises.

Rothbard, Murray N. The Case Against the Fed. LC 94-73591. 158p. (Orig.). 1994. pap. 9.95 (*0-945466-17-X*) Ludwig von Mises.

— Classical Economics Vol. II: An Austrian Perspective on the History of Economic Thought. 544p. 1995. 120.00 (*1-85278-962-X*) E Elgar.

***Rothbard, Murray N.** Conceived in Liberty, 4 vols., Set. 1668p. 2000. 100.00 (*0-945466-26-9*) Ludwig von Mises.

Rothbard, Murray N. Economic Thought Before Adam Smith Vol. I: An Austrian Perspective on the History of Economic Thought. 576p. 1995. 120.00 (*1-85278-961-1*) E Elgar.

***Rothbard, Murray N.** Education: Free & Compulsory. 64p. 1999. pap. 5.95 (*0-945466-22-6*) Ludwig von Mises.

Rothbard, Murray N. The Essential von Mises. 44p. 1980. pap. 3.95 (*0-910884-33-1*) Libertarian Press.

— The Ethics of Liberty. Hoppe, Hans-Hermann, ed. & intro. by. LC 98-10058. 320p. 1998. text 25.00 (*0-8147-7506-3*) NYU Pr.

— For a New Liberty: The Libertarian Manifesto. 3rd rev. ed. 333p. 1985. pap. 12.95 (*0-930073-02-9*) Fox & Wilkes.

— The Logic of Action One: Method, Money & the Austrian School. LC 96-37189. (Economists of the Twentieth Century Ser.). 480p. 1997. 90.00 (*1-85898-015-1*) E Elgar.

— The Logic of Action Two: Applications & Criticism from the Austrian School. LC 96-37189. (Economists of the Twentieth Century Ser.). 432p. 1997. 85.00 (*1-85898-570-6*) E Elgar.

— Making Economic Sense. LC 95-78335. 439p. (Orig.). 1995. pap. 19.95 (*0-945466-18-8*) Ludwig von Mises.

— Man, Economy & State: A Treatise on Economic Principles. 2nd rev. ed. 987p. (C). 1993. reprint ed. pap. text 24.95 (*0-945466-15-3*) Ludwig von Mises.

— What Has Government Done to Our Money? 119p. (Orig.). 1990. reprint ed. pap. text 6.95 (*0-945466-10-2*) Ludwig von Mises.

Rothbard, Murray N., ed. The Review of Austrian Economics, 1990, Vol. 4. (C). 1990. lib. bdg. 86.00 (*0-7923-9064-4*) Kluwer Academic.

Rothbard, Murray N. & Hess, Karl, eds. Libertarian Forum, 1969-1971. LC 77-172217. (Right Wing Individualist Tradition in America Ser.). 1979. reprint ed. 23.95 (*0-405-00427-3*) Ayer.

Rothbard, Murray N. & Sylvester, Isaiah W. What Is Money? An Original Arno Press Compilation. LC 74-172227. (Right Wing Individualist Tradition in America Ser.). 1972. reprint ed. 13.95 (*0-405-00447-8*) Ayer.

Rothbard, Murray N. & Tuccille, Jerome, eds. The Right Wing Individualist Tradition in America, 38 bks. 1972. 812.00 (*0-405-00410-9*) Ayer.

Rothbard, Shmuel. Koi Breeding. (Illus.). 64p. 1997. 12.95 (*0-7938-0216-4*, WW-050) TFH Pubns.

Rothbardt, Don & Harris, Paul N. Love & Attachment: or Falling in Love Is B. S. An Unauthorized Psychological Approach. LC 92-34014. 208p. (Orig.). 1992. pap. 11.95 (*0-915180-35-9*) Harrowood Bks.

Rothbart, Andrea. The Theory of Remainders. 1995. pap. 19.95 (*0-939765-82-9*, G168) Janson Pubns.

Rothbart, Betty. Multiple Blessings: From Pregnancy Through Childhood, a Guide for Parents of Twins, Triplets, or More. LC 93-36250. 381p. 1994. pap. 12.00 (*0-688-11642-6*, Hearst) Hearst Commns.

Rothbart, Daniel. Concise Intro Logic. 176p. (C). 1995. pap. text, student ed. 25.95 (*0-7872-0958-9*) Kendall-Hunt.

— Explaining the Growth of Scientific Knowledge: Metaphors, Models & Meanings. LC 96-51652. (Problems in Contemporary Philosophy Ser.: Vol. 37). 172p. 1997. text 79.95 (*0-7734-8721-2*) E Mellen.

— Science, Reason & Reality. LC 97-72809. 1997. pap. text 46.00 (*0-15-503529-0*, Pub. by Harcourt Coll Pubs) Harcourt.

Rothbart, Harold A. Cybernetic Creativity. LC 78-175238. 240p. 1972. 14.95 (*0-8315-0118-9*) Speller.

— Mechanical Systems Reference Guide. 1989. 34.50 (*0-07-054025-X*) McGraw.

Rothbart, Harold A., ed. Mechanical Design Handbook. (Illus.). 1472p. 1995. 125.00 (*0-07-054038-1*) McGraw.

Rothbart, Mary K., jt. auth. see Ruff, Holly A.

Rothbart, Mary Klevjord, jt. auth. see Ruff, Holly Alliger.

Rothbaum, Barbara O., jt. auth. see Foa, Edna B.

***Rothbaun, Barbara O.** Reclaiming Your Life after Rape: A Cognitive-Behavioral Therapy for PTSD. 148p. 2000. pap., wbk. ed. 22.00 (*0-12-784456-2*) Acad Pr.

Rothberg, Abraham. The Four Corners of the House. Stories. LC 81-10464. (Illinois Short Fiction Ser.). 120p. 1981. 9.95 (*0-252-00926-6*); text 14.95 (*0-252-00922-3*) U of Ill Pr.

Rothberg, Abraham, jt. auth. see Simon, Solomon.

Rothberg, David L. Insecurity & Success in Organizational Life: Sources of Personal Motivation among Leaders & Managers. LC 81-11881. (Illus.). 213p. 1981. 55.00 (*0-275-90712-0*, C0712, Praeger Pubs) Greenwood.

Rothberg, Donald J. & Kelly, Sean M., eds. Ken Wilber in Dialogue: Conversations with Leading Transpersonal Thinkers. LC 97-35286. (Illus.). 304p. 1998. pap. 16.95 (*0-8356-0766-6*, Quest) Theos Pub Hse.

Rothberg, Harvey. The First Seventy-Five Years: A History of Princeton Hospital. 140p. 1995. 20.00 (*0-9647986-0-3*) Med Ctr Princeton Foun.

Rothberg, Joel. Poems of the Big Sur. (Illus.). 114p. (Orig.). 1989. pap. 12.95 (*0-9610386-0-8*) Dragons Tail Pr.

Rothberg, L., jt. ed. see Alfano, R. R.

Rothberg, Lewis J., jt. ed. see Vardeny, Z. Valy.

Rothberg, Morey. John Franklin Jameson & the Development of Humanistic Scholarship in America: The . . ., Vol. 2. 1996. 55.00 (*0-8203-1713-6*) U of Ga Pr.

Rothberg, Morey & Goggin, Jacqueline, eds. John Franklin Jameson & the Development of Humanistic Scholarship in America: Selected Essays, Vol. 1. LC 92-8221. (Illus.). 432p. 1992. 45.00 (*0-8203-1446-3*) U of Ga Pr.

***Rothberg, O.** Air-Operated Valves in United States Nuclear Power Plants. 335p. 2000. per. 31.00 (*0-16-059121-X*) USGPO.

Rothbert, Otto A. History of Muhlenberg County. (Illus.). 496p. 1997. reprint ed. lib. bdg. 52.00 (*0-8328-6738-1*) Higginson Bk Co.

Rothblatt, Donald N. & Sancton, Andrew, eds. Metropolitan Governance Revisited: American-Canadian Intergovernmental Perspectives. LC 98-24288. 530p. 1998. 29.95 (*0-87772-381-8*) UCB IGS.

Rothblatt, Donald N., et al. Suburbia. LC 78-19797. (Praeger Special Studies). 234p. 1979. 55.00 (*0-275-90414-8*, C0414, Praeger Pubs) Greenwood.

Rothblatt, Henry B. The Art of Cross Examination. 1971. student ed. 35.00 (*1-55917-014-X*, 881); audio 50.00 (*1-55917-012-3*) Natl Prac Inst.

Rothblatt, Henry B., et al. How to Stop the Pain of Arthritis. LC 84-61541. 140p. (Orig.). 1985. pap. 4.95 (*0-936320-23-0*) Compact Books.

Rothblatt, Henry B., jt. auth. see Bailey, F. Lee.

Rothblatt, J., et al, eds. Guidebook to the Secretory Pathway. (Illus.). 320p. 1995. 95.00 (*0-19-859942-0*); pap. text 45.00 (*0-19-859941-2*) OUP.

Rothblatt, Martin A. Radiodetermination Satellite Services & Standards. LC 87-9141. (Artech House Telecommunications Library). 201p. 1987. reprint ed. pap. 62.40 (*0-608-02367-1*, 206300900004) Bks Demand.

Rothblatt, Martine, jt. auth. see Kirk, Sheila.

Rothblatt, Martine A. Unzipped Genes: Taking Charge of Baby-Making. LC 96-35970. (America in Transition Ser.). 192p. 1997. pap. 18.95 (*1-56639-554-2*) Temple U Pr.

— Unzipped Genes: Taking Charge of Baby-Making. LC 96-35970. (America in Transition Ser.). 192p. 1997. 49.95 (*1-56639-522-4*) Temple U Pr.

Rothblatt, Sheldon. The Modern University & Its Discontents: The Fate of Newman's Legacies in Britain & America. 475p. 1997. text 64.95 (*0-521-45331-3*) Cambridge U Pr.

— The Revolution of the Dons: Cambridge & Society in Victorian England. LC 80-41865. 325p. reprint ed. pap. 92.70 (*0-608-17526-9*, 2030618) Bks Demand.

Rothblatt, Sheldon & Wittrock, Bjorn, eds. The European & American University since 1800: Historical & Sociological Essays. 382p. (C). 1993. text 64.95 (*0-521-43165-4*) Cambridge U Pr.

Rothblatt, Sheldon, ed. see Clifford, Geraldine J.

Rothblatt, Sheldon, ed. see May, Henry F.

Rothblum, Esther D., ed. Classics in Lesbian Studies. LC 96-38180. (Journal of Lesbian Studies: Vol. 1, Nos. 1/2). 286p. (C). 1996. pap. 24.95 (*1-56023-093-2*, Harrington Park) Haworth Pr.

— Classics in Lesbian Studies. LC 96-38180. (Journal of Lesbian Studies: Vol. 1, Nos. 1/2). 286p. (C). 1997. 39.95 (*0-7890-0014-8*, Haworth Pastrl) Haworth Pr.

— Women & Sex Therapy. LC 88-11068. (Women & Therapy Ser.: Vol. 7, No. 2-3). (Illus.). 300p. 1988. pap. text 19.95 (*0-918393-54-X*, Harrington Park) Haworth Pr.

Rothblum, Esther D., et al, eds. Women in the Antarctic. LC 97-39233. (Illus.). 250p. 1998. pap. 19.95 (*1-56023-914-X*, Harrington Park) Haworth Pr.

***Rothblum, Esther D., et al, eds.** Women in the Antarctic. LC 97-39233. (Illus.). 250p. 1998. 39.95 (*0-7890-0247-7*, Harrington Park) Haworth Pr.

Rothblum, Esther D & Bond, Lynne A. Preventing Heterosexism & Homophobia. LC 96-4511. (Primary Prevention of Psychopathology Ser.: Vol. 17). 360p. 1996. 55.00 (*0-7619-0022-5*); pap. 24.95 (*0-7619-0023-3*) Sage.

Rothblum, Esther D. & Brehony, Kathleen A., eds. Boston Marriages: Romantic but Asexual Relationships among Contemporary Lesbians. LC 93-4281. 216p. 1993. 40.00 (*0-87023-875-2*); pap. 16.95 (*0-87023-876-0*) U of Mass Pr.

Rothblum, Esther D. & Brown, Laura S., eds. Fat Oppression & Psychotherapy: A Feminist Perspective. LC 89-19860. (Women & Therapy Ser.: Vol. 8, No. 3). 103p. 1990. text 39.95 (*0-86656-954-5*) Haworth Pr.

Rothblum, Esther D. & Cole, Ellen. Lesbianism: Affirming Nontraditional Roles. LC 88-32028. (Women & Therapy Ser.: Vol. 8, Nos. 1-2). (Illus.). 224p. 1989. text 49.95 (*0-86656-809-3*) Haworth Pr.

— Loving Boldly: Issues Facing Lesbians. LC 88-21415. (Women & Therapy Ser.: Vol. 8, Nos. 1-2). (Illus.). 224p. 1989. pap. text 14.95 (*0-918393-58-2*, Harrington Park) Haworth Pr.

— Professional Training for Feminist Therapists: Personal Memoirs. LC 90-26555. (Women & Therapy Ser.). 129p. 1991. text 39.95 (*1-56024-123-3*) Haworth Pr.

Rothblum, Esther D. & Cole, Ellen, eds. Another Silenced Trauma: Twelve Feminist Therapists & Activists Respond to One Woman's Recovery from War. LC 86-9481. 124p. 1986. pap. 9.95 (*0-918393-29-9*, Harrington Park) Haworth Pr.

— Treating Women's Fear of Failure. LC 87-25134. (Women & Therapy Ser.: Vol. 6, No. 3). 105p. 1988. text 29.95 (*0-86656-676-7*) Haworth Pr.

— Treating Women's Fear of Failure: From Worry to Enlightenment. LC 87-25132. (Women & Therapy Ser.: Vol. 6, No. 3). 105p. 1988. pap. text 9.95 (*0-918393-41-8*, Harrington Park) Haworth Pr.

— A Woman's Recovery from the Trauma of War: Twelve Responses from Feminist Therapists & Activists. 124p. 1986. 3.95 (*0-86656-561-2*) Haworth Pr.

— Women's Mental Health in Africa. (Women & Therapy Ser.). (Illus.). 98p. 1990. text 3.95 (*1-56024-043-1*); pap. text 9.95 (*0-918393-86-8*) Haworth Pr.

Rothblum, Esther D., jt. ed. see Brown, Laura S.

Rothblum, Esther D., jt. ed. see Cole, Ellen.

Rothblum, Esther D., jt. ed. see Hill, Marcia.

Rothblum, Esther D., jt. ed. see Mintz, Beth.

Rothblum, Esther D., jt. ed. see Weinstock, Jacqueline S.

Rothbrmich, Terry P., ed. Bible Story Activities, Vol. 3. 1999. pap. text 15.99 (*0-8272-9056-X*) Chalice Pr.

Rothbrust, Florian K. Guderian's XIX Panzer Corps & the Battle of France: Breakthrough in the Ardennes, May 1940. LC 89-38182. 224p. 1990. 55.00 (*0-275-93473-X*, C3473, Greenwood Pr) Greenwood.

Rothchild, B. J., ed. Global Fisheries: Perspectives for the 1980's. (Environmental Management Ser.). (Illus.). 289p. 1983. 124.00 (*0-387-90772-6*) Spr-Verlag.

Rothchild, Donald, ed. Ghana: The Political Economy of Recovery. LC 90-26072. (SAIS African Studies Library). 287p. (C). 1991. pap. text 18.95 (*1-55587-284-0*) L Rienner.

Rothchild, Donald & Curry, Robert L., Jr. Scarcity, Choice, & Public Policy in Middle Africa. LC 76-50255. 1978. pap. 15.00 (*0-520-03534-8*, Pub. by U CA Pr) Cal Prin Full Svc.

Rothchild, Donald & Harbeson, John W. Africa in World Politics: Globalization & the Changing State System. 3rd ed. LC 99-48912. 352p. 1999. pap. 25.00 (*0-8133-3613-9*) Westview.

Rothchild, Donald, jt. auth. see Lake, David.

Rothchild, Donald, jt. ed. see Harbeson, John W.

Rothchild, Donald, jt. ed. see Keller, Edmond J.

Rothchild, Donald S. Managing Ethnic Conflict in Africa: Pressures & Incentives for Cooperation. LC 97-4763. 343p. 1997. 49.95 (*0-8157-7594-6*) Brookings.

Rothchild, Donald S., jt. auth. see Lake, David A.

Rothchild, Gillian. Dear Mom & Dad: What Kids of Divorce Really Want to Say to Their Parents. LC 99-12399. 128p. (Orig.). 1999. per. 10.00 (*0-671-02788-3*, PB Trade Paper) PB.

Rothchild, Joan, et al, eds. Research in Philosophy & Technology Vol. 13: Technology & Feminism. 395p. 1993. 78.50 (*1-55938-566-9*) Jai Pr.

Rothchild, John. The Bear Book: Survie & Profit in Ferocious Makets. LC 97-52583. 304p. 1998. 24.95 (*0-471-19718-1*) Wiley.

— Fool & His Money: The Odyssey of an Average Investor. (Wiley Investment Classics Ser.). 272p. 1998. 34.95 (*0-471-25151-8*) Wiley.

***Rothchild, John.** Fool & His Money: The Odyssey of an Average Investor. (Wiley Investment Classics Ser.). 272p. 1998. pap. 19.95 (*0-471-25138-0*) Wiley.

— Up for Grabs: A Trip Through Time & Space in the Sunshine State. 2000. reprint ed. pap. 19.95 (*0-8130-1829-3*) U Press Fla.

Rothchild, John, jt. auth. see Douglas, Marjory S.

Rothchild, John, jt. auth. see Lynch, Peter.

Rothchild, Nina, jt. auth. see Watkins, Bonnie.

Rothchild, Seymour, ed. Advances in Tracer Methodology: A Collection of Papers Presented at the Sixth, Seventh & Eighth Symposia on Tracer Methodology & Other Papers Selected by the Editor. LC 62-13475. 329p. reprint ed. pap. 102.00 (*0-8357-5189-9*, 201940800002) Bks Demand.

Rothchild, Seymour, ed. see Advances in Tracer Methodology.

Rothchild, Sylvia. Family Stories for Every Generation. LC 89-5561. 229p. reprint ed. pap. 71.00 (*0-608-10553-8*, 207117300009) Bks Demand.

Rothe, Andrea, jt. ed. see Dardes, Kathleen.

***Rothe, Barbara.** Rescue Ring. LC 99-93889. 1999. pap. 14.95 (*0-533-13183-9*) Vantage.

***Rothe, Claude R.** 100 Steps to Better Health. LC 99-96681. 2000. pap. 11.95 (*0-533-13318-1*) Vantage.

***Rothe, Dietmar.** In Search of Truth & Freedom: A Path from Ignorance to Awareness. unabridged ed. LC 99-76710. (Illus.). xvi, 266p. 2000. 26.95 (*0-9677453-2-2*) Avila Bks.

Rothe, E. H. Introduction to Various Aspects of Degree Theory in Banach Spaces. LC 86-8038. (Mathematical Surveys & Monographs: Vol. 23). 242p. 1986. text 77.00 (*0-8218-1522-9*, SURV/23) Am Math.

Rothe, F. Global Solutions of Reaction-Diffusion Systems. (Lecture Notes in Mathematics Ser.: Vol. 1072). v, 216p. 1984. 37.95 (*0-387-13365-8*) Spr-Verlag.

Rothe, Gunter M. Electrophoresis of Enzymes: Laboratory Methods. LC 94-35142. (Laboratory Ser.). 1994. write for info. (*3-540-58114-6*) Spr-Verlag.

— Electrophoresis of Enzymes: Laboratory Methods. LC 94-35142. (Laboratory Ser.). 1994. 79.95 (*0-387-58114-6*) Spr-Verlag.

Rothe, H. J. Lattice Gauge Theories. 396p. (C). 1992. text 86.00 (*981-02-0606-2*); pap. text 46.00 (*981-02-0607-0*) World Scientific Pub.

Rothe, Hans, ed. Daumier on War. LC 77-9349. (Quality Paperbacks Ser.). (Illus.). 1977. pap. 6.95 (*0-306-80079-9*) Da Capo.

Rothe, Heinz J. Lattice Gauge Theories: An Introduction. 2nd ed. Vol. 59. 528p. pap. 26.00 (*981-02-3742-1*) World Scientific Pub.

Rothe, J. Peter. Beyond Traffic Safety. 366p. (C). 1993. text 44.95 (*1-56000-095-3*) Transaction Pubs.

— The Safety of Elderly Drivers: Yesterday's Young in Today's Traffic. 250p. 1989. pap. 24.95 (*0-88738-728-4*) Transaction Pubs.

— The Trucker's World: Risk, Safety, & Mobility. 240p. 1991. 44.95 (*1-56000-023-6*) Transaction Pubs.

— The Trucker's World: Risk, Safety, & Mobility. 240p. (C). 1991. pap. 24.95 (*1-56000-551-3*) Transaction Pubs.

Rothe, J. Peter, ed. Challenging the Old Order: Towards New Directions in Traffic Safety Theory. 250p. 1990. pap. 24.95 (*0-88738-828-0*) Transaction Pubs.

— Rethinking Young Drivers. 292p. 1989. pap. 21.95 (*0-88738-785-3*) Transaction Pubs.

Rothe, J. Peter & Cooper, P. J., eds. Motorcyclists: Image & Reality. 222p. 1989. pap. 21.95 (*0-88738-784-5*) Transaction Pubs.

Rothe, J. Peter & Cooper, Peter J. Never Say Always: Perspectives on Seat Belt Use. 192p. 1989. pap. 24.95 (*0-88738-775-6*) Transaction Pubs.

Rothe, Len. The Bare Truth: Stars of Burlesque from the '40s & '50s. 112p. 1998. pap. 19.95 (*0-7643-0603-0*) Schiffer.

— The Queens of Burlesque: Vintage Photographs from the 1940s & 1950s. LC 97-80161. (Illus.). 112p. 1998. pap. 19.95 (*0-7643-0449-6*) Schiffer.

Rothe, Manfred. Introduction to Aroma Research. (C). 1988. text 173.50 (*90-277-2078-9*) Kluwer Academic.

Rothe, P. H., ed. see Basic Mechanisms in Two-phase Flow & Heat Transfer.

Rothe, Peter. Kanarische Inseln: Lanzarote, Fuerteventura, Gran Canaria, Tenerife, Gomera, La Palma, Hierro. 2nd rev. ed. (Sammlung Geologischer Fuehrer Ser.: Band 81). (GER., Illus.). xiv, 308p. 1996. spiral bd. 35.00 (*3-443-15064-0*, Pub. by Gebruder Borntraeger) Balogh.

Rothe, Robert. Acadia: The Story Behind the Scenery. LC 78-78121. (Illus.). 48p. (Orig.). 1979. pap. 7.95 (*0-916122-57-3*) KC Pubns.

Rotheim, Philip. Agbiotech: Genetically Altered Traits in Crops - Food Products & Food Ingredients. 124p. 1998. 3250.00 (*1-56965-125-6*, GA-104) BCC.

— Bulk Pharmaceutical Actives. LC 97-145022. 215p. 1997. 3400.00 (*1-56965-367-4*, B-108) BCC.

— Cytokines & Growth Factors. 243rd ed. LC 96-128210. 1995. 2750.00 (*1-56965-035-7*, C-194) BCC.

— Inert Ingredients for Drugs. LC 98-143452. 285p. 1997. 3750.00 (*1-56965-373-9*, C-068N) BCC.

— Investment Opportunities in China. LC 96-136090. 310p. 1995. 2650.00 (*1-56965-033-0*, C-142) BCC.

— Opportunities in Chiral Technology: Emphasizing Enabling Products. LC 96-143425. 290p. 1995. 2950.00 (*1-56965-031-4*, C079R) BCC.

— Plant-Derived Drugs: Products, Technologies, Applications. 324p. 1998. 3450.00 (*1-56965-392-5*, B-121) BCC.

— Protein Drugs: Manufacturing Technologies. LC 98-120872. (Report Ser.: No. B-114). 274p. 1997. 3450.00 (*1-56965-384-4*) BCC.

Rotheim, Philip, contrib. by. Genetic Platform Technologies: Materials & Applications. 293p. 1995. 2950.00 (*1-56965-016-0*, C-199) BCC.

Rotheim, Philip & Wakeford. Commercial Biotechnology Reviews. 294p. 1995. 1500.00 (*1-56965-323-2*, DBI94) BCC.

Rotheim, Roy, ed. New Keynesian Economics. LC 96-54816. (Routledge Frontiers of Political Economy Ser.: Vol. 9). (Illus.). 408p. (C). 1998. 90.00 (*0-415-12388-7*) Routledge.

Rothel, David. An Ambush of Ghosts: A Guide to Great Western Film Locations. LC 90-84532. 306p. 1991. 40.00 (*0-944019-10-2*) Empire NC.

— The Gene Autry Book: A Reference - Trivia - Scrapbook. LC 87-82382. 294p. 1988. pap. 25.00 (*0-944019-03-X*) Empire NC.

***Rothel, David.** Richard Boone: A Knight without Armor in a Savage Land. LC 99-69178. (Illus.). 274p. 2000. 35.00 (*0-944019-29-3*) Empire NC.

Rothel, David. The Roy Rogers Book: A Reference-Trivia-Scrapbook. LC 87-8183. 224p. 1987. pap. 25.00 (*0-944019-01-3*) Empire NC.

— Those Great Cowboy Sidekicks. LC 84-10513. 338p. 1984. 49.50 (*0-8108-1707-1*) Scarecrow.

— Tim Holt. (Illus.). 290p. 1994. text 30.00 (*0-944019-13-7*) Empire NC.

Rothel, David, jt. auth. see Thornton, Chuck.

Rothenbeck-Neff, Nancy, ed. see Hedge, Christine.

Rothenberg. Race Class & Gender. 4th ed. 1998. pap. text 5.00 (*0-312-17961-8*) St Martin.

— Race Class Gender: Dictionary. 1997. pap. text 34.50 (*0-312-18513-8*); pap. text 28.00 (*0-312-18514-6*) St Martin.

Rothenberg, et al. Basic Prehospital Care. (Illus.). 688p. 1991. student ed., wbk. ed. 12.95 (*0-8016-3418-0*) Mosby Inc.

Rothenberg, Albert. Creativity & Madness: New Findings & Old Stereotypes. 208p. 1994. reprint ed. pap. text 14.95 (*0-8018-4977-2*) Johns Hopkins.

— The Emerging Goddess: The Creative Process in Art, Science, & Other Fields. LC 78-26486. 1993. lib. bdg. 22.50 (*0-226-72948-6*) U Ch Pr.

— The Emerging Goddess: The Creative Process in Art, Science, & Other Fields. LC 78-26486. (Midway Reprint Ser.). (Illus.). xii, 452p. 1998. pap. text 30.00 (*0-226-72950-8*) U Ch Pr.

An Asterisk (*) at the beginning of an entry indicates that the title is appearing for the first time.

An Asterisk (*) at the beginning of an entry indicates that the title is appearing for the first time.

R

Rother, K. & Till, G. O., eds. The Complement System. (Illus.). 540p. 1988. 130.95 (0-387-18205-5) Spr-Verlag.
Rother, K., et al. The Complement System. 2nd rev. ed. LC 97-1035. 1997. write for info. (3-540-61894-5) Spr-Verlag.
Rother, K. O., ed. see Collegium Internationale Allergologicum Symposium.
Rother, U., jt. ed. see Rother, K.
Rother, Wolfgang. Der Kunsttempel an der Bruhlschen Terrasse: Das Akademie-& Ausstellungsgebaude von Constantin Lipsius in Dresden. (GER., Illus.). 104p. 1994. pap. text 9.00 (3-364-00292-4) Gordon & Breach.
Rotheram-Borus, Mary J., et al, eds. Planning to Live: Evaluating & Treating Suicidal Teens in Community Settings. (Illus.). 408p. (C). 1990. 24.95 (1-878848-00-3, 119) Natl Res Ctr.
Rotheram, Mary, jt. auth. see Phinney, Jean S.
Rotherham, G. A. It's Really Quite Safe. (Illus.). 304p. 1985. 18.00 (0-89745-107-4) Sunflower U Pr.
Rotherham, G. A., ed. It's Really Quite Safe. 304p. (C). 1990. pap. 48.00 (0-920497-07-1, Pub. by Picton) St Mut.
Rotherham, J. B., et al. The Lord's Supper: Historical Writings on Its Meaning to the Body of Christ. Gresham, Charles & Lawson, Tom, eds. 243p. (C). 1993. 13.99 (0-89900-603-5) College Pr Pub.
Rotherham, Joseph B. The Emphasized Bible. LC 59-7560. 1208p. 1994. reprint ed. 49.99 (0-8254-3601-X, Kregel Class) Kregel.
Rotherham, Lee, jt. auth. see White, Christopher.
Rothermel, Dan. Starting Points: How to Set up & Run a Writing Workshop. LC 96-20406. 1996. pap. write for info. (1-56090-109-8) Natl Middle Schl.
Rothermel, Jerry L. Human - a Novel. 207p. (C). 1987. reprint ed. pap. 5.95 (0-944386-05-9) SOM Pub.
— Meditation the Answer to Your Prayers. 99p. (C). 1987. reprint ed. pap. 4.95 (0-944386-01-6) SOM Pub.
— Symbols of Dreams. 95p. (Orig.). (C). 1987. reprint ed. pap. 4.95 (0-944386-03-2) SOM Pub.
Rothermel, Kurt & Hohl, Fritz. Mobile Agents: 2nd International Workshop, MA '98, Stuttgart, Germany, September 9-11, 1998: Proceedings, Vol. 147. LC 98-39444. (Lecture Notes in Computer Science Ser.). 1998. pap. 49.00 (3-540-64959-X) Spr-Verlag.
Rothermel, Kurt & Popescu-Zeletin, R. Mobile Agents: First International Workshop, MA 97, Berlin, Germany, April 1997: Proceedings, Vol. 121. LC 97-13203. (Lecture Notes in Computer Science Ser.). 1997. pap. write for info. (3-540-62803-7) Spr-Verlag.
Rothermel, Richard C., et al. Fire Growth Maps for the 1988 Greater Yellowstone Area Fires. (Illus.). 68p. 1997. reprint ed. 16.00 (0-89904-589-8, Bear Meadows Resrch Grp); reprint ed. pap. 10.00 (0-89904-590-1, Bear Meadows Resrch Grp) Crumb Elbow Pub.
Rothermel, Richard C., jt. auth. see Latham, Don J.
Rothermell, Fred. Fifth Avenue. LC 76-134978. (Short Story Index Reprint Ser.). 1977. 20.95 (0-8369-3708-2) Ayer.
Rothermich, John A., ed. see Schanker, Harry H.
Rothermund, Dietmar. Asian Trade & European Expansion in the Age of Mercantilism. 1981. 17.50 (0-8364-0812-8, Pub. by Manohar) S Asia.
— An Economic History of India. 224p. 1988. text 49.95 (0-7099-4228-1) Routledge.
— An Economic History of India: From Pre-Colonial Times to 1991. 2nd ed. 224p. (C). 1993. pap. 25.99 (0-415-08871-2) Routledge.
— The German Intellectual Quest for India. 73p. 1987. 8.00 (81-85054-16-9, Pub. by Manohar) S Asia.
— The Global Impact of the Great Depression, 1929-1939. LC 95-25780. 192p. (C). 1996. pap. 18.99 (0-415-11819-0) Routledge.
— The Indian Economy Under British Rule. 1983. 17.50 (0-8364-1021-1, Pub. by Manohar) S Asia.
Rothermund, Dietmar, et al, eds. Urban Growth & Rural Stagnation: Studies in the Economy of an Indian Coalfield & Its Hinterland. 1980. 36.00 (0-8364-0662-1, Pub. by Manohar) S Asia.
Rothermund, Dietmar, et al. Regional Desparities in India: Rural & Industrial Dimensions. (C). 1991. 22.00 (0-8364-2734-3, Pub. by Manohar) S Asia.
Rothermund, Dietmar, jt. auth. see Kulke, Herman.
Rothermund, Dietmar, jt. auth. see Kulke, Hermann.
Rothero, Chris. Strawberry Fair. 96p. (J). (gr. 1-6). write for info. (0-7136-2676-3, Pub. by A & C Blk) Midpt Trade.
Rothero, Christopher. The Armies of Agincourt. (Men-at-Arms Ser.: No. 113). (Illus.). 48p. pap. 11.95 (0-85045-394-1, 9046, Pub. by Ospry) Stackpole.
— Armies of Crecy & Poitiers. (Men-at-Arms Ser.: No. 111). (Illus.). 48p. pap. 11.95 (0-85045-393-3, 9044, Pub. by Ospry) Stackpole.
— The Scottish & Welsh War, 1250-1400. (Men-at-Arms Ser.: No. 151). (Illus.). 48p. pap. 11.95 (0-85045-542-1, 9083, Pub. by Ospry) Stackpole.
Rotheroe, Dominic. London Inn Signs. (Album Ser.: No. 257). (Illus.). 32p. 1989. pap. 6.25 (0-7478-0088-X, Pub. by Shire Pubns) Parkwest Pubns.
Rothert, Eugene A. & Daubert, James R. Horticultural Therapy at a Physical Rehabilitation Facility. (Illus.). 130p. (Orig.). (C). 1981. pap. 10.00 (0-939914-02-6) Chi Horticult.
— Horticultural Therapy for Nursing Homes, Senior Centers, Retirement Living. (Illus.). 130p. (Orig.). 1981. pap. 10.00 (0-939914-01-8) Chi Horticult.
Rothert, Eugene A., Jr., jt. auth. see Daubert, James R.
Rothert, Gene. The Enabling Garden: Creating Barrier-Free Gardens. LC 93-41968. (Illus.). 160p. 1994. pap. 13.95 (0-87833-847-0) Taylor Pub.
Rothert, Otto A. A History of Muhlenberg County Kentucky. (Illus.). 496p. 1996. pap. 34.50 (0-7884-0454-7, R573) Heritage Bk.
— A History of Muhlenberg County (Kentucky) 496p. 1996. reprint ed. pap. 39.95 (0-8063-4628-0, 9415) Clearfield Co.
— The Outlaws of Cave-in-Rock. LC 70-140371. (Select Bibliographies Reprint Ser.). 1977. 22.95 (0-8369-5614-1) Ayer.
— The Outlaws of Cave-in-Rock. (Shawnee Classics Ser.). (C). 1995. pap. 12.95 (0-8093-2034-7) S Ill U Pr.
— Story of a Poet: Madison Cawein. LC 76-146871. (Select Bibliographies Reprint Ser.). 1977. reprint ed. 42.95 (0-8369-5640-0) Ayer.
Rothery, Agnes E. Joyful Gardener. LC 77-99647. (Essay Index Reprint Ser.). 1977. 21.95 (0-8369-2128-3) Ayer.
Rothery, Andrew, ed. see Language & Reading in Mathematics Group Staff.
Rothery, Brian. BS 7750: Implementing the Environment Management Standard. 237p. 1993. 74.95 (0-566-07392-7, Pub. by Gower) Ashgate Pub Co.
— ISO 14000 & ISO 9000. LC 95-22035. 278p. 1996. 83.95 (0-566-07648-9, Pub. by Gower) Ashgate Pub Co.
— ISO 9000. 2nd ed. 220p. 1993. 74.95 (0-566-07402-8, Pub. by Gower) Ashgate Pub Co.
— Standards & Certification in Europe. 216p. 1996. 78.95 (0-566-07644-6, Pub. by Gower) Ashgate Pub Co.
— Standards in the Services Industry. LC 96-38968. 200p. 1997. text 78.95 (0-566-07837-6, Pub. by Gower) Ashgate Pub Co.
Rothery, Brian & Robertson, Ian. The Truth about Outsourcing. 200p. 1995. 78.95 (0-566-07515-6, Pub. by Gower) Ashgate Pub Co.
Rothery, David A. Geology. (Study Guides Ser.). 224p. 1998. pap., student ed. 12.95 (0-8442-0035-2, 00352, Teach Yrslf) NTC Contemp Pub Co.
— Satellites of the Outer Planets: Worlds in Their Own Right. 2nd ed. LC QB401.R67 1999. (Illus.). 264p. 1999. pap. 45.00 (0-19-512555-X) OUP.
***Rothery, David A.** Teach Yourself the Planets. (Teach Yourself Ser.). (Illus.). 192p. 2000. pap. 10.95 (0-658-00486-7, 004867, Teach Yrslf) NTC Contemp Pub Co.
Rothery, M. & Cameron, G., eds. Child Maltreatment: Expanded Concepts of Helping. 336p. 1990. text 69.95 (0-8058-0455-2) L Erlbaum Assocs.
***Rothery, M. A. & Enns, George.** Clinical Practice with Families: Supporting Creativity & Competence. LC 00-40783. 2000. pap. write for info. (0-7890-1085-2) Haworth Pr.
Rothery, P., jt. auth. see Brown, D.
Rothery, Sean. A Field Guide to the Buildings of Ireland: Illustrating the Smaller Buildings of Town & Count. LC 97-184583. (Illus.). 240p. 1997. 53.95 (1-874675-86-4); pap. 25.95 (1-874675-81-3) Dufour.
— Ireland & the New Architecture, 1900-1940. 1996. 69.95 (0-946640-58-0, Pub. by Lilliput Pr) Irish Bks Media.
Rothes, John L. Relation of Proceedings Concerning the Affairs of the Kirk of Scotland. LC 79-174966. (Bannatyne Club, Edinburgh. Publications: No. 37). reprint ed. 38.50 (0-404-52743-4) AMS Pr.
Rotheva, Brian, jt. auth. see Lawson-Hall, Toni.
Rothfarb, Ed. In the Land of Taj Mahal: The World of the Fabulous Mughals. LC 97-8281. 243p. (YA). (gr. 7 up). 1998. 21.95 (0-8050-5299-2) H Holt & Co.
Rothfarb, Lee A., ed. see Kurth, Ernst.
Rothfeder, Jeffrey, et al. The People vs. Big Tobacco: How the States Took on the Cigarette Giants. LC 97-42358. (Illus.). 334p. 1998. 23.95 (1-57660-057-2, Pub. by Bloomberg NJ) Norton.
Rothfeld, Beverly. Pediatric Health Certification: Exam Review. LC 98-22075. 196p. (C). 1998. pap. text 39.95 (0-8385-8137-4, A-8137-0) Appleton & Lange.
Rothfeld, Glenn & LeVert, Suzanne. Ginkgo Biloba: An Herbal Fountain of Youth for Your Brain. LC 99-163046. 256p. 1998. mass mkt. 5.99 (0-440-22625-2) Dell.
— Natural Medicine for Back Pain: The Best Alternative Methods for Banishing Backache from Acupressure & Chiropractic to Nutrition & Yoga. LC 95-31025. (Illus.). 224p. (Orig.). 1996. pap. 11.95 (0-87596-288-2) Rodale Pr Inc.
Rothfeld, Glenn, et al. Natural Medicine for Heart Disease: The Best Alternative Methods to Prevent & Treat High Cholesterol, High Blood Pressure, Stroke, Chest Pain, & Other Circulatory Problems. LC 95-24445. 233p. (Orig.). 1996. pap. 11.95 (0-87596-289-0) Rodale Pr Inc.
***Rothfeld, Glenn S.** Folic Acid & the Amazing B Vitamins. 2000. mass mkt. 6.99 (0-425-17369-0) Berkley Pub.
Rothfeld, Glenn S. & LeVert, Suanne. Natural Medicine for Arthritis: The Best Alternative Methods for Relieving Pain & Stiffness: from Food & Herbs to Acupuncture & Homeopathy. 288p. 1996. pap. 13.95 (0-87596-287-4) Rodale Pr Inc.
Rothfeld, Glenn S. & LeVert, Suzanne. Natural Medicine for Allergies: The Best Alternative Methods for Quick Relief. 288p. 1996. pap. 13.95 (0-87596-286-6) Rodale Pr Inc.
— Natural Medicine for Back Pain. large type ed. LC 96-39213. (Spec-Hall Ser.). 328p. 1997. lib. bdg. 23.95 (0-7838-2026-7, G K Hall Lrg Type) Mac Lib Ref.
Rothfeld, Otto. With Pen & Rifle in Kashmir. (C). 1993. reprint ed. 18.00 (81-7041-823-2, Pub. by Anmol) S Asia.
Rothfeld, Steven. French Dreams. LC 92-50934. (Illus.). 96p. 1993. 19.95 (1-56305-469-8, 3469) Workman Pub.
— Irish Dreams. 1998. 17.95 (0-8118-1985-X) Chronicle Bks.
— Italian Dreams. LC 95-9105. (Illus.). 86p. 1995. 19.95 (0-00-225066-7) Collins SF.
Rothfield. Mapping the Local. (C). 1999. write for info. (0-415-06057-5); pap. write for info. (0-415-06058-3) Routledge.
Rothfield, Lawrence. Vital Signs: Medical Realism in Nineteenth-Century Fiction. (Literature in History Ser.). 250p. 1992. text 37.50 (0-691-06896-8, Pub. by Princeton U Pr); pap. text 15.95 (0-691-02954-7, Pub. by Princeton U Pr) Cal Prin Full Svc.
Rothfield, Tom. Classical Comedy - An Armoury of Laughter, Democracy's Bastion of Defence: Introducing a Law of Opposites. LC 99-17577. 288p. 1999. 42.00 (0-7618-1365-9) U Pr of Amer.
Rothfork, Judy & Drilling, Eileen. Listening to God's Word - Year A: Activities & Stories. 176p. 1998. pap. 15.00 (1-56854-226-7, LCATA) Liturgy Tr Pubns.
— Listening to God's Word - Year A: Adult's Journal. 60p. (Orig.). 1998. pap. 5.00 (1-56854-227-5, AJORNA) Liturgy Tr Pubns.
— Listening to God's Word - Year A: Child's Journal. 60p. (Orig.). (J). (gr. 1-4). 1998. pap. 5.00 (1-56854-228-3, CJORNA) Liturgy Tr Pubns.
— Listening to God's Word - Year B: Activities & Stories. 176p. 1996. pap. 15.00 (1-56854-177-5, LCATB) Liturgy Tr Pubns.
— Listening to God's Word - Year B: Adult Journal. 60p. (Orig.). 1996. pap., wbk. ed. 5.00 (1-56854-206-2, ADJORN) Liturgy Tr Pubns.
— Listening to God's Word - Year B: Child's Journal. 60p. (Orig.). (J). (gr. 1-4). 1996. pap., wbk. ed. 5.00 (1-56854-207-0, CHJORN) Liturgy Tr Pubns.
— Listening to God's Word - Year C: Activities & Stories. 176p. 1997. pap. 15.00 (1-56854-209-7, LCATC) Liturgy Tr Pubns.
— Listening to God's Word - Year C: Adult's Journal. 60p. (Orig.). 1997. pap. 5.00 (1-56854-210-0, AJORNC) Liturgy Tr Pubns.
— Listening to God's Word - Year C: Child's Journal. 60p. (Orig.). (J). (gr. 1-4). 1997. pap. 5.00 (1-56854-211-9, CJORNC) Liturgy Tr Pubns.
Rothfus, Robert R. Working Concepts of Fluid Flow. (Illus.). 96p. (Orig.). (C). pap. 3.75 (0-685-23655-2) Bek Tech.
Rothgarber, Herbert. The Ensemble Recorder, Bk. 2. 1975. 4.00 (0-913334-23-5, CM1027) Consort Music.
— Let's Folk Dance. 16p. 1980. pap. 3.25 (0-918812-10-0, SE 0440) MMB Music.
— Make a Glad Sound. 1974. 5.00 (0-913334-17-0, CM1021) Consort Music.
Rothgarber, Herbert, contrib. by. The Drunken Sailor. 1975. 4.50 (0-913334-28-6, CM1035) Consort Music.
Rothgeb, Anita B. Short Stories. LC 95-67130. 1995. 8.95 (0-8158-0512-8) Chris Mass.
Rothgeb, Carrie L., ed. Abstracts of the Collected Works of C. G. Jung. LC 78-603478. 150p. 1993. pap. text 25.00 (1-85575-035-X, Pub. by H Karnac Bks Ltd) Other Pr LLC.
— Abstracts of the Standard Edition of the Complete Psychological Works of Sigmund Freud. LC 73-2144. 770p. (C). 1973. 85.00 (0-8236-0030-0) Intl Univs Pr.
— Abstracts of the Standard Edition of the Complete Works of Sigmund Freud. LC 94-70895. 315p. 1987. 35.00 (0-87668-135-6) Aronson.
Rothgeb, John, ed. see Schenker, Heinrich.
Rothgeb, John, ed. & tr. see Schenker, Heinrich.
Rothgeb, John, tr. see Jonas, Oswald.
Rothgeb, John M., Jr. Foreign Investment & Political Conflict in Developing Countries. LC 96-16280. 160p. 1996. 57.95 (0-275-94548-0, Praeger Pubs) Greenwood.
— Myths & Realities of Foreign Investment in Poor Countries: The Modern Leviathan in the Third World. LC 88-34026. 162p. 1989. 57.95 (0-275-93255-9, C3255, Praeger Pubs) Greenwood.
Rothgeb, Wayne P. New Guinea Skies: A Fighter Pilot's View of World War II. LC 92-2916. (Illus.). 278p. 1992. 39.95 (0-8138-0836-7) Iowa St U Pr.
Rothgerber, Harry, ed. see Gilbert, Brother.
Rothhammer, Francisco, jt. ed. see Schull, William J.
Rothholz, Amy. Iced Tigers. 72p. 1987. 10.00 (0-943959-00-4) Amagansett Pr.
Rothkegel. Knowledge & Object Knowledge. 1993. text 59.00 (0-86187-136-7) St Martin.
Rothko, Mark. Mark Rothko, 1903-1970. (Illus.). 205p. 1997. pap. 45.00 (1-55670-550-6) Stewart Tabori & Chang.
Rothkopf, David, jt. auth. see Johnstone, Christopher.
Rothkopf, David, jt. ed. see Purcell, Susan Kaufman.
Rothkopf, David J. The Price of Peace: Emergency Economic Intervention & U. S. Foreign Policy. LC 98-17009. 114p. 1998. pap. 10.95 (0-87003-150-3) Carnegie Endow.
Rothkopf, Ernst Z., ed. see Review of Research in Education Staff.
Rothkopf, Michael M. Standards & Practice of Homecare Therapeutics. 2nd ed. LC 96-20733. (Illus.). 440p. 1997. pap. 49.00 (0-683-07375-3) Lppncott W & W.
Rothkopf, Michael M. & Askanazi, Jeffrey. Intensive Home Care. (Illus.). 352p. 1992. 70.00 (0-683-07389-3) Lppncott W & W.
Rothkopf, Michelle, ed. see Blackwell, Donald A.
Rothkopf, Nancy & Cantor, Gilbert M. Pennsylvania Estates Practice, Vol. 1. LC 79-91161. (Practice Systems Library Manual). ring bd. 125.00 (0-317-00577-4) West Group.
— Pennsylvania Estates Practice, Vol. 1. LC 79-91161. (Practice Systems Library Manual). 1991. suppl. ed. 65.00 (0-317-03207-0) West Group.
***Rothkrug, Lionel.** Encyclopedia of Irish Spirituality. 2000. lib. bdg. 60.00 (1-57607-146-4) ABC-CLIO.
Rothkrug, Lionel & Taylor, Richard P. Death Masks, Relics, & Tombs: An Encyclopedia of Burial Traditions. 324p. 1997. 55.00 (0-87436-938-X, FN-1721) ABC-CLIO.
— Heavens, Hells, & Other Worlds: An Encyclopedia of the Afterlife. 324p. 1997. 55.00 (0-87436-939-8, FN-1720) ABC-CLIO.
Rothkrug, Paul & Olsen, Robert, eds. Mending the Earth: A World for Our Grandchildren. LC 90-23408. 219p. 1990. pap. 9.95 (1-55643-091-4) North Atlantic.
Rothleder, Dianne. The Work of Friendship: Rorty, His Critics, & the Project of Solidarity. LC 98-8132. (SUNY Series in the Philosophy of the Social Sciences). (Illus.). 163p. (C). 1999. pap. text 19.95 (0-7914-4128-8) State U NY Pr.
— The Work of Friendship: Rorty, His Critics, & the Project of Solidarity. LC 98-8132. (SUNY Series in the Philosophy of the Social Sciences). (Illus.). 160p. (C). 1999. text 59.50 (0-7914-4127-X) State U NY Pr.
Rothleder, Joseph. Specifications & Tolerances for Reference Standards & Field Standard Weights & Measures: 6, Specifications & Tolerances for Thermometers. 14p. 1997. pap. 1.75 (0-16-054743-1) USGPO.
Rothlein, Liz & Kelly, Walter. Holocaust. (Thematic Units Ser.). 80p. (J). (gr. 5-8). 1997. pap. 9.95 (1-55734-210-5) Tchr Create Mat.
Rothlein, Liz & Vaughn, Sharon. Learning Through Literature: Native Americans. (Learning Through Literature Ser.). (Illus.). 144p. (J). (gr. 3-5). 1997. pap., wbk. ed. 14.95 (1-55734-476-0) Tchr Create Mat.
Rothlein, Liz, et al. The Complete Guide to Thematic Units: Creating the Integrated Curriculum. (Illus.). 250p. (Orig.). (C). 1995. pap. text 33.95 (0-926842-42-0) CG Pubs Inc.
— More Thematic Units for Creating the Integrated Curriculum. 200p. (J). (gr. k-6). 1996. pap. 27.95 (0-926842-53-6) CG Pubs Inc.
Rothlein, Liz C. & Christman, Terri. Read It Again! A Guide for Teaching Reading Through Literature, K-2, Bk. 1. (Illus.). 116p. (Orig.). 1988. pap. 9.95 (0-673-38199-4, GoodYrBooks) Addson-Wesley Educ.
— Read It Again, More: Grades K-2, Bk. 1. 1990. pap., student ed. 9.95 (0-673-46373-7, GoodYrBooks) Addson-Wesley Educ.
— Read It Again, More: Grades 3-5, Bk. 2. 1991. pap., student ed. 9.95 (0-673-36007-5, GoodYrBooks) Addson-Wesley Educ.
Rothlein, Liz C. & Christmas, Terri. Read It Again Bk. 2: Grades 3-5. 1990. pap., student ed. 9.95 (0-673-46290-0, GoodYrBooks) Addson-Wesley Educ.
Rothlein, Liz C. & Meinbach, Anita M. The Literature Connection: Using Children's Books in the Classroom, K-Grade 8. 1990. pap. 24.95 (0-673-38450-0, GoodYrBooks) Addson-Wesley Educ.
— Take Ten Steps to Successful Research: Grades 5-8. (Illus.). 82p. (Orig.). 1988. pap. 9.95 (0-673-38087-4, GoodYrBooks) Addson-Wesley Educ.
Rothlein, Liz C. & Miller, Libby. Read It Again! Introducing Literature to Young Children, Preschool - Kindergarten, Bk. 1. (Illus.). 112p. (Orig.). (J). (ps). 1991. pap. 9.95 (0-673-36008-3, GoodYrBooks) Addson-Wesley Educ.
— Read It Again! Preschool - Kindergarten, Bk. 2. (Illus.). 144p. (Orig.). (J). (ps). 1993. pap. 9.95 (0-673-36042-3, GoodYrBooks) Addson-Wesley Educ.
Rothlein, Liz C. & Wild, Terri C. Read It Again! Multicultural Books for the Intermediate Grades. (Illus.). 144p. (Orig.). (J). (gr. 3-5). 1993. pap. 9.95 (0-673-36081-4, GoodYrBooks) Addson-Wesley Educ.
— Read It Again! Multicultural Books for the Primary Grades, Bk. 1. (Illus.). 144p. (Orig.). (J). 1993. pap. 9.95 (0-673-36064-4, GoodYrBooks) Addson-Wesley Educ.
Rothlein, Liz C., jt. auth. see Meinbach, Anita M.
Rothlein, Liz C., jt. auth. see Vaughn, Sharon.
Rothlein, Valerie, ed. see Hou, Tien.
Rothlisberg, Barbara A., jt. auth. see D'Amato, Rik C.
Rothlisberger, Marcel. Claude Lorrain: The Paintings: Critical Catalogue & Illustrations, 2 vols., Set. LC 79-83839. (Illus.). 1979. reprint ed. lib. bdg. 150.00 (0-87817-244-0) Hacker.
Rothman. Physical Therapy Assistant License Exam. (Physical Therapy Ser.). (C). 2000. 29.95 (0-8273-8082-8) Delmar.
— Prevention Practice. 1992. text 78.95 (0-7216-3261-0, W B Saunders Co) Harcrt Hlth Sci Grp.
— Reopening the American West. LC 97-21138. 1998. 35.00 (0-8165-1600-6); pap. 15.95 (0-8165-1625-1) U of Ariz Pr.
— Self Awareness. LC 98-21919. 155p. 1998. pap. text, wbk. ed. 24.00 (0-205-29029-9) Allyn.
— Stepping Out into Field. 230p. 1999. pap. text 32.00 (0-205-31332-9) Allyn.
Rothman, Alan. Poems for All Seasons. 1998. pap. write for info. (1-58235-028-0) Watermrk Pr.
— Poetic Memories. 1998. pap. write for info. (1-58235-106-6) Watermrk Pr.
— Portugal in Africa: The Last Hundred Years. LC 81-150129. 27.00 (0-582-64379-1) Longman.
Rothman, Barbara Katz. Encyclopedia of Childbearing: Critical Perspectives. LC 92-14975. (Illus.). 472p. 1992. 74.50 (0-89774-648-1) Oryx Pr.
— Genetic Maps & Human Imaginations: The Limits of Science in Understanding Who We Are. LC 98-18800. 288p. 1998. 24.95 (0-393-04703-2) Norton.
***Rothman, Barbara Katz.** Recreating Motherhood. LC 00-32349. 312p. (C). 2000. pap. text 22.00 (0-8135-2874-7) Rutgers U Pr.
Rothman, Barbara Katz. The Tentative Pregnancy: How Amniocentesis Changes the Experience of Motherhood. LC 93-205351. 288p. 1993. pap. 9.95 (0-393-30998-3) Norton.

An Asterisk (*) at the beginning of an entry indicates that the title is appearing for the first time.

R

An Asterisk (*) at the beginning of an entry indicates that the title is appearing for the first time.

R

Matters as the Mind Fluid, the Behavior of the Stock Market & the Disposition of a Quantum Mechanical Sphinx, to Name a Few. 336p. 1999. pap. text 15.00 (*0-7382-0169-3*, Pub. by Perseus Pubng) HarpC.

Rothman, W. A. & Title, Monroe M. Health Facility Malpractice Cases: A Management Prevention Guide. 187p. 1995. lib. bdg. 145.00 (*1-56072-227-4*) Nova Sci Pubs.

Rothman, William. Documentary Film Classics. (Cambridge Studies in Film). (Illus.). 233p. (C). 1997. text 69.95 (*0-521-45067-5*); pap. text 18.95 (*0-521-45681-9*) Cambridge U Pr.

— Hitchcock: The Murderous Gaze. (Harvard Film Studies). (Illus.). 383p. 1982. pap. 25.95 (*0-674-40411-4*) HUP.

— The I of the Camera: Essays in Film Criticism, History & Aesthetics. (Cambridge Studies in Film). (Illus.). 232p. 1988. text 74.95 (*0-521-36048-X*); pap. text 19.95 (*0-521-36828-6*) Cambridge U Pr.

***Rothman, William & Keane, Marian.** Cavell's "The World Viewed" A Philosophical Perspective on Film. (Contemporary Film & Television Ser.). (Illus.). 320p. 2000. 49.95 (*0-8143-2895-4*); pap. 19.95 (*0-8143-2896-2*) Wayne St U Pr.

Rothman, William A. A Bibliography of Collective Bargaining in Hospitals & Related Facilities, 2 vols. Incl. Vol. 2. Bibliography of Collective Bargaining in Hospitals & Related Facilities. 1970. (*0-87736-318-8*); Vol. 1. 1959-1968. 1970. 10.00 (*0-87736-301-3*); Vol. 2. 1969-1971. 1970. 10.00 (*0-87736-320-X*); 1970. 20.00 (*0-318-56089-5*) U of Mich Inst Labor.

Rothmann, Ralf. Knife Edge. Mitchell, Breon, tr. from GER. LC 91-43449. 128p. 1992. 19.95 (*0-8112-1204-1*, Pub. by New Directions); pap. 9.95 (*0-8112-1210-6*, NDP744, Pub. by New Directions) Norton.

Rothmann, S. Charles, ed. Constructive Uses of Atomic Energy. LC 73-128304. (Essay Index Reprint Ser.). 1977. 23.95 (*0-8369-2129-1*) Ayer.

Rothmann, Susan A. Sperm Confirm: Comprehensive Morphology Atlas of Sperm. (Illus.). 127p. 1997. sl. 363.00 (*0-9660540-0-8*, SC100) Fertil Solns.

Rothmann, Susan A., ed. Sperm Confirm: Comprehensive Morphology Atlas of Sperm. (Illus.). 127p. 1997. 375.00 (*0-9660540-1-6*, SC101) Fertil Solns.

Rothmann, Susan A., jt. auth. see Kinzer, Donna R.

Rothmeier, Arnold F. Pan the Low Waters. 219p. 1999. pap. 12.95 (*1-891929-25-9*) Four Seasons.

Rothmeier, Jeffrey, ed. Proceedings: MUMPS Users' Group Meeting. 1976. 20.00 (*0-918118-03-4*) M Technol.

Rothmiller, Mike. L. A. Secret Police. 1992. mass mkt. 5.99 (*0-671-79657-7*) PB.

Rothmiller, Mike & Goldman, Ivan G. L. A. Secret Police. 1992. pap. 5.99 (*0-685-61109-4*) PB.

Rothmund, M., et al, eds. Carcinoid Tumors. (Journal: Digestion: Vol. 55, Suppl. 3, 1994). (Illus.). iv, 116p. 1995. pap. 49.75 (*3-8055-6121-0*) S Karger.

Rothmund, M. & Wells, S. A., Jr., eds. Parathyroid Surgery. (Progress in Surgery Ser.: Vol. 18). (Illus.). x, 250p. 1986. 154.00 (*3-8055-4217-8*) S Karger.

Rothmyer, Karen. Winning Pulitzers: The Stories Behind Some of the Best News Coverage of Our Time. 256p. 1991. text 36.50 (*0-231-07028-4*) Col U Pr.

Rothney, Murray, jt. auth. see Findley, A. M.

Rothnie, W., jt. auth. see Lahore, J.

Rothon, R. N., ed. Particulate Filled Polymer Composites. 1996. (*0-582-08782-1*) Addison-Wesley.

Rothovius, Andrew E., jt. auth. see Hughes, John C.

Rothra, Elizabeth O. Florida's Pioneer Naturalist: The Life of Charles Torrey Simpson. (Illus.). 240p. 1995. 29.95 (*0-8130-1374-7*) U Press Fla.

Rothrock, Carson. Training the High School Orchestra. LC 71-148489. 231 P.p. 1971. 8.95 (*0-13-926816-2*, Parker Publishing Co) P-H.

Rothrock, Cynthia, jt. auth. see Chung, George.

Rothrock, G. L. Development of a Smaller Automobile Transmission. (Technical Papers: Vol. P189). (Illus.). 22p. 1939. pap. text 30.00 (*1-55589-405-4*) AGMA.

Rothrock, Gail C., jt. ed. see Coleman, Margaret M.

Rothrock, George A. The Huguenots: A Biography of a Minority. LC 78-23476. (Illus.). 228p. 1979. text 37.95 (*0-88229-277-3*) Burnham Inc.

Rothrock, George A. & Jones, Tom B. Europe; a Brief History Vol. I: Prehistory to 1815. 2nd rev. ed. LC 81-43503. (Illus.). 410p. 1981. reprint ed. pap. text 23.00 (*0-8191-2070-7*) U Pr of Amer.

Rothrock, George A., jt. auth. see Hebbert, John.

Rothrock, Jane C. Perioperative Nursing Care Planning. 2nd ed. (Illus.). 656p. (C). (gr. 13). 1996. pap. text 42.95 (*0-8151-7147-1*, 24557) Mosby Inc.

— The RN First Assistant. 3rd ed. LC 98-20816. 512p. 1998. pap. text 44.95 (*0-7817-1501-6*) Lppncott W & W.

Rothrock, Jane C., ed. The RN First Assistant: An Expanded Perioperative Nursing Role. 2nd ed. LC 92-48997. 416p. 1993. text 43.95 (*0-397-55014-6*) Lppncott W & W.

Rothrock, Jane C., jt. auth. see Meeker, Margaret H.

Rothrock, Jane C., jt. auth. see Rothrock, Joseph T.

Rothrock, Jane C., ed. see AORN Staff.

Rothrock, Joseph T. & Rothrock, Jane C. Chesapeake Odysseys: An 1883 Cruise Revisited. LC 84-40343. (Illus.). 138p. reprint ed. pap. 42.80 (*0-608-20037-9*, 207130900010) Bks Demand.

Rothrock, Mary U., ed. The French Broad-Holston Country: A History of Knox County, Tennessee. (Illus.). 573p. 1972. 11.00 (*0-941199-02-9*) ETHS.

Rothrock, Robert W. & D'Amore, Gabriella. The Illustrated Guide to Better Sex for People with Chronic Pain. 19p. 1991. pap. 8.95 (*0-9632602-0-0*) Rothrock & DAmore.

— The Illustrated Guide to Better Sex for People with Chronic Pain. 2nd ed. (Illus.). 50p. 1992. pap. 11.95 (*0-9632602-1-9*) Rothrock & DAmore.

Rothrock, Steven G. Tarascon Adult Emergency Pocketbook. rev. ed. 128p. 1998. pap. 9.95 (*1-882742-10-9*) Tarascon Pub.

— Tarascon Pediatric Emergency Pocketbook. 3rd rev. ed. 128p. 1998. pap. 9.95 (*1-882742-11-7*) Tarascon Pub.

***Roths, Regina.** Kansas - Vast Horizons. 144p. 1999. 34.95 (*1-883987-08-3*, Pub. by Riverbend Bks) Bookhouse.

***Roths, Regina & Metz, Kim.** Rapid City & the Black Hills. (Illus.). 288p. 1999. 34.95 (*1-883987-09-1*, Pub. by Riverbend Bks) Bookhouse.

Rothschield, Paul. Holocaust Pawns. (Ben-Gurion Bks. & Media Production Ser.). 1998. pap. 31.00 (*0-915133-15-6*) Gindi Pr.

Rothschild. Biological Treatment in Psychiatry. (C). 1999. text. write for info. (*0-7216-7164-0*, W B Saunders Co) Harcrt Hlth Sci Grp.

Rothschild. The Sea: Ocean Science of Fisheries, Vol. 15. 500p. 1998. 110.00 (*0-471-18900-6*) Wiley.

Rothschild, jt. auth. see Lambert.

Rothschild, A. M., ed. Contributions to Autacoid Pharmacology: A Festschrift in Honour of Mauricio Rocha e Silva. LC 92-10713. (Agents & Actions Supplements Ser.: Vol. 36). (Illus.). x, 286p. 1992. 81.50 (*0-8176-2617-4*) Birkhauser.

***Rothschild, Amalie R.** Fillmore East Live!, 1. 156p. 1999. 40.00 (*1-56025-244-8*) Thunder Mtn.

***Rothschild, Amalie R. & Gruber, Ruth Ellen.** Live at the Fillmore East: A Photographic Memoir. (Illus.). 2000. reprint ed. pap. 24.95 (*1-56025-279-0*, Thunders Mouth) Avalon NY.

Rothschild, Anthony J., jt. auth. see Sederer, Lloyd I.

Rothschild, Brian J. Dynamics of Marine Fish Populations. LC 86-9877. 293p. 1986. reprint ed. pap. 90.90 (*0-7837-2325-3*, 205741300004) Bks Demand.

Rothschild, Bruce J., ed. Toward a Theory on Biological-Physical Interactions in the World Ocean. (C). 1988. text 321.00 (*90-277-2765-1*) Kluwer Academic.

Rothschild, Bruce M. & Martin, Larry. Paleopathology: Disease in the Fossil Record. 400p. 1992. 148.95 (*0-8493-8897-X*, R134) CRC Pr.

Rothschild, D. Aviva. Graphic Novels: A Bibliographic Guide to Book-Length Comics. xxii, 246p. 1995. lib. bdg. 30.00 (*1-56308-086-9*) Libs Unl.

Rothschild, David, ed. Protecting What's Ours: Indigenous Peoples & Biodiversity. LC 96-71965.Tr. of Profegiendo lo Nuestro: Pueblos Indigenas y Biodiversidad. 1997. 10.83 (*0-9635396-0-4*) S & Meso-Am Ind.

Rothschild, Deborah, et al. Graphic Design in the Mechanical Age: Selections from the Merrill C. Berman Collection. LC 97-81268. (Illus.). 224p. 1998. 50.00 (*0-300-07494-8*) Yale U Pr.

Rothschild, Deborah M. Picasso's Parade: From Page to Stage. (Illus.). 280p. 1991. 90.00 (*0-85667-392-7*, Pub. by P Wilson) Scala Books.

— Yardbird Suite. LC 94-938. (Illus.). 72p. 1995. pap. text 18.95 (*0-913697-19-5*) Williams Art.

Rothschild, Deborah M., ed. James Turrell. LC 91-50616. (Illus.). 48p. (Orig.). 1991. pap. text 12.95 (*0-913697-12-5*) Williams Art.

Rothschild, Deborah M., jt. auth. see Balken, Debra B.

Rothschild, Deborah M., jt. auth. see Mandle, Julia B.

***Rothschild, Deborah Menaker, et al.** Graphic Design in the Mechanical Age: Selections from the Merrill C. Berman Collection. LC 97-81268. (Illus.). 1998. write for info. (*0-913697-23-0*) Williams Art.

Rothschild, Debra Reinking, jt. auth. see Rothschild, Peter.

***Rothschild, Dick.** Better Health: Simple, Sensible Strategies. (Illus.). 192p. 2000. pap. 12.95 (*0-9674108-1-9*, BH-1, Pub. by Standish Pr) ACCESS Pubs Network.

Rothschild, Edmund De, see De Rothschild, Edmund.

Rothschild, Edward F., jt. auth. see Sweeney, James J.

Rothschild, Frances, ed. see Denner, Richard E.

Rothschild, Frank D. State V. Lewis Case File. LC 99-169122. 101 p. 1998. 22.95 (*1-55681-615-4*) Natl Inst Trial Ad.

***Rothschild, Friedrich S.** Creation & Evolution. LC 99-47533. 360p. 1999. pap. 29.95 (*0-7658-0686-X*) Transaction Pubs.

Rothschild, Fritz A., ed. Jewish Perspectives on Christianity: Leo Baeck, Martin Buber, Franz Rosenweig, Will Herberg, Abraham J. Heschel. LC 96-21216. 376p. 1996. pap. 24.95 (*0-8264-0895-8*) Continuum.

Rothschild, Jeffrey. Bestower of Light: A Portrait Of Dr. Javad Nurbakh, Master of the Nimatullahi Sufi Order. LC 98-37912. 1999. 20.00 (*0-933546-98-X*) KNP.

Rothschild, Jeffrey, ed. see Nurbakhsh, Javad & Lewisehn, Leonard.

Rothschild, Joan. Teaching Technology from a Feminist Perspective: A Practical Guide. (Athene Ser.). 200p. 1988. 36.50 (*0-08-034234-5*, Pergamon Pr); pap. 17.95 (*0-08-034233-7*, Pergamon Pr) Elsevier.

Rothschild, Joan, ed. Machina Ex Dea: Feminist Perspectives on Technology. (Athene Ser.). 264p. 1983. text 48.50 (*0-08-029404-9*, Pergamon Pr); pap. text 19.95 (*0-08-029403-0*, Pergamon Pr) Elsevier.

Rothschild, Joan, ed. see Cheng, Alethea.

***Rothschild, Joel Michael.** Signals: A True Story of Life after Life. LC 99-49354. 160p. 2000. 17.95 (*1-57731-150-7*) New Wrld Lib.

Rothschild, John, tr. see Assouline, Pierre.

Rothschild, John, tr. see Vitale, Serena.

Rothschild, Jon, tr. see de Saint-Cheron, Michael & Wiesel, Elie.

Rothschild, Jon, tr. see Ding, Ya.

Rothschild, Jon, tr. see Kadare, Ismail.

Rothschild, Jon, tr. see Parboni, Ricardo.

Rothschild, Jon, tr. see Rodinson, Maxime.

Rothschild, Jon, tr. see Wiesel, Elie.

Rothschild, Jon, tr. see Wiesel, Elie & De Saint-Cheron, Philippe.

Rothschild, Joseph. Communist Party of Bulgaria. LC 72-174967. reprint ed. 34.50 (*0-404-07164-3*) AMS Pr.

— East Central Europe Between the Two World Wars. LC 74-8327. (History of East Central Europe Ser.: Vol. 9). (Illus.). 438p. 1990. pap. 27.50 (*0-295-95357-8*) U of Wash Pr.

— Return to Diversity. 3rd ed. LC 98-29737. (Illus.). 338p. 1999. pap. 24.95 (*0-19-511993-2*) OUP.

— Return to Diversity: A Political History of East Central Europe since World War II. 2nd ed. LC 92-35420. (Illus.). 320p. 1993. pap. text 21.95 (*0-19-507382-7*) OUP.

— Return to Diversity: A Political History of East Central Europe Since World War II. 3rd ed. LC 98-29737. (Illus.). 352p. 1999. text 45.00 (*0-19-511992-4*) OUP.

Rothschild, Kristin, jt. auth. see Inglis, Stephen.

Rothschild, Kurt W. Ethics & Economic Theory: Ideas - Models - Dilemmas. 176p. 1993. 85.00 (*1-85278-675-2*) E Elgar.

Rothschild, Lincoln. Susan Kahn. LC 79-5388. (Illus.). 164p. 1980. 45.00 (*0-87982-031-4*) Art Alliance.

— To Keep Art Alive: The Effort of Kenneth Hayes Miller, American Painter (1876-1952) (Illus.). 208p. 1974. 40.00 (*0-87982-012-8*) Art Alliance.

Rothschild, M. A., jt. ed. see Rosenoer, V.

Rothschild, M. R. & Ruvinsky, A., eds. The Genetics of the Pig. (A CAB International Publication). 634p. 1998. text 160.00 (*0-85199-229-3*) OUP.

Rothschild, Mary A. A Case of Black & White: Northern Volunteers & the Southern Freedom Summers, 1964-1965, 69. LC 82-6175. (Contributions in Afro-American & African Studies: No. 69). 213p. 1982. 55.00 (*0-313-23430-2*, RBL/) Greenwood.

Rothschild, Mary L. & Hronek, Pamela C. Doing What the Day Brought: An Oral History of Arizona Women. LC 91-20354. (Illus.). 174p. (Orig.). 1992. 43.50 (*0-8165-1032-6*); pap. 17.95 (*0-8165-1276-0*) U of Ariz Pr.

Rothschild, Michael. Advertising: From Fundamentals to Strategies. LC 86-80487. (Illus.). 776p. (C). 1987. text 71.16 (*0-669-07213-3*); teacher ed. 2.66 (*0-669-07212-5*) HM Trade Div.

— Marketing Communications: From Fundamentals to Strategies. LC 86-80486. (Illus.). 765p. (C). 1987. text 68.76 (*0-669-07210-9*) HM Trade Div.

— Marketing Communications: From Fundamentals to Strategies. LC 86-80486. (Illus.). 765p. (C). 2000. pap. text, teacher ed. 2.66 (*0-669-07209-5*) HM Trade Div.

— Rothschild Short Stories, Bk. 2. 1999. text. write for info. (*0-670-81375-3*) Viking Penguin.

— Wondermonger. 1999. pap. 8.00 (*0-14-015266-0*, Viking) Viking Penguin.

***Rothschild, Michael & Osborn, Hazel.** Sarah's First Day: A Story for Children in Childcare. (Illus.). 32p. (J). (ps-1). 1999. pap. 6.95 (*0-9671177-0-4*) Tea Pot Pr.

Rothschild, Michael, jt. ed. see Colfelter, Charles T.

Rothschild, Michael, jt. ed. see McAlister, Leigh.

Rothschild, Michael L. Bionomics: Economy As Ecosystem. 448p. 1995. pap. 17.95 (*0-8050-1979-0*, Owl) H Holt & Co.

Rothschild, Miriam. Animals & Man: The Romane Lecture for 1984-5. 108p. 1987. pap. 15.95 (*0-19-854210-0*) OUP.

— Dear Lord Rothschild: Birds, Butterflies & History. (Illus.). 398p. 1983. write for info. (*0-86689-019-X*) Balaban Intl Sci Serv.

Rothschild, Miriam, et al. The Rothschild Gardens. LC 96-23746. (Illus.). 192p. 1997. 35.00 (*0-8109-3790-5*, Pub. by Abrams) Time Warner.

Rothschild, Miriam, jt. auth. see Hopkins, G. H.

Rothschild, Monique, ed. see Tobias, Paul H. & Sauter, Susan.

Rothschild, Nan A. New York City Neighborhoods: The Eighteenth Century. 264p. 1990. text 65.00 (*0-12-598725-0*) Acad Pr.

Rothschild, Nan A., ed. see Strong, William D.

Rothschild, Nannette F., et al. Encounters with Modern Art: The Reminiscences of Nannette F. Rothschild: Works from the Rothschild Family Collections. Marcus, George H., ed. LC 96-32373. (Illus.). 216p. 1996. 46.00 (*0-87633-107-X*); pap. 22.50 (*0-87633-108-8*) Phila Mus Art.

***Rothschild, Peter & Rothschild, Debra Reinking.** Open MRI. LC 99-42876. 383p. 1999. write for info. (*0-7817-2173-3*, Lippnctt) Lppncott W & W.

Rothschild, Phillipine. Mouton Rothschild: Paintings for the Labels. 1991. write for info. (*0-8212-1856-5*) Little.

Rothschild, Richard C. The Emerging Religion of Science. LC 88-12010. 176p. 1989. 45.00 (*0-275-93097-1*, C3097, Praeger Pubs) Greenwood.

Rothschild, Richard E., et al. High Velocity Neutron Stars & Gamma-Ray Bursts. (AIP Press Conference Proceedings Ser.: No. 366). (Illus.). 304p. 1996. 140.00 (*1-56396-593-3*, CP 366, AIP Pr) Spr-Verlag.

Rothschild, Salomon De, see De Rothschild, Salomon.

Rothschild-Sherwin, Shelley, jt. auth. see Batra, Neelam.

***Rothschild, Susan B. & Fotheringham, Nick.** Beachcomber's Guide to Gulf Coast Marine Life: Texas, Louisiana, Mississippi, Alabama & Florida. 3rd ed. (Illus.). 200p. 2000. pap. write for info. (*0-89123-075-0*, Lone Star Books) Gulf Pub.

Rothschild, Tom. The Inevitable Fall. LC 97-90858. 171p. 1998. 16.95 (*0-533-12494-8*) Vantage.

— The Neptune Expedition. 1995. 15.95 (*0-533-11295-8*) Vantage.

Rothschild, Walter. Dynamics of Molecular Liquids. 432p. (C). 1984. reprint ed. text 64.95 (*0-471-73971-5*) Krieger.

— Tales of the Chutzper Rebbe: A Selection from the Acidic Anthology. (Illus.). 80p. 1997. 16.50 (*1-881283-12-7*) Alef Design.

Rothschild, Walter G. Fractals in Chemistry. LC 98-10104. 248p. 1998. 69.95 (*0-471-17968-X*, Wiley-Interscience) Wiley.

Rothschild-Whitt, Joyce, jt. ed. see Lindenfeld, Frank.

Rothschuh, Karl E. History of Physiology. Risse, Gunter B., tr. from GER. LC 74-158126. Orig. Title: Geschichte der Physiologie. (Illus.). 400p. 1973. 43.50 (*0-88275-069-0*) Krieger.

— History of Physiology. Risse, Gunter B., tr. from GER. LC 74-158126. Orig. Title: Geschichte der Physiologie. (Illus.). 400p. 1980. reprint ed. pap. 28.50 (*0-89874-254-4*) Krieger.

Rothsein, Paul F. Evidence in A Nutshell: State & Federal Rules. 2nd ed. (Nutshell Ser.). 514p. (C). 1981. reprint ed. pap. text 16.00 (*0-8299-2131-1*) West Pub.

Rothstein. Events & Grammar. LC 98-14156. 1998. lib. bdg. 132.00 (*0-7923-4940-7*) Kluwer Academic.

***Rothstein.** Special Education Law. 3rd ed. 2001. pap., teacher ed. 26.00 (*0-8013-1963-3*) Longman.

Rothstein, jt. auth. see Grant Staff.

Rothstein, A. The Enzymology of the Cell Surface. (Protoplasmatologia Ser.: Vol. 2e, Pts. 4-5). (Illus.). iv, 116p. 1954. 24.80 (*0-387-80345-9*) Spr-Verlag.

***Rothstein, A.** Psychoanalytic Technique & the Creation of Analytic Patients. 184p. 1998. pap. 25.50 (*1-85575-205-0*, Pub. by H Karnac Bks Ltd) Other Pr LLC.

Rothstein, Andrew. British Foreign Policy & Its Critics, 1830-1950. 128p. 1969. 19.95 (*0-8464-0212-2*) Beekman Pubs.

Rothstein, Arden, et al. Learning Disorders: An Integration of Neuropsychological & Psychoanalytic Considerations. 398p. 1988. 55.00 (*0-8236-2956-2*) Intl Univs Pr.

Rothstein, Arden Aibel & Glenn, Jules. Learning Disabilities & Psychic Conflict: A Psychoanalytic Casebook. LC 98-51468. 520p. 1999. 78.00 (*0-8236-2952-X*, 02952) Intl Univs Pr.

Rothstein, Arnold. Narcissistic Pursuit of Perfection. 2nd rev. ed. LC 84-25159. 327p. 1985. 50.00 (*0-8236-3494-9*, 03493) Intl Univs Pr.

— The Narcissistic Pursuit of Perfection. 2nd rev. ed. 327p. 1999. pap. 29.95 (*0-8236-8157-2*, 23494) Intl Univs Pr.

— Psychoanalytic Technique & the Creation of Analytic Patients. LC 95-46202. 137p. 1995. 27.50 (*0-8236-5057-X*, RC506) Intl Univs Pr.

— Psychoanalytic Technique & the Creation of Analytic Patients. 2nd ed. LC 97-42836. 1997. 29.95 (*0-8236-5058-8*) Intl Univs Pr.

— The Structural Hypothesis: An Evolutionary Hypothesis. LC 83-18490. vii, 194p. 1984. 31.50 (*0-8236-6175-X*) Intl Univs Pr.

Rothstein, Arnold, ed. How Does Treatment Help? On the Modes of Therapeutic Action of Psychoanalytic Psychotherapy. LC 88-13604. (Workshop Series of the American Psychoanalytic Association: Monograph 4). 242p. 1988. 35.00 (*0-8236-2362-9*) Intl Univs Pr.

— The Interpretation of Dreams in Clinical Work. (American Psychoanalytic Association Workshop Ser.: Monograph 3). 1987. 35.00 (*0-8236-2910-4*) Intl Univs Pr.

— Models of the Mind: Their Relationship to Clinical Work. LC 85-10844. (Monograph 1 of the American Psychanalytic Association Ser.). x, 160p. 1985. 27.50 (*0-8236-3410-8*) Intl Univs Pr.

— The Moscow Lectures on Psychoanalysis. LC 91-30974. 186p. (C). 1991. 30.00 (*0-8236-3435-3*) Intl Univs Pr.

— The Reconstruction of Trauma: Monograph II. LC 86-10672. (Workshop Series of the American Psychoanalytic Association). 280p. (C). 1986. 40.00 (*0-8236-5786-8*) Intl Univs Pr.

Rothstein, Arnold, et al. Teaching for Thinking: Theory, Strategies & Activities for the Classroom. 2nd ed. 240p. (C). 1986. pap. 18.95 (*0-8077-2814-4*) Tchrs Coll.

Rothstein, Arnold, jt. ed. see Dowling, Scott.

Rothstein, Arnold, jt. ed. see Jacobs, Theodore J.

Rothstein, Arnold M. The Jesus Idea. LC 93-39806. 135p. 1993. 25.95 (*0-87975-862-7*) Prometheus Bks.

— Re-Thinking Biblical Story & Myth: Selected Lectures at the Theodor Herzl Institute 1986-1995. 104p. (Orig.). 1995. pap. text. write for info. (*0-9639999-1-5*) Jay St Pubs.

— Re-Thinking Biblical Story & Myth: Selected Lectures at the Theodor Herzl Institute, 1986-1995. LC 98-7749. 104p. 1998. 44.00 (*0-7618-1166-4*); pap. 24.50 (*0-7618-1167-2*) U Pr of Amer.

Rothstein, Arthur. The Depression Years As Photographed by Arthur Rothstein. LC 77-91384. (Illus.). 119p. 1978. pap. 12.95 (*0-486-23590-4*) Dover.

Rothstein, Bo. Just Institutions Matter: The Moral & Political Logic of the Universal Welfare State. LC 97-27001. (Theories of Institutional Design Ser.). 270p. (C). 1998. pap. text 19.95 (*0-521-59893-1*) Cambridge U Pr.

— The Social Democratic State: Bureaucracy & Social Reforms in Swedish Labor Market & School Policy. LC 95-2869. (Pitt Series in Policy & Institutional). 231p. 1996. text 39.95 (*0-8229-3881-2*) U of Pittsburgh Pr.

— The Social Democratic State: The Swedish Model & the Bureaucratic Problem of Social Reforms. (Pitt Series in Policy & Institutional Studies). 231p. 1998. pap. 19.95 (*0-8229-5674-8*) U of Pittsburgh Pr.

Rothstein, Chaya L. But Then I Remembered. 1991. 11.95 (*0-87306-558-1*) Feldheim.

— Mentchkins Make Friends. (J). (gr. 4-8). 1988. pap. 7.95 (*0-87306-453-4*) Feldheim.

— The Mentchkins Make Shabbos. (Sifrei Rimon Ser.). (Illus.). (J). (ps-2). 1986. pap. 2.95 (*0-87306-401-1*) Feldheim.

R

An Asterisk (*) at the beginning of an entry indicates that the title is appearing for the first time.

R

*__Rothwell, William J.__ Effective Succession Planning: Ensuring Leadership Continuity & Building Talent from Within. 2000. 65.00 (0-8144-7080-7) AMACOM.

Rothwell, William J. Emerging Issues in HRD Sourcebook. 200p. 1995. pap. 44.95 (0-87425-266-0) HRD Press.

Rothwell, William J. Mastering the Instructional Design Process: A Systematic Approach. 2nd ed. 1997. 59.95 (0-471-36513-0) Wiley.

*__Rothwell, William J., ed.__ ASTD Models for Human Performance Improvement: Roles, Competencies & Outputs. LC 99-73433. (ASTD Models Ser.). 120p. 1999. pap. 70.00 (1-56286-126-3) Am Soc Train & Devel.

Rothwell, William J., et al, eds. Improving Performance in Organizations: Eleven Case Studies from the Real World of Training. LC 98-74117. (In Action Ser.). 202p. 1998. pap. 50.00 (1-56286-100-X) Am Soc Train & Devel.

Rothwell, William J. & Cookson, Peter S. Beyond Instruction: Comprehensive Program Planning for Business & Education. LC 96-53566. (Jossey-Bass Business & Management Ser.). 1997. 34.95 (0-7879-0328-0) Jossey-Bass.

Rothwell, William J. & Kazanas, Hercules C. Building In-House Management & Leadership Development Programs: Their Creation, Management, & Continuous Improvement. LC 99-14846. 296p. 1999. 69.50 (1-56720-258-6, Quorum Bks) Greenwood.

— The Complete AMA Guide to Management Development. 336p. 1993. 65.00 (0-8144-5079-2) AMACOM.

— Human Resource Development: A Strategic Approach. 1993. ring bd. 39.95 (0-87425-238-5) HRD Press.

— Improving on-the-Job Training: How to Establish & Operate a Comprehensive OJT Program. LC 94-7847. (Management Ser.). 186p. 1994. text 32.95 (1-55542-665-4) Jossey-Bass.

— Planning & Managing Human Resources. 1993. ring bd. 34.95 (0-87425-246-6) HRD Press.

Rothwell, William J. & Phillips, Jack J., eds. Linking HRD Programs with Organizational Strategy: Twelve Case Studies from the Real World of Training. LC 98-71679. (In Action Ser.). 221 p. 1998. pap. 50.00 (1-56286-087-9) Am Soc Train & Devel.

Rothwell, William J. & Sredl, Henry J. The ASTD Reference Guide to Professional Human Resource Development Roles & Competencies. 2nd ed. 1000p. 1992. 89.95 (0-87425-177-X) HRD Press.

*__Rothwell, William J., et al.__ ASTD Models for Workplace Learning & Performance: Roles, Competencies & Outputs. LC 98-74603. 134p. 1999. pap. 70.00 (1-56286-110-7) Am Soc Train & Devel.

Rothwell, William J., et al. Practicing Organization Development: A Guide for Consultants. LC 94-69887. 512p. 1995. text 59.95 (0-88390-379-2) Jossey-Bass.

— The Strategic Human Resource Leader: How to Prepare Your Organization for the Six Key Trends Shaping the Future. LC 98-18574. 376p. 1998. 49.95 (0-89106-122-3, 7792, Pub. by Consulting Psychol) Natl Bk Netwk.

Rothwell, William S. The Vocabulary of Physics. 188p. (Orig.). 1988. pap. text 13.95 (0-89420-250-2, 230500) Natl Book.

Rotilio, G. Oxidative Damage & Related Enzymes, Vol. 2. (Life Chemistry Reports). x, 436p. 1984. pap. text 225.00 (3-7186-0221-0) Gordon & Breach.

Rotker, Susana. The American Chronicles of Jose Marti: Journalism & Modernity in Spanish America. Semler, Katherine & French, Jennifer, trs. from SPA. LC 99-41912. (Reencounters with Colonialism Ser.). 256p. 2000. pap. 19.95 (0-87451-902-0); text 50.00 (0-87451-901-2) U Pr of New Eng.

Rotker, Susana, ed. see De Mier, Fray S.

Rotkirch, Anna, jt. ed. see Haavio-Mannila, Elina.

Rotman. Shark! 44.95 (1-893263-02-9) Ipso Facto.

Rotman, A., ed. see Weizman Institute of Science Staff.

*__Rotman, B.__ Mathematics as Sign: Writing, Imagining, Counting. LC 00-23291. 2000. pap. write for info. (0-8047-3684-7) Stanford U Pr.

Rotman, Brian. Ad Infinitum - the Ghost in Turing's Machine: Taking God Out of Mathematics & Putting the Body Back In: An Essay in Corporeal Semiotics. LC 92-26420. 224p. 1993. 39.50 (0-8047-2127-0); pap. 14.95 (0-8047-2128-9) Stanford U Pr.

— Signifying Nothing: The Semiotics of Zero. LC 87-15632. 210p. 1988. pap. 12.95 (0-318-32465-2) St Martin.

— Signifying Nothing: The Semiotics of Zero. (Illus.). 111p. (C). 1993. reprint ed. pap. 12.95 (0-8047-2129-7) Stanford U Pr.

Rotman, Dan, et al. A Game of Revenge. (Orig.). 1996. pap. 10.95 (0-9637533-4-7) Magnus Bks.

Rotman, Edgardo. Beyond Punishment: A New View on the Rehabilitation of Criminal Offenders. 26. LC 89-37996. (Contributions in Criminology & Penology Ser.: No. 26). 227p. 1990. 55.00 (0-313-26493-7, RCI/, Greenwood Pr) Greenwood.

Rotman, J. Galois Theory. 2nd ed. (Universitext Ser.). (Illus.). 154p. 1998. pap. 35.95 (0-387-98541-7) Spr-Verlag.

Rotman, Jayne. If Your Doctor's Busy, Call on God: A Spiritual Journey Through Ecological Illness. 190p. (Orig.). pap. write for info. (0-931515-05-X) Triumph Pr.

Rotman, Jeffrey L., photos by. Coral Reef: A City That Never Sleeps. LC 95-6635. (Illus.). 64p. (J). (gr. 4). 1996. 17.99 (0-525-65193-4, Dutton Child) Peng Put Young Read.

Rotman, Jeffrey L., photos by. Sharks: Challengers of the Deep. (Illus.). (J). (gr. 6). 1995. 9.28 (0-395-73271-9) HM.

*__Rotman, Joseph J.__ First Course in Abstract Algebra. 2nd ed. LC 99-88794. (Illus.). 488p. 2000. 89.33 (0-13-011584-3) P-H.

Rotman, Joseph J. Galois Theory. xii, 108p. 1994. 35.95 (0-387-97305-2) Spr-Verlag.

— An Introduction to Algebraic Topology. (Graduate Texts in Mathematics Ser.: Vol. 119). (Illus.). xiii, 433p. 1994. reprint ed. 59.95 (0-387-96678-1) Spr-Verlag.

— An Introduction to Homological Algebra. (Pure & Applied Mathematics Ser.). 1979. text 99.00 (0-12-599250-5) Acad Pr.

— An Introduction to the Theory of Groups. 3rd ed. 500p. (C). 1984. text 56.25 (0-697-06882-X, WCB McGr Hill) McGrw-H Hghr Educ.

— An Introduction to the Theory of Groups. 4th ed. LC 94-6507. (Graduate Texts in Mathematics Ser.). (Illus.). 513p. 1994. 59.95 (0-387-94285-8) Spr-Verlag.

— Journey into Mathematics: The World of Proof. LC 97-19520. 237p. (C). 1997. 77.33 (0-13-842360-1) P-H.

Rotman, Leonard I. Parallel Paths: Fiduciary Doctrine & the Crown-Native Relationship in Canada. 336p. 1996. text 50.00 (0-8020-0821-6); pap. text 19.95 (0-8020-7813-3) U of Toronto Pr.

Rotman, Leslie, jt. auth. see Lampert, Rachel.

Rotman, M., et al, eds. Concomitant Continuous Infusion Chemotherapy & Radiation. (Medical Radiology, Diagnostic Imaging & Radiation Oncology Ser.). (Illus.). xiv, 304p. 1991. 174.00 (0-387-52545-9) Spr-Verlag.

Rotman, M., jt. ed. see Rosenthal, C. J.

Rotman, Marvin, jt. auth. see Rosenthal, C. Julian.

Rotman, Morris B. Opportunities in Public Relations Careers. 1993. pap. 10.95 (0-8442-6487-3, VGM Career) NTC Contemp Pub Co.

— Opportunities in Public Relations Careers. LC 94-49547. (Opportunities In . . . Ser.). (Illus.). 160p. 1995. pap. 11.95 (0-8442-4419-8, 44198, VGM Career) NTC Contemp Pub Co.

— Opportunities in Public Relations Careers. LC 94-49547. (VGM Opportunities Ser.). (Illus.). 160p. 1995. 14.95 (0-8442-4417-1, 44171, VGM Career) NTC Contemp Pub Co.

Rotman, Stanley R., ed. Wide-Gap Luminescent Materials: Theory & Applications. LC 96-39299. (Electronic Materials, Science & Technology Ser.). 384p. 1996. text 187.50 (0-7923-9837-8) Kluwer Academic.

Rotman, Stanley R., jt. ed. see Shladov, Itzah.

Rotmans, Jan. Image: An Integrated Model to Assess the Greenhouse Effect. (C). 1990. text 185.50 (0-7923-0957-X) Kluwer Academic.

Rotmans, Jan & De Vries, Bert, eds. Perspectives on Global Change: The TARGETS Approach. LC 97-229056. (Illus.). 479p. 1997. text 69.95 (0-521-62176-3) Cambridge U Pr.

Rotmans, Jan, jt. auth. see Martens, Willem J.

Rotmansh. Basic Drafting Technology. (Drafting Ser.). 1980. pap., teacher ed. 12.50 (0-8273-1294-6) Delmar.

Rotner, jt. auth. see Allen.

Rotner, Shelley. Action Alphabet: A Is for Arching & Action, too! LC 94-32212. (Illus.). 40p. (J). (ps-2). 1996. 16.00 (0-689-80086-X, Mac Bks Young Read) S&S Childrens.

*__Rotner, Shelley.__ The A.D.D. Book for Kids. LC 99-46220. 32p. (J). (gr. k-3). 2000. 22.90 (0-7613-1722-8) Millbrook Pr.

— A.D.D. Book for Kids. (Illus.). (J). 2000. pap. 7.95 (0-7613-1436-9) Millbrook Pr.

Rotner, Shelley. Boats Afloat. LC 98-3675. (Illus.). 32p. (J). (gr. k-2). 1998. 15.95 (0-531-30112-5); lib. bdg. 16.99 (0-531-33112-1) Orchard Bks Watts.

*__Rotner, Shelley.__ Feeling Thankful. (Illus.). (J). 2000. pap. 5.95 (0-7613-1437-7) Millbrook Pr.

— Lots of Dads. (Picture Puffin Ser.). (Illus.). (J). 2000. pap. 5.99 (0-14-056516-7, PuffinBks) Peng Put Young Read.

— Lots of Dads. (Illus.). (J). 2000. 11.44 (0-606-18422-8) Turtleback.

Rotner, Shelley. Wheels Around. (Illus.). 32p. (J). (ps-3). 1995. 13.95 (0-395-71815-5) HM.

*__Rotner, Shelley & Calcagnino, Steve.__ Body Book. LC 99-34866. (Illus.). 32p. (J). (ps-1). 2000. 15.95 (0-531-30256-3) Orchard Bks Watts.

— The Body Book. LC 99-34866. 32p. (J). (ps-1). 2000. lib. bdg. 16.99 (0-531-33256-X) Orchard Bks Watts.

Rotner, Shelley & Hellums, Julia P. Hold the Anchovies! A Book about Pizza. LC 96-3999. (Illus.). 32p. (J). (ps-3). 1996. 15.95 (0-531-09507-X); lib. bdg. 16.99 (0-531-08857-X) Orchard Bks Watts.

Rotner, Shelley & Kelly, Sheila M. About Twins. LC 98-3060. (Illus.). (J). (ps-2). 1999. 16.95 (0-7894-2556-4, D K Ink) DK Pub Inc.

— Lots of Dads. LC 96-33714. (Illus.). 24p. (J). 1997. 12.99 (0-8037-2086-6, Dial Yng Read); 12.89 (0-8037-2089-0, Dial Yng Read) Peng Put Young Read.

Rotner, Shelley & Kreisler, Ken. Citybook. LC 93-6350. (Illus.). 32p. (J). (ps-1). 1994. 15.95 (0-531-06837-4); lib. bdg. 16.99 (0-531-08687-9) Orchard Bks Watts.

— Citybook. LC 93-6350. (Illus.). 32p. (J). (ps-1). 1998. pap. 6.95 (0-531-07106-5) Orchard Bks Watts.

— Faces. LC 93-46758. (Illus.). 32p. (J). (ps-1). 1994. mass mkt. 14.95 (0-02-777887-8, Pub. by Macmillan) S&S Trade.

— Nature Spy. LC 91-38430. (Illus.). 32p. (J). (ps-1). 1992. lib. bdg. 14.95 (0-02-777885-1, Mac Bks Young Read) S&S Childrens.

— Ocean Day. LC 92-6114. (Illus.). 32p. (J). (ps-1). 1993. text 14.95 (0-02-777886-X, Mac Bks Young Read) S&S Childrens.

Rotner, Shelley & Olivo, Richard. Close, Closer, Closest. (Illus.). (J). (ps-2). 1997. 13.00 (0-614-29088-0) Atheneum Yung Read.

Rotner, Shelley, et al. Pick a Pet. LC 98-33752. (Illus.). 32p. (J). (ps-k). 1999. 15.95 (0-531-30147-8); lib. bdg. 16.99 (0-531-33147-4) Orchard Bks Watts.

Rotner, Shelley, jt. auth. see Allen, Marjorie N.

Rotner, Shelley, jt. auth. see Olivo, C. Thomas.

Rotner, Shelley, jt. auth. see Woodhull, Anne.

Roto, Robert R. Casino Craps: Making Sense of Professional Play. LC 99-28332. 1999. pap. 12.00 (1-56980-137-1) Barricade Bks.

Rotola, Albert C., ed. & tr. see Stoquerus, Gaspar.

Rotondi, Giovanni. Leges Publicae Populi Romani. (Olms Paperbacks Ser.: Bd. 25). vii, 544p. 1990. reprint ed. pap. write for info. (3-487-01173-5) G Olms Pubs.

Rotondi, Michael & Reeve, Margaret. Design Process at SCI-Arc: From the Center. LC 96-40517. (Illus.). 162p. 1997. 60.00 (1-885254-34-2, Pub. by Monacelli Pr) Penguin Putnam.

Rotondi, Paul, tr. see Forte, Bruno.

Rotondo, Antonio, ed. Camillo Renato: Opere, Documenti E Testimonianze. LC 72-3454. (Corpus Reformatorum Italicorum & Biblioteca Ser.). (ITA & LAT., Illus.). 353p. 1968. 40.00 (0-87580-034-3) N Ill U Pr.

Rotondo, James H. & Williams, Paul D. Connecticut Product Liability Law. LC 98-194578. 332p. 1998. pap. 75.00 (1-878698-49-4) Atlantic Law.

Rotondo, Susan, ed. see Schuster, Michael L.

Rotovis. Illustrators 39. 1998. 57.50 (2-88046-347-5, Rotovision) Watsn-Guptill.

Rotovision. Art Directors' Index to Illustrators 18. 300p. 1999. 70.00 (2-88046-320-3) Watsn-Guptill.

Rotovision S. A. Staff. The Annual of the American Advertising Federation. (Illus.). 592p. 1997. 70.00 (0-8230-0509-7) Watsn-Guptill.

— Architecture: The Architecture of the Skyscrapers. 1996. pap. text 35.00 (0-8230-6538-3) Watsn-Guptill.

— Creating Special Effects. (Pro-Photo Ser.). (Illus.). 160p. 1996. pap. text 35.00 (0-8230-6501-4) Watsn-Guptill.

— Decoration: Brightly Lit Space. (Illus.). 160p. 1996. pap. text 35.00 (0-8230-6539-1) Watsn-Guptill.

— Design 2: Industrial Design. (Illus.). 160p. 1996. pap. text 35.00 (0-8230-6540-5) Watsn-Guptill.

— Environmental Restoration. (Illus.). 160p. 1996. pap. text 35.00 (0-8230-6497-2) Watsn-Guptill.

— 50 Chairs. (Illus.). 160p. 1996. pap. text 35.00 (0-8230-6505-7) Watsn-Guptill.

— Houses: Rustic & Country Houses. (Illus.). 160p. 1996. pap. text 39.95 (0-8230-6523-5) Watsn-Guptill.

— Indoor Shots: Pro-Lighting. (Pro-Lighting Ser.). (Illus.). 160p. 1995. pap. 29.95 (0-8230-6465-4, Amphoto) Watsn-Guptill.

RotoVision S. A. Staff. Interior Design: Kitchens & Bathrooms. (Illus.). 160p. 1996. pap. 39.95 (0-8230-2500-4) Watsn-Guptill.

Rotovision S. A. Staff. Interiors. (Illus.). 160p. 1996. pap. text 35.00 (0-8230-6496-4) Watsn-Guptill.

— Lingerie Shots: Pro-Lighting. (Pro-Lighting Ser.). (Illus.). 160p. 1995. pap. 29.95 (0-8230-6466-2, Amphoto) Watsn-Guptill.

— New Bridges. (Illus.). 160p. 1996. pap. text 35.00 (0-8230-6498-0) Watsn-Guptill.

— New European Architecture. (Illus.). 160p. 1996. pap. text 35.00 (0-8230-6491-3) Watsn-Guptill.

— Office Furniture. (Illus.). 160p. 1996. pap. text 39.95 (0-8230-6559-6) Watsn-Guptill.

— Office Spaces. (Commercial Spaces Ser.). (Illus.). 160p. 1995. pap. 35.00 (0-8230-6474-3, Whitney Lib) Watsn-Guptill.

— Packaging Design. (Illus.). 160p. 1996. pap. text 35.00 (0-8230-6502-2) Watsn-Guptill.

— Pro-Lighting: Food Shots. (Illus.). 160p. 1995. pap. text 29.95 (0-8230-6432-8, Rotovision) Watsn-Guptill.

— Pro-Lighting: Glamour Shots. (Illus.). 160p. 1995. pap. text 29.95 (0-8230-6431-X, Rotovision) Watsn-Guptill.

— Pro-Lighting: Nudes. (Illus.). 160p. 1997. pap. text 35.00 (0-8230-6520-0, Amphoto) Watsn-Guptill.

— Pro-Lighting: Portraits. (Illus.). 160p. 1997. pap. text 35.00 (0-8230-6522-7, Amphoto) Watsn-Guptill.

— Pro-Lighting: Product Shots. (Illus.). 160p. 1995. pap. text 29.95 (0-8230-6433-6) Watsn-Guptill.

— Pro-Lighting: Still Life. (Illus.). 160p. 1997. pap. text 35.00 (0-8230-6521-9, Amphoto) Watsn-Guptill.

— Residential. (Illus.). 160p. 1996. pap. text 35.00 (0-8230-6492-1) Watsn-Guptill.

— Restaurants. (Illus.). 160p. 1996. pap. text 39.95 (0-8230-6556-1) Watsn-Guptill.

— Shop Windows. (Commercial Spaces Ser.). (Illus.). 160p. 1995. pap. 35.00 (0-8230-6472-7, Whitney Lib) Watsn-Guptill.

— Shop Windows: Cosmetics. (Illus.). 160p. 1996. pap. text 39.95 (0-8230-6558-8) Watsn-Guptill.

— Special Effects: Pro-Lighting. (Pro-Lighting Ser.). (Illus.). 160p. 1995. pap. 29.95 (0-8230-6467-0, Amphoto) Watsn-Guptill.

— Studio Portrait Photography. (Pro-Photo Ser.). (Illus.). 160p. 1995. pap. 29.95 (0-8230-6468-9, Amphoto) Watsn-Guptill.

— Wedding Photography. (Pro-Photo Ser.). (Illus.). 160p. 1995. pap. 29.95 (0-8230-6469-7, Amphoto) Watsn-Guptill.

— Working with Computer Type Vol. 3: Color & Type. (Illus.). 160p. 1996. pap. text 35.00 (0-8230-6500-6) Watsn-Guptill.

Rotovision S. A. Staff, compiled by. Graphic Designers' Index, No. 10. 10th ed. (Illus.). 170p. 1996. 69.00 (0-8230-6424-7, Rotovision) Watsn-Guptill.

— Working with Computer Type: Books, Magazines & Newsletters, 1. 160p. 1995. pap. 29.50 (0-8230-6478-6, Rotovision) Watsn-Guptill.

— Working with Computer Type: Logo Types, Stationery Systems & Visual Communications, 2. 160p. 1995. pap. 29.50 (0-8230-6479-4, Rotovision) Watsn-Guptill.

Rotovision Staff. Abitare 13. 276p. 1999. 55.00 (2-88046-402-1, Rotovision) Watsn-Guptill.

Rotovision Staff. Addy, Bk. 3. 1997. 70.00 (2-88046-309-2, Rotovision) Watsn-Guptill.

— Art Directors Annual. 78th ed. 466p. 2000. 75.00 (2-88046-471-4, Rotovision) Watsn-Guptill.

Rotovision Staff. Art Directors Annual 77. 560p. 1999. 75.00 incl. cd-rom (2-88046-398-X, Rotovision) Watsn-Guptill.

— Art Directors' Index to Illustrators 17. (Illus.). 352p. 1997. 69.00 (2-88046-305-X, Rotovision) Watsn-Guptill.

— Art Directors' Index to Photographers 22 Vol. I: Europe, Vol. 1. (Art Directors' Index to Photographers Ser.). (Illus.). 350p. 1997. 69.00 (2-88046-302-5, Rotovision) Watsn-Guptill.

*__Rotovision Staff.__ Art Directors' Index to Photographers 23, 2 vols. 600p. 1999. 140.00 (2-88046-413-7, Rotovision) Watsn-Guptill.

— Book 4. 464p. 1999. 70.00 (2-88046-401-3, Rotovision) Watsn-Guptill.

Rotovision Staff. Epica 11. 368p. 1999. 55.00 (2-88046-399-8, Rotovision) Watsn-Guptill.

— European Design Annual 4. 128p. 1999. 39.95 (2-88046-395-5) Watsn-Guptill.

— Europe/The Americas, Asia, Australasia. (Art Directors' Index to Photographers Ser.: No. 22). (Illus.). 680p. 1997. 137.00 (2-88046-301-7) Watsn-Guptill.

— Graphic Design & TV Advertising. LC 98-211515. (Illus.). 178p. 1997. pap. 55.00 (2-88046-314-9, Rotovision) Watsn-Guptill.

— Graphic Designers' Index, Vol. 11. (Illus.). 320p. 1997. 69.00 (2-88046-288-6, Rotovision) Watsn-Guptill.

— Graphic Designers' Index 12. 320p. 1999. 70.00 (2-88046-321-1, Rotovision) Watsn-Guptill.

— Graphics. (Illus.). 160p. 1997. pap. 35.00 (2-88046-315-7, Rotovision) Watsn-Guptill.

— Hypergraphics: Design for the Internet. (Illus.). 160p. 1997. pap. 35.00 (2-88046-313-0, Rotovision) Watsn-Guptill.

*__Rotovision Staff.__ Illustrators 41. LC 59-10849. (Illus.). 2000. 49.95 (2-88046-466-8, Rotovision) Watsn-Guptill.

— One Show Interactive 2. 272p. 1999. 45.00 (2-88046-474-9, Rotovision) Watsn-Guptill.

Rotovision Staff. One Show Interactive 1. 192p. 1999. 45.00 (2-88046-430-7, Rotovision) Watsn-Guptill.

*__Rotovision Staff.__ One Show 21. 409p. 1999. 79.95 (2-88046-475-7, Rotovision) Watsn-Guptill.

Rotovision Staff. One Show 20. 500p. 1999. 79.00 (2-88046-400-5, Rotovision) Watsn-Guptill.

— Pro-Illustration: Advertising. (Illus.). 160p. 1997. pap. 37.50 (2-88046-310-6, Rotovision) Watsn-Guptill.

Rotovision Staff, ed. Images 22: The Best of British Illustration. (Illus.). 1998. pap. 20.00 (2-88046-359-9) Watsn-Guptill.

Rotovision Staff, jt. auth. see Print Staff.

Rotroff, Susan I. Hellenistic Pottery, Athenian & Imported Moldmade Bowls. LC 91-43755. (Athenian Agora Ser.: Vol. 22). (Illus.). xvi, 136p. 1982. 40.00 (0-87661-222-2) Am Sch Athens.

— Hellenistic Pottery, Athenian & Imported Wheelmade Table Ware & Related Materials. LC 96-47458. (Athenian Agora Ser.: Vol. 29). (Illus.). xxxviii, 574p. 1997. 175.00 (0-87661-229-X) Am Sch Athens.

Rotroff, Susan I. & Lamberton, Robert. Birds of the Athenian Agora. (Excavations of the Athenian Agora Picture Bks.: No. 22). (Illus.). 32p. 1985. pap. 3.00 (0-87661-627-9) Am Sch Athens.

Rotroff, Susan I. & Oakley, John W. Debris from a Public Dining Place in the Athenian Agora. (Hesperia Supplement Ser.: No. 25). (Illus.). 116p. 1992. pap. 35.00 (0-87661-525-6) Am Sch Athens.

Rotrosen, John, jt. ed. see Stanley, Michael.

Rotrou. Cosroes. Watts, ed. (Exeter French Texts Ser.: Vol. 51). (FRE.). 142p. Date not set. pap. text 19.95 (0-85989-154-2, Pub. by Univ Exeter Pr) Northwestern U Pr.

— L' Innocente Infidelite. Gethner, Perry, ed. (Exeter French Texts Ser.: Vol. 57). (FRE.). 128p. Date not set. pap. text 19.95 (0-85989-221-2, Pub. by Univ Exeter Pr) Northwestern U Pr.

— La Soeur. Kite, ed. (Exeter French Texts Ser.: No. 88). (FRE.). 136p. Date not set. pap. text 19.95 (0-85989-398-7) Univ Exeter Pr.

— Venceslas, EFT LXXIX. Watts, D. A., ed. (FRE.). 136p. (C). pap. 19.95 (0-85989-361-8, Pub. by Univ Exeter Pr) Northwestern U Pr.

Rotruck, Richard E. Flight Notes for General Aviation Bk. 1: VFR. 2nd unabridged ed. (Illus.). 96p. 1996. pap. 14.95 (0-9654474-0-5, FN4GAB1E2V1) Clear Approach.

— Flight Notes for General Aviation Bk. 2: IFR. unabridged ed. (Illus.). 124p. (Orig.). 1995. pap. 16.95 (0-9654474-1-3, FN4GAB2V1) Clear Approach.

Rots, J. G., ed. Structural Masonry: An Experimental/ Numerical Basis for Practical Design Rules. (CUR Report Ser.: No. 171). (Illus.). 166p. (C). 1997. text 113.00 (90-5410-680-8, Pub. by A A Balkema) Ashgate Pub Co.

Rotsfein, Abraham, jt. auth. see Polyani, Karl.

Rotsler, William. Plot-It-Yourself Adventure: Goonies Cavern of Horror. Arico, Diane, ed. 128p. (Orig.). (J). (gr. 3-7). 1985. pap. 3.95 (0-671-60135-0) S&S Trade.

— The Star Trek II, 3 vols., Set. gif. ed. (J). boxed set 9.50 (0-317-12429-3) S&S Trade.

Rotsler, William, jt. auth. see Benford, Gregory.

Rotstein, Enrique, et al. Handbook of Food Engineering Practice. LC 96-53959. 736p. 1997. boxed set 134.95 (0-8493-8694-2) CRC Pr.

Rotstein, J., ed. Immunosuppression Systematic Lupus Erythematosus. (Rheumatology Ser.: Vol. 5). (Illus.). 1974. 100.00 (3-8055-1540-5) S Karger.

Rotstein, Maurice. The Quest for a Democratic World. 240p. 1998. 60.00 (0-391-04079-0); pap. 18.50 (0-391-04077-4) Humanities.

*__Rotstein, Maurice.__ The Quest for a Democratic World. LC 99-51810. 288p. 2000. 54.00 (0-7618-1568-6); pap. 34.50 (0-7618-1569-4) U Pr of Amer.

An Asterisk (*) at the beginning of an entry indicates that the title is appearing for the first time.

Rotstein, Nancy-Gay. Shattering Glass. LC 95-25705. 352p. 1996. 22.00 (*0-374-26223-3*) FS&G.
— Shattering Glass. 1997. pap. 19.99 (*0-7710-7589-8*) McCland & Stewart.
Rotstein, Ronald D. The Future: Trends & Developments Through the 21st Century. 1989. 19.95 (*0-8184-0505-8*) Carol Pub Group.
Rott, Hans, jt. ed. see Fuhrmann, Andre.
Rott, Jean, ed. Correspondance de Martin Bucer Tome II (1524-1526) (Studies in Medieval & Reformation Thought: No. 43). (FRE & LAT., Illus.). xxi, 294p. (C). 1988. 103.00 (*90-04-08636-6*) Brill Academic Pubs.
Rott, R. & Goebel, W. Molecular Basis of Viral & Microbial Pathogenesis. (Colloquium Mosbach Ser.: Vol. 38). (Illus.). 280p. 1988. 69.00 (*0-387-18606-9*) Spr-Verlag.
***Rotte, Joanna.** Acting with Adler. 176p. 2000. 25.00 (*0-87910-299-3*); pap. 14.95 (*0-87910-298-5*) Limelight Edns.
Rotte, Joanna. Scene Change: A Theatre Diary Prague, Moscow, Leningrad Spring 1991. LC 94-67. (Illus.). 176p. (Orig.). 1994. 25.00 (*0-87910-175-X*); pap. 12.95 (*0-87910-171-7*) Limelight Edns.
Rotte, Joanna & Yamamoto, Koji. Vision: A Holistic Guide to Healing the Eyesight. LC 84-80538. 152p. (Orig.). 1986. pap. 18.00 (*0-87040-622-1*) Japan Pubns USA.
Rotteck, Karl, ed. Dictionnaire Allemand-Francais, Francais-Allemand. (FRE & GER.). 980p. 1970. pap. 10.95 (*0-7859-0753-X*, M-6115) Fr & Eur.
Rotteck, Karl & Kister, G. Dictionnaire Allemand-Francais et Francais-Allemand. (FRE & GER.). 1978. 19.95 (*0-7859-8004-0*, 2-7370-0085-8) Fr & Eur.
Rottem, S., jt. ed. see Ron, E. Z.
Rottem, Shraga, jt. auth. see Timor-Trishsch, I. E.
Rottenberg. El of Argu/World of Ideas. 1997. pap. text 47.70 (*0-312-17799-2*) St Martin.
— El of Argu/World of Ideas. 1997. 149.75 (*0-312-17798-4*) St Martin.
— Elements of Argument. 6th ed. 1999. pap. text 39.95 (*0-312-19576-1*) St Martin.
— Structure Argument for Writing Research, Vol. 1. 1997. pap. text. write for info. (*0-312-18322-4*) St Martin.
— Structure of Argument. 3rd ed. 1999. pap. text 26.95 (*0-312-19578-8*) St Martin.
Rottenberg, Annette T. Elements of Argument. 5th ed. 1996. pap. text 5.00 (*0-312-15032-6*); pap. text 2.25 (*0-312-15033-4*) St Martin.
— Elements of Argument: Pocket Style Manual. 1996. pap. text 28.80 (*0-312-13752-4*) St Martin.
— The Structure of Argument. 5th ed. 1996. pap. text. write for info. (*0-312-15034-2*); pap. text 5.00 (*0-312-15035-0*) St Martin.
Rottenberg, Dan. Finding Our Fathers: A Guidebook to Jewish Genealogy. LC 85-82512. xxii, 401p. 1998. reprint ed. pap. 19.95 (*0-8063-1151-7*, 5000) Genealog Pub.
Rottenberg, Dan. The Inheritor's Handbook: A Definitive Guide for Beneficiaries. LC 98-34093. (Personal Bookshelf Ser.). (Illus.). 288p. 1998. 23.95 (*1-57660-051-3*, Pub. by Bloomberg NJ) Norton.
***Rottenberg, Dan.** The Inheritor's Handbook: A Definitive Guide for Beneficiaries. 240p. 2000. per. 13.00 (*0-684-86908-X*) S&S Trade.
Rottenberg, Dan, ed. Middletown Jews: The Tenuous Survival of an American Jewish Community. LC 96-22779. (Illus.). 192p. 1998. pap. 12.95 (*0-253-21206-5*) Ind U Pr.
Rottenberg, David, jt. auth. see Shuman, Jeffrey C.
Rottenberg, Elizabeth, tr. see Blanchot, Maurice.
Rottenberg, Simon. The Cost of Regulated Pricing: A Critical Analysis of Auto Insurance Premium Rate - Setting in Massachusetts. LC 89-22939. (Pioneer Paper Ser.: No. 2). 50p. (Orig.). 1989. pap. 10.00 (*0-929930-02-9*) Pioneer Inst.
Rottenberg, Simon, ed. The Economics of Legal Minimum Wages. LC 80-26563. (AEI Symposia Ser.: No. 81A). (Illus.). 552p. reprint ed. pap. 171.20 (*0-8357-4470-1*, 203731400008) Bks Demand.
— The Economics of Medical Malpractice. LC 78-6364. (Illus.). 302p. reprint ed. pap. 93.70 (*0-8357-4471-X*, 203731500008) Bks Demand.
— The Political Economy of Poverty, Equity, & Growth: Costa Rica & Uruguay. (Comparative Study Ser.). (Illus.). 440p. 1993. text 49.95 (*0-19-520883-8*, 60883) OUP.
Rottenburg, Annette T. Structure Argument. 5th ed. LC 96-84941. 407p. 1996. pap. text 26.95 (*0-312-13412-6*) St Martin.
Rottensteiner, Franz. The Best of Austrian Science Fiction. LC 98-46873. (Studies in Austrian Literarure, Culture & Thought). 2000. pap. write for info. (*1-57241-078-7*) Ariadne CA.
— The Fantasy Book: An Illustrated History from Dracula to Tolkien LC 78-2994. 160p. 1978. write for info. (*0-02-053560-0*) Free Pr.
— The Fantasy Book: The Ghostly, the Gothic, the Magical, the Unreal LC 79-306396. 160p. 1978. write for info. (*0-500-27119-4*) Thames Hudson.
Rottensteiner, Franz, ed. View from Another Shore: European Science Fiction. LC 99-228141. 240p. 1998. pap. 16.95 (*0-85323-942-8*, Pub. by Liverpool Univ Pr) Intl Spec Bk.
— View from Another Shore: European Science Fiction. 2nd ed. LC 99-228141. 240p. 1998. 32.95 (*0-85323-932-0*, Pub. by Liverpool Univ Pr) Intl Spec Bk.
Rottensteiner, Franz, ed. see Lem, Stanislaw.
Rotter. Guide for Economic Design of Metal Silos. (Civil Engineering Ser.). 256p. (C). (gr. 13). 1998. pap. 92.00 (*0-419-23460-8*, E & FN Spon) Routledge.
***Rotter, Andrew J.** Comrades at Odds: Culture & Indo-U. S. Relations, 1947-1964. 2000. 55.00 (*0-8014-3449-1*) Cornell U Pr.
— Comrades at Odds: Culture & Indo-U. S. Relations, 1947-1964. LC 00-9283. (Illus.). 2000. pap. 19.95 (*0-8014-8460-X*) Cornell U Pr.
Rotter, Andrew J. Light at the End of the Tunnel: A Vietnam War Anthology. rev. ed. LC 98-40989. 576p. 1999. 55.00 (*0-8420-2712-2*); pap. text 22.95 (*0-8420-2713-0*) Scholarly Res Inc.
— The Path to Vietnam: Origins of the American Commitment to Southeast Asia. LC 87-47603. 304p. (C). 1987. pap. text 17.95 (*0-8014-9620-9*) Cornell U Pr.
Rotter, Charles. Monarch Butterflies. (Nature Books Ser.). (Illus.). 32p. (J). (gr. 2-6). 1993. lib. bdg. 22.79 (*0-89565-840-2*) Childs World.
— Seals & Sea Lions. (Nature Books Ser.). (Illus.). 32p. (J). (gr. 2-6). 1991. lib. bdg. 22.79 (*0-89565-714-7*) Childs World.
Rotter, Joseph & Bailey, Walter. Transitions: Education & Employment. 204p. (C). 1996. pap. text, per. 44.95 (*0-7872-2711-0*, 41271101) Kendall-Hunt.
Rotter, Julian B. Clinical Psychology. 2nd ed. LC 74-110493. (Foundations of Modern Psychology Ser.). (Illus.). 1971. pap. 8.95 (*0-685-03791-6*) P-H.
Rotterdam Conference Staff. Human Gene Mapping: Proceedings of the Rotterdam Conference, 2nd, 1974. Bergsma, Daniel, ed. LC 75-8204. (March of Dimes Ser.: Vol. 11, No. 3). 1976. 20.00 (*0-686-14571-2*) March of Dimes.
— Human Gene Mapping Two: Proceedings of the Rotterdam Conference, 1974 - Journal: Cytogenetics & Cell Genetics, Vol. 14, Nos. 3-6. Bergsma, Daniel, ed. (Illus.). 332p. 1975. pap. 68.75 (*3-8055-2251-7*) S Karger.
Rotterdam, Heidrum. Progress in AIDS Pathology. 1989. 75.00 (*0-938607-21-9*) Field & Wood Inc Medical.
— Progress in AIDS Pathology, Vol. 2. 1990. 109.00 (*0-938607-35-9*) Field & Wood Inc Medical.
Rotterdam, Heidrun, et al. Biopsy Diagnosis of the Digestive Tract, 2 vols., Set. 2nd ed. (Biopsy Interpretation Ser.). 872p. 1992. text 168.00 (*0-88167-968-2*) Lppncott W & W.
Rotteveel, Jacqueline. Incest: The Pain & the Healing. 93p. (YA). (gr. 7-12). 1990. pap. 6.95 (*1-57515-004-2*) PPI Pubng.
Rottgen, Karl-Heinz, jt. auth. see Mensching, Herausgegeben V.
Rottger, H., jt. auth. see Von der Hardt, Peter.
Rottger, Heinz, jt. auth. see Genthon, J. P.
Rottger, Heinz, jt. auth. see Von Der Hardt, Peter.
Rottger, Heinz, jt. ed. see Von der Hardt, Peter.
Rottger, J. & Wickwar, V. B. Thermosphere-Ionosphere-Middle Atmosphere Coupling & Dynamics. (Advances in Space Research (RJ) Ser.: Vol. 18). 160p. 1995. 97.75 (*0-08-042667-0*, Pergamon Pr) Elsevier.
Rottgers, Steven. Outstanding in His Field. LC 95-68405. (Illus.). 27p. (Orig.). 1995. pap. 8.95 (*1-882792-10-6*) Proctor Pubns.
Rottier, Jerry. Implementing & Improving Teaming: A Handbook for Middle Level Leaders. LC 96-8797. 1996. write for info. (*1-56090-110-1*) Natl Middle Schl.
Rottier, Jerry & Ogan, Beverly J. Cooperative Learning in Middle-Level Schools. 112p. 1991. pap. 11.95 (*0-8106-3068-0*) NEA.
Rottkemper, Michael. Deliktische Aubenhaftung der Leitungsorganmitglieder Rechtsfahiger Korperschaften. (GER.). 218p. 1996. 42.95 (*3-631-30424-2*) P Lang Pubng.
Rottlevy, Uriel. Behavior & Motivation: Index of Modern Information. LC 90-31679. 150p. 1990. 47.50 (*1-55914-140-9*); pap. 44.50 (*1-55914-141-7*) ABBE Pubs Assn.
***Rottman, David.** The Career As the Path to the Soul. 2001. 24.95 (*0-670-89163-0*) Viking Penguin.
Rottman, David B., et al. State Court Organization, 1993. (Illus.). 399p. (Orig.). (C). 1995. pap. text 45.00 (*0-7881-2267-3*) DIANE Pub.
Rottman, Fred & Gross, Elaine. Halston: An American Original. LC 99-19332. 256p. 1999. 50.00 (*0-06-019318-2*) HarpC.
Rottman, Gordon. U.S. Army Special Forces: Airborne Rangers. (Warfare & Weapons Ser.). 1999. 20.00 (*0-531-12014-7*) Watts.
— U.S. Navy Special Forces: Special boat units. 1999. 20.00 (*0-531-12015-5*) Watts.
Rottman, Gordon, et al. The Official Lite History & Cookbook of the Gulf War. (Illus.). 160p. (Orig.). 1991. pap. 6.95 (*0-9623992-1-3*) Electric Strawberry.
Rottman, Gordon L. Armies of the Gulf War. (Elite Ser.: No. 45). (Illus.). 64p. pap. 12.95 (*1-85532-277-3*, 9460, Pub. by Ospry) Stackpole.
— German Combat Equipments, 1939-1945, Vol. 234. (Men-at-Arms Ser.). 1991. pap. 12.95 (*0-85045-952-4*, Pub. by Ospry) Motorbooks Intl.
— German Combat Equipments 1939-451. (Men-at-Arms Ser.: No. 234). (Illus.). 48p. pap. 11.95 (*1-85532-952-2*, 9192, Pub. by Ospry) Stackpole.
— Inside the U. S. Army Today. (Elite Ser.: No. 20). (Illus.). 64p. 1989. pap. 12.95 (*0-85045-855-2*, 9420) Stackpole.
— Panama. (Elite Ser.: No. 37). (Illus.). 64p. pap. 12.95 (*1-85532-156-4*, 9452, Pub. by Ospry) Stackpole.
— U. S. Army Air Force One. (Elite Ser.: No. 46). (Illus.). 64p. pap. 12.95 (*1-85532-294-3*, 9461, Pub. by Ospry) Stackpole.
— U. S. Army Air Force Two. (Elite Ser.). (Illus.). 64p. 1994. pap. 12.95 (*1-85532-339-7*, 9466, Pub. by Ospry) Stackpole.
— U. S. Army Airborne, 1940-1990: The First Fifty Years. (Elite Ser.: No. 31). (Illus.). 64p. 1990. pap. 12.95 (*0-85045-948-6*, 9431, Pub. by Ospry) Stackpole.
— U. S. Army Combat Equipments. (Men-at-Arms Ser.: No. 205). (Illus.). 48p. 1989. pap. 11.95 (*0-85045-842-0*, 9138) Stackpole.
— U. S. Army Rangers & LRRP Units, 1942-87. (Elite Ser.: No. 13). (Illus.). 64p. pap. 12.95 (*0-85045-795-5*, 9412, Pub. by Ospry) Stackpole.
— U. S. Army Special Forces, 1952-84. (Elite Ser.: No. 4). (Illus.). 64p. pap. 12.95 (*0-85045-610-X*, 9403, Pub. by Ospry) Stackpole.
— Vietnam Airborne. (Elite Ser.: No. 29). (Illus.). 64p. 1990. pap. 12.95 (*0-85045-941-9*, 9429, Pub. by Ospry) Stackpole.
— Warsaw Pact Ground Forces. (Elite Ser.: No. 10). (Illus.). 64p. pap. 12.95 (*0-85045-730-0*, 9409, Pub. by Ospry) Stackpole.
— World Special Forces Insignia. (Elite Ser.: No. 22). (Illus.). 64p. pap. 12.95 (*0-85045-865-X*, 9422, Pub. by Ospry) Stackpole.
Rottman, John M. & Wilson, Paul S., eds. Seasons of Preaching: 160 Best Sermons from the Preaching Resource Word & Witness. 270p. (Orig.). 1996. pap. 20.00 (*0-940169-12-6*) Liturgical Pubns.
Rottman, Michael. The Basic First Aid Card Deck. (Illus.). (Orig.). 1998. pap. 14.95 (*1-57532-035-5*) Press-Tige Pub.
Rottman, Ray, jt. auth. see Wood, Lowell T.
Rottman, S. L. Head above Water. LC 99-26030. 192p. (YA). (gr. 7-11). 1999. 14.95 (*1-56145-185-1*) Peachtree Pubs.
***Rottman, S. L.** Hero. LC 99-27762. (Illus.). (J). 2000. pap. 5.99 (*0-14-130701-3*) Peng Put Young Read.
— Rough Waters. LC 97-39434. (Illus.). 192p. (YA). (gr. 7-11). 1998. 14.95 (*1-56145-172-X*) Peachtree Pubs.
***Rottman, S. L.** Rough Waters. LC 99-27767. (Illus.). (YA). 2000. pap. 5.99 (*0-14-130703-X*) Peng Put Young Read.
Rottman, Susan L. Hero. LC 97-3139. 142p. (YA). (gr. 7-11). 1997. 14.95 (*1-56145-159-2*) Peachtree Pubs.
Rottman, Vicki. The Coffee Break Book: Brief Diversions for Your Busy Day. LC 94-96366. (Illus.). 112p. (Orig.). 1994. pap. 12.95 (*0-9642517-0-1*) VR Prodns.
Rottmann, Gordon. U. S. Marine Corps, 1941-45. (Elite Ser.). (Illus.). 64p. 1995. pap. 12.95 (*1-85532-497-0*, Pub. by Ospry) Stackpole.
Rottmann, Larry. Voices from the Ho Chi Minh Trail. LC 93-71258. (Illus.). 224p. (Orig.). 1993. pap. 19.95 (*1-880391-06-6*) Event Horizon.
Rottnek, Matthew. Sissies & Tomboys: Gender Nonconformity & Homosexual Childhood. LC 98-53735. 1999. pap. 18.95 (*0-8147-7484-9*) NYU Pr.
Rottnek, Matthew, ed. Sissies & Tomboys: Gender Nonconformity & Homosexual Childhood. LC 98-53735. 344p. 1999. text 55.00 (*0-8147-7483-0*) NYU Pr.
Rotton, Wendy & Salvadeo, Michele B. The Ill-Tempered Crane. (Illus.). 48p. (J). (gr. 3-5). 1994. pap. 6.95 (*1-56721-060-0*) Twnty-Fifth Cent Pr.
Rotton, Wendy, et al. Leftover Magic. 96p. (Orig.). 1994. pap. 15.95 (*1-56721-084-8*) Twnty-Fifth Cent Pr.
Rotts, J., jt. auth. see Van Mier, J.
Rottschaefer, Henry. The Constitution & Socio-Economic Change. LC 77-173667. (American Constitutional & Legal History Ser). 253p. 1971. reprint ed. lib. bdg. 35.00 (*0-306-70410-2*) Da Capo.
— Constitution & Socio-Economic Change. LC 49-2548. (Michigan Legal Publications). xiii, 253p. 1986. reprint ed. lib. bdg. 42.00 (*0-89941-542-3*, 304710) W S Hein.
Rottschaefer, William A. The Biology & Psychology of Moral Agency. LC 97-8764. (Studies in Philosophy & Biology). 320p. (C). 1997. text 59.95 (*0-521-59265-8*) Cambridge U Pr.
Rottzoll, Dirk U. Abraham Ibn Ersas Kommentar zur Urgeschichte: Mit einem Anhang: Raschbams Kommentar zum Ersten Kapitel der Urgeschichte. (Studia Judaica: Band 15). (GER.). xxxiii, 243p. (C). 1996. lib. bdg. 126.15 (*3-11-015068-9*) De Gruyter.
— Rabbinischer Kommentar Zum Buch Genesis: Darstellung der Rezeption des Buches Genesis in Mischna & Talmud unter Angabe Tragumischer & Midreschischer Paralleltexte. (Studia Judaica Ser.: Bank 14). (GER.). x, 542p. (C). 1993. lib. bdg. 132.00 (*3-11-014231-7*) Mouton.
— Studien Zur Redaktion und Komposition des Amosbuchs. (Beiheft zur Zeitschrift fuer die Alttestamentliche Wissenschaft Ser.: Vol. 243). (GER.). x, 319p. (C). 1996. lib. bdg. 124.45 (*3-11-015290-1*, 114/96) De Gruyter.
Rottzoll, Dirk U., jt. auth. see Eingeleitet.
Rotunda, D. P. Motif-Index of the Italian Novella in Prose. LC 72-6778. (Studies in Italian Literature: No. 46). 1972. reprint ed. lib. bdg. 75.00 (*0-8383-1653-0*) M S G Haskell Hse.
Rotunda, Ronald D. Black Letter on Professional Responsibility. 4th ed. LC 95-30770. (Black Letter Ser.). 449p. (C). 1995. pap. 24.50 incl. disk (*0-314-06469-9*) West Pub.
— Constitutional Law. LC 86-26555. 609p. 1987. pap. text, teacher ed. write for info. (*0-314-66077-1*) West Pub.
— Modern Constitutional Law: Cases & Notes. 4th ed. LC 93-9233. (American Casebook Ser.). 1126p. 1993. text 48.50 (*0-314-01816-6*) West Pub.
— Modern Constitutional Law: Cases & Notes, 1995 Supplement To. 4th ed. (American Casebook Ser.). 100p. (C). 1995. pap. text 12.50 (*0-314-06875-9*) West Pub.
— Modern Constitutional Law: Cases & Notes, 1996 Supplement To. 4th ed. (American Casebook Ser.). 176p. 1996. pap. text. write for info. (*0-314-09939-5*) West Pub.
— Modern Constitutional Law: Cases & Notes, 1997 Supplement To. 5th ed. (American Casebook Ser.). 150p. (C). 1997. pap. text. write for info. (*0-314-21185-3*) West Pub.
— Modern Constitutional Law: Cases & Notes (5th Edition) 5th ed. LC 97-5642. (Paralegal). 1198p. (C). 1997. text 60.25 (*0-314-21140-3*) West Pub.
— 1998 Supplement to Modern Constitutional Law Cases & Notes. 5th ed. (American Casebks.). 192p. 1998. pap. text 13.25 (*0-314-23253-2*) West Pub.
— The Politics of Language: Liberalism As Word & Symbol. LC 85-24548. 148p. reprint ed. pap. 45.90 (*0-8357-3406-4*, 203966300013) Bks Demand.
Rotunda, Ronald D., jt. auth. see Morgan, Thomas D.
Rotunda, Ronald D., jt. auth. see Nowak, John E.
Rotunda, Ronald D., ed. see Morgan, Thomas D.
Rotundo, E. Anthony. American Manhood: Transformations in Masculinity from the Revolution to the Modern Era. LC 92-53247. 400p. 1994. reprint ed. pap. 16.00 (*0-465-00169-6*, Pub. by Basic) HarpC.
Rotundo, John L., jt. auth. see Ericson, Don.
Rotundo, L. Battle for Stalingrad: The 1943 Soviet General Staff Study. (Illus.). 342p. 1989. 47.00 (*0-08-035974-4*, 3574M) Brasseys.
Rotundo, Louis C. Into the Unknown: The X-1 Story. LC 93-15989. (Illus.). 352p. 1994. 29.95 (*1-56098-305-1*) Smithsonian.
Rotunno, Betsy, jt. auth. see Rotunno, Rocco.
Rotunno, Betsy, jt. auth. see Rotunno, Roccy.
Rotunno, Catalina A., jt. auth. see Cereijido, Marcelino.
Rotunno, Rocco & Rotunno, Betsy. How Snowshoe Saves Christmas. (Stamptime Stories Ser.). (Illus.). 12p. (Orig.). (J). (gr. 2-6). 1993. boxed set 7.00 (*1-881980-05-7*) Noteworthy.
— The Incredible Crash Dummies: The Dashboard Sandwich. (Stamptime Stories Ser.). (Illus.). 12p. (Orig.). (J). (gr. 2-6). 1993. student ed., boxed set 7.00 (*1-881980-06-5*) Noteworthy.
— Little Bear's Best Birthday. (Stamptime Stories Ser.). (Illus.). 12p. (J). (gr. 2-6). 1992. 7.00 (*1-881980-00-6*) Noteworthy.
— The Story of Christmas Tree Lane. (Stamptime Stories Ser.). (Illus.). 12p. (Orig.). (J). (gr. 2-6). 1993. boxed set 7.00 (*1-881980-04-9*) Noteworthy.
— Tessa Becomes a Ballerina. (Stamptime Stories Ser.). (Illus.). 12p. (J). (gr. 2-6). 1992. 7.00 (*1-881980-01-4*) Noteworthy.
— A Trick for Magic Bunny. (Stamptime Stories Ser.). (Illus.). 12p. (J). (gr. 2-6). 1992. 7.00 (*1-881980-02-2*) Noteworthy.
Rotunno, Roccy & Rotunno, Betsy. Dennis the Dinosaur Moves to Crystal Pond. (Stamptime Stories Ser.). (Illus.). 12p. (J). (gr. 2-6). 1992. 7.00 (*1-881980-03-0*) Noteworthy.
Rotunno, Ron. Full Tilt to the NFL: Steel Valley Heroes. unabridged ed. (Illus.). 120p. (Orig.). Date not set. 5.95 (*0-936369-51-5*) Son-Rise Pubns.
Rotunno, Ron T. Jack Lambert: Tough As Steel. abr. ed. LC 97-92180. (Illus.). 160p. (Orig.). 1997. pap. 9.95 (*0-936369-54-X*) Son-Rise Pubns.
***Roturra, Daniel.** Macaroni on Tuesdays. 198p. 2000. pap. 10.95 (*1-929416-24-5*) Magner Pubg.
Rotwein, Eugene, ed. & intro. see Hume, David.
Rotwitt, Jeffrey B., jt. auth. see Nasuti, James F.
Roty, Martine. Dictionnaire Russe-Francais des Termes en Usage Dans l'Eglise Russe. 2nd ed. (FRE & RUS.). 160p. 1983. pap. 24.95 (*0-7859-7961-1*, 2720401935) Fr & Eur.
Rotz, Anna O. Heritage Hill Farm Cookbook. 96p. 1980. 7.95 (*0-9605108-0-X*) Rotz.
Rotzel, Grace. The School in Rose Valley: A Parent Venture in Education. LC 70-144200. (Illus.). 159p. (C). reprint ed. 49.30 (*0-8357-9284-6*, 201573900097) Bks Demand.
Rotzer, Florian. Conversations with French Philosophers. Aylesworth, Gary E., tr. from GER. LC 93-30819. 120p. (C). 1995. pap. 12.50 (*0-391-03847-8*); text 39.95 (*0-391-03846-X*) Humanities.
Rotzetter, Anton, et al. Gospel Living: St. Francis of Assisi Yesterday & Today. (Franciscan Pathways Ser.). 308p. 1994. pap. 20.00 (*1-57659-061-5*) Franciscan Inst.
Rotzoll, Kim B. Advertising in Contemporary Society. 2nd ed. (C). 1989. pap. text. write for info. (*0-318-65184-X*, SJ70BA) S-W Pub.
Rotzoll, Kim B., ed. Proceedings of the 1989 Conference of the American Academy of Advertising. 1989. pap. 25.00 (*0-931030-12-9*) Am Acad Advert.
Rotzoll, Kim B., et al. Advertising in Contemporary Society: Perspectives Toward Understanding. 3rd ed. LC 95-41806. (Illus.). 280p. 1996. pap. text 14.95 (*0-252-06542-5*) U of Ill Pr.
Rotzsche, H. Stationary Phases in Gas Chromatography. (Journal of Chromatography Library: Vol. 48). 410p. 1991. 250.75 (*0-444-98733-9*) Elsevier.
Roual & Ancient Golf Club Staff. British Open Championship, 1996. 1996. 24.95 (*1-874557-22-5*, Pub. by Hazelton) Motorbooks Intl.
Rouan, Chris. Basic Biology Questions for GCSE. 278p. (YA). (gr. 9-11). 1998. pap. 23.00 (*0-7487-1726-9*) St Mut.
***Rouanet, Henry, et al.** New Ways in Statistical Methodology: From Significance Tests to Bayesian Inference. LC 98-42942. (European University Studies: Series 6, Vol. 618). xviii, 276p. 1998. 44.95 (*3-906760-68-5*, Pub. by P Lang) P Lang Pubng.
Rouanet, Leo. Coleccion De Autos, Farsas y Coloquios Del Siglo, 4 vols., Set, XVI. xxviii, 2124p. 1979. reprint ed. write for info. incl. 3.5 hd (*3-487-06804-4*) G Olms Pubs.
Rouard, Danielle, jt. auth. see Dibango, Manu.
Rouard, Marguerite, jt. auth. see Simon, Jacques.
Rouart, Denis, ed. Berthe Morisot: Correspondence. Hubbard, Betty W., tr. from FRE. 288p. pap. 10.95 (*0-918825-62-8*) Moyer Bell.
Rouaud, Jean. Fields of Glory. Manheim, Ralph, tr. from FRE. 160p. 1993. reprint ed. pap. 9.70 (*1-55970-216-8*, Pub. by Arcade Pub Inc) Time Warner.

— Of Illustrious Men. Wright, Barbara, tr. from FRE. LC 94-13979. 160p. 1994. 19.45 (*1-55970-265-6*, Pub. by Arcade Pub Inc) Time Warner.

— Of Illustrious Men. Wright, Barbara, tr. from FRE. 160p. 1995. pap. 10.45 (*1-55970-319-9*, Pub. by Arcade Pub Inc) Time Warner.

— The World More or Less. Wright, Barbara, tr. from FRE. LC 97-30001.Tr. of Monde, Plus ou Monis. 192p. 1998. 22.45 (*1-55970-405-5*, Pub. by Arcade Pub Inc) Time Warner.

Rouault, Isabelle. Rouault's Complete Paintings, 2 vols., Set. (ENG & FRE., Illus.). 1988. 1500.00 (*1-55660-031-3*) A Wofsy Fine Arts.

Rouault, Isabelle, jt. auth. see Chapon, Francois.

Rouault, Oliver. Elements pour un Logiciel Assyriologique. (Computer Aided Research in Near Eastern Studies: Vol. 1, Pt. 2). 82p. 1984. pap. 11.00 (*0-89003-185-1*) Undena Pubns.

Rouault, Oliver & Buccellati, Giorgio. Terqa Preliminary Report No. 12: Digital Plotting of Archaeological Floor Plans. (Computer Aided Research in Near Eastern Studies: Vol. 1, Pt. 1). 40p. 1983. pap. text 9.00 (*0-89003-146-0*) Undena Pubns.

Rouault, Olivier. Terqa Final Reports: L'Archive de Puzurum. LC 81-71741. (Bibliotheca Mesopotamica Ser.: Vol. 16). (AKK, ENG & FRE., Illus.). xxii, 112p. 1984. pap. 26.00 (*0-89003-102-9*) Undena Pubns.

Roubal, Diane, ed. see Hill, Susan G.

Roubal, Diane, ed. see Podolsky, Nancy.

Rouban, Luc, ed. Citizens & the New Governance: Beyond New Public Management - EGPA Yearbook. (International Institute of Administrative Sciences Monographs: Vol. 10). 1999. 69.00 (*0-9673355-3-1*) IOS Press.

Roubatis, Yiannis P. Tangled Webs: The U. S. in Greece, 1947-1967. LC 87-60390. 228p. (Orig.). 1987. pap. 12.00 (*0-918618-34-7*) Pella Pub.

Roubaud, Jacques. The Great Fire of London. Di Bernardi, Dominic, tr. from FRE. (Illus.). 330p. 1992. reprint ed. pap. 12.95 (*0-916583-89-9*) Dalkey Arch.

— Hortense in Exile. Di Bernardi, Dominic, tr. from FRE. LC 91-29759. 211p. 1992. 19.95 (*1-56478-001-5*) Dalkey Arch.

— Hortense Is Abducted. Di Bernardi, Dominic, tr. from FRE. LC 88-30390. 230p. 1989. 19.95 (*0-916583-38-4*) Dalkey Arch.

— Plurality of Worlds of Lewis. Waldrop, Rosmarie, tr. from FRE. LC 94-7327. 109p. (Orig.). 1995. pap. 9.95 (*1-56478-069-4*) Dalkey Arch.

— The Princess Hoppy: or The Tale of Labrador. Hoepffner, Bernard, tr. from FRE. LC 93-18995. (Illus.). 133p. (Orig.). 1993. pap. 9.95 (*1-56478-032-5*) Dalkey Arch.

— Some Thing Black. Waldrop, Rosmarie, tr. from FRE. LC 89-35216. (Illus.). 112p. 1999. reprint ed. pap. 12.50 (*1-56478-206-9*) Dalkey Arch.

***Roubaud, Jacques & Di Bernardi, Dominic.** Hortense in Exile. LC 91-29759. 211p. 2000. pap. 11.95 (*1-56478-255-7*) Dalkey Arch.

— Hortense Is Abducted. LC 88-30390. 229p. 2000. pap. 12.50 (*1-56478-256-5*) Dalkey Arch.

Roubaud, Jacques, ed. see Perec, Georges.

Roubelakis-Angelakis, K. A. & Tran Thanh Van, K. Morphogenesis in Plants: Molecular Approaches, Vol. 253. LC 93-20954. (NATO ASI Ser.: Vol. 256). (Illus.). 292p. (C). 1993. text 110.00 (*0-306-44597-2*, Kluwer Plenum) Kluwer Academic.

Roubens, M. & Vincke, P. Preference Modelling. (Lecture Notes in Economics & Mathematical Systems Ser.: Vol. 250). (Illus.). viii, 94p. 1985. 29.50 (*0-387-15685-2*) Spr-Verlag.

Roubens, M., jt. ed. see Kacprzyk, Janusz.

Roubens, Marc, jt. auth. see Fodor, Janos.

Roubens, Marc, jt. auth. see Meskens, Nadine.

Rouberg, A. A., et al. Aaker Saga, a Family History. 206p. 1997. reprint ed. pap. 33.50 (*0-8328-7193-1*); reprint ed. lib. bdg. 43.50 (*0-8328-7192-3*) Higginson Bk Co.

Roubicek, Henry L. Doing Business & Professional Speech Communications. 3rd ed. 204p. 1995. per. 21.00 (*0-8403-8204-9*) Kendall-Hunt.

Roubicek, Marcel. Special Corps of Austria & Czechoslovakia, 1918-1945. 3rd rev. ed. (Military Monograph Ser.: Vol. 302). (Illus.). 37p. 1997. 14.95 (*1-57638-054-8*, M302H); pap. 4.95 (*1-57638-038-6*, M302S) Merriam Pr.

Roubicek, Tomas. Relaxation in Optimization Theory & Variational Calculus. LC 96-31728. (Series in Nonlinear Analysis & Applications: Vol. 4). xiv, 474p. (C). 1997. text 158.95 (*3-11-014542-1*) De Gruyter.

Roubickova, Eva M., jt. auth. see Roubickova, Mandlova.

Roubickova, Mandlova & Roubickova, Eva M. We're Alive & Life Goes On: A Theresienstadt Diary. Alexander, Zaia, tr. LC 97-18576. (YA). (gr. 9 up). 1998. 16.95 (*0-8050-5352-2*) H Holt & Co.

Roubiczek, Paul. Existentialism: For & Against. LC 64-21562. 206p. reprint ed. pap. 58.80 (*0-608-30599-5*, 2022466) Bks Demand.

Roubik, David W. Ecology & Natural History of Tropical Bees. (Cambridge Tropical Biology Ser.). (Illus.). 524p. (C). 1992. pap. text 37.95 (*0-521-42909-9*) Cambridge U Pr.

Roubin, Gary S., et al, eds. Interventional Cardiovascular Medicine: Principles & Practice. (Illus.). 976p. 1993. text 199.00 (*0-443-08834-9*) Church.

Roubin, Gary S. & Slyer, S., eds. Coronary Artery Stenting. (Interventional Cardiology Ser.). 400p. 1997. 95.00 (*0-86542-283-4*) Blackwell Sci.

Roubine, E., et al, eds. Mathematics Applied to Physics. (Illus.). 1970. 86.95 (*0-387-04965-7*) Spr-Verlag.

Roubine, E. & Bolomey, J. C. Antennas Vol. 1: General Principles. LC 66-56953. 218p. 1987. 137.00 (*0-89116-278-X*) Hemisp Pub.

Roubini, Nouriel, jt. auth. see Alesina, Alberto.

Roucek, Joseph S. Balkan Politics: International Relations in No Man's Land. LC 75-106696. (Illus.). 298p. 1971. reprint ed. lib. bdg. 65.00 (*0-8371-3370-X*, ROBP, Greenwood Pr) Greenwood.

— Contemporary Roumania & Her Problems: A Study in Modern Nationalism. LC 74-135831. (Eastern Europe Collection). 1971. reprint ed. 30.95 (*0-405-02773-7*) Ayer.

— Social Control for the 1980s: A Handbook for Order in a Democratic Society, 31. LC 77-91112. (Contributions in Sociology Ser.: No. 31). 386p. 1978. 69.50 (*0-313-20048-3*, RSC/, Greenwood Pr) Greenwood.

Roucek, Joseph S., ed. Challenge of Science Education. LC 77-128305. (Essay Index Reprint Ser.). 1977. 29.95 (*0-8369-2070-8*) Ayer.

— Juvenile Delinquency. LC 70-128306. (Essay Index Reprint Ser.). 1977. 26.95 (*0-8369-1848-7*) Ayer.

Roucek, Joseph S. & Belok, Michael V. The United States & the Persian Gulf: An ANVIL Original. LC 84-19366. (Anvil Ser.). 208p. (C). 1985. reprint ed. pap. text 11.50 (*0-89874-574-8*) Krieger.

Roucek, Joseph S. & Eisenberg, Bernard, eds. America's Ethnic Politics, 5. LC 81-986. (Contributions in Ethnic Studies: No. 5). (Illus.). 403p. 1982. 79.50 (*0-313-22024-7*, ROA/, Greenwood Pr) Greenwood.

Roucek, Joseph S. & Lottich, Kenneth. Behind the Iron Curtain. LC 64-153290. 631p. 1986. 10.00 (*0-939482-51-7*, 0072, Noontide Pr) Legion Survival.

Rouch, James. The Zone No. 2: Blind Fire. 1985. mass mkt. 2.50 (*0-8217-1588-7*, Zebra Kensgtn) Kensgtn Pub Corp.

Rouch, Lawrence L. The Vernor's Story: From Gnomes to Now. (Illus.). (C). text. write for info. (*0-472-09697-4*); pap. text. write for info. (*0-472-06697-8*) U of Mich Pr.

Rouchdy, Aleya. Nubians & the Nubian Language in Contemporary Egypt: A Case of Cultural & Linguistic Contact. LC 90-19286. (Studies in Semitic Languages & Linguistics: No. 15). xiv, 83p. 1991. 64.50 (*90-04-09197-1*) Brill Academic Pubs.

— Variation on a Theme: Bilingualism, a Case Study. LC 76-47344. (Language Science Monographs: Vol. 17). 1977. pap. text 12.00 (*0-87750-209-9*) Res Inst Inner Asian Studies.

Rouchdy, Aleya, ed. The Arabic Language in America. LC 91-30156. 350p. 1992. pap. 21.95 (*0-8143-2284-0*) Wayne St U Pr.

Rouchdy, Asleya, ed. The Arabic Language in America. 350p. 1996. pap. 19.95 (*0-614-21636-2*, 56) Kazi Pubns.

Rouche, Daniel, jt. auth. see Bellahsen, Fabien.

Rouchota, Villy & Jucker, Andreas H., eds. Current Issues in Relevance Theory. LC 98-18678. (Pragmatics & Beyond New Ser.: Vol. 58). xii, 368p. 1998. 75.00 (*1-55619-821-3*) J Benjamins Pubng Co.

Rouck, A. De, see Francois, J. & De Rouck, A., eds.

Roucoules. Terminologie Fondamentale en Odonto-Stomatologie et Lexique: Francais-Anglais, Anglais-Francais. (ENG & FRE.). 259p. 1977. 35.95 (*0-8288-5524-2*, M6492) Fr & Eur.

Roucoules, Gil & Perlemuter, Leon. Dictionnaire Pratique des Soins et du Soutien a Domicile. (FRE.). 1990. write for info. (*0-7859-7829-1*, 2-225-81308-6) Fr & Eur.

Roucoux, A. & Crommelinck, M. Physiological & Pathological Aspects of Eye Movements. 1982. text 249.00 (*90-6193-730-2*) Kluwer Academic.

Roud, Paul C. Making Miracles: Exploration into the Dynamics of Self-Healing. 1990. pap. 9.95 (*0-446-39118-2*) Warner Bks.

Roud, Richard. Passion for Films: Henri Langlois & the Cinematheque Francaise. LC 99-14614. (Illus.). 218p. 1999. pap. text 16.95 (*0-8018-6206-X*) Johns Hopkins.

Roud, Steve, jt. auth. see Simpson, Jacqueline.

Roudane. American Drama Since 1960. 1997. pap. 18.00 (*0-8057-1619-X*, Twyne) Mac Lib Ref.

Roudane, M. C., ed. Public Issues, Private Tensions: Contemporary American Drama. LC 91-58147. (Georgia State Literary Studies: No. 9). 1993. 55.00 (*0-404-63209-2*) AMS Pr.

***Roudane, Matthew C.** American Drama Since 1960: A Critical History. 298p. 2000. reprint ed. 25.00 (*0-7881-9328-7*) DIANE Pub.

Roudane, Matthew C. American Drama Since 1960. (Illus.). 250p. 1996. per. 28.95 (*0-8057-8954-5*, Twyne) Mac Lib Ref.

— Who's Afraid of Virginia Woolf? Necessary Fictions, Terrifying Realities. (Masterwork Studies: No. 34). 142p. 1989. 23.95 (*0-8057-8059-9*, MWS-34); pap. 18.00 (*0-8057-8105-6*) Macmillan.

Roudane, Matthew C., ed. Approaches to Teaching Miller's Death of a Salesman. LC 94-32025. (Approaches to Teaching World Literature Ser.: No. 52). xii, 178p. (Orig.). 1995. pap. 18.00 (*0-87352-728-3*); lib. bdg. 37.50 (*0-87352-727-5*) Modern Lang.

— The Cambridge Companion to Tennessee Williams. LC 96-40036. (Cambridge Companions to Literature Ser.). (Illus.). 302p. (C). 1998. text 59.95 (*0-521-49533-4*); pap. text 18.95 (*0-521-49883-X*) Cambridge U Pr.

Roudiez, Leon, tr. see Kristeva, Julia.

Roudiez, Leon S. French Fiction Revisited. LC 90-14081. 350p. (Orig.). 1991. pap. 14.95 (*0-916583-73-2*) Dalkey Arch.

Roudiez, Leon S., ed. see Kristeva, Julia.

Roudiez, Leon S., tr. see Kristeva, Julia.

Roudinesco, Elisabeth. Dictionnaire de Psychanalyse. (FRE.). 1200p. 1997. 125.00 (*0-7859-9473-4*) Fr & Eur.

— Jacques Lacan & Co. A History of Psychoanalysis in France, 1925-1985. LC 89-78164. (Illus.). 788p. 1990. 45.00 (*0-226-72997-4*) U Ch Pr.

— Madness & Revolution: The Lives & Legends of Theroigne de Mericourt. Thom, Martin, tr. (Illus.). 296p. (gr. 13). 1992. pap. 20.00 (*0-86091-597-2*, A9770, Pub. by Verso) Norton.

Roudinesco, Elizabeth. Jacques Lacan: An Outline of a Life & a History of a System of Thought. 1999. pap. 19.50 (*0-231-10147-3*) Col U Pr.

— Jacques Lacan: His Life & Work. Bray, Barbara, tr. LC 96-30125. (European Perspectives Ser.). 464p. 1997. 39.00 (*0-231-10146-5*) Col U Pr.

***Roudometof, Victor.** Macedonian Question: Cultural, Historiography, Politics. 320p. 2000. 42.00 (*0-88033-451-7*, 553, Pub. by East Eur Monographs) Col U Pr.

Roudometof, Victor, jt. ed. see Epitropoulos, Mike-Frank G.

Roudybush, Tom, jt. auth. see Grindol, Diane.

Roueche & Graves, Virginia H. Business Mathematics. 7th ed. 1996. pap. text, student ed. 26.00 (*0-13-723578-X*) P-H.

Roueche, Berton. Greener Grass & Some People Who Found It. LC 78-160927. (Biography Index Reprint Ser.). 1977. reprint ed. 19.95 (*0-8369-8090-5*) Ayer.

— The Medical Detectives. 448p. 1991. pap. 14.95 (*0-452-26588-6*, Truman Talley) St Martin.

— Sea to Shining Sea: People, Travels, Places. 288p. 1987. mass mkt. 4.50 (*0-380-70265-7*, Avon Bks) Morrow Avon.

Roueche, Berton, et al. Electroshock Treatment over Four Decades: The Case Against. Morgan, Robert F., ed. 99p. (C). 1999. pap. 56.00 (*1-885679-02-5*) Morgan Fnd Pubs.

Roueche, Charlotte & Erim, Kenan T., eds. Aphrodisias Papers. Recent Work on Architecture & Sculpture: Including the Papers Given at the Second International Aphrodisias Colloquium Held at King's College London on 14 November, 1987. (JRA Supplementary Ser.: No. 1). (ENG & FRE., Illus.). 160p. 1990. 59.75 (*1-887829-01-6*) Jour Roman Arch.

Roueche, Charlotte & Smith, R. R., eds. Aphrodisias Papers 3. The Setting & Quarries, Mythological & Other Sculptural Decoration, Architectural Development, Portico of Tiberius, & Tetrapylon: Including the Papers Given at the Fourth International Aphrodisias Colloquium. (Journal of Roman Archaeology Supplementary Ser.: No. 20). (ENG, FRE & GER., Illus.). 224p. 1996. 79.50 (*1-887829-20-2*) Jour Roman Arch.

Roueche, Charlotte, jt. ed. see Beaton, Roderick.

Roueche, John E. & Baker, George A., III. Access & Excellence: The Open-Door College. 1987. pap. 33.00 (*0-87117-257-7*, 1001) Comm Coll Pr Am Assn Comm Coll.

Roueche, John E. & Kirk, R. Wade. Catching Up: Remedial Education. LC 73-1851. (Jossey-Bass Higher Education Ser.). 122p. reprint ed. 37.90 (*0-8357-9299-4*, 201374600088) Bks Demand.

Roueche, John E. & Pitman, John C. A Modest Proposal: Students Can Learn. LC 73-184956. (Jossey-Bass Higher Education Ser.). 160p. reprint ed. 49.60 (*0-8357-9336-2*, 201386400088) Bks Demand.

Roueche, John E. & Roueche, Suanne D. Between a Rock & a Hard Place: The At-Risk Student in the Open-Door College. 294p. 1993. pap. 33.00 (*0-87117-259-3*, 1354) Comm Coll Pr Am Assn Comm Coll.

— High Stakes, High Performance: Making Remediial Education Work. LC 99-483507. (Illus.). 70p. 1999. pap. 19.00 (*0-87117-321-2*, 1433) Comm Coll Pr Am Assn Comm Coll.

Roueche, John E., et al. The Company We Keep: Collaboration in the Community College. 406p. 1995. pap. 33.00 (*0-87117-282-8*, 1378) Comm Coll Pr Am Assn Comm Coll.

— Embracing the Tiger: The Effectiveness Debate & the Community College. LC 97-176644. 180p. 1997. pap. 32.00 (*0-87117-306-9*, 1407) Comm Coll Pr Am Assn Comm Coll.

— Shared Vision: Transformational Leadership in American Community Colleges. 1989. 33.00 (*0-87117-190-2*, 1100) Comm Coll Pr Am Assn Comm Coll.

— Strangers in Their Own Land: Part-Time Faculty in American Community Colleges. LC 95-173038. 196p. 1995. pap. 32.00 (*0-87117-283-6*, 1377) Comm Coll Pr Am Assn Comm Coll.

Roueche, Nelda W. & Graves, Virginia H. Business Mathematics. 7th ed. LC 96-10831. 704p. (C). 1996. 95.00 (*0-13-500000-9*) P-H.

— Business Mathematics: A Collegiate Approach. 8th ed. LC 99-88768. (Illus.). 672p. 2000. 76.00 (*0-13-084730-5*) P-H.

Roueche, Suanne D., jt. auth. see Roueche, John E.

Rouede, Denise, jt. auth. see Rouede, Pierre.

Rouede, Pierre & Rouede, Denise. Dictionnaire Italien-Francais et Francais-Italien: Italian - French, French - Italian Dictionary. (FRE & ITA.). 1256p. 1970. 55.00 (*0-8288-6526-4*, M-6493) Fr & Eur.

Rouen, Ren. China's Economic Performance in an International Perspective. LC 98-121141. 166p. 1997. pap. 32.00 (*92-64-15581-3*, 41-97-10-1, Pub. by Org for Econ) OECD.

Rouet, Albert. Liturgy & the Arts. Philibert, Paul, tr. from FRE. LC 96-41896. (FRE & ENG.). 192p. (Orig.). 1997. pap. text 19.95 (*0-8146-2393-X*, Liturg Pr Bks) Liturgical Pr.

Rouet, Marcel. Dictionnaire de la Culture Physique. (FRE.). 304p. 1975. 39.95 (*0-8288-5846-2*, M6494) Fr & Eur.

***Rouette, H. K.** Encyclopedia of Textile Finishing, 3 vols. 3000p. 2000. 1495.00 incl. cd-rom (*3-540-65490-9*); cd-rom 699.00 (*3-540-14765-9*) Spr-Verlag.

— Encyclopedia of Textile Finishing, 3 vols. 3000p. 2000. 999.00 (*3-540-65031-8*) Spr-Verlag.

Rouffet, Denis, jt. auth. see Morgan, Walter L.

Rouffignac, Ann E. De, see De Rouffignac, Ann E.

***Rouge Et Noir Staff.** Winning at Casino Gaming: New, Revised, Expanded & Updated Edition. rev. expanded ed. (Illus.). 168p. 2000. 35.00 (*0-9701977-0-5*) Rge Et Noir.

Rouge, J. de. Geographie Ancienne de la Basse Egypte. (Illus.). 188p. reprint ed. lib. bdg. 38.50 (*0-685-13354-0*, Pub. by AM Hakkert) Coronet Bks.

Rouge, Jacques-Marie. Petit Dictionnaire du Parler de Touraine. (FRE.). 91p. 1991. pap. 32.95 (*0-7859-8094-6*, 2854432258) Fr & Eur.

Rouge, Janine, jt. auth. see Moureau, Magdeleine.

Rougeau, Darlene H. Bride's Organizer. 1993. mass mkt. 5.99 (*0-345-37923-3*) Ballantine Pub Grp.

Rougeau, Darlene H. & Hudak, Deanna M. The Bride's Organizer. 1993. mass mkt. 5.99 (*0-345-90224-6*) Ballantine Pub Grp.

Rougemont, Claire. The National Dream Book. 188p. 1996. pap. 15.00 (*0-89540-247-5*, SB-247) Sun Pub.

Rougemont, Denis. The Devil's Share. LC 79-8118. reprint ed. 37.50 (*0-404-18431-6*) AMS Pr.

Rougemont, Denis De, see De Rougemont, Denis, ed.

Rouger, ed. see Perrault, Charles.

Rouger, P., jt. ed. see Cartron, J. P.

Rouget, Gilbert. Music & Trance: A Theory of the Relations Between Music & Possession. Biebuyck, Brunhilde, tr. LC 85-1107. (Illus.). xx, 416p. 1985. pap. text 24.00 (*0-226-73006-9*) U Ch Pr.

— Music & Trance: A Theory of the Relations Between Music & Possession. Biebuyck, Brunhilde, tr. LC 85-1107. (Illus.). xx, 236p. 1996. lib. bdg. 72.00 (*0-226-73005-0*) U Ch Pr.

Rougeyron, Andre. Agents for Escape: Inside the French Resistance, 1939-1945. McConnell, Marie-Antoinette, tr. LC 95-23387. (Illus.). 248p. (C). 1996. 24.95 (*0-8071-2019-7*) La State U Pr.

Rough Guide Staff. Hindi. (Rough Guide Phrasebooks Ser.). 272p. 1997. pap. 6.00 (*1-85828-252-7*, Penguin Bks) Viking Penguin.

— Indonesian. (Rough Guide Phrasebooks Ser.). 272p. 1997. pap. 6.00 (*1-85828-250-0*, Penguin Bks) Viking Penguin.

— Russian. (Rough Guide Phrasebooks Ser.). 272p. 1997. pap. 6.00 (*1-85828-251-9*, Penguin Bks) Viking Penguin.

***Rough Guides Staff.** Amsterdam. 6th ed. (Travel Ser.). (Illus.). 2000. pap. 14.95 (*1-85828-512-7*, Pub. by Rough Guides) Penguin Putnam.

— Andalucia. 3rd ed. (Travel Ser.). 2000. pap. 16.95 (*1-85828-545-3*, Pub. by Rough Guides) Penguin Putnam.

Rough Guides Staff. Barcelona. 4th ed. 288p. 1999. pap. 14.95 (*1-85828-412-0*, Pub. by Rough Guides) Penguin Putnam.

***Rough Guides Staff.** Beijing. (Miniguides Ser.). 2000. pap. 11.95 (*1-85828-519-4*, Pub. by Rough Guides) Penguin Putnam.

— Brazil: The Rough Guide. 4th ed. 2000. pap. 23.95 (*1-85828-564-X*, Rough Guides) Viking Penguin.

— Britain. (Illus.). 1120p. 2000. pap. 23.95 (*1-85828-513-5*, Rough Guides) Viking Penguin.

Rough Guides Staff. Brittany & Normandy. 6th ed. 416p. 1999. pap. 16.95 (*1-85828-425-2*, Pub. by Rough Guides) Penguin Putnam.

***Rough Guides Staff.** Brussels. (Miniguides Ser.). (Illus.). 320p. 1999. pap. 11.95 (*1-85828-411-2*, Pub. by Rough Guides) Penguin Putnam.

Rough Guides Staff. Bulgaria. 3rd ed. 432p. 1999. pap. 16.95 (*1-85828-422-8*, Pub. by Rough Guides) Penguin Putnam.

***Rough Guides Staff.** California. 6th ed. (Travel Ser.). 2000. pap. 18.95 (*1-85828-539-9*, Pub. by Rough Guides) Penguin Putnam.

— Capetown: Mini Rough Guide. 2000. pap. 11.95 (*1-85828-548-8*, Rough Guides) Viking Penguin.

Rough Guides Staff. Central America. (Rough Guide Ser.). (Illus.). 656p. 1998. pap. 19.95 (*1-85828-335-3*, Pub. by Rough Guides) Penguin Putnam.

***Rough Guides Staff.** Classical Music: 100 Essential Cd's. 208p. 1999. pap. 8.95 (*1-85828-489-9*, Pub. by Rough Guides) Penguin Putnam.

— Corsica. 3rd ed. (Travel Ser.). (Illus.). 2000. pap. 16.95 (*1-85828-600-X*, Pub. by Rough Guides) Penguin Putnam.

— Country Music. (Music Reference Ser.). 2000. pap. 24.95 (*1-85828-534-8*, Pub. by Rough Guides) Penguin Putnam.

— Croatia: The Rough Guide. 2000. pap. 16.95 (*1-85828-544-5*, Rough Guides) Viking Penguin.

— Cuba. (Illus.). 512p. 2000. pap. 17.95 (*1-85828-520-8*, Rough Guides) Viking Penguin.

— Czech & Slovak Republics. 5th ed. (Travel Ser.). (Illus.). 2000. pap. 18.95 (*1-85828-529-1*, Pub. by Rough Guides) Penguin Putnam.

Rough Guides Staff. Dodecanese & the East Aegean Islands. 2nd ed. 432p. 1999. pap. 16.95 (*1-85828-417-1*, Pub. by Rough Guides) Penguin Putnam.

***Rough Guides Staff.** Ecuador: The Rough Guide. 2000. pap. 18.95 (*1-85828-552-6*, Rough Guides) Viking Penguin.

— Egypt. 4th ed. (Travel Ser.). (Illus.). 2000. pap. 18.95 (*1-85828-522-4*, Pub. by Rough Guides) Penguin Putnam.

— English Football: A Fan's Handbook. 1999. pap. 19.95 (*1-85828-455-4*, Pub. by Rough Guides) Penguin Putnam.

— English Football: The Rough Guide. 2nd ed. 2000. pap. 21.95 (*1-85828-557-7*, Rough Guides) Viking Penguin.

Rough Guides Staff. English Roots Music. 1998. audio compact disk 14.95 (*1-85828-375-2*) Penguin Putnam.

An Asterisk (*) at the beginning of an entry indicates that the title is appearing for the first time.

*Rough Guides Staff. European Football: The Rough Guide. 4th ed. 2000. pap. 21.95 (*1-85828-568-2*, Rough Guides) Viking Penguin.
— European Languages Dictionary Phrasebook. 496p. 2000. pap. 8.50 (*1-85828-466-X*, Pub. by Rough Guides) Penguin Putnam.
— Florence. (Miniguides Ser.). 288p. 1999. pap. 11.95 (*1-85828-471-6*, Pub. by Rough Guides) Penguin Putnam.
Rough Guides Staff. France. 6th ed. 1104p. 1999. pap. 19.95 (*1-85828-415-5*, Pub. by Rough Guides) Penguin Putnam.
***Rough Guides Staff.** German. 2nd ed. (Phrasebooks Ser.). 256p. 2000. pap. 5.00 (*1-85828-610-7*, Pub. by Rough Guides) Penguin Putnam.
— Hotels & Restaurants of France 2000. 3rd ed. (Illus.). 960p. 2000. pap. 19.95 (*1-85828-531-3*, Rough Guides) Viking Penguin.
Rough Guides Staff. Hotels & Restos de France: 1999-2000. 2nd ed. 2nd ed. 704p. 1999. pap. 19.95 (*1-85828-409-0*) Penguin Putnam.
— Hungarian: A Rough Guide Phrasebook. LC 98-218752. (Rough Guide Phrasebooks Ser.). (HUN.). 255p. 1998. pap. 6.00 (*1-85828-304-3*, Penguin Bks) Viking Penguin.
— Indonesia. 1008p. 1999. pap. 25.95 (*1-85828-429-5*, Pub. by Rough Guides) Penguin Putnam.
***Rough Guides Staff.** Ionian Islands. 2nd ed. (Travel Ser.). (Illus.). 2000. pap. 14.95 (*1-85828-530-5*, Pub. by Rough Guides) Penguin Putnam.
Rough Guides Staff. Italy. 4th ed. 1056p. 1999. pap. 19.95 (*1-85828-413-9*, Pub. by Rough Guides) Penguin Putnam.
***Rough Guides Staff.** Jamaica: The Rough Guide. 2nd ed. 2000. pap. 16.95 (*1-85828-554-2*, Rough Guides) Viking Penguin.
— Lake District. (Travel Ser.). (Illus.). 2000. pap. 14.95 (*1-85828-533-X*, Pub. by Rough Guides) Penguin Putnam.
— Madrid. 2nd ed. (Miniguides Ser.). (Illus.). 2000. pap. 9.95 (*1-85828-535-6*, Pub. by Rough Guides) Penguin Putnam.
Rough Guides Staff. Mallorca & Menorca. 2nd ed. 304p. 1999. pap. 16.95 (*1-85828-408-2*, Pub. by Rough Guides) Penguin Putnam.
***Rough Guides Staff.** Mandarin Chinese. 2nd ed. (Phrasebooks Ser.). (Illus.). 288p. 2000. pap. 6.50 (*1-85828-607-7*, Pub. by Rough Guides) Penguin Putnam.
— Mexican Spanish. 2nd ed. (Phrasebooks Ser.). (Illus.). 272p. 2000. pap. 5.00 (*1-85828-609-3*, Pub. by Rough Guides) Penguin Putnam.
— Miami & the Florida Keys. (Miniguides Ser.). 2000. pap. 9.95 (*1-85828-547-X*, Pub. by Rough Guides) Penguin Putnam.
— Mini Rough Guide Edinburgh. 2nd ed. (Illus.). 2000. pap. 9.95 (*1-85828-505-4*) Viking Penguin.
— Mini Rough Guide to Boston. 2nd ed. (Miniguides Ser.). (Illus.). 352p. 2000. pap. 9.95 (*1-85828-521-6*, Pub. by Rough Guides) Penguin Putnam.
— Mini Rough Guide to Dublin. 2nd ed. (Illus.). 336p. 2000. pap. 9.95 (*1-85828-504-6*, Pub. by Rough Guides) Penguin Putnam.
Rough Guides Staff. Mini Rough Guide to Honolulu: Including Waikiki & All of Oahu. 208p. 1999. pap. 9.95 (*1-85828-402-3*) Penguin Putnam.
***Rough Guides Staff.** Mini Rough Guide to Jerusalem 2000. (Miniguides Ser.). (Illus.). 2000. pap. 9.95 (*1-85828-579-8*, Rough Guides) Viking Penguin.
— Mini Rough Guide to Lisbon. 2nd ed. (Illus.). 2000. pap. 9.95 (*1-85828-514-3*, Rough Guides) Viking Penguin.
Rough Guides Staff. Mini Rough Guide to Maui. 240p. 1999. pap. 9.95 (*1-85828-401-5*) Penguin Putnam.
— Mini Rough Guide to the Big Island of Hawaii. 2nd ed. (Illus.). 256p. 1999. pap. 9.95 (*1-85828-485-6*) Penguin Putnam.
***Rough Guides Staff.** Mini Rough Guide to Toronto. (Miniguides Ser.). 544p. 1999. pap. 9.95 (*1-85828-414-7*, Pub. by Rough Guides) Penguin Putnam.
Rough Guides Staff. Music of Eastern Europe. (Orig.). 1998. audio compact disk 14.95 (*1-85828-368-X*) Penguin Putnam.
— Native American Music Directory. 1999. audio compact disk 14.95 (*1-85828-372-8*) Penguin Putnam.
— New England. 544p. 1999. pap. 17.95 (*1-85828-426-0*, Pub. by Rough Guides) Penguin Putnam.
***Rough Guides Staff.** New Zealand: The Rough Guide. 2nd ed. 2000. pap. 19.95 (*1-85828-555-0*, Rough Guides) Viking Penguin.
— Norway. 2nd ed. (Illus.). 368p. 2000. pap. 17.95 (*1-85828-524-0*, Rough Guides) Viking Penguin.
— Opera: A Complete Guide to the Operas, Composers, Artists & Recordings. 2nd ed. (Music Reference Ser.). (Illus.). 704p. 1999. pap. 24.95 (*1-85828-456-2*, Pub. by Rough Guides) Penguin Putnam.
— Opera: 100 Essential CDs. (Music Reference Ser.). 1999. pap. text 8.95 (*1-85828-451-1*, Pub. by Rough Guides) Penguin Putnam.
Rough Guides Staff. Paris. 7th ed. 464p. 1999. pap. 14.95 (*1-85828-407-4*, Pub. by Rough Guides) Penguin Putnam.
***Rough Guides Staff.** Peru. 4th ed. (Travel Ser.). (Illus.). 2000. pap. 17.95 (*1-85828-536-4*, Pub. by Rough Guides) Penguin Putnam.
Rough Guides Staff. Poland. 4th ed. 704p. 1999. pap. 18.95 (*1-85828-423-6*, Pub. by Rough Guides) Penguin Putnam.
— Portuguese Fado. 1998. audio compact disk 14.95 (*1-85828-369-8*) Penguin Putnam.
***Rough Guides Staff.** Prague. 4th ed. (Illus.). 320p. 2000. pap. 14.95 (*1-85828-525-9*, Rough Guides) Viking Penguin.
— Reggae: 100 Essential CDs. 1999. pap. 8.95 (*1-85828-450-3*) Rough Guides.
— Rock. 2nd ed. (Music Reference Ser.). 1999. pap. text 26.95 (*1-85828-457-0*, Pub. by Rough Guides) Penguin Putnam.
— Rock: 100 Essential CDs. 208p. 1999. pap. 8.95 (*1-85828-490-2*, Pub. by Rough Guides) Penguin Putnam.
— Rome. (Illus.). 352p. 2000. pap. 9.95 (*1-85828-599-2*, Rough Guides) Viking Penguin.
— Rough Guide England. 4th ed. (Illus.). 2000. pap. 19.95 (*1-85828-506-2*) Viking Penguin.
— Rough Guide Jazz. 2nd ed. (Illus.). 2000. pap. 26.95 (*1-85828-528-3*, Rough Guides) Viking Penguin.
— Rough Guide London Restaurants 2000. (Illus.). 2000. pap. 11.95 (*1-85828-509-7*, Rough Guides) Viking Penguin.
— Rough Guide Scotland. 4th ed. (Illus.). 656p. 2000. pap. 16.95 (*1-85828-508-9*) Viking Penguin.
Rough Guides Staff. Rough Guide Swahili Phrasebook. (Rough Guide Phrasebooks Ser.). (SWA.). 1998. pap. 6.00 (*1-85828-320-5*, Penguin Bks) Viking Penguin.
***Rough Guides Staff.** The Rough Guide to Blues: 100 Essential CDs. 2000. 8.95 (*1-85828-560-7*, Rough Guides) Viking Penguin.
Rough Guides Staff. Rough Guide to Britain. 2nd ed. (Rough Guide Ser.). (Illus.). 1056p. (Orig.). 1998. pap. text 23.95 (*1-85828-312-4*, Pub. by Rough Guides) Penguin Putnam.
***Rough Guides Staff.** Rough Guide to China. 2nd ed. (Illus.). 2000. pap. 25.95 (*1-85828-503-8*, Rough Guides) Viking Penguin.
Rough Guides Staff. The Rough Guide to Czech. 224p. (Orig.). 1995. pap. 5.00 (*1-85828-148-2*, Penguin Bks) Viking Penguin.
— The Rough Guide to Europe, 2000. 6th ed. (Illus.). 1312p. 1999. 24.95 (*1-85828-462-7*, Pub. by Rough Guides) Penguin Putnam.
— The Rough Guide to Florida. 4th ed. 432p. 1999. pap. 17.95 (*1-85828-403-1*) Penguin Putnam.
***Rough Guides Staff.** Rough Guide to Greece. 8th ed. (Illus.). 2000. pap. 19.95 (*1-85828-515-1*, Rough Guides) Viking Penguin.
Rough Guides Staff. Rough Guide to Greek Islands. 2nd ed. (Rough Guides Ser.). 464p. 1998. pap. 17.95 (*1-85828-310-8*, Penguin Bks) Viking Penguin.
***Rough Guides Staff.** Rough Guide to Las Vegas. (Miniguides Ser.). (Illus.). 240p. 2000. pap. 9.95 (*1-85828-463-5*, Pub. by Rough Guides) Penguin Putnam.
— The Rough Guide to Music of Indonesia. 2000. cd-rom 14.95 (*1-85828-478-3*, Rough Guides) Viking Penguin.
— Rough Guide to New York. 7th ed. 2000. pap. text 15.95 (*1-85828-507-0*, Pub. by Rough Guides) Penguin Putnam.
Rough Guides Staff. Rough Guide to Pacific Northwest. 2nd ed. (Rough Guides Ser.). 656p. 1998. pap. 19.95 (*1-85828-326-4*, Penguin Bks) Viking Penguin.
— The Rough Guide to Polish. (Rough Guides Ser.). 224p. 1996. pap. 6.00 (*1-85828-174-1*, Penguin Bks) Viking Penguin.
***Rough Guides Staff.** Rough Guide to Portugal. 9th ed. (Illus.). 2000. pap. 17.95 (*1-85828-516-X*) Viking Penguin.
— Rough Guide to Reggae 100. (Illus.). 1999. pap. 8.95 (*1-85828-567-4*, Pub. by Rough Guides) Penguin Putnam.
— The Rough Guide to San Francisco. 5th ed. 2000. pap. 14.95 (*1-85828-526-7*, Rough Guides) Viking Penguin.
— Rough Guide to Sardinia. (Illus.). 2000. pap. 16.95 (*1-85828-502-X*, Rough Guides) Viking Penguin.
— Rough Guide to the Scottish Highlands & the Islands. (Illus.). 2000. pap. 14.95 (*1-85828-511-9*, Rough Guides) Viking Penguin.
— Rough Guide to the U. S. A. 5th ed. (Illus.). 2000. pap. 19.95 (*1-85828-527-5*, Rough Guides) Viking Penguin.
— Rough Guide to the Year 2000: The Essential Travel Guide to 2000's Festivals, Projects & Mega Events. 3rd ed. (Illus.). 2000. pap. 8.95 (*1-85828-510-0*, Rough Guides) Viking Penguin.
Rough Guides Staff. The Rough Guide to Turkish. LC 96-147794. (Rough Guides Ser.). 224p. 1996. pap. 5.00 (*1-85828-173-3*, Penguin Bks) Viking Penguin.
***Rough Guides Staff.** Rough Guide to Tuscany & Umbria. 4th ed. (Illus.). 2000. pap. 18.95 (*1-85828-518-6*, Rough Guides) Viking Penguin.
Rough Guides Staff. The Rough Guide to Vietnam. LC 96-179019. (Rough Guides Ser.). 224p. 1996. pap. 5.00 (*1-85828-172-5*, Penguin Bks) Viking Penguin.
***Rough Guides Staff.** Rough Guide to Washington D. C. 2nd ed. 2000. pap. 14.95 (*1-85828-465-1*, Pub. by Rough Guides) Penguin Putnam.
— The Rough Guide to World Music. 2000. audio compact disk 14.95 (*1-85828-645-X*, Rough Guides) Viking Penguin.
— The Rough Guide to World Music, Vol. 2. 2000. audio compact disk 14.95 (*1-85828-646-8*, Rough Guides) Viking Penguin.
— Saxophone Tipbook. (Tipbooks Ser.). (Illus.). 2000. pap. 9.95 (*1-85828-649-2*, Pub. by Rough Guides) Penguin Putnam.
— Scandinavia: Denmark, Norway, Sweden, Finland. 5th ed. (Travel Ser.). (Illus.). 2000. pap. 23.95 (*1-85828-517-8*, Pub. by Rough Guides) Penguin Putnam.
Rough Guides Staff. Seattle. (Mini Rough Guide Ser.). 12p. 1998. pap. 9.95 (*1-85828-324-8*, Penguin Bks) Viking Penguin.
— Sicily. 4th ed. 448p. 1999. pap. 17.95 (*1-85828-424-4*, Pub. by Rough Guides) Penguin Putnam.
***Rough Guides Staff.** Soul: The 100 Essential CDs. 2000. pap. 8.95 (*1-85828-562-3*, Rough Guides) Viking Penguin.
— Southwest USA: The Rough Guide. 2nd ed. 2000. pap. 17.95 (*1-85828-556-9*, Rough Guides) Viking Penguin.
Rough Guides Staff. Spain. 8th ed. 912p. 1999. pap. 19.95 (*1-85828-419-8*, Pub. by Rough Guides) Penguin Putnam.
***Rough Guides Staff.** Sweden. 2nd ed. (Travel Ser.). (Illus.). 2000. pap. 17.95 (*1-85828-537-2*, Pub. by Rough Guides) Penguin Putnam.
— Switzerland. (Travel Ser.). (Illus.). 2000. pap. 18.95 (*1-85828-538-0*, Pub. by Rough Guides) Penguin Putnam.
— Thailand: Rough Guide Phrasebook. 2nd ed. 288p. 1996. pap. 6.50 (*1-85828-608-5*, Pub. by Rough Guides) Penguin Putnam.
— Turkey. 4th ed. (Travel Ser.). (Illus.). 2000. pap. 19.95 (*1-85828-542-9*, Pub. by Rough Guides) Penguin Putnam.
— Rough Guide Internet 2000. 5th ed. (Reference Ser.). (C). 2000. pap. 9.95 (*1-85828-442-2*, Pub. by Rough Guides) Penguin Putnam.
— Europe 2001: The Rough Guide. 7th ed. 2000. pap. 24.95 (*1-85828-572-0*, Rough Guides) Viking Penguin.
— 2001 Internet & the World Wide Web. 6th ed. (Reference Ser.). 2000. pap. 9.95 (*1-85828-551-8*, Pub. by Rough Guides) Penguin Putnam.
— Vietnam. 3rd ed. (Travel Ser.). 2000. pap. 18.95 (*1-85828-550-X*, Pub. by Rough Guides) Penguin Putnam.
— Wales. 3rd ed. (Travel Ser.). (Illus.). 2000. pap. 17.95 (*1-85828-543-7*, Pub. by Rough Guides) Penguin Putnam.
— World Music: Latin & North America, Caribbean, India, Asia & the Pacific. 2nd ed. (Music Reference Ser.). 2000. pap. 26.95 (*1-85828-636-0*, Pub. by Rough Guides) Penguin Putnam.
Rough Guides Staff. World Music: The Definitive Guide to World Music, from Salsa to Soukous, Cajun to Calypso. 2nd ed. Broughton, Simon et al, eds. (Rough Guide Ser.). (Illus.). 848p. 1998. pap. text 24.95 (*1-85828-334-5*, Pub. by Rough Guides) Penguin Putnam.
— World Music 2. 2000. audio compact disk 14.95 (*1-85828-370-1*) Penguin Putnam.
***Rough Guides Staff.** Zimbabwe: Includes Botswana's National Parks & Okavango Delta. 4th ed. (Travel Ser.). (Illus.). 2000. pap. 18.95 (*1-85828-532-1*, Pub. by Rough Guides) Penguin Putnam.
Rough Guides Staff, ed. Classical Music on CD: An A-Z of Composers & Key Recordings. 2nd ed. (Rough Guide Ser.). (Illus.). 608p. 1998. pap. 23.95 (*1-85828-257-8*, Pub. by Rough Guides); pap. 23.95 (*1-85828-333-7*, Pub. by Rough Guides) Penguin Putnam.
***Rough Guides Staff, ed.** World Music Vol. 1: Africa, Europe & the Middle East. 2nd ed. (Rough Guides Ser.). (Illus.). 2000. pap. 26.95 (*1-85828-635-2*, Rough Guides) Viking Penguin.
Rough Guides Staff & Humphreys, Rob. Rough Guide to Prague. 3rd ed. (Rough Guide Ser.). (Illus.). 320p. 1998. pap. text 14.95 (*1-85828-318-3*, Pub. by Rough Guides) Penguin Putnam.
— Rough Guide to the Czech & Slovak Republics. 4th ed. (Rough Guide Ser.). (Illus.). 560p. 1998. pap. text 18.95 (*1-85828-317-5*, Pub. by Rough Guides) Penguin Putnam.
***Rough Guides Staff, et al.** Greek Islands. 3rd ed. (Illus.). 528p. 2000. pap. 17.95 (*1-85828-523-2*, Rough Guides) Viking Penguin.
Rough Guides Staff, et al. Rough Guide to Canada. 3rd ed. (Rough Guides Ser.). (Illus.). 16p. 1998. pap. 19.95 (*1-85828-311-6*, Penguin Bks) Viking Penguin.
***Rough Guides Staff, et al.** Rough Guide to Holland. 2nd ed. (Travel Ser.). (Illus.). 416p. 2000. pap. 17.95 (*1-85828-541-0*, Pub. by Rough Guides) Penguin Putnam.
Rough, Jackie, ed. Miniversity: Ideas for Student Activities & Projects. 32p. (Orig.). 1989. pap. 10.00 (*0-88210-237-0*, 6208902) Natl Assn Student.
Rough, Jackie, ed. see Rogers, Linda T.
Rough Notes Co., Inc., Staff. The Letter Book. 211p. 1991. 38.25 (*1-877723-77-0*, 29008) Rough Notes.
Rough Notes Co., Inc Staff, ed. Business Owners Policy Guide - 1996. 1996. pap. 36.25 (*1-56461-165-5*, 30155) Rough Notes.
Rough Stones Company, Inc., Publishing Division Staff. Diamond Consumers Report: Blue Book Value. (Illus.). 100p. Date not set. pap. write for info. (*0-9675148-1-9*) Rough Stones Co Inc.
***Roughan, Howard.** The Up & Comer. LC 00-32490. 2001. write for info. (*0-446-52666-5*) Warner Bks.
***Roughead, William.** Classic Crimes. (Classics). (Illus.). 600p. 2000. pap. 14.95 (*0-940322-46-3*, Pub. by NY Rev Bks) Midpt Trade.
Roughead, William, ed. Burke & Hare. (Notable British Trials Ser.). x, 280p. 1995. reprint ed. 88.00 (*1-56169-132-1*, 14642) Gaunt.
— Trial of Captain Porteous, No. 1. (Notable British Trials Ser.). 366p. 1995. reprint ed. 114.00 (*1-56169-118-6*) Gaunt.
— Trial of Deacon Brodie, No. 1. 2nd ed. (Notable British Trials Ser.). 283p. 1995. reprint ed. 87.00 (*1-56169-127-5*, 14632) Gaunt.
— Trial of Dr. Pritchard. (Notable British Trials Ser.). 343p. 1995. reprint ed. 107.00 (*1-56169-139-9*) Gaunt.
— Trial of John Donald Merrett. (Notable British Trials Ser.). x, 326p. 1995. reprint ed. 102.00 (*1-56169-173-9*) Gaunt.
— Trial of John Watson Laurie: The Arran Murder. (Notable British Trials Ser.). x, 284p. 1995. reprint ed. 89.00 (*1-56169-149-6*) Gaunt.
— Trial of Katharine Nairn. (Notable British Trials Ser.). xiii, 257p. 1995. reprint ed. 82.00 (*1-56169-124-0*) Gaunt.
— Trial of Mary Blandy. (Notable British Trials Ser.). 210p. 1995. reprint ed. 67.00 (*1-56169-121-6*, 14614) Gaunt.
— Trial of Mrs. M'Lachlan. (Notable British Trials Ser.). c, 338p. 1995. reprint ed. 132.00 (*1-56169-137-2*) Gaunt.
— Trial of Oscar Slater. (Notable British Trials Ser.). lxxx, 320p. 1995. reprint ed. 121.00 (*1-56169-160-7*) Gaunt.
Roughead, William, ed. see Galt, John.
Roughgarden, Jonathan. Anolis Lizards of the Caribbean: Ecology, Evolution & Plate Tectonics. (Oxford Series in Ecology & Evolution). (Illus.). 226p. 1995. pap. text 40.00 (*0-19-509605-3*) OUP.
Roughgarden, Jonathan. Anolis Lizards of the Caribbean: Ecology, Evolution & Plate Tectonics. (Oxford Series in Ecology & Evolution). (Illus.). 226p. 1995. text 70.00 (*0-19-506731-2*) OUP.
Roughgarden, Jonathan. Primer of Ecological Theory. LC 97-5917. 456p. 1997. pap. text 58.00 (*0-13-442062-4*) P-H.
— Theory of Population Genetics & Evolutionary Ecology: An Introduction. LC 95-20698. 612p. (C). 1995. text 41.20 (*0-13-441965-0*) P-H.
Roughgarden, Jonathan, et al, eds. Perspectives in Ecological Theory. 425p. 1989. pap. text 29.50 (*0-691-08508-0*, Pub. by Princeton U Pr) Cal Prin Full Svc.
Roughhead, William. Twelve Scots Trails. 320p. 1997. pap. 48.00 (*1-873644-39-6*, Pub. by Mercat Pr Bks) St Mut.
Roughley, Alan. James Joyce & Critical Theory: An Introduction. LC 91-34377. 304p. (C). 1992. text 52.50 (*0-472-09489-0*, 09489); pap. text 19.95 (*0-472-06489-4*, 06489) U of Mich Pr.
— Reading Derrida Reading Joyce. LC 99-19693. 176p. 1999. 49.95 (*0-8130-1684-3*) U Press Fla.
***Roughley, Rob.** Scary Secrets. LC 98-61388. (Secrets Ser.). (Illus.). 20p. (J). (ps-3). 1999. 9.98 (*0-7651-0921-2*) Smithmark.
Roughton, Evelyn & Roughton, Tony. Classic Catfish: From the Crown at the Antique Mall. (Illus.). 160p. 1993. write for info. (*0-9635571-0-6*) Ant Mall & Crown.
Roughton, James E. Confined Space Entry: Complying with the Standard. 180p. 1994. pap. text 79.00 (*0-86587-406-9*) Gov Insts.
— Ergonomic Problems in the Workplace: A Guide to Effective Management. 234p. 1996. pap. text 59.00 (*0-86587-474-3*) Gov Insts.
***Roughton, James E. & Whiting, Nancy E.** Safety Training Basics: A Handbook for Safety Training Program Development. (Illus.). 300p. 2000. 79.00 (*0-86587-699-1*, 699) Gov Insts.
Roughton, Roger, ed. Contemporary Poetry & Prose. (Illus.). 274p. 1968. 35.00 (*0-7146-2106-4*, Pub. by F Cass Pubs) Intl Spec Bk.
Roughton, Sheila. Breaking & Training Your Horse. (Illus.). 176p. (Orig.). 1996. pap. 19.95 (*0-7063-7485-1*, Pub. by WrLock) Sterling.
— Ward Lock Riding School: Eventing. (Illus.). 96p. 1998. pap. 10.95 (*0-7063-7426-6*, Pub. by WrLock) Sterling.
Roughton, Tony, jt. auth. see Roughton, Evelyn.
Rougier, Andre, et al, eds. In Vitro Skin Toxicology Vol. 10: Irritation, Phototoxicity, Sensitization. (Alternative Methods in Toxicology Ser.: No. 10). (Illus.). 448p. 1994. 185.00 (*0-913113-65-4*) M Liebert.
Rougier, Phillip A. Site Engineering Practice. 1984. pap. text. write for info. (*0-582-41236-6*, Pub. by Addison-Wesley) Longman.
Rougle, Charles, ed. see Babel, I.
Rougle, Charles, tr. see Bogdanov, Alexander.
Rougle, Charles, tr. see Groys, Boris.
Rougny, Paula B. Happiness Is a Kitchen in Maine. (Illus.). 250p. 1998. pap. write for info. (*0-9660852-0-5*) Peapatch Pr.
Rouhana, Nadim N. Palestinian Citizens in an Ethnic Jewish State: Identities in Conflict. LC 96-51073. 312p. 1997. 32.00 (*0-300-06685-6*) Yale U Pr.
Rouhani. College Algebra. 304p. (C). 1998. pap. text, student ed. 17.75 (*0-536-01524-4*) Pearson Custom.
— Intermediate Algebra. 2nd ed. 252p. 1998. pap. text, student ed. 15.75 (*0-536-01429-9*) Pearson Custom.
Rouhani, Behnaz. Intermediate Algebra. 190p. (C). 1996. text 16.60 (*0-536-59286-1*) Pearson Custom.
Rouhani, Fazullah. Black Tents. (Middle Eastern Ser.: No. 19). Orig. Title: Chadur-ha-ye Siah. (Illus.). 350p. (Orig.). 1986. pap. 17.00 (*0-936665-06-8*) Jahan Bk Co.
Rouhani, Fu'ad, tr. see Aeschylus.
Rouhi, Leyla. Mediation & Love: A Study of the Medieval Go-Between in Key Romance & Near Eastern Texts. LC 98-53963. (Studies in Intellectual History). 320p. 1999. 112.50 (*90-04-11268-5*) Brill Academic Pubs.
Rouhi, Shafii. Scent of Saffron. 1997. pap. 19.95 (*1-85727-088-6*, Pub. by Scarlet Pr) LPC InBook.
Rouhiainen, Veikko, jt. ed. see Malmn, Y.
Rouhiainen, Veikko, jt. ed. see Suokas, Jouko.
Rouhier, Kathleen M. Lifelong Reading, Bk. 2. (C). 1993. pap. text 6.50 (*0-13-016098-9*) P-H.
— Lifelong Reading, Bk. 3. (C). 1994. pap. text 6.50 (*0-13-016106-3*) P-H.
— Lifelong Reading, Bk. 4. 1994. pap. text 12.67 (*0-13-532292-8*) P-H.
— Lifelong Reading No. 1: A Basic Course. 128p. 1993. pap. text 6.50 (*0-13-016080-6*) P-H.
***Rouhier-Willoughby, J.** Readings in Russian Folklor. 112p. 2000. write for info. (*1-58692-017-0*) Copyright Mgmt.
Rouillac, Didier. Cement Evaluation Logging Handbook. 1994. 380.00 (*2-7708-0677-7*, Pub. by Edits Technip) Enfield Pubs NH.

R

— Cement Evaluation Logging Handbook. LC 95-152771. (Illus.). 172p. (C). 1994. 380.00 (*2-7108-0677-0*, Pub. by Edits Technip) Enfield Pubs NH.

Rouillard, Clarence D. The Turk in French History, Thought & Literature, 1520-1660. LC 71-180375. reprint ed. 67.50 (*0-404-56321-X*) AMS Pr.

Rouillard, Dom P. Diccionario de los Santos de Cada Dia. 2nd ed. (SPA.). 336p. 1989. pap. write for info. (*0-7859-5125-3*) Fr & Eur.

***Rouillard, Dominique.** Building the Slope: California Hillside Houses, 1920-1960. LC 99-44577. (California Architecture & Architects Ser.). (Illus.). 1999. pap. 24.50 (*0-940512-21-1*) Hennessey.

Rouillard, Larrie A. Goals & Goal Setting: Planning to Succeed. 2nd rev. ed. LC 97-77463. (Crisp 50-Minute Ser.). (Illus.). 88p. 1997. pap. 10.95 (*1-56052-476-6*) Crisp Pubns.

Rouillard, Philippe. Diccionari dels Sants de Cada Dia. (CAT.). 442p. 1965. pap. 12.95 (*0-7859-5852-5*, 8428100616) Fr & Eur.

Rouillard, Philippe, ed. see Braghin, Andrea & Caruana, Edmund.

***Rouillard, Wendy W.** Barnaby-Seasons in the Park. (The Barnaby Ser.: Vol. 5). (Illus.). 32p. (J). 2000. 15.95 (*0-9642836-9-7*) Barnaby.

Rouillard, Wendy W. Barnaby's Aspen Coloring Book. 16p. (J). (ps-4). 1996. pap. 2.50 (*0-9642836-5-4*) Barnaby.

— Barnaby's Cape Cod Coloring Book. 16p. (J). (ps-4). 1996. pap. 2.50 (*0-9642836-4-6*) Barnaby.

— Barnaby's Faraway Land. LC 94-70710. (Illus.). 28p. (J). (ps-4). 1993. pap. 8.95 (*0-9642836-0-3*) Barnaby.

— Barnaby's Kite Ride. large type ed. (Illus.). 32p. (J). (gr. 1-3). 1998. 15.95 (*0-9642836-6-2*) Barnaby.

— Barnaby's Legend: The Nantucket Love Story of Wonoma & Autopscot. LC 96-96421. (Illus.). (J). (ps-4). 1996. pap. 8.95 (*0-9642836-3-8*) Barnaby.

— Barnaby's Martha's Vineyard Coloring Book. 24p. (J). (ps-4). 1995. pap. 5.95 (*0-9642836-2-X*) Barnaby.

— Barnaby's Nantucket Coloring Book. (Illus.). 32p. (J). (ps-4). 1994. pap. 5.95 (*0-9642836-1-1*) Barnaby.

— A Penny for Barnaby. large type ed. (Illus.). 32p. (J). (gr. 1-3). 1998. 15.95 (*0-9642836-7-0*) Barnaby.

Rouiller, Gregoire, jt. ed. see Bovon, Francois.

Rouillon, F., jt. auth. see Montgomery, S. A.

Rouit, Huguette & Humbert, Jean-Marcel, eds. A la Recherche de la Memoire: Le Patrimoine Culturel Actes du Colloque Organise par la Section des Bibliotheques d'Art de l'IFLA, Paris, 16-19 Aout 1989. (IFLA Publications: Vol. 62). 330p. 1992. lib. bdg. 65.00 (*3-598-21790-0*) K G Saur Verlag.

Rouix, William. The Role of Parents in School to Work Transition. (Education Reform & School-to-Work Transition Ser.). 22p. 1995. pap. text, teacher ed. 12.00 (*0-614-24524-9*) Natl Inst Work.

Roukema, Richard W. The Soul in Distress: What Every Pastoral Counselor Should Know about Emotional & Mental Illness. LC 96-48818. 274p. 1997. 49.95 (*0-7890-0168-3*, Haworth Pastrl); pap. 19.95 (*0-7890-0198-5*, Haworth Pastrl) Haworth Pr.

— What Every Patient, Family, Friend, & Caregiver Needs to Know about Psychiatry. 408p. 1998. 25.95 (*0-88048-806-9*, 8806) Am Psychiatric.

***Roukema, Riemer.** Gnosis & Faith in Early Christianity: An Introduction to Gnosticism. LC 99-47261. 224p. 1999. pap. 23.00 (*1-56338-299-7*) TPI PA.

Roukes, Nicholas. Art Synectics. (Illus.). 156p. (YA). (gr. 9-12). 1982. pap. 20.75 (*0-87192-151-0*) Davis Mass.

— Design Synectics: Stimulating Creativity in Design. LC 88-70675. (Illus.). 224p. (YA). (gr. 9-12). 1988. pap. 28.05 (*0-87192-198-7*) Davis Mass.

— Humor in Art: A Celebration of Visual Wit. LC 96-86386. (Illus.). 176p. (YA). (gr. 9-12). 1997. 33.80 (*0-87192-304-1*) Davis Mass.

— Sculpture in Paper. LC 92-72329. (Illus.). 160p. (YA). (gr. 9-12). 1993. 31.15 (*0-87192-246-0*) Davis Mass.

Roukis, George S. American Labor & the Conservative Republicans, 1946-1948: A Study in Economic & Political Conflict. LC 88-10266. (Modern American History Ser.). 392p. 1988. 20.00 (*0-8240-4338-3*) Garland.

Roukis, George S., et al, eds. Global Corporate Intelligence: Opportunities, Technologies & Threats in the 1990s. LC 89-27240. 360p. 1990. 79.50 (*0-89930-220-3*, RMC/, Quorum Bks) Greenwood.

Roukis, George S. & Montana, Patrick J., eds. Workforce Management in the Arabian Peninsula: Forces Affecting Development, 67. LC 85-24772. (Contributions in Economics & Economic History Ser.: No. 67). 228p. 1986. 59.95 (*0-313-24209-7*) Greenwood.

Roukis, George S., jt. ed. see Montana, Patrick J.

Roulac, John. Hemp Foods & Oils for Health: Your Guide to Cooking, Nutrition, & Body Care. 1999. pap. 6.95 (*1-886874-05-0*) HEMPTECH.

Roulac, John W. Backyard Composting: Your Complete Guide to Recycling Yard Clippings. 9th rev. ed. LC 91-73105. (Illus.). 96p. 1997. pap. 6.95 (*0-9629768-3-0*) Harmonious Tech.

— Hemp Horizons: The Comeback of the World's Most Promising Plant. LC 97-18376. 200p. 1997. pap. 18.95 (*0-930031-93-8*) Chelsea Green Pub.

— Industrial Hemp: Practical Products - Paper to Fabric to Cosmetics. 2nd rev. ed. (Illus.). 48p. Date not set. pap. 4.95 (*1-886874-00-X*) Harmonious Tech.

Roulac, Stephen E. Ethics in Real Estate LC 99-12831. (Research Issues in Real Estate Ser.). 1999. write for info. (*0-7923-8228-5*) Kluwer Academic.

***Rouland, L. P. & Schapira, A. V. H.** Clinical Cases in Neurologic Disease. (Illus.). 224p. 2000. pap. text 55.00 (*0-7506-4304-8*) Buttrwrth-Heinemann.

Rouland, Linda, jt. auth. see Rouland, Steven.

Rouland, Norbert. Legal Anthropology. Planel, Philippe G., tr. from FRE. 364p. 1995. 45.00 (*0-8047-1931-4*) Stanford U Pr.

Rouland, Steve. Heywood-Wakefield Modern Furniture. (Illus.). 244p. 1994. pap. 18.95 (*0-89145-624-4*, 3906) Collector Bks.

Rouland, Steven & Rouland, Linda. Knoll Furniture: 1938-1960. (Illus.). 160p. 1999. 39.95 (*0-7643-0937-4*) Schiffer.

Roule, Louis. Fishes: Their Journeys & Migrations. Elphinstone, Conrad, tr. (Illus.). 304p. 1996. reprint ed. pap. 15.00 (*1-56836-103-3*, Kodansha Globe) Kodansha.

Rouleau, Bill. Banker's Blood. 2001. pap. 10.95 (*0-9627860-1-2*) Lone Oak MN.

Roulet, Jean-Francois. Degradation of Dental Polymers. (Illus.). xiv, 228p. 1986. 172.25 (*3-8055-4320-4*) S Karger.

Roulet, Jean-Francois & Herder, Stefan. Bonded Ceramic Inlays. (Illus.). 103p. 1991. text 64.00 (*0-86715-244-3*) Quint Pub Co.

Roulet, Jean-Francois, jt. auth. see Degrange, Michel.

***Roulet, Laura.** Contemporary Puerto Rican Installation Art: The Guagua Aberea, the Trojan Horse & the Termite. LC 00-42333. (Illus.). 2000. pap. write for info. (*0-8477-0197-2*) U of PR Pr.

Roulier, Richard P. Bank Governance Contracts: Establishing Goals & Accountability in Bank Restructuring. (World Bank Discussion Papers: Vol. 308). 38p. 1995. pap. 22.00 (*0-8213-3472-7*, 13472) World Bank.

Roulin, Gilles. Le Livre de la Nuit: Une Composition Egyptienne de l'Au-Dela: I Partie: Traduction et Commentaire. (Orbis Biblicus et Orientalis Ser.: Vol. 147/1). (FRE.). 409p. 1996. text 126.00 (*3-7278-1054-8*, Pub. by Presses Univ Fribourg) Eisenbrauns.

Roulston, Christine & Regis, Louis. Virtue, Gender & the Authentic Self in Eighteenth-Century Fiction: Richardson, Rousseau & Laclos Tabago. LC 97-37804. 320p. 1998. 49.95 (*0-8130-1581-2*) U Press Fla.

Roulston, David J. Bipolar Semiconductor Devices. 448p. (C). 1989. 98.13 (*0-07-054120-5*) McGraw.

— An Introduction to the Physics of Semiconductor Devices. (The Oxford Series in Electrical & Computer Engineering). (Illus.). 320p. (C). 1998. text 84.00 (*0-19-511477-9*) OUP.

Roulston, F. R., jt. auth. see Horgan.

Roulston, Helen, ed. Love & Nature, Unity & Doubling in the Novels of Maupassant. (American Univ. Studies: Romance Languages & Literature: Ser. 2, Vol. 79). XIV, 152p. 1989. 28.50 (*0-8204-0635-X*) P Lang Pubng.

Roulston, Helen H., jt. auth. see Roulston, Robert.

Roulston, J. E. & Leonard, R. C. Serological Tumour Markers: An Introduction. LC 92-49368. (Illus.). 192p. 1993. text 89.00 (*0-443-04511-9*) Church.

Roulston, Kathleen, ed. see Heyge, Lorna L. & Sillick, Audrey.

Roulston, Kathleen, ed. see Swears, Linda & Heyge, Lorna L.

Roulston, Robert & Roulston, Helen H. The Winding Road to West Egg: The Artistic Development of F. Scott Fitzgerald. LC 94-20157. 1995. 37.50 (*0-8387-5280-2*) Bucknell U Pr.

Roulstone. Enabling Technology: Disabled DHRS. LC 97-33099. (Disability, Human Rights, & Society Ser.). 1998. pap. 28.95 (*0-335-19801-5*) OpUniv Pr.

Roulstone, Alan. Enabling Technology: Disabled People, Work & New Technology. LC 97-33099. (Disability, Human Rights, & Society Ser.). 159p. 1998. 85.00 (*0-335-19802-3*) OpUniv Pr.

Roulstone, Tom. Fleeing Babylon. pap. 13.95 (*1-55517-383-7*) CFI Dist.

Roulstone, Tom. One Against the Wilderness. 1996. pap. 12.98 (*1-55517-267-9*) CFI Dist.

Roult, Neil J. A Catalog of the Russian War Loan Posters of 1916 & 1917. (Illus.). 36p. (Orig.). 1993. pap. 12.50 (*0-9639726-0-X*) N J Roult.

Roumain, Jacques. Masters of the Dew. LC 98-140605. (Caribbean Writers Ser.). 192p. (C). 1978. pap. 10.95 (*0-435-98745-3*, 98745) Heinemann.

— When the Tom-Tom Beats: Selected Poems. Fungaroli, Joann, ed. LC 94-72476. 96p. pap. 11.95 (*0-9632363-8-5*) Azul Edits.

Roumani, Judith, tr. see De Felice, Renzo.

Roumeliotis, Michael D. A Study of Epistemology in Legal History. LC 94-594. (Avebury Series in Philosophy). 1994. 67.95 (*1-85628-697-5*, Pub. by Avebry) Ashgate Pub Co.

Roumenin, Chavdar S., ed. Solid State Magnetic Sensors. LC 94-26842. 434p. 1994. 168.75 (*0-444-89401-2*) Elsevier.

Rounce, J. F., jt. auth. see Lowe, T. L.

Round, ed. see Tirso De Molina.

***Round, David K.** Truth or Treaty? Common Sense Questions about the Treaty of Waitaugi. (Illus.). 160p. 1998. pap. 19.95 (*0-908812-72-8*, Pub. by Canterbury Univ) Accents Pubns.

Round, David K., ed. The Australian Trade Practices Act, 1974: Proscriptions & Prescriptions for a More Competitive Economy. (Studies in Industrial Organization: Vol. 19). 1995. lib. bdg. 119.00 (*0-7923-3228-8*) Kluwer Academic.

Round, F. E. Algae & the Aquatic Environment (Contributions in Honour of J. W. G. Lind, CBE, FRS) Contributions in Honour of J. W. G. Lund. (Illus.). 460p. 1988. 120.00 (*0-948737-06-9*, Pub. by Biopress) Balogh.

Round, F. E. & Chaoman, D. J., eds. Progress in Phycological Research, Vol. 7. (Illus.). 330p. 1990. lib. bdg. 90.00 (*0-948737-13-1*, Pub. by Biopress) Balogh.

Round, F. E. & Chapman, D. J. Progress in Phycological Research, Vol. 5. (Illus.). 299p. 1987. lib. bdg. 90.00 (*0-948737-03-4*, Pub. by Biopress) Balogh.

— Progress in Phycological Research, Vol. 6. (Illus.). 286p. 1988. lib. bdg. 90.00 (*0-948737-07-7*, Pub. by Biopress) Balogh.

Round, F. E. & Chapman, D. J., eds. Progress in Phycological Research. (Progress in Phycological Research Ser.: Vol. 8). (Illus.). 278p. 1992. lib. bdg. 90.00 (*0-948737-17-4*, Pub. by Biopress) Balogh.

— Progress in Phycological Research, Vol. 4. (Illus.). 481p. 1986. lib. bdg. 90.00 (*0-948737-00-X*, Pub. by Biopress) Balogh.

— Progress in Phycological Research, Vol. 9. (Illus.). 376p. 1993. lib. bdg. 120.00 (*0-948737-19-0*, Pub. by Biopress) Balogh.

— Progress in Phycological Research, Vol. 10. (Illus.). 209p. 1994. lib. bdg. 128.00 (*0-948737-20-4*, Pub. by Biopress) Balogh.

— Progress in Phycological Research, Vol. 11. 1995. 120.00 (*0-948737-40-9*, Pub. by Biopress) Balogh.

— Progress in Phycological Research, Vol. 12. 324p. 1997. 120.00 (*0-948737-50-6*, Pub. by Biopress) Balogh.

***Round, F. E. & Chapman, D. J., eds.** Progress in Phycological Research, Vol. 13. (Illus.). 201p. 1999. 99.00 (*0-948737-55-7*, Pub. by Biopress) Balogh.

Round, F. E., et al. Diatoms. (Illus.). 757p. (C). 1990. text 305.00 (*0-521-36318-7*) Cambridge U Pr.

Round, G., jt. auth. see Tyler, J.

Round, George F., ed. Freight Pipelines. 50p. 1990. 126.00 (*0-89116-886-9*) Hemisp Pub.

***Round, Graham.** Historia de David. (SPA.). (J). (ps-3). 1999. pap. 4.99 (*0-7899-0721-6*) Spanish Hse Distributors.

— Historia de Moises. (SPA.). (J). (ps-3). 1999. pap. 4.99 (*0-7899-0722-4*) Spanish Hse Distributors.

Round, Graham, jt. auth. see Pipe, Rhona.

Round, Graham, jt. auth. see Tyler, Jenny.

Round, Graham, jt. auth. see Water, Mark.

Round, Graham, jt. auth. see Waters, Gaby.

Round, J. H. Feudal England: Historical Studies on the Eleventh & Twelfth Centuries. 587p. (Orig.). 1994. pap. text 35.00 (*0-7884-0033-9*) Heritage Bk.

Round, J. Horace. Studies in Peerage & Family History. 496p. 1996. reprint ed. pap. 39.95 (*0-8063-0426-X*, 5015) Clearfield Co.

Round, J. M., jt. auth. see Jones, Dorothy A.

Round, Jeffrey. A Cage of Bones. 224p. 1997. pap. 14.95 (*0-85449-252-6*, Pub. by Gay Mens Pr) LPC InBook.

Round, Jeffrey I., ed. The European Economy in Perspective. 314p. 1994. 70.00 (*0-7083-1240-3*, Pub. by Univ Wales Pr) Paul & Co Pubs.

Round, Joan M., jt. auth. see Clayton, Barbara E.

Round, John H. Family Origins & Other Studies. Page, William, ed. LC 79-124474. 377p. 1998. reprint ed. pap. 35.00 (*0-8063-0424-3*) Clearfield Co.

— Feudal England: Historical Studies on the Eleventh & Twelfth Centuries. LC 78-21143. 444p. 1979. reprint ed. lib. bdg. 35.00 (*0-313-21239-2*, ROEN, Greenwood Pr) Greenwood.

— Peerage & Pedigree: Studies in Peerage Law & Family History, 2 Vols. LC 76-124476. 770p. 1998. reprint ed. pap. 60.00 (*0-8063-0425-1*) Clearfield Co.

Round, Jonathan. Paediatrics: Key Questions Answered. LC 98-41105. (Key Questions Answered Ser.). 308p. 1999. pap. text 29.95 (*0-19-262904-2*) OUP.

***Round Lake Publishing Staff.** Ads Plus. 1999. pap. text. write for info. (*0-929543-61-0*) Round Lake Pub.

***Round, Michael A.** Grounded: Reagan & the PATCO Crash. rev. ed. LC 99-31680. (Studies in the History of American Law). 144p. 1999. 45.00 (*0-8153-3506-7*) Garland.

Round, N. G., ed. see De Molina.

Round, Nicholas. The Greatest Man Uncrowned: A Study of the Fall of Don Alvaro De Luna. (Monagrafias A Ser.: Vol. CXI). 302p. 1986. 58.00 (*0-7293-0211-3*, Pub. by Tamesis Bks Ltd) Boydell & Brewer.

Round, Nicholas, ed. see Garcia Lorca, Federico.

Round, Nicholas G., ed. see De Molina, Tirso.

Round, Nicholas G., ed. see Plato.

Round, Phillip H. By Nature & by Custom Cursed: Transatlantic Civil Discourse & New England Cultural Production, 1620-1660. LC 98-50672. (Civil Society Ser.). 335p. 1999. pap. 21.00 (*0-87451-929-2*); text 45.00 (*0-87451-928-4*) U Pr of New Eng.

Round Table Conference on Government Regulation of. Government Regulation of Accounting & Information. Abdel-Khalik, Rashad, ed. LC 79-26555. (University of Florida Accounting Ser.: No. 11). 328p. reprint ed. pap. 101.70 (*0-8357-6712-4*, 203534400095) Bks Demand.

Roundell, Juie A. Montague. Cowdray: The History of a Great English House (Seat of the Montagues, with Some Genealogy) (Illus.). 178p. 1997. reprint ed. pap. 25.00 (*0-8328-9473-7*); reprint ed. lib. bdg. 35.00 (*0-8328-9472-9*) Higginson Bk Co.

Rounder Records Staff. Cajun Dance Hall Special - Fiddle Edition. 64p. 1995. pap. 24.95 incl. audio compact disk (*0-7866-1286-X*, 95364CDP); pap. 19.95 incl. audio (*0-7866-1287-8*, 95364P) Mel Bay.

— Cajun Dance Hall Special/Accordion Edition. 72p. 1995. pap. 19.95 incl. audio (*0-7866-1148-0*, 95313P); pap. 24.95 incl. audio compact disk (*0-7866-1147-2*, 95313CDP) Mel Bay.

— Cajun Spice for Accordian. 52p. 1996. pap. 19.95 incl. audio (*0-7866-1690-3*, 95711P); pap. 24.95 incl. audio compact disk (*0-7866-1689-X*, 95711CDP); pap. 9.95 (*0-7866-1688-1*, 95711) Mel Bay.

Roundhill, Clare, jt. auth. see King, Penny.

Roundhill, D. M. Photochemistry & Photophysics of Metal Complexes. (Modern Inorganic Chemistry Ser.). (Illus.). 368p. (C). 1994. text 95.00 (*0-306-44694-4*, Kluwer Plenum) Kluwer Academic.

Roundhill, D. M. & Fackler, J. P. Optoelectronic Properties of Inorganic Compounds. LC 98-7495. (Modern Inorganic Chemistry Ser.). (Illus.). 416p. (C). 1998. text 115.00 (*0-306-45557-9*, Kluwer Plenum) Kluwer Academic.

Rounds. International Criminal Justice: Issues in Global Perspective. LC 99-22899. 306p. 1999. 46.00 (*0-205-29067-1*) Allyn.

— Trust Handbook. 7th ed. LC 94-75308. 1994. 110.00 (*0-316-35073-7*, Aspen Law & Bus) Aspen Pub.

— Trustee Handbook 1995. 1995. 75.00 (*0-316-35011-7*, Aspen Law & Bus) Aspen Pub.

***Rounds, Charles E.** Loring a Trustee's Handbook. 1024p. 1999. boxed set 145.00 (*0-7355-0443-1*) Aspen Pub.

Rounds, Charles E., Jr. & Hayes, Eric P. Loring: A Trustee's Handbook. annuals 384p. pap. 95.00 (*0-316-35243-8*, 52438) Aspen Law.

Rounds, Cheryl. Dreams & Whispers. 176p. 1999. 17.95 (*1-56167-479-6*) Am Literary Pr.

Rounds, David. Celebrisi's Journey. 173p. (Orig.). 1976. pap. 4.00 (*0-917512-14-6*) Buddhist Text.

— The Four & the One: In Praise of String Quartets. LC 98-67097. 216p. 1998. pap. 17.50 (*1-882897-26-9*) Lost Coast.

***Rounds, Glen.** Beaver. LC 98-28803. (J). (ps-3). 1999. 15.95 (*0-8234-1440-X*) Holiday.

Rounds, Glen. The Cowboy Trade. (Illus.). (J). (gr. 4-7). 1994. pap. 6.95 (*0-8234-1083-8*) Holiday.

— The Cowboy Trade. (Illus.). 96p. (J). (gr. 4-6). 1994. reprint ed. 15.95 (*0-8234-1075-7*) Holiday.

— Cowboys. LC 90-46501. (Illus.). 32p. (J). (gr. k-3). 1991. lib. bdg. 16.95 (*0-8234-0867-1*) Holiday.

— Cowboys. (J). (ps-3). 1991. pap. 5.95 (*0-8234-1061-7*) Holiday.

— Ol' Paul, the Mighty Logger. LC 75-22163. (Illus.). 96p. (J). (gr. 4-6). 1988. pap. 5.95 (*0-8234-0713-6*) Holiday.

— Once We Had a Horse. rev. ed. (Illus.). 32p. (J). (ps-3). 1996. 15.95 (*0-8234-1241-5*); pap. 6.95 (*0-8234-1243-1*) Holiday.

— The Prairie Schooners. (Illus.). (J). (gr. 4-7). 1994. pap. 6.95 (*0-8234-1087-0*) Holiday.

— The Prairie Schooners. (Illus.). 96p. (J). (gr. 4-6). 1994. reprint ed. 15.95 (*0-8234-1086-2*) Holiday.

— Sod Houses on the Great Plains. LC 94-27390. (Illus.). 32p. (J). (gr. k-3). 1995. lib. bdg. 16.95 (*0-8234-1162-1*) Holiday.

— Sod Houses on the Great Plains. (Illus.). 32p. (J). (ps-3). 1995. pap. 6.95 (*0-8234-1263-6*) Holiday.

— The Treeless Plains. (Illus.). (J). (gr. 4-7). 1994. pap. 6.95 (*0-8234-1085-4*) Holiday.

— The Treeless Plains. (Illus.). 96p. (J). (gr. 4-6). 1994. reprint ed. 15.95 (*0-8234-1084-6*) Holiday.

— Wild Horses. LC 92-73608. (Illus.). 32p. (J). (gr. k-3). 1993. lib. bdg. 14.95 (*0-8234-1019-6*) Holiday.

Rounds, Glen. I Know an Old Lady Who Swallowed a Fly. LC 89-46244. 32p. (J). (gr. k-3). 1990. lib. bdg. 16.95 (*0-8234-0814-0*) Holiday.

Rounds, Glen. The Blind Colt. LC 89-1779. 84p. (J). (gr. 4-6). 1989. reprint ed. 16.95 (*0-8234-0010-7*); reprint ed. pap. 5.95 (*0-8234-0758-6*) Holiday.

Rounds, Glen. Washday on Noah's Ark: A Story of Noah's Ark. LC 91-4507. 32p. (J). (gr. k-3). 1985. pap. 5.95 (*0-8234-0880-9*) Holiday.

Rounds, Glen. The Three Billy Goats Gruff. LC 92-23951. 32p. (J). (gr. k-3). 1993. lib. bdg. 15.95 (*0-8234-1015-3*) Holiday.

— The Three Billy Goats Gruff. LC 92-23951. 32p. (J). (ps-3). 1993. pap. 5.95 (*0-8234-1136-2*) Holiday.

Rounds, H. L. Abstracts of Bristol County, Massachusetts Probate Records, 1745-1762. 365p. 22.50 (*0-8063-1226-2*, 5022) Clearfield Co.

Rounds, Joseph B. The Time Was Right: A History of the Buffalo & Erie County Public Library, 1940-1975. Mahaney, Michael C., ed. (Illus.). x, 172p. 1986. 11.95 (*0-9615896-0-4*) Grosvenor Soc.

Rounds, Laura & Matthews, Michael, eds. Total Quality Management in Academic Libraries: Initial Implementation Efforts; Proceedings of the 1st International Conference on TQM & Academic Libraries. LC 96-105102. 348p. 1995. 60.00 (*0-918006-75-9*) ARL.

Rounds, Michael. Ontario: An Illustrated History. LC 97-78256. (Illus.). 1999. 39.95 (*1-886483-16-7*) Heritge Media.

Rounds, Michael F. Fishin' with a Net: How to Use the Internet for Business & Pleasure. 5th ed. LC 98-71021. (Illus.). 112p. 1998. pap. 19.95 (*0-9629944-6-4*) CPM Systems.

— Mike Rounds' Quick Tips for the Internet. 2p. 1998. pap. 9.95 (*1-891440-08-X*) CPM Systems.

Rounds, Michael F. & Miller, Nancy. Inventing for Money. LC 97-75120. (Illus.). 112p. 1997. pap. 19.95 (*0-9629944-7-2*) CPM Systems.

— Marketing the One Person Business. LC 97-94834. (Illus.). 112p. 1998. pap. 19.95 (*0-9629944-3-X*) CPM Systems.

— Mechanics of Mail Order. 4th rev. ed. (Illus.). 80p. (Orig.). 1996. pap. 19.95 (*0-9629944-2-1*) CPM Systems.

Rounds, R. Stowell. Men & Birds in South America, 1492 to 1900. LC 89-43069. (Illus.). 204p. 1989. pap. 14.95 (*0-936609-16-8*) QED Ft Bragg.

Rounds, Richard S. Basic Budgeting Practices for Librarians. 2nd ed. LC 93-47476. 180p. 1994. pap. 30.00 (*0-8389-0630-3*) ALA.

Rounds, Stewart A., jt. auth. see Bonn, Bernadine A.

Rounds, Stowell & O'Connell, Joseph J. How to Save Time & Taxes Preparing Fiduciary Income Tax Returns. 2nd ed. (How to Save Time & Taxes Ser.). 1985. ring bd. 230.00 incl. cd-rom (*0-8205-1204-4*) Bender.

An Asterisk (*) at the beginning of an entry indicates that the title is appearing for the first time.

Roundtree, Cathleen. On Women Turning Sixty: Embracing the Age of Fulfillment. LC 97-5889. 1997. 25.00 (*0-517-70757-8*) Harmony Bks.

***Roundtree, Robert Collins & Colman, Carol.** Immunotics: A Revolutionary Way to Fight Infection, Beat Chronic Illness & Stay Well. 224p. 2000. 19.95 (*0-399-14504-4*) Putnam Pub Group.

Roundy, Bruce A., et al, eds. Wild Land Shrub & Arid Land Restoration Symposium: Proceedings. (Illus.). 384p. (Orig.). (C). 1996. pap. text 50.00 (*0-7881-3067-6*) DIANE Pub.

Roundy, Elizabeth, jt. auth. see Tree, Christina.

Roundy, Shaun B. Gone but Not Forgotten. (Not Forgotten Ser.: No. 1). 110p. 1998. pap. 5.95 (*1-893594-00-9*) Univ of Life.

Rouner, L. S., ed. Philosophy, Religion, & the Coming World Civilization: Essays in Honour of William Ernst Hocking. 526p. 1966. lib. bdg. 126.50 (*90-247-0070-1*, Pub. by M Nijhoff) Kluwer Academic.

Rouner, Leroy S. Loneliness. LC 97-45632. (Boston University Studies in Philosophy & Religion: No. 19). 301p. 1998. 35.00 (*0-268-01318-7*) U of Notre Dame Pr.

— Within Human Experience: The Philosophy of William Ernest Hocking. LC 71-75433. 395p. 1969. reprint ed. pap. 122.50 (*0-7837-4186-3*, 205903600012) Bks Demand.

Rouner, Leroy S., ed. Celebrating Peace. LC 90-36381. (Boston University Studies in Philosophy & Religion: Vol. 11). 256p. (C). 1990. text 37.00 (*0-268-00779-9*) U of Notre Dame Pr.

— The Changing Face of Friendship. LC 94-15462. (Boston University Studies in Philosophy & Religion: Vol. 15). (C). 1994. text 34.50 (*0-268-00804-3*) U of Notre Dame Pr.

— Civil Religion & Political Theology. LC 86-11242. (Boston University Studies in Philosophy & Religion: Vol. 8). 240p. (C). 1986. text 34.50 (*0-268-00757-8*) U of Notre Dame Pr.

— Civil Religion & Political Theology. LC 86-11242. (Boston University Studies in Philosophy & Religion: Vol. 8). (C). 1994. reprint ed. pap. text 13.00 (*0-268-00806-X*) U of Notre Dame Pr.

***Rouner, Leroy S., ed.** Civility. (Boston University Studies in Philosophy & Religion: Vol. 21). 232p. 2000. 30.00 (*0-268-02255-0*, Pub. by U of Notre Dame Pr) Chicago Distribution Ctr.

Rouner, Leroy S., ed. Human Rights & the World's Religions. LC 88-17303. (Boston University Studies in Philosophy & Religion: Vol. 9). (C). 1994. reprint ed. pap. text 13.00 (*0-268-01107-9*) U of Notre Dame Pr.

— In Pursuit of Happiness. LC 95-16518. (Boston University Studies in Philosophy & Religion: Vol. 16). (C). 1995. text 34.95 (*0-268-01174-5*) U of Notre Dame Pr.

— The Longing for Home. LC 96-30449. (Boston University Studies in Philosophy & Religion: Vol. 17). 248p. (C). 1997. text 34.00 (*0-268-01310-1*) U of Notre Dame Pr.

— Meaning, Truth & God. LC 82-7023. (Boston University Studies in Philosophy & Religion: Vol. 3). (C). 1994. reprint ed. pap. text 13.00 (*0-268-01415-9*) U of Notre Dame Pr.

— On Community. LC 91-50573. (Boston University Studies in Philosophy & Religion: Vol. 12). (C). 1991. text 34.50 (*0-268-01507-4*) U of Notre Dame Pr.

— On Freedom. LC 89-33164. (Boston University Studies in Philosophy & Religion: Vol. 10). (C). 1989. text 34.50 (*0-268-01502-3*) U of Notre Dame Pr.

— On Nature. LC 84-7502. (Boston University Studies in Philosophy & Religion: Vol. 6). 224p. (C). 1984. text 33.50 (*0-268-01499-X*) U of Notre Dame Pr.

***Rouner, Leroy S., ed.** Religion, Politics & Peace. LC 98-48108. Vol. 20. 232p. 1999. 34.00 (*0-268-01664-X*, Pub. by U of Notre Dame Pr) Chicago Distribution Ctr.

Rouner, Leroy S., ed. Religious Pluralism. LC 84-7431. (Boston University Studies in Philosophy & Religion: Vol. 5). 256p. (C). 1984. text 37.00 (*0-268-01626-7*) U of Notre Dame Pr.

— Selves, People, & Persons: What Does It Mean to Be a Self? LC 92-53748. (Boston University Studies in Philosophy & Religion: Vol. 13). (C). 1992. text 37.00 (*0-268-01747-6*) U of Notre Dame Pr.

Rouner, Leroy S. & Darling-Smith, Barbara, eds. Is There a Human Nature? LC 97-20808. (Boston University Studies in Philosophy & Religion). 232p. (C). 1997. 30.00 (*0-268-01181-8*) U of Notre Dame Pr.

Rouner, Leroy S. & Langford, James R., eds. Philosophy, Religion, & Contemporary Life: Essays on Perennial Problems. (C). 1995. pap. text 10.95 (*0-268-03807-4*) U of Notre Dame Pr.

Rouner, Leroy S., jt. ed. see Dickie, Robert B.

Rouner, Leroy S., jt. ed. see Olson, Alan M.

Rounick, Jack A. Pennsylvania Matrimonial Practice, 4 vols. LC 81-85429. (Pennsylvania Practice Systems Library). 1982. ring bd. 400.00 (*0-317-00357-7*) West Group.

— Pennsylvania Matrimonial Practice, 4 vols. LC 81-85429. (Pennsylvania Practice Systems Library). 1993. suppl. ed. 175.00 (*0-317-03160-0*) West Group.

Rounsaville, Bruce J., jt. ed. see Kranzler, Henry R.

Rounsefell, G. A. & Everhart, W. Harry. Fishery Science: Its Methods & Applications. 444p. 1953. pap. 175.00 (*0-7855-0356-0*, Pub. by Intl Bks & Periodicals) St Mut.

Rounsevell, Mark D. & Loveland, Peter J., eds. Soil Responses to Climate Change. LC 94-35237. (NATO ASI Series I: Global Environmental Change: Vol. 23). 1994. write for info. (*0-387-58373-4*) Spr-Verlag.

Rounseville, A. W. The Poetry of the Orient. 1973. 59.95 (*0-8490-0865-4*) Gordon Pr.

Rounsley, Chloe A., jt. auth. see Brown, Mildred L.

Rountree. Diversity Amidst Globalization. LC 99-52981. 752p. 1999. text 69.33 (*0-13-376427-3*) P-H.

Rountree, Albert & Rountree, Ann. The Heavens Opened: Revealing a Fresh Vision of God's Love for You. LC 98-40738. 208p. 1999. pap. 12.99 (*0-88419-598-8*) Creation House.

Rountree, Ann, jt. auth. see Rountree, Albert.

Rountree, Cathleen. Heart of Marriage. 2000. pap. 11.00 (*0-06-250843-1*) HarperTrade.

— On Women Turning Fifty: Celebrating Mid-Life Discoveries. LC 92-54617. 224p. 1994. reprint ed. pap. 17.00 (*0-06-250731-1*, Pub. by Harper SF) HarpC.

— On Women Turning Forty: Coming Into Our Fullness. (Illus.). 214p. 1991. pap. 16.00 (*0-89594-517-7*) Crossing Pr.

— On Women Turning 70: Honoring the Voices of Wisdom. LC 98-40145. (Illus.). 243p. 1999. 25.00 (*0-7879-4512-9*) Jossey-Bass.

***Rountree, Cathleen.** On Women Turning 70: Honoring the Voices of Wisdom. large type ed. LC 00-30290. 2000. write for info. (*0-7862-2563-7*) Thorndike Pr.

Rountree, Cathleen. On Women Turning 60: Embracing the Age of Fulfillment. (Illus.). 288p. 1998. pap. 15.00 (*0-609-80228-3*) Harmony Bks.

***Rountree, Cathleen.** On Women Turning 30: Making Choices, Finding Meaning. LC 99-50520. 2000. 26.00 (*0-7879-5036-X*) Jossey-Bass.

Rountree, Charlotte. Seoul Sketches: A Visual Sketch of the Yi Dynasty. (Illus.). 84p. 1985. 22.50 (*0-930878-43-4*) Hollym Intl.

Rountree, Estelle & Halverstadt, Hugh F., eds. Sometimes They Cry: A Study-Action Book. rev. ed. LC 72-129096. (Illus.). 144p. reprint ed. pap. 44.70 (*0-7837-1957-4*, 204217400001) Bks Demand.

Rountree, George. A Govan Childhood. 250p. (C). 1989. pap. text 30.00 (*0-85976-385-4*, Pub. by J Donald) St Mut.

***Rountree, Helen C.** Beyond the Village: A Colonial Parkway Guide to the Local Indians' Use of Natural Resources. 1999. pap. 3.95 (*0-9648727-1-4*) H C Rountree.

Rountree, Helen C. Pocahontas's People: The Powhatan Indians of Virginia Through Four Centuries. LC 90-33598. (Civilization of the American Indian Ser.: Vol. 196). (Illus.). 416p. 1996. pap. 14.95 (*0-8061-2849-6*) U of Okla Pr.

— The Powhatan Indians of Virginia: Their Traditional Culture. LC 88-27905. (Civilization of the American Indian Ser.: Vol. 193). (Illus.). 232p. 1992. pap. 13.95 (*0-8061-2455-5*) U of Okla Pr.

— Young Pocahontas in the Indian World. (Illus.). 52p. (J). (gr. 4-6). 1995. pap. 8.95 (*0-9648727-0-6*) H C Rountree.

Rountree, Helen C., ed. Powhatan Foreign Relations, 1500-1722. LC 92-21942. (Illus.). 328p. 1993. text 35.00 (*0-8139-1409-4*) U Pr of Va.

Rountree, Helen C. & Davidson, Thomas E. Eastern Shore Indians of Virginia & Maryland. LC 97-2651. 352p. 1998. pap. 16.95 (*0-8139-1801-4*) U Pr of Va.

— Eastern Shore Indians of Virginia & Maryland. LC 97-2651. 352p. 1998. text 49.50 (*0-8139-1734-4*) U Pr of Va.

Rountree, Melissa. Jasper Johns: Collecting Prints. (Illus.). 32p. (Orig.). 1993. pap. 15.00 (*0-914489-13-5*) Univ Miss-KC Art.

Rountree, Melissa, et al. Jeff Colby: A Catalog of a Retrospective Exhibition at the Illinois Art Gallery in Chicago-November 4, 1994 Through January 6, 1995. LC 96-8589. 1996. write for info. (*0-89792-150-X*) Ill St Museum.

Rountree, Paul P., jt. auth. see McCunney, Robert J.

Rountree, Susan H. Christmas Decorations from Williamsburg. LC 91-24638. (Illus.). 144p. 1991. 19.95 (*0-87935-085-7*) Colonial Williamsburg.

— Dollhouses, Miniature Kitchens & Shops from the Abby Aldrich Rockefeller Folk Art Center. LC 95-36507. (Illus.). 96p. 1995. 24.95 (*0-87935-159-4*) Colonial Williamsburg.

— Entertaining Ideas from Williamsburg. LC 93-23178. (Illus.). 155p. 1993. 19.95 (*0-87935-095-4*) Colonial Williamsburg.

Rountree, Thomas J. Emma Notes. (Cliffs Notes Ser.). 88p. 1967. pap. 4.95 (*0-8220-0434-8*, Cliff) IDG Bks.

— Last of the Mohicans Notes. (Cliffs Notes Ser.). 64p. 1965. pap. 4.95 (*0-8220-0717-7*, Cliff) IDG Bks.

— This Mighty Sum of Things: Wordsworth's Theme of Benevolent Necessity. LC 65-12244. reprint ed. 27.00 (*0-8357-9621-3*, 2103214) Bks Demand.

Rountree, Thomas J., ed. Critics on Emerson. LC 73-77552. (Readings in Literary Criticism Ser.: No. 20). 128p. 1973. 19.95 (*0-87024-237-7*) U of Miami Pr.

— Critics on Hawthorne. LC 78-159297. (Readings in Literary Criticism Ser.: No. 16). 1972. 19.95 (*0-87024-209-1*) U of Miami Pr.

— Critics on Melville. LC 74-143456. (Readings in Literary Criticism Ser.: No. 12). 1972. pap. 19.95 (*0-87024-193-1*) U of Miami Pr.

Roupe, Diane. The Blue Country Ribbon Cookbook: New Standard of Midwest Cooking to the New Standard of American Cooking. LC 97-43569. 960p. 1998. 35.00 (*0-517-70442-0*) C Potter.

— The Blue Ribbon Country Cookbook: The New Standard of Midwest Cooking. LC 97-43569. 1997. pap. 35.00 (*0-517-88679-0*) C Potter.

Roupp, Heidi, ed. Teaching World History: A Resource Book. LC 96-23391. (Sources & Studies in World History). 288p. (C). (gr. 13). 1996. text 74.95 (*1-56324-419-5*); pap. text 38.95 (*1-56324-420-9*) M E Sharpe.

Roupp, Heidi & Hitchens, Marilynn. How to Prepare for SAT II: World History. LC 95-46634. 1996. 13.95 (*0-8120-9294-5*) Barron.

Rouquerol. Adsorption by Powder Pourous Solids. 16p. (C). 1998. text 95.00 (*0-12-598920-2*) Acad Pr.

Rouquerol, J., et al, eds. Characterization of Porous Solids III: Proceedings of the IUPAC Symposium (COPS III), Marseille, France, May 9-12, 1993. LC 94-27695. 816p. 1994. 304.50 (*0-444-81491-4*) Elsevier.

Rouquette, F. M. Ecology, Production, & Management of Lolium for Forage in the U. S. A. LC 97-67558. (Special Publication Ser.: Vol. 24). 138p. 1997. 25.00 (*0-89118-542-9*) Crop Sci Soc Am.

Rouquette, Jean. Litterature D'Oc. (FRE.). 125p. 1968. 9.95 (*0-8288-7417-4*) Fr & Eur.

Rouquette, Max. Green Paradise. MacGregor, William B., tr. LC 95-1139. 280p. 1995. pap. 19.95 (*0-472-06543-2*, 06543) U of Mich Pr.

— Green Paradise. MacGregor, William B., tr. LC 95-1139. 280p. 1995. text 47.50 (*0-472-09543-9*, 09543) U of Mich Pr.

Rouqui. Guerras y Paz en America Central. (SPA.). pap. 14.99 (*968-16-4309-7*, Pub. by Fondo) Continental Bk.

Rouquie, Alain. The Military & the State in Latin America. Sigmund, Paul E., tr. 520p. 1987. 60.00 (*0-520-05559-4*, Pub. by U CA Pr) Cal Prin Full Svc.

Rouquie, Alain, contrib. by. Las Fuerzas Politicas en America Central (Political Forces in Central America) (SPA.). 275p. 1994. pap. 13.99 (*968-16-4358-5*, Pub. by Fondo) Continental Bk.

Rouquier, Magali. Vocabulaire d'Ancien Francais. (FRE.). 127p. 1992. pap. 22.95 (*0-7859-0969-9*, 2091906549) Fr & Eur.

Rouquite, Ann-Marie. Specialized Dictionary of Beverages: English, French, German. (ENG, FRE & GER.). 400p. 1986. 275.00 (*0-7859-9966-3*) Fr & Eur.

Roure. F., ed. Peri-Tethyan Platforms: Proceedings of the IFP-Peritethys Research Conference, Aries, France, 1993. LC 95-153171. (Illus.). 294p. 1994. 480.00 (*2-7108-0679-7*, Pub. by Edits Technip) Enfield Pubs NH.

Roure. F. & Ellouz, N., eds. Geodynamic Evolution of Sedimentary Basins: International Symposium, May 18-23, 1992, Moscow. LC 97-116842. 480p. 1995. pap. 580.00 (*2-7108-0692-4*, Pub. by Edits Technip) Enfield Pubs NH.

Roure, Luis A. The Brotherhood of Five. LC 98-90662. 1999. pap. 13.95 (*0-533-12873-0*) Vantage.

Rourke. International Politics. 7th ed. LC 98-74368. 1998. text 31.74 (*0-697-38594-9*) McGrw-H Hghr Educ.

— International Politics World Statistics. 1996. teacher ed. 20.00 (*0-697-32381-1*, WCB McGr Hill) McGrw-H Hghr Educ.

— Taking Sides Online. 1999. pap. 6.32 (*0-07-234626-4*) McGraw.

— World Politics. 7th ed. 1996. teacher ed. 14.06 (*0-697-31395-6*, WCB McGr Hill) McGrw-H Hghr Educ.

Rourke, Arlene C. Accessories. (Looking Good Ser.: Set I). (Illus.). 32p. (YA). (gr. 5 up). 1987. lib. bdg. 21.27 (*0-86625-281-9*) Rourke Pubns.

— Clothing. (Looking Good Ser.: Set I). (Illus.). 32p. (YA). (gr. 5 up). 1987. lib. bdg. 21.27 (*0-86625-277-0*) Rourke Pubns.

— Decorating Your Room. (Looking Good Ser.: Set II). (Illus.). 32p. (J). (gr. 5 up). 1987. lib. bdg. 21.27 (*0-86625-286-X*) Rourke Pubns.

— Los Dientes y los Trenos. (Buena Presencia Ser.). (SPA.). 32p. (J). 1995. lib. bdg. 19.93 (*0-86625-291-6*) Rourke Pubns.

— Diet & Exercise. (Looking Good Ser.: Set I). (Illus.). 32p. (YA). (gr. 5 up). 1987. lib. bdg. 21.27 (*0-86625-280-0*) Rourke Pubns.

— La Dieta y el Ejercicio. (Buena Presencia Ser.).Tr. of Diet & Exercise. 32p. (J). 1989. lib. bdg. 19.93 (*0-86625-295-9*) Rourke Pubns.

— Hair. (Looking Good Ser.: Set I). (Illus.). 32p. (YA). (gr. 5 up). 1987. lib. bdg. 21.27 (*0-86625-278-9*) Rourke Pubns.

— Hands & Feet. (Looking Good Ser.). (Illus.). 32p. (YA). (gr. 5 up). 1987. lib. bdg. 21.27 (*0-86625-279-7*) Rourke Pubns.

— La Piel. (Buena Presencia Ser.).Tr. of Skin. (SPA.). 32p. (J). 1989. lib. bdg. 19.93 (*0-86625-294-0*) Rourke Pubns.

— Skin. (Looking Good Ser.: Set I). (Illus.). 32p. (J). (gr. 5 up). 1987. lib. bdg. 21.27 (*0-86625-276-2*) Rourke Pubns.

Rourke, Byron P. Nonverbal Learning Disabilities: The Syndrome & the Model. LC 89-1958. 253p. 1989. lib. bdg. 35.00 (*0-89862-378-2*) Guilford Pubns.

— Syndrome of Nonverbal Learning Disabilities: Neurodevelopmental Manifestations. LC 95-3981. 518p. 1995. lib. bdg. 55.00 (*0-89862-155-0*) Guilford Pubns.

Rourke, Byron P., ed. Neuropsychological Validation of Learning Disability Subtypes. LC 90-3912. 398p. 1990. lib. bdg. 45.00 (*0-89862-446-0*) Guilford Pubns.

— Neuropsychology of Learning Disabilities: Essentials of Subtype Analysis. LC 84-10860. 351p. 1985. lib. bdg. 45.00 (*0-89862-644-7*) Guilford Pubns.

Rourke, Byron P., et al, eds. Methodological & Biostatistical Foundations of Clinical Neuropsychology. xii, 556p. 1992. 81.50 (*90-265-1165-5*); pap. 41.00 (*90-265-1245-7*) Swets.

Rourke, Byron P. & Del Dotto, Jerel E. Learning Disabilities: A Neuropsychological Perspective. (Developmental Clinical Psychology & Psychiatry Ser.: Vol. 30). 160p. (C). 1994. text 42.00 (*0-8039-5353-4*); pap. text 18.95 (*0-8039-5354-2*) Sage.

Rourke, Byron P. & Fuerst, Darren R. Learning Disabilities & Psychosocial Functioning: A Neuropsychological Perspective. LC 91-16388. 198p. 1991. lib. bdg. 32.00 (*0-89862-767-2*) Guilford Pubns.

Rourke, Byron P., et al. Child Neuropsychology: An Introduction to Theory, Research, & Clinical Practice. LC 83-1657. 389p. 1991. reprint ed. pap. text 30.00 (*0-89862-468-1*) Guilford Pubns.

Rourke, Byron P., jt. ed. see Adams, Kenneth.

Rourke, C. P. & Sanderson, B. J. Introduction to Piecewise-Linear Topology. (Springer Study Edition Ser.). (Illus.). 130p. 1982. 29.95 (*0-387-11102-6*) Spr-Verlag.

Rourke, Constance. Audubon. 1993. reprint ed. lib. bdg. 89.00 (*0-7812-5826-X*) Rprt Serv.

— Davy Crockett. LC 98-10024. (Illus.). xxv, 276p. 1998. pap. 12.95 (*0-8032-8967-7*, Bison Books) U of Nebr Pr.

Rourke, Constance & Lhamon, W. T. American Humor: A Study of the National Character. rev. ed. LC 85-26428. 376p. 1986. reprint ed. pap. 16.95 (*0-8130-0837-9*) U Press Fla.

Rourke, Constance M. Troupers of the Gold Coast: or The Rise of Lotta Crabtree. 1992. reprint ed. lib. bdg. 75.00 (*0-7812-5082-X*) Rprt Serv.

Rourke, Dennis J. The American Home Builder & the Housing Industry: A Textbook in Residential Building Management. 2nd ed. (Illus.). 405p. 1994. 70.00 (*0-9641670-0-X*) Mgmt Practice.

— Construction Management for the Residential Project Manager. LC 96-158590. 528p. 1996. 49.95 (*0-9641670-1-8*) Mgmt Practice.

Rourke, Francis E. Bureaucracy & Foreign Policy. LC 73-186516. (Washington Center of Foreign Policy Research, Studies in International Affairs: Vol. 17). 96p. 1972. reprint ed. pap. 30.00 (*0-608-03746-X*, 206457100009) Bks Demand.

— Bureaucracy, Politics & Public Policy. 3rd ed. (C). 1984. pap. text 26.13 (*0-673-39475-1*) Addson-Wesley Educ.

Rourke, Francis E., ed. Bureaucratic Power in National Policy Making. 4th ed. (C). 1986. pap. text 33.53 (*0-673-39474-3*) Addson-Wesley Educ.

***Rourke, James.** Mayor of Aln. LC 99-215243. 1999. pap. text 12.95 (*0-9521558-9-3*) Parthian Bks.

***Rourke, John.** Upgrading, Troubleshooting & Maintaining PCs: Complete Reference. (Complete Reference Ser.). 2000. pap. 49.99 (*0-07-212516-0*) Osborne-McGraw.

Rourke, John T. Clashing Views on Controversial Issues in World Politics. 8th ed. (Taking Sides Ser.). (Illus.). 400p. 1998. pap. text 13.00 (*0-697-39107-8*, Dshkn McG-Hill) McGrw-H Hghr Educ.

— Course Kit: International Politics on the World Stage/Taking Sides: World Politics. 5th ed. (C). 1995. text. write for info. (*0-697-31445-6*) Brown & Benchmark.

— International Politics on the World Stage. 5th ed. 629p. (C). 1995. text 39.15 (*1-56134-382-X*, Dshkn McG-Hill) McGrw-H Hghr Educ.

— International Politics on the World Stage. 6th ed. LC 97-65111. 704p. 1997. pap. text. write for info. (*0-697-32740-X*) Brown & Benchmark.

— Taking Sides: Clashing Views on Controversial Issues. 7th ed. LC 95-83864. 384p. (C). 1996. text. write for info. (*0-697-31296-8*, WCB McGr Hill) McGrw-H Hghr Educ.

— Taking Sides: Clashing Views on Controversial Issues. 7th ed. 384p. (C). 1997. text. write for info. (*0-697-39277-5*, WCB McGr Hill) McGrw-H Hghr Educ.

Rourke, John T., ed. Taking Sides: Clashing Views on Controversial Issues in World Politics. 6th ed. LC 94-33209. (Illus.). 408p. (C). 1995. text 13.95 (*1-56134-324-2*, Dshkn McG-Hill) McGrw-H Hghr Educ.

Rourke, John T. & Boyer, Mark A. World Politics: International Politics on the World Stage, Brief. 2nd ed. (Illus.). 496p. 1998. pap. text 37.00 (*0-07-292901-4*, Dshkn McG-Hill) McGrw-H Hghr Educ.

Rourke, John T. & Carter, Ralph G. Making American Foreign Policy. 2nd ed. 614p. (C). 1996. text. write for info. (*0-697-32682-9*) Brown & Benchmark.

Rourke, John T., et al. Direct Democracy & International Politics: Deciding International Issues Through Referendums. LC 92-8773. 202p. 1992. lib. bdg. 40.00 (*1-55587-263-8*) L Rienner.

Rourke, John T., et al. Making American Foreign Policy. LC 93-73227. (Illus.). 512p. (C). 1994. text 34.95 (*1-56134-116-9*, Dshkn McG-Hill) McGrw-H Hghr Educ.

Rourke, John T., jt. auth. see Boyer, Mark A.

Rourke, John T., jt. auth. see Harf, James E.

***Rourke, Kelley, ed.** Career Guide for Singers. 5th ed. 294p. 2000. 70.00 (*1-885131-00-3*) Opera Amer.

Rourke, Mary & Gwathmey, Emily. Amazing Grace in America: Our Spiritual National Anthem. LC 96-25221. (Illus.). 128p. 1996. 26.95 (*1-883318-30-0*) Angel City Pr.

Rourke, Nancy E. A Difference of Reason. LC 96-46099. 336p. 1996. 63.50 (*0-7618-0590-7*); pap. 34.50 (*0-7618-0591-5*) U Pr of Amer.

Rourke, Norman, ed. I Saw the Elephant: The Civil Experiences of Bailey George McCellan, Company D, 10th Alabama Infantry Regiment. LC 94-39798. (Illus.). 50p. 1995. pap. 6.95 (*0-942597-85-0*, Burd St Pr) White Mane Pub.

Rourke, Norman E. War Comes to Alaska: The Dutch Harbor Attack, June 3-4, 1942. LC 96-53353. (Illus.). 166p. 1997. pap. 12.95 (*1-57249-028-4*, Burd St Pr) White Mane Pub.

Rourke-O'Briant, Judith, jt. auth. see Harte, Lawrence.

Rourke, Richard W. Cape Cod & the Islands: An Artist's Sketchbook. rev. ed. (Illus.). 52p. 1994. pap. 8.50 (*1-884824-08-0*) Tryon Pubng.

Rourke, Thomas R. A Conscience As Large As the World: Yves R. Simon Versus the Catholic Neoconservatives. LC 96-21007. (Religious Forces in the Modern Political World Ser.). 240p. 1996. 62.50 (*0-8476-8325-7*); pap. 24.95 (*0-8476-8326-5*) Rowman.

Rous, J. & Peset, Z. Devetsil Czech Avant-Garde Art: Architecture & Design of the 1920s & 30s. 115p. 1990. pap. 45.00 (*0-905836-70-7*, Pub. by Museum Modern Art) St Mut.

An Asterisk (*) at the beginning of an entry indicates that the title is appearing for the first time.

R

Rous, John. Diary of John Rous, Incumbent of Santon Downham, Suffolk, from 1625 to 1642. Green, Mary A., ed. (Camden Society, London. Publications, First Ser.: No. 66). reprint ed. 35.00 (*0-404-50166-4*) AMS Pr.

Rous, S. N. Understanding Urology. (Perspectives in Medicine Ser.: No. 5). (Illus.). 1973. 16.75 (*3-8055-0000-9*) S Karger.

Rous, Stephen N. The Prostate Book. rev. ed. 288p. 1995. pap. 13.00 (*0-393-30864-2*) Norton.

— The Prostate Book: Sound Advice on Symptoms & Treatment. (Illus.). 256p. 1992. 22.95 (*0-393-03387-2*) Norton.

— Urology: A Core Textbook. 2nd ed. LC 95-39429. (Illus.). 365p. 1996. pap. text 46.95 (*0-86542-493-4*) Blackwell Sci.

— Urology: Core Textbook. Date not set. pap. write for info. (*0-393-71033-5*) Norton.

— Urology Annual, 1987, Vol. 1. (Illus.). 336p. (C). 1987. pap. text 90.00 (*0-8385-9318-6*, A9318-5) Appleton & Lange.

— Urology Annual, 1990, Vol. 4. (Illus.). 300p. (C). 1989. pap. text 95.00 (*0-8385-9322-4*, A9322-7, Apple Lange Med) McGraw.

— Urology Annual, 1991, Vol. 5. (Illus.). 288p. (C). 1990. pap. text 95.00 (*0-8385-9323-2*, A9323-5, Apple Lange Med) McGraw.

Rous, Stephen N. Urology Annual 1996, Vol. 10. 368p. 1996. 95.00 (*0-86542-488-8*) Blackwell Sci.

Rous, Stephen N. Urology Annual 1996, Vol. 10. Date not set. write for info. (*0-393-71034-3*) Norton.

Rous, Stephen N., ed. Urology Annual, 1997, Vol. 11. (Illus.). 321p. 1997. 125.00 (*0-86542-567-1*) Blackwell Sci.

Rous, Stephen N., jt. auth. see Zobel, Hiller B.

***Rous, Yva.** Know Thyself. 1999. pap. write for info. (*1-58235-169-4*) Watermrk Pr.

Rousar, I., et al. Electrochemical Engineering I-II, 2 vols., Vol. 1. (Chemical Engineering Monographs: No. 21 A&B). 354p. 1986. 188.25 (*0-444-99563-3*) Elsevier.

— Electrochemical Engineering I-II, 2 vols., Vol. 2. (Chemical Engineering Monographs: No. 21 A&B). 338p. 1986. 162.00 (*0-444-99548-X*) Elsevier.

Rousch, Jim. From Eros to Venus. 46p. 1997. pap. 8.00 (*0-8059-3929-6*) Dorrance.

Rouse. Human Problem Solving in Failure Situations. write for info. (*0-444-00876-4*) Elsevier.

— Txt/fly Prg Ibm P/cmp Ucsd:f77. (C). 1984. pap. text 2.00 (*0-03-069474-4*) Harcourt Coll Pubs.

Rouse & Cardoso, Ersillo. Dictionnaire Portugais. (FRE & POR.). 1820p. (YA). (gr. 9-12). 1963. 49.95 (*0-685-57714-7*, M-6495) Fr & Eur.

Rouse, Andy. Photographing Animals in the Wild. (Illus.). 1998. 19.95 (*0-86343-362-6*, Pub. by Hove Foto) Watsn-Guptill.

Rouse, Anne. Sunset Grill: Poems. 64p. 1993. pap. 12.95 (*1-85224-219-1*, Pub. by Bloodaxe Bks) Dufour.

— Timing. LC 98-140085. 64p. 1998. pap. 15.95 (*1-85224-404-6*, Pub. by Bloodaxe Bks) Dufour.

Rouse, Barry T. & Lopez, Carlos, eds. Immunobiology of Herpes Simplex Virus Infection. 176p. 1984. 105.00 (*0-8493-6037-4*, RC147, CRC Reprint) Franklin.

Rouse, Beatrice A., ed. Substance Abuse & Mental Health Statistics Sourcebook. (Illus.). 193p. 1996. pap. text 35.00 (*0-7881-2985-6*) DIANE Pub.

Rouse, Beatrice A., jt. auth. see Melnick, Daniel.

Rouse, Bill, tr. see Stiltner, Edgar, Jr.

Rouse, Blair. Ellen Glasgow. LC 62-16821. (Twayne's United States Authors Ser.). 1962. pap. text 4.95 (*0-8290-0010-0*); lib. bdg. 20.95 (*0-89197-745-7*) Irvington.

Rouse, Carolyn & Katera. Quick & Easy Ideas & Materials: To Help the Nonverbal Child "Talk" at Home. (Illus.). 200p. 1997. pap. 29.00 (*1-884135-33-1*, M420) Mayer-Johnson.

Rouse, Cecilia, jt. auth. see Ashenfelter, Orley.

Rouse, Charles E. Philosophy As Method & Process. 104p. (Orig.). 1990. pap. 10.00 (*0-9626282-0-4*) C E Rouse.

Rouse, E. Clive, ed. Medieval Wall Paintings. (Illus.). 80p. 1989. pap. 12.50 (*0-7478-0144-4*, Pub. by Shire Pubns) Parkwest Pubns.

Rouse, Elizabeth. Understanding Fashion. (Illus.). 256p. (C). 1989. pap. text 34.95 (*0-632-01891-7*) Blackwell Sci.

Rouse, Geraldine & Birch, Carol. Socialization & Sex Education. (C). 1991. pap. text 99.00 (*1-56304-031-X*) J Stanfield.

Rouse, Hunter. Elementary Mechanics of Fluids. LC 78-57159. (Illus.). 376p. 1978. reprint ed. pap. 11.95 (*0-486-63699-2*) Dover.

Rouse, Irving. Prehistory in Haiti: A Study in Method. LC 64-21834. (Yale University Publications in Anthropology Reprints Ser.: No. 21). 202p. 1964. pap. 20.00 (*0-87536-504-3*) HRAFP.

— A Survey of Indian River Archeology, Florida. LC 76-43813. (Yale Univ. Publications in Anthropology: No. 45). 376p. reprint ed. 52.50 (*0-404-15668-1*) AMS Pr.

— The Tainos: Rise & Decline of the People Who Greeted Columbus. (Illus.). 232p. (C). 1993. pap. 14.00 (*0-300-05696-6*) Yale U Pr.

Rouse, Irving & Alegria, Ricardo E. Excavations at Maria de la Cruz Cave & Hacienda Grande Village Site, Loiza, Puerto Rico. (Publications in Anthropology: No. 80). (Illus.). viii, 133p. (Orig.). 1990. pap. 13.50 (*0-913516-16-3*) Yale U Anthro.

***Rouse, Irving & Morse, Birgit Faber.** Excavations at the Indian Creek Site, Antiqua, West Indies. (YUPA Ser.: Vol. 82). (Illus.). 70p. (C). 1999. pap. 18.50 (*0-913516-19-8*) Yale U Anthro.

Rouse, Jacqueline A. Lugenia Burns Hope: Black Southern Reformer. LC 88-17521. (Brown Thrasher Bks.). (Illus.). 198p. 1992. reprint ed. pap. 15.95 (*0-8203-1464-1*) U of Ga Pr.

Rouse, Jay. Two Hearts Now One. 1995. pap. 14.95 (*1-57320-089-1*) PraiseGathering.

Rouse, Jeff. The Young Swimmer. LC 97-12474. (Young Enthusiast Ser.). (Illus.). 40p. (J). (gr. 3-8). 1997. 15.95 (*0-7894-1533-X*) DK Pub Inc.

***Rouse, Jeff.** Young Swimmer. LC 99-51398. (Young Enthusiast Ser.). (J). (gr. 3-7). 2000. 9.95 (*0-7894-5432-7*) DK Pub Inc.

Rouse, John. Brecht & the West German Theatre: The Practice & Politics of Interpretation. Brockett, Oscar G., ed. LC 89-20165. (Theatre & Dramatic Studies: No. 62). 235p. 1989. reprint ed. pap. 72.90 (*0-8357-2006-3*, 207076100004) Bks Demand.

Rouse, John, Jr., jt. auth. see Berkley, George E.

Rouse, Joseph. Engaging Science: How to Understand Its Practices Philosophically. 280p. 1996. text 42.50 (*0-8014-3193-X*); pap. text 17.95 (*0-8014-8289-5*) Cornell U Pr.

— Knowledge & Power: Toward a Political Philosophy of Science. LC 87-47604. 304p. (C). 1987. 37.50 (*0-8014-1959-X*); pap. text 15.95 (*0-8014-9713-2*) Cornell U Pr.

Rouse, Kate. Classic Cameras. 1994. 10.98 (*0-7858-0177-4*); 10.98 (*0-7858-0152-9*) Bk Sales Inc.

Rouse, Ken. Putting Money in Its Place. 164p. 1993. per. 14.95 (*0-8403-9115-3*) Kendall-Hunt.

Rouse, Linda P. You Are Not Alone. 2nd abr. ed. 1993. pap. 12.95 (*1-55691-089-4*, 899x) Learning Pubns.

Rouse, Martyn & McLaughlin, Margaret J. Special Education & School Reform in United States & Britain. LC 99-11555. (Illus.). 208p. 1999. pap. 27.99 (*0-415-19757-0*) Routledge.

Rouse, Mary, jt. auth. see Rouse, Richard.

Rouse, Mary, ed. see Hu, Shih.

Rouse, Mary A. & Rouse, Richard H. Authentic Witnesses: Approaches to Medieval Texts & Manuscripts. LC 89-40389. (Mediaeval Studies: Vol. 27). (C). 1993. pap. text 34.50 (*0-268-00623-7*) U of Notre Dame Pr.

Rouse, Mary A., jt. ed. see Rouse, Richard H.

***Rouse, Michael.** Business Communication. (ITBP Textbooks Ser.). 2000. pap. 34.95 (*1-86152-544-3*) Thomson Learn.

— Drinking Water 1997: A Report by the Chief Inspector, Drinking Water Inspectorate. xx, 210p. 1998. 67.00 (*0-11-753468-4*, Pub. by Statnry Office) Balogh.

Rouse, Michael, jt. auth. see Scheiman, Mitchell M.

Rouse, Michael D., jt. auth. see Cabot, Susan M.

Rouse, Michael W. Coastal Resorts of East Anglia. 192p. (C). 1988. pap. 70.00 (*0-86138-010-X*, Pub. by T Dalton) St Mut.

Rouse, Michael W. & Ettinger, Ellen R. Clinical Decision Making in Optometry. 440p. 1996. pap. text 49.50 (*0-7506-9571-4*) Buttrwrth-Heinemann.

Rouse, Michael W., jt. auth. see Scheiman, Mitchell M.

Rouse, Nicholas. Applied Lending Techniques. 242p. 1999. pap. 70.00 (*0-85297-537-6*, Pub. by Chartered Bank) St Mut.

— Bankers Lending Techniques. 168p. (C). 1990. pap. 125.00 (*0-85297-228-8*, Pub. by Chartered Bank) St Mut.

Rouse, Parke, Jr. Along Virginia's Golden Shores: Glimpses of Tidewater Life. 1995. pap. 19.95 (*0-87517-079-X*) Dietz.

— Below the James Lies Dixie. (Illus.). 1968. pap. 7.50 (*0-87517-048-X*) Dietz.

Rouse, Parke. Cows on the Campus. 1987. reprint ed. 8.50 (*0-87517-047-1*) Dietz.

— The Good Old Days in Hampton & Newport News. 1986. pap. 14.95 (*0-87517-056-0*) Dietz.

Rouse, Parke, Jr. The Great Wagon Road: From Philadelphia to the South. 1992. pap. 13.95 (*0-87517-065-X*) Dietz.

— A House for a President. 264p. 1983. 14.95 (*0-87517-050-1*) Dietz.

— The James - Where a Nation Began. 1991. pap. 17.95 (*0-87517-062-5*) Dietz.

Rouse, Parke. James Blair of Virginia. LC 70-159559. 368p. reprint ed. pap. 114.10 (*0-8357-4420-5*, 203724000008) Bks Demand.

Rouse, Parke, Jr. Living by Design: Leslie Cheek & the Arts. LC 85-73016. (Illus.). 197p. 1985. 29.95 (*0-9615670-0-7*) Soc Alu Wm.

— We Happy Wasps: Virginia in the Days of Jim Crow & Harry Byrd. (Illus.). 244p. (Orig.). 1996. pap. 17.95 (*0-87517-091-9*) Dietz.

Rouse, Parke, Jr., ed. see West, George B.

***Rouse, Richard & Rouse, Mary.** The Paris Book Trade in the Middle Ages 1200-1500. (Illus.). 800p. 1999. text 225.00 (*1-872501-41-9*, Pub. by Harvey Miller) Gordon & Breach.

Rouse, Richard & Rouse, Susan. The Last Week. 1985. 1.00 (*0-89536-726-2*, 5810) CSS OH.

Rouse, Richard H. & Rouse, Mary A., eds. Authentic Witnesses: Approaches to Medieval Texts & Manuscripts. LC 89-40389. (Mediaeval Studies: No. 27). (C). 1990. text 69.00 (*0-268-00622-9*) U of Notre Dame Pr.

Rouse, Richard H., jt. auth. see Rouse, Mary A.

Rouse, Richard H., ed. see Ferrari, Mirella.

Rouse, Richard O., jt. ed. see Schwartz, Fred.

Rouse, Sarah, jt. auth. see National Library of Ireland Staff.

Rouse, Steve. Rouse & Company: Booked! LC 98-60425. (Illus.). 112p. 1998. pap. 16.95 (*1-891521-02-0*) Woodholme Hse.

Rouse, Steven. MMPI Treatment. Date not set. pap. 9.95 (*0-8166-3026-7*) U of Minn Pr.

— Personnel. Date not set. pap. 6.00 (*0-8166-2796-7*) U of Minn Pr.

Rouse, Susan, jt. auth. see Rouse, Richard.

Rouse, Ted. Contemporary Christian Music, Where's the Controversy? 24p. 1995. pap. 2.50 (*1-892239-03-5*) New Creation.

— "Dear Mr. Evolutionist, Please Answer Me This" 56p. 1997. pap. 5.00 (*1-892239-04-3*) New Creation.

— Eternal Security - A Deadly Web of Deception. Date not set. pap. write for info. (*1-892239-06-X*) New Creation.

***Rouse, Ted.** Faith & the Pharisees: Sincere Critics Are Sincerely Wrong about the Word of Faith Teachings. rev. ed. LC 99-95566. 400p. 2000. pap. 13.99 (*1-890900-03-6*) Insight Intl.

Rouse, Ted. The Key to the Mystery of Life. 2nd ed. 78p. 1990. reprint ed. pap. 5.00 (*1-892239-02-7*) New Creation.

— True Grace & False Grace. Date not set. pap. write for info. (*1-892239-05-1*) New Creation.

— A Two Step Journey Back to God. 31p. 1994. reprint ed. pap. 4.00 (*1-892239-01-9*) New Creation.

— The Word of Faith Which We Preach. 394p. 1998. pap. write for info. (*1-892239-00-0*) New Creation.

***Rouse, Toni.** How to Use Parts of Speech. Arquilevich, Gabriel, ed. (Illus.). 48p. (YA). (gr. 6-8). 1999. pap., teacher ed. 7.95 (*1-57690-500-4*, TCM2500) Tchr Create Mat.

Rouse, W. D., jt. tr. see Bendall, Cecil.

Rouse, W. H. Greek Votive Offerings. 1997. 45.00 (*0-89005-558-0*) Ares.

Rouse, W. H. & Warmington, E. H., trs. The Satyricon. (Loeb Classical Library: No. 15). 15.50 (*0-674-99016-1*) HUP.

Rouse, W. H., jt. ed. see Bendall, Cecil.

Rouse, W. H., tr. see Xenophon.

Rouse, W. H. D. Great Dialogues of Plato: Complete Texts of the Republic, Apology, Crito Phaido, Ion & Meno, Vol. 1. (Signet Classics Ser.). 1999. mass mkt. 6.95 (*0-451-52745-3*, Sig Classics) NAL.

Rouse, W.H.D. Gods, Heroes & Men of Ancient Greece. 1957. mass mkt. 6.99 (*0-451-62800-4*) NAL.

Rouse, W.H.D., tr. see Homer.

Rouse, William, ed. see National Research Council Staff.

Rouse, William B. Catalysts for Change: Concepts & Principles for Enabling Innovation. LC 93-364. (Series in Systems Engineering). 272p. 1993. 108.95 (*0-471-59196-3*) Wiley.

— Design for Success: A Human-Centered Approach to Designing Successful Products & Systems. LC 90-45055. (Systems Engineering Ser.). 304p. 1991. 109.95 (*0-471-52483-2*) Wiley.

— Don't Jump to Solutions: Thirteen Delusions That Undermine Strategic Thinking--& How to Overcome Them. LC 97-33871. (Business & Management Ser.). 1998. 28.95 (*0-7879-0998-X*) Jossey-Bass.

— Start Where You Are: Matching Your Strategy to Your Marketplace. LC 95-47030. (Business & Management Ser.). 222p. 1996. 30.95 (*0-7879-0247-0*) Jossey-Bass.

— Strategies for Innovation: Creating Successful Products, Systems, & Organizations. LC 91-42515. (Series in Systems Engineering). 272p. 1992. 109.95 (*0-471-55904-0*) Wiley.

— Systems Engineering Models of Human Machine Interactions. (Systems Science & Engineering Ser.: Vol. 6). 152p. 1980. 60.25 (*0-444-00366-5*) P-H.

Rouse, William B., ed. Human Technology in Complex Systems, Vol. 3. 247p. 1987. 90.25 (*0-89232-659-X*) Jai Pr.

— Human Technology in Complex Systems, Vol. 4. 267p. 1988. 90.25 (*0-89232-753-7*) Jai Pr.

— Human/Technology Interaction in Complex Systems, Vol. 5. 299p. 1989. 90.25 (*1-55938-011-X*) Jai Pr.

— Human/Technology Interaction in Complex Systems, Vol. 6. 250p. 1993. 90.25 (*1-55938-192-2*) Jai Pr.

— Human/Technology Interaction in Complex Systems, Vol. 7. 324p. 1995. 90.25 (*1-55938-843-9*) Jai Pr.

— Human/Technology Interaction in Complex Systems, Vol. 8. 1996. 90.25 (*0-7623-0013-2*) Jai Pr.

— Human/Technology Interaction in Complex Systems, Vol. 9. 1999. 90.25 (*0-7623-0177-5*) Jai Pr.

Rouse, William B., jt. ed. see Rasmussen, Jens.

Rouse, William B., jt. ed. see Sage, Andrew P.

Rouse, William H. Greek Votive Offerings: An Essay in the History of Greek Religion. LC 75-10654. (Ancient Religion & Mythology Ser.). (Illus.). 1976. reprint ed. 52.95 (*0-405-07262-7*) Ayer.

— Greek Votive Offerings: An Essay in the History of Greek Religion. xviii, 463p. 1976. reprint ed. 96.20 (*3-487-05828-6*) G Olms Pubs.

Rouseau, Denise M., jt. auth. see Leana, Carrie R.

Rouseff, Russell L. & Leahy, Margaret M., eds. Fruit Flavors: Biogenesis, Characterization, & Authentication. LC 95-8847. (Symposium Ser.: No. 596). (Illus.). 296p. 1995. text 95.00 (*0-8412-3227-X*, Pub. by Am Chemical) OUP.

Rouseff, Russell L., jt. auth. see Ting, S. V.

Rouself, R., ed. Bitterness in Foods & Beverages. (Developments in Food Science Ser.: No. 25). 356p. 1990. 205.00 (*0-444-88175-1*) Elsevier.

Rousey, Dennis C. Policing the Southern City: New Orleans, 1805-1889. LC 95-50128. (Illus.). 288p. (C). 1997. text 35.00 (*0-8071-2046-4*) La State U Pr.

Roush, Chris. Inside Home Depot: How One Company Revolutionized an Industry through the Relentless Pursuit of Growth. LC 98-47998. 256p. 1999. 24.95 (*0-07-134095-5*) McGraw.

***Roush, David W.** Juvenile Detention Training Needs Assessment: Research Report. 58p. 2000. pap. text 20.00 (*0-7881-8937-9*) DIANE Pub.

Roush, David W. & Wyss, Trudy. A Resource Manual for Juvenile Detention & Corrections: Effective & Innovative Programs. 164p. 1998. reprint ed. pap. text 35.00 (*0-7881-7319-7*) DIANE Pub.

***Roush, Fred William.** Transfer in Generalized Cohomology Theories. 180p. 1999. pap. 32.00 (*963-05-7650-3*, Pub. by Akade Kiado) Intl Spec Bk.

Roush, Fred William, jt. auth. see Kim, Ki H.

Roush, Fred William, jt. auth. see Kim, Ki Hang.

Roush, George, et al. Cancer Risks & Incidence Trends: The Connecticut Perspective. (Illus.). 435p. 1987. 176.00 (*0-89116-412-X*) Hemisp Pub.

***Roush, Jackson.** Screening for Hearing Loss & Otitis Media in Children. (Illus.). 200p. 2001. pap. 40.00 (*0-7693-0000-6*, Pub. by Singular Publishing) Thomson Learn.

Roush, Jackson & Matkin, Noel, eds. Infants & Toddlers with Hearing Loss: Family Centered Assessment & Intervention. 360p. 1994. 38.50 (*0-912752-28-9*) York Pr.

Roush, John, et al. Scandinavian Defense Portuguese Variation: Portuguese Variation. (Illus.). 111p. 1998. pap. 7.95 (*0-945470-70-3*) Chess Ent.

Roush, John H., Jr. Enjoying Fishing Lake Tahoe: The Truckee River & Pyramid Lake. LC 87-70065. (Illus.). 375p. 1987. 21.00 (*0-9600830-3-0*) J H Roush.

— Management Audits of Branch Claims Offices of National Insurance Companies. LC 74-31546. 197p. 1975. pap. 21.00 (*0-9600830-1-4*) J H Roush.

***Roush, John H., Jr., ed.** World War II Reminiscences. 3rd ed. 2000. pap. 25.00 (*0-9600830-4-9*) J H Roush.

***Roush, John H., Jr. & Islam, Shuja Vl.** Hunting Dangerous Game with the Maharajas: Tales of Big Game Hunting in the Days of the Raj. LC 00-90808. (Illus.). 312p. 2000. 50.00 (*0-9600830-2-2*) J H Roush.

Roush, L. L. Rouch: History of the Roush Family in America, from Its Founding by John Adam Rausch in 1736 to the Present (1928) (Illus.). 738p. 1995. reprint ed. pap. 109.00 (*0-8328-4828-X*); reprint ed. lib. bdg. 119.00 (*0-8328-4827-1*) Higginson Bk Co.

Roush, Marvin L., jt. auth. see Wang, John X.

Roush, Nadine. Get Moving: The Transportation Activity Book. (J). (gr. 4-6). 1991. pap. text 11.97 (*0-937659-52-5*) GCT.

Roush, Patricia B., ed. The Design, Sampling, Handling, & Applications of Infrared Microscopes. LC 87-14345. (Special Technical Publication Ser.: No. 949). (Illus.). viii, 115p. 1987. 24.00 (*0-8031-0953-9*, STP949) ASTM.

Roush, Robert. Improving Teaching Gerontology & Geriatrics. Harris, Diana K., ed. (Issues in Aging Ser.). 350p. Date not set. text 52.50 (*0-8153-1729-8*) Garland.

Roush, Ronald C. Bottling Ships & Houses. (Illus.). 224p. (Orig.). 1985. 22.95 (*0-8306-0975-X*, 1975); pap. 17.95 (*0-8306-1975-5*, 1975P) McGraw-Hill Prof.

Roush, Sheryl. Newsletters for the 90s. 1992. write for info. (*1-880878-02-X*) Creative Comns.

Roush, W. R., jt. auth. see Pearson, Anthony J.

***Roush, W.R.** Handbook of Reagents for Organic Synthesis, Activating Agents & Protecting Groups. Pearson, Anthony J., ed. LC 98-53088. 528p. 1999. 115.00 (*0-471-97927-9*) Wiley.

Rousmaniere, John. The Annapolis Book of Seamanship. 2nd rev. ed. 432p. 1989. 32.50 (*0-671-67447-1*) S&S Trade.

***Rousmaniere, John.** The Annapolis Book of Seamanship: Third Edition Completely Revised Expanded & Updated. 3rd rev. ed. LC 99-21737. (Illus.). 416p. 1999. 40.00 (*0-684-85420-1*) S&S Trade.

Rousmaniere, John. A Bridge to Dialogue: The Story of Jewish-Christian Relations. LC 91-30794. 1991. pap. 8.95 (*0-8091-3284-2*) Paulist Pr.

— Fastnet, Force Ten. (Illus.). 288p. 2000. pap. 14.95 (*0-393-30865-0*) Norton.

— The Illustrated Dictionary of Boating Terms: 1,900 Essential Terms for Sailors & Powerboaters. LC 97-45938. (Illus.). 160p. 1998. 23.95 (*0-393-04649-4*) Norton.

— The Life & Times of the Equitable. LC 98-127561. (Illus.). 496p. 1995. write for info. (*0-9648761-2-4*) D L & J.

— The Low Black Schooner: Yacht America, 1851-1945. (Illus.). 71p. 1998. pap. text 20.00 (*0-7881-5274-2*) DIANE Pub.

— The Low Black Schooner: Yacht America, 1851-1945. 80p. (C). 1990. text 59.00 (*0-7855-7002-0*, Pub. by Fernhurst Bks) St Mut.

— The Norton Boater's Log: An Innovative Log, Guest Register, & Boater's Data Manual. LC 96-39784. 96p. 1997. pap. 22.00 (*0-393-31660-2*) Norton.

Rousmaniere, John, et al. A Picture History of the America's Cup. 1989. 39.95 (*0-393-02819-4*) Norton.

Rousmaniere, John, ed. see Cruising Club of America Technical Committee, et al.

Rousmaniere, Kate. City Teachers: Teaching & School Reform in Historical Perspective. LC 96-43883. 192p. (C). 1996. text 44.00 (*0-8077-3589-2*); pap. text 21.95 (*0-8077-3588-4*) Tchrs Coll.

***Rousmaniere, Kate, et al, eds.** Silences & Images: The Social History of the Classroom. LC 98-53608. (History of Schools & Schooling Ser.: Vol. 7). (Illus.). 274p. (C). 1999. pap. text 29.95 (*0-8204-3926-6*) P Lang Pubng.

Rousmaniere, Kate, et al. Discipline, Moral Regulation & Schooling: A Social History. Beauchamp, Edward, ed. LC 97-11679. (Studies in the History of Education: No. 4). 312p. 1997. text 72.00 (*0-8153-1606-2*) Garland.

Rousmaniere, Leah R. & Larom, Peter. Anchored Within the Vail: A Pictorial History of the Seamen's Church Institute. (Illus.). 135p. (Orig.). 1995. pap. 18.00 (*0-9643657-0-7*) Seamens Church.

An Asterisk (*) at the beginning of an entry indicates that the title is appearing for the first time.

— Anchored Within the Vail: A Pictorial History of the Seamen's Church Institute. deluxe ed. (Illus.). 135p. (Orig.). 1995. 75.00 (0-9643657-1-5) Seamens Church.
Rousopoulos, Deno, jt. auth. see Millage, Philip J.
Rouss, Sylvia. Sammy Spider's First Passover. (Illus.). 32p. (J). (ps-2). 1995. pap. 6.95 (0-929371-82-8) Kar-Ben.
***Rouss, Sylvia.** Sammy Spider's First Purim. LC 99-56681. (Illus.). 32p. (J). (ps-2). 2000. pap. 6.95 (1-58013-062-3) Kar-Ben.
Rouss, Sylvia. Sammy Spider's First Rosh Hashanah. (Illus.). 32p. (J). (ps-2). 1996. pap. 6.95 (0-929371-99-2) Kar-Ben.
— Sammy Spider's First Shabbat. LC 97-2616. (Illus.). 32p. (J). (ps-2). 1997. 14.95 (1-58013-007-0); pap. 5.95 (1-58013-006-2) Kar-Ben.
Rouss, Sylvia A. Fun with Jewish Holiday Rhymes. LC 91-40931. (Illus.). (J). (ps). 1992. 10.95 (0-8074-0463-2, 101981) UAHC.
— Sammy Spider's First Hanukkah. LC 92-39639. (Illus.). (J). (ps-2). 1993. pap. 6.95 (0-929371-46-1) Kar-Ben.
Roussa, Nick. Basketball Legends of All Times, Vol. 2. (Sports Legends Ser.). (Illus.). 216p. 1999. lib. bdg. 24.95 (1-56674-283-8) Forest Hse.
Roussakis, Emmanuel N. Commercial Banking in an Era of Deregulation. 3rd ed. LC 96-33187. 456p. 1997. text 65.00 (0-275-95693-8, Praeger Pubs) Greenwood.
***Roussakis, Emmanuel N.** Literature & the Land. 2000. 25.00 (0-86709-568-7, Pub. by Boynton Cook Pubs) Heinemann.
Roussakis, Emmanuel N. Managing Commercial Banks. LC 77-4380. (Special Studies). 202p. 1977. 35.00 (0-275-90274-9, C0274, Praeger Pubs) Greenwood.
Roussarie, R. H., et al. Bifurcations of Planar Vector Fields: Nilpotent Singularities & Abelian Integrals. Dold, A. et al, eds. (Lecture Notes in Mathematics Ser.: Vol. 1480). (Illus.). viii, 226p. 1991. 41.95 (0-387-54521-2) Spr-Verlag.
Roussarie, R. H., jt. ed. see Francoise, J. P.
Roussarie, Robert, jt. auth. see Dumortier, Freddy.
Roussarie, Robert H. Bifurcations of Planar Vector Fields & Hilbert's Sixteenth Problem. LC 98-7674. (Progress in Mathematics Ser.). 1998. write for info. (0-8176-5900-5); 78.00 (3-7643-5900-5) Birkhauser.
Roussas. An Introduction to Probability & Statistical Inference. 448p. 2000. write for info. (0-12-599020-0) Acad Pr.
Roussas, George, ed. Nonparametric Functional Estimation & Related Topics. (C). 1991. text 341.00 (0-7923-1226-0) Kluwer Academic.
Roussas, George G. A Course in Mathematical Statistics. 2nd ed. LC 96-42115. (Illus.). 572p. 1997. text 59.95 (0-12-599315-3) Acad Pr.
Rousseas, Stephen. Post Keynesian Monetary Economics. 2nd ed. LC 92-9112. 136p. (Orig.). (C). (gr. 13). 1992. text 64.95 (1-56324-082-3) M E Sharpe.
Rousseas, Stephen. Post Keynesian Monetary Economics. 2nd ed. LC 92-9112. 136p. (Orig.). (C). (gr. 13). 1992. pap. text 34.95 (1-56324-095-5) M E Sharpe.
Rousseau, Bonney J. The E-Log Reunion. LC 98-11031. 180p. 1998. pap. 7.00 (0-86663-219-0) Ide Hse.
— The Plano Seasons. iv, 147p. (YA). (gr. 7-12). 1999. pap. 11.00 (0-9667395-4-X) In the BAG.
Rousseau, Bonney Jo. Color Coded Camping. (Illus.). 52p. 1998. spiral bd. 7.00 (0-9667395-2-3) In the BAG.
— Recipes Lost Through Generations - A Sampler. (Illus.). 112p. 1998. spiral bd. 10.00 (0-9667395-0-7) In the BAG.
Rousseau, C., jt. auth. see Lozansky, E.
Rousseau, David & Wasley, James. Healthy by Design: Building & Remodeling Solutions for Creating Healthy Homes. 2nd rev. ed. LC 99-29708. (Illus.). 384p. 1999. pap. 24.95 (0-88179-177-6) Hartley & Marks.
Rousseau, David, et al. Your Home, Your Health & Well Being. LC 87-7080. (Illus.). 300p. 1988. pap. 14.95 (0-89815-223-2) Ten Speed Pr.
Rousseau, Denise M. Psychological Contracts in Organizations: Understanding Written & Unwritten Agreements. LC 95-11730. (Illus.). 242p. 1995. 48.00 (0-8039-7104-4); pap. 21.95 (0-8039-7105-2) Sage.
Rousseau, Denise M., jt. ed. see Arthur, Michael B.
Rousseau, Francois-Olivier. L' Enfant d'Edouard. (FRE.). 1984. pap. 11.95 (0-7859-4214-9) Fr & Eur.
Rousseau, G. S. Goldsmith: The Critical Heritage. (Critical Heritage Ser.). 412p. 1974. 69.50 (0-7100-7720-3, Routledge Thoemms) Routledge.
— Pre- & Postmodern Discourses on the Enlightenment, 3 vols., Set. LC 90-19452. 976p. 1991. text 200.00 (0-7190-3549-X, Pub. by Manchester Univ Pr) St Martin.
Rousseau, G. S., ed. The Languages of Psyche: Mind & Body in Enlightenment Thought. LC 90-34872. (Publications from the Clark Library Professorship, UCLA: No. 12). (Illus.). 494p. 1991. 58.00 (0-520-07044-5, Pub. by U CA Pr); pap. 18.95 (0-520-07119-0, Pub. by U CA Pr) Cal Prin Full Svc.
— The Letters & Papers of Sir John Hill, 1714-1775. LC 81-68993. (Studies in the Eighteenth Century: No. 6). (Illus.). 264p. 1990. 39.50 (0-404-61472-8) AMS Pr.
Rousseau, G. S., jt. auth. see Porter, Roy.
Rousseau, George S. Sexual Underworlds of the Enlightenment. Porter, Roy, ed. LC 87-27893. (Illus.). 304p. reprint ed. pap. 94.30 (0-608-06016-X, 206634400008) Bks Demand.
— Tobias Smollett. 210p. 1982. 24.95 (0-567-09330-1, Pub. by T & T Clark) Bks Intl VA.
***Rousseau, Henri.** Rousseau. (Illus.). 2000. pap. 1.00 (0-486-41067-6) Dover.
Rousseau, J. J. Basic Crystallography. James, A., tr. from FRE. LC 97-44185. 426p. 1998. 198.00 (0-471-97048-4); pap. 79.95 (0-471-97049-2) Wiley.
Rousseau, Jean-Jacques. Basic Political Writings. Cress, Donald A., tr. from FRE. LC 87-23610. (HPC Classics Ser.). 249p. (C). 1987. pap. text 6.95 (0-87220-047-7); lib. bdg. 29.95 (0-87220-048-5) Hackett Pub.
— Charles Burney: The Cunning Man: Taken from the Devin du Village of Jean-Jacques Rousseau. fac. ed. Kaufman, Charlotte & Grant, Kerry S., eds. (Recent Researches in Music of the Classic Era Ser.: No. RRC50P). (Illus.). 1998. pap. 50.00 (0-89579-400-4) A-R Eds.
— A Complete Dictionary of Music. LC 72-1664. reprint ed. 55.00 (0-404-08335-8) AMS Pr.
— Les Confessions, 2 vols. Koenig, Catherine, ed. (FRE.). 384p. 1973. pap. 10.95 (0-7859-1630-X, 2070363767) Fr & Eur.
— Les Confessions. Voisine, ed. (Coll. Prestige). (FRE.). 512p. 1973. pap. 10.95 (0-7859-1631-8, 2070363775) Fr & Eur.
— Les Confessions. Voisine, ed. (FRE.). 1981. pap. 45.00 (0-7859-1497-8, 2705002529) Fr & Eur.
— Confessions. 1992. 20.00 (0-679-41334-0) Everymns Lib.
— Confessions. 1094p. 1964. 16.95 (0-8288-7479-4) Fr & Eur.
***Rousseau, Jean-Jacques.** Confessions. Coleman, Patrick, ed. Scholar, Angela, tr. (Oxford World's Classics Ser.). 720p. 2000. pap. 10.95 (0-19-282275-6) OUP.
Rousseau, Jean-Jacques. Confessions. Cohen, J. M., tr. & intro. by. (Classics Ser.). 608p. 1953. pap. 11.95 (0-14-044033-X, Penguin Classics) Viking Penguin.
— Confessions. (Classics of World Literature Ser.). 1998. pap. 5.95 (1-85326-465-2, 4652WW, Pub. by Wrdsworth Edits) NTC Contemp Pub Co.
— Confessions, Tome 1. (Folio Ser.: No. 376). (FRE.). pap. 9.95 (2-07-036376-7) Schoenhof.
— Confessions, Tome 2. (Folio Ser.: No. 377). (FRE.). 1990. pap. 9.95 (2-07-036377-5) Schoenhof.
— The Confessions & Correspondence, Including the Letters to Malesherbes. Kelly, Christopher et al, eds. LC 94-47021. (Collected Writings of Rousseau: Vol. 5). (Illus.). 736p. 1995. pap. 25.00 (0-87451-836-9); text 80.00 (0-87451-707-9) U Pr of New Eng.
— Contrato Social. De los Rios, Fernando, tr. (Nueva Austral Ser.: Vol. 165). (SPA.). 1991. pap. text 24.95 (84-239-1965-X) Elliots Bks.
— Deux Lettres a Monsieur le Marechal Duc de Luxembourg. (FRE., Illus.). 122p. 1977. pap. 49.95 (0-7859-5567-4) Fr & Eur.
***Rousseau, Jean-Jacques.** Dictionnaire de la Musique. (FRE.). 1998. 295.00 (0-320-00285-3) Fr & Eur.
Rousseau, Jean-Jacques. Discours sur les Sciences et les Arts. (Folio Ser.: No. 1874). (FRE.). pap. 12.95 (2-07-037874-8) Schoenhof.
— Discours sur les Sciences et les Arts: Avec: Discours sur l'Origine et l'Inegalite. (FRE.). 510p. 1955. pap. 10.95 (0-7859-1427-7, 2080702432) Fr & Eur.
— Discours sur l'Origine et les Fondements de l'Inegalite Parmi les Hommes. (Folio Essais Ser.: No. 18). (FRE.). 185p. 1985. pap. 11.95 (2-07-032541-5) Schoenhof.
— Discours sur l'Origine et les Fondements de l'Inegalite Parmi les Hommes: Avec: La Reine Fantastique. (FRE.). 192p. 1973. pap. 17.95 (0-7859-5568-2); pap. 4.95 (0-686-55343-8) Fr & Eur.
— A Discourse on Inequality. Cranston, Maurice, tr. & anno. by. (Classics Ser.). 208p. 1985. pap. 9.95 (0-14-044439-4, Penguin Classics) Viking Penguin.
— Discourse on the Origin of Inequality. Cress, Donald A., tr. from FRE. LC 92-20421.Tr. of Discours Sur l'Origine et les Fondements de l'Inegalite Parmi les Hommes. 112p. (C). 1992. pap. text 5.95 (0-87220-150-3); lib. bdg. 27.95 (0-87220-151-1) Hackett Pub.
— Discourse on the Origins of Inequality (Second Discourse), Polemics, & Political Economy. Masters, Roger D. & Kelly, Christopher, eds. & trs. by. from FRE. LC 92-53866. (Collected Writings of Rousseau: Vol. 3). (Illus.). 242p. 1993. 50.00 (0-87451-603-X) U Pr of New Eng.
— Discourse on the Sciences & Arts (First Discourse) & Polemics. Masters, Roger D. & Kelly, Christopher, eds. & trs. by. from FRE. LC 91-50820. (Collected Writings of Rousseau: Vol. 2). (Illus.). 259p. 1992. 50.00 (0-87451-580-7) U Pr of New Eng.
— The Discourses & Other Early Political Writings: On the Sciences & Arts (1st Discourse) & Polemics; On the Origin of Inequality (2nd Discourse) & Polemics; Letter to Voltaire on Providence; Essay on the Origin of Languages; War; Discourse on the Virtue a Hero Most Needs; Method in the Composition of a Book. Gourevitch, Victor, ed. & tr. by. (Cambridge Texts in the History of Political Thought Ser.). 494p. (C). 1997. text 54.95 (0-521-41381-8); pap. text 14.95 (0-521-42445-3) Cambridge U Pr.
***Rousseau, Jean-Jacques.** Discouse on Political Economy & the Social Contract. (Oxford World Classics Ser.). 246p. 1999. pap. 6.95 (0-19-283597-1) OUP.
Rousseau, Jean-Jacques. Du Contrat Social. (Coll. Prestige). 21.95 (0-685-34055-4) Fr & Eur.
— Du Contrat Social. Burgelin, Pierre, ed. 215p. 1971. 3.95 (0-686-55344-6) Fr & Eur.
— Du Contrat Social. (FRE.). 254p. 1985. pap. 10.95 (0-7859-1268-1, 2040161007) Fr & Eur.
— Du Contrat Social. Grimsley, Ronald, ed. (FRE.). (C). 1972. 24.00 (0-19-815710-X) OUP.
— Du Contrat Social/Discours Sur l'Origine et les Fondements de l'Inegalite Parmi les Hommes. unabridged ed. (FRE.). Date not set. reprint ed. pap. 7.95 (2-87714-343-0, Pub. by Bookking Intl) Distribks Inc.
— Emile ou de l'Education. Launay, Michel, ed. (FRE.). 636p. 1966. 5.95 (0-685-55346-2) Fr & Eur.
— Emile ou de l'Education. Richard, ed. (FRE.). 189p. 1986. pap. 10.95 (0-7859-1269-X, 2040166300) Fr & Eur.
— Emile ou de l'Education: College Prestige. Richard, ed. (FRE.). 27.95 (0-685-34056-2) Fr & Eur.
— Essai sur l'Origine des Langues. (FRE.). 1990. 13.95 (0-686-55347-0, 2070325431); pap. 11.95 (0-7859-1359-9) Fr & Eur.
— Essai sur l'Origine des Langues. (Folio Essais Ser.: No. 135). (FRE.). pap. 11.95 (2-07-032543-1) Schoenhof.
— Essay on the Origin of Languages & Writings Related to Music. Scott, John T. et al, eds. LC 98-8043. (Collected Writings of Rousseau: Vol. 7). 656p. 1999. 55.00 (0-87451-839-3) U Pr of New Eng.
— The Essential Rousseau. 1974. pap. 13.95 (0-452-01031-4, Plume) Dutton Plume.
— First & Second Discourses. Masters, Roger D., ed. 248p. 1969. pap. text 11.95 (0-312-69440-7) St Martin.
— The Government of Poland. Kendall, Willmoore, ed. & tr. by. from FRE. LC 85-5463. (HPC Classics Ser.). 158p. (C). 1985. reprint ed. pap. 8.95 (0-915145-95-2) Hackett Pub.
— The Government of Poland. Kendall, Willmoore & Mansfield, Harvey C., Jr., eds. & trs. by. from FRE. LC 85-5463. (HPC Classics Ser.). 158p. (C). 1985. reprint ed. lib. bdg. 29.95 (0-915145-96-0) Hackett Pub.
— Jean Jacques Entre Socrate et Caton. (FRE.). 112p. 1972. pap. 12.95 (0-7859-5476-7) Fr & Eur.
— Jean-Jacques Rousseau: Le Devin du Village (Full Score) Kaufman, Charlotte, ed. (Recent Researches in Music of the Classic Era Ser.: No. RRC50). (Illus.). 1998. pap. 65.00 (0-89579-399-7) A-R Eds.
— Jean-Jacques Rousseau: Le Devin du Village (Piano-Vocal Score) Kaufman, Charlotte, ed. (Recent Researches in Music of the Classic Era Ser.: No. C50KEY). (Illus.). 1998. pap. 20.00 (0-89579-409-8) A-R Eds.
— Julie Ou, La Nouvelle Heloise. Pomeau, Rene, ed. (Coll. Prestige). 35.95 (0-685-34057-0) Fr & Eur.
— Julie Ou, La Nouvelle Heloise. Launay, Michel, ed. 640p. 1967. 5.95 (0-686-55351-9) Fr & Eur.
— Julie Ou, La Nouvelle Heloise. Pomeau, Rene, ed. (FRE.). 640p. 1967. pap. 14.95 (0-7859-1383-1, 2070701487) Fr & Eur.
— Julie or The New Heloise: Letters of Two Lovers Who Live in a Small Town at the Foot of the Alps. Masters, Roger D. et al, eds. Stewart, Philip & Vache, Jean, trs. from FRE. LC 97-9172. (Collected Writings of Rousseau: Vol. 6). (Illus.). 760p. 1997. pap. 25.00 (0-87451-825-3) U Pr of New Eng.
— Lettre a M. d'Alembert sur les Spectacles. (FRE.). 254p. 1967. pap. 10.95 (0-7859-1420-X, 2080701606) Fr & Eur.
— Lettres Philosphiques. (FRE.). 232p. 1974. pap. 29.95 (0-686-55353-5, 271160666X) Fr & Eur.
— La Nouvelle Heloise, 2 vols., 1. (FRE.). 1993. pap. 19.95 (0-7859-2932-0) Fr & Eur.
— La Nouvelle Heloise, 2 vols., 2. (FRE.). 1993. pap. 19.95 (0-7859-2933-9) Fr & Eur.
— La Nouvelle Heloise: Julie, or the New Eloise. McDowell, Judith H., tr. LC 67-27114. (FRE.). 428p. 1986. reprint ed. pap. 14.95 (0-271-00602-1) Pa St U Pr.
Rousseau, Jean-Jacques. Oeuvres Completes, Tome II. Raymont, Andre, ed. (FRE.). 1961. lib. bdg. 130.00 (0-7859-3954-7) Fr & Eur.
— Oeuvres Completes, Tome II. Gagnebin & Raymont, Andre, eds. (Pleiade Ser.). (FRE.). 1964. 88.95 (2-07-010489-3) Schoenhof.
— Oeuvres Completes, Tome III. Gagnebin & Raymont, Andre, eds. (Pleiade Ser.). (FRE.). 1964. 89.95 (2-07-010490-7) Schoenhof.
— Oeuvres Completes, Tome III. deluxe ed. (FRE.). 2224p. 1964. 125.00 (0-7859-1622-9, 2070104907) Fr & Eur.
— Oeuvres Completes, Tome IV. deluxe ed. (FRE.). 2184p. 1969. write for info. (0-7859-1623-7, 2070104915) Fr & Eur.
Rousseau, Jean-Jacques. On the Social Contract. Masters, Roger D., ed. Masters, Judith R., tr. LC 77-86291. 245p. 1978. pap. text 11.95 (0-312-69446-6) St Martin.
— On the Social Contract. rev. ed. Cress, Donald A., ed. & tr. by. LC 88-28260. 112p. (C). 1988. pap. 5.95 (0-87220-068-X); lib. bdg. 24.95 (0-87220-069-8) Hackett Pub.
— Politics & the Arts: Letter to M. D'Alembert on the Theatre. Bloom, Allan, tr. 196p. 1968. reprint ed. pap. text 11.95 (0-8014-9071-5) Cornell U Pr.
— Profession de Foi du Vicaire Savoyard. Robinet, Andre, ed. (FRE.). 1978. pap. 24.95 (0-685-73323-8, 2711606678) Fr & Eur.
— Les Reveries du Promeneur Solitaire. (FRE.). 288p. 1972. pap. 10.95 (0-7859-3989-X, 2070361861) Fr & Eur.
— Les Reveries du Promeneur Solitaire. De Sacy, S. Sylvestre, ed. (FRE.). 288p. 1972. write for info. (0-318-63590-9) Fr & Eur.
— Les Reveries du Promeneur Solitaire. Sacy, S. Sylvestre de, ed. (Folio Ser.: No. 186). (FRE.). 288p. 1972. 6.95 (2-07-036186-1) Schoenhof.
— Les Reveries du Promeneur Solitaire. unabridged ed. (FRE.). pap. 5.95 (2-87714-224-8, Pub. by Bookking Intl) Distribks Inc.
— The Reveries of the Solitary Walker. France, Peter, tr. from FRE. & intro. by. (Classics Ser.). 160p. 1980. pap. 9.95 (0-14-044363-0, Penguin Classics) Viking Penguin.
— The Reveries of the Solitary Walker. Butterworth, Charles E., tr. from FRE. & notes by. LC 92-28212. 288p. (C). 1992. reprint ed. pap. text 8.95 (0-87220-162-7); reprint ed. lib. bdg. 29.95 (0-87220-163-5) Hackett Pub.
***Rousseau, Jean-Jacques.** The Reveries of the Solitary Walker, Botanical Writings & Letter to Franquieres. Kelly, Christopher & Masters, Roger D., eds. Butterworth, Charles et al, trs. from FRE. LC 99-39783. (Collected Writings of Rousseau Ser.: Vol. 8). 377p. 2000. 65.00 (1-58465-007-9) U Pr of New Eng.
Rousseau, Jean-Jacques. Rousseau, Judge of Jean-Jacques: Dialogues. Masters, Roger D. et al, eds. Kelly, Christopher et al, trs. from FRE. LC 89-40234. (Collected Writings of Rousseau: Vol. 1). (Illus.). 309p. 1990. 60.00 (0-87451-495-9) U Pr of New Eng.
— Rousseau on International Relations. Hoffman, Stanley & Fidler, David P., eds. 292p. 1991. text 55.00 (0-19-827321-5) OUP.
— Rousseau's Political Writings. Ritter, Alan, ed. Bondanella, Julia C., tr. LC 87-24056. (Critical Editions Ser.). (C). 1987. pap. text 12.50 (0-393-95651-2) Norton.
— The Social Contract. (C). 1997. pap. text. write for info. (0-321-02593-8) Addson-Wesley Educ.
***Rousseau, Jean-Jacques.** Social Contract. Cranston, Maurice, tr. & intro. by. (Classics Ser.). 192p. 1998. pap. 5.33 (0-14-044201-4) Addson-Wesley Educ.
Rousseau, Jean-Jacques. Social Contract. 20.95 (0-8488-0840-1) Amereon Ltd.
— Social Contract. Frankell, Charles, ed. (Library of Classics: No. 1). 160p. 1970. pap. 13.95 (0-02-851150-6) Hafner.
— Social Contract. Cole, G. D., tr. LC 88-60152. (Great Books in Philosophy). 137p. (C). 1988. pap. 5.95 (0-87975-444-3) Prometheus Bks.
— Social Contract. (Classics of World Literature Ser.). 1998. pap. 5.95 (1-85326-781-3, 7813WW, Pub. by Wrdsworth Edits) NTC Contemp Pub Co.
— Social Contract & Discourse on the Origin of Inequality. Crocker, Lester G., ed. 288p. 1989. mass mkt. 5.99 (0-671-68956-8, WSP) PB.
— The Social Contract & Discourses. Brumfitt, J. H., ed. Cole, G. D., tr. 422p. 1993. pap. 6.95 (0-460-87357-1, Everyman's Classic Lib) Tuttle Pubng.
Rousseau, Jean-Jacques. The Social Contract & Other Later Political Writings: Including a Discourse on Political Economy; Portions of the Geneva Ms.; the Government of Poland; Selected Letters. Gourevitch, Victor, ed. (Cambridge Texts in the History of Political Thought Ser.). 398p. (C). 1997. text 44.95 (0-521-41382-6); pap. text 12.95 (0-521-42446-1) Cambridge U Pr.
Rousseau, Jean-Jacques. The Social Contract & the Discourses. Cole, G. D., tr. LC 93-22368. 1993. 17.00 (0-679-42302-8) Everymns Lib.
— Social Contract, Discourse on the Virtue Most Necessary for a Hero, Political Fragments, & Geneva Manuscript. Masters, Roger D. & Kelly, Christopher, eds. & trs. by. from FRE. LC 94-4496. (Collected Writings of Rousseau: Vol. 4). (Illus.). 306p. 1994. 60.00 (0-87451-646-3) U Pr of New Eng.
Rousseau, Jean-Jacques & Furbank, P. N. Confessions. 1992. 20.00 (0-679-40998-X) Everymns Lib.
Rousseau, Jean-Jacques & Herder, Johann G. On the Origin of Language. Moran, John H. & Gode, Alexander, trs. from FRE. LC 85-20945. x, 186p. 1986. pap. text 9.95 (0-226-73012-3) U Ch Pr.
Rousseau, Jean-Jacques, et al. Jean-Jacques Rousseau, Political Writings. LC 87-24056. 1987. write for info. (0-393-02479-2) Norton.
Rousseau, Jerome. Central Borneo: Ethnic Identity & Social Life in a Stratified Society. (Illus.). 394p. 1990. text 85.00 (0-19-827716-4) OUP.
***Rousseau, Jerome.** Kayan Religion: Ritual Life & Religious Reform in Central Borneo. (Illus.). 352p. 1998. pap. 44.00 (90-6718-132-3, Pub. by KITLV Pr) Book Bin.
Rousseau, John J., et al. Jesus & His World: An Archaeological & Cultural Dictionary. LC 94-12733. 504p. 1995. pap. 36.00 (0-8006-2805-5, 1-2805, Fortress Pr) Augsburg Fortress.
Rousseau, Julie W. Alice Bay Cookbook. LC 85-63063. (Illus.). 256p. (Orig.). 1985. pap. 12.95 (0-931849-02-0) Quartzite Bks.
Rousseau, Louis-Jean. English - French Lexicon of the Mining Industry Two: Mineral Processing. (ENG & FRE.). 83p. 1981. pap. 39.95 (0-8288-9400-0) Fr & Eur.
Rousseau, Louis-Jean, jt. auth. see Auger, Pierre.
***Rousseau, M.** Nisoldipine Coat-Core. LC 99-33461. (Illus.). 100p. 1999. pap. 41.00 (3-540-66049-6) Spr-Verlag.
Rousseau, Marc. Vietnam. 1998. 19.99 (3-8228-7758-1) Taschen Amer.
Rousseau, Mark O. & Zariski, Raphael. Regionalism & Regional Devolution in Comparative Perspective. LC 87-11617. 303p. 1987. 69.50 (0-275-92546-3, C2546, Praeger Pubs) Greenwood.
Rousseau, Mary. Community: The Tie That Binds. 188p. (C). 1991. lib. bdg. 47.50 (0-8191-8209-5) U Pr of Amer.
Rousseau, Mary F., tr. Liber de Pomo: The Apple or Aristotle's Death. LC 68-28028. (Medieval Philosophical Texts in Translation Ser.: No. 18). 1968. pap. 5.00 (0-87462-218-2) Marquette.
Rousseau, May. Everyone Is Dressing Up! (Illus.). 12p. (J). (ps). 1991. bds. 4.95 (0-916291-38-3) Kane-Miller Bk.
Rousseau, Philip. Basil of Caesarea. LC 93-3552. (Transformation of the Classical Heritage Ser.: Vol. 20). 1994. 65.00 (0-520-08238-9, Pub. by U CA Pr) Cal Prin Full Svc.
— Basil of Caesarea. (Transformation of the Classical Heritage Ser.). 1998. pap. text 19.95 (0-520-21381-5, Pub. by U CA Pr) Cal Prin Full Svc.
***Rousseau, Philip.** Pachomius: The Making of a Community in Fourth-Century Egypt, Vol. 6. 250p. 1999. pap. 19.95 (0-520-21959-7, Pub. by U CA Pr) Cal Prin Full Svc.
Rousseau, Philip, jt. ed. see Hagg, Tomas.
Rousseau, Richard W., ed. Christianity & Islam: The Struggling Dialogue. (Modern Theological Themes: Selections from the Literature Ser.: Vol. 4). 220p. (Orig.). 1985. pap. 17.95 (0-940866-03-X) U Scranton Pr.
— Christianity & Judaism: The Deepening Dialogue.

(Modern Theological Themes: Selections from the Literature Ser.: Vol. 3). (Orig.). 1983. pap. 15.00 (*0-940866-02-1*) U Scranton Pr.

— Christianity & the Religions of the East: Models for a Dynamic Relationship. (Modern Theological Themes: Selections from the Literature Ser.: Vol. 2). 174p. (Orig.). (C). 1982. pap. 15.00 (*0-940866-01-3*) U Scranton Pr.

R

Rousseau, Ronald W. Handbook of Separation Process Technology. LC 86-28134. 1024p. 1987. 250.00 (*0-471-89558-X*) Wiley.

Rousseau, Ronald W., jt. auth. see Felder, Richard M.

Rousseau, Serge, jt. auth. see Pichette, Marise.

***Rousseau, William.** Teach Yourself Linux Programming in 21 Days. (Teach Yourself Ser.). (Illus.). 752p. 1999. pap. 29.99 (*0-672-31597-1*) Sams.

Rousseaux, Colin G., jt. auth. see Haschek, Wanda M.

Rousseaux, Colin G., jt. ed. see Haschek, Wanda M.

Rousseeuw, Peter J. & Leroy, Annick M. Robust Regression & Outlier Detection. LC 87-8234. (Probability & Mathematical Statistics Ser.). 352p. 1987. 140.00 (*0-471-85233-3*) Wiley.

Roussel, A. Liberalism & Catholicism. Daniels, Coenraad, tr. from FRE. LC 99-164535. Orig. Title: Liberalisme et Catholicisme. 135p. 1998. pap. 6.95 (*0-935952-53-5*) Angelus Pr.

Roussel, Fernand. Le Moniteur d'Orientation Rogerienne. fac. ed. LC 72-366473. (FRE.). 249p. reprint ed. pap. 77.20 (*0-7837-6953-9*, 204678200003) Bks Demand.

Roussel, Hubert. The Houston Symphony Orchestra, 1913-1971. LC 74-38924. 273p. reprint ed. pap. 84.70 (*0-8357-7760-X*, 203611800002) Bks Demand.

Roussel, Jean C., jt. auth. see Roussel, Paule.

Roussel, Mike. Clay. (Craft Projects Ser.). (Illus.). 32p. (J). (gr. 2-6). 1990. lib. bdg. 22.60 (*0-86592-485-6*) Rourke Enter.

— Scrap Materials. (Craft Projects Ser.). (Illus.). 32p. (J). (gr. 2-6). 1990. 11.95 (*0-685-36305-8*) Rourke Corp.

Roussel, Mike, et al. Craft Projects, 3 bks., Set. (Illus.). 192p. (J). (gr. 2-6). 1990. lib. bdg. 67.80 (*0-86592-482-1*) Rourke Enter.

Roussel, Monique. Biographie Legendaire D'Achille. (FRE.). x, 505p. 1991. pap. 112.00 (*90-256-0993-7*, Pub. by AM Hakkert) BookLink Distributors.

Roussel, Paule & Roussel, Jean C. The Art of Furniture Decoration. (Illus.). 80p. 1996. pap. 19.95 (*0-233-98951-X*, Pub. by Andre Deutsch) Trafalgar.

Roussel, Philip A., et al. Third Generation R & D: Managing the Link to Corporate Strategy. 224p. 1991. 29.95 (*0-87584-252-6*) Harvard Busn.

Roussel, Raymond. How I Wrote Certain of My Books. Winkfield, Trevor, ed. 288p. 1995. pap. 15.95 (*1-878972-14-6*) Exact Change.

— Impressions of Africa. 224p. (Orig.). reprint ed. pap. 13.95 (*0-7145-0289-8*) Riverrun NY.

— Raymond Roussel: Life, Death & Works. Brotchie, Alastair, ed. 1987. pap. 13.00 (*0-947757-14-7*, Pub. by Atlas Pr) Serpents Tail.

— Selections from Certain of His Books. 224p. 1991. pap. 14.95 (*0-947757-26-0*) Serpents Tail.

Roussel, Raymond, jt. auth. see Padgett, Ron.

Roussel, Royal. The Metaphysics of Darkness: A Study in the Unity & Development of Conrad's Fiction. LC 74-146458. 208p. reprint ed. pap. 64.50 (*0-8357-9277-3*, 201100400071) Bks Demand.

Rousselet-Blanc, Josette, jt. auth. see Rousselet-Blanc, Pierre.

Rousselet-Blanc, Pierre. Dictionary of Animals: Dictionnaire des Animaux. (ENG & FRE.). 250p. 1981. 19.95 (*0-8288-4443-7*, M9771) Fr & Eur.

— Larousse des Animaux Familiers Insolites. (FRE.). 1976. 24.95 (*0-8288-5723-7*, M6334) Fr & Eur.

Rousselet-Blanc, Pierre, ed. Larousse des Poissons D'Aquarium. (FRE.). 120p. 1975. 59.95 (*0-8288-5912-4*, M6336) Fr & Eur.

— Larousse du Chevel. (FRE.). 1976. 85.00 (*0-8288-5726-1*, F12080) Fr & Eur.

Rousselet-Blanc, Pierre & Rousselet-Blanc, Josette. Dictionnaire du Chien. (FRE.). 267p. 1976. 49.95 (*0-8288-5648-6*, M6647) Fr & Eur.

Roussell, Aage. Norse Building Customs in the Scottish Isles. LC 77-87681. reprint ed. 34.50 (*0-404-16477-3*) AMS Pr.

Roussell, Jeroid O. Dealing with Grief: Theirs & Ours. LC 99-17443. 153p. 1999. pap. 9.95 (*0-8189-0823-8*) Alba.

Rousselot, Jean, ed. see Reverdy, Pierre.

Rousselot, Lucien. Napoleon's Elite Cavalry: Cavalry of the Imperial Guard, 1804-1815. 208p. 1999. 85.00 (*1-85367-371-4*, Pub. by Greenhill Bks) Stackpole.

Rousselot, Pierre. The Eyes of Faith: With Rousselot's "Answer to Two Attacks" Donceel, Joseph, ed. Dulles, Avery, tr. from FRE. LC 90-82352. 117p. 1990. reprint ed. 27.50 (*0-8232-1288-2*) Fordham.

Rousselot, Pierre & Tallon, Andrew. Intelligence: Sense of Being, Sense of the Other, Sense of God. LC 98-25398. (Studies in Philosophy). 1998. write for info. (*0-87462-615-3*) Marquette.

Rousselow, Jessica L. & Winquist, Alan H. God's Ordinary People, No Ordinary Heritage. LC 96-61465. xvi, 345p. 1996. write for info. (*0-9621187-4-5*) Taylor Univ.

Rousset, Paul. Les Origines et les Caracteres de la Premier Croisade. LC 76-29837. reprint ed. 37.50 (*0-404-15428-X*) AMS Pr.

Rousset, Pierre R. Reflections from a French Childhood. Swann Publications Staff, ed. (Illus.). x, 60p. 1997. pap. 7.50 (*0-9645451-9-5*, Swann Pubns) F Swann Pubns.

Roussie, Gerald. Award Enterprises. (C). 1991. pap. text. write for info. (*0-7730-5060-4*) Addison-Wes.

Roussier, Pierre J. Memoire sur la Musique des Anciens. fac. ed. (Monuments of Music & Music Literature in Facsimile, II Ser.: Vol. 41). (Illus.). 1966. lib. bdg. 42.50 (*0-8450-2241-5*) Broude.

Roussin, Andre, jt. auth. see Mitford, Nancy.

Rousso, Harilyn, et al. Disabled, Female, & Proud! Stories of Ten Women with Disabilities. LC 93-26049. (Illus.). 1993. pap. 12.95 (*0-89789-358-1*, Bergin & Garvey) Greenwood.

Rousso, Henry. The Vichy Syndrome: History & Memory in France since 1914. 400p. (C). 1994. pap. text 18.00 (*0-674-93539-X*) HUP.

— The Vichy Syndrome: History & Memory in France since 1944. Goldhammer, Arthur, tr. (Illus.). 384p. (C). 1991. 49.95 (*0-674-93538-1*) HUP.

Rousso, Henry, jt. auth. see Conan, Eric.

Rousso, Nira. The Passover Gourmet. (Illus.). 192p. 1987. 22.95 (*0-915361-66-3*) Lambda Pubs.

Rousso, Robyn, jt. auth. see Cohen, Robyn.

Roussopoulos, et al. The Anarchist Papers. Poussopoulos, Dimitrios I., ed. 175p. 1986. 41.99 (*0-920057-57-8*, Pub. by Black Rose); pap. 12.99 (*0-920057-58-6*, Pub. by Black Rose) Consort Bk Sales.

Roussopoulos, Dimitrios I. The Coming of World War Three: A New Agenda: From Resistance to Social Change, Vol. 2. 200p. 1990. write for info. (*0-920057-83-7*); pap. write for info. (*0-920057-85-3*) Black Rose.

— The Coming of World War Three: From Protest to Resistance & the International War System, Vol. 1. 299p. 1986. 43.99 (*0-920057-03-9*, Pub. by Black Rose); pap. 14.99 (*0-920057-02-0*, Pub. by Black Rose) Consort Bk Sales.

— Dissidence: Essays Against the Mainstream. LC 92-72630. 250p. 1993. 48.99 (*1-895431-41-7*, Pub. by Black Rose); pap. 19.99 (*1-895431-40-9*, Pub. by Black Rose) Consort Bk Sales.

— Green Politics: Agenda for a Free Society. LC 90-83631. 250p. (Orig.). 1992. text. write for info. (*0-921689-75-6*); pap. text. write for info. (*0-921689-74-8*) Black Rose.

— 1984 & After. Hewitt, Marsha, ed. 234p. 1984. 43.99 (*0-920057-28-4*, Pub. by Black Rose); pap. 14.95 (*0-920057-29-2*, Pub. by Black Rose) Consort Bk Sales.

— Political Ecology: Beyond Environmentalism. LC 93-72749. 180p. 1994. 44.99 (*1-895431-81-6*, Pub. by Black Rose); pap. 15.99 (*1-895431-80-8*, Pub. by Black Rose) Consort Bk Sales.

***Roussopoulos, Dimitrios I.** The Public Place: Citizen Participation in the Neighbourhood & the City. 2000. 48.99 (*1-55164-157-7*) Black Rose.

Roussopoulos, Dimitrios I., ed. The Anarchist Papers II. 192p. (Orig.). (C). 1992. 41.99 (*0-921689-37-3*, Pub. by Black Rose); pap. 12.99 (*0-921689-36-5*, Pub. by Black Rose) Consort Bk Sales.

— The Anarchist Papers III. 168p. (Orig.). (C). 1990. 41.99 (*0-921689-53-5*, Pub. by Black Rose); pap. 12.99 (*0-921689-52-7*, Pub. by Black Rose) Consort Bk Sales.

— Canada & Radical Social Change. 220p. 1973. write for info. (*0-919618-10-3*); pap. write for info. (*0-919618-09-X*) Black Rose.

— The City & Radical Social Change. 344p. 1982. write for info. (*0-919618-83-9*); pap. write for info. (*0-919618-82-0*) Black Rose.

— Our Generation Against Nuclear War. 476p. 1983. 43.99 (*0-920057-15-2*, Pub. by Black Rose); pap. 14.99 (*0-920057-04-7*, Pub. by Black Rose) Consort Bk Sales.

— The Political Economy of the State. 196p. 1973. 35.99 (*0-919618-02-2*, Pub. by Black Rose); pap. 6.99 (*0-919618-01-4*, Pub. by Black Rose) Consort Bk Sales.

— Quebec & Radical Social Change. 210p. 1974. write for info. (*0-919618-52-9*); pap. write for info. (*0-919618-51-0*) Black Rose.

— Radical Papers. 160p. 1987. 41.99 (*0-920057-87-X*, Pub. by Black Rose); pap. 12.99 (*0-920057-86-1*, Pub. by Black Rose) Consort Bk Sales.

— Radical Papers, No. 2. 168p. 1987. 41.99 (*0-921689-13-6*, Pub. by Black Rose); pap. 12.99 (*0-921689-12-8*, Pub. by Black Rose) Consort Bk Sales.

— The Sixties & the Legacy of the New Left. 210p. 1998. 48.99 (*1-55164-021-X*, Pub. by Black Rose); pap. 19.99 (*1-55164-020-1*, Pub. by Black Rose) Consort Bk Sales.

Roussopoulos, Dimitrios I., tr. & intro. see Leonard, Jean-Francois & Leveillee, Jacques.

Roussopoulos, Dimitrios J. The New Left in Canada. 2nd ed. LC HN0018.R6. (Black Rose Bks.: Vol. 1). 156p. 1971. reprint ed. pap. 48.40 (*0-608-00457-X*, 206127600007) Bks Demand.

— The Public Place: Citizen Participation in the Neighbourhood & the City. 200p. 2000. pap. 19.99 (*1-55164-156-9*) Consort Bk Sales.

***Roussopoulos, Peter J., ed.** Burning Issues & Smoke Screens: Heat & Light in Southern Forests. (Illus.). 116p. 2000. reprint ed. pap. text 25.00 (*0-7881-8649-3*) DIANE Pub.

Roussos. The Thorax, Pt. C. 2nd expanded rev. ed. (Lung Biology in Health & Disease Ser.: Vol. 85, Pt. C). (Illus.). 2892p. 1995. text 495.00 (*0-8247-9601-2*) Dekker.

— The Thorax, Pt. A. 2nd expanded rev. ed. LC 97-6745. (Lung Biology in Health & Disease Ser.: Vol. 85, Pt. A). (Illus.). 1080p. 1995. text 495.00 (*0-8247-9504-0*) Dekker.

— The Thorax, Pt. B. 2nd expanded rev. ed. (Lung Biology in Health & Disease Ser.: Vol. 85, Pt. B). (Illus.). 1995. text 495.00 (*0-8247-9600-4*) Dekker.

Roussos, Charis & Macklem, Peter T., eds. The Thorax, Pt. A. LC 85-25254. (Lung Biology in Health & Disease Ser.: No. 29). 655p. reprint ed. pap. 200.00 (*0-7837-0322-8*, 204064200001) Bks Demand.

— The Thorax, Pt. B. LC 85-25254. (Lung Biology in Health & Disease Ser.: No. 29). 955p. reprint ed. pap. 200.00 (*0-7837-0323-6*, 204064200002) Bks Demand.

Roussos, S., et al, eds. Advances in Solid State Fermentation: Proceedings of 2nd International Symposium on Solid State Fermentation, FMS-95, Montpellier, France. LC 97-33656. 672p. 1997. text 331.50 (*0-7923-4732-3*) Kluwer Academic.

Roussy De Sales, R. Easy French Reader. (Easy... Readers Ser.). (FRE., Illus.). 224p. 1994. pap. 12.95 (*0-8442-1001-3*, 10013, Natl Textbk Co) NTC Contemp Pub Co.

— French Verb Drills. 142p. 1989. pap. 6.95 (*0-8442-1032-3*, Natl Textbk Co) NTC Contemp Pub Co.

— Jeux de Grammaire. (FRE., Illus.). 64p. (J). (gr. 5 up). 1995. pap. 4.95 (*0-8442-1380-2*, Natl Textbk Co) NTC Contemp Pub Co.

Roussy De Sales, Raoul De, see De Roussy De Sales, Raoul.

Roussy, G. & Pearce, J. A. Foundations & Industrial Applications of Microwave & Radio Frequency Fields: Physical & Chemical Processes. LC 94-36676. 492p. 1995. 210.00 (*0-471-93849-1*) Wiley.

Roussy, R. De Sales. Easy French Grammar Puzzles. (Easy...Word Games & Ser.). (FRE., Illus.). 64p. 1994. pap. 4.95 (*0-8442-1322-5*, 13225, Natl Textbk Co) NTC Contemp Pub Co.

Roustang, Francois. Dire Mastery: Discipleship from Freud to Lacan. Lukacher, Ned, tr. from FRE. LC 86-20572. 162p. 1986. pap. text 7.50 (*0-88048-259-1*, 8259) Am Psychiatric.

— Dire Mastery: Discipleship from Freud to Lacan. Lukacher, Ned, tr. from FRE. LC 82-6552. 160p. 1982. text 30.00 (*0-8018-2675-6*) Johns Hopkins.

***Roustang, Francois.** How to Make a Paranoid Laugh: Or, What is Psychoanalysis? LC 99-32950. 1999. pap. 17.50 (*0-8122-1708-X*) U of Pa Pr.

— How to Make a Paranoid Laugh, or, What Is Psychoanalysis LC 99-36953. (Critical Authors & Issues Ser.). 1999. write for info. (*0-8122-3525-8*) U of Pa Pr.

Roustang, Francois. Psychoanalysis Never Lets Go. Lukacher, Ned, tr. from FRE. LC 82-10042. 176p. (C). 1982. text 30.00 (*0-8018-2674-8*) Johns Hopkins.

— The Quadrille of Gender: Casanova's 'Memoirs' Vila, Anne C., tr. from FRE. LC 87-27807. 184p. 1988. 32.50 (*0-8047-1456-8*) Stanford U Pr.

Roustiau, Judith. Messengers of the New Millennium: "A Walk with the Angels" (Illus.). v, 59p. 1998. 19.95 (*0-9665246-0-8*) Roustiau Ent.

Rout. Self-Assessment Picture Test. 1996. mass mkt. 32.95 (*0-7234-2422-5*) Wolfe Pubng AZ.

***Rout.** Understanding Stress in Doctors' Families. 144p. 2000. 59.95 (*1-85972-591-0*) Ashgate Pub Co.

Rout, Katharina, tr. see Streeruwitz, Marlene.

Rout, Kathleen. Eldridge Cleaver. (Twayne's United States Authors Ser.: No. 583). 288p. (C). 1991. 24.95 (*0-8057-7620-6*) Macmillan.

Rout, Leslie B. & Bratzel, John. The Shadow War: German Espionage & United States Counterespionage in Latin America During World War II. LC 85-29563. (Foreign Intelligence Book Ser.). 496p. 1986. lib. bdg. 69.50 (*0-313-27005-8*, U7005, Greenwood Pr) Greenwood.

Rout, Nancy E., jt. ed. see Buckley, Ellen.

Rout, Paul. Francis & Bonaventure. Vardy, Peter, ed. LC 96-52492. (Great Christian Thinkers Ser.). 112p. 1997. reprint ed. pap. 9.00 (*0-7648-0113-9*, Liguori Triumph) Liguori Pubns.

Rout, Pravakar. Environmental Concept Development in Children. (C). 1988. 31.00 (*81-7024-206-1*, Pub. by Ashish Pub Hse) S Asia.

Rout, Robin. Men's Maintenance Manual. LC 98-43183. 1999. pap. text 19.95 (*0-7892-0547-5*) Abbeville Pr.

Routburg, Marcia. On Becoming a Special Parent: A Mini-Support Group in a Book. (Illus.). 130p. (Orig.). 1987. pap. 9.00 (*0-9619347-0-0*) Parent Prof Pubns.

Route, Anthony J. Flies for Alaska: A Guide to Buying & Tying. LC 91-77326. (Illus.). 188p. 1991. pap. 18.95 (*1-55566-087-8*, Sprng Creek Pr) Johnson Bks.

— Flyfishing Alaska. rev. ed. LC 95-250. (Illus.). 240p. 1995. pap. 17.95 (*1-55566-150-5*, Sprng Creek Pr) Johnson Bks.

— Kenai River, AK. LC 94-227073. (River Journal Ser.: Vol. 2, No. 1). (Illus.). 48p. 1994. pap. 15.95 (*1-878175-64-5*) F Amato Pubns.

Routh. Impact Poverty. (JCCP Ser.: Vol. 23, No. 4). 1994. 24.50 (*0-8058-9958-8*) L Erlbaum Assocs.

Routh, C. R., ed. Who's Who in Tudor England. LC 90-63661. (Who's Who in British History Ser.). (Illus.). 494p. 1990. 59.95 (*1-55862-133-4*) St James Pr.

Routh, D. K. Clinical Psychology since 1917: Science, Practice, & Organization. LC 93-50551. (Applied Clinical Psychology Ser.). (Illus.). 300p. (C). 1994. 59.50 (*0-306-44452-6*, Kluwer Plenum) Kluwer Academic.

Routh, David, jt. auth. see Devine, Mike.

Routh, David, jt. auth. see Newhouse, Tom.

Routh, Donald K., ed. Disruptive Behavior Disorders in Childhood. (Illus.). 256p. (C). 1994. 45.00 (*0-306-44695-2*, Plenum Trade) Perseus Pubng.

— Learning, Speech, & the Complex Effects of Punishment: Essays Honoring George J. Wischner. LC 82-18075. 248p. 1982. 49.50 (*0-306-40960-7*, Plenum Trade) Perseus Pubng.

Routh, Donald K. & DeRubeis, Robert J., eds. The Science of Clinical Psychology: Accomplishments & Future Directions. LC 98-39998. 323p. 1998. 39.95 (*1-55798-520-0*, 431-8790) Am Psychol.

Routh, Donald K., jt. ed. see Wolraich, Mark L.

Routh, H. V. Money, Morals & Manners As Revealed in Modern Literature. 1972. 59.95 (*0-8490-0662-7*) Gordon Pr.

Routh, Harold V. God, Man & Epic Poetry: A Study in Comparative Literature, 2 vols., Set. LC 69-10152. (Illus.). 1968. reprint ed. lib. bdg. 75.00 (*0-8371-9948-4*, ROEP, Greenwood Pr) Greenwood.

— God, Man & Epic Poetry: A Study in Comparative Literature, 2 vols., Vol. 1. LC 69-10152. (Illus.). 1968. reprint ed. lib. bdg. 45.00 (*0-8371-0206-5*, ROEA, Greenwood Pr) Greenwood.

— God, Man & Epic Poetry: A Study in Comparative Literature, 2 vols., Vol. 2. LC 69-10152. (Illus.). 1968. reprint ed. lib. bdg. 45.00 (*0-8371-0880-2*, ROEB, Greenwood Pr) Greenwood.

— Towards the Twentieth Century. LC 69-17587. (Essay Index Reprint Ser.). 1977. 21.95 (*0-8369-0091-X*) Ayer.

Routh, Martin J., ed. see Burnet, Gilbert.

Routh, Martinus J. Reliaquiae Sacrae, 5 vols. lv, 2416p. 1974. reprint ed. write for info. (*3-487-05142-7*) G Olms Pubs.

Routh, Paul & Kladder, Ronald. Welfare Benefits Guide, 1990-91. 1993. pap. 128.00 (*0-685-31929-6*) West Group.

Routh, Paul J., jt. auth. see Kladder, Ronald A.

Routhier-Graf, Diane, jt. auth. see Schroeder, Betty.

Routhier-Graf, Diane, jt. auth. see Schroeder, Betty L.

***Routhier, Nicole.** Cooking under Wraps: Recipes & Step-by-Step Techniques. (Illus.). 382p. 1999. text 27.00 (*0-7881-5994-1*) DIANE Pub.

Routhier, Nicole. Cooking under Wraps: The Art of Wrapping Hors D'Oeuvres, Main Courses, & Desserts. 1996. pap. 18.00 (*0-688-14610-4*, Hearst) Hearst Commns.

***Routhier, Nicole.** The Foods of Vietnam. (Illus.). 256p. 1999. pap. 27.50 (*1-55670-959-5*) STC Pubns.

Routhier, Nicole. The Foods of Vietnam. LC 89-11320. (Illus.). 240p. 1989. 40.00 (*1-55670-095-4*) Stewart Tabori & Chang.

— Nicole Routhier's Fruit Cookbook. (Illus.). 480p. 1996. 25.95 (*0-7611-0506-9*, 10506); pap. 15.95 (*1-56305-565-1*, 3565) Workman Pub.

Routiaux, Claudine. The Hen with the Wooden Leg. (Child's World Library). (Illus.). 32p. (J). (gr. k-5). 1992. lib. bdg. 18.50 (*0-89565-751-1*) Childs World.

Routier, Marcelle, jt. auth. see Fenelon, Fania.

Routledge. Arabic-English, English-Arabic Computer Dictionary. (ARA & ENG.). 350p. 1986. 125.00 (*0-8288-0227-0*, F62951) Fr & Eur.

— Arabic-English, English-Arabic Dictionary of Civil Engineering. (ARA & ENG.). 1986. 150.00 (*0-7859-0639-8*, F76990) Fr & Eur.

— Colloquial French. 1985. pap. 12.95 (*0-7100-0450-8*, Routledge Thoemms) Routledge.

***Routledge (Firm) Staff.** The Concise Routledge Encyclopedia of Philosophy. LC 99-52692. 1104p. 2000. 40.00 (*0-415-22364-4*) Routledge.

Routledge Chapman & Hall Inc. Staff. Performance & Management of Complex Communication Networks. text 159.50 (*0-412-84250-5*) Routledge.

Routledge Chapman Hall, Inc Staff. Applications of Super Critical Fluids in Industrial Analysis. text 202.00 (*0-7514-0057-2*) Routledge.

— Atlantic Salmon Planning for the Future. (C). text 210.50 (*0-7099-5108-6*, Pub. by C Helm) Routldge.

— Gulls & Plovers the Ecology of Mixed-Species Feeding Groups. (C). text 202.00 (*0-7099-3230-8*) C Helm.

Routledge Chapman Hall, Inc Staff, ed. Database Security IX: Status & Prospects. text 159.50 (*0-412-72920-2*) Routledge.

Routledge Chapman Hall, Inc Staff, ed. Handbook of Inductively Coupled Plasma Mass Spectrometry. text 233.50 (*0-7514-0277-X*) B Acad & Prof.

Routledge Chapman Hall, Inc Staff, ed. Handdbook of Silicate Rock Analysis. pap. 180.50 (*0-7514-0287-7*) B Acad & Prof.

— Principles & Applications of Nonlinear Optical Materials. text 210.50 (*0-7514-0085-8*) B Acad & Prof.

— Super Critical Fluid Extraction & Its Use in Chromatographic. text 168.00 (*0-7514-0089-0*) B Acad & Prof.

Routledge Chapman Hall, Inc. Staff. Environmental Contamination & Remediation Practices at Former. pap. text 80.00 (*0-7923-5248-3*) Routledge.

Routledge Chapman Hall, Inc. Staff. Naturally Occurring Quinones. 4th ed. 1996. text. write for info. (*0-7514-0248-6*) Kluwer Academic.

Routledge, Chapman, Hall Ltd Staff. Bulk Solids Handlingan Introduction to the Practice & Technology. text 265.50 (*0-7514-0295-8*) Routledge.

— Grazing in Temperate Eco Systemslarge Herbivores & the Ecology of the New Forest. text 147.00 (*0-7099-4036-X*) Routledge.

— Instrumental Analysis in the Biological Sciences. pap. text 83.00 (*0-7514-0111-0*) Routledge.

— New Methods of Polymer Synthesis. text 189.50 (*0-7514-0142-0*) Routledge.

— Poucher's Perfumes, Cosmetics & Soaps The Raw Material of Prefume. 9th ed. text 159.50 (*0-7514-0301-6*) Routledge.

Routledge, Chapman, Hall Ltd Staff. Recruitment, Colonisation & Physical-Chemical Forcing In. text 202.50 (*0-7923-5273-4*) Kluwer Academic.

Routledge, Chapman, Hall Ltd Staff. Specialty Polymers. 2nd ed. text 122.00 (*0-7514-0358-X*) Routledge.

Routledge, Chapman, Hall Ltd Staff, ed. Ecological Indicators, 2 Vols. text 690.50 (*0-412-73970-4*) Routledge.

— Ethnobotany Evolution of a Discipline. text 95.50 (*0-412-72270-4*) Routledge.

— Genetic Rearrangement the Fifth John Innes Symposium. (C). text 168.00 (*0-7099-0779-6*, Pub. by C Helm) Routldge.

An Asterisk (*) at the beginning of an entry indicates that the title is appearing for the first time.

— In Action: A Practical Approach to Continuous Performance Improvement. pap. text 58.50 (*0-412-71530-9*) Routledge.
— An Introduction to Coastal Ecology. pap. text 58.50 (*0-7514-0109-9*) Routledge.
— Quantitative Ecological Theory: An Introduction to Basic Models. (C). text 95.50 (*0-7099-2289-2*) C Helm.
— Recent Advances in Aquaculture. (Recent Advances in Aquaculture Ser.). (C). text 210.50 (*0-7099-3592-7*, Pub. by C Helm) Routldge.
— Salmon: Economics & Marketing. (C). text 147.00 (*0-7099-3344-4*) Routledge.
— Seed Dormancy & Germination. pap. text 63.50 (*0-7514-0108-0*) Routledge.
— Simplified for Services: Practical Tools for Continuous Quality Improvement. pap. 104.50 (*0-412-44740-1*) Routledge.
— Spice Simulation of Power Electronics Circuits. pap. text 74.50 (*0-412-75140-2*) Routledge.
— Techniques in Molecular Biology. (C). text 74.50 (*0-7099-2755-X*) C Helm.
— VLSI: Integrated Systems on Silicon. text 212.50 (*0-412-82370-5*) Routledge.
Routledge, J. Instructions for Engineers' Slide Rule. (Illus.). 32p. 1990. reprint ed. pap. 4.00 (*1-879335-17-4*) Astragal Pr.
Routledge, K., jt. auth. see Routledge, W. S.
Routledge, Katherine. The Mystery of Easter Island. 1997. pap. 16.95 (*0-932813-48-8*) Adventures Unltd.
— The Mystery of Easter Island: The Story of an Expedition. LC 77-18690. reprint ed. 84.50 (*0-404-14231-1*) AMS Pr.
Routledge, Marg, jt. auth. see Young, Donna.
Routledge, Marie & Jackson, Marion E. Pudlo: Thirty Years of Drawing. (Illus.). 176p. 1995. pap. 24.95 (*0-88884-603-7*) U Ch Pr.
Routledge, N. W. History of the Royal Regiment of Artillery: Anti-Aircraft Artillery, 1914-1955. (Illus.). 500p. 1994. 66.00 (*1-85753-099-3*, Pub. by Brasseys) Brasseys.
Routledge, Paul. John Hume: A Biography. LC 99-194308. viii, 327 p. 1997. write for info. (*0-00-638739-X*) HarpC.
Routledge, Paul. Terrains of Resistance: Nonviolent Social Movements & the Contestation of Place in India. 200p. 1993. 52.95 (*0-275-94517-0*, C4517, Praeger Pubs) Greenwood.
Routledge, Philip. Cycling Ireland: Ireland's Friendly People & Hospital Terrain Make It a Favorite Cycling Destination. LC 97-9349. (Illus.). 224p. 1997. pap. 14.95 (*0-933201-80-X*) MBI Pubg.
Routledge Staff. Danish Dictionary: Danish-English, English-Danish. LC 93-40631. 720p. 1995. pap. 29.99 (*0-415-10803-9*) Routledge.
Routledge Staff, ed. Adaptations: From Text to Screen Screen to Text. LC 98-49576. 1999. text. write for info. (*0-415-16737-X*) Routledge.
***Routledge Staff, ed.** Adaptations: From Text to Screen Screen to Text. LC 98-49576. 1999. pap. 21.99 (*0-415-16738-8*) Routledge.
Routledge Staff, ed. Fiction of Bioethics. LC 98-43178. 1999. 69.99 (*0-415-91988-6*) Routledge.
Routledge, W. S. & Routledge, K. With a Prehistoric People: A Kikuyu of British East Africa. (Illus.). 392p. 1968. reprint ed. 49.50 (*0-7146-1716-4*, Pub. by F Cass Pubs) Intl Spec Bk.
Routley, Erik. Christian Hymns Observed: When in Our Music God Is Glorified. LC 82-61841. 121p. (Orig.). (C). 1982. pap. text 12.95 (*0-911009-00-0*) Prestige Pubns.
— Church Music & the Christian Faith. LC 78-110219. 156p. 1978. pap. 11.95 (*0-916642-10-0*) Agape IL.
— The Divine Formula. LC 85-63336. 128p. (Orig.). 1985. pap. text 14.95 (*0-911009-03-5*) Prestige Pubns.
— The English Carol. LC 73-9129. (Illus.). 272p. 1973. reprint ed. lib. bdg. 35.00 (*0-8371-6989-5*, ROEC, Greenwood Pr) Greenwood.
— The Musical Wesleys. LC 75-36511. (Illus.). 272p. 1976. reprint ed. lib. bdg. 77.50 (*0-8371-8644-7*, ROMW, Greenwood Pr) Greenwood.
— A Short History of English Church Music. 160p. (C). 1997. pap. text 16.95 (*0-916642-63-1*, 1995) Hope Pub.
Routley, Erik & Tindall, Adrienne. Encounter with Erik Routley: Erik Routley, BD, MA, PhD, FRSCM, FWCC, FHSA. LC 97-67961. (Illus.). 374p. 1997. pap. 27.00 (*1-889079-17-0*) Darcey Pr.
Routley, Erik & Young, Carlton R. Music Leadership in the Church. 136p. 1985. reprint ed. pap. text 11.95 (*0-916642-24-0*) Agape IL.
Routley, Erik, ed. see Reformed Church in America Staff.
Routley, Jane. Aramaya. LC 99-94757. 288p. 1999. pap. 13.50 (*0-380-79428-4*, Eos) Morrow Avon.
***Routley, Jane.** Aramaya. 352p. 2000. mass mkt. 6.99 (*0-380-79460-8*, Avon Bks) Morrow Avon.
Routley, Jane. Fire Angels. 512p. 1999. mass mkt. 6.99 (*0-380-79427-6*, Avon Bks) Morrow Avon.
— Mage Heart. 480p. 2000. reprint ed. mass mkt. 5.99 (*0-380-78127-1*, Avon Bks) Morrow Avon.
Routley, Richard. Exploring Meinong's Jungle & Beyond. (Monograph Ser.: No. 3). xxvii, 1035p. (C). 1980. lib. bdg. 49.00 (*0-909596-36-0*) Ridgeview.
— Relevant Logics & Their Rivals, One, No. 1. 460p. (C). 1983. pap. text 30.00 (*0-917930-66-5*); lib. bdg. 49.00 (*0-917930-80-0*) Ridgeview.
***Routman, Mark J.** Understanding Politics: Political Positions, Political Realities, False Consciousness. 120p. 2000. pap. 12.50 (*1-886699-30-5*) Five Corners.
***Routman, Regie.** Conversations: Strategies for Teaching, Learning & Evalating. 656p. 1999. pap. text 35.00 (*0-325-00109-X*) Heinemann.
Routman, Regie. Invitations: Changing As Teachers & Learners K-12. rev. ed. LC 94-29709. 758p. 1994. pap. text 36.00 (*0-435-08836-X*, 08836) Heinemann.
— Invitations: Changing As Teachers & Learners K-12. rev. ed. LC 94-29709. 758p. 1994. 38.50 (*0-435-08837-8*, 08837) Heinemann.
***Routman, Regie.** Kids' Poems: Teaching Kindergartners to Love Writing Poetry. (Kids' Poems Ser.). 64p. (J). 2000. pap. 15.99 (*0-590-01797-7*) Scholastic Inc.
Routman, Regie. Literacy at the Crossroads: Crucial Talk about Reading, Writing & Other Teaching Dilemmas. LC 96-12254. 222p. 1996. pap. text 21.00 (*0-435-07210-2*) Heinemann.
***Routman, Regie.** Teaching First Graders to Love Writing Poetry. (Illus.). 64p. (J). (gr. 1). 2000. pap. 15.99 (*0-590-22734-3*) Scholastic Inc.
— Teaching Second Graders to Love Writing Poetry. (Kids' Poems Ser.). 64p. (J). (gr. 2). 2000. pap. 15.99 (*0-590-22732-7*) Scholastic Inc.
— Teaching Third & Fourth Graders to Love Writing Poetry. (Illus.). 64p. (J). (gr. 3-4). 2000. pap. text 15.99 (*0-590-22735-1*) Scholastic Inc.
Routman, Regie. Transitions: From Literature to Literacy. LC 88-4379. 352p. (Orig.). (C). 1988. pap. 23.00 (*0-435-08467-4*, 08467) Heinemann.
Routman, Regie, et al. The Blue Pages: Resources for Teachers from Invitations: Changing As Teachers & Learners K-12. LC 94-31701. 256p. 1994. pap. text 18.00 (*0-435-08835-1*, 08835) Heinemann.
Routray, jt. auth. see Pradhan, U. C.
Routson, Ken. Internal Life: I Do Beleive in Spirit. LC 98-61171. 200p. 1998. pap. 12.95 (*1-891067-02-8*) Tulip Press.
Routson, Kenneth L. Beliefology: Raise Your Consciousness to Wealth, Health, & Happiness. LC 97-61108. 160p. 1997. pap. 14.95 (*1-891067-01-X*) Tulip Press.
Routson, Kenneth L. & Stewart, Leslie. Beliefology Workbook. (Illus.). 75p. 1997. pap. 9.95 (*1-891067-00-1*) Tulip Press.
Routt, Liam, jt. auth. see Stafford, Greg.
Routt, Liam, ed. see Hind, Chris, et al.
Routtenberg, A., jt. auth. see Gispen, W. H.
Routtenberg, Max J. One in a Minyan & Other Studies. 1979. pap. 6.95 (*0-87068-342-X*) Ktav.
Rouveirol, Celine, jt. ed. see Nedellec, Claire.
Rouvelas, Marilyn. A Guide to Greek Traditions & Customs in America. Papaioannou, George, ed. LC 93-72728. (Illus.). 336p. 1993. 25.00 (*0-9638051-0-X*) Nea Attiki Pr.
Rouverol, Alicia J. & Cole, Stephen A. I Was Content & Not Content: The Story of Linda Lord & the Closing of Penobscot Poultry. LC 99-25059. 240p. 2000. 34.95 (*0-8093-2237-4*) S Ill U Pr.
***Rouverol, Jean.** Refugees from Hollywood: A Journal of the Blacklist Years. LC 00-9135. 2000. 24.95 (*0-8263-2266-2*) U of NM Pr.
Rouverol, Jean. Writing for Daytime Drama. 368p. 1992. pap. 44.95 (*0-240-80102-4*, Focal) Buttrwrth-Heinemann.
Rouverol, W. S. & Pearce, W. J. The Reduction of Gear Pair Transmission Error by Minimizing Mesh Stiffness Variation. (Fall Technical Meeting Papers 88FTM11). (Illus.). 20p. 1988. pap. text 30.00 (*1-55589-516-6*) AGMA.
Rouverol, William, jt. auth. see Wyeth, Mark.
Rouvray, D. H., ed. Computational Chemical Graph Theory. 329p. (C). 1990. text 165.00 (*0-941743-84-5*) Nova Sci Pubs.
Rouvray, D. H., jt. ed. see Bonchev, Danail.
Rouvray, D. H., jt. ed. see Bonchev, D.
Rouvray, Dennis H., ed. Fuzzy Logic in Chemistry. LC 96-50417. (Illus.). 364p. 1997. text 80.00 (*0-12-598910-5*) Morgan Kaufmann.
Rouvray, Dennis H., jt. ed. see Bonchev, Danail.
Rouwen, A. J. Corneal Alterations with Contact Lens Wear. (Illus.). 168p. 1992. lib. bdg. 46.00 (*90-6299-080-0*, Pub. by Kugler) Kugler Pubns.
Rouwendal, Jan. Choice & Allocation Models for the Housing Market. (C). 1989. lib. bdg. 182.50 (*0-7923-0466-7*) Kluwer Academic.
Roux, jt. auth. see Weinberger.
Roux, A. P., jt. ed. see Coetzee, P. H.
Roux, B., jt. ed. see Merz, K. M.
Roux, Barbara & Gordon, Coco. The Opaque Glass. 30p. (Orig.). 1985. 50.00 (*0-931956-25-0*) Water Mark.
Roux, Benoit, jt. ed. see Merz, Kenneth M., Jr.
Roux, C. & Coatrieux, J. L., eds. Contemporary Perspectives in Three-Dimensional Biomedical Imaging. (Studies in Health Technology & Informatics: Vol. 30). 350p. (YA). (gr. 12). 1997. 115.00 (*90-5199-260-2*, 260-2) IOS Press.
Roux, C. J. Fertility Management: Contraception in Practice. 1995. pap. 23.00 (*0-7021-3254-3*, Pub. by Juta & Co) Intl Spec Bk.
Roux, Claude. Etude Ecologique et Phytosociologique des Peuplements Licheniques Saxicoles-Calcicoles du Sud-Est de la France. (Bibliotheca Lichenologica Ser.: Vol. 15). (FRE., Illus.). 558p. 1981. text 136.00 (*3-7682-1301-3*) Lubrecht & Cramer.
Roux, Dominique De, see De Roux, Dominique.
Roux, Edward. Time Longer Than Rope: A History of the Black Man's Struggle for Freedom in South Africa. 2nd ed. 488p. 1967. pap. 14.95 (*0-299-03204-3*) U of Wis Pr.
Roux, Georges. Ancient Iraq. 3rd ed. (Illus.). 576p. 1993. pap. 15.95 (*0-14-012523-X*, Penguin Bks) Viking Penguin.
— Le Temps Des Plenitudes; Conquete De L'harmonie Interieure. 1999. pap. text 9.95 (*2-8251-0397-7*) Age Homme Edits.
Roux, Henry, ed. see Mittleberger, Ernest.
Roux, J. A. & McCay, T. D., eds. Spacecraft Contamination: Sources & Prevention. LC 84-12401. (PAAS Ser.: Vol. 91). 333p. 1984. 74.95 (*0-915928-85-X*, Y-91) AIAA.
Roux, J. A., jt. ed. see McCay, T. D.
***Roux, Marie-Genevieve & Charpy, Elisabeth.** Saint Catherine Laboure: Mary's Messenger. (Along the Paths of the Gospel Ser.). (Illus.). 74p. (YA). (gr. 5-9). 2000. 9.95 (*0-8198-7037-4*) Pauline Bks.
Roux, Michel. Michel Roux: Sauces. LC 96-20167. (Illus.). 176p. 1996. 35.00 (*0-8478-1970-1*, Pub. by Rizzoli Intl) St Martin.
— Michel Roux's Finest Desserts. LC 95-35427. (Illus.). 192p. 1995. 45.00 (*0-8478-1857-8*, Pub. by Rizzoli Intl) St Martin.
Roux, Pak Le, see Le Roux, Pak.
Roux, S., jt. ed. see Herrmann, H. J.
Roux, V., ed. The Potters Wheel. (C). 1989. 44.00 (*81-204-0436-X*) S Asia.
Rouxel, Francis, jt. auth. see Davet, Pierre.
Rouxel, J., et al, eds. Soft Chemistry Routes to New Materials. (Materials Science Forum Ser.: Vols. 152 & 153). 422p. 1994. 183.00 (*0-87849-677-7*, Pub. by Trans T Pub) Enfield Pubs NH.
Rouxel, Jean. Crystal Chemistry & Properties of Materials with Quasi-One-Dimensional Structures. 1986. text 206.50 (*90-277-2057-6*) Kluwer Academic.
Rouxeville, Annie. Parlons Affaires. 160p. 1998. pap. 24.50 (*1-85075-388-1*, Pub. by Sheffield Acad) CUP Services.
Rouxeville, Annie, jt. auth. see Jubb, Margaret A.
Rouyer, Alwyn R. Turning Water into Politics. LC 99-31477. 2000. text 59.95 (*0-312-22611-X*) St Martin.
Rouzer, Paul F. Writing Another's Dream: The Poetry of Wen Tingyun. LC 92-33907. 276p. (C). 1993. 39.50 (*0-8047-2165-3*) Stanford U Pr.
Rouzic, Pierre Le, see Le Rouzic, Pierre.
Rouzier, Pierre & White, Tammy. The Sports Medicine Patient Advisor. (Illus.). 412p. 1999. pap. 59.95 (*0-9671831-0-3*) Sportsmed Pr.
Rov, A. B. & Trudinger, P. A. The Biochemistry of Inorganic Compounds of Sulphur. LC 78-79056. 414p. reprint ed. pap. 118.00 (*0-8357-7218-7*, 2025595) Bks Demand.
Rovainen, Carl M., ed. Neurobiology of Jawless Fishes: 7th Annual Karger Workshop, San Diego, November 1995. (Journal Ser.: Vol. 48, No. 5, 1996). (Illus.). 76p. 1996. pap. 45.25 (*3-8055-6404-X*) S Karger.
Rovan, B., ed. SOFSEM '98: Theory & Practice of Informatics: Proceedings of the 25th Seminar on Current Trends in Theory & Practice of Informatics, Jasn A, Slovakia, November 21-27, 1998. LC 98-48082. (Lecture Notes in Computer Science Ser.). xi, 453p. 1998. pap. 69.00 (*3-540-65260-4*) Spr-Verlag.
Rovan, B., et al, eds. Mathematical Foundations of Computer Science, 1990: Banska Bystrica, Czechoslovakia, August 27-31, 1990 Proceedings. (Lecture Notes in Computer Science Ser.). viii, 544p. 1990. 50.95 (*0-387-52953-5*) Spr-Verlag.
Rovane, Carol A. The Bounds of Agency: An Essay in Revisionary Metaphysics. LC 97-17514. 304p. 1998. text 37.50 (*0-691-01716-6*, Pub. by Princeton U Pr) Cal Prin Full Svc.
Rovang, Paul R. Refashioning "Knights & Ladies Gentle Deeds" The Intertextuality of Spenser's Faerie Queene & Malory's Morte d'Arthur. LC 95-16880. 160p. 1996. 32.50 (*0-8386-3598-9*) Fairleigh Dickinson.
Rovanpera, Brad. Walnut Creek: First One Hundred Fifty Years, a Pictorial History. Parks, Lori, ed. LC 99-73078. (Illus.). 150p. 1999. 39.95 (*1-886483-34-5*, Pub. by Heritge Media) Sunbelt Pubns.
Rovasio, Michael, jt. auth. see Stalcup, Jeff.
***Roveda, Gabriele & Garavini, Daniel.** The Goose. (Illus.). 150p. 1999. 12.95 (*3-8290-1464-3*, 520875) Konemann.
— Pigs & Pork. (Illus.). 183p. 1999. 12.95 (*3-8290-1463-5*, 520874) Konemann.
Roveda, Gabriele & Garavini, Daniel. The Squash. (Illus.). 143p. 1999. 12.95 (*3-8290-1462-7*, 520876) Konemann.
Rovee-Collier, Carolyn, et al, eds. Progress in Infancy Research. 264p. 2000. write for info. (*0-8058-3493-1*) L Erlbaum Assocs.
Rovee-Collier, Carolyn & Lipsitt, Lewis P., eds. Advances in Infancy Research, Vol. 5. 240p. 1988. text 78.50 (*0-89391-378-2*) Ablx Pub.
— Advances in Infancy Research, Vol. 6. 336p. (C). 1990. text 78.50 (*0-89391-512-2*) Ablx Pub.
Rovee-Collier, Carolyn & Lipsitt, Lewis P, eds. Advances in Infancy Research, Vol. 9. (Illus.). 424p. 1995. 78.50 (*1-56750-126-5*) Ablx Pub.
Rovee-Collier, Carolyn, jt. ed. see Lipsett, Lewis P.
Rovee-Collier, Carolyn, jt. ed. see Lipsitt, Lewis P.
***Rovee-Collier, Carolyn K., et al.** The Development of Implicit & Explicit Memory. LC 00-34218. (Advances in Consciousness Research Ser.). 2000. pap. write for info. (*1-55619-724-1*) J Benjamins Pubng Co.
Rovelli, Riccardo, jt. auth. see Angeloni, Ignazio.
Roven, Milton D. Non-Disabling Surgical Rehabilitation of the Forefoot. LC 76-176177. (Illus.). 416p. 1976. 32.50 (*0-87527-123-5*) Green.
Rovenal, Cynthia, ed. see Maye, Jennifer.
Rovenger, Holli & Bosshardt, Alexa. Today's Specials. 328p. 1991. pap. 14.95 (*0-9630382-0-6*) Nutrit Mktg.
Rovenskii, Vladimir. Foliations on Riemannian Manifolds: Synthetic Methods. LC 96-5737. 268p. 1997. 79.50 (*0-8176-3806-7*) Birkhauser.
— Foliations on Riemannian Manifolds & Submanifolds. LC 96-5737. 280p. 1997. write for info. (*3-7643-3806-7*) Birkhauser.
— Geometry of Curves & Surfaces with Maple. LC 99-12491. (Illus.). 320p. 2000. 49.95 (*0-8176-4074-6*, Pub. by Birkhauser) Spr-Verlag.
***Rovenskii, Vladimir Y.** Geometry of Curves & Surfaces with Maple. LC 99-12491. 1999. write for info. (*3-7643-4074-6*) Birkhauser.
Rover, Michelle. French for Business Studies. (ENG & FRE.). 1980. pap. 14.95 (*0-8288-1549-6*, M9207) Fr & Eur.
Rover, Red, jt. auth. see Lee, Butch.
Rovere-Fenati, Beatrice. Vocabulary Trainer: Italian. LC 97-72611. 56p. 1997. 8.95 incl. audio (*0-7641-7124-0*) Barron.
Rovere, Richard H. The American Establishment & Other Reports, Opinions, & Speculations. LC 80-22247. 308p. 1981. reprint ed. lib. bdg. 59.75 (*0-313-22646-6*, ROAE, Greenwood Pr) Greenwood.
— Senator Joe McCarthy. LC 95-40975. 288p. (C). 1996. pap. 14.95 (*0-520-20472-7*, Pub. by U CA Pr) Cal Prin Full Svc.
Rovere, Richard H. & Schlesinger, Arthur Meier, Jr. Final Reports: Personal Reflections on Politics & History in Our Time. LC 86-7735. (Wesleyan Paperback Ser.). 264p. reprint ed. pap. 81.90 (*0-7837-0220-5*, 204052800017) Bks Demand.
Rovere, Richard H., jt. auth. see Schlesinger, Arthur Meier, Jr.
Rovers, jt. auth. see McBean.
Rovers, John P., ed. A Practical Guide to Pharmaceutical Care. LC 98-8812. 242p. 1998. pap. 40.00 (*0-917330-90-0*) Am Pharm Assn.
Roversi, Paolo. Nudes. (Illus.). 144p. 1997. 45.00 (*3-931141-57-8*) Dist Art Pubs.
— Nudi. (Illus.). 128p. 1999. 49.95 (*3-88243-662-X*, Pub. by Steidl) Dist Art Pubs.
Roverso, I. S. The Birth of the Poet. 1985. pap. 3.50 (*0-913054-14-3*) Poet Gal Pr.
— The Musician. 1975. pap. 3.50 (*0-913054-08-9*) Poet Gal Pr.
— Plastics Are Fluid Again. 1971. pap. 3.50 (*0-913054-05-4*) Poet Gal Pr.
Roverts, John H. C. H. Graun & Lotti. (Handel Sources Ser.). 410p. 1987. text 30.00 (*0-8240-6479-8*) Garland.
— Narrative & Voice in Post-War Poetry. LC 98-37694. 11p. (C). 1999. pap. 33.53 (*0-582-23350-X*) Addison-Wesley.
Rovet, Joanne, jt. ed. see Hauser, Peter.
Rovetch, Lissa. Cora & the Elephants. (Illus.). (J). (ps-3). 1997. pap. 4.99 (*0-614-28893-2*, PuffinBks) Peng Put Young Read.
Rovetch, Lissa. Cora & the Elephants, 1. (J). 1997. 10.19 (*0-606-11221-9*, Pub. by Turtleback) Demco.
— Sweet Dreams, Little One. (J). 2001. mass mkt. 4.99 (*0-375-80624-5*, Pub. by Random Bks Yng Read) Random.
***Rovetch, Lissa & McNeill, Shannon.** Ook the Book. LC 00-8942. 2001. pap. write for info. (*0-8118-2660-0*) Chronicle Bks.
Rovetti, Paul F., intro. Dwight W. Tryon: A Retrospective Exhibition, 1971. (Illus.). 48p. 1971. 3.00 (*0-918386-05-5*) W Benton Mus.
***Rovick, Margaret.** A Child of the Troubles. 546p. 2000. pap. write for info. (*0-7541-0760-4*, Pub. by Minerva Pr) Unity Dist.
***Rovin.** Medicine Meets Business. 2000. boxed set 55.00 (*0-8342-1612-4*) Aspen Pub.
Rovin, Jeff. Adventure Heroes: Legendary Characters from Odysseus to James Bond. LC 93-46603. 320p. 1994. 35.00 (*0-8160-2881-8*) Facts on File.
— Adventure Heroes: Legendary Characters from Odysseus to James Bond. (Illus.). 320p. 1995. pap. 19.95 (*0-8160-2886-9*) Facts on File.
— Aliens, Robots, & Spaceships. LC 94-24273. (Illus.). 384p. (YA). (gr. 5 up). 1995. 35.00 (*0-8160-3107-X*) Facts on File.
— Aliens, Robots, & Spaceships. LC 94-24273. (Illus.). 352p. 1996. pap. 21.95 (*0-8160-3113-4*) Facts on File.
— The Book of Dumb Movie Blurbs. 96p. (Orig.). 1995. pap. 8.00 (*0-425-14616-2*) Berkley Pub.
— Broken Arrow. 272p. (Orig.). 1996. mass mkt. 5.99 (*1-57297-085-5*) Blvd Books.
— Dino-Mite Dinosaur Jokes. Ashby, Ruth, ed. (Illus.). 96p. (J). 1994. pap. 2.99 (*0-671-88258-9*, Minstrel Bks) PB.
Rovin, Jeff. Dino-Mite Dinosaur Jokes. 1994. 8.09 (*0-606-06322-6*, Pub. by Turtleback) Demco.
Rovin, Jeff. Encyclopedia of Monsters. (Illus.). 400p. 1989. 35.00 (*0-8160-1824-3*) Facts on File.
— The Encyclopedia of Monsters. (Illus.). 400p. 1990. pap. 19.95 (*0-8160-2303-4*) Facts on File.
***Rovin, Jeff.** Fatalis. LC 00-25474. 384p. 2000. text 25.95 (*0-312-24103-8*) St Martin.
Rovin, Jeff. Five Hundred Hilarious Jokes for Kids. 144p. (Orig.). (J). 1990. mass mkt. 4.99 (*0-451-16549-7*, Sig) NAL.
— 500 Hilarious Jokes for Kids. (J). 1990. 10.09 (*0-606-03285-1*, Pub. by Turtleback) Demco.
— The Game. 1997. mass mkt. 5.99 (*1-57297-328-5*) Blvd Books.
— Gamemaster. 1994. pap. 59.88 (*0-312-95456-5*); pap. 59.88 (*0-312-95488-3*) St Martin.
— Gamemaster: Computer Video Game Guide. 1995. pap. 59.90 (*0-312-95523-5*) St Martin.
— Gamemaster Vol. 1: Conquering Super Nintendo Games. 1994. mass mkt. 4.99 (*0-312-95437-9*) St Martin.
— GameMaster Complete Video Game Guide 1995. 1995. mass mkt. 5.99 (*0-312-95439-5*) St Martin.
— Gamemasters Vol. 1: Conquering Sega Genesis Games. 1994. mass mkt. 4.99 (*0-312-95438-7*) St Martin.
— How to Win at Nintendo Games, 3 vols., Set. 1991. pap. write for info. (*0-312-92696-0*); pap. 11.89 (*0-312-92697-9*) St Martin.
— In Search of Trivia. 1984. mass mkt. 6.99 (*0-451-16250-1*) NAL.
— Mortal Kombat. (Orig.). 1995. mass mkt. 4.99 (*1-57297-059-6*) Blvd Books.

R

— One Thousand & One Great Jokes. 1989. mass mkt. 5.99 (0-451-15979-9, Sig) NAL.

— 1001 Great Jokes. 1987. mass mkt. 5.99 (0-451-16829-1) NAL.

— A Pictorial History of Science Fiction Films. (Illus.). 1976. pap. 12.95 (0-8065-0537-0, Citadel Pr) Carol Pub Group.

— Return of the Wolfman. 352p. 1998. pap. 6.99 (0-425-16576-0) Blvd Books.

— The Second Good News - Bad News Joke Book. 1999. pap. 3.99 (0-451-17760-6, Sig) NAL.

***Rovin, Jeff.** Stealth War: A Novel of America's Stealth Warriors. 2000. mass mkt. 6.99 (0-515-12724-8, Jove) Berkley Pub.

Rovin, Jeff. Vespers. LC 98-19398. 320p. 1998. text 23.95 (0-312-19351-3) St Martin.

— Vespers. 304p. 1999. mass mkt. 6.99 (0-312-96993-7) St Martin.

***Rovin, Jeff.** Vespers Floor Display: Say Your Prayers. 1999. mass mkt. 223.68 (0-312-97196-6) St Martin.

Rovin, Jeff & Tracy, Kathy. The Essential Jackie Chan Source Book. LC 97-18378. 1997. per. 16.00 (0-671-00843-9) PB.

Rovin, Jeff, jt. auth. see West, Adam.

Rovine, Arthur W., et al. U. S. Treaties . . . Digests . . . Digest of United States Practice in International Law, 10 vols., Set. xxi, 618p. 1990. reprint ed. 995.00 (1-57588-372-4, 201250) W S Hein.

Rovine, Arthur W., jt. ed. see Hanessian, Grant.

Rovine, Harven. Silence in Shakespeare: Drama, Power, & Gender. 112p. 1987. pap. 59.98 (0-7734-1998-5) E Mellen.

Rovine, Michael J. & Von Eye, Alexander. Applied Computational Statistics Longitudinal Research. 237p. (C). 1991. pap. text 53.00 (0-12-599450-8) Acad Pr.

***Rovine, Victoria.** Renewing Tradition: The Revitalization of Bogolanin Mali & Abroad. (Illus.). 14p. 2000. pap. 5.00 (0-87414-121-4) U IA Pubns Dept.

Rovinski & Zastocki. Home Care: A Technical Manual for the Professional. 1989. pap. text 47.00 (0-7216-2449-9, W B Saunders Co) Harcrt Hlth Sci Grp.

Rovinski, jt. auth. see Zastocki.

Rovinski, Yanina, jt. ed. see Barzetti, Valerie.

Rovinson, Solon. Facts for Farmers. (Notable American Authors Ser.). 1999. reprint ed. lib. bdg. 125.00 (0-7812-8805-3) Rprt Serv.

— Guano: A Treatise of Practical Information for Farmers. (Notable American Authors Ser.). 1999. reprint ed. lib. bdg. 125.00 (0-7812-8803-7) Rprt Serv.

— Hot Corn-Life Scenes in New York. (Notable American Authors Ser.). 1999. reprint ed. lib. bdg. 125.00 (0-7812-8804-5) Rprt Serv.

— How to Live: Saving & Wasting: or Domestic Economy Illustrated by the Life of Two Families of Opposite Character (Novel) (Notable American Authors Ser.). 1999. reprint ed. lib. bdg. 125.00 (0-7812-8807-X) Rprt Serv.

— Me-won-i-toc: A Tale of Frontier Life & Indian Character. (Notable American Authors Ser.). 1999. reprint ed. lib. bdg. 125.00 (0-7812-8806-1) Rprt Serv.

— Selected Writings. (Notable American Authors Ser.). 1999. reprint ed. lib. bdg. 125.00 (0-7812-8808-8) Rprt Serv.

— The Will: A Tale of the Lake of the Red Cedars & Sabbona. (Notable American Authors Ser.). 1999. reprint ed. lib. bdg. 125.00 (0-7812-8802-9) Rprt Serv.

Rovinson, W. Heath. Aladdin & Other Tales from the Arabian Nights. LC 93-55071. (Everyman's Library of Children's Classics). (J). 1993. 12.95 (0-679-42533-0) Knopf.

Rovira, Albert. Wax Crayon. (I Draw, I Paint Ser.). (Illus.). 48p. (J). (gr. 3 up). 1991. pap. 7.95 (0-8120-4718-4) Barron.

Rovira, Catherine. Semblanza y Circunstancia de Manuel Gonzalez Prada. LC 93-72951. (SPA.). 142p. (Orig.). 1993. pap. 19.00 (0-89729-704-0) Ediciones.

Rovira de Jesus, Armando. El Nino Excepcional. (SPA.). 342p. 1991. pap. write for info. (0-929441-16-8) Pubns Puertorriquenas.

Rovira, Jose C., ed. see Hernandez, Miguel.

Rovirosa, Dolores. Jorge Manach: Bibliografia. (Bibliography & Reference Ser.: No. 13). 261p. (Orig.). 1985. pap. 15.00 (0-917617-04-5) SALALM.

Rovit, Earl H. Saul Bellow. LC 67-26665. (University of Minnesota Pamphlets on American Writers Ser.: No. 65). 46p. reprint ed. pap. 30.00 (0-608-14133-X, 205593400039) Bks Demand.

Rovit, Earl H., jt. auth. see Brenner, Gerry.

***Rovit, Rebecca & Goldfarb, Alvin, eds.** Theatrical Performance During the Holocaust: Texts, Documents, Memoirs. LC 99-29416. (PAJ Bks). 312p. 1999. 39.95 (0-8018-6167-5) Johns Hopkins.

Rovit, Richard L., et al. Trigeminal Neuralgia. (Illus.). 218p. 1990. 85.00 (0-683-07393-1) Lppncott W & W.

***Rovithakis, George A. & Christodoulou, Manoulis A.** Adaptive Control with Recurrent High-Order Neural Networks: Theory & Industrial Applications. LC 99-47344. (Advances in Industrial Control Ser.). (Illus.). 200p. 2000. 79.00 (1-85233-623-4, Pub. by Spr-Verlag) Spr-Verlag.

Rovner, Irwin & Lewenstein, Suzanne H. Maya Stone Tools of Dzibilchaltun, Yucatan, & Becau & Chicanna, Campedie. LC 97-19488. (Publication Ser.: No. 65). 1997. write for info. (0-939238-95-0) Tulane MARI.

Rovner, Jerome S., jt. ed. see Witt, Peter N.

***Rovner, Julie.** Health Care Policy & Politics A to Z. LC 99-40972. (Ready Reference Encyclopedia of American Government Ser.). 244p. 1999. 55.00 (1-56802-437-1) CQ Pr.

Rovner, Mark J. Defense Dollars & Sense: A Common Cause Guide to the Defense Budget Process. (Illus.). 96p. (Orig.). 1983. pap. 4.50 (0-914389-00-9) Common Cause.

Rovner, Uri A. You Can Teach Yourself Blues Piano. (You Can Teach Yourself Ser.). 96p. 1995. pap. 9.95 (0-7866-0232-5, MB95280) Mel Bay.

— You Can Teach Yourself Jazz Piano. 120p. 1998. pap. 9.95 (0-7866-3229-1, 96876) Mel Bay.

— You Can Teach Yourself Jazz Piano. 120p. 1999. pap. 24.95 incl. audio compact disk (0-7866-3231-3, 96876) Mel Bay.

Rovner, Uri Ayn. You Can Teach Yourself Blues Piano. 96p. 1995. pap. 18.95 incl. audio (0-7866-1254-1, 95280P); pap. 24.95 incl. audio compact disk (0-7866-1253-3, 95280CDP) Mel Bay.

Rovnyak, James, jt. auth. see Rosenblum, Marvin.

Row, A. T., jt. ed. see Alter, Judy.

Row, A. Tracy, ed. Frontier Tucson: Hispanic Contributions. (Illus.). 85p. 1987. reprint ed. pap. 9.95 (0-910037-22-1) AZ Hist Soc.

Row, B. Suryarain. History of Vijayanagar: The Never to Be Forgotten Empire. (C). 1993. reprint ed. 27.50 (81-206-0860-7, Pub. by Asian Educ Servs) S Asia.

Row, Ernest F., tr. see Gide, Charles.

Row, H. J., ed. see Anderson, George B.

Row, John & Row, William. Historie of the Kirk of Scotland, 2 vols. LC 70-174969. (Maitland Club, Glasgow. Publications: No. 55). reprint ed. 115.00 (0-404-53039-7) AMS Pr.

Row, Matthew, jt. auth. see Cannon, Ariel.

Row, Richard D., ed. Standard Vocal Repertoire Bk. 2: For High Voice. (Illus.). 80p. 1963. pap. 10.50 (0-8258-0253-9, RB-71) Fischer Inc NY.

Row, Sanjiva. Negotiable Instruments Acts. (C). 1988. 150.00 (0-7855-3546-2) St Mut.

Row, T. Subba. Consciousness & Immortality. (Sangam Texts Ser.). 96p. (Orig.). 1983. pap. 12.75 (0-88695-012-0) Concord Grove.

— Notes on the Bhagavad-Gita. LC 77-88628. 182p. 1978. reprint ed. 15.95 (0-911500-81-2); reprint ed. pap. 10.95 (0-911500-82-0) Theos U Pr.

Row, T. Sundara. Geometric Exercises in Paper Folding. (Illus.). 148p. 1966. pap. 4.95 (0-486-21594-6) Dover.

Row, William, jt. auth. see Row, John.

Rowallan, Lord. Rowallan. (Illus.). 1977. 24.95 (0-8464-0802-3) Beekman Pubs.

Rowan, A. James. Seizures & Epilepsy in the Elderly. LC 96-28927. 343p. 1996. text 99.00 (0-7506-9622-2) Buttrwrth-Heinemann.

Rowan, A. James, jt. auth. see Schachter, Steven C.

Rowan, A. James, jt. ed. see Gates, John R.

Rowan, Alex A. A Stitch in Time. LC 96-19097. 55p. (Orig.). 1996. pap. 5.00 (0-88734-361-9) Players Pr.

Rowan, Alistair. North Leinster. (Illus.). 544p. text 65.00 (0-14-071085-X, Pub. by Pnguin Bks Ltd) Trafalgar.

Rowan, Alistair, jt. ed. see Gow, Ian.

Rowan, Andrew N. Of Mice, Models, & Men: A Critical Evaluation of Animal Research. LC 83-4986. 323p. 1984. text 21.50 (0-87395-776-8) State U NY Pr.

Rowan, Andrew N., ed. Animals & People Sharing the World. LC 88-40114. (Illus.). 206p. reprint ed. pap. 63.90 (0-608-09095-6, 206972900005) Bks Demand.

Rowan, Archibald Hamilton. The Autobiography of Archibald Hamilton Rowan. LC 73-166125. xvi, 475p. 1972. write for info. (0-7165-0011-6) Irish Acad Pr.

Rowan, Bonnie G. & Wood, Cynthia. Scholars' Guide to Washington, D. C., for Media Collections. (Woodrow Wilson Center Press Ser.). (Illus.). 208p. (C). 1994. pap. text 19.95 (0-943875-55-2) Johns Hopkins.

— Scholars' Guide to Washington, D.C., for Media Collections. (Woodrow Wilson Center Press Ser.). 208p. (C). 1994. text 45.00 (0-943875-54-4) Johns Hopkins.

Rowan, Brian. Behind the Lines: The Story of the IRA & Loyalist Ceasefires. LC 95-229078. 224p. 1996. pap. 19.95 (0-85640-564-7, Pub. by Blackstaff Pr) Dufour.

Rowan, Carl T. South of Freedom. LC 97-7075. 270p. 1997. pap. 14.95 (0-8071-2170-3) La State U Pr.

Rowan, Chris, jt. auth. see Leininger, Laura.

Rowan, David. Glossary of the 90s: A Cultural Primer. 224p. 1998. pap. 18.95 (1-85375-282-7) Prion.

— Jack-Up Based Extended Well Test System. 1989. 125.00 (90-6314-522-5, Pub. by Lorne & MacLean Marine) St Mut.

— Jack-Up Based Extended Well Test System. (C). 1989. 95.00 (0-89771-725-2, Pub. by Lorne & MacLean Marine) St Mut.

***Rowan, Edward L.** The Joy of Self-Pleasuring: Why Feel Guilty about Feeling Good? 205p. 2000. pap. 16.95 (1-57392-795-3) Prometheus Bks.

Rowan, Eric. Art in Wales, AD1850-1980: An Illustrated History. (Illus.). 194p. 1997. pap. 25.00 (0-7083-1408-2, Pub. by Univ Wales Pr) Paul & Co Pubs.

Rowan, Eric & Wallace, David, compiled by. The Really Wild Guide to Britain: A Guide to Wildlife Activities for Children over 200 Sites Included. (Illus.). 289p. 1995. pap. 12.95 (0-563-36788-1, BBC-Parkwest) Parkwest Pubns.

Rowan, Hester. The Linden Tree. large type ed. 320p. 1985. 27.99 (0-7089-1331-8) Ulverscroft.

— Overture in Venice. large type ed. 320p. 1985. 27.99 (0-7089-1353-9) Ulverscroft.

— Snowfall. large type ed. 352p. 1985. 27.99 (0-7089-1395-4) Ulverscroft.

Rowan, J. O. Physics & the Circulation. fac. ed. LC 81-12790. (Medical Physics Handbks.: No. 9). (Illus.). 132p. 1981. reprint ed. pap. 41.00 (0-7837-7999-2, 204775500008) Bks Demand.

Rowan, James P. Ants. (Insects Discovery Library). 24p. (J). (gr. k-4). 1991. lib. bdg. 10.95 (0-86593-289-1) Rourke Corp.

— Butterflies & Moths. LC 83-7216. (New True Books Ser.). (Illus.). 48p. (J). (gr. k-4). 1983. pap. 5.50 (0-516-41692-8) Childrens.

— Dragonflies. (Insects Discovery Library). 24p. (J). (gr. k-4). 1991. lib. bdg. 10.95 (0-86593-287-5) Rourke Corp.

— Grasshoppers. LC 93-7586. (Insects Discovery Library). 24p. (J). (gr. k-4). 1993. lib. bdg. 10.95 (0-86593-286-7) Rourke Corp.

— Honeybees. (Insects Discovery Library). 24p. (J). (gr. k-4). 1991. lib. bdg. 10.95 (0-86593-290-5) Rourke Corp.

— Ladybugs. (Insects Discovery Library). 24p. (J). (gr. k-4). 1991. lib. bdg. 10.95 (0-86593-291-3) Rourke Corp.

Rowan, Jim. Call Center Continuity Management 1999. LC 99-186622. 444p. 1998. ring bd. 295.00 (0-8493-9982-3) CRC Pr.

Rowan, John. Breakthroughs & Integragation. 244p. 1992. 49.95 (1-56593-579-9, 0310) Singular Publishing.

— Discovering Your Subpersonalities: Our Inner World & the People in It. LC 93-14812. (Illus.). 192p. (C). 1993. pap. 22.99 (0-415-07366-9, A7634) Routledge.

— Healing the Male Psyche: Therapy As Initiation. LC 96-337. 296p. (C). 1997. 85.00 (0-415-10048-8); pap. 25.99 (0-415-10049-6) Routledge.

— Horned God: Feminism & Men As Wounding & Healing. 1987. pap. 13.95 (0-7102-0674-7, Routledge Thoemms) Routledge.

— The Plural Self: Multiplicity in Everyday Life LC 98-61585. 278 p. 1999. write for info. (0-7619-6076-7) Sage.

— The Reality Game: A Guide to Humanistic Counselling & Therapy. 2nd rev. ed. LC 97-46440. 256p. (C). 1998. 80.00 (0-415-16433-8); pap. 24.99 (0-415-16434-6) Routledge.

— Subpersonalities: The People Inside Us. 256p. (C). 1990. pap. 24.99 (0-415-04329-8) Routledge.

— The Transpersonal: Psychotherapy & Counselling. LC 92-15268. (Illus.). 304p. (C). (gr. 13). 1993. pap. 25.99 (0-415-05362-5, A7787) Routledge.

Rowan, John, jt. auth. see Holland, Carol.

Rowan, John, jt. ed. see Reason, Peter.

Rowan, John P., tr. see Aquinas, Thomas, Saint.

Rowan, John R. Conflicts of Rights: Moral Theory & Social Policy Implications. LC 99-21203. 240p. 1999. 62.00 (0-8133-9122-9, Pub. by Westview) HarpC.

Rowan, June H., jt. auth. see Rowan, Peter.

Rowan, Kate. I Know How My Cells Make Me Grow. LC 98-45215. (Sam's Science Ser.). (Illus.). 32p. (J). (ps-3). 1999. 9.99 (0-7636-0502-6, Pub. by Candlewick Pr) Penguin Putnam.

— Sam's Science: I Know How We Fight Germs. LC 98-19626. (Illus.). 32p. (J). (gr. k-2). 1999. 9.99 (0-7636-0503-4) Candlewick Pr.

***Rowan, Kate & McEwen, Katharine.** I Know Why I Brush My Teeth. LC 93-30291. (Sam's Science Ser.). (Illus.). 32p. (J). (gr. k-2). 1999. 9.99 (0-7636-0504-2, Pub. by Candlewick Pr) Penguin Putnam.

Rowan-Kedge, jt. auth. see Rawson.

Rowan, Leonie, et al. Shifting Borders. 1996. pap. 66.00 (0-949823-63-5, Pub. by Deakin Univ) St Mut.

Rowan, N. R. Women in the Marines: The Book Camp Challenge. LC 93-9706. (Illus.). (YA). (gr. 5 up). 1993. lib. bdg. 23.93 (0-8225-1430-3, Lerner Publctns) Lerner Pub.

Rowan, Paula S. Remember This. LC 99-162448. (World Tree Ser.). (Illus.). (J). (gr. 2-5). 1998. 18.95 (0-9654682-5-9) Savannah Coll.

Rowan, Pete. Big Head! A Book about Your Brain & Head. LC 97-39009. (Illus.). 44p. (J). (gr. 5-9). 1998. 20.00 (0-679-89018-1, Pub. by Random Bks Yng Read) Random.

Rowan, Peter & Rowan, June H. Mountain Summers: Tales of Hiking & Exploration in the White Mountains from 1878 to 1886 As Seen Through the Eyes of Women. (Illus.). 273p. 1995. pap. 16.95 (0-9648801-0-5) Gulfside Pr.

Rowan, Richard L., ed. Collective Bargaining: Survival in the '70's? Proceedings of a Conference. LC 75-189564. (Labor Relations & Public Policy Ser.: No. 5). 499p. reprint ed. pap. 154.70 (0-8357-3150-2, 203941300012) Bks Demand.

Rowan, Richard L. & Barr, Robert E. Employee Relations Trends & Practices in the Textile Industry. LC 86-82726. (Major Industrial Research Unit Studies: No. 65). (Illus.). 142p. 1987. reprint ed. pap. 44.10 (0-608-04370-2, 206515100001) Bks Demand.

Rowan, Richard L. & Northrup, Herbert R. Educating the Employed Disadvantaged for Upgrading: A Report on Remedial Education Programs in the Paper Industry. LC 76-184335. (Manpower & Human Resources Studies: No. 2). 184p. reprint ed. pap. 57.10 (0-8357-3157-X, 203942000012) Bks Demand.

Rowan, Richard L. & O'Brien, Rae A. Multinational Union Organizations in the Manufacturing Industries. LC 80-53989. (Multinational Industrial Relations Ser.: No. 7). (Illus.). 232p. (Orig.). 1980. reprint ed. pap. 72.00 (0-608-04368-0, 206514900001) Bks Demand.

Rowan, Richard L., et al. Multinational Union Organizations in the White-Collar, Service, & Communications Industries. LC 83-48900. (Multinational Industrial Relations Ser.: No. 7). (Illus.). 506p. 1983. reprint ed. pap. 156.90 (0-608-04369-9, 206515000001) Bks Demand.

Rowan, Richard L., jt. auth. see Campbell, Duncan C.

Rowan, Richard L., jt. auth. see Northrup, Herbert R.

Rowan, Richard L., jt. auth. see Perry, Charles R.

Rowan, Richard L., jt. ed. see Northrup, Herbert R.

***Rowan, Robert.** Control High Blood Pressure Without Drugs: A Complete Hypertension Handbook. 2001. pap. 12.00 (0-684-87328-1, Fireside) S&S Trade Pap.

Rowan, Robert L. How to Control High Blood Pressure Without Drugs. 320p. 1987. mass mkt. 5.99 (0-8041-0144-2) Ivy Books.

— Men & Their Sex. LC 80-25539. (Illus.). 168p. 1982. pap. 12.95 (0-8290-0446-7) Irvington.

Rowan, Robin H. & Perry, Clark. The Insiders' Guide to Florida's Great Northwest. 2nd ed. LC 97-210392. (Insiders' Guide Travel Ser.). (Illus.). 451p. 1995. pap. 14.95 (0-912367-70-9, The Insiders Guide) Falcon Pub Inc.

Rowan-Robinson, Jeremy, jt. auth. see Brand, Clive.

Rowan-Robinson, M. Fire-Ice: Nuclear Winter. 1985. pap. text. write for info. (0-582-44698-8, Pub. by Addison-Wesley) Longman.

Rowan-Robinson, Michael. Cosmology. 3rd ed. (Illus.). 184p. 1996. pap. text 32.00 (0-19-851884-6) OUP.

— Cosmology. 3rd ed. (Illus.). 184p. (C). 1996. text 65.00 (0-19-851885-4) OUP.

***Rowan-Robinson, Michael.** The Nine Numbers of the Cosmos. LC 99-42817. (Illus.). 192p. 1999. 24.95 (0-19-850444-6) OUP.

Rowan-Robinson, Michael. Ripples in the Cosmos: A View Behind the Scenes of the New Cosmology. LC 93-1590. (Illus.). 232p. 1998. reprint ed. 23.00 (0-7167-4503-8) OUP.

***Rowan, Ronald R.** Attua the Aleut. LC 99-91323. 1999. 25.00 (0-7388-0746-X); pap. 18.00 (0-7388-0747-8) Xlibris Corp.

— Will Power: A Novel. LC 99-91579. 1999. 25.00 (0-7388-0902-0); pap. 18.00 (0-7388-0903-9) Xlibris Corp.

Rowan, Roy. Connections, Vol. 1. 1989. 18.95 (0-316-75976-7) Little.

***Rowan, Roy.** Surfcaster's Quest: Seeking Stripers, Blues & Solitude at the Edge of the Surging Sea. LC 99-32030. 160p. 1999. 22.95 (1-55821-981-1) Lyons Pr.

Rowan, Roy & Janis, Brooke. First Dogs: American Presidents & Their Best Friends. LC 97-6172. (Illus.). 160p. 1997. 17.95 (1-56512-143-0, 72143) Algonquin Bks.

Rowan, Steve, ed. & tr. see Boernstein, Henry.

Rowan, Steven, ed. see Boernstein, Henry.

Rowan, Steven, ed. see Goetz, Hans-Werner.

Rowan, Steven, tr. see Boernstein, Henry.

Rowan, Steven, tr. see Grundmann, Herbert.

Rowan, Steven, tr. see Kaufmann, Wilhelm.

Rowan, Steven, tr. see Klauprecht, Emil.

Rowan, Steven W. & Western Reserve Historical Society Staff. Cleveland & Its Germans. LC 97-52732. (Werner D. Mueller Reprint Ser.). 1998. write for info. (0-911704-49-3) Western Res Pr.

Rowan, Steven W., tr. see Western Reserve Historical Society Staff.

Rowan, Thomas E. & Bourne, Barbara. Thinking Like Mathematicians: Putting the K-4 NCTM Standards into Practice. LC 93-43901. 134p. (YA). (gr. k). 1994. pap. text 19.00 (0-435-08343-0, 08343) Heinemann.

Rowan, Thomas E. & Morrow, Lorna J., eds. Implementing the K-8 Curriculum & Evaluation Standards: Readings from the "Arithmetic Teacher" LC 92-30628. (Illus.). 105p. 1992. pap. 11.95 (0-87353-351-8) NCTM.

Rowan, Tim & O'Hanlon, Bill. Solution-Oriented Therapy for Chronic & Severe Mental Illness. LC 98-14865. 177p. 1998. 47.50 (0-471-18362-8) Wiley.

Rowan, Victoria. Eat New York. pap. 15.00 (1-84166-035-3, Pub. by Ellipsis) Norton.

— Shop New York. pap. 15.00 (1-84166-033-7, Pub. by Ellipsis) Norton.

Rowan, Walter, jt. auth. see King, L. R.

***Rowan, William.** Incident at Roan High Bluff. LC 00-191097. 268p. 2000. pap. 14.50 (0-9662860-2-2) Cenografix.

Rowan, William. On the Spring Tide: A Special Kind of Courage. LC 98-72212. x, 201p. 1998. pap. 12.95 (0-9662860-4-9) Cenografix.

— Tales from Towhee Inn. LC 98-96952. (Illus.). 179p. 1999. pap. 18.50 (0-9662860-5-7) Cenografix.

— Together Met, Together Bound: Hymn Settings by William Rowan. 80p. 1994. pap. 9.95 (0-9622553-5-1, 125-030) Selah Pub Co.

Rowan, William L., ed. Atomic Processes in Plasmas. (AIP Conference Proceedings Ser.: No. 322). 224p. 1995. text 95.00 (1-56396-411-2) Am Inst Physics.

***Rowan, Wingham.** Net Benefit: Guaranteed Electronic Markets: The Ultimate Potential of Online Trade. 1999. text 35.00 (0-312-22291-2) St Martin.

Rowand, David. Pictorial History of Paisley. 1980. pap. 40.00 (0-907526-55-1, Pub. by Alloway Publ) St Mut.

Rowand, E. C., Jr. We Know the Words: We Need Lives That Match. 224p. 1998. pap. text 15.00 (0-9644609-5-5) Srchlight Pr.

***Rowand, Phyllis.** Is It Night. 32p. (J). (ps-2). 2001. 14.95 (0-06-027916-8) HarpC Child Bks.

Rowat, Donald C. The Ombudsman Plan: The Worldwide Spread of an Idea. rev. ed. 208p. (Orig.). (C). 1986. pap. text 22.00 (0-8191-5040-1) U Pr of Amer.

— Public Administration in Developed Democracies: A Comparative Study. (Public Administration & Public Policy Ser.: Vol. 32). (Illus.). 528p. 1987. text 145.00 (0-8247-7807-3) Dekker.

Rowat, Donald C., ed. International Handbook on Local Government Reorganization: Contemporary Developments. LC 79-54063. (Illus.). 626p. 1980. lib. bdg. 105.00 (0-313-21269-4, RHL/, Greenwood Pr) Greenwood.

— The Ombudsman: Citizen's Defender. LC K 3416.R. 401p. reprint ed. pap. 124.40 (0-608-12869-4, 202366400033) Bks Demand.

An Asterisk (*) at the beginning of an entry indicates that the title is appearing for the first time.

R

*Rowat, Malcolm & Astigarraga, Jose. Latin American Insolvency Systems: A Comparative Assessment. LC 98-48419. 103p. 1999. pap. 22.00 (0-8213-4399-8) World Bank.

Rowat, Malcolm, et al. Competition Policy & MERCOSUR. (Technical Paper Ser.: No. 385). 130p. 1997. pap. 22.00 (0-8213-4055-7, 14055) World Bank.

— Judicial Reform in Latin America & the Caribbean. LC 95-6392. (World Bank Technical Papers: No. 280). 256p. 1995. pap. 22.00 (0-8213-3206-6, 13206) World Bank.

*Rowbotham. Chronic Pain. 2000. 14.95 (1-85317-878-0, Pub. by Martin Dunitz) Blackwell Sci.

Rowbotham, D., jt. auth. see Nimmo, Walter S.

Rowbotham, David. The Ebony Gates: New & Wayside Poems. LC 97-166330. xii, 79p. 1996. pap. 12.95 (1-875998-05-5, Pub. by Central Queensland) Accents Pubns.

Rowbotham, John F. Troubadours & Courts of Love. 352p. 1998. reprint ed. pap. 24.95 (0-7661-0432-X) Kessinger Pub.

*Rowbotham, Michael. Goodbye America! Globalization, Debt & the Dollar Empire. 224p. 2000. pap. 22.50 (1-897766-56-4, Pub. by Jon Carpenter) Paul & Co Pubs.

Rowbotham, Michael. The Grip Death: A Study of Modern Money, Debt Slavery & Destructive Economics. LC 98-203034. 336p. 1998. pap. 29.95 (1-897766-40-8, Pub. by Jon Carpenter) Paul & Co Pubs.

Rowbotham, Sheila. A Century of Women: The History of Women in Britain & the United States. 752p. 1997. 34.95 (0-670-87420-5) Viking Penguin.

— Century of Women: The History of Women in Britain & the United States. 1999. pap. 16.95 (0-14-023282-6) Viking Penguin.

— A Century of Women: The History of Women in Britain & the United States in the Twentieth Century. LC 98-36626. 1999. pap. 16.95 (0-14-027902-4) Viking Penguin.

— Friends of Alice Wheeldon. (New Feminist Library). 256p. (C). 1988. 26.00 (0-85345-729-8, Pub. by Monthly Rev); pap. 12.00 (0-85345-728-X, Pub. by Monthly Rev) NYU Pr.

Rowbotham, Sheila. Hidden from History. 182p. 1992. 49.95 (0-902818-29-5, Pub. by Pluto GBR) Stylus Pub VA.

Rowbotham, Sheila. Hidden from History: 300 Years of Women's Oppression & the Fight Against It. 182p. (C). pap. 16.95 (0-904383-56-3, Pub. by Pluto GBR) Stylus Pub VA.

— Hidden from History: 300 Years of Women's Oppression & the Fight Against It. 182p. 1996. 49.95 (0-7453-1166-0, Pub. by Pluto GBR) Stylus Pub VA.

*Rowbotham, Sheila. Hidden from History: 300 Years of Women's Oppression & the Fight Against It. 3rd ed. 182p. 1999. reprint ed. pap. text 17.00 (0-7881-6754-5) DIANE Pub.

Rowbotham, Sheila. Threads Through Time: Writings on History & Autobiography. LC 99-216757. 488p. 1999. pap. 13.95 (0-14-027554-1) Viking Penguin.

— Women in Movement: Feminism & Social Action. LC 92-12239. (Revolutionary Thought & Radical Movements Ser.). 390p. (C). 1992. pap. 19.99 (0-415-90652-0, A7619) Routledge.

Rowbotham, Sheila & Mitter Swasti, eds. Dignity & Daily Bread: New Forms of Economic Organising among Poor Women in the Third World & the First. LC 93-7363. 256p. (C). 1993. pap. 27.99 (0-415-09586-7, B2209) Routledge.

Rowbotham, Sheila, jt. ed. see Mitter Swasti.

Rowbotham, Shelia. Hidden from History: 300 Years of Women's Oppression & the Fight Against It. 182p. 1996. pap. text 16.95 (0-7453-1165-2, Pub. by Pluto GBR) Stylus Pub VA.

*Rowbottom, Derek. Miniature Dolls' Houses in 1/24th Scale: A Complete Guide to Making & Furnishing Houses. (Illus.). 2000. 29.95 (0-7153-0836-X) D & C Pub.

Rowbottom, Frederick, jt. auth. see Chapman, Johnathan.

Rowbottom, Ralph & Billis, David. Organisational Design: The Work Levels Approach. 1987. text 78.95 (0-566-05408-6, Pub. by Avebry) Ashgate Pub Co.

Rowden, Geoffrey, jt. auth. see Lewis, Martin G.

Rowden, Thomas, tr. see Lawson, Myldred.

Rowder, Luanne. Glass Heartstrings. 201p. 1997. mass mkt. 5.99 (1-55197-560-2) Partners Pubs Grp.

Rowdon, Maurice. The Spanish Terror: Spanish Imperialism in the Sixteenth Century LC 74-196578. 335 p. 1974. 3.95 (0-09-458070-7) Trafalgar.

— The Spanish Terror: Spanish Imperialism in the Sixteenth Century. LC 74-196578. 343p. reprint ed. pap. 106.40 (0-608-13603-4, 205126500093) Bks Demand.

Rowe. Barrier Systems for Waste Disposal Facilities. 2nd ed. 1997. pap. write for info. (0-419-22640-0) Thomson Learn.

— Barrier Systems for Waste Disposal Facilities. 2nd ed. 1998. pap. write for info. (0-419-22630-3) Thomson Learn.

Rowe. Essential Welder: Flux Core. (Welding Ser.). (C). 2000. pap. 19.95 (0-8273-7604-9); pap., lab manual ed. 13.95 (0-8273-7605-7) Delmar.

— Essential Welder: Gas Metal Arc Welding Classroom. LC 98-29584. (Welding Ser.). (C). 2000. pap. 19.95 (0-8273-7608-1) Delmar.

— Essential Welder: Gas Metal Arc Welding Laboratory. (Welding Ser.). (C). 2000. pap. 13.95 (0-8273-7609-X) Delmar.

— Essential Welder: Phase 1. (C). 1998. text 25.00 (0-8273-7607-3) Delmar.

— Giant Dinosaurs. 32p. (J). (ps-2). 1989. pap. 19.95 (0-590-73275-7) Scholastic Inc.

— Handbook of Pediatric Surgery. 1998. pap. text. write for info. (0-316-75989-9) Lppncott W & W.

— Iris Murdoch Revisited. 1998. 22.95 (0-8057-4620-X, Twyne) Mac Lib Ref.

— Philosophy of Religion. 3rd ed. LC 97-71995. (C). 1997. pap. text 47.50 (0-15-503687-4, Pub. by Harcourt Coll Pubs) Harcourt.

— Philosophy of Religion: An Introduction. 3rd ed. 2000. pap. text 26.50 (0-534-57425-4) Thomson Learn.

— Vascular Access Surgery. (C). 1999. pap. text 60.00 (0-8385-9353-4) P-H.

— Welding Series. (C). 1999. pap. 12.95 (0-8273-7615-4) Delmar.

— Welding Series: Gas Tung Metal Arc Welding. (C). 1999. 26.95 (0-8273-7616-2) Delmar.

Rowe, jt. auth. see Banks.

Rowe, jt. auth. see Camfield.

Rowe, jt. auth. see Gerhardt.

Rowe, jt. auth. see Harding, S. E.

Rowe, jt. auth. see O'Neil.

Rowe, jt. auth. see Ricci.

Rowe, A. Jack. In the Light of His Glory. 196p. 1999. pap. 9.95 (0-9621384-2-8) Rowe Evangelistic Minist.

Rowe, Matthew. John Wells. LC 99-177572. (Illus.). 64p. 1999. pap. text 19.95 (1-85437-271-8) Tate Pubng.

Rowe, Alan. Aliens on Earth: Puzzles, Jokes, & Things to Make & Do. (Illus.). 32p. (J). (ps-3). 1994. pap. 2.99 (1-56402-407-5) Candlewick Pr.

— The Topography & History of Beth-shan: With Details of the Egyptian & Other Inscriptions Found on the Site. LC 31-13812. (Publications of the Palestine Section of the Museum of the University of Pennsylvania: Vol. 1). 144p. reprint ed. pap. 44.70 (0-608-13638-7, 205203000026) Bks Demand.

Rowe, Alan J. Strategic Management. 4th ed. (C). 1994. pap. text. write for info. (0-201-60082-X) Addison-Wesley.

— Strategic Management & Business Policy: A Methodological Approach. 3rd ed. (C). 1989. pap. text 54.95 (0-201-15736-5) Addison-Wesley.

Rowe, Alan J. & Davis, Sue A. Intelligent Information Systems: Meeting the Challenge of the Knowledge Era. LC 95-46277. 200p. 1996. 57.95 (0-89930-912-7, Quorum Bks) Greenwood.

Rowe, Alan J. & Mason, Richard O. Strategic Management & Business Policy: A Methodological Approach. 2nd ed. Dickel, Karl E., ed. 700p. 1985. pap. text. write for info. (0-201-06087-6) Addison-Wesley.

Rowe, Alan J., et al. Cases in Strategic Management. (C). 1986. teacher ed. write for info. (0-201-06098-1); pap. text. write for info. (0-201-16899-5, 85-18612) Addison-Wesley.

— Strategic Management: A Methodological Approach. 2nd ed. 396p. (C). 1986. teacher ed. write for info. (0-318-59831-0); pap. text. write for info. (0-201-16898-7) Addison-Wesley.

— Strategic Management & Business Policy: A Methodological Approach. 1982. text 20.75 (0-201-06387-5) Addison-Wesley.

Rowe, Alan J., jt. auth. see Willison, M.

Rowe, Alice. Where Have All the Smart Women Gone? Smith, Margaret D., ed. LC 96-76263. 84p. (Orig.). 1996. pap. 11.95 (1-883697-50-6) Hara Pub.

Rowe, Allan, jt. auth. see Harris, Tim.

*Rowe, Allen M. Old West Hurley Revisited: A Nostalgic Tour. (Illus.). 210p. 1999. pap. write for info. (0-910746-31-1) Hope Farm.

Rowe, Amy & Rowe, Philip. Ernest the Fierce Mouse. rev. ed. (Quality Time Easy Readers Ser.). (Illus.). 32p. (J). (gr. k-2). 1990. reprint ed. lib. bdg. 12.95 (1-878363-08-5) Forest Hse.

Rowe, Anita & Rowe, Larry. Oak Creek. LC 98-88259. (Images of America Ser.). 1998. write for info. (0-7524-1373-2) Arcadia Publng.

Rowe, Anita, jt. auth. see Gardenswartz, Lee.

Rowe, Ann P. Costumes & Featherwork of the Lords of Chimor. LC 84-50103. (Illus.). 192p. 1984. pap. 35.00 (0-87405-023-5) Textile Mus.

Rowe, Ann P., ed. The Junius B. Bird Conference on Andean Textiles. LC 86-51317. (Illus.). 384p. 1986. pap. 35.00 (0-87405-025-1) Textile Mus.

Rowe, Ann P., et al, eds. The Junius B. Bird Pre-Columbian Textile Conference. LC 79-63729. (Illus.). 278p. 1979. 35.00 (0-318-42011-2) Textile Mus.

— Junius B. Bird Pre-Columbian Textile Conference, May 19 & 20, 1973. LC 79-63729. (Illus.). 280p. 1979. 30.00 (0-88402-086-X) Dumbarton Oaks.

Rowe, Ann Pollard. Costume & Identity in Highland Ecuador. LC 98-24521. (Illus.). 305p. 1999. pap. 50.00 (0-295-97742-6) U of Wash Pr.

Rowe, Anne. The Secret Name of Ra. (Myths & Legends Ser.). (Illus.). (J). 1998. (1-57572-016-7) Heinemann Lib.

Rowe, Anne E. The Idea of Florida in the American Literary Imagination. (Florida Sand Dollar Bk.). (Illus.). 176p. 1992. reprint ed. pap. 17.95 (0-8130-1107-8) U Press Fla.

Rowe, B. R., et al. Dissociative Recombination: Theory, Experiment & Applications. (NATO ASI Ser.: Vol. 313). (Illus.). 292p. (C). 1993. text 110.00 (0-306-44568-9, Kluwer Plenum) Kluwer Academic.

Rowe, Barney. Catching More Flounder - Fluke. (Illus.). 36p. (Orig.). 1982. pap. 2.75 (0-940844-74-5) Wellspring.

— Catching More Pacific Salt Water Fish. 36p. (Orig.). 1993. pap. 3.80 (0-940844-81-8) Wellspring.

— Saltwater Fishing. (Illus.). 36p. (Orig.). 1983. pap. 3.80 (0-940844-55-9) Wellspring.

Rowe, Basil. Under My Wings. (Airlines History Project Ser.). reprint ed. 30.00 (0-404-19333-1) AMS Pr.

Rowe, Bruce M. The College Survival Guide. 3rd ed. LC 94-34060. 101p. (C). 1994. mass mkt. 8.50 (0-314-04511-2) West Pub.

— College Survival Guide. 4th ed. LC 98-174344. (Psychology Ser.). 1998. mass mkt. 13.95 (0-534-35569-2) Brooks-Cole.

— College Survival Guide: Hints & References to Aid College Students. 2nd ed. Perlee, Clyde, ed. 98p. (C). 1992. pap. text 8.25 (0-314-00363-0) West Pub.

Rowe, Bruce M., jt. auth. see Stein, Philip L.

Rowe, C. J. Phaedo. LC 92-33958. (Greek & Latin Classics Ser.). 313p. (C). 1993. pap. text 24.95 (0-521-31318-X) Cambridge U Pr.

— Plato: Symposium. (Classical Texts Ser.). 228p. 1998. 59.95 (0-85668-614-X) David Brown.

*Rowe, C. J., ed. Plato: Syposium. (Classical Texts Ser.). 228p. 1998. pap. 28.00 (0-85668-615-8) David Brown.

Rowe, C. J., ed. see Plato.

Rowe, C. J., ed. & tr. see Plato.

Rowe, Carter R. Lest We Forget: Orthopaedics at the Massachusetts General Hospital, 1900-1995. LC 96-5704. 1996. 30.00 (0-87233-119-9) Bauhan.

Rowe, Carter R., ed. The Shoulder. (Illus.). 1988p. 1987. text 195.00 (0-443-08457-2) Church.

Rowe, Christopher. Introduccion a la Etica. (Breviarios Ser.). (SPA.). pap. 7.99 (968-16-0340-0, Pub. by Fondo) Continental Bk.

*Rowe, Christopher & Schofield, Malcolm, eds. The Cambridge History of Greek & Roman Political Thought. (Cambridge History of Political Thought Ser.). (Illus.). 750p. 2000. 125.00 (0-521-48136-8) Cambridge U Pr.

Rowe, Christopher & Thompson, Jane. People & Chips: The Human Implications of Information Technology. 3rd ed. LC 96-42124. 1996. pap. write for info. (0-07-709345-3) McGraw.

Rowe, Christopher, tr. see Plato.

Rowe, Christopher, tr. & intro. see Plato.

Rowe, Colin. Architecture of Good Intentions: Towards a Possible Retrospect. (Illus.). 144p. 1994. pap. 35.00 (1-85490-307-1) Academy Ed UK.

— As I Was Saying Vol. 1: Recollections & Miscellaneous Essays: Texas, Pre-Texas, Cambridge, Vol. 1. Caragonne, Alexander, ed. LC 95-15191. (Illus.). 213p. (C). 1995. 35.00 (0-262-18167-3) MIT Pr.

— As I Was Saying Vol. 2: Recollections & Miscellaneous Essays: Cornelliana, Vol. 2. Caragonne, Alexander, ed. (Illus.). 388p. (C). 1995. 40.00 (0-262-18168-1) MIT Pr.

— As I Was Saying Vol. 3: Recollections & Miscellaneous Essays: Urbanistics, Vol. 3. Caragonne, Alexander, ed. (Illus.). 372p. (C). 1995. 40.00 (0-262-18169-X) MIT Pr.

— As I Was Saying Vols. 1-3: Recollections & Miscellaneous Essays. Cargonne, Alexander, ed. 1995. 110.00 (0-262-18172-X) MIT Pr.

— As I Was Saying-Three Volume Set. 1999. 47.50 (0-262-68113-7) MIT Pr.

— Cornelliana. (As I Was Saying Ser.: Vol. 2). (Illus.). 388p. 1999. reprint ed. pap. 20.00 (0-262-68111-0) MIT Pr.

— Mathematics of the Ideal Villa & Other Essays. (Illus.). 233p. (C). 1982. pap. text 17.50 (0-262-68037-8) MIT Pr.

— Texas, Pre-Texas, Cambridge. Caragonne, Alexander, ed. (As I Was Saying Ser.: Vol. 1). (Illus.). 213p. 1999. reprint ed. pap. 19.50 (0-262-68110-2) MIT Pr.

— Urbanistics. (As I Was Saying Ser.: Vol. 3). (Illus.). 376p. 1999. reprint ed. pap. 20.00 (0-262-68112-9) MIT Pr.

Rowe, Colin & Koetter, Fred. Collage City. 1984. pap. text 21.95 (0-262-68042-4) MIT Pr.

Rowe, Colin, et al. Transparency. LC 97-4294. (Illus.). 132p. 1997. pap. 19.95 (3-7643-5615-4) Princeton Arch.

— Transparenz. (GER., Illus.). 132p. 1997. pap. 19.95 (3-7643-5614-6, Pub. by Birkhauser) Princeton Arch.

Rowe, Crayton E. & MacIsaac, David S. Empathic Attunement: The "Technique" of Psychoanalytic Self Psychology. LC 88-8069. 328p. 1989. 50.00 (0-87668-857-1) Aronson.

Rowe, Cyprian, jt. ed. see Bensinger, Gad J.

Rowe, D., jt. auth. see Peavy, H. S.

Rowe, D. J., ed. Dynamic Structure of Nuclear States: Proceedings of 1971 Mont Tremblant International Summer School. LC 75-186282. 599p. reprint ed. pap. 185.70 (0-608-10106-0, 201439100090) Bks Demand.

Rowe, D. M., ed. CRC Handbook of Thermoelectrics. 720p. 1995. boxed set 199.95 (0-8493-0146-7, 146) CRC Pr.

— First European Conference on Thermoelectrics. (Materials & Devices Ser.: No. 7). 430p. 1988. boxed set 119.00 (0-86341-134-7, ED007) INSPEC Inc.

Rowe, David. Popular Cultures: Rock Music, Sport & the Politics of Pleasure. (Media, Culture & Society Ser.). 224p. 1995. 69.95 (0-8039-7700-X); pap. 25.95 (0-8039-7701-8) Sage.

*Rowe, David. Wine Dictionary. (Collins Gem Ser.). (Illus.). 256p. 2000. pap. 7.95 (0-00-472202-7, Pub. by HarpC) Trafalgar.

Rowe, David & McCleary, John, eds. The History of Modern Mathematics, Vol. 2. 325p. 1989. text 71.00 (0-12-599662-4) Acad Pr.

Rowe, David, jt. auth. see Gray, Jeremy.

Rowe, David, jt. ed. see Borrowdale, Andrew.

Rowe, David C. The Limits of Family Influence: Genes, Experience & Behavior. LC 93-21876. 232p. 1995. pap. text 21.00 (0-89862-148-8, 2148) Guilford Pubns.

Rowe, David E., jt. auth. see Parshall, Karen H.

Rowe, David E., jt. ed. see Knobloch, Eberhard.

Rowe, David J. Faith at Work: A Celebration of All We Do. LC 94-22304. 112p. 1994. pap. 11.00 (1-880837-80-3) Smyth & Helwys.

— Head Dress of the British Heavy Cavalry (Dragoons) 1842-1922. (Illus.). 256p. 1999. write for info. (0-7643-0957-9) Schiffer.

Rowe, David M. Manipulating the Market: Understanding Economic Sanctions, Institutional Change, & the Political Unity of White Rhodesia. (Illus.). 284p. (C). text 52.50 (0-472-11187-6, 11187) U of Mich Pr.

Rowe, David M., jt. ed. see Nye, Joseph S., Jr.

Rowe, Debi M. Introduction to the Siddur Vol. 1: The Brakhah System. (Illus.). 96p. (J). (gr. 4-5). 1990. student ed. 5.95 (0-933873-58-1) Torah Aura.

— Introduction to the Siddur Vol. 2: The Shema & Its Blessings. (Illus.). 164p. (J). (gr. 5-6). 1991. student ed. 5.95 (0-933873-60-3) Torah Aura.

Rowe, Debi M. Introduction to the Siddur Vol. 3: Amidah, Torah Service & Concluding Prayers. Grishaver, Joel Lurie, ed. & illus. by. 143p. (Orig.). (J). (gr. 6-7). 1992. pap. text 6.95 (0-933873-75-1) Torah Aura.

Rowe, Debi M. Introduction to the Siddur Vol. 3: Amidah, Torah Service & Concluding Prayers Teacher's Guide. Grishaver, Joel Lurie, ed. & illus. by. 150p. (Orig.). pap. text, teacher ed. 16.95 (0-933873-77-8) Torah Aura.

Rowe, Debi Mahrer, jt. auth. see Mahrer, Lawrence N.

Rowe, Deborah. Preschoolers As Authors: Literacy Learning in the Social World of the Classroom. Green, Judith, ed. LC 93-1672. (Language & Social Processes Ser.). 288p. (C). 1993. text 57.50 (1-881303-71-3); pap. text 23.95 (1-881303-72-1) Hampton Pr NJ.

Rowe, Dennis. Considered Responses to Contemporary Terrorism in Democratic Societies. 56p. (C). 1988. pap. 4.95 (0-942511-06-9) OICJ.

Rowe, Dennis, ed. International Drug Trafficking. 178p. (C). 1988. pap. 9.95 (0-942511-15-8) OICJ.

Rowe, Dennis, intro. International Drug Trafficking. 168p. (C). 1988. 18.95 (0-942511-16-6) OICJ.

Rowe, Desiree E. He Leadeth Me, Vol. 1. 104p. (Orig.). 1995. pap. 9.95 (1-890526-00-2, 1930) Katrilyn Pub.

— He Leadeth Me, Vol. 2. 2nd ed. (Orig.). 1996. pap. 9.95 (1-890526-01-0, 1931) Katrilyn Pub.

Rowe, Desiree E., contrib. by. The House Where Nancy Lived, Bk. 1. 1997. pap. 9.95 (1-890526-02-9, 1932) Katrilyn Pub.

Rowe, Don & Citizenship Foundation Staff. Citizenship for All. 160p. 1998. pap. 83.00 (0-7487-3196-2) St Mut.

Rowe, Donald R. & Mohamed Abdel Magid, Isam. Handbook of Wastewater Reclamation & Reuse. 576p. (C). 1995. boxed set 139.95 (0-87371-671-X, L671) Lewis Pubs.

Rowe, Donald W. Through Nature to Eternity: Chaucer's "Legend of Good Women" LC 87-5993. 228p. 1988. reprint ed. pap. 70.70 (0-608-02132-6, 206280100003) Bks Demand.

Rowe, Dorothy. Depression: The Way Out of Your Prison. (Illus.). 242p. 1984. pap. 10.95 (0-7100-9586-4, Routledge Thoemms) Routledge.

— Depression: The Way Out of Your Prison. 1985. pap. text 15.95 (0-415-03456-6) Routledge.

— Depression: The Way Out of Your Prison. 2nd ed. LC 96-593. 272p. 1996. pap. 16.99 (0-415-14482-5) Routledge.

Rowe, Dorothy. The Experience of Depression. LC 77-9609. 292p. reprint ed. pap. 90.60 (0-608-30236-8, 202240600026) Bks Demand.

Rowe, Dwayne W., jt. auth. see Sisson, Hal C.

Rowe, Ednor, ed. see Kapitza, S. P. & Melekhin, V. N.

Rowe, Edwin, jt. auth. see Yagar, Sam.

Rowe, Erna. Giant Dinosaurs. (Illus.). 32p. (J). (ps-3). 1975. pap. 4.99 (0-590-40262-5) Scholastic Inc.

Rowe, F. W. & Gatto, John T. Echinodermata. (Zoological Catalogue of Australia Ser.: Vol. 33). (Illus.). 523p. 1995. 74.95 (0-643-05696-3, Pub. by CSIRO) Accents Pubns.

Rowe, Fiona J. Clinical Orthoptics. (Illus.). 336p. (Orig.). 1997. pap. text 69.95 (0-632-04274-5) Blackwell Sci.

Rowe, Fran, ed. see Levitch, Edward J.

Rowe, Frank & Jones, Glynn. Junior Soccer: A Session by Session Approach. 208p. 1996. pap. text 22.95 (0-7507-0500-0, Falmer Pr) Taylor & Francis.

Rowe, Fred A. The Career Connection for College Education: A Guide to College Majors & Related Career Opportunities. LC 94-15662. 268p. (Orig.). 1994. pap. 16.95 (1-56370-142-1, CCCE) JIST Works.

— The Career Connection for Technical Education: A Guide to Technical Training & Related Career Opportunities. LC 94-16434. 174p. (Orig.). 1994. pap. 14.95 (1-56370-143-X, CCTE) JIST Works.

Rowe, Frederick J. AP Chemistry. 2nd ed. LC 93-18320. 224p. 1993. pap. 14.00 (0-671-84778-3, Arco) Macmillan Gen Ref.

— AP Chemistry: Advanced Placement Examination. 3rd ed. LC 97-70071. (Illus.). 240p. 1997. pap. 16.95 (0-02-861708-8, Arc) IDG Bks.

Rowe, Frederick M., et al, eds. Enterprise Law of the Eighties: European & American Perspectives on Competition & Industrial Organization. LC 80-67958. 254p. (Orig.). 1980. pap. text 15.00 (0-89707-018-6, 5030033) Amer Bar Assn.

Rowe, G. C., jt. auth. see Ramsay, R. M.

Rowe, G. S. Embattled Bench: The Pennsylvania Supreme Court & the Forging of a Democratic Society, 1684-1809. LC 93-47888. (C). 1994. 45.00 (0-87413-526-5) U Delaware Pr.

Rowe, G. W., et al, eds. Finite Element Plasticity & Metalforming Analysis. (Illus.). 323p. (C). 1991. text 120.00 (0-521-38362-5) Cambridge U Pr.

Rowe, Gaelene. Guiding Young Artists: Curriculum Ideas for Teachers. (Illus.). 89p. (Orig.). (C). 1989. pap. text 18.00 (0-435-08499-2, 08499) Heinemann.

Rowe, Gail S. Thomas McKean: The Shaping of an American Republicanism. LC 77-94085. (Illus.). 517p. reprint ed. pap. 160.30 (0-8357-5500-2, 203511500093) Bks Demand.

An Asterisk (*) at the beginning of an entry indicates that the title is appearing for the first time.

R

Rowe, Garry W. Building & Using a Groundwater Database. 1991. lib. bdg. 99.95 (*0-87371-404-0*, L404) Lewis Pubs.

Rowe, Gavin. Fairy Tales. 96p. (J). (gr. 1-6). 1996. 9.98 (*1-85854-370-3*) Brimax Bks.

Rowe, Gavin, jt. illus. see Waite, Judy.

Rowe, Genevieve B., ed. see Rowe, Josiah P., Jr.

Rowe, George E. Distinguishing Jonson: Imitation, Rivalry, & the Direction of a Dramatic Career. LC 87-13198. 232p. 1988. reprint ed. pap. 72.00 (*0-608-02139-3*, 206280800003) Bks Demand.

— Thomas Middleton & the New Comedy Tradition. LC 79-4289. 252p. reprint ed. pap. 78.20 (*0-7837-6179-1*, 204590100009) Bks Demand.

Rowe, George E., et al, eds. Family Strengths Eight-Nine: Pathways to Well-Being. 1987. pap. 10.00 (*0-934949-03-4*) U Nebr Dept Human.

— Family Strengths 6: Enhancement of Interaction. 1985. pap. text 10.00 (*0-934949-01-8*) U Nebr Dept Human.

— Family Strengths 7: Vital Connections. 1986. pap. 10.00 (*0-934949-02-6*) U Nebr Dept Human.

Rowe, George S., ed. see Williams, Thomas & Calvert, James.

Rowe, Gerard P., jt. auth. see Rashkind, Alan B.

Rowe, Gilbert T., ed. Deep-Sea Biology. LC QH0091.. (Sea Ser.: No. 8). 572p. 1983. reprint ed. pap. 177.40 (*0-7837-2806-9*, 205766600006) Bks Demand.

Rowe, Gilbert T. & Pariente, Vita, eds. Deep-Sea Food Chains & the Global Carbon Cycle. (C). 1992. text 208.00 (*0-7923-1608-8*) Kluwer Academic.

Rowe, Glen W. Theoretical Models in Biology: The Original of Life, the Immune System, & the Brain. LC 93-40873. (Illus.). 440p. 1994. 69.00 (*0-19-859688-X*) OUP.

***Rowe, Glenn.** The Essence of Java Programming. LC 99-25292. (Essence of Computing Ser.). 1999. write for info. (*0-13-011377-8*) P-H.

— Introduction to Data Structures & Algorithms with C++ 371p. 1996. pap. 63.00 (*0-13-579178-2*) P-H.

Rowe, Glenn. Introduction to Data Structures & Algorithms with Java. LC 97-41673. 445p. 1997. pap. 59.00 (*0-13-857749-8*) P-H.

— Theoretical Models in Biology: The Origin of Life, the Immune System & the Brain. LC 93-40873. (Illus.). 436p. 1998. reprint ed. pap. text 45.00 (*0-19-859687-1*) OUP.

Rowe, Gordon J. The Magic Spectacles. LC 98-85756. (Illus.). 32p. (J). 1998. pap. 8.95 (*1-56167-444-3*) Am Literary Pr.

***Rowe, Gordon J.** Showdown at Pecos. (Illus.). 32p. (J). (ps-3). 2000. 11.95 (*1-57197-192-0*) Pentland Pr.

Rowe, H. A., ed. Intelligence: Reconceptualization & Measurement. 312p. (C). 1991. text 65.00 (*0-8058-0942-2*) L Erlbaum Assocs.

***Rowe, Harrison E.** Electromagnetic Propagation in One-Dimensional Random Media. LC 98-28787. 233p. 1999. 69.95 (*0-471-11003-5*) Wiley.

Rowe, Helga A. Learning with Personal Computers. (C). 1992. 90.00 (*0-86431-129-X*, Pub. by Aust Council Educ Res) St Mut.

— Problem Solving & Intelligence. 416p. (C). 1985. text 79.95 (*0-89859-347-6*) L Erlbaum Assocs.

— Problem Solving & Intelligence. LC 84-18855. (Illus.). 406p. 1985. reprint ed. pap. 125.90 (*0-608-05703-7*, 206621800007) Bks Demand.

Rowe, Henry K. Modern Pathfinders of Christianity: The Lives & Deeds of Seven Centuries of Christian Leaders. LC 68-16973. (Essay Index Reprint Ser.). 1977. 19.95 (*0-8369-0839-2*) Ayer.

Rowe, Hortense M., jt. ed. see Joseph, Gloria I.

Rowe, J. Fostering in the Eighties. (C). 1989. 60.00 (*0-903534-48-7*, Pub. by Brit Ag for Adopt & Fost) St Mut.

Rowe, J. & Lambert, L. Children Who Wait (Extracts) (C). 1989. 65.00 (*0-903534-31-2*, Pub. by Brit Ag for Adopt & Fost) St Mut.

Rowe, J., et al. Child Care Now: A Survey of Placement Patterns. (C). 1989. 75.00 (*0-903534-85-1*, Pub. by Brit Ag for Adopt & Fost) St Mut.

— Long-Term Fostering & the Children Act: A Study of Foster Parents Who Went on to Adopt. (C). 1989. 60.00 (*0-903534-49-5*, Pub. by Brit Ag for Adopt & Fost) St Mut.

Rowe, J. G., ed. Aspects of Late Medieval Government & Society: Essays Presented to J. R. Lander. 278p. 1986. text 40.00 (*0-8020-5695-4*) U of Toronto Pr.

Rowe, J. H., et al. The Kroeber Anthropological Society Papers. (Publications of the Kroeber Anthropological Society: No. 12). (Illus.). 105p. (C). 1955. reprint ed. pap. text 11.56 (*1-55567-474-7*) Coyote Press.

Rowe, J. H., ed. see Baumhoff, Martin A.

Rowe, J. H., ed. see Cook, S. F.

Rowe, J. H., ed. see Downs, James F.

Rowe, J. H., ed. see Fand, Robert & Murphy, Yolanda.

Rowe, J. H., ed. see Freed, Stanley A.

Rowe, J. H., ed. see Kroeber, A. L.

Rowe, J. H., ed. see Kroeber, A. L. & Barrett, Samuel A.

Rowe, J. H., ed. see Massey, W. C. & Osborne, C. M.

Rowe, J. M. Diagnosis & Therapy of Acute Leukemia in Adults. 144p. 1995. text 50.00 (*3-7186-5559-4*, Harwood Acad Pubs) Gordon & Breach.

Rowe, J. N. An Investigation of the Effects of Solar Flares & Stratospheric Warmings on the Lower Ionosphere. LC 72-135091. 90p. 1970. 15.00 (*0-403-04533-9*) Scholarly.

Rowe, J. Phillip, jt. auth. see Gray, John T.

Rowe, J. W., ed. Natural Products of Woody Plants. (Wood Science Ser.). (Illus.). 1280p. 1990. 645.95 (*0-387-50300-5*) Spr-Verlag.

Rowe, Jack. No - It's Not the Devil: It's You. 80p. (Orig.). 1990. spiral bd. 3.00 (*0-9621384-1-X*) Rowe Evangelistic Minist.

— The Strait Way, Vol. 1. (Illus.). 128p. (Orig.). 1988. spiral bd. 4.95 (*0-9621384-0-1*) Rowe Evangelistic Minist.

Rowe, James G., Jr. Love to All, Jim: A Young Man's Letters from Vietnam. Prescott, Gary R., ed. LC 88-35579. (Illus.). 128p. (Orig.). 1989. pap. 9.95 (*0-89407-096-7*) Strawberry Hill.

Rowe, James N. Five Years to Freedom. 480p. 1984. mass mkt. 6.99 (*0-345-31460-3*, Ballantine) Ballantine Pub Grp.

Rowe, Jane, jt. auth. see Hewitt, Sally.

Rowe, Jane, jt. auth. see Howitt, Sally.

***Rowe, Jeannette.** Whose Ears? LC 98-75757. (Illus.). 16p. (J). (ps-k). 1999. 7.95 (*0-316-75932-5*) Little.

— Whose Feet? LC 98-75758. (Illus.). 16p. (J). (ps-k). 1999. 7.95 (*0-316-75934-1*) Little.

— Whose Nose? LC 98-75756. (Illus.). 16p. (J). (ps-k). 1999. 7.95 (*0-316-75933-3*) Little.

***Rowe, Jennifer.** Something Wicked. 304p. 1999. mass mkt. 5.99 (*0-345-42795-5*) Ballantine Pub Grp.

Rowe, Jennifer. Stranglehold. large type ed. LC 94-49410. 338p. 1995. lib. bdg. 19.95 (*0-7838-1247-7*, G K Hall Lrg Type) Mac Lib Ref.

— Suspect. 1999. mass mkt. 5.99 (*0-345-42793-9*) Ballantine Pub Grp.

Rowe, Jeremy. Photographers in Arizona, 1850-1920: A History & Directory. limited ed. (Illus.). 136p. 1997. boxed set 125.00 (*1-887694-06-4*) C Mautz Pubng.

— Photographers in Arizona 1950-1920: A History & Directory. Mossinger, Rosemarie & Leavitt, Cathie, eds. (Illus.). 136p. (Orig.). 1997. 35.00 (*1-887694-05-6*) C Mautz Pubng.

Rowe, John. The Hard-Rock Men: Cornish Immigrants & the North American Mining Frontier LC 74-193879. xii, 322p. 1974. write for info. (*0-85323-120-6*) Liverpool Univ Pr.

— Letters & Diary of John Rowe: Boston Merchant, 1759 to 1762. Cunningham, Anne R., ed. LC 76-76564. (Eyewitness Accounts of the American Revolution Ser.). (Illus.). 453p. 1969. reprint ed. 28.95 (*0-405-01148-2*) Ayer.

— Rabbit Moon. LC 92-6047. (Illus.). 28p. (J). 1992. pap. 14.95 (*0-88708-246-7*, Picture Book Studio) S&S Childrens.

Rowe, John, ed. see Carpenter, Allan & Maginnis, Matthew.

Rowe, John, jt. ed. see Wetle, Terrie.

***Rowe, John A.** Favorite Stories by John A. Rowe: 3 Complete Tales. LC 99-24800. (Illus.). 96p. (J). (ps up). 1999. 12.98 (*0-7651-1685-5*) Smithmark.

Rowe, John A. Jack the Dog. (Illus.). 28p. (J). (gr. k up). 1993. 14.95 (*0-88708-266-1*, Picture Book Studio) S&S Childrens.

— Monkey Trouble. LC 99-17364. (Illus.). 32p. (J). (gr. k-3). 1999. lib. bdg. 15.88 (*0-7358-1034-6*, Pub. by North-South Bks NYC) Chronicle Bks.

***Rowe, John A.** Monkey Trouble. LC 99-17364. (Illus.). 32p. (J). (gr. k-3). 1999. 15.95 (*0-7358-1033-8*, Pub. by North-South Bks NYC) Chronicle Bks.

Rowe, John A. Smudge. LC 97-8737. (Illus.). 36p. (J). (gr. k-3). 1997. 16.95 (*1-55858-788-8*, Pub. by North-South Bks NYC); lib. bdg. 16.88 (*1-55858-789-6*, Pub. by North-South Bks NYC) Chronicle Bks.

Rowe, John A. The Gingerbread Man: An Old English Folktale. LC 95-36755. 32p. (J). (ps-1). 1996. 15.95 (*1-55858-542-7*, Pub. by North-South Bks NYC); lib. bdg. 15.88 (*1-55858-543-5*, Pub. by North-South Bks NYC) Chronicle Bks.

— The Gingerbread Man: An Old English Folktale. LC 95-36755. 32p. (J). (ps-1). 1998. pap. 6.95 (*1-55858-906-6*, Pub. by North-South Bks NYC) Chronicle Bks.

Rowe, John C. At Emerson's Tomb: The Politics of Classic American Literature. LC 96-24554. 320p. 1996. 52.00 (*0-231-05894-2*); pap. 17.50 (*0-231-05895-0*) Col U Pr.

***Rowe, John C.** Culture & the Problem of the Disciplines. LC 97-44499. 240p. 1998. pap. 18.50 (*0-231-11243-2*); lib. bdg. 49.50 (*0-231-11242-4*) Col U Pr.

Rowe, John C. The Other Henry James. LC 98-18977. (New Americanists Ser.). 1998. 49.95 (*0-8223-2128-9*); pap. 17.95 (*0-8223-2147-5*) Duke.

Rowe, John C. The Theoretical Dimensions of Henry James. LC 84-40158. (Wisconsin Project on American Writers Ser.: No. 2). 304p. 1985. pap. 17.95 (*0-299-09974-1*) U of Wis Pr.

Rowe, John C. Through the Custom-House: Nineteenth-Century American Fiction & Modern Theory. LC 81-20866. 235p. 1982. reprint ed. pap. 72.90 (*0-608-03747-8*, 206457200009) Bks Demand.

Rowe, John C., ed. New Essays on the Education of Henry Adams. LC 95-21110. (American Novel Ser.). 176p. (C). 1996. text 32.95 (*0-521-44551-5*); pap. text 14.95 (*0-521-44573-6*) Cambridge U Pr.

Rowe, John C. & Berg, Richard, eds. The Vietnam War & American Culture. (Social Foundations of Aesthetic Forms Ser.). 320p. (C). 1992. pap. 19.00 (*0-231-06733-X*) Col U Pr.

Rowe, John C., jt. auth. see Emerson, Ralph Waldo.

Rowe, John C., jt. ed. see McWhirter, David.

***Rowe, John Carlos.** Literary Culture & Us Imperialism: From the Revolution to World War II. 368p. 2000. pap. 19.95 (*0-19-513151-7*); text 55.00 (*0-19-513150-9*) OUP.

— Post-Nationalist American Studies. LC 99-56775. 280p. 2000. 45.00 (*0-520-22438-8*, Pub. by U CA Pr) Cal Prin Full Svc.

— Post-Nationalist American Studies. LC 99-56775. (Illus.). 280p. 2000. pap. 17.95 (*0-520-22439-6*, Pub. by U CA Pr) Cal Prin Full Svc.

Rowe, John D. Animal Nutrition: You May Be Poisoning Your Pet Unknowingly, a Little Each Day. (Illus.). 200p. 1997. pap. 12.95 (*0-9655196-0-0*) Setter Pubns.

Rowe, John F. Newington, New Hampshire: A Heritage of Independence since 1630. LC 87-2235. (Illus.). 336p. 1987. 18.00 (*0-914659-25-1*) Phoenix Pub.

Rowe, John L. & Etier, A. Faborn. Typewriting Drills for Speed & Accuracy. 4th ed. LC 76-50096. 1977. text 12.96 (*0-07-054151-5*) McGraw.

Rowe, John L., et al. Gregg Typing. 2nd ed. Incl. Book 1, General Typing. 1967. text 11.76 (*0-07-054105-1*); (One Ninety-One Series). 1967. write for info. (*0-318-54172-6*) McGraw.

— Typing Three Hundred, 2 vols., Vol. 1: General Course. (Illus.). 288p. (gr. 9-12). 1972. text 24.24 (*0-07-054090-X*) McGraw.

Rowe, John R., et al. The New Model Me. (gr. 8-12). 1983. teacher ed. 13.95 (*0-8077-2733-4*); text, student ed. 10.95 (*0-8077-2732-6*) Tchrs Coll.

Rowe, John S., jt. auth. see Morison, Samuel L.

Rowe, John W. Primary Commodities in International Trade. LC 65-18930. 236p. (Orig.). reprint ed. pap. 67.30 (*0-608-11103-1*, 2022467) Bks Demand.

— Successful Aging: The MacArthur Foundation Study Shows How the Lifestyle Choices You Make Now--More Than Heredity--Determine Your Health & Vitality. 1999. pap. write for info. (*0-375-70043-9*) Vin Bks.

— The Transformation of Electric Utilities: Restructuring, Yes Deregulation, No. LC 99-182056. 33p. 1998. pap. 9.95 (*0-8447-7118-X*) Am Enterprise.

— Wages in Practice & Theory. LC 70-76356. x, 277p. 1969. reprint ed. 39.50 (*0-678-06502-0*) Kelley.

Rowe, John W. & Ahronheim, Judith C., eds. Annual Review of Gerontology & Geriatrics Vol. 12: Medications & the Elderly. 232p. 1992. 46.00 (*0-8261-6494-3*) Springer Pub.

Rowe, John W. & Besdine, Richard W. Geriatric Medicine. 2nd ed. (Illus.). 750p. 1988. 115.00 (*0-316-75969-4*, Little Brwn Med Div) Lppncott W & W.

Rowe, John W. & Kahn, Robert L. Successful Aging: The MacArthur Foundation Study Shows How the Lifestyle Choices You Make Now--More Than Heredity--Determine Your Health & Vitality. 1999. pap. 12.95 (*0-440-50863-0*) Dell.

— Successful Aging: The MacArthur Foundation Study Shows How the Lifestyle Choices You Make Now--More Than Heredity--Determine Your Health & Vitality. LC 97-36900. 288p. 1998. 26.50 (*0-375-40045-1*) Pantheon.

Rowe, Jon, jt. auth. see Partridge, Derek.

Rowe, Jonathan, jt. auth. see Cahn, Edgar S.

Rowe, Joseph H., jt. auth. see Attali, Jacques.

Rowe, Joseph H., tr. see Corbin, Henry.

Rowe, Joseph M., jt. auth. see Camfield, Thomas M.

Rowe, Josiah P., Jr. Letters from a World War I Aviator. Rowe, Genevieve B. & Doran, Diana R., eds. LC 86-90456. (Illus.). 200p. 1986. 15.95 (*0-9616886-0-2*) Sinclaire Pr.

Rowe, Julian. Making Sounds. (Illus.). 32p. (J). (gr. 3-6). 1994. pap. 4.95 (*0-516-48136-3*) Childrens.

— Music. LC 96-17979. (Science Encounters Ser.). (J). 1998. 19.92 (*1-57572-091-4*) Heinemann Lib.

— Recreation. LC 96-33352. (Science Encounters Ser.). (J). 1998. 21.36 (*1-57572-092-2*) Heinemann Lib.

— Science & Technology. (Legacies Ser.). (Illus.). 48p. (J). (gr. 4-6). 1995. lib. bdg. 24.26 (*1-56847-395-8*) Raintree Steck-V.

— Sports. LC 96-33351. (Science Encounters Ser.). (J). 1998. 21.36 (*1-57572-089-2*) Heinemann Lib.

— Transportation. LC 96-27560. (Science Encounters Ser.). (J). 1998. 22.79 (*1-57572-087-6*) Heinemann Lib.

Rowe, Julian & Perham, Molly. Amazing Magnets. LC 94-16942. (First Science Ser.). (Illus.). 32p. (J). (gr. 1-4). 1994. pap. 4.95 (*0-516-48137-1*) Childrens.

— Resources. (MapWorlds Ser.). (J). 1997. lib. bdg. 20.00 (*0-531-14387-2*) Watts.

Rowe, Julian, jt. auth. see Burns, Peggy.

Rowe, Julian, jt. auth. see Oxlade, Chris.

Rowe, Julian, jt. auth. see Perham, Molly.

Rowe, K. Management Techniques for Civil Engineering Construction. (Illus.). x, 268p. 1975. 63.00 (*0-85334-613-5*) Elsevier.

Rowe, Karen E. Saint & Singer: Edward Taylor's Typology & the Poetics of Meditation. (Cambridge Studies in American Literature & Culture: No. 18). 370p. 1986. text 69.95 (*0-521-30865-8*) Cambridge U Pr.

Rowe, Kathleen. The Unruly Woman: Gender & the Genres of Laughter. LC 94-13656. (Texas Film Studies). (Illus.). 272p. 1995. pap. 17.95 (*0-292-77069-3*); text 37.50 (*0-292-79072-4*) U of Tex Pr.

— Women's Issues. 40p. (Orig.). 1986. pap. 3.00 (*0-89486-361-4*, 5498B) Hazelden.

Rowe, Kenneth E. Methodist Union Catalog: Pre-1976 Imprints, Vol. V. LC 75-33190. 371p. 1981. 35.00 (*0-8108-1454-4*) Scarecrow.

— The Postal History & Markings of the Forwarding Agents. Hartmann, Leonard H., ed. LC 96-75098. (Illus.). 288p. 1996. 47.50 (*0-917528-12-3*) L H Hartmann.

— The Postal History of the Forwarding Agents. Hartmann, Leonard H., ed. LC 84-80011. (Illus.). 296p. 1984. 35.00 (*0-917528-06-9*) L H Hartmann.

— United Methodist Studies, Basic Bibliographies. 3rd ed. 96p. 1992. pap. 7.95 (*0-687-43165-4*) Abingdon.

Rowe, Kenneth E., ed. Methodist Union Catalog: Pre-1976 Imprints, 20 vols., Vol. I, A[00ad]bj. LC 75-33190. 438p. 1975. 35.00 (*0-8108-0880-3*) Scarecrow.

— Methodist Union Catalog: Pre-1976 Imprints, Vol. II: Bl[00ad]cha. LC 75-33190. 422p. 1976. 35.00 (*0-8108-0920-6*) Scarecrow.

— Methodist Union Catalog: Pre-1976 Imprints, Vol. III, Che[00ad]Dix. LC 75-33190. 431p. 1978. 35.00 (*0-8108-1067-0*) Scarecrow.

— Methodist Union Catalog: Pre-1976 Imprints, Vol. IV, Do[00ad]Fy. LC 75-33190. 436p. 1979. 40.00 (*0-8108-1225-8*) Scarecrow.

— Methodist Union Catalog: Pre-1976 Imprints, Vol. VI. LC 75-33190. 360p. 1985. 37.50 (*0-8108-1725-X*) Scarecrow.

— Methodist Union Catalog Vol. VII: J-Le: Pre-1976 Imprints. 419p. 1994. 52.00 (*0-8108-2669-0*) Scarecrow.

— The Place of Wesley in the Christian Tradition: Essays Delevered at Drew University in Celebration of the Commencement of the Publication of the Oxford Edition of the Works of John Wesley. LC 76-27659. 168p. 1976. 26.50 (*0-8108-0981-8*) Scarecrow.

Rowe, Kenneth E., et al, eds. To Remember & Celebrate: Worship Resources for Heritage Events. 65p. (Orig.). 1996. pap. 7.00 (*1-880927-19-5*) Gen Comm Arch.

Rowe, Kenneth E. & Matthews, Rex, eds. United Methodist Studies: Basic Bibliographies. 4th ed. LC 98-13831. (Wesleyan/Methodist Studies). 120p. (Orig.). 1997. pap. 9.95 (*0-687-24994-5*) Abingdon.

Rowe, Kenneth E., ed. see Dieter, Melvin E.

Rowe, Kenneth E., ed. see Huber, Donald L.

Rowe, Kenneth E., ed. see Kaufman, Paul L.

Rowe, Kenneth E., ed. see Rubinstein, Murray A.

Rowe, Kenneth L. Communications in Marketing. (Occupational Manuals & Projects in Marketing Ser.). (Illus.). 1978. text 12.28 (*0-07-054154-X*) McGraw.

Rowe, Kenneth W. Mathew Carey, a Study in American Economic Development. LC 78-64151. (Johns Hopkins University. Studies in the Social Sciences. Thirtieth Ser. 1912: 4). 144p. 1982. reprint ed. 37.50 (*0-404-61261-X*) AMS Pr.

Rowe, L. J. Radiology of the Spine. (Illus.). 800p. 1998. write for info. (*0-443-08968-X*) Church.

Rowe, Larry, jt. auth. see Rowe, Anita.

Rowe, Laura. The Life & Progress of Henry Quick of Zennor. (C). 1989. 22.00 (*0-907566-43-X*, Pub. by Dyllansow Truran) St Mut.

Rowe-Leete, Susan, jt. auth. see Kidel, Mark.

Rowe-Leete, Susan, jt. ed. see Kidel, Mark.

Rowe, Leo S. The United States & Puerto Rico. LC 74-14249. (Puerto Rican Experience Ser.). 290p. 1975. reprint ed. 23.95 (*0-405-06235-4*) Ayer.

Rowe, Lindsay J., jt. auth. see Yochum, Terry R.

Rowe, Lois. On Call: A Devotional for Nurses. LC 58-7316. 230p. 1988. pap. 9.99 (*0-8010-7749-4*) Baker Bks.

Rowe, M. Jessica. This Is Always Finished (David Dunlap) LC 89-81319. (Illus.). 42p. (Orig.). 1989. pap. 12.00 (*0-9614615-9-4*) Edmundson.

***Rowe, M. Jessica & Leveton, Deborah.** Iowa Artists 1998. 69p. 1998. pap. 20.00 (*1-879003-21-X*) Edmundson.

Rowe, M. Jessica, jt. auth. see Cromwell-Lacy, Sherry.

Rowe, M. Jessica, jt. auth. see Danoff, I. Michael.

Rowe, Maggie, ed. see Ireland, John E.

Rowe, Marian B., ed. Highlights of Westbrook History. (Illus.). 242p. 1995. reprint ed. lib. bdg. 34.50 (*0-8328-5036-5*) Higginson Bk Co.

Rowe, Martin, ed. The Way of Compassion: Survival Strategies for a World in Crisis. 256p. 1998. pap. 16.95 (*0-9664056-0-9*) Stealth Technol.

Rowe, Marvin W. & Hyman, Marian, eds. Advances in Analytical Geochemistry, Vol. 1. 257p. 1994. 109.50 (*1-55938-332-1*) Jai Pr.

— Advances in Analytical Geochemistry, Vol. 2. 329p. 1995. 109.50 (*1-55938-785-8*) Jai Pr.

Rowe, Marvin W., jt. ed. see Hyman, Marian.

Rowe, Mary. Knitted Tams. LC 89-7438. (Illus.). 104p. (Orig.). 1989. pap. 12.95 (*0-934026-48-3*) Interweave.

***Rowe, Maurice.** Track Record: Images of Motor Sport 1950-1980. (Illus.). 192p. 1999. 39.95 (*0-7603-0792-X*, 129168AP, Pub. by MBI Pubg) Motorbooks Intl.

— Track Record: Images of Motor Sport, 1950-1980. (Illus.). 192p. 1999. 39.95 (*1-902655-00-1*, Pub. by Queensgate Pubns) Motorbooks Intl.

Rowe, Michael. Countertrade. 3rd ed. 1997. 215.00 (*1-85564-580-7*, Pub. by Euromoney) Am Educ Systs.

— Crossing the Border: Encounters Between Homeless People & Outreach Workers / LC 98-42986. 208p. 1999. pap. 17.95 (*0-520-21883-3*, Pub. by U CA Pr) Cal Prin Full Svc.

— Crossing The Border: Encounters Between Homeless People & Outreach Workers. LC 98-42986. 208p. 1999. 45.00 (*0-520-21831-0*, Pub. by U CA Pr) Cal Prin Full Svc.

— Letters of Credit. 2nd ed. 311p. 1997. pap. 215.00 (*1-85564-579-3*, Pub. by Euromoney) Am Educ Systs.

— Looking For Brothers: Essays. 196p. 1999. pap. text 15.00 (*0-88962-671-5*) Mosaic.

— The Racialisation of Disorder in Twentieth Century Britain. LC 98-71405. (Research in Ethnic Relations Ser.). 220p. 1998. text 65.95 (*1-84014-528-5*, Pub. by Ashgate Pub) Ashgate Pub Co.

— Trade & Project Finance in Emerging Markets. 260p. 1995. 170.00 (*1-85564-387-1*, Pub. by Euromoney) Am Educ Systs.

— Writing below the Belt: Conversations with Erotic Authors. LC 96-228055. 1995. 19.95 (*1-56333-363-5*, R Kasak Bks) Masquerade.

— Writing below the Belt: Conversations with Erotic Authors. 1997. reprint ed. mass mkt. 7.95 (*1-56333-540-9*, Hard Candy) Masquerade.

Rowe, Michael & Roche, Thomas, eds. Sons of Darkness: Tales of Men, Blood & Immortality. 180p. 1996. pap. 12.95 (*1-57344-059-0*) Cleis Pr.

Rowe, Michael, jt. auth. see Hughes, Richard.

Rowe, Michael Langham, jt. auth. see Stanley, George Edward.

An Asterisk (*) at the beginning of an entry indicates that the title is appearing for the first time.

R

An Asterisk (*) at the beginning of an entry indicates that the title is appearing for the first time.

Rowell, Harry & Landis, Carolyn P. Contracting for Computing: A Checklist of Terms & Clauses for Use in Contracting with Vendors for Computing Resources, Vol. I. 156p. 1973. 16.00 (0-318-14016-0); 9.00 (0-318-14017-9) EDUCOM.

Rowell, Henry T., ed. see Carcopino, Jerome.

Rowell, J. Cy. The Church's Educational Space: Creating Learning Environments for Teaching & Learning. 80p. (Orig.). 1989. pap. 6.99 (0-8272-0454-X) Chalice Pr.

Rowell, JoAnn C. Understanding Medical Insurance. 3rd ed. (Medical Assisting Ser.). 384p. 1996. text 35.95 (0-8273-7268-X) Delmar.

Rowell, Joann C. Understanding Medical Insurance: A Step-by-Step Guide. 2nd ed. LC 93-2680. 336p. 1994. pap. 29.95 (0-8273-4966-1) Delmar.

***Rowell, John.** Magnify Your Vision for the Small Church, 1. 1998. pap. 14.99 (0-9668853-0-9) Northside Comm.

Rowell, John W. Yankee Cavalrymen: Through the Civil War with the Ninth Pennsylvania Calvary. LC 70-126939. 296p. 1971. reprint ed. pap. 91.80 (0-608-00260-7, 201617200001) Bks Demand.

Rowell, Jonathan. Malaysia. LC 96-17968. (Economically Developing Countries Ser.). (J). 1997. lib. bdg. 24.26 (0-8172-4531-6) Raintree Steck-V.

Rowell, Judy, ed. The First Hundred Years, 1853-1953: Bowdon, Georgia. (Illus.). 222p. 1990. reprint ed. text 40.00 (0-88107-176-5) Curtis Media.

***Rowell, Katherine L.** Dead Hands. LC 99-39447. 1999. 45.00 (0-8047-3385-6) Stanford U Pr.

Rowell, Katherine L., ed. Clinical Computers in Nuclear Medicine. LC 91-5207. (Illus.). 86p. 1992. 49.00 (0-932004-40-7) Soc Nuclear Med.

Rowell, Lewis. Music & Musical Thought in Early India. 1998. 68.00 (81-215-0867-3, Pub. by M Manoharial) Coronet Bks.

— Music & Musical Thought in Early India. (Chicago Studies in Ethnomusicology). 384p. 1992. lib. bdg. 68.00 (0-226-73032-8) U Ch Pr.

— Music & Musical Thought in Early India. (Chicago Studies in Ethnomusicology). 428p. 1998. pap. text 27.50 (0-226-73033-6) U Ch Pr.

— Thinking about Music: An Introduction to the Philosophy of Music. LC 82-21979. (Illus.). 304p. 1984. pap. text 18.95 (0-87023-461-7) U of Mass Pr.

Rowell, Lewis, jt. ed. see Fraser, J. T.

Rowell, Lois. American Organ Music on Records. LC 76-360159. 122p. 1976. pap. 9.00 (0-913746-08-8) Organ Lit.

Rowell, Loring B. Human Cardiovascular Control. (Illus.). 520p. 1993. text 69.50 (0-19-507362-2) OUP.

— Human Circulation: Regulation During Physical Stress. (Illus.). 426p. (C). 1986. text 59.95 (0-19-504075-9) OUP.

Rowell, Loring B. & Shepherd, John T., eds. Handbook of Physiology Section 12: Exercise: Regulation & Integration of Multiple Systems. (American Physiological Society Book). (Illus.). 1224p. 1996. text 195.00 (0-19-509174-4) OUP.

Rowell, Margit. Antonin Artaud: Works on Paper. (Illus.). 168p. 1996. 35.00 (0-87070-118-5, 0-8109-6168-7, Pub. by Mus of Modern Art) Abrams.

— The Captured Imagination. LC 87-70555. (Illus.). 96p. 1987. pap. text 27.95 (0-8122-1289-4) U of Pa Pr.

— Julio Gonzalez: A Retrospective. LC 82-62612. (Illus.). 216p. 1983. pap. 18.50 (0-89207-039-0) S R Guggenheim.

— New Images from Spain. Flint, Lucy, tr. LC 79-92992. (Illus.). 144p. (Orig.). 1980. pap. 8.50 (0-89207-023-4) S R Guggenheim.

— Objects of Desire: The Modern Still Life. (Illus.). 232p. 1997. 49.50 (0-8109-6172-5, Pub. by Abrams) Time Warner.

— Objects of Desire: The Modern Still Life. (Illus.). 232p. 1997. 50.00 (0-87070-111-8, 0-8109-6172-5, Pub. by Mus of Modern Art); pap. 24.95 (0-87070-110-X) Mus of Modern Art.

— The Planar Dimension: Europe, 1912-1932. LC 78-74711. 1981. reprint ed. pap. 12.95 (0-89207-017-X) S R Guggenheim.

— Sigmar Polke: Works on Paper, 1963-1974. LC 98-68390. (Illus.). 192p. 1999. 49.50 (0-8109-6196-2, Pub. by Abrams) Time Warner.

***Rowell, Margit.** Sigmar Polke: Works on Paper, 1963-1974. 176p. 1999. 50.00 (0-87070-082-0, Pub. by Mus of Modern Art) Abrams.

— Sigmar Polke: Works on Paper, 1963-74. LC 98-68390. 176p. 1999. pap. 24.95 (0-87070-083-9) Mus of Modern Art.

Rowell, Margit, ed. Antonin Artaud: Works on Paper. (Illus.). 168p. 1996. 35.00 (0-8109-6168-7, Pub. by Abrams) Time Warner.

— Joan Miro: Selected Writings & Interviews. (Documents of Twentieth Century Art Ser.). (Illus.). 350p. (C). 1986. 36.00 (0-8057-9956-7) Macmillan.

Rowell, Margit & Rudenstine, Angelica Z. Art of the Avant-Garde in Russia: Selections from the George Costakis Collection. LC 81-52858. (Illus.). 320p. 1981. pap. 17.00 (0-686-81458-4) S R Guggenheim.

***Rowell, Michael.** SAP R/3 Consultants Bible. LC 99-88434. 800p. 2000. pap. text 39.99 (0-7645-4631-7) IDG Bks.

— Understanding EAI: Enterprise Application Integration. (Illus.). 450p. 2000. pap. 34.99 (0-672-31941-1) Sams.

Rowell, R. M. Chemistry of Solid Wood. 614p. (C). 1986. 475.00 (0-7855-6874-3, Pub. by Intl Bk Distr) St Mut.

— Chemistry of Solid Wood. 614p. (C). 1986. reprint ed. 210.00 (81-7089-040-3, Pub. by Intl Bk Distr) St Mut.

Rowell, Raymond J. Ornamental Conifers for Australian Gardens. (Illus.). 320p. 1996. 44.95 (0-86840-239-7, Pub. by New South Wales Univ Pr) Intl Spec Bk.

— Ornamental Flowering Shrubs in Australia. (Illus.). 334p. 1991. 37.95 (0-86840-084-X, Pub. by New South Wales Univ Pr) Intl Spec Bk.

— Ornamental Flowering Trees in Australia. (Illus.). 321p. 1991. 37.95 (0-86840-124-2, Pub. by New South Wales Univ Pr) Intl Spec Bk.

— Ornamental Plants in Australia. 4th ed. (Illus.). 244p. 1992. 37.95 (0-86840-372-5, Pub. by New South Wales Univ Pr) Intl Spec Bk.

Rowell, Roger, ed. The Chemistry of Solid Wood: Based on a Short Course & Symposium Sponsored by the Division of Cellulose, Paper & Textile Chemistry at the 185th Meeting of the American Chemical Society, Seattle, WA, March 20-25, 1983. LC 83-22451. (Advances in Chemistry Ser.: No. 207). (Illus.). 624p. 1984. reprint ed. pap. 193.50 (0-608-06782-2, 206697900009) Bks Demand.

***Rowell, Roger, ed.** 5th International Conference on Woodfiber - Plastic Composites Proceedings. 324p. 1999. pap. 65.00 (1-892529-07-6, 7263) Forest Prod.

Rowell, Roger & Sanadi, Anand, eds. 4th International Conference on Woodfiber-Plastic Composites. (Illus.). 334p. 1997. pap. 65.00 (0-935018-95-6, 7277) Forest Prod.

Rowell, Roger M., ed. The Chemistry of Solid Wood. LC 83-22451. (Advances in Chemistry Ser.: No. 207). 614p. 1984. text 85.00 (0-8412-0796-8, Pub. by Am Chemical) OUP.

Rowell, Roger M., et al, eds. Emerging Technologies for Materials & Chemicals from Biomass. LC 91-36048. (ACS Symposium Ser.: No. 476). (Illus.). 480p. 1991. text 110.00 (0-8412-2171-5, Pub. by Am Chemical) OUP.

Rowell, Roger M. & Barbour, R. James, eds. Archaeological Wood: Properties, Chemistry & Preservation. LC 89-39451. (Advances in Chemistry Ser.: No. 225). 473p. 1989. text 85.00 (0-8412-1623-1, Pub. by Am Chemical) OUP.

— Archaeological Wood: Properties, Chemistry, & Preservation: Developed from a Symposium Sponsored by the Cellulose, Paper, & Textile Division at the 196th National Meeting of the American Chemical Society, Los Angeles, CA, September 25-30, 1988. LC 89-39451. (Advances in Chemistry Ser.: No. 225). (Illus.). 487p. reprint ed. pap. 151.00 (0-608-06791-1, 206698800009) Bks Demand.

Rowell, Roger M., et al. Paper & Composites from Agro-Based Resources. LC 96-8877. 384p. 1996. lib. bdg. 110.00 (1-56670-235-6) Lewis Pubs.

Rowell, Roland. Counterfeiting & Forgery - a Practical Guide to the Law. 294p. 1986. boxed set 100.00 (0-406-10110-8, U.K., MICHIE) LEXIS Pub.

Rowell, Roland & Hancock, Jane. Regulating the Sale of Property. 136p. 1993. pap. 43.00 (1-85811-019-X, Pub. by CLT Prof) Gaunt.

Rowell, S. C. Lithuania Ascending: A Pagan Empire Within East-Central Europe, 1295-1345. (Cambridge Studies in Medieval Life & Thought: No. 25). (Illus.). 415p. (C). 1994. text 74.95 (0-521-45011-X) Cambridge U Pr.

Rowell, Unni H., ed. see Geoscience Information Society Staff.

Rowen, David. Sport, Culture, & the Media: The Unruly Trinity. LC 99-33226. 192p. 1999. pap. text 24.95 (0-335-20202-0) OpUniv Pr.

Rowen, Henry S. Behind East Asian Growth: The Political & Social Foundations of Prosperity. LC 97-26883. 376p. (C). 1997. pap. 29.99 (0-415-16520-2) Routledge.

— Behind East Asian Growth: The Political & Social Foundations of Prosperity. LC 97-26883. 376p. (C). 1998. 90.00 (0-415-16519-9) Routledge.

***Rowen, Henry S.** Catch Up: Why Poor Countries Are Becoming Richer, Democratic, Increasingly Peaceable & Sometimes More Dangerous. unabridged ed. (Illus.). 50p. 1999. pap. 7.50 (0-9653935-8-5) Asia-Pacific Res.

Rowen, Henry S., ed. Options for U. S. Energy Policy. 317p. 1977. pap. text 24.95 (0-917616-20-0) Transaction Pubs.

Rowen, Henry S., et al, eds. Defense Conversion, Economic Reform & the Outlook for Russian & Ukrainian Economics. LC 94-6786. 1994. text 55.00 (0-312-12158-X) St Martin.

Rowen, Henry S. & Wolf, Charles, Jr. Impoverished Superpower: Perestroika & the Soviet Military Burden. LC 89-29818. 1990. 29.95 (1-55815-070-6); pap. 19.95 (1-55815-066-8) ICS Pr.

Rowen, Henry S. & Wolf, Charles, eds. The Future of the Soviet Empire. LC 87-20737. 350p. 1988. pap. 19.95 (0-312-01348-5) ICS Pr.

Rowen, Herbert H. History of Early Modern Europe, 1500-1815. 1960. pap. 15.95 (0-672-60697-6, Bobbs) Macmillan.

— John de Witt, Grand Pensionary of Holland, 1625-1672. LC 76-45909. 964p. 1978. reprint ed. pap. 200.00 (0-7837-8596-8, 204941100011) Bks Demand.

— The Princes of Orange: The Stadholders in the Dutch Republic. (Studies in Early Modern History). (Illus.). 264p. (C). 1990. pap. text 19.95 (0-521-39653-0) Cambridge U Pr.

Rowen, Herbert H., tr. see Schulte Nordholt, Jan W.

Rowen, Larry. Beyond Winning: Group Centered Games & Sports. (J). (gr. 2-6). 1990. pap. 10.99 (0-8224-3380-X) Fearon Teacher Aids.

Rowen, Louis. Algebra: Groups, Rings, & Fields. LC 93-39371. (Illus.). 264p. (C). 1995. text 59.00 (1-56881-028-8) AK Peters.

Rowen, Louis, ed. Ring Theory 1989 in Honor of S. A. Amitsur. (Israel Mathematical Conference Proceedings Ser.: Vol. 1). 430p. 1990. reprint ed. pap. 32.00 (0-685-70699-0, IMCP/1C) Am Math.

Rowen, Louis H. Ring Theory. 623p. (C). 1991. text, student ed. 82.00 (0-12-599840-6) Acad Pr.

Rowen, Rachel, tr. see Frieder, Emanuel.

Rowen, Rachel, tr. see Platonov, Vladimir & Rapinchuk, Andrei.

Rowen, Ruth H. Early Chamber Music: Music Book Index. 188p. 1993. reprint ed. lib. bdg. 69.00 (0-7812-9641-2) Rprt Serv.

— Symphonic & Chamber Music Score & Parts Bank Thematic Catalogue of the Facsimile Archive of 18th & Early 19th Century Autographs, Manuscripts, & Printed Copies at the Ph.D Program in Music of the Graduate School of the City University of New York. LC 95-39268. (Thematic Catalogues Ser.: Vol. 24). 1996. 62.00 (0-945193-84-X) Pendragon NY.

Rowen, Ruth H., jt. auth. see Katz, Adele T.

Rowena, Lawson. Anderson County Kentucky 1830-1850 Censuses. iii, 78p. (Orig.). 1987. pap. 11.50 (1-55613-075-9) Heritage Bk.

Rower, Alexander S. Calder Sculpture. 80p. 1998. 19.95 (0-7893-0134-2, Pub. by Universe) St Martin.

***Rower, Alexander S. C., et al.** Calder in Connecticut. (Illus.). 176p. 2000. text 40.00 (0-8478-2249-4) Rizzoli Intl.

Rower, Ann. Armed Response. (High Risk Ser.). 200p. 1995. pap. 12.99 (1-85242-415-X, High Risk Bks) Serpents Tail.

— If You're a Girl. (Native Agents Ser.). 270p. 1990. pap. 6.00 (0-936756-60-8) Autonomedia.

Rower, Ann, et al. Chance: The Catalogue. (Illus.). 44p. 1996. pap. 10.00 (1-889195-05-7) Smart Art Pr.

Rower, Holton. Nettles. (Illus.). 40p. 1991. pap. 35.00 (0-9623585-6-8) Flockophobic Pr.

— Nettles. limited ed. (Illus.). 40p. 1991. 55.00 (0-9623585-5-X) Flockophobic Pr.

Rower, J. R., jt. auth. see Stevens, Benjamin H.

Rower, Jack. The Absentee Landlord: A Survival Guide for the Absent Owner. 76p. (Orig.). 1993. pap. text 12.50 (0-9653817-0-6) Mellwood Pub.

— The Absentee Landlord's Survival Guide. 2nd ed. United Homeowners Association Staff, ed. 99p. 1997. pap. 14.95 (0-9653817-1-4, 0200) Mellwood Pub.

Rower, Richard. The Over-the-Road Driver's Training Manual. 170p. 1999. spiral bd. 32.50 (0-9653817-3-0) Mellwood Pub.

Rowes, P. G. Taxation, 1995. 528p. 1995. pap. 59.95 (1-85805-126-6, Pub. by DP Publns) St Mut.

***Rowh, Mark.** Careers for Crafty People: And Other Dexterous Types. LC 99-47856. (Careers for You Ser.). 192p. 2000. 14.95 (0-658-00211-2, 002112) NTC Contemp Pub Co.

Rowh, Mark. Careers for Crafty People: And Other Dextrous Types. LC 93-16030. (Illus.). 150p. 1994. pap. 9.95 (0-8442-4107-5, VGM Career) NTC Contemp Pub Co.

— Careers for Crafty People: And Other Dextrous Types. LC 93-16030. (Illus.). 150p. 1994. 14.95 (0-8442-4106-7, VGM Career) NTC Contemp Pub Co.

***Rowh, Mark.** Careers for Crafty People & Other Dexterous Types. LC 99-47856. (Careers for You Ser.). 192p. 2000. pap. 9.95 (0-658-00212-0, 002120, VGM Career) NTC Contemp Pub Co.

Rowh, Mark. Coping with Stress in College. 172p. (C). 1989. pap. 9.95 (0-87447-334-9) College Bd.

— Crafts. LC 95-50611. (VGM Career Portraits Ser.). (Illus.). 96p. (gr. 7 up). 1996. 13.95 (0-8442-4378-7, 43787) NTC Contemp Pub Co.

— Drafting Careers. (Opportunities in...Ser.). (Illus.). 160p. 1991. 13.95 (0-8442-6143-2, Passprt Bks); pap. 10.95 (0-8442-6144-0, Passprt Bks) NTC Contemp Pub Co.

***Rowh, Mark.** Fund-Raising Careers. (Opportunities in . . . Ser.). 2000. 14.95 (0-658-00055-1, VGM Career); pap. 11.95 (0-658-00485-9, VGM Career) NTC Contemp Pub Co.

Rowh, Mark. Great Jobs for Chemistry Majors. LC 98-46898. (Great Jobs for... Ser.). 208p. 1999. pap. 11.95 (0-8442-1915-0, 19150, VGM Career) NTC Contemp Pub Co.

— How to Improve Your Grammar & Usage. LC 93-31276. (Speak Out! Write On! Ser.). (Illus.). 96p. (YA). (gr. 7-12). 1994. lib. bdg. 24.00 (0-531-11177-6) Watts.

— How to Improve Your Grammar & Usage. (Speak Out, Write On! Ser.). (Illus.). 96p. (YA). (gr. 7-12). 1994. pap. 7.95 (0-531-15729-6) Watts.

— Opportunities in Drafting Careers. LC 93-10586. (Opportunities In . . . Ser.). (Illus.). 160p. pap. 12.95 (0-8442-4083-4, 297OIDR, VGM Career) NTC Contemp Pub Co.

— Opportunities in Drafting Careers. LC 93-10586. (Opportunities in...Ser.). (Illus.). 160p. 1994. 14.95 (0-8442-4082-6, 40826, VGM Career) NTC Contemp Pub Co.

— Opportunities in Electronics Careers. (Opportunities In . . . Ser.). (Illus.). 160p. pap. 12.95 (0-8442-8184-0, 297OIEL, VGM Career) NTC Contemp Pub Co.

— Opportunities in Electronics Careers. (Opportunities in...Ser.). (Illus.). 160p. 1992. 14.95 (0-8442-8183-2, VGM Career) NTC Contemp Pub Co.

— Opportunities in Electronics Careers. LC 98-42440. (Opportunities in...Ser.). 160p. 1999. 14.95 (0-8442-1841-3, 18413, VGM Career) NTC Contemp Pub Co.

— Opportunities in Electronics Careers. rev. ed. LC 98-42440. (Opportunities in...Ser.). 160p. 1999. pap. 11.95 (0-8442-1845-6, 18456, VGM Career) NTC Contemp Pub Co.

— Opportunities in Installation & Repair Careers. LC 93-47510. (Opportunities In . . . Ser.). (Illus.). 160p. 1994. pap. 11.95 (0-8442-4136-9, 41369, VGM Career) NTC Contemp Pub Co.

— Opportunities in Installation & Repair Careers. LC 93-47510. (Opportunities in...Ser.). (Illus.). 160p. 1995. 14.95 (0-8442-4135-0, 41350, VGM Career) NTC Contemp Pub Co.

— Opportunities in Metal Working Careers. LC 90-50730. (Opportunities In . . . Ser.). (Illus.). 160p. (YA). (gr. 7 up). pap. 12.95 (0-8442-8538-2, 297OIMW, VGM Career) NTC Contemp Pub Co.

— Opportunities in Metal Working Careers. LC 90-50730. (Opportunities in...Ser.). (Illus.). 160p. (YA). (gr. 7 up). 1994. 14.95 (0-8442-8537-4, VGM Career) NTC Contemp Pub Co.

***Rowh, Mark.** Opportunities in Metalworking Careers. LC 99-53372. (Opportunities in... Ser.). 160p. 2000. 14.95 (0-658-00198-1, 001981, VGM Career) NTC Contemp Pub Co.

— Opportunities in Metalworking Careers. rev. ed. LC 99-53372. (Opportunities in... Ser.). 160p. 2000. pap. 11.95 (0-658-00200-7, 002007) NTC Contemp Pub Co.

Rowh, Mark. Opportunities in Warehousing Careers. LC 92-16776. (Opportunities in...Ser.). (Illus.). 160p. 1994. 14.95 (0-8442-4034-6, VGM Career) NTC Contemp Pub Co.

— Opportunities in Waste Management Careers. (Opportunities In . . . Ser.). (Illus.). 160p. pap. 11.95 (0-8442-4019-2, 40192, VGM Career) NTC Contemp Pub Co.

— Opportunities in Welding Careers. LC 96-9351. (Opportunities in... Ser.). (Illus.). 160p. pap. 11.95 (0-8442-4669-7, 46697, Natl Textbk Co) NTC Contemp Pub Co.

— Opportunities in Welding Careers. LC 96-9351. (Opportunities in... Ser.). (Illus.). 160p. 1996. 14.95 (0-8442-4668-9, 46689, Natl Textbk Co) NTC Contemp Pub Co.

— Political Science Majors. LC 98-7263. (Great Jobs for... Ser.). 208p. 1998. pap. 11.95 (0-8442-4724-3, 47243) NTC Contemp Pub Co.

— Slam Dunk Cover Letters That Score Every Time. LC 97-1853. 144p. 1997. pap. 7.95 (0-8442-8198-0, 81980) NTC Contemp Pub Co.

— W. E. B. Du Bois: Champion of Civil Rights. LC 98-50787. (African-American Biographies Ser.). (Illus.). 128p. (YA). (gr. 6 up). 1999. lib. bdg. 20.95 (0-7660-1209-3) Enslow Pubs.

— Welding Careers. (Opportunities in...Ser.). 160p. 1992. pap. 10.95 (0-8442-8599-4, VGM Career) NTC Contemp Pub Co.

— Welding Careers. (Opportunities in...Ser.). 160p. 1994. 13.95 (0-8442-8598-6, VGM Career) NTC Contemp Pub Co.

— Winning Government Grants & Contracts for Your Small Business. 191p. 1991. 16.95 (0-07-054142-6) McGraw.

Rowh, Mark, jt. auth. see Heitzmann, W.

Rowh, Mark, jt. auth. see Heitzmann, William R.

Rowhani, Fazlollah. Elegy. 2nd rev. ed. (Illus.). 56p. 1989. reprint ed. pap. text 4.00 (0-685-26489-0) Farabi Pubs.

Rowhani, Shahrokh, ed. see Johnson, A. Ivan & ASTM Committee D-18 on Soil & Rock.

Rowinska, Leokadia. Poklosie: Gleanning. (Illus.). 200p. (Orig.). 1987. pap. 10.95 (0-930401-07-7) Artex Pub.

Rowinski, Jim & Rowinski, Kate. L. L. Bean Outdoor Photography Handbook. LC 99-17165. (Illus.). 162p. (Orig.). 1999. pap. 18.95 (1-55821-879-3) Lyons Pr.

Rowinski, Kate. Cats in the Dark. LC 97-31124. (Illus.). 32p. (J). (ps-3). 1998. 14.95 (0-89272-427-7) Down East.

— Ellie Bear & the Fly-Away Fly. LC 93-25260. (Illus.). 32p. (J). (gr. 1-4). 1993. 14.95 (0-89272-335-1) Down East.

— L. L. Bear's Island Adventure. LC 92-71972. (Illus.). 32p. (J). (ps-4). 1992. 4.95 (0-89272-320-3) Down East.

***Rowinski, Kate, ed.** The Quotable Cook. (Illus.). 256p. 2000. 20.00 (1-58574-164-7) Lyons Pr.

Rowinski, Kate, jt. auth. see Rowinski, Jim.

Rowinski, Leokadia. That the Nightingale Return: Memoir of the Polish Resistance, the Warsaw Uprising & German P. O. W. Camps. (Illus.). 180p. 1999. lib. bdg. 32.50 (0-7864-0513-9) McFarland & Co.

Rowinsky, Erick K., jt. ed. see McGuire, William P.

Rowitz, L., ed. Mental Retardation in the Year 2000. (Disorders of Human Learning, Behavior, & Communication Ser.). (Illus.). 344p. 1992. 123.00 (0-387-97474-1) Spr-Verlag.

Rowitz, Louis. Public Health Leadership for the 21st Century. 275p. 2000. 50.00 (0-8342-0738-9) Aspen Pub.

Rowitz, Louis, et al. Socio-Behavioral Sciences & Public Health Practice. 300p. 39.95 (0-8342-0627-7) Aspen Pub.

Rowitz, Mary & Brauckmann-Towns, Krista. The Tortoise & the Hare: A Tale of Perseverance. LC 97-220751. (Illus.). 1997. write for info. (0-7853-2132-2) Pubns Intl Ltd.

Rowl, Wilson. Where Is the Red Fern? (Illus.). (J). 1986. mass mkt. 6.95 (0-553-16672-7) BDD Bks Young Read.

Rowland. Applied Genetics. (UK - Science Ser.). 1990. pap. 26.95 (0-17-438511-0) S-W Pub.

***Rowland.** When Elvis Met Jerry. 2000. mass mkt. 18.00 (0-306-80965-6, Pub. by Da Capo) HarpC.

Rowland, A. Westley. Key Resources on Institutional Advancement: A Guide to the Field & Its Literature. LC 86-10296. (Jossey-Bass Higher Education Ser.). 269p. reprint ed. pap. 83.40 (0-7837-2543-4, 204270200006) Bks Demand.

Rowland, A. Westley, ed. Handbook of Institutional Advancement: A Practical Guide to College & University Relations, Fund Raising, Alumni Relations, Government Relations, Publications, & Executive Management for Continued Advancement. LC 76-50722. (Jossey-Bass Higher Education Ser.). 589p. reprint ed. pap. 182.60 (0-608-16911-0, 202776700056) Bks Demand.

Rowland, Adam B., jt. auth. see Rowland, Heidi F.

Rowland, Alan. Using WordPerfect 6.0 for DOS. 200p. (C). 1995. pap. text 18.76 (0-395-72128-8) HM.

An Asterisk (*) at the beginning of an entry indicates that the title is appearing for the first time.

— Using WordPerfect 6.1 for Windows. 224p. (C). 1995. pap. text 18.76 (0-395-72132-6) HM.

Rowland, Amy Z. How I Learned to Make Friends. (Illus.). 44p. (J). (gr. 1-6). 1995. pap. 17.95 (1-882732-29-4) Childswork.

— Traditional Reiki for Our Times: Practical Methods for Personal & Planetary Healing. LC 98-10603. (Illus.). 256p. 1998. pap. 19.95 (0-89281-777-1, Inner Trad) Inner Tradit.

Rowland, Art. Machine & Assembler Language Simulation. 112p. (C). 1994. pap. text 20.55 (1-56226-195-9) CAT Pub.

Rowland, Arthur R. & Dorsey, James E. Bibliography of the Writings on Georgia History, Nineteen Hundred to Nineteen Seventy. LC 77-21733. 1978. 25.00 (0-87152-254-3) Reprint.

Rowland, B. Selections from the Man from Snowy River. 24p. 1997. pap. 8.95 (0-7935-7779-9) H Leonard.

Rowland, Barbara, jt. auth. see Rippey, Elizabeth.

Rowland, Barbara M. Ordered Liberty & the Constitutional Framework: The Political Thought of Friedrich A. Hayek, 176. LC 87-278. (Contributions in Political Science Ser.: No. 176). 156p. 1987. 49.95 (0-313-25609-8, RLI/, Greenwood Pr) Greenwood.

Rowland, Beatrice L., jt. auth. see Rowland, Howard S.

Rowland, Beatrice L., jt. ed. see Rowland, Howard S.

Rowland, Ben. Allison's Affair with the High School Principal. LC 92-239897. 141p. 1993. reprint ed. 21.95 (0-9636632-0-8) GI Pub.

Rowland, Benjamin, Jr. Ancient Art from Afghanistan: Treasures of the Kabul Museum. LC 74-27419. (Asia Society Ser.). (Illus.). 1976. reprint ed. lib. bdg. 33.95 (0-405-06567-1) Ayer.

— The Evolution of the Buddha Image. LC 74-27420. (Asia Society Ser.). (Illus.). 1976. reprint ed. lib. bdg. 27.95 (0-405-06568-X) Ayer.

Rowland, Benjamin M., jt. auth. see Callao, David P.

Rowland, Beryl. Birds with Human Souls: A Guide to Bird Symbolism. LC 77-4230. 232p. reprint ed. pap. 72.00 (0-7837-3025-X, 204291500006) Bks Demand.

— Blind Beasts: Chaucer's Animal World. LC 77-104839. (Illus.). 206p. reprint ed. pap. 63.90 (0-7837-0569-7, 204091300019) Bks Demand.

Rowland, Beryl, ed. Companion to Chaucer Studies. rev. ed. 528p. 1979. pap. text 22.95 (0-19-502489-3) OUP.

Rowland, Beryl, ed. see Birney, Earle.

Rowland, Beth, ed. Quick Games for Children's Ministry: 100 Games. LC 92-33256. 1992. 14.99 (1-55945-157-2) Group Pub.

Rowland, Bob, ed. see Tindell, Charles.

Rowland, Bob, ed. see Watrous, Richard.

Rowland, Bobbie H., ed. see Houtman, Sally.

Rowland, C. K. & Carp, Robert A. Politics & Judgment in Federal District Courts. LC 95-46680. 240p. (C). 1996. 29.95 (0-7006-0776-5) U Pr of KS.

Rowland, C. K., jt. auth. see Carp, Robert A.

Rowland, Charles & Tamsitt, Gary. Hutley's Australian Wills Precedents. 4th ed. 286p. 1989. 65.00 (0-409-49488-7, AT, MICHIE); pap. 44.00 (0-409-30321-6, AT, MICHIE) LEXIS Pub.

Rowland, Charles, et al. Wills, Probate & Administrative Law in New South Wales. 3rd ed. 1200p. 1996. 169.00 (0-455-21364-X, Pub. by LawBk Co); pap. 135.00 (0-455-21365-8, Pub. by LawBk Co) Gaunt.

Rowland, Cherry, jt. auth. see Friedrich, Elizabeth.

Rowland, Christopher. Radical Christianity: A Reading of Recovery. LC 88-12402. 207p. 1988. reprint ed. pap. 64.20 (0-7837-9824-5, 206055300005) Bks Demand.

Rowland, Christopher. Revelation. (Commentary Ser.). 1997. pap. text 16.00 (0-7162-0493-2) Epworth Pr.

Rowland, Christopher, ed. The Cambridge Companion to Liberation Theology. LC 98-20489. (Companions to Religion Ser.). (Illus.). 160p. (C). 1999. 59.95 (0-521-46144-8); pap. 19.95 (0-521-46707-1) Cambridge U Pr.

Rowland, Christopher & Fletcher-Louis, Crispin H., eds. Understanding, Studying & Reading: New Testament Essays in Honour of John Ashton. LC 98-121854. (JSNTS Ser.: Vol. 153). 267p. 1998. 75.00 (1-85075-828-X, Pub. by Sheffield Acad) CUP Services.

Rowland, Cynthia, tr. see Cristiani, Leon.

Rowland, Daniel. Competing to Win: How to Succeed in Business by Really Trying. Beckley, John L., ed. (Illus.). 158p. 1983. 14.95 (0-910187-01-0) Economics Pr.

Rowland, David. A History of Pianoforte Pedalling. LC 92-37065. (Cambridge Musical Texts & Monographs). 206p. (C). 1994. text 64.95 (0-521-40266-2) Cambridge U Pr.

Rowland, David, ed. The Cambridge Companion to the Piano. LC 97-41860. (Cambridge Companions to Music Ser.). (Illus.). 325p. (C). 1999. 64.95 (0-521-47470-1); pap. text 22.95 (0-521-47986-X) Cambridge U Pr.

Rowland, David, tr. see Whitlock, Keith, ed.

Rowland, Della. The Case of the Barking Dog. (Clue Jr. Ser.: No. 11). 80p. (J). (gr. 2-4). 1997. pap. text 3.50 (0-590-13786-7) Scholastic Inc.

Rowland, Della. The Case of the Chocolate Fingerprints. (Clue Jr. Ser.: No. 3). (J). (gr. 4-7). 1995. pap. 2.99 (0-590-26217-3) Scholastic Inc.

— The Case of the Clubhouse Thief. (Clue Jr. Ser.: No. 8). (J). (gr. 2-4). 1997. pap. 3.50 (0-590-86634-6) Scholastic Inc.

— The Case of the Karate Chop. (Clue Jr. Ser.: No. 9). (J). (gr. 2-4). 1997. pap. text 3.50 (0-590-86635-4, Little Apple) Scholastic Inc.

— The Case of the Missing Movie. (Clue Jr. Ser.: No. 4). (J). (gr. 4-7). 1995. pap. 2.99 (0-590-26218-1) Scholastic Inc.

— The Case of the Mystery Ghost. (Clue Jr. Ser.: No. 7). (J). (gr. 2-4). 1996. pap. text 2.99 (0-590-86633-8) Scholastic Inc.

— The Case of the Runaway Turtle. (Clue Jr. Ser.: No. 6). (J). (gr. 4-7). 1996. pap. text 2.99 (0-590-62373-7) Scholastic Inc.

— The Case of the Secret Password. (Clue Jr. Ser.: No. 10). (J). (gr. 2-4). 1997. pap. text 3.50 (0-590-13785-9, Little Apple) Scholastic Inc.

— The Case of the Soccer Camp Mystery. (Clue Jr. Ser.: No. 13). (J). (gr. 2-4). 1998. pap. 3.50 (0-590-13788-3, Little Apple) Scholastic Inc.

— The Case of the Winning Skateboard. (Clue Jr. Ser.: No. 12). (J). (gr. 2-4). 1998. pap. text 3.50 (0-590-13787-5) Scholastic Inc.

— The Case of the Zoo Clue. (Clue Jr. Ser.: No. 5). (Illus.). (J). (gr. 4-7). 1996. pap. text 2.99 (0-590-62372-9) Scholastic Inc.

— Christmas: A Holiday Treasury. LC 94-71121. (Illus.). 16p. 1994. 4.95 (0-8362-3086-8) Andrews & McMeel.

— Little Red Riding Hood: The Wolf's Tale. LC 93-42781. (Upside Down Tales Ser.). (Illus.). (J). 1994. pap. 8.95 (0-8065-1526-0, Citadel Pr) Carol Pub Group.

— Little Red Riding Hood & the Wolf's Tale. (J). (ps-3). 1991. 13.95 (1-55972-072-7, Birch Ln Pr) Carol Pub Group.

— Martin Luther King, Jr. The Dream of Peaceful Revolution. Gallin, Richard, ed. (Civil Rights Ser.). (Illus.). 128p. (J). (gr. 5 up). 1990. lib. bdg. 12.95 (0-382-09924-9) Silver Burdett Pr.

— Martin Luther King, Jr. The Dream of Peaceful Revolution. Gallin, Richard, ed. (Civil Rights Ser.). (Illus.). 128p. (YA). (gr. 5 up). 1990. pap. 7.95 (0-382-24062-6) Silver Burdett Pr.

— Martin Luther King, Jr. The Dream of Peaceful Revolution. (History of the Civil Rights Movement Ser.). (J). 1990. 13.15 (0-606-04742-5, Pub. by Turtleback) Demco.

— The Story of Sacajawea: Guide to Lewis & Clark. 96p. (J). (gr. k-6). 1989. pap. 3.99 (0-440-40215-8, YB BDD) BDD Bks Young Read.

Rowland, Della, ed. Christmas: A Holiday Treasury. LC 93-16663. (Illus.). 32p. (J). 1993. 6.95 (0-8362-4938-0) Andrews & McMeel.

Rowland, Desmond & Bailey, James. The Law Enforcement Handbook. LC 84-18840. 294p. reprint ed. pap. 91.20 (0-7837-6686-6, 204630200011) Bks Demand.

Rowland, Diana. Japanese Business Etiquette. 2nd rev. ed. 304p. (Orig.). 1993. mass mkt. 14.99 (0-446-39518-8, Pub. by Warner Bks) Little.

Rowland, Diana, jt. auth. see Engholm, Christopher.

Rowland, Diane & Lyons, Barbara, eds. Financing Home Care: Improving Protection for Disabled Elderly People. LC 91-20809. (Johns Hopkins Studies in Health Care Finance & Administration: Vol. 4). (Illus.). 276p. 1991. reprint ed. pap. 85.60 (0-608-07389-X, 206761600009) Bks Demand.

Rowland, Diane, et al. Medicaid & Managed Care: Lessons from the Literature. 88p. 1995. write for info. (0-944525-21-0) H J Kaiser.

— Medicaid at the Crossroads: A Report of the Kaiser Commission on the Future of Medicaid. 90p. (Orig.). 1992. pap. 5.00 (0-944525-10-5) H J Kaiser.

— Medicaid Financing Crisis: Balancing Responsibilities, Priorities, & Dollars. 222p. (C). 1994. pap. 21.95 (0-87168-514-0, 93-04S) Transaction Pubs.

Rowland, Diane, jt. auth. see Davis, Karen.

Rowland, Diane, jt. auth. see Macdonald, Elizabeth.

Rowland, Donald E. John Rowland & Williams Workman: Southern California Pioneers of 1841. LC 99-17972. (Western Frontiersmen Ser.: Vol. XXVII). (Illus.). 224p. 1999. 32.00 (0-87062-290-0) A H Clark.

Rowland, Donald J. Whites Crossing. LC 96-92135. (Illus.). viii, 231p. 1996. 20.00 (0-9653407-0-8) Sunset Publns.

Rowland, Dunbar. History of Mississippi, the Heart of the South, Vol. I. (Illus.). 933p. 1994. reprint ed. lib. bdg. 95.00 (0-8328-4265-6) Higginson Bk Co.

— History of Mississippi, the Heart of the South, Vol. II. (Illus.). 905p. 1994. reprint ed. lib. bdg. 95.00 (0-8328-4266-4) Higginson Bk Co.

— Military History of Mississippi, 1803-1898. LC 78-2454. 704p. 1999. reprint ed. 47.50 (0-87152-266-7) Reprint.

— Military History Official & Statistical Register of the State of Mississippi, Military History Only. 565p. 1995. reprint ed. lib. bdg. 59.50 (0-8328-6546-X) Higginson Bk Co.

— Official & Statistical Register of the State of Mississippi. 1317p. 1995. reprint ed. lib. bdg. 125.00 (0-8328-5050-0) Higginson Bk Co.

Rowland, Dunbar, ed. Mississippi: Sketches of Counties, Towns, Events, Institutions & Persons Arranged in Cyclopedic Form, 4 vols., 1. LC 76-73. 1976. reprint ed. 37.50 (0-87152-220-9) Reprint.

— Mississippi: Sketches of Counties, Towns, Events, Institutions & Persons Arranged in Cyclopedic Form, 4 vols., 2. LC 76-73. 1976. reprint ed. 37.50 (0-87152-221-7) Reprint.

— Mississippi: Sketches of Counties, Towns, Events, Institutions & Persons Arranged in Cyclopedic Form, 4 vols., Vol. 3. LC 76-73. 1976. reprint ed. 37.50 (0-87152-222-5) Reprint.

— Mississippi: Sketches of Counties, Towns, Events, Institutions & Persons Arranged in Cyclopedic Form, 4 vols., Vol. 4. LC 76-73. 1976. reprint ed. suppl. ed. 37.50 (0-87152-223-3) Reprint.

Rowland, Dunbar, ed. see Claiborne, William C.

Rowland, Dunbar, ed. see Davis, Jefferson.

Rowland, Dunbar, ed. see Mississippi Department of Archives and History Sta.

Rowland, Edna. How to Obtain a Birth Certificate. 1990. pap. 17.00 (0-86690-370-4, 3041-014) Am Fed Astrologers.

— True Crime Astrology: Famous Murders & Suicides. LC 96-19695. (Popular Astrology Ser.). (Illus.). 224p. (Orig.). 1996. pap. 14.95 (1-56718-588-6) Llewellyn Pubns.

Rowland, Eleanor H., ed. The Psychological Experiences Connected with Different Parts of Speech. (Psychology Monographs General & Applied: Vol. 8). 1974. reprint ed. pap. 55.00 (0-8115-1407-2) Periodicals Srv.

Rowland-Entwistle, Theodore. The Pop-Up Atlas of the World. (Illus.). 18p. (J). (gr. 3 up). 1988. pap. 12.95 (0-671-65898-0) S&S Bks Yung.

— Rivers & Lakes. (Our World Ser.). (Illus.). 48p. (J). (gr. 5-8). 1999. lib. bdg. 20.00 (0-382-09499-9) Silver Burdett Pr.

Rowland-Entwistle, Theodore & O'Donoghue, Michael. Rocks & Minerals of the World. (Science Nature Guides Ser.). (Illus.). 80p. (J). (gr. 4-7). 1998. reprint ed. 12.95 (1-57145-379-2, Silver Dolph) Advantage Pubs.

Rowland-Entwistle, Theodore, ed. see Abbot, R. Tucker.

Rowland, Eron. Andrew Jackson's Campaign Against the British. LC 72-146870. (Select Bibliographies Reprint Ser.). (Illus.). 1977. reprint ed. 37.95 (0-8369-5637-0) Ayer.

***Rowland, Eron.** Mississippi Territory in the War of 1812. 249p. 1999. 25.00 (0-8063-0301-8) Clearfield Co.

Rowland, F., jt. auth. see Marshall, L.

Rowland, Fytton & Meadows, Jack, eds. New Models & Opportunities: Electronic Publishing '97 Conference Proceedings. (Illus.). 300p. 1997. 60.00 (1-891365-00-2) ICCC Pr.

— Towards the Information Rich Society: Electronic Publishing '98 Conference Proceedings. (Illus.). 300p. 1997. 60.00 (1-891365-02-9) ICCC Pr.

***Rowland, Fytton & Rhodes, Peter, eds.** Information Sources in Chemistry. 5th ed. 360p. 2000. 100.00 (1-85739-282-5) Bowker-Saur.

***Rowland, Gordon.** A Tripartite Seed: The Future Creating Capacity of Designing, Learning & Systems. LC 99-24833. (Advances in Systems Theory, Complexity & the Human Sciences Ser.). 256p. (C). 1999. 49.50 (1-57273-191-5); pap. 21.95 (1-57273-192-3) Hampton Pr NJ.

Rowland, Heidi F. & Rowland, Adam B. Hospital Consents Manual, Vol. 1. LC 92-22018. 1992. ring bd. 249.00 (0-8342-0328-6, S50) Aspen Pub.

Rowland, Herbert. Matthias Claudius: Language as "Infamous Funnel" & Its Imperatives. LC 96-29134. (Illus.). 335p. 1997. 48.50 (0-8386-3686-1) Fairleigh Dickinson.

Rowland, Howard. Let's Read the Arabic Newspapers: Arabic Reader. 1997. pap. 19.95 (0-86685-673-0) Intl Bk Ctr.

***Rowland, Howard D.** Barking Her Way to the Top: A Collie Pursues a Career in the Civil Service. (Illus.). 296p. 2000. pap. 18.95 (1-877809-81-0) Park Pl Pubns.

Rowland, Howard S. Ambulatory Care Quality Assurance Manual. 1990. ring bd. 199.00 (0-8342-0134-8, S24) Aspen Pub.

— Hospital Administration Handbook. LC 83-9236. 768p. (C). 1991. 149.00 (0-89443-941-3) Aspen Pub.

— Hospital Risk Management: Forms, Checklists & Guidelines, 2 vols., Set. 1997. ring bd. 275.00 (0-8342-0121-6) Aspen Pub.

— Hospitals & Health Systems Quality Management. 2 vols., Set. 1997. ring bd. 359.00 (0-8342-0072-4) Aspen Pub.

— Operating Room Administration Manual: Checklists, Guidelines & Forms. 650p. 1991. 152.00 (0-8342-0174-7, S31) Aspen Pub.

Rowland, Howard S. & Rowland, Beatrice L. Manual of Hospital Administration. LC 92-10857. ring bd. 249.00 (0-8342-0324-3) Aspen Pub.

— Nursing Administration Handbook. 4th ed. LC 96-39566. 768p. 1997. 80.00 (0-8342-0926-8, 20926) Aspen Pub.

— The Nursing Department Forms Manual. 500p. 1993. 199.00 (0-8342-0334-0, S58) Aspen Pub.

Rowland, Howard S. & Rowland, Beatrice L., eds. Manual of Nursing Quality Assurance. ring bd. 289.00 (0-87189-875-6, S08) Aspen Pub.

Rowland, Howard S., et al. Hospital Legal Forms, Checklists & Guidelines, 2 vols. LC 86-17391. ring bd. 440.00 (0-87189-053-4) Aspen Pub.

Rowland, I. Timor: Including the Islands of Roti & Ndao. LC 93-186479. (World Bibliographical Ser.). 160p. 1992. lib. bdg. 67.50 (1-85109-159-9) ABC-CLIO.

Rowland, Ian R. Nutrition, Toxicity & Cancer. 464p. 1991. lib. bdg. 159.00 (0-8493-8812-0, QP141) CRC Pr.

— Nutrition, Toxicity & Cancer. 450p. 1990. 62.50 (0-936923-47-4) Telford Pr.

Rowland, Ingrid D. The Culture of the High Renaissance: Ancients & Moderns in Sixteenth-Century Rome. LC 97-29765. (Illus.). 448p. (C). 1998. text 65.00 (0-521-58145-1) Cambridge U Pr.

***Rowland, Ingrid D.** The Culture of the High Renaissance: Ancients & Moderns in Sixteenth-Century Rome. 446p. (C). 2000. pap. Price not set. (0-521-79441-2) Cambridge U Pr.

— Place of Antique Early Modern Europe. 2000. pap. 22.00 (0-935573-28-3) U Ch Pr.

***Rowland, Ingrid D., ed.** Vitruvius: Ten Books of Architecture. LC 98-11716. (Illus.). 317p. (C). 1999. 80.00 (0-521-55364-4) Cambridge U Pr.

***Rowland, Ingrid D. & University of Chicago Staff.** The Ecstatic Journey: Athanasius Kircher in Baroque Rome. LC 00-27481. (Illus.). 2000. write for info. (0-943056-25-X) Univ Chi Lib.

Rowland, J. F., jt. ed. see Bottle, R. T.

Rowland, Jay, et al. Pocket Guide to Fly Fishing for Steelhead. (Illus.). 28p. 1994. spiral bd. 12.95 (0-9633024-9-3) Greycliff Pub.

Rowland, Jenny, ed. Early Welsh Saga Poetry: A Study & Edition of the Englynion. 698p. 1990. 170.00 (0-85991-275-2) Boydell & Brewer.

Rowland, John. Mysteries of Science. LC 78-105035. (Essay Index Reprint Ser.). 1977. 21.95 (0-8369-1624-7) Ayer.

Rowland, John H., jt. auth. see Hanna, J. Ray.

Rowland, Jon T. Faint Praise & Civil Leer: The "Decline" of Eighteenth-Century Panegyric. LC 94-17432. 190p. 1995. 32.50 (0-87413-543-5) U Delaware Pr.

— "Swords in Myrtle Dress'd" Toward a Rhetoric of Sodom: Gay Readings of Homosexual Politics & Poetics in the Eighteenth Century. LC 97-21641. 248p. 1998. 41.50 (0-8386-3760-4) Fairleigh Dickinson.

Rowland-Jones, Anthony. Playing Recorder Sonatas: Technique & Interpretation. (Illus.). 240p. (C). 1992. 59.95 (0-19-879002-3); pap. text 29.95 (0-19-879001-5) OUP.

Rowland-Jones, Anthony, jt. ed. see Thomson, John M.

***Rowland-Jones, Sarah & McMichael, Andrew J.** Lymphocytes: A Practical Approach. 2nd ed. LC 99-54711. 384p. 2000. write for info. (0-19-963817-9); 55.00 (0-19-963816-0) OUP.

Rowland, K. Nicole, ed. see Miller, Frances D.

Rowland, Kendrith M., jt. ed. see Ferris, Gerald R.

***Rowland, Laura J.** Samurai's Wife. LC 99-87939. 261p. 2000. text 23.95 (0-312-20325-X, Minotaur) St Martin.

Rowland, Laura Joh. Bundori. 368p. 1997. mass mkt. 5.99 (0-06-101197-5, Harp PBks) HarpC.

— The Concubine's Tattoo. LC 98-7910. 336p. 1998. text 23.95 (0-312-19252-5) St Martin.

***Rowland, Laura Joh.** The Concubine's Tattoo. LC 98-7910. 384p. 2000. mass mkt. 6.50 (0-312-96922-8) St Martin.

Rowland, Laura Joh. Shinju. 384p. mass mkt. write for info. (0-06-101035-9, Harp PBks) HarpC.

— Shinju. 384p. 1997. mass mkt. 5.99 (0-06-100950-4) HarpC.

Rowland, Lawrence S. Window on the Atlantic: The Rise & Fall of Santa Elena South Carolina's Spanish City. Brimelow, Judith M., ed. (Illus.). 32p. 1990. pap. 5.00 (1-880067-03-X) SC Dept of Arch & Hist.

Rowland, Lawrence S., et al. The History of Beaufort County, South Carolina: Vol. 1 : 1514-1861. LC 96-10078. (Illus.). 592p. 1996. 39.95 (1-57003-090-1) U of SC Pr.

Rowland, Leon. Santa Cruz: The Early Years. Gant, Michael S., ed. LC 80-81418. (Illus.). 273p. 1980. pap. 7.95 (0-934136-04-1) Otter B Bks.

Rowland, Leslie, jt. auth. see Berlin, Ira.

Rowland, Leslie S., jt. ed. see Berlin, Ira.

Rowland, Lewis P. Current Neurologic Drugs. 2nd ed. 382p. 1998. pap. 49.00 (0-683-30475-5) Lppncott W & W.

Rowland, Lewis P. Merritt's Neurology. 10th ed. 1,024p. text 89.00 (0-683-30474-7) Lppncott W & W.

— Merritt's Neurology: Companion Handbook. 10th ed. 500p. pap. text 32.95 (0-683-30496-8) Lppncott W & W.

Rowland, Lewis P., ed. Amyotrophic Lateral Sclerosis & Other Motor Neuron Diseases. LC 91-6871. (Advances in Neurology Ser.: No. 56). 591p. 1991. pap. 183.30 (0-608-05601-4, 206605900006) Bks Demand.

— Human Motor Neuron Diseases. LC 81-40378. (Advances in Neurology Ser.: No. 36). (Illus.). 591p. 1982. reprint ed. pap. 183.30 (0-608-00634-3, 206122200007) Bks Demand.

— Merritt's Textbook of Neurology. 9th ed. (Illus.). 1000p. 1995. 79.50 (0-683-07400-8) Lppncott W & W.

Rowland, Lewis P. & Klein, Donald F., eds. Current Neurologic Drugs. 360p. 1996. pap. text 53.00 (1-878132-72-5) Current Med.

Rowland, Lewis P., jt. ed. see Klein, Donald F.

Rowland, Lori, jt. auth. see Pierce, Kathy.

Rowland, Lucy M. Release of Genetically Engineered Organisms: Planning Aspects. LC 95-38449. (CPL Bibliographies Ser.: Vol. 324). 33p. 1995. pap. 10.00 (0-86602-324-0, Sage Prdcls Pr) Sage.

Rowland, Mabel, ed. Bert Williams, Son of Laughter. LC 72-84693. 218p. 1969. reprint ed. lib. bdg. 59.50 (0-8371-1667-8, ROW&) Greenwood.

Rowland, Malcolm, et al, eds. Variability in Drug Therapy: Description, Estimation, & Control: A Sandoz Workshop. LC 85-1888. 270p. 1985. reprint ed. pap. 83.70 (0-608-04735-X, 206545600004) Bks Demand.

Rowland, Malcolm & Tozer, Thomas N. Clinical Pharmacokinetics: Concepts & Applications. 3rd ed. LC 94-26305. (Illus.). 608p. 1995. 55.00 (0-683-07404-0) Lppncott W & W.

***Rowland, Marcus L.** The Challenger Years: Forgotten Futures Adventures for George E. Challenger's Mysteries. (Illus.). 2000. pap. 18.00 (0-9668926-7-4) Heliograph Inc.

— George E. Challenger's Mysterious World: A Forgotten Futures Worldbook. (Illus.). 2000. pap. 18.00 (0-9668926-6-6) Heliograph Inc.

— Masters of the Graviton: Forgotten Futures Adventures for Log Of. (Illus.). 2000. pap. 18.00 (0-9668926-5-8) Heliograph Inc.

Rowland, Margaret, ed. see Kaufman, Julie.

***Rowland, Marilyn & Brenner, Diane, eds.** Beyond Book Indexing: How to Get Started in Web Indexing, Embedded Indexing, & Other Computer-Based Media. 1999. 31.25 (1-57387-081-1) Info Today Inc.

Rowland, Mary. Best Practices for Financial Advisors. LC 96-52818. (Bloomberg Professional Library). 336p. 1997. 40.00 (1-57660-006-8, Pub. by Bloomberg NJ) Norton.

— A Commonsense Guide to Mutual Funds. LC 96-83201. (Bloomberg Personal Bookshelf Ser.). (Illus.). 240p. 1996. 19.95 (1-57660-000-9, Pub. by Bloomberg NJ) Norton.

R

R

— A Commonsense Guide to Your 401(k) LC 97-35143. (Bloomberg Personal Bookshelf Ser.). (Illus.). 240p. 1997. 19.95 (*1-57660-019-X*, Pub. by Bloomberg NJ) Norton.

— The New Commonsense Guide to Mutual Funds. rev. ed. LC 98-36088. (Bloomberg Press Ser.). (Illus.). 336p. 1998. pap. 15.95 (*1-57660-063-7*, Pub. by Bloomberg NJ) Norton.

Rowland, Mary C. As Long As Life: The Memoirs of a Frontier Woman Doctor. 1996. mass mkt. write for info. (*0-449-22511-9*, Crest) Fawcett.

Rowland, Mary C. & Loomis, F. A. As Long As Life: The Memoirs of a Frontier Woman Doctor, Mary Canaga Rowland, 1873-1966. LC 94-66409. (Illus.). 192p. (Orig.). 1994. pap. 11.95 (*0-9641357-0-1*) Storm Peak.

Rowland, May. Dare to Believe! LC 89-50842. 1961. 3.98 (*0-87159-024-7*) Unity Bks.

— The Magic of the Word. LC 73-180756. 182p. 1972. 3.48 (*0-87159-094-8*) Unity Bks.

Rowland, Melanie J., jt. auth. see Bean, Michael J.

Rowland, Michael D. Absolute Happiness: The Way to a Life of Complete Fulfillment. LC 95-1312. 256p. 1995. pap. 12.95 (*1-56170-219-6*, 172) Hay House.

***Rowland, Michael D.** S. A. F. E. Handbook: School Administrator Facility Examination. 53p. 1999. pap. 8.00 (*0-87367-819-2*) Phi Delta Kappa.

Rowland, Michael L. & Forthofer, Ronald N. Investigation of Nonresponse Bias: Hispanic Health & Nutrition Examination Survey. LC 93-29686. (Vital & Health Statistics Ser. 2: Data Evaluation & Methods Research: No. 119). 5.50 (*0-8406-0485-8*) Natl Ctr Health Stats.

***Rowland, Nancy & Goss, Stephen.** Evidence-Based Counselling & Psychological Therapies: Research & Applications. LC 00-21257. 2000. pap. write for info. (*0-415-20507-7*) Routledge.

Rowland, Nancy & Tolley, Keith. Evaluating the Cost-Effectiveness of Counselling in Health Care. 256p. (C). 1995. pap. 27.99 (*0-415-07661-7*, C0326) Routledge.

— Evaluating the Cost-Effectiveness of Counselling in Health Care. LC 94-47491. 256p. (C). (gr. 13). 1995. 85.00 (*0-415-07660-9*, C0325) Routledge.

Rowland, Natalie B. Valley of Maize: Breads, Muffins, Treats. Ruggles, Laurel, ed. LC 98-65134. (Illus.). 144p. 1998. pap. 12.95 (*0-918860-56-3*, 8250) G Ohsawa.

Rowland, O. W. A History of Van Buren County, Michigan, 2 vols., Set. (Illus.). 1158p. 1993. reprint ed. lib. bdg. 115.00 (*0-8328-3484-X*) Higginson Bk Co.

Rowland, Patrick. Property Investments & Their Financing. 288p. 1993. pap. 55.00 (*0-455-21167-1*, Pub. by LawBk Co) Gaunt.

Rowland, Peter. Birds of Australia. (Eco-Travel Guides Ser.). (Illus.). 144p. 1998. pap. 15.95 (*0-88359-035-2*, Pub. by R Curtis Pubng) Chelsea Green Pub.

— The Life & Times of Thomas Day, 1748-1789 - English Philanthropist & Author: Virtue Almost Personified. LC 95-31872. (Studies in British History: Vol. 39). (Illus.). 468p. 1996. text 109.95 (*0-7734-8844-8*) E Mellen.

— A Photographic Guide to Mammals of Australia. (Eco-Travel Guides Ser.). (Illus.). 144p. 1998. pap. 15.95 (*0-88359-032-8*, Pub. by R Curtis Pubng) Chelsea Green Pub.

Rowland, Phyllis C. How to Write "Time of Your Life" Stories in Ten Easy Steps. (Illus.). 272p. (Orig.). (C). 1996. pap. text 19.95 (*1-889668-02-8*) S & D.

***Rowland, Pleasant T.** American Girl Planner. 1999. pap. 11.95 (*1-56247-802-8*); text 11.95 (*1-56247-800-1*); text 11.95 (*1-56247-801-X*); text 11.95 (*1-56247-745-5*) Pleasant Co.

Rowland, Pleasant T. American Girl Planner Purple. 1998. 10.95 (*1-56247-618-1*) Pleasant Co.

Rowland, Ralph S., et al. Kellenbergers & Shearers of Pennsylvania, Maryland, & Points West. LC 85-60465. xi, 287p. 1985. 15.00 (*0-9605746-3-8*) R & S Rowland.

***Rowland, Randy.** The Sins We Love: Embracing Brokenness, Hoping for Wholeness. LC 00-26204. 224p. 2000. 17.95 (*0-385-49703-2*) Doubleday.

Rowland, Rebecca, ed. see Karwoshi, Glenn.

Rowland, Richard, ed. see Marlowe, Christopher.

Rowland, Richard H., jt. auth. see Lewis, Robert A.

***Rowland, Robert.** Analyzing Rhetoric: A Handbook for the Informed Citizen in a New Millennium. 468p. (C). 1999. pap. text 78.95 (*0-7872-6274-9*, 41627401) Kendall-Hunt.

Rowland, Robert. Rhetoric & Social Influence. 260p. (C). 1996. pap. text, per. 41.95 (*0-7872-2605-X*) Kendall-Hunt.

— Rhetoric & Social Influence. 2nd ed. 310p. (C). 1997. per. 45.95 (*0-7872-4195-4*) Kendall-Hunt.

Rowland, Robert, jt. auth. see Iyer, Praema V.

Rowland, Robert C. The Rhetoric of Menachem Begin: The Myth of Redemption Through Return. 330p. (Orig.). 1985. pap. text 25.50 (*0-8191-4736-2*); lib. bdg. 55.50 (*0-8191-4735-4*) U Pr of Amer.

— U. S. Policy & the Global Environment. 160p. 1992. pap. 22.60 (*0-8442-5163-1*, NTC Business Bks) NTC Contemp Pub Co.

— United States Policy on Immigration: An Overview of the Issues Affecting the Immigration Policy of the United States. 148p. 1995. pap. 23.95 (*0-8442-5837-7*) NTC Contemp Pub Co.

Rowland, Robert O. For The People: A Recipe for Saving Democracy & Freedom. 362p. 19.95 (*0-615-11189-0*) Rowland Bks.

Regardless of your political affiliation, be it Republican, Democrat or disenfranchised, this book is for you. As our country enters the 21st century the U.S. Constitution has been torn apart by an overzealous & over-extended federal government. Each day, many of our constitutional rights are weakened. These rights include: our right to freely worship God, our right be free from illegal search & seizure & our right to own & control private property. Billions of out tax dollars are wasted every year by inefficient federal agencies that serve no purpose. In addition, billions more are actually spent on eroding our consitutional rights & placing private property under governmental control. If it surprises you that the federal government is buying up land all across America (millions of acres a year), then it is time you opened your eyes & read the truth contained in these pages. I urge all true-blooded Americans to read this book. It is the culmination of years of research against the "New World Order" of Socialism that has developed in our country & around the world. The fight must begin now it begins with the pen. This book will give you the information & guidance you need to demand accountability from our public officials. We can achieve the dream of our foundling fathers if we begin to dismantle the oppressive juggernaut our federal government has become. This way, we can ensure that the freedom our forefathers founded & millions died to protect, will remain for future generations to come. Read this book for yourself, your family & your church. Read it "For the People". ***Publisher Paid Annotation.***

***Rowland, Robin.** The Creative Guide to Research: How to Find What You Need... Online or Offline. 256p. 2000. pap. 16.99 (*1-56414-442-9*) Career Pr Inc.

Rowland, Robin. Researching on the Internet: The Complete Guide to Organizing Searching & Qualifying... 1995. pap. 29.95 (*0-7615-0063-4*) Prima Pub.

Rowland, Robyn. Living Laboratories: Women & Reproductive Technology. LC 92-13199. 384p. 1992. 37.95 (*0-253-34999-0*); pap. 6.95 (*0-253-20760-6*, MB-760) Ind U Pr.

— Perverse Serenity. 96p. 1993. pap. 12.95 (*1-875559-13-2*, Pub. by SpiniFex Pr) LPC InBook.

— Woman Herself: A Transdisciplinary Perspective on Women's Identity. 240p. 1990. pap. 19.95 (*0-19-554475-7*) OUP.

— Women Who Do & Women Who Don't: Join the Women's Movement. (Illus.). 224p. (Orig.). 1984. pap. 9.95 (*0-7102-0296-2*, Routledge Thoemms) Routledge.

***Rowland, Russell.** In Open Spaces. 2001. write for info. (*0-688-17270-9*, Wm Morrow) Morrow Avon.

Rowland, Sanders & Terrell, Bob. Papa Coke: 65 Years Selling Coca-Cola. LC 86-9526. (Illus.). 224p. 1986. 10.95 (*0-914875-14-0*) Bright Mtn Bks.

Rowland, Sharon S. Pathology & Microbiology. LC 94-14073. 416p. 1994. pap. text, lab manual ed. 32.00 (*0-316-76049-8*, Little Brwn Med Div) Lppncott W & W.

Rowland, Shirley D. Looking for Normal. 1997. pap. 56.95 (*1-57553-596-3*) Watermrk Pr.

Rowland, Sid. A Career in Crime. (Illus.). 75p. (Orig.). 1987. pap. 7.00 (*0-937158-03-8*) Del Valley.

— The Hopes of Cats. (Illus.). 80p. 1993. pap. 8.00 (*0-937158-06-2*) Del Valley.

— An Invitation to Dinner. (Illus.). 70p. (Orig.). 1985. pap. 5.00 (*0-937158-02-X*) Del Valley.

— Ludwig the Tomato. (Illus.). 76p. 1990. pap. 8.00 (*0-937158-05-4*) Del Valley.

— Passion Play. (Illus.). 80p. (Orig.). 1996. pap. 10.00 (*0-937158-07-0*) Del Valley.

— The Queen of Spades. (Illus.). 86p. 1999. pap. 10.00 (*0-937158-00-3*) Del Valley.

Rowland, Sidney T., jt. auth. see Harlan, Joan C.

Rowland, Stanley P., ed. Water in Polymers. LC 80-13860. (ACS Symposium Ser.: No. 127). 1980. 65.95 (*0-8412-0559-0*) Am Chemical.

— Water in Polymers. LC 80-13860. (ACS Symposium Ser.: Vol. 127). 606p. 1980. reprint ed. pap. 187.90 (*0-608-03064-3*, 206351700007) Bks Demand.

Rowland, Stephen. The Enquiring Classroom: An Approach to Understanding Children's Learning. (Curriculum Series for Teaching). 160p. 1984. pap. 29.95 (*0-905273-99-0*, Falmer Pr) Taylor & Francis.

— The Enquiring Tutor: Explorations in Professional Learning. LC 93-26438. 180p. 1993. 75.00 (*0-7507-0210-9*, Falmer Pr) Taylor & Francis.

***Rowland, Stephen.** The Enquiring University Teacher. LC 99-50127. 176p. 2000. pap. 34.95 (*0-335-20507-0*) OpUniv Pr.

Rowland, Stephen M. & Duebendorfer, Ernest M. Structural Analysis & Synthesis: A Laboratory Course in Structural Geology. 2nd ed. LC 93-28089. (Illus.). 304p. 1994. pap. 38.95 (*0-86542-366-0*) Blackwell Sci.

— Structural Analysis & Synthesis: Answer Book. LC 93-28089. 1994. write for info. (*0-86542-436-5*) Blackwell Sci.

***Rowland, Susan.** C.g. Jung & Literary Theory: The Challenge from Fiction. LC 98-55202. 1999. text 59.95 (*0-312-22275-0*) St Martin.

— From Agatha Christie to Ruth Rendell. LC 00-42202. 2000. write for info. (*0-333-67450-2*) St Martin.

Rowland, Susan, jt. auth. see Rosenthal, Lisa.

Rowland, T. J. & Beck, Paul A., eds. Magnetic & Inelastic Scattering of Neutrons by Metals. LC 67-29670. (Metallurgical Society Conference Ser.: Vol. 43). 239p. reprint ed. pap. 74.10 (*0-608-11352-2*, 200153200079) Bks Demand.

Rowland, T. J., ed. see Metallurgical Society of AIME Staff.

***Rowland, Thomas.** God Acts, We React: An Approach to Liturgical Prayer. 2nd ed. 154p. 1998. pap. 11.95 (*0-921440-51-0*) Madonna Hse.

Rowland, Thomas J. George B. McClellan & Civil War History: In the Shadow of Grant & Sherman. LC 98-13967. (Illus.). 264p. 1998. text 28.00 (*0-87338-603-5*) Kent St U Pr.

Rowland, Thomas W. Developmental Exercise Physiology. LC 96-10886. (Illus.). 280p. 1996. text 39.00 (*0-87322-640-2*, BROW0640) Human Kinetics.

— Exercise & Children's Health. 3rd ed. LC 89-71708. (Illus.). 368p. 1990. pap. text 19.00 (*0-87322-810-3*, BROW0810) Human Kinetics.

Rowland, Thomas W., ed. Pediatric Laboratory Exercise Testing: Clinical Guidelines. LC 92-1575. (Illus.). 216p. 1992. text 33.00 (*0-87322-380-2*, BROW0380) Human Kinetics.

Rowland, Tim. The Pragmatics of Mathematics Education: Vagueness in Mathematical Discourse. LC 99-26513. (Studies in Mathematics Education). (Illus.). 242p. 1999. 90.00 (*0-7507-1012-8*, Pub. by Falmer Pr UK); pap. 28.95 (*0-7507-1013-6*, Pub. by Falmer Pr UK) Taylor & Francis.

Rowland, Tom & Riley, Noel. A-Z Guide to Cleaning, Conserving & Repairing Antiques. (Illus.). 190p. 1998. 29.95 (*0-09-474250-2*, Pub. by Constable & Co) Trafalgar.

— A-Z Guide to Cleaning, Conserving & Repairing Antiques. (Illus.). 192p. 1998. pap. 15.95 (*0-09-478360-8*, Pub. by Constable & Co) Trafalgar.

Rowland, V. R., jt. auth. see Langford, D. A.

Rowland, W. F. Campus Ministries. 250p. (Orig.). 1991. pap. 9.95 (*0-940999-72-2*, C-2172) Star Bible.

Rowland, Wade. Spirit of the Web: The Age of Information from Telegraph to Internet. LC 98-203597. 416p. 1997. 34.95 (*1-895897-98-X*) Somerville Hse.

Rowland, Wade, jt. auth. see MacInnis, Jeff.

***Rowland-Warne, L.** Costume. (Eyewitness Books). (Illus.). (J). (gr. 4-7). 2000. 19.99 (*0-7894-6584-1*) DK Pub Inc.

— Costume. (Eyewitness Books). (J). (gr. 4-7). 2000. 15.95 (*0-7894-5586-2*) DK Pub Inc.

Rowland, Willard D., Jr. Interpreting Television: Current Research Perspectives. Watkins, Bruce O., ed. LC 84-17714. (Sage Annual Reviews of Communication Research Ser.: No. 12). (Illus.). 293p. 1984. reprint ed. pap. 90.90 (*0-608-01157-6*, 205945700001) Bks Demand.

Rowland, Willard D. The Politics of TV Violence: Policy Uses of Communication Research. LC 82-23009. (People & Communication Ser.: No. 16). 320p. 1983. reprint ed. pap. 99.20 (*0-608-01502-4*, 205954600001) Bks Demand.

Rowland, William G., Jr. Literature & the Marketplace: Romantic Writers & Their Audiences in Great Britain & the United States. LC 96-33836. xv, 232p. 1996. text 50.00 (*0-8032-3918-1*) U of Nebr Pr.

Rowlands. Recent Advances in Cardiology, Vol. 12. 12th ed. 1995. text 89.00 (*0-443-05199-2*, W B Saunders Co) Harcrt Hlth Sci Grp.

Rowlands, jt. auth. see Smape.

Rowlands, jt. auth. see Snape.

Rowlands, Arril. More Tales from the Ark. (Illus.). 160p. (Orig.). (J). (gr. 3-5). 1995. pap. 4.99 (*0-7459-3035-2*) Lion USA.

Rowlands, Avril. The Animals' Christmas: And Other Stories. (Illus.). 128p. (J). (gr. 3-7). 1997. 4.99 (*0-7459-3699-7*) Lion USA.

***Rowlands, Avril.** Animals' Easter. (Illus.). (J). 2000. pap. 5.99 (*0-7459-4097-8*) Lion USA.

Rowlands, Avril. The Continuity Handbook: A Guide for Single Camera Shooting. 3rd ed. LC 94-27790. 161p. 1994. pap. 29.95 (*0-240-51391-6*, Focal) Buttrwrth-Heinemann.

***Rowlands, Avril.** The Continuity Supervisor. 4th ed. (Media Manuals Ser.). (Illus.). 192p. 2000. pap. 34.95 (*0-240-51613-3*, Focal) Buttrwrth-Heinemann.

Rowlands, Avril. Tales from the Ark. 160p. (J). (ps-3). 1995. pap. 4.99 (*0-7459-2375-5*) Lion USA.

— The Television PA's Handbook. 2nd ed. LC 93-3718. 240p. 1993. pap. 39.95 (*0-240-51353-3*, Focal) Buttrwrth-Heinemann.

***Rowlands, Barbara.** Asthma & Allergies. LC 99-16029. (Alternative Answers to Ser.). 2000. 22.95 (*0-7621-0246-2*, Pub. by RD Assn) Penguin Putnam.

Rowlands, Betty. Copycat. 1999. 25.00 (*0-7278-5499-2*) Severn Hse.

— Death at Dearley Manor. 224p. 1998. 24.00 (*0-7278-5381-3*) Severn Hse.

***Rowlands, Betty.** Death at Dearley Manor. large type ed. 384p. 1999. 31.99 (*0-7089-4112-5*, Linford) Ulverscroft.

Rowlands, Betty. Exhaustive Enquiries: A Melissa Craig Mystery. 252p. 1994. 19.95 (*0-8027-3180-5*) Walker & Co.

— Finishing Touch: A Melissa Craig Mystery. 253p. 1992. 19.95 (*0-8027-3209-7*) Walker & Co.

— A Hive of Bees. large type ed. (Ulverscroft Large Print Ser.). 400p. 1998. 29.99 (*0-7089-3933-3*) Ulverscroft.

— An Inconsiderate Death. 256p. 1997. 25.00 (*0-7278-5233-7*) Severn Hse.

Rowlands, Betty. An Inconsiderate Death. large type ed. 400p. 31.99 (*0-7089-4042-0*) Ulverscroft.

Rowlands, Betty. Over the Edge: A Melissa Craig Mystery. LC 92-40543. 252p. 1993. 19.95 (*0-8027-3228-3*) Walker & Co.

Rowlands, D. Problem Solving in Science & Technology: Workplace, No. 2. (C). 1989. 220.00 (*0-09-172781-2*, Pub. by S Thornes Pubs) St Mut.

Rowlands, D., jt. auth. see Snape, G.

Rowlands, D. J. Electrocardiography Pocket Book. 160p. (C). 1993. pap. text 22.00 (*0-7923-8805-4*) Kluwer Academic.

Rowlands, Derek, jt. auth. see Turkie, Wajdi.

Rowlands, Derek J., ed. Recent Advances in Cardiology - 11. (Illus.). 224p. (Orig.). 1993. pap. text 79.95 (*0-443-04565-8*) Church.

Rowlands, E. C. Teach Yourself Yorruba. (Teach Yourself Ser.). 1992. 15.95 (*0-8288-8414-5*) Fr & Eur.

— Teach Yourself Yoruba: A Complete Course for Beginners. (YOR., Illus.). 288p. 1994. pap. 16.95 (*0-8442-3843-0*, Teach Yrslf) NTC Contemp Pub Co.

Rowlands, Eliot W. Georgia Museum of Art Bulletin, Fall 1990 Vol. 16: Two Saints from the Workshop of Fra Filippo Lippi, Their Companion Panels. 60p. 1991. pap. 3.00 (*0-685-66928-9*) Georgia Museum of Art.

Rowlands, G., jt. auth. see Infeld, E.

Rowlands, Gareth. The Gardener's Guide to Growing Dahlias. LC 99-16738. (Gardener's Guide Ser.). (Illus.). 160p. 1999. 29.95 (*0-88192-434-2*) Timber.

Rowlands, George, jt. auth. see Infeld, E.

Rowlands, Gerald. Coming Alive in the Spirit: The Spirit-led Life. (Basic Bible Study Ser.). Orig. Title: The Holy Spirit & His Fruit. 64p. 1985. pap. 3.95 (*0-930756-90-8*, 521019) Aglow Communs.

— The Holy Spirit & His Gifts: A Study of the Spiritual Gifts. Sekowsky, Joanne, ed. (Basic Bible Study Ser.). 64p. 1984. pap. 3.95 (*0-930756-83-5*, 521017) Aglow Communs.

***Rowlands, Ian H.** A Trilogy of Appropriation. 204p. 1999. pap. 14.95 (*1-902638-01-8*, Pub. by Parthian) Dufour.

Rowlands, Ian H. Understanding Information Policy. LC 97-30014. (British Library Research). 1997. 60.00 (*1-85739-179-9*) Bowker-Saur.

Rowlands, J. E., jt. auth. see Elliot, G. J.

Rowlands, Jim. One Hour Kites. 1989. pap. 14.95 (*0-312-03218-8*) St Martin.

— Soft Kites & Windsocks. LC 92-26426. 1993. pap. 14.95 (*0-312-08966-X*) St Martin.

Rowlands, Jo. Questioning Empowerment: Working with Women in Honduras. LC 97-222505. 208p. (C). 1997. 15.95 (*0-85598-362-0*, Pub. by Oxfam Pub) Stylus Pub VA.

Rowlands, John. Hercules Segers. LC 78-26815. (Illus.). 120p. 1979. 30.00 (*0-8076-0909-9*, Pub. by Braziller) Norton.

***Rowlands, John & Rowlands, Sheila.** Welsh Family History: A Guide to Research. 2nd ed. (Illus.). 325p. 1999. pap. 19.95 (*0-8063-1620-9*) Genealog Pub.

***Rowlands, John & Rowlands, Sheila, eds.** Second Stages in Researching Welsh Ancestry. LC 99-73353. 348p. 1999. 21.95 (*0-8063-1619-5*) Genealog Pub.

Rowlands, John, jt. auth. see Jones, Glyn.

Rowlands, John J. Cache Lake Country: Life in the North Woods. LC 98-14503. (Illus.). 280p. 1998. reprint ed. pap. 14.00 (*0-88150-421-1*, Pub. by Countryman) Norton.

***Rowlands, Kenneth W.** The Friars: A History of the British Medieval Friars. (Illus.). 392p. 1999. 33.50 (*1-85776-399-8*, Pub. by Book Guild Ltd) Trans-Atl Phila.

***Rowlands, Mark.** The Body in Mind: Understanding Cognitive Processes. LC 98-45620. (Cambridge Studies in Philosophy). 260p. 1999. 59.95 (*0-521-65274-X*) Cambridge U Pr.

— The Environmental Crisis: Understanding the Value of Nature. LC 99-59239. 2000. text 59.95 (*0-312-23235-7*) St Martin.

Rowlands, Mark. Supervenience & Materialism. 144p. 1995. 56.95 (*1-85972-096-X*, Pub. by Avebry) Ashgate Pub Co.

Rowlands, Michael & Kristanson, K., eds. Structure & Social Transformation in Archaeology. LC 99-166566. (Material Cultures Ser.). (Illus.). x, 438p. (C). (gr. 13). 1998. 110.00 (*0-415-06789-8*, B0309) Routledge.

Rowlands, O., jt. auth. see Adcock, M. R.

***Rowlands, Penelope.** Weekend Houses. LC 00-29535. (Illus.). 2000. 40.00 (*0-8118-2543-4*) Chronicle Bks.

Rowlands, Richard. The Post for Divers Partes of the World, to Travaile from One Notable Citie unto an Other, 2 pts. LC 77-7422. (English Experience Ser.: No. 889). 1977. reprint ed. 20.00 (*90-221-0889-9*) Walter J Johnson.

— A Restitution of Decayed Intelligence: In Antiquities, Concerning the...English Nation. by the Studie & Travaile of R. Verstegen. Dedicated Unto the Kings Most Excellent Majestie. LC 79-84134. (English Experience Ser.: No. 952). 380p. 1979. reprint ed. lib. bdg. 35.00 (*90-221-0952-6*) Walter J Johnson.

Rowlands, Sam, et al. Managing Family Planning in General Practice. LC 97-10270. 1997. write for info. (*1-85775-205-8*, Radcliffe Med Pr) Scovill Paterson.

Rowlands, Samuel. Uncollected Poems, 1604-1617. LC 78-119867. 210p. 1970. 50.00 (*0-8201-1074-4*) Schol Facsimiles.

Rowlands, Sheila, jt. auth. see Rowlands, John.

Rowlands, Sheila, jt. ed. see Rowlands, John.

Rowlands, V. M. Fair Rosalind. large type ed. (Ulverscroft Large Print Ser.). 352p. 1997. 27.99 (*0-7089-3869-8*) Ulverscroft.

— The Lady & the Highwayman. large type ed. 320p. 1994. 27.99 (*0-7089-3139-1*) Ulverscroft.

Rowlands, William A. Anglesey, Wales a Research Reference. LC 91-90538. 285p. 1991. pap. 25.00 (*0-9630454-0-7*) MBR Co.

Rowlandson, Jane. Landowners & Tenants in Roman Egypt: The Social Relations of Agriculture in the Oxyrhynchite Nome. (Oxford Classical Monographs). (Illus.). 398p. (C). 1996. text 80.00 (*0-19-814735-X*, Clarendon Pr) OUP.

Rowlandson, Jane, ed. Women & Society in Greek & Roman Egypt: A Sourcebook. LC 97-32001. (Illus.). 428p. (C). 1999. text 64.95 (*0-521-58212-1*); pap. text 24.95 (*0-521-58815-4*) Cambridge U Pr.

Rowlandson, L. G. & Schwarz, J. S. Radio Refractivity & Meteorological Data Plots from Radiosonde Launches Trade Winds. LC 77-135079. 224p. 1970. 29.00 (*0-403-04534-7*) Scholarly.

Rowlandson, Mary. The Captive: The True Story of the Captivity of Mrs. Mary Rowlandson among the Indians & God's Faithfulness to Her in Her Time of Trial. rev. ed. (Illus.). 96p. 1988. reprint ed. 14.95 (*0-929408-00-4*, E87R895R69) Amer Eagle Pubns Inc.

— The Captive: The True Story of the Captivity of Mrs. Mary Rowlandson among the Indians & God's Faithfulness to Her in Her Time of Trial. rev. ed. (Illus.). 64p. 1991. pap. 6.95 (*0-929408-03-9*) Amer Eagle Pubns Inc.

— The Narrative of the Captivity & the Restoration of Mrs. Mary Rowlandson. 96p. 1998. pap. 9.95 (*0-939218-20-8*) Chapman Billies.

Rowlandson, Mary, et al. Classic American Autobiographies. Andrews, William L., ed. & intro. by. 464p. (Orig.). 1992. mass mkt. 6.99 (*0-451-62852-7*, Ment) NAL.

Rowlandson, Mary W. The Narrative of the Captivity & Restoration of Mrs. Mary Rowlandson. (American Biography Ser.). 96p. 1991. reprint ed. lib. bdg. 59.00 (*0-7812-8332-9*) Rprt Serv.

Rowlandson, Thomas. Loyal Volunteers of London & Environs Infantry & Cavalry in Their Respective Uniforms. 1981. 325.00 (*0-238-78977-2*) St Mut.

Rowlatt, Charles, jt. ed. see Hodges, Gisele M.

Rowlatt, K. Reprographic Methods. 1986. pap. text. write for info. (*0-582-41324-9*, Pub. by Addison-Wesley) Longman.

Rowles, C., et al. AI, 1993: Proceedings of the Sixth Australian Joint Conference on Artificial Intelligence. 450p. 1993. text 114.00 (*981-02-1526-6*) World Scientific Pub.

Rowles, Genevieve. Adventure Guide to Idaho. (Illus.). 420p. (Orig.). 1997. pap. 16.95 (*1-55650-789-5*) Hunter NJ.

— Montana. (Adventure Guide Ser.). (Illus.). 550p. 1999. pap. 17.95 (*1-55650-856-5*) Hunter NJ.

Rowles, Graham D., et al, eds. Long Term Care for the Rural Elderly: New Directions in Services, Research, & Policy. LC 96-28439. (Illus.). 216p. 1996. 39.95 (*0-8261-9380-3*) Springer Pub.

Rowles, Graham D., jt. ed. see Reinharz, Shulamit.

Rowles, Raymond. Drilling for Water: A Practical Manual. 2nd ed. 192p. 1995. pap. 51.95 (*1-85628-984-2*, Pub. by Avebry) Ashgate Pub Co.

Rowlett, Elsebet S., et al. Neolithic Levels on the Titelberg, Luxembourg. 2nd ed. LC 76-623772. (Museum Briefs Ser.: No. 18). iii, 61p. 1980. pap. 4.00 (*0-913134-83-X*) Mus Anthro MO.

Rowlett, Frank B. The Story of Magic: Memoirs of an American Cryptologic Pioneer. LC 98-73252. (Illus.). 266p. 1998. 32.80 (*0-89412-273-8*) Aegean Park Pr.

Rowlett, Lori L. Joshua & the Rhetoric of Violence: A New Historicist Analysis. (JSOT Supplement Ser.: No. 226). 197p. 1996. 57.50 (*1-85075-627-9*, Pub. by Sheffield Acad) CUP Services.

Rowlett, Martha. Responding to God. 160p. 1996. pap. 10.00 (*0-8358-0783-5*, UR783) Upper Room Bks.

***Rowlett, Martha Graybeal.** Responding to God: A Guide to Prayer Leader's Guide. LC 00-20984. 2000. write for info. (*0-8358-0926-9*) Upper Room Bks.

Rowlett, Paul. Sentential Negation in French. 256p. 1998. text 75.00 (*0-19-511924-X*); pap. text 29.95 (*0-19-512591-6*) OUP.

Rowley. Basic Clinical Science. 1991. 115.00 (*1-56593-037-1*, 0440) Singular Publishing.

— Richard Wright. 2001. text 37.50 (*0-8050-4776-X*) St Martin.

Rowley, jt. auth. see Wells.

Rowley, A., jt. auth. see Watt, F.

Rowley, A. F., et al. Eicosanoids & Related Compounds in Plants & Animals. LC 98-87898. 228p. 1998. 85.00 (*0-691-00902-3*, Pub. by Princeton U Pr) Cal Prin Full Svc.

Rowley, A. F., jt. ed. see Ratcliffe, N. A.

Rowley, Alexandra, jt. ed. see Cheim, John.

Rowley, Andrew, et al, eds. Eicosanoids & Related Compounds in Plants & Animals. (Portland Press Research Monograph Ser.: No. 11). (Illus.). 240p. 1998. text 119.00 (*1-85578-108-5*, Pub. by Portland Pr Ltd) Ashgate Pub Co.

Rowley, Arden A. Korea-POW: A Thousand Days with Life on Hold, 1950-1953. (Illus.). 227p. 1997. 49.95 (*1-883981-03-4*) Tanner Pub.

— Korea-POW: A Thousand Days with Life on Hold, 1950-1953. rev. ed. (Illus.). 232p. 1997. 39.95 (*1-883981-04-2*) Tanner Pub.

Rowley, B. A., tr. see Steiner, Rudolf.

***Rowley, B. J.** Missing Children. (Light Traveler Adventure Ser.: Vol. 3). 256p. (YA). 2000. pap. 13.95 (*0-9700103-3-8*) Goldn Wings.

— My Body Fell Off! A Novel. (Light Traveler Adventure Ser.: Vol. 1). 206p. (YA). 2000. pap. 11.95 (*0-9700103-1-1*) Goldn Wings.

— Silver Hawk's Revenge. (Light Traveler Adventure Ser.: Vol. 2). 256p. (YA). 2000. pap. 12.95 (*0-9700103-2-X*) Goldn Wings.

Rowley, Barbara. Baby Days: Activities, Ideas, & Games for Enjoying Daily Life with a Child under Three. LC 99-21945. 256p. 2000. pap. text 14.95 (*0-7868-8452-5*, Pub. by Hyperion) Time Warner.

***Rowley, Brent.** Light Traveler: The Adventure Begins : A Novel. LC 98-220290. 185 P. ;p. 1998. write for info. (*1-57734-310-7*) Covenant Comms.

Rowley, Brent. Out for Revenge. LC 98-29766. (J). 1998. 11.95 (*1-57734-312-3*) Covenant Comms.

Rowley, Charles K. Liberty & the State. (Shaftesbury Papers: Vol. 4). 112p. 1993. pap. 13.00 (*1-85278-853-4*) E Elgar.

— The Right to Justice: The Political Economy of Legal Services in the United States. (John Locke Ser.). 432p. 1992. text 100.00 (*1-85278-526-8*) E Elgar.

Rowley, Charles K., ed. Classical Liberalism & Civil Society. LC 97-41481. (John Locke Ser.). 504p. (C). 1998. 100.00 (*1-85898-660-5*) E Elgar.

— Constitutional Political Economy in a Public Choice Perspective. LC 98-121272. 1997. lib. bdg. 137.50 (*0-7923-4497-9*) Kluwer Academic.

— The Political Economy of the Minimal State. LC 95-40192. (Shaftesbury Papers). 348p. 1996. 95.00 (*1-85898-199-9*) E Elgar.

— Property Rights & the Limits of Democracy. (Shaftesbury Papers). 404p. 1993. 100.00 (*1-85278-529-2*) E Elgar.

— Public Choice Theory, 3 vols., Set. (International Library of Critical Writings in Economics: Vol. 24). 1616p. 1993. 560.00 (*1-85278-160-2*) E Elgar.

Rowley, Charles K., ed. Social Choice Theory, 3 vols. (International Library of Critical Writings in Economics: Vol. 27). 1716p. 1993. 560.00 (*1-85278-159-9*) E Elgar.

Rowley, Charles K., et al, eds. The Next Twenty-Five Years of Public Choice. LC 93-21577. (DIVS-Diverse Ser.). 232p. (C). 1993. lib. bdg. 145.50 (*0-7923-2450-1*) Kluwer Academic.

— The Political Economy of Rent Seeking. 1988. lib. bdg. 192.50 (*0-89838-241-6*) Kluwer Academic.

Rowley, Charles K., et al. Trade Protection in the United States. LC 95-7195. (John Locke Ser.). (Illus.). 368p. 1995. 100.00 (*1-85898-198-0*) E Elgar.

Rowley, Chris, ed. Human Resource Management in the Asia Pacific Region: Convergence Questioned. LC 97-42862. 216p. 1998. 42.50 (*0-7146-4849-3*, Pub. by F Cass Pubs) Intl Spec Bk.

— Human Resources Management in the Asia Pacific Region: Convergence Questioned. LC 97-42862. 216p. 1998. pap. 18.50 (*0-7146-4407-2*, Pub. by F Cass Pubs) Intl Spec Bk.

Rowley, Chris & Bae, Johngseok, eds. Korean Businesses: Internal & External Industrialization. LC 98-26372. (Studies in Asia Pacific: Vol. 5). 148p. 1998. 44.50 (*0-7146-4924-4*, Pub. by F Cass Pubs); pap. 22.50 (*0-7146-4483-8*, Pub. by F Cass Pubs) Intl Spec Bk.

***Rowley, Chris & Benson, John.** Globalization & Labour in the Asia Pacific. LC 00-31563. (Studies in Asia Pacific Business). 2000. write for info. (*0-7146-8089-3*, Pub. by F Cass Pubs) Intl Spec Bk.

***Rowley, Chris & Fitzgerald, Robert, eds.** Managed in Hong Kong: Adaptive Systems, Entrepreneurship & Human Resources. LC 99-57241. (Studies in Asia Pacific Business Ser.: Vol. 8). (Illus.). 144p. 2000. 57.50 (*0-7146-5026-9*, Pub. by F Cass Pubs); pap. 24.50 (*0-7146-8082-6*, Pub. by F Cass Pubs) Intl Spec Bk.

Rowley, Chris & Lewis, Mark. Greater China: Political Economy, Inward Investment, & Business Culture. LC 96-2924. 220p. 1996. text 30.00 (*0-7146-4739-X*, Pub. by F Cass Pubs) Intl Spec Bk.

Rowley, Chris & Lewis, Mark, eds. Greater China: Political Economy, Inward Investment, & Business Culture. LC 96-2924. 220p. 1996. pap. 19.50 (*0-7146-4296-7*, Pub. by F Cass Pubs) Intl Spec Bk.

***Rowley, Christopher.** The Ancient Enemy. (Arna Ser.: No. 1). 2000. mass mkt. 6.99 (*0-451-45772-2*, ROC) NAL.

Rowley, Christopher. Dragon Ultimate. 1999. mass mkt. 6.99 (*0-451-45548-7*, ROC) NAL.

— Dragons of Argonath. 1998. mass mkt. 6.99 (*0-451-45547-9*, ROC) NAL.

Rowley, Christopher, jt. ed. see Fitzgerald, Robert.

Rowley, Christopher B. Basil Broketail. 480p. 1992. mass mkt. 6.99 (*0-451-45206-2*, ROC) NAL.

— A Dragon at World's End. 1997. mass mkt. 6.99 (*0-451-45546-0*, ROC) NAL.

— Dragons of War. 464p. (Orig.). 1994. mass mkt. 6.99 (*0-451-45342-5*, ROC) NAL.

— A Sword for a Dragon. LC 93-199280. 480p. (Orig.). 1993. mass mkt. 6.99 (*0-451-45235-6*, ROC) NAL.

— Wizard of the Floating City. 1996. mass mkt. 5.99 (*0-451-45469-3*, ROC) NAL.

Rowley-Conwy, Peter. Arctic Archaeology. 1999. pap. 27.99 (*0-415-19810-0*) Routledge.

Rowley-Conwy, Peter, jt. ed. see Luff, Rosemary.

Rowley, Cynthia & Rosenzweig, Ilene. Swell: A Girl's Guide to the Good Life. LC 99-24242. 160p. 1999. 23.95 (*0-446-52456-5*, Pub. by Warner Bks) Little.

Rowley, D. I. & Dent, John A. The Musculoskeletal System: An Integrated Textbook of Diagnosis & Medical Surgical Management of Musculoskeletal Disorders. LC 96-85637. (Illus.). 352p. 1997. pap. text 19.99 (*0-412-62700-0*, Pub. by E A) OUP.

Rowley, Daniel J., et al. Strategic Change in Colleges & Universities: Planning to Survive & Prosper. LC 96-25370. (Higher & Adult Education Ser.). 1997. 34.95 (*0-7879-0348-5*) Jossey-Bass.

— Strategic Choices for the Academy: How Demand for Lifelong Learning Will Re-Create Higher Education. LC 97-44074. (Higher & Adult Education Ser.). 1998. 34.95 (*0-7879-4067-4*) Jossey-Bass.

Rowley, David, jt. auth. see Purser, Harry.

Rowley, David G. Millenarian Bolshevism, 1900 to 1920. (Modern European History Ser.). 392p. 1987. text 15.00 (*0-8240-8061-0*) Garland.

Rowley, David I. & Clift, Benedict, eds. Skeletal Trauma in Old Age. LC 94-70928. (Illus.). 240p. (gr. 13). 1994. text 65.00 (*0-412-48750-0*, Pub. by E A) OUP.

Rowley, David T. Hypnosis & Hypnotherapy. LC 86-71023. 208p. 1986. 24.95 (*0-914783-13-0*); pap. 17.95 (*0-914783-15-7*) Charles.

Rowley, Derek G. The Nevada Corporation Handbook: Effectively Using Nevada Corporations for Privacy, Asset Protection, & Tax Strategies. 7th ed. 336p. 1998. pap. 69.95 (*1-886683-01-8*) Strategic NV.

***Rowley, Derek G.** The Nevada Corporation Handbook: Effectively Using nevada Corporations for Privacy, Asset, Protection & Tax Strategies. 8th ed. (Eighth Edition). 352p. 2000. pap. 69.95 (*1-886683-03-4*) Strategic NV.

Rowley, Doris. Nostalgia. 48p. 1984. 19.00 (*0-7212-0693-X*, Pub. by Regency Pr GBR) St Mut.

***Rowley, Elaine.** Jean Moss Book of Sculptured Knits: 40 Great Designs Inspired by Decorative Art of the 20th Century. 1999. 29.95 (*0-9646391-9-X*) XRX Inc.

Rowley, Elaine. Socks, Socks, Socks: 70 Winning Patterns From Knitter's Year of the Sock Contest. 1998. pap. 19.95 (*0-9646391-5-7*) XRX Inc.

Rowley, Elaine, ed. The Great American Afghan: A Special Knitter's Magazine Publication. (Illus.). 32p. (Orig.). 1997. pap. 8.95 (*0-9646391-2-2*) XRX Inc.

Rowley, Elaine, ed. see Melville, Sally.

Rowley, Elaine, ed. see Zilborg, Anne.

Rowley, Elton H. Time Before Space: An Airman's Odyssey...from Biplanes to Rockets. (Illus.). 238p. 1994. pap. 25.95 (*0-89745-174-0*) Sunflower U Pr.

Rowley, Eric E. Hyperinflation in Germany: Perceptions of a Process. LC 93-45454. (Illus.). 189p. 1994. 86.95 (*1-85928-039-0*, Pub. by Scolar Pr) Ashgate Pub Co.

Rowley, Frank B. & Algren, Axel B. Thermal Conductivity of Building Materials. LC 37-27901. (University of Minnesota Engineering Experimentation Bulletin Ser.: No. 12). 144p. reprint ed. pap. 44.70 (*0-608-14153-4*, 205590700039) Bks Demand.

Rowley, Fred, jt. compiled by see Hemmasi, Harriette.

***Rowley, G. G.** Yosano Akiko & the Tale of Genji. LC 99-89978. (Michigan Monograph Series in Japanese Studies: Vol. 28). (Illus.). xi, 221p. (C). 2000. text 32.95 (*0-939512-98-X*) U MI Japan.

Rowley, George. Principles of Chinese Painting. 2nd rev. ed. LC ND1040.R6. (Princeton Monographs in Art & Archaeology: Vol. 24). (Illus.). 105p. 1959. reprint ed. pap. 32.60 (*0-608-07636-8*, 205995200010) Bks Demand.

Rowley, Gill. The Book of Music. (Illus.). 192p. 1998. pap. 19.95 (*1-57715-037-6*) Knckerbocker.

Rowley, Gorden. Candiciform & Pachycaul Succulents. Schwartz, Herman & LaFon, Ron, eds. (Illus.). 282p. 1980. 80.00 (*0-912647-03-5*) Strawberry.

Rowley, Graham, et al, eds. Law & Practice for Paraegals. 200p. 1999. pap. (*0-7487-2508-3*) S Thornes Pubs.

Rowley, Graham, et al. Law for Legal Executives Pt. 1: Year Two. 2nd ed. 350p. pap. 38.00 (*1-85431-358-4*, Pub. by Blackstone Pr) Gaunt.

— Law for Legal Executives Pt. 1: Year Two. 3rd ed. 400p. 1996. pap. 40.00 (*1-85431-590-0*, Pub. by Blackstone Pr) Gaunt.

Rowley, Graham W. Cold Comfort: My Love Affair with the Arctic. LC 97-161178. (McGill-Queen's Native & Northern Ser.: Vol. 13). (Illus.). 300p. (C). 1996. 49.95 (*0-7735-1393-0*, 71104, Pub. by McG-Queens Univ Pr) CUP Services.

— Cold Comfort: My Love Affair with the Arctic. (Illus.). 288p. 1998. pap. 19.95 (*0-7735-1823-1*) McG-Queens Univ Pr.

Rowley-Greene, Clare J. Creative Feet Technical Guide & Workbook, Vol. 1. Wood, Therese M., ed. (Illus.). 266p. 1996. ring bd. 49.95 (*0-9653164-0-8*, WKBK-1) C J Inspirations.

Rowley, H. H. The Book of Job. (New Century Bible Ser.). 281p. 1976. pap. 24.50 (*0-551-00859-8*, Pub. by Sheffield Acad) CUP Services.

Rowley, H. H. From Joseph to Joshua, 1948: Biblical Traditions in the Light of Archaeology. (Schweich Lectures on Biblical Archaeology). 1970. 9.98 (*0-19-725857-3*) David Brown.

— Job. rev. ed. (New Century Bible Ser.). 302p. 1976. 9.95 (*0-551-00596-3*) Attic Pr.

— Rediscovery of the Old Testament. 224p. 1946. 14.00 (*0-227-67576-2*) Attic Pr.

— The Relevance of Apocalyptic. 3rd rev. ed. LC 64-12221. 240p. 1980. reprint ed. pap. text 9.50 (*0-87921-061-3*) Attic Pr.

Rowley, H H, jt. ed. see Black, Matthew.

Rowley, Harold H. From Moses to Qumran. LC 74-128307. (Essay Index Reprint Ser.). 1977. 20.95 (*0-8369-2130-5*) Ayer.

— Re-Discovery of the Old Testament. LC 75-76912. (Essay Index Reprint Ser.). 1977. 21.95 (*0-8369-1154-7*) Ayer.

— The Unity of the Bible. LC 78-2684. 201p. 1978. reprint ed. lib. bdg. 38.50 (*0-313-20346-6*, ROUB, Greenwood Pr) Greenwood.

Rowley, Hazel. Christina Stead: A Biography. LC 94-14236. 1995. 37.50 (*0-8050-3411-0*); pap. 18.95 (*0-8050-4262-8*) H Holt & Co.

Rowley, Hazel, jt. auth. see Ommundsenand, Wenche.

Rowley, Ian. Behavioural Ecology of Galahs. 188p. (C). 1999. pap. 160.00 (*0-949324-27-2*, Pub. by Surrey Beatty & Sons) St Mut.

Rowley, Ian & Russell, Eleanor. Fairy-wrens & Grasswrens: Maluridae. LC 96-52084. (Bird Families of the World Ser.). (Illus.). 312p. (C). 1997. text 75.00 (*0-19-854690-4*) OUP.

Rowley, J. C. & Trivedi, P. K. Econometrics of Investment. LC 74-32176. (Wiley Monographs in Applied Econometrics). (Illus.). 217p. reprint ed. pap. 67.30 (*0-8357-4322-5*, 203712100007) Bks Demand.

Rowley, J. C., jt. ed. see Hamouda, Omar F.

Rowley, J. Carter, jt. auth. see Moran, David T.

Rowley, J. W. & Baker, Donald I. International Mergers: The Antitrust Process , 2 Vol. 2nd ed. LC 99-159971. 1996. write for info. (*0-421-52220-8*) Sweet & Maxwell.

***Rowley, James B. & Hart, Patricia M.** High-Performance Mentoring: A Multimedia Program for Training Mentor Teachers. (One-Off Ser.). 1999. 795.00 incl. VHS, cd-rom (*0-7619-7521-7*) Sage.

Rowley, James B. & Hart, Patricia M. Recruiting & Training Successful Substitute Teachers: A Multimedia Training Program, Incl. notebook, matrix. (Illus.). 1998. teacher ed. 795.00 incl. sl., cd-rom (*0-8039-6774-8*) Corwin Pr.

— Recruiting & Training Successful Substitute Teachers: Facilitator's Guide. (Illus.). 200p. 1998. pap., teacher ed. 39.95 (*0-8039-6776-4*) Corwin Pr.

— Recruiting & Training Successful Substitute Teachers: Participant's Notebook. (Illus.). 136p. 1998. pap. 19.95 (*0-8039-6775-6*) Corwin Pr.

Rowley, James B., jt. auth. see Hart, Patricia M.

Rowley, James W., ed. see Hizer, Evelyn R.

Rowley, James W., ed. see Plymale, Sallie H.

Rowley, James W., ed. see Rice, Otis K. & Brown, Stephen W.

Rowley, James W., ed. see Williams, Tony L.

Rowley, Jennifer. The Electronic Library. 4th ed. (Illus.). 396p. 1998. 65.00 (*1-85604-149-2*, Pub. by Library Association) Bernan Associates.

— Organizing Knowledge. 2nd ed. 450p. 1992. pap. 34.95 (*1-85742-005-5*, Pub. by Gower) Ashgate Pub Co.

***Rowley, Jennifer & Farrow, John.** Organizing Knowledge: An Introduction to Managing Access to Information. 3rd ed. LC 99-45648. 416p. 2000. pap. 39.95 (*0-566-08047-8*, Pub. by Gower) Ashgate Pub Co.

Rowley, Jennifer & Fisher, Shelagh. Bookshelf: A Guide for Librarians & Systems Managers. 273p. 1992. 76.95 (*1-85742-008-X*, Pub. by Gower) Ashgate Pub Co.

Rowley, Jennifer & Slack, Frances. Designing Public Access Systems. LC 98-5387. 272p. 1998. pap. 69.95 (*0-566-08070-2*, Pub. by Gower) Ashgate Pub Co.

Rowley, Jenny E. & Rowley, Peter J. Operations Research: A Tool for Library Management. LC 81-12899. (Illus.). 151p. (Orig.). 1981. reprint ed. pap. 46.90 (*0-7837-9687-0*, 206041700005) Bks Demand.

Rowley, John. Harriet Tubman. LC 97-13730. (Lives & Times Ser.). 24p. (J). (gr. 2-4). 1998. 18.50 (*1-57572-558-4*) Heinemann Lib.

— Roald Dahl. LC 98-23293. (Profiles Ser.). (Illus.). 56p. (J). 1998. write for info. (*1-57572-693-9*) Heinemann Lib.

Rowley, Keith. Keith Rowley's Woodturning Projects. (Illus.). 176p. 1997. pap. 17.95 (*1-86108-013-1*, Pub. by Guild Master) Sterling.

— Woodturning: A Foundation Course. (Illus.). 151p. 1992. pap. 19.95 (*0-946819-20-3*, Pub. by Guild Master) Sterling.

— Woodturning: A Foundation Course. (Illus.). 176p. 1999. pap. 19.95 (*1-86108-114-6*, Pub. by Guild Master) Sterling.

Rowley-Kelly, Fern L. & Reigel, Donald H., eds. Teaching the Student with Spina Bifida. 496p. (Orig.). (C). 1992. pap. text 40.00 (*1-55766-064-6*) P H Brookes.

Rowley, Michael. Kana Pict-o-Graphix: Mnemonics for Japanese Hiragana & Katakana. LC 94-48537. (Illus.). 72p. (Orig.). 1995. pap. 6.00 (*1-880656-18-3*) Stone Bridge Pr.

— Kanji Pict-O-Graphix: Over One Thousand Japanese Kanji & Kana Mnemonics. LC 91-23153. (Illus.). 216p. (Orig.). 1992. pap. 19.95 (*0-9628137-0-2*) Stone Bridge Pr.

Rowley, Michael C., ed. see Peters Corporation, Gerald Peters Gallery Staff.

***Rowley, Nic & Hartvig, Kirsten.** Energy Foods. (Illus.). 72p. 2000. 12.95 (*0-89087-978-8*) Celestial Arts.

Rowley, Nic & Hartvig, Kirsten. 10 Days to Better Health. (Illus.). 1999. pap. 14.95 (*0-7499-1816-0*, Pub. by Piatkus Bks) London Brdge.

Rowley, Peter J., jt. auth. see Rowley, Jenny E.

***Rowley, Philip.** Fly Pattern for Stillwaters. 2000. pap. 29.95 (*1-57188-195-6*, BLF) F Amato Pubns.

Rowley, Robin, jt. auth. see Hamouda, Omar F.

Rowley, Roger. The Wetlands Series. 1992. 7.50 (*0-614-18207-7*) Visual Studies.

Rowley, Sam R. Discovering Falconry: A Comprehensive Guide to Contemporary Falconry. LC 85-61152. (Illus.). 160p. (Orig.). 1985. pap. text 11.95 (*0-934271-00-3*) New Dawn.

Rowley, Samuel. When You See Me You Know Me. LC 70-133730. (Tudor Facsimile Texts. Old English Plays Ser.: No. 106). reprint ed. 59.50 (*0-404-53406-6*) AMS Pr.

Rowley, Sue, ed. Craft & Contemporary Theory. LC 98-130083. 224p. 1997. pap. 29.95 (*1-86448-313-X*, Pub. by Allen & Unwin Pty) Paul & Co Pubs.

Rowley, Thomas D., et al. Rural Development Research: A Foundation for Policy, 170. LC 95-22979. (Contributions in Economics & Economic History Ser.: Vol. 170). 264p. 1996. 67.95 (*0-313-29726-6*, Greenwood Pr) Greenwood.

Rowley, Thomas E. Atari BASIC: Learning by Using. 73p. 7.95 (*0-936200-35-9*) Blue Cat.

Rowley, Trevor. The Normans. (Illus.). 208p. 1999. 32.50 (*0-7524-1434-8*, Pub. by Tempus Pubng) Arcadia Publng.

***Rowley, Trevor.** The Normans. (Illus.). 176p. 2000. pap. 24.99 (*0-7524-1496-8*, Pub. by Tempus Pubng) Arcadia Publng.

Rowley, Trevor, ed. The Origins of Open Field Agriculture. (Illus.). 258p. 1981. 44.00 (*0-389-20102-2*, OROPEC) B&N Imports.

Rowley, Trevor & Wood, John. Deserted Villages. (Archaeology Ser.: Vol. 23). (Illus.). 72p. pap. 10.50 (*0-7478-0283-1*, Pub. by Shire Pubns) Parkwest Pubns.

R

R

Rowley, William & Heywood, Thomas. The Thracian Wonder. Nolan, Michael, ed. LC 98-106202. 1997. pap. 29.95 (*3-7052-0091-7*, Pub. by Poetry Salzburg) Intl Spec Bk.

Rowley, William, jt. auth. see Middleton, Thomas.

Rowley, William, jt. auth. see Shakespeare, William.

Rowley, William D. M. L. Wilson & the Campaign for the Domestic Allotment. LC 69-19106. 233p. reprint ed. pap. 72.30 (*0-8357-2952-4*, 203920800011) Bks Demand.

— A New Wonder, a Woman Never Vext: An Old-Spelling, Critical Edition. Cheatham, George, ed. LC 92-27581. (Renaissance & Baroque Studies & Texts: Vol. 6). XII, 264p. (C). 1993. text 49.95 (*0-8204-1916-8*) P Lang Pubng.

— Reclaiming the Arid West: The Career of Francis G. Newlands. LC 95-34788. (American West in the Twentieth Century Ser.). 216p. 1996. 27.50 (*0-253-33002-5*) Ind U Pr.

— Reno - Tahoe Country: An Illustrated History of Western Nevada. LC 97-78261. 1999. 39.95 (*1-886483-18-3*) Heritge Media.

— U. S. Forest Service Grazing & Rangelands: A History. LC 85-40048. (Environmental History Ser.: No. 8). (Illus.). 288p. 1985. 31.95 (*0-89096-218-9*) Tex A&M Univ Pr.

Rowley, William D., jt. auth. see Elliott, Russell R.

Rowley, William D., jt. auth. see Middleton, Thomas.

Rowley, Wm., jt. auth. see Middleton, Thomas.

***Rowling, J. K.** Harry Potter a l'Ecole des Sorciers. 3rd ed. (Harry Potter Ser.: Year 1).Tr. of Harry Potter & the Sorcerer's Stone. (FRE., Illus.). (YA). (gr. 4-7). 1998. pap. 14.95 (*2-07-050142-6*) Distribks Inc.

Rowling, J. K. Harry Potter & the Chamber of Secrets. LC 98-46370. (Harry Potter Ser.: Year 2). (Illus.). 320p. (YA). (gr. 4-7). 1999. 19.95 (*0-439-06486-4*, Pub. by Scholastic Inc) Penguin Putnam.

***Rowling, J. K.** Harry Potter & the Chamber of Secrets. (Harry Potter Ser.). (Illus.). 352p. (J). (gr. 4-7). 2000. pap. 6.99 (*0-439-06487-2*) Scholastic Inc.

— Harry Potter & the Chamber of Secrets. large type ed. (Harry Potter Ser.: Year 2). (Illus.). (YA). (gr. 8-12). 2000. 23.95 (*0-7862-2273-5*) Thorndike Pr.

— Harry Potter & the Goblet of Fire. (Harry Potter Ser.: Year 4). (Illus.). 752p. (J). (gr. 4-7). 2000. 25.95 (*0-439-13959-7*, A A Levine) Scholastic Inc.

— Harry Potter & the Prisoner of Azkaban. LC 99-23982. (Harry Potter Ser.: Year 3). (Illus.). 435p. (YA). (gr. 4-7). 1999. 19.95 (*0-439-13635-0*, Scholastic Hardcover) Scholastic Inc.

— Harry Potter & the Prisoner of Azkaban. LC 99-23982. (Harry Potter Ser.: Year 3). (Illus.). (YA). (gr. 3 up). 2000. pap. write for info. (*0-439-13636-9*, A A Levine) Scholastic Inc.

— Harry Potter & the Prisoner of Azkaban. large type ed. LC 99-48322. (Harry Potter Ser.: Year 3). (Illus.). 582p. (J). (gr. 4-7). 2000. 23.95 (*0-7862-2274-3*) Thorndike Pr.

— Harry Potter & the Sorcerer's Stone. (Harry Potter Ser.: Year 1). (Illus.). (YA). (gr. 3 up). 1997. pap. 4.99 (*0-7475-3274-5*) Blmsbury Pub.

— Harry Potter & the Sorcerer's Stone. (Harry Potter Ser.: Year 1). (YA). (gr. 3 up). 0.00 (*950-04-1957-2*) Emece.

Rowling, J. K. Harry Potter & the Sorcerer's Stone. LC 97-39059. (Harry Potter Ser.: Year 1). (Illus.). 320p. (YA). (gr. 3-7). 1998. 19.95 (*0-590-35340-3*, A A Levine) Scholastic Inc.

— Harry Potter & the Sorcerer's Stone. LC 97-39059. (Harry Potter Ser.: Year 1). (Illus.). 312p. (YA). (gr. 3-7). 1999. pap. 6.99 (*0-590-35342-X*) Scholastic Inc.

Rowling, J .K. Harry Potter & the Sorcerer's Stone. (Harry Potter Ser.: Year 1). 320p. (YA). (gr. 3 up). pap. 5.99 (*0-8072-1547-3*) Listening Lib.

***Rowling, J. K.** Harry Potter & the Sorcerer's Stone. large type ed. LC 99-50266. (Harry Potter Ser.: Year 1). (Illus.). 414p. (YA). (gr. 4-7). 1999. 23.95 (*0-7862-2272-7*) Thorndike Pr.

— Harry Potter Boxed Set. (Harry Potter Ser.: Years 1-3). (Illus.). (YA). (gr. 3 up). 1999. boxed set 55.85 (*0-439-13316-5*) Scholastic Inc.

— Harry Potter Coffret: Harry Potter a L'Ecole Des Sorciers, Harry Potter et la Chambre des Secret, Harry Potter et le Prisonnier d'Azkaban, 3 vols. (Harry Potter Ser.: Year 1-3). (FRE.). (YA). (gr. 3 up). 1999. pap. 43.95 (*2-07-052929-0*) Gallimard Edns.

— Harry Potter et la Chambre des Secrets. (Harry Potter Ser.: Year 2).Tr. of Harry Potter & the Chamber of Secrets. (FRE., Illus.). (YA). (gr. 4-7). 1999. pap. 14.95 (*2-07-052455-8*) Distribks Inc.

— Harry Potter et le Prisonnier d'Azkaban. (Harry Potter Ser.: Year 3).Tr. of Harry Potter & the Prisoner of Azkaban. (FRE.). (YA). (gr. 3 up). 1999. pap. 14.95 (*2-07-052818-9*) Gallimard Edns.

— Harry Potter und der Gefange von Azkaban. (Harry Potter Ser.: Year 3).Tr. of Harry Potter & the Prisoner of Azkaban. (GER.). (YA). (gr. 3 up). 1999. 31.95 (*3-551-55169-3*) Carlsen Verlag.

— Harry Potter und der Stein der Weisen. (Harry Potter Ser.: Year 1).Tr. of Harry Potter & the Sorcerer's Stone. (GER.). (YA). (gr. 3 up). 1999. 27.95 (*3-551-55167-7*) Carlsen Verlag.

— Harry Potter und die Kammer Schreckens. (Harry Potter Ser.: Year 2).Tr. of Harry Potter & the Chamber of Secrets. (GER.). (YA). (gr. 3 up). 1999. 27.95 (*3-551-55168-5*) Carlsen Verlag.

— Harry Potter y el Prisionero de Azkaban. (Harry Potter Ser.: Year 3).Tr. of Harry Potter & the Prisoner of Azkaban. (SPA.). (YA). (gr. 3 up). 2000. 17.95 (*84-7888-519-6*) Lectorum Pubns.

Rowling, Louise, jt. auth. see Glassrock, Geoffrey T.

Rowling, Marjorie. Life in Medieval Times. 1973. pap. 10.95 (*0-399-50258-0*, Perigee Bks) Berkley Pub.

Rowlingson, Karen, et al. Social Security Fraud: The Role of Penalties. LC 98-129695. (Department of Social Security Research Report.). vii, 188 p. 1997. write for info. (*0-11-762471-3*) Statnry Office.

Rowlingson, John C., jt. ed. see Hamill, Robin J.

Rowlingson, K. & Berthoud, R. Disability, Benefits & Employment. (DSS Research Report Ser.). 1996. 65.00 (*0-11-762398-9*, HM623989, Pub. by Statnry Office) Bernan Associates.

Rowlinson, J. S. Liquids & Liquid Mixtures. 2nd ed. LC 79-75522. 372p. 1969. 37.50 (*0-306-30694-8*, Plenum Trade) Perseus Pubng.

Rowlinson, Mark. Schubert. 1998. 47.50 (*0-375-40073-7*) Everymns Lib.

Rowlinson, Matthew. Tennyson's Fixations: Psychoanalysis & the Topics of the Early Poetry. (Victorian Literature & Culture Ser.). 224p. (C). 1994. text 37.50 (*0-8139-1478-7*) U Pr of Va.

Rowlinson, Peter, ed. Surveys in Combinatorics, 1995. (London Mathematical Society Lecture Note Ser.: No. 218). (Illus.). 239p. (C). 1995. pap. text 47.95 (*0-521-49797-3*) Cambridge U Pr.

Rowlinson, Stephen M., jt. auth. see Walker, Tony.

Rowlinson, Steve & McDermott, Peter, eds. Procurement Systems: A Guide to Best Practice in Construction. LC 98-49878. (Illus.). 264p. (C). (gr. 13). 1999. 100.00 (*0-419-24100-0*, D6635, E & FN Spon) Routledge.

Rowlinson, William. French Grammar. (Paperback Reference Ser.). 288p. 1994. reprint ed. pap. 7.95 (*0-19-282894-0*) OUP.

— German Grammar. (Paperback Reference Ser.). 302p. 1994. reprint ed. pap. 7.95 (*0-19-280020-5*) OUP.

— Ten Thousand French Words. LC 94-9758. (Paperback Reference Ser.). 336p. 1994. reprint ed. pap. 8.95 (*0-19-282895-9*) OUP.

— Ten Thousand German Words. LC 93-45641. (Paperback Reference Ser.). 384p. 1994. pap. 7.95 (*0-19-283095-3*) OUP.

Rowlinson, William, et al. The Oxford Paperback French Dictionary & Grammar. (FRE.). 806p. 1995. pap. 13.95 (*0-19-864529-5*) OUP.

— The Oxford Paperback German Dictionary & Grammar. (GER.). 862p. 1995. pap. 13.95 (*0-19-864530-9*) OUP.

Rowlinson, William, tr. see Brecht, Bertolt.

Rowlison, Bruce A. Creative Hospitality As a Means of Evangelism. rev. ed. LC 81-84182. (Illus.). 145p. 1984. pap. 8.99 (*0-938462-03-2*) Green Leaf CA.

Rowlison, Bruce A. & Hinn, George. Let's Talk about Your Wedding & Marriage. 3rd ed. 48p. 1994. pap. 3.95 (*0-938462-17-2*) Green Leaf CA.

Rowlison, Bruce A., jt. auth. see Wiebe, Ronald W.

Rowlson, Rachel & Staub, Dusty. Self Taught-Self Help. Williams, Tim, ed. 75p. (Orig.). 1984. pap. 7.95 (*0-9614201-0-3*) Dragonlord Pr.

Rowman and Little Field Inc, jt. auth. see Besterman, Theodore.

***Rowney, A. Charles, et al.** Sustaining Urban Water Resources in the 21st Century: Proceedings, September 7-12, 1997, Malmo, Sweden. LC 99-13264. ix, 574p. 1999. 69.00 (*0-7844-0424-0*) Am Soc Civil Eng.

Rowney, Don K. Transition to Technocracy: The Structural Origins of the Soviet Administrative State. LC 88-47925. (Cornell Studies in Soviet History & Science). 264p. 1989. text 39.95 (*0-8014-2183-7*) Cornell U Pr.

Rowney, Don K., ed. Imperial Power & Development: Papers on Pre-Revolutionary Russian History: Selected Papers of the Third World Congress for Soviet & East European Studies. 187p. (Orig.). 1990. pap. 23.95 (*0-89357-209-8*) Slavica.

— Soviet Quantitative History. LC 83-19196. (New Approaches to Social Science History Ser.: No. 4). (Illus.). 216p. reprint ed. pap. 67.00 (*0-8357-8506-8*, 203479300091) Bks Demand.

Rowney, Rosemarie & Holzemer, Stephen, eds. The New Public Health Redesigning Care for Social Responsiblity. (Council of Community Health Services Monograph Ser.: Vol. II). 150p. 1997. 23.95 (*0-88737-747-5*, 19-7475, NLN Pr) Natl League Nurse.

***Rowntree.** Between Friends. 2000. pap. 12.95 (*0-552-99506-1*, Pub. by Transworld Publishers Ltd) Trafalgar.

— Innocent Diversion. 2000. pap. 12.95 (*0-552-99814-1*, Pub. by Transworld Publishers Ltd) Trafalgar.

— Outside Looking In. 2000. 25.95 (*0-385-40564-2*, Pub. by Transworld Publishers Ltd) Trafalgar.

— Quiet War of Rebecca Sheldon. (J). 2000. pap. 12.95 (*0-552-99325-5*, Pub. by Transworld Publishers Ltd) Trafalgar.

Rowntree, B. Seebohm, Jr. The Human Factor in Business. Chandler, Alfred D., ed. LC 79-7553. (History of Management Thought & Practice Ser.). 1980. reprint ed. lib. bdg. 19.95 (*0-405-12339-6*) Ayer.

Rowntree, B. Seebohm. Old People: Report of a Survey Committee on the Problems of Aging & the Care of Old People. Stein, Leon, ed. LC 79-8682. (Growing Old Ser.). (Illus.). 1980. reprint ed. lib. bdg. 23.95 (*0-405-12799-5*) Ayer.

Rowntree, B. Seebohm & Kendall, May. How the Labourer Lives: A Study of the Rural Problem. LC 74-25780. (European Sociology Ser.). 342p. 1975. reprint ed. 28.95 (*0-405-06533-7*) Ayer.

***Rowntree, C. Brightwen.** Rowntrees of Riseborough. 1999. pap. 45.00 (*1-85072-115-7*, Pub. by W Sessions) St Mut.

Rowntree, C. Brightwen & Sessions, E. M. Rowntrees of Riseborough: A Genealogy. (C). 1986. 125.00 (*0-900657-67-7*, Pub. by W Sessions) St Mut.

Rowntree, Derek. Assessing Students. 2nd rev. ed. 280p. 1989. pap. 29.95 (*1-85091-300-5*, Pub. by Kogan Pg) Stylus Pub VA.

Rowntree, Derek. Exploring Open & Distance Learning. (Open & Distance Learning Ser.). 304p. 1992. pap. 29.95 (*0-7494-0813-8*, Kogan Pg Educ) Stylus Pub VA.

— Learn How to Study. 2nd ed. (J). 1976. pap. 12.95 (*0-8464-0548-2*) Beekman Pubs.

Rowntree, Derek. Making Materials-Based Learning Work. 144p. 1997. pap. 25.00 (*0-7494-2240-8*, Kogan Pg Educ) Stylus Pub VA.

Rowntree, Derek. Statistics Without Tears: A Primer for Non-Mathematicians. 199p. (C). 1981. pap. text 42.00 (*0-02-404090-8*, Macmillan Coll) P-H.

Rowntree, J. W. & Binns, H. B. A History of the Adult School Movement. 88p. (C). 1985. 65.00 (*0-7855-2395-2*, Pub. by Univ Nottingham); 65.00 (*1-85041-007-0*, Pub. by Univ Nottingham) St Mut.

Rowntree, K. Outside Looking In. 292p. 1996. pap. 10.95 (*0-552-99606-8*) Bantam.

Rowntree, K., jt. ed. see Fox.

Rowntree, Kathleen. Brief Shining. 320p. 1998. mass mkt. write for info. (*0-552-99584-3*, Pub. by Corgi Bks Ltd) Doubleday.

— The Haunting of Willow Dasset. 288p. 1989. 17.95 (*0-316-75975-9*) Little.

***Rowntree, Kathleen.** An Innocent Diversion. large type ed. 376p. 1999. 31.99 (*0-7089-4137-0*) Ulverscroft.

Rowntree, Kathleen. Laurie & Claire. 480p. 1996. pap. 12.95 (*0-552-99608-4*) Bantam.

***Rowntree, Kathleen.** Laurie & Claire. 2000. 27.95 (*0-385-40565-0*, Pub. by Transworld Publishers Ltd) Trafalgar.

— Mr. Brightly's Evening Off. (J). 2000. pap. 10.95 (*0-552-99733-1*, Pub. by Transworld Publishers Ltd) Trafalgar.

Rowntree, Kathleen. Mr. Brightly's Evening Off. large type ed. 1998. 26.95 (*0-7531-5856-6*) T T Beeler.

— Prize for Sister Catherine. 1998. mass mkt. 14.95 (*0-552-99732-3*) Bantam.

***Rowntree, Kathleen.** Tell Mrs. Poole I'm Sorry. (J). 2000. pap. 12.95 (*0-552-99561-4*, Pub. by Transworld Publishers Ltd) Trafalgar.

Rowntree, L. B., et al. Journal of California & Great Basin Anthropology. fac. ed. (Malki Museum, Journal of California & Great Basin Anthropology Ser.: Vol. 7:1). (Illus.). 146p. (C). 1985. reprint ed. pap. text 16.25 (*1-55567-773-8*) Coyote Press.

***Rowntree, Lester, et al.** Diversity Amid Globalization & Geotutor Building Literature. 752p. 1999. pap. 81.33 (*0-13-088423-5*, Prentice Hall) P-H.

Rowny, Edward L., et al. Strategic Force Modernization & Arms Control. LC 85-10579. (National Security Papers: No. 6). 1986. 7.50 (*0-89549-075-7*) Inst Foreign Policy Anal.

Rowold, Katharina, ed. Gender & Science: Late Nineteenth-Century Debates on the Female Mind & Body. LC 96-214623. (Key Issues Ser.: No. 9). 300p. 1996. 72.00 (*1-85506-411-1*); pap. 24.00 (*1-85506-410-3*) Bks Intl VA.

Rowold, Milam C., jt. auth. see Sitton, Thad.

***Rowsden, Mark.** The Art of Identity: Creating & Managing a Successful Corporate Identity. 208p. 2000. 79.95 (*0-566-08318-3*) Ashgate Pub Co.

***Rowse.** Bosworth Field & the War of the Roses. 1998. pap. 12.99 (*1-85326-691-4*, Pub. by Wrdsworth Edits) Combined Pub.

Rowse, A. L. The Controversial Colensos. 152p. (C). 1989. 100.00 (*1-85022-047-6*, Pub. by Dyllansow Truran) St Mut.

***Rowse, A. L.** The Elizabethan Renaissance Vol. I: The Life of the Society. (Illus.). 352p. 2000. reprint ed. pap. 17.95 (*1-56663-315-X*, Pub. by I R Dee) Natl Bk Netwk.

— The Elizabethan Renaissance Vol. II: The Cultural Achievement. (Illus.). 432p. 2000. reprint ed. pap. 17.95 (*1-56663-316-8*, Pub. by I R Dee) Natl Bk Netwk.

Rowse, A. L. England of Elizabeth. LC 78-53293. 562p. 1978. reprint ed. pap. 16.50 (*0-299-07724-1*) U of Wis Pr.

— Homosexuals in History. LC 97-10275. (Illus.). 400p. 1997. pap. 14.95 (*0-7867-0423-3*) Carroll & Graf.

— Matthew Arnold: Poet & Prophet. (Illus.). 210p. (C). 1986. reprint ed. lib. bdg. 36.00 (*0-8191-5120-3*) U Pr of Amer.

— Memories of Men & Women American & British. LC 83-16875. 266p. (Orig.). (C). 1983. reprint ed. pap. text 11.25 (*0-8191-3583-6*); reprint ed. lib. bdg. 20.25 (*0-8191-3582-8*) U Pr of Amer.

— The Poet Auden: A Personal Memoir. LC 87-149279. 138p. 1987. write for info. (*0-413-40390-4*) Heinemann.

— Prompting the Age: Poems Early & Late. (C). 1989. text 60.00 (*1-85022-056-5*, Pub. by Dyllansow Truran) St Mut.

— Tudor Cornwall. (C). 1989. 140.00 (*1-85022-058-1*, Pub. by Dyllansow Truran) St Mut.

Rowse, A. L., ed. The Contemporary Shakespeare: Volume VII-King Henry VI, Part One, King Henry VI, Part Two, King Henry VI, Part Three, King John, Pericles, Titus Andronicus. LC 84-5105. (Modern Text with Introduction Ser.). 724p. (C). 1987. lib. bdg. 27.50 (*0-8191-3947-5*) U Pr of Amer.

— The Contemporary Shakespeare Series Vol. III: Hamlet, Julius Caesar, Merchant of Venice, A Midsummer Night's Dream, Romeo & Juliet, The Tempest. LC 84-5105. 690p. (C). 1984. lib. bdg. 27.50 (*0-8191-3922-X*) U Pr of Amer.

Rowse, A. L., ed. see Shakespeare, William.

Rowse, A. L., ed. & intro. see Shakespeare, William.

Rowse, Alfred L. An Elizabethan Garland. LC 76-161760. reprint ed. 20.00 (*0-404-07965-2*) AMS Pr.

— The Elizabethans & America. LC 78-5090. (Illus.). 221p. 1978. reprint ed. lib. bdg. 35.00 (*0-8371-9350-8*, ROELA, Greenwood Pr) Greenwood.

— The England of Elizabeth: The Structure of Society. LC 78-53293. 559p. reprint ed. pap. 173.30 (*0-608-09923-6*, 206926100003) Bks Demand.

Rowse, Alfred L. & Harrison, George B. Queen Elizabeth & Her Subjects. LC 79-76913. (Essay Index Reprint Ser.). 1977. 16.95 (*0-8369-1895-9*) Ayer.

Rowse, Alfred L., ed. see Thomson, Gladys S.

***Rowse, Arthur E.** The Ultimate Coup: How the News Monster Took over Washington. LC 00-25333. 2000. write for info. (*1-56751-193-7*) Common Courage.

Rowse, Judy & Wojda, Raymond. Women Behind Bars. LC 96-25770. (Illus.). 95p. (Orig.). 1997. pap. 22.95 (*1-56991-049-9*) Am Correctional.

Rowse, Tim. After Mabo: Interpreting Indigenous Traditions. 168p. 1996. 19.95 (*0-522-84492-8*, Pub. by Melbourne Univ Pr) Paul & Co Pubs.

***Rowse, Tim.** Obliged to Be Difficult: Nugget Coombs' Legacy in Indigenous Affairs. LC 99-55004. 272p. (C). 2000. 64.95 (*0-521-77353-9*); pap. 24.95 (*0-521-77410-1*) Cambridge U Pr.

Rowse, Tim. White Flour, White Power: From Rations to Citizenship in Central Australia. LC 97-51616. (Illus.). 232p. (C). 1998. 64.95 (*0-521-62457-6*) Cambridge U Pr.

Rowsemitt, Carol, et al. The Timing & Patterns of Molt in Microtus Breweri. (Occasional Papers: No. 34). 11p. 1975. pap. 1.00 (*0-317-04913-5*) U KS Nat Hist Mus.

Rowsey, Katheryn, jt. auth. see Knox, Carol.

Rowshan, Arthur. Stress: An Owner's Manual - Positive Techniques for Taking Charge. 192p. 1997. pap. 10.95 (*1-85168-140-X*, Pub. by Onewrld Pubns) Penguin Putnam.

— Telling Tales: How to Use Stories to Help Your Children Overcome Their Problems. 160p. 1997. pap. 10.95 (*1-85168-139-6*, Pub. by Onewrld Pubns) Penguin Putnam.

Rowsome, Frank, Jr. The Verse by the Side of the Road. 1993. reprint ed. lib. bdg. 18.95 (*1-56849-088-7*) Buccaneer Bks.

— The Verse by the Side of the Road. 1979. reprint ed. pap. 10.95 (*0-452-26762-5*, Plume) Dutton Plume.

Rowson, Everett. A Muslim Philosopher on the Soul & Its Fate: Al-Amiri's Kitab al-Amad ala L-Abad. 375p. 1996. 42.50 (*0-614-21210-3*, 2) Kazi Pubns.

Rowson, Everett, tr. see Al-Tabari.

Rowson, Everett K. A Muslim Philosopher on the Soul & Its Fate: Al-Amiri's Kitab al-Amad 'ala l'abad. (Amer. Oriental Ser.: Vol. 70). vi, 375p. 1988. 42.50 (*0-940490-70-6*) Am Orient Soc.

Rowson, Everett K., tr. The History of al-Tabari Vol. 22: The Marwanid Restoration: The Caliphate of 'Abd al-Malik: A.D. 693-701 - A.H. 74-81. LC 88-16086. (SUNY Series in Near Eastern Studies). 228p. (C). 1987. pap. text 21.95 (*0-88706-976-2*) State U NY Pr.

— The History of al-Tabari Vol. 22: The Marwanid Restoration: The Caliphate of 'Abd al-Malik: A.D. 693-701 - A.H. 74-81. LC 88-16086. (SUNY Series in Near Eastern Studies). 228p. (C). 1989. text 49.50 (*0-88706-975-4*) State U NY Pr.

Rowson, Everett K & Bonebakker, Seeger A. A Computerized Listing of Biographical Data from the Yatimat al-dahr by al-Tha'alibi. LC 79-67633. viii, 101p. 1980. pap. 24.00 (*0-89003-044-8*) Undena Pubns.

Rowson, Everett K., jt. auth. see Wright, J. W.

Rowson, John & Slaney, Adrian. Dentistry. Scott, Sir Walter, ed. LC 96-229460. (Medico-Legal Practitioner Ser.). 118p. 1996. 69.90 (*1-85941-212-2*, Pub. by Cavendish Pubng) Gaunt.

Rowson, Jonathan. Gambit Guide to the Grunfeld. 1998. pap. text 19.95 (*1-901983-09-9*) Gambit.

***Rowson, Jonathan.** The Seven Deadly Chess Sins. 2000. pap. 18.95 (*1-901983-36-6*, Pub. by Gambit) BHB Intl.

Rowson, K. E., jt. auth. see Mahy, Brian W.

Rowson, Martin. The Life & Opinions of Tristram Shandy, Gentleman. LC 96-49506. (Illus.). 176p. 1997. 26.95 (*0-87951-768-9*, Pub. by Overlook Pr) Penguin Putnam.

Rowson, Richard. Introduction to Personal & Professional Ethics: Morality Explained. LC 99-41633. 1999. pap. 23.95 (*1-85302-750-2*) Jessica Kingsley.

***Rowson, Susanna Haswell.** Americans in England. (Notable American Authors Ser.). 1999. reprint ed. lib. bdg. 125.00 (*0-7812-8846-0*) Rprt Serv.

— Charlotte: A Tale of Truth. (Notable American Authors Ser.). 1999. reprint ed. lib. bdg. 125.00 (*0-7812-8837-1*) Rprt Serv.

Rowson, Susanna Haswell. Charlotte Temple. 160p. 1987. pap. text 9.95 (*0-19-504238-7*) OUP.

— Charlotte Temple: A Tale of Truth. Kirk, Clara M. & Kirk, Rudolf, eds. (Masterworks of Literature Ser.). 1964. pap. 10.95 (*0-8084-0073-8*) NCUP.

— Charlotte Temple: A Tale of Truth. (BCL1-PS American Literature Ser.). 1992. reprint ed. lib. bdg. 99.00 (*0-7812-6846-X*) Rprt Serv.

— Charlotte Temple & Lucy Temple. Douglas, Ann, ed. & intro. by. 336p. 1991. pap. 12.95 (*0-14-039080-4*, Penguin Classics) Viking Penguin.

— Charlotte's Daughter: Or the Three Orphans. LC 72-78812. reprint ed. 39.00 (*0-403-01983-4*) Somerset Pub.

— Charlotte's Temple, a Tale of Truth. LC 72-78814. reprint ed. 39.00 (*0-403-01984-2*) Somerset Pub.

***Rowson, Susanna Haswell.** Essays & Poems - Poems on Varius Subjects. (Notable American Authors Ser.). 1999. reprint ed. lib. bdg. 125.00 (*0-7812-8840-1*) Rprt Serv.

— The Female Patriot (Adapted from Massinger's the Bondman) (Notable American Authors Ser.). 1999. reprint ed. lib. bdg. 125.00 (*0-7812-8845-2*) Rprt Serv.

Rowson, Susanna Haswell. Lucy Temple. Levendusk, Christine, ed. (Masterworks of Literature Ser.). 1991. 12.95 (*0-8084-0433-4*) NCUP.

An Asterisk (*) at the beginning of an entry indicates that the title is appearing for the first time.

R

***Rowson, Susanna Haswell.** Mary: Or The Test of Honour. (Notable American Authors Ser.). 1999. reprint ed. lib. bdg. 125.00 (*0-7812-8836-3*) Rprt Serv.

— Miscellaneous Poems. (Notable American Authors Ser.). 1999. reprint ed. lib. bdg. 125.00 (*0-7812-8842-8*) Rprt Serv.

— Plays Slaves in Algiers. (Notable American Authors Ser.). 1999. reprint ed. lib. bdg. 125.00 (*0-7812-8843-6*) Rprt Serv.

— Rebecca: Or, The Fille de Chambre. (Notable American Authors Ser.). 1999. reprint ed. lib. bdg. 125.00 (*0-7812-8838-X*) Rprt Serv.

— Reuben & Rachel. (Notable American Authors Ser.). 1999. reprint ed. lib. bdg. 125.00 (*0-7812-8839-8*) Rprt Serv.

Rowson, Susanna Haswell. Reuben & Rachel: or Tales of Old Times, 2 vols. in 1. LC 78-64089. reprint ed. 37.50 (*0-404-17074-9*) AMS Pr.

— Sarah: or The Exemplary Wife. LC 78-64090. reprint ed. 37.50 (*0-404-17165-6*) AMS Pr.

— Trials of the Human Heart, 4 vols. in 2. LC 78-64091. reprint ed. 75.00 (*0-404-17360-8*) AMS Pr.

***Rowson, Susanna Haswell.** A Trip to Parnassus. (Notable American Authors Ser.). 1999. reprint ed. lib. bdg. 125.00 (*0-7812-8841-X*) Rprt Serv.

— Victoria, 1786: The Inquisitor: or, Invisible Rambler. (Notable American Authors Ser.). 1999. reprint ed. lib. bdg. 125.00 (*0-7812-8835-5*) Rprt Serv.

— The Volunteer. (Notable American Authors Ser.). 1999. reprint ed. lib. bdg. 125.00 (*0-7812-8844-4*) Rprt Serv.

Rowter, Philip D. The Hunting Instinct: Safari Chronicles from the Republic of South Africa & Namibia 1990-1998. (Illus.). 243p. 1999. 29.95 (*1-57157-158-2*) Safari Pr.

— The Hunting Instinct: Safari Chronicles from the Republic of South Africa & Namibia, 1990-1998. limited ed. (Illus.). 243p. 1999. 50.00 (*1-57157-092-6*) Safari Pr.

Rowthorn, Anne. Caring for Creation: Toward an Ethic of Responsibility. LC 89-32725. 176p. (Orig.). 1990. pap. 11.95 (*0-8192-1506-6*) Morehouse Pub.

***Rowthorn, Anne.** Earth & All the Stars: Reconnecting with Nature Through Hymns, Stories, Poems, & Prayers from the World's Great Religions & Cultures. LC 99-49439. 312p. 2000. pap. 15.95 (*1-57731-106-X*, Pub. by New Wrld Lib) Publishers Group.

Rowthorn, Anne. Samuel Seabury: A Bicentennial Biography. 160p. 1984. 14.95 (*0-8164-0517-4*) Harper SF.

Rowthorn, Anne, et al. Godworks: Evangelism at Work with Young People. LC 97-37762. 144p. 1997. pap. 17.95 (*0-8192-1731-X*) Morehouse Pub.

Rowthorn, Bob. Capitalism Conflict & Inflation. (C). 1980. pap. 18.50 (*0-85315-539-9*, Pub. by Lawrence & Wishart) NYU Pr.

Rowthorn, Chris. Lonely Planet Malaysia, Singapore & Brunei: Travel Survival Kit. 7th ed. LC 97-649684. (Lonely Planet Travel Guides Ser.). (Illus.). 608p. 1999. pap. text 17.95 (*0-86442-618-6*) Lonely Planet.

— Lonely Planet Tokyo. LC 99-192646. (Illus.). 248p. 1998. pap. 14.95 (*0-86442-567-8*) Lonely Planet.

Rowthorn, Chris, et al. Lonely Planet Malaisie et Singapour. 3rd ed. 608p. 1999. pap. 29.95 (*2-84070-093-X*) Lonely Planet.

Rowthorn, Chris, jt. auth. see Cruttenden, Pete.

Rowthorn, Jeffery & Schulz-Widmar, Russell, eds. A New Hymnal for Colleges & Schools. LC 91-5026. 512p. (C). 1992. 25.00 (*0-300-05113-1*) Yale U Pr.

Rowthorn, Jeffery W. The Wideness of God's Mercy: Litanies to Enlarge Our Prayer, 2 vols. 1985. 15.95 (*0-86683-794-9*); 15.95 (*0-86683-795-7*) Harper SF.

— The Wideness of God's Mercy: Litanies to Enlarge Our Prayer. rev. ed. LC 95-2357. 256p. 1995. pap. 19.95 (*0-8192-1606-2*) Morehouse Pub.

Rowthorn, Jeffrey W. The Wideness of God's Mercy: Litanies to Enlarge Our Prayer, 2 vols. 1985. 29.95 (*0-86683-789-2*) Harper SF.

Rowthorn, Robert, jt. ed. see Chang, Ha-Joon.

Rowthorn, Robert, jt. ed. see Pagano, Ugo.

Rowton, Paul, jt. ed. see Rycraft, Carol.

Rowzee, Janet Z. & Watson, James A. The Song of the Shepherd Boy. 20p. (J). (gr. 4-8). 1993. pap. 6.95 (*0-9638941-0-2*) Eagles Three.

Roxbee-Cox, P. Atoms & Molecules. (Understanding Science Ser.). (Illus.). 32p. (YA). (gr. 7-13). 1993. pap. 7.95 (*0-7460-0988-7*, Usborne) EDC.

— Atoms & Molecules. (Understanding Science Ser.). (Illus.). 32p. (J). (gr. 7-12). 1999. lib. bdg. 15.95 (*0-88110-589-9*, Usborne) EDC.

***Roxbee-Cox, P.** Ted in a Red Bed. (Easy Words to Read Ser.). (Illus.). 16p. (J). (ps-3). 1999. pap. 7.95 (*0-7460-3023-1*, Usborne) EDC.

Roxbee-Cox, P. What Were Castles For? (Starting Point History Ser.). (Illus.). 24p. (J). (gr. 1 up). 1995. pap. 4.95 (*0-7460-1341-8*, Usborne); lib. bdg. 12.95 (*0-88110-729-8*, Usborne) EDC.

— Who Were the First People? (Starting Point History Ser.). (Illus.). 24p. (J). (gr. 1-4). 1995. pap. 4.95 (*0-7460-1343-4*, Usborne) EDC.

— Who Were the First People? (Starting Point History Ser.). (Illus.). 24p. (J). (gr. 1 up). 1995. lib. bdg. 12.95 (*0-88110-730-1*, Usborne) EDC.

Roxbee-Cox, Phil. Nightmare at Mystery Mansion. (Spinechillers Ser.). (Illus.). 48p. (J). (gr. 4-7). 1996. pap. 5.95 (*0-7460-2089-9*, Usborne) EDC.

Roxbee-Cox, Phil. Nightmare at Mystery Mansion. (Spinechillers Ser.). (Illus.). 48p. (J). (gr. 4 up). 1996. lib. bdg. 13.95 (*0-88110-824-3*, Usborne) EDC.

— El Reino de los Juguetes. (Young Puzzles Ser.). (SPA., Illus.). 32p. (ps-3). 1999. 14.95 (*1-58086-215-2*) EDC.

— Who Stole the Black Diamond? (Solve It Yourself Ser.). 48p. (YA). (gr. 7 up). 1996. lib. bdg. 15.95 (*0-88110-829-4*, Usborne) EDC.

— Who Stole the Black Diamond? LC 96-17476. (Solve It Yourself Ser.). (Illus.). 48p. (YA). (gr. 7 up). 1996. pap. 7.95 (*0-7460-2053-8*, Usborne) EDC.

Roxbee-Cox, Phil & Tyler, Jenny. Magic Toyshop. (Young Puzzles Ser.). (Illus.). 32p. (J). (gr. k up). 1998. lib. bdg. 14.95 (*1-58086-122-9*, Usborne) EDC.

— Magic Toyshop. (Young Puzzles Ser.). (Illus.). 32p. (J). (ps up). 1998. pap. 6.95 (*0-7460-2847-4*, Usborne) EDC.

Roxberg, Joan M., jt. auth. see Montoya, Candace G.

Roxberg, Joan Mariner, see Glass Montoya, Candace & Mariner Roxberg, Joan.

Roxborough, Ian, jt. ed. see Bethell, Leslie.

***Roxborough, John.** Thomas Chalmers: Enthusiast for Mission. (Rutherford Studies in Historical Theology). 324p. 1999. pap. 40.00 (*0-946068-49-6*, Pub. by Rutherford Hse) OM Literature.

Roxborough, Judy, ed. see Rodriguez, Gloria & Casado, Silvia.

Roxburgh, Alan J. The Missionary Congregation, Leadership & Liminality. LC 96-49154. (Christian Mission & Modern Culture Ser.). 80p. 1997. pap. 7.00 (*1-56338-190-7*) TPI PA.

— Reaching a New Generation: Strategies for Tomorrow's Church. 140p. 1998. reprint ed. pap. 15.95 (*1-57383-100-X*) Regent College.

***Roxburgh, Barry, ed.** Fishing Forays: A Distinguished Companion to the Rivers, Lochs & Still Waters of Great Britain & Ireland. 4th rev. ed. (Illus.). 224p. 2000. 19.95 (*1-871349-23-0*, Pub. by Kensington West) Midpt Trade.

Roxburgh, Ian W., et al, eds. Physical Processes in Astrophysics: Proceedings of a Meeting in Honour of Evry Schatzman Held in Paris, France, 22-24 September 1993, Vol. XII. LC 95-37623. (Lecture Notes in Physics Ser.: Vol. 458). 249p. 1995. 80.95 (*3-540-60259-3*) Spr-Verlag.

Roxburgh, Kenneth B. E. Thomas Gillespie & the Orgins of the Relief Church in 18th Century Scotland. LC 99-210725. (International Theological Studies: Vol. 3). XVI, 272p. 1999. 42.95 (*0-8204-4228-3*) P Lang Pubng.

Roxburgh, Nigel. Policy Responses to Resource Depletion: The Case of Mercury. Altman, Edward I. & Walter, Ingo I., eds. LC 77-24395. (Contemporary Studies in Economic & Financial Analysis: Vol. 21). 219p. 1980. 78.50 (*0-89232-093-1*) Jai Pr.

Roxburgh, R. Icones Roxburghianae: or Drawings of Indian Plants. (C). 1988. 170.00 (*0-7855-3240-4*, Pub. by Scientific) St Mut.

Roxburgh, Ronald F. The Origins of Lincoln's Inn. LC 85-81798. (Cambridge Studies in English Legal History). 102p. 1986. reprint ed. 35.00 (*0-912004-52-5*) Gaunt.

Roxburgh, William. Flora Indica: Description of Indian Plants. Carey, ed. (Illus.). lxiv, 775p. 1974. reprint ed. 50.00 (*0-88065-182-2*) Scholarly Pubns.

— Plants of the Coast of Coromandel, 3 vols. (C). 1988. text 2000.00 (*0-7855-6002-5*, Pub. by Scientific) St Mut.

— Plants of the Coast of Coromandel: Selected from Drawings & Descriptions Presented to the Hon. Court of Directors of the East India Company, under the Order of Sir Joseph Banks, 3 vols. (Illus.). 20p. 1982. reprint ed. lib. bdg. 1200.00 (*0-685-44091-5*) Lubrecht & Cramer.

***Roxbury Park Staff.** Best of Scary Stories for Stormy Nights. (Illus.). (J). 2000. pap. 5.95 (*0-7373-0431-6*, Roxbury Park) Lowell Hse.

— Scary Classics: Stories from the Greatest Horror Writers of All Time. (Illus.). (J). 2000. pap. 9.95 (*0-7373-0438-3*, Roxbury Park) Lowell Hse.

Roxe, Linda A. Personnel Management for the Smaller Company: A Hands-on Manual. LC 79-10867. 256p. reprint ed. pap. 79.40 (*0-608-12965-8*, 202392000034) Bks Demand.

Roxin, E. O. Control Theory & Its Applications. (Stability & Control: Vol. 4). 160p. 1997. text 42.00 (*2-919875-22-1*, ECU54) Gordon & Breach.

Roxin, Emilio O. Modern Optimal Control: A Conference in Honor of Solomon Lefschetz & Joseph P. La Salle. (Lecture Notes in Pure & Applied Mathematics Ser.: Vol. 119). (Illus.). 464p. 1989. pap. text 170.00 (*0-8247-8168-6*) Dekker.

Roxin, Emilio D., jt. auth. see Liu, Pan-Tai.

Roxton, James. The Markets Directory, 1991: Focus Facilities, Test Kitchens, Malls, Moderators by Location in Every Major Market in the United States. 261p. 1990. pap. 40.00 (*0-9628135-0-8*) Dobbs Dirs.

Roxton, Tiniki, ed. Recommended Videos for Schools. 2nd ed. 300p. 1992. lib. bdg. 55.00 (*0-87436-688-7*) ABC-CLIO.

Roxxie. Girljock. LC 96-47871. (Illus.). 240p. 1998. pap. 16.95 (*0-312-15134-9*) St Martin.

Roy. Among the Great. 1993. pap. text 10.95 (*1-879649-02-0*) Osiris Pr.

— Basic Technical Writing. (C). 1995. pap. text. write for info. (*0-15-502033-1*) Harcourt Coll Pubs.

— Basic Technical Writing. (C). 1995. pap. text, teacher ed. 28.00 (*0-15-502172-9*) Harcourt Coll Pubs.

— Bhagavad Gita: A Revelation. 1993. pap. text 10.50 (*1-879649-03-9*) Osiris Pr.

— Combinatorial Programming. 1975. text 148.50 (*90-277-0625-5*) Kluwer Academic.

— Diversity & Dominance in Indian Politics: Diversity, Deprivation & the Congress, Vol. 2. 240p. 1990. 26.00 (*0-8039-9660-8*) Sage.

— Master Techniques in Ophthalmalic Surgery. (Illus.). 1277p. 1995. 225.00 (*0-683-07410-5*) Lppncott W & W.

Roy & Klatte. Compact Dictionary: German. (ENG & GER.). 1408p. 1993. vinyl bd. 15.95 (*0-88729-071-X*) Langenscheidt.

Roy, jt. auth. see Chanda.

Roy, A. E. Orbital Motion. 3rd rev. ed. (Illus.). 548p. 1988. 239.00 (*0-85274-228-2*); pap. 56.00 (*0-85274-229-0*) IOP Pub.

— Predictability, Stability & Chaos in N-Body Dynamical Systems. (NATO ASI Ser.: Vol. 272). (Illus.). 616p. (C). 1991. text 155.00 (*0-306-44034-2*, Plenum Trade) Perseus Pubng.

Roy, A. E. & Clarke, D. Astronomy: Principles & Practice. 3rd ed. (Illus.). 376p. 1988. 158.00 (*0-85274-394-7*) IOP Pub.

— Astronomy: Principles & Practice. 3rd ed. LC 87-32403. (Illus.). 376p. 1988. pap. 40.00 (*0-85274-393-9*) IOP Pub.

— Astronomy: Structure of the Universe. 3rd ed. (Illus.). 316p. 1989. 158.00 (*0-85274-082-4*); pap. 40.00 (*0-85274-083-2*) IOP Pub.

Roy, A. E. & Steves, B. A. From Newton to Chaos: Modern Techniques for Understanding & Coping with Chaos in N-Body Dynamical Systems. LC 95-1181. (NATO ASI Ser.: Vol. 336). (Illus.). 602p. (C). 1995. text 149.50 (*0-306-44904-8*) Plenum.

Roy, A. E., jt. auth. see Steves, Bonnie A.

***Roy, A. K., et al, eds.** Phytodiversification & Human Welfare: Dedicated to Late Prof. K. S. Bilgrami, FNA (1933-96) LC 99-931560. 329 p. 1998. pap. 200.00 (*81-7533-077-5*, Pub. by Print Hse) St Mut.

Roy, A. K. & Clark, J. H., eds. Gene Regulation by Steroid Hormones. (Illus.). 400p. 1980. 175.00 (*0-387-90464-6*) Spr-Verlag.

— Gene Regulation by Steroid Hormones II. (Illus.). 384p. 1983. 205.00 (*0-387-90784-X*) Spr-Verlag.

— Gene Regulation by Steroid Hormones III. (Illus.). 335p. 1987. 223.00 (*0-387-96436-3*) Spr-Verlag.

— Gene Regulation by Steroid Hormones IV. (Illus.). xi, 239p. 1989. 117.00 (*0-387-96999-3*) Spr-Verlag.

Roy, A. K. & Sinha, K. K. Recent Advances in Phytopathological Researches. 211p. 1995. pap. 150.00 (*81-85880-76-X*, Pub. by Print Hse) St Mut.

Roy, A. K. & Sinha, K. K., eds. Recent Advances in Phytopathological Researches. 211p. 1995. pap. 130.00 (*0-7855-2726-5*, Pub. by Print Hse) St Mut.

Roy, A. K., jt. auth. see Harper, Malcolm.

Roy, A. S., jt. ed. see Smith, I. M.

Roy, Abhijit & Roy, Rakesh. How to Invest in India. 1997. pap. 17.50 (*81-7476-149-7*, Pub. by UBS Pubs) S Asia.

Roy, Ajit K. The Historical Evolution of Corporation Tax in India. (C). 1987. 62.50 (*0-8364-2130-2*) S Asia.

Roy, Alain. Dictionnaire Raisonne et Illustre du Theatre A l'Italienne. (FRE.). 1992. 65.00 (*0-7859-8166-7*, 2-86943-357-3) Fr & Eur.

Roy, Alec, ed. Hysteria. LC 80-42308. 332p. reprint ed. pap. 103.00 (*0-608-15825-9*, 203129700074) Bks Demand.

Roy, Alene A. Cooking with Sourdough: A Tribute to the Oregon Trail Pioneers. (Illus.). 1995. spiral bd. 7.95 (*0-9635069-2-7*) Closer Walk.

— In His Gardens, Bk. 1. 72p. (Orig.). 1992. pap. 7.95 (*0-9635069-0-0*) Closer Walk.

— Winter in His Garden: Essays of Faith & Family. LC 94-69070. (In His Gardens Ser.: Bk. 2). (Illus.). 116p. (Orig.). 1995. pap. 7.95 (*0-9635069-1-9*) Closer Walk.

Roy, Alice M., jt. ed. see Buranen, Lise.

Roy, Andre. The Passions of Mr. Desire. 82p. pap. 8.00 (*0-919349-64-1*) Guernica Editions.

Roy, Andrew. Fallen Soldier: The Memoir of a Civil War Casualty. LC 96-47714. 1996. pap. text 14.95 (*1-880216-40-X*, Elliott Clark) Black Belt Communs.

Roy, Anilbaran, ed. The Message of the Gita. 311p. 1985. 15.95 (*0-318-37180-4*) Asia Bk Corp.

Roy, Anilbaran, ed. The Message of the Gita. 5th ed. 306p. 1993. pap. 10.95 (*81-7058-305-5*, Pub. by SAA) E-W Cultural Ctr.

Roy, Anilbaran, ed. see Aurobindo, Sri.

Roy, Aniruddha, ed. Technology in Ancient & Medieval India. 170p. 1986. 46.00 (*81-85055-95-5*, Pub. by Minerva) S Asia.

Roy, Anjali. A Monograph on Polyporaceae of India. LC 96-904929. 1996. pap. 163.00 (*81-7089-213-9*, Pub. by Intl Bk Distr) St Mut.

Roy, Ann S. Mommy, What Is a Dysfunctional Family? Random Tales of Wayward Folks. Carmical, Phillip, ed. 150p. 1998. pap. 12.95 (*0-89896-436-9*) Larksdale.

Roy, Anup K., jt. auth. see Gottman, John.

***Roy, Anuradha.** Patterns of Feminist Consciousness in Indian Women Writers: A Study of Anita Desai's Cry, the Peacock, Nayantara Sahgal's Storm in Chandigarh, Attia Hosain's Sunlight on a Broken Column, Rama Mehta's Inside the Haveli, Shashi Despande's That Long Silence. LC 99-932114. 152p. 1999. write for info. (*81-7551-064-1*, Pub. by Prestige) Advent Bks Div.

Roy, Archie E., ed. Long-Term Dynamical Behaviour of Natural & Artificial N-Body Systems. (C). 1988. text 256.50 (*90-277-2801-1*) Kluwer Academic.

Roy, Arthur J., ed. see Flint, Albert S.

***Roy, Arundhati.** Cost of Living. LC 99-41156. 144p. 1999. pap. 11.95 (*0-375-75614-0*) Random.

— The God of Small Things. LC 97-32562. 336p. 1998. pap. 14.00 (*0-06-097749-3*, HarperFlamingo) HarpC.

Roy, Arundhati. The God of Small Things. large type ed. LC 97-34118. 471p. 1997. 25.95 (*0-7838-8296-3*, G K Hall Lrg Type) Mac Lib Ref.

Roy, Arundhati. God of Small Things: Choudhury,&Sarita, Set. abr. ed. 1997. audio 25.00 (*0-694-51960-X*, Caedmon) HarperAudio.

Roy, Arundhati. The Soviet Intervention in Afghanistan: Causes, Consequences & India's Response. 140p. 1987. text 22.50 (*81-7045-006-3*, Pub. by Assoc Pub Hse) Advent Bks Div.

Roy, Ashim K. & Gidwani, N. N. A Dictionary of Indology Vol. 3: L-R. 1986. 24.00 (*81-204-0036-4*, Pub. by Oxford IBH) S Asia.

Roy, Ashok, ed. Artists' Pigments: A Handbook of Their History & Characteristics, Vol. 2. (A National Gallery of Art USA Publication). (Illus.). 232p. 1997. pap. 29.95 (*0-89468-260-1*) OUP.

Roy, Asim. Islam in South Asia: A Regional Perspective. LC 96-902360. (C). 1996. 30.00 (*81-7003-193-1*, Pub. by S Asia Pubs) S Asia.

— The Islamic Syncretistic Tradition in Bengal. LC 83-42574. 336p. 1983. reprint ed. pap. 104.20 (*0-608-02936-X*, 206400200008) Bks Demand.

Roy, B. Rabindranath Tagore. 1972. 59.95 (*0-8490-0924-3*) Gordon Pr.

Roy, B., ed. see NATO Advanced Study Institute Staff.

Roy, B. C., jt. auth. see Datta, Ashim K.

Roy, Benoy B. Socio-Economic Impact of Sati in Bengal & the Role of Raja Rammohun Roy. (C). 1987. 31.00 (*81-85109-70-2*, Pub. by Naya Prokash) S Asia.

Roy, Bernard. Multicriteria Methodology for Decision Aiding. (Nonconvex Optimization & Its Applications Ser.). 320p. (C). 1996. lib. bdg. 156.00 (*0-7923-4166-X*) Kluwer Academic.

Roy, Beth. Bitters in the Honey: Tales of Hope & Disappointment Across Divides of Race & Time. LC 99-23950. 1999. 32.00 (*1-55728-553-5*); pap. 20.00 (*1-55728-554-3*) U of Ark Pr.

— Some Trouble with Cows: Making Sense of Social Conflict. LC 93-25761. (C). 1994. 48.00 (*0-520-08341-5*, Pub. by U CA Pr); pap. 16.95 (*0-520-08342-3*, Pub. by U CA Pr) Cal Prin Full Svc.

Roy, Bhasker. The Defeat or Distant Drumbeats. LC 98-907293. 216p. 1998. write for info. (*81-241-0027-6*) Har-Anand Pubns.

***Roy-Bhattacharya, Joydeep.** The Gabriel Club. LC 99-932517. 396 p. 1998. write for info. (*0-14-028299-8*, Penguin Classics) Viking Penguin.

Roy, Bimalendu N. Crystal Growth from Melts: Applications to Growth of Groups 1 & 2 Crystals. LC 91-18377. (Illus.). 344p. 1992. reprint ed. pap. 106.70 (*0-608-07297-4*, 206752500009) Bks Demand.

Roy, Buddhaved. Marriage Rituals & Songs of Bengal. 1985. 6.50 (*0-8364-1290-7*, Pub. by Mukhopadhyaya) S Asia.

Roy, Cal. Bubble, the Birds, & the Noise. (Illus.). (J). (gr. k-4). 1968. 8.95 (*0-8392-3069-9*) Astor-Honor.

— Friend Can Be. (Illus.). (J). (gr. 2 up). 1969. 9.95 (*0-8392-3075-3*) Astor-Honor.

— Time Is Day. (Illus.). (J). (gr. k-3). 1968. 9.95 (*0-8392-3065-6*) Astor-Honor.

— What Every Young Wizard Should Know. (Illus.). (J). (gr. 2 up). 1963. 8.95 (*0-8392-3043-5*) Astor-Honor.

Roy, Callista. The Roy Adaptation Model: The Definitive Statement. 2nd ed. LC 98-33477. (C). 1998. pap. text 34.95 (*0-8385-8248-6*) Appleton & Lange.

Roy, Camille. Cold Heaven. LC 93-84574. 89p. 1993. 9.00 (*1-882022-15-7*) O Bks.

— The Rosy Medallions: Selected Work. Dienstfrey, Patricia, ed. LC 95-2637. 72p. (Orig.). (C). 1995. pap. text 10.00 (*0-932716-35-0*) Kelsey St Pr.

— Swarm. unabridged ed. (Illus.). 122p. 1998. pap. 8.50 (*0-9607630-3-1*) Black Star.

***Roy-Campbell, Zaline M.** Empowerment Through Language: The African Experience in Tanzania & Beyond. LC 99-23972. 1999. pap. write for info. (*0-86543-765-3*) Africa World.

Roy, Carrista & Andrews, Heather A. The Roy Adaptation Model: The Definitive Statement. 2nd ed. (Illus.). 472p. (C). 1991. pap. text 36.95 (*0-8385-2272-6*, A2272-1) Appleton & Lange.

Roy Chaudary, P. C. Gandhi & His Contemporaries. 271p. 1986. 34.95 (*81-207-0115-1*) Asia Bk Corp.

Roy Chowdhury, Profulla. The North East: Roots of Insurgency. 1986. 8.50 (*0-8364-1869-7*, Pub. by Firma KLM) S Asia.

***Roy, Christian.** Encyclopedia of Traditional Festivals. 2001. lib. bdg. 70.00 (*1-57607-089-1*) ABC-CLIO.

Roy, Christina. Sunshine Country. (Illus.). 1847p. (YA). (gr. 7-10). 1967. pap. 6.70 (*0-7399-0130-3*, 2421) Rod & Staff.

***Roy, Christopher D.** Kilengi: African Art from the Bareiss Family Collection. (Illus.). 428p. 1999. 75.00 (*0-295-97822-8*) U of Wash Pr.

Roy, Christopher D. Selections from the Julian & Irma Brody Collection. LC 88-70384. (Illus.). 40p. (Orig.). 1988. pap. 10.00 (*0-9614615-3-5*) Edmundson.

Roy, Clarence H. The Operation & Maintenance of Surface Finishing Wastewater Treatment Systems. 199p. 1988. 60.00 (*0-936569-04-2*); pap. 40.00 (*0-318-35444-6*) Am Electro Surface.

Roy, Claude. Balthus. LC 96-85463. (Illus.). 272p. 1996. 65.00 (*0-8212-2345-3*, Pub. by Bulfinch Pr) Little.

— Chat Qui Parlait Malgre Lui. (Folio - Junior Ser.: No. 194). (FRE., Illus.). 87p. (J). (gr. 5-10). 1982. pap. 8.95 (*2-07-033615-8*) Schoenhof.

— Distant Friend. Harter, Hugh A., tr. LC 90-30540. (French Expressions Ser.). 176p. 1990. 19.95 (*0-8419-1196-7*) Holmes & Meier.

— Enfantasques. (Folio - Junior Ser.: No. 87). (FRE.). (J). (gr. 5-10). 1979. pap. 6.95 (*2-07-033087-7*) Schoenhof.

— Maison Qui S'Envole. (Folio - Junior Ser.: No. 1). (FRE., Illus.). 90p. (J). (gr. 5-10). 1977. pap. 7.95 (*2-07-033001-X*) Schoenhof.

— Le Malheur d'Aimer. (FRE.). 1974. pap. 10.95 (*0-7859-4029-4*) Fr & Eur.

— Moi-Je. (FRE.). 497p. 1978. pap. 13.95 (*0-7859-4107-X*, 2070370666) Fr & Eur.

— Nous. (FRE.). 576p. 1980. pap. 15.95 (*0-7859-4141-X*, 2070372472) Fr & Eur.

— La Nuit Est le Manteau des Pauvres. (FRE.). 1976. pap. 10.95 (*0-7859-4053-7*) Fr & Eur.

— Permis de Sejour. (FRE.). 1985. pap. 14.95 (*0-7859-4238-6*) Fr & Eur.

Roy, Claude, intro. Marc Riboud: Photographs at Home & Abroad. (Illus.). 120p. 1988. 45.00 (*0-8109-1566-9*, Pub. by Abrams) Time Warner.

R

Roy, Claude, jt. auth. see Chateaubriand, Francois-Rene de.

Roy, Claude C. Pediatric Clinical Gastroenterology. 4th ed. (Illus.). 970p. 1991. 89.95 (*0-8016-6216-8*) Mosby Inc.

Roy, Claude C., et al, eds. Pediatric Clinical Gastroenterology. 4th ed. LC 94-12633. (Illus.). 960p. (C). (gr. 13). 1995. text 120.00 (*0-8151-7406-3*, 24171) Mosby Inc.

Roy, Claudine, jt. auth. see Bourdeau, Pierre-Yves.

***Roy, Cynthia B.** Innovative Practices for Teaching Sign Language Interpreters. LC 99-59244. 2000. 34.95 (*1-56368-088-2*) Gallaudet Univ Pr.

Roy, Cynthia B. Interpreting As a Discourse Process. LC 99-13649. (Oxford Studies in Sociolinguistics). 152p. 1999. text 35.00 (*0-19-511948-7*) OUP.

Roy, D. C., ed. Northeastern Section Field Guide. (DNAG Centennial Field Guides Ser.: No. 5). (Illus.). 517p. 1987. 21.75 (*0-8137-5405-4*) Geol Soc.

Roy, D. C. & Skehan, J. W., eds. The Acadian Orogeny: Recent Studies in New England, Maritime Canada, & the Autochthonous Foreland. (Special Papers: No. 275). 1993. pap. 21.25 (*0-8137-2275-6*) Geol Soc.

Roy, D. J., et al. Bioscience - Society: Report of the Schering Workshop, Berlin 1990, November 25-30. 420p. 1991. 315.00 (*0-471-93152-7*, Wiley-Liss) Wiley.

Roy, D. M. & Idorn, G. M. Concrete Microstructure. 179p. (C). 1993. pap. text 15.00 (*0-309-05254-8*, SHRP-C-340) SHRP.

Roy, D. M., et al. Concrete Microstructure: Recommended Revisions to Test Methods. 107p. (C). 1993. pap. text 15.00 (*0-309-05601-2*, SHRP-C-339) SHRP.

Roy, D. N. Applied Fluid Mechanics. 1988. text 104.00 (*0-470-21314-0*) P-H.

Roy, D. P. Heat. 1985. 100.00 (*0-7855-0736-1*, Pub. by Current Dist) St Mut.

Roy, D. P. & Roy, P. Phenomenology of the Standard Model & Beyond: Workshop on Hep. Phenomenology. 728p. 1989. text 130.00 (*9971-5-0909-1*) World Scientific Pub.

Roy, Daniel, jt. auth. see Briand, Lo C.

Roy, David, ed. see Jenness, Kirik.

***Roy, David E.** Toward a Process Psychology: A Model of Integration. LC 00-190306. 252p. 2000. 54.50 (*1-929673-00-0*) Adobe Creat.

— Toward a Process Psychology: A Model of Integration. xviii, 232p. (C). 2000. pap. 24.95 (*1-929673-01-9*) Adobe Creat.

Roy, David T. Kuo Mo-Jo: The Early Years. LC 77-123569. (Harvard East Asian Ser.: No. 55). 258p. reprint ed. pap. 80.00 (*0-7837-2326-1*, 205741400004) Bks Demand.

Roy, David T., tr. The Plum in the Golden Vase: Chin P'ing Mei The Gathering, Vol. 1. LC 92-45054. (Library of Asian Translations). (Illus.). 544p. 1993. text 65.00 (*0-691-06932-8*, Pub. by Princeton U Pr) Cal Prin Full Svc.

Roy, David Tod. Gathering, Vol. 1. 714p. 1993. pap. text 24.95 (*0-691-01614-3*, Pub. by Princeton U Pr) Cal Prin Full Svc.

Roy, Debal K. Women, New Technology & Development: Changing Nature of Gender Relations in Rural India. (C). 1995. 30.00 (*81-7304-102-4*, Pub. by Manohar) S Asia.

Roy, Denny. China's Foreign Relations. LC 97-51889. 276p. 1998. 64.00 (*0-8476-9012-1*); pap. 21.95 (*0-8476-9013-X*) Rowman.

— The New Security Agenda in the Asia-Pacific Region. LC 97-11429. 256p. 1997. text 59.95 (*0-312-17371-7*) St Martin.

Roy, Denny, jt. auth. see Christie, Kenneth.

***Roy, Dewayne.** Welding for Arts & Crafts. LC 99-89024. 2000. pap. 13.50 (*0-7668-1896-9*) Thomson Learn.

Roy, Dewayne, jt. auth. see Jeffus, Larry.

Roy, Dilip. Environment Management with Indian Experience. LC 98-909195. 1998. 72.00 (*81-7024-961-9*, Pub. by Ashish Pub Hse) S Asia.

Roy, Dilip, ed. Strategic Management: Indian Experience. LC 97-906574. 311p. 1997. 45.00 (*81-212-0546-8*, Pub. by Gyan Publishing Hse) Nataraj Bks.

Roy, Dilip K. A Quantum Measurement Approach to Tunnelling: Tunnelling by Quantum Measurement. 200p. 1993. text 48.00 (*981-02-1223-2*) World Scientific Pub.

— Quantum Mechanical Tunnelling & Its Applications. 400p. 1986. text 77.00 (*9971-5-0024-8*) World Scientific Pub.

Roy, Dipak. Microbiology Lab Guide. 72p. (C). 1995. pap. text, per. 15.95 (*0-7872-0993-7*) Kendall-Hunt.

Roy, Dipti K. Leftist Politics in India: M. N. Roy & the Radical Democratic Party. (C). 1989. 25.50 (*81-85195-18-8*, Pub. by Minerva) S Asia.

— Trade Union Movement in India: Role of M. N. Roy. 1990. 17.50 (*81-85195-28-5*, Pub. by Minerva) S Asia.

Roy, Donald. Quota Restriction & Goldbricking in a Machine Shop. (Reprint Series in Social Sciences). (C). 1993. reprint ed. pap. text 5.00 (*0-8290-2670-3*, S-244) Irvington.

— The Reuniting of America: Eleven Multicultural Dialogues. (Major Concepts in Politics & Political Theory ser.: Vol. 11). X, 264p. (C). 1996. pap. text 29.95 (*0-8204-3118-4*) P Lang Pubng.

Roy, Donald H. Public Policy Dialogues. 240p. (Orig.). (C). 1994. pap. text 28.50 (*0-8191-9336-4*); lib. bdg. 49.50 (*0-8191-9335-6*) U Pr of Amer.

Roy, Donna S. & Flores, Kathleen. What's for Breakfast? Light & Easy Morning Meals for Busy People. Winchester, Faith & Hachfeld, Linda, eds. (Illus.). 286p. 1994. pap. 13.95 (*0-9620471-4-7*) Appletree MN.

Roy, E. Harold. In Remembrance of Me. LC 96-199803. 96p. (Orig.). 1996. pap. 7.99 (*0-8280-1054-4*) Review & Herald.

Roy, Emil & Roy, Sandra. Images: Reading for Writing. LC 96-77397. 320p. (C). 1996. pap. text 37.00 (*0-15-503166-X*, Pub. by Harcourt Coll Pubs) Harcourt.

Roy, Eric A., jt. ed. see Elliott, Digby.

Roy, Erik M., ed. Ergonomics Process Manual. (Illus.). 174p. 1993. 199.00 (*0-931690-53-6*) Genium Pub.

— Hazwoper Compliance System, 2 vols. 1992. 199.00 (*0-931690-49-8*); teacher ed. write for info. (*0-931690-50-1*) Genium Pub.

Roy, F. Hampton & Russell, Charles. The Encyclopedia of Aging & the Elderly. (Illus.). 320p. 1992. lib. bdg. 50.00 (*0-8160-1869-3*) Facts on File.

Roy, F. Hampton & Tindall, Renee, eds. Master the Techniques of Ophthalmic Surgery. LC 94-7614. (Illus.). 1994. write for info. (*0-8121-1679-8*) Lppncott W & W.

Roy F. Weston, Inc. Staff. The Road to ISO 1400. LC 95-51289. 64p. 1996. text 13.95 (*0-7863-0866-4*, Irwn Prfssnl) McGraw-Hill Prof.

Roy, Frederick H. Ocular Differential Diagnosis. 5th ed. LC 92-10384. 900p. 1992. pap. text 62.50 (*0-8121-1594-5*) Lppncott W & W.

— Ocular Differential Diagnosis. 6th ed. LC 96-13229. (Illus.). 768p. 1996. pap. 65.00 (*0-683-07415-6*) Lppncott W & W.

Roy, G. & Schmor, P., eds. Polarized Proton Ion Sources: Conference Proceedings, TRIUMF, Vancouver, 1983. LC 84-71235. (AIP Conference Proceedings Ser.: No. 117). 209p. 1984. lib. bdg. 37.00 (*0-88318-316-1*) Am Inst Physics.

Roy, G. D. Propulsion Combustion: Fuels to Emissions. LC 97-24299. (Combustion Ser.). 376p. 1997. 95.00 (*1-56032-431-7*) Taylor & Francis.

Roy, G. J. Instrumentation & Control. 168p. 1994. pap. text 34.95 (*0-7506-1837-X*) Buttrwrth-Heinemann.

Roy, G. P. Flora of Madhya Pradesh (Chhatarpur & Damoh) (C). 1992. 80.00 (*81-7024-457-9*, Pub. by Ashish Pub Hse) S Asia.

— Grasses of Madhya Pradesh. (C). 1988. text 50.00 (*0-7855-3152-1*, Pub. by Scientific) St Mut.

Roy, G. Ross, ed. see Burns, Robert.

Roy, Gabrielle. Cashier. 285p. 1996. pap. text 7.95 (*0-7710-9855-3*) McCland & Stewart.

— Garden in the Wind. 185p. 1996. pap. text 5.95 (*0-7710-9857-X*) McCland & Stewart.

— The Road Past Altamont. 154p. 1996. pap. text 6.95 (*0-7710-9856-1*) McCland & Stewart.

— The Road Past Altamont. Marshall, Joyce, tr. LC 93-14195. vi, 147p. 1993. pap. 7.95 (*0-8032-8948-0*, Bison Books) U of Nebr Pr.

— Street of Riches. Binsse, Harry, tr. LC 93-8661. viii, 247p. 1993. pap. 8.95 (*0-8032-8947-2*, Bison Books) U of Nebr Pr.

— The Tin Flute. 392p. 1996. pap. 7.95 (*0-7710-9860-X*) McCland & Stewart.

— Where Nests the Water Hen. 192p. 1996. pap. text 7.95 (*0-7710-9854-5*) McCland & Stewart.

— Windflower. 161p. 1996. pap. text 5.95 (*0-7710-9879-0*) McCland & Stewart.

Roy, Gaylord C. Le, see Le Roy, Gaylord C.

***Roy, Geoffrey.** North Canada - Yukon, Northwest Territories, Nunavut: The Bradt Travel Guide. (Illus.). 2000. pap. 18.95 (*1-84162-003-3*) Globe Pequot.

Roy, Gerald E. Blending the Old & the New: Quilts by Paul D. Pilgrim. LC 97-11395. (Illus.). 80p. 1997. pap. 16.95 (*1-57432-702-X*, 4918, Am Quilters Soc) Collector Bks.

Roy, Girish C. Value Conflict in Study of Social Change in India. 272p. 1983. 30.95 (*0-318-36870-6*) Asia Bk Corp.

Roy, Glenn. Activated Carbon Applications in the Food & Pharmaceutical Industries. LC 94-61026. 200p. 1994. text 84.95 (*1-56676-198-0*) Technomic.

Roy, Glenn, ed. Modifying Bitterness: Mechanism, Ingredients, & Applications. LC 97-60221. 350p. 1997. text 169.95 (*1-56676-491-2*) Technomic.

Roy, Greg. Becoming Financially Free: Proven Principles for Achieving Financial Independence. 160p. 1996. pap. 12.95 (*0-9651638-0-6*, Nehemiah Pr) Nehemiah Sol.

Roy, Greg. Hungry for Success. 178p. 1997. pap. 14.95 (*0-9651638-7-3*) Nehemiah Sol.

— The Magic of Duplication: Leverage Your Time & Multiply Your Profits. 160p. 1997. 18.95 (*0-9651638-6-5*) Nehemiah Sol.

Roy, Gregor. Monarch Notes on Cervantes' Don Quixote. (Orig.). (C). 3.95 (*0-671-00553-7*, Arco) Macmillan Gen Ref.

— Monarch Notes on Graham Greene's Major Novels. (Orig.). (C). 4.25 (*0-671-00838-2*, Arco) Macmillan Gen Ref.

— Monarch Notes on Kafka's The Trial, The Castle & Other Works. (Orig.). (C). 3.95 (*0-671-00847-1*, Arco) Macmillan Gen Ref.

— Monarch Notes on Pope's Rape of the Lock & Other Poems. (Orig.). (C). 4.25 (*0-671-00788-2*, Arco) Macmillan Gen Ref.

Roy, Gregor, tr. see Derrey, Francois.

Roy, Helen. Rumpelstiltskin. LC 95-8420. 24p. (J). (gr. 1-4). 1995. 13.95 (*1-57255-000-7*) Mondo Pubng.

Roy, Ian, ed. Richard Symond's Diary of the Marches of the Royal Army. LC 97-27995. (Camden Classic Reprints Ser.: No. 3). 340p. (C). 1998. reprint ed. text 64.95 (*0-521-62308-1*); reprint ed. pap. text 24.95 (*0-521-62656-0*) Cambridge U Pr.

***Roy, Ian & Doiron, Julie.** The Longest Winter. (Illus.). 64p. 1999. pap. 14.00 (*0-921411-95-2*) Genl Dist Srvs.

Roy, Indrani B. Kalighat: Its Impact on Socio-Cultural Life of Hindus. 1993. 20.00 (*81-212-0401-1*, Pub. by Gian Publng Hse) S Asia.

Roy, Indrapramit. The Very Hungry Lion. deluxe limited ed. 24p. (YA). (ps up). 1996. 29.95 (*1-55037-481-8*, Pub. by Annick) Firefly Bks Ltd.

Roy, J. Dictionnaire Professional du BTP. (FRE.). 1998. 110.00 (*0-320-00308-6*) Fr & Eur.

Roy, J. & Paterson, H. A Faith for the Year Two Thousand. 88p. (C). 1990. pap. text 45.00 (*0-7152-0639-7*) St Mut.

Roy, J., et al. Time Scales of Biological Responses to Water Contraints: The Case of Mediterranean Biota. 242p. 1995. 85.00 (*90-5103-107-6*, Pub. by SPB Acad Pub) Balogh.

Roy, J. C., et al. Progress in Electrodermal Research. LC 93-11397. (NATO ASI Ser.: Vol. 249). (Illus.). 360p. (C). 1993. text 110.00 (*0-306-44536-0*, Kluwer Plenum) Kluwer Academic.

Roy, J. C., jt. ed. see Pethica, James.

Roy, J. H. The Calf. 4th ed. LC 79-42840. (Studies in the Agricultural & Food Sciences). 1980. 95.00 (*0-408-70941-3*) Buttrwrth-Heinemann.

Roy, J. H. & Weston, B., eds. Politique Urbaine a Montreal. (FRE.). 374p. 1990. pap. 15.00 (*2-89135-038-3*) Guernica Editions.

Roy, Jacqueline. Daughter Like Me. (Illus.). 192p. (J). pap. 9.95 (*0-14-037927-4*, Pub. by Pnguin Bks Ltd) Trafalgar.

Roy, Jacques. Didactologie et Phonetique Appropriative. (American University Studies: Linguistics: Ser. XIII, Vol. 8). (FRE.). XVIII, 202p. (C). 1989. text 33.00 (*0-8204-0754-2*) P Lang Pubng.

***Roy, Jacques.** Informix Dynamic Server 2000: Server-Side Programming in C. LC 99-44857. (Illus.). 432p. 1999. pap. text 54.00 (*0-13-013709-X*) P-H.

Roy, Jacques & Garnier, Eric, eds. A Whole Plant Perspective on Carbon-Nitrogen Interactions. (Illus.). 1994. 94.00 (*90-5103-086-X*, Pub. by SPB Acad Pub) Balogh.

Roy, James. Almost Wednesday. (YA). 1996. pap. 12.95 (*0-7022-2826-5*, Pub. by Univ Queensland Pr) Intl Spec Bk.

***Roy, James.** Captain Mack. 1999. pap. 13.95 (*0-7022-3107-X*, Pub. by Univ Queensland Pr) Intl Spec Bk.

Roy, James. Full Moon Racing. LC 98-219250. (YA). 1998. pap. 12.95 (*0-7022-2974-1*, Pub. by Univ Queensland Pr) Intl Spec Bk.

Roy, James A. Cowper & His Poetry. LC 76-120982. (Poetry & Life Ser.). reprint ed. 27.50 (*0-404-52530-X*) AMS Pr.

Roy, James A. Le, see Le Roy, James A.

Roy, James C. Islands of Storm. LC 90-48646. 320p. 1991. 30.00 (*0-8023-1293-4*) Dufour.

— Islands of Storm. LC 90-48646. (Illus.). 320p. 1994. pap. 17.95 (*0-8023-1301-9*) Dufour.

— The Road Wet, the Wind Close: Celtic Ireland. LC 85-31100. 220p. 1986. reprint ed. 30.00 (*0-8023-1281-0*) Dufour.

— The Road Wet, the Wind Close: Celtic Ireland. LC 85-31100. (Illus.). 220p. 1995. reprint ed. pap. 17.95 (*0-8023-1283-7*) Dufour.

— The Vanished Kingdom: Travels Through the History of Prussia. LC 99-14278. (Illus.). 272p. 1999. 28.00 (*0-8133-3667-8*, Pub. by Westview) HarpC.

***Roy, James C.** Vanished Kingdom: Travels Through the History of Prussia. (Illus.). 2000. pap. 18.00 (*0-8133-3793-3*) Westview.

Roy, Jayanta, ed. Macroeconomic Management & Fiscal Decentralization. (EDI Seminar Ser.). 264p. 1996. pap. 22.00 (*0-8213-3409-3*, 13409) World Bank.

Roy, Jean-Hugues & Weston, Brendan, eds. Montreal. LC 90-81637. 250p. 1996. 43.99 (*0-921689-71-3*, Pub. by Black Rose); pap. 14.99 (*0-921689-70-5*, Pub. by Black Rose) Consort Bk Sales.

Roy, Jean-Yves, jt. auth. see Haineault, Doris-Louise.

***Roy, Jennifer Rozines.** Romantic Breakup: It's Not the End of the World. LC 99-40900. (Teen Issues Ser.). (Illus.). 64p. (YA). (gr. 6 up). 2000. lib. bdg. 17.95 (*0-7660-1361-8*) Enslow Pubs.

Roy, Jessie H. & Turner, Geneva C. Pioneers of Long Ago. (Illus.). (J). 1990. 12.95 (*0-87498-008-9*) Assoc Pubs DC.

Roy, Jim. Real World Whitetail Behavior. Boddington, Craig, ed. (Whitetail Secrets Ser.: No. 9). (Illus.). 190p. 1996. lthr. 17.95 (*1-56416-159-5*) Derrydale Pr.

Roy, Joanna. Delicious Holiday Chocolate & Cookies: With Sweet Holiday Music CD. LC 99-182123. (BookNotes Ser.). 56p. 1998. 13.99 incl. cd-rom (*0-88088-408-8*) Peter Pauper.

Roy, Joaquin. Cuba y Espana: Perscepciones y Relaciones. (Biblioteca Cubana Contemporanea Ser.). (SPA.). 100p. (Orig.). 1988. pap. 9.95 (*84-359-0542-X*, Pub. by Editorial Playor) Ediciones.

Roy, Joaquin, ed. The Reconstruction of Central America: The Role of the European Community. 424p. (C). 1992. pap. 24.95 (*0-935501-46-0*) U Miami N-S Ctr.

***Roy, Jody M.** Rhetorical Campaigns of the 19th Century Anti-Catholics & Catholics in America. LC 99-48972. (Studies in American Religion: Vol. 71). 228p. 1999. text 89.95 (*0-7734-7908-2*) E Mellen.

Roy, John R., jt. ed. see Hayashi, Yoshitsugu.

Roy, Joyashree. Demand for Energy in Indian Industries: A Quantitative Approach. (C). 1992. 21.00 (*81-7035-106-5*, Pub. by Daya Pub Hse) S Asia.

Roy, Jules. The Battle of Dienbienphu. 384p. 1984. pap. 10.95 (*0-88184-034-3*) Carroll & Graf.

Roy, K. & Tisdell, C. Tourism in India & India's Economic Development. LC 98-39202. 222p. 1998. 69.00 (*1-56072-612-1*) Nova Sci Pubs.

Roy, K. C., jt. auth. see Clark, Cal.

Roy, K. C., jt. auth. see Tisdell, C. A.

Roy, K. K., et al, eds. Deep Electromagnetic Exploration. LC 98-49121. (Lecture Notes in Earth Science Ser.: Vol. 83). (Illus.). x, 652p. 1999. pap. 130.00 (*3-540-63503-3*) Spr-Verlag.

Roy, Kanchan, ed. Education & Health Problems in Tribal Development. (C). 1989. 15.00 (*81-7022-236-2*, Pub. by Concept) S Asia.

Roy, Kartik, jt. auth. see Vecchio, Nerina C.

Roy, Kartik C., et al, eds. Economic Development & Women in the World Community. 256p. 1999. pap. 22.95 (*0-275-96631-3*, Praeger Pubs) Greenwood.

Roy, Kartik C. & Clark, Cal M., eds. Technological Change & Rural Development in Poor Countries: Neglected Issues. 188p. 1995. 21.00 (*0-19-563583-3*) OUP.

Roy, Kartik C., et al. Economic Development & Women in the World Community. LC 95-23225. 256p. 1996. 65.00 (*0-275-95134-0*, Praeger Pubs) Greenwood.

Roy, Kaushik & Prasad, Sharat. Low Power CMOS VLSI Circuit Design. LC 98-19426. 359p. 2000. 79.95 (*0-471-11488-X*) Wiley.

Roy, Ken, ed. see Shakespeare, William.

Roy, Ken, ed. & notes see Shakespeare, William.

Roy, Kevin. Baptism Reconciliation & Unity. x, 204p. 1997. reprint ed. pap. 30.00 (*0-85364-815-8*, Pub. by Paternoster Pub) OM Literature.

***Roy, Kirby, III.** Love Letters: A Novel. LC 98-55254. 383p. (Orig.). 1999. pap. 18.95 (*0-9644932-7-6*, NanKira Bks) Kujichagulia Pr.

Roy, Kristina. Only a Servant. 129p. 1991. pap. 4.50 (*0-7399-0143-5*, 2331) Rod & Staff.

Roy, Kumkum. The Emergence of Monarchy in North India, Eighth to Fifth Centuries B.C. (As Reflected in the Brahmanical Tradition) 356p. 1995. 32.00 (*0-19-563416-0*) OUP.

Roy, Larnders. Bits of Experience. 109p. 1992. pap. 5.99 (*0-9634432-0-8*) Croy & Assocs.

Roy, Loriene & Sheldon, Brooke E. Education for Librarianship in the U. S. A. LC 97-33046. (Education for Library & Information Professionals). 224p. 1998. 99.50 (*0-7201-2232-5*) Continuum.

Roy, Lucinda. Blood Sisters. 2000. 13.00 (*0-06-093207-4*) HarpC.

***Roy, Lucinda.** The Hotel Alleluia: A Novel. LC 99-53121. 368p. 2000. 25.00 (*0-06-019395-6*) HarpC.

Roy, Lucinda. The Humming Birds. LC 95-38457. 150p. 1995. pap. 12.95 (*0-933377-38-X*); lib. bdg. 22.95 (*0-933377-39-8*, Pub. by Eighth Mount Pr) Consort Bk Sales.

— Lady Moses: A Novel. LC 97-33216. 400p. 1998. 24.00 (*0-06-018244-X*) HarpC.

— Lady Moses: A Novel. 400p. 1999. pap. 13.00 (*0-06-093084-5*) HarpC.

Roy, Lynette. Brown Girl in the Ring: Rosemary Brown, a Biography for Young People. 80p. 1995. per. write for info. (*0-920813-52-6*) Sister Vis Pr.

Roy, Lynette A., tr. see Budar, Valjeanne, ed.

Roy, M., jt. auth. see Allan, R. J.

Roy, M. M. Agroforestry Systems for Sustainable Land Use. 292p. 1995. text 72.00 (*1-886106-19-3*) Science Pubs.

Roy, M. N. Fragments of a Prisoner's Diary: India's Message. reprint ed. 18.00 (*0-8364-0912-4*, Pub. by Ajanta) S Asia.

— M. N. Roy's Memoirs. 1985. 17.50 (*0-8364-1296-6*, Pub. by Ajanta) S Asia.

— Materialism. 1982. reprint ed. 18.50 (*0-8364-0914-0*, Pub. by Ajanta) S Asia.

— New Orientation: Lectures Delivered at the Political Study Camp Held at Dehradun from May 8th-18th, 1946. 1999. 7.00 (*0-8364-5684-X*) S Asia.

— Selected Works of M. N. Roy, 1932-1936, Vol. IV. Ray, Sibnarayan, ed. (Illus.). 676p. 1997. 35.00 (*0-19-563768-2*) OUP.

— Selected Works of M. N. Roy, 1927-1932, Vol. III. Ray, Sibnarayan, ed. (Illus.). 664p. 1991. 35.00 (*0-19-562640-0*) OUP.

— The Way to Durable Peace. (C). 1986. 6.50 (*0-8364-2198-1*, Pub. by Minerva) S Asia.

Roy, M. N., jt. auth. see Spratt, Phillip.

Roy, Manisha. Bengali Women. LC 74-33521. 200p. 1992. pap. text 10.95 (*0-226-73042-5*) U Ch Pr.

— Bengali Women. LC 92-14268. (Illus.). xviii, 232p. 1992. pap. text 22.00 (*0-226-73043-3*) U Ch Pr.

Roy, Manisha, jt. ed. see Ross, Lena B.

Roy, Margaret. I Fed My Children Summer: Adirondack/Olympic Poems. 65p. 1995. pap. 5.00 (*0-9645264-0-9*) Black Fly Pr.

— The Principles of Homeopathic Philosophy. LC 93-14982. 150p. 1993. pap. text. write for info. (*0-344-30482-5*) Church.

Roy, Marie L., jt. auth. see Wood, Robert.

***Roy, Marilyn.** EyeRobics: How to Improve Your Eyesight: Healthy Eyes & Better Vision ...The Natural Way. (Illus.). 128p. 1999. pap. 12.95 (*0-7225-3846-4*, Pub. by Thorsons MD) Natl Bk Netwk.

Roy, Martha R., jt. auth. see Withers, Richard.

Roy, Martine, jt. auth. see Dieudonne, Adeline.

Roy, Maurice. The Parish & Democracy in French Canada. LC 52-1123. (University of Toronto, Duncan & John Gray Memorial Lecture Ser.). 37p. reprint ed. pap. 30.00 (*0-608-16348-1*, 202654600050) Bks Demand.

***Roy, Meenu.** Elections 1998: A Continuity in Coalition. LC 98-917642. 307 p. 1999. write for info. (*81-86803-40-8*) S Asia.

Roy, Meenu. India Votes: Elections 1996, a Critical Analysis. (C). 1996. 27.00 (*81-7100-900-X*, Pub. by Deep & Deep Pubns) S Asia.

— Thousand Days of Indo-U. S. Diplomacy: The Kennedy-Nehru Era. (C). 1993. 20.00 (*81-7100-580-2*, Pub. by Deep & Deep Pubns) S Asia.

Roy, Michael, et al. Persian Limes in North America: An Economic Analysis of the Production & Marketing Channels. LC 96-84267. (Illus.). (Orig.). 1996. pap. 25.00 (*0-944961-02-9*) FL Sci Source.

Roy, Mike, jt. auth. see Omarr, Sydney.

Roy, N., tr. see Hager, W. H.

An Asterisk (*) at the beginning of an entry indicates that the title is appearing for the first time.

Roy, Namba. No Black Sparrows: A Vivid Portrait of Jamaica in the 1930s. (Caribbean Writers Ser.). 224p. (Orig.). (C). 1989. pap. 7.95 (*0-435-98812-3*, 98812) Heinemann.

Roy, Namiba. Black Albino. (Caribbean Writers Ser.). (C). 1995. pap. 16.80 (*0-582-78563-4*, TG7158) Longman.

Roy, Nancy R. Duncan: Descendants of William Duncan the Elder. 276p. 1992. reprint ed. pap. 42.50 (*0-8328-2467-4*); reprint ed. lib. bdg. 52.50 (*0-8328-2466-6*) Higginson Bk Co.

***Roy, Nina.** Tea & Spices. 192p. 2000. pap. 10.95 (*0-7867-0718-6*) Carroll & Graf.

Roy, Noel, jt. ed. see Schrank, William E.

Roy, Olivier. Afghanistan Vol. 1: From Holy War to Civil War. LC 94-18404. (Leon B. Poullada Memorial Lecture Ser.). (Illus.). 142p. 1995. 24.95 (*0-87850-076-6*) Darwin Pr.

— The Failure of Political Islam. Volk, Carol, tr. LC 94-18782. 208p. 1994. text 22.95 (*0-674-29140-9*, ROYFAI) HUP.

— The Failure of Political Islam. Volk, Carol, tr. 256p. 1996. pap. 17.00 (*0-674-29141-7*) HUP.

— Islam & Resistance in Afghanistan. 2nd ed. (Cambridge Middle East Library: No. 8). 282p. (C). 1990. pap. text 21.95 (*0-521-39700-6*) Cambridge U Pr.

***Roy, Olivier.** The New Central Asia: The Creation of Nations. LC 00-37219. 2000. pap. write for info. (*0-8147-7554-3*) NYU Pr.

Roy, P. Mussolini & the Cult of Italian Youth. 1972. 250.00 (*0-8490-0685-6*) Gordon Pr.

Roy, P. & Gorman, B. M., eds. Bluetongue Viruses. (Current Topics in Microbiology & Immunology Ser.: Vol. 162). (Illus.). 192p. 1990. 114.00 (*0-387-51922-X*) Spr-Verlag.

Roy, P., jt. auth. see Roy, D. P.

Roy, P. C. The Coin Age of Northern India. 1980. 27.50 (*0-8364-0641-9*, Pub. by Abhinav) S Asia.

— Indo-U. S. Economic Relations. 206p. 1986. 26.00 (*0-8364-1895-6*, Pub. by Deep & Deep Pubns) S Asia.

Roy, P. N. Dictionary of Economics. (C). 1989. 45.00 (*0-89771-426-1*, Pub. by Current Dist) St Mut.

Roy, Parama. Indian Traffic: Identities in Question in Colonial & Postcolonial India. LC 96-42104. 1997. 45.00 (*0-520-20486-7*, Pub. by U CA Pr) Cal Prin Full Svc.

— Indian Traffic: Identities in Question in Colonial & Postcolonial India. LC 96-42104. 237p. 1998. 16.95 (*0-520-20487-5*, Pub. by U CA Pr) Cal Prin Full Svc.

Roy, Pat, jt. auth. see Royall, Sandy.

Roy, Patricia. Lucky Stars. 384p. 1998. mass mkt. 5.99 (*0-446-60504-2*, Pub. by Warner Bks) Little.

— The Wedding Knot. 352p. 1999. mass mkt. 6.50 (*0-446-60503-4*, Pub. by Warner Bks) Little.

Roy, Patricia E., et al. Mutual Hostages: Canadian & Japanese During the Second World War. 320p. 1990. 24.95 (*0-8020-5774-8*) U of Toronto Pr.

— Mutual Hostages: Canadian & Japanese During the Second World War. 298p. 1992. pap. text 18.95 (*0-8020-7366-2*) U of Toronto Pr.

Roy, Paul-Emile. Lectures Quebecoises et Independance. 1998. write for info. (*2-89415-238-8*) Edits Meridien.

Roy, Paulette M., jt. auth. see Rezendes, Paul.

Roy, Peter A. & Cinquanti, Michael. Workplace Safety Pocket Guide. rev. ed. (Illus.). 64p. 1994. pap. text. write for info. (*0-931690-37-4*) Genium Pub.

Roy, Peter Van, see Van Roy, Peter.

Roy, Pierre G. Isle of Orleans. (Illus.). 510p. 1997. reprint ed. pap. 34.95 (*1-886560-93-5*, 09407) Quintin Pub RI.

Roy, Pierre-Georges. Fremont: La Famille Fremont. (FRE.). 71p. 1997. reprint ed. pap. 14.00 (*0-8328-8658-0*); reprint ed. lib. bdg. 24.00 (*0-8328-8657-2*) Higginson Bk Co.

Roy, Pierre Georges, ed. An Index of Marriage Contracts & Inventories after Death Deposited in the Archives of Quebec. 1997. 39.95 (*1-886560-60-9*) Quintin Pub RI.

Roy, Prodipto, et al. Rural Employment Programmes: Longitudinal Analysis. 1990. text 25.00 (*0-7069-5297-9*, Pub. by Vikas) S Asia.

Roy, Prodipto, jt. auth. see Bijlani, H. U.

Roy Publishing Systems, Inc. Staff. The Dining & Doing Guide. rev. ed. (Illus.). 552p. 1995. pap. 11.95 (*1-887353-00-3*) Roy Pubng Systs.

Roy, R. Chronic Pain & the Family: A Problem-Centered Perspective. (Illus.). 256p. 1989. 32.95 (*0-89885-443-1*, Kluwer Acad Hman Sci) Kluwer Academic.

— Foreign Exchange Regulation Act, 1973. 3rd ed. (C). 1989. 350.00 (*0-7855-3711-2*) St Mut.

***Roy, R.** Industrial Knowledge Management: A Micro-Level Approach. LC 00-44029. 2000. write for info. (*1-85233-339-1*) Spr-Verlag.

Roy, R., et al, eds. Advances in Soft Computing: Engineering Design & Manufacturing. LC 98-41923. (Lecture Notes in Control & Information Sciences). xiii, 638p. 1998. pap. 179.00 (*1-85233-062-7*) Spr-Verlag.

— Soft Computing in Engineering Design & Manufacturing. LC 97-31959. xix, 455p. 1997. pap. 89.95 (*3-540-76214-0*) Spr-Verlag.

Roy, R., jt. auth. see Thomas, M. R.

Roy, R. N., jt. auth. see Dudal, R.

Roy, R. R., jt. auth. see Reed, Robert D.

Roy, Rahul, jt. auth. see Meester, Ronald.

***Roy, Raja Ram.** Vedic Physics: Scientific Origin of Hinduism. 268p. 1999. 14.95 (*0-9684120-0-9*) Gol Egg.

***Roy, Raja Rammohun.** The Essential Writings of Raja Rammohan Ray. Robertson, Bruce Carlisle, ed. LC 99-932755. 344p. 1999. write for info. (*0-19-564731-9*) OUP.

Roy, Rajat. Simulation of Manufacturing Systems. (C). 2000. text. write for info. (*0-201-39847-8*) Addison-Wesley.

Roy, Rakesh, jt. auth. see Roy, Abhijit.

Roy, Ramashray. Beyond EGO's Domain: Being & Order in the Veda. LC 98-915919. 345 p. 1999. write for info. (*81-7541-013-2*, Pub. by Shipra Pubns) Nataraj Bks.

***Roy, Ramashray.** Dalits, Development & Democracy. LC 99-932531. vi, 184 p. 1999. write for info. (*81-7541-028-0*, Pub. by Shipra Pubns) S Asia.

Roy, Ramashray. Politics of International Economic Relations. 234p. 1982. 24.95 (*0-318-37261-4*) Asia Bk Corp.

— Self & Society: A Study of Gandhian Thought. 205p. 1985. text 25.00 (*0-8039-9484-2*) Sage.

— The Uncertain Verdict: A Study of the 1969 Elections in Four Indian States. rev. ed. LC 75-328407. (Illus.). 313p. reprint ed. pap. 97.10 (*0-608-18504-3*, 203151300075) Bks Demand.

— Understanding Gandhi. (C). 1996. 27.00 (*81-202-0423-9*, Pub. by Ajanta) S Asia.

— World of Development: A Theoretical Dead End. 1993. 21.00 (*81-202-0372-0*, Pub. by Ajanta) S Asia.

***Roy, Ramashray & Wallace, Paul.** Indian Politics & the 1998 Election: Regionalism, Hindutva & State Politics LC 99-37985. 1999. write for info. (*0-7619-9388-6*) Sage.

Roy, Ranjan. Childhood Abuse & Chronic Pain: A Curious Relationship. LC 98-176843. 176p. 1998. text 45.00 (*0-8020-0739-2*); pap. text 18.95 (*0-8020-7790-0*) U of Toronto Pr.

— The Social Context of the Chronic Pain Sufferer. 176p. 1992. text 50.00 (*0-8020-2860-8*); pap. text 19.95 (*0-8020-7360-3*) U of Toronto Pr.

Roy, Ranjan, ed. Chronic Pain in Old Age: An Integrated Biopsychosocial Perspective. 272p. 1995. pap. 19.95 (*0-8020-7359-X*); text 50.00 (*0-8020-2859-4*) U of Toronto Pr.

Roy, Ranjit. A Primer on the Taguchi Method. LC 89-14736. (Illus.). 247p. 1990. 58.00 (*0-87263-468-X*) SME.

***Roy, Ranjit K.** Design of Experiments Using the Taguchi Approach: 16 Steps to Product & Process Improvement. LC 00-36841. 2001. write for info. (*0-471-36101-1*) Wiley.

Roy, Rathin, jt. ed. see Mackintosh, Maureen.

Roy, Regis, jt. auth. see Massicotte, Edouard Z.

Roy, Rob. The Complete Book of Cordwood Masonry Housebuilding: The Earthwood Method. LC 91-41313. (Illus.). 264p. 1992. pap. 17.95 (*0-8069-8590-9*) Sterling.

— Complete Book of Underground Houses: How to Build a Low Cost Home. LC 94-16840. (Illus.). 148p. 1994. pap. 14.95 (*0-8069-0728-2*) Sterling.

— The Sauna. LC 96-2761. (Illus.). 120p. 1996. pap. 20.00 (*0-930031-87-3*) Chelsea Green Pub.

***Roy, Rob.** Stone Circles: A Modern Builder's Guide to the Megalithic Revival. LC 99-33259. (Illus.). 320p. 1999. pap. 35.00 (*1-890132-03-9*) Chelsea Green Pub.

Roy, Robert A., jt. auth. see Accrocco, Joseph O.

Roy, Robert A., ed. see Conforti, John V.

Roy, Robert H. The Administrative Process. LC 58-7212. (Illus.). 248p. reprint ed. pap. 76.90 (*0-608-06126-3*, 206645900008) Bks Demand.

— The Cultures of Management. LC 76-47385. (Illus.). 448p. reprint ed. pap. 138.90 (*0-608-06127-1*, 206646000008) Bks Demand.

— Operations Technology: Systems & Evolution. LC 86-7139. (Illus.). 271p. reprint ed. pap. 84.10 (*0-608-06137-9*, 206647000008) Bks Demand.

Roy, Robert H. & MacNeill, James H. Horizons for a Profession: The Common Body of Knowledge for Certified Public Accountants. LC 67-4826. (Illus.). 368p. reprint ed. pap. 114.10 (*0-608-17974-4*, 202657400050) Bks Demand.

Roy, Robert L. Mortgage-Free! Radical Strategies for Home Ownership. LC 98-10080. (Real Goods Solar Living Book Ser.). (Illus.). 280p. 1998. pap. 24.95 (*0-930031-98-9*) Chelsea Green Pub.

Roy, Robin & Wield, David, eds. Product Design & Technological Innovation. 320p. 1986. 79.95 (*0-335-15110-8*); pap. 34.95 (*0-335-15109-4*) OpUniv Pr.

Roy, Rocco B. Remember. (Illus.). 44p. 1999. pap. 5.99 (*0-9672359-0-1*) Eternal Way.

Roy, Roland R. & Ishihara, Akihiko, eds. Functional Implications of the Design of Skeletal Muscles. (Acta Anatomica Ser.: Vol. 159, No. 2-3, 1997). (Illus.). 98p. 1998. pap. 83.50 (*3-8055-6682-4*) S Karger.

Roy, Ron. The Absent Author. LC 97-2030. (A to Z Mysteries Ser.: No. 1). (Illus.). 80p. (J). (gr. k). 1997. pap. 3.99 (*0-679-88168-9*) Random.

— The Absent Author. (A to Z Mysteries Ser.: No. 1). (Illus.). (J). (gr. k). 1997. 9.09 (*0-606-12612-0*, Pub. by Turtleback) Demco.

***Roy, Ron.** The Bald Bandit. (A to Z Mysteries Ser.: No. 2). (J). (gr. k-3). 1999. (*0-613-04691-9*) Econo-Clad Bks.

Roy, Ron. The Bald Bandit. LC 96-40473. (A to Z Mysteries Ser.: No. 2). (Illus.). 80p. (J). (gr. 2-5). 1997. pap. 3.99 (*0-679-88449-1*) Random.

— The Bald Bandit. LC 96-40473. (A to Z Mysteries Ser.: No. 2). (Illus.). 80p. (J). (gr. k-5). 1997. lib. bdg. 11.99 (*0-679-98449-6*) Random.

— The Bald Bandit. (A to Z Mysteries Ser.: No. 2). (Illus.). (J). (gr. k-3). 1997. 9.19 (*0-606-12613-9*, Pub. by Turtleback) Demco.

— The Canary Caper. LC 97-15564. (A to Z Mysteries Ser.: No. 3). (Illus.). 80p. (J). (gr. k-3). 1998. lib. bdg. 11.99 (*0-679-98593-X*) Random.

— The Canary Caper. LC 97-15564. (A to Z Mysteries Ser.: No. 3). (Illus.). 80p. (J). (gr. 2-5). 1998. pap. 3.99 (*0-679-88593-5*) Random.

***Roy, Ron.** The Canary Caper, 3. (A to Z Mysteries Ser.: No. 3). (J). (gr. k-3). 1998. 9.09 (*0-606-12864-6*, Pub. by Turtleback) Demco.

Roy, Ron. The Deadly Dungeon. LC 97-27566. (A to Z Mysteries Ser.: No. 4). (Illus.). 96p. (J). (gr. k-5). 1998. lib. bdg. 11.99 (*0-679-98755-X*) Random.

— The Deadly Dungeon. LC 97-27566. (A to Z Mysteries Ser.: No. 4). (Illus.). 96p. (J). (gr. 2-5). 1998. pap. 3.99 (*0-679-88755-5*) Random.

***Roy, Ron.** The Deadly Dungeon, 4. (A to Z Mysteries Ser.: No. 4). (J). (gr. k-3). 1998. 9.09 (*0-606-12865-4*, Pub. by Turtleback) Demco.

— The Empty Envelope. (A to Z Mysteries Ser.: No. 5). (Illus.). (J). (gr. k-3). 1999. 11.10 (*0-613-07707-5*) Econo-Clad Bks.

Roy, Ron. The Empty Envelope. LC 97-31711. (A to Z Mysteries Ser.: No. 5). (Illus.). 79p. (J). (gr. k-3). 1998. pap. 3.99 (*0-679-89054-8*) Random.

— The Empty Envelope. LC 97-31711. (A to Z Mysteries Ser.: No. 5). (Illus.). (J). (gr. k-5). 1998. lib. bdg. 11.99 (*0-679-99054-2*) Random.

***Roy, Ron.** The Empty Envelope. (A to Z Mysteries Ser.: No. 5). (Illus.). (J). (gr. k-3). 1998. 9.09 (*0-606-13949-4*, Pub. by Turtleback) Demco.

— The Falcon's Feathers. (A to Z Mysteries Ser.: No. 6). (Illus.). (J). (gr. k-3). 1999. 11.10 (*0-613-11527-9*) Econo-Clad Bks.

Roy, Ron. The Falcon's Feathers. LC 98-10784. (A to Z Mysteries Ser.: No. 6). (Illus.). 96p. (J). (gr. k-5). 1998. lib. bdg. 11.99 (*0-679-99055-0*, Pub. by Random Bks Yng Read) Random.

— The Falcon's Feathers. LC 98-10784. (A to Z Mysteries Ser.: No. 6). (Illus.). 96p. (J). (gr. 2-5). 1998. pap. 3.99 (*0-679-89055-6*, Pub. by Random Bks Yng Read) Random.

— The Goose's Gold. LC 98-46152. (A to Z Mysteries Ser.: No. 7). (Illus.). 96p. (J). (gr. k-5). 1999. lib. bdg. 11.99 (*0-679-99078-X*, Pub. by Random Bks Yng Read) Random.

— The Goose's Gold. LC 98-46152. (A to Z Mysteries Ser.: No. 7). (Illus.). 96p. (J). (gr. 2-5). 1999. pap. 3.99 (*0-679-89078-5*, Pub. by Random Bks Yng Read) Random.

— The Haunted Hotel. LC 98-46856. (A to Z Mysteries Ser.: No. 8). (Illus.). 96p. (J). (gr. k-3). 1999. pap. 3.99 (*0-679-89079-3*) Random.

— The Haunted Hotel. LC 98-46856. (A to Z Mysteries Ser.: No. 8). (Illus.). 89p. (J). (gr. 2-4). 1999. lib. bdg. 11.99 (*0-679-99079-8*) Random.

— The Invisible Island. LC 99-18346. (A to Z Mysteries Ser.: No. 9). (Illus.). 96p. (J). (gr. k-3). 1999. lib. bdg. 11.99 (*0-679-99457-2*, Pub. by Random Bks Yng Read) Random.

***Roy, Ron.** The Invisible Island. LC 99-18346. (A to Z Mysteries Ser.: No. 9). (Illus.). 96p. (J). (gr. 2-5). 1999. pap. 3.99 (*0-679-89457-8*, Pub. by Random Bks Yng Read) Random.

— The Jaguar's Jewel. LC 99-40056. (A to Z Mysteries Ser.: No. 10). (Illus.). 96p. (J). (gr. k-3). 2000. pap. 3.99 (*0-679-89458-6*, Pub. by Random Bks Yng Read) Random.

— The Jaguar's Jewel. LC 99-40056. (A to Z Mysteries Ser.: No. 10). (Illus.). 96p. (J). (gr. 2-5). 2000. lib. bdg. 11.99 (*0-679-99458-0*, Pub. by Random Bks Yng Read) Random.

— Jaguar's Jewel. (A to Z Mysteries Ser.: Vol. 10). (Illus.). (J). 2000. 9.34 (*0-606-18480-5*) Turtleback.

— The Kidnapped King. LC 99-89549. (A to Z Mysteries Ser.: No. 11). (Illus.). 96p. (J). (gr. k-3). 2000. pap. 3.99 (*0-679-89459-4*, Pub. by Random Bks Yng Read) Random.

— The Kidnapped King. LC 99-89549. (A to Z Mysteries Ser.: Vol. 11). (Illus.). 96p. (J). (gr. k-3). 2000. lib. bdg. 11.99 (*0-679-99459-9*, Pub. by Random Bks Yng Read) Random.

— Kidnapped King, 11. (A to Z Mysteries Ser.). (Illus.). (J). 2000. 9.44 (*0-606-18481-3*) Turtleback.

— Lucky Lottery. (A to Z Mysteries Ser.: Vol. 12). (Illus.). (J). 2000. pap. 3.99 (*0-679-89460-8*) Random.

— Lucky Lottery. (A to Z Mysteries Ser.: Vol. 12). (Illus.). (J). 2000. 11.99 (*0-679-99460-2*) Random Bks Yng Read.

— Missing Mummy. (J). 2001. mass mkt. 11.99 (*0-375-90268-6*, Pub. by Random Bks Yng Read); mass mkt. 3.99 (*0-375-80268-1*, Pub. by Random Bks Yng Read) Random.

Roy, Ron. Someone is Following Pip Ramsey. (Stepping Stone Bks.). (J). 1996. 9.19 (*0-606-11858-6*, Pub. by Turtleback) Demco.

***Roy, Ron & Woodruff, Liza.** Who Cloned the President? LC 00-39325. (Road to Reading Ser.). (J). 2001. pap. write for info. (*0-307-46510-1*, Goldn Books) Gldn Bks Pub Co.

Roy, Ronald. Frankie Is Staying Back, 001. (Illus.). 64p. (J). (gr. 2-5). 1981. 8.95 (*0-395-31025-3*, Clarion Bks) HM.

Roy, Ronald. Whose Hat Is That? (Illus.). 40p. (J). (ps-3). 1990. pap. 6.95 (*0-395-54778-4*, Clarion Bks) HM.

Roy, Ronald, jt. auth. see Laubenstein, Karen.

Roy, Russell A. Physical Science: An Integrated Approach Laboratory Manual. 2nd ed. 117p. (C). 1990. pap. text 18.95 (*0-89892-071-X*) Contemp Pub Co of Raleigh.

Roy, Russell A., jt. auth. see Ferrari, Angelo.

Roy, Rustum, et al, eds. New Diamond Science & Technology: Proceedings of the 2nd International Conference, Materials Research Society Conference Proceedings, Washington, D. C., U. S. A., September 17-19, 1990, Vol. NDST-2. 1111p. 1991. text 17.50 (*1-55899-111-5*, NDST-2) Materials Res.

Roy, S., jt. auth. see Lehnert, B.

Roy, S. B. Early Aryans of India: 3100-1400 B. C. (C). 1989. 35.00 (*81-7013-052-2*, Pub. by Navarang) S Asia.

Roy, S. K. Evidence in Criminal Court Practice. (C). 1990. 140.00 (*0-89771-151-3*) St Mut.

Roy, S. M., et al, eds. Developments in Theoretical Physics. 1989. 32.00 (*81-204-0470-X*, Pub. by Oxford IBH) S Asia.

***Roy, Sally.** Essential Edinburgh. (AAA Essential Guides Ser.). (Illus.). 128p. 2000. pap. 8.95 (*0-658-00372-0*, 003720, Passprt Bks) NTC Contemp Pub Co.

Roy, Samaren. Calcutta, Society & Change, 1690-1990. (C). 1991. 31.50 (*81-7167-046-6*, Pub. by Rupa) S Asia.

— India's First Communist. (C). 1988. 12.75 (*81-85195-10-2*, Pub. by Minerva) S Asia.

— The Twice-Born Heretic: MN Roy & Comintern. 1986. 27.50 (*0-8364-1576-0*) S Asia.

R

Roy, Samuel. Elvis: Prophet of Power. 2nd ed. (Illus.). 1985. pap. 11.95 (*0-8283-1898-0*) Branden Bks.

— Elvis, Prophet of Power: The Truth about the Man, His Music & the Phenomenon of This Century. (Illus.). 195p. 1998. pap. text 12.00 (*0-7881-5764-7*) DIANE Pub.

Roy, Samuel & Aspell, Tom. The Essential Elvis: The Life & Legacy of the King As Revealed Through 112 of His Most Significant Songs. LC 98-29204. 256p. 1998. pap. 14.95 (*1-55853-693-0*) Rutledge Hill Pr.

Roy, Sander, jt. auth. see Berson, Dvera.

Roy, Sandra, jt. auth. see Roy, Emil.

Roy, Sara. The Gaza Strip: The Political Economy of De-Development. 290p. 1995. pap. 17.95 (*0-88728-261-X*) Inst Palestine.

Roy, Shaibal. Sybase Performance Tuning. 622p. (C). 1996. 72.00 (*0-13-442997-4*) P-H.

Roy, Shaibal, et al. Sybase Database Administrator's Reference Library. 1996. pap. text 119.95 (*0-13-624719-9*, Prentice Hall) P-H.

— Sybase EDM Performance Tuning. 2nd ed. 2001. 59.00 (*0-13-021497-3*) P-H.

Roy, Shibani & Rizvi, S. H. Tribal Customary Laws of North East India. (C). 1990. text 27.00 (*81-7018-586-6*, Pub. by BR Pub) S Asia.

Roy, Shivani, jt. auth. see Rizvi, S. H.

Roy, Shukla. Indian Political Thought: Impact of Russian Revolution. 1988. 21.00 (*81-85195-08-0*, Pub. by Minerva) S Asia.

Roy, Sisir. Statistical Geometry & Applications to Microphysics Cosmology. LC 97-50114. (Fundamental Theories of Physics Ser.). 260p. 1998. 112.00 (*0-7923-4907-5*) Kluwer Academic.

Roy, Skip, compiled by. Southcentral Alaskan Salmon Streams: An Atlas. (ENG.). 96p. 1987. per. 13.00 (*1-878100-96-3*) Todd Commns.

Roy, Steven A. How Fire Got Into the Rocks & Trees: A Story Based on Indian Legend. LC 95-62110. (American Heritage Ser.). (Illus.). 17p. (Orig.). (J). (gr. 3 up). 1996. pap. 3.95 (*1-877976-17-2*, 406-0020) Tipi Pr.

This traditional Native American legend tells the story of Nee-kil-stlas & how he brought fire to the Indians long ago. The book's realistic & lifelike illustrations bring warmth to this creative recounting of Nee-kil-stlas' struggles with the Bad Fairy Chief & how he outsmarts him by using magic powers. He becomes a hero to the Indian people because it was through Nee-kil-stlas that the Indians of long ago were able to make fire by rubbing rocks & wood together. A delightful story for young & old as well. Order from: Tipi Press, St. Joseph's Indian School, North Main St., Chamberlain, SD 57326, 605-734-3300, 800-229-5684. *Publisher Paid Annotation.*

–How the Baby Deer Got Spots: A Story Based on Indian Legend. LC 95-62109. (American Heritage Ser.). (Illus.). 14p. (Orig.). (J). (gr. 3 up). 1995. pap. 3.95 (*1-877976-16-4*, 406-0019) Tipi Pr.

This beautifully illustrated children's book tells the traditional Lakota (Sioux) Legend of HOW THE BABY DEER GOT SPOTS. The story describes the friendly spirit's encounters with the animals & how he bestowed upon them the natural gifts as a means of protection. The Friendly Spirit soon discovers his error when he becomes aware of the baby deer's vulnerability. The wise spirit corrects his mistake using wisdom & creativity. Order from: Tipi Press, St. Joseph's Indian School, North Main St., Chamberlain, SD 57326; 605-734-3300, 800-229-5684. *Publisher Paid Annotation.*

Roy, Subroto. The Philosophy of Economics: A Treatise on Reason, Value & Economic. 256p. 1989. 37.50 (*0-415-03592-9*, A3633) Routledge.

Roy, Subroto & James, William E., eds. Foundations of India's Political Economy: Towards an Agenda for the 1990s. (Illus.). 304p. (C). 1992. text 36.00 (*0-8039-9411-7*) Sage.

Roy, Subrotto, jt. ed. see James, William E.

Roy, Sumit. Agriculture & Technology in Developing Countries: India & Nigeria. (Illus.). 232p. (C). 1991. 27.50 (*0-8039-9662-4*) Sage.

Roy, Sumit, jt. auth. see Singer, H. W.

Roy, Sumita, jt. auth. see Sivaramkrishna, M.

Roy, Sumita, jt. ed. see Sivaramkrishna, M.

Roy, Susan & Steele, Jeremy, eds. Young Imagination: Writing & Artwork by Children of New South Wales. (Illus.). 96p. (Orig.). (C). 1988. pap. 13.50 (0-909955-79-4, 00597) Heinemann.

Roy, Tapti. The Politics of a Popular Uprising: Bundelkhand in 1857. (Illus.). 302p. 1995. text 28.00 (0-19-563612-0) OUP.

Roy, Tirthankar. Artisans & Industrialization: Indian Weaving in the Twentieth Century. (Illus.). 256p. 1994. 24.95 (0-19-563100-5) OUP.

— Traditional Industry in the Economy of Colonial India. LC 98-44110. (Cambridge Studies in Indian History & Society: No. 5). (Illus.). 288p. 1999. 64.95 (0-521-65012-7) Cambridge U Pr.

Roy, Tirthankar, ed. Cloth & Commerce: Textiles in Colonial India. LC 96-595. 338p. 1996. 49.95 (0-8039-9300-5) Sage.

Roy, Tom. A Scot Gallery Eccentric: Wry Tales of a Little-Known Realm. LC 92-30161. (Orig.). 1993. 14.95 (1-879094-22-3) Momentum Bks.

Roy, Travis & Swift, E. M. Eleven Seconds: A Story of Tragedy, Courage & Triumph. LC 97-25213. (Illus.). 224p. 1998. 20.00 (0-446-52188-4, Pub. by Warner Bks) Little.

Roy, Tui De, see De Roy, Tui.

Roy, Vijayesh, jt. ed. see Stratton, Kathleen.

Roy, Vijayesh D., ed. see Ballard, Scott L.

Roy, Virginia C. Charlottesville for Seniors: A Guide to Activities & Services in Jefferson's Country. (Illus.). 256p. (Orig.). 1997. pap. 14.95 (0-9641731-2-3) Featherstne Inc.

Roy, William. Rede Me & Be Nott Wrothe for I Say No Thynge but Trothe. LC 76-38221. (English Experience Ser.: No. 485). 144p. 1972. reprint ed. 25.00 (90-221-0485-0) Walter J Johnson.

Roy, William G. Socializing Capital. 360p. 1999. pap. text 18.95 (0-691-01034-X, Pub. by Princeton U Pr) Cal Prin Full Svc.

— Socializing Capital: The Rise of the Large Industrial Corporation in America. LC 96-8672. 338p. 1997. text 35.00 (0-691-04353-1, Pub. by Princeton U Pr) Cal Prin Full Svc.

Roy, William N. & Braun, David W. LaMoine Lumber & Trading Co. Narrow-Gauge Logging on the Shasta-Trinity Divide. LC 92-90822. (Timberbeast Special Publications: Nos. 28-29). 1992. pap. 12.50 (0-9634695-0-9) Timberbeast.

Royak-Schaler, Renee, jt. auth. see Keita, Gwendolyn P.

Royakkers, Lamber M. Extending Deontic Logic for the Formalisation of Legal Rules. LC 98-9205. (Law & Philosophy Library). 1998. write for info. (0-7923-4982-2) Kluwer Academic.

Royal & Ancient Golf Club of St. Andrews, Scotland & Glover, John. Golf: A Celebration of 100 Years of the Rules of Play. (Illus.). 192p. 1998. 38.95 (1-57243-284-5) Triumph Bks.

Royal & Ancient Golf Club of St. Andrews, Scotland, jt. auth. see United States Golf Association Staff.

***Royal & Ancient Golf Club Staff.** The British Open Golf Championship, 1998. (Illus.). 112p. 1998. text 29.95 (1-56554-410-2) Pelican.

— The British Open Golf Championship, 1999. (Illus.). 112p. 2000. 29.95 (1-56554-715-2) Pelican.

***Royal Academy of Dancing Staff.** Royal Academy of Dancing Step-by-Step Ballet Class: An Illustrated Guide to the Official Ballet Syllabus. (Illus.). 1999. pap. 19.95 (0-09-186531-X) Random.

Royal Academy of Dancing Staff. Step-By-Step Ballet Class. (Illus.). 144p. (J). 1994. pap. 14.95 (0-8092-3499-8, 349980, Contemporary Bks) NTC Contemp Pub Co.

Royal Academy of Letters, History, & Antiquities S. Medieval Wooden Sculpture in Sweden, 5 vols., Set. Anderson, A. & Thordeman, B., eds. (Illus.). 1168p. (Orig.). 1966. pap. text 195.00 (0-685-13807-0) Coronet Bks.

Royal Aeronautical Society Staff. A List of the Books, Periodicals & Pamphlets in the Library of the Royal Aeronautical Society: With Which Is Incorporated the Institution of Aeronautical Engineers. Gilbert, James B., ed. LC 79-7295. (Flight: Its First Seventy-Five Years Ser.). 1980. reprint ed. lib. bdg. 26.95 (0-405-12202-0) Ayer.

Royal Anthropological Institute of Great Britain &. A Catalogue of the Library of Sir Richard Burton, K. C. M. G., Held by the Royal Anthropological Institute. Kirkpatrick, B. J., ed. LC 80-473753. 182p. reprint ed. pap. 56.50 (0-7837-6667-X, 204627900011) Bks Demand.

Royal Australian Air Force Historical Section Staf. Units of the Royal Australian Air Force Vol. 1: A Concise History: Introduction, Bases, Supporting Organisations. LC 94-31303. (Illus.). 243p. (Orig.). 1995. pap. 24.95 (0-644-42792-2, 9431303, Pub. by AGPS Pr) Intl Spec Bk.

— Units of the Royal Australian Air Force Vol. 2: A Concise History: Fighter Units. LC 94-31315. 187p. (Orig.). 1995. pap. 24.95 (0-644-42794-9, 9431315, Pub. by AGPS Pr) Intl Spec Bk.

— Units of the Royal Australian Air Force Vol. 3: A Concise History: Bomber Units. LC 94-31327. (Illus.). 191p. (Orig.). 1995. pap. 24.95 (0-644-42795-7, 9431327, Pub. by AGPS Pr) Intl Spec Bk.

— Units of the Royal Australian Air Force Vol. 4: Maritime & Transport Units. LC 94-31339. (Illus.). 221p. (Orig.). 1995. pap. 24.95 (0-644-42796-5, 9431339, Pub. by AGPS Pr) Intl Spec Bk.

— Units of the Royal Australian Air Force Vol. 5: A Concise History: Radar Units. LC 94-31340. (Illus.). 190p. (Orig.). 1995. pap. 24.95 (0-644-42797-3, 9431340, Pub. by AGPS Pr) Intl Spec Bk.

— Units of the Royal Australian Air Force Vol. 6: A Concise History: Logistics Units. LC 94-31352. (Illus.). 176p. (Orig.). 1995. pap. 24.95 (0-644-42798-1, 9431352, Pub. by AGPS Pr) Intl Spec Bk.

— Units of the Royal Australian Air Force Vol. 7: A Concise History: Maintenance Units. LC 94-31364. (Illus.). 157p. (Orig.). 1995. pap. 24.95 (0-644-42799-X, 9431364, Pub. by AGPS Pr) Intl Spec Bk.

— Units of the Royal Australian Air Force Vol. 8: A Concise History: Training Units. LC 94-31376. (Illus.). 237p. (Orig.). 1995. pap. 24.95 (0-644-42800-7, 9431376, Pub. by AGPS Pr) Intl Spec Bk.

— Units of the Royal Australian Air Force Vol. 9: A Concise History: Ancillary Units. LC 94-3139. (Illus.). 255p. (Orig.). 1995. pap. 24.95 (0-644-42802-3, 943139X, Pub. by AGPS Pr) Intl Spec Bk.

— Units of the Royal Australian Air Force Vol. 10: A Concise History: Units of the Air Staff, Aircraft, Bibliography. LC 94-31388. (Illus.). 150p. (Orig.). 1995. pap. 24.95 (0-644-42801-5, 9431388, Pub. by AGPS Pr) Intl Spec Bk.

Royal Barry Wills Associates Staff. Houses for Good Living. (Illus.). 144p. 1993. 37.50 (0-942655-07-9) Archit CT.

Royal Botanic Garden, Calcutta Staff. The Aconites of India: A Monograph by Otto Stapf, with A Sketch of the Life of Francis Hamilton (Once Buchanan), Vol. X, Pt. 2. (Illus.). lxxv, 197p. 69.00 (0-88065-014-1) Scholarly Pubns.

Royal Botanic Garden, Calcutta Staff & King, George. The Species of Artocarpus Indigenous to the British India: And the Indo-Malayan Species of Quercus & Castnopsis, 2 pts., Vol. II. (Illus.). 107p. 1979. reprint ed. 80.00 (0-88065-010-9) Scholarly Pubns.

Royal Botanic Garden, Calcutta Staff & Prain, D. The Species of Dalbargia of South Eastern Asia. (Annals of Royal Botanic Garden, Calcutta Ser.: Vol. X, Pt. 1). (Illus.). 114p. 1979. reprint ed. 100.00 (0-88065-013-3) Scholarly Pubns.

Royal Botanic Garden, Calcutta Staff, et al. A Century of New & Rare Indian Plants, Vol. V, Pt. II. (Illus.). 1971. reprint ed. 50.00 (0-88065-011-7) Scholarly Pubns.

— A Second Century of New & Rare Indian Plants, Vol. IX, Pt. 1. (Illus.). 80p. 1972. reprint ed. 50.00 (0-88065-012-5) Scholarly Pubns.

Royal Botanic Gardens Kew Staff, jt. auth. see Davis, Aaron P.

Royal Botanic Gardens Kew Staff, jt. auth. see Guy's & St. Thomas Hospital Staff.

Royal Botanic Gardens Kew Staff, jt. auth. see Stiff, Ruth.

Royal Canadian Air Force Staff. Royal Canadian Air Force Exercise Plans for Physical Fitness. 80p. 1978. pap. 7.00 (0-671-24651-8) S&S Trade.

Royal Canadian Commission Staff. The Defection of Igor Gouzenko, Vol. 1. 99p. (C). 1984. pap. 16.80 (0-89412-066-2) Aegean Park Pr.

Royal Canadian Commission Staff. The Defection of Igor Gouzenko, Vol. 2. 447p. (C). 1984. pap. 16.80 (0-89412-067-0) Aegean Park Pr.

— The Defection of Igor Gouzenko, Vol. 3. 196p. (C). 1984. pap. 16.80 (0-89412-068-9) Aegean Park Pr.

Royal Canadian Mounted Police Staff. International Illustrated Vocabulary of Dactyloscopy (Fingerprinting) French & English with 6 Language Index. (DUT, ENG, FRE, GER & ITA.). 1991. 125.00 (0-8288-6909-X) Fr & Eur.

Royal, Cathy, jt. auth. see Hammond, Sue A.

Royal, Charlotte. Invitation to Sin. (Orig.). 1997. mass mkt. 9.95 (0-352-33217-4, Pub. by BLA4) London Brdge.

Royal, Claudia, tr. see Amselle, Jean-Loup.

Royal College of Midwives Staff. Successful Breastfeeding. 2nd ed. (Illus.). 88p. 1991. pap. text 13.95 (0-443-04460-0) Church.

Royal College of Physicians of London Staff & Greenwood, Major. Medical Statistics from Graunt to Farr: Proceedings of the Royal College of Physicians of London, February, 1943. Rosenkrantz, Barbara G., ed. LC 76-25665. (Public Health in America Ser.). (Illus.). 1977. reprint ed. lib. bdg. 17.95 (0-405-09820-0) Ayer.

Royal College of Physicians Staff. A Great & Growing Evil? The Medical Consequences of Alcohol Abuse. 144p. (C). 1987. text 45.00 (0-422-61140-9, Pub. by Tavistock) Routldge.

— Topics in Therapeutics. Breckenridge, A. M., ed. 1974. pap. text 45.00 (0-7855-7134-5) St Mut.

— Topics in Therapeutics, 1976. Shanks, R. G., ed. 1976. pap. text 65.00 (0-7855-7135-3) St Mut.

Royal College of Physicians Staff, jt. auth. see Advanced Medicine Symposia Staff.

Royal College of Psychiatrists, Education Committe. List of Books Suitable for a Psychiatric Library. rev. ed. LC Z 6664.. (Special Publication: No. 3). 68p. reprint ed. pap. 30.00 (0-7837-0997-8, 204130300020) Bks Demand.

Royal College of Psychiatrists Staff. The Misuse of Psychotropic Drugs. Murray, Robin et al, eds. LC RM0146.M67. (Special Publication: No. 1). 116p. reprint ed. pap. 36.00 (0-7837-0998-6, 204130400020) Bks Demand.

Royal College of Surgeons of England, Institute of. Leukotrienes & Other Lipoxygenase Products: Proceedings of the Annual Symposium of the Institute of Basic Medical Sciences, Royal College of Surgeons of England, 25-26 October 1982. Piper, Priscilla J., ed. LC 83-175919. (Prostaglandins Ser.: No. 3). (Illus.). 367p. reprint ed. pap. 113.80 (0-8357-7081-8, 203334600085) Bks Demand.

Royal Commission Aboriginal People Staff, ed. Bridging the Cultural Divide: A Report on Aboriginal People & Criminal Justice in Canada. LC 96-183194. 315p. 1996. pap. 32.95 (0-660-16283-0, Pub. by Canadian Govt Pub) Accents Pubns.

Royal Commission on Aboriginal Peoples Staff, ed. Public Policy & Aboriginal Peoples Series, 1965-1992 Vol. 1: Soliloquy & Dialogue: Overview of Major Trends in Public Policy Relating to Aboriginal Peoples. 2nd ed. 353p. 1996. pap. 39.95 (0-660-16644-5, Pub. by Canadian Govt Pub) Accents Pubns.

Royal Commission on Bilingualism & Biculturalism. Preliminary Report: Education of the Royal Commission on Bilingualism & Biculturalism, 3 vols. Cordasco, Francesco, ed. LC 77-17707. (Bilingual-Bicultural Education in the U. S. Ser.). 1978. reprint ed. lib. bdg. 70.95 (0-405-11109-6) Ayer.

***Royal Commission on Environmental Pollution.** Setting Environmental Standards. LC 98-221329. 1998. write for info. (0-10-140532-4) Statnry Office.

Royal Commission on Environmental Pollution. Transport & the Environment: The Royal Commission on Environmental Pollution Report. (Illus.). 344p. 1996. pap. 14.95 (0-19-826065-2) OUP.

***Royal Commission on Historical Manuscripts Staff.** Archives at the Millennium. 84p. 1999. pap. 25.00 (0-11-702664-6, Pub. by Statnry Office) Balogh.

— Historical Manuscripts Annual Review, 1998-1999. 72p. 1999. pap. 25.00 (0-11-440278-7, Pub. by Statnry Office) Balogh.

Royal Commission on Historical Manuscripts Staff. Papers of British Churchmen, 1780-1940. (Guides to Sources for British History Ser.: No. 6). 96p. 1987. 16.00 (0-11-440212-4, HM208, Pub. by Statnry Office) Balogh.

— Principal Family & Estate Collections Pt. 1: Families A-K. 1996. pap. 60.00 (0-11-440265-5) Statnry Office.

— Principal Family & Estate Collections Pt. 2: Families L-Z. 1999. pap. 75.00 (0-11-440276-0, Pub. by Statnry Office) Balogh.

— Private Papers of British Colonial Governors, 1782-1900. (Guides to Sources for British History Ser.: No. 5). 66p. 1986. 12.00 (0-11-440206-X, HM494, Pub. by Statnry Office) Balogh.

— Private Papers of British Diplomats, 1782-1900. (Guides to Sources for British History Ser.: No. 4). 80p. 1985. 12.00 (0-11-440188-8, HM495, Pub. by Statnry Office) Balogh.

Royal Commission on Historical Monuments. An Inventory of the Historical Monuments in the County of Northampton Vol. 6: Architectural Monuments in North Northamptonshire. (Illus.). ciii, 196p. 1985. 40.00 (0-11-700996-2, Pub. by Statnry Office) Balogh.

Royal Commission on Historical Monuments. Stonehenge & Its Environs. (RCHM Inventory Vols Ser.). (Illus.). 50p. 1979. pap. 15.00 (0-85224-379-0, Pub. by Edinburgh U Pr) Col U Pr.

Royal Commission on New Reproductive Technologies. Proceed with Care: Final Report of the Royal Commission on New Reproductive Technologies. 26p. (Orig.). 1993. pap. 16.85 (0-660-58996-6, Pub. by Canadian Govt Pub) Accents Pubns.

— Proceed with Care: Final Report of the Royal Commission on New Reproductive Technologies. (Illus.). 1275p. (Orig.). 1993. pap. 67.60 (0-660-15359-9, Pub. by Canadian Govt Pub) Accents Pubns.

Royal Commission on Police Powers & Procedures. Report of the Royal Commission on Police Powers & Procedure. LC 73-156283. (Police in Great Britain Ser.). 1971. reprint ed. 16.95 (0-405-03394-X) Ayer.

Royal Commission on the Ancient & Historial Monume. Tolbooths & Town-houses: Civic Architecture in Scotland to 1833. LC 97-179580. (Illus.). 241p. 1996. 88.00 (0-11-495799-1, Pub. by Statnry Office) Balogh.

Royal Commission on the Historical Monuments of En. Docklands in the Making: The Redevelopment of the Isle of Dogs 1981-1995. LC 96-152795. (Illus.). 160p. (C). 1995. pap. 25.00 (0-485-48500-1, Pub. by Athlone Pr) Humanities.

Royal Commission upon the Duties of the Metropolit. Minutes of Evidence of the Royal Commission upon the Duties of the Metropolitan Police, 3 vols. LC 70-156285. (Police in Great Britain Ser.). 1971. reprint ed. 217.95 (0-405-03396-6) Ayer.

Royal Commonwealth Society Staff & Simpson, D. H. First Supplement to the Subject Catalogue of the Royal Commonwealth Society. 1977. 320.00 (0-8161-0075-6, G K Hall & Co) Mac Lib Ref.

Royal Cortissoz & Leonard Clayton Gallery Staff. Childe Hassam's Etchings & Drypoints: A Catalogue Raisonne. rev. ed. (Illus.). 450p. 1989. 95.00 (1-55660-029-1) A Wofsy Fine Arts.

***Royal, Dan.** Spearman's Grass. large type ed. 256p. 1999. pap. 18.99 (0-7089-5555-X, Linford) Ulverscroft.

Royal Dutch-Shell Group of Companies Staff. The Petroleum Handbook. 6th rev. ed. 710p. 1983. 303.25 (0-444-42118-1) Elsevier.

Royal Entomological Society of London Staff. Catalog of the Library of the Royal Entomological Society of London. (Printed Book Catalogs). 1980. 650.00 (0-8161-0315-1, G K Hall & Co) Mac Lib Ref.

Royal Fine Art Commission. Improving Design in the High Street: An RFAC Guide. 2nd ed. LC 97-186386. 84p. 1997. pap. text 19.95 (0-7506-3453-7) Buttrwrth-Heinemann.

Royal Geography Society. The Lands of Cazembe: Lacerda's Journey to Cazembe in 1798. Burton, Richard F., tr. LC 69-18974. (Illus.). vii, 272p. 1969. reprint ed. 19.75 (0-8371-0894-2, BUC&, Greenwood Pr) Greenwood.

Royal Gustavus Adolphus Society Staff, ed. Scandinavian Yearbook of Folklore, Vol. 45. 152p. 1990. 48.00 (91-22-01333-4) Coronet Bks.

Royal Historical Society Staff. Royal Historical Society Transactions, Vol. 5, 1995. (Royal Historical Society Transactions Ser.: No. 6). 276p. (C). 1996. text 35.95 (0-521-55200-1) Cambridge U Pr.

— Royal Historical Society Transactions Vol. 6: Sixth Series, Vol. 6. 273p. (C). 1997. text 39.95 (0-521-58330-6) Cambridge U Pr.

— Royal Historical Society Transactions Vol. 7: Sixth Series, Vol. 7. (Illus.). 361p. (C). 1998. text 44.95 (0-521-62262-X) Cambridge U Pr.

Royal Historical Society Staff, ed. Royal Historical Society Transactions, 1998 Vol. 8: Sixth Series. 392p. (C). 1999. text 44.95 (0-521-65009-7) Cambridge U Pr.

***Royal Horticultural Society Staff, ed.** Essential Gardening Techniques: Over 1,500 Step-by-Step Illustrations. (Illus.). 256p. 2000. pap. 24.95 (1-84000-013-9) Mitchell Beazley.

Royal India, Pakistan, jt. auth. see Herringham, Christiana J.

Royal Inst. of Chartered Surveyors Staff. Commercial Property Management. 1995. pap. 30.00 (0-85406-694-2, Pub. by R-I-C-S Bks) St Mut.

Royal Institute of International Affairs. British Foreign Policy: Some Relevant Documents, January, 1950 - April, 1955. LC 78-4467. 1978. reprint ed. lib. bdg. 65.00 (0-313-20370-9, RIBF, Greenwood Pr) Greenwood.

— British Yearbook of International Law. Jennings, R. Y. & Waldock, Humphrey, eds. Incl. Vol. 42. 386p. 1969. 27.50 (0-19-214658-0); (Royal Institute of International Affairs Ser.). write for info. (0-318-54809-7) OUP.

— Chronology & Index of the Second World War, 1938-1945. LC 89-48664. 448p. 1990. lib. bdg. 105.00 (0-313-28072-X, RCQ/, Greenwood Pr) Greenwood.

— Index to Periodical Articles, 1950 to 1964, in the Library of the Royal Institute of International Affairs. 1990. 290.00 (0-8161-1566-4, G K Hall & Co) Mac Lib Ref.

— Index to Periodical Articles, 1979-1989, in the Library of the Royal Institute of International Affairs. (Monographs). 1990. 290.00 (0-8161-1784-5, G K Hall & Co) Mac Lib Ref.

— Reports on Nationalism by a Study Group of Members of the Royal Institute of International Affairs: Proceedings. 360p. 1963. 30.00 (0-7146-1571-4, Pub. by F Cass Pubs) Intl Spec Bk.

— The Republics of South America. LC 76-29396. reprint ed. 39.50 (0-404-15350-X) AMS Pr.

Royal Institute of International Affairs, ed. Index to Periodical Articles, 1973-1978. (Library Reference Ser.). 1979. 170.00 (0-8161-0281-3, G K Hall & Co) Mac Lib Ref.

Royal Institute of International Affairs, jt. auth. see Lynch, Dov.

Royal Institute of International Affairs Staff. Britain in Western Europe: WEU & the Atlantic Alliance. LC 78-2451. 1978. reprint ed. lib. bdg. 62.50 (0-313-20348-2, RIBW, Greenwood Pr) Greenwood.

— South-Eastern Europe: A Political & Economic Survey. LC 81-7168. 203p. 1982. reprint ed. lib. bdg. 35.00 (0-313-23195-8, ROSU, Greenwood Pr) Greenwood.

Royal Institute of International Affairs Staff & Gini, Corraco. Report on the Problem of Raw Materials & Foodstuffs. LC 82-48298. (World Economy Ser.). 325p. 1982. lib. bdg. 39.00 (0-8240-5353-2) Garland.

Royal Institute Staff, ed. see Commission on Britain & Europe Staff.

Royal Irish Academy Staff. Todd Lecture Series, Set, Vols. 1-17. reprint ed. 388.00 (0-404-60560-5) AMS Pr.

Royal, Jenny, jt. ed. see Hardingham, Alison.

***Royal, Lauren.** Emerald. 2000. mass mkt. 6.50 (0-451-20142-6, Sig) NAL.

Royal Life Saving Society-Australia Staff. Lifeguarding Manual. (Illus.). 228p. (gr. 13). 1994. pap. text. write for info. (0-8151-7321-0, 25244) Mosby Inc.

— Resuscitation & Emergency Care. 96p. (C). (gr. 13). 1994. pap. text. write for info. (0-8151-7322-9) Mosby Inc.

— Swimming & Lifesaving Manual. (Illus.). 228p. (gr. 13). 1994. pap. text. write for info. (0-8151-7324-5, 25247) Mosby Inc.

Royal, Lyssa. Millennium: Tools for the Coming Changes. 205p. 1999. pap. 13.95 (0-9631320-3-2, Pub. by Royal Priest) ACCESS Pubs Network.

Royal, Lyssa & Priest, Keith. Preparing for Contact: A Metamorphosis of Consciousness. 192p. (Orig.). 1994. pap. 12.95 (0-9631320-2-4) Royal Priest.

— Prism of Lyra: An Exploration of Human Galactic Heritage. rev. ed. 114p. 1991. reprint ed. pap. 11.95 (0-9631320-0-8) Royal Priest.

— Visitors from Within: Extraterrestrial Encounters & Species Evolution. 2nd rev. ed. LC 99-17177. 192p. 1999. pap. 14.95 (1-893183-04-1, Pub. by Granite Pub) ACCESS Pubs Network.

Royal, Marcella. Youth Crime-Violence & the Cause. LC 94-94495. (Illus.). 208p. (Orig.). 1994. pap. 12.95 (0-9642111-0-6) BARRONS WA.

Royal, Marshal. Charlie Christian. (Bayou Jazz Ser.). 1998. 30.00 (0-304-70035-5) Continuum.

Royal, Marshal & Gordon, Claire P. Marshal Royal: Jazz Survivor. (Bayou Jazz Ser.). 224p. 2000. 27.95 (0-304-33836-2) Continuum.

Royal, Mickey. The Pimp Game. Foote, Stacie, ed. (Illus.). 96p. (YA). pap. 14.95 (0-9700587-0-5) Sharif Pubng.

Royal Microscopical Society (Great Britain) Staff, et al. Microscopy of Semiconducting Materials, 1997: Proceedings of the Royal Microscopical Society Conference Held at Oxford University, 7-10 April, 1997. LC 97-42765. (Institute of Physics Conference Ser.). 1997. 420.00 (0-7503-0464-2) IOP Pub.

Royal Microscopy Society, Nomenclature Committee S. RMS Dictionary of Light Microscopy. (Royal Microscopy Society Microscopy Handbooks Ser.: No. 15). (Illus.). 152p. 1989. 35.00 (0-19-856421-X) OUP.

Royal Musical Association Staff. Index to Papers Read Before the Members...1874-1944. 56p. 1993. reprint ed. lib. bdg. 69.00 (0-7812-9683-8) Rprt Serv.

Royal National Institute for the Blind Staff. Early Years: A Series. 1996. pap. 22.95 (*0-89128-310-2*, Pub. by Royal Natl Inst) Am Foun Blind.

Royal Ontario Museum Staff. Homage to Heaven, Homage to Earth: Chinese Treasures of the Royal Ontario Museum. (Illus.). 256p. 1992. text 95.00 (*0-8020-5876-0*) U of Toronto Pr.

Royal, Penny C. Curativement Votre. (Health Education Ser.). 128p. 1983. pap. 8.95 (*0-9609226-2-8*) Sound Nutri.

— Herbally Yours. 3rd ed. (Health Education Ser.). 128p. (C). 1982. pap. 7.95 (*0-9609226-1-X*) Sound Nutri.

— Yerbamente Suyo. 3rd ed. 130p. 1987. pap. 7.95 (*0-9609226-3-6*) Sound Nutri.

***Royal, Robert.** Catholic Martyrs of the Twentieth Century: A Comprehensive World History. (Illus.). 400p. 2000. 39.95 (*0-8245-1846-2*, Pub. by Crossroad NY) Natl Bk Netwk.

Royal, Robert. Fourteen-Ninety-Two & All That: Political Manipulations of History. 214p. (C). 1992. 18.95 (*0-89633-174-1*) Ethics & Public Policy.

— The Virgin & the Dynamo: The Use & Abuse of Religion in the Environmental Debate. LC 98-50276. 271p. 1999. pap. 25.00 (*0-8028-4468-5*) Eerdmans.

Royal, Robert, ed. Challenge & Response: Critiques of the Catholic Bishops' Draft Letter on the U. S. Economy. 87p. 1985. pap. 12.00 (*0-89633-091-5*) Ethics & Public Policy.

— Jacques Maritain & the Jews. LC 93-4633. (American Maritain Association Publications). (C). 1993. pap. text 17.50 (*0-268-01193-1*) U of Notre Dame Pr.

Royal, Robert, jt. ed. see Falcoff, Mark.

Royal, Robert, ed. see Hambrick-Stowe, Charles E.

Royal, Robert, jt. ed. see Nemoianu, Virgil.

Royal, Robert, jt. ed. see Weigel, George.

Royal, Robert, tr. see Torrell, Jean-Pierre.

Royal Scottish Geographical Society Staff. Land Assessment in Scotland: Proceedings of the Royal Scottish Geographical Society Symposium, University of Edinburgh, May, 1979. Thomas, M. F. & Coppock, J. T., eds. (Illus.). 156p. 1980. 27.00 (*0-08-025716-X*, Pergamon Pr) Elsevier.

Royal Society for the Prevention of Accidents Staff. Tolley's Health & Safety at Work Handbook 1999 Eleventh Edition. 11th rev. ed. 1998. pap. 295.00 (*1-86012-823-8*) Tolley Pubng.

Royal Society of Chemistry. Electrochemistry, Vol. 7. 1989. 104.00 (*0-85186-870-3*) CRC Pr.

Royal Society of Chemistry Staff. Agrochemicals Handbook. 3rd ed. 1991. 446.00 (*0-85186-464-3*) CRC Pr.

— Aliphatic & Related Natural Product Chemistry, Vol. 1. 1989. 92.00 (*0-85186-642-5*) CRC Pr.

— Aliphatic & Related Natural Product Chemistry, Vol. 2. 1989. 128.00 (*0-85186-652-2*) CRC Pr.

— Aliphatic & Related Natural Product Chemistry, Vol. 3. 1989. 110.00 (*0-85186-662-X*) CRC Pr.

— Alkaloids, Vol. 9. 1989. 102.00 (*0-85186-660-3*) CRC Pr.

— Alkaloids, Vol. 11. 1989. 163.00 (*0-85186-347-7*) CRC Pr.

— Alkaloids, Vol. 12. 1989. 178.00 (*0-85186-357-4*) CRC Pr.

— Amino Acids & Peptides, Vol. 18. 1987. 175.00 (*0-85186-164-4*) CRC Pr.

— Analysis of Airborne Pollutants in Working Atmospheres. 1989. 44.00 (*0-85186-860-6*) CRC Pr.

— Annual Reports on Analytical Atomic Spectroscopy, Vol. 3. 1989. 32.00 (*0-85990-253-6*) CRC Pr.

— Annual Reports on Analytical Atomic Spectroscopy, Vol. 4. 1989. 46.00 (*0-85990-254-4*) CRC Pr.

— Annual Reports on Analytical Atomic Spectroscopy, Vol. 5. 1989. 52.00 (*0-85186-757-X*) CRC Pr.

— Annual Reports on Analytical Atomic Spectroscopy, Vol. 6. 1989. 70.00 (*0-85186-747-2*) CRC Pr.

— Annual Reports on Analytical Atomic Spectroscopy, Vol. 7. 1989. 64.00 (*0-85186-737-5*) CRC Pr.

— Annual Reports on Analytical Atomic Spectroscopy, Vol. 10. 1989. 104.00 (*0-85186-717-0*) CRC Pr.

— Annual Reports on Analytical Atomic Spectroscopy, Vol. 11. 1989. 141.00 (*0-85186-707-3*) CRC Pr.

— Annual Reports on Analytical Atomic Spectroscopy, Vol. 12. 1989. 122.00 (*0-85186-697-2*) CRC Pr.

— Aromatic & Heteroaromatic Chemistry, Vol. 7. 1989. 126.00 (*0-85186-600-X*) CRC Pr.

— Biosynthesis, Vol. 6. 1989. 128.00 (*0-85186-990-4*) CRC Pr.

— Biosynthesis, Vol. 7. 1989. 86.00 (*0-85186-553-4*) CRC Pr.

— Carbohydrate Chemistry, Vol. 13. 1989. 286.00 (*0-85186-112-1*) CRC Pr.

— Carbohydrate Chemistry, Vol. 14, Pt. 1. 1989. 153.00 (*0-85186-122-9*) CRC Pr.

— Carbohydrate Chemistry, Vol. 15, Pt. 1. 1989. 87.00 (*0-85186-142-3*) CRC Pr.

— Carbohydrate Chemistry, Vol. 20, Pt. 1. 1989. 186.00 (*0-85186-242-X*) CRC Pr.

— Carbohydrate Chemistry, Vol. 21, Pt. 1. 1989. 208.00 (*0-85186-232-2*) CRC Pr.

— Catalysis, Vol. 1. 1991. 131.00 (*0-85186-534-8*) CRC Pr.

— Catalysis, Vol. 2. 1991. 131.00 (*0-85186-544-5*) CRC Pr.

— Catalysis, Vol. 3. 1991. 131.00 (*0-85186-720-0*) CRC Pr.

— Catalysis, Vol. 4. 1991. 131.00 (*0-85186-554-2*) CRC Pr.

— Catalysis, Vol. 5. 1989. 197.00 (*0-85186-564-X*) CRC Pr.

— Catalysis, Vol. 6. 1989. 142.00 (*0-85186-574-7*) CRC Pr.

— Catalysis, Vol. 7. 1988. 186.00 (*0-85186-584-4*) CRC Pr.

— Challenges/Contemporary Dairy Analytical Techniques, No. 49. 1989. 53.00 (*0-85186-925-4*) CRC Pr.

— Chemical Physics of Solids & Their Surfaces, Vol. 8. 1988. 141.00 (*0-85186-740-5*) CRC Pr.

— Chemical Regulation of Biological Mechanisms, No. 42. 1989. 44.00 (*0-85186-855-X*) CRC Pr.

— Chemical Safety Data Sheets Vol. 4, Pt. 1, A-L: Toxic Chemicals. 1991. 122.00 (*0-85186-311-6*) CRC Pr.

— Chemical Safety Data Sheets Vol. 4, Pt. 2, M-Z: Toxic Chemicals. 1992. 122.00 (*0-85186-321-3*) CRC Pr.

— Chemicals in the Oil Industry, No. 45. 2nd ed. 1989. 44.00 (*0-85186-885-1*) CRC Pr.

— Chemistry & Agriculture, No. 36. 1989. 28.00 (*0-85186-680-8*) CRC Pr.

— Chemistry & the Needs of Society, No. 26. 1989. 22.00 (*0-85186-218-7*) CRC Pr.

— Colloid Science, Vol. 2. 1990. 70.00 (*0-85186-518-6*) CRC Pr.

— Colloid Science, Vol. 3. 1989. 82.00 (*0-85186-528-3*) CRC Pr.

— Colloid Science, Vol. 4. 1989. 154.00 (*0-85186-538-0*) CRC Pr.

— Composition of Foods. 5th ed. 1991. 83.00 (*0-85186-391-4*) CRC Pr.

— Conservation of Resources, No. 27. 1989. 30.00 (*0-85186-208-X*) CRC Pr.

— Dictionary of Substances & Their Effects, Vol. 6. 1995. 350.00 (*0-85186-330-2*) CRC Pr.

— Dictionary of Substances & Their Effects, Vol. 7. 1995. 350.00 (*0-85186-340-X*) CRC Pr.

— Eight Peak Index, 7. 4th ed. 1992. 2095.00 (*0-85186-417-1*) CRC Pr.

— Electrochemistry, Vol. 8. 1989. 168.00 (*0-85186-067-2*) CRC Pr.

— Electrochemistry, Vol. 9. 1989. 168.00 (*0-85186-077-X*) CRC Pr.

— Electrochemistry, Vol. 10. 1989. 176.00 (*0-85186-087-7*) CRC Pr.

— Electron Spin Resonance, Vol. 4. 1988. 109.00 (*0-85186-781-2*) CRC Pr.

— Electron Spin Resonance, Vol. 6. 1988. 197.00 (*0-85186-801-0*) CRC Pr.

— Electron Spin Resonance, Vol. 7. 1988. 252.00 (*0-85186-811-8*) CRC Pr.

— Electron Spin Resonance, Vol. 8. 1988. 197.00 (*0-85186-821-5*) CRC Pr.

— Electron Spin Resonance, Vol. 9. 1988. 197.00 (*0-85186-831-2*) CRC Pr.

— Electronic Structure & Magnetism of Inorganic Compounds, Vol. 7. 1988. 132.00 (*0-85186-301-9*) CRC Pr.

— Electrothermal Atomization for Atomic Absorption Spectrometry. 1989. 52.00 (*0-85186-777-4*) CRC Pr.

— Energy & Chemistry, No. 41. 1988. 34.00 (*0-85186-845-2*) CRC Pr.

— Environmental Chemistry, Vol. 2. 1989. 106.00 (*0-85186-765-0*) CRC Pr.

— Environmental Chemistry, Vol. 3. 1989. 108.00 (*0-85186-775-8*) CRC Pr.

— Essays on Free Radical Chemistry, No. 24. 1989. 34.00 (*0-85186-009-5*) CRC Pr.

— European Directory of Agrochemical Products, Vol. III. 2nd ed. 1989. 186.00 (*0-85186-633-6*) CRC Pr.

— European Directory of Agrochemical Products Vol. I: Fungicides. 4th ed. 1990. 260.95 (*0-85186-933-5*) CRC Pr.

— European Directory of Agrochemical Products Vol. II: Herbicides. 4th ed. 1990. 260.95 (*0-85186-943-2*) CRC Pr.

— European Directory of Agrochemical Products Vol. III: Insecticides. 4th ed. 1990. 260.95 (*0-85186-953-X*) CRC Pr.

— European Directory of Agrochemical Products Vol. IV: Plant Growth Regulators. 4th ed. 1990. 260.95 (*0-85186-963-7*) CRC Pr.

— European Directory of Agrochemical Products, 1984 Pt. 2: Herbicides. 1984. 110.00 (*0-85186-573-9*); 110.00 (*0-85186-563-1*) CRC Pr.

— Fifty Years of the Faraday Society, 1903-1953. 1992. 8.00 (*0-85186-649-2*) CRC Pr.

— Foreign Compound Metabolism in Mammals, Vol. 6. 1989. 185.00 (*0-85186-058-3*) CRC Pr.

— Gas Kinetics & Energy Transfer, Vol. 2. 1988. 92.00 (*0-85186-766-9*) CRC Pr.

— Gas Kinetics & Energy Transfer, Vol. 3. 1988. 92.00 (*0-85186-776-6*) CRC Pr.

— Gas Kinetics & Energy Transfer, Vol. 4. 1988. 130.00 (*0-85186-786-3*) CRC Pr.

— General Synthetic Methods, Vol. 3. 1993. 146.00 (*0-85186-730-8*) CRC Pr.

— General Synthetic Methods, Vol. 5. 1990. 252.00 (*0-08-518686-4*) CRC Pr.

— General Synthetic Methods, Vol. 6. 1989. 274.00 (*0-85186-874-6*) CRC Pr.

— General Synthetic Methods, Vol. 7. 1989. 252.00 (*0-85186-884-3*) CRC Pr.

— General Synthetic Methods, Vol. 8. 1989. 352.00 (*0-85186-894-0*) CRC Pr.

— General Synthetic Methods, Vol. 9. 1989. 352.00 (*0-85186-904-1*) CRC Pr.

— Guidance on Laboratory Fume Cupboards. 1990. 32.00 (*0-85186-329-9*) CRC Pr.

— Health & Safety/Chem Lab-Where Do We Go from Here?, No. 51. 1988. 61.00 (*0-85186-945-9*) CRC Pr.

— Heterocyclic Chemistry, Vol. 1. 1989. 218.00 (*0-85186-970-X*) CRC Pr.

— Heterocyclic Chemistry, Vol. 2. 1989. 229.00 (*0-85186-813-4*) CRC Pr.

— Heterocyclic Chemistry, Vol. 3. 1989. 229.00 (*0-85186-823-1*) CRC Pr.

— High Temperature Chemistry/Inorganic/Ceramic Materials, No. 30. 1989. 50.00 (*0-85186-168-7*) CRC Pr.

— Index for Reviews in Analytical Chemistry, 1983. 1989. 26.00 (*0-85186-586-0*) CRC Pr.

— Index of Chemistry Films. 7th ed. 1989. 42.00 (*0-85186-499-6*) CRC Pr.

— Index of Reviews in Organic Chemistry. 1989. suppl. ed. 22.00 (*0-85186-549-6*) CRC Pr.

— Index of Reviews in Organic Chemistry, No. 83. 1989. 50.00 (*0-85186-569-0*) CRC Pr.

— Index of Reviews in Organic Chemistry, No. 84. 1989. 50.00 (*0-85186-579-8*) CRC Pr.

— Index of Reviews in Organic Chemistry, No. 85. 1988. 53.00 (*0-85186-589-5*) CRC Pr.

— Index of Reviews in Organic Chemistry, Nos. 81-82. 1989. 50.00 (*0-85186-559-3*) CRC Pr.

— Industrial Use of Thermochemical Data, No. 34. 1989. 44.00 (*0-85186-930-0*) CRC Pr.

— Industry & the Environment in Perspective, No. 46. (Orig.). 1988. 34.00 (*0-85186-895-9*) CRC Pr.

— Inorganic Biochemistry, Vol. 1. 1988. 106.00 (*0-85186-570-4*) CRC Pr.

— Inorganic Biochemistry, Vol. 2. 1988. 134.00 (*0-85186-555-0*) CRC Pr.

— Inorganic Biochemistry, Vol. 3. 1988. 183.00 (*0-85186-565-8*) CRC Pr.

— Inorganic Reaction Mechanisms, Vol. 7. 1988. 210.00 (*0-85186-315-9*) CRC Pr.

— Interfacial Kinetics in Solution. 1992. 69.00 (*0-85186-628-X*) CRC Pr.

— International Conference on Co-Ordination Chemistry, No. 13. 1989. 13.00 (*0-85186-079-6*) CRC Pr.

— International Symposium on Inorganic Polymers, No. 15. 1990. 11.00 (*0-85186-089-3*) CRC Pr.

— Ion-Ion & Ion-Solvent Interaction. 1992. 34.00 (*0-85186-958-0*) CRC Pr.

— Isotopes: Essential Chemistry & Applications, No. 68. 2nd ed. 1988. 127.00 (*0-85186-746-4*) CRC Pr.

— Long Term Neurotoxic Effects of Paint Solvents. 1990. 55.00 (*0-85186-339-6*) CRC Pr.

— Macromolecular Chemistry, Vol. 1. 1991. 128.00 (*0-85186-840-1*) CRC Pr.

— Macromolecular Chemistry, Vol. 2. 1989. 192.00 (*0-85186-866-5*) CRC Pr.

— Macromolecular Chemistry, Vol. 3. 1989. 236.00 (*0-85186-876-2*) CRC Pr.

— Mathematical Formulae for Reference. 1989. write for info. (*0-85404-006-4*) CRC Pr.

— Measurement Technology/Carcinogenic Agents/Workplace Air. 1989. 83.00 (*0-85186-098-2*) CRC Pr.

— Modern Inorganic Chemicals Industry, No. 31. 1989. 34.00 (*0-85186-158-X*) CRC Pr.

— Molecular Spectroscopy, Vol. 6. 1988. 126.00 (*0-85186-556-9*) CRC Pr.

— Organic Chlorine Solvents: Health Risk to Workers. (Orig.). 1987. 153.00 (*0-85186-078-8*) CRC Pr.

— Organic Compounds of Sulphur, Selenium & Tellurium, Vol. 6. 1989. 194.00 (*0-85186-299-3*) CRC Pr.

— Organometallic Chemistry, Vol. 18. 1989. 362.00 (*0-85186-661-1*) CRC Pr.

— Oxygen & Life, No. 39. 1989. 30.00 (*0-85186-825-8*) CRC Pr.

— Oxygen & the Conversion of Future Feedstocks, No. 48. 1988. 48.00 (*0-85186-915-7*) CRC Pr.

— Oxygen in the Metal & Gaseous Fuel Industries, No. 32. 1989. 28.00 (*0-85186-138-5*) CRC Pr.

— Particle Size Analysis. 1989. 28.00 (*0-85990-104-1*) CRC Pr.

— Practicing Chemists: A History of the Society for Analytic Chemistry. 1989. 22.00 (*0-85990-100-9*) CRC Pr.

— Proceedings of the International Congress on Catalysis, 5th, 2 Vols. 1989. 122.00 (*0-85186-188-1*) CRC Pr.

— Properties & Applications of Zeolites, No. 33. 1988. 44.00 (*0-85186-670-0*) CRC Pr.

— Reaction Kinetics, Vol. I. 1988. 51.00 (*0-85186-756-1*) CRC Pr.

— Recent Advances in Chemistry of B-Lactam Antibiotics, No. 38. 2nd ed. 1989. 46.00 (*0-85186-815-0*) CRC Pr.

— Recent Advances in Chemistry of B-Lactam Technology, No. 28. 1989. 65.00 (*0-85186-198-9*) CRC Pr.

— Recent Advances in the Chemistry of Meat, No. 47. 1989. 49.00 (*0-85186-905-X*) CRC Pr.

— Safe Practices in Chemical Laboratories. 1989. 49.00 (*0-85186-309-4*) CRC Pr.

— Selected Annual Reviews of the Analytical Sciences, Vol. 1. 1989. 24.00 (*0-85990-201-3*) CRC Pr.

— Selected Annual Reviews of the Analytical Sciences, Vol. 2. 1989. 24.00 (*0-85990-202-1*) CRC Pr.

— Selected Annual Reviews of the Analytical Sciences, Vol. 3. 1989. 28.00 (*0-85990-203-X*) CRC Pr.

— Selected Annual Reviews on the Analytical Sciences, Vol. 4. 1989. 40.00 (*0-85990-204-8*) CRC Pr.

— Seminars in Organic Systhesis, Vol. 3. 1993. 121.00 (*88-86208-09-X*) CRC Pr.

— Separation of Gases: BOC Priestley Conference. 5th, No. 80. 1990. 131.00 (*0-85186-637-9*) CRC Pr.

— Solvents in Common Use: Health Risks to Workers. 1989. 187.00 (*0-85186-088-5*) CRC Pr.

— Specialty Inorganic Chemicals, No. 40. 1989. 50.00 (*0-85186-835-5*) CRC Pr.

— Surface Chemistry of Oxides. 1992. 28.00 (*0-85990-386-9*) CRC Pr.

— Symposium on Organic Reaction Mechanisms, No. 19. 1990. 14.00 (*0-85186-139-3*) CRC Pr.

— Symposium on Recent Advances in the Chemistry of Colouring Matters, No. 4. 1989. 7.00 (*0-85185-029-X*) CRC Pr.

— Symposium on the Alkali Metals, No. 22. 1989. 20.00 (*0-85186-169-5*) CRC Pr.

— Symposium on the Solution Properties/Natural Polymers, No. 23. 1989. 17.00 (*0-85186-179-2*) CRC Pr.

— Terpenoids & Steroids, Vol. 12. 1989. 166.00 (*0-85186-356-6*) CRC Pr.

— Theoretical Chemistry, Vol. 4. 1988. 112.00 (*0-85186-784-7*) CRC Pr.

Royal Society of Chemistry Staff, jt. auth. see HSEC Staff.

Royal Society of Chemistry U. K. Staff. Annual Reports on Analytical Atomic Spectroscopy, Vol. 9. 1989. 100.00 (*0-85186-727-8*) CRC Pr.

Royal Society of Literature of the United Kingdom. The Eighteen-Eighties: Essays by Fellows of the Royal Society of Literature. (BCL1-PR English Literature Ser.). 271p. 1992. reprint ed. lib. bdg. 79.00 (*0-7812-7054-5*) Rprt Serv.

Royal Society of Literature, United Kingdom Staff. Essays by Divers Hands, Vol. 14. Lytton, ed. (Essay Index in Reprint Ser.). 1978. reprint ed. 25.00 (*0-8486-3027-0*) Roth Pub Inc.

— Essays by Divers Hands, Vol. 16. Gooch, G. P., ed. (Essay Index in Reprint Ser.). 1978. reprint ed. 25.00 (*0-8486-3028-9*) Roth Pub Inc.

— Essays by Divers Hands, Vol. 17. Meyerstein, E. H., ed. (Essay Index in Reprint Ser.). 1978. 25.00 (*0-8486-3029-7*) Roth Pub Inc.

— Essays by Divers Hands, Vol. 18. Ervine, St. John G., ed. (Essay Index in Reprint Ser.). 1978. reprint ed. 25.00 (*0-8486-3030-0*) Roth Pub Inc.

Royal Society of London Staff, et al. Optical Bi-Stability, Dynamical Nonlinearity & Photonic Logic: Proceedings of a Royal Society Discussion Meeting Held on 21-22, March 1984, Organized by S. D. Smith, A. Miller & B. S. Wherrett. Miller, Arthur et al, eds. (Illus.). 261p. 1985. text 86.50 (*0-85403-239-8*) Royal Soc London.

Royal Society of Marine Artists Staff. A Celebration of Marine Art: Fifty Years of the Royal Society of Marine Artists. LC 96-229698. (Illus.). 176p. 1996. 55.00 (*0-7137-2564-8*, Pub. by Blandford Pr) Sterling.

Royal Society Staff, ed. see Young, J. Z., et al.

Royal, Suzanne, tr. see Hyde, Dayton O.

Royal Swedish Academy of Music Staff, ed. Trends & Perspectives in Musicology: Proceedings of the World Music Conference. (Illus.). 166p. (Orig.). 1983. pap. text 37.50 (*91-85428-42-6*) Coronet Bks.

Royal Swedish Academy of Sciences Staff. Chemistry & Geochemistry of Solutions at High Temperatures & Pressures: Proceedings of the Royal Swedish Academy of Sciences, Nobel Symposium, Bjorkborns Herrgard, Karlskoga, Sweden, Sept., 1979. Rickard, David & Wickman, Frans E., eds. (Physics & Chemistry of the Earth Series; International Series in Earth Sciences: Vols. 13 & 37). (Illus.). 600p. 1982. 205.00 (*0-08-026285-6*, Pergamon Pr) Elsevier.

— Nuclear War: The Aftermath - Special Ambio Publication, Vol. 11. 3rd ed. Peterson, J. & Hinrichsen, D., eds. (Illus.). 204p. 1982. pap. text 98.00 (*0-08-028176-1*, Pub. by Pergamon Repr) Franklin.

Royal, Ted, jt. auth. see Royal, William N.

Royal, Travis W., ed. see National Institute on Drug Abuse Staff, et al.

Royal Tyrrell Museum of Palaeontology Staff & Budgen, Dennis. The Land Before Us: A Geological History of Alberta. Nikiforuk, Andrew, ed. (Illus.). 96p. (gr. 4-7). 1994. pap. 17.95 (*0-88995-123-3*, Pub. by Red Deer) Genl Dist Srvs.

Royal Tyrrell Museum of Palaeontology Staff & Wishart, Pat. The Land Before Us: The Making of Ancient Alberta. Nikiforuk, Andrew, ed. 1994. pap. 17.95 (*1-55105-053-6*) Lone Pine.

Royal United Services Institute for Defense Studies, jt. auth. see Quinlan, Michael.

Royal United Services Institute Staff. International Weapon Developments: A Survey of Current Developments in Weapon Systems. 4th ed. (Illus.). 203p. 1980. pap. 19.00 (*0-08-027028-X*, Pergamon Pr) Elsevier.

— Nuclear Attack - Civil Defense: Aspects of Civil Defense in the Nuclear Age. (Illus.). 292p. 1983. 28.00 (*0-08-027041-7*, Pergamon Pr); pap. 13.95 (*0-08-027042-5*, Pergamon Pr) Elsevier.

— Rusi & Brassey's Defence Yearbook 1983. 93rd ed. (Brassey's Defence Yearbook Ser.). 400p. 1983. 60.50 (*0-08-028346-2*, Pergamon Pr); pap. 24.50 (*0-08-028347-0*, Pergamon Pr) Elsevier.

— Rusi & Brassey's Defence Yearbook 1985. 95th ed. (Brassey's Defence Yearbook Ser.). 388p. 1985. 46.00 (*0-08-031168-7*, Pergamon Pr); pap. 20.50 (*0-08-031169-5*, Pergamon Pr) Elsevier.

— RUSI-Brassey's Defence Yearbook. 94th ed. (Brassey's Defence Yearbook Ser.). 350p. 1984. 60.50 (*0-08-030552-0*, Pergamon Pr); pap. 19.25 (*0-08-031176-8*, Pergamon Pr) Elsevier.

— RUSI-Brassey's Defence Yearbook, 1974-75. 85th ed. (Brassey's Defence Yearbook Ser.). (Illus.). 338p. 1974. 30.50 (*0-08-027000-X*, Pergamon Pr) Elsevier.

— RUSI-Brassey's Defence Yearbook, 1975-76. 86th ed. (Brassey's Defence Yearbook Ser.). 418p. 1975. 30.50 (*0-08-027001-8*, Pergamon Pr) Elsevier.

— RUSI-Brassey's Defence Yearbook, 1976-77. 87th ed. (Brassey's Defence Yearbook Ser.). 377p. 28.00 (*0-317-66873-0*, Pergamon Pr) Elsevier.

— RUSI-Brassey's Defence Yearbook, 1977-78. 88th ed. (Brassey's Defence Yearbook Ser.). 430p. 1977. 30.50 (*0-08-027003-4*, Pergamon Pr) Elsevier.

— RUSI-Brassey's Defence Yearbook, 1978-79. 89th ed. (Brassey's Defence Yearbook Ser.). 365p. 1978. 44.00 (*0-08-027004-2*, Pergamon Pr) Elsevier.

— RUSI-Brassey's Defence Yearbook, 1979-80. 90th ed. (Brassey's Defence Yearbook Ser.). 355p. 1979. 44.00 (*0-08-027005-0*, Pergamon Pr) Elsevier.

— RUSI-Brassey's Defence Yearbook, 1981. 91st ed. 376p. 1980. 55.00 (*0-08-027006-9*, Pergamon Pr) Elsevier.

— Rusi-Brassey's Defence Yearbook 1982. 92nd ed. 365p. 1981. 48.50 (*0-08-027039-5*, Pergamon Pr); pap. 30.50 (*0-08-027040-9*, Pergamon Pr) Elsevier.

— RUSI-Brassey's Defence Yearbook 1986. 96th ed. 350p. 1986. 48.50 (*0-08-031210-1*, Pergamon Pr); pap. 24.00 (*0-08-031220-9*, Pergamon Pr) Elsevier.

R

— RUSI-Brassey's Defence Yearbook 1987. 97th ed. 350p. 1987. 50.00 (*0-08-033607-8*, Pergamon Pr); pap. 24.00 (*0-08-033608-6*, Pergamon Pr) Elsevier.

— RUSI-Brassey's Defence Yearbook 1988. 98th ed. (Brassey's Defence Yearbook Ser.). 350p. 1988. 61.00 (*0-08-035815-2*, Pergamon Pr); pap. 33.00 (*0-08-035816-0*, Pergamon Pr) Elsevier.

Royal United Services Institute Staff, ed. Future of Armoured Warfare. 135p. 1987. 18.71 (*0-08-034738-X*, Pergamon Pr); pap. 8.91 (*0-08-034739-8*, Pergamon Pr) Elsevier.

Royal United Services Institute Staff, jt. auth. see Stationery Office Staff.

Royal, Weld, ed. see Honda, Sadaharn.

Royal, William N. & Royal, Ted. Checkered Flag: Favorite Auto-Racing Stories of Great Drivers & Owners. (Illus.). 240p. (Orig.). Date not set. pap. 24.95 (*1-57488-146-9*) Brasseys.

Royall, Anne. Mrs. Royall's America, 1828 to 1831, 7 vols. in 6. Incl. Pt. 2. Mrs. Royall's Pennsylvania: or Travels Continued in the United States., 2 vols. LC 72-37720. 16.00 Pt. 3. Mrs. Royall's Southern Tour: or Second Series of the Black Book., 2 vols. LC 72-37720. 16.00 LC 72-37720. reprint ed. 95.00 (*0-404-56830-0*) AMS Pr.

— The Tennessean. LC 78-64092. reprint ed. 37.50 (*0-404-17166-4*) AMS Pr.

Royall, David. Project Delivery Systems. 224p. 15.00 (*0-614-05190-8*, PEC09931.5M) ASFE.

— Teach Yourself Quattro Pro for Windows. (Illus.). 240p. 1995. pap. 11.95 (*0-8442-3949-6*, Teach Yrslf) NTC Contemp Pub Co.

Royall, David, jt. auth. see Royall, Jacky.

Royall, Jacky & Royall, David. Teach Yourself Lotus 1-2-3 for Windows. (Illus.). 212p. 1994. pap. 11.95 (*0-8442-3959-3*, Teach Yrslf) NTC Contemp Pub Co.

Royall, Mary Julia C. Mount Pleasant, South Carolina: A Victorian Village. (Images of America Ser.). (Illus.). 128p. 1996. pap. 16.99 (*0-7524-0531-4*) Arcadia Publng.

Royall, R. Statistical Evidence: A Likelihood Paradigm. LC 97-66011. 192p. 1997. lib. bdg. 64.95 (*0-412-04411-0*) Chapman & Hall.

Royall, Sandy & Roy, Pat. Jonathan Park & the Secret of the Hidden Cave. LC 99-64019. 112p. 1999. pap. 8.99 (*0-89051-263-9*) Master Bks.

***Royals, Melanie.** Trompe L'Oeil Murals Using Stencils. (Illus.). 128p. 2001. pap. 24.99 (*1-58180-028-2*, North Lght Bks) F & W Pubns Inc.

***Royals, Susan.** Missouri: Fun Facts & Games. (Fun Facts & Games Bks.). (Illus.). 64p. (J). 2000. pap. text 5.59 (*1-892920-21-2*) G H B Pubs.

Royals, William T., et al, eds. Flammability & Sensitivity of Materials in Oxygen-Enriched Atmospheres. (STP Ser.: Vol. 1319). (Illus.). 486p. 1997. 89.00 (*0-8031-2401-5*, STP1319) ASTM.

Royalty, Robert. The Streets of Heaven: The Ideology of Wealth in the Apocalypse of John. LC 98-41237. 1998. write for info. (*0-08-655609-6*) Elsevier.

Royalty, Robert M., Jr. The Streets of Heaven: The Ideology of Wealth in the Apocalypse of John. 288p. 1998. text 27.95 (*0-86554-609-6*, H465) Mercer Univ Pr.

Royama, Masamichi. Foreign Policy of Japan: 1914-1939. LC 73-3930. 182p. 1973. reprint ed. lib. bdg. 35.00 (*0-8371-6853-8*, ROFP, Greenwood Pr) Greenwood.

Royama, Shoichi, jt. auth. see Cargill, Thomas F.

Royama, T. Analytical Population Dynamics. (Population & Community Biology Ser.). (Illus.). 392p. 1996. pap. write for info. (*0-412-75570-X*) Kluwer Academic.

Roybal, Beth A. Hepatitis C: A Personal Guide to Good Health. 2nd rev. ed. 168p. 1999. pap. 13.95 (*1-56975-183-8*) Ulysses Pr.

Roybal, Beth A. & Skowronski, Gayle. Sex Herbs: Nature's Sexual Enhancers for Men & Women. 328p. 1999. pap. 14.95 (*1-56975-185-4*) Ulysses Pr.

Roybal, Beth P., jt. auth. see Skowronski, Gayle.

***Roybal, Bill, ed.** Advanced Telescope Design, Fabrication & Control. (Illus.). 1999. pap. text 62.00 (*0-8194-3271-7*) SPIE.

Roybal, Debbie. Eternity Is Only a Step Away: Facts & Knowledge. 44p. (Orig.). 1996. pap. 4.95 (*0-7880-0667-3*) CSS OH.

Roybal, Laura. Billy. LC 93-4837. 240p. (YA). (gr. 7 up). 1994. 14.95 (*0-395-67649-5*) HM.

— Billy. 240p. (YA). (gr. 7 up). 1999. pap. 5.95 (*0-395-96062-2*) HM.

Roybal, Michael A. The Maxims of Madness. 137p. (Orig.). 1993. pap. 8.00 (*0-9639456-0-2*) Maximedia NM.

Royce. Alcoholism & Other Drug Problems. 2nd ed. 1995. 34.00 (*0-02-874049-1*) Free Pr.

Royce, Anya. Movement & Meaning: Creativity & Interpretation in Ballet & Mime. LC 83-48526. (Illus.). 254p. 1984. pap. 78.80 (*0-608-05042-3*, 205970300004) Bks Demand.

Royce, Beverly. Notes on Double Knitting. rev. ed. Swansen, Meg, ed. (Illus.). 85p. 1994. pap. 17.00 (*0-942018-06-0*) Schoolhouse WI.

Royce, Brenda S. Donna Reed: A Bio-Bibliography, 16. LC 90-44109. (Bio-Bibliographies in the Performing Arts Ser.). 160p. 1990. lib. bdg. 45.00 (*0-313-26806-1*, RDB, Greenwood Pr) Greenwood.

— Hogan's Heroes: A Comprehensive Reference to the 1965-1971 Television Comedy Series, with Cast Biographies & an Episode Guide. LC 92-50947. (Illus.). 303p. 1993. lib. bdg. 42.50 (*0-89950-796-4*) McFarland & Co.

— Hogan's Heroes: Behind the Scenes at Stalag 13. (Illus.). 272p. 1998. pap. 14.95 (*1-58063-031-6*) Renaissance.

— Lauren Bacall: A Bio-Bibliography, 30. LC 92-12500. (Bio-Bibliographies in the Performing Arts Ser.: No. 30). 312p. 1992. lib. bdg. 55.00 (*0-313-27831-8*, RLL/, Greenwood Pr) Greenwood.

— Party of Five: The Unofficial Companion. LC 97-34225. (Illus.). 256p. 1997. pap. 14.95 (*1-58063-000-6*) Renaissance.

— Rock Hudson: A Bio-Bibliography, 61. LC 94-39511. (Bio-Bibliographies in the Performing Arts Ser.: Vol. 61). 336p. 1995. lib. bdg. 65.00 (*0-313-28672-8*, Greenwood Pr) Greenwood.

Royce, Caroline H. Westborough Bessboro: History of Westport, Essex County. (Illus.). 616p. 1997. reprint ed. lib. bdg. 64.00 (*0-8328-6279-7*) Higginson Bk Co.

Royce, Charles C., ed. Indian Land Cessions in the United States. LC 78-146416. (First American Frontier Ser.). (Illus.). 1975. reprint ed. 82.95 (*0-405-02880-6*) Ayer.

Royce, Delanie, jt. auth. see Pazdur, Richard.

Royce, Easton. Voltage. (X-Files Ser.). 1996. 9.60 (*0-606-10095-4*, Pub. by Turtleback) Demco.

Royce, Easton. X Files: Bad Sign, No. 3. (X-Files Ser.). 144p. (YA). (gr. 12 up). 1997. pap. 4.50 (*0-06-447170-5*, HarpTrophy) HarpC Child Bks.

— X Files: Dark Matter, No. 10. (X Files Ser.: Vol. 10). 128p. (J). (gr. 12 up). 1999. pap. 4.50 (*0-06-447182-9*, HarpEntertain) Morrow Avon.

— X Files: Voltage, No. 8. (X-Files Ser.: Vol. 8). (Illus.). 112p. (J). (gr. 5 up). 1996. pap. 4.50 (*0-06-440643-1*, HarpTrophy) HarpC Child Bks.

Royce, Edward. The Origins of Southern Sharecropping. LC 93-18076. (Labor & Social Change Ser.). 288p. 1993. 69.95 (*1-56639-069-9*) Temple U Pr.

***Royce, Edward R., ed.** The Impact of U. S. Development Assistance in Africa: Congressional Hearings. 111p. (C). 1999. reprint ed. pap. text 25.00 (*0-7881-8287-0*) DIANE Pub.

Royce, Greyland. Advanced CICS/VS Command Level Programming for OS/390. Thomas, Mark, ed. (Illus.). 600p. 1998. spiral bd. 52.95 (*1-928778-07-0*, M01AAA3A-001AD) Royce Pubg.

— CICS/VS Programmer's Desk Reference for OS/390. Thomas, Mark, ed. (Illus.). 1100p. 1998. spiral bd. 109.95 (*1-928778-08-9*, M01GAA3A-001V1) Royce Pubg.

— DB2 Database Administration Tool for Database Administrators, Vol. I. Thomas, Mark, ed. (Illus.). 1200p. 1999. spiral bd. 72.50 (*1-928778-01-1*, M01AAA2A-001V1) Royce Pubg.

— DB2 Database Administration Tool for Database Administrators, Vol. II. Thomas, Mark, ed. (Illus.). 1200p. 1999. spiral bd. 72.50 (*1-928778-02-X*, M01AAA2A-001V2) Royce Pubg.

— DB2 Database Administration Tool for Database Administrators, Vols. I & II. Thomas, Mark, ed. (Illus.). 1200p. 1999. spiral bd. 129.95 (*1-928778-03-8*, M01AAA2A-001V3) Royce Pubg.

— DB2 Performance Tuning - Optimizing for OS/390: A Complete Guide to Optimizing Your DB2 OS/390 Software. Thomas, Mark, ed. (Illus.). 450p. 1999. spiral bd. 72.95 (*1-928778-00-3*, M01SAA2A-001) Royce Pubg.

— Introduction to CICS/VS Command Level Programming for OS/390: The Complete Guide, Vol. I. Thomas, Mark, ed. (Illus.). 600p. 1998. spiral bd. 42.95 (*1-928778-04-6*, M01AAA3A-001V1) Royce Pubg.

— Introduction to CICS/VS Command Level Programming for OS/390: The Complete Guide, Vol. II. Thomas, Mark, ed. (Illus.). 600p. 1998. spiral bd. 42.95 (*1-928778-05-4*, M01AAA3A-001V2) Royce Pubg.

— Introduction to CICS/VS Command Level Programming for OS/390: The Complete Guide, Vols. I & II. Thomas, Mark, ed. (Illus.). 1200p. 1998. spiral bd. 69.99 (*1-928778-06-2*, M01AAA3A-001V3) Royce Pubg.

— PeopleSoft Pro - A Complete Guide. Thomas, Mark, ed. (Illus.). 800p. 1999. spiral bd. 79.95 (*1-928778-09-7*, M01APEIA-001V1) Royce Pubg.

Royce, Jack. Bewitched by the Stage. 1998. 19.95 (*1-884953-09-3*) Eaton St Pr.

***Royce, Jack.** Bewitched by the Stage. 2000. mass mkt. 7.95 (*1-884953-04-2*) Eaton St Pr.

Royce, Jack. Dressed to Murder. 1995. 7.95 (*1-884953-02-6*) Eaton St Pr.

— Murder at the Kabuki. 1994. 6.95 (*1-884953-01-8*) Eaton St Pr.

— Troubled Paradise. 204p. 1999. 23.95 (*1-884953-11-5*) Eaton St Pr.

***Royce, Jack.** Wallpaper Murders. 2000. pap. 7.95 (*1-884953-13-1*) Eaton St Pr.

Royce, Jack. Way to the Towers of Silence. LC 97-60212. (Illus.). 1997. pap. 7.95 (*1-884953-03-4*, WTOS-0004) Eaton St Pr.

Royce, Jack & Mitchell, John D. The Train Stopped at Domodossola. LC 94-70382. (Orig.). 1993. pap. text 6.95 (*1-884953-00-X*) Eaton St Pr.

Royce, James, jt. auth. see Bissell, LeClair.

Royce, James E. Alcohol Problems & Alcoholism: A Comprehensive Survey. 2nd rev. ed. 480p. 1989. 35.00 (*0-02-927541-5*) Free Pr.

Royce, James E. & Scratchley, David. Alcoholism & Other Drug Problems. 400p. 1996. 35.00 (*0-684-82314-4*) Free Pr.

***Royce, John, et al.** ServiceSim: Administrator's Guide. (Illus.). 37p. 1998. pap. text 95.00 (*1-885837-27-5*) Interpret Sftware.

Royce, Joseph R. & Mos, Leendert P., eds. Humanistic Psychology: Concepts & Criticisms. (PATH in Psychology Ser.). 332p. 1981. 49.50 (*0-306-40596-2*, Plenum Trade) Perseus Pubng.

— Theoretical Advances in Behavior Genetics, No. 2. (NATO Advanced Study Institute Ser.). 722p. 1981. lib. bdg. 211.50 (*90-286-0569-X*) Kluwer Academic.

Royce, Joseph R., ed. see Banff Conference on Theoretical Psychology Staff.

Royce, Joseph R., jt. ed. see Mos, Leendert P.

Royce, Josiah. California from the Conquest in 1846 to the Second Vigilance Committee in San Francisco (1856) 1992. reprint ed. lib. bdg. 75.00 (*0-7812-5083-8*) Rprt Serv.

— California, from the Conquest in 1846 to the Second Vigilance Committee in San Francisco, 1856: A Study of American Character. LC 72-3762. (American Commonwealths Ser.: No. 7). reprint ed. 49.50 (*0-404-57207-3*) AMS Pr.

Royce, Josiah. Conception of Immortality. 1988. reprint ed. lib. bdg. 59.00 (*0-7812-0089-X*) Rprt Serv.

— The Feud of Oakfield Creek: A Novel of California Life. LC 71-104560. reprint ed. lib. bdg. 32.50 (*0-8398-1770-3*) Irvington.

Royce, Josiah. Fugitive Essays. LC 68-16974. (Essay Index Reprint Ser.). 1977. 23.95 (*0-8369-0840-6*) Ayer.

— Herbert Spencer: An Estimate & Review Together with a Chapter of Personal Reminiscences. 1977. 16.95 (*0-8369-7121-3*, 7955) Ayer.

— Hope of the Great Community. LC 67-26777. (Essay Index Reprint Ser.). 1977. 18.95 (*0-8369-0841-4*) Ayer.

— Metaphysics. Hocking, William E. et al, eds. LC 97-47449. (SUNY Series in Philosophy). 352p. (C). 1998. text 73.50 (*0-7914-3865-1*); pap. text 24.95 (*0-7914-3866-X*) State U NY Pr.

— Outlines of Psychology: An Elementary Treatise, with Some Practical Applications. LC 75-3334. reprint ed. 41.50 (*0-404-59337-2*) AMS Pr.

— The Philosophy of Josiah Royce. Roth, John K., ed. & intro. by. LC 82-2932. (HPC Classics Ser.). 429p. (C). 1982. reprint ed. pap. text 14.95 (*0-915145-41-3*); reprint ed. lib. bdg. 34.95 (*0-915145-42-1*) Hackett Pub.

— Race Questions, Provincialism, & Other American Problems. LC 67-23266. (Essay Index Reprint Ser.). 1977. 25.95 (*0-8369-0842-2*) Ayer.

— The Religious Philosophy of Josiah Royce. Brown, Stuart G., ed. LC 76-4496. 239p. 1976. reprint ed. lib. bdg. 35.00 (*0-8371-8810-5*, RORP, Greenwood Pr) Greenwood.

— The Spirit of Modern Philosophy. 519p. 1983. reprint ed. pap. 10.95 (*0-486-24432-6*) Dover.

— War & Insurance. LC 75-3336. reprint ed. 34.50 (*0-404-59339-9*) AMS Pr.

— World & the Individual, Vol. 1. 1990. 14.50 (*0-8446-2842-5*) Peter Smith.

***Royce, Josiah.** The World & the Individual: Nature, Man, & the Moral Order (1904) 500p. 1998. reprint ed. pap. 35.00 (*0-7661-0224-6*) Kessinger Pub.

Royce, Kenneth. The Ambassador's Son. 1994. 20.00 (*0-7278-4713-9*) Severn Hse.

— The Ambassador's Son. large type ed. 528p. 1996. 27.99 (*0-7089-3524-9*) Ulverscroft.

— Channel Assault. large type ed. 480p. 1984. 27.99 (*0-7089-1131-5*) Ulverscroft.

— The Crypto Man. large type ed. 528p. 1988. 27.99 (*0-7089-1841-7*) Ulverscroft.

— Exchange of Doves. 320p. 1992. mass mkt. 4.99 (*1-55817-606-3*, Pinncle Kensgtn) Kensgtn Pub Corp.

— Ghostman. 256p. 1998. 25.00 (*0-7278-5295-7*) Severn Hse.

***Royce, Kenneth.** Ghostman. large type ed. 368p. 1999. 31.99 (*0-7089-4063-3*) Ulverscroft.

— The Judas Trail. 424p. 2000. 31.99 (*0-7089-4234-2*) Ulverscroft.

Royce, Kenneth. No Way Back. large type ed. 528p. 1988. 27.99 (*0-7089-1778-X*) Ulverscroft.

— Patriots. large type ed. 518p. 1989. 27.99 (*0-7089-1967-7*) Ulverscroft.

— Shadows. 288p. 1996. 22.00 (*0-7278-4878-X*) Severn Hse.

— Shadows. large type ed. LC 96-52557. 275p. 1997. pap. 20.95 (*0-7862-1023-0*) Thorndike Pr.

— The Stalin Account. large type ed. 576p. 1986. 11.50 (*0-7089-8328-6*, Charnwood) Ulverscroft.

— Ten Thousand Days. large type ed. 464p. 1984. 27.99 (*0-7089-1175-7*) Ulverscroft.

— The Third Arm. large type ed. 416p. 1985. 27.99 (*0-7089-1332-6*) Ulverscroft.

Royce, Kenneth W. Hologram of Liberty: The Constitution's Shocking Alliance with Big Government. LC 97-73818. (Illus.). 256p. 1997. pap. 19.95 (*1-888766-03-4*) Javelin Pr.

Royce, Kenneth W., ed. see Party, Boston T.

Royce, Michael. Beat the Car Salesman. 160p. 1998. mass mkt. 5.99 (*0-380-79759-3*, Avon Bks) Morrow Avon.

— Beat the Car Salesman: Become an Expert Car Buyer in Five Easy Steps. LC 95-92427. 120p. 1996. pap. 8.95 (*0-9648400-4-9*) Powersrce Pr.

Royce, Patrick M. Royce's Powerboating Illustrated: The Best of All Powerboating Worlds, Vol. 1. 6th ed. LC 94-207903. (Royce's Powerboating Training Ser.). (Illus.). 416p. 1994. pap. text 15.00 (*0-911284-02-8*) Royce Pubns.

— Royce's Powerboating Illustrated Workbook: 27 Basic Concepts. (Royce's Powerboating Training Ser.). (Illus.). 48p. 1994. pap. text, wbk. ed. 5.00 (*0-911284-03-6*) Royce Pubns.

— Royce's Sailing Illustrated: The Best of All Sailing Worlds, Modern & Traditional, 2 vols. LC 97-163565. (Sailing Illustrated Ser.: Vol. 2). (Illus.). 160p. 1997. pap. text 15.00 (*0-911284-07-9*) Royce Pubns.

— Royce's Sailing Illustrated: The Sailor's Bible since 1956, 2 vols. 9th rev. ed. LC 82-6925. (Sailing Illustrated Ser.: Vol. 1). (Illus.). 368p. 1998. pap. text 15.00 (*0-911284-08-7*) Royce Pubns.

— Royce's Sailing Illustrated Course: Provides Lectures That Can Be Read Word for Word, Vol. 1. (Sailing Illustrated Ser.). (Illus.). 100p. (Orig.). 1993. pap. text, teacher ed. 7.00 (*0-911284-01-X*) Royce Pubns.

— Royce's Sailing Illustrated Course Workbook: The Easiest Way to Learn the Complex Sailing Language. (Illus.). 52p. 1998. pap. text, wbk. ed. 5.00 (*0-911284-05-2*) Royce Pubns.

Royce, Peter M. & Steinmann, Beat, eds. Connective Tissue & Its Disorders: Molecular, Genetic, & Medical Aspects. LC 00-92. 724p. 1992. 465.00 (*0-471-58819-9*, Wiley-Liss) Wiley.

Royce, Robert. Managed Care: Practice & Progress. LC 96-29999. 1997. write for info. (*1-85775-280-5*, Radcliffe Med Pr) Scovill Paterson.

Royce, Samuel. Deterioration & Race Education with Practical Application to the Condition of the People & Industry. LC 72-180587. (Medicine & Society in America Ser.). 596p. 1972. reprint ed. 39.95 (*0-405-03967-0*) Ayer.

Royce, Sarah. A Frontier Lady: Recollections of the Gold Rush & Early California. Gabriel, Ralph H., ed. LC 76-44263. (Illus.). xvi, 144p. 1977. reprint ed. pap. 7.95 (*0-8032-5856-9*, Bison Books) U of Nebr Pr.

— Sarah Royce & the American West. Shuter, Jane, ed. & intro. by. (History Eyewitness Ser.). (Illus.). 48p. (J). (gr. 7-8). 1996. lib. bdg. 24.26 (*0-8114-8286-3*) Raintree Steck-V.

Royce, Sherry & Zook, Doris. Read English, Bk. 1. (Speak English Ser.). (Illus.). 80p. (Orig.). 1993. pap. text 7.95 (*0-8325-0504-8*, Natl Textbk Co) NTC Contemp Pub Co.

Royce, Sherry, jt. auth. see Hershberger, Jane.

Royce, Walker. Controlled Software Project Management. LC 98-20071. 448p. (C). 1998. 49.95 (*0-201-30958-0*) Peachpit Pr.

Royce, William, jt. auth. see Donaldson, Maureen.

Royce, William F. Fishery Development. 248p. 1987. text 52.00 (*0-12-600955-4*) Acad Pr.

Royce, William F., ed. Introduction to the Practice of Fishery Science. 2nd rev. ed. LC 95-12388. (Illus.). 448p. 1995. text 54.95 (*0-12-600952-X*) Acad Pr.

***Roychaudhuri, Bimalakanta.** Dictionary of Hindustani Classical Music. 2000. 24.00 (*81-208-1708-7*, Pub. by Motilal Bnarsidass) S Asia.

Roychaudhury, D. P. Advance Acoustics. 1985. 100.00 (*0-7855-0723-X*, Pub. by Current Dist) St Mut.

Roychoudhury, Anita. Teaching & Learning Science: Critical & Alternative Views. Kincheloe, Joe & Steinberg, Shirley R., eds. (Critical Education Practice Ser.). 300p. Date not set. text 45.00 (*0-8153-1726-3*); pap. text 18.95 (*0-8153-2327-1*) Garland.

Roychowdhury, R. & Bhattacharyya, B. Cost & Management Accountancy (M&T) (C). 1989. 80.00 (*0-89771-436-9*, Pub. by Current Dist) St Mut.

Roychowdhury, R., jt. auth. see Mukherji, M.

Roychowdhury, Vwani P., et al, eds. Theoretical Advances in Neural Computation & Learning. LC 94-34334. 496p. (C). 1994. text 169.00 (*0-7923-9478-X*) Kluwer Academic.

Roychowdhury, Vwani P., et al. Computational Paradigms for Nanoelectronics. 1998. 54.95 (*1-55860-340-9*) Morgan Kaufmann.

— Discrete Neural Computation: A Theoretical Foundation. (C). 1995. text 44.20 (*0-13-300708-1*) P-H.

Roycraft, Roland. Fill Your Watercolors with Light & Color. (Illus.). 144p. 1990. 28.99 (*0-89134-338-5*, 30221, North Lght Bks) F & W Pubns Inc.

Roycroft, A. John, ed. see Blandford, Hugh.

Roycroft, A. John, ed. see Kasparyan, Genrikh.

***Roycroft, Judith.** Confessional. (Black Lace Ser.). 1999. mass mkt. 6.95 (*0-352-33421-5*) BLA4.

Roycrofters Staff. Roycroft Furniture Catalog, 1906. LC 93-49373. Orig. Title: A Catalog of Roycrofters Furniture & Other Things. (Illus.). 64p. 1994. reprint ed. pap. 6.95 (*0-486-28113-2*) Dover.

Royden, H. L. Real Analysis. 3rd ed. 434p. (C). 1988. 90.67 (*0-02-404151-3*, Macmillan Coll) P-H.

Royden, Leigh H. & Horvath, Ferenc, eds. The Pannonian Basin: A Study in Basin Evolution. LC 88-21095. (AAPG Memoir Ser.: Vol. 45). (Illus.). 463p. 1988. reprint ed. pap. 143.60 (*0-608-07374-1*, 206760200001) Bks Demand.

— The Pannonian Basin Maps: A Study in Basin Evolution. LC 88-21095. (AAPG Memoir Ser.: Vol. 45). (Illus.). 81p. reprint ed. pap. 30.00 (*0-608-07375-X*, 206760200002) Bks Demand.

Roydhouse, Eric, jt. ed. see Davies, Andrew.

Roydhouse, Noel. Underwater Ear & Nose Care. rev. ed. (Illus.). 78p. (C). 1994. 14.95 (*0-941332-23-3*, D055) Best Pub Co.

Royds, Kathleen E. Coleridge & His Poetry. LC 76-120990. (Poetry & Life Ser.). reprint ed. 27.50 (*0-404-52532-6*) AMS Pr.

— Elizabeth Barrett Browning & Her Poetry. LC 73-148799. (Poetry & Life Ser.). reprint ed. 27.50 (*0-404-52531-8*) AMS Pr.

Roye, William. A Brief Dialogue Between a Christian Father & His Stubborn Son. Parker, Douglas & Krajewski, Bruce, eds. 312p. 1999. text 60.00 (*0-8020-4389-5*) U of Toronto Pr.

Roye, William, jt. auth. see Barlowe, Jerome.

Royeen, Charlotte B. A Research Primer for Occupational & Physical Therapy. 360p. (Orig.). (C). 1997. pap. text 55.00 (*1-56900-063-8*); lib. bdg. 60.00 (*1-56900-062-X*) Am Occup Therapy.

Royeen, Charlotte B., ed. AOTA Self Study Series: Neuroscience & Occupation: Links to Practice. 1997. pap. text 290.00 (*0-910317-82-8*) Am Occup Therapy.

Royeen, Charlotte B., jt. ed. see Crist, Patricia.

Royem, Robert T. An American Classic: The Durango & Silverton Narrow Gauge Railroad. (Illus.). 152p. 1995. 39.95 (*0-9643430-0-2*); pap. 24.95 (*0-9643430-1-0*) Limelight Pr.

An Asterisk (*) at the beginning of an entry indicates that the title is appearing for the first time.

Royen, Christoph. Osteuropa: Reformen & Wandel. 2nd ed. (GER.). 168p. 1990. pap. 23.00 (*3-7890-1948-8*, Pub. by Nomos Verlags) Intl Bk Import.

Royen, Rene A. Van, see Van Royen, Rene A.

Royer, Ariela. Life with Chronic Illness: Social & Psychological Dimensions. LC 98-11133. 232p. 1998. 55.00 (*0-275-96123-0*, Praeger Pubs) Greenwood.

Royer, Bud, jt. auth. see Royer, Karen.

Royer, Charles T., ed. Campaign for President: The Managers Look at 1992. 352p. 1994. pap. 19.95 (*1-884186-00-9*) Hollis Pub.

Royer-Collard, F. B. Skeleton Clocks. (Illus.). 165p. 1981. 49.50 (*0-7198-0110-9*, Pub. by NAG Press) Antique Collect.

***Royer, D. & Dieulesaint, E.** Elastic Waves in Solids I: Free & Guided Propagation. Morgan, D. P., tr. from FRE. LC 99-34758. (Illus.). 360p. 1999. 82.00 (*3-540-65932-3*) Spr-Verlag.

— Elastic Waves in Solids II: Generation, Acousto-Optic Interaction, Applications. Lyle, S., tr. from FRE. LC 99-34758. (Illus.). 460p. 1999. 89.95 (*3-540-65931-5*) Spr-Verlag.

Royer, D., jt. auth. see Dieulesaint, E.

Royer, Denise W. Summary Groundwater Resources of Lebanon County, Pennsylvania. (Water Resource Reports: No. 55). (Illus.). 84p. (Orig.). 1983. pap. 15.30 (*0-8182-0026-X*) Commonweal PA.

Royer, Denise W. & Socolow, Arthur A., prefs. Summary of Groundwater Resources of Perry County, Pennsylvania. (Water Resource Reports: No. 59). (Illus.). 70p. 1984. pap. 16.25 (*0-8182-0059-6*) Commonweal PA.

Royer, Diana, jt. ed. see Inness, Sherrie A.

Royer, Fanchon. The Life of St. Anthony Mary Claret. LC 85-52248. 302p. (Orig.). 1992. reprint ed. pap. 15.00 (*0-89555-288-4*) TAN Bks Pubs.

Royer, France & Dickinson, Richard. Weeds of Canada: And the Northern United States. (Illus.). 434p. 1999. pap. 21.95 (*0-88864-311-X*) Lone Pine.

Royer, France, jt. auth. see Dickinson, Richard.

Royer, G. P. Fundamentals of Enzymology: Rate Enhancement, Specificity, Control & Application. LC 81-11359. 242p. 1986. reprint ed. 36.95 (*0-471-04675-2*) Krieger.

Royer, Gary L. Models for Fulfilling Missions: Discovering Strategies for Passing on the Bread. 203p. 1997. pap. text 9.95 (*0-9656825-0-1*) G L Royer.

Royer, Gene. School Board Leadership, 2000. 200p. 1995. 21.95 (*0-9638758-9-2*) Brockton Pubng.

Royer, J. J., jt. auth. see Bardinet, Claude.

Royer, J. S. A Connotational Theory of Program Structure. (Lecture Notes in Computer Science Ser.: Vol. 273). v, 186p. 1987. 30.00 (*0-387-18253-5*) Spr-Verlag.

Royer, Jack P. & Convery, Frank J., eds. Nonindustrial Private Forests: Data & Information Needs: Conference Proceedings, April 17-18, 1980, Duke University, Durham, North Carolina. LC SD0143.N65. (Illus.). 136p. reprint ed. pap. 42.20 (*0-7837-6037-X*, 204585000008) Bks Demand.

Royer, Jack P. & Risbrudt, Christopher D., eds. Nonindustrial Private Forests: A Review of Economic & Policy Studies: Symposium Proceedings, April 19-20, 1983. LC SD0387.W6N66. (Illus.). 406p. reprint ed. pap. 125.90 (*0-8357-8252-2*, 203395800087) Bks Demand.

Royer, James S. & Case, John. Subrecursive Programming Systems: Complexity & Succinctness. LC 94-26443. (Progress in Theoretical Computer Science Ser.). viii, 252p. 1994. 54.50 (*0-8176-3767-2*) Birkhauser.

Royer, Jean. Interviews to Literature. Sloatet, Daniel, tr. from FRE. LC 94-72972. (Essay Ser.: No. 19). (Illus.). 196p. 1995. pap. 18.00 (*1-55071-008-7*) Guernica Editions.

— Quebec en Poesie. (Folio - Junior Ser). (FRE.). pap. 9.95 (*2-07-034059-7*) Schoenhof.

Royer, Jean M. Synthese Eurosiberienne, Phytosociologique et Phytogeographique de la Classe des Festuco-Brometea. (Dissertationes Botanicae Ser.: Band 178). (FRE., Illus.). vi, 296p. 1991. pap. 83.00 (*3-443-64090-7*, Pub. by Gebruder Borntraeger) Balogh.

Royer, Jeffrey P. Handbook of Software & Hardware: Interfacing for IBM PCs. (Illus.). 240p. 1987. pap. 30.95 (*0-13-381849-7*); text 33.00 (*0-317-44717-3*) P-H.

Royer, Jeffrey S. & Rogers, Richard T., eds. The Industrialization of Agriculture: Vertical Coordination in the U. S. Food System. 346p. 1998. text 72.95 (*1-84014-382-7*, Pub. by Ashgate Pub) Ashgate Pub Co.

Royer, Jessica, ed. see Ocken, Kathleen Ann Duesel.

Royer, Karen & Hons, Tami. Random Thoughts: To Help You Get a Life! Hons, Frank, ed. & photos by by. (Illus.). 70p. 1998. pap. 7.95 (*1-57502-959-6*, PO2631) Morris Pubng.

Royer, Karen & Royer, Bud. Royers' Round Top Cafe: A Rural Odessey. LC 95-61736. 176p. text. write for info. (*0-9647729-0-6*) Royers Domain.

Royer, Kenneth. Retailing Flowers Profitability. (Illus.). 480p. 1998. 29.95 (*0-9664598-0-6*) Royer Pub.

Royer, King. Desk Book for Construction Superintendents. 2nd ed. (Illus.). 1980. text 27.50 (*0-685-03826-2*) P-H.

Royer, M., et al. Preparation of Strontium Iodate Monohydrate. Neidig, H. Anthony, ed. (Modular Laboratory Program in Chemistry Ser.). 12p. (C). 1988. pap. text 1.50 (*0-87540-347-6*, SYNT 347-6) Chem Educ Res.

— Synthesis of Strontium Iodate Monohydrate. Neidig, H. Anthony, ed. (Modular Laboratory Program in Chemistry Ser.). 12p. (C). 1987. pap. text 1.50 (*0-87540-341-7*, SYNT 341-7) Chem Educ Res.

Royer, Marc. Happiness in 30 Days or Less. 94p. 1998. pap. 7.95 (*1-57502-816-6*, PO2244) Morris Pubng.

***Royer, Marc.** Hell No! 180p. 1999. pap. write for info. (*0-7392-0408-4*, PO3654) Morris Pubng.

Royer, Marc. Practical Patience. 99p. 1999. pap. 8.95 (*0-7392-0083-6*, P02950) Morris Pubng.

— Rejection: Turning Your Lemons into Lemonade. 192p. 1997. pap. 8.95 (*1-57502-618-X*, P01771) Morris Pubng.

Royer, Marie. Camping Cuisine: The Ultimate Cookbook for the Avid Camper. large type ed. LC 94-79775. 164p. 1994. pap. text 13.95 (*0-9644266-0-9*) Mossy Crk OR.

Royer, Marie Hamel. The Saxon Story. (History Ser.: Vol. 2). (Illus.). xiv, 340p. 1982. pap. 13.95 (*0-939576-04-X*) Whatcom County Historical Society.

Royer, P., et al. Nephrologie Pediatrique. 3rd ed. (Collection Pediatrie Ser.). (FRE., Illus.). 652p. 1983. lib. bdg. 75.00 (*2-257-12397-2*) S M P F Inc.

Royer, Ronald A. Butterflies of North Dakota: An Atlas & Guide. (Illus.). 192p. (Orig.). (C). 1988. pap. text 14.95 (*0-9619635-0-6*) Minot St U.

Royer, Rosanne G., et al. PR Prototypes: A Guidebook for Promoting Foreign Language Study to the Public. LC 81-15482. (Language in Education Ser.). vii, 98p. 1981. write for info. (*0-87281-161-1*) Ctr Appl Ling.

Royer, Victor. Casino (tm) Magazine's Play Smart & Win: How to Beat Most Popular Casino Games. 272p. 1994. per. 12.00 (*0-671-88024-1*, Fireside) S&S Trade Pap.

Royer, Victor H. Casino Games Made Easy: Newest Games & Most up to Date Strategies. (Illus.). 320p. 1999. pap. 12.95 (*1-891337-06-8*, Pub. by Premier Pub NV) ACCESS Pubs Network.

Royer, Warren. Memories of the Heart: Rural Schools of Illinois. LC 96-79694. (Illus.). 224p. 2000. pap. 17.95 (*1-878044-17-6*) Mayhaven Pub.

Royes, Heather. The Caribbean Raj. LC 97-212154. 57p. 1997. 20.00 (*976-8100-86-9*, Pub. by Ian Randle) Paul & Co Pubs.

Royet-Journoud, Claude. A Descriptive Method. Waldrop, Keith, tr. from FRE. 30p. (Orig.). 1995. pap. 7.00 (*0-942996-23-2*) Post Apollo Pr.

— I.E. Serie D'Ecriture Supplement No 1. Waldrop, Keith, tr. from FRE. (Serie d'Ecriture Supplement: No. 1). 30p. (Orig.). 1995. pap. 5.00 (*1-886224-08-0*) Burning Deck.

Royidis, Emmanuel, tr. & adapted by see Durrell, Lawrence.

Royka, Paul. Mission Furniture: From the American Arts & Crafts Movement. LC 97-80044. (Illus.). 256p. 1997. 69.95 (*0-88740-987-3*) Schiffer.

Royka, Paul A. Fireworks: New England Art Pottery of the Arts & Crafts Movement. LC 97-24474. (Schiffer Book for Collectors Ser.). (Illus.). 192p. 1997. 69.95 (*0-88740-988-1*) Schiffer.

***Royko, David.** Voices of Children of Divrce: Their Own Words on Feeling Caught in the Middle, Visitation & Keeping Commitments, Mon & Dat & Dating & Sex, Remarriage & Stepfamilies, Their Own Future Marriages. 224p. 2000. pap. 12.95 (*0-312-25469-5*) St Martin.

Royko, Mike. Boss: Richard J. Daley of Chicago. 1988. pap. 12.95 (*0-452-26167-8*, Plume) Dutton Plume.

— One More Time. LC 98-46699. (Illus.). 295p. 1999. 22.00 (*0-226-73071-9*) U Ch Pr.

***Royko, Mike.** One More Time: The Best of Mike Royko. LC 98-46699. (Illus.). 304p. 1999. pap. 12.00 (*0-226-73072-7*) U Ch Pr.

— Second Time Around. 1999. 22.00 (*0-226-73073-5*) U Ch Pr.

Roylance, Dale. European Graphic Arts: The Art of the Book from Guttenberg to Picasso. (Illus.). 199p. 1986. pap. 10.00 (*0-87811-030-5*) Princeton Lib.

Roylance, Dale & Finlay, Nancy, compiled by. Pride of Place: Early American Views from the Collection of Leonard L. Milberg '53. (Illus.). 66p. 1983. pap. 10.00 (*0-87811-029-1*) Princeton Lib.

Roylance, David. Mechanics of Materials. LC 95-43057. 336p. 1995. text 102.95 (*0-471-59399-0*, Wiley-Interscience) Wiley.

Roylance, Susan, ed. see Ellsworth, Sterling G.

Roylance, Susan, ed. see Jones, Gracia N.

Roylance, William H. Complete Book of Insults, Boasts & Riddles. (C). 1971. pap. text 10.95 (*0-13-157479-5*, Reward) P-H.

Royle. Chartism. 2nd ed. 1995. pap. text 15.20 (*0-582-35569-9*) Addison-Wesley.

Royle. Regional Identity. LC 98-2900. 252p. 2000. text 79.95 (*0-7190-5028-6*, Pub. by Manchester Univ Pr) St Martin.

Royle, A., jt. auth. see Unett, E.

Royle, A. G., tr. see Gy, Pierre.

Royle, Derek, jt. auth. see Cooper, Emanuel.

Royle, Duncan, jt. auth. see Hares, John.

Royle, Edward. Chartism SSH Series. 3rd ed. LC 96-7738. (Seminar Studies in History). (C). 1996. pap. text 13.00 (*0-582-29080-5*) Addison-Wesley.

— Modern Britain: A Social History, 1750-1985. 400p. (C). 1995. pap. text 25.00 (*0-7131-6477-8*, Pub. by E A) St Martin.

— Modern Britain: A Social History, 1750-1997. 2nd ed. 496p. 1997. pap. text 24.95 (*0-340-57944-7*) OUP.

— Robert Owen & the Commencement of the Millennium: The Harmony Community at Queenwood Farm, Hampshire, 1839-1845. 256p. 1998. text 79.95 (*0-7190-5426-5*, Pub. by Manchester Univ Pr) St Martin.

Royle, Edward & Walvin, James. English Radicals & Reformers, 1760-1848. fac. ed. LC 82-40179. 233p. 1982. pap. 72.30 (*0-7837-7599-7*, 204735200007) Bks Demand.

Royle, Edwin M. The Squaw Man: A Comedy Drama in Four Acts. (BCL1-PS American Literature Ser.). 90p. 1992. reprint ed. lib. bdg. 59.00 (*0-7812-6847-8*) Rprt Serv.

Royle, Edwin M. & Faversham, Julie O. The Squaw Man: A Comedy Drama in Four Acts. LC 77-104559. 294p. (C). 1988. reprint ed. pap. text 7.95 (*0-8290-2142-6*); reprint ed. lib. bdg. 31.00 (*0-8398-1769-X*) Irvington.

Royle, Howard A. Evolution - Evolution Vol. II: Sound Bites & Insights. LC 97-68238. 160p. 1997. pap. 6.50 (*0-9649118-1-7*) Canyn Pubng.

***Royle, Howard A.** Future - Future Vol. 3: Sound Bites & Insights. LC 99-74817. 160p. 1999. pap. 6.50 (*0-9649118-2-5*, Pub. by Canyn Pubng) Partners Pubs Grp.

Royle, Howard A. Science - Science: Sound Bites & Insights. 160p. (Orig.). 1996. pap. 6.50 (*0-9649118-0-9*) Canyn Pubng.

Royle, J. F. Fibrous Plants of India. (C). 1988. 120.00 (*0-7855-3307-9*, Pub. by Scientific) St Mut.

— Illustrations of Botany & of the Himalayan Mountains & Flora of Cashmere - 1883, 2 vols., II:plates. lxxviii, 468p. 1970. reprint ed. write for info. (*0-318-55692-8*) Scholarly Pubns.

— Illustrations of Botany & of the Himalayan Mountains & Flora of Cashmere - 1883, 2 vols., Vol. I: Text. lxxviii, 468p. 1970. reprint ed. 120.00 (*0-88065-183-0*) Scholarly Pubns.

Royle, Jo. Boxers Today. (Book of the Breed). (Illus.). 176p. 1994. 24.95 (*0-948955-08-2*, Pub. by Ringpr Bks) Seven Hills Bk.

Royle, Kent & Terry, Cliff. Hawaiian Design: Strategies for Energy Efficient Architecture. (Illus.). 59p. (Orig.). (C). 1993. pap. text 20.00 (*0-7881-0120-X*) DIANE Pub.

Royle, Lee, ed. see Pratt, Douglas R.

Royle, Nicholas. After Derrida. LC 94-5404. 176p. 1995. text 19.95 (*0-7190-4379-4*, Pub. by Manchester Univ Pr) St Martin.

— A Book of Two Halves. 288p. 1997. pap. text 11.95 (*0-575-40097-8*) V Gollancz.

***Royle, Nicholas.** E. M. Forster. (Writers & Their Works Ser.). 112p. 1999. pap. text 19.00 (*0-7463-0841-8*, Pub. by Northcote House) U Pr of Miss.

Royle, Nicholas, jt. auth. see Bennett, Andrew.

Royle, Richard. Briefcase on Land Law. (Cavendish Briefcase Ser.). 228p. 1995. pap. 20.00 (*1-85941-248-3*, Pub. by Cavendish Pubng) Gaunt.

Royle, Roger & Woods, Gary. Mother Teresa: A Life of Pictures. LC 92-52654. 160p. (Orig.). 1995. pap. 14.95 (*0-89870-584-3*) Ignatius Pr.

Royle, Stephen, jt. ed. see Boal, Frederick W.

Royle, Susan G. Carry on Osteopathy. 1992. 14.95 (*0-533-10176-X*) Vantage.

Royle, T. Mainstream Companion of Scottish Literature. text 29.95 (*1-85158-583-4*, Pub. by Mainstream Pubng) Trafalgar.

Royle, Trevor. The Best Years of Their Lives: The National Service Experience, 1945-1963. (Illus.). 304p. 1998. pap. 27.50 (*0-7195-5688-0*, Pub. by John Murray) Trafalgar.

***Royle, Trevor.** Crimea: The Great Crimean War 1854-1856. (Illus.). 564p. 2000. text 35.00 (*0-312-23079-6*) St Martin.

— Crimea: The Great Crimean War, 1854-1856. 512p. 2001. 5.95 (*0-316-64849-3*, Pub. by Little) Time Warner.

Royle, Trevor. The Last Days of the Raj. (Illus.). 304p. 1998. pap. 22.95 (*0-7195-5686-4*, Pub. by John Murray) Trafalgar.

— Winds of Change: The End of Empire in Africa. LC 97-122530. (Illus.). 288p. 1998. 40.00 (*0-7195-5352-0*, Pub. by John Murray) Trafalgar.

Royle, Trevor, ed. In Flanders Fields: Scottish Poetry & Prose of the First World War. 272p. 1992. pap. 22.95 (*1-85158-303-3*, Pub. by Mainstream Pubng) Trafalgar.

Royle, Trevor, ed. see Kipling, Rudyard.

Royle, Trevor, ed. see Stevenson, Robert Louis.

Roymans, N., ed. From the Sword to the Plough: Three Studies on the Earliest Romanisation of Northern Gaul. 260p. (C). 1997. text 54.50 (*90-5356-237-0*, 56237, Pub. by Amsterdam U Pr) U of Mich Pr.

Roymans, N., jt. ed. see Theuws, F.

***Royo, Luis.** Dreams. Manning, Anabel, tr. from SPA. (Illus.). 80p. 1999. pap. 18.95 (*1-56163-241-4*) NBM.

Royo, Luis. Malefic. (Illus.). 80p. 1997. pap. 18.95 (*1-56163-181-7*) NBM.

***Royo, Luis.** Prohibited. 1999. 12.95 (*1-882931-51-3*) Heavy Metal Magazine.

Royo, Luis. Secrets. (Illus.). 80p. 1996. pap. 18.95 (*1-56163-162-0*) NBM.

— III Millennium. Mojica, Yvonne, tr. from SPA. LC 99-169508. (Illus.). 80p. 1998. pap. 18.95 (*1-56163-204-X*) NBM.

— Women. (Illus.). 80p. 1997. pap. 18.95 (*1-56163-171-X*) NBM.

***Royo, Sebastin.** Social Democracy to Neoliberalism: The Consequences of Part. LC 99-41530. 2000. text 55.00 (*0-312-22390-0*) St Martin.

Roys, Deloris T. & Roys, Pat. Protocol for Phallometric Assessment: A Clinician's Guide. Bear, Euan, ed. 78p. (Orig.). 1999. pap., student ed. 10.00 (*1-884444-11-3*) Safer Soc.

Roys, Pat, jt. auth. see Roys, Deloris T.

Roys, R. L., et al. Contributions to American Anthropology & History: The Indians of Cozumel, Personal Names of the Maya of Yucatan & Maize Cultivation in Guatemala. (Yucatan Ser.). 1979. lib. bdg. 69.95 (*0-8490-2903-1*) Gordon Pr.

Roys, Ralph L. The Ethno-Botany of the Maya (with a New Introduction & Supplement Bibliography by Sheila Cosminsky) LC 76-29024. (ISHI Reprints on Latin America & the Caribbean Ser.). 414p. reprint ed. pap. 128.40 (*0-608-15019-3*, 202571000046) Bks Demand.

— The Titles of Ebtun. LC 76-44711. (Carnegie Institution of Washington. Publications: No. 505). (Illus.). 512p. reprint ed. 110.00 (*0-404-15918-4*) AMS Pr.

Roysdon, Christine & White, Howard D., eds. Expert Systems in Reference Services. LC 88-39835. (Reference Librarian Ser.: No. 23). (Illus.). 238p. 1989. text 49.95 (*0-86656-839-5*) Haworth Pr.

Royse. An Introduction to Data Analysis for Social Workers. (C). 1999. pap. text 53.33 (*0-205-28903-7*, Longwood Div) Allyn.

Royse, David. How Do I Know It's Abuse? Identifying & Countering Emotional Mistreatment from Friends & Family Members. LC 94-11495. 248p. (C). 1994. pap. 37.95 (*0-398-06350-8*); text 54.95 (*0-398-05921-7*) C C Thomas.

***Royse, David.** Research Methods in Social Work. 3rd ed. LC 98-44273. (Nelson-Hall Series in Social Work). 400p. 1999. pap. 51.95 (*0-8304-1533-5*) Thomson Learn.

Royse, David & Thyer, Bruce A. Program Evaluation: An Introduction. 2nd ed. 230p. 1996. pap. text 49.95 (*0-8304-1415-0*) Thomson Learn.

***Royse, David D.** Program Evaluation: An Introduction. 3rd ed. LC 00-33740. 2000. write for info. (*0-8304-1536-X*) Burnham Inc.

— Teaching Tips for College & University Instructors: A Practical Guide. LC 00-38976. (Illus.). 2001. pap. write for info. (*0-205-29839-7*) Allyn.

***Royse, David D., et al.** Field Instruction: A Guide for Social Work Students. 3rd ed. LC 98-9686. (Illus.). 145p. (C). 1998. pap. text 38.00 (*0-8013-3044-0*) Allyn.

Royse, James R. The Spurious Texts of Philo of Alexandria: A Study of Textual Transmission & Corruption with Indexes to the Major Collections of Greek Fragments. (Arbeiten zur Literatur und Geschichte des Hellenistischen Judentums Ser.: No. 22). xiii, 252p. 1991. 97.00 (*90-04-09511-X*) Brill Academic Pubs.

***Royse, Lariann.** Innocence Into Autumn. 1999. write for info. (*1-58235-520-7*) Watermrk Pr.

Royster. Ida B. Wells. 228p. 1996. pap. text 11.95 (*0-312-11695-0*) St Martin.

— Writing & the Public Good: A Casebook. (C). 1999. text. write for info. (*0-321-01586-X*) Addison-Wesley Educ.

***Royster Beito, Linda.** Leadership Effectiveness in Community Policing. LC 99-67018. 1999. pap. 6.00 (*1-55605-290-1*) Wyndham Hall.

Royster, Charles. The Destructive War: William Tecumseh Sherman, Stonewall Jackson, & the Americans. LC 92-56370. 531p. 1993. pap. 17.00 (*0-679-73878-9*) Vin Bks.

— The Fabulous History of the Dismal Swamp Company: A Story of George Washington's Times. LC 98-42773. 1999. 35.00 (*0-679-43345-7*) Knopf.

— Light-Horse Harry Lee & the Legacy of the American Revolution. LC 82-9620. (Illus.). 336p. 1994. pap. 16.95 (*0-8071-1910-5*) La State U Pr.

— A Revolutionary People at War: The Continental Army & American Character, 1775-1783. 463p. (C). 1996. pap. 22.50 (*0-8078-4606-6*) U of NC Pr.

Royster, Charles, ed. see Barnes, Ian.

Royster, Charles, ed. see Sherman, William T.

Royster, Dmitri. The Kingdom of God: The Sermon on the Mount. LC 92-29952. 128p. 1993. pap. 8.95 (*0-88141-116-7*) St Vladimirs.

— The Miracles of Christ. LC 98-56027. 1999. write for info. (*0-88141-193-0*) St Vladimirs.

— The Parables: Biblical, Patristic & Liturgical Interpretation. LC 96-36367. 1996. 8.95 (*0-88141-067-5*) St Vladimirs.

Royster, Glenn. The Slave Master's Religion: Breaking the Last Bonds of Slavery. 152p. 1993. pap. 7.00 (*0-9638214-4-X*) Kabila Communs.

***Royster, Jacqueline Jones.** Traces of a Stream: Literacy & Social Change among African-American Women. LC 99-50942. 2000. 45.00 (*0-8229-4122-8*) U of Pittsburgh Pr.

— Traces of a Stream: Literacy & Social Change among African-American Women. LC 99-50942. (Illus.). 352p. 2000. pap. 19.95 (*0-8229-5725-6*) U of Pittsburgh Pr.

Royster, John, jt. ed. see Simpson, Allan.

Royster, Julia D. & Royster, Larry H. Hearing Conservation Programs: Practical Guidelines for Success. (Illus.). 136p. 1990. lib. bdg. 85.00 (*0-87371-307-9*, L307) Lewis Pubs.

Royster, Larry H., jt. auth. see Royster, Julia D.

Royster, Philip M. Songs & Dances: Selected Poems. LC 80-85233. 61p. (YA). (gr. 9-12). 1981. per. 5.00 (*0-916418-28-6*) Lotus.

Royster, Salibelle. Bleak House Notes. (Cliffs Notes Ser.). 96p. 1966. pap. 4.95 (*0-8220-0247-7*, Cliff) IDG Bks.

— Main Street Notes. (Cliffs Notes Ser.). 64p. 1965. pap. 4.95 (*0-8220-0798-3*, Cliff) IDG Bks.

— Much Ado about Nothing Notes. (Cliffs Notes Ser.). 56p. 1963. pap. 4.95 (*0-8220-0060-1*, Cliff) IDG Bks.

Royston. Baby Animals Eye Openers. (J). 1998. 7.95 (*0-87628-160-9*) Ctr Appl Res.

— Dinosaurs Eye Openers. (J). 1998. pap. 7.95 (*0-87628-162-5*) Ctr Appl Res.

— Jungle Animals Eye Openers. (J). 1998. 8.99 (*0-87628-471-3*) S&S Trade.

Royston, Angela. The A to Z Book of Cars. (Illus.). 32p. 1995. pap. text 5.95 (*0-8120-9267-8*) Barron.

Royston, Angela. A-to-Z Book of Cars. LC 90-19496. 1991. 11.15 (*0-606-08964-0*, Pub. by Turtleback) Demco.

— Alcohol. LC 99-88167. (Learn to Say No! Ser.). 2000. lib. bdg. write for info. (*1-57572-236-4*) Heinemann Lib.

— Bean. LC 97-39693. (J). (ps-4). 1998. 19.92 (*1-57572-612-2*) Heinemann Lib.

Royston, Angela. Birth & Reproduction. LC 96-27553. (Body Systems Ser.). (J). 1998. (*1-57572-099-X*) Heinemann Lib.

— Boats & Ships. LC 97-19339. (Inside & Out Ser.). (Illus.). 24p. (J). 1998. write for info. (*1-57572-170-8*) Heinemann Lib.

***Royston, Angela.** Butterfly. LC 98-10572. (J). 1998. 19.92 (*1-57572-697-1*) Heinemann Lib.

R

Royston, Angela. Cars. LC 91-16122. (Eye Openers Ser.). (Illus.). 24p. (J). (ps-k). 1991. mass mkt. 7.95 (*0-689-71517-X*) Aladdin.
— Cars. LC 97-29181. (Inside And Out). (Illus.). 24p. (J). 1998. write for info. (*1-57572-171-6*) Heinemann Lib.
***Royston, Angela.** Cities. LC 97-30493. (Inside & Out Ser.). (Illus.). 24p. (J). 1998. 19.92 (*1-57572-172-4*) Heinemann Lib.
— Clean & Healthy. LC 99-14555. 1999. write for info. (*1-57572-981-4*) Heinemann Lib.
Royston, Angela. Diggers & Dump Trucks. LC 91-16119. (Eye Openers Ser.). (Illus.). 24p. (J). (ps-k). 1991. 8.99 (*0-689-71516-1*) Aladdin.
— Dinosaurs. LC 91-16121. (Eye Openers Ser.). (Illus.). 24p. (J). (ps-k). 1991. mass mkt. 7.95 (*0-689-71518-8*) Aladdin.
— The Earth. LC 97-19334. (Inside & Out Ser.). (Illus.). 24p. (J). 1998. write for info. (*1-57572-179-1*) Heinemann Lib.
***Royston, Angela.** Eat Well. LC 99-14553. (Illus.). 32p. (J). (gr. k-2). 1999. lib. bdg. 13.95 (*1-57572-982-2*) Heinemann Lib.
Royston, Angela. Eating & Digestion. LC 96-27554. (Body Systems Ser.). (J). 1998. (*1-57572-098-1*) Heinemann Lib.
— Emergency Rescue. LC 97-16132. (Illus.). 24p. (J). 1998. write for info. (*1-57572-173-2*) Heinemann Lib.
— Fire Fighter! LC 97-36342. (Eyewitness Readers). 32p. (J). (gr. 1-3). 1998. pap. 3.95 (*0-7894-2960-8*) DK Pub Inc.
Royston, Angela. Fire Fighters. (Eyewitness Readers). 0032p. (J). (gr. 1-3). 12.95 (*0-7894-4255-8*) DK Pub Inc.
— A First Atlas. LC 94-27714. (First Encyclopedia Ser.). (Illus.). 96p. (J). (ps-3). 2000. pap. 7.95 (*0-590-47528-2*) Scholastic Inc.
Royston, Angela. Flying Machines. LC 97-19350. (Inside & Out Ser.). (Illus.). 24p. (J). 1998. write for info. (*1-57572-175-9*) Heinemann Lib.
***Royston, Angela.** Frog. LC 97-39692. (Illus.). 32p. (J). (ps-4). 1998. 19.92 (*1-57572-613-0*) Heinemann Lib.
— A Healthy Body. LC 99-14554. (Illus.). 32p. (J). (gr. k-2). 1999. lib. bdg. 13.95 (*1-57572-983-0*) Heinemann Lib.
Royston, Angela. Healthy Me. (Illus.). 24p. (J). (ps-3). 1995. 13.95 (*0-8120-6423-2*) Barron.
— Horses & Ponies. LC 97-19348. (In the Wild Ser.). (Illus.). 24p. (J). 1998. write for info. (*1-57572-176-7*) Heinemann Lib.
— How Plants Grow. LC 98-45519. (Plants Ser.). (Illus.). 32p. (J). (gr. k-3). 1999. lib. bdg. 13.95 (*1-57572-824-9*) Heinemann Lib.
***Royston, Angela.** Inhalents. LC 99-88154. (Learn to Say No! Ser.). (Illus.). (J). 2000. lib. bdg. write for info. (*1-57572-237-2*) Heinemann Lib.
Royston, Angela. Insects & Crawly Creatures. LC 92-12356. (Illus.). 24p. (J). (ps-k). 1992. 8.99 (*0-689-71645-1*) Litle Simon.
— Jungle Animals. LC 91-16120. (Illus.). 24p. (J). (ps-k). 1991. 8.99 (*0-689-71519-6*) Litle Simon.
— Kangaroo. LC 97-39696. (Illus.). 32p. (J). (gr. 1-3). 1998. 13.95 (*1-57572-615-7*) Heinemann Lib.
***Royston, Angela.** Levers. LC 00-35002. (Machines in Action Ser.). (Illus.). (J). 2000. lib. bdg. write for info. (*1-57572-319-0*) Heinemann Lib.
— Life Cycle of a Chicken. LC 98-10754. (J). 1998. 19.92 (*1-57572-698-X*) Heinemann Lib.
— Life Cycle of a Dog. LC 99-46854. 2000. lib. bdg. write for info. (*1-57572-209-7*) Heinemann Lib.
— Life Cycle of a Mushroom. LC 99-46105. 2000. lib. bdg. write for info. (*1-57572-210-0*) Heinemann Lib.
— Life Cycle of a Salmon. LC 99-46104. 2000. lib. bdg. write for info. (*1-57572-212-7*) Heinemann Lib.
— Life Cycle of an Oak Tree. LC 99-46855. 2000. lib. bdg. write for info. (*1-57572-211-9*) Heinemann Lib.
Royston, Angela. Mammals, 11 vols. LC 94-27458. (Science Nature Guides Ser.). (Illus.). 80p. (J). (gr. 1-8). 1995. 12.95 (*1-57145-016-5*, Silver Dolph) Advantage Pubs.
— Maps & Symbols. LC 97-46959. (Geography Starts Here Ser.). (J). 1998. write for info. (*0-8172-5113-8*) Raintree Steck-V.
— Maps & Symbols. LC 97-46959. (Geography Starts Here Ser.). 1998. write for info. (*0-7502-1987-4*) Raintree Steck-V.
***Royston, Angela.** Marijuana. LC 99-88168. (Learn to Say No! Ser.). (Illus.). (J). 2000. lib. bdg. write for info. (*1-57572-238-0*) Heinemann Lib.
— Mighty Machines. LC 00-25792. 2000. pap. 10.95 (*0-7534-5315-0*, Kingfisher) LKC.
Royston, Angela. Pets. LC 97-19349. (Inside & Out Ser.). (Illus.). 24p. (J). 1998. write for info. (*1-57572-177-5*) Heinemann Lib.
— Plants & Us. LC 98-42810. (Plants Ser.). 32p. (J). 1999. lib. bdg. write for info. (*1-57572-825-7*) Heinemann Lib.
***Royston, Angela.** Pulleys & Gears. LC 00-29593. (Machines in Action Ser.). (Illus.). 2000. lib. bdg. write for info. (*1-57572-320-4*) Heinemann Lib.
— Ramps & Wedges. LC 00-29594. (Machines in Action Ser.). (Illus.). 2000. lib. bdg. write for info. (*1-57572-321-2*) Heinemann Lib.
Royston, Angela. Recycling. LC 98-17741. (Environment Starts Here Ser.). (J). 1999. 22.83 (*0-8172-5353-X*) Raintree Steck-V.
***Royston, Angela.** Safety First. LC 99-14559. (Illus.). 2000. write for info. (*1-57572-984-9*) Heinemann Lib.
— Screws. LC 00-29592. (Machines in Action Ser.). (Illus.). 2000. lib. bdg. write for info. (*1-57572-322-0*) Heinemann Lib.
— Space Station: Accident on Mir. (Eyewitness Readers). 48p. (gr. 2-4). 2000. 12.95 (*0-7894-6685-6*, D K Ink) DK Pub Inc.
— Space Station: Accident on Mir. (Dorling Kindersley Readers). (Illus.). 48p. (gr. 2-4). 2000. pap. 3.95 (*0-7894-6686-4*, D K Ink) DK Pub Inc.
— Springs. LC 00-35023. (Machines in Action Ser.). (Illus.). (J). 2000. lib. bdg. write for info. (*1-57572-323-9*) Heinemann Lib.
Royston, Angela. Stars & Planets. LC 97-42625. (Inside & Out Ser.). (Illus.). 24p. (J). 1998. write for info. (*1-57572-182-1*) Heinemann Lib.
***Royston, Angela.** Strange Plants. LC 98-44518. (Illus.). 32p. (J). (gr. k-3). 1999. lib. bdg. 13.95 (*1-57572-829-X*) Heinemann Lib.
Royston, Angela. Sunflower. LC 98-10733. (Illus.). 32p. (J). 1998. write for info. (*1-57572-699-8*) Heinemann Lib.
— Thinking & Feeling. LC 96-29403. (Body Systems Ser.). (J). 1998. 21.36 (*1-57572-095-7*) Heinemann Lib.
***Royston, Angela.** Tobacco. LC 99-88145. (Learn to Say No! Ser.). (Illus.). (J). 2000. write for info. (*1-57572-239-9*) Heinemann Lib.
Royston, Angela. Tractors. LC 97-41189. (Inside & Out Ser.). (Illus.). 24p. (J). 1998. write for info. (*1-57572-180-5*) Heinemann Lib.
— Trains: Eye Openers. Aladdin, ed. LC 92-12351. (Eye Openers Ser.). (Illus.). 24p. (J). (ps-k). 1992. mass mkt. 8.99 (*0-689-71647-8*) Aladdin.
— Transportation. LC 98-18253. (Environment Starts Here Ser.). 32 p. (J). 1999. 22.83 (*0-8172-5352-1*) Raintree Steck-V.
Royston, Angela. Truck Trouble. (Eyewitness Readers). 32p. (J). (ps-1). 12.95 (*0-7894-4254-X*) DK Pub Inc.
Royston, Angela. Truck Trouble. (Eyewitness Readers). 32p. (J). (ps-1). 1998. pap. 3.95 (*0-7894-2958-6*) DK Pub Inc.
— Trucks. LC 97-19337. (Inside & Out Ser.). (Illus.). 24p. (J). 1998. write for info. (*1-57572-181-3*) Heinemann Lib.
***Royston, Angela.** Under the Sea. LC 97-19333. (Inside & Out Ser.). (Illus.). 24p. (J). 1998. 19.92 (*1-57572-178-3*) Heinemann Lib.
— Volcanoes. (On the Spot Ser.). 16p. (gr. 4-6). 2000. 7.99 (*1-57584-319-6*) Rdrs Digest.
Royston, Angela. Weather Around You. LC 97-17987. (Geography Starts Here Ser.). 1998. 22.83 (*0-8172-5115-4*) Raintree Steck-V.
***Royston, Angela.** Wheels & Cranks. LC 00-35024. (Machines in Action Ser.). (Illus.). (J). 2000. lib. bdg. write for info. (*1-57572-324-7*) Heinemann Lib.
Royston, Angela. Where Do Babies Come From? (J). 1996. 9.95 (*0-7894-0579-2*) DK Pub Inc.
— Where People Live. LC 97-29909. (Geography Starts Here Ser.). (J). 1998. 22.83 (*0-8172-5116-2*) Raintree Steck-V.
— You & Your Body. LC 94-16304. (One Hundred One Questions & Answers Ser.). (Illus.). 48p. (J). (gr. 4-9). 1994. 11.95 (*0-8160-3217-3*) Facts on File.
Royston, Angela, ed. Birds, 11 vols. LC 93-48675. (Science Nature Guides Ser.). (Illus.). 80p. (J). (gr. 3-6). 1994. 12.95 (*1-85028-261-7*, Thunder Bay) Advantage Pubs.
***Royston, Angela, narrated by.** Guinea Pig. LC 97-39689. (Illus.). 32p. (J). (gr. 1-3). 1998. 19.92 (*1-57572-614-9*) Heinemann Lib.
***Royston, Angela, et al.** On the Spot Discovery Books (Package-Slipcase) (Illus.). 48p. (J). (gr. 1-2). 2000. write for info. (*1-57584-703-5*, Pub. by Rdrs Digest) S&S Trade.
Royston, Angela, jt. auth. see Hardie, Jackie.
Royston, Angela, jt. auth. see Hook, Sue.
Royston, Angela, jt. auth. see Reader's Digest Editors.
Royston, Angela, ed. see Forey, Pam.
Royston, Angela, tr. see Lazier, Christine.
Royston, David. Hemostasis in Anesthesia. 300p. 2001. pap. 75.00 (*0-7506-9580-3*) Buttrwrth-Heinemann.
Royston, E. & Armstrong, S. Preventing Maternal Deaths. 233p. 1989. 40.00 (*92-4-156128-9*) World Health.
Royston, E., jt. compiled by see AbouZahr, C.
Royston, Mike. Finding a Voice: Study Techniques for A-Level English. (Illus.). 224p. (YA). (gr. 11 up). 1998. pap. 35.00 (*0-7487-3373-6*, Pub. by S Thornes Pubs) Trans-Atl Phila.
Royston, Mike, ed. Short Stories by Charles Dickens. (Thornes Classic Short Stories Ser.). (Illus.). 90p. (Orig.). 1997. pap. 10.95 (*0-7487-3095-8*, Pub. by S Thornes Pubs) Trans-Atl Phila.
— Short Stories by Edgar Allen Poe. (Thornes Classic Short Stories Ser.). (Orig.). 1997. pap. 10.95 (*0-7487-3096-6*, Pub. by S Thornes Pubs) Trans-Atl Phila.
— Short Stories by Guy de Maupassant. (Thornes Classic Short Stories Ser.). (Illus.). 92p. 1995. pap. 10.95 (*0-7487-2240-8*, Pub. by S Thornes Pubs) Trans-Atl Phila.
— Short Stories by H. G. Wells. (Thornes Classic Short Stories Ser.). (Orig.). 1997. pap. 10.95 (*0-7487-3132-6*, Pub. by S Thornes Pubs) Trans-Atl Phila.
— Short Stories by Kate Chopin, Elizabeth Gaskell & Olive Schreiner. (Thornes Classic Short Stories Ser.). (Illus.). 112p. (YA). (gr. 6-11). 1998. pap. 17.95 (*0-7487-3356-6*, Pub. by S Thornes Pubs) Trans-Atl Phila.
— Short Stories by Katherine Mansfield. (Thornes Classic Short Stories Ser.). (Illus.). 91p. 1995. pap. 10.95 (*0-7487-2199-1*, Pub. by S Thornes Pubs) Trans-Atl Phila.
— Short Stories by Oscar Wilde. (Thornes Classic Short Stories Ser.). (Illus.). 89p. 1996. pap. 10.95 (*0-7487-2482-6*, Pub. by S Thornes Pubs) Trans-Atl Phila.
— Short Stories by Thomas Hardy. (Thornes Classic Short Stories Ser.). (Illus.). 92p. 1995. pap. 10.95 (*0-7487-2241-6*, Pub. by S Thornes Pubs) Trans-Atl Phila.
Royston, Mike, jt. ed. see Matthews, Sarah.
Royston, Peter L., jt. auth. see Koon, William H.
***Roystonn, Angela.** Apple. LC 98-10753. (J). 1998. 19.92 (*1-57572-696-3*) Heinemann Lib.
Royt, Paulette. Interactive Learning Guide for Microbiology. 336p. (C). 1998. spiral bd. 39.95 (*0-7872-5047-3*, 41504701) Kendall-Hunt.
Roza, Marguerite. A Toolkit Using Data to Improve Schools: Raise Student Achievement by Incorporating Data Analysis in School Planning. rev. ed. 41p. 1998. pap. 35.00 (*0-89292-288-5*) Educ Dev Ctr.
Rozak, Chester, jt. auth. see Matthews, Jay.
Rozakis, Christos L. & Stagos, Petros N. The Turkish Straits. LC 86-28581. (International Straits of the World Ser.: Vol. 9). 1987. lib. bdg. 99.00 (*90-247-3464-9*) Kluwer Academic.
Rozakis, Laurie. AP English Literature & Composition: Advanced Placement Examination. 4th ed. (Illus.). 320p. 1997. pap. 14.95 (*0-02-861715-0*, Arc) IDG Bks.
— Celebrate! Holidays Around the World. LC 92-81915. (Illus.). (J). (ps-4). 1993. pap. 5.95 (*0-88160-217-5*, LW107) Learning Wks.
— Complete Idiot's Guide to Creative Writing. 352p. 1997. 16.95 (*0-02-861734-7*) Macmillan Gen Ref.
— Complete Idiot's Guide to Making Money in Freelancing. LC 97-80972. (Illus.). 360p. 1997. pap. 16.95 (*0-02-862119-0*) Macmillan Gen Ref.
— Complete Idiot's Guide to Speaking in Public with Confidence. 352p. 1995. 16.95 (*0-02-861038-5*) Macmillan Gen Ref.
— Complete Idiot's Guide to Writing Well. 352p. 2000. pap. text 16.95 (*0-02-863694-5*) S&S Trade.
— Power Reading. 1996. 12.95 (*0-02-861367-8*) Macmillan.
— Steven Jobs. LC 92-43268. (Masters of Invention Ser.). (J). (gr. 5 up). 1993. 11.95 (*0-685-66327-2*) Rourke Corp.
— Steven Jobs: Computer Genius. LC 92-43268. (Masters of Invention Ser.). 48p. (J). (gr. 4-8). 1993. lib. bdg. 21.27 (*0-86592-001-X*) Rourke Enter.
Rozakis, Laurie, et al. Magic Johnson, 6 bks., Set I, Reading Level 8. (Winning Spirit Ser.). (Illus.). 48p. (J). (gr. 4-8). 1988. lib. bdg. 21.27 (*0-86592-025-7*) Rourke Enter.
***Rozakis, Laurie E.** Big Book of Dates: A Chronology of the Most Important People, Events & Achievements of All Time. 504p. 2000. pap. 21.95 (*0-07-136102-2*) McGraw.
Rozakis, Laurie E. Buying & Selling Collectibles. LC 96-80407. 342p. 1997. pap. 16.95 (*0-02-861595-6*) Macmillan Gen Ref.
— The Complete Idiot's Guide to American Literature. 432p. 1999. pap. text 16.95 (*0-02-863378-4*, Pub. by Macmillan Gen Ref) S&S Trade.
***Rozakis, Laurie E.** The Complete Idiot's Guide to Buying & Selling Collectibles. 2nd ed. (Illus.). 360p. 2000. 18.95 (*0-02-863836-0*) Macmillan.
Rozakis, Laurie E. Critical Thinking. 1991. pap. 14.95 (*0-590-49157-1*) Scholastic Inc.
— Dick Rutan & Jeana Yeager: Flying Non-Stop Around the World. Glassman, Bruce, ed. LC 94-20399. (Illus.). 48p. (J). (gr. 2-5). 1994. lib. bdg. 9.45 (*1-56711-087-8*) Blackbirch.
— 50 Ways to Meet & Drop Your Lover. 1997. pap. 7.95 (*0-02-861520-4*, Arco) Macmillan Gen Ref.
— Homelessness: Can We Solve the Problem? (Issues of Our Time Ser.). (Illus.). 64p. (YA). (gr. 5-8). 1995. lib. bdg. 18.90 (*0-8050-3878-7*) TFC Bks NY.
— How to Interpret Poetry. 2nd ed. 134p. 1997. 9.95 (*0-02-862189-1*, Arc) IDG Bks.
— Laura Ingalls Wilder: Activities Based on Research from the Laura Ingalls Wilder Homes. 1993. pap. 10.95 (*0-590-49271-3*) Scholastic Inc.
— Mary Kay: Cosmetics Queen. LC 92-45124. (Made in America Ser.). 48p. (J). (gr. 4-8). 1993. lib. bdg. 21.27 (*0-86592-040-0*) Rourke Enter.
***Rozakis, Laurie E.** Master AP English Literature & the Composition Test. 2000. pap. 15.99 (*0-7645-6184-7*, Arco) Macmillan Gen Ref.
— 101 Fresh & Fun Critical Thinking Activities: Engaging Activities & Reproducibles to Develop Kids' Higher-Level Thinking Skills. 128p. 1998. pap. 12.95 (*0-590-37523-7*) Scholastic Inc.
Rozakis, Laurie E. Power Reading. 224p. 1995. 12.95 (*0-02-860562-4*, Arc) IDG Bks.
— Public Speaking. 2nd ed. (Complete Idiot's Guides (Lifestyle) Ser.). (Illus.). 358p. 1999. pap. 16.95 (*0-02-863383-0*, Pub. by Macmillan Gen Ref) S&S Trade.
— Schaum's Quick Guide to Writing Great Research Papers. LC 99-13669. 160p. 1999. pap. 10.95 (*0-07-012300-4*, Schaums Outlne) McGraw-Hill Prof.
— Shakespeare. (Complete Idiot's Guide Ser.). (Illus.). 380p. 1999. pap. 16.95 (*0-02-862905-1*) Macmillan Gen Ref.
— Teen Pregnancy: Why Are Kids Having Babies? (Issues of Our Time Ser.). (Illus.). 64p. (J). (gr. 5-8). 1995. lib. bdg. 18.90 (*0-8050-2569-3*) TFC Bks NY.
Rozakis, Laurie E. & Rozakis, Samantha. Who Are You? Teen Magazine. 1998. pap. 5.99 (*0-671-01193-6*) S&S Trade.
Rozakis, Laurie E., jt. auth. see Zipes, Jack D.
Rozakis, Laurie E., ed. see Princeton Institute Staff.
Rozakis, Laurie N. AP English Literature & Composition. 3rd ed. (AP Exam Guides Ser.). 320p. 1993. pap. 13.00 (*0-671-84784-8*, Arco) Macmillan Gen Ref.
— How to Write Poetry. 3rd ed. 150p. 1997. pap. 9.95 (*0-02-862207-3*, Arc) IDG Bks.
— The Joy Luck Club Notes. (Cliffs Notes Ser.). 80p. 1994. pap. text 4.95 (*0-8220-0685-5*, Cliff) IDG Bks.
***Rozakis, Laurie N.** The Literate Executive: Learn How to Write Like a Leader. 304p. 1999. 19.95 (*0-07-135288-0*) McGraw.
Rozakis, Laurie N. Webster's New World Power Reading. 1995. pap. 12.95 (*0-671-51897-6*) S&S Trade.
Rozakis, Laurie N., jt. auth. see Martin, Sally.
Rozakis, Samantha, jt. auth. see Rozakis, Laurie E.
Rozan, S. J. A Bitter Feast. LC 98-21558. 320p. 1998. text 23.95 (*0-312-19259-2*) St Martin.
— A Bitter Feast. 72p. 1999. mass mkt. 5.99 (*0-312-97011-0*, St Martins Paperbacks) St Martin.
— A Bitter Feast. large type ed. LC 98-51092. 539p. 1999. 26.95 (*0-7862-1773-1*) Thorndike Pr.
— China Trade. 1995. mass mkt. 5.99 (*0-312-95590-1*) St Martin.
— Concourse: A Bill Smith-Lydia Chin Mystery. LC 95-34741. 288p. 1995. 21.95 (*0-312-13453-3*) St Martin.
— Concourse: A Bill Smith-Lydia Chin Mystery. 3rd ed. Vol. 2. 304p. 1996. mass mkt. 5.99 (*0-312-95944-3*) St Martin.
— Mandarin Plaid. LC 96-8499. Vol. 3. 288p. 1996. text 22.95 (*0-312-14674-4*) St Martin.
— Mandarin Plaid. 1997. mass mkt. 5.99 (*0-614-27790-6*) St Martin.
— Mandarin Plaid, Vol. 1. 288p. 1997. mass mkt. 5.99 (*0-312-96283-5*) St Martin.
— No Colder Place. large type ed. LC 97-39743. (CD Ser.). 473p. 1997. lib. bdg. 26.95 (*0-7862-1251-9*) Thorndike Pr.
— No Colder Place, Vol. 1. Vol. 1. 304p. 1998. pap. 5.99 (*0-312-96664-4*, Pub. by Tor Bks) St Martin.
Rozan, S. J. Stone Quarry. LC 99-35869. 288p. 1999. text 23.95 (*0-312-20912-6*, Minotaur) St Martin.
***Rozan, S. J.** Stone Quarry. 2001. pap. write for info. (*0-312-97703-4*, St Martins Paperbacks) St Martin.
Rozanne, S. Beyond Our Wildest Dreams: A History of OA As Seen by a Co-Founder. LC 96-70336. 210p. (Orig.). 1996. pap. 10.99 (*1-889681-00-8*) Overeaters Anym.
Rozanov, I. U. Random Fields & Stochastic Partial Differential Equations. LC 97-46148. (Mathematics & Its Applications Ser.). 229p. 1998. 105.00 (*0-7923-4984-9*) Kluwer Academic.
Rozanov, J. A., jt. auth. see Prohorov, Y. V.
Rozanov, J. A., ed. see Steklov Institute of Mathematics, Academy of Scien.
Rozanov, Y. A. Probability Theory: A Concise Course. rev. ed. Silverman, Richard A., tr. from RUS. LC 77-78592. 148p. 1977. reprint ed. pap. text 7.95 (*0-486-63544-9*) Dover.
Rozanov, Yu A. Probability Theory, Random Processes & Mathematical Statistics. (Mathematics & Its Applications Ser.: Vol. 344). 268p. (C). 1995. text 161.50 (*0-7923-3764-6*) Kluwer Academic.
Rozanov, Yuri A. Introduction to the Theory of Random Processes. (Soviet Mathematics Ser.). viii, 117p. 1987. 59.95 (*0-387-17874-0*) Spr-Verlag.
— Markov Random Fields. Elson, C. M., tr. from RUS. (Illus.). 201p. 1982. 118.95 (*0-387-90708-4*) Spr-Verlag.
Rozanov, Yuri A., jt. auth. see Ibragimov, I. A.
Rozanska, M. & Rybicki, K., eds. Proceedings of the 15th International Conference on Physics Held in Collison, 1995. LC 96-3255. 540p. 1996. write for info. (*981-02-2587-3*) World Scientific Pub.
Rozanski, Mordechai, ed. Records of the Department of State Relating to the Internal Affairs of China, 1910-1949: A Descriptive Guide & Subject Index to Microcopy No. 329. LC 79-13351. 61p. 1979. lib. bdg. 30.00 (*0-8420-2133-7*) Scholarly Res Inc.
Rozantsev, E. G. Free Nitroxyl Radicals. Ulrich, H., ed. LC 69-12541. (Illus.). 263p. 1970. reprint ed. pap. 81.60 (*0-608-05755-X*, 205971900007) Bks Demand.
Rozario, Diane. The Immunization Resource Guide: Where to Find Answers to All Your Questions about Childhood Immunizations. 3rd rev. ed. LC 98-65312. 90p. (Orig.). 1998. pap. 12.95 (*0-9643366-4-2*) Patter Pubns.
***Rozario, Diane.** The Immunization Resource Guide: Where to Find Answers to All Your Questions about Childhood Immunizations. 4th ed. LC 00-91401. 200p. (Orig.). 2000. pap. 12.95 (*0-9643366-5-0*) Patter Pubns.
Rozario, M. Rita. Trafficking in Women & Children in India: Sexual Exploitation & Sale. 1988. 22.00 (*0-317-90858-8*, Pub. by Uppal Pub Hse) S Asia.
Rozarkis, Laurie. Complete Idiot's Guide to Grammar & Style. LC 97-73151. 352p. 1997. 16.95 (*0-02-861956-0*) Macmillan Gen Ref.
Rozas, Diane. Chicken Breasts: 116 New & Classic Recipes for the Fairest Part of the Fowl. (Particular Palate Ser.). (Illus.). 96p. 1996. pap. 10.00 (*0-517-88705-3*, Crown) Crown Pub Group.
— Low-Fat Chicken Breasts: 120 Healthy & Delicious Recipes for Skinless, Boneless Chicken Breasts. (Particular Palate Ser.). (Illus.). 144p. 1996. 10.00 (*0-517-88634-0*, Crown) Crown Pub Group.
— More Chicken Breasts: 91 New & Classic Recipes for the Fairest Part of the Fowl. (Illus.). 128p. 1996. pap. 10.00 (*0-517-88706-1*, Crown) Crown Pub Group.
Rozas, Diane, jt. auth. see Gottehrer, Anita Bourne.
Rozas, Diane, jt. auth. see Leach, Robin.
Rozbicki, Michal J. The Complete Colonial Gentleman: Cultural Legitimacy in Plantation America. LC 97-22568. 256p. 1998. text 35.00 (*0-8139-1750-6*) U Pr of Va.
— Transformation of the English Cultural Ethos in Colonial America: Maryland, 1634-1720. LC 88-14399. 232p. (C). 1988. lib. bdg. 41.50 (*0-8191-7048-8*) U Pr of Amer.
Rozday, Bill. High Ground: Peak Hikes of the Mid Atlantic States, Vol. I. LC 98-90349. (Illus.). 140p. 1998. pap. 15.95 (*0-9664875-0-8*) Virgin Pines.
Rozdestvenskii, B. L. & Janenko, N. N. Systems of Quasilinear Equations & Their Applications to Gas Dynamics. LC 82-24488. (Translations of Mathematical Monographs: Vol. 55). 676p. 1983. text 198.00 (*0-8218-4509-8*, MMONO/55) Am Math.

An Asterisk (*) at the beginning of an entry indicates that the title is appearing for the first time.

***Roze, Anne.** Fields of Memory: A Testimony to the Great War. (Illus.). 232p. 2000. 34.95 (*0-304-35324-8*) Continuum.

Roze, C. & Bernades, P., eds. European Pancreatic Club, EPC Twenty-Fifth Meeting, Paris, October 1993: Abstracts. (Journal: Digestion: Vol. 54, No. 5, 1993). (Illus.). 62p. 1993. pap. 85.25 (*3-8055-5876-7*) S Karger.

Roze, Janis A. Coral Snakes of the Americas: Biology, Identification, & Venoms. LC 93-1912. 340p. 1996. 95.00 (*0-89464-847-0*) Krieger.

Roze, Maris. Technical Communication: The Practical Craft. 3rd ed. LC 95-5164. 290p. (C). 1996. pap. text 54.00 (*0-13-455874-X*) P-H.

Roze, Uldis. The North American Porcupine. (Illus.). 224p. 1989. pap. 15.95 (*0-87474-787-2*) Smithsonian.

Rozelaar, Marc. Lukrez - Versuch Einer Deutung. (GER.). xvi, 267p. 1988. reprint ed. write for info. (*3-487-09026-0*) G Olms Pubs.

Rozell, Erik & Pablo, Mary. MCSE TestPrep: TCP/IP. 2nd ed. LC 98-88578. 400p. 1998. pap. 19.99 (*0-7357-0025-7*) New Riders Pub.

Rozell, Gail. A Reed in His Hand: Ordinary People Doing Astounding Things Through God's Anointing. LC 99-165193. 210p. (Orig.). 1997. pap. 9.99 (*1-884369-64-2*) McDougal Pubng.

Rozell, Mark J. Executive Privilege: The Dilemma of Secrecy & Democratic Accountability. LC 94-6801. (Interpreting American Politics Ser.). 1994. text 49.95 (*0-8018-4899-7*); pap. text 15.95 (*0-8018-4900-4*) Johns Hopkins.

***Rozell, Mark J., et al.** George Washington & the Origins of the American Presidency. LC 99-54740. 232p. 2000. 65.00 (*0-275-96867-7*, Praeger Pubs) Greenwood.

Rozell, Mark J. In Contempt of Congress: Postwar Press Coverage on Capitol Hill. LC 96-16277. (Series in Political Communication). 160p. 1996. 49.95 (*0-275-95690-3*, Praeger Pubs) Greenwood.

— The Press & the Bush Presidency. LC 96-10429. (Presidential Studies). 200p. 1996. 57.95 (*0-275-95653-9*, Praeger Pubs) Greenwood.

— The Press & the Ford Presidency. LC 92-8700. 264p. (C). 1992. text 49.50 (*0-472-10350-4*, 10350) U of Mich Pr.

Rozell, Mark J. & Pederson, William D., eds. FDR & the Modern Presidency: Leadership & Legacy. LC 96-53620. 248p. 1997. 59.95 (*0-275-95873-6*, Praeger Pubs) Greenwood.

Rozell, Mark J. & Wilcox, Clyde. Interest Groups in American Campaigns: The New Face of Electioneering. LC 98-38324. 170p. 1998. pap. text 20.95 (*1-56802-392-8*) Congr Quarterly.

— Second Coming: The New Christian Right in Virginia Politics. LC 95-44562. 304p. (C). 1996. 32.95 (*0-8018-5297-8*) Johns Hopkins.

***Rozell, Mark J. & Wilcox, Clyde, eds.** The Clinton Scandal & the Future of American Government. LC 99-36836. 256p. 2000. pap. 18.95 (*0-87840-777-4*); text 55.00 (*0-87840-776-6*) Georgetown U Pr.

Rozell, Mark J. & Wilcox, Clyde, eds. God at the Grass Roots 1996: The Christian Right in the American Elections. LC 97-19042. 250p. 1997. 63.50 (*0-8476-8610-8*); pap. 24.95 (*0-8476-8611-6*) Rowman.

Rozell, Mark J., jt. ed. see Bullock, Charles S., III.

Rozell, Mark J., jt. ed. see Wilcox, Clyde.

***Rozell, Ned.** Walking My Dog, Jane: From Valdez to Prudhoe Bay along the Trans-Alaska Pipeline. LC 99-50435. (Emerging Writers in Creative Nonfiction Ser.). (Illus.). 350p. 2000. text 24.95 (*0-8207-0314-1*) Duquesne.

Rozell, O. B. The Freeway: A One-Act Play. 24p. 1976. pap. 3.25 (*0-88680-059-5*) I E Clark.

— Nathan the Nervous: A One-Act Comedy. (Illus.). 24p. (J). (gr. 6-12). 1977. pap. 3.25 (*0-88680-136-2*) I E Clark.

— Of Winners, Losers, & Games: A Drama About Life. (Illus.). 24p. 1976. pap. 3.25 (*0-88680-145-1*) I E Clark.

Rozell, Paula. Plotting Pictures: Coordinate Graphing & Number Skills. Gideon, Joan, ed. (Illus.). 64p. (J). (gr. 5-8). 1994. student ed. 10.95 (*0-86651-854-1*) Seymour Pubns.

Rozelle, Harold. Drift on the River. Rozelle, Pauline, ed. LC 88-60412. 208p. (Orig.). 1989. pap. 9.95 (*0-941903-00-1*) Ransom Hill.

Rozelle, Lew. Origami in King Arthurs Court: An Adventure in Folding. LC 97-5636. 1997. pap. 15.95 (*0-312-15619-7*, St Martin Griffin) St Martin.

***Rozelle, Lew.** Origami Ornaments. (Illus.). 160p. 2000. pap. 17.95 (*0-312-26369-4*) St Martin.

Rozelle, Lew. Origami Rockets: Spinners, Zoomers, Floaters & More. LC 98-31678. 192p. 1999. pap. 17.95 (*0-312-19944-9*) St Martin.

Rozelle, Pauline, ed. see Rozelle, Harold.

Rozelle, Robert V., ed. Gold of Greece: Jewelry & Ornaments from the Benaki Museum. LC 90-80359. (Illus.). 112p. (Orig.). 1990. pap. 19.95 (*0-936227-07-9*) Dallas Mus.

Rozelle, Robert V., ed. see Wardlaw, Alvia J., et al.

Rozelle, Ron. Into That Good Night. LC 97-43463. 192p. 1998. text 22.00 (*0-374-17711-2*) FS&G.

***Rozelle, Ron.** Into That Good Night. large type ed. LC 99-89598. (Nonfiction Ser.). 2000. 27.95 (*0-7838-8963-1*, G K Hall Lrg Type) Mac Lib Ref.

— The Windows of Heaven: A Novel of Galveston's Great Storm of 1900. 256p. 2000. pap. 16.95 (*1-881515-27-3*, Pub. by TX Review Pr) Tex A&M Univ Pr.

Rozelle, Scott, jt. auth. see Nyberg, Albert.

Rozells, Gia. Super Paint 3: Everything You Need to Know. (Illus.). 320p. (Orig.). 1992. pap. 24.95 (*1-55958-098-4*) Prima Pub.

Rozema. Medical Matters: A Handbook for Medical Secretaries. 3rd ed. 1997. pap. 0.00 (*0-582-80907-X*) Addison-Wesley.

Rozema, David, jt. auth. see Fendt, Gene.

***Rozema, J., ed.** Stratospheric Ozone Depletion: The Effects of Enhanced UV-B Radiation on Terrestrial Ecosystems. (Illus.). 352p. 1999. 100.00 (*90-5782-047-1*, Pub. by Backhuys Pubs) Balogh.

Rozema, J., et al, eds. CO B2 S & Biosphere. LC 92-37361. (Advances in Vegetation Science Ser.: No. 14). 488p. (C). 1993. text 426.00 (*0-7923-2044-1*) Kluwer Academic.

— UV-B & Biosphere. LC 96-54602. (Advances in Vegetation Science Ser.: No. 17). 230p. 1997. lib. bdg. 208.00 (*0-7923-4422-7*) Kluwer Academic.

Rozema, J. & Verkleij, J. A., eds. Ecological Responses to Environmental Stresses. (C). 1991. text 309.50 (*0-7923-0762-3*) Kluwer Academic.

***Rozema, Patricia.** Mansfield Park: A Screenplay. LC 00-37026. 2000. 10.95 (*0-7868-8603-X*, Pub. by Hyperion) Time Warner.

Rozema, Vicki. Footsteps of the Cherokees: A Guide to the Eastern Homelands of the Cherokee Nation. LC 95-18092. (Illus.). 396p. (Orig.). 1995. pap. 17.95 (*0-89587-133-5*) Blair.

Rozemond, Marleen. Descartes's Dualism. LC 97-42399. 320p. 1999. 45.00 (*0-674-19840-9*) HUP.

Rozen, Arthur. Monarch Notes on Flaubert's Madame Bovary & Three Tales. (Orig.). (C). 3.95 (*0-671-00560-X*, Arco) Macmillan Gen Ref.

Rozen, Kenneth C. The Archaeological Survey of the Northern Tucson 138 KV Transmission Line System: The Northern Tucson Basin & Lower Santa Cruz Valley, Arizona. (Archaeological Ser.: No. 132). (Illus.). 71p. 1979. pap. 5.95 (*1-889747-09-2*) Ariz St Mus.

Rozen, Marvin E. The Economics of Organizational Choice: Workers, Jobs, Labor Markets & Implicit Contracting. 216p. 1991. text 52.50 (*0-472-10278-8*, 10278) U of Mich Pr.

— The Economics of Work Reorganization. LC 82-22358. 240p. 1983. 55.00 (*0-275-91069-5*, C1069, Praeger Pubs) Greenwood.

Rozen, Minna. Haskoy Cemetery Typology of Stones. x, 271p. 1994. text 150.00 (*0-9602686-7-7*, Pub. by Center Judaic Studies) Eisenbrauns.

— Jewish Identity & Society in the 17th Century: Reflections on the Life & Work of Refael Mordekhai Malki. Wachsman, Goldie, tr. (Texts & Studies in Medieval & Early Modern Judaism: No. 6). 190p. 1992. 87.50 (*3-16-145770-6*, Pub. by JCB Mohr) Coronet Bks.

Rozen, P., et al, eds. Gastrointestinal Cancer: Advances in Basic Sciences. (Frontiers of Gastrointestinal Research Ser.: Vol. 4). (Illus.). 1979. 82.75 (*3-8055-2903-1*) S Karger.

— Gastrointestinal Cancer: Advances in Diagnostics Techniques & Therapy. (Frontiers of Gastrointestinal Research Ser.: Vol. 5). (Illus.). 1979. 82.75 (*3-8055-2905-8*) S Karger.

— Large Bowel Cancer: Policy, Prevention, Research & Treatment. (Frontiers of Gastrointestinal Research Ser.: Vol. 18). (Illus.). viii, 302p. 1991. 242.75 (*3-8055-5269-6*) S Karger.

Rozen, P. & De Dombal, F. T., eds. Computer Aid in Gastroenterology. (Frontiers of Gastrointestinal Research Ser.: Vol. 7). (Illus.). viii, 196p. 1984. 71.50 (*3-8055-3770-0*) S Karger.

Rozen, P. & Winawer, S. J., eds. Secondary Prevention of Colorectal Cancer. (Frontiers of Gastrointestinal Research Ser.: Vol. 10). (Illus.). xiv, 274p. 1986. 172.50 (*3-8055-4252-6*) S Karger.

Rozen, P., jt. ed. see Horwitz, C.

Rozen, P., ed. see International Conference on Gastrointestinal Cance.

Rozen, Peter, jt. auth. see Creighton, Breen.

Rozen, Sydney C., jt. auth. see Bernstein, Albert J.

Rozen, Sydney C., jt. auth. see Eastman, Meg.

Rozen, Todd D., jt. auth. see Silberstein, Steven D.

Rozenbaum, Henri. Dictionary of Gynecology: Dictionnaire de Gynecologie. (ENG & FRE.). 312p. 1981. 85.00 (*0-8288-1826-6*) Fr & Eur.

Rozenberg, G. Handbook of Formal Languages Vol. 1: Word, Language, Grammar. LC 96-47134. 912p. 1997. 99.50 (*3-540-60420-0*) Spr-Verlag.

— Handbook of Formal Languages Vol. 2: Linear Modeling Background & Application. LC 96-47134. 584p. 1997. 89.50 (*3-540-60648-3*) Spr-Verlag.

— Handbook of Formal Languages Vol. 3: Beyond Words. LC 96-47134. 584p. 1997. 89.50 (*3-540-60649-1*) Spr-Verlag.

Rozenberg, G. & Sallomaa, Arto. Developments in Language Theory: At the Crossroads of Mathematics, Computer Science & Biology. (Series in Computer Science). 504p. 1994. text 121.00 (*981-02-1645-9*) World Scientific Pub.

Rozenberg, G., ed. see Spears, W.

Rozenberg, Georgii V. Twilight: A Study in Atmospheric Optics. LC 65-11345. 368p. reprint ed. pap. 114.10 (*0-608-12931-3*, 202470200038) Bks Demand.

Rozenberg, Gillian. Microscopic Haematology: A Practical Guide for the Laboratory. 160p. 1997. pap. text 31.00 (*90-5702-247-8*, Harwood Acad Pubs) Gordon & Breach.

— Microscopic Haematology: A Practical Guide to the Haematology Laboratory. 160p. 1996. text 78.00 (*90-5702-093-9*, Harwood Acad Pubs) Gordon & Breach.

Rozenberg, Grzegorz, ed. Advances in Petri Nets, 1984. (Lecture Notes in Computer Science Ser.: Vol. 188). vii, 467p. 1985. pap. 45.00 (*0-387-15204-0*) Spr-Verlag.

— Advances in Petri Nets, 1985. (Lecture Notes in Computer Science Ser.: Vol. 222). vi, 498p. 1986. 53.00 (*0-387-16480-4*) Spr-Verlag.

— Advances in Petri Nets, 1987. (Lecture Notes in Computer Science Ser.: Vol. 266). vi, 451p. 1987. 52.00 (*0-387-18086-9*) Spr-Verlag.

— Advances in Petri Nets, 1988. (Lecture Notes in Computer Science Ser.: Vol. 340). vi, 439p. 1988. 47.00 (*0-387-50580-6*) Spr-Verlag.

— Advances in Petri Nets, 1993, Vol. 674. vii, 457p. 1993. 65.95 (*0-387-56689-9*) Spr-Verlag.

Rozenberg, Grzegorz, et al, eds. Advances in Petri Nets, 1989. (Lecture Notes in Computer Science Ser.: Vol. 424). vi, 524p. 1990. 60.00 (*0-387-52494-0*) Spr-Verlag.

— Advances in Petri Nets, 1990. (Lecture Notes in Computer Science Ser.: Vol. 483). vi, 515p. 1991. 63.00 (*0-387-53863-1*) Spr-Verlag.

— Advances in Petri Nets, 1991. (Lecture Notes in Computer Science Ser.: Vol. 524). viii, 572p. 1991. 58.95 (*0-387-54398-8*) Spr-Verlag.

— Advances in Petri Nets, 1992. (Lecture Notes in Computer Science Ser.: Vol. 609). viii, 472p. 1992. 62.95 (*0-387-55610-9*) Spr-Verlag.

Rozenberg, Grzegorz & Salomaa, Arto. Current Trends in Theoretical. (Series in Computer Science). 630p. 1993. text 109.00 (*981-02-1462-6*) World Scientific Pub.

— Handbook of Formal Languages. LC 96-47134. 1997. 259.50 (*3-540-61486-9*) Spr-Verlag.

Rozenberg, Grzegorz & Salomaa, Arto, eds. The Book of L. xv, 468p. 1985. 59.95 (*0-387-16022-1*) Spr-Verlag.

— Lindenmayer Systems: Impacts on Theoretical Computer Science, Computer Graphics, & Developmental Biology. LC 92-14822. ix, 514p. 1992. write for info. (*3-540-55320-7*); 114.95 (*0-387-55320-7*) Spr-Verlag.

Rozenberg, Grzegorz, jt. ed. see Deikert, Volker.

Rozenberg, Grzegorz, jt. ed. see Jensen, K.

***Rozenberg, Jacques J.** From the Unconscious to Ethics. LC 97-44053. (San Francisco State University Series in Philosophy: Vol. 12). XXIV, 158p. (C). 1999. text 45.00 (*0-8204-3860-X*) P Lang Pubng.

Rozenblat, Anatoly. Collected Works of A. I. Rozenblat. 72p. 1998. pap. 9.00 (*0-8059-4218-1*) Dorrance.

— Rozenblat's Innovations for the Twenty-First Century. (Illus.). 112p. 1999. pap. 13.00 (*0-8059-4655-1*) Dorrance.

Rozenblit, Bruce. Audio Reality: Myths Debunked Truths Revealed. Schiller, Karla, ed. LC 98-91127. (Illus.). 126p. 1999. pap. 29.95 (*0-9669611-0-2*) Transcend.

Rozenblit, Jerzy & Buchenrieder, Klaus, eds. Codesign: Computer-Aided Software/Hardware Engineering. LC 94-22820. 464p. 1994. 89.95 (*0-7803-1049-7*, PC4028) Inst Electrical.

***Rozenblit, Marsha L.** Reconstructing a National Identity: The Jews of Habsburg Austria During World War I. LC 99-53423. (Illus.). 304p. 2000. text. write for info. (*0-19-513465-6*) OUP.

***Rozenblit, Moshe.** Security for Telecommunications Network Management. LC 99-38975. (Series on Network Management). 1999. 69.95 (*0-7803-3490-6*) Inst Electrical.

Rozenblum, G. V., tr. see Babich, Vasili M., et al.

Rozencvejg, V. Ju. Linguistic Interference & Convergent Change. (Janua Linguarum, Series Minor: No. 99). (Illus.). 58p. 1976. pap. text 64.60 (*90-279-3414-2*) Mouton.

Rozencwaig, Roman & Walji, Hasnain. The Melatonin & Aging Sourcebook. LC 96-39113. (Illus.). 220p. 1997. text 79.95 (*0-934252-76-9*, Pub. by Hohm Pr) SCB Distributors.

Rozencweig, M., jt. ed. see Funes, H. Cortes.

Rozencweig, Marcel, et al, eds. New Anticancer Drugs: Mitoxantrone & Bisantrene. LC 82-42744. (Monograph Series of the European Organization for Research on Treatment of Cancer: No. 12). (Illus.). 210p. 1983. reprint ed. pap. 65.10 (*0-7837-9553-X*, 206030200005) Bks Demand.

Rozencweig, Marcel, jt. ed. see Muggia, Franco M.

Rozengurt, Michael. The Soviet Water Crisis: Exposing an Environmental Disaster, Vol. 17. (C). 1999. pap. text 32.50 (*0-8133-8117-7*) Westview.

Rozens, Aleksandrs. Environmental Destruction. LC 93-41213. (When Disaster Strikes Ser.). (Illus.). 64p. (J). (gr. 5-8). 1995. lib. bdg. 18.90 (*0-8050-3098-0*) TFC Bks NY.

— Floods. (When Disaster Strikes Ser.). (Illus.). 64p. (J). (gr. 5-8). 1995. lib. bdg. 22.90 (*0-8050-3097-2*) TFC Bks NY.

Rozenshtein, David, et al. Tree & Graph Processing in SQL. Bondur, Tom, ed. 1998. mass mkt. 31.95 (*0-9649812-3-8*) SQL Forum.

Rozensky, Ronald H., et al. Psychological Assessment in Medical Settings. LC 97-24814. (Applied Clinical Psychology Ser.). (Illus.). 340p. (C). 1997. 49.50 (*0-306-45551-X*, Plenum Trade) Perseus Pubng.

Rozensky, Ronald H., jt. ed. see Resnick, Robert J.

Rozental, D. E. Dictionary of the Difficulties of the Russian Language. 3rd ed. (ENG & RUS.). 704p. 1984. 35.00 (*0-8288-2006-6*, M15156) Fr & Eur.

Rozental, I. L., jt. auth. see Nikitin, Yu P.

Rozenzweig. Der Stern der Erlosung. 553p. 1977. lib. bdg. 168.50 (*90-247-1766-3*, Pub. by M Nijhoff) Kluwer Academic.

Rozett, Martha T. The Doctrine of Election & the Emergence of Elizabethan Tragedy. LC 84-42565. 340p. 1984. reprint ed. pap. 105.40 (*0-608-02902-5*, 206396600008) Bks Demand.

— Talking Back to Shakespeare. LC 93-45821. 1995. 35.00 (*0-87413-529-X*) U Delaware Pr.

Rozewicz, Tadeusz. The Card Index. 11.95 (*0-7145-0061-5*); pap. 6.95 (*0-7145-0062-3*) M Boyars Pubs.

— Mariage Blanc & the Hunger Artist Departs: Two Plays. Czerniawski, Adam, tr. from POL. LC 82-12859. 112p. 1983. 13.50 (*0-7145-2775-0*); pap. 7.95 (*0-7145-2776-9*) M Boyars Pubs.

— Reading the Apocalypse in Bed: Selected Plays & Short Dramas. LC 98-25180. (POL.). 224p. 1998. pap. text 14.95 (*0-7145-3037-9*) M Boyars Pubs.

Rozewicz, Tadeusz. The Survivor & Other Poems. Krynski, Magnus J. & Maguire, Robert A., trs. LC 76-3034. (Lockert Library of Poetry in Translation). 180p. reprint ed. pap. 55.80 (*0-8357-4202-4*, 203698100006) Bks Demand.

Rozewicz, Tadeusz. The Trap. Czerniawski, Adam, tr. (Polish Theatre Archive Ser.). (Illus.). 115p. 1997. text 23.00 (*3-7186-5855-0*, Harwood Acad Pubs); pap. text 15.00 (*3-7186-5856-9*, Harwood Acad Pubs) Gordon & Breach.

— Unease. Contoski, Victor, tr. 160p. 1980. pap. 5.00 (*0-89823-013-6*) New Rivers Pr.

Rozewicz, Tadeusz & Czerniawski, Adam. They Came to See a Poet: Selected Poems. 232p. 1991. 34.95 (*0-85646-238-1*, Pub. by Anvil Press) Dufour.

Rozgonyi, George A., ed. see International Symposium on Very Large Scale Integr.

Rozgonyi, George A., ed. see Topical Conference on Characterization Techniques for Semi-Conductor Materials & Devices Staff.

Rozgonyi, Jay. Preston Sturges's Vision of America: Critical Analyses of Fourteen Films. LC 94-24196. (Illus.). 207p. 1995. lib. bdg. 34.50 (*0-89950-985-1*) McFarland & Co.

Rozgonyi, Tamas, jt. auth. see Tannenbaum, Arnold S.

Rozgonyi, Tibor G. & Golosinski, Tad S., eds. Continuous Surface Mining: Equipment, Operation & Design. (Proceedings of the 2nd International Symposium on Continuous Surface Mining, Austin Texas, October 2-5, 1988 Ser.). (Illus.). x, 225p. 1988. lib. bdg. 155.00 (*90-6191-858-8*, Pub. by A A Balkema) Ashgate Pub Co.

***Rozhansky, Vladimir. A. & Tsendin, Lev D.** Transport Phenomena in Partially Ionized Plasma. 416p. 2000. text 120.00 (*90-5699-038-1*, G & B Science) Gordon & Breach.

***Rozhdestvensky, K. V.** Aerodynamics of a Lifting System in Extreme Ground Effect. x, 347p. 2000. (*3-540-66277-4*) Spr-Verlag.

Rozhkov, Anatoly S. & Mikhailova, Tatyana A. The Effect of Fluorine-Containing Emissions on Conifers. LC 92-21023. (Illus.). 200p. 1993. 174.95 (*0-387-54735-5*) Spr-Verlag.

Rozhkovskaya, Tamara, tr. see Godunov, S. K.

Rozhkovskaya, Tamara, tr. see Osmolovskii, V. G.

Rozhon, Tracie. The Cheapskate Millionaire's Guide to Bargain Hunting in the Big Apple. LC 99-25227. 1999. pap. 14.00 (*0-8129-3108-4*, Times Bks) Crown Pub Group.

Rozich, Alan F. Design & Operation - Activated Sludge Processes Using Respirometry. 208p. 1992. lib. bdg. 95.00 (*0-87371-449-0*, L449) Lewis Pubs.

Rozier, Dana. Whatcom County with Kids Vol. 1: Places to Go & Things to Do. (Illus.). 160p. (Orig.). 1999. pap. 12.95 (*0-9670750-0-9*, Pub. by Coho Pr) Partners-West.

Rozier, John, ed. The Granite Farm Letters: The Civil War Correspondence of Edgeworth & Sallie Bird. LC 88-13978. 368p. 1988. 35.00 (*0-8203-1042-5*) U of Ga Pr.

Rozier, Louise, tr. see Pasqualino, Fortunato.

Roziere, Gael. Artist's Alphabet: A Child's Activity Book for Language, Movement & Painting. 28p. (J). (ps-4). 1988. pap., student ed. 5.95 (*0-9619004-2-3*) M Press HI.

Rozin, Elisabeth. Crossroads Cooking: The Meeting & Mating of Ethnic Cuisines from Burma to Texas. LC 98-53226. 288p. 1999. 27.50 (*0-670-87338-1*, Viking) Viking Penguin.

Rozin, Elizabeth. Blue Corn & Chocolate. 1992. 25.00 (*0-394-58308-6*) Knopf.

— Ethnic Cuisine: How to Create the Authentic Flavors of 30 International Cuisines. rev. ed. 288p. 1992. pap. 14.95 (*0-14-046931-1*, Penguin Bks) Viking Penguin.

— Universal Kitchen. 1997. pap. 13.95 (*0-14-025782-9*, Penguin Bks) Viking Penguin.

Rozin, Mordechai. The Rich & the Poor: Jewish Philanthropy & Social Control in Nineteenth-Century London. LC 98-43070. xi, 268p. 1999. 59.95 (*1-898723-79-6*) Intl Spec Bk.

— The Rich & the Poor: Jewish Philanthropy & Social Control in Nineteenth-Century London. 224p. 1997. pap. 24.95 (*1-898723-80-X*, Pub. by Sussex Acad Pr) Intl Spec Bk.

Rozin, Paul, ed. Morality & Health. LC 96-52813. 432p. (C). 1997. 80.00 (*0-415-91581-3*); pap. 25.99 (*0-415-91582-1*) Routledge.

***Rozin, Seth.** The Artvark: A Zoo & a Museum. (Illus.). 64p. 1999. pap. 18.95 (*0-9674390-0-0*) Blind Dog Bks.

Roziner, Felix. A Certain Finkelmeyer. Heim, Michael H., tr. 362p. pap. 16.95 (*0-8101-1263-9*, Hydra Bks) Northwestern U Pr.

Rozinier, Felix, et al. The Times of Turmoil: A Collection of Stories. Yanishevsky, Arkady, tr. from RUS. LC 93-40496. (Illus.). 176p. (Orig.). 1994. pap. 12.00 (*1-55779-065-5*) Hermitage Pubs.

Rozis, J. F. Drying Foodstuffs: Techniques, Processes, Equipment - Technical Guidebook. (Illus.). 311p. 1997. pap. 45.00 (*90-73348-75-7*) Balogh.

Rozis, Jean-Francois. Solar Heating in Cold Regions. 184p. (Orig.). 1996. pap. 19.50 (*1-85339-329-0*, Pub. by Intermed Tech) Stylus Pub VA.

Rozkosny, R. A Biosystematic Study of the European Stratiomyidae (Diptera) 1982. text 261.50 (*90-6193-132-0*) Kluwer Academic.

— The Sciomyzidae (Diptera) of Fennoscandia & Denmark. (Fauna Entomologica Scandinavica Ser.: No. 14). (Illus.). 224p. 1984. text 47.00 (*90-04-07592-5*) Lubrecht & Cramer.

— The Stratiomyoidea (Diptera) of Fennoscandia & Denmark. (Fauna Entomologica Scandinavica Ser.: No. 1). (Illus.). 151p. 1973. pap. 25.50 (*87-87491-00-1*) Lubrecht & Cramer.

R

***Rozmajzl, Michon.** Music Fundamentals, Methods & Materials for the Elementary Classroom Teacher. 3rd ed. 416p. (Orig.). (C). 1999. pap. text. write for info. (0-8013-3082-3) Longman.

Rozmajzl, Michon & Boyer-White, Rene. Music Fundamentals, Methods & Materials for the Elementary Classroom Teacher. 2nd ed. LC 95-9934. (Orig.). (C). 1996. pap. text 62.81 (0-8013-1580-8) Longman.

Rozmajzl, Michon & Castleberry, Rosalie. Rhythm & Melody Concepts: A Sequential Approach for Children. LC 95-166827. 144p. (J). (gr. k-6). 1995. spiral bd. 25.95 (1-881641-13-9) Pencil Point.

Rozman, Deborah, jt. auth. see Hills, Christopher.

Rozman, Deborah, ed. see Hills, Christopher.

Rozman, Deborah A. Meditating with Children: The Art of Concentration & Centering. rev. ed. LC 93-44420. (Illus.). 154p. 1994. pap. 16.95 (1-879052-24-5) Planetary Pubns.

Rozman, Deborah A., ed. see Childre, Doc Lew.

Rozman, Gilbert. The Chinese Debate about Soviet Socialism, 1978-1985. LC 86-25166. 411p. reprint ed. pap. 127.50 (0-608-02910-6, 206397400008) Bks Demand.

***Rozman, Gilbert.** Japan & Russia: The Tortuous Path to Normalization 1949-1999. LC 99-47763. 2000. text 39.95 (0-312-22877-5) St Martin.

Rozman, Gilbert. Japan's Response to the Gorbachev Era, 1985-1991: A Rising Superpower Views a Declining One. 370p. 1992. text 39.50 (0-691-03189-4, Pub. by Princeton U Pr) Cal Prin Full Svc.

— A Mirror for Socialism: Soviet Criticisms of China. LC 84-42902. 307p. 1985. reprint ed. pap. 95.20 (0-7837-9436-3, 206017800004) Bks Demand.

— Urban Networks in Russia, 1750-1800, & Premodern Periodization. LC 75-3472. 349p. reprint ed. pap. 108.20 (0-8357-6932-1, 203799100009) Bks Demand.

Rozman, Gilbert, ed. The East Asian Region: Confucian Heritage & Its Modern Adaptation. 231p. 1991. text 42.50 (0-691-05597-1, Pub. by Princeton U Pr); pap. text 17.95 (0-691-02485-5, Pub. by Princeton U Pr) Cal Prin Full Svc.

— The Modernization of China. (Illus.). 1981. 29.95 (0-02-927480-X) Free Pr.

— Soviet Studies of Premodern China: Assessments of Recent Scholarship. LC 84-7742. (Michigan Monographs in Chinese Studies: No. 50). 247p. (C). 1984. text 35.00 (0-89264-052-9); pap. text 20.00 (0-89264-053-7) Ctr Chinese Studies.

Rozman, Gilbert, et al, eds. Dismantling Communism: Common Causes & Regional Variations. LC 92-15892. 304p. 1992. text 38.00 (0-943875-35-8) Johns Hopkins.

Rozman, Gregorij. S Pota v Ameriko: Voyage to the U. S. A. in 1935. (Studia Slovenica Ser.: SP.S. 7). (SLV., Illus.). 110p. (Orig.). 1997. pap. 8.00 (0-614-25686-0) Studia Slovenica.

***Rozmanjzl & Boyer-Alexander.** Music Fundamentals, Methods & Materials for the Elementary Classroom Teacher. 3rd ed. 1999. spiral bd. 70.00 (0-13-088109-0) P-H.

***Rozmarin, Rarhel.** Mamma Used to Say: Pearls of Wisdom from the World of Yiddish. LC 00-39303. 2000. write for info. (1-58330-423-1) Feldheim.

***Rozmiarek, Rebecca J.** Meeting Writing Standards: Pursuasive Writing. 144p. 2000. pap. 14.95 (1-57690-990-5) Tchr Create Mat.

Rozmovits, Linda. Shakespeare & the Politics of Culture in Late Victorian England. LC 97-49966. 172p. 1998. text 29.95 (0-8018-5836-4) Johns Hopkins.

***Rozmus, Lidia.** Dwadziescia Widokow Z Kreciej Gory: Ostatnia Haibun-ga W Dwudzieskym Wieku.Tr. of Twenty Views from Mole Hill. (POL., Illus.). 27p. 1999. pap. 18.00 (1-929116-03-9) Deep North.

— Twenty Views from Mole Hill: The Last Haibun-ga of the Twentieth Century. 27p. 1999. pap. 18.00 (1-929116-02-0) Deep North.

Rozmus, W. & Tuszynski, J. A., eds. Nonlinear & Chaotic Phenomena in Plasmas, Solids & Fluids, Edmonton, Alberta, Canada, July 16-27, 1990. 640p. 1991. text 118.00 (981-02-0386-1) World Scientific Pub.

Rozmyn, Mia. Freedom in Design. Reinstatler, Laura M., ed. (Illus.). 90p. 1995. pap. 24.95 (1-56477-102-4, B218) Martingale & Co.

Rozmyn, Norma M. Words in the Wind. 1997. pap. 56.95 (1-57553-563-7) Watermrk Pr.

Rozner, Barry. Mark Grace: Winning with Grace. Rains, Rob, ed. (Super Star Ser.). 96p. (J). 1999. pap. 4.95 (1-58261-056-8) Sprts Pubng.

Rozner, Barry, jt. auth. see Stone, Steve.

Roznoy, Rich, ed. Packet: Speed, More Speed & Applications. LC 97-180549. 1997. pap. 15.00 (0-87259-605-2) Am Radio.

Rozo-Moorhouse, Teresa, ed. Diosas en Bronce: Poesia Contemporanea de la Mujer. (Illus.). 400p. 1995. pap. write for info. (1-886480-11-7) Edici Latidos.

Rozo-Moorhouse, Teresa, ed. & tr. see Rossetti, Ana.

Rozo, Stella Luz. Exito Sin Limites. LC 99-36054. (SPA., Illus.). 240p. 1999. pap. text 8.95 (1-56718-590-8) Llewellyn Pubns.

Rozo, Teresa, jt. auth. see Debicki, Andrew.

Rozova, A. V. Biostratigraphic Zoning Trilobites of the Upper Cambrian & Lower Ordovician of the Northwestern Siberian Platform. Chakravarthy, R. S., tr. from RUS. (ENG.). 279p. (C). 1984. text 123.00 (90-6191-434-5, Pub. by A A Balkema) Ashgate Pub Co.

Rozovksy, Fay E. Consent. 1994. 75.00 (0-316-76047-1) Little.

Rozovskii, B. L. Stochastic Evolution Systems: Linear Theory & Applications to Non-Linear Filtering. (Mathematics & Its Applications, Soviet Ser.). (C). 1990. text 218.00 (0-7923-0037-8) Kluwer Academic.

Rozovskii, B. L. & Sowers, R. B., eds. Stochastic Partial Differential Equations & Their Applications: Proceedings of IFIP WG 7-1 International Conference, June 6-8, 1991, University of North Carolina at Charlotte, NC. (Lecture Notes in Control & Information Sciences: Vol. 176). (Illus.). iv, 251p. 1992. 90.95 (0-387-55292-8) Spr-Verlag.

Rozovskii, Boris, jt. ed. see Carmona, Rene A.

Rozovsky, F. A. Liability & Risk Management in Home Health Care. LC 97-44706. 368p. 1998. 149.00 (0-8342-1067-3) Aspen Pub.

Rozovsky, Fay, jt. auth. see RiskCare Staff.

Rozovsky, Fay A. Consent Set. 2nd ed. 1990. 145.00 (0-316-76059-5, Aspen Law & Bus) Aspen Pub.

— Consent to Treatment: A Practical Guide. LC 83-81948. 669p. 1984. 80.00 (0-316-76073-0, Aspen Law & Bus) Aspen Pub.

— Consent to Treatment: A Practical Guide. 2nd ed. 670p. 1998. 149.00 (0-8342-1105-X, S676) Aspen Pub.

— Consent to Treatment: A Practical Guide. 2nd ed. 750p. 1998. 149.00 (0-316-76057-9, Y0314, Aspen Law & Bus) Aspen Pub.

— Corporate Compliance in Home Health: Establishing a Plan, Managing the Risks. LC 98-24887. 528p. 1998. pap. 49.00 (0-8342-1173-4, 11734) Aspen Pub.

Rozovsky, Fay A., et al. Medical Staff Credentialing: A Practical Guide. LC 93-33354. (Illus.). 132p. 1993. pap. 49.00 (1-55648-112-8, 145102) AHPI.

Rozovsky, Fay A., jt. auth. see Benda, Charles G.

Rozovsky, Fay E. Home Health Law. 1993. 125.00 (0-316-76076-5, Aspen Law & Bus) Aspen Pub.

— 96 Home Health, Vol. 1. 1996. 65.00 (0-316-76103-6, Little Brwn Med Div) Lppncott W & W.

Rozovsky, Fay E. & Rozovsky, Lorne E. Home Health Care Law Parts 1-3: Liability & Risk Management, Set. 340p. 1994. 125.00 (0-316-76100-1, Little Brwn Med Div) Lppncott W & W.

Rozovsky, Lorne. Canadian Patient's. LC 94-227688. 256p. 1994. pap. 18.95 (0-385-25449-0) Doubleday.

Rozovsky, Lorne A. Canadian Dental Law. 152p. 1987. boxed set 56.00 (0-409-86335-1, MICHIE) LEXIS Pub.

Rozovsky, Lorne E., jt. auth. see Rozovsky, Fay E.

Rozsa, Gyorgy. Scientific Information & Society. 1973. bds. 27.25 (90-279-7181-1) Mouton.

Rozsa, K. & Salanki, Janos. Neurobiology of Invertebrates, Transmitters, Modulators & Receptors: Proceedings of the Satellite Symposium of the 2nd World Congress of Neuroscience, Held at the Balaton Limnological Research Institute of Hungarian Academy of Science in Tihany, 22-26 August, 1987. (Symposia Biologica Hungarica Ser.: No. 36). (Illus.). 768p. (C). 1988. 207.00 (963-05-4958-1, Pub. by Akade Kiado) St Mut.

Rozsa, K. S., ed. see Salanki, J.

Rozsa, P., jt. auth. see Greenspan, D.

Rozsa, Sandor. Nuclear Measurements in Industry. 310p. (C). 1989. 150.00 (963-05-5219-1, Pub. by Akade Kiado) St Mut.

Rozum, Fred & Rozum, Mary. David D. Law: Bloomington-Normal's Veteran Streetcar Man. Morgan, Jim, ed. 24p. (Orig.). 1995. pap. write for info. (1-885001-10-X) Via Press.

Rozum, Mary, jt. auth. see Rozum, Fred.

Rozvany, G. I., ed. Topology Optimization in Structural Mechanics. (CISM International Centre for Mechanical Sciences Ser.: No. 374). (Illus.). vii, 322p. 1997. pap. text 80.00 (3-211-82907-5) Spr-Verlag.

Rozvany, George I. Optimal Design of Flexural Systems. 200p. 1976. 136.00 (0-08-020517-8, Pub. by Pergamon Repr) Franklin.

— Structural Design Via Optimality Criteria: The Prager Approach to Structural Optimization. (C). 1989. text 266.50 (90-247-3613-7) Kluwer Academic.

Rozvany, George I., ed. Optimization of Large Structural Systems: Proceedings of the NATO - DFG Advanced Study Institute, Berchtesgaden, Germany, 23 September-4 October 1991, 2 vols., Set. LC 92-43799. (NATO Advanced Science Institutes Series: Mathematical & Physical Sciences: No. 231). 1244p. (C). 1993. lib. bdg. 481.00 (0-7923-2130-8) Kluwer Academic.

— Optimization of Large Structural Systems: Proceedings of the NATO - DFG Advanced Study Institute, Berchtesgaden, Germany, 23 September-4 October 1991, 2 vols., Vol. I. LC 92-43799. (NATO Advanced Science Institutes Series: Mathematical & Physical Sciences: No. 231). 1244p. (C). 1993. lib. bdg. 580.50 (0-7923-2128-6) Kluwer Academic.

— Optimization of Large Structural Systems: Proceedings of the NATO - DFG Advanced Study Institute, Berchtesgaden, Germany, 23 September-4 October 1991, 2 vols., Vol. II. LC 92-43799. (NATO Advanced Science Institutes Series: Mathematical & Physical Sciences: No. 231). 1244p. (C). 1993. lib. bdg. write for info. (0-7923-2129-4) Kluwer Academic.

— Shape & Layout Optimization of Structural Systems & Optimality Criteria Methods. (CISM International Centre for Mechanical Sciences Ser.: Vol. 325). (Illus.). vi, 496p. 1995. 99.00 (0-387-82363-8) Spr-Verlag.

Rozvany, George I. & Karihaloo, Bhushan L., eds. Structural Optimization. (C). 1988. text 245.00 (90-247-3771-0) Kluwer Academic.

Rozvany, George I., jt. ed. see Olhoff, Niels.

Rozwaski, Chaim Z. Flight from Commitment: An Explanation of Paradoxes in Jewish Life. LC 96-13665. 224p. 1997. pap. 40.00 (1-56821-941-5) Aronson.

— Jewish Meditations on the Meaning of Death. LC 93-31385. 232p. 1994. 30.00 (1-56821-081-7) Aronson.

Rozwenc, Edwin C. Cooperatives Come to America: The History of the Protective Union Store Movement 1845-1867. LC 74-31009. (American Utopian Adventure Ser.). (Illus.). viii, 151p. 1975. reprint ed. lib. bdg. 35.00 (0-87991-004-6) Porcupine Pr.

Rozwenc, Edwin C., ed. The New Deal: Revolution or Evolution? rev. ed. (Problems in American Civilization Ser.). 113p. (C). 1959. pap. text 18.36 (0-669-23838-4) HM Trade Div.

Rozwenc, Edwin C., et al. The Restless Americans: The Challenge of Change in American History, Vol. 2. LC 76-180833. 74p. (C). 1997. reprint ed. pap. text 13.00 (0-536-00735-7) Pearson Custom.

Rozycki, Edward G. & Clabaugh, Gary K. The Plagiarism Book: A Student's Manual. 51p. 1999. pap., student ed. 7.95 (1-929463-00-6) NewFound.

Rozycki, Edward G., jt. auth. see Clabaugh, Gary K.

Rozycki, Tony. The Saint Bonaventure's Day Affair & 7 More Weird Stories. 104p. (Orig.). 1990. pap. text 10.00 (0-685-29065-4) Black Riv MN.

Rozycki, William. Mongol Elements in Manchu. LC 94-65580. (Uralic & Altaic Ser.: Vol. 157). 255p. 1994. 29.90 (0-933070-31-4) Ind U Res Inst.

— Mongolian-English Parallel Text. LC 94-69716. 1995. 49.00 (1-881265-13-7) Dunwoody Pr.

Rozycki, William & Dwyer, Rex. A Reverse Index of Manchu. Sinor, Denis, ed. LC 81-52901. (Uralic & Altaic Ser.: Vol. 140). 189p. (Orig.). 1981. 14.00 (0-933070-08-X) Res Inst Inner Asian Studies.

Rozzell, J. David & Wagner, Fritz, eds. Bioanalytic Production of Amino Acids & Derivatives. 411p. 1993. 125.00 (0-471-03717-6) Wiley.

Rozzi, T. & Mongiardo, M. Open Electromagnetic Waveguides. (IEE Electromagnetic Waves Ser.: No. 43). 387p. 1997. 95.00 (0-85296-896-5) INSPEC Inc.

***Rozzi, Tullio & Farina, Marco.** Advanced Electromagnetic Analysis of Passive & Active Planar Structures. (IEE Electromagnetic Waves Ser.: No. 46). 264p. 1999. 79.00 (0-85296-763-2) INSPEC Inc.

RPA Singer Staff. Adequacy of Hemodialysis: Clinical Practice Guideline, No. 1. 112p. 1996. pap. text, per. 21.95 (0-7872-1880-4) Kendall-Hunt.

RPP International Staff, jt. auth. see Berman, Paul.

Rpss, Paula P., tr. see Chekhov, Anton.

RRinglstetter, Maria, tr. see Perkins, Anne T.

RS Means Company, Inc. Staff & Association of Facilities Engineers Staff. Facilities Operations & Engineering Reference. (Illus.). 550p. 1999. 99.95 (0-87629-462-X, 67318) R S Means.

***Rsa.** Redefining Work. 72p. 1998. pap. 43.95 (0-566-08192-X) Ashgate Pub Co.

RSA Inquiry Staff. Tomorrow's Company. 36p. 1995. pap. 43.95 (0-566-07814-7, Pub. by Gower) Ashgate Pub Co.

***RSA Staff.** On Design & Innovation: A Selection of Lecturers Organized by the Royal Society for the Encouragement of Arts, Manufactures & Commerce. (RSA Lecture Ser.). 144p. 1999. 61.95 (0-566-08107-5, Pub. by Ashgate Pub) Ashgate Pub Co.

— On Work & Leadership: A Selection of Lecturers Organized by the Royal Society for the Encouragement of Arts, Manufactures & Commerce. (RSA Lecture Ser.). 90p. 1999. 61.95 (0-566-08108-3, Pub. by Ashgate Pub) Ashgate Pub Co.

RSA Staff, ed. The Arts Matter. 142p. 1997. pap. 22.95 (0-566-07977-1, Pub. by Gower) Ashgate Pub Co.

***RSA Staff, ed.** On Community & Environment. 160p. 1999. 61.95 (0-566-08106-7, Pub. by Gower) Ashgate Pub Co.

RSI Promotion. Assorted Inside Series. 1998. 19.95 (0-7148-3853-5) Phaidon Press.

RSI Promotion Staff. Mastering Fall Assortments. 1997. pap. text 35.99 (0-7821-2217-5) Sybex.

— O'Reilly Nutshell Assortment. 1997. pap. 19.95 (1-56592-374-X) OReilly & Assocs.

RSI Promotions. NY Public Library. 1997. 72.00 (0-15-100379-3) Dryden Pr.

***RSI Promotions Staff.** Arts & Ideas Assortment. (Illus.). 1999. 24.95 (0-7148-3978-7) Phaidon Pr.

RSI Promotions Staff. Star Wars: Incredible Cross Sections, 1. (Star Wars Ser.). 1998. 19.95 (5-551-78735-4) DK Pub Inc.

***RSI Promotions Staff.** Star Wars Visual Dictionary. (Star Wars Ser.). (Illus.). 1998. 19.95 (5-551-78733-8) DK Pub Inc.

RSI Promotions Staff, ed. RSI Assorted Nutritional Therapy. 1998. pap. 14.95 (0-8092-2677-4) NTC Contemp Pub Co.

***RSI Promotions Staff, ed.** RSI Style Assortment. (Illus.). 2000. pap. 29.95 (0-7148-4016-5) Phaidon Pr.

***RSM McGladrey Inc. Staff, ed.** Mandated Benefits: 2000 Compliance Guide, 1. 1104p. 1999. pap. text 165.00 (0-7355-0491-1) Panel Pubs.

***RSM McGladrey Inc. Staff & Negroni & Winston PLLC Staff.** Mortgage Banker's Guide to Regulatory Compliance. 2nd ed. (C). 1999. ring bd. 400.00 (1-57599-061-X, PB2-110112-SO-P, Real Est Fin Pr) Mortgage Bankers.

Rstavik, Dag & Pittford, Thomas R. Essential Endodontology: Prevention & Treatment of Apical Periodontitis. LC 98-25953. 1998. write for info. (0-632-04089-0) Blackwell Sci.

Rtischel, Wolfgang A. GerontoKinetics: PharmacoKinetics of Drugs in the Elderly. 225p. 1989. 45.00 (0-685-44558-5) Telford Pr.

RTNA Members. RadTech '98 North America Conference Proceedings. (Illus.). xi, 756p. 1998. pap. text 150.00 (1-878664-18-2) RadTech Intl North Amer.

Ru, Kwang, jt. auth. see Taylor, Chuck.

Ru, Yi-Ling. The Family Novel: Toward a Generic Definition. LC 91-27580. (American University Studies: General Literature: Ser. XIX, Vol. 28). 221p. (C). 1992. text 40.95 (0-8204-1567-7) P Lang Pubng.

Rua, Pedro J. Bolivar ante Marx y Otros Ensayos. (Norte Ser.). 148p. 1978. pap. 6.95 (0-940238-05-5) Ediciones Huracan.

Rua, Pedro J., ed. Introduccion a las Ciencias Sociales. LC 81-69790. 432p. 1982. reprint ed. pap. 12.25 (0-940238-64-0) Ediciones Huracan.

Ruachbauer, Otto, ed. Ancestral Voices: The Big House in Anglo-Irish Literature. (Anglistische und Amerikanistische Texte und Studien Ser.: Vol. 6). 307p. 1992. lib. bdg. 60.00 (0-685-66950-5) G Olms Pubs.

Ruan, D., ed. Fuzzy Logic Foundations & Industrial Applications. LC 96-31534. (International Series in Intelligent Technologies). 352p. (C). 1996. text 145.00 (0-7923-9774-6) Kluwer Academic.

— Fuzzy Set Theory & Advanced Mathematical Applications. LC 95-18108. (International Series in Intelligent Technologies: Vol. 4). 344p. (C). 1995. text 133.00 (0-7923-9586-7) Kluwer Academic.

Ruan, D. & Kerre, Etienne E. Foundations & Applications of Possibility Theory; Proceedings of FAPT '95: Ghent, Belgium, 13-15 December 1995. De Cooman, Gert, ed. (Advances in Fuzzy Systems Ser.). 250p. 1995. text 78.00 (981-02-2289-0) World Scientific Pub.

Ruan, D., et al. Fuzzy Logic & Intelligent Technologies in Nuclear Science: Proceedings of the First International FLINS Workshop, Mol, Belgium, September 14-16, 1994. 304p. 1994. text 99.00 (981-02-2003-0) World Scientific Pub.

***Ruan, Da, ed.** Fuzzy Systems & Soft Computing in Nuclear Engineering. LC 99-52051. (Studies in Fuzziness & Soft Computing). (Illus.). xiv, 479p. 1999. 108.00 (3-7908-1251-X, Pub. by Physica-Verlag) Spr-Verlag.

Ruan, Da, et al, eds. Fuzzy Logic & Intelligent Technologies for Nuclear Science & Industry: Proceedings of the 3rd International FLINS Workshop. 450p. 1998. 88.00 (981-02-3532-1) World Scientific Pub.

Ruan, Daonal. Intelligent Systems & Soft Computing for Nuclear Science & Industry: Proceedings of the 2nd International Flins Workshop, Mol, Belgium, September 25-27, 1996. LC 96-23425. 420p. 1996. write for info. (981-02-2738-8) World Scientific Pub.

Ruan, F. F. Sex in China: Studies in Sexology in Chinese Culture. (Perspectives in Sexuality Ser.). (Illus.). 225p. (C). 1991. text 42.50 (0-306-43860-7, Kluwer Plenum) Kluwer Academic.

Ruan, Ming. Essays on the Character of the Communist Party of China. 188p. 1994. pap. text 11.00 (1-879771-08-X) Global Pub NJ.

Ruan, Shigui, et al, eds. Differential Equations with Applications to Biology. LC 98-33721. (Fields Institute Communications Ser.: Vol. 21). 509p. 1998. 129.00 (0-8218-0944-X) Am Math.

Ruan, Zhong-Jin, jt. auth. see Effros, Edward G.

Ruane, Christine. Gender, Class & the Professionalization of Russian City Teachers, 1860-1914. (Pitt Series in Russian & East European). 258p. (C). 1994. text 59.95 (0-8229-3864-2) U of Pittsburgh Pr.

— War & Revolution in Vietnam. LC 98-127223. (Introductions to History Ser.). 1998. pap. 11.95 (1-85728-323-6, Pub. by UCL Pr Ltd) Taylor & Francis.

Ruane, G. La Eucaristia. (Greatest Healing Gifts Ser.: Vol. 1). (SPA.). 176p. (Orig.). 1995. pap. text 8.95 (1-885857-15-2) Four Wnds Pubng.

Ruane, Janet M. & Cerulo, Karen A. Second Thoughts: Seeing Conventional Wisdom Through the Sociological Eye. LC 96-45365. 218p. 1997. pap. 15.95 (0-7619-8505-0) Sage.

Ruane, Joanna. Boats, Boats, Boats. (My First Reader Ser.). (Illus.). 28p. (J). (ps-2). 1990. pap. 3.95 (0-516-45351-3) Childrens.

Ruane, John, jt. auth. see Campbell, Earl.

***Ruane, Joseph.** After the Good Friday Agreement: Analyzing Political Change in Northern Ireland. Todd, Jennifer, ed. 234p. 2000. pap. 29.95 (1-900621-26-6, Pub. by Univ Coll Dublin Pr) Dufour.

Ruane, Joseph & Todd, Jennifer. The Dynamics of Conflict in Northern Ireland: Power, Conflict & Emancipation. 381p. (C). 1996. text 59.95 (0-521-56018-7); pap. text 21.95 (0-521-56879-X) Cambridge U Pr.

***Ruane, Kevin.** The Rise & Fall of the European Defence Community: Anglo-American Relations & the Crisis of European Defence, 1950-54. LC 00-27836. (Cold War History Ser.). 2000. write for info. (0-312-23482-1) St Martin.

Ruani, G., jt. auth. see Taliani, C.

Ruano, A. E. P., on Algorithms & Architectures for, et al. Algorithms & Architectures for Real-Time Control 1997, AARTC '97: A Postprint Volume from the 4th IFAC Workshop, Vilamoura, Portugal, 9-11 April 1997. LC 97-27640. 1997. write for info. (0-08-042930-0, Pergamon Pr) Elsevier.

Ruano, Argimiro. Etica Fundamental: Los Valores del Bien y del Mal. 174p. (C). 1991. pap. 10.00 (1-881375-15-3) Libreria Univ.

— Etica Profesional: Perspectiva Puertorriquena. 101p. (C). 1986. pap. 10.00 (1-881375-14-5) Libreria Univ.

Ruano De La Haza, Jose M., ed. see Calderon de la Barca, Pedro.

Ruano De La Haza, Jose M., ed. see de Vega, Lope.

Ruardij, P., jt. ed. see Baretta, J. W.

Ruark, Gibbons. Keeping Company. LC 83-43. (Poetry & Fiction Ser.). 80p. 1983. text 14.95 (0-8018-3041-9) Johns Hopkins.

— Rescue the Perishing. LC 90-47142. 64p. 1991. pap. 7.95 (0-8071-1668-8); text 15.95 (0-8071-1667-X) La State U Pr.

Ruark, Jim, ed. see Bisagno, John R.

Ruark, John, jt. auth. see Gonda, Thomas A.

Ruark, Robert. The Honey Badger. 1994. reprint ed. lib. bdg. 39.95 (1-56849-326-6) Buccaneer Bks.

— Horn of the Hunter. 1994. reprint ed. lib. bdg. 39.95 (1-56849-327-4) Buccaneer Bks.

— Horn of the Hunter: The Story of an African Hunt. 1995. 35.00 (1-57157-023-3) Safari Pr.

An Asterisk (*) at the beginning of an entry indicates that the title is appearing for the first time.

— I Didn't Know It Was Loaded. 1994. reprint ed. lib. bdg. 39.95 (*1-56849-328-2*) Buccaneer Bks.
— Lost Classics. 1996. 35.00 (*1-57157-022-5*) Safari Pr.
— The Old Man & the Boy. LC 57-10425. 320p. 1995. 24.95 (*0-8050-0239-1*); pap. 12.95 (*0-8050-2669-X*) H Holt & Co.
— The Old Man & the Boy. large type ed. LC 94-5764. 417p. 1994. reprint ed. lib. bdg. 21.95 (*0-8161-5966-1*, G K Hall Lrg Type) Mac Lib Ref.
— Old Man's Boy Grows Older. 300p. 1995. 22.00 (*0-8050-2980-X*); pap. 12.95 (*0-8050-2974-5*) H Holt & Co.
— Poor No More. 1994. reprint ed. lib. bdg. 39.95 (*1-56849-329-0*) Buccaneer Bks.
— Something of Value. 574p. 1991. reprint ed. lib. bdg. 45.95 (*0-89966-816-X*) Buccaneer Bks.
— Uhuru. 1993. reprint ed. lib. bdg. 45.95 (*1-56849-025-9*) Buccaneer Bks.
Ruark, Robert C. Grenadine Etching: Her Life & Loves. 23.95 (*0-89190-954-0*) Amereon Ltd.
— Grenadine's Spawn. 22.95 (*0-89190-957-5*) Amereon Ltd.
— I Didn't Know It Was Loaded. 22.95 (*0-89190-958-3*) Amereon Ltd.
— Robert Ruark's Africa. McIntosh, Michael, ed. LC 90-86286. (Illus.). 256p. 1991. 32.00 (*0-924357-20-7*, 11420-A) Countrysport Pr.
Ruaro, Luir J. Amazonas: A Brazilian Adventure Story. Pidcoke, Heather F., ed. & tr. by. from POR. LC 98-13772. 340p. 1998. pap. 17.95 (*0-932727-93-X*) Hope Pub Hse.
Ruas, Charles, ed. see Young, Marguerite.
Ruas, Charles, tr. see Assouline, Pierre.
Ruasse, Jean-Pierre. Lexique de Nutrition: Les Mots pour Comprendre. (FRE.). 45p. 1993. pap. 15.95 (*0-7859-5668-9*, 2908502100) Fr & Eur.
Rub, Timothy, et al. A Gift to the College: The Mr. & Mrs. Adolph Weil, Jr. Collection of Master Prints. LC 98-36752. 1998. 40.00 (*0-944722-20-2*) Hood Mus Art.
***Rub, Timothy, et al.** A Gift to the College: The Mr. & Mrs. Adolph Weil, Jr. Collection of Master Prints. LC 98-36752. 1998. pap. 25.00 (*0-944722-21-0*) Hood Mus Art.
Rub, Timothy, et al. Two Views of Italy: Master Prints by Canaletto & Piranesi. (Illus.). 1995. pap. 14.00 (*0-614-12958-3*) Hood Mus Art.
***Rubach, A.** An Introduction to Ear Acupuncture. (Illus.). 248p. 2000. 59.00 (*0-86577-937-6*) Thieme Med Pubs.
Rubach, Bonita K., ed. see Ross, James, et al.
Rubach, Jerzy. The Lexical Phonology of Slovak. LC 92-38746. (Phonology of the World's Languages Ser.). (Illus.). 328p. 1993. text 75.00 (*0-19-824000-7*, Clarendon Pr) OUP.
***Rubach, Michael J.** Institutional Shareholder Activism: The Changing Face of Corporate Ownership. LC 99-49476. (Studies on the Financial Sector of the American Economy). 1999. write for info. (*0-8153-3502-4*) Garland.
Ruback, R. B., jt. auth. see Greenberg, M. S.
Ruback, R. Barry & Weiner, Neil A., eds. Interpersonal Violent Behaviors: Social & Cultural Aspects. LC 94-23169. (Illus.). 200p. 1995. 31.95 (*0-8261-8510-X*) Springer Pub.
Ruback, Stephen. New Wheels Without Getting the Shaft. vii, 71p. 1998. pap. 19.95 (*0-9651551-4-5*) Dynamic Pubng.
— Zoned Out: The Ultimate Irreverent Nutritional Guide Book. LC 98-96945. (Illus.). 100p. 1998. pap. 19.95 (*0-9651551-5-3*) Dynamic Pubng.
***Rubacki, James.** The Essential Guide to Prescription Drugs 2001: Everything You Need to Know for Safe Drug Use. 1216p. 2000. 50.00 (*0-06-019857-5*); pap. 20.00 (*0-06-095816-2*) HarpC.
Rubado, Clarence A. Problems of the City School Superintendent in the Field of Arithmetic. LC 71-177217. (Columbia University. Teachers College. Contributions to Education Ser.: No. 406). reprint ed. 37.50 (*0-404-55406-7*) AMS Pr.
Rubagumya, Casmir M., ed. Language in Education in Africa: Tanzanian Perspectives. (Multilingual Matters Ser.: No. 57). 154p. 1990. 74.95 (*1-85359-063-0*, Pub. by Multilingual Matters); pap. 29.95 (*1-85359-062-2*, Pub. by Multilingual Matters) Taylor & Francis.
— Teaching & Researching Language in African Classrooms. LC 93-29931. (Multilingual Matters Ser.: Vol. 98). 214p. 1994. 79.00 (*1-85359-200-5*, Pub. by Multilingual Matters); pap. 29.95 (*1-85359-199-8*, Pub. by Multilingual Matters) Taylor & Francis.
***Rubahn, H.G.** Laser Applications in Surface Science & Technology. LC 98-51716. 346p. 1999. 155.00 (*0-471-98449-3*) Wiley.
Rubajlo, V. L., et al, eds. Liquid-Phase Oxidation of Unsaturated Compounds. 227p. 1993. text 145.00 (*1-56072-119-7*) Nova Sci Pubs.
Rubakov, V. R., et al. Quarks '90: Proceedings of the International Seminar. 572p. 1991. text 151.00 (*981-02-0441-8*) World Scientific Pub.
Rubalcaba, Jill. A Place in the Sun. LC 96-38635. 96p. (J). (gr. 3-7). 1997. 13.95 (*0-395-82645-4*) HM.
— Place in the Sun. LC 98-16336. (Puffin Novels Ser.). 96p. (J). (gr. 3-7). 1998. pap. 4.99 (*0-14-130123-6*) Peng Put Young Read.
— Saint Vitus' Dance. LC 96-1260. 112p. (J). (gr. 4-9). 1996. 13.95 (*0-395-72768-5*, Clarion Bks) HM.
***Rubalcaba, Jill.** The Wadjet Eye. LC 99-57744. (Illus.). 128p. (J). (gr. 4-8). 2000. 15.00 (*0-395-68942-2*, Clarion Bks) HM.
***Rubalcaba, Stacy Rae.** In the Kitchen with the Chippendales: More Than 70 Romantic Recipes to Tempt, Tease & Tantalize. 128p. 1999. 14.98 (*0-7624-0569-4*) Running Pr.
***Rubalcava, Pedro.** Hoy Nos Reunimos. 2000. pap. write for info. (*1-58459-015-7*) Wrld Lib Pubns.
Rubalcava, Peter. Deo Gratias (Songbook) 1997. pap. 7.95 (*0-915531-74-7*) OR Catholic.
Rubaloff, Joa, jt. ed. see Huttner, Susanne.
Rubaltelli, Firmino F., ed. Metabolic Problems of the Newborn: Journal: Biology of the Neonate, Vol. 58, Suppl. 1, 1990. (Illus.). iv, 108p. 1990. pap. 35.00 (*3-8055-5304-8*) S Karger.
Rubano, Anthony, et al. Girl with the Scarf: Conservation of a Sculpture at Allerton Park. (Illus.). 22p. 1996. pap. write for info. (*1-883015-16-2*) Krannert Art.
Rubano, Gregory L., jt. auth. see Anderson, Philip M.
Rubano, Judith. Culture & Behavior in Hawaii: An Annotated Bibliography. LC 79-634604. (Hawaii Ser.: No. 3). 159p. reprint ed. pap. 49.30 (*0-608-13861-4*, 202044500018) Bks Demand.
Rubano, Susan & Flicker, Frances. Cucina Casolinga Italiana (Italian Home Style Cooking) Party-in-a-Packet. (Illus.). 1998. 19.95 (*1-891988-01-8*) Dining In-Novations.
— L' Esprit de France - French Home Style Cooking: Party-in-a-Packet. (Illus.). 1998. 19.95 (*1-891988-00-X*) Dining In-Novations.
— Gefsis Tis Hellas (The Flavors of Greece) Party-in-a-Packet. (Illus.). 1998. 19.95 (*1-891988-02-6*) Dining In-Novations.
— Hooray for Hollywood, California Cuisine: Party-in-a-Packet. (Illus.). 1998. 19.95 (*1-891988-03-4*) Dining In-Novations.
— Wake up & Smell the Coffee, Brunch: Party-in-a-Packet. (Illus.). 1998. 19.95 (*1-891988-04-2*) Dining In-Novations.
Rubanov, L. I., jt. auth. see Fain, V. S.
Rubanowice, Robert J. Crisis in Consciousness: The Thought of Ernst Troeltsch. LC 81-16085. xxiii, 177p. 1983. 49.95 (*0-8130-0721-6*) U Press Fla.
Rubanyi, G. M. & Vanhoutte, P. M., eds. Endothelium-Derived Contracting Factors. (Illus.). x, 238p. 1990. 177.50 (*3-8055-5092-8*) S Karger.
— Endothelium-Derived Relaxing Factors. (Illus.). x, 336p. 1990. 245.25 (*3-8055-5091-X*) S Karger.
***Rubanyi, Gabor, ed.** Pathophysiology & Clinical Applications of Nitric Oxide. (Endothelial Cell Research Ser.). 396p. 1999. text 220.00 (*90-5702-415-2*, Harwood Acad Pubs) Gordon & Breach.
Rubanyi, Gabor & Kauffman, Raymond, eds. Estrogen & the Vessel Wall. (Endothelial Cell Research Ser.). 288p. 1998. text 90.00 (*90-5702-283-4*, Harwood Acad Pubs) Gordon & Breach.
Rubanyi, Gabor M. Endothelin. (Clinical Physiology Series - An American Physiological Society Book). (Illus.). 306p. 1992. text 70.00 (*0-19-506641-3*) OUP.
***Rubanyi, Gabor M., et al, eds.** Therapeutic Angiogenesis: From Basic Science to the Clinic. LC 99-34989. (Ernst Schering Research Foundation Workshop Ser.: Vol. 28). (Illus.). xi, 186p. 1999. 79.00 (*3-540-65693-6*) Spr-Verlag.
Rubanyi, Gabor M. & Dzau, Victor J., eds. The Endothelium in Clinical Practice. LC 96-49906. (Fundamental & Clinical Cardiology Ser.: Vol. 29). (Illus.). 576p. 1997. text 210.00 (*0-8247-9809-0*) Dekker.
Rubanyi, Gabor M., jt. ed. see Ryan, Una S.
Rubash, Joyce. The Master Dictionary of Food & Wine. 2nd ed. (Culinary Arts Ser.). 458p. 1996. 41.95 (*0-442-02242-5*, VNR) Wiley.
Rubash, Joyce. The Master Dictionary of Food & Wine. 2nd ed. (Culinary Arts Ser.). 464p. 1996. 44.95 (*0-471-28756-3*, VNR) Wiley.
Rubatzky, V. E. World Vegetables. 704p. 1997. 79.00 (*0-8342-1687-6*) Aspen Pub.
Rubatzky, V. E., et al. Carrots & Related Vegetable Umbelliferae. LC 99-26900. (CABI Publishing Ser.). (Illus.). 304p. 1999. pap. text 50.00 (*0-85199-129-7*) OUP.
Rubatzky, Vincent E. & Yamaguchi, Masatoshi. World Vegetables: Principles, Production, & Nutritive Values. 2nd ed. LC 96-23732. 704p. (C). (gr. 13). 1997. 79.00 (*0-412-11221-3*) Kluwer Academic.
Rubbi, C. Light Microscopy: Essential Data. LC 94-9543. (Essential Data Ser.). 128p. 1994. pap. 43.95 (*0-471-94270-7*) Wiley.
Rubbini, Alice & Weiermair, Peter. Liberations Contemporary Multimedia Art: Representation of Feeling. (Illus.). 144p. 1998. pap. 29.95 (*88-8158-171-X*, Pub. by Charta) Dist Art Pubs.
Rubble Mound Structures Committee of the Waterway, & Administracao do Porto de Sines, Sines, Portugal. Reconstruction of the West Breakwater at Port Sines, Portugal. LC 94-30076. 452p. 1994. 44.00 (*0-7844-0044-X*) Am Soc Civil Eng.
Rubbo, Anthony, jt. auth. see Yepremian, Garo.
Rubbra, Edmund. Gustav Holst: Music Book Index. 48p. 1993. reprint ed. lib. bdg. 59.00 (*0-7812-9601-3*) Rprt Serv.
Rube, B. Johnny & Yuma County Historical Society Staff. A Wooden Road Through the Hollow of God's Hand: Taming the American Sahara. LC 96-48295. 1996. 18.95 (*1-884172-14-8*) Yuma Cnty Hist.
Rubek, Erno. My Cube. 1999. pap. write for info. (*0-14-006250-5*, Penguin Bks) Viking Penguin.
Rubel. The Reading List: Contemporary. LC 98-12456. (Illus.). 352p. 1998. 14.95 (*0-8050-5527-4*); 30.00 (*0-8050-5868-0*) H Holt & Co.
Rubel & Rosman. Your Own Pigs You May Not Eat. (Australian National University Press Ser.). 1996. write for info. (*0-08-033012-6*, Pergamon Pr) Elsevier.
Rubel, et al. Atlas of Diagnostic Radiology of Exotic Pets. 1991. text 182.00 (*0-7216-3493-1*, W B Saunders Co) Harcrt Hlth Sci Grp.
Rubel, Arthur J., et al, eds. Susto: A Folk Illness. (Comparative Studies of Health Systems & Medical Care: Vol. 12). (Illus.). 195p. 1991. reprint ed. pap. 15.95 (*0-520-07634-6*, Pub. by U CA Pr) Cal Prin Full Svc.
***Rubel, Barbara.** But I Didn't Say Goodbye: For Parents & Professionals Helping Child Suicide Survivors. LC 99-96975. 112p. 2000. pap. 14.95i (*1-892906-00-7*) Griefwork Ctr.
Rubel, Darrell. Maude's Ice Cream. deluxe ed. (Set 1 Ser.: Vol. 3). (Illus.). 20p. (J). (ps-3). 1997. pap. 2.50 (*1-890567-02-7*) Berry Bks Ltd.
— Strawberry Meets Rex. deluxe ed. (Set 1 Ser.: Vol. 2). (Illus.). 20p. (J). (ps-3). 1997. pap. 2.50 (*1-890567-01-9*) Berry Bks Ltd.
Rubel, David. America's War of Independence: A Concise Illustrated History of the American Revolution. (Illus.). 48p. (Orig.). 1993. pap. 7.95 (*1-881889-39-4*) Silver Moon.
— Elvis Presely: The Rise of Rock & Roll. (YA). 1992. pap. 5.70 (*0-395-63566-7*) HM.
— Elvis Presley: The Rise of Rock & Roll. (New Directions Ser.). (Illus.). 96p. (YA). (gr. 7 up). 1991. pap. 5.95 (*1-56294-829-6*) Millbrook Pr.
— Fannie Lou Hamer: From Sharecropping to Politics. Gallin, Richard, ed. (History of the Civil Rights Movement Ser.). (Illus.). 128p. (J). (gr. 5 up). 1990. lib. bdg. 12.95 (*0-382-09923-0*) Silver Burdett Pr.
— Fannie Lou Hamer: From Sharecropping to Politics. Gallin, Richard, ed. (History of the Civil Rights Movement Ser.). (Illus.). 128p. (YA). (gr. 5 up). 1990. pap. 7.95 (*0-382-24061-8*) Silver Burdett Pr.
— How to Drive an Indy Race Car. LC 92-4545. (Masters of Motion Ser.). (Illus.). 48p. (J). (gr. 4-7). 1992. pap. 6.95 (*1-56261-062-7*) Avalon Travel.
— Mr. President: The Human Side of America's Chief Executives. LC 97-41135. (Illus.). 256p. (YA). (gr. 11). 1998. 24.95 (*0-7835-5253-X*) Time-Life.
***Rubel, David.** Scholastic Atlas of the United States. LC 99-26960. (Illus.). 144p. (YA). (gr. 3 up). 2000. 19.95 (*0-590-72562-9*) Scholastic Inc.
Rubel, David. The Scholastic Encyclopedia of the Presidents & Their Times. rev. ed. LC 93-11810. (Illus.). 224p. (J). (gr. 7 up). 1994. 17.95 (*0-590-49366-3*, Scholastic Ref) Scholastic Inc.
— Science. LC 94-46529. (Kid's Encyclopedia Ser.). (Illus.). 192p. (J). (gr. 2 up). 1995. 18.95 (*0-590-49367-1*) Scholastic Inc.
— The United States in the 19th Century. (Scholastic Timelines Ser.). 192p. (J). (gr. 4-7). 1996. 18.95 (*0-590-72564-5*, Scholastic Ref) Scholastic Inc.
— The United States in the 20th Century. LC 94-45702. (Scholastic Timelines Ser.). (Illus.). 192p. (YA). (gr. 4 up). 1995. 16.95 (*0-590-27134-2*, Scholastic Ref) Scholastic Inc.
Rubel, Edwin W., et al. Development of the Auditory System. LC 97-6235. (Handbook of Auditory Research Ser.). 504p. 1997. 89.00 (*0-387-94984-4*) Spr-Verlag.
Rubel, Edwin W., jt. ed. see Werner, Lynne A.
Rubel, Gene, ed. Encyclopedia of Connectors Master Index. 730p. 1997. per., ring bd. 89.00 (*0-935531-72-6*) Edwards CA.
Rubel, Gene, ed. see Wiseman, Ed.
Rubel, Gene, ed. see Wiseman, Edward.
Rubel, John. Oft in the Stilly Night. (Illus.). 396p. Date not set. pap. write for info. (*0-7392-0336-3*, PO3506) Morris Pubng.
Rubel, Lee A. Entire & Meromorphic Functions. 187p. 1996. 39.00 (*0-387-94510-5*) Spr-Verlag.
Rubel, Lee A., jt. auth. see Luecking, D. H.
Rubel, M. M. Savage & Barbarian: Historical Attitudes in the Criticism of Homer & Ossian in Britian, 1760-1800. (Verhandelingen der Koninklijke Nederlandse Akademie van Wetenschappen, Afd. Letterkunde, Nieuwe Reeks Ser.: No. 96). 128p. 1978. pap. text 34.50 (*0-7204-8442-1*) Elsevier.
Rubel, Mac, ed. see Egger, Markus.
***Rubel, Nicole.** A Cowboy Named Ernestine. LC 00-38338. (Illus.). (J). 2001. write for info. (*0-8037-2152-8*, Dial Yng Read) Peng Put Young Read.
Rubel, Nicole. Goldie. LC 88-32796. (Illus.). 32p. (J). (ps-2). 1989. 11.95 (*0-06-025096-8*) HarpC Child Bks.
— Goldie's Nap. LC 90-4401. (Illus.). 32p. (J). (ps-2). 1991. 14.95 (*0-06-025106-9*) HarpC Child Bks.
— No School for Penelope Pig. LC 97-20931. (Illus.). (J). 1997. pap. 3.50 (*0-8167-4300-2*) Troll Communs.
Rubel, Paula, jt. auth. see Rosman, Abraham.
Rubel, Paula G. Kalmyk Mongols: A Study of Continuity & Change. LC 66-63901. (Uralic & Altaic Ser.: Vol. 64). 282p. (Orig.). 1967. pap. text. write for info. (*0-87750-068-1*) Curzon Pr Ltd.
Rubel, Paula G. & Rosman, Abraham. Your Own Pigs You May Not Eat: A Comparative Study of New Guinea Societies. LC 78-7544. (Illus.). 382p. reprint ed. pap. 118.50 (*0-608-09519-2*, 205432000005) Bks Demand.
Rubel, Paula G., jt. auth. see Rosman, Abraham.
Rubel, Thom, jt. auth. see Kayne, Jay.
Rubel, William. The Stone Soup Book of Friendship Stories. LC 98-15481. (Illus.). 128p. (J). (gr. 3-8). 1998. pap. 8.95 (*1-883672-76-7*) Tricycle Pr.
***Rubel, William & Mandel, Gerry, eds.** Animal Stories by Young Writers. 96p. (J). 2000. 18.95 (*1-58246-025-6*) Tricycle Pr.
— Animal Stories by Young Writers. LC 99-39889. 96p. (J). (gr. 3-8). 2000. pap. 9.95 (*1-58246-017-5*) Tricycle Pr.
Rubell, Victor. Specialty Directory Publishing. 2000. 3rd rev. ed. Kopp, Linda, ed. (Illus.). 147p. 2000. 2495.00 (*0-88709-122-9*) Simba Info Inc.
Rubelmann, Stephen. Encyclopedia of the AirBrush, Black White Retouching, Vol. 3. LC 81-67960. 108p. 1984. 23.50 (*0-88108-006-3*) Art Dir.
Rubelmann, Stephen D., ed. Encyclopedia of the Airbrush, Vol. 1. LC 81-67960. (Illus.). 96p. 1992. reprint ed. pap. text 22.50 (*0-88108-100-0*) Art Dir.
Rubelmann, Steven. Encyclopedia of the Airbrush, 3 vols., 2. LC 81-67960. (Illus.). (C). 1982. 23.50 (*0-910158-76-2*) Art Dir.
— Encyclopedia of the Airbrush, Set. LC 81-67960. (Illus.). (C). 1982. student ed. 67.50 (*0-686-87028-X*) Art Dir.
Ruben & Lehr. Excellence in Higher Education. 140p. (C). 1997. per. 12.95 (*0-7872-3879-1*) Kendall-Hunt.
Ruben, Ann M. How I Grew up Feeling Some Day I Could Be President of the U. S. A. (Illus.). 40p. (Orig.). (J). (gr. 1-3). 1993. pap. 4.95 (*0-9608400-9-5*) Women Are Wonderful.
Ruben, Brent. Excellence in Higher Education. 52p. (C). 1997. per. 10.95 (*0-7872-3877-5*) Kendall-Hunt.
Ruben, Brent D. Communicating with Patients. 128p. (C). 1992. per. 12.00 (*0-8403-7430-5*) Kendall-Hunt.
— The Face of Higher Education: Quality & Service Excellence on the Front Line. 124p. (C). 1996. pap. text, per. 10.95 (*0-7872-2182-1*) Kendall-Hunt.
— Study Guide for Communication & Human Behavior. 96p. (C). 1996. spiral bd. 14.43 (*0-8403-9050-5*) Kendall-Hunt.
Ruben, Brent D., ed. Communication Yearbook, Vol. 2. 587p. 1978. 49.95 (*0-87855-282-0*) Transaction Pubs.
— Information & Behavior, Vol. I. 614p. (C). 1985. text 54.95 (*0-88738-007-7*) Transaction Pubs.
— Information & Behavior, Vol. 2. 600p. 1987. 54.95 (*0-88738-106-5*) Transaction Pubs.
— Quality in Higher Education. 300p. (C). 1994. 39.95 (*1-56000-190-9*); pap. 24.95 (*1-56000-795-8*) Transaction Pubs.
Ruben, Brent D. & Budd, Richard W., eds. Interdisciplinary Approaches to Human Communication. 2nd ed. 173p. 1979. pap. text 16.95 (*0-8104-5125-5*) Transaction Pubs.
Ruben, Brent D. & Lievrouw, Leah A., eds. Mediation, Information, & Communication. (Information & Behavior Ser.: Vol. 3). 496p. 1989. 49.95 (*0-88738-278-9*) Transaction Pubs.
Ruben, Brent D. & Stewart, Lea. Communication & Human Behavior. 4th ed. LC 97-27360. 496p. 1997. pap. text 52.00 (*0-205-26769-6*) Allyn.
Ruben, Brent D. & Stewart, Lea P. Communication & Human Behavior. 4th ed. 1997. pap. text, student ed. 23.00 (*0-205-26770-X*, T6770-6) Allyn.
— Communication & Human Behavior. 4th ed. 176p. (C). 1998. teacher ed., spiral bd. write for info. (*0-205-27983-X*, T7983-4) Allyn.
Ruben, Brent D., jt. ed. see Budd, Richard W.
Ruben, Brent D., jt. ed. see Kubey, Robert.
Ruben, Brent D., jt. ed. see Schement, Jorge R.
Ruben, David H., ed. Explanation. LC 92-33929. (Oxford Readings in Philosophy Ser.). 376p. 1993. text 55.00 (*0-19-875129-X*) OUP.
Ruben, David-Hillel. The Metaphysics of the Social World. 189p. (C). 1985. text 24.00 (*0-685-46216-1*) B&N Imports.
Ruben, Douglas. Avoidance Syndrome: Doing Things out of Fear. 183p. (C). 1992. pap. 22.50 (*0-87527-502-8*) Green.
Ruben, Douglas H. Drug Abuse & the Elderly: An Annotated Bibliography. LC 83-20463. 269p. 1984. 26.50 (*0-8108-1677-6*) Scarecrow.
— Family Addiction: An Analytical Guide. LC 92-27787. (Reference Books on Family Issues: Vol. 21). 384p. 1993. text 66.00 (*0-8153-0031-X*) Garland.
— Publicity for Mental Health Clinicians: Using TV, Radio, & Print Media to Enhance Your Public Image. LC 95-6249. (Illus.). 222p. (C). 1995. lib. bdg. 39.95 (*1-56024-953-6*) Haworth Pr.
— Writing for Money in Mental Health. LC 96-51806. (Illus.). 290p. 1997. 49.95 (*0-7890-0101-2*); pap. 24.95 (*0-7890-0240-X*) Haworth Pr.
Ruben, Douglas H., compiled by. Philosophy Journals & Serials: An Analytical Guide, 2. LC 84-29021. (Annotated Bibliographies of Serials: A Subject Approach Ser.: No. 2). 147p. 1985. lib. bdg. 55.00 (*0-313-23958-4*, RPJ/, Greenwood Pr) Greenwood.
Ruben, Douglas H., et al, eds. Current Advances in Inpatient Psychiatric Care: A Handbook. LC 92-49214. 384p. 1993. lib. bdg. 85.00 (*0-313-28046-0*, RCP/, Greenwood Pr) Greenwood.
Ruben, Douglas H. & Delprato, Dennis J., eds. New Ideas in Therapy: Introduction to an Interdisciplinary Approach, 10. LC 86-31922. (Contributions in Psychology Ser.: No. 10). (Illus.). 235p. 1987. 59.95 (*0-313-24845-1*, RNI/, Greenwood Pr) Greenwood.
Ruben, Douglas H. & Stout, Chris E., eds. Transitions: Handbook of Managed Care for Inpatient to Outpatient Treatment. LC 92-45144. 184p. 1993. 62.95 (*0-275-94064-0*, C4064, Praeger Pubs) Greenwood.
Ruben, Douglas H., jt. auth. see Macciomei, Nancy R.
Ruben, Jay, ed. see Salzman, Tony.
Ruben, Laurens N. & Gershwin, M. Eric, eds. Immune Regulation: Evolutionary & Biological Significance. LC 82-9994. (Immunology Ser.: No. 17). 351p. reprint ed. pap. 108.90 (*0-7837-3356-9*, 204331400008) Bks Demand.
Ruben, Margarete. Parent Guidance in the Nursery School. LC 60-8066. 72p. 1970. reprint ed. 27.50 (*0-8236-4000-0*); reprint ed. pap. 24.95 (*0-8236-8180-7*, 24000) Intl Univs Pr.
Ruben, Montague, jt. auth. see Hamano, Hikaru.
Ruben, Nicholas E., jt. auth. see Werth, Jacques.
Ruben, Patrica. True or False? LC 77-25285. (Illus.). 32p. (J). (gr. k-3). 1978. 11.95 (*0-397-31791-3*) HarpC Child Bks.

R

Ruben, R. Lynne. Instructional Media: Design & Production. 484p. (C). 1996. pap. text, spiral bd. 47.95 (*0-7872-0416-1*, 41041601) Kendall-Hunt.

***Ruben, Richard.** The Farmer's Market Cookbook: 100 Seasonal Dishes Made from Nature's Freshest Ingredients. LC 00-42324. 144p. 2000. 19.95 (*1-58574-131-0*) Lyons Pr.

Ruben, Robert J., jt. ed. see Alberti, Peter W.

Ruben, Samuel. Necessity's Children: Memoirs of an Independent Inventor. LC 89-17290. (Illus.). 160p. 1990. 17.95 (*0-932576-75-3*) Breitenbush Bks.

Rubenberg, Cheryl, jt. ed. see Alnasrawi, Abbas.

Rubenberg, Cheryl A. Israel & the American National Interest: A Critical Examination. 464p. 1989. reprint ed. pap. text 13.95 (*0-252-06074-1*) U of Ill Pr.

Rubenchik, A. & Witkowski, S., eds. Physics of Laser Plasma. (Handbook of Plasma Physics Ser.: Vol. 3). x, 654p. 1991. 300.00 (*0-444-87426-7*) Elsevier.

Rubenfein, Louisa, tr. see Ozawa, Ichiro.

Rubenfeld, Alan. Supertraders: Secrets & Successes of Wall Street's Best & Brightest. 1995. pap. 19.95 (*1-55738-810-5*, Irwn Prfssnl) McGraw-Hill Prof.

— SuperTraders: Secrets & Successes of Wall Street's Best & Brightest. rev. ed. 225p. 1992. text 24.95 (*1-55738-284-0*, Irwn Prfssnl) McGraw-Hill Prof.

Rubenfeld, Florence. Biography of Clement Greenberg: A Life. LC 97-36452. 448p. 1998. 29.50 (*0-684-19110-5*) S&S Trade.

Rubenfeld, Frank. The Peace Manual: A Guide to Personal-Political Integration. (Illus.). 85p. 1986. pap. 7.95 (*0-9616424-0-8*) Lion Lamb Pr.

Rubenfeld, Fred, jt. auth. see Smulkis, Michael.

Rubenfeld, Gordon D., jt. ed. see Curtis, J. Randall.

***Rubenfeld, Ilana.** The Listening Hand: Self-Healing Through the Rubenfeld Synergy Method of Talk & Touch. LC 00-37842. 320p. 2000. 25.95 (*0-553-11144-2*) Bantam.

Rubenfeld, Lester A., jt. auth. see Amazigo, John C.

Rubenfeld, M. Gaie. Critical Thinking in Nursing: An Interactive Approach. 336p. 1994. pap. text 23.95 (*0-397-55099-5*) Lppncott W & W.

Rubenfeld, M. Gaie & Scheffer, Barbara K. Critical Thinking in Nursing: An Interactive Approach. 2nd ed. LC 98-46410. 438p. 1999. pap. write for info. (*0-7817-1634-9*, Lippnctt) Lppncott W & W.

Rubenfeld, Sheldon. Could It Be My Thyroid? Kobos, Kathy, ed. (Illus.). 193p. 1996. pap. 18.00 (*0-9660398-0-7*) S Rubenfeld.

Rubenking, Neil J. Can Do DOS. (Illus.). 1993. pap. 12.95 (*1-56276-147-1*, Ziff-Davis Pr) Que.

— Can Do DOS & Display. 1993. 51.80 (*1-56276-162-5*, Ziff-Davis Pr) Que.

— Can Do Windows. 1993. pap. 5.95 (*1-56276-163-3*, Ziff-Davis Pr) Que.

— Delphi Programming for Dummies. (For Dummies Ser.). 400p. 1995. pap. 19.99 (*1-56884-200-7*) IDG Bks.

— Delphi Programming for Dummies. 2nd ed. (For Dummies Ser.). 448p. 1996. pap. 24.99 (*1-56884-621-5*) IDG Bks.

Rubenking, Neil J. Delphi 3 for Dummies. 3rd ed. LC 97-70740. (For Dummies Ser.). 448p. 1997. pap. 24.99 (*0-7645-0179-8*) IDG Bks.

Rubenking, Neil J. PC Magazine DOS Batch File Lab Notes. (Lab Notes Ser.). 309p. 1992. pap. 29.95 incl. disk (*1-56276-067-X*, Ziff-Davis Pr) Que.

— PC Magazine Guide to Turbo Pascal Techniques & Utilities. (Techniques & Utilities Ser.). 892p. (Orig.). 1991. pap. 39.95 incl. disk (*1-56276-010-6*, Ziff-Davis Pr) Que.

— PC Magazine Turbo Pascal 6.0 for Windows Techniques & Utilities. (Techniques & Utilities Ser.). (Illus.). 1100p. (Orig.). 1992. pap. 39.95 incl. disk (*1-56276-035-1*, Ziff-Davis Pr) Que.

Rubens, Alfred. A History of Jewish Costume. 221p. 1967. 55.00 (*0-317-61338-3*, Pub. by P Owen Ltd) Dufour.

— A History of Jewish Costume. rev. ed. 221p. 1973. reprint ed. 75.00 (*0-7206-0588-1*, Pub. by P Owen Ltd) Dufour.

Rubens, David, tr. see Shioda, Gozo & Shioda, Yasuhisa.

Rubens, Doris. Bread & Rice. (American Autobiography Ser.). 235p. 1995. reprint ed. lib. bdg. 79.00 (*0-7812-8633-6*) Rprt Serv.

Rubens, Horatio S. Liberty: The Story of Cuba. LC 72-111732. (American Imperialism: Viewpoints of United States Foreign Policy, 1898-1941 Ser.). 1970. reprint ed. 26.95 (*0-405-02049-X*) Ayer.

— Liberty, the Story of Cuba. LC 79-107075. reprint ed. 21.50 (*0-404-00633-7*) AMS Pr.

Rubens, James J., jt. auth. see Mintz, Robert J.

Rubens, Jeff. The Bridge World Magazine: Swiss Match Challenge - Learn How to Bid & Play Like a Winner & Have Fun Too! LC 92-74745. 240p. 1992. pap. 11.95 (*0-685-63269-5*) Lawrence & Leong Pub.

— The Secrets of Winning Bridge. 241p. 1981. reprint ed. pap. 5.95 (*0-486-24076-2*) Dover.

— Win at Poker. 224p. 1984. reprint ed. pap. 6.95 (*0-486-24626-4*) Dover.

Rubens, Peter Paul. Drawings of Rubens. Longstreet, Stephen, ed. (Master Draughtsman Ser.). (Illus.). (Orig.). 1964. pap. 4.95 (*0-87505-186-3*) Borden.

— Palazzi di Genova, 2 vols in 1. LC 68-21226. (Illus.). 1972. reprint ed. 66.95 (*0-405-08901-5*) Ayer.

— Pompa Introitus: Ferdinandi Austriaci Cum Antiverpiam Adventu Suo Bearet, 15 Kal. Maii Anno 1665. LC 68-21225. (LAT., Illus.). 1972. 71.95 (*0-405-08902-3*) Ayer.

— Rubens Drawings. (Illus.). 48p. 1989. pap. 4.95 (*0-486-25963-3*) Dover.

Rubens, Philip. Science & Technical Writing: A Manual of Style. LC 91-36422. 544p. 1995. pap. 19.95 (*0-8050-3091-3*) H Holt & Co.

***Rubens, Philip.** Science & Technical Writing: A Manual of Style. 2nd ed. LC 00-32837. (Illus.). 2001. pap. write for info. (*0-415-92551-7*) Routledge.

Rubens, Philip, ed. Science & Technical Writing: A Manual of Style. 512p. 1995. 40.00 (*0-8050-1831-X*) H Holt & Co.

Rubens, R., ed. see Dunlop, R.

Rubens, Robert, jt. auth. see Mundy, Gregory R.

Rubens, Tom. Spinozan Power in a Naturalistic Perspective: And Other Essays. 265p. 1997. pap. 18.95 (*1-85756-218-6*, Pub. by Janus Pubng) Paul & Co Pubs.

Rubenson, David & Anderson, John R. California Base Closure: Lessons for DoD's Cleanup Program. LC 95-42191. 109p. (Orig.). 1995. pap. text 9.00 (*0-8330-2327-6*, MR-621-OSD) Rand Corp.

Rubenson, David, et al. Does the Army Need (Have) a National Land Strategy. LC 99-26759. (Illus.). iv, 104p. 1999. pap. 28.00 (*0-8330-2733-6*, MR-1064-A) Rand Corp.

— Marching to Different Drummers: Evolution of the Army's Environmental Program. LC 94-28610. 1994. pap. 15.00 (*0-8330-1564-8*, MR-453-A) Rand Corp.

— McGregor Renewal & the Current Air Defense Mission. LC 98-47603. (Illus.). 108p. 1998. pap. 15.00 (*0-8330-2669-0*, MR-1010-A) Rand Corp.

— More Than 25 Million Acres? DOD As a Federal, Natural & Cultural Resource Manager. LC 96-17909. 130p. 1996. pap. text 15.00 (*0-8330-2363-2*, MR-715-OSD) Rand Corp.

Rubenson, David, jt. auth. see Mitchell, Donald.

***Rubenson, Ellen.** When Aging Parents Can't Live Alone: A Practical Family Guide. LC 00-23248. (Illus.). 288p. 2000. pap. 16.95 (*0-7373-0320-4*, 03204W, Pub. by Lowell Hse) NTC Contemp Pub Co.

Rubenson, Samuel. The Letters of St. Antony: Monasticism & the Making of a Saint. LC 95-24837. (Studies in Antiquity & Christianity). 256p. (C). 1998. pap. 22.00 (*0-8006-2910-8*) TPI PA.

Rubenson, Sven. The Survival of Ethiopian Independence. LC 78-1367. (Illus.). 437p. 1978. pap. 35.00 (*0-8419-0375-1*, Africana) Holmes & Meier.

Rubenstein. The Cultural Landscape: An Introduction to Human Geography. 6th ed. LC 98-7272. 543p. (C). 1998. 74.67 (*0-13-079778-2*) P-H.

— Mediated Minds, Mediated Lives. (Speech & Theater Ser.). Date not set. pap. 28.00 (*0-534-52416-8*) Course Tech.

— A New Direction in Conflict Resolution. 1999. text. write for info. (*0-312-10371-9*) St Martin.

Rubenstein. Scientific American Medicine. 1994. pap. text 187.95 (*0-89454-020-3*) Scientific Am Inc.

Rubenstein & Lacron-Foster. The Social Dynamics of Peace & Conflict. 220p. (C). 1997. per. 30.95 (*0-7872-4414-7*, 41441401) Kendall-Hunt.

Rubenstein, Albert H. & Schwartzel, Heinz, eds. Intelligent Workstations for Professionals: Proceedings of a Joint Symposium, Siemens AG, Northwestern University, March 1992. LC 93-9853. 1995. 165.00 (*0-387-56546-9*) Spr-Verlag.

Rubenstein, Alvin Z., jt. ed. see Blank, Stephen J.

Rubenstein, Anne. Bad Language, Naked Ladies, & Other Threats to the Nation: A Political History of Comic Books in Mexico. LC 98-7517. 1998. pap. 17.95 (*0-8223-2141-6*) Duke.

— Bad Language, Naked Ladies & Other Threats to the Nation: A Political History of Comic Books in Mexico. LC 98-7517. 1998. 49.95 (*0-8223-2108-4*) Duke.

Rubenstein, Ben, jt. ed. see Levitt, Morton.

Rubenstein, Betty R., et al. What Kind of God? Essays in Honor of Richard L. Rubenstein. Feibel, Hannah R. et al, eds. LC 95-23284. (Studies in the Shoah: Vol. 11). 524p. (C). 1995. lib. bdg. 64.50 (*0-7618-0036-0*) U Pr of Amer.

Rubenstein, Bruce A. & Ziewacz, Lawrence E. Michigan: A History of the Great Lakes State. 2nd rev. ed. (Illus.). 282p. (C). 1995. pap. text 21.95 (*0-88295-919-0*) Harlan Davidson.

— Payoffs in the Cloakroom: The Greening of the Michigan Legislature, 1938-1946. LC 94-48041. 1995. 28.00 (*0-87013-387-X*) Mich St U Pr.

Rubenstein, Carin. The Sacrificial Mother: Escaping the Trap of Self-Denial. 256p. 1999. reprint ed. pap. 12.95 (*0-7868-8410-X*, Pub. by Hyperion) Time Warner.

Rubenstein, Charles F. AutoCAD: The Drawing Tool. 1992. pap., teacher ed. 21.00 (*0-8273-4887-8*) Delmar.

— AutoCAD Command Practice Workbook. 60p. 1993. pap., wbk. ed. 17.95 (*0-8273-6034-7*) Delmar.

Rubenstein, Charles F., jt. auth. see Richter, Herbert W.

Rubenstein, Charlotte S. American Women Artists: From Early Indian Times to the Present. (Illus.). 608p. 1982. pap. 15.95 (*0-380-61101-5*, Avon Bks) Morrow Avon.

Rubenstein, Daniel B. Environmental Accounting for the Sustainable Corporation: Strategies & Techniques. LC 93-50066. 224p. 1994. 59.95 (*0-89930-866-X*, Quorum Bks) Greenwood.

Rubenstein, Daniel I. & Wrangham, Richard W. Ecological Aspects of Social Evolution: Birds & Mammals. LC 86-9371. (Illus.). 562p. 1986. reprint ed. pap. 174.30 (*0-608-07159-5*, 206738400009) Bks Demand.

Rubenstein, David, et al. Lecture Notes on Clinical Medicine. 5th ed. LC 97-10914. (Lecture Notes Ser.). (Illus.). 320p. (C). 1997. pap. text 32.95 (*0-86542-925-1*) Blackwell Sci.

Rubenstein, Diane. What's Left? The Ecole Normale Superieure & the Right. LC 90-50096. (Rhetoric of the Human Sciences Ser.). 256p. (C). 1991. pap. text 19.95 (*0-299-12564-5*) U of Wis Pr.

Rubenstein, Edward. An Awakening from the Trances of Everyday Life: A Journey to Empowerment. D'ville, Linda G., ed. LC 98-97923. 177p. 1999. pap. 12.95 (*0-9668700-0-X*) Stillpt NC.

Rubenstein, Edwin. The Right Data. LC 93-85579. 409p. (Orig.). (C). 1993. pap. text 17.95 (*0-9627841-3-3*) Natl Review.

Rubenstein, Edwin S., jt. auth. see London, Herbert.

Rubenstein, Eli, ed. For You Who Died I Must Live On... Reflections on the March of the Living. (Illus.). 128p. 1996. reprint ed. 24.95 (*0-88962-577-8*); reprint ed. pap. 17.95 (*0-88962-510-7*) Mosaic.

Rubenstein, Eli A., et al, eds. Media, Social Science, & Social Policy for Children. LC 83-1393. (Child & Family Policy Ser.: Vol. 5). 256p. 1985. text 73.25 (*0-89391-229-8*) Ablx Pub.

Rubenstein, Eliza & Kalina, Shari. The Adoption Option: Choosing & Raising the Shelter Dog for You. (Illus.). 192p. 1996. 12.95 (*0-87605-425-4*) Howell Bks.

Rubenstein, Ellen. Your Specialty Store: How to Start & Run a Money-Making Store. LC 98-92725. (Illus.). 208p. 1998. pap. 19.95 (*0-9662193-0-9*) Duck Pr AZ.

Rubenstein, Faith J., jt. auth. see Eaker, Mark R.

Rubenstein, Gillian. Under the Cat's Eye: A Tale of Morph & Mystery. 208p. (J). (gr. 4-7). 2000. pap. 4.99 (*0-689-82288-X*) Aladdin.

Rubenstein, Hal. Paisley Goes with Nothing: A Man's Guide to Style. 240p. 1997. pap. 11.95 (*0-385-48393-7*, Main St Bks) Doubleday.

Rubenstein, Harriet, jt. auth. see Wallerstein, Nina.

Rubenstein, Harry R., jt. auth. see Bird, William L.

Rubenstein, Harvey M. A Guide to Site Planning & Landscape Construction. 4th ed. LC 95-24630. (Illus.). 424p. 1996. 90.00 (*0-471-12932-1*) Wiley.

— Pedestrian Malls, Streetscapes, & Urban Spaces. LC 92-2897. 288p. 1992. 99.00 (*0-471-54680-1*) Wiley.

Rubenstein, Helge, ed. The Oxford Book of Marriage. 400p. 1990. 35.00 (*0-19-214150-3*) OUP.

***Rubenstein, Herbert R. & Grundy, Tony.** Breakthrough Incorporation: High Growth Strategies for the Entrepreneurial Organization. (Illus.). 242p. 1999. 29.95 (*0-273-63885-8*, Pub. by F T P-H) Natl Bk Netwk.

Rubenstein, Hilary, ed. see Raphael, Caroline.

Rubenstein, Howard, tr. see Aeschylus.

Rubenstein, Howard S., ed. Songs of the Seder: A Music Book to Accompany the Passover Haggadah - Twenty-Three Songs, Prayers, & Chants - Traditional & Contemporary - Transliteration & English - Keys That Are Easy to Sing & Play - Chords for Piano & Guitar. 70p. (Orig.). (J). 1994. pap. 9.95 (*0-9638886-1-7*) Granite Hills Pr.

Rubenstein, Howard S. & Rubenstein, Judith S. Becoming Free: A Biblically Oriented Haggadah for Passover: The Permanent Relevance of the Ancient Lesson. LC 93-73663. 200p. (J). 1993. pap. 9.95 (*0-9638886-0-9*) Granite Hills Pr.

— Becoming Free: A New Look at the Ancient Lesson - A Haggadah for Passover (with Notes) 2nd adapted ed. LC 98-75746. 176p. 1999. pap. text 19.95 (*0-9638886-8-4*) Granite Hills Pr.

Rubenstein, Irwin, et al, eds. Genetic Improvement of Crops: Emergent Techniques. LC 80-23560. 254p. reprint ed. pap. 78.80 (*0-7837-2922-7*, 205753200006) Bks Demand.

Rubenstein, Israel, jt. ed. see Bard, Allen J.

Rubenstein, Israel, ed. see Mankiw, Dorothy.

Rubenstein, James M. The Changing Geography of the U. S. Automobile Industry. (Illus.). 336p. (C). (gr. 13). 1992. 90.00 (*0-415-05544-X*, A6907) Routledge.

— The Cultural Landscape: An Intro to Human Geography. (Illus.). 608p. (C). 1993. write for info. (*0-318-69912-5*) Macmillan.

Rubenstein, James M. & Bacon, Robert. The Cultural Landscape: An Introduction to Human Geography. (Illus.). 501p. (C). 1983. pap. text, teacher ed. write for info. (*0-314-71118-X*) West Pub.

***Rubenstein, Jeffrey L.** Talmudic Stories: Narrative Art, Composition & Culture. LC 99-10877. 408p. 1999. 49.95 (*0-8018-6146-2*) Johns Hopkins.

Rubenstein, Jill, ed. see Hogg, James.

Rubenstein, Joshua. Tangled Loyalties: The Life & Times of Ilya Ehrenburg. LC 98-40775. (Judaic Studies). 35p. 1999. pap. 24.95 (*0-8173-0963-2*) U of Ala Pr.

Rubenstein, Judith S., jt. auth. see Rubenstein, Howard S.

Rubenstein, Julie, ed. German/English Dictionary. rev. ed. (GER & ENG.). 672p. 1993. per. 5.99 (*0-671-86419-X*) PB.

Rubenstein, Julie, ed. see Baker, Mark.

Rubenstein, Julie, ed. see Barrett, Ron & Brown, Patty.

Rubenstein, Julie, ed. see Beals, Melba Pettillo.

Rubenstein, Julie, ed. see Blum, Howard.

Rubenstein, Julie, ed. see Bradley, Marion Zimmer.

Rubenstein, Julie, ed. see Brown, Todd D.

Rubenstein, Julie, ed. see Clark, Mary Higgins.

Rubenstein, Julie, ed. see Collins, Jackie.

Rubenstein, Julie, ed. see Collins, Joan.

Rubenstein, Julie, ed. see Comfort, Alex.

Rubenstein, Julie, ed. see Conran, Shirley.

Rubenstein, Julie, ed. see Craig, Jean.

Rubenstein, Julie, ed. see Danvers, Dennis.

Rubenstein, Julie, ed. see Davis, Patti.

Rubenstein, Julie, ed. see Fairchild, John.

Rubenstein, Julie, ed. see Fisher, Jeffrey A.

Rubenstein, Julie, ed. see Fletcher, Connie.

Rubenstein, Julie, ed. see French, Thomas.

Rubenstein, Julie, ed. see Friday, Nancy.

Rubenstein, Julie, ed. see Gage, Elizabeth.

Rubenstein, Julie, ed. see Goddard, Robert.

Rubenstein, Julie, ed. see Goldsmith, Olivia.

Rubenstein, Julie, ed. see Higgins, Jack.

Rubenstein, Julie, ed. see Hoffman, Eileen.

Rubenstein, Julie, ed. see Hoffman, Ronald L.

Rubenstein, Julie, ed. see Jacobs, Nancy B.

Rubenstein, Julie, ed. see Jenkins, Dan.

Rubenstein, Julie, jt. ed. see Kaye, J. Leonard.

Rubenstein, Julie, ed. see Kelley, Kitty.

Rubenstein, Julie, ed. see Kelley, Virginia C. & Morgan, James.

Rubenstein, Julie, ed. see Kushner, Harold J.

Rubenstein, Julie, ed. see Latt, Mimi.

Rubenstein, Julie, ed. see Levine, Katherine G.

Rubenstein, Julie, ed. see Lindvall, Michael L.

Rubenstein, Julie, ed. see Lutz, John.

Rubenstein, Julie, ed. see Maas, Peter.

Rubenstein, Julie, ed. see Marston, Stephanie.

Rubenstein, Julie, ed. see McGinniss, Joe.

Rubenstein, Julie, ed. see McGuire, Christine.

Rubenstein, Julie, ed. see Michael, Judith, pseud.

Rubenstein, Julie, ed. see Montecino, Marcel.

Rubenstein, Julie, ed. see Morton, Andrew.

Rubenstein, Julie, ed. see Moser, Marvin, et al.

Rubenstein, Julie, ed. see Murano, Vincent & Hammer, Richard.

Rubenstein, Julie, ed. see Nin, Anais.

Rubenstein, Julie, ed. see Nixon, Richard M.

Rubenstein, Julie, ed. see O'Donnell, John R.

Rubenstein, Julie, ed. see O'Frank, Milo.

Rubenstein, Julie, ed. see Pope, Jamie.

Rubenstein, Julie, ed. see Pritikin, Robert C.

Rubenstein, Julie, ed. see Quine, Judith B.

Rubenstein, Julie, ed. see Rogers, Jacqueline.

Rubenstein, Julie, ed. see Ross, Elizabeth & Sachs, Judith.

Rubenstein, Julie, ed. see Rossner, Judith.

Rubenstein, Julie, ed. see Rule, Ann.

Rubenstein, Julie, ed. see Safer, Jeanne A.

Rubenstein, Julie, ed. see Seligman, Martin E.

Rubenstein, Julie, ed. see Sheehy, Gail.

Rubenstein, Julie, ed. see Smalley, Gary & Trent, John.

Rubenstein, Julie, ed. see Smith, C. W.

Rubenstein, Julie, ed. see Smith, Winnie.

Rubenstein, Julie, ed. see Steel, Danielle.

Rubenstein, Julie, ed. see Stoll, Clifford.

Rubenstein, Julie, ed. see Stone, Gene.

Rubenstein, Julie, ed. see Summers, Anthony.

Rubenstein, Julie, ed. see Tarshis, Barry.

Rubenstein, Julie, ed. see Tempest, John.

Rubenstein, Julie, ed. see Tifft, Susan E. & Jones, Alex S.

Rubenstein, Julie, ed. see Tremain, Rose.

Rubenstein, Julie, ed. see Wadler, Joyce.

Rubenstein, Julie, ed. see Walker, Alice.

Rubenstein, Julie, ed. see Webb, James H., Jr.

Rubenstein, Julie, ed. see Wolfe, Linda.

Rubenstein, Julie, ed. see Woodward, Bob.

Rubenstein, Julie, ed. see Woolley, Persia.

Rubenstein, Julie, ed. see York, Michael.

Rubenstein, Ken. Biochip Technologies & Applications. DiClemente, Susan C., ed. LC 98-233805. 1997. spiral bd. 4950.00 (*1-57936-097-1*, 1901, Drug & Market Dev) IBC USA.

Rubenstein, L. Touring Prose: Writings on Golf. 11th ed. 1994. pap. 13.00 (*0-394-22331-4*) Random.

Rubenstein, L. I. The Stefan Problem. Solomon, A., tr. LC 75-168253. (Translations of Mathematical Monographs: Vol. 27). 419p. 1971. text 77.00 (*0-8218-1577-6*, MMONO/27) Am Math.

Rubenstein, Laurence Z. & Wieland, Darryl, eds. Improving Care in the Nursing Home: Comprehensive Reviews of Clinical Research. (Illus.). 296p. (C). 1993. text 52.00 (*0-8039-4306-7*); pap. text 24.00 (*0-8039-4307-5*) Sage.

Rubenstein, Len. Most Beautiful Villages of New England. 1998. pap. 12.95 (*0-500-95049-0*, Pub. by Thames Hudson) Norton.

Rubenstein, Lenny, jt. ed. see Georgakas, Dan.

Rubenstein, Leonard S., jt. auth. see Levy, Robert M.

***Rubenstein, Lisa.** Improving Depression Outcomes in Primary Care No. 15: A User's Guide to Implementing the Partners in Care Approach. 32p. 2000. pap. 12.00 (*0-8330-2840-5*) iUniversecom.

Rubenstein, Lona. From Away. Murphy, Rick, ed. (Illus.). 352p. 1997. pap. 14.95 (*0-9659552-0-6*) Arete Press.

Rubenstein, Lorne. Links: An Exploration into the Mind, Heart, & Soul of Golf. 176p. 1993. pap. 10.95 (*1-55958-279-0*) Prima Pub.

Rubenstein, Lorne, jt. auth. see Knudson, George.

Rubenstein, Mark. Derivatives: A Powerplus Picture Book: Futures, Options & Dynamic Strategies. 382p. (C). 1998. pap. text 75.00 (*0-9665860-5-0*) In-The-Money.

Rubenstein, Max D. You & Your Hormones. 1960. 15.95 (*0-8084-0387-7*) NCUP.

Rubenstein, Melvin & Burks, Jayne. The Unchanging You in a Changing World. (Illus.). 128p. (Orig.). 1996. pap. 12.95 (*0-9655143-0-7*) Blick & Staff.

Rubenstein, Michael, jt. auth. see De Vries, Ineke M.

Rubenstein, Nicolle. The Illusive Wizard of Oz. 23p. (J). (gr. k-5). 1997. mass mkt. 4.00 (*1-58193-165-4*) Brown Bag Prods.

— Snow White & Her Friends. 29p. (J). (gr. k-5). 1997. mass mkt. 4.00 (*1-58193-183-2*) Brown Bag Prods.

Rubenstein, Paul M. & Maloney, Martin J. Writing for the Media: Film, Television, Video & Radio. 2nd ed. (Illus.). 352p. (C). 1987. pap. text 79.00 (*0-13-971508-8*) P-H.

Rubenstein, Raeanne. Gone Country: Portraits of New Country Music's Stars. (Orig.). 1997. pap. 32.00 (*0-614-27475-3*, Schirmer Books) Mac Lib Ref.

Rubenstein, Raphael. The Basement of the Cafe Rilke. LC 96-37249. (House of Outside First Book Ser.). 80p. 1997. 10.00 (*1-889097-07-1*) Hard Pr MA.

— Postcards from Alphaville. 1999. pap. 13.95 (*1-889097-35-7*, Pub. by Hard Pr MA) Consort Bk Sales.

Rubenstein, Richard. The Cunning of History. 128p. 1987. pap. 13.00 (*0-06-132068-4*, TB2068, Torch) HarpC.

An Asterisk (*) at the beginning of an entry indicates that the title is appearing for the first time.

***Rubenstein, Richard.** When Jesus Became God: The Epic Fight over Christ's Divinity in the Last Days of Rome. LC 98-52097. 288p. 1999. 26.00 (0-15-100368-8) Harcourt.

Rubenstein, Richard E. Comrade Valentine: The Life of Yevno Azef, Russian Terrorist & Master Spy. LC 93-37988. 1994. 24.95 (0-15-152895-0) Harcourt.

— Comrade Valentine: The True Story of Azef the Spy -- The Most Dangerous Man in Russia at the Time of the Last Czars. 316p. 1998. text 25.00 (0-7881-5633-0) DIANE Pub.

***Rubenstein, Richard E.** When Jesus Became God: The Struggle to Define Christianity During the Last Days of Rome. 288p. 2000. pap. 14.00 (0-15-601315-0) Harcourt.

Rubenstein, Richard E., ed. see Bivins, Frank J.

Rubenstein, Richard E., ed. see Brinton, J. W.

Rubenstein, Richard E., ed. see Caldwell, Erskine & Bourke-White, Margaret.

Rubenstein, Richard E., ed. see Commission on Country Life, Jr.

Rubenstein, Richard E., ed. see Cooperative Central Exchange Staff.

Rubenstein, Richard E., ed. see Dies, Edward J.

Rubenstein, Richard E., ed. see Education & Labor Committee.

Rubenstein, Richard E., ed. see Federal Trade Commission.

Rubenstein, Richard E., jt. ed. see Fogelson, Robert M.

Rubenstein, Richard E., ed. see Hill, John, Jr.

Rubenstein, Richard E., ed. see Howe, Frederic C.

Rubenstein, Richard E., ed. see Kerr, William H.

Rubenstein, Richard E., ed. see Kinney, J. P.

Rubenstein, Richard E., ed. see Lord, Russell.

Rubenstein, Richard E., ed. see Loucks, Henry L.

Rubenstein, Richard E., jt. ed. see McCurry, Dan C.

Rubenstein, Richard E., ed. see Murphy, Jerre C.

Rubenstein, Richard E., ed. see Rochester, Anne.

Rubenstein, Richard E., ed. see Russell, Charles E.

Rubenstein, Richard E., ed. see Simonsen, Sigurd J.

Rubenstein, Richard E., ed. see Todes, Charlotte.

Rubenstein, Richard E., ed. see U. S. Department of Labor, Bureau of Statistics St.

Rubenstein, Richard E., ed. see Wallace, Henry C.

Rubenstein, Richard E., ed. see Watson, Thomas E.

Rubenstein, Richard E., ed. see White, Roland A.

Rubenstein, Richard E., ed. see Whitney, Caspar.

Rubenstein, Richard L. After Auschwitz: History, Theology, & Contemporary Judaism. 2nd ed. (Jewish Studies). 416p. 1992. text 52.00 (0-8018-4284-0) Johns Hopkins.

Rubenstein, Richard L., ed. The Dissolving Alliance: The U. S. & the Future of Europe. LC 86-25191. 216p. 1987. 22.95 (0-88702-216-2); pap. 12.95 (0-88702-217-0) Washington Inst Pr.

— Modernization: The Humanist Response to Its Promise & Problems. LC 82-83241. 353p. (C). 1986. pap. 14.95 (0-89226-031-9) Paragon Hse.

Rubenstein, Richard L., jt. auth. see Roth, John K.

Rubenstein, Robert A. & Foster, Mary L., eds. Peace & War: Cross-Cultural Perspectives. 350p. (C). 1985. pap. 21.95 (0-88738-619-9) Transaction Pubs.

Rubenstein, Roberta. Boundaries of the Self: Gender, Culture, Fiction. LC 86-11252. 272p. 1987. text 29.95 (0-252-01355-7) U of Ill Pr.

Rubenstein, Roberta & Larson, Charles R. Worlds of Fiction. (Illus.). 1472p. (Orig.). (C). 1992. pap. text 57.00 (0-02-404185-8, Macmillan Coll) P-H.

Rubenstein, Roni, ed. see Eisenstein, Laurence J. & Santoli, Al.

Rubenstein, Roni, ed. see Santoli, Al & Eisenstein, Laurence J.

Rubenstein, Sondra M. Surveying Public Opinion. LC 94-16428. 425p. 1994. 50.95 (0-534-17856-1) Wadsworth Pub.

Rubenstein, Susanne. Go Public! Encouraging Student Writers to Publish. LC 97-43721. 221p. 1998. pap. 25.95 (0-8141-1862-3) NCTE.

Rubenstein, W. D. Capitalism, Culture & Decline in Britain: 1750-1990. LC 93-33085. 240p. (C). 1994. pap. 18.99 (0-415-03719-0, A6027) Routledge.

Rubenstein, Warren & Talbot, Yves. Medical Teaching in Ambulatory Care: A Practical Guide. LC 91-5183. (Medical Education Ser.: Vol. 15). 144p. 1992. 27.95 (0-8261-7690-9) Springer Pub.

Rubenstein, William B. Lesbians, Gay Men & the Law: Cases & Materials. 2nd ed. LC 96-46482. (American Casebook Ser.). 918p. (C). 1996. 60.25 (0-314-20383-4) West Pub.

Rubenstein, William B., et al. The Rights of People Who Are HIV Positive: The Basic ACLU Guide to the Rights of People Living with HIV Disease & AIDS. LC 95-52122. 488p. (C). 1996. pap. 13.95 (0-8093-1992-6) S Ill U Pr.

Rubenstone, jt. auth. see Dalby.

Rubenstone, Jessie. Weaving for Beginners. LC 75-163009. (Illus.). 80p. (J). (gr. 5-8). 1975. 8.95 (0-397-31635-6) HarpC Child Bks.

Rubenstone, Sally & Dalby, Sidonia. College Admissions: A Crash Course for Panicked Parents. 2nd ed. 230p. 1997. 12.95 (0-02-861931-5, Arc) IDG Bks.

Rubenzer, Rex. You're a Real Cheesehead If... 1998. pap. 5.95 (0-9670616-0-1) Rex Productions.

Ruber, Peter. The Last Bookman: A Biography of Vincent Starrett. 2nd rev. expanded enl. ed. (Vincent Starrett Memorial Library Ser.: Vol. 3). 172p. 1995. text 24.00 (1-896032-66-4) Battered Silicon.

***Ruber, Peter A.** Arkham's Masters of Horror: A 60th Anniversary Anthology Retrospective of the First 30 Years of Arkham House. Arkham House Staff, ed. LC 00-26189. (Illus.). 2000. write for info. (0-87054-177-3) Arkham.

Ruber, Peter A., ed. see Wakefield, Herbert Russell.

Ruberg, Cynthia Lief, jt. auth. see Birch, Robert William.

Ruberry, Mary. Historias Biblicas EM Three-D. Flores van Damme, Patricia, tr. from ENG. (POR., Illus.). 64p. 1994. pap. 13.95 (0-9641811-0-X) Three-D Revel.

— Three-D Bible Stories. 64p. 1994. pap. text 15.95 (0-9641811-4-2) Three-D Revel.

— 3-D Book of Angels: A Collection. Collins, Norma, ed. (Illus.). 32p. (YA). (gr. 12). 1995. text 12.95 (0-9641811-8-5) Three-D Revel.

Ruberry, William J., jt. auth. see Arnavas, Donald P.

Ruberson, J. R., ed. Handbook of Pest Management. LC 99-35345. (Books in Soils, Plants & the Environment). (Illus.). 864p. 1999. text 225.00 (0-8247-9433-8) Dekker.

Ruberson, J. R., jt. auth. see Coll, M.

Rubert Candau, Jose M., jt. ed. see Lasso de La Vega, Javier.

Rubert de Ventos, Xavier. Heresies of Modern Art. Bernstein, J. S., tr. LC 79-19613. (Illus.). 276p. reprint ed. pap. 85.60 (0-8357-4578-3, 203748700008) Bks Demand.

Rubert, Steven C. A Most Promising Weed: A History of Tobacco Farming & Labor in Colonial Zimbabwe, 1890-1945. LC 98-19136. (Monographs in International Studies, Africa). xvi, 255p. 1998. pap. text 26.00 (0-89680-203-5) Ohio U Pr.

Rubert, Steven C. & Rasmussen, R. Kent. Historical Dictionary of Zimbabwe. 3rd ed. (African Historical Dictionaries Ser.: No. 46). (Illus.). 560p. 1998. 89.50 (0-8108-3471-5) Scarecrow.

Rubert, Steven C., jt. auth. see Rasmussen, R. Kent.

Ruberte, Ruth M., jt. auth. see Martin, Franklin W.

Ruberti, A., ed. Realization Theory. LC 76-21964. 1977. pap. 23.00 (0-08-021276-X, Pergamon Pr) Elsevier.

Rubertis, Barbara De, see De Rubertis, Barbara.

Rubery, Jill. Women & European Employment. LC 97-6093. (Frontiers of Political Economy Ser.). (Illus.). 352p. (C). 1997. 100.00 (0-415-16985-2) Routledge.

Rubery, Jill, ed. Women & Recession. (International Library of Economics). 288p. 1988. text 55.00 (0-7102-0701-8, Routledge Thoemms); pap. text 19.95 (0-7102-1337-9, Routledge Thoemms) Routledge.

Rubery, Jill & Wilkinson, Frank, eds. Employer Strategy & the Labour Market. (Social Change & Economic Life Initiative Ser.). 408p. 1994. 69.00 (0-19-827894-2) OUP.

Rubery, Jill, et al. Women's Employment in Europe: Trends & Prospects. LC 98-47473. 350p. 1999. pap. 29.99 (0-415-19854-2) Routledge.

Rubesa, Domagoj. Lifetime Prediction & Constitutive Modelling for Creep-Fatigue Interaction. LC 97-107878. (Materialkundlich-Technische Reihe Ser.: No. 13). (Illus.). 151p. 1996. 37.70 (3-443-23015-6, Pub. by Gebruder Borntraeger) Balogh.

***Rubey, Arnold.** Fallen Brother in Blue: The Tragic Death of Police Officer Mark Stall. 240p. 1999. pap. 15.00 (1-892525-15-1) ACW Press.

Rubey, Harry, et al. The Engineer & Professional Management. 3rd ed. LC 70-137090. (Illus.). 399p. reprint ed. pap. 123.70 (0-608-18766-6, 202978000065) Bks Demand.

Rubi, J. M. & Perez-Vicente, Conrado. Complex Behaviour of Glassy Systems: Proceedings of the XIV Sitges Conference, Sitges, Barcelona, Spain, 10-14 June 1996. LC 97-13334. (Lecture Notes in Physics). ix, 465p. 1997. text. write for info. (3-540-63069-4) Spr-Verlag.

Rubia, Geraldine. Skating among the Graves. 96p. 1991. pap. 5.55 (0-920021-97-2) Creative Bk Pub.

Rubia, Tomas Diaz de la, see Diaz de la Rubia, Tomas.

Rubicam, Milton. Eckel Family of Maryland, Penna, Tenn., No. Carolina & Delaware. (Illus.). 70p. 1997. reprint ed. pap. 14.00 (0-8328-8434-0); reprint ed. lib. bdg. 24.00 (0-8328-8433-2) Higginson Bk Co.

Rubie, D. C., jt. ed. see Thompson, A. B.

Rubie, Peter. The Elements of Storytelling: How to Write Compelling Fiction. LC 96-128077. 173p. 1995. pap. 15.95 (0-471-13045-1) Wiley.

***Rubie, Peter.** The Everything Get Published Book. LC 00-23952. (Illus.). 336p. 2000. pap. 12.95 (1-58062-315-8) Adams Media.

Rubie, Peter, jt. auth. see Provost, Gary.

Rubie, Peter, jt. ed. see Reyes, Luis.

Rubies, Joan, jt. ed. see Bugge, Henriette.

Rubies, Joan-Pau, jt. ed. see Elsner, Jas.

***Rubietta, Jane.** Fabulous After 50: Finding Fulfillment for Tomorrow. 2000. pap. 10.99 (0-89221-497-X) New Leaf.

Rubietta, Jane. Quiet Places: A Woman's Guide to Personal Retreat. LC 97-33849. 192p. 1997. pap. 9.99 (0-7642-2001-2) Bethany Hse.

***Rubietta, Jane.** Still Waters. LC 99-6553. 176p. 1999. pap. text 9.99 (0-7642-2200-7) Bethany Hse.

Rubiez, Ghassan, et al. Justice & the Intifada: Palestinians & Israelis Speak Out. 160p. 1991. pap. 10.95 (0-377-00237-2) Friendship Pr.

Rubik, Beverly. Life at the Edge of Science: An Anthology of Papers by Beverly Rubik. LC 96-94315. (Illus.). 185p. (Orig.). 1996. pap. 16.00 (0-9652401-0-X, BR1) Inst Frontier Sci.

Rubik, Beverly, intro. The Interrelationship Between Mind & Matter. 281p. (Orig.). 1992. pap. 20.00 (0-9633272-0-8) Temple U Frontier Sci.

Rubik, Frieder, jt. auth. see Frankl, Paolo.

Rubik, Margarete. The Novels of Mrs. Oliphant: A Subversive View of Traditional Themes. LC 93-13111. (Writing about Women: Feminist Literary Studies: Vol. 8). 343p. (C). 1994. text 54.95 (0-8204-2209-6) P Lang Pubng.

Rubin. The Art of the Shuffle. 64p. 1996. pap. 19.95 (0-7935-4206-5, 00695005) H Leonard.

Rubin. Communication Research. 5th ed. LC 99-16080. (Speech & Theater Ser.). 1999. pap. 35.95 (0-534-56169-1) Wadsworth Pub.

— Emily in Love. 1997. pap. 5.00 (0-15-200957-4) Harcourt.

— Frommer's Family Travel Guide Washington, D. C., with Kids. 2nd ed. 1996. pap. 14.95 (0-671-51930-1) S&S Trade.

***Rubin.** Gaining Word Power. 5th ed. LC 99-13673. 401p. 1999. pap. text 41.00 (0-205-29863-X, Longwood Div) Allyn.

— Grandma Doralee Patinkins Jewi. 288p. 1999. pap. 14.95 (0-312-24445-2) St Martin.

Rubin. History of Economic Thought. 440p. pap. 22.95 (0-7453-0301-3, Pub. by Pluto GBR) Stylus Pub VA.

— The Limbo Road. Date not set. 22.50 (0-8050-5665-3); pap. write for info. (0-8050-5666-1, Owl) H Holt & Co.

— Mammography: The Requisites. (Illus.). 384p. (C). (gr. 13). 2000. text 79.00 (0-8151-7481-0, 27477) Mosby Inc.

— Math Logic with Applications. (C). 1990. pap. text, teacher ed. 34.00 (0-03-012809-9) Harcourt Coll Pubs.

— Oncologic Imaging. 2nd ed. 1999. text. write for info. (0-7216-7494-1, W B Saunders Co) Harcrt Hlth Sci Grp.

— "Primitivism" in 20th Century Art: Affinity of the Tribal & the Modern, 2 vols. 1995. pap. text. write for info. (0-8109-6134-2) Abrams.

— Psychology. (C). Date not set. pap. 59.16 (0-395-65554-4) HM.

— Psychology. (C). 1992. pap. text 59.16 (0-395-65553-6); pap. text, student ed. 17.96 (0-395-60552-0) HM.

— Psychology. (C). 1993. pap., teacher ed., suppl. ed. 3.96 (0-395-60553-9) HM.

— Psychology. (C). 1993. pap. 3.16 (0-395-60551-2) HM.

— Social Psychology of Bargaining & Negotiation. 359p. 1975. 65.00 (0-12-601250-4) Acad Pr.

***Rubin.** The Swallowing Manual. LC 99-46383. 1999. pap. 70.95 (0-7693-0070-7) Thomson Learn.

Rubin. World Encyclopedia of Contemporary Theatre Vol. 6: World Theatre Bibliography - Cumulative Index. annot. ed. (Illus.). 520p. (C). 1999. 140.00 (0-415-05934-8, B0400) Routledge.

Rubin, et al. Construction Claims: Prevention & Resolution. 3rd ed. LC 99-22909. 416p. 1999. 69.95 (0-471-34863-5) Wiley.

Rubin, jt. auth. see Levin.

Rubin, Abba. Images in Transition: The English Jew in English Literature, 1660-1830, 4. LC 83-22730. (Contributions to the Study of World Literature Ser.: No. 4). 157p. 1984. 45.00 (0-313-23779-4, RUJ/, Greenwood Pr) Greenwood.

***Rubin, Alan.** Diabetes Cookbook for Dummies. 384p. 2000. pap. 19.99 (0-7645-5230-9) IDG Bks.

Rubin, Alan, ed. Prentice-Hall Federal Tax Course, 1986. 1440p. (C). 1985. text, student ed. 34.95 (0-13-312794-X) P-H.

Rubin, Alan, ed. see Prentice-Hall Staff.

Rubin, Alan A. New Drugs: Discovery & Development. (Drugs & the Pharmaceutical Sciences Ser.: Vol. 5). (Illus.). 328p. 1978. text 165.00 (0-8247-6634-2) Dekker.

Rubin, Alan A., ed. Search for New Drugs. LC 74-187516. (Medicinal Research Ser.: No. 6). (Illus.). 464p. reprint ed. pap. 143.90 (0-7837-0931-5, 204123600019) Bks Demand.

Rubin, Alan A., intro. The Complete Guide to America's National Parks, 1994-1995. 6th rev. ed. LC 89-63985. 1990. pap. 14.95 (0-9603410-6-4) Natl Pk Found.

Rubin, Alan L. Diabetes for Dummies. (For Dummies Ser.). 384p. 1999. pap. 19.99 (0-7645-5154-X, Dummies Trade Pr) IDG Bks.

Rubin, Albert L., ed. see Cheich, Jhoong S., et al.

Rubin, Alexis P., ed. Scattered among the Nations: Documents Affecting Jewish History 49 to 1975. LC 94-17497. 360p. 1995. 40.00 (1-56821-237-2) Aronson.

Rubin, Alfred P. Ethics & Authority in International Law. LC 96-45060. (Cambridge Studies in International & Comparative Law). 256p. (C). 1997. text 59.95 (0-521-58202-4) Cambridge U Pr.

— The Law of Piracy. 2nd rev. ed. LC 96-53043. 504p. 1998. 115.00 (1-57105-035-3) Transnatl Pubs.

Rubin, Allen. Research Methods for Social Work. (Social Work Ser.). 1989. pap. write for info. (0-534-10057-0) Brooks-Cole.

Rubin, Allen & Babbie. Research Methods for Social Work. 3rd ed. 1996. mass mkt. write for info. (0-534-34499-2) Thomson Learn.

Rubin, Allen & Babbie, Earl. Research Methods for Social Work. 507p. (C). 1989. pap. 45.00 (0-534-10056-2) Brooks-Cole.

— Research Methods for Social Work. 2nd ed. 752p. (C). 1993. text 56.95 (0-534-17478-7) Brooks-Cole.

Rubin, Allen & Babbie, Earl. Research Methods for Social Work. 3rd ed. LC 96-17903. (Social Work Ser.). 750p. (C). 1996. 76.95 (0-534-26388-7) Brooks-Cole.

Rubin, Allen & Babbie, Earl. Research Methods for Social Work: Study Guide. 3rd ed. LC 96-31385. (C). 1996. mass mkt., student ed. 15.00 (0-534-34498-4) Brooks-Cole.

***Rubin, Allen & Babbie, Earl R.** Research Methods for Social Work. 4th ed. LC 00-32466. 2000. write for info. (0-534-36217-6) Wadsworth Pub.

Rubin, Andee & Mokros, Jan. Data: Kids, Cata, & Ads: Statistics. rev. ed. Anderson, Catherine & Cory, Beverly, eds. (Investigations in Number, Data, & Space Ser.). (Illus.). 158p. (YA). (gr. 5 up). 1997. pap. text 22.95 (1-57232-804-5, 47051) Seymour Pubns.

Rubin, Andee, et al. Data: Kids, Cats, & Ads: Statistics. Anderson, Catherine et al, eds. (Investigations in Number, Data, & Space Ser.). (Illus.). 154p. (Orig.). 1995. teacher ed. 22.95 (0-86651-994-7, DS21430) Seymour Pubns.

Rubin, Andee, jt. auth. see Bruce, Bertrum.

Rubin, Andee, jt. auth. see Russell, Susan J.

Rubin, Andrew, jt. ed. see Bayoumi, Moustafa.

Rubin, Andrew, jt. ed. see Gibson, Nigel C.

Rubin, Anne. The Valley of the Shadow. (C). pap. text. write for info. (0-393-97431-6) Norton.

Rubin, Arnold. Art As Technology: The Arts of Africa, Oceania, Native America & Southern California. Pearlstone, Zena, ed. (Illus.). 184p. 1990. pap. text 24.95 (0-914589-04-0) Hillcrest Pr.

— The Sculptor's Eye: The African Art Collection of Chaim Gross. (Illus.). 1976. 9.00 (0-686-25966-1) Mus African Art.

Rubin, Arnold & Bianchi, Robert S. Marks of Civilization: Artistic Transformations of the Human Body. LC 88-195361. (Illus.). 280p. (C). 1988. pap. 35.00 (0-930741-12-9); text 49.00 (0-930741-13-7) UCLA Fowler Mus.

Rubin, Arnold & Waxman, Samuel. The Leukemia Cell. (Uniscience Ser.). 192p. 1979. 112.00 (0-8493-5009-3, RC643, CRC Reprint) Franklin.

Rubin, Arthur. Intelligent Building Technology in Japan. (Illus.). 59p. (C). 1998. reprint ed. pap. text 20.00 (0-7881-4893-1) DIANE Pub.

Rubin, Audrey S., ed. see Heller, Jack.

Rubin, Audrey S., ed. see Liles, Parker, et al.

Rubin, Aviel D., et al. Web Security Sourcebook. LC 97-16374. 368p. 1997. pap. 34.99 (0-471-18148-X) Wiley.

Rubin, B. A., jt. ed. see Van Duuren, B. L.

Rubin, Barbara B., tr. from LAT. The Dictionaries of John de Garlande. 98p. (C). 1981. 10.00 (0-87291-155-1) Coronado Pr.

Rubin, Barnett R. The Fragmentation of Afghanistan: State Formation & Collapse in the International System. LC 94-21189. 370p. 1994. 42.00 (0-300-05963-9) Yale U Pr.

— The Search for Peace in Afghanistan: From Buffer State to Failed State. LC 95-15694. 1996. 32.00 (0-300-06376-8) Yale U Pr.

Rubin, Barnett R., ed. Preventive Action: Cases & Strategies. LC 97-41268. 247p. 1997. pap. 11.95 (0-87078-412-9) Century Foundation.

Rubin, Barnett R. & Snyder, Jack L. Post-Soviet Political Order: Conflict & State Building. LC 97-36987. (Illus.). 224p. (C). 1998. 80.00 (0-415-17068-0); pap. 25.99 (0-415-17069-9) Routledge.

Rubin, Barnett R., jt. auth. see Center for Preventive Action Staff.

Rubin, Barry. Cauldron of Turmoil: America in the Middle East. 1992. write for info. (0-15-116128-3) Harcourt.

— Four-Piece Passover Pak, Set. (Illus.). 32p. 1989. pap. 17.99 incl. audio (1-880226-50-2) M J Pubs.

— Great Powers in the Middle East, 1941-1947: The Road to the Cold War. 254p. 1980. 49.50 (0-7146-3141-8, Pub. by F Cass Pubs) Intl Spec Bk.

— Islamic Fundamentalism in Egyptian Politics. 1993. 39.95 (0-333-54374-2, Pub. by Macmillan) Humanities.

— Islamic Fundamentalism in Egyptian Politics. LC 90-8060. 180p. 1990. text 39.95 (0-312-04571-9) St Martin.

— Modern Dictators: Third World Coup Makers, Strongmen, & Populist Tyrants. 1989. 8.95 (0-317-02814-6) NAL.

— Revolution Until Victory? The Politics & History of the PLO. LC 93-31651. 287p. 1994. text 24.95 (0-674-76803-5) HUP.

— Revolution until Victory? The Politics & History of the PLO. (Illus.). 288p. 1996. pap. 16.50 (0-674-76804-3) HUP.

***Rubin, Barry.** Trae las Roscas Judias Que Yo Traigo el Evangelio. (SPA.). 2000. pap. 8.99 (0-8297-2410-9) Vida Pubs.

Rubin, Barry. The Transformation of Palestinian Politics: From Revolution to State-Building. LC 99-34447. 288p. 1999. 29.95 (0-674-00071-4) HUP.

— U. S. Policy Towards Radical Middle East States & U. S. Policy. LC 92-44064. (Policy Papers Ser.: No. 35). 61p. 1992. pap. 8.00 (0-944029-22-1) Wash Inst NEP.

Rubin, Barry, et al, eds. From War to Peace: Arab-Israeli Relations, 1973-1993. LC 94-38055. 224p. (C). 1994. text 40.00 (0-8147-7462-8) NYU Pr.

***Rubin, Barry & Rubin, Steffi.** Haggadah Preparation Guide. (SPA.). 1998. pap. 2.99 (1-880226-72-3) M J Pubs.

— Messianic Passover Haggadah. (SPA.). 1998. pap. 4.99 (1-880226-59-6) M J Pubs.

Rubin, Barry & Rubin, Steffi. The Sabbath: Entering God's Rest. LC 99-229097. (Illus.). 48p. 1998. pap. 4.99 (1-880226-74-X) M J Pubs.

Rubin, Barry & Rubin, Steffi K. The Messianic Passover Seder Preparation Guide: Instructions, Recipes & Music for a Messianic Passover Seder. 20p. 1989. pap. 2.99 (1-880226-24-3) M J Pubs.

Rubin, Barry & Rubin, Steffi K. The Messianic Passover Haggadah. 32p. 1989. pap. 4.99 (1-880226-07-3) M J Pubs.

Rubin, Barry, et al. Gulfwatch Anthology: The Day by Day Analysis of the Gulf Crisis. LC 61-17900. 158p. 1991. pap. 10.00 (0-944029-09-4) Wash Inst NEP.

Rubin, Barry, jt. auth. see Blum, Laura.

Rubin, Barry, jt. ed. see Baram, Amatzia.

Rubin, Barry, jt. ed. see Laqueur, Walter.

R

An Asterisk (*) at the beginning of an entry indicates that the title is appearing for the first time.

R

Rubin, Barry, jt. ed. see Lustick, Ian S.

Rubin, Barry A. You Bring the Bagels, I'll Bring the Gospel: Sharing the Messiah with Your Jewish Neighbor. rev. ed. (Illus.). 256p. 1997. pap. 12.99 (1-880226-65-0) M J Pubs.

***Rubin, Barry M. & Keaney, Thomas A.** U. S. Allies in a Changing World. LC 00-34574. (Studies in International Security). 2000. write for info. (0-7146-5078-1, Pub. by F Cass Pubs) Intl Spec Bk.

Rubin, Barry R. A Citizen's Guide to Politics in America: How the System Works & How to Work the System. LC 96-46521. 304p. (C). (gr. 13). 1997. 40.95 (0-7656-0028-5); pap. 24.95 (0-7656-0029-3) M E Sharpe.

***Rubin, Barry R.** A Citizen's Guide to Politics in America: How the System Works & How to Work the System. 2nd expanded ed. (Illus.). 352p. 2000. text 42.95 (0-7656-0627-5); pap. text 23.95 (0-7656-0628-3) M E Sharpe.

Rubin, Bernard, ed. Questioning Media Ethics. 320p. 1978. pap., student ed. 19.95 (0-03-046126-X, Praeger Pubs) Greenwood.

Rubin, Bernard, jt. auth. see Backstrom, Gayle.

Rubin, Berthold. Das Zeitalter Iustinians, Band 2. (Illus.). x, 315p. (C). 1995. lib. bdg. 152.30 (3-11-003411-5) De Gruyter.

Rubin, Beth. Frommer's Washington D.C. with Kids. 3rd ed. 304p. 1996. 15.95 (0-02-860923-9, P-H Travel) Prntice Hall Bks.

Rubin, Beth, jt. auth. see Frommer's Staff.

Rubin, Beth A. Shifts in the Social Contract: Understanding Change in American Society. LC 95-13200. (Illus.). 224p. (Orig.). (C). 1995. pap. 17.95 (0-8039-9040-5) Pine Forge.

Rubin, Betsy. Grammar Write Away Bk. 1: Edge on English, Bk. 1. 185p. 1987. pap. 9.60 (0-8092-4807-7) NTC Contemp Pub Co.

— Grammar Write Away Bk. 2: Edge on English, Bk. 2. 185p. 1987. pap. 9.60 (0-8092-4806-9) NTC Contemp Pub Co.

Rubin, Betsy, ed. All Spelled Out, Bk. C. 80p. 1986. pap. 9.00 (0-8092-4965-0) NTC Contemp Pub Co.

— All Spelled Out, Bk. A. 80p. 1985. pap. 9.00 (0-8092-5201-5) NTC Contemp Pub Co.

— All Spelled Out, Bk. B. 80p. 1985. pap. 9.00 (0-8092-5200-7) NTC Contemp Pub Co.

— Contemporary's Edge on English: All Spelled Out D. 80p. (Orig.). 1986. pap. 9.00 (0-8092-4964-2) NTC Contemp Pub Co.

— Exercising Your English Bk. 1: Basic Sentence Structure, Grammar, Usage, Bk. 1. 70p. 1990. pap. 7.93 (0-8092-4081-5) NTC Contemp Pub Co.

— Exercising Your English Bk. 2: Spelling, Capitalization, Punctuation, Bk. 2. (Exercises in English). 70p. 1990. pap. 7.93 (0-8092-4080-7) NTC Contemp Pub Co.

— Exercising Your English Bk. 3: Sentence Types, Style & Diction, Paragraph Structure, Bk. 3. 70p. 1990. pap. 7.93 (0-8092-4079-3) NTC Contemp Pub Co.

Rubin, Betty L., jt. ed. see Deane, H. W.

Rubin, Bonnie M. Fifty on Fifty: Wisdom, Inspiration & Reflections on Lives Well Lived. LC 97-18087. (Illus.). 160p. 1998. 30.00 (0-446-52369-0, Pub. by Warner Bks) Little.

Rubin, Bonnie M. & Mason, Marcy. Quick Escapes from Chicago: 25 Weekend Trips from the Windy City. 3rd ed. LC 97-49972. (Quick Escapes Ser.). (Illus.). 224p. 1998. pap. 14.95 (0-7627-0195-1) Globe Pequot.

***Rubin, Bonnie Miller & Mason, Marcy.** Quick Escapes - Chicago: 26 Weekend Getaways in & Around the Windy City. 4th ed. LC 00-25055. (Quick Escapes Ser.). (Illus.). 320p. 2000. pap. 15.95 (0-7627-0628-7) Globe Pequot.

Rubin, Boris. Fractional Integrals & Potentials. 1996. 120.00 (0-582-25341-1) Addison-Wesley.

Rubin, Bruce J. Jacob's Ladder. (Screenplay Ser.). 192p. 1990. pap. 12.95 (1-55783-086-X) Applause Theatre Bk Pubs.

Rubin, Bruce K. Conquering Childhood Asthma. 1995. 12.95 (0-9697781-7-1) Login Pubs Consort.

Rubin, Bruce K., et al. Conquering Childhood Asthma: An Illustrated Guide to Understanding the Treatment & Control of Childhood Asthma. LC 98-206940. (Illus.). iv, 114p. 1998. write for info. (1-896998-02-X) Decker Art.

Rubin, Byron, et al, eds. Lipases Pt. A: Biotechnology, Pt. A. (Methods in Enzymology Ser.: Vol. 284). (Illus.). 408p. 1997. text 89.95 (0-12-182185-4) Morgan Kaufmann.

Rubin, Carol. Working Model for Windows. 1995. pap. text, student ed. 64.00 (0-201-82110-9) Addison-Wesley.

Rubin, Caroline, ed. see Barnes, Jill & Asuka, Ken.

Rubin, Caroline, ed. see Barnes, Jill & Ishinabe, Fusako.

Rubin, Caroline, ed. see Barnes, Jill & Kanabe, Junkichi.

Rubin, Caroline, ed. see Barnes, Jill & Tsurmi, Masao.

Rubin, Caroline, ed. see Litchfield, Ada B.

Rubin, Caroline, ed. see Simon, Norma.

Rubin, Chana S. A Time to Heal. 235p. (C). 1991. 17.95 (1-56062-067-6) CIS Comm.

— A Time to Live. (Illus.). 269p. (YA). (gr. 9-12). 1988. 16.95 (0-935063-48-X) CIS Comm.

— Tomorrow May Be Too Late: An Assimilated Journalist's Involvement in the Notorious Dreyfus Trial Reunites Him with His Jewish Heritage. 15.99 (0-89906-619-4, TOMH); pap. 12.99 (0-89906-620-8, TOMP) Mesorah Pubns.

Rubin, Charles. Don't Let Your Kids Kill You: A Guide for Parents of Drug & Alcohol Addicted Children. LC 96-43239. 192p. 1996. pap. 12.95 (1-85230-863-X, Pub. by Element MA) Penguin Putnam.

Rubin, Charles. The Macintosh Bible Guide to ClarisWorks 4. (Illus.). 520p. (C). 1995. pap. 24.95 (0-201-88406-2) Peachpit Pr.

Rubin, Charles & Parssinen, Diane. Managing Your Business with QuickBooks 6. 2nd ed. LC 98-228290. 312p. (C). 1998. pap. text 19.95 (0-201-35356-3, Pub. by Peachpit Pr) Addison-Wesley.

Rubin, Charles, jt. auth. see Levinson, Jay C.

Rubin, Charles, jt. auth. see Rubin, Leslie.

Rubin, Charles T. The Green Crusade: Rethinking the Roots of Environmentalism. 320p. 1994. 22.95 (0-02-927525-3) Free Pr.

— The Green Crusade: Rethinking the Roots of Environmentalism. 320p. 1998. pap. 16.95 (0-8476-8817-8) Rowman.

***Rubin, Charles T., ed.** Conservation Reconsidered: Nature, Virtue & American Liberal Democracy. (The Political Economy Forum Ser.). 272p. 2000. pap. 24.95 (0-8476-9717-7); text 65.00 (0-8476-9716-9) Rowman.

Rubin, Claire B., et al. Community Recovery from a Major Disaster. (Program on Environment & Behavior Monograph Ser.: No. 41). 295p. (Orig.). (C). 1985. pap. 20.00 (0-685-28115-9) Natural Hazards.

— Summary of Major Natural Disaster Incidents in the U. S., 1965-85. (Special Publications: No. 17). 47p. 1986. 20.00 (0-614-01776-9) Natural Hazards.

Rubin, Cynthia E., selected by. ABC Americana from the National Gallery of Art. (Illus.). 26p. (J). (ps up). 1989. 11.95 (0-15-200660-5, Gulliver Bks) Harcourt.

Rubin, D. Modes Stats Infer Causal Effect. (C). (gr. 13). 1997. write for info. (0-412-31770-2) Chapman & Hall.

Rubin, D. E. Hidden Horses Two. (Illus.). 100p. 1994. pap. 17.95 (0-939481-40-5) Half Halt Pr.

Rubin, Dale F. Public Subsidies to Private Corporations: Stop Violating the Colorado Constitution. (Issue Paper #7-96 Ser.). 11p. 1996. pap. text 8.00 (1-57655-151-2) Independ Inst.

Rubin, Daniel. How a Communist Club Functions. 1971. pap. 0.40 (0-87898-067-9) New Outlook.

Rubin, Daniel, jt. ed. see Krippner, Stanley.

***Rubin, Dave.** Acoustic Country Blues Guitar: Delta Blues Before Robert Johnson. 80p. 2000. otabind 16.95 (0-7935-7225-8) H Leonard.

— B B King Guitar School. 48p. 1997. pap. 12.95 (0-7935-6504-9) H Leonard.

Rubin, Dave. Blues Power Trios. 64p. 1996. pap. 19.95 incl. audio compact disk (0-7935-4589-7, 00695028) H Leonard.

— Inside the Blues: 1942-1982. 176p. 1995. otabind 24.95 (0-7935-3611-1) H Leonard.

Rubin, David, tr. from HIN. The Return of Sarasvati: Translations of the Poetry of Prasad, Nirala, Pant & Mahadevi. LC 93-20404. (Studies on South Asia: No. 7). 201p. 1983. 25.00 (0-936115-08-4) U Penn South Asia.

Rubin, David & Sangster, Gary. Old Glory: The American Flag in Contemporary Art. (Illus.). 64p. 1994. pap. text. write for info. (1-880353-07-5) Cleveland Ctr.

Rubin, David, jt. auth. see Rubin, Mark.

Rubin, David, jt. ed. see Dvell, Persis.

Rubin, David, ed. & tr. see Premchand.

Rubin, David, tr. see Premchand, A.

Rubin, David B. School Board Member Liability under Section 1983. Gittens, Naomi E., ed. 44p. 1992. pap. text 15.00 (0-88364-134-8, 06-136) Natl Sch Boards.

Rubin, David B., ed. The Radiation Biology of the Vascular Endothelium. LC 97-34506. (Illus.). 272p. 1997. text 179.95 (0-8493-4840-4) CRC Pr.

Rubin, David C. Memory in Oral Traditions: The Cognitive Psychology of Counting-out Rhymes, Ballads & Epic. LC 94-8997. (Illus.). 400p. 1995. text 60.00 (0-19-508211-7) OUP.

— Memory in Oral Traditions: The Cognitive Psychology of Epic, Ballads & Counting-Out Rhymes. (Illus.). 400p. 1997. reprint ed. pap. text 26.00 (0-19-512032-9) OUP.

Rubin, David C., ed. Autobiographical Memory: Theoretical & Applied Perspectives. (Illus.). 312p. 1988. pap. text 26.95 (0-521-36850-2) Cambridge U Pr.

— Remembering Our Past: Studies in Autobiographical Memory. (Illus.). 458p. (C). 1996. text 59.95 (0-521-46145-6) Cambridge U Pr.

— Remembering Our Past: Studies in Autobiographical Memory. (Illus.). 448p. (C). 1999. pap. text 21.95 (0-521-65723-7) Cambridge U Pr.

Rubin, David G., tr. from NEP. Nepali Visions, Nepali Dreams: The Poetry of Laxmiprasad Devkota. (Modern Asian Literature Ser.). 192p. 1980. text 50.00 (0-231-05014-3) Col U Pr.

— A Season on the Earth: Selected Poems of Nirala. LC 76-40026. 1976. text 50.50 (0-231-04160-8) Col U Pr.

— A Season on the Earth: Selected Poems of Nirala. LC 76-40026. 1977. pap. text 19.50 (0-231-04161-6) Col U Pr.

Rubin, David H. & Barkin, Roger M. Pediatric Emergency Medicine: Self-Assessment & Review. 2nd ed. LC 98-6926. 1998. 29.95 (1-55664-453-1) Mosby Inc.

Rubin, David L. The Knot of Artifice: A Poetic of the French Lyric in the Early 17th Century. LC 80-26260. 119p. reprint ed. pap. 36.90 (0-608-09872-8, 206983700006) Bks Demand.

Rubin, David L., ed. Continuum: Problems in French Literature from the Renaissance to the Early Enlightenment, 5 vols., Set. LC 87-45806. 1989. write for info. (0-404-63750-7) AMS Pr.

— EMF: Studies in Early Modern France, Set. (Illus.). (C). 1994. 39.95 (0-9634355-2-3) Rookwood Pr.

— EMF! Studies in Early Modern France: Utopia 2 (18th Century), Vol. 5. 200p. 1998. lib. bdg. 25.95 (1-886365-13-X) Rookwood Pr.

— EMF Studies in Early Modern France Vol. 1: Word & Image. (Illus.). 248p. (C). 1994. lib. bdg. 39.95 (0-9634355-3-1) Rookwood Pr.

— EMF Studies in Early Modern France Vol. 3: Signs of the Early Modern. unabridged ed. (EMF Studies in Early Modern France: No. 3). 257p. (C). 1996. lib. bdg. 39.95 (1-886365-02-4) Rookwood Pr.

— EMF Studies in Early Modern France Vol. 3: Signs of the Early Modern II. 250p. (C). 1997. lib. bdg. 39.95 (1-886365-07-5) Rookwood Pr.

— Sun King: The Ascendancy of French Culture During the Reign of Louis XIV. LC 90-55041. (Illus.). 248p. 1992. 42.50 (0-918016-94-0) Folger Bks.

Rubin, David L. & Arndt, Richard T., eds. The Fulbright Difference, 1948-1992. 508p. (C). 1995. pap. text 29.95 (1-56000-861-X) Transaction Pubs.

Rubin, David L. & McKinley, Mary B., eds. Convergences: Rhetoric & Poetic in Seventeenth-Century France. LC 89-30177. (Illus.). 262p. reprint ed. pap. 81.30 (0-608-09873-6, 2069838) Bks Demand.

Rubin, David L., jt. ed. see Arndt, Richard T.

Rubin, David L., jt. ed. see Drell, Persis S.

Rubin, David L., jt. ed. see Fenoaltea, Doranne.

Rubin, David Lee, ed. Emf: Studies in Early Modern France: Utopia 16th & 17th Century. (Illus.). 248p. (C). 1994. pap. 22.95 (0-9634355-6-6) Rookwood Pr.

Rubin, David M. Cross-Bedding, Bedforms & Paleocurrents. LC 89-138314. (Concepts in Sedimentology & Paleontology Ser.: No. 1). 195p. 1987. reprint ed. pap. 60.50 (0-7837-8314-0, 204909800001) Bks Demand.

— Desktop Musician: Orchestrating Music on Your Computer. 452p. 1994. pap. 39.95 (0-07-881209-7) McGraw.

Rubin, David S. Computer Assisted: The Computer in Contemporary Art. LC 87-82883. (Illus.). 24p. (Orig.). 1987. pap. text 4.00 (0-941972-06-2) Freedman.

— Contemporary Triptychs. LC 82-80232. (Illus.). 72p. 1982. 6.00 (0-915478-15-3) Montgomery Gallery.

— Cruciformed: Images of the Cross Since 1980. (Illus.). 64p. 1991. pap. text 15.00 (1-880353-00-8) Cleveland Ctr.

— Cynthia Carlson: Installations, 1979-1989 (A Decade, More or Less) (Illus.). 40p. (Orig.). 1989. pap. text 10.00 (0-941972-08-9) Freedman.

— Donald Lipski: Poetic Sculpture. LC 89-82748. (Illus.). 56p. (Orig.). 1990. pap. text 12.00 (0-941972-10-0) Freedman.

— Ellen Brooks: Nature As Artifice. (Illus.). 32p. 1993. pap. text 15.00 (1-880353-03-2) Cleveland Ctr.

— Gary Bower: Abstract Paintings, 1969-1993. (Illus.). 36p. 1993. pap. text 15.00 (1-880353-05-9) Cleveland Ctr.

Rubin, David S. It's Only Rock & Roll: Rock & Roll Currents in Contemporary Art. LC 95-61896. (Illus.). 156p. (Orig.). 1996. pap. 29.95 (3-7913-1627-3, Pub. by Prestel) te Neues.

Rubin, David S. 1998 Phoenix Triennial. LC 98-33837. (Illus.). 88p. 1998. pap. write for info. (0-910407-35-5) Phoenix Art.

— Petah Coyne. (Illus.). 36p. 1992. pap. text 10.00 (1-880353-02-4) Cleveland Ctr.

— William Baziotes: A Commemorative Exhibition. Bross, Louise S. & Martin, Lys, eds. LC 87-80348. (Illus.). 24p. (Orig.). 1987. pap. text 10.00 (0-941972-05-4) Freedman.

Rubin, David S. & Kiberd, James B. James Kiberd Drawings: Meyer Shapiro Artist Award 1. Richardson, Eve, ed. (Illus.). 48p. 1999. pap. 20.00 (0-9670698-0-7) Water Island.

Rubin, David S., jt. auth. see Albee, Edward.

Rubin, David S., jt. auth. see Levin, Richard I.

Rubin, David S., jt. auth. see Tannenbaum, Judith E.

Rubin, Davida. Sir Kenelm Digby, F. R. S. An Annotated Bibliography. (Illus.). 130p. 1991. 95.00 (0-930405-29-3) Norman SF.

Rubin, Deborah E. Horse Trivia: A Hippofile's Delight. LC 95-45068. 1995. pap. 16.95 (0-939481-45-6) Half Halt Pr.

Rubin, Devora. Daughters of Destiny: Women Who Revolutionized Jewish Life & Torah Education. (ArtScroll History Ser.). (Illus.). 240p. 1988. 14.95 (0-89906-494-9); pap. 11.95 (0-89906-495-7) Mesorah Pubns.

Rubin, Diana K. Visions of Enchantment. LC 91-90088. (Illus.). 80p. 1991. pap. 6.95 (1-878116-09-6) JVC Bks.

Rubin, Diana Kwiatkowski. Breath of the Spirit: A Collection of Short Stories. pap. 7.95 (1-879183-41-2) Bristol Banner.

— A Gathered Meadow. 96p. 2000. pap. 9.99 (1-892668-19-X) Prospect Pr.

Rubin, Don, ed. Canadian Theatre History: Selected Readings. 1996. write for info. (0-7730-5542-8) Addison-Wesley.

***Rubin, Don, ed.** World Encyclopedia of Contemporary Theatre, 6 vols., set. (World Encyclopedia of Contemporary Theatre Ser.). (C). 2000. text 890.00 (0-415-23205-8) Routledge.

Rubin, Don, ed. World Encyclopedia of Contemporary Theatre Vol. 1: Europe. (Illus.). 1064p. (C). (gr. 13). 1995. 190.00 (0-415-05928-3, B0376) Routledge.

Rubin, Donald B. Multiple Impulation for Nonresponse in Surveys. 9th ed. LC 89-28935. (Probability & Mathematical Statistics Ser.). 288p. 1987. 135.00 (0-471-08705-X) Wiley.

Rubin, Donald L., ed. Composing Social Identity in Writing Style. 256p. 1995. pap. 29.95 (0-8058-1384-5); text 59.95 (0-8058-1383-7) L Erlbaum Assocs.

Rubin, Donnalee. Gender Influences: Reading Student Texts. LC 92-26313. (Studies in Writing & Rhetoric). 120p. (Orig.). (C). 1993. pap. 14.95 (0-8093-1866-0) S Ill U Pr.

Rubin, Doralee P. Grandma Doralee Patinkin's Jewish Family Cookbook: More Than 150 Treasured Recipes from My Kitchen to Yours. LC 97-20906. (Illus.). 240p. 1997. text 23.95 (0-312-16856-X) St Martin.

Rubin, Dorothy. Comprehension Power: Reading-Thinking Strategies for Adults, Bk. 1. LC 94-38282. 1994. 5.95 (0-13-184847-X) P-H.

Rubin, Dorothy. Diagnosis & Correction in Reading Instruction. 3rd ed. LC 96-7396. 500p. 1996. pap. text 69.00 (0-205-20023-0) Allyn.

Rubin, Dorothy. Diagnosis & Correction in Reading Instruction. 3rd ed. (C). 1996. pap., teacher ed. write for info. (0-205-26288-0, T6288-9) Allyn.

— Power English Eight: Basic Language Skills for Adults. (C). 1989. pap. text 5.85 (0-13-688516-0) P-H.

— Power English Five: Basic Language Skills for Adults. (C). 1989. pap. text 5.85 (0-13-688482-2) P-H.

— Power English Four: Basic Language Skills for Adults. (C). 1989. pap. text 5.85 (0-13-688474-1) P-H.

— Power English Nine: Basic Language Skills for Adults. (C). 1990. pap. text 5.85 (0-13-688524-1) P-H.

— Power English One: Basic Language Skills for Adults. 128p. (C). 1989. pap. text 5.85 (0-13-688441-5) P-H.

— Power English Seven: Basic Language Skills for Adults. (C). 1989. pap. text 5.85 (0-13-688508-X) P-H.

— Power English Six: Basic Language Skills for Adults. (C). 1989. pap. text 5.85 (0-13-688490-3) P-H.

— Power English Three: Basic Language Skills for Adults. (C). 1989. pap. text 5.85 (0-13-688466-0) P-H.

— Power English Two: Basic Language Skills for Adults. (C). 1989. pap. text 5.85 (0-13-688458-X) P-H.

— Power Vocabulary Five: Basic Word Strategies for Adults. 128p. 1992. pap. text 5.55 (0-13-681214-7) P-H.

— Power Vocabulary Four: Basic Word Strategies for Adults. 128p. 1992. pap. text 5.55 (0-13-681206-6) P-H.

— Power Vocabulary One: Basic Word Strategies for Adults. 112p. (C). 1992. pap. text 12.50 (0-13-678244-2) P-H.

— Power Vocabulary Three: Basic Word Strategies for Adults. 96p. (C). 1992. pap. text 12.50 (0-13-681198-1) P-H.

— Power Vocabulary Two: Basic Word Strategies for Adults. 96p. (C). 1992. pap. text 5.55 (0-13-678251-5) P-H.

— A Practical Approach to Teaching Reading. 2nd ed. LC 92-21969. 512p. 1992. 79.00 (0-205-14215-X) Allyn.

— Reading & Learning Power. 3rd ed. 360p. (C). 1999. pap. text 30.60 (0-536-57654-8) Pearson Custom.

— Teaching Elementary Language Arts: A Balanced Approach. 6th ed. LC 99-19744. 470p. (C). 1999. pap. text 65.00 (0-205-29372-7, Longwood Div) Allyn.

— Vocabulary Expansion. 2nd ed. 416p. (C). 1990. pap. text 50.00 (0-02-404245-5, Macmillan Coll) P-H.

Rubin-Dorsky, Jeffrey. Adrift in the Old World: The Psychological Pilgrimage of Washington Irving. (Illus.). xx, 328p. 1998. 39.00 (0-226-73094-8) U Ch Pr.

Rubin-Dorsky, Jeffrey & Fishkin, Shelley F., eds. People of the Book: Thirty Scholars Reflect on Their Jewish Identity. LC 95-44454. (Wisconsin Studies in American Autobiography). 520p. 1996. 49.95 (0-299-15010-0); pap. 24.95 (0-299-15014-3) U of Wis Pr.

Rubin, Drew. The Adjustment: A Novel. 212p. 1998. pap. 19.95 (1-57579-121-8) Pine Hill Pr.

Rubin, Edmund J. Abstract Functioning in the Blind. LC 64-2911. (American Foundation for the Blind Research Ser.: No. 11). 64p. reprint ed. pap. 30.00 (0-7837-0128-4, 204041100016) Bks Demand.

***Rubin, Edward.** Minimizing Harm. 224p. 1999. pap. 24.00 (0-8133-6804-9) Westview.

Rubin, Edward L. & Cooter, Robert. The Payment System: Cases, Materials & Issues. 2nd ed. (American Casebook Ser.). 992p. (C). 1994. 57.50 (0-314-03545-1) West Pub.

— The Payment System, Cases, Materials & Issues, Teacher's Manual to Accompany. (American Casebook Ser.). 195p. 1995. pap. text, teacher ed. write for info. (0-314-07605-0) West Pub.

Rubin, Edward L., jt. auth. see Feeley, Malcolm M.

Rubin, Elaine R., ed. Mission Management Vol. 2: A New Synthesis. LC 98-19149. 1998. pap. 30.00 (1-879694-12-3) AAH Ctrs.

Rubin, Eli Z., et al. Cognitive Perceptual Motor Dysfunction: From Research to Practice. LC 77-157415. (Lafayette Clinic Monographs in Psychiatry: No. 5). 173p. reprint ed. pap. 53.70 (0-608-16553-0, 202766200055) Bks Demand.

Rubin, Eli Z., jt. auth. see Llorens, Lela A.

Rubin, Emanuel. Pathology. 3rd ed. LC 98-3831. 18p. 1998. text 71.95 (0-397-58422-9) Lppncott W & W.

Rubin, Emanuel, et al, eds. Pathology. 2nd ed. LC 93-15103. (Illus.). 1578p. 1993. text 69.50 (0-397-51047-0) Lppncott W & W.

Rubin, Emanuel & Damjanov, Ivan, eds. Pathology Reviews - 1989. (Illus.). 307p. 1989. 89.50 (0-89603-162-4) Humana.

— Pathology Reviews, 1990. (Illus.). 268p. 1990. 99.50 (0-89603-195-0) Humana.

Rubin, Emanuel & Farber, John L. Essential Pathology. 3rd ed. 800p. text. write for info. (0-7817-2395-7) Lppncott W & W.

Rubin, Emanuel & Farber, John L., eds. Essential Pathology. 2nd ed. LC 94-46367. (Illus.). 832p. 1995. text 49.95 (0-397-51487-5) Lppncott W & W.

Rubin, Emanuel, et al. Pathology. LC 65-8626. (Illus.). 1824p. 1988. text 62.50 (0-397-50698-8, Lippnctt) Lppncott W & W.

Rubin, Emanuel, jt. auth. see Damjanov, Ivan.

Rubin, Ernest, jt. auth. see Kuznets, Simon Smith.

Rubin, Eva & Simpson, Jean F. Breast Specimen Radiography. (Illus.). 304p. 1997. text 95.00 (0-397-51667-3) Lppncott W & W.

Rubin, Eva R. Abortion, Politics, & the Courts: Roe vs. Wade & Its Aftermath, 89. LC 86-22847. (Contributions in American Studies: No. 89). 264p. 1987. 59.95 (0-313-25614-4, RBA/, Greenwood Pr) Greenwood.

— The Supreme Court & the American Family: Ideology &

An Asterisk (*) at the beginning of an entry indicates that the title is appearing for the first time.

Issues, 85. LC 85-21865. (Contributions in American Studies: No. 85). 251p. 1986. 57.95 (*0-313-25157-6*, RSU/, Greenwood Pr) Greenwood.

Rubin, Eva R., ed. The Abortion Controversy: A Documentary History. LC 93-25068. (Primary Documents in American History & Contemporary Issues Ser.: Vol. 1). 336p. 1994. text 49.95 (*0-313-28476-8*, RAY/, Greenwood Pr) Greenwood.

Rubin, Eva R., ed. The Abortion Controversy: A Documentary History. LC 93-25068. 336p. 1998. pap. 24.95 (*0-275-96526-0*, Praeger Pubs) Greenwood.

Rubin, Frances. A Basic Guide to Evaluation for Development Workers. (Practical Handbooks). 96p. (C). 1995. pap. 7.95 (*0-85598-275-6*, Pub. by Oxfam Pub) Stylus Pub VA.

Rubin, G. R. Private Property, Government Requisition & the Constitution, 1914-1927. LC 93-48977. 276p. 1994. 60.00 (*1-85285-098-1*) Hambledon Press.

— War, Law, & Labor: The Munitions Acts, State Regulation, & the Unions 1915-1921. (Illus.). 288p. 1988. text 75.00 (*0-19-825538-1*) OUP.

Rubin, G. R. & Sugarman, David, eds. Rubin & Sugarman: Law, Economy & Society - Essays in the History of English Law. 1984. 78.00 (*0-86205-085-5*, MICHIE); pap. 58.00 (*0-86205-098-7*, MICHIE) LEXIS Pub.

Rubin, Gary E. The Asylum Challenge to Western Nations. Tripp, Rosemary E., ed. (Illus.). 19p. 1984. pap. 2.00 (*0-685-10162-2*) US Comm Refugees.

— The Newest Americans: Report of the American Jewish Committee's Task Force on the Acculturation of Immigrants to American Life. LC 87-70998. 36p. 1987. pap. 5.00 (*0-87495-089-9*) Am Jewish Comm.

Rubin, Gaviel, tr. see Mykoff, M. H., et al, eds.

Rubin, Gay. On a Good Day. (Orig.). Date not set. pap. 14.95 (*0-911051-96-1*) Plain View.

Rubin, Geoffrey M. & Overstreet, George A. The Applicability of Credit Scoring in Credit Unions. 32p. 1996. pap. 100.00 (*1-880572-21-4*) Filene Res.

Rubin, Geoffrey M., jt. auth. see Overstreet, George A., Jr.

Rubin, Gerry R. Durban, 1942: A British Troopship Revolt. LC 92-3361. 158p. 1992. 40.00 (*1-85285-080-9*) Hambledon Press.

Rubin, Gerry R., jt. ed. see O'Donovan, Katherine.

Rubin, Gertrude. A Beating of Wings. Spelius, Carol, ed. 92p. (Orig.). 1991. pap. 7.95 (*0-941363-09-0*) Lake Shore Pub.

— The Passover Poems. (Illus.). 64p. (Orig.). 1991. pap. 8.00 (*1-879260-00-X*) Evanston Pub.

Rubin, Greg, jt. auth. see Hungin, Pali.

***Rubin, Gretchen Craft.** Power Money Fame Sex: A Users Guide. 304p. 2000. 25.95 (*0-671-04128-2*) PB.

Rubin, H. Ted. Behind the Black Robes: Juvenile Court Judges & the Court. LC 85-11923. (Sage Library of Social Research: No. 160). 248p. reprint ed. pap. 76.90 (*0-7837-4575-3*, 204410400003) Bks Demand.

Rubin, Hank. Collaboration Skills for Educators & Nonprofit Leaders. LC 98-6173. 128p. 1998. pap. 19.95 (*0-925065-49-8*) Lyceum IL.

Rubin, Hank. Spain's Cause Was Mine: A Memoir of an American Medic in the Spanish Civil War. LC 97-15733. (Illus.). 176p. 1997. 29.95 (*0-8093-2159-9*) S Ill U Pr.

***Rubin, Hank.** Spain's Cause Was Mine: A Memoir of an American Medic in the Spanish Civil War. 2000. pap. text 17.95 (*0-8093-2317-6*) S Ill U Pr.

Rubin, Harriet. The Princessa: Machiavelli for Women. 208p. 1998. pap. 9.95 (*0-440-50832-0*, Dell Trade Pbks) Dell.

Rubin, Harriet. Soloing: Realizing Your Life's Ambition. LC 99-37322. 352p. 1999. 23.00 (*0-06-662014-7*) HarpC.

***Rubin, Harriet.** Soloing: Realizing Your Life's Ambition. 2001. pap. write for info. (*0-06-662016-3*) HarpC.

Rubin, Harvey W. Dictionary of Insurance Terms. 3rd ed. LC 95-6527. 640p. 1995. pap. 11.95 (*0-8120-3379-5*) Barron.

***Rubin, Harvey W.** Dictionary of Insurance Terms. 4th ed. LC 99-46788. (Business Dictionaries Ser.). 512p. 2000. 12.95 (*0-7641-1262-7*) Barron.

***Rubin, Harvey W. & Wood, David H., eds.** DNA Based Computers III. LC 98-55491. (Dimacs Series in Discrete Mathematics & Theoretical Computer Science). 375p. 1999. 79.00 (*0-8218-0842-7*) Am Math.

Rubin, Haya R. & Owens, Amanda J. Progress Report: An Investigation to Determine Whether the Built Environment Affects Patient's Medical Outcomes. 48p. (C). 1996. pap. text 19.00 (*0-9638938-3-1*) Ctr for Hlth.

— Status Report: An Investigation to Determine Whether the Built Environment Affects Patients' Medical Outcomes. 48p. (C). 1997. pap. 33.00 (*0-9638938-4-X*) Ctr for Hlth.

Rubin, Henry. Transformations. 1996. 19.95 (*0-226-73091-3*) U Ch Pr.

Rubin, Herbert. Integrating Rural Development: The Problem & a Solution. 1980. pap. text 2.50 (*0-89249-031-4*) Intl Development.

Rubin, Herbert, et al. International Economic Law 1996. annuals text 42.00 (*0-8205-2725-4*) Bender.

Rubin, Herbert J. Community Organization & Development. 2nd ed. LC 91-22943. 448p. 1991. pap. text 67.00 (*0-675-21235-9*, Merrill Coll) P-H.

***Rubin, Herbert J.** Community Organization & Development. 3rd ed. (C). 1999. pap. text 36.00 (*0-205-26116-7*, Macmillan Coll) P-H.

— Renewing Hope within Neighborhoods of Despair: The Community-Based Development Model. LC 99-39478. (C). 2000. text 73.50 (*0-7914-4553-4*); pap. text 24.95 (*0-7914-4554-2*) State U NY Pr.

Rubin, Herbert J., jt. auth. see Rubin, Irene B.

Rubin, Hillel, et al, eds. Soil & Aquifer Pollution: Non-Aqueous Phase Liquids - Contamination & Reclamation. LC 97-29318. (Illus.). 390p. 1998. 189.00 (*3-540-62586-0*) Spr-Verlag.

Rubin, Howard. Practical Guide to the Design & Implementation of Information Systems Measurement Programs. (C). 2001. boxed set 38.00 (*0-13-681784-X*) P-H.

Rubin, Howard & Robbins, Brian. Evaluating Success of a Y 2000 Project. unabridged ed. LC 98-70637. 135p. 1998. pap. 24.95 (*0-9620413-7-8*, 109) Info Econ Pr.

Rubin, I. B., jt. auth. see Bayne, C. K.

Rubin, I. I. Essays on Marx's Theory of Value. Samardzija, Milos & Perlman, Fredy, trs. from RUS. Orig. Title: Ocherki po Teorii Stoimosti Marksa. 275p. 1973. 47.99 (*0-919618-11-1*, Pub. by Black Rose); pap. 18.99 (*0-919618-18-9*, Pub. by Black Rose) Consort Bk Sales.

Rubin, I. Leslie & Crocker, Allen C. Developmental Disabilities: Delivery of Medical Care for Children & Adults. LC 87-2840. 526p. reprint ed. pap. 163.10 (*0-7837-2743-7*, 204312300006) Bks Demand.

Rubin, Ira L., et al. Treatment of Heart Disease in the Adult. 2nd ed. LC 79-175466. 522p. reprint ed. pap. 161.90 (*0-608-12693-4*, 205600800043) Bks Demand.

Rubin, Irene, jt. ed. see Levine, Charles H.

Rubin, Irene B. & Rubin, Herbert J. Qualitative Interviewing: The Art of Hearing Data. 302p. (C). 1995. 52.00 (*0-8039-5095-0*); pap. 24.00 (*0-8039-5096-9*) Sage.

Rubin, Irene S. Class, Tax, & Power: Municipal Budgeting in the United States. LC 98-8975. 256p. (C). 1998. pap. 29.95 (*1-56643-062-3*, Chatham House Pub) Seven Bridges.

— The Politics of Public Budgeting: Getting & Spending, Borrowing & Balancing. 3rd ed. LC 96-32924. (Illus.). 320p. (Orig.). (C). 1996. pap. text 29.95 (*1-56643-033-X*, Chatham House Pub) Seven Bridges.

— The Politics of Public Budgeting: Getting & Spending, Borrowing & Balancing. 4th ed. LC 99-86159. (Illus.). 320p. (Orig.). 2000. pap. text 29.95 (*1-889119-42-3*, Chatham House Pub) Seven Bridges.

— Running in the Red: The Political Dynamics of Urban Fiscal Stress. LC 81-9329. 171p. (C). 1983. text 20.50 (*0-87395-564-1*) State U NY Pr.

Rubin, Irene S., ed. New Directions in Budget Theory. LC 87-9977. (SUNY Series in Public Administration). 207p. (C). 1988. text 20.50 (*0-88706-624-0*); pap. text 21.95 (*0-88706-625-9*) State U NY Pr.

Rubin, Irvin I. Handbook of Plastics Materials & Technology. LC 89-48281. 1792p. 1990. 295.00 (*0-471-09634-2*) Wiley.

— Injection Molding: Theory & Practice. (SPE Monographs: Vol. 1). 672p. 1973. 195.00 (*0-471-74445-X*) Wiley.

Rubin, Irwin. ABCs of Effective Feedback: A Guide for Caring Professionals. LC 97-14970. 1997. 29.95 (*0-7879-1077-5*) Jossey-Bass.

Rubin, Irwin M. & Fernandez, C. Raymond. My Pulse Is Not What It Used to Be: The Leadership Challenges in Health Care. LC 91-65593. 104p. (Orig.). 1991. pap. 40.00 (*0-9629561-0-4*) Temenos Found.

Rubin, Irwin M., et al. Task-Oriented Team Development. (Illus.). 1978. ring bd. 85.00 (*0-07-054196-5*) McGraw.

Rubin, Israel. Satmar: Two Generations of an Urban Island. 2nd ed. LC 95-51537. (Illus.). 314p. (C). 1997. text 39.95 (*0-8204-0759-3*) P Lang Pubng.

Rubin, J. Language Planning in the United States. (International Journal of the Sociology of Language Ser.: No. 11). 1977. 60.00 (*90-279-7694-5*) Mouton.

Rubin, J. Z., jt. auth. see Brockner, J.

Rubin, James. Courbet. (Art & Ideas Ser.). (Illus.). 352p. 1997. pap. 19.95 (*0-7148-3180-8*, Pub. by Phaidon Press) Phaidon Pr.

Rubin, James H. Impressionism. LC 99-494999. 446p. 1999. pap. 24.95 (*0-7148-3826-8*) Phaidon Press.

— Manet's Silence & the Poetics of Bouquets. LC 93-38505. (Illus.). 192p. 1994. 44.50 (*0-674-54802-7*) HUP.

— Manet's Silence & the Poetics of Bouquets. LC 93-38505. (Essays in Art & Culture Ser.). (Illus.). 256p. (C). 1995. text 25.95 (*0-674-54803-5*) HUP.

— Realism & Social Vision in Courbet & Proudhon. LC 80-17559. (Princeton Essays on the Arts Ser.: No. 10). (Illus.). 230p. 1980. reprint ed. pap. 71.30 (*0-608-02742-1*, 206340700004) Bks Demand.

Rubin, Janet & Merrion, Margaret. Drama & Music: Creative Activities for Young Children. LC 94-24087. (Illus.). 196p. (J). (gr. k-3). 1995. lib. bdg. 26.95 (*0-89334-244-0*, 2440X34) Humanics Ltd.

***Rubin, Janet E.** Voices: Plays for Studying the Holocaust. LC 99-20979. 336p. 1999. text 35.00 (*0-8108-3655-6*) Scarecrow.

Rubin, Janet E. & Merrion, Margaret. Creative Drama & Music Methods: Introductory Activities for Children. LC 96-13082. xiv, 216p. (Orig.). 1996. pap. text 30.00 (*0-208-02428-X*, Linnet Bks) Shoe String.

Rubin, Janet E., jt. auth. see Merrion, Margaret.

Rubin, Janet E., ed. see Kraus, Joanna H.

***Rubin, Janice.** Looking Back, Moving on: Memoir as Prologue. 191p. 2000. pap. write for info. (*1-889534-44-7*) Jay St Pubs.

Rubin, Jay. Making Sense of Japanese: What the Textbooks Don't Tell You. (Power Japanese Ser.). 1998. pap. text 13.00 (*4-7700-2310-3*, Pub. by Kodansha Intl) Kodansha.

***Rubin, Jay.** Modern Japanese Writers. (Scribner Writers Ser.). 2000. 125.00 (*0-684-80598-7*) Gale.

Rubin, Jay, tr. see Murakami, Haruki.

Rubin, Jay, tr. see Natsume Soseki, pseud.

Rubin, Jean. Mathematical Logic: Application & Theory. 417p. (C). 1990. text 81.50 (*0-03-012808-0*) SCP.

Rubin, Jean E., jt. auth. see Howard, Paul.

Rubin, Jeanne S. Frank Lloyd Wright & the Froebel Kindergarten. LC 98-25781. 1999. 49.95 (*0-8093-2132-7*) S Ill U Pr.

Rubin, Jeff. Lonely Planet Antarctica. (Illus.). 352p. 1996. pap. 17.95 (*0-86442-415-9*) Lonely Planet.

***Rubin, Jeff.** Lonely Planet Antarctica. 2nd ed. (Travel Guides Ser.). (Illus.). 384p. 2000. pap. 19.95 (*0-86442-772-7*) Lonely Planet.

Rubin, Jeffrey. Handbook of Usability Testing: How to Plan, Design, & Conduct Effective Tests. (Technical Communication Library). 352p. 1994. pap. 44.99 (*0-471-59403-2*) Wiley.

Rubin, Jeffrey & LaPorte, Valerie, eds. Alternatives in Rehabilitating the Handicapped: A Policy Analysis. LC 81-4144. 244p. 1982. 35.95 (*0-89885-010-X*, Kluwer Acad Hman Sci) Kluwer Academic.

Rubin, Jeffrey, jt. ed. see LaPorte, Valerie.

Rubin, Jeffrey B. A Psychoanalysis for Our Time: Exploring the Blindness of the Seeing I. LC 98-58002. 230p. 1998. text 35.00 (*0-8147-7491-1*) NYU Pr.

— Psychotherapy & Buddhism: Toward an Integration. (Issues in the Practice of Psychology Ser.). (Illus.). 197p. (C). 1996. 47.00 (*0-306-45441-6*, Plenum Trade) Perseus Pubng.

Rubin, Jeffrey W. Decentering the Regime: Ethnicity, Radicalism, & Democracy in Juchitan, Mexico. LC 97-13515. 1997. pap. 17.95 (*0-8223-2063-0*); lib. bdg. 54.95 (*0-8223-2050-9*) Duke.

Rubin, Jeffrey Z., ed. Dynamics of Third-Party Intervention: Kissinger in the Middle East. LC 80-28763. 303p. 1981. 49.95 (*0-275-90714-7*, C0714, Praeger Pubs) Greenwood.

Rubin, Jeffrey Z., et al. Social Conflict: Escalation, Stalemate, & Settlement. 2nd ed. LC 93-24557. 288p. (C). 1994. 37.19 (*0-07-054211-2*) McGraw.

Rubin, Jeffrey Z., jt. auth. see Bunker, Barbara B.

Rubin, Jeffrey Z., jt. auth. see Zartman, I. W.

Rubin, Jeffrey Z., jt. ed. see Breslin, J. William.

Rubin, Jeffrey Z., jt. ed. see Faure, Guy O.

Rubin, Jeffrey Z., jt. ed. see Kellerman, Barbara.

***Rubin, Jennifer, et al.** The Management of Epistaxis. 3rd rev. ed. LC 99-34051. (Self-Instructional Ser.). (Illus.). 64p. 1999. pap. text 25.00 (*1-56772-073-0*) AAO-HNS.

Rubin, Jerome. New York Naturally, 1989: A Resource Directory for Natural Living in the Tri-State Area. 168p. (Orig.). 1988. pap. write for info. (*0-318-65041-X*) City Spirit Pubns.

— Old Boston Fare in Food & Pictures. (Illus.). 128p. (Orig.). 1997. pap. 13.50 (*0-88278-047-6*) Yankee Products.

— Old Cape Cod Fare in Food & Pictures. (Illus.). 128p. (Orig.). 1997. pap. 13.50 (*0-88278-046-8*) Yankee Products.

Rubin, Jerome & Donaldson, Stephen, eds. Connecticut Naturally, 1990: A Resource Directory for Natural Living in the Tri-State Area, Including New York & New Jersey. (Orig.). 1990. pap. 4.95 (*0-9622953-3-7*) City Spirit Pubns.

— New Jersey Naturally, 1990: A Resource Directory for Natural Living in the Tri-State Area, Including New York & Connecticut. (Orig.). 1990. pap. 4.95 (*0-9622953-2-9*) City Spirit Pubns.

— New York Naturally, 1990: A Resource Directory for Natural Living in the Tri-State Area, Including New Jersey & Connecticut. (Orig.). 1990. pap. 4.95 (*0-9622953-1-0*) City Spirit Pubns.

Rubin, Jim. Porkchop to the Rescue. LC PZ7.R83125Po 1998. (Doug Chronicles: No. 2). (Illus.). 64p. (J). (gr. 2-4). 1998. pap. 3.99 (*0-7868-4231-8*, Pub. by Disney Pr) Time Warner.

Rubin, Joan. How to Be a More Successful Language Learner: Toward Learner Autonomy. 2nd ed. LC 93-42857. 128p. (J). 1994. mass mkt. 26.95 (*0-8384-4734-1*) Heinle & Heinle.

Rubin, Joan, et al, eds. Language Planning Processes. (Contributions to the Sociology of Language Ser.: No. 21). 1977. text 43.85 (*90-279-7714-3*) Mouton.

Rubin, Joan, et al. English Works! LC 95-1983. 144p. 1995. pap. text 14.69 (*0-201-87681-7*) Addison-Wesley.

Rubin, Joan, jt. ed. see Shuy, Roger W.

Rubin, Joan S. Constance Rourke & American Culture. LC 79-9272. (Illus.). xv, 244p. 1980. 37.50 (*0-8078-1402-4*) U of NC Pr.

— The Making of Middlebrow Culture. LC 91-22241. (Illus.). xxii, 416p. (C). 1992. pap. 19.95 (*0-8078-4354-7*) U of NC Pr.

— They Flash upon That Inward Eye: Poetry Recitation & American Readers. 15p. 1997. pap. 5.00 (*0-944026-76-1*) Am Antiquarian.

Rubin, Joanna, et al. Almanac of Virginia Politics, 1998. 1998. 24.99 (*0-917560-32-9*) Woman Activist.

Rubin, John. The Law of Self Defense in North Carolina, 1996. LC 96-177889. 215p. (Orig.). (C). 1996. pap. text 18.00 (*1-56011-245-X*, 95.14) Institute Government.

Rubin, John & Hughes, Thomasin. North Carolina Public Defender Manual. (C). 1998. pap. text 25.00 (*1-56011-339-1*) Institute Government.

Rubin, John & Loeb, Ben F., Jr. Punishments for North Carolina Crimes & Motor Vehicle Offenses. 1999. pap. 15.00 (*1-56011-359-6*) Institute Government.

Rubin, John S., ed. see Korovin, Sergey K. & Gould.

Rubin, Jonathan M. & Chandler, William F. Ultrasound in Neurosurgery. LC 88-43078. 223p. reprint ed. pap. 69.20 (*0-608-03443-6*, 206414400008) Bks Demand.

Rubin, Joseph. New York Collections. LC 80-81138. (Practice Systems Library Manual). ring bd. 120.00 (*0-317-00518-9*) West Group.

— New York Collections. LC 80-81138. (Practice Systems Library Manual). 1993. suppl. ed. 75.00 (*0-317-04327-7*) West Group.

Rubin, Joseph L. Heartburst. LC 88-82305. 125p. (Orig.). 1988. pap. 11.95 (*0-9621100-0-0*) Heartburst.

Rubin, Judith A. The Art of Art Therapy. LC 84-9344. 224p. 1986. text 35.95 (*0-87630-371-8*) Brunner-Mazel.

— Art Therapy: An Introduction. LC 98-35409. (Basic Principles into Practice Ser.). 1998. boxed set 29.95 (*0-87630-897-3*) Brunner-Mazel.

Rubin, Judith A. Child Art Therapy: Understanding & Helping Children Grow Through Art. 2nd ed. (Illus.). 320p. 1984. pap. 59.95 (*0-471-28951-5*, VNR) Wiley.

Rubin, Judith A. Child Art Therapy: Understanding & Helping Children Through Art. 2nd ed. (Illus.). 336p. 1984. pap. 48.95 (*0-442-27767-9*, VNR) Wiley.

Rubin, Judith A., ed. Approaches to Art Therapy: Theory & Technique. LC 86-26376. 362p. 1987. text 35.95 (*0-87630-452-8*) Brunner-Mazel.

Rubin, Julius H. The Other Side of Joy: Religious Melancholy among the Bruderhof. LC 97-24740. 288p. 2000. text 45.00 (*0-19-511943-6*) OUP.

— Religious Melancholy & Protestant Experience in America. (Religion in America Ser.). 320p. 1994. text 55.00 (*0-19-508301-6*) OUP.

Rubin, K., et al, eds. High-Density Magnetic Recording & Integrated Magneto-Optics - Materials & Devices Vol. 517: Proceedings Materials Research Society Symposium. LC 98-29133. 669p. 1998. text 86.00 (*1-55899-423-8*) Materials Res.

Rubin, Karen. Flying High in Travel: A Complete Guide to Careers in the Travel Industry. 2nd expanded ed. LC 91-26084. 336p. 1992. pap. 24.95 (*0-471-55173-2*) Wiley.

***Rubin, Karl.** Euler Systems. (Annals of Mathematics Studies: Vol. 147). 240p. 2000. 69.50 (*0-691-05075-9*) Princeton U Pr.

— Euler Systems. (Annals of Mathematics Studies: Vol. 147). (Illus.). 240p. 2000. pap. 24.95 (*0-691-05076-7*) Princeton U Pr.

Rubin, Ken. Crossing the Desert: A Motorized Novel. LC 98-96692. (Illus.). 232p. 1999. pap. 16.95 (*0-9668043-0-9*) Mesa Vista.

Rubin, Kenneth H. & Asendorpf, Jens, eds. Social Withdrawal, Inhibition, & Shyness in Childhood. 368p. 1993. pap. 39.95 (*0-8058-1220-2*); text 79.95 (*0-8058-1219-9*) L Erlbaum Assocs.

Rubin, Kenneth H., jt. ed. see Pepler, Debra.

Rubin, Kenneth I., jt. auth. see Doll, Amy.

Rubin, Kenneth S., jt. auth. see Goldberg, Adele.

Rubin-Kurtzman, Jane R. The Socioeconomic Determinants of Fertility in Mexico: Changing Perspectives. (Monographs: No. 23). 66p. (Orig.). (C). 1987. pap. 7.50 (*0-935391-73-8*, MN-23) UCSD Ctr US-Mex.

Rubin, Kyna, tr. see Ruowang, Wang.

Rubin, L. Families on the Fault Line. 304p. 1995. pap. 14.00 (*0-06-092229-X*) HarpC.

Rubin, L. F., jt. auth. see Saunders, L. Z.

Rubin, L. G., et al, eds. Resistance, Electronic & Magnetic Thermometry: Controls & Calibration; Bridges, Pt. 2. LC 62-19138. 794p. 1972. pap. 200.00 (*0-608-08466-2*, 205213300002) Bks Demand.

Rubin, Larry. Unanswered Calls: A Book of Poems. LC 97-74330. 84p. 1997. spiral bd. 12.95 (*0-7872-4376-0*) Kendall-Hunt.

Rubin, Laurie F., jt. auth. see Moriearty, Scott C.

Rubin, Lawrence A. Mighty Mac: The Official Picture History of the Mackinac Bridge. LC 58-13847. (Illus.). 148p. 1986. reprint ed. pap. 13.95 (*0-8143-1817-7*) Wayne St U Pr.

Rubin, Leigh. Amusing Arrangements. LC 84-90632. (Notable Quotes Ser.: Vol. III). (Illus.). 80p. (Orig.). 1985. pap. text 5.95 (*0-943384-04-4*) Rubes Pubns.

— Calves Can Be So Cruel. (Illus.). 90p. 1990. pap. 5.95 (*0-452-26509-6*) Rubes Pubns.

— Encore! LC 83-90153. (Notable Quotes Ser.: Vol. II). (Illus.). 80p. (C). 1983. pap. 5.95 (*0-943384-03-6*) Rubes Pubns.

— Notable Quotes. (Orig.). 1981. pap. 5.95 (*0-941364-00-3*) Rubes Pubns.

— Notable Quotes. LC 81-69508. (Notable Quotes Ser.: Vol. I). (Illus.). 80p. (Orig.). (J). (gr. 4 up). 1981. pap. 5.95 (*0-943384-00-1*) Rubes Pubns.

— Rubes Bible Cartoons. 144p. 1999. pap. 8.95 (*1-56563-423-3*) Hendrickson MA.

— Rubes Then & Now: Cartoons for the Millennium & Beyond! (Illus.). 100p. 1999. pap. 8.95 (*0-9644695-4-5*) Image Maker Pub.

— Sharks Are People Too! LC 82-99813. (Illus.). 80p. 1982. pap. 4.95 (*0-943384-02-8*) Rubes Pubns.

Rubin, Leslie & Rubin, Charles. The Quest for Justice. 3rd ed. 332p. (C). 1992. pap. text 52.00 (*0-536-58152-5*) Pearson Custom.

Rubin, Leslie G., ed. Justice vs. Law in Greek Political Thought. LC 96-38949. 288p. 1997. 66.00 (*0-8476-8422-9*); pap. 25.95 (*0-8476-8423-7*) Rowman.

Rubin, Lewis J., ed. Pulmonary Heart Disease. 1984. text 200.00 (*0-89838-632-2*) Kluwer Academic.

Rubin, Lewis J. & Rich, Stuart, eds. Primary Pulmonary Hypertension. LC 96-36758. (Lung Biology in Health & Disease Ser.: Vol. 99). (Illus.). 384p. 1996. text 170.00 (*0-8247-9505-9*) Dekker.

Rubin, Lillian B. Busing & Backlash: White Against White in an Urban School District. 1972. pap. 9.95 (*0-520-02257-2*, Pub. by U CA Pr) Cal Prin Full Svc.

— Intimate Strangers: Men & Women Together. LC 82-48678. 240p. 1990. pap. 13.50 (*0-06-091134-4*, CN 1134, Perennial) HarperTrade.

— Just Friends: The Role of Friendship in Our Lives. LC 84-43074. 256p. 1990. reprint ed. pap. 13.00 (*0-06-091349-5*, PL 1349, Perennial) HarperTrade.

R

***Rubin, Lillian B.** Tangled Lives: Daughters, Mothers, & the Crucible of Aging. LC 00-8458. 2000. 24.00 (*0-8070-6794-6*) Beacon Pr.

Rubin, Lillian B. The Transcendent Child: Tales of Triumph over the Past. 240p. 1997. pap. 12.50 (*0-06-097720-5*, Perennial) HarperTrade.

Rubin, Louis, jt. ed. see Epstein, George.

Rubin, Louis D. The Boll Weevil & the Triple Play. 1979. 5.00 (*0-937684-00-7*) Tradd St Pr.

— The Heat of the Sun. LC 95-77242. 448p. 1995. 21.95 (*1-56352-233-0*) Longstreet.

— The Wary Fugitives: Four Poets & the South. LC 77-25479. (Walter Lynwood Fleming Lectures in Southern History Ser.). 400p. 1978. reprint ed. pap. 124.00 (*0-7837-9867-9*, 206059300006) Bks Demand.

— William Elliott Shoots a Bear: Essays on the Southern Literary Imagination. fac. ed. LC 75-5352. 295p. 1975. reprint ed. pap. 91.50 (*0-7837-7820-1*, 204757600007) Bks Demand.

Rubin, Louis D., Sr. & Duncan, Jim. The Weather Wizard's Cloud Book. (Illus.). 87p. 1984. pap. 8.95 (*0-912697-10-5*) Algonquin Bks.

Rubin, Louis D. & Mills, Jerry L. Writer's Companion. LC 95-158. 1088p. (C). 1995. 39.95 (*0-8071-1992-X*) La State U Pr.

Rubin, Louis D. & Mills, Jerry L., eds. A Writer's Companion: A Handy Compendium of Useful But Hard-To-Find Information on History, Literature, Art, Science, Travel, Philosophy, & Much More. LC 96-45543. 1008p. 1997. pap. 24.00 (*0-06-273472-5*, Harper Ref) HarpC.

Rubin, Louis Decimus, Jr. Algonquin Literary Quiz Book. 96p. 1990. pap. 7.95 (*0-945575-50-5*) Algonquin Bks.

— Babe Ruth's Ghost: And Other Historical & Literary Speculations. LC 95-52732. 224p. 1996. 30.00 (*0-295-97529-6*) U of Wash Pr.

Rubin, Louis Decimus, Jr Babe Ruth's Ghost: And Other Historical & Literary Speculations. LC 95-52732. 224p. 1996. pap. 14.95 (*0-295-97530-X*) U of Wash Pr.

Rubin, Louis Decimus, Jr A Gallery of Southerners. LC 82-64. xx, 233p. 1982. pap. text 16.95 (*0-8071-1160-0*) La State U Pr.

— Golden Weather. LC 61-6740. (Voices of the South Ser.). 303p. 1995. pap. 12.95 (*0-8071-2009-X*) La State U Pr.

***Rubin, Louis Decimus, Jr.** A Memory of Trains: The Boll Weevil & Others. LC 00-9043. (Illus.). 2000. pap. 24.95 (*1-57003-382-X*) U of SC Pr.

Rubin, Louis Decimus, Jr. Mockingbird in the Gum Tree: A Literary Gallimaufry. LC 90-27597. 281p. 1991. 27.50 (*0-8071-1680-7*) La State U Pr.

— Seaports of the South. LC 98-66376. (Illus.). 276p. 1998. 25.00 (*1-56352-499-6*) Longstreet.

— Small Craft Advisory: A Book about the Building of a Boat. LC 91-19545. 416p. 1991. pap. 12.00 (*0-87113-533-7*, Atlntc Mnthly) Grove-Atltic.

— Virginia: A History. (States & the Nation Ser.). (Illus.). 1984. pap. 7.95 (*0-393-30137-0*) Norton.

Rubin, Louis Decimus, Jr., ed. The American South: Portrait of a Culture. LC 79-12316. (Southern Literary Studies). 389p. 1980. reprint ed. pap. 120.60 (*0-7837-9873-3*, 206059900006) Bks Demand.

— An Apple for My Teacher: Twelve Writers Tell about Teachers Who Made All the Difference. (Illus.). 186p. 1987. pap. 10.95 (*0-912697-57-1*) Algonquin Bks.

— A Bibliographical Guide to the Study of Southern Literature. LC 69-17627. (Southern Literary Studies). 375p. reprint ed. pap. 116.30 (*0-8357-7168-7*, 201959100013) Bks Demand.

***Rubin, Louis Decimus, Jr., ed.** The Quotable Baseball Fanatic. LC 99-45877. 2000. 20.00 (*1-58574-012-8*) Lyons Pr.

Rubin, Louis Decimus, Jr., et al, eds. The History of Southern Literature. LC 85-10183. xiv, 626p. 1990. pap. 19.95 (*0-8071-1643-2*) La State U Pr.

Rubin, Louis Decimus, Jr & Holman, C. Hugh, eds. Southern Literary Study: Problems & Possibilities. LC 75-11553. 250p. reprint ed. pap. 77.50 (*0-8357-3874-4*, 203660600004) Bks Demand.

Rubin, Louis Decimus, Jr. & Jacobs, Robert D. South: Modern Southern Literature. LC 73-16744. 434p. 1974. reprint ed. lib. bdg. 65.00 (*0-8371-7224-1*, RUS, Greenwood Pr) Greenwood.

Rubin, Louis J. Artistry in Teaching. 192p. (C). 1984. pap. 24.69 (*0-07-554606-X*) McGraw.

Rubin, M. J., ed. Studies in Antarctic Meteorology. LC 66-6578. (Antarctic Research Ser.: Vol. 9). (Illus.). 231p. 1966. 18.00 (*0-87590-109-3*) Am Geophysical.

Rubin, Manning. 60 Ways to Relieve Stress in 60 Seconds. LC 92-50932. (Illus.). 128p. 1993. pap. 5.95 (*1-56305-338-1*, 3338) Workman Pub.

Rubin, Manning, jt. auth. see Katz, Lawrence.

Rubin, Marcus & Richardson, Ray. The Microeconomics of the Shorter Working Week. 192p. 1997. text 59.95 (*1-85972-482-5*, Pub. by Avebry) Ashgate Pub Co.

Rubin, Marilyn B. Nursing Care for Myocardial Infarction: Physiological Basis of Cardiovascular Nursing. LC 76-6218. (Illus.). 200p. 1977. 14.50 (*0-87527-151-0*) Green.

Rubin, Mark. The Beginning of Responsibilty. 68p. 1992. pap. 12.00 (*0-937669-48-2*) Owl Creek Pr.

Rubin, Mark & Daniel, Alan. The Orchestra. (Illus.). 48p. (J). (gr. 1-3). 1992. pap. 8.95 (*0-920668-99-2*) Firefly Bks Ltd.

Rubin, Mark & Rubin, David. The Cellulite Prophecy: An Adventure. 48p. (Orig.). 1995. pap. 5.95 (*0-9645015-0-3*, Light-Heart Bks) Lumina Pub.

Rubin, Mark G. Manual of Chemical Peels: Superficial & Medium Depth. 200p. 1995. text 104.00 (*0-397-51506-5*) Lppncott W & W.

Rubin, Mark R. & Papacosma, S. Victor, eds. Europe's Neutral & Nonaligned States Between Nato & the Warsaw Pact. LC 87-33545. 246p. 1989. 45.00 (*0-8420-2269-4*) Scholarly Res Inc.

Rubin, Martin. Showstoppers: Busby Berkeley & the Tradition of Spectacle. Belton, John, ed. LC 92-37956. (Film & Culture Ser.). 352p. (C). 1993. 40.50 (*0-231-08054-9*) Col U Pr.

— Thrillers. LC 98-38139. (Genres in American Cinema Ser.). (Illus.). 300p. (C). 1999. text 59.95 (*0-521-58183-4*); pap. text 18.95 (*0-521-58839-1*) Cambridge U Pr.

Rubin, Martin, ed. Computerization & Automation in Health Facilities: Computerization & Automation. 296p. 1984. 167.00 (*0-8493-5143-X*, RC268, CRC Reprint) Franklin.

Rubin, Marvin K., contrib. by. Word of Mouth: A Manhattan Dentist Tells All... Well, Almost. 1998. 24.95 (*1-890091-06-5*) Trialtantic Bks.

Rubin, Matatyahu. The Reconstruction of Trees from Their Automorphism Groups. LC 93-11577. (Contemporary Mathematics Ser.: Vol. 151). 274p. 1993. pap. 56.00 (*0-8218-5187-X*, CONM/151) Am Math.

Rubin, Maury. Book of Tarts: Form, Function & Flavor at the City Bakery. LC 94-32734. (Illus.). 128p. 1995. 25.00 (*0-688-12254-X*, Wm Morrow) Morrow Avon.

Rubin, Max. Comp City: A Guide to Free Las Vegas Vacations. 296p. (Orig.). 1994. 39.95 (*0-929712-35-8*) Huntington Pr.

— Comp City: A Guide to Free Las Vegas Vacations. 2nd ed. 300p. (Orig.). 1999. pap. 19.95 (*0-929712-36-6*) Huntington Pr.

Rubin, Melvin L. Optics for Clinicians. 25th anniversary ed. LC 72-97862. (Illus.). 1993. 38.00 (*0-937404-34-9*) Triad Pub FL.

Rubin, Melvin L., jt. auth. see Milder, Benjamin.

Rubin, Melvin L., jt. auth. see Winograd, Lawrence.

Rubin, Melvin L., ed. see Cassin, Barbara & Solomon, Sheila A.

Rubin, Michael. Architectural Ceramics - Eight Concepts. Van Shaik, Terry, ed. LC 85-50004. (Illus.). 28p. (Orig.). 1985. pap. 5.00 (*0-936316-10-1*) Wash U Gallery.

— Nonlinear: A Guide to Digital Film & Video Editing. 3rd ed. LC 95-40791. (Illus.). 320p. (Orig.). (C). 1995. pap. 29.95 (*0-937404-84-5*) Triad Pub FL.

***Rubin, Michael & Diamond, Ron.** Nonlinear: A Field Guide to Digital & Video Editing. 4th rev. ed. (Illus.). 400p. (C). 2000. pap. 39.95 (*0-937404-85-3*) Triad Pub FL.

Rubin, Michael R. Private Rights, Public Wrongs: The Computer & Personal Privacy. Dervin, Brenda, ed. LC 88-19345. (Communication & Information Science Ser.). 168p. 1989. text 73.25 (*0-89391-518-1*) Ablx Pub.

Rubin, Michael R., et al. The Knowledge Industry in the United States, 1960-1980. LC 85-43307. 232p. 1986. reprint ed. pap. 72.00 (*0-608-04628-0*, 206531500003) Bks Demand.

Rubin, Mickey, ed. see Zidonis, Nancy A. & Soderberg, Marie K.

Rubin, Milton A. Plumming in America: The Game: Poor Little Unfortunate Me. (Illus.). 90p. 1989. pap. write for info. (*0-9624702-0-1*) Behav Psychol Servs.

Rubin, Milton D., ed. Man in Systems. (Illus.). xii, 496p. (C). 1971. text 323.00 (*0-677-14060-6*) Gordon & Breach.

Rubin, Miri. Corpus Christi: The Eucharist in Late Medieval Culture. (Illus.). 446p. (C). 1992. pap. text 24.95 (*0-521-43805-5*) Cambridge U Pr.

— Gentile Tales: The Narrative Assault on Late Medieval Jews. LC 98-49996. (Illus.). 257p. 1999. 30.00 (*0-300-07612-6*) Yale U Pr.

Rubin, Miri, ed. The Work of Jacques le Goff & the Challenges of Medieval History. LC 96-46634. 272p. 1997. 90.00 (*0-85115-622-3*) Boydell & Brewer.

Rubin, Morton. Plantation County. (Orig.). 1951. pap. 12.95 (*0-8084-0247-1*) NCUP.

Rubin, Murray. Federal-State Relations in Unemployment Insurance: A Balance of Power. LC 83-17118. 258p. 1983. 22.00 (*0-88099-013-9*); 12.00 (*0-88099-012-0*) W E Upjohn.

Rubin, N. N. & Cotran, E., eds. Annual Survey of African Law, Vol. 3: 1969. 416p. 1973. 59.50 (*0-7146-2948-0*, Pub. by F Cass Pubs) Intl Spec Bk.

— Readings in African Law, 2 vols. 351p. 1970. 95.00 (*0-7146-2602-3*, Pub. by F Cass Pubs) Intl Spec Bk.

Rubin, Nancy. Ask Me If I Care: Voices from an American High School. (Illus.). 464p. (YA). (gr. 9 up). 1994. pap. 21.95 (*0-89815-597-5*) Ten Speed Pr.

— Isabella of Castile: The First Renaissance Queen. 2nd ed. (Illus.). 480p. 1992. pap. 16.95 (*0-312-08511-7*) St Martin.

Rubin, Nathan. Rock & Roll: Art & Anti-Art. 252p. (C). 1995. per. 30.95 (*0-8403-8666-4*) Kendall-Hunt.

***Rubin, Neal.** Michigan Curiosities: The Most Outlandish People, Places & Things in the Great State of Michigan. (Illus.). 224p. 2000. pap. text 12.95 (*0-7627-0601-5*) Globe Pequot.

Rubin, Olis. The Design of Automatic Control Systems. LC 86-71824. (Artech House Communications & Electronic Defense Library). (Illus.). 397p. 1986. reprint ed. pap. 123.10 (*0-7837-9699-4*, 206043000005) Bks Demand.

Rubin, P., jt. ed. see Vegh, B.

Rubin, Patricia L. Giorgio Vasari: Art & History. LC 94-1254. (Illus.). 448p. 1995. 45.00 (*0-300-04909-9*) Yale U Pr.

Rubin, Patricia L., jt. ed. see Ciappelli, Giovanni.

***Rubin, Patricia Lee.** Florence in the 1470's. (Illus.). 288p. 1999. 50.00 (*0-300-08171-5*) Yale U Pr.

Rubin, Paul, jt. auth. see Enstice, Wayne.

Rubin, Paul, jt. auth. see McChesney, Fred.

Rubin, Paul H. Business Firms & the Common Law: The Evolution of Efficient Rules. LC 83-11028. 189p. 1983. 49.95 (*0-275-91070-9*, C1070, Praeger Pubs) Greenwood.

— Managing Business Transactions: Controlling the Cost of Coordinating, Communicating, & Decision Making. 225p. 1990. 32.95 (*0-02-927595-4*) Free Pr.

— Managing Business Transactions: Controlling the Cost of Coordinating, Communicating, & Decision Making. 225p. 1993. pap. 19.95 (*0-02-927596-2*) Free Pr.

***Rubin, Paul H.** Promises, Promises: Contracts in Russia & Other Post-Communist Economies. LC 97-38256. (Shaftesbury Papers: Vol. 11). 96p. (C). 1998. pap. 15.00 (*1-85898-558-7*) E Elgar.

Rubin, Paul H. Tort Reform by Contract. LC 92-38918. 100p. (Orig.). 1993. 29.75 (*0-8447-3829-8*, AEI Pr); pap. 9.75 (*0-8447-3828-X*, AEI Pr) Am Enterprise.

Rubin, Paul H., jt. auth. see Kau, James B.

Rubin, Paul H., jt. ed. see Higgins, Richard S.

Rubin, Peter, ed. Controversies in Therapeutics. (Illus.). 78p. 1991. pap. text 8.00 (*0-7279-0299-7*, Pub. by BMJ Pub) Login Brothers Bk Co.

***Rubin, Peter, ed.** Prescribing in Pregnancy. 3rd ed. 198p. 2002. pap. text 35.95 (*0-7279-1449-9*) BMJ Pub.

Rubin, Philip F. Clinical Oncology. 8th ed. 1999. text. write for info. incl. cd-rom (*0-7216-7496-8*, W B Saunders Co) Harcrt Hlth Sci Grp.

— Clinical Oncology for Physicians & Students: A Multidisciplinary Approach. 7th ed. (Illus.). 804p. 1993. pap. text 25.00 (*0-7216-3761-2*, W B Saunders Co) Harcrt Hlth Sci Grp.

Rubin, Phyllis B. & Tregay, Jeanine L. Play with Them - Theraplay Groups in the Classroom: A Technique for Professionals Who Work with Children. (Illus.). 206p. 1989. pap. 33.95 (*0-398-06715-5*) C C Thomas.

— Play with Them - Theraplay Groups in the Classroom: A Technique for Professionals Who Work with Children. (Illus.). 206p. (C). 1989. text 41.95 (*0-398-05579-3*) C C Thomas.

Rubin, R., et al, eds. Transport & Relaxation in Random Materials: Proceedings of the Third NBS Conference on Transport & Relaxation in Random Materials, October 15-17, 1985, Maryland. 425p. 1986. pap. 45.00 (*9971-5-0134-1*); text 110.00 (*9971-5-0133-3*) World Scientific Pub.

Rubin, R. & Leopold, L. Hematologic Pathophysiology. (Pathophysiology Ser.). (C). 1997. pap. 24.95 (*1-889325-04-X*) Fence Crk Pubng.

Rubin, R. H. & Young, L. S., eds. Clinical Approach to Infection in the Compromised Host. 3rd ed. (Illus.). 780p. (C). 1994. text 145.00 (*0-306-44617-0*, Kluwer Plenum) Kluwer Academic.

***Rubin, Rachel.** Jewish Gangsters of Modern Literature. LC 99-6761. 2000. 29.95 (*0-252-02539-3*) U of Ill Pr.

***Rubin, Rachel & Melnick, Jeffrey, eds.** American Popular Music: New Approaches to the Twentieth Century. 2001. pap. 17.95 (*1-55849-268-2*) U of Mass Pr.

Rubin, Ramon. La Bruma lo Vuelve Azul. 1997. pap. 5.99 (*968-16-5444-7*) Fondo CA.

Rubin, Ramon. El Callado Dolor de los Tzotziles. (SPA.). pap. 7.99 (*968-16-3387-3*, Pub. by Fondo) Continental Bk.

— La Canoa Perdida (The Lost Canoe) Novela Mestiza (Mestizo Novel) (SPA.). 337p. 1993. 16.99 (*968-16-4121-3*, Pub. by Fondo) Continental Bk.

— El Canto de la Grilla (The Song of the Cricket) (SPA.). 163p. 1985. pap. 8.99 (*968-16-1898-X*, Pub. by Fondo) Continental Bk.

— Cuentos Del Mundo Mestizo (Stories of the Mestizo World) (SPA.). 331p. 1985. pap. 12.99 (*968-16-1999-4*, Pub. by Fondo) Continental Bk.

Rubin, Raoul. Understanding Com+ LC 98-43598. (Microsoft Technology Ser.). 320p. 1998. pap. text 49.99 (*0-13-095966-9*) P-H.

Rubin, Rebecca B., et al, eds. Communication Research Measures: A Sourcebook. LC 93-23402. (Communication Ser.). 400p. 1994. lib. bdg. 45.00 (*0-89862-291-3*, C2291) Guilford Pubns.

Rubin, Rebecca B., et al. Communication Research: Strategies & Sources. 233p. (C). 1985. pap. 17.95 (*0-534-05514-1*) Wadsworth Pub.

— Communication Research: Strategies & Sources. 2nd ed. 270p. (C). 1989. pap. write for info. (*0-534-12144-6*) Wadsworth Pub.

— Communication Research: Strategies & Sources. 3rd ed. 318p. (C). 1992. mass mkt. 14.75 (*0-534-17862-6*) Wadsworth Pub.

— Communication Research: Strategies & Sources. 4th ed. (C). 1995. pap. 22.50 (*0-534-50646-1*) Wadsworth Pub.

***Rubin, Rehav.** Image & Reality: Jerusalem in Maps & Views. (Israel Studies in Historical Geography: Vol. 8). (Illus.). 181p. 1999. text 39.00 (*965-493-012-9*, Pub. by Magnes Pr) Eisenbrauns.

Rubin, Renee. Avoiding Liability Risk: An Attorney's Advice to Library Trustees & Others. 30p. (Orig.). 1994. pap. text 17.00 (*0-8389-3448-X*) ALA.

Rubin, Rhea J. Intergenerational Programming: A How-to-Do-It Manual for Librarians. LC 93-28617. (How-to-Do-It Manuals for Libraries Ser.: No. 36). 198p. 1993. pap. 35.00 (*1-55570-157-4*) Neal-Schuman.

— Of a Certain Age: A Guide to Contemporary Fiction Featuring Older Adults. 308p. 1990. lib. bdg. 45.00 (*0-87436-547-3*) ABC-CLIO.

Rubin, Rhea J. & McGovern, Gail. Working with Older Adults: A Handbook for Libraries. 3rd ed. 1990. pap. text 17.50 (*0-929722-37-X*) CA State Library Fndtn.

Rubin, Rhea J. & Suvak, Daniel. Libraries Inside: A Practical Guide for Prison Librarians. Lee, Richard, ed. & illus. by. LC 94-43076. 243p. 1995. lib. bdg. 41.50 (*0-7864-0061-7*) McFarland & Co.

***Rubin, Rhea Joyce.** Defusing the Angry Patron: A How-to-Do-It Manual for Librarians. LC 99-48199. (How-to-Do-It Manuals for Librarians Ser.: Vol. 100). 99p. 2000. pap. 45.00 (*1-55570-372-0*) Neal-Schuman.

Rubin, Richard. Foundations of Library & Information Science. LC 97-49205. 530p. 1998. pap. text 45.00 (*1-55570-309-7*) Neal-Schuman.

— Human Resource Management in Libraries: Theory & Practice. 344p. 1991. pap. 55.00 (*1-55570-087-X*) Neal-Schuman.

Rubin, Richard, ed. Critical Issues in Library Personnel Management. (Allerton Park Institute Ser.: No. 29). 1989. 10.00 (*0-87845-081-5*) U of Ill Grad Sch.

Rubin, Richard, et al. Psyching Out Diabetes. 2nd rev. ed. 312p. 1997. pap. 16.00 (*1-56565-808-6*, Anodyne) Lowell Hse.

— Psyching Out Diabetes: A Positive Approach to Your Negative Emotions. 288p. 1992. 22.95 (*0-929923-97-9*) Lowell Hse.

— Psyching Out Diabetes: A Positive Approach to Your Negative Emotions. 312p. 1993. pap. 16.00 (*1-56565-088-3*, Anodyne) Lowell Hse.

Rubin, Richard, jt. auth. see Brackenridge, Betty Page.

Rubin, Richard E. Hiring Library Employees: A How-to-Do-It Manual. LC 93-36114. (How-to-Do-It Manuals for Libraries Ser.: No. 37). 205p. 1993. 45.00 (*1-55570-159-0*) Neal-Schuman.

Rubin, Richard H., et al. Medicine: A Primary Care Approach. LC 95-21763. (Saunders Text & Review Ser.). (Illus.). 517p. 1996. pap. text 33.95 (*0-7216-5200-X*, W B Saunders Co) Harcrt Hlth Sci Grp.

Rubin, Richard R. Psyching out Diabetes: A Positive Approach to Your Negative Emotions. 3rd ed. 384p. 1999. pap. 16.95 (*0-7373-0258-5*, 02585W) NTC Contemp Pub Co.

Rubin, Richard R., et al. Reflections on Diabetes. LC 96-6157. 104p. 1996. pap. 9.95 (*0-945448-65-1*, 00651Q, Pub. by Am Diabetes) NTC Contemp Pub Co.

***Rubin, Rick.** Naked Against the Rain: The People of the Lower Columbia River, 1770-1830. (Illus.). 448p. (YA). (gr. 10 up). 1999. 29.95 (*1-883287-00-6*) Far Shore Pr.

Rubin, Robert A., ed. Poetry Out Loud. 240p. 1995. pap. 9.95 (*1-56512-122-8*, 72122) Algonquin Bks.

— The Weather Wizard's 5-Year Weather Diary. (Illus.). 400p. 1991. 13.95 (*0-945575-85-8*, 71585) Algonquin Bks.

Rubin, Robert A., et al. Construction Claims: Prevention & Resolution. 2nd ed. (Illus.). 352p. (gr. 13). 1992. mass mkt. 69.95 (*0-442-00441-9*) Chapman & Hall.

***Rubin, Robert Alden.** On the Beaten Path: An Appalachian Pilgrimage. LC 99-56989. 256p. 2000. 24.95 (*1-58574-023-3*) Lyons Pr.

Rubin, Roger H., jt. ed. see Macklin, Eleanor D.

***Rubin, Ron, compiled by.** Rudy, Rudy, Rudy: The Real & the Rational. 208p. 2000. pap. 10.95 (*0-8419-1410-9*) Holmes & Meier.

Rubin, Ronald & Young, Charles M. Formal Logic: A Model of English. LC 88-33383. 393p. (C). 1989. pap. text 49.95 (*0-87484-891-1*, 891) Mayfield Pub.

— Formal Logic, Solutions Manual: A Model of English. (C). 1989. pap. text, teacher ed. write for info. (*0-87484-913-6*, 913) Mayfield Pub.

Rubin, Ronald, tr. see Biffle, Christopher.

Rubin, Ronald, tr. see Descartes, Rene.

Rubin, Ronald P., ed. Calcium & Cellular Secretion. LC 82-7489. 288p. 1982. 65.00 (*0-306-40978-X*, Plenum Trade) Perseus Pubng.

Rubin, Ronald P., et al, eds. Calcium in Biological Systems. LC 84-18246. 760p. 1985. 145.00 (*0-306-41747-2*, Plenum Trade) Perseus Pubng.

Rubin, Ronald P. & Laychock, Suzanne. Lipid Second Messengers. LC 98-50105. (Methods in Life Sciences - Signal Transduction Ser.). 160p. 1998. per. 94.95 (*0-8493-3383-0*) CRC Pr.

Rubin, Rose M. & Nieswiadomy, Michael. Expenditures of Older Americans. LC 97-19755. 176p. 1997. 55.00 (*0-275-95874-4*, Praeger Pubs) Greenwood.

Rubin, Rose M. & Riney, Bobye J. Working Wives & Dual-Earner Families. LC 93-5441. 176p. 1993. 52.95 (*0-275-94682-7*, Praeger Pubs) Greenwood.

— Working Wives & Dual-Earner Families. LC 93-5441. 176p. 1995. pap. 19.95 (*0-275-95338-6*, Praeger Pubs) Greenwood.

Rubin, Rose N. & Stillman, Michael. Russian Songbook. 112p. 1989. pap. 8.95 (*0-486-26118-2*) Dover.

***Rubin, Ruth.** Voices of a People: The Story of Yiddish Folksong. LC 00-39216. 568p. 2000. 23.95 (*0-252-06918-8*) U of Ill Pr.

***Rubin, S., ed.** 1st International Conference on Information Reuse & Integration: IRI-99 Proceedings: Nov. 4-6, 1999, Atlanta, GA, U. S. A. (C). 1999. write for info. (*1-880843-31-5*) Int Soc Comp App.

Rubin, S., jt. auth. see Bozarth, J.

Rubin, S. G., ed. see Computers in Aerodynamics Symposium Staff.

Rubin, Sally. The Great Brain. (Novel-Ties Ser.). (J). (gr. 3-5). 1989. pap. text, teacher ed., student ed. 15.95 (*0-88122-048-5*) Lrn Links.

Rubin, Sally Jo, jt. auth. see Von Graevenitz, Alexander.

***Rubin, Sandra M.** Look Fear In The Face: From Adolescence to Adulthood Against All Odds. 206p. 1998. pap. 11.95 (*0-9657402-0-X*) Rubin & Kraus.

Rubin, Saul. Offbeat Marijuana: The Life & Times of the World's Grooviest Plant. LC 99-13285. (Illus.). 2p. 1999. pap. 19.95 (*1-891661-05-1*, 1051, Offbeat) Snta Monica.

— Offbeat Museums: The Curators & Collections of America's Most Unusual Museums. LC 97-16766. (Illus.). 240p. 1997. pap. 19.95 (*0-9639946-4-6*, 46-4-6) Snta Monica.

An Asterisk (*) at the beginning of an entry indicates that the title is appearing for the first time.

Rubin, Seymour J. Private Foreign Investment: Legal & Economic Realities. LC 56-7594. 120p. reprint ed. pap. 37.20 (*0-608-13620-4*, 202075100018) Bks Demand.

Rubin, Seymour J. & Alexander, Dean C. NAFTA & the Environment. LC 96-40979. (NAFTA Law & Policy Ser.). 1996. 295.00 (*90-411-0033-4*) Kluwer Law Intl.

Rubin, Seymour J. & Hufbauer, Gary C., eds. Emerging Standards of International Trade & Investment: Multinational Codes & Corporate Conduct. LC 83-13859. 212p. 1984. 65.00 (*0-86598-133-7*) Rowman.

Rubin, Seymour J. & Nelson, Richard W. International Investment Disputes: Avoidance & Settlement, No. 20. (Studies in Transnational Legal Policy). 1985. 8.50 (*0-317-01188-X*) Am Soc Intl Law.

Rubin, Seymour J. & Wallace, Don, Jr., eds. Transnational Corporations & Innovatory Activities. LC 93-15972. (United Nations Library on Transnational Corporations: Vol. 17). 1994. write for info. (*0-415-08550-0*) Routledge.

Rubin, Sol, jt. ed. see Surrency, Erwin C.

***Rubin, Stanford E. & Roessler, Richard.** Foundations of the Vocational Rehabilitation Process. 5th ed. LC 00-37294. 2000. write for info. (*0-89079-854-0*) PRO-ED.

Rubin, Stanford E. & Roessler, Richard T. Foundations of the Vocational Rehabilitation Process. 4th ed. LC 94-6130. 460p. (C). 1995. pap. text 37.00 (*0-89079-601-7*, 6786) PRO-ED.

Rubin, Stanford E., jt. auth. see Roessler, Richard.

Rubin, Stanford E., jt. auth. see Roessler, Richard T.

Rubin, Steffi, jt. auth. see Rubin, Barry.

Rubin, Steffi K. It Is Good: Growing up in a Messianic Jewish Family, a Story to Read & Color. (Illus.). (J). 1989. pap. 2.99 (*1-880226-06-5*) M J Pubs.

Rubin, Steffi K., jt. auth. see Rubin, Barry.

Rubin, Steffi K., jt. illus. see Rubin, Barry.

Rubin, Stephen, jt. auth. see Biggs, John S.

Rubin, Stephen C. Ovarian Cancer. text. write for info. (*0-7817-2408-2*) Lppncott W & W.

Rubin, Stephen C., ed. Chemotherapy of Gynecologic Cancers: Society of Gynecologic Oncologists Handbook. LC 95-50021. 240p. 1996. pap. text 31.00 (*0-397-51736-X*) Lppncott W & W.

Rubin, Stephen C. & Hoskins, William J., eds. Cervical Cancer & Preinvasive Neoplasia. LC 95-26460. 512p. 1996. text 160.00 (*0-397-51645-2*) Lppncott W & W.

Rubin, Stephen M. & Clarizio, Tony V. Consumer's Credit Guide. 104p. (Orig.). 1994. pap. text 19.95 (*0-9640055-0-6*) Applied Telemedia.

Rubin, Steven J. The Complete James Bond Movies Encyclopedia. rev. ed. LC 97-100543. (Illus.). 512p. 1995. pap. 25.00 (*0-8092-3268-5*, 326850, Contemporary Bks) NTC Contemp Pub Co.

— Reel Exposure: How to Publicize & Promote Today's Motion Pictures. (Illus.). 337p. (C). 1992. pap. 19.95 (*0-911747-20-6*) Broadway Pr.

— Writing Our Lives: Autobiographies of American Jews, 1890-1990. LC 91-3599. 384p. 1991. text 24.95 (*0-8276-0393-2*) JPS Phila.

Rubin, Steven J., ed. Telling & Remembering: A Century of American Jewish Poetry. 528p. 1998. pap. 20.00 (*0-8070-6839-X*) Beacon Pr.

Rubin, Steven M. Computer Aids for VLSI Design. LC 86-26571. (VLSI Systems Ser.). (Illus.). 458p. (C). 1987. text 49.50 (*0-201-05824-3*) Addison-Wesley.

Rubin, Susan B. When Doctors Say No: The Battleground of Medical Futility. LC 98-6798. (Medical Ethics Ser.). 240p. 1998. 24.95 (*0-253-33463-2*) Ind U Pr.

***Rubin, Susan B. & Zoloth, Laurie, eds.** Margin of Error: The Ethics of Mistakes in Clinical Medicine. 384p. 2000. pap. 29.95 (*1-55572-053-6*) Univ Pub Group.

— Margin of Error: The Ethics of Mistakes in Clinical Medicine. 384p. (C). 2000. lib. bdg. 65.00 (*1-55572-078-1*) Univ Pub Group.

Rubin, Susan G. Emily Good as Gold. LC 93-13192. (Illus.). 180p. (J). (gr. 5-9). 1993. 10.95 (*0-15-276632-4*, Harcourt Child Bks); pap. 3.95 (*0-15-276633-2*, Harcourt Child Bks) Harcourt.

***Rubin, Susan G.** Fireflies in the Dark. LC 99-12282. 48p. (J). 2000. 18.95 (*0-8234-1461-2*) Holiday.

Rubin, Susan G. Frank Lloyd Wright. LC 93-48523. (First Impressions Ser.). (Illus.). 92p. (J). 1994. 19.95 (*0-8109-3974-6*, Pub. by Abrams) Time Warner.

— The Rainbow Fields. LC 92-46875. (Illus.). 40p. (J). (gr. k-4). 1993. 14.95 (*1-56844-004-9*) Enchante Pub.

— The Rainbow Fields. 2nd rev. ed. Hoy, Gudrun & Martin, Bobi, eds. (Emotional Literacy Ser.). (Illus.). 40p. (J). (gr. k-5). 1995. 14.95 (*1-56844-104-5*) Enchante Pub.

***Rubin, Susan G.** Toilets, Toasters, & Telephones: The How & Why of Everyday Objects. LC 97-28650. (Illus.). 132p. (YA). (gr. 5-8). 1998. 20.00 (*0-15-201421-7*) Harcourt.

***Rubin, Susan Goldman.** Margaret Bourke-White: Her Pictures Were Her Life. LC 98-53967. (Illus.). 96p. (YA). (gr. 5-8). 1999. 19.95 (*0-8109-4381-6*, Pub. by Abrams) Time Warner.

— There Goes the Neighborhood: 10 Buildings People Loved to Hate. LC 00-36953. (Illus.). 2001. write for info. (*0-8234-1435-3*) Holiday.

— The Whiz Kids Plugged In. LC 97-220901. (Hands-On Science Ser.). (Illus.). 32p. (J). 1997. write for info. (*0-590-06583-1*) Scholastic Inc.

Rubin, Sylvia P. It's Not Too Late for a Baby: For Men & Women over Thirty-Five. (Illus.). 272p. 1980. 14.95 (*0-13-507046-5*, Spectrum IN) Macmillan Gen Ref.

Rubin, Theodore I. Angry Book. 216p. 1998. per. 11.00 (*0-684-84201-7*, Touchstone) S&S Trade Pap.

— Compassion & Self-Hate: An Alternative to Despair. 288p. 1998. per. 12.00 (*0-684-84199-1*, Touchstone) S&S Trade Pap.

— Jordi - Lisa & David. 18.95 (*0-89190-588-X*) Amereon Ltd.

— One to One: Understanding Personal Relationships. LC 99-21604. 1999. pap. 11.95 (*0-312-87184-8*, Pub. by Forge NYC) St Martin.

— Overcoming Indecisiveness. 208p. 1986. mass mkt. 4.99 (*0-380-69977-X*, Avon Bks) Morrow Avon.

Rubin, Theodore Isaac. David & Lisa. 1998. pap. 11.95 (*0-312-87003-5*, Pub. by Forge NYC) St Martin.

— Lisa & David/Jordi/Little Ralphie & the Creature. LC 97-33049. 224p. 1998. 22.95 (*0-312-86372-1*, Pub. by Forge NYC); pap. 11.95 (*0-312-86373-X*, Pub. by Forge NYC) St Martin.

Rubin, Tony. User Interface Design for Computer Systems. 1988. text 41.95 (*0-470-21172-5*) P-H.

Rubin, U., jt. ed. see Reed, R.

Rubin, Uri. Between Bible & Quran: The Children of Israel & the Islamic Self-Image. LC 99-23119. (Studies in Late Antiquity & Early Islam). 1999. 29.95 (*0-87850-134-7*) Darwin Pr.

— The Eye of the Beholder: The Life of Muhammad As Viewed by the Early Muslims: A Textual Analysis. LC 94-49175. (Studies in Late Antiquity & Early Islam: No. 5). ix, 289p. 1995. 27.50 (*0-87850-110-X*) Darwin Pr.

Rubin, Uri, ed. The Life of Muhammad. LC 98-6041. (Formation of the Classical Islamic World Ser.: Vol. 4). 1p. 1998. text 129.95 (*0-86078-703-6*, BP75.L53, Pub. by Ashgate Pub) Ashgate Pub Co.

Rubin, Uri & Wasserstein, David J., eds. Dhimmis & Others: Jews & Christians & the World of Classical Islam. (Israel Oriental Studies: Vol. 17). 257p. 1997. text 49.50 (*1-57506-026-4*) Eisenbrauns.

Rubin, Vera. Bright Galaxies, Dark Matters. LC 96-25122. (Masters of Modern Physics Ser.). (Illus.). 236p. 1997. 29.95 (*1-56396-231-4*) Spr-Verlag.

Rubin, Vera, ed. Cannabis & Culture. (World Anthropology Ser.). (Illus.). xiv, 598p. 1975. 53.10 (*90-279-7669-4*) Mouton.

Rubin, Vera & Comitas, Lambros. Ganja in Jamaica. (New Babylon Studies in the Social Sciences: No.26). 206p. 1975. text 24.65 (*90-279-7731-3*) Mouton.

Rubin, Vera, ed. see American Association for the Advancement of Science Staff.

Rubin, Victor, jt. auth. see Maxwell, Nan L.

Rubin, Vitalifi. Individual & State in Ancient China: Essays on Four Chinese Philosophers. LC 76-4516. 179p. reprint ed. pap. 55.50 (*0-8357-7779-0*, 203613900002) Bks Demand.

Rubin, W. & Brookler, K. Dizziness: Etiologic Approach to Management. (Illus.). 256p. 1991. text 59.00 (*0-86577-391-2*) Thieme Med Pubs.

Rubin, W. L., jt. auth. see DiFranco, J. V.

Rubin, William. Frank Stella. (Illus.). 1992. pap. 22.50 (*0-8109-6107-5*, Pub. by Abrams) Time Warner.

— Painted Steel: The Late Work of David Smith. (Illus.). 60p. 1998. pap. 30.00 (*1-880154-23-4*) Gagosian Gallery.

— Picasso & Braque: Pioneering Cubism. (Illus.). 464p. 1989. 70.00 (*0-87070-675-6*, 0-8109-6065-6, Pub. by Mus of Modern Art) Abrams.

Rubin, William, ed. Picasso & Portraiture: Representation & Transformation. (Illus.). 496p. 1999. text 50.00 (*0-7881-6076-1*) DIANE Pub.

Rubin, William S. Frank Stella: 1970-1987. (Illus.). 208p. 1987. 45.00 (*0-87070-593-8*, 0-8109-6074-5); pap. 22.50 (*0-87070-599-7*, 0-8109-6107-5, Pub. by Mus of Modern Art) Abrams.

— Modern Sacred Art & the Church of Assy. LC 61-15469. (Illus.). 245p. reprint ed. pap. 76.00 (*0-608-18600-7*, 205185800011) Bks Demand.

— Picasso & Braque: A Symposium. (Illus.). 360p. 1992. 35.00 (*0-8109-6115-6*, Pub. by Abrams); pap. 19.95 (*0-8109-6117-2*, Pub. by Abrams) Time Warner.

— Picasso & Braque: Pioneering Cubism. (Illus.). 1990. 70.00 (*0-8109-6065-6*, Pub. by Abrams); pap. 34.95 (*0-685-58430-5*, 0-8109-6120-2) Abrams.

— Picasso & Portraiture: Representation & Transformation. (Illus.). 496p. 1996. 75.00 (*0-87070-143-6*, 0-8109-6140-1); pap. 35.00 (*0-87070-142-8*) Mus of Modern Art.

— Primitivism in 20th Century Art: Affinity of the Tribal & the Modern. (Illus.). 706p. 1990. 125.00 (*0-8109-6067-2*, Pub. by Abrams) Time Warner.

Rubin, William S., ed. Primitivism in 20th Century Art: Affinity of the Tribal & the Modern, 2 vols. (Illus.). 706p. 1990. pap. 65.00 (*0-8109-6068-0*, Pub. by Abrams) Time Warner.

Rubin, William S., ed. Primitivism in Twentieth Century Art: Affinity of the Tribal & the Modern. (Illus.). 706p. 1984. 125.00 (*0-87070-518-0*, 0-8109-6067-2, Pub. by Mus of Modern Art); pap. 65.00 (*0-87070-534-2*, 0-8109-6068-0, Pub. by Mus of Modern Art) Abrams.

Rubin, William S. & Armstrong, Matthew. The William S. Paley Collection. (Illus.). 192p. 1992. 45.00 (*0-87070-170-3*); pap. 27.50 (*0-87070-193-2*) Mus of Modern Art.

Rubin, William S., et al. Les Demoiselles D'Avignon. Elderfield, John, ed. (Studies in Modern Art: No. 3). (Illus.). 224p. 1994. 40.00 (*0-87070-162-2*, 0-8109-6125-3, Pub. by Mus of Modern Art) Abrams.

***Rubin Wolf, Rachel, ed.** Keys to Painting: Fruit & Flowers. LC 99-55195. (Keys to Painting Ser.). (Illus.). 128p. 2000. pap. 19.99 (*1-58180-003-7*, North Lght Bks) F & W Pubns Inc.

Rubin, Z. Psychology. (C). 1992. text 65.96 (*0-395-60550-4*) HM.

Rubin, Z., jt. ed. see Hartup, William W.

Rubin, Zick. Children's Friendship. (Developing Child Ser.). (Illus.). 165p. 1980. pap. text 11.50 (*0-674-11619-4*) HUP.

Rubin, Zick, ed. Doing Unto Others: Joining, Molding, Conforming, Helping, Loving. (Patterns of Social Behavior Ser.). 160p. 1975. pap. 3.45 (*0-13-217596-7*, Spectrum IN) Macmillan Gen Ref.

***Rubina, Dina.** Here Comes the Messiah! 2000. pap. 16.95 (*0-939010-60-7*) Zephyr Pr.

Rubincam, Barclay, jt. auth. see Sheppard, Beverly.

Rubincam, Milton. Evidence: An Exemplary Study, a Craig Family Case History. LC 81-86218. 41p. (Orig.). 1981. pap. text 6.00 (*0-915156-49-0*, SP 49) Natl Genealogical.

— Pitfalls in Genealogical Research. 2nd ed. LC 87-70105. (Illus.). 74p. 1987. reprint ed. pap. 7.95 (*0-916489-28-0*, 143) Ancestry.

Rubinchik, Iu. Persian-Russian Dictionary, 2 vols. 1564p. (C). 1983. 195.00 (*0-7855-6493-4*, Pub. by Collets) St Mut.

Rubincik, J. Persian-Russian Dictionary, 2 vols. (PER & RUS.). 1664p. 1985. 150.00 (*0-8288-1126-1*, F47750) Fr & Eur.

Rubine, David. Climber's Guide to Pinnacles National Monument. 2nd ed. LC 97-132996. (Illus.). 254p. (Orig.). 1995. pap. 25.00 (*0-934641-89-7*) Falcon Pub Inc.

Rubinetti, Donald. Cappy the Lonely Camel. LC 95-9690. (Illus.). 32p. (J). (gr. 1-3). 1996. 13.95 (*0-382-39150-0*, Silver Pr NJ); pap. 5.95 (*0-382-39152-7*); lib. bdg. 15.95 (*0-382-39151-9*) Silver Burdett Pr.

Rubinfeld, Daniel L., jt. auth. see Pindyck, Robert S.

Rubinfeld, Daniel L., jt. ed. see Quigley, John M.

Rubinfeld, William A. Planning Your College Education. 160p. 1994. pap. 6.95 (*0-8442-6673-6*, Passprt Bks) NTC Contemp Pub Co.

Rubinfeld, Yisroel M. Yedios Klalios: Basic Torah Knowledge Booklet. (HEB.). 1997. pap. 3.75 (*1-878895-06-0*, A258) Torah Umesorah.

Rubinfield, Daniel L., jt. auth. see Pindyck, Robert S.

Rubinfien, Leo, photos by. A Map of the East. (Illus.). 132p. 1992. pap. 25.00 (*0-87923-943-3*) Godine.

Rubinfien, Louisa, tr. see Ozawa, Ichiro.

Rubinger, Bruce, ed. Applied Artificial Intelligence in Japan: Current Status, Key Research & Industrial Performers, Strategic Focus. 280p. 1988. 560.00 (*0-89116-744-7*) Hemisp Pub.

Rubinger, Catherine, jt. ed. see Bonnel, Roland.

Rubinger, Richard. Private Academies of Tokugawa Japan. LC 81-47950. (Illus.). 300p. 1982. reprint ed. pap. 93.00 (*0-608-02591-7*, 206324800004) Bks Demand.

Rubinger, Richard, jt. auth. see Watt, Yasuko I.

Rubinger, Richard, ed. see Motoyama, Yukihiko.

Rubingh, Donn N. & Holland, Paul M., eds. Cationic Surfactants: Physical Chemistry. (Surfactant Science Ser.: Vol. 37). (Illus.). 544p. 1990. text 199.00 (*0-8247-8357-3*) Dekker.

Rubingh, Donn N., jt. ed. see Holland, Paul M.

Rubington, Earl & Weinberg, Martin S. Deviance: The Interactionist Perspective. 7th ed. LC 98-4974. 448p. 1998. pap. text 46.00 (*0-205-27780-2*) Allyn.

— The Study of Social Problems: Seven Perspectives. 5th ed. (Illus.). 384p. (C). 1995. pap. text 28.95 (*0-19-508367-9*) OUP.

Rubini, Alessandro. Linux Device Drivers. Oram, Andy, ed. LC 98-134181. 442p. (Orig.). 1998. pap. 29.95 (*1-56592-292-1*) OReilly & Assocs.

Rubini, Alice & Weiermair, Peter. Tony Oursler. (Illus.). 64p. 1998. pap. 24.95 (*88-8158-168-X*, Pub. by Charta) Dist Art Pubs.

Rubini, Michel. Merlin & the Dragons. (J). (gr. k-6). 1993. pap. 9.95 incl. VHS (*1-879496-49-6*, 54003-3) Lightyear Entrtnmnt.

Rubino, Anthony. 1001 Ways to Procrastinate. Carle, Cliff, ed. 1994. pap. 4.99 (*0-918259-58-4*) CCC Pubns.

Rubino, Carl. Ilocano-English, English-Ilocano Dictionary & Phrasebook. LC 98-12437. 450p. 1998. pap. 14.95 (*0-7818-0642-9*) Hippocrene Bks.

Rubino, Carl R. Ilocano Dictionary & Grammar: Ilocano-English, English-Ilocano. (PALI Language Texts). 674p. 2000. pap. 40.00 (*0-8248-2068-6*) UH Pr.

Rubino, Carl R. Gavez, see Gavez Rubino, Carl R.

Rubino, Debra. Keepers of Secrets & Truths Otherwise Unknown. (Illus.). 40p. 1994. 11.00 (*0-9624021-8-4*) Ursinus College.

Rubino, Jane. Cheat the Devil. 352p. 1998. 24.95 (*1-885173-56-3*) Write Way.

— Death of a DJ. 225p. 1995. 20.95 (*1-885173-09-1*) Write Way.

— Fruitcake. 384p. 1997. 24.95 (*1-885173-29-6*) Write Way.

***Rubino, Jane.** Plot Twist. 304p. 2000. 24.95 (*1-885173-80-6*, Pub. by Write Way) Midpt Trade.

***Rubino, Jane, et al.** Homicide for the Holidays: Fruitcake; Milwaukee Winters Can Be Murder; A Perfect Time for Murder. (WWL Mystery Ser.). 2000. mass mkt. 6.99 (*0-373-26362-7*, 1-26362-3, Wrldwide Lib) Harlequin Bks.

***Rubino, Jimmy, Jr. & Taylor, Ted.** Ralph's Italian Restaurant, 100 Years & 100 Recipes. LC 00-190870. 2000. 25.00 (*0-7388-2059-8*); pap. 18.00 (*0-7388-2060-1*) Xlibris Corp.

***Rubino, Joe.** The Magic Lantern: A Fable about Leadership, Personal Excellence & Empowerment. (Illus.). 170p. 2000. pap. 14.95 (*0-9678529-0-0*) Vision Works.

Rubino, John. Main Street, Not Wall Street: Investing Close to Home, the Smart Way to Make More Money. LC 97-47694. 320p. 1998. 25.00 (*0-688-15421-2*, Wm Morrow) Morrow Avon.

Rubino, John A. Communicating Compensation Programs: An Approach to Providing Information to Employees. (Building Blocks Ser.: Vol. 4). (Illus.). 20p. (Orig.). 1992. pap. 24.95 (*1-57963-007-3*, A0004) Am Compensation.

Rubino, Lisa. Beat the Clock Cooking No. 1: Take the Easy Way Out of the Kitchen with the Short Cut Cooks. Oleksiw, Barbara, ed. LC 96-90562. (Illus.). 243p. (Orig.). 1998. pap. 18.95 (*0-9654204-7-7*) TeriLee Prods.

Rubino, Paul, jt. auth. see Stein, Victor.

Rubino, Paul, ed. see Simpson, Brad.

***Rubino, Paul W.** Body Parts. LC 99-91266. 2000. 25.00 (*0-7388-0720-6*); pap. 18.00 (*0-7388-0721-4*) Xlibris Corp.

Rubino, Peter. The Portrait in Clay. LC 97-17653. (Illus.). 160p. 1997. pap. 24.95 (*0-8230-4102-6*) Watsn-Guptill.

Rubino, Ray. It's Not All Coffee & Donuts: A Read for Police Officers & Those Who Dare to Learn What Makes Them Tick & Ticked Off. LC 99-93011. 218p. 1998. write for info. (*0-9668280-0-3*) Asphalt Warriors.

Rubino, S., jt. auth. see Perez-Bendito, D.

Rubino-Sammartano, M. International Arbitration Law. 550p. 1990. 110.00 (*90-6544-432-7*) Kluwer Law Intl.

Rubino-Sammartano, M., ed. Warranties in Cross-Border Acquisitions. LC 93-23307. (International Bar Association Ser.). 480p. (C). 1993. lib. bdg. 183.50 (*1-85333-946-6*, Pub. by Graham & Trotman) Kluwer Academic.

Rubino-Sammartano, M. & Morse, C. G. Public Policy in Transnational Relationships. 1990. ring bd. 97.00 (*90-6544-955-8*) Kluwer Law Intl.

Rubinof, Arthur G., jt. auth. see Matthews, Robert O.

Rubinoff, Arthur G. Canada & South Asia: Political & Strategic Relations. (C). 1992. text 32.00 (*1-895214-02-5*, Pub. by Ctre South Asian); pap. text 23.00 (*1-895214-01-7*, Pub. by Ctre South Asian) S Asia.

— The Construction of a Political Community: Integration & Identity in GOA. LC 98-7052. 1998. 32.00 (*0-7619-9259-6*) Sage.

Rubinoff, Aviva. Ima I'm Bored. 160p. 1994. 14.95 (*1-56871-052-6*) Targum Pr.

Rubinoff, Darlene A. Dance of the Russian Peasant: Zaboomi. (Illus.). 321p. (Orig.). 1994. pap. text 14.95 (*1-885740-01-8*) Raza Pubng.

Rubinoff, Elaine. The Art of Teaching: Practical Strategies for Effective Chinuch. LC 95-25504. 1996. 29.95 (*0-87306-739-8*) Feldheim.

Rubinoff, Lionel. Collingwood & the Reform of Metaphysics: A Study in the Philosophy of Mind. LC 73-19150. 427p. reprint ed. pap. 132.40 (*0-608-30613-4*, 202051900018) Bks Demand.

Rubinoff, Lionel, jt. auth. see Van der Dussen, W. J.

Rubinoff, Michael W. Principle or Pragmatism: Interest Groups, PACs, & Campaign Contributions in 1984. write for info. (*0-318-61041-8*) Free Congr Res.

Rubinov, A. M., jt. auth. see Dem'yanov, V. F.

***Rubinov, Aleksandr Moiseevich.** Abstract Convexity & Global Optimization. LC 00-39102. (Nonconvex Optimization & Its Applications Ser.). (Illus.). 2000. write for info. (*0-7923-6323-X*, Kluwer Plenum) Kluwer Academic.

Rubinov, Aleksandr Moiseevich, jt. auth. see Dem'kilanov, V. F.

Rubinov, Alexander M., jt. auth. see Demyanov, Vladimir F.

***Rubinov-Jacobson, Philip.** Drinking Lightning: Art, Creativity & Transformation. LC 00-37157. (Illus.). 2000. 50.00 (*1-57062-746-0*, Pub. by Shambhala Pubns) Random.

Rubinow, Isaac M. Economic Conditions of the Jews in Russia. LC 74-29519. (Modern Jewish Experience Ser.). 1975. reprint ed. 18.95 (*0-405-06744-5*) Ayer.

— The Quest for Security. LC 75-17241. (Social Problems & Social Policy Ser.). 1976. reprint ed. 52.95 (*0-405-07512-X*) Ayer.

— Social Insurance. LC 76-89761. (American Labor, from Conspiracy to Collective Bargaining Ser., No. 1). 525p. 1974. reprint ed. 30.95 (*0-405-02146-1*) Ayer.

Rubinow, Isaac M. & Stein, Leon, eds. The Aged & the Depression. Incl. Care of the Aged. LC 79-8683. (Illus.). 1980. reprint ed. lib. bdg. 17.95 (*0-405-12800-2*); LC 71-169363. (Family in America Ser.). 41.95 (*0-405-03881-X*) Ayer.

Rubinow, Sol I. Mathematical Problems in the Biological Sciences. (CBMS-NSF Regional Conference Ser.: No. 10). vii, 90p. 1973. pap. text 21.00 (*0-89871-008-1*) Soc Indus-Appl Math.

Rubinowitz, Chaim D. The History of the Jewish People - From Nechemia to the Present, 2 vols. Carmel, Shlomo, tr. from HEB. 602p. 1997. 45.00 (*1-885220-19-7*) Moznaim.

— The History of the Jewish People - From Nechemia to the Present Vol. 2: The Last Millennium. Carmel, Shlomo, tr. from HEB. 558p. 1997. 22.50 (*1-885220-20-0*) Moznaim.

***Rubinowitz, Leonard S. & Rosenbaum, James E.** Crossing the Class & Color Lines: From Public Housing to White Suburbia. LC 99-53847. 240p. 2000. 25.00 (*0-226-73089-1*) U Ch Pr.

Rubins, David K. The Human Figure. (Illus.). 1975. pap. 15.95 (*0-14-004243-1*, Penguin Bks) Viking Penguin.

Rubins, Diane T. Building Positive Parent-Child Communications. (For Parents Only Ser.). 16p. 1994. 1.95 (*1-56688-185-4*) Bur For At-Risk.

— Dealing with Your Child's Feelings. (For Parents Only Ser.). 16p. 1994. 1.95 (*1-56688-187-0*) Bur For At-Risk.

— Encouraging a Positive Attitude. (For Parents Only Ser.). 16p. 1994. 1.95 (*1-56688-189-7*) Bur For At-Risk.

— Getting along Better with Your Child. (For Parents Only Ser.). 16p. 1994. 1.95 (*1-56688-186-2*) Bur For At-Risk.

— Keeping Your Child Drug-Free. (For Parents Only Ser.). 16p. (Orig.). 1994. 1.95 (*1-56688-193-5*) Bur For At-Risk.

R

An Asterisk (*) at the beginning of an entry indicates that the title is appearing for the first time.

— Teaching Your Child Responsibility. (For Parents Only Ser.). 16p. 1994. 1.95 (1-56688-192-7) Bur For At-Risk.

— Teaching Your Child the Value of Friendship. (For Parents Only Ser.). 16p. 1994. 1.95 (1-56688-194-3) Bur For At-Risk.

— Teaching Your Child to Appreciate Diversity. (For Parents Only Ser.). 16p. 1994. 1.95 (1-56688-195-1) Bur For At-Risk.

Rubins, J., et al. Brownstone. 101p. 1987. pap. 6.95 (0-88145-054-5) Broadway Play.

Rubins, Maria. Crossroad of Arts Crossroad of Cultures: Ecphrasis in Russian. text. write for info. (0-312-22951-8) St Martin.

Rubins, Maria, tr. see Etkind, Alexander.

Rubins, Noah, tr. see Etkind, Alexander.

Rubinski, Yuri. Beyond HTML. 1996. 29.95 (0-614-14488-4) P-H.

Rubinsky, Holley. At First I Hope for Rescue. LC 97-33369. 256p. 1998. text 22.00 (0-312-18043-8) St Martin.

— At First I Hope for Rescue. LC 98-51201. 245p. 1999. pap. 12.00 (0-312-19967-8, Picador USA) St Martin.

Rubinsky, Susan, et al. An EMT Prepares: One Hundred Role-Playing Scenarios. 311p. (C). 1993. ring bd. 59.95 (1-884225-00-4) Communs Skills.

Rubinsohn, W. Z. Spartacus' Uprising & Soviet Historical Writing. 56p. 1987. pap. 4.95 (0-9511243-1-5, Pub. by Oxbow Bks) David Brown.

Rubinson, Judith F. & Rubinson, Kenneth A. Contemporary Chemical Analysis. LC 97-52137. 613p. (C). 1998. 105.00 (0-13-519331-1, Prentice Hall) P-H.

— Contemporary Instrumental Analysis. LC 99-33308. 840p. (C). 1999. 110.67 (0-13-790726-5, Macmillan Coll) P-H.

Rubinson, Kenneth A., jt. auth. see Rubinson, Judith F.

Rubinson, Laura, jt. auth. see Neutens, James J.

Rubinson, Mirian. Mystery of the Blanket: A Fictional Tale of Life . . . (of Truth) 200p. 1998. pap. 12.00 (0-9668684-0-4) Robinson Publ.

Rubinson, Richard, ed. Dynamics of World Development. LC 81-1437. (Political Economy of the World-System Annuals Ser.: No. 4). 264p. reprint ed. pap. 81.90 (0-8357-8507-6, 203479400091) Bks Demand.

Rubinson, Richard, jt. ed. see Fuller, Bruce.

Rubinson, Teresa C. & Terplan, Kornel. Network Design: Management & Technical Perspectives. LC 98-6583. 416p. 1998. boxed set 79.95 (0-8493-3404-7) CRC Pr.

***Rubinstein.** Dress Codes. 2nd ed. 2000. 30.00 (0-8133-6795-6, Pub. by Westview) HarpC.

Rubinstein. Pharmaceutical Tech: Control. 1990. boxed set. write for info. (0-318-68276-1) P-H.

— Philo: Semitism & the Readmission of the Jews to England, 1603-1655. LC 98-52706. 1999. text 59.95 (0-312-22205-X) St Martin.

— Society's Child Date not set. write for info. (0-8133-6670-4) HarpC.

Rubinstein, jt. auth. see Russell.

Rubinstein, A. Autobiography, 1829-1889. LC 68-25303. (Studies in Music: No. 42). 1969. reprint ed. lib. bdg. 75.00 (0-8383-0315-3) M S G Haskell Hse.

Rubinstein, Akiba. Rubinstein's Chess Masterpieces. Kmoch, Hans, ed. Winkelman, Barnie F., tr. 192p. 1941. pap. 6.95 (0-486-20617-3) Dover.

Rubinstein, Allen & Korf, Bruce R. Neurofibramatosis. (Illus.). 320p. 1990. text 75.00 (0-86577-154-5) Thieme Med Pubs.

Rubinstein, Alvin Z. Soviet Policy Toward Turkey, Iran & Afghanistan: The Dynamics of Influence. LC 82-7513. 200p. 1982. 45.00 (0-275-90891-7, C0891, Praeger Pubs) Greenwood.

— The Soviet Union & the Iran-Iraq War. (Pew Case Studies in International Affairs). 50p. (C). 1991. pap. text 3.50 (1-56927-352-9) Geo U Inst Dplmcy.

— The Soviets in International Organizations: Changing Policy Toward Developing Countries, 1953-1963. LC 64-12184. 400p. 1964. reprint ed. pap. 124.00 (0-7837-9437-1, 206017900004) Bks Demand.

Rubinstein, Alvin Z., ed. America's National Interest in a Post-Cold War World: Issues & Dilemmas. LC 93-33417. 352p. (C). 1994. 30.31 (0-07-054162-0) McGraw.

***Rubinstein, Alvin Z., et al, eds.** Clinton Foreign Policy Reader: Presidential Speeches with Commentary. LC 99-59587. 294p. 1999. text 64.95 (0-7656-0583-X) M E Sharpe.

— Clinton Foreign Policy Reader: Presidential Speeches with Commentary. 294p. 1999. reprint ed. pap. text 24.95 (0-7656-0584-8) M E Sharpe.

Rubinstein, Alvin Z. & Smith, Donald E. P., eds. Anti-Americanism in the Third World: Implications for U. S. Foreign Policy. (Foreign Policy Research Institute Ser.). 284p. 1984. 65.00 (0-275-91257-4, C1257, Praeger Pubs) Greenwood.

Rubinstein, Alvin Z. & Smolansky, Oles M., eds. Regional Power Rivalries in the New Eurasia: Russia, Turkey, & Iran. LC 95-6805. 304p. (C). 1995. text 81.95 (1-56324-622-8) M E Sharpe.

Rubinstein, Alvin Z., jt. auth. see Petro, Nicolai N.

Rubinstein, Alvin Z., ed. see Duncan, W. Raymond.

Rubinstein, Alvin Z., jt. ed. see Rieber, Alfred J.

Rubinstein, Alvin Z., ed. see Tahir-Kheli, Shirin.

***Rubinstein, Amnon.** From Herzl to Rabin: The Changing Image of Zionism. 304p. 2000. 32.95 (0-8419-1408-7) Holmes & Meier.

Rubinstein, Annette. Great Tradition in English Literature from Shakespeare to Shaw, 2 Vols, Set. 3rd ed. LC 69-19792. 1969. pap. 35.00 (0-85345-096-X, Pub. by Monthly Rev) NYU Pr.

Rubinstein, Annette T., et al, eds. Vito Marcantonio: Selected Debates, Speeches & Writings 1935-1950. LC 73-12402. (Illus.). xii, 494p. 1973. reprint ed. 49.50 (0-678-01365-9) Kelley.

Rubinstein, Anton. A Conversation on Music. Morgan, tr. from RUS. LC 81-12547. (Music Ser.). 146p. 1982. reprint ed. lib. bdg. 23.50 (0-306-76121-1) Da Capo.

Rubinstein, Anton, ed. Autobiography of Anton Rubinstein, 1829-1889. 1988. reprint ed. lib. bdg. 59.00 (0-7812-0097-0) Rprt Serv.

***Rubinstein, Ariel.** Economics & Language. (Churchill Lectures in Economics). 134p. (C). 2000. text Price not set. (0-521-59306-9); pap. text Price not set. (0-521-78990-7) Cambridge U Pr.

Rubinstein, Ariel. Game Theory in Economics. (International Library of Critical Writings in Economics: Vol. 5). 680p. 1990. text 270.00 (1-85278-169-6) E Elgar.

— Modeling Bounded Rationality. LC 97-40481. (Zeuthen Lecture Book Ser.). 220p. 1997. 29.95 (0-262-18187-8) MIT Pr.

— Modeling Bounded Rationality. LC 97-40481. (Zeuthen Lecture Bks.). (Illus.). 224p. 1997. pap. text 16.95 (0-262-68100-5) MIT Pr.

Rubinstein, Ariel, jt. auth. see Osborne, Martin J.

Rubinstein, Charlotte S. American Women Sculptors: A History of Women Working in Three Dimensions. (Monographs) (Illus.). 600p. (C). 1990. 60.00 (0-8161-8732-0, G K Hall & Co) Mac Lib Ref.

Rubinstein, Danny. The Mystery of Arafat. Leon, Dan, tr. 140p. (C). 1998. text 18.00 (0-7881-5430-3) DIANE Pub.

— The Mystery of Arafat. LC 95-9748. 144p. 1995. 18.00 (1-883642-10-8) Steerforth Pr.

***Rubinstein, David.** But He'll Remember: An Autobiography. 356p. 1999. pap. 45.00 (1-85072-220-X, Pub. by W Sessions) St Mut.

Rubinstein, David, jt. auth. see Martin, David E.

Rubinstein, Donald H., intro. Pacific History: Papers from the 8th Pacific History Association Conference. (Illus.). vi, 476p. (Orig.). (C). 1992. pap. 12.00 (1-878453-14-9) Univ Guam MAR Ctr.

Rubinstein, E. Filmguide to The General. LC 72-88637. (Filmguide Ser.: No. 5). 93p. reprint ed. pap. 30.00 (0-608-16111-X, 201763800007) Bks Demand.

Rubinstein, E., jt. ed. see Affron, Mirella J.

Rubinstein, Eli A., ed. see Conference on Research in Psychotherapy Staff.

Rubinstein, Erna F. After the Holocaust: The Long Road to Freedom. LC 95-21102. (Illus.). viii, 192p. (YA). (gr. 8 up). 1995. pap. text 17.50 (0-208-02421-2, Archon Bks) Shoe String.

— The Survivor in Us All: Four Young Sisters in the Holocaust. 185p. 1986. pap. 15.00 (0-208-02128-0, Archon Bks) Shoe String.

— The Survivor in Us All: Four Young Sisters in the Holocaust. LC 86-10844. v, 187p. (YA). (gr. 8 up). 1986. pap. text 15.00 (0-208-02129-9, Archon Bks) Shoe String.

Rubinstein, Ernest. An Episode of Jewish Romanticism: Franz Rosenzweig's The Star of Redemption. LC 99-17920. (SUNY Series in Judaica). 288p. (C). 1999. pap. text 21.95 (0-7914-4276-4) State U NY Pr.

— An Episode of Jewish Romanticism: Franz Rosenzweig's The Star of Redemption. LC 99-17920. (SUNY Series in Judaica). 288p. (C). 1999. text 65.50 (0-7914-4275-6) State U NY Pr.

Rubinstein, Frankie. A Dictionary of Shakespeare's Sexual Puns & Their Significance. 2nd rev. ed. 334p. (C). 1989. pap. 18.95 (0-945726-35-X) Scholars Bookshelf.

***Rubinstein, Gary.** Reluctant Disciplinarian: Advice on Classroom Management from a Softy Who Became a Successful Teacher. (Illus.). 143p. 1999. pap. 14.95 (1-877673-36-6) Cottonwood Pr.

Rubinstein, Gillian. Foxspell. LC 95-186956. 190 p. (J). 1995. write for info. (1-875657-32-0) Hyland Hse.

Rubinstein, Gillian. Foxspell. 224p. (YA). (gr. 5 up). 1996. 16.00 (0-689-80602-7) S&S Bks Yung.

— Galax-Arena. LC 95-4100. 176p. (YA). (gr. 7 up). 1995. mass mkt. 15.00 (0-689-80136-X) S&S Bks Yung.

— Galax-Arena. 208p. (J). (gr. 7). 1997. per. 3.99 (0-689-81235-3) S&S Childrens.

— Galax-Arena. (J). 1997. 9.09 (0-606-11358-4, Pub. by Turtleback) Demco.

— Galax-Arena. (YA). (gr. 5 up). 1997. reprint ed. pap. 3.99 (0-614-29087-2) Aladdin.

— Sharon, Keep Your Hair on LC 97-201323. (J). 1996. write for info. (0-09-183008-7) Random.

— Skymaze. MacDonald, Patricia, ed. 240p. (J). (gr. 5 up). 1993. reprint ed. mass mkt. 2.99 (0-671-76988-X, Archway) PB.

— Under the Cat's Eye: A Tale of Morph & Mystery. LC 97-32643. 208p. (J). (gr. 4-6). 1998. per. 16.00 (0-689-81800-9) S&S Childrens.

Rubinstein, Hilary. Great Britain. (Europe's Wonderful Little Hotels & Inns Ser.). 400p. 1997. pap. 16.99 (0-312-16825-X) St Martin.

Rubinstein, Hilary C., jt. auth. see Rubinstein, W. D.

Rubinstein, Isaak. Electro-Diffusion of Ions. LC 90-38332. (Studies in Applied Mathematics: No. 11). ix, 254p. 1990. 59.50 (0-89871-245-9) Soc Indus-Appl Math.

Rubinstein, Israel, ed. Physical Electrochemistry: Science & Technology. (Monographs in Electroanalytical Chemistry & Electrochemistry: Vol. 7). (Illus.). 608p. 1995. text 150.00 (0-8247-9452-4) Dekker.

Rubinstein, Israel, jt. ed. see Bard, Allen J.

Rubinstein, Jonathan. City Police. 498p. 1980. pap. 15.00 (0-374-51555-7) FS&G.

Rubinstein, Joseph & Slife, Brent D., eds. Taking Sides: Clashing Views on Controversial Psychological Issues. 8th rev. ed. LC 93-48692. (Illus.). 408p. (C). 1994. text 13.95 (1-56134-294-7, Dshkn McG-Hill) McGrw-H Hghr Educ.

Rubinstein, Judah, ed. see Brown, Albert M.

Rubinstein, Julie, ed. see Eppolito, Lou & Drury, Bob.

Rubinstein, Julie, ed. see Goldsmith, Olivia.

Rubinstein, Julie, ed. see Natow, Annette B. & Heslin, Jo-Ann.

Rubinstein, Julius B. Column Flotation: Processes, Designs & Practices. (Process Engineering for the Chemical Ser.). xii, 300p. 1995. text 105.00 (2-88124-917-5) Gordon & Breach.

Rubinstein, Leon. The First Swallows. LC 83-45138. (Illus.). 216p. 1986. 14.95 (0-8453-4758-6, Cornwall Bks) Assoc Univ Prs.

Rubinstein, Leonard. The Great Spy Films. (Illus.). 256p. 1981. pap. 7.95 (0-8065-0775-6, Citadel Pr) Carol Pub Group.

Rubinstein, Lorne, jt. auth. see Price, Nick.

Rubinstein, M. C., jt. ed. see Krischer, W.

Rubinstein, M. H. Pharmaceutical Technology: Controlled Drug Release. LC 87-2847. (Pharmaceutical Technology Ser.). 126p. 1987. text 65.95 (0-470-20881-3) P-H.

Rubinstein, M. H., ed. Pharmaceutical Technology: Drug Stability. 1989. text 69.95 (0-470-21411-2) P-H.

Rubinstein, Mark, jt. auth. see Cox, John C.

***Rubinstein, Marv.** Net-Wit.Com: A Smorgasbord of E-Mail & Internet Wit Blended with Humorous Incidents from the Author's Wild & Woolly Life. LC 00-27906. (Illus.). 232p. 2000. pap. 17.50 (1-887563-52-0, Pub. by Schreiber Pub) Natl Bk Netwk.

Rubinstein, Marv. 21st Century American English Compendium: A Portable Guidebook for Translators, Interpreters, Writers, Editors & Advanced Language Students. LC 97-65718. 350p. 1997. pap. 19.95 (1-887563-38-5) Schreiber Pub.

***Rubinstein, Marv.** 21st Century American English Compendium: A Portable Guidebook for Translators, Interpreters, Writers, Editors & Advanced Language Students. 2nd rev. ed. LC 00-32956. xviii, 382p. 2000. 24.95 (1-887563-56-3, Pub. by Schreiber Pub) Natl Bk Netwk.

Rubinstein, Meyer R. & Schwabsky, Barry. Walton Ford & Julie Jones. Riley, Jan, ed. (Illus.). 48p. (C). 1993. pap. 25.00 (0-917562-63-1) Contemp Arts.

Rubinstein, Michael. Pharmaceutical Technology: Tableting Technology, Vol. 1. 200p. 1988. text 62.95 (0-470-21001-X) P-H.

— Rembrandt & Angels. 47p. 1982. pap. 6.00 (0-904674-18-5, Pub. by Octagon Pr) ISHK.

Rubinstein, Michael, jt. auth. see Parker, Rowland.

***Rubinstein, Moshe F. & Firstenberg, Iris R.** The Minding Organization: Bring the Future to the Present & Turn Creative Ideas into Business Solutions. LC 99-22803. 224p. 1999. 27.95 (0-471-34781-7) Wiley.

Rubinstein, Moshe F. & Firstenberg, Iris R. Patterns of Problem Solving. 2nd ed. LC 94-7371. (C). 1994. text 51.80 (0-13-122706-8) Prntice Hall Bks.

Rubinstein, Moshe F., jt. auth. see Hurty, Walter C.

Rubinstein, Murray A. The Origins of the Anglo-American Missionary Enterprise in China, 1807. Rowe, Kenneth E., ed. (ATLA Monographs: No. 33). 400p. 1996. 59.50 (0-8108-2770-0) Scarecrow.

Rubinstein, Murray A., ed. The Other Taiwan, 1945 to the Present. LC 94-16058. 496p. (C). (gr. 13). 1994. text 88.95 (1-56324-192-7, East Gate Bk); pap. text 34.95 (1-56324-193-5, East Gate Bk) M E Sharpe.

— The Protestant Community on Modern Taiwan: Mission, Seminary, & Church. LC 90-31312. (Taiwan in the Modern World). 214p. (C). (gr. 13). 1991. text 79.95 (0-87332-658-X, East Gate Bk) M E Sharpe.

— Taiwan: A New History. LC 98-6043. (Taiwan in the Modern World Ser.). 536p. (C). (gr. 13). 1999. text 73.95 (1-56324-815-8, East Gate Bk) M E Sharpe.

— Taiwan: A New History. LC 98-6043. (Taiwan in the Modern World Ser.). (Illus.). 536p. (C). (gr. 13). 1999. pap. text 27.95 (1-56324-816-6, East Gate Bk) M E Sharpe.

Rubinstein, Nicolai. The Government of Florence under the Medici, 1434-94. 2nd ed. LC 96-43871. (Oxford-Warburg Studies). 424p. 1998. text 87.00 (0-19-817418-7) OUP.

Rubinstein, Nicolai, ed. Florentine Studies: Politics & Society in Renaissance Florence. LC 69-122553. 585p. reprint ed. 181.40 (0-8357-9458-X, 201027600068) Bks Demand.

Rubinstein, Nicoli. The Palazzo Vecchio, 1298-1532: Government, Architecture, & Imagery in the Civic Palace of the Florentine Republic. (Oxford-Warburg Studies). (Illus.). 172p. 1995. text 89.00 (0-19-920602-3) OUP.

Rubinstein, Norman. The Invisibly Wounded. 224p. 1993. 45.00 (1-870360-00-1) St Mut.

Rubinstein, Paul, jt. auth. see Whittlesey, Lee H.

Rubinstein, R. & Santoro, A. Experimental Physics. 304p. (C). 1989. text 102.00 (9971-5-0759-5) World Scientific Pub.

Rubinstein, Raechelle & Conner, Linda H., eds. Staying Local in the Global Village: Bali in the Twentieth Century. LC 99-27856. (Illus.). 376p. 1999. text 47.00 (0-8248-2117-3) UH Pr.

Rubinstein, Reuven, et al. Modern Simulation & Modeling. LC 97-11869. (Series in Probability & Statistics). 384p. 1998. 89.95 (0-471-17077-1) Wiley.

Rubinstein, Reuven Y. Monte Carlo Optimization, Simulation & Sensitivity of Queueing Networks. LC 92-13121. 272p. (C). 1992, reprint ed. lib. bdg. 54.00 (0-89464-764-4) Krieger.

— Simulation & The Monte Carlo Method. LC 81-1873. (Probability & Mathematical Statistics Ser.). 304p. 1981. 138.95 (0-471-08917-6) Wiley.

Rubinstein, Robert E. Hints for Teaching Success in Middle School. (Illus.). xiv, 169p. 1994. pap. text 19.00 (1-56308-124-5) Teacher Ideas Pr.

Rubinstein, Robert L. Singular Paths: Old Men Living Alone. LC 85-19063. 1988. pap. text 20.50 (0-231-06207-9) Col U Pr.

Rubinstein, Robert L., ed. Anthropology & Aging: Comprehensive Reviews. (C). 1990. lib. bdg. 135.00 (0-7923-0743-7) Kluwer Academic.

***Rubinstein, Robert L., et al, eds.** The Many Dimensions of Aging. LC 99-31415. 256p. 1999. 42.95 (0-8261-1247-1) Springer Pub.

Rubinstein, Robert L. & Lawton, M. Powell. Depression in Long Term & Residential Care: Advance in Research & Treatment. LC 97-16281. 272p. 1997. 47.95 (0-8261-9550-4) Springer Pub.

Rubinstein, Robert L., et al. Elders Living Alone: Frailty & the Perception of Choice. 184p. 1992. lib. bdg. 41.95 (0-202-36083-0) Aldine de Gruyter.

Rubinstein, Robert L., jt. auth. see Black, Helen K.

Rubinstein, Robert L., jt. auth. see Lawton, M. Powell.

Rubinstein, Ruth. Dress Codes: Meanings & Messages in American Culture. LC 94-32808. (C). 1994. pap. 30.00 (0-8133-2283-9, Pub. by Westview) HarpC.

Rubinstein, Sally, ed. see Larson, Paul C.

Rubinstein, Sarah P., jt. auth. see Brook, Michael.

Rubinstein, Sidney P., ed. Participative Systems at Work: Creating Quality & Employment Security. LC 86-20044. 180p. 1987. 30.95 (0-89885-338-9, Kluwer Acad Hman Sci) Kluwer Academic.

Rubinstein, W. D. Britain's Century: A Political & Social History, 1815-1905. LC 98-8219. (Arnold Publications). 368p. 1998. text 80.00 (0-340-57533-6) OUP.

— Britain's Century: A Political & Social History, 1815-1905. LC 98-8219. (Arnold Publications). (Illus.). 368p. 1998. pap. text 19.95 (0-340-57534-4) OUP.

— Men of Property: The Very Wealthy in Britain since the Industrial Revolution. LC 80-54836. (Illus.). 261p. reprint ed. pap. 81.00 (0-8357-7950-5, 205702500002) Bks Demand.

Rubinstein, W. D. & Rubinstein, Hilary C. Menders of the Mind: A History of the Royal Australian & New Zealand College of Psychiatrists 1946-1996. (Illus.). 288p. 1997. text 49.50 (0-19-553953-2) OUP.

Rubinstein, William D. The Myth of Rescue: Why the Democracies Could Not Have Saved More Jews from the Nazis. LC 97-203027. 288p. 1997. 32.99 (0-415-12455-7) Routledge.

— Myth of Rescue: Why the Democracies Could Not Have Saved More Jews from the Nazis. LC 99-27372. 1999. pap. 20.99 (0-415-21249-9) Routledge.

***Rubinsztein, D. C.** Analysis of Triplet Repeat Disorders. 327p. 2000. 110.00 (0-12-220431-X) Acad Pr.

Rubinyl, Paul. Unchaining the Chain of Command. Christopher, Bill, ed. LC 97-68249. (Management Library: No. 14). 88p. 1997. pap. 12.95 (1-56052-440-5) Crisp Pubns.

Rubio, Samuel. Classical Polyphony. LC 73-157996. xvi, xvi, 178 p. 1972. write for info. (0-631-11740-7) Blackwell Pubs.

***Rubio, Abel.** Stolen Heritage: 1998 Edition. LC 98-112334. (Illus.). 248p. 1998. 18.95 (1-57168-170-1) Sunbelt Media.

Rubio, Alfredo. Adventures in Being. 124p. 1993. pap. 12.95 (0-85244-212-2, 6301, Pub. by Gra1cewing) Morehouse Pub.

Rubio, Antonio, jt. auth. see Jackson, Eugene.

Rubio-Boitel, Fernando. Spanish Short Stories & Poems. 1979. pap. 1.50 (0-686-23892-3) Rubio-Boitel.

Rubio Cremades, Enrique, ed. see Fernan, Caballero.

Rubio, Daniel, jt. auth. see Gaos, Ignacio.

Rubio, David. Hay una Filosofia En el Quijote. (SPA.). 168p. 1924. 1.00 (0-318-14272-4) Hispanic Inst.

— Symbolism & Classicism in Modern Literature. 1972. 59.95 (0-8490-1167-1) Gordon Pr.

Rubio, Enrique, ed. see Valera, Juan.

Rubio, Fanny, ed. see Alonso, Damaso.

Rubio, Gwyn Hyman. Icy Sparks. 320p. 1999. pap. 12.95 (0-14-028014-6) Viking Penguin.

Rubio, J. E. Control & Optimization: The Linear Treatment of Nonlinear Problems. LC 85-15256. (Nonlinear Science: Theory & Applications Ser.). 250p. (C). 1988. text 65.00 (0-7190-1841-2, Pub. by Manchester Univ Pr) St Martin.

— Optimization & Nonstandard Analysis. LC 94-21446. (Pure & Applied Mathematics Ser.: Vol. 184). (Illus.). 376p. 1994. text 175.00 (0-8247-9281-5) Dekker.

Rubio, J. L., et al, eds. Risk Analysis. (Computational Studies: Vol. 2). 336p. 1998. 159.00 (1-85312-604-7, 6047, Pub. by WIT Pr) Computational Mech MA.

Rubio, J. Lopez. Celos Del Aire. (SPA.). 125p. 1982. 9.50 (0-8288-7159-0) Fr & Eur.

— In August We Play the Pyrenees. Halsey, Martha T., ed. Holt, Marion P., tr. LC 92-72823. (Contemporary Spanish Plays Ser.: No. 2). x, 69p. 1993. pap. 6.00 (0-9631212-1-9) Estreno.

Rubio, Jesus M. Aspectroscopia Infrarroja. 2nd rev. ed. (Serie de Quimica: No. 12). 80p. (C). 1981. pap. text 3.50 (0-8270-1419-8) OAS.

Rubio Jimenez, Jesus, ed. see Del Valle-Inclan, Ramon.

Rubio-Jimenez, Jesus, tr. see De Alarcon, Pedro A.

Rubio, Lourdes, tr. Un Curso Basico de Lenguaje Americano de Senas. 1991. spiral bd. 29.95 (0-932666-35-3) T J Pubs.

Rubio, Luis. Como Va Afectar a Mexico el Tratado de Libre Comercio (How Mexico Will Be Affected by NAFTA) (SPA.). 335p. 1992. pap. 8.99 (968-16-3960-X, Pub. by Fondo) Continental Bk.

Rubio, Luis, jt. ed. see Purcell, Susan K.

Rubio, Luis F. & Gil-Diaz, Francisco. A Mexican Response: A Twentieth Century Fund Paper. 72p. (Orig.). 1987. pap. 9.00 (0-87078-215-0) Century Foundation.

Rubio, Maggie & Durnberg, Steffi. A New Beginning. 144p. (C). 1994. pap. text, per. 31.95 (0-8403-9931-6, 40993101) Kendall-Hunt.

An Asterisk (*) at the beginning of an entry indicates that the title is appearing for the first time.

Rubio, Manny. Rattlesnake: Portrait of a Predator. LC 98-22935. (Illus.). 240p. 1998. 49.95 (*1-56098-808-8*) Smithsonian.

***Rubio, Manny.** Scorpions: A Complete Pet Owner's Manual. LC 99-31708. (Complete Pet Owner's Manuals Ser.). 104p. 2000. 6.95 (*0-7641-1224-4*) Barron.

***Rubio-Marin, Ruth.** Immigration as a Democratic Challenge: Citizenship & Inclusion in Germany & the United States. LC 99-16899. 320p. (C). 2000. 57.95 (*0-521-77152-8*); pap. 21.95 (*0-521-77770-4*) Cambridge U Pr.

Rubio, Mary & Waterston, Elizabeth. Writing a Life: L. M. Montgomery. LC 95-173250. (Illus.). 133p. 1995. pap. 9.95 (*1-55022-220-1*) LPC InBook.

— Writing a Life: L. M. Montgomery. large type ed. (Illus.). 188p. 1995. pap. 15.95 (*1-55022-239-2*, Pub. by ECW) Genl Dist Srvs.

***Rubio, Mary & Waterston, Elizabeth, eds.** Selected Journals of L. M. Montgomery, 1889-1910, Vol. 1. (Illus.). 424p. 2000. pap. 16.95 (*0-19-541512-4*) OUP.

Rubio, Mary, ed. see Montgomery, L. M.

Rubio, Pedro. The Lamps of Fire. Prouty, Graciela P., tr. from SPA. (Illus.). 115p. (Orig.). pap. 8.95 (*0-9637601-0-6*) Mount Ctr.

Rubio, Thalia. Slices of Life: Writing from North America. 160p. (C). 1993. 30.40 (*0-13-813296-8*) P-H.

Rubissow, Ariel. Cliff House & Lands End: San Francisco's Seaside Retreat. (Illus.). 48p. 1993. pap. 7.95 (*1-883869-12-9*) Gldn Gate Natl Parks Assoc.

— John Muir National Historic Site. Priehs, T. J., ed. LC 90-62309. (Illus.). 16p. (Orig.). 1990. pap. 3.95 (*0-911408-91-6*) SW Pks Mnmts.

***Rubiz, Vicki & Dubois, Ellen C.** Unequal Sisters: A Multicultural Reader in U. S. Women's History. 3rd ed. LC 99-16825. 640p. 2000. pap. write for info. (*0-415-92517-7*) Routledge.

Rublack, Ulinka. The Crimes of Women in Early Modern Germany. LC 98-3196. (Oxford Studies in Social History). (Illus.). 304p. 1999. text 70.00 (*0-19-820637-2*) OUP.

***Ruble, Blair A.** Fragmented Space in the Russian Federation. 2000. 48.00 (*0-8018-6570-0*) Johns Hopkins.

Ruble, Blair A. Leningrad: Shaping a Soviet City. 1990. 55.00 (*0-520-06534-4*, Pub. by U CA Pr) Cal Prin Full Svc.

— Money Sings: The Changing Politics of Urban Space in Post-Soviet Yaroslavl. (Woodrow Wilson Center Press Ser.). (Illus.). 176p. (C). 1995. text 64.95 (*0-521-48242-9*) Cambridge U Pr.

Ruble, Blair A., jt. auth. see Kahan, Arcadius.

Ruble, Blair A., jt. auth. see Pravda, Alex.

Ruble, Blair A., jt. ed. see Brumfield, William C.

Ruble, David A. Practical Analysis & Design for Client-Server & GUI Systems. LC 97-9895. 542p. (C). 1997. 54.67 (*0-13-521758-X*) P-H.

Ruble, Diane N., et al, eds. The Social Psychology of Mental Health: Basic Mechanisms & Applications. LC 92-1540. 365p. 1992. lib. bdg. 46.95 (*0-89862-136-4*) Guilford Pubns.

Ruble, Richard, ed. Christian Perspectives on Psychology. LC 75-15956. 147p. (C). 1975. pap. text 18.95 (*0-8422-0456-3*) Irvington.

Ruble, Shirley. DUI Handbook for Paralegals. LC 94-77356. 150p. 1994. pap. text 20.00 (*1-878703-03-X*) Legal Pubns.

— France: A Memoir. (Illus.). 120p. (Orig.). 1997. pap. 14.95 (*1-878703-04-8*) Legal Pubns.

— Spain & Portugal: The Iberian Peninsula. (Illus.). 150p. 1998. pap. 14.95 (*1-878703-05-6*) Legal Pubns.

— Welcome to Israel: A Bridges for Peace Study Tour. (Illus.). 110p. (Orig.). 1993. pap. 10.00 (*1-878703-01-3*) Legal Pubns.

***Rublein.** Fear of Flying. 276p. (C). 1998. pap. text 31.20 (*0-536-01581-3*) Pearson Custom.

— Fear of Flying. 2nd ed. 284p. 1999. pap. text 28.00 (*0-536-02805-2*) Pearson Custom.

Rubloff, Gary & Lucovsky, Gerald, eds. Deposition & Growth: Limits for Microelectronics: Proceedings of a Topical Conference at Anaheim, California in November 1987. (Conference Proceedings Ser.: No. 167). (Illus.). 402p. 1988. 70.00 (*0-88318-367-6*) Am Inst Physics.

Rubly-Burggraff, Roberta. Magnum Opus: My Own Journal. (Illus.). 72p. (Orig.). (YA). (gr. 7-12). 1999. pap. 5.95 (*0-937997-14-5*) Hi-Time Pflaum.

Rubner, Alex. The Economy of Israel. 307p. 1959. 35.00 (*0-7146-1249-9*, Pub. by F Cass Pubs) Intl Spec Bk.

— The Might of the Multinationals: The Rise & Fall of the Corporate Legend. LC 89-26526. 312p. 1990. 55.00 (*0-275-93531-0*, C3531, Greenwood Pr) Greenwood.

Rubnitsky, David, jt. auth. see Parr, Rob.

Rubotkin. Beyond the Apocalypse: The Transmutation of Personal Experience into Intuitive & Prophetic Wisdom. LC 98-166936. (Illus.). ix, 160p. 1997. pap. 12.95 (*0-9660613-0-6*) Foxs Cloth.

Rubottom, Richard R. & Murphy, J. C. Spain & the United States: Since World War II. LC 83-19247. 163p. 1984. 47.95 (*0-275-91259-0*, C1259, Praeger Pubs) Greenwood.

***Rubottom, Verda.** StepOne A guide for Teachers: Elementary. (StepOne). 15p. 2000. pap. 1.95 (*0-88243-287-7*, 02-0287) Gospel Pub.

Rubovits, Norma. Marbled Vignettes: Including Muir Dawson & Norma Rubovits in Conversation. 8p. 1992. 125.00 (*0-87093-278-0*); 600.00 (*0-87093-279-9*) Dawsons.

Rubovits-Seitz, Philip F. Depth-Psychological Understanding: The Methodologic Grounding of Clinical Interpretations. LC 98-5988. 480p. 1998. 69.95 (*0-88163-279-1*) Analytic Pr.

— Kohut's Freudian Vision. LC 98-47795. 264p. 1999. 49.95 (*0-88163-284-8*) Analytic Pr.

Rubow, Lynn N., ed. Fluidized Bed Combustion, 1993: FBC's Role in the World Energy Mix. LC 87-70969. 1388p. 1993. pap. 144.00 (*0-7918-0681-2*, I00344) ASME.

Rubow, P. V. Shakespeare's Hamlet. LC 79-174974. (DAN.). reprint ed. 34.50 (*0-404-05448-X*) AMS Pr.

Rubrich, Larry & Watson, Madelyn. Implementing World Class Manufacturing: A Bridge to Your Manufacturing Survival. Rubrich, Shirley, ed. LC 98-90427. (Illus.). 440p. 1998. spiral bd. 84.00 (*0-9662906-0-7*) WCM Assocs.

Rubrich, Shirley, ed. see Rubrich, Larry & Watson, Madelyn.

Rubright, Lynn. Beyond the Beanstalk: The Playful Way to Learn Through Storytelling & the Arts. LC 96-9057. 176p. 1996. pap. text 21.00 (*0-435-07028-2*) Heinemann.

Rubright, Lynnell, jt. auth. see Griffiths, Mel.

Rubright, Robert. Walks & Rambles in & Around St. Louis. LC 95-16437. (Walks & Rambles Ser.). (Illus.). 264p. (Orig.). 1995. pap. 15.00 (*0-88150-344-4*, Pub. by Countryman) Norton.

***Rubright, Robert.** Weekend Walks in St. Louis & Beyond. 2000. pap. 14.95 (*0-88150-448-3*, Pub. by Countryman) Norton.

Rubsamen, Bitsy A. Gentle Rain: Reflections on the Mercy of God. LC 97-44056. (Illus.). 144p. 1998. 14.99 (*0-8054-5454-3*) Broadman.

Rubsamen, David S. Diagnostic Errors in Primary Care: 84 Case Illustrations. xii, 218p. 1999. 29.00 (*0-933994-21-4*) Comstock Bon.

Rubsamen, Gisela. The Orsini Inventories. LC 80-83121. 224p. 1980. pap. 46.00 (*0-89236-010-0*, Pub. by J P Getty Trust) OUP.

Rubsamen, Traudel. Morphologische, Embryologische und Systematische Untersuchungen An Burmanniaceae und Corsiaceae. (Dissertationes Botanicae Ser.: Band 92). (GER., Illus.). 512p. 1986. pap. 95.00 (*3-443-64004-4*, Pub. by Gebruder Borntraeger) Balogh.

Rubsamen, Walter H. Literary Sources of Secular Music in Italy, 1500. LC 72-4482. (Music Ser.). 82p. 1972. reprint ed. lib. bdg. 21.50 (*0-306-70496-X*) Da Capo.

— Music Research in Italian Libraries. 1993. reprint ed. lib. bdg. 89.00 (*0-7812-9699-4*) Rprt Serv.

Rubsamen-Weustenfeld, Traudel. Morphologische, Embryologische und Systematische IUntersuchungen an Triuridaceae. (Bibliotheca Botanica: Vol. 140). (GER., Illus.). iv, 113p. 1991. 105.00 (*3-510-48011-2*, Pub. by E Schweizerbartsche) Balogh.

Rubstov, V. V. Learning in Children: Organization & Development of Cooperation Actions. 250p. 1991. pap. text 110.00 (*1-56072-005-0*) Nova Sci Pubs.

Rubtsov, I. A. Blackflies (Simuliidae) LC 89-71184. (Fauna of the U. S. S. R. Diptera Ser.: Vol. 6, Pt. 6). (Illus.). xxviii, 1042p. 1990. lib. bdg. 236.00 (*90-04-08871-7*) Brill Academic Pubs.

Ruby. Meta Incognita. Date not set. 30.00 (*0-8050-5215-1*); pap. 18.00 (*0-8050-5214-3*) H Holt & Co.

Ruby, Amanda. Lighten Up! With Non Fat-Low Fat Recipes. 215p. pap. text. write for info. (*0-9644820-0-2*) Amegard.

***Ruby-Baird, Janet.** Color & Two-Dimensional Design A Computer-Enhanced Course. 1999. pap. 50.00 (*1-57249-124-8*) White Mane Pub.

— Color & Two-Dimensional Design Superpaint Guide & Tutorials. 1999. pap. 29.95 (*1-57249-117-5*) White Mane Pub.

Ruby, Carl, jt. auth. see Fajardo, Renee.

Ruby, Clayton C. & Martin, Dianne L. Criminal Sentencing Digest. 380p. 1993. ring bd. 150.00 (*0-409-91241-7*, MICHIE) LEXIS Pub.

Ruby, Daniel. Schema und Variation. (Europaische Hochschulschriften Ser.: Reihe 1, Bd. 1638). (Illus.). 115p. 1998. pap. 26.95 (*3-631-49725-3*) P Lang Pubng.

Ruby, Doug. The Gift: The Crop Circles Deciphered. (Illus.). 192p. 1995. 32.95 (*1-878398-14-8*) Blue Note Pubns.

Ruby, E. A. The Human Figure: A Photographic Reference for Artists. 1974. pap. 29.95 (*0-442-27148-4*, VNR) Wiley.

— The Human Figure: A Photographic Reference for Artists. 338p. 1979. pap. 32.95 (*0-471-28949-3*, VNR) Wiley.

***Ruby, Jay.** Picturing Culture: Explorations in Film & Anthropology. 1999. pap. text 19.00 (*0-226-73099-9*) U Ch Pr.

— Picturing Culture: Explorations in Film & Anthropology. (Illus.). 1999. lib. bdg. 44.00 (*0-226-73098-0*) U Ch Pr.

Ruby, Jay. Secure the Shadow: Death & Photography in America. LC 94-23118. (Illus.). 232p. 1995. 42.50 (*0-262-18164-9*) MIT Pr.

— Secure the Shadow: Death & Photography in America. (Illus.). 232p. 1999. pap. 22.00 (*0-262-68109-9*) MIT Pr.

— The World of Francis Cooper: Nineteenth-Century Pennsylvania Photographer. LC 98-6993. 1998. 60.00 (*0-271-01762-7*) Pa St U Pr.

Ruby, Jay, ed. The Cinema of John Marshall. LC 92-28923. (Visual Anthropology Ser.: Vol. 3). 282p. 1993. text 77.00 (*3-7186-0557-0*); pap. text 32.00 (*3-7186-0558-9*) Gordon & Breach.

Ruby, Jeff, jt. ed. see Ebent, Aaron M.

Ruby, Leona. That Nun from Saint Luis: To Catch a Snake. (Illus.). 140p. 1996. pap. 10.00 (*0-8059-3726-9*) Dorrance.

Ruby, Lois. Skin Deep. LC 93-13707. 224p. (YA). (gr. 7-9). 1994. 14.95 (*0-590-47699-8*) Scholastic Inc.

— Skin Deep. (J). (gr. 7). 1996. pap. text 4.99 (*0-590-47700-5*) Scholastic Inc.

— Skin Deep. 1994. 10.09 (*0-606-09864-X*, Pub. by Turtleback) Demco.

***Ruby, Lois.** Soon Be Free. LC 99-47319. 240p. (J). (gr. 4-7). 2000. per. 17.00 (*0-689-83266-4*) S&S Childrens.

Ruby, Lois. Steal Away Home. 208p. (J). 1999. pap. 4.50 (*0-689-82435-1*) Aladdin.

— Steal Away Home. LC 93-47300. (Illus.). 176p. (J). (gr. 3-7). 1994. mass mkt. 16.00 (*0-02-777883-5*) Macmillan.

***Ruby, Lois.** Swindletop. LC 00-28833. (Illus.). (J). 2000. write for info. (*1-57168-393-3*, Eakin Pr) Sunbelt Media.

***Ruby, Mary K., ed.** Poetry for Students, Vol. 5. 350p. 1999. text 60.00 (*0-7876-3566-9*, GML00299-113189, Gale Res Intl) Gale.

Ruby, Ralph, et al. Microsoft Works Applications. rev. ed. 1991. pap. text 13.95 (*1-56118-540-X*); pap. text, teacher ed. 8.00 (*1-56118-541-8*) Paradigm MN.

Ruby, Ralph, jt. auth. see Ladd, Paula.

Ruby, Robert H. Jericho. 1995. 25.00 (*0-8050-2799-8*) H Holt & Co.

— Ruby in the Rough. LC 76-40031. 1976. 12.95 (*0-88289-099-9*) Pelican.

Ruby, Robert H. Ruby in the Rough. LC 76-40031. (Illus.). 194p. 1976. pap. 12.95 (*1-56554-632-6*) Pelican.

Ruby, Robert H. & Brown, John A. The Cayuse Indians: Imperial Tribesmen of Old Oregon. (Illus.). 345p. (Orig.). 1989. reprint ed. pap. text 10.95 (*0-914019-21-X*) NW Interpretive.

— The Chinook Indians: Traders of the Lower Columbia River. LC 75-40148. (Civilization of the American Indian Ser.: Vol. 138). (Illus.). 400p. 1988. pap. 19.95 (*0-8061-2107-6*) U of Okla Pr.

— Dreamer-Prophets of the Columbia Plateau: Smohalla & Skolaskin. LC 89-5292. (Illus.). 272p. 1989. 24.95 (*0-8061-2183-1*) U of Okla Pr.

— A Guide to the Indian Tribes of the Pacific Northwest. LC 85-22470. (Civilization of the American Indian Ser.: Vol. 173). (Illus.). 312p. 1992. pap. 19.95 (*0-8061-2479-2*) U of Okla Pr.

— Half-Sun on the Columbia: A Biography of Chief Moses. LC 94-37092. (Civilization of the American Indian Ser.: Vol. 80). (Illus.). 416p. 1995. pap. 18.95 (*0-8061-2738-4*) U of Okla Pr.

— Indians of the Pacific Northwest: A History. LC 80-5946. (Civilization of the American Indian Ser.: Vol. 158). (Illus.). 300p. 1988. pap. 22.95 (*0-8061-2113-0*) U of Okla Pr.

— John Slocum & the Indian Shaker Church. LC 95-52252. (Illus.). 320p. 1996. 34.95 (*0-8061-2865-8*) U of Okla Pr.

— The Spokane Indians: Children of the Sun. LC 79-108797. (Civilization of the American Indian Ser.: Vol. 104). (Illus.). 346p. 1982. pap. 18.95 (*0-8061-1757-5*) U of Okla Pr.

Ruby, Thelma, jt. auth. see Frye, Peter.

Rubycz, Rom, jt. auth. see Barker, Lynton.

Rucckert, Carla L., jt. auth. see Elkins, Don.

Ruccolo, Michael A. The NAFTA Register. 3rd ed. (Illus.). 180p. 1996. pap. 150.00 (*0-9651569-0-7*) Global Contact.

Ruch, Richard, jt. auth. see Sato, Tatsuo.

Ruch, Theodore C. Bibliographia Primatologica Pt. 1: A Classified Bibliography of Primates Other Than Man: Anatomy, Embryology, & Quantitative Morphology, Physiology & Psychobiology. Primate Phylogeny & Miscellanea. 1941. 250.00 (*0-614-00151-X*) Elliots Bks.

Ruch, Velma. The Signature of God. 1986. pap. 5.00 (*0-8309-0428-X*) Herald Pub Hse.

— Summoned to Pilgrimage: The Temple As Focus of a Pilgrim People. LC 94-10322. 1994. pap. 6.00 (*0-8309-0667-3*) Herald Pub Hse.

***Ruch, Velma.** Transforming Power of Prayer. LC 98-43211. 1998. write for info. (*0-8309-0820-X*) Herald Pub Hse.

Ruch, W. The Sense of Humor: Explorations of a Personality Characteristic. LC 98-15494. (Humor Research Ser.). 498p. 1998. 132.00 (*3-11-016207-5*) De Gruyter.

Ruch, William A. White Collar Productivity, Vol 23. (Studies in Productivity: Highlights of the Literature Ser.). (Orig.). pap. 55.00 (*0-89361-033-X*) Work in Amer.

Ruch, William J. Atlas of Common Subluxations of the Human Spine. LC 96-46124. 256p. 1997. boxed set 104.95 (*0-8493-3117-X*) CRC Pr.

Ruch, William V. Corporate Communications: A Comparison of Japanese & American Practices. LC 84-1973. (Illus.). 298p. 1984. 65.00 (*0-89930-028-6*, RCC/, Quorum Bks) Greenwood.

Ruchelle, Marion, jt. auth. see Emmel, Ruth.

Ruchelman, Leonard. A Workbook in Program Design for Public Managers. LC 85-9936. (SUNY Series in Public Administration). 123p. (C). 1985. pap. text 18.95 (*0-88706-025-0*) State U NY Pr.

***Ruchelman, Leonard I.** Cities in the Third Wave: The Technological Transformation of Urban America. LC 99-37119. 1999. pap. write for info. (*0-8304-1564-5*) Burnham Inc.

Ruchelman, Leonard I. The Formulation & Presentation of Alternatives for Public Programs. (Learning Packages in the Policy Sciences Ser.: No. 25). (Illus.). 42p. (Orig.). 1984. pap. text 8.50 (*0-936826-20-7*) PS Assocs Croton.

— Political Careers: Recruitment Through the Legislature. LC 70-99325. 216p. 1975. 25.00 (*0-8386-7613-8*) Fairleigh Dickinson.

Ruchelman, Leonard I., ed. Big City Mayors: The Crisis in Urban Politics. LC 80-15673. 371p. 1981. reprint ed. lib. bdg. 75.00 (*0-313-22605-9*, RUBC, Greenwood Pr) Greenwood.

Ruchhoft, Robert H. Backpack Loops & Long Day Trail Hikes in Southern Ohio. Sears, Linda, ed. (Illus.). 260p. (Orig.). 1984. pap. text 12.95 (*0-940029-01-4*) Pucelle Pr.

— Exploring North Manitou, South Manitou, High & Garden Islands of the Lake Michigan Archipelago. Dews, Cynthia & McCabe, Edith, eds. (Illus.). 357p. (Orig.). 1991. pap. 14.95 (*0-940029-02-2*) Pucelle Pr.

— Kentucky's Land of the Arches. rev. ed. Sears, Linda, ed. (Illus.). 1986. pap. text 9.95 (*0-9476-9856-0*) Pucelle Pr.

Ruchlin, Hirsch S., jt. auth. see Finkel, Madelon L.

Ruchlis, Hy. How Do You Know It's True? Discovering the Difference Between Science & Superstition. LC 90-28449. (Young Readers Ser.). (Illus.). 112p. (Orig.). (J). 1991. pap. 13.95 (*0-87975-657-8*) Prometheus Bks.

Ruchlis, Hy & Oddo, Sandra. Clear Thinking: A Practical Introduction. LC 90-35711. (Illus.). 275p. (Orig.). 1990. pap. 17.95 (*0-87975-594-6*) Prometheus Bks.

Ruchlis, Hy, jt. auth. see Herbert, Don.

Ruchlis, Hy, ed. see Pollack, Cecelia & Lane, Patrick R.

***Rucht, Dieter, et al, contrib. by.** Acts of Dissent: New Developments in the Study of Protest. LC 99-45880. 352p. 2000. text 665.00 (*0-8476-9856-4*) Rowman.

***Rucht, Dieter, et al.** Acts of Dissent: New Developments in the Study of Protest. LC 99-45880. 1999. pap. 29.95 (*0-8476-9857-2*) Rowman.

Ruchwarger, Gary. From Triumph to Challenge. (C). 1996. pap. text 35.00 (*0-8133-8485-0*) Westview.

— People in Power: Forging a Grassroots Democracy in Nicaragua. LC 87-12623. 351p. 1987. 69.50 (*0-89789-129-5*, Bergin & Garvey); pap. 24.95 (*0-89789-130-9*, Bergin & Garvey) Greenwood.

Ruck, jt. auth. see Deluc, Yves.

Ruck, Anne. Pearl. 1986. pap. 4.95 (*9971-972-37-9*) OMF Bks.

— This Child Must Die: A Biography of Anne Ruck. 148p. 1991. pap. 5.95 (*981-3009-01-2*) OMF Bks.

Ruck-Braun, Karola, jt. auth. see Kunz, Horst.

Ruck, Carl & Staples, Danny. The World of Classical Myth: Gods & Goddesses, Heroines & Heroes. LC 93-74701. (Illus.). 366p. (C). 1994. pap. 25.95 (*0-89089-575-9*) Carolina Acad Pr.

Ruck, Carl A. Ancient Greek: A New Approach. 2nd ed. 270p. 1979. pap. text 31.50 (*0-262-68031-9*) MIT Pr.

— Intensive Latin: First Year & Review. LC 97-6301. (ENG & LAT.). 208p. 1997. pap. 19.95 (*0-89089-912-6*) Carolina Acad Pr.

Ruck, Carlton, et al. The Feasibility of Vertical Evacuation: Behavioral, Legal, Political & Structural Considerations. (Monograph: No. 52). 1991. pap. 20.00 (*1-877943-05-3*) Natural Hazards.

Ruck, E. H. An Index of Themes & Motifs in 12th-Century French Arthurian Poetry. (Arthurian Studies: No. XXV). 208p. (C). 1991. 75.00 (*0-85991-335-X*) Boydell & Brewer.

Ruck, George, et al. Radar Cross Section Handbook, 2 vols. LC 68-26774. 949p. 1970. 72.00 (*0-306-30343-4*) Peninsula CA.

Ruck, Hendrick W. & Ellis, John A., eds. Military Training Technology: Systematic Approaches. LC 85-9459. 253p. 1985. 49.95 (*0-275-90008-8*, C0008, Praeger Pubs) Greenwood.

Ruck, John. The Cross-Leased Chardonnay Cellphone Paradise LC 97-162224. vi, 154 p. 1996. write for info. (*1-86950-200-0*) HarpC.

Ruck, Rob. Sandlot Seasons: Sport in Black Pittsburgh. LC 92-46304. 280p. 1993. pap. text 15.95 (*0-252-06342-2*) U of Ill Pr.

— The Tropic of Baseball: Baseball in the Dominican Republic. 232p. 1993. pap. 10.95 (*0-88184-876-X*) Carroll & Graf.

— The Tropic of Baseball: Baseball in the Dominican Republic. (Baseball & American Society Ser.). (Illus.). 175p. 1991. lib. bdg. 37.50 (*0-88736-707-0*) Mecklermedia.

— The Tropic of Baseball: Baseball in the Dominican Republic. LC 98-45479. (Illus.). 240p. 1999. pap. 12.00 (*0-8032-8978-2*, Bison Books) U of Nebr Pr.

Ruck, Ruth J. Along Came a Llama. large type ed. 384p. 1983. 27.99 (*0-7089-0935-3*) Ulverscroft.

***Ruck, Susan.** Bloom Now: A Garden Journal for Life. (Illus.). 168p. 2000. 17.35 (*0-9662934-3-6*, Pub. by Sunflower Promo) Quality Bks IL.

Ruck, Susan. Jonathan's Garden. LC 98-90086. (Illus.). 48p. (J). (gr. k-4). 1998. 13.75 (*0-9662934-0-1*) Sunflower Promo.

— Jonathan's Garden. LC 98-90883. (Illus.). 48p. (J). (gr. k-4). 1998. reprint ed. 17.35 incl. audio (*0-9662934-1-X*) Sunflower Promo.

***Rucka, Greg.** Batman: No Man's Land. 208p. (J). 2000. pap. text 12.95 (*1-56389-599-4*, Pub. by DC Comics) Time Warner.

— Batman: No Man's Land. LC 99-57478. 448p. 2000. 23.95 (*0-671-03828-1*) PB.

— Batman: No Man's Land. (Illus.). (J). 2000. 9.34 (*0-606-18364-7*) Turtleback.

Rucka, Greg. Keeper. 368p. 1997. mass mkt. 5.99 (*0-553-57428-0*, Crimeline) Bantam.

— Shooting at Midnight. LC 99-19814. 368p. 1999. 23.95 (*0-553-10720-8*) Bantam.

***Rucka, Greg.** Shooting at Midnight. 432p. 2000. mass mkt. 5.99 (*0-553-57827-8*) Bantam.

Rucka, Greg. Smoker. 432p. 1999. mass mkt. 5.99 (*0-553-57829-4*) Bantam.

— Whiteout. Rich, Jamie S., ed. (Illus.). 126p. 1999. pap. 10.95 (*0-9667127-1-4*) Oni Pr Inc.

***Rucka, Greg.** Whiteout Vol. 2: Melt. Rich, Jamie S., ed. (Illus.). 110p. 2000. pap. 11.95 (*1-929998-03-1*) Oni Pr Inc.

Rucka, Gregory. Finder. 352p. 1998. mass mkt. 5.99 (*0-553-57429-9*) Bantam.

— 1990's Handbook: Modern Background for Cthulhu. rev. ed. Sellers, Janice, ed. (Call of Cthulhu Roleplaying Game Ser.). (Illus.). 80p. (Orig.). 1995. pap. 12.95 (*1-56882-048-8*, 2355) Chaosium.

Ruckauer, Jaime S., jt. ed. see Gausa, Manuel.

R

R

Ruckdashel, Candy. A Literary Travel Log: Integrating Literature & Global Awareness. Keeling, Jan, ed. (Illus.). 64p. (Orig.). (J). (gr. 1-6). 1993. pap. text 8.95 (*0-86530-256-1*) Incentive Pubns.

Ruckdeschel, John. Myths & Facts About Lung Cancer. (Illus.). 1999. pap. 9.95 (*1-891483-04-8*) PRR.

***Rucker.** Hacker & the Ants. 2000. 20.00 (*0-380-97236-0*) Morrow Avon.

***Rucker, Brian.** Voices from My Heart: Odes to Tania, Vols. 1 & 2 limited ed. 125p. (Orig.). 1999. pap. 30.00 (*1-882695-12-7*) Patagonia Pr.

Rucker, Brian R. Brick Road to Boom Town: The Story of Santa Rosa County's "Old Brick Road" (Illus.). 58p. (Orig.). 1993. pap. 5.50 (*1-882695-07-0*) Patagonia Pr.

— Encyclopedia of Education in Antebellum Pensacola. LC 99-204499. (Illus.). 149p. 1999. pap. 19.95 (*1-882695-10-0*) Patagonia Pr.

— Jackson Morton: West Florida's Soldier, Senator, & Secessionist. (Illus.). 52p. (Orig.). 1990. mass mkt. 5.95 (*1-882695-00-3*) Patagonia Pr.

Rucker, Brian R., compiled by. Index to Deaths & Marriages in Pensacola Newspapers, 1821-1865. 126p. (Orig.). 1990. pap. 19.00 (*1-882695-01-1*) Patagonia Pr.

Rucker, Brian R., jt. auth. see Bingham, F. F.

Rucker, Brian R., ed. see Bingham, F. F.

Rucker, Brian R., ed. see Brackenridge, Henry M.

Rucker, Bronwyn. Teenscenes: Theatre Peer Educator Training Project on Relationship Violence & Racism. unabridged ed. Russo, Rick, ed. 43p. (Orig.). 1994. pap. 5.00 (*0-9657394-0-6*) Meltdown Inc.

***Rucker, Della.** From the McCauslin to Jab Switch: A History of Logging in Oconto County. deluxe ed. Nichols, Diane, ed. & footn. by. (Illus.). 107p. 1999. 24.95 (*0-9676727-0-8*) Oconto Cnty Econ.

Rucker, E. H. Hoyle: Genealogy of Peiter Heyl (Hoyle) & His Descendants, 1100-1936, with Intermarried Families of Arnold, Bess, Byrd, Cansler, et al. (Illus.). 1539p. 1991. reprint ed. pap. 198.00 (*0-8328-1772-4*); reprint ed. lib. bdg. 208.00 (*0-8328-1771-6*) Higginson Bk Co.

Rucker, Edward W. The Complete Unabridged Information Manual & Reference Guide to the Oklahoma Non-Coal Mining Industry. Tommerlin, Gayle, ed. 198p. 1985. pap. 24.95 (*0-9614352-0-8*) Edw Rucker Ent.

— Rucker's Personal Guide to Successful Money Making Opportunities & Credit Information. LC 86-90451. 245p. 1987. pap. 29.95 (*0-9614352-1-6*) Edw Rucker Ent.

Rucker, Herbert J., jt. auth. see Henderson, Melvin.

Rucker, John. Seasonal Guide to the Natural Year: North Carolina, South Carolina & Tennessee. (Seasonal Guides to the Natural Year Ser.). (Illus.). 360p. (Orig.). 1996. pap. 16.95 (*1-55591-270-2*) Fulcrum Pub.

***Rucker, Karen S.** Comprehensive Chronic Pain Evaluation: A User's Manual. (Illus.). 176p. 2000. pap. 30.00 (*0-7506-7121-1*) Buttrwrth-Heinemann.

Rucker, Karen S., et al. Low Back Pain: A Symptom-Based Approach to Diagnosis & Treatment. (Illus.). 368p. 2000. 40.00 (*0-7506-9485-8*) Buttrwrth-Heinemann.

Rucker, Karen S., jt. ed. see Lillegard, Wade A.

Rucker, Kathy D. Adult Education in the Parish: A Practical Handbook. 92p. 1990. pap. 4.95 (*0-86716-125-6*) St Anthony Mess Pr.

Rucker, L. B. Rucker: Genealogy of the Rucker Family, with Bush Genealogy. 148p. 1995. reprint ed. pap. 24.00 (*0-8328-4830-1*); reprint ed. lib. bdg. 34.00 (*0-8328-4829-8*) Higginson Bk Co.

Rucker, Linda, jt. ed. see Rucker, Randy.

Rucker, Mark, ed. Baseball for the Fun of It. 1997. pap. 9.95 (*0-910137-69-2*) Soc Am Baseball Res.

Rucker, Mark, jt. auth. see Bjarkman, Peter C.

Rucker, Mark, jt. auth. see Ritter, Lawrence S.

Rucker, Mark, jt. ed. see Thorn, John.

Rucker, Mark, jt. ed. see Tiemann, Robert L.

***Rucker, Michael, et al.** The Illustration: The Revelation of St. John the Divine, Chapters 4 & 5:1-5. (Illus.). 248p. 2000. pap. write for info. (*0-9677794-0-5*) Fifty-Four Hund Vessels.

Rucker, Naomi & Lombardi, Karen. Subject Relations: Unconscious Experience & Relational Psychoanalysis. LC 97-16984. 256p. (C). 1997. 75.00 (*0-415-91422-1*); pap. 23.99 (*0-415-91423-X*) Routledge.

Rucker, Neima, jt. auth. see Rogers, Karen M.

Rucker, Randy & Rucker, Linda, eds. The Rock & Roll Birthday Book. 144p. (Orig.). 1991. pap. 9.95 (*0-944445-03-9*) Musi-Key.

Rucker, Robert L. Lex-I-Con. (Chaplets Ser.). 12p. 1996. pap. 2.50 (*0-916155-33-1*) Trout Creek.

Rucker, Robert M. Producing & Directing Drama for the Church. 208p. Date not set. pap. 19.99 (*0-8341-9726-X*) Nazarene.

Rucker, Rudolf V. Geometry, Relativity & the Fourth Dimension. LC 76-22240. (Illus.). 133p. 1977. pap. text 5.95 (*0-486-23400-2*) Dover.

Rucker, Rudy. All the Visions. (Doubles Ser.). (Illus.). 224p. 1993. pap. 16.95 (*0-938075-12-8*) Ocean View Bks.

Rucker, Rudy. All the Visions. deluxe limited ed. (Doubles Ser.). (Illus.). 224p. 1993. boxed set 59.95 (*0-938075-37-3*) Ocean View Bks.

— All the Visions & the Secret of Life, 2 vols. deluxe limited ed. (Illus.). 1993. boxed set 99.95 (*0-938075-09-8*) Ocean View Bks.

— Freeware. LC 96-47375. 304p. 1997. pap. 13.00 (*0-380-79278-8*, Avon Bks) Morrow Avon.

— Freeware. LC 96-47375. 272p. 1998. mass mkt. 5.99 (*0-380-78159-X*, Avon Bks) Morrow Avon.

***Rucker, Rudy.** Gnarl! Stories. 565p. 2000. 35.00 (*1-56858-158-0*, Pub. by FWEW); pap. 30.00 (*1-56858-159-9*, Pub. by FWEW) Publishers Group.

Rucker, Rudy. The Hacker & the Ants. LC 93-43500. 1994. 20.00 (*0-688-13416-5*, Avon Bks) Morrow Avon.

— The Hacker & the Ants. 320p. 1995. mass mkt. 4.99 (*0-380-71844-8*, Avon Bks) Morrow Avon.

— The Hollow Earth. 304p. 1992. reprint ed. mass mkt. 3.99 (*0-380-75535-1*, Avon Bks) Morrow Avon.

— Infinity & the Mind: The Science & Philosophy of the Infinite. (Princeton Science Library). 352p. 1995. pap. 14.95 (*0-691-00172-3*, Pub. by Princeton U Pr) Cal Prin Full Svc.

— Live Robots. LC 93-90822. 368p. 1994. mass mkt. 5.99 (*0-380-77543-3*, Avon Bks) Morrow Avon.

— Mind Tools: The Five Levels of Mathematical Reality. (Illus.). 352p. 1988. pap. 14.00 (*0-395-46810-8*) HM.

***Rucker, Rudy.** Realware. LC 00-20152. 320p. 2000. pap. 14.00 (*0-380-80877-3*, Avon Bks) Morrow Avon.

Rucker, Rudy. Saucer Wisdom. LC 99-22076. 304p. 1999. 23.95 (*0-312-86884-7*, Pub. by Forge NYC) St Martin.

— The Secret of Life. deluxe limited ed. 250p. 1985. boxed set 59.95 (*0-938075-55-1*) Ocean View Bks.

***Rucker, Rudy.** Seek! Selected Non-Fiction. 356p. 1999. pap. 16.95 (*1-56858-138-6*) FWEW.

Rucker, Rudy. Seek! Selected Nonfiction. LC 99-10706. 356p. 1999. 35.00 (*1-56858-133-5*) FWEW.

— Software. 176p. (Orig.). 1987. mass mkt. 5.99 (*0-380-70177-4*, Avon Bks) Morrow Avon.

— Wetware. 192p. 1988. mass mkt. 5.99 (*0-380-70178-2*, Avon Bks) Morrow Avon.

— White Light. LC 97-15079. 272p. 1997. pap. 12.95 (*1-888869-17-8*) Wired Bks.

Rucker, Rudy, et al, eds. Semiotext(e)SF. 384p. Date not set. 12.00 (*0-936756-43-8*) Autonomedia.

Rucker, Rudy, et al. The Fourth Dimension: A Guided Tour of Higher Universes, 001. (Illus.). 228p. 1985. pap. 15.00 (*0-395-39388-4*) HM.

Rucker, Walt, jt. auth. see Ockenga, Earl.

Ruckert, Friedrich. Hamasa Oder die Altesten Arabischen Volkslieder, 2 pts., Set. 826p. reprint ed. write for info. (*0-318-71558-9*) G Olms Pubs.

Ruckert, George & Akbar Khan, Ali. Rag Chandranandan. (Classical Music of North India Ser.: Vol. II, No. 2). 53p. 1996. pap. 22.95 (*0-930997-05-0*) East Bay Bks.

— Rag Darbari Kanra. (Classical Music of North India Ser.: Vol. II, No. 1). 95p. 1996. pap. 39.95 (*0-930997-04-2*) East Bay Bks.

— Rag Kirwani. (Classical Music of North India Ser.: Vol. II, No. 3). 43p. 1996. pap. 19.95 (*0-930997-06-9*) East Bay Bks.

Ruckert, George & Khan, Ali A. The First Years' Study. (Classical Music of North India Ser.: Vol. 1, No. 1). xiii, 367p. 1991. pap. 59.95 (*0-930997-02-6*) East Bay Bks.

Ruckert, George, jt. auth. see Khan, Ali A.

Ruckert, Janet. L'Animal Therapeute, Ou, Comment Votre Animal de Compagnie Peut Vous Aider a Resoudre Vos Problemes. Reavis, Marguerite, tr. (FRE.). 245p. 1994. 19.95 (*2-920083-87-2*) Edns Roseau.

— The Four Footed Therapist: How Your Pet Can Help You Solve Your Problems. LC 86-23123. 256p. 1987. pap. 7.95 (*0-89815-185-6*) Ten Speed Pr.

Ruckert, Tilman. Der Intellektuelle Verbrechensschaden Bei Carl-theodor Welcker. 171p. 1998. 39.95 (*3-631-33973-9*) P Lang Pubng.

Ruckheim, Ulrich, jt. auth. see Weiner, Lawrence.

***Rucki, Alexander.** Fascinating (Australian) Family Life Collection. LC 99-93743. 2000. pap. 10.95 (*0-533-13278-9*) Vantage.

Rucki, Ani. When the Earth Wakes. LC 97-8187. (Illus.). 32p. (J). (ps-2). 1998. 15.95 (*0-590-05951-3*) Scholastic Inc.

Ruckle, Gene. Multifamily Selective Rehabilitation No. 2: Housing Production Manual. Cashman, Jude & Werwath, Peter, eds. (Housing Production Manuals Ser.). 1990. student ed. 35.00 (*0-942901-03-7*) Enterprise Fnd.

Ruckle, James E. Distinctive Qualities of Third Sector Organizations. LC 92-32113. (Non-profit Institutions in America Ser.). 168p. 1992. text 10.00 (*0-8153-0905-8*) Garland.

Ruckley, C. V., et al, eds. Venous Disease: Epidemiology, Management & Delivery of Care. LC 98-35856. (Illus.). ix, 278p. 1999. 149.00 (*1-85233-070-8*) Spr-Verlag.

Rucklidge, W. Efficient Visual Recognition Using the Hausdorff Distance. LC 96-48288. (Lecture Notes in Computer Science Ser.: Vol. 1173). 178p. 1996. 36.00 (*3-540-61993-3*) Spr-Verlag.

Ruckman, Bret & Ruckman, Stuart. Rock Climbing in the Wasatch Range. 2nd rev. ed. LC 98-15007. (Illus.). 1997. pap. 30.00 (*1-57540-090-1*) Falcon Pub Inc.

Ruckman, Bret, jt. auth. see Ruckman, Stuart.

Ruckman, Ivy. The Hunger Scream. LC 83-6522. 200p. (J). (gr. 6 up). 1983. 14.95 (*0-8027-6514-9*) Walker & Co.

***Ruckman, Ivy.** In Care of Cassie Tucker. 176p. (J). 2000. pap. 4.50 (*0-440-41406-7*) Dell Yearling.

Ruckman, Ivy. Night of the Twister. 1986. 10.05 (*0-606-02536-7*, Pub. by Turtleback) Demco.

— Night of the Twisters. LC 83-46168. 160p. (J). (gr. 3-6). 1984. lib. bdg. 15.89 (*0-690-04409-7*) HarpC Child Bks.

— Night of the Twisters. LC 83-46168. (Trophy Bk.). 160p. (J). (gr. 4-7). 1986. reprint ed. pap. 4.95 (*0-06-440176-6*, HarpTrophy) HarpC Child Bks.

— No Way Out. LC 87-47817. (Trophy Keypoint Bk.). 224p. (YA). (gr. 7 up). 1989. reprint ed. mass mkt. 4.95 (*0-06-447003-2*, HarpTrophy) HarpC Child Bks.

— Spell It M-U-R-D-E-R. 160p. (J). (gr. 4-7). 1994. pap. 3.50 (*0-553-48175-4*) Bantam.

Ruckman, Jo Ann. The Moscow Business Elite, 1840-1905: A Social & Cultural Portrait of Two Generations. LC 83-23732. 275p. 1984. 32.00 (*0-87580-096-3*) N Ill U Pr.

Ruckman, Peter S. The Clownsville Carnival. LC 99-168676. 315 p. 1998. write for info. (*1-58026-097-7*) Bible Bapt Bookstore.

Ruckman, Stuart & Ruckman, Bret. Climbers Guide to American Fork Canyon Rock Canyon. LC 97-134543. (Illus.). 200p. (Orig.). 1995. pap. 18.00 (*0-934641-88-9*) Falcon Pub Inc.

— Wasatch Range. (Classic Rock Climbs Ser.: Vol. 11). (Illus.). (Orig.). 1997. pap. 10.95 (*1-57540-036-7*) Falcon Pub Inc.

Ruckman, Stuart, jt. auth. see Ruckman, Bret.

Ruckpaul, Klaus & Rein, Horst, eds. Cytochrome P-450. 398p. 1985. 88.00 (*0-85066-337-7*); pap. text 27.00 (*0-85066-970-7*) Taylor & Francis.

— Cytochrome Substrates. (Frontiers in Biotransformation Ser.: Vol. 6). 192p. 1991. text 150.00 (*3-05-501284-4*, Pub. by Akademie Verlag) Wiley.

— Membrane Organization & Phospholipid Interaction of Cytochrome P-450. (Frontiers in Biotransformation Ser.: Vol. 5). 210p. 1991. lib. bdg. 155.00 (*3-05-500461-2*, Pub. by Akademie Verlag) Wiley.

— Microbial & Plant Cytochrome P-450: Biochemical Characteristics, Genetic Engineering & Practical Implications. (Frontiers in Biotransformation Ser.: Vol. 4). 280p. 1991. 90.00 (*0-7484-0029-X*, Pub. by Tay Francis Ltd) Taylor & Francis.

— Molecular Mechanisms of Adrenal Steroidogenesis & Aspects of Regulation & Application. (Frontiers in Biotransformation Ser.: Vol. 3). 251p. 1991. 90.00 (*0-7484-0025-7*, Pub. by Tay Francis Ltd) Taylor & Francis.

— Principles, Mechanisms & Biological Consequences of Induction. (Frontiers in Biotransformation Ser.: Vol. 2). 352p. 1991. 90.00 (*0-85066-799-2*, Pub. by Tay Francis Ltd) Taylor & Francis.

— Relationships Between Structure & Function of Cytochrome P-450: Experiments, Calculations, Models. (Frontiers in Biotransformation Ser.: Vol. 7). 370p. 1993. 140.00 (*0-685-67332-4*, Pub. by Akademie Verlag) Wiley.

Ruckstuhl, Eugen. Die Literarische Einheit des Johannesevangeliums: Der Gegenwartige Stand der Einschlagigen Forschungen: Mit Einem Vorwort von Martin Hengel. (Novum Testamentum et Orbis Antiquus Ser.: Vol. 5). (GER.). 331p. 1987. text 61.75 (*3-7278-0542-0*, Pub. by Presses Univ Fribourg) Eisenbrauns.

Ruckstuhl, Eugen & Dschulnigg, Peter. Stilkritik und Verfasserfrage Im Johannesevangelium: Die Johanneischen Sprachmerkmale Auf Dem Hintergrund des Neuen Testaments und des Zeitgenossischen Hellenistischen Schrifttums. (Novum Testamentum et Orbis Antiquus Ser.: Vol. 17). (GER.). 282p. 1991. text 53.25 (*3-7278-0740-7*, Pub. by Presses Univ Fribourg) Eisenbrauns.

Ruckstuhl, Irma. Old Provincetown in Early Photographs. (Illus.). 96p. (Orig.). 1987. pap. 11.95 (*0-486-25410-0*) Dover.

Ruckstuhl, William J. Financial Planning Applications. 15th ed. LC 98-71839. 836p. (C). 1998. text 68.00 (*1-57996-006-5*) Amer College.

Ruckstuhl, William J., jt. auth. see Langdon, Thomas P.

Ruckwick, Christian A., ed. Iowa University Studies in Psychology. (Psychological Monographs General & Applied: Vol. 43). 1969. reprint ed. pap. 55.00 (*0-8115-1442-0*) Periodicals Srv.

— Iowa University Studies in Psychology, No. 13. (Psychology Monographs General & Applied: Vol. 40). 1969. reprint ed. pap. 55.00 (*0-8115-1439-0*) Periodicals Srv.

— Studies in the Psychology of Art. (Psychology Monographs General & Applied: Vol. 45). 1974. reprint ed. 55.00 (*0-8115-1444-7*) Periodicals Srv.

Rud, Anthony G., Jr. & Oldendorf, Walter P., eds. A Place for Teacher Renewal: Challenging the Intellect, Creating Education Reform. 176p. (C). 1992. text 35.00 (*0-8077-3147-1*); pap. text 17.95 (*0-8077-3146-3*) Tchrs Coll.

— A Place for Teacher Renewal: Challenging the Intellect, Creating Educational Reform. LC 91-28670. 176p. reprint ed. pap. 54.60 (*0-608-20009-3*, 207128500010) Bks Demand.

Rud, Anthony G., Jr., jt. ed. see Garrison, James W.

***Rud, Jeff.** Skywalking: How Ten Young Basketball Stars Soared to the Pros. 144p. (J). 2000. pap. 9.95 (*1-896095-46-1*) Polstar Bk.

***Rud, Olivia C.** Data Mining, Cookbook: Modeling Data for Marketing, Risk & Customer Relationship Management. 416p. 2000. pap. 49.99 (*0-471-38564-6*) Wiley.

Ruda, Howard. Asset-Based Financing: A Transactional Guide, 4 vols. LC 84-72027. 1985. ring bd. 570.00 (*0-8205-1059-9*) Bender.

Ruda, Jeffrey. The Art of Drawing: Old Masters from the Crocker Art Museum. LC 92-71560. (Illus.). 200p. (Orig.). 1992. pap. 50.00 (*0-939896-00-1*) Flint Inst Arts.

— Fra Filippo Lippi: Life & Work. 352p. 1999. pap. 39.95 (*0-7148-3889-6*) Phaidon Pr.

— Fra Filippo Lippi: Life & Work with a Complete Catalogue. (Illus.). 560p. 1997. 195.00 (*0-7148-2362-7*, Pub. by Phaidon Press) Phaidon Pr.

***Ruda, Jose Maria & Armas Barea, Calixto A.** Liber Amicorum "In Memoriam" of Judge Jose Maria Ruda. LC 00-25768. 2000. write for info. (*90-411-1367-3*) Kluwer Law Intl.

***Rudacille, Deborah.** The Scalpel & the Butterfly: The War Between Animal Research & Animal Protection. 320p. 2000. text 25.00 (*0-374-25420-6*) FS&G.

Rudacille, Wendell C. Identifying Lies in Disguise, Vol. 1: A Practical Guide to Detecting Deception in Verbal Behavior. 312p. (C). 1993. 35.00 (*1-877858-27-7*, ILID-WR) Amer Focus Pub.

Rudakov, A. N., ed. Helices & Exceptional Vector Bundles: Seminaire Rudakov. (London Mathematical Society Lecture Note Ser.: No. 148). 149p. (C). 1990. pap. text 31.95 (*0-521-38811-2*) Cambridge U Pr.

Rudakova, I. Leaner's Dictionary of Polytechnical Terms: Russian-English-French-German. 4th rev. ed. (FRE, GER & RUS.). 448p. 1988. 35.00 (*0-7859-7154-8*) Fr & Eur.

Rudakova, I. F. General Technical Lexicon. 3rd ed. (ENG, FRE, GER & RUS.). 448p. 1985. 39.95 (*0-8288-0686-1*, M 15525) Fr & Eur.

Rudall, B. H. Computers & Cybernetics, Vol. 11. (Cybernetics & Systems Ser., Abacus Bks.). x, 188p. 1981. text 135.00 (*0-85626-173-4*) Gordon & Breach.

Rudall, B. H. & Corns, T. N. Computers & Literature. (Computer Language Programmes Ser., Abacus Bks.). (Illus.). x, 130p. 1987. text 75.00 (*0-85626-340-0*) Gordon & Breach.

Rudall, Nicholas, jt. auth. see Marlowe, Christopher.

Rudall, Nicholas, intro. see Von Kleist, Heinrich.

Rudall, Nicholas, tr. see Aristophanes.

Rudall, Nicholas, tr. see Euripides.

Rudall, Nicholas, tr. see Ibsen, Henrik.

Rudall, Nicholas, tr. see Sophocles.

Rudall, Nicholas, tr. & intro. see Euripides.

Rudall, P. J., et al, eds. Monocotyledons: Systematics & Evolution, 2 vols. Incl. Vol. 1. xxii, 750p. 1995. (*0-947643-83-4*, Pub. by Royal Botnic Grdns); Vol. 2. xxii, 750p. 1995. (*0-947643-84-2*, Pub. by Royal Botnic Grdns); 1995. Set pap. 90.00 (*0-947643-85-0*, Pub. by Royal Botnic Grdns) Balogh.

Rudall, P. J., jt. auth. see Owens, S. J.

Rudall, Paula. Anatomy of Flowering Plants: An Introduction to Structure & Development. 2nd ed. LC 92-13493. (Illus.). 120p. (C). 1992. pap. text 21.95 (*0-521-42154-3*) Cambridge U Pr.

— Anatomy of the Monocotyledons Vol. 8: Iridaceae. (Illus.). 134p. 1995. text 135.00 (*0-19-854504-5*) OUP.

Rudanko, Juhani. Complementation & Case Grammar: A Syntactic & Semantic Study of Selected Patterns of Complementation in Present-Day English. LC 88-20983. (SUNY Series in Linguistics). 173p. (C). 1989. text 74.50 (*0-88706-931-2*); pap. text 24.95 (*0-88706-932-0*) State U NY Pr.

— Diachronic Studies of English Complementation Patterns: Eighteenth Century Evidence in Tracing the Development of Verbs & Adjectives Selecting Prepositions & Complement Clauses. LC 99-26022. 152p. 1999. 39.50 (*0-7618-1407-8*) U Pr of Amer.

— Linguistic Analysis & Text Interpretation: Essays on the Bill of Rights & on Keats, Shakespeare & Dreiser. LC 97-9489. 144p. 1997. 49.00 (*0-7618-0734-9*); pap. 26.50 (*0-7618-0735-7*) U Pr of Amer.

— Pragmatic Approaches to Shakespeare: Essays on Othello, Coriolanus & Timon of Athens. 222p. (C). 1993. lib. bdg. 43.00 (*0-8191-9107-8*) U Pr of Amer.

— Prepositions & Complement Clauses: A Syntactic & Semantic Study of Verbs Governing Prepositions & Complement Clauses in Present-Day English. LC 95-22230. (SUNY Series in Linguistics). 211p. (C). 1996. text 59.50 (*0-7914-2873-7*); pap. text 19.95 (*0-7914-2874-5*) State U NY Pr.

Rudanko, M. Juhani. Change & Continuity in the English Language: Studies on Complementation over the Past Three Hundred Years. LC 97-53064. (Illus.). 184p. (C). 1998. 39.00 (*0-7618-1039-0*) U Pr of Amer.

Rudarmel. Peak Experiences: Write 'Em Down. 1994. pap. text 9.95 (*1-880133-44-X*) AHA Calligraphy.

Rudas, Marie, ed. see Kaszas, John.

Rudas, Tamas. Odds Ratios in the Analysis of Contingency Tables. LC 97-33790. (Sage University Papers). 1997. pap. write for info. (*0-7619-0362-3*) Sage.

Rudat, Wolfgang E. Alchemy in "The Sun Also Rises" Hidden Gold in Hemingway's Narrative. LC 92-25021. 288p. 1992. text 89.95 (*0-7734-9579-7*) E Mellen.

— Earnest Exuberance in Chaucer's Poetics: Textual Games in the Canterbury Tales. LC 93-34113. 348p. 1993. 99.95 (*0-7734-9381-6*) E Mellen.

— A Rotten Way to Be Wounded: The Tragicomedy of the Sun Also Rises. LC 90-5903. (American University Studies: American Literature: Ser. XXIV, Vol. 21). X, 214p. (C). 1991. text 38.95 (*0-8204-1282-1*) P Lang Pubng.

Rudatis, Renato. Classic Pizza & Pasta Recipes. (Illus.). 1989. 17.95 (*0-572-01450-3*, Pub. by W Foulsham) Trans-Atl Phila.

— Pizza & Pasta Recipes: Appetising, Exciting & Inexpensive Italian Dishes. (Illus.). 1991. 24.50 (*0-572-01691-3*, Pub. by W Foulsham) Trans-Atl Phila.

— Regional Italian Specialties. Allison, Sonia, ed. (Gourmet Cookshelf Ser.). (Illus.). 64p. 1992. 13.95 (*0-572-01707-3*, Pub. by W Foulsham) Trans-Atl Phila.

Rudavsky, Joseph. To Live with Hope, to Die with Dignity: Spiritual Resistance in the Ghettos & Camps. LC 96-340. 288p. 1997. 30.00 (*1-56821-940-7*) Aronson.

Rudavsky, T. M. Time Matters: Time, Creation, & Cosmology in Medieval Jewish Philosophy. LC 99-88797. (C). 2000. text 68.50 (*0-7914-4453-8*); pap. text 22.95 (*0-7914-4454-6*) State U NY Pr.

Rudavsky, T. M., ed. Gender & Judaism: The Transformation of Tradition. 320p. (C). 1995. text 47.50 (*0-8147-7452-0*) NYU Pr.

— Gender & Judaism: The Transformation of Tradition. 320p. (C). 1995. pap. text 19.50 (*0-8147-7453-9*) NYU Pr.

Rudavsky, Tamar, ed. Divine Omniscience & Omnipotence in Medieval Philosophy. 299p. 1984. text 179.50 (*90-277-1750-8*) Kluwer Academic.

An Asterisk (*) at the beginning of an entry indicates that the title is appearing for the first time.

Rudaz, S. & Walsh, T., eds. Sixth Workshop on Grand Unification: Proceedings of the Workshop held at Minneapolis, April, 1985. 500p. 1986. pap. 55.00 (*9971-978-84-9*); text 124.00 (*9971-978-83-0*) World Scientific Pub.

Rudd, A., tr. see Benker, Hans.

Rudd, A. B., ed. see Stacy, Pocahontas H.

Rudd, Andrea & Taylor, Darien, eds. Positive Women: Voices of Women Living with AIDS. (Illus.). 276p. 1992. pap. 14.95 (*0-929005-30-9*, Pub. by Sec Story Pr) LPC InBook.

Rudd, Andrew & Clasing, Henry J., Jr. Modern Portfolio Theory: The Principles of Investment Management. 525p. 1988. pap. 50.00 (*0-9620194-0-2*) A Rudd.

Rudd, Anthony. Kierkegaard & the Limits of the Ethical. 198p. 1997. pap. text 26.00 (*0-19-875218-0*) OUP.

— Mastering C. 371p. 1994. pap. 24.95 (*0-471-60820-3*) Wiley.

— Mastering C++ 486p. 1994. pap. 24.95 (*0-471-06565-X*) Wiley.

— Practical Usage of ISPF Dialog Manager. 2nd rev. ed. 381p. 1996. pap. 69.95 (*3-540-19950-0*) Spr-Verlag.

Rudd, Anthony S. Implementing Practical DB2 Applications. 2nd ed. LC 96-18942. 206p. 1996. pap. 74.95 (*3-540-19953-5*) Spr-Verlag.

— Practical Usage of ISPF Dialog Manager. 1989. text 32.95 (*0-470-21574-7*) P-H.

— Practical Usage of MVS REXX. 2nd rev. ed. (Illus.). xiv, 310p. 1996. pap. 59.95 (*3-540-19952-7*) Spr-Verlag.

***Rudd, Anthony S.** Practical Usage of TSO REXX. 3rd rev. ed. LC 00-20844. (Illus.). xvi, 362p. 2000. pap. 79.95 (*1-85233-261-1*) Spr-Verlag.

Rudd, Barry. Stock Patterns for Day Trading. 224p. 1998. 95.00 (*0-934380-41-4*, 1208) Traders Pr.

— Stock Patterns for Day Trading, Vol. 2. Vol. 2. (Illus.). 224p. 1999. 95.00 (*0-934380-57-0*) Traders Pr.

Rudd, Betty, ed. see Gluchowsky, Paul M.

Rudd, C. D. Liquid Moulding Technologies: Resin Transfer Moulding, Structural Reaction Injection Moulding, & Related Processing Techniques. LC 97-19335. 1997. 75.00 (*0-7680-0016-5*, R-204) Soc Auto Engineers.

Rudd, C. D., et al. Liquid Moulding Technologies: Resin Transfer Moulding, Structural Reaction Injection Moulding & Related. 464p. 1997. boxed set 170.00 (*1-85573-242-4*, Pub. by Woodhead Pubng) Am Educ Systs.

***Rudd, Carol.** The Complete Illustrated Guide to Flower Remedies: A Practical Approach to Healing with 400 Essences from Around the World. (Illus.). 2000. pap. 24.95 (*1-86204-366-3*, Pub. by Element MA) Penguin Putnam.

Rudd, Carol. Flower Essences. LC 98-6434. (Illustrated Guide Ser.). (Illus.). 1998. pap. 19.95 (*1-86204-167-9*, Pub. by Element MA) Penguin Putnam.

Rudd, Chris & Roper, Brian, eds. The Political Economy of New Zealand. 2nd ed. LC 97-200086. (Illus.). 324p. 1997. pap. text 45.00 (*0-19-558331-0*) OUP.

Rudd, Chris, jt. ed. see Roper, Brian.

Rudd, Connie. Grand Canyon--North Rim: The Story Behind the Scenery. LC 89-45019. (Illus.). 48p. (Orig.). 1989. pap. 7.95 (*0-88714-033-5*) KC Pubns.

— In Pictures Grand Canyon: The Continuing Story. LC 90-60038. (Illus.). 48p. (Orig.). 1990. pap. 7.95 (*0-88714-046-7*) KC Pubns.

— In Pictures Grand Canyon: The Continuing Story. (KOR., Illus.). 48p. (Orig.). 1990. pap. 8.95 (*0-88714-720-8*) KC Pubns.

— In Pictures Grand Canyon: The Continuing Story. Le Bras, Yvon, tr. (FRE., Illus.). 48p. (Orig.). 1990. pap. 8.95 (*0-88714-717-8*) KC Pubns.

— In Pictures Grand Canyon: The Continuing Story. Petzinger, Saori, tr. (JPN., Illus.). 48p. (Orig.). 1990. pap. 8.95 (*0-88714-718-6*) KC Pubns.

— In Pictures Grand Canyon: The Continuing Story. (GER., Illus.). 48p. (Orig.). 1990. pap. 8.95 (*0-88714-716-X*) KC Pubns.

— In Pictures Grand Canyon: The Continuing Story. Marapodi, Carlos, tr. (SPA., Illus.). 48p. (Orig.). 1992. pap. 8.95 (*0-88714-719-4*) KC Pubns.

— In Pictures Grand Canyon: The Continuing Story. Lee, Frances Y., tr. (CHI., Illus.). 48p. (Orig.). 1993. pap. 8.95 (*0-88714-721-6*) KC Pubns.

— In Pictures Grand Canyon: The Continuing Story. Comollo, Adriano, tr. (ITA., Illus.). 48p. (Orig.). 1993. pap. 8.95 (*0-88714-722-4*) KC Pubns.

— In Pictures Grand Canyon: The Continuing Story. Popov, Alex, tr. (RUS., Illus.). 48p. (Orig.). 1994. pap. 8.95 (*0-88714-785-2*) KC Pubns.

Rudd, Daniel & Bond, Theophilus. From Slavery to Wealth: The Life of Scott Bond. LC 73-173615. (Black Heritage Library Collection). 1977. reprint ed. 33.95 (*0-8369-8907-4*) Ayer.

***Rudd, David.** Enid Blyton & the Mystery of Children's Literature. LC 99-59251. 2000. 59.95 (*0-312-23212-8*) St Martin.

Rudd, David. Introduction to Software Design & Development with ADA. LC 93-37696. 812p. (C). 1994. mass mkt. 70.95 (*0-314-02829-3*) West Pub.

***Rudd, David.** Prosperity from Technology: A New Approach to Industrial Production, Money & the Environment. LC 99-201234. x, 409 p. 1999. write for info. (*1-85776-362-9*, Pub. by Book Guild Ltd) Gannon.

***Rudd, David E.** Burning from the Inside. (Illus.). 170p. 1998. pap. 17.00 (*0-9673400-2-0*) Cycleback Pr.

— The Illustrated History of Baseball Cards: The 1800's. (Illus.). 130p. (Orig.). 1999. pap. 20.00 (*0-9673400-0-4*) Cycleback Pr.

— The Illustrated History of Baseball Cards, 1900-1915 Vol. II. (Illus.). 215p. 1999. pap. text 25.00 (*0-9673400-1-2*) Cycleback Pr.

***Rudd, Denis P. & Marshall, Lincoln H.** Introduction to Casino & Gaming Operations. 2nd ed. LC 99-30911. (Illus.). 262p. 1999. 62.00 (*0-13-979568-5*) P-H.

Rudd, E. A New Look at Postgraduate Failure. 144p. 1985. pap. 38.00 (*1-85059-009-5*) Taylor & Francis.

***Rudd, E. J. & Ota, K., eds.** Environmental Aspects of Electrochemical Technology. 248p. 2000. 65.00 (*1-56677-262-1*, PV 99-39) Electrochem Soc.

Rudd, Gail. John Danced. 40p. (Orig.). 1982. pap. 9.95 (*0-917658-20-5*) BPW & P.

Rudd, Gillian. Managing Language in "Piers Plowman" (Piers Plowman Studies: Vol. 9). 260p. (C). 1994. 75.00 (*0-85991-392-9*, DS Brewer) Boydell & Brewer.

Rudd, Jill & Gough, Val, eds. Charlotte Perkins Gilman: Optimist Reformer. LC 99-29216. 330p. 1999. text 37.95 (*0-87745-695-X*); pap. text 17.95 (*0-87745-696-8*) U of Iowa Pr.

Rudd, Jill, jt. ed. see Gough, Val.

Rudd, Leigh, jt. auth. see Fuller, Sheila.

Rudd, M. Eugene, jt. auth. see Cahan, David.

Rudd, Margaret. The Lone Heretic. LC 75-31688. 370p. 1976. reprint ed. 75.00 (*0-87752-181-6*) Gordian.

Rudd, Margaret E. Divided Image. LC 73-118003. (Studies in Blake: No. 3). 1970. reprint ed. lib. bdg. 75.00 (*0-8383-1015-X*) M S G Haskell Hse.

Rudd, Merri. Life Planning in New Mexico: Your Guide to State Law on Powers of Attorney, Right to Die, Nursing Home Benefits, Wills, Trusts & Probate. 3rd rev. ed. LC 92-70603. 238p. 2000. pap. 16.95 (*0-9632173-1-3*) Abogada Pr.

Rudd, Niall. The Classical Tradition in Operation. (Robson Classical Lectures). 204p. 1994. text 55.00 (*0-8020-0570-5*) U of Toronto Pr.

— Pale Green, Light Orange: A Portrait of Bourgois Ireland, 1930-1950. LC 94-184818. 168p. 1994. pap. 18.95 (*1-874675-21-X*) Dufour.

— The Satires of Horace. (Bristol Classical Paperbacks Ser.). 336p. 1994. pap. 25.95 (*0-86292-041-8*, Pub. by Brist Class Pr) Focus Pub-R Pullins.

— The Satires of Horace: A Study. LC 66-11031. 330p. reprint ed. pap. 94.10 (*0-608-12497-4*, 2024525) Bks Demand.

Rudd, Niall, ed. Horace Two Thousand: A Celebration: Essays for the Bimillennium. LC 93-11057. (Illus.). 150p. (C). 1993. text 42.50 (*0-472-10490-X*, 10490) U of Mich Pr.

Rudd, Niall, tr. The Satires. (Illus.). 288p. 1991. text 95.00 (*0-19-814756-2*, 1643) OUP.

Rudd, Niall & Courtney, E. Juvenal: Satires 1, 3, 10. rev. ed. (LAT.). 100p. (C). 1998. pap. 18.95 (*0-906515-03-3*, Pub. by Brist Class Pr) Focus Pub-R Pullins.

Rudd, Niall & Courtney, E. C. Juvenal Satires, Nos. I, III, X. 91p. 1984. reprint ed. 13.00 (*0-86516-039-2*) Bolchazy-Carducci.

Rudd, Niall, et al. The Satires of Horace & Persius. (Classics Ser.). 304p. 1974. pap. 11.95 (*0-14-044279-0*, Penguin Classics) Viking Penguin.

Rudd, Niall, jt. auth. see Mayer, Roland H.

Rudd, Niall, ed. see Horace.

Rudd, Niall, tr. see Cicero, Marcus Tullius.

Rudd, Niall, tr. see Juvenal.

Rudd, Norman N. An Irish Rudd Family, 1760-1988: Rudd Origins & Other Irish Rudds: Progeny of Gordon Rudd & Alicia Wellwood, Rathsarn Parish, Queens County, Ireland. 552p. 1992. 25.00 (*0-9632992-0-4*) Rudd Family Res.

Rudd, P. T., jt. auth. see Davies, Pamela A.

Rudd, Peggy J. Crossdressers: And Those Who Share Their Lives. LC 95-68067. (Illus.). 126p. 1995. pap. 14.95 (*0-9626762-3-3*) PM Pubs.

***Rudd, Peggy J.** Crossdressers: And Those Who Share Their Lives. 2nd rev. ed. LC 00-132539. 128p. 2000. pap. 14.95 (*0-9626762-7-6*) PM Pubs.

Rudd, Peggy J. Crossdressing with Dignity: The Case for Transcending Gender Lines. 2nd ed. LC 98-68036. 190p. (Orig.). 1999. pap. 14.95 (*0-9626762-6-8*) PM Pubs.

— My Husband Wears My Clothes. 2nd ed. LC 98-67950. 174p. 1999. pap. text 14.95 (*0-9626762-5-X*) P M Publng.

— Who's Really from Venus: The Tale of Two Genders. LC 98-65013. (Illus.). 172p. 1998. pap. 15.95 (*0-9626762-4-1*) PM Pubs.

Rudd, Peter & Nicoll, Angus, eds. British Pediatric Association Manual on Infections & Immunizations in Children. 2nd ed. (Illus.). 320p. 1991. pap. 27.50 (*0-19-262118-1*) OUP.

Rudd, Rebecca S., jt. auth. see Sizer, Nancy F.

Rudd, Robert L. Pesticides & the Living Landscape. LC 64-14506. 336p. reprint ed. pap. 104.20 (*0-608-14279-4*, 201565300095) Bks Demand.

Rudd, Sheila P. Coloring Charleston. (Coloring the Low Country Ser.). (Illus.). 32p. (J). (gr. 1-8). 1994. pap. text 4.95 (*1-880795-75-2*) MBT Ent P&P.

Rudd, Sheila P., ed. George Gershwin. (Composer Highlights Ser.). (Illus.). 32p. (J). (gr. 1-8). 1995. pap. text 4.95 (*1-880795-10-8*) MBT Ent P&P.

Rudd, Shirley. Time Manage Your Reading. 173p. 1990. text 51.95 (*0-566-02762-3*, Pub. by Gower); pap. text 22.95 (*0-566-02976-6*, Pub. by Gower) Ashgate Pub Co.

Rudd, Steele. On Our Selection: The Original Dad & Dave Stories. 1995. pap. 16.95 (*0-7022-2844-3*, Pub. by Univ Queensland Pr) Intl Spec Bk.

— A Steele Rudd Selection: The Best Dad & Dave Stories with Other Rudd Classics. Moorhouse, Frank, ed. LC 86-975. (Illus.). 240p. (Orig.). 1987. pap. 15.95 (*0-7022-1978-9*, Pub. by Univ Queensland Pr) Intl Spec Bk.

Rudd, Terry R. 1929 Again? rev. ed. (Illus.). 450p. (C). 1988. reprint ed. 27.50 (*0-9620011-0-4*) Bell Curve Rsch.

***Rudd, Tony.** It Was Fun! (Illus.). 352p. 2000. 39.95 (*1-85960-666-0*, 130661AE, Pub. by Haynes Manuals) Motorbooks Intl.

Ruddel, David T. Quebec City, 1765-1832: The Evolution of a Colonial Town. (Mercury Ser.: History No. 41). (Illus.). 292p. 1988. pap. 24.95 (*0-660-10771-6*, Pub. by CN Mus Civilization) U of Wash Pr.

Ruddell, Anita, jt. auth. see Brown, Cheryl.

Ruddell, Martha R. Teaching Content Reading & Writing. 2nd ed. (C). 1996. pap., teacher ed. write for info. (*0-205-26658-4*, T6658-3) Allyn.

Ruddell, Martha Rapp. Teaching Content Reading & Writing. 2nd ed. (Illus.). 432p. 1997. teacher ed. 73.95 (*0-471-36557-2*) Wiley.

— Teaching Content Reading & Writing. 3rd ed. 2001. 52.95 (*0-471-36674-9*) Wiley.

Ruddell, Nancy. Mystery of the Maya: The Golden Age of the Classic Maya. (Illus.). 56p. 1995. pap. 8.95 (*0-660-14036-5*, Pub. by CN Mus Civilization) U of Wash Pr.

— Mystery of the Maya: The Golden Age of the Classic Maya. (Illus.). 56p. 1996. 8.95 (*0-660-14040-3*, Pub. by CN Mus Civilization) U of Wash Pr.

— Raven's Village: The Myths, Arts, & Traditions of Native People from the Pacific Northwest Coast. LC 96-131905. (Illus.). 64p. 1996. pap. 8.95 (*0-660-14035-7*, Pub. by CN Mus Civilization) U of Wash Pr.

Ruddell, Robert B. Teaching Children to Read & Write: Becoming an Influential Teacher. 2nd ed. LC 98-13645. 503p. 1998. 76.00 (*0-205-27494-3*) Allyn.

Ruddell, Robert B., et al, eds. Theoretical Models & Processes of Reading. 4th ed. 1296p. 1994. pap. 75.00 (*0-87207-437-4*) Intl Reading.

Ruddell, Robert B., jt. ed. see Singer, Harry.

Ruddell, Tom. 11 Words for Winning: Finding Certain Success in Uncertain Times. LC 99-94719. (Illus.). 248p. 1999. pap. 14.95 (*0-9649284-6-9*) Capstar.

***Ruddell, Tom.** 11 Words for Winning: Finding Certain Success in Uncertain Times. LC 99-94719. (Illus.). 248p. 1999. 21.95 (*0-9649284-5-0*) Capstar.

Ruddell, Tom. The MECCA Factor: 5 Imperatives for a Successful Life. 2nd ed. LC 96-96446. (Illus.). 288p. 1996. 14.95 (*0-9649284-1-8*) Capstar.

Rudden, B. & Yeats, J. M. Disclosure in Insurance: The Changing Scene & Judicial Review in England. (Lectures on the Common Law Ser.: Vol. 3). 60p. 1991. pap. 28.00 (*90-6544-540-4*) Kluwer Law Intl.

Rudden, Bernard. Basic Community Cases. 2nd ed. 410p. 1997. pap. text (*0-19-876438-3*) OUP.

— Basic Japanese Laws. Oda, Hiroshi et al, eds. LC 97-4160. (Modern Japanese Law Ser.). 524p. (C). 1997. text 115.00 (*0-19-825686-8*) OUP.

— The New River: A Legal History. (Illus.). 1985. 39.00 (*0-19-825497-0*) OUP.

Rudden, Bernard, ed. Basic Community Cases. 276p. 1990. reprint ed. pap. 38.00 (*0-19-876211-9*) OUP.

Rudden, Bernard & Phelan, Diarmuid R. Basic Community Cases. 2nd ed. 410p. 1998. text 77.00 (*0-19-876439-1*) OUP.

***Rudden, Bernard & Wyatt, Derrick, eds.** Basic Community Laws. 7th ed. LC 99-16149. 408p. 2000. write for info. (*0-19-876554-1*) OUP.

Rudden, Bernard & Wyatt, Derrick A., eds. Basic Community Laws. 6th ed. 720p. 1996. text 89.00 (*0-19-876428-6*); pap. text 26.00 (*0-19-876427-8*) OUP.

Rudden, Bernard, jt. auth. see Lawson, Frederick H.

Rudden, M. N. & Wilson, J. Elements of Solid State Physics. 2nd ed. LC 92-36621. 278p. 1993. pap. 62.95 (*0-471-92973-5*) Wiley.

Rudder, C., jt. auth. see Maury, Emmerick-Armand.

Rudder, Catherine E., jt. ed. see Engel, Elizabeth Weaver.

Rudder, Chantal De, see Maury, Emmerick-Armand & De Rudder, Chantal.

Rudder, Edith A. Douglas: My Father's Family, Douglas-Haden-Churchill-Blakey-George-Perkins-Oglesby-Attkisson & Allied Families. (Illus.). 119p. 1997. reprint ed. pap. 18.50 (*0-8328-8346-8*); reprint ed. lib. bdg. 28.50 (*0-8328-8345-X*) Higginson Bk Co.

Rudder Editors. Good Sailing: An Illustrated Course on Sailing. (Illus.). (J). (gr. 7 up). 1976. pap. 5.95 (*0-679-50630-6*) McKay.

Rudder, Lena E. King of the World & the Subterranean Kingdom & The Earth Is Hollow at the North & South Poles. 150p. (Orig.). 1988. write for info. (*0-937581-03-8*) Zarathustrotemo Pr.

— White Roots & the Mysteries of God. (Illus.). 144p. (Orig.). 1986. pap. write for info. (*0-937581-00-3*) Zarathustrotemo Pr.

Rudder, Mary, jt. auth. see Sebring, Ellen.

Rudder, N. K. Greek Coinage of Southern Italy & Sicily. (Illus.). 1997. lib. bdg. 60.00 (*0-907605-82-6*) S J Durst.

Rudder, Robert, tr. see Galdos, Benito Perez.

Rudder, Robert S., tr. see Castellanos, Rosario.

Rudder, Robert S., tr. see Gonzalez, Francisco Rojas.

Rudder, Robert S., tr. see Rossi, Cristina Peri.

Rudder, Walter J. At Risk: The Vo-Tech Student in Suburban Society. 150p. 1994. pap. 29.95 (*0-938198-01-7*) Weidner & Sons.

Ruddick, Bob, jt. auth. see Greer, Gary.

Ruddick, Bob, jt. auth. see Greer, Gery.

Ruddick, Bruce. Poems. LC 93-46450. 60p. (Orig.). 1994. pap. 10.95 (*1-878818-26-0*, Pub. by Sheep Meadow) U Pr of New Eng.

Ruddick, Lisa. Reading Gertrude Stein: Body, Text, Gnosis. LC 89-46133. (Reading Women Writing Ser.). 288p. 1990. 39.95 (*0-8014-2363-1*) Cornell U Pr.

— Reading Gertrude Stein: Body, Text, Gnosis. LC 89-46133. (Reading Women Writing Ser.). 288p. 1991. reprint ed. pap. text 16.95 (*0-8014-9957-7*) Cornell U Pr.

Ruddick, Nicholas. British Science Fiction: A Chronology, 1478-1990, 35. LC 92-6409. (Bibliographies & Indexes in World Literature Ser.: No. 35). 296p. 1992. lib. bdg. 69.50 (*0-313-28002-9*, RBF, Greenwood Pr) Greenwood.

— Christopher Priest. LC 88-16046. (Starmont Reader's Guide Ser.: Vol. 50). x, 104p. 1989. pap. 17.00 (*1-55742-109-9*) Millefleurs.

— Ultimate Island: On the Nature of British Science Fiction, 55. LC 92-24136. (Contributions to the Study of Science Fiction & Fantasy Ser.: No. 55). 216p. 1993. 55.00 (*0-313-27373-1*, RUC, Greenwood Pr) Greenwood.

Ruddick, Nicholas, ed. State of the Fantastic: Studies in the Theory & Practice of Fantastic Literature & Film: Selected Essays from the Eleventh International Conference on the Fantastic in the Arts, 1990, 50. LC 91-46867. (Contributions to the Study of Science Fiction & Fantasy Ser.: No. 50). 232p. 1992. 59.95 (*0-313-27853-9*, RSF, Greenwood Pr) Greenwood.

Ruddick, Robert, jt. auth. see Greer, Gary.

Ruddick, Robert, jt. auth. see Greer, Gery.

Ruddick, Sara. Maternal Thinking: Toward a Politics of Peace. 2nd rev. ed. 320p. 1994. pap. 18.00 (*0-8070-1409-5*) Beacon Pr.

Ruddick, Susan M. Young & Homeless in Hollywood: Mapping Social Identities. LC 94-21839. 272p. (C). (gr. 13). 1995. pap. 18.99 (*0-415-91031-5*, B3865) Routledge.

Ruddiman, Catherine, jt. auth. see Aird, Hazel B.

***Ruddiman, William F.** Earth's Climatic History. 2001. pap. text. write for info. (*0-7167-3741-8*) W H Freeman.

Ruddiman, William F., ed. Tectonic Uplift & Climate Change. LC 97-32123. 558p. (C). 1997. text 115.00 (*0-306-45642-7*, Kluwer Plenum) Kluwer Academic.

Ruddle & Johnson. Palm Sago. (Australian National University Press Ser.). 1996. pap. write for info. (*0-08-033013-4*, Pergamon Pr) Elsevier.

Ruddle, Bud. Fishin' Tips. LC 96-68136. (Illus.). 55p. (Orig.). 1996. pap. 10.95 (*1-57197-025-8*) Pentland Pr.

Ruddle, H., jt. ed. see O'Connor, J.

Ruddle, Kenneth. The Coastal Zone: Man's Response to Change. viii, 556p. 1988. text 182.00 (*3-7186-0482-5*) Gordon & Breach.

— The Yukpa Cultivation System: A Study of Shifting Cultivation in Colombia & Venezuela. LC 73-78557. (Ibero-Americana Ser.: No. 52). (Illus.). 234p. reprint ed. pap. 72.60 (*0-608-18178-1*, 203289600081) Bks Demand.

Ruddle, Kenneth, jt. auth. see Manshard, W.

Ruddock, E. H. Vitalogy. (Illus.). 128p. 1995. reprint ed. pap. 8.95 (*1-55709-404-7*) Applewood.

Ruddock, William T. Linen Threads & Broom Twines Vol. 1: An Irish & American Album & Directory of the People of the Dunbarton Mill, Greenwich, New York, 1879-1952. LC 98-146872. (Illus.). 179p. 1997. pap. text 14.50 (*0-7884-0770-8*, R811) Heritage Bk.

Ruddolo, Lisa M., jt. auth. see Smith, Susan B.

Ruddon, Raymond W. Cancer Biology. 3rd ed. (Illus.). 544p. 1995. pap. text 52.50 (*0-19-509691-6*) OUP.

Rudduck, Jean. Developing a Gender Policy in Secondary Schools. LC 93-4049. 160p. 1994. 96.95 (*0-335-19153-3*); pap. 29.95 (*0-335-19152-5*) OpUniv Pr.

Rudduck, Jean, ed. see Stenhouse, Lawrence.

Ruddy, Anna C., see McLeod, Christian, pseud.

Ruddy, Christine A., jt. auth. see Dooling-Plecki, Eileen M.

Ruddy, Christopher. The Strange Death of Vincent Foster: An Investigation. LC 97-22737. (Illus.). 256p. 1997. 25.00 (*0-684-83837-0*) Free Pr.

Ruddy, F., jt. auth. see Deak, F.

Ruddy, J., jt. auth. see Bowers, D.

Ruddy, James F. Photograde: A Photographic Grading Encyclopedia for United States Coins. rev. ed. (Illus.). 208p. 1988. pap. 9.95 (*0-943161-04-5*) Bowers & Merena.

— Photograde: A Photographic Grading Encyclopedia for United States Coins. 17th rev. ed. (Illus.). 208p. 1988. 19.95 (*0-943161-09-6*) Bowers & Merena.

***Ruddy, John J.** Reinventing New London. (Images of America Ser.). (Illus.). 128p. 2000. pap. 18.99 (*0-7385-0480-7*) Arcadia Publng.

Ruddy, John L. New London. (Images of America Ser.). (Illus.). 128p. 1998. pap. 16.99 (*0-7524-0949-2*) Arcadia Publng.

Ruddy, Judy. Job Descriptions Encyclopedia. 1996. 199.95 (*1-55645-047-8*) Busn Legal Reports.

Ruddy, Robin. French Provincial Furniture. LC 97-38783. 128p. 1998. 29.95 (*0-7643-0205-1*) Schiffer.

Ruddy, T. Michael. The Cautious Diplomat: Charles E. Bohlen & the Soviet Union, 1929-1969. LC 86-4705. (Illus.). 234p. reprint ed. pap. 72.60 (*0-608-10529-5*, 207114900009) Bks Demand.

Ruddy, T. Michael, ed. Charting an Independent Course: Finland's Place in the Cold War & in U. S. Foreign Policy. LC 98-5995. 228p. 1998. pap. text 14.95 (*0-941690-84-9*) Regina Bks.

Ruddy, William. Braille for a Storm of Loss: Poems. 1978. 6.95 (*0-685-50207-4*); pap. 3.50 (*0-685-50208-2*) Oyez.

Rude, Carolyn & Dragga, Sam. Technical Editing. 2nd ed. (Series in Technical Communication). 96p. (C). 1997. pap. text, teacher ed. write for info. (*0-205-27855-8*, T7855-4) Allyn.

Rude, Carolyn D. Technical Editing. 2nd ed. Draggo, Sam, ed. LC 97-24302. 422p. 1997. pap. text 49.00 (*0-205-20032-X*) P-H.

Rude, Christina & Rue, Debbie. Great Adventures for Kitsap Peninsula. (Illus.). xi, 152p. 1997. pap. 9.95 (*0-9657914-0-8*) Building Kitsap.

R

Rude, Donald W., ed. A Critical Edition of Sir Thomas Elyot's "The Boke Named the Governour" LC 92-3303. (Renaissance Imagination Ser.). 472p. 1992. text 20.00 (*0-8153-0458-7*) Garland.

Rude, Edna, tr. see McIntyre, Sally.

Rude, George. The Crowd in History: A Study of Popular Disturbances in France & England, 1730-1848. (Illus.). 288p. 1998. pap. 19.95 (*1-897959-21-4*, Pub. by Serif) IPG Chicago.

— Crowd in the French Revolution. (Illus.). 276p. 1967. reprint ed. pap. text 20.95 (*0-19-500370-5*) OUP.

— The Crowd in the French Revolution. LC 86-3166. 295p. 1986. reprint ed. lib. bdg. 89.50 (*0-313-25168-1*, RUCR, Greenwood Pr) Greenwood.

— Europe in the Eighteenth Century: Aristocracy & the Bourgeois Challenge. 292p. 1985. pap. 18.00 (*0-674-26921-7*) HUP.

— The French Revolution: Its Causes, Its History & Its Legacy after 200 Years. LC 88-10707. 224p. 1991. reprint ed. pap. 14.00 (*0-8021-3272-3*, Grove) Grove-Atltic.

— Ideology & Popular Protest. (C). 1980. pap. 18.50 (*0-85315-514-3*, Pub. by Lawrence & Wishart) NYU Pr.

— Ideology & Popular Protest. LC 94-32657. 190p. 1995. pap. text 16.95 (*0-8078-4514-0*) U of NC Pr.

Rude, Kelli, jt. ed. see Peterson, Janet.

Rude, Marc, jt. auth. see Dahlia, Blag.

Rude, Paul. Souls to Soles: A Self-Help Exploration of Reflexology. LC 97-71445. (Illus.). 160p. (Orig.). 1997. pap. 12.95 (*0-914955-51-9*) Lotus Pr.

Rude, Paul, et al. Integrated Pest Management for Cotton. 2nd ed. LC 84-51158. (Illus.). 164p. 1996. pap. 30.00 (*1-879906-30-9*, 3305) ANR Pubns CA.

Rude, Robert. An Act of Deception: Alaska Native Corporations since ANSCA. 120p. 1995. pap. 12.00 (*0-9634000-8-8*) Salmon Run.

— An Act of Deception: Discussions on A.N.S.C.A. 220p. (Orig.). 1996. pap. 16.00 (*1-887573-02-X*) Salmon Run.

Rude, Steve. Steve Rude Sketchbook. Nesheim, Eric, ed. (Illus.). 136p. 1989. pap. 14.95 (*0-87816-047-7*) Kitchen Sink.

Rude, Steve, jt. auth. see Baron, Mike.

Rudeanu, S., ed. see Institute of Management Sciences Staff & Econometric Institute Staff.

Rudebeck, Lars. Guinea-Bissau: A Study of Political Mobilization. 227p. 1974. write for info. (*91-7106-080-4*, Pub. by Nordic Africa) Transaction Pubs.

— Guinea-Bissau: Folket, Partiet Och Staten. Om Den Frediga Kampen For Utveckling. 152p. 1977. write for info. (*91-7106-120-7*, Pub. by Nordic Africa) Transaction Pubs.

— Problemes de Pouvoir Populaire et de Developpement: Transition Difficile en Guinee-Bissau. (Research Report Ser.: No. 63). 73p. 1982. write for info. (*91-7106-208-4*, Pub. by Nordic Africa) Transaction Pubs.

Rudebeck, Lars, ed. When Democracy Makes Sense: Studies in the Democratic Potential of Third World Popular Movements. 399p. (Orig.). 1992. pap. 62.50 (*91-506-0928-9*) Coronet Bks.

Rudebeck, Lars, jt. auth. see Lopes, Carlos.

Rudebeck, Lars, jt. ed. see Negash, Tekeste.

Rudebusch, Glenn D., jt. auth. see Diebold, Francis X.

Rudebusch, George. Socrates, Pleasure & Value. LC 98-36534. 192p. 1999. text 35.00 (*0-19-512855-9*) OUP.

Rudeen, Kenneth. Jackie Robinson. LC 75-139100. (Illus.). 64p. (J). (gr. 2-5). 1996. pap. 4.25 (*0-06-442042-6*, HarpTrophy) HarpC Child Bks.

— Jackie Robinson. LC 75-139100. 1996. 9.15 (*0-606-09484-9*, Pub. by Turtleback) Demco.

— Muhammad Ali. LC 76-12093. (Crowell Biography Ser.). (Illus.). 40p. (J). (gr. 1-4). 1976. lib. bdg. 12.89 (*0-690-01128-8*) HarpC Child Bks.

— Swiftest. (Illus.). 1966. 5.50 (*0-393-07443-9*) Norton.

— Wilt Chamberlain. LC 74-94800. (Crowell Biography Ser.). (Illus.). (J). (gr. 2-5). 1970. 11.74 (*0-690-89458-9*); lib. bdg. 11.89 (*0-690-01134-2*) HarpC Child Bks.

Rudeen, Louisa. Against the Sea: Great Adventure Stories from the Pages of Motorboating & Sailing. LC 98-22222. 288p. 1998. pap. 14.00 (*0-380-79861-1*, Avon Bks) Morrow Avon.

Rudel, Anthony, jt. auth. see Joel, Billy.

Rudel, Anthony J. Tales from the Opera. 379p. 1985. pap. 9.95 (*0-685-43051-0*, Fireside) S&S Trade Pap.

Rudel, Jaufre & Pickens, Rupert T. Songs of Jaufre Rudel. pap. text 38.29 (*0-88844-041-3*) Brill Academic Pubs.

Rudel, Rachel. Cooking Healthy & Fast. large type ed. 1994. 14.95 (*0-9642510-0-0*) Apple a Day.

Rudel, Rachel A. Cooking Healthy, Fast & Super Fast: Recipes & Helpful Hints for Cooks Who Don't Have Time to Cook Healthy. large type ed. 241p. 1994. pap. 9.96 (*0-9642510-1-9*) Apple a Day.

Rudel, Thomas K. & Horowitz, Bruce. Tropical Deforestation: Small Farmers & Land Clearing in the Ecuadorian Amazon. LC 92-44356. (Cases & Methods in Biological Diversity Ser.). 1993. pap. 28.00 (*0-231-08045-X*) Col U Pr.

— Tropical Deforestation: Small Farmers & Land Clearing in the Ecuadorian Amazon. LC 92-44356. (Cases & Methods in Biological Diversity Ser.). 1993. 58.50 (*0-231-08044-1*) Col U Pr.

Rudel, Weston W. Reflections. 1997. pap. 56.95 (*1-57553-588-2*) Watermrk Pr.

Rudell, Fredrica. Consumer Food Selection & Nutrition Information. LC 79-10149. (Praeger Special Studies). 167p. 1979. 47.95 (*0-275-90415-6*, C0415, Praeger Pubs) Greenwood.

Rudell, Michael I. Behind the Scenes: Practical Entertainment Law. LC 83-22201. 275p. 1984. 48.00 (*0-15-004363-5*) Harcourt.

Rudelle, Carla P. Butter - Analysis, Composition, Uses & Flavorings: Index of New Information with Authors, Subjects, Research Categories & References. rev. ed. 145p. (Orig.). 1997. 47.50 (*0-7883-1491-2*); pap. 44.50 (*0-7883-1492-0*) ABBE Pubs Assn.

Rudelle, Christian. Dictionnaire des Termes Juridiques. (FRE.). 221p. 1992. pap. 45.00 (*0-7859-8202-7*, 2883990662) Fr & Eur.

Rudelson, Justin. Oasis Identities: Uyghur Nationalism along China's Silk Road. LC 97-11066. (Illus.). 224p. 1998. pap. 17.50 (*0-231-10787-0*) Col U Pr.

— Oasis Identities: Uyghur Nationalism along China's Silk Road. LC 97-11066. (Illus.). 224p. 1998. 45.00 (*0-231-10786-2*) Col U Pr.

Rudelson, Justin Ben-Adam. Mandarin: Phrasebook. 4th ed. LC 97-109758. (CHI., Illus.). 250p. 1996. pap. 5.95 (*0-86442-344-6*) Lonely Planet.

Rudelson, Justin Ben-Adam, jt. auth. see Wistinetzki, Klara Ilane.

Rudelson, Justin J. Central Asia: Language Survival Kit. (Illus.). 240p. (Orig.). 1998. pap. 5.95 (*0-86442-419-1*) Lonely Planet.

***Ruden, Ronald A.** The Craving Brain: Achieving & maintaining the proper levels of serotonin & dopamine is the keyto breaking free from* dru*overeating* sm* gambdiction. 240p. 2000. pap. 13.00 (*0-06-092899-9*, Perennial) HarperTrade.

Ruden, Ronald A. & Byalick, Marcia. The Craving Brain: The BioBalance Approach to Controlling Addiction. LC 96-49607. 224p. 1997. 23.00 (*0-06-018698-4*) HarpC.

Ruden, Sanford I., jt. auth. see Cramer, Martin R.

Ruden, Sarah, tr. see Petronius.

Rudenberg, Reinhold. Electrical Shock Waves in Power Systems: Traveling Waves in Lumped & Distributed Circuit Elements. LC 68-14272. (Illus.). 350p. 1968. 43.00 (*0-674-24350-1*) HUP.

Rudenberg, Werner. Chinesisch-Deutsches Woerterbuch. 3rd ed. (CHI & GER.). 821p. 1963. 395.00 (*0-7859-8264-7*, 3110000202) Fr & Eur.

Rudenbush, G. D. The Estimation of Macroeconomic Disequilibruim Models with Regime Classification Information. (Lecture Notes in Economics & Mathematical Systems Ser.: Vol. 288). vii, 128p. 1987. 31.00 (*0-387-17757-4*) Spr-Verlag.

Rudenga, Liz, jt. auth. see Bergeron, Bette S.

Rudengren, Jan. Peasants by Preference? Socio-Economic & Environmental Aspects of Rural Development in Tanzania. 385p. 1981. write for info. (*91-7258-132-8*, Pub. by Nordic Africa) Transaction Pubs.

Rudenko, B. T. Grammatika Gruzinskogo Jazyka: Grammar of the Georgian Language. (Janua Linguarum, Series Anastatica: No. 7). 1972. pap. 57.70 (*3-10-800126-4*) Mouton.

***Rudenko, Innokenty.** Cisco Routers for IP Networking Black Book. LC 00-29055. 2000. write for info. (*1-57610-610-1*) Coriolis Grp.

Rudenko, Innokenty. Cisco Routers for IP Routing: Little Black Book. 1. LC 99-25844. 1999. pap. text 29.99 (*1-57610-421-4*) Coriolis Grp.

Rudenko, Mykola. The Cross. 1986. 10.00 (*0-318-21433-4*) St Sophia Religious.

Rudenko, Y. N., ed. Power Systems of East European Countries: Problems & Methods for Control & Development. LC 93-23936. 353p. 1993. 110.00 (*1-56700-013-4*) Begell Hse.

Rudenko, Y. N., jt. auth. see Melentiev, A.

Rudenko, Y. N., ed. see Izmailov, L. D., et al.

Rudenko, Y. N., ed. see Levin, L. I., et al.

Rudenko, Y. N., ed. see Sokolov, E. Y., et al.

Rudenko, Y. N., ed. see Zinger, N. M., et al.

Rudensky, Morris R. & Riley, Don. Gonif: Red Rudensky. LC 71-139587. 1970. 20.00 (*0-87832-002-4*) Piper.

Rudenstine, Angelica Z. The Guggenheim Museum Collection: Paintings 1880-1945, 2 vols. LC 75-37356. (Illus.). 1976. pap. 42.00 (*0-685-70089-5*) S R Guggenheim.

— The Guggenheim Museum Collection: Paintings 1880-1945, 2 vols., Set. LC 75-37356. (Illus.). 1976. 85.00 (*0-89207-002-1*) S R Guggenheim.

— Modern Painting, Drawing & Sculpture: Collected by Emily & Joseph Pulitzer, Jr., Vol. 4. (Catalog of the Emily & Joseph Pulitzer, Jr., Collection: Vol. IV). (Illus.). 372p. (Orig.). 1988. pap. 4.95 (*0-916724-67-0*, 4670) Harvard Art Mus.

Rudenstine, Angelica Z., jt. auth. see Rowell, Margit.

Rudenstine, David. The Day the Presses Stopped: A History of the Pentagon Papers Case. LC 95-44464. (Illus.). 278p. (C). 1996. 45.00 (*0-520-08672-4*, Pub. by U CA Pr) Cal Prin Full Svc.

— The Day the Presses Stopped: A History of the Pentagon Papers Case. 278p. 1998. pap. text 17.95 (*0-520-21382-3*, Pub. by U CA Pr) Cal Prin Full Svc.

Rudenstine, Neil, jt. auth. see Bowen, William.

Ruder, Cynthia A. Making History for Stalin: The Story of the Belomor Canal. LC 97-24059. 192p. 1998. 49.95 (*0-8130-1567-7*) U Press Fla.

Ruder, Hanns. Atoms in Strong Magnetic Fields: Quantum Mechanical Treatment & Applications in Astrophysics & Quantum Chaos. LC 94-23259. 1994. write for info. (*3-540-57699-1*) Spr-Verlag.

— Atoms in Strong Magnetic Fields: Quantum Mechanical Treatment & Applications in Astrophysics & Quantum Chaos. LC 94-23259. 1994. 79.95 (*0-387-57699-1*) Spr-Verlag.

Ruder, Jesse H. BASIC for the HP 3000. LC 85-12044. 240p. reprint ed. pap. 74.40 (*0-7837-2379-2*, 204006500006) Bks Demand.

Ruder, Linda N., ed. Enhancing Capacities & Confronting Controversies in Criminal Justice: Proceedings of the 1993 National Conference. 166p. (Orig.). (C). 1994. pap. text 45.00 (*0-7881-1376-3*) DIANE Pub.

Ruderman, Anne C. The Pleasures of Virtue: Political Thought in the Novels of Jane Austin. LC 95-32349. 214p. (C). 1995. pap. text 25.95 (*0-8476-8101-7*); lib. bdg. 65.00 (*0-8476-8100-9*) Rowman.

Ruderman, Arthur, jt. auth. see Ruderman, Larry.

Ruderman, David, jt. auth. see Hallo, William.

Ruderman, David, jt. ed. see Hallo, William.

***Ruderman, David B.** Jewish Enlightenment in an English Key: Anglo-Jewry's Construction of Modern Jewish Thought. LC 00-27869. (Illus.). 280p. 2000. 39.50 (*0-691-04883-5*) Princeton U Pr.

Ruderman, David B. Jewish Thought & Scientific Discovery in Early Modern Europe. LC 94-30520. 1995. 37.50 (*0-300-06112-9*) Yale U Pr.

— Kabbalah, Magic, & Science: The Cultural Universe of a Sixteenth-Century Jewish Physician. LC 87-35271. 256p. 1988. 44.50 (*0-674-49660-4*) HUP.

— The World of a Renaissance Jew: The Life & Thought of Abraham Ben Mordecai Farissol. LC 81-2551. (Monographs of the Hebrew Union College: No. 6). 283p. reprint ed. pap. 87.80 (*0-7837-2998-7*, 204294300006) Bks Demand.

Ruderman, David B., ed. Essential Paper on Jewish Culture in Renaissance & Baroque Italy. (Essential Papers in Jewish Studies). 512p. (C). 1992. text 75.00 (*0-8147-7419-9*); pap. text 27.50 (*0-8147-7420-2*) NYU Pr.

— Preachers of the Italian Ghetto. (C). 1992. 45.00 (*0-520-07735-0*, Pub. by U CA Pr) Cal Prin Full Svc.

Ruderman, David B., jt. ed. see Myers, David N.

Ruderman, Harry, ed. Mathematical Buds, Vol. I. (Illus.). 1978. pap. text 2.50 (*0-940790-01-7*) Mu Alpha Theta.

— Mathematical Buds, Vol. V. 1992. 2.50 (*0-940790-05-X*) Mu Alpha Theta.

Ruderman, Harry D. Tac-Tickle: Pure Strategy. 1966. 3.00 (*0-911624-06-6*) Wffn Proof.

Ruderman, Larry & Ruderman, Arthur. In-Store Signage Graphics: Connecting with Your Customer. (Illus.). 112p. 1998. pap. 24.95 (*0-944094-31-7*, 24) ST Pubns.

Ruderman, Marian N. & Ohlott, Patricia J. The Realities of Management Promotion. LC 93-43611. (Technical Reports: No. 157G). 52p. 1993. pap. 15.00 (*0-912879-88-2*) Ctr Creat Leader.

Ruderman, Marian N., et al. Managerial Promotion: The Dynamics for Men & Women. LC 95-52022. 28p. 1996. pap. text 15.00 (*1-882197-13-5*) Ctr Creat Leader.

— Selected Research on Work Team Diversity. LC 95-34408. 183p. 1996. pap. text 24.95 (*1-882197-08-9*) Ctr Creat Leader.

Ruderman, Marian N., jt. ed. see Jackson, Susan E.

Ruderman, Neil, et al, eds. Hyperglycemia, Diabetes & the Vascular Disease. (Clinical Physiology Series - An American Physiological Society Book). (Illus.). 320p. 1992. text 90.00 (*0-19-506773-8*) OUP.

Ruderman, Renee. Poems from the Rooms Below. LC 95-34861. (Illus.). 72p. (Orig.). 1995. pap. 11.95 (*0-938075-58-6*) Ocean View Bks.

Ruderman, S., ed. see Riley, R.

Ruderman, Terry J. Stanley M. Isaacs, the Conscience of New York. 1981. 38.95 (*0-405-14105-X*) Ayer.

Rudert, Eileen R. The Validity of Testing in Education & Employment. 192p. 1997. reprint ed. pap. text 40.00 (*0-7881-4590-8*) DIANE Pub.

Rudert, H. & Werner, J. A., eds. Lasers in Otorhinolaryngology, & in Head & Neck Surgery. (Advances in OtoRhinoLaryngology Ser.: Vol. 49). (Illus.). xii, 264p. 1995. 215.75 (*3-8055-6087-7*) S Karger.

Rudes, Blair A. Tuscarora-English - English-Tuscarora Dictionary. 496p. 1998. text 75.00 (*0-8020-4336-4*) U of Toronto Pr.

Rudestam, Kjell E. & Newton, Rae R. Surviving Your Dissertation: A Comprehensive Guide to Content & Process. 208p. (C). 1992. text 48.00 (*0-8039-4562-0*); pap. text 21.00 (*0-8039-4563-9*) Sage.

Rudestam, Kjell E., jt. auth. see Newton, Rae R.

***Rudestam, Kjell Erik & Newton, Rae R.** Surviving Your Dissertation: A Comprehensive Guide to Content & Process. LC 00-9854. 2000. pap. write for info. (*0-7619-1962-7*) Sage.

Rudge, A. W., et al, eds. The Handbook of Antenna Design, Vol. I. (Electromagnetic Waves Ser.: Nos. 15 & 16). 708p. 1983. boxed set 145.00 (*0-906048-82-6*, EW015) INSPEC Inc.

— The Handbook of Antenna Design, Vol. II. (Electromagnetic Waves Ser.: Nos. 15 & 16). 960p. 1983. boxed set 177.00 (*0-906048-87-7*, EW016) INSPEC Inc.

***Rudge, Bill.** The ABC's of False Teachings & Extreme Groups. expanded rev. ed. 54p. 1999. pap. 2.00 (*1-889809-10-1*) Liv Truth.

Rudge, Bill. Beware! Deception & Delusion in the Church. LC 96-78378. 1996. pap. write for info. (*1-889809-00-4*) Liv Truth.

— Conquering Stress Before it Conquers You. expanded ed. 24p. 2000. reprint ed. pap. 2.00 (*1-889809-12-8*) Liv Truth.

— Death, Dying, & Eternity. expanded rev. ed. 27p. 2000. pap. 2.00 (*1-889809-14-4*) Liv Truth.

— Faith Through the Fire. 37p. 2000. pap. 2.00 (*1-889809-07-1*) Liv Truth.

***Rudge, Bill.** Fasting for Sensitivity & Power. 56p. 1999. pap. 4.00 (*1-889809-05-5*) Liv Truth.

Rudge, Bill. The Last Days: What's Ahead for the Body of Christ, the Apostate Church, & the World. LC 98-65516. 120p. 1998. pap. 7.00 (*1-889809-02-0*) Liv Truth.

— Overcoming Sexual Immorality. expanded rev. ed. 42p. 2000. pap. 2.00 (*1-889809-13-6*) Liv Truth.

— Overcoming the Giants in Your Life. 73p. 1999. pap. 6.00 (*1-889809-08-X*) Liv Truth.

— Peer Pressure. 28p. 1996. pap. 2.00 (*1-889809-15-2*) Liv Truth.

— Reaching Your Maximum Potential in Christ. rev. ed. LC 98-65515. 144p. 1998. pap. 7.00 (*1-889809-01-2*) Liv Truth.

— Self-Defense from a Biblical Perspective. 50p. 2000. pap. 3.00 (*1-889809-09-8*) Liv Truth.

— Spiritual Warfare & Victory in Christ. expanded ed. 44p. 2000. reprint ed. pap. 5.00 (*1-889809-06-3*) Liv Truth.

— Strength Through Weakness. 48p. 1998. pap. 2.00 (*1-889809-04-7*) Liv Truth.

— Who Is This Jesus? Overwhelming Evidence for Those Who Want to Know the Real Truth! expanded ed. 60p. 1998. reprint ed. pap. 6.00 (*1-889809-03-9*) Liv Truth.

— Why I Quit Karate. 42p. 1994. pap. 3.00 (*1-889809-11-X*) Liv Truth.

***Rudge, Geraldine.** Garden Crafts: A Practical Guide to Creating Handcrafted Features for Your Garden. (Illus.). 160p. 2000. 35.00 (*1-58574-055-1*) Lyons Pr.

***Rudge, Janet & Nicol, F.** Cutting the Cost of Cold: Affordable Warmth for Healthier Homes. LC 00-21310. 2000. write for info. (*0-419-25050-6*, E & FN Spon) Routledge.

Rudge, M., jt. ed. see Crowe, A.

Rudge, Mary. Going to China - And Other Places. LC 87-60437. (Mucho Somos Ser.: No. 11). 32p. (Orig.). 1987. pap. 1.50 (*0-914370-56-1*) Mothers Hen.

***Rudgers, David F.** Creating the Secret State: The Origins of the Central Intelligence Agency, 1943-1947. LC 99-89870. 272p. 2000. text 35.00 (*0-7006-1024-3*) U Pr of KS.

Rudgley, Richard. The Encyclopedia of Psychoactive Substances. LC 98-51585. (Illus.). 320p. 1999. text 25.95 (*0-312-19868-X*) St Martin.

***Rudgley, Richard.** Encyclopedia of Psychoative Substances. (Illus.). 320p. 2000. pap. 15.95 (*0-312-26317-1*) St Martin.

Rudgley, Richard. Essential Substances: A Cultural History of Intoxicants in Society. Urda, John, ed. (Kodansha Globe Trade Paperback Ser.). (Illus.). 208p. 1995. pap. 12.00 (*1-56836-075-4*, Kodansha Globe) Kodansha.

— The Lost Civilizations of the Stone Age. LC 98-37079. 320p. 1998. 26.00 (*0-684-85580-1*) S&S Trade.

***Rudgley, Richard.** The Lost Civilizations of the Stone Age. 320p. 2000. per. 15.00 (*0-684-86270-0*) S&S Trade.

Rudhyar, Dane. The Astrological Houses: The Spectrum of Individual Experience. LC 74-180105. 208p. 1986. reprint ed. pap. 12.95 (*0-916360-24-5*) CRCS Pubns CA.

— Astrological Insights into the Spiritual Life. 154p. 1979. pap. 10.95 (*0-943358-09-4*) Aurora Press.

— Astrological Mandala: The Cycle of Transformations & Its 360 Symbolic Phases. 1974. pap. 12.00 (*0-394-71992-1*) Vin Bks.

— Astrological Triptych. 296p. 1978. pap. 14.00 (*0-943358-10-8*) Aurora Press.

— The Astrology of Personality. 445p. 1991. 21.95 (*0-943358-25-6*) Aurora Press.

Rudhyar, Dane. The Astrology of Transformation a Multilevel Approach. 230p. pap. 14.00 (*0-943358-49-3*) Aurora Press.

Rudhyar, Dane. Beyond Individualism: The Psychology of Transformation. LC 78-64906. 1979. pap. 4.75 (*0-8356-0518-3*, Quest) Theos Pub Hse.

— Culture, Crisis & Creativity. LC 76-43008. 1977. pap. 4.25 (*0-8356-0487-X*, Quest) Theos Pub Hse.

— The Galactic Dimension of Astrology. 214p. 1975. pap. 10.95 (*0-943358-13-2*) Aurora Press.

— The Lunation Cycle: A Key to the Understanding of Personality. 208p. 1986. pap. 16.95 (*0-943358-26-4*) Aurora Press.

— Person Centered Astrology. 385p. 1983. 14.00 (*0-943358-02-7*) Aurora Press.

— The Planetarization of Consciousness. (Dane Rudhyar Ser.). 318p. 1977. pap. 22.95 (*0-943358-16-7*) Aurora Press.

— Rhythm of Wholeness: A Total Affirmation of Being. LC 83-70689. 268p. 1983. pap. 7.50 (*0-8356-0578-7*) Theos Pub Hse.

Rudhyar, Dane, jt. auth. see Rael, Leyla.

***Rudi, Thomas.** Christian Philipp Koester, 1784-1851 Maler und Restaurator: Monographie Mit Kritischem Oeuvreverzeichnis. (Europaische Hochschulschriften, Reihe 28). 440p. 1999. 67.95 (*3-631-32446-4*) P Lang Pubng.

Rudich, Joe. Windows NT Server 5: The System Administrator's Guide. 556p. 1997. pap., pap. text 49.95 incl. cd-rom (*0-07-913285-5*) McGraw.

Rudich, Vasily. Dissidence & Literature under Nero: The Price of Rhetoricization. LC 96-32615. 408p. (C). 1997. 90.00 (*0-415-09501-8*) Routledge.

— Political Dissidence under Nero. LC 92-7604. 388p. (C). (gr. 13). 1993. 80.00 (*0-415-06951-3*; A7048) Routledge.

Rudick, Michael, jt. auth. see Raleigh, Walter.

Rudick, Michael, ed. see Ringler, William A., Jr.

Rudick, R. A., et al, eds. Treatment of Multiple Sclerosis: Trial Design, Results & Future Perspectives. (Clinical Medicine & the Nervous System Ser.). (Illus.). xviii, 313p. 1992. 150.00 (*0-387-19683-8*) Spr-Verlag.

Rudick, R. A., jt. ed. see Goodkin, D. E.

Rudick, Richard A. & Goodkin, Donald E. Treatment of Multiple Sclerosis: Trial Design, Results, & Future Perspectives. (Clinical Medicine & the Nervous System Ser.). 290p. 1991. 145.00 (*3-540-19683-8*) Spr-Verlag.

Rudie, Carol V. Discover Acts: Road to Rome - Leader. (Discover Your Bible Ser.). (Illus.). 49p. 1999. pap. 3.95 (*1-56212-400-5*, 1960-0555) CRC Pubns.

— Discover Acts: Road to Rome - Study. (Discover Your Bible Ser.). (Illus.). 28p. 1999. pap. 2.75 (*1-56212-401-3*, 1960-0550) CRC Pubns.

An Asterisk (*) at the beginning of an entry indicates that the title is appearing for the first time.

— Discover Acts: The Gentile Connection - Leader Guide. (Illus.). 94p. 1998. pap., teacher ed. 6.95 (*1-56212-372-6*, 1970-0545) CRC Pubns.
— Discover Acts: The Gentile Connection - Study Guide. 50p. 1998. pap. 4.25 (*1-56212-387-4*, 1960-0540) CRC Pubns.
— Discover Psalms: Hope When We're Hurting. (Discover Your Bible Ser.). 1995. pap., teacher ed. 3.95 (*1-56212-092-1*) CRC Pubns.
— Exodus: On the Way (Leader) 112p. 1998. pap. 6.95 (*1-56212-348-3*, 1960-0495) CRC Pubns.
Rudie, Carol Veldman. Discover Acts: The Early Church: Leader's Guide. 66p. 1998. pap., teacher ed. 4.95 (*1-56212-358-0*) CRC Pubns.
***Rudie, Carol Veldman.** Encuentros Espirituales. Pimentel, Alejandro, ed. Lumpuy, Luis Bernal, tr. (Animo! Ser.).Tr. of Close Encounters of a Spiritual Kind. (SPA.). 60p. 1999. 8.95 (*1-55883-116-9*) Libros Desafio.
— Exodus 1-15 Out of Oppression: Leader Guide. (Discover Your Bible Ser.). 112 p. 1997. pap., teacher ed. 6.45 (*1-56212-237-1*,) CRC Pubns.
— Exodus 1-15 Out of Oppression: Student Guide. (Discover Your Bible Ser.). 43p. pap., student ed. 3.95 (*1-56212-238-X*) CRC Pubns.
— Genesis - Abraham & Sarah: Leader Guide. (Discover Your Bible Ser.). 38p. pap., teacher ed. 6.45 (*1-56212-145-6*) CRC Pubns.
— Genesis - Creation to Abraham: Study Guide. (Discover Your Bible Ser.). 47p. pap., student ed. 2.95 (*1-56212-228-2*) CRC Pubns.
Rudie, Ingrid. Visible Women in East Coast Malay Society: On the Reproduction of Gender in Ceremonial, School & Market. 337p. 1994. 18.00 (*82-00-21919-4*) Scandnvan Univ Pr.
Rudig, Doug. Big Bend Adventure Guide. Pearson, John R. & Deckert, Frank J., eds. (Illus.). 32p. (Orig.). (J). (gr. k-6). 1983. pap. 2.00 (*0-912001-10-0*) Big Bend.
***Rudig, Wolfgang, ed.** Environmental Policy, 2 vols. LC 99-16004. (International Library of Comparative Public Policy). 1280p. 1999. write for info. (*1-85278-950-6*) E Elgar.
Rudig, Wolfgang, ed. Green Politics I - 1990. 386p. (C). 1991. 31.95 (*0-8093-1734-6*) S Ill U Pr.
— Green Politics II. 248p. 1993. pap. text 42.00 (*0-7486-0271-2*, Pub. by Edinburgh U Pr) Col U Pr.
Rudiger, G. Differential Rotation & Stellar Convection - Sun & Solar Type Stars. (Fluid Mechanics of Astrophysics & Geophysics Ser.). 328p. 1989. text 334.00 (*2-88124-066-6*) Gordon & Breach.
Rudiger, Horst. Goethe und Europa: Essays und Aufsatze 1944-1983. (Komparatistische Studien: Band 14). xiv, 331p. (C). 1990. lib. bdg. 26.15 (*3-11-011805-X*) De Gruyter.
— Wesen und Wandlungen des Humanismus. 323p. 1966. write for info. (*0-318-71278-4*) G Olms Pubs.
Rudiger, Margit. 388 Great Hairstyles. LC 97-51848. (Illus.). 128p. 1998. 12.95 (*0-8069-9401-0*) Sterling.
Rudiger, R., jt. auth. see Haensch, Guenther.
Rudikoff, Sonya. Ancestral Houses: Virginia Woolf & the Aristocracy. LC 99-26806. (Illus.). 328p. 1999. 35.00 (*0-930664-18-3*) SPOSS.
***Rudin.** A Cocktail History of America. 2001. write for info. (*0-15-100383-1*) Harcourt.
— Russian Petroleum Refinery Handbook. 214p. 1998. 189.00 (*1-56700-110-6*) Begell Hse.
Rudin, Leonid I. & Bramble, Simon K., eds. Investigative Image Processing, Vol. 2942. LC 96-69892. 190p. 1997. 56.00 (*0-8194-2344-0*) SPIE.
Rudin, Leonid I., et al. Investigative & Trial Image Processing: 13-14 July, 1995, San Diego, California LC 95-68582. vii, 262 p. 1995. write for info. (*0-8194-1926-5*) SPIE.
Rudin, A. James & Wilson, Marvin R., eds. A Time to Speak: The Evangelical-Jewish Encounter. LC 87-16770. 218p. (Orig.). reprint ed. pap. 67.60 (*0-7837-3187-6*, 204279100006) Bks Demand.
Rudin, Afred. The Elements of Polymer Science & Engineering. 2nd ed. LC 98-11623. (Illus.). 509p. 1998. boxed set 65.00 (*0-12-601685-2*) Acad Pr.
Rudin, Alfred. The Elements of Polymer Science & Engineering: An Introductory Text for Engineers & Chemists. 1982. text 81.00 (*0-12-601680-1*) Acad Pr.
***Rudin-Brasciu, Holly.** Grill Power: Everything You Need to Know to Make Great, Healthy Meals with Your Indoor Tabletop Electric Grill. (Illus.). 2000. pap. 19.95 (*1-928998-37-2*) Q V C Pubg.
Rudin, Catherine. Aspects of Bulgarian Syntax: Complementizers & WH Constructions. iv, 232p. (Orig.). 1986. pap. 22.95 (*0-89357-156-3*) Slavica.
Rudin, Catherine, jt. auth. see Gribble, Lyubomira P.
Rudin, Donald O. & Felix, Clara. Omega-3 Oils: Why You Can't Afford to Live Without Essential Oils. 224p. 1996. pap. 11.95 (*0-89529-721-3*, Avery) Penguin Putnam.
Rudin, Ernst. Tender Accents of Sound: Spanish in the Chicano Novel in English. 262p. (Orig.). 1996. pap. 22.00 (*0-927534-52-5*) Biling Rev-Pr.
Rudin, Jacob P. Very Truly Yours. 1971. 10.00 (*0-8197-0279-X*) Bloch.
***Rudin, Jacob P. & Abramson, Lillian S., eds.** Haggadah for Children: Their Family & Friends. (Illus.). 46p. (J). 1999. pap. 3.95 (*0-8197-0664-7*) Bloch.
Rudin, James, et al. Twenty Years of Jewish-Catholic Relations. 336p. (Orig.). 1986. pap. 11.95 (*0-8091-2762-8*) Paulist Pr.
Rudin, Jeremy R. & Papell, David. Macroeconomics: Study Guide. pap. 12.00 (*0-393-96590-2*) Norton.
Rudin, Josef. Psychotherapy & Religion. Reinecke, Elisabeth & Bailey, Paul C., trs. LC 68-12291. 258p. 1968. reprint ed. pap. 80.00 (*0-608-00880-X*, 206167400010) Bks Demand.
Rudin, M. E. Lectures on Set Theoretic Topology. LC 74-31124. (CBMS Regional Conference Series in Mathematics: No. 23). 76p. 1975. reprint ed. pap. 16.00 (*0-8218-1673-X*, CBMS/23) Am Math.
Rudin, Marcia R., ed. Cults on Campus: Continuing Challenge. 2nd rev. ed. 140p. (Orig.). 1996. pap. 12.00 (*0-931337-07-0*) Am Family Foun.
Rudin, Norah. Dictionary of Modern Biology. LC 96-24180. 1997. pap. 15.95 (*0-8120-9516-2*) Barron.
Rudin, Norah, jt. auth. see Inman, Keith.
Rudin-O'Brasky, Talia. The Patriarchs in Hebron & Sodom (Genesis 18-19) A Study of the Structure & Composition of a Biblical Story. (Jerusalem Biblical Studies: Vol. 2). (HEB.). 156p. 1982. pap. text 12.00 (*0-685-49415-2*, Pub. by Simor Ltd) Eisenbrauns.
Rudin, Ronald. Banking en Francais: The French Banks of Quebec, 1835-1925. (Social History of Canada Ser.: No. 38). 216p. 1985. pap. 10.95 (*0-8020-6579-1*); pap. text 27.50 (*0-8020-2560-9*) U of Toronto Pr.
— In Whose Interest? Quebec's Caisses Populaires, 1900-1945. 208p. (C). 1990. text 65.00 (*0-7735-0759-0*, Pub. by McG-Queens Univ Pr) CUP Services.
— Making History in Twentieth-Century Quebec. LC 98-150395. (Illus.). 270p. 1997. text 50.00 (*0-8020-0853-4*); pap. text 18.95 (*0-8020-7838-9*) U of Toronto Pr.
***Rudin, Stephen.** Body. 1999. 9.95 (*0-7611-1519-6*) Workman Pub.
Rudin, W. New Constructions of Functions Holomorphic in the Unit: Ball of C to the N Power. LC 86-1205. (CBMS Regional Conference Series in Mathematics: No. 63). 78p. 1986. pap. 19.00 (*0-8218-0713-7*, CBMS/63) Am Math.
Rudin, Walter. Fourier Analysis on Groups. (Classics Library). 296p. 1990. pap. 99.95 (*0-471-52364-X*) Wiley.
— Fourier Analysis on Groups. LC 62-12211. (INterscience Tracts in Pure & Applied Mathematics Ser.: No. 12). 295p. reprint ed. pap. 91.50 (*0-608-17414-9*, 205644400067) Bks Demand.
— Functional Analysis. 2nd ed. 448p. (C). 1991. 86.56 (*0-07-054236-8*) McGraw.
— Lectures on the Edge-of-the-Wedge Theorem. LC 73-145640. (CBMS Regional Conference Series in Mathematics: No. 6). 30p. 1971. pap. 16.00 (*0-8218-1655-1*, CBMS/6) Am Math.
— Principles of Mathematical Analysis. 3rd ed. (International Series in Pure & Applied Mathematics). 325p. (C). 1976. 90.94 (*0-07-054235-X*) McGraw.
— Real & Complex Analysis. 3rd ed. (Higher Mathematics Ser.). 483p. (C). 1986. 93.13 (*0-07-054234-1*) McGraw.
— The Way I Remember It. LC 96-27190. (History of Mathematics Ser.: Vol. 12). 191p. 1996. pap. 29.00 (*0-8218-0633-5*, HMATH/12) Am Math.
***Ruding, Eric.** Middle Management in Action: Practical Approaches to School Improvement. LC 00-28424. 2000. pap. write for info. (*0-415-23155-8*) Routledge.
Ruding, P. R. Experimental Endolymphatic Hydrops. (Illus.). 89p. 1988. pap. 29.00 (*90-5103-011-8*, Pub. by SPB Acad Pub) Balogh.
Rudinger, E., ed. see Bohr, Niels.
Rudinger, E., jt. ed. see Kalckar, J.
Rudinger, Joel. How to Bingo 75 Ways: A Complete Guide to American Bingo Patterns. (Bingo Guide Ser.: No. 1). 48p. 1976. pap. 4.00 (*0-918342-02-3*) Cambric.
— Lovers & Celebrations. (Orig.). 1984. pap. 7.95 (*0-918342-20-1*) Cambric.
Rudinger, Joel, ed. Cambric Poetry Project One. 1978. pap. 6.95 (*0-918342-06-6*) Cambric.
— Poetry Project, Vol. 4. (Poetry Projects Ser.). 104p. (Orig.). 1985. pap. 7.00 (*0-918342-22-8*) Cambric.
— Poetry Project CPP, Vol. 3. 128p. (Orig.). (C). 1983. pap. 7.95 (*0-918342-16-3*) Cambric.
Rudinger, Jonathan. Effective Pet Massage for Dogs: Manual. large type ed. (Illus.). 155p. 1998. mass mkt. 34.95 (*0-9664826-2-X*) Effective Pet.
Rudinow. Invitation to Critical Thinking. 3rd ed. (C). 1993. pap. text, teacher ed. 5.50 (*0-15-501628-8*) Harcourt Coll Pubs.
— Inviting Critical Thinking. 3rd ed. LC 93-77822. (C). 1993. pap. text 51.50 (*0-15-500374-7*, Pub. by Harcourt Coll Pubs) Harcourt.
Rudinow, Joel. Invitation to Critical Thinking. 4th ed. LC 98-72953. (Illus.). 304p. (C). 1998. pap. text 45.00 (*0-15-505562-3*, Pub. by Harcourt Coll Pubs) Harcourt.
— Invitation to Critical Thinking: Test Bank. 3rd ed. (C). 1994. text 40.00 (*0-15-501771-3*, Pub. by Harcourt Coll Pubs) Harcourt.
— LogicWorks. (C). 1994. pap. text, student ed. 17.00 (*0-15-501942-2*) Harcourt Coll Pubs.
Rudinsky, Joseph. Challenge of the Steppes: Roots of the Cold War. 10.00 (*0-8315-0070-0*) Speller.
Rudinsky, Norma L. Incipient Feminists: Women Writers in the Slovak National Revival. 285p. 1991. 27.95 (*0-89357-220-9*) Slavica.
Rudis, Deborah D., jt. auth. see DeGraaf, Richard M.
***Rudisill, J. J., et al.** The Boys Against the Girls. (Wimzie's House Bks.). 24p. (J). 1999. pap. 3.99 (*0-88724-515-3*, CD-4840) Carson-Dellos.
— Get in Shape, Jonas! (Wimzie's House Bks.). 24p. (J). 1999. pap. 3.99 (*0-88724-517-X*, CD-4841) Carson-Dellos.
— Horace's Hidden Pictures. (Wimzie's House Bks.). 32p. (J). 1999. pap. 2.99 (*0-88724-483-1*, CD-4851) Carson-Dellos.
— Jonas's Puzzles & Games. 32p. (J). 1999. pap. 2.99 (*0-88724-484-X*, CD-4852) Carson-Dellos.
— LouLou's Dot-to-Dot. 32p. (J). 1999. pap. 2.99 (*0-88724-485-8*) Carson-Dellos.
— LouLou's Lemonade Stand. (Wimzie's House Bks.). 24p. (J). 1999. pap. 3.99 (*0-88724-541-2*, CD-4847) Carson-Dellos.
— No More Chores. (Wimzie's House Bks.). 24p. (J). 1999. pap. 3.99 (*0-88724-542-0*, CD-4848) Carson-Dellos.
— Scaredy Cats. (Wimzie's House Bks.). 24p. (J). 1999. pap. 3.99 (*0-88724-518-8*, CD-4842) Carson-Dellos.
— Shaggy's Visit. (Wimzie's House Bks.). 24p. (J). 1999. pap. 3.99 (*0-88724-540-4*, CD-4846) Carson-Dellos.
— Welcome to Wimzie's House. (Wimzie's House Bks.). 24p. (J). 1999. pap. 3.99 (*0-88724-461-0*) Carson-Dellos.
— Wimzie's Alphabet. (Wimzie's House Bks.). 32p. (J). 1999. pap. 2.99 (*0-88724-513-7*, CD-4854) Carson-Dellos.
— Wimzie's Beach Trip. (Wimzie's House Bks.). 24p. (J). 1999. pap. 3.99 (*0-88724-543-9*, CD-4849) Carson-Dellos.
— Wimzie's Birthday Fun & Games. (Wimzie's House Bks.). 32p. 1999. pap. 2.99 (*0-88724-514-5*, CD-4855) Carson-Dellos.
— Wimzie's Mazes. (Wimzie's House Bks.). 32p. (J). 1999. pap. 2.99 (*0-88724-482-3*, CD-4850) Carson-Dellos.
Rudisill, Marianne, et al. Human Computer Interface Design: Success Cases, Emerging Methods & Real-World Context. LC 95-20362. 408p. 1995. pap. text 48.95 (*1-55860-310-7*) Morgan Kaufmann.
***Rudisill, Marie.** Fruitcake: Christmas Memories of Capote & Sook. 2000. 15.95 (*1-892514-81-8*) Hill St Pr.
***Rudisill, Marie & Simmons, James C.** The Southern Haunting of Truman Capote. LC 00-43087. (Illus.). 2000. write for info. (*1-58182-136-0*) Cumberland Hse.
Rudisill, Mary E. & Jackson, Andrew S. Theory & Application of Motor Learning. (Illus.). 175p. (C). 1992. write for info. (*0-9634528-0-0*) MacJR.
Rudisill, Richard. Mirror Image: The Influence of the Daguerreotype on American Society. LC 79-137880. 354p. reprint ed. pap. 109.80 (*0-608-12048-0*, 202467800038) Bks Demand.
***Ruditis, Paul.** Roswell Pop Quiz. 96p. (J). 2000. 4.99 (*0-7434-1199-4*, Pocket Pulse) PB.
Rudka, Andrzej & Mizsei, Kalman. East Central Europe Between Disintegration & Reintegration: Is CEFTA the Solution. 1995. write for info. (*0-913449-40-7*) Inst EW Stud.
Rudka, Andrzej, jt. auth. see Mizsei, Kalman.
Rudka, Andrzej, jt. ed. see Mizsei, Kalman.
Rudkin, Charles N., tr. see De Petit-Thouars, Abel.
Rudkin, David. The Saxon Shore. (Methuen Modern Plays Ser.). 52p. (C). 1988. pap. 8.95 (*0-413-14100-4*, A0255) Heinemann.
Rudkin, Olive D. Thomas Spence & His Connections. LC 65-26376. (Reprints of Economic Classics Ser.). 256p. 1966. reprint ed. 37.50 (*0-678-00178-2*) Kelley.
Rudkin, Tami. His Silhouette: Devotions to Help Your Prayer Life. 124p. 1998. pap. 10.00 (*0-939513-46-3*) Joy Pub SJC.
Rudko, Che. Hide-and-seek Hippo. (Illus.). 9p. (gr. k-3). 2000. bds. 4.99 (*1-57584-397-8*) Rdrs Digest.
***Rudko, Che.** Hungry Dinosaur. (Chompers Ser.). (Illus.). 9p. (gr. k-3). 2000. bds. 4.99 (*1-57584-396-X*) Rdrs Digest.
Rudko, Che. Mighty Joe Young. LC PZ7.M6995735Wal 1998. (Golden Look-Look Bks.). 24p. 1998. pap. 3.29 (*0-307-13183-1*, 13183, Goldn Books) Gldn Bks Pub Co.
— Rescue on Parrot Island. (Fisher-Price Magic Wheels Ser.). (Illus.). 12p. (J). (ps-1). 1999. bds. 7.99 (*1-57584-322-6*, Pub. by Rdrs Digest) Random.
***Rudko, Che.** Tricky Tiger. (Chompers Ser.). (Illus.). 9p. (gr. k-3). 2000. bds. 4.99 (*1-57584-394-3*) Rdrs Digest.
Rudko, Frances H. John Marshall & International Law: Statesman & Chief Justice, 280. LC 91-11333. (Contributions in Political Science Ser.: No. 280). 152p. 1991. 49.95 (*0-313-27932-2*, RJM/, Greenwood Pr) Greenwood.
— Truman's Court: A Study in Judicial Restraint, 45. LC 88-5664. (Contributions in Legal Studies: No. 45). 186p. 1988. 45.00 (*0-313-26316-7*, RTC/, Greenwood Pr) Greenwood.
Rudland, D. L. Effects of Cyclic & Dynamic Loading on the Fracture Resistance of Nuclear Piping Steels: Technical Report, October 1992-April 1996. 203p. 1997. per. 20.00 (*0-16-062799-0*) USGPO.
— Fracture Toughness Evaluations of TP304 Stainless Steel Pipes: Technical Report, January 1994-November 1996. 122p. 1997. per. 11.00 (*0-16-062810-5*) USGPO.
Rudland, S., et al, eds. Mammary Development & Cancer. LC 98-110810. (Biochemical Society Symposium Ser.: Vol. 63). (Illus.). 319p. (C). 1997. text 95.00 (*1-85578-087-9*, Pub. by Portland Pr Ltd) Ashgate Pub Co.
Rudler-Barnett, Carol S. & Suckley, Luann M. The Last Word in Medical Technology. 239p. 1985. pap. 28.95 (*0-316-76094-3*, Little Brwn Med Div) Lppncott W & W.
Rudler, Gustave, ed. see Racine, Jean.
Rudley, Marcia M., jt. auth. see Rudley, Otto C.
Rudley, Otto C. & Rudley, Marcia M. Philosophies, Missions, Goals. 82p. (C). 1990. pap. text 19.95 (*0-9626259-0-6*) Con Mar Pub.
Rudlin, John. The Commedia dell'Arte in the Twentieth Century. LC 93-13426. (Illus.). 288p. (gr. 13). 1994. pap. 22.99 (*0-415-04770-6*) Routledge.
***Rudlin, Pernille.** The History of Mitsubishi Corporation in London. LC 99-54970. 224p. 2000. 90.00 (*0-415-22872-7*) Routledge.
Rudloe, Jack. Easy Money. 1999. pap. write for info. (*0-670-28697-4*) Viking Penguin.
— Search for the Great Turtle Mother. LC 94-44849. (Illus.). 272p. 1995. 17.95 (*1-56164-072-7*) Pineapple Pr.
Rudloff, DeLoyd E., jt. auth. see Ainsworth, Jim T.
Rudloff, Michael & Schmeitzner, Mike. Solche Schadlinge Gibt Es Auch In Leipzig: Sozialdemokraten und die SED. 220p. 1997. 42.95 (*3-631-47385-0*) P Lang Pubng.
***Rudloff, Sandra.** Cooking with Your Kids. (Illus.). 144p. 2000. pap. 8.95 (*1-55867-250-8*, Nitty Gritty Ckbks) Bristol Pub Ent CA.
Rudloff, Sandra. Flexible Fare: Personalize Recipes with Countless Variations. (Illus.). 176p. 1999. pap. 12.95 (*1-55867-228-1*) Bristol Pub Ent CA.
***Rudloff, Sandra.** Pinch of Time: Meals in Less Than 30 Minutes. (Illus.). 128p. 2000. pap. 8.95 (*1-55867-251-6*, Nitty Gritty Ckbks) Bristol Pub Ent CA.
Rudloff, Thomas M. Ausgewahlte Rechtsfragen der Inkassounternehmen. (Europaische Hochschulschriften: Reihe 2: Bd. 2075). (GER.). 193p. 1996. pap. 42.95 (*3-631-30864-7*) P Lang Pubng.
Rudman. Allied Health Professions Admission Test (AHPAT) (Admission Test Ser.: ATS-99). 1994. pap. 23.95 (*0-8373-5099-9*) Nat Learn.
— ARRT Examination in Cardiovascular - Interventional Technology (CIT) (Admission Test Ser.: Vol. ATS-117). 1997. pap. 49.95 (*0-8373-5817-5*, ATS117) Nat Learn.
— ARRT Examination in Computed Tomography (CT) (Admission Test Ser.: ATS-116). pap. 49.95 (*0-8373-5816-7*) Nat Learn.
— ARRT Examination in Mammography (MAM) (Admission Test Ser.). Date not set. pap. 49.95 (*0-8373-5818-3*, ATS118) Nat Learn.
— California Achievement Test (CAT) (Admission Test Ser.: ATS-101). pap. 29.95 (*0-8373-5801-9*, ATS-101) Nat Learn.
— Foreign Medical Graduates Examination in Medical Science (FMGEMS), 2 pts. in 1 vol. (Admission Test Ser.: ATS-74). pap. 69.95 (*0-8373-5074-3*) Nat Learn.
— Geography. (Undergraduate Program Field Tests (UPFT) Ser.: Vol. UPFT-10). 1994. pap. 23.95 (*0-8373-6010-2*) Nat Learn.
— Given the Crime. 1998. mass mkt. 6.50 (*0-671-00152-3*) S&S Trade.
— Home Health Nurse. (Certified Nurse Examination Ser.). 1997. pap. 23.95 (*0-8373-6126-5*, CN26) Nat Learn.
— Inpatient Obstetric Nursing. (Certified Nurse Examination Ser.: CN-20). pap. 23.95 (*0-8373-6120-6*) Nat Learn.
— Low Risk Neonatal Nursing. (Certified Nurse Examination Ser.: CN-22). pap. 23.95 (*0-8373-6122-2*) Nat Learn.
— Magnetic Resonance Imaging Technologist (MRI) (Admission Test Ser.: ATS-115). pap. 49.95 (*0-8373-5815-9*) Nat Learn.
— Master Fire Supression Piping Contractor. (Career Examination Ser.: C-3765). 1985. pap. 23.95 (*0-8373-3765-8*) Nat Learn.
— National Dental Boards (NDB), Pt. I. (Admission Test Ser.: ATS-36A). 1996. pap. 49.95 (*0-8373-6955-X*) Nat Learn.
— National Veterinary Boards (NBE) (NVB), 3 pts. in 1 vol. (Admission Test Ser.: ATS-50). pap. 69.95 (*0-8373-5050-6*) Nat Learn.
— National Veterinary Boards (NBE) (NVB) Anatomy, Physiology, Pathology, Pt. 1. (Admission Test Ser.: ATS-50A). pap. 39.95 (*0-8373-6960-6*) Nat Learn.
— Neonatal Intensive Care Nursing. (Certified Nurse Examination Ser.: CN-25). pap. 23.95 (*0-8373-6125-7*) Nat Learn.
— Neonatal Nurse Practitioner. (Certified Nurse Examination Ser.: CN-21). pap. 23.95 (*0-8373-6121-4*) Nat Learn.
— OB/GYN Nurse Practitioner. (Certified Nurse Examination Ser.: CN-19). pap. 23.95 (*0-8373-6119-2*) Nat Learn.
— Reproductive Endocrinology/Infertility Nursing. (Certified Nurse Examination Ser.: CN-23). pap. 23.95 (*0-8373-6123-0*) Nat Learn.
— Respiratory Therapy Technician. (Career Examination Ser.: C-3422). 1994. pap. 29.95 (*0-8373-3422-5*) Nat Learn.
— U. S. Medical License Examination, 3 vols. in 1. (Admission Test Ser.: ATS-104). 1994. pap. 89.95 (*0-8373-5804-3*) Nat Learn.
— U. S. Medical Licensing Examination Step III: Patient Management. (Admission Test Ser.: ATS-104C). 1996. pap. 49.95 (*0-8373-6969-X*) Nat Learn.
— Writing. (College Board SAT II Subject Test Ser.). 1997. pap. 23.95 (*0-8373-6316-0*, SATII-16) Nat Learn.
Rudman, Andrew I., jt. ed. see Tulchin, Joseph S.
Rudman, Bernadette, jt. auth. see Bentley, Colin.
Rudman, Carol. Frames of Reference: How Men & Woman Can Overcome Communication Barriers - & Increase Their Effectiveness at Work. LC 95-30147. 208p. 1995. 22.95 (*1-56079-532-8*, Petersons Pacesetter) Petersons.
Rudman, Daniel, ed. Take It to the Hoop. (Illus.). 300p. (Orig.). 1980. 25.00 (*0-913028-80-0*) North Atlantic.
Rudman, David, jt. auth. see Shinde, Subhash.
Rudman, Gerald J., jt. auth. see Bergmann, Sherrel.
Rudman, Jack. Able Seaman. (Career Examination Ser.: C-1). 1994. pap. 29.95 (*0-8373-0001-0*) Nat Learn.
— Abnormal Psychology. (ACT Proficiency Examination Program Ser.: PEP-53). 1994. 39.95 (*0-8373-5928-7*); pap. 23.95 (*0-8373-5903-1*) Nat Learn.
— Abstract Reasoning. (General Aptitude & Abilities Ser.: CS-26). 1994. pap. 23.95 (*0-8373-6726-3*) Nat Learn.
— Account Clerk. (Career Examination Ser.: C-2). 1994. pap. 23.95 (*0-8373-0002-9*) Nat Learn.
— Account Clerk-Stenographer. (Career Examination Ser.: C-3220). 1994. pap. 23.95 (*0-8373-3220-6*) Nat Learn.
— Account Clerk-Typist. (Career Examination Ser.: C-3221). 1994. pap. 23.95 (*0-8373-3221-4*) Nat Learn.
— Accountant. (Career Examination Ser.: C-3). 1994. pap. 29.95 (*0-8373-0003-7*) Nat Learn.
— Accountant-Auditor. (Career Examination Ser.: C-4). 1994. pap. 34.95 (*0-8373-0004-5*) Nat Learn.
— Accountant-Auditor Trainee. (Career Examination Ser.: C-2993). 1994. pap. 27.95 (*0-8373-2993-0*) Nat Learn.

R

R

— Accountant I. (Career Examination Ser.: C-2966). 1994. pap. 29.95 (*0-8373-2966-3*) Nat Learn.

— Accountant II. (Career Examination Ser.: C-2967). 1994. pap. 34.95 (*0-8373-2967-1*) Nat Learn.

— Accountant III. (Career Examination Ser.: C-2968). 1994. pap. 34.95 (*0-8373-2968-X*) Nat Learn.

— Accountant IV. (Career Examination Ser.: C-2969). 1994. pap. 39.95 (*0-8373-2969-8*) Nat Learn.

— Accounting. (Regents College Proficiency Examination Ser.: Vol. 1). 43.95 (*0-8373-5451-X*) Nat Learn.

— Accounting. (Regents College Proficiency Examination Ser.: CPEP-1). 1994. pap. 23.95 (*0-8373-5401-3*) Nat Learn.

— Accounting: Advanced Accounting. (ACT Proficiency Examination Program Ser.: PEP-13). 1994. pap. 23.95 (*0-8373-5513-3*) Nat Learn.

— Accounting & Auditing Clerk. (Career Examination Ser.: C-5). 1994. pap. 23.95 (*0-8373-0005-3*) Nat Learn.

— Accounting & Business Practice, Sr. H. S. (Teachers License Examination Ser.: T-1). 1994. pap. 27.95 (*0-8373-8001-4*) Nat Learn.

— Accounting Assistant. (Career Examination Ser.: C-1071). 1994. pap. 27.95 (*0-8373-1071-7*) Nat Learn.

— Accounting Executive. (Career Examination Ser.: C-1072). 1994. pap. 34.95 (*0-8373-1072-5*) Nat Learn.

— Accounting I. (Regents External Degree Ser.: REDP-1). 1994. pap. 23.95 (*0-8373-5601-6*) Nat Learn.

— Accounting II. (Regents External Degree (REDP) Ser.: Vol. 2). 43.95 (*0-8373-5652-0*) Nat Learn.

— Accounting II. (Regents External Degree Ser.: REDP-2). 1994. pap. 23.95 (*0-8373-5602-4*) Nat Learn.

— Accounting III. (Regents External Degree (REDP) Ser.: Vol. 3). 43.95 (*0-8373-5653-9*) Nat Learn.

— Accounting III. (Regents External Degree Ser.: REDP-3). 1994. pap. 23.95 (*0-8373-5603-2*) Nat Learn.

— Accounting Machine Operator. (Career Examination Ser.: C-1073). 1994. pap. 23.95 (*0-8373-1073-3*) Nat Learn.

— Accounting Technician. (Career Examination Ser.: No. C-2252). 1994. pap. 27.95 (*0-8373-2252-9*) Nat Learn.

— Accounting Trainee. (Career Examination Ser.: C-6). 1994. pap. 23.95 (*0-8373-0006-1*) Nat Learn.

— Accounts Investigator. (Career Examination Ser.: C-1862). 1994. pap. 27.95 (*0-8373-1862-9*) Nat Learn.

— ACT Assessment Examination for College Entrance (ACT) (Admission Test Ser.: Vol. 44). 43.95 (*0-8373-5144-8*) Nat Learn.

— ACT Assessment Examination for College Entrance (ACT) (Admission Test Ser.: ATS-44). 1994. pap. 23.95 (*0-8373-5044-1*) Nat Learn.

— ACT Proficiency Examination Program (PEP) 1994. pap. write for info. (*0-8373-5500-1*) Nat Learn.

— Activities Aide. (Career Examination Ser.: C-3101). 1994. pap. 23.95 (*0-8373-3101-3*) Nat Learn.

— Activities Director. (Career Examination Ser.: C-2949). 1994. pap. 34.95 (*0-8373-2949-3*) Nat Learn.

— Activities Specialist. (Career Examination Ser.: C-1074). 1994. pap. 27.95 (*0-8373-1074-1*) Nat Learn.

— Actuarial Clerk. (Career Examination Ser.: C-2417). 1994. pap. 27.95 (*0-8373-2417-3*) Nat Learn.

— Actuary. (Career Examination Ser.: C-7). 1994. pap. 39.95 (*0-8373-0007-X*) Nat Learn.

— Addiction Counselor. (Career Examination Ser.: C-2150). 1994. pap. 29.95 (*0-8373-2150-6*) Nat Learn.

— Addiction Specialist. (Career Examination Ser.: C-1075). 1994. pap. 29.95 (*0-8373-1075-X*) Nat Learn.

— Addressing Machine Operator. (Career Examination Ser.: C-1892). 1994. pap. 23.95 (*0-8373-1892-0*) Nat Learn.

— Addressing Machine Supervisor. (Career Examination Ser.: C-1893). 1994. pap. 27.95 (*0-8373-1893-9*) Nat Learn.

— Addressograph Machine Operator. (Career Examination Ser.: C-1076). 1994. pap. 23.95 (*0-8373-1076-8*) Nat Learn.

— Adjudicator. (Career Examination Ser.: C-1087). 1994. pap. 39.95 (*0-8373-1087-3*) Nat Learn.

— Administrative Accountant. (Career Examination Ser.: C-1078). 1994. pap. 39.95 (*0-8373-1078-4*) Nat Learn.

— Administrative Aide. (Career Examination Ser.: C-8). 1994. pap. 27.95 (*0-8373-0008-8*) Nat Learn.

— Administrative Analyst. (Career Examination Ser.: C-2144). 1994. pap. 34.95 (*0-8373-2144-1*) Nat Learn.

— Administrative Assessor. (Career Examination Ser.: C-2596). 1994. pap. 34.95 (*0-8373-2596-X*) Nat Learn.

— Administrative Assistant. (Career Examination Ser.: C-9). 1994. pap. 27.95 (*0-8373-0009-6*) Nat Learn.

— Administrative Assistant I. (Career Examination Ser.: C-1848). 1994. pap. 27.95 (*0-8373-1848-3*) Nat Learn.

— Administrative Assistant II. (Career Examination Ser.: C-1849). 1994. pap. 29.95 (*0-8373-1849-1*) Nat Learn.

— Administrative Associate. (Career Examination Ser.: C-67). 1994. pap. 29.95 (*0-8373-0067-3*) Nat Learn.

— Administrative Attorney. (Career Examination Ser.: C-2597). 1994. pap. 39.95 (*0-8373-2597-8*) Nat Learn.

— Administrative Auditor of Accounts. (Career Examination Ser.: C-2598). 1994. pap. 39.95 (*0-8373-2598-6*) Nat Learn.

— Administrative Business Promotion Coordinator. (Career Examination Ser.: C-2599). 1994. pap. 39.95 (*0-8373-2599-4*) Nat Learn.

— Administrative Careers Examination. (Career Examination Ser.: C-69). 1994. pap. 27.95 (*0-8373-0069-X*) Nat Learn.

— Administrative Claim Examiner. (Career Examination Ser.: C-2600). 1994. pap. 29.95 (*0-8373-2600-1*) Nat Learn.

— Administrative Clerk. (Career Examination Ser.: C-2014). 1994. pap. 27.95 (*0-8373-2014-3*) Nat Learn.

— Administrative Clerk (U.S.P.S.) (Career Examination Ser.: C-2101). 1994. pap. 27.95 (*0-8373-2101-8*) Nat Learn.

— Administrative Consultant. (Career Examination Ser.: C-2089). 1994. pap. 34.95 (*0-8373-2089-5*) Nat Learn.

— Administrative Education Analyst. (Career Examination Ser.: C-3317). 1994. pap. 39.95 (*0-8373-3317-2*) Nat Learn.

— Administrative Engineer. (Career Examination Ser.: C-2601). 1994. pap. 34.95 (*0-8373-2601-X*) Nat Learn.

— Administrative Fire Alarm Dispatcher. (Career Examination Ser.: C-2602). 1994. pap. 34.95 (*0-8373-2602-8*) Nat Learn.

— Administrative Fire Marshal (Uniformed) (Career Examination Ser.: C-2603). 1994. pap. 44.95 (*0-8373-2603-6*) Nat Learn.

— Administrative Housing Inspector. (Career Examination Ser.: C-2604). 1994. pap. 39.95 (*0-8373-2604-4*) Nat Learn.

— Administrative Housing Manager. (Career Examination Ser.: C-1799). 1994. pap. 39.95 (*0-8373-1799-1*) Nat Learn.

— Administrative Housing Superintendent. (Career Examination Ser.: C-1800). 1994. pap. 34.95 (*0-8373-1800-9*) Nat Learn.

— Administrative Investigator. (Career Examination Ser.: C-1924). 1994. pap. 34.95 (*0-8373-1924-2*) Nat Learn.

— Administrative Labor Relations Specialist. (Career Examination Ser.: C-2027). 1994. pap. 44.95 (*0-8373-2027-5*) Nat Learn.

— Administrative Management Auditor. (Career Examination Ser.: No. C-3516). 1994. pap. 39.95 (*0-8373-3516-7*) Nat Learn.

— Administrative Manager. (Career Examination Ser.: C-1754). 1994. pap. 34.95 (*0-8373-1754-1*) Nat Learn.

— Administrative Officer. (Career Examination Ser.: C-1079). 1994. pap. 29.95 (*0-8373-1079-2*) Nat Learn.

— Administrative Officer I. (Career Examination Ser.: C-1850). 1994. pap. 29.95 (*0-8373-1850-5*) Nat Learn.

— Administrative Officer II. (Career Examination Ser.: C-1852). 1994. pap. 34.95 (*0-8373-1852-1*) Nat Learn.

— Administrative Park & Recreation Manager. (Career Examination Ser.: C-2606). 1994. pap. 39.95 (*0-8373-2606-0*) Nat Learn.

— Administrative Personnel Examiner. (Career Examination Ser.: C-70). 1994. pap. 39.95 (*0-8373-0070-3*) Nat Learn.

— Administrative Project Coordinator. (Career Examination Ser.: C-1080). 1994. pap. 34.95 (*0-8373-1080-6*) Nat Learn.

— Administrative Public Information Specialist. (Career Examination Ser.: C-2607). 1994. pap. 34.95 (*0-8373-2607-9*) Nat Learn.

— Administrative Secretary. (Career Examination Ser.: C-1081). 1994. pap. 27.95 (*0-8373-1081-4*) Nat Learn.

— Administrative Service Officer. (Career Examination Ser.: C-10). 1994. pap. 29.95 (*0-8373-0010-X*) Nat Learn.

— Administrative Services Clerk. (Career Examination Ser.: C-2869). 1994. pap. 27.95 (*0-8373-2869-1*) Nat Learn.

— Administrative Services Manager. (Career Examination Ser.: C-2712). 1994. pap. 34.95 (*0-8373-2712-1*) Nat Learn.

— Administrative Space Analyst. (Career Examination Ser.: No. C-3517). 1994. pap. 39.95 (*0-8373-3517-5*) Nat Learn.

— Administrative Staff Analyst. (Career Examination Ser.: C-1553). 1994. pap. 34.95 (*0-8373-1553-0*) Nat Learn.

— Administrative Superintendent of Buildings & Grounds. (Career Examination Ser.: C-1707). 1994. pap. 34.95 (*0-8373-1707-X*) Nat Learn.

— Administrative Superintendent of Highway Operations. (Career Examination Ser.: C-2608). 1994. pap. 39.95 (*0-8373-2608-7*) Nat Learn.

— Administrative Supervisor of Building Maintenance. (Career Examination Ser.: C-3617). 1994. pap. 34.95 (*0-8373-3617-1*) Nat Learn.

— Administrative Trainee. (Career Examination Ser.: C-1082). 1994. pap. 27.95 (*0-8373-1082-2*) Nat Learn.

— Administrator. (Career Examination Ser.: C-1077). 1994. pap. 29.95 (*0-8373-1077-6*) Nat Learn.

— Administrator I. (Career Examination Ser.: C-1769). 1994. pap. 29.95 (*0-8373-1769-X*) Nat Learn.

— Administrator II. (Career Examination Ser.: C-1691). 1994. pap. 34.95 (*0-8373-1691-X*) Nat Learn.

— Administrator III. (Career Examination Ser.: C-2175). 1994. pap. 39.95 (*0-8373-2175-1*) Nat Learn.

— Administrator IV. (Career Examination Ser.: C-2176). 1994. pap. 39.95 (*0-8373-2176-X*) Nat Learn.

— Admission Test Series. 1994. pap. write for info. (*0-8373-5000-X*) Nat Learn.

— Admissions Officer. (Career Examination Ser.: C-1083). 1994. pap. 29.95 (*0-8373-1083-0*) Nat Learn.

— Admitting Clerk. (Career Examination Ser.: C-71). 1994. pap. 23.95 (*0-8373-0071-1*) Nat Learn.

— Adult Nurse Practitioner. (Certified Nurse Examination Ser.: CN-1). 1994. 39.95 (*0-8373-6151-6*); pap. 23.95 (*0-8373-6101-X*) Nat Learn.

— Adult Nursing. (Regents College Proficiency Examination Ser.: Vol. 35). 43.95 (*0-8373-5485-4*) Nat Learn.

— Adult Nursing. (ACT Proficiency Examination Program (PEP) Ser.: Vol. 39). 43.95 (*0-8373-5589-3*) Nat Learn.

— Adult Nursing. (ACT Proficiency Examination Program Ser.: PEP-39). 1994. pap. 23.95 (*0-8373-5539-7*) Nat Learn.

— Adult Nursing. (Regents College Proficiency Examination Ser.: Vol. CPEP-35). 1994. pap. 23.95 (*0-8373-5435-8*) Nat Learn.

— Advanced Accounting. (ACT Proficiency Examination Program Ser.: PEP-13). 1994. 39.95 (*0-8373-5563-X*) Nat Learn.

— Advanced Spelling. (General Aptitude & Abilities Ser.: Vol. CS-54). 1997. pap. 19.95 (*0-8373-6754-9*) Nat Learn.

— Aerospace Engineer. (Career Examination Ser.: C-72). 1994. pap. 34.95 (*0-8373-0072-X*) Nat Learn.

— Affirmative Action Officer. (Career Examination Ser.: C-2647). 1994. pap. 29.95 (*0-8373-2647-8*) Nat Learn.

— Affirmative Action Specialist. (Career Examination Ser.: C-2581). 1991. pap. 29.95 (*0-8373-2581-1*) Nat Learn.

— African & Afro-American History. (ACT Proficiency Examination Program (PEP) Ser.: Vol. 1). 43.95 (*0-8373-5551-6*) Nat Learn.

— African & Afro-American History. (Regents College Proficiency Examination Ser.: Vol. 36). 43.95 (*0-8373-5486-2*) Nat Learn.

— African & Afro-American History. (ACT Proficiency Examination Program Ser.: PEP-1). 1994. pap. 23.95 (*0-8373-5501-X*) Nat Learn.

— African & Afro-American History. (Regents College Proficiency Examination Ser.: Vol. CPEP-36). 1994. pap. 23.95 (*0-8373-5436-6*) Nat Learn.

— Afro-American History. (College Level Examination Ser.: CLEP-36). 1994. 39.95 (*0-8373-5386-6*); pap. 23.95 (*0-8373-5336-X*) Nat Learn.

— Aging Services Representative. (Career Examination Ser.: C-2880). 1994. pap. 27.95 (*0-8373-2880-2*) Nat Learn.

— Agriculture. (National Teacher Examination Ser.: NT-20). 1994. pap. 23.95 (*0-8373-8430-3*) Nat Learn.

— AIDS Counselor. (Career Examination Ser.: C-3619). 1994. pap. 29.95 (*0-8373-3619-8*) Nat Learn.

— Air Conditioning & Refrigeration. (Occupational Competency Examination (OCE) Ser.: Vol. 1). 47.95 (*0-8373-5751-9*) Nat Learn.

— Air Conditioning & Refrigeration. (Occupational Competency Examination Ser.: OCE-1). 1994. pap. 27.95 (*0-8373-5701-2*) Nat Learn.

— Air Conditioning, Heating & Refrigeration Mechanic. (Career Examination Ser.: C-73). 1994. pap. 29.95 (*0-8373-0073-8*) Nat Learn.

— Air Pollution Control Chemist. (Career Examination Ser.: C-1084). 1994. pap. 29.95 (*0-8373-1084-9*) Nat Learn.

— Air Pollution Control Engineer. LC 94-38034. (Career Examination Ser.: C-76). 1994. pap. 34.95 (*0-8373-0076-2*) Nat Learn.

— Air Pollution Control Engineering Trainee. (Career Examination Ser.: C-1926). 1994. pap. 27.95 (*0-8373-1926-9*) Nat Learn.

— Air Pollution Control Technician. (Career Examination Ser.: C-1085). 1991. pap. 29.95 (*0-8373-1085-7*) Nat Learn.

— Air Pollution Inspector. (Career Examination Ser.: C-11). 1994. pap. 29.95 (*0-8373-0011-8*) Nat Learn.

— Air Pollution Laboratory Maintainer. (Career Examination Ser.: C-1086). 1994. pap. 29.95 (*0-8373-1086-5*) Nat Learn.

— Air Traffic Control Specialist (ATCS) (Career Examination Ser.: C-68). 1994. pap. 29.95 (*0-8373-0068-1*) Nat Learn.

— Airbrake Maintainer. (Career Examination Ser.: C-12). 1994. pap. 23.95 (*0-8373-0012-6*) Nat Learn.

— Airframe or Powerplant Mechanics. (Occupational Competency Examination Ser.: OCE-2). 1994. pap. 27.95 (*0-8373-5702-0, OCE-2*) Nat Learn.

— Airport Attendant. (Career Examination Ser.: C-306). 1994. pap. 23.95 (*0-8373-0306-0*) Nat Learn.

— Airport Maintenance Supervisor. (Career Examination Ser.: C-3381). 1994. pap. 27.95 (*0-8373-3381-4*) Nat Learn.

— Airport Security Guard. (Career Examination Ser.: C-456). 1994. pap. 23.95 (*0-8373-0456-3*) Nat Learn.

— Airport Security Supervisor. (Career Examination Ser.: C-2153). 1994. pap. 29.95 (*0-8373-2153-0*) Nat Learn.

— Airport Supervisor. (Career Examination Ser.: C-3219). 1994. pap. 29.95 (*0-8373-3219-2*) Nat Learn.

— Alcoholism Counselor. (Career Examination Ser.: C-2145). 1994. pap. 29.95 (*0-8373-2145-X*) Nat Learn.

— Alcoholism Rehabilitation Consultant. (Career Examination Ser.: C-2772). 1994. pap. 29.95 (*0-8373-2772-5*) Nat Learn.

— Allied Health Aptitude Tests (AHAT) (Admission Test Ser.: ATS-78). 1994. pap. 23.95 (*0-8373-5078-6*) Nat Learn.

— Allied Health Entrance Examination (AHEE) (Admission Test Ser.: ATS-79). 1994. pap. 23.95 (*0-8373-5079-4*) Nat Learn.

— Allied Health Professions Admission Test (AHPAT) (Admission Test Ser.: Vol. 99). 43.95 (*0-8373-5199-5*) Nat Learn.

— Alphabetic Key Punch Operator, (IBM) (Career Examination Ser.: C-13). 1994. pap. 23.95 (*0-8373-0013-4*) Nat Learn.

— Ambulance Attendant. (Career Examination Ser.: C-1088). 1994. pap. 29.95 (*0-8373-1088-1*) Nat Learn.

— Ambulance Corpsman. (Career Examination Ser.: C-2650). 1994. pap. 29.95 (*0-8373-2650-8*) Nat Learn.

— Ambulance Driver. (Career Examination Ser.: C-1089). 1994. pap. 27.95 (*0-8373-1089-X*) Nat Learn.

— Ambulatory Women's Health Care Nursing. (Certified Nurse Examination Ser.: CN-24). pap. 23.95 (*0-8373-6124-9*) Nat Learn.

— American Government. (College Level Examination (CLEP) Ser.: Vol. 1). 43.95 (*0-8373-5351-3*) Nat Learn.

— American Government. (Regents College Proficiency Examination Ser.: Vol. 2). 43.95 (*0-8373-5452-8*) Nat Learn.

— American Government. (Regents College Proficiency Examination Ser.: CPEP-2). 1994. pap. 23.95 (*0-8373-5402-1*) Nat Learn.

— American Government. (College Level Examination (CLEP) Ser.: Vol. CLEP-1). 1994. pap. 23.95 (*0-8373-5301-7*) Nat Learn.

— American History. (College Level Examination (CLEP) Ser.: Vol. 2). 43.95 (*0-8373-5352-1*) Nat Learn.

— American History. (Regents College Proficiency Examination Ser.: Vol. 3). 43.95 (*0-8373-5453-6*) Nat Learn.

— American History. (College Level Examination Ser.: CLEP-2). 1994. pap. 23.95 (*0-8373-5302-5*) Nat Learn.

— American History. (Regents College Proficiency Examination Ser.: Vol. CPEP-3). 1994. pap. 23.95 (*0-8373-5403-X*) Nat Learn.

— American Literature. (College Level Examination (CLEP) Ser.: Vol. 3). 43.95 (*0-8373-5353-X*) Nat Learn.

— American Literature. (Regents College Proficiency Examination Ser.: Vol. 4). 43.95 (*0-8373-5454-4*) Nat Learn.

— American Literature. (College Level Examination Ser.: CLEP-3). 1994. pap. 23.95 (*0-8373-5303-3*) Nat Learn.

— American Literature. (Regents College Proficiency Examination Ser.: Vol. CPEP-4). 1994. pap. 23.95 (*0-8373-5404-8*) Nat Learn.

— American Literature: Civil War to the Present. (Regents College Proficiency Examination Ser.: Vol. 27). 43.95 (*0-8373-5477-3*) Nat Learn.

— American Literature: Civil War to the Present. (Regents College Proficiency Examination Ser.: CPEP-27). 1994. pap. 23.95 (*0-8373-5427-7*) Nat Learn.

— American Literature: The Beginnings to the Civil War. (ACT Proficiency Examination Program (PEP) Ser.: Vol. 2). 43.95 (*0-8373-5552-4*) Nat Learn.

— American Literature: The Beginnings to the Civil War. (Regents College Proficiency Examination Ser.: Vol. 26). 43.95 (*0-8373-5476-5*) Nat Learn.

— American Literature: The Beginnings to the Civil War. (Regents College Proficiency Examination Ser.: CPEP-26). 1994. pap. 23.95 (*0-8373-5426-9*) Nat Learn.

— American Literature: The Beginnings to the Civil War. (ACT Proficiency Examination Program (PEP) Ser.: Vol. PEP-2). 1994. pap. 23.95 (*0-8373-5502-8*) Nat Learn.

— American Literature: The Civil War to the Present. (ACT Proficiency Examination Program (PEP) Ser.: Vol. 3). 43.95 (*0-8373-5553-2*) Nat Learn.

— American Literature: The Civil War to the Present. (ACT Proficiency Examination Program Ser.: PEP-3). 1994. pap. 23.95 (*0-8373-5503-6*) Nat Learn.

— AMRA-AHIMA Medical Record Administrator National Registration Examination (RRA) (Admission Test Ser.: Vol. 84). 49.95 (*0-8373-5184-7*) Nat Learn.

— AMRA-AHIMA Medical Record Technician National Registration Examination (ART) (Admission Test Ser.: Vol. 85). 49.95 (*0-8373-5185-5*) Nat Learn.

— AMRA/AHIMA Medical Record Administrator National Registration Examination (RRA) (Admission Test Ser.: ATS-84). 1994. pap. 29.95 (*0-8373-5084-0*) Nat Learn.

— AMRA/AHIMA Medical Record Technician National Registration Examination (ART) (Admission Test Ser.: ATS-85). 1994. pap. 29.95 (*0-8373-5085-9*) Nat Learn.

— Analysis & Interpretation of Literature. (College Level Examination Ser.: CLEP-4). 1994. pap. 23.95 (*0-8373-5304-1*) Nat Learn.

— Anatomy & Physiology. (Regents College Proficiency Examination Ser.: Vol. 37). 43.95 (*0-8373-5487-0*) Nat Learn.

— Anatomy & Physiology. (ACT Proficiency Examination Program Ser.: PEP-4). 1994. pap. 23.95 (*0-8373-5504-4*) Nat Learn.

— Anatomy & Physiology. (Regents College Proficiency Examination Ser.: Vol. CPEP-37). 1994. pap. 23.95 (*0-8373-5437-4*) Nat Learn.

— Anatomy, Physiology & Microbiology. (College Level Examination Ser.: CLEP-38). 1994. pap. 23.95 (*0-8373-5338-6*) Nat Learn.

— Anatomy, Physiology, & Microbiology. (College Level Examination (CLEP) Ser.: Vol. 38). 43.95 (*0-8373-5388-2*) Nat Learn.

— Anesthesiologist. (Career Examination Ser.: C-1090). 1994. pap. 49.95 (*0-8373-1090-3*) Nat Learn.

— Animal Caretaker. (Career Examination Ser.: C-1091). 1994. pap. 23.95 (*0-8373-1091-1*) Nat Learn.

— Animal Health Aide. (Career Examination Ser.: C-75). 1994. pap. 29.95 (*0-8373-0075-4*) Nat Learn.

— Animal Health Technician Licensing Examination. (Career Examination Ser.: C-3039). 1994. pap. 39.95 (*0-8373-3039-4*) Nat Learn.

— Animal Shelter Officer. (Career Examination Ser.: C-2361). 1994. pap. 23.95 (*0-8373-2361-4*) Nat Learn.

— Animal Shelter Supervisor. (Career Examination Ser.: C-2363). 1994. pap. 29.95 (*0-8373-2363-0*) Nat Learn.

— Animal Warden. (Career Examination Ser.: C-1844). 1994. pap. 23.95 (*0-8373-1844-0*) Nat Learn.

— Announcer. (Career Examination Ser.: C-14). 1994. pap. 29.95 (*0-8373-0014-2*) Nat Learn.

— Appliance Repair. (Occupational Competency Examination (OCE) Ser.: Vol. 3). 47.95 (*0-8373-5753-5*) Nat Learn.

— Appliance Repair. (Occupational Competency Examination Ser.: OCE-3). 1994. pap. 27.95 (*0-8373-5703-9*) Nat Learn.

— Appraisal Investigator. (Career Examination Ser.: C-452). 1994. pap. 29.95 (*0-8373-0452-0*) Nat Learn.

— Appraiser. (Career Examination Ser.: C-15). 1994. pap. 23.95 (*0-8373-0015-0*) Nat Learn.

— Apprentice. (Career Examination Ser.: C-16). 1994. pap. 23.95 (*0-8373-0016-9*) Nat Learn.

— Architect. (Career Examination Ser.: C-17). 1994. pap. 39.95 (*0-8373-0017-7*) Nat Learn.

— Architectural Drafting. (Occupational Competency Examination Ser.: OCE-4). 1994. pap. 27.95 (*0-8373-5704-7*) Nat Learn.

— Architectural Draftsman. (Career Examination Ser.: C-1092). 1994. pap. 27.95 (*0-8373-1092-X*) Nat Learn.

— Architectural Estimator. (Career Examination Ser.: C-3114). 1994. pap. 34.95 (*0-8373-3114-5*) Nat Learn.

— Architectural Specifications Writer. (Career Examination Ser.: C-3222). 1994. pap. 34.95 (*0-8373-3222-2*) Nat Learn.

An Asterisk (*) at the beginning of an entry indicates that the title is appearing for the first time.

— Area Examination - Biological Sciences. (Graduate Record Examination (GRE) Ser.: Vol. 41). 43.95 (*0-8373-5291-6*) Nat Learn.
— Area Maintenance Technician (USPS) (Career Examination Ser.: C-3429). 1994. pap. 27.95 (*0-8373-3429-2*) Nat Learn.
— Area Services Coordinator. (Career Examination Ser.: C-18). 1994. pap. 34.95 (*0-8373-0018-5*) Nat Learn.
— Armature Winder. (Career Examination Ser.: C-2481). 1994. pap. 29.95 (*0-8373-2481-5*) Nat Learn.
— Armed Forces Tests (AFT-ASVAB) (Admission Test Ser.: Vol. 34). 49.95 (*0-8373-5134-0*) Nat Learn.
— Armed Forces Tests (AFT-ASVAB) (Admission Test Ser.: ATS-34). 1994. pap. 29.95 (*0-8373-5034-4*) Nat Learn.
— Art Education. (National Teacher Examination Ser.: NT-13). 1994. pap. 23.95 (*0-8373-8423-0*) Nat Learn.
— Art History. (Undergraduate Program Field Tests (UPFT) Ser.: Vol. 1). 43.95 (*0-8373-6051-X*) Nat Learn.
— Art History. (Undergraduate Program Field Tests Ser.: UPFT-1). 1994. pap. 23.95 (*0-8373-6001-3*) Nat Learn.
— Art History. (Advanced Placement Test (AP) Ser.: Vol. AP-1). 1997. pap. 23.95 (*0-8373-6201-6*) Nat Learn.
— Art of the Western World. (Dantes Subject Standardized Tests Ser.: DANTES-61). pap. 23.95 (*0-8373-6661-5*) Nat Learn.
— Asphalt Worker. (Career Examination Ser.: C-19). 1994. pap. 23.95 (*0-8373-0019-3*) Nat Learn.
— Assessment Aide. (Career Examination Ser.: C-2180). 1994. pap. 23.95 (*0-8373-2180-8*) Nat Learn.
— Assessment & Tax Accounting Supervisor. (Career Examination Ser.: C-3270). 1994. pap. 39.95 (*0-8373-3270-2*) Nat Learn.
— Assessment Assistant. (Career Examination Ser.: C-2181). 1994. pap. 23.95 (*0-8373-2181-6*) Nat Learn.
— Assessment Clerk. (Career Examination Ser.: C-2920). 1994. pap. 19.95 (*0-8373-2920-5*) Nat Learn.
— Assessor. (Career Examination Ser.: C-20). 1994. pap. 23.95 (*0-8373-0020-7*) Nat Learn.
— Assets Analyst. (Career Examination Ser.: C-1851). 1994. pap. 27.95 (*0-8373-1851-3*) Nat Learn.
— Assistant Accountant. (Career Examination Ser.: C-21). 1994. pap. 27.95 (*0-8373-0021-5*) Nat Learn.
— Assistant Accountant-Auditor. (Career Examination Ser.: C-2077). 1994. pap. 27.95 (*0-8373-2077-1*) Nat Learn.
— Assistant Actuary. (Career Examination Ser.: C-22). 1994. pap. 34.95 (*0-8373-0022-3*) Nat Learn.
— Assistant Administrative Director. (Teachers License Examination (TLE) Ser.: S-12). 1994. pap. 49.95 (*0-8373-8112-6*) Nat Learn.
— Assistant Administrator. (Career Examination Ser.: C-1093). 1994. pap. 27.95 (*0-8373-1093-8*) Nat Learn.
— Assistant Air Pollution Control Engineer. (Career Examination Ser.: C-1094). 1994. pap. 29.95 (*0-8373-1094-6*) Nat Learn.
— Assistant Architect. (Career Examination Ser.: C-77). 1994. pap. 34.95 (*0-8373-0077-0*) Nat Learn.
— Assistant Architectural Draftsman. (Career Examination Ser.: C-1095). 1994. pap. 27.95 (*0-8373-1095-4*) Nat Learn.
— Assistant Area Manager. (Career Examination Ser.: C-1096). 1994. pap. 29.95 (*0-8373-1096-2*) Nat Learn.
— Assistant Area Manager of School Maintenance. (Career Examination Ser.: No. C-3523). 1994. pap. 29.95 (*0-8373-3523-X*) Nat Learn.
— Assistant Area Services Coordinator. (Career Examination Ser.: C-78). 1994. pap. 29.95 (*0-8373-0078-9*) Nat Learn.
— Assistant Assessor. (Career Examination Ser.: C-23). 1994. pap. 23.95 (*0-8373-0023-1*) Nat Learn.
— Assistant Attorney. (Career Examination Ser.: C-24). 1994. pap. 34.95 (*0-8373-0024-X*) Nat Learn.
— Assistant Automotive Shop Supervisor. (Career Examination Ser.: C-529). 1994. pap. 27.95 (*0-8373-0529-2*) Nat Learn.
— Assistant Bacteriologist. (Career Examination Ser.: C-25). 1994. pap. 27.95 (*0-8373-0025-8*) Nat Learn.
— Assistant Bridge & Tunnel Maintainer. (Career Examination Ser.: C-27). 1994. pap. 23.95 (*0-8373-0027-4*) Nat Learn.
— Assistant Bridge Operator. (Career Examination Ser.: C-26). 1994. pap. 27.95 (*0-8373-0026-6*) Nat Learn.
— Assistant Bridge Operator Trainee. (Career Examination Ser.: C-79). 1994. pap. 23.95 (*0-8373-0079-7*) Nat Learn.
— Assistant Budget Analyst. (Career Examination Ser.: C-1736). 1994. pap. 34.95 (*0-8373-1736-3*) Nat Learn.
— Assistant Budget Director. (Career Examination Ser.: C-2991). 1994. pap. 39.95 (*0-8373-2991-4*) Nat Learn.
— Assistant Budget Examiner. (Career Examination Ser.: C-28). 1994. pap. 29.95 (*0-8373-0028-2*) Nat Learn.
— Assistant Building Construction Engineer. (Career Examination Ser.: C-3169). 1994. pap. 29.95 (*0-8373-3169-2*) Nat Learn.
— Assistant Building Custodian. (Career Examination Ser.: C-66). 1994. pap. 23.95 (*0-8373-0066-5*) Nat Learn.
— Assistant Building Electrical Engineer. (Career Examination Ser.: C-1909). 1994. pap. 29.95 (*0-8373-1909-9*) Nat Learn.
— Assistant Building Mechanical Engineer. (Career Examination Ser.: C-2570). 1994. pap. 29.95 (*0-8373-2570-6*) Nat Learn.
— Assistant Building Structural Engineer. (Career Examination Ser.: C-2567). 1994. pap. 34.95 (*0-8373-2567-6*) Nat Learn.
— Assistant Buildings Superintendent. (Career Examination Ser.: C-1097). 1994. pap. 29.95 (*0-8373-1097-0*) Nat Learn.
— Assistant Business Manager. (Career Examination Ser.: C-528). 1994. pap. 29.95 (*0-8373-0528-4*) Nat Learn.
— Assistant Business Officer. (Career Examination Ser.: C-2075). 1994. pap. 29.95 (*0-8373-2075-5*) Nat Learn.
— Assistant Buyer. (Career Examination Ser.: C-29). 1994. pap. 23.95 (*0-8373-0029-0*) Nat Learn.
— Assistant Captain. (Career Examination Ser.: No. C-3524). 1994. pap. 29.95 (*0-8373-3524-8*) Nat Learn.
— Assistant Cashier. (Career Examination Ser.: C-30). 1994. pap. 19.95 (*0-8373-0030-4*) Nat Learn.
— Assistant Chemical Engineer. (Career Examination Ser.: C-31). 1994. pap. 29.95 (*0-8373-0031-2*) Nat Learn.
— Assistant Chemist. (Career Examination Ser.: C-32). 1994. pap. 27.95 (*0-8373-0032-0*) Nat Learn.
— Assistant Civil Engineer. (Career Examination Ser.: C-33). 1994. pap. 29.95 (*0-8373-0033-9*) Nat Learn.
— Assistant Civil Engineer (Structures) (Career Examination Ser.: C-1910). 1994. pap. 34.95 (*0-8373-1910-2*) Nat Learn.
— Assistant Claims Examiner. (Career Examination Ser.: C-1098). 1994. pap. 27.95 (*0-8373-1098-9*) Nat Learn.
— Assistant Clerk. (Career Examination Ser.: C-1099). 1994. pap. 19.95 (*0-8373-1099-7*) Nat Learn.
— Assistant Community Development Project Supervisor. (Career Examination Ser.: C-907). 1994. pap. 34.95 (*0-8373-0907-7*) Nat Learn.
— Assistant Community Organization Specialist (Urban Renewal) (Career Examination Ser.: C-1100). 1994. pap. 29.95 (*0-8373-1100-4*) Nat Learn.
— Assistant Cook. (Career Examination Ser.: C-1101). 1994. pap. 27.95 (*0-8373-1101-2*) Nat Learn.
— Assistant Coordinator of Volunteer Services. (Career Examination Ser.: C-3140). 1994. pap. 29.95 (*0-8373-3140-4*) Nat Learn.
— Assistant Court Clerk. (Career Examination Ser.: C-34). 1994. pap. 27.95 (*0-8373-0034-7*) Nat Learn.
— Assistant Custodial Work Supervisor. (Career Examination Ser.: C-2916). 1994. pap. 27.95 (*0-8373-2916-7*) Nat Learn.
— Assistant Custodian. (Career Examination Ser.: C-35). 1994. pap. 23.95 (*0-8373-0035-5*) Nat Learn.
— Assistant Custodian-Engineer. (Career Examination Ser.: C-36). 1994. pap. 27.95 (*0-8373-0036-3*) Nat Learn.
— Assistant Departmental Attorney. (Career Examination Ser.: C-2233). 1994. pap. 39.95 (*0-8373-2233-2*) Nat Learn.
— Assistant Deputy Superintendent of Women's Prisons. (Career Examination Ser.: C-1697). 1994. pap. 44.95 (*0-8373-1697-9*) Nat Learn.
— Assistant Deputy Warden. (Career Examination Ser.: C-1698). 1994. pap. 44.95 (*0-8373-1698-7*) Nat Learn.
— Assistant Director. (Career Examination Ser.: C-1102). 1994. pap. 39.95 (*0-8373-1102-0*) Nat Learn.
— Assistant Director (Child Welfare) (Career Examination Ser.: C-1809). 1994. pap. 39.95 (*0-8373-1809-2*) Nat Learn.
— Assistant Director of Building & Housing. (Career Examination Ser.: C-3086). 1994. pap. 44.95 (*0-8373-3086-6*) Nat Learn.
— Assistant Director of Custodial & Security Services. (Career Examination Ser.: C-2922). 1994. pap. 39.95 (*0-8373-2922-1*) Nat Learn.
— Assistant Director of Maintenance (Sewer District) (Career Examination Ser.: C-2908). 1994. pap. 39.95 (*0-8373-2908-6*) Nat Learn.
— Assistant Director of Nursing Care. (Career Examination Ser.: C-2858). 1994. pap. 39.95 (*0-8373-2858-6*) Nat Learn.
— Assistant Director of Social Services. (Career Examination Ser.: C-2798). 1994. pap. 39.95 (*0-8373-2798-9*) Nat Learn.
— Assistant Director of Traffic Control. (Career Examination Ser.: C-1876). 1994. pap. 39.95 (*0-8373-1876-9*) Nat Learn.
— Assistant Director of Traffic Safety. (Career Examination Ser.: C-458). 1994. pap. 39.95 (*0-8373-0458-X*) Nat Learn.
— Assistant Director (Welfare) (Career Examination Ser.: C-1802). 1994. pap. 39.95 (*0-8373-1802-5*) Nat Learn.
— Assistant District Attorney. (Career Examination Ser.: C-1103). 1994. pap. 34.95 (*0-8373-1103-9*) Nat Learn.
— Assistant Electrical Engineer. (Career Examination Ser.: C-37). 1994. pap. 29.95 (*0-8373-0037-1*) Nat Learn.
— Assistant Electronic Technician. (Career Examination Ser.: C-1982). 1994. pap. 27.95 (*0-8373-1982-X*) Nat Learn.
— Assistant Employment & Training Program Administrator. (Career Examination Ser.: C-3075). 1994. pap. 39.95 (*0-8373-3075-0*) Nat Learn.
— Assistant Engineering Technician. (Career Examination Ser.: C-931). 1994. pap. 27.95 (*0-8373-0931-X*) Nat Learn.
— Assistant Federal & State Aid Coordinator. (Career Examination Ser.: C-1104). 1994. pap. 34.95 (*0-8373-1104-7*) Nat Learn.
— Assistant Fire Marshal. (Career Examination Ser.: C-1105). 1994. pap. 34.95 (*0-8373-1105-5*) Nat Learn.
— Assistant Floor Supervisor. (Career Examination Ser.: C-1106). 1994. pap. 29.95 (*0-8373-1106-3*) Nat Learn.
— Assistant Foreman. (Career Examination Ser.: C-38). 1994. pap. 29.95 (*0-8373-0038-X*) Nat Learn.
— Assistant Foreman (Department of Sanitation) (Career Examination Ser.: C-39). 1994. pap. 29.95 (*0-8373-0039-8*) Nat Learn.
— Assistant Gardener. (Career Examination Ser.: C-40). 1994. pap. 23.95 (*0-8373-0040-1*) Nat Learn.
— Assistant General Superintendent. (Career Examination Ser.: C-2109). 1994. pap. 39.95 (*0-8373-2109-3*) Nat Learn.
— Assistant Head Custodian. (Career Examination Ser.: C-1822). 1994. pap. 34.95 (*0-8373-1822-X*) Nat Learn.
— Assistant Health Insurance Administrator. (Career Examination Ser.: C-358). 1994. pap. 34.95 (*0-8373-0358-3*) Nat Learn.
— Assistant Heating & Ventilating Engineer. (Career Examination Ser.: C-1912). 1994. pap. 29.95 (*0-8373-1912-9*) Nat Learn.
— Assistant Hospital Administrator. (Career Examination Ser.: C-1107). 1994. pap. 34.95 (*0-8373-1107-1*) Nat Learn.
— Assistant Housing Manager. (Career Examination Ser.: C-41). 1994. pap. 29.95 (*0-8373-0041-X*) Nat Learn.
— Assistant Labor Relations Specialist. (Career Examination Ser.: C-2057). 1994. pap. 34.95 (*0-8373-2057-7*) Nat Learn.
— Assistant Land Surveyor. (Career Examination Ser.: C-3031). 1994. pap. 29.95 (*0-8373-3031-9*) Nat Learn.
— Assistant Landscape Architect. (Career Examination Ser.: C-42). 1994. pap. 29.95 (*0-8373-0042-8*) Nat Learn.
— Assistant Landscape Engineer. (Career Examination Ser.: C-43). 1994. pap. 29.95 (*0-8373-0043-6*) Nat Learn.
— Assistant Library Director. (Career Examination Ser.: C-1108). 1994. pap. 34.95 (*0-8373-1108-X*) Nat Learn.
— Assistant Library Director I. (Career Examination Ser.: C-2783). 1994. pap. 34.95 (*0-8373-2783-0*) Nat Learn.
— Assistant Library Director II. (Career Examination Ser.: C-2784). 1994. pap. 34.95 (*0-8373-2784-9*) Nat Learn.
— Assistant Library Director III. (Career Examination Ser.: C-2785). 1994. pap. 34.95 (*0-8373-2785-7*) Nat Learn.
— Assistant Library Director IV. (Career Examination Ser.: C-2786). 1994. pap. 34.95 (*0-8373-2786-5*) Nat Learn.
— Assistant Library Director V. (Career Examination Ser.: C-2787). 1994. pap. 34.95 (*0-8373-2787-3*) Nat Learn.
— Assistant Management Analyst. (Career Examination Ser.: C-2094). 1994. pap. 34.95 (*0-8373-2094-1*) Nat Learn.
— Assistant Mechanical Construction Engineer. (Career Examination Ser.: C-2706). 1994. pap. 29.95 (*0-8373-2706-7*) Nat Learn.
— Assistant Mechanical Engineer. (Career Examination Ser.: C-44). 1994. pap. 29.95 (*0-8373-0044-4*) Nat Learn.
— Assistant Microbiologist. (Career Examination Ser.: C-1811). 1994. pap. 29.95 (*0-8373-1811-4*) Nat Learn.
— Assistant Office Services Supervisor. (Career Examination Ser.: C-3048). 1994. pap. 29.95 (*0-8373-3048-3*) Nat Learn.
— Assistant Park Supervisor. (Career Examination Ser.: C-1564). 1994. pap. 29.95 (*0-8373-1564-6*) Nat Learn.
— Assistant Pathologist. (Career Examination Ser.: C-1109). 1994. pap. 44.95 (*0-8373-1109-8*) Nat Learn.
— Assistant Payroll Supervisor. (Career Examination Ser.: C-1110). 1994. pap. 29.95 (*0-8373-1110-1*) Nat Learn.
— Assistant Personnel Examiner. (Career Examination Ser.: C-1661). 1994. pap. 34.95 (*0-8373-1661-8*) Nat Learn.
— Assistant Physicist. (Career Examination Ser.: C-2087). 1994. pap. 34.95 (*0-8373-2087-9*) Nat Learn.
— Assistant Plan Examiner. (Career Examination Ser.: C-932). 1994. pap. 29.95 (*0-8373-0932-8*) Nat Learn.
— Assistant Planner. (Career Examination Ser.: C-933). 1994. pap. 29.95 (*0-8373-0933-6*) Nat Learn.
— Assistant Plant Facilities Administrator. (Career Examination Ser.: C-2757). 1994. pap. 39.95 (*0-8373-2757-1*) Nat Learn.
— Assistant Plumbing Engineer. (Career Examination Ser.: C-2705). 1994. pap. 34.95 (*0-8373-2705-9*) Nat Learn.
— Assistant Power Plant Operator. (Career Examination Ser.: C-1905). 1994. pap. 27.95 (*0-8373-1905-6*) Nat Learn.
— Assistant Press Secretary. (Career Examination Ser.: C-1111). 1994. pap. 27.95 (*0-8373-1111-X*) Nat Learn.
— Assistant Principal, Elementary School. (Teachers License Examination Ser.: S-1). 1994. pap. 49.95 (*0-8373-8101-0*) Nat Learn.
— Assistant Principal, Jr. H. S. (Teachers License Examination Ser.: S-2). 1994. pap. 49.95 (*0-8373-8102-9*) Nat Learn.
— Assistant Procurement Coordinator. (Career Examination Ser.: C-916). 1994. pap. 34.95 (*0-8373-0916-6*) Nat Learn.
— Assistant Program Manager. (Career Examination Ser.: C-934). 1994. pap. 34.95 (*0-8373-0934-4*) Nat Learn.
— Assistant Program Specialist (Correction) (Career Examination Ser.: C-1996). 1994. pap. 39.95 (*0-8373-1996-X*) Nat Learn.
— Assistant Project Coordinator. (Career Examination Ser.: C-2590). 1994. pap. 29.95 (*0-8373-2590-0*) Nat Learn.
— Assistant Public Buildings Manager. (Career Examination Ser.: C-2718). 1994. pap. 29.95 (*0-8373-2718-0*) Nat Learn.
— Assistant Public Health Engineer. (Career Examination Ser.: C-2232). 1994. pap. 29.95 (*0-8373-2232-4*) Nat Learn.
— Assistant Purchasing Agent. (Career Examination Ser.: C-935). 1994. pap. 23.95 (*0-8373-0935-2*) Nat Learn.
— Assistant Radiologist. (Career Examination Ser.: C-1112). 1994. pap. 44.95 (*0-8373-1112-8*) Nat Learn.
— Assistant Real Estate Agent. (Career Examination Ser.: C-2178). 1994. pap. 23.95 (*0-8373-2178-6*) Nat Learn.
— Assistant Real Estate Appraiser. (Career Examination Ser.: C-3365). 1994. pap. 23.95 (*0-8373-3365-2*) Nat Learn.
— Assistant Recreation Supervisor. (Career Examination Ser.: C-45). 1994. pap. 29.95 (*0-8373-0045-2*) Nat Learn.
— Assistant Rent Examiner. (Career Examination Ser.: C-936). 1994. pap. 23.95 (*0-8373-0936-0*) Nat Learn.
— Assistant Resident Buildings Superintendent. (Career Examination Ser.: C-1058). 1994. pap. 29.95 (*0-8373-1058-X*) Nat Learn.
— Assistant Retirement Benefits Examiner. (Career Examination Ser.: C-1557). 1994. pap. 29.95 (*0-8373-1557-3*) Nat Learn.
— Assistant Sanitary Engineer. (Career Examination Ser.: C-1969). 1994. pap. 29.95 (*0-8373-1969-2*) Nat Learn.
— Assistant School Custodian-Engineer. (Career Examination Ser.: C-46). 1994. pap. 27.95 (*0-8373-0046-0*) Nat Learn.
— Assistant School Transportation Supervisor. (Career Examination Ser.: C-112). 1994. pap. 29.95 (*0-8373-0112-2*) Nat Learn.
— Assistant Signal Circuit Engineer. (Career Examination Ser.: C-47). 1994. pap. 29.95 (*0-8373-0047-9*) Nat Learn.
— Assistant Social Worker. (Career Examination Ser.: C-1113). 1994. pap. 23.95 (*0-8373-1113-6*) Nat Learn.
— Assistant State Accounts Auditor/Examiner of Municipal Affairs. (Career Examination Ser.: C-1991). 1994. pap. 39.95 (*0-8373-1991-9*) Nat Learn.
— Assistant Station Supervisor. (Career Examination Ser.: C-48). 1994. pap. 23.95 (*0-8373-0048-7*) Nat Learn.
— Assistant Stationary Engineer. (Career Examination Ser.: C-2279). 1994. pap. 29.95 (*0-8373-2279-0*) Nat Learn.
— Assistant Statistician. (Career Examination Ser.: C-49). 1994. pap. 34.95 (*0-8373-0049-5*) Nat Learn.
— Assistant Stockman. (Career Examination Ser.: C-50). 1994. pap. 23.95 (*0-8373-0050-9*) Nat Learn.
— Assistant Superintendent (Buses & Shops) (Career Examination Ser.: C-1725). 1994. pap. 34.95 (*0-8373-1725-8*) Nat Learn.
— Assistant Superintendent (Cars & Shops) (Career Examination Ser.: C-2015). 1994. pap. 34.95 (*0-8373-2015-1*) Nat Learn.
— Assistant Superintendent of Alarms. (Career Examination Ser.: C-2964). 1994. pap. 39.95 (*0-8373-2964-7*) Nat Learn.
— Assistant Superintendent of Buildings & Grounds. (Career Examination Ser.: C-937). 1994. pap. 29.95 (*0-8373-0937-9*) Nat Learn.
— Assistant Superintendent of Construction. (Career Examination Ser.: C-1114). 1994. pap. 34.95 (*0-8373-1114-4*) Nat Learn.
— Assistant Superintendent of Public Works. (Career Examination Ser.: C-2306). 1994. pap. 34.95 (*0-8373-2306-1*) Nat Learn.
— Assistant Superintendent of Sanitation. (Career Examination Ser.: C-2456). 1994. pap. 34.95 (*0-8373-2456-4*) Nat Learn.
— Assistant Superintendent of Water Works. (Career Examination Ser.: C-2003). 1994. pap. 34.95 (*0-8373-2003-8*) Nat Learn.
— Assistant Superintendent (Power) (Career Examination Ser.: C-2016). 1994. pap. 34.95 (*0-8373-2016-X*) Nat Learn.
— Assistant Superintendent (Signals) (Career Examination Ser.: C-2017). 1994. pap. 34.95 (*0-8373-2017-8*) Nat Learn.
— Assistant Superintendent (Structures) (Career Examination Ser.: C-2018). 1994. pap. 34.95 (*0-8373-2018-6*) Nat Learn.
— Assistant Superintendent (Surface Transportation) (Career Examination Ser.: C-1770). 1994. pap. 34.95 (*0-8373-1770-3*) Nat Learn.
— Assistant Superintendent (Track) (Career Examination Ser.: C-2019). 1994. pap. 34.95 (*0-8373-2019-4*) Nat Learn.
— Assistant Supervisor (Air Conditioning, Rolling Stock) (Career Examination Ser.: C-2063). 1994. pap. 29.95 (*0-8373-2063-1*) Nat Learn.
— Assistant Supervisor (Buses & Shops) (Career Examination Ser.: C-1115). 1994. pap. 29.95 (*0-8373-1115-2*) Nat Learn.
— Assistant Supervisor (Cars & Shops) (Career Examination Ser.: C-1975). 1994. pap. 29.95 (*0-8373-1975-7*) Nat Learn.
— Assistant Supervisor (Child Welfare) (Career Examination Ser.: C-51). 1994. pap. 29.95 (*0-8373-0051-7*) Nat Learn.
— Assistant Supervisor (Electrical Power) (Career Examination Ser.: C-1976). 1994. pap. 29.95 (*0-8373-1976-5*) Nat Learn.
— Assistant Supervisor (Electronic Equipment) (Career Examination Ser.: C-2192). 1994. pap. 29.95 (*0-8373-2192-1*) Nat Learn.
— Assistant Supervisor (Elevators & Escalators) (Career Examination Ser.: C-1727). 1994. pap. 29.95 (*0-8373-1727-4*) Nat Learn.
— Assistant Supervisor (Lighting) (Career Examination Ser.: C-2006). 1994. pap. 29.95 (*0-8373-2006-2*) Nat Learn.
— Assistant Supervisor of Electrical Installations. (Career Examination Ser.: C-1116). 1994. pap. 29.95 (*0-8373-1116-0*) Nat Learn.
— Assistant Supervisor of Mechanical Installations. (Career Examination Ser.: C-1117). 1994. pap. 29.95 (*0-8373-1117-9*) Nat Learn.
— Assistant Supervisor of Youth Services. (Career Examination Ser.: C-1659). 1994. pap. 29.95 (*0-8373-1659-6*) Nat Learn.
— Assistant Supervisor (Power Distribution) (Career Examination Ser.: C-1777). 1994. pap. 29.95 (*0-8373-1777-0*) Nat Learn.
— Assistant Supervisor (Stores, Materials & Supplies) (Career Examination Ser.: C-1814). 1994. pap. 29.95 (*0-8373-1814-9*) Nat Learn.
— Assistant Supervisor (Structures) (Career Examination Ser.: C-1977). 1994. pap. 29.95 (*0-8373-1977-3*) Nat Learn.
— Assistant Supervisor (Structures) - Group C. (Career Examination Ser.: C-1972). 1994. pap. 29.95 (*0-8373-1972-2*) Nat Learn.
— Assistant Supervisor (Track) (Career Examination Ser.: C-1728). 1994. pap. 29.95 (*0-8373-1728-2*) Nat Learn.
— Assistant Supervisor (Turnstiles) (Career Examination Ser.: C-2007). 1994. pap. 29.95 (*0-8373-2007-0*) Nat Learn.
— Assistant Supervisor (Ventilation & Drainage) (Career Examination Ser.: C-2091). 1994. pap. 29.95 (*0-8373-2091-7*) Nat Learn.

R

— Assistant Supervisor (Welfare) (Career Examination Ser.: C-52). 1994. pap. 29.95 (*0-8373-0052-5*) Nat Learn.
— Assistant Surveyor. (Career Examination Ser.: C-1792). 1994. pap. 29.95 (*0-8373-1792-4*) Nat Learn.
— Assistant Tax Valuation Engineer. (Career Examination Ser.: C-3196). 1994. pap. 27.95 (*0-8373-3196-X*) Nat Learn.
— Assistant Teacher. (Career Examination Ser.: C-1118). 1994. pap. 23.95 (*0-8373-1118-7*) Nat Learn.
— Assistant Tenant Supervisor. (Career Examination Ser.: C-542). 1994. pap. 27.95 (*0-8373-0542-X*) Nat Learn.
— Assistant to Assessor. (Career Examination Ser.: C-2182). 1994. pap. 27.95 (*0-8373-2182-4*) Nat Learn.
— Assistant to City Clerk. (Career Examination Ser.: C-930). 1994. pap. 23.95 (*0-8373-0930-1*) Nat Learn.
— Assistant to Commissioner. (Career Examination Ser.: C-1119). 1994. pap. 39.95 (*0-8373-1119-5*) Nat Learn.
— Assistant to Director. (Career Examination Ser.: C-3092). 1994. pap. 39.95 (*0-8373-3092-0*) Nat Learn.
— Assistant to Director, Bureau of Vehicle Maintenance. (Career Examination Ser.: C-3111). 1994. pap. 39.95 (*0-8373-3111-0*) Nat Learn.
— Assistant to Planning Director. (Career Examination Ser.: C-3155). 1994. pap. 39.95 (*0-8373-3155-2*) Nat Learn.
— Assistant to Superintendent. (Career Examination Ser.: C-2210). 1994. pap. 39.95 (*0-8373-2210-3*) Nat Learn.
— Assistant to the Town Comptroller. (Career Examination Ser.: C-3128). 1994. pap. 39.95 (*0-8373-3128-5*) Nat Learn.
— Assistant Town Engineer. (Career Examination Ser.: C-211). 1994. pap. 34.95 (*0-8373-0211-0*) Nat Learn.
— Assistant Train Dispatcher. (Career Examination Ser.: C-53). 1994. pap. 23.95 (*0-8373-0053-3*) Nat Learn.
— Assistant Transit Management Analyst. (Career Examination Ser.: C-3280). 1994. pap. 29.95 (*0-8373-3280-X*) Nat Learn.
— Assistant Urban Designer. (Career Examination Ser.: C-1120). 1994. pap. 27.95 (*0-8373-1120-9*) Nat Learn.
— Assistant Warden. (Career Examination Ser.: C-1121). 1994. pap. 44.95 (*0-8373-1121-7*) Nat Learn.
— Assistant Water Maintenance Foreman. (Career Examination Ser.: C-2919). 1994. pap. 29.95 (*0-8373-2919-1*) Nat Learn.
— Assistant Water Service Foreman. (Career Examination Ser.: C-2924). 1994. pap. 29.95 (*0-8373-2924-8*) Nat Learn.
— Assistant Workmen's Compensation Examiner. (Career Examination Ser.: C-1643). 1994. pap. 29.95 (*0-8373-1643-X*) Nat Learn.
— Assistant Youth Corps Project Director. (Career Examination Ser.: C-2207). 1994. pap. 34.95 (*0-8373-2207-3*) Nat Learn.
— Assistant Youth Guidance Technician. (Career Examination Ser.: C-938). 1994. pap. 29.95 (*0-8373-0938-7*) Nat Learn.
— Associate Accountant. (Career Examination Ser.: C-1798). 1994. pap. 34.95 (*0-8373-1798-3*) Nat Learn.
— Associate Administrator. (Career Examination Ser.: C-1122). 1994. pap. 29.95 (*0-8373-1122-5*) Nat Learn.
— Associate Advisor, PEDC (U. S. P. S.) (Career Examination Ser.: C-2118). 1994. pap. 34.95 (*0-8373-2118-2*) Nat Learn.
— Associate Analytical Chemist. (Career Examination Ser.: C-3194). 1994. pap. 34.95 (*0-8373-3194-3*) Nat Learn.
— Associate Attorney. (Career Examination Ser.: C-2269). 1994. pap. 39.95 (*0-8373-2269-3*) Nat Learn.
— Associate Biostatistician. (Career Examination Ser.: C-2292). 1994. pap. 39.95 (*0-8373-2292-8*) Nat Learn.
— Associate Budget Analyst. (Career Examination Ser.: C-3172). 1994. pap. 39.95 (*0-8373-3172-2*) Nat Learn.
— Associate Business Promotion Coordinator. (Career Examination Ser.: C-2526). 1994. pap. 39.95 (*0-8373-2526-9*) Nat Learn.
— Associate Capital Program Analyst. (Career Examination Ser.: C-2039). 1994. pap. 39.95 (*0-8373-2039-9*) Nat Learn.
— Associate Cashier. (Career Examination Ser.: C-2005). 1994. pap. 23.95 (*0-8373-2005-4*) Nat Learn.
— Associate Chemist. (Career Examination Ser.: C-3362). 1994. pap. 34.95 (*0-8373-3362-8*) Nat Learn.
— Associate Civil Engineer (Structures) (Career Examination Ser.: C-1911). 1994. pap. 39.95 (*0-8373-1911-0*) Nat Learn.
— Associate Claim Examiner. (Career Examination Ser.: C-3504). 1994. pap. 34.95 (*0-8373-3504-3*) Nat Learn.
— Associate Computer Programmer. (Career Examination Ser.: C-2206). 1994. pap. 34.95 (*0-8373-2206-5*) Nat Learn.
— Associate Computer Programmer/Analyst. (Career Examination Ser.: C-3218). 1994. pap. 34.95 (*0-8373-3218-4*) Nat Learn.
— Associate Computer Systems Analyst. (Career Examination Ser.: C-939). 1994. pap. 34.95 (*0-8373-0939-5*) Nat Learn.
— Associate Court Clerk. (Career Examination Ser.: C-2587). 1994. pap. 29.95 (*0-8373-2587-0*) Nat Learn.
— Associate Economist. (Career Examination Ser.: C-2497). 1994. pap. 39.95 (*0-8373-2497-1*) Nat Learn.
— Associate Education Analyst. (Career Examination Ser.: C-3046). 1994. pap. 39.95 (*0-8373-3046-7*) Nat Learn.
— Associate Education Officer. (Career Examination Ser.: C-3051). 1994. pap. 39.95 (*0-8373-3051-3*) Nat Learn.
— Associate Engineering Technician. (Career Examination Ser.: C-2467). 1994. pap. 34.95 (*0-8373-2467-X*) Nat Learn.
— Associate Environmental Analyst. (Career Examination Ser.: C-3033). 1994. pap. 39.95 (*0-8373-3033-5*) Nat Learn.
— Associate Graphic Artist. (Career Examination Ser.: C-1525). 1994. pap. 29.95 (*0-8373-1525-5*) Nat Learn.
— Associate Industrial Hygienist. (Career Examination Ser.: C-3037). 1994. pap. 44.95 (*0-8373-3037-8*) Nat Learn.
— Associate Information & Referral Coordinator. (Career Examination Ser.: C-2926). 1994. pap. 34.95 (*0-8373-2926-4*) Nat Learn.
— Associate Inspector (Construction) (Career Examination Ser.: No. C-3502). 1994. pap. 34.95 (*0-8373-3502-7*) Nat Learn.
— Associate Inspector (Electrical) (Career Examination Ser.: C-3360). 1994. pap. 34.95 (*0-8373-3360-1*) Nat Learn.
— Associate Inspector (Highways & Sewers) (Career Examination Ser.: C-3519). 1994. pap. 34.95 (*0-8373-3519-1*) Nat Learn.
— Associate Inspector (Housing) (Career Examination Ser.: C-3011). 1994. pap. 34.95 (*0-8373-3011-4*) Nat Learn.
— Associate Inspector (Plumbing) (Career Examination Ser.: C-3666). pap. 34.95 (*0-8373-3666-X*) Nat Learn.
— Associate Investigator. (Career Examination Ser.: No. C-3503). 1994. pap. 34.95 (*0-8373-3503-5*) Nat Learn.
— Associate Labor Relations Specialist. (Career Examination Ser.: C-1946). 1994. pap. 39.95 (*0-8373-1946-3*) Nat Learn.
— Associate Management Analyst. (Career Examination Ser.: C-1234). 1994. pap. 39.95 (*0-8373-1234-5*) Nat Learn.
— Associate Manpower Program Coordinator. (Career Examination Ser.: C-2317). 1994. pap. 39.95 (*0-8373-2317-7*) Nat Learn.
— Associate Marketing Representative. (Career Examination Ser.: C-2040). 1994. pap. 34.95 (*0-8373-2040-2*) Nat Learn.
— Associate Medical Examiner. (Career Examination Ser.: C-2722). 1994. pap. 44.95 (*0-8373-2722-9*) Nat Learn.
— Associate Methods Analyst. (Career Examination Ser.: C-1735). 1994. pap. 39.95 (*0-8373-1735-5*) Nat Learn.
— Associate Occupational Analyst. (Career Examination Ser.: C-2550). 1994. pap. 39.95 (*0-8373-2550-1*) Nat Learn.
— Associate Park Service Worker. (Career Examination Ser.: C-2469). 1994. pap. 29.95 (*0-8373-2469-6*) Nat Learn.
— Associate Personnel Administrator. (Career Examination Ser.: C-3322). 1994. pap. 39.95 (*0-8373-3322-9*) Nat Learn.
— Associate Public Health Sanitarian. (Career Examination Ser.: C-3690). pap. 34.95 (*0-8373-3690-2*) Nat Learn.
— Associate Public Information Specialist. (Career Examination Ser.: C-3520). 1994. pap. 34.95 (*0-8373-3520-5*) Nat Learn.
— Associate Public Records Officer. (Career Examination Ser.: No. C-3521). 1994. pap. 29.95 (*0-8373-3521-3*) Nat Learn.
— Associate Quality Assurance Specialist. (Career Examination Ser.: C-3522). 1994. pap. 39.95 (*0-8373-3522-1*) Nat Learn.
— Associate Real Property Manager. (Career Examination Ser.: C-2890). 1994. pap. 34.95 (*0-8373-2890-X*) Nat Learn.
— Associate Sanitation Enforcement Agent. (Career Examination Ser.: C-3216). 1994. pap. 29.95 (*0-8373-3216-8*) Nat Learn.
— Associate Social Services Management Specialist. (Career Examination Ser.: C-454). 1994. pap. 39.95 (*0-8373-0454-7*) Nat Learn.
— Associate Space Analyst. (Career Examination Ser.: No. C-3518). 1994. pap. 39.95 (*0-8373-3518-3*) Nat Learn.
— Associate Staff Analyst. (Career Examination Ser.: C-1552). 1994. pap. 39.95 (*0-8373-1552-2*) Nat Learn.
— Associate Statistician. (Career Examination Ser.: C-940). 1994. pap. 39.95 (*0-8373-0940-9*) Nat Learn.
— Associate Superintendent of Construction. (Career Examination Ser.: C-1518). 1994. pap. 34.95 (*0-8373-1518-2*) Nat Learn.
— Associate Tax Auditor. (Career Examination Ser.: C-2314). 1994. pap. 34.95 (*0-8373-2314-2*) Nat Learn.
— Associate Traffic Enforcement Agent. (Career Examination Ser.: C-215). 1994. pap. 34.95 (*0-8373-0215-3*) Nat Learn.
— Associate Transit Management Analyst. (Career Examination Ser.: C-3423). 1994. pap. 34.95 (*0-8373-3423-3*) Nat Learn.
— Associate Urban Park Ranger. (Career Examination Ser.: C-3179). 1994. pap. 29.95 (*0-8373-3179-X*) Nat Learn.
— Associate Water Use Inspector. (Career Examination Ser.: C-3583). 1994. pap. 29.95 (*0-8373-3583-3*) Nat Learn.
— Associate Word Processor. (Career Examination Ser.: C-3183). 1994. pap. 29.95 (*0-8373-3183-8*) Nat Learn.
— Associate Worker's Compensation Review Analyst. (Career Examination Ser.: C-309). 1994. pap. 34.95 (*0-8373-0309-5*) Nat Learn.
— Associate Workmen's Compensation Examiner. (Career Examination Ser.: C-1547). 1994. pap. 34.95 (*0-8373-1547-6*) Nat Learn.
— Astronomer. (Career Examination Ser.: C-54). 1994. pap. 34.95 (*0-8373-0054-1*) Nat Learn.
— Astronomy. (Dantes Subject Standardized Tests Ser.: Vol. DANTES-1). 1994. pap. 23.95 (*0-8373-6601-1*) Nat Learn.
— Attendance Teacher. (Teachers License Examination Ser.: T-2a). 1994. pap. 27.95 (*0-8373-8002-2*) Nat Learn.
— Attendance Teacher (Spanish) (Teachers License Examination Ser.: T-2b). 1994. pap. 27.95 (*0-685-49789-5*) Nat Learn.
— Attendant. (Career Examination Ser.: C-55). 1994. pap. 19.95 (*0-8373-0055-X*) Nat Learn.
— Attorney. (Career Examination Ser.: C-56). 1994. pap. 39.95 (*0-8373-0056-8*) Nat Learn.
— Attorney - Departmental. (Career Examination Ser.: C-2234). 1994. pap. 44.95 (*0-8373-2234-0*) Nat Learn.
— Attorney Trainee. (Career Examination Ser.: C-57). 1994. pap. 29.95 (*0-8373-0057-6*) Nat Learn.
— Audience Promotion Assistant. (Career Examination Ser.: C-1123). 1994. pap. 29.95 (*0-8373-1123-3*) Nat Learn.
— Audio-Visual Aide. (Career Examination Ser.: C-2903). 1994. pap. 23.95 (*0-8373-2903-5*) Nat Learn.
— Audio-Visual Aide Technician. (Career Examination Ser.: C-58). 1994. pap. 23.95 (*0-8373-0058-4*) Nat Learn.
— Audio-Visual Programs Specialist. (Career Examination Ser.: C-3209). 1994. pap. 29.95 (*0-8373-3209-5*) Nat Learn.
— Audio-Visual Specialist. (Career Examination Ser.: C-1826). 1994. pap. 23.95 (*0-8373-1826-2*) Nat Learn.
— Audio-Visual Technician. (Career Examination Ser.: C-1894). 1994. pap. 23.95 (*0-8373-1894-7*) Nat Learn.
— Audiologist. (Career Examination Ser.: C-1124). 1994. pap. 27.95 (*0-8373-1124-1*) Nat Learn.
— Audiologist - Speech Pathologist. (Career Examination Ser.: C-59). 1994. pap. 27.95 (*0-8373-0059-2*) Nat Learn.
— Audiology. (National Teacher Examination Ser.: NT-34). 1994. pap. 23.95 (*0-8373-8444-3*) Nat Learn.
— Audit Clerk. (Career Examination Ser.: C-1907). 1994. pap. 23.95 (*0-8373-1907-2*) Nat Learn.
— Auditing. (ACT Proficiency Examination Program (PEP) Ser.: Vol. 14). 43.95 (*0-8373-5564-8*) Nat Learn.
— Auditing. (Dantes Subject Standardized Tests (DANTES) Ser.: Vol. 69). 43.95 (*0-8373-6569-4*) Nat Learn.
— Auditing. (ACT Proficiency Examination Program Ser.: PEP-14). 1994. pap. 23.95 (*0-8373-5514-1*) Nat Learn.
— Auditing. (Dantes Subject Standardized Tests (DANTES) Ser.: No. 69). 1997. 23.95 (*0-8373-6669-0*) Nat Learn.
— Auditing Assistant. (Career Examination Ser.: C-2092). 1994. pap. 27.95 (*0-8373-2092-5*) Nat Learn.
— Auditor. (Career Examination Ser.: C-60). 1994. pap. 29.95 (*0-8373-0060-6*) Nat Learn.
— Auditor Trainee. (Career Examination Ser.: C-2404). 1994. pap. 27.95 (*0-8373-2404-1*) Nat Learn.
— Auto Body Repair. (Occupational Competency Examination (OCE) Ser.: Vol. 5). 47.95 (*0-8373-5755-1*) Nat Learn.
— Auto Body Repair. (Occupational Competency Examination Ser.: OCE-5). 1994. pap. 29.95 (*0-8373-5705-5*) Nat Learn.
— Auto Body Repairman. (Career Examination Ser.: C-1125). 1994. pap. 23.95 (*0-8373-1125-X*) Nat Learn.
— Auto Engineman. (Career Examination Ser.: C-61). 1994. pap. 23.95 (*0-8373-0061-4*) Nat Learn.
— Auto Equipment Inspector. (Career Examination Ser.: C-1126). 1994. pap. 27.95 (*0-8373-1126-8*) Nat Learn.
— Auto Machinist. (Career Examination Ser.: C-62). 1994. pap. 23.95 (*0-8373-0062-2*) Nat Learn.
— Auto Maintenance Coordinator. (Career Examination Ser.: C-1127). 1994. pap. 29.95 (*0-8373-1127-6*) Nat Learn.
— Auto Mechanic. (Career Examination Ser.: C-63). 1994. pap. 23.95 (*0-8373-0063-0*) Nat Learn.
— Auto Mechanic (Diesel) (Career Examination Ser.: C-64). 1994. pap. 23.95 (*0-8373-0064-9*) Nat Learn.
— Auto Mechanics. (Occupational Competency Examination (OCE) Ser.: Vol. 7). 47.95 (*0-8373-5757-8*) Nat Learn.
— Auto Mechanics. (Dantes Subject Standardized Tests Ser.: DANTES 2). 1994. pap. 23.95 (*0-8373-6602-X*) Nat Learn.
— Auto Mechanics. (Occupational Competency Examination (OCE) Ser.: Vol. OCE-7). 1994. pap. 27.95 (*0-8373-5707-1*) Nat Learn.
— Auto Parts Storekeeper. (Career Examination Ser.: C-1128). 1994. pap. 23.95 (*0-8373-1128-4*) Nat Learn.
— Auto Shop Foreman. (Career Examination Ser.: C-1129). 1994. pap. 29.95 (*0-8373-1129-2*) Nat Learn.
— Auto Shop Supervisor. (Career Examination Ser.: C-1130). 1994. pap. 29.95 (*0-8373-1130-6*) Nat Learn.
— Automatic Heating. (Occupational Competency Examination Ser.: OCE-6). 1994. pap. 27.95 (*0-8373-5706-3*) Nat Learn.
— Automotive Electrical - Electronics. (Dantes Subject Standardized Tests (DANTES) Ser.: Vol. 39). 43.95 (*0-8373-6539-2*) Nat Learn.
— Automotive Electrical/Electronics. (Dantes Subject Standardized Tests Ser.: DANTES 39). 1994. pap. 23.95 (*0-8373-6639-9*) Nat Learn.
— Automotive Facilities Inspector. (Career Examination Ser.: C-2213). 1994. pap. 27.95 (*0-8373-2213-8*) Nat Learn.
— Automotive Maintenance Supervisor. (Career Examination Ser.: C-2096). 1994. pap. 29.95 (*0-8373-2096-8*) Nat Learn.
— Automotive Mechanic (USPS) (Career Examination Ser.: C-1131). 1994. pap. 23.95 (*0-8373-1131-4*) Nat Learn.
— Automotive Parts Supervisor. (Career Examination Ser.: C-2841). 1994. pap. 27.95 (*0-8373-2841-1*) Nat Learn.
— Automotive Serviceman. (Career Examination Ser.: C-65). 1994. pap. 23.95 (*0-8373-0065-7*) Nat Learn.
— Automotive Workbook. (Workbook (W) Ser.: Vol. 2820). 43.95 (*0-8373-7926-1*) Nat Learn.
— Automotive Workbook. (Workbook Ser.: W-2820). 1994. pap. 23.95 (*0-8373-7901-6*) Nat Learn.
— Auxiliary Teacher, Elementay School. (Teachers License Examination Ser.: T-3). pap. 27.95 (*0-8373-8003-0*) Nat Learn.
— Bacteriologist. (Career Examination Ser.: C-80). 1994. pap. 29.95 (*0-8373-0080-0*) Nat Learn.
— Bailiff. (Career Examination Ser.: C-3693). pap. 23.95 (*0-8373-3693-7*) Nat Learn.
— Baker. (Career Examination Ser.: C-1132). 1994. pap. 23.95 (*0-8373-1132-2*) Nat Learn.
— Ballot Clerk. (Career Examination Ser.: C-1133). 1994. pap. 23.95 (*0-8373-1133-0*) Nat Learn.
— Bank Examiner. (Career Examination Ser.: C-105). 1994. pap. 29.95 (*0-8373-0105-X*) Nat Learn.
— Bank Examiner Trainee. (Career Examination Ser.: Vol. C-292). 1994. pap. 27.95 (*0-8373-0292-7*) Nat Learn.
— Bank Tellers. (Career Examination Ser.: C-293). 1994. pap. 23.95 (*0-8373-0293-5*) Nat Learn.
— Barber. (Career Examination Ser.: C-1134). 1994. pap. 29.95 (*0-8373-1134-9*) Nat Learn.
— Basic Marketing. (DANTES Ser.: DANTES-3). 1994. pap. 23.95 (*0-8373-6603-8*) Nat Learn.
— Basic Scholastic Aptitude Test (BSAT) (General Aptitude & Abilities Ser.: CS-49). 1994. pap. 29.95 (*0-8373-6749-2*) Nat Learn.
— Basic Skills Assessment Program (BSAP) (Admission Test Ser.: Vol. 59). 43.95 (*0-8373-5159-6*) Nat Learn.
— Basic Skills Assessment Program (BSAP) (Admission Test Ser.: ATS-59). 1994. pap. 23.95 (*0-8373-5059-X*) Nat Learn.
— Basic Statistics. (DANTES Ser.: DANTES-4). 1994. pap. 23.95 (*0-8373-6604-6*) Nat Learn.
— Basin Machine Operator. (Career Examination Ser.: C-2517). 1994. pap. 29.95 (*0-8373-2517-X*) Nat Learn.
— Battalion Chief, Fire Department. (Career Examination Ser.: C-81). 1994. pap. 34.95 (*0-8373-0081-9*) Nat Learn.
— Bay Constable. (Career Examination Ser.: C-2524). 1994. pap. 29.95 (*0-8373-2524-2*) Nat Learn.
— Bay Constable II. (Career Examination Ser.: C-885). 1994. pap. 34.95 (*0-8373-0885-2*) Nat Learn.
— Bay Management Specialist. (Career Examination Ser.: C-1165). 1994. pap. 29.95 (*0-8373-1165-9*) Nat Learn.
— Beach Supervisor. (Career Examination Ser.: C-836). 1994. pap. 29.95 (*0-8373-0836-4*) Nat Learn.
— Beginning Clerical Worker. (Career Examination Ser.: No. C-3505). 1994. pap. 19.95 (*0-8373-3505-1*) Nat Learn.
— Beginning German. (DANTES Ser.: DANTES-5). (GER.). 1994. pap. 23.95 (*0-8373-6605-4*) Nat Learn.
— Beginning Italian. (Dantes Subject Standardized Tests (DANTES) Ser.: Vol. 54). 43.95 (*0-8373-6554-6*) Nat Learn.
— Beginning Italian. (Dantes Subject Standardized Tests Ser.: DANTES-54). 1994. pap. 23.95 (*0-8373-6654-2*) Nat Learn.
— Beginning Office Worker. (Career Examination Ser.: C-82). 1994. pap. 19.95 (*0-8373-0082-7*) Nat Learn.
— Beginning Spanish. (DANTES Ser.: DANTES-6). 1994. pap. 23.95 (*0-8373-6606-2*) Nat Learn.
— Behavioral Sciences for Nurses. (College Level Examination Ser.: CLEP-39). 1994. pap. 23.95 (*0-8373-5339-4*) Nat Learn.
— Beverage Control Inspector. (Career Examination Ser.: C-83). 1994. pap. 29.95 (*0-8373-0083-5*) Nat Learn.
— Beverage Control Investigator. (Career Examination Ser.: C-918). 1994. pap. 27.95 (*0-8373-0918-2*) Nat Learn.
— Bilingual Common Branches (1-6) (Spanish), Elementary School. (Teachers License Examination Ser.: T-68). 1994. pap. 27.95 (*0-8373-8068-5*) Nat Learn.
— Bilingual Teacher in School & Community Relations. (Teachers License Examination Ser.: T-66). 1994. pap. 27.95 (*0-8373-8066-9*) Nat Learn.
— Bilingual Teacher (Jr. & Sr. High School) (Teachers License Examination Ser.: T-70). 1994. pap. 27.95 (*0-8373-8070-7*) Nat Learn.
— Bindery Worker. (Career Examination Ser.: C-84). 1994. pap. 23.95 (*0-8373-0084-3*) Nat Learn.
— Bingo Control Investigator. (Career Examination Ser.: C-106). 1994. pap. 27.95 (*0-8373-0106-8*) Nat Learn.
— Bingo Inspector. (Career Examination Ser.: C-846). 1994. pap. 27.95 (*0-8373-0846-1*) Nat Learn.
— Biochemist. (Career Examination Ser.: C-85). 1994. pap. 29.95 (*0-8373-0085-1*) Nat Learn.
— Biochemist Trainee. (Career Examination Ser.: C-1171). 1994. pap. 27.95 (*0-8373-1171-3*) Nat Learn.
— Biological Aide. (Career Examination Ser.: C-86). 1994. pap. 27.95 (*0-8373-0086-X*) Nat Learn.
— Biological Sciences - Area Examination. (Graduate Record Area Examination Ser.: GRE-41). 1994. pap. 23.95 (*0-8373-5241-X*) Nat Learn.
— Biologist. (Career Examination Ser.: C-2013). 1994. pap. 29.95 (*0-8373-2013-5*) Nat Learn.
— Biology. (Graduate Record Examination (GRE) Ser.: Vol. 1). 43.95 (*0-8373-5251-7*) Nat Learn.
— Biology. (Undergraduate Program Field Tests (UPFT) Ser.: Vol. 2). 43.95 (*0-8373-6052-8*) Nat Learn.
— Biology. (Regents College Proficiency Examination Ser.: Vol. 5). 43.95 (*0-8373-5455-2*) Nat Learn.
— Biology. (Regents College Proficiency Examination Ser.: CPEP-5). 1994. pap. 23.95 (*0-8373-5405-6*) Nat Learn.
— Biology. (Graduate Record Examination (GRE) Ser.: Vol. GRE-1). 1994. pap. 23.95 (*0-8373-5201-0*) Nat Learn.
— Biology. (Undergraduate Program Field Tests Ser.: Vol. UPFT-2). 1994. pap. 23.95 (*0-8373-6002-1*) Nat Learn.
— Biology & General Science. (National Teacher Examination Ser.: NT-3). 1994. pap. 23.95 (*0-8373-8413-3*) Nat Learn.
— Biology & General Science Sr. H. S. (Teachers License Examination Ser.: T-4). 1994. pap. 27.95 (*0-8373-8004-9*) Nat Learn.
— Biostatistician. (Career Examination Ser.: C-1135). 1994. pap. 29.95 (*0-8373-1135-7*) Nat Learn.
— Blacksmith. (Career Examination Ser.: C-107). 1994. pap. 27.95 (*0-8373-0107-6*) Nat Learn.
— Blacksmith's Helper. (Career Examination Ser.: C-108). 1994. pap. 23.95 (*0-8373-0108-4*) Nat Learn.
— Blind. (Teachers License Examination Ser.: T-5). 1994. pap. 27.95 (*0-8373-8005-7*) Nat Learn.
— Blueprint Machine Operator. (Career Examination Ser.: C-1136). 1994. pap. 27.95 (*0-8373-1136-5*) Nat Learn.
— Blueprinter. (Career Examination Ser.: C-1621). 1994. pap. 27.95 (*0-8373-1621-9*) Nat Learn.
— Board Member. (Career Examination Ser.: C-1137). 1994. pap. 39.95 (*0-8373-1137-3*) Nat Learn.
— Body Repair Inspector. (Career Examination Ser.: C-3281). 1994. pap. 23.95 (*0-8373-3281-8*) Nat Learn.
— Boiler Inspector. (Career Examination Ser.: C-87). 1994. pap. 29.95 (*0-8373-0087-8*) Nat Learn.

An Asterisk (*) at the beginning of an entry indicates that the title is appearing for the first time.

R

— Certified Professional Social Worker (CPSW) (Admission Test Ser.: ATS-88). 1994. pap. 23.95 (0-8373-5088-3) Nat Learn.
— Certified Protection Professional Examination (CPP) (Admission Test Ser.: Vol. 68). 59.95 (0-8373-5168-5) Nat Learn.
— Certified Protection Professional Examination (CPP) (Admission Test Ser.: ATS-68). 1994. pap. 39.95 (0-8373-5068-9) Nat Learn.
— Certified Public Accountant Examination (CPA) (Admission Test Ser.: Vol. 71). 89.95 (0-8373-5171-5) Nat Learn.
— Certified Public Accountant Examination (CPA) (Admission Test Ser.: ATS-71). 1994. pap. 69.95 (0-8373-5071-9) Nat Learn.
— Certified Safety Professional Examination (CSP) (Admission Test Ser.: Vol. 72). 69.95 (0-8373-5172-3) Nat Learn.
— Certified Safety Professional Examination (CSP) (Admission Test Ser.: ATS-72). 1994. pap. 49.95 (0-8373-5072-7) Nat Learn.
— Certified Shorthand Reporter. (Career Examination Ser.: C-133). 1994. pap. 27.95 (0-8373-0133-5) Nat Learn.
— Certified Social Worker (CSW) (Career Examination Ser.: C-178). 1994. pap. 29.95 (0-8373-0178-5) Nat Learn.
— Chairman, Academic Subjects (English & Social Studies) (Teachers License Examination Ser.: CH-1). 1994. pap. 39.95 (0-8373-8151-7) Nat Learn.
— Chairman, Accounting & Business Practice. (Teachers License Examination Ser.: CH-2). 1994. pap. 39.95 (0-8373-8152-5) Nat Learn.
— Chairman, Civil Service Commission. (Career Examination Ser.: C-1164). 1994. pap. 49.95 (0-8373-1164-0) Nat Learn.
— Chairman, Distributive Education (Merchandising & Salesmanship), Sr. H. S. (Teachers License Examination Ser.: CH-3). 1994. pap. 39.95 (0-8373-8153-3) Nat Learn.
— Chairman, English, Jr. H. S. (Teachers License Examination Ser.: CH-4). 1994. pap. 39.95 (0-8373-8154-1) Nat Learn.
— Chairman, English, Sr. H. S. (Teachers License Examination Ser.: CH-5). 1994. pap. 39.95 (0-8373-8155-X) Nat Learn.
— Chairman, Fine Arts, Sr. H. S. (Teachers License Examination Ser.: CH-7). 1994. pap. 39.95 (0-8373-8157-6) Nat Learn.
— Chairman, Foreign Languages, Jr. H. S. (Teachers License Examination Ser.: CH-8). 1994. pap. 39.95 (0-8373-8158-4) Nat Learn.
— Chairman, Foreign Languages, Sr. H. S. (Teachers License Examination Ser.: CH-9). 1994. pap. 39.95 (0-8373-8159-2) Nat Learn.
— Chairman, Health & Physical Education, Jr. H. S. (Teachers License Examination Ser.: CH-10). 1994. pap. 39.95 (0-8373-8160-6) Nat Learn.
— Chairman, Health & Physical Education, Sr. H. S. (Teachers License Examination Ser.: CH-11). 1994. pap. 39.95 (0-8373-8161-4) Nat Learn.
— Chairman, Home Economics, Jr. H. S. (Teachers License Examination Ser.: CH-12). 1994. pap. 39.95 (0-8373-8162-2) Nat Learn.
— Chairman, Home Economics, Sr. H. S. (Teachers License Examination Ser.: CH-13). 1994. pap. 39.95 (0-8373-8163-0) Nat Learn.
— Chairman, Industrial Arts, Jr. H. S. (Teachers License Examination Ser.: CH-14). 1994. pap. 39.95 (0-8373-8164-9) Nat Learn.
— Chairman, Industrial Arts, Sr. H. S. (Teachers License Examination Ser.: CH-15). 1994. pap. 39.95 (0-8373-8165-7) Nat Learn.
— Chairman, Mathematics, Jr. H. S. (Teachers License Examination Ser.: CH-16). 1994. pap. 39.95 (0-8373-8166-5) Nat Learn.
— Chairman, Mathematics, Sr. H. S. (Teachers License Examination Ser.: CH-17). 1994. pap. 39.95 (0-8373-8167-3) Nat Learn.
— Chairman, Music, Jr. H. S. (Teachers License Examination Ser.: CH-18). 1994. pap. 39.95 (0-8373-8168-1) Nat Learn.
— Chairman, Music, Sr. H. S. (Teachers License Examination Ser.: CH-19). 1994. pap. 39.95 (0-8373-8169-X) Nat Learn.
— Chairman, Nursing. (Teachers License Examination Ser.: CH-31). 1994. pap. 39.95 (0-8373-8181-9) Nat Learn.
— Chairman, Related Technical Subjects (Biological & Chemical), Sr. H. S. (Teachers License Examination Ser.: CH-20). 1994. pap. 39.95 (0-8373-8170-3) Nat Learn.
— Chairman, Related Technical Subjects (Mechanical, Structural, Electrical), Sr. H. S. (Teachers License Examination Ser.: CH-21). 1994. pap. 39.95 (0-8373-8171-1) Nat Learn.
— Chairman, Sciences, Jr. H. S. (Teachers License Examination Ser.: CH-22). 1994. pap. 39.95 (0-8373-8172-X) Nat Learn.
— Chairman, Sciences, Sr. H. S. (Teachers License Examination Ser.: CH-23). 1994. pap. 39.95 (0-8373-8173-8) Nat Learn.
— Chairman, Shop Subjects, Sr. H. S. (Teachers License Examination Ser.: CH-24). 1994. pap. 39.95 (0-8373-8174-6) Nat Learn.
— Chairman, Social Studies, Jr. H. S. (Teachers License Examination Ser.: CH-25). 1994. pap. 39.95 (0-8373-8175-4) Nat Learn.
— Chairman, Social Studies, Sr. H. S. (Teachers License Examination Ser.: CH-26). 1994. pap. 39.95 (0-8373-8176-2) Nat Learn.
— Chairman, Speech, Sr. H. S. (Teachers License Examination Ser.: CH-27). 1994. pap. 39.95 (0-8373-8177-0) Nat Learn.
— Chairman, Stenography & Typewriting (Gregg & Pitman), Sr. H. S. (Teachers License Examination Ser.: CH-28). 1994. pap. 39.95 (0-8373-8178-9) Nat Learn.
— Chairman, Teacher-Trainer, Language Arts & Social Studies, I. S. & Jr. H. S. (Teachers License Examination Ser.: CH-30). 1994. pap. 39.95 (0-8373-8180-0) Nat Learn.
— Chairman, Teacher-Trainer, Math & Science, I. S. & Jr. H. S. (Teachers License Examination Ser.: CH-29). 1994. pap. 39.95 (0-8373-8179-7) Nat Learn.
— Chauffeur. (Career Examination Ser.: C-1166). 1994. pap. 23.95 (0-8373-1166-7) Nat Learn.
— Chemical Engineer. (Career Examination Ser.: C-134). 1994. pap. 29.95 (0-8373-0134-3) Nat Learn.
— Chemical Engineering Trainee. (Career Examination Ser.: C-3131). 1994. pap. 27.95 (0-8373-3131-5) Nat Learn.
— Chemist. (Career Examination Ser.: C-135). 1994. pap. 29.95 (0-8373-0135-1) Nat Learn.
— Chemist I (Environmental Control) (Career Examination Ser.: C-2983). 1994. pap. 29.95 (0-8373-2983-3) Nat Learn.
— Chemist II (Enviromental Control) (Career Examination Ser.: C-2984). 1994. pap. 29.95 (0-8373-2984-1) Nat Learn.
— Chemist Trainee. (Career Examination Ser.: C-1186). 1994. pap. 27.95 (0-8373-1186-1) Nat Learn.
— Chemistry. (Graduate Record Examination (GRE) Ser.: Vol. 2). 43.95 (0-8373-5252-5) Nat Learn.
— Chemistry. (Undergraduate Program Field Tests (UPFT) Ser.: Vol. 4). 43.95 (0-8373-6054-4) Nat Learn.
— Chemistry. (Regents College Proficiency Examination Ser.: Vol. 6). 43.95 (0-8373-5456-0) Nat Learn.
— Chemistry. (Undergraduate Program Field Tests Ser.: UPFT-4). 1994. pap. 23.95 (0-8373-6004-8) Nat Learn.
— Chemistry. (Regents College Proficiency Examination Ser.: Vol. CPEP-6). 1994. pap. 23.95 (0-8373-5406-4) Nat Learn.
— Chemistry. (Graduate Record Examination (GRE) Ser.: Vol. GRE-2). 1994. pap. 23.95 (0-8373-5202-9) Nat Learn.
— Chemistry & General Science. (National Teacher Examination Ser.: NT-7A). 1994. pap. 23.95 (0-8373-8409-5) Nat Learn.
— Chemistry & General Science, Senior High School. (Teachers License Examination Ser.: T-6). 1994. pap. 27.95 (0-8373-8006-5) Nat Learn.
— Chemistry, Physics & General Science. (National Teacher Examination Ser.: NT-7). 1994. pap. 23.95 (0-8373-8417-6) Nat Learn.
— Chief Account Clerk. (Career Examination Ser.: C-2707). 1994. pap. 29.95 (0-8373-2707-5) Nat Learn.
— Chief Accountant. (Career Examination Ser.: C-1565). 1994. pap. 39.95 (0-8373-1565-4) Nat Learn.
— Chief Auditor. (Career Examination Ser.: C-2348). 1994. pap. 39.95 (0-8373-2348-7) Nat Learn.
— Chief Beverage Control Investigator. (Career Examination Ser.: C-2825). 1994. pap. 34.95 (0-8373-2825-X) Nat Learn.
— Chief Biostatistician. (Career Examination Ser.: C-1167). 1994. pap. 39.95 (0-8373-1167-5) Nat Learn.
— Chief Budget Examiner. (Career Examination Ser.: C-2667). 1994. pap. 39.95 (0-8373-2667-2) Nat Learn.
— Chief Building Inspector. (Career Examination Ser.: C-2847). 1994. pap. 39.95 (0-8373-2847-0) Nat Learn.
— Chief Buildings Engineer. (Career Examination Ser.: C-1168). 1994. pap. 39.95 (0-8373-1168-3) Nat Learn.
— Chief Cartographer-Draftsman. (Career Examination Ser.: C-1169). 1994. pap. 34.95 (0-8373-1169-1) Nat Learn.
— Chief Civil Engineer. (Career Examination Ser.: C-1170). 1994. pap. 39.95 (0-8373-1170-5) Nat Learn.
— Chief Clerk. (Career Examination Ser.: C-189). 1994. pap. 29.95 (0-8373-0189-0) Nat Learn.
— Chief Clerk Surrogate. (Career Examination Ser.: C-2131). 1994. pap. 34.95 (0-8373-2131-X) Nat Learn.
— Chief Compensation Investigator. (Career Examination Ser.: C-3229). 1994. pap. 34.95 (0-8373-3229-X) Nat Learn.
— Chief Compliance Investigator. (Career Examination Ser.: C-2423). 1994. pap. 34.95 (0-8373-2423-8) Nat Learn.
— Chief Consumer Affairs Investigator. (Career Examination Ser.: C-2378). 1994. pap. 34.95 (0-8373-2378-9) Nat Learn.
— Chief Custodian. (Career Examination Ser.: C-2555). 1994. pap. 34.95 (0-8373-2555-2) Nat Learn.
— Chief Data Processing Control Clerk. (Career Examination Ser.: C-2486). 1994. pap. 29.95 (0-8373-2486-6) Nat Learn.
— Chief Data Processing Equipment Operator. (Career Examination Ser.: C-2304). 1994. pap. 34.95 (0-8373-2304-5) Nat Learn.
— Chief Deputy County Attorney. (Career Examination Ser.: C-1172). 1994. pap. 44.95 (0-8373-1172-1) Nat Learn.
— Chief Deputy Sheriff. (Career Examination Ser.: C-1173). 1994. pap. 34.95 (0-8373-1173-X) Nat Learn.
— Chief Dietitian. (Career Examination Ser.: C-1174). 1994. pap. 34.95 (0-8373-1174-8) Nat Learn.
— Chief Draftsman. (Career Examination Ser.: C-1577). 1994. pap. 39.95 (0-8373-1577-8) Nat Learn.
— Chief Electronic Computer Operator. (Career Examination Ser.: C-1550). 1994. pap. 34.95 (0-8373-1550-6) Nat Learn.
— Chief Elevator Starter. (Career Examination Ser.: C-1175). 1994. pap. 29.95 (0-8373-1175-6) Nat Learn.
— Chief Engineer. (Career Examination Ser.: C-1176). 1994. pap. 44.95 (0-8373-1176-4) Nat Learn.
— Chief Excise Tax Investigator. (Career Examination Ser.: C-2420). 1994. pap. 34.95 (0-8373-2420-3) Nat Learn.
— Chief Executive Officer. (Career Examination Ser.: C-2828). 1994. pap. 44.95 (0-8373-2828-4) Nat Learn.
— Chief Field Accountant. (Career Examination Ser.: C-1571). 1994. pap. 39.95 (0-8373-1571-9) Nat Learn.
— Chief File Clerk. (Career Examination Ser.: C-453). 1994. pap. 29.95 (0-8373-0453-9) Nat Learn.
— Chief Fire Marshal. (Career Examination Ser.: C-3431). 1994. pap. 39.95 (0-8373-3431-4) Nat Learn.
— Chief Groundskeeper. (Career Examination Ser.: C-1574). 1994. pap. 29.95 (0-8373-1574-3) Nat Learn.
— Chief Institution Safety Officer. (Career Examination Ser.: C-2120). 1994. pap. 34.95 (0-8373-2120-4) Nat Learn.
— Chief Investigator. (Career Examination Ser.: C-1401). 1994. pap. 34.95 (0-8373-1401-1) Nat Learn.
— Chief Key Punch Operator. (Career Examination Ser.: C-2104). 1994. pap. 29.95 (0-8373-2104-2) Nat Learn.
— Chief Labor Standards Investigator. (Career Examination Ser.: C-3127). 1994. pap. 39.95 (0-8373-3127-7) Nat Learn.
— Chief Law Assistant. (Career Examination Ser.: C-1177). 1994. pap. 34.95 (0-8373-1177-2) Nat Learn.
— Chief Law Stenographer. (Career Examination Ser.: C-941). 1994. pap. 29.95 (0-8373-0941-7) Nat Learn.
— Chief Management Analyst. (Career Examination Ser.: C-1178). 1994. pap. 44.95 (0-8373-1178-0) Nat Learn.
— Chief Marine Engineer. (Career Examination Ser.: C-1794). 1994. pap. 39.95 (0-8373-1794-0) Nat Learn.
— Chief Marketing Representative. (Career Examination Ser.: C-2041). 1994. pap. 34.95 (0-8373-2041-0) Nat Learn.
— Chief Marshal. (Career Examination Ser.: C-1179). 1994. pap. 34.95 (0-8373-1179-9) Nat Learn.
— Chief Meat Inspector. (Career Examination Ser.: C-2042). 1994. pap. 34.95 (0-8373-2042-9) Nat Learn.
— Chief Medical Examiner. (Career Examination Ser.: C-1180). 1994. pap. 59.95 (0-8373-1180-2) Nat Learn.
— Chief Multiple Residence Inspector. (Career Examination Ser.: C-2844). 1994. pap. 39.95 (0-8373-2844-6) Nat Learn.
— Chief of Police. (Career Examination Ser.: C-2148). 1994. pap. 49.95 (0-8373-2148-4) Nat Learn.
— Chief of Staff (Sheriff) (Career Examination Ser.: C-2502). 1994. pap. 39.95 (0-8373-2502-1) Nat Learn.
— Chief of Stenographic Services. (Career Examination Ser.: C-943). 1994. pap. 34.95 (0-8373-0943-3) Nat Learn.
— Chief Office Manager. (Career Examination Ser.: C-2400). 1994. pap. 39.95 (0-8373-2400-9) Nat Learn.
— Chief Personnel Administrator. (Career Examination Ser.: C-942). 1994. pap. 49.95 (0-8373-0942-5) Nat Learn.
— Chief Physical Therapist. (Career Examination Ser.: C-3384). 1994. pap. 39.95 (0-8373-3384-9) Nat Learn.
— Chief Police Surgeon. (Career Examination Ser.: C-1181). 1994. pap. 49.95 (0-8373-1181-0) Nat Learn.
— Chief Probation Officer. (Career Examination Ser.: C-1593). 1994. pap. 34.95 (0-8373-1593-X) Nat Learn.
— Chief Process Server. (Career Examination Ser.: C-1182). 1994. pap. 29.95 (0-8373-1182-9) Nat Learn.
— Chief Psychologist. (Career Examination Ser.: C-2194). 1994. pap. 44.95 (0-8373-2194-8) Nat Learn.
— Chief Public Health Nutritionist. (Career Examination Ser.: C-1567). 1994. pap. 34.95 (0-8373-1567-0) Nat Learn.
— Chief Purchasing Agent. (Career Examination Ser.: C-3323). 1994. pap. 34.95 (0-8373-3323-7) Nat Learn.
— Chief Recreation Therapist. (Career Examination Ser.: C-3279). 1994. pap. 39.95 (0-8373-3279-6) Nat Learn.
— Chief Registrar. (Career Examination Ser.: C-1183). 1994. pap. 34.95 (0-8373-1183-7) Nat Learn.
— Chief Safety & Security Officer. (Career Examination Ser.: C-3629). pap. 39.95 (0-8373-3629-5) Nat Learn.
— Chief Schedule Maker. (Career Examination Ser.: C-1729). 1994. pap. 39.95 (0-8373-1729-0) Nat Learn.
— Chief Security Officer. (Career Examination Ser.: C-1185). 1994. pap. 34.95 (0-8373-1185-3) Nat Learn.
— Chief Special Investigator. (Career Examination Ser.: C-1591). 1994. pap. 39.95 (0-8373-1591-3) Nat Learn.
— Chief Stationary Engineer. (Career Examination Ser.: C-1184). 1994. pap. 39.95 (0-8373-1184-5) Nat Learn.
— Chief Supervisor of Mechanical Installations. (Career Examination Ser.: C-2482). 1994. pap. 39.95 (0-8373-2482-3) Nat Learn.
— Chief Support Investigator. (Career Examination Ser.: C-2767). 1994. pap. 39.95 (0-8373-2767-9) Nat Learn.
— Chief Surface Line Dispatcher. (Career Examination Ser.: C-944). 1994. pap. 29.95 (0-8373-0944-1) Nat Learn.
— Chief Water Pollution Control Inspector. (Career Examination Ser.: C-1187). 1994. pap. 39.95 (0-8373-1187-X) Nat Learn.
— Chief Water Treatment Plant Operator. (Career Examination Ser.: C-2149). 1994. pap. 39.95 (0-8373-2149-2) Nat Learn.
— Child & Adolescent Nurse. (Certified Nurse Examination Ser.: CN-7). 1994. pap. 23.95 (0-8373-6107-9) Nat Learn.
— Child Protective Services Specialist. (Career Examination Ser.: C-3295). 1994. pap. 29.95 (0-8373-3295-8) Nat Learn.
— Child Protective Supervisor. (Career Examination Ser.: C-3701). 1991. pap. 34.95 (0-8373-3701-1) Nat Learn.
— Child Support Specialist. (Career Examination Ser.: C-3433). 1994. pap. 29.95 (0-8373-3433-0) Nat Learn.
— Children with Limited Vision. (Teachers License Examination Ser.: T-7). 1994. pap. 27.95 (0-8373-8007-3) Nat Learn.
— Children's Counselor. (Career Examination Ser.: C-1604). 1994. pap. 29.95 (0-8373-1604-9) Nat Learn.
— Citizen Participation Specialist. (Career Examination Ser.: C-3669). pap. 29.95 (0-8373-3669-4) Nat Learn.
— City Chamberlain. (Career Examination Ser.: C-2981). 1994. pap. 34.95 (0-8373-2981-7) Nat Learn.
— City Comptroller. (Career Examination Ser.: C-1746). 1994. pap. 39.95 (0-8373-1746-0) Nat Learn.
— City Surveyor. (Career Examination Ser.: C-1188). 1994. pap. 29.95 (0-8373-1188-8) Nat Learn.
— Civil Engineer. (Career Examination Ser.: C-136). 1994. pap. 29.95 (0-8373-0136-X) Nat Learn.
— Civil Engineer I. (Career Examination Ser.: C-2158). 1994. reprint ed. pap. 29.95 (0-8373-2158-1) Nat Learn.
— Civil Engineer I, II, III, IV, V. (Career Examination Ser.: C-2000). 1994. pap. 49.95 (0-8373-2000-3) Nat Learn.
— Civil Engineer II. (Career Examination Ser.: C-2159). 1994. reprint ed. pap. 29.95 (0-8373-2159-X) Nat Learn.
— Civil Engineer III. (Career Examination Ser.: C-2160). 1994. reprint ed. pap. 34.95 (0-8373-2160-3) Nat Learn.
— Civil Engineer IV. (Career Examination Ser.: C-2161). 1994. reprint ed. pap. 34.95 (0-8373-2161-1) Nat Learn.
— Civil Engineer (Materials) (Career Examination Ser.: C-3224). 1994. pap. 29.95 (0-8373-3224-9) Nat Learn.
— Civil Engineer (Physical Research) (Career Examination Ser.: C-3225). 1994. pap. 29.95 (0-8373-3225-7) Nat Learn.
— Civil Engineer (Planning) (Career Examination Ser.: C-3226). 1994. pap. 29.95 (0-8373-3226-5) Nat Learn.
— Civil Engineer (Traffic) (Career Examination Ser.: C-3227). 1994. pap. 29.95 (0-8373-3227-3) Nat Learn.
— Civil Engineer V. (Career Examination Ser.: C-2162). 1994. reprint ed. pap. 34.95 (0-8373-2162-X) Nat Learn.
— Civil Engineering Draftsman. (Career Examination Ser.: C-137). 1994. pap. 27.95 (0-8373-0137-8) Nat Learn.
— Civil Engineering Draftsman I. (Career Examination Ser.: C-2154). 1994. pap. 27.95 (0-8373-2154-9) Nat Learn.
— Civil Engineering Draftsman II. (Career Examination Ser.: C-2155). 1994. pap. 29.95 (0-8373-2155-7) Nat Learn.
— Civil Engineering Draftsman III. (Career Examination Ser.: C-2156). 1994. pap. 29.95 (0-8373-2156-5) Nat Learn.
— Civil Engineering Trainee. (Career Examination Ser.: C-945). 1994. pap. 27.95 (0-8373-0945-X) Nat Learn.
— Civil Service Administration, Management & Supervision. (General Aptitude & Abilities Ser.: CS-3). 1994. pap. 29.95 (0-8373-6703-4) Nat Learn.
— Civil Service Arithmetic. (General Aptitude & Abilities Ser.: CS-6). 1994. pap. 19.95 (0-8373-6706-9) Nat Learn.
— Civil Service Clerical Abilities. (General Aptitude & Abilities Ser.: CS-12). 1994. pap. 19.95 (0-8373-6712-3) Nat Learn.
— Civil Service General & Mental Abilities. (General Aptitude & Abilities Ser.: CS-16). 1994. pap. 23.95 (0-8373-6716-6) Nat Learn.
— Civil Service Grammar & Usage. (General Aptitude & Abilities Ser.: CS-7). 1994. pap. 23.95 (0-8373-6707-7) Nat Learn.
— Civil Service Graphs, Charts & Tables. (General Aptitude & Abilities Ser.: CS-11). 1994. pap. 23.95 (0-8373-6711-5) Nat Learn.
— Civil Service Home Study Course. (General Aptitude & Abilities Ser.: CS-1). 1994. pap. 23.95 (0-8373-6701-8) Nat Learn.
— Civil Service Mechanical Aptitude. (General Aptitude & Abilities Ser.: CS-15). 1994. pap. 23.95 (0-8373-6715-8) Nat Learn.
— Civil Service Promotion Course. (General Aptitude & Abilities Ser.: CS-2). 1994. pap. 27.95 (0-8373-6702-6) Nat Learn.
— Civil Service Reading Comprehension. (General Aptitude & Abilities Ser.: CS-8). 1994. pap. 23.95 (0-8373-6708-5) Nat Learn.
— Civil Service Secretary. (General Aptitude & Abilities Ser.: CS-4). 1994. pap. 23.95 (0-8373-6704-2) Nat Learn.
— Civil Service Spelling. (General Aptitude & Abilities Ser.: CS-9). 1994. pap. 19.95 (0-8373-6709-3) Nat Learn.
— Civil Service Test Practice Book for 100 Civil Service Jobs. (General Aptitude & Abilities Ser.: CS-5). 1994. pap. 29.95 (0-8373-6705-0) Nat Learn.
— Civil Service Verbal Abilities. (General Aptitude & Abilities Ser.: CS-13). 1994. pap. 19.95 (0-8373-6713-1) Nat Learn.
— Civil Service Verbal & Clerical Abilities. (General Aptitude & Abilities Ser.: CS-14). 1994. pap. 23.95 (0-8373-6714-X) Nat Learn.
— Civil Service Vocabulary. (General Aptitude & Abilities Ser.: CS-10). 1994. pap. 19.95 (0-8373-6710-7) Nat Learn.
— The Civil War & Reconstruction. (Dantes Subject Standardized Tests (DANTES) Ser.: Vol. 70). 43.95 (0-8373-6570-8) Nat Learn.
— The Civil War & Reconstruction, No. 70. Date not set. 23.95 (0-8373-6670-4) Nat Learn.
— Claim Examiner. (Career Examination Ser.: C-139). 1994. pap. 27.95 (0-8373-0139-4) Nat Learn.
— Claims Clerk. (Career Examination Ser.: C-138). 1994. pap. 23.95 (0-8373-0138-6) Nat Learn.
— Claims Examiner. (Career Examination Ser.: C-140). 1994. pap. 27.95 (0-8373-0140-8) Nat Learn.
— Claims Examiner Aide. (Career Examination Ser.: C-948). 1994. pap. 23.95 (0-8373-0948-4) Nat Learn.
— Claims Investigator. (Career Examination Ser.: C-3324). 1994. pap. 27.95 (0-8373-3324-5) Nat Learn.
— Claims Settlement Agent. (Career Examination Ser.: C-1189). 1994. pap. 27.95 (0-8373-1189-6) Nat Learn.
— Cleaner, Custodian USPS. (Career Examination Ser.: C-3315). 1994. pap. 27.95 (0-8373-3315-6) Nat Learn.
— Cleaner-Helper. (Career Examination Ser.: C-1195). 1994. pap. 23.95 (0-8373-1195-0) Nat Learn.
— Cleaner (T. A.) (Career Examination Ser.: C-946). 1994. pap. 23.95 (0-8373-0946-8) Nat Learn.
— Clerical & Administrative Support Positions. (Career Examination Ser.: C-314). 1994. pap. 23.95 (0-8373-0314-1) Nat Learn.

An Asterisk (*) at the beginning of an entry indicates that the title is appearing for the first time.

R

— Clerical Positions G-5. (Career Examination Ser.: C-1943). 1994. pap. 23.95 (*0-8373-1943-9*) Nat Learn.
— Clerical Training Supervisor. (Career Examination Ser.: C-1194). 1994. pap. 29.95 (*0-8373-1194-2*) Nat Learn.
— Clerk. (Career Examination Ser.: C-142). 1994. pap. 19.95 (*0-8373-0142-4*) Nat Learn.
— Clerk - Part-Time. (Career Examination Ser.: C-1191). 1994. pap. 19.95 (*0-8373-1191-8*) Nat Learn.
— Clerk-Carrier (U. S. P. S.) (Career Examination Ser.: C-143). 1994. pap. 19.95 (*0-8373-0143-2*) Nat Learn.
— Clerk GS1-4. (Career Examination Ser.: C-144). 1994. pap. 19.95 (*0-8373-0144-0*) Nat Learn.
— Clerk GS5-7. (Career Examination Ser.: C-145). 1994. pap. 19.95 (*0-8373-0145-9*) Nat Learn.
— Clerk I. (Career Examination Ser.: C-3271). 1994. pap. 19.95 (*0-8373-3271-0*) Nat Learn.
— Clerk II. (Career Examination Ser.: C-3272). 1994. pap. 23.95 (*0-8373-3272-9*) Nat Learn.
— Clerk III. (Career Examination Ser.: C-3273). 1994. pap. 27.95 (*0-8373-3273-7*) Nat Learn.
— Clerk (Income Maintenance) (Career Examination Ser.: C-1642). 1994. reprint ed. pap. 23.95 (*0-8373-1642-1*) Nat Learn.
— Clerk IV. (Career Examination Ser.: C-3274). 1994. pap. 29.95 (*0-8373-3274-5*) Nat Learn.
— Clerk-Laborer. (Career Examination Ser.: C-1190). 1994. pap. 23.95 (*0-8373-1190-X*) Nat Learn.
— Clerk of the Works. (Career Examination Ser.: C-3230). 1994. pap. 27.95 (*0-8373-3230-3*) Nat Learn.
— Clerk-Seasonal. (Career Examination Ser.: C-1192). 1994. pap. 19.95 (*0-8373-1192-6*) Nat Learn.
— Clerk-Stenographer. (Career Examination Ser.: C-146). 1994. pap. 19.95 (*0-8373-0146-7*) Nat Learn.
— Clerk-Stenographer I. (Career Examination Ser.: C-2339). 1994. pap. 19.95 (*0-8373-2339-8*) Nat Learn.
— Clerk-Stenographer II. (Career Examination Ser.: C-1650). 1994. pap. 23.95 (*0-8373-1650-2*) Nat Learn.
— Clerk-Stenographer III. (Career Examination Ser.: C-1651). 1994. pap. 27.95 (*0-8373-1651-0*) Nat Learn.
— Clerk-Stenographer IV. (Career Examination Ser.: C-1652). 1994. pap. 29.95 (*0-8373-1652-9*) Nat Learn.
— Clerk-Technician (U. S. P. S.) (Career Examination Ser.: C-1633). 1994. reprint ed. pap. 27.95 (*0-8373-1633-2*) Nat Learn.
— Clerk-Typist. (Career Examination Ser.: C-147). 1994. pap. 19.95 (*0-8373-0147-5*) Nat Learn.
— Clerk-Typist II. (Career Examination Ser.: C-3572). 1994. pap. 23.95 (*0-8373-3572-8*) Nat Learn.
— Clerk-Typist Trainee. (Career Examination Ser.: C-1193). 1994. pap. 19.95 (*0-8373-1193-4*) Nat Learn.
— Climatology - Meteorology. (DANTES Ser.: DANTES-9). 1994. pap. 23.95 (*0-8373-6609-7*) Nat Learn.
— Climber & Pruner. (Career Examination Ser.: C-148). 1994. pap. 23.95 (*0-8373-0148-3*) Nat Learn.
— Clinic Administrator. (Career Examination Ser.: C-915). 1994. pap. 39.95 (*0-8373-0915-8*) Nat Learn.
— Clinic Supervisor (Drug Abuse) (Career Examination Ser.: C-3007). 1994. pap. 39.95 (*0-8373-3007-6*) Nat Learn.
— Clinical Chemistry. (College Level Examination Ser.: CLEP-32). 1994. pap. 23.95 (*0-8373-5332-7*) Nat Learn.
— Clinical Laboratory Investigator. (Career Examination Ser.: C-2098). 1994. pap. 39.95 (*0-8373-2098-4*) Nat Learn.
— Clinical Nurse. (Career Examination Ser.: C-947). 1994. pap. 29.95 (*0-8373-0947-6*) Nat Learn.
— Clinical Psychologist. (Career Examination Ser.: C-149). 1994. pap. 34.95 (*0-8373-0149-1*) Nat Learn.
— Clinical Psychologist Intern. (Career Examination Ser.: C-1196). 1994. pap. 29.95 (*0-8373-1196-9*) Nat Learn.
— Clinical Specialist in Adult Psychiatric & Mental Health Nursing. (Certified Nurse Examination Ser.: CN-14). 1994. pap. 23.95 (*0-8373-6114-1*) Nat Learn.
— Clinical Specialist in Child & Adolescent Psychiatric & Mental Health Nursing. (Certified Nurse Examination Ser.: CN-15). 1994. pap. 23.95 (*0-8373-6115-X*) Nat Learn.
— Clinical Specialist in Medical-Surgical Nursing. (Certified Nurse Examination Ser.: CN-13). 1994. pap. 23.95 (*0-8373-6113-3*) Nat Learn.
— Clinician. (Career Examination Ser.: C-150). 1994. pap. 34.95 (*0-8373-0150-5*) Nat Learn.
— Clinician, Part-Time. (Career Examination Ser.: C-1197). 1994. pap. 29.95 (*0-8373-1197-7*) Nat Learn.
— Clock Repairer. (Career Examination Ser.: C-151). 1994. pap. 39.95 (*0-8373-0151-3*) Nat Learn.
— Clothing Attendant. (Career Examination Ser.: C-1198). 1994. pap. 23.95 (*0-8373-1198-5*) Nat Learn.
— Coastal Resources Specialist. (Career Examination Ser.: Vol. C-3813). 1997. pap. 29.95 (*0-8373-3813-1*) Nat Learn.
— Code Compliance Assistant. (Career Examination Ser.: C-3186). 1994. pap. 29.95 (*0-8373-3186-2*) Nat Learn.
— Code Compliance Coordinator. (Career Examination Ser.: C-3569). 1994. pap. 39.95 (*0-8373-3569-8*) Nat Learn.
— Code Compliance Supervisor. (Career Examination Ser.: C-3187). 1994. pap. 39.95 (*0-8373-3187-0*) Nat Learn.
— Code Enforcement Officer. (Career Examination Ser.: C-3424). 1994. pap. 34.95 (*0-8373-3424-1*) Nat Learn.
— Coding. (General Aptitude & Abilities Ser.: CS-44). 1994. pap. 19.95 (*0-8373-6744-1*) Nat Learn.
— Collection & Civil Prosecution Specialist. (Career Examination Ser.: C-3702). 1991. pap. 29.95 (*0-8373-3702-X*) Nat Learn.
— Collection Clerk. (Career Examination Ser.: C-3096). 1994. pap. 23.95 (*0-8373-3096-3*) Nat Learn.
— Collection Supervisor (Revenue) (Career Examination Ser.: C-3672). pap. 27.95 (*0-8373-3672-4*) Nat Learn.
— College Accounting Assistant. (Career Examination Ser.: Vol. C-3809). 1997. pap. 23.95 (*0-8373-3809-3*) Nat Learn.
— College Administrative Assistant. (Career Examination Ser.: C-152). 1994. pap. 27.95 (*0-8373-0152-1*) Nat Learn.
— College Administrative Associate. (Career Examination Ser.: C-2658). 1994. pap. 29.95 (*0-8373-2658-3*) Nat Learn.
— College Algebra. (College Level Examination (CLEP) Ser.: Vol. 6). 43.95 (*0-8373-5356-4*) Nat Learn.
— College Algebra. (College Level Examination Ser.: CLEP-6). 1994. pap. 23.95 (*0-8373-5306-8*) Nat Learn.
— College Algebra-Trigonometry. (College Level Examination Ser.: CLEP-7). 1994. pap. 23.95 (*0-8373-5307-6*) Nat Learn.
— College Algebras - Trigonometry. (College Level Examination (CLEP) Ser.: Vol. 7). 43.95 (*0-8373-5357-2*) Nat Learn.
— College & University Basic Competency Tests (BCT-C&U) (Admission Test Ser.: Vol. 58). 43.95 (*0-8373-5158-8*) Nat Learn.
— College & University Basic Competency Tests (BCT-C&U) (Admission Test Ser.: ATS-58). 1994. pap. 23.95 (*0-8373-5058-1*) Nat Learn.
— College Chemistry. (Dantes Subject Standardized Tests Ser.: DANTES-10). 1994. pap. 23.95 (*0-8373-6610-0*) Nat Learn.
— College Composition. (College Level Examination (CLEP) Ser.: Vol. 11). 43.95 (*0-8373-5361-0*) Nat Learn.
— College Composition. (College Level Examination Ser.: CLEP-11). 1994. pap. 23.95 (*0-8373-5311-4*) Nat Learn.
— College French. (College Level Examination Ser.: CLEP-44). 1994. reprint ed. pap. 23.95 (*0-8373-5344-0*) Nat Learn.
— College German. (College Level Examination Ser.: CLEP-45). 1994. reprint ed. pap. 23.95 (*0-8373-5345-9*) Nat Learn.
— College Graduate Careers Examination. (Career Examination Ser.: C-3703). 1994. pap. 29.95 (*0-8373-3703-8*) Nat Learn.
— College Level Academic Skills Test (CLAST) (Admission Test Ser.: ATS-111). pap. 29.95 (*0-8373-5811-6*) Nat Learn.
— College Level Examination. 1997. pap. text 20.01 (*0-8373-5350-5*) Nat Learn.
— College Level Examination Program - General Examination (CLEP) One Volume Combined Edition. (Admission Test Ser.: No. ATS-9). pap. 27.95 (*0-8373-5009-3*, ATS-9) Nat Learn.
— College-Level Examination Series. (Entire Ser.). 1994. pap. write for info. (*0-8373-5300-9*) Nat Learn.
— College Office Assistant A. (Career Examination Ser.: C-153). 1994. pap. 23.95 (*0-8373-0153-X*) Nat Learn.
— College Office Assistant B. (Career Examination Ser.: C-154). 1994. pap. 23.95 (*0-8373-0154-8*) Nat Learn.
— College Secretarial Assistant A. (Career Examination Ser.: C-155). 1994. pap. 23.95 (*0-8373-0155-6*) Nat Learn.
— College Secretarial Assistant B. (Career Examination Ser.: C-156). 1994. pap. 23.95 (*0-8373-0156-4*) Nat Learn.
— College Spanish. (College Level Examination Ser.: CLEP-46). 1994. reprint ed. pap. 23.95 (*0-8373-5346-7*) Nat Learn.
— Colleges of Podiatry Admission Test (CPAT) (Admission Test Ser.: Vol. 37). 49.95 (*0-8373-5137-5*) Nat Learn.
— Colleges of Podiatry Admission Test (CPAT) (Admission Test Ser.: ATS-37). 1994. reprint ed. pap. 29.95 (*0-8373-5037-9*) Nat Learn.
— Commercial & Advertising Art. (Occupational Competency Examination (OCE) Ser.: Vol. 11). 47.95 (*0-8373-5761-6*) Nat Learn.
— Commercial & Advertising Art. (Occupational Competency Examination Ser.: OCE-11). 1994. pap. 27.95 (*0-8373-5711-X*) Nat Learn.
— Commercial Driver's License (CDL) (Career Examination Ser.: Vol. C-295). 1997. pap. 29.95 (*0-8373-0295-1*) Nat Learn.
— Commercial Photography. (Occupational Competency Examination (OCE) Ser.: Vol. 12). 47.95 (*0-8373-5762-4*) Nat Learn.
— Commercial Photography. (Occupational Competency Examination Ser.: OCE-12). 1994. pap. 27.95 (*0-8373-5712-8*) Nat Learn.
— Commercial Valuation Specialist. (Career Examination Ser.: C-3289). 1994. pap. 29.95 (*0-8373-3289-3*) Nat Learn.
— Commissary Clerk I. (Career Examination Ser.: C-216). 1994. pap. 23.95 (*0-8373-0216-1*) Nat Learn.
— Commissary Clerk II. (Career Examination Ser.: C-217). 1994. pap. 27.95 (*0-8373-0217-X*) Nat Learn.
— Commissary Clerk III. (Career Examination Ser.: C-218). 1994. pap. 27.95 (*0-8373-0218-8*) Nat Learn.
— Commissary Clerk IV. (Career Examination Ser.: C-219). 1994. pap. 29.95 (*0-8373-0219-6*) Nat Learn.
— Commission on Graduates of Foreign Nursing Schools Qualifying Examinations (CGFNS) (Admission Test Ser.: ATS-90). 1994. pap. 39.95 (*0-8373-5090-5*) Nat Learn.
— Commissioner. (Career Examination Ser.: C-1199). 1994. pap. 39.95 (*0-8373-1199-3*) Nat Learn.
— Commissioner of Correction. (Career Examination Ser.: C-1203). 1994. pap. 49.95 (*0-8373-1203-5*) Nat Learn.
— Commissioner of Deeds. (Career Examination Ser.: C-157). 1994. pap. 49.95 (*0-8373-0157-2*) Nat Learn.
— Commissioner of General Services. (Career Examination Ser.: C-1858). 1994. pap. 49.95 (*0-8373-1858-0*) Nat Learn.
— Commissioner of Jurors. (Career Examination Ser.: C-1204). 1994. pap. 49.95 (*0-8373-1204-3*) Nat Learn.
— Commissioner of Police. (Career Examination Ser.: C-1200). 1994. pap. 49.95 (*0-8373-1200-0*) Nat Learn.
— Commissioner of Recreation & Community Services. (Career Examination Ser.: C-1890). 1994. pap. 49.95 (*0-8373-1890-4*) Nat Learn.
— Commissioner of Social Services. (Career Examination Ser.: C-1205). 1994. pap. 49.95 (*0-8373-1205-1*) Nat Learn.
— Common Branches (1-6), Elementary School. (Teachers License Examination Ser.: T-9). 1994. pap. 27.95 (*0-8373-8009-X*) Nat Learn.
— Commonalities in Nursing Care: Area A. (Regents External Degree (REDP) Ser.: Vol. 17). 43.95 (*0-8373-5667-9*) Nat Learn.
— Commonalities in Nursing Care: Area A. (Regents External Degree Ser.: REDP-17). 1994. pap. 23.95 (*0-8373-5617-2*) Nat Learn.
— Commonalities in Nursing Care: Area B. (Regents External Degree (REDP) Ser.: Vol. 18). 43.95 (*0-8373-5668-7*) Nat Learn.
— Commonalities in Nursing Care: Area B. (Regents External Degree Ser.: REDP-18). 1994. pap. 23.95 (*0-8373-5618-0*) Nat Learn.
— Commonalities in Nursing Care, Area A. (ACT Proficiency Examination Program (PEP) Ser.: Vol. 41). 43.95 (*0-8373-5591-5*) Nat Learn.
— Commonalities in Nursing Care, Area A. (ACT Proficiency Examination Program Ser.: PEP-41). 1994. pap. 23.95 (*0-8373-5541-9*) Nat Learn.
— Commonalities in Nursing Care, Area B. (ACT Proficiency Examination Program (PEP) Ser.: Vol. 42). 43.95 (*0-8373-5592-3*) Nat Learn.
— Commonalities in Nursing Care, Area B. (ACT Proficiency Examination Program Ser.: PEP-42). 1994. pap. 23.95 (*0-8373-5542-7*) Nat Learn.
— Communications Aide. (Career Examination Ser.: C-1201). 1994. pap. 23.95 (*0-8373-1201-9*) Nat Learn.
— Communications Analyst. (Career Examination Ser.: C-1202). 1994. pap. 29.95 (*0-8373-1202-7*) Nat Learn.
— Communications & Education. (Regents College Proficiency Examination Ser.: Vol. 20). 43.95 (*0-8373-5470-6*) Nat Learn.
— Communications & Education. (Regents College Proficiency Examination Ser.: CPEP-20). 1994. pap. 23.95 (*0-8373-5420-X*) Nat Learn.
— Communications Operator. (Career Examination Ser.: C-2296). 1994. reprint ed. pap. 23.95 (*0-8373-2296-0*) Nat Learn.
— Communications Specialist. (Career Examination Ser.: C-3586). 1994. pap. 27.95 (*0-8373-3586-8*) Nat Learn.
— Communications Technician. (Career Examination Ser.: C-2186). 1994. pap. 27.95 (*0-8373-2186-7*) Nat Learn.
— Community Centers (Physical Education) (Teachers License Examination Ser.: T-10). 1994. pap. 27.95 (*0-8373-8010-3*) Nat Learn.
— Community Development Administrator. (Career Examination Ser.: C-1420). 1994. pap. 39.95 (*0-8373-1420-8*) Nat Learn.
— Community Development Assistant. (Career Examination Ser.: C-904). 1994. pap. 27.95 (*0-8373-0904-2*) Nat Learn.
— Community Development Housing Analyst. (Career Examination Ser.: C-905). 1994. pap. 34.95 (*0-8373-0905-0*) Nat Learn.
— Community Development Program Analyst. (Career Examination Ser.: C-903). 1994. pap. 34.95 (*0-8373-0903-4*) Nat Learn.
— Community Development Program Technician. (Career Examination Ser.: C-902). 1994. pap. 29.95 (*0-8373-0902-6*) Nat Learn.
— Community Development Project Director. (Career Examination Ser.: C-909). 1994. pap. 39.95 (*0-8373-0909-3*) Nat Learn.
— Community Development Project Supervisor. (Career Examination Ser.: C-908). 1994. pap. 34.95 (*0-8373-0908-5*) Nat Learn.
— Community Development Specialist. (Career Examination Ser.: C-1421). 1994. pap. 29.95 (*0-8373-1421-6*) Nat Learn.
— Community Health Nurse. (Certified Nurse Examination Ser.: CN-4). 1994. pap. 23.95 (*0-8373-6104-4*) Nat Learn.
— Community Improvement Coordinator. (Career Examination Ser.: C-906). 1994. pap. 34.95 (*0-8373-0906-9*) Nat Learn.
— Community Liason Worker. (Career Examination Ser.: C-2976). 1994. pap. 23.95 (*0-8373-2976-0*) Nat Learn.
— Community Mental Health Nurse. (Career Examination Ser.: C-3223). 1994. pap. 34.95 (*0-8373-3223-0*) Nat Learn.
— Community Organization Specialist. (Career Examination Ser.: C-3292). 1994. pap. 27.95 (*0-8373-3292-3*) Nat Learn.
— Community Organization Specialist (Urban Renewal) (Career Examination Ser.: C-1206). pap. 29.95 (*0-8373-1206-X*) Nat Learn.
— Community Relations Assistant. (Career Examination Ser.: C-1207). 1994. pap. 23.95 (*0-8373-1207-8*) Nat Learn.
— Community Relations Specialist. (Career Examination Ser.: No. C-3535). 1994. pap. 27.95 (*0-8373-3535-3*) Nat Learn.
— Community Residence Aide. (Career Examination Ser.: C-3135). 1994. pap. 23.95 (*0-8373-3135-8*) Nat Learn.
— Community Service Aide. (Career Examination Ser.: C-1402). 1994. pap. 23.95 (*0-8373-1402-X*) Nat Learn.
— Community Service Officer. (Career Examination Ser.: C-1404). pap. 23.95 (*0-8373-1404-6*) Nat Learn.
— Community Service Worker. (Career Examination Ser.: C-2675). 1994. pap. 23.95 (*0-8373-2675-3*) Nat Learn.
— Community Services Assistant. (Career Examination Ser.: C-1403). 1994. pap. 23.95 (*0-8373-1403-8*) Nat Learn.
— Community Services Coordinator. (Career Examination Ser.: C-3306). 1994. pap. 34.95 (*0-8373-3306-7*) Nat Learn.
— Compensation Claims Auditor. (Career Examination Ser.: C-2126). 1994. reprint ed. pap. 29.95 (*0-8373-2126-3*) Nat Learn.
— Compensation Claims Clerk. (Career Examination Ser.: C-866). 1994. pap. 23.95 (*0-8373-0866-6*) Nat Learn.
— Compensation Claims Examiner. (Career Examination Ser.: C-2133). 1994. reprint ed. pap. 27.95 (*0-8373-2133-6*) Nat Learn.
— Compensation Claims Examiner Trainee. (Career Examination Ser.: C-879). 1994. pap. 23.95 (*0-8373-0879-8*) Nat Learn.
— Compensation Claims Investigator. (Career Examination Ser.: C-949). 1994. pap. 27.95 (*0-8373-0949-2*) Nat Learn.
— Compensation Claims Legal Investigator. (Career Examination Ser.: C-2100). 1994. pap. 27.95 (*0-8373-2100-X*) Nat Learn.
— Compensation Claims Referee. (Career Examination Ser.: C-3631). pap. 39.95 (*0-8373-3631-7*) Nat Learn.
— Compensation Investigator. (Career Examination Ser.: C-950). 1994. pap. 27.95 (*0-8373-0950-6*) Nat Learn.
— Complaint Investigator. (Career Examination Ser.: C-1863). 1994. pap. 27.95 (*0-8373-1863-7*) Nat Learn.
— Compliance Investigator. (Career Examination Ser.: C-2421). 1994. pap. 27.95 (*0-8373-2421-1*) Nat Learn.
— Composing Machine Operator. (Career Examination Ser.: C-1223). 1994. pap. 23.95 (*0-8373-1223-X*) Nat Learn.
— Compositor (Job) (Career Examination Ser.: C-2649). 1994. pap. 23.95 (*0-8373-2649-4*) Nat Learn.
— Comprehensive Employment & Training Act (CETA) Trainee. (Career Examination Ser.: C-2505). 1994. pap. 27.95 (*0-8373-2505-6*) Nat Learn.
— Computer Aide. (Career Examination Ser.: C-1208). 1994. pap. 23.95 (*0-8373-1208-6*) Nat Learn.
— Computer Aptitude Test (CAT) (Career Examination Ser.: C-180). 1994. pap. 23.95 (*0-8373-0180-7*) Nat Learn.
— Computer Associate (Applications Programming) (Career Examination Ser.: C-2470). 1994. pap. 29.95 (*0-8373-2470-X*) Nat Learn.
— Computer Associate (Operations) (Career Examination Ser.: C-2471). 1994. pap. 29.95 (*0-8373-2471-8*) Nat Learn.
— Computer Associate (Software) (Career Examination Ser.: C-3002). 1994. pap. 29.95 (*0-8373-3002-5*) Nat Learn.
— Computer Associate (Systems Programming) (Career Examination Ser.: C-2472). 1994. pap. 29.95 (*0-8373-2472-6*) Nat Learn.
— Computer Associate (Technical Support) (Career Examination Ser.: C-2473). 1994. pap. 29.95 (*0-8373-2473-4*) Nat Learn.
— Computer Control Supervisor. (Career Examination Ser.: C-3001). 1994. pap. 34.95 (*0-8373-3001-7*) Nat Learn.
— Computer Equipment Analyst. (Career Examination Ser.: C-1209). 1994. pap. 29.95 (*0-8373-1209-4*) Nat Learn.
— Computer Graphics Mapping Specialist. (Career Examination Ser.: C-3231). 1994. pap. 29.95 (*0-8373-3231-1*) Nat Learn.
— Computer Literacy: Data Processing. (National Teacher Examination Ser.: NT-49). 1994. pap. 23.95 (*0-8373-8459-1*) Nat Learn.
— Computer Operator. (Career Examination Ser.: C-158). 1994. pap. 23.95 (*0-8373-0158-0*) Nat Learn.
— Computer Operator II. (Career Examination Ser.: C-3151). 1994. pap. 27.95 (*0-8373-3151-X*) Nat Learn.
— Computer Operator III. (Career Examination Ser.: C-3152). 1994. pap. 29.95 (*0-8373-3152-8*) Nat Learn.
— Computer Operator IV. (Career Examination Ser.: C-3153). 1994. pap. 29.95 (*0-8373-3153-6*) Nat Learn.
— Computer Operator Trainee. (Career Examination Ser.: C-878). 1994. pap. 23.95 (*0-8373-0878-X*) Nat Learn.
— Computer Programmer. (Career Examination Ser.: C-159). 1994. pap. 27.95 (*0-8373-0159-9*) Nat Learn.
— Computer Programmer Analyst. (Career Examination Ser.: C-2474). 1994. pap. 27.95 (*0-8373-2474-2*) Nat Learn.
— Computer Programmer Analyst Trainee. (Career Examination Ser.: C-2475). 1994. pap. 23.95 (*0-8373-2475-0*) Nat Learn.
— Computer Programmer Trainee. (Career Examination Ser.: C-160). 1994. pap. 23.95 (*0-8373-0160-2*) Nat Learn.
— Computer Programming Supervisor. (Career Examination Ser.: C-1961). 1994. pap. 34.95 (*0-8373-1961-7*) Nat Learn.
— Computer Science. (Graduate Record Examination Ser.: GRE-21). 1994. pap. 23.95 (*0-8373-5221-5*) Nat Learn.
— Computer Specialist. (Career Examination Ser.: C-161). 1994. pap. 27.95 (*0-8373-0161-0*) Nat Learn.
— Computer Specialist (Applications Programming) (Career Examination Ser.: C-2874). 1994. pap. 29.95 (*0-8373-2874-8*) Nat Learn.
— Computer Specialist (Data Base Administration) (Career Examination Ser.: C-2876). 1994. pap. 29.95 (*0-8373-2876-4*) Nat Learn.
— Computer Specialist (Systems Programming) (Career Examination Ser.: C-2875). 1994. pap. 29.95 (*0-8373-2875-6*) Nat Learn.
— Computer Systems Analyst. (Career Examination Ser.: C-162). 1994. pap. 27.95 (*0-8373-0162-9*) Nat Learn.
— Computer Systems Analyst Trainee. (Career Examination Ser.: C-951). 1994. pap. 23.95 (*0-8373-0951-4*) Nat Learn.
— Computer Systems Manager. (Career Examination Ser.: C-1668). 1994. pap. 34.95 (*0-8373-1668-5*) Nat Learn.
— Computer Technical Assistant. (Career Examination Ser.: C-1210). 1994. pap. 27.95 (*0-8373-1210-8*) Nat Learn.
— Computer Technician. (Career Examination Ser.: C-952). 1994. pap. 29.95 (*0-8373-0952-2*) Nat Learn.
— Computer Technician. (Teacher's License Examination (TLE) Ser.: Vol. T-67). 1994. pap. 27.95 (*0-8373-8067-7*) Nat Learn.

— Computers & Data Processing. (College Level Examination (CLEP) Ser.: Vol. 8). 43.95 (*0-8373-5358-0*) Nat Learn.
— Computers & Data Processing. (College Level Examination Ser.: CLEP-8). 1994. pap. 23.95 (*0-8373-5308-4*) Nat Learn.
— Conductor. (Career Examination Ser.: C-163). 1994. pap. 19.95 (*0-8373-0163-7*) Nat Learn.
— Confidential Attendant. (Career Examination Ser.: C-1211). 1994. pap. 23.95 (*0-8373-1211-6*) Nat Learn.
— Confidential Investigator. (Career Examination Ser.: C-2806). 1994. pap. 27.95 (*0-8373-2806-3*) Nat Learn.
— Confidential Reporter. (Career Examination Ser.: C-1212). 1994. pap. 23.95 (*0-8373-1212-4*) Nat Learn.
— Confidential Secretary. (Career Examination Ser.: C-3023). 1994. pap. 23.95 (*0-8373-3023-8*) Nat Learn.
— Conservation Aide. (Career Examination Ser.: C-3704). 1991. pap. 27.95 (*0-8373-3704-6*) Nat Learn.
— Conservation Biologist. (Career Examination Ser.: C-3126). 1994. pap. 29.95 (*0-8373-3126-9*) Nat Learn.
— Conservation Operations Supervisor. (Career Examination Ser.: C-3591). 1994. pap. 34.95 (*0-8373-3591-4*) Nat Learn.
— Construction Analyst. (Career Examination Ser.: C-1216). 1994. pap. 34.95 (*0-8373-1216-7*) Nat Learn.
— Construction Cost Specialist. (Career Examination Ser.: C-2060). 1994. reprint ed. pap. 34.95 (*0-8373-2060-7*) Nat Learn.
— Construction Equipment Mechanic. (Career Examination Ser.: C-3435). 1994. pap. 27.95 (*0-8373-3435-7*) Nat Learn.
— Construction Equipment Repair Production Coordinator. (Career Examination Ser.: C-3436). 1994. pap. 34.95 (*0-8373-3436-5*) Nat Learn.
— Construction Inspector. (Career Examination Ser.: C-164). 1994. pap. 29.95 (*0-8373-0164-5*) Nat Learn.
— Construction Inspector No. I. (Career Examination Ser.: C-3441). 1994. pap. 29.95 (*0-8373-3441-1*) Nat Learn.
— Construction Inspector No. II. (Career Examination Ser.: C-3042). 1994. pap. 34.95 (*0-8373-3042-4*) Nat Learn.
— Construction Inspector No. III. (Career Examination Ser.: C-3443). 1994. pap. 34.95 (*0-8373-3443-8*) Nat Learn.
— Construction Inspector Trainee. (Career Examination Ser.: C-3167). 1994. pap. 27.95 (*0-8373-3167-6*) Nat Learn.
— Construction Manager. (Career Examination Ser.: C-1789). 1994. pap. 39.95 (*0-8373-1789-4*) Nat Learn.
— Construction Project Manager Intern. (Career Examination Ser.: C-3734). 1991. pap. 29.95 (*0-8373-3734-8*) Nat Learn.
— Consultant. (Career Examination Ser.: C-953). 1994. pap. 34.95 (*0-8373-0953-0*) Nat Learn.
— Consultant (Early Childhood Education) (Career Examination Ser.: C-954). 1994. pap. 34.95 (*0-8373-0954-9*) Nat Learn.
— Consultant in Audiology. (Career Examination Ser.: C-1213). 1994. pap. 34.95 (*0-8373-1213-2*) Nat Learn.
— Consumer Affairs Inspector. (Career Examination Ser.: C-1655). 1994. pap. 27.95 (*0-8373-1655-3*) Nat Learn.
— Consumer Affairs Investigator. (Career Examination Ser.: C-1214). 1994. pap. 27.95 (*0-8373-1214-0*) Nat Learn.
— Consumer Affairs Research Assistant. (Career Examination Ser.: C-1215). 1994. pap. 27.95 (*0-8373-1215-9*) Nat Learn.
— Consumer Affairs Specialist. (Career Examination Ser.: C-1864). 1994. reprint ed. pap. 27.95 (*0-8373-1864-5*) Nat Learn.
— Consumer Frauds Representative. (Career Examination Ser.: C-876). 1994. pap. 27.95 (*0-8373-0876-3*) Nat Learn.
— Consumer Services Representative. (Career Examination Ser.: Vol. C-3812). 1997. pap. 34.95 (*0-8373-3812-3*) Nat Learn.
— Contemporary Western Europe. (Dantes Subject Standardized Tests (DANTES) Ser.: Vol. 71). 43.95 (*0-8373-6571-6*) Nat Learn.
— Contemporary Western Europe. (Dantes Subject Standardized Tests (DANTES) Ser.: Vol. DANTES-71). 1997. pap. 23.95 (*0-8373-6671-2*) Nat Learn.
— Contract Coordinator. (Career Examination Ser.: C-3439). 1994. pap. 29.95 (*0-8373-3439-X*) Nat Learn.
— Contract Specialist. (Career Examination Ser.: C-955). 1994. pap. 27.95 (*0-8373-0955-7*) Nat Learn.
— Contracts Examiner. (Career Examination Ser.: C-888). 1994. pap. 27.95 (*0-8373-0888-7*) Nat Learn.
— Contracts Technician. (Career Examination Ser.: C-834). 1994. pap. 27.95 (*0-8373-0834-8*) Nat Learn.
— Control Room Supervisor. (Career Examination Ser.: C-3705). 1994. pap. 34.95 (*0-8373-3705-4*) Nat Learn.
— Cook. (Career Examination Ser.: C-1218). 1994. pap. 27.95 (*0-8373-1218-3*) Nat Learn.
— Coordinator of Child Support Enforcement. (Career Examination Ser.: C-927). 1994. pap. 39.95 (*0-8373-0927-1*) Nat Learn.
— Coordinator of Community Mental Health Services. (Career Examination Ser.: C-1228). 1994. pap. 39.95 (*0-8373-1228-0*) Nat Learn.
— Coordinator of Drainage Designing. (Career Examination Ser.: C-3124). 1994. pap. 39.95 (*0-8373-3124-2*) Nat Learn.
— Coordinator of Drug Abuse Educational Programs. (Career Examination Ser.: C-1767). 1994. pap. 39.95 (*0-8373-1767-3*) Nat Learn.
— Coordinator of Educational Affairs. (Career Examination Ser.: C-2209). 1994. pap. 39.95 (*0-8373-2209-X*) Nat Learn.
— Coordinator of Human Services. (Career Examination Ser.: C-3706). 1994. pap. 39.95 (*0-8373-3706-2*) Nat Learn.
— Coordinator of Laboratory Services. (Career Examination Ser.: C-1227). 1994. pap. 39.95 (*0-8373-1227-2*) Nat Learn.
— Coordinator of Nursing Education. (Career Examination Ser.: C-1843). 1994. pap. 39.95 (*0-8373-1843-2*) Nat Learn.
— Coordinator of Surveying Services. (Career Examination Ser.: C-3022). 1994. pap. 39.95 (*0-8373-3022-X*) Nat Learn.
— Coordinator of Volunteer Services. (Career Examination Ser.: C-3110). 1994. pap. 34.95 (*0-8373-3110-2*) Nat Learn.
— Coordinator, Senior Citizen Planning & Research. (Career Examination Ser.: C-2939). 1994. pap. 39.95 (*0-8373-2939-6*) Nat Learn.
— Corporate Finance. (ACT Proficiency Examination Program Ser.: PEP-15). 1994. pap. 23.95 (*0-8373-5515-X*) Nat Learn.
— Correction Captain. (Career Examination Ser.: C-165). 1994. pap. 29.95 (*0-8373-0165-3*) Nat Learn.
— Correction Counselor. (Career Examination Ser.: C-2593). 1994. pap. 29.95 (*0-8373-2593-5*) Nat Learn.
— Correction Counselor Trainee. (Career Examination Ser.: C-2999). 1994. pap. 27.95 (*0-8373-2999-X*) Nat Learn.
— Correction Hospital Officer (Men) (Career Examination Ser.: C-956a). 1994. pap. 27.95 (*0-8373-0956-5*) Nat Learn.
— Correction Hospital Officer (Women) (Career Examination Ser.: C-956b). 1994. pap. 27.95 (*0-685-03521-2*) Nat Learn.
— Correction Lieutenant. (Career Examination Ser.: C-166). 1994. pap. 29.95 (*0-8373-0166-1*) Nat Learn.
— Correction Matron. (Career Examination Ser.: C-1219). 1994. pap. 23.95 (*0-8373-1219-1*) Nat Learn.
— Correction Officer. (Career Examination Ser.: C-3019). 1994. pap. 23.95 (*0-8373-3019-X*) Nat Learn.
— Correction Officer I. (Career Examination Ser.: C-837). 1994. pap. 23.95 (*0-8373-0837-2*) Nat Learn.
— Correction Officer II. (Career Examination Ser.: C-838). 1994. pap. 27.95 (*0-8373-0838-0*) Nat Learn.
— Correction Officer III. (Career Examination Ser.: C-839). 1994. pap. 27.95 (*0-8373-0839-9*) Nat Learn.
— Correction Officer IV. (Career Examination Ser.: C-840). 1994. pap. 29.95 (*0-8373-0840-2*) Nat Learn.
— Correction Officer (Men) (Career Examination Ser.: C-167). 1994. pap. 23.95 (*0-8373-0167-X*) Nat Learn.
— Correction Officer Trainee. (Career Examination Ser.: C-957). 1994. pap. 23.95 (*0-8373-0957-3*) Nat Learn.
— Correction Officer (Women) (Career Examination Ser.: C-168). 1994. pap. 23.95 (*0-8373-0168-8*) Nat Learn.
— Correction Promotion Course. (General Aptitude & Abilities Ser.: CS-25). 1994. pap. 39.95 (*0-8373-6725-5*) Nat Learn.
— Correction Sergeant. (Career Examination Ser.: C-169). 1994. pap. 27.95 (*0-8373-0169-6*) Nat Learn.
— Correction Youth Camp Officer (Men) (Career Examination Ser.: C-958a). 1994. pap. 23.95 (*0-8373-0958-1*) Nat Learn.
— Correction Youth Camp Officer (Women) (Career Examination Ser.: C-958b). 1994. pap. 23.95 (*0-685-03522-0*) Nat Learn.
— Correctional Alternatives Program Representative. (Career Examination Ser.: C-3622). pap. 34.95 (*0-8373-3622-8*) Nat Learn.
— Correctional Treatment Specialist. (Career Examination Ser.: C-959). 1994. pap. 34.95 (*0-8373-0959-X*) Nat Learn.
— Corrective & Remedial Instruction in Reading. (Regents College Proficiency Examination Ser.: Vol. 31). 43.95 (*0-8373-5481-1*) Nat Learn.
— Corrective & Remedial Instruction in Reading. (ACT Proficiency Examination Program (PEP) Ser.: Vol. 32). 43.95 (*0-8373-5582-6*) Nat Learn.
— Corrective & Remedial Instruction in Reading. (ACT Proficiency Examination Program Ser.: PEP-32). 1994. pap. 23.95 (*0-8373-5532-X*) Nat Learn.
— Corrective & Remedial Instruction in Reading. (Regents College Proficiency Examination Ser.: Vol. CPEP-31). 1994. pap. 23.95 (*0-8373-5431-5*) Nat Learn.
— Corrective Therapist. (Career Examination Ser.: C-960). 1994. pap. 29.95 (*0-8373-0960-3*) Nat Learn.
— Correctness & Effectiveness of English Expression (G. E. D.) (General Aptitude & Abilities Ser.: CS-35). 1994. pap. 17.95 (*0-8373-6735-2*) Nat Learn.
— Cosmetologist. (Career Examination Ser.: C-2251). 1994. pap. 29.95 (*0-8373-2251-0*) Nat Learn.
— Cosmetology. Date not set. 43.95 (*0-8373-5763-2*) Nat Learn.
— Cosmetology. (Occupational Competency Examination Ser.: OCE-13). 1994. pap. 27.95 (*0-8373-5713-6*) Nat Learn.
— Cosmetology. (Teacher's License Examination (TLE) Ser.: Vol. T-71). 1994. pap. 27.95 (*0-8373-8071-5*) Nat Learn.
— Cost Accounting & Analysis. (ACT Proficiency Examination Program Ser.). 39.95 (*0-8373-5562-1*) Nat Learn.
— Cost Accounting & Analysis. (ACT Proficiency Examination Program Ser.: PEP-12). 1994. pap. 23.95 (*0-8373-5512-5*) Nat Learn.
— Cost & Statistical Analyst. (Career Examination Ser.: C-3561). 1994. pap. 39.95 (*0-8373-3561-2*) Nat Learn.
— Counselor. (Career Examination Ser.: C-1162). 1994. pap. 29.95 (*0-8373-1162-4*) Nat Learn.
— County Attorney. (Career Examination Ser.: C-1220). 1994. pap. 39.95 (*0-8373-1220-5*) Nat Learn.
— County Clerk. (Career Examination Ser.: C-2114). 1994. pap. 29.95 (*0-8373-2114-X*) Nat Learn.
— County Comptroller. (Career Examination Ser.: C-1222). 1994. pap. 39.95 (*0-8373-1222-1*) Nat Learn.
— County Director of Accounting. (Career Examination Ser.: C-1960). 1994. pap. 39.95 (*0-8373-1960-9*) Nat Learn.
— County Executive. (Career Examination Ser.: C-1224). 1994. pap. 49.95 (*0-8373-1224-8*) Nat Learn.
— County Treasurer. (Career Examination Ser.: C-1225). 1994. pap. 39.95 (*0-8373-1225-6*) Nat Learn.
— Court Assistant. (Career Examination Ser.: C-1226). 1994. pap. 23.95 (*0-8373-1226-4*) Nat Learn.
— Court Assistant I. (Career Examination Ser.: C-961). 1994. pap. 23.95 (*0-8373-0961-1*) Nat Learn.
— Court Assistant II. (Career Examination Ser.: C-962). 1994. pap. 27.95 (*0-8373-0962-X*) Nat Learn.
— Court Attendant. (Career Examination Ser.: C-170). 1994. pap. 23.95 (*0-8373-0170-X*) Nat Learn.
— Court Clerk. (Career Examination Ser.: C-171). 1994. pap. 27.95 (*0-8373-0171-8*) Nat Learn.
— Court Clerk I. (Career Examination Ser.: C-963). 1994. pap. 27.95 (*0-8373-0963-8*) Nat Learn.
— Court Clerk II. (Career Examination Ser.: C-964). 1994. pap. 29.95 (*0-8373-0964-6*) Nat Learn.
— Court Consultation Specialist. (Career Examination Ser.: C-3707). 1994. pap. 34.95 (*0-8373-3707-0*) Nat Learn.
— Court Hearing Reporter. (Career Examination Ser.: C-172). 1994. pap. 23.95 (*0-8373-0172-6*) Nat Learn.
— Court Law Stenographer. (Career Examination Ser.: C-173). 1994. pap. 23.95 (*0-8373-0173-4*) Nat Learn.
— Court Office Assistant. (Career Examination Ser.: C-965). 1994. pap. 23.95 (*0-8373-0965-4*) Nat Learn.
— Court Officer. (Career Examination Ser.: C-966). 1994. pap. 23.95 (*0-8373-0966-2*) Nat Learn.
— Court Officer Sergeant. (Career Examination Ser.: No. C-3508). 1994. pap. 27.95 (*0-8373-3508-6*) Nat Learn.
— Court Records Supervisor. (Career Examination Ser.: C-3160). 1994. pap. 29.95 (*0-8373-3160-9*) Nat Learn.
— Court Reporter. (Career Examination Ser.: C-174). 1994. pap. 23.95 (*0-8373-0174-2*) Nat Learn.
— Court Reporter, I. (Career Examination Ser.: C-967). 1994. pap. 23.95 (*0-8373-0967-0*) Nat Learn.
— Court Reporter, II. (Career Examination Ser.: C-968). 1994. pap. 27.95 (*0-8373-0968-9*) Nat Learn.
— Court Security Supervisor. (Career Examination Ser.: C-3632). pap. 29.95 (*0-8373-3632-5*) Nat Learn.
— Crane Operator (Any Motive Power Except Steam) (AMPES) (Career Examination Ser.: C-1749). 1994. pap. 27.95 (*0-8373-1749-5*) Nat Learn.
— Credit & Collection Coordinator. (Career Examination Ser.: C-3107). 1994. pap. 34.95 (*0-8373-3107-2*) Nat Learn.
— Crime & Delinquency Prevention Specialist. (Career Examination Ser.: C-3212). 1994. pap. 34.95 (*0-8373-3212-5*) Nat Learn.
— Crime Victims' Advocate. (Career Examination Ser.: C-3497). 1994. pap. 34.95 (*0-8373-3497-7*) Nat Learn.
— Crime Victims Program Monitor. (Career Examination Ser.: C-3438). 1994. pap. 34.95 (*0-8373-3438-1*) Nat Learn.
— Criminal Identification Technician. (Career Examination Ser.: C-3105). 1994. pap. 29.95 (*0-8373-3105-6*) Nat Learn.
— Criminal Investigation. (Regents College Proficiency Examination Ser.: Vol. 30). 43.95 (*0-8373-5480-3*) Nat Learn.
— Criminal Investigation. (ACT Proficiency Examination Program (PEP) Ser.: Vol. 9). 43.95 (*0-8373-5559-1*) Nat Learn.
— Criminal Investigation. (ACT Proficiency Examination Program Ser.: PEP-9). 1994. pap. 23.95 (*0-8373-5509-5*) Nat Learn.
— Criminal Investigation. (Regents College Proficiency Examination Ser.: Vol. CPEP-30). 1994. pap. 23.95 (*0-8373-5430-7*) Nat Learn.
— Criminal Investigator. (Career Examination Ser.: C-1229). 1994. pap. 29.95 (*0-8373-1229-9*) Nat Learn.
— Criminal Law Investigator. (Career Examination Ser.: C-969). 1994. pap. 29.95 (*0-8373-0969-7*) Nat Learn.
— Criminalist. (Career Examination Ser.: No. C-3511). 1994. pap. 39.95 (*0-8373-3511-6*) Nat Learn.
— Criminology. (Dantes Subject Standardized Tests Ser.: Vol. DANTES-11). 1994. pap. 23.95 (*0-8373-6611-9*) Nat Learn.
— Criminology, Criminal Justice. (DANTES Ser.: Vol. DANTES-11). 1994. 39.95 (*0-8373-6511-2*) Nat Learn.
— Crisis Intervention Worker. (Career Examination Ser.: C-3708). 1994. pap. 27.95 (*0-8373-3708-9*) Nat Learn.
— Critical Care Nurse. (Certified Nurse Examination Ser.: CN-18). pap. 23.95 (*0-8373-6118-4*) Nat Learn.
— Cultural Affairs Supervisor. (Career Examination Ser.: C-2860). 1994. pap. 29.95 (*0-8373-2860-8*) Nat Learn.
— Cultural Program Assistant. (Career Examination Ser.: No. C-3540). 1994. pap. 27.95 (*0-8373-3540-X*) Nat Learn.
— Custodial Assistant. (Career Examination Ser.: Vol. C-141). 1994. pap. 19.95 (*0-8373-0141-6*) Nat Learn.
— Custodial Foreman. (Career Examination Ser.: C-970). 1994. pap. 27.95 (*0-8373-0970-0*) Nat Learn.
— Custodial Laborer (USPS) (Career Examination Ser.: C-3316). 1994. pap. 23.95 (*0-8373-3316-4*) Nat Learn.
— Custodial Work Supervisor. (Career Examination Ser.: C-1231). 1994. pap. 29.95 (*0-8373-1231-0*) Nat Learn.
— Custodial Worker. (Career Examination Ser.: C-1230). 1994. pap. 23.95 (*0-8373-1230-2*) Nat Learn.
— Custodian. (Career Examination Ser.: C-175). 1994. pap. 23.95 (*0-8373-0175-0*) Nat Learn.
— Custodian-Engineer. (Career Examination Ser.: C-176). 1994. pap. 27.95 (*0-8373-0176-9*) Nat Learn.
— Customer Service Representative. (Career Examination Ser.: C-3605). 1994. pap. 29.95 (*0-8373-3605-8*) Nat Learn.
— Customhouse Brokers License Examination (CBLE) (Admission Test Ser.: ATS-7). 1994. pap. 49.95 (*0-8373-5007-7*) Nat Learn.
— Customhouse Brokers' License Examination (CBLE) (Admission Test Ser.: Vol. 7). 69.95 (*0-8373-5107-3*) Nat Learn.
— Customs Aide. (Career Examination Ser.: C-3442). 1994. pap. 23.95 (*0-8373-3442-X*) Nat Learn.
— Customs Inspector. (Career Examination Ser.: C-177). 1994. pap. 27.95 (*0-8373-0177-7*) Nat Learn.
— Customs Security Officer (Sky Marshal) (Career Examination Ser.: C-1611). 1994. pap. 27.95 (*0-8373-1611-1*) Nat Learn.
— Dairy Products Specialist. (Career Examination Ser.: C-3117). 1994. pap. 29.95 (*0-8373-3117-X*) Nat Learn.
— Dance, Jr. H. S. (Teachers License Examination Ser.: T-64). 1994. pap. 27.95 (*0-8373-8064-2*) Nat Learn.
— Data Base Coordinator. (Career Examination Ser.: C-3232). 1994. pap. 34.95 (*0-8373-3232-X*) Nat Learn.
— Data Base Manager. (Career Examination Ser.: C-2873). 1994. pap. 34.95 (*0-8373-2873-X*) Nat Learn.
— Data Base Programmer Analyst. (Career Examination Ser.: C-3233). 1994. pap. 29.95 (*0-8373-3233-8*) Nat Learn.
— Data Collection Clerk. (Career Examination Ser.: C-1233). 1994. pap. 23.95 (*0-8373-1233-7*) Nat Learn.
— Data Communications Specialist. (Career Examination Ser.: C-3234). 1994. pap. 29.95 (*0-8373-3234-6*) Nat Learn.
— Data Control Assistant. (Career Examination Ser.: C-2889). 1994. pap. 23.95 (*0-8373-2889-6*) Nat Learn.
— Data Control Specialist. (Career Examination Ser.: C-901). 1994. pap. 27.95 (*0-8373-0901-8*) Nat Learn.
— Data Conversion Operator (USPS) (Career Examination Ser.: C-1609). 1994. pap. 29.95 (*0-8373-1609-X*) Nat Learn.
— Data Entry Clerk. (Career Examination Ser.: C-3339). 1994. pap. 23.95 (*0-8373-3339-3*) Nat Learn.
— Data Entry Machine Operator. (Career Examination Ser.: C-2409). 1994. pap. 23.95 (*0-8373-2409-2*) Nat Learn.
— Data Entry Supervisor. (Career Examination Ser.: C-1232). 1994. pap. 29.95 (*0-8373-1232-9*) Nat Learn.
— Data Processing. (Occupational Competency Examination (OCE) Ser.: Vol. 14). 47.95 (*0-8373-5764-0*) Nat Learn.
— Data Processing. (Occupational Competency Examination Ser.: OCE-14). 1994. pap. 27.95 (*0-8373-5714-4*) Nat Learn.
— Data Processing Clerk I. (Career Examination Ser.: C-536). 1994. pap. 23.95 (*0-8373-0536-5*) Nat Learn.
— Data Processing Clerk II. (Career Examination Ser.: C-537). 1994. pap. 27.95 (*0-8373-0537-3*) Nat Learn.
— Data Processing Clerk III. (Career Examination Ser.: C-538). 1994. pap. 27.95 (*0-8373-0538-1*) Nat Learn.
— Data Processing Control Clerk. (Career Examination Ser.: C-2483). 1994. pap. 23.95 (*0-8373-2483-1*) Nat Learn.
— Data Processing Equipment Operator. (Career Examination Ser.: C-2301). 1994. pap. 23.95 (*0-8373-2301-0*) Nat Learn.
— Data Processing Operations Coordinator. (Career Examination Ser.: C-2759). 1994. pap. 34.95 (*0-8373-2759-8*) Nat Learn.
— Data Processing Operations Supervisor. (Career Examination Ser.: C-2347). 1994. pap. 29.95 (*0-8373-2347-9*) Nat Learn.
— Data Processing Specialist. (Career Examination Ser.: C-2242). 1994. pap. 29.95 (*0-8373-2242-1*) Nat Learn.
— Data Transcriber. (Career Examination Ser.: C-1634). 1994. reprint ed. pap. 23.95 (*0-8373-1634-0*) Nat Learn.
— Day Care Center Aide. (Career Examination Ser.: C-1235). 1994. pap. 23.95 (*0-8373-1235-3*) Nat Learn.
— Deaf & Hard of Hearing. (Teachers License Examination Ser.: T-11). 1994. pap. 27.95 (*0-8373-8011-1*) Nat Learn.
— Deckhand. (Career Examination Ser.: C-190). 1994. pap. 29.95 (*0-8373-0190-4*) Nat Learn.
— Demolition Inspector. (Career Examination Ser.: C-191). 1994. pap. 29.95 (*0-8373-0191-2*) Nat Learn.
— Dental Admission Test (DAT) (Admission Test Ser.: Vol. 12). 43.95 (*0-8373-5112-X*) Nat Learn.
— Dental Admission Test (DAT) (Admission Test Ser.: ATS-12). 1994. pap. 29.95 (*0-8373-5012-3*) Nat Learn.
— Dental Assistant. (Career Examination Ser.: C-205). 1994. pap. 29.95 (*0-8373-0205-6*) Nat Learn.
— Dental Assisting. (Occupational Competency Examination (OCE) Ser.: Vol. 15). 47.95 (*0-8373-5765-9*) Nat Learn.
— Dental Assisting. (Occupational Competency Examination Ser.: OCE-15). 1994. pap. 27.95 (*0-8373-5715-2*) Nat Learn.
— Dental Auxiliary Education Examination in Dental Materials. (College Level Examination Ser.: CLEP-47). 1994. pap. 23.95 (*0-8373-5347-5*) Nat Learn.
— Dental Auxiliary Education Examination in Head, Neck & Oral Anatomy. (College Level Examination Ser.: CLEP-48). 1994. pap. 23.95 (*0-8373-5348-3*) Nat Learn.
— Dental Auxiliary Education Examination in Oral Radiography. (College Level Examination Ser.: CLEP-49). 1994. pap. 23.95 (*0-8373-5349-1*) Nat Learn.
— Dental Auxiliary Education Examination in Tooth Morphology & Function. (College Level Examination Ser.: CLEP-50). 1994. pap. 23.95 (*0-8373-5950-3*) Nat Learn.
— Dental Hygiene Aptitude Test (DHAT) (Admission Test Ser.: Vol. 32). 49.95 (*0-8373-5132-4*) Nat Learn.
— Dental Hygiene Aptitude Test (DHAT) (Admission Test Ser.: ATS-32). 1994. pap. 29.95 (*0-8373-5032-8*) Nat Learn.
— Dental Hygienist. (Career Examination Ser.: C-192). 1994. pap. 29.95 (*0-8373-0192-0*) Nat Learn.
— Dentist. (Career Examination Ser.: C-193). 1994. pap. 49.95 (*0-8373-0193-9*) Nat Learn.
— Denver Proficiency & Review Program (PRP) (Admission Test Ser.: Vol. 66). 43.95 (*0-8373-5166-9*) Nat Learn.
— Denver Proficiency & Review Program (PRP) (Admission Test Ser.: ATS-66). 1994. pap. 23.95 (*0-8373-5066-2*) Nat Learn.
— Department Librarian. (Career Examination Ser.: C-194). 1994. pap. 27.95 (*0-8373-0194-7*) Nat Learn.

— Department Library Aide. (Career Examination Ser.: C-206). 1994. pap. 23.95 (*0-8373-0206-4*) Nat Learn.
— Department Senior Librarian. (Career Examination Ser.: C-1622). 1994. pap. 29.95 (*0-8373-1622-7*) Nat Learn.
— Deputy. (Career Examination Ser.: C-1236). 1994. pap. 29.95 (*0-8373-1236-1*) Nat Learn.
— Deputy Assessor. (Career Examination Ser.: C-1237). 1994. pap. 23.95 (*0-8373-1237-X*) Nat Learn.
— Deputy Chief Clerk. (Career Examination Ser.: C-1238). 1994. pap. 29.95 (*0-8373-1238-8*) Nat Learn.
— Deputy Chief, Fire Department. (Career Examination Ser.: C-195). 1994. pap. 34.95 (*0-8373-0195-5*) Nat Learn.
— Deputy Chief Fire Marshal (Uniformed) (Career Examination Ser.: C-2169). 1994. pap. 39.95 (*0-8373-2169-7*) Nat Learn.
— Deputy Chief Marshal. (Career Examination Ser.: C-1239). 1994. pap. 34.95 (*0-8373-1239-6*) Nat Learn.
— Deputy Chief Medical Examiner. (Career Examination Ser.: C-2723). 1994. pap. 59.95 (*0-8373-2723-7*) Nat Learn.
— Deputy Chief Registrar. (Career Examination Ser.: C-1240). 1994. pap. 34.95 (*0-8373-1240-X*) Nat Learn.
— Deputy City Chamberlain. (Career Examination Ser.: C-2982). 1994. pap. 34.95 (*0-8373-2982-5*) Nat Learn.
— Deputy Commissioner. (Career Examination Ser.: C-1241). 1994. pap. 39.95 (*0-8373-1241-8*) Nat Learn.
— Deputy Commissioner of Commerce & Industry. (Career Examination Ser.: C-1990). 1994. pap. 39.95 (*0-8373-1990-0*) Nat Learn.
— Deputy Commissioner of General Services. (Career Examination Ser.: C-1859). 1994. pap. 39.95 (*0-8373-1859-9*) Nat Learn.
— Deputy Commissioner of Jurors. (Career Examination Ser.: C-1242). 1994. pap. 39.95 (*0-8373-1242-6*) Nat Learn.
— Deputy Commissioner of Recreation & Community Services. (Career Examination Ser.: C-1891). 1994. pap. 39.95 (*0-8373-1891-2*) Nat Learn.
— Deputy Comptroller. (Career Examination Ser.: C-1243). 1994. pap. 39.95 (*0-8373-1243-4*) Nat Learn.
— Deputy County Attorney. (Career Examination Ser.: C-1244). 1994. pap. 39.95 (*0-8373-1244-2*) Nat Learn.
— Deputy County Clerk. (Career Examination Ser.: C-1772). 1994. pap. 29.95 (*0-8373-1772-X*) Nat Learn.
— Deputy Director of Administration. (Career Examination Ser.: C-1853). 1994. pap. 39.95 (*0-8373-1853-X*) Nat Learn.
— Deputy Director of Planning. (Career Examination Ser.: C-1708). 1994. pap. 39.95 (*0-8373-1708-8*) Nat Learn.
— Deputy Medical Examiner. (Career Examination Ser.: C-1245). 1994. pap. 44.95 (*0-8373-1245-0*) Nat Learn.
— Deputy Probation Director. (Career Examination Ser.: C-2263). 1994. pap. 39.95 (*0-8373-2263-4*) Nat Learn.
— Deputy Probation Director IV. (Career Examination Ser.: C-1900). 1994. pap. 39.95 (*0-8373-1900-5*) Nat Learn.
— Deputy Registrar. (Career Examination Ser.: C-1246). 1994. pap. 29.95 (*0-8373-1246-9*) Nat Learn.
— Deputy Sheriff. (Career Examination Ser.: C-204). 1994. pap. 23.95 (*0-8373-0204-8*) Nat Learn.
— Deputy Superintendent of Highways. (Career Examination Ser.: C-2319). 1994. pap. 39.95 (*0-8373-2319-3*) Nat Learn.
— Deputy Superintendent of Women's Prisons. (Career Examination Ser.: C-1763). 1994. pap. 49.95 (*0-8373-1763-0*) Nat Learn.
— Deputy Town Assessor. (Career Examination Ser.: C-2184). 1994. pap. 27.95 (*0-8373-2184-0*) Nat Learn.
— Deputy Town Clerk. (Career Examination Ser.: C-1855). 1994. reprint ed. pap. 29.95 (*0-8373-1855-6*) Nat Learn.
— Deputy United States Marshal. (Career Examination Ser.: C-1620). 1994. pap. 27.95 (*0-8373-1620-0*) Nat Learn.
— Deputy Warden. (Career Examination Ser.: C-1762). 1994. reprint ed. pap. 49.95 (*0-8373-1762-2*) Nat Learn.
— Detective Investigator. (Career Examination Ser.: C-1247). 1994. pap. 34.95 (*0-8373-1247-7*) Nat Learn.
— Developmental Disabilities Program Aide. (Career Examination Ser.: C-864). 1994. pap. 23.95 (*0-8373-0864-X*) Nat Learn.
— Developmental Disabilities Program Specialist. (Career Examination Ser.: C-3368). 1994. pap. 27.95 (*0-8373-3368-7*) Nat Learn.
— Developmental Specialist. (Career Examination Ser.: C-923). 1994. pap. 27.95 (*0-8373-0923-9*) Nat Learn.
— Diagnosis & Remediation of Reading Problems. (Regents College Proficiency Examination Ser.: Vol. 38). 43.95 (*0-8373-5488-9*) Nat Learn.
— Diagnosis & Remediation of Reading Problems. (Regents College Proficiency Examination Ser.: CPEP-38). 1994. pap. 23.95 (*0-8373-5438-2*) Nat Learn.
— Dictating Machine Transcriber. (Career Examination Ser.: C-1248). 1994. pap. 23.95 (*0-8373-1248-5*) Nat Learn.
— Diesel Engine Repair. (Occupational Competency Examination (OCE) Ser.: Vol. 16). 47.95 (*0-8373-5766-7*) Nat Learn.
— Diesel Engine Repair. (Occupational Competency Examination Ser.: OCE-16). 1994. pap. 27.95 (*0-8373-5716-0*) Nat Learn.
— Dietitian. (Career Examination Ser.: C-196). 1994. pap. 27.95 (*0-8373-0196-3*) Nat Learn.
— Differences in Nursing Care: Area A. (Regents External Degree (REDP) Ser.: Vol. 21). 43.95 (*0-8373-5671-7*) Nat Learn.
— Differences in Nursing Care: Area A. REDP-21. 1994. pap. 23.95 (*0-8373-5621-0*) Nat Learn.
— Differences in Nursing Care: Area A. (ACT Proficiency Examination Program (PEP) Ser.: Vol. PEP-43). 1994. pap. 23.95 (*0-8373-5543-5*) Nat Learn.
— Differences in Nursing Care: Area B. (Regents External Degree (REDP) Ser.: Vol. 22). 43.95 (*0-8373-5672-5*) Nat Learn.
— Differences in Nursing Care: Area B. 1994. pap. 23.95 (*0-8373-5622-9*) Nat Learn.
— Differences in Nursing Care: Area B. (ACT Proficiency Examination Program (PEP) Ser.: Vol. PEP-44). 1994. pap. 23.95 (*0-8373-5544-3*) Nat Learn.
— Differences in Nursing Care: Area C. (Regents External Degree (REDP) Ser.: Vol. 23). 43.95 (*0-8373-5673-3*) Nat Learn.
— Differences in Nursing Care: Area C. REDP-23. 1994. pap. 23.95 (*0-8373-5623-7*) Nat Learn.
— Differences in Nursing Care: Area C. (ACT Proficiency Examination Program (PEP) Ser.: Vol. PEP-45). 1994. pap. 23.95 (*0-8373-5545-1*) Nat Learn.
— Differences in Nursing Care, Area A. (ACT Proficiency Examination Program (PEP) Ser.: Vol. 43). 43.95 (*0-8373-5593-1*) Nat Learn.
— Differences in Nursing Care, Area B. (ACT Proficiency Examination Program (PEP) Ser.: Vol. 44). 43.95 (*0-8373-5594-X*) Nat Learn.
— Differences in Nursing Care, Area C. (ACT Proficiency Examination Program (PEP) Ser.: Vol. 45). 43.95 (*0-8373-5595-8*) Nat Learn.
— Differential Aptitude Tests (DATS) (Admission Test Ser.: ATS-112). pap. 29.95 (*0-8373-5812-4*) Nat Learn.
— Differential Equations. (Dantes Subject Standardized Tests Ser.: DANTES-12). 1994. pap. 23.95 (*0-8373-6612-7*) Nat Learn.
— Differential Equations. (DANTES Ser.: Vol. DANTES-12). 1994. 39.95 (*0-8373-6512-0*) Nat Learn.
— Digital Cable Technologist (DCT) (Career Examination Ser.: Vol. C-3823). 1997. pap. 29.95 (*0-8373-3823-9*) Nat Learn.
— Digital Computer Operator. (Career Examination Ser.: C-197). 1994. pap. 23.95 (*0-8373-0197-1*) Nat Learn.
— Digital Computer Programmer. (Career Examination Ser.: C-198). 1994. pap. 27.95 (*0-8373-0198-X*) Nat Learn.
— Digital Computer Specialist. (Career Examination Ser.: C-199). 1994. pap. 27.95 (*0-8373-0199-8*) Nat Learn.
— Digital Computer Systems Analyst. (Career Examination Ser.: C-200). 1994. pap. 27.95 (*0-8373-0200-5*) Nat Learn.
— Digital Computer Systems Operator. (Career Examination Ser.: C-1249). 1994. pap. 23.95 (*0-8373-1249-3*) Nat Learn.
— Digital Computer Systems Programmer. (Career Examination Ser.: C-1250). 1994. pap. 27.95 (*0-8373-1250-7*) Nat Learn.
— Digital Computer Systems Specialist. (Career Examination Ser.: C-1251). 1994. pap. 27.95 (*0-8373-1251-5*) Nat Learn.
— Digital Computer Systems Technician. (Career Examination Ser.: C-1252). 1994. pap. 29.95 (*0-8373-1252-3*) Nat Learn.
— Director. (Career Examination Ser.: C-1253). 1994. pap. 39.95 (*0-8373-1253-1*) Nat Learn.
— Director of Administration. (Career Examination Ser.: C-2189). 1994. pap. 44.95 (*0-8373-2189-1*) Nat Learn.
— Director of Administrative Services. (Career Examination Ser.: C-2177). 1994. pap. 44.95 (*0-8373-2177-8*) Nat Learn.
— Director of Advertising. (Career Examination Ser.: C-1865). 1994. pap. 39.95 (*0-8373-1865-3*) Nat Learn.
— Director of Animal Shelter & Control. (Career Examination Ser.: C-548). 1994. pap. 39.95 (*0-8373-0548-9*) Nat Learn.
— Director of Building & Housing. (Career Examination Ser.: C-3087). 1994. pap. 44.95 (*0-8373-3087-4*) Nat Learn.
— Director of Cemeteries. (Career Examination Ser.: C-2794). 1994. pap. 39.95 (*0-8373-2794-6*) Nat Learn.
— Director of Child Care Program. (Career Examination Ser.: C-3709). 1994. pap. 39.95 (*0-8373-3709-7*) Nat Learn.
— Director of Child Support Enforcement Bureau. (Career Examination Ser.: C-928). 1994. pap. 39.95 (*0-8373-0928-X*) Nat Learn.
— Director of Citizens' Affairs. (Career Examination Ser.: C-3710). 1994. pap. 39.95 (*0-8373-3710-0*) Nat Learn.
— Director of Community Development. (Career Examination Ser.: C-2813). 1994. pap. 39.95 (*0-8373-2813-6*) Nat Learn.
— Director of Community Relations. (Career Examination Ser.: C-1856). 1994. pap. 39.95 (*0-8373-1856-4*) Nat Learn.
— Director of Conservation. (Career Examination Ser.: C-1296). 1994. pap. 39.95 (*0-8373-1296-5*) Nat Learn.
— Director of Custodial & Security Services. (Career Examination Ser.: C-2923). 1994. pap. 39.95 (*0-8373-2923-X*) Nat Learn.
— Director of Data Entry Operations. (Career Examination Ser.: C-3286). 1994. pap. 39.95 (*0-8373-3286-9*) Nat Learn.
— Director of Data Processing. (Career Examination Ser.: C-2518). 1994. pap. 39.95 (*0-8373-2518-8*) Nat Learn.
— Director of Drug Treatment Services. (Career Examination Ser.: C-2821). 1994. pap. 39.95 (*0-8373-2821-7*) Nat Learn.
— Director of Engineering, Building & Housing. (Career Examination Ser.: C-2391). 1994. pap. 44.95 (*0-8373-2391-6*) Nat Learn.
— Director of Environmental Health Services. (Career Examination Ser.: C-3136). 1994. pap. 39.95 (*0-8373-3136-6*) Nat Learn.
— Director of Facilities Management. (Career Examination Ser.: C-3358). 1994. pap. 44.95 (*0-8373-3358-X*) Nat Learn.
— Director of Facilities Planning. (Career Examination Ser.: C-3437). 1994. pap. 39.95 (*0-8373-3437-3*) Nat Learn.
— Director of Fire Safety. (Career Examination Ser.: C-2396). 1994. pap. 39.95 (*0-8373-2396-7*) Nat Learn.
— Director of Graphics & Production. (Career Examination Ser.: C-1795). 1994. pap. 39.95 (*0-8373-1795-9*) Nat Learn.
— Director of Human Development. (Career Examination Ser.: C-3235). 1994. pap. 44.95 (*0-8373-3235-4*) Nat Learn.
— Director of Industrial Development. (Career Examination Ser.: C-2857). 1994. pap. 44.95 (*0-8373-2857-8*) Nat Learn.
— Director of Library. (Career Examination Ser.: C-1254). 1994. pap. 39.95 (*0-8373-1254-X*) Nat Learn.
— Director of Maintenance. (Career Examination Ser.: C-2812). 1994. pap. 39.95 (*0-8373-2812-8*) Nat Learn.
— Director of Materials Testing. (Career Examination Ser.: C-3236). 1994. pap. 44.95 (*0-8373-3236-2*) Nat Learn.
— Director of Nursing Care. (Career Examination Ser.: C-2859). 1994. pap. 39.95 (*0-8373-2859-4*) Nat Learn.
— Director of Office Services. (Career Examination Ser.: C-1857). 1994. pap. 39.95 (*0-8373-1857-2*) Nat Learn.
— Director of Office Systems. (Career Examination Ser.: C-3348). 1994. pap. 39.95 (*0-8373-3348-2*) Nat Learn.
— Director of Operations. (Career Examination Ser.: C-1827). 1994. pap. 39.95 (*0-8373-1827-0*) Nat Learn.
— Director of Parks & Recreation. (Career Examination Ser.: C-3349). 1994. pap. 39.95 (*0-8373-3349-0*) Nat Learn.
— Director of Patient Services. (Career Examination Ser.: C-2724). 1994. pap. 39.95 (*0-8373-2724-5*) Nat Learn.
— Director of Personnel. (Career Examination Ser.: C-2083). 1994. reprint ed. pap. 44.95 (*0-8373-2083-6*) Nat Learn.
— Director of Physical Development. (Career Examination Ser.: C-914). 1994. pap. 44.95 (*0-8373-0914-X*) Nat Learn.
— Director of Program Planning. (Career Examination Ser.: C-2408). 1994. pap. 44.95 (*0-8373-2408-4*) Nat Learn.
— Director of Public Information. (Career Examination Ser.: C-1866). 1994. pap. 39.95 (*0-8373-1866-1*) Nat Learn.
— Director of Purchasing. (Career Examination Ser.: C-1950). 1994. pap. 39.95 (*0-8373-1950-1*) Nat Learn.
— Director of Registrants. (Career Examination Ser.: C-1255). 1994. pap. 39.95 (*0-8373-1255-8*) Nat Learn.
— Director of Research & Evaluation. (Career Examination Ser.: C-2891). 1994. pap. 44.95 (*0-8373-2891-8*) Nat Learn.
— Director of School Facilities & Operations. (Career Examination Ser.: C-2072). 1994. pap. 39.95 (*0-8373-2072-0*) Nat Learn.
— Director of Security. (Career Examination Ser.: C-2444). 1994. pap. 39.95 (*0-8373-2444-0*) Nat Learn.
— Director of Senior Citizens Services. (Career Examination Ser.: C-3329). 1994. pap. 39.95 (*0-8373-3329-6*) Nat Learn.
— Director of Social Services. (Career Examination Ser.: C-2666). 1994. pap. 44.95 (*0-8373-2666-4*) Nat Learn.
— Director of Traffic Control. (Career Examination Ser.: C-1877). 1994. pap. 39.95 (*0-8373-1877-7*) Nat Learn.
— Director of Traffic Safety. (Career Examination Ser.: C-527). 1994. pap. 39.95 (*0-8373-0527-6*) Nat Learn.
— Director of Training. (Career Examination Ser.: C-2460). 1994. pap. 44.95 (*0-8373-2460-2*) Nat Learn.
— Director of Transportation Operations. (Career Examination Ser.: C-114). 1994. pap. 39.95 (*0-8373-0114-9*) Nat Learn.
— Director of Weights & Measures. (Career Examination Ser.: C-3350). 1994. pap. 39.95 (*0-8373-3350-4*) Nat Learn.
— Director of Youth Bureau. (Career Examination Ser.: C-2325). 1994. pap. 39.95 (*0-8373-2325-8*) Nat Learn.
— Dishwasher. (Career Examination Ser.: C-1256). 1994. pap. 23.95 (*0-8373-1256-6*) Nat Learn.
— Dispatcher. (Career Examination Ser.: C-213). 1994. pap. 23.95 (*0-8373-0213-7*) Nat Learn.
— Dispensing & Handling Motor Fuel License. (Career Examination Ser.: C-3763). pap. 23.95 (*0-8373-3763-1*) Nat Learn.
— Distribution Clerk - Machine (U. S. P. S.) (Career Examination Ser.: C-2255). 1994. pap. 19.95 (*0-8373-2255-3*) Nat Learn.
— Distributive Education (Merchandising & Salesmanship), Sr. H. S. (Teachers License Examination Ser.: T-12). 1994. pap. 27.95 (*0-8373-8012-X*) Nat Learn.
— District Administrator, Public Health. (Career Examination Ser.: C-3006). 1994. pap. 44.95 (*0-8373-3006-8*) Nat Learn.
— District Attorney. (Career Examination Ser.: C-1257). 1994. pap. 49.95 (*0-8373-1257-4*) Nat Learn.
— District Business Officer. (Career Examination Ser.: C-1726). 1994. pap. 34.95 (*0-8373-1726-6*) Nat Learn.
— District Director (Social Services) (Career Examination Ser.: C-2990). 1994. pap. 39.95 (*0-8373-2990-6*) Nat Learn.
— District Foreman (Department of Sanitation) (Career Examination Ser.: C-207). 1994. pap. 29.95 (*0-8373-0207-2*) Nat Learn.
— District Foreman (Highway Maintenance) (Career Examination Ser.: C-1978). 1994. pap. 29.95 (*0-8373-1978-1*) Nat Learn.
— District Foreman (Sewer Maintenance) (Career Examination Ser.: C-1815). 1994. pap. 29.95 (*0-8373-1815-7*) Nat Learn.
— District Foreman (Water Supply) (Career Examination Ser.: C-2037). 1994. pap. 29.95 (*0-8373-2037-2*) Nat Learn.
— District Foreman (Watershed Maintenance) (Career Examination Ser.: C-428). 1994. pap. 29.95 (*0-8373-0428-8*) Nat Learn.
— District Superintendent (Department of Sanitation) (Career Examination Ser.: C-201). 1994. pap. 34.95 (*0-8373-0201-3*) Nat Learn.
— District Supervisor of School Custodians. (Career Examination Ser.: C-2349). 1994. pap. 29.95 (*0-8373-2349-5*) Nat Learn.
— District Supervisor (Water & Sewer Systems) (Career Examination Ser.: C-3044). 1994. pap. 29.95 (*0-8373-3044-0*) Nat Learn.
— Dockbuilder. (Career Examination Ser.: C-1696). 1994. pap. 27.95 (*0-8373-1696-0*) Nat Learn.
— Dog Control Officer. (Career Examination Ser.: C-547). 1994. pap. 23.95 (*0-8373-0547-0*) Nat Learn.
— Dog Control Officer II. (Career Examination Ser.: C-3038). 1994. pap. 27.95 (*0-8373-3038-6*) Nat Learn.
— Dog Enumerator Coordinator. (Career Examination Ser.: C-3496). 1994. pap. 29.95 (*0-8373-3496-9*) Nat Learn.
— Dog Warden. (Career Examination Ser.: C-2645). 1994. pap. 23.95 (*0-8373-2645-1*) Nat Learn.
— Domestic Worker. (Career Examination Ser.: C-1258). 1994. pap. 23.95 (*0-8373-1258-2*) Nat Learn.
— Drafting Aide. (Career Examination Ser.: C-202). 1994. pap. 23.95 (*0-8373-0202-1*) Nat Learn.
— Drafting Technician. (Career Examination Ser.: C-2678). 1994. pap. 23.95 (*0-8373-2678-8*) Nat Learn.
— Draftsman. (Career Examination Ser.: C-203). 1994. pap. 23.95 (*0-8373-0203-X*) Nat Learn.
— Drama & Theatre. (Undergraduate Program Field Tests (UPFT) Ser.: Vol. 5). 43.95 (*0-8373-6055-2*) Nat Learn.
— Drama & Theatre. (Undergraduate Program Field Tests Ser.: UPFT-5). 1994. pap. 23.95 (*0-8373-6005-6*) Nat Learn.
— Dressmaking. (Occupational Competency Examination (OCE) Ser.: Vol. 17). 47.95 (*0-8373-5767-5*) Nat Learn.
— Dressmaking. (Occupational Competency Examination Ser.: OCE-17). 1994. pap. 27.95 (*0-8373-5717-9*) Nat Learn.
— Drilling Supervisor. (Career Examination Ser.: C-3326). 1994. pap. 29.95 (*0-8373-3326-1*) Nat Learn.
— Driver License Written Examination. (Career Examination Ser.: C-1635). 1994. pap. 23.95 (*0-8373-1635-9*) Nat Learn.
— Drug Abuse Counselor. (Career Examination Ser.: C-2725). 1994. pap. 29.95 (*0-8373-2725-3*) Nat Learn.
— Drug Abuse Education Group Leader. (Career Examination Ser.: C-1259). 1994. pap. 29.95 (*0-8373-1259-0*) Nat Learn.
— Drug Abuse Educator. (Career Examination Ser.: C-1597). 1994. pap. 29.95 (*0-8373-1597-2*) Nat Learn.
— Drug Abuse Group Worker. (Career Examination Ser.: C-1260). 1994. pap. 27.95 (*0-8373-1260-4*) Nat Learn.
— Drug Abuse Rehabilitation Counselor. (Career Examination Ser.: C-2929). 1994. pap. 29.95 (*0-8373-2929-9*) Nat Learn.
— Drug Abuse Secretarial Aide. (Career Examination Ser.: C-1261). 1994. pap. 23.95 (*0-8373-1261-2*) Nat Learn.
— Drug Abuse Technician. (Career Examination Ser.: C-1405). 1994. pap. 27.95 (*0-8373-1405-4*) Nat Learn.
— Drug Abuse Technician Trainee. (Career Examination Ser.: C-1406). 1994. pap. 23.95 (*0-8373-1406-2*) Nat Learn.
— Drug & Alcohol Abuse. (Dantes Subject Standardized Tests (DANTES) Ser.: Vol. 78). 43.95 (*0-8373-6578-3*) Nat Learn.
— Drug & Alcohol Community Coordinator. (Career Examination Ser.: C-2776). 1994. pap. 34.95 (*0-8373-2776-8*) Nat Learn.
— Drug & Alcohol Counselor. (Career Examination Ser.: C-2741). 1994. pap. 29.95 (*0-8373-2741-5*) Nat Learn.
— Drug & Alcohol Program Coordinator. (Career Examination Ser.: C-2775). 1994. pap. 34.95 (*0-8373-2775-X*) Nat Learn.
— Duplicating Equipment Operator. (Career Examination Ser.: C-208). 1994. pap. 23.95 (*0-8373-0208-0*) Nat Learn.
— Duplicating Machine Operator. (Career Examination Ser.: C-1407). 1994. pap. 23.95 (*0-8373-1407-0*) Nat Learn.
— Duplicating Machine Supervisor. (Career Examination Ser.: C-1408). 1994. pap. 27.95 (*0-8373-1408-9*) Nat Learn.
— Early Childhood Education (KG-3) (National Teacher Examination Ser.: NT-2). 1994. pap. 23.95 (*0-8373-8412-5*) Nat Learn.
— Early Childhood, Elementary School (Pre-Kg.-2) (Teachers License Examination Ser.: T-13). 1994. pap. 27.95 (*0-8373-8013-8*) Nat Learn.
— Early Intervention Coordinator. (Career Examination Ser.: C-3711). 1994. pap. 34.95 (*0-8373-3711-9*) Nat Learn.
— Earth Science. (ACT Proficiency Examination Program (PEP) Ser.: Vol. 5). 43.95 (*0-8373-5555-9*) Nat Learn.
— Earth Science. (Regents College Proficiency Examination Ser.: Vol. 7). 43.95 (*0-8373-5457-9*) Nat Learn.
— Earth Science. (College Proficiency Examination Ser.: CPEP-7). 1994. pap. 23.95 (*0-8373-5407-2*) Nat Learn.
— Earth Science. (ACT Proficiency Examination Program (PEP) Ser.: Vol. PEP-5). 1994. pap. 23.95 (*0-8373-5505-2*) Nat Learn.
— Earth Science & General Science, Sr. H. S. (Teachers License Examination Ser.: T-14). 1994. pap. 27.95 (*0-8373-8014-6*) Nat Learn.
— Econometrician. (Career Examination Ser.: C-3652). pap. 34.95 (*0-8373-3652-X*) Nat Learn.
— Economic Development Program Specialist. (Career Examination Ser.: C-3444). 1994. pap. 39.95 (*0-8373-3444-6*) Nat Learn.
— Economic Opportunity Program Specialist. (Career Examination Ser.: C-2545). 1994. pap. 34.95 (*0-8373-2545-5*) Nat Learn.
— Economics. (National Teacher Examination Ser.: NT-53). pap. 23.95 (*0-8373-8473-7*) Nat Learn.
— Economics. (Graduate Record Examination (GRE) Ser.: Vol. 3). 43.95 (*0-8373-5253-3*) Nat Learn.
— Economics. (Undergraduate Program Field Tests (UPFT) Ser.: Vol. 6). 43.95 (*0-8373-6056-0*) Nat Learn.
— Economics. (Regents College Proficiency Examination Ser.: Vol. 8). 43.95 (*0-8373-5458-7*) Nat Learn.

R

— Economics. (Regents College Proficiency Examination Ser.: CPEP-8). 1994. pap. 23.95 (*0-8373-5408-0*) Nat Learn.
— Economics. (Graduate Record Examination (GRE) Ser.: Vol. GRE-3). 1994. pap. 23.95 (*0-8373-5203-7*) Nat Learn.
— Economics. (Undergraduate Program Field Tests (UPFT) Ser.: Vol. UPFT-6). 1994. pap. 23.95 (*0-8373-6006-4*) Nat Learn.
— Economist. (Career Examination Ser.: C-1262). 1994. pap. 34.95 (*0-8373-1262-0*) Nat Learn.
— Editorial Assistant. (Career Examination Ser.: C-220). 1994. pap. 27.95 (*0-8373-0220-X*) Nat Learn.
— Editorial Clerk. (Career Examination Ser.: C-2564). 1994. pap. 23.95 (*0-8373-2564-1*) Nat Learn.
— Education. (Graduate Record Examination (GRE) Ser.: Vol. 4). 43.95 (*0-8373-5254-1*) Nat Learn.
— Education. (Undergraduate Program Field Tests (UPFT) Ser.: Vol. 7). 43.95 (*0-8373-6057-9*) Nat Learn.
— Education. (Graduate Record Examination Ser.: GRE-4). 1994. pap. 23.95 (*0-8373-5204-5*) Nat Learn.
— Education. (Teacher's License Examination (TLE) Ser.: Vol. G-1). 1994. pap. 27.95 (*0-8373-8191-6*) Nat Learn.
— Education. (Undergraduate Program Field Tests (UPFT) Ser.: Vol. UPFT-7). 1994. pap. 23.95 (*0-8373-6007-2*) Nat Learn.
— Education Analyst. (Career Examination Ser.: C-3045). 1994. pap. 39.95 (*0-8373-3045-9*) Nat Learn.
— Education Counselor. (Career Examination Ser.: C-2739). 1994. pap. 39.95 (*0-8373-2739-3*) Nat Learn.
— Education Director. (Career Examination Ser.: C-2506). 1994. pap. 49.95 (*0-8373-2506-4*) Nat Learn.
— Education in an Urban Setting. (National Teacher Examination Ser.: NT-31). 1994. pap. 23.95 (*0-8373-8441-9*) Nat Learn.
— Education in the Elementary School (1-8) (National Teacher Examination Ser.: NT-1). 1994. pap. 23.95 (*0-8373-8411-7*) Nat Learn.
— Education of the Mentally Retarded. (National Teacher Examination Ser.: NT-24). 1994. pap. 23.95 (*0-8373-8434-6*) Nat Learn.
— Education Officer. (Career Examination Ser.: C-3050). 1994. pap. 39.95 (*0-8373-3050-5*) Nat Learn.
— Education Program Assistant. (Career Examination Ser.: C-865). 1994. pap. 34.95 (*0-8373-0865-8*) Nat Learn.
— Education Supervisor. (Career Examination Ser.: C-2508). 1994. pap. 34.95 (*0-8373-2508-0*) Nat Learn.
— Education Supervisor (Developmental Disabilities) (Career Examination Ser.: C-2511). 1994. pap. 39.95 (*0-8373-2511-0*) Nat Learn.
— Education Supervisor (Special Subjects) (Career Examination Ser.: C-2509). 1994. pap. 39.95 (*0-8373-2509-9*) Nat Learn.
— Education Supervisor (Vocational) (Career Examination Ser.: C-2510). 1994. pap. 39.95 (*0-8373-2510-2*) Nat Learn.
— Educational Commission for Foreign Medical Graduates English Test (ECFMG-ET) (Admission Test Ser.: Vol. 43). 49.95 (*0-8373-5143-X*) Nat Learn.
— Educational Commission for Foreign Medical Graduates English Test (ECFMG-ET) (Admission Test Ser.: ATS-43). 1994. pap. 29.95 (*0-8373-5043-3*) Nat Learn.
— Educational Commission for Foreign Medical Graduates Examination (ECFMG) (Admission Test Ser.: Vol. 24). 89.95 (*0-8373-5124-3*) Nat Learn.
— Educational Commission for Foreign Medical Graduates Examination (ECFMG) (Admission Test Ser.: ATS-24). 1994. pap. 69.95 (*0-8373-5024-7*) Nat Learn.
— Educational Commission for Foreign Veterinary Graduates Exam (ECFVG), 3 pts. in 1 vol. (Admission Test Ser.: ATS-49). 1994. pap. 69.95 (*0-8373-5049-2*) Nat Learn.
— Educational Commission for Foreign Veterinary Graduates Examination (ECFVG) Pt. I: Anatomy, Physiology, Pathology. (Admission Test Ser.: Vol. 49A). 59.95 (*0-8373-6982-7*) Nat Learn.
— Educational Commission for Foreign Veterinary Graduates Examination (ECFVG) Pt. I: Anatomy, Physiology, Pathology. (Admission Test Ser.: ATS-49A). 1994. pap. 39.95 (*0-8373-6957-6*) Nat Learn.
— Educational Commission for Foreign Veterinary Graduates Examination (ECFVG) Pt. II: Pharmacology, Therapeutics, Parasitology, Hygiene. (Admission Test Ser.: Vol. 49B). 59.95 (*0-8373-6983-5*) Nat Learn.
— Educational Commission for Foreign Veterinary Graduates Examination (ECFVG) Pt. II: Pharmacology, Therapeutics, Parasitology, Hygiene. (Admission Test Ser.: ATS-49B). 1994. pap. 39.95 (*0-8373-6958-4*) Nat Learn.
— Educational Commission for Foreign Veterinary Graduates Examination (ECFVG) Pt. III: Physical Diagnosis, Medicine, Surgery. (Admission Test Ser.: Vol. 49C). 59.95 (*0-8373-6984-3*) Nat Learn.
— Educational Commission for Foreign Veterinary Graduates Examination (ECFVG) Pt. III: Physical Diagnosis, Medicine, Surgery. (Admission Test Ser.: ATS-49C). 1994. pap. 39.95 (*0-8373-6959-2*) Nat Learn.
— Educational Psychology. (ACT Proficiency Examination Program (PEP) Ser.: Vol. 28). 43.95 (*0-8373-5578-8*) Nat Learn.
— Educational Psychology. (College Level Examination (CLEP) Ser.: Vol. 9). 43.95 (*0-8373-5359-9*); 43.95 (*0-8373-5459-5*) Nat Learn.
— Educational Psychology. (College Level Examination Ser.: CLEP-9). 1994. pap. 23.95 (*0-8373-5309-2*) Nat Learn.
— Educational Psychology. (Regents College Proficiency Examination Ser.: Vol. CPEP-9). 1994. pap. 23.95 (*0-8373-5409-9*) Nat Learn.
— Educational Psychology. (Dantes Subject Standardized Tests (DANTES) Ser.: Vol. DANTES-13). 1994. pap. 23.95 (*0-8373-6613-5*) Nat Learn.
— Educational Psychology. (ACT Proficiency Examination Program (PEP) Ser.: Vol. PEP-28). 1994. pap. 23.95 (*0-8373-5528-1*) Nat Learn.
— EEG Technician. (Career Examination Ser.: C-1263). 1994. pap. 39.95 (*0-8373-1263-9*) Nat Learn.
— EKG Technician. (Career Examination Ser.: C-1264). 1994. pap. 39.95 (*0-8373-1264-7*) Nat Learn.
— Election Inspector. (Career Examination Ser.: C-1265). 1994. pap. 29.95 (*0-8373-1265-5*) Nat Learn.
— Election Registrar. (Career Examination Ser.: C-1266). 1994. pap. 27.95 (*0-8373-1266-3*) Nat Learn.
— Electric Accounting Machine Operator. (Career Examination Ser.: C-238). 1994. pap. 23.95 (*0-8373-0238-2*) Nat Learn.
— Electric Circuits. (Dantes Subject Standardized Tests (DANTES) Ser.: Vol. 41). 43.95 (*0-8373-6541-4*) Nat Learn.
— Electric Circuits. (Dantes Subject Standardized Tests Ser.: DANTES-41). 1994. pap. 23.95 (*0-8373-6641-0*) Nat Learn.
— Electric Meter Tester. (Career Examination Ser.: C-2249). 1994. pap. 29.95 (*0-8373-2249-9*) Nat Learn.
— Electric Station Operator. (Career Examination Ser.: C-3291). 1994. pap. 29.95 (*0-8373-3291-5*) Nat Learn.
— Electrical Contractor. (Career Examination Ser.: C-3598). 1994. pap. 34.95 (*0-8373-3598-1*) Nat Learn.
— Electrical Engineer. (Career Examination Ser.: C-221). 1994. pap. 34.95 (*0-8373-0221-8*) Nat Learn.
— Electrical Engineering Draftsman. (Career Examination Ser.: C-222). 1994. pap. 27.95 (*0-8373-0222-6*) Nat Learn.
— Electrical Engineering Trainee. (Career Examination Ser.: C-239). 1994. pap. 27.95 (*0-8373-0239-0*) Nat Learn.
— Electrical Inspector. (Career Examination Ser.: C-223). 1994. pap. 34.95 (*0-8373-0223-4*) Nat Learn.
— Electrical Installation. (Occupational Competency Examination (OCE) Ser.: Vol. 18). 47.95 (*0-8373-5768-3*) Nat Learn.
— Electrical Installation. (Occupational Competency Examination Ser.: OCE-18). 1994. pap. 27.95 (*0-8373-5718-7*) Nat Learn.
— Electrical Service Supervisor. (Career Examination Ser.: C-1267). 1994. pap. 34.95 (*0-8373-1267-1*) Nat Learn.
— Electrician. (Career Examination Ser.: C-224). 1994. pap. 27.95 (*0-8373-0224-2*) Nat Learn.
— Electrician (Automobile) (Career Examination Ser.: C-1268). 1994. pap. 27.95 (*0-8373-1268-X*) Nat Learn.
— Electrician's Helper. (Career Examination Ser.: C-225). 1994. pap. 23.95 (*0-8373-0225-0*) Nat Learn.
— Electricity Workbook. (Workbook (W) Ser.: Vol. 2870). 43.95 (*0-8373-7927-X*) Nat Learn.
— Electricity Workbook. (Workbook Ser.: W-2870). 1994. pap. 23.95 (*0-8373-7902-4*) Nat Learn.
— Electro-Mechanical Examination (U.S.P.S.) (Career Examination Ser.: C-1607). 1994. pap. 27.95 (*0-8373-1607-3*) Nat Learn.
— Electrocardiograph Technician. (Career Examination Ser.: C-1269). 1994. pap. 39.95 (*0-8373-1269-8*) Nat Learn.
— Electronic Computer Operator. (Career Examination Ser.: C-241). 1994. pap. 23.95 (*0-8373-0241-2*) Nat Learn.
— Electronic Computer Trainee. (Career Examination Ser.: C-242). 1994. pap. 23.95 (*0-8373-0242-0*) Nat Learn.
— Electronic Devices. (Dantes Subject Standardized Tests (DANTES) Ser.: Vol. 42). 43.95 (*0-8373-6542-2*) Nat Learn.
— Electronic Devices. (Dantes Subject Standardized Tests Ser.: DANTES-42). 1994. pap. 23.95 (*0-8373-6642-9*) Nat Learn.
— Electronic Engineer. (Career Examination Ser.: C-226). 1994. pap. 34.95 (*0-8373-0226-9*) Nat Learn.
— Electronic Equipment Maintainer. (Career Examination Ser.: C-227). 1994. pap. 27.95 (*0-8373-0227-7*) Nat Learn.
— Electronic Equipment Repairer. (Career Examination Ser.: C-243). 1994. pap. 27.95 (*0-8373-0243-9*) Nat Learn.
— Electronic Measuring Instruments. (Dantes Subject Standardized Tests Ser.: DANTES-14). 1994. pap. 23.95 (*0-8373-6614-3*) Nat Learn.
— Electronic Mechanic. (Career Examination Ser.: C-228). 1994. pap. 27.95 (*0-8373-0228-5*) Nat Learn.
— Electronic Occupations. (Teachers License Examination Ser.: T-73). 1994. pap. 27.95 (*0-8373-8073-1*) Nat Learn.
— Electronic Technician (USPS) (Career Examination Ser.: C-229). 1994. pap. 27.95 (*0-8373-0229-3*) Nat Learn.
— Electronics Communication. (Occupational Competency Examination (OCE) Ser.: Vol. 19). 47.95 (*0-8373-5769-1*) Nat Learn.
— Electronics Communication. (Occupational Competency Examination Ser.: OCE-19). 1994. pap. 27.95 (*0-8373-5719-5*) Nat Learn.
— Elementary Computer Programming. (College Level Examination Ser.: CLEP-10). 1994. pap. 23.95 (*0-8373-5310-6*) Nat Learn.
— Elementary School Basic Competency Tests (BCT-ES) (Admission Test Ser.: Vol. 56). 43.95 (*0-8373-5156-1*) Nat Learn.
— Elementary School Basic Competency Tests (BCT-ES) (Admission Test Ser.: ATS-56). 1994. pap. 23.95 (*0-8373-5056-5*) Nat Learn.
— Elementary Schools: Pre K-6. (Teachers Lesson Plan Bk.: E-1). 1994. boxed set 9.95 (*0-8373-7951-2*) Nat Learn.
— Elevator Inspector. (Career Examination Ser.: C-244). 1994. pap. 29.95 (*0-8373-0244-7*) Nat Learn.
— Elevator Mechanic. (Career Examination Ser.: C-1056). 1994. pap. 23.95 (*0-8373-1056-3*) Nat Learn.
— Elevator Mechanic (U. S. P. S.) (Career Examination Ser.: C-1684). 1994. pap. 23.95 (*0-8373-1684-7*) Nat Learn.
— Elevator Mechanic's Helper. (Career Examination Ser.: C-237). 1994. pap. 23.95 (*0-8373-0237-4*) Nat Learn.
— Elevator Operator. (Career Examination Ser.: C-230). 1994. pap. 23.95 (*0-8373-0230-7*) Nat Learn.
— Elevator Starter. (Career Examination Ser.: C-1270). 1994. pap. 23.95 (*0-8373-1270-1*) Nat Learn.
— Eligibility Specialist. (Career Examination Ser.: C-2958). 1994. pap. 23.95 (*0-8373-2958-2*) Nat Learn.
— Emergency Communications Specialist. (Career Examination Ser.: C-2878). 1994. pap. 27.95 (*0-8373-2878-0*) Nat Learn.
— Emergency Complaint Operator. (Career Examination Ser.: C-1057). 1994. pap. 23.95 (*0-8373-1057-1*) Nat Learn.
— Emergency Medical Technicians - Paramedic Examination (EMT) (Admission Test Ser.: Vol. 70). 69.95 (*0-8373-5170-7*) Nat Learn.
— Emergency Medical Technicians-Paramedic Examination (EMT) (Admission Test Ser.: ATS-70). 1994. pap. 49.95 (*0-8373-5070-0*) Nat Learn.
— Emotionally Handicapped Children. (Teachers License Examination Ser.: T-69). 1994. pap. 27.95 (*0-8373-8069-3*) Nat Learn.
— Employee Assistance Program Coordinator. (Career Examination Ser.: C-3667). pap. 34.95 (*0-8373-3667-8*) Nat Learn.
— Employee Assistance Program Worker. (Career Examination Ser.: C-3712). 1994. pap. 29.95 (*0-8373-3712-7*) Nat Learn.
— Employee Benefits Supervisor. (Career Examination Ser.: C-2810). 1994. pap. 34.95 (*0-8373-2810-1*) Nat Learn.
— Employee Relations Director. (Career Examination Ser.: C-3597). pap. 39.95 (*0-8373-3597-3*) Nat Learn.
— Employment & Training Assistant. (Career Examination Ser.: C-3713). 1994. pap. 29.95 (*0-8373-3713-5*) Nat Learn.
— Employment & Training Coordinator. (Career Examination Ser.: C-2884). 1994. pap. 44.95 (*0-8373-2884-5*) Nat Learn.
— Employment & Training Fiscal Auditor. (Career Examination Ser.: C-3385). 1994. pap. 44.95 (*0-8373-3385-7*) Nat Learn.
— Employment & Training Programs Administrator. (Career Examination Ser.: C-3076). 1994. pap. 44.95 (*0-8373-3076-9*) Nat Learn.
— Employment Consultant (Testing) (Career Examination Ser.: C-2463). 1994. pap. 39.95 (*0-8373-2463-7*) Nat Learn.
— Employment Counselor. (Career Examination Ser.: C-245). 1994. pap. 29.95 (*0-8373-0245-5*) Nat Learn.
— Employment Counselor Trainee. (Career Examination Ser.: C-246). 1994. pap. 27.95 (*0-8373-0246-3*) Nat Learn.
— Employment Interviewer. (Career Examination Ser.: C-231). 1994. pap. 29.95 (*0-8373-0231-5*) Nat Learn.
— Employment Manager. (Career Examination Ser.: C-2582). 1994. pap. 39.95 (*0-8373-2582-X*) Nat Learn.
— Employment Security Claims Trainee. (Career Examination Ser.: C-3144). 1994. pap. 23.95 (*0-8373-3144-7*) Nat Learn.
— Employment Security Clerk. (Career Examination Ser.: C-2350). 1994. pap. 23.95 (*0-8373-2350-9*) Nat Learn.
— Employment Security Manager. (Career Examination Ser.: C-3188). 1994. pap. 39.95 (*0-8373-3188-9*) Nat Learn.
— Employment Security Placement Trainee. (Career Examination Ser.: C-2229). 1994. pap. 23.95 (*0-8373-2229-4*) Nat Learn.
— Energy Assistance Review Aide. (Career Examination Ser.: C-3308). 1994. pap. 27.95 (*0-8373-3308-3*) Nat Learn.
— Energy Assistance Review Supervisor. (Career Examination Ser.: C-3309). 1994. pap. 29.95 (*0-8373-3309-1*) Nat Learn.
— Energy Conservation Analyst. (Career Examination Ser.: C-2035). 1994. pap. 29.95 (*0-8373-2035-6*) Nat Learn.
— Engineer. (Career Examination Ser.: C-240). 1994. pap. 39.95 (*0-8373-0240-4*) Nat Learn.
— Engineering. (Graduate Record Examination (GRE) Ser.: Vol. 5). 43.95 (*0-8373-5255-X*) Nat Learn.
— Engineering. (Undergraduate Program Field Tests (UPFT) Ser.: Vol. 8). 43.95 (*0-8373-6058-7*) Nat Learn.
— Engineering. (Graduate Record Examination Ser.: GRE-5). 1994. pap. 23.95 (*0-8373-5205-3*) Nat Learn.
— Engineering. (Undergraduate Program Field Tests (UPFT) Ser.: Vol. UPFT-8). 1994. pap. 23.95 (*0-8373-6008-0*) Nat Learn.
— Engineering Administrative Technician. (Career Examination Ser.: C-1271). 1994. pap. 34.95 (*0-8373-1271-X*) Nat Learn.
— Engineering Aid & Science Assistant. (Career Examination Ser.: C-232). 1994. pap. 29.95 (*0-8373-0232-3*) Nat Learn.
— Engineering Aide. (Career Examination Ser.: C-233). 1994. pap. 23.95 (*0-8373-0233-1*) Nat Learn.
— Engineering Assistant. (Career Examination Ser.: C-234). 1994. pap. 27.95 (*0-8373-0234-X*) Nat Learn.
— Engineering Draftsman. (Career Examination Ser.: C-247). 1994. pap. 27.95 (*0-8373-0247-1*) Nat Learn.
— Engineering Inspector. (Career Examination Ser.: C-1861). 1994. reprint ed. pap. 39.95 (*0-8373-1861-0*) Nat Learn.
— Engineering Materials Technician. (Career Examination Ser.: C-315). 1994. pap. 27.95 (*0-8373-0315-X*) Nat Learn.
— Engineering Technician. (Career Examination Ser.: C-235). 1994. pap. 23.95 (*0-8373-0235-8*) Nat Learn.
— Engineering Technician (Drafting) (Career Examination Ser.: C-991). 1994. pap. 23.95 (*0-8373-0991-3*) Nat Learn.
— Engineering Technician (Environmental Quality) (Career Examination Ser.: C-3237). 1994. pap. 27.95 (*0-8373-3237-0*) Nat Learn.
— Engineering Technician Trainee. (Career Examination Ser.: C-248). 1994. pap. 23.95 (*0-8373-0248-X*) Nat Learn.
— Engineering Trainee. (Career Examination Ser.: C-1272). 1994. pap. 27.95 (*0-8373-1272-8*) Nat Learn.
— Engineman (U. S. P. S.) (Career Examination Ser.: C-2371). 1994. pap. 27.95 (*0-8373-2371-1*) Nat Learn.
— English & Citizenship. (Teachers License Examination Ser.: T-17). 1994. pap. 27.95 (*0-8373-8017-0*) Nat Learn.
— English As a Second Language. (National Teacher Examination Ser.: NT-47). 1994. pap. 23.95 (*0-8373-8457-5*) Nat Learn.
— English as a Second Language (Day Elementary Schools) (Teachers License Examination Ser.: T-65a). 1994. pap. 27.95 (*0-8373-8065-0*) Nat Learn.
— English as a Second Language (Secondary Schools) (Teachers License Examination Ser.: T-65b). 1994. pap. 27.95 (*0-685-49790-9*) Nat Learn.
— English Composition. (College Level Examination (CLEP) Ser.: Vol. ATS-9A). 43.95 (*0-8373-5295-9*) Nat Learn.
— English Composition. (College-Level Examination Series (General Examinations): ATS-9A). 1994. pap. 23.95 (*0-8373-5245-2*) Nat Learn.
— English, Jr. H. S. (Teachers License Examination Ser.: T-15). 1994. pap. 27.95 (*0-8373-8015-4*) Nat Learn.
— English Language & Literature. (National Teacher Examination Ser.: NT-4). 1994. pap. 23.95 (*0-8373-8414-1*) Nat Learn.
— English Literature. (College Level Examination (CLEP) Ser.: Vol. 12). 43.95 (*0-8373-5362-9*) Nat Learn.
— English Literature. (College Level Examination Ser.: CLEP-12). 1994. pap. 23.95 (*0-8373-5312-2*) Nat Learn.
— English, Sr. H. S. (Teachers License Examination Ser.: T-16). 1994. pap. 27.95 (*0-8373-8016-2*) Nat Learn.
— Entomologist. (Career Examination Ser.: C-249). 1994. pap. 34.95 (*0-8373-0249-8*) Nat Learn.
— Environment & Humanity. (Dantes Subject Standardized Tests (DANTES) Ser.: Vol. 72). 43.95 (*0-8373-6572-4*) Nat Learn.
— Environment & Humanity. (Dantes Subject Standardized Test (DANTES) Ser.: Vol. DANTES-72). 1997. pap. 23.95 (*0-8373-6672-0*) Nat Learn.
— Environmental Analyst. (Career Examination Ser.: C-2659). 1994. pap. 34.95 (*0-8373-2659-1*) Nat Learn.
— Environmental Assistant. (Career Examination Ser.: C-1583). 1994. pap. 27.95 (*0-8373-1583-2*) Nat Learn.
— Environmental Chemist I. (Career Examination Ser.: C-2985). 1994. pap. 29.95 (*0-8373-2985-X*) Nat Learn.
— Environmental Chemist II. (Career Examination Ser.: C-2986). 1994. pap. 29.95 (*0-8373-2986-8*) Nat Learn.
— Environmental Conservation Investigator. (Career Examination Ser.: C-3214). 1994. pap. 29.95 (*0-8373-3214-1*) Nat Learn.
— Environmental Conservation Officer. (Career Examination Ser.: C-2428). 1994. pap. 29.95 (*0-8373-2428-9*) Nat Learn.
— Environmental Conservation Officer Trainee. (Career Examination Ser.: C-1759). 1994. pap. 27.95 (*0-8373-1759-2*) Nat Learn.
— Environmental Control Specialist. (Career Examination Ser.: C-2429). 1994. pap. 29.95 (*0-8373-2429-7*) Nat Learn.
— Environmental Control Specialist Trainee. (Career Examination Ser.: C-2067). 1994. reprint ed. pap. 27.95 (*0-8373-2067-4*) Nat Learn.
— Environmental Control Technician. (Career Examination Ser.: C-3582). 1994. pap. 29.95 (*0-8373-3582-5*) Nat Learn.
— Environmental Education. (National Teacher Examination Ser.: NT-54). pap. 23.95 (*0-8373-8474-5*) Nat Learn.
— Environmental Educator. (Career Examination Ser.: C-3241). 1994. pap. 34.95 (*0-8373-3241-9*) Nat Learn.
— Environmental Enforcement Specialist. (Career Examination Ser.: C-3328). 1994. pap. 29.95 (*0-8373-3328-8*) Nat Learn.
— Environmental Engineer. (Career Examination Ser.: C-3673). pap. 34.95 (*0-8373-3673-2*) Nat Learn.
— Environmental Health Aide. (Career Examination Ser.: C-1959). 1994. pap. 29.95 (*0-8373-1959-5*) Nat Learn.
— Environmental Health Specialist. (Career Examination Ser.: C-3714). 1994. pap. 39.95 (*0-8373-3714-3*) Nat Learn.
— Environmental Health Technician. (Career Examination Ser.: C-2652). 1994. pap. 29.95 (*0-8373-2652-4*) Nat Learn.
— Environmental Planner. (Career Examination Ser.: C-2662). 1994. pap. 34.95 (*0-8373-2662-1*) Nat Learn.
— Environmental Program Specialist Trainee. (Career Examination Ser.: C-3621). 1994. pap. 29.95 (*0-8373-3621-X*) Nat Learn.
— Environmental Projects Coordinator. (Career Examination Ser.: C-3633). pap. 34.95 (*0-8373-3633-3*) Nat Learn.
— Environmental Protection Director. (Career Examination Ser.: C-2849). 1994. pap. 39.95 (*0-8373-2849-7*) Nat Learn.
— Environmental Radiation Specialist. (Career Examination Ser.: C-3715). 1994. pap. 34.95 (*0-8373-3715-1*) Nat Learn.
— Environmental Technician. (Career Examination Ser.: C-3311). 1994. pap. 29.95 (*0-8373-3311-3*) Nat Learn.
— Environmentalist. (Career Examination Ser.: C-1584). 1994. pap. 29.95 (*0-8373-1584-0*) Nat Learn.
— Equalization Rates Analyst. (Career Examination Ser.: C-3240). 1994. pap. 34.95 (*0-8373-3240-0*) Nat Learn.
— Equipment Foreman. (Career Examination Ser.: C-1273). 1994. pap. 29.95 (*0-8373-1273-6*) Nat Learn.
— Equipment Operator. (Career Examination Ser.: C-1274). 1994. pap. 27.95 (*0-8373-1274-4*) Nat Learn.
— Equipment Specialist. (Career Examination Ser.: C-971). 1994. pap. 27.95 (*0-8373-0971-9*) Nat Learn.
— Equipment Supervisor. (Career Examination Ser.: C-3071). 1994. pap. 29.95 (*0-8373-3071-8*) Nat Learn.

An Asterisk (*) at the beginning of an entry indicates that the title is appearing for the first time.

— Estimator. (Career Examination Ser.: C-1275). 1994. pap. 34.95 (0-8373-1275-2) Nat Learn.
— Ethics in America. (Dantes Subject Standardized Tests Ser.: Vol. DANTES-8). 1994. 39.95 (0-8373-6658-5) Nat Learn.
— European History. (Regents College Proficiency Examination Ser.: Vol. 10). 43.95 (0-8373-5460-9) Nat Learn.
— European History. (Regents College Proficiency Examination Ser.: CPEP-10). 1994. pap. 23.95 (0-8373-5410-2) Nat Learn.
— Every-Day Spanish for Police Officers. (General Aptitude & Abilities Ser.: CS-31). 1994. pap. 29.95 (0-8373-6731-X) Nat Learn.
— Evidence Control Clerk. (Career Examination Ser.: C-3149). 1994. pap. 27.95 (0-8373-3149-8) Nat Learn.
— Evidence Technician. (Career Examination Ser.: C-2748). 1994. pap. 29.95 (0-8373-2748-2) Nat Learn.
— Examen de Equavalencia para el Diploma de Escuela Superior (EEE) (Admission Test Ser.: Vol. 22). 59.95 (0-8373-5122-7) Nat Learn.
— Examen de Equivalencia Para el Diploma de Escuela Superior (EEE) (Admission Test Ser.: ATS-22). 1994. reprint ed. pap. 39.95 (0-8373-5022-0) Nat Learn.
— Examiner, Board of Examiners. (Teachers License Examination Ser.: GT-10). 1994. pap. 49.95 (0-8373-8130-4) Nat Learn.
— Examiner (Intermittent) (Career Examination Ser.: C-2622). 1994. pap. 39.95 (0-8373-2622-2) Nat Learn.
— Examiner of Municipal Affairs. (Career Examination Ser.: C-2726). 1994. pap. 39.95 (0-8373-2726-1) Nat Learn.
— Examiner, Social Services. (Career Examination Ser.: C-2138). 1994. reprint ed. pap. 23.95 (0-8373-2138-7) Nat Learn.
— Excise Tax Investigator. (Career Examination Ser.: C-972). 1994. pap. 27.95 (0-8373-0972-7) Nat Learn.
— Executive Assistant. (Career Examination Ser.: C-1276). 1994. pap. 27.95 (0-8373-1276-0) Nat Learn.
— Executive Director. (Career Examination Ser.: C-1277). 1994. pap. 39.95 (0-8373-1277-9) Nat Learn.
— Executive Director of Youth Bureau. (Career Examination Ser.: C-416). 1994. pap. 39.95 (0-8373-0416-4) Nat Learn.
— Executive Officer. (Career Examination Ser.: C-1278). 1994. pap. 34.95 (0-8373-1278-7) Nat Learn.
— Executive Secretary. (Career Examination Ser.: C-1279). 1994. pap. 27.95 (0-8373-1279-5) Nat Learn.
— Executive Staff Assistant. (Career Examination Ser.: C-1280). 1994. pap. 27.95 (0-8373-1280-9) Nat Learn.
— Exhibits Technician. (Career Examination Ser.: No. C-1281). 1994. pap. 27.95 (0-8373-1281-7) Nat Learn.
— Exterminator. (Career Examination Ser.: C-236). 1994. pap. 27.95 (0-8373-0236-6) Nat Learn.
— F. C. C. Amateur License Examinations (AL) (Admission Test Ser.: Vol. 83). 47.95 (0-8373-5183-9) Nat Learn.
— F. C. C. Commercial Radio Operator License Examination (CRO) (Admission Test Ser.: Vol. 73). 49.95 (0-8373-5173-1) Nat Learn.
— Facilities Planner. (Career Examination Ser.: Vol. C-3816). 1997. pap. 34.95 (0-8373-3816-6) Nat Learn.
— Facility Management Assistant. (Career Examination Ser.: C-387). 1994. pap. 29.95 (0-8373-0387-7) Nat Learn.
— Factory Inspector. (Career Examination Ser.: C-283). 1994. pap. 29.95 (0-8373-0283-8) Nat Learn.
— Family & Children Services Specialist. (Career Examination Ser.: C-3549). 1994. pap. 29.95 (0-8373-3549-3) Nat Learn.
— Family Nurse Practitioner. (Certified Nurse Examination Ser.: CN-2). 1994. pap. 23.95 (0-8373-6102-8) Nat Learn.
— Family Planning Aide. (Career Examination Ser.: C-3369). 1994. pap. 27.95 (0-8373-3369-5) Nat Learn.
— Farm Products Grading Inspector. (Career Examination Ser.: C-3137). 1994. pap. 29.95 (0-8373-3137-4) Nat Learn.
— F.C.C. Amateur License Examinations (AL) (Admission Test Ser.: ATS-83). 1994. pap. 27.95 (0-8373-5083-2) Nat Learn.
— F.C.C. Commmercial Radio Operator License Examination (CRO) (Admission Test Ser.: ATS-73). 1994. pap. 29.95 (0-8373-5073-5) Nat Learn.
— F.C.C. General Radiotelephone Operator (RTO) (Admission Test Ser.: ATS-114). pap. 29.95 (0-8373-5814-0) Nat Learn.
— Federal Administrative & Management Examination. (Career Examination Ser.: C-250). 1994. pap. 27.95 (0-8373-0250-1) Nat Learn.
— Federal & State Aid Claims Technician. (Career Examination Ser.: C-3297). 1994. pap. 29.95 (0-8373-3297-4) Nat Learn.
— Federal & State Aid Coordinator. (Career Examination Ser.: C-1282). 1994. pap. 34.95 (0-8373-1282-5) Nat Learn.
— Federal Construction Project Coordinator. (Career Examination Ser.: C-2879). 1994. pap. 39.95 (0-8373-2879-9) Nat Learn.
— Federal Guard. (Career Examination Ser.: C-251). 1994. pap. 23.95 (0-8373-0251-X) Nat Learn.
— Federal Mine Inspector. (Career Examination Ser.: C-1283). 1994. pap. 29.95 (0-8373-1283-3) Nat Learn.
— Federal Office Assistant. (Career Examination Ser.: C-252). 1994. pap. 23.95 (0-8373-0252-8) Nat Learn.
— Federal Protective Officer. (Career Examination Ser.: C-1612). 1994. pap. 27.95 (0-8373-1612-X) Nat Learn.
— Federal Service Entrance Examination (FSEE) (Admission Test Ser.: ATS-16). 1994. pap. 23.95 (0-8373-5016-6) Nat Learn.
— Federal Service Entrance Examination (FSEE) (Career Examination Ser.: Vol. C-253). 1994. pap. 23.95 (0-8373-0253-6) Nat Learn.
— Federal Service Management Intern Examination. (Career Examination Ser.: C-285). 1994. pap. 23.95 (0-8373-0285-4) Nat Learn.
— Federation Licensing Examination (FLEX) (Admission Test Ser.: Vol. 31). 89.95 (0-8373-5131-6) Nat Learn.
— Federation Licensing Examination (FLEX) (Admission Test Ser.: ATS-31). 1994. pap. 69.95 (0-8373-5031-X) Nat Learn.
— Ferry Agent. (Career Examination Ser.: C-3370). 1994. pap. 27.95 (0-8373-3370-9) Nat Learn.
— Ferry Terminal Supervisor. (Career Examination Ser.: C-2142). 1994. reprint ed. pap. 29.95 (0-8373-2142-5) Nat Learn.
— Field Accountant. (Career Examination Ser.: C-1568). 1994. pap. 29.95 (0-8373-1568-9) Nat Learn.
— Field Auditor. (Career Examination Ser.: C-1284). 1994. pap. 29.95 (0-8373-1284-1) Nat Learn.
— Field Investigator. (Career Examination Ser.: C-1285). 1994. pap. 27.95 (0-8373-1285-X) Nat Learn.
— Field Representative. (Career Examination Ser.: C-2115). 1994. reprint ed. pap. 27.95 (0-8373-2115-8) Nat Learn.
— Field Representative (Code Compliance) (Career Examination Ser.: C-3354). 1994. pap. 34.95 (0-8373-3354-7) Nat Learn.
— Field Representative, Senior Citizen Services Project. (Career Examination Ser.: C-2948). 1994. pap. 29.95 (0-8373-2948-5) Nat Learn.
— Field Systems Coordinator. (Career Examination Ser.: C-2243). 1994. pap. 34.95 (0-8373-2243-X) Nat Learn.
— File Clerk. (Career Examination Ser.: C-254). 1994. pap. 19.95 (0-8373-0254-4) Nat Learn.
— Filing. (General Aptitude & Abilities Ser.: CS-45). 1994. pap. 19.95 (0-8373-6745-X) Nat Learn.
— Film Editor. (Career Examination Ser.: C-1286). 1994. pap. 23.95 (0-8373-1286-8) Nat Learn.
— Finance I. (Regents External Degree (REDP) Ser.: Vol. 4). 43.95 (0-8373-5654-7) Nat Learn.
— Finance I. (Regents External Degree Ser.: REDP-4). 1994. pap. 23.95 (0-8373-5604-0) Nat Learn.
— Finance II. (Regents External Degree (REDP) Ser.: Vol. 5). 43.95 (0-8373-5655-5) Nat Learn.
— Finance II. (Regents External Degree Ser.: REDP-5). 1994. pap. 23.95 (0-8373-5605-9) Nat Learn.
— Finance III. (Regents External Degree (REDP) Ser.: Vol. 6). 43.95 (0-8373-5656-3) Nat Learn.
— Finance III. (Regents External Degree Ser.: REDP-6). 1994. pap. 23.95 (0-8373-5606-7) Nat Learn.
— Financial Accounting. (Dantes Subject Standardized Tests Ser.: DANTES-15). 1994. pap. 23.95 (0-8373-6615-1) Nat Learn.
— Financial Analyst. (Career Examination Ser.: C-2642). 1994. pap. 34.95 (0-8373-2642-7) Nat Learn.
— Financial Clerk. (Career Examination Ser.: C-3716). 1994. pap. 23.95 (0-8373-3716-X) Nat Learn.
— Financial Investigator. (Career Examination Ser.: C-873). 1994. pap. 29.95 (0-8373-0873-9) Nat Learn.
— Financial Officer. (Career Examination Ser.: C-3512). 1994. pap. 34.95 (0-8373-3512-4) Nat Learn.
— Fine Arts, Jr. H. S. (Teachers License Examination Ser.: T-18). 1994. pap. 27.95 (0-8373-8018-9) Nat Learn.
— Fine Arts, Sr. H. S. (Teachers License Examination Ser.: T-19). 1994. pap. 27.95 (0-8373-8019-7) Nat Learn.
— Fingerprint Technician. (Career Examination Ser.: C-255). 1994. pap. 27.95 (0-8373-0255-2) Nat Learn.
— Fingerprint Technician Trainee. (Career Examination Ser.: C-286). 1994. pap. 23.95 (0-8373-0286-2) Nat Learn.
— Fire Administration & Supervision. (General Aptitude & Abilities Ser.: No. CS-38). pap. 39.95 (0-8373-6738-7, CS-38) Nat Learn.
— Fire Alarm Dispatcher. (Career Examination Ser.: C-256). 1994. pap. 23.95 (0-8373-0256-0) Nat Learn.
— Fire & Safety Representative. (Career Examination Ser.: C-3242). 1994. pap. 29.95 (0-8373-3242-7) Nat Learn.
— Fire Communications Technician. (Career Examination Ser.: C-1217). 1994. pap. 29.95 (0-8373-1217-5) Nat Learn.
— Fire Control Mechanic. (Career Examination Ser.: C-257). 1994. pap. 27.95 (0-8373-0257-9) Nat Learn.
— Fire Engine Driver. (Career Examination Ser.: C-3446). 1994. pap. 27.95 (0-8373-3446-2) Nat Learn.
— Fire Fighter. (Career Examination Ser.: C-1287). 1994. pap. 23.95 (0-8373-1287-6) Nat Learn.
— Fire Guard License. (Career Examination Ser.: C-3764). pap. 23.95 (0-8373-3764-X) Nat Learn.
— Fire Inspector. (Career Examination Ser.: C-1288). 1994. pap. 34.95 (0-8373-1288-4) Nat Learn.
— Fire Marshal. (Career Examination Ser.: C-2401). 1994. pap. 34.95 (0-8373-2401-7) Nat Learn.
— Fire Medic. (Career Examination Ser.: C-296). 1994. pap. 29.95 (0-8373-0296-X) Nat Learn.
— Fire Officer. (Career Examination Ser.: C-1578). 1994. pap. 29.95 (0-8373-1578-6) Nat Learn.
— Fire Prevention Inspector. (Career Examination Ser.: C-287). 1994. pap. 34.95 (0-8373-0287-0) Nat Learn.
— Fire Promotion Course. (General Aptitude & Abilities Ser.: CS-21). 1994. pap. 39.95 (0-8373-6721-2) Nat Learn.
— Fire Protection Inspector. (Career Examination Ser.: C-3717). 1994. pap. 34.95 (0-8373-3717-8) Nat Learn.
— Fire Protection Specialist. (Career Examination Ser.: C-3447). 1994. pap. 34.95 (0-8373-3447-0) Nat Learn.
— Fire Safety Officer. (Career Examination Ser.: C-2230). 1994. pap. 29.95 (0-8373-2230-8) Nat Learn.
— Fire Safety Technician. (Career Examination Ser.: C-3243). 1994. pap. 29.95 (0-8373-3243-5) Nat Learn.
— Firehouse Attendant. (Career Examination Ser.: C-3386). 1994. pap. 23.95 (0-8373-3386-5) Nat Learn.
— Fireman Examinations - All States. (Career Examination Ser.: C-258). 1994. pap. 23.95 (0-8373-0258-7) Nat Learn.
— Fireman, Fire Department. (Career Examination Ser.: C-259). 1994. pap. 23.95 (0-8373-0259-5) Nat Learn.
— Fireman-Laborer. (Career Examination Ser.: C-1289). 1994. pap. 27.95 (0-8373-1289-2) Nat Learn.
— Fiscal Administrator. (Career Examination Ser.: C-2612). 1994. pap. 39.95 (0-8373-2612-5) Nat Learn.
— Fiscal Analyst. (Career Examination Ser.: C-3341). 1994. pap. 34.95 (0-8373-3341-5) Nat Learn.
— Fiscal Clerk. (Career Examination Ser.: C-3718). 1994. pap. 23.95 (0-8373-3718-6) Nat Learn.
— Fiscal Director. (Career Examination Ser.: C-1290). 1994. pap. 39.95 (0-8373-1290-6) Nat Learn.
— Fiscal Manager. (Career Examination Ser.: C-2686). 1995. pap. 39.95 (0-8373-2686-9) Nat Learn.
— Fiscal Officer. (Career Examination Ser.: C-1409). 1994. pap. 34.95 (0-8373-1409-7) Nat Learn.
— Fish & Wildlife Technician. (Career Examination Ser.: C-3159). 1994. pap. 27.95 (0-8373-3159-5) Nat Learn.
— Flight Attendant Skills Test (FAST) (Career Examination Ser.: C-3338). 1994. pap. 23.95 (0-8373-3338-5) Nat Learn.
— Floating Plant Supervisor. (Career Examination Ser.: C-3658). pap. 29.95 (0-8373-3658-9) Nat Learn.
— Florida Functional Literacy Test (FLT) (Admission Test Ser.: Vol. 54). 43.95 (0-8373-5154-5) Nat Learn.
— Florida Functional Literacy Test (FLT) (Admission Test Ser.: ATS-54). 1994. pap. 23.95 (0-8373-5054-9) Nat Learn.
— Florist. (Career Examination Ser.: C-1410). 1994. pap. 29.95 (0-8373-1410-0) Nat Learn.
— Food Inspector. (Career Examination Ser.: C-2543). 1994. pap. 29.95 (0-8373-2543-9) Nat Learn.
— Food Inspector Trainee. (Career Examination Ser.: C-2998). 1994. pap. 27.95 (0-8373-2998-1) Nat Learn.
— Food Service Management Specialist. (Career Examination Ser.: C-3624). pap. 34.95 (0-8373-3624-4) Nat Learn.
— Food Service Manager. (Career Examination Ser.: C-3564). 1994. pap. 34.95 (0-8373-3564-7) Nat Learn.
— Food Service Specialist. (Career Examination Ser.: C-3513). 1994. pap. 29.95 (0-8373-3513-2) Nat Learn.
— Food Service Supervisor. (Career Examination Ser.: C-1411). 1994. pap. 29.95 (0-8373-1411-9) Nat Learn.
— Food Service Worker. (Career Examination Ser.: C-260). 1994. pap. 27.95 (0-8373-0260-9) Nat Learn.
— Ford M - Triple S Assessment Test (FORD) (Admission Test Ser.: Vol. 107). 49.95 (0-8373-5857-4) Nat Learn.
— Ford M-Triple S Assessment Test (Ford) (Admission Test Ser.: ATS-107). 1994. pap. 29.95 (0-8373-5807-8) Nat Learn.
— Foreign Language - French. (Regents External Degree Ser.: REDP-27). 1994. pap. 23.95 (0-8373-5627-X) Nat Learn.
— Foreign Language - German. (Regents External Degree Ser.: REDP-28). 1994. pap. 23.95 (0-8373-5628-8) Nat Learn.
— Foreign Language - Italian. (Regents External Degree Ser.: REDP-29). 1994. pap. 23.95 (0-8373-5629-6) Nat Learn.
— Foreign Language - Spanish. (Regents External Degree Ser.: REDP-30). 1994. pap. 23.95 (0-8373-5630-X) Nat Learn.
— Foreign Language Pedagogy. (National Teacher Examination Ser.: NT-55). pap. 23.95 (0-8373-8475-3) Nat Learn.
— Foreign Medical Graduates Examination in Medical Science (FMGEMS) Pt. I: Basic Medical Sciences. (Admission Test Ser.: Vol. 74A). 69.95 (0-8373-6990-8) Nat Learn.
— Foreign Medical Graduates Examination in Medical Science (FMGEMS) Pt. I: Basic Medical Sciences. (Admission Test Ser.: ATS-74A). 1994. pap. 49.95 (0-8373-6965-7) Nat Learn.
— Foreign Medical Graduates Examination in Medical Science (FMGEMS) Pt. II: Clinical Sciences. (Admission Test Ser.: Vol. 74B). 69.95 (0-8373-6991-6) Nat Learn.
— Foreign Medical Graduates Examination in Medical Science (FMGEMS) Pt. II: Clinical Sciences, Pt. 2. (Admission Test Ser.: ATS-74B). 1994. pap. 49.95 (0-8373-6966-5) Nat Learn.
— Foreign Pharmacy Graduates Equivalency Examination (FPGEE) (Admission Test Ser.: Vol. 82). 69.95 (0-8373-5182-0) Nat Learn.
— Foreign Pharmacy Graduates Equivalency Examination (FPGEE) (Admission Test Ser.: ATS-82). 1994. pap. 49.95 (0-8373-5082-4) Nat Learn.
— Foreign Service Officer. (Career Examination Ser.: C-261). 1994. pap. 29.95 (0-8373-0261-7) Nat Learn.
— Foreman. (Career Examination Ser.: C-262). 1994. pap. 29.95 (0-8373-0262-5) Nat Learn.
— Foreman Asphalt Worker. (Career Examination Ser.: C-2080). 1994. reprint ed. pap. 29.95 (0-8373-2080-1) Nat Learn.
— Foreman Auto Mechanic. (Career Examination Ser.: C-263). 1994. pap. 29.95 (0-8373-0263-3) Nat Learn.
— Foreman Blacksmith. (Career Examination Ser.: C-1709). 1994. pap. 29.95 (0-8373-1709-6) Nat Learn.
— Foreman Bricklayer. (Career Examination Ser.: C-2020). 1994. pap. 29.95 (0-8373-2020-8) Nat Learn.
— Foreman Bridge Painter. (Career Examination Ser.: C-1412). 1994. pap. 29.95 (0-8373-1412-7) Nat Learn.
— Foreman (Buses & Shops) (Career Examination Ser.: C-264). 1994. pap. 29.95 (0-8373-0264-1) Nat Learn.
— Foreman Cable Splicer. (Career Examination Ser.: C-2021). 1994. pap. 29.95 (0-8373-2021-6) Nat Learn.
— Foreman Carpenter. (Career Examination Ser.: C-1779). 1994. pap. 29.95 (0-8373-1779-7) Nat Learn.
— Foreman (Cars & Shops) (Career Examination Ser.: C-265). 1994. pap. 29.95 (0-8373-0265-X) Nat Learn.
— Foreman (Department of Sanitation) (Career Examination Ser.: C-266). 1994. pap. 29.95 (0-8373-0266-8) Nat Learn.
— Foreman Dockbuilder. (Career Examination Ser.: C-2022). 1994. pap. 29.95 (0-8373-2022-4) Nat Learn.
— Foreman (Electrical Power) (Career Examination Ser.: C-267). 1994. pap. 29.95 (0-8373-0267-6) Nat Learn.
— Foreman Electrician. (Career Examination Ser.: C-1710). 1994. pap. 29.95 (0-8373-1710-X) Nat Learn.
— Foreman (Electronic Equipment) (Career Examination Ser.: C-2032). 1994. pap. 29.95 (0-8373-2032-1) Nat Learn.
— Foreman Elevator Mechanic. (Career Examination Ser.: C-2165). 1994. reprint ed. pap. 29.95 (0-8373-2165-4) Nat Learn.
— Foreman (Elevators & Escalators) (Career Examination Ser.: C-1413). 1994. pap. 29.95 (0-8373-1413-5) Nat Learn.
— Foreman Furniture Maintainer. (Career Examination Ser.: C-2023). 1994. pap. 29.95 (0-8373-2023-2) Nat Learn.
— Foreman (Highways & Sewers) (Career Examination Ser.: C-2190). 1994. pap. 29.95 (0-8373-2190-5) Nat Learn.
— Foreman, Laborer-Janitor (U. S. P. S.) (Career Examination Ser.: C-1686). 1994. pap. 29.95 (0-8373-1686-3) Nat Learn.
— Foreman Lineman. (Career Examination Ser.: C-2024). 1994. pap. 29.95 (0-8373-2024-0) Nat Learn.
— Foreman Locksmith. (Career Examination Ser.: C-2223). 1994. pap. 29.95 (0-8373-2223-5) Nat Learn.
— Foreman Machinist. (Career Examination Ser.: C-1414). 1994. pap. 29.95 (0-8373-1414-3) Nat Learn.
— Foreman, Maintenance (MPE) (U. S. P. S.) (Career Examination Ser.: C-1786). 1994. pap. 29.95 (0-8373-1786-X) Nat Learn.
— Foreman of Gardeners. (Career Examination Ser.: C-268). 1994. pap. 29.95 (0-8373-0268-4) Nat Learn.
— Foreman of Housing Caretakers. (Career Examination Ser.: C-269). 1994. pap. 29.95 (0-8373-0269-2) Nat Learn.
— Foreman of Housing Exterminators. (Career Examination Ser.: C-2514). 1994. pap. 29.95 (0-8373-2514-5) Nat Learn.
— Foreman of Laborers. (Career Examination Ser.: C-270). 1994. pap. 29.95 (0-8373-0270-6) Nat Learn.
— Foreman of Lighting. (Career Examination Ser.: C-271). 1994. pap. 29.95 (0-8373-0271-4) Nat Learn.
— Foreman of Mechanics. (Career Examination Ser.: C-1605). 1994. reprint ed. pap. 29.95 (0-8373-1605-7) Nat Learn.
— Foreman of Mechanics (Motor Vehicles) (Career Examination Ser.: C-272). 1994. pap. 29.95 (0-8373-0272-2) Nat Learn.
— Foreman Painter. (Career Examination Ser.: C-273). 1994. pap. 29.95 (0-8373-0273-0) Nat Learn.
— Foreman Plasterer. (Career Examination Ser.: C-2270). 1994. reprint ed. pap. 29.95 (0-8373-2270-7) Nat Learn.
— Foreman Plumber. (Career Examination Ser.: C-1415). 1994. pap. 29.95 (0-8373-1415-1) Nat Learn.
— Foreman (Power Cables) (Career Examination Ser.: C-2034). 1994. pap. 29.95 (0-8373-2034-8) Nat Learn.
— Foreman (Power Distribution) (Career Examination Ser.: C-274). 1994. pap. 29.95 (0-8373-0274-9) Nat Learn.
— Foreman (Railroad Watchman) (Career Examination Ser.: C-275). 1994. pap. 29.95 (0-8373-0275-7) Nat Learn.
— Foreman Roofer. (Career Examination Ser.: C-1416). 1994. pap. 29.95 (0-8373-1416-X) Nat Learn.
— Foreman (Sewer Maintenance) (Career Examination Ser.: C-1816). 1994. pap. 29.95 (0-8373-1816-5) Nat Learn.
— Foreman Sheet Metal Worker. (Career Examination Ser.: C-1711). 1994. pap. 29.95 (0-8373-1711-8) Nat Learn.
— Foreman (Signals) (Career Examination Ser.: C-276). 1994. pap. 29.95 (0-8373-0276-5) Nat Learn.
— Foreman Steamfitter. (Career Examination Ser.: C-2025). 1994. pap. 29.95 (0-8373-2025-9) Nat Learn.
— Foreman (Stores, Materials & Supplies) (Career Examination Ser.: C-1625). 1994. pap. 29.95 (0-8373-1625-1) Nat Learn.
— Foreman (Structures) (Career Examination Ser.: C-288). 1994. pap. 29.95 (0-8373-0288-9) Nat Learn.
— Foreman (Structures - Group A) (Carpentry) (Career Examination Ser.: C-1322). 1994. pap. 29.95 (0-8373-1322-8) Nat Learn.
— Foreman (Structures - Group B) (Masonry) (Career Examination Ser.: C-1323). 1994. pap. 29.95 (0-8373-1323-6) Nat Learn.
— Foreman (Structures - Group C) (Iron Work) (Career Examination Ser.: C-1324). 1994. pap. 29.95 (0-8373-1324-4) Nat Learn.
— Foreman (Structures - Group D) (Sheet Metal) (Career Examination Ser.: C-2277). 1994. reprint ed. pap. 29.95 (0-8373-2277-4) Nat Learn.
— Foreman (Structures - Group E) (Plumbing) (Career Examination Ser.: C-2278). 1994. reprint ed. pap. 29.95 (0-8373-2278-2) Nat Learn.
— Foreman (Structures - Group F) (Painting) (Career Examination Ser.: C-1325). 1994. pap. 29.95 (0-8373-1325-2) Nat Learn.
— Foreman (Structures - Group H) (Air Conditioning & Heating) (Career Examination Ser.: C-3494). 1994. pap. 29.95 (0-8373-3494-2) Nat Learn.
— Foreman (Telephones) (Career Examination Ser.: C-1970). 1994. pap. 29.95 (0-8373-1970-6) Nat Learn.
— Foreman (Track) (Career Examination Ser.: C-277). 1994. pap. 29.95 (0-8373-0277-3) Nat Learn.
— Foreman Traffic Device Maintenance. (Career Examination Ser.: C-1712). 1994. pap. 29.95 (0-8373-1712-6) Nat Learn.
— Foreman (Turnstiles) (Career Examination Ser.: C-2033). 1994. pap. 29.95 (0-8373-2033-X) Nat Learn.

R

— Foreman (Ventilation & Drainage) (Career Examination Ser.: C-278). 1994. pap. 29.95 (*0-8373-0278-1*) Nat Learn.
— Foreman (Water Supply) (Career Examination Ser.: C-279). 1994. pap. 29.95 (*0-8373-0279-X*) Nat Learn.
— Foreman (Watershed Maintenance) (Career Examination Ser.: C-280). 1994. pap. 29.95 (*0-8373-0280-3*) Nat Learn.
— Forensic Medical Investigator. (Career Examination Ser.: C-2936). 1994. pap. 39.95 (*0-8373-2936-1*) Nat Learn.
— Forensic Mental Health Assistant. (Career Examination Ser.: C-3058). 1994. pap. 29.95 (*0-8373-3058-0*) Nat Learn.
— Forensic Program Aide. (Career Examination Ser.: C-3719). 1994. pap. 27.95 (*0-8373-3719-4*) Nat Learn.
— Forensic Scientist I (Toxicology) (Career Examination Ser.: C-2937). 1994. pap. 34.95 (*0-8373-2937-X*) Nat Learn.
— Forensic Scientist II (Toxicology) (Career Examination Ser.: C-2938). 1994. pap. 34.95 (*0-8373-2938-8*) Nat Learn.
— Forensic Scientist Trainee. (Career Examination Ser.: C-3448). 1994. pap. 29.95 (*0-8373-3448-9*) Nat Learn.
— Forest Ranger. (Career Examination Ser.: C-281). 1994. pap. 27.95 (*0-8373-0281-1*) Nat Learn.
— Forester. (Career Examination Ser.: C-289). 1994. pap. 27.95 (*0-8373-0289-7*) Nat Learn.
— Forester Trainee. (Career Examination Ser.: C-3084). 1994. pap. 23.95 (*0-8373-3084-X*) Nat Learn.
— Forestry Technician. (Career Examination Ser.: C-1424). 1994. pap. 27.95 (*0-8373-1424-0*) Nat Learn.
— Forms Technician. (Career Examination Ser.: C-2406). 1994. pap. 34.95 (*0-8373-2406-8*) Nat Learn.
— Foundations of Gerontology. (ACT Proficiency Examination Program Ser.: PEP-54). 1994. pap. 23.95 (*0-8373-5904-X*) Nat Learn.
— Freight Rate Specialist. (Career Examination Ser.: C-973). 1994. pap. 27.95 (*0-8373-0973-5*) Nat Learn.
— French. (Graduate Record Examination (GRE) Ser.: Vol. 6). 43.95 (*0-8373-5256-8*) Nat Learn.
— French. (Undergraduate Program Field Tests (UPFT) Ser.: Vol. 9). 43.95 (*0-8373-6059-5*) Nat Learn.
— French. (Graduate Record Examination Ser.: GRE-6). 1994. pap. 23.95 (*0-8373-5206-1*) Nat Learn.
— French. (Undergraduate Program Field Tests (UPFT) Ser.: Vol. UPFT-9). 1994. pap. 23.95 (*0-8373-6009-9*) Nat Learn.
— French. (Advanced Placement Test (AP) Ser.: Vol. AP-8). 1997. pap. 23.95 (*0-8373-6208-3*) Nat Learn.
— French, Jr. H. S. (Teachers License Examination Ser.: T-20). 1994. pap. 27.95 (*0-8373-8020-0*) Nat Learn.
— French, Sr. H. S. (Teachers License Examination Ser.: T-21). 1994. pap. 27.95 (*0-8373-8021-9*) Nat Learn.
— Freshman English. (Regents College Proficiency Examination Ser.: Vol. 11). 43.95 (*0-8373-5461-7*) Nat Learn.
— Freshman English. (ACT Proficiency Examination Program (PEP) Ser.: Vol. 6). 43.95 (*0-8373-5556-7*) Nat Learn.
— Freshman English. (Regents College Proficiency Examination Ser.: CPEP-11). 1994. pap. 23.95 (*0-8373-5411-0*) Nat Learn.
— Freshman English. (College Level Examination (CLEP) Ser.: Vol. CLEP-31). 1994. pap. 23.95 (*0-8373-5331-9*) Nat Learn.
— Freshman English. (ACT Proficiency Examination Program (PEP) Ser.: Vol. PEP-6). 1994. pap. 23.95 (*0-8373-5506-0*) Nat Learn.
— Freshman Skills Assessment Program Admission Test (FSAP) (Admission Test Ser.: ATS-113). pap. 29.95 (*0-8373-5813-2*) Nat Learn.
— Fundamentals of Counseling. (Dantes Subject Standardized Tests Ser.: DANTES-65). 1994. pap. 23.95 (*0-8373-6665-8*) Nat Learn.
— Fundamentals of Nursing. (Regents College Proficiency Examination Ser.: Vol. 12). 43.95 (*0-8373-5462-5*) Nat Learn.
— Fundamentals of Nursing. (College Level Examination (CLEP) Ser.: Vol. 30). 43.95 (*0-8373-5380-7*) Nat Learn.
— Fundamentals of Nursing. (Regents College Proficiency Examination Ser.: CPEP-12). 1994. pap. 23.95 (*0-8373-5412-9*) Nat Learn.
— Fundamentals of Nursing. (College Level Examination (CLEP) Ser.: Vol. CLEP-30). 1994. pap. 23.95 (*0-8373-5330-0*) Nat Learn.
— Fundamentals of Nursing. (ACT Proficiency Examination Program (PEP) Ser.: Vol. PEP-36). 1994. pap. 23.95 (*0-8373-5536-2*) Nat Learn.
— Funeral Directing Investigator. (Career Examination Ser.: C-3112). 1994. pap. 29.95 (*0-8373-3112-9*) Nat Learn.
— Furniture Maintainer. (Career Examination Ser.: C-1059). 1994. pap. 23.95 (*0-8373-1059-8*) Nat Learn.
— Furniture Maintainer's Helper. (Career Examination Ser.: C-282). 1994. pap. 23.95 (*0-8373-0282-X*) Nat Learn.
— Game Management. (Career Examination Ser.: C-1291). 1994. pap. 27.95 (*0-8373-1291-4*) Nat Learn.
— Game Warden. (Career Examination Ser.: C-2012). 1994. pap. 27.95 (*0-8373-2012-7*) Nat Learn.
— Gang Foreman. (Career Examination Ser.: Vol. C-290). 1994. pap. 29.95 (*0-8373-0290-0*) Nat Learn.
— Gang Foreman (Structures) (Career Examination Ser.: Vol. C-291). 1994. pap. 29.95 (*0-8373-0291-9*) Nat Learn.
— Garage Foreman. (Career Examination Ser.: C-1603). 1994. pap. 29.95 (*0-8373-1603-0*) Nat Learn.
— Garageman. (Career Examination Ser.: C-1292). 1994. pap. 23.95 (*0-8373-1292-2*) Nat Learn.
— Garageman-Driver (U. S. P. S.) (Career Examination Ser.: C-1757). 1994. reprint ed. pap. 23.95 (*0-8373-1757-6*) Nat Learn.
— Garageman (U. S. P. S.) (Career Examination Ser.: C-1497). 1994. pap. 23.95 (*0-8373-1497-6*) Nat Learn.
— Gardener. (Career Examination Ser.: C-297). 1994. pap. 23.95 (*0-8373-0297-8*) Nat Learn.
— Garment Trades. (Teachers License Examination Ser.: T-72). 1994. pap. 27.95 (*0-8373-8072-3*) Nat Learn.
— Gas & Electric Welder. (Career Examination Ser.: C-1293). 1994. pap. 27.95 (*0-8373-1293-0*) Nat Learn.
— Gasoline Roller Engineer. (Career Examination Ser.: C-1294). 1994. pap. 29.95 (*0-8373-1294-9*) Nat Learn.
— General Anthropology. (Dantes Subject Standardized Tests (DANTES) Ser.: Vol. DANTES-16). 1997. pap. 23.95 (*0-8373-6616-X*) Nat Learn.
— General Aptitude & Abilities Series (CS) 1994. pap. write for info. (*0-8373-6700-X*) Nat Learn.
— General Aptitude Test (Battery) (General Aptitude & Abilities Ser.: No. CS-29). pap. 23.95 (*0-8373-6729-8*, CS-29) Nat Learn.
— General Biology. (College Level Examination (CLEP) Ser.: Vol. 5). 43.95 (*0-8373-5355-6*) Nat Learn.
— General Biology. (College Level Examination Ser.: CLEP-5). 1994. pap. 23.95 (*0-8373-5305-X*) Nat Learn.
— General Chemistry. (College Level Examination (CLEP) Ser.: Vol. 13). 43.95 (*0-8373-5363-7*) Nat Learn.
— General Chemistry. (College Level Examination Ser.: CLEP-13). 1994. pap. 23.95 (*0-8373-5313-0*) Nat Learn.
— General Clerical & Typing Careers Test. (Career Examination Ser.: C-3720). 1994. pap. 23.95 (*0-8373-3720-8*) Nat Learn.
— General Construction Supervisor. (Career Examination Ser.: C-3721). 1994. pap. 34.95 (*0-8373-3721-6*) Nat Learn.
— General Engineer. (Career Examination Ser.: C-298). 1994. pap. 39.95 (*0-8373-0298-6*) Nat Learn.
— General Geophysics. (Dantes Subject Standardized Tests Ser.: DANTES-17). 1994. pap. 23.95 (*0-8373-6617-8*) Nat Learn.
— General Industrial Training Supervisor. (Career Examination Ser.: C-2893). 1994. pap. 39.95 (*0-8373-2893-4*) Nat Learn.
— General Knowledge (Combined) (National Teacher Examination Ser.: NC-8). 1994. pap. 23.95 (*0-8373-8468-0*) Nat Learn.
— General Maintainer. (Career Examination Ser.: C-3449). 1994. pap. 27.95 (*0-8373-3449-7*) Nat Learn.
— General Management Ability Battery (GMAB) (Career Examination Ser.: No. C-3532). 1994. pap. 34.95 (*0-8373-3532-9*) Nat Learn.
— General Mathematical Ability (G. E. D.) (General Aptitude & Abilities Ser.: CS-33). 1994. pap. 17.95 (*0-8373-6733-6*) Nat Learn.
— General Mechanic (USPS) (Career Examination Ser.: C-835). 1994. pap. 27.95 (*0-8373-0835-6*) Nat Learn.
— General Park Foreman. (Career Examination Ser.: C-299). 1994. pap. 29.95 (*0-8373-0299-4*) Nat Learn.
— General Park Manager. (Career Examination Ser.: C-386). 1994. pap. 29.95 (*0-8373-0386-9*) Nat Learn.
— General Printing. (Occupational Competency Examination (OCE) Ser.: Vol. 20). 47.95 (*0-8373-5770-5*) Nat Learn.
— General Printing. (Occupational Competency Examination Ser.: OCE-20). 1994. pap. 27.95 (*0-8373-5720-9*) Nat Learn.
— General Psychology. (College Level Examination (CLEP) Ser.: Vol. 14). 43.95 (*0-8373-5364-5*) Nat Learn.
— General Psychology. (College Level Examination Ser.: CLEP-14). 1994. pap. 23.95 (*0-8373-5314-9*) Nat Learn.
— General Science. (National Teacher Examination Ser.: NT-48). 1994. pap. 23.95 (*0-8373-8458-3*) Nat Learn.
— General Science, Jr. H. S. (Teachers License Examination Ser.: T-22). 1994. pap. 27.95 (*0-8373-8022-7*) Nat Learn.
— General Services Manager. (Career Examination Ser.: C-3244). 1994. pap. 34.95 (*0-8373-3244-3*) Nat Learn.
— General Superintendent. (Career Examination Ser.: C-2110). 1994. reprint ed. pap. 34.95 (*0-8373-2110-7*) Nat Learn.
— General Superintendent (Sanitation) (Career Examination Ser.: C-2097). 1994. pap. 29.95 (*0-8373-2097-6*) Nat Learn.
— General Supervisor. (Career Examination Ser.: C-1295). 1994. pap. 29.95 (*0-8373-1295-7*) Nat Learn.
— General Supervisor of Building Maintenance (Construction) (Career Examination Ser.: C-3364). 1994. pap. 29.95 (*0-8373-3364-4*) Nat Learn.
— General Supervisor of Building Maintenance (Electrical) (Career Examination Ser.: C-3417). 1994. pap. 29.95 (*0-8373-3417-9*) Nat Learn.
— General Supervisor of Building Maintenance (Mechanical) (Career Examination Ser.: C-3418). 1994. pap. 29.95 (*0-8373-3418-7*) Nat Learn.
— General Supervisor of School Maintenance (Construction) (Career Examination Ser.: C-1675). 1994. pap. 29.95 (*0-8373-1675-8*) Nat Learn.
— General Supervisor of School Maintenance (Electrical) (Career Examination Ser.: C-2116). 1994. reprint ed. pap. 29.95 (*0-8373-2116-6*) Nat Learn.
— General Supervisor of School Maintenance (Mechanical) (Career Examination Ser.: C-1676). 1994. pap. 29.95 (*0-8373-1676-6*) Nat Learn.
— Geodesist. (Career Examination Ser.: C-300). 1994. pap. 27.95 (*0-8373-0300-1*) Nat Learn.
— Geography. (Undergraduate Program Field Tests (UPFT) Ser.: Vol. 10). 43.95 (*0-8373-6060-9*) Nat Learn.
— Geography. (Graduate Record Examination (GRE) Ser.: Vol. 7). 43.95 (*0-8373-5257-6*) Nat Learn.
— Geography. (Graduate Record Examination Ser.: GRE-7). 1994. pap. 23.95 (*0-8373-5207-X*) Nat Learn.
— Geography: Human/Cultural. (Dantes Subject Standardized Tests Ser.: No. Dantes-62). pap. 23.95 (*0-8373-6662-3*, Dantes-62) Nat Learn.
— Geologist. (Career Examination Ser.: C-301). 1994. pap. 27.95 (*0-8373-0301-X*) Nat Learn.
— Geology. (Undergraduate Program Field Tests (UPFT) Ser.: Vol. 11). 43.95 (*0-8373-6061-7*) Nat Learn.
— Geology. (Regents College Proficiency Examination Ser.: Vol. 13). 43.95 (*0-8373-5463-3*) Nat Learn.
— Geology. (College Level Examination (CLEP) Ser.: Vol. 15). 43.95 (*0-8373-5365-3*) Nat Learn.
— Geology. (Graduate Record Examination (GRE) Ser.: Vol. 8). 43.95 (*0-8373-5258-4*) Nat Learn.
— Geology. (College Level Examination (CLEP) Ser.: Vol. CLEP-15). 1994. pap. 23.95 (*0-8373-5315-7*) Nat Learn.
— Geology. (Regents College Proficiency Examination Ser.: Vol. CPEP-13). 1994. pap. 23.95 (*0-8373-5413-7*) Nat Learn.
— Geology. (Graduate Record Examination (GRE) Ser.: Vol. GRE-8). 1994. pap. 23.95 (*0-8373-5208-8*) Nat Learn.
— Geology. (Undergraduate Program Field Tests (UPFT) Ser.: Vol. UPFT-11). 1995. pap. 23.95 (*0-8373-6011-0*) Nat Learn.
— Geology (Physical) (Dantes Subject Standardized Tests Ser.: DANTES-18). 1994. pap. 23.95 (*0-8373-6618-6*) Nat Learn.
— Geophysicist. (Career Examination Ser.: C-302). 1994. pap. 27.95 (*0-8373-0302-8*) Nat Learn.
— German. (Undergraduate Program Field Tests (UPFT) Ser.: Vol. 12). 43.95 (*0-8373-6062-5*) Nat Learn.
— German. (Graduate Record Examination (GRE) Ser.: Vol. 9). 43.95 (*0-8373-5259-2*) Nat Learn.
— German. (Graduate Record Examination Ser.: GRE-9). 1994. pap. 23.95 (*0-8373-5209-6*) Nat Learn.
— German. (National Teacher Examination (NTE) Ser.: Vol. NT-32). 1994. pap. 23.95 (*0-8373-8442-7*) Nat Learn.
— German. (Undergraduate Program Field Tests (UPFT) Ser.: Vol. UPFT-12). 1994. pap. 23.95 (*0-8373-6012-9*) Nat Learn.
— Gerontological Nurse. (Certified Nurse Examination Ser.: CN-5). 1994. pap. 23.95 (*0-8373-6105-2*) Nat Learn.
— Gerontological Nurse Practitioner. (Certified Nurse Examination Ser.: CN-6). 1994. pap. 23.95 (*0-8373-6106-0*) Nat Learn.
— Glazier. (Career Examination Ser.: C-303). 1994. pap. 27.95 (*0-8373-0303-6*) Nat Learn.
— GMC Apprentice Program Battery Tests (GMC) (Admission Test Ser.: Vol. 94). 49.95 (*0-8373-5194-4*) Nat Learn.
— GMC Apprentice Program Battery Tests (GMC) (Admission Test Ser.: ATS-94). 1994. pap. 29.95 (*0-8373-5094-8*) Nat Learn.
— Golf Course Supervisor. (Career Examination Ser.: C-2774). 1994. pap. 29.95 (*0-8373-2774-1*) Nat Learn.
— Government/Political Science. (National Teacher Examination Ser.: NT-57). 1994. pap. 23.95 (*0-8373-8477-X*) Nat Learn.
— Graduate Management Admission Test (GMAT) (Admission Test Ser.: Vol. 14). 43.95 (*0-8373-5114-6*) Nat Learn.
— Graduate Management Admission Test (GMAT) (Admission Test Ser.: ATS-14). 1994. pap. 23.95 (*0-8373-5014-X*) Nat Learn.
— Graduate Record Examination General (Aptitude) Test (GRE) (Admission Test Ser.: ATS-10). 1994. pap. 23.95 (*0-8373-5010-7*) Nat Learn.
— Graduate Record Examination-General (Aptitude) Test (GRE) (Admission Test Ser.: Vol. 10). 43.95 (*0-8373-5110-3*) Nat Learn.
— Graduate Record Examination Series. 1994. pap. write for info. (*0-8373-5200-2*) Nat Learn.
— Graduate School Foreign Language Test (GSFLT) - French. (Admission Test Ser.: ATS-28A). pap. 23.95 (*0-8373-6952-5*) Nat Learn.
— Graduate School Foreign Language Test (GSFLT) - German. (Admission Test Ser.: Vol. 28B). 43.95 (*0-8373-6978-9*) Nat Learn.
— Graduate School Foreign Language Test (GSFLT) - German. (Admission Test Ser.: ATS-28B). 1994. pap. 23.95 (*0-8373-6953-3*) Nat Learn.
— Graduate School Foreign Language Test (GSFLT) - Spanish. (Admission Test Ser.: Vol. 28C). 43.95 (*0-8373-6979-7*) Nat Learn.
— Graduate School Foreign Language Test (GSFLT) - Spanish. (Admission Test Ser.: ATS-28C). 1994. pap. 23.95 (*0-8373-6954-1*) Nat Learn.
— Grammar. (Teachers License Examination Ser.: G-2). 1994. pap. 27.95 (*0-8373-8192-4*) Nat Learn.
— Grants Analyst. (Career Examination Ser.: C-2832). 1994. pap. 34.95 (*0-8373-2832-2*) Nat Learn.
— Grants Coordinator. (Career Examination Ser.: C-2797). 1994. pap. 34.95 (*0-8373-2797-0*) Nat Learn.
— Grants in Aid Program Assistant. (Career Examination Ser.: C-3542). 1994. pap. 29.95 (*0-8373-3542-6*) Nat Learn.
— Grants Technician. (Career Examination Ser.: C-3174). 1994. pap. 29.95 (*0-8373-3174-9*) Nat Learn.
— Graphic Arts Specialist. (Career Examination Ser.: C-2672). 1994. pap. 27.95 (*0-8373-2672-9*) Nat Learn.
— Graphics Supervisor. (Career Examination Ser.: C-3325). 1994. pap. 29.95 (*0-8373-3325-3*) Nat Learn.
— Greenskeeper. (Career Examination Ser.: C-2656). 1994. pap. 23.95 (*0-8373-2656-7*) Nat Learn.
— Grounds Superintendent. (Career Examination Ser.: C-3357). 1994. pap. 29.95 (*0-8373-3357-1*) Nat Learn.
— Groundskeeper. (Career Examination Ser.: C-1298). 1994. pap. 23.95 (*0-8373-1298-1*) Nat Learn.
— Group Health Insurance Specialist. (Career Examination Ser.: C-1299). pap. 29.95 (*0-8373-1299-X*) Nat Learn.
— Group Health Insurance Supervisor. (Career Examination Ser.: C-3059). 1994. pap. 34.95 (*0-8373-3059-9*) Nat Learn.
— Group Worker. (Career Examination Ser.: C-1300). 1994. pap. 27.95 (*0-8373-1300-7*) Nat Learn.
— Guard Patrolman. (Career Examination Ser.: C-304). 1994. pap. 23.95 (*0-8373-0304-4*) Nat Learn.
— Guidance Counselor. (Career Examination Ser.: C-305). 1994. pap. 29.95 (*0-8373-0305-2*) Nat Learn.
— Guidance Counselor: Combined Edition. (National Teacher Examination (NTE) Ser.: Vol. NT-16). 1994. pap. 23.95 (*0-8373-8456-7*) Nat Learn.
— Guidance Counselor, Elementary School. (National Teacher Examination Ser.: NT-16a). 1994. pap. 23.95 (*0-8373-8426-5*) Nat Learn.
— Guidance Counselor, Elementary School. (Teachers License Examination (TLE) Ser.: Vol. GT-1). 1994. pap. 27.95 (*0-8373-8121-5*) Nat Learn.
— Guidance Counselor, Junior H. S. (Teachers License Examination Ser.: GT-2). 1994. pap. 27.95 (*0-8373-8122-3*) Nat Learn.
— Guidance Counselor, Junior H. S. (National Teacher Examination Ser.: NT-16b). 1994. pap. 23.95 (*0-8373-8427-3*) Nat Learn.
— Guidance Counselor, Senior H. S. (Teachers License Examination Ser.: GT-3). 1994. pap. 27.95 (*0-8373-8123-1*) Nat Learn.
— Guidance Counselor, Senior H. S. (National Teacher Examination Ser.: NT-16c). 1994. pap. 23.95 (*0-8373-8428-1*) Nat Learn.
— Habilitation Specialist. (Career Examination Ser.: C-2900). 1994. pap. 27.95 (*0-8373-2900-0*) Nat Learn.
— Handbook of Real Estate (HRE) (Encyclopedia of Terms) (Admission Test Ser.: Vol. 5). 43.95 (*0-8373-5105-7*) Nat Learn.
— Handbook of Real Estate (HRE) (Encyclopedia of Terms) (Admission Test Ser.: ATS-5). 1994. pap. 29.95 (*0-8373-5005-0*) Nat Learn.
— Handbook of Tests. (General Aptitude & Abilities Ser.: CS-17). 1994. pap. 23.95 (*0-8373-6717-4*) Nat Learn.
— Handbook of the Stock Market (HOS) (Glossary of Terms) (Admission Test Ser.: ATS-2). 1994. pap. 13.95 (*0-8373-5002-6*) Nat Learn.
— Handicapped Children's Services Specialist. (Career Examination Ser.: C-3722). 1994. pap. 29.95 (*0-8373-3722-4*) Nat Learn.
— Handicapped Service Aide. (Career Examination Ser.: C-3305). 1994. pap. 27.95 (*0-8373-3305-9*) Nat Learn.
— Harbormaster. (Career Examination Ser.: C-3245). 1994. pap. 29.95 (*0-8373-3245-1*) Nat Learn.
— Hawaii Credit-by-Examination Program (CEP) (Admission Test Ser.: Vol. 62). 43.95 (*0-8373-5162-6*) Nat Learn.
— Hawaii Credit-by-Examination Program (CEP) (Admission Test Ser.: ATS-62). 1994. pap. 23.95 (*0-8373-5062-X*) Nat Learn.
— Hazardous Waste Facility Monitor. (Career Examination Ser.: C-3115). 1994. pap. 34.95 (*0-8373-3115-3*) Nat Learn.
— Head Account-Audit Clerk. (Career Examination Ser.: C-2009). 1994. pap. 29.95 (*0-8373-2009-7*) Nat Learn.
— Head Automotive Mechanic. (Career Examination Ser.: C-1302). 1994. pap. 34.95 (*0-8373-1302-3*) Nat Learn.
— Head Bus Driver. (Career Examination Ser.: C-2198). 1994. pap. 29.95 (*0-8373-2198-0*) Nat Learn.
— Head Clerk. (Career Examination Ser.: C-347). 1994. pap. 29.95 (*0-8373-0347-8*) Nat Learn.
— Head Clerk (Payroll) (Career Examination Ser.: C-1908). 1994. pap. 29.95 (*0-8373-1908-0*) Nat Learn.
— Head Clerk Surrogate. (Career Examination Ser.: C-2130). 1994. reprint ed. pap. 34.95 (*0-8373-2130-1*) Nat Learn.
— Head Custodian. (Career Examination Ser.: C-1958). 1994. pap. 29.95 (*0-8373-1958-7*) Nat Learn.
— Head Custodian I. (Career Examination Ser.: C-1823). 1994. pap. 29.95 (*0-8373-1823-8*) Nat Learn.
— Head Custodian II. (Career Examination Ser.: C-1824). 1994. pap. 34.95 (*0-8373-1824-6*) Nat Learn.
— Head Custodian III. (Career Examination Ser.: C-1825). 1994. pap. 34.95 (*0-8373-1825-4*) Nat Learn.
— Head Dietitian. (Career Examination Ser.: C-320). 1994. pap. 34.95 (*0-8373-0320-6*) Nat Learn.
— Head Janitor. (Career Examination Ser.: C-2066). 1994. reprint ed. pap. 29.95 (*0-8373-2066-6*) Nat Learn.
— Head Laundry Supervisor. (Career Examination Ser.: C-2426). 1994. pap. 34.95 (*0-8373-2426-2*) Nat Learn.
— Head Maintenance Supervisor. (Career Examination Ser.: C-2043). 1994. pap. 34.95 (*0-8373-2043-7*) Nat Learn.
— Head Nurse. (Career Examination Ser.: C-321). 1994. pap. 39.95 (*0-8373-0321-4*) Nat Learn.
— Head Process Server. (Career Examination Ser.: C-348). 1994. pap. 29.95 (*0-8373-0348-6*) Nat Learn.
— Head Process Server & Court Aide. (Career Examination Ser.: C-349). 1994. pap. 34.95 (*0-8373-0349-4*) Nat Learn.
— Head School Lunch Manager. (Career Examination Ser.: C-2172). 1994. reprint ed. pap. 34.95 (*0-8373-2172-7*) Nat Learn.
— Head Stationary Engineer. (Career Examination Ser.: C-1720). 1994. pap. 39.95 (*0-8373-1720-7*) Nat Learn.
— Health Aide. (Career Examination Ser.: C-1301). 1994. pap. 27.95 (*0-8373-1301-5*) Nat Learn.
— Health & Physical Education, Jr. H. S. (Teachers License Examination Ser.: T-24). 1994. pap. 27.95 (*0-8373-8024-3*) Nat Learn.
— Health & Physical Education, Sr. H. S. (Teachers License Examination Ser.: T-25). 1994. pap. 27.95 (*0-8373-8025-1*) Nat Learn.
— Health Benefits Clerk. (Career Examination Ser.: C-3558). 1994. pap. 27.95 (*0-8373-3558-2*) Nat Learn.
— Health Care Fiscal Analyst. (Career Examination Ser.: C-3620). 1994. pap. 34.95 (*0-8373-3620-1*) Nat Learn.
— Health Care Surveyor. (Career Examination Ser.: C-3361). 1994. pap. 34.95 (*0-8373-3361-X*) Nat Learn.

— Health Conservation. (Teachers License Examination Ser.: T-23). 1994. pap. 27.95 (*0-8373-8023-5*) Nat Learn.
— Health Department Investigator. (Career Examination Ser.: C-3074). 1994. pap. 29.95 (*0-8373-3074-2*) Nat Learn.
— Health Education. (National Teacher Examination Ser.: NT-38). 1994. pap. 23.95 (*0-8373-8448-6*) Nat Learn.
— Health Education Media Specialist. (Career Examination Ser.: C-3657). pap. 27.95 (*0-8373-3657-0*) Nat Learn.
— Health Facilities Manager. (Career Examination Ser.: C-3634). pap. 34.95 (*0-8373-3634-1*) Nat Learn.
— Health Facilities Planner. (Career Examination Ser.: No. C-3531). 1994. pap. 34.95 (*0-8373-3531-0*) Nat Learn.
— Health Facility Management Assistant. (Career Examination Ser.: C-3387). 1994. pap. 29.95 (*0-8373-3387-3*) Nat Learn.
— Health I. (Regents College Proficiency Examination Ser.: CPEP-17). 1994. pap. 23.95 (*0-8373-5417-X*) Nat Learn.
— Health I: Personal Health, Physical Aspects. (ACT Proficiency Examination Program Ser.: PEP-33). 1994. pap. 23.95 (*0-8373-5533-8*) Nat Learn.
— Health II. (Regents College Proficiency Examination Ser.: No. CPEP-18). 1994. pap. 23.95 (*0-8373-5418-8*) Nat Learn.
— Health II: Personal Health, Emotional-Social Aspects. (ACT Proficiency Examination Program Ser.: No. PEP-34). 1994. pap. 23.95 (*0-8373-5534-6*) Nat Learn.
— Health III. (Regents College Proficiency Examination Ser.: CPEP-19). 1994. pap. 23.95 (*0-8373-5419-6*) Nat Learn.
— Health III: Public & Environmental Health. (ACT Proficiency Examination Program Ser.: PEP-35). 1994. pap. 23.95 (*0-8373-5535-4*) Nat Learn.
— Health Inspector. (Career Examination Ser.: C-322). 1994. pap. 29.95 (*0-8373-0322-2*) Nat Learn.
— Health Insurance Administrator. (Career Examination Ser.: C-2687). 1994. pap. 39.95 (*0-8373-2687-7*) Nat Learn.
— Health, Jr. H. S. (Teachers License Examination Ser.: T-24a). 1994. pap. 27.95 (*0-8373-8094-4*) Nat Learn.
— Health Occupations Aptitude Examination (HOAE) (Admission Test Ser.: Vol. 98). 49.95 (*0-8373-5198-7*) Nat Learn.
— Health Occupations Aptitude Examination (HOAE) (Admission Test Ser.: ATS-98). 1994. pap. 29.95 (*0-8373-5098-0*) Nat Learn.
— Health Planner. (Career Examination Ser.: C-3027). 1994. pap. 34.95 (*0-8373-3027-0*) Nat Learn.
— Health Planner Trainee. (Career Examination Ser.: C-3026). 1994. pap. 29.95 (*0-8373-3026-2*) Nat Learn.
— Health Program Administrator. (Career Examination Ser.: C-3601). 1994. pap. 39.95 (*0-8373-3601-5*) Nat Learn.
— Health Program Aide. (Career Examination Ser.: C-3588). 1994. pap. 27.95 (*0-8373-3588-4*) Nat Learn.
— Health Program Analyst. (Career Examination Ser.: C-3723). 1994. pap. 34.95 (*0-8373-3723-2*) Nat Learn.
— Health Program Investigations Specialist. (Career Examination Ser.: C-3388). 1994. pap. 34.95 (*0-8373-3388-1*) Nat Learn.
— Health Restoration: Area I. (Regents External Degree (REDP) Ser.: Vol. 31). 43.95 (*0-8373-5681-4*) Nat Learn.
— Health Restoration: Area I. (ACT Proficiency Examination Program (PEP) Ser.: Vol. 51). 43.95 (*0-8373-5926-0*) Nat Learn.
— Health Restoration: Area I. (ACT Proficiency Examination Program Ser.: PEP-51). 1994. pap. 23.95 (*0-8373-5901-5*) Nat Learn.
— Health Restoration: Area I. (Regents External Degree (REDP) Ser.: Vol. REDP-31). 1994. pap. 23.95 (*0-8373-5631-8*) Nat Learn.
— Health Restoration: Area II. (Regents External Degree (REDP) Ser.: Vol. 32). 43.95 (*0-8373-5682-2*) Nat Learn.
— Health Restoration: Area II. (ACT Proficiency Examination Program (PEP) Ser.: Vol. 52). 43.95 (*0-8373-5927-9*) Nat Learn.
— Health Restoration: Area II. (ACT Proficiency Examination Program Ser.: PEP-52). 1994. pap. 23.95 (*0-8373-5902-3*) Nat Learn.
— Health Restoration: Area II. (Regents External Degree (REDP) Ser.: Vol. REDP-32). 1994. pap. 23.95 (*0-8373-5632-6*) Nat Learn.
— Health, Safety & Environment Occupations. (Career Examination Ser.: C-3554). 1994. pap. 27.95 (*0-8373-3554-X*) Nat Learn.
— Health Service Nurse. (Career Examination Ser.: C-350). 1994. pap. 27.95 (*0-8373-0350-8*) Nat Learn.
— Health Services Manager. (Career Examination Ser.: C-3178). 1994. pap. 39.95 (*0-8373-3178-1*) Nat Learn.
— Health, Sr. H. S. (Teachers License Examination Ser.: T-24b). 1994. pap. 27.95 (*0-8373-8095-2*) Nat Learn.
— Health Support: Area I. (ACT Proficiency Examination Program Ser.: PEP-48). 1994. pap. 23.95 (*0-8373-5548-6*) Nat Learn.
— Health Support: Area I. (Regents External Degree (REDP) Ser.: Vol. REDP-24). 1994. pap. 23.95 (*0-8373-5624-5*) Nat Learn.
— Health Support: Area II. (ACT Proficiency Examination Program Ser.: PEP-49). 1994. pap. 23.95 (*0-8373-5549-4*) Nat Learn.
— Health Support: Area II. (Regents External Degree (REDP) Ser.: Vol. REDP-25). 1994. pap. 23.95 (*0-8373-5625-3*) Nat Learn.
— Hearing Administrative Services Coordinator. (Career Examination Ser.: C-1743). 1994. reprint ed. pap. 39.95 (*0-8373-1743-6*) Nat Learn.
— Hearing Examiner. (Career Examination Ser.: C-351). 1994. pap. 34.95 (*0-8373-0351-6*) Nat Learn.
— Hearing Officer. (Career Examination Ser.: C-1758). 1994. reprint ed. pap. 34.95 (*0-8373-1758-4*) Nat Learn.
— Hearing Reporter. (Career Examination Ser.: C-2795). 1994. pap. 23.95 (*0-8373-2795-4*) Nat Learn.
— Heating Plant Technician. (Career Examination Ser.: C-329). 1994. pap. 27.95 (*0-8373-0329-X*) Nat Learn.
— Heavy Equipment Mechanic. (Career Examination Ser.: C-1310). 1994. pap. 27.95 (*0-8373-1310-4*) Nat Learn.
— Heavy Equipment Repair Supervisor. (Career Examination Ser.: C-2614). 1994. pap. 29.95 (*0-8373-2614-1*) Nat Learn.
— Hebrew, Jr. & Sr. H. S. (Teachers License Examination Ser.: T-26). 1994. pap. 27.95 (*0-8373-8026-X*) Nat Learn.
— Hematology. (College Level Examination Ser.: CLEP-33). 1994. pap. 23.95 (*0-8373-5333-5*) Nat Learn.
— Here's to Your Health. (Dantes Subject Standardized Tests (DANTES) Ser.: Vol. 73). 43.95 (*0-8373-6573-2*) Nat Learn.
— Here's to Your Health. (DANTES Ser.: No. 73). 1991. 23.95 (*0-8373-6673-9*) Nat Learn.
— High Pressure Plant Tender. (Career Examination Ser.: C-3277). 1994. pap. 27.95 (*0-8373-3277-X*) Nat Learn.
— High Risk Perinatal Nurse. (Certified Nurse Examination Ser.: CN-10). 1994. pap. 23.95 (*0-8373-6110-9*) Nat Learn.
— High School APL Survey (APL/HS) (Admission Test Ser.: Vol. ATS-60A). 1994. pap. 23.95 (*0-8373-6963-0*) Nat Learn.
— High School Basic Competency Tests (BCT/HS) (Admission Test Ser.: ATS-57). 1994. pap. 23.95 (*0-8373-5057-3*) Nat Learn.
— High School Equivalency Diploma Examination (EE) (Admission Test Ser.: ATS-17). 1994. pap. 23.95 (*0-8373-5017-4*) Nat Learn.
— High School Equivalency Diploma Examination (HSEDE) (General Aptitude & Abilities Ser.: CS-50). 1994. pap. 23.95 (*0-8373-6750-6*) Nat Learn.
— High School Equivalency Diploma Workbook (HSEDE) (General Aptitude & Abilities Ser.: CS-51). 1994. pap. 23.95 (*0-8373-6751-4*) Nat Learn.
— High Voltage Specialist. (Career Examination Ser.: C-3389). 1994. pap. 29.95 (*0-8373-3389-X*) Nat Learn.
— Highway Construction Coordinator. (Career Examination Ser.: C-2804). 1994. pap. 34.95 (*0-8373-2804-7*) Nat Learn.
— Highway Construction Supervisor. (Career Examination Ser.: C-3072). 1994. pap. 34.95 (*0-8373-3072-6*) Nat Learn.
— Highway Engineer. (Career Examination Ser.: C-2521). 1994. pap. 34.95 (*0-8373-2521-8*) Nat Learn.
— Highway Equipment Supervisor. (Career Examination Ser.: C-2805). 1994. pap. 29.95 (*0-8373-2805-5*) Nat Learn.
— Highway General Foreman. (Career Examination Ser.: C-2308). 1994. pap. 29.95 (*0-8373-2308-8*) Nat Learn.
— Highway Maintenance Specialist. (Career Examination Ser.: C-1330). 1994. pap. 29.95 (*0-8373-1330-9*) Nat Learn.
— Highway Maintenance Supervisor. (Career Examination Ser.: C-2212). 1994. pap. 29.95 (*0-8373-2212-X*) Nat Learn.
— Highway Patrolman. (Career Examination Ser.: C-3450). 1994. pap. 27.95 (*0-8373-3450-0*) Nat Learn.
— Highway Reports & Inventory Assistant. (Career Examination Ser.: C-3134). 1994. pap. 27.95 (*0-8373-3134-X*) Nat Learn.
— Highway Safety Aide. (Career Examination Ser.: C-3680). pap. 29.95 (*0-8373-3680-5*) Nat Learn.
— Highway Transportation Specialist. (Career Examination Ser.: C-2248). 1994. pap. 29.95 (*0-8373-2248-0*) Nat Learn.
— Highway Zone Foreman. (Career Examination Ser.: C-2307). 1994. reprint ed. pap. 29.95 (*0-8373-2307-X*) Nat Learn.
— Histology Technician. (Career Examination Ser.: C-2837). 1994. pap. 29.95 (*0-8373-2837-3*) Nat Learn.
— Historian. (Career Examination Ser.: C-3163). 1994. pap. 29.95 (*0-8373-3163-3*) Nat Learn.
— Historic Site Manager. (Career Examination Ser.: C-2373). 1994. pap. 29.95 (*0-8373-2373-8*) Nat Learn.
— History. (Undergraduate Program Field Tests (UPFT) Ser.: Vol. 13). 43.95 (*0-8373-6063-3*) Nat Learn.
— History. (Graduate Record Examination Ser.: GRE-10). 1994. pap. 23.95 (*0-8373-5210-X*) Nat Learn.
— History. (Undergraduate Program Field Tests (UPFT) Ser.: Vol. UPFT-13). 1994. pap. 23.95 (*0-8373-6013-7*) Nat Learn.
— History of American Education. (College Level Examination Ser.: CLEP-16). 1994. pap. 23.95 (*0-8373-5316-5*) Nat Learn.
— History of American Education. (Regents College Proficiency Examination Ser.: Vol. CPEP-21). 1994. pap. 23.95 (*0-8373-5421-8*) Nat Learn.
— History of American Education. (ACT Proficiency Examination Program (PEP) Ser.: Vol. PEP-29). 1994. pap. 23.95 (*0-8373-5529-X*) Nat Learn.
— A History of the Vietnam War. (Dantes Subject Standardized Tests (DANTES) Ser.: Vol. 67). 43.95 (*0-8373-6567-8*) Nat Learn.
— Hoisting Machine Operator. (Career Examination Ser.: C-2257). 1994. reprint ed. pap. 27.95 (*0-8373-2257-X*) Nat Learn.
— Hoists & Rigging Inspector. (Career Examination Ser.: C-323). 1994. pap. 27.95 (*0-8373-0323-0*) Nat Learn.
— Home Economics Education. (National Teacher Examination Ser.: NT-12). 1994. pap. 23.95 (*0-8373-8422-2*) Nat Learn.
— Home Economics, Junior High School. (Teachers License Examination Ser.: T-28). 1994. pap. 27.95 (*0-8373-8028-6*) Nat Learn.
— Home Economics, Senior High School. (Teachers License Examination Ser.: T-29). 1994. pap. 27.95 (*0-8373-8029-4*) Nat Learn.
— Home Economist. (Career Examination Ser.: C-324). 1994. pap. 27.95 (*0-8373-0324-9*) Nat Learn.
— Home Economist Trainee. (Career Examination Ser.: C-352). 1994. pap. 23.95 (*0-8373-0352-4*) Nat Learn.
— Home Health Aide. (Career Examination Ser.: C-3635). pap. 27.95 (*0-8373-3635-X*) Nat Learn.
— Home Health Nurse. (Certified Nurse Examination (CN) Ser.: Vol. 26). 43.95 (*0-8373-6176-1*) Nat Learn.
— Homebound. (Teachers License Examination Ser.: T-27). 1994. pap. 27.95 (*0-8373-8027-8*) Nat Learn.
— Homemaker. (Career Examination Ser.: C-1303). 1994. pap. 27.95 (*0-8373-1303-1*) Nat Learn.
— Horticultural Inspector. (Career Examination Ser.: C-1304). 1994. pap. 29.95 (*0-8373-1304-X*) Nat Learn.
— Horticulturist. (Career Examination Ser.: C-1305). 1994. pap. 29.95 (*0-8373-1305-8*) Nat Learn.
— Hospice Coordinator. (Career Examination Ser.: C-3034). 1994. pap. 29.95 (*0-8373-3034-3*) Nat Learn.
— Hospital Administration Consultant. (Career Examination Ser.: C-2768). 1994. pap. 39.95 (*0-8373-2768-7*) Nat Learn.
— Hospital Administration Intern. (Career Examination Ser.: C-1967). 1994. pap. 29.95 (*0-8373-1967-6*) Nat Learn.
— Hospital Administrator. (Career Examination Ser.: C-1654). 1994. pap. 34.95 (*0-8373-1654-5*) Nat Learn.
— Hospital Attendant. (Career Examination Ser.: C-325). 1994. pap. 23.95 (*0-8373-0325-7*) Nat Learn.
— Hospital Care Investigator. (Career Examination Ser.: C-326). 1994. pap. 27.95 (*0-8373-0326-5*) Nat Learn.
— Hospital Care Investigator Trainee. (Career Examination Ser.: C-327). 1994. pap. 23.95 (*0-8373-0327-3*) Nat Learn.
— Hospital Case Investigator. (Career Examination Ser.: C-1889). 1994. pap. 27.95 (*0-8373-1889-0*) Nat Learn.
— Hospital Clerk. (Career Examination Ser.: C-328). 1994. pap. 23.95 (*0-8373-0328-1*) Nat Learn.
— Hospital Controller. (Career Examination Ser.: C-1760). 1994. reprint ed. pap. 34.95 (*0-8373-1760-6*) Nat Learn.
— Hospital Patient Services Clerk. (Career Examination Ser.: C-3610). 1994. pap. 27.95 (*0-8373-3610-4*) Nat Learn.
— Hospital Reimbursement Specialist. (Career Examination Ser.: C-1297). 1994. pap. 27.95 (*0-8373-1297-3*) Nat Learn.
— Hospital Safety Officer. (Career Examination Ser.: C-118). 1994. pap. 27.95 (*0-8373-0118-1*) Nat Learn.
— Hospital Safety Officer Trainee. (Career Examination Ser.: C-119). 1994. pap. 23.95 (*0-8373-0119-X*) Nat Learn.
— Hospital Security Officer. (Career Examination Ser.: C-353). 1994. pap. 23.95 (*0-8373-0353-2*) Nat Learn.
— Hotline Coordinator. (Career Examination Ser.: C-3533). 1994. pap. 29.95 (*0-8373-3533-7*) Nat Learn.
— House Painter. (Career Examination Ser.: C-354). 1994. pap. 23.95 (*0-8373-0354-0*) Nat Learn.
— Housekeeper. (Career Examination Ser.: C-330). 1994. pap. 23.95 (*0-8373-0330-3*) Nat Learn.
— Housemother. (Career Examination Ser.: C-1306). 1994. pap. 27.95 (*0-8373-1306-6*) Nat Learn.
— Housing & Community Development Assistant. (Career Examination Ser.: C-2537). 1994. pap. 27.95 (*0-8373-2537-4*) Nat Learn.
— Housing & Community Development Representative. (Career Examination Ser.: C-2539). 1994. pap. 29.95 (*0-8373-2539-0*) Nat Learn.
— Housing Assistant. (Career Examination Ser.: C-331). 1994. pap. 27.95 (*0-8373-0331-1*) Nat Learn.
— Housing Captain. (Career Examination Ser.: C-332). 1994. pap. 39.95 (*0-8373-0332-X*) Nat Learn.
— Housing Caretaker. (Career Examination Ser.: C-333). 1994. pap. 23.95 (*0-8373-0333-8*) Nat Learn.
— Housing Community Activities Coordinator. (Career Examination Ser.: C-334). 1994. pap. 34.95 (*0-8373-0334-6*) Nat Learn.
— Housing Construction Inspector. (Career Examination Ser.: C-335). 1994. pap. 29.95 (*0-8373-0335-4*) Nat Learn.
— Housing Consumer Representative. (Career Examination Ser.: C-3145). 1994. pap. 27.95 (*0-8373-3145-5*) Nat Learn.
— Housing Exterminator. (Career Examination Ser.: C-2283). 1994. pap. 27.95 (*0-8373-2283-9*) Nat Learn.
— Housing Fireman. (Career Examination Ser.: C-336). 1994. pap. 27.95 (*0-8373-0336-2*) Nat Learn.
— Housing Groundsman. (Career Examination Ser.: C-337). 1994. pap. 23.95 (*0-8373-0337-0*) Nat Learn.
— Housing Guard. (Career Examination Ser.: C-338). 1994. pap. 23.95 (*0-8373-0338-9*) Nat Learn.
— Housing Inspector. (Career Examination Ser.: C-339). 1994. pap. 29.95 (*0-8373-0339-7*) Nat Learn.
— Housing Lieutenant. (Career Examination Ser.: C-340). 1994. pap. 34.95 (*0-8373-0340-0*) Nat Learn.
— Housing Maintenance Helper. (Career Examination Ser.: C-355). 1994. pap. 23.95 (*0-8373-0355-9*) Nat Learn.
— Housing Management Assistant. (Career Examination Ser.: C-2290). 1995. reprint ed. pap. 27.95 (*0-8373-2290-1*) Nat Learn.
— Housing Management Representative. (Career Examination Ser.: C-2291). 1995. pap. 29.95 (*0-8373-2291-X*) Nat Learn.
— Housing Manager. (Career Examination Ser.: C-341). 1994. pap. 29.95 (*0-8373-0341-9*) Nat Learn.
— Housing Patrolman. (Career Examination Ser.: C-342). 1994. pap. 23.95 (*0-8373-0342-7*) Nat Learn.
— Housing, Planning & Redevelopment Aide. (Career Examination Ser.: C-343). 1994. pap. 29.95 (*0-8373-0343-5*) Nat Learn.
— Housing Rehabilitation Manager. (Career Examination Ser.: C-3452). 1994. pap. 39.95 (*0-8373-3452-7*) Nat Learn.
— Housing Sergeant. (Career Examination Ser.: C-344). 1994. pap. 29.95 (*0-8373-0344-3*) Nat Learn.
— Housing Supervisor. (Career Examination Ser.: C-3313). 1994. pap. 34.95 (*0-8373-3313-X*) Nat Learn.
— Housing Supplyman. (Career Examination Ser.: C-345). 1994. pap. 23.95 (*0-8373-0345-1*) Nat Learn.
— Housing Teller. (Career Examination Ser.: C-346). 1994. pap. 23.95 (*0-8373-0346-X*) Nat Learn.
— How to Prepare for a Civil Service Examination (TEXT) (General Aptitude & Abilities Ser.: CS-42). 1994. pap. 9.95 (*0-8373-6742-5*) Nat Learn.
— Human Growth & Development. (College Level Examination Ser.: CLEP-17). 1994. pap. 23.95 (*0-8373-5317-3*) Nat Learn.
— Human Relations Aide. (Career Examination Ser.: C-1307). 1994. pap. 23.95 (*0-8373-1307-4*) Nat Learn.
— Human Relations Representative. (Career Examination Ser.: C-1308). 1994. pap. 27.95 (*0-8373-1308-2*) Nat Learn.
— Human Relations Specialist. (Career Examination Ser.: C-1614). 1994. pap. 27.95 (*0-8373-1614-6*) Nat Learn.
— Human Relations Training Officer. (Career Examination Ser.: C-1309). 1994. pap. 34.95 (*0-8373-1309-0*) Nat Learn.
— Human Resources Aide. (Career Examination Ser.: C-1785). 1994. pap. 23.95 (*0-8373-1785-1*) Nat Learn.
— Human Resources Specialist. (Career Examination Ser.: C-356). 1994. pap. 27.95 (*0-8373-0356-7*) Nat Learn.
— Human Resources Technician. (Career Examination Ser.: C-2071). 1994. pap. 27.95 (*0-8373-2071-2*) Nat Learn.
— Human Rights Investigator. (Career Examination Ser.: C-2228). 1994. pap. 27.95 (*0-8373-2228-6*) Nat Learn.
— Human Rights Specialist. (Career Examination Ser.: C-3453). 1994. pap. 27.95 (*0-8373-3453-5*) Nat Learn.
— Human Services Technician. (Career Examination Ser.: C-3687). pap. 27.95 (*0-8373-3687-2*) Nat Learn.
— Humanities. (College Level Examination (CLEP) Ser.: Vol. ATS-9B). 43.95 (*0-8373-5296-7*) Nat Learn.
— Humanities. (College Level Examination (CLEP) Ser.: Vol. ATS-9B). 1994. pap. 23.95 (*0-8373-5246-0*) Nat Learn.
— Humanities - Area Examination. (Graduate Record Examination Ser.: GRE-42). 1995. pap. 23.95 (*0-8373-5242-8*) Nat Learn.
— Hydraulic Engineer. (Career Examination Ser.: C-357). 1994. pap. 39.95 (*0-8373-0357-5*) Nat Learn.
— Hydrogeologist. (Career Examination Ser.: C-3390). 1994. pap. 39.95 (*0-8373-3390-3*) Nat Learn.
— IBM Tabulator Operator. (Career Examination Ser.: C-1920). 1994. pap. 23.95 (*0-8373-1920-X*) Nat Learn.
— IBM Tabulator Operator Trainee. (Career Examination Ser.: C-360). 1994. pap. 19.95 (*0-8373-0360-5*) Nat Learn.
— Identification Clerk. (Career Examination Ser.: C-361). 1994. pap. 23.95 (*0-8373-0361-3*) Nat Learn.
— Identification Officer. (Career Examination Ser.: C-1986). 1994. pap. 29.95 (*0-8373-1986-2*) Nat Learn.
— Identification Specialist. (Career Examination Ser.: C-2294). 1994. pap. 29.95 (*0-8373-2294-4*) Nat Learn.
— Illustrator. (Career Examination Ser.: C-379). 1994. pap. 29.95 (*0-8373-0379-6*) Nat Learn.
— Illustrator Aide. (Career Examination Ser.: C-2930). 1994. pap. 27.95 (*0-8373-2930-2*) Nat Learn.
— Immigration Patrol Inspector. (Career Examination Ser.: C-362). 1994. pap. 27.95 (*0-8373-0362-1*) Nat Learn.
— Immunohematology & Blood Banking. (College Level Examination Ser.: CLEP-34). 1994. pap. 23.95 (*0-8373-5334-3*) Nat Learn.
— Incinerator Plant Foreman. (Career Examination Ser.: C-2163). 1994. reprint ed. pap. 29.95 (*0-8373-2163-8*) Nat Learn.
— Incinerator Plant Maintenance Foreman. (Career Examination Ser.: C-2773). 1994. pap. 29.95 (*0-8373-2773-3*) Nat Learn.
— Incinerator Plant Supervisor. (Career Examination Ser.: C-2164). 1994. reprint ed. pap. 29.95 (*0-8373-2164-6*) Nat Learn.
— Incinerator Stationary Engineer. (Career Examination Ser.: C-2636). 1994. pap. 29.95 (*0-8373-2636-2*) Nat Learn.
— Income Maintenance Specialist. (Career Examination Ser.: C-3557). 1994. pap. 27.95 (*0-8373-3557-4*) Nat Learn.
— Income Maintenance Supervisor. (Career Examination Ser.: C-3724). 1994. pap. 29.95 (*0-8373-3724-0*) Nat Learn.
— Income Maintenance Worker. (Career Examination Ser.: C-3725). 1994. pap. 23.95 (*0-8373-3725-9*) Nat Learn.
— Indian Education - Elementary Teacher. (Career Examination Ser.: C-1311). 1994. pap. 27.95 (*0-8373-1311-2*) Nat Learn.
— Indian Education - Guidance Counselor. (Career Examination Ser.: C-1312). 1994. pap. 27.95 (*0-8373-1312-0*) Nat Learn.
— Indian Education - Secondary Teacher. (Career Examination Ser.: C-1313). 1994. pap. 27.95 (*0-8373-1313-9*) Nat Learn.
— Industrial Arts, Jr. H. S. (Teachers License Examination Ser.: T-30). 1994. pap. 27.95 (*0-8373-8030-8*) Nat Learn.
— Industrial Arts, Sr. H. S. (Teachers License Examination Ser.: T-31). 1994. pap. 27.95 (*0-8373-8031-6*) Nat Learn.
— Industrial Consultant. (Career Examination Ser.: C-2771). 1994. pap. 39.95 (*0-8373-2771-7*) Nat Learn.
— Industrial Development Assistant. (Career Examination Ser.: C-2848). 1994. pap. 34.95 (*0-8373-2848-9*) Nat Learn.
— Industrial Electronics. (Occupational Competency Examination Ser.: OCE-21). 1994. pap. 27.95 (*0-8373-5721-7*) Nat Learn.
— Industrial Engineer. (Career Examination Ser.: C-380). 1994. pap. 34.95 (*0-8373-0380-X*) Nat Learn.

R

— Industrial Equipment Mechanic (USPS) (Career Examination Ser.: C-3359). 1994. pap. 27.95 (*0-8373-3359-8*) Nat Learn.
— Industrial Foreman. (Career Examination Ser.: C-1956). 1994. pap. 29.95 (*0-8373-1956-0*) Nat Learn.
— Industrial Hygienist. (Career Examination Ser.: C-381). 1994. pap. 39.95 (*0-8373-0381-8*) Nat Learn.
— Industrial Hygienist Trainee. (Career Examination Ser.: C-3035). 1994. pap. 34.95 (*0-8373-3035-1*) Nat Learn.
— Industrial Training Supervisor. (Career Examination Ser.: C-2839). 1994. pap. 39.95 (*0-8373-2839-X*) Nat Learn.
— Industrial Waste Control Specialist. (Career Examination Ser.: C-3454). 1994. pap. 34.95 (*0-8373-3454-3*) Nat Learn.
— Infection Control Nurse. (Career Examination Ser.: C-3213). 1994. pap. 29.95 (*0-8373-3213-3*) Nat Learn.
— Information & Graphics Technician. (Career Examination Ser.: Vol. C-3818). 1997. pap. 29.95 (*0-8373-3818-2*) Nat Learn.
— Information & Referral Aide. (Career Examination Ser.: C-2892). 1994. pap. 23.95 (*0-8373-2892-6*) Nat Learn.
— Information & Referral Coordinator. (Career Examination Ser.: C-2927). 1994. pap. 29.95 (*0-8373-2927-2*) Nat Learn.
— Information Assistant. (Career Examination Ser.: C-363). 1994. pap. 27.95 (*0-8373-0363-X*) Nat Learn.
— Information Booth Attendant. (Career Examination Ser.: C-1314). 1994. pap. 23.95 (*0-8373-1314-7*) Nat Learn.
— Information Media Specialist. (Career Examination Ser.: C-1315). 1994. pap. 27.95 (*0-8373-1315-5*) Nat Learn.
— Information Services Specialist. (Career Examination Ser.: C-3603). 1994. pap. 34.95 (*0-8373-3603-1*) Nat Learn.
— Information Specialist. (Career Examination Ser.: C-1316). 1994. pap. 27.95 (*0-8373-1316-3*) Nat Learn.
— Information Specialist I. (Career Examination Ser.: C-1867). 1994. pap. 27.95 (*0-8373-1867-X*) Nat Learn.
— Information Specialist II. (Career Examination Ser.: C-1868). 1994. pap. 29.95 (*0-8373-1868-8*) Nat Learn.
— Information Specialist Trainee. (Career Examination Ser.: C-1687). 1994. pap. 23.95 (*0-8373-1687-1*) Nat Learn.
— Initial-Level Supervisor Examination (U.S.P.S.) (Career Examination Ser.: C-1788). 1994. pap. 29.95 (*0-8373-1788-6*) Nat Learn.
— Inmate Records Coordinator. (Career Examination Ser.: C-3726). 1994. pap. 34.95 (*0-8373-3726-7*) Nat Learn.
— Inspector. (Career Examination Ser.: C-364). 1994. pap. 27.95 (*0-8373-0364-8*) Nat Learn.
— Inspector (Construction) (Career Examination Ser.: C-2994). 1994. pap. 29.95 (*0-8373-2994-9*) Nat Learn.
— Inspector (Highways & Sewers) (Career Examination Ser.: C-366). 1994. pap. 29.95 (*0-8373-0366-4*) Nat Learn.
— Inspector (Housing) (Career Examination Ser.: C-2975). 1994. pap. 29.95 (*0-8373-2975-2*) Nat Learn.
— Inspector of Carpentry & Masonry. (Career Examination Ser.: C-365). 1994. pap. 29.95 (*0-8373-0365-6*) Nat Learn.
— Inspector of Fire Alarm Boxes. (Career Examination Ser.: C-2515). 1994. pap. 29.95 (*0-8373-2515-3*) Nat Learn.
— Inspector of Low Pressure Boilers. (Career Examination Ser.: C-367). 1994. pap. 29.95 (*0-8373-0367-2*) Nat Learn.
— Inspector of Markets, Weights, & Measures. (Career Examination Ser.: C-368). 1994. pap. 27.95 (*0-8373-0368-0*) Nat Learn.
— Install & Repair Underground Storage Tanks (License) (Career Examination Ser.: C-369). 1994. pap. 29.95 (*0-8373-0369-9*) Nat Learn.
— Install Oil Burner Equipment (License) (Career Examination Ser.: C-1317). 1994. pap. 27.95 (*0-8373-1317-1*) Nat Learn.
— Institution Food Administrator. (Career Examination Ser.: C-2121). 1994. reprint ed. pap. 34.95 (*0-8373-2121-2*) Nat Learn.
— Institution Safety Officer. (Career Examination Ser.: C-370). 1994. pap. 29.95 (*0-8373-0370-2*) Nat Learn.
— Institution Steward. (Career Examination Ser.: C-2626). 1994. pap. 29.95 (*0-8373-2626-5*) Nat Learn.
— Institutional Inspector. (Career Examination Ser.: C-382). 1994. pap. 29.95 (*0-8373-0382-6*) Nat Learn.
— Institutional Trades Instructor. (Career Examination Ser.: C-371). 1994. pap. 29.95 (*0-8373-0371-0*) Nat Learn.
— Instructor Certification Examination (ICE) (Admission Test Ser.: Vol. 123). 59.95 (*0-8373-5873-6*) Nat Learn.
— Instructor Certification Examination (ICE) (Admission Test Ser.: Vol. ATS-123). 1997. pap. 39.95 (*0-8373-5823-X*) Nat Learn.
— Instructor of the Blind. (Career Examination Ser.: C-2838). 1994. pap. 29.95 (*0-8373-2838-1*) Nat Learn.
— Instrumentation Technician. (Career Examination Ser.: C-2366). 1994. pap. 29.95 (*0-8373-2366-5*) Nat Learn.
— Instrumentman. (Career Examination Ser.: C-1318). 1994. pap. 29.95 (*0-8373-1318-X*) Nat Learn.
— Insurance Agent - Insurance Broker. (Career Examination Ser.: C-373). 1994. pap. 29.95 (*0-8373-0373-7*) Nat Learn.
— Insurance Agent - Insurance Broker (Accident & Health) (Career Examination Ser.: C-372). 1994. pap. 29.95 (*0-8373-0372-9*) Nat Learn.
— Insurance Agent - Insurance Broker (Fire & Casualty) (Career Examination Ser.: C-374). 1994. pap. 29.95 (*0-8373-0374-5*) Nat Learn.
— Insurance Broker. (Career Examination Ser.: C-388). 1994. pap. 29.95 (*0-8373-0388-5*) Nat Learn.
— Insurance Contract Analyst. (Career Examination Ser.: C-3246). 1994. pap. 29.95 (*0-8373-3246-X*) Nat Learn.
— Insurance Examiner. (Career Examination Ser.: C-2694). 1994. pap. 29.95 (*0-8373-2694-X*) Nat Learn.
— Insurance Fund Field Services Representative. (Career Examination Ser.: C-2166). 1994. reprint ed. pap. 27.95 (*0-8373-2166-2*) Nat Learn.
— Insurance Fund Hearing Representative. (Career Examination Ser.: C-1546). 1994. pap. 27.95 (*0-8373-1546-8*) Nat Learn.
— Insurance Fund Hearing Representative Trainee. (Career Examination Ser.: C-880). 1994. pap. 23.95 (*0-8373-0880-1*) Nat Learn.
— Insurance Investigator. (Career Examination Ser.: C-3539). 1994. pap. 29.95 (*0-8373-3539-6*) Nat Learn.
— Insurance Manager. (Career Examination Ser.: C-1598). 1994. pap. 29.95 (*0-8373-1598-0*) Nat Learn.
— Insurance Salesman. (Career Examination Ser.: C-389). 1994. pap. 29.95 (*0-8373-0389-3*) Nat Learn.
— Intergovernmental Analyst. (Career Examination Ser.: C-3507). 1994. pap. 34.95 (*0-8373-3507-8*) Nat Learn.
— Intermediate Accounting. (ACT Proficiency Examination Program Ser.: PEP-11). 1994. pap. 23.95 (*0-8373-5511-7*, PEP-12) Nat Learn.
— Intermediate Algebra. (Dantes Subject Standardized Tests Ser.: DANTES-19). 1994. pap. 23.95 (*0-8373-6619-4*) Nat Learn.
— Intermediate Business Law. (ACT Proficiency Examination Program Ser.: PEP-17). 1994. pap. 23.95 (*0-8373-5517-6*) Nat Learn.
— Intermediate Care Facility Program Manager. (Career Examination Ser.: C-3247). 1994. pap. 29.95 (*0-8373-3247-8*) Nat Learn.
— Intermediate Schools. (Teachers Lesson Plan Bk.: IS-1). (J). (gr. 5-8). 1994. pap. 6.95 (*0-8373-7952-0*) Nat Learn.
— Internal Auditor. (Career Examination Ser.: C-375). 1994. pap. 29.95 (*0-8373-0375-3*) Nat Learn.
— Internal Revenue Agent. (Career Examination Ser.: C-376). 1994. pap. 27.95 (*0-8373-0376-1*) Nat Learn.
— Internal Revenue Officer. (Career Examination Ser.: Vol. 3392). 1994. pap. 27.95 (*0-8373-3392-X*) Nat Learn.
— Interpreter (Spanish) (Career Examination Ser.: C-2239). 1994. pap. 29.95 (*0-8373-2239-1*) Nat Learn.
— Interviewing. (General Aptitude & Abilities Ser.: CS-40). 1994. pap. 29.95 (*0-8373-6740-9*) Nat Learn.
— Introduction Cost Accounting. (DANTES Ser.: No. 75). 1991. 23.95 (*0-8373-6675-5*) Nat Learn.
— Introduction Cost Accounting. (Dantes Subject Standardized Tests Ser.: DANTES-25). 1994. pap. 23.95 (*0-8373-6625-9*) Nat Learn.
— Introduction to Air Conditioning, Refrigeration & Heating. (Dantes Subject Standardized Tests Ser.: DANTES-20). 1994. pap. 23.95 (*0-8373-6620-8*) Nat Learn.
— Introduction to Anatomy & Physiology. (Regents College Proficiency Examination Ser.: CPEP-28). 1994. reprint ed. pap. 23.95 (*0-8373-5428-5*) Nat Learn.
— Introduction to Business. (Dantes Subject Standardized Tests Ser.: DANTES-21). 1994. pap. 23.95 (*0-8373-6621-6*) Nat Learn.
— Introduction to Business Management (Principles Of) (College Level Examination Ser.: CLEP-18). 1994. pap. 23.95 (*0-8373-5318-1*) Nat Learn.
— Introduction to Carpentry. (Dantes Subject Standardized Tests (DANTES) Ser.: Vol. 40). 43.95 (*0-8373-6540-6*) Nat Learn.
— Introduction to Carpentry. (Dantes Subject Standardized Tests Ser.: DANTES-40). 1994. pap. 23.95 (*0-8373-6640-2*) Nat Learn.
— Introduction to Computers with Basic Programming. (Dantes Subject Standardized Tests (DANTES) Ser.: Vol. 50). 43.95 (*0-8373-6550-3*) Nat Learn.
— Introduction to Computers with Basic Programming. (Dantes Subject Standardized Tests Ser.: DANTES-50). 1994. pap. 23.95 (*0-8373-6650-X*) Nat Learn.
— Introduction to Criminal Justice. (ACT Proficiency Examination Program Ser.: PEP-8). 1994. pap. 23.95 (*0-8373-5508-7*) Nat Learn.
— Introduction to Criminal Justice. (Regents College Examination (CPEP) Ser.: Vol. CPEP-29). 1994. reprint ed. pap. 23.95 (*0-8373-5429-3*) Nat Learn.
— Introduction to Education (Foundations Of) (Dantes Subject Standardized Tests Ser.: DANTES-22). 1994. pap. 23.95 (*0-8373-6622-4*) Nat Learn.
— Introduction to Electronics. (Dantes Subject Standardized Tests Ser.: DANTES-23). 1994. pap. 23.95 (*0-8373-6623-2*) Nat Learn.
— Introduction to Forestry. (Dantes Subject Standardized Tests Ser.: DANTES-24). 1994. pap. 23.95 (*0-8373-6624-0*) Nat Learn.
— Introduction to Management. (Dantes Subject Standardized Tests Ser.: DANTES-26). 1994. 39.95 (*0-8373-6526-0*); pap. 23.95 (*0-8373-6626-7*) Nat Learn.
— An Introduction to the Modern Middle East. (Dantes Subject Standardized Tests (DANTES) Ser.: Vol. 68). 43.95 (*0-8373-6568-6*) Nat Learn.
— An Introduction to the Modern Middle East. (Dantes Subject Standardized Test (DANTES) Ser.: No. 68). 1991. 23.95 (*0-8373-6668-2*) Nat Learn.
— Introduction to the Teaching of Reading. (National Teacher Examination Ser.: NT-39). 1994. pap. 23.95 (*0-8373-8449-4*) Nat Learn.
— Introduction to World Religions. (Dantes Subject Standardized Tests (DANTES) Ser.: Vol. 74). 43.95 (*0-8373-6574-0*) Nat Learn.
— Introduction to World Religions. (Dantes Subject Standardized Tests (DANTES) Ser.: Vol. DANTES-74). 1997. pap. 23.95 (*0-8373-6674-7*) Nat Learn.
— Introductory Accounting. (ACT Proficiency Examination Program Ser.: PEP-10). 1994. pap. 23.95 (*0-8373-5510-9*) Nat Learn.
— Introductory Accounting. (College Level Examination (CLEP) Ser.: Vol. CLEP-19). 1994. pap. 23.95 (*0-8373-5319-X*) Nat Learn.
— Introductory Business Law. (College Level Examination Ser.: CLEP-20). 1994. pap. 23.95 (*0-8373-5320-3*) Nat Learn.
— Introductory College Algebra. (Dantes Subject Standardized Tests Ser.: DANTES-55). 1994. pap. 23.95 (*0-8373-6655-0*) Nat Learn.
— Introductory Cost Accounting. (Dantes Subject Standardized Tests (DANTES) Ser.: Vol. 75). 43.95 (*0-8373-6575-9*) Nat Learn.
— Introductory Economics. (College Level Examination (CLEP) Ser.: Vol. CLEP-22). 1994. pap. 23.95 (*0-8373-5322-X*) Nat Learn.
— Introductory Macroeconomics. (College Level Examination Ser.: CLEP-41). 1994. pap. 23.95 (*0-8373-5341-6*) Nat Learn.
— Introductory Marketing. (College Level Examination Ser.: CLEP-23). 1994. pap. 23.95 (*0-8373-5323-8*) Nat Learn.
— Introductory Micro- & Macroeconomics. (College Level Examination Ser.: CLEP-42). 1994. reprint ed. pap. 23.95 (*0-8373-5342-4*) Nat Learn.
— Introductory Microeconomics. (College Level Examination Ser.: CLEP-40). 1994. reprint ed. pap. 23.95 (*0-8373-5340-8*) Nat Learn.
— Introductory Sociology. (College Level Examination Ser.: CLEP-24). 1994. pap. 23.95 (*0-8373-5324-6*) Nat Learn.
— Inventory Control Clerk. (Career Examination Ser.: C-2616). 1994. pap. 23.95 (*0-8373-2616-8*) Nat Learn.
— Inventory Control Supervisor. (Career Examination Ser.: C-3562). 1994. pap. 27.95 (*0-8373-3562-0*) Nat Learn.
— The Investigator. (Career Examination Ser.: C-377). 1994. pap. 27.95 (*0-8373-0377-X*) Nat Learn.
— Investigator-Inspector. (Career Examination Ser.: C-378). 1994. pap. 29.95 (*0-8373-0378-8*) Nat Learn.
— Investigator Trainee. (Career Examination Ser.: C-3456). 1994. pap. 23.95 (*0-8373-3456-X*) Nat Learn.
— Investment Analysis Trainee. (Career Examination Ser.: C-1438). 1994. pap. 29.95 (*0-8373-1438-0*) Nat Learn.
— Investment Analyst. (Career Examination Ser.: C-2333). 1994. pap. 39.95 (*0-8373-2333-9*) Nat Learn.
— Investment Officer. (Career Examination Ser.: C-2978). 1994. pap. 34.95 (*0-8373-2978-7*) Nat Learn.
— Investment Officer Trainee. (Career Examination Ser.: C-2977). 1994. pap. 29.95 (*0-8373-2977-9*) Nat Learn.
— Italian. (National Teacher Examination Ser.: NT-50). 1994. pap. 23.95 (*0-8373-8460-5*) Nat Learn.
— Italian, Sr. H. S. (Teachers License Examination Ser.: No. T-32b). pap. 27.95 (*0-8373-8032-4*, T-32b) Nat Learn.
— Jail Guard. (Career Examination Ser.: C-406). 1994. pap. 23.95 (*0-8373-0406-7*) Nat Learn.
— Jail Matron. (Career Examination Ser.: C-1329). 1994. pap. 23.95 (*0-8373-1329-5*) Nat Learn.
— Jail Training Supervisor. (Career Examination Ser.: C-1331). 1994. pap. 29.95 (*0-8373-1331-7*) Nat Learn.
— Jailer-Clerk. (Career Examination Ser.: C-1332). 1994. pap. 23.95 (*0-8373-1332-5*) Nat Learn.
— Job Corps Teacher. (Career Examination Ser.: C-407). 1994. pap. 29.95 (*0-8373-0407-5*) Nat Learn.
— Job Developer for Manpower Programs. (Career Examination Ser.: C-2865). 1994. pap. 34.95 (*0-8373-2865-9*) Nat Learn.
— Job Developer for the Handicapped. (Career Examination Ser.: C-1333). 1994. pap. 34.95 (*0-8373-1333-3*) Nat Learn.
— Job Training Specialist. (Career Examination Ser.: C-2697). 1994. pap. 34.95 (*0-8373-2697-4*) Nat Learn.
— Joiner. (Career Examination Ser.: C-408). 1994. pap. 27.95 (*0-8373-0408-3*) Nat Learn.
— Journeyman. (Career Examination Ser.: C-409). 1994. pap. 27.95 (*0-8373-0409-1*) Nat Learn.
— Journeyman in the Printing Crafts. (Career Examination Ser.: C-410). 1994. pap. 27.95 (*0-8373-0410-5*) Nat Learn.
— Junior Account Clerk. (Career Examination Ser.: C-515). 1994. pap. 23.95 (*0-8373-0515-2*) Nat Learn.
— Junior Accountant. (Career Examination Ser.: C-3727). 1994. pap. 27.95 (*0-8373-3727-5*) Nat Learn.
— Junior Administrative Assistant. (Career Examination Ser.: C-832). 1994. pap. 27.95 (*0-8373-0832-1*) Nat Learn.
— Junior Air Pollution Control Engineer. (Career Examination Ser.: C-1334). 1994. pap. 27.95 (*0-8373-1334-1*) Nat Learn.
— Junior Architect. (Career Examination Ser.: C-411). 1994. pap. 27.95 (*0-8373-0411-3*) Nat Learn.
— Junior Area Services Coordinator. (Career Examination Ser.: C-390). 1994. pap. 29.95 (*0-8373-0390-7*) Nat Learn.
— Junior Attorney. (Career Examination Ser.: C-391). 1994. pap. 29.95 (*0-8373-0391-5*) Nat Learn.
— Junior Bacteriologist. (Career Examination Ser.: C-392). 1994. pap. 27.95 (*0-8373-0392-3*) Nat Learn.
— Junior Building Custodian. (Career Examination Ser.: C-412). 1994. pap. 23.95 (*0-8373-0412-1*) Nat Learn.
— Junior Chemical Engineer. (Career Examination Ser.: C-393). 1994. pap. 27.95 (*0-8373-0393-1*) Nat Learn.
— Junior Chemist. (Career Examination Ser.: C-394). 1994. pap. 27.95 (*0-8373-0394-X*) Nat Learn.
— Junior Civil Engineer. (Career Examination Ser.: C-395). 1994. pap. 27.95 (*0-8373-0395-8*) Nat Learn.
— Junior Civil Engineer Trainee. (Career Examination Ser.: C-212). 1994. pap. 23.95 (*0-8373-0212-9*) Nat Learn.
— Junior Draftsman. (Career Examination Ser.: C-396). 1994. pap. 27.95 (*0-8373-0396-6*) Nat Learn.
— Junior Electrical Engineer. (Career Examination Ser.: C-397). 1994. pap. 27.95 (*0-8373-0397-4*) Nat Learn.
— Junior Engineer. (Career Examination Ser.: C-413). 1994. pap. 23.95 (*0-8373-0413-X*) Nat Learn.
— Junior Federal Assistant. (Career Examination Ser.: C-398). 1994. reprint ed. pap. 27.95 (*0-8373-0398-2*) Nat Learn.
— Junior Foreign Service Officer. (Career Examination Ser.: C-399). 1994. pap. 27.95 (*0-8373-0399-0*) Nat Learn.
— Junior Geologist. (Career Examination Ser.: C-414). 1994. pap. 27.95 (*0-8373-0414-8*) Nat Learn.
— Junior High School. (Teachers Lesson Plan Bk.: J-1). 1994. pap. 6.95 (*0-8373-7953-9*) Nat Learn.
— Junior Hospital Administrator. (Career Examination Ser.: C-400). 1994. pap. 29.95 (*0-8373-0400-8*) Nat Learn.
— Junior Insurance Examiner. (Career Examination Ser.: C-2069). 1994. reprint ed. pap. 27.95 (*0-8373-2069-0*) Nat Learn.
— Junior Intern. (Career Examination Ser.: C-1335). 1994. pap. 27.95 (*0-8373-1335-X*) Nat Learn.
— Junior Landscape Architect. (Career Examination Ser.: C-401). 1994. pap. 27.95 (*0-8373-0401-6*) Nat Learn.
— Junior Librarian. (Career Examination Ser.: C-1820). 1994. reprint ed. pap. 23.95 (*0-8373-1820-3*) Nat Learn.
— Junior Mechanical Engineer. (Career Examination Ser.: C-402). 1994. pap. 27.95 (*0-8373-0402-4*) Nat Learn.
— Junior Methods Analyst. (Career Examination Ser.: C-403). 1994. pap. 34.95 (*0-8373-0403-2*) Nat Learn.
— Junior Personnel Examiner. (Career Examination Ser.: C-404). 1994. pap. 34.95 (*0-8373-0404-0*) Nat Learn.
— Junior Physicist. (Career Examination Ser.: C-405). 1994. pap. 29.95 (*0-8373-0405-9*) Nat Learn.
— Junior Planner. (Career Examination Ser.: C-415). 1994. pap. 27.95 (*0-8373-0415-6*) Nat Learn.
— Junior Quantitative Analyst. (Career Examination Ser.: C-1797). 1994. pap. 29.95 (*0-8373-1797-5*) Nat Learn.
— Junior Rent Examiner. (Career Examination Ser.: C-2099). 1994. reprint ed. pap. 23.95 (*0-8373-2099-2*) Nat Learn.
— Justice Court Clerk. (Career Examination Ser.: C-3393). 1994. pap. 27.95 (*0-8373-3393-8*) Nat Learn.
— Juvenile Counselor. (Career Examination Ser.: C-2026). 1994. pap. 29.95 (*0-8373-2026-7*) Nat Learn.
— Kennel Foreman. (Career Examination Ser.: C-3129). 1994. pap. 27.95 (*0-8373-3129-3*) Nat Learn.
— Key Punch Operator. (Career Examination Ser.: C-420). 1994. pap. 23.95 (*0-8373-0420-2*) Nat Learn.
— Key Punch Supervisor. (Career Examination Ser.: C-2102). 1994. reprint ed. pap. 29.95 (*0-8373-2102-6*) Nat Learn.
— Keyboard Specialist. (Career Examination Ser.: C-3493). 1994. pap. 23.95 (*0-8373-3493-4*) Nat Learn.
— Kitchen Supervisor. (Career Examination Ser.: C-1336). 1994. pap. 27.95 (*0-8373-1336-8*) Nat Learn.
— Labor-Management Practices Adjuster. (Career Examination Ser.: C-433). 1994. pap. 39.95 (*0-8373-0433-4*) Nat Learn.
— Labor Mediation Trainee. (Career Examination Ser.: C-2851). 1994. pap. 34.95 (*0-8373-2851-9*) Nat Learn.
— Labor Mediator. (Career Examination Ser.: C-2850). 1994. pap. 39.95 (*0-8373-2850-0*) Nat Learn.
— Labor Relations. (ACT Proficiency Examination Program (PEP) Ser.: Vol. 22). 43.95 (*0-8373-5572-9*) Nat Learn.
— Labor Relations. (ACT Proficiency Examination Program Ser.: PEP-22). 1994. pap. 23.95 (*0-8373-5522-2*) Nat Learn.
— Labor Relations Analyst. (Career Examination Ser.: C-3457). 1994. pap. 39.95 (*0-8373-3457-8*) Nat Learn.
— Labor Relations Assistant. (Career Examination Ser.: C-1338). 1994. pap. 29.95 (*0-8373-1338-4*) Nat Learn.
— Labor Relations Representative. (Career Examination Ser.: C-3310). 1994. pap. 29.95 (*0-8373-3310-5*) Nat Learn.
— Labor Relations Technician. (Career Examination Ser.: C-3215). 1994. pap. 29.95 (*0-8373-3215-X*) Nat Learn.
— Labor Safety Technician. (Career Examination Ser.: C-1595). 1994. pap. 29.95 (*0-8373-1595-6*) Nat Learn.
— Labor Specialist. (Career Examination Ser.: C-2146). 1994. reprint ed. pap. 29.95 (*0-8373-2146-8*) Nat Learn.
— Labor Standards Investigator. (Career Examination Ser.: C-3210). 1994. pap. 27.95 (*0-8373-3210-9*) Nat Learn.
— Labor Technician. (Career Examination Ser.: C-1587). 1994. pap. 29.95 (*0-8373-1587-5*) Nat Learn.
— Laboratory Aide. (Career Examination Ser.: C-430). 1994. pap. 23.95 (*0-8373-0430-X*) Nat Learn.
— Laboratory Assistant. (Career Examination Ser.: C-1879). 1994. reprint ed. pap. 27.95 (*0-8373-1879-3*) Nat Learn.
— Laboratory Assistant (Bacteriology) (Career Examination Ser.: C-431). 1994. pap. 27.95 (*0-8373-0431-8*) Nat Learn.
— Laboratory Assistant (Chemistry) (Career Examination Ser.: C-432). 1994. pap. 27.95 (*0-8373-0432-6*) Nat Learn.
— Laboratory Equipment Specialist. (Career Examination Ser.: C-2297). 1994. reprint ed. pap. 27.95 (*0-8373-2297-9*) Nat Learn.
— Laboratory Helper (Men) (Career Examination Ser.: C-446). 1994. pap. 23.95 (*0-8373-0446-6*) Nat Learn.
— Laboratory Helper (Women) (Career Examination Ser.: C-447). 1994. pap. 23.95 (*0-8373-0447-4*) Nat Learn.
— Laboratory Specialist (Biology), Sr. H. S. (Teachers License Examination Ser.: T-34). 1994. pap. 27.95 (*0-8373-8034-0*) Nat Learn.
— Laboratory Specialist, Jr. H. S. (Teachers License Examination Ser.: T-33). 1994. pap. 27.95 (*0-8373-8033-2*) Nat Learn.
— Laboratory Specialist (Physical Sciences), Sr. H. S. (Teachers License Examination Ser.: T-35). 1994. pap. 27.95 (*0-8373-8035-9*) Nat Learn.
— Laboratory Supervisor. (Career Examination Ser.: C-3198). 1994. pap. 34.95 (*0-8373-3198-6*) Nat Learn.
— Laboratory Technician. (Career Examination Ser.: C-1734). 1994. pap. 27.95 (*0-8373-1734-7*) Nat Learn.
— Laboratory Technician, Secondary Schools. (Teachers License Examination Ser.: T-36). 1994. pap. 27.95 (*0-8373-8036-7*) Nat Learn.
— Laboratory Technician Trainee. (Career Examination Ser.: C-2909). 1994. pap. 23.95 (*0-8373-2909-4*) Nat Learn.
— Laborer. (Career Examination Ser.: C-434). 1994. pap. 23.95 (*0-8373-0434-2*) Nat Learn.
— Laborer Foreman. (Career Examination Ser.: C-1337). 1994. pap. 29.95 (*0-8373-1337-6*) Nat Learn.

An Asterisk (*) at the beginning of an entry indicates that the title is appearing for the first time.

— Laborer Supervisor. (Career Examination Ser.: C-3458). 1994. pap. 29.95 (*0-8373-3458-6*) Nat Learn.
— Land & Claims Adjuster. (Career Examination Ser.: C-3459). 1994. pap. 29.95 (*0-8373-3459-4*) Nat Learn.
— Land Management Specialist. (Career Examination Ser.: C-2618). 1994. pap. 29.95 (*0-8373-2618-4*) Nat Learn.
— Land Surveyor. (Career Examination Ser.: C-3029). 1994. pap. 29.95 (*0-8373-3029-7*) Nat Learn.
— Land Surveyor Trainee. (Career Examination Ser.: C-3030). 1994. pap. 27.95 (*0-8373-3030-0*) Nat Learn.
— Landscape Architect. (Career Examination Ser.: C-2392). 1994. pap. 29.95 (*0-8373-2392-4*) Nat Learn.
— Latin. (National Teacher Examination Ser.: NT-18). 1994. pap. 23.95 (*0-8373-8408-7*) Nat Learn.
— Latin. (Advanced Placement Test (AP) Ser.: Vol. AP-13). 1997. pap. 23.95 (*0-8373-6213-X*) Nat Learn.
— Latin, Sr. H. S. (Teachers License Examination Ser.: T-37). 1994. pap. 27.95 (*0-8373-8037-5*) Nat Learn.
— Laundry Foreman. (Career Examination Ser.: C-2244). 1994. pap. 29.95 (*0-8373-2244-8*) Nat Learn.
— Laundry Manager. (Career Examination Ser.: C-2427). 1994. pap. 34.95 (*0-8373-2427-0*) Nat Learn.
— Laundry Supervisor. (Career Examination Ser.: C-1339). 1994. pap. 29.95 (*0-8373-1339-2*) Nat Learn.
— Laundry Washman. (Career Examination Ser.: C-1340). 1994. pap. 23.95 (*0-8373-1340-6*) Nat Learn.
— Laundry Worker. (Career Examination Ser.: C-435). 1994. pap. 23.95 (*0-8373-0435-0*) Nat Learn.
— Law Assistant. (Career Examination Ser.: C-1341). 1994. pap. 27.95 (*0-8373-1341-4*) Nat Learn.
— Law Clerk. (Career Examination Ser.: C-448). 1994. pap. 27.95 (*0-8373-0448-2*) Nat Learn.
— Law Department Investigator. (Career Examination Ser.: C-849). 1994. pap. 29.95 (*0-8373-0849-6*) Nat Learn.
— Law Enforcement & Investigation Occupations. (Career Examination Ser.: C-3551). 1994. pap. 27.95 (*0-8373-3551-5*) Nat Learn.
— Law Enforcement Candidate Record. (Career Examination Ser.: C-3600). 1994. pap. 29.95 (*0-8373-3600-7*) Nat Learn.
— Law Library Clerk. (Career Examination Ser.: C-2888). 1994. pap. 23.95 (*0-8373-2888-8*) Nat Learn.
— Law School Admission Test (LSAT) (Admission Test Ser.: Vol. 13). 43.95 (*0-8373-5113-8*) Nat Learn.
— Law School Admission Test (LSAT) (Admission Test Ser.: No. ATS-13). 300p. 1994. pap. 23.95 (*0-8373-5013-1*) Nat Learn.
— Law Stenographer. (Career Examination Ser.: C-436). 1994. pap. 23.95 (*0-8373-0436-9*) Nat Learn.
— Leader (Lighting) (Career Examination Ser.: C-3085). 1994. pap. 27.95 (*0-8373-3085-8*) Nat Learn.
— Learning Ability Test (LAT) (Career Examination Ser.: C-1062). 1994. pap. 23.95 (*0-8373-1062-8*) Nat Learn.
— Leasing Agent. (Career Examination Ser.: C-1992). 1994. pap. 29.95 (*0-8373-1992-7*) Nat Learn.
— Legal Assistant. (Career Examination Ser.: C-2980). 1994. pap. 27.95 (*0-8373-2980-9*) Nat Learn.
— Legal Assistant I. (Career Examination Ser.: C-2988). 1994. pap. 27.95 (*0-8373-2988-4*) Nat Learn.
— Legal Assistant Trainee. (Career Examination Ser.: C-2979). 1994. pap. 23.95 (*0-8373-2979-5*) Nat Learn.
— Legal Assistant II. (Career Examination Ser.: C-2989). 1994. pap. 29.95 (*0-8373-2989-2*) Nat Learn.
— Legal Careers. (Career Examination Ser.: C-3284). 1994. pap. 27.95 (*0-8373-3284-2*) Nat Learn.
— Legal Clerk. (Career Examination Ser.: C-3394). 1994. pap. 23.95 (*0-8373-3394-6*) Nat Learn.
— Legal Coordinator. (Career Examination Ser.: C-2651). 1994. pap. 39.95 (*0-8373-2651-6*) Nat Learn.
— Legal Secretarial Assistant. (Career Examination Ser.: C-3545). 1994. pap. 23.95 (*0-8373-3545-0*) Nat Learn.
— Legal Secretary. (Career Examination Ser.: C-1343). 1994. pap. 23.95 (*0-8373-1343-0*) Nat Learn.
— Legal Stenographer. (Career Examination Ser.: C-1344). 1994. pap. 23.95 (*0-8373-1344-9*) Nat Learn.
— Legislative Analyst. (Career Examination Ser.: C-3065). 1994. pap. 34.95 (*0-8373-3065-3*) Nat Learn.
— Letter Box Mechanic (USPS) (Career Examination Ser.: C-3367). 1994. pap. 27.95 (*0-8373-3367-9*) Nat Learn.
— Letterpress Pressman. (Career Examination Ser.: C-437). 1994. pap. 27.95 (*0-8373-0437-7*) Nat Learn.
— Liability Claims Supervisor. (Career Examination Ser.: C-3509). 1994. pap. 34.95 (*0-8373-3509-4*) Nat Learn.
— Liberal Arts & Sciences Test (LAST) (Admission Test Ser.: Vol. 119). 49.95 (*0-8373-5869-8*) Nat Learn.
— Liberal Arts & Sciences Test (LAST) (Admission Test Ser.: Vol. ATS-119). 1997. pap. 29.95 (*0-8373-5819-1*) Nat Learn.
— Librarian. (Career Examination Ser.: C-438). 1994. pap. 27.95 (*0-8373-0438-5*) Nat Learn.
— Librarian V. (Career Examination Ser.: C-2792). 1994. pap. 29.95 (*0-8373-2792-X*) Nat Learn.
— Librarian IV. (Career Examination Ser.: C-2791). 1994. pap. 29.95 (*0-8373-2791-1*) Nat Learn.
— Librarian I. (Career Examination Ser.: C-2788). 1994. pap. 27.95 (*0-8373-2788-1*) Nat Learn.
— Librarian III. (Career Examination Ser.: C-2790). 1994. pap. 29.95 (*0-8373-2790-3*) Nat Learn.
— Librarian Trainee. (Career Examination Ser.: C-2864). 1994. pap. 23.95 (*0-8373-2864-0*) Nat Learn.
— Librarian II. (Career Examination Ser.: C-2789). 1994. pap. 29.95 (*0-8373-2789-X*) Nat Learn.
— Library Assistant. (Career Examination Ser.: C-1345). 1994. pap. 23.95 (*0-8373-1345-7*) Nat Learn.
— Library Clerk. (Career Examination Ser.: C-1931). 1994. pap. 23.95 (*0-8373-1931-5*) Nat Learn.
— Library Director. (Career Examination Ser.: C-1346). 1994. pap. 34.95 (*0-8373-1346-5*) Nat Learn.
— Library Director I. (Career Examination Ser.: C-1929). 1994. pap. 34.95 (*0-8373-1929-3*) Nat Learn.
— Library Director II. (Career Examination Ser.: C-2779). 1994. pap. 34.95 (*0-8373-2779-2*) Nat Learn.
— Library Director III. (Career Examination Ser.: C-2780). 1994. pap. 39.95 (*0-8373-2780-6*) Nat Learn.
— Library Director IV. (Career Examination Ser.: C-2781). 1994. pap. 39.95 (*0-8373-2781-4*) Nat Learn.
— Library Director V. (Career Examination Ser.: C-2782). 1994. pap. 39.95 (*0-8373-2782-2*) Nat Learn.
— Library, Elementary School. (Teachers License Examination Ser.: T-38). 1994. pap. 27.95 (*0-8373-8038-3*) Nat Learn.
— Library, Secondary Schools. (Teachers License Examination Ser.: T-39). 1994. pap. 27.95- (*0-8373-8039-1*) Nat Learn.
— Library Technician. (Career Examination Ser.: C-2544). 1994. pap. 23.95 (*0-8373-2544-7*) Nat Learn.
— License Inspector. (Career Examination Ser.: C-439). 1994. pap. 27.95 (*0-8373-0439-3*) Nat Learn.
— License Investigator. (Career Examination Ser.: C-449). 1994. pap. 27.95 (*0-8373-0449-0*) Nat Learn.
— License Investigator (Spanish Speaking) (Career Examination Ser.: C-2286). 1994. reprint ed. pap. 29.95 (*0-8373-2286-3*) Nat Learn.
— Licensed Practical Nurse. (Career Examination Ser.: C-440). 1994. pap. 27.95 (*0-8373-0440-7*) Nat Learn.
— Licensing Inspector Trainee. (Career Examination Ser.: C-3122). 1994. pap. 23.95 (*0-8373-3122-6*) Nat Learn.
— Licensing Services Aide. (Career Examination Ser.: C-3120). 1994. pap. 23.95 (*0-8373-3120-X*) Nat Learn.
— Lieutenant, Fire Department. (Career Examination Ser.: C-441). 1994. pap. 34.95 (*0-8373-0441-5*) Nat Learn.
— Lieutenant, Police Department. (Career Examination Ser.: C-442). 1994. pap. 34.95 (*0-8373-0442-3*) Nat Learn.
— Life Insurance Agent. (Career Examination Ser.: C-443). 1994. pap. 29.95 (*0-8373-0443-1*) Nat Learn.
— Life Skills Counselor. (Career Examination Ser.: C-2917). 1994. pap. 29.95 (*0-8373-2917-5*) Nat Learn.
— Lifeguard. (Career Examination Ser.: C-2300). 1994. reprint ed. pap. 29.95 (*0-8373-2300-2*) Nat Learn.
— Light Maintainer. (Career Examination Ser.: C-444). 1994. pap. 23.95 (*0-8373-0444-X*) Nat Learn.
— Lighting Inspector. (Career Examination Ser.: C-2134). 1994. reprint ed. pap. 29.95 (*0-8373-2134-4*) Nat Learn.
— Linear Algebra. (Dantes Subject Standardized Tests Ser.: DANTES-27). 1994. pap. 23.95 (*0-8373-6627-5*) Nat Learn.
— Lineman. (Career Examination Ser.: C-1347). 1994. pap. 23.95 (*0-8373-1347-3*) Nat Learn.
— Lineman (Electrical Power) (Career Examination Ser.: C-450). 1994. pap. 23.95 (*0-8373-0450-4*) Nat Learn.
— Literature. (Undergraduate Program Field Tests (UPFT) Ser.: Vol. 14). 43.95 (*0-8373-6064-1*) Nat Learn.
— Literature. (Undergraduate Program Field Tests Ser.: UPFT-14). 1994. pap. 23.95 (*0-8373-6014-5*) Nat Learn.
— Literature. (Teachers License Examination (TLE) Ser.: Vol. G-3). 1994. pap. 27.95 (*0-8373-8193-2*) Nat Learn.
— Literature in English. (Graduate Record Examination Ser.: GRE-11). 1994. pap. 23.95 (*0-8373-5211-8*) Nat Learn.
— Lithographic Pressman. (Career Examination Ser.: C-445). 1994. pap. 27.95 (*0-8373-0445-8*) Nat Learn.
— Loan Advisor. (Career Examination Ser.: C-1321). 1994. pap. 27.95 (*0-8373-1321-X*) Nat Learn.
— Locksmith. (Career Examination Ser.: C-1348). 1994. pap. 23.95 (*0-8373-1348-1*) Nat Learn.
— Logical Reasoning. (General Aptitude & Abilities Ser.: Vol. CS-47). 1994. pap. 27.95 (*0-8373-6747-6*) Nat Learn.
— Lottery Inspector. (Career Examination Ser.: C-451). 1994. pap. 27.95 (*0-8373-0451-2*) Nat Learn.
— Lottery Marketing Aide. (Career Examination Ser.: C-3165). 1994. pap. 27.95 (*0-8373-3165-X*) Nat Learn.
— Lottery Marketing Representative. (Career Examination Ser.: C-3166). 1994. pap. 27.95 (*0-8373-3166-8*) Nat Learn.
— Machine Drafting. (Occupational Competency Examination Ser.: OCE-24). 1994. pap. 27.95 (*0-8373-5724-1*) Nat Learn.
— Machine Shop Workbook. (Workbook (W) Ser.: Vol. 2920). 43.95 (*0-8373-7928-8*) Nat Learn.
— Machine Shop Workbook. (Workbook Ser.: W-2920). 1994. pap. 23.95 (*0-8373-7903-2*) Nat Learn.
— Machine Trades. (Occupational Competency Examination Ser.: OCE-22). 1994. pap. 27.95 (*0-8373-5722-5*) Nat Learn.
— Machinist. (Career Examination Ser.: C-460). 1994. pap. 23.95 (*0-8373-0460-1*) Nat Learn.
— Machinist's Helper. (Career Examination Ser.: C-461). 1994. pap. 23.95 (*0-8373-0461-X*) Nat Learn.
— Macroeconomics. (Advanced Placement Test (AP) Ser.: Vol. AP-6). 1997. pap. 23.95 (*0-8373-6206-7*) Nat Learn.
— Magnetic Tape Librarian. (Career Examination Ser.: C-2872). 1994. pap. 27.95 (*0-8373-2872-1*) Nat Learn.
— Mail & Supply Clerk. (Career Examination Ser.: C-3162). 1994. pap. 23.95 (*0-8373-3162-5*) Nat Learn.
— Mail Clerk. (Career Examination Ser.: C-2280). 1994. reprint ed. pap. 19.95 (*0-8373-2280-4*) Nat Learn.
— Mail Division Supervisor. (Career Examination Ser.: C-2624). 1994. pap. 29.95 (*0-8373-2624-9*) Nat Learn.
— Mail Handler (U. S. P. S.) (Career Examination Ser.: C-462). 1994. pap. 19.95 (*0-8373-0462-8*) Nat Learn.
— Mail Processing Equipment Operator. (Career Examination Ser.: C-3460). 1994. pap. 27.95 (*0-8373-3460-8*) Nat Learn.
— Maintainer's Helper - Group A. (Career Examination Ser.: C-465). 1994. pap. 23.95 (*0-8373-0465-2*) Nat Learn.
— Maintainer's Helper - Group B. (Career Examination Ser.: C-466). 1994. pap. 23.95 (*0-8373-0466-0*) Nat Learn.
— Maintainer's Helper - Group C. (Career Examination Ser.: C-467). 1994. pap. 23.95 (*0-8373-0467-9*) Nat Learn.
— Maintainer's Helper - Group D. (Career Examination Ser.: C-468). 1994. pap. 23.95 (*0-8373-0468-7*) Nat Learn.
— Maintainer's Helper - Group E. (Career Examination Ser.: C-469). 1994. pap. 23.95 (*0-8373-0469-5*) Nat Learn.
— Maintenance Carpenter. (Career Examination Ser.: C-1349). 1994. pap. 23.95 (*0-8373-1349-X*) Nat Learn.
— Maintenance Carpenter Foreman. (Career Examination Ser.: C-1350). 1994. pap. 29.95 (*0-8373-1350-3*) Nat Learn
— Maintenance Crew Chief. (Career Examination Ser.: C-3461). 1994. pap. 34.95 (*0-8373-3461-6*) Nat Learn.
— Maintenance, Custodial Branch Initial-Level Supervisor Examination (U. S. P. S.) (Career Examination Ser.: C-1775). 1994. pap. 34.95 (*0-8373-1775-4*) Nat Learn.
— Maintenance Development Program Aptitude Test USPS. (Career Examination Ser.: C-3609). 1994. pap. 34.95 (*0-8373-3609-0*) Nat Learn.
— Maintenance Electrician. (Career Examination Ser.: C-1351). 1994. pap. 27.95 (*0-8373-1351-1*) Nat Learn.
— Maintenance Electrician Foreman. (Career Examination Ser.: C-1352). 1994. pap. 29.95 (*0-8373-1352-X*) Nat Learn.
— Maintenance Locksmith. (Career Examination Ser.: C-1353). 1994. pap. 23.95 (*0-8373-1353-8*) Nat Learn.
— Maintenance Machinist. (Career Examination Ser.: C-1354). 1994. pap. 23.95 (*0-8373-1354-6*) Nat Learn.
— Maintenance Man Trainee. (Career Examination Ser.: C-464). 1994. pap. 23.95 (*0-8373-0464-4*) Nat Learn.
— Maintenance Man (Worker) (Career Examination Ser.: C-463). 1994. pap. 23.95 (*0-8373-0463-6*) Nat Learn.
— Maintenance Mason. (Career Examination Ser.: C-1355). 1994. pap. 23.95 (*0-8373-1355-4*) Nat Learn.
— Maintenance Mason Foreman. (Career Examination Ser.: C-1356). 1994. pap. 29.95 (*0-8373-1356-2*) Nat Learn.
— Maintenance Mechanic. (Career Examination Ser.: C-1357). 1994. pap. 23.95 (*0-8373-1357-0*) Nat Learn.
— Maintenance Mechanic (Automated Mail Processing Equipment) (A.M.P.E) (U.S.P.S.) (Career Examination Ser.: C-1606). 1994. pap. 27.95 (*0-8373-1606-5*) Nat Learn.
— Maintenance Painter. (Career Examination Ser.: C-1358). 1994. pap. 23.95 (*0-8373-1358-9*) Nat Learn.
— Maintenance Painter Foreman. (Career Examination Ser.: C-1359). 1994. pap. 29.95 (*0-8373-1359-7*) Nat Learn.
— Maintenance Plumber. (Career Examination Ser.: C-1360). 1994. pap. 27.95 (*0-8373-1360-0*) Nat Learn.
— Maintenance Plumber Foreman. (Career Examination Ser.: C-1361). 1994. pap. 29.95 (*0-8373-1361-9*) Nat Learn.
— Maintenance Supervisor. (Career Examination Ser.: C-2044). 1994. pap. 29.95 (*0-8373-2044-5*) Nat Learn.
— Maintenance Supervisor (Track Equipment) (Career Examination Ser.: C-3546-9). 1994. pap. 29.95 (*0-8373-3546-9*) Nat Learn.
— Maintenance Welder. (Career Examination Ser.: C-1362). 1994. pap. 23.95 (*0-8373-1362-7*) Nat Learn.
— Management Analysis Trainee. (Career Examination Ser.: C-470). 1994. pap. 27.95 (*0-8373-0470-9*) Nat Learn.
— Management Analyst. (Career Examination Ser.: C-1061). 1994. pap. 34.95 (*0-8373-1061-X*) Nat Learn.
— Management Analyst Aide. (Career Examination Ser.: C-1721). 1994. reprint ed. pap. 29.95 (*0-8373-1721-5*) Nat Learn.
— Management Auditor. (Career Examination Ser.: C-3217). 1994. pap. 34.95 (*0-8373-3217-6*) Nat Learn.
— Management Auditor Trainee. (Career Examination Ser.: C-3285). 1994. pap. 29.95 (*0-8373-3285-0*) Nat Learn.
— Management Information Systems. (Dantes Subject Standardized Tests (DANTES) Ser.: Vol. 77). 43.95 (*0-8373-6577-5*) Nat Learn.
— Management Information Systems Specialist. (Career Examination Ser.: C-3579). 1994. pap. 39.95 (*0-8373-3579-5*) Nat Learn.
— Management Intern. (Career Examination Ser.: C-1927). 1994. reprint ed. pap. 27.95 (*0-8373-1927-7*) Nat Learn.
— Management of Human Resources I. (Regents External Degree (REDP) Ser.: Vol. 7). 43.95 (*0-8373-5657-1*) Nat Learn.
— Management of Human Resources I. (Regents External Degree Ser.: REDP-7). 1994. pap. 23.95 (*0-8373-5607-5*) Nat Learn.
— Management of Human Resources II. (Regents External Degree (REDP) Ser.: Vol. 8). 43.95 (*0-8373-5658-X*) Nat Learn.
— Management of Human Resources II. (Regents External Degree Ser.: REDP-8). 1994. pap. 23.95 (*0-8373-5608-3*) Nat Learn.
— Management of Human Resources III. (Regents External Degree (REDP) Ser.: Vol. 9). 43.95 (*0-8373-5659-8*) Nat Learn.
— Management of Human Resources III. (Regents External Degree Ser.: REDP-9). 1994. pap. 23.95 (*0-8373-5609-1*) Nat Learn.
— Management Specialist Trainee. (Career Examination Ser.: C-3608). 1994. pap. 27.95 (*0-8373-3608-2*) Nat Learn.
— Management Technician. (Career Examination Ser.: C-2751). 1994. pap. 27.95 (*0-8373-2751-2*) Nat Learn.
— Management Trainee (U. S. P. S.) (Career Examination Ser.: C-1690). 1994. pap. 29.95 (*0-8373-1690-1*) Nat Learn.
— Manager Computer Operations. (Career Examination Ser.: C-2241). 1994. pap. 34.95 (*0-8373-2241-3*) Nat Learn.
— Manpower Counselor. (Career Examination Ser.: C-2435). 1994. pap. 34.95 (*0-8373-2435-1*) Nat Learn.
— Manpower Development Specialist. (Career Examination Ser.: C-2688). 1994. pap. 34.95 (*0-8373-2688-5*) Nat Learn.
— Manpower Grants Technician. (Career Examination Ser.: C-2822). 1994. pap. 29.95 (*0-8373-2822-5*) Nat Learn.
— Manpower Information & Liaison Specialist. (Career Examination Ser.: C-2807). 1994. pap. 39.95 (*0-8373-2807-1*) Nat Learn.
— Manpower Program Administrator. (Career Examination Ser.: C-2671). 1994. pap. 39.95 (*0-8373-2671-0*) Nat Learn.
— Manpower Program Coordinator. (Career Examination Ser.: C-2316). 1994. pap. 39.95 (*0-8373-2316-9*) Nat Learn.
— Manpower Training Coordinator. (Career Examination Ser.: C-1554). 1994. pap. 39.95 (*0-8373-1554-9*) Nat Learn.
— Map & Coordinate Supervisor. (Career Examination Ser.: C-3330). 1994. pap. 34.95 (*0-8373-3330-X*) Nat Learn.
— Map Drafter. (Career Examination Ser.: C-3729). 1994. pap. 27.95 (*0-8373-3729-1*) Nat Learn.
— Map Reading. (General Aptitude & Abilities Ser.: Vol. 59). pap. 19.95 (*0-8373-6759-X*) Nat Learn.
— Map Room Clerk. (Career Examination Ser.: C-3730). 1994. pap. 23.95 (*0-8373-3730-5*) Nat Learn.
— Mapping Technician. (Career Examination Ser.: C-3462). 1994. pap. 27.95 (*0-8373-3462-4*) Nat Learn.
— Mapping Technologist. (Career Examination Ser.: C-3463). 1994. pap. 29.95 (*0-8373-3463-2*) Nat Learn.
— Marine Engineer. (Career Examination Ser.: C-1363). 1994. pap. 29.95 (*0-8373-1363-5*) Nat Learn.
— Marine Maintenance Foreman. (Career Examination Ser.: C-3070). 1994. pap. 29.95 (*0-8373-3070-X*) Nat Learn.
— Marine Oiler. (Career Examination Ser.: C-471). 1994. pap. 27.95 (*0-8373-0471-7*) Nat Learn.
— Marine Resources Technician. (Career Examination Ser.: C-1369). 1994. pap. 29.95 (*0-8373-1369-4*) Nat Learn.
— Marine Stoker. (Career Examination Ser.: C-472). 1994. pap. 23.95 (*0-8373-0472-5*) Nat Learn.
— Mark-Up Clerk (U. S. P. S.) (Career Examination Ser.: C-2459). 1994. pap. 19.95 (*0-8373-2459-9*) Nat Learn.
— Marketing & Distributive Education. (National Teacher Examination Ser.: NT-46). 1994. pap. 23.95 (*0-8373-8466-4*) Nat Learn.
— Marketing I. (Regents External Degree (REDP) Ser.: Vol. 10). 43.95 (*0-8373-5660-1*) Nat Learn.
— Marketing I. (Regents External Degree Ser.: REDP-10). 1994. pap. 23.95 (*0-8373-5610-5*) Nat Learn.
— Marketing Representative. (Career Examination Ser.: C-2465). 1994. pap. 29.95 (*0-8373-2465-3*) Nat Learn.
— Marketing III. (Regents External Degree (REDP) Ser.: Vol. 12). 43.95 (*0-8373-5662-8*) Nat Learn.
— Marketing III. (Regents External Degree Ser.: REDP-12). 1994. pap. 23.95 (*0-8373-5612-1*) Nat Learn.
— Marketing II. (Regents External Degree (REDP) Ser.: Vol. 11). 43.95 (*0-8373-5661-X*) Nat Learn.
— Marketing II. (Regents External Degree Ser.: REDP-11). 1994. pap. 23.95 (*0-8373-5611-3*) Nat Learn.
— Maryland Basic Mastery Test for Reading (BMT-R) (Admission Test Ser.: Vol. 63). 43.95 (*0-8373-5163-4*) Nat Learn.
— Maryland Basic Mastery Test for Reading (BMT-R) (Admission Test Ser.: ATS-63). 1994. pap. 23.95 (*0-8373-5063-8*) Nat Learn.
— Mason. (Career Examination Ser.: C-473). 1994. pap. 23.95 (*0-8373-0473-3*) Nat Learn.
— Masonry. (Occupational Competency Examination (OCE) Ser.: Vol. 23). 47.95 (*0-8373-5773-X*) Nat Learn.
— Masonry. (Occupational Competency Examination Ser.: OCE-23). 1994. pap. 27.95 (*0-8373-5723-3*) Nat Learn.
— Mason's Helper. (Career Examination Ser.: C-474). 1994. pap. 23.95 (*0-8373-0474-1*) Nat Learn.
— Master Electrician. (Career Examination Ser.: C-475). 1994. pap. 29.95 (*0-8373-0475-X*) Nat Learn.
— Master Plumber. (Career Examination Ser.: C-476). 1994. pap. 29.95 (*0-8373-0476-8*) Nat Learn.
— Master Rigger. (Career Examination Ser.: C-477). 1994. pap. 27.95 (*0-8373-0477-6*) Nat Learn.
— Master Sign Hanger. (Career Examination Ser.: C-478). 1994. pap. 27.95 (*0-8373-0478-4*) Nat Learn.
— Mate. (Career Examination Ser.: C-3156). 1994. pap. 29.95 (*0-8373-3156-0*) Nat Learn.
— Material Control Clerk I. (Career Examination Ser.: C-3088). 1994. pap. 23.95 (*0-8373-3088-2*) Nat Learn.
— Material Control Clerk II. (Career Examination Ser.: C-3089). 1994. pap. 27.95 (*0-8373-3089-0*) Nat Learn.
— Material Control Clerk III. (Career Examination Ser.: C-3090). 1994. pap. 27.95 (*0-8373-3090-4*) Nat Learn.
— Material Control Clerk IV. (Career Examination Ser.: C-3091). 1994. pap. 29.95 (*0-8373-3091-2*) Nat Learn.
— Materials Engineer. (Career Examination Ser.: C-1780). 1994. pap. 39.95 (*0-8373-1780-0*) Nat Learn.
— Materials Manager. (Career Examination Ser.: C-3395). 1994. pap. 34.95 (*0-8373-3395-4*) Nat Learn.
— Materials Testing Technician. (Career Examination Ser.: C-1834). 1994. pap. 34.95 (*0-8373-1834-3*) Nat Learn.
— Maternal & Child Health Nurse. (Certified Nurse Examination Ser.: CN-9). 1994. pap. 23.95 (*0-8373-6109-5*) Nat Learn.
— Maternal & Child Nursing - Associate. (Regents College Proficiency Examination Ser.: Vol. 22). 43.95 (*0-8373-5472-2*) Nat Learn.
— Maternal & Child Nursing - Baccalaureate. (Regents College Proficiency Examination Ser.: Vol. 23). 43.95 (*0-8373-5473-0*) Nat Learn.
— Maternal & Child Nursing, Associate. (Regents College Proficiency Examination Ser.: CPEP-22). 1994. pap. 23.95 (*0-8373-5422-6*) Nat Learn.
— Maternal & Child Nursing, Associate Degree. (ACT Proficiency Examination Program (PEP) Ser.: Vol. 37). 43.95 (*0-8373-5587-7*) Nat Learn.
— Maternal & Child Nursing, Associate Degree. (ACT Proficiency Examination Program Ser.: PEP-37). 1994. pap. 23.95 (*0-8373-5537-0*) Nat Learn.

R

— Maternal & Child Nursing, Baccalaureate. (Regents College Proficiency Examination Ser.: CPEP-23). 1994. pap. 23.95 (*0-8373-5423-4*) Nat Learn.
— Maternal & Child Nursing, Baccalaureate Degree. (ACT Proficiency Examination Program (PEP) Ser.: Vol. 38). 43.95 (*0-8373-5588-5*) Nat Learn.
— Maternal & Child Nursing, Baccalaureate Degree. (ACT Proficiency Examination Program Ser.: PEP-38). 1994. pap. 23.95 (*0-8373-5538-9*) Nat Learn.
— Mathematician. (Career Examination Ser.: C-479). 1994. pap. 29.95 (*0-8373-0479-2*) Nat Learn.
— Mathematics. (Graduate Record Examination (GRE) Ser.: Vol. 12). 43.95 (*0-8373-5262-2*) Nat Learn.
— Mathematics. (Undergraduate Program Field Tests (UPFT) Ser.: Vol. 15). 43.95 (*0-8373-6065-X*) Nat Learn.
— Mathematics. (Graduate Record Examination Ser.: GRE-12). 1994. pap. 23.95 (*0-8373-5212-6*) Nat Learn.
— Mathematics. (Teachers License Examination (TLE) Ser.: Vol. G-4). 1994. pap. 27.95 (*0-8373-8194-0*) Nat Learn.
— Mathematics. (Undergraduate Program Field Tests (UPFT) Ser.: Vol. UPFT-15). 1994. pap. 23.95 (*0-8373-6015-3*) Nat Learn.
— Mathematics Aide. (Career Examination Ser.: C-480). 1994. pap. 27.95 (*0-8373-0480-6*) Nat Learn.
— Mathematics, Jr. H.S. (Teachers License Examination Ser.: T-40). 1994. pap. 27.95 (*0-8373-8040-5*) Nat Learn.
— Mathematics, Sr. H.S. (Teachers License Examination Ser.: T-41). 1994. pap. 27.95 (*0-8373-8041-3*) Nat Learn.
— Meat Cutter. (Career Examination Ser.: C-516). 1994. pap. 27.95 (*0-8373-0516-0*) Nat Learn.
— Meat Inspector. (Career Examination Ser.: C-517). 1994. pap. 27.95 (*0-8373-0517-9*) Nat Learn.
— Meat Inspector-Poultry Inspector. (Career Examination Ser.: C-513). 1994. pap. 29.95 (*0-8373-0513-6*) Nat Learn.
— Meat Inspector Trainee. (Career Examination Ser.: C-518). 1994. pap. 23.95 (*0-8373-0518-7*) Nat Learn.
— Mechanical Engineer. (Career Examination Ser.: C-481). 1994. pap. 29.95 (*0-8373-0481-4*) Nat Learn.
— Mechanical Engineering Draftsman. (Career Examination Ser.: Vol. C-482). 1994. pap. 27.95 (*0-8373-0482-2*) Nat Learn.
— Mechanical Engineering Trainee. (Career Examination Ser.: C-519). 1994. pap. 23.95 (*0-8373-0519-5*) Nat Learn.
— Mechanical Equipment Inspector. (Career Examination Ser.: C-2045). 1994. pap. 34.95 (*0-8373-2045-3*) Nat Learn.
— Mechanical Estimator. (Career Examination Ser.: C-3113). 1994. pap. 27.95 (*0-8373-3113-7*) Nat Learn.
— Mechanical Maintainer - Group A. (Career Examination Ser.: C-483). 1994. pap. 23.95 (*0-8373-0483-0*) Nat Learn.
— Mechanical Maintainer - Group B. (Career Examination Ser.: C-484). 1994. pap. 23.95 (*0-8373-0484-9*) Nat Learn.
— Mechanical Maintainer - Group C. (Career Examination Ser.: C-485). 1994. pap. 23.95 (*0-8373-0485-7*) Nat Learn.
— Mechanical Maintenance Supervisor. (Career Examination Ser.: C-2793). 1994. pap. 29.95 (*0-8373-2793-8*) Nat Learn.
— Mechanical Specifications Writer. (Career Examination Ser.: C-3248). 1994. pap. 29.95 (*0-8373-3248-6*) Nat Learn.
— Mechanical Stores Clerk. (Career Examination Ser.: C-3080). 1994. pap. 23.95 (*0-8373-3080-7*) Nat Learn.
— Mechanical Technology. (Occupational Competency Examination (OCE) Ser.: Vol. 25). 47.95 (*0-8373-5775-6*) Nat Learn.
— Mechanical Technology. (Occupational Competency Examination Ser.: OCE-25). 1994. pap. 27.95 (*0-8373-5725-X*) Nat Learn.
— Media Services Technician. (Career Examination Ser.: C-3181). 1994. pap. 29.95 (*0-8373-3181-1*) Nat Learn.
— Media Specialist. (Career Examination Ser.: C-2894). 1994. pap. 29.95 (*0-8373-2894-2*) Nat Learn.
— Media Specialist - Library & Audio-Visual Services (Library Media Specialist) (National Teacher Examination Ser.: NT-29). 1994. pap. 23.95 (*0-8373-8439-7*) Nat Learn.
— Mediator (Labor Relations) (Career Examination Ser.: C-520). 1994. pap. 39.95 (*0-8373-0520-9*) Nat Learn.
— Medicaid Claims Examiner. (Career Examination Ser.: C-2691). 1994. pap. 27.95 (*0-8373-2691-5*) Nat Learn.
— Medicaid Review Analyst. (Career Examination Ser.: C-3207). 1994. pap. 27.95 (*0-8373-3207-9*) Nat Learn.
— Medical Aide. (Career Examination Ser.: C-1364). 1994. pap. 23.95 (*0-8373-1364-3*) Nat Learn.
— Medical Assistant. (Career Examination Ser.: C-1365). 1994. pap. 23.95 (*0-8373-1365-1*) Nat Learn.
— Medical Assisting. (Occupational Competency Examination (OCE) Ser.: Vol. 26). 47.95 (*0-8373-5776-4*) Nat Learn.
— Medical Assisting. (Occupational Competency Examination Ser.: OCE-26). 1994. pap. 27.95 (*0-8373-5726-8*) Nat Learn.
— Medical Care Representative. (Career Examination Ser.: C-3147). 1994. pap. 29.95 (*0-8373-3147-1*) Nat Learn.
— Medical Clerk. (Career Examination Ser.: C-1796). 1994. pap. 23.95 (*0-8373-1796-7*) Nat Learn.
— Medical College Admission Test (MCAT) (Admission Test Ser.: Vol. 11). 43.95 (*0-8373-5111-1*) Nat Learn.
— Medical College Admission Test (MCAT) (Admission Test Ser.: ATS-11). 1994. pap. 23.95 (*0-8373-5011-5*) Nat Learn.
— Medical Conduct Investigator. (Career Examination Ser.: C-2287). 1994. reprint ed. pap. 27.95 (*0-8373-2287-1*) Nat Learn.
— Medical Emergency Dispatcher. (Career Examination Ser.: C-2331). 1994. pap. 27.95 (*0-8373-2331-2*) Nat Learn.
— Medical Equipment Technician. (Career Examination Ser.: C-2654). 1994. pap. 29.95 (*0-8373-2654-0*) Nat Learn.
— Medical Examiner. (Career Examination Ser.: C-486). 1994. pap. 49.95 (*0-8373-0486-5*) Nat Learn.
— Medical Facilities Auditor. (Career Examination Ser.: C-2058). 1994. reprint ed. pap. 39.95 (*0-8373-2058-5*) Nat Learn.
— Medical Inspector. (Career Examination Ser.: C-487). 1994. pap. 44.95 (*0-8373-0487-3*) Nat Learn.
— Medical Laboratory Technician. (Career Examination Ser.: C-2323). 1994. pap. 27.95 (*0-8373-2323-1*) Nat Learn.
— Medical Laboratory Technician (Substance Abuse) (Career Examination Ser.: C-3119). 1994. pap. 29.95 (*0-8373-3119-6*) Nat Learn.
— Medical Officer. (Career Examination Ser.: C-488). 1994. pap. 39.95 (*0-8373-0488-1*) Nat Learn.
— Medical Officer (Departmental) (Career Examination Ser.: C-489). 1994. pap. 39.95 (*0-8373-0489-X*) Nat Learn.
— Medical Photographer. (Career Examination Ser.: C-1366). 1994. pap. 29.95 (*0-8373-1366-X*) Nat Learn.
— Medical Purchasing Specialist. (Career Examination Ser.: C-2448). 1994. pap. 27.95 (*0-8373-2448-3*) Nat Learn.
— Medical Radiology Technician. (Career Examination Ser.: C-1367). 1994. pap. 27.95 (*0-8373-1367-8*) Nat Learn.
— Medical Radiology Technologist. (Career Examination Ser.: C-490). 1994. pap. 29.95 (*0-8373-0490-3*) Nat Learn.
— Medical Record Librarian. (Career Examination Ser.: C-491). 1994. pap. 27.95 (*0-8373-0491-1*) Nat Learn.
— Medical Record Technician. (Career Examination Ser.: C-2329). 1994. pap. 27.95 (*0-8373-2329-0*) Nat Learn.
— Medical Records Assistant. (Career Examination Ser.: C-2952). 1994. pap. 27.95 (*0-8373-2952-3*) Nat Learn.
— Medical Records Clerk. (Career Examination Ser.: C-2309). 1994. reprint ed. pap. 27.95 (*0-8373-2309-6*) Nat Learn.
— Medical Records Supervisor. (Career Examination Ser.: C-3731). 1994. pap. 34.95 (*0-8373-3731-3*) Nat Learn.
— Medical Relations Officer. (Career Examination Ser.: C-3351). 1994. pap. 34.95 (*0-8373-3351-2*) Nat Learn.
— Medical Sciences Knowledge Profile Examination (MSKP) (Admission Test Ser.: Vol. 86). 89.95 (*0-8373-5186-3*) Nat Learn.
— Medical Sciences Knowledge Profile Examination (MSKP) (Admission Test Ser.: ATS-86). 1994. pap. 69.95 (*0-8373-5086-7*) Nat Learn.
— Medical Services Specialist. (Career Examination Ser.: C-2746). 1994. pap. 34.95 (*0-8373-2746-6*) Nat Learn.
— Medical Social Work Assistant. (Career Examination Ser.: C-3168). 1994. pap. 27.95 (*0-8373-3168-4*) Nat Learn.
— Medical Social Work Coordinator. (Career Examination Ser.: C-2578). 1994. pap. 34.95 (*0-8373-2578-1*) Nat Learn.
— Medical Social Worker. (Career Examination Ser.: C-521). 1994. pap. 29.95 (*0-8373-0521-7*) Nat Learn.
— Medical Specialist. (Career Examination Ser.: C-1965). 1994. reprint ed. pap. 39.95 (*0-8373-1965-X*) Nat Learn.
— Medical Stenographer. (Career Examination Ser.: C-1368). 1994. pap. 23.95 (*0-8373-1368-6*) Nat Learn.
— Medical Supply Supervisor. (Career Examination Ser.: C-3106). 1994. pap. 29.95 (*0-8373-3106-4*) Nat Learn.
— Medical Supply Technician. (Career Examination Ser.: C-3353). 1994. pap. 27.95 (*0-8373-3353-9*) Nat Learn.
— Medical-Surgical Nurse. (Certified Nurse Examination Ser.: CN-11). 1994. pap. 23.95 (*0-8373-6111-7*) Nat Learn.
— Medical Surgical Nursing. (Regents College Proficiency Examination Ser.: CPEP-24). 1994. pap. 23.95 (*0-8373-5424-2*) Nat Learn.
— Medical-Surgical Nursing. (College Level Examination Ser.: CLEP-37). 1994. pap. 23.95 (*0-8373-5337-8*) Nat Learn.
— Medical Technical Assistant. (Career Examination Ser.: C-492). 1994. pap. 27.95 (*0-8373-0492-X*) Nat Learn.
— Medical Technician. (Career Examination Ser.: C-512). 1994. pap. 29.95 (*0-8373-0512-8*) Nat Learn.
— Medical Technician Instructor. (Career Examination Ser.: C-1370). 1994. pap. 39.95 (*0-8373-1370-8*) Nat Learn.
— Medical Technician Trainee. (Career Examination Ser.: C-1371). 1994. pap. 27.95 (*0-8373-1371-6*) Nat Learn.
— Medical Technologist. (Career Examination Ser.: C-493). 1994. pap. 29.95 (*0-8373-0493-8*) Nat Learn.
— Medical Transcribing Machine Operator. (Career Examination Ser.: C-3203). 1994. pap. 23.95 (*0-8373-3203-6*) Nat Learn.
— Medical Typist. (Career Examination Ser.: C-3396). 1994. pap. 23.95 (*0-8373-3396-2*) Nat Learn.
— Menagerie Keeper. (Career Examination Ser.: C-494). 1994. pap. 23.95 (*0-8373-0494-6*) Nat Learn.
— Men's Physical Education. (National Teacher Examination Ser.: NT-36). 1994. pap. 23.95 (*0-8373-8446-X*) Nat Learn.
— Mental Health Aide. (Career Examination Ser.: C-1372). 1994. pap. 23.95 (*0-8373-1372-4*) Nat Learn.
— Mental Health Assistant. (Career Examination Ser.: C-3397). 1994. pap. 23.95 (*0-8373-3397-0*) Nat Learn.
— Mental Health Geriatric Consultant. (Career Examination Ser.: C-1582). 1994. pap. 39.95 (*0-8373-1582-4*) Nat Learn.
— Mental Health Group Leader. (Career Examination Ser.: C-3054). 1994. pap. 34.95 (*0-8373-3054-8*) Nat Learn.
— Mental Hygiene Nursing Program Coordinator. (Career Examination Ser.: C-2665). 1994. pap. 34.95 (*0-8373-2665-6*) Nat Learn.
— Mental Hygiene Staff Development Specialist I. (Career Examination Ser.: C-3489). 1994. pap. 29.95 (*0-8373-3489-6*) Nat Learn.
— Mental Hygiene Staff Development Specialist II. (Career Examination Ser.: C-2490). 1994. pap. 29.95 (*0-8373-2490-4*) Nat Learn.
— Mental Hygiene Staff Development Specialist III. (Career Examination Ser.: C-2491). 1994. pap. 34.95 (*0-8373-2491-2*) Nat Learn.
— Mental Hygiene Staff Development Specialist IV. (Career Examination Ser.: C-2492). 1994. pap. 34.95 (*0-8373-2492-0*) Nat Learn.
— Mental Hygiene Therapy Aide. (Career Examination Ser.: C-3056). 1994. pap. 23.95 (*0-8373-3056-4*) Nat Learn.
— Mental Hygiene Therapy Assistant. (Career Examination Ser.: C-2188). 1994. pap. 27.95 (*0-8373-2188-3*) Nat Learn.
— Mental Hygiene Treatment Team Leader. (Career Examination Ser.: C-1885). 1994. pap. 29.95 (*0-8373-1885-8*) Nat Learn.
— Messenger. (Career Examination Ser.: C-495). 1994. pap. 23.95 (*0-8373-0495-4*) Nat Learn.
— Metallurgist. (Career Examination Ser.: C-496). 1994. pap. 34.95 (*0-8373-0496-2*) Nat Learn.
— Meteorologist. (Career Examination Ser.: C-497). 1994. pap. 34.95 (*0-8373-0497-0*) Nat Learn.
— Meter Maid. (Career Examination Ser.: C-498). 1994. pap. 23.95 (*0-8373-0498-9*) Nat Learn.
— Methods Analyst. (Career Examination Ser.: C-499). 1994. pap. 34.95 (*0-8373-0499-7*) Nat Learn.
— Microbiologist. (Career Examination Ser.: C-2477). 1994. pap. 29.95 (*0-8373-2477-7*) Nat Learn.
— Microbiology. (College Level Examination (CLEP) Ser.: Vol. 35). 43.95 (*0-8373-5385-8*) Nat Learn.
— Microbiology. (ACT Proficiency Examination Program Ser.: PEP-55). 1994. pap. 23.95 (*0-8373-5905-8*) Nat Learn.
— Microbiology. (College Level Examination (CLEP) Ser.: Vol. CLEP-35). 1994. pap. 23.95 (*0-8373-5335-1*) Nat Learn.
— Microconputer Operator. (Career Examination Ser.: C-3733). 1994. pap. 27.95 (*0-8373-3733-X*) Nat Learn.
— Microcomputer Technician. (Career Examination Ser.: Vol. C-3821). 1997. pap. 29.95 (*0-8373-3821-2*) Nat Learn.
— Microcomputer/Audio Visual Repair Supervisor. (Career Examination Ser.: No. C-3732). 1994. pap. 34.95 (*0-8373-3732-1*) Nat Learn.
— Microeconomics. (Advanced Placement (AP) Test Ser.: No. AP-5). Date not set. pap. 23.95 (*0-8373-6205-9*) Nat Learn.
— Micrographics Operator. (Career Examination Ser.: C-2157). 1994. reprint ed. pap. 23.95 (*0-8373-2157-3*) Nat Learn.
— Micrographics Technician. (Career Examination Ser.: C-2761). 1994. pap. 23.95 (*0-8373-2761-X*) Nat Learn.
— Middle Level Positions. (Career Examination Ser.: C-511). 1994. pap. 27.95 (*0-8373-0511-X*) Nat Learn.
— Miller Analogies Test, (MAT) (Admission Test Ser.: ATS-18). 300p. 1994. pap. 29.95 (*0-8373-5018-2*) Nat Learn.
— Missouri Basic Essential Skills Test (BEST) (Admission Test Ser.: ATS-64). 1994. pap. 23.95 (*0-8373-5064-6*) Nat Learn.
— Money & Banking. (Dantes Subject Standardized Tests Ser.: DANTES-28). 1994. pap. 23.95 (*0-8373-6628-3*) Nat Learn.
— Money & Banking. (DANTES Ser.: No. 28). 1994. 39.95 (*0-8373-6528-7*) Nat Learn.
— Money & Banking. (College Level Examination (CLEP) Ser.: Vol. CLEP-25). 1994. pap. 23.95 (*0-8373-5325-4*) Nat Learn.
— Mortgage Administrator. (Career Examination Ser.: C-2311). 1994. reprint ed. pap. 29.95 (*0-8373-2311-8*) Nat Learn.
— Mortgage Analyst. (Career Examination Ser.: C-2653). 1994. pap. 29.95 (*0-8373-2653-2*) Nat Learn.
— Mortgage Tax Clerk. (Career Examination Ser.: C-929). 1994. pap. 23.95 (*0-8373-0929-8*) Nat Learn.
— Mortuary Caretaker. (Career Examination Ser.: C-500). 1994. pap. 23.95 (*0-8373-0500-4*) Nat Learn.
— Mortuary Technician. (Career Examination Ser.: C-514). 1994. pap. 23.95 (*0-8373-0514-4*) Nat Learn.
— Mosquito Control Inspector. (Career Examination Ser.: C-2912). 1994. pap. 29.95 (*0-8373-2912-4*) Nat Learn.
— Motion Picture Operator. (Career Examination Ser.: C-501). 1994. pap. 23.95 (*0-8373-0501-2*) Nat Learn.
— Motor Carrier Investigator. (Career Examination Ser.: C-523). 1994. pap. 27.95 (*0-8373-0523-3*) Nat Learn.
— Motor Equipment Maintenance Foreman. (Career Examination Ser.: C-2084). 1994. reprint ed. pap. 29.95 (*0-8373-2084-4*) Nat Learn.
— Motor Equipment Maintenance Supervisor. (Career Examination Ser.: C-3298). 1994. pap. 29.95 (*0-8373-3298-2*) Nat Learn.
— Motor Equipment Manager. (Career Examination Ser.: C-359). 1994. pap. 34.95 (*0-8373-0359-1*) Nat Learn.
— Motor Equipment Mechanic. (Career Examination Ser.: C-459). 1994. pap. 23.95 (*0-8373-0459-8*) Nat Learn.
— Motor Equipment Partsman. (Career Examination Ser.: C-1790). 1994. pap. 23.95 (*0-8373-1790-8*) Nat Learn.
— Motor Equipment Records Assistant. (Career Examination Ser.: C-3206). 1994. pap. 27.95 (*0-8373-3206-0*) Nat Learn.
— Motor Equipment Repairman. (Career Examination Ser.: C-524). 1994. pap. 23.95 (*0-8373-0524-1*) Nat Learn.
— Motor Equipment Specialist. (Career Examination Ser.: C-3299). 1994. pap. 27.95 (*0-8373-3299-0*) Nat Learn.
— Motor Grader Operator. (Career Examination Ser.: C-502). 1994. pap. 27.95 (*0-8373-0502-0*) Nat Learn.
— Motor Vehicle Bureau Supervisor. (Career Examination Ser.: C-3574). 1994. pap. 34.95 (*0-8373-3574-4*) Nat Learn.
— Motor Vehicle Cashier. (Career Examination Ser.: C-1722). 1994. pap. 19.95 (*0-8373-1722-3*) Nat Learn.
— Motor Vehicle Dispatcher. (Career Examination Ser.: C-503). 1994. pap. 23.95 (*0-8373-0503-9*) Nat Learn.
— Motor Vehicle Foreman. (Career Examination Ser.: C-1781). 1994. pap. 29.95 (*0-8373-1781-9*) Nat Learn.
— Motor Vehicle Inspector. (Career Examination Ser.: C-2384). 1994. pap. 27.95 (*0-8373-2384-3*) Nat Learn.
— Motor Vehicle Investigator. (Career Examination Ser.: C-504). 1994. pap. 27.95 (*0-8373-0504-7*) Nat Learn.
— Motor Vehicle License Clerk. (Career Examination Ser.: C-505). 1994. pap. 23.95 (*0-8373-0505-5*) Nat Learn.
— Motor Vehicle License Examiner. (Career Examination Ser.: C-506). 1994. pap. 23.95 (*0-8373-0506-3*) Nat Learn.
— Motor Vehicle License Examiner 1. (Career Examination Ser.: C-1937). 1994. pap. 27.95 (*0-8373-1937-4*) Nat Learn.
— Motor Vehicle Licensing Supervisor. (Career Examination Ser.: C-2809). 1994. pap. 29.95 (*0-8373-2809-8*) Nat Learn.
— Motor Vehicle Officer. (Career Examination Ser.: C-2031). 1994. pap. 27.95 (*0-8373-2031-3*) Nat Learn.
— Motor Vehicle Operator. (Career Examination Ser.: C-507). 1994. pap. 23.95 (*0-8373-0507-1*) Nat Learn.
— Motor Vehicle Operator (U. S. P. S.) (Career Examination Ser.: C-508). 1994. pap. 23.95 (*0-8373-0508-X*) Nat Learn.
— Motor Vehicle Program Manager. (Career Examination Ser.: C-311). 1994. pap. 34.95 (*0-8373-0311-7*) Nat Learn.
— Motor Vehicle Referee. (Career Examination Ser.: C-2330). 1994. pap. 34.95 (*0-8373-2330-4*) Nat Learn.
— Motor Vehicle Representative. (Career Examination Ser.: C-3258). 1994. pap. 23.95 (*0-8373-3258-3*) Nat Learn.
— Motor Vehicle Supervisor. (Career Examination Ser.: C-3544-2). 1994. pap. 29.95 (*0-8373-3544-2*) Nat Learn.
— Motorman. (Career Examination Ser.: C-509). 1994. pap. 23.95 (*0-8373-0509-8*) Nat Learn.
— Motorman Instructor. (Career Examination Ser.: C-510). 1994. pap. 27.95 (*0-8373-0510-1*) Nat Learn.
— Mower Maintenance Mechanic. (Career Examination Ser.: C-1373). 1994. pap. 23.95 (*0-8373-1373-2*) Nat Learn.
— Multi-Keyboard Operator. (Career Examination Ser.: C-455). 1994. pap. 23.95 (*0-8373-0455-5*) Nat Learn.
— Multi-Keyboard Operator II. (Career Examination Ser.: C-3073). 1994. pap. 27.95 (*0-8373-3073-4*) Nat Learn.
— Multiple Residence Inspector. (Career Examination Ser.: C-2842). 1994. pap. 29.95 (*0-8373-2842-X*) Nat Learn.
— Multiple Residence Inspector II. (Career Examination Ser.: C-3078). 1994. pap. 34.95 (*0-8373-3078-5*) Nat Learn.
— Multiple Subject Assessment for Teachers (MSAT) (National Teacher Examination Ser.: Vol. NT-9). 1994. pap. 23.95 (*0-8373-8469-9*) Nat Learn.
— Multistate Bar Examination (MBE) (Admission Test Ser.: ATS-8). 300p. 1994. pap. 39.95 (*0-8373-5008-5*) Nat Learn.
— Municipal Bonds Coordinator. (Career Examination Ser.: C-1342). 1994. pap. 34.95 (*0-8373-1342-2*) Nat Learn.
— Museum Attendant. (Career Examination Ser.: C-1374). 1994. pap. 23.95 (*0-8373-1374-0*) Nat Learn.
— Museum Curator. (Career Examination Ser.: C-1375). 1994. pap. 27.95 (*0-8373-1375-9*) Nat Learn.
— Museum Director. (Career Examination Ser.: C-2372). 1994. pap. 34.95 (*0-8373-2372-X*) Nat Learn.
— Museum Instructor. (Career Examination Ser.: C-1705). 1994. pap. 27.95 (*0-8373-1705-3*) Nat Learn.
— Museum Intern. (Career Examination Ser.: C-1376). 1994. pap. 23.95 (*0-8373-1376-7*) Nat Learn.
— Museum Laboratory Technician. (Career Examination Ser.: C-1377). 1994. pap. 27.95 (*0-8373-1377-5*) Nat Learn.
— Museum Supervisor. (Career Examination Ser.: C-2941). 1994. pap. 29.95 (*0-8373-2941-8*) Nat Learn.
— Museum Technician. (Career Examination Ser.: C-522). 1994. pap. 27.95 (*0-8373-0522-5*) Nat Learn.
— Music. (Undergraduate Program Field Tests (UPFT) Ser.: Vol. 16). 43.95 (*0-8373-6066-8*) Nat Learn.
— Music. (Graduate Record Examination Ser.: GRE-13). 1994. pap. 23.95 (*0-8373-5213-4*) Nat Learn.
— Music. (Undergraduate Program Field Tests (UPFT) Ser.: Vol. UPFT-16). 1994. pap. 23.95 (*0-8373-6016-1*) Nat Learn.
— Music Education. (National Teacher Examination Ser.: NT-11). 1994. pap. 23.95 (*0-8373-8421-4*) Nat Learn.
— Music, Jr. H. S. (Teachers License Examination Ser.: T-42). 1994. pap. 27.95 (*0-8373-8042-1*) Nat Learn.
— Music, Sr. H. S. (Teachers License Examination Ser.: T-43). 1994. pap. 27.95 (*0-8373-8043-X*) Nat Learn.
— Music Theory. (Advanced Placement Test (AP) Ser.: Vol. AP-15). 1997. pap. 23.95 (*0-8373-6215-6*) Nat Learn.
— Musical Supervisor. (Career Examination Ser.: C-525). 1994. pap. 29.95 (*0-8373-0525-X*) Nat Learn.
— Narcotics Education Assistant. (Career Examination Ser.: C-2503). 1994. pap. 29.95 (*0-8373-2503-X*) Nat Learn.
— Narcotics Education Specialist. (Career Examination Ser.: C-847). 1994. pap. 29.95 (*0-8373-0847-X*) Nat Learn.
— Narcotics Investigator. (Career Examination Ser.: C-1600). 1994. pap. 34.95 (*0-8373-1600-6*) Nat Learn.
— Narcotics Security Assistant. (Career Examination Ser.: C-1378). 1994. pap. 27.95 (*0-8373-1378-3*) Nat Learn.
— NASD Series 6 Examination: Annuities & Mutual Funds. (Admission Test Ser.: Vol. 97). 59.95 (*0-8373-5197-9*) Nat Learn.
— NASD Series 6 Examination: Annuities & Mutual Funds. (Admission Test Ser.: ATS-97). 1994. pap. 39.95 (*0-8373-5097-2*) Nat Learn.
— National Certifying Examination for Physician's Assistants (PA) (Admission Test Ser.: ATS-91). 1994. pap. 29.95 (*0-8373-5091-3*) Nat Learn.

An Asterisk (*) at the beginning of an entry indicates that the title is appearing for the first time.

— The National Council Licensure Examination for Practical Nurses (NCLEX-PN) (Admission Test Ser.: ATS-76). 1994. pap. 29.95 (*0-8373-5076-X*) Nat Learn.
— The National Council Licensure Examination for Registered Nurses (NCLEX-RN) (Admission Test Ser.: ATS-75). 300p. 1994. pap. 29.95 (*0-8373-5075-1*) Nat Learn.
— National Counselor Examination (NCE) (Admission Test Ser.: Vol. 102). 59.95 (*0-8373-5852-3*) Nat Learn.
— National Dental Assistant Boards (NDAB) (Admission Test Ser.: Vol. 87). 59.95 (*0-8373-5187-1*) Nat Learn.
— National Dental Assistant Boards (NDAB) (Admission Test Ser.: ATS-87). 1994. pap. 39.95 (*0-8373-5087-5*) Nat Learn.
— National Dental Boards (NDB), 2 vols. in 1. (Admission Test Ser.: Vol. 36). 89.95 (*0-8373-5136-7*) Nat Learn.
— National Dental Boards (NDB), 2 pts. in 1 vol. (Admission Test Ser.: ATS-36). 1996. pap. 69.95 (*0-8373-5036-0*) Nat Learn.
— National Dental Boards (NDB), Pt. II. (Admission Test Ser.: Vol. 36B). 69.95 (*0-8373-6981-9*) Nat Learn.
— National Dental Boards (NDB), Pt. II. (Admission Test Ser.: ATS-36B). 1994. pap. 49.95 (*0-8373-6956-8*) Nat Learn.
— National Dental Hygiene Boards (NDHB) (Admission Test Ser.: Vol. 51). 59.95 (*0-8373-5151-0*) Nat Learn.
— National Dental Hygiene Boards (NDHB) (Admission Test Ser.: ATS-51). 1994. pap. 39.95 (*0-8373-5051-4*) Nat Learn.
— National Highway Traffic Safety Administration's Truck Operator Qualification Examination (NTSATOQ) (Admission Test Ser.: ATS-96). 1994. pap. 29.95 (*0-8373-5096-4*) Nat Learn.
— National Medical Boards (NMB), 2 vols. in 1. (Admission Test Ser.: Vol. 23). 89.95 (*0-8373-5123-5*) Nat Learn.
— National Medical Boards (NMB), 2 pts. in 1 vol. (Admission Test Ser.: Vol. ATS-23). 1994. pap. 69.95 (*0-8373-5023-9*) Nat Learn.
— National Medical Boards (NMB), Pt. I. (Admission Test Ser.: Vol. 23A). 69.95 (*0-8373-6975-4*) Nat Learn.
— National Medical Boards (NMB), Pt. I. (Admission Test Ser.: ATS-23A). 1994. pap. 49.95 (*0-8373-6950-9*) Nat Learn.
— National Medical Boards (NMB), Pt. II. (Admission Test Ser.: Vol. 23B). 69.95 (*0-8373-6976-2*) Nat Learn.
— National Medical Boards (NMB), Pt. II. (Admission Test Ser.: Vol. ATS-23B). 1994. pap. 49.95 (*0-8373-6951-7*) Nat Learn.
— National Pharmacy Boards (NPB) (Admission Test Ser.: Vol. 47). 69.95 (*0-8373-5147-2*) Nat Learn.
— National Pharmacy Boards (NPB) (Admission Test Ser.: ATS-47). 1994. pap. 49.95 (*0-8373-5047-6*) Nat Learn.
— National Psychology Boards (NPsyB) (Admission Test Ser.: Vol. 89). 69.95 (*0-8373-5189-8*) Nat Learn.
— National Psychology Boards (NPsyB) (Admission Test Ser.: ATS-89). 1994. pap. 49.95 (*0-8373-5089-1*) Nat Learn.
— National Teacher Examination (Core Battery) (NTE) (Admission Test Ser.: Vol. 15). 47.95 (*0-8373-5115-4*) Nat Learn.
— National Teacher Examination (Core Battery) (NTE) Combined Edition. (Admission Test Ser.: ATS-15). 300p. 1994. pap. 27.95 (*0-8373-5015-8*) Nat Learn.
— National Teacher Examination Passbook Series. (Entire Ser.). 1994. pap. write for info. (*0-8373-8400-1*) Nat Learn.
— National Veterinary Boards (NBE) (NVB) Pt. II: Pharmacology, Therapeutics, Parasitology, Hygiene. (Admission Test Ser.: Vol. 50B). 59.95 (*0-8373-6986-X*) Nat Learn.
— National Veterinary Boards (NBE) (NVB) Pt. II: Pharmacology, Therapeutics, Parasitology, Hygiene, Pt. 2. (Admission Test Ser.: ATS-50B). 1994. pap. 39.95 (*0-8373-6961-4*) Nat Learn.
— National Veterinary Boards (NBE) (NVB) Pt. III: Physical Diagnosis, Medicine, Surgery, Pt. 3. (Admission Test Ser.: ATS-50C). 1994. pap. 39.95 (*0-8373-6962-2*) Nat Learn.
— National Veterinary Boards (NBE) (NVE) Pt. III: Physical Diagnosis, Medicine, Surgery. (Admission Test Ser.: Vol. 50C). 59.95 (*0-8373-6987-8*) Nat Learn.
— Natural Sciences. (College Level Examination (CLEP) Ser.: Vol. ATS-9D). 43.95 (*0-8373-5298-3*) Nat Learn.
— Natural Sciences. (College-Level Examination Series (General Examinations): ATS-9D). 1994. pap. 23.95 (*0-8373-5248-7*) Nat Learn.
— Naturalist. (Career Examination Ser.: C-1379). 1994. pap. 29.95 (*0-8373-1379-1*) Nat Learn.
— NCR No. 3100 Operator. (Career Examination Ser.: C-530). 1994. pap. 19.95 (*0-8373-0530-6*) Nat Learn.
— Nebraska Assessment Battery of Essential Learning Skills (N-ABELS) (Admission Test Ser.: Vol. 65). 43.95 (*0-8373-5165-0*) Nat Learn.
— Nebraska Assessment Battery of Essential Learning Skills (N-ABELS) (Admission Test Ser.: ATS-65). 1994. pap. 23.95 (*0-8373-5065-4*) Nat Learn.
— Neighborhood Aide. (Career Examination Ser.: C-2910). 1994. pap. 23.95 (*0-8373-2910-8*) Nat Learn.
— Nevada Competency-Based High School Diploma Program. (Admission Test Ser.: ATS-67). 1994. pap. 23.95 (*0-8373-5067-0*) Nat Learn.
— Nevada Competency-Based High School Diploma Program (CHSD) (Admission Test Ser.: Vol. 67). 43.95 (*0-8373-5167-7*) Nat Learn.
— New York Basic Competency Tests (BCT-NY) (Admission Test Ser.: Vol. 55). 43.95 (*0-8373-5155-3*) Nat Learn.
— New York Basic Competency Tests (BCT-NY) (Admission Test Ser.: ATS-55). 1994. pap. 23.95 (*0-8373-5055-7*) Nat Learn.
— New York State Bar Examination (NYBE) (Admission Test Ser.: ATS-25). 1994. pap. 49.95 (*0-8373-5025-5*) Nat Learn.
— Nonverbal Reasoning. (General Aptitude & Abilities Ser.: CS-27). 1994. pap. 23.95 (*0-8373-6727-1*) Nat Learn.
— Notary Public. (Career Examination Ser.: C-531). 1994. pap. 19.95 (*0-8373-0531-4*) Nat Learn.
— Numerical & Alphabetical Progressions & Abstract Reasoning. (General Aptitude & Abilities Ser.: CS-30). 1994. pap. 23.95 (*0-8373-6730-1*) Nat Learn.
— Nurse. (Career Examination Ser.: C-532). 1994. pap. 27.95 (*0-8373-0532-2*) Nat Learn.
— Nurse Administrator. (Career Examination Ser.: C-2913). 1994. pap. 34.95 (*0-8373-2913-2*) Nat Learn.
— Nurse GS4-GS7. (Career Examination Ser.: C-533). 1994. pap. 27.95 (*0-8373-0533-0*) Nat Learn.
— Nurse Instructor. (Career Examination Ser.: C-2108). 1994. reprint ed. pap. 34.95 (*0-8373-2108-5*) Nat Learn.
— Nursery Supervisor. (Career Examination Ser.: C-3575). 1994. pap. 29.95 (*0-8373-3575-2*) Nat Learn.
— Nurse's Aide. (Career Examination Ser.: C-535). 1994. pap. 23.95 (*0-8373-0535-7*) Nat Learn.
— Nursing Administration. (Certified Nurse Examination Ser.: CN-16). 1994. pap. 23.95 (*0-8373-6116-8*) Nat Learn.
— Nursing Administration (Advanced) (Certified Nurse Examination Ser.: CN-17). 1994. pap. 23.95 (*0-8373-6117-6*) Nat Learn.
— Nursing Assistant. (Career Examination Ser.: C-534). 1994. pap. 23.95 (*0-8373-0534-9*) Nat Learn.
— Nursing Care Coordinator. (Career Examination Ser.: C-3735). 1994. pap. 39.95 (*0-8373-3735-6*) Nat Learn.
— Nursing Health Care. (Regents External Degree (REDP) Ser.: Vol. 19). 43.95 (*0-8373-5669-5*) Nat Learn.
— Nursing Health Care. (ACT Proficiency Examination Program (PEP) Ser.: Vol. 46). 43.95 (*0-8373-5596-6*) Nat Learn.
— Nursing Health Care. (Regents External Degree Ser.: REDP-19). 1994. pap. 23.95 (*0-8373-5619-9*) Nat Learn.
— Nursing Health Care. (ACT Proficiency Examination Program (PEP) Ser.: Vol. PEP-46). 1994. pap. 23.95 (*0-8373-5546-X*) Nat Learn.
— Nursing Home Administrator. (Career Examination Ser.: C-3205). 1994. pap. 39.95 (*0-8373-3205-2*) Nat Learn.
— Nursing School Entrance Examinations for Practical Nurse (PN) (Admission Test Ser.: Vol. 20). 43.95 (*0-8373-5120-0*) Nat Learn.
— Nursing School Entrance Examinations for Practical Nurse (PN) (Admission Test Ser.: ATS-20). 1994. pap. 23.95 (*0-8373-5020-4*) Nat Learn.
— Nursing School Entrance Examinations for Registered & Graduate Nurses (RN) (Admission Test Ser.: ATS-19). 1994. pap. 23.95 (*0-8373-5019-0*) Nat Learn.
— Nursing, Sr. H. S. (Teachers License Examination Ser.: T-44). 1994. pap. 27.95 (*0-8373-8044-8*) Nat Learn.
— Nursing Station Clerk Trainee. (Career Examination Ser.: C-3158). 1994. pap. 23.95 (*0-8373-3158-7*) Nat Learn.
— Nutrition Assistant. (Career Examination Ser.: C-3303). 1994. pap. 23.95 (*0-8373-3303-2*) Nat Learn.
— Nutrition Education Consultant. (Career Examination Ser.: C-2740). 1994. pap. 34.95 (*0-8373-2740-7*) Nat Learn.
— Nutrition Program Representative. (Career Examination Ser.: Vol. C-3808). 1997. pap. 29.95 (*0-8373-3808-5*) Nat Learn.
— Nutrition Services Consultant. (Career Examination Ser.: C-2836). 1994. pap. 34.95 (*0-8373-2836-5*) Nat Learn.
— Nutrition Services Supervisor. (Career Examination Ser.: C-1384). 1994. pap. 29.95 (*0-8373-1384-8*) Nat Learn.
— Nutritionist. (Career Examination Ser.: C-2326). 1994. pap. 27.95 (*0-8373-2326-6*) Nat Learn.
— Nutritionist I. (Career Examination Ser.: C-3004). 1994. pap. 27.95 (*0-8373-3004-1*) Nat Learn.
— Nutritionist II. (Career Examination Ser.: C-3005). 1994. pap. 29.95 (*0-8373-3005-X*) Nat Learn.
— Occupancy Director. (Career Examination Ser.: C-3736). 1994. pap. 39.95 (*0-8373-3736-4*) Nat Learn.
— Occupational Analyst. (Career Examination Ser.: C-2548). 1994. pap. 29.95 (*0-8373-2548-X*) Nat Learn.
— Occupational Competency Examination - General Examination (OCE) (Occupational Competency Examination (OCE) Ser.: Vol. ATS-33). 49.95 (*0-8373-5133-2*) Nat Learn.
— Occupational Competency Examination - General Examination (OCE) (Admission Test Ser.: ATS-33). 1994. pap. 29.95 (*0-8373-5033-6*) Nat Learn.
— Occupational Competency Examination Series. 1994. pap. write for info. (*0-8373-5700-4*) Nat Learn.
— Occupational Licensing Specialist. (Career Examination Ser.: C-3737). 1994. pap. 27.95 (*0-8373-3737-2*) Nat Learn.
— Occupational Strategy, Nursing. (ACT Proficiency Examination Program (PEP) Ser.: Vol. 47). 43.95 (*0-8373-5597-4*) Nat Learn.
— Occupational Strategy, Nursing. (ACT Proficiency Examination Program Ser.: PEP-47). 1994. pap. 23.95 (*0-8373-5547-8*) Nat Learn.
— Occupational Strategy, Nursing. (Regents External Degree Ser.: REDP-20). 1994. pap. 23.95 (*0-8373-5620-2*) Nat Learn.
— Occupational Strategy (Nursing) (Regents External Degree (REDP) Ser.: Vol. 20). 43.95 (*0-8373-5670-9*) Nat Learn.
— Occupational Therapist. (Career Examination Ser.: C-558). 1994. pap. 29.95 (*0-8373-0558-6*) Nat Learn.
— Occupational Therapist Aide. (Career Examination Ser.: C-1380). 1994. pap. 27.95 (*0-8373-1380-5*) Nat Learn.
— Occupational Therapist Assistant. (Career Examination Ser.: C-1381). 1994. pap. 27.95 (*0-8373-1381-3*) Nat Learn.
— Oceanographer. (Career Examination Ser.: C-550). 1994. pap. 27.95 (*0-8373-0550-0*) Nat Learn.
— Office Aide. (Career Examination Ser.: C-1065). 1994. pap. 19.95 (*0-8373-1065-2*) Nat Learn.
— Office & Science Assistant. (Career Examination Ser.: C-552). 1994. pap. 29.95 (*0-8373-0552-7*) Nat Learn.
— Office Appliance Operator. (Career Examination Ser.: C-551). 1994. pap. 23.95 (*0-8373-0551-9*) Nat Learn.
— Office Assistant. (Career Examination Ser.: C-1382). 1994. pap. 19.95 (*0-8373-1382-1*) Nat Learn.
— Office Associate. (Career Examination Ser.). pap. 19.95 (*0-8373-2450-5*, C2450) Nat Learn.
— Office Machine Aide. (Career Examination Ser.: C-1579). 1994. pap. 19.95 (*0-8373-1579-4*) Nat Learn.
— Office Machine Associate. (Career Examination Ser.: C-2451). 1994. pap. 23.95 (*0-8373-2451-3*) Nat Learn.
— Office Machine Operating, Sr. H. S. (Teachers License Examination Ser.: T-45). 1994. pap. 27.95 (*0-8373-8045-6*) Nat Learn.
— Office Machine Operator. (Career Examination Ser.: C-559). 1994. pap. 23.95 (*0-8373-0559-4*) Nat Learn.
— Office Manager. (Career Examination Ser.: C-2398). 1994. pap. 29.95 (*0-8373-2398-3*) Nat Learn.
— Office Services Supervisor. (Career Examination Ser.: C-2196). 1994. pap. 29.95 (*0-8373-2196-4*) Nat Learn.
— Office Systems Analyst. (Career Examination Ser.: C-3100). 1994. pap. 34.95 (*0-8373-3100-5*) Nat Learn.
— Office Typist. (Career Examination Ser.: C-3373). 1994. pap. 19.95 (*0-8373-3373-3*) Nat Learn.
— Officer Candidate School Admission Test (OCS) (Admission Test Ser.: Vol. 53). 43.95 (*0-8373-5153-7*) Nat Learn.
— Officer Candidate School Admission Test (OCS) (Admission Test Ser.: ATS-53). 1994. pap. 23.95 (*0-8373-5053-0*) Nat Learn.
— Offset Lithography. (Occupational Competency Examination (OCE) Ser.: Vol. 27). 47.95 (*0-8373-5777-2*) Nat Learn.
— Offset Lithography. (Occupational Competency Examination Ser.: OCE-27). 1994. pap. 27.95 (*0-8373-5727-6*) Nat Learn.
— Offset Photographer. (Career Examination Ser.: C-560). 1994. pap. 27.95 (*0-8373-0560-8*) Nat Learn.
— Offset Pressman. (Career Examination Ser.: C-561). 1994. pap. 27.95 (*0-8373-0561-6*) Nat Learn.
— Offset Printing Machine Operator. (Career Examination Ser.: C-562). 1994. pap. 27.95 (*0-8373-0562-4*) Nat Learn.
— Offtrack Betting Operations Analyst. (Career Examination Ser.: C-3302). 1994. pap. 29.95 (*0-8373-3302-4*) Nat Learn.
— Oiler. (Career Examination Ser.: C-553). 1994. pap. 27.95 (*0-8373-0553-5*) Nat Learn.
— Operating Engineer (Stationary) (Career Examination Ser.: C-555). 1994. pap. 29.95 (*0-8373-0555-1*) Nat Learn.
— Operations & Maintenance Trainee. (Career Examination Ser.: C-554). 1994. pap. 27.95 (*0-8373-0554-3*) Nat Learn.
— Operations Flight Clerk. (Career Examination Ser.: C-564). 1994. pap. 23.95 (*0-8373-0564-0*) Nat Learn.
— Operations Management I. (Regents External Degree (REDP) Ser.: Vol. 13). 43.95 (*0-8373-5663-6*) Nat Learn.
— Operations Management I. (Regents External Degree Ser.: REDP-13). 1994. pap. 23.95 (*0-8373-5613-X*) Nat Learn.
— Operations Management III. (Regents External Degree (REDP) Ser.: Vol. 15). 43.95 (*0-8373-5665-2*) Nat Learn.
— Operations Management III. (Regents External Degree Ser.: REDP-15). 1994. pap. 23.95 (*0-8373-5615-6*) Nat Learn.
— Operations Management II. (Regents External Degree (REDP) Ser.: Vol. 14). 43.95 (*0-8373-5664-4*) Nat Learn.
— Operations Management II. (Regents External Degree Ser.: REDP-14). 1994. pap. 23.95 (*0-8373-5614-8*) Nat Learn.
— Operations Officer. (Career Examination Ser.: C-3069). 1994. pap. 34.95 (*0-8373-3069-6*) Nat Learn.
— Operations Research Analyst. (Career Examination Ser.: C-556). 1994. pap. 34.95 (*0-8373-0556-X*) Nat Learn.
— Operations Review Specialist. (Career Examination Ser.: C-3260). 1994. pap. 34.95 (*0-8373-3260-5*) Nat Learn.
— Ophthalmic Aide. (Career Examination Ser.: C-563). 1994. pap. 23.95 (*0-8373-0563-2*) Nat Learn.
— Optometrist. (Career Examination Ser.: C-557). 1994. pap. 29.95 (*0-8373-0557-8*) Nat Learn.
— Optometry Admission Test. (Admission Test Ser.: ATS-27). 1997. reprint ed. pap. 23.95 (*0-8373-5027-1*) Nat Learn.
— Optometry Admission Test (OAT) (Admission Test Ser.: Vol. 27). 43.95 (*0-8373-5127-8*) Nat Learn.
— Ordinance Enforcement Officer. (Career Examination Ser.: C-3068). 1994. pap. 29.95 (*0-8373-3068-8*) Nat Learn.
— Ordinance Inspector. (Career Examination Ser.: C-2852). 1994. pap. 29.95 (*0-8373-2852-7*) Nat Learn.
— Organizational Behavior. (ACT Proficiency Examination Program (PEP) Ser.: Vol. 19). 43.95 (*0-8373-5569-9*) Nat Learn.
— Organizational Behavior. (Dantes Subject Standardized Tests (DANTES) Ser.: Vol. 49). 43.95 (*0-8373-6549-X*) Nat Learn.
— Organizational Behavior. (ACT Proficiency Examination Program Ser.: PEP-19). 1994. pap. 23.95 (*0-8373-5519-2*) Nat Learn.
— Organizational Behavior. (Dantes Subject Standardized Tests (DANTES) Ser.: Vol. DANTES-49). 1994. pap. 23.95 (*0-8373-6649-6*) Nat Learn.
— Ornamental Horticulture. (Occupational Competency Examination (OCE) Ser.: Vol. 28). 47.95 (*0-8373-5778-0*) Nat Learn.
— Ornamental Horticulture. (Occupational Competency Examination Ser.: OCE-28). 1994. pap. 27.95 (*0-8373-5728-4*) Nat Learn.
— Orthopedic Nurse. (Certified Nurse Examination (CN) Ser.: Vol. 27). 43.95 (*0-8373-6177-X*) Nat Learn.
— Orthopedic Nurse. (Certified Nurse Examination Ser.: Vol. CN-27). 1997. pap. 23.95 (*0-8373-6127-3*) Nat Learn.
— Outreach Worker. (Career Examination Ser.: C-3559). 1994. pap. 23.95 (*0-8373-3559-0*) Nat Learn.
— Packer. (Career Examination Ser.: C-1647). 1994. reprint ed. pap. 19.95 (*0-8373-1647-2*) Nat Learn.
— Painter. (Career Examination Ser.: C-570). 1994. pap. 23.95 (*0-8373-0570-5*) Nat Learn.
— Painting Inspector. (Career Examination Ser.: C-1778). 1994. pap. 27.95 (*0-8373-1778-9*) Nat Learn.
— Para-Professional Careers in Mental Hygiene. (Career Examination Ser.: C-3055). 1994. pap. 23.95 (*0-8373-3055-6*) Nat Learn.
— Paralegal Aide. (Career Examination Ser.: C-2245). 1994. pap. 27.95 (*0-8373-2245-6*) Nat Learn.
— Pari-Mutuel Examiner. (Career Examination Ser.: C-644). 1994. pap. 23.95 (*0-8373-0644-2*) Nat Learn.
— Park Attendant. (Career Examination Ser.: C-1541). 1994. pap. 23.95 (*0-8373-1541-7*) Nat Learn.
— Park Construction Coordinator. (Career Examination Ser.: C-3278). 1994. pap. 34.95 (*0-8373-3278-8*) Nat Learn.
— Park Engineer. (Career Examination Ser.: C-3191). 1994. pap. 34.95 (*0-8373-3191-9*) Nat Learn.
— Park Foreman. (Career Examination Ser.: C-571). 1994. pap. 29.95 (*0-8373-0571-3*) Nat Learn.
— Park Maintenance Supervisor. (Career Examination Ser.: C-2942). 1994. pap. 29.95 (*0-8373-2942-6*) Nat Learn.
— Park Manager. (Career Examination Ser.: C-2247). 1994. pap. 29.95 (*0-8373-2247-2*) Nat Learn.
— Park Manager I. (Career Examination Ser.: C-383). 1994. pap. 29.95 (*0-8373-0383-4*) Nat Learn.
— Park Manager III. (Career Examination Ser.: C-385). 1994. pap. 29.95 (*0-8373-0385-0*) Nat Learn.
— Park Manager II. (Career Examination Ser.: C-384). 1994. pap. 29.95 (*0-8373-0384-2*) Nat Learn.
— Park Patrolman. (Career Examination Ser.: C-1688). 1994. pap. 23.95 (*0-8373-1688-X*) Nat Learn.
— Park Ranger. (Career Examination Ser.: C-650). 1994. pap. 23.95 (*0-8373-0650-7*) Nat Learn.
— Park Service Worker. (Career Examination Ser.: C-2468). 1994. pap. 23.95 (*0-8373-2468-8*) Nat Learn.
— Park Superintendent. (Career Examination Ser.: C-2268). 1994. reprint ed. pap. 29.95 (*0-8373-2268-5*) Nat Learn.
— Park Supervisor. (Career Examination Ser.: C-1563). 1994. pap. 29.95 (*0-8373-1563-8*) Nat Learn.
— Parking Enforcement Agent. (Career Examination Ser.: C-572). 1994. pap. 23.95 (*0-8373-0572-1*) Nat Learn.
— Parking Meter Attendant. (Career Examination Ser.: C-1063). 1994. pap. 23.95 (*0-8373-1063-6*) Nat Learn.
— Parking Meter Collector. (Career Examination Ser.: C-573). 1994. pap. 23.95 (*0-8373-0573-X*) Nat Learn.
— Parking Meter Supervisor. (Career Examination Ser.: C-2592). 1994. pap. 29.95 (*0-8373-2592-7*) Nat Learn.
— Parole Officer. (Career Examination Ser.: C-574). 1994. pap. 27.95 (*0-8373-0574-8*) Nat Learn.
— Party Chief. (Career Examination Ser.: C-2167). 1994. reprint ed. pap. 34.95 (*0-8373-2167-0*) Nat Learn.
— Pathologist. (Career Examination Ser.: C-645). 1994. pap. 49.95 (*0-8373-0645-0*) Nat Learn.
— Patrolman Examinations - All States. (Career Examination Ser.: C-575). 1994. pap. 23.95 (*0-8373-0575-6*) Nat Learn.
— Patrolman, Police Department. (Career Examination Ser.: C-576). 1994. pap. 23.95 (*0-8373-0576-4*) Nat Learn.
— Patrolman-Policewoman. (Career Examination Ser.: C-1922). 1994. pap. 23.95 (*0-8373-1922-6*) Nat Learn.
— Payroll Auditor. (Career Examination Ser.: C-2074). 1994. reprint ed. pap. 29.95 (*0-8373-2074-7*) Nat Learn.
— Payroll Clerk. (Career Examination Ser.: C-1596). 1994. pap. 23.95 (*0-8373-1596-4*) Nat Learn.
— Payroll Supervisor. (Career Examination Ser.: C-3154). 1994. pap. 29.95 (*0-8373-3154-4*) Nat Learn.
— PBX Equipment Installer & Repairer. (Career Examination Ser.: C-1385). 1994. pap. 27.95 (*0-8373-1385-6*) Nat Learn.
— Peace Corps Examination. (Career Examination Ser.: C-646). 1994. pap. 23.95 (*0-8373-0646-9*) Nat Learn.
— Pediatric Nurse Practitioner. (Certified Nurse Examination Ser.: CN-8). 1994. pap. 23.95 (*0-8373-6108-7*) Nat Learn.
— Personal Finance. (Dantes Subject Standardized Tests (DANTES) Ser.: Vol. 76). 43.95 (*0-8373-6576-7*) Nat Learn.
— Personal Finance. (DANTES Ser.: No. 26). 1991. 23.95 (*0-8373-6676-3*) Nat Learn.
— Personnel - Human Resource Management. (Dantes Subject Standardized Tests (DANTES) Ser.: Vol. 48). 43.95 (*0-8373-6548-1*) Nat Learn.
— Personnel, Administration & Computer Occupations. (Career Examination Ser.: C-3555). 1994. pap. 27.95 (*0-8373-3555-8*) Nat Learn.
— Personnel Administrator. (Career Examination Ser.: C-647). 1994. pap. 39.95 (*0-8373-0647-7*) Nat Learn.
— Personnel Analyst. (Career Examination Ser.: C-2344). 1994. pap. 34.95 (*0-8373-2344-4*) Nat Learn.
— Personnel Analyst Trainee. (Career Examination Ser.: C-2395). 1994. pap. 27.95 (*0-8373-2395-9*) Nat Learn.
— Personnel Assistant. (Career Examination Ser.: C-577). 1994. pap. 29.95 (*0-8373-0577-2*) Nat Learn.
— Personnel Associate. (Career Examination Ser.: C-648). 1994. pap. 29.95 (*0-8373-0648-5*) Nat Learn.

R

— Personnel Clerk. (Career Examination Ser.: C-2461). 1994. pap. 23.95 (*0-8373-2461-0*) Nat Learn.
— Personnel Examiner. (Career Examination Ser.: C-578). 1994. pap. 29.95 (*0-8373-0578-0*) Nat Learn.
— Personnel Examining Trainee. (Career Examination Ser.: C-579). 1994. pap. 27.95 (*0-8373-0579-9*) Nat Learn.
— Personnel-Human Resource Management. (Dantes Subject Standardized Tests Ser.: DANTES-48). 1994. pap. 23.95 (*0-8373-6648-8*) Nat Learn.
— Personnel Management. (ACT Proficiency Examination Program (PEP) Ser.: Vol. 20). 43.95 (*0-8373-5570-2*) Nat Learn.
— Personnel Management. (ACT Proficiency Examination Program Ser.: PEP-20). 1994. pap. 23.95 (*0-8373-5520-6*) Nat Learn.
— Personnel Manager. (Career Examination Ser.: C-2112). 1994. reprint ed. pap. 39.95 (*0-8373-2112-3*) Nat Learn.
— Personnel Officer. (Career Examination Ser.: C-2343). 1994. pap. 29.95 (*0-8373-2343-6*) Nat Learn.
— Personnel Specialist. (Career Examination Ser.: C-1386). 1994. pap. 29.95 (*0-8373-1386-4*) Nat Learn.
— Personnel Systems Analyst. (Career Examination Ser.: C-1387). 1994. pap. 34.95 (*0-8373-1387-2*) Nat Learn.
— Personnel Technician. (Career Examination Ser.: C-1944). 1994. pap. 29.95 (*0-8373-1944-7*) Nat Learn.
— Personnel Technician Trainee. (Career Examination Ser.: C-2274). 1994. pap. 27.95 (*0-8373-2274-X*) Nat Learn.
— Personnel Transactions Supervisor. (Career Examination Ser.: C-3150). 1994. pap. 29.95 (*0-8373-3150-1*) Nat Learn.
— Pest Control Aide. (Career Examination Ser.: C-2030). 1994. pap. 23.95 (*0-8373-2030-5*) Nat Learn.
— Pest Control Supervisor. (Career Examination Ser.: C-3094). 1994. pap. 29.95 (*0-8373-3094-7*) Nat Learn.
— Pesticide Control Inspector. (Career Examination Ser.: C-2561). 1994. pap. 29.95 (*0-8373-2561-7*) Nat Learn.
— Pharmaceutical Examiner. (Career Examination Ser.: C-1839). 1994. pap. 39.95 (*0-8373-1839-4*) Nat Learn.
— Pharmacist. (Career Examination Ser.: C-580). 1994. pap. 29.95 (*0-8373-0580-2*) Nat Learn.
— Pharmacist I. (Career Examination Ser.: C-1836). 1994. pap. 29.95 (*0-8373-1836-X*) Nat Learn.
— Pharmacist III. (Career Examination Ser.: C-1838). 1994. pap. 34.95 (*0-8373-1838-6*) Nat Learn.
— Pharmacist Trainee. (Career Examination Ser.: C-649). 1994. pap. 23.95 (*0-8373-0649-3*) Nat Learn.
— Pharmacist II. (Career Examination Ser.: C-1837). 1994. pap. 34.95 (*0-8373-1837-8*) Nat Learn.
— Pharmacologist. (Career Examination Ser.: C-581). 1994. pap. 39.95 (*0-8373-0581-0*) Nat Learn.
— Pharmacy Aide. (Career Examination Ser.: C-2576). 1994. pap. 23.95 (*0-8373-2576-5*) Nat Learn.
— Pharmacy Assistant. (Career Examination Ser.: C-1388). 1994. pap. 23.95 (*0-8373-1388-0*) Nat Learn.
— Pharmacy Assistant II. (Career Examination Ser.: C-2943). 1994. pap. 27.95 (*0-8373-2943-4*) Nat Learn.
— Pharmacy College Admission Test. (Admission Test Ser.: ATS-52). 1994. pap. 23.95 (*0-8373-5052-2*) Nat Learn.
— Pharmacy College Admission Test (PCAT) (Admission Test Ser.: Vol. 52). 43.95 (*0-8373-5152-9*) Nat Learn.
— Pharmacy Inspector. (Career Examination Ser.: C-2536). 1994. pap. 34.95 (*0-8373-2536-6*) Nat Learn.
— Pharmacy Technician. (Career Examination Ser.: Vol. C-3822). 1997. pap. 23.95 (*0-8373-3822-0*) Nat Learn.
— Philosophy. (Graduate Record Examination (GRE) Ser.: Vol. 14). 43.95 (*0-8373-5264-9*) Nat Learn.
— Philosophy. (Undergraduate Program Field Tests (UPFT) Ser.: Vol. 17). 43.95 (*0-8373-6067-6*) Nat Learn.
— Philosophy. (Graduate Record Examination Ser.: GRE-14). 1994. pap. 23.95 (*0-8373-5214-2*) Nat Learn.
— Philosophy. (Undergraduate Program Field Tests (UPFT) Ser.: Vol. UPFT-17). 1994. pap. 23.95 (*0-8373-6017-X*) Nat Learn.
— Philosophy of Education. (ACT Proficiency Examination Program (PEP) Ser.: Vol. 30). 43.95 (*0-8373-5580-X*) Nat Learn.
— Philosophy of Education. (Regents College Proficiency Examination Ser.: Vol. 32). 43.95 (*0-8373-5482-X*) Nat Learn.
— Philosophy of Education. (ACT Proficiency Examination Program Ser.: PEP-30). 1994. pap. 23.95 (*0-8373-5530-3*) Nat Learn.
— Philosophy of Education. (Regents College Proficiency Examination Ser.: Vol. CPEP-32). 1994. reprint ed. pap. 23.95 (*0-8373-5432-3*) Nat Learn.
— Photo Laboratory Technician. (Career Examination Ser.: C-1389). 1994. pap. 27.95 (*0-8373-1389-9*) Nat Learn.
— Photo Machine Operator. (Career Examination Ser.: C-1390). 1994. pap. 19.95 (*0-8373-1390-2*) Nat Learn.
— Photo Specialist. (Career Examination Ser.: C-1391). 1994. pap. 23.95 (*0-8373-1391-0*) Nat Learn.
— Photocopy Machine Operator. (Career Examination Ser.: C-2971). 1994. pap. 19.95 (*0-8373-2971-X*) Nat Learn.
— Photographer. (Career Examination Ser.: C-582). 1994. pap. 29.95 (*0-8373-0582-9*) Nat Learn.
— Photographic Specialist I. (Career Examination Ser.: C-1870). 1994. pap. 23.95 (*0-8373-1870-X*) Nat Learn.
— Photographic Specialist II. (Career Examination Ser.: C-1871). 1994. pap. 23.95 (*0-8373-1871-8*) Nat Learn.
— Photographic Technician. (Career Examination Ser.: C-1872). 1994. pap. 23.95 (*0-8373-1872-6*) Nat Learn.
— Photostat Operator. (Career Examination Ser.: C-1878). 1994. pap. 19.95 (*0-8373-1878-5*) Nat Learn.
— Physical Education. (Undergraduate Program Field Tests (UPFT) Ser.: Vol. 18). 43.95 (*0-8373-6068-4*) Nat Learn.
— Physical Education. (Graduate Record Examination (GRE) Ser.: Vol. 20). 43.95 (*0-8373-5270-3*) Nat Learn.
— Physical Education. (National Teacher Examination Ser.: NT-9). 1994. pap. 23.95 (*0-8373-8419-2*) Nat Learn.
— Physical Education. (Graduate Record Examination (GRE) Ser.: Vol. GRE-20). 1994. pap. 23.95 (*0-8373-5220-7*) Nat Learn.
— Physical Education. (Undergraduate Program Field Tests (UPFT) Ser.: Vol. UPFT-18). 1994. pap. 23.95 (*0-8373-6018-8*) Nat Learn.
— Physical Geology. (ACT Proficiency Examination Program Ser.: No. PEP-56). 1994. 39.95 (*0-8373-5931-7*) Nat Learn.
— Physical Geology. (ACT Proficiency Examination Program Ser.: PEP-56). 1994. pap. 23.95 (*0-8373-5906-6*) Nat Learn.
— Physical Science. (Dantes Subject Standardized Tests (DANTES) Ser.: Vol. 30). 43.95 (*0-8373-6530-9*) Nat Learn.
— Physical Science. (Dantes Subject Standardized Tests Ser.: DANTES-30). 1994. pap. 23.95 (*0-8373-6630-5*) Nat Learn.
— Physical Science Aide. (Career Examination Ser.: C-583). 1994. pap. 27.95 (*0-8373-0583-7*) Nat Learn.
— Physical Science Technician. (Career Examination Ser.: C-584). 1994. pap. 27.95 (*0-8373-0584-5*) Nat Learn.
— Physical Sciences - Area Examination. (Graduate Record Examination Ser.: GRE-43). 1994. pap. 23.95 (*0-8373-5243-6*) Nat Learn.
— Physical Therapist. (Career Examination Ser.: C-585). 1994. pap. 29.95 (*0-8373-0585-3*) Nat Learn.
— Physician. (Career Examination Ser.: C-1392). 1994. pap. 44.95 (*0-8373-1392-9*) Nat Learn.
— Physician's Assistant. (Career Examination Ser.: C-2557). 1994. pap. 29.95 (*0-8373-2557-9*) Nat Learn.
— Physicist. (Career Examination Ser.: C-586). 1994. pap. 34.95 (*0-8373-0586-1*) Nat Learn.
— Physics. (Graduate Record Examination (GRE) Ser.: Vol. 15). 43.95 (*0-8373-5265-7*) Nat Learn.
— Physics. (Undergraduate Program Field Tests (UPFT) Ser.: Vol. 19). 43.95 (*0-8373-6069-2*) Nat Learn.
— Physics. (DANTES Ser.). 1994. 39.95 (*0-8373-6531-7*) Nat Learn.
— Physics. (Graduate Record Examination Ser.: GRE-15). 1994. pap. 23.95 (*0-8373-5215-0*) Nat Learn.
— Physics. (Undergraduate Program Field Tests Ser.: UPFT-19). 1994. pap. 23.95 (*0-8373-6019-6*) Nat Learn.
— Physics. (Dantes Subject Standardized Tests (DANTES) Ser.: Vol. DANTES-31). 1994. pap. 23.95 (*0-8373-6631-3*) Nat Learn.
— Physics & General Science, Sr. H. S. (Teachers License Examination Ser.: T-46). 1994. pap. 27.95 (*0-8373-8046-4*) Nat Learn.
— Physics B. (Advanced Placement Test (AP) Ser.: Vol. AP-16). 1997. pap. 23.95 (*0-8373-6216-4*) Nat Learn.
— Physics C (Electricity & Magnetism) (Advanced Placement Test (AP) Ser.: Vol. AP-18). 1997. pap. 23.95 (*0-8373-6218-0*) Nat Learn.
— Physics C (Mechanics) (Advanced Placement Test (AP) Ser.: Vol. AP-17). 1997. pap. 23.95 (*0-8373-6217-2*) Nat Learn.
— Pile Driving Engineer. (Career Examination Ser.: C-2558). 1994. pap. 34.95 (*0-8373-2558-7*) Nat Learn.
— Pipe Caulker. (Career Examination Ser.: C-641). 1994. pap. 23.95 (*0-8373-0641-8*) Nat Learn.
— Pipefitter. (Career Examination Ser.: C-587). 1994. pap. 23.95 (*0-8373-0587-X*) Nat Learn.
— Placement Representative I. (Career Examination Ser.: C-868). 1994. pap. 27.95 (*0-8373-0868-2*) Nat Learn.
— Placement Representative II. (Career Examination Ser.: C-869). 1994. pap. 29.95 (*0-8373-0869-0*) Nat Learn.
— Plan Examiner. (Career Examination Ser.: C-651). 1994. pap. 29.95 (*0-8373-0651-5*) Nat Learn.
— Plane Trigonometry. (Dantes Subject Standardized Tests Ser.: DANTES-29). 1994. pap. 23.95 (*0-8373-6629-1*) Nat Learn.
— Plane Trigonometry. (DANTES Ser.: No. 29). 1994. 39.95 (*0-8373-6529-5*) Nat Learn.
— Planner. (Career Examination Ser.: C-588). 1994. pap. 27.95 (*0-8373-0588-8*) Nat Learn.
— Planner & Analyst Trainee. (Career Examination Ser.: C-2996). 1994. pap. 29.95 (*0-8373-2996-5*) Nat Learn.
— Planner (Criminal Justice) (Career Examination Ser.: C-3020). 1994. pap. 34.95 (*0-8373-3020-3*) Nat Learn.
— Planner Trainee. (Career Examination Ser.: C-2778). 1994. pap. 23.95 (*0-8373-2778-4*) Nat Learn.
— Planner Youth Services. (Career Examination Ser.: C-3003). 1994. pap. 29.95 (*0-8373-3003-3*) Nat Learn.
— Planning Aide. (Career Examination Ser.: C-2770). 1994. pap. 23.95 (*0-8373-2770-9*) Nat Learn.
— Planning & Evaluation Assistant. (Career Examination Ser.: C-549). 1994. pap. 29.95 (*0-8373-0549-7*) Nat Learn.
— Planning Director. (Career Examination Ser.: C-3401). 1994. pap. 39.95 (*0-8373-3401-2*) Nat Learn.
— Planning Technician. (Career Examination Ser.: C-3185). 1994. pap. 27.95 (*0-8373-3185-4*) Nat Learn.
— Plant Facilities Administrator. (Career Examination Ser.: C-2758). 1994. pap. 39.95 (*0-8373-2758-X*) Nat Learn.
— Plant Maintenance Engineer. (Career Examination Ser.: C-2480). 1994. pap. 34.95 (*0-8373-2480-7*) Nat Learn.
— Plant Maintenance Mechanic. (Career Examination Ser.: C-1393). 1994. pap. 27.95 (*0-8373-1393-7*) Nat Learn.
— Plant Maintenance Supervisor. (Career Examination Ser.: C-1559). 1994. pap. 27.95 (*0-8373-1559-X*) Nat Learn.
— Plant Superintendent. (Career Examination Ser.: C-1935). 1994. reprint ed. pap. 34.95 (*0-8373-1935-8*) Nat Learn.
— Plant Superintendent A. (Career Examination Ser.: C-2046). 1994. pap. 34.95 (*0-8373-2046-1*) Nat Learn.
— Plant Superintendent B. (Career Examination Ser.: C-2047). 1994. pap. 34.95 (*0-8373-2047-X*) Nat Learn.
— Plant Superintendent C. (Career Examination Ser.: C-2048). 1994. pap. 34.95 (*0-8373-2048-8*) Nat Learn.
— Plasterer. (Career Examination Ser.: C-589). 1994. pap. 23.95 (*0-8373-0589-6*) Nat Learn.
— Playground Director. (Career Examination Ser.: C-590). 1994. pap. 34.95 (*0-8373-0590-X*) Nat Learn.
— Playgrounds (Health Education), Men. (Teachers License Examination Ser.: T-47a). 1994. pap. 27.95 (*0-8373-8047-2*) Nat Learn.
— Playgrounds (Health Education), Women. (Teachers License Examination Ser.: T-47b). 1994. pap. 27.95 (*0-685-49791-7*) Nat Learn.
— Playgrounds (Kindergarten) (Teachers License Examination Ser.: T-48). 1994. pap. 27.95 (*0-8373-8048-0*) Nat Learn.
— Playgrounds (Swimming) (Teachers License Examination Ser.: T-49). 1994. pap. 27.95 (*0-8373-8049-9*) Nat Learn.
— Plumber. (Career Examination Ser.: C-591). 1994. pap. 27.95 (*0-8373-0591-8*) Nat Learn.
— Plumber's Helper. (Career Examination Ser.: C-592). 1994. pap. 23.95 (*0-8373-0592-6*) Nat Learn.
— Plumbing. (Occupational Competency Examination (OCE) Ser.: Vol. 29). 47.95 (*0-8373-5779-9*) Nat Learn.
— Plumbing. (Occupational Competency Examination Ser.: OCE-29). 1994. pap. 27.95 (*0-8373-5729-2*) Nat Learn.
— Plumbing Engineer. (Career Examination Ser.: C-2713). 1994. pap. 34.95 (*0-8373-2713-X*) Nat Learn.
— Plumbing Inspector. (Career Examination Ser.: C-593). 1994. pap. 29.95 (*0-8373-0593-4*) Nat Learn.
— Plumbing Supervisor. (Career Examination Ser.: C-2583). 1994. pap. 34.95 (*0-8373-2583-8*) Nat Learn.
— Plumbing Workbook. (Workbook (W) Ser.: Vol. 3160). 43.95 (*0-8373-7930-X*) Nat Learn.
— Plumbing Workbook. (Workbook Ser.: W-3160). 1994. pap. 23.95 (*0-8373-7905-9*) Nat Learn.
— Police Administration & Supervision. (General Aptitude & Abilities Ser.: No. CS-32). pap. 39.95 (*0-8373-6732-8*, CS-32) Nat Learn.
— Police Administrative Aide. (Career Examination Ser.: C-640). 1994. pap. 23.95 (*0-8373-0640-X*) Nat Learn.
— Police Attendant. (Career Examination Ser.: C-982). 1994. pap. 23.95 (*0-8373-0982-4*) Nat Learn.
— Police Cadet. (Career Examination Ser.: C-594). 1994. pap. 23.95 (*0-8373-0594-2*) Nat Learn.
— Police Captain. (Career Examination Ser.: C-2803). 1994. pap. 39.95 (*0-8373-2803-9*) Nat Learn.
— Police Chief. (Career Examination Ser.: C-2754). 1994. pap. 44.95 (*0-8373-2754-7*) Nat Learn.
— Police Clerk. (Career Examination Ser.: C-639). 1994. pap. 23.95 (*0-8373-0639-6*) Nat Learn.
— Police Communications & Teletype Operator. (Career Examination Ser.: C-1847). 1994. pap. 23.95 (*0-8373-1847-5*) Nat Learn.
— Police Communications & Teletype Operator Supervisor. (Career Examination Ser.: C-1437). 1994. pap. 29.95 (*0-8373-1437-2*) Nat Learn.
— Police Communications Technician. (Career Examination Ser.: C-3526). 1994. pap. 23.95 (*0-8373-3526-4*) Nat Learn.
— Police Dispatcher. (Career Examination Ser.: C-2256). 1994. reprint ed. pap. 23.95 (*0-8373-2256-1*) Nat Learn.
— Police Inspector. (Career Examination Ser.: C-1383). 1994. pap. 39.95 (*0-8373-1383-X*) Nat Learn.
— Police Lieutenant. (Career Examination Ser.: C-2802). 1994. pap. 34.95 (*0-8373-2802-0*) Nat Learn.
— Police Officer. (Career Examination Ser.: C-1939). 1994. reprint ed. pap. 23.95 (*0-8373-1939-0*) Nat Learn.
— Police Officer, Los Angeles Police Department. (Career Examination Ser.: C-2441). 1994. pap. 23.95 (*0-8373-2441-6*) Nat Learn.
— Police Officer, Nassau County Police Department. (Career Examination Ser.: C-1755). 1994. pap. 23.95 (*0-8373-1755-X*) Nat Learn.
— Police Officer, New York Police Department. (Career Examination Ser.: C-1739). 1994. reprint ed. pap. 23.95 (*0-8373-1739-8*) Nat Learn.
— Police Officer, Suffolk County Police Department. (Career Examination Ser.: C-1741). 1994. reprint ed. pap. 23.95 (*0-8373-1741-X*) Nat Learn.
— Police Operations Aide. (Career Examination Ser.: C-3402). 1994. pap. 23.95 (*0-8373-3402-0*) Nat Learn.
— Police Patrolman. (Career Examination Ser.: C-595). 1994. pap. 23.95 (*0-8373-0595-0*) Nat Learn.
— Police Promotion Course. (General Aptitude & Abilities Ser.: No. CS-18). pap. 39.95 (*0-8373-6718-2*, CS-18) Nat Learn.
— Police Reading Comprehension. (General Aptitude & Abilities Ser.: No. CS-23). pap. 23.95 (*0-8373-6723-9*, CS-23) Nat Learn.
— Police Surgeon. (Career Examination Ser.: C-596). 1994. pap. 49.95 (*0-8373-0596-9*) Nat Learn.
— Police Trainee. (Career Examination Ser.: C-597). 1994. pap. 23.95 (*0-8373-0597-7*) Nat Learn.
— Policewoman. (Career Examination Ser.: C-598). 1994. pap. 23.95 (*0-8373-0598-5*) Nat Learn.
— Political Science. (Graduate Record Examination (GRE) Ser.: Vol. 16). 43.95 (*0-8373-5266-5*) Nat Learn.
— Political Science. (Undergraduate Program Field Tests (UPFT) Ser.: Vol. 20). 43.95 (*0-8373-6070-6*) Nat Learn.
— Political Science. (Graduate Record Examination Ser.: GRE-16). 1994. pap. 23.95 (*0-8373-5216-9*) Nat Learn.
— Political Science. (Undergraduate Program Field Tests (UPFT) Ser.: Vol. UPFT-20). 1994. pap. 23.95 (*0-8373-6020-X*) Nat Learn.
— Pollution Control Specialist. (Career Examination Ser.: C-3738). 1994. pap. 29.95 (*0-8373-3738-0*) Nat Learn.
— Portable Engineer - (Any Motive Power Except Steam) (AMPES) (Career Examination Ser.: C-599). 1994. pap. 29.95 (*0-8373-0599-3*) Nat Learn.
— Portable Engineer (Steam) (Career Examination Ser.: C-600). 1994. pap. 29.95 (*0-8373-0600-0*) Nat Learn.
— Position Classification Specialist. (Career Examination Ser.: C-601). 1994. pap. 29.95 (*0-8373-0601-9*) Nat Learn.
— Postal Arithmetic. (General Aptitude & Abilities Ser.: No. CS-20). pap. 19.95 (*0-8373-6720-4*, CS-20) Nat Learn.
— Postal Inspector (U. S. P. S.) (Career Examination Ser.: C-602). 1994. pap. 27.95 (*0-8373-0602-7*) Nat Learn.
— Postal Police Officer (U.S.P.S.) (Career Examination Ser.: C-2211). 1994. pap. 27.95 (*0-8373-2211-1*) Nat Learn.
— Postal Supervisor (U. S. P. S.) (Career Examination Ser.: C-603). 1994. pap. 29.95 (*0-8373-0603-5*) Nat Learn.
— Postal System Examiner (U. S. P. S.) (Career Examination Ser.: C-2079). 1994. reprint ed. pap. 34.95 (*0-8373-2079-8*) Nat Learn.
— Postal Transportation Clerk (U. S. P. S.) (Career Examination Ser.: C-604). 1994. pap. 23.95 (*0-8373-0604-3*) Nat Learn.
— Postmaster, 1st, 2nd, & 3rd Classes (U. S. P. S.) (Career Examination Ser.: C-605). 1994. pap. 29.95 (*0-8373-0605-1*) Nat Learn.
— Postmaster, 4th Class (U. S. P. S.) (Career Examination Ser.: C-606). 1994. pap. 27.95 (*0-8373-0606-X*) Nat Learn.
— Power Cable Maintainer. (Career Examination Ser.: C-653). 1994. pap. 23.95 (*0-8373-0653-1*) Nat Learn.
— Power Distribution Maintainer. (Career Examination Ser.: C-1394). 1994. pap. 23.95 (*0-8373-1394-5*) Nat Learn.
— Power Electronic Maintainer. (Career Examination Ser.: C-3180). 1994. pap. 23.95 (*0-8373-3180-3*) Nat Learn.
— Power Maintainer - Group A. (Career Examination Ser.: C-607). 1994. pap. 23.95 (*0-8373-0607-8*) Nat Learn.
— Power Maintainer - Group B. (Career Examination Ser.: C-608). 1994. pap. 23.95 (*0-8373-0608-6*) Nat Learn.
— Power Maintainer - Group C. (Career Examination Ser.: C-609). 1994. pap. 23.95 (*0-8373-0609-4*) Nat Learn.
— Power Plant Operator. (Career Examination Ser.: C-1395). 1994. pap. 27.95 (*0-8373-1395-3*) Nat Learn.
— Power Plant Supervisor. (Career Examination Ser.: C-3403). 1994. pap. 29.95 (*0-8373-3403-9*) Nat Learn.
— Practical Nurse. (Career Examination Ser.: C-642). 1994. pap. 27.95 (*0-8373-0642-6*) Nat Learn.
— Practice & Drill for the Clerk, Typist & Stenographer Examinations. (General Aptitude & Abilities Ser.: No. CS-19). pap. 23.95 (*0-8373-6719-0*, CS-19) Nat Learn.
— Pre-Employment Counselor. (Career Examination Ser.: C-1396). 1994. pap. 29.95 (*0-8373-1396-1*) Nat Learn.
— Pre-Law Equivalency Examination (PL) (Admission Test Ser.: Vol. 40). 49.95 (*0-8373-5140-5*) Nat Learn.
— Pre-Law Equivalency Examination (PL) (Admission Test Ser.: ATS-40). 1994. pap. 29.95 (*0-8373-5040-9*) Nat Learn.
— Pre Professional Skills Test (PPST) (Admission Test Ser.: Vol. 95). 43.95 (*0-8373-5195-2*) Nat Learn.
— Precis of Postal Service Manual. (General Aptitude & Abilities Ser.: No. CS-22). pap. 19.95 (*0-8373-6722-0*, CS-22) Nat Learn.
— Preparing Written Material. (General Aptitude & Abilities Ser.: No. CS-37). pap. 23.95 (*0-8373-6737-9*, CS-37) Nat Learn.
— Press Operator. (Career Examination Ser.: C-3190). 1994. pap. 27.95 (*0-8373-3190-0*) Nat Learn.
— Presser. (Career Examination Ser.: C-1397). 1994. pap. 27.95 (*0-8373-1397-X*) Nat Learn.
— Preventive Maintenance Supervisor. (Career Examination Ser.: C-3499). 1994. pap. 29.95 (*0-8373-3499-3*) Nat Learn.
— Principal, Academic High School. (Teachers License Examination Ser.: S-5). 1994. pap. 49.95 (*0-8373-8105-3*) Nat Learn.
— Principal Account-Audit Clerk. (Career Examination Ser.: C-2008). 1994. pap. 27.95 (*0-8373-2008-9*) Nat Learn.
— Principal Account Clerk. (Career Examination Ser.: C-655). 1994. pap. 27.95 (*0-8373-0655-8*) Nat Learn.
— Principal Accountant. (Career Examination Ser.: C-654). 1994. pap. 34.95 (*0-8373-0654-X*) Nat Learn.
— Principal Actuarial Clerk. (Career Examination Ser.: C-2424). 1994. pap. 29.95 (*0-8373-2424-6*) Nat Learn.
— Principal Actuary. (Career Examination Ser.: C-610). 1994. pap. 49.95 (*0-8373-0610-8*) Nat Learn.
— Principal Addiction Specialist. (Career Examination Ser.: C-1398). 1994. pap. 34.95 (*0-8373-1398-8*) Nat Learn.
— Principal Administrative Analyst. (Career Examination Ser.: C-2710). 1994. pap. 39.95 (*0-8373-2710-5*) Nat Learn.
— Principal Administrative Associate. (Career Examination Ser.: C-2394). 1994. pap. 29.95 (*0-8373-2394-0*) Nat Learn.
— Principal Administrative Services Clerk. (Career Examination Ser.: C-2871). 1994. pap. 29.95 (*0-8373-2871-3*) Nat Learn.
— Principal Admitting Clerk. (Career Examination Ser.: C-656). 1994. pap. 27.95 (*0-8373-0656-6*) Nat Learn.
— Principal Affirmative Action Officer. (Career Examination Ser.: C-2689). 1994. pap. 34.95 (*0-8373-2689-3*) Nat Learn.
— Principal Alcoholism Rehabilitaion Counselor. (Career Examination Ser.: C-2796). 1994. pap. 34.95 (*0-8373-2796-2*) Nat Learn.
— Principal Attorney. (Career Examination Ser.: C-1913). 1994. pap. 44.95 (*0-8373-1913-7*) Nat Learn.
— Principal Audit Clerk. (Career Examination Ser.: C-657). 1994. pap. 27.95 (*0-8373-0657-4*) Nat Learn.
— Principal Auditor. (Career Examination Ser.: C-2405). 1994. pap. 39.95 (*0-8373-2405-X*) Nat Learn.
— Principal Bank Examiner. (Career Examination Ser.: C-658). 1994. pap. 34.95 (*0-8373-0658-2*) Nat Learn.
— Principal Bookkeeper. (Career Examination Ser.: C-1756). 1994. reprint ed. pap. 29.95 (*0-8373-1756-8*) Nat Learn.
— Principal Budget Analyst. (Career Examination Ser.: C-2416). 1994. pap. 39.95 (*0-8373-2416-5*) Nat Learn.

An Asterisk (*) at the beginning of an entry indicates that the title is appearing for the first time.

— Principal Budget Examiner. (Career Examination Ser.: C-1637). 1994. reprint ed. pap. 39.95 (*0-8373-1637-5*) Nat Learn.
— Principal Budget Officer. (Career Examination Ser.: C-2685). 1994. pap. 39.95 (*0-8373-2685-0*) Nat Learn.
— Principal Building Inspector. (Career Examination Ser.: C-2853). 1994. pap. 34.95 (*0-8373-2853-5*) Nat Learn.
— Principal Buyer. (Career Examination Ser.: C-3419). 1994. pap. 29.95 (*0-8373-3419-5*) Nat Learn.
— Principal Cashier. (Career Examination Ser.: C-1974). 1994. pap. 23.95 (*0-8373-1974-9*) Nat Learn.
— Principal Chemist. (Career Examination Ser.: C-2403). 1994. pap. 34.95 (*0-8373-2403-3*) Nat Learn.
— Principal Children's Counselor. (Career Examination Ser.: C-1602). 1994. pap. 34.95 (*0-8373-1602-2*) Nat Learn.
— Principal Civil Engineer. (Career Examination Ser.: C-318). 1994. pap. 34.95 (*0-8373-0318-4*) Nat Learn.
— Principal Clerk. (Career Examination Ser.: C-611). 1994. pap. 23.95 (*0-8373-0611-6*) Nat Learn.
— Principal Clerk (Personnel) (Career Examination Ser.: C-1399). 1994. pap. 27.95 (*0-8373-1399-6*) Nat Learn.
— Principal Clerk-Stenographer. (Career Examination Ser.: C-3327). 1994. pap. 23.95 (*0-8373-3327-X*) Nat Learn.
— Principal Clerk Surrogate. (Career Examination Ser.: C-2129). 1994. reprint ed. pap. 29.95 (*0-8373-2129-8*) Nat Learn.
— Principal Commissary Clerk. (Career Examination Ser.: C-2049). 1994. pap. 27.95 (*0-8373-2049-6*) Nat Learn.
— Principal Communications Technician. (Career Examination Ser.: C-2413). 1994. pap. 34.95 (*0-8373-2413-0*) Nat Learn.
— Principal, Comprehensive High School. (Teachers License Examination Ser.: S-11). 1994. pap. 49.95 (*0-8373-8111-8*) Nat Learn.
— Principal Computer Programmer. (Career Examination Ser.: C-1626). 1994. pap. 34.95 (*0-8373-1626-X*) Nat Learn.
— Principal Construction Inspector. (Career Examination Ser.: C-1400). 1994. pap. 34.95 (*0-8373-1400-3*) Nat Learn.
— Principal Consumer Affairs Inspector. (Career Examination Ser.: C-1658). 1994. reprint ed. pap. 29.95 (*0-8373-1658-8*) Nat Learn.
— Principal Consumer Affairs Investigator. (Career Examination Ser.: C-2377). 1994. pap. 29.95 (*0-8373-2377-0*) Nat Learn.
— Principal Court Clerk. (Career Examination Ser.: C-2588). 1994. pap. 29.95 (*0-8373-2588-9*) Nat Learn.
— Principal Custodial Foreman. (Career Examination Ser.: C-2560). 1994. pap. 29.95 (*0-8373-2560-9*) Nat Learn.
— Principal Data Entry Machine Operator. (Career Examination Ser.: C-2866). 1994. pap. 29.95 (*0-8373-2866-7*) Nat Learn.
— Principal Data Processing Control Clerk. (Career Examination Ser.: C-2485). 1994. pap. 29.95 (*0-8373-2485-8*) Nat Learn.
— Principal Data Processing Equipment Operator. (Career Examination Ser.: C-2303). 1994. reprint ed. pap. 29.95 (*0-8373-2303-7*) Nat Learn.
— Principal Developmental Specialist. (Career Examination Ser.: C-925). 1994. pap. 34.95 (*0-8373-0925-5*) Nat Learn.
— Principal Drafting Technician. (Career Examination Ser.: C-2680). 1994. pap. 29.95 (*0-8373-2680-X*) Nat Learn.
— Principal Draftsman. (Career Examination Ser.: C-1576). 1994. pap. 29.95 (*0-8373-1576-X*) Nat Learn.
— Principal Drug & Alcohol Counselor. (Career Examination Ser.: C-2743). 1994. pap. 34.95 (*0-8373-2743-1*) Nat Learn.
— Principal Editorial Clerk. (Career Examination Ser.: C-2566). 1994. pap. 29.95 (*0-8373-2566-8*) Nat Learn.
— Principal, Elementary School. (Teachers License Examination Ser.: S-3). 1994. pap. 49.95 (*0-8373-8103-7*) Nat Learn.
— Principal Employment Security Clerk. (Career Examination Ser.: C-2352). 1994. pap. 29.95 (*0-8373-2352-5*) Nat Learn.
— Principal Engineering Aide. (Career Examination Ser.: C-1561). 1994. pap. 29.95 (*0-8373-1561-1*) Nat Learn.
— Principal Engineering Inspector. (Career Examination Ser.: C-911). 1994. pap. 39.95 (*0-8373-0911-5*) Nat Learn.
— Principal Engineering Technician. (Career Examination Ser.: C-1425). 1994. pap. 29.95 (*0-8373-1425-9*) Nat Learn.
— Principal Engineering Technician (Drafting) (Career Examination Ser.: C-1954). 1994. pap. 29.95 (*0-8373-1954-4*) Nat Learn.
— Principal Engineering Technician (Environmental Quality) (Career Examination Ser.: C-3239). 1994. pap. 34.95 (*0-8373-3239-7*) Nat Learn.
— Principal Environmental Analyst. (Career Examination Ser.: C-2661). 1994. pap. 39.95 (*0-8373-2661-3*) Nat Learn.
— Principal Environmental Planner. (Career Examination Ser.: C-2664). 1994. pap. 39.95 (*0-8373-2664-8*) Nat Learn.
— Principal Evidence Technician. (Career Examination Ser.: C-2750). 1994. pap. 34.95 (*0-8373-2750-4*) Nat Learn.
— Principal Examiner of Municipal Affairs. (Career Examination Ser.: C-2727). 1994. pap. 44.95 (*0-8373-2727-X*) Nat Learn.
— Principal Executive Officer. (Career Examination Ser.: C-2827). 1994. pap. 39.95 (*0-8373-2827-6*) Nat Learn.
— Principal Field Accountant. (Career Examination Ser.: C-1570). 1994. pap. 34.95 (*0-8373-1570-0*) Nat Learn.
— Principal File Clerk. (Career Examination Ser.: C-659). 1994. pap. 23.95 (*0-8373-0659-0*) Nat Learn.
— Principal Financial Analyst. (Career Examination Ser.: C-2644). 1994. pap. 44.95 (*0-8373-2644-3*) Nat Learn.
— Principal Forestry Technician. (Career Examination Ser.: C-2716). 1994. pap. 29.95 (*0-8373-2716-4*) Nat Learn.
— Principal Grants Analyst. (Career Examination Ser.: C-2835). 1994. pap. 39.95 (*0-8373-2835-7*) Nat Learn.
— Principal Groundskeeper. (Career Examination Ser.: C-1573). 1994. pap. 29.95 (*0-8373-1573-5*) Nat Learn.
— Principal Home Economist. (Career Examination Ser.: C-1627). 1994. pap. 34.95 (*0-8373-1627-8*) Nat Learn.
— Principal Hospital Care Investigator. (Career Examination Ser.: C-612). 1994. pap. 34.95 (*0-8373-0612-4*) Nat Learn.
— Principal Housing Inspector. (Career Examination Ser.: C-1426). 1994. reprint ed. pap. 34.95 (*0-8373-1426-7*) Nat Learn.
— Principal Human Resources Specialist. (Career Examination Ser.: C-974). 1994. pap. 34.95 (*0-8373-0974-3*) Nat Learn.
— Principal Illustrator. (Career Examination Ser.: C-1713). 1994. pap. 34.95 (*0-8373-1713-4*) Nat Learn.
— Principal Insurance Examiner. (Career Examination Ser.: C-2696). 1994. pap. 34.95 (*0-8373-2696-6*) Nat Learn.
— Principal Investigator. (Career Examination Ser.: C-1791). 1994. pap. 34.95 (*0-8373-1791-6*) Nat Learn.
— Principal, Junior High School. (Teachers License Examination Ser.: S-4). 1994. pap. 49.95 (*0-8373-8104-5*) Nat Learn.
— Principal Juvenile Counselor. (Career Examination Ser.: C-422). 1994. pap. 34.95 (*0-8373-0422-9*) Nat Learn.
— Principal Key Punch Operator. (Career Examination Ser.: C-2103). 1994. pap. 27.95 (*0-8373-2103-4*) Nat Learn.
— Principal Labor-Management Practices Adjustor. (Career Examination Ser.: C-613). 1994. pap. 44.95 (*0-8373-0613-2*) Nat Learn.
— Principal Labor Relations Analyst. (Career Examination Ser.: C-2231). 1994. pap. 44.95 (*0-8373-2231-6*) Nat Learn.
— Principal Labor Specialist. (Career Examination Ser.: C-2670). 1994. pap. 39.95 (*0-8373-2670-2*) Nat Learn.
— Principal Laboratory Animal Caretaker. (Career Examination Ser.: Vol. C-3794). 1997. pap. 29.95 (*0-8373-3794-1*) Nat Learn.
— Principal Laboratory Technician. (Career Examination Ser.: C-3014). 1994. pap. 34.95 (*0-8373-3014-9*) Nat Learn.
— Principal Land Management Specialist. (Career Examination Ser.: C-2620). 1994. pap. 39.95 (*0-8373-2620-6*) Nat Learn.
— Principal Librarian. (Career Examination Ser.: C-2915). 1994. pap. 29.95 (*0-8373-2915-9*) Nat Learn.
— Principal Library Clerk. (Career Examination Ser.: C-1932). 1994. pap. 27.95 (*0-8373-1932-3*) Nat Learn.
— Principal Mail & Supply Clerk. (Career Examination Ser.: C-975). 1994. pap. 27.95 (*0-8373-0975-1*) Nat Learn.
— Principal Management Analyst. (Career Examination Ser.: C-1737). 1994. pap. 39.95 (*0-8373-1737-1*) Nat Learn.
— Principal Management Technician. (Career Examination Ser.: C-2753). 1994. pap. 34.95 (*0-8373-2753-9*) Nat Learn.
— Principal Manpower Development Specialist. (Career Examination Ser.: C-2819). 1994. pap. 39.95 (*0-8373-2819-5*) Nat Learn.
— Principal Mechanical Engineer. (Career Examination Ser.: C-3249). 1994. pap. 39.95 (*0-8373-3249-4*) Nat Learn.
— Principal Methods Analyst. (Career Examination Ser.: C-1738). 1994. pap. 39.95 (*0-8373-1738-X*) Nat Learn.
— Principal Motor Vehicle License Examiner. (Career Examination Ser.: Vol. C-3799). 1997. pap. 34.95 (*0-8373-3799-2*) Nat Learn.
— Principal Museum Curator. (Career Examination Ser.: C-2375). 1994. pap. 34.95 (*0-8373-2375-4*) Nat Learn.
— Principal Occupational Analyst. (Career Examination Ser.: C-2535). 1994. pap. 34.95 (*0-8373-2535-8*) Nat Learn.
— Principal Office Assistant. (Career Examination Ser.: C-2595). 1994. pap. 23.95 (*0-8373-2595-1*) Nat Learn.
— Principal Office Stenographer. (Career Examination Ser.: C-3377). 1994. pap. 23.95 (*0-8373-3377-6*) Nat Learn.
— Principal Office Typist. (Career Examination Ser.: C-3375). 1994. pap. 23.95 (*0-8373-3375-X*) Nat Learn.
— Principal Park Supervisor. (Career Examination Ser.: C-2355). 1994. pap. 29.95 (*0-8373-2355-X*) Nat Learn.
— Principal Personnel Administrator. (Career Examination Ser.: C-2411). 1994. pap. 44.95 (*0-8373-2411-4*) Nat Learn.
— Principal Personnel Analyst. (Career Examination Ser.: C-2346). 1994. pap. 39.95 (*0-8373-2346-0*) Nat Learn.
— Principal Personnel Clerk. (Career Examination Ser.: C-2944). 1994. pap. 27.95 (*0-8373-2944-2*) Nat Learn.
— Principal Personnel Examiner. (Career Examination Ser.: C-1915). 1994. pap. 39.95 (*0-8373-1915-3*) Nat Learn.
— Principal Planner. (Career Examination Ser.: C-1764). 1994. reprint ed. pap. 34.95 (*0-8373-1764-9*) Nat Learn.
— Principal Planner (Education) (Career Examination Ser.: C-1669). 1994. pap. 39.95 (*0-8373-1669-3*) Nat Learn.
— Principal Planner (Manpower) (Career Examination Ser.: C-1599). 1994. pap. 39.95 (*0-8373-1599-9*) Nat Learn.
— Principal Probation Officer. (Career Examination Ser.: C-1427). 1994. pap. 29.95 (*0-8373-1427-5*) Nat Learn.
— Principal Program Evaluation Specialist. (Career Examination Ser.: C-2701). 1994. pap. 39.95 (*0-8373-2701-6*) Nat Learn.
— Principal Program Examiner. (Career Examination Ser.: C-2756). 1994. pap. 39.95 (*0-8373-2756-3*) Nat Learn.
— Principal Program Research Analyst. (Career Examination Ser.: C-2218). 1994. reprint ed. pap. 39.95 (*0-8373-2218-9*) Nat Learn.
— Principal Program Specialist. (Career Examination Ser.: C-2863). 1994. pap. 39.95 (*0-8373-2863-2*) Nat Learn.
— Principal Program Specialist (Correction) (Career Examination Ser.: C-2259). 1994. reprint ed. pap. 39.95 (*0-8373-2259-6*) Nat Learn.
— Principal Programmer Analyst. (Career Examination Ser.: C-3739). 1994. pap. 34.95 (*0-8373-3739-9*) Nat Learn.
— Principal Public Health Engineer. (Career Examination Ser.: C-3099). 1994. pap. 39.95 (*0-8373-3099-8*) Nat Learn.
— Principal Public Health Nutritionist. (Career Examination Ser.: C-1566). 1994. pap. 34.95 (*0-8373-1566-2*) Nat Learn.
— Principal Public Health Representative. (Career Examination Ser.: C-3025). 1994. pap. 34.95 (*0-8373-3025-4*) Nat Learn.
— Principal Purchase Inspector. (Career Examination Ser.: C-1747). 1994. reprint ed. pap. 34.95 (*0-8373-1747-9*) Nat Learn.
— Principal Purchasing Agent. (Career Examination Ser.: C-912). 1994. pap. 29.95 (*0-8373-0912-3*) Nat Learn.
— Principal Quantitative Analyst. (Career Examination Ser.: C-1715). 1994. pap. 39.95 (*0-8373-1715-0*) Nat Learn.
— Principal Real Estate Manager. (Career Examination Ser.: C-1628). 1994. pap. 34.95 (*0-8373-1628-6*) Nat Learn.
— Principal Records Center Assistant. (Career Examination Ser.: C-1914). 1994. pap. 29.95 (*0-8373-1914-5*) Nat Learn.
— Principal Rent Examiner. (Career Examination Ser.: C-2093). 1994. reprint ed. pap. 34.95 (*0-8373-2093-3*) Nat Learn.
— Principal Research Analyst. (Career Examination Ser.: C-2353). 1994. pap. 39.95 (*0-8373-2353-3*) Nat Learn.
— Principal Right-Of-Way Aide. (Career Examination Ser.: C-2737). 1994. pap. 29.95 (*0-8373-2737-7*) Nat Learn.
— Principal Safety Coordinator. (Career Examination Ser.: C-2669). 1994. pap. 39.95 (*0-8373-2669-9*) Nat Learn.
— Principal Sanitary Engineer. (Career Examination Ser.: C-1819). 1994. pap. 39.95 (*0-8373-1819-X*) Nat Learn.
— Principal Senior Citizens' Program Coordinator. (Career Examination Ser.: C-2799). 1994. pap. 34.95 (*0-8373-2799-7*) Nat Learn.
— Principal, Six Hundred School. (Teachers License Examination Ser.: S-7). 1994. pap. 49.95 (*0-8373-8107-X*) Nat Learn.
— Principal Social Welfare Examiner. (Career Examination Ser.: C-2495). 1994. pap. 29.95 (*0-8373-2495-5*) Nat Learn.
— Principal Special Investigator. (Career Examination Ser.: C-1590). 1994. pap. 34.95 (*0-8373-1590-5*) Nat Learn.
— Principal Special Officer. (Career Examination Ser.: C-3420). 1994. pap. 29.95 (*0-8373-3420-9*) Nat Learn.
— Principal Staff Development Specialist. (Career Examination Ser.: C-2703). 1994. pap. 39.95 (*0-8373-2703-2*) Nat Learn.
— Principal Stationary Engineer. (Career Examination Ser.: C-1719). 1994. pap. 39.95 (*0-8373-1719-3*) Nat Learn.
— Principal Statistician. (Career Examination Ser.: C-976). 1994. pap. 39.95 (*0-8373-0976-X*) Nat Learn.
— Principal Statistics Clerk. (Career Examination Ser.: C-977). 1994. pap. 27.95 (*0-8373-0977-8*) Nat Learn.
— Principal Stenographer. (Career Examination Ser.: C-614). 1994. pap. 23.95 (*0-8373-0614-0*) Nat Learn.
— Principal Stenographer (Law) (Career Examination Ser.: C-3294). 1994. pap. 27.95 (*0-8373-3294-X*) Nat Learn.
— Principal Storekeeper. (Career Examination Ser.: C-3013). 1994. pap. 29.95 (*0-8373-3013-0*) Nat Learn.
— Principal Stores Clerk. (Career Examination Ser.: C-978). 1994. pap. 27.95 (*0-8373-0978-6*) Nat Learn.
— Principal Systems Analyst. (Career Examination Ser.: C-2388). 1994. pap. 39.95 (*0-8373-2388-6*) Nat Learn.
— Principal Tax Compliance Agent. (Career Examination Ser.: C-2954). 1994. pap. 34.95 (*0-8373-2954-X*) Nat Learn.
— Principal Telephone Operator. (Career Examination Ser.: C-2493). 1994. pap. 27.95 (*0-8373-2493-9*) Nat Learn.
— Principal Typist. (Career Examination Ser.: C-615). 1994. pap. 23.95 (*0-8373-0615-9*) Nat Learn.
— Principal Unemployment Insurance Hearing Representative. (Career Examination Ser.: C-2730). 1994. pap. 34.95 (*0-8373-2730-X*) Nat Learn.
— Principal Unemployment Insurance Investigator. (Career Examination Ser.: C-2831). 1994. pap. 34.95 (*0-8373-2831-4*) Nat Learn.
— Principal, Vocational High School. (Teachers License Examination Ser.: S-6). 1994. pap. 49.95 (*0-8373-8106-1*) Nat Learn.
— Principal Water Plant Supervisor. (Career Examination Ser.: C-2960). 1994. pap. 34.95 (*0-8373-2960-4*) Nat Learn.
— Principal Workers' Compensation Review Analyst. (Career Examination Ser.: C-310). 1994. pap. 34.95 (*0-8373-0310-9*) Nat Learn.
— Principal Workmen's Compensation Examiner. (Career Examination Ser.: C-1548). 1994. pap. 34.95 (*0-8373-1548-4*) Nat Learn.
— Principal X-Ray Technician. (Career Examination Ser.: C-979). 1994. pap. 29.95 (*0-8373-0979-4*) Nat Learn.
— Principal, Youth & Adult Center. (Teachers License Examination Ser.: S-8). 1994. pap. 49.95 (*0-8373-8108-8*) Nat Learn.
— Principal Zoning Inspector. (Career Examination Ser.: C-2854). 1994. pap. 34.95 (*0-8373-2854-3*) Nat Learn.
— Principles of Economics. (Dantes Subject Standardized Tests Ser.: DANTES-32). 1994. pap. 23.95 (*0-8373-6632-1*) Nat Learn.
— Principles of Economics. (DANTES Ser.: No. 32). 1994. 39.95 (*0-8373-6532-5*) Nat Learn.
— Principles of Electronic Communication Systems. (Dantes Subject Standardized Tests Ser.: DANTES-44). 1994. pap. 23.95 (*0-8373-6644-5*) Nat Learn.
— Principles of Finance. (Dantes Subject Standardized Tests (DANTES) Ser.: Vol. 46). 43.95 (*0-8373-6546-5*) Nat Learn.
— Principles of Finance. (Dantes Subject Standardized Tests Ser.: DANTES-46). 1994. pap. 23.95 (*0-8373-6646-1*) Nat Learn.
— Principles of Financial Accounting. (Dantes Subject Standardized Tests (DANTES) Ser.: Vol. 47). 43.95 (*0-8373-6547-3*) Nat Learn.
— Principles of Financial Accounting. (Dantes Subject Standardized Tests Ser.: DANTES-47). 1994. pap. 23.95 (*0-8373-6647-X*) Nat Learn.
— Principles of Guidance. (Dantes Subject Standardized Tests Ser.: DANTES-33). 1994. pap. 23.95 (*0-8373-6633-X*) Nat Learn.
— Principles of Guidance. (DANTES Ser.: No. 33). 1994. 39.95 (*0-8373-6533-3*) Nat Learn.
— Principles of Management (Human Resources) (ACT Proficiency Examination Program (PEP) Ser.: Vol. 18). 43.95 (*0-8373-5568-0*) Nat Learn.
— Principles of Management (Human Resources) (ACT Proficiency Examination Program Ser.: PEP-18). 1994. pap. 23.95 (*0-8373-5518-4*) Nat Learn.
— Principles of Marketing. (ACT Proficiency Examination Program (PEP) Ser.: Vol. 21). 43.95 (*0-8373-5571-0*) Nat Learn.
— Principles of Marketing. (ACT Proficiency Examination Program Ser.: PEP-21). 1994. pap. 23.95 (*0-8373-5521-4*) Nat Learn.
— Principles of Public Speaking. (Dantes Subject Standardized Tests (DANTES) Ser.: Vol. DANTES-59). pap. 23.95 (*0-8373-6659-3*) Nat Learn.
— Principles of Refrigeration. (Dantes Subject Standardized Tests (DANTES) Ser.: Vol. 45). 43.95 (*0-8373-6545-7*) Nat Learn.
— Principles of Refrigeration. (Dantes Subject Standardized Tests Ser.: DANTES-45). 1994. pap. 23.95 (*0-8373-6645-3*) Nat Learn.
— Printer. (Career Examination Ser.: C-616). 1994. pap. 23.95 (*0-8373-0616-7*) Nat Learn.
— Printer-Proofreader. (Career Examination Ser.: C-617). 1994. pap. 29.95 (*0-8373-0617-5*) Nat Learn.
— Prison Guard. (Career Examination Ser.: C-618). 1984. pap. 23.95 (*0-8373-0618-3*) Nat Learn.
— Private Investigator. (Career Examination Ser.: C-2462). 1994. pap. 27.95 (*0-8373-2462-9*) Nat Learn.
— Probation Assistant. (Career Examination Ser.: C-2577). 1994. pap. 27.95 (*0-8373-2577-3*) Nat Learn.
— Probation Consultant. (Career Examination Ser.: C-980). 1994. pap. 29.95 (*0-8373-0980-8*) Nat Learn.
— Probation Counselor. (Career Examination Ser.: C-1981). 1994. pap. 29.95 (*0-8373-1981-1*) Nat Learn.
— Probation Director. (Career Examination Ser.: C-2266). 1994. reprint ed. pap. 39.95 (*0-8373-2266-9*) Nat Learn.
— Probation Employment Officer. (Career Examination Ser.: C-1428). 1994. pap. 29.95 (*0-8373-1428-3*) Nat Learn.
— Probation Investigator. (Career Examination Ser.: C-981). 1994. pap. 29.95 (*0-8373-0981-6*) Nat Learn.
— Probation Officer. (Career Examination Ser.: C-619). 1994. pap. 27.95 (*0-8373-0619-1*) Nat Learn.
— Probation Officer Trainee. (Career Examination Ser.: C-1429). 1994. pap. 23.95 (*0-8373-1429-1*) Nat Learn.
— Probation Supervisor. (Career Examination Ser.: C-2262). 1994. reprint ed. pap. 29.95 (*0-8373-2262-6*) Nat Learn.
— Probation Supervisor I. (Career Examination Ser.: C-1828). 1994. pap. 29.95 (*0-8373-1828-9*) Nat Learn.
— Probation Supervisor II. (Career Examination Ser.: C-1829). 1994. pap. 29.95 (*0-8373-1829-7*) Nat Learn.
— Probation Training Director. (Career Examination Ser.: C-3283). 1994. pap. 39.95 (*0-8373-3283-4*) Nat Learn.
— Process Server. (Career Examination Ser.: C-620). 1994. pap. 23.95 (*0-8373-0620-5*) Nat Learn.
— Processing Technician. (Career Examination Ser.: C-3534). 1994. pap. 27.95 (*0-8373-3534-5*) Nat Learn.
— Procurement Agent. (Career Examination Ser.: C-621). 1994. pap. 23.95 (*0-8373-0621-3*) Nat Learn.
— Procurement Clerk. (Career Examination Ser.: C-2623). 1994. pap. 23.95 (*0-8373-2623-0*) Nat Learn.
— Procurement Coordinator. (Career Examination Ser.: C-2368). 1994. pap. 34.95 (*0-8373-2368-1*) Nat Learn.
— Procurement Supervisor. (Career Examination Ser.: C-2711). 1994. pap. 29.95 (*0-8373-2711-3*) Nat Learn.
— Production - Operations Management. (ACT Proficiency Examination Program (PEP) Ser.: Vol. 24). 43.95 (*0-8373-5574-5*) Nat Learn.
— Production-Operations Management. (ACT Proficiency Examination Program Ser.: PEP-24). 1994. pap. 23.95 (*0-8373-5524-9*, PEP-24) Nat Learn.
— Professional & Administrative Career Examination (PACE) (Admission Test Ser.). 43.95 (*0-8373-5126-X*) Nat Learn.
— Professional & Administrative Career Examination (PACE) (General Aptitude & Abilities Ser.: No. CS-28). pap. 23.95 (*0-8373-6728-X*, CS-28) Nat Learn.
— Professional & Administrative Career Examination (PACE) (Admission Test Ser.: Vol. ATS-26). 1994. pap. 23.95 (*0-8373-5026-3*) Nat Learn.
— Professional Careers in Administrative & Technical Services. (Career Examination Ser.: C-2068). 1994. pap. 23.95 (*0-8373-2068-2*) Nat Learn.
— Professional Careers in the Natural Sciences. (Career Examination Ser.: C-2386). 1994. pap. 23.95 (*0-8373-2386-X*) Nat Learn.
— Professional Careers Test (PCT) (Career Examination Ser.: C-622). 1994. pap. 23.95 (*0-8373-0622-1*) Nat Learn.
— Professional Conduct Investigator. (Career Examination Ser.: C-2315). 1994. reprint ed. pap. 27.95 (*0-8373-2315-0*) Nat Learn.
— Professional Engineer (PE) (Admission Test Ser.: Vol. 35). 89.95 (*0-8373-5135-9*) Nat Learn.
— Professional Engineer (PE) (Admission Test Ser.: ATS-35). 1994. pap. 69.95 (*0-8373-5035-2*) Nat Learn.
— Professional Entry Test (PET) (Career Examination Ser.: C-3404). 1994. pap. 23.95 (*0-8373-3404-7*) Nat Learn.

R

— Professional Knowledge (Combined) (National Teacher Examination Ser.: NC-7). 1994. pap. 23.95 (*0-8373-8467-2*) Nat Learn.
— Professional Library Examination. (Career Examination Ser.: C-623). 1994. pap. 29.95 (*0-8373-0623-X*) Nat Learn.
— Professional Nurse. (Career Examination Ser.: C-624). 1994. pap. 29.95 (*0-8373-0624-8*) Nat Learn.
— Professional Strategies, Nursing. (ACT Proficiency Examination Program (PEP) Ser.: Vol. 50). 43.95 (*0-8373-5925-2*) Nat Learn.
— Professional Strategies, Nursing. (ACT Proficiency Examination Program Ser.: PEP-50). 1994. pap. 23.95 (*0-8373-5900-7*) Nat Learn.
— Professional Strategies, Nursing. (Regents External Degree (REDP) Ser.: Vol. REDP-26). 1994. pap. 23.95 (*0-8373-5626-1*) Nat Learn.
— Professional Strategies (Nursing) (Regents External Degree (REDP) Ser.: Vol. 26). 43.95 (*0-8373-5676-8*) Nat Learn.
— Professional Trainee. (Career Examination Ser.: C-625). 1994. pap. 23.95 (*0-8373-0625-6*) Nat Learn.
— Program Administrator. (Career Examination Ser.: C-2868). 1994. pap. 34.95 (*0-8373-2868-3*) Nat Learn.
— Program Evaluation Specialist. (Career Examination Ser.: C-2699). 1994. pap. 34.95 (*0-8373-2699-0*) Nat Learn.
— Program Examiner. (Career Examination Ser.: C-2655). 1994. pap. 34.95 (*0-8373-2655-9*) Nat Learn.
— Program Manager. (Career Examination Ser.: C-985). 1994. pap. 34.95 (*0-8373-0985-9*) Nat Learn.
— Program Outreach Specialist. (Career Examination Ser.: C-3405). 1994. pap. 29.95 (*0-8373-3405-5*) Nat Learn.
— Program Research Analyst. (Career Examination Ser.: C-1704). 1994. pap. 34.95 (*0-8373-1704-5*) Nat Learn.
— Program Research Specialist. (Career Examination Ser.: C-3200). 1994. pap. 34.95 (*0-8373-3200-1*) Nat Learn.
— Program Specialist. (Career Examination Ser.: C-2861). 1994. pap. 34.95 (*0-8373-2861-6*) Nat Learn.
— Program Specialist (Aging Services) (Career Examination Ser.: C-2820). 1994. pap. 29.95 (*0-8373-2820-9*) Nat Learn.
— Program Specialist (Correction) (Career Examination Ser.: C-1997). 1994. pap. 34.95 (*0-8373-1997-8*) Nat Learn.
— Programmer. (Career Examination Ser.: C-1430). 1994. pap. 27.95 (*0-8373-1430-5*) Nat Learn.
— Programmer Aptitude Test (PAT) (Career Examination Ser.: C-643). 1994. pap. 23.95 (*0-8373-0643-4*) Nat Learn.
— Programmer Trainee. (Career Examination Ser.: C-1431). 1994. pap. 23.95 (*0-8373-1431-3*) Nat Learn.
— Programmer/Programmer Analyst. (Career Examination Ser.: C-1439). 1994. pap. 27.95 (*0-8373-1439-9*) Nat Learn.
— Project Coordinator. (Career Examination Ser.: C-2589). 1994. pap. 29.95 (*0-8373-2589-7*) Nat Learn.
— Project Development Coordinator. (Career Examination Ser.: C-1432). 1994. pap. 29.95 (*0-8373-1432-1*) Nat Learn.
— Project Manager. (Career Examination Ser.: C-1433). 1994. pap. 29.95 (*0-8373-1433-X*) Nat Learn.
— Project Services Specialist. (Career Examination Ser.: C-1660). 1994. pap. 29.95 (*0-8373-1660-X*) Nat Learn.
— Promotion Test Battery. (Career Examination Ser.: Vol. C-3815). 1997. pap. 29.95 (*0-8373-3815-8*) Nat Learn.
— Property Clerk. (Career Examination Ser.: C-3465). 1994. pap. 23.95 (*0-8373-3465-9*) Nat Learn.
— Psychiatric - Mental Health Nursing. (Regents College Proficiency Examination Ser.: Vol. 34). 43.95 (*0-8373-5484-6*) Nat Learn.
— Psychiatric - Mental Health Nursing. (ACT Proficiency Examination Program (PEP) Ser.: Vol. 40). 43.95 (*0-8373-5590-7*) Nat Learn.
— Psychiatric & Mental Health Nurse. (Certified Nurse Examination Ser.: CN-12). 1994. pap. 23.95 (*0-8373-6112-5*) Nat Learn.
— Psychiatric Attendant. (Career Examination Ser.: C-1434). 1994. pap. 23.95 (*0-8373-1434-8*) Nat Learn.
— Psychiatric-Mental Health Nursing. (Regents College Proficiency Examination Ser.: CPEP-34). 1994. pap. 23.95 (*0-8373-5434-X*) Nat Learn.
— Psychiatric-Mental Health Nursing. (ACT Proficiency Examination Program (PEP) Ser.: Vol. PEP-40). 1994. pap. 23.95 (*0-8373-5540-0*) Nat Learn.
— Psychiatric Nurse. (Career Examination Ser.: C-986). 1994. pap. 29.95 (*0-8373-0986-7*) Nat Learn.
— Psychiatric Senior Attendant. (Career Examination Ser.: C-1435). 1994. pap. 27.95 (*0-8373-1435-6*) Nat Learn.
— Psychiatric Social Work Assistant. (Career Examination Ser.: C-2414). 1994. pap. 27.95 (*0-8373-2414-9*) Nat Learn.
— Psychiatric Social Work Supervisor. (Career Examination Ser.: C-2357). 1994. pap. 34.95 (*0-8373-2357-6*) Nat Learn.
— Psychiatric Social Worker. (Career Examination Ser.: C-987). 1994. pap. 29.95 (*0-8373-0987-5*) Nat Learn.
— Psychiatric Social Worker Trainee. (Career Examination Ser.: C-988). 1994. pap. 23.95 (*0-8373-0988-3*) Nat Learn.
— Psychiatric Staff Attendant. (Career Examination Ser.: C-1436). 1994. pap. 23.95 (*0-8373-1436-4*) Nat Learn.
— Psychiatric Therapy Aide. (Career Examination Ser.: C-2124). 1994. reprint ed. pap. 23.95 (*0-8373-2124-7*) Nat Learn.
— Psychiatrist. (Career Examination Ser.: C-626). 1994. pap. 49.95 (*0-8373-0626-4*) Nat Learn.
— Psychologist. (Career Examination Ser.: C-627). 1994. pap. 34.95 (*0-8373-0627-2*) Nat Learn.
— Psychologist Trainee. (Career Examination Ser.: C-2621). 1994. pap. 29.95 (*0-8373-2621-4*) Nat Learn.
— Psychology. (Graduate Record Examination (GRE) Ser.: Vol. 17). 43.95 (*0-8373-5267-3*) Nat Learn.
— Psychology. (Undergraduate Program Field Tests (UPFT) Ser.: Vol. 21). 43.95 (*0-8373-6071-4*) Nat Learn.
— Psychology. (Graduate Record Examination Ser.: GRE-17). 1994. pap. 23.95 (*0-8373-5217-7*) Nat Learn.
— Psychology. (National Teacher Examination (NTE) Ser.: Vol. NT-42). 1994. pap. 23.95 (*0-8373-8452-4*) Nat Learn.
— Psychology. (Undergraduate Program Field Tests (UPFT) Ser.: Vol. UPFT-21). 1994. pap. 23.95 (*0-8373-6021-8*) Nat Learn.
— Psychology Assistant. (Career Examination Ser.: C-1774). 1994. pap. 29.95 (*0-8373-1774-6*) Nat Learn.
— Psychology Assistant I. (Career Examination Ser.: C-919). 1994. pap. 29.95 (*0-8373-0919-0*) Nat Learn.
— Psychology Assistant III. (Career Examination Ser.: C-922). 1994. pap. 34.95 (*0-8373-0922-0*) Nat Learn.
— Psychology Assistant II. (Career Examination Ser.: C-921). 1994. pap. 34.95 (*0-8373-0921-2*) Nat Learn.
— Psychology of Adjustment. (Dantes Subject Standardized Tests Ser.: DANTES-34). 1994. pap. 23.95 (*0-8373-6634-8*) Nat Learn.
— Psychology of Adjustment. (DANTES Ser.: No. 34). 1994. 39.95 (*0-8373-6534-1*) Nat Learn.
— Psychometrician. (Career Examination Ser.: C-1830). 1994. pap. 39.95 (*0-8373-1830-0*) Nat Learn.
— Public Administration Intern. (Career Examination Ser.: C-628). 1994. pap. 23.95 (*0-8373-0628-0*) Nat Learn.
— Public Administrator. (Career Examination Ser.: C-1440). 1994. pap. 29.95 (*0-8373-1440-2*) Nat Learn.
— Public Buildings Manager. (Career Examination Ser.: C-2719). 1994. pap. 29.95 (*0-8373-2719-9*) Nat Learn.
— Public Health Administrator. (Career Examination Ser.: C-2082). 1994. reprint ed. pap. 39.95 (*0-8373-2082-8*) Nat Learn.
— Public Health Adviser. (Career Examination Ser.: C-3093). 1994. pap. 27.95 (*0-8373-3093-9*) Nat Learn.
— Public Health Aide. (Career Examination Ser.: C-1441). 1994. pap. 23.95 (*0-8373-1441-0*) Nat Learn.
— Public Health Aide I. (Career Examination Ser.: C-2334). 1994. pap. 27.95 (*0-8373-2334-7*) Nat Learn.
— Public Health Aide II. (Career Examination Ser.: C-1812). 1994. pap. 29.95 (*0-8373-1812-2*) Nat Learn.
— Public Health Assistant. (Career Examination Ser.: C-629). 1994. pap. 23.95 (*0-8373-0629-9*) Nat Learn.
— Public Health Consultant. (Career Examination Ser.: C-312). 1994. pap. 34.95 (*0-8373-0312-5*) Nat Learn.
— Public Health Director. (Career Examination Ser.: C-2240). 1994. pap. 39.95 (*0-8373-2240-5*) Nat Learn.
— Public Health Education Trainee. (Career Examination Ser.: C-983). 1994. pap. 27.95 (*0-8373-0983-2*) Nat Learn.
— Public Health Educator. (Career Examination Ser.: C-630). 1994. pap. 29.95 (*0-8373-0630-2*) Nat Learn.
— Public Health Educator 1. (Career Examination Ser.: C-2354). 1994. pap. 34.95 (*0-8373-2354-1*) Nat Learn.
— Public Health Engineer. (Career Examination Ser.: C-1979). 1994. pap. 29.95 (*0-8373-1979-X*) Nat Learn.
— Public Health Engineer Trainee. (Career Examination Ser.: C-1881). 1994. pap. 27.95 (*0-8373-1881-5*) Nat Learn.
— Public Health Epidemiologist. (Career Examination Ser.: C-2246). 1994. pap. 34.95 (*0-8373-2246-4*) Nat Learn.
— Public Health Inspector. (Career Examination Ser.: C-1753). 1994. pap. 29.95 (*0-8373-1753-3*) Nat Learn.
— Public Health Nurse. (Career Examination Ser.: C-631). 1994. pap. 27.95 (*0-8373-0631-0*) Nat Learn.
— Public Health Nutritionist. (Career Examination Ser.: C-632). 1994. pap. 27.95 (*0-8373-0632-9*) Nat Learn.
— Public Health Representative. (Career Examination Ser.: C-2369). 1994. pap. 27.95 (*0-8373-2369-X*) Nat Learn.
— Public Health Representative I. (Career Examination Ser.: C-2972). 1994. pap. 27.95 (*0-8373-2972-8*) Nat Learn.
— Public Health Representative II. (Career Examination Ser.: C-2973). 1994. pap. 29.95 (*0-8373-2973-6*) Nat Learn.
— Public Health Sanitarian. (Career Examination Ser.: C-633). 1994. pap. 27.95 (*0-8373-0633-7*) Nat Learn.
— Public Health Sanitarian Trainee. (Career Examination Ser.: C-984). 1994. pap. 23.95 (*0-8373-0984-0*) Nat Learn.
— Public Health Scientist. (Career Examination Ser.: C-634). 1994. pap. 34.95 (*0-8373-0634-5*) Nat Learn.
— Public Health Social Work Assistant. (Career Examination Ser.: C-1442). 1994. pap. 27.95 (*0-8373-1442-9*) Nat Learn.
— Public Health Technician. (Career Examination Ser.: C-2226). 1994. pap. 27.95 (*0-8373-2226-X*) Nat Learn.
— Public Information Assistant. (Career Examination Ser.: C-2956). 1994. pap. 27.95 (*0-8373-2956-6*) Nat Learn.
— Public Information Officer. (Career Examination Ser.: C-2950). 1994. pap. 29.95 (*0-8373-2950-7*) Nat Learn.
— Public Information Specialist. (Career Examination Ser.: C-2111). 1994. pap. 29.95 (*0-8373-2111-5*) Nat Learn.
— Public Librarian. (Career Examination Ser.: C-989). 1994. pap. 27.95 (*0-8373-0989-1*) Nat Learn.
— Public Relations Assistant. (Career Examination Ser.: C-635). 1994. pap. 27.95 (*0-8373-0635-3*) Nat Learn.
— Public Relations Director. (Career Examination Ser.: C-1901). 1994. pap. 34.95 (*0-8373-1901-3*) Nat Learn.
— Public Relations Specialist. (Career Examination Ser.: C-2934). 1994. pap. 29.95 (*0-8373-2934-5*) Nat Learn.
— Public Safety Aide. (Career Examination Ser.: C-3740). 1994. pap. 23.95 (*0-8373-3740-2*) Nat Learn.
— Public Safety Dispatcher I. (Career Examination Ser.: C-116). 1994. pap. 23.95 (*0-8373-0116-5*) Nat Learn.
— Public Safety Dispatcher II. (Career Examination Ser.: C-117). 1994. pap. 27.95 (*0-8373-0117-3*) Nat Learn.
— Public Safety Officer IV. (Career Examination Ser.: C-3053). 1994. pap. 29.95 (*0-8373-3053-X*) Nat Learn.
— Public Safety Officer I. (Career Examination Ser.: C-2895). 1994. pap. 23.95 (*0-8373-2895-0*) Nat Learn.
— Public Safety Officer III. (Career Examination Ser.: C-2897). 1994. pap. 29.95 (*0-8373-2897-7*) Nat Learn.
— Public Safety Officer II. (Career Examination Ser.: C-2896). 1994. pap. 27.95 (*0-8373-2896-9*) Nat Learn.
— Public Services Officer. (Career Examination Ser.: C-636). 1994. pap. 29.95 (*0-8373-0636-1*) Nat Learn.
— Public Work Wage Investigator. (Career Examination Ser.: C-990). 1994. pap. 29.95 (*0-8373-0990-5*) Nat Learn.
— Publications Editor. (Career Examination Ser.: C-3146). 1994. pap. 29.95 (*0-8373-3146-3*) Nat Learn.
— Pump Station Operator. (Career Examination Ser.: C-2442). 1994. pap. 27.95 (*0-8373-2442-4*) Nat Learn.
— Purchase Inspector. (Career Examination Ser.: C-637). 1994. pap. 27.95 (*0-8373-0637-X*) Nat Learn.
— Purchase Inspector (Shop Steel) (Career Examination Ser.: C-2258). 1994. reprint ed. pap. 29.95 (*0-8373-2258-8*) Nat Learn.
— Purchase Specifications Assistant. (Career Examination Ser.: C-2542). 1994. pap. 23.95 (*0-8373-2542-0*) Nat Learn.
— Purchasing Agent. (Career Examination Ser.: C-638). 1994. pap. 23.95 (*0-8373-0638-8*) Nat Learn.
— Purchasing Agent (Food) (Career Examination Ser.: C-2731). 1994. pap. 27.95 (*0-8373-2731-8*) Nat Learn.
— Purchasing Agent (Lumber) (Career Examination Ser.: C-2732). 1994. pap. 27.95 (*0-8373-2732-6*) Nat Learn.
— Purchasing Agent (Medical) (Career Examination Ser.: C-2733). 1994. pap. 27.95 (*0-8373-2733-4*) Nat Learn.
— Purchasing Agent (Printing) (Career Examination Ser.: C-2734). 1994. pap. 27.95 (*0-8373-2734-2*) Nat Learn.
— Purchasing Supervisor. (Career Examination Ser.: C-2720). 1994. pap. 29.95 (*0-8373-2720-2*) Nat Learn.
— Purchasing Technician. (Career Examination Ser.: C-913). 1994. pap. 23.95 (*0-8373-0913-1*) Nat Learn.
— Q & A on Drug Education. (General Aptitude & Abilities Ser.: CS-24). 1994. pap. 29.95 (*0-8373-6724-7*) Nat Learn.
— Q & A on the Real Estate License Examinations (RE) (Admission Test Ser.: ATS-6). 1994. pap. 23.95 (*0-8373-5006-9*) Nat Learn.
— Q. & A. on the Real Estate License Examinations (RE) (Admission Test Ser.: Vol. 6). 43.95 (*0-8373-5106-5*) Nat Learn.
— Qualifying Examination/Management Service. (General Aptitude & Abilities Ser.: CS-39). 1994. pap. 29.95 (*0-8373-6739-5*) Nat Learn.
— Quality Assurance Nurse. (Career Examination Ser.: C-3742). 1994. pap. 29.95 (*0-8373-3742-9*) Nat Learn.
— Quality Control Inspector (U. S. P. S.) (Career Examination Ser.: C-2458). 1994. pap. 39.95 (*0-8373-2458-0*) Nat Learn.
— Quality Control Investigator. (Career Examination Ser.: C-2137). 1994. pap. 34.95 (*0-8373-2137-9*) Nat Learn.
— Quality Control Specialist. (Career Examination Ser.: C-1618). 1994. pap. 34.95 (*0-8373-1618-9*) Nat Learn.
— Quantitative Analyst. (Career Examination Ser.: C-1714). 1994. pap. 29.95 (*0-8373-1714-2*) Nat Learn.
— Quantity Food Preparation. (Occupational Competency Examination (OCE) Ser.: Vol. 30). 47.95 (*0-8373-5780-2*) Nat Learn.
— Quantity Food Preparation. (Occupational Competency Examination Ser.: OCE-30). 1994. pap. 27.95 (*0-8373-5730-6*) Nat Learn.
— Racing & Wagering Assistant. (Career Examination Ser.: C-2714). 1994. pap. 23.95 (*0-8373-2714-8*) Nat Learn.
— Radiation Technician. (Career Examination Ser.: C-681). 1994. pap. 29.95 (*0-8373-0681-7*) Nat Learn.
— Radio & Telegraph Operator. (Career Examination Ser.: C-1443). 1994. pap. 27.95 (*0-8373-1443-7*) Nat Learn.
— Radio & Television Engineer. (Career Examination Ser.: C-1444). 1994. pap. 29.95 (*0-8373-1444-5*) Nat Learn.
— Radio & Television Mechanic. (Career Examination Ser.: C-1445). 1994. pap. 27.95 (*0-8373-1445-3*) Nat Learn.
— Radio & Television Technician. (Career Examination Ser.: C-1446). 1994. pap. 27.95 (*0-8373-1446-1*) Nat Learn.
— Radio Broadcast Technician. (Career Examination Ser.: C-682). 1994. pap. 27.95 (*0-8373-0682-5*) Nat Learn.
— Radio Dispatcher. (Career Examination Ser.: C-540). 1994. pap. 23.95 (*0-8373-0540-3*) Nat Learn.
— Radio Mechanic. (Career Examination Ser.: C-660). 1994. pap. 27.95 (*0-8373-0660-4*) Nat Learn.
— Radio Operator. (Career Examination Ser.: C-683). 1994. pap. 27.95 (*0-8373-0683-3*) Nat Learn.
— Radio Servicing. (Dantes Subject Standardized Tests Ser.: DANTES-35). 1994. pap. 23.95 (*0-8373-6635-6*) Nat Learn.
— Radio Station Manager. (Career Examination Ser.: C-2935). 1994. pap. 34.95 (*0-8373-2935-3*) Nat Learn.
— Radio Technologist. (Career Examination Ser.: C-1957). 1994. pap. 27.95 (*0-8373-1957-9*) Nat Learn.
— Radio Telephone Operator. (Career Examination Ser.: C-2883). 1994. pap. 27.95 (*0-8373-2883-7*) Nat Learn.
— Radiologic Technologist. (Career Examination Ser.: C-1544). 1994. pap. 29.95 (*0-8373-1544-1*) Nat Learn.
— Radiological Health Specialist. (Career Examination Ser.: C-3118). 1994. pap. 34.95 (*0-8373-3118-8*) Nat Learn.
— Radiological Officer. (Career Examination Ser.: C-3406). 1994. pap. 34.95 (*0-8373-3406-3*) Nat Learn.
— Radiologist. (Career Examination Ser.: C-1447). 1994. pap. 39.95 (*0-8373-1447-X*) Nat Learn.
— Railroad Caretaker. (Career Examination Ser.: C-684). 1994. pap. 23.95 (*0-8373-0684-1*) Nat Learn.
— Railroad Clerk. (Career Examination Ser.: C-661). 1994. pap. 23.95 (*0-8373-0661-2*) Nat Learn.
— Railroad Equipment Inspector. (Career Examination Ser.: C-210). 1994. pap. 27.95 (*0-8373-0210-2*) Nat Learn.
— Railroad Inspector. (Career Examination Ser.: C-685). 1994. pap. 27.95 (*0-8373-0685-X*) Nat Learn.
— Railroad Porter. (Career Examination Ser.: C-662). 1994. pap. 23.95 (*0-8373-0662-0*) Nat Learn.
— Railroad Signal Specialist. (Career Examination Ser.: C-663). 1994. pap. 27.95 (*0-8373-0663-9*) Nat Learn.
— Railroad Stock Assistant. (Career Examination Ser.: C-1448). 1994. pap. 23.95 (*0-8373-1448-8*) Nat Learn.
— Railroad Stockman. (Career Examination Ser.: C-664). 1994. pap. 23.95 (*0-8373-0664-7*) Nat Learn.
— Railroad Track & Structure Inspector. (Career Examination Ser.: C-209). 1994. pap. 27.95 (*0-8373-0209-9*) Nat Learn.
— Range Conservationist. (Career Examination Ser.: C-686). 1994. pap. 29.95 (*0-8373-0686-8*) Nat Learn.
— Ranger, U. S. Park Service. (Career Examination Ser.: C-665). 1994. pap. 27.95 (*0-8373-0665-5*) Nat Learn.
— Reading Instruction: Application. (ACT Proficiency Examination Program (PEP) Ser.: Vol. 25). 43.95 (*0-8373-5575-3*) Nat Learn.
— Reading Instruction: Application. (ACT Proficiency Examination Program Ser.: PEP-25). 1994. pap. 23.95 (*0-8373-5525-7*) Nat Learn.
— Reading Instruction: Theoretical Foundations. (ACT Proficiency Examination Program (PEP) Ser.: Vol. 26). 43.95 (*0-8373-5576-1*) Nat Learn.
— Reading Instruction: Theoretical Foundations. (ACT Proficiency Examination Program Ser.: PEP-26). 1994. pap. 23.95 (*0-8373-5526-5*) Nat Learn.
— Reading Instruction in the Elementary School. (Regents College Proficiency Examination Ser.: Vol. 25). 43.95 (*0-8373-5475-7*) Nat Learn.
— Reading Instruction in the Elementary School. (ACT Proficiency Examination Program (PEP) Ser.: Vol. 31). 43.95 (*0-8373-5581-8*) Nat Learn.
— Reading Instruction in the Elementary School. (Regents College Proficiency Examination Ser.: CPEP-25). 1994. pap. 23.95 (*0-8373-5425-0*) Nat Learn.
— Reading Instruction in the Elementary School. (ACT Proficiency Examination Program (PEP) Ser.: Vol. PEP-31). 1994. pap. 23.95 (*0-8373-5531-1*) Nat Learn.
— Reading Interpretation in Social Studies, Natural Sciences, & Literature (G. E. D.) (General Aptitude & Abilities Ser.: CS-34). 1994. pap. 17.95 (*0-8373-6734-4*) Nat Learn.
— Reading Specialist. (National Teacher Examination Ser.: NT-30). 1994. pap. 23.95 (*0-8373-8440-0*) Nat Learn.
— Real Estate Agent. (Career Examination Ser.: C-2179). 1994. pap. 23.95 (*0-8373-2179-4*) Nat Learn.
— Real Estate Aide. (Career Examination Ser.: C-687). 1994. pap. 23.95 (*0-8373-0687-6*) Nat Learn.
— Real Estate Appraiser. (Career Examination Ser.: C-1640). 1994. reprint ed. pap. 23.95 (*0-8373-1640-5*) Nat Learn.
— Real Estate Assistant. (Career Examination Ser.: C-688). 1994. pap. 23.95 (*0-8373-0688-4*) Nat Learn.
— Real Estate Broker. (Admission Test Ser.: ATS-3). 1994. pap. 23.95 (*0-8373-5003-4*) Nat Learn.
— Real Estate Broker. (Career Examination Ser.: C-666). 1994. pap. 23.95 (*0-8373-0666-3*) Nat Learn.
— Real Estate Broker (REB) (Admission Test Ser.: Vol. 3). 43.95 (*0-8373-5103-0*) Nat Learn.
— Real Estate Management Trainee. (Career Examination Ser.: C-667). 1994. pap. 23.95 (*0-8373-0667-1*) Nat Learn.
— Real Estate Manager. (Career Examination Ser.: C-689). 1994. pap. 29.95 (*0-8373-0689-2*) Nat Learn.
— Real Estate Salesman. (Admission Test Ser.: ATS-4). 1994. pap. 23.95 (*0-8373-5004-2*) Nat Learn.
— Real Estate Salesman. (Career Examination Ser.: C-668). 1994. pap. 23.95 (*0-8373-0668-X*) Nat Learn.
— Real Estate Salesman (RES) (Admission Test Ser.: Vol. 4). 43.95 (*0-8373-5104-9*) Nat Learn.
— Real Property Appraisal Technician. (Career Examination Ser.: C-2185). 1994. pap. 23.95 (*0-8373-2185-9*) Nat Learn.
— Real Property Appraiser. (Career Examination Ser.: C-841). 1994. pap. 23.95 (*0-8373-0841-0*) Nat Learn.
— Real Property Appraiser - Arbitrator Supervisor. (Career Examination Ser.: C-3276). 1994. pap. 39.95 (*0-8373-3276-1*) Nat Learn.
— Real Property Appraiser IV. (Career Examination Ser.: C-845). 1994. pap. 29.95 (*0-8373-0845-3*) Nat Learn.
— Real Property Appraiser I. (Career Examination Ser.: C-842). 1994. pap. 23.95 (*0-8373-0842-9*) Nat Learn.
— Real Property Appraiser III. (Career Examination Ser.: C-844). 1994. pap. 29.95 (*0-8373-0844-5*) Nat Learn.
— Real Property Appraiser II. (Career Examination Ser.: C-843). 1994. pap. 27.95 (*0-8373-0843-7*) Nat Learn.
— Real Property Assessor. (Career Examination Ser.: C-2199). 1994. pap. 23.95 (*0-8373-2199-9*) Nat Learn.
— Real Property Assistant. (Career Examination Ser.: C-699). 1994. pap. 23.95 (*0-8373-0699-X*) Nat Learn.
— Real Property Examiner. (Career Examination Ser.: C-3345). 1994. pap. 27.95 (*0-8373-3345-8*) Nat Learn.
— Real Property Information System Specialist. (Career Examination Ser.: C-3138). 1994. pap. 29.95 (*0-8373-3138-2*) Nat Learn.
— Real Property Manager. (Career Examination Ser.: C-698). 1994. pap. 29.95 (*0-8373-0698-1*) Nat Learn.
— Real Property Recorder. (Career Examination Ser.: C-3102). 1994. pap. 27.95 (*0-8373-3102-1*) Nat Learn.
— Real Property Tax Examiner. (Career Examination Ser.: C-1835). 1994. pap. 27.95 (*0-8373-1835-1*) Nat Learn.
— Real Property Tax Specialist. (Career Examination Ser.: C-2227). 1994. pap. 29.95 (*0-8373-2227-8*) Nat Learn.
— Real Property Tax Supervisor. (Career Examination Ser.: C-3604). 1994. pap. 34.95 (*0-8373-3604-X*) Nat Learn.
— Receptionist. (Career Examination Ser.: C-1636). 1994. reprint ed. pap. 19.95 (*0-8373-1636-7*) Nat Learn.
— Record Keeping. (General Aptitude & Abilities Ser.: Vol. 60). pap. 19.95 (*0-8373-6760-3*) Nat Learn.

— Senior Bookkeeping Machine Operator. (Career Examination Ser.: C-3097). 1994. pap. 27.95 (*0-8373-3097-1*) Nat Learn.
— Senior Bridge & Tunnel Maintainer. (Career Examination Ser.: C-1472). 1997. pap. 29.95 (*0-8373-1472-0*) Nat Learn.
— Senior Budget Analyst. (Career Examination Ser.: C-2415). 1994. pap. 39.95 (*0-8373-2415-7*) Nat Learn.
— Senior Budget Examiner. (Career Examination Ser.: C-2528). 1994. pap. 34.95 (*0-8373-2528-5*) Nat Learn.
— Senior Budget Officer. (Career Examination Ser.: C-2683). 1994. pap. 34.95 (*0-8373-2683-4*) Nat Learn.
— Senior Building Construction Engineer. (Career Examination Ser.: C-3171). 1994. pap. 39.95 (*0-8373-3171-4*) Nat Learn.
— Senior Building Custodian. (Career Examination Ser.: C-997). 1994. pap. 27.95 (*0-8373-0997-2*) Nat Learn.
— Senior Building Electrical Engineer. (Career Examination Ser.: C-1916). 1994. pap. 39.95 (*0-8373-1916-1*) Nat Learn.
— Senior Building Guard. (Career Examination Ser.: C-2529). 1994. pap. 27.95 (*0-8373-2529-3*) Nat Learn.
— Senior Building Inspector. (Career Examination Ser.: C-2113). 1994. reprint ed. pap. 34.95 (*0-8373-2113-1*) Nat Learn.
— Senior Building Mechanical Engineer. (Career Examination Ser.: C-2572). 1994. pap. 39.95 (*0-8373-2572-2*) Nat Learn.
— Senior Building Rehabilitation Specialist. (Career Examination Ser.: C-1933). 1994. pap. 39.95 (*0-8373-1933-1*) Nat Learn.
— Senior Building Structural Engineer. (Career Examination Ser.: C-2569). 1994. pap. 39.95 (*0-8373-2569-2*) Nat Learn.
— Senior Business Consultant. (Career Examination Ser.: C-1983). 1994. pap. 39.95 (*0-8373-1983-8*) Nat Learn.
— Senior Business Machine Operator. (Career Examination Ser.: C-1896). 1994. pap. 27.95 (*0-8373-1896-3*) Nat Learn.
— Senior Business Manager. (Career Examination Ser.: C-2359). 1994. pap. 39.95 (*0-8373-2359-2*) Nat Learn.
— Senior Buyer. (Career Examination Ser.: C-2254). 1994. reprint ed. pap. 29.95 (*0-8373-2254-5*) Nat Learn.
— Senior Campus Security Officer. (Career Examination Ser.: C-2265). 1994. reprint ed. pap. 27.95 (*0-8373-2265-0*) Nat Learn.
— Senior Capital Police Officer. (Career Examination Ser.: C-2070). 1994. reprint ed. pap. 29.95 (*0-8373-2070-4*) Nat Learn.
— Senior Caseworker. (Career Examination Ser.: C-2931). 1994. pap. 27.95 (*0-8373-2931-0*) Nat Learn.
— Senior Cashier. (Career Examination Ser.: C-860). 1994. pap. 23.95 (*0-8373-0860-7*) Nat Learn.
— Senior Chemist. (Career Examination Ser.: C-2402). 1994. pap. 29.95 (*0-8373-2402-5*) Nat Learn.
— Senior Children's Counselor. (Career Examination Ser.: C-1601). 1994. reprint ed. pap. 34.95 (*0-8373-1601-4*) Nat Learn.
— Senior Citizen Aide. (Career Examination Ser.: C-1473). 1994. pap. 23.95 (*0-8373-1473-9*) Nat Learn.
— Senior Citizens' Activities Specialist. (Career Examination Ser.: C-900). 1994. pap. 23.95 (*0-8373-0900-X*) Nat Learn.
— Senior Citizens' Club Leader. (Career Examination Ser.: C-2745). 1994. pap. 23.95 (*0-8373-2745-8*) Nat Learn.
— Senior Citizens' Information & Referral Specialist. (Career Examination Ser.: C-2814). 1994. pap. 27.95 (*0-8373-2814-4*) Nat Learn.
— Senior Citizens' Program Coordinator. (Career Examination Ser.: C-2811). 1994. pap. 29.95 (*0-8373-2811-X*) Nat Learn.
— Senior Citizens' Program Supervisor. (Career Examination Ser.: C-2360). 1994. pap. 29.95 (*0-8373-2360-6*) Nat Learn.
— Senior Citizens' Services Coordinator. (Career Examination Ser.: C-2117). 1994. reprint ed. pap. 29.95 (*0-8373-2117-4*) Nat Learn.
— Senior Civil Engineer. (Career Examination Ser.: C-998). 1994. pap. 29.95 (*0-8373-0998-0*) Nat Learn.
— Senior Civil Engineer (Structures) (Career Examination Ser.: C-1917). 1994. pap. 34.95 (*0-8373-1917-X*) Nat Learn.
— Senior Claim Examiner. (Career Examination Ser.: C-1716). 1994. pap. 29.95 (*0-8373-1716-9*) Nat Learn.
— Senior Clerical Series. (Career Examination Ser.: C-3473). 1994. pap. 23.95 (*0-8373-3473-X*) Nat Learn.
— Senior Clerk. (Career Examination Ser.: C-707). 1994. pap. 23.95 (*0-8373-0707-4*) Nat Learn.
— Senior Clerk-Stenographer. (Career Examination Ser.: C-2633). 1994. pap. 23.95 (*0-8373-2633-8*) Nat Learn.
— Senior Clerk (Surrogate) (Career Examination Ser.: C-2128). 1994. reprint ed. pap. 29.95 (*0-8373-2128-X*) Nat Learn.
— Senior Clerk-Typist. (Career Examination Ser.: C-1936). 1994. pap. 23.95 (*0-8373-1936-6*) Nat Learn.
— Senior Clinical Psychologist. (Career Examination Ser.: C-1906). 1994. pap. 39.95 (*0-8373-1906-4*) Nat Learn.
— Senior Code Enforcement Officer. (Career Examination Ser.: C-3602). 1994. pap. 39.95 (*0-8373-3602-3*) Nat Learn.
— Senior Commissary Clerk. (Career Examination Ser.: C-2050). 1994. pap. 27.95 (*0-8373-2050-X*) Nat Learn.
— Senior Communications Technician. (Career Examination Ser.: C-2412). 1994. pap. 29.95 (*0-8373-2412-2*) Nat Learn.
— Senior Community Liaison Worker. (Career Examination Ser.: C-2995). 1994. pap. 27.95 (*0-8373-2995-7*) Nat Learn.
— Senior Community Narcotic Education Representative. (Career Examination Ser.: C-1942). 1994. pap. 34.95 (*0-8373-1942-0*) Nat Learn.
— Senior Community Service Worker. (Career Examination Ser.: C-2676). 1994. pap. 27.95 (*0-8373-2676-1*) Nat Learn.
— Senior Compensation Claims Auditor. (Career Examination Ser.: C-2127). 1994. reprint ed. pap. 34.95 (*0-8373-2127-1*) Nat Learn.
— Senior Compensation Claims Clerk. (Career Examination Ser.: C-867). 1994. pap. 27.95 (*0-8373-0867-4*) Nat Learn.
— Senior Compensation Claims Examiner. (Career Examination Ser.: C-1702). 1994. pap. 29.95 (*0-8373-1702-9*) Nat Learn.
— Senior Compensation Claims Investigator. (Career Examination Ser.: C-2613). 1994. pap. 29.95 (*0-8373-2613-3*) Nat Learn.
— Senior Compensation Investigator. (Career Examination Ser.: C-2609). 1994. pap. 29.95 (*0-8373-2609-5*) Nat Learn.
— Senior Compliance Investigator. (Career Examination Ser.: C-2422). 1994. pap. 29.95 (*0-8373-2422-X*) Nat Learn.
— Senior Computer Operator. (Career Examination Ser.: C-708). 1994. pap. 27.95 (*0-8373-0708-2*) Nat Learn.
— Senior Computer Programmer. (Career Examination Ser.: C-1630). 1994. pap. 29.95 (*0-8373-1630-8*) Nat Learn.
— Senior Computer Programmer-Analyst. (Career Examination Ser.: C-1030). 1994. pap. 29.95 (*0-8373-1030-X*) Nat Learn.
— Senior Computer Systems Analyst. (Career Examination Ser.: C-999). 1994. pap. 29.95 (*0-8373-0999-9*) Nat Learn.
— Senior Construction Inspector. (Career Examination Ser.: C-709). 1994. pap. 34.95 (*0-8373-0709-0*) Nat Learn.
— Senior Consumer Affairs Inspector. (Career Examination Ser.: C-1656). 1994. pap. 29.95 (*0-8373-1656-1*) Nat Learn.
— Senior Consumer Affairs Investigator. (Career Examination Ser.: C-2376). 1994. pap. 29.95 (*0-8373-2376-2*) Nat Learn.
— Senior Consumer Frauds Representative. (Career Examination Ser.: C-877). 1994. pap. 29.95 (*0-8373-0877-1*) Nat Learn.
— Senior Contracts Examiner. (Career Examination Ser.: C-3536). 1994. pap. 29.95 (*0-8373-3536-1*) Nat Learn.
— Senior Correction Counselor. (Career Examination Ser.: C-3263). 1994. pap. 34.95 (*0-8373-3263-X*) Nat Learn.
— Senior Court Clerk. (Career Examination Ser.: C-2704). 1994. pap. 29.95 (*0-8373-2704-0*) Nat Learn.
— Senior Court Officer. (Career Examination Ser.: C-710). 1994. pap. 27.95 (*0-8373-0710-4*) Nat Learn.
— Senior Court Reporter. (Career Examination Ser.: C-3543). 1994. pap. 27.95 (*0-8373-3543-4*) Nat Learn.
— Senior Custodial Assistant. (Career Examination Ser.: Vol. C-1001). 1994. pap. 23.95 (*0-8373-1001-6*) Nat Learn.
— Senior Custodial Foreman. (Career Examination Ser.: C-2271). 1994. reprint ed. pap. 29.95 (*0-8373-2271-5*) Nat Learn.
— Senior Data Entry Clerk. (Career Examination Ser.: C-3506). 1994. pap. 27.95 (*0-8373-3506-X*) Nat Learn.
— Senior Data Entry Machine Operator. (Career Examination Ser.: C-3063). 1994. pap. 27.95 (*0-8373-3063-7*) Nat Learn.
— Senior Data Processing Control Clerk. (Career Examination Ser.: C-2484). 1994. pap. 27.95 (*0-8373-2484-X*) Nat Learn.
— Senior Data Processing Equipment Operator. (Career Examination Ser.: C-2302). 1994. reprint ed. pap. 27.95 (*0-8373-2302-9*) Nat Learn.
— Senior Demolition Inspector. (Career Examination Ser.: C-1475). 1994. pap. 34.95 (*0-8373-1475-5*) Nat Learn.
— Senior Dental Hygienist. (Career Examination Ser.: C-2855). 1994. pap. 34.95 (*0-8373-2855-1*) Nat Learn.
— Senior Dentist. (Career Examination Ser.: C-711). 1994. pap. 54.95 (*0-8373-0711-2*) Nat Learn.
— Senior Deputy Sheriff. (Career Examination Ser.: C-1665). 1994. pap. 27.95 (*0-8373-1665-0*) Nat Learn.
— Senior Detective Investigator. (Career Examination Ser.: C-2038). 1994. pap. 39.95 (*0-8373-2038-0*) Nat Learn.
— Senior Dietitian. (Career Examination Ser.: C-1985). 1994. pap. 29.95 (*0-8373-1985-4*) Nat Learn.
— Senior Dog Warden. (Career Examination Ser.: C-2646). 1994. pap. 27.95 (*0-8373-2646-X*) Nat Learn.
— Senior Drafting Technician. (Career Examination Ser.: C-2679). 1994. pap. 27.95 (*0-8373-2679-6*) Nat Learn.
— Senior Draftsman. (Career Examination Ser.: C-1575). 1994. pap. 27.95 (*0-8373-1575-1*) Nat Learn.
— Senior Drug Abuse Educator. (Career Examination Ser.: C-2520). 1994. pap. 34.95 (*0-8373-2520-X*) Nat Learn.
— Senior Drug Abuse Rehabilitation Counselor. (Career Examination Ser.: C-2928). 1994. pap. 34.95 (*0-8373-2928-0*) Nat Learn.
— Senior Drug & Alcohol Counselor. (Career Examination Ser.: C-2742). 1994. pap. 34.95 (*0-8373-2742-3*) Nat Learn.
— Senior Duplicating Machine Operator. (Career Examination Ser.: C-1899). 1994. pap. 23.95 (*0-8373-1899-8*) Nat Learn.
— Senior Economist. (Career Examination Ser.: C-3252). 1994. pap. 34.95 (*0-8373-3252-4*) Nat Learn.
— Senior Editorial Clerk. (Career Examination Ser.: C-2565). 1994. pap. 27.95 (*0-8373-2565-X*) Nat Learn.
— Senior Electrical Engineer. (Career Examination Ser.: C-1631). 1994. pap. 39.95 (*0-8373-1631-6*) Nat Learn.
— Senior Electrical Inspector. (Career Examination Ser.: C-712). 1994. pap. 34.95 (*0-8373-0712-0*) Nat Learn.
— Senior Electronic Computer Operator. (Career Examination Ser.: C-1002). 1994. pap. 27.95 (*0-8373-1002-4*) Nat Learn.
— Senior Elevator Inspector. (Career Examination Ser.: C-1717). 1994. pap. 34.95 (*0-8373-1717-7*) Nat Learn.
— Senior Employment Counselor. (Career Examination Ser.: C-1003). 1994. pap. 34.95 (*0-8373-1003-2*) Nat Learn.
— Senior Employment Interviewer. (Career Examination Ser.: C-2284). 1994. reprint ed. pap. 34.95 (*0-8373-2284-7*) Nat Learn.
— Senior Employment Security Clerk. (Career Examination Ser.: C-2351). 1994. pap. 27.95 (*0-8373-2351-7*) Nat Learn.
— Senior Engineer. (Career Examination Ser.: C-1476). 1994. pap. 44.95 (*0-8373-1476-3*) Nat Learn.
— Senior Engineering Aide. (Career Examination Ser.: C-1560). 1994. pap. 27.95 (*0-8373-1560-3*) Nat Learn.
— Senior Engineering Inspector. (Career Examination Ser.: C-2808). 1994. pap. 44.95 (*0-8373-2808-X*) Nat Learn.
— Senior Engineering Materials Technician. (Career Examination Ser.: C-316). 1994. pap. 29.95 (*0-8373-0316-8*) Nat Learn.
— Senior Engineering Technician. (Career Examination Ser.: C-1004). 1994. pap. 27.95 (*0-8373-1004-0*) Nat Learn.
— Senior Engineering Technician (Drafting) (Career Examination Ser.: C-1005). 1994. pap. 27.95 (*0-8373-1005-9*) Nat Learn.
— Senior Engineering Technician (Environmental Quality) (Career Examination Ser.: C-3238). 1994. pap. 29.95 (*0-8373-3238-9*) Nat Learn.
— Senior Environmental Analyst. (Career Examination Ser.: C-2660). 1994. pap. 39.95 (*0-8373-2660-5*) Nat Learn.
— Senior Environmental Control Technician. (Career Examination Ser.: C-3363). 1994. pap. 34.95 (*0-8373-3363-6*) Nat Learn.
— Senior Environmental Planner. (Career Examination Ser.: C-2663). 1994. pap. 39.95 (*0-8373-2663-X*) Nat Learn.
— Senior Environmentalist. (Career Examination Ser.: C-1585). 1994. pap. 34.95 (*0-8373-1585-9*) Nat Learn.
— Senior Evidence Technician. (Career Examination Ser.: C-2749). 1994. pap. 34.95 (*0-8373-2749-0*) Nat Learn.
— Senior Examiner, Social Services. (Career Examination Ser.: C-2139). 1994. reprint ed. pap. 27.95 (*0-8373-2139-5*) Nat Learn.
— Senior Excise Tax Investigator. (Career Examination Ser.: C-2419). 1994. pap. 29.95 (*0-8373-2419-X*) Nat Learn.
— Senior Executive Officer. (Career Examination Ser.: C-2826). 1994. pap. 39.95 (*0-8373-2826-8*) Nat Learn.
— Senior Field Accountant. (Career Examination Ser.: C-1569). 1994. pap. 34.95 (*0-8373-1569-7*) Nat Learn.
— Senior Field Representative (Human Rights) (Career Examination Ser.: C-2563). 1994. pap. 29.95 (*0-8373-2563-3*) Nat Learn.
— Senior File Clerk. (Career Examination Ser.: C-713). 1940. pap. 23.95 (*0-8373-0713-9*) Nat Learn.
— Senior Financial Analyst. (Career Examination Ser.: C-2643). 1994. pap. 39.95 (*0-8373-2643-5*) Nat Learn.
— Senior Fingerprint Technician. (Career Examination Ser.: C-2073). 1994. reprint ed. pap. 29.95 (*0-8373-2073-9*) Nat Learn.
— Senior Fire Prevention Inspector. (Career Examination Ser.: C-1765). 1994. reprint ed. pap. 34.95 (*0-8373-1765-7*) Nat Learn.
— Senior Food Inspector. (Career Examination Ser.: C-2051). 1994. pap. 34.95 (*0-8373-2051-8*) Nat Learn.
— Senior Forestry Technician. (Career Examination Ser.: C-2715). 1994. pap. 29.95 (*0-8373-2715-6*) Nat Learn.
— Senior Geologist. (Career Examination Ser.: C-1006). 1994. pap. 29.95 (*0-8373-1006-7*) Nat Learn.
— Senior Grants Analyst. (Career Examination Ser.: C-2833). 1994. pap. 39.95 (*0-8373-2833-0*) Nat Learn.
— Senior Groundskeeper. (Career Examination Ser.: C-1572). 1994. pap. 29.95 (*0-8373-1572-7*) Nat Learn.
— Senior Harbormaster. (Career Examination Ser.: C-3474). 1994. pap. 34.95 (*0-8373-3474-8*) Nat Learn.
— Senior Health Planner. (Career Examination Ser.: C-3028). 1994. pap. 39.95 (*0-8373-3028-9*) Nat Learn.
— Senior Heating & Ventilating Engineer. (Career Examination Ser.: C-1918). 1994. pap. 34.95 (*0-8373-1918-8*) Nat Learn.
— Senior High School. (Teachers Lesson Plan Bk.: S-1). 1994. pap. 6.95 (*0-8373-7954-7*) Nat Learn.
— Senior Highway Engineer. (Career Examination Ser.: C-2522). 1994. pap. 39.95 (*0-8373-2522-6*) Nat Learn.
— Senior Highway Maintenance Supervisor. (Career Examination Ser.: C-2631). 1994. pap. 34.95 (*0-8373-2631-1*) Nat Learn.
— Senior Highway Transportation Specialist. (Career Examination Ser.: C-1477). 1994. pap. 34.95 (*0-8373-1477-1*) Nat Learn.
— Senior Hospital Administration Consultant. (Career Examination Ser.: C-2769). 1994. pap. 44.95 (*0-8373-2769-5*) Nat Learn.
— Senior Hospital Care Investigator. (Career Examination Ser.: C-715). 1994. pap. 29.95 (*0-8373-0715-5*) Nat Learn.
— Senior Hospital Case Investigator. (Career Examination Ser.: C-1888). 1994. reprint ed. pap. 29.95 (*0-8373-1888-2*) Nat Learn.
— Senior Housekeeper. (Career Examination Ser.: C-1007). 1994. pap. 29.95 (*0-8373-1007-5*) Nat Learn.
— Senior Housing Inspector. (Career Examination Ser.: C-792). 1994. pap. 34.95 (*0-8373-0792-9*) Nat Learn.
— Senior Housing Management Assistant. (Career Examination Ser.: C-2538). 1994. pap. 29.95 (*0-8373-2538-2*) Nat Learn.
— Senior Housing Management Representative. (Career Examination Ser.: C-2540). 1994. pap. 34.95 (*0-8373-2540-4*) Nat Learn.
— Senior Housing Teller. (Career Examination Ser.: C-714). 1994. pap. 27.95 (*0-8373-0714-7*) Nat Learn.
— Senior Human Relations Representative. (Career Examination Ser.: C-2584). 1994. pap. 29.95 (*0-8373-2584-6*) Nat Learn.
— Senior Human Resources Specialist. (Career Examination Ser.: C-1064). 1994. pap. 29.95 (*0-8373-1064-4*) Nat Learn.
— Senior Human Resources Technician. (Career Examination Ser.: C-1478). 1994. pap. 29.95 (*0-8373-1478-X*) Nat Learn.
— Senior Human Rights Investigator. (Career Examination Ser.: C-1417). 1994. pap. 29.95 (*0-8373-1417-8*) Nat Learn.
— Senior Identification Clerk. (Career Examination Ser.: C-2293). 1994. pap. 27.95 (*0-8373-2293-6*) Nat Learn.
— Senior Identification Officer. (Career Examination Ser.: C-1987). 1994. pap. 34.95 (*0-8373-1987-0*) Nat Learn.
— Senior Identification Specialist. (Career Examination Ser.: C-2512). 1994. pap. 34.95 (*0-8373-2512-9*) Nat Learn.
— Senior Illustrator. (Career Examination Ser.: C-1008). 1994. pap. 34.95 (*0-8373-1008-3*) Nat Learn.
— Senior Incinerator Stationary Engineer. (Career Examination Ser.: C-2637). 1994. pap. 34.95 (*0-8373-2637-0*) Nat Learn.
— Senior Industrial Hygienist. (Career Examination Ser.: C-3036). 1994. pap. 44.95 (*0-8373-3036-X*) Nat Learn.
— Senior Inspector Meat & Poultry. (Career Examination Ser.: C-1771). 1994. pap. 34.95 (*0-8373-1771-1*) Nat Learn.
— Senior Inspector of Fire Alarm Boxes. (Career Examination Ser.: C-2516). 1994. pap. 34.95 (*0-8373-2516-1*) Nat Learn.
— Senior Inspector of Low Pressure Boilers. (Career Examination Ser.: C-2272). 1994. reprint ed. pap. 34.95 (*0-8373-2272-3*) Nat Learn.
— Senior Inspector of Markets, Weights & Measures. (Career Examination Ser.: C-716). 1994. pap. 29.95 (*0-8373-0716-3*) Nat Learn.
— Senior Institution Safety Officer. (Career Examination Ser.: C-2119). 1994. reprint ed. pap. 34.95 (*0-8373-2119-0*) Nat Learn.
— Senior Instrumentation Technician. (Career Examination Ser.: C-3256). 1994. pap. 34.95 (*0-8373-3256-7*) Nat Learn.
— Senior Insurance Examiner. (Career Examination Ser.: C-2685). 1994. pap. 34.95 (*0-8373-2695-8*) Nat Learn.
— Senior Internal Auditor. (Career Examination Ser.: C-1009). 1994. pap. 34.95 (*0-8373-1009-1*) Nat Learn.
— Senior Investigator. (Career Examination Ser.: C-1010). 1994. pap. 29.95 (*0-8373-1010-5*) Nat Learn.
— Senior Investment Analyst. (Career Examination Ser.: C-1623). 1994. pap. 44.95 (*0-8373-1623-5*) Nat Learn.
— Senior Justice Court Clerk. (Career Examination Ser.: C-3615). 1994. pap. 29.95 (*0-8373-3615-5*) Nat Learn.
— Senior Juvenile Counselor. (Career Examination Ser.: C-421). 1994. pap. 34.95 (*0-8373-0421-0*) Nat Learn.
— Senior Key Punch Operator. (Career Examination Ser.: C-717). 1994. pap. 27.95 (*0-8373-0717-1*) Nat Learn.
— Senior Labor-Management Practices Adjuster. (Career Examination Ser.: C-718). 1994. pap. 44.95 (*0-8373-0718-X*) Nat Learn.
— Senior Labor Specialist. (Career Examination Ser.: C-2381). 1994. pap. 34.95 (*0-8373-2381-9*) Nat Learn.
— Senior Laboratory Technician. (Career Examination Ser.: C-1693). 1994. pap. 29.95 (*0-8373-1693-6*) Nat Learn.
— Senior Laboratory Technician (Biochemistry) (Career Examination Ser.: C-3081). 1994. pap. 34.95 (*0-8373-3081-5*) Nat Learn.
— Senior Laboratory Technician (Chemistry) (Career Examination Ser.: C-3082). 1994. pap. 34.95 (*0-8373-3082-3*) Nat Learn.
— Senior Laboratory Technician (Food Chemistry) (Career Examination Ser.: C-3253). 1994. pap. 34.95 (*0-8373-3253-2*) Nat Learn.
— Senior Laboratory Technician (Microbiology) (Career Examination Ser.: C-3083). 1994. pap. 34.95 (*0-8373-3083-1*) Nat Learn.
— Senior Land Management Specialist. (Career Examination Ser.: C-2619). 1994. pap. 34.95 (*0-8373-2619-2*) Nat Learn.
— Senior Landscape Architect. (Career Examination Ser.: C-1479). 1994. pap. 34.95 (*0-8373-1479-8*) Nat Learn.
— Senior Laundry Supervisor. (Career Examination Ser.: C-2220). 1994. pap. 34.95 (*0-8373-2220-0*) Nat Learn.
— Senior Laundry Worker. (Career Examination Ser.: C-719). 1994. pap. 27.95 (*0-8373-0719-8*) Nat Learn.
— Senior Leasing Agent. (Career Examination Ser.: C-2494). 1994. pap. 34.95 (*0-8373-2494-7*) Nat Learn.
— Senior Legal Stenographer. (Career Examination Ser.: C-2634). 1994. pap. 29.95 (*0-8373-2634-6*) Nat Learn.
— Senior Level Positions. (Career Examination Ser.: C-720). 1994. pap. 29.95 (*0-8373-0720-1*) Nat Learn.
— Senior Librarian. (Career Examination Ser.: C-1011). 1994. pap. 29.95 (*0-8373-1011-3*) Nat Learn.
— Senior Librarian I. (Career Examination Ser.: C-1821). 1994. pap. 29.95 (*0-8373-1821-1*) Nat Learn.
— Senior Library Clerk. (Career Examination Ser.: C-1930). 1994. pap. 27.95 (*0-8373-1930-7*) Nat Learn.
— Senior License Investigator. (Career Examination Ser.: C-2530). 1994. pap. 27.95 (*0-8373-2530-7*) Nat Learn.
— Senior Licensed Practical Nurse. (Career Examination Ser.: C-3500). 1994. pap. 29.95 (*0-8373-3500-0*) Nat Learn.
— Senior Mail Clerk. (Career Examination Ser.: C-1053). 1994. pap. 23.95 (*0-8373-1053-9*) Nat Learn.
— Senior Maintenance Supervisor. (Career Examination Ser.: C-2052). 1994. pap. 29.95 (*0-8373-2052-6*) Nat Learn.
— Senior Management Analyst. (Career Examination Ser.: C-1782). 1994. pap. 39.95 (*0-8373-1782-7*) Nat Learn.
— Senior Management Technician. (Career Examination Ser.: C-2752). 1994. pap. 29.95 (*0-8373-2752-0*) Nat Learn.
— Senior Manpower Counselor. (Career Examination Ser.: C-2436). 1994. pap. 39.95 (*0-8373-2436-X*) Nat Learn.

— Senior Marketing Representative. (Career Examination Ser.: C-2053). 1994. reprint ed. pap. 34.95 (*0-8373-2053-4*) Nat Learn.
— Senior Mathematician. (Career Examination Ser.: C-2078). 1994. reprint ed. pap. 34.95 (*0-8373-2078-X*) Nat Learn.
— Senior Meat Cutter. (Career Examination Ser.: C-1012). 1994. pap. 29.95 (*0-8373-1012-1*) Nat Learn.
— Senior Meat Inspector. (Career Examination Ser.: C-2054). 1994. pap. 29.95 (*0-8373-2054-2*) Nat Learn.
— Senior Mechanical Engineer. (Career Examination Ser.: C-1648). 1994. reprint ed. pap. 34.95 (*0-8373-1648-0*) Nat Learn.
— Senior Mechanical Stores Clerk. (Career Examination Ser.: C-3060). 1994. pap. 27.95 (*0-8373-3060-2*) Nat Learn.
— Senior Medicaid Claims Examiner. (Career Examination Ser.: C-2692). 1994. pap. 29.95 (*0-8373-2692-3*) Nat Learn.
— Senior Medical Conduct Investigator. (Career Examination Ser.: C-2610). 1994. pap. 29.95 (*0-8373-2610-9*) Nat Learn.
— Senior Medical Emergency Dispatcher. (Career Examination Ser.: C-2332). 1994. pap. 29.95 (*0-8373-2332-0*) Nat Learn.
— Senior Medical Laboratory Technician. (Career Examination Ser.: C-2496). 1994. pap. 29.95 (*0-8373-2496-3*) Nat Learn.
— Senior Medical Records Clerk. (Career Examination Ser.: C-2310). 1994. reprint ed. pap. 29.95 (*0-8373-2310-X*) Nat Learn.
— Senior Medical Records Librarian. (Career Examination Ser.: C-1013). 1994. pap. 29.95 (*0-8373-1013-X*) Nat Learn.
— Senior Medical Services Specialist. (Career Examination Ser.: C-2747). 1994. pap. 39.95 (*0-8373-2747-4*) Nat Learn.
— Senior Medical Social Worker. (Career Examination Ser.: C-2629). 1994. pap. 34.95 (*0-8373-2629-X*) Nat Learn.
— Senior Medical Stenographer. (Career Examination Ser.: C-2940). 1994. pap. 27.95 (*0-8373-2940-X*) Nat Learn.
— Senior Menagerie Keeper. (Career Examination Ser.: C-1971). 1994. pap. 27.95 (*0-8373-1971-4*) Nat Learn.
— Senior Mental Health Worker. (Career Examination Ser.: C-1925). 1994. pap. 29.95 (*0-8373-1925-0*) Nat Learn.
— Senior Meteorologist. (Career Examination Ser.: C-2201). 1994. pap. 34.95 (*0-8373-2201-4*) Nat Learn.
— Senior Methods Analyst. (Career Examination Ser.: C-1014). 1994. pap. 39.95 (*0-8373-1014-8*) Nat Learn.
— Senior Microbiologist. (Career Examination Ser.: C-1945). 1994. pap. 34.95 (*0-8373-1945-5*) Nat Learn.
— Senior Micrographics Operator. (Career Examination Ser.: C-2760). 1994. pap. 27.95 (*0-8373-2760-1*) Nat Learn.
— Senior Micrographics Technician. (Career Examination Ser.: C-2762). 1994. pap. 27.95 (*0-8373-2762-8*) Nat Learn.
— Senior Mortuary Caretaker. (Career Examination Ser.: C-721). 1994. pap. 27.95 (*0-8373-0721-X*) Nat Learn.
— Senior Motor Vehicle License Clerk. (Career Examination Ser.: C-2611). 1994. pap. 27.95 (*0-8373-2611-7*) Nat Learn.
— Senior Motor Vehicle Supervisor. (Career Examination Ser.: C-3527). 1994. pap. 34.95 (*0-8373-3527-2*) Nat Learn.
— Senior Multiple Residence Inspector. (Career Examination Ser.: C-2843). 1994. pap. 34.95 (*0-8373-2843-8*) Nat Learn.
— Senior Museum Curator. (Career Examination Ser.: C-2374). 1994. pap. 29.95 (*0-8373-2374-6*) Nat Learn.
— Senior Museum Instructor. (Career Examination Ser.: C-1016). 1994. pap. 29.95 (*0-8373-1016-4*) Nat Learn.
— Senior Narcotics Investigator. (Career Examination Ser.: C-2531). 1994. pap. 39.95 (*0-8373-2531-5*) Nat Learn.
— Senior Neighborhood Aide. (Career Examination Ser.: C-2911). 1994. pap. 27.95 (*0-8373-2911-6*) Nat Learn.
— Senior Nutritionist. (Career Examination Ser.: C-1419). 1994. pap. 29.95 (*0-8373-1419-4*) Nat Learn.
— Senior Occupational Analyst. (Career Examination Ser.: C-2549). 1994. pap. 34.95 (*0-8373-2549-8*) Nat Learn.
— Senior Occupational Therapist. (Career Examination Ser.: C-2174). 1994. pap. 34.95 (*0-8373-2174-3*) Nat Learn.
— Senior Office Appliance Operator. (Career Examination Ser.: C-1677). 1994. pap. 27.95 (*0-8373-1677-4*) Nat Learn.
— Senior Office Assistant. (Career Examination Ser.: C-2594). 1994. pap. 23.95 (*0-8373-2594-3*) Nat Learn.
— Senior Office Machine Operator. (Career Examination Ser.: C-1480). 1994. pap. 27.95 (*0-8373-1480-1*) Nat Learn.
— Senior Office Manager. (Career Examination Ser.: C-2399). 1994. pap. 34.95 (*0-8373-2399-1*) Nat Learn.
— Senior Office Stenographer. (Career Examination Ser.: C-3376). 1994. pap. 23.95 (*0-8373-3376-8*) Nat Learn.
— Senior Office Typist. (Career Examination Ser.: C-3374). 1994. pap. 23.95 (*0-8373-3374-1*) Nat Learn.
— Senior Office Worker. (Career Examination Ser.: C-2519). 1994. pap. 23.95 (*0-8373-2519-6*) Nat Learn.
— Senior Offset Printing Machine Operator. (Career Examination Ser.: C-3334). 1994. pap. 27.95 (*0-8373-3334-2*) Nat Learn.
— Senior Operations Review Specialist. (Career Examination Ser.: C-3261). 1994. pap. 39.95 (*0-8373-3261-3*) Nat Learn.
— Senior Park Attendant. (Career Examination Ser.: C-1542). 1994. pap. 27.95 (*0-8373-1542-5*) Nat Learn.
— Senior Park Engineer. (Career Examination Ser.: C-3192). 1994. pap. 39.95 (*0-8373-3192-7*) Nat Learn.
— Senior Park Foreman. (Career Examination Ser.: C-1562). 1994. pap. 29.95 (*0-8373-1562-X*) Nat Learn.
— Senior Park Supervisor. (Career Examination Ser.: C-2356). 1994. pap. 29.95 (*0-8373-2356-8*) Nat Learn.
— Senior Parking Enforcement Agent. (Career Examination Ser.: C-793). 1994. pap. 27.95 (*0-8373-0793-7*) Nat Learn.
— Senior Parole Officer. (Career Examination Ser.: C-2466). 1994. pap. 29.95 (*0-8373-2466-1*) Nat Learn.
— Senior Payroll Audit Clerk. (Career Examination Ser.: C-2085). 1994. reprint ed. pap. 27.95 (*0-8373-2085-2*) Nat Learn.
— Senior Personnel Administrator. (Career Examination Ser.: C-2410). 1994. pap. 44.95 (*0-8373-2410-6*) Nat Learn.
— Senior Personnel Analyst. (Career Examination Ser.: C-2345). 1994. pap. 39.95 (*0-8373-2345-2*) Nat Learn.
— Senior Personnel Clerk. (Career Examination Ser.: C-2867). 1994. pap. 27.95 (*0-8373-2867-5*) Nat Learn.
— Senior Personnel Examiner. (Career Examination Ser.: C-1017). 1994. pap. 34.95 (*0-8373-1017-2*, C-1017) Nat Learn.
— Senior Pesticide Control Inspector. (Career Examination Ser.: C-2562). 1994. pap. 34.95 (*0-8373-2562-5*) Nat Learn.
— Senior Pharmacist. (Career Examination Ser.: C-722). 1994. pap. 34.95 (*0-8373-0722-8*) Nat Learn.
— Senior Pharmacy Inspector. (Career Examination Ser.: C-2532). 1994. pap. 39.95 (*0-8373-2532-3*) Nat Learn.
— Senior Photographic Machine Operator. (Career Examination Ser.: C-2882). 1994. pap. 23.95 (*0-8373-2882-9*) Nat Learn.
— Senior Physical Therapist. (Career Examination Ser.: C-1018). 1994. pap. 29.95 (*0-8373-1018-0*) Nat Learn.
— Senior Plan Examiner. (Career Examination Ser.: C-1481). 1994. pap. 34.95 (*0-8373-1481-X*) Nat Learn.
— Senior Planner. (Career Examination Ser.: C-1019). 1994. pap. 34.95 (*0-8373-1019-9*) Nat Learn.
— Senior Plumbing Inspector. (Career Examination Ser.: C-1740). 1994. pap. 34.95 (*0-8373-1740-1*) Nat Learn.
— Senior Police Administrative Aide. (Career Examination Ser.: C-1020). 1994. pap. 27.95 (*0-8373-1020-2*) Nat Learn.
— Senior Probation Officer. (Career Examination Ser.: C-1594). 1994. pap. 29.95 (*0-8373-1594-8*) Nat Learn.
— Senior Professional Conduct Investigator. (Career Examination Ser.: C-2298). 1994. reprint ed. pap. 29.95 (*0-8373-2298-7*) Nat Learn.
— Senior Program Evaluation Specialist. (Career Examination Ser.: C-2700). 1994. pap. 39.95 (*0-8373-2700-8*) Nat Learn.
— Senior Program Examiner. (Career Examination Ser.: C-2755). 1994. pap. 39.95 (*0-8373-2755-5*) Nat Learn.
— Senior Program Research Analyst. (Career Examination Ser.: C-2219). 1994. reprint ed. pap. 39.95 (*0-8373-2219-7*) Nat Learn.
— Senior Program Specialist. (Career Examination Ser.: C-2862). 1994. pap. 39.95 (*0-8373-2862-4*) Nat Learn.
— Senior Program Specialist (Correction) (Career Examination Ser.: C-1998). 1994. pap. 39.95 (*0-8373-1998-6*) Nat Learn.
— Senior Programmer. (Career Examination Ser.: C-2580). 1994. pap. 34.95 (*0-8373-2580-3*) Nat Learn.
— Senior Project Coordinator. (Career Examination Ser.: C-1482). 1994. pap. 34.95 (*0-8373-1482-8*) Nat Learn.
— Senior Project Development Coordinator. (Career Examination Ser.: C-2898). 1994. pap. 34.95 (*0-8373-2898-5*) Nat Learn.
— Senior Project Services Specialist. (Career Examination Ser.: C-1662). 1994. pap. 34.95 (*0-8373-1662-6*) Nat Learn.
— Senior Psychiatric Social Worker. (Career Examination Ser.: C-2487). 1994. pap. 34.95 (*0-8373-2487-4*) Nat Learn.
— Senior Psychologist. (Career Examination Ser.: C-2173). 1994. pap. 39.95 (*0-8373-2173-5*) Nat Learn.
— Senior Public Health Adviser. (Career Examination Ser.: C-3175). 1994. pap. 29.95 (*0-8373-3175-7*) Nat Learn.
— Senior Public Health Educator. (Career Examination Ser.: C-3475). 1994. pap. 34.95 (*0-8373-3475-6*) Nat Learn.
— Senior Public Health Engineer. (Career Examination Ser.: C-3346). 1994. pap. 34.95 (*0-8373-3346-6*) Nat Learn.
— Senior Public Health Nutritionist. (Career Examination Ser.: C-1592). 1994. pap. 29.95 (*0-8373-1592-1*) Nat Learn.
— Senior Public Health Representative. (Career Examination Ser.: C-2385). 1994. pap. 29.95 (*0-8373-2385-1*) Nat Learn.
— Senior Public Health Sanitarian. (Career Examination Ser.: C-2002). 1994. pap. 29.95 (*0-8373-2002-X*) Nat Learn.
— Senior Public Information Assistant. (Career Examination Ser.: C-2957). 1994. pap. 29.95 (*0-8373-2957-4*) Nat Learn.
— Senior Pump Operator. (Career Examination Ser.: C-2951). 1994. pap. 29.95 (*0-8373-2951-5*) Nat Learn.
— Senior Purchase Inspector. (Career Examination Ser.: C-1483). 1994. pap. 29.95 (*0-8373-1483-6*) Nat Learn.
— Senior Quantitative Analyst. (Career Examination Ser.: C-1718). 1994. pap. 34.95 (*0-8373-1718-5*) Nat Learn.
— Senior Radio Operator. (Career Examination Ser.: C-2551). 1994. pap. 29.95 (*0-8373-2551-X*) Nat Learn.
— Senior Radiologic Technologist. (Career Examination Ser.: C-1545). 1994. pap. 34.95 (*0-8373-1545-X*) Nat Learn.
— Senior Real Estate Agent. (Career Examination Ser.: C-1941). 1994. pap. 27.95 (*0-8373-1941-2*) Nat Learn.
— Senior Real Estate Appraiser. (Career Examination Ser.: C-569). 1994. pap. 27.95 (*0-8373-0569-1*) Nat Learn.
— Senior Real Estate Manager. (Career Examination Ser.: C-1021). 1994. pap. 34.95 (*0-8373-1021-0*) Nat Learn.
— Senior Real Property Recorder. (Career Examination Ser.: C-3103). 1994. pap. 29.95 (*0-8373-3103-X*) Nat Learn.
— Senior Records Center Assistant. (Career Examination Ser.: C-1919). 1994. pap. 27.95 (*0-8373-1919-6*) Nat Learn.
— Senior Recreation Leader. (Career Examination Ser.: C-1938). 1994. pap. 29.95 (*0-8373-1938-2*) Nat Learn.
— Senior Recreation Therapist. (Career Examination Ser.: C-2974). 1994. pap. 29.95 (*0-8373-2974-4*) Nat Learn.
— Senior Rehabilitation Counselor. (Career Examination Ser.: C-1952). 1994. pap. 34.95 (*0-8373-1952-8*) Nat Learn
— Senior Rent Examiner. (Career Examination Ser.: C-1022). 1994. pap. 27.95 (*0-8373-1022-9*) Nat Learn.
— Senior Rent Inspector. (Career Examination Ser.: C-2721). 1994. pap. 27.95 (*0-8373-2721-0*) Nat Learn.
— Senior Rent Research Associate. (Career Examination Ser.: C-1023). 1994. pap. 34.95 (*0-8373-1023-7*) Nat Learn
— Senior Research Analyst. (Career Examination Ser.: C-1543). 1994. pap. 39.95 (*0-8373-1543-3*) Nat Learn.
— Senior Research Assistant. (Career Examination Ser.: C-2717). 1994. pap. 34.95 (*0-8373-2717-2*) Nat Learn.
— Senior Right-of-Way Aide. (Career Examination Ser.: C-2736). 1994. pap. 29.95 (*0-8373-2736-9*) Nat Learn.
— Senior Safety & Health Engineer. (Career Examination Ser.: C-3204). 1994. pap. 39.95 (*0-8373-3204-4*) Nat Learn.
— Senior Safety Coordinator. (Career Examination Ser.: C-2668). 1994. pap. 39.95 (*0-8373-2668-0*) Nat Learn.
— Senior Sanitarian. (Career Examination Ser.: C-2430). 1994. pap. 29.95 (*0-8373-2430-0*) Nat Learn.
— Senior Sanitary Engineer. (Career Examination Ser.: C-2446). 1994. pap. 34.95 (*0-8373-2446-7*) Nat Learn.
— Senior Security Hospital Treatment Assistant. (Career Examination Ser.: C-1617). 1994. pap. 27.95 (*0-8373-1617-0*) Nat Learn.
— Senior Security Officer. (Career Examination Ser.: C-2449). 1994. pap. 27.95 (*0-8373-2449-1*) Nat Learn.
— Senior Sewage Treatment Plant Operator. (Career Examination Ser.: C-1556). 1994. pap. 29.95 (*0-8373-1556-5*) Nat Learn.
— Senior Sewage Treatment Worker. (Career Examination Ser.: C-791). 1994. pap. 29.95 (*0-8373-0791-0*) Nat Learn.
— Senior Shorthand Reporter. (Career Examination Ser.: C-724). 1994. pap. 27.95 (*0-8373-0724-4*) Nat Learn.
— Senior Social Case Worker. (Career Examination Ser.: C-1555). 1994. pap. 27.95 (*0-8373-1555-7*) Nat Learn.
— Senior Social Services Employment Specialist. (Career Examination Ser.: C-2817). 1994. pap. 34.95 (*0-8373-2817-9*) Nat Learn.
— Senior Social Services Management Specialist. (Career Examination Ser.: C-2579). 1994. pap. 39.95 (*0-8373-2579-X*) Nat Learn.
— Senior Social Services Medical Assistance Specialist. (Career Examination Ser.: C-2432). 1994. pap. 39.95 (*0-8373-2432-7*) Nat Learn.
— Senior Social Services Program Specialist. (Career Examination Ser.: C-2236). 1994. pap. 39.95 (*0-8373-2236-7*) Nat Learn.
— Senior Social Welfare Examiner. (Career Examination Ser.: C-2320). 1994. pap. 27.95 (*0-8373-2320-7*) Nat Learn.
— Senior Social Welfare Examiner (Spanish Speaking) (Career Examination Ser.: C-2321). 1994. pap. 29.95 (*0-8373-2321-5*) Nat Learn.
— Senior Social Worker. (Career Examination Ser.: C-2488). 1994 pap. 27.95 (*0-8373-2488-2*) Nat Learn.
— Senior Special Investigator. (Career Examination Ser.: C-1589). 1994. pap. 34.95 (*0-8373-1589-1*) Nat Learn.
— Senior Special Officer. (Career Examination Ser.: C-725). 1994 pap. 27.95 (*0-8373-0725-2*) Nat Learn.
— Senior Speech & Hearing Therapist. (Career Examination Ser.: C-2273). 1994. reprint ed. pap. 34.95 (*0-8373-2273-1*) Nat Learn.
— Senior Staff Development Specialist. (Career Examination Ser.: C-2702). 1994. pap. 39.95 (*0-8373-2702-4*) Nat Learn.
— Senior Stationary Engineer. (Career Examination Ser.: C-1024). 1994. pap. 29.95 (*0-8373-1024-5*) Nat Learn.
— Senior Stationary Engineer (Electric) (Career Examination Ser.: C-2433). 1994. pap. 29.95 (*0-8373-2433-5*) Nat Learn.
— Senior Statistician. (Career Examination Ser.: C-1025). 1994. pap. 34.95 (*0-8373-1025-3*) Nat Learn.
— Senior Stenographer. (Career Examination Ser.: C-726). 1994. pap. 23.95 (*0-8373-0726-0*) Nat Learn.
— Senior Storekeeper. (Career Examination Ser.: C-3009). 1994. pap. 27.95 (*0-8373-3009-2*) Nat Learn.
— Senior Stores Clerk. (Career Examination Ser.: C-2383). 1994. pap. 27.95 (*0-8373-2383-5*) Nat Learn.
— Senior Street Club Worker. (Career Examination Ser.: C-727). 1994. pap. 29.95 (*0-8373-0727-9*) Nat Learn.
— Senior Superintendent (Department of Sanitation) (Career Examination Ser.: C-1026). 1994. pap. 39.95 (*0-8373-1026-1*) Nat Learn.
— Senior Superintendent of Construction. (Career Examination Ser.: C-541). 1994. pap. 39.95 (*0-8373-0541-1*) Nat Learn.
— Senior Supervisor of Mechanical Installations. (Career Examination Ser.: C-1679). 1994. pap. 34.95 (*0-8373-1679-0*) Nat Learn.
— Senior Supervisor of Park Operations. (Career Examination Ser.: C-1694). 1994. pap. 34.95 (*0-8373-1694-4*) Nat Learn.
— Senior Support Collector. (Career Examination Ser.: C-3211). 1994. pap. 27.95 (*0-8373-3211-7*) Nat Learn.
— Senior Surface Line Dispatcher. (Career Examination Ser.: C-728). 1994. pap. 27.95 (*0-8373-0728-7*) Nat Learn.
— Senior Systems Analyst. (Career Examination Ser.: C-2389). 1994. pap. 34.95 (*0-8373-2389-4*) Nat Learn.
— Senior Tabulator Operator. (Career Examination Ser.: C-1678). 1994. pap. 27.95 (*0-8373-1678-2*) Nat Learn.
— Senior Tax Cashier. (Career Examination Ser.: C-2095). 1994. pap. 23.95 (*0-8373-2095-X*) Nat Learn.
— Senior Tax Compliance Agent. (Career Examination Ser.: C-2953). 1994. pap. 29.95 (*0-8373-2953-1*) Nat Learn.
— Senior Tax Valuation Engineer. (Career Examination Ser.: C-3197). 1994. pap. 29.95 (*0-8373-3197-8*) Nat Learn.
— Senior Taxi & Limousine Inspector. (Career Examination Ser.: C-2553). 1994. pap. 27.95 (*0-8373-2553-6*) Nat Learn.
— Senior Telephone Inspector. (Career Examination Ser.: C-2217). 1994. reprint ed. pap. 29.95 (*0-8373-2217-0*) Nat Learn.
— Senior Telephone Operator. (Career Examination Ser.: C-1027). 1994. pap. 23.95 (*0-8373-1027-X*) Nat Learn.
— Senior Tenant Supervisor. (Career Examination Ser.: C-544). 1994. pap. 34.95 (*0-8373-0544-6*) Nat Learn.
— Senior Title Examiner. (Career Examination Ser.: C-2250). 1994. pap. 27.95 (*0-8373-2250-2*) Nat Learn.
— Senior Title Searcher. (Career Examination Ser.: C-2086). 1994. reprint ed. pap. 27.95 (*0-8373-2086-0*) Nat Learn.
— Senior Traffic Control Inspector. (Career Examination Ser.: C-729). 1994. pap. 29.95 (*0-8373-0729-5*) Nat Learn.
— Senior Traffic Supervisor. (Career Examination Ser.: C-2628). 1994. pap. 34.95 (*0-8373-2628-1*) Nat Learn.
— Senior Training Officer. (Career Examination Ser.: C-1485). 1994. pap. 39.95 (*0-8373-1485-2*) Nat Learn.
— Senior Training Technician. (Career Examination Ser.: C-1486). 1994. pap. 39.95 (*0-8373-1486-0*) Nat Learn.
— Senior Training Technician (Police) (Career Examination Ser.: C-418). 1994. pap. 44.95 (*0-8373-0418-0*) Nat Learn.
— Senior Transportation Analyst. (Career Examination Ser.: C-3202). 1994. pap. 34.95 (*0-8373-3202-8*) Nat Learn.
— Senior Transportation Inspector. (Career Examination Ser.: C-1487). 1994. pap. 34.95 (*0-8373-1487-9*) Nat Learn.
— Senior Typist. (Career Examination Ser.: C-730). 1994. pap. 23.95 (*0-8373-0730-9*) Nat Learn.
— Senior Underwriting Clerk. (Career Examination Ser.: C-2987). 1994. pap. 27.95 (*0-8373-2987-6*) Nat Learn.
— Senior Unemployment Insurance Claims Examiner. (Career Examination Ser.: C-2285). 1994. reprint ed. pap. 29.95 (*0-8373-2285-5*) Nat Learn.
— Senior Unemployment Insurance Hearing Representative. (Career Examination Ser.: C-2729). 1994. pap. 34.95 (*0-8373-2729-6*) Nat Learn.
— Senior Unemployment Insurance Investigator. (Career Examination Ser.: C-2830). 1994. pap. 34.95 (*0-8373-2830-6*) Nat Learn.
— Senior Vocational Counselor. (Career Examination Ser.: C-2438). 1994. pap. 34.95 (*0-8373-2438-6*) Nat Learn.
— Senior Water Plant Operator. (Career Examination Ser.: C-1638). 1994. pap. 29.95 (*0-8373-1638-3*) Nat Learn.
— Senior Water Plant Supervisor. (Career Examination Ser.: C-2959). 1994. pap. 34.95 (*0-8373-2959-0*) Nat Learn.
— Senior Water Use Inspector. (Career Examination Ser.: C-1639). 1994. pap. 27.95 (*0-8373-1639-1*) Nat Learn.
— Senior X-Ray Technician. (Career Examination Ser.: C-731). 1994. pap. 27.95 (*0-8373-0731-7*) Nat Learn.
— Senior Youth Division Counselor. (Career Examination Ser.: C-2500). 1994. pap. 34.95 (*0-8373-2500-5*) Nat Learn.
— Senior Youth Group Worker. (Career Examination Ser.: C-2585). 1994. pap. 29.95 (*0-8373-2585-4*) Nat Learn.
— Senior Zoning Inspector. (Career Examination Ser.: C-2341). 1994. pap. 34.95 (*0-8373-2341-X*) Nat Learn.
— Sergeant - Police Department. (Career Examination Ser.: C-733). 1994. pap. 29.95 (*0-8373-0733-3*) Nat Learn.
— Sergeant Bridge & Tunnel Authority. (Career Examination Ser.: C-732). 1994. pap. 29.95 (*0-8373-0732-5*) Nat Learn.
— Sergeant, Sheriff's Department. (Career Examination Ser.: C-874). 1994. pap. 29.95 (*0-8373-0874-7*) Nat Learn.
— Service Inspector. (Career Examination Ser.: C-3501). 1994. pap. 29.95 (*0-8373-3501-9*) Nat Learn.
— Service Operations Supervisor. (Career Examination Ser.: C-1880). 1994. pap. 29.95 (*0-8373-1880-7*) Nat Learn.
— Sewage District Superintendent. (Career Examination Ser.: C-3343). 1994. pap. 39.95 (*0-8373-3343-1*) Nat Learn.
— Sewage Plant Operations Supervisor. (Career Examination Ser.: C-3017). 1994. pap. 34.95 (*0-8373-3017-3*) Nat Learn.
— Sewage Plant Operator. (Career Examination Ser.: C-2443). 1994. pap. 27.95 (*0-8373-2443-2*) Nat Learn.
— Sewage Plant Operator Trainee. (Career Examination Ser.: C-2281). 1994. reprint ed. pap. 23.95 (*0-8373-2281-2*) Nat Learn.
— Sewage Pump Operator. (Career Examination Ser.: C-3018). 1994. pap. 29.95 (*0-8373-3018-1*) Nat Learn.
— Sewage Treatment Operator. (Career Examination Ser.: C-1488). 1994. pap. 27.95 (*0-8373-1488-7*) Nat Learn.
— Sewage Treatment Operator Trainee. (Career Examination Ser.: C-1489). 1994. pap. 23.95 (*0-8373-1489-5*) Nat Learn.
— Sewage Treatment Plant Supervisor. (Career Examination Ser.: C-1490). 1994. pap. 34.95 (*0-8373-1490-9*) Nat Learn.
— Sewage Treatment Worker. (Career Examination Ser.: C-734). 1994. pap. 27.95 (*0-8373-0734-1*) Nat Learn.
— Sewage Treatment Worker Trainee. (Career Examination Ser.: C-735). 1994. pap. 23.95 (*0-8373-0735-X*) Nat Learn.
— Sewer Inspector. (Career Examination Ser.: C-2454). 1994. pap. 29.95 (*0-8373-2454-8*) Nat Learn.
— Shakespeare. (ACT Proficiency Examination Program (PEP) Ser.: Vol. 7). 43.95 (*0-8373-5557-5*) Nat Learn.
— Shakespeare. (ACT Proficiency Examination Program Ser.: PEP-7). 1994. pap. 23.95 (*0-8373-5507-9*) Nat Learn.

R

R

— Shakespeare. (Regents College Proficiency Examination Ser.: Vol. CPEP-33). 1994. reprint ed. pap. 23.95 (*0-8373-5433-1*) Nat Learn.
— Sheet Metal Fabrication. (Occupational Competency Examination (OCE) Ser.: Vol. 31). 47.95 (*0-8373-5781-0*) Nat Learn.
— Sheet Metal Fabrication. (Occupational Competency Examination Ser.: OCE-31). 1994. pap. 27.95 (*0-8373-5731-4*) Nat Learn.
— Sheet Metal Worker. (Career Examination Ser.: C-736). 1994. pap. 23.95 (*0-8373-0736-8*) Nat Learn.
— Shelter Inspector (Civil Defense) (Career Examination Ser.: C-737). 1994. pap. 34.95 (*0-8373-0737-6*) Nat Learn.
— Sheriff. (Career Examination Ser.: C-794). 1994. pap. 27.95 (*0-8373-0794-5*) Nat Learn.
— Shipfitter. (Career Examination Ser.: C-1031). 1994. pap. 27.95 (*0-8373-1031-8*) Nat Learn.
— Shipment Clerk. (Career Examination Ser.: C-738). 1994. pap. 23.95 (*0-8373-0738-4*) Nat Learn.
— Shop Carpenter. (Career Examination Ser.: C-739). 1994. pap. 23.95 (*0-8373-0739-2*) Nat Learn.
— Shop Clerk. (Career Examination Ser.: C-740). 1994. pap. 23.95 (*0-8373-0740-6*) Nat Learn.
— Shop Mathematics. (General Aptitude & Abilities Ser.: No. CS-36). 1994. pap. 23.95 (*0-8373-6736-0*) Nat Learn.
— Shop Subjects. (Teachers License Examination Ser.: T-53). 1994. pap. 27.95 (*0-8373-8053-7*) Nat Learn.
— Shorthand Reporter. (Career Examination Ser.: C-741). 1994. pap. 23.95 (*0-8373-0741-4*) Nat Learn.
— Sign Painter. (Career Examination Ser.: C-2090). 1994. reprint ed. pap. 27.95 (*0-8373-2090-9*) Nat Learn.
— Signal Electrician. (Career Examination Ser.: C-2440). 1994. pap. 27.95 (*0-8373-2440-8*) Nat Learn.
— Signal Maintainer. (Career Examination Ser.: C-742). 1994. pap. 23.95 (*0-8373-0742-2*) Nat Learn.
— Site Plan Reviewer. (Career Examination Ser.: C-3251). 1994. pap. 34.95 (*0-8373-3251-6*) Nat Learn.
— Small Engine Repair. (Occupational Competency Examination (OCE) Ser.: Vol. 32). 47.95 (*0-8373-5782-9*) Nat Learn.
— Small Engine Repair. (Occupational Competency Examination Ser.: OCE-32). 1994. pap. 27.95 (*0-8373-5732-2*) Nat Learn.
— Social Case Worker. (Career Examination Ser.: C-795). 1994. pap. 23.95 (*0-8373-0795-3*) Nat Learn.
— Social Health Investigator. (Career Examination Ser.: C-2970). 1994. pap. 29.95 (*0-8373-2970-1*) Nat Learn.
— Social Insurance Claims Representative. (Career Examination Ser.: C-3372). 1994. pap. 27.95 (*0-8373-3372-5*) Nat Learn.
— Social Investigator. (Career Examination Ser.: C-743). 1994. pap. 27.95 (*0-8373-0743-0*) Nat Learn.
— Social Investigator Trainee. (Career Examination Ser.: C-744). 1994. pap. 23.95 (*0-8373-0744-9*) Nat Learn.
— Social Sciences - Area Examination. (Graduate Record Examination Ser.: GRE-44). 1994. pap. 23.95 (*0-8373-5244-4*) Nat Learn.
— Social Sciences & History. (College Level Examination (CLEP) Ser.: Vol. ATS-9E). 43.95 (*0-8373-5299-1*) Nat Learn.
— Social Sciences & History. (College-Level Examination Series (General Examinations): ATS-9E). 1994. pap. 23.95 (*0-8373-5249-5*) Nat Learn.
— Social Service Entry Test. (Career Examination Ser.: Vol. C-3824). 1997. pap. 23.95 (*0-8373-3824-7*) Nat Learn.
— Social Service Representative. (Career Examination Ser.: C-745). 1994. pap. 23.95 (*0-8373-0745-7*) Nat Learn.
— Social Services Administrative Planner. (Career Examination Ser.: C-3066). 1994. pap. 34.95 (*0-8373-3066-1*) Nat Learn.
— Social Services Aide. (Career Examination Ser.: C-3319). 1994. pap. 23.95 (*0-8373-3319-9*) Nat Learn.
— Social Services Collection Representative. (Career Examination Ser.: C-3304). 1994. pap. 27.95 (*0-8373-3304-0*) Nat Learn.
— Social Services Disability Aide. (Career Examination Ser.: C-3259). 1994. pap. 23.95 (*0-8373-3259-1*) Nat Learn.
— Social Services Disability Analyst. (Career Examination Ser.: C-859). 1994. pap. 27.95 (*0-8373-0859-3*) Nat Learn.
— Social Services Employment Specialist. (Career Examination Ser.: C-2816). 1994. pap. 29.95 (*0-8373-2816-0*) Nat Learn.
— Social Services Human Resources Development Specialist. (Career Examination Ser.: C-3189). 1994. pap. 34.95 (*0-8373-3189-7*) Nat Learn.
— Social Services Management Specialist. (Career Examination Ser.: C-1994). 1994. pap. 34.95 (*0-8373-1994-3*) Nat Learn.
— Social Services Management Trainee. (Career Examination Ser.: C-1993). 1994. pap. 29.95 (*0-8373-1993-5*) Nat Learn.
— Social Services Medical Assistance Specialist. (Career Examination Ser.: C-2431). 1994. pap. 34.95 (*0-8373-2431-9*) Nat Learn.
— Social Services Program Coordinator. (Career Examination Ser.: C-3566). 1994. pap. 34.95 (*0-8373-3566-3*) Nat Learn.
— Social Services Program Specialist. (Career Examination Ser.: C-2235). 1994. pap. 34.95 (*0-8373-2235-9*) Nat Learn.
— Social Services Specialist. (Career Examination Ser.: No. C-3747). pap. 29.95 (*0-8373-3747-X*) Nat Learn.
— Social Services Specialist Trainee. (Career Examination Ser.: C-3547). 1994. pap. 27.95 (*0-8373-3547-7*) Nat Learn.
— Social Services Systems Manager. (Career Examination Ser.: C-2992). 1994. pap. 39.95 (*0-8373-2992-2*) Nat Learn.
— Social Studies, Jr. H. S. (Teachers License Examination Ser.: T-54). 1994. pap. 27.95 (*0-8373-8054-5*) Nat Learn.
— Social Studies, Sr. H. S. (Teachers License Examination Ser.: T-55). 1994. pap. 27.95 (*0-8373-8055-3*) Nat Learn.
— Social Welfare Examiner. (Career Examination Ser.: C-2132). 1994. reprint ed. pap. 23.95 (*0-8373-2132-8*) Nat Learn.
— Social Welfare Examiner: (Spanish Speaking) (Career Examination Ser.: C-2136). 1994. reprint ed. pap. 27.95 (*0-8373-2136-0*) Nat Learn.
— Social Work Assistant. (Career Examination Ser.: C-796). 1994. pap. 23.95 (*0-8373-0796-1*) Nat Learn.
— Social Work Training Director. (Career Examination Ser.: C-3476). 1994. pap. 39.95 (*0-8373-3476-4*) Nat Learn.
— Social Worker. (Career Examination Ser.: C-746). 1994. pap. 23.95 (*0-8373-0746-5*) Nat Learn.
— Sociology. (Regents College Proficiency Examination Ser.: Vol. 14). 43.95 (*0-8373-5464-1*) Nat Learn.
— Sociology. (Graduate Record Examination (GRE) Ser.: Vol. 18). 43.95 (*0-8373-5268-1*) Nat Learn.
— Sociology. (Undergraduate Program Field Tests (UPFT) Ser.: Vol. 23). 43.95 (*0-8373-6073-0*) Nat Learn.
— Sociology. (Regents College Proficiency Examination Ser.: CPEP-14). 1994. pap. 23.95 (*0-8373-5414-5*) Nat Learn.
— Sociology. (Graduate Record Examination (GRE) Ser.: Vol. GRE-18). 1994. pap. 23.95 (*0-8373-5218-5*) Nat Learn.
— Sociology. (Undergraduate Program Field Tests (UPFT) Ser.: Vol. UPFT-23). 1994. pap. 23.95 (*0-8373-6023-4*) Nat Learn.
— Soil Conservationist. (Career Examination Ser.: C-1032). 1994. pap. 29.95 (*0-8373-1032-6*) Nat Learn.
— Soil Scientist. (Career Examination Ser.: C-1033). 1994. pap. 29.95 (*0-8373-1033-4*) Nat Learn.
— Solid Waste Construction & Maintenance Supervisor. (Career Examination Ser.: C-3606). 1994. pap. 34.95 (*0-8373-3606-6*) Nat Learn.
— Space Manager. (Career Examination Ser.: C-1055). 1994. pap. 34.95 (*0-8373-1055-5*) Nat Learn.
— Spanish. (Graduate Record Examination (GRE) Ser.: Vol. 19). 43.95 (*0-8373-5269-X*) Nat Learn.
— Spanish. (Undergraduate Program Field Tests (UPFT) Ser.: Vol. 24). 43.95 (*0-8373-6074-9*) Nat Learn.
— Spanish. (National Teacher Examination Ser.: NT-14). 1994. pap. 23.95 (*0-8373-8424-9*) Nat Learn.
— Spanish. (Graduate Record Examination (GRE) Ser.: Vol. GRE-19). 1994. pap. 23.95 (*0-8373-5219-3*) Nat Learn.
— Spanish. (Undergraduate Program Field Tests (UPFT) Ser.: Vol. UPFT-24). 1994. pap. 23.95 (*0-8373-6024-2*) Nat Learn.
— Spanish. (Advanced Placement Test (AP) Ser.: Vol. AP-20). 1997. pap. 23.95 (*0-8373-6220-2*) Nat Learn.
— Spanish, Jr. H. S. (Teachers License Examination Ser.: T-56). 1994. pap. 27.95 (*0-8373-8056-1*) Nat Learn.
— Spanish, Sr. H. S. (Teachers License Examination Ser.: T-57). 1994. pap. 27.95 (*0-8373-8057-X*) Nat Learn.
— Special Agent (Department of Justice) (Career Examination Ser.: C-3287). 1994. pap. 29.95 (*0-8373-3287-7*) Nat Learn.
— Special Agent (FBI) (Career Examination Ser.: C-1060). 1994. pap. 29.95 (*0-8373-1060-1*) Nat Learn.
— Special Agent (INS) (Career Examination Ser.: C-3490). 1994. pap. 29.95 (*0-8373-3490-X*) Nat Learn.
— Special Agent (Wildlife) (Career Examination Ser.: C-2221). 1994. pap. 29.95 (*0-8373-2221-9*) Nat Learn.
— Special Education. (National Teacher Examination Ser.: NT-41). 1994. pap. 23.95 (*0-8373-8451-6*) Nat Learn.
— Special Electrical License. (Career Examination Ser.: C-1492). 1994. pap. 34.95 (*0-8373-1492-5*) Nat Learn.
— Special Enrollment Examination (IRS) (Career Examination Ser.: C-747). 1994. pap. 49.95 (*0-8373-0747-3*) Nat Learn.
— Special Investigations Inspector. (Career Examination Ser.: C-748). 1994. pap. 29.95 (*0-8373-0748-1*) Nat Learn.
— Special Investigator. (Career Examination Ser.: C-1588). 1994. pap. 29.95 (*0-8373-1588-3*) Nat Learn.
— Special Officer. (Career Examination Ser.: C-749). 1994. pap. 23.95 (*0-8373-0749-X*) Nat Learn.
— Special Projects Coordinator. (Career Examination Ser.: C-2933). 1994. pap. 34.95 (*0-8373-2933-7*) Nat Learn.
— Special Rigger. (Career Examination Ser.: C-750). 1994. pap. 27.95 (*0-8373-0750-3*) Nat Learn.
— Special Services Manager. (Career Examination Ser.: C-2147). 1994. reprint ed. pap. 39.95 (*0-8373-2147-6*) Nat Learn.
— Special Sign Hanger. (Career Examination Ser.: C-751). 1994. pap. 27.95 (*0-8373-0751-1*) Nat Learn.
— Specialist, Aging Services. (Career Examination Ser.: C-3565). 1994. pap. 29.95 (*0-8373-3565-5*) Nat Learn.
— Specialist in Adult Services. (Career Examination Ser.: C-3548). 1994. pap. 29.95 (*0-8373-3548-5*) Nat Learn.
— Specialist in Education. (Career Examination Ser.: C-752). 1994. pap. 34.95 (*0-8373-0752-X*) Nat Learn.
— Speech & Hearing Therapist. (Career Examination Ser.: C-754). 1994. pap. 27.95 (*0-8373-0754-6*) Nat Learn.
— Speech & Language Pathology. (National Teacher Examination Ser.: NT-33). 1994. pap. 23.95 (*0-8373-8443-5*) Nat Learn.
— Speech Audiologist. (Career Examination Ser.: C-753). 1994. pap. 27.95 (*0-8373-0753-8*) Nat Learn.
— Speech Communication. (National Teacher Examination Ser.: NT-35). 1994. pap. 23.95 (*0-8373-8445-1*) Nat Learn.
— Speech Improvement. (Teachers License Examination Ser.: T-59). 1994. pap. 27.95 (*0-8373-8059-6*) Nat Learn.
— Speech Pathologist. (Career Examination Ser.: C-755). 1994. pap. 27.95 (*0-8373-0755-4*) Nat Learn.
— Speech Pathology & Audiology. (Undergraduate Program Field Tests (UPFT) Ser.: Vol. 25). 43.95 (*0-8373-6075-7*) Nat Learn.
— Speech Pathology & Audiology. (Undergraduate Program Field Tests Ser.: UPFT-25). 1994. pap. 23.95 (*0-8373-6025-0*) Nat Learn.
— Speech, Sr. H. S. (Teachers License Examination Ser.: T-58). 1994. pap. 27.95 (*0-8373-8058-8*) Nat Learn.
— Speech Technician. (Career Examination Ser.: C-1034). 1994. pap. 27.95 (*0-8373-1034-2*) Nat Learn.
— Staff Analyst. (Career Examination Ser.: C-1551). 1994. pap. 34.95 (*0-8373-1551-4*) Nat Learn.
— Staff Development Coordinator. (Career Examination Ser.: C-2171). 1994. reprint ed. pap. 34.95 (*0-8373-2171-9*) Nat Learn.
— Staff Development Specialist. (Career Examination Ser.: C-2489). 1994. pap. 34.95 (*0-8373-2489-0*) Nat Learn.
— Staff Nurse. (Career Examination Ser.: C-756). 1994. pap. 23.95 (*0-8373-0756-2*) Nat Learn.
— Staff Physician. (Career Examination Ser.: C-1493). 1994. pap. 44.95 (*0-8373-1493-3*) Nat Learn.
— Staff Services Analyst. (Career Examination Ser.: Vol. C-3810). 1997. pap. 34.95 (*0-8373-3810-7*) Nat Learn.
— Standards Compliance Analyst. (Career Examination Ser.: C-3109). 1994. pap. 27.95 (*0-8373-3109-9*) Nat Learn.
— State Accounts Auditor: Examiner of Municipal Affairs. (Career Examination Ser.: C-2367). 1994. pap. 39.95 (*0-8373-2367-3*) Nat Learn.
— State Nursing Boards for Practical Nurse (SNB-PN) (Admission Test Ser.: Vol. 46). 49.95 (*0-8373-5146-4*) Nat Learn.
— State Nursing Boards for Practical Nurse (SNB-PN) (Admission Test Ser.: ATS-46). 1994. pap. 29.95 (*0-8373-5046-8*) Nat Learn.
— State Nursing Boards for Registered Nurse (SNB-RN) (Admission Test Ser.: Vol. 45). 49.95 (*0-8373-5145-6*) Nat Learn.
— State Nursing Boards for Registered Nurse (SNB-RN) (Admission Test Ser.: ATS-45). 1994. pap. 29.95 (*0-8373-5045-X*) Nat Learn.
— State Policewoman. (Career Examination Ser.: C-1692). 1994. pap. 23.95 (*0-8373-1692-8*) Nat Learn.
— State Trooper. (Career Examination Ser.: C-757). 1994. pap. 23.95 (*0-8373-0757-0*) Nat Learn.
— State University Program Aide. (Career Examination Ser.: C-3541). 1994. pap. 27.95 (*0-8373-3541-8*) Nat Learn.
— Station Supervisor. (Career Examination Ser.: C-2105). 1994. reprint ed. pap. 23.95 (*0-8373-2105-0*) Nat Learn.
— Stationary Engineer. (Career Examination Ser.: C-758). 1994. pap. 27.95 (*0-8373-0758-9*) Nat Learn.
— Stationary Engineer (Electric) (Career Examination Ser.: C-759). 1994. pap. 27.95 (*0-8373-0759-7*) Nat Learn.
— Stationary Engineer 1. (Career Examination Ser.: C-1903). 1994. pap. 27.95 (*0-8373-1903-X*) Nat Learn.
— Stationary Engineer 2. (Career Examination Ser.: C-1904). 1994. pap. 29.95 (*0-8373-1904-8*) Nat Learn.
— Stationary Fireman. (Career Examination Ser.: C-760). 1994. pap. 27.95 (*0-8373-0760-0*) Nat Learn.
— Statistical Clerk. (Career Examination Ser.: C-762). 1994. pap. 23.95 (*0-8373-0762-7*) Nat Learn.
— Statistician. (Career Examination Ser.: C-761). 1994. pap. 29.95 (*0-8373-0761-9*) Nat Learn.
— Statistics. (College Level Examination (CLEP) Ser.: Vol. 26). 43.95 (*0-8373-5376-9*) Nat Learn.
— Statistics. (ACT Proficiency Examination Program Ser.: PEP-57). 1994. pap. 23.95 (*0-8373-5907-4*) Nat Learn.
— Statistics. (College Level Examination (CLEP) Ser.: Vol. CLEP-26). 1994. pap. 23.95 (*0-8373-5326-2*) Nat Learn.
— Statistics. (Regents College Proficiency Examination Ser.: Vol. CPEP-15). 1994. pap. 23.95 (*0-8373-5415-3*) Nat Learn.
— Statistics. (Advanced Placement Test (AP) Ser.: Vol. AP-21). 1997. pap. 23.95 (*0-8373-6221-0*) Nat Learn.
— Steam Fireman. (Career Examination Ser.: C-1035). 1994. pap. 27.95 (*0-8373-1035-0*) Nat Learn.
— Steam Fireman - Stationary Fireman. (Career Examination Ser.: C-1902). 1994. pap. 29.95 (*0-8373-1902-1*) Nat Learn.
— Steam Fitter. (Career Examination Ser.: C-763). 1994. pap. 27.95 (*0-8373-0763-5*) Nat Learn.
— Steam Fitter's Helper. (Career Examination Ser.: C-764). 1994. pap. 23.95 (*0-8373-0764-3*) Nat Learn.
— Steel Construction Inspector. (Career Examination Ser.: C-765). 1994. pap. 29.95 (*0-8373-0765-1*) Nat Learn.
— Stenographer. (Career Examination Ser.: C-766). 1994. pap. 19.95 (*0-8373-0766-X*) Nat Learn.
— Stenographer: Law. (Career Examination Ser.: C-1036). 1994. pap. 23.95 (*0-8373-1036-9*) Nat Learn.
— Stenographer-Secretary. (Career Examination Ser.: C-2559). 1994. pap. 23.95 (*0-8373-2559-5*) Nat Learn.
— Stenographer-Typist. (Career Examination Ser.: C-1966). 1994. pap. 19.95 (*0-8373-1966-8*) Nat Learn.
— Stenographer-Typist GS5-7. (Career Examination Ser.: C-768). 1994. pap. 23.95 (*0-8373-0768-6*) Nat Learn.
— Stenographer-Typist GS1-4. (Career Examination Ser.: C-767). 1994. pap. 19.95 (*0-8373-0767-8*) Nat Learn.
— Stenographic Secretarial Associate. (Career Examination Ser.: C-2452). 1994. pap. 23.95 (*0-8373-2452-1*) Nat Learn.
— Stenographic Secretary. (Career Examination Ser.: C-1653). 1994. pap. 23.95 (*0-8373-1653-7*) Nat Learn.
— Stenographic Specialist. (Career Examination Ser.: C-2453). 1994. pap. 23.95 (*0-8373-2453-X*) Nat Learn.
— Stenography & Typewriting (Gregg & Pitman), Sr. H. S. (Teachers License Examination Ser.: T-60). 1994. pap. 27.95 (*0-8373-8060-X*) Nat Learn.
— Stock Clerk. (Career Examination Ser.: C-2617). 1994. pap. 23.95 (*0-8373-2617-6*) Nat Learn.
— Stockman. (Career Examination Ser.: C-769). 1994. pap. 23.95 (*0-8373-0769-4*) Nat Learn.
— Stockroom Worker. (Career Examination Ser.: C-770). 1994. pap. 23.95 (*0-8373-0770-8*) Nat Learn.
— Storekeeper. (Career Examination Ser.: C-771). 1994. pap. 23.95 (*0-8373-0771-6*) Nat Learn.
— Storekeeper I. (Career Examination Ser.: C-2901). 1994. pap. 23.95 (*0-8373-2901-9*) Nat Learn.
— Storekeeper II. (Career Examination Ser.: C-2902). 1994. pap. 27.95 (*0-8373-2902-7*) Nat Learn.
— Stores Assistant. (Career Examination Ser.: C-3344). 1994. pap. 23.95 (*0-8373-3344-X*) Nat Learn.
— Stores Clerk. (Career Examination Ser.: C-1494). 1994. pap. 23.95 (*0-8373-1494-1*) Nat Learn.
— Street Club Worker. (Career Examination Ser.: C-1038). 1994. pap. 27.95 (*0-8373-1038-5*) Nat Learn.
— Street Light Inspections Foreman. (Career Examination Ser.: C-2961). 1994. pap. 29.95 (*0-8373-2961-2*) Nat Learn.
— Street Lighting Installation Worker. (Career Examination Ser.: C-3108). 1994. pap. 27.95 (*0-8373-3108-0*) Nat Learn.
— Structural Engineer. (Career Examination Ser.: C-3335). 1994. pap. 39.95 (*0-8373-3335-0*) Nat Learn.
— Structural Welder. (Career Examination Ser.: C-773). 1994. pap. 23.95 (*0-8373-0773-2*) Nat Learn.
— Structure Maintainer. (Career Examination Ser.: C-772). 1994. pap. 23.95 (*0-8373-0772-4*) Nat Learn.
— Structure Maintainer, Group A (Carpentry) (Career Examination Ser.: C-1495). 1994. pap. 23.95 (*0-8373-1495-X*) Nat Learn.
— Structure Maintainer, Group B (Masonry) (Career Examination Ser.: C-1730). 1994. pap. 23.95 (*0-8373-1730-4*) Nat Learn.
— Structure Maintainer, Group C (Iron Work) (Career Examination Ser.: C-1731). 1994. pap. 23.95 (*0-8373-1731-2*) Nat Learn.
— Structure Maintainer, Group D (Sheet Metal) (Career Examination Ser.: C-1732). 1994. pap. 23.95 (*0-8373-1732-0*) Nat Learn.
— Structure Maintainer, Group E (Plumbing) (Career Examination Ser.: C-1733). 1994. pap. 23.95 (*0-8373-1733-9*) Nat Learn.
— Structure Maintainer, Group F (Sign Painting) (Career Examination Ser.: C-1776). 1994. reprint ed. pap. 23.95 (*0-8373-1776-2*) Nat Learn.
— Structure Maintainer, Group G (Painting) (Career Examination Ser.: C-3528). 1994. pap. 23.95 (*0-8373-3528-0*) Nat Learn.
— Structure Maintainer, Group H (Air Conditioning & Heating) (Career Examination Ser.: C-1422). 1994. pap. 23.95 (*0-8373-1422-4*) Nat Learn.
— Structure Maintainer-Groups A, B, C, D & E. (Career Examination Ser.: C-2064). 1994. reprint ed. pap. 23.95 (*0-8373-2064-X*) Nat Learn.
— Structure Maintainer Trainee, Group A (Carpentry) (Career Examination Ser.: C-1670). 1994. pap. 23.95 (*0-8373-1670-7*) Nat Learn.
— Structure Maintainer Trainee, Group B (Masonry) (Career Examination Ser.: C-1671). 1994. pap. 23.95 (*0-8373-1671-5*) Nat Learn.
— Structure Maintainer Trainee, Group C (Iron Work) (Career Examination Ser.: C-1672). 1994. pap. 23.95 (*0-8373-1672-3*) Nat Learn.
— Structure Maintainer Trainee, Group D (Sheet Metal) (Career Examination Ser.: C-1673). 1994. pap. 23.95 (*0-8373-1673-1*) Nat Learn.
— Structure Maintainer Trainee, Group E (Plumbing) (Career Examination Ser.: C-1674). 1994. pap. 23.95 (*0-8373-1674-X*) Nat Learn.
— Structure Maintainer Trainee, Group G (Painting) (Career Examination Ser.: C-3529). 1994. pap. 23.95 (*0-8373-3529-9*) Nat Learn.
— Structure Maintainer Trainee, Group H (Air Conditioning & Heating) (Career Examination Ser.: C-1491). 1994. pap. 23.95 (*0-8373-1491-7*) Nat Learn.
— Student Aide. (Career Examination Ser.: C-1496). 1994. pap. 23.95 (*0-8373-1496-8*) Nat Learn.
— Student Trainee. (Career Examination Ser.: C-1039). 1994. pap. 23.95 (*0-8373-1039-3*) Nat Learn.
— Substance Abuse Accounts Auditor. (Career Examination Ser.: C-3478). 1994. pap. 29.95 (*0-8373-3478-0*) Nat Learn.
— Substance Abuse Counselor. (Career Examination Ser.: C-3563). 1994. pap. 29.95 (*0-8373-3563-9*) Nat Learn.
— Substance Abuse Prevention Coordinator. (Career Examination Ser.: C-3750). 1994. pap. 34.95 (*0-8373-3750-X*) Nat Learn.
— Substance Abuse Program Specialist. (Career Examination Ser.: C-3336). 1994. pap. 29.95 (*0-8373-3336-9*) Nat Learn.
— Substance Abuse Treatment Program Assistant. (Career Examination Ser.: C-3479). 1994. pap. 27.95 (*0-8373-3479-9*) Nat Learn.
— Summer Aide. (Career Examination Ser.: C-1498). 1994. pap. 23.95 (*0-8373-1498-4*) Nat Learn.
— Summer Employment Examination. (Career Examination Ser.: C-1663). 1994. reprint ed. pap. 23.95 (*0-8373-1663-4*) Nat Learn.
— Summer Intern. (Career Examination Ser.: C-1499). 1994. pap. 23.95 (*0-8373-1499-2*) Nat Learn.
— Superintendent Building Service (U. S. P. S.) (Career Examination Ser.: C-1685). 1994. pap. 34.95 (*0-8373-1685-5*) Nat Learn.
— Superintendent for Administrative Services. (Career Examination Ser.: C-2815). 1994. pap. 34.95 (*0-8373-2815-2*) Nat Learn.
— Superintendent of Alarms. (Career Examination Ser.: C-2965). 1994. pap. 34.95 (*0-8373-2965-5*) Nat Learn.
— Superintendent of Building Inspection. (Career Examination Ser.: C-2282). 1994. reprint ed. pap. 39.95 (*0-8373-2282-0*) Nat Learn.

An Asterisk (*) at the beginning of an entry indicates that the title is appearing for the first time.

— Superintendent of Buildings & Grounds. (Career Examination Ser.: C-1773). 1994. pap. 29.95 (*0-8373-1773-8*) Nat Learn.
— Superintendent of Construction. (Career Examination Ser.: C-1500). 1994. pap. 34.95 (*0-8373-1500-X*) Nat Learn.
— Superintendent of Heating & Ventilation. (Career Examination Ser.: C-2380). 1994. pap. 39.95 (*0-8373-2380-0*) Nat Learn.
— Superintendent of Highways. (Career Examination Ser.: C-2318). 1994. pap. 39.95 (*0-8373-2318-5*) Nat Learn.
— Superintendent of Laundries. (Career Examination Ser.: C-1882). 1994. pap. 34.95 (*0-8373-1882-3*) Nat Learn.
— Superintendent of Plant Operations. (Career Examination Ser.: C-2478). 1994. pap. 39.95 (*0-8373-2478-5*) Nat Learn.
— Superintendent of Public Works. (Career Examination Ser.: C-2305). 1994. reprint ed. pap. 39.95 (*0-8373-2305-3*) Nat Learn.
— Superintendent of Recreation. (Career Examination Ser.: C-652). 1994. pap. 34.95 (*0-8373-0652-3*) Nat Learn.
— Superintendent of Sanitation. (Career Examination Ser.: C-2457). 1994. pap. 34.95 (*0-8373-2457-2*) Nat Learn.
— Superintendent of Sewer Service. (Career Examination Ser.: C-2141). 1994. reprint ed. pap. 39.95 (*0-8373-2141-7*) Nat Learn.
— Superintendent of Sewers. (Career Examination Ser.: C-2276). 1994. reprint ed. pap. 39.95 (*0-8373-2276-6*) Nat Learn.
— Superintendent of Street Lighting. (Career Examination Ser.: C-3125). 1994. pap. 39.95 (*0-8373-3125-0*) Nat Learn.
— Superintendent of Wastewater Treatment Plant. (Career Examination Ser.: C-2963). 1994. pap. 39.95 (*0-8373-2963-9*) Nat Learn.
— Superintendent of Women's Prisons. (Career Examination Ser.: C-1744). 1994. reprint ed. pap. 49.95 (*0-8373-1744-4*) Nat Learn.
— Supervising Account Clerk. (Career Examination Ser.: C-1884). 1994. pap. 27.95 (*0-8373-1884-X*) Nat Learn.
— Supervising Accountant. (Career Examination Ser.: C-1040). 1994. pap. 34.95 (*0-8373-1040-7*) Nat Learn.
— Supervising Addiction Specialist. (Career Examination Ser.: C-1501). 1994. pap. 34.95 (*0-8373-1501-8*) Nat Learn.
— Supervising Admitting Clerk. (Career Examination Ser.: C-1041). 1994. pap. 27.95 (*0-8373-1041-5*) Nat Learn.
— Supervising Air Pollution Inspector. (Career Examination Ser.: C-1502). 1994. pap. 34.95 (*0-8373-1502-6*) Nat Learn.
— Supervising Appraiser. (Career Examination Ser.: C-1699). 1994. pap. 29.95 (*0-8373-1699-5*) Nat Learn.
— Supervising Appraiser (Real Estate) (Career Examination Ser.: C-1680). 1994. pap. 29.95 (*0-8373-1680-4*) Nat Learn.
— Supervising Assessor. (Career Examination Ser.: C-1042). 1994. pap. 29.95 (*0-8373-1042-3*) Nat Learn.
— Supervising Audiologist. (Career Examination Ser.: C-2237). 1994. pap. 34.95 (*0-8373-2237-5*) Nat Learn.
— Supervising Audit Clerk. (Career Examination Ser.: C-887). 1994. pap. 27.95 (*0-8373-0887-9*) Nat Learn.
— Supervising Auditor. (Career Examination Ser.: C-2681). 1994. pap. 39.95 (*0-8373-2681-8*) Nat Learn.
— Supervising Automotive Facilities Inspector. (Career Examination Ser.: C-2215). 1994. pap. 29.95 (*0-8373-2215-4*) Nat Learn.
— Supervising Automotive Mechanic. (Career Examination Ser.: C-2575). 1994. pap. 29.95 (*0-8373-2575-7*) Nat Learn.
— Supervising Beverage Control Investigator. (Career Examination Ser.: C-2824). 1994. pap. 29.95 (*0-8373-2824-1*) Nat Learn.
— Supervising Bookkeeper. (Career Examination Ser.: C-2682). 1994. pap. 27.95 (*0-8373-2682-6*) Nat Learn.
— Supervising Building Inspector. (Career Examination Ser.: C-2840). 1994. pap. 34.95 (*0-8373-2840-3*) Nat Learn.
— Supervising Building Plan Examiner. (Career Examination Ser.: C-862). 1994. pap. 34.95 (*0-8373-0862-3*) Nat Learn.
— Supervising Campus Security Officer. (Career Examination Ser.: C-1703). 1994. pap. 27.95 (*0-8373-1703-7*) Nat Learn.
— Supervising Cashier. (Career Examination Ser.: C-774). 1994. pap. 23.95 (*0-8373-0774-0*) Nat Learn.
— Supervising Children's Counselor. (Career Examination Ser.: C-2010). 1994. pap. 34.95 (*0-8373-2010-0*) Nat Learn.
— Supervising Claim Examiner. (Career Examination Ser.: C-2322). 1994. pap. 29.95 (*0-8373-2322-3*) Nat Learn.
— Supervising Clerk. (Career Examination Ser.: C-775). 1994. pap. 23.95 (*0-8373-0775-9*) Nat Learn.
— Supervising Clerk (Income Maintenance) (Career Examination Ser.: C-1706). 1994. pap. 27.95 (*0-8373-1706-1*) Nat Learn.
— Supervising Community Service Worker. (Career Examination Ser.: C-2677). 1994. pap. 27.95 (*0-8373-2677-X*) Nat Learn.
— Supervising Computer Operator. (Career Examination Ser.: C-776). 1994. pap. 29.95 (*0-8373-0776-7*) Nat Learn.
— Supervising Construction Inspector. (Career Examination Ser.: C-1043). 1994. pap. 34.95 (*0-8373-1043-1*) Nat Learn.
— Supervising Consumer Affairs Inspector. (Career Examination Ser.: C-1657). 1994. pap. 29.95 (*0-8373-1657-X*) Nat Learn.
— Supervising Court Officer. (Career Examination Ser.: C-1503). 1994. pap. 27.95 (*0-8373-1503-4*) Nat Learn.
— Supervising Custodial Foreman. (Career Examination Ser.: C-1044). 1994. pap. 29.95 (*0-8373-1044-X*) Nat Learn.
— Supervising Demolition Inspector. (Career Examination Ser.: C-777). 1994. pap. 34.95 (*0-8373-0777-5*) Nat Learn.
— Supervising Deputy Sheriff. (Career Examination Ser.: C-1666). 1994. pap. 29.95 (*0-8373-1666-9*) Nat Learn.
— Supervising Developmental Specialist. (Career Examination Ser.: C-924). 1994. pap. 29.95 (*0-8373-0924-7*) Nat Learn.
— Supervising Dietitian. (Career Examination Ser.: C-1968). 1994. pap. 29.95 (*0-8373-1968-4*) Nat Learn.
— Supervising Drug & Alcohol Community Coordinator. (Career Examination Ser.: C-2777). 1994. pap. 39.95 (*0-8373-2777-6*) Nat Learn.
— Supervising Economist. (Career Examination Ser.: C-2202). 1994. pap. 34.95 (*0-8373-2202-2*) Nat Learn.
— Supervising Electrical Inspector. (Career Examination Ser.: C-778). 1994. pap. 39.95 (*0-8373-0778-3*) Nat Learn.
— Supervising Electronic Computer Operator. (Career Examination Ser.: C-1549). 1994. pap. 29.95 (*0-8373-1549-2*) Nat Learn.
— Supervising Elevator Inspector. (Career Examination Ser.: C-1955). 1994. pap. 34.95 (*0-8373-1955-2*) Nat Learn.
— Supervising Emergency Medical Service Specialist. (Career Examination Ser.: C-3480). 1994. pap. 34.95 (*0-8373-3480-2*) Nat Learn.
— Supervising Employment Consultant (Testing) (Career Examination Ser.: C-2464). 1994. pap. 44.95 (*0-8373-2464-5*) Nat Learn.
— Supervising Environmentalist. (Career Examination Ser.: C-1586). 1994. pap. 34.95 (*0-8373-1586-7*) Nat Learn.
— Supervising Examiner, Social Services. (Career Examination Ser.: C-2140). 1994. reprint ed. pap. 29.95 (*0-8373-2140-9*) Nat Learn.
— Supervising Fire Alarm Dispatcher. (Career Examination Ser.: C-1695). 1994. pap. 27.95 (*0-8373-1695-2*) Nat Learn.
— Supervising Fire Marshal (Uniformed) (Career Examination Ser.: C-1817). 1994. pap. 39.95 (*0-8373-1817-3*) Nat Learn.
— Supervising Food Inspector. (Career Examination Ser.: C-2055). 1994. pap. 34.95 (*0-8373-2055-0*) Nat Learn.
— Supervising Glazier. (Career Examination Ser.: C-3751). 1994. pap. 29.95 (*0-8373-3751-8*) Nat Learn.
— Supervising Grants Analyst. (Career Examination Ser.: C-2834). 1994. pap. 39.95 (*0-8373-2834-9*) Nat Learn.
— Supervising Hearing Examiner. (Career Examination Ser.: C-2327). 1994. pap. 39.95 (*0-8373-2327-4*) Nat Learn.
— Supervising Hearing Officer. (Career Examination Ser.: C-2328). 1994. pap. 39.95 (*0-8373-2328-2*) Nat Learn.
— Supervising Highway Engineer. (Career Examination Ser.: C-2523). 1994. pap. 39.95 (*0-8373-2523-4*) Nat Learn.
— Supervising Highway Maintenance Supervisor. (Career Examination Ser.: C-2632). 1994. pap. 34.95 (*0-8373-2632-X*) Nat Learn.
— Supervising Hospital Care Investigator. (Career Examination Ser.: C-779). 1994. pap. 29.95 (*0-8373-0779-1*) Nat Learn.
— Supervising Housing Groundsman. (Career Examination Ser.: C-780). 1994. pap. 29.95 (*0-8373-0780-5*) Nat Learn.
— Supervising Housing Inspector. (Career Examination Ser.: C-1045). 1994. pap. 34.95 (*0-8373-1045-8*) Nat Learn.
— Supervising Housing Sergeant. (Career Examination Ser.: C-1667). 1994. pap. 39.95 (*0-8373-1667-7*) Nat Learn.
— Supervising Housing Teller. (Career Examination Ser.: C-781). 1994. pap. 27.95 (*0-8373-0781-3*) Nat Learn.
— Supervising Human Resources Specialist. (Career Examination Ser.: C-1046). 1994. pap. 34.95 (*0-8373-1046-6*) Nat Learn.
— Supervising Human Rights Specialist. (Career Examination Ser.: C-1613). 1994. pap. 29.95 (*0-8373-1613-8*) Nat Learn.
— Supervising Identification Specialist. (Career Examination Ser.: C-2513). 1994. pap. 34.95 (*0-8373-2513-7*) Nat Learn.
— Supervising Incinerator Stationary Engineer. (Career Examination Ser.: C-2638). 1994. pap. 34.95 (*0-8373-2638-9*) Nat Learn.
— Supervising Inspector of Markets, Weights & Measures. (Career Examination Ser.: C-1047). 1994. pap. 34.95 (*0-8373-1047-4*) Nat Learn.
— Supervising Investigator. (Career Examination Ser.: C-2106). 1994. reprint ed. pap. 29.95 (*0-8373-2106-9*) Nat Learn.
— Supervising Janitor. (Career Examination Ser.: C-2065). 1994. reprint ed. pap. 29.95 (*0-8373-2065-8*) Nat Learn.
— Supervising Labor Specialist. (Career Examination Ser.: C-2382). 1994. pap. 39.95 (*0-8373-2382-7*) Nat Learn.
— Supervising Laundry Worker. (Career Examination Ser.: C-2200). 1994. pap. 29.95 (*0-8373-2200-6*) Nat Learn.
— Supervising Legal Stenographer. (Career Examination Ser.: C-2635). 1994. pap. 29.95 (*0-8373-2635-4*) Nat Learn.
— Supervising Manpower Counselor. (Career Examination Ser.: C-2437). 1994. pap. 39.95 (*0-8373-2437-8*) Nat Learn.
— Supervising Meat Inspector. (Career Examination Ser.: C-2056). 1994. pap. 34.95 (*0-8373-2056-9*) Nat Learn.
— Supervising Medicaid Claims Examiner. (Career Examination Ser.: C-2693). 1994. pap. 34.95 (*0-8373-2693-1*) Nat Learn.
— Supervising Medical Care Representative. (Career Examination Ser.: C-3148). 1994. pap. 34.95 (*0-8373-3148-X*) Nat Learn.
— Supervising Medical Services Specialist. (Career Examination Ser.: C-3616). 1994. pap. 39.95 (*0-8373-3616-3*) Nat Learn.
— Supervising Medical Social Worker. (Career Examination Ser.: C-2630). 1994. pap. 34.95 (*0-8373-2630-3*) Nat Learn.
— Supervising Mortgage Administrator. (Career Examination Ser.: C-2312). 1994. reprint ed. pap. 34.95 (*0-8373-2312-6*) Nat Learn.
— Supervising Motor Vehicle License Examiner. (Career Examination Ser.: C-2390). 1994. pap. 27.95 (*0-8373-2390-8*) Nat Learn.
— Supervising Museum Instructor. (Career Examination Ser.: C-1048). 1994. pap. 29.95 (*0-8373-1048-2*) Nat Learn.
— Supervising Nurse. (Career Examination Ser.: C-1883). 1994. pap. 29.95 (*0-8373-1883-1*) Nat Learn.
— Supervising Painter. (Career Examination Ser.: C-3254). 1994. pap. 29.95 (*0-8373-3254-0*) Nat Learn.
— Supervising Parking Enforcement Agent. (Career Examination Ser.: C-2143). 1994. reprint ed. pap. 27.95 (*0-8373-2143-3*) Nat Learn.
— Supervising Parking Meter Collector. (Career Examination Ser.: C-782). 1994. pap. 27.95 (*0-8373-0782-1*) Nat Learn.
— Supervising Photographer. (Career Examination Ser.: C-2504). 1994. pap. 34.95 (*0-8373-2504-8*) Nat Learn.
— Supervising Physical Therapist. (Career Examination Ser.: C-2904). 1994. pap. 34.95 (*0-8373-2904-3*) Nat Learn.
— Supervising Physician & Surgeon. (Career Examination Ser.: C-2195). 1994. pap. 49.95 (*0-8373-2195-6*) Nat Learn.
— Supervising Plumbing Inspector. (Career Examination Ser.: C-1049). 1994. pap. 34.95 (*0-8373-1049-0*) Nat Learn.
— Supervising Police Communications Technician. (Career Examination Ser.: C-3618). 1994. pap. 27.95 (*0-8373-3618-X*) Nat Learn.
— Supervising Probation Officer. (Career Examination Ser.: C-2591). 1994. pap. 29.95 (*0-8373-2591-9*) Nat Learn.
— Supervising Professional Conduct Investigator. (Career Examination Ser.: C-2299). 1994. reprint ed. pap. 29.95 (*0-8373-2299-5*) Nat Learn.
— Supervising Program Research Specialist. (Career Examination Ser.: C-3201). 1994. pap. 39.95 (*0-8373-3201-X*) Nat Learn.
— Supervising Public Health Adviser. (Career Examination Ser.: C-3176). 1994. pap. 29.95 (*0-8373-3176-5*) Nat Learn.
— Supervising Public Health Nurse. (Career Examination Ser.: C-1748). 1994. reprint ed. pap. 29.95 (*0-8373-1748-7*) Nat Learn.
— Supervising Public Health Sanitarian. (Career Examination Ser.: C-2275). 1994. reprint ed. pap. 34.95 (*0-8373-2275-8*) Nat Learn.
— Supervising Real Estate Manager. (Career Examination Ser.: C-1860). 1994. pap. 34.95 (*0-8373-1860-2*) Nat Learn.
— Supervising Rent Examiner. (Career Examination Ser.: C-1818). 1994. pap. 29.95 (*0-8373-1818-1*) Nat Learn.
— Supervising Sanitary Engineer. (Career Examination Ser.: C-2447). 1994. pap. 39.95 (*0-8373-2447-5*) Nat Learn.
— Supervising Sanitation Inspector. (Career Examination Ser.: C-2455). 1994. pap. 34.95 (*0-8373-2455-6*) Nat Learn.
— Supervising Security Officer. (Career Examination Ser.: C-2205). 1994. pap. 29.95 (*0-8373-2205-7*) Nat Learn.
— Supervising Senior Citizens' Club Leader. (Career Examination Ser.: C-2829). 1994. pap. 29.95 (*0-8373-2829-2*) Nat Learn.
— Supervising Social Welfare Examiner. (Career Examination Ser.: C-2379). 1994. pap. 29.95 (*0-8373-2379-7*) Nat Learn.
— Supervising Special Officer. (Career Examination Ser.: C-1756). 1994. pap. 29.95 (*0-8373-1766-5*) Nat Learn.
— Supervising Stenographer. (Career Examination Ser.: C-783). 1994. pap. 23.95 (*0-8373-0783-X*) Nat Learn.
— Supervising Storekeeper. (Career Examination Ser.: C-861). 1994. pap. 29.95 (*0-8373-0861-5*) Nat Learn.
— Supervising Street Club Worker. (Career Examination Ser.: C-1050). 1994. pap. 29.95 (*0-8373-1050-4*) Nat Learn.
— Supervising Support Investigator. (Career Examination Ser.: C-2766). 1994. pap. 29.95 (*0-8373-2766-0*) Nat Learn.
— Supervising Systems Analyst. (Career Examination Ser.: C-2387). 1994. pap. 34.95 (*0-8373-2387-8*) Nat Learn.
— Supervising Tabulator Operator. (Career Examination Ser.: C-1681). 1994. pap. 29.95 (*0-8373-1681-2*) Nat Learn.
— Supervising Taxi & Limosine Inspector. (Career Examination Ser.: C-2554). 1994. pap. 29.95 (*0-8373-2554-4*) Nat Learn.
— Supervising Therapist. (Career Examination Ser.: C-2253). 1994. pap. 34.95 (*0-8373-2253-7*) Nat Learn.
— Supervising Typist. (Career Examination Ser.: C-1928). 1994. pap. 23.95 (*0-8373-1928-5*) Nat Learn.
— Supervising Vocational Counselor. (Career Examination Ser.: C-2439). 1994. pap. 34.95 (*0-8373-2439-4*) Nat Learn.
— Supervising Water Use Inspector. (Career Examination Ser.: C-1051). 1994. pap. 29.95 (*0-8373-1051-2*) Nat Learn.
— Supervising Youth Division Counselor. (Career Examination Ser.: C-2501). 1994. pap. 34.95 (*0-8373-2501-3*) Nat Learn.
— Supervision Test. (Teachers License Examination Ser.: S-9). 1994. pap. 49.95 (*0-8373-8109-6*) Nat Learn.
— Supervisor. (Career Examination Ser.: C-3510). 1994. pap. 29.95 (*0-8373-3510-8*) Nat Learn.
— Supervisor (Buses & Shops) (Career Examination Ser.: C-1504). 1994. pap. 29.95 (*0-8373-1504-2*) Nat Learn.
— Supervisor (Cars & Shops) (Career Examination Ser.: C-1723). 1994. pap. 29.95 (*0-8373-1723-1*) Nat Learn.
— Supervisor (Child Welfare) (Career Examination Ser.: C-784). 1994. pap. 29.95 (*0-8373-0784-8*) Nat Learn.
— Supervisor (Electrical Power) (Career Examination Ser.: C-2238). 1994. pap. 29.95 (*0-8373-2238-3*) Nat Learn.
— Supervisor (Electronic Equipment) (Career Examination Ser.: C-2193). 1994. pap. 29.95 (*0-8373-2193-X*) Nat Learn.
— Supervisor (Elevators & Escalators) (Career Examination Ser.: C-1934). 1994. pap. 29.95 (*0-8373-1934-X*) Nat Learn.
— Supervisor, General Equipment Repair. (Career Examination Ser.: C-1458). 1994. pap. 34.95 (*0-8373-1458-5*) Nat Learn.
— Supervisor (Lighting) (Career Examination Ser.: C-1724). 1994. pap. 29.95 (*0-8373-1724-X*) Nat Learn.
— Supervisor (Medical & Psychiatric Social Work) (Career Examination Ser.: C-1052). 1994. pap. 34.95 (*0-8373-1052-0*) Nat Learn.
— Supervisor of Building Custodians. (Career Examination Ser.: C-1015). 1994. pap. 29.95 (*0-8373-1015-6*) Nat Learn.
— Supervisor of Conservation Areas. (Career Examination Ser.: C-3123). 1994. pap. 34.95 (*0-8373-3123-4*) Nat Learn.
— Supervisor of Construction Inspection Services. (Career Examination Ser.: C-3139). 1994. pap. 39.95 (*0-8373-3139-0*) Nat Learn.
— Supervisor of Electrical Installations. (Career Examination Ser.: C-1507). 1994. pap. 29.95 (*0-8373-1507-7*) Nat Learn.
— Supervisor of Facilities Planning. (Career Examination Ser.: C-3021). 1994. pap. 34.95 (*0-8373-3021-1*) Nat Learn.
— Supervisor of Housing Caretakers. (Career Examination Ser.: C-3010). 1994. pap. 29.95 (*0-8373-3010-6*) Nat Learn.
— Supervisor of Licensing. (Career Examination Ser.: C-2191). 1994. pap. 29.95 (*0-8373-2191-3*) Nat Learn.
— Supervisor of Marina Maintenance. (Career Examination Ser.: C-3130). 1994. pap. 29.95 (*0-8373-3130-7*) Nat Learn.
— Supervisor of Mechanical Installations. (Career Examination Ser.: C-1508). 1994. pap. 29.95 (*0-8373-1508-5*) Nat Learn.
— Supervisor of Mechanics (Mechanical Equipment) (Career Examination Ser.: C-1484). 1994. pap. 29.95 (*0-8373-1484-4*) Nat Learn.
— Supervisor of Mechanics (Motor Vehicles) (Career Examination Ser.: C-3047). 1994. pap. 29.95 (*0-8373-3047-5*) Nat Learn.
— Supervisor of Menagerie. (Career Examination Ser.: C-1792). 1994. pap. 29.95 (*0-8373-1793-2*) Nat Learn.
— Supervisor of Motor Repair. (Career Examination Ser.: C-1875). 1994. pap. 29.95 (*0-8373-1875-0*) Nat Learn.
— Supervisor of Motor Transport. (Career Examination Ser.: C-1509). 1994. pap. 29.95 (*0-8373-1509-3*) Nat Learn.
— Supervisor of Office Services. (Career Examination Ser.: C-2533). 1994. pap. 29.95 (*0-8373-2533-1*) Nat Learn.
— Supervisor of Operations. (Career Examination Ser.: C-1028). 1994. pap. 34.95 (*0-8373-1028-8*) Nat Learn.
— Supervisor of Park Operations. (Career Examination Ser.: C-1752). 1994. pap. 29.95 (*0-8373-1752-5*) Nat Learn.
— Supervisor of Professional Licensing. (Career Examination Ser.: C-1029). 1994. pap. 29.95 (*0-8373-1029-6*) Nat Learn.
— Supervisor of Public Parking. (Career Examination Ser.: C-1418). 1994. pap. 29.95 (*0-8373-1418-6*) Nat Learn.
— Supervisor of School Maintenance (Construction) (Career Examination Ser.: C-1510). 1994. pap. 29.95 (*0-8373-1510-7*) Nat Learn.
— Supervisor of School Maintenance (Mechanical) (Career Examination Ser.: C-1511). 1994. pap. 29.95 (*0-8373-1511-5*) Nat Learn.
— Supervisor of Tax Compliance Field Operations. (Career Examination Ser.: C-2955). 1994. pap. 34.95 (*0-8373-2955-8*) Nat Learn.
— Supervisor of Traffic Device Maintainers. (Career Examination Ser.: C-3052). 1994. pap. 29.95 (*0-8373-3052-1*) Nat Learn.
— Supervisor of Transportation. (Career Examination Ser.: C-1813). 1994. pap. 29.95 (*0-8373-1813-0*) Nat Learn.
— Supervisor of Vocational Rehabilitation Unit. (Career Examination Ser.: C-1742). 1994. pap. 34.95 (*0-8373-1742-8*) Nat Learn.
— Supervisor of Volunteer Services. (Career Examination Ser.: Vol. C-3814). 1997. pap. 29.95 (*0-8373-3814-X*) Nat Learn.
— Supervisor of Youth Services. (Career Examination Ser.: C-1682). 1994. pap. 29.95 (*0-8373-1682-0*) Nat Learn.
— Supervisor I (Child Welfare) (Career Examination Ser.: C-1806). 1994. pap. 29.95 (*0-8373-1806-8*) Nat Learn.
— Supervisor I (Welfare) (Career Examination Ser.: C-1803). 1994. pap. 29.95 (*0-8373-1803-3*) Nat Learn.
— Supervisor (Power Distribution) (Career Examination Ser.: C-423). 1994. pap. 29.95 (*0-8373-0423-7*) Nat Learn.
— Supervisor (Signals) (Career Examination Ser.: C-2062). 1994. pap. 29.95 (*0-8373-2062-3*) Nat Learn.
— Supervisor (Social Work) (Career Examination Ser.: C-1000). 1994. pap. 29.95 (*0-8373-1000-8*) Nat Learn.
— Supervisor (Stores, Materials & Supplies) (Career Examination Ser.: C-1505). 1994. pap. 29.95 (*0-8373-1505-0*) Nat Learn.
— Supervisor (Structures) (Career Examination Ser.: C-424). 1994. pap. 29.95 (*0-8373-0424-5*) Nat Learn.
— Supervisor (Structures - Group C) (Iron Work) (Career Examination Ser.: C-425). 1994. pap. 29.95 (*0-8373-0425-3*) Nat Learn.
— Supervisor (Telephones) (Career Examination Ser.: C-426). 1994. pap. 29.95 (*0-8373-0426-1*) Nat Learn.
— Supervisor III (Child Welfare) (Career Examination Ser.: C-1808). 1994. pap. 34.95 (*0-8373-1808-4*) Nat Learn.
— Supervisor III (Social Service) (Career Examination Ser.: C-1951). 1994. pap. 34.95 (*0-8373-1951-X*) Nat Learn.
— Supervisor III (Welfare) (Career Examination Ser.: C-1805). 1994. pap. 34.95 (*0-8373-1805-X*) Nat Learn.

R

R

— Supervisor (Track) (Career Examination Ser.: C-1953). 1994. reprint ed. pap. 29.95 (*0-8373-1953-6*) Nat Learn.

— Supervisor (Turnstiles) (Career Examination Ser.: C-427). 1994. pap. 29.95 (*0-8373-0427-X*) Nat Learn.

— Supervisor II (Child Welfare) (Career Examination Ser.: C-1807). 1994. pap. 34.95 (*0-8373-1807-6*) Nat Learn.

— Supervisor II (Welfare) (Career Examination Ser.: C-1804). 1994. pap. 34.95 (*0-8373-1804-1*) Nat Learn.

— Supervisor (Ventilation & Drainage) (Career Examination Ser.: C-1506). 1994. pap. 29.95 (*0-8373-1506-9*) Nat Learn.

— Supervisor (Water & Sewer Systems) (Career Examination Ser.: C-2907). 1994. pap. 29.95 (*0-8373-2907-8*) Nat Learn.

— Supervisor (Welfare) (Career Examination Ser.: C-0785). 1994. pap. 29.95 (*0-8373-0785-6*) Nat Learn.

— Supervisor's Handbook of Mnemonic Devices. (Teachers License Examination Ser.: S-10). 1994. pap. 49.95 (*0-8373-8110-X*) Nat Learn.

— Supervisory Electric Engineer. (Career Examination Ser.: C-786). 1994. pap. 39.95 (*0-8373-0786-4*) Nat Learn.

— Supervisory General Engineer. (Career Examination Ser.: C-787). 1994. pap. 44.95 (*0-8373-0787-2*) Nat Learn.

— Supply Clerk. (Career Examination Ser.: C-3340). 1994. pap. 23.95 (*0-8373-3340-7*) Nat Learn.

— Support Collector. (Career Examination Ser.: C-2800). 1994. pap. 23.95 (*0-8373-2800-4*) Nat Learn.

— Support Investigator. (Career Examination Ser.: C-2765). 1994. pap. 27.95 (*0-8373-2765-2*) Nat Learn.

— Surface Line Dispatcher. (Career Examination Ser.: C-788). 1994. pap. 23.95 (*0-8373-0788-0*) Nat Learn.

— Surface Line Operator. (Career Examination Ser.: C-789). 1994. pap. 19.95 (*0-8373-0789-9*) Nat Learn.

— Surgeon. (Career Examination Ser.: C-790). 1994. pap. 44.95 (*0-8373-0790-2*) Nat Learn.

— Surrogate's Court Clerk. (Career Examination Ser.: C-2135). 1994. reprint ed. pap. 27.95 (*0-8373-2135-2*) Nat Learn.

— Surveyor. (Career Examination Ser.: C-3032). 1994. pap. 29.95 (*0-8373-3032-7*) Nat Learn.

— Swimming & Health Instruction, Sr. H. S. (Teachers License Examination Ser.: T-62). 1994. pap. 27.95 (*0-8373-8062-6*) Nat Learn.

— Swimming Pool Operator. (Career Examination Ser.: Vol. C-3819). 1997. pap. 27.95 (*0-8373-3819-0*) Nat Learn.

— Switchboard Operator. (Career Examination Ser.: C-883). 1994. pap. 19.95 (*0-8373-0883-6*) Nat Learn.

— Switchboard Supervisor. (Career Examination Ser.: C-884). 1994. pap. 27.95 (*0-8373-0884-4*) Nat Learn.

— Systems Analyst. (Career Examination Ser.: C-2168). 1994. reprint ed. pap. 29.95 (*0-8373-2168-9*) Nat Learn.

— Systems Control Clerk. (Career Examination Ser.: C-3571). 1994. pap. 23.95 (*0-8373-3571-X*) Nat Learn.

— Systems Programmer. (Career Examination Ser.: C-2187). 1994. pap. 27.95 (*0-8373-2187-5*) Nat Learn.

— Systems Support Aide. (Career Examination Ser.: Vol. C-3811). 1997. pap. 29.95 (*0-8373-3811-5*) Nat Learn.

— Tabulator Operator. (Career Examination Ser.: C-800). 1994. pap. 23.95 (*0-8373-0800-3*) Nat Learn.

— Tailor. (Career Examination Ser.: C-1512). 1994. pap. 34.95 (*0-8373-1512-3*) Nat Learn.

— Tariff Examiner. (Career Examination Ser.: C-828). 1994. pap. 27.95 (*0-8373-0828-3*) Nat Learn.

— Tax Auditor. (Career Examination Ser.: C-2313). 1994. reprint ed. pap. 29.95 (*0-8373-2313-4*) Nat Learn.

— Tax Cashier. (Career Examination Ser.: C-2573). 1994. pap. 19.95 (*0-8373-2573-0*) Nat Learn.

— Tax Collector. (Career Examination Ser.: C-801). 1994. pap. 23.95 (*0-8373-0801-1*) Nat Learn.

— Tax Compliance Agent. (Career Examination Ser.: C-2122). 1994. reprint ed. pap. 27.95 (*0-8373-2122-0*) Nat Learn.

— Tax Compliance Agent (Spanish Speaking) (Career Examination Ser.: C-2123). 1994. reprint ed. pap. 29.95 (*0-8373-2123-9*) Nat Learn.

— Tax Compliance Representative. (Career Examination Ser.: C-2997). 1994. pap. 27.95 (*0-8373-2997-3*) Nat Learn.

— Tax Examiner. (Career Examination Ser.: C-802). 1994. pap. 27.95 (*0-8373-0802-X*) Nat Learn.

— Tax Examiner Trainee. (Career Examination Ser.: C-803). 1994. pap. 23.95 (*0-8373-0803-8*) Nat Learn.

— Tax Map Technician. (Career Examination Ser.: C-3199). 1994. pap. 29.95 (*0-8373-3199-4*) Nat Learn.

— Tax Processing Manager. (Career Examination Ser.: C-3173). 1994. pap. 34.95 (*0-8373-3173-0*) Nat Learn.

— Tax Technician. (Career Examination Ser.: C-2370). 1994. pap. 27.95 (*0-8373-2370-3*) Nat Learn.

— Tax Technician Trainee. (Career Examination Ser.: C-214). 1994. pap. 23.95 (*0-8373-0214-5*) Nat Learn.

— Taxi & Limousine Inspector. (Career Examination Ser.: C-2552). 1994. pap. 23.95 (*0-8373-2552-8*) Nat Learn.

— Taxpayer Service Representative. (Career Examination Ser.: C-833). 1994. pap. 27.95 (*0-8373-0833-X*) Nat Learn.

— Teacher. (Career Examination Ser.: C-2267). 1994. reprint ed. pap. 27.95 (*0-8373-2267-7*) Nat Learn.

— Teachers License Examination Passbook Series. (Entire Ser.). 1994. pap. write for info. (*0-8373-8000-6*) Nat Learn.

— Teachers' Retirement System Information Representative. (Career Examination Ser.: C-3482). 1994. pap. 29.95 (*0-8373-3482-9*) Nat Learn.

— Teaching Assistant. (Career Examination Ser.: C-2845). 1994. pap. 23.95 (*0-8373-2845-4*) Nat Learn.

— Teaching Emotionally Disturbed. (National Teacher Examination Ser.: NT-43). 1994. pap. 23.95 (*0-8373-8453-2*) Nat Learn.

— Teaching Health Conservation. (National Teacher Examination Ser.: NT-23). 1994. pap. 23.95 (*0-8373-8433-8*) Nat Learn.

— Teaching Hearing Handicapped. (National Teacher Examination Ser.: NT-28). 1994. pap. 23.95 (*0-8373-8438-9*) Nat Learn.

— Teaching Learning Disabled. (National Teacher Examination Ser.: NT-44). 1994. pap. 23.95 (*0-8373-8454-0*) Nat Learn.

— Teaching Speech Handicapped. (National Teacher Examination Ser.: NT-26). 1994. pap. 23.95 (*0-8373-8436-2*) Nat Learn.

— Teaching Visually Handicapped. (National Teacher Examination Ser.: NT-27). 1994. pap. 23.95 (*0-8373-8437-0*) Nat Learn.

— Technical Aid in Science & Engineering. (Career Examination Ser.: C-829). 1994. pap. 29.95 (*0-8373-0829-1*) Nat Learn.

— Technical Aide. (Career Examination Ser.: C-1514). 1994. pap. 27.95 (*0-8373-1514-X*) Nat Learn.

— Technical & Professional Assistant. (Career Examination Ser.: C-805). 1994. pap. 29.95 (*0-8373-0805-4*) Nat Learn.

— Technical Assistant. (Career Examination Ser.: C-1515). 1994. pap. 27.95 (*0-8373-1515-8*) Nat Learn.

— Technical Careers Test. (Career Examination Ser.: C-804). 1994. pap. 27.95 (*0-8373-0804-6*) Nat Learn.

— Technical Coordinator. (Career Examination Ser.: C-3614). 1994. pap. 34.95 (*0-8373-3614-7*) Nat Learn.

— Technical Drawing & Graphics. (Dantes Subject Standardized Tests Ser.: DANTES-36). 1994. pap. 23.95 (*0-8373-6636-4*) Nat Learn.

— Technical Mathematics. (Dantes Subject Standardized Tests Ser.: DANTES-37). 1994. pap. 23.95 (*0-8373-6637-2*) Nat Learn.

— Technical Support Aide. (Career Examination Ser.: C-2476). 1994. pap. 29.95 (*0-8373-2476-9*) Nat Learn.

— Technical Writing. (Dantes Subject Standardized Tests (DANTES) Ser.: Vol. 43). 43.95 (*0-8373-6543-0*) Nat Learn.

— Technical Writing. (Dantes Subject Standardized Tests Ser.: DANTES-43). 1994. pap. 23.95 (*0-8373-6643-7*) Nat Learn.

— Technology (Industrial Arts) Education. (National Teacher Examination Ser.: NT-5). 1994. pap. 23.95 (*0-8373-8415-X*) Nat Learn.

Rudman, Jack. Telecommunications Aide. (Career Examination Ser.: C-2877). 1994. pap. 23.95 (*0-8373-2877-2*) Nat Learn.

Rudman, Jack. Telecommunications Analyst. (Career Examination Ser.: C-3000). 1994. pap. 29.95 (*0-8373-3000-9*) Nat Learn.

— Telecommunications Analyst Trainee. (Career Examination Ser.: C-3483). 1994. pap. 27.95 (*0-8373-3483-7*) Nat Learn.

— Telecommunications Qualification Test (TQT) (Career Examination Ser.: Vol. C-3820). 1997. pap. 27.95 (*0-8373-3820-4*) Nat Learn.

— Telecommunications Specialist. (Career Examination Ser.: C-3410). 1994. pap. 27.95 (*0-8373-3410-1*) Nat Learn.

— Telecommunications Technician. (Career Examination Ser.: C-3411). 1994. pap. 27.95 (*0-8373-3411-X*) Nat Learn.

— Telemetric Systems Specialist. (Career Examination Ser.: C-1940). 1994. pap. 34.95 (*0-8373-1940-4*) Nat Learn.

— Telephone Ability Battery (TAB) (Career Examination Ser.: C-3371). 1994. pap. 23.95 (*0-8373-3371-7*) Nat Learn.

— Telephone Cable Maintainer. (Career Examination Ser.: C-830). 1994. pap. 23.95 (*0-8373-0830-5*) Nat Learn.

— Telephone Inspector. (Career Examination Ser.: C-3599). 1994. pap. 27.95 (*0-8373-3599-X*) Nat Learn.

— Telephone Maintainer. (Career Examination Ser.: C-807). 1994. pap. 23.95 (*0-8373-0807-0*) Nat Learn.

— Telephone Operator. (Career Examination Ser.: C-806). 1994. pap. 19.95 (*0-8373-0806-2*) Nat Learn.

— Telephone Services Supervisor. (Career Examination Ser.: C-2586). 1994. pap. 27.95 (*0-8373-2586-2*) Nat Learn.

— Teletypist. (Career Examination Ser.: C-831). 1994. pap. 23.95 (*0-8373-0831-3*) Nat Learn.

— Television Servicing. (Dantes Subject Standardized Tests Ser.: DANTES-38). 1994. pap. 23.95 (*0-8373-6638-0*) Nat Learn.

— Tenant Supervisor. (Career Examination Ser.: C-543). 1994. pap. 29.95 (*0-8373-0543-8*) Nat Learn.

— Test of English As a Foreign Language (TOEFL) (Admission Test Ser.: ATS-30). 1994. pap. 29.95 (*0-8373-5030-1*) Nat Learn.

— Test of General Educational Development (GED) (Admission Test Ser.: ATS-61). 1994. pap. 23.95 (*0-8373-5061-1*) Nat Learn.

— Test Your Knowledge Series. 1994. write for info. (*0-8373-7200-3*); pap. write for info. (*0-8373-7000-0*) Nat Learn.

— Tests & Measurement Specialist. (Career Examination Ser.: C-3484). 1994. pap. 39.95 (*0-8373-3484-5*) Nat Learn.

— Tests & Measurements. (College Level Examination Ser.: CLEP-27). 1994. pap. 23.95 (*0-8373-5327-0*) Nat Learn.

— Therapeutic Activities Specialist. (Career Examination Ser.: C-889). 1994. pap. 29.95 (*0-8373-0889-5*) Nat Learn.

— Thermostat Repairer. (Career Examination Ser.: C-3408). 1994. pap. 23.95 (*0-8373-3408-X*) Nat Learn.

— Ticket Agent. (Career Examination Ser.: C-808). 1994. pap. 23.95 (*0-8373-0808-9*) Nat Learn.

— Timekeeper. (Career Examination Ser.: C-3485). 1994. pap. 23.95 (*0-8373-3485-3*) Nat Learn.

— Title Examiner. (Career Examination Ser.: C-809). 1994. pap. 23.95 (*0-8373-0809-7*) Nat Learn.

— Title Searcher. (Career Examination Ser.: C-1516). 1994. pap. 23.95 (*0-8373-1516-6*) Nat Learn.

— Toll Collector. (Career Examination Ser.: C-810). 1994. pap. 23.95 (*0-8373-0810-0*) Nat Learn.

— Toll Equipment Maintenance Supervisor. (Career Examination Ser.: C-2547). 1994. pap. 29.95 (*0-8373-2547-1*) Nat Learn.

— Toll Equipment Mechanic. (Career Examination Ser.: C-2546). 1994. pap. 27.95 (*0-8373-2546-3*) Nat Learn.

— Toll Section Supervisor. (Career Examination Ser.: C-1947). 1994. pap. 29.95 (*0-8373-1947-1*) Nat Learn.

— Tool & Parts Clerk (USPS) (Career Examination Ser.: C-1610). 1994. pap. 27.95 (*0-8373-1610-3*) Nat Learn.

— Toolmaker. (Career Examination Ser.: C-1517). 1994. pap. 29.95 (*0-8373-1517-4*) Nat Learn.

— Towerman. (Career Examination Ser.: C-811). 1994. pap. 23.95 (*0-8373-0811-9*) Nat Learn.

— Town Clerk. (Career Examination Ser.: C-1854). 1994. pap. 27.95 (*0-8373-1854-8*) Nat Learn.

— Town Engineer. (Career Examination Ser.: C-2001). 1994. pap. 34.95 (*0-8373-2001-1*) Nat Learn.

— Town Investigator. (Career Examination Ser.: C-3067). 1994. pap. 29.95 (*0-8373-3067-X*) Nat Learn.

— Town Maintenance Supervisor. (Career Examination Ser.: C-2764). 1994. pap. 29.95 (*0-8373-2764-4*) Nat Learn.

— Track Equipment Maintainer. (Career Examination Ser.: C-3307). 1994. pap. 23.95 (*0-8373-3307-5*) Nat Learn.

— Trackman. (Career Examination Ser.: C-1066). 1994. pap. 23.95 (*0-8373-1066-0*) Nat Learn.

— Tractor Operator. (Career Examination Ser.: C-827). 1994. pap. 23.95 (*0-8373-0827-5*) Nat Learn.

— Tractor-Trailer Operator. (Career Examination Ser.: C-1519). 1994. pap. 23.95 (*0-8373-1519-0*) Nat Learn.

— Trade Shop Assistant. (Career Examination Ser.: C-3296). 1994. pap. 27.95 (*0-8373-3296-6*) Nat Learn.

— Trade Shop Manager. (Career Examination Ser.: C-3043). 1994. pap. 34.95 (*0-8373-3043-2*) Nat Learn.

— Trades & Industrial Education. (National Teacher Examination Ser.: NT-22). 1994. pap. 23.95 (*0-8373-8432-X*) Nat Learn.

— Traffic & Park Officer. (Career Examination Ser.: C-1689). 1994. pap. 23.95 (*0-8373-1689-8*) Nat Learn.

— Traffic Control Agent. (Career Examination Ser.: C-1750). 1994. reprint ed. pap. 23.95 (*0-8373-1750-9*) Nat Learn.

— Traffic Control Inspector. (Career Examination Ser.: C-812). 1994. pap. 27.95 (*0-8373-0812-7*) Nat Learn.

— Traffic Device Maintainer. (Career Examination Ser.: C-813). 1994. pap. 23.95 (*0-8373-0813-5*) Nat Learn.

— Traffic Device Maintainer Trainee. (Career Examination Ser.: C-814). 1994. pap. 23.95 (*0-8373-0814-3*) Nat Learn.

— Traffic Enforcement Agent. (Career Examination Ser.: C-2407). 1994. pap. 23.95 (*0-8373-2407-6*) Nat Learn.

— Traffic Engineer. (Career Examination Ser.: C-1520). 1994. pap. 29.95 (*0-8373-1520-4*) Nat Learn.

— Traffic Engineer I. (Career Examination Ser.: C-1886). 1994. pap. 29.95 (*0-8373-1886-6*) Nat Learn.

— Traffic Recorder. (Career Examination Ser.: C-1521). 1994. pap. 27.95 (*0-8373-1521-2*) Nat Learn.

— Traffic Supervisor. (Career Examination Ser.: C-2627). 1994. pap. 29.95 (*0-8373-2627-3*) Nat Learn.

— Traffic Technician. (Career Examination Ser.: C-1522). 1994. pap. 27.95 (*0-8373-1522-0*) Nat Learn.

— Traffic Technician I. (Career Examination Ser.: C-2335). 1994. pap. 27.95 (*0-8373-2335-5*) Nat Learn.

— Traffic Technician III. (Career Examination Ser.: C-1887). 1994. pap. 29.95 (*0-8373-1887-4*) Nat Learn.

— Traffic Technician Trainee. (Career Examination Ser.: C-3269). 1994. pap. 23.95 (*0-8373-3269-9*) Nat Learn.

— Traffic Technician II. (Career Examination Ser.: C-2336). 1994. pap. 29.95 (*0-8373-2336-3*) Nat Learn.

— Train Dispatcher. (Career Examination Ser.: C-815). 1994. pap. 23.95 (*0-8373-0815-1*) Nat Learn.

— Train Operator. (Career Examination Ser.: C-1068). 1994. pap. 23.95 (*0-8373-1068-7*) Nat Learn.

— Trainee. (Career Examination Ser.: C-816). 1994. pap. 23.95 (*0-8373-0816-X*) Nat Learn.

— Training & Safety Officer. (Career Examination Ser.: C-3491). 1994. pap. 34.95 (*0-8373-3491-8*) Nat Learn.

— Training Coordinator. (Career Examination Ser.: C-3257). 1994. pap. 39.95 (*0-8373-3257-5*) Nat Learn.

— Training Development Specialist. (Career Examination Ser.: C-3495). 1994. pap. 34.95 (*0-8373-3495-0*) Nat Learn.

— Training Officer. (Career Examination Ser.: C-1523). 1994. pap. 34.95 (*0-8373-1523-9*) Nat Learn.

— Training Specialist. (Career Examination Ser.: C-2337). 1994. pap. 34.95 (*0-8373-2337-1*) Nat Learn.

— Training Specialist I. (Career Examination Ser.: C-2338). 1994. pap. 34.95 (*0-8373-2338-X*) Nat Learn.

— Training Specialist II. (Career Examination Ser.: C-1768). 1994. reprint ed. pap. 39.95 (*0-8373-1768-1*) Nat Learn.

— Training Technician. (Career Examination Ser.: C-1524). 1994. pap. 34.95 (*0-8373-1524-7*) Nat Learn.

— Training Technician (Police) (Career Examination Ser.: C-417). 1994. pap. 39.95 (*0-8373-0417-2*) Nat Learn.

— Trainmaster. (Career Examination Ser.: C-817). 1994. pap. 23.95 (*0-8373-0817-8*) Nat Learn.

— Transcribing Machine Operator. (Career Examination Ser.: C-1067). 1994. pap. 23.95 (*0-8373-1067-9*) Nat Learn.

— Transcribing Typist. (Career Examination Ser.: C-818). 1994. pap. 23.95 (*0-8373-0818-6*) Nat Learn.

— Transit Captain. (Career Examination Ser.: C-819). 1994. pap. 39.95 (*0-8373-0819-4*) Nat Learn.

— Transit Electrical Helper Series. (Career Examination Ser.: C-1963). 1994. pap. 23.95 (*0-8373-1963-3*) Nat Learn.

— Transit Lieutenant. (Career Examination Ser.: C-820). 1994. pap. 34.95 (*0-8373-0820-8*) Nat Learn.

— Transit Management Analyst. (Career Examination Ser.: C-2028). 1994. pap. 34.95 (*0-8373-2028-3*) Nat Learn.

— Transit Management Analyst Trainee. (Career Examination Ser.: C-3228). 1994. reprint ed. pap. 29.95 (*0-8373-3228-1*) Nat Learn.

— Transit Patrolman. (Career Examination Ser.: C-821). 1994. pap. 23.95 (*0-8373-0821-6*) Nat Learn.

— Transit Property Protection Agent. (Career Examination Ser.: C-2397). 1994. pap. 23.95 (*0-8373-2397-5*) Nat Learn.

— Transit Sergeant. (Career Examination Ser.: C-822). 1994. pap. 34.95 (*0-8373-0822-4*) Nat Learn.

— Transit System Manager. (Career Examination Ser.: C-539). 1994. pap. 39.95 (*0-8373-0539-X*) Nat Learn.

— Transportation Analyst. (Career Examination Ser.: C-3380). 1994. pap. 29.95 (*0-8373-3380-6*) Nat Learn.

— Transportation Assistant. (Career Examination Ser.: C-2358). 1994. pap. 27.95 (*0-8373-2358-4*) Nat Learn.

— Transportation Health & Safety Representative. (Career Examination Ser.: C-3379). 1994. pap. 29.95 (*0-8373-3379-2*) Nat Learn.

— Transportation Planning Aide. (Career Examination Ser.: C-2846). 1994. pap. 27.95 (*0-8373-2846-2*) Nat Learn.

— Transportation Specialist. (Career Examination Ser.: C-2479). 1994. pap. 29.95 (*0-8373-2479-3*) Nat Learn.

— Transportation Supervisor. (Career Examination Ser.: C-2738). 1994. pap. 29.95 (*0-8373-2738-5*) Nat Learn.

— Travel Information Aide. (Career Examination Ser.: C-3486). 1994. pap. 27.95 (*0-8373-3486-1*) Nat Learn.

— Treasury Enforcement Agent. (Career Examination Ser.: C-823). 1994. pap. 27.95 (*0-8373-0823-2*) Nat Learn.

— Treatment Unit Clerk. (Career Examination Ser.: C-319). 1994. pap. 23.95 (*0-8373-0319-2*) Nat Learn.

— Tree Pruner Supervisor. (Career Examination Ser.: C-3049). 1994. pap. 29.95 (*0-8373-3049-1*) Nat Learn.

— Tree Trimmer. (Career Examination Ser.: C-1526). 1994. pap. 23.95 (*0-8373-1526-3*) Nat Learn.

— Tree Trimmer Foreman. (Career Examination Ser.: C-2574). 1994. pap. 27.95 (*0-8373-2574-9*) Nat Learn.

— Trigonometry. (College Level Examination Ser.: CLEP-28). 1994. pap. 23.95 (*0-8373-5328-9*) Nat Learn.

— Truck Driver. (Career Examination Ser.: C-1161). 1994. pap. 23.95 (*0-8373-1161-6*) Nat Learn.

— Tunnel Maintainer. (Career Examination Ser.: C-824). 1994. pap. 23.95 (*0-8373-0824-0*) Nat Learn.

— Turnstile Maintainer. (Career Examination Ser.: C-825). 1994. pap. 23.95 (*0-8373-0825-9*) Nat Learn.

— Typewriter Repairman (Electric) (Career Examination Ser.: C-1646). 1994. pap. 27.95 (*0-8373-1646-4*) Nat Learn.

— Typewriter Repairman (Manual) (Career Examination Ser.: C-1645). 1994. reprint ed. pap. 27.95 (*0-8373-1645-6*) Nat Learn.

— Typewriting, Jr. H. S. (Teachers License Examination Ser.: T-63). 1994. pap. 27.95 (*0-8373-8063-4*) Nat Learn.

— Typist. (Career Examination Ser.: C-826). 1994. pap. 19.95 (*0-8373-0826-7*) Nat Learn.

— U. S. Medical License Examination Step I: Basic Medical Sciences. (Admission Test Ser.: ATS-104A). 1994. pap. 49.95 (*0-8373-6967-3*) Nat Learn.

— U. S. Medical License Examination Step II: Clinical Sciences. (Admission Test Ser.: ATS-104B). 1994. pap. 49.95 (*0-8373-6968-1*) Nat Learn.

— U. S. Medical Licensing Exam (USMLE) Step I: Basic Medical Sciences. (Admission Test Ser.: Vol. 104A). 69.95 (*0-8373-6992-4*) Nat Learn.

— U. S. Medical Licensing Exam (USMLE) Step II: Clinical Sciences. (Admission Test Ser.: Vol. 104B). 69.95 (*0-8373-6993-2*) Nat Learn.

— U. S. Medical Licensing Examination (USMLE), 2 vols. in 1. (Admission Test Ser.: Vol. 104). 109.95 (*0-8373-5854-X*) Nat Learn.

— Undergraduate Program Field Test Series. 1994. pap. write for info. (*0-8373-6000-5*) Nat Learn.

— Underwriter. (Career Examination Ser.: C-2011). 1994. pap. 29.95 (*0-8373-2011-9*) Nat Learn.

— Unemployment Insurance Accounts Examiner. (Career Examination Ser.: C-3164). 1994. pap. 27.95 (*0-8373-3164-1*) Nat Learn.

— Unemployment Insurance Claims Clerk. (Career Examination Ser.: C-850). 1994. pap. 23.95 (*0-8373-0850-X*) Nat Learn.

— Unemployment Insurance Claims Examiner. (Career Examination Ser.: C-851). 1994. pap. 27.95 (*0-8373-0851-8*) Nat Learn.

— Unemployment Insurance Hearing Representative. (Career Examination Ser.: C-2728). 1994. pap. 29.95 (*0-8373-2728-8*) Nat Learn.

— Unemployment Insurance Investigator. (Career Examination Ser.: C-2364). 1994. pap. 29.95 (*0-8373-2364-9*) Nat Learn.

— Unemployment Insurance Referee. (Career Examination Ser.: C-917). 1994. pap. 34.95 (*0-8373-0917-4*) Nat Learn.

— Unemployment Insurance Reviewing Examiner. (Career Examination Ser.: C-3041). 1994. pap. 29.95 (*0-8373-3041-6*) Nat Learn.

— Uniformed Court Officer. (Career Examination Ser.: C-852). 1994. pap. 23.95 (*0-8373-0852-6*) Nat Learn.

— United States Citizenship Examination. (Career Examination Ser.: C-3487). 1994. pap. 23.95 (*0-8373-3487-X*) Nat Learn.

— United States Marshal. (Career Examination Ser.: C-853). 1994. pap. 27.95 (*0-8373-0853-4*) Nat Learn.

— United States Park Police Officer. (Career Examination Ser.: C-1989). 1994. pap. 23.95 (*0-8373-1989-7*) Nat Learn.

— Urban Designer. (Career Examination Ser.: C-1527). 1994. pap. 27.95 (*0-8373-1527-1*) Nat Learn.

— Urban Forester. (Career Examination Ser.: C-2905). 1994. pap. 27.95 (*0-8373-2905-1*) Nat Learn.

— Urban Park Officer. (Career Examination Ser.: C-1995). 1994. pap. 23.95 (*0-8373-1995-1*) Nat Learn.

— Urban Park Patrol Sergeant. (Career Examination Ser.: C-2541). 1994. pap. 29.95 (*0-8373-2541-2*) Nat Learn.

— Urban Park Ranger. (Career Examination Ser.: C-3267). 1994. pap. 23.95 (*0-8373-3267-2*) Nat Learn.
— Urban Planner. (Career Examination Ser.: C-854). 1994. pap. 27.95 (*0-8373-0854-2*) Nat Learn.
— Utilities Service Worker. (Career Examination Ser.: C-3161). 1994. pap. 27.95 (*0-8373-3161-7*) Nat Learn.
— Utilization Review Coordinator. (Career Examination Ser.: C-3262). 1994. pap. 27.95 (*0-8373-3262-1*) Nat Learn.
— Varitype Operator. (Career Examination Ser.: C-872). 1994. pap. 23.95 (*0-8373-0872-0*) Nat Learn.
— Vector Control Assistant. (Career Examination Ser.: C-3481). 1994. pap. 23.95 (*0-8373-3481-0*) Nat Learn.
— Vector Control Supervisor. (Career Examination Ser.: C-2763). 1994. pap. 27.95 (*0-8373-2763-6*) Nat Learn.
— Ventilation & Drainage Maintainer. (Career Examination Ser.: C-1528). 1994. pap. 23.95 (*0-8373-1528-X*) Nat Learn.
— Veteran Counselor. (Career Examination Ser.: C-2690). 1994. pap. 29.95 (*0-8373-2690-7*) Nat Learn.
— Veterans Claims Examiner. (Career Examination Ser.: C-3288). 1994. pap. 27.95 (*0-8373-3288-5*) Nat Learn.
— Veterinarian. (Career Examination Ser.: C-870). 1994. pap. 49.95 (*0-8373-0870-4*) Nat Learn.
— Veterinarian Trainee. (Career Examination Ser.: C-1529). 1994. pap. 39.95 (*0-8373-1529-8*) Nat Learn.
— Veterinary College Admission Test (College) (VCAT) (Admission Test Ser.: ATS-29). 1994. pap. 23.95 (*0-8373-5029-8*) Nat Learn.
— Veterinary Medical Officer. (Career Examination Ser.: C-875). 1994. pap. 49.95 (*0-8373-0875-5*) Nat Learn.
— Veterinary Science Officer. (Career Examination Ser.: C-871). 1994. pap. 49.95 (*0-8373-0871-2*) Nat Learn.
— Victims' Services Coordinator. (Career Examination Ser.: C-3537). 1994. pap. 29.95 (*0-8373-3537-X*) Nat Learn.
— Visa Qualifying Examination (VQE) (Admission Test Ser.: ATS-48). 1994. pap. 69.95 (*0-8373-5048-4*) Nat Learn.
— Visiting Teacher. (National Teacher Examination Ser.: NT-21). 1994. pap. 23.95 (*0-8373-8431-1*) Nat Learn.
— Vocabulary. (Teachers License Examination Ser.: G-5). 1994. pap. 27.95 (*0-8373-8195-9*) Nat Learn.
— Vocational Counselor. (Career Examination Ser.: C-1530). 1994. pap. 29.95 (*0-8373-1530-1*) Nat Learn.
— Vocational Counselor Trainee. (Career Examination Ser.: C-1531). 1994. pap. 27.95 (*0-8373-1531-X*) Nat Learn.
— Vocational Guidance Counselor. (Career Examination Ser.: C-1532). 1994. pap. 29.95 (*0-8373-1532-8*) Nat Learn.
— Vocational Rehabilitation Counselor. (Career Examination Ser.: C-2425). 1994. pap. 29.95 (*0-8373-2425-4*) Nat Learn.
— Vocational Rehabilitation Counselor Assistant. (Career Examination Ser.: C-3040). 1994. pap. 27.95 (*0-8373-3040-8*) Nat Learn.
— Vocational Rehabilitation Counselor Trainee. (Career Examination Ser.: C-858). 1994. pap. 27.95 (*0-8373-0858-5*) Nat Learn.
— Vocational Specialist. (Career Examination Ser.: C-3293). 1994. pap. 29.95 (*0-8373-3293-1*) Nat Learn.
— Vocational Training Supervisor. (Career Examination Ser.: C-2673). 1994. pap. 34.95 (*0-8373-2673-7*) Nat Learn.
— Voucher Examiner. (Career Examination Ser.: C-3265). 1994. pap. 23.95 (*0-8373-3265-6*) Nat Learn.
— Warden. (Career Examination Ser.: C-894). 1994. pap. 49.95 (*0-8373-0894-1*) Nat Learn.
— Warehouse Examiner. (Career Examination Ser.: C-895). 1994. pap. 27.95 (*0-8373-0895-X*) Nat Learn.
— Warehouse Supervisor. (Career Examination Ser.: C-926). 1994. pap. 29.95 (*0-8373-0926-3*) Nat Learn.
— Warehouseman. (Career Examination Ser.: C-890). 1994. pap. 23.95 (*0-8373-0890-9*) Nat Learn.
— Warrant & Transfer Officer. (Career Examination Ser.: Vol. C-3817). 1997. pap. 27.95 (*0-8373-3817-4*) Nat Learn.
— Wastewater Technician. (Career Examination Ser.: C-3412). 1994. pap. 27.95 (*0-8373-3412-8*) Nat Learn.
— Wastewater Treatment Plant Maintenance Supervisor. (Career Examination Ser.: C-3064). 1994. pap. 34.95 (*0-8373-3064-5*) Nat Learn.
— Watchman. (Career Examination Ser.: C-891). 1994. pap. 23.95 (*0-8373-0891-7*) Nat Learn.
— Water Basin Supervisor. (Career Examination Ser.: C-3492). 1994. pap. 29.95 (*0-8373-3492-6*) Nat Learn.
— Water District Clerk. (Career Examination Ser.: C-3378). 1994. pap. 23.95 (*0-8373-3378-4*) Nat Learn.
— Water District Superintendent. (Career Examination Ser.: C-3342). 1994. pap. 39.95 (*0-8373-3342-3*) Nat Learn.
— Water District Supervisor. (Career Examination Ser.: C-2625). 1994. pap. 34.95 (*0-8373-2625-7*) Nat Learn.
— Water Maintainance Foreman. (Career Examination Ser.: C-2925). 1994. pap. 29.95 (*0-8373-2925-6*) Nat Learn.
— Water Maintainance Man. (Career Examination Ser.: C-2657). 1994. pap. 27.95 (*0-8373-2657-5*) Nat Learn.
— Water Management Program Coordinator. (Career Examination Ser.: C-3208). 1994. pap. 39.95 (*0-8373-3208-7*) Nat Learn.
— Water Meter Reader. (Career Examination Ser.: C-2224). 1994. pap. 23.95 (*0-8373-2224-3*) Nat Learn.
— Water Meterman. (Career Examination Ser.: C-2225). 1994. pap. 23.95 (*0-8373-2225-1*) Nat Learn.
— Water Plant Operator. (Career Examination Ser.: C-897). 1994. pap. 27.95 (*0-8373-0897-6*) Nat Learn.
— Water Plant Operator Trainee. (Career Examination Ser.: C-886). 1994. pap. 23.95 (*0-8373-0886-0*) Nat Learn.
— Water Plant Supervisor. (Career Examination Ser.: C-2445). 1994. pap. 34.95 (*0-8373-2445-9*) Nat Learn.
— Water Program Specialist. (Career Examination Ser.: C-3488). 1994. pap. 34.95 (*0-8373-3488-8*) Nat Learn.
— Water Quality Control Specialist. (Career Examination Ser.: C-3337). 1994. pap. 34.95 (*0-8373-3337-7*) Nat Learn.
— Water Service Foreman. (Career Examination Ser.: C-2918). 1994. pap. 29.95 (*0-8373-2918-3*) Nat Learn.
— Water Superintendent. (Career Examination Ser.: C-1534). 1994. pap. 39.95 (*0-8373-1534-4*) Nat Learn.
— Water Tender. (Career Examination Ser.: C-1649). 1994. reprint ed. pap. 27.95 (*0-8373-1649-9*) Nat Learn.
— Water Use Inspector. (Career Examination Ser.: C-898). 1994. pap. 23.95 (*0-8373-0898-4*) Nat Learn.
— Watershed Maintainer. (Career Examination Ser.: C-284). 1994. pap. 23.95 (*0-8373-0284-6*) Nat Learn.
— Waterways Management Supervisor. (Career Examination Ser.: C-3414). 1994. pap. 34.95 (*0-8373-3414-4*) Nat Learn.
— Weigher. (Career Examination Ser.: C-2674). 1994. pap. 23.95 (*0-8373-2674-5*) Nat Learn.
— Welder. (Career Examination Ser.: C-892). 1994. pap. 23.95 (*0-8373-0892-5*) Nat Learn.
— Welding. (Occupational Competency Examination Ser.: OCE-33). 1994. pap. 27.95 (*0-8373-5733-0*) Nat Learn.
— Welding Engineer. (Career Examination Ser.: C-1533). 1994. pap. 27.95 (*0-8373-1533-6*) Nat Learn.
— Welfare Housing Consultant. (Career Examination Ser.: C-3331). 1994. pap. 34.95 (*0-8373-3331-8*) Nat Learn.
— Welfare Management System Coordinator. (Career Examination Ser.: C-3024). 1994. pap. 39.95 (*0-8373-3024-6*) Nat Learn.
— Welfare Representative. (Career Examination Ser.: C-899). 1994. pap. 23.95 (*0-8373-0899-2*) Nat Learn.
— Welfare Resources Supervisor. (Career Examination Ser.: C-3332). 1994. pap. 29.95 (*0-8373-3332-6*) Nat Learn.
— Western Civilization. (College Level Examination Ser.: CLEP-29). 1994. pap. 23.95 (*0-8373-5329-7*) Nat Learn.
— Western Civilization. (Regents College Proficiency Examination Ser.: Vol. CPEP-16). 1994. pap. 23.95 (*0-8373-5416-1*) Nat Learn.
— What Do You Know about Accounting? (Test Your Knowledge Ser.: Q-1). 1994. pap. 23.95 (*0-8373-7001-9*) Nat Learn.
— What Do You Know about Afro-American History? (Test Your Knowledge Ser.: Q-2). 1994. pap. 23.95 (*0-8373-7002-7*) Nat Learn.
— What Do You Know about Air Conditioning, Refrigeration & Heating? (Test Your Knowledge Ser.: Q-3). 1994. pap. 29.95 (*0-8373-7003-5*) Nat Learn.
— What Do You Know about American Government? (Test Your Knowledge Ser.: No. Q-4). 1994. pap. 23.95 (*0-8373-7004-3*) Nat Learn.
— What Do You Know about American History? (Test Your Knowledge Ser.: No. Q-5). 1994. pap. 23.95 (*0-8373-7005-1*) Nat Learn.
— What Do You Know about American Literature? (Test Your Knowledge Ser.: No. Q-6). 1994. pap. 23.95 (*0-8373-7006-X*) Nat Learn.
— What Do You Know about Anatomic Sciences? (Test Your Knowledge Ser.: No. Q-7). 1994. pap. 23.95 (*0-8373-7007-8*) Nat Learn.
— What Do You Know about Anthropology? (Test Your Knowledge Ser.: No. Q-8). 1994. pap. 23.95 (*0-8373-7008-6*) Nat Learn.
— What Do You Know about Appliance Repair? (Test Your Knowledge Ser.: No. Q-9). 1994. pap. 23.95 (*0-8373-7009-4*) Nat Learn.
— What Do You Know about Art History? (Test Your Knowledge Ser.: No. Q-10). 1994. pap. 23.95 (*0-8373-7010-8*) Nat Learn.
— What Do You Know about Astronomy? (Test Your Knowledge Ser.: No. Q-11). 1994. pap. 23.95 (*0-8373-7011-6*) Nat Learn.
— What Do You Know about Auto Mechanics? (Test Your Knowledge Ser.: No. Q-12). 1994. pap. 23.95 (*0-8373-7012-4*) Nat Learn.
— What Do You Know about Bacteriology? (Test Your Knowledge Ser.: No. Q-13). 1994. pap. 23.95 (*0-8373-7013-2*) Nat Learn.
— What Do You Know about Biochemistry/Physiology? (Test Your Knowledge Ser.: No. Q-14). 1994. pap. 23.95 (*0-8373-7014-0*) Nat Learn.
— What Do You Know about Biological Sciences? (Test Your Knowledge Ser.: No. Q-15). 1994. pap. 23.95 (*0-8373-7015-9*) Nat Learn.
— What Do You Know about Biology? (Test Your Knowledge Ser.: No. Q-16). 1994. pap. 23.95 (*0-8373-7016-7*) Nat Learn.
— What Do You Know about Building Maintenance? (Test Your Knowledge Ser.: No. Q-17). 1994. pap. 23.95 (*0-8373-7017-5*) Nat Learn.
— What Do You Know about Business Law? (Test Your Knowledge Ser.: No. Q-18). 1994. pap. 23.95 (*0-8373-7018-3*) Nat Learn.
— What Do You Know about Cabinet Making & Millwork? (Test Your Knowledge Ser.: No. Q-19). 1994. pap. 23.95 (*0-8373-7019-1*) Nat Learn.
— What Do You Know about Calculus? (Test Your Knowledge Ser.: No. Q-20). 1994. pap. 23.95 (*0-8373-7020-5*) Nat Learn.
— What Do You Know about Calculus with Analytical Geometry? (Test Your Knowledge Ser.: No. Q-21). 1994. pap. 23.95 (*0-8373-7021-3*) Nat Learn.
— What Do You Know about Carpentry? (Test Your Knowledge Ser.: No. Q-22). 1994. pap. 23.95 (*0-8373-7022-1*) Nat Learn.
— What Do You Know about Chemical Engineering? (Test Your Knowledge Ser.: No. Q-23). 1994. pap. 23.95 (*0-8373-7023-X*) Nat Learn.
— What Do You Know about Chemistry? (Test Your Knowledge Ser.: No. Q-24). 1994. pap. 23.95 (*0-8373-7024-8*) Nat Learn.
— What Do You Know about Civil Engineering? (Test Your Knowledge Ser.: No. Q-25). 1994. pap. 23.95 (*0-8373-7025-6*) Nat Learn.
— What Do You Know about Civil Practice Law & Rules (CPLR)? (Test Your Knowledge Ser.: No. Q-26). 1994. pap. 23.95 (*0-8373-7026-4*) Nat Learn.
— What Do You Know about Clinical Chemistry? (Test Your Knowledge Ser.: No. Q-27). 1994. pap. 23.95 (*0-8373-7027-2*) Nat Learn.
— What Do You Know about College Algebra? (Test Your Knowledge Ser.: No. Q-28). 1994. pap. 23.95 (*0-8373-7028-0*) Nat Learn.
— What Do You Know about College Algebra-Trigonometry? (Test Your Knowledge Ser.: No. Q-29). 1994. pap. 23.95 (*0-8373-7029-9*) Nat Learn.
— What Do You Know about Commercial & Advertising Art? (Test Your Knowledge Ser.: No. Q-30). 1994. pap. 23.95 (*0-8373-7030-2*) Nat Learn.
— What Do You Know about Computer Programming? (Test Your Knowledge Ser.: No. Q-31). 1994. pap. 23.95 (*0-8373-7031-0*) Nat Learn.
— What Do You Know about Computer Science? (Test Your Knowledge Ser.: No. Q-32). 1994. pap. 23.95 (*0-8373-7032-9*) Nat Learn.
— What Do You Know about Cooking? (Test Your Knowledge Ser.: No. Q-33). 1994. pap. 23.95 (*0-8373-7033-7*) Nat Learn.
— What Do You Know about Cosmetology? (Test Your Knowledge Ser.: No. Q-34). 1994. pap. 23.95 (*0-8373-7034-5*) Nat Learn.
— What Do You Know about Criminal Investigation? (Test Your Knowledge Ser.: No. Q-35). 1994. pap. 23.95 (*0-8373-7035-3*) Nat Learn.
— What Do You Know about Criminal Procedure? (Test Your Knowledge Ser.: No. Q-36). 1994. pap. 23.95 (*0-8373-7036-1*) Nat Learn.
— What Do You Know about Criminology? (Test Your Knowledge Ser.: No. Q-37). 1994. pap. 23.95 (*0-8373-7037-X*) Nat Learn.
— What Do You Know about Data Processing? (Test Your Knowledge Ser.: No. Q-38). 1994. pap. 23.95 (*0-8373-7038-8*) Nat Learn.
— What Do You Know about Dental Anatomy? (Test Your Knowledge Ser.: No. Q-39). 1994. pap. 23.95 (*0-8373-7039-6*) Nat Learn.
— What Do You Know about Dental Pharmacology? (Test Your Knowledge Ser.: No. Q-40). 1994. pap. 23.95 (*0-8373-7040-X*) Nat Learn.
— What Do You Know about Diesel Engine Repair? (Test Your Knowledge Ser.: No. Q-41). 1994. pap. 23.95 (*0-8373-7041-8*) Nat Learn.
— What Do You Know about Drafting? (Test Your Knowledge Ser.: No. Q-42). 1994. pap. 23.95 (*0-8373-7042-6*) Nat Learn.
— What Do You Know about Drama & Theatre? (Test Your Knowledge Ser.: No. Q-43). 1994. pap. 23.95 (*0-8373-7043-4*) Nat Learn.
— What Do You Know about Dressmaking? (Test Your Knowledge Ser.: No. Q-44). 1994. pap. 23.95 (*0-8373-7044-2*) Nat Learn.
— What Do You Know about Driving? (Test Your Knowledge Ser.: No. Q-45). 1994. pap. 23.95 (*0-8373-7045-0*) Nat Learn.
— What Do You Know about Earth Science? (Test Your Knowledge Ser.: No. Q-46). 1994. pap. 23.95 (*0-8373-7046-9*) Nat Learn.
— What Do You Know about Economics? (Test Your Knowledge Ser.: No. Q-47). 1994. pap. 23.95 (*0-8373-7047-7*) Nat Learn.
— What Do You Know about Education? (Test Your Knowledge Ser.: No. Q-48). 1994. pap. 23.95 (*0-8373-7048-5*) Nat Learn.
— What Do You Know about Educational Psychology? (Test Your Knowledge Ser.: No. Q-49). 1994. pap. 23.95 (*0-8373-7049-3*) Nat Learn.
— What Do You Know about Electrical Engineering? (Test Your Knowledge Ser.: No. Q-50). 1994. pap. 23.95 (*0-8373-7050-7*) Nat Learn.
— What Do You Know about Electrical Installation? (Test Your Knowledge Ser.: No. Q-51). 1994. pap. 23.95 (*0-8373-7051-5*) Nat Learn.
— What Do You Know about Electrocardiography? (Test Your Knowledge Ser.: No. Q-52). 1994. pap. 39.95 (*0-8373-7052-3*) Nat Learn.
— What Do You Know about Electronics? (Test Your Knowledge Ser.: No. Q-53). 1994. pap. 23.95 (*0-8373-7053-1*) Nat Learn.
— What Do You Know about Endodontics/Periodontics? (Test Your Knowledge Ser.: No. Q-54). 1994. pap. 23.95 (*0-8373-7054-X*) Nat Learn.
— What Do You Know about English Literature? (Test Your Knowledge Ser.: No. Q-55). 1994. pap. 23.95 (*0-8373-7055-8*) Nat Learn.
— What Do You Know about First Aid? (Test Your Knowledge Ser.: No. Q-56). 1994. pap. 23.95 (*0-8373-7056-6*) Nat Learn.
— What Do You Know about Food Service? (Test Your Knowledge Ser.: No. Q-57). 1994. pap. 23.95 (*0-8373-7057-4*) Nat Learn.
— What Do You Know about French? (Test Your Knowledge Ser.: No. Q-58). 1994. pap. 23.95 (*0-8373-7058-2*) Nat Learn.
— What Do You Know about Fundamentals of Nursing? (Test Your Knowledge Ser.: No. Q-59). 1994. pap. 23.95 (*0-8373-7059-0*) Nat Learn.
— What Do You Know about Gardening? (Test Your Knowledge Ser.: No. Q-60). 1994. pap. 23.95 (*0-8373-7060-4*) Nat Learn.
— What Do You Know about Geography? (Test Your Knowledge Ser.: No. Q-61). 1994. pap. 23.95 (*0-8373-7061-2*) Nat Learn.
— What Do You Know about Geology? (Test Your Knowledge Ser.: No. Q-62). 1994. pap. 23.95 (*0-8373-7062-0*) Nat Learn.
— What Do You Know about Geometry? (Test Your Knowledge Ser.: No. Q-63). 1994. pap. 23.95 (*0-8373-7063-9*) Nat Learn.
— What Do You Know about Geophysics? (Test Your Knowledge Ser.: No. Q-64). 1994. pap. 23.95 (*0-8373-7064-7*) Nat Learn.
— What Do You Know about German? (Test Your Knowledge Ser.: No. Q-65). 1994. pap. 23.95 (*0-8373-7065-5*) Nat Learn.
— What Do You Know about Guidance & Counseling? (Test Your Knowledge Ser.: No. Q-66). 1994. pap. 23.95 (*0-8373-7066-3*) Nat Learn.
— What Do You Know about Health? (Test Your Knowledge Ser.: No. Q-67). 1994. pap. 23.95 (*0-8373-7067-1*) Nat Learn.
— What Do You Know about Hematology? (Test Your Knowledge Ser.: No. Q-68). 1994. pap. 23.95 (*0-8373-7068-X*) Nat Learn.
— What Do You Know about History? (Test Your Knowledge Ser.: No. Q-69). 1994. pap. 23.95 (*0-8373-7069-8*) Nat Learn.
— What Do You Know about Home Economics? (Test Your Knowledge Ser.: No. Q-70). 1994. pap. 23.95 (*0-8373-7070-1*) Nat Learn.
— What Do You Know about Humanities? (Test Your Knowledge Ser.: No. Q-71). 1994. pap. 23.95 (*0-8373-7071-X*) Nat Learn.
— What Do You Know about Immunohematology & Blood Banking? (Test Your Knowledge Ser.: No. Q-72). 1994. pap. 23.95 (*0-8373-7072-8*) Nat Learn.
— What Do You Know about Inorganic Chemistry? (Test Your Knowledge Ser.: No. Q-73). 1994. pap. 23.95 (*0-8373-7073-6*) Nat Learn.
— What Do You Know about Intermediate Algebra? (Test Your Knowledge Ser.: No. Q-74). 1994. pap. 23.95 (*0-8373-7074-4*) Nat Learn.
— What Do You Know about Italian? (Test Your Knowledge Ser.: No. Q-75). 1994. pap. 23.95 (*0-8373-7075-2*) Nat Learn.
— What Do You Know about Latin? (Test Your Knowledge Ser.: No. Q-76). 1994. pap. 23.95 (*0-8373-7076-0*) Nat Learn.
— What Do You Know about Law Enforcement? (Test Your Knowledge Ser.: No. Q-77). 1994. pap. 23.95 (*0-8373-7077-9*) Nat Learn.
— What Do You Know about Library Science? (Test Your Knowledge Ser.: No. Q-78). 1994. pap. 23.95 (*0-8373-7078-7*) Nat Learn.
— What Do You Know about Literature? (Test Your Knowledge Ser.: No. Q-79). 1994. pap. 23.95 (*0-8373-7079-5*) Nat Learn.
— What Do You Know about Machine Trades? (Test Your Knowledge Ser.: No. Q-80). 1994. pap. 23.95 (*0-8373-7080-9*) Nat Learn.
— What Do You Know about Marketing? (Test Your Knowledge Ser.: No. Q-81). 1994. pap. 23.95 (*0-8373-7081-7*) Nat Learn.
— What Do you Know about Masonry & Bricklaying? (Test Your Knowledge Ser.: No. Q-82). 1994. pap. 23.95 (*0-8373-7082-5*) Nat Learn.
— What Do You Know about Mechanical Engineering? (Test Your Knowledge Ser.: No. Q-83). 1994. pap. 23.95 (*0-8373-7083-3*) Nat Learn.
— What Do You Know about Meteorology? (Test Your Knowledge Ser.: No. Q-84). 1994. pap. 23.95 (*0-8373-7084-1*) Nat Learn.
— What Do You Know about Microbiology/Pathology? (Test Your Knowledge Ser.: No. Q-85). 1994. pap. 23.95 (*0-8373-7085-X*) Nat Learn.
— What Do You Know about Money & Banking? (Test Your Knowledge Ser.: No. Q-86). 1994. pap. 23.95 (*0-8373-7086-8*) Nat Learn.
— What Do You Know about Music? (Test Your Knowledge Ser.: No. Q-87). 1994. pap. 23.95 (*0-8373-7087-6*) Nat Learn.
— What Do You Know about Offset Lithography? (Test Your Knowledge Ser.: No. Q-88). 1994. pap. 23.95 (*0-8373-7088-4*) Nat Learn.
— What Do You Know about Operative Dentistry? (Test Your Knowledge Ser.: No. Q-89). 1994. pap. 23.95 (*0-8373-7089-2*) Nat Learn.
— What Do You Know about Oral Pathology/Radiography? (Test Your Knowledge Ser.: No. Q-90). 1994. pap. 23.95 (*0-8373-7090-6*) Nat Learn.
— What Do You Know about Oral Surgery & Anaesthesia? (Test Your Knowledge Ser.: No. Q-91). 1994. pap. 23.95 (*0-8373-7091-4*) Nat Learn.
— What Do You Know about Organic Chemistry? (Test Your Knowledge Ser.: No. Q-92). 1994. pap. 23.95 (*0-8373-7092-2*) Nat Learn.
— What Do You Know about Orthodontics/Pedodontics? (Test Your Knowledge Ser.: No. Q-93). 1994. pap. 23.95 (*0-8373-7093-0*) Nat Learn.
— What Do You Know about Penal Law? (Test Your Knowledge Ser.: No. Q-94). 1994. pap. 23.95 (*0-8373-7094-9*) Nat Learn.
— What Do You Know about Pharmacology? (Test Your Knowledge Ser.: No. Q-95). 1994. pap. 23.95 (*0-8373-7095-7*) Nat Learn.
— What Do You Know about Philosophy? (Test Your Knowledge Ser.: No. Q-96). 1994. pap. 23.95 (*0-8373-7096-5*) Nat Learn.
— What Do You Know about Photography? (Test Your Knowledge Ser.: No. Q-97). 1994. pap. 23.95 (*0-8373-7097-3*) Nat Learn.
— What Do You Know about Physical Education? (Test Your Knowledge Ser.: No. Q-98). 1994. pap. 23.95 (*0-8373-7098-1*) Nat Learn.
— What Do You Know about Physical Sciences? (Test Your Knowledge Ser.: No. Q-99). 1994. pap. 23.95 (*0-8373-7099-X*) Nat Learn.
— What Do You Know about Physics? (Test Your Knowledge Ser.: No. Q-100). 1994. pap. 23.95 (*0-8373-7100-7*) Nat Learn.

R

— What Do You Know about Plumbing? (Test Your Knowledge Ser.: No. Q-102). 1994. pap. 23.95 (*0-8373-7102-3*) Nat Learn.
— What Do You Know about Political Science? (Test Your Knowledge Ser.: No. Q-101). 1994. pap. 23.95 (*0-8373-7101-5*) Nat Learn.
— What Do You Know about Printing? (Test Your Knowledge Ser.: No. Q-103). 1994. pap. 23.95 (*0-8373-7103-1*) Nat Learn.
— What Do You Know about Prosthodontics? (Test Your Knowledge Ser.: No. Q-104). 1994. pap. 23.95 (*0-8373-7104-X*) Nat Learn.
— What Do You Know about Psychology? (Test Your Knowledge Ser.: No. Q-105). 1994. pap. 23.95 (*0-8373-7105-8*) Nat Learn.
— What Do You Know about Radio & TV Servicing? (Test Your Knowledge Ser.: No. Q-106). 1994. pap. 23.95 (*0-8373-7106-6*) Nat Learn.
— What Do You Know about Shakespeare? (Test Your Knowledge Ser.: No. Q-107). 1994. pap. 23.95 (*0-8373-7107-4*) Nat Learn.
— What Do You Know about Sheet Metal Work? (Test Your Knowledge Ser.: No. Q-108). 1994. pap. 23.95 (*0-8373-7108-2*) Nat Learn.
— What Do You Know about Small Engine Repair? (Test Your Knowledge Ser.: No. Q-109). 1994. pap. 23.95 (*0-8373-7109-0*) Nat Learn.
— What Do You Know about Social Sciences? (Test Your Knowledge Ser.: No. Q-110). 1994. pap. 23.95 (*0-8373-7110-4*) Nat Learn.
— What Do You Know about Sociology? (Test Your Knowledge Ser.: No. Q-111). 1994. pap. 23.95 (*0-8373-7111-2*) Nat Learn.
— What Do You Know about Spanish? (Test Your Knowledge Ser.: No. Q-112). 1994. pap. 23.95 (*0-8373-7112-0*) Nat Learn.
— What Do You Know about Statistics? (Test Your Knowledge Ser.: No. Q-113). 1994. pap. 23.95 (*0-8373-7113-9*) Nat Learn.
— What Do You Know about Trigonometry? (Test Your Knowledge Ser.: No. Q-114). 1994. pap. 23.95 (*0-8373-7114-7*) Nat Learn.
— What Do You Know about Welding? (Test Your Knowledge Ser.: No. Q-115). 1994. pap. 23.95 (*0-8373-7115-5*) Nat Learn.
— What Do You Know about Western Civilization? (Test Your Knowledge Ser.: No. Q-116). 1994. pap. 23.95 (*0-8373-7116-3*) Nat Learn.
— Wildlife Specialist. (Career Examination Ser.: C-896). 1994. pap. 27.95 (*0-8373-0896-8*) Nat Learn.
— Window Cleaner. (Career Examination Ser.: C-893). 1994. pap. 19.95 (*0-8373-0893-3*) Nat Learn.
— Window Clerk (USPS) (Career Examination Ser.: C-3314). 1994. pap. 23.95 (*0-8373-3314-8*) Nat Learn.
— Window Washer. (Career Examination Ser.: C-1535). 1994. pap. 19.95 (*0-8373-1535-2*) Nat Learn.
— Wiper (Uniformed) (Career Examination Ser.: C-1632). 1994. pap. 27.95 (*0-8373-1632-4*) Nat Learn.
— Women's Physical Education. (National Teacher Examination Ser.: NT-37). 1994. pap. 23.95 (*0-8373-8447-8*) Nat Learn.
— Word Processing Supervisor. (Career Examination Ser.: C-3570). 1994. pap. 27.95 (*0-8373-3570-1*) Nat Learn.
— Word Processor. (Career Examination Ser.: C-3184). 1994. pap. 23.95 (*0-8373-3184-6*) Nat Learn.
— Workbook Series. 1994. pap. write for info. (*0-8373-7900-8*) Nat Learn.
— Worker's Compensation Review Analyst. (Career Examination Ser.: C-308). 1994. pap. 29.95 (*0-8373-0308-7*) Nat Learn.
— Workers' Compensation Social Worker I. (Career Examination Ser.: C-1319). 1994. pap. 27.95 (*0-8373-1319-8*) Nat Learn.
— Workers' Compensation Social Worker II. (Career Examination Ser.: C-1320). 1994. pap. 29.95 (*0-8373-1320-1*) Nat Learn.
— Workmen's Compensation Examiner. (Career Examination Ser.: C-1644). 1994. reprint ed. pap. 27.95 (*0-8373-1644-8*) Nat Learn.
— Writing & Public Information Occupations. (Career Examination Ser.: C-3556). 1994. pap. 27.95 (*0-8373-3556-6*) Nat Learn.
— Written English Paper, Elem. School, Jr. & Sr. H. S. (Teachers License Examination Ser.: T-61). 1994. pap. 27.95 (*0-8373-8061-8*) Nat Learn.
— X-Ray Coordinator. (Career Examination Ser.: C-1536). 1994. pap. 34.95 (*0-8373-1536-0*) Nat Learn.
— X-Ray Technician. (Career Examination Ser.: C-910). 1994. pap. 27.95 (*0-8373-0910-7*) Nat Learn.
— X-Ray Technician I. (Career Examination Ser.: C-1840). 1994. pap. 27.95 (*0-8373-1840-8*) Nat Learn.
— X-Ray Technician III. (Career Examination Ser.: C-1842). 1994. pap. 29.95 (*0-8373-1842-4*) Nat Learn.
— X-Ray Technician II. (Career Examination Ser.: C-1841). 1994. pap. 29.95 (*0-8373-1841-6*) Nat Learn.
— Youth Corps Project Director. (Career Examination Ser.: C-2208). 1994. pap. 39.95 (*0-8373-2208-1*) Nat Learn.
— Youth Corps Recruiter. (Career Examination Ser.: C-1537). 1994. pap. 29.95 (*0-8373-1537-9*) Nat Learn.
— Youth Counselor. (Career Examination Ser.: C-2906). 1994. pap. 29.95 (*0-8373-2906-X*) Nat Learn.
— Youth Division Counselor. (Career Examination Ser.: C-2107). 1994. pap. 29.95 (*0-8373-2107-7*) Nat Learn.
— Youth Education Coordinator. (Career Examination Ser.: C-2534). 1994. pap. 34.95 (*0-8373-2534-X*) Nat Learn.
— Youth Employment Program Specialist. (Career Examination Ser.: C-3538). 1994. pap. 34.95 (*0-8373-3538-8*) Nat Learn.
— Youth Group Supervisor. (Career Examination Ser.: C-1540). 1994. pap. 29.95 (*0-8373-1540-9*) Nat Learn.
— Youth Group Worker. (Career Examination Ser.: C-1538). 1994. pap. 27.95 (*0-8373-1538-7*) Nat Learn.
— Youth Group Worker Aide. (Career Examination Ser.: C-1539). 1994. pap. 23.95 (*0-8373-1539-5*) Nat Learn.
— Youth Guidance Technician. (Career Examination Ser.: C-920). 1994. pap. 29.95 (*0-8373-0920-4*) Nat Learn.
— Youth Services Coordinator. (Career Examination Ser.: C-2324). 1994. pap. 34.95 (*0-8373-2324-X*) Nat Learn.
— Youth Services Specialist. (Career Examination Ser.: C-1641). 1994. reprint ed. pap. 27.95 (*0-8373-1641-3*) Nat Learn.
— Zoning Inspector. (Career Examination Ser.: C-2340). 1994. pap. 29.95 (*0-8373-2340-1*) Nat Learn.
— Zoning Inspector II. (Career Examination Ser.: C-3079). 1994. pap. 34.95 (*0-8373-3079-3*) Nat Learn.

Rudman, Jack, ed. see Standish, Burt L.

Rudman, Mark. By Contraries & Other Poems. LC 86-64043. (Collected Poems Ser.). 162p. (Orig.). 1987. 25.00 (*0-915032-92-9*) Natl Poet Foun.
— By Contraries & Other Poems. LC 86-64043. (Collected Poems Ser.). 162p. (Orig.). 1989. pap. 12.95 (*0-915032-93-7*) Natl Poet Foun.
— Diverse Voices: Essays on Poets & Poetry. 282p. (C). 1993. 26.95 (*0-934257-67-1*); pap. 18.95 (*0-934257-68-X*) Story Line.
— In the Neighboring Cell. 1982. 5.00 (*0-686-34454-5*) S Duyvil.
— The Millennium Hotel. LC 96-26572. (Wesleyan Poetry Ser.). 201p. 1996. pap. 14.95 (*0-8195-2230-9*, Wesleyan Univ Pr); text 35.00 (*0-8195-2229-5*, Wesleyan Univ Pr) U Pr of New Eng.
— The Nowhere Steps. LC 90-30054. 139p. 1990. pap. 13.95 (*0-935296-90-5*, Pub. by Sheep Meadow); text 27.50 (*0-935296-93-X*, Pub. by Sheep Meadow) U Pr of New Eng.
— Provoked in Venice. LC 98-47527. (Wesleyan Poetry Ser.). 212p. 1999. pap. 14.95 (*0-8195-6354-4*, Wesleyan Univ Pr); text 30.00 (*0-8195-6353-6*, Wesleyan Univ Pr) U Pr of New Eng.
— Realm of Unknowing: Meditations on Art, Suicide, & Other Transformations. LC 94-39701. 193p. 1995. pap. 15.95 (*0-8195-1224-9*, Wesleyan Univ Pr); text 35.00 (*0-8195-2220-1*, Wesleyan Univ Pr) U Pr of New Eng.
— Rider. LC 93-38326. (Wesleyan Poetry Ser.). 122p. 1994. pap. 13.95 (*0-8195-1217-6*, Wesleyan Univ Pr) U Pr of New Eng.

Rudman, Mark, ed. Literature & the Visual Arts: A Special Issue of Pequod. (Illus.). 303p. (Orig.). 1990. pap. 17.95 (*1-878818-01-5*, Pub. by Sheep Meadow) U Pr of New Eng.

Rudman, Mark, tr. see Pasternak, Boris.

Rudman, Masha K. Children's Literature. 2nd ed. LC 83-22217. 448p. (C). 1984. text 34.95 (*0-582-28398-1*, 71430) Longman.
— Children's Literature: An Issues Approach. 3rd rev. ed. LC 94-6627. 512p. (C). 1994. pap. text 52.00 (*0-8013-0537-3*, 78414) Longman.

Rudman, Reuben, ed. Diffraction Aspects of Orientationally Disordered (Plastic) Crystals. (Transactions of the American Crystallographic Association Ser.: Vol. 17). 114p. 1981. pap. 25.00 (*0-937140-26-0*) Polycrystal Bk Serv.

Rudman, Stanley. Concepts of Person & Christian Ethics. LC 96-53048. (New Studies in Christian Ethics: Vol. 11). 421p. (C). 1998. text 69.95 (*0-521-58171-0*) Cambridge U Pr.

Rudman, Theo. The Complete Guide to Cigars: How & Where to Find Them, Select Them & Smoke Them. (Illus.). 350p. (Orig.). 1996. pap. 14.95 (*1-57243-149-0*) Triumph Bks.
— Rudman's Cigar Buying Guide: Selecting & Savoring the Perfect Cigar for Any Occasion. 400p. 1997. pap. 14.95 (*1-57243-233-0*) Triumph Bks.
— Rudman's Complete Guide to Cigars: How to Find, Select & Smoke Them. rev. ed. 366p. 1997. pap. 14.95 (*1-57243-245-4*) Triumph Bks.

Rudman, Tim. Master Photographer's Lith Printing Course: A Definitive Guide to Creative Lith Printing. 128p. 1999. pap. 24.95 (*0-8174-4539-0*) Watsn-Guptill.
— The Photographer's Master Printing Course. (Illus.). 160p. 1998. text 29.95 (*0-240-80324-8*, Focal) Buttrwrth-Heinemann.

Rudman, Warren B., jt. auth. see Brown, Harold.

Rudman, William J. Performance Improvement in Health Information Services. Biello, Lisa, ed. LC 96-46878. 224p. 1997. text 44.00 (*0-7216-6009-6*, W B Saunders Co) Harcrt Hlth Sci Grp.

Rudmann, Sally V., ed. Textbook of Blood Banking & Transfusion Medicine. LC 93-49788. 1994. text. write for info. (*0-7216-3453-2*, W B Saunders Co) Harcrt Hlth Sci Grp.

Rudner, Barry. The Bumblebee & the Ram. LC 89-81585. (Illus.). 32p. (Orig.). (J). (gr. k-6). 1990. pap. 5.95 (*0-925928-03-8*) Tiny Thought.
— Filet of Soil. 25p. (J). 1995. pap. 6.95 (*0-9642206-3-6*) Windword Pr.
— The Handstand. (Illus.). 32p. (J). 1991. pap. 5.95 (*0-925928-05-4*) Tiny Thought.
— The Littlest Tall Fellow. Carraro, J. M., ed. (Illus.). 32p. (J). (gr. k-6). 1989. pap. 5.95 (*0-925928-00-3*) Tiny Thought.
— My Friends That Rhyme with Orange. LC 95-90526. 29p. (J). (ps). 1995. pap. 6.95 (*0-9642206-2-8*) Windword Pr.
— Nonsense. (Illus.). 32p. (J). (gr. k-6). 1991. pap. 5.95 (*0-925928-04-6*) Tiny Thought.
— Special Ed. 28p. (J). 1999. pap. 7.95 (*0-9642206-4-4*, Pub. by Windword Pr) ACCESS Pubs Network.

***Rudner, Barry.** Special Ed. large type ed. LC 98-90743. (Illus.). 28p. (J). (gr. k-6). 2000. 7.95 (*0-9642206-6-0*, Pub. by Windword Pr) ACCESS Pubs Network.

Rudner, Barry. Will I Still Have to Make My Bed in the Morning? (Illus.). 30p. (Orig.). (J). (gr. k-6). 1992. pap. 5.95 (*0-925928-10-0*) Tiny Thought.
— You're the Apple of My Face. 2nd ed. 30p. (Orig.). (J). (gr. k-6). 1995. pap. 4.95 (*0-9642206-0-1*) Windword Pr.
— You're the Apple of My Face, 20 bks., Set. 2nd ed. (Illus.). 30p. (Orig.). (J). (gr. k-6). 1995. pap. 49.60 (*0-9642206-1-X*) Windword Pr.

Rudner, David W. Caste & Capitalism in Colonial India: The Nattukottai Chettiars. 390p. 1995. 42.50 (*0-614-07890-3*, Pub. by M Manoharial) Coronet Bks.
— Caste & Capitalism in Colonial India: The Nattukottai Chettiars. LC 92-38124. 1994. 55.00 (*0-520-07236-7*, Pub. by U CA Pr); pap. 19.95 (*0-520-08350-4*, Pub. by U CA Pr) Cal Prin Full Svc.

Rudner, Ione, jt. auth. see Rudner, Jalmar.

Rudner, Jalmar & Rudner, Ione. The Hunter & His Art: A Survey of Rock Art in Southern Africa. (Illus.). 1974. 32.00 (*0-685-03456-9*) Munger Africana Lib.

Rudner, Lawrence. Memory's Tailor. Kessel, John & Ketchin, Susan, eds. LC 98-15895. 156p. 1998. 25.00 (*1-57806-090-7*) U Pr of Miss.

Rudner, Richard S. & Scheffler, Israel, eds. Logic & Art: Essays in Honor of Nelson Goodman. LC 76-140799. x, 332p. (C). 1972. lib. bdg. 20.00 (*0-672-51639-X*) Ridgeview.

***Rudner, Ruth.** A Chorus of Buffalo. LC 99-88014. 192p. 2000. 22.95 (*1-58080-049-1*) Burford Bks.

Rudner, Ruth. Greetings from Wisdom, Montana. LC 89-33077. 172p. 1989. 15.95 (*1-55591-045-9*) Fulcrum Pub.
— Walking. LC 95-1520. (Outdoor Pursuits Ser.). (Illus.). 128p. (Orig.). 1995. pap. 13.95 (*0-87322-668-2*, PRUD0668) Human Kinetics.

Rudnev, V. K. Digging of Soils by Earthmovers with Powered Parts. Sivaramakrishnan, M. M., tr. from RUS. 144p. (C). 1985. text 116.00 (*90-6191-450-7*, Pub. by A A Balkema) Ashgate Pub Co.

Rudney, Robert, ed. Peace Research in Western Europe: A Directory Guide. 45p. (Orig.). 1989. pap. text 4.00 (*1-878597-05-1*) Access Sec Info Serv.

Rudney, Robert & Reychler, Luc, eds. European Security Beyond the Year 2000. LC 87-12494. 317p. 1988. 55.00 (*0-275-92625-7*, C2625, Praeger Pubs) Greenwood.

Rudney, Robert, jt. ed. see Bailey, Kathleen.

Rudnick & Wolfe Staff. Structuring Commercial Real Estate Workouts: Alternatives to Foreclosure. Lieberman, Donna H., ed. 602p. ring bd. 130.00 (*0-13-151853-4*, 58799) Aspen Law.

Rudnick, Dorothea, ed. see Puck, Theodore T., et al.

Rudnick, Hans H., ed. Ingardeniana II: New Studies in the Philosophy of Roman Ingarden with a New International Ingarden Bibliography. 320p. (C). 1990. lib. bdg. 191.50 (*0-7923-0627-9*, Pub. by Kluwer Academic) Kluwer Academic.

Rudnick, Jesse A., jt. auth. see Krulik, Stephen.

Rudnick, Karen, et al. International Newcomer's Guide to Boston. 126p. 1999. pap. 18.95 (*0-9672934-1-3*) Interchange Inst.
— Moving to Boston: Relocating from Around the World. 126p. 1999. pap. write for info. (*0-9672934-0-5*) Interchange Inst.

Rudnick, Leslie & Shubkin, Ronald, eds. Synthetic Lubricants & High-Performance Functional Fluids. 2nd expanded rev. ed. LC 99-18803. (Chemical Industries Ser.). (Illus.). 904p. 1999. text 235.00 (*0-8247-0194-1*, 0194-1) Dekker.

Rudnick, Lewis G. How to Be a Franchisor. 20p. 1999. 12.50 (*0-317-66113-2*) Intl Franchise Assn.

Rudnick, Lewis G., jt. auth. see Lowell, H. Bret.

Rudnick, Lois, jt. ed. see Heller, Adele.

Rudnick, Lois P. Utopian Vistas: The Mabel Dodge Luhan House & the American Counterculture. (Illus.). xiv, 401p. 1998. pap. text 17.95 (*0-8263-1926-2*) U of NM Pr.

Rudnick, Lois Palken. Mabel Dodge Luhan: New Woman, New Worlds. LC 84-7415. (Illus.). 384p. 1987. reprint ed. pap. 19.95 (*0-8263-0995-X*) U of NM Pr.

Rudnick, Lois Palken, ed. Intimate Memories: The Autobiography of Mabel Dodge Luhan. LC 99-24085. 384p. 1999. pap. 17.95 (*0-8263-2106-2*) U of NM Pr.
— Intimate Memories: The Autobiography of Mabel Dodge Luhan. abr. ed. LC 99-24085. (Illus.). 384p. 1999. 45.00 (*0-8263-1857-6*) U of NM Pr.

Rudnick, Milton L. Christianity Is for You. 110p. 1968. pap. 6.60 (*0-570-03503-1*, 14-1271) Concordia.

***Rudnick, Norman.** The Murder of Eleaner Lindquist. (New Voices in American Fiction Ser.). 200p. 2000. pap. 14.95 (*1-883938-80-5*) Dry Bones Pr.

Rudnick, Norman, jt. ed. see Gong, Victor.

Rudnick, Paul. I Hate Hamlet. 1992. pap. 5.25 (*0-8222-0546-7*) Dramatists Play.
— I'll Take It. 304p. 1990. mass mkt. 5.99 (*0-345-36225-X*) Ballantine Pub Grp.
— Jeffrey. 1995. pap. 5.25 (*0-8222-1402-4*) Dramatists Play.

Rudnick, Paul. The Most Fabulous Story Ever Told. pap. 5.95 (*0-8222-1720-1*) Dramatists Play.
— Most Fabulous Story Ever Told: And Mr. Charles, Currently of Palm Beach. 2000. pap. 12.95 (*1-58567-052-9*, Pub. by Overlook Pr) Penguin Putnam.

Rudnick, Paul. The Naked Truth. 1999. pap. 7.95 (*0-452-27423-0*, Plume) Dutton Plume.
— Social Disease. LC 97-7192. 1997. pap. 11.95 (*0-312-15659-6*) St Martin.

Rudnick, Paul D., et al. Illinois Real Estate Forms, 3 vols. 1800p. 1993. suppl. ed. 87.50 (*0-685-74614-3*, MICHIE) LEXIS Pub.

***Rudnick, Paul D., et al.** Illinois Real Estate Forms, Issue 8. 150p. 1999. ring bd. write for info. (*0-327-01688-4*, 8113116) LEXIS Pub.

Rudnick, Terry. Foghorn Outdoors: Washington Boating & Water Sports. 550p. 2000. pap. 19.95 (*1-57354-071-4*, Foghorn Outdoors) Avalon Travel.
— Foghorn Outdoors: Washington Fishing: The Complete Guide to More Than 1,000 Fishing Spots on Streams, Rivers, Lakes, & Salt Water. 3rd ed. (Illus.). 520p. 2000. pap. 19.95 (*1-57354-084-6*, Foghorn Outdoors) Avalon Travel.

Rudnick, Terry, jt. auth. see Batin, Christopher M.

Rudnick, Ursula. Post-Shoa Religious Metaphors: The Image of God in the Poetry of Nelly Sachs. LC 95-37056. XI, 296p. 1995. pap. 57.95 (*0-8204-2929-5*, 68702) P Lang Pubng.

***Rudnicka, Alicja & Birch, Jennie.** Diabetic Eye Disease: Identification & Co-Management. (Illus.). 176p. 2000. pap. 55.00 (*0-7506-3781-1*) Buttrwrth-Heinemann.

Rudnicki, Adolf. Les Fenetres d'Or et Autres Recits. (FRE.). 1979. pap. 11.95 (*0-7859-4111-8*) Fr & Eur.

Rudnicki, Barbara, jt. auth. see Woolgar, Josh.

Rudnicki, Barbara A. Pack Your Own Parachute: The Three Secrets to Being Successful No Matter Who You Work For. LC 96-92863. (Illus.). xx, 100p. (Orig.). 1996. pap. 11.95 (*1-890013-00-5*) Sebastian Prods.

Rudnicki, Konrad. The Cosmologists Second: The Riddle of Time in Theories of the Universe. Lipson, Michael, tr. from GER. 128p. (Orig.). 1991. pap. 12.95 (*0-940262-41-X*, Lindisfarne) Anthroposophic.

Rudnicki, Robert W. Percyscapes: The Fugue State in Twentieth-Century Southern Fiction. LC 98-44082. (Southern Literary Studies). 176p. 1999. text 30.00 (*0-8071-2344-7*) La State U Pr.

Rudnicki, Stefan, compiled by. The Actor's Book of Monologues for Women. 336p. (Orig.). 1991. pap. 12.95 (*0-14-015787-5*, Penguin Bks) Viking Penguin.

Rudnicki, Stefan, intro. The Actor's Book of Classical Monologues. 320p. 1988. pap. 11.95 (*0-14-010676-6*, Penguin Bks) Viking Penguin.

Rudnicki, Stefan & Mitchell, Julian. Wilde: The Novel. LC 98-165773. 215p. 1997. write for info. (*0-7528-1160-6*) Orion.

Rudnicki, Stefan, ed. see Shakespeare, William.

Rudnik-Smalbraak, Marijke. Samuel Richardson: Minute Particulars Within the Large Design. LC 83-241191. (Germanic & Anglistic Studies of the University of Leiden). 291p. 1983. 64.00 (*90-04-07005-2*) Brill Academic Pubs.

Rudnitsky, jt. auth. see Parr.

Rudnitsky, Alan N., jt. auth. see Posner, George J.

Rudnitsky, David. Rob Parr's Post Pregnancy Workout. (Orig.). 1997. pap. 13.00 (*0-614-20757-6*) Berkley Pub.

Rudnitsky, David, jt. auth. see Bakker, Tammy F.

***Rudnitsky, Konstantin.** Russian & Soviet Theatre: Tradition & the Avant-Garde. LC 99-66013. (Illus.). 320p. 2000. pap. 39.95 (*0-500-28195-5*, Pub. by Thames Hudson) Norton.

Rudnitsky, V. Russian & Soviet Theatre Tradition & the Avantgarde. (C). 1990. 400.00 (*0-7855-4454-2*, Pub. by Collets) St Mut.

Rudnytsky, Ivan L. & Himka, John-Paul, eds. Rethinking Ukrainian History. LC 81-91218. x, 268p. 14.95 (*0-920862-12-8*) Ukrainian Acad.
— Rethinking Ukrainian History. LC 81-91218. x, 268p. 1981. pap. 9.95 (*0-920862-14-4*) Ukrainian Acad.

Rudnytsky, Peter L. Ferenczi's Turn in Psychoanalysis. pap. text 20.00 (*0-8147-7545-4*) NYU Pr.

Rudnytsky, Peter L. Freud & Oedipus. (Psychoanalysis & Culture Ser.). 416p. (C). 1992. pap. 20.50 (*0-231-06353-9*) Col U Pr.
— The Psychoanalytic Vocation: Rank, Winnicott, & the Legacy of Freud. 224p. (C). 1991. 40.00 (*0-300-05067-4*) Yale U Pr.

Rudnytsky, Peter L., et al, eds. Ferenczi's Turn in Psychoanalysis. LC 96-10022. 450p. (C). 1996. text 50.00 (*0-8147-7475-X*) NYU Pr.
— Transitional Objects & Potential Spaces: Literary Uses of D. W. Winnicott. LC 92-43907. (Psychoanalysis & Culture Ser.). 315p. (C). 1993. text 57.50 (*0-231-07572-3*) Col U Pr.

***Rudnytsky, Peter L. & Gordon, Andrew.** Psychoanalyses/Feminisms. LC 99-45447. 237p. (C). 1999. text 54.50 (*0-7914-4377-9*) State U NY Pr.

***Rudnytsky, Peter L. & Gordon, Andrew M., eds.** Psychoanalyses & Feminisms. LC 99-45447. (C). 1999. pap. text 17.95 (*0-7914-4378-7*) State U NY Pr.

Rudnytsky, Peter L. & Spitz, Ellen H., eds. Freud & Forbidden Knowledge. 200p. (C). 1995. pap. text 18.50 (*0-8147-7460-1*) NYU Pr.

Rudnytsky, Peter L., jt. ed. see Logan, Marie-Rose.

Rudnytzky, Irene I., tr. see Kosyk, Wolodymyr.

Rudnytzky, Leonid, jt. ed. see Labunka, Miroslav.

Rudo, J., jt. auth. see Immenga, U.

***Rudock.** Masonry Bridges, Viaducts & Aqueducts. 400p. 2000. 156.00 (*0-86078-751-6*) Ashgate Pub Co.

Rudoe, Judy. Decorative Arts, 1850-1950: A Catalogue of the British Museum. (Illus.). 336p. 1994. pap. text 45.00 (*0-7141-0567-8*) Antique Collect.

Rudoe, Judy, et al. Cartier: 1900-1939. LC 96-47813. (Illus.). 320p. 1997. 75.00 (*0-8109-4047-7*, Pub. by Abrams) Time Warner.

Rudoff, Alvin. The Paths to Social Deviance & Conformity: A Model of the Process. LC 91-39309. 144p. 1992. lib. bdg. 69.95 (*0-7734-9438-3*) E Mellen.
— Societies in Space. (American University Studies XI: Vol. 69). XII, 209p. (C). 1996. text 42.95 (*0-8204-3078-1*) P Lang Pubng.

***Rudoff, Alvin & Esselstyn, T. C.** Homicide in Fact & Fiction: An Analytical Study of the Statistical Reality & It's Literary Portrayal. 240p. 2000. pap. 32.00 (*1-55605-310-X*) Wyndham Hall.

Rudoff, Carol. Allergy Baker. 3rd ed. LC 89-85111. (Illus.). 128p. 1990. pap. 8.95 (*0-944569-00-5*) Allergy Pubns.

An Asterisk (*) at the beginning of an entry indicates that the title is appearing for the first time.

R

— Allergy Cookie Jar. LC 85-60322. (Illus.). 128p. 1985. pap. 8.95 (*0-9616708-3-5*) Allergy Pubns.

— The Allergy Gourmet: A Collection of Wheat-Free, Milk-Free, Egg-Free, Corn-Free & Soy-Free Recipes. LC 83-61902. (Illus.). 225p. 1983. pap. 12.95 (*0-930048-11-3*) Allergy Pubns.

— The Allergy Oven. LC 88-70472. (Allergy Kitchen Ser.: Vol. 3). (Illus.). 112p. (Orig.). 1988. pap. 7.95 (*0-9616708-9-4*) Allergy Pubns.

— Allergy Products Directory, 1998 Vol. 5: Food Allergy Resources. 20p. 1998. spiral bd. 14.00 (*0-944569-07-2*) Allergy Pubns.

— Allergy Products Directory, 1995-1996, 4 vols., Set. Blessing-Moore, Joann, ed. 1995. pap. 108.80 (*0-944569-02-1*) Allergy Pubns.

— Allergy Products Directory, 1995-1996 Vol. 1: Controlling Your Environment. Blessing-Moore, Joann, ed. LC 95-75930. 270p. 1995. pap. 34.95 (*0-944569-03-X*) Allergy Pubns.

— Allergy Products Directory, 1995-1996 Vol. 3: Allergy Asthma Finding Help. Blessing-Moore, Joann, ed. LC 95-79543. 229p. 1995. pap. 29.95 (*0-944569-04-8*) Allergy Pubns.

— Allergy Products Directory, 1995-1996 Vol. 4: Protecting Your Skin. Fowler, Joseph F., Jr., ed. LC 95-75928. 149p. 1995. pap. 19.95 (*0-944569-06-4*) Allergy Pubns.

Rudoff, James D. The Creative Cookie. LC 87-72388. (Allergy Kitchen Ser.: Vol. 2). (Illus.). 112p. (Orig.). 1988. pap. 7.95 (*0-9616708-8-6*) Allergy Pubns.

Rudofsky, B. Architecture Without Architects. 1p. 1996. pap. 25.00 (*0-902620-78-9*) Wiley.

Rudofsky, Bernard. Architecture Without Architects: A Short Introduction to Non-Pedigreed Architecture. LC 87-10778. (Illus.). 151p. 1987. reprint ed. pap. 17.95 (*0-8263-1004-4*) U of NM Pr.

— The Prodigious Builders. (Illus.). 383p. (C). 1977. text 59.50 (*0-8290-0986-8*) Irvington.

Rudofsky, Herbert. Trakehnen Horses. (Breed Ser.). 1977. pap. 4.95 (*0-88376-011-8*) Dreenan Pr.

— Young Horses. (Breed Ser.). 1977. pap. 4.95 (*0-88376-009-6*) Dreenan Pr.

Rudolf, Andorka. Homo-Socio Oeconomicus: Ereekezesek, Emlekezesek. 1995. pap. 60.00 (*963-05-6923-X*, Pub. by Akade Kiado) St Mut.

Rudolf, Anthony. Wine from Two Glasses (Poetry & Politics, Trust & Mistrust in Language) 1991. pap. 9.00 (*1-870921-03-8*) SPD-Small Pr Dist.

Rudolf, Anthony, ed. I'm Not Even a Grown-up: The Diary of Jerzy Feliks Urman. 1991. pap. 9.00 (*0-9513753-3-4*) SPD-Small Pr Dist.

Rudolf, Anthony, ed. see Bonnefoy, Yves.

Rudolf, Anthony, jt. ed. see Schwartz, Howard.

Rudolf, Bernd & Ougizawa, Toshiaki. Equation of State Theories & Their Application to Polymers, Blends & Solutions. (Series on Chemical Engineering & Chemical Technology). 250p. 1999. 42.00 (*1-86094-121-4*) World Scientific Pub.

Rudolf, C. & Dezsone, S. Dictionary of Technical Information: Meteorology. 596p. (C). 1986. 120.00 (*0-7855-6756-9*, Pub. by Collets); 120.00 (*0-89771-916-6*, Pub. by Collets) St Mut.

Rudolf, David S. & Maher, Thomas K. State vs. Wyatt. 100p. 1995. pap. 22.95 (*1-55681-476-3*) Natl Inst Trial Ad.

Rudolf, Gloria. Panama's Poor: Victims, Agents, & Historymakers. LC 99-13978. 1999. 49.95 (*0-8130-1680-0*) U Press Fla.

Rudolf, Hans U., jt. ed. see Heinzer, Felix.

Rudolf, Irene. Bedros: A Novel. LC 82-80009. 292p. 1983. pap. 7.45 (*0-937884-07-3*, Bennington Bks) Hystry Mystry.

***Rudolf, Jakhel.** Modern Sports Karate: Basics of Techniques & Tactics. 1998. pap. text 17.95 (*3-89124-428-2*) Meyer & Meyer.

Rudolf, Kathleen B. The Effect of Reading Instruction on Achievement in Eighth Grade Social Studies. LC 75-177218. (Columbia University. Teachers College. Contributions to Education Ser.: No. 945). reprint ed. 37.50 (*0-404-55945-X*) AMS Pr.

Rudolf, Mary C. J., jt. auth. see Levene, Malcolm I.

Rudolf, Max. The Grammar of Conducting: A Comprehensive Guide to Baton Technique & Interpretation. 3rd ed. LC 93-12310. (Illus.). 481p. 1993. 45.00 (*0-02-872221-3*, Schirmer Books) Mac Lib Ref.

Rudolf, R., jt. auth. see Lowndes, L.

Rudolf, Ralph, jt. auth. see Homes, A. M.

***Rudolf Steiner Press Staff.** Rosicrucian Wisdom. 2000. pap. 14.95 (*1-85584-063-4*) R Steiner Pr.

***Rudolph.** Pediatric Rotation Value Pak. 1999. 59.95 (*0-8385-8186-2*, Apple Lange Med) McGraw.

— Reversing the Gaze. 650p. 2000. 60.00 (*0-8133-3626-0*) Westview.

— Rudolph's Pediatrics. 21st ed. 1999. pap. text, student ed. 55.00 (*0-8385-8286-9*) Appleton & Lange.

Rudolph. Rudolph's Pediatrics. 21st ed. (C). 2001. 99.95 (*0-8385-8285-0*) Appleton & Lange.

Rudolph & Kamei. Rudolph's Fundamentals of Pediatrics. 2nd ed. (C). 1998. pap. text 44.95 (*0-8385-8236-2*, A-8236-0, Apple Lange Med) McGraw.

Rudolph, Abraham. Rudolph's Pediatrics. 20th ed. (Illus.). 2337p. (C). 1995. pap. text 115.00 (*0-8385-8492-6*, A8492-9, Apple Lange Med) McGraw.

Rudolph, Abraham M. Color Atlas of Neonatology. 1997. write for info. (*0-7216-6716-3*, W B Saunders Co) Harcrt Hlth Sci Grp.

— Resale Thrift Store Junkie's Guide. 1992. pap. 9.95 (*0-9628752-3-6*) Fifty-Six Palms.

Rudolph, Abraham M. & Kamei, Robert. Rudolph's Fundamentals of Pediatrics. (Illus.). 650p. (C). 1994. pap. text 39.95 (*0-8385-8233-8*, A8233-7) Appleton & Lange.

Rudolph, Abraham M., et al. The Library Literate. 136p. 1996. spiral bd. 15.95 (*0-7872-1668-2*) Kendall-Hunt.

Rudolph, Alan S., et al, eds. Red Blood Cell Substitutes: Basic Principles & Applications. LC 97-31069. (Illus.). 504p. 1997. text 175.00 (*0-8247-0058-9*) Dekker.

Rudolph, Albert, see Rudrananda, Swami, pseud.

Rudolph, Arnold J. Atlas of the Newborn, 5 vols. (Illus.). 1200p. 1997. boxed set 299.00 incl. cd-rom (*1-55009-062-3*) DEKR.

— Dermatology & Perinatal Infection. (Atlas of the Newborn Ser.: Vol. 4). (Illus.). 1997. boxed set 89.95 incl. cd-rom (*1-55009-034-8*) DEKR.

— Head & Neck, Eye, & Central Nervous System. (Atlas of the Newborn Ser.: Vol. 3). (Illus.). 1997. boxed set 89.95 incl. cd-rom (*1-55009-033-X*) DEKR.

— Musculoskeletal Disorders & Congenital Deformities. (Atlas of the Newborn Ser.: Vol. 2). (Illus.). 1997. boxed set 89.95 incl. cd-rom (*1-55009-032-1*) DEKR.

Rudolph, Arnold J. Neonatal & Perinatal Medicine. (Atlas of the Newborn Ser.: Vol. 1). (Illus.). 160p. 1996. boxed set 89.95 incl. cd-rom (*1-55009-031-3*) DEKR.

Rudolph, Arnold J. Thorax, Abdomen, Blood, Endocrine & Metabolic Disorders. (Atlas of the Newborn Ser.: Vol. 5). (Illus.). 1997. boxed set 89.95 incl. cd-rom (*1-55009-035-6*) DEKR.

Rudolph, B., jt. ed. see Pohl, H.

Rudolph, Barbara. Disconnected: How Six People from AT&T Discovered the New Meaning of Work in a Downsized Corporate America. LC 97-46187. 240p. 1998. 25.00 (*0-684-84266-1*) Free Pr.

***Rudolph, Bestow R.** Playmate & the Carpetbaggers. LC 99-96751. 2000. 18.95 (*0-533-13336-X*) Vantage.

Rudolph, Betsy B. Betsy's Blue Plate Specials: Meals Like Moms...Now Low-Fat, Delicious & Fast! Fish, Kimberley S., ed. LC 96-92868. 79p. 1996. 15.95 (*0-9655228-0-6*) BBR Pub.

***Rudolph, Bonnie A.** Brief Collaborative Therapy: A Practical Guide for Practitioners. 184p. 1999. pap. 18.95 (*0-275-96745-X*, Praeger Pubs) Greenwood.

Rudolph, Bonnie A. Brief Collabortive Therapy: A Practical Guide for Practitioners. LC 96-2202. 184p. 1996. 55.00 (*0-275-95469-2*, Praeger Pubs) Greenwood.

Rudolph, Camilla B., tr. see Di Crescenzo, Casimiro.

Rudolph, Catherine E., ed. see Schultz, Karen, et al.

Rudolph, Catherine E., tr. see Perissinotto, Giorgia, ed.

Rudolph, Cathy F. Remembery Chips. (Illus.). 34p. (J). (ps-3). 1994. 15.00 (*0-9642360-0-1*) Wayward Fluffy.

Rudolph, Claire S. & Borker, Susan R. Regionalization: Issues in Intensive Care for High Risk Newborns & their Families. LC 87-15136. 216p. 1987. 65.00 (*0-275-92547-1*, C2547, Praeger Pubs) Greenwood.

Rudolph, Conrad. Artistic Change at St-Denis: Abbot Suger's Program & the Early Twelfth-Century Controversy over Art. 139p. 1990. text 29.50 (*0-691-04068-0*, Pub. by Princeton U Pr) Cal Prin Full Svc.

— Artistic Change at St-Denis: Abbot Suger's Program & the Early Twelfth-Century Controversy over Art. LC 89-10606. (Princeton Essays on the Arts Ser.). (Illus.). 144p. reprint ed. pap. 44.70 (*0-608-09111-1*, 206974300005) Bks Demand.

— Violence & Daily Life: Reading, Art, & Polemics in the Citeaux Moralia in Job. LC 96-22197. (Illus.). 196p. 1997. text 39.50 (*0-691-02673-4*, Pub. by Princeton U Pr) Cal Prin Full Svc.

Rudolph, D. Restricted Orbit Equivalence. LC 84-28119. (Memoirs Ser.: No. 323). 149p. 1986. reprint ed. pap. text 26.00 (*0-8218-2324-8*, MEMO/54/323) Am Math.

Rudolph, D., jt. ed. see Schmahl, G.

Rudolph, David J., ed. The Voice of the Lord: A Messianic Jewish Daily Devotional. LC 99-179098. (Illus.). 416p. 1998. pap. 19.99 (*1-880226-70-7*) M J Pubs.

Rudolph, Dietmar. Das AutoCAD Lexikon. (GER.). 589p. 1991. 135.00 (*0-7859-8697-9*, 387686240x) Fr & Eur.

***Rudolph, Dietmar.** Mastering Autocad 2000 Objects. 4th ed. 416p. 1999. 49.99 (*0-7821-2562-X*) Sybex.

***Rudolph, Dirk.** Spark. 2000. pap. 44.00 (*3-931126-33-1*) Die Gestalten.

Rudolph, Donna K. & Rudolph, G. A. Historical Dictionary of Venezuela, 2 vols. 2nd enl. rev. ed. 986p. 1996. 110.00 (*0-8108-3029-9*) Scarecrow.

***Rudolph, Dorothy.** Avons Bottles Vol. 6: By Any Other Name. 2nd rev. unabridged ed. LC 74-30220. (Illus.). 60p. 1999. reprint ed. pap. 10.00 (*0-913772-04-6*) Avons Res.

Rudolph, Elisabeth. Contrast: Adversative & Concessive Relations & Their Expressions in English, German, Spanish, Portuguese on Sentence & Text Level. LC 96-7760. (Research in Text Theory Ser.: Vol. 23). xx, 544p. (Orig.). (C). 1996. text 191.10 (*3-11-014955-9*, 103/96) De Gruyter.

Rudolph, Enno & Stamatescu, Ion-Opimpiu, eds. Philosophy Mathematics & Modern Physics: A Dialogue. LC 94-8282. (Illus.). 242p. 1995. 53.95 (*0-387-57683-5*) Spr-Verlag.

Rudolph, Frederick. The American College & University: A History. LC 90-40967. 616p. 1991. pap. 18.00 (*0-8203-1284-3*) U of Ga Pr.

— Curriculum: A History of the American Undergraduate Course of Study since 1636. fac. ed. LC 77-84319. (Carnegie Council Ser.). 380p. 1977. reprint ed. pap. 117.80 (*0-7837-8050-8*, 204780300008) Bks Demand.

— Curriculum: A History of the American Undergraduate Course of Study Since 1636. LC 77-84319. (Higher & Adult Education Ser.). 392p. (C). 1993. reprint ed. pap. text 28.00 (*1-55542-535-6*) Jossey-Bass.

Rudolph, Frederick, ed. Mark Hopkins & the Log: Williams College, 1836-1872. 2nd rev. ed. (Illus.). 288p. 1996. pap. 19.95 (*0-915081-03-2*) Williams Coll.

— Perspectives: A Williams Anthology. LC 83-51219. 340p. 1983. 17.50 (*0-915081-00-8*) Williams Coll.

Rudolph, Frederick B. & McIntire, Larry V., eds. Biotechnology: Science, Engineering, & Ethical Challenges for the 21st Century. 296p. (C). 1996. pap. 34.95 (*0-309-05282-3*, Joseph Henry Pr) Natl Acad Pr.

Rudolph, G. A. & Williams, Evan N. Linnaeana. LC 72-636354. (Libraries Bibliography: No. 7). 1970. pap. 5.00 (*0-686-20815-3*) KSU.

Rudolph, G. A., jt. auth. see Rudolph, Donna K.

Rudolph, Gunter & Schafer, Jurgen. Deutschunterricht in Den Neuen Bundeslandern Seit, 1990: Aspekte, Tenderzen, Probleme. (GER.). 1996. 42.95 (*3-631-49317-7*) P Lang Pubng.

Rudolph, J. Langenscheidt Handbook of Business English: Handbuch der Englischen Wirtschaftssprache. (ENG & GER.). 415p. 1986. 110.00 (*0-8288-0078-2*, M7374) Fr & Eur.

Rudolph, J. & Koppmann, Ralf. Atmospheric Measurements During Popcorn. LC 98-32182. 246 p. 1999. 126.00 (*0-7923-5531-8*) Kluwer Academic.

Rudolph, James D. Peru: The Evolution of a Crisis. LC 91-23655. (Politics in Latin America Ser.). 192p. 1992. 59.95 (*0-275-94146-9*, C4146, Praeger Pubs); pap. 17.95 (*0-275-94181-7*, B4181, Praeger Pubs) Greenwood.

Rudolph, James S. Make Your Own Working Paper Clock. LC 83-47570. 40p. 1983. pap. 14.00 (*0-06-091066-6*, CN1066, Perennial) HarperTrade.

Rudolph, John W. Las Olas. LC 87-80761. (Illus.). 101p. (Orig.). (YA). 1987. pap. 9.00 (*0-941611-09-4*) Shasta San Rafael.

Rudolph, Jorg M. Cankao Xiaoxi: Foreign News in the Propaganda System of the People's Republic of China. (Occasional Papers-Reprints Series in Contemporary Asian Studies: No. 6-1984 (65)). 174p. (Orig.). 1984. pap. text 5.00 (*0-942182-67-7*) Occasional Papers.

— Media-Coverage on Taiwan in the People's Republic of China. (Occasional Papers-Reprints Series in Contemporary Asian Studies: No. 3-1983 (56)). 77p. (Orig.). 1983. pap. text 3.50 (*0-942182-55-3*) U MD Law.

Rudolph, Joseph R., Jr. Energy. LC 95-3370. (Magill Bibliographies Ser.). 185p. 1995. 32.50 (*0-8108-3011-6*) Scarecrow.

Rudolph, Joseph R., Jr. & Thompson, Robert J., eds. Ethnoterritorial Politics, Policy, & the Western World. LC 89-30268. 262p. 1989. lib. bdg. 47.00 (*1-55587-095-3*) L Rienner.

Rudolph, Jurgen. Reconstructing Identities: A Social History of Babas in Singapore. LC 98-72630. 507p. 1998. text 80.95 (*1-84014-357-6*, Pub. by Ashgate Pub) Ashgate Pub Co.

***Rudolph, Jutta J.** Imaginationstherapie Bei Patienten Mit Primarem Kopfschmerz: Eine Analyse Der Wirkkomponenten Bei Imaginativer Transformation Von Gedachtnisinhalten. (Illus.). 236p. 1999. 40.95 (*3-631-34497-X*) P Lang Pubng.

***Rudolph, Kenny.** Under Hemingway's Michigan Sky: Selected Poems, Prose & Short Plays by Kenny Rudolph. LC 00-190050. (Illus.). 145p. 2000. pap. 12.00 (*0-9678088-0-4*) Woodburn Ave Bks.

Rudolph, Kevin. Bible Tour Guide: A 365 Day Spiritual Journey. LC 94-66386. (Illus.). 380p. 1994. 19.95 (*0-927577-01-1*) Rich Pub Co.

Rudolph, Klaus-Peter. Pseudomonas Syringae Pathovars & Related Pathogens. LC 97-19457. (Developments in Plant Pathology Ser.: Vol. 9). 663p. 1997. text 327.50 (*0-7923-4601-7*) Kluwer Academic.

Rudolph, Kurt. Geschichte und Probleme der Religionswissenschaft. LC 91-26964. (Numen Supplements Ser.: Vol. 53). (GER.). xiv, 446p. 1992. 173.50 (*90-04-09503-9*) Brill Academic Pubs.

— Gnosis: The Nature & History of Gnosticism. LC 81-47437. 432p. 1987. pap. 23.00 (*0-06-067018-5*, PL 4122, Pub. by Harper SF) HarpC.

— Gnosis Und Sp Atantike Religionsgeschichte: Gesammelte Aufs Atze. LC 96-26930. (Nag Hammadi & Manichaean Studies). 1996. 265.00 (*90-04-10625-1*) Brill Academic Pubs.

Rudolph, L., jt. auth. see Lerman, G.

Rudolph, L., jt. ed. see Feitelson, D. G.

Rudolph, L. C. Francis Asbury. 240p. (Orig.). 1983. pap. 0.99 (*0-687-13461-7*) Abingdon.

— Hoosier Faiths: A History of Indiana's Churches & Religious Groups. LC 94-43452. 688p. 1995. 89.95 (*0-253-32882-9*) Ind U Pr.

— Hoosier Zion: The Presbyterian in Early Indiana. LC 62-8261. (Yale Publications in Religion: No. 5). (Illus.). 196p. reprint ed. pap. 60.80 (*0-608-30078-0*, 200900800071) Bks Demand.

Rudolph, L. C. & Endelman, Judith E. Religion in Indiana: A Guide to Historical Resources. LC 84-43186. 247p. reprint ed. pap. 76.60 (*0-7837-4204-5*, 205905400012) Bks Demand.

Rudolph, Larry, jt. auth. see Feitelson, Dror G.

Rudolph, Lee. Blackjack Consensus: How to Take the B. S. Out of Basic Strategy. 112p. (Orig.). 1989. pap. 7.95 (*0-9624047-0-5*) Gamblers Analysis.

— The Country Changes. LC 78-60470. 72p. 1978. pap. 3.95 (*0-914086-23-5*) Alice James Bks.

— Curses, & Songs & Poems. LC 74-81380. 72p. 1974. pap. 3.95 (*0-914086-04-9*) Alice James Bks.

Rudolph, Leighton & Simpson, Ethel C., eds. Selected Letters of John Gould Fletcher. LC 95-39410. (John Gould Fletcher Ser.: Vol. 7). (Illus.). 384p. 1996. text 50.00 (*1-55728-329-X*) U of Ark Pr.

Rudolph, Lieba. The Best Call of All. LC 98-4446. (Illus.). (J). 1998. 12.00 (*0-8266-0025-5*, Merkos LInyonei Chinuch) Kehot Pubn Soc.

Rudolph, Linda B., jt. auth. see Thompson, Charles L.

Rudolph, Lloyd, ed. Cultural Policy in India. 1984. 12.50 (*0-8364-1243-5*, Pub. by Chanakya) S Asia.

Rudolph, Lloyd I. & Rudolph, Susanne H. Gandhi: The Traditional Roots of Charisma. LC 83-1179. (Modernity of Tradition Ser.: Pt. 2). 104p. (C). 1983. pap. text 9.95 (*0-226-73136-7*) U Ch Pr.

— In Pursuit of Lakshmi: The Political Economy of the Indian State. LC 86-24903. (Illus.). xviii, 548p. (C). 1987. pap. text 23.50 (*0-226-73139-1*) U Ch Pr.

— In Pursuit of Lakshmi: The Political Economy of the Indian State. LC 86-24903. (Illus.). xviii, 548p. (C). 1996. lib. bdg. 49.95 (*0-226-73138-3*) U Ch Pr.

— The Modernity of Tradition: Political Development in India. LC 67-25527. (Midway Reprint Ser.). x, 316p. (C). 1984. pap. text 25.00 (*0-226-73137-5*) U Ch Pr.

Rudolph, Lloyd I., jt. ed. see Rudolph, Susanne H.

***Rudolph, Marian.** Lovina's Song: A Pioneer Girl's Journey with the Donner Party. LC 99-61583. (Illus.). 187p. (YA). (gr. 5-8). 1999. pap. 11.95 (*1-928595-01-4*) Citron Bay.

Rudolph, Marian. Lovina's Song: A Pioneer Girl's Journey with the Donner Party. (Illus.). 192p. (J). 1998. pap. 11.95 (*1-883965-43-8*) Rattle OK Pubns.

Rudolph, Monika. Naum Slutzky: Meister Am Bauhaus Goldschmied und Designer. (GER., Illus.). 240p. 95.00 (*3-925369-06-6*, Pub. by Arnoldsche Art Pubs) Antique Collect.

Rudolph, Nancy. Workyards: Playgrounds Planned for Adventure. LC 74-5187. (Illus.). 71p. reprint ed. pap. 30.00 (*0-8357-3033-6*, 203928000011) Bks Demand.

Rudolph, Nancy L. Paper Animal Masks from Northwest Tribal Tales. LC 95-39222. (Illus.). 80p. (J). 1996. 19.95 (*0-8069-4383-1*) Sterling.

Rudolph, Paul & Futagawa, Yukio. Paul Rudolph: Architectural Drawings. (Illus.). 218p. 1981. 55.00 (*0-8038-0208-0*) Archit CT.

Rudolph, Richard L. Banking & Industrialization in Austria-Hungary: The Role of Banks in the Industrialization of the Czech Crownlands, 1873-1914. LC 75-2736. 303p. reprint ed. pap. 86.40 (*0-8357-5963-6*, 2024524) Bks Demand.

Rudolph, Richard L. & Good, David A., eds. Nationalism & Empire: The Habsburg Monarchy & the Soviet Union. 320p. 1992. text 49.95 (*0-312-06892-1*) St Martin.

Rudolph, Richard L., jt. ed. see Zipes, Jack.

Rudolph, Robert. The Boys from New Jersey: How the Mob Beat the Feds. 431p. 1995. pap. 16.95 (*0-8135-2154-8*) Rutgers U Pr.

Rudolph, Ross. Chronic Problem Wound. 1983. 67.00 (*0-316-76110-9*) Little.

Rudolph, Ross, et al. Skin Grafting. 1979. 42.95 (*0-316-76109-5*, Little Brwn Med Div) Lppncott W & W.

Rudolph, Stormy. Many Horses (Sequel to Quest for Courage) (Indian Culture Ser.). (Illus.). 79p. (J). (gr. 4-10). 1987. pap. 8.95 (*0-89992-112-4*) Coun India Ed.

Rudolph, Susanne H. & Piscatori, James P., eds. Transnational Religion & Fading States. LC 96-35187. 288p. (C). 1996. pap. text 27.00 (*0-8133-2768-7*, Pub. by Westview) HarpC.

Rudolph, Susanne H. & Rudolph, Lloyd I., eds. Education & Politics in India: Studies in Organization, Society, & Policy. LC 71-186675. 480p. reprint ed. pap. 148.80 (*0-7837-1526-9*, 204180300024) Bks Demand.

Rudolph, Susanne H., jt. auth. see Rudolph, Lloyd I.

Rudolph, Susanne H., ed. see Piscatori, James P.

Rudolph, Teresa P. Lithic Procurement & Manufacturing Sequences at SBA-1542, Vandenberg Air Force Base, California. (Illus.). 111p. (C). 1984. reprint ed. pap. text 12.19 (*1-55567-447-X*) Coyote Press.

Rudolph, Thomas & Richmond, Floyd. Technology Strategies for Music Education. Dunday, John & Pinchock, George, eds. 70p. 1997. spiral bd. 14.95 (*0-9661110-0-1*) Tech Inst Music.

Rudolph, Thomas D., ed. see ERDA Technical Information Center Staff.

Rudolph, Thomas E. Music & the Apple II: Applications for Music Education, Composition, & Performance. (Illus.). 175p. (Orig.). 1984. pap. text 17.95 (*0-9615386-0-0*) Unsinn Pubns.

Rudolph, Ulrich. Al-M Atur Id I und die Sunnitische Theologie In Samarkand. LC 96-19206. (Islamic Philosophy, Theology & Science, Studies & Texts Ser.). xii, 396p. 1996. 117.50 (*90-04-10023-7*) Brill Academic Pubs.

Rudolph, W. & Wilhelmi, B. Light Pulse Compression. Letokhov, V. S., ed. (Laser Science & Technology Ser.: Vol. 3). viii, 132p. 1989. pap. text 162.00 (*3-7186-4888-1*) Gordon & Breach.

Rudolph, Wilhelm. Hebraisches Woerterbuch Zu Jeremia. 2nd ed. (GER & HEB.). 46p. 1953. 19.95 (*0-7859-8278-7*, 3113902533) Fr & Eur.

Rudolph, William B., jt. auth. see Bittinger, Marvin L.

Rudolph, Wolf. A Golden Legacy: Ancient Jewelry from the Burton Y. Berry Collection. (Illus.). 320p. 1994. pap. 39.95 (*0-253-20913-7*); text 59.95 (*0-253-34980-X*) Ind U Pr.

Rudolph, Wolfgang, jt. auth. see Diels, Jean-Claude.

Rudolphi, jt. auth. see Doring, G.

Rudomin, Pablo, et al, eds. Neuroscience: From Neural Networks to Artificial Intelligence - Proceedings of a U. S.-Mexico Seminar Held in the City of Xalapa in the State of Veracruz in December 9-11, 1991. LC 93-18575. (Research Notes in Neural Computing Ser.: Vol. 4). 1993. 78.95 (*0-387-56501-9*) Spr-Verlag.

Rudorf, W. D., jt. auth. see Dunn, A. D.

Rudorf, Welhelm, jt. auth. see Roemer, Theodor.

Rudova, Larissa. Pasternak's Short Fiction & the Cultural Vanguard. LC 93-22860. (Middlebury Studies in Russian Language & Literature: Vol. 6). 167p. (C). 1994. text 35.95 (*0-8204-2273-8*) P Lang Pubng.

R

— Understanding Boris Pasternak. LC 96-45786. (Understanding Modern European Literature Ser.). 1997. text 29.95 (*1-57003-143-6*) U of SC Pr.

Rudovsky, David, et al. The Rights of Prisoners: A Comprehensive Guide to the Legal Rights of Prisoners under Current Law. 4th rev. ed. LC 87-23577. 127p. 1988. pap. 9.95 (*0-8093-1452-5*) S Ill U Pr.

Rudovsky, David, jt. auth. see Avery, Michael.

Rudow, Leonard H. Ultimate Sportfishing: Tips, Tricks, & Tactics for the Serious Angler. LC 98-27234. (Illus.). 136p. 1998. pap. 16.95 (*0-07-058039-1*) McGraw.

Rudowicz, C., et al, eds. Modern Applications of EPR-ESR - From Biophysics to Materials Science: The First Asia-Pacific EPR-ESR Symposium. 750p. 1998. 69.00 (*981-3083-23-9*, Pub. by Spr-Verlag) Spr-Verlag.

Rudowski, jt. auth. see Hofmeister.

Rudowski, Joyce, jt. auth. see Hofmeister, Joseph F.

Rudowski, Victor A. The Prince: A Historical Critique. (MWS Ser.: No. 82). 180p. (C). 1992. per. 13.95 (*0-8057-8555-8*, Twyne) Mac Lib Ref.

— The Prince: A Historical Critique. (MWS Ser.: No. 82). 180p. (C). 1992. 23.95 (*0-8057-8079-3*, Twyne) Mac Lib Ref.

Rudowski, Witold, et al. Burn Therapy & Research. LC 74-29339. (Illus.). 351p. reprint ed. pap. 108.90 (*0-8357-7481-3*, 202075200018) Bks Demand.

Rudra, Ashok. Political Economy of Indian Agriculture. (C). 1992. 28.50 (*0-685-61702-5*, Pub. by KP Bagchi) S Asia.

— Prasanta Chandra Mahalanobis: A Biography. LC 96-906245. (Illus.). 510p. (C). 1997. 45.00 (*0-19-563679-1*) OUP.

Rudrananda, Swami, pseud. Rudi: Entering Infinity. Rosen, Cheryl B., ed. LC 92-45648. xiii, 210p. 1994. pap. 16.95 (*0-915801-41-8*) Rudra Pr.

— Rudi in His Own Words. LC 90-20083. 197p. (Orig.). 1990. pap. 14.95 (*0-915801-20-5*) Rudra Pr.

Rudrum, Alan, ed. Essential Articles for the Study of Henry Vaughan. LC 87-11377. (Essential Articles Ser.). xii, 332p. (C). 1987. lib. bdg. 47.50 (*0-208-02045-4*, Archon Bks) Shoe String.

Rudrum, Alan, ed. see Vaughan, Henry.

Rudstein, David, et al. Criminal Constitutional Law, 3 vols., Set. 1990. ring bd. write for info. (*0-8205-1098-X*, 098) Bender.

Rudt de Collenberg, W. H. Familles de l'Orient Latin, XIIe-XIVe Siecles. (Collected Studies: No. CS176). (FRE.). 326p. (C). 1983. reprint ed. lib. bdg. 124.95 (*0-86078-124-0*, Pub. by Variorum) Ashgate Pub Co.

Rudwick. Georges Cuvier & Fossil Bones. 1998. pap. text 19.00 (*0-226-73107-3*) U Ch Pr.

Rudwick, Elliott, jt. auth. see Meier, August.

Rudwick, Elliott M. Race Riot at East St. Louis, July 2, 1917. LC 82-1940. (Blacks in the New World Ser.). 322p. reprint ed. pap. 99.90 (*0-8357-7503-8*, 203446100090) Bks Demand.

Rudwick, Martin J. Georges Cuvier & Fossil Bones. LC 97-15628. 320p. 1997. 34.95 (*0-226-73106-5*) U Ch Pr.

— The Great Devonian Controversy: The Shaping of Scientific Knowledge among Gentlemanly Specialists. LC 84-16199. (Science & Its Conceptual Foundations Ser.). (Illus.). 528p. 1985. 45.00 (*0-226-73101-4*) U Ch Pr.

— The Great Devonian Controversy: The Shaping of Scientific Knowledge among Gentlemanly Specialists. LC 84-16199. (Science & Its Conceptual Foundations Ser.). (Illus.). 538p. 1988. pap. text 24.95 (*0-226-73102-2*) U Ch Pr.

— The Meaning of Fossils: Episodes in the History of Palaeontology. 2nd ed. LC 84-28080. (Illus.). 304p. (C). 1985. pap. text 19.00 (*0-226-73103-0*) U Ch Pr.

— Scenes from Deep Time: Early Pictorial Representations of the Prehistoric World. LC 91-47677. (Illus.). 294p. 1992. 49.50 (*0-226-73104-9*) U Ch Pr.

— Scenes from Deep Time: Early Pictorial Representations of the Prehistoric World. xiv, 294p. 1995. pap. 20.00 (*0-226-73105-7*) U Ch Pr.

Rudwin, M. Satanism in French Romanticism. 1972. 59.59 (*0-8490-0993-6*) Gordon Pr.

Rudwin, Maximilian J. The Devil in Legend & Literature. LC 71-111780. (Illus.). reprint ed. 29.50 (*0-404-05451-X*) AMS Pr.

Rudy, Ann. Mom Spelled Backwards Is Tired. LC 79-55442. 190p. 1980. 9.95 (*0-672-52627-1*, Bobbs) Macmillan.

Rudy, Bernardo. Ion Channels. Ivenson, Linda E. et al, eds. (Methods in Enzymology Ser.: Vol. 207). (Illus.). 917p. 1997. 59.95 (*0-12-601695-X*) Morgan Kaufmann.

Rudy, Bernardo & Seeburg, Peter, eds. Molecular & Functional Diversity of Ion Channels & Receptors. LC 99-13744. (Annals of the New York Academy of Sciences Ser.). 1998. pap. 140.00 (*1-57331-177-4*) NY Acad Sci.

— Molecular & Functional Diversity of Ion Channels & Receptors. LC 99-13744. (Annals of the New York Academy of Sciences Ser.). 1999. 140.00 (*1-57331-176-6*) NY Acad Sci.

Rudy, Carol-Ann. Coral Gables, Gateway to the Sun. George, Paul S., ed. (Hometown Heritage Ser.). (Illus.). 32p. (Orig.). (J). (gr. 2-4). Date not set. pap. 3.50 (*1-889300-03-9*); pap., teacher ed. 10.00 (*0-614-30044-4*) Dormouse Prods.

— Crossing to Freedom. George, Paul S., ed. (Hometown Heritage Ser.). (Illus.). 48p. (Orig.). (J). (gr. 2-4). Date not set. pap. 4.95 (*1-889300-02-0*); pap., teacher ed. 10.00 (*0-614-30043-6*) Dormouse Prods.

— The Little Theater That Could: And the Story of Key Biscayne. LC 96-85492. (Hometown Heritage Ser.: Vol. 1). (Illus.). 32p. (Orig.). (J). (gr. 3-4). 1996. pap. 3.50 (*1-889300-00-4*) Dormouse Prods.

— Opa-Locka, Baghdad of the South. George, Paul S., ed. LC 96-93118. (Hometown Heritage Ser.: Vol. 2). (Illus.). 32p. (Orig.). (J). (gr. 2-4). 1996. pap. 3.50 (*1-889300-01-2*) Dormouse Prods.

Rudy, D. L. Voices Through Time & Distant Places. 36p. (Orig.). 1993. pap. 6.00 (*0-9637386-0-7*) Willdor Pr.

Rudy, Dale, jt. auth. see Rudy, Diane.

Rudy, David R. Becoming Alcoholic: Alcoholics Anonymous & the Reality of Alcoholism. LC 85-11750. 192p. 1986. 21.95 (*0-8093-1244-1*); pap. 12.95 (*0-8093-1245-X*) S Ill U Pr.

Rudy, David R. & Kurowski, Kurt. Family Medicine. LC 96-37442. (House Officer Ser.). 656p. 1997. pap. 24.95 (*0-683-18243-9*) Lppncott W & W.

***Rudy, Diane & Rudy, Dale.** Antiqs4u, Inc. Buyers/Sellers Guide, eBay Auctions & More. Bacon, Virginia, ed. 76p. 1999. pap. 9.95 (*0-9671729-0-X*) Antiqsfouru.

Rudy, Doris, intro. Worship & Daily Life: A Resource for Worship Planners. LC 98-70466. 112p. 1999. pap. 15.95 (*0-88177-245-3*, DR245) Discipleship Res.

Rudy, Ellen B. & Gray, Ruth V. Handbook of Health Assessment. 2nd ed. 304p. 1985. pap. text 13.95 (*0-89303-493-2*, Appleton-Century-Crofts) P-H.

Rudy, Ellen B. & Gray, V. Ruth. Handbook of Health Assessment. 3rd ed. (Illus.). 305p. (C). 1991. pap. text 24.95 (*0-8385-3602-6*, A3602-8) Appleton & Lange.

Rudy-Froese, Allan, jt. auth. see Snyder, Eleanor.

Rudy-Gervais, Darla, tr. see Boustani, Rafic & Fargues, Philippe.

Rudy, Jack R. Archeological Survey of Western Utah. (Utah Anthropological Papers: No. 12). reprint ed. 34.50 (*0-404-60612-1*) AMS Pr.

Rudy, Jack R. & Stirland, Robert D. An Archeological Reconnaissance in Washington County, Utah. fac. ed. (University of Utah, Department of Anthropology, Anthropological Papers: No. 9). (Illus.). 81p. (C). 1950. reprint ed. pap. text 9.38 (*1-55567-862-9*) Coyote Press.

Rudy, John. Moneywise Meditations: To Be Found Faithful in God's Audit. LC 89-2191. (Illus.). 144p. (Orig.). 1989. pap. 7.99 (*0-8361-3486-9*) Herald Pr.

Rudy, John G. Wordsworth & the Zen Mind: The Poetry of Self-Emptying. LC 95-19528. 284p. (C). 1996. pap. text 19.95 (*0-7914-2904-0*) State U NY Pr.

— Wordsworth & the Zen Mind: The Poetry of Self-Emptying. LC 95-19528. 284p. (C). 1996. text 59.50 (*0-7914-2903-2*) State U NY Pr.

Rudy, Kathy. Sex & the Church: Gender, Homosexuality & the Transformation of Christian Ethics. 1998. pap. 14.00 (*0-8070-1035-9*) Beacon Pr.

Rudy, Lisa. Ocean Life: A Theme Unit Developed with the New Jersey State Aquarium. 1994. pap. 9.95 (*0-590-49508-9*) Scholastic Inc.

Rudy, Martin & Salcedo, Gregory B. IFW Paradox 4 Programming Secrets. 2nd ed. (PC World Ser.). 940p. 1993. pap. 44.95 incl. disk (*1-878058-54-1*) IDG Bks.

Rudy, S. Willis. The College of the City of New York: A History, 1847-1947. Metzger, Walter P., ed. LC 76-55189. (Academic Profession Ser.). (Illus.). 1977. lib. bdg. 42.95 (*0-405-10014-0*) Ayer.

— Total War & Twentieth-Century Higher Learning: Universities of the Western World in the First & Second World Wars. LC 90-55172. 136p. 1991. 30.00 (*0-8386-3409-5*) Fairleigh Dickinson.

— The Universities of Europe. LC 82-49281. 176p. 1984. 22.50 (*0-685-07997-X*) Fairleigh Dickinson.

— The Universities of Europe, 1100-1914: A History. 176p. 1984. 29.50 (*0-8386-3177-0*) Fairleigh Dickinson.

Rudy, Stephen, ed. Roman Jakobson: A Complete Bibliography of His Writings. xii, 188p. 1990. lib. bdg. 67.70 (*0-89925-068-8*) Mouton.

— Roman Jakobson Selected Writings, Vol. VIII. 685p. (C). 1988. lib. bdg. 242.35 (*0-89925-175-7*) Mouton.

— Selected Writings Vol. VIII: Major Works 1976-1980. xxiv, 685p. 1988. 211.00 (*3-11-010379-6*) De Gruyter.

Rudy, Stephen & Waugh, Linda R., eds. Selected Writings Vol. VII: Contributions to Comparative Mythology: Studies in Linguistics & Philosophy, 1972-1982. xxiv, 405p. 1985. 111.00 (*3-11-010617-5*) De Gruyter.

Rudy, Stephen, jt. ed. see Jackson, Robert L.

Rudy, Stephen, ed. see Jakobson, Roman.

Rudy, Stephen, jt. ed. see Waugh, Linda R.

Rudy, Theresa M. The Legal Resource Directory: Your Guide to Help Hotlines & Hot Websites. 185p. 1997. 10.00 (*0-910073-23-6*) HALT DC.

Rudy, Theresa M., jt. auth. see Dimeo, Jean.

***Rudy, Vicky.** Call Me Jillian. LC 99-91767. 2000. 25.00 (*0-7388-1246-3*); pap. 18.00 (*0-7388-1247-1*) Xlibris Corp.

Rudy, Willis. The Campus & a Nation in Crisis: From the American Revolution to Vietnam. LC 96-45748. 272p. 1996. 42.50 (*0-8386-3658-6*) Fairleigh Dickinson.

Rudy, Willis, jt. auth. see Brubacher, John S.

Rudyak, Yu. B. On Thom Spectra, Orientability & Cobordism. LC 97-32730. (Monographs in Mathematics). xii, 583p. (C). 1998. 129.00 (*3-540-62043-5*) Spr-Verlag.

Rudzikas, Z., et al, eds. Ultrafast Phenomena in Spectroscopy: Proceedings of the 5th International Symposium. 536p. (C). 1988. text 138.00 (*9971-5-0616-5*) World Scientific Pub.

Rudzikas, Zenonas. Theoretical Atomic Spectroscopy. LC 96-18913. (Cambridge Monographs on Atomic, Molecular, & Chemical Physics Ser.: Vol. 7). (Illus.). 448p. (C). 1998. text 125.00 (*0-521-44425-X*) Cambridge U Pr.

Rudzinski, W. & Everett, D. H. Adsorption of Gases on Heterogeneous Surfaces. (Illus.). 624p. 1991. text 205.00 (*0-12-601690-9*) Acad Pr.

Rudzinski, W., et al. Equilibria & Dynamics of Gas Absorption on Heterogeneous Solid Surfaces, Vol. 104. LC 96-49552. (Studies in Surface Science & Catalysis). 908p. 1996. 390.75 (*0-444-82243-7*) Elsevier.

Rudzitis, Gundars. Residential Location Determinants of the Older Population. LC 82-10966. (University of Chicago, Department of Geography, Research Paper Ser.: No. 202). 130p. 1982. reprint ed. pap. 40.30 (*0-608-02286-1*, 206292700004) Bks Demand.

— Wilderness & the Changing American West. LC 96-15426. 240p. 1996. pap. 54.95 (*0-471-13396-5*, Wiley-Liss) Wiley.

Rudzka-Ostyn, Brygida, jt. ed. see Geiger, Richard A.

Rue. Management. 9th ed. LC 99-26770. 496p. 1999. pap. 52.50 (*0-07-228885-X*) McGraw.

Rue & Croese. National Assessment Institute Manual para el Manejo de Alimentos Saludables. (Illus.). 224p. (C). 1994. pap. text 25.95 (*0-13-135238-5*) P-H.

Rue & Hjorth-Pkg. Management: Skills & App/Career Handbook/Bu. 7th ed. 1996. 60.00 (*0-256-22694-6*) McGraw.

Rue, Andre La, see La Rue, Andre.

Rue, Colin De la, see De la Rue, Colin, ed.

Rue, Debbie, jt. auth. see Rude, Christina.

Rue, Geraldine, jt. compiled by see Rue, Richard.

Rue, III, Leonard Lee. Elephants: A Portrait of the Animal World, 1. 1998. pap. text 10.98 (*1-880908-22-0*) Todtri Prods.

Rue, J. Home-Based Businesses: Over 250 Ways to Earn Your Fortune. 208p. 1995. pap. 14.95 (*0-915665-35-2*) Premier Publishers.

***Rue, Leonard L., III.** Deer Hunter's Encyclopedia. (Illus.). 2000. 29.95 (*1-58574-128-0*) Lyons Pr.

Rue, Leonard L. The Deer of North America. 1989. 32.95 (*1-55654-051-5*) Times Mir Mag Bk Div.

Rue, Leonard L., III. The Deer of North America. (Illus.). 544p. 1997. 35.00 (*1-55821-577-8*) Lyons Pr.

— How I Photograph Wildlife & Nature. LC 96-178224. (Illus.). 288p. 1996. pap. 19.95 (*0-393-31370-0*, Norton Paperbks) Norton.

Rue, Leonard L., Jr. How to Photograph Animals in the Wild. (Illus.). 144p. 1996. pap. 16.95 (*0-8117-2451-4*) Stackpole.

Rue, Leonard L., III. Leonard Lee Rue III's Whitetails: Answers to All Your Questions on Life Cycle, Feeding Patterns, Antlers, Scrapes & Rubs, Behavior During the Rut, & Habitat. LC 90-27656. (Illus.). 288p. 1991. 34.95 (*0-8117-1938-3*) Stackpole.

Rue, Leonard Lee, III. Alligators & Crocodiles: A Portrait of the Animal World, 1. 1998. pap. text 10.98 (*1-880908-21-2*) Todtri Prods.

— Birds of Prey: A Portrait of the Animal World, 1. (Illus.). 80p. 1998. pap. text 10.98 (*1-880908-17-4*) Todtri Prods.

***Rue, Leonard Lee, III.** Leonard Lee Rue III's Way of the Whitetail. LC 00-24654. (Illus.). 160p. 2000. 35.00 (*0-89658-417-8*) Voyageur Pr.

Rue, Leonard Lee, III. Wolves: A Portrait of the Animal World, 1. 1998. pap. text 10.98 (*1-880908-33-6*) Todtri Prods.

Rue, Leslie W. Management: Skills & Application. 8th ed. LC 96-45341. 576p. (C). 1996. per. 39.95 (*0-256-22737-3*, Irwn McGrw-H) McGrw-H Hghr Educ.

— Supervision. 6th ed. LC 98-20986. 480p. (C). 1998. pap. 67.81 (*0-256-27173-9*) McGraw.

Rue, Leslie W. & Byars, Betsy C. Management. 5th ed. (C). 1989. student ed. 18.95 (*0-256-07568-9*, Irwn McGrw-H) McGrw-H Hghr Educ.

Rue, Leslie W. & Byars, Lloyd L. Management. 5th ed. (C). 1989. text 54.95 (*0-256-06896-8*, Irwn McGrw-H) McGrw-H Hghr Educ.

— Management: Skills & Application. 6th ed. 608p. (C). 1991. text 39.95 (*0-256-08702-4*, Irwn McGrw-H) McGrw-H Hghr Educ.

— Supervision: Key Link to Productivity. 3rd ed. (C). 1990. pap. text, student ed. 17.95 (*0-256-08192-1*, Irwn McGrw-H) McGrw-H Hghr Educ.

— Supervision, Key Link to Productivity. 5th ed. LC 95-8206. 480p. (C). 1995. text 54.50 (*0-256-17068-1*, Irwn McGrw-H) McGrw-H Hghr Educ.

Rue, Leslie W., jt. auth. see Byars, Lloyd.

Rue, Leslie W., jt. auth. see Byars, Lloyd L.

Rue, Loyal. By the Grace of Guile: The Role of Deception in Natural History & Human Affairs. LC 93-32877. (Illus.). 368p. 1994. 30.00 (*0-19-507508-0*) OUP.

— Everybody's Story: Wising up to the Epic of Evolution. LC 99-13703. (SUNY Series in Philosophy & Biology). (Illus.). 170p. (C). 1999. text 49.50 (*0-7914-4391-4*); pap. text 16.95 (*0-7914-4392-2*) State U NY Pr.

Rue, Nancy. The Accused. LC 95-10950. (Christian Heritage Ser.: Vol. 4). 202p. (J). (gr. 3-7). 1998. pap. 5.99 (*1-56179-398-1*) Focus Family.

— The Ally. LC 97-25411. (Christian Heritage Ser.). 192p. (J). (gr. 3-7). 1998. pap. 5.99 (*1-56179-561-5*) Focus Family.

— "B" Is for Bad at Getting into Harvard. LC 98-228468. (Raise the Flag Ser.: Bk. 2). 224p. (YA). (gr. 6-12). 1998. pap. 6.95 (*1-57856-033-0*) Waterbrook Pr.

— The Battle. LC 97-2494. (Christian Heritage Ser.). 192p. (J). (gr. 3-7). 1998. pap. 5.99 (*1-56179-542-9*) Focus Family.

***Rue, Nancy.** Beauty Book: It's a God Thing. (Young Women of Faith Library). (Illus.). (J). 2000. pap. 7.99 (*0-310-70014-0*, Zonderkidz) Zondervan.

— Body Book: It's a God Thing. (Young Women of Faith Library). (Illus.). (J). 2000. pap. 7.99 (*0-310-70015-9*, Zonderkidz) Zondervan.

Rue, Nancy. The Burden. LC 96-44973. (Christian Heritage Ser.: Vol. 3). 192p. (J). (gr. 5-7). 1998. pap. 5.99 (*1-56179-517-8*) Focus Family.

***Rue, Nancy.** The Caper. LC 99-56189. (Christian Heritage Ser.: Vol. 5). 192p. (J). (gr. 3-7). 2000. pap. 5.99 (*1-56179-837-1*) Bethany Hse.

Rue, Nancy. The Capture. LC 99-27161. (Christian Heritage Ser.). 192p. (J). (gr. 3-7). 1999. pap. text 5.99 (*1-56179-810-X*) Bethany Hse.

— The Chase. LC 99-20084. (Christian Heritage Ser.: Vol. 2). 192p. (J). (gr. 3-7). 1999. pap. text 5.99 (*1-56179-735-9*) Focus Family.

— Christian Heritage Series: The Charleston Years Boxed Set: The Misfit; The Ally; The Threat; The Trap; The Hostage; The Escape, 6 vols., Set. (Christian Heritage Ser.). (J). (gr. 4-7). 1998. boxed set 35.99 (*1-56179-696-4*) Bethany Hse.

***Rue, Nancy.** Christian Heritage Series: The Chicago Years Boxed Set: The Trick; The Chase; The Capture; The Stunt; The Caper; The Pursuit, 6 vols., Set. (Christian Heritage Ser.). (J). (gr. 3-7). 2000. pap., boxed set 35.99 (*1-56179-877-0*) Bethany Hse.

Rue, Nancy. Christian Heritage Series: The Salem Years Boxed Set: The Rescue; The Stowaway; The Guardian; The Accused; The Samaritan; The Secret, 6 vols., Set. (Christian Heritage Ser.). (J). (gr. 3-7). 1998. boxed set 35.99 (*1-56179-694-8*) Bethany Hse.

— Christian Heritage Series: The Williamsburg Years Boxed Set: The Rebel; The Theif; The Burden; The Prisoner; The Invasion; The Battle, 6 vols., Set. (Christian Heritage Ser.). (J). (gr. 4-7). 1998. boxed set 35.99 (*1-56179-695-6*) Bethany Hse.

— Christian Heritage Teaching Guide: The Charleston Years. 128p. 1998. pap. 7.99 (*1-56179-645-X*) Bethany Hse.

***Rue, Nancy.** Christian Heritage Teaching Guide: The Chicago Years. 96p. (gr. 3-7). 2000. pap., teacher ed. 7.99 (*1-56179-857-6*) Bethany Hse.

Rue, Nancy. Christian Heritage Teaching Guide: The Salem Years. LC 98-27229. 96p. 1998. pap. 7.99 (*1-56179-640-9*) Focus Family.

— Christian Heritage Teaching Guide: The Williamsburg Years. 96p. 1998. pap. 7.99 (*1-56179-641-7*) Bethany Hse.

— Do I Have to Paint You a Picture? LC 98-230260. (Raise the Flag Ser.: Bk. 4). 224p. (J). (gr. 7-12). 1998. pap. 6.95 (*1-57856-035-7*) Waterbrook Pr.

— Don't Count on Homecoming Queen. LC 98-230229. (Raise the Flag Ser.: Bk. 1). 224p. (J). (gr. 7-12). 1998. pap. 2.95 (*1-57856-032-2*) Waterbrook Pr.

— The Escape. LC 98-25554. (Christian Heritage Ser.). 192p. (J). (gr. 3-7). 1998. pap. 5.99 (*1-56179-639-5*) Bethany Hse.

— Friends Don't Let Friends Date Jason. LC 99-10708. (Raise the Flag Ser.: Bk. 5). 224p. (J). (gr. 8-12). 1999. pap. 6.95 (*1-57856-087-X*) Waterbrook Pr.

— The Guardian. LC 94-41919. (Christian Heritage Ser.: Vol. 3). 192p. (J). (gr. 3-7). 1998. pap. 5.99 (*1-56179-348-5*) Focus Family.

— Guys & Other Things That Fry Your Brains. LC 98-45163. 1999. pap. 10.99 (*1-56955-126-X*) Servant.

***Rue, Nancy.** Here's Lily! (Young Women of Faith Library). (Illus.). (J). 2000. pap. text 2.97 (*0-310-23248-1*, Zonderkidz) Zondervan.

Rue, Nancy. The Hostage. LC 98-25553. (Christian Heritage Ser.: Vol. 5). 28p. (J). (gr. 3-7). 1998. pap. 5.99 (*1-56179-638-7*) Bethany Hse.

— I Only Binge on Holy Hungers. (Raise the Flag Ser.: Bk. 3). 224p. (YA). (gr. 6-12). 1998. pap. 6.95 (*1-57856-034-9*) Waterbrook Pr.

— The Invasion. LC 97-5400. (Christian Heritage Ser.: Vol. 5). 192p. (J). (gr. 3-7). 1998. pap. 5.99 (*1-56179-541-0*) Focus Family.

***Rue, Nancy.** Lily Robbins, M. D. Medical Dabbler. (Young Women of Faith Library). (Illus.). (J). 2000. pap. 4.99 (*0-310-23249-X*, Zonderkidz) Zondervan.

Rue, Nancy. The Misfit. LC 97-24445. (Christian Heritage Ser.: Vol. 1). 192p. (J). (gr. 3-13). 1998. pap. 5.99 (*1-56179-560-7*) Focus Family.

— The Prisoner. LC 96-38992. (Christian Heritage Ser.: Vol. 4). 192p. (J). (gr. 5-7). 1998. pap. 5.99 (*1-56179-518-6*) Focus Family.

***Rue, Nancy.** The Pursuit. LC 99-55398. (Christian Heritage Ser.: Vol. 4). 192p. (J). (gr. 3-7). 2000. pap. 5.99 (*1-56179-856-8*) Bethany Hse.

Rue, Nancy. The Rebel. LC 96-8549. (Christian Heritage Ser.: Vol. 1). 192p. (J). (gr. 3-7). 1998. pap. 5.99 (*1-56179-478-3*) Focus Family.

— The Rescue. LC 94-41917. (Christian Heritage Ser.: Vol. 1). 192p. (J). (gr. 3-7). 1998. pap. 5.99 (*1-56179-346-9*) Focus Family.

— The Samaritan. LC 95-25701. (Christian Heritage Ser.: Vol. 5). 224p. (Orig.). (J). (gr. 3-7). 1998. pap. 5.99 (*1-56179-442-2*) Focus Family.

— The Secret. LC 95-25700. (Christian Heritage Ser.). 192p. (Orig.). (J). (gr. 3-7). 1998. pap. 5.99 (*1-56179-443-0*) Focus Family.

— The Stowaway. LC 94-41918. (Christian Heritage Ser.: Vol. 2). 28p. (J). (gr. 3-7). 1998. pap. 5.99 (*1-56179-347-7*) Focus Family.

— The Stunt. LC 99-30013. (Christian Heritage Ser.). 192p. (J). (gr. 3-7). 1999. pap. text 5.99 (*1-56179-833-9*) Bethany Hse.

— The Thief. LC 96-8551. (Christian Heritage Ser.: Vol. 2). 192p. (J). (gr. 3-7). 1998. pap. 5.99 (*1-56179-479-1*) Focus Family.

— The Threat. LC 97-51659. (Christian Heritage Ser.: Vol. 3). 28p. (J). (gr. 3-7). 1998. pap. 5.99 (*1-56179-566-6*) Focus Family.

— The Trap. LC 97-51660. (Christian Heritage Ser.). 28p. (J). (gr. 3-7). 1998. pap. 5.99 (*1-56179-567-4*) Focus Family.

— The Trick. LC 99-19627. (Christian Heritage Ser.: Vol. 1). 192p. (J). (gr. 3-7). 1999. pap. text 5.99 (*1-56179-734-0*) Focus Family.

— When Is Perfect, Perfect Enough? LC 99-10709. (Raise the Flag Ser.: Bk. 6). 224p. (YA). (gr. 6-12). 1999. pap. 6.95 (*1-57856-088-8*) Waterbrook Pr.

Rue, Nancy & McSwane, David Z. The Essentials of Safe Food Management & Sanitation. LC 97-20689. 373p. 1997. pap. 44.00 (*0-13-532136-0*) P-H.

An Asterisk (*) at the beginning of an entry indicates that the title is appearing for the first time.

***Rue, Nancy N.** Choosing a Career in Hotels, Motels & Resorts. rev. ed. (World of Work Ser.). (Illus.). 64p. (YA). (gr. 7-12). 1999. 16.95 (*0-8239-2999-X*) Rosen Group.

Rue, Nancy N. Coping with An Illiterate Parent. Rosen, Roger, ed. (Coping Ser.). 64p. (YA). (gr. 7-12). 1990. lib. bdg. 17.95 (*0-8239-1070-9*) Rosen Group.

— Everything You Need to Know about Abusive Relationships. (Need to Know Library). (Illus.). 64p. (YA). (gr. 8-12). 1998. lib. bdg. 17.95 (*0-8239-2832-2*) Rosen Group.

— Everything You Need to Know about Getting Your Period. LC 94-42067. (Need to Know Library). (Illus.). 64p. (YA). (gr. 7-12). 1995. lib. bdg. 17.95 (*0-8239-1870-X*) Rosen Group.

— Everything You Need to Know about Peer Mediation. LC 96-34712. (Need to Know Library). (Illus.). 64p. (YA). (gr. 7-12). 1997. lib. bdg. 17.95 (*0-8239-2435-1*, D2435-1) Rosen Group.

— Hotels/Motels/Resorts. (World of Work Ser.). (Illus.). 64p. (YA). (gr. 7-12). 1997. lib. bdg. 16.95 (*0-8239-2273-1*) Rosen Group.

Rue, Richard & Rue, Geraldine, compiled by. In Song & Sorrow: The Daily Journal of Thomas H. B. McCain. 1998. 24.95 (*1-57860-019-7*); pap. 17.95 (*1-57860-020-0*) Guild Pr IN.

Rue, Richard M. De La, see Marsh, John H. & De La Rue, Richard M., eds.

***Rue, Stephen.** Voodoo Divorce: Put a Hex on Your Ex Through Preparation & Knowledge. 320p. 1998. 23.95 (*0-8281-1290-8*) American Heritage Inc.

Rue Van Hook, La, see Van Hook, La Rue, tr.

Rue, Wendy & Abarbanel, Karin. The Dollar Bill Knows No Sex: Savvy Business Secrets & Lessons from the Founder of the National Association for Female Executives. LC 96-51761. (Illus.). 160p. 1997. 21.95 (*0-07-057787-0*) McGraw.

Rueb, Wendy, ed. see Duley, Irene, et al.

Rueb, Wendy, ed. see Guay-Woodford, Lisa, et al.

Ruebel, James S., ed. Caesar & the Crisis of the Roman Aristocracy: A Civil War Reader. LC 93-21007. (Oklahoma Series in Classical Culture: Vol. 18). (Illus.). 216p. 1994. 22.95 (*0-8061-2590-X*) U of Okla Pr.

Ruebelman, Kerry L., ed. Snake River Plain - Yellowstone Volcanic Province. (IGC Field Trip Guidebooks Ser.). 1989. 21.00 (*0-87590-627-3*, T305) Am Geophysical.

Rueben, B. G. & Burstall, M. L. The Chemical Economy: A Guide to the Technology & Economics of the Chemistry Industry. LC 73-85210. 552p. 1973. reprint ed. pap. 171.20 (*0-608-04760-0*, 201960400013) Bks Demand.

Rueben, Douglas H. Publicity for Mental Health Clinicians: Using TV, Radio, & Print Media to Enchance Your Public. LC 95-6249. 238p. 1997. pap. text 22.95 (*0-7890-0411-9*) Haworth Pr.

Rueben, Kim S., jt. auth. see Poterba, James M.

Rueben, Steven C. Children of Character: Leading Your Children to Ethical Choices in Everyday Life. Canter, Marlene et al, eds. 197p. (Orig.). 1996. pap. text 12.95 (*1-57271-011-X*) Canter & Assocs.

Ruebens, John & Gary, J. H., eds. Proceedings of the 10th Oil Shale Symposium. LC 75-17946. (Illus.). 256p. 1977. pap. 3.50 (*0-918062-01-2*) Colo Sch Mines.

Ruebner, Boris H. Diagnostic Pathology of Liver & Biliary Tract. 2nd ed. 1991. 164.00 (*1-56032-060-5*) Hemisp Pub.

***Ruebner, Ralph.** Illinois Criminal Procedure, 2 vols. 3rd ed. Incl. Vol. 1. Illinois Criminal Procedure. 3rd ed. 1999. (*0-327-04990-1*, 8108320); Vol. 2. Illinois Criminal Procedure. 3rd ed. 1999. (*0-327-04992-8*, 8108420); 1000p. 1999. 185.00 (*0-327-04989-8*, 8109111) LEXIS Pub.

Ruebner, Ralph. Illinois Criminal Procedure, Issue 4. 500p. 1999. ring bd. write for info. (*0-327-01000-2*, 8109514) LEXIS Pub.

— Illinois Criminal Trial Evidence. 2nd ed. 350p. 1993. suppl. ed. 42.50 (*0-685-74470-1*, MICHIE); ring bd. 85.00 (*1-56257-713-1*, MICHIE) LEXIS Pub.

Ruebner, Ralph, ed. see Rinella, Richard A.

Ruechardt, Christoph, jt. ed. see Janich, Peter.

Ruechardt, Eduard. Light, Visible & Invisible. LC 58-5904. (Ann Arbor Science Library). 201p. reprint ed. pap. 62.40 (*0-608-11839-7*, 205564300029) Bks Demand.

Rueckert, Carla L. A Channeling Handbook. 118p. 1987. pap. 6.95 (*0-945007-07-8*) L-L Resrch.

Rueckert, Carla L., jt. auth. see Elkins, Don.

Rueckert, George L. Global Double Zero: The INF Treaty from Its Origins to Implementation, 135. LC 92-30019. (Contributions in Military Studies Ser.: No. 135). 248p. 1993. 57.95 (*0-313-28695-7*, RGB/, Greenwood Pr) Greenwood.

— On-Site Inspection in Theory & Practice: A Primer on Modern Arms Control Regimes. LC 97-23346. 296p. 1998. 69.50 (*0-275-96047-1*, Praeger Pubs) Greenwood.

Rueckert, William H. Encounters with Kenneth Burke. LC 93-15560. 256p. 1994. text 39.95 (*0-252-02054-5*); pap. text 15.95 (*0-252-06350-3*) U of Ill Pr.

— Glenway Wescott. Bowman, Sylvia E., ed. LC 65-18906. (Twayne's United States Authors Ser.). 172p. (C). 1965. lib. bdg. 20.95 (*0-8290-1709-7*) Irvington.

Rueckert, William H., ed. Critical Responses to Kenneth Burke, 1924-1966. LC 71-75973. 541p. reprint ed. pap. 167.80 (*0-608-14152-6*, 205590800039) Bks Demand.

Rueckl, Gotthard, jt. auth. see Kunze, Horst.

Rued, Tim. Fiddling in Sonoma County. McCurry, Tom, ed. (Illus.). 32p. (Orig.). 1989. pap. write for info. (*0-318-66628-6*) Cult Arts Council Sonoma Cty.

Rueda. Las Aceitunas y Otros Pasos: A, Level Books. text 7.95 (*0-88436-923-4*) EMC-Paradigm.

***Rueda, Paul E.** Die Verfassungsgerichtliche Unvereinbarerklarung Verfassungswidriger Gesetze: Untersuchungen Zur Entwicklung und Funktion Dieser Rechtsfigur Im Deutschen Recht und Zu Ihrer Ubertragbarkeit Ins Costaricanische Recht. (GER.). 187p. 1999. 41.00 (*3-631-33432-X*) P Lang Pubng.

Rueda, Aude. Cocina Sin Colesterol. (SPA.). 1997. pap. text 7.98 (*970-643-047-4*) Selector.

Rueda, Barbara F., tr. see Rueda, Edward A., ed.

Rueda, Edward A., ed. Colombia, Sangil, Gods, Gold, Sex & Violence: Presence of a People, Reminiscence of the City of Sangil. unabridged ed. Rueda-Vasquez, Eduardo & Rueda, Barbara F., trs. from SPA. Orig. Title: Presencia de un Pueblo. 208p. 1999. pap. 19.99 (*0-9665288-0-8*) E R Vasquez.

Rueda, Enrique T. & Schwartz, Michael. Gays, AIDS & You. LC 87-24527. (Illus.). 118p. 1987. 7.95 (*0-8159-5624-X*) Devin.

Rueda, Lupicinio I., jt. ed. see Ibanez-Gracia, Tomas.

Rueda, Marta F. De, see De Rueda, Marta F.

Rueda, Salvador. El Ritmo. Palenque, ed. (Exeter Hispanic Text Ser.: No. 53). (SPA.). 150p. Date not set. pap. text 17.95 (*0-85989-401-0*, Pub. by Univ Exeter Pr) Northwestern U Pr.

Rueda-Vasquez, Eduardo, tr. see Rueda, Edward A., ed.

Ruede, Howard. Sod-House Days: Letters from a Kansas Homesteader, 1877. Ise, J., ed. LC 66-17858. 248p. reprint ed. 53.00 (*0-8154-0200-7*) Cooper Sq.

Ruede, Ulrich. Mathematical & Computational Techniques for Multilevel Adaptive Methods. LC 93-28379. (Frontiers in Applied Mathematics Ser.: No. 13). xii, 140p. 1993. pap. 29.00 (*0-89871-320-X*) Soc Indus-Appl Math.

Ruedenberg, Werner. Chinesisch-Deutsches Woerterbuch. 3rd ed. (CHI & GER.). 821p. (C). 1963. 173.50 (*3-11-000020-2*) De Gruyter.

Ruedi, T., et al. Surgical Approaches for Internal Fixation. (Illus.). 180p. 1983. 154.00 (*0-387-12809-3*) Spr-Verlag.

***Ruedi, T. P. & Murphy, W. M.** AO Principles of Fracture Management. (Illus.). 1000p. 2000. pap. 369.00 (*0-86577-886-8*) Thieme Med Pubs.

Ruediger, E., jt. auth. see Strauss, Eduard.

Ruediger, Horst. Kleines Literarisches Lexikon: Small Lexicon of Literature, 4 vols., Set. 4th ed. (GER.). 1972. 150.00 (*0-8288-6401-2*, M-7504) Fr & Eur.

Ruediger, Horst, ed. Die Gattungen in der vergleichenden Literaturwissenschaft. (Komparatistische Studien: Vol. 4, Beihefte zur Zeitschrift 'Arcadia'). 92p. (C). 1973. 11.20 (*3-11-004496-X*) De Gruyter.

Ruediger, Horst, et al, eds. Zur Theorie der Vergleichenden Literaturwissenschaft. 87p. (C). 1971. 15.40 (*3-11-003622-3*) De Gruyter.

Ruedt, Lucy W., tr. see Boehlke, LeRoy & Silldorff, Donald.

Ruedy, Elisabeth & Nirenberg, Sue. Where Do I Put the Decimal Point? How to Conquer Math Anxiety & Let Numbers Work for You. 1992. pap. 9.00 (*0-380-71596-1*, Avon Bks) Morrow Avon.

Ruedy, John. Modern Algeria: The Origins & Development of a Nation. LC 92-4637. 320p. 1992. pap. 17.95 (*0-253-20746-0*, MB-746) Ind U Pr.

Ruedy, John, jt. auth. see Marshall, Shane A.

Ruef, Dorothy N. Health Education in Senior High Schools. LC 79-177219. (Columbia University, Teachers College - Contributions to Education Ser.: No. 636). reprint ed. 37.50 (*0-404-55636-1*) AMS Pr.

Ruef, Hans. Sprichwort und Sprache: Am Beispiel des Sprichworts im Schweizerdeutschen. (Studia Linguistica Germanica: No. 36). (GER.). x, 303p. (C). 1995. lib. bdg. 124.60 (*3-11-014494-8*) De Gruyter.

Ruef, Kerry. The Private Eye: Looking-Thinking by Analogy - A Guide to Developing the Interdisciplinary Mind. (Illus.). 240p. (Orig.). 1992. pap. text 18.95 (*0-9605434-1-4*) Private Eye.

— The Private Eye Loupe (5X) 1992. 3.95 (*0-9605434-2-2*) Private Eye.

Ruef, Kerry, et al, eds. The Crystal Set: Poems, Fiction, Memoirs-an Anthology Of Older Voices. (Illus.). 88p. (Orig.). 1980. pap. 3.95 (*0-9605434-0-6*) Private Eye.

Rueff, Bob. Minnesota Heat: The Heat Minnesotans Get When They Go Someplace Else. (Illus.). 176p. (Orig.). 1997. pap. 14.95 (*0-9656395-0-9*) RM Pub.

Rueff, Dominique. La Biblia de las Vitaminas. 299p. 1998. pap. text 9.95 (*84-8327-004-8*) E Martinez Roca.

Rueff, Marcel & Jeger, Max. Sets & Boolean Algebra. Howson, A. G., ed. LC 72-189267. (Mathematical Studies: A Series for Teachers & Students: No. 4). 192p. reprint ed. pap. 59.60 (*0-608-11936-9*, 202332900032) Bks Demand.

Ruefle, Mary. The Adamant. LC 88-38575. (Iowa Poetry Prize Ser.). 87p. 1989. 17.95 (*0-87745-235-0*); pap. 11.95 (*0-87745-236-9*) U of Iowa Pr.

— Cold Pluto. LC 95-67961. (Poetry Ser.). 72p. (C). 1996. 20.95 (*0-88748-220-1*); pap. 11.95 (*0-88748-221-X*) Carnegie-Mellon.

***Ruefle, Mary.** Post Meridian. LC 98-71943. (Poetry Ser.). 88p. 2000. 24.95 (*0-88748-315-1*, Pub. by Carnegie-Mellon); pap. 12.95 (*0-88748-302-X*, Pub. by Carnegie-Mellon) CUP Services.

Ruefli, Timothy. Ordinal Time Series Analysis: Methodology & Applications in Management Strategy & Policy, 1. LC 90-30011. 280p. 1990. 55.00 (*0-89930-571-7*, Quorum Bks) Greenwood.

Ruefli, Timothy W., jt. auth. see Collins, James M.

Ruegamer, Lana, jt. auth. see Thornbrough, Emma Lou.

Rueger, Doris, jt. auth. see Gordon, Howard A.

Rueger, J. M. Electronic Distance Measurement. (Illus.). 265p. 1990. 63.95 (*0-387-51523-2*, 3434) Spr-Verlag.

— Electronic Distance Measurement: An Introduction. 4th ed. LC 96-16952. 1996. pap. write for info. (*0-387-61159-2*); pap. 74.95 (*3-540-61159-2*) Spr-Verlag.

Ruegg, Arthur, ed. Le Corbusier - Polychromie Architecturale: The "Claviers de Couleurs" from 1931 & 1959, 3 vols. (Illus.). 1997. boxed set 225.00 (*3-7643-5612-X*, Pub. by Birkhauser) Princeton Arch.

***Ruegg, Arthur & Burri, Rene.** Le Corbusier, Photographed by Rene Burri/Magnum. LC 99-25201. (Illus.). 1999. 80.00 (*3-7643-5999-4*, Pub. by Birkhauser) Princeton Arch.

Ruegg, David S. Buddha-Nature, Mind & the Problem of Gradualism in a Comparative Perspective. 1989. 50.00 (*0-7286-0152-4*, Pub. by Sch Orient & African Stud) S Asia.

Ruegg, David S., et al, eds. Earliest Buddhism & Madhyamaka. (Panels of the VIIth World Sanskrit Conference - Kern Institute, Leiden: August 23-29, 1987 Ser.: Vol. II). 114p. 1990. 53.50 (*90-04-09246-3*) Brill Academic Pubs.

Ruegg, Erwin. Urbanitat und Stadtentwicklung. (Europaische Urbanitat-Politik der Stadte Ser.). (GER.). 224p. 1996. text 56.00 (*90-5708-005-2*); pap. text 16.00 (*90-5708-006-0*) Gordon & Breach.

Ruegg, Frank & Bianchina, Paul. You Can't Plant Tomatoes in Central Park: The Urban Dropouts Guide to Rural Relocation. LC 90-53281. 303p. 1990. 18.95 (*0-88282-060-5*); pap. 13.95 (*0-88282-107-5*) New Horizon NJ.

Ruegg, Johann C. Calcium in Muscle Activation. (Zoophysiology Ser.: Vol. 19). (Illus.). 320p. 1986. 129.00 (*0-387-17117-7*) Spr-Verlag.

— Calcium in Muscle Activation. (Zoophysiology Ser.: Vol. 19). (Illus.). 300p. 1988. reprint ed. pap. 69.00 (*0-387-18278-0*) Spr-Verlag.

— Calcium in Muscle Contraction: Cellular & Molecular Physiology. 2nd ed. LC 92-20353. Orig. Title: Calcium in Muscle Activation. (Illus.). 352p. 1992. 118.95 (*0-387-55544-7*) Spr-Verlag.

Ruegg, Johann C., ed. Peptides As Probes in Muscle Research. (Illus.). 188p. 1991. 119.95 (*0-387-53653-1*) Spr-Verlag.

Ruegg, Ruedi. Basic Typography: Handbook for Technique & Design. LC 89-31190. (Illus.). 176p. 1989. text 32.95 (*0-442-23913-0*, VNR) Wiley.

Ruegsegger, Ronald W., ed. Reflections on Francis Schaeffer. 336p. 1986. pap. 13.45 (*0-310-37091-4*, 12355P) Zondervan.

Ruehl, Peter. American Downunder. Allen & Unwin, eds. 152p. (Orig.). 1992. pap. text 14.95 (*0-04-442320-9*, Pub. by Allen & Unwin Pty) Paul & Co Pubs.

Ruehli, A. E., ed. Circuit Analysis, Simulation & Design. (Advances in CAD for VLSI Ser.: Vol. 3, Part 2). 400p. 1987. 72.25 (*0-444-87889-0*, North Holland) Elsevier.

— Circuit Analysis, Simulation & Design: General Aspects of Circuit Analysis & Design. 332p. 1986. 78.50 (*0-444-87893-9*, North Holland) Elsevier.

Ruehlmann, Virginia J., jt. auth. see Rice, Helen Steiner.

Ruehr, Thomas A., ed. see Hartel, Peter G., et al.

Ruehrwein, Dick & North, Julie. Discover Rivers: A Discovery Book. (Illus.). 32p. (J). (gr. 5-7). 1995. pap. 3.75 (*0-915992-73-6*) Eastern National.

Ruehrwein, Richard L. Discover Florida in the New World. (Illus.). 32p. 1997. pap. 4.95 (*1-888213-08-6*) Eastern National.

Ruel, Francine. Des Graffiti A Suivre. (Novels in the Roman Plus Ser.). (FRE.). 160p. (YA). (gr. 8 up). 1991. pap. 8.95 (*2-89021-166-5*, Pub. by La Courte Ech) Firefly Bks Ltd.

— Mon Pere et Moi. (Novels in the Roman Plus Ser.). (FRE., Illus.). 160p. (YA). (gr. 8 up). 1993. pap. 8.95 (*2-89021-192-4*, Pub. by La Courte Ech) Firefly Bks Ltd.

Ruel, Jeannot. Fly Fishing: Equipment & Techniques. (Illus.). 140p. (Orig.). 1997. pap. 24.95 (*1-55209-100-7*) Firefly Bks Ltd.

Ruel, Malcolm J. Belief, Ritual & the Securing of Life: Reflective Essays on a Bantu Religion. LC 96-39014. (Studies of Religion in Africa: Vol. 18). x, 270p. 1997. 106.00 (*90-04-10640-5*, NLG135) Brill Academic Pubs.

Ruele, Judy. How to Teach Hobby Ceramics. 1989. pap. 9.95 (*0-916809-36-6*) Scott Pubns MI.

Ruell, David. No Stone Unturned: Saving Outdoor Sculpture. 34p. 1994. pap. write for info. (*0-9643014-0-7*) NH Pres Alliance.

Ruell, Patrick. Death of a Dormouse. 288p. 1987. 15.45 (*0-89296-260-7*, Pub. by Mysterious Pr) Little.

— The Long Kill. 256p. 1989. reprint ed. pap. 3.50 (*0-380-70742-X*, Avon Bks) Morrow Avon.

— The Only Game. large type ed. 467p. 1993. 27.99 (*0-7505-0451-X*, Pub. by Mgna Lrg Print) Ulverscroft.

— Urn Burial. 224p. 1994. 19.50 (*0-7451-8628-9*, Black Dagger) Chivers N Amer.

Ruelle, David. Chance & Chaos. (Science Library). (Illus.). 202p. (C). 1991. text 39.50 (*0-691-08574-9*, Pub. by Princeton U Pr); pap. text 11.95 (*0-691-02100-7*, Pub. by Princeton U Pr) Cal Prin Full Svc.

— Chaotic Evolution & Strange Attractors. (Lezioni Lincee Lectures). (Illus.). 112p. 1989. pap. text 20.95 (*0-521-36830-8*) Cambridge U Pr.

— Dynamical Zeta Functions for Piecewise Monotone Maps of the Interval. LC 94-6986. (CRM Monograph Ser.: Vol. 4). 62p. 1994. text 19.00 (*0-8218-6991-4*, CRMM/4) Am Math.

***Ruelle, David.** Statistical Mechanics Rigorous Results. 1999. 32.00 (*981-02-3862-2*) World Scientific Pub.

Ruelle, David. Turbulence, Strange Attractors & Chaos. 450p. 1995. text 86.00 (*981-02-2310-2*); pap. text 48.00 (*981-02-2311-0*) World Scientific Pub.

Ruelle, Karen G. The Book of Baths. LC 96-23760. (Illus.). 10p. (J). 1997. pap. 4.95 (*0-15-201003-3*) Harcourt.

— Seventy-Five Fun Things to Make & Do by Yourself. (Illus.). 80p. (J). (gr. 3-7). 1995. pap. 6.95 (*0-8069-0332-5*) Sterling.

***Ruelle, Karen Gray.** Snow Valentines. LC 99-46315. (Illus.). 48p. (J). (gr. k-3). 2000. 14.95 (*0-8234-1533-3*) Holiday.

Ruelle, Karen Gray. The Thanksgiving Beast Feast Level 2: A Holiday House Reader. LC 98-51339. (Illus.). 32p. (J). 1999. 14.95 (*0-8234-1511-2*) Holiday.

Ruello, Catherine, ed. Manual: Art in General, 1993 & 1994. (Illus.). 96p. (Orig.). 1994. pap. 15.00 (*1-883967-02-3*) Art in General.

Ruemke, P., ed. Therapy of Advanced Melanoma. (Pigment Cell Ser.: Vol. 10). (Illus.). viii, 230p. 1990. 172.25 (*3-8055-5032-4*) S Karger.

Ruepke, Joerg. Kalender & Oeffentlichkeit: Die Geschichte der Repraesentation & Religioesen Qualifikation von Zeit in Rom. (Religionsgeschichtliche Versuche und Vorarbeiten Ser.: Bd 40). (GER.). 740p. (C). 1995. lib. bdg. 260.00 (*3-11-014514-6*) De Gruyter.

Ruepp, Krista. Horses in the Fog. James, J. Alison, tr. LC 97-8736. (Illus.). 64p. (J). (gr. 1-4). 1997. 13.95 (*1-55858-804-3*, Pub. by North-South Bks NYC); 13.88 (*1-55858-805-1*, Pub. by North-South Bks NYC) Chronicle Bks.

— Horses in the Fog. James, J. Alison, tr. LC 97-8736. (Illus.). 64p. (J). (gr. 1-4). 1999. pap. 5.95 (*0-7358-1101-6*, Pub. by North-South Bks NYC) Chronicle Bks.

***Ruepp, Krista.** Horses in the Fog. (Illus.). (J). 1999. 11.40 (*0-606-18321-3*) Turtleback.

Ruepp, Krista. Midnight Rider. James, J. Alison, tr. LC 95-12321. (Illus.). 64p. (J). (gr. 2-4). 1995. 13.95 (*1-55858-494-3*, Pub. by North-South Bks NYC); lib. bdg. 13.88 (*1-55858-495-1*, Pub. by North-South Bks NYC) Chronicle Bks.

— Midnight Rider. James, J. Alison, tr. LC 95-12321. (Illus.). 64p. (J). (gr. 2-4). 1996. pap. 5.95 (*1-55858-620-2*, Pub. by North-South Bks NYC) Chronicle Bks.

Rueppel, R. A. Analysis & Design of Stream Ciphers. (Communications & Control Engineering Ser.). (Illus.). 260p. 1986. 108.95 (*0-387-16870-2*) Spr-Verlag.

Rueppel, R. A., ed. Advances in Cryptology - EUROCRYPT '92: Workshop on the Theory & Application of Cryptographic Techniques, Balatonfured, Hungary, May 24-28, 1992 Proceedings. LC 92-46271. (Lecture Notes in Computer Science Ser.: Vol. 658). 1993. 73.95 (*0-387-56413-6*) Spr-Verlag.

Rueppell, H. & Rueppell, Marlies. Intelligenzfoerderung - Moeglichkeiten und Grenzen. Schmitz-Scherzer, R., ed. (Psychologische Praxis Ser.: Band 49). (Illus.). 105p. 1976. 19.25 (*3-8055-2303-3*) S Karger.

Rueppell, Marlies, jt. auth. see Rueppell, H.

Ruers, T. J., jt. ed. see Jakimowicz, J. J.

Rues, D., jt. ed. see Oswatitsch, K.

Ruesch, H., et al. Creep & Shrinkage: Their Effect on the Behavior of Concrete Structures. (Illus.). 284p. 1983. 179.95 (*0-387-90669-X*) Spr-Verlag.

Ruesch, Hans. Naked Empress: or The Great Medical Fraud. 3rd rev. ed. (Illus.). 202p. 1982. pap. text 10.00 (*3-905280-02-7*, Pub. by Civis) U of Mich Pr.

— Slaughter of the Innocent. 446p. 1992. reprint ed. pap. 4.95 (*0-9610016-0-7*) CIVIS-Civitas.

— Top of the World. 1991. mass mkt. 4.50 (*0-671-73928-X*) PB.

Ruesch, Jurgen. Semiotic Approaches to Human Relations. 1972. 141.55 (*90-279-2299-3*) Mouton.

Ruesch, Peter. Spielt die Schule eine Rolle? Schulische Bedingungen Ungleicher Bildungschancen von Immigrantenkindern - Eine Mehrebenenanalyse. (Explorationen Ser.: Bd. 18). (GER.). 352p. 1998. 49.95 (*3-906760-16-2*) P Lang Pubng.

Rueschemeyer, Dietrich. Lawyers & Their Society: A Comparative Study of the Legal Profession in Germany & the United States. LC 72-93953. 268p. reprint ed. pap. 83.10 (*0-7837-2327-X*, 205741500004) Bks Demand.

— Power & the Division of Labour. LC 85-51798. viii, 260p. 1986. pap. 14.95 (*0-8047-1325-1*) Stanford U Pr.

Rueschemeyer, Dietrich, et al, eds. Participation & Democracy East & West: Comparisons & Interpretations. LC 97-50400. 304p. (C). (gr. 13). 1998. text 73.95 (*0-7656-0229-6*) M E Sharpe.

— Participation & Democracy East & West: Comparisons & Interpretations. LC 97-50400. (Illus.). 304p. 1998. pap. text 32.95 (*0-7656-0230-X*) M E Sharpe.

Rueschemeyer, Dietrich & Skocpol, Theda, eds. States, Special Knowledge, & the Origins of Modern Social Policies. LC 95-17924. 328p. 1996. text 60.00 (*0-691-03444-3*, Pub. by Princeton U Pr); pap. text 19.95 (*0-691-00112-X*, Pub. by Princeton U Pr) Cal Prin Full Svc.

Rueschemeyer, Dietrich, et al. Capitalist Development & Democracy. (Illus.). 400p. 1992. pap. text 19.95 (*0-226-73144-8*); lib. bdg. 52.00 (*0-226-73142-1*) U Ch Pr.

Rueschemeyer, Dietrich, jt. ed. see Putterman, Louis.

Rueschemeyer, Marilyn, ed. Women in the Politics of Post-Communist Eastern Europe. LC 93-13580. 272p. (gr. 13). 1994. text 77.95 (*1-56324-168-4*) M E Sharpe.

Rueschemeyer, Marilyn, ed. Women in the Politics of Post-Communist Eastern Europe. LC 93-13580. 272p. (C). (gr. 13). 1994. pap. text 36.95 (*1-56324-169-2*) M E Sharpe.

Rueschemeyer, Marilyn, ed. Women in the Politics of Postcommunist Eastern Europe. 2nd expanded rev. ed. LC 98-15195. 320p. (C). (gr. 13). 1998. pap. text 28.95 (*0-7656-0296-2*) M E Sharpe.

Rueschemeyer, Marilyn, et al, eds. Left Parties & Social Policy in Post-Communist Europe. (Eastern Europe after Communism Ser.). 280p. 1999. pap. 25.00 (*0-8133-3569-8*, Pub. by Westview); text 69.00 (*0-8133-3568-X*, Pub. by Westview) HarpC.

R

R

Rueschemeyer, Marilyn & Lemke, Christiane, eds. Quality of Life in the German Democratic Republic: Changes & Developments in a State Socialist Society. LC 88-4089. 256p. (C). (gr. 13). 1989. text 85.95 (*0-87332-484-6*) M E Sharpe.

Rueschemeyer, Marilyn, et al. Soviet Emigre Artists. LC 84-23558. 184p. (C). (gr. 13). 1985. pap. text 42.95 (*0-87332-810-8*) M E Sharpe.

Rueschhoff, Norlin G. International Accounting & Financial Reporting. LC 76-12871. (Special Studies). 172p. 1976. 57.95 (*0-275-90250-1*, C0250, Praeger Pubs) Greenwood.

Rueschmann, Eva. Sisters on Screen: Siblings in Contemporary Cinema. (Culture & the Moving Image Ser.). (Illus.). 304p. 2000. 69.50 (*1-56639-746-4*); pap. 22.95 (*1-56639-747-2*) Temple U Pr.

Rueschmeyer, Marilyn, ed. Women in the Politics of Postcommunist Eastern Europe. 2nd expanded rev. ed. LC 98-15195. 320p. (C). (gr. 13). 1998. text 68.95 (*0-7656-0295-4*) M E Sharpe.

Rueschoff, Phil H. & Swartz, M. Evelyn. Teaching Art in the Elementary School: Enhancing Visual Perception. LC 78-75641. (Illus.). 345p. reprint ed. pap. 107.00 (*0-608-11196-1*, 205551800023) Bks Demand.

Ruesga, Santos M., jt. ed. see Van Der Laan, Lambert.

Ruesing, Tony. Better Questions Better Answers: Staying on Target. LC 97-75175. v, 133p. (Orig.). 1997. pap. 14.95 (*0-9660560-0-0*) Ancil Ents.

Ruess, Everett. On Desert Trails with Everett Ruess: Commemorative Edition. Bergera, Gary J., ed. (Illus.). 144p. 2000. 17.95 (*0-87905-825-0*) Gibbs Smith Pub.

— The Wilderness Journals of Everett Ruess. Rusho, W. L., ed. LC 98-17502. (Illus.). 208p. 1998. pap. 14.95 (*0-87905-863-3*) Gibbs Smith Pub.

Ruestow, E. G. The Microscope in the Dutch Republic: The Shaping of Discovery. (Illus.). 360p. (C). 1996. text 59.95 (*0-521-47078-1*) Cambridge U Pr.

Ruete, Emily. Memoirs of an Arabian Princess from Zanzibar. rev. ed. Wiener, Markus W., tr. from GER. LC 89-9064. (Topics in World History Ser.). (Illus.). 326p. (C). 1989. reprint ed. text 39.95 (*1-55876-011-3*) Wiener Pubs Inc.

— Memoirs of an Arabian Princess from Zanzibar. rev. ed. Wiener, Markus W., tr. from GER. LC 89-9064. (Topics in World History Ser.). (Illus.). 326p. (C). 1990. reprint ed. pap. text 18.95 (*1-55876-007-5*) Wiener Pubs Inc.

Ruete, Emily, jt. auth. see Salme, Sayyida.

Rueter, Alvin. The Freedom to Be Wrong. 1985. 6.55 (*0-89536-749-1*, 5855) CSS OH.

— Making Good Preaching Better: A Step-by-Step Guide to Scripture-Based People-Centered Preaching. LC 96-42563. 280p. 1997. pap. 19.95 (*0-8146-2215-1*) Liturgical Pr.

***Rueter, Ted.** The 267 Stupidest Things Republicans Ever Said/The 267 Stupidest Things Democrats Ever Said: Flip-Book. LC 99-59995. 120p. 2000. pap. 8.95 (*0-609-80635-1*, HUM006000, Three Riv Pr) Crown Pub Group.

Rueter, Theodore, ed. The Politics of Race: African Americans & the Political System. LC 95-5901. 416p. (gr. 13). 1995. text 77.95 (*1-56324-564-7*) M E Sharpe.

— The Politics of Race: African Americans & the Political System. LC 95-5901. 416p. (C). (gr. 13). 1995. pap. text 26.95 (*1-56324-565-5*) M E Sharpe.

— The United States in the World Political Economy. LC 93-1129. 320p. (C). 1994. 33.44 (*0-07-054259-7*) McGraw.

Rueter, Theodore, jt. auth. see Bitzer, Lloyd F.

Ruetersworden, Udo. Dominium Terrae: Studien Zur Genese Einer Alttestamentlichen Vorstellung. (Beiheft zur Zeitschrift fuer die Alttestamentliche Wissenschaft Ser.: No. 215). x, 205p. 1993. lib. bdg. 95.40 (*3-11-013948-0*) De Gruyter.

Rueth, Robert M. The Next Presidency - Leadership. LC 97-67141. 176p. 1998. 18.95 (*1-57197-072-X*) Pentland Pr.

***Ruether, Rosemary Radford.** Christianity, Family & the Rise of the West. 2000. 28.50 (*0-8070-5404-6*) Beacon Pr.

Ruether, Rosemary Radford. Faith & Fratricide: The Theological Roots of Anti-Semitism. 1984. 12.95 (*0-8164-2263-X*) Harper SF.

— Faith & Fratricide: The Theological Roots of Anti-Semitism. 294p. 1996. pap. 25.00 (*0-9653517-5-0*) Wipf & Stock.

— Gaia & God: An Ecofeminist Theology of Earth Healing. LC 91-58911. (Illus.). 320p. 1994. reprint ed. pap. 17.00 (*0-06-066967-5*, Pub. by Harper SF) HarpC.

— Introducing Redemption in Christian Feminism. (Introductions in Feminist Theology Ser.: Vol. 1). 136p. 1998. pap. 19.95 (*1-85075-888-3*, Pub. by Sheffield Acad) CUP Services.

— Liberation Theology: Human Hope Confronts Christian History & American Power. LC 72-92263. 202p. reprint ed. 62.70 (*0-8357-9487-3*, 201521200092) Bks Demand.

— New Woman, New Earth: Sexist Ideologies & Human Liberation. LC 95-16969. 256p. (C). 1995. pap. 14.00 (*0-8070-6503-X*) Beacon Pr.

***Ruether, Rosemary Radford.** Religion & Sexism: Images of Women in the Jewish & Christian Traditions. 356p. 1998. pap. 27.00 (*1-57910-116-X*) Wipf & Stock.

Ruether, Rosemary Radford. Sexism & God-Talk: Toward a Feminist Theology. LC 92-33119. 320p. (Orig.). 1993. pap. 17.00 (*0-8070-1205-X*) Beacon Pr.

— Womanguides: Readings Toward a Feminist Theology. 2nd ed. 304p. 1996. reprint ed. pap. 15.00 (*0-8070-1235-1*) Beacon Pr.

— Women & Redemption: A Theological History. LC 98-11783. 1998. 45.00 (*0-8006-2947-7*, 1-2947, Fortress Pr); pap. text 20.00 (*0-8006-2945-0*, 1-2945, Fortress Pr) Augsburg Fortress.

Ruether, Rosemary Radford, ed. Women Healing Earth: Third World Women on Ecology, Feminism & Religion. LC 96-528. (Ecology & Justice Ser.). 175p. 1996. pap. 17.00 (*1-57075-057-2*) Orbis Bks.

Ruether, Rosemary Radford & McLaughlin, Eleanor. Women of Spirit: Female Leadership in the Jewish & Christian Traditions. 400p. 1998. pap. 28.00 (*1-57910-109-7*) Wipf & Stock.

Ruether, Rosemary Radford, jt. auth. see Hall, Douglas J.

Ruether, Rosemary Radford, jt. auth. see Merton, Thomas.

Ruether, Rosemary Radford, jt. ed. see Hessel, Dieter T.

Ruether, Ursula, et al, eds. Paraneoplastic Syndromes. LC 97-46075. (Beitraege Zur Onkologie, Contributions to Oncology Ser.: Vol. 52, 1998). (Illus.). viii, 260p. 1998. 143.50 (*3-8055-6570-4*) S Karger.

Ruette, F., ed. Quantum Chemistry Approaches to Chemisorption & Heterogeneous Catalysis. (C). 1992. text 185.00 (*0-7923-1543-X*) Kluwer Academic.

Ruetten. Comprehending Academic Lectures. (J). 1991. audio 91.95 (*0-8384-3360-X*) Heinle & Heinle.

— Comprehending Academic Lectures. (J). 1996. mass mkt. 23.95 (*0-8384-3359-6*) Heinle & Heinle.

— Developing Composition Skills. LC 96-34769. (Miscellaneous/Catalogs Ser.). 300p. (J). 1997. pap. text 28.95 (*0-8384-6932-9*) Heinle & Heinle.

Ruetten, Charles W. Keyboarding: It's Fun to Use a Keyboard on the Typewriter or Computer. (Illus.). 131p. (J). (gr. 4 up). 1992. pap. text 12.95 (*1-881842-02-9*) Sundial Pub.

— Type with the Left or Right Hand on the Typewriter or Computer Keyboard. (Illus.). 95p. (Orig.). (YA). (gr. 5 up). 1993. pap. text 12.92 (*1-881842-03-7*) Sundial Pub.

Ruetten, Mary K., jt. auth. see Smalley, Regina L.

Ruettgers, H., ed. Immunotherapy of Vaginal Infections. (Journal: Gynaekologische Rundschau: Vol. 24, Suppl. 3, 1984). (Illus.). iv, 92p. 1985. pap. 28.00 (*3-8055-4072-8*) S Karger.

— Trichomoniasis. (Journal: Gynaekologische Rundschau: Vol. 22, Suppl. 2). (Illus.). viii, 92p. 1983. pap. 24.50 (*3-8055-3646-1*) S Karger.

— Trichomoniasis. (Journal: Gynaekologische Rundschau: Vol. 23, Suppl. 2, 1983). (Illus.). iv, 92p. 1983. pap. 24.50 (*3-8055-3751-4*) S Karger.

Ruettgers, Ken. The Home Field Advantage: Modeling Your Life Where the Score Really Counts. 224p. 1995. pap. 10.99 (*0-88070-799-2*, Multnomah Bks) Multnomah Pubs.

Ruettiger, Rudy & Celizic, Michael. Rudy's Rules: Game Plans for Life from the Real Rudy! LC 94-21231. (Illus.). 180p. 1994. 19.95 (*1-56796-056-1*) Rudy Intl.

Ruettiger, Rudy, et al. Rudy's Lessons for Young Champions: Choices & Challenges. (Illus.). 195p. (Orig.). (J). (gr. 4-6). 1997. pap. 14.95 (*0-9658119-0-5*) Rudy Intl.

Ruettner, J. R., et al, eds. Inflammatory Vascular Diseases-Endo-Myocardial Fibrosis-Pulmonary Hypertension: Proceedings - Conference of the International Society of Geographical Pathology, 12th, Zurich, September 1975. (Pathologia et Microbiologica Ser.: Vol. 43, No. 1-2). (Illus.). 180p. 1976. 68.00 (*3-8055-2311-4*) S Karger.

Ruettner, J. R., ed. see International Society of Geographical Pathology St.

Ruetz, Michael. Cosmos: Photographs 1971-1996. (Illus.). 156p. 1997. 29.95 (*3-88243-481-3*) Dist Art Pubs.

— Scottish Symphony. 1991. write for info. (*0-316-88887-7*) Little.

Ruetzler, Klaus & MacIntyre, Ian G., eds. The Atlantic Barrier Reef Ecosystem at Carrie Bow Cay, Belize Vol. I: Structure & Communities. LC 81-607039. (Illus.). 554p. (C). 1986. text 35.00 (*0-87474-850-X*) Smithsonian.

Rueveni, Roni, jt. auth. see Rabeeya, David.

Rueveni, Uri. Applications of Networking in Family & Community: A Special Issue of Journal of Family Therapy, Vol. 6, No. 2. 80p. 1984. pap. 14.95 (*0-89885-246-3*, Kluwer Acad Hman Sci) Kluwer Academic.

Rueveni, Uri. Networking Families in Crisis: Intervention Strategies with Families & Social Networks. LC 78-8024. 162p. 1979. 32.95 (*0-87705-374-X*, Kluwer Acad Hman Sci) Kluwer Academic.

Rueveni, Uri, et al, eds. Therapeutic Intervention: Healing Strategies for Human Systems. LC 81-13501. 285p. 1982. 35.95 (*0-89885-086-X*, Kluwer Acad Hman Sci) Kluwer Academic.

Ruevert, Sigmund. Crimson Hairs. 192p. 1999. mass mkt. 7.95 (*1-56201-118-9*) Blue Moon Bks.

Ruezulli, Joseph S., jt. auth. see Reis, Sally M.

***Ruf, Beatrix.** Ugo Rondinone: Guided by Voices. 2000. 45.00 (*3-7757-9006-3*) Gerd Hatje.

Ruf, Bob & Ruf, Pat. Fairy Lamps: Elegance in Candle Lighting. (Illus.). 240p. 1996. 59.95 (*0-88740-975-X*) Schiffer.

Ruf, Carolyn. Guinea Pigs. (Illus.). 80p. 1984. pap. 6.95 (*0-86622-987-6*, PB-113) TFH Pubns.

Ruf, Francois & Siswoputranto, P. S., eds. Cocoa Cycles: The Economics of Cocoa Supply. 400p. 1995. pap. 199.00 (*1-85573-215-7*, Pub. by Woodhead Pubng) Am Educ Systs.

Ruf, Frederick J. The Creation of Chaos: William James & the Stylistic Making of a Disorderly World. LC 90-44858. (SUNY Series in Rhetoric & Theology). 185p. (C). 1991. pap. text 21.95 (*0-7914-0702-0*) State U NY Pr.

— Entangled Voices: Genre & the Religious Construction of the Self. LC 96-41281. 136p. 1997. text 32.00 (*0-19-510263-0*) OUP.

Ruf, Gregory A. Cadres & Kin: Making a Socialist Village in West China, 1921-1991. LC 98-16522. xvii, 249p. 1998. pap. write for info. (*0-8047-3533-6*) Stanford U Pr.

— Cadres & Kin: Making a Socialist Village in West China, 1921-1991. LC 98-16522. (Illus.). 288p. 1999. 49.50 (*0-8047-3377-5*) Stanford U Pr.

Ruf, Henry, ed. Religion, Ontotheology & Deconstruction. (God: The Contemporary Discussion Ser.). 353p. 1991. 27.95 (*0-913757-98-5*); pap. 14.95 (*0-89226-066-1*) Paragon Hse.

Ruf, K. B. & Tolis, George, eds. Advances in Neuroendocrine Physiology. (Frontiers of Hormone Research Ser.: Vol. 10). (Illus.). vi, 142p. 1982. 85.25 (*3-8055-2949-X*) S Karger.

Ruf, Katharine. Bildung Hat (k)ein Geschlecht: Uber Erzogene und Erziehende Frauen. (GER., Illus.). 191p. 1998. 45.95 (*3-631-32649-1*) P Lang Pubng.

Ruf, Kathleen. Quality Control, Quality Assurance: Manual for Food & Nutrition Services. LC 88-22662. 418p. 1989. 220.00 (*0-87189-793-8*) Aspen Pub.

Ruf, Pat, jt. auth. see Ruf, Bob.

Ruf, Tobias, et al. Phonon Raman Scattering in Semniconductors, Quantum Wells & Superlattices, Vol. 142. Hshler, G., ed. LC 97-39897. (Springer Tracts in Modern Physics Ser.). (Illus.). 240p. 1997. 129.00 (*3-540-63301-4*) Spr-Verlag.

Rufe, Laurie, jt. auth. see Kahin, Sharon.

Rufe, Robert. Rock & Roll Flyer. 96p. 1990. pap. text 8.00 (*0-9627196-0-9*) Aremar Pubns.

Rufenacht, Claude. Fundamentals of Esthetics. (Illus.). 372p. 1990. text 156.00 (*0-86715-230-3*) Quint Pub Co.

Rufenacht, Claude R. Principles of Esthetic Integration. (Illus.). 300p. 128.00 (*0-86715-369-5*) Quint Pub Co.

Rufenbarger, Connie, ed. Just Peachey: Cooking up a Cure. (Illus.). 320p. 1995. 15.00 (*0-9646719-0-5*) WWABC.

Rufer, Joseph. Composition with Twelve Notes Related Only to One Another. rev. ed. LC 78-9838. (Illus.). 186p. 1979. reprint ed. lib. bdg. 35.00 (*0-313-21236-8*, RUCT, Greenwood Pr) Greenwood.

Rufey, Celia, jt. auth. see Schoeser, Mary.

Ruff. How to Prosper. 1999. mass mkt. 3.50 (*0-446-96936-2*, Pub. by Warner Bks) Little.

Ruff, A. R. Commercial & Industrial Law. (C). 1984. 110.00 (*0-7855-4253-1*, Pub. by Witherby & Co) St Mut.

Ruff, A. W. & Bayer, Raymond G., eds. Tribology: Wear Test Selection for Design & Application. LC 93-37460. (Special Technical Publication: Vol. 1199). (Illus.). 185p. 1993. text 46.00 (*0-8031-1856-2*, STP1199) ASTM.

Ruff, Allen. "We Called Each Other Comrade" Charles H. Kerr & Company, Radical Publishers. LC 96-1008. 336p. 1997. text 49.95 (*0-252-02277-7*); pap. text 19.95 (*0-252-06582-4*) U of Ill Pr.

Ruff, Ann. Backroads of Florida. LC 91-29924. 180p. 1992. pap. 9.95 (*0-88415-008-9*, 5008) Gulf Pub.

— Outlaws in Petticoats. (Women of the West Ser.). 1995. pap. 12.95 (*1-55622-315-3*, Rep of TX Pr) Wordware Pub.

Ruff, Anne, ed. Principles of Law for Managers. LC 94-37890. (Series in the Principles of Management). 304p. (C). 1996. pap. 16.99 (*0-415-07378-2*, B4298) Thomson Learn.

Ruff, Babs. Turning Grief Around: A Journey in Reason & Rhyme. (Illus.). 64p. 1998. pap. 9.95 (*1-888468-20-3*) Dawn Dancer.

Ruff, Barry & Bodio, Gene. Softimage. 1997. pap. 49.99 (*0-614-28449-X*) Coriolis Grp.

Ruff, Barry C. Softimage 3D Design Guide. 10th ed. LC 98-125227. (Illus.). 282p. (C). 1997. 39.99 (*1-57610-147-9*) Coriolis Grp.

Ruff, Christopher. Aging & Osteoporosis in Native Americans from Pecos Pueblo, New Mexico: Behavioral & Biomechanical Effects. LC 91-2397. (Evolution of North American Indians Ser.: Vol. 20). 435p. 1991. text 10.00 (*0-8240-2515-6*) Garland.

Ruff, Debbie, jt. auth. see Kienzle, Patricia T.

Ruff, Doris, ed. see Baudelaire, Charles.

Ruff, Ferenc & Csizmadia, I. G. Organic Reactions: Equilibria, Kinetics, & Mechanism. LC 94-6367. (Studies in Organic Chemistry: Vol. 50). 482p. 1994. 249.00 (*0-444-88174-3*) Elsevier.

Ruff, Holly A. & Rothbart, Mary K. Attention in Early Development: Themes & Variations. (Illus.). 312p. 1996. text 45.00 (*0-19-507143-3*) OUP.

***Ruff, Holly Alliger & Rothbart, Mary Klevjord.** Attention in Early Development: Themes & Variations. (Illus.). 312p. 2000. pap. text 27.50 (*0-19-513632-2*) OUP.

Ruff, Howard. How to Prosper During the Hard Times Ahead: A Crash Course for the American Family in the New Millennium. LC 98-50851. 380p. 1999. 24.95 (*0-89526-313-0*) Regnery Pub.

Ruff, Jack J. An Analysis of Mortgage Lending Patterns in Omaha. 84p. (Orig.). 1983. pap. 4.50 (*1-55719-095-X*) U NE CPAR.

— Community Development for the City of Norfolk, Nebraska. 28p. (Orig.). 1980. pap. 2.50 (*1-55719-033-X*) U NE CPAR.

— Nebraska Program for Technology Transfer: An Operational Framework. 15p. (Orig.). 1980. pap. 1.50 (*1-55719-034-8*) U NE CPAR.

— Residential Investment & Insurance Practices. 54p. (Orig.). 1984. pap. 4.00 (*1-55719-030-5*) U NE CPAR.

— Rural Development Strategies for Southcentral Nebraska. 176p. (Orig.). 1982. pap. 11.50 (*1-55719-035-6*) U NE CPAR.

Ruff, Jack J. & Coffin, Peggy. Homeowner Insurance Availability & Cost in Omaha. 76p. (Orig.). 1983. pap. 4.00 (*1-55719-091-7*) U NE CPAR.

Ruff, Jack J. & Hein, Peggy. Builders & Lenders Attitudes: The Nebraska Mortgage Finance Fund Use of FHA 235 Housing. 32p. 1979. pap. 2.50 (*1-55719-097-6*) U NE CPAR.

Ruff, Jack J. & Krager, Anne. Cooperative Purchasing for Local Government. 44p. (Orig.). 1984. pap. 3.00 (*1-55719-085-2*) U NE CPAR.

Ruff, Jack J. & Piper, R. K. Omaha's Neighborhood Housing Services Area: A Physical Conditions Inventory. 80p. (Orig.). 1982. pap. 6.50 (*1-55719-032-1*) U NE CPAR.

— Potentials for Ridesharing in Southwest Iowa. 66p. (Orig.). 1982. pap. 4.50 (*1-55719-036-4*) U NE CPAR.

Ruff, Jack J., jt. auth. see Hanlon, Gene.

Ruff, Jerry, Sr. Jerry Ruff's Notebook Vol. 1: A Collection of His Best Columns, 1974-1987. Ruff, Mary K., ed. 240p. (Orig.). 1996. pap. 9.95 (*0-9654889-0-X*) Ruff Hse.

Ruff, Ken. Little Speedy Jo: The Antelope Fawn. Martin, Anne M., ed. LC 98-94880. (Illus.). 88p. (J). 1998. pap. write for info. (*1-57579-141-2*) Pine Hill Pr.

Ruff, Larry J. & Kanamori, Hiroo. Subduction Zones, Pt. II. 376p. 1989. 34.50 (*0-8176-2272-1*) Birkhauser.

Ruff, Larry J. & Kanomori, Hiroo. Subduction Zones, Pt. I. 352p. 1989. 34.50 (*0-8176-1928-3*) Birkhauser.

Ruff, Laura B. & Weitzer, Mary K. Understanding & Using MS-DOS - PC-DOS: The First Steps. 2nd ed. Leyh, ed. 118p. (C). 1989. pap. text 19.50 (*0-314-50330-7*) West Pub.

— Understanding & Using PFS: File-Report. (Illus.). 253p. (Orig.). (C). 1986. pap. text 28.75 (*0-314-96215-8*) West Pub.

***Ruff, Loren K.** Imitation/imagination: The Art of the Theatre. 500p. (C). 1999. per. 78.95 (*0-7872-6073-8*, 41607301) Kendall-Hunt.

Ruff, Mary K., ed. see Ruff, Jerry, Sr.

Ruff, Matt. Fool on the Hill: A Novel. 416p. 1998. reprint ed. pap. 12.00 (*0-8021-3535-8*, Grove) Grove-Atltic.

— Sewer, Gas & Electric: The Public Works Trilogy. 576p. 1998. mass mkt. 6.99 (*0-446-60642-1*, Pub. by Warner Bks) Little.

Ruff, Nancy, jt. ed. see Smithson, Isaiah.

Ruff, Nathan, jt. auth. see Kline, John.

Ruff, Richard, jt. auth. see Rackham, Neil.

Ruff, Robert. Aborting Planned Parenthood. 189p. (C). reprint ed. pap. 9.95 (*0-919225-32-2*) Life Cycle Bks.

Ruff, Shawn S. Go the Way Your Blood Beats. 480p. 1995. 30.00 (*0-8050-4736-0*) H Holt & Co.

***Ruff, Sue & Wilson, Don E.** Bats. LC 99-58684. (Animal Ways Ser.). (Illus.). (J). 2001. 28.50 (*0-7614-1137-2*, Benchmark NY) Marshall Cavendish.

Ruff, Sue, ed. see American Society of Mammalogists Staff.

Ruff, Susan A., jt. auth. see Roman, Jaime Rene.

Ruff, Susan L. Ready to Use Holiday Small Frames. 1997. pap. 5.95 (*0-486-29623-7*) Dover.

Ruff, Thomas P. Classroom Ready Activities for Teaching History & Geography in Grades 7-12. LC 97-15531. 276p. (C). 1997. pap. text 30.00 (*0-205-26375-5*) P-H.

— A Guide for Teaching Social Studies in Grades K-8: Information, Ideas & Resources for Classroom Teachers. LC 93-19503. 253p. (C). 1993. pap. text 43.00 (*0-205-14606-6*, Longwood Div) Allyn.

Ruffa, Anthony. Darwinism & Determinism: The Role of Direction in Evolution. 1983. 25.95 (*0-8283-1732-1*) Branden Bks.

***Ruffa, Stephen A. & Perozziello, Michael J.** Breaking the Cost Barrier: A Proven Approach to Managing & Implementing Lean Manufacturing. LC 00-27329. (NSFRE-Wiley Fund Development Ser.). 304p. 2000. text 49.95 (*0-471-38136-5*) Wiley.

Ruffalo, Richard & Moretti, Mike. PEP: The Seven P's to Positively Enhance Performance. LC 96-77150. 128p. (Orig.). 1996. pap. 11.95 (*1-883697-23-9*) Hara Pub.

Ruffault, Charlotte. Animals Underground. Matthews, Sarah, tr. from FRE. LC 87-34616. (Young Discovery Library). (Illus.). 38p. (J). (gr. k-5). 1988. 5.95 (*0-944589-03-0*, 030) Young Discovery Lib.

Ruffcorn, Kevin E. Rural Evangelism: Catching the Vision. LC 93-36830. 128p. 1994. pap. 12.99 (*0-8066-2642-9*, 9-2642) Augsburg Fortress.

Ruffel, Denis. Croustades, Quenelles, Souffles, Beignets, Individual Hot Dishes, Mixed Salads, Fish in Aspic. (Professional Caterer Ser.). 320p. 1997. text 69.95 (*0-470-25009-7*) Halsted Pr.

— Individual Cold Dishes, Pates, Terrines, Galantines & Ballotines, Aspics, Pizzas & Quiches. (Professional Caterer Ser.). 320p. 1997. text 69.95 (*0-470-25008-9*) Halsted Pr.

— Meat & Game: Sauces & Base, Planning, Execution, Display & Decoration for Buffets & Receptions. (Professional Caterer Ser.). 320p. 1997. text 69.95 (*0-470-25010-0*) Halsted Pr.

— Pastry Cold Dishes Croustades. 1999. 239.95 (*0-471-32145-1*) Wiley.

— Pastry, Hors d'Oeuvres, Mini-Sandwiches, Canapes, Assorted Snacks, Hot Hors d'Oeuvres. (Professional Caterer Ser.). 244p. 1997. text 69.95 (*0-470-25007-0*) Halsted Pr.

Ruffer, Jonathan G. Big Shots: Edwardian Shooting Parties. 1992. 75.00 (*1-870948-38-6*, Pub. by Quiller Pr) St Mut.

Ruffer, Marc A. Studies in the Paleopathology of Egypt. Moodie, Roy L., ed. LC 75-23758. reprint ed. 135.00 (*0-404-13364-9*) AMS Pr.

Ruffhead, Owen. The Life of Alexander Pope. (Anglistica & Americana Ser.: No. 5). 586p. 1968. 89.70 (*0-317-05061-3*, 05101959) G Olms Pubs.

Ruffier, Peter R. Toxic Substances in Municipal Wastewaters. 240p. 1991. lib. bdg. 85.00 (*0-87371-533-0*, L533) Lewis Pubs.

An Asterisk (*) at the beginning of an entry indicates that the title is appearing for the first time.

Ruffin. Principles of Macroeconomics & Study Guide Pkg. 6th ed. (C). 1997. 65.95 (*0-321-80119-9*) Addison-Wesley.

Ruffin, ed. Test Bank Principal Economics. 1997. pap. text 11.00 (*0-673-53877-X*) P-H.

Ruffin, C. Bernard. Last Words: A Dictionary of Deathbed Quotations. LC 95-3196. 269p. 1995. lib. bdg. 42.50 (*0-7864-0043-9*) McFarland & Co.

— Padre Pio. 2nd rev. expanded ed. LC 81-81525. (Illus.). 444p. (Orig.). 1991. pap. 13.95 (*0-87973-673-9*, 673) Our Sunday Visitor.

— Profiles of Faith: The Religious Beliefs of Eminent Americans. LC 97-15972. 416p. (Orig.). 1997. pap. 18.00 (*0-7648-0106-6*, Liguori Triumph) Liguori Pubns.

— The Shroud of Turin. LC 99-70509. 192p. 1999. pap. 14.95 (*0-87973-617-8*) Our Sunday Visitor.

— The Twelve: The Lives of the Apostles after Calvary. LC 97-69275. 192p. 1998. pap. 9.95 (*0-87973-926-6*) Our Sunday Visitor.

Ruffin, Clyde, jt. auth. see Patterson, Carole.

Ruffin, E. Anticipations of the Future. LC 70-38021. (Black Heritage Library Collection). 1977. reprint ed. 32.95 (*0-8369-8988-0*) Ayer.

Ruffin, Edmund. Diary of Edmund Ruffin Vol. 1: Toward Independence: October, 1856-April, 1861. Scarborough, William K., ed. LC 75-165069. (Library of Southern Civilization). (Illus.). xlviii, 664p. 1972. text 90.00 (*0-8071-0948-7*) La State U Pr.

— Diary of Edmund Ruffin Vol. 2: The Years of Hope: April, 1861-June, 1863. LC 75-165069. (Library of Southern Civilization). xxxvi, 706p. 1977. text 90.00 (*0-8071-0183-4*) La State U Pr.

— Diary of Edmund Ruffin Vol. 3: A Dream Shattered: June, 1863-June, 1865. Scarborough, William K., ed. LC 75-165069. (Library of Southern Civilization). 896p. 1989. text 95.00 (*0-8071-1418-9*) La State U Pr.

— Essay on Calcareous Manures. Sitterson, J. Carlyle, ed. LC 61-6352. (John Harvard Library). (Illus.). 234p. 1961. 24.00 (*0-674-26201-8*) HUP.

— Nature's Management: Writings on Landscape & Reform, 1822-1852. Kirby, Jack T., ed. LC 99-39150. (Illus.). 424p. 1999. pap. 70.00 (*0-8203-2162-1*) U of Ga Pr.

Ruffin, Frances & Ruffin, John. Blue Ridge China Today: A Comprehensive Identification & Price Guide for Today's Collector. LC 96-41048. 216p. (gr. 10). 1997. pap. 34.95 (*0-7643-0206-X*) Schiffer.

— Blue Ridge China Traditions. LC 99-60441. (Illus.). 224p. 1999. pap. 34.95 (*0-7643-0822-X*) Schiffer.

Ruffin, John, jt. auth. see Ruffin, Frances.

***Ruffin, M. Holt.** Civil Society in Central Asia. LC 98-33178. (Illus.). 320p. 1999. pap. text 19.95 (*0-295-97795-7*) U of Wash Pr.

Ruffin, M. Holt, et al. The Post-Soviet Handbook: A Guide to Grassroots Organizations & Internet Resources. 2nd rev. ed. LC 98-54115. 396p. 1999. pap. 19.95 (*0-295-97794-9*) U of Wash Pr.

Ruffin, Marshall. Digital Doctors. LC 98-89673. 220p. 1999. pap. 45.00 (*0-924674-63-6*) Am Coll Phys Execs.

Ruffin, Patricia. Capitalism & Socialism in Cuba: A Study of Dependency, Development & Underdevelopment. LC 89-24072. (International Political Economy Ser.). 210p. 1990. text 45.00 (*0-312-04044-X*) St Martin.

Ruffin, Paul. Circling. (American Regional Bks.). 87p. (Orig.). 1997. pap. 7.99 (*0-9651359-0-X*) Browder Springs.

— The Man Who Would Be God. LC 93-5225. (Southwest Life & Letters Ser.). 168p. (Orig.). 1993. pap. 10.95 (*0-87074-363-5*) SMU Press.

— The Man Who Would Be God: Stories. LC 93-5225. (Southwest Life & Letters Ser.). 168p. 1993. 22.50 (*0-87074-354-6*) SMU Press.

Ruffin, Paul, jt. ed. see Garrett, George P.

Ruffin, Paul D., ed. see Brown, Glenn.

Ruffin, Roy. S/G Principle Macroecon. 6th ed. (C). 1997. pap. text, student ed. 28.00 (*0-673-99492-9*) Addison-Wesley.

— S/G Principle Microecon. 6th ed. (C). 1997. pap. text, student ed. 29.40 (*0-673-99494-5*) Addison-Wesley.

Ruffin, Roy, ed. S/G Principle Economics. 6th ed. 448p. (C). 1997. pap. text, student ed. 39.00 (*0-673-99489-9*) Addison-Wesley.

Ruffin, Roy J. & Gregory, Paul R. Macroeconomics. (C). 1997. pap. text, student ed. 25.33 (*0-673-46588-8*) Addson-Wesley Educ.

— Microeconomics. (C). 1997. student ed. 26.00 (*0-673-46585-3*) Addson-Wesley Educ.

— Principles Macroeconomics. 6th ed. LC 96-17800. (C). 1997. pap. text 70.00 (*0-673-99491-0*) Addson-Wesley Educ.

— Principles Microeconomics. 6th ed. LC 96-15001. (C). 1997. pap. text 70.00 (*0-673-99493-7*) Addson-Wesley Educ.

— Principles of Economics. 5th ed. LC 92-23589. (C). 1992. text 68.12 (*0-673-46590-X*) Addson-Wesley Educ.

— Principles of Economics. 5th ed. (C). 1993. pap. text, student ed. 23.12 (*0-673-46591-8*); disk 118.00 (*0-673-53880-X*) Addson-Wesley Educ.

***Ruffin, Roy J. & Gregory, Paul R.** Principles of Economics. 7th ed. 2001. 90.00 (*0-321-07730-X*) Addison-Wesley.

Ruffin, Roy J., jt. auth. see Gregory, Paul.

Ruffin, Roy J., jt. auth. see Gregory, Paul R.

Ruffin, Thomas. Papers of Thomas Ruffin, 4 vols. Hamilton, J. G., ed. LC 74-174788. reprint ed. 225.00 (*0-404-04630-4*) AMS Pr.

Ruffinatto, Aldo, ed. see Berces, Gonzalo D.

***Ruffing, Janet K.** Spiritual Direction: Beyond the Beginnings. LC 00-28558. 192p. 2000. pap. 12.95 (*0-8091-3958-8*) Paulist Pr.

Ruffini, John. Doctor Antonio: A Tale. LC 79-8193. reprint ed. 44.50 (*0-404-62109-0*) AMS Pr.

Ruffini, Julio L. Advances in Medical Social Science, Vol. 2. xii, 402p. 1984. text 196.00 (*0-677-06490-X*) Gordon & Breach.

Ruffini, Pierre-Bruno, jt. auth. see Lee, Sang-Gon.

Ruffini, R. & Keiser, M. General Relativity: Proceedings of the 7th Marcel Grossmann Meeting, 2 Vols. 1600p. 1997. text 314.00 (*981-02-2064-2*) World Scientific Pub.

Ruffini, R., jt. ed. see Gurzadyan, V. G.

Ruffini, Remo. Astrophysics from Spacelab. Bernacca, Pier L., ed. (Astrophysics & Space Science Library: No. 81). 720p. 1980. text 155.50 (*90-277-1064-3*) Kluwer Academic.

Ruffini, Remo & Ciufolini, Ignazio. Relativistic Gravitational Experiments in Space: First William Fairbank Meeting. (Advanced Series in Astrophysics & Cosmology). 500p. 1993. text 121.00 (*981-02-1263-1*) World Scientific Pub.

Ruffini, Remo, jt. auth. see Lizhi, Fang.

Ruffini, Remo, jt. ed. see Gursky, H.

Ruffini, Remo, ed. see Lizhi, Fang.

Ruffini, Remo, jt. ed. see Lizhi, Fang.

Ruffino, Giovanna Folonar. Chianti Family Cooking. 1999. 30.00 (*0-8129-3138-6*, Times Bks) Crown Pub Group.

Ruffins, Reynold. Misoso: Once upon a Time Tales from Africa. LC 92-43288. 96p. (J). (gr. k-5). 1994. 19.00 (*0-679-83430-3*, Pub. by Knopf Bks Yng Read) Random.

Ruffins, Reynold, jt. auth. see Cartier, Wesley.

Ruffle, John. Glimpses of Ancient Egypt: Studies in Honour of H. W. Fairman. 1979. 69.95 (*0-85668-147-4*, Pub. by Aris & Phillips) David Brown.

Ruffle, John, ed. see Goring, Elizabeth & Reeves, Nicholas.

***Ruffman, Alan.** Titanic Remembered: The Unsinkable Ship & Halifax. (Illus.). 72p. 2000. pap. 12.95 (*0-88780-467-5*, Pub. by Formac Publ Co) Seven Hills Bk.

Ruffner, Budge. All Hell Needs Is Water. (Illus.). 96p. reprint ed. pap. 27.40 (*0-8357-5312-3*, 2025555) Bks Demand.

— Ruff Country. (Illus.). 198p. 1994. pap. 14.95 (*0-9624499-3-8*) Prickly AZ.

Ruffner, Ginny, et al. Glass: Material in the Service of Meaning. (Illus.). 72p. 1991. 17.95 (*0-295-97161-4*) Tacoma Art Mus.

Ruffner, Henry. Judith Bensaddi: A Tale. LC 83-9858. (Library of Southern Civilization). 222p. 1984. text 30.00 (*0-8071-1129-5*) La State U Pr.

— Judith Bensaddi: A Tale & Seclusaval: or The Sequel to the Tale of Judith Bensaddi. fac. ed. Pemberton, J. Michael, ed. LC 83-9858. (Library of Southern Civilization). 236p. 1984. reprint ed. pap. 73.20 (*0-7837-7924-0*, 204768000008) Bks Demand.

***Ruffner, Kevin C.** Corona: America's First Satellite Program. 378p. 1999. per. 32.00 (*0-16-058824-3*) USGPO.

Ruffner, Kevin C. Forty-Fourth Virginia Infantry. (Illus.). 121p. 1987. 19.95 (*0-930919-47-5*) H E Howard.

— Maryland's Blue & Gray: A Border State's Union & Confederate Junior Officer Corps. LC 97-7078. (Illus.). 464p. 1997. 34.95 (*0-8071-2135-5*) La State U Pr.

Ruffner, Kevin C., jt. auth. see Driver, Robert J.

Ruffner, Sara. That Beautiful Future. LC 97-65999. 250p. 1998. pap. 14.50 (*0-88739-157-5*) Creat Arts Bk.

Ruffner, Trenna E. Personal Lace: A Collection of Bobbin Lace Patterns. 32p. 1993. student ed. 10.00 (*0-9636953-0-4*) Alembic Arts.

Ruffo, Armand G. Grey Owl: The Mystery of Archie Belaney. LC 97-169903. (Illus.). 224p. 1997. pap. 12.95 (*1-55050-109-7*, Pub. by Coteau) Genl Dist Srvs.

Ruffo, Sandro. Enciclopedia Monografica de Ciencias Naturales, 5 vols., Set. (SPA.). 2500p. 1974. 250.00 (*0-8288-6035-1*, S50568) Fr & Eur.

Ruffo, Titta. La Mia Parabola, Memorie. Farkas, Andrew, ed. LC 76-29966. (Opera Biographies Ser.).Tr. of My Parable, Reminiscences. (ITA., Illus.). 1977. reprint ed. lib. bdg. 39.95 (*0-405-09705-0*) Ayer.

— Ruffo: My Parabola. (Great Voices Ser.: Vol. 1). (Illus.). 490p. 1995. 38.00 (*1-880909-39-1*) Baskerville.

Ruffo, Vincenzo. Vincenzo Ruffo: Seven Masses I. Lockwood, Lewis, ed. (Recent Researches in Music of the Renaissance Ser.: Vol. RRR32). (Illus.). xiv, 125p. 1979. pap. 45.00 (*0-89579-119-6*, RRR32) A-R Eds.

— Vincenzo Ruffo: Seven Masses II. Lockwood, Lewis, ed. (Recent Researches in Music of the Renaissance Ser.: Vol. RRR33). (Illus.). 118p. 1979. pap. 40.00 (*0-89579-120-X*, RRR33) A-R Eds.

***Ruffolo, Jennifer.** Should the Sun Set on State Agency Consultations under the Endangered Species Act?, Vol. 2. 14p. 1998. pap. write for info. (*1-58703-088-8*, CRB Note 5) CA St Libry.

— TDMLs: The Revolution in Water Quality Regulation. 50p. 1999. pap. write for info. (*1-58703-102-7*, CRB-99-005) CA St Libry.

— TMDL's: The Revolution in Water Quality Regulation. 50p. (C). 2000. pap. text 20.00 (*0-7881-8669-8*) DIANE Pub.

Ruffolo, R. R., ed. Alpha-Adrenoceptors: Molecular Biology, Biochemistry & Pharmacology. (Progress in Basic & Clinical Pharmacology Ser.: Vol. 8). (Illus.). xiv, 226p. 1991. 205.25 (*3-8055-5390-0*) S Karger.

— Beta-Adrenoceptors: Molecular Biology, Biochemistry & Pharmacology. (Progress in Basic & Clinical Pharmacology Ser.: Vol. 7). (Illus.). x, 240p. 1991. 213.25 (*3-8055-5366-8*) S Karger.

Ruffolo, Robert R., Jr., ed. Adrenoceptors: Structure, Function & Pharmacology. 280p. 1995. text 105.00 (*3-7186-5644-2*, Harwood Acad Pubs) Gordon & Breach.

— The Alpha-1 Adrenergic Receptors. LC 87-17006. (Receptors Ser.). 568p. 1988. 135.00 (*0-89603-110-1*) Humana.

— Angiotensin II Receptors: Medicinal Chemistry, Vol. II. 256p. 1994. lib. bdg. 139.00 (*0-8493-8545-8*) CRC Pr.

Ruffolo, Robert R., ed. Ansiotensin in Receptors, Vol. 1. 192p. 1994. lib. bdg. 119.00 (*0-8493-8380-3*) CRC Pr.

Ruffolo, Robert R., Jr., ed. Endothelin Receptors From the Gene to the Human: From the Gene to the Brain. LC 94-40203. (Pharmacology & Toxicology: Basic & Clinical Aspects Ser.). 304p. 1995. ring bd. 224.95 (*0-8493-5938-4*, 5938) CRC Pr.

Ruffolo, Robert R., Jr., et al, eds. Cell Cycle Regulation. (New Horizons in Therapeutics Ser.). 192p. 1997. text 52.00 (*90-5702-204-4*, Harwood Acad Pubs) Gordon & Breach.

***Ruffolo, Robert R., Jr., et al, eds.** Inflammatory Cells & Mediators in CNS Diseases. (New Horizons in Therapeutics Ser.: Vol. 2). (Illus.). 540p. 1999. text 95.00 (*90-5702-296-6*, Harwood Acad Pubs) Gordon & Breach.

Ruffolo, Robert R., Jr. & Hollinger, Mannfred A., eds. Inflammation: Mediators & Pathways. LC 94-44223. 224p. 1995. boxed set 149.95 (*0-8493-9473-2*, 9473) CRC Pr.

Ruffy, Rodolphe, tr. see Fischer, Wilhelm & Ritter, P.

Rufi, John. The Small High School. LC 70-177214. (Columbia University. Teachers College. Contributions to Education Ser.: No. 236). reprint ed. 37.50 (*0-404-55236-6*) AMS Pr.

***Rufin, Jean.** The Abyssinian: A Novel. 448p. 2000. reprint ed. pap. 14.95 (*0-393-32109-6*) Norton.

— The Siege of Isfahan. 26.95 (*0-393-04988-4*) Norton.

Rufin, Jean-Christophe. The Abyssinian: A Novel. LC 99-25126. 448p. 1999. 25.95 (*0-393-04716-4*) Norton.

***Rufin, Jean-Christophe.** L'Abyssin. 2000. pap. 17.95 (*2-07-040697-0*) Gallimard Edns.

Rufinus. The Church History of Rufinus of Aquileia: Books 10 & 11. Amidon, Philip R., tr. LC 96-41365. 160p. 1997. text 45.00 (*0-19-511031-5*) OUP.

Rufkin, Reno, jt. auth. see Ohanian, Hans C.

Rufolo, Anthony M., jt. ed. see Hirsch, Werner Z.

Rufsvold, Margaret I. Guides to Educational Media: Films, Filmstrips, Multimedia Kits, Programmed Instruction Materials, Recordings on Discs & Tapes, Slides, Transparencies, Videotapes. 4th ed. LC 77-5058. 167p. 1977. reprint ed. pap. 51.80 (*0-608-01735-3*, 206239200002) Bks Demand.

Rufus, Anneli. Magnificent Corpses: Searching Through Europe for St. Peter's Head, St. Claire's Heart, St. Stephen's Hand, & Other Saintly Relics. LC 99-15317. (Illus.). 320p. 1999. pap. 14.95 (*1-56924-687-4*) Marlowe & Co.

Rufus, Anneli, jt. auth. see Lawson, Kristan.

Rufus, Quintus C. The History of Alexander. Yardley, John & Heckel, Waldemar, trs. (Classics Ser.). 352p. 1984. pap. 11.95 (*0-14-044412-2*, Penguin Classics) Viking Penguin.

Rug, W. & Tomaszewski, Adam. Grammatik mit Sinn und Verstand: 20 Kapitel Deutsche Grammatik fuer Fortgeschrittene: Lehr- und Uebungsbuch. (GER.). 320p. (C). 1993. pap. text 36.00 (*3-12-675335-3*, Pub. by Klett Edition) Intl Bk Import.

— Grammatik mit Sinn und Verstand: 20 Kapitel Deutsche Grammatik fuer Fortgeschrittene: Loesungsheft. (GER.). 55p. (C). 1993. pap. text 10.00 (*3-12-675334-5*, Pub. by Klett Edition) Intl Bk Import.

Rug, W., et al. 50 Praktische Tips zum Deutschlernen: Amerikanisches Englisch. (GER.). 56p. (C). 1994. pap. text 9.00 (*3-12-675384-1*, Pub. by Klett Edition) Intl Bk Import.

Rug, W., jt. auth. see Papp, I.

Ruga, Barbara A. & Kopka, Daniel D., eds. Michigan Wrongful Discharge & Employment Discrimination Law. rev. ed. LC 90-81125. 540p. 1990. ring bd., suppl. ed. 110.00 (*0-685-22730-8*, 90-016) U MI Law CLE.

— Michigan Wrongful Discharge & Employment Discrimination Law. rev. ed. LC 90-81125. 540p. 1993. suppl. ed. 40.00 (*0-685-44340-X*, 93-014) U MI Law CLE.

Rugaas, Bendik, ed. Library Information Science Education for the 21st Century: The Tromso Conference. LC 93-4497. 163p. 1993. 55.00 (*1-55570-148-5*) Neal-Schuman.

***Rugaas, Bendik, et al.** Management Basics for Information Professionals. LC 99-86970. 560p. 2000. pap. 55.00 (*1-55570-370-4*) Neal-Schuman.

Rugaleva, Anelya. Advanced Russian 1: Student Manual. (OSU Foreign Language Publications). (RUS., Illus.). 210p. (C). 1980. pap. text, student ed. 17.50 (*0-87415-089-2*, 37) Foreign Lang.

— Advanced Russian 2: Student Manual. (OSU Foreign Language Publications: No. 38). (RUS., Illus.). 185p. (C). 1980. pap. text, student ed. 16.00 (*0-87415-091-4*) Foreign Lang.

— Advanced Russian 1: Instructor Manual. (OSU Foreign Language Publications: No. 37). (RUS., Illus.). 171p. (Orig.). (C). 1980. pap., teacher ed. 16.50 (*0-87415-090-6*, 37A) Foreign Lang.

— Advanced Russian 2: Instructor Manual. (OSU Foreign Language Publications: No. 38). (RUS., Illus.). 183p. (C). 1980. pap., teacher ed. 17.50 (*0-87415-092-2*, 38A) Foreign Lang.

— Reading Russian 1: Instructor Manual. (OSU Foreign Language Publications). (RUS., Illus.). 249p. (Orig.). (C). 1984. pap., teacher ed. 12.50 (*0-87415-001-9*, 7A) Foreign Lang.

— Reading Russian 1: Student Manual. (OSU Foreign Language Publications). (RUS., Illus.). 249p. (C). 1984. pap. text, student ed. 20.50 (*0-87415-000-0*, 7) Foreign Lang.

— Reading Russian 3: Instructor Manual. (RUS., Illus.). 101p. (C). 1986. pap., teacher ed. 11.50 (*0-87415-110-4*, 46A) Foreign Lang.

— Reading Russian 3: Student Manual. (RUS., Illus.). 208p. (C). 1986. pap. text, student ed. 17.50 (*0-87415-109-0*, 46) Foreign Lang.

Rugaleva, Anelya, et al. Reading Russian 2: Instructor Manual. (OSU Foreign Language Publications). (RUS., Illus.). 308p. (C). 1984. pap., teacher ed. 8.50 (*0-87415-003-5*, 8A) Foreign Lang.

— Reading Russian 2: Student Manual. (OSU Foreign Language Publications). (RUS., Illus.). 308p. (Orig.). (C). 1984. pap. text, student ed. 25.00 (*0-87415-002-7*, 8) Foreign Lang.

— Russian 104.51, Bk. 2, Lessons 5-8. (ENG & RUS.). 99p. 1997. spiral bd. 10.00 (*0-87415-335-2*, RU04) Foreign Lang.

— Russian 101.51 Bk. 1, Lessons 1-4: Student Manual for Individualized Instruction. (ENG & RUS.). 83p. 1997. student ed., spiral bd. 8.50 (*0-87415-330-1*, RU01) Foreign Lang.

— Russian 103.51, Bk. 2, Lessons 1-4. (ENG & RUS.). 108p. 1997. spiral bd. 10.00 (*0-87415-334-4*, RU03) Foreign Lang.

— Russian 102.51 Bk. 1, Lessons 5-8, Bk. 1, Lessons 5-8. (ENG & RUS.). 79p. 1997. spiral bd. 8.50 (*0-87415-331-X*, RU02) Foreign Lang.

Rugama, Leonel, et al. The Earth Is a Satellite of the Moon: La Tierra Es un Satelite de la Luna. Miles, Sara et al, trs. from SPA. LC 85-62201. (ENG & SPA., Illus.). 139p. (Orig.). 1987. 19.95 (*0-915306-54-9*); pap. 9.95 (*0-915306-50-6*) Curbstone.

Rugby Football Union Staff. The RFU Handbook of Safe Rugby. unabridged ed. (Illus.). 128p. 1998. pap. 20.95 (*0-7136-4520-2*, Pub. by A & C Blk) Midpt Trade.

— The Rugby Union Referee's Manual. (Illus.). 128p. 1998. pap. 20.95 (*0-7136-4614-4*) Adlard Coles.

Ruge, Arnold. Neue Vorschule der Aesthetik: Das Komische Mit Einem Komischen Anhange. (GER.). 274p. 1975. reprint ed. write for info. (*3-487-05675-5*) G Olms Pubs.

Ruge, Daniel & Wiltse, Leon L., eds. Spinal Disorders: Diagnosis & Treatment. LC 77-1875. (Illus.). 458p. reprint ed. pap. 142.00 (*0-8357-7655-7*, 205698100096) Bks Demand.

Ruge, Gerda. Wortbedeutung und Termassoziation. (Sprache und Computer Ser.: Vol. 14). (GER.). 246p. 1995. write for info. (*3-487-09964-0*) G Olms Pubs.

Ruge, Ingolf, jt. auth. see Ryssel, Heiner.

Ruge, Kenneth C. Where Do I Go from Here? An Inspirational Guide to Making Authentic Career & Life Choices. LC 97-49363. 240p. 1998. pap. 12.95 (*0-07-058984-4*, BusinessWeek Bks) McGraw.

Ruge, Sophus. Der Literatur Zur Geschichte der Erdkunde Vom Mittelalter An. 299p. 1979. reprint ed. write for info. (*3-487-06730-7*) G Olms Pubs.

Ruge, Valis F., ed. Life along the Hudson: Wood Engravings of Hudson River Subjects from Harper's Weekly, 1859-1903. (Illus.). 180p. 1994. 45.00 (*0-87951-523-6*, Pub. by Overlook Pr) Penguin Putnam.

Rugel, Robert P. Dealing with the Problem of Low Self-Esteem: Common Characteristics & Treatment in Individual, Marital-Family & Group Psychotherapy. LC 94-33872. 228p. (C). 1994. text 48.95 (*0-398-05936-5*) C C Thomas.

— Dealing with the Problem of Low Self-Esteem: Common Characteristics & Treatment in Individual, Marital-Family & Group Psychotherapy. LC 94-33872. (Illus.). 228p. (C). 1995. pap. 35.95 (*0-398-05951-9*) C C Thomas.

— Husband-Focused Marital Therapy: An Approach to Dealing with Marital Distress. LC 97-20409. (Illus.). 230p. 1997. text 49.95 (*0-398-06792-9*); pap. text 35.95 (*0-398-06793-7*) C C Thomas.

***Rugeley, Terry.** Of Wonders & Wise Men: Religion & Popular Cultures in Southeast Mexico, 1800-1876. LC 00-29909. (Illus.). 384p. 2000. pap. 26.95 (*0-292-77107-X*) U of Tex Pr.

— Of Wonders & Wise Men: Religion & Popular Cultures in Southeast Mexico, 1800-1876. 2001. 55.00 (*0-292-77106-1*) U of Tex Pr.

Rugeley, Terry. Yucatan's Maya Peasantry & the Origins of the Caste War. LC 95-42405. (Illus.). 272p. 1996. pap. 19.95 (*0-292-77078-2*); text 40.00 (*0-292-77074-X*) U of Tex Pr.

Rugenstein, Ed, ed. see Esarde, Edward E.

Rugenstein, Julie, ed. see King, Kathleen W.

Ruger, H. P., ed. see Barthelemy, D.

Rugg, Cheryl A., jt. auth. see Jaynes, Judith H.

Rugg, E. R. The Descendants of John Rugg. 586p. 1989. reprint ed. pap. 88.00 (*0-8328-1035-5*); reprint ed. lib. bdg. 96.00 (*0-8328-1034-7*) Higginson Bk Co.

— Rugg: The Descendents of John Rugg. 580p. 1990. reprint ed. pap. 86.00 (*0-8328-1623-X*); reprint ed. lib. bdg. 94.00 (*0-8328-1622-1*) Higginson Bk Co.

Rugg, Ellen R. The Descendants of John Rugg. 580p. 1989. reprint ed. pap. 89.00 (*0-8328-1408-3*); reprint ed. lib. bdg. 99.00 (*0-8328-1407-5*) Higginson Bk Co.

Rugg, Frederick E. Financial Aid in Less Than 2000 Words. 5p. 1999. pap. 6.95 (*1-883062-31-4*, 5) Ruggs Recommend.

— Forty Tips on the Colleges. 5th ed. 19p. 1999. pap. 9.95 (*1-883062-29-2*, 3) Ruggs Recommend.

— Rugg's Recommendations on the Colleges. 16th ed. 170p. (YA). 1999. pap. 20.95 (*1-883062-27-6*, 1) Ruggs Recommend.

***Rugg, Frederick E.** Rugg's Recommendations on the Colleges. 17th rev. ed. LC 89-62896. 178p. (gr. 11-12). 2000. pap. 20.95 (*1-883062-32-2*) Ruggs Recommend.

Rugg, Frederick E. Thirty Questions & Answers. 5th ed. 23p. 1999. pap. 9.95 (*1-883062-30-6*, 4) Ruggs Recommend.

An Asterisk (*) at the beginning of an entry indicates that the title is appearing for the first time.

R

— 20 More Tips on the Colleges. 5th ed. 8p. 1999. pap. 8.95 (1-883062-28-4, 2) Ruggs Recommend.
Rugg-Gunn, A. J. Nutrition & Dental Health. LC 92-49776. (Illus.). 488p. 1993. 87.50 (0-19-262109-2) OUP.
Rugg-Gunn, Andrew J., ed. Sugarless: Towards the Year 2000. 208p. 1994. 73.00 (0-85186-495-3, R6495) CRC Pr.
Rugg-Gunn, Andrew J. & Nunn, June H. Nutrition, Diet & Oral Health. LC 99-11561. (Illus.). 208p. 1999. pap. text 59.50 (0-19-262937-9) OUP.
Rugg, Harold & Shumaker, Ann. Child-Centered School: An Appraisal of the New Education. LC 75-89227. (American Education: Its Men, Institutions, & Ideas. Series 1). 1974. reprint ed. 24.95 (0-405-01466-X) Ayer.
Rugg, Harold, et al. Curriculum-Making: Past & Present. LC 71-89228. (American Education: Its Men, Institutions, & Ideas. Series 1). 1974. reprint ed. 24.95 (0-405-01464-3) Ayer.
— Foundations of Curriculum-Making. LC 75-89229. (American Education: Its Men, Institutions, & Ideas. Series 1). 1979. reprint ed. 23.95 (0-405-01465-1) Ayer.
Rugg, Julie. Young People, Housing & Social Policy LC 98-50860. 1999. pap. write for info. (0-415-18580-7) Routledge.
***Rugg, Julie.** Young People, Housing & Social Policy LC 98-50860. 1999. write for info. (0-415-18579-3) Routledge.
Rugg, Kenneth, jt. auth. see Kahan, Stanley.
Rugg, Linda H. Picturing Ourselves: Photography & Autobiography. LC 97-3996. 286p. 1997. pap. 17.95 (0-226-73147-2) U Ch Pr.
— Picturing Ourselves: Photography & Autobiography. LC 97-3996. 286p. 1997. lib. bdg. 46.00 (0-226-73146-4) U Ch Pr.
Rugg, Linda H., tr. see Enzensberger, Hans M.
Rugg, Linda H., tr. see Swartz, Richard.
Rugg, Linda Haverty, tr. see Lindqvist, Sven.
Rugg, Michael D., ed. Cognitive Neuroscience. LC 96-39229. (Studies in Cognition Ser.). 402p. 1997. 55.00 (0-262-18181-9) MIT Pr.
— Cognitive Neuroscience. LC 96-39229. (Studies in Cognition Ser.). 402p. 1997. pap. text 27.50 (0-262-68094-7) MIT Pr.
Rugg, Michael D. & Coles, Michael G., eds. Electrophysiology of Mind: Event-Related Brain Potentials & Cognition. (Oxford Psychology Ser.: No. 25). (Illus.). 238p. 1996. pap. text 34.95 (0-19-852416-1) OUP.
Rugg, Sharon. When Death Knocks at the Schoolhouse Door. (Illus.). 38p. (J). (gr. k-6). 1998. text 25.00 (0-9652410-2-5) S Rugg.
Rugg, Sharon, et al. Memories Live Forever: A Memory Book for Grieving Children. 3rd rev. ed. (Illus.). 35p. (Orig.). (J). (gr. k-8). 1996. pap. 5.00 (0-9652410-0-9) S Rugg.
— Los Recuerdos Viven Eternamente: Un Libro de Recuerdos para Ninos Afligidos por una Muerta. 3rd ed.Tr. of Memories Live Forever: A Memory Book for Grieving Children. (ENG & SPA., Illus.). 35p. (Orig.). (J). (gr. k-8). 1997. pap. 5.00 (0-9652410-1-7) S Rugg.
Rugg, Tom. Word for Windows 2: The Complete Reference. LC 94-168949. 912p. 1993. pap. text 29.95 (0-07-881948-2) McGraw.
Rugg, Tom & Feldman, Phil. Using BASIC. 2nd ed. (Illus.). 930p. 1993. 27.95 (1-56529-140-9) Que.
Rugg, Winnifred K. Unafraid. LC 73-114891. (Select Bibliographies Reprint Ser.). 1977. 19.95 (0-8369-5295-2) Ayer.
Rugg, Winnifred K., jt. auth. see Leonardo, Bianca.
Rugge, John, jt. auth. see Davidson, James W.
Rugge, Peter. Zur Deregulierung des Europaischen Erdgasmarktes, Vol. XI. (Europaische Hochschulschriften: Reihe 5: Bd. 1747). (GER., Illus.). 291p. 1995. pap. 57.95 (3-631-48481-X) P Lang Pubng.
Rugge, Sue & Glossbrenner, Alfred. The Information Broker's Handbook. 3rd ed. LC 96-53298. (Illus.). 608p. 1997. 49.95 (0-07-057870-2); pap. 34.95 (0-07-057871-0) McGraw.
Ruggeberg, Dieter. Franz Bardon: Questions & Answers. Hanswille, Gerhard, tr. from GER. Orig. Title: Fragen an Meister Arion (Franz Bardon). 100p. 1998. per. 14.95 (1-885928-11-4) Merkur Pubng.
Ruggeri, A. & Motta, P. M., eds. Ultrastructure of the Connective Tissue Matrix. 228p. 1984. text 159.00 (0-89838-600-4) Kluwer Academic.
***Ruggeri, David.** A Handful of Dust. 1999. pap. write for info. (1-58235-236-4) Watermrk Pr.
Ruggeri, David L. A River of Time. 270p. mass mkt. 4.99 (1-896329-48-9) Picasso Publ.
Ruggeri, Fabrizio, jt. auth. see Rios-Insua, David.
Ruggeri, G. C. & Hermanutz, Derek. Leviathan Revisited: The Growth of Government Spending in Canada Since 1961. LC 97-18353. (Illus.). 112p. 1997. text 55.95 (1-85972-447-7, Pub. by Avebry) Ashgate Pub Co.
Ruggeri, G. C. & Vincent, Carole. An Economic Analysis of Income Tax Reforms. LC 98-72628. 232p. 1998. text 59.95 (1-84014-531-5, Pub. by Ashgate Pub) Ashgate Pub Co.
Ruggeri, Raffaele, jt. auth. see Nicolle, David.
Ruggeri, T., jt. auth. see Rionero, S.
Ruggeri, Tommaso, jt. auth. see Muller, Ingo.
Ruggeri, Tommaso, jt. auth. see Myeller, Ingo.
Ruggeri, Z. M., ed. Von Willebrand Factor & the Mechanisms of Platelet Function. (Biotechnology Intelligence Unit Ser.). (Illus.). xi, 253p. 1998. 179.00 (3-540-64709-0) Spr-Verlag.
Ruggeri, Zaverio, jt. auth. see Zimmerman.
Ruggerio, David. David Ruggerio's Italian Kitchen: Family Recipes from the Old Country. LC 98-50971. (Illus.). 248p. 2000. 30.00 (1-57965-115-1, 85115) Artisan.
— Little Italy Cookbook. LC 97-15261. (Illus.). 232p. 1997. 29.95 (1-885183-54-2) Artisan.
Ruggerio, John. Neville Chamberlain & British Rearmament: Pride, Prejudice & Politics, 71. LC 99-14841. (Contributions to the Study of World History Ser.: No. 71). 272p. 1999. 65.00 (0-313-31050-5, Greenwood Pr) Greenwood.
Ruggerio, Lisa, ed. see Strangio, Linda, et al.
Ruggero. The Academy. 1998. mass mkt. write for info. (0-671-89171-5) S&S Trade.
Ruggero, Ed. The Academy: A Novel of West Point. LC 97-26832. 448p. 1997. 24.00 (0-671-89169-3) PB.
— Breaking Ranks. LC 95-30739. 413p. 1995. 23.00 (0-671-89170-7, PB Hardcover) PB.
— Breaking Ranks. 1996. mass mkt. 6.99 (0-671-89172-3) PB.
— The Common Defense. McCarthy, Paul, ed. 432p. 1992. reprint ed. mass mkt. 5.99 (0-671-73009-6) PB.
— Firefall. McCarthy, Paul, ed. 480p. 1995. mass mkt. 5.99 (0-671-73011-8) PB.
— Inside West Point. Date not set. 27.50 (0-06-019317-4); pap. 15.00 (0-06-093133-7) HarpC.
— Thirty-Eight North Yankee. 1990. 18.95 (0-317-99663-0) PB.
— Thirty-Eight North Yankee. McCarthy, Paul, ed. 480p. 1991. reprint ed. mass mkt. 5.99 (0-671-70022-7) PB.
Ruggiano-Schmidt, Patricia. Cultural Conflict & Struggle: Literacy Learning in a Kindergarten Program. LC 96-54246. (Rethinking Childhood Ser.: Vol. 5). (Illus.). XV, 160p. (C). 1998. pap. text 29.95 (0-8204-3757-3) P Lang Pubng.
Ruggie, John. Winning the Peace: America & World Order in the New Era. 288p. 1998. pap. 17.50 (0-231-10427-8) Col U Pr.
Ruggie, John, ed. see Wagner, Richard, et al.
Ruggie, John G. Constructing the World Polity: Essays on International Institutionalization. LC 98-192711. (New International Relations Ser.). 336p. (C). 1998. 75.00 (0-415-09990-0); pap. 22.99 (0-415-09991-9) Routledge.
— Winning the Peace: America & World Order in the New Era. LC 96-7385. (Illus.). 288p. 1996. 29.50 (0-231-10426-X) Col U Pr.
Ruggie, John G., ed. The Antinomies of Interdependence. LC 82-2123. (Political Economy of International Change Ser.). 392p. 1983. text 76.00 (0-231-05724-5); pap. text 25.50 (0-231-05725-3) Col U Pr.
— Multilateralism Matters: The Theory & Praxis of an Institutional Forum. LC 92-31586. (New Directions in World Politics Ser.). 400p. (C). 1993. text 73.50 (0-231-07980-X); pap. text 23.00 (0-231-07981-8) Col U Pr.
Ruggie, John G., jt. ed. see Bhagwati, Jagdish N.
Ruggie, John G., ed. see Cox, Robert W.
Ruggie, John G., ed. see Litfin, Karen.
Ruggie, John G., ed. see Taylor, Paul.
Ruggie, Mary. Realignments in the Welfare State: Health Policy in the United States, Britain, & Canada. LC 96-10966. (Illus.). 336p. 1996. 47.50 (0-231-10484-7); pap. 19.50 (0-231-10485-5) Col U Pr.
— The State & Working Women: A Comparative Study of Britain & Sweden. LC 84-42563. 376p. 1984. reprint ed. pap. 116.60 (0-7837-9283-2, 206002200004) Bks Demand.
Ruggieri, Claude-Fortune. Principles of Pyrotechnics. deluxe ed. Carlton, Stuart, tr. 364p. 1995. text 114.00 (0-9643114-0-2) MP Assocs.
— Principles of Pyrotechnics. limited ed. Carlton, Stuart, tr. 364p. 1995. text 750.00 (0-9643114-1-0) MP Assocs.
Ruggieri, Ford F. The Poor Man's Guide to Self Publishing. LC 84-1107. 164p. 1984. 24.95 (0-931588-15-4) Allegany Mtn Pr.
Ruggieri, Giuseppe & Tomka, Miklos, eds. The Church in Fragments: Toward What Kind of Unity? 150p. 1997. pap. 15.00 (1-57075-128-5) Orbis Bks.
***Ruggieri, Helen.** Glimmer Girls. 40p. 1999. pap. 8.00 (0-932412-16-5) Mayapple Pr.
Ruggieri, Helen. The Poetess. LC 79-18883. 1980. 8.00 (0-931588-09-X); pap. 3.50 (0-931588-10-3) Allegany Mtn Pr.
Ruggieri, L., ed. see AIDS Foundation Dayton Staff & Volunteers.
Ruggieri, M., ed. Mobile & Personal Satellite Communications 3: Proceeding of the 3rd European Workshop on Mobile/Personal Satcoms. LC 98-44133. (Illus.). xii, 428p. 1998. pap. 109.00 (1-85233-045-7) Spr-Verlag.
***Ruggieri, Paul.** Profiting from Human Genome Stocks: Bigger Than the Internet. 145p. 2000. pap. 39.95 (1-893756-07-6) M Gordon Pubng.
Ruggieri, Paul. The Surgery Handbook: A Guide for Patients & Families. (Illus.). 152p. 1999. pap. 14.95 (1-886039-38-0) Addicus Bks.
Ruggieri, Paul F. Answers for Troubled Times. 5th ed. (Catholic Apologetics Ser.: Vol. CAS-1). (Illus.). ix, 63p. 1999. pap. 7.50 (0-916843-20-3) Order of Legion.
Ruggieri Staff. Catalogue des Livres Rares et Precieux Composant la Bibliotheque de M. E. F. D. Ruggieri. 277p. 1998. reprint ed. 75.00 (1-57898-087-9) Martino Pubng.
Ruggiero. Eurodrugs. LC 94-29846. 224p. 1994. pap. 23.00 (1-85728-102-0, Pub. by UCL Pr Ltd) Taylor & Francis.
— Eurodrugs: Drug Use, Markets & Trafficking in Europe. LC 94-29846. 224p. 1994. 65.00 (1-85728-101-2, Pub. by UCL Pr Ltd) Taylor & Francis.
— Superconductor Devices Handbook. 450p. 1998. write for info. (0-12-601713-1) Acad Pr.
— Thinking Sociologically: A Critical Thinking Activities Manual. 2nd ed. 89p. 1998. pap. write for info. (0-205-27818-3) Allyn.
— Valery Larbaud et l'Italie. 26.25 (0-685-34263-8) Fr & Eur.
Ruggiero, Adriane. The Baltic Countries: Estonia, Latvia & Lithuania. LC 96-41447. (Discovering Our Heritage Ser.). (J). 1998. 19.95 (0-382-39472-0, Dillon Silver Burdett); pap. write for info. (0-382-39538-7, Dillon Silver Burdett) Silver Burdett Pr.
— Korea: Bridge Between East & West. LC 98-31737. (Discovering Our Heritage Ser.). 1999. 23.00 (0-382-39891-2, Dillon Silver Burdett) Silver Burdett Pr.
Ruggiero, Alessandro G., ed. Stability of Particle Motion in Storage Rings. (AIP Conference Proceedings Ser.: Vol. 292, No. 54). 516p. 1993. text 502.00 (1-56396-225-X) Am Inst Physics.
Ruggiero, Elessandro G., ed. Hadron Colliders at the Highest Energy & Luminosity: Proceedings of the 34th Workshop of the INFN Project Eric, Italy 4-13 November, 1996. LC 98-221684. (Science & Culture Ser.). 308p. 1998. 78.00 (981-02-3361-2) World Scientific Pub.
Ruggiero, Greg. Microradio & Democracy: (Low) Power to the People. LC 99-11326. (Open Media Pamphlet Ser.: Vol. 10). 64p. 1999. pap. text 5.95 (1-58322-000-3, Pub. by Seven Stories) Publishers Group.
Ruggiero, Greg & Sahulka, Stuart, eds. The New American Crisis: Radical Analyses of the Problems Facing America Today. 272p. 1996. pap. 13.95 (1-56584-317-7, Pub. by New Press NY) Norton.
— Open Fire: The Open Magazine Pamphlet Series Anthology, Vol. 1. LC 92-50758. 320p. 1993. pap. 12.95 (1-56584-056-9, Pub. by New Press NY) Norton.
Ruggiero, Greg, ed. see Cooper, Marc, et al.
Ruggiero, Guido. Binding Passions: Tales of Magic, Marriage & Power at the End of the Renaissance. LC 92-24005. 296p. 1993. pap. text 24.00 (0-19-508320-2) OUP.
— The Boundaries of Eros: Sex Crime & Sexuality in Renaissance Venice. (Studies in the History of Sexuality). (Illus.). 240p. 1989. reprint ed. pap. text 19.95 (0-19-505696-5) OUP.
— Violence in Early Renaissance Venice. LC 79-25650. (Crime, Law, & Deviance Ser.). 250p. reprint ed. pap. 77.50 (0-8357-7951-3, 205702600002) Bks Demand.
Ruggiero, Guido, jt. ed. see Muir, Edward.
Ruggiero, Kristin H. And Here the World Ends: The Life of an Argentine Village. LC 87-20311. 248p. 1988. 39.50 (0-8047-1379-0) Stanford U Pr.
Ruggiero, Leonard F., et al, eds. American Marten, Fisher, Lynx, & Wolverine in the Western United States. (Illus.). 198p. 1997. reprint ed. 28.00 (0-89904-581-2); reprint ed. pap. 20.00 (0-89904-582-0) Crumb Elbow Pub.
***Ruggiero, Leonard F., et al.** Ecology & Conservation of Lynx in the United States. LC 99-59214. 480p. 2000. 59.95 (0-87081-577-6, Pub. by Univ Pr Colo); pap. 59.95 (0-87081-580-6, Pub. by Univ Pr Colo) U of Okla Pr.
***Ruggiero, Michael A. & Christopher, Thomas.** Annuals with Style: Inspired Design Ideas from Classic to Cutting Edge. LC 99-47133. (Illus.). 224p. 2000. 29.95 (1-56158-201-8) Taunton.
Ruggiero, Murray A. Cybernetic Trading Strategies: Developing a Profitable Trading System with State-of-the-Art Technologies. LC 96-53326. (Wiley Trading Advantage Ser.). 336p. 1997. 59.95 (0-471-14920-9) Wiley.
Ruggiero, Murray A., jt. auth. see Toghraie, Adrienne L.
Ruggiero, Renato, jt. ed. see Stephenson, Larry W.
Ruggiero, Timothy, ed. The Excelsior Guide to Mail Communication. (Illus.). 600p. 1997. pap. 95.00 (0-9660765-0-8, EX-0002) Excelsior PA.
Ruggiero, Vincent R. The Art of Thinking: A Guide to Critical & Creative Thought. 5th ed. LC 97-29. 281p. (C). 1997. pap. text 38.00 (0-321-01263-1) Addison-Wesley Educ.
— Becoming a Critical Thinker, 2 vols. 2nd ed. 160p. (C). 1995. pap. text 9.56 (0-395-77250-8) HM.
— Beyond Feelings: A Guide to Critical Thinking. 5th ed. LC 97-18648. 223p. 1997. pap. text 25.95 (1-55934-835-6, 1835) Mayfield Pub.
— Beyond Feelings Instructor's Manual. 5th rev. ed. (C). 1997. pap. text, teacher ed. write for info. (1-55934-981-6, 1981) Mayfield Pub.
— A Guide to Sociological Thinking. 160p. 1995. 28.00 (0-8039-5741-6); pap. 13.95 (0-8039-5742-4) Sage.
— Lessonpack: For Creative & Critical Thinking. 327p. 1990. 380.00 (0-9629083-0-4) Mindbuilding.
— Thinking Critically about Attitudes: A Strategy for Motivating Students to Learn. 125p. (YA). (gr. 6-9). 1998. pap. text, wbk. ed. 6.95 (0-205-27001-8, T7001-5, Longwood Div) Allyn.
— Thinking Critically about Ethical Issues. 4th ed. LC 96-7989. 224p. 1996. pap. text 25.95 (1-55934-654-X, 1654) Mayfield Pub.
Ruggiero, Vincent R., jt. auth. see Vesper, Joan F.
***Ruggiero, Vincent Ryan.** The Art of Thinking: A Guide to Critical & Creative Thought. 6th ed. LC 00-27272. 2000. write for info. (0-321-07637-0) Longman.
— Beyond Feelings: A Guide to Critical Thinking. 6th ed. LC 00-37224. 2000. pap. write for info. (0-7674-1589-2) Mayfield Pub.
— Changing Attitudes: A Strategy for Motivating Students to Learn. LC 97-43213. 125p. (C). 1998. pap. text 23.00 (0-205-26972-9) Allyn.
— Thinking Critically about Ethical Issues. 5th ed. LC 00-38689. 2000. pap. write for info. (0-7674-1582-5) Mayfield Pub.
***Ruggiero, Vincenzo.** Crime & Markets: Crimes in the Street & Crimes of the Elite. LC 99-86722. 220p. 2000. 74.00 (0-19-826838-6) OUP.
Ruggiero, Vincenzo. Organized & Corporate Crime in Europe: Offers That Can't be Refused. (Socio-Legal Studies). (Illus.). 208p. 1996. 83.95 (1-85521-522-5, Pub. by Dartmth Pub) Ashgate Pub Co.
Ruggiero, Vincenzo, et al, eds. Western European Penal Systems: A Critical Anatomy. 256p. 1995. 69.95 (0-8039-7720-4); pap. 25.95 (0-8039-7721-2) Sage.
Ruggiers, Paul G. Florence in the Age of Dante. LC 64-20761. (Centers of Civilization Ser.: No. 15). 203p. reprint ed. 63.00 (0-8357-9727-9, 201626300002) Bks Demand.
Ruggiers, Paul G., ed. Editing Chaucer: The Great Tradition. LC 84-1872. 301p. 1984. 29.95 (0-937664-58-8) Pilgrim Bks OK.
Ruggiers, Paul G., ed. see Chaucer, Geoffrey.
Ruggles, Glenn. Voices on the Water: An Oral & Pictorial History of Antrim County's Chain of Lakes. (Illus.). 340p. 1998. pap. 19.95 (0-9662149-0-0) Blue Heron MI.
Ruggles, Alison. Lories & Lorikeets: The Brush-Tongued Parrots & Their Care. (Illus.). 272p. 1996. 34.95 (0-7137-2268-1, Pub. by Blandford Pr) Sterling.
Ruggles, Allen M. A Diagnostic Test of Aptitude for Clerical Office Work Based on an Analysis of Clerical Operations. LC 74-177215. (Columbia University. Teachers College. Contributions to Education Ser.: No. 148). reprint ed. 37.50 (0-404-55148-3) AMS Pr.
Ruggles, C. L., ed. Formal Methods in Standards: A Report from the BCS Working Group. xi, 135p. 1990. 54.95 (0-387-19577-7) Spr-Verlag.
Ruggles, Clive L. Astronomy in Prehistoric Britain & Ireland. LC 98-40922. (Illus.). 288p. 1999. 65.00 (0-300-07814-5) Yale U Pr.
Ruggles, D. Fairchild, ed. Women, Patronage, & Self-Representation in Islamic Societies. LC 99-54125. (C). 2000. text 59.50 (0-7914-4469-4); pap. text 19.95 (0-7914-4470-8) State U NY Pr.
Ruggles, E. Stoddard. Ruggles Family of England & America. (Illus.). 232p. 1995. reprint ed. pap. 36.00 (0-8328-4942-1); reprint ed. lib. bdg. 46.00 (0-8328-4941-3) Higginson Bk Co.
Ruggles, Eleanor. Prince of Players: Edwin Booth. 27.95 (0-89190-565-0) Amereon Ltd.
Ruggles, Ellen. The New England Beach Guide. Brox, Andrea & Wood, Beverly J., eds. (Illus.). 336p. (Orig.). 1996. pap. 11.95 (0-9636123-2-8) Pleasant St Pr.
Ruggles, Fairchild D. Gardens, Landscape, & Vision in the Palaces of Islamic Spain. LC 98-18914. (Illus.). 264p. 1999. 65.00 (0-271-01851-8) Pa St U Pr.
Ruggles, Frederick W. Certain Paper Clips from the People's Republic of China: An International Trade Investigation. (Illus.). 81p. (Orig.). (C). 1994. pap. text 50.00 (0-7881-1505-7) DIANE Pub.
Ruggles, Grace, ed. see Harper-Deiters, Cyndi.
Ruggles, Grace, ed. see Harper-Dieters, Cyndi.
Ruggles, Kathryn E. Dialogues in Academia I: Introduction to a New Faith for Mankind. LC 91-66271. 247p. (Orig.). 1991. pap. 12.00 (0-9623596-1-0) Natl Spir Assy HI.
Ruggles, Laurel, ed. see Albert, Rachel.
Ruggles, Laurel, ed. see Ferre, Julia.
Ruggles, Laurel, ed. see Henkel, Pamela & Koch, Lee.
Ruggles, Laurel, ed. see Lawson, Margaret & Monte, Tom.
Ruggles, Laurel, ed. see Ohsawa, George, Macrobiotic Foundation Staff.
Ruggles, Laurel, ed. see Rowland, Natalie B.
Ruggles, Melville J. & Mostecky, Vaclav. Russian & East European Publications in the Libraries of the United States, No. 11--11. LC 73-437. (Illus.). 396p. 1973. reprint ed. lib. bdg. 69.50 (0-8371-6767-1, RURE, Greenwood Pr) Greenwood.
Ruggles, Myles A. The Audience Reflected in the Medium of Law: A Critique of the Political Economy of Speech Rights in the United States. 208p. 1994. pap. 39.50 (0-89391-993-4); text 73.25 (0-89391-881-4) Ablx Pub.
Ruggles, Nancy D., ed. Role of the Computer in Economic & Social Research in Latin America. (Other Conferences Ser.: No. 8). 409p. 1975. 106.90 (0-87014-260-7) Natl Bur Econ Res.
Ruggles, Nancy D. & Ruggles, Richard. Design of Economic Accounts. (General Ser.: No. 89). 196p. 1970. text 52.00 (0-87014-204-6) Natl Bur Econ Res.
***Ruggles, Nancy D. & Ruggles, Richard.** Macro & Micro Data Analyses & Their Integration. LC 99-17050. 576p. 1999. 115.00 (1-85898-991-4) E Elgar.
— National Accounting & Economic Policy: The United States & the Un Systems. LC 99-17050. 576p. 1999. 115.00 (1-85898-992-2) E Elgar.
— Pricing Systems, Indexes & Price Behavior. LC 99-17051. 528p. 1999. 115.00 (1-85898-993-0) E Elgar.
Ruggles, Philip K. Computer Dividends: Management Information Systems for the Graphic Arts. LC 94-92296. 122p. (Orig.). (C). 1995. pap. text 39.00 (0-9638203-2-X) Prtng Mgmt Srvs.
— Desktop Dividends: Managing Electronic Prepress for Profit. (Illus.). 188p. (Orig.). 1993. pap. 23.95 (0-9638203-0-3) Prtng Mgmt Srvs.
— Printing Estimating. 3rd ed. 528p. 1990. text 48.95 (0-8273-3805-8) Delmar.
— Printing Estimating. 4th ed. (Graphic Communications Ser.). 800p. (C). 1996. mass mkt. 78.95 (0-8273-6439-3) Delmar.
— Printing Estimating Workbook. 3rd ed. 48p. (C). reprint ed. pap. write for info. (0-9638203-1-1) Prtng Mgmt Srvs.
— Printing Estimating Workbook. 4th rev. ed. 64p. 1996. pap. 20.00 (0-9638203-3-8) Prtng Mgmt Srvs.
Ruggles Radclife, Rebecca. Dance Naked in Your Living Room: Handling Stress & Finding Joy. LC 96-90896. (Illus.). 192p. (Orig.). 1997. pap. 12.95 (0-9636607-1-3) EASE.
Ruggles Radcliffe, Rebecca. Enlightened Eating: Understanding & Changing Your Relationship with Food. 172p. 1996. 18.95 (0-9636607-0-5) EASE.
Ruggles, Richard, jt. auth. see Ruggles, Nancy D.

An Asterisk (*) at the beginning of an entry indicates that the title is appearing for the first time.

R

An Asterisk (*) at the beginning of an entry indicates that the title is appearing for the first time.

R

Ruhnau, Helena E. & Van Der Naillen, A. In the Sanctuary - Exalted Order of the Magi: Exalted Order of the Magi. (Illus.). 142p. 1984. pap. 13.95 (*0-941036-21-9*) Colleasius Pr.

Ruhnke, Amiyo & Wurzburger, Anando. Body Wisdom: An Easy-to-Use Handbook of Simple Exercises & Self-Massage Techniques for Busy People. LC 95-25026. 157p. 1996. 16.95 (*0-8048-3081-9*) Tuttle Pubng.

Ruhnke, Elmer, ed. & intro. see Simonetta, Joseph R.

Ruhnke, Lothar H. & Deepak, Adarsh, eds. Hygroscopic Aerosols. LC 84-9529. (Illus.). 375p. (C). 1984. 66.00 (*0-937194-02-6*) A Deepak Pub.

Ruhnke, Lothar H. & Latham, John, eds. Proceedings in Atmospheric Electricity. LC 83-10096. (Illus.). 427p. 1983. 53.00 (*0-937194-04-2*) A Deepak Pub.

Ruhnke, Robert. Sponsor Couple Program for Christian Marriage Preparation - Dialogue Packet: For Better & Forever. 96p. 1981. pap. 5.95 (*0-89243-144-X*) Liguori Pubns.

— Sponsor Couple Program for Christian Marriage Preparation - Manual: For Better & For Ever. 32p. 1981. pap. 5.95 (*0-89243-143-1*) Liguori Pubns.

***Ruhnke, Robert A.** For Better & For Ever 3.2. (Illus.). 200p. (YA). 1999. pap. 10.00 (*0-9677223-0-6*) Redemptorists.

***Ruhoff, Ron, et al, photos by.** High Rails over Cumbres: A Pictorial History. (Illus.). 32p. 1999. pap. 5.00 (*1-892717-06-9*, MISB 102) Sanborn Ltd.

Ruhr, Mario Von der, see Tessin, Timothy & Von Der Ruhr, Mario, eds.

Ruhrberg, Karl, et al. Art of the 20th Century, 2 vols. deluxe ed. Walter, Ingo F., ed. (Illus.). 840p. 1998. boxed set 79.99 (*3-8228-8576-2*) Taschen Amer.

***Rui, Huang Guo, ed.** Silk Reeling (Cocoon Silk Study) 461p. 1998. 85.00 (*1-57808-038-X*) Science Pubs.

Rui, Jiang, jt. auth. see Qianli, Sun.

Rui, Manuel. Yes, Comrade! Sousa, Ronald W., tr. LC 92-32341. (Emergent Literatures Ser.: Vol. 11). 176p. (C). 1993. 19.95 (*0-8166-1966-2*) U of Minn Pr.

Ruibal, Carmen C., jt. auth. see Wohl, Gary.

Ruibal, Julio. Ungido. 1998. pap. 6.99 (*0-8297-1685-8*) Vida Pubs.

Ruifang Wang. Macroeconomic Management under the Economic Reform. 59.95 (*1-85972-563-5*) Ashgate Pub Co.

Ruigh, Robert E. Parliament of 1624: Politics & Foreign Policy. LC 72-135548. (Historical Studies: No. 87). (Illus.). 448p. 1971. 27.50 (*0-674-65225-8*) HUP.

Ruigrok, J. J. Short-Wavelength Magnetic Recording: New Methods & Analysis. 566p. 1990. 190.25 (*0-946395-56-X*) Elsevier.

Ruigrok, Winfried & Van Tulder, Rob. The Logic of International Restructuring: The Management of Dependencies in Rival Industrial Complexes. LC 95-20711. (Illus.). 360p. (C). 1996. 90.00 (*0-415-12238-4*) Routledge.

— The Logic of International Restructuring: The Management of Dependencies in Rival Industrial Complexes. LC 95-20711. (Illus.). 360p. (C). 1996. pap. 27.99 (*0-415-12239-2*) Routledge.

Ruihley, Glenn R. An Anthology of Great U. S. Women Poets 1850-1990: Temples & Palaces. (Illus.). 606p. 1997. 50.00 (*0-9655735-0-8*) Mosaic Fnd.

RuijGrok, G. J. Elements of Airplane Performance. 462p. 1990. 97.50 (*90-6275-608-5*, Pub. by Delft U Pr) Coronet Bks.

Ruijs, J. H. Diagnosis of Cholecystoses. 1977. pap. text 94.00 (*90-247-1932-1*) Kluwer Academic.

Ruijsenaars, B., tr. see Van Den Berg, A. J., et al.

Ruilan, Lu, tr. Handbook of Regulations on Environmental Protection in China. 413p. 1995. pap. 250.00 (*0-915707-77-2*) Resources Future.

Ruin, Hans. Enigmatic Origins: Tracing the Theme of Historicity Through Heidegger's Works. (Stockholm Studies in Philosophy: No. 15). 294p. (Orig.). 1994. pap. 49.50 (*91-22-01621-X*) Coronet Bks.

Ruin, Inger. Grammar & the Advanced Learner: On Learning & Teaching a Second Language. (Studia Anglistica Upsaliensia Ser.: No. 96). 128p. 1996. pap. 39.50 (*91-554-3833-4*, Pub. by Uppsala Univ Acta Univ Uppsaliensis) Coronet Bks.

Ruinian, Li, ed. Modern Electrostatics: International Conference on Modern Electrostatics, October 21-25, 1988, Beijing, China. (International Academic Publishers Ser.). xviii, 569 p. 1989. 170.00 (*0-08-037029-2*, Pergamon Pr) Elsevier.

Ruiqing Du. Chinese Higher Education: A Decade of Reform & Development (1978-88) LC 91-24251. 176p. 1992. text 59.95 (*0-312-06071-8*) St Martin.

Ruis. Nicaragua for Beginners. (Illus.). 160p. 1984. pap. 7.95 (*0-86316-067-0*) Writers & Readers.

Ruitenbeek, Hendrik M. Homosexuality & Creative Genius. 1965. 25.00 (*0-8392-1149-X*) Astor-Honor.

Ruitenbeek, Hendrik M., ed. The First Freudians. rev. ed. LC 73-77278. 288p. 1973. 50.00 (*0-87668-694-3*) Aronson.

— Psychoanalysis & Male Sexuality. 1966. pap. 15.95 (*0-8084-0256-0*) NCUP.

Ruitenbeek, Hendrik M., ed. Freud As We Knew Him. LC 72-6471. (Illus.). 525p. reprint ed. pap. 162.80 (*0-608-10573-2*, 207119300009) Bks Demand.

Ruitenbeek, K. Carpentry & Building in Late Imperial China: A Study of the Fifteenth-Century Carpenter's Manual Lu Ban Jing. (Sinica Leidensia Ser.: No. 23). 500p. 1992. 141.50 (*90-04-09258-7*) Brill Academic Pubs.

Ruitenbeek, Klaas. Carpentry & Building in Late Imperial China: A Study of the Fifteenth-Century Carpenter's Manual, Lu Ban Jing. 2nd rev. ed. LC 96-317. (Sinica Leidensia Ser.: No. 23). (CHI & ENG.). xviii, 520p. 1996. 178.00 (*90-04-10529-8*) Brill Academic Pubs.

Ruitenberg, Bert, jt. auth. see Isaac, Anne R.

Ruiter, A., ed. Fish & Fishery Products: Composition, Nutritive Properties & Stability. (Illus.). 400p. 1995. text 120.00 (*0-85198-927-6*) OUP.

Ruiter, Barbara & Ruiter, Cindy. Pink Is Perfect for Pigs. (Illus.). 32p. (Orig.). (J). 1993. pap. 5.95 (*1-56883-019-X*) Colonial Pr AL.

Ruiter, Cindy, jt. auth. see Ruiter, Barbara.

***Ruiter, David E.** Generic Key to the Adult Ocellate Limnephiloidea of the Western Hemisphere: Insecta: Trichoptera. (Miscellaneous Contributions Ser.: Vol. 5). 40p. (C). 2000. 10.00 (*0-86727-135-3*) Ohio Bio Survey.

Ruiter, David E. The Genus Limnephilus Leach (Trichoptera: Limnephilidae) of the New World. LC 95-69879. (Bulletin New Ser.: Vol. 11, No. 1). 1995. pap. text 25.00 (*0-86727-117-5*) Ohio Bio Survey.

Ruiter, Dick W. Institutional Legal Facts: Legal Powers & Their Effects. (Law & Philosophy Library). 200p. (C). 1993. lib. bdg. 122.00 (*0-7923-2441-2*, Pub. by Kluwer Academic) Kluwer Academic.

Ruiter, Dirk J., et al, eds. Application of Nonclonal Antibodies in Tumor Pathology. (Developments in Oncology Ser.). 1987. lib. bdg. 225.50 (*0-89838-853-8*) Kluwer Academic.

— Cutaneous Melanoma & Precursor Lesions. (Developments in Oncology Ser.). 1984. text 185.50 (*0-89838-689-6*) Kluwer Academic.

Ruiter, Frans, jt. auth. see Fokkema, Douwe.

Ruitter, M. M. De, see De Ruitter, M. M., ed.

Ruivenkamp, Guido, jt. auth. see Richards, Paul.

Ruivo, Mario, ed. Marine Pollution & Sea Life. 1978. 100.00 (*0-7855-6936-7*) St Mut.

Ruiz, A., jt. auth. see Rodrigo, T.

Ruiz, Alphonse. The Prayers of John of the Cross. 3rd ed. 128p. 1994. pap. 9.95 (*1-56548-073-2*) New City.

Ruiz, Ana, jt. auth. see Gonzalez, Ralfka.

Ruiz, Andres L. Animals on the Inside: A Book of Discovery & Learning. (Illus.). 96p. (J). 1995. pap. 10.95 (*0-8069-0831-9*) Sterling.

— Blood Circulation. LC 96-9201. (Cycles of Life Ser.). (Illus.). 32p. (J). 1996. 12.95 (*0-8069-9331-6*) Sterling.

— Evolution. LC 96-25863. (Cycles of Life Ser.). (Illus.). 32p. (J). 1996. 12.95 (*0-8069-9329-4*) Sterling.

— The Fight for Survival. LC 96-37954. (Cycles of Life Ser.). (Illus.). 32p. (J). 1997. 12.95 (*0-8069-9743-5*) Sterling.

— The Life of a Cell. LC 96-37952. (Cycles of Life Ser.). (Illus.). 32p. (J). 1997. 12.95 (*0-8069-9741-9*) Sterling.

— Metamorphosis. LC 96-9200. (Cycles of Life Ser.). (Illus.). 32p. (J). 1996. 12.95 (*0-8069-9325-1*) Sterling.

— The Origin of the Universe. Tizon, Natalia, tr. LC 96-37980. (Sequences of Earth & Space Ser.). (Illus.). 32p. (J). 1997. 12.95 (*0-8069-9744-3*) Sterling.

— Rain. LC 96-25866. (Sequences of Earth & Space Ser.). (Illus.). 32p. (J). 1996. 12.95 (*0-8069-9333-2*) Sterling.

— Rivers. (Sequences of Earth & Space Ser.). (Illus.). 32p. (J). 1996. 12.95 (*0-8069-9310-3*) Sterling.

— Seasons. (Sequences of Earth & Space Ser.). (Illus.). 32p. (J). 1996. 12.95 (*0-8069-9335-9*) Sterling.

— Stars. (Sequences of Earth & Space Ser.). (Illus.). 32p. (J). 1996. 12.95 (*0-8069-9337-5*) Sterling.

— Trees. LC 96-25740. (Cycles of Life Ser.). (Illus.). 32p. (J). 1996. 12.95 (*0-8069-9327-8*) Sterling.

— Volcanoes & Earthquakes. LC 96-37981. (Sequences of Earth & Space Ser.). (Illus.). 32p. (J). 1997. 12.95 (*0-8069-9745-1*) Sterling.

Ruiz, Antonio, jt. auth. see Trenchard, Ernesto.

Ruiz, Antonio Machado y, see Machado y Ruiz, Antonio.

Ruiz, Arturo & Molinos, Manuel. The Archaeology of the Iberians: Archaeological Analysis of a Historical Process. LC 97-44332. (Illus.). 350p. (C). 1999. text 69.95 (*0-521-56402-6*) Cambridge U Pr.

Ruiz Barrionuevo, Carmen, ed. see Dario, Ruben.

Ruiz, Blanca R. Privacy in Telecommunications European & an American Approach. LC 96-22773. 1997. 134.00 (*90-411-0274-4*) Kluwer Law Intl.

Ruiz, C. & Koenigsburger, F. Design for Strength & Production. x, 270p. 1970. text 355.00 (*0-677-62050-0*) Gordon & Breach.

Ruiz-Cobo, Maria Reyes, jt. ed. see Castillo, Enrique.

Ruiz, Dana C. De, see De Ruiz, Dana C.

Ruiz de Adana, R. Manual de Diagnostico y Terapeutica Medica en Atencion Primaria. 2nd ed. (SPA.). 1221p. 1996. pap. 52.00 (*84-7978-255-2*, Pub. by Ediciones Diaz) IBD Ltd.

Ruiz de Alarcon, Hernando. Treatise on the Heathen Superstitions that Today Live among the Indians Native to this Day in New Spain, 1629. Andrews, J. Richard & Hassig, Ross, eds. LC 83-47842. (Civilization of the American Indian Ser.: Vol. 164). (Illus.). 540p. 1987. pap. 24.95 (*0-8061-2031-2*) U of Okla Pr.

Ruiz De Alarcon, Juan. La Verdad Sospechosa. Martin Martinez, Juan M., ed. (Nueva Austral Ser.: Vol. 173). (SPA.). 1991. pap. text 11.95 (*84-239-1973-0*) Elliots Bks.

Ruiz de Alarcon, Juan. La Verdad Sospechosa. (SPA.). pap. 11.95 (*84-376-0076-6*, Pub. by Ediciones Catedra) Continental Bk.

Ruiz De Alarcon, Juan. La Verdad Sospechosa, No. 68. (SPA.). 165p. 1969. write for info. (*0-8288-8557-5*) Fr & Eur.

Ruiz de Burton, Maria A. The Squatter & the Don. 2nd ed. Sanchez, Rosaura & Pita, Beatrice, eds. 381p. 1997. pap. 14.00 (*1-55885-185-2*) Arte Publico.

— Who Would Have Thought It? Sanchez, Rosaura & Pita, Beatrice, eds. LC 95-11585. 298p. 1995. pap. 12.95 (*1-55885-081-3*) Arte Publico.

Ruiz De Elvira, A. Mitologia Clasica. 2nd ed. (SPA.). 540p. 1993. 100.00 (*84-249-0204-1*) Elliots Bks.

Ruiz de la Pena, Alvaro, ed. see Palacio Valdes, Armando.

Ruiz del Vizo, Hortensia. El Marques de Mantua. 1971. pap. 5.00 (*0-89729-138-7*) Ediciones.

Ruiz del Vizo, Hortensia, ed. Black Poetry of the Americas. (ENG & SPA.). 1972. pap. 12.00 (*0-89729-008-9*) Ediciones.

Ruiz, Don Miguel. Los Cuatro Acuerdos: Una Guia Practica para la Libertad Personal. (Toltec Wisdom Ser.).Tr. of Four Agreements. (SPA.). 160p. 1999. pap. 10.95 (*1-878424-36-X*, Pub. by Amber-Allen Pub) Publishers Group.

— The Four Agreements: A Practical Guide to Personal Freedom. LC 97-18256. (Toltec Wisdom Ser.). 160p. 1997. pap. 12.95 (*1-878424-31-9*) Amber-Allen Pub.

***Ruiz, Don Miguel.** The Four Agreements Daily Companion Guide. 160p. 2000. 12.95 (*1-878424-48-3*, Pub. by Amber-Allen Pub) Publishers Group.

Ruiz, Don Miguel. The Mastery of Love: A Practical Guide to the Art of Relationship. LC 99-18199. (Toltec Wisdom Ser.). 224p. 1999. pap. 14.00 (*1-878424-42-4*) Amber-Allen Pub.

Ruiz, Don Miguel. The Medicine Bag: The Ancient Mystery of the Mind. Date not set. Price not set. (*1-878424-45-9*) Amber-Allen Pub.

Ruiz, Dorothy S., ed. Handbook of Mental Health & Mental Disorder among Black Americans. LC 89-71401. 352p. 1990. lib. bdg. 65.00 (*0-313-26330-2*, SRZ/, Greenwood Pr) Greenwood.

Ruiz, Elizabeth. Dating Dummies: or The Inevitable Extinction of the Homo Sapiens. 62p. (Orig.). 1997. pap. 4.95 (*1-885901-21-6*) Presbyters Peartree.

Ruiz, Enrique L. Cartas a la Carte. Pita, Juana R., ed. LC 90-84526. (Coleccion Clasicos Cubanos). (SPA.). 146p. (Orig.). 1991. pap. 15.00 (*0-89729-581-1*) Ediciones.

— El Pan de los Muertos. 2nd ed. LC 88-80745. (Coleccion Clasicos Cubanos). (SPA., Illus.). 225p. 1988. reprint ed. pap. 12.00 (*0-89729-482-3*) Ediciones.

Ruiz-Escalante, Jose A., ed. Foundations of Bilingual Education. 200p. (Orig.). 1997. pap. text 10.00 (*1-891074-02-4*) TX Assn Bilingual.

Ruiz, Estela. Our Lady of the America's: The Messages of the Blessed Virgin Mary As Received by Estela Ruiz of South Phoenix, AZ. 224p. 1994. pap. 9.95 (*1-891903-16-0*) St Andrew Prodns.

Ruiz, Geraldo. Selena: The Last Song. 1995. mass mkt. 5.99 (*1-887599-01-0*) El Diario Bks.

Ruiz Goldstein, Gisele, ed. see Goldstein, Jerome A.

Ruiz, Gracie, tr. see Zimmer, Luke.

Ruiz, Guadalupe, tr. see McGlone, Mary.

Ruiz, H. & Pavon, J. Flora Peruviana et Chilensis, 3 vols. in 1. (Illus.). 1965. reprint ed. 360.00 (*3-7682-0283-6*) Lubrecht & Cramer.

Ruiz, H. Rafael, jt. auth. see Gallegos-Ruiz, M. Antonieta.

Ruiz-Herrera, Jose. Fungal Cell Wall: Structure, Synthesis & Assembly. 256p. 1991. lib. bdg. 199.00 (*0-8493-6672-0*, QK601) CRC Pr.

Ruiz, Hip-olito, et al. The Journals of Hippolito Ruiz: Spanish Botanist in Peru & Chile, 1777-1788. Schultes, Richard E. & De Jaramillo-Arango, Maria J., trs. from SPA. LC 97-11251. (Illus.). 367p. 1998. 44.95 (*0-88192-407-5*) Timber.

Ruiz Iriarte, Victor. Carrusell. Holt, Marion P., ed. LC 76-125615. (SPA.). (Orig.). (C). 1970. pap. text 7.95 (*0-89197-063-0*) Irvington.

Ruiz, J. Mathematical Results in Statistical Mechanics; Proceedings of the Satellite Colloquium Statphys. 450p. 1999. 98.00 (*981-02-3863-0*) World Scientific Pub.

***Ruiz, Jean-Pierre.** Ezekiel. (Berit Olam (The Everlasting Covenant) Ser.). 2000. 0.00 (*0-8146-5067-8*) Liturgical Pr.

Ruiz, Jesus M., jt. auth. see Andradas, Carlos.

Ruiz, Jim. The Black Hood of the Ku Klux Klan. LC 97-17879. 450p. 1997. pap. 49.95 (*1-57292-043-2*) Austin & Winfield.

— The Black Hood of the Ku Klux Klan. LC 97-17879. 600p. 1998. 79.95 (*1-57292-044-0*) Austin & Winfield.

Ruiz Jodar, Carlos. Diccionario Espanol-Aleman, Aleman-Espanol Militar. (GER & SPA.). 375p. 1975. pap. 24.95 (*0-8288-5820-9*, S50101) Fr & Eur.

Ruiz, Jose M., see Azorin, pseud.

***Ruiz, Joseph J.** The Little Ghost Who Wouldn't Go Away: A Story for Children. (SPA & ENG., Illus.). 96p. (J). (gr. 2-8). 2000. pap. 10.95 (*0-86534-303-9*) Sunstone Pr.

Ruiz, Joseph J. Little Juan Learns a Lesson: A Story for Children. Adelo, Samuel, tr. LC 97-28150. (ENG & SPA., Illus.). 64p. (Orig.). (J). (gr. 3-8). 1997. pap. 8.95 (*0-86534-267-9*) Sunstone Pr.

Ruiz, Juan. The Book of Good Love. 1999. pap. 8.95 (*0-460-87762-3*) Tuttle Pubng.

— The Book of True Love: Bilingual Edition. Zahareas, Anthony N., ed. Daly, Saralyn R., tr. from SPA. & intro. by. LC 77-12820. (C). 1978. 29.95 (*0-271-00523-8*) Pa St U Pr.

— Libro de Buen Amor: Edicion Facsimil del Manuscrito Gayoso (1389) (Real Academia Ediciones Ser.). (SPA.). 1993. 500.00 (*84-600-6149-3*) Elliots Bks.

— Libro Del Arcipreste, Tambien Llamado Libro de Buen Amor: Edicion Sinoptica. (Spanish Ser.: No. 44). (SPA.). lxvi, 230p. (C). 1989. 20.00 (*0-940639-28-9*) Hispanic Seminary.

Ruiz, Juan D. La Migracion Indocumentada de Mexico a Los Estados Unidos (Indocumented Migration from Mexico) Un Nuevo Enfoque. LC 85-187805. (Seccion de Obras de Economia). (SPA.). 208p. 1984. pap. 9.99 (*968-16-1742-8*, Pub. by Fondo) Continental Bk.

Ruiz, Juan P., et al. Alta Colombia. 1997. text 50.00 (*958-9393-26-8*) St Martin.

Ruiz, Judy. Talking Razzmatazz: Poems by Judy Ruiz. 64p. 1991. pap. 10.95 (*0-8262-0772-3*); text 18.95 (*0-8262-0771-5*) U of Mo Pr.

Ruiz, Karen & Mohler, Sarah, eds. Creative Ideas for Home Cell Groups. 48p. 1996. pap. 4.95 (*1-886973-15-6*) Dove Chr Fel.

Ruiz, Lester E., ed. see Falk, Richard A.

Ruiz, Lester Edwin J., jt. ed. see Wapner, Paul.

Ruiz, Luisa, tr. see Contreras, Francisco.

Ruiz, M. A. & Cheremisinoff, Paul N. Pocket Guidebook on Environmental Auditing. 2nd ed. (Illus.). 109p. 1989. 24.95 (*0-925760-31-5*) SciTech Pubs.

Ruiz-Maldonado, Ramon, ed. see Congress of Pediatric Dermatology, 2nd, Mexico Cit.

Ruiz, Maria C. Literatura y Politica: El "Libro de los Estados" y el "Libro de las Armas" de Don Juan Manuel. 1990. 37.50 (*0-916379-63-9*) Scripta.

Ruiz, Mary S. & Amend, Karen S. Handwriting Analysis. 1980. pap. 12.95 (*0-87877-050-X*) Newcastle Pub.

Ruiz, Mary S., jt. auth. see Amend, Karen K.

Ruiz Massieu, Jose F. Proceso Democratico de Mexico. (SPA.). pap. 8.99 (*968-16-4424-7*, Pub. by Fondo) Continental Bk.

Ruiz, Michael & Booker, Randy. Astronomy Labs for the Personal Computer. 100p. (C). 1996. pap. text, spiral bd. 26.95 (*0-7872-2357-3*) Kendall-Hunt.

Ruiz, Mona & Boucher, Geoff. Two Badges: The Lives of Mona Ruiz. 288p. 1997. 22.95 (*1-55885-202-6*) Arte Publico.

Ruiz Morcillo, Maria J. Que Tal? An Introductory Course. 3rd ed. (C). 1991. pap. text 60.62 (*0-07-909968-8*) McGraw.

Ruiz, Nagual Miguel, jt. auth. see Nelson, Mary C.

Ruiz, Octavio, et al. Las Caras de Mexico. Fernandez, Manuel et al, trs. (Many Faces of Mexico Supplement Ser.). (ENG & SPA., Illus.). 90p. (Orig.). (C). 1996. pap. 25.00 (*0-9617743-7-1*) Res Ctr Amer.

Ruiz, Pablo, ed. Gordon's Photography Price Annual International, 1996. annuals 184p. 1996. ring bd. 55.00 (*0-931036-52-6*) Gordon s Art.

— Gordon's Print Price Annual, 1994. annuals 1078p. 1994. 95.00 (*0-931036-13-5*) Gordon s Art.

— Gordon's Print Price Annual, 1996. annuals 1238p. 1996. 135.00 (*0-931036-08-9*) Gordon s Art.

***Ruiz, Pedro, ed.** Ethnicity & Psychopharmacology. (Review of Psychiatry Ser.: Vol. 19, No. 4). 192p. 2000. pap. 28.50 (*0-88048-274-5*) Am Psychiatric.

Ruiz, Pedro J. Senderos de mi Destino. (SPA.). 80p. 1984. pap. 5.00 (*0-685-08592-9*) SLUSA.

Ruiz, Pedro M., jt. ed. see Van Der Hammen, Thomas.

Ruiz, Ramon, ed. Proceedings of the Seminar on Natural Family Planning & Family Life Education. 320p. (C). 1990. pap. text 32.50 (*962-209-260-8*, Pub. by HK Univ Pr) Coronet Bks.

Ruiz, Ramon E. The Great Rebellion: Mexico 1905-1924. (C). 1982. pap. text 17.50 (*0-393-95129-4*) Norton.

— Labor & the Ambivalent Revolutionaries: Mexico, 1911-1923. LC 75-29087. 162p. reprint ed. pap. 50.30 (*0-608-14764-8*, 202586700046) Bks Demand.

***Ruiz, Ramon E.** On the Rim of Mexico: Encounters of the Rich & Poor. LC 98-23319. 272p. 1998. 27.00 (*0-8133-3499-3*, Pub. by Westview) HarpC.

Ruiz, Ramon E. The People of Sonora & Yankee Capitalists. LC 87-30133. (PROFMEX Ser.). 326p. 1988. 43.50 (*0-8165-1012-1*) U of Ariz Pr.

— Triumphs & Tragedy: A History of the Mexican People. 512p. 1993. pap. 18.95 (*0-393-31066-3*) Norton.

***Ruiz, Ramon Eduardo.** On the Rim of Mexico: Encounters of the Rich & Poor. 1999. pap. 16.00 (*0-8133-3734-8*, Pub. by Westview) HarpC.

Ruiz, Raoul. Poetics of Cinema. 128p. 1995. pap. 19.50 (*2-906571-38-5*, Pub. by Editions Dis Voir) Dist Art Pubs.

***Ruiz, Reynaldo.** Hispanic Poetry in Los Angeles, 1850-1900: La Poesia Angelina. LC 00-32455. (Hispanic Literature Ser.: Vol. 56). 484p. 2000. 109.95 (*0-7734-7747-0*) E Mellen.

Ruiz, Roberto, jt. ed. see Bijou, Sidney W.

Ruiz-Rogers, Olga, jt. auth. see Rogers, Peter T.

Ruiz, Ronald. Happy Birthday Jesus. LC 93-45643. 320p. 1994. 9.95 (*1-55885-108-9*) Arte Publico.

Ruiz, Ronald L. Giuseppe Rocco. LC 98-12848. 368p. 1998. pap. 12.95 (*1-55885-228-X*) Arte Publico.

Ruiz, Shirley. Journey to High Places: A Spiritual Evolution. Peterson, Kim, ed. (Illus.). 400p. (Orig.). 1987. pap. 12.95 (*0-944020-00-3*) Shastar Pr.

Ruiz Silva, Carlos, ed. see Rivas, Duque de.

Ruiz, Sonia Lombardo de, see Lombardo de Ruiz, Sonia.

Ruiz, Susan, jt. auth. see Page, Claudia.

Ruiz, Suzanne. A Dog Owner's Guide to Grooming Your Dog. (Illus.). 118p. 1995. 10.95 (*1-56465-136-3*, 16021) Tetra Pr.

Ruiz, Teofilo F. The City & the Realm: Burgos & Castile, 1080-1492. (Collected Studies: No. CS375). 551p. 1992. 109.95 (*0-86078-329-4*, Pub. by Variorum) Ashgate Pub Co.

— Crisis & Continuity: Land & Town in Late Medieval Castile. LC 93-35573. (Middle Ages Ser.). (Illus.). 368p. (C). 1994. text 48.95 (*0-8122-3228-3*) U of Pa Pr.

Ruiz Torres, Erich. English-Spanish Dictionary of Medical Terms. 8th ed. (ENG & SPA.). 652p. 1995. 125.00 (*0-7859-9751-2*) Fr & Eur.

Ruiz Torres, Francisco. English-Spanish, Spanish-English Medical Vocabulary: Vocabulario Ingles-Espanol, Espanol-Ingles de Medicina. (ENG & SPA.). 300p. 1979. pap. 24.95 (*0-8288-4845-9*, S50091) Fr & Eur.

Ruiz, Vicki L. Cannery Women, Cannery Lives: Mexican Women, Unionization, & the California Food Processing Industry, 1930-1950. LC 87-13878. (Illus.). 194p. 1987. pap. 14.95 (*0-8263-0988-7*) U of NM Pr.

— From out of the Shadows: Mexican Women in Twentieth-Century America. (Illus.). 288p. 1999. pap. 15.95 (*0-19-513099-5*) OUP.

An Asterisk (*) at the beginning of an entry indicates that the title is appearing for the first time.

— From Out of the Shadows: Mexican Women in 20th Century America. LC 97-9387. (Illus.). 288p. (C). 1998. 30.00 (*0-19-511483-3*) OUP.

***Ruiz, Vicki L.** Unequal Sisters: A Multicultural Reader in U.S. Women's History. 3rd ed. LC 99-16825. 2000. text 85.00 (*0-415-92516-9*) Routledge.

***Ruiz, Vicki L., ed.** Las Obreras: Chicana Politics of Work & Family. (Aztlan Anthology Ser.: Vol. 1). 328p. 2000. reprint ed. pap. 25.00 (*0-89551-094-4*) UCLA Chicano Studies.

Ruiz, Vicki L. & DuBois, Ellen C., eds. Unequal Sisters: A Multicultural Reader in U. S. Women's History. 2nd ed. LC 94-2430. 1994. write for info. (*0-415-90905-8*); pap. write for info. (*0-415-90906-6*) Routledge.

Ruiz, Vicki L. & Tiano, Susan. Women on the U. S. Mexico Border: Responses to Change. LC 86-22305. (Thematic Studies in Latin America). 256p. 1987. text 44.95 (*0-04-497038-2*); pap. text 15.95 (*0-04-497039-0*) Routledge.

Ruiz, Vicki L., jt. ed. see DuBois, Ellen C.

Ruiz, Wendy, ed. see Ellison, George Vernon & Young, Loy.

***RUIZRAZO, TSOLAGIU M A.** Spirit of the White Wolf Woman. (Illus.). 1999. pap. text 19.95 (*3-00-002730-0*) World Educ.

Ruja, Harry, ed. see Russell, Bertrand.

Rujula, A. de, ed. A Unified View of the Macro- & Micro-Cosmos. 680p. (C). 1987. pap. 64.00 (*9971-5-0394-8*); text 153.00 (*9971-5-0393-X*) World Scientific Pub.

Rukang, Wu, jt. ed. see Olsen, John W.

***Rukes, Brian.** Illustrated Buyers Guide Minneapolis-Moline Tractors. (Illustrated Buyer's Guide Ser.). (Illus.). 128p. 2000. pap. 17.95 (*0-7603-0739-3*, 129813AP, Pub. by MBI Pubg) Motorbooks Intl.

Rukes, Brian & Kraushaar, Andrew. John Deere Model A. (Original Ser.). (Illus.). 128p. 2000. 24.95 (*0-7603-0218-9*, Pub. by MBI Pubg) Motorbooks Intl.

Rukeyser. Common Sense. 333p. (C). 1999. 34.95 (*0-471-33212-7*) Wiley.

***Rukeyser.** The Common Sense of Money & Investments. LC 99-30159. (Wiley Investment Classics). 352p. (C). 1999. pap. 19.95 (*0-471-33213-5*) Wiley.

Rukeyser, Louis. Louis Rukeyser's Book of Lists: The Best, the Worst, & the Funniest from the Worlds of Business, Finance, & Politics. LC 97-23136. 320p. 1997. 25.00 (*0-8050-5126-0*) H Holt & Co.

— Louis Rukeyser's Book of Lists: The Best, the Worst & the Funniest from the Worlds of Business, Finance & Politics. 288p. 1999. pap. 14.95 (*0-8050-5127-9*, Owl) H Holt & Co.

***Rukeyser, Muriel.** Houdini: A Verse Drama to Be Spoken or Sung. 2000. pap. 14.95 (*1-930464-00-2*) Paris Pr MA.

Rukeyser, Muriel. The Life of Poetry. LC 96-22476. 256p. 1996. pap. 14.95 (*0-9638183-3-3*) Paris Pr MA.

— The Orgy. rev. ed. LC 97-23632. 216p. 1997. reprint ed. pap. 14.95 (*0-9638183-2-5*) Paris Pr MA.

— Out of Silence: Selected Poems. Daniels, Kate, ed. 192p. 1992. 28.00 (*0-916384-11-X*, TriQuart) Northwestern U Pr.

— Out of Silence: Selected Poems. Daniels, Kate, ed. 192p. 1994. pap. 14.95 (*0-8101-5015-8*) Northwestern U Pr.

— Theory of Flight. LC 74-144741. (Yale Series of Younger Poets: No. 34). reprint ed. 18.00 (*0-404-53834-7*) AMS Pr.

— Willard Gibbs. LC 87-12394. (Illus.). xiv, 465p. 1988. reprint ed. 35.00 (*0-918024-57-9*); reprint ed. pap. 25.00 (*0-918024-56-0*) Ox Bow.

Rukeyser, Muriel, ed. see Levi, Jan H.

Rukeyser, Muriel, tr. see Ekelof, Gunnar.

Rukeyser, Muriel, tr. & pref. see Paz, Octavio.

Rukl, Antonin. Atlas of the Moon. Rackham, T. W., ed. (Illus.). 224p. 1990. reprint ed. 34.95 (*0-913135-17-8*, 18539) Kalmbach.

— Constellation Guidebook. Kadecka, Slavos, tr. LC 98-22850. (Illus.). 224p. 1998. 17.95 (*0-8069-4299-1*) Sterling.

— Constellation Guidebook. 224p. 1999. pap. text 14.95 (*0-8069-3979-6*) Sterling.

Rukmani, T. S. Sankara: The Man & His Philosophy. (C). 1991. text 3.50 (*81-85425-33-7*, Pub. by Manohar) S Asia.

Rukmani, T. S., tr. Yogavarttika of Vijnanabhiksu Vol. 3: Vibhutipada. 1988. 26.00 (*81-215-0057-5*, Pub. by M Manoharial) Coronet Bks.

Rukstad, Michael G. Corporate Decision Making in the World Economy. 2nd ed. (C). 1999. pap. text 53.50 (*0-03-011304-0*) Harcourt Coll Pubs.

— Corporate Decision Making in World Economics. 640p. (C). 1992. pap. text 71.00 (*0-03-076526-9*) Dryden Pr.

— Macroeconomic Decision Making. 4th ed. (C). Date not set. pap. text, teacher ed. 29.75 (*0-03-012099-3*) Harcourt Coll Pubs.

— Macroeconomic Decision Making. 4th ed. (C). 1999. pap. text 44.00 (*0-03-007334-0*, Pub. by Harcourt Coll Pubs) Harcourt.

— Macroeconomic Decision Making in the World Economy. 3rd ed. 720p. (C). 1992. pap. text 81.00 (*0-03-074733-3*) Dryden Pr.

— Macroeconomic Decision Making in the World Economy. 3rd ed. 481p. (C). 1993. pap. text, teacher ed. 27.50 (*0-03-076346-0*) Dryden Pr.

Rukstalis, Susan. How Many Steps Before the Queen? LC 92-60664. (Illus.). 32p. (J). (ps-4). 1992. 14.95 (*0-9628914-2-8*) Padakami Pr.

Rukuza, E. W. West Coast Turnaround. 1990. mass mkt. 4.50 (*0-445-21002-8*, Pub. by Warner Bks) Little.

Rul, Francisco G. Materiales Liticos y Ceramicos Encontrados en las Cercanias del Monolito Coyolxauhqui. (SPA., Illus.). 65p. 1997. pap. 10.00 (*968-29-5118-6*, IN88, Pub. by Dir Gen Pubicaiones) UPLAAP.

Ruland, Heiner. Expanding Tonal Awareness: A Musical Exploration of the Evolution of Consciousness Guided by the Monochord. Orig. Title: Ein Weg Zur Erweiterung Des Toneyllebens. 188p. 1992. 56.95 (*1-85584-170-3*, Pub. by R Steiner Pr) Anthroposophic.

Ruland, Martin. Lexicon Alchemiae. (GER.). 1997. reprint ed. 158.00 (*3-487-00631-6*) G Olms Pubs.

Ruland, Richard & Bradbury, Malcolm. From Puritanism to Postmodernism: A History of American Literature. 496p. 1992. reprint ed. pap. 16.95 (*0-14-014435-8*, Penguin Bks) Viking Penguin.

Ruland-Thorne, Kate. Experience Sedona, Legends & Legacies. Blake, Bennie, ed. LC 89-51796. (Illus.). 114p. (Orig.). 1989. pap. 8.95 (*0-9628329-0-1*) Thorne Enterprises.

— The Yavapai People of the Red Rocks: People of the Sun. Caillou, Aliza, ed. (Illus.). 102p. (Orig.). 1993. pap. 6.95 (*0-9628329-5-2*) Thorne Enterprises.

Ruland, Vernon. Eight Sacred Horizons: The Religious Imagination East & West. 240p. 1985. write for info. (*0-317-18117-3*) Macmillan.

— Horizons of Criticism: An Assessment of Religious-Literary Options. LC 75-20162. 275p. reprint ed. pap. 85.30 (*0-608-14073-2*, 202420300035) Bks Demand.

— Imagining the Sacred: Soundings in World Religions. LC 98-28478. (Faith Meets Faith Ser.). (Illus.). 270p. 1998. pap. 24.00 (*1-57075-209-5*) Orbis Bks.

— Sacred Lies & Silences: A Psychology of Religious Disguise. LC 93-34712. 168p. (Orig.). 1994. pap. text 10.95 (*0-8146-5847-4*, M Glazier) Liturgical Pr.

Ruland, William. The Accounting System: A Self Study Guide. 2nd ed. LC 99-58638. (SWC-Accounting Ser.). 150p. 2000. pap. 25.95 (*0-324-02361-8*) Sth-Wstrn College.

Ruland, William. The Accounting System: A Self-study Preparation for Introductory Accounting. LC 97-202334. (Illus.). 1997. pap. write for info. (*0-538-88597-1*) Sth-Wstrn College.

Rulandus, Martinus. A Lexicon of Alchemy: or Alchemical Dictionary. 466p. 1992. reprint ed. pap. 30.00 (*0-922802-82-3*) Kessinger Pub.

Rulau, Russell. Discovering America: The Coin Collecting Connection. LC 89-85218. (Illus.). 328p. 1989. pap. 19.95 (*0-87341-129-3*, DA01) Krause Pubns.

— Hard Times Tokens, 1832-1844. 6th ed. LC 80-82710. 120p. 1996. pap. 19.95 (*0-87341-414-4*, HT06) Krause Pubns.

***Rulau, Russell.** Latin American Tokens. 2nd ed. LC 92-71453. (Illus.). 480p. 2000. pap. 37.95 (*0-87341-566-3*) Krause Pubns.

Rulau, Russell. Latin American Tokens: A Guide Book & Catalog 1700-1920. LC 92-71453. (Illus.). 410p. 1992. pap. 29.95 (*0-87341-200-1*, TL01) Krause Pubns.

— Standard Catalog of United States Tokens 1700-1900. 2nd ed. LC 93-80096. (Illus.). 944p. 1997. pap. 47.95 (*0-87341-479-9*, ST02) Krause Pubns.

— Standard Catalog of United States Tokens 1700-1900. 3rd ed. LC 99-462560. (Illus.). 1040p. 1999. pap. 49.95 (*0-87341-565-5*) Krause Pubns.

Rulau, Russell & Fuld, George. Medallic Portraits of Washington. 2nd ed. LC 98-87365. (Illus.). 432p. 1999. 34.95 (*0-87341-681-3*) Krause Pubns.

Rule, Albert R., jt. ed. see Petruk, William.

Rule, Amy, ed. Carleton Watkins: Selected Texts & Bibliography. LC 92-42581. 200p. 1993. 95.00 (*0-8161-0578-2*, Hall Reference) Macmillan.

Rule, Amy & Lorenz, Richard, eds. Imogen Cunningham: Selected Texts & Bibliography. (World Photographers Reference Ser.). (Illus.). 200p. 1993. 95.00 (*0-8161-0575-8*, G K Hall & Co) Mac Lib Ref.

Rule, Ann. And Never Let Her Go: Thomas Capano: The Deadly Seducer. LC 99-47339. 480p. 1999. 25.00 (*0-684-81048-4*) S&S Trade.

***Rule, Ann.** . . . And Never Let Her Go: Thomas Capano, the Deadly Seducer. large type ed. LC 99-462230. (Mystery Ser.). 2000. 29.95 (*0-7862-2429-0*) Thorndike Pr.

— And Never Let Her Go Bk. 3: Thomas Capano: The Deadly Seducer. (Illus.). 688p. 2000. mass mkt. 7.99 (*0-671-86871-3*, Pocket Star Bks) PB.

Rule, Ann. Bitter Harvest: A Woman's Fury, a Mother's Sacrifice. (Illus.). 482p. 1999. mass mkt. 7.99 (*0-671-86869-1*) PB.

— Bitter Harvest: A Woman's Fury, a Mother's Sacrifice. 1998. 23.00 (*0-684-86868-7*) S&S Trade.

— Bitter Harvest: A Woman's Fury, a Mother's Sacrifice. LC 97-49677. (Illus.). 320p. 1998. 22.50 (*0-684-81047-6*) S&S Trade.

— Bitter Harvest: A Woman's Fury, a Mother's Sacrifice. large type ed. LC 98-18428. 565p. 1998. 28.95 (*0-7838-0250-1*, G K Hall & Co) Mac Lib Ref.

— Bitter Harvest International. 1998. per. 6.99 (*0-671-02047-1*) PB.

— The Crime Files: A Rose for Her Grave You Belong to Me Forever in the Heart. 1104p. 1997. 14.00 (*0-671-01751-9*, PB Hardcover) PB.

— Dead by Sunset: Perfect Husband, Perfect Killer? 1999. pap. 9.98 (*0-671-04454-0*) PB.

— Dead by Sunset: Perfect Husband, Perfect Killer? 544p. 1996. per. 6.99 (*0-671-00113-2*) S&S Trade.

— Empty Promises: Case Files. 416p. 2001. mass mkt. 7.99 (*0-671-02533-3*, Pocket Star Bks) PB.

— End of The Dream: The Golden Boy Who Never Grew Up & Other True Cases. (Ann Rule's Crime Files Ser.: No. 5). 523p. 1999. mass mkt. 7.99 (*0-671-79357-8*) PB.

***Rule, Ann.** End of the Dream: The Golden Boy Who Never Grew Up & Other True Cases. large type ed. LC 99-12936. 1999. 29.95 (*0-7862-1907-6*) Thorndike Pr.

Rule, Ann. Everything She Ever Wanted. Rubenstein, Julie, ed. 560p. 1993. reprint ed. per. 6.99 (*0-671-69071-X*) PB.

— Everything She Ever Wanted: A True Story of Obsessive Love, Murder, & Betrayal. (Illus.). 384p. 1992. pap. 23.00 (*0-671-69070-1*) S&S Trade.

— A Fever in the Heart: And Other True Cases. (Ann Rule's Crime Files Ser.: Vol. 3). 480p. 1996. per. 6.99 (*0-671-79355-1*, PB Trade Paper) PB.

— If You Really Loved Me. Rubenstein, Julie, ed. 624p. 1992. reprint ed. mass mkt. 6.99 (*0-671-76920-0*) PB.

— In the Name of Love. large type ed. LC 98-15158. 1998. 28.95 (*0-7862-1462-7*) Thorndike Pr.

— In the Name of Love: And Other True Cases. (Ann Rule's True Crime Files Ser.: Vol. 4). 1998. per. 6.99 (*0-671-79356-X*) PB.

— Lesbian Images. (C). 1989. pap. 16.95 (*0-7453-0366-8*) Westview.

— Possession: A Novel. 1997. per. 5.99 (*0-671-52788-6*) PB.

— A Rage to Kill: And Other True Stories, Vol. 6. (Ann Rule's Crime Files Ser.). (Illus.). 382p. 1999. mass mkt. 7.99 (*0-671-02534-1*, Pocket Star Bks) PB.

***Rule, Ann.** A Rage to Kill & Other True Cases: Ann Rule's Crime Files. large type ed. LC 99-52365. 1999. 29.95 (*0-7838-8826-0*, G K Hall Lrg Type) Mac Lib Ref.

Rule, Ann. A Rose for Her Grave. (Ann Rule's Crime Files Ser.: Vol. 1). 528p. 1993. per. 6.99 (*0-671-79353-5*) PB.

— A Rose for Her Grave. 1996. per. 6.99 (*0-671-53798-9*) PB.

— Small Sacrifices. 496p. 1988. mass mkt. 7.99 (*0-451-16660-4*, Sig); mass mkt. 5.99 (*0-451-18779-2*, Sig) NAL.

— The Stranger Beside Me. (Illus.). 512p. 1981. mass mkt. 7.99 (*0-451-16493-8*, Sig) NAL.

***Rule, Ann.** Stranger Beside Me. 20th anniversary ed. 2000. 25.95 (*0-393-05029-7*) Norton.

Rule, Ann. You Belong to Me & Other True Cases: Ann Rule's Crime Files, Vol. 2. Rubenstein, Julie, ed. (Illus.). 480p. (Orig.). 1994. per. 6.99 (*0-671-79354-3*) PB.

Rule, Ann & Ladd, Veronica. Dead by Sunset: Perfect Husband, Perfect Killer? abr. ed. (First Love Ser.). 158p. (J). 1995. pap. 17.00 incl. audio (*0-671-53408-4*) Silhouette.

Rule, Ann, see Stack, Andy, pseud.

Rule, B. J. Polar Knight: The Mystery of Sir John Franklin. LC 98-22705. 1998. pap. 14.95 (*1-877633-40-2*) Luthers.

Rule, Colter. Uncovering the Sources of Love & Hate: A Theory of Human Behavior. LC 95-1450. 288p. 1995. 26.95 (*0-86534-102-8*); pap. 18.95 (*0-86534-229-6*) Sunstone Pr.

Rule, Greg. Electro Shock! Groundbreakers of Synth Music. LC 99-22704. (Illus.). 256p. 1999. pap. 17.95 (*0-87930-582-7*) Miller Freeman.

Rule, James & Veacht, Robert. Ethical Questions in Dentistry. LC 92-48228. 282p. 1993. pap. text 28.00 (*0-86715-203-6*) Quint Pub Co.

Rule, James B. Theory & Progress in Social Science. (Illus.). 271p. (C). 1997. text 59.95 (*0-521-57365-3*); pap. text 18.95 (*0-521-57494-3*) Cambridge U Pr.

Rule, Jane. After the Fire. LC 89-34014. 256p. 1989. pap. 8.95 (*0-941483-45-2*) Naiad Pr.

— Against the Season. 224p. 1984. reprint ed. pap. 8.95 (*0-930044-48-7*) Naiad Pr.

— Desert of the Heart. 224p. 1985. pap. 12.95 (*0-930044-73-8*) Naiad Pr.

— The Desert of the Heart. LC 75-12344. (Homosexuality Ser.). 1979. reprint ed. 25.95 (*0-405-07386-0*) Ayer.

— A Hot-Eyed Moderate. LC 84-22831. 256p. 1985. pap. 7.95 (*0-930044-57-6*) Naiad Pr.

— Inland Passage. 288p. 1985. pap. 10.95 (*0-930044-56-8*) Naiad Pr.

— Memory Board. 336p. 1987. pap. 12.95 (*0-941483-02-9*) Naiad Pr.

— Outlander. LC 80-84221. (Illus.). 224p. (Orig.). 1981. pap. 8.95 (*0-930044-17-7*) Naiad Pr.

— Theme for Diverse Instruments. 208p. 1990. pap. 8.95 (*0-941483-63-0*) Naiad Pr.

— Theme for Diverse Instruments. 192p. reprint ed. pap. 12.95 (*0-88922-060-3*) LPC InBook.

— This Is Not for You. 304p. 1982. reprint ed. pap. 8.95 (*0-930044-25-8*) Naiad Pr.

— The Young in One Another's Arms. 224p. 1984. reprint ed. pap. 9.95 (*0-930044-53-3*) Naiad Pr.

Rule, Jeffrey S. Dynamic HTML: The HTML Developer's Guide. LC 98-38784. 288p. (C). 1998. pap. text 39.95 (*0-201-37961-9*) Addison-Wesley.

Rule, John. Albion's People: 1714-1815. LC 91-21964. (Social & Economic History of England Ser.). 269p. (C). 1995. pap. 48.00 (*0-582-08916-6*, 79212) Longman.

— The Labouring Classes in Early Industrial England, 1750-1850. LC 85-16665. (Themes in British Social History Ser.). 432p. (C). 1989. pap. 98.00 (*0-582-49172-X*, 73511) Longman.

— The Vital Century: England's Developing Economy, 1714-1815 (Social & Economic History of England) (Social & Economic History of England Ser.). 334p. (C). 1991. pap. text 30.50 (*0-582-49425-7*, 79211) Longman.

— The Vital Century, 1714-1815. 1992. text. write for info. (*0-582-49424-9*, Pub. by Addison-Wesley) Longman.

Rule, John, ed. Crime, Protest & Popular Politics in Southern England, 1740-1850. LC 96-29453. 224p. 1997. 55.00 (*1-85285-076-0*) Hambledon Press.

Rule, John & Malcolmson, Robert, eds. Protest & Survival: Essays in E. P. Thompson. LC 93-15823. 432p. 1993. 30.00 (*1-56584-114-X*, Pub. by New Press NY) Norton.

Rule, John C., ed. Louis XIV & the Craft of Kingship. LC 72-79845. 500p. 1970. reprint ed. pap. 155.00 (*0-608-00918-0*, 206171200011) Bks Demand.

Rule, Keith. 3D Graphics File Formats. 1996. 39.95 (*0-614-20262-0*) Addison-Wesley.

Rule, Lareina. Name Your Baby. rev. ed. 256p. (Orig.). 1986. mass mkt. 4.99 (*0-553-27145-8*) Bantam.

Rule, Leslie. Kill Me Again. 1996. mass mkt. 5.99 (*0-515-11939-3*, Jove) Berkley Pub.

— Whispers from the Grave. 272p. (Orig.). (YA). 1995. mass mkt. 5.99 (*0-425-14777-0*) Berkley Pub.

Rule, Luauna. An Insider's Secrets to Becoming a Flight Attendant. LC 97-90017. (Illus.). 150p. 1997. pap. 19.95 (*0-9656438-4-0*) Flight Attendant.

Rule, Margaret, ed. Edward Albee at Home & Abroad: A Bibliography. LC 73-158245. (Studies in Modern Literature: No. 1). reprint ed. 29.50 (*0-404-07945-8*) AMS Pr.

Rule, Martin, ed. Eadmeri Historia Novorum in Anglia, et Opuscula Duo de Vita Sancti Anselmi et Quibusdam Miraculis Ejus: Edition from the Manuscript in the Library of Corpus Christi College, Cambridge. (Rolls Ser.: No. 81). 1972. reprint ed. 70.00 (*0-8115-1151-0*) Periodicals Srv.

Rule, Michael, ed. see Nolan, Jack & Fardray, Dayton.

Rule, Paul A. K'ung-Tzu or Confucius? The Jesuit Interpretation of Confucianism. 292p. (Orig.). 1987. pap. text 19.95 (*0-86861-913-2*) Routledge.

Rule, Rebecca. The Best Revenge: Short Stories. LC 94-40944. (Hardscrabble Bks.). 208p. 1995. 19.95 (*0-87451-702-8*) U Pr of New Eng.

Rule, Rebecca & Wheeler, Susan. Creating the Story: Guides for Writers. LC 92-30964. 280p. (C). 1993. pap. 15.95 (*0-435-08765-7*) Heinemann.

***Rule, Rebecca & Wheeler, Susan.** True Stories: Guides for Writing from Your Life. LC 99-41956. 296p. 2000. 16.95 (*0-325-00046-8*) Heinemann.

Rule Regulatory Handbook Staff. California's Permit by Rule Regulatory Handbook. 260p. 1992. 29.95 (*0-934615-38-1*) Gulf Pub.

Rule, Richard. Flyfishing Lakes: Waterproof Guide. 35p. 1998. pap. 5.95 (*0-9587143-5-5*) F Amato Pubns.

— Flyfishing Rivers: Waterproof Guide. 35p. 1998. pap. 5.95 (*0-9587143-6-3*) F Amato Pubns.

Rule, Robin. Baseball Prayers. 16p. (Orig.). 1990. pap. 3.00 (*1-879082-02-0*) Rainy Day CA.

— The String Creek Saga, 1990-1997. 31p. 1997. pap. 5.00 (*0-614-30307-9*) Rainy Day CA.

Rule, Robin, jt. ed. see Essman, Daniel.

***Rule, Roger C.** Franchise Redbook: Easy-to-use Facts & Figures. LC 99-37189. 750p. 1999. pap. text 34.95 (*1-55571-484-6*) PSI Resch.

Rule, Roger C. No Money down Financing for Franchising. LC 98-45404. 240p. 1999. pap. 19.95 (*1-55571-462-5*, NMDFP, Oasis Pr) PSI Resch.

— Rule Book of Business Plans for Startups. 300p. 2000. pap. 18.95 (*1-55571-519-2*) PSI Resch.

Rule, Warren R., jt. auth. see Bauserman, Joseph M.

Rule, William, III. Milestones in Mission. Sugue, Barbara R., ed. LC 98-65598. (Illus.). 352p. 1998. pap. 22.95 (*1-57736-092-3*) Providence Hse.

Rule, Wilma & Noonan, Norma, eds. Russian Women in Politics & Society, 157. LC 96-10766. (Contributions in Women's Studies: Vol. 157). 200p. 1996. 62.95 (*0-313-29363-5*, Greenwood Pr) Greenwood.

Rule, Wilma & Zimmerman, Joseph F., eds. Electoral Systems in Comparative Perspective: Their Impact on Women & Minorities, 338. LC 93-28034. (Contributions in Political Science Ser.: No. 338). 280p. 1994. 65.00 (*0-313-28633-7*, Greenwood Pr) Greenwood.

— United States Electoral Systems: Their Impact on Women & Minorities. LC 91-29608. (Contributions in Political Science Ser.: No. 294). 264p. 1992. pap. 22.95 (*0-275-94240-6*, B4240, Greenwood Pr) Greenwood.

— United States Electoral Systems: Their Impact on Women & Minorities, 294. LC 91-34481. (Contributions in Political Science Ser.: No. 294). 264p. 1992. 65.00 (*0-313-27730-3*, ZIU/, Greenwood Pr) Greenwood.

Rule, Wilma, jt. ed. see Zimmerman, Joseph F.

Ruled. The Lord Is Near to All. 1997. 7.98 (*0-7824-7905-7*) Antioch Pub Co.

— Praise Him. 1997. 7.98 (*0-7824-7906-5*) Antioch Pub Co.

Ruleh, Ted J., ed. Wisconsin Seasons: Classic Tales of Life Outdoors. (Illus.). 256p. 1998. 22.95 (*0-9653381-5-0*) Cabin Bkshelf.

Ruler, Arnold Van, see Van Ruler, Arnold.

Ruler, John. Worldwide Riding Vacations: A Global Guide to Holidays on Horseback. 2nd ed. (Illus.). 383p. 1999. pap. text 21.95 (*0-9653558-3-7*, Pub. by Compleat Trvllr) Seven Hills Bk.

Ruler, John & Sacks, Arthur. Riding Holidays Worldwide: A Global View. (Illus.). x, 400p. 1998. pap. 21.95 (*0-9653558-2-9*) Compleat Trvllr.

Ruler, John, jt. auth. see Sacks, Arthur.

Ruler, Keith. 3D Graphics File Formats. 480p. (C). 1996. pap. text 39.95 (*0-201-48835-3*) Addison-Wesley.

***Ruley, Angela M.** Blue Ridge Mountaineers: The Tolley Family of Rockbridge County, VA; including those who migrated to Bedford, Botetourt, Alleghany, Augusta & Beyond. LC 99-71788. (Illus.). 456p. 1999. 59.95 (*0-9671723-0-6*) Legacy VA.

— Rockbridge Researcher's Handbook. 182p. 1998. pap. 29.95 (*0-9671723-2-2*) Legacy VA.

***Ruley, Angela M., ed.** Revolutionary Pension Applications: Rockbridge County, VA. 188p. 1998. pap. 20.95 (*0-9671723-1-4*) Legacy VA.

***Ruley, John D.** Palm PCs with Windows CE. (Mastering Ser.). 432p. 2000. pap. 29.99 (*0-7821-2651-0*) Sybex.

Ruley, John D., et al. Networking Windows NT 4.0: Workstation & Server. 3rd ed. LC 96-46445. 688p. 1997. pap. 34.95 (*0-471-17502-1*) Wiley.

R

R

Rulfo, Juan. The Burning Plain & Other Stories. Schade, George D., tr. from SPA. LC 67-25698. (Texas Pan American Ser.). (Illus.). 191p. 1967. pap. 10.95 (*0-292-70132-2*) U of Tex Pr.
— Llano en Llamas. 1999. pap. 10.95 (*0-14-025581-8*, Viking) Viking Penguin.
— El Llano en Llamas. LC 88-190446. (Coleccion Popular Ser.). (SPA.). 1992. pap. 9.99 (*968-16-0207-2*) Fondo.
— El Llano en Llamas. (SPA.). 1989. 5.50 (*0-8288-2574-2*) Fr & Eur.
— Obras (Complete Works) (SPA.). 341p. 1987. 16.99 (*968-16-2174-3*, Pub. by Fondo) Continental Bk.
— Pedro Paramo. (SPA.). pap. 13.95 (*84-376-0418-4*, Pub. by Ediciones Catedra) Continental Bk.
— Pedro Paramo. 1991. pap. 9.99 (*968-16-0502-0*) Fondo.
— Pedro Paramo. (SPA.). 1989. 6.50 (*0-8288-2575-0*) Fr & Eur.
— Pedro Paramo. Paden, Margaret S., tr. from SPA. LC 90-2821. 136p. 1990. pap. 11.00 (*0-8021-3390-8*, Grove) Grove-Atltic.
— Pedro Paramo, el llano en Llamas. (SPA.). pap. 11.95 (*84-322-0474-9*, Pub. by E Seix Barral) Continental Bk.
Rulfo, Juan, et al. Inframundo: El Mexico de Juan Rulfo. Bremer, Juan J., ed. (SPA., Illus.). 160p. 1983. pap. text 18.00 (*0-910061-15-7*, 1501) Ediciones Norte.
Rulhiere, Claude De, see De Rulhiere, Claude.
Rulien, Diane E. & Cardinale, Gary. The Orange County Experience: A Pictorial History of Orange County California. (Illus.). 228p. 1987. pap. 23.95 (*0-932967-07-8*) Pacific Shoreline.
Rulien, Diane E., et al. The Orange County Experience. 2nd ed. (Orange County Centennial Edition Ser.). (Illus.). 250p. 1989. pap. text 27.95 (*0-932967-13-2*) Pacific Shoreline.
— Paws to Remember. (Illus.). 80p. 1998. 25.00 (*0-9669801-0-7*) Chameleon Ent.
— U. S. History & Government, Cornerstone Documents. 360p. (C). 1992. pap. text 31.19 (*1-56226-094-4*) CAT Pub.
Rull, R. N. Simian Viruses. (Virology Monographs: Vol. 2). (Illus.). iv, 124p. 1968. 25.00 (*0-387-80890-6*) Spr-Verlag.
***Rulleau, Jean-Marc.** Baptism of Desire: A Patristic Commentary (What the Fathers Teach) LC 99-35177. 72p. 1999. pap. 5.45 (*0-935952-74-8*) Angelus Pr.
Rulli, Angelo, ed. Musical Boxes & Other Musical Marvels. (Illus.). 500p. 1991. pap. 15.00 (*0-915000-02-4*) Musical Box Soc.
Rulliere, C., ed. Femtosecond Laser Pulses: Principles & Experiments. (Illus.). 300p. 1998. 59.95 (*3-540-63663-3*) Spr-Verlag.
Rullman, Hans P., tr. see Omrcanin, Margaret S.
Rullman, R. R. & Rullman, S. S. The Mother: A Suburban Horror Story. 290p. (Orig.). 1993. pap. text 8.95 (*0-9615938-5-7*) Banner Bks.
Rullman, S. S., jt. auth. see Rullman, R. R.
Rullo, Thomas A., ed. Advances in Computer Programming Management, Vol. 1. LC 81-640183. (Heyden Advances Library in EDP Management). 254p. reprint ed. pap. 78.80 (*0-8357-5151-1*, 203269100080) Bks Demand.
— Advances in Computer Security Management, Vol. 1. LC 81-641060. (Heyden Advances Library in EDP Management). 263p. reprint ed. pap. 81.60 (*0-8357-5152-X*, 203268800080) Bks Demand.
— Advances in Data Base Management, Vol. 1. LC 81-640184. (Heyden Advances Library in EDP Management). 223p. reprint ed. pap. 69.20 (*0-8357-5154-6*, 203268700080) Bks Demand.
— Advances in Data Communications Management, Vol. 1. LC 81-641056. (Heyden Advances Library in EDP Management). 261p. reprint ed. pap. 81.00 (*0-8357-5155-4*, 203269000080) Bks Demand.
— Advances in Data Processing Management, Vol. 1. LC 81-640185. (Heyden Advances Library in EDP Management). (Illus.). 218p. reprint ed. pap. 67.60 (*0-8357-5156-2*, 203268600001) Bks Demand.
— Advances in Distributed Processing Management, Vol. 1. LC 81-641059. (Heyden Advances Library in EDP Management). 217p. reprint ed. pap. 67.30 (*0-8357-5157-0*, 203268900080) Bks Demand.
Rulnick, Mary Jo. Write Well & Sell: How-To Articles. (Blueprint Ser.). 92p. 1998. pap. 9.95 (*1-892356-01-5*) Jam-Packed.
***Rulnick, Mary Jo & Schneider, Judith Burnett.** Write Well & Sell: Self-Publishing Made Simple. 90p. 1999. pap. 9.95 (*1-892356-03-1*) Jam-Packed.
Ruloff, Dieter, jt. auth. see Frei, Daniel.
Rulon, Bart. Artist's Photo Reference: Birds. LC 98-27746. (Artist's Photo Reference Ser.). (Illus.). 144p. 1999. 28.99 (*0-89134-859-X*, North Lght Bks) F & W Pubns Inc.
— Painting Birds Step by Step. LC 95-35786. (Illus.). 144p. 1996. 28.99 (*0-89134-632-5*, North Lght Bks) F & W Pubns Inc.
Rulon, Curt M., jt. auth. see Griggs, Silas.
Rulon, Philip R., et al. Keeping Christmas: The Celebration of an American Holiday. LC 90-43295. (Illus.). viii, 319p. (C). 1990. lib. bdg. 32.50 (*0-208-02278-3*, Archon Bks) Shoe String.
— Letters from the Hill Country: The Correspondence Between Rebekah & Lyndon Baines Johnson. LC 82-19369. 1982. 17.00 (*0-914476-97-1*) Thorp Springs.
Rulon, Philip R., ed. see Richardson, Gladwell.
Rulseh, Ted & Petrie, Chuck, eds. Harvest Moon: An Anthology of Wisconsin Writers. 224p. 1993. 19.95 (*1-883755-00-X*) Lost Riv Pr.
Rulseh, Ted J., ed. Michigan Seasons: Classic Tales of Life Outdoors. LC 97-69590. (Illus.). 246p. 1997. 22.95 (*0-9653381-3-4*) Cabin Bkshelf.
Rulseh, Ted J., ed. see Ellis, Mel.

Rumack, et al. Diagnostic Ultrasound. 2nd ed. LC 97-41915. (Illus.). 1952p. (C). (gr. 13). 1997. text 250.00 (*0-8151-8683-5*, 28974) Mosby Inc.
Rumack, Barry H. Handbook of Mushroom Poisoning. 464p. 1994. boxed set 178.95 (*0-8493-0194-7*) CRC Pr.
Rumack, Carol M., et al. Pocket Atlas of Pediatric Ultrasound. 120p. 1990. pap. text 16.95 (*0-88167-620-9*) Lppncott W & W.
Rumaihi, Muhammad. Beyond Oil: Unity & Development in the Gulf. pap. 9.95 (*0-86356-032-6*, Pub. by Saqi) Intl Spec Bk.
Rumaker, Michael. Gringos & Other Stories: A New Edition. deluxe ed. LC 90-63313. 280p. 1991. reprint ed. 25.00 (*0-933598-27-0*) NC Wesleyan Pr.
— Gringos & Other Stories: A New Edition. LC 90-63313. 280p. 1991. reprint ed. pap. 12.95 (*0-933598-26-2*) NC Wesleyan Pr.
— Robert Duncan in San Francisco. 84p. (Orig.). 1996. pap. 8.95 (*0-912516-13-5*) Grey Fox.
— To Kill a Cardinal. 160p. 1992. text 11.95 (*0-9632962-2-1*) A Mann Kaye.
Rumalshah, Mano. Pakistan. (Focus On Ser.). (Illus.). 32p. (YA). (gr. 7-10). 1991. write for info. (*0-237-60193-1*) EVN1 UK.
***Ruman, Jeannie Madelyn.** As They Walk among Us: An Amazing Look at Nature-Within-Nature. Sanford, Rob, ed. (Illus.). 108p. 2000. pap. 19.95 (*1-57077-970-8*, Writers Direct) Titlewaves.
Rumary, Mark. The Dry Garden: A Practical Guide to Planning & Planting. LC 95-18312. (Wayside Gardens Collection). (Illus.). 128p. 1995. 19.95 (*0-8069-3831-5*) Sterling.
***Rumaty, Renven, et al, eds.** Li Be B, Cosmic Rays & Related X- & Gamma-Rays, Vol. 171. (ASP Conference Series Proceedings). 279p. (C). 1999. text 52.00 (*1-886733-93-7*) Astron Soc Pacific.
Rumawas, F., jt. ed. see Flach, M.
Rumayor, Armando, photos by. Manifesto Photography. (Illus.). 1994. write for info. (*0-614-04252-6*) Focal Point Pr.
Rumbach, John. Friends & Neighbors: A Tribute to the People of Dubois County. Baumann, J. Bruce, ed. (Illus.). 112p. 1995. 26.95 (*1-884850-05-7*) Scripps Howard.
***Rumball, Edwin.** Rare Bibles: An Introduction for Collectors & a Descriptive Checklist. 1999. pap. text 25.00 (*1-57074-387-8*) Greyden Pr.
***Rumball-Petre, Edwin.** Rare Bibles: An Introduction for Collectors & a Descriptive Checklist. 2000. 45.00 (*1-57898-199-9*) Martino Pubng.
Rumbarger, J. H. A Fatigue Life & Reliability Model for Gears. (Technical Papers: Vol. P229.16). (Illus.). 48p. 1972. pap. text 30.00 (*1-55589-283-3*) AGMA.
Rumbarger, J. H., jt. auth. see Shapiro, W.
Rumbarger, John J. Drug & Alcohol Prohibition. (Clio Companion Ser.). 1995. lib. bdg. 55.00 (*0-87436-793-X*) ABC-CLIO.
— Profits, Power, & Prohibition: American Alcohol Reform & the Industrializing of America, 1800-1930. LC 88-1884. (SUNY Series in New Social Studies on Alcohol & Drugs). 272p. 1989. text 24.50 (*0-88706-782-4*) State U NY Pr.
Rumbaugh, Calvin L., et al, eds. Cerebrovascular Disease: Imaging & International Treatment Options. LC 94-27327. (Illus.). 544p. 1995. 225.00 (*0-89640-259-2*) Igaku-Shoin.
Rumbaugh, Duane M., jt. ed. see Velichkovsky, Boris M.
Rumbaugh, James. OMT Insights: Perspectives on Modeling from the Journal of Object-Oriented Programming. LC 96-18006. (SIGS Reference Library: No. 6). 412p. (C). 1996. pap. 44.95 (*0-13-846965-2*) Cambridge U Pr.
— UML Reference Guide. LC 98-33392. 576p. (C). 1998. 54.95 (*0-201-30998-X*) Addison-Wesley.
Rumbaugh, James & Blaha, Stephen. Object Oriented Modeling & Design. 1991. pap. text, student ed. 31.60 (*0-13-629858-3*) P-H.
Rumbaugh, James O., jt. ed. see Ritchey, Joseph D.
Rumbaugh, Jim. Object-Oriented Modeling & Design. 528p. 1990. 69.00 (*0-13-629841-9*) P-H.
Rumbaugh, Margaret G. Conducting Market Research. (Career Learning Ser.). 88p. 1997. pap. 29.95 (*0-940343-83-5*, CMRM) Natl Contract Mgmt.
Rumbaugh, Margaret G., ed. see Bowen, Barbara C. & Reid, Tom.
Rumbaugh, Sue S. Kanzi: The Ape at the Brink of the Human Mind. LC 94-9038. 299p. 1996. pap. 15.95 (*0-471-15959-X*) Wiley.
Rumbaught, Duane M., ed. Gibbon & Siamang: A Series of Volumes on the Lesser Apes, 4 vols., Set. Incl. Vol. 1. Evolution, Ecology, Behavior & Captive Maintenance. 1972. 117.50 (*3-8055-1362-3*); Vol. 2. Anatomy, Dentition, Taxonomy & Molecular Evolution & Behavior. 1973. 117.50 (*3-8055-1341-0*); Vol. 3. Natural History, Social Behavior, Reproduction, Vocalizations, Prehension. 1974. 113.25 (*3-8055-1602-9*); Vol. 4. Suspensory Behavior, Locomotion, & Other Behaviors of Captive Gibbons: Cognition. 1975. 204.50 (*3-8055-1658-4*); (Illus.). 552.25 (*3-8055-2308-4*) S Karger.
Rumbaut, Ruben, jt. auth. see Pedraza, Silvia.
Rumbaut, Ruben D. Esa Palabra. LC 80-70306. (Coleccion Espejo de Paciencia). (SPA.). 63p. (Orig.). 1981. pap. 5.95 (*0-89729-258-8*) Ediciones.
Rumbaut, Ruben G., jt. auth. see Portes, Alejandro.
Rumberger, Russell W. Overeducation in the U. S. Labor Market. LC 80-24648. 148p. 1981. 57.95 (*0-275-90715-5*, C0715, Praeger Pubs) Greenwood.
Rumberger, Russell W. & Levin, Henry M. Computers in Small Business. 50p. (Orig.). 1986. pap. text 6.00 (*0-940791-04-8*) NFIB Found.

Rumberger, Russell W., jt. ed. see Burke, Gerald.
Rumble, Alexander. The Reign of Cnut: The King of England, Denmark & Norway. (Illus.). 352p. 1999. pap. 32.95 (*0-7185-0205-1*) Continuum.
Rumble, Alexander, ed. The Reign of Cnut. LC 94-16870. (Studies in the Early History of Britain). 1994. 46.50 (*0-8386-3605-5*) Fairleigh Dickinson.
Rumble, Alexander R., jt. ed. see Hill, David.
Rumble, Dale. And Then the End Shall Come. 154p. (Orig.). 1991. pap. 9.99 (*1-56043-063-X*) Destiny Image.
— Behold the Harvest. LC 99-166409. 192p. 1998. pap. 10.99 (*1-56043-192-X*, Revival Pr) Destiny Image.
— The Crucible of the Future. 168p. (Orig.). 1989. pap. 10.99 (*0-914903-89-6*) Destiny Image.
— The Diakonate. 240p. (Orig.). 1990. pap. 7.99 (*1-56043-020-6*) Destiny Image.
***Rumble, Dale.** Grafting in the Natural Branches: One New Man: The Body of Messiah. unabridged ed. (Illus.). 75p. 1999. pap. write for info. (*0-9674710-1-X*) Fountain of Life.
Rumble, Donald. Apostolic & Prophetic Foundations: Giving the Lord Back His Church. LC 96-45752. 160p. (Orig.). 1996. pap. 10.00 (*1-883551-53-6*, 53-6) Attic Studio Pub.
Rumble, Greville. The Costs & Economics of Open & Distance Learning. 224p. 1997. pap. 35.00 (*0-7494-1519-3*, Kogan Pg Educ) Stylus Pub VA.
Rumble, J. R. & Smith, F. J. Database Systems in Science & Engineering. (Illus.). 304p. 1990. 109.00 (*0-7503-0048-5*) IOP Pub.
Rumble, J. R., Jr., jt. ed. see Glazman, J. S.
Rumble, L. A Brief Life of Christ. 54p. 1992. reprint ed. pap. 2.00 (*0-89555-096-2*) TAN Bks Pubs.
Rumble, Leslie. The Incredible Creed of the Jehovah Witnesses. 1977. reprint ed. pap. 1.50 (*0-89555-025-3*) TAN Bks Pubs.
Rumble, Leslie & Carty, Charles M. Radio Replies, 3 vols. LC 79-51938. 1979. reprint ed. pap. 42.00 (*0-89555-159-4*) TAN Bks Pubs.
— Radio Replies, 3 vols., 1. LC 79-51938. 1979. reprint ed. pap. write for info. (*0-89555-089-X*) TAN Bks Pubs.
— Radio Replies, 3 vols., 2. LC 79-51938. 1979. reprint ed. pap. write for info. (*0-89555-090-3*) TAN Bks Pubs.
— Radio Replies, 3 vols., 3. LC 79-51938. 1979. reprint ed. pap. write for info. (*0-89555-091-1*) TAN Bks Pubs.
Rumble, Leslie, jt. auth. see Carty, Charles M.
Rumble, P. Barry. Full Moon. LC 94-39517. 14p. (J). 1995. pap. 5.00 (*0-88734-422-4*) Players Pr.
Rumble, Patricia B. The Archer & the Princess: A Comedy Based on a Russian Folk Tale. (Stage Magic Play Ser.). (Illus.). 48p. (Orig.). (J). (gr. 4-10). 1990. pap. 3.50 (*0-88680-334-9*) I E Clark.
— Aunt Sophie's Latkes. 12p. 1995. pap. 5.00 (*0-88734-348-1*) Players Pr.
— Circus Boy. 29p. (Orig.). (J). (gr. 3-8). 1993. pap. 3.00 (*1-57514-110-8*, 1100) Encore Perform Pub.
— Las Fabulas Chisostas de Esopo. Mena, Alicia, tr. (Multicultural Theatre Ser.). Orig. Title: Aesops Funny Fables. (ENG & SPA.). 37p. (Orig.). (J). (gr. k-8). 1994. pap. 3.00 (*1-57514-103-5*, 1132) Encore Perform Pub.
— The Mother Goose Comedy Revue. 30p. (Orig.). (J). (gr. k-6). 1994. pap. 3.00 (*1-57514-222-8*, 1101) Encore Perform Pub.
— The Night the Animals Talked. 36p. (YA). 1992. pap. 3.00 (*1-57514-179-5*, 1105) Encore Perform Pub.
Rumble, Patricia B. & Aesop. Aesop's Funny Fables. 32p. (Orig.). (J). (gr. k-8). 1993. pap. 3.00 (*1-57514-204-X*, 1107) Encore Perform Pub.
Rumble, Patrick & Testa, Bart, eds. Pier Paolo Pasolini: Contemporary Perspectives. LC 95-120658. 258p. 1993. text 50.00 (*0-8020-2966-3*) U of Toronto Pr.
— Pier Paolo Pasolini: Contemporary Perspectives. LC 95-120658. (Major Italian Authors Ser.: No. 1). 256p. 1993. pap. text 17.95 (*0-8020-7737-4*) U of Toronto Pr.
Rumble, Patrick A. Allegories of Contamination: Pier Paolo Pasolini's Trilogy of Life. (Italian Studies). (Illus.). 200p. 1995. text 50.00 (*0-8020-0428-8*); pap. text 17.95 (*0-8020-7219-4*) U of Toronto Pr.
Rumble, Thomas C., ed. The Breton Lays in Middle English. LC 65-11629. (Waynebooks Ser.: No. 25). (Illus.). 300p. 1965. reprint ed. pap. 17.95 (*0-8143-1265-9*) Wayne St U Pr.
Rumble, Wilfrid E., ed. see Austin, John.
Rumbley, Rose-Mary. Unauthorized History of Dallas. (Illus.). 192p. 1991. pap. 14.95 (*0-89015-833-9*) Sunbelt Media.
— What? No Chili? LC 94-39639. (Illus.). 144p. (J). (gr. 5-6). 1994. 14.95 (*0-89015-992-0*, Eakin Pr) Sunbelt Media.
Rumbold. Ethics in Nursing Practice. 3rd ed. LC 98-31648. xi, 275p. 1999. pap. text 24.00 (*0-7020-2312-4*, W B Saunders Co) Harcrt Hlth Sci Grp.
Rumbold, Margaret E. Traducteur Huguenot: Peirre Coste. LC 90-34363. (American University Studies: Romance Languages & Literature: Ser. II, Vol. 140). (Illus.). VIII, 192p. (C). 1991. text 36.95 (*0-8204-1270-8*) P Lang Pubng.
Rumbold, Valerie. Women's Place in Pope's World. (Cambridge Studies in Eighteenth-Century English Literature & Thought: No. 2). (Illus.). 336p. (C). 1989. text 69.95 (*0-521-36308-X*) Cambridge U Pr.
Rumbold, Valerie & Fenlon, Iain, eds. A Short-Title Catalogue of Music Printed Before 1825 in the Fitzwilliam Museum, Cambridge. (Illus.). 190p. (C). 1992. text 95.00 (*0-521-41535-7*) Cambridge U Pr.
Rumbold, Valerie, ed. see Pope, Alexander.
Rumboli, M., jt. auth. see De la Penn, M.
Rumburg, H. Rondel. The Last Earthly Meeting of Lee & Jackson: A Few Days in May 1863. (Illus.). 52p. (Orig.). (C). 1997. pap. 5.00 (*0-9639730-3-7*) Soc Bibl & So Stud.

— Some Southern Documents of the People Called Baptists. 276p. 1995. 24.95 (*0-9639730-1-0*) Soc Bibl & So Stud.
— Stonewall Jackson's Verse. 147p. 1992. 16.95 (*0-9639730-0-2*) Soc Bibl & So Stud.
— The Universal Dominion of Christ: A Study in Psalm 2. 159p. (YA). 1996. 16.95 (*0-9639730-2-9*) Soc Bibl & So Stud.
Rumclt. Fundamental Issues Strategy. 656p. 1994. 45.00 (*0-07-103590-7*) McGraw.
Rumelhart & Martin. Cognitive Science. (Illus.). 430p. 1999. 69.95 (*0-12-601730-1*) Acad Pr.
Rumelhart, David E., et al. Parallel Distributed Processing: Explorations in the Microstructure of Cognition, 2 vols., Set. 1190p. 1987. pap. text 55.00 (*0-262-63112-1*, Bradford Bks) MIT Pr.
— Parallel Distributed Processing: Explorations in the Microstructure of Cognition, Vol. 2: Psychological & Biological Models. Vol. 2. (Illus.). 623p. 1987. pap. text 33.00 (*0-262-63110-5*, Bradford Bks) MIT Pr.
Rumelhart, David E., jt. auth. see McClelland, James L.
Rumelhart, David E., jt. ed. see Chauvin, Yves.
Rumelhart, David E., jt. ed. see Gluck, Mark A.
Rumelt. Fundamental Issues Strategy. 656p. 1995. pap. 24.95 (*0-07-103647-4*) McGraw.
Rumelt, Richard P. Strategy, Structure & Economic Performance. 1986. pap. text 14.95 (*0-07-103265-7*) McGraw.
Rumelt, Richard P., et al, eds. Fundamental Issues in Strategy: A Research Agenda. LC 93-38541. 656p. (C). 1994. 45.00 (*0-87584-343-3*) Harvard Busn.
— Fundamental Issues in Strategy: A Research Agenda. 656p. 1996. pap. 24.95 (*0-87584-645-9*) Harvard Busn.
Rumely, R. S. Capacity Theory on Algebraic Curves. (Lecture Notes in Mathematics Ser.: Vol. 1378). iii, 437p. 1989. 56.95 (*0-387-51410-4*, 3278) Spr-Verlag.
***Rumely, Robert S., et al.** Existence of the Sectional Capacity. LC 00-20861. (Memoirs of the American Mathematical Society Ser.). 2000. write for info. (*0-8218-2058-3*) Am Math.
Rumens, Carol. Best China Sky. 64p. 1996. pap. 16.95 (*1-85224-337-6*, Pub. by Bloodaxe Bks) Dufour.
— A Greening of the Snow Beach: A Readers' & Writers' Guide to the Poetry Scene. 1988. pap. 14.95 (*1-85224-062-8*) Dufour.
— Holding Pattern, 1. LC 99-176212. 128p. 1999. pap. text 16.95 (*0-85640-638-4*) Blackstaff Pr.
— The Miracle Diet. 64p. 1998. pap. 15.95 (*1-85224-418-6*, Pub. by Bloodaxe Bks) Dufour.
— Thinking of Skins: New & Selected Poems. 160p. 1994. pap. 18.95 (*1-85224-280-9*, Pub. by Bloodaxe Bks) Dufour.
Rumens, Carol, intro. New Women Poets. 176p. (Orig.). 1990. pap. 17.95 (*1-85224-145-4*, Pub. by Bloodaxe Bks) Dufour.
Rumens, Carol, ed. see Bartlett, Elizabeth.
Rumer, Boris, ed. Central Asia in Transition: Dilemmas of Political & Economic Development. LC 96-8137. 308p. (C). (gr. 13). 1996. text 81.95 (*1-56324-766-6*) M E Sharpe.
***Rumer, Boris, ed.** Central Asia & the New Global Economy: Critical Problems, Critical Choices. (Illus.). 288p. 2000. 66.95 (*0-7656-0629-1*) M E Sharpe.
Rumer, Boris & Zhukov, Stansislav, eds. Central Asia: The Challenges of Independence. LC 98-15194. 324p. (gr. 13). 1998. text 69.95 (*0-7656-0254-7*) M E Sharpe.
Rumer, Eugene B. The Building Blocks of Russia's Future Military Doctrine. LC 93-42246. 1994. pap. text 15.00 (*0-8330-1483-8*, MR-359-A) Rand Corp.
— The Ideological Crisis in the Russian Military. LC 93-38437. xi, 27p. 1994. pap. 15.00 (*0-8330-1473-0*, MR-335) Rand Corp.
— Russian National Security & Foreign Policy in Transition. LC 94-42678. x, 68p. 1995. pap. text 15.00 (*0-8330-1615-6*, MR-512-AF) Rand Corp.
***Rumer, Patricia & National Council of the Churches of Christ in the United States of America Staff.** Pillars of Peace for the 21st Century: Study Guide. LC 99-24264. 1999. write for info. (*0-377-00329-8*) Friendship Pr.
Rumer, Ralph R. & Ryan, Michael E., eds. Barrier Containment Technologies for Environmental Remediation Applications. LC 95-30532. 170p. 1995. 84.95 (*0-471-13272-1*, Wiley-Interscience) Wiley.
Rumer, Ralph R., jt. ed. see Cotroneo, George V.
Rumer, Thomas. Unearthing the Land: The Story of Ohio's Scioto Marsh. LC 99-38410. (Ohio History & Culture Ser.). (Illus.). 1999. 39.95 (*1-884836-51-8*); pap. 22.95 (*1-884836-52-6*) U Akron Pr.
***Rumerman, Judy A.** NASA Historical Data: NASA Space Applications, Aeronautics & Space Research & Technology, Tracking & Data Acquisition/Support Operations, Commercial Programs & Resources, 1979-1988, Vol. 6. 641p. 2000. boxed set 46.00 (*0-16-050266-7*) USGPO.
Rumery, Kenneth R. Introduction to Musical Design, Vol. I. 480p. (C). 1991. text. write for info. (*0-697-10719-1*) Brown & Benchmark.
— Introduction to Musical Design, Vol. II. 432p. (C). 1992. text. write for info. (*0-697-11648-4*) Brown & Benchmark.
Rumford, Benjamin T. Collected Works of Count Rumford, 5 vols. Brown, Sanborn C., ed. Incl. Vol. 1. Nature of Heat. LC 68-17633. (Illus.). 521p. 1968. 49.95 (*0-674-13951-8*); Vol. 4. Light & Armament. LC 68-17633. (Illus.). 511p. 1970. 42.50 (*0-674-13954-2*); Vol. 5. Public Institutions. LC 68-17633. (Illus.). 524p. 1970. 39.95 (*0-674-13955-0*); LC 68-17633. write for info. (*0-318-53031-7*) HUP.
***Rumford, Chris.** European Cohesion? Contradictions in European Integration. LC 99-52070. 2000. text 68.00 (*0-312-22961-5*) St Martin.

An Asterisk (*) at the beginning of an entry indicates that the title is appearing for the first time.

Rumford, Douglas. Scared to Life. LC 94-29603. 180p. 1994. pap. 9.99 (*1-56476-413-3*, 6-3413, Victor Bks) Chariot Victor.

Rumford, Douglas J. Questions God Asks, Questions Satan Asks. LC 98-6793. 1998. 10.99 (*0-8423-5119-1*) Tyndale Hse.

— Soulshaping: Taking Care of Your Spiritual Life Through Godly Disciplines. LC 96-20351. 462p. 1996. pap. 10.99 (*0-8423-3593-5*) Tyndale Hse.

***Rumford, Douglas J.** What about Heaven & Hell? LC 99-86460. 2000. pap. 5.99 (*0-8423-7405-1*) Tyndale Hse.

— What about Spiritual Warfare? The Bible's Answers to Your Questions about God, Angels, Satan & 2000. pap. 5.99 (*0-8423-7404-3*) Tyndale Hse.

— What about Unanswered Prayer? LC 99-86461. 2000. pap. 5.99 (*0-8423-7403-5*) Tyndale Hse.

Rumford, James. The Cloudmakers. (Illus.). 32p. (J). (ps-4). 1996. 15.95 (*0-395-76505-6*) HM.

— The Island-below-the-Star. LC 97-9568. (Illus.). 32p. (J). (gr. k-3). 1998. 15.00 (*0-395-85159-9*) HM.

***Rumford, James.** Seeker of Knowledge: The Man Who Deciphered Egyptian Hieroglyphs. LC 99-37254. 32p. (J). (gr. k-4). 2000. 15.00 (*0-395-97934-X*) HM.

Rumford, James. When Silver Needles Swam: The Story of Tutu's Quilt. LC 97-76246. (ENG & HAW., Illus.). 30p. (J). (gr. 1-6). 1998. 10.95 (*1-891839-00-4*) Manoa Pr HI.

***Rumgay, Judith.** The Addicted Offender: Developments in Policy & Practice. LC 00-31113. 2000. write for info. (*0-312-23537-2*) St Martin.

Rumgay, Judith & Campling, Jo. Crime, Punishment & the Drinking Offender. LC 98-7076. 1998. text 59.95 (*0-312-21679-3*) St Martin.

Rumi, Jalal Al-Din. Birdsong: Fifty-Three Short Poems by Rumi. Barks, Coleman, tr. & intro. by. 64p. (Orig.). 1993. pap. 9.00 (*0-9618916-7-X*) Maypop.

— Daylight: A Daybook of Spiritual Guidance. (Illus.). 208p. 1990. pap. 16.00 (*0-939660-36-9*) Threshold CA.

— Delicious Laughter: Rambunctious Teaching Stories from the Mathnawi of Jelaluddin Rumi. Barks, Coleman, tr. 129p. 1990. 7.50 (*0-9618916-1-0*) Maypop.

— Feeling the Shoulder of the Lion: Poems & Teaching Stories from the Mathnawi. Barks, Coleman, tr. LC 91-4749. 104p. 1991. pap. 10.00 (*0-939660-37-7*) Threshold CA.

***Rumi, Jalal Al-Din.** Feeling the Shoulder of the Lion: Selected Poetry & Teaching Stories of Rumi. LC 99-42871. 120p. 2000. pap. 22.00 (*1-57062-522-0*, Pub. by Shambhala Pubns) Random.

— Kalilah & Dimnah Stories for Young Adults. (Illus.). 2000. pap. text 12.95 (*1-930637-07-1*) ABC Intl Grp.

Rumi, Jalal Al-Din. Like This. Barks, Coleman, tr. 130p. 1990. pap. 7.50 (*0-9618916-2-9*) Maypop.

***Rumi, Jalal Al-Din.** Love Is a Stranger: Selected Lyric Poetry of Jalaluddin Rumi. Helminski, Kabir, tr. LC 99-49893. 96p. 2000. pap. 10.95 (*1-57062-527-1*, Pub. by Shambhala Pubns) Random.

Rumi, Jalal Al-Din. Love Is a Stranger: Selected Lyric Poetry of Jalaluddin Rumi. Helminski, Kabir E., tr. & intro. by. 96p. 1993. pap. 10.00 (*0-939660-32-6*) Threshold CA.

— Masnavi Mawlana Rumi. Nicholson, Reynold A., tr. 1200p. 1996. 165.00 (*0-614-21309-6*, 758) Kazi Pubns.

— Mystical Poems of Rumi. Arberry, Arthur J., tr. from PER. LC 68-29935. vi, 208p. 1974. pap. 13.00 (*0-226-73151-0*, P584) U Ch Pr.

— Mystical Poems of Rumi, Vol. 1. Arberry, Arthur J., tr. 202p. 1996. pap. 21.90 (*0-614-21320-7*, 877) Kazi Pubns.

— Mystical Poems of Rumi, Vol. 2. Arberry, A. J., tr. 202p. 1996. pap. 10.95 (*0-614-21321-5*, 877) Kazi Pubns.

— One-Handed Basket Weaving: Poems on the Theme of Work from the Mathnawi. Barks, Coleman, tr. from PER. & intro. by. 136p. (C). 1992. pap. 9.00 (*0-9618916-3-7*) Maypop.

— Open Secret. Moyne, John & Barks, Coleman, trs. from ENG. LC 99-31399. 1999. pap. 10.95 (*1-57062-529-8*, Pub. by Shambhala Pubns) Random.

— Rumi: Divan-i Kebir. Ergin, Nevit O., tr. 418p. 1996. pap. 25.00 (*0-614-21336-3*, 1376) Kazi Pubns.

— Rumi Daylight: A Daybook of Spiritual Guidance. Helminski, Camille & Helminski, Kabir, trs. 224p. 1996. 19.00 (*0-614-21335-5*, 1091) Kazi Pubns.

— Rumi for Children Vol. I: Wisdom of the Selfless: Classics from the Mathnawi of Maulana Jalauddin Rumi. rev. ed. (Illus.). 44p. (YA). (gr. 5-8). 1999. text 9.00 (*1-56316-306-3*) Iqra Intl Ed Fdtn.

***Rumi, Jalal Al-Din.** Rumi Stories for Young Adults. (Illus.). (YA). 2000. pap. text 12.95 (*1-930637-04-7*) ABC Intl Grp.

— Ruminations. Partovi, Zahra, tr. 64p. 1998. per. 15.00 (*0-935581-00-6*) Vincent Fitzgerald & Co.

Rumi, Jalal Al-Din. Say I Am You: Poetry Interspersed with Stories of Rumi & Shams. Barks, Coleman & Moyne, John, trs. 128p. (Orig.). 1994. pap. 12.00 (*1-884237-00-2*) Maypop.

— Teachings of Rumi. Whinfield, E. H., tr. 330p. 1996. 39.95 (*0-614-21370-3*, 1223) Kazi Pubns.

— Teachings of Rumi: The Masnaui. Whinfield, E. H., tr. 330p. 1994. pap. 24.95 (*0-86304-067-5*, Pub. by Octagon Pr) ISHK.

— These Branching Moments: Forty Odes. Barks, Coleman & Moyne, John, trs. from PER. LC 87-36429. 52p. (Orig.). 1988. pap. 10.00 (*0-914278-50-9*) Copper Beech.

— We Are Three. Barks, Coleman, tr. 132p. 1987. pap. 7.50 (*0-9618916-0-2*) Maypop.

— When Grapes Turn to Wine. Bly, Robert, tr. (PER., Illus.). 24p. 1986. reprint ed. pap. 4.00 (*0-938756-16-8*) Yellow Moon.

Rumi, Julie. Coming Together: Integrating Math & Language in a Sheltered Approach, Bk. 1. 160p. 1994. pap. text 19.53 (*0-13-210451-2*) P-H.

— Coming Together: Integrating Math & Language in a Sheltered Approach, Bk. 2. 160p. 1994. pap. text 19.53 (*0-13-146606-2*) P-H.

Rumi, Melvana. Crazy As We Are. Ergin, Nevit O., tr. from PER. LC 92-54952. 88p. (Orig.). 1992. pap. 9.95 (*0-934252-30-0*, Pub. by Hohm Pr) SCB Distributors.

— Divan - I Kebir, Vol. 4. 418p. 1997. pap. text 19.95 (*1-887991-02-6*) Echo Pubns CA.

— Mevlana Celaleddin Rumi: Divan-I Kebir. 418p. 1997. pap. text 19.95 (*1-887991-01-8*) Echo Pubns CA.

— Mevlana Celaleddin Rumi: Divan-I Kebir, Meter 2. 418p. 1996. pap. text 19.95 (*1-887991-00-X*) Echo Pubns CA.

— Open Secret: Versions of Rumi. Barks, Coleman, tr. LC 83-50052. 96p. 1984. reprint ed. pap. 11.00 (*0-939660-06-7*) Threshold CA.

— Unseen Rain: Quatrains of Rumi. Moyne, John & Barks, Coleman, trs. from PER. LC 86-50782. 96p. 1986. 15.00 (*0-939660-17-2*); pap. 10.00 (*0-939660-16-4*) Threshold CA.

Rumiantsev, A., jt. ed. see Collet's Holdings, Ltd. Staff.

Rumiko Takahashi. Lum: Uruseiyatsura, Graphic Novel, Vol. 1. Seiji Horibuchi, ed. Satoru Fujii & Jones, Gerard, trs. from JPN. (Illus.). 194p. 1990. pap. 14.95 (*0-929279-64-6*) Viz Commns Inc.

— Lum: Uruseiyatsura, Graphic Novel, Vol. 2. Seiji Horibuchi, ed. Satoru Fujii & Jones, Gerard, trs. from JPN. (Illus.). 214p. 1990. pap. 14.95 (*0-929279-63-8*) Viz Commns Inc.

— Rumic World. Seiji Horibuchi, ed. Satoru Fujii, tr. from JPN. (Illus.). 150p. (Orig.). pap. 14.95 (*0-929279-83-2*) Viz Commns Inc.

Ruminer, Cliff. Blazing Bellyboats & Other Angling Misadventures. 1993. 17.95 (*1-879034-06-9*) MS River Pub.

Rumler, John & McGarry, Thomas. The Insiders' Guide to Portland. (Insiders' Guide Travel Ser.). (Illus.). 328p. 1999. pap. 15.95 (*1-57380-078-3*, The Insiders Guide) Falcon Pub Inc.

***Rumley, Dennis.** The Geopolitics of Australia's Regional Relations. LC 99-41413. (Geojournal Library). 1999. write for info. (*0-7923-5916-X*) Kluwer Academic.

Rumley, Dennis, et al, eds. Global Geopolitical Change & the Asia Pacific: A Regional Perspective. 360p. 1996. text 78.95 (*1-85972-269-5*, Pub. by Avebry) Ashgate Pub Co.

Rumley, Hilary, jt. auth. see McNair, William.

***Rumley, Katrina.** Denise Green, No. 6. (Illus.). 60p. 1998. text 29.50 (*90-5704-151-0*) Gordon & Breach.

Rumley, Mildred M., ed. see Day, Jean.

Rumman, Ali, jt. auth. see Mansour, Awad.

Rumman, Wadi S. Statically Indeterminate Structures. LC 90-22897. 504p. 1991. 140.00 (*0-471-09345-9*) Wiley.

Rumme, Daigaku, tr. see Harada, Sekkei.

***Rummel, Erika.** The Confessionalization of Humanism in Reformation Germany. LC 99-42481. 224p. 2000. write for info. (*0-19-513712-4*) OUP.

Rummel, Erika. Erasmus & His Catholic Critics, 2 vols., Vols. 1 & 2. (Bibliotheca Humanistica & Reformatorica Ser.). 277p. 1989. 150.00 (*90-6004-401-0*, Pub. by B De Graaf) Coronet Bks.

— Erasmus' Annotations on the New Testament: From Philologist to Theologian. (Erasmus Studies). 246p. 1986. text 40.00 (*0-8020-5683-0*) U of Toronto Pr.

— Erasmus as a Translator of the Classics. (Erasmus Studies: No. 7). 191p. 1985. pap. text 35.00 (*0-8020-5653-9*) U of Toronto Pr.

— The Humanist-Scholastic Debate in the Renaissance & Reformation. LC 94-34983. (Historical Studies: No. 120). 264p. 1995. 45.00 (*0-674-42250-3*, RUMHUM) HUP.

— Humanist-Scholastic Debate in the Renaissance & Reformation. 264p. 1998. pap. text 18.95 (*0-674-42251-1*) HUP.

***Rummel, Erika.** Jimenez de Cisneros: On the Threshold of Spain's Golden Age. LC 99-54901. (Medieval & Renaissance Texts & Studies: Vol. 212). (Illus.). 160p. 1999. 22.00 (*0-86698-254-X*) MRTS.

Rummel, Erika, ed. Editing Texts from the Age of Erasmus. (Conference on Editorial Problems Ser.). (Illus.). 128p. 1996. text 35.00 (*0-8020-0797-X*) U of Toronto Pr.

— Erasmus on Women. 272p. 1996. pap. text 19.95 (*0-8020-7808-7*) U of Toronto Pr.

— The Erasmus Reader. 432p. 1995. pap. text 19.95 (*0-8020-6806-5*) U of Toronto Pr.

Rummel, Erika, ed. from GER. Scheming Papists & Lutheran Fools: Five Reformation Satires. LC 92-34382. 122p. (C). 1993. 25.00 (*0-8232-1482-6*); pap. 15.00 (*0-8232-1483-4*) Fordham.

Rummel, Erika, ed. see Erasmus, Desiderius.

Rummel, Erika, ed. & tr. see Erasmus, Desiderius.

***Rummel, George A., 3rd.** Cavalry on the Roads to Gettysburg: Kilpatrick at Hanover & Hunterstown. LC 99-45935. (Illus.). 562p. 2000. 40.00 (*1-57249-174-4*) White Mane Pub.

Rummel, George A., III. 72 Days at Gettysburg: Organization of the 10th Regiment, New York Volunteer Cavalry. LC 97-18120. 254p. 1998. 30.00 (*1-57249-086-1*) White Mane Pub.

Rummel, J. D., et al, eds. Space & Its Exploration. (Space Biology & Medicine Ser.: Vol. 1). 338p. 1993. 99.95 (*1-56347-061-6*, 61-6) AIAA.

***Rummel, Jack.** Frida Kahlo: A Spiritual Biography. (Lives & Legacies Ser.). (Illus.). 192p. 2000. 19.95 (*0-8245-2353-9*, Pub. by Crossroad NY) Natl Bk Netwk.

Rummel, Jack. Langston Hughes: Poet. Huggins, Nathan I., ed. LC 87-10920. (Black Americans of Achievement Ser.). (Illus.). 111p. (YA). (gr. 5 up). 1987. lib. bdg. 19.95 (*1-55546-595-1*) Chelsea Hse.

— Langston Hughes: Poet. Huggins, Nathan I., ed. LC 87-10920. (Black Americans of Achievement Ser.). (Illus.). 111p. (YA). (gr. 5 up). 1989. pap. 8.95 (*0-7910-0201-2*) Chelsea Hse.

— Malcolm X: Biography of Black Civil Rights Leader. (Black American Ser.). (Illus.). 192p. (YA). 1990. mass mkt. 3.95 (*0-87067-554-0*, Melrose Sq) Holloway.

— Malcolm X: Militant Black Leader. Huggins, Nathan I., ed. (Black Americans of Achievement Ser.). (Illus.). 124p. (YA). (gr. 5 up). 1989. lib. bdg. 19.95 (*1-55546-600-1*) Chelsea Hse.

— Malcolm X: Militant Black Leader. Huggins, Nathan I., ed. (Black Americans of Achievement Ser.). (Illus.). 124p. (YA). (gr. 5 up). 1989. pap. 9.95 (*0-7910-0227-5*) Chelsea Hse.

— Mexico: Major World Nations. (Major World Nations Ser.). (Illus.). 144p. (YA). (gr. 5 up). 1999. lib. bdg. 19.95 (*0-7910-4763-5*) Chelsea Hse.

— Muhammad Ali: Heavyweight Champion. Huggins, Nathan I., ed. (Black Americans of Achievement Ser.). (Illus.). 124p. (Orig.). (YA). (gr. 5 up). 1988. lib. bdg. 19.95 (*1-55546-569-2*) Chelsea Hse.

— Muhammad Ali: Heavyweight Champion. Huggins, Nathan I., ed. (Black Americans of Achievement Ser.). (Illus.). 124p. (Orig.). (YA). (gr. 5 up). 1989. pap. 8.95 (*0-7910-0210-1*) Chelsea Hse.

— Robert Oppenheimer: Dark Prince. annot. ed. (Makers of Modern Science Ser.). (Illus.). 144p. (YA). (gr. 7-12). 1992. lib. bdg. 19.95 (*0-8160-2598-3*) Facts on File.

Rummel, K. G. & Dougherty, J. J. A Criterion for On-Condition Transmissions & Its Application to the CH-47C. (Technical Papers: Vol. P109.28). (Illus.). 31p. 1972. pap. text 30.00 (*1-55589-198-5*) AGMA.

Rummel, Mary. God's Love for Happiness: A Return to Family Values. LC 92-91032. (Illus.). 64p. (Orig.). (J). (gr. k up). 1992. pap. 9.95 (*0-9635091-0-1*) Olive Brnch.

Rummel, Mary K. This Body She's Entered: A Collection of Poems. 67p. 1990. pap. 6.00 (*0-89823-115-9*) New Rivers Pr.

Rummel, Mary K. & Quintero, Elizabeth P. Teachers' Reading/Teachers' Lives. LC 96-36918. (SUNY Series, Urban Voices, Urban Visions). 225p. (C). 1997. text 57.50 (*0-7914-3485-0*) State U NY Pr.

Rummel, Mary K., et al. Teachers' Reading/Teachers' Lives. LC 96-36918. (SUNY Series, Urban Voices, Urban Visions). 225p. (C). 1997. pap. text 18.95 (*0-7914-3486-9*) State U NY Pr.

Rummel, Mary K., jt. auth. see Quintero, Elizabeth.

Rummel, Merle, jt. auth. see Henning, Elma.

Rummel, R. Death by Government. 510p. 1997. pap. text 29.95 (*1-56000-927-6*) Transaction Pubs.

Rummel, R. J. China's Bloody Century: Genocide & Mass Murder since 1900. 196p. (C). 1991. 44.95 (*0-88738-417-X*) Transaction Pubs.

— The Conflict Helix: Principles & Practices of Interpersonal, Social & International Conflict & Cooperation. 297p. (C). 1990. 44.95 (*0-88738-389-0*) Transaction Pubs.

— Death by Government: Genocide & Mass Murder since 1900. LC 93-21279. 510p. (C). 1994. 54.95 (*1-56000-145-3*) Transaction Pubs.

— Democide: Nazi Genocide & Mass Murder. 150p. (C). 1991. text 39.95 (*1-56000-004-X*) Transaction Pubs.

— Lethal Politics: Soviet Genocide & Mass Murder since 1917. 172p. (C). 1990. 39.95 (*0-88738-333-5*) Transaction Pubs.

— Lethal Politics: Soviet Genocide & Mass Murder since 1917. 172p. 1996. pap. text 24.95 (*1-56000-887-3*) Transaction Pubs.

— Power Kills: Democracy As a Method of Nonviolence. LC 96-45040. 187p. 1997. text 32.95 (*1-56000-297-2*) Transaction Pubs.

Rummel, Reiner, et al, eds. Gravity, Gradiometry & Gravimetry. (International Association of Geodesy Symposia Ser.: Vol. 103). x, 181p. 1990. 79.95 (*0-387-97267-6*) Spr-Verlag.

Rummel, Reiner & Sanso, F., eds. Satellite Altimetry in Geodesy & Oceanography. LC 93-17952. (Lecture Notes in Earth Sciences Ser.: Vol. 50). 1993. 118.95 (*0-387-56818-2*) Spr-Verlag.

Rummel, Reiner, jt. ed. see Sanso, F.

Rummel, Rudolph J. Applied Factor Analysis. 617p. 1970. pap. 32.95 (*0-8101-0824-0*) Northwestern U Pr.

— The Dimensionality of Nations Project: Attributes of Nations & Behavior of Nation Dyads, 1950-1965. LC 75-40620. 1975. write for info. (*0-89138-121-X*) ICPSR.

***Rummel, Rudolph J.** Statistics of Democide: Genocide & Mass Murder since 1900. 544p. 1999. 52.95 (*3-8258-4010-7*, Pub. by CE24) Transaction Pubs.

Rummel, Rudolph J. & Tanter, Raymond. Dimensions of Conflict Behavior Within & Between Nations, 1955-1960. 1974. write for info. (*0-89138-072-8*) ICPSR.

Rummel, Ward D. & Matzkanin, George A. Nondestructive Evaluation (NDE) Capabilities Data Book. (Illus.). iii, 338p. 1996. 100.00 (*1-890596-03-5*) TX Res Inst.

Rummell, Mary Kay. The Long Journey into North, Vol. 65. (Juniper Books Ser.). 78p. 1998. pap. 8.50 (*1-55780-153-3*) Juniper Pr ME.

Rummery, Gerard, ed. see Pungier, Jean.

Rummler & Odiorne, George S. Training & Development: A Guide for Professionals. 472p. 1988. 55.00 (*0-685-67146-1*, 5287) CCH INC.

Rummler, Geary A. & Brache, Alan P. Improving Performance: How to Manage the White Space on the Organization Chart. LC 89-43299. (Management Ser.). 247p. 1990. text 32.95 (*1-55542-214-4*) Jossey-Bass.

— Improving Performance: How to Manage the White Space on the Organization Chart. 2nd ed. LC 94-48105. (Management Ser.). 221p. 1995. text 36.95 (*0-7879-0090-7*) Jossey-Bass.

Rummo, Paul-Eerik. September Sun. Barkan, Stanley H., ed. Poom, Ritva, tr. (Review Chapbook Ser.: No. 16: Estonian Poetry 1).Tr. of Estonian & Eng.. 16p. 1989. reprint ed. 15.00 (*0-89304-822-4*, CCC143); reprint ed. pap. 5.00 (*0-89304-815-1*); reprint ed. pap. 5.00 (*0-89304-824-0*) Cross-Cultrl NY.

— September Sun: Mini. Barkan, Stanley H., ed. Poom, Ritva, tr. (Review Chapbook Ser.: No. 16: Estonian Poetry 1).Tr. of Estonian & Eng.. 16p. 1989. reprint ed. 15.00 (*0-89304-823-2*) Cross-Cultrl NY.

Rummonds, Richard-Gabriel. Printing on the Iron Handpress. LC 97-26661. 1997. pap. 49.95 (*1-884718-40-X*) Oak Knoll.

Rumney, Avis. Dying to Please: Anorexia Nervosa & Its Cure. LC 83-9443. 128p. (Orig.). 1983. pap. 25.00 (*0-89950-083-8*) McFarland & Co.

Rumney, Donna. My Picture Book about Me. (Illus.). 20p. (J). (ps). 1988. write for info. (*0-318-64233-6*) My Picture Bks.

Rumney, Jay & Murphy, Joseph P. Probation & Social Adjustment. LC 68-28593. 285p. 1968. reprint ed. lib. bdg. 75.00 (*0-8371-0208-1*, RUPS, Greenwood Pr) Greenwood.

Rumney, Laurence & Altman, Jack. Peggy Guggenheim: A Collector's Album. (Illus.). 176p. 1996. 45.00 (*2-08-013610-0*, Pub. by Flammarion) Abbeville Pr.

Rumohr, Karl F. Von, see Von Rumohr, Karl F.

Rumold, Rainer, ed. see Jolas, Eugene.

Rumor, M., et al, eds. Geographical Information: From Research to Application Through Cooperation. LC 96-7571. 1347p. (YA). (gr. 12). 1996. pap. 158.00 (*90-5199-268-8*, 268-8) IOS Press.

Rump, Ariane, tr. see Wang, Pi.

Rump, Eric S., ed. & intro. see Sheridan, Richard Brinsley.

Rump, Gabriele, jt. ed. see Roth, Lutz.

Rump, Gerhard, tr. see Poling, Clark V.

Rump, Gerhard C. Pferde, und Jagdbilder in der Englischen Kunst. (GER., Illus.). 396p. 1983. write for info. (*3-487-07425-7*) G Olms Pubs.

***Rump, Hans H.** Examination of Water, Waste Water & Soil. 236p. 2000. pap., lab manual ed. 55.00 (*3-527-29825-8*) Wiley.

Rump, Martin. Vergleichende Untersuchungen Extensiver und Intensiver Weidebetriebe Mit Rindern und Schafen Aus Grunlandwirtschaftlicher und Okologischer Sicht An Acht Standorten. LC 94-5089. (GER.). 312p. 1994. pap. 99.95 (*0-7734-4048-8*) E Mellen.

Rump, Nan. Puppets & Masks: Stagecraft & Storytelling. LC 94-73962. (Illus.). 192p. (J). (gr. k-6). 1995. spiral bd. 20.75 (*0-87192-298-3*) Davis Mass.

Rump, Paul C. State of the Environment Reporting: Source Book of Methods & Approaches. (Environment Information & Assessment Technical Report Ser.: No. 1). 144p. 20.00 (*92-807-1583-6*) UN.

Rumpe, Bernhard, jt. ed. see France, R.

Rumpel, Johannes. Lexicon Pindaricum. 498p. 1961. reprint ed. write for info. (*0-318-71017-X*) G Olms Pubs.

— Lexicon Theocriteum. 319p. 1961. reprint ed. write for info. (*0-318-72072-8*) G Olms Pubs.

— Lexicon Theocriteum. 319p. 1973. reprint ed. write for info. (*0-318-71018-8*) G Olms Pubs.

Rumpf, Dorothea. Bildung und Religion: Prinzipienwissenschaftliche und Schulpadagogische Untersuchungen Zu Ihrem Korrelativen Zusammenhang. 184p. 1997. write for info. (*3-487-10461-X*) G Olms Pubs.

Rumpf, Eva A., jt. auth. see Grottkau, Beverly J.

Rumpf, Georg E. & Beekman, E. M. The Ambonese Curiosity Cabinet. LC 98-40046. (Illus.). 704p. 1999. 45.00 (*0-300-07534-0*) Yale U Pr.

Rumpf, Howard A. Corporate Liquidations for the Lawyer & Accountant. 5th ed. LC 82-5298. 256p. 1982. text 39.50 (*0-13-174383-X*, Busn) P-H.

Rumph, T. W. Diligence, a Key to Survival & Success: Lessons from Proverbial Pests. 1996. pap. text 3.95 (*1-885342-28-4*) Creative Ways.

Rumphius. The Poison Tree: Selected Writings of Rumphius on the Natural History of the Indies. Beekman, E. M., tr. from DUT. LC 81-7605. (Library of the Indies). (Illus.). 272p. 1981. lib. bdg. 32.50 (*0-87023-329-7*) U of Mass Pr.

***Rumple, Jethro.** History of Rowan County, North Carolina. (Illus.). 428p. 1999. pap. 31.00 (*0-7884-1203-5*, R856) Heritage Bk.

— History of Rowan County, North Carolina. 434p. 2000. reprint ed. 46.50 (*0-7404-0047-9*) Higginson Bk Co.

Rumreich, Mark. Car Stereo Cookbook: How to Design, Choose & Install Car Stereo Systems. LC 98-26979. 320p. 1998. pap. 24.95 (*0-07-058083-9*) McGraw.

Rumrich, John P. Matter of Glory: A New Preface to "Paradise Lost" LC 87-40158. 220p. 1987. reprint ed. pap. 68.20 (*0-608-00911-3*, 206170500010) Bks Demand.

— Milton Unbound: Controversy & Reinterpretation. (Illus.). 204p. (C). 1996. text 54.95 (*0-521-55173-0*) Cambridge U Pr.

Rumrill, Alan F. J. A. French's Cheshire County. LC 98-87446. (Images of America Ser.). 128p. 1998. pap. 18.99 (*0-7385-0015-1*) Arcadia Publng.

— Keene. (Images of America Ser.). 1995. pap. 16.99 (*0-7524-0210-2*) Arcadia Publng.

Rumrill, Phillip D., Jr. Employment Issues & Multiple Sclerosis. LC 96-22536. (Illus.). 180p. (Orig.). 1996. pap. 29.95 (*1-888799-03-X*) Demos Medical.

Rumrill, Phillip D., Jr., jt. auth. see Bellini, James L.

Rumsby, G. & Farrow, S., eds. Molecular Endocrinology: Genetic Analysis of Hormones & Their Receptors. (Human Molecular Genetics Ser.). (Illus.). 300p. 1997. 130.00 (*1-85996-235-1*, Pub. by Bios Sci) Bks Intl VA.

R

*Rumsby, Gill. Molecular Endocrinology: Genetic Analysis of Hormones & Their Receptors. (Illus.). 264p. 1999. 105.00 (0-12-220440-9) Acad Pr.
Rumscheidt. Revelation & Theology. 1996. 37.95 (0-521-08365-6, Pub. by T & T Clark) Bks Intl VA.
Rumscheidt, Barbara, tr. see Schotroff, Luise, et al.
Rumscheidt, Barbara, tr. see Schottroff, Luise.
Rumscheidt, Barbara, tr. see Soelle, Dorothee.
Rumscheidt, H. Martin. Karl Barth in Review: Posthumous Works Introduced & Assessed. LC 81-5881. (Pittsburgh Theological Monographs: No. 30). xxviii, 118p. (Orig.). 1981. pap. 10.00 (0-915138-45-X) Pickwick.
Rumscheidt, H. Martin, ed. The Way of Theology in Karl Barth: Essays & Comments. LC 86-15069. (Princeton Theological Monographs: No. 8). 1986. pap. 12.00 (0-915138-61-1) Pickwick.
Rumscheidt, H. Martin & De Gruchy, John, eds. Adolf Von Harnach: Liberal Theology at Its Height. (Making of Modern Theology). 352p. 1995. pap. 19.95 (0-00-599130-7, Pub. by T & T Clark) Bks Intl VA.
Rumscheidt, H. Martin, tr. see Bonhoeffer, Dietrich.
Rumscheidt, Martin, tr. see Schotroff, Luise, et al.
Rumscheidt, Martin, tr. see Schottroff, Luise.
Rumscheidt, Martin, tr. see Soelle, Dorothee.
Rumscheidt, Martin, tr. see Zellweger-Barth, Max.
Rumsewicz, Michael, jt. ed. see Everitt, David.
Rumsey, Alan, jt. auth. see Merlan, Francesca C.
*Rumsey, Andrew. Homing In. 44p. 1998. reprint ed. pap. 7.99 (1-900507-72-2, Pub. by Solway) OM Literature.
Rumsey, Anne, ed. see Hemley, Robin.
Rumsey, Barbara M., jt. auth. see Martin, Jane D.
Rumsey, Dusty. Gifts I Almost Got You: One Hundred One Great Gifts & Perfect Excuses Why You Didn't Get Them. LC 92-80468. (Illus.). 115p. (Orig.). 1992. pap. 7.95 (0-929957-06-7, Push-Pull Pr) JSA Pubns.
— UnCivil War. (Illus.). 64p. (Orig.). 1992. pap. 8.95 (0-941711-19-6) Wyrick & Co.
— You Know You're an Old Fart When: Recognizing the Tell-Tale Signs of Old Age. Carle, Cliff, ed. 1993. pap. 4.95 (0-918259-52-5) CCC Pubns.
Rumsey, Francis. The Audio Workstation Handbook. LC 96-174205. (Illus.). 286p. 1996. pap. text 44.95 (0-240-51450-5, Focal) Buttrwrth-Heinemann.
— MIDI Systems & Control. 2nd expanded ed. LC 94-191382. 256p. 2000. pap. text 42.95 (0-240-51370-3, Focal) Buttrwrth-Heinemann.
— Sound & Recording: An Introduction. 3rd ed. LC 97-179681. (Illus.). 384p. 2000. pap. text 39.95 (0-240-51487-4) Buttrwrth-Heinemann.
— Stereo Sound for Television. LC 89-35568. (Illus.). 111p. reprint ed. pap. 34.50 (0-608-06244-8, 206657300008) Bks Demand.
Rumsey, Francis & Watkinson, John. The Digital Interface Handbook. 2nd ed. (Illus.). 288p. 1995. pap. 49.95 (0-240-51396-7, Focal) Buttrwrth-Heinemann.
Rumsey, H. St. John, ed. see Aikin, W. A.
Rumsey, Henry W. Essays on State Medicine. Rosenkrantz, Barbara G., ed. LC 76-40641. (Public Health in America Ser.). 1977. reprint ed. lib. bdg. 35.95 (0-405-09829-4) Ayer.
Rumsey, Jill. Victorian Relief Moulded Jugs. (Illus.). 48p. 1987. pap. 12.95 (0-903685-20-5, Pub. by R Dennis) Antique Collect.
Rumsey, Judith, jt. ed. see Ernst, Monique.
Rumsey, Judith M., jt. ed. see Lyon, G. Reid.
Rumsey, Kimberly A. & Rieger, Paula T. Biological Response Modifiers: A Self-Instruction Manual for Health Professionals. LC 92-81530. 134p. 1992. 39.95 (0-944496-30-X) Precept Pr.
Rumsey, Michael G., et al, eds. Personnel Selection & Classification. 504p. 1994. text 49.95 (0-8058-1644-5) L Erlbaum Assocs.
Rumsey, Monica S., ed. see Brownell, Charles E., et al.
Rumsey, N., jt. auth. see Bull, R.
Rumsey, Peter L. Acts of God & the People, 1620-1730. LC 86-19292. (Studies in Religion: No. 2). 181p. reprint ed. pap. 56.20 (0-8357-1761-5, 207052100097) Bks Demand.
*Rumsey, Tessa. Assembling the Shepherd. LC 99-31497. (Contemporary Poetry Ser.). 80p. 1999. pap. 15.95 (0-8203-2168-0) U of Ga Pr.
Rumsey, Theron S., jt. ed. see Steffens, George L.
Rumsey, Thomas R. Men & Women of the Renaissance & Reformation, 1300-1600. 487p. (Orig.). (gr. 9-12). 1981. pap. text 15.95 (0-88334-145-X) Longman.
Rumsey, William, jt. ed. see Hutchings, Noel.
Rumsheidt, Barbara. No Room for Grace: Pastoral Theology & Dehumanization in the Global Economy. LC 98-28236. 152p. 1998. pap. 18.00 (0-8028-4547-9) Eerdmans.
Rumwell, Claudia & McPharlin, Michalene. Vascular Technology: An Illustrated Review. LC 99-86818. (Illus.). 322p. 2000. pap. text 64.95 (0-941022-45-5, 11026) Davies Pubng.
*Rumwell, Claudia & McPharlin, Michalene, eds. Vascular Laboratory Policies & Procedures Manual-Windows 95, 98, NT. 1998. ring bd. 795.00 incl. disk (0-941022-49-8) Davies Pubng.
Rumwell, Claudia B. Educational Slide Graphics for the Vascular Laboratory. 20p. 1988. ring bd. 115.00 (0-941022-13-7) Davies Pubng.
Rumwell, Claudia B., ed. Vascular Laboratory Operations Manual: A Guide to Survival. 2nd rev. ed. LC 92-48990. (Illus.). 350p. 1997. ring bd. 295.00 (0-941022-24-2) Davies Pubng.
Rumwell, Claudia B. & McPharlin, Michalene. Vascular Technology: An Illustrated Review for the Registry Exam. (Illus.). 267p. 1995. pap. text 59.95 (0-941022-43-9) Davies Pubng.
Rumwell, Claudia B. & McPharlin, Michalene, eds. Vascular Laboratory Policies & Procedures Manual-MSR 1.1. 1995. ring bd. 795.00 incl. disk (0-941022-41-2) Davies Pubng.
— Vascular Laboratory Policies & Procedures Manual-Windows 2.1.1. 1995. ring bd. 795.00 incl. disk (0-941022-42-0) Davies Pubng.
Rumyantsev, A. M., et al. Soviet Economic Reform: Progress & Problems. 247p. 1975. 22.95 (0-8464-0867-8) Beekman Pubs.
Rumyantsev, P. I., jt. auth. see Stanislavski, Constantin.
Rumyantsev, P. P. Growth & Hyperplasia of Cardiac Muscle Cells, 3. (Soviet Medical Reviews Supplement Ser.). 376p. 1991. text 283.00 (3-7186-4958-6, Harwood Acad Pubs) Gordon & Breach.
Rumyantsev, V. G., jt. auth. see Ivaschenko, A. V.
Rumyantsev, V. V. & Karapatyan, A. V., eds. Modern Methods of Analytical Mechanics & Their Applications. (CISM International Centre for Mechanical Sciences Ser.: No. 387). (Illus.). vii, 344p. 1998. pap. 78.95 (3-211-83138-X) Spr-Verlag.
Rumyantsev, Yevgeni. Indian Ocean & Asian Security. (C). 1988. 15.00 (0-8364-2385-2, Pub. by Allied Pubs) S Asia.
*Run, Reverend. It's Like That: A Spiritual Momoir. LC 00-29685. (Illus.). 320p. 2000. text 23.95 (0-312-20467-1) St Martin.
Runblom, Harald & Norman, Hans, eds. From Sweden to America: A History of the Migration. (Illus.). 391p. 1976. text 57.50 (91-554-0355-7) Coronet Bks.
Runchock-Droste, Rita, ed. Ralph's Ready Reference DOS CD-ROM. 1995. 400.00 incl. cd-rom (0-7876-0257-4, 109075) Gale.
Runci, Paul. 2020 Vision Vol. 21: The Energy World in the Next Quarter Century. Riggs, John A., tr. (Annual Summer Policy Forum Ser.: Vol. 21). (Illus.). 196p. 1997. pap. 15.00 (0-89843-219-7) The Aspen Inst.
Runcie, Robert A. Seasons of the Spirit: The Archbishop of Canterbury at Home & Abroad. LC 83-1734. 272p. reprint ed. pap. 84.40 (0-608-14511-4, 202534200043) Bks Demand.
Runciman. Applications of Functional Progress. LC 94-23269. (C). 1994. write for info. (1-85728-377-5, Pub. by UCL Pr Ltd) Taylor & Francis.
Runciman. Relative Deprivation & Social Justice. 1993. 61.95 (0-7512-0131-6) Ashgate Pub Co.
Runciman. The St. Martin's Workbook. 3rd ed. 1995. pap. text, teacher ed. 5.00 (0-312-10245-3) St Martin.
— St. Martins. 4th ed. 1999. pap. text, wbk. ed. 23.95 (0-312-18851-X) St Martin.
Runciman, David. Pluralism & the Personality of the State. (Ideas in Context Ser.: Vol. 47). 297p. (C). 1997. text 59.95 (0-521-55191-9) Cambridge U Pr.
Runciman, Lex. The Admirations. LC 88-31219. 72p. 1989. 15.95 (0-89924-062-3); pap. 8.50 (0-89924-061-5) Lynx Hse.
— Luck. deluxe limited ed. 72p. 1981. pap. 12.00 (0-937669-02-4) Owl Creek Pr.
— The St. Martin's Workbook. 3rd ed. 592p. 1995. pap. text 23.95 (0-312-10216-X) St Martin.
Runciman, Lex, jt. auth. see Anderson, Chris.
Runciman, Rosy, jt. auth. see Amery, Colin.
Runciman, Steven. The Eastern Schism. LC 78-63367. (Crusades & Military Orders Ser.: Second Series). 200p. reprint ed. 34.50 (0-404-16247-9) AMS Pr.
— The Emperor Romanus Lecapenus & His Reign: A Study of Tenth Century Byzantium. 284p. 1988. pap. text 24.95 (0-521-35722-5) Cambridge U Pr.
— The Fall of Constantinople, 1453. (Canto Book Ser.). (Illus.). 270p. (C). 1990. pap. 12.95 (0-521-39832-0) Cambridge U Pr.
— The First Crusade. (Canto Book Ser.). 209p. (C). 1992. pap. 11.95 (0-521-42705-3) Cambridge U Pr.
— The Great Church in Captivity: A Study of the Patriarchate of Constantinople from the Eve of the Turkish Conquest to the Greek War of Independence. 455p. 1986. pap. text 29.95 (0-521-31310-4) Cambridge U Pr.
— The Great Church in Captivity: A Study of the Patriarchate of Constantinople from the Eve of the Turkish Conquest to the Greek War of Independence. LC 68-29330. 465p. reprint ed. pap. 132.60 (0-608-12502-4, 2024531) Bks Demand.
— History of the Crusades, 3 vols., 1. (Illus.). 394p. (C). 1987. pap. text 22.95 (0-521-34770-X) Cambridge U Pr.
— History of the Crusades, 3 vols., 2. (Illus.). 538p. (C). 1987. pap. text 22.95 (0-521-34771-8) Cambridge U Pr.
— History of the Crusades, 3 vols., 3. (Illus.). 542p. (C). 1987. pap. text 22.95 (0-521-34772-6) Cambridge U Pr.
— History of the Crusades, 3 vols., Set. (C). 1996. pap. text 54.95 (0-521-35997-X) Cambridge U Pr.
— History of the Crusades, 3 vols., Vol. I. 391p. 1951. 54.95 (0-521-06161-X) Cambridge U Pr.
— History of the Crusades, Vol. 2: 1100-1187. 546p. 1952. text 59.95 (0-521-06162-8) Cambridge U Pr.
— History of the Crusades, Vol. 3. 542p. 1954. text 59.95 (0-521-06163-6) Cambridge U Pr.
— The Medieval Manichee: A Study of the Christian Dualist Heresy. LC 82-4123. 224p. 1982. pap. text 22.95 (0-521-28926-2) Cambridge U Pr.
— The Sicilian Vespers: A History of the Mediterranean World in the Later Thirteenth Century. (Canto Book Ser.). (Illus.). 368p. (C). 1992. pap. 12.95 (0-521-43774-1) Cambridge U Pr.
*Runciman, W. G. The Social Animal. 240p. 2000. pap. 17.95 (0-472-06730-3, 06730); text 39.50 (0-472-09730-X, 09730) U of Mich Pr.
Runciman, W. G. A Treatise on Social Theory: Applied Social Theory, Vol. 3. 348p. (C). 1997. text 69.95 (0-521-24960-0); pap. text 27.95 (0-521-58801-4) Cambridge U Pr.
Runciman, Walter G. Social Science & Political Theory. 2nd ed. LC 69-16286. 208p. reprint ed. pap. 59.30 (0-608-12499-0, 2024528) Bks Demand.
— A Treatise on Social Theory: The Methodology of Social Theory, 2 vols., 1. LC 82-4493. (Illus.). 362p. 1983. pap. text 25.95 (0-521-27251-3) Cambridge U Pr.
Runciman, Walter G., jt. ed. see Smith, John M.
Runciman, Walter G., ed. see Weber, Max.
Runck, Robert. JFK: The Words of John F. Kennedy. 64p. 2000. 4.95 (1-58066-002-9, Covered Brdge Pr) Douglas Charles Ltd.
Runck, Robert F., jt. ed. see Roth, Edward S.
Runck, Robert R., ed. Premachining Planning & Tool Presetting. LC 67-28208. (American Society of Tool & Manufacturing Engineers Manufacturing Data Ser.). 82p. 1967. reprint ed. pap. 30.00 (0-608-09975-9, 201600500097) Bks Demand.
Runco. Encyclopedia of Creativity. 850p. (C). 1999. text. write for info. (0-12-227076-2); text. write for info. (0-12-227077-0) Acad Pr.
Runco, Mark A. Creativity, Art, & Artists. 189p. 1997. pap. 20.00 (0-8058-9864-6) L Erlbaum Assocs.
— Creativity As an Educational Objective for Disadvantaged Students. (Illus.). 105p. (Orig.). (C). 1994. pap. text 35.00 (0-7881-0440-3) DIANE Pub.
— The Creativity Research Handbook, Vol. 1. LC 96-31262. (Perspectives on Creativity Ser.). 352p. 1997. text 75.00 (1-881303-73-X); pap. text 27.95 (1-881303-74-8) Hampton Pr NJ.
— Divergent Thinking. (Creativity Research Ser.). 240p. (C). 1991. pap. 39.50 (0-89391-716-8); text 73.25 (0-89391-700-1) Ablx Pub.
Runco, Mark A., ed. Attributional Approach to Creativity. 155p. 1995. pap. 20.00 (0-8058-9930-8) L Erlbaum Assocs.
— Creativity & Deviance: A Special Issue of Creativity Research Journal. 81p. 1999. pap. 20.00 (0-8058-9803-4) L Erlbaum Assocs.
— The Creativity Research Handbook, Vol. 2. (Perspectives on Creativity Ser.). 464p. 1999. text 85.00 (1-57273-132-X); pap. text 32.50 (1-57273-133-8) Hampton Pr NJ.
— Critical Creative Processes. (Perspectives on Creativity Ser.). 384p. 1999. text 79.50 (1-57273-134-6); pap. text 27.50 (1-57273-135-4) Hampton Pr NJ.
*Runco, Mark A., ed. Longitudinal Studies of Creativity: A Special Issue of Creativity Research Journal. 72p. 1999. pap. 20.00 (0-8058-9802-6) L Erlbaum Assocs.
Runco, Mark A., ed. Problem Finding, Problem Solving, & Creativity. LC 94-1974. (Creativity Research Ser.). 320p. 1994. pap. 39.50 (1-56750-013-7); text 73.25 (0-89391-975-6) Ablx Pub.
Runco, Mark A. & Albert, Robert S., eds. Theories of Creativity. (Focus Editions Ser.: Vol. 115). (Illus.). 320p. (C). 1990. pap. 26.00 (0-8039-3545-5) Sage.
— Theories of Creativity. LC 90-31971. (Sage Focus Editions Ser.: No. 115). 276p. 1990. reprint ed. pap. 85.60 (0-608-01537-7, 205958100002) Bks Demand.
— Theories of Creativity. 2nd rev. ed. (Perspectives on Creativity Ser.). 288p. 1999. text 59.50 (1-57273-136-2); pap. text 22.95 (1-57273-137-0) Hampton Pr NJ.
*Runco, Mark A. & Pritzker, Steven, eds. Encyclopedia of Creativity, 2 vols. LC 99-61534. (Illus.). 1904p. (C). 1999. text 350.00 (0-12-227075-4) Acad Pr.
Runco, Mark A., ed. see Abelman, Bob.
Runco, Mark A., ed. see Andreasen, Nancy C., et al.
Runco, Mark A., ed. see Bailin, Sharon.
Runco, Mark A., ed. see Barron, Frank.
Runco, Mark A., ed. see Gedo, John E. & Gedo, Mary M.
Runco, Mark A., ed. see Jausovic, Norbert.
Runco, Mark A., jt. ed. see Milgram, Robert M.
Runco, Mark A., jt. ed. see Milgram, Roberta M.
Runco, Mark A., jt. ed. see Shaw, Melvin P.
Runco, Mark A., ed. see Wakefield, John F.
Runco, Mark A., ed. see Walkefield, John F.
Runcorn, David. Rumors of Life: Reflections on the Resurrection Appearances. pap. write for info. (0-232-52088-7) S Asia.
— Touch Wood: Meeting the Cross in the World Today. pap. write for info. (0-232-51943-9) S Asia.
Runcorn, S. K., ed. International Dictionary of Geophysics, 2 vols. (Illus.). 1728p. 1967. 970.00 (0-08-011834-8, Pergamon Pr) Elsevier.
— The Physics of the Planets: Their Origin, Evolution & Structure. LC 87-10465. 468p. reprint ed. pap. 145.10 (0-8357-6944-5, 203900300009) Bks Demand.
Runcorn, S. K., et al, eds. Smaller Solar System Bodies & Orbits: Proceedings of Symposium 3, Workshops II, III & XXVI & the Topical Meetings of the COSPAR Interdisciplinary Scientific Commission B & P of the COSPAR 27th Plenary Meeting Held in Espoo, Finland, July, 1988. (Advances in Space Research Ser.: Vol. 10). (Illus.). 434p. 1989. pap. 190.25 (0-08-040163-5, Pergamon Pr) Elsevier.
Runcorn, S. K., ed. see International Astronomical Union Staff.
Runcorn, S. K., jt. ed. see Rosenberg, G. D.
Rund & Brown. Chemistry 104B. 3rd ed. 98p. (C). 1997. spiral bd., lab manual ed. 15.95 (0-7872-4355-8, 41435501) Kendall-Hunt.
Rund, Douglas, et al. Essentials of Emergency Medicine. 2nd ed. LC 96-17608. (Illus.). 912p. (C). (gr. 13). 1996. pap. text 59.95 (0-8151-7146-3, 24599) Mosby Inc.
Rund, H. Differential Geometry & Gauge Fields. 1994. text 68.00 (981-02-1230-5) World Scientific Pub.
Rundall, Thomas G., et al. After Restructuring: Empowerment Strategies at Work in America's Hospitals. LC 98-17784. (Business & Management Ser.). 288p. 1998. 42.95 (0-7879-4029-1) Jossey-Bass.
Runde, Austin W. The Happy Wanderer. (Illus.). xii, 209p. (Orig.). 1996. 5.00 (0-9655294-0-1) N Runde Digital Artist.
Runde, Raymond E. & Britton, Gregory. Depression: The Dark Night of the Soul. 100p. 1990. pap. write for info. (0-9628401-0-6) Millers Pr.
Rundekl, P. W., et al, eds. Stable Isotopes in Ecological Research. (Ecological Studies: Vol. 68). (Illus.). 545p. 1988. 108.00 (0-387-96712-5) Spr-Verlag.
Rundel, P. W., et al, eds. Landscape Degradation & Biodiversity in Mediterranean-Type Ecosystems. LC 98-8218. (Ecological Studies: Vol. 136). (Illus.). xxvi, 432p. 1998. 169.00 (3-540-64475-X) Spr-Verlag.
Rundel, P. W. & Gibson, A. C. Ecological Communities & Processes in a Mojave Desert Ecosystem: Rock Valley, Nevada. (Illus.). 387p. (C). 1996. text 129.95 (0-521-46541-9) Cambridge U Pr.
Rundel, P. W., et al. Tropical Alpine Environments: Plant Form & Function. (Illus.). 390p. (C). 1994. text 105.00 (0-521-42089-X) Cambridge U Pr.
Rundel, Philip W. An Annotated Bibliography of West Indian Plant Ecology. (Illus.). 72p. 1974. 10.00 (0-318-14610-X) Isl Resources.
Rundell, James R. & Wise, Michael G., eds. The American Psychiatric Press Textbook of Consultation-Liaison Psychiatry. 1184p. 1996. text 145.00 (0-88048-336-9, 8336) Am Psychiatric.
*Rundell, James R. & Wise, Michael G., eds. Concise Guide to Consultation Psychiatry. 3rd ed. 352p. 2000. pap. 22.95 (0-88048-394-6) Am Psychiatric.
Rundell, James R., et al. Essentials of Consultation-liaison Psychiatry: Based on the American Psychiatric Press Textbook of Consultation-liaison Psychiatry. LC 98-54234. 1999. 60.00 (0-88048-801-8) Am Psychiatric.
Rundell, John. Between Totalitarianism & Postmodernity: A Thesis Eleven Reader. Beilharz, Peter et al, eds. (Illus.). 276p. 1992. pap. text 16.00 (0-262-52179-2) MIT Pr.
Rundell, John, jt. auth. see Baubock, Rainer.
Rundell, John, jt. ed. see Robinson, Gillian.
Rundell, John F., jt. auth. see Mennell, Stephen.
*Rundell, Maria E. A New System of Domestic Cookery by a Lady: Mrs. Maria Eliza Rundell's Original 1806 Classic - Fort Niagara Edition. Bowler, R. Arthur, ed. (Illus.). 320p. 1998. reprint ed. 14.95 (0-941967-20-4) Old Fort Niagara Assn.
Rundell, Mary G. Texas Gardener's Guide to Growing Tomatoes. 128p. (Orig.). 1984. pap. text 6.95 (0-914641-00-X) TX Gardener Pr.
Rundell, Michael. The Dictionary of Cricket. (Illus.). 224p. 1995. 25.00 (0-19-866198-3) OUP.
*Rundell, Michael. The Dictionary of Cricket. 2nd ed. (Illus.). 218p. 2000. reprint ed. text 25.00 (0-7881-6965-3) DIANE Pub.
Rundell, Nancy T. Iran: Front Row Balcony. LC 81-68157. (Illus.). 248p. 1981. 12.95 (0-940928-01-9) Felsun Pr.
Rundell, Richard W. The Rising Son: The Manifestation of the Sons of God. 124p. 1996. pap. 7.95 (0-89228-117-0) Impact Christian.
Rundell, Robert & Rundell, Roberta. Kids Care, Vol. 1: K-2. 1989. teacher ed. 40.00 (1-56117-012-7) Telesis CA.
— Kids Care, Vol. 2: 3-4. 1989. teacher ed. 35.00 (1-56117-013-5) Telesis CA.
— Kids Care, Vol. 3: 5-6. 1989. teacher ed. 35.00 (1-56117-017-8) Telesis CA.
— Kids Care, Vol. 4: Teens Care. 1993. teacher ed. 35.00 (1-56117-015-1) Telesis CA.
— Kids Care: Preschool - First Grade. (J). (ps). 1989. 15.00 (1-56117-014-3) Telesis CA.
Rundell, Roberta, jt. auth. see Rundell, Robert.
Rundell, W., et al, eds. Inverse Problems in Partial Differential Equations. LC 89-26348. (Proceedings in Applied Mathematics Ser.: No. 42). xi, 214p. 1990. pap. 41.50 (0-89871-252-1) Soc Indus-Appl Math.
Rundell, Walter. Black Market Money: The Collapse of U. S. Military Currency Control in World War II. LC 64-15879. 139p. reprint ed. pap. 43.10 (0-8357-7292-6, 205188200013) Bks Demand.
Rundell, William, jt. auth. see Engl, Heinz W.
Rundell, William, jt. ed. see Engl, Heinz W.
Rundgaard, H., jt. ed. see De Weck, Alain L.
Rundin, Ulf, ed. Perspectives on Multilateral Assistance: A Review by the Nordic U. N. Project. 317p. (Orig.). 1990. pap. 79.00 (91-22-01405-5) Coronet Bks.
— The United Nations: Issues & Options. (Five Studies on the Role of the UN in the Economic & Social Fields Commissioned by the Nordic UN Project). 358p. (Orig.). 1991. pap. 77.50 (91-22-01426-8) Coronet Bks.
— The United Nations in Development: Reform Issues in the Economic & Social Fields (Final Report by the Nordic UN Project) 111p. (Orig.). 1991. pap. 49.00 (91-22-01437-3) Coronet Bks.
Rundkvist, D. V. & Gillen, Con. Precambrian Ore Deposits of the East European & Siberian Cratons. LC 97-38578. (Developments in Economic Geology Ser.). 1997. write for info. (0-444-82657-2) Elsevier.
Rundle. MRI Study Guide & Exam Review. (C). 1997. pap. text, student ed. write for info. (0-7216-6880-1, W B Saunders Co) Harcrt Hlth Sci Grp.
Rundle, Anne. Honoring Patient Preferences: A Guide to Complying with Multicultural Patient Requirements. LC 99-6601. 300p. 1999. 249.95 (0-7879-4650-8) Jossey-Bass.
Rundle, Bede. Mind in Action. LC 97-18544. 314p. (C). 1997. text 70.00 (0-19-823691-3) OUP.
— Perception, Sensation & Verification. 266p. 1972. text 34.00 (0-19-824390-1) OUP.
Rundle, David, ed. Hutchison Encyclopedia of the Renaissance. (Illus.). 448p. 1999. 65.00 (0-8133-3670-8) HarpC.

An Asterisk (*) at the beginning of an entry indicates that the title is appearing for the first time.

Rundle, John. Reduction & Prediction of Natural Disasters. LC 95-51857. Vol. 25. 304p. (C). 1996. pap. 38.00 (*0-201-87049-5*) Addison-Wesley.
— SFI Reduction & Prediction of Natural Disasters-H. 320p. (C). 1996. 61.00 (*0-201-87048-7*) Addison-Wesley.
***Rundle, John, et al.** Geocomplexity & the Physics of Earthquakes. LC 00-30618. (Geophysical Monographs). 2000. write for info. (*0-87590-978-7*) Am Geophysical.
Rundle, R. N. International Affairs, 1890-1939. LC 79-12170. (Illus.). 162p. (C). 1980. 29.50 (*0-8419-0516-9*) Holmes & Meier.
Rundle, Randy. Automotive Cooling System Basics. LC 98-87287. (Illus.). 224p. 1999. pap. 19.95 (*0-87341-680-5*, ACLS) Krause Pubns.
— Wired for Success: Auto Electrical Made Easy. LC 95-77302. (Illus.). 224p. 1995. pap. 19.95 (*0-87341-402-0*, AEM01) Krause Pubns.
Rundle, Stanley. Cracking the Language Code: French. 271p. 1983. pap. 19.95 (*0-87243-110-X*) Templegate.
— Cracking the Language Code: German. 332p. 1982. pap. 19.95 (*0-87243-107-X*) Templegate.
— Cracking the Language Code: Spanish. 265p. 1974. pap. 19.95 (*0-87243-109-6*) Templegate.
Rundle, Vesta M. Jenny the Guard Goose. (Illus.). 24p. (Orig.). (J). (gr. k-4). 1993. pap. 5.95 (*1-882672-00-3*) V M Rundle.
— Snow Calf. (Illus.). 36p. (Orig.). (J). (gr. 4-8). 1993. pap. 4.50 (*1-882672-01-1*) V M Rundle.
Rundle, Vivienne, jt. ed. see Collins, Thomas.
Rundles, Jeff, ed. Colorado Economy, 93-94. 100p. 1993. 14.00 (*0-9638170-0-0*) CO Econ Rpts.
Rundlett, Ellsworth T. Maximizing Damages in Small Personal Injury Cases. 344p. 1991. ring bd. 119.00 (*0-938065-55-6*) James Pub Santa Ana.
Rundquist, E. Day Geckos. (Illus.). 64p. 1995. pap. 9.95 (*0-7938-0267-9*, RE126) TFH Pubns.
— Reptiles & Amphibians: Care in Captivity. (Illus.). 192p. 1994. 29.95 (*0-7938-0298-9*, TS211) TFH Pubns.
Rundquist, Edward & Sletto, Raymond. Personality in the Depression. Vol. 12. LC 72-142315. (University of Minnesota Institute of Child Welfare Monographs: No. 12). (Illus.). 398p. 1975. reprint ed. lib. bdg. 55.00 (*0-8371-5903-2*, CWRP, Greenwood Pr) Greenwood.
Rundquist, Eric. Reptile & Amphibian Parasites. (Illus.). 64p. 1995. pap. 9.95 (*0-7938-0276-8*, RE123) TFH Pubns.
Rundquist, Eric M. Reptile & Amphibian Parasites. LC 98-22376. (Basic Domestic Reptile & Amphibian Library). (Illus.). 64p. (YA). (gr. 3 up). 1999. lib. bdg. 17.95 (*0-7910-5080-7*) Chelsea Hse.
Rundquist, Thomas J. The Artist-Writer Path: Suggestions on How Creative Persons Should Live. unabridged ed. (Illus.). 76p. (Orig.). 1996. pap. 19.95 (*1-884239-12-9*) Nova Media.
— Detroit Undercover. 50p. (Orig.). 1995. pap. 7.95 (*1-884239-08-0*) Nova Media.
— Eugenics in Michigan Without Due Process: Coercised Sterilization in the 1960's & 1970's in Michigan Hospitals. unabridged ed. (Illus.). 60p. (Orig.). 1996. 29.95 (*1-884239-09-9*) Nova Media.
Rundquist, Thomas J., ed. AIDS Trivia: Update for 90's Updated. 3rd ed. 1995. disk 39.95 (*1-884239-02-1*) Nova Media.
— AIDS Trivia: Update for 90's Updated. 3rd ed. (Illus.). 42p. 1995. pap. text, teacher ed. 14.95 (*1-884239-01-3*) Nova Media.
— Cultural Diversity Test. unabridged ed. (Illus.). 30p. 1997. pap. 29.95 (*1-884239-16-1*) Nova Media.
— Drug Abuse Treatment Using Biochemistry: Specialized Vitamins, Herbs & Nutrition with Counseling Plus Urinalysis. unabridged ed. (Illus.). 70p. 1996. 19.95 (*1-884239-10-2*); pap. 12.95 (*1-884239-11-0*) Nova Media.
— Drugs, Sex in Religions: TR's Autobiography 1962-1992. 54p. (Orig.). (C). 1993. pap. 29.95 (*0-9618567-7-7*) Nova Media.
— Erotic Cyclic Forecast: Psychological Prediction Formula. (Illus.). 130p. 1998. pap., wbk. ed. 29.95 (*1-884239-22-6*) Nova Media.
— Home Hospice after Your Home: A Michigan Law Case. (Illus.). 130p. (C). 1998. pap. 29.95 (*1-884239-24-2*) Nova Media.
— Racial Attitude Test: PC Windows 1.0 Version. (Illus.). 45p. 1996. pap., teacher ed. 39.95 incl. disk (*1-884239-03-X*) Nova Media.
— Sales, Persuasion Presentations: A Psychological Analysis. 6p. (Orig.). 1994. pap. 6.95 (*0-9618567-9-3*) Nova Media.
— Sexual Cyclic Forecast. (Illus.). 130p. 1998. pap. 29.95 (*1-884239-23-4*) Nova Media.
— Special Forces Handbook: For Business Management & Marketing. (Illus.). 100p. (Orig.). 1996. pap. 19.95 (*1-884239-14-5*) Nova Media.
— Teacher (Substitute) Survival Activities Kit Vol. 1: Emergency Activities Material on Class Control Guide. (Illus.). 101p. 1998. pap. text 29.95 (*1-884239-21-8*) Nova Media.
— Viagra for Women: Aids (Psychological, Nutritional & Pharmacology) for Women's Sexuality. unabridged ed. (Illus.). 47p. 1999. pap. text 19.95 (*1-884239-19-6*) Nova Media.
Rundquist, Thomas J., ed. Drug Culture Monopoly. 42p. (Orig.). 1995. pap. text 30.95 (*1-884239-04-8*) Nova Media.
Rundquist, Thomas J., intro. Drugs, Sex & Religions: An Uncensored Bibliography. rev. ed. 4p. (C). 1989. pap. text 4.95 (*0-9618567-4-2*) Nova Media.
— Sterilization (Involuntary) A Case Study. (Illus.). 54p. (Orig.). (C). 1993. pap. 29.95 (*0-9618567-8-5*) Nova Media.
Rundquist, Thomas J. & Guild, Robert W., Jr. Drugs, Sex & Rock-n-Roll. (Illus.). 15p. (Orig.). (YA). (gr. 7-12). 1988. pap. text 19.95 (*0-9618567-3-4*) Nova Media.
Rundquist, Thomas J. & Parent, Frederick. Horse Is Boss: Drug Culture Education & Prevention Game. 2nd ed. (Illus.). 42p. (Orig.). (YA). (gr. 7-12). 1988. pap. text 30.50 (*0-9618567-1-8*) Nova Media.
Rundqvist, D. V. & Mitrofanov, F. P., eds. Precambrian Geology of the U. S. S. R. LC 92-8594. 528p. 1993. 218.00 (*0-444-89380-6*) Elsevier.
Rundus. Joseph Mitchell. 1997. 22.95 (*0-8057-4574-2*) Mac Lib Ref.
Rune, Thomas. The Elven Ways Bk. 1: The Ways of Magic. 272p. (Orig.). 1996. mass mkt. 5.50 (*0-380-77980-3*, Avon Bks) Morrow Avon.
Runes, D. D. & Schrickel, H. G., eds. Art in a Post War World. LC 75-90603. (Essay Index Reprint Ser.). 1977. 17.95 (*0-8369-1272-1*) Ayer.
Runes, Dagobert D. Dictionary of Judaism. 236p. 1981. 8.95 (*0-8065-0787-X*, Citadel Pr) Carol Pub Group.
— Lost Legends of Israel. 1997. 6.99 (*0-517-18077-4*) Random Hse Value.
— Wisdom of FDR. 1993. pap. 7.95 (*0-8065-1462-0*, Citadel Pr) Carol Pub Group.
Runes, Dagobert D., ed. Concise Dictionary of Judaism. LC 77-88933. 124p. 1982. reprint ed. lib. bdg. 75.00 (*0-8371-2109-4*, AERUDJ, Greenwood Pr) Greenwood.
— Dictionary of Philosophy. enl. rev. ed. LC 81-80240. 360p. (C). 1984. pap. 14.95 (*0-8226-0392-6*) Littlefield.
— The Wisdom of the Torah. 1966. pap. 2.25 (*0-8065-0015-8*, 236, Citadel Pr) Carol Pub Group.
Runestad, J. A., jt. auth. see Pedersen, J. H.
Runey, Mim L., ed. Charleston Hospitality. 2nd ed. 1993. 19.95 (*0-9639364-0-9*) Johnson & Wales.
Runfola, Charles, ed. see Clover, Richard.
Runfola, Maria & Bash, Lee, eds. Research Symposium on the Male Adolescent Voice. (Proceedings Ser.). (Illus.). 182p. (Orig.). 1984. pap. 14.95 (*0-931111-00-5*) SUNY Buff Music.
Runfola, Maria, jt. compiled by see Rutkowski, Joanne.
Rung, Mark, jt. auth. see Lata, Jennifer.
Rungapadiachy. Interpersonal Communication & Psychology for Health Care. 304p. 1998. pap. text 37.50 (*0-7506-4080-4*) Buttrwrth-Heinemann.
***Rungard, Sue & French, Ylva, eds.** Marketing & Public Relations Handbook for Museums, Galleries & Heritage Attractions. 304p. 2000. pap. 44.95 (*0-7425-0407-7*) AltaMira Pr.
Runge. Clinical MRI. 2000. text 79.00 (*0-7216-8036-4*, W B Saunders Co) Harcrt Hlth Sci Grp.
Runge, Anita. Literarische Praxis von Frauen Um, 1800. (Germanistische Texte und Studien: Bd. 55). 267p. 1997. 40.00 (*3-487-10259-5*) G Olms Pubs.
Runge, C. Ford, ed. The Future of the North American Granary: Politics, Economics & Resource Constraints in North American Agriculture. LC 85-23905. (Illus.). 258p. 1986. reprint ed. pap. 80.00 (*0-608-00159-7*, 206094000006) Bks Demand.
Runge, C. Ford & World Resources Institute Staff. Sustainable Trade Expansion in Latin America & the Caribbean: Analysis & Assessment. LC 97-80170. 50 p. 1997. 20.00 (*1-56973-227-2*) World Resources Inst.
Runge, C. Ford, et al. Freer Trade, Protected Environment: Balancing Trade Liberalization & Environmental Interests. 146p. 1993. pap. 17.95 (*0-87609-154-0*) Coun Foreign.
Runge, C. Ford, jt. auth. see Cochrane, Willard W.
Runge, E. C., et al, eds. Utilization, Treatment, & Disposal of Waste on Land. 318p. 1986. 21.00 (*0-89118-781-2*) Soil Sci Soc Am.
Runge, Ian. Mining Economics & Strategy. LC 98-24661. (Illus.). 312p. 1998. pap. 83.00 (*0-87335-165-7*, 165-7) SMM&E Inc.
***Runge, Ian C.** Capital & Uncertainty: The Capital Investment Process in a Market Economy. LC 00-35345. 2000. write for info. (*1-84064-288-2*) E Elgar.
***Runge, Jonathan.** Rum & Reggae's Caribbean. 2nd ed. 720p. 2000. pap. 22.95 (*1-893675-02-5*, Pub. by Rum & Reggae) Midpt Trade.
Runge, Jonathan. Rum & Reggae's Caribbean, 2000. (Rum & Reggae Ser.). 720p. 1999. pap. 22.95 (*1-893675-00-9*) Rum & Reggae.
***Runge, Jonathan.** Rum & Reggae's Hawaii. 432p. 2000. pap. 19.95 (*1-893675-01-7*) Rum & Reggae.
Runge, Laura. Gender & Language in British Literary Criticism, 1660-1790. LC 96-40456. 244p. (C). 1997. text 59.95 (*0-521-57009-3*) Cambridge U Pr.
Runge, M. Bones & Joints. (Exercises in Radiological Diagnosis Ser.). (Illus.). 210p. 1987. 34.95 (*0-387-16544-4*) Spr-Verlag.
***Runge, Robert.** Collectors Encyclopedia of Stangl Dinnerware. 224p. 1999. 24.95 (*1-57432-152-8*) Collector Bks.
Runge, Roger, ed. 1998 Official P. G. A. Golf Directory of the South Central Section, Vol. 3. (Illus.). 144p. 1997. pap. 8.95 (*0-9662780-0-3*) Resource Design.
Runge, Roger, ed. see Frace, Mark.
Runge, Senta M. Face Lifting by Exercise. 10th rev. ed. LC 56-6321. (Illus.). 1992. 25.00 (*0-9601042-1-6*) Allegro Pub.
***Runge, Tina.** Treasures of the Heart. 1999. mass mkt. 5.99 (*0-515-12680-2*, Jove) Berkley Pub.
Runge, Val M. Contrast Media in Magnetic Resonance Imaging. (Illus.). 176p. 1991. text 65.00 (*0-397-51270-8*) Lppncott W & W.
— Magnetic Resonance of the Brain, Head & Neck. LC 93-24586. (Illus.). 608p. 1993. text 189.00 (*0-397-51244-9*) Lppncott W & W.
— Review of Neuroradiology. 160p. 1995. pap. text 45.00 (*0-7216-5134-8*, W B Saunders Co) Harcrt Hlth Sci Grp.
Runge, Val M., ed. Contrast-Enhanced Clinical Magnet Resonance Imaging. LC 95-30288. (Illus.). 192p. (C). 1996. 40.00 (*0-8131-1944-8*) U Pr of Ky.
— Magnetic Resonance Imaging: Clinical Principles. LC 91-35577. (Illus.). 439p. 1992. reprint ed. pap. 136.10 (*0-608-05878-5*, 205984400007) Bks Demand.
Runge, Val M., et al, eds. Clinical Magnetic Resonance Imaging. LC 89-12810. (Illus.). 604p. 1990. reprint ed. pap. 187.30 (*0-608-05879-3*, 205984500007) Bks Demand.
Runge, Val M., et al. Magnetic Resonance Imaging of the Spine. (Illus.). 550p. 1994. text 150.00 (*0-397-51290-2*) Lppncott W & W.
Runger, George C., jt. auth. see Montgomery, Douglas C.
Rungta, Ravi, ed. Inclusions & Their Influence on Material Behavior: Proceedings of a Symposium Held in Conjunction with the 1988 World Materials Congress, Chicago, IL, USA, 24-30 September 1988. LC 88-71672. (Illus.). 207p. reprint ed. pap. 64.20 (*0-8357-4089-7*, 203685500005) Bks Demand.
Runia, Anthony P., tr. see Ter Hark, Michel.
Runia, D. T. Philo of Alexandria & the Timaeus of Plato. xii, 617p. 1986. 171.00 (*90-04-07477-5*, PHA, 44) Brill Academic Pubs.
Runia, David T. Exegesis & Philosophy: Studies on Philo of Alexandria. 320p. 1991. text 109.95 (*0-86078-287-5*, Pub. by Variorum) Ashgate Pub Co.
— Philo in Early Christian Literature: A Survey. LC 93-28508. (Compendia Rerum Iudaicarum ad Novum Testamentum Ser.: Vol. 3). 320p. 1993. 50.00 (*0-8006-2828-4*, Fortress Pr) Augsburg Fortress.
— Philo of Alexandria & the Church Fathers: A Collection of Papers. (Vigiliae Christianae Ser.: No. 32). 300p. 1995. 110.00 (*90-04-10355-4*) Brill Academic Pubs.
Runia, David T., jt. auth. see Mansfeld, J. J.
Runia, David T., jt. auth. see Radice, Roberto.
Runion, Garth E. Golden Section. LC 92-231874. 14.95 (*0-86651-510-0*) Seymour Pubns.
Runion, Garth E. & Lockwood, James R. Deductive Systems: Finite & Non-Euclidean Geometries. LC 78-17827. (Illus.). 90p. 1978. pap. 10.95 (*0-87353-129-9*) NCTM.
Runions, Debbie. Sabrina's Gifts: A Fairy Tale about Learning to See with Your Heart. (Illus.). 64p. (Orig.). 1996. pap. 10.00 (*0-9653297-0-4*) Hero Pub TN.
Runk, Emma T. Barcroft Family Records: An Account of the Family in England & the Descendants of Ambrose Barcroft, the Emigrant, of Solebury, Penn. (Illus.). 334p. 1988. reprint ed. pap. 53.00 (*0-8328-0187-9*); reprint ed. lib. bdg. 63.00 (*0-8328-0186-0*) Higginson Bk Co.
Runk, Wesley T. God Loves Us All. (Orig.). 1989. pap. 7.50 (*1-55673-114-0*, 9825) CSS OH.
— Jesus the Light: Coloring Book. 1993. pap. 1.25 (*1-55673-828-5*) CSS OH.
— Jesus, the Light of Our Lives. LC 96-121026. 1994. pap. 5.50 (*1-55673-523-5*) CSS OH.
— Jesus, the Servant King: Six Children's Object Lessons for Len: Coloring Book. (J). 1993. pap. 1.25 (*1-55673-604-5*) CSS OH.
— Object Lessons from the Bible. (Object Lessons Ser.). 96p. (YA). (gr. 10). 1980. pap. 6.99 (*0-8010-7698-6*) Baker Bks.
— Our Father, Friend of Little Children: Children's Object Lessons Based on the Lord's Prayer. 2nd ed. 24p. (Orig.). 1995. pap. 4.95 (*0-7880-0372-0*) CSS OH.
— Speaking with Signs: Children's Object Lessons for Lent & Easter. 2nd ed. (Illus.). 24p. (Orig.). 1995. pap. 4.95 (*0-7880-0371-2*) CSS OH.
— We Are the Church: 52 Second Lesson Text Children's Object Lessons. LC 94-8316. 1994. 10.95 (*0-7880-0100-0*) CSS OH.
***Runke, Gayle.** Fitness for Living Laboratory Manual. 3rd rev. ed. 95p. 1998. pap. 14.95 (*1-57879-000-X*) E Bowers Pub.
Runkel, Charles P., et al. The Illinois Law Enforcement Officer: The Basic Training Course, 2 vols. (Illus.). 860p. (Orig.). (C). 1989. pap. text 60.00 (*0-8211-1721-1*) McCutchan.
Runkel, David R., ed. Campaign for President: The Managers Look at '88. LC 89-6767. 316p. 1989. 55.00 (*0-86569-194-0*, Auburn Hse); pap. 22.95 (*0-86569-195-9*, Auburn Hse) Greenwood.
Runkel, Janet, ed. Virginia Administrative Law Appendix: 1998 Edition. 1998. pap. write for info. (*0-327-06144-8*, 49092-16) LEXIS Pub.
Runkel, Margaret, jt. auth. see Runkel, Philip.
Runkel, Philip, et al, eds. The Changing College Classroom. LC 70-92896. (Jossey-Bass Higher Education Ser.). 380p. reprint ed. pap. 117.80 (*0-8357-9301-X*, 201386200092) Bks Demand.
Runkel, Philip & Runkel, Margaret. Guide to Usage for Writers & Students in the Social Studies. LC 83-19179. (Helix Bks.: No. 382). (Illus.). 168p. 1984. 32.50 (*0-86598-132-9*); pap. 14.00 (*0-8226-0382-9*) Rowman.
Runkel, Philip J. Casting Nets & Testing Specimens: Two Grand Methods of Psychology. LC 89-48665. 208p. 1990. 57.95 (*0-275-93533-7*, C3533, Greenwood Pr) Greenwood.
Runkel, Philip J., jt. auth. see Schmuck, Richard A.
Runkel, Phillip M. Alfred Lunt & Lynn Fontanne: A Bibliography. (Illus.). (C). 1978. pap. 4.50 (*0-916120-03-1*) Carroll Coll.
Runkel, Sylvan T. & Bull, Alvin F. Wildflowers of the Iowa Woodlands. LC 86-27589. (Illus.). 272p. 1987. reprint ed. pap. 24.95 (*0-8138-1929-6*) Iowa St U Pr.
Runkel, Sylvan T. & Roosa, Dean M. Wildflowers of the Tallgrass Prairie: The Upper Midwest. (Illus.). 292p. (Orig.). 1988. pap. 24.95 (*0-8138-1979-2*) Iowa St U Pr.
Runkel, Sylvan T., jt. auth. see Roosa, Dean M.
Runkis, Walt, jt. auth. see LaPuma, Karen.
Runkle, jt. auth. see Street.
Runkle, Anna. In Good Conscience: A Practical Emotional, & Spiritual Guide to Deciding Whether to Have an Abortion. LC 98-25319. (Psychology Ser.). 160p. 1998. mass mkt. 16.00 (*0-7879-4149-2*) Jossey-Bass.
Runkle, Gerald. A History of Western Political Theory. LC 68-21652. 682p. reprint ed. pap. 200.00 (*0-608-12780-9*, 202347800032) Bks Demand.
Runkles, Janet, jt. auth. see Runkles, Richard.
Runkles, Richard & Runkles, Janet. His Guiding Hand: Seeking God's Best for Our Children. Bagnull, Marlene, ed. (Illus.). 96p. 1997. pap. write for info. (*0-9656251-1-7*) Makarios.

R

Runnalls, ed. Le Mystere de Sainte Venice. (Exeter French Texts Ser.: Vol. 38). (FRE.). 60p. Date not set. pap. text 19.95 (*0-85989-186-0*, Pub. by Univ Exeter Pr) Northwestern U Pr.
Runnalls, David, jt. auth. see Doering, Ronald L.
Runnalls, David, jt. auth. see English, H. Edward.
Runnalls, Graham, jt. ed. see Bennett, Philip.
Runne, John. Par for the Course. 1995. 13.95 (*0-87197-433-9*) Favorite Recipes.
Runnebaum, B., et al, eds. Future Aspects in Contraception Pt. II: Female Contraception. 1985. text 322.00 (*0-85200-906-2*) Kluwer Academic.
— Secretion & Action of Gonadotropins. (Illus.). 105p. 1984. 47.95 (*0-387-13854-4*) Spr-Verlag.
Runnebaum, B. & Rabe, T. Gynecological Endocrinology & Reproductive Medicine, 2 vols. LC 96-36079. (Illus.). 1230p. 1997. 479.00 (*3-540-60930-X*) Spr-Verlag.
Runnebaum, B., jt. ed. see Rabe, T.
***Runnells, M. T.** A Genealogy of Runnells & Reynolds Families in America with Records & Brief Memorials of the Earliest Ancestors So Far as Known & Many of Their Descendants, Bearing the Same & Other Names. 371p. 1999. reprint ed. pap. 28.50 (*0-7884-1324-4*) Heritage Bk.
Runnells, R. R. Infection Control in the Former Wet Finger Environment. (Illus.). 182p. (C). pap. text. write for info. (*0-936751-09-6*) Infection Control.
— Practical How-Tos of Dental Infection Control. 82p. (C). 1987. pap. text. write for info. (*0-936751-03-7*) Infection Control.
Runnells, Robert R. AIDS in the Dental Office? The Story of Kimberly Bergalis & Dr. David Acer. Newman, Katherine, ed. (Illus.). 325p. 1993. 29.95 (*0-936751-11-8*) Infection Control.
— Infection Control in the Former Wet Finger Environment. 3rd ed. (Illus.). 274p. 1994. pap., student ed. 29.95 (*0-936751-12-6*) Infection Control.
Runnels, Curtis, et al, eds. Artifact & Assemblage Vol. 1: The Finds from a Regional Survey of the Southern Argolid, Greece: The Prehistoric & Early Iron Age Pottery & the Lithic Artifacts. LC 94-25691. xii, 476p. 1995. 75.00 (*0-8047-2065-7*) Stanford U Pr.
Runnels, Curtis, jt. auth. see Evely, Don.
Runnels, Curtis N., jt. auth. see Van Andel, Tjeerd H.
Runnels, Gayle S., jt. auth. see Lay, Artie K.
Runnels, LaJeanne, ed. see Watson, Carol.
Runnels, Louise C. Memories of Louise Coe Runnels: Alias "Bonito Lau" unabridged ed. LC 97-75329. (Illus.). 162p. 1996. pap. 12.00 (*1-887523-14-6*) Human Systs Res.
Runnels, M. T. A Genealogy of the Runnels & Reynolds Family in America. 371p. 1989. reprint ed. pap. 56.00 (*0-8328-1039-8*); reprint ed. lib. bdg. 64.00 (*0-8328-1038-X*) Higginson Bk Co.
— The History of Sanbornton, New Hampshire, Vol. 1. (Illus.). 570p. 1988. reprint ed. lib. bdg. 57.00 (*0-8328-0074-0*, NH0021) Higginson Bk Co.
Runnenbaum, B., et al, eds. Future Aspects in Contraception Pt. I: Male Contraception. 1985. text 322.00 (*0-85200-893-7*) Kluwer Academic.
Runner, Jeffrey T. Noun Phrase Licensing. rev. ed. LC 98-21435. (Outstanding Dissertations in Linguistics Ser.). 264p. 1998. 62.00 (*0-8153-3134-7*) Garland.
Runner's World Editors. The Complete Marathoner. LC 78-362. (Illus.). 425p. 1978. 11.95 (*0-89037-097-4*); pap. 8.95 (*0-686-85633-3*) Anderson World.
— The Complete Runner. LC 74-83666. (Illus.). 391p. 1974. 7.95 (*0-89037-041-9*) Anderson World.
— The Complete Woman Runner. LC 78-58048. (Illus.). 440p. 1979. 12.00 (*0-89037-143-1*) Anderson World.
— New Exercises for Runners. LC 78-460. (Illus.). 176p. 1978. pap. 4.95 (*0-89037-151-2*) Anderson World.
— New Guide to Distance Running. rev. ed. (Illus.). 400p. 1983. reprint ed. 11.95 (*0-89037-133-4*); reprint ed. pap. 8.95 (*0-89037-270-5*) Anderson World.
— Runners after Forty. 1980. pap. 4.95 (*0-02-499690-4*, Macmillan Coll) P-H.
— The Runner's Diet: New & Revised. rev. ed. LC 78-455. (Illus.). 134p. 1978. pap. 3.95 (*0-89037-152-0*) Anderson World.
— Runner's Training Guide. (Illus.). 96p. 1978. pap. 3.95 (*0-89037-026-5*) Anderson World.
— Runners Training Guide. 1978. pap. 3.95 (*0-02-499440-5*, Macmillan Coll) P-H.
— Runner's World Training Diary. 1979. spiral bd. 6.95 (*0-89037-153-9*) Anderson World.
— Running after Forty. rev. ed. LC 78-68620. (Illus.). 160p. 1980. pap. 4.95 (*0-89037-205-5*) Anderson World.
— Stretching Book. (Runner's World Ser.). 1982. pap. 9.95 (*0-02-499610-6*, Macmillan Coll) P-H.
— Training Diary. (Runner's World Ser.). 1978. pap. 6.95 (*0-02-499620-3*, Macmillan Coll) P-H.
Runnersworld Staff. Runners World Training Diary. 172p. 1995. 8.95 (*0-02-860820-8*) Macmillan.
Runnggaldier, Edmund. Zeichen und Bezeichnetes: Sprachphilosophische Untersuchungen zum Problem der Referenz. (Grundlagen der Kommunikation-Bibliotheksausgabe Ser.). (GER.). xii, 363p. 1985. 97.70 (*3-11-010107-6*) De Gruyter.

An Asterisk (*) at the beginning of an entry indicates that the title is appearing for the first time.

R

Running-Bear, Stephen. The White Rose, Sparrow & Unicorn. (Illus.). 36p. (J). 1997. 14.95 (*0-9653175-0-1*) Voices of Wellness.

***Running Deer, Pearl.** The Clock Struck Twelve. 120p. 1999. pap. 500.00 (*0-9674983-1-7*) Mayokko.

Running, John. Honor Dance: Native American Photographs. LC 85-16444. (Illus.). 176p. 1995. pap. 24.95 (*0-87417-277-2*) U of Nev Pr.

— The Unknown: A Monument by R. V. Greeves. LC 86-61592. (Illus.). (Orig.). (C). 1986. pap. 9.75 (*0-9616999-0-6*) R V Greeves.

Running, Leona G. & Freedman, David N. William Foxwell Albright: A 20th Century Genius. LC 75-11180. 466p. (C). 1991. pap. 14.99 (*0-8467-0071-9*) Andrews Univ Pr.

Running, Leona G., jt. ed. see Geraty, Lawrence T.

***Running Press Staff.** Ancient Mystery of Tangrams: 500 Magnetic Variations on the World's Classic Puzzles. (Illus.). 80p. 2000. 16.95 (*0-7624-0740-9*) Running Pr.

— Angels A Joyous Celebration, Mini Edition. 1999. 4.95 (*0-7624-0605-4*) Running Pr.

Running Press Staff. Angels Notebook: An Illustrated Journal, with Quotes. 96p. 1997. pap. 5.95 (*0-7624-0055-2*) Running Pr.

***Running Press Staff.** Animals. (Fit-a-Shape Ser.). (Illus.). (J). 2000. 6.95 (*0-7624-0818-9*) Running Pr.

— Big Trucks. (Fit-a-Shape Ser.). (Illus.). (J). 2000. 6.95 (*0-7624-0813-8*) Running Pr.

Running Press Staff. Bride's Journal: A Personal Diary of Plans, Hopes, & Dreams. (Illus.). 144p. 1998. 14.95 (*0-7624-0266-0*) Running Pr.

***Running Press Staff.** Bugs. (Fit-a-Shape Ser.). (Illus.). (J). 2000. 6.95 (*0-7624-0817-0*) Running Pr.

— Butterflies: Mini Edition. (Illus.). (J). 2000. 4.95 (*0-7624-0757-3*) Running Press Min.

— Cat Collection. 1999. 19.95 (*0-7624-0635-6*) Running Pr.

— Cats Mini Edition. (Little Scribbles Ser.). 1999. 4.95 (*0-7624-0661-5*) Running Pr.

— Christmas Miniature Editions Gift Set. 1999. pap. 17.95 (*0-7624-0666-6*) Running Press Min.

— Colors. (Fit-a-Shape Ser.). (Illus.). (J). 2000. 6.95 (*0-7624-0816-2*) Running Pr.

— Cyclopedia: The Visual Desk Reference, with More Than 20,000 Facts & 800 Illustrations. (Illus.). 2000. 19.98 (*0-7624-0875-8*) Running Pr.

— Dinosaurs. (Fit-a-Shape Ser.). (Illus.). (J). 2000. 6.95 (*0-7624-0815-4*) Running Pr.

— Disney's Library of Timeless Tales Mini Edition. 1999. 21.95 (*0-7624-0674-7*) Running Pr.

— Disney's Treasury of Classic Adventures. 1999. 21.95 (*0-7624-0630-5*) Running Pr.

— The Encyclopedia of Knitting: A Step-by-Step Visual Guide, with an Inspirational Gallery of Finished Products. (Illus.). 2000. 24.95 (*0-7624-0805-7*) Running Pr.

Running Press Staff. The Expectant Father's Handbook. (Illus.). 64p. 1997. 9.95 (*0-7624-0192-3*) Running Pr.

***Running Press Staff.** Faith, Hope & Light: The Art of the Stained Glass Window. 128p. 1999. 19.98 (*0-7624-0593-7*) Running Pr.

— Flowers Mini Edition. (Little Scribbles Ser.). 1999. 4.95 (*0-7624-0662-3*) Running Pr.

— Gifts of Love. 1999. 19.95 (*0-7624-0636-4*) Running Pr.

— Graduation: Mini Edition. 2000. pap. 4.95 (*0-7624-0705-0*, Courage) Running Pr.

— Kiss: A Romantic Treasury. 2000. 19.98 (*0-7624-0877-4*) Running Pr.

— Library of Classic Women's Literature. 2000. pap. 15.95 (*0-7624-0873-1*) Running Pr.

— Little Book of Sign Language: Mini Edition. 2000. pap. 4.95 (*0-7624-0706-9*, Courage) Running Pr.

— Love Quotations from the Heart, Mini Edition. 1999. 4.95 (*0-7624-0665-8*) Running Pr.

— Meditations: A New Guide Book to Simple Wisdom, with Book & Meditation Cards. 128p. 2000. 9.98 (*0-7624-0771-9*) Running Pr.

Running Press Staff. Meditations: A Woman's Personal Journal, with Quotations. 144p. 1997. 14.95 (*0-7624-0052-8*) Running Pr.

***Running Press Staff.** Nutcracker: Mini Edition. 1999. 4.95 (*0-7624-0604-6*) Running Pr.

— Nutcracker: Mini Edition. 1999. 7.95 (*0-7624-0629-1*) Running Press Min.

— Nutcracker Keepsake With Nutcracker Figurine. 1999. 17.98 (*0-7624-0667-4*) Running Pr.

Running Press Staff. Peace Notebook: An Illustrated Journal, with Quotes. (Illus.). 96p. 1998. pap. 5.95 (*0-7624-0268-7*) Running Pr.

***Running Press Staff.** Pets. (Fit-A-Shape Ser.). 1999. 5.95 (*0-7624-0608-9*) Running Pr.

— Philadelphia: A Photographic Celebration. (Illus.). 128p. 2000. 13.98 (*0-7624-0683-6*, Courage) Running Pr.

— Quotable Women: A Celebration. 2000. 19.98 (*0-7624-0876-6*) Running Pr.

— Shapes. (Fit-a-Shape Ser.). (Illus.). (J). 2000. 6.95 (*0-7624-0814-6*) Running Pr.

— Shoes! A Personal Journal, with Heart & Sole. 2000. pap. 5.95 (*0-7624-0696-8*) Running Pr.

Running Press Staff. Simple Pleasures: A Journal of Life's Joys. 144p. 1996. 14.95 (*1-56138-755-X*) Running Pr.

***Running Press Staff.** Simple Pleasures Mini Edition. (Little Scribbles Ser.). 1999. 4.95 (*0-7624-0602-X*) Running Pr.

Running Press Staff. Sisters. 60p. 1997. 8.95 (*0-7624-0076-5*) Running Pr.

***Running Press Staff.** Unicorns 3-D Journal. (Illus.). (J). 2000. 14.95 (*0-7624-0460-4*) Running Pr.

— Vampires 3-D Journal. (Illus.). 128p. (gr. 3 up). 2000. 14.95 (*0-7624-0459-0*) Running Pr.

— Very Muppet Christmas Mini Edition. 1999. 4.95 (*0-7624-0590-2*) Running Pr.

— Weather. (Fit-A-Shape Ser.). 1999. 5.95 (*0-7624-0609-7*) Running Pr.

— Wine Spectator's Champagne. (Wine Spectator's Ser.). 1999. 4.95 (*0-7624-0654-2*) Running Pr.

— Wine Spectator's Little Book of Wine. (Wine Spectator's Ser.). 1999. 4.95 (*0-7624-0653-4*) Running Pr.

— Wine Spectator's Pocket Guide to Wine. 64p. 1999. 5.95 (*1-881659-55-0*, Wine Spectator) M Shanken Comm.

Running Press Staff. Wishes: A Personal Journal of Hopes & Dreams. (Illus.). 96p. 1996. pap. text 5.95 (*1-56138-701-0*) Running Pr.

— A Woman's Journal: A Blank Book with Quotes by Women. (Illus.). 192p. 1985. 14.95 (*0-89471-406-6*) Running Pr.

Running Press Staff, ed. Art of the Kiss: A Postcard Book. (Illus.). 1996. pap. 8.95 (*1-56138-726-6*) Running Pr.

— Beverly Clark's Wedding Collection. (Tender Notions Ser.). (Illus.). 2000. pap. 19.95 (*0-7624-0756-5*) Running Pr.

— Bless This Home: Everyday Blessings, Graces & Poems from Around the World with Home. 2000. pap. 17.95 (*0-7624-0796-4*) Running Pr.

— Celebration of Motherhood. (Tender Notions Ser.). (Illus.). 2000. 19.95 (*0-7624-0755-7*) Running Pr.

Running Press Staff, ed. Friendship Notes. (Notes Ser.). (Illus.). 80p. (Orig.). 1994. pap. 4.95 (*1-56138-482-8*) Running Pr.

— Georgia O'Keeffe: A Postcard Book. (Postcard Bks.). (Illus.). 64p. 1993. pap. 8.95 (*1-56138-163-2*) Running Pr.

— Marilyn Monroe: A Postcard Book. (Postcard Bks.). (Illus.). 64p. (Orig.). 1989. pap. text 8.95 (*0-89471-766-9*) Running Pr.

— Martini. (Illus.). 60p. 1998. pap. 8.95 (*0-7624-0371-3*) Running Pr.

— Matisse: A Postcard Book. (Postcard Bks.). (Illus.). 64p. (Orig.). 1989. pap. text 8.95 (*0-89471-711-1*) Running Pr.

— New Beginnings: A Notebook of Infinite Possibilities. (Illus.). 96p. (Orig.). 1991. pap. 5.95 (*1-56138-066-0*) Running Pr.

— Original Mother Goose. deluxe ed. LC 91-51057. (Illus.). 136p. (J). (ps-3). 1992. 15.95 (*1-56138-113-6*) Running Pr.

— Quotable Woman: Witty, Poignant & Insightful Observations from Notable Women. LC 91-52546. 92p. 1991. 12.95 (*1-56138-015-6*) Running Pr.

— Shoes. (Illus.). 60p. 1998. pap. 8.95 (*0-7624-0370-5*) Running Pr.

***Running Press Staff, ed.** 3D Mother Goose Nursery Rhymes. (Illus.). (J). 2001. 19.95 (*0-7624-0782-4*) Running Pr.

Running Press Staff, ed. Traveler's Diary. (Portable Diary Ser.). (Illus.). 144p. 1989. 11.95 (*0-89471-783-9*) Running Pr.

***Running Press Staff, ed.** Woman: Photos by the Magnum Cooperative & Essays from Prominent Feminist Writers. (Illus.). 2000. 29.95 (*0-7624-0356-X*) Running Pr.

Running Press Staff, ed. Women's Notes. (Notes Ser.). (Illus.). 80p. (Orig.). 1994. pap. 4.95 (*1-56138-481-X*) Running Pr.

Running Press Staff & Plaut, David. Baseball Wit & Wisdom: Miniature Edition. (Illus.). 144p. 1999. 4.95 (*0-7624-0512-0*) Running Press Min.

Running Press Staff, ed. see Smith, Lou E.

Running, Steven W., jt. ed. see Waring, Richard H.

Running, Thorpe. The Critical Poem: Borges, Paz, & Other Language-Centered Poets in Latin America. LC 95-45747. 192p. 1996. 32.50 (*0-8387-5319-1*) Bucknell U Pr.

***Running Times Magazine Staff, ed.** Guide to Breakthrough Running. LC 00-27146. (Illus.). 368p. 2000. pap. 19.95 (*0-7360-0217-0*) Human Kinetics.

Runnings, Anna. An Experimental Analysis of Two Bone Tools from the Manis Site, Sequim, Washington. xi, 84p. (C). 1984. pap. 10.63 (*1-55567-019-9*) Coyote Press.

Runnings, John & Bennett, Sue. I'm from Palestine... LC 82-243211. (Illus.). 40p. 1982. pap. 6.00 (*0-912021-00-4*) Grey Bk.

***RunningWolf, Michael B. & Smith, Patricia Clark.** On the Trail of Elder Brother: Glous'gap Stories of the Micmac Indians. LC 99-87597. (Illus.). 160p. 2000. 17.95 (*0-89255-248-4*, Pub. by Persea Bks) Norton.

Runnion, Dale F. & Runnion, June A. The Saddle & Sirloin Portrait Collection. 120p. 1992. pap. 10.00 (*0-9634756-0-6*) N Am Int Livestock.

***Runnion, Dale F., et al.** The Saddle & Sirloin Portrait Collection: A Biographical Catalog, Kentucky Fair & Exposition Center, Louisville, Kentucky. LC 98-67867. (Illus.). 119p. 1998. write for info. (*0-9634756-1-4*) N Am Int Livestock.

Runnion, June A., jt. auth. see Runnion, Dale F.

Runnion, June A., ed. see Goff, Dick, et al.

Runnion, William C. Structured Programming in Assembly Language for the IBM PC. 690p. (C). 1988. text 56.95 incl. disk (*0-534-91480-2*) PWS Pubs.

— Structured Programming in Assembly Language for the IBM PC. 2nd ed. LC 94-286. 1994. mass mkt. 95.95 (*0-534-93268-1*) PWS Pubs.

Runnymede Trust Staff. Equality Assurance in Schools. 72p. 1993. pap. 9.00 (*0-948080-91-4*, Trentham Bks) Stylus Pub VA.

Runolfson, Rodney & Schoemeh, Karen. The Consolidated Services Desk. 350p. (C). 1999. pap. 49.95 (*0-12-602870-2*) Acad Pr.

Runowicz, C. D. To Be Alive: A Woman's Guide to a Full Life After Cancer. 272p. 1996. pap. 14.95 (*0-8050-2959-1*, Owl) H Holt & Co.

Runowicz, Carolyn. Gynecologic Oncology. (Vademecum Ser.). 2001. spiral bd. 45.00 (*1-57059-582-8*) Landes Bioscience.

— To Be Alive. 1995. 22.50 (*0-8050-2958-3*) H Holt & Co.

Runowicz, Carolyn, jt. auth. see Cherry, Sheldon H.

Runowicz, Carolyn D., jt. auth. see Cherry, Sheldon H.

Runowitz, Carolyn, et al. The American Cancer Society: A Thorough & Compassionate Resource for Patients & Their Families. LC 98-39231. (Illus.). 336p. 1999. pap. 14.95 (*0-679-77814-4*) Random.

Runquist, Phillip. Ready-to-Use Outline Maps of U. S. States & Regions: 161 Different Copyright-Free Maps Printed One Side. (Clip Art Ser.). (Illus.). 64p. pap. 5.95 (*0-486-28056-X*) Dover.

Runquist, Phillip R. Ready-to-Use Contemporary Mortised Cuts. (Clip Art Ser.). (Illus.). 64p. pap. text 4.95 (*0-486-26334-7*) Dover.

— Ready-to-Use Illustrations of Cars, Trucks, Trains, Ships & Planes. (Clip Art Ser.). (Illus.). 64p. pap. 5.95 (*0-486-25768-1*) Dover.

— Ready-to-Use Pictographs of People. (Clip Art Ser.). (Illus.). 64p. pap. 4.95 (*0-486-27365-2*) Dover.

Runquist, Willie. Baseball by the Numbers: How Statistics are Collected, What They Mean, & How They Reveal the Game. LC 94-8901. 196p. 1995. pap. 24.95 (*0-7864-0006-4*) McFarland & Co.

Runser, Dennis J. Industrial-Academic Interfacing. LC 83-27558. (ACS Symposium Ser.: Vol. 244). 175p. 1984. reprint ed. pap. 54.30 (*0-608-03124-0*, 206357700007) Bks Demand.

— Maintaining & Troubleshooting HPLC Systems: A Users Guide. LC 80-25444. 184p. 1981. 89.95 (*0-471-06479-3*) Wiley.

Runser, Dennis J., ed. Industrial-Academic Interfacing. LC 83-27558. (ACS Symposium Ser.: No. 244). 176p. 1984. lib. bdg. 38.95 (*0-8412-0825-5*) Am Chemical.

Runst, Thomas & Sickel, Winfried. Sobolev Spaces of Fractional Order, Nemytskij Operators, & Nonlinear Partial Differential Equations. LC 96-31730. (Nonlinear Analysis & Applications Ser.). x, 547p. (C). 1996. text 158.95 (*3-11-015113-8*) De Gruyter.

Runstadler, P., ed. see Joint Fluids Engineering Gas Turbine Conference &.

***Runstein, Linda J.** Life Switch. 157p. 1999. pap. 13.95 (*0-7414-0123-1*) Buy Books.

Runsten, David & LeVeen, Phillip. Mechanization & Mexican Labor in California Agriculture. (Monographs: No. 6). 135p. (Orig.). (C). 1981. ring bd. 7.50 (*0-935391-44-4*, MN-06) UCSD Ctr US-Mex.

Runt, James P. & Fitzgerald, John J., eds. Dielectric Spectroscopy of Polymeric Materials: Fundamentals & Applications. LC 97-7622. (ACS Professional Reference Book Ser. ; An American Chemical Society Publication). (Illus.). 464p. 1997. text 124.95 (*0-8412-3335-7*, Pub. by Am Chemical) OUP.

Runte, Alfred E. National Parks: The American Experience. 3rd ed. LC 96-37399. (Illus.). xxiii, 379p. 1997. pap. 16.00 (*0-8032-8963-4*) U of Nebr Pr.

— Trains of Discovery: Western Railroads & the National Parks. limited rev. ed. (Illus.). 96p. 1993. 60.00 (*1-879373-74-2*) Roberts Rinehart.

— Trains of Discovery: Western Railroads & the National Parks. 3rd rev. ed. (Illus.). 96p. 1993. 35.00 (*1-879373-69-6*) Roberts Rinehart.

— Trains of Discovery: Western Railroads & the National Parks. 4th rev. ed. (Illus.). 112p. 1998. pap. 19.95 (*1-57098-231-7*, R Rinehart Intl) Roberts Rinehart.

— Yosemite: The Embattled Wilderness. LC 89-35128. (Illus.). xii, 319p. 1990. pap. 14.95 (*0-8032-8941-3*, Bison Books) U of Nebr Pr.

Runte, Hans R. & Runte, Roseann, eds. Oralite et Litterature-Orality & Literature: Actes du XIe Congres de L'Aaaociation Internationale de Litterature Comparee-Proceedings of the XIth Congress of the International Comparative Association. 260p. 1991. 39.80 (*0-8204-1372-0*) P Lang Pubng.

Runte, Roseann, jt. ed. see Runte, Hans R.

Runtz, Michael. The Howls of August: Encounters with Algonquin Wolves. LC 99-183488. (Illus.). 128p. 1997. pap. text 13.50 (*1-55046-195-8*, Pub. by Boston Mills) Genl Dist Srvs.

— Moose Country: Saga of the Woodland Moose. (Illus.). 112p. 1999. 39.95 (*0-7737-2469-9*) Genl Dist Srvs.

Runtz, Michael W. Moose Country: A Saga of the Woodland Moose. 112p. 1996. pap. 24.95 (*0-7737-5766-X*) Stoddart Publ.

Runtz, Michael W. Wild Flowers: Beauty & The Beasts. LC 97-136015. (Illus.). 120p. text 16.00 (*1-55046-106-0*, Pub. by Boston Mills) Genl Dist Srvs.

— Wild Things: The Hidden World Of Animals. LC 97-136008. (Illus.). 120p. 1996. text 16.00 (*1-55046-140-0*, Pub. by Boston Mills) Genl Dist Srvs.

— Wild Wings: The Hidden World Of Birds. LC 97-136013. (Illus.). 120p. 1996. text 16.00 (*1-55046-184-2*, Pub. by Boston Mills) Genl Dist Srvs.

Runtz, Vic. Here Today: Twenty-Five Years of Cartoons. 1983. 19.95 (*0-89101-060-2*); pap. 9.95 (*0-89101-059-9*) U Maine Pr.

Runyan. Precalculus: Making Connections. 752p. 1998. pap. text 44.00 (*0-13-095674-0*) P-H.

— Precalculus Whetstone. 1999. pap. text, student ed. 10.00 (*0-13-934282-6*) P-H.

Runyan, Anne S., jt. auth. see Marchand, Marianne H.

Runyan, Anne Sisson, jt. auth. see Peterson, V. Spike.

Runyan, Anne Sisson, jt. ed. see Marchand, Marianne H.

Runyan, Cathy C. Knuckles Down! A Fun Guide to Marble Play. 3rd ed. (Illus.). 36p. (J). (gr. 1-6). 1990. reprint ed. pap. 5.95 (*0-935295-01-1*) Right Brain.

Runyan, Donna H., jt. auth. see Hull, M. Alison.

Runyan, Holly, jt. auth. see Runyan, Lawrence.

Runyan, Lawrence & Runyan, Holly. Precalculus: A Functional Approach. 1991. text. write for info. (*0-07-909943-2*) McGraw.

Runyan, Robyn. You Can Come Back. 1996. pap. 12.95 (*1-885487-22-3*) Brownell & Carroll.

Runyan, Ruth A., jt. auth. see Wilson, Ewen.

Runyan-Svacina, Cathy. What Goes Around . . . LC 98-65695. 608p. 1998. pap. 19.95 (*1-890622-29-X*) Leathers Pub.

Runyan, Timothy J., ed. Ships, Seafaring & Society: Essays in Maritime History. LC 87-17769. 382p. 1987. pap. 18.95 (*0-8143-1991-2*) Wayne St U Pr.

Runyan, Timothy J., et al, eds. Ships, Seafaring & Society: Essays in Maritime History. LC 87-14226. (Illus.). 382p. reprint ed. pap. 118.50 (*0-608-10610-0*, 2071232) Bks Demand.

Runyan, W. R. Silicon Semiconductor Technology. LC 64-24607. (Texas Instruments Electronics Ser.). (Illus.). 284p. reprint ed. pap. 81.00 (*0-608-10237-7*, 2055600) Bks Demand.

Runyan, W. R. & Shaffner, T. J. Semiconductor Measurements & Instrumentation. 2nd ed. LC 97-26081. (Illus.). 454p. 1998. 70.00 (*0-07-057697-1*) McGraw.

Runyan, William M. Life Histories & Psychobiography: Explorations in Theory & Method. (Illus.). 302p. 1984. pap. text 21.95 (*0-19-503486-4*) OUP.

Runyan, William M., ed. Psychology & Historical Interpretation. (Illus.). 320p. 1988. pap. text 22.95 (*0-19-505328-1*) OUP.

Runyeon, Richard. Creating a Life-Long-Love Relationship: Primary Relationship Primer. 1997. 16.95 (*0-9659866-0-8*) Grace Matters.

Runyon, Beverly B. The Overloving Parent: Making Love Work for You & Your Child. 160p. 1992. pap. 10.95 (*0-87833-803-9*) Taylor Pub.

Runyon, Carroll. The Book of Solomon's Magick. LC 96-92734. (Illus.). 232p. 1996. pap. 24.95 (*0-9654881-1-X*) C H S Inc.

Runyon, Cheryl C. & Davis, Asiyih. Developing a Multipurpose Canister System for Spent Nuclear Fuel. (State Legislative Reports: Vol. 19, No. 4). 3p. 1994. 15.00 (*1-55516-095-6*, 7302-1904) Natl Conf State Legis.

Runyon, Cheryl C. & Helland, John. Wetlands Mitigation & Mitigation Banking. LC 97-190583. 24p. 1995. 10.00 (*1-55516-403-X*, 4342) Natl Conf State Legis.

Runyon, Cheryl C. & Morandi, Larry. Protecting Estuaries: The Mix of Land & Sea. 30p. 1993. 10.00 (*1-55516-376-9*, 4338) Natl Conf State Legis.

Runyon, D. Damon Runyon Reader. 25.95 (*0-89190-781-5*) Amereon Ltd.

Runyon, Damon. Bloodhounds Broadway. 2000. mass mkt. 3.95 (*0-380-70653-9*, Avon Bks) Morrow Avon.

— Blue Plate Special. 19.95 (*0-89190-360-7*) Amereon Ltd.

— Broadway, Mon Village. (FRE.). 1982. pap. 11.95 (*0-7859-4165-7*) Fr & Eur.

— Le Complexe de Broadway. (FRE.). 320p. 1982. pap. 11.95 (*0-7859-4169-X*, 2070373886) Fr & Eur.

— Damon Runyon Favorites. reprint ed. lib. bdg. 22.95 (*0-89190-440-9*, Rivercity Pr) Amereon Ltd.

— Damon Runyon Omnibus. 1976. reprint ed. lib. bdg. 32.95 (*0-89190-441-7*, Rivercity Pr) Amereon Ltd.

— Damon Runyon Omnibus. 1993. reprint ed. lib. bdg. 28.95 (*1-56849-217-0*) Buccaneer Bks.

— Guys & Dolls. reprint ed. lib. bdg. 20.95 (*0-89190-438-7*, Rivercity Pr) Amereon Ltd.

— Guys & Dolls: The Stories of Damon Runyon. LC 92-27639. 480p. 1992. pap. 14.95 (*0-14-017659-4*, Penguin Bks) Viking Penguin.

— In Our Town. 126p. Date not set. 17.95 (*0-8488-2593-4*) Amereon Ltd.

— Jack Johnson: In the Ring - & Out - the Autobiography of Jack Johnson. (Illus.). 272p. 1992. pap. 10.95 (*0-8065-1358-6*, Citadel Pr) Carol Pub Group.

— Little Miss Marker. reprint ed. lib. bdg. 19.95 (*0-89190-436-0*, Rivercity Pr) Amereon Ltd.

— Money from Home. 19.95 (*0-89190-361-5*) Amereon Ltd.

— Poems for Men. 22.95 (*0-8488-1145-3*) Amereon Ltd.

— Ring-Tailed, Red-Eyed Sons O' Trouble. 24.95 (*0-8488-0144-X*) Amereon Ltd.

— Slight Case of Murder. 17.95 (*0-8488-1143-7*) Amereon Ltd.

— Slow Horses & Fast Women. (Illus.). reprint ed. lib. bdg. 22.95 (*0-89190-439-5*, Rivercity Pr) Amereon Ltd.

— Tents of Trouble: Verse of D. Runyon. 17.95 (*0-8488-0841-X*) Amereon Ltd.

— Trials & Other Tribulations. 23.95 (*0-8488-1619-6*) Amereon Ltd.

— Troopers, Tramps & Other Loose Characters. 23.95 (*0-8488-0145-8*) Amereon Ltd.

Runyon, Daniel V. Ferguson: Her Tractor-Biography. (Illus.). 128p. 1995. pap. 10.00 (*1-878559-03-6*) Saltbox Pr.

Runyon, Daniel V., ed. World Mission People: The Best of the Missionary Tidings, 1990-95. 400p. 1995. pap. 15.00 (*1-878559-04-4*) Saltbox Pr.

Runyon, Daniel V., jt. auth. see Snyder, Howard A.

Runyon, Daniel V., ed. see Cox, Betty E.

Runyon, Daniel V., ed. see Locke, David R. & Maurer, Kent L.

Runyon, Daniel V., ed. see Watson, C. Hoyt.

Runyon, Kenneth E. Consumer Behavior. Stewart, David W., ed. (C). 1998. text. write for info. (*0-321-01412-X*) Addson-Wesley Educ.

Runyon, Linda. Backyard Wild Food Recipes. 2nd ed. Dixon, Althea, ed. (Illus.). 16p. 1996. pap. 6.50 (*0-936699-38-8*) Wild Foods Co.

— A Basic Middle Eastern Desert Survival Guide: Of Common Edible Wild Foods. rev. ed. Kurdish Museum Staff, ed. (Illus.). 42p. 1997. pap., ring bd. 10.00 (*0-936699-88-4*) Wild Foods Co.

— Crabgrass Muffins & Pine Needle Tea: How to Identify, Enjoy, & Cook the Cornucopia of Wild Foods Growing Among us. LC 93-25247. 1994. 20.00 (*0-517-88033-4*) Harmony Bks.

An Asterisk (*) at the beginning of an entry indicates that the title is appearing for the first time.

— A Survival Acre - Fifty Nationwide Wild Foods & Medicines. (Illus.). 43p. (Orig.). 1985. pap. 10.00 (*0-918517-03-6*) Wild Foods Co.

Runyon, Mildred M. Are Clowns Hatched? Life of Chucko the Clown. LC 93-80477. (Illus.). 180p. (Orig.). 1994. pap. 19.95 (*1-884431-09-7*) Gold Ring Pubng.

Runyon, Randolph. Fowles, Irving & Barthes: Canonical Variations on an Apocryphal Theme. LC 81-11125. (Illus.). 135p. reprint ed. pap. 41.90 (*0-608-09875-2*, 206984100006) Bks Demand.

Runyon, Randolph P. The Braided Dream: Robert Penn Warren's Late Poetry. LC 89-48187. 264p. 1990. text 30.00 (*0-8131-1722-4*) U Pr of Ky.

— Reading Raymond Carver. LC 91-36790. 246p. 1992. 45.00 (*0-8156-2563-4*) Syracuse U Pr.

— Reading Raymond Carver. LC 91-36790. 246p. (C). 1993. reprint ed. pap. text 19.95 (*0-8156-2631-2*) Syracuse U Pr.

— The Taciturn Text: The Fiction of Robert Penn Warren. LC 89-30177. 262p. reprint ed. pap. 81.30 (*0-608-09874-4*, 206983900006) Bks Demand.

Runyon, Randolph Paul. Delia Webster & the Underground Railroad. (Illus.). 264p. 1999. pap. 18.00 (*0-8131-0974-4*) U Pr of Ky.

Runyon, Richard P. Descriptive Statistics: A Contemporary Approach. LC 76-15467. (Statistics Ser.). (C). 1977. pap. text. write for info. (*0-201-06652-1*) Addison-Wesley.

— Winning with Statistics: A Painless First Look at Numbers, Ratios, Percentages, Means & Inference. (Statistics Ser.). (Illus.). 1977. pap. text. write for info. (*0-201-06654-8*) Addison-Wesley.

Runyon, Richard P. & Pittenger, David J. Fundamentals of Behavioral Statistics. 8th ed. (C). 1995. pap., student ed. 26.25 (*0-07-054988-5*) McGraw.

Runyon, Richard P., et al. Behavioral Statistics: The Core. (C). 1994. pap., student ed. 25.00 (*0-07-054926-5*); pap., student ed. 52.50 (*0-07-911433-4*) McGraw.

— Fundamentals of Behavioral Statistics. 8th rev. ed. LC 95-38509. 624p. (C). 1995. 79.69 (*0-07-054985-0*) McGraw.

***Runyon, Richard P., et al.** Fundamentals of Behavioral Statistics. 9th ed. LC 99-14482. 2000. write for info. (*0-07-228641-5*) McGrw-H Highr Educ.

Runyon, Richard P., jt. auth. see Haber, Audrey.

Runyon, Theodore. The New Creation: John Wesley's Theology Today. LC 97-42936. 288p. 1998. pap. 20.95 (*0-687-09602-2*) Abingdon.

Runyon, Theodore H., ed. Theology, Politics, & Peace. LC 89-15977. 223p. 1989. reprint ed. pap. 69.20 (*0-7837-9838-5*, 206056700005) Bks Demand.

***Runzo, Joseph.** Global Philosophy of Religion. 2000. pap. 14.95 (*1-85168-235-X*, Pub. by Onewrld Pubns) Penguin Putnam.

— Love, Sex & Gender in the World Religions. 2000. pap. 19.95 (*1-85168-223-6*, Pub. by Onewrld Pubns) Penguin Putnam.

Runzo, Joseph. Worldviews & Perceiving God. LC 93-26988. 1993. text 45.00 (*0-312-10379-4*) St Martin.

Runzo, Joseph & Ihara, Graig K., eds. Religious Experience & Religious Belief: Essays in the Epistemology of Religion. LC 86-1614. 160p. (C). 1986. pap. text 19.50 (*0-8191-5293-5*) U Pr of Amer.

Ruocchio, Albert C. & Klein, Maury D. Track Layout & Accessory Manual for Lionel Trains. (Illus.). 1979. pap. 3.95 (*0-934580-08-1*, K-4) MDK Inc.

Ruocco, L. A. Document Zippo. 188p. 1999. pap. 16.00 (*1-887128-29-8*) Soft Skull Pr.

Ruof, George C. Christmas Stories. 1994. 10.00 (*0-533-10983-3*) Vantage.

Ruoff, A. LaVonne. American Indian Literatures: An Introduction, Bibliographic Review & Selected Bibliography. LC 90-13438. (Illus.). viii, 200p. 1990. pap. 19.75 (*0-87352-192-7*, B106P); lib. bdg. 45.00 (*0-87352-191-9*) Modern Lang.

Ruoff, A. LaVonne, Jr. & Ward, Jerry W., Jr., eds. Redefining American Literary History. LC 90-6530. (Committee on Literatures & Languages of America Ser.). iv, 406p. 1990. pap. 19.75 (*0-87352-188-9*, B105P); lib. bdg. 45.00 (*0-87352-187-0*, B105C) Modern Lang.

Ruoff, A. Lavonne, jt. auth. see Johnson, E. Pauline.

Ruoff, A. LaVonne, ed. see Copway, George.

Ruoff, A. LaVonne, ed. & intro. see Callahan, S. Alice.

Ruoff, Abby. Making Rustic Originals: Turning Furniture Finds into Folk Art. LC 98-35415. (Illus.). 216p. 1999. pap. 24.95 (*0-88179-155-5*) Hartley & Marks.

— Making Twig Furniture & Household Things. 3rd rev. ed. LC 99-43782. (Illus.). 320p. 2000. pap. 24.95 (*0-88179-185-7*, Pub. by Hartley & Marks) Andrews & McMeel.

— Making Twig Garden Furniture. LC 96-52936. (Illus.). 208p. 1997. pap. 24.95 (*0-88179-144-X*) Hartley & Marks.

***Ruoff, Abby.** Making Twig Garden Furniture. 2nd ed. (Illus.). 2000. 24.95 (*0-88179-186-5*) Hartley & Marks.

— Rustic Country: Handmade Accents for the Home. (Illus.). 160p. 2000. 34.95 (*0-87905-979-6*) Gibbs Smith Pub.

Ruoff-Appel, Andrea, ed. see Vollman, June.

Ruoff, Arthur L. Introduction to Materials Science. LC 79-4668. 718p. 1979. reprint ed. lib. bdg. 64.50 (*0-88275-960-4*) Krieger.

Ruoff, Carl F. & Skaar, Steven B., eds. Teleoperation & Robotics in Space. (Illus.). 502p. 1994. 99.95 (*1-56347-095-0*, V-161(890)) AIAA.

Ruoff, E. G., ed. Death Throes of a Dynasty: Letters & Diaries of Charles & Bessie Ewing, Missionaries to China. LC 90-35339. (Illus.). 286p. 1990. 29.00 (*0-87338-414-8*) Kent St U Pr.

Ruoff, Gene W. Wordsworth & Coleridge: The Making of the Major Lyrics, 1802-1804. LC 88-28292. 320p. (C). 1989. pap. text 19.00 (*0-8135-1399-5*) Rutgers U Pr.

Ruoff, Gene W., ed. The Romantics & Us: Essays on Literature & Culture. 275p. (Orig.). (C). 1990. pap. 19.00 (*0-8135-1499-1*); text 45.00 (*0-8135-1498-3*) Rutgers U Pr.

Ruoff, Gene W., jt. ed. see Kroeber, Karl.

Ruoff, Lou. Parables of Conversion: Lectionary Stories That Will Change Your Life. LC 96-40258. 128p. (Orig.). 1997. pap. text 10.95 (*0-89390-403-1*) Resource Pubns.

Ruoff, Mona. From the Dragon's Cloud: Vietnamese Folk Tales. (Illus.). 63p. (Orig.). 1984. reprint ed. pap. 5.00 (*0-9619969-5-1*) Blue Horse Pr.

Ruoff, R., jt. auth. see Kadish, K.

Ruoff, R. S., jt. auth. see Kadish, K. M.

Ruoff, R. S., jt. ed. see Kadish, K. M.

Ruoff, Rodney S., jt. ed. see Kadish, Karl M.

Ruoff, Shari, ed. see Vollman, June.

Ruoff, Theodore, jt. compiled by see Fourmat's Editorial Staff.

Ruokanen, Miikka. The Catholic Doctrine of Non-Christian Religions According to the Second Vatican Council. LC 91-46332. (Studies in Christian Mission: Vol. 7). 169p. 1992. 67.50 (*90-04-09517-9*) Brill Academic Pubs.

Ruokonen, Kyllikki. India Information Sources, Economics & Business. (Concepts in Communication Informatics & Librarianship Ser.: No. 38). (C). 1992. text 26.00 (*81-7022-437-3*, Pub. by Concept) S Asia.

Ruokonen, T., ed. Fault Detection, Supervision & Safety for Technical Processes 1994. LC 94-37925. 790p. 1994. pap. 120.50 (*0-08-042222-5*, Pergamon Pr) Elsevier.

Ruopp, Phillips. Private Testimony & Public Policy. (C). 1959. pap. 4.00 (*0-87574-105-3*) Pendle Hill.

Ruopp, Richard R., et al, eds. Labnet: Toward a Community of Practice. (Technology & Education Ser.). 384p. 1993. pap. 45.00 (*0-8058-1294-6*); text 89.95 (*0-8058-1263-6*) L Erlbaum Assocs.

Ruosla, jt. see Weinberg.

Ruoslahti, Erkki, et al, eds. Extracellular Matrix Components. (Methods in Enzymology Ser.: Vol. 245). (Illus.). 638p. 1995. text 94.00 (*0-12-182146-3*) Acad Pr.

Ruoss, Martin. A Policy & Procedure Manual for Church & Synagogue Libraries: A Do-It-Yourself Guide. LC 79-28676. (Guide Ser.: No. 9). 14p. 1998. pap. 9.00 (*0-915324-17-2*) CSLA.

Ruoti, Richard. Aquatic Rehabilitation. LC 96-2682. 400p. 1996. text 49.00 (*0-397-55152-5*) Lppncott W & W.

Ruotolo, George L. A Format for Successful Accident Reconstruction Report Writing. 40p. (C). 1993. pap. text 14.95 (*1-884566-13-8*) Inst Police Tech.

Ruotolo, Lucio P. The Interrupted Moment: A View of Virginia Woolf's Novels. LC 86-6002. 280p. 1986. pap. 13.95 (*0-8047-1523-8*) Stanford U Pr.

— Six Existential Heroes: The Politics of Faith. LC 72-86386. 173p. reprint ed. pap. 53.70 (*0-7837-4187-1*, 205903700012) Bks Demand.

Ruotolo, Lucio P., ed. see Woolf, Virginia.

Ruotsala, Jim. Pilots of the Panhandle: Aviation in Southeast Alaska, the Early Years, 1920-1935. LC 97-91980. (Illus.). 120p. 1997. pap. 29.95 (*0-9658830-0-0*) Seadrome Pr.

Ruowang, Wang. Hunger Trilogy. Rubin, Kyna & Kasoff, Ira E., trs. from CHI. LC 91-9017. 176p. (C). (gr. 13). 1991. 61.95 (*0-87332-739-X*, East Gate Bk) M E Sharpe.

— Hunger Trilogy. Rubin, Kyna & Kasoff, Ira, trs. from CHI. LC 91-9017. 176p. (C). (gr. 13). 1992. pap. 22.50 (*0-87332-740-3*, East Gate Bk) M E Sharpe.

Ruoxi, Chen. Democracy Wall & the Unofficial Journals. (Current Chinese Language Project Ser.: No. 20). 119p. 1983. pap. text 5.00 (*0-912966-57-2*) IEAS.

— The Short Stories of Chen Ruoxi, Translated from the Original Chinese: A Writer at the Crossroads. Kao, Hsin-sheng C., ed. LC 92-29960. 420p. 1992. 109.95 (*0-7734-9190-2*) E Mellen.

Ruoxi, Chen, jt. auth. see Dittmer, Lowell.

Ruozi, R. & Anderloni, L., eds. Banking Privatisation in Europe: The Process & the Consequences on Stategies & Organizational Structures. LC 99-31191. (Illus.). xiv, 321p. 1999. 89.95 (*3-540-65788-6*) Spr-Verlag.

Rupa, ed. see Sen, Geeti.

Rupa Vitasa Dasa, pseud. A Ray of Vishnu: The Biography of a Saktyavesa. (Lives of Vaisnava Acaryas Ser.: Vol. 1). (Illus.). 291p. (Orig.). (C). 1988. pap. 9.95 (*0-923519-01-7*) New Jaipur.

***Ruparelia, Nayan.** MQSeries Messaging. (Illus.). 400p. 2000. pap. 59.95 (*1-884777-98-8*, Pub. by Manning Pubns) IPG Chicago.

RuPaul. Lettin' It All Hang Out: An Autobiography. (Illus.). 240p. (J). 1995. 19.45 (*0-7868-6156-8*, Pub. by Hyperion) Time Warner.

RuPaul. Lettin' It All Hang Out: An Autobiography. Cashion, David, ed. LC 94-43503. (Illus.). 240p. (J). 1996. reprint ed. pap. 10.45 (*0-7868-8165-8*, Pub. by Hyperion) Time Warner.

Rupel, Cynthia A. Select Poems of Cynthia A. Y. Rupel. 28p. 1997. pap. 10.00 (*0-944551-20-3*) Sundance Pr TX.

Rupen, Robert A. Mongols of the Twentieth Century. LC 63-64522. (Uralic & Altaic Ser.: Vol. 37-Pt. 2). (Orig.). 1964. pap. text. write for info. (*0-87750-062-2*) Mongolia.

Ruperell, Tinu, jt. ed. see Markham, Ian S.

Rupert, David, jt. auth. see Lesch, William C.

Rupert, Hoover. Why Didn't Noah Swat Both Mosquitoes? Plus Other Humorous Stories for Clergy. LC 93-44439. 100p. 1994. pap. 11.95 (*1-55673-519-7*) CSS OH.

Rupert, James. Mini: The Complete Story. (Illus.). 200p. 1997. 35.95 (*1-86126-047-4*, Pub. by Crolwood) Motorbooks Intl.

Rupert, Janet E. The African Mask. LC 93-7726. 144p. (J). 1994. 15.00 (*0-395-67295-3*, Clarion Bks) HM.

***Rupert, Mark.** Ideologies of Globalization: Contending Visions of a New World Order. LC 00-38258. 2000. pap. write for info. (*0-415-18925-X*) Routledge.

Rupert, Mark. Producing Hegemony: The Politics of Mass Production & American Global Power. (Studies in International Relations: No. 38). (Illus.). 277p. (C). 1995. pap. text 19.95 (*0-521-46650-4*) Cambridge U Pr.

Rupert, Raymond H. New Era of Investment Banking: Industry Structure, Trends & Performance. 400p. 1993. 75.00 (*1-55738-454-1*, Irwn Prfssnl) McGraw-Hill Prof.

Rupert, Rona. Straw Sense. LC 92-8775. (Illus.). (J). 1993. pap. 14.00 (*0-671-77047-0*) S&S Bks Yung.

Ruperti, Alexander. Astrological Passages: The Planetary Pattern of Growth. 274p. 1999. pap. 14.95 (*0-935127-75-5*, Pub. by ACS Pubns) ACCESS Pubs Network.

Ruperti, George, jt. auth. see Tribbeko, John.

Rupesinge, Kumar & Mumtaz, Khawar, eds. Internal Conflicts in South Asia. LC 96-142007. 256p. (C). 1996. 65.00 (*0-8039-7752-2*) Sage.

Rupesinghe, Kumar. Ethnicity & Power in the Contemporary World. LC 97-108072. 200p. 35.00 (*92-808-0908-3*, UNUP-0908) UN.

Rupesinghe, Kumar, ed. Conflict Resolution in Uganda. LC 89-30799. 316p. 1989. text 29.95 (*0-8214-0929-8*) Ohio U Pr.

Rupesinghe, Kumar, et al, eds. Ethnicity & Conflict in a Post-Communist World: The Soviet Union, Eastern Europe, & China. LC 92-11320. 1992. text 69.95 (*0-312-08565-6*) St Martin.

Rupesinghe, Kumar & Anderlini, Sanam Naraghi. Civil Wars, Civil Peace: An Introduction to Conflict Resolution. LC 97-44921. 192p. 1998. 49.95 (*0-7453-1242-X*, Pub. by Pluto GBR); pap. 16.95 (*0-7453-1237-3*, Pub. by Pluto GBR) Stylus Pub VA.

Rupesunghe, Kumar, et al. Ethnic Conflict & Human Rights in Sri Lanka Volume 2: An Annoted Bibliography: 1989-1992. annot. ed. LC 89-2077. 313p. 1993. 75.00 (*1-873836-80-5*, Pub. by H Zell Pubs) Seven Hills Bk.

Rupieper, Herman J. The Cuno Government & Reparations, 1922-1923. (Studies in Contemporary History: No. 1). 1979. pap. text 155.50 (*90-247-2114-8*) Kluwer Academic.

Rupinska, M., jt. auth. see Maronski, J.

Rupke, Nicolaas A. Richard Owen: Victorian Naturalist. LC 93-5739. (Illus.). 480p. 1994. 50.00 (*0-300-05820-9*) Yale U Pr.

Rupke, Nicolaas A., ed. Vivisection in Historical Perspective. LC 87-8992. 373p. 1987. 85.00 (*0-7099-4236-2*, Pub. by C Helm) Routldge.

Ruple, Joelyn. Antonio Buero Vallejo: The First Fifteen Years. 1971. 12.95 (*0-88303-006-3*); pap. 8.95 (*0-685-73210-X*) E Torres & Sons.

Rupley. Take Excel for Windows to the Edge. 1995. 39.95 (*1-56276-109-9*, Ziff-Davis Pr) Que.

Rupley, Agnes E. Manual of Avian Practice. Donley, Stephanie, ed. LC 96-34618. (Illus.). 576p. 1997. pap. text 49.00 (*0-7216-4083-4*, W B Saunders Co) Harcrt Hlth Sci Grp.

Rupley, Frances. A Walking Tour of the University at Buffalo: And Other Area Architectural Treasures. LC 93-12107. (Illus.). 119p. (Orig.). (C). 1993. pap. 15.95 (*0-87975-813-9*) Prometheus Bks.

Rupley, Lawrence, jt. auth. see Mcfarland, Daniel M.

Rupley, Sebastian. Portable Computing Official Laptop Field Manual. LC 90-84499. 205p. 1994. 14.95 (*1-878058-10-X*) IDG Bks.

Rupley, William. Phonics Research & Instruction. 104p. (C). 1995. pap. text, ring bd. 20.95 (*0-7872-1499-X*, 41149901) Kendall-Hunt.

Rupley, William H. & Blair, Timothy R. Teaching Reading: Diagnosis, Direct Instruction Practice. 2nd ed. 256p. (C). 1990. pap. text 41.00 (*0-675-20891-2*, Merrill Coll) P-H.

Ruplin, Ferdinand A. & Russell, John R. Basic German: A Programmed Course. (C). 1969. reprint ed. pap. text 8.95 (*0-89197-535-7*); reprint ed. 0.65 (*0-8290-1410-1*) Irvington.

Rupnow, Marcia E. & Miller, Richard K. Bioremediation. (Survey on Technology & Markets Ser.: No. 226). 50p. 1994. pap. text 200.00 (*1-55865-257-4*) Future Tech Surveys.

— Environmental Test Laboratories. (Survey on Technology & Markets Ser.: No. 222). 50p. 1994. pap. text 200.00 (*1-55865-256-6*) Future Tech Surveys.

— Geographic Information Systems. (Survey on Technology & Markets Ser.: No. 233). 50p. 1994. pap. text 200.00 (*1-55865-264-7*) Future Tech Surveys.

— Incinerator Construction. (Survey on Technology & Markets Ser.: No. 231). 50p. 1994. pap. text 200.00 (*1-55865-262-0*) Future Tech Surveys.

— Independent Power Production. (Survey on Technology & Markets Ser.: No. 232). 50p. (Orig.). 1994. pap. text 200.00 (*1-55865-263-9*) Future Tech Surveys.

— Industrial Wastewater Treatment. (Survey on Technology & Markets Ser.: No. 229). 50p. 1994. 200.00 (*1-55865-260-4*) Future Tech Surveys.

— Municipal Wastewater Treatment. (Survey on Technology & Markets Ser.: No. 230). 50p. 1994. 200.00 (*1-55865-261-2*) Future Tech Surveys.

Rupnow, Marcia E., jt. auth. see Miller, Richard K.

Rupow, Marcia E. & Miller, Richard K. Groundwater Remediation. (Survey on Technology & Markets Ser.: No. 228). 50p. 1994. 200.00 (*1-55865-259-0*) Future Tech Surveys.

Rupp, Anne N. Celebrating the Advent-Christmas Season. 50p. (Orig.). 1989. pap. 9.25 (*0-940754-79-7*) Ed Ministries.

— Christmas Everywhere. 80p. 1994. pap. 12.95 (*1-877871-67-2*, 2570) Ed Ministries.

— Growing Together: Understanding & Nurturing Your Child's Faith Journey. LC 95-83740. 261p. 1996. pap. 11.95 (*0-87303-238-1*) Faith & Life.

— Walking Towards Pentecost. 157p. 1996. pap. 14.95 (*1-877871-95-8*, 2686) Ed Ministries.

Rupp, David W., ed. Western Cyprus - Connections: An Archaeological Symposium Held at Brock University, St. Catharines, Ontario, Canada. (Studies in Mediterranean Archaeology: Vol. LXXVII). (Illus.). 240p. (Orig.). 1987. pap. 95.00 (*91-86098-57-8*, Pub. by P Astroms) Coronet Bks.

Rupp, Diana. Pennsylvania: A Guide to Backcountry Travel & Adventure. 415p. 1999. pap. 16.00 (*1-893695-00-X*) Out There Pr.

Rupp, E. Gordon, ed. see Erasmus, Desiderius.

Rupp, Ernest G. Six Makers of English Religion, 1500-1700. (Essay Index Reprint Ser.). 1977. reprint ed. 19.95 (*0-518-10159-2*) Ayer.

Rupp, Galen, jt. auth. see Tennant, Kirk.

Rupp, George H. A Wavering Friendship: Russia & Austria, 1876-1878. LC 76-8455. (Perspectives in European History Ser.: No. 11). xiv, 599p. 1976. reprint ed. lib. bdg. 57.50 (*0-87991-617-6*) Porcupine Pr.

Rupp, Gerhard. Wozu Kultur? Zur Funktion Von Sprache, Literatur und Unterricht. (GER., Illus.). 310p. 1997. 63.95 (*3-631-30753-5*) P Lang Pubng.

Rupp, Gordon. Religion in England, 1688-1781. LC 85-23886. (History of the Christian Church Ser.). 520p. 1987. 105.00 (*0-19-826918-8*) OUP.

Rupp, Gretchen L. & Jones, Roy R., Sr., eds. Characterizing Heterogeneous Wastes: Methods & Recommendations. LC 92-35493. 176p. 1992. lib. bdg. 79.95 (*0-8493-8720-5*, TD793) CRC Pr.

Rupp, Heinz & International Society for Molecular Nutrition & Th. The Excess Catecholamine Syndrome: From Cause to Therapy, Symposium-Stuttgart, Germany, June 29, 1995. LC 96-39362. 1996. lib. bdg. write for info. (*0-7923-4328-X*) Kluwer Academic.

Rupp, Heinz, jt. ed. see Maurer, Friedrich.

Rupp, I. D. Early History of Western Pennsylvania & of the West: And of the Western Expeditions & Campaigns from MDCCLIV to MDCCCXXXIII. LC 95-80270. (Great Pennsylvania Frontier Ser.: Vol. 5). (Illus.). 776p. 1995. reprint ed. 44.95 (*1-889037-04-4*, 5) Wennawoods.

Rupp, I. Daniel. History of Lancaster County, Pennsylvania: To Which Is Prefixed a Brief Sketch of the Early History of Pennsylvania. (Illus.). 570p. 1990. reprint ed. pap. 27.50 (*1-55613-295-6*) Heritage Bk.

— History of Northampton, Lehigh, Monroe, Carbon, & Schuylkill Counties. (Illus.). 568p. 1992. reprint ed. lib. bdg. 59.00 (*0-8328-2253-1*) Higginson Bk Co.

Rupp, Israel D. He Pasa Ekklesia: An Original History of the Religious Denominations at Present Existing in the United States Containing Authentic Accounts of Their Rise, Progress, Statistics. 1977. 33.95 (*0-8369-7149-3*, 7981) Ayer.

— History of Northampton, Lehigh, Monroe, Carbon, & Schuylkill Counties. LC 71-146417. (First American Frontier Ser.). (Illus.). 1971. reprint ed. 45.95 (*0-405-02881-4*) Ayer.

— The Religious Denominations in the United States: Their Past History, Present Condition, & Doctrines. LC 72-2943. reprint ed. 115.00 (*0-404-10709-5*) AMS Pr.

Rupp, J., ed. see Hierosolymitanus, Cyrillus.

Rupp, James E., jt. compiled by see Rupp, Nadine.

Rupp, Jean. Flawless Grammar at Your Fingertips: An Instant Guide to Perfect Grammar for Everybody in Business. Orig. Title: Grammar Gremlins: An Instant Guide to Perfect Grammar for Everybody in Business. (Illus.). 124p. 1998. reprint ed. pap. 10.00 (*1-885221-99-1*) BookPartners.

Rupp, Joyce. The Cup of Our Life: A Guide for Spiritual Growth. LC 97-19768. (Illus.). 184p. 1997. pap. 12.95 (*0-87793-625-0*) Ave Maria.

— Dear Heart, Come Home: The Path of Midlife Spirituality. 208p. (Orig.). 1996. pap. text 13.95 (*0-8245-1556-0*) Crossroad NY.

— Fresh Bread: And Other Gifts of Spiritual Nourishment. LC 85-70020. 160p. 1985. pap. 9.95 (*0-87793-283-2*) Ave Maria.

— Little Pieces of Light: Darkness & Personal Growth. LC 94-30803. (Illumination Bks.). 80p. 1994. pap. 5.95 (*0-8091-3512-4*) Paulist Pr.

— May I Have This Dance? LC 92-71817. (Illus.). 184p. (Orig.). 1992. pap. 11.95 (*0-87793-480-0*) Ave Maria.

***Rupp, Joyce.** Out of the Ordinary: Prayers, Poems & Reflections for Every Season. LC 99-52395. 256p. 2000. pap. 13.95 (*0-87793-920-9*) Ave Maria.

Rupp, Joyce. Prayers to Sophia: A Companion to "The Star in My Heart" LC 99-56817. (Illus.). 128p. 2000. pap. 12.95 (*1-880913-42-9*) Innisfree Pr.

— Praying Our Goodbyes. LC 87-72291. 184p. 1988. pap. 9.95 (*0-87793-370-7*) Ave Maria.

— Praying Our Goodbyes. 1992. reprint ed. mass mkt. 4.99 (*0-8041-1060-3*) Ivy Books.

— The Star in My Heart: Experiencing Sophia, Inner Wisdom. LC 90-41108. (Illus.). 128p. (Orig.). 1990. pap. 11.95 (*0-931055-75-X*) Innisfree Pr.

— Your Sorrow Is My Sorrow: Hope & Strength in Times of Suffering. LC 98-31344. 184p. 1999. pap. 13.95 (*0-8245-1566-8*) Crossroad NY.

Rupp, Joyce, jt. auth. see Hutchison, Joyce.

Rupp, Kalman. Entrepreneurs in Red: Structure & Organizational Innovation in the Centrally Planned Economy. LC 82-3389. 260p. (C). 1983. text 20.50 (*0-87395-635-4*) State U NY Pr.

Rupp, Kalman & Stapleton, David C. Growth in Disability Benefits: Explanations & Policy Implications. LC 98-24695. 450p. (C). 1998. text 43.00 (*0-88099-188-7*); pap. text 25.00 (*0-88099-187-9*) W E Upjohn.

R

Rupp, Leila J. A Desired Past: A Short History of Same-Sex Love in America. LC 98-56542. 1996. pap. 15.00 (*0-226-73156-1*) U Ch Pr.

— A Desired Past: A Short History of Same-Sex Love in America. LC 98-56542. (Illus.). 224p. 1999. 22.00 (*0-226-73155-3*) U Ch Pr.

— Mobilizing Women for War: German & American Propaganda. LC 77-85562. (Illus.). 256p. reprint ed. pap. 79.40 (*0-8357-3698-9*, 203642200003) Bks Demand.

***Rupp, Leila J.** What Makes a Man a Man. 1999. 25.00 (*0-226-73158-8*) U Ch Pr.

Rupp, Leila J. Worlds of Women: The Makings of an International Women's Movement. LC 97-14449. 328p. 1998. text 55.00 (*0-691-01676-3*, Pub. by Princeton U Pr); pap. text 19.95 (*0-691-01675-5*, Pub. by Princeton U Pr) Cal Prin Full Svc.

Rupp, Leila J. & Taylor, Verta. Survival in the Doldrums: The American Women's Rights Movement. LC 89-28829. (Illus.). 304p. reprint ed. pap. 94.30 (*0-608-09876-0*, 206984200006) Bks Demand.

***Rupp, Myron, ed.** Quotations of Chairman Jesse. 136p. 2000. pap. 9.00 (*1-886913-39-0*, Pub. by Ruminator Bks) Consort Bk Sales.

Rupp, N. Daniel, jt. ed. see Walling, Regis M.

Rupp, Nadine & Rupp, James E., compiled by. Ozumacin Chinantec Texts Vol. 2: Folklore Texts in Mexican Indian Languages. LC 93-86273. (Language Data, Amerindian Ser.: No. 11). 96p. 1994. pap. 12.50 (*0-88312-624-9*) S I L Intl.

Rupp, R. F., jt. auth. see Wujek, E. D.

Rupp, Randall G., jt. ed. see Oka, Melvin S.

Rupp, Rebecca. Blue Corn & Square Tomatoes: Unusual Facts about Common Garden Vegetables. Burns, Deborah, ed. LC 87-45009. (Illus.). 232p. (Orig.). 1987. pap. 12.95 (*0-88266-505-7*, Garden Way Pub) Storey Bks.

— Blue Corn & Square Tomatoes: Unusual Facts about Common Garden Vegetables. Burns, Deborah, ed. LC 87-45009. (Illus.). 232p. (Orig.). 1988. 19.95 (*0-88266-504-9*, Garden Way Pub) Storey Bks.

— The Dragon of Lonely Island. LC 97-47759. 160p. (J). (gr. 3). 1998. 16.99 (*0-7636-0408-9*) Candlewick Pr.

— Everything You Never Learned about Birds. LC 94-21014. (Everything You Never Learned About Ser.). (Illus.). 144p. 1995. pap. 14.95 (*0-88266-345-3*, Storey Pub) Storey Bks.

— Getting Started on Home Learning: How & Why to Create a Classroom at Home. LC 99-12789. 1999. pap. 11.00 (*0-609-80343-3*, Crown) Crown Pub Group.

— Good Stuff: Learning Tools for All Ages. rev. ed. 386p. 1994. pap. 14.75 (*0-945097-20-4*) Home Educ Pr.

— Home Learning Companion. LC 98-38440. 1998. pap. 29.95 (*0-609-80109-0*, Crown) Crown Pub Group.

***Rupp, Rebecca.** Home Learning Year by Year: How to Design a Homeschool Curriculum from Preschool Through High School. LC 00-23312. 224p. 2000. pap. 11.00 (*0-609-80585-1*, EDU017000, Three Riv Pr) Crown Pub Group.

Rupp, Rebecca. How We Remember & Why We Forget. LC 98-30860. 320p. 1998. pap. 14.00 (*0-609-80227-5*, Crown) Crown Pub Group.

Rupp, Rebecca A. Barbie Doll Accessories, Treasury of. LC 96-169680. (Illus.). 144p. 1996. pap. 19.95 (*0-87588-450-4*) Hobby Hse.

Rupp, Rebecca Ann. Barbie Doll Treasures. LC 98-185501. (Illus.). 128p. 1997. 24.95 (*0-87588-505-5*) Hobby Hse.

Rupp, Richard H., ed. Critics on Emily Dickinson. LC 77-143454. (Readings in Literary Criticism Ser.: No. 14). 1986. pap. 19.95 (*0-87024-318-7*) U of Miami Pr.

— Critics on Whitman. LC 78-143457. (Readings in Literary Criticism Ser.: No. 13). 1972. 19.95 (*0-87024-195-8*) U of Miami Pr.

— The Marble Faun: or The Romance of Monte Beni. LC 73-134464. 1971. pap. 7.60 (*0-672-61026-4*, Bobbs) Macmillan.

Rupp, Robert O. James A. Garfield: A Bibliography, 20. LC 97-33146. (Bibliographies of the Presidents of the United States Ser.: 20). 216p. 1997. lib. bdg. 65.00 (*0-313-28178-5*, Greenwood Pr) Greenwood.

Rupp, Robert O., jt. auth. see Remini, Robert V.

***Rupp-Serrano, Karen.** Collection Management: Preparing Today's Bibliographies for Tomorrow's Libraries. LC 00-21761. 95p. 2000. pap. text 19.95 (*0-7890-1003-8*) Haworth Pr.

***Rupp-Serrano, Karen, ed.** Collection Management: Preparing Today's Bibliographies for Tomorrow's Libraries. LC 00-21761. 95p. 2000. 29.95 (*0-7890-1002-X*) Haworth Pr.

Rupp, Stephen. Allegories of Kingship: Calderon & the Anti-Machiavellian Tradition. LC 94-41635. (Studies in Romance Literatures). 1996. 32.50 (*0-271-01456-3*) Pa St U Pr.

Rupp, Steven J. The Christian's Reward. LC 99-168826. 243 p. 1998. write for info. (*0-9666538-0-7*) Family of God.

Rupp, William, et al. The Commodore 64 Game Construction Toolkit. (Illus.). 250p. 1984. 14.95 (*0-8359-0775-9*) P-H.

Ruppard, Lynn, jt. auth. see Pyne, Lynette.

Ruppard, Lynn, ed. see Cunningham, Patricia & Hall, Dorothy.

Ruppard, Lynn, ed. see Hall, Amanda, et al.

Ruppard, Lynn H. Capital & Lowercase Letters. (Basic Skills Ser.). (Illus.). 32p. (J). (gr. k). 1997. pap. text 4.95 (*0-88724-400-9*, CD2100) Carson-Dellos.

— Consonant Sounds. (Basic Skills Ser.). (Illus.). 32p. (J). (gr. k). 1997. pap. text 4.95 (*0-88724-401-7*, CD-2101) Carson-Dellos.

— Making Sentences. (Basic Skills Ser.). (Illus.). 32p. (J). (gr. 3). 1997. pap. text 4.95 (*0-88724-417-3*, CD-2117) Carson-Dellos.

— Sight Words. (Basic Skills Ser.). (Illus.). 32p. (J). (gr. k). 1997. pap. text 4.95 (*0-88724-402-5*, CD-2102) Carson-Dellos.

— Subtraction 0 to 20. (Basic Skills Ser.). (Illus.). 32p. (J). (gr. 1-2). 1997. pap. text 4.95 (*0-88724-391-6*, CD-2126) Carson-Dellos.

Ruppart, Lynn. Shapes & Patterns. (Basic Skills Ser.). (Illus.). 32p. (J). (gr. k). 1997. pap. text 4.95 (*0-88724-389-4*, CD-2124) Carson-Dellos.

Ruppe, Juan V. Barney's Happy Valentine's Day. LC 97-72793. (Barney Ser.). 24p. (J). (ps-k). 1997. pap. 3.25 (*1-57064-294-X*, 97752, Barney Publ) Lyrick Pub.

Ruppe, Reynold. The Acoma Culture Province: An Archeological Concept. LC 90-21599. (Evolution of North American Indians Ser.: Vol. 21). 320p. 1991. reprint ed. text 10.00 (*0-8240-6110-1*) Garland.

Ruppel, Aloys. Johannes Gutenberg: Sein Leben und Sein Werk. 2nd ed. (GER., Illus.). 140p. 1967. reprint ed. text 132.50 (*90-6004-157-7*, Pub. by B De Graaf) Coronet Bks.

Ruppel, Fred J. & Kellogg, Earl D., eds. National & Regional Self-Sufficiency Goals: Implications for International Agriculture. LC 90-25593. 254p. 1991. lib. bdg. 45.00 (*1-55587-152-6*) L Rienner.

Ruppel, Gregg. Manual of Pulmonary Function Testing. 7th ed. LC 97-26485. (Illus.). 384p. (C). (gr. 13). 1997. pap. text 36.00 (*0-8151-2299-3*, 27686) Mosby Inc.

***Ruppel, Karl A.** Theologie und Wirtschaft: Konzepte Protestantischer Wirtschaftsethik Zwischen Aufklarung und Industrialisierung. (Theologische Texte und Studien Ser.: Bd. 7). (GER.). xii, 368p. 1999. 65.00 (*3-487-10926-3*, Pub. by G Olms Verlag) Lubrecht & Cramer.

Ruppel, Maxine. Vostaas: White Buffalo's Story of the Plains Indians. (Indian Culture Ser.). (J). (gr. 4-10). pap. 4.95 (*0-89992-001-2*) Coun India Ed.

— Vostaas: White Buffalo's Story of the Plains Indians. (Indian Culture Ser.). 80p. (J). (gr. 4-10). 1995. pap. 6.95 (*0-89992-137-X*) Coun India Ed.

Ruppel, Richard R. Gottfried Keller: Poet, Pedagogue & Humanist. (Studies in Modern German Literature: Vol. 12). XIV, 282p. (C). 1988. text 42.50 (*0-8204-0453-5*) P Lang Pubng.

— Gottfried Keller & His Critics: A Case Study in Scholarly Criticism. LC 98-20320. (Literary Criticism in Perspective Ser.). 188p. (C). 1998. 55.00 (*1-57113-055-1*) Camden Hse.

Ruppel, S. C. & Cander, H. S. Effects of Facies & Diagenesis on Reservoir Heterogeneity: Emma San Andres Field, West Texas. (Reports of Investigations: RI 178). (Illus.). 67p. 1988. pap. 6.75 (*0-317-03113-9*) Bur Econ Geology.

Ruppel, S. C. & Holtz, M. H. Depositional & Diagenetic Facies Patterns & Reservoir Development in Silurian & Devonian Rocks of the Permian Basin. (Reports of Investigations: Vol. RI 216). (Illus.). 89p. 1994. pap. 6.00 (*0-614-01865-X*) Bur Econ Geology.

Ruppel, S. C. & Hovorka, S. D. Chert Reservoir Development in the Devonian Thirtyone Formation: Three Bar Field, West Texas. (Reports of Investigations: No. 230). (Illus.). 50p. (Orig.). 1995. pap. 7.50 (*0-614-11608-2*) Bur Econ Geology.

Ruppel, S. C., et al. Controls on Reservoir Heterogeneity in Permian Shallow-Water-Platform Carbonate Reservoirs, Permian Basin: Implications for Improved Recovery. (Geological Circular Ser.: No. 95-2). (Illus.). 30p. 1995. pap. 4.50 (*0-614-11615-5*) Bur Econ Geology.

***Ruppel, Warren.** GAAP for Governments Field Guide 2000: Including GASB---34 New GASB Reporting Model. 256p. 2000. pap. 22.95 (*0-471-38256-6*) Wiley.

Ruppel, Warren. Miller Not-for-Profit Organization Audits. 1998. pap. 130.00 (*0-15-606215-1*) Harcourt Coll Pubs.

— Miller Not-for-Profit Organization Audits: Electronic Workpapers & Reference Guide. (Illus.). 851p. 1999. pap. 137.00 incl. cd-rom (*0-15-606875-3*) Harcourt.

***Ruppel, Warren.** 2001 Miller Not-for-Profit Organization Audits: Electronic Workpapers & Reference Guide. 900p. 2000. pap. 149.00 (*0-15-607190-8*) Harcourt.

Ruppel, Warren. Wiley GAAP for Governments 1999: Interpretation & Applications of Generally Accepted Accounting Principles for State & Local Governments 1999. 99th ed. (Illus.). 576p. 1999. pap. text 65.00 (*0-471-29588-4*) Wiley.

***Ruppel, Warren.** Wiley GAAP for Governments 2000: Interpretation & Application of Generally Accepted Accounting Principles for State & Local Governments. 573p. 2000. pap. 69.00 (*0-471-35110-5*) Wiley.

***Ruppel/GGAAP 99 Staff.** GAAP for Governments 99: Interpretation & Application of Generally: Accepted Accounting Principles for State & Local Governments. 99th ed. 1999. 134.00 incl. cd-rom (*0-471-19550-2*) Wiley.

Ruppen, Francia. The Hollywood Vegetarian Cookbook: Lean, Healthy Meals from America's Celebrity Kitchens. (Illus.). 224p. 1995. 16.95 (*1-55972-288-6*, Birch Ln Pr) Carol Pub Group.

Ruppen, Paul. Einstieg in die Formale Logik: Ein Lern - Und Ubungsbuch fur Nichtmathematiker. 368p. 1996. 39.95 (*3-906756-85-8*) P Lang Pubng.

***Ruppenthal, Roland G.** United States Army in World War 2: European Theater of Operations, Logistical Support of the Armies, Sept 1944-May 1945. 540p. 1999. boxed set 21.00 (*0-16-018660-9*) USGPO.

Ruppenthal, Stephen, jt. intro. see Easwaran, Eknath.

Ruppersberg, Allen. The Secret of Life & Death: Nineteen Sixty-Nine to Nineteen Eighty-Four, Vol. 1. Brown, Julia, ed. LC 84-63020. (Illus.). 127p. (C). 1985. pap. 50.00 (*0-914357-07-7*) Los Angeles Mus Contemp.

***Ruppersburg, Hugh, ed.** Georgia Voices, Vol. 3. 500p. 1999. 40.00 (*0-8203-2167-2*) U of Ga Pr.

— Georgia Voices Vol. 3: Poetry. 500p. 2000. pap. 19.95 (*0-8203-2177-X*) U of Ga Pr.

Ruppersburg, Hugh M. Robert Penn Warren & the American Imagination. LC 89-20451. 216p. 1990. 35.00 (*0-8203-1215-0*) U of Ga Pr.

Ruppersburg, Hugh M., ed. Georgia Voices: Fiction, Vol. 1. LC 91-36688. 528p. 1992. 40.00 (*0-8203-1432-3*); pap. 19.95 (*0-8203-1433-1*) U of Ga Pr.

— Georgia Voices Vol. 2: Nonfiction. LC 91-36688. 592p. 1994. 40.00 (*0-8203-1625-3*); pap. 19.95 (*0-8203-1626-1*) U of Ga Pr.

***Ruppersburg, Hugh M. & Engles, Tim.** Critical Essays on Don Delillo. LC 00-24507. (Critical Essays on American Literature Ser.). 2000. write for info. (*0-7838-0458-X*, G K Hall & Co) Mac Lib Ref.

Ruppert, Alex D. Biology of Alligators & Crocodiles: Index of New Information & Research Bible. LC 95-17181. 1995. write for info. (*0-7883-0752-5*); pap. write for info. (*0-7883-0753-3*) ABBE Pubs Assn.

***Ruppert, Brian D.** Jewel in the Ashes: Buddha Relics & Power in Early Medieval Japan. LC 99-88187. (Harvard East Asian Monographs: Vol. 188). (Illus.). 420p. 2000. 49.50 (*0-674-00245-8*) HUP.

Ruppert, Bryan, tr. see Loth.

***Ruppert, E.** Biology 104 Handout Package. 112p. 1999. 10.00 (*1-886855-25-0*) Tavenner Pub.

Ruppert, Edward E. & Barnes, Robert D. Invertebrate Zoology. 6th ed. LC 93-85930. 1056p. (C). 1993. text 93.50 (*0-03-026668-8*, Pub. by SCP) Harcourt.

Ruppert, Edward E. & Fox, Richard S. Seashore Animals of the Southeast. LC 87-27349. (Illus.). 429p. 1988. pap. text 29.95 (*0-87249-535-3*) U of SC Pr.

Ruppert, Edward E., jt. auth. see Harrison, Frederick W.

Ruppert, Edward E., jt. ed. see Harrison, Frederick W.

Ruppert, Ette. Intro to Biology 103 Handout Package. (Illus.). 105p. (C). 1996. wbk. ed. 9.00 (*1-886855-58-7*) Tavenner Pub.

Ruppert, Fidelis & Gruen, Anselm. Christ in the Brother: According to the Rule of St. Benedict. rev. ed. Lauer, Alphonse M., ed. Roettger, Gregory J., tr. from GER. (Schuyler Spiritual Ser.: Vol. 2). 60p. 1992. pap. text 3.60 (*1-56788-001-0*, 10-002) BMH Pubns.

Ruppert, Godehard, jt. ed. see Irsigler, Hubert.

Ruppert, Hans & Hofer, Conrad, eds. Zeitschrift fur Bucherfreunde, 1897-1936: Gesamtregister, 3 vols. in 1. vi, 665p. 1964. reprint ed. write for info. (*0-318-71881-2*) G Olms Pubs.

Ruppert, James. D'Arcy McNickle. LC 87-73496. (Western Writers Ser.: No. 83). (Illus.). 55p. (Orig.). 1988. pap. 4.95 (*0-88430-082-X*) Boise St U W Writ Ser.

— Guide to Poetry Explication: American Poetry, Vol. 1. 225p. 1989. 45.00 (*0-8161-8919-6*, Hall Reference) Macmillan.

— Mediation in Contemporary Native American Fiction. LC 94-47465. (American Indian Literature & Critical Studies: Vol. 15). 192p. 1995. 29.95 (*0-8061-2749-X*) U of Okla Pr.

— Mediation in Contemporary Native American Fiction. LC 97-47465. (American Indian Literature & Critical Studies Ser.: Vol. 15). xiii, 174p. 1997. pap. 11.95 (*0-8061-2993-X*) U of Okla Pr.

— VW Golf: The Complete Story. (Illus.). 200p. 1996. 24.98 (*1-85223-996-4*, Pub. by Cro1wood) Motorbooks Intl.

Ruppert, James, jt. auth. see Purdy, John L.

Ruppert, Janette K. First Aid: Index of Modern Information. rev. ed. LC 91-7266. 150p. 1991. 47.50 (*1-55914-352-5*); pap. 44.50 (*1-55914-353-3*) ABBE Pubs Assn.

— First Aid & Emergencies: Index of Modern Authors & Subjects in Current Research. 160p. 1991. 47.50 (*1-55914-466-1*); pap. 44.50 (*1-55914-467-X*) ABBE Pubs Assn.

Ruppert, Jeanne, ed. Gender: Literary & Cinematic Representation. (Florida State University Annual Conference on Literature & Film Ser.). 144p. (C). 1994. pap. text 17.95 (*0-8130-1911-7*) U Press Fla.

Ruppert, Karl. Chichen Itza: Architectural Notes & Plans. LC 77-11519. (Carnegie Institution of Washington. Publications: No. 595). reprint ed. 42.50 (*0-404-16279-7*) AMS Pr.

Ruppert, Karl & Denison, John H., Jr. Archaeological Reconnaissance in Campeche, Quintana Roo, & Peten. LC 77-11517. (Carnegie Institution of Washington. Publications: No. 543). reprint ed. 44.00 (*0-404-16277-0*) AMS Pr.

Ruppert, Kathleen C. Plant Fun: Crafts & Games for All Ages. (Illus.). 60p. (Orig.). 1996. pap. text 7.00 (*0-916287-20-3*, SP207) Univ Fla Food.

Ruppert, Kathleen C. & Black, Robert J., eds. Florida Lawn Handbook: An Environmental Approach to Care & Maintenance of Your Lawn. 2nd ed. LC 98-25888. 1997. pap. 19.95 (*0-8130-1643-6*) U Press Fla.

Ruppert, Kathleen C., jt. ed. see Black, Robert J.

Ruppert, Kathleen C., ed. see Dunn, R. A., et al.

Ruppert, Marion C. Projects Patterns & Poems for Early Education. LC 87-31202. (Illus.). 175p. (Orig.). 1989. lib. bdg. 29.95 (*0-89334-226-2*, 2262030) Humanics Ltd.

***Ruppert, Martha.** The Dating Trap: Helping Your Children Make Wise Choices in Their Relationships. LC 00-33870. 2000. pap. write for info. (*0-8024-6946-9*) Moody.

Ruppert, Peter. Walden II. 1976. 3.50 (*0-671-00973-7*, Arco) Macmillan Gen Ref.

Ruppert, Peter, ed. see Florida State University Conference on Literature.

Ruppert, Stefan, jt. auth. see Schneewind, Klaus.

Ruppert, Susan D. & Kernicki, Jeanette. Dolan's Critical Care Nursing: Clinical Management Through the Nursing Process. 2nd ed. 1123p. 1996. text 61.95 (*0-8036-0025-9*) Davis Co.

Ruppert, Trisha. Search for the Word: Over 65 Biblical Puzzles for all Ages. LC 91-77489. 96p. (Orig.). 1993. pap. 3.95 (*1-883654-00-9*) Bethlehem Star.

Ruppert, W. Compact Semitopological Semigroups: An Intrinsic Theory. (Lecture Notes in Mathematics Ser.: Vol. 1079). v, 260p. 1984. 42.95 (*0-387-13387-9*) Spr-Verlag.

Ruppert, Wolfgang, jt. auth. see Hofmann, Karl H.

Ruppin, Arthur. The Jewish Fate & Future. Dickes, E. W., tr. LC 76-97300. (Illus.). 386p. 1972. reprint ed. lib. bdg. 35.00 (*0-8371-2628-2*, RUJF, Greenwood Pr) Greenwood.

— The Jews in the Modern World. LC 73-2225. (Jewish People; History, Religion, Literature Ser.). 1973. reprint ed. 40.95 (*0-405-05287-1*) Ayer.

— Three Decades of Palestine: Speeches & Papers on the Upbuilding of the Jewish National Home. LC 70-97301. (Illus.). 342p. 1975. reprint ed. lib. bdg. 38.50 (*0-8371-2629-0*, RUPA, Greenwood Pr) Greenwood.

Rupple, Dan, et al. Isaac Air Freight: The Works: Sketches from the Premier Christian Comedy Group. Wray, Rhonda, ed. LC 96-19906. 320p. (YA). (gr. 9 up). 1997. pap. 15.95 (*1-56608-034-7*, B215) Meriwether Pub.

Ruppli, Michel. The Decca Labels: A Discography, 6 vols., 63. LC 95-47140. (Discographies Ser.: Vol. 63). 6106p. 1996. lib. bdg. 595.00 (*0-313-27370-7*, Greenwood Pr) Greenwood.

— The Decca Labels: A Discography Volume 2 - the Eastern & Southern Sessions (1934-1942), Vol. 2. LC 95-47140. (Discographies Ser.: Vol. 63). 1018p. 1996. lib. bdg. 225.00 (*0-313-29985-4*, Greenwood Pr) Greenwood.

— The Decca Labels: A Discography Volume 3 - the Eastern Sessions (1943-1956), Vol. 2. LC 95-47140. (Discographies Ser.: Vol. 63). 1018p. 1996. lib. bdg. 225.00 (*0-313-29986-2*, Greenwood Pr) Greenwood.

— The Decca Labels: A Discography Volume 4 - the Eastern Sessions (1956-1973), Vol. 4. LC 95-47140. (Discographies Ser.: Vol. 63). 1046p. 1996. lib. bdg. 225.00 (*0-313-29987-0*, Greenwood Pr) Greenwood.

— The Decca Labels: A Discography Volume 5 - Country Recordings, Classical Recordings & Reissues, Vol. 5. LC 95-47140. (Discographies Ser.: Vol. 63). 982p. 1996. lib. bdg. 225.00 (*0-313-29988-9*, Greenwood Pr) Greenwood.

— The Decca Labels: A Discography Volume 6 - Record Numerical Listings & General Artist Index, Vol. 6. LC 95-47140. (Discographies Ser.: Vol. 63). 990p. 1996. lib. bdg. 225.00 (*0-313-29989-7*, Greenwood Pr) Greenwood.

— The Decca Labels Vol. 1: A Discography: The California Sessions, Vol. 1. LC 95-47140. (Discographies Ser.: Vol. 63). 1054p. 1996. lib. bdg. 225.00 (*0-313-29984-6*, Greenwood Pr) Greenwood.

— The King Labels: A Discography, 2 vols., 18. LC 85-17655. (Discographies Ser.: No. 18). 1418p. 1985. lib. bdg. 195.00 (*0-313-24771-4*, RKL/) Greenwood.

— The King Labels: A Discography, 2 vols., Vol. 1. LC 85-17655. (Discographies Ser.: No. 18). xviii, 1381p. 1985. lib. bdg. 125.00 (*0-313-25145-2*, RML/01) Greenwood.

— The King Labels: A Discography, 2 vols., Vol. 2. LC 85-17655. (Discographies Ser.: No. 18). xviii, 1381p. 1985. lib. bdg. 125.00 (*0-313-25146-0*, RKL/02) Greenwood.

— The Savoy Label: A Discography, 2. LC 79-7727. (Discographies Ser.: No. 2). (Illus.). 442p. 1980. lib. bdg. 105.00 (*0-313-21199-X*, RUS/, Greenwood Pr) Greenwood.

Ruppli, Michel, compiled by. The Aladdin-Imperial Labels: A Discography, 42. LC 90-22696. (Discographies Ser.: No. 42). 760p. 1991. lib. bdg. 99.50 (*0-313-27821-0*, RAH, Greenwood Pr) Greenwood.

— Atlantic Records: A Discography, 4 vols., 1. LC 78-75237. 1979. lib. bdg. 275.00 (*0-313-21170-1*, RAL/) Greenwood.

— Atlantic Records: A Discography, 4 vols., Vol. 1. LC 78-75237. 1979. lib. bdg. 95.00 (*0-313-21171-X*, RAL/1) Greenwood.

— Atlantic Records: A Discography, 4 vols., Vol. 2. LC 78-75237. 1979. lib. bdg. 95.00 (*0-313-21172-8*, RAL/2) Greenwood.

— Atlantic Records: A Discography, 4 vols., Vol. 3. LC 78-75237. 1979. lib. bdg. 95.00 (*0-313-21173-6*, RAL/3) Greenwood.

— Atlantic Records: A Discography, 4 vols., Vol. 4. LC 78-75237. 1979. lib. bdg. 95.00 (*0-313-21174-4*, RAL/4) Greenwood.

— The Chess Labels: A Discography, 2 vols., 7. LC 82-25148. (Discographies Ser.: No. 7). 752p. 1983. lib. bdg. 125.00 (*0-313-23471-X*, RCL/) Greenwood.

— The Chess Labels: A Discography, 2 vols., Vol. 1. LC 82-25148. (Discographies Ser.: No. 7). xviii, 743p. 1983. lib. bdg. 75.00 (*0-313-23980-0*, RCL/01) Greenwood.

— The Chess Labels: A Discography, 2 vols., Vol. 2. LC 82-25148. (Discographies Ser.: No. 7). xviii, 743p. 1983. lib. bdg. 75.00 (*0-313-23981-9*, RCL/02) Greenwood.

— The Clef-Verve Labels: A Discography, 2 vols., 26. LC 86-19530. (Discographies Ser.: No. 26). 894p. 1986. lib. bdg. 165.00 (*0-313-25294-7*, RCV/) Greenwood.

— The Clef-Verve Labels: A Discography, 2 vols., Vol. 1. LC 86-19530. (Discographies Ser.: No. 26). 894p. 1986. lib. bdg. 105.00 (*0-313-25693-4*, RCV/01) Greenwood.

— The Clef-Verve Labels Vol. 2: A Discography, 2 vols., Vol. 2. LC 86-19530. (Discographies Ser.: No. 26). 894p. 1986. lib. bdg. 105.00 (*0-313-25694-2*, RCV/02) Greenwood.

— The Prestige Label: A Discography, 3. LC 79-8294. (Discographies Ser.: No. 3). 390p. 1980. lib. bdg. 95.00 (*0-313-22019-0*, RPL/, Greenwood Pr) Greenwood.

An Asterisk (*) at the beginning of an entry indicates that the title is appearing for the first time.

Ruppli, Michel, ed. The Blue Note Label: A Discography, 29. LC 88-162. (Discographies Ser.: No. 29). 532p. 1988. lib. bdg. 95.00 (*0-313-22018-2*, RBN/, Greenwood Pr) Greenwood.

Ruppli, Michel & Novitsky, Ed, compiled by. The MGM Labels: A Discography, 75. LC 98-9602. (Discographies Ser.: Vol. 75). 2736p. 1998. lib. bdg. 325.00 (*0-313-30052-6*, Greenwood Pr) Greenwood.

— The MGM Labels: A Discography, 1946-1960, Vol. 1. LC 98-9602. (Discographies Ser.: 75). 1016p. 1998. lib. bdg. 135.00 (*0-313-30778-4*, Greenwood Pr) Greenwood.

— The MGM Labels Vol. 2: A Discography, 1961-1982, Vol. 2. LC 98-9602. (Discographies Ser.: 75). 984p. 1998. lib. bdg. 135.00 (*0-313-30779-2*, Greenwood Pr) Greenwood.

— The MGM Labels Vol. 3: A Discography: Additional Recordings/Record & Artist Indexes, Vol. 3. LC 98-9602. (Discographies Ser.: 75). 864p. 1998. lib. bdg. 135.00 (*0-313-30780-6*, Greenwood Pr) Greenwood.

Rupprecht, C. E., et al. Current Topics in Microbiology & Immunology No. 187. 360p. 1994. 149.95 (*0-387-57194-9*) Spr-Verlag.

Rupprecht, Carol S., ed. The Dream & the Text: Essays on Literature & Language. LC 92-4560. (SUNY Series in Dream Studies). 325p. (C). 1993. text 64.50 (*0-7914-1361-6*); pap. text 21.95 (*0-7914-1362-4*) State U NY Pr.

Rupprecht, Carol S., jt. ed. see Lauter, Estella.

Rupprecht, Caroline, tr. see Zurn, Unica.

Rupprecht, David & Rupprecht, Ruth. Radical Hospitality. LC 83-3259. 110p. 1983. pap. 4.99 (*0-87552-420-6*) P & R Pubng.

Rupprecht, David, et al. Radical Hospitality: Leader's Guide. 1985. pap. 2.99 (*0-87552-419-2*) P & R Pubng.

Rupprecht, Eva-Maria. Kritikvergessene Spekulation: Das Religions- und Theologieverstandnis der Spekulativen Theologie Ph. K. Marheinekes. (Beitrage zur Rationalen Theologie Ser.: Bd. 3). (GER.). 345p. 1993. 55.95 (*3-631-45975-0*) P Lang Pubng.

Rupprecht, H. A., jt. auth. see Pestman, P. W.

Rupprecht, H. S. & Weimann, G., eds. Gallium Arsenide & Related Compounds, 1993: Proceedings of the 20th International Symposium, 29 August-2 September 1993, Freiburg in Braunschweig, Germany. (Institute of Physics Conference Ser.: No. 136). (Illus.). 864p. 1994. 276.00 (*0-7503-0295-X*) IOP Pub.

***Rupprecht, Karen.** Miss Prudence Pennypack's a Month of Manners. (Illus.). 40p. (J). (ps-4). 2000. pap. (*1-893116-13-1*) Baltimore Sun.

— Miss Prudence Pennypack's Perfectly Proper. (Illus.). 68p. (J). (ps-4). 1999. 16.95 (*1-893116-09-3*) Baltimore Sun.

Rupprecht, Konrad. Der Tempel Von Jerusalem. (Beiheft zur Zeitschrift fuer die Alttestamentliche Wissenschaft Ser.: No. 144). (C). 1976. text 60.80 (*3-11-006619-X*) De Gruyter.

Rupprecht, Larry, ed. Conductive Polymers & Plastics in Industrial Applications. LC 98-89320. 302p. 1999. 160.00 (*1-884207-77-4*) William Andrew.

Rupprecht, Ruth, jt. auth. see Rupprecht, David.

Ruprail, Nirmal. Bibliography on India in 2000 A. D. (C). 1991. 28.00 (*0-8364-2739-4*, Pub. by Abhinav) S Asia.

Ruprecht. Mary M. Ruprecht Speaks on End-User Computing. (KU - Office Procedures Ser.). (C). 1991. 385.50 (*0-538-70785-2*) S-W Pub.

— Ruprecht on End-User Computing, Lecture 3. (KU - Office Procedures Ser.). (C). 1991. 142.50 (*0-538-70788-7*) S-W Pub.

Ruprecht, Alvina & Taiana, Cecilia, eds. The Reordering of Culture: Latin America, the Caribbean & Canada in the Hood. 400p. 1995. pap. 27.95 (*0-88629-269-7*, Pub. by McG-Queens Univ Pr) CUP Services.

Ruprecht, F. J. Phycologia Ochotiensis: Tange des Ochotskischen Meeres (From Middendorff's Sibirische Reise) (Illus.). 1978. reprint ed. lib. bdg. 120.00 (*3-7682-1184-3*) Lubrecht & Cramer.

Ruprecht, F. J., jt. auth. see Postels, A.

Ruprecht, H., jt. ed. see Parret, Herman.

Ruprecht, H. G., jt. ed. see Parret, Herman.

Ruprecht, J., et al, eds. Catalogue of Star Clusters & Associations, Supplement 1. 190p. 1981. 195.00 (*963-05-2472-4*, Pub. by Akade Kiado) St Mut.

Ruprecht, J., et al. Catalogue of Star Clusters & Associations: Supplement 1. 440p. 1981. 325.00 (*0-569-08698-1*) St Mut.

Ruprecht, Louis A., Jr. Afterwords: Hellenism, Modernism, & the Myth of Decadence. LC 95-20798. 260p. (C). 1996. text 65.50 (*0-7914-2933-4*); pap. text 21.95 (*0-7914-2934-2*) State U NY Pr.

— Symposia: Plato, the Erotic, & Moral Value. LC 98-31973. 160p. (C). 1999. text 47.50 (*0-7914-4263-2*); pap. text 15.95 (*0-7914-4264-0*) State U NY Pr.

— Tragic Posture & Tragic Vision: Against the Modern Failure of Nerve. 288p. (C). 1994. 29.95 (*0-8264-0686-6*) Continuum.

***Ruprecht, T.** Toronto's Many Faces: A Multicultural Guide to Festivals, Restaurants, Museums & Sites of Ove. 420p. 1999. pap. text 14.95 (*1-55082-201-2*) Quarry Pr.

Ruprecht, Thomas M. Felix Boenheim - Arzt, Politiker, Historiker. (Wissenschaftliche Abhandlungen des Salomon Ludwig Steinheim-Instituts Fur Deutsch-Judische Geschichte Ser.: Vol. 7). (GER.). 550p. 1992. write for info. (*3-487-09538-6*) G Olms Pubs.

Rupreht, J., et al, eds. Anaesthesia: Essays on Its History. (Illus.). 430p. 1985. 93.95 (*0-387-13255-4*) Spr-Verlag.

Ruptic, Cynthia, jt. auth. see Hill, Bonnie C.

Ruqvist, Anders. Peasant Struggle & Action Research in Colombia. (Uppsala University Research Report Series, 1986: No. 3). 396p. (Orig.). 1986. pap. text 50.00 (*0-317-57954-1*) Coronet Bks.

Rural Economic Development Center Staff. North Carolina Aquaculture Report. 128p. (Orig.). 1989. pap. text 5.00 (*0-945597-12-6*) NC Biotech Ctr.

Rurinf, L. & Dixit, K., eds. Bikas-Binash Development-Destruction: The Change in Life & Environment of the Himalaya. 400p. (C). 1990. 150.00 (*0-89771-049-5*, Pub. by Ratna Pustak Bhandar) St Mut.

Rurode, Louise W. From the Hills & My Heart. 69p. 1967. pap. 5.00 (*0-614-24774-8*) Tesseract SD.

Rurup, Reinhard. Germany & the Rise of Bourgeois Society. Hein, Ruth, tr. from GER. 256p. 1988. text 35.00 (*0-674-35308-0*) HUP.

Rurup, Reinhard, ed. The Problem of Revolution in Germany, 1789-1989. (German Historical Perspectives Ser.). 256p. 2000. 65.00 (*1-85973-276-3*, Pub. by Berg Pubs) NYU Pr.

Rury, John L. Education & Women's Work: Female Schooling & the Division of Labor in Urban America, 1870-1930. LC 90-38325. (SUNY Series on Women & Work). 296p. (C). 1991. text 24.50 (*0-7914-0617-2*) State U NY Pr.

Rury, John L. & Cassell, Frank A., eds. Seeds of Crisis: Public Schooling in Milwaukee since 1920. LC 93-18827. (Illus.). 389p. (Orig.). (C). 1993. pap. text 19.95 (*0-299-13814-3*) U of Wis Pr.

***Ruryk, Jean.** Next Week Will Be Better: A Cat Wilde Mystery. 1999. per. 4.99 (*0-373-26333-3*) Harlequin Bks.

Ruryk, Jean. Next Week Will Be Better: A Cat Wilde Mystery. LC 97-37119. 256p. 1998. text 21.95 (*0-312-18144-2*) St Martin.

Rus, D., jt. auth. see Rus, R.

Rus, D., jt. auth. see Rus, T.

Rus, Daniela, jt. auth. see Rus, Teodor.

***Rus, Mayer.** Lauren Rottet: The Substance of Style. 144p. 1999. pap. 40.00 (*0-9662230-1-2*, Pub. by Edizioni Pr) Antique Collect.

Rus, Mayer. Loft. LC 98-37001. (Illus.). 240p. 1998. 55.00 (*1-58093-013-1*, Pub. by Monacelli Pr) Penguin Putnam.

Rus, R. & Rus, D. System Software & Software Systems: Systems Methodology for System Software. 388p. 1993. text 48.00 (*981-02-1254-2*) World Scientific Pub.

Rus, T. & Rus, D. System Software & Software Systems: Programming Support Environment. 250p. 1998. text 46.00 (*981-02-1256-9*) World Scientific Pub.

***Rus, Teodor.** Algebraic Methodology & Software Technology: 8th International Conference, AMAST 2000, Iowa City, Iowa, U. S. A., May 20-27, 2000 : Proceedings / International Conference on Algebraic Methodology & Software Technology Staff, ed. LC 00-32203. (Lecture Notes in Computer Science). 2000. pap. write for info. (*3-540-67530-2*) Spr-Verlag.

Rus, Teodor. Data Structures & Operating Systems. LC 77-3262. (Wiley Series in Computing). 376p. reprint ed. pap. 116.60 (*0-608-12339-0*, 202437700037) Bks Demand.

Rus, Teodor & Rattray, Charles. Theories & Experiences for Real-Time System Development. (AMAST Computing Ser.). 444p. 1995. text 99.00 (*981-02-1923-7*) World Scientific Pub.

Rus, Teodor & Rus, Daniela. Execution Support Environment. (System Software & Software Systems: Vol. 2). 444p. 1994. text 59.00 (*981-02-1255-0*) World Scientific Pub.

Rus, Theodor, et al, eds. Transformation-Based Reactive Systems Development: 4th International AMAST Workshop on Real-Time Systems & Concurrent & Distributed Software, ARTS'97, Palma, Mallorca, Spain, May 21-23, 1997, Proceedings. LC 97-20858. (Lecture Notes in Computer Science Ser.: No. 1231). xi, 431p. 1997. pap. 67.00 (*3-540-63010-4*) Spr-Verlag.

Rus, Veljko, jt. ed. see Russell, Raymond.

Rusackas, Francesca. Friendship Crafts. (Girls Wanna Have Fun! Ser.). (Illus.). 64p. (J). (gr. 2-6). 1999. pap. 9.95 (*0-7373-0161-9*, 01619W) NTC Contemp Pub Co.

— 60 Super Simple Friendship Crafts. LC 98-75620. (60 Super Simple Ser.). (Illus.). 80p. (J). (gr. 3-6). 1999. pap. 6.95 (*0-7373-0062-0*, 00620W) NTC Contemp Pub Co.

Rusackas, Francesca, jt. auth. see Pearce, Q. L.

Rusak, Halina R., jt. auth. see Puniello, Francoise S.

Rusakova, A. Nesterov, Mikhail. 220p. (C). 1990. 118.00 (*0-89771-822-4*, Pub. by Collets) St Mut.

Rusanov, Anatolii I. Micellization in Surfactant Solutions. (Chemistry Reviews Ser.: Vol. 22, No. 1). 326p. 1998. pap. text 88.00 (*90-5702-297-4*, Harwood Acad Pubs) Gordon & Breach.

Rusanov, Anatolii I. & Prokhorov, V. A. Interfacial Tensiometry. LC 96-18110. (Studies in Interface Science: Vol. 3). 420p. 1996. text 262.50 (*0-444-82128-7*) Elsevier.

***Rusaw.** Leading Public Organizations. (C). 1999. pap. text. write for info. (*0-15-508462-3*) Harcourt Coll Pubs.

Rusaw, A. Carol. Transforming the Character of Public Organizations: Techniques for Change Agents. LC 97-20730. 264p. 1998. 65.00 (*1-56720-103-2*, Quorum Bks) Greenwood.

Rusbridger, James. The Intelligence Game: Illusions & Delusions of International Espionage. (Illus.). 294p. (C). 1992. 24.95 (*1-56131-008-5*, NAB) I R Dee.

Rusbridger, James & Nave, Eric. Betrayal at Pearl Harbor: How Churchill Lured Roosevelt into World War II. (Illus.). 303p. 19.95 (*0-685-52042-0*) Summit Bks.

Rusbuldt, Richard E. Basic Leader Skills: Handbook for Church Leaders. 64p. 1981. pap. 11.00 (*0-8170-0920-5*) Judson.

— Evangelism on Purpose. 48p. 1980. pap. 7.00 (*0-8170-0894-2*) Judson.

— Leader's Guide to a Workbook on Biblical Stewardship. 1994. pap., teacher ed. 6.00 (*0-8028-0830-1*) Eerdmans.

Rusbuldt, Richard E., et al. Medidas Principales en la Planificacion de la Iglesia Local: Key Steps in Local Church Planning. Rodriguez, Oscar E., tr. (SPA.). 134p. 1981. pap. 6.00 (*0-8170-0933-7*) Judson.

***Rusca, Giuliano.** Soccer: Coaching Soccer. (Illus.). 197p. (J). (gr. 1-5). 1999. pap. 14.95 (*1-890946-31-1*) Reedswain.

Ruscalleda, Jorge M. La Poesia de Nicolas Guillen: Cuatro Elementos Sustanciales. LC 76-1828. 310p. (C). 1975. 5.00 (*0-8477-0518-8*); pap. 4.00 (*0-8477-0519-6*) U of PR Pr.

Ruscello. Cleft Palate & Craniofacial Anomalies. (Dental Assisting Procedures Ser.). 1995. text 34.95 (*0-8273-5688-9*) Delmar.

***Ruscello, Dennis M.** Test & Measurements in Speech-Language Pathology. (Illus.). 396p. 2000. 55.00 (*0-7506-7003-7*) Buttrwrth-Heinemann.

Ruscello, Dennis M., jt. auth. see Philips, Betty J.

Rusch. Fuentes. (C). 1995. pap. text 31.96 (*0-395-68837-X*) HM.

— Fuentes: Conversacion Y Gramatica. (C). 1995. 39.16 (*0-395-68836-1*) HM.

Rusch, Debbie, et al. Fuentes. (SPA.). (C). 1996. pap., teacher ed. 11.96 (*0-395-74579-9*) HM.

— Fuentes. annot. ed. (SPA.). (C). 1995. pap., teacher ed. 40.36 incl. audio (*0-395-74576-4*) HM.

— Fuentes. annot. ed. (SPA.). (C). 1996. pap., teacher ed. 33.16 (*0-395-74578-0*) HM.

Rusch, Frank R. Supported Employment: Models, Methods & Issues. (Illus.). 400p. (C). 1990. text 39.95 (*0-685-30431-0*) Sycamore Pub.

Rusch, Frank R., et al, eds. Transition from School to Adult Life. 400p. (C). 1991. text 49.95 (*0-9625233-4-8*) Sycamore Pub.

Rusch, Frank R. & Rusch, Janis C. Transition from School to Adult Life. LC 97-36935. (Special Education Ser.). (C). 1997. 65.95 (*0-534-34432-1*) Wadsworth Pub.

Rusch, Frederic E., jt. ed. see Newlin, Keith.

Rusch, Frederik L., ed. A Jean Toomer Reader: Selected Unpublished Writings. LC 93-16374. 320p. 1993. pap. text 27.95 (*0-19-508329-6*) OUP.

Rusch, Frederik L., jt. compiled by see Natoli, Joseph P.

Rusch, Gloria. Professional Singer's Handbook. 216p. 1998. per. 19.95 (*0-7935-8851-0*) H Leonard.

Rusch, H. P., jt. ed. see Dove, W. F.

Rusch, Harold W., jt. auth. see Spinosa, Frank.

Rusch, Janis C., jt. auth. see Rusch, Frank R.

Rusch, K. K., jt. auth. see Devlin, D. W.

Rusch, Kris. Hitler's Angel. LC 97-916. 224p. 1998. text 20.95 (*0-312-15498-4*) St Martin.

Rusch, Kristine. Star Wars Diplomatic Corps Entrance Exam. LC 97-92947. 1997. pap. 12.00 (*0-345-41412-8*, Del Rey) Ballantine Pub Grp.

Rusch, Kristine K. Alien Influences. 352p. 1997. mass mkt. 5.99 (*0-553-56998-8*, Spectra) Bantam.

— The Black Queen. 448p. 1999. mass mkt. 6.50 (*0-553-58115-5*) Bantam.

— The Changeling. (Fey Ser.: Vol. 2). 640p. 1996. mass mkt. 5.99 (*0-553-56895-7*, Spectra) Bantam.

— The Rival. (Fey Ser.: No. 3). 592p. 1997. mass mkt. 6.50 (*0-553-56896-5*, Spectra) Bantam.

— The Sacrifice: The First Book of the Fey. 688p. 1995. mass mkt. 6.99 (*0-553-56894-9*, Spectra) Bantam.

***Rusch, Kristine K. & Smith, Dean W.** X-Men. 256p. 2000. mass mkt. 6.99 (*0-345-44095-1*, Del Rey) Ballantine Pub Grp.

Rusch, Kristine K., jt. auth. see Anderson, Kevin J.

Rusch, Kristine K., jt. auth. see Smith, Dean W.

Rusch, Kristine K., jt. auth. see Smith, Dean Wesley.

***Rusch, Kristine Kathryn.** The Black King. (Black Throne Ser.). 2000. mass mkt. 6.50 (*0-553-58118-X*) Bantam.

Rusch, Kristine Kathryn. The New Rebellion. LC 96-8073. (Star Wars Ser.: 1). 400p. 1996. 22.95 (*0-553-10093-9*, Spectra) Bantam.

— The New Rebellion. (Star Wars Ser.). 1996. 22.95 (*0-614-20653-7*) Bantam.

— The New Rebellion. LC 96-8073. (Star Wars Ser.). 532p. 1997. mass mkt. 5.99 (*0-553-57414-0*, Spectra) Bantam.

— The New Rebellion. (Star Wars Ser.). 1997. 11.09 (*0-606-11894-2*, Pub. by Turtleback) Demco.

— Star Wars Diplomatic Corps Entrance Exam. (Star Wars Ser.). 1997. pap. 12.00 (*0-614-27311-0*, Del Rey) Ballantine Pub Grp.

***Rusch, Kristine Kathryn.** Tenth Planet: Final Assault. 2000. mass mkt. 6.50 (*0-345-42142-6*) Ballantine Pub Grp.

Rusch, Kristine Kathryn. The Victory: Book of the Fey. (Fey Ser.: Vol. 5). 512p. 1998. mass mkt. 6.50 (*0-553-57714-X*, Spectra) Bantam.

Rusch, Kristine Kathryn & Smith, Dean Wesley. Thin Air. (Star Trek Ser.: No. 5). 304p. 2000. per. 6.50 (*0-671-78577-X*, Star Trek) PB.

Rusch, Kristine Kathryn, jt. auth. see Smith, Dean Wesley.

Rusch, Kristine Kathryn, jt. ed. see Smith, Dean Wesley.

Rusch, Patricia H. Foodservice Policies & Procedures for Residential & Intermediate Care Facilities. LC 97-33560. 1997. write for info. (*0-88091-156-5*) Am Dietetic Assn.

Rusch, Robert D. Jazz Talk. (Illus.). 192p. 1984. 14.95 (*0-8184-0357-8*) Carol Pub Group.

— Jazztalk: Basie. (Jazztalk Ser.). (Orig.). 1997. pap. 50.00 (*1-881993-28-0*) Cadence Jazz.

Rusch, Robert J., jt. auth. see Lister, Eugene C.

Rusch, Shari. Stumbling Blocks to Stepping Stones. (Illus.). 272p. (Orig.). 1991. pap. 11.95 (*0-9629392-0-X*) Arc WA.

Rusch, Wilbert H., Sr. The Argument: Creationism vs. Evolutionism. (Creation Research Society Monograph Ser.: No. 3). (Illus.). 86p. (Orig.). (C). 1984. pap. 8.00 (*0-940384-04-3*) Creation Research.

— Origins: What Is at Stake? (Creation Research Society Monographs: No. 5). (Illus.). 73p. (Orig.). 1991. pap. text 8.00 (*0-940384-10-8*) Creation Research.

Rusch, Wilbert H., Sr. & Klotz, John W. Did Charles Darwin Become a Christian? 44p. (Orig.). 1988. pap. text 4.00 (*0-940384-05-1*) Creation Research.

Rusch, Willard J. The Language of the East Midlands & the Development of Standard English: A Study in Diacronic Phonology. LC 91-31826. (Berkeley Insights in Linguistics & Semiotics Ser.: Vol. 8). 197p. (C). 1992. text 41.95 (*0-8204-1582-0*) P Lang Pubng.

Rusch, William G., ed. The Trinitarian Controversy. LC 79-8889. (Sources of Early Christian Thought Ser.). 182p. 1980. pap. 17.00 (*0-8006-1410-0*, 1-1410, Fortress Pr) Augsburg Fortress.

Rusch, William G. & Gros, Jeffrey, eds. Deepening Communion: International Ecumenical Documents with Roman Catholic Participation. LC 98-191020. 627p. 1998. pap. 29.95 (*1-57455-164-7*) US Catholic.

Rusch, William G., jt. auth. see Norgren, William A.

Rusch, William G., jt. ed. see Gros, Jeffrey.

Rusch, William G., jt. ed. see Norgren, William A.

Rusch, William G., jt. ed. see Norris, Richard A., Jr.

***Ruscha, Ed.** They Called Her Styrene. (Illus.). 2000. 19.95 (*0-7148-4011-4*) Phaidon Pr.

***Ruscha, Edward.** Edward/Ruscha: Editions, 1959-1999. LC 99-22720. (Illus.). 288p. 1999. 85.00 (*0-935640-60-6*, Pub. by Walker Art Ctr) Dist Art Pubs.

Ruschak, Lynette. Annie Ate Apples. LC 97-36200. (Illus.). (J). 1998. 14.95 (*0-7894-2478-9*) DK Pub Inc.

— Nature by the Numbers. (Illus.). 12p. (J). (ps-1). 1994. 12.95 (*0-671-88610-X*) Litle Simon.

— Who's Hiding? (Illus.). 22p. (J). (ps-1). 1991. pap. 8.95 (*0-671-73957-3*) S&S Bks Yung.

Ruschau, John J., et al, eds. Special Applications & Advanced Techniques for Crack Size Determination: Symposium on Special Applications & Advanced Techniques for Crack Size Determination (1993: Atlanta, GA), STP 1251. LC 94-49349. (Special Technical Publication Ser.: No. 1251). (Illus.). 163p. 1995. pap. 62.00 (*0-8031-2003-6*, STP1251) ASTM.

Rusche, Sue. A Guide to the Drug Legalization Movement: How You Can Stop It. (Illus.). 112p. 1997. pap. 10.00 (*1-880958-06-6*) Natl Fam Act.

Rusche, Sue & Kemp, Paula. Tobacco. (You Have the Right to Know Ser.: No. 3). 130p. 1992. pap. write for info. (*1-880958-02-3*) Natl Fam Act.

— You Have the Right to Know Vol. 1: Cocaine. 140p. 1990. pap. write for info. (*1-880958-00-7*) Natl Fam Act.

— You Have the Right to Know Vol. 2: Alcohol. 175p. 1991. pap. write for info. (*1-880958-01-5*) Natl Fam Act.

— You Have the Right to Know about Drugs. (You Have the Right to Know Ser.: No. 5). 114p. (J). (gr. 5). 1995. pap. write for info. (*1-880958-05-8*) Natl Fam Act.

Rusche, Sue, jt. auth. see Friedman, David P.

Ruschel, Alaides P., jt. ed. see Vose, Peter B.

Ruschendorf, Ludoer, et al, eds. Distributions with Fixed Marginals & Related Topics. LC 96-77773. (Lecture Notes - Monograph Ser.: No. 28). (Illus.). 364p. 1997. pap. 52.00 (*0-940600-40-4*) Inst Math.

Ruscheweyh, S., et al, eds. Computational Methods & Function Theory: Proceedings of a Conference Held in Valparaiso, Chile, March 13-18, 1989. (Lecture Notes in Mathematics Ser.: Vol. 1435). vi, 211p. 1990. 35.00 (*0-387-52768-0*) Spr-Verlag.

Ruschlikon, ed. see Baptist Theological Seminary Faculty Staff.

Ruschoff, Bernd & Schmitz, Ulrich. Kommunikation und Lernen Mit Alten und Neuen Medien. (Forum Angewandte Linguistik Ser.: Bd. 30). (GER., Illus.). 143p. 1996. 32.95 (*3-631-30462-5*) P Lang Pubng.

Rusciano, Frank L. Isolation & Paradox: Defining "The Public" in Modern Political Analysis, 233. LC 88-29626. (Contributions in Political Science Ser.: No. 233). 183p. 1989. 49.95 (*0-313-26492-9*, RBX/, Greenwood Pr) Greenwood.

Rusciano, Frank Loius. World Opinion & the Emerging International Order. LC 97-50040. (Praeger Series in Political Communication). 208p. 1998. 55.00 (*0-275-95449-8*, Praeger Pubs) Greenwood.

Ruscica, Marybeth B., jt. auth. see Fitzpatrick, Carolyn H.

Ruscin, Terry. Mission Memoirs: A Collection of Photographs, Illustrations & Late Twentieth-Century Reflections of California's Past. LC 99-20322. (Illus.). 200p. 1999. 50.00 (*0-932653-30-8*) Sunbelt Pubns.

Rusco, Elmer, ed. & intro. see Liebling, A. J.

Rusco, Elmer R. Good Time Coming? Black Nevadans in the Nineteenth Century, 15. LC 75-16969. (Contributions in Afro-American & African Studies: No. 15). (Illus.). 230p. 1976. 55.00 (*0-8371-8286-7*, RGT/, Greenwood Pr) Greenwood.

***Rusco, Elmer R.** Legislation & Background of the Indian Reorganization Act. LC 00-8554. (Wilbur S. Shepperson Series in History & Humanities). 360p. 2000. 44.95 (*0-87417-345-0*) U of Nev Pr.

Rusco, F. W. & Walls, W. D. Clearing the Air: Vehicular Emissions Policy for Hong Kong. LC 97-153763. 122p. (Orig.). (C). 1997. pap. text 17.95 (*962-201-657-X*, Pub. by Chinese Univ) U of Mich Pr.

Ruscombe-King, Gillie, jt. auth. see Hurst, Sheila.

Rusconi, Roberto, ed. The Book of Prophecies by Christopher Columbus. Sullivan, Blair, tr. from LAT. LC 96-49651. 280p. (C). 1996. 48.00 (*0-520-20047-0*, Pub. by U CA Pr) Cal Prin Full Svc.

Rusconi, Roberto, jt. ed. see Bornstein, Daniel.

Rusczyk, Richard, jt. auth. see Lehoczky, Sandor.

R

An Asterisk (*) at the beginning of an entry indicates that the title is appearing for the first time.

Rusczyk, Richard, jt. auth. see Leholzky, Sandor.

Rusdorf, Richard, jt. auth. see Goodwin, Daniel.

Ruse, Arnold, ed. & intro. see Gendusa, Sam.

Ruse, Ch., jt. auth. see Hornby, A. S.

***Ruse, Michael.** Can a Darwinian be a Christian? The Relationship Between Science & Religion. (Illus.). 272p. 2000. 24.95 (*0-521-63144-0*) Cambridge U Pr.

Ruse, Michael. The Darwinian Paradigm: Essays on Its History, Philosophy & Religious Implications. 272p. 1989. 25.00 (*0-415-00300-8*) Routledge.

— The Darwinian Revolution: Science Red in Tooth & Claw. LC 78-25826. 336p. 1981. pap. text 14.95 (*0-226-73165-0*) U Ch Pr.

— The Darwinian Revolution: Science Red in Tooth & Claw. LC 78-25826. 1992. lib. bdg. 25.00 (*0-226-73164-2*) U Ch Pr.

***Ruse, Michael.** The Darwinian Revolution: Science Red in Tooth & Claw. 2nd ed. LC 99-23377. xvi, 358p. 1999. pap. text 18.00 (*0-226-73169-3*); lib. bdg. 45.00 (*0-226-73168-5*) U Ch Pr.

— The Evolution Wars. 2000. lib. bdg. 55.00 (*1-57607-185-5*) ABC-CLIO.

Ruse, Michael. Evolutionary Naturalism: Selected Essays. LC 94-18435. (Illus.). 320p. (C). 1995. 75.00 (*0-415-08997-2*, C0350) Routledge.

— Is Science Sexist? And Other Problems in the Biomedical Sciences. 318p. 1981. lib. bdg. 93.00 (*90-277-1249-2*, D Reidel) Kluwer Academic.

— Is Science Sexist? And Other Problems in the Biomedical Sciences. (University of Western Ontario Series in Philosophy of Science: No. 17). 318p. 1981. pap. text 51.50 (*90-277-1250-6*) Kluwer Academic.

— Monad to Man: The Concept of Progress in Evolutionary Biology. (Illus.). 640p. 1996. 51.95 (*0-674-58220-9*) HUP.

— Mystery of Mysteries: Is Evolution a Social Construction? LC 98-41969. 320p. 1999. 27.50 (*0-674-46706-X*) HUP.

— Nature Animated. 287p. 1982. lib. bdg. 135.00 (*90-277-1403-7*, D Reidel) Kluwer Academic.

— The Philosophy of Biology. Edwards, Paul, ed. (Philosophical Topics Ser.). 368p. (C). 1988. pap. text 15.00 (*0-02-404492-X*, Macmillan Coll) P-H.

— The Philosophy of Biology. LC 97-36460. 392p. 1998. pap. text 18.95 (*1-57392-185-8*) Prometheus Bks.

— Philosophy of Biology Today. LC 88-15377. (SUNY Series in Philosophy & Biology). 155p. (C). 1988. pap. text 16.95 (*0-88706-911-8*) State U NY Pr.

— Sociobiology: Sense or Nonsense. rev. ed. (Episteme Ser.: No. 8). 244p. 1984. pap. text 57.00 (*90-277-1798-2*, D Reidel) Kluwer Academic.

— Sociobiology: Sense or Nonsense. 2nd rev. ed. (Episteme Ser.: No. 8). 248p. 1984. lib. bdg. 89.00 (*90-277-1797-4*, D Reidel) Kluwer Academic.

— Taking Darwin Seriously: A Naturalistic Approach to Philosophy. LC 98-38272. (Illus.). 340p. 1998. reprint ed. pap. 18.95 (*1-57392-242-0*) Prometheus Bks.

Ruse, Michael, ed. But Is It Science? The Philosophical Question in the Creation/Evolution Controversy. LC 96-4218. (Illus.). 406p. 1996. pap. 22.95 (*1-57392-087-8*) Prometheus Bks.

— What the Philosophy of Biology Is: Essays for David Hull. 348p. (C). 1989. text 191.50 (*90-247-3778-8*) Kluwer Academic.

***Ruse, Michael & Sheppard, Aryne, eds.** Cloning: Responsible Science Or Technomadness? 300p. 2000. pap. 19.00 (*1-57392-836-4*) Prometheus Bks.

Ruse, Michael, jt. ed. see Hull, David L.

Ruse, Michael, jt. ed. see Maienschein, Jane.

Rusek, Jamie. Exotic Butterflies Charted Designs. (Needlecraft Ser.). (Illus.). 32p. (Orig.). 1991. pap. 3.95 (*0-486-26708-3*) Dover.

Rusel, Demaria. SimCity 3000: Prima's Official Strategy Guide. LC 97-67477. 304p. 1998. pap. 19.99 (*0-7615-1124-5*) Prima Pub.

Rusell, William. Scientific Horseshoeing. 2nd ed. LC 87-82868. 490p. 1995. 45.00 (*0-944707-01-7*) Loose Change.

Rusen, Jorn. Studies in Metahistory. Duvenage, Pieter, ed. & intro. by. 240p. 1999. pap. 19.95 (*0-7969-1520-2*) Berghahn Bks.

Ruser, Kevin, jt. auth. see Minahan, John C., Jr.

Rusezyk, Richard & Lehoczky, Sandor. The Art of Problem Solving Vol. I: The Basics Solutions. Date not set. 8.00 (*1-885875-00-2*) Mu Alpha Theta.

Rush, A., ed. Records of Kuwait, 1899-1965, 14 vols. (Illus.). 8000p. (C). 1989. reprint ed. lib. bdg. 2495.00 (*1-85207-200-8*, Pub. by Archive Editions) N Ross.

Rush, A. D., ed. Records of Islam in Arabia & the Holy Places, 1803-1971, 10 vols. 7000p. 1997. reprint ed. lib. bdg. 2495.00 (*1-85207-860-X*, Pub. by Archive Editions) N Ross.

— Records of the Hajj: A Documentary History of the Pilgrimage to Mecca, 10 vols. (ARA & ENG., Illus.). 6000p. 1993. reprint ed. lib. bdg. 2495.00 (*1-85207-430-2*, Pub. by Archive Editions) N Ross.

— Records of the Hashimite Dynasties, 15 vols. 10,000p. 1994. reprint ed. lib. bdg. 3995.00 (*1-85207-590-2*, Pub. by Archive Editions) N Ross.

Rush, A. John. Beating Depression. LC 84-13564. (Illus.). 155p. reprint ed. pap. 48.10 (*0-8357-4248-2*, 203703700007) Bks Demand.

Rush, A. John, ed. Mood & Anxiety Disorders. 379p. 1997. pap. 49.95 (*0-683-30516-6*) Lppncott W & W.

— Mood Disorders: Systematic Medication Management. LC 97-21357. (Modern Problems of Pharmacopsychiatry Ser.: Vol. 25, 1996). (Illus.). viii, 262p. 1997. 224.50 (*3-8055-6223-3*) S Karger.

— Short-Term Psychotherapies for Depression: Behavioral, Interpersonal, Cognitive, & Psychodynamic Approaches. LC 81-7058. 351p. reprint ed. pap. 108.90 (*0-608-07582-5*, 205989700010) Bks Demand.

Rush, A. John, jt. auth. see Basco, Monica R.

Rush, A. John, jt. auth. see Thase, Michael.

Rush, Ann, ed. see Pilgrim, Peace.

***Rush, Ann Kent.** Massage for Total Well-Being: A Hands-On Guide to Reviving Body, Mind & Spirit. (Illus.). 2000. 25.00 (*0-7893-0490-2*) Universe.

Rush, Anne K. The Back Rub Book: A Guide to the Simple Pleasures of Back Rubs. 1989. pap. 13.00 (*0-394-75962-1*) Vin Bks.

***Rush, Anne K.** Classic Cameos & Incomparable Intaglios: Yesterday & Today. (Illus.). 48p. 1999. pap. 14.95 (*0-931452-04-X*, Jules & Jems) Greta Bear.

Rush, Anne K. Romantic Massage. 1991. pap. 14.00 (*0-380-75985-3*, Avon Bks) Morrow Avon.

Rush, Anne Kent. Bodywork Basics: A Guide to the Powers & Pleasures of Your Body. LC 99-36563. (Omega Institute Mind, Body & Spirit Bks.). 224p. 2000. pap. 12.95 (*0-440-50870-3*, Dell Trade Pbks) Dell.

***Rush, Barbara.** The Jewish Year: Celebrating the Holidays. LC 00-29718. 2000. write for info. (*1-58479-030-X*) Stewart Tabori & Chang.

Rush, Barbara, ed. The Sabbath Lion: A Jewish Folktale from Algeria. LC 91-35766. (Illus.). 32p. (J). (gr. k-4). 1992. 14.00 (*0-06-020853-8*); lib. bdg. 13.89 (*0-06-020854-6*) HarpC Child Bks.

***Rush, Barbara & Schwartzs, Cherie K.** The Kids' Catalog of Passover: A Worldwide Celebration: Stories, Songs, Customs, Crafts, Food & Fun from Around the World. LC 99-35118. 226p. (J). 2000. 15.95 (*0-8276-0687-7*) JPS Phila.

Rush, Barbara, jt. auth. see Schwartz, Howard.

Rush, Barry. Extreme Love. rev. ed. (Inter Acta Ser.). (Illus.). 6p. (C). 1996. teacher ed., ring bd. 1.25 (*1-57334-013-8*, 741-008t, Inter Acta); student ed., ring bd. 3.25 (*1-57334-012-X*, 741-008S, Inter Acta) WSN Pr.

— Philippians IV. (Inter Acta Logos Ser.). (Illus.). 2p. (C). 1994. student ed., ring bd. 2.75 (*1-885702-68-X*, 741-058s, Inter Acta) WSN Pr.

— Philippians IV, 4 bks., Set. (Inter Acta Logos Ser.). (Illus.). 2p. (C). 1994. teacher ed., ring bd. 3.50 (*1-885702-69-8*, 741-055t, Inter Acta) WSN Pr.

— Philippians I. (Inter Acta Logos Ser.). (Illus.). 2p. (C). 1994. student ed., ring bd. 2.75 (*1-885702-36-1*, 741-055s, Inter Acta) WSN Pr.

— Philippians I, 4 bks., Set. (Inter Acta Logos Ser.). (Illus.). 2p. (C). 1994. teacher ed., ring bd. 3.50 (*1-885702-37-X*, 741-055t, Inter Acta) WSN Pr.

— Philippians III. (Inter Acta Logos Ser.). (Illus.). 2p. (C). 1994. teacher ed., ring bd. 3.50 (*1-885702-67-1*, 741-055t, Inter Acta); student ed., ring bd. 2.75 (*1-885702-66-3*, 741-057s, Inter Acta) WSN Pr.

— Philippians II. (Inter Acta Logos Ser.). (Illus.). 2p. (C). 1994. student ed., ring bd. 2.75 (*1-885702-62-0*, 741-056s, Inter Acta) WSN Pr.

— Philippians II, 4 bks., Set. (Inter Acta Logos Ser.). (Illus.). 2p. (C). 1994. teacher ed., ring bd. 3.50 (*1-885702-63-9*, Inter Acta) WSN Pr.

Rush, Benjamin. An Account of the Bilious Remitting Yellow Fever as It Appeared in the City of Philadelphia. (Notable American Authors Ser.). 1999. reprint ed. lib. bdg. 125.00 (*0-7812-8852-5*) Rprt Serv.

— An Account of the Life & Character of Christopher Ludwick: Baker-General of the Army of the U. S. During the Revolutionary War. 1972. reprint ed. 19.50 (*0-8422-8133-9*) Irvington.

— An Address to the Inhabitants of the British Settlements in American upon Slave-Keeping. (Notable American Authors Ser.). 1999. reprint ed. lib. bdg. 125.00 (*0-7812-8849-5*) Rprt Serv.

— An Address to the Inhabitants of the British Settlements, on the Slavery of the Negroes in America. 2nd ed. (Anti-Slavery Crusade in America Ser.). 92p. 1980. reprint ed. 11.95 (*0-405-00656-X*) Ayer.

— The Autobiography of Benjamin Rush: His Travels Through Life. Corner, George W., ed. LC 72-100241. 399p. 1970. reprint ed. lib. bdg. 65.00 (*0-8371-3037-9*, RUAR, Greenwood Pr) Greenwood.

— Benjamin Rush's Lectures on the Mind. Carlson, Eric T. et al, eds. LC 80-70300. (American Philosophical Society, Memoirs Ser.: No. 144). 755p. reprint ed. pap. 200.00 (*0-7837-2682-1*, 204305900006) Bks Demand.

— Essays: Literary, Moral & Philosophical. LC 88-80672. 230p. 1988. 26.50 (*0-912756-22-5*) Union Coll.

— Essays: Literary, Moral & Philosophical. (Notable American Authors Ser.). 1999. reprint ed. lib. bdg. 125.00 (*0-7812-8850-9*) Rprt Serv.

— An Medical Inquiries & Observations. (Notable American Authors Ser.). 1999. reprint ed. lib. bdg. 125.00 (*0-7812-8851-7*) Rprt Serv.

— Medical Inquiries & Observations, 4 vols., Set. 4th ed. LC 76-180588. (Medicine & Society in America Ser.). 1070p. 1972. reprint ed. 65.95 (*0-405-03968-9*) Ayer.

— Medical Inquiries & Observations, 4 vols., Vol. 1. 4th ed. LC 76-180588. (Medicine & Society in America Ser.). 1070p. 1972. reprint ed. 33.95 (*0-405-03969-7*) Ayer.

— Medical Inquiries & Observations, 4 vols., Vol. 2. 4th ed. LC 76-180588. (Medicine & Society in America Ser.). 1070p. 1972. reprint ed. 33.95 (*0-405-03970-0*) Ayer.

— Medical Inquiries & Observations upon the Diseases of the Mind. (Notable American Authors Ser.). 1999. reprint ed. lib. bdg. 125.00 (*0-7812-8853-3*) Rprt Serv.

— Sermons to Gentlemen upon Temperance & Exercise. (Notable American Authors Ser.). 1999. reprint ed. lib. bdg. 125.00 (*0-7812-8848-7*) Rprt Serv.

— A Syllabus of a Course of Lectures on Chemistry. (Notable American Authors Ser.). 1999. reprint ed. lib. bdg. 125.00 (*0-7812-8847-9*) Rprt Serv.

Rush, Benjamin, jt. auth. see Adams, John.

Rush, Beverly & Wittman, Lassie. The Complete Book of Seminole Patchwork. rev. ed. Orig. Title: The Complete Book of Seminole Patchwork: From Traditional Methods to Contemporary Uses. (Illus.). 128p. 1993. reprint ed. pap. 7.95 (*0-486-27617-1*) Dover.

Rush, C. A Resurrection of a Kind. 112p. 1984. pap. text 12.00 (*0-08-030400-1*, Pergamon Pr) Elsevier.

— Two Christmas Stories. (Illus.). 54p. 1988. pap. 8.00 (*0-08-036586-8*, Pergamon Pr) Elsevier.

Rush, C. M., jt. ed. see Sherwood, J. L.

Rush, Caroline. Slopes. LC 96-18785. (Simple Science Ser.). (Illus.). 32p. (J). (ps-4). 1997. lib. bdg. 19.97 (*0-8172-4502-2*) Raintree Steck-V.

— Wheels & Cogs. LC 96-21231. (Simple Science Ser.). (Illus.). 32p. (J). (ps-4). 1997. lib. bdg. 19.97 (*0-8172-4500-6*) Raintree Steck-V.

Rush, Caroline E. North & South: Slavery - Its Contrasts. LC 70-149877. (Black Heritage Library Collection). 1977. 28.95 (*0-8369-8757-8*) Ayer.

Rush, Catharine, tr. see Farre, Henry.

Rush, Charles M. & Michels, Gerald J., Jr. Proceedings High Plains Disease Symposium. (Illus.). 77p. (Orig.). 1995. pap. text 10.00 (*0-926195-01-8*, AREC 96-19) TX AES.

Rush, Cheryl B. Circling Home. 85p. 1990. 22.50 (*0-916379-59-0*) Scripta.

Rush, Christopher. Into the Ebb: A New Collection of East Neuk Stories. 176p. 1989. pap. 19.95 (*0-08-036590-6*, Pub. by Aberdeen U Pr) Macmillan.

— Last Lesson of the Afternoon. 320p. 1997. pap. 13.95 (*0-86241-649-3*, Pub. by Canongate Books) Interlink Pub.

— A Twelvemonth & a Day. (Canongate Scottish Classics Ser.). 308p. 1999. pap. 12.95 (*0-86241-439-3*, Pub. by Canongate Books) Interlink Pub.

— A Twelvemonth & a Day. 196p. 1985. text 25.00 (*0-08-032428-2*, Pergamon Pr) Elsevier.

— A Twelvemonth & a Day. 296p. 1986. pap. text 11.95 (*0-08-032469-X*, R145, R150, K150, P110, Pergamon Pr) Elsevier.

— Venus Peter Saves the Whale. LC 92-7808. (Illus.). 32p. (J). (gr. 4-7). 1992. 14.95 (*0-88289-928-7*) Pelican.

Rush, Christopher & Shaw, John F. With Sharp Compassion: Norman Dott: Freeman Surgeon of Edinburgh. (Illus.). 1990. 35.00 (*0-08-037975-3*, Pub. by Aberdeen U Pr) Macmillan.

Rush, D. A. & Siljander, R. P. Fundamentals of Civil & Private Investigation. (Illus.). 172p. 1984. pap. 22.95 (*0-398-06411-3*) C C Thomas.

— Fundamentals of Civil & Private Investigation. (Illus.). 172p. (C). 1984. 35.95 (*0-398-04932-7*) C C Thomas.

Rush, Dee Dee. No Excuses: Moses. (Inter Acta Ser.). (Illus.). 6p. (C). 1994. teacher ed., ring bd. 1.25 (*1-885702-23-X*, 741-019t, Inter Acta); student ed., ring bd. 3.25 (*1-885702-22-1*, 741-019s, Inter Acta) WSN Pr.

Rush, Dee N. The Satanic Nurses. (Illus.). 168p. (Orig.). 1990. pap. 12.95 (*0-9627950-0-3*) ISOS PC.

Rush, Edna T. Memories. 1998. pap. write for info. (*1-57553-791-5*) Watermrk Pr.

Rush, Florence. The Best-Kept Secret: Sexual Abuse of Children. 238p. 1991. pap. 9.95 (*0-8306-3907-1*) McGraw-Hill Prof.

Rush, George. Prisons & Jails, Inside American Prisons. LC 97-65246. (Illus.). 205p. (C). 1997. pap. 19.95 (*0-942728-79-3*) Copperhouse.

Rush, George & Torres, Sam. Dictionary of Criminology. 200p. (C). 1997. pap. 19.95 (*0-942728-83-1*) Copperhouse.

Rush, George, jt. auth. see Whisenand, Paul.

Rush, George E. Dictionary of Criminal Justice. 4th ed. LC 85-73890. (Illus.). 432p. (C). 1994. text 14.95 (*1-56134-297-1*, Dshkn McG-Hill) McGrw-H Hghr Educ.

Rush, George E., jt. auth. see Champion, Dean J.

Rush, George E., jt. ed. see Ryan, Patrick J.

Rush, Harold M. Behavioral Science: Concepts & Management Application. (Studies in Personnel Policy: No. 216). 174p. (Orig.). 1969. pap. text 40.00 (*0-8237-0003-8*) Conference Bd.

Rush, Helene & Emmons, Rachael. Sweaters by Hand: Designs for Spinners & Knitters. LC 88-32898. (Illus.). 160p. 1988. pap. 17.95 (*0-934026-37-8*) Interweave.

Rush, Helene M. Head to Toe: Thirty Original Designs for Hats, Mittens & Other Accessories. LC 89-81052. (Illus.). 72p. 1989. pap. 9.95 (*0-89272-276-2*) Down East.

Rush, Howard, jt. auth. see Hoffman, Kurt.

Rush, James. The Collected Works of James Rush, 4 vols. Bernstein, Melvin H., ed. 1925p. 1974. 115.00 (*0-87730-008-9*) M & S Pr.

— Time Frames. 304p. 1988. 16.95 (*0-8065-1083-8*, Citadel Pr) Carol Pub Group.

Rush, James E., jt. auth. see Davis, Charles H.

***Rush, James J.** Cousin Harry. (Illus.). 249p. (J). 2000. pap. 17.10 (*1-58721-037-1*) First Bks Lib.

Rush, James J. Durner's Spring. 1980. 9.95 (*0-8065-0732-2*, Citadel Pr) Carol Pub Group.

— Naked in the Streets. 256p. 1985. 14.95 (*0-8065-0951-1*, Citadel Pr) Carol Pub Group.

Rush, James R. Opium to Java: Revenue Farming & Chinese Enterprise in Colonial Indonesia, 1860-1910. LC 89-45974. (Asia East by South Ser.). (Illus.). 280p. 1990. text 45.00 (*0-8014-2218-3*) Cornell U Pr.

Rush, Jean C., jt. auth. see Hobbs, Jack A.

Rush, Jeff, jt. auth. see Dancyger, Ken.

Rush, John & Altshuler, Kenneth Z., eds. Depression: Basic Mechanisms, Diagnosis, & Treatment. LC 84-19318. (Illus.). 254p. 1986. reprint ed. pap. 78.80 (*0-608-07572-8*, 205988700010) Bks Demand.

Rush, John & Anderson, Abbe. The Man with the Bird on His Head: The Amazing Fulfillment of a Mysterious Island Prophecy. (International Adventures Ser.). 192p. 1997. pap. 8.99 (*1-57658-005-9*) YWAM Pub.

Rush, John A. Clinical Anthropology: An Application of Anthropological Concepts Within Clinical Settings. LC 96-2203. 312p. 1996. 79.50 (*0-275-95571-0*, Praeger Pubs); pap. 24.95 (*0-275-95572-9*, Praeger Pubs) Greenwood.

— Stress & Emotional Health: Applications of Clinical Anthropology. LC 99-11414. (Illus.). 232p. 1999. 69.50 (*0-86569-290-4*, T290, Auburn Hse) Greenwood.

***Rush, John A.** Stress & Emotional Health: Applications of Clinical Anthropology. LC 99-11414. (Illus.). 232p. 1999. pap. 22.95 (*0-86569-291-2*, T290, Auburn Hse) Greenwood.

Rush, Joseph H. New Directions in Parapsychological Research. LC 64-22612. (Parapsychological Monographs: No. 4). 1964. pap. 5.00 (*0-912328-07-X*) Parapsych Foun.

***Rush, Keith A.** Ringknockers. 344p. 1999. 22.95 (*0-9673676-0-3*) Diezel Pr.

Rush, Ken. The Seltzer Man. LC 91-40905. (Illus.). 32p. (J). (ps-3). 1993. lib. bdg. 14.95 (*0-02-777917-3*, Mac Bks Young Read) S&S Childrens.

— What about Emma? LC 95-53730. (Illus.). 32p. (J). (ps-2). 1996. 15.95 (*0-531-09534-7*); lib. bdg. 16.99 (*0-531-08884-7*) Orchard Bks Watts.

Rush, Kenneth, et al. The President, the Congress, & Foreign Policy: A Joint Project of the Association of Former Members of Congress & the Atlantic Council of the United States. LC 86-1634. 1986. 52.00 (*0-8191-5283-8*) U Pr of Amer.

Rush, Laurence W. HMM 165: White Beach to Vietnam. 128p. reprint ed. pap. write for info. (*0-318-64842-3*) L & R Art.

Rush, Mallory. Between the Sheets. (Temptation Ser.). 1996. per. 3.50 (*0-373-25707-4*, 1-25707-0) Harlequin Bks.

— Kiss of the Beast. LC 95-22312. 218p. 1995. per. 3.25 (*0-373-25658-2*, 1-25658-5) Harlequin Bks.

— Love Game. LC 96-323. 250p. 1995. per. 4.99 (*0-373-83313-X*, 1-83313-6) Harlequin Bks.

— Love Games: Secret Fantasies. 1995. pap. 2.99 (*0-614-00493-4*, 1-25622-1) Harlequin Bks.

— Love Play. 1999. per. 5.99 (*0-373-83359-8*, 1-83359-9) Harlequin Bks.

— Love Slave. (Temptation Ser.). 1993. mass mkt. 2.99 (*0-373-25548-9*, 1-25548-8) Harlequin Bks.

Rush, Mark. Study Guide to Accompany Barro - Macroeconomics. 5th ed. (Illus.). 227p. 1998. pap. text, student ed. 17.50 (*0-262-68103-X*) MIT Pr.

Rush, Mark & Badger-Dole, Carol. Principles of MicroEconomics. 2nd ed. 240p. (C). 1995. pap. text, spiral bd. 23.95 (*0-7872-0343-2*) Kendall-Hunt.

Rush, Mark E. Does Redistricting Make a Difference? Partisan Representation & Electoral Behavior. LC 93-6670. 232p. (C). 1993. text 35.00 (*0-8018-4579-3*) Johns Hopkins.

Rush, Mark E., ed. Voting Rights & Redistricting in the United States, 384. LC 98-11108. (Contributions in Political Science Ser.). 328p. 1998. 69.50 (*0-313-29948-X*, Greenwood Pr) Greenwood.

Rush, Mary L. The Language of Directions: A Programmed Workbook. LC 77-87703. 1977. pap. text 14.95 (*0-88200-113-2*, C1321) Alexander Graham.

Rush, Michael. New Media in the Late 20th Century Art. LC 99-70940. (World of Art Ser.). (Illus.). 224p. (Orig.). 1999. pap. 14.95 (*0-500-20329-6*, Pub. by Thames Hudson) Norton.

Rush, Michael, ed. Parliament & Pressure Politics. (Illus.). 320p. 1990. 65.00 (*0-19-827576-5*) OUP.

Rush, Michael, jt. auth. see Althoff, Phillip.

Rush, Myron. Administracion: Un Enfoque Biblico - Vida Cristiana.Tr. of Management: A Biblical Approach - Christ Life. (SPA.). 222p. 1983. pap. 6.99 (*1-56063-357-3*, 490215) Editorial Unilit.

— Agotado! Ayudas/Vidas Desequilibradas.Tr. of Burnout. (SPA.). 153p. 1987. pap. 5.99 (*1-56063-242-9*, 497706) Editorial Unilit.

— Political Succession in the U. S. S. R. LC 65-14778. xv, 223p. 1965. text 64.50 (*0-231-02825-3*) Col U Pr.

Rush, Myron D. Management: A Biblical Approach. 240p. 1983. pap. 10.99 (*0-88207-607-8*, 6-2607, Victor Bks) Chariot Victor.

Rush, N. Orwin. Battle of Pensacola. (Florida Classics Ser.). (Illus.). 157p. (Orig.). 1981. reprint ed. 14.95 (*0-912451-05-X*); reprint ed. pap. 9.95 (*0-912451-06-8*) Florida Classics.

Rush, N. Orwin, et al. Special Collections: What They Mean to Librarians, Professors, & Collectors. LC 72-93783. 1972. 5.00 (*0-9607778-4-9*) Friends Fla St.

Rush, Norman. Mating. LC 92-50106. 480p. 1992. pap. 13.00 (*0-679-73709-X*) Vin Bks.

— Whites: Stories. LC 92-50099. 1992. pap. 12.00 (*0-679-73816-9*) Vin Bks.

Rush, Pat. Teddy Bears. (Collins Gem Ser.). 1997. pap. 8.00 (*0-00-471007-X*) Collins.

Rush, Peggy F. The Willis Family of the Northern Neck in VA, 1669-1737. LC 98-154733. 205p. 1998. pap. 19.00 (*0-7884-0832-1*, R873) Heritage Bk.

Rush, Peter, ed. Theoretical Roman Archaeology: 2nd Conference Proceedings. 203p. (C). 1995. text 72.95 (*1-85628-713-0*, Pub. by Avebry) Ashgate Pub Co.

Rush, Peter, et al, eds. Criminal Legal Doctrine. LC 97-19615. 238p. (C). 1997. text 82.95 (*1-85521-969-7*, Pub. by Dartmth Pub) Ashgate Pub Co.

Rush, R. Timothy, et al. Occupational Literacy Education. LC 86-778. (Illus.). 167p. reprint ed. pap. 51.80 (*0-8357-4305-5*, 203710200007) Bks Demand.

Rush, R. W. Lancashire & Yorkshire Passenger Stock. 96p. (C). 1985. 39.00 (*0-85361-306-0*) St Mut.

An Asterisk (*) at the beginning of an entry indicates that the title is appearing for the first time.

— North Staffordshire Railway Locomotives & Rolling Stock. 72p. (C). 1985. 39.00 (*0-85361-275-7*) St Mut.

Rush, R. W. & Price, M. R. Garstang & Knott End Railway. 92p. (C). 1985. 39.00 (*0-85361-318-4*) St Mut.

Rush, Ramona, et al, eds. Communications at the Crossroads: The Gender Gap Connection. LC 88-26757. (Communication & Information Science Ser.). 352p. (C). 1989. text 73.25 (*0-89391-481-9*) Ablx Pub.

Rush, Ramona R., et al, eds. Communications at the Crossroads: The Gender Gap Connection. LC 88-26757. (Communication & Information Science Ser.). 352p. (C). 1989. pap. 39.50 (*0-89391-569-6*) Ablx Pub.

Rush, Rebecca. Kelroy. Nelson, Dana, ed. (Early American Women Writers Ser.). 224p. 1993. pap. 12.95 (*0-19-507703-2*) OUP.

— Kelroy. LC 78-64093. reprint ed. 37.50 (*0-404-17167-2*) AMS Pr.

Rush, Richard D., ed. The Building Systems Integration Handbook: The American Institute of Architects. (Illus.). 458p. 1991. reprint ed. pap. text 46.95 (*0-7506-9198-0*, Butterwrth Archit) Buttrwrth-Heinemann.

Rush, Richard D., jt. auth. see Piper, Robert J.

Rush, Robert A. Neurotrophin Protocols. (Methods in Molecular Biology Ser.). 256p. 2000. 89.00 (*0-89603-699-5*) Humana.

Rush, Robert L. NCO Guide. 6th ed. LC 98-44321. (Illus.). 336p. 1999. pap. text 18.95 (*0-8117-2859-5*) Stackpole.

Rush, S., ed. see Body Surface Mapping of Cardiac Fields Symposium S.

***Rush, Sarah L., ed.** The Language of Trees: An Illustrated Workbook Introducing NLP Communication Skills. (Illus.). xxii, 245p. 2000. pap., wbk. ed. 24.95 (*0-9700272-1-4*) Rushs Arts.

Rush, Sean C. The Decaying American Campus: A Ticking Time Bomb. 136p. 1988. 30.00 (*0-913359-47-5*); 25.00 (*0-318-39805-2*) APPA VA.

Rush, Sean C., jt. auth. see Applied Management Engineering Staff.

Rush, Sean C., ed. see Coopers & Lybrand LLP Staff, et al.

Rush, Sean C., jt. ed. see Johnson, Sandra L.

Rush, Sean C., jt. ed. see Oblinger, Diana G.

Rush, Sella, ed. see Duggal, Vijay.

***Rush, Sharon.** Loving Across the Color Line: A White Adoptive Mother Learns about Race. LC 99-89362. 192p. 2000. 23.95 (*0-8476-9912-9*) Rowman.

Rush, Sheila, jt. auth. see Clark, Chris.

Rush, Solveiga. Oliver Newberry Chaffee (1881-1944) LC 91-65383. (Illus.). 44p. (Orig.). 1991. pap. 10.00 (*0-915577-22-4*) Taft Museum.

Rush, Steve. Ready to Be Revealed. 152p. (Orig.). 1996. pap. 8.99 (*1-57502-369-5*, PO1178) Morris Pubng.

Rush, Susan D. & Durham, Katherine C. The Alabama Heritage Cookbook. LC 83-82791. (Illus.). 164p. 1984. 19.95 (*0-9612868-1-4*); spiral bd. 12.95 (*0-9612868-0-6*) Heritage Pubns.

Rush, Terry. God Will Make a Way: When There Seems to Be No Way. 166p. 1995. 12.99 (*1-878990-40-3*) Howard Pub LA.

— The Miracle of Mercy: Filling the World with the Love of God. LC 99-19367. 200p. 1999. 14.99 (*1-58229-010-5*) Howard Pub LA.

Rush, Theressa G., et al. Black American Writers Past & Present: A Biographical & Bibliographical Dictionary, 2 vols. LC 74-28400. 865p. 1975. 85.00 (*0-8108-0785-8*) Scarecrow.

Rush, Thetis B. Hattie Saussy: Georgia Painter. LC 83-80323. (Illus.). 38p. (Orig.). 1983. pap. 20.00 (*0-9632836-2-6*) R M Hicklin.

Rush, Thomas. The Future of Local Telephone Companies in the U. S. (Illus.). 161p. 1994. 2450.00 (*1-56965-057-8*) BCC.

— The Rush to New Television Delivery & Reception Options. LC 98-120772. 136p. 1997. 2950.00 (*1-56965-084-5*, G-193) BCC.

Rush, Thomas, contrib. by. Personal Navigation Systems. 139p. 1996. 2850.00 (*1-56965-075-6*, G-182) BCC.

Rush, Tom. Residential Internet Provider Systems: Cable, Telephone, Satellite, & Wireless. 118p. 1998. 3150.00 (*1-56965-095-0*, G-216) BCC.

Rush, W. F., et al, eds. Integrating Microelectronics into Gas Distribution. 490p. 1987. 75.00 (*0-910091-62-5*) Inst Gas Tech.

Rusham, G. B., et al. A Short History of Anaesthesia: The First 150 Years. LC 96-31494. 218p. 1996. pap. text 37.50 (*0-7506-3066-3*) Buttrwrth-Heinemann.

Rushbrook, F. Fire Aboard. (C). 1987. 175.00 (*0-85174-331-5*) St Mut.

Rushbrook, Frank. Ship Fires & the Law: Through the Eyes of a Firefighter. 450p. 1995. 125.00 (*1-85044-838-8*) LLP.

Rushbrook, Philip & Pugh, Michael. Solid Waste Landfills in Middle & Lower-Income Countries: A Technical Guide to Planning, Design & Operation. 267p. 1999. 30.00 (*0-8213-4457-9*, 14457) World Bank.

***Rushby, Kevin.** Chasing the Mountain of Light: Across India on the Trail of the Koh-i-Noor Diamond. LC 99-36877. 272p. 2000. text 24.95 (*0-312-22813-9*) St Martin.

— Eating the Flowers of Paradise: One Man's Journey Through Ethiopia & Yemen. LC 99-10666. (Illus.). 322p. 1999. text 24.95 (*0-312-21794-3*) St Martin.

***Rushby, Kevin.** Eating the Flowers of Paradise: One Man's Journey Through Ethiopia & Yemen. (Illus.). 336p. 2000. pap. 16.95 (*0-312-22969-0*) St Martin.

Rushcamp, Sharon. Cultural Differences in Business. (Illus.). 265p. (Orig.). (C). 1997. pap. text 35.00 (*1-886855-75-7*) Tavenner Pub.

***Rushd, Ibn.** The Distinguished Jurist's Primer Vol. I: Bidayat al-Mujtahid wa Nihayat al-Muqtasid. Nyazee, Imran, tr. (Great Books of Islamic Civilization Ser.). 660p. 2000. pap. 35.00 (*1-85964-138-5*) Garnet Publishing Co.

— The Distinguished Jurist's Primer Vol. II: Bidayat al-Mujtahid wa Nihayat al-Muqtasid. Nyazee, Imran, tr. (Great Books of Islamic Civilization Ser.). 676p. 2000. pap. 35.00 (*1-85964-139-3*) Garnet Publishing Co.

Rushd, Ibn, ed. & tr. see Bland, Kalman P.

Rushdie, Salman. East, West: Stories. 224p. 1996. pap. 11.00 (*0-679-75789-9*) Vin Bks.

— Grimus: A Novel. LC 78-65232. 320p. 1982. 27.95 (*0-87951-093-5*, Pub. by Overlook Pr); pap. 9.95 (*0-87951-138-9*, Pub. by Overlook Pr) Penguin Putnam.

— The Ground Beneath Her Feet. LC 98-42407. 592p. 1999. 26.00 (*0-8050-5308-5*) H Holt & Co.

***Rushdie, Salman.** The Ground Beneath Her Feet: A Novel. LC 99-88361. 592p. 2000. pap. 16.00 (*0-312-25499-7*, Picador USA) St Martin.

Rushdie, Salman. The Ground Beneath Her Feet: A Novel. large type ed. LC 99-32533. (Core Ser.). 2000. pap. 30.00 (*0-7838-8712-4*, G K Hall Lrg Type) Mac Lib Ref.

***Rushdie, Salman.** The Ground Beneath Her Feet: A Novel. large type ed. LC 99-32533. 1999. 30.95 (*0-7838-8713-2*) Thorndike Pr.

Rushdie, Salman. Haroun & the Sea of Stories. 96p. 1999. pap. 13.00 (*0-571-19693-4*) Faber & Faber.

— Haroun & the Sea of Stories. 1999. pap. 4.99 (*0-14-037636-4*) Viking Penguin.

— Haroun & the Sea of Stories. 204p. 1991. reprint ed. pap. 12.95 (*0-14-015737-9*, Penguin Bks) Viking Penguin.

— Imaginary Homelands: Essays & Criticism 1981-1991. 448p. 1992. pap. 14.95 (*0-14-014036-0*) Viking Penguin.

— The Jaguar Smile: A Nicaraguan Journey. LC 97-794. 176p. 1997. pap. 12.00 (*0-8050-5311-5*) H Holt & Co.

— The Jaguar Smile: A Nicaraguan Journey. 1987. 12.95 (*0-317-56603-2*) Viking Penguin.

— Midnight's Children. 620p. 1995. 20.00 (*0-679-44462-9*) Knopf.

— Midnight's Children. 552p. (C). 1999. pap. 14.95 (*0-14-013270-8*) Viking Penguin.

***Rushdie, Salman.** Midnight's Children 1980. 544p. 2000. pap. 15.95 (*0-14-028339-0*) Viking Penguin.

Rushdie, Salman. The Moor's Last Sigh. LC 95-24392. 448p. 1996. 25.00 (*0-679-42049-5*) Pantheon.

— The Moor's Last Sigh. 1997. pap. 14.00 (*0-679-74466-5*) Pantheon.

— The Moor's Last Sigh. Date not set. pap. 13.00 (*0-614-26587-8*) Vin Bks.

— The Satanic Verses. 1992. pap. 14.00 (*0-9632707-0-2*) Consortium DE.

— The Satanic Verses. LC 88-40266. 496p. 1989. 27.95 (*0-670-82537-9*) Viking Penguin.

***Rushdie, Salman.** Satanic Verses. 2000. pap. 16.00 (*0-312-27082-8*, Picador USA) St Martin.

Rushdie, Salman. The Satanic Verses: A Novel. LC 97-795. 561p. 1997. pap. 15.00 (*0-8050-5309-3*, Owl) H Holt & Co.

Rushdie, Salman. Shame. 1984. pap. 9.95 (*0-394-72665-0*) Random.

— Shame. 2000. pap. 14.00 (*0-312-27093-3*, Picador USA) St Martin.

Rushdie, Salman. Shame: A Novel. LC 97-5633. 320p. 1997. pap. 12.00 (*0-8050-5310-7*, Owl) H Holt & Co.

— The Wizard of Oz: BFI Film Classics. (Illus.). 72p. 1992. pap. 9.95 (*0-85170-300-3*, Pub. by British Film Inst) Ind U Pr.

Rushdie, Salman & West, Elizabeth. Mirrorwork: 50 Years of Indian Writing, 1947-1997. LC 97-19595. 1997. pap. 15.00 (*0-8050-5710-2*) H Holt & Co.

Rushdie, Salman & West, Elizabeth, eds. Mirrorwork: 50 Years of Indian Writing, 1947-1997. LC 97-19595. 566p. 1997. 30.00 (*0-8050-5709-9*) H Holt & Co.

Rushdie, Salman, et al. Suitcase Vol. 2: A Journal of Transcultural Traffic. annuals (Illus.). 376p. (Orig.). 1997. pap. 20.00 (*0-9659565-1-2*) Suitcase.

Rushdj, Averroes E. Averroes: Middle Commentary on Aristotle's Categories & De Interpretation. unabridged ed. Butterworth, Charles E., tr. from ARA. & intro. by. LC 97-37675. 213p. 1997. reprint ed. 35.00 (*1-890318-01-9*) St Augustines Pr.

Rushdoony, Haig A. Exploring Our World With Maps. (J). (gr. k-6). 1995. pap. 13.99 (*0-8224-4396-1*) Fearon Teacher Aids.

— Language of Maps: A Map Skills Program for Grades 4-6. (Makemaster Bk.). (J). (gr. 4-6). 1983. pap. 12.99 (*0-8224-4242-6*) Fearon Teacher Aids.

Rushdoony, Rousas J. By What Standard: An Analysis of the Philosophy of Cornelius Van Til. 212p. 1995. reprint ed. text. write for info. (*1-879998-05-X*) Ross Hse Bks.

— The Institutes of Biblical Law. LC 72-79485. 1973. 34.99 (*0-87552-410-9*) P & R Pubng.

— The Messianic Character of American Education. 192p. 1995. reprint ed. text. write for info. (*1-879998-06-8*) Ross Hse Bks.

— Politics of Guilt & Pity. 400p. 1995. reprint ed. text. write for info. (*1-879998-07-6*) Ross Hse Bks.

— Romans & Galatians. 446p. 1997. reprint ed. text. write for info. (*1-879998-10-6*) Ross Hse Bks.

— Roots of Reconstruction. 1124p. 1991. text. write for info. (*1-879998-00-9*) Ross Hse Bks.

— Systematic Theology, 2 vols. LC 94-65571. 1301p. 1994. text. write for info. (*1-879998-03-3*) Ross Hse Bks.

Rushdy, Ashraf H. The Empty Garden: The Subject of Late Milton. LC 92-9975. 533p. 1992. reprint ed. pap. 165.30 (*0-608-07896-4*, 206787700010) Bks Demand.

— Neo-Slave Narratives: Studies in the Social Logic of a Literary Form. LC 98-27667. (Race & American Culture Ser.). 296p. 1999. text 45.00 (*0-19-512533-9*) OUP.

Rushefsky, Mark E. Public Policy in the United States: Toward the 21st Century. 2nd ed. LC 95-45292. (Political Science Ser.). 400p. (C). 1996. pap. text 62.00 (*0-534-24996-5*) Harcourt.

Rushefsky, Mark E. & Patel, Kant. Politics, Power & Policy Making: The Case of Health Care Reform in the 1990s. LC 97-33625. 316p. (C). (gr. 13). 1998. text 70.95 (*1-56324-955-3*) M E Sharpe.

***Rushefsky, Mark E., et al.** Politics, Power & Policy Making: The Case of Health Care Reform in the 1990s. LC 97-33625. 316p. (C). (gr. 13). 1998. pap. text 30.95 (*1-56324-956-1*) M E Sharpe.

Rushefsky, Mark E., jt. auth. see Patel, Kant.

Rusher, Annette W. African American Women Administrators. 120p. (C). 1996. lib. bdg. 48.50 (*0-7618-0249-5*); pap. text 28.00 (*0-7618-0250-9*) U Pr of Amer.

Rusher, Bobby. How to Line up Your Fourth Putt. LC 97-5059. 1997. write for info. (*0-88166-284-4*) Meadowbrook.

— How to Line Up Your Fourth Putt. LC 97-5059. 112p. 1997. 7.00 (*0-671-52126-8*) S&S Trade.

Rusher, William A. How to Win Arguments. LC 85-13344. 216p. 1985. reprint ed. pap. text 17.75 (*0-8191-4771-0*) U Pr of Amer.

— The Rise of the Right. rev. ed. 256p. (C). 1993. pap. text 14.95 (*0-9627841-2-5*) Natl Review.

Rusher, William A. & Masugi, Ken, eds. The Ambiguous Legacy of the Enlightenment. LC 95-15728. 236p. (C). 1995. pap. text 28.50 (*0-8191-9957-5*); lib. bdg. 52.00 (*0-8191-9956-7*) U Pr of Amer.

Rushery, Shirley. Ballroom Dance. 1996. pap. 34.95 (*0-945483-58-9*) E Bowers Pub.

***Rushfield, Richard.** On Spec: Novel of Young Hollywood. LC 99-54821. 192p. 2000. text 21.95 (*0-312-24226-3*) St Martin.

Rushford, Carrolle A. Special Emphasis Program Managers Handbook. rev. ed. (Illus.). 300p. (Orig.). (C). 1990. ring bd. 89.95 (*1-877645-00-1*) Rushford & Assocs.

Rushford, Jerry. Christians on the Oregon Trail: Churches of Christ & Christian Churches in Early Oregon, 1842-1882. LC 97-12265. 1997. 29.99 (*0-89900-777-5*) College Pr Pub.

Rushford, Patricia. Desperate Measures #11. (Jenny McGrady Mysteries Ser.: Vol. 11). 192p. (YA). 1998. mass mkt. 4.99 (*0-7642-2080-2*, 202080) Bethany Hse.

***Rushford, Patricia.** Forgotten. LC 99-50486. (Jennie McGrady Ser.: 13). (J). 2000. mass mkt. 4.99 (*0-7642-2121-3*) Bethany Hse.

Rushford, Patricia. Jennie McGrady, Vols. 1-5. (Jenny McGrady Mysteries Ser.). (YA). 1995. pap., boxed set 24.95 (*1-55661-799-2*, 252799) Bethany Hse.

— Jennie McGrady Mysteries, Vols. 6-10. (Jennie McGrady Mystery Ser.). (YA). 1997. boxed set 24.99 (*0-7642-8196-8*, 258196) Bethany Hse.

Rushford, Patricia. When Shadows Fall. (Helen Bradley Mysteries Ser.: No. 4). pap. 9.99 (*0-7642-1733-X*) Bethany Hse.

Rushford, Patricia H. Abandoned. (Jennie McGrady Mysteries Ser.). 176p. 1999. mass mkt. 4.99 (*0-7642-2120-5*) Bethany Hse.

— Betrayed. (Jennie McGrady Mystery Ser.: Vol. 7). 192p. (Orig.). (YA). (gr. 7-10). 1996. mass mkt. 4.99 (*1-55661-560-4*, Hampshire MN) Bethany Hse.

— Deceived. LC 94-33038. (Jennie McGrady Mystery Ser.: No. 4). 192p. (YA). (gr. 7-10). 1994. mass mkt. 4.99 (*1-55661-334-2*) Bethany Hse.

***Rushford, Patricia H.** Desperate Measures. large type ed. LC 99-58243. (Christian Mystery Ser.). 2000. 23.95 (*0-7862-2374-X*) Thorndike Pr.

Rushford, Patricia H. Dying to Win, Vol. 6. LC 95-33332. (Jennie McGrady Mystery Ser.). 192p. (YA). (gr. 7 up). 1995. mass mkt. 4.99 (*1-55661-559-0*) Bethany Hse.

— From the Ashes, 10. LC 97-21124. (Jennie Mcgrady Mystery Ser.). 192p. (YA). 1997. mass mkt. 4.99 (*1-55661-563-9*) Bethany Hse.

— Haunting Refrain. (Helen Bradley Mysteries Ser.). 256p. 1998. pap. 9.99 (*1-55661-732-1*) Bethany Hse.

— Haunting Refrain. large type ed. LC 98-55242. 1999. 23.95 (*0-7862-1799-5*) Thorndike Pr.

— In Too Deep. (Jenny McGrady Mysteries Ser.: No. 8). 28p (YA). (gr. 7-10). 1996. mass mkt. 4.99 (*1-55661-561-2*) Bethany Hse.

— Morningsong. LC 97-33860. (Portraits Ser.). 256p. 1998. pap 8.99 (*1-55661-993-6*) Bethany Hse.

— Now I Lay Me down to Sleep. LC 96-45848. (Helen Bradley Mysteries Ser.: No. 1). 24p. 1997. pap. 8.99 (*1-55661-730-5*) Bethany Hse.

— Over the Edge, Vol. 9. LC 97-4713. (Jennie McGrady Mystery Ser.). 16p. (J). (gr. 7). 1997. mass mkt. 4.99 (*1-55661-562-0*) Bethany Hse.

— Pursued. LC 93-74536. (Jennie McGrady Ser.: Vol. 3). 176p. (YA). (gr. 7-10). 1994. mass mkt. 4.99 (*1-55661-333-4*) Bethany Hse.

— Red Sky in Mourning. LC 97-21117. (Helen Bradley Mysteries Ser.). 24p. 1997. pap. 9.99 (*1-55661-731-3*) Bethany Hse.

— Red Sky in Mourning. large type ed. LC 98-42038. 1999. 22.95 (*0-7862-1693-X*) Thorndike Pr.

— Silent Witness. (Jennie McGrady Mystery Ser.: No. 2). 176p. (YA). (gr. 7 up). 1993. mass mkt. 4.99 (*1-55661-332-6*) Bethany Hse.

— Too Many Secrets. (Jennie McGrady Mystery Ser.: No. 1). 176p. (YA). (gr. 7-10). 1993. mass mkt. 4.99 (*1-55661-331-8*) Bethany Hse.

— What Kids Need Most in a Mom. 2nd rev. ed. LC 99-18716. 208p. 1999. pap. 9.99 (*0-8007-5697-5*) Revell.

***Rushford, Patricia H.** When Shadows Fall. LC 00-8487. (Helen Bradley Mysteries Ser.). 320p. 2000. pap. 9.99 (*1-55661-733-X*) Bethany Hse.

Rushford, Patricia H. Without a Trace. (Jennie McGrady Mystery Ser.: No. 5). 192p. (J). (gr. 7-10). 1995. mass mkt. 4.99 (*1-55661-558-2*) Bethany Hse.

Rushford, Patricia H., jt. auth. see Lush, Jean.

Rushforth, G. McN. Latin Historical Inscriptions. xxxii, 144p. 1980. pap. 25.00 (*0-89005-179-8*) Ares.

— Latin Historical Inscriptions. LC 70-107831. (Select Bibliographies Reprint Ser.). 1977. 21.95 (*0-8369-5196-4*) Ayer.

Rushforth, J. M. & Morris, J. L. Computers & Computing. LC 72-8616. (Introductory Mathematics for Scientists & Engineers Ser.). 269p. reprint ed. pap. 83.40 (*0-608-30318-6*, 202210400024) Bks Demand.

***Rushforth, Keith.** Trees of Britain & Europe. (Collins Wild Guide Ser.). (Illus.). 1332p. 2000. pap. 29.95 (*0-00-220013-9*, Pub. by HarpC) Trafalgar.

Rushforth, Keith D. Conifers. fac. ed. LC 87-28965. (Illus.). 240p. reprint ed. pap. 74.40 (*0-7837-8153-9*, 204785800008) Bks Demand.

— Pocket Guide to Trees. 1981. 7.95 (*0-686-73804-7*) S&S Trade.

Rushforth, Peter. Kindergarten. LC 87-45454. 208p. 1989. pap. 10.95 (*0-87923-701-5*) Godine.

Rushforth, S. R., jt. auth. see Clark, R. L.

Rushforth, S. R., jt. auth. see Grimes, Judith A.

Rushforth, S. R., jt. auth. see Kaczmarska.

Rushforth, S. R., jt. auth. see Lawson, L. L.

Rushforth, Scott. A Hopi Social History: Anthropological Perspectives on Sociocultural Persistence & Change. (Illus.). 320p. (Orig.). (C). 1992. pap. 18.95 (*0-292-73067-5*); text 35.00 (*0-292-73066-7*) U of Tex Pr.

Rushforth, Scott & Chisholm, James S. Cultural Persistence: Continuity in Meaning & Moral Responsibility among the Bearlake Athapaskans. LC 91-17616. (Illus.). 187p. 1991. 40.95 (*0-8165-1241-8*) U of Ariz Pr.

Rushg. Dictionary of Criminal Justice. 5th ed. 432p. 1999. pap. 20.00 (*0-07-030709-1*) McGraw.

***Rushin, John W.** Science Fair Projects. (YA). (gr. 5). 1999. 9.95 (*1-58037-100-0*, Pub. by M Twain Media) Carson-Dellos.

Rushin, Kate. The Black Back-Ups. LC 92-46886. 96p. (Orig.). 1993. pap. 9.95 (*1-56341-025-7*); lib. bdg. 20.95 (*1-56341-026-5*) Firebrand Bks.

Rushin, Pat. Puzzling Through the News. 130p. 1991. pap. 11.95 (*0-913123-33-1*) Galileo.

Rushin, Steve. Road Swing: One Fan's Journey into the Soul of American Sports. 256p. 1999. pap. 12.95 (*0-385-48392-9*) Doubleday.

Rushing, Andrea B., jt. ed. see Terborg-Penn, Rosalyn.

Rushing, Anthony. Along the Road to Glory: A Compilation & Biography of the Soldier, Company & Regiment of the Confederate Army from Saline County. (Illus.). 103p. 1985. ring bd. 14.25 (*0-945183-01-1*) Saline Cnty Hist Heritage Soc.

Rushing, Charles W., jt. auth. see Doerner, William G.

Rushing, Donna, jt. auth. see Brewer, Karen.

Rushing, F. C. Vibration Problems in Engineering. (Technical Papers: Vol. P248). (Illus.). 16p. (Orig.). 1944. pap. text 30.00 incl. audio compact disk (*1-55589-380-5*) AGMA.

Rushing, Felder. Gardening Southern Style. LC 86-33997. 230p. (Orig.). 1987. pap. 17.95 (*0-87805-390-5*) U Pr of Miss.

***Rushing, Felder.** New Junior Garden Book. Barash, Cathy Wilkinson, ed. LC 98-68021. (Illus.). 112p. (J). (ps-3). 1999. 15.95 (*0-696-20849-0*) Meredith Bks.

Rushing, Felder. Scarecrows: Making Harvest Figures & Other Yard Folks. LC 98-3817. (Illus.). 112p. 1998. pap. 19.95 (*1-58017-067-6*) Storey Bks.

Rushing, Felder, jt. auth. see Bender, Steve.

Rushing, Jack. Mountain & Sorrel Land Tales. 40p. Date not set. pap. 5.00 (*1-891538-01-2*) River Dragon.

— Tales from the Blue Hills. 48p. 1999. pap. 9.95 (*1-891538-00-4*) River Dragon.

***Rushing, Jack.** Tales from the Tribes Vol. 1: Folklore of the Eastern Woodlands Indians. 80p. 1999. 19.95 (*1-891538-02-0*); pap. 9.95 (*1-891538-03-9*) River Dragon.

Rushing, James A., Jr. Images of Adventure: Ywain in the Visual Arts. LC 95-8878. (Middle Ages Ser.). (Illus.). 320p. 1995. 39.95 (*0-8122-3293-3*) U of Pa Pr.

Rushing, Jane G. Against the Moon. LC 91-3111. (Texas Tradition Ser.: No. 17). 222p. 1991. reprint ed. pap. 14.95 (*0-87565-094-5*) Tex Christian.

— Starting from Pyron. (Illus.). xi, 153p. (C). 1992. 25.00 (*0-89672-283-X*) Tex Tech Univ Pr.

— Walnut Grove. xiv, 255p. 1992. reprint ed. pap. 12.00 (*0-89672-278-3*) Tex Tech Univ Pr.

R

An Asterisk (*) at the beginning of an entry indicates that the title is appearing for the first time.

Rushing, Janice H. & Frentz, Thomas S. Projecting the Shadow: The Cyborg Hero in American Film. LC 95-30431. 274p. 1995. lib. bdg. 45.00 (0-226-73166-9) U Ch Pr.

— Projecting the Shadow: The Cyborg Hero in American Film. LC 95-30431. (Illus.). 224p. 1995. pap. 14.95 (0-226-73167-7) U Ch Pr.

Rushing, Janice W. A Humorous Walk on Wall Street. (Illus.). 328p. 1998. pap. 10.95 (1-890669-06-7) Biofeedback Ctr.

Rushing, Phillip. Empty Sleeves: A Story of Tragedy & Triumph. 158p. (Orig.). 1994. pap. 6.99 (0-88270-685-3) Bridge-Logos.

Rushing, R. D. Vibration Problems in Engineering. (Technical Papers: Vol. P109.01A). (Illus.). 14p. 1944. pap. text 30.00 (1-55589-371-6) AGMA.

Rushing, Robert. Lamia Anemia. 280p. 1988. pap. 8.95 (0-89697-287-9) Intl Univ Pr.

Rushing, Sandra M. The Magdalene Legacy: A Presbyterian Minister Examines the Wounded Icon of Sexuality. LC 93-40160. 240p. 1994. 59.95 (0-89789-388-3, Bergin & Garvey) Greenwood.

Rushing, Steve. Legal Insanity: Disorder in the Court. (Illus.). 90p. (Orig.). 1993. pap. 10.00 (0-88092-076-9) Royal Fireworks.

Rushing, W. Jackson. Native American Art & the New York Avante-Garde: A History of Cultural Primitivism. Goetzmann, William H., ed. LC 94-14250. (American Studies). (Illus.). 288p. (C). 1995. text 39.95 (0-292-75547-3) U of Tex Pr.

— Native American Art in the Twentieth Century. LC 98-48803. (Illus.). 1999. 85.00 (0-415-13747-0) Routledge.

Rushing, W. Jackson, ed. Native American Art in the Twentieth Century: Makers, Meanings & Histories. LC 98-48803. (Illus.). 214p. 1999. pap. 29.99 (0-415-13748-9) Routledge.

Rushing, W. Jackson, intro. St. James Guide to Native North American Artists. LC 97-18453. (Illus.). 691p. 1997. 155.00 (1-55862-221-7, 00155966) St James Pr.

Rushing, W. Jackson, jt. auth. see Bernstein, Bruce.

Rushing, William A. Social Functions & Economic Aspects of Health Insurance. (S. S. Huebner International Ser.). 1987. lib. bdg. 72.00 (0-89838-219-X) Huebner Foun Insur.

***Rushkoff, Douglas.** Coercion. 2000. pap. 14.00 (1-57322-829-X, Riverhd Trade) Berkley Pub.

Rushkoff, Douglas. Coercion: Why We Listen to What "They" Say. LC 99-18230. 336p. 1999. 24.95 (1-57322-115-5, Riverhead Books) Putnam Pub Group.

— Ecstasy Club. 1997. 17.50 (0-614-27933-X) Harper SF.

***Rushkoff, Douglas.** Ecstasy Club. LC 98-10736. 320p. 1998. reprint ed. pap. 13.00 (1-57322-702-1, Riverhd Trade) Berkley Pub.

Rushkoff, Douglas. Media Virus! 368p. 1996. pap. 12.00 (0-345-39774-6) Ballantine Pub Grp.

— Playing the Future: How Kid's Culture Can Teach Us to Thrive in an Age of Chaos. LC 99-28145. 1999. pap. text 14.00 (1-57322-764-1, Riverhead Books) Putnam Pub Group.

Rushkovskaia, M. A., ed. see Pasternak, Boris & Bobrov, Sergei.

Rushman. Lees Synopsis of Anaesthesia. 816p. pap. text. write for info. (0-7506-1608-3) Buttrwrth-Heinemann.

Rushman, jt. auth. see McCormick.

***Rushman, G. B.** Lee's Synopsis of Anaesthesia. 12th ed. LC 99-25482. 750p. 1999. pap. text 47.50 (0-7506-3247-X) Buttrwrth-Heinemann.

Rushmer, Dixie. Whidbey Island Sketchbook. LC 84-14629. (Illus.). 64p. (Orig.). 1985. pap. 9.95 (0-88240-266-8, Alaska NW Bks) Gr Arts Ctr Pub.

Rushmer, Nancy & Schuyler, Valerie, eds. Trainer's Handbook: What Infant-Family Specialists Need to Know & How to Teach It. (Early Intervention Ser.). 90p. (C). 1993. 45.00 (1-883204-00-3) Hearing & Speech.

Rushmer, Nancy, jt. auth. see Schuyler, Valerie.

Rushmore, Stephen. The Computerized Income Approach to Hotel-Motel Valuations & Market Studies. 428p. 1990. 21.00 (0-922154-02-3) Appraisal Inst.

— Hotel Investments: A Guide for Lenders & Owners. annuals LC 89-52143. (Illus.). 425p. (C). 1990. ring bd., suppl. ed. 145.00 (0-7913-0379-9) Warren Gorham & Lamont.

— Hotels & Motels: A Guide to Market Analysis, Investment Analysis, & Valuations. LC 92-17619. 1992. 35.00 (0-922154-06-6) Appraisal Inst.

Rusho, Josie & Ogan, Rene. Grab Your Tails & Ride the Trails. (Illus.). v, 218p. 1997. spiral bd. 19.95 (0-9668532-0-2) Horse of Course.

Rusho, W. L. Everett Ruess: A Vagabond for Beauty. LC 83-643. (Illus.). 240p. 1985. pap. 14.95 (0-87905-210-4) Gibbs Smith Pub.

— Lee's Ferry: Desert River Crossing. 3rd rev. ed. (Illus.). 196p. (C). 1998. pap. 16.95 (0-9656645-1-1) Tower Prods.

— Powell's Canyon Voyage. LC 70-64908. (Wild & Woolly West Ser., No. 11). (Illus.). 52p. 1969. pap. 4.00 (0-910584-12-5) Filter.

Rusho, W. L., ed. see Ruess, Everett.

Rushton, A. & Oxley, J. Handbook of Logistics & Distribution Management. 339p. (C). 1989. 350.00 (0-7855-4610-3, Pub. by Inst Pur & Supply) St Mut.

Rushton, A., et al. New Parents for Older Children. (C). 1989. 50.00 (0-903534-79-7, Pub. by Brit Ag for Adopt & Fost) St Mut.

— Solid-Liquid Filtration & Separation Technology: An Introduction. (Illus.). 539p. 1996. 260.00 (3-527-28613-6, Wiley-VCH) Wiley.

Rushton, Alan R. Genetics & Medicine in the United States, 1800 to 1922. LC 93-35943. 1994. text 45.00 (0-8018-4781-8) Johns Hopkins.

***Rushton, Alan R.** Handbook of Logistics & Distribution Manage. 2000. pap. 44.00 (0-7494-3365-5) Kogan Page Ltd.

Rushton, Albert, ed. Mathematical Models & Design Methods in Solid-Liquid Separation. 1985. text 184.00 (90-247-3140-2) Kluwer Academic.

Rushton, Alice. History of the Town of Orting (1854-1981) enl. ed. (Illus.). 358p. 1989. reprint ed. pap. 29.95 (0-945433-13-1) Herit Quest.

Rushton, Alice, ed. Bell-Tower Biographies, Vol. 1. (Illus.). 217p. 1989. pap. 5.95 (0-945433-14-X) Herit Quest.

— Bell-Tower Biographies, Vol. 2. (Illus.). 76p. 1989. pap. 4.95 (0-945433-15-8) Herit Quest.

***Rushton, Andrew.** VHDL for Logic Synthesis. 2nd ed. LC 98-9176. 390p. 1998. 74.95 (0-471-98325-X) Wiley.

Rushton, Andrew. VHDL for Logic Synthesis: An Introductory Guide for Achieving Design Requirements. LC 95-30321. 1996. 50.00 (0-07-709092-6) McGraw.

Rushton, Anna & Bond, Shirley. Natural Progesterone: The Natural Way to Alleviate Symptoms of Menopause, PMS & Other Hormone-Related Problems. 1999. pap. 15.00 (0-7225-3766-2) Thorsons PA.

Rushton, Colin. Spectator in Hell: A British Soldier's Extraordinary Story. 1998. pap. text 9.95 (1-901442-06-3, Pub. by Pharaoh Pr) Seven Hills Bk.

Rushton, David N., ed. Handbook of Neuro-Urology. LC 94-12979. (Neurological Disease & Therapy Ser.: Vol. 28). (Illus.). 424p. 1994. text 180.00 (0-8247-9248-3) Dekker.

Rushton, Donnetta Gibby. Hand in Hand - YW: Lesson Handouts. pap. 12.98 (1-55517-305-5) CFI Dist.

Rushton, Dorgan. The FFrench Letters: Of Godwyn Ainsley Ffrench. (Illus.). 88p. 1998. 14.95 (0-233-99033-X, Pub. by Andre Deutsch) Trafalgar.

Rushton, Francis E. Family Support in Community Pediatrics: Confronting New Challenges. LC 98-11137. 232p. 1998. 59.95 (0-275-96190-7, Praeger Pubs) Greenwood.

Rushton, Gerard, jt. ed. see Onsrud, Harlan J.

Rushton, J. Philippe, jt. ed. see Jackson, Douglas N.

Rushton, J. Phillipe. Race, Evolution, & Behavior: A Life History Perspective. LC 93-21282. 398p. (C). 1994. 39.95 (1-56000-146-1) Transaction Pubs.

Rushton, Julian. Berlioz, Romeo et Juliette. LC 93-32505. (Cambridge Music Handbooks Ser.). (Illus.). 129p. (C). 1994. text 39.95 (0-521-37397-2); pap. text 12.95 (0-521-37767-6) Cambridge U Pr.

— Classical Music: A Concise History from Gluck to Beethoven. LC 86-50223. (World of Art Ser.). 192p. (Orig.). 1986. pap. 14.95 (0-500-20210-9, Pub. by Thames Hudson) Norton.

— Elgar: "Enigma" Variations. LC 98-22042. (Music Handbks.). (Illus.). 128p. (C). 1999. text 44.95 (0-521-63175-0); pap. text 12.95 (0-521-63637-X) Cambridge U Pr.

Rushton, Julian, ed. see Philidor, Francois-Andre D.

Rushton, Julian, ed. see Piccinni, Niccolo.

Rushton, K. R. & Redshaw, S. C. Seepage & Groundwater Flow: Numerical Analysis by Analog & Digital Methods. LC 78-23359. (Wiley Series in Geotechnical Engineering). 351p. reprint ed. pap. 108.90 (0-8357-7017-6, 203362200086) Bks Demand.

Rushton, Lucy. Birth Customs. LC 92-42174. (Comparing Religions Ser.). (Illus.). 32p. (J). (gr. 4-8). 1993. lib. bdg. 22.83 (1-56847-030-4) Raintree Steck-V.

— Death Customs. (Comparing Religions Ser.). (Illus.). 32p. (J). (gr. 4-8). 1993. lib. bdg. 22.83 (0-8172-5282-7) Raintree Steck-V.

Rushton, Pauline, ed. European Musical Instruments in Liverpool Museum. (Illus.). 1993. 110.00 (0-906367-68-9, Pub. by Natl Mus & Galls) St Mut.

Rushton, Peter, jt. auth. see Morgan, Gwenda.

Rushton, Peter H. The Jin Ping Mei & the Non-Linear Dimensions of the Traditional Chinese Novel. LC 93-37252. (Illus.). 436p. 1993. text 109.95 (0-7734-9831-1) E Mellen.

Rushton, Peters, jt. auth. see Norton, Daniel S.

Rushton, Rosie. How Could You Do This to Me, Mum? 1999. 3.99 (0-7868-1388-1, Pub. by Hyprn Ppbks) Little.

— I Think I'll Just Curl up & Die. LC 98-83036. 253p. (YA). (gr. 7-10). 1999. mass mkt. 3.99 (0-7868-1389-X, Pub. by Hyperion) Time Warner.

— Just Don't Make a Scene, Mum! LC 98-898069. 231p. (YA). (gr. 7-10). 1999. pap. text 3.99 (0-7868-1370-9, Pub. by Hyperion) Time Warner.

***Rushton, Rosie.** Melissa. (Fab 5 Ser.). 224p. (YA). (gr. 5-9). 2000. pap. 4.99 (0-7868-1502-7) Hyprn Ppbks.

Rushton, Rosie. Olivia. 224p. (gr. 5-9). 2000. mass mkt. 3.99 (0-7868-1392-X, Pub. by Hyprn Ppbks) Little.

— Poppy. 224p. (J). (gr. 5-9). 2000. mass mkt. 3.99 (0-7868-1391-1, Pub. by Hyprn Ppbks) Little.

***Rushton, Rosie.** Sophie. (Fab 5 Ser.). 224p. (YA). (gr. 5-9). 2000. pap. 4.99 (0-7868-0691-5) Hyprn Ppbks.

— What a Week to Break Free. (Illus.). 128p. (J). pap. 7.95 (0-14-038762-5, Pub. by Pnguin Bks Ltd) Trafalgar.

— What a Week to Fall in Love. (Illus.). 128p. (J). pap. 7.95 (0-14-038760-9, Pub. by Pnguin Bks Ltd) Trafalgar.

— What a Week to Make It Big. (Illus.). 128p. (J). pap. 7.95 (0-14-038761-7, Pub. by Pnguin Bks Ltd) Trafalgar.

Rushton, Rosie. Where Do We Go from Here? 224p. (J). 1999. pap. text 3.99 (0-7868-1390-3, Pub. by Hyperion) Time Warner.

Rushton, William. Shakespeare an Archer. LC 73-7501. (Studies in Shakespeare: No. 24). 1973. reprint ed. lib. bdg. 75.00 (0-8383-1696-4) M S G Haskell Hse.

Rushton, William L. Shakespeare a Lawyer. LC 72-174790. reprint ed. 24.50 (0-404-05452-8) AMS Pr.

— Shakespeare & the Arte of English Poesie. LC 70-174792. 1973. reprint ed. 27.50 (0-404-05458-7) AMS Pr.

— Shakespeare's Euphuism. LC 77-174794. reprint ed. 29.50 (0-404-05454-4) AMS Pr.

— Shakespeare's Legal Maxims. LC 70-174795. reprint ed. 24.50 (0-404-05456-0) AMS Pr.

Rushton, Willie, jt. auth. see Rae, Simon.

Rushworth, F. D., et al. Purposes in Education. 38p. 1974. pap. 6.00 (0-904674-01-0, Pub. by Octagon Pr) ISHK.

Rushworth, Francis A. & Tunstall, David P. Nuclear Magnetic Resonance. LC 72-89713. xii, 254p. 1973. text 306.00 (0-677-04820-3) Gordon & Breach.

Rushworth, Peter, et al. Selected References on the Geology & Coal Resources of the Central & Western Colorado Coal Fields & Regions. (Information Ser.: No. 25). 141p. (Orig.). 1989. pap. 8.00 (1-884216-20-X) Colo Geol Survey.

Rushworth, Stan. Sam Woods: American Healing. LC 92-81553. 1993. pap. 11.95 (0-88268-122-2) Station Hill Pr.

Rushworth, Stanley E. Sam Woods. Greenwood, Peter, ed. LC 92-81553. 176p. (Orig.). (C). 1992. pap. 14.95 (0-9632574-9-8) Talk Leaves.

Rusi, Alpo M. Dangerous Peace: New Rivalry in World Politics. LC 97-13206. 208p. 1997. text 59.00 (0-8133-2258-8, Pub. by Westview) HarpC.

— Dangerous Peace: New Rivalry in World Politics. 208p. 1997. pap. text 25.00 (0-8133-3496-9, Pub. by Westview) HarpC.

RUSI Staff. RUSI & Brassey's Defence Yearbook, 1990. 100th ed. 450p. 1990. 56.00 (0-08-037336-4, Pergamon Pr); pap. 15.25 (0-08-037338-0, Pergamon Pr) Elsevier.

— RUSI-Brassey's Defence Yearbook, 1989. LC 75-641843. (Brassey's Defence Yearbook Ser.). 361p. 1988. 63.00 (0-08-036698-8, Pergamon Pr) Elsevier.

Rusicka, M. Therese, jt. ed. see Weckmueller, Beth L.

Rusiecki, Stephen M. The Key to the Bulge: The Battle for Losheimergraben. LC 96-21317. 224p. 1996. 55.00 (0-275-95302-5, Praeger Pubs) Greenwood.

Rusike, Elias. Zimbabwe. (Profiles of Africa Ser.). 1996. text 26.50 (0-86531-754-2) Westview.

Rusin, Jo Bryan. Volunteers Wanted: A Practical Guide for Getting & Keeping Volunteers. LC 99-61522. 168p. (Orig.). 1999. pap. 10.95 (0-9665175-2-0) Magnolia Mansions.

Rusin, Richard P. & Fischman, Gary S., eds. Bioceramics: Materials & Applications II. LC 96-295. (Ceramic Transactions Ser.: Vol. 63). 1996. 95.00 (1-57498-006-8, CT063) Am Ceramic.

Rusinko, Elaine, ed. & tr. see Duknovych, Aleksandr.

Rusinko, Susan. British Drama, 1950 to Present. (Critical History of British Drama Ser.). 285p. (C). 1989. 32.00 (0-8057-8952-9, Twyne) Mac Lib Ref.

— Joe Orton. LC 95-10064. (English Authors Ser.: Vol. 515). 1995. 32.00 (0-8057-7034-8, Twyne) Mac Lib Ref.

— The Plays of Benn Levy: Between Conrad & Shaw. LC 94-10592. (Illus.). 224p. 1994. 36.50 (0-8386-3556-3) Fairleigh Dickinson.

Rusinko, Susan, ed. see Weintraub, Stanley.

Rusinoff, Samuel E. Automation in Practice. LC 57-13299. 269p. reprint ed. pap. 83.40 (0-8357-5916-4, 205204600030) Bks Demand.

— Practical Descriptive Geometry. LC 47-24789. 268p. 1947. reprint ed. pap. 83.10 (0-608-11843-5, 200456200043) Bks Demand.

— Tool Engineering. LC 59-13786. (Illus.). 335p. reprint ed. pap. 103.90 (0-608-11614-9, 200456600043) Bks Demand.

Rusinov, V. S., ed. Electrophysiology of the Central Nervous System. Haigh, Basil & Doty, Robert W., trs. from RUS. LC 69-12542. (Illus.). 528p. 1970. reprint ed. pap. 163.70 (0-608-05482-8, 206595100006) Bks Demand.

Rusinov, V. S., jt. ed. see Livanov, M. N.

Rusinow, Dennison, ed. Yugoslavia: A Fractured Federalism. LC 88-14356. (Woodrow Wilson Center Perspectives Ser.). (Illus.). 198p. (Orig.). (C). 1988. pap. text 14.25 (0-943875-07-2); lib. bdg. 32.00 (0-943875-08-0) W Wilson Ctr Pr.

Rusinowitch, M., jt. ed. see Narendran, Paliath.

Rusinowitch, Michael & Remy, J. L., eds. Conditional Term Rewriting Systems: Third International Workshop, CTRS-92, Pont-a-Mousson, France, July 8-10, 1992, Proceedings. LC 92-44413. (Lecture Notes in Computer Science Ser.: Vol. 656). 1993. 73.95 (0-387-56393-8) Spr-Verlag.

Rusk, Claude E. Tales of a Western Mountaineer: A Record of Mountain Experiences on the Pacific Coast. (American Biography Ser.). 309p. 1991. reprint ed. lib. bdg. 79.00 (0-7812-8333-7) Rprt Serv.

Rusk, Dave. Rocky Mountain Day Hikes: Featuring 24 Hikes in Rocky Mountain National Park. 2nd ed. (Illus.). 68p. 1998. reprint ed. pap. 4.95 (0-9671535-0-6) Barefoot Pubs.

Rusk, David. Baltimore Unbound: A Strategy for Regional Renewal. 177p. 1995. pap. 14.95 (0-8018-5078-9) Johns Hopkins.

— Cities Without Suburbs. 135p. 1993. pap. text 13.95 (0-943875-50-1) W Wilson Ctr Pr.

— Cities Without Suburbs. 2nd ed. 168p. 1995. text 29.00 (0-943875-74-9); pap. text 14.95 (0-943875-73-0) Johns Hopkins.

— Inside Game-Outside Game: Winning Strategies for Saving Urban America. LC 98-25430. 384p. 1999. 29.95 (0-8157-7650-0) Brookings.

***Rusk, James R., Jr.** The Face in the Surface. LC 98-89363. (Oceanids Ser.: Vol. 1). 254p. 1998. pap. 6.99 (1-893181-10-3) Le Gesse Stevens.

Rusk, Jeff E. Legal Services to the Poor: The Dream, the Reality, the Future. (Institute & Seminar Proceedings Ser.). 120p. 1992. pap. 10.50 (0-89940-103-1) LBJ Sch Pub Aff.

***Rusk, Jerrold G.** Statistical History of American Elections. 2000. 54.95 (1-56802-364-2) CQ Pr.

Rusk, John. On Time & on Budget: A Home Renovation Survival Guide. 320p. 1997. pap. 11.95 (0-385-47511-X) Doubleday.

Rusk, R. L., ed. see Emerson, Ralph Waldo.

Rusk, Ralph L. The Literature of the Middle Western Frontier, 2 vols. (BCL1-PS American Literature Ser.). 1992. reprint ed. lib. bdg. 150.00 (0-7812-6627-0) Rprt Serv.

Rusk, Ralph L., ed. see Lazarus, Emma.

Rusk, Robert R. & Scotland, James. Doctrines of the Great Educators. 5th ed. LC 78-12874. 1979. pap. text 16.00 (0-312-21492-8) St Martin.

Rusk, Rogers D. Atoms, Men & Stars: A Survey of the Latest Developments of Physical Science & Their Relation to Life. LC 70-156712. (Essay Index Reprint Ser.). 1977. reprint ed. 26.95 (0-8369-2332-4) Ayer.

Rusk, Tom. Get Out of Your Own Way! Escape from Mind Traps. LC 95-48124. 320p. 1996. pap. 12.95 (1-56170-276-5) Hay House.

— Instead of Therapy. 256p. 1993. pap. 12.00 (1-56170-059-2, 135T) Hay House.

Rusk, Tom & Miller, D. Patrick. Instead of Therapy: Help Yourself Change & Change the Help You're Getting. LC 91-70545. 256p. (Orig.). 1991. 20.00 (1-56170-021-5, 135H) Hay House.

Rusk, Tom & Miller, D. Patrick. The Power of Ethical Persuasion: Winning Through Understanding at Work & at Home. 240p. 1994. pap. 9.95 (0-14-017214-9, Penguin Bks) Viking Penguin.

Rusk, Tom & Read, Randy. I Want to Change, but I Don't Know How. 2nd ed. 384p. 1981. reprint ed. pap. 13.95 (0-8431-0491-0, Price Stern) Peng Put Young Read.

Ruska. Microelectronic Processing. 1987. 27.50 (0-07-054281-3) McGraw.

Ruska, W. S. Microelectronic Processes: An Introduction to the Manufacture of Integrated Circuits. (McGraw-Hill Series in Computer Engineering). 488p. (C). 1987. text 77.74 (0-07-054280-5) McGraw.

Ruskai, Mary Beth, et al. Wavelets & Their Applications. (C). 1992. 75.00 (0-86720-225-4) Jones & Bartlett.

Ruskan, John. Emotional Clearing: A/Groundbreaking East/West Guide to Unconditional Happiness. LC 99-44628. (Illus.). 352p. 2000. 25.00 (0-7679-0406-0) Broadway BDD.

Ruskay, John S. & Szonyi, David M., eds. Deepening a Commitment: Zionism & the Conservative/Masorti Movement. 15.95 (0-614-13103-0) Ktav.

Ruskay, Joseph A. & Osserman, Richard A. Halfway to Tax Reform. LC 78-126216. 317p. reprint ed. pap. 98.30 (0-608-30008-X, 205520700011) Bks Demand.

Ruskay, Sophie. Horse Cars & Cobblestones. (American Autobiography Ser.). 240p. 1995. reprint ed. lib. bdg. 79.00 (0-7812-8634-4) Rprt Serv.

Ruskeep, A. Heikki. Mathematica Navigator: Graphics & Methods of Applied Mathematics. LC 98-22863. (Illus.). 848p. 1998. pap. text 44.95 incl. cd-rom (0-12-603640-3) Acad Pr.

Ruskell, Arnold. Breaking the Ice: An Arctic Odyssey. LC 98-114427. (Illus.). 160p. 1997. pap. 16.95 (0-9698752-9-0) Sh1oreline.

Ruskiewicz, John, jt. auth. see Lunsford, Andrea.

Ruskin & Saili. Himalayan Leaf & Flower. 1996. pap. 25.00 (0-7855-7413-1, Pub. by Ratna Pustak Bhandar) St Mut.

Ruskin, Adina L. The Art of Remembering. LC 98-222976. 1998. pap. 3.25 (0-8222-1607-8) Dramatists Play.

Ruskin, Anna Marie, ed. see Roberts, Kenneth J.

Ruskin, Arnold M. & Estes, W. Eugene. What Every Engineer Should Know about Project Management. 2nd expanded rev. ed. LC 94-39689. (What Every Engineer Should Know Ser.: Vol. 33). (Illus.). 296p. 1994. text 49.75 (0-8247-8953-9) Dekker.

Ruskin, Asa P., ed. Current Therapy in Psychiatry: Physical Medicine & Rehabilitation. (Illus.). 608p. 1984. text 140.00 (0-7216-7853-X, W B Saunders Co) Harcrt Hlth Sci Grp.

Ruskin, Cindy. The Quilt: Stories from the Names Project. (Illus.). 1988. 22.95 (0-317-67839-6) PB.

Ruskin, Ellen, jt. auth. see Sigman, Marian.

Ruskin, F. R., ed. Lost Crops of Africa Vol. I: Grains. (Illus.). 383p. (C). 1999. reprint ed. pap. text 50.00 (0-7881-7512-2) DIANE Pub.

Ruskin, H., jt. ed. see Sivan, A. A.

Ruskin, Hillel. Leisure: Toward a Theory & Policy. LC 83-48608. 192p. 1984. 33.50 (0-8386-3134-7) Fairleigh Dickinson.

Ruskin, Hillel & Sivan, Atara, eds. Leisure Education Towards the 21st Century. 289p. (Orig.). (C). 1995. pap. text 19.45 (0-9648003-0-6, Dept Rec Mgmt) Brigham.

Ruskin, John. Art Criticism. Herbert, R. L., ed. 1990. 16.50 (0-8446-0694-4) Peter Smith.

— The Brantwood Diary of John Ruskin: Together with Selected Related Letters & Sketches of Persons Mentioned. Viljoen, Helen G., ed. LC 72-99844. 650p. reprint ed. pap. 200.00 (0-8357-7382-5, 202204900024) Bks Demand.

Ruskin, John. The Complete Works of John Ruskin, 39 vols. Incl. Bible of Amiens; Valle Crucis; The Art of England; The Pleasurers of England. 1999. reprint ed. lib. bdg. 98.00 (1-58201-373-X); Bibliography, Catalogue of Ruskin's Drawings, Addena et Corrigenda. 1999. reprint ed. lib. bdg. 98.00 (1-58201-378-0); Bibliotheca Pastorum, The Economist of Xenophon, Rock Honeycomb. 1999. reprint ed. lib. bdg. 98.00 (1-58201-371-3); Cestus of Aglaia, the Queen of the Air. 1999. reprint ed. lib. bdg. 98.00 (1-58201-359-4); Deucalion & Other Studies in Rocks & Stones. 1999. reprint ed. lib. bdg. 98.00 (1-58201-366-7); Early Prose Writings, 1834-1843. 550p. 1999. reprint ed. lib. bdg. 98.00 (1-58201-341-1); Fors Clavigera Letters Pt. 1: 1-36. 1999. reprint ed. lib. bdg. 98.00 (1-58201-367-5); Fors Clavigera Letters Pt. 2: 37-72. 1999. reprint ed. lib. bdg. 98.00 (1-58201-368-3); Fors Clavigera Letters Pt.

An Asterisk (*) at the beginning of an entry indicates that the title is appearing for the first time.

3: 73-96. 1999. reprint ed. lib. bdg. 98.00 (*1-58201-369-1*); General Index. 1999. reprint ed. lib. bdg. 98.00 (*1-58201-379-9*); Giotto, His Works in Padua, The Cavalli Monuments, Guide to the Academy, St. Mark's Rest. 1999. reprint ed. lib. bdg. 98.00 (*1-58201-364-0*); Guild & Museum of St. George. 1999. reprint ed. lib. bdg. 98.00 (*1-58201-370-5*); Harbours of England. 646p. 1999. reprint ed. lib. bdg. 98.00 (*1-58201-353-5*); Joy Forever. 487p. 1999. reprint ed. lib. bdg. 98.00 (*1-58201-356-X*); Lectures on Architecture & Painting. 603p. 1999. reprint ed. lib. bdg. 98.00 (*1-58201-352-7*); Lectures on Art, Artra Pentelici. 1999. reprint ed. lib. bdg. 98.00 (*1-58201-360-8*); Letters of John Ruskin Pt. 1: 1827-1869. 1999. reprint ed. lib. bdg. 98.00 (*1-58201-376-4*); Letters of John Ruskin Pt. 2: 1870-1889. 1999. reprint ed. lib. bdg. 98.00 (*1-58201-377-2*); Love's Meinie & Proserpina. 1999. reprint ed. lib. bdg. 98.00 (*1-58201-365-9*); Notes on Prout & Hunt & Other Art Criticisms. 499p. 1999. reprint ed. lib. bdg. 98.00 (*1-58201-354-3*); Poems. 541p. 1999. reprint ed. lib. bdg. 98.00 (*1-58201-342-X*); Praeterita & Dilecta. 1999. reprint ed. lib. bdg. 98.00 (*1-58201-375-6*); Ruskin Art Collection at Oxford. 1999. reprint ed. lib. bdg. 98.00 (*1-58201-361-6*); Seven Lamps. 1999. lib. bdg. 98.00 (*1-58201-348-9*); Stones of Venice. 1999. lib. bdg. 98.00 (*1-58201-349-7*); Storm-Cloud of the Nineteenth Century; On the Old Road; Arrows of the Chace; Ruskiniana. 1999. reprint ed. lib. bdg. 98.00 (*1-58201-374-8*); Studies of Peasant Life; The Story of Ida; Roadside; Songs of Tuscany. 1999. reprint ed. lib. bdg. 98.00 (*1-58201-372-1*); Unto This Last Munera Pulveris Time & Tide. 565p. 1999. reprint ed. lib. bdg. 98.00 (*1-58201-357-8*); Val D'Arno, The Schools of Florence, Mornings in Florence, The Shepherd's Tower. 1999. reprint ed. lib. bdg. 98.00 (*1-58201-363-2*); Pt. 1. Modern Painters. 607p. 1999. reprint ed. lib. bdg. 98.00 (*1-58201-343-8*); Pt. 2. Modern Painters. 399p. 1999. reprint ed. lib. bdg. 98.00 (*1-58201-344-6*); Pt. 2. Stones of Venice. 470p. 1999. reprint ed. lib. bdg. 98.00 (*1-58201-350-0*); Pt. 3. Modern Painters. 439p. 1999. reprint ed. lib. bdg. 98.00 (*1-58201-345-4*); Pt. 3. Stones of Venice. 436p. 1999. reprint ed. lib. bdg. 98.00 (*1-58201-351-9*); Pt. 4. Modern Painters. 407p. 1999. reprint ed. lib. bdg. 98.00 (*1-58201-346-2*); Pt. 5. Modern Painters. 495p. 1999. reprint ed. lib. bdg. 98.00 (*1-58201-347-0*); Set lib. bdg. 3822.00 (*1-58201-340-3*) Classic Bks.

Ruskin, John. The Elements of Drawing. (Illus.). 228p. 1971. pap. 6.95 (*0-486-22730-8*) Dover.

— The Elements of Drawing. (Illus.). 1997. pap. text 19.95 (*0-8230-1602-1*) Watsn-Guptill.

— The Elements of Drawing. LC 74-115264. 1970. reprint ed. 75.00 (*0-403-00307-5*) Scholarly.

— The Genius of John Ruskin: Selections from His Writings. Rosenberg, John D., ed. LC 97-31013. (Victorian Literature & Culture Ser.). 576p. 1998. reprint ed. pap. 19.50 (*0-8139-1789-1*) U Pr of Va.

— The Gulf of Years: Letters from John Ruskin to Kathleen Olander. Unwin, Rayner, ed. & pref. by. LC 77-18837. 98p. 1978. reprint ed. lib. bdg. 35.00 (*0-313-20188-9*, RUGY, Greenwood Pr) Greenwood.

— King of Golden River. (J). Date not set. 11.95 (*0-399-21514-X*) Putnam Pub Group.

— The King of the Golden River. 17.95 (*0-8488-0620-4*) Amereon Ltd.

*__Ruskin, John.__ The King of the Golden River. LC 99-13463. (Treasures Ser.). (Illus.). 96p. (J). (gr. 3-7). 2000. text 11.99 (*0-7636-0845-9*) Candlewick Pr.

Ruskin, John. The King of the Golden River. (Illus.). 64p. 1995. 12.50 (*0-939218-09-7*) Chapman Billies.

— The King of the Golden River or the Black Brothers. LC 74-82199. (Illus.). 56p. (J). (gr. 1 up). 1974. reprint ed. pap. 3.50 (*0-486-20066-3*) Dover.

— The Lamp of Beauty: Writings on Art. rev. ed. Evans, Joan, ed. & selected by by. (Arts & Letters Ser.). (Illus.). (C). 1995. pap. 14.95 (*0-7148-3358-4*, Pub. by Phaidon Press) Phaidon Pr.

— The Laws of Fesole: Principles of Drawing & Painting from the Tuscan Masters. LC 95-83004. (Illus.). 208p. 1996. pap. 18.95 (*1-880559-44-7*) Allworth Pr.

— Lectures on Art. LC 96-84638. (Illus.). 224p. (Orig.). 1997. pap. 18.95 (*1-880559-54-4*) Allworth Pr.

— The Literary Criticism of John Ruskin. Bloom, Harold, ed. & selected by by. (Quality Paperbacks Ser.). xxvii, 398p. 1987. pap. 12.95 (*0-306-80294-5*) Da Capo.

— Mornings in Florence. 1994. lib. bdg. 21.95 (*1-56849-424-6*) Buccaneer Bks.

— Mornings in Florence: Being Simple Studies of Christian Art for English Travellers. LC 71-11568. 271p. 1972. reprint ed. 69.00 (*0-403-00306-7*) Scholarly.

— Munera Pulveris: Six Essays on the Elements of Political Economy. LC 69-14065. 218p. 1969. reprint ed. lib. bdg. 35.00 (*0-8371-0642-7*, RUMP, Greenwood Pr) Greenwood.

— The Poetry of Architecture. LC 74-148294. reprint ed. 29.50 (*0-404-05463-3*) AMS Pr.

— The Poetry of Architecture. LC 78-115265. (Illus.). 274p. 1972. reprint ed. 69.00 (*0-403-00305-9*) Scholarly.

— Poetry of Architecture. 300p. 1998. reprint ed. lib. bdg. 79.00 (*0-7812-7707-8*) Rprt Serv.

*__Ruskin, John.__ The Poetry of Architecture: Cottage, Villa Etc. to Which Is Added Suggestions on Works of Art. LC 99-68874. (Illus.). 246p. 1999. reprint ed. pap. 24.95 (*1-930423-00-4*) Brohan Pr.

Ruskin, John. The Poetry of Architecture or the Architecture of the Nations of Europe. 1972. 59.95 (*0-8490-0859-X*) Gordon Pr.

— Queen of the Air: A Study of Greek Myths. 1969. pap. 22.00 (*0-8196-1392-4*) Biblo.

— Ruskin As Literary Critic. (BCL1-PR English Literature Ser.). 291p. 1992. reprint ed. lib. bdg. 79.00 (*0-7812-7633-0*) Rprt Serv.

— Ruskin As Literary Critic: Selections. Ball, A. H., ed. LC 69-14066. 291p. 1969. reprint ed. lib. bdg. 65.00 (*0-8371-1149-8*, RULC, Greenwood Pr) Greenwood.

— Ruskin's Letters from Venice 1841 to 1852, Vol. 129--129. Bradley, John L., ed. LC 78-6260. (Yale Studies in English: Vol. 129). 330p. 1978. reprint ed. lib. bdg. 49.50 (*0-313-20456-X*, RULE, Greenwood Pr) Greenwood.

— St. Mark's Rest, the History of Venice. (BCL1-PR English Literature Ser.). 236p. 1992. reprint ed. lib. bdg. 79.00 (*0-7812-7635-7*) Rprt Serv.

— Selected Writings. Davis, Philip, ed. 360p. 1995. pap. 8.50 (*0-460-87460-8*, Everyman's Classic Lib) Tuttle Pubng.

— Selections & Essays. 1988. reprint ed. lib. bdg. 69.00 (*0-7812-0370-8*) Rprt Serv.

— Selections & Essays. Roe, Frederick W., ed. & intro. by. LC 77-145274. 1971. reprint ed. 69.00 (*0-403-01189-2*) Scholarly.

— Sesame & Lilies: The Two Paths & the King of the Golden River. LC 70-145275. (Illus.). 1971. reprint ed. 69.00 (*0-403-01190-6*) Scholarly.

— The Seven Lamps of Architecture. (Illus.). 264p. 1989. pap. 8.95 (*0-486-26145-X*) Dover.

— The Seven Lamps of Architecture. 1991. 23.50 (*0-8446-6469-3*) Peter Smith.

— Seven Lamps of Architecture. 282p. 1998. reprint ed. pap. 19.95 (*0-7661-0716-7*) Kessinger Pub.

— The Stones of Venice. Links, J. G., ed. (Quality Paperbacks Ser.). 256p. 1985. reprint ed. pap. 11.95 (*0-306-80244-9*) Da Capo.

— Unto This Last: Four Essays on the First Principles of Political Economy. Hubenka, Lloyd J., ed. & intro. by. LC 67-12118. 143p. 1967. pap. 44.40 (*0-608-04826-7*, 206548300004) Bks Demand.

Ruskin, John. Unto This Last & Other Stories. Wilmer, Clive, ed. & intro. by. (Classics Ser.). 368p. 1986. pap. 12.95 (*0-14-043211-6*, Penguin Classics) Viking Penguin.

Ruskin, John. Winnington Letters: John Ruskin's Correspondence with Margaret Alexis Bell & the Children at Winnington Hall. Burd, Van A., ed. LC 68-28692. (Illus.). 736p. 1969. 58.00 (*0-674-95365-7*) Belknap Pr.

— Works, 39 vols., Set. (BCL1-PR English Literature Ser.). 1992. reprint ed. lib. bdg. 3510.00 (*0-7812-7632-2*) Rprt Serv.

*__Ruskin, John & Beck, Bill.__ The Laws of Fesole: Principles of Drawing & Painting from the Tuscan Masters. (Illus.). 223p. 1999. reprint ed. pap. text 19.00 (*0-7881-6711-1*) DIANE Pub.

Ruskin, John J. The Ruskin Family Letters: The Correspondence of John James Ruskin, His Wife, & Their Son, John, 1801-1843, 2 vols. Burd, Van A., ed. Incl. Vol. 1. 1801 to 1837. 1973. Vol. 2. 1837 to 1843. 1973. (Illus.). 792p. 1973. Set text 100.00 (*0-8014-0725-7*) Cornell U Pr.

Ruskin, Judith, ed. see Sojka, Nancy.

Ruskin, Karen B., jt. auth. see Achilles, Charles M.

Ruskin, Keith, et al. Introduction to Anesthesiology. (Illus.). 500p. 1999. pap. text 32.00 (*0-07-006304-4*) McGraw-Hill HPD.

Ruskin, Paul E. & Talbot, John A., eds. Aging & Posttraumatic Stress Disorder. 288p. 1996. text 39.50 (*0-88048-513-2*, 8513) Am Psychiatric.

Ruskin, Robert S., jt. auth. see Johnson, Kent R.

Ruskin, Robert S., jt. auth. see Sherman, J. Gilmour.

Ruskin, Ronald, jt. ed. see Greben, Stanley E.

Ruskin, Thelma, et al. Indians of the Tidewater Country of Maryland, Virginia, Delaware & North Carolina. 3rd ed. LC 96-31588. (Illus.). 132p. (J). 1997. 15.00 (*0-917882-45-8*) MD Hist Pr.

Ruskin, Yvonne S. High on Rebellion: Inside the Underground at Max's Kansas City. LC 98-5533. (Illus.). 288p. 1998. 24.95 (*1-56025-183-2*, Thunders Mouth) Avalon NY.

Ruskosky, Nita H. Microsoft Word 6.0 for Windows. 1994. pap. text, teacher ed. 19.00 (*1-56118-734-8*) Paradigm MN.

Ruskowski, Leo F. French Emigre Priests in the United States (1791-1815) LC 73-3586. (Catholic University of America. Studies in Romance Languages & Literatures: No. 32). reprint ed. 32.00 (*0-404-57782-2*) AMS Pr.

Ruskuc, Nikola, jt. ed. see Howie, John M.

Rusler, William, ed. Standard History of Allen County: Authentic Narrative of the Past, with Particular Attention to the Modern Era, 2 vols. (Illus.). 1997. reprint ed. lib. bdg. 100.00 (*0-8328-6290-8*) Higginson Bk Co.

Rusling. Linux Kernel. (ITCP-UK Computer Science Ser.). (C). 1998. pap. 34.99 (*1-85032-338-0*, VNR) Wiley.

Rusling, J. F. Rusling Family. (Illus.). 160p. 1991. reprint ed. pap. 24.00 (*0-8328-1889-5*); reprint ed. lib. bdg. 34.00 (*0-8328-1888-7*) Higginson Bk Co.

Rusling, James F. & Kumosinski, Thomas F. Nonlinear Computer Modeling of Chemical & Biochemical Data. LC 95-30376. (Illus.). 268p. 1996. text 64.95 (*0-12-604490-2*) Acad Pr.

Rusmore, Jean. The Bay Area Ridge Trail. LC 95-35393. 200p. (Orig.). 1995. pap. 14.95 (*0-89997-166-0*) Wilderness Pr.

Rusmore, Jean, et al. Peninsula Trails: Outdoor Adventures on the San Francisco Peninsula. 3rd rev. ed. LC 96-46624. (Illus.). 304p. 1997. pap. 14.95 (*0-89997-197-0*) Wilderness Pr.

Rusmore, Jean, jt. auth. see Spangle, Frances.

Rusnack, Richard, 2nd. 101 Things to Do in Door County. 1996. pap. 6.95 (*0-932212-91-3*) Avery Color.

Rusnack, Richard. 101 Things to Do in Traverse City. 1997. pap. 6.95 (*0-932212-95-6*) Avery Color.

Rusnak. Airland Regions & Processes. 800p. 1998. pap. text 70.00 (*0-536-01316-0*) Pearson Custom.

Rusnak, Paul D. Now That I'm Saved . . . 16 Ways to Experience God. LC 95-77538. 142p. (Orig.). 1996. pap. 6.99 (*0-88270-684-5*) Bridge-Logos.

Rusnak-Smith, Sandra & Moffat, Marilyn. Physical Therapy of the Thorax. (Illus.). 256p. 1999. spiral bd. 34.95 (*0-397-55272-6*) Lppncott W & W.

Rusnak, Timothy. An Integrated Approach to Character Education. LC 97-21186. (Illus.). 192p. 1997. 55.95 (*0-7619-0437-9*); pap. 24.95 (*0-7619-0438-7*) Corwin Pr.

Rusnbrook, Rosalyn. Where Did I Go Wrong? (Illus.). 96p. (C). 1996. pap. 39.95 (*0-85439-418-4*, Pub. by St Paul Pubns) St Mut.

Ruso. Teen Magazine Schoolyear Astrology a Cosmic Guide for 1998-1999. 1998. mass mkt. 5.99 (*0-671-01192-8*) S&S Trade.

Rusong, Wu, et al. Sun Zi's Art of War & Health Care: Military Science & Medical Science. Duanzhi, She & Bin, Li, trs. 412p. 1997. pap. 22.95 (*7-80005-376-8*, Pub. by New World Pr) Cheng & Tsui.

Ruspantini, Anthony. Prayer-a-Phrases. 112p. 1997. pap. 9.99 (*1-56043-286-1*, Treasure Hse) Destiny Image.

Ruspoli, Mario. The Cave of Lascaux: The Final Photographs. (Illus.). 208p. 1987. 60.00 (*0-8109-1267-8*, Pub. by Abrams) Time Warner.

Rusque, Rosana & Segal, Linda. English, English, English: The Past Tense of Irregular Verbs. (Illus.). 52p. 1996. pap. text 16.50 (*1-882483-40-5*) Alta Bk Ctr.

Russ. Lessons for Today. 1999. text. write for info. (*0-312-48168-3*) St Martin.

— Material Science. (General Engineering Ser.). (C). 1995. 29.95 (*0-534-95052-3*) PWS Pubs.

— Materials Science: A Multimedia Approach-Win. (General Engineering Ser.). (C). 1996. pap. 29.95 (*0-534-95736-6*) Wadsworth Pub.

Russ, Adryan, jt. auth. see Wallace, Arnie.

Russ, Adryan, ed. see Carroll, Alex L.

Russ, Adryan, ed. see Fay, Jim & Fay, Charles.

Russ, Alfred. Revelation: Illuminated Through Other Scripture. 80p. (Orig.). 1996. pap. 8.00 (*1-57502-300-8*, P1030) Morris Pubng.

Russ, Biff. Black Method: Poems. (Winner of the 1991 Marianne Moore Poetry Prize Ser.). (Orig.). 1991. pap. 9.95 (*0-9627460-1-0*) Helicon Nine Eds.

Russ, Charles. The German Language Today: A Linguistic Introduction. LC 93-51009. (Illus.). 350p. (C). 1994. pap. 25.99 (*0-415-10439-4*, B2289) Routledge.

— The German Language Today: A Linguistic Introduction. LC 93-51009. (Illus.). 350p. (C). (gr. 13). 1994. 85.00 (*0-415-10438-6*, B2285) Routledge.

Russ, Charles, ed. The Dialects of Modern German: A Linguistic Survey. 2nd ed. 496p. 1990. 67.50 (*0-8047-1547-5*) Stanford U Pr.

Russ, Charles V. Studies in Historical German Phonology: A Phonological Comparison of MHG & NHG with Reference to Modern Dialects. (European University Studies: German Language & Literature: Ser. 1, Vol. 616). 214p. 1982. pap. 38.00 (*3-261-05070-5*) P Lang Pubng.

Russ, David. The Complete Oahu Guidebook. 2nd rev. ed. (Illus.). 152p. 1998. pap. 9.95 (*0-916841-68-5*) Indian Chief.

Russ, David J. The Complete Big Island of Hawaii Guidebook. (Hawaii Ser.). (Illus.). 152p. 1997. pap. 9.95 (*0-916841-63-4*) Indian Chief.

— The Complete Kauai Guidebook. 2nd ed. (Illus.). 136p. 1995. pap. 8.95 (*0-916841-52-9*) Indian Chief.

— Complete Maui, Molokai & Lanai Guidebook. 2nd ed. (Hawaii Ser.). (Illus.). 152p. 1994. pap. 9.95 (*0-916841-51-0*) Indian Chief.

Russ, Diane & Rogers, Shirle. The Beautiful Bernese Mountain Dog. LC 92-46693. (Illus.). 226p. 1994. text 39.95 (*0-931866-55-3*) Alpine Pubns.

Russ, Donald J., jt. auth. see Blackman, Irving L.

Russ-Eft, Darlene, et al, eds. Human Resources Development Review: Research & Implications. 512p. 1996. 69.95 (*0-7619-0560-X*); pap. 32.95 (*0-7619-0561-8*) Sage.

Russ Flint & Associates Staff, jt. auth. see Sande, Corlette.

Russ, Harlow W. Project Alberta: The Preparation of Atomic Bombs for Use in World War II. (Illus.). 200p. (Orig.). 1990. pap. 34.95 (*0-944482-01-5*) Except Bks NM.

Russ, Hume R. How to Write Jokes (By the Numbers) in 20 Funny Lessons. (Illus.). 432p. (Orig.). 1991. pap. 22.00 (*0-9628231-0-4*) Fun-E-Prodns.

Russ, J. C. Computer-Assisted Microscopy: The Measurement & Analysis of Images. LC 89-70945. (Illus.). 466p. (C). 1990. text 79.50 (*0-306-43410-5*, Kluwer Plenum) Kluwer Academic.

— Fractal Surfaces. LC 93-45023. (Illus.). 320p. (C). 1994. text 59.50 (*0-306-44702-9*, Kluwer Plenum) Kluwer Academic.

— Practical Stereology. (Illus.). 194p. (C). 1986. text 59.50 (*0-306-42460-6*, Kluwer Plenum) Kluwer Academic.

Russ, Jacqueline. Dictionnaire de Philosophie. (FRE.). 383p. 1991. pap. 45.00 (*0-7859-7709-0*, 2040193014) Fr & Eur.

Russ, Jeff. Screen Printer's Tip Book. (Illus.). 52p. 1996. pap. 9.95 (*0-944094-18-X*) ST Pubns.

Russ, Jenny. German Grammar. rev. ed. (GER.). 256p. 1999. pap. 11.95 (*0-8442-3799-X*) NTC Contemp Pub Co.

*__Russ, Joanna.__ The Female Man. 2000. pap. 13.00 (*0-8070-6299-5*) Beacon Pr.

Russ, Joanna. The Female Man. LC 86-47511. 225p. 1987. reprint ed. pap. 12.00 (*0-8070-6313-4*) Beacon Pr.

— How to Suppress Women's Writing. LC 83-5910. 167p. (C). 1983. pap. 9.95 (*0-292-72445-4*) U of Tex Pr.

— To Write Like a Woman: Essays in Feminism & Science Fiction. LC 95-3576. 200p. 1995. 27.95 (*0-253-32914-0*); pap. 13.95 (*0-253-20983-8*) Ind U Pr.

— What Are We Fighting For? Sex, Race, Class & the Futute of Feminism. LC 96-36688. 560p. 1998. text 27.95 (*0-312-15198-5*) St Martin.

Russ, John C. Computer Assisted Microscopy: The Measurement & Analysis of Images. LC 89-69855. (Illus.). 350p. (Orig.). (C). 1988. pap. text 50.00 (*1-56049-006-3*) NCSU CE IES.

— Image Processing Handbook. 464p. 1992. 89.95 (*0-8493-4233-3*, PA1632) CRC Pr.

— The Image Processing Handbook. 2nd ed. LC 94-27648. 688p. 1994. boxed set 115.95 (*0-8493-2516-1*, 2516) CRC Pr.

— The Image Processing Handbook. 3rd ed. LC 98-35413. 1998. write for info. (*3-540-64747-3*); boxed set 129.95 (*0-8493-2532-3*) CRC Pr.

Russ, Larry. The Complete Mancala Games Book: How to Play the World's Oldest Board Games. rev. ed. LC 99-30964. (Illus.). 128p. 1999. reprint ed. pap. 14.95 (*1-56924-683-1*, Pub. by Marlowe & Co) Publishers Group.

Russ, Lawrence. The Burning-Ground. (Poetry Chapbook Ser.). 32p. (Orig.). 1981. pap. 7.00 (*0-937669-01-6*) Owl Creek Pr.

Russ, Lee, et al. Attorney's Medical Advisor-Atlas, 10 vols., Set. LC 94-60666. 1994. ring bd. 1650.00 (*0-614-07290-5*) West Group.

Russ, Marion. Courts, Counselors & Correspondents: A Media Relations Analysis of the Legal System. LC 97-42938. xxx, 233p. 1998. 60.00 (*0-8377-1181-9*, Rothman) W S Hein.

Russ, Marion, et al, eds. German Dictionary of Philosophical Worterbuch Philosophischer Fachbe Englisch, Set. LC 98-133753. (Routledge Bilingual Specialist Dictionaries Ser.). (GER.). 450p. (C). 1998. 280.00 (*0-415-17890-8*) Routledge.

*__Russ, Martin.__ Breakout: The Chosin Reservoir Campaign, Korea, 1950. 2000. pap. 14.95 (*0-14-029259-4*) Viking Penguin.

Russ, Martin. The Last Parallel: A Marine's War Journal. LC 99-19089. 352p. 1999. pap. 15.00 (*0-88064-237-8*) Fromm Intl Pub.

— The Last Parallel: A Marine's War Journal. 1973. write for info. (*0-8371-6770-1*) Greenwood.

— Sound Synthesis & Sampling. LC 97-129131. (Illus.). 224p. 2000. pap. text 36.95 (*0-240-51429-7*, Focal) Buttrwrth-Heinemann.

Russ, Mel. Sea Angling: Kent to Cornwall. (Illus.). 208p. 1992. pap. 8.95 (*0-09-174244-7*, Pub. by S Paul) Trafalgar.

Russ, Michael. Musorgsky: "Pictures at an Exhibition" (Cambridge Music Handbooks Ser.). (Illus.). 111p. (C). 1992. pap. text 13.95 (*0-521-38607-1*) Cambridge U Pr.

Russ, Michael J. 401K Investing Made Easy: A Quick & Easy Guide to Help You: Understand Investing; Choose the Right Investments. (Illus.). 35p. 1997. pap., wbk. ed. 9.95 (*0-9658454-0-0*) Russ Inov.

Russ, Richard T. Jaguar V-12 E-Type: A Guide to Authenticity. (Illus.). 210p. 1991. 49.95 (*0-9629958-0-0*) Exec Twin Av.

Russ, Robert A., jt. ed. see Kramer, Victor A.

Russ, Sandra. Affect & Creativity: The Role of Affect & Play in the Creative Process. (Spielberger: Personality Assessment Ser.). 160p. 1993. text 36.00 (*0-8058-0986-4*) L Erlbaum Assocs.

Russ, Sandra W. Affect, Creative Experience & Psychological Adjustment. LC 98-22837. (Series in Clinical & Community Psychology). 1998. 59.95 (*0-87630-917-1*); pap. 29.95 (*0-87630-918-X*) Brunner-Mazel.

*__Russ, Sandra Walker & Ollendick, Thomas H., eds.__ Handbook of Psychotherapies with Children & Families. LC 99-40702. (Issues in Clinical Child Psychology Ser.). 600p. 1999. write for info. (*0-306-46098-X*, Kluwer Plenum) Kluwer Academic.

*__Russ, Tom.__ Redeveloping Brownfields: Landscape Architects, Site Planners & Developers. 1999. 79.95 (*0-07-135311-9*) McGraw.

Russ, Tony. Alaska Bowhunting Records. Lauber, Lon E., ed. (Illus.). 128p. 1999. 25.00 (*0-9659998-1-5*) Alaskan Bowhunters.

— The Manual for Successful Hunters: Why 10of the Hunters Harvest 90of the Game. (Illus.). 400p. (Orig.). 1999. pap. 24.95 (*0-9639869-1-0*) Northern Pubng.

— Sheep Hunting in Alaska: The Dall Sheep Hunters' Guide. LC 93-86886. (Illus.). 160p. (Orig.). 1994. pap. text 19.95 (*0-9639869-0-2*) Northern Pubng.

Russ, Tony, ed. see Swanson, Ron.

Russ, Tony, ed. & photos by see Wilson, Jack E.

Russ, Wilbert D. Traditional African American Women, Who Made a Difference in Life. large type ed. Debruhl, Duneen, ed. (Illus.). vii, 51p. (J). (ps-8). 1997. pap. text 5.00 (*0-9670510-0-2*) Four-D Success.

Russ, William A., Jr. The Hawaiian Republic, 1894-98: And Its Struggle to Win Annexation. LC 91-43886. 416p. 1993. reprint ed. 40.00 (*0-945636-44-X*); reprint ed. pap. 16.95 (*0-945636-52-0*) Susquehanna U Pr.

— The Hawaiian Revolution, 1893-94. LC 91-41517. 392p. 1993. reprint ed. 40.00 (*0-945636-43-1*) Susquehanna U Pr.

Russack, Benjamin, ed. Wine Country: A Literary Companion. LC 98-40387. 256p. 1998. pap. 15.95 (*1-890771-10-4*) Heyday Bks.

*__Russack, Joy.__ Those Wonderful Children. (Illus.). 32p. (J). 2000. pap. 8.00 (*0-8059-4831-7*) Dorrance.

Russack, Joy C. Thoughtful Thomas. (J). 1998. pap. 7.95 (*0-533-12722-X*) Vantage.

Russakoff, Andrew, jt. auth. see Marpet, Mark.

Russakoff, L. Mark, jt. auth. see Oldham, John M.

Russakoff, Sylvia. Getting Started with Microsoft Applications: Microsoft Word 6.0 for Windows, Microsoft Excel 5.0. 624p. 1996. pap. text 26.50 (*0-471-16524-7*) Wiley.

Russakoff, Sylvia. Getting Started with Microsoft Word 6.0 for Windows. (Getting Started Ser.). 200p. 1995. pap. text. write for info. incl. 3.5 hd (*0-471-12567-9*) Wiley.

Russakoff, Sylvia & Bacon, Marie L. Getting Started with Windows 95, Vol. 5. LC 97-134535. 192p. 1996. pap. 21.95 (*0-471-15943-3*) Wiley.

Russakoff, Sylvia & Gaylord, Henry. Getting Started with Windows 3.1 & Getting Started with Microsoft Access 2.0 for Windows & Getting Started with Microsoft Powerpoint 4.0 for Windows. 576p. 1996. pap. text 62.85 (*0-471-17802-0*) Wiley.

Russakoff, Sylvia, et al. Getting Started with Microsoft Word 6.0 for Windows. 200p. 1995. text, pap. text 21.95 incl. disk (*0-471-12054-5*) Wiley.

Russakovsky, Vladimir, jt. auth. see Turner, Raymond.

Russcol, Herbert & Oehmich-Russcol, Nancy. The Hunting Season: Palestine 1945-1948. LC 88-19230. 256p. 1989. lib. bdg. 16.95 (*0-943247-05-5*) UCS Press.

Russe. Artificial Intelligence: A Modern Approach. 2nd ed. 944p. (C). 2001. 64.00 (*0-13-790395-2*, Macmillan Coll) P-H.

Russek, H., ed. Essentials of Adult Ambulatory Care. LC 96-28283. (Illus.). 650p. 1973. pap. 37.50 (*0-683-07456-3*) Lppncott W & W.

Russek, Janet, jt. auth. see Scheinbaum, David.

Russel. Leadership in Recreation. 2nd ed. 384p. 2000. 52.81 (*0-07-012330-6*) McGraw.

— Understanding Bacterial Action. 1990. pap. write for info. (*0-318-68274-5*) P-H.

Russel, jt. auth. see Reiter.

Russel, B. Religion y Ciencia. (Breviarios Ser.). (SPA.). pap. 6.99 (*968-16-0938-7*, Pub. by Fondo) Continental Bk.

Russel, Charlie. Murphy's Laws of DOS. 2nd ed. LC 93-85947. 356p. 1993. pap. 16.99 (*0-7821-1424-5*) Sybex.

— SCO OpenServer: The Windows Network Solution. LC 96-24172. 400p. 1996. pap. text 26.20 (*0-13-459421-5*) P-H.

— UNIX & Linux Answers! Certified Tech Support. LC 98-127230. 1998. pap. text 24.99 (*0-07-882446-X*) Osborne-McGraw.

Russel, Charlie & Crawford, Sharon. The ABCs of Windows NT Workstation 4. LC 96-69915. 384p. 1996. pap. text 19.99 (*0-7821-1999-9*) Sybex.

— Running Microsoft Windows NT Server 4.0. LC 97-128659. 1996. pap. text 39.95 (*1-57231-333-1*) Microsoft.

— Upgrading to Windows 98. LC 98-84007. 464p. 1998. pap. text 19.99 (*0-7821-2190-X*) Sybex.

Russel, George E. Collected Poems. 1988. reprint ed. lib. bdg. 59.00 (*0-7812-0480-1*) Rprt Serv.

Russel, George W. Collected Poems. LC 73-131821. 1970. reprint ed. 29.00 (*0-403-00708-9*) Scholarly.

Russel, H. To Remember & Heal: Theological & Psychological Reflections on Truth & Reconciliation. LC 97-152771. 1997. pap. text 19.95 (*0-7981-3644-8*) Human & Rousseau.

Russel, Henry B. International Monetary Conferences: Their Purposes, Character & Results with a Study of the Conditions of Currency & Finance in Europe & America, Vol. 10. LC 74-359. 477p. 1974. reprint ed. 37.95 (*0-405-05920-5*) Ayer.

Russel, J. C. & Morse, William E. United States Navy in World War I with over 600 Photos. 1977. lib. bdg. 175.00 (*0-8490-2785-3*) Gordon Pr.

Russel, Jeffrey B. Witchcraft in the Middle Ages. (Illus.). 1976. pap. 5.95 (*0-8065-0504-4*, Citadel Pr) Carol Pub Group.

Russel, John, intro. Jennifer Bartlett: In the Garden. (Contemporary Artists Ser.). (Illus.). 208p. 1982. 49.50 (*0-8109-0709-7*, Pub. by Abrams) Time Warner.

Russel, K. W. & Pisa, Maria G. Agriculture, Libraries & Information. (C). 1992. text 200.00 (*81-7233-034-0*, Pub. by Scientific Pubs) St Mut.

Russel, Myra T., intro. James Joyce's Chamber Music: The Lost Song Settings. LC 92-23654. (Illus.). 144p. (C). 1993. pap. 21.95 (*0-253-34994-X*) Ind U Pr.

Russel, P., ed. see International Pigment Cell Conference Staff.

Russel, R. P., ed. Guide to Books on AIDS. (Illus.). 107p. 1994. text 95.00 (*1-56072-179-0*) Nova Sci Pubs.

Russel, Robert R. Critical Studies in Antebellum Sectionalism: Essays in American Political & Economic History, 7. LC 78-105977. (Contributions in American History Ser.: No. 7). 223p. 1972. 55.00 (*0-8371-3304-1*, RAS/, Greenwood Pr) Greenwood.

Russel, W. B., et al. Colloidal Dispersions. (Cambridge Monographs on Mechanics & Applied Mathematics). (Illus.). 543p. (C). 1992. pap. text 49.95 (*0-521-42600-6*) Cambridge U Pr.

Russel, William B. The Dynamics of Collodial Systems: 1984 Olaf A. Hougen Lectures. LC 86-40060. (Illus.). 136p. 1987. text 24.95 (*0-299-10530-X*) U of Wis Pr.

Russell. Art in the World. 3rd ed. 1989. mass mkt. 28.00 (*0-03-016924-0*) H Holt & Co.

— Art in the World. 4th ed. (C). 1993. pap. text, teacher ed. 10.50 (*0-03-094060-5*) Harcourt Coll Pubs.

— Brown Harvest. LC 99-22211. 1999. text. write for info. (*0-312-20284-9*) St Martin.

— Classical Thermodynamics. 944p. 1995. teacher ed. 34.00 (*0-03-075394-5*) OUP.

— Education & the Good Life. 1985. pap. 5.95 (*0-87140-012-X*) Liveright.

***Russell.** Fundamentals of Genetics & the Biology Place. 2nd ed. 2000. pap. 77.00 (*0-321-04868-7*) Benjamin-Cummings.

Russell. Inquiry into Meaning & Truth. 368p. (C). 1996. pap. 22.99 (*0-415-13600-8*) Routledge.

— Interpersonal Is Between. 1993. pap. 41.25 (*0-8087-6713-5*) Pearson Custom.

— Language & Behavior. 1993. pap. 41.25 (*0-8087-6712-7*) Pearson Custom.

— Logic. 2nd ed. 1998. pap. text 26.00 (*0-471-32102-8*) Wiley.

— The Origins of Organic Chemistry, 1800-1900. 1992. 18.00 (*0-85186-440-6*) CRC Pr.

— Pastimes: Context Contemporary. 1995. teacher ed. 9.68 (*0-697-22726-X*) McGraw.

— Patricia MacLachlan. LC 97-7224. 1997. 32.00 (*0-8057-4575-0*, Twyne) Mac Lib Ref.

— Prospects of Eternity. 188p. 1982. 10.95 (*0-85435-394-1*, Pub. by C W Daniel) Natl Bk Netwk.

— Prospects of Industrial Civilization. LC 96-222613. 264p. (C). 1996. 60.00 (*0-415-13602-4*) Routledge.

Russell. Quick & Easy Marketing that Works. 120p. 1996. pap. 39.95 (*0-566-07838-4*) Ashgate Pub Co.

Russell. Recreation Leadership. 1985. 13.75 (*0-697-41038-2*, WCB McGr Hill) McGrw-H Hghr Educ.

— Reinventing Public Administration. (Political Science Ser.). 2000. mass mkt. 26.00 (*0-534-54999-3*) Wadsworth Pub.

— Russian for Chessplayers. 1995. pap. 12.95 (*0-938650-44-0*) Thinkers Pr.

— Scott O'Dell. LC 99-19718. 1999. 28.95 (*0-8057-1682-3*) S&S Trade.

***Russell.** Sex & Beauty. 2000. 23.00 (*0-7382-0208-8*, Pub. by Perseus Pubng) HarpC.

Russell. Telecommunications Pocket Ref. 352p. 2000. pap. 29.95 (*0-07-135140-X*) McGraw.

***Russell.** Telecommunications Protocol. 2nd ed. LC 99-54596. 1999. 49.95 (*0-07-134915-4*) McGraw.

— Voted Out. text 60.00 (*0-8147-7543-8*); pap. text 20.00 (*0-8147-7544-6*) NYU Pr.

— Women of Taste: Recipes & Profiles of Famous Women Chefs. (Illus.). 224p. (C). 1999. pap. 19.95 (*0-471-33179-1*) Wiley.

Russell. Writing at Work. (C). 1994. pap. text 20.00 (*0-07-054956-7*) McGraw.

Russell, ed. Genetic: Study Guide & Solution Manual. (C). 1996. text, student ed. 80.63 (*0-673-67650-1*) Addison-Wesley.

Russell & Cater. Family Puzzle & Game Book. 1999. 4.99 (*0-517-20569-6*) Random Hse Value.

Russell & Monaghan. Keeping Pets: A Classroom Guide. 1990. pap. text. write for info. (*0-582-87036-4*, Pub. by Addison-Wesley) Longman.

Russell & Rubinstein. Pathology of Tumours of the Nervous System. 5th ed. 974p. 1989. 249.00 (*0-683-07462-8*) Lppncott W & W.

Russell & Zamboni. Manual of Free Flaps. (Illus.). 320p. (C). (gr. 13). 1999. text 195.00 (*0-8151-9013-1*, 29110) Mosby Inc.

Russell, et al. Cumberland & No. Yarmouth Register, 1904 (Town Histories & Directories) 100p. 1997. reprint ed. pap. 17.00 (*0-8328-5830-7*) Higginson Bk Co.

Russell, jt. auth. see Bucklow.

Russell, jt. auth. see Garbis.

Russell, jt. auth. see Jamison.

Russell, jt. compiled by see Mitchell.

Russell, A. Berman, jt. ed. see Cross, Charlotte M.

Russell, A. D., et al, eds. Principles & Practice of Disinfection, Preservation & Sterilization. 2nd ed. (Illus.). 656p. 1992. 165.00 (*0-632-02625-1*) Blackwell Sci.

Russell, A. D. & Chopra, Ian. Understanding Bacterial Resistance & Antibacterial Action. 1990. text 61.95 (*0-470-21651-4*) P-H.

Russell, A. D., et al. Principles & Practice of Disinfection, Preservation & Sterilisation. 3rd ed. LC 98-14781. (Illus.). 826p. 1999. 185.00 (*0-632-04194-3*) Blackwell Sci.

Russell, A. D., jt. auth. see Hugo, W. B.

Russell, A. E. Song & Its Fountains. 112p. 1991. reprint ed. pap. 10.95 (*0-943914-52-3*) Larson Pubns.

Russell, A. J. God Calling. 252p. 1996. pap. 3.97 (*1-55748-777-4*) Barbour Pub.

— God Calling. LC 72-78545. 208p. (gr. 11). 1993. mass mkt. 6.99 (*0-8007-8096-5*, Spire) Revell.

Russell, A. J., ed. God Calling. (Inspirational Library Ser.). 249p. 1989. lthr. 4.97 (*1-55748-110-5*) Barbour Pub.

— God Calling. 384p. 1997. lthr. 9.97 (*1-57748-096-1*) Barbour Pub.

— God Calling. (Essential Christian Library Ser.). 288p. 1998. 9.97 (*1-57748-266-2*) Barbour Pub.

***Russell, A. J., ed.** God Calling. (Illus.). 292p. 1999. 14.97 (*1-57748-657-9*) Barbour Pub.

Russell, A. J., ed. God Calling. LC 72-78545. 208p. 1981. mass mkt. 5.99 (*0-515-09026-3*, Jove) Berkley Pub.

***Russell, A. J., ed.** God Calling. deluxe ed. (Deluxe Christian Classics). 272p. 2000. 9.97 (*1-57748-917-9*) Barbour Pub.

Russell, A. J., ed. God Calling Journal. deluxe ed. 384p. 1996. bond lthr. 19.97 (*1-55748-899-1*) Barbour Pub.

Russell, A. K. Liberal Landslide: The General Election of 1906. 260p. 1973. 79.50 (*0-208-01389-X*) Elliots Bks.

Russell, A. Lewis. Corporate & Industrial Security. LC 80-15789. (Illus.). 285p. reprint ed. pap. 88.40 (*0-608-18151-X*, 203284000081) Bks Demand.

***Russell, A. Sue.** Conversion, Identity, & Power: The Impact of Christianity on Power Relationships & Social Exchanges. LC 99-23659. 200p. 1999. pap. 29.50 (*0-7618-1440-X*) U Pr of Amer.

— Conversion, Identity & Power: The Impact of Christianity on Power Relationships & Social Exchanges. LC 99-23659. 200p. 1999. 52.00 (*0-7618-1439-6*) U Pr of Amer.

Russell, Addison P. Library Notes. rev. ed. LC 72-4599. (Essay Index Reprint Ser.). 1977. reprint ed. 24.95 (*0-8369-2971-3*) Ayer.

Russell, Alan. The Fat Innkeeper. 352p. 1995. 19.95 (*0-89296-539-8*) Mysterious Pr.

— The Fat Innkeeper. 304p. 1996. mass mkt. 5.99 (*0-446-40349-0*, Pub. by Warner Bks) Little.

— The Hotel Detective. 304p. 1995. mass mkt. 5.50 (*0-446-40348-2*, Pub. by Warner Bks) Little.

— No Sign of Murder. 240p. 1993. mass mkt. 4.99 (*0-380-71656-9*, Avon Bks) Morrow Avon.

Russell, Alan. No Sign of Murder. 192p. 1990. 17.95 (*0-8027-5767-7*) Walker & Co.

Russell, Alan. Shame. LC 97-50508. 304p. 1998. 22.50 (*0-684-81527-3*) S&S Trade.

Russell, Alan, jt. ed. see Clayton, Anthony.

Russell, Alan J., jt. ed. see Dordick, Jonathan S.

Russell, Alan K. Battle Tanks & Support Vehicles. LC 93-36814. (Greenhill Military Manuals Ser.). 160p. 1994. 19.95 (*1-85367-174-6*) Stackpole.

— The Book of the Dead: Thirteen Classic Tales of the Supernatural. LC 86-209354. 382 p. 1986. write for info. (*1-85079-035-3*) NEW3 UK.

— Modern Battle Tanks & Support Vehicles. LC 97-16371. (Greenhill Military Manuals Ser.). 1998. write for info. (*1-85367-258-0*, Pub. by Greenhill Bks) Stackpole.

— Rivals of Sherlock Holmes. 1993. 8.98 (*1-55521-974-8*) Bk Sales Inc.

Russell, Alan P. Hematology. (Clinical Laboratory Manual Ser.). (Illus.). 224p. (C). 1996. mass mkt. 31.95 (*0-8273-6373-7*) Delmar.

Russell, Alanson E. & Russell, Joan M. The Seminary. 2nd ed. 128p. (Orig.). (C). 1987. pap. 12.95 (*0-9619115-0-6*) Seminary Pubn.

***Russell, Alec.** Big Men, Little People: The Leaders Who Defined Africa. 2000. 28.95 (*0-8147-7542-X*) NYU Pr.

Russell, Alene B. Advances in Statewide Higher Education Data Systems. 1995. 10.00 (*0-614-13547-8*) SHEEO.

— Faculty Workload: State & System Perspectives. 84p. 1992. pap. 7.50 (*0-614-30589-6*, PS-92-1) Ed Comm States.

— Faculty Workload: State & System Perspectives. (Series on Faculty Productivity). 1992. 10.00 (*0-614-13564-8*) SHEEO.

Russell, Alene B. & Christal, Melodie E., eds. Compendium of National Data Sources on Higher Education. 1996. 20.00 (*0-614-13560-5*) SHEEO.

Russell, Alene B., et al. An Annotated Bibliography on Student Preparation for College & the Workplace. (SHEEO/ECS Monograph Ser.). 1995. 15.00 (*0-614-13549-4*) SHEEO.

Russell, Alene B., jt. auth. see Epper, Rhonda M.

Russell, Alice. Growth of Occupational Welfare in Britain. 300p. 1991. text 77.95 (*1-85628-121-3*, Pub. by Avebry) Ashgate Pub Co.

Russell, Alison. Crossing Boundaries: Postmodern Travel Literature. text. write for info. (*0-312-23388-4*) St Martin.

Russell, Allan M., jt. auth. see Gerhart, Mary.

Russell, Allen S., tr. see Pachman, Ludek.

Russell, Amber. Pets Need Scrapbooks Too! A Start-to-Finish Guide for Creating a Lasting Memory of Your Family Pet. (Illus.). 80p. 1999. pap. 15.95 (*0-9666639-1-8*, Pub. by Ambers Albums) Partners Pubs Grp.

— Scrapbooking with Amber: A Step-by-Step Guide to Organizing, Creating, & Completing. (Illus.). 96p. 1998. pap. 19.95 (*0-9666639-9-3*) Ambers Albums.

Russell, Amy R., ed. see Herrick, Lucy K.

***Russell, Andrew, et al, eds.** Contraception Across Cultures: Technologies, Choices, Constraints. (Cross-Cultural Perspectives on Women Ser.). (Illus.). 224p. 2000. 65.00 (*1-85973-381-6*, Pub. by Berg Pubs); pap. 19.50 (*1-85973-386-7*, Pub. by Berg Pubs) NYU Pr.

Russell, Andrew, jt. auth. see Edgar, Ian R.

Russell, Andrew, jt. ed. see Edgar, Iain.

***Russell, Andrew G.** Mac OS X Administrator's Guide. 500p. 2000. pap. 39.99 (*0-7615-2415-0*) Prima Pub.

Russell, Andrew J. Russell's Civil War Photographs: 115 Historic Prints. (Illus.). 128p. 1982. pap. 9.95 (*0-486-24283-8*) North South Trader.

— Russell's Union Pacific Railroad Photographs. (Illus.). 96p. 1997. reprint ed. pap. text 11.95 (*0-486-29667-9*) Dover.

Russell, Andy. Andy Russell: A Steeler Odyssey. (Illus.). 250p. 1998. 22.95 (*1-57167-235-4*) Sports Pub.

***Russell, Andy.** Andy Russell's Campfire Stories. (Illus.). 328p. (J). 2000. pap. 15.95 (*0-7710-7884-6*) McCland & Stewart.

Russell, Andy. Andy Russell's Campfire Yarns. LC 99-167082. (Illus.). 1999. 23.95 (*0-7710-7882-X*) McCland & Stewart.

Russell, Andy. The Canadian Cowboy: Stories of Cows, Cowboys & Cayuses. (Illus.). 288p. 1996. pap. 16.99 (*0-7710-7881-1*) McCland & Stewart.

Russell, Andy. Great Bear Adventures: True Tales from the Wild. LC 93-45667. (Illus.). 282p. (Orig.). 1990. pap. 14.95 (*0-89658-078-4*) Voyageur Pr.

***Russell, Andy.** Grizzly Country. (Illus.). 2000. pap. 16.95 (*1-58574-024-1*) Lyons Pr.

Russell, Andy. Grizzly Country. (Illus.). 320p. 1986. reprint ed. pap. 16.95 (*0-941130-12-6*) Lyons Pr.

***Russell, Andy.** The Life of a River. (Douglas Gibson Bks.). 192p. 2000. reprint ed. pap. 15.95 (*0-7710-7876-5*) McCland & Stewart.

Russell, Andy. Memoirs of a Mountain Man. 305p. 1984. mass mkt. 5.95 (*0-88780-156-0*, Pub. by Formac Publ Co) Formac Dist Ltd.

***Russell, Andy.** Trails of a Wilderness Wanderer: True Stories from the Western Frontier. 2000. pap. 16.95 (*1-58574-183-3*) Lyons Pr.

Russell, Anita. Self-Esteem. Schulz, William, ed. (Options: Guidance for Grades 1). 88p. (Orig.). (gr. 1-8). 1989. pap., teacher ed. 8.00 (*0-920541-51-8*) Peguis Pubs Ltd.

Russell, Anita, et al. Suicide. (Options: Guidance for Grades 1). 112p. (gr. 1-8). 1989. pap., teacher ed. 8.00 (*0-920541-65-8*) Peguis Pubs Ltd.

Russell, Anne. Daring Disciples: Embark on an Exciting Journey of Discovery Children's Journal. (1994 50-Day Spiritual Adventure Ser.). (Illus.). 64p. (Orig.). (J). (gr. 3-6). 1993. pap. text, student ed. 4.99 (*1-879050-16-1*) Chapel of Air.

— Discoveries in God's Family. (1992 50-Day Spiritual Adventure Ser.). (Illus.). 64p. (Orig.). (J). (gr. 3-6). 1991. pap. text, student ed. 4.95 (*1-879050-05-6*) Chapel of Air.

— Fear Busters: Join the Kids Courageous Rescue Team Children's Journal. (1995 50-Day Spiritual Adventure Ser.). (Illus.). 64p. (Orig.). (J). (gr. 3-6). 1994. pap. text, student ed. 4.95 (*1-879050-49-8*) Chapel of Air.

— Kids Courageous: Traveling the Path of True Winners. (1993 50-Day Spiritual Adventure Ser.). (Illus.). 64p. (Orig.). (J). (gr. 3-6). 1992. pap. text, student ed. 4.99 (*1-879050-09-9*) Chapel of Air.

Russell, Anne, ed. The Rover: Aphra Behn. 220p. 1994. pap. 9.95 (*1-55111-037-7*) Broadview Pr.

Russell, Anne, ed. see Behn, Aphra.

Russell, Anne, jt. ed. see Comensoli, Viviana.

Russell, Archibald. A Span of Wings: An Autobiography. 202p. 1993. 19.00 (*1-56091-401-7*, R-132) Soc Auto Engineers.

Russell, Armand & Trubitt, Allen R. The Shaping of Musical Elements, Vol. 1. 410p. (C). 1992. 35.00 (*0-02-872080-6*, Schirmer Books); pap., teacher ed. write for info. (*0-02-872201-9*, Schirmer Books) Mac Lib Ref.

— The Shaping of Musical Elements, Vol. 2. 494p. (C). 1992. 35.00 (*0-02-872120-9*, Schirmer Books) Mac Lib Ref.

— The Shaping of Musical Elements Workbook, Vol. 1. 337p. (C). 1992. wbk. ed. 19.00 (*0-02-872090-3*, Schirmer Books) Mac Lib Ref.

— The Shaping of Musical Elements Workbook, Vol. 2. 429p. (C). 1992. wbk. ed. 19.00 (*0-02-872200-0*, Schirmer Books) Mac Lib Ref.

Russell, Armida M. & Hayles, Robert. The Diversity Directive: Why Some Initiatives Fail & What to Do about It. LC 96-35438. 144p. 1996. text 24.95 (*0-7863-0819-2*, Irwn Prfssnl) McGraw-Hill Prof.

Russell, Arthur J. Their Religion. LC 78-128308. (Essay Index Reprint Ser.). 1977. 23.95 (*0-8369-2131-3*) Ayer.

Russell, B. La Philosophie de Leibniz. (Reimpressions G & B Ser.). 250p. 1971. pap. 72.00 (*0-685-47123-3*) Gordon & Breach.

— Running Microsoft Word 2000. LC 98-50600. 900p. 1998. 39.99 (*1-57231-943-7*) Microsoft.

Russell, Barbara. Blue Lightning. LC 96-30908. (J). (gr. 3-7). 1997. 14.99 (*0-670-87023-4*) Viking Penguin.

Russell, Barbara C. 7-Day Art Workshop. Bradsaw, Bonnie A., ed. & des. by. (Illus.). 100p. (Orig.). (YA). (gr. 8 up). 1996. pap. 24.95 (*0-9642945-0-8*) Studio Press.

Russell, Barbara S. Infection Control & OSHA Essentials. 3rd ed. LC 99-161718. 111p. (Orig.). 1998. pap. text 23.00 (*1-879772-12-4*) Health Studies.

Russell, Barbara T. Last Left Standing. LC 94-16732. 128p. (J). (gr. 4-6). 1996. 14.95 (*0-395-71037-5*) Ticknor & Flds Bks Yng Read.

— Last Left Standing. 1998. 9.60 (*0-606-13563-4*, Pub. by Turtleback) Demco.

— Remembering Stone. LC 98-41151. (Illus.). (J). 1999. write for info. (*0-7894-2583-1*) DK Pub Inc.

— The Taker's Stone. LC 98-24022. 240p. (J). 1999. 16.95 (*0-7894-2568-8*) DK Pub Inc.

Russell, Barry. Bankruptcy Evidence Manual. 850p. 1993. pap. text. write for info. (*0-314-02223-6*) West Pub.

— Bankruptcy Evidence Manual: 1994-1995 Edition. 1000p. 1994. pap. text. write for info. (*0-314-04509-0*) West Pub.

— Bankruptcy Evidence Manual: 1997 Edition. 1150p. (C). 1997. pap. text. write for info. (*0-314-22337-1*) West Pub.

— Bankruptcy Evidence Manual 1995-96 Edition. 1040p. 1995. pap. text. write for info. (*0-314-07586-0*) West Pub.

Russell, Ben. Laundries - Are They a Good Business to Get Into? Answers to the Most Often-Asked Questions about the Self-Service Laundry Industry. LC 95-94298. 220p. (Orig.). 1995. pap. 21.95 (*0-9645877-0-X*) Burnside Pub.

Russell, Bert. Calked Boots & Other Northwest Writings. 4th ed. (Folklore Ser.). 1979. 9.95 (*0-930344-03-0*); pap. 6.95 (*0-930344-00-6*) Lacon Pubs.

— Hardships & Happy Times. LC 78-75104. (Oral History Ser.: No. 1). 1982. 9.95 (*0-930344-04-9*); pap. 7.95 (*0-930344-01-4*) Lacon Pubs.

— North Fork of the Coeur d'Alene. (Oral History Ser.: No. 3). (Illus.). 448p. 1985. 12.95 (*0-930344-07-3*); pap. 9.95 (*0-930344-06-5*) Lacon Pubs.

— Swiftwater People. (Oral History Ser.: No. 2). 1979. 11.95 (*0-930344-05-7*); pap. 8.95 (*0-930344-02-2*) Lacon Pubs.

Russell, Bert & Russell, Marie. Rock Burst. LC 97-9491. (Living the West Ser.). 425p. 1998. 39.95 (*0-89301-197-5*) U of Idaho Pr.

— Rock Burst: Another Bert Russell Book. LC 94-77720. (Oral History Ser.: Bk. 4). (Illus.). (Orig.). pap. write for info. (*0-930344-11-1*) Lacon Pubs.

Russell, Bertrand. Analysis of Mind. LC 96-163298. 320p. (C). 1995. pap. 22.99 (*0-415-09097-0*) Routledge.

— The Art of Philosophizing & Other Essays. (Quality Paperback Ser.: No. 273). 119p. 1977. reprint ed. pap. 9.95 (*0-8226-0273-3*) Littlefield.

— Atheism: Collected Essays, 1943-1949. LC 71-169217. (Atheist Viewpoint Ser.). 232p. 1976. reprint ed. 22.95 (*0-405-03808-9*) Ayer.

An Asterisk (*) at the beginning of an entry indicates that the title is appearing for the first time.

— Authority & the Individual. 2nd ed. LC 96-171065. 96p. (C). 1985. pap. 14.99 (*0-415-11956-1*) Routledge.

— Autobiography. LC 98-19555. 766p. (C). 1998. 50.00 (*0-415-18985-3*) Routledge.

— Autobiography of Bertrand Russell. (Unwin Paperbacks Ser.). 1978. pap. 16.95 (*0-04-921022-X*) Routledge.

— Autobiography of Bertrand Russell: Vol. 2, 1914-1944. 1968. 34.95 (*0-04-921009-2*) Routledge.

— Bertrand Russell on Ethics, Sex, & Marriage. Seckel, Al, ed. LC 87-60825. (Great Books in Philosophy). 352p. (Orig.). 1987. pap. 19.95 (*0-87975-400-1*) Prometheus Bks.

— Bertrand Russell on God & Religion. Seckel, Al, ed. LC 85-63409. (Great Books in Philosophy). 350p. 1986. pap. 19.95 (*0-87975-323-4*) Prometheus Bks.

— Bertrand Russell Speaks His Mind. LC 74-3626. (Illus.). 173p. 1974. reprint ed. lib. bdg. 35.00 (*0-8371-7445-7*, RUBR, Greenwood Pr) Greenwood.

— Bolshevism: Practice & Theory. LC 72-4296. (World Affairs Ser.: National & International Viewpoints). 192p. 1979. reprint ed. 19.95 (*0-405-04587-5*) Ayer.

— Cambridge Essays, 1888-99. Blackwell, Kenneth et al, eds. (Collected Papers of Bertrand Russell: Vol. 1). 588p. (C). (gr. 13). 1988. 175.00 (*0-04-920067-4*, A9409) Routledge.

— Collected Papers of Bertrand Russell, Vol. 5. (C). 1999. 165.00 (*0-415-09407-0*) Routledge.

— Collected Papers of Bertrand Russell, Vol. 15. (C). 1999. text. write for info. (*0-04-920081-X*) Routledge.

— Collected Papers of Bertrand Russell, Vol. 16. (C). 1999. text. write for info. (*0-04-920082-8*) Routledge.

— Collected Papers of Bertrand Russell, Vol. 17. (C). 1999. text. write for info. (*0-04-920083-6*) Routledge.

— Collected Papers of Bertrand Russell, Vol. 18. (C). 1999. text. write for info. (*0-04-920084-4*) Routledge.

— Collected Papers of Bertrand Russell, Vol. 19. (C). 1999. text. write for info. (*0-04-920085-2*) Routledge.

— Collected Papers of Bertrand Russell, Vol. 20. (C). 1999. text. write for info. (*0-04-920086-0*) Routledge.

— Collected Papers of Bertrand Russell, Vol. 21. (C). 1999. text. write for info. (*0-04-920087-9*) Routledge.

— Collected Papers of Bertrand Russell, Vol. 22. (C). 1999. text. write for info. (*0-04-920088-7*) Routledge.

— Collected Papers of Bertrand Russell, Vol. 23. (C). 1999. text. write for info. (*0-04-920089-5*) Routledge.

— Collected Papers of Bertrand Russell, Vol. 24. (C). 1999. text. write for info. (*0-04-920090-9*) Routledge.

— Collected Papers of Bertrand Russell, Vol. 26. (C). 1999. text. write for info. (*0-04-920092-5*) Routledge.

— Collected Papers of Bertrand Russell, Vol. 27. (C). 1999. text. write for info. (*0-04-920093-3*) Routledge.

— Collected Papers of Bertrand Russell, Vol. 28. (C). 1999. text. write for info. (*0-04-920094-1*) Routledge.

— Collected Papers of Bertrand Russell Volume 25, Vol. 25. (C). 1999. text. write for info. (*0-04-920091-7*) Routledge.

— The Conquest of Happiness. 256p. 1996. reprint ed. pap. 11.00 (*0-87140-162-2*, Pub. by Liveright) Norton.

— La Conquista de la Felicidad. (Nueva Austral Ser.: Vol. 189). (SPA.). 1991. pap. text 24.95 (*84-239-1989-7*) Elliots Bks.

— Contemplation & Action, 1902-14, Vol. 7. 654p. (C). 1988. 190.00 (*0-415-10462-9*) Routledge.

— Diccionario del Hombre Contemporaneo. (SPA.). pap. 17.50 (*0-686-56655-6*) Fr & Eur.

— Education & the Social Order. 160p. (C). 1988. pap. 17.99 (*0-415-07916-0*) Routledge.

— An Essay on the Foundations of Geometry. LC 95-45882. 224p. (C). 1996. pap. 24.99 (*0-415-14146-X*) Routledge.

— Essays on Language, Mind & Matter, 1919-1926, Vol. 9. Slater, John G., ed. 704p. (C). 1988. 175.00 (*0-415-09917-X*) Routledge.

— Essays on Language, Mind & Matter, 1919-1926, Vol. 9. Frohmann, Bernd & Slater, John G., eds. LC 88-32. (Collected Papers of Bertrand Russell). 704p. (C). (gr. 13). 1988. text 150.00 (*0-04-920075-5*, A9417) Routledge.

— Fact & Fiction. 288p. (C). 1994. pap. 18.99 (*0-415-11461-6*, B4554) Routledge.

— Foundations of Logic, 1903-05. Urquhart, Alasdair & Lewis, Albert C., eds. LC 93-5603. (The Collected Papers of Bertrand Russell: Vol. 4). (Illus.). 796p. (C). 1994. 175.00 (*0-415-09406-2*) Routledge.

— A Fresh Look at Empiricism, 1927-46. Slater, John G. & Kollner, Peter, eds. LC 96-11344. (Collected Papers of Bertrand Russell: No. 10). 936p. (C). 1996. 200.00 (*0-415-09408-9*) Routledge.

— Has Man a Future? LC 84-12766. 128p. 1984. reprint ed. lib. bdg. 38.50 (*0-313-24382-4*, RHMF, Greenwood Pr) Greenwood.

— History of Western Philosophy. 896p. 1967. per. 22.00 (*0-671-20158-1*) S&S Trade.

— History of Western Philosophy: And Its Connection with Political & Social Circumstances. 848p. (C). 1993. pap. 24.99 (*0-415-07854-7*) Routledge.

— Human Knowledge. 540p. (C). 1994. pap. 27.99 (*0-415-08302-8*, B4573) Routledge.

— Impact of Science on Society. 128p. (C). 1985. pap. 16.99 (*0-415-10906-X*) Routledge.

— Impact of Science on Society. LC 68-54290. reprint ed. 20.00 (*0-404-05466-8*) AMS Pr.

— In Praise of Idleness. 176p. (C). 1985. pap. 15.99 (*0-415-10924-8*) Routledge.

— In Praise of Idleness & Other Essays. (Unwin Paperbacks Ser.). 231p. 1981. reprint ed. pap. 7.95 (*0-04-304006-3*) Routledge.

— Inquiry into Meaning & Truth. (Unwin Paperbacks Ser.). (Orig.). 1980. pap. 7.95 (*0-04-121019-0*) Routledge.

— Introduction to Mathematical Philosophy. LC 93-21477. viii, 208p. 1993. reprint ed. pap. text 7.95 (*0-486-27724-0*) Dover.

— Introduction to Mathematical Philosophy. LC 93-12357. 208p. (C). 1993. reprint ed. pap. 20.99 (*0-415-09604-9*, B0413) Routledge.

— Justice in Wartime. LC 73-18081. (English Literature Ser.: No. 33). 1974. lib. bdg. 75.00 (*0-8383-1738-3*) M S G Haskell Hse.

— Logic & Knowledge: Essays, 1901 to 1950. Marsh, Robert C., ed. 392p. 1988. pap. text 21.95 (*0-04-440260-0*) Routledge.

— Logical & Philosophical Papers, 1909-1913. Slater, John G. & Frohmann, Bernd, eds. LC 92-2380. (Collected Papers of Bertrand Russell: Vol. 6). (Illus.). 682p. (C). (gr. 13). 1992. 175.00 (*0-415-08446-6*, A9414) Routledge.

— Marriage & Morals. LC 70-114377. 1970. pap. 13.95 (*0-87140-211-4*, Pub. by Liveright) Norton.

— Mortals & Others: American Essays, 1931-1935. 2nd ed. Ruja, Harry, ed. 192p. (C). 1996. pap. 20.99 (*0-415-12585-5*) Routledge.

— Mortals & Others: American Essays 1931-1935, Vol. 2. Ruja, Harry, ed. 192p. (C). 1998. 65.00 (*0-415-17866-5*) Routledge.

— Mortals & Others Vol. II: American Essays, 1931-1935, Vol. II. 192p. (C). 1998. pap. 20.99 (*0-415-17867-3*) Routledge.

— My Philosophical Development. (Unwin Paperbacks Ser.). 1975. pap. 9.95 (*0-04-192030-9*) Routledge.

— My Philosophical Development. LC 96-163548. 224p. (C). 1995. pap. 17.99 (*0-415-13601-6*) Routledge.

— Our Knowledge of the External World: As a Field for Scientific Method in Philosophy. LC 93-16365. 256p. (C). 1993. reprint ed. pap. 18.99 (*0-415-09605-7*, B0417) Routledge.

— An Outline of Philosophy. 264p. (C). 1996. 60.00 (*0-415-14030-7*); pap. 17.99 (*0-415-14117-6*) Routledge.

— Philosophical Essays. LC 94-5628. 160p. (C). 1994. reprint ed. pap. 19.99 (*0-415-10579-X*) Routledge.

— Philosophical Papers, 1896-99. Griffin, Nicholas, ed. (The Collected Papers of Bertrand Russell: Vol. 2). 672p. (C). 1990. 175.00 (*0-415-09863-7*) Routledge.

— The Philosophy of Leibniz. 2nd ed. 200p. 1989. 27.50 (*0-89341-548-0*, Longwood Academic) Hollowbrook.

— The Philosophy of Leibniz. 3rd ed. 352p. (C). 1992. pap. 27.99 (*0-415-08296-X*, B0541) Routledge.

— The Philosophy of Logical Atomism & Other Essays, 1914-19. Slater, John G., ed. (Collected Papers of Bertrand Russell: Vol. 8). (Illus.). 418p. (C). (gr. 13). 1988. 175.00 (*0-04-920074-7*, A9416) Routledge.

— Political Ideals. 80p. (C). 1988. pap. 14.99 (*0-415-10907-8*) Routledge.

— Political Ideals. (Unwin Paperbacks Ser.). 1980. reprint ed. pap. 9.95 (*0-04-320120-2*) Routledge.

— Power: A New Social Analysis. 216p. (C). 1993. pap. 16.99 (*0-415-09456-9*, B2534) Routledge.

— The Principles of Mathematics. (Illus.). 576p. 1996. reprint ed. pap. 17.95 (*0-393-31404-9*, Norton Paperbks) Norton.

— Principles of Social Reconstruction. 2nd ed. LC 97-171658. 192p. (Orig.). (C). 1997. pap. 18.99 (*0-415-14349-7*) Routledge.

— The Problem of China. 266p. 1993. reprint ed. 72.50 (*0-85124-552-8*, Pub. by Spkesman); reprint ed. pap. 29.50 (*0-85124-553-6*, Pub. by Spkesman) Coronet Bks.

***Russell, Bertrand.** The Problems of Philosophy. LC 98-33214. 1999. pap. text 4.95 (*0-486-40674-1*) Dover.

Russell, Bertrand. The Problems of Philosophy. LC 97-2432. 192p. 1997. pap. 8.95 (*0-19-511552-X*) OUP.

— The Problems of Philosophy. LC 88-61328. (Great Books in Philosophy). 163p. (C). 1988. pap. 8.95 (*0-87975-497-4*) Prometheus Bks.

— The Problems of Philosophy. large type ed. LC 97-30369. 168p. 1997. text 22.95 (*1-56000-539-4*) Transaction Pubs.

— The Problems of Philosophy. LC 90-81389. (HPC Classics Ser.). 168p. (C). 1990. reprint ed. pap. text 7.95 (*0-87220-098-1*); reprint ed. lib. bdg. 24.95 (*0-87220-099-X*) Hackett Pub.

***Russell, Bertrand.** The Problems of Philosophy. 2nd ed. LC 98-7017. 1998. pap. write for info. (*0-19-289298-3*) OUP.

Russell, Bertrand. Prospects of Industrial Civilization. 1996. lib. bdg. 251.75 (*0-8490-5942-9*) Gordon Pr.

— Religion & Science. 2nd ed. LC 96-48939. 272p. 1997. pap. 13.95 (*0-19-511551-1*) OUP.

— Roads to Freedom. (C). 1970. pap. 11.95 (*0-415-09893-9*); pap. 12.99 (*0-415-15430-8*) Routledge.

— Roads to Freedom: Socialism, Anarchism & Syndication. (Unwin Paperbacks Ser.). 1966. pap. 9.95 (*0-04-335033-X*) Routledge.

— Sceptical Essays. (Unwin Paperbacks Ser.). 1960. pap. 19.95 (*0-04-104003-1*) Routledge.

— Sceptical Essays. 192p. (C). 1988. pap. 16.99 (*0-415-07919-5*) Routledge.

— Theory of Knowledge: The 1913 Manuscript. Eames, Elizabeth R. & Blackwell, Kenneth, eds. 264p. (C). 1992. pap. 20.99 (*0-415-08298-6*, A7942) Routledge.

— Theory of Knowledge: The 1913 Manuscript, Vol. 7. Eames, Elizabeth R., ed. 314p. (C). 1988. 180.00 (*0-415-10450-5*) Routledge.

— Toward the Principles of Mathematics, 1900-1902. Moore, Gregory H., ed. LC 93-3505. (Collected Papers of Bertrand Russell: Vol. 3). (Illus.). 960p. (C). 1994. 200.00 (*0-415-09405-4*, A9411) Routledge.

— Unpopular Essays. LC 96-231281. 208p. (C). 1996. pap. 16.99 (*0-415-11963-4*) Routledge.

— Why I Am Not a Christian. 268p. (C). 1967. per. 12.00 (*0-671-20323-1*) S&S Trade Pap.

— Why Men Fight: A Method of Abolishing the International Duel. LC 72-164623. (Select Bibliographies Reprint Ser.). 1977. reprint ed. 23.95 (*0-8369-5906-X*) Ayer.

Russell, Bertrand & Marsh, Robert C., eds. Logic & Knowledge. 400p. (C). 1988. pap. 25.99 (*0-415-09074-1*) Routledge.

Russell, Bertrand & Pigden, Charles. Russell on Ethics: Selections from the Writings of Bertrand Russell. LC 97-42586. 224p. (C). 1998. pap. 20.99 (*0-415-15660-2*) Routledge.

— Russell on Ethics: Selections from the Writings of Bertrand Russell. LC 97-42586. 272p. (C). 1999. 65.00 (*0-415-15659-9*) Routledge.

Russell, Bertrand & Russell, Dora. Prospects of Industrial Civilization. LC 96-222613. 264p. (C). 1996. pap. 18.99 (*0-415-13133-2*) Routledge.

Russell, Bertrand, et al. If I Could Preach Just Once. LC 73-167364. (Essay Index Reprint Ser.). 1977. reprint ed. 19.95 (*0-8369-2457-6*) Ayer.

— The Last Philosophical Testament, 1947-68. LC 96-40868. (Collected Papers of Bertrand Russell). (Illus.). 880p. (C). 1997. 195.00 (*0-415-09409-7*) Routledge.

— Russell on Religion: Selections from the Writings of Bertrand Russell. LC 98-30931. 1999. 65.00 (*0-415-18091-0*); pap. 20.99 (*0-415-18092-9*) Routledge.

Russell, Bertrand, jt. auth. see Nearing, Scott.

Russell, Bertrand, jt. auth. see Whitehead, Alfred North.

Russell, Bertrand R. Common Sense & Nuclear Warfare. LC 68-54291. 1995. reprint ed. 18.00 (*0-404-05465-X*) AMS Pr.

— War Crimes in Vietnam. LC 67-23969. 178p. reprint ed. pap. 55.20 (*0-608-30489-1*, 200170800004) Bks Demand.

Russell, Beth. Beth Russell's Traditional Needlepoint: Glorious Rugs, Cushions & Pictures. (Illus.). 128p. 1999. pap. 19.95 (*0-7153-0960-9*, Pub. by D & C Pub) Sterling.

— Victorian Needlepoint. (Illus.). 112p. 1996. pap. 19.95 (*1-85470-258-0*, Pub. by Collins & Br) Trafalgar.

Russell, Betty G. Silent Sisters: An Ethnography of Homeless Women. (Health Care for Women International Publication). 160p. 1991. 33.95 (*1-56032-098-2*) Hemisp Pub.

Russell, Beverly. Architecture & Design, 1970-1990: New Ideas in America. (Illus.). 144p. 1989. 29.95 (*0-685-28261-9*) Abrams.

— 40 under 40: A Guide to New Young Talent with Seductive Ideas for Living Today. (Illus.). 220p. 1996. reprint ed. pap. 34.99 (*1-883065-05-4*) Rockport Vitae Pub.

— Women of Taste: Recipes & Profiles of Famous Women Chefs. LC 97-13168. (Illus.). 224p. 1997. 35.00 (*0-471-17943-4*) Wiley.

Russell, Bill. Decorative Furniture Finishes with Vinegar Paint. LC 98-41274. (Illus.). 128p. 1999. pap. 24.99 (*0-89134-870-0*, 31363, North Lght Bks) F & W Pubns Inc.

Russell, Bob. More with Less: Work Reorganization in the Canadian Mining Industry. (Studies in Comparative Political Economy & Public Policy Ser.). (Illus.). 352p. 1998. text 55.00 (*0-8020-4354-2*); pap. text 21.95 (*0-8020-8178-9*) U of Toronto Pr.

— My Year in the Word, 1999: Through the Gospels with Bob Russell. Eichenberger, Jim, ed. 208p. 1998. pap. 14.99 (*0-7847-0800-2*, 11-41000) Standard Pub.

***Russell, Bob & Russell, Rusty.** When God Builds a Church: 10 Principles for Growing a Church God's Way. x, 288p. 2000. 19.99 (*1-58229-125-X*) Howard Pub LA.

Russell, Bob, jt. auth. see Cain, Danny.

Russell, Bob, jt. auth. see Collison, Linda.

Russell, Brian. Introduction to Seismic Inversion Methods. (Course Notes Ser.: No. 2). 90p. (Orig.). 1988. pap. text 20.00 (*0-931830-65-6*, 252A) Soc Expl Geophys.

Russell, Bruce, ed. Freedom, Rights & Pornography: A Collection of Papers by Fred R. Berger. (Philosophical Studies in Philosophy Ser.). 242p. (C). 1990. lib. bdg. 135.00 (*0-7923-1034-9*, Pub. by Kluwer Academic) Kluwer Academic.

Russell, Bruce, jt. auth. see Magoldi, Mary.

Russell, Bruce J., jt. auth. see Rainis, Kenneth G.

Russell, Byron A. It Was Like This. LC 87-71286. (Illus.). 240p. 1987. pap. 11.95 (*0-931170-33-8*) Ctr Western Studies.

Russell, C. One Hundred Predictions for the Baby Boom: The Next 50 Years. (Illus.). 250p. (C). 1987. 17.95 (*0-306-42527-0*, Plenum Trade) Perseus Pubng.

***Russell, C. A.** Chemistry, Society & Environment: A New History of the British Chemical Industry. 320p. 1999. 120.00 (*0-85404-599-6*, Pub. by Royal Soc Chem) Spr-Verlag.

Russell, C. Greg. Equations & Formulas for the Traffic Accident Investigator & Reconstructionist. LC 99-19745. 136p. 1999. spiral bd. 39.00 (*0-913875-69-4*) Lawyers & Judges.

Russell, C. H. AIDS in America. xi, 147p. 1991. 79.95 (*0-387-97462-8*) Spr-Verlag.

Russell, C. H. & Megaard, I. The General Social Survey, 1972-1986. (Recent Research in Psychology Ser.). xxix, 228p. 1990. 71.95 (*0-387-96746-X*) Spr-Verlag.

Russell, C. M. Charles M. Russell Postcard Book. 1995. pap. 8.95 (*1-56044-358-8*) Falcon Pub Inc.

Russell, C. T. Results of the IASTP Program. (Advances in Space Research Ser.: Vol. 20). 606p. 1998. pap. 201.00 (*0-08-043301-4*, Pergamon Pr) Elsevier.

— Venus Aeronomy. (C). 1991. lib. bdg. 266.50 (*0-7923-1091-8*) Kluwer Academic.

Russell, C. T., ed. Active Experiments in Space Plasmas. (Advances in Space Research Ser.: Vol. 1, No. 2). (Illus.). 468p. 1981. pap. 72.00 (*0-08-027158-8*, Pergamon Pr) Elsevier.

— The Galileo Mission. LC 92-9943. 600p. (C). 1992. text 335.50 (*0-7923-1719-X*) Kluwer Academic.

— The Magnetosheath: Proceedings of the Topical Meeting of the COSPAR Interdisciplinary Scientific Commission D (Meeting D6) of the COSPAR 29th Plenary Meeting Held in Washington, D. C., U. S. A., 28 August-5 September, 1992. (Advances in Space Research Ser.: Vol. 14). (Illus.). 142p. 1994. pap. 165.00 (*0-08-042484-8*) Elsevier.

— Multipoint Magnetospheric Measurements: Proceedings of Symposium 8 of the COSPAR 27th Plenary Meeting Held in Espoo, Finland, 18-29 July, 1988. (Advances in Space Research Ser.: Vol. 8). (Illus.). 472p. 1989. pap. 170.00 (*0-08-037373-9*, Pergamon Pr) Elsevier.

— The Near Earth Asteroid Rendezvous Mission. LC 97-52154. 320p. 1998. 185.00 (*0-7923-4957-1*) Kluwer Academic.

— Physics of Collisionless Shocks. (Advances in Space Research (RJ) Ser.: Vol. 15). 542p. 1995. pap. 194.50 (*0-08-042558-5*, Pergamon Pr) Elsevier.

— Physics of Magnetic Flux Ropes. (Geophysical Monograph Ser.: Vol. 58). 752p. 1990. 60.00 (*0-87590-026-7*) Am Geophysical.

Russell, C. T., jt. ed. see Southwood, D. J.

Russell, C. V. & Willig, P. L. German Tests Without Translation. 1978. pap. text 3.70 (*0-08-022868-2*, Pergamon Pr) Elsevier.

Russell, C. W. Income Taxation of Natural Resources: (1996 Edition) rev. ed. 904p. 1995. pap. text 95.00 (*0-7811-0127-1*) Res Inst Am.

— Income Taxation of Natural Resources, 1998. rev. ed. 944p. 1998. text 99.00 (*0-7811-0174-3*) Res Inst Am.

— Income Taxation of Natural Resources, 1999. rev. ed. 944p. 1999. text 99.00 (*0-7811-0208-1*) Res Inst Am.

— Income Taxation of Natural Resources, 1993. 800p. 1992. text 95.00 (*0-7811-0066-6*) Res Inst Am.

Russell, C. W. & KPMG Peat Marwick Staff. Income Taxation of Natural Resources: 1997 Edition. rev. ed. 928p. 1997. pap. text 99.00 (*0-7811-0151-4*) Res Inst Am.

Russell, C. W. & Marwick, Peat. Income Taxation of Natural Resources, 1994. rev. ed. 800p. 1993. text 92.00 (*0-7811-0082-8*) Res Inst Am.

***Russell, C. W., et al.** Income Taxation of Natural Resources, 2000: Partners of KPMG Peat Marwick LLP. rev. ed. 976p. 2000. pap. 99.00 (*0-7811-0228-6*) Res Inst Am.

Russell, C. W., jt. auth. see KPMG Peat Marwick Staff.

Russell, Carl P. Firearms, Traps & Tools of the Mountain Men. LC 77-81984. (Illus.). 456p. 1977. reprint ed. pap. 16.95 (*0-8263-0465-6*) U of NM Pr.

Russell, Carlos E. An Old Woman Remembers: The Recollected History of West Indians in Panama 1855-1955. (Illus.). 50p. (Orig.). 1995. pap. text 10.00 (*1-878433-20-2*) Caribbean Diaspora Pr.

Russell, Carol A. Silver Dollar. 57p. (Orig.). 1995. pap. 8.95 (*0-931122-81-3*) West End.

Russell, Carol K. The Tapestry Handbook: An Illustrated Manual of Traditional Techniques. Taylor, Carol, ed. (Illus.). 176p. 1990. 26.95 (*0-937274-54-2*) Lark Books.

Russell, CarolAnn. Feast. (Illus.). 58p. (Orig.). 1993. pap. 9.95 (*0-926147-04-8*) Loonfeather.

— The Red Envelope. LC 85-9163. (University of Central Florida Contemporary Poetry Ser.). 94p. (Orig.). 1985. pap. 10.95 (*0-8130-0828-X*) U Press Fla.

Russell, Carolyn, jt. auth. see Russell, Mike.

Russell, Carroll, jt. auth. see Horst, Louis.

Russell, Carron-Ann. Opinion Writing & Drafting in Contract Law. 193p. 1996. pap. 22.00 (*1-85941-030-8*, Pub. by Cavendish Pubng) Gaunt.

Russell, Catherine. Experimental Ethnography: The Work of Film in the Age of Video. LC 98-46549. (Illus.). 408p. 1999. 64.95 (*0-8223-2287-0*); pap. 21.95 (*0-8223-2319-2*) Duke.

— Narrative Mortality: Death, Closure & New Wave Cinemas. LC 94-17542. 288p. 1994. pap. 19.95 (*0-8166-2486-0*); text 49.95 (*0-8166-2485-2*) U of Minn Pr.

Russell, Charles. Five on the Black Hand Side: A Play. LC 73-82643. (Illus.). 96p. 1973. 15.95 (*0-89388-092-2*) Okpaku Communications.

— The Improvement of the City Elementary School Teacher in Service. LC 78-177216. (Columbia University. Teachers College. Contributions to Education Ser.: No. 128). reprint ed. 37.50 (*0-404-55128-9*) AMS Pr.

— Spirit Bear: Encounters with the White Bear of the Western Rainforest. (Illus.). 144p. (Orig.). 1999. pap. 22.95 (*1-55013-649-6*) Firefly Bks Ltd.

Russell, Charles, ed. The Avant-Garde Today: An International Anthology. LC 80-23922. 286p. 1981. text 29.95 (*0-252-00851-0*) U of Ill Pr.

Russell, Charles, jt. auth. see Maitland-Walker, Julian.

Russell, Charles, jt. auth. see Roy, F. Hampton.

Russell, Charles C. The Don Juan Legend Before Mozart: With a Collection of Eighteenth-Century Opera Librettos. 528p. 1993. text 75.00 (*0-472-10413-6*, 10413) U of Mich Pr.

Russell, Charles E. The American Orchestra & Theodore Thomas. LC 76-139146. (Illus.). 344p. (C). 1971. reprint ed. lib. bdg. 59.75 (*0-8371-5762-5*, RUAO, Greenwood Pr) Greenwood.

— The American Orchestra & Theodore Thomas. 344p. 1990. reprint ed. lib. bdg. 79.00 (*0-7812-9116-X*) Rprt Serv.

— The Greatest Trust in the World. McCurry, Dan C. & Rubenstein, Richard E., eds. LC 74-30650. (American Farmers & the Rise of Agribusiness Ser.). 1975. reprint ed. 25.95 (*0-405-06822-0*) Ayer.

— Haym Salomon & the Revolution. LC 77-114892. (Select Bibliographies Reprint Ser.). 1977. 24.95 (*0-8369-5296-0*) Ayer.

— Haym Salomon & the Revolution. 1993. reprint ed. lib. bdg. 89.00 (*0-7812-5827-8*) Rprt Serv.

— The Story of the Nonpartisan League: A Chapter in

R

American Evolution. McCurry, Dan C. & Rubenstein, Richard E., eds. LC 74-30651. (American Farmers & the Rise of Agribusiness Ser.). (Illus.). 1975. reprint ed. 35.95 (*0-405-06823-9*) Ayer.

— Thomas Chatterton. LC 70-130258. (English Literature Ser.: No. 33). 1970. reprint ed. lib. bdg. 75.00 (*0-8383-1162-8*) M S G Haskell Hse.

***Russell, Charles G.** Culture, Language & Behavior. LC 99-43092. 313p. (C). 1999. pap. text 29.95 (*0-918970-47-4*) Intl Gen Semantics.

Russell, Charles M. Charlie Russell Journal. Lambert, Kirby, ed. LC 98-132229. (Illus.). 128p. 1997. 12.95 (*0-917298-36-5*) MT Hist Soc.

— Paintings & Sketches. (Illus.). (Orig.). pap. write for info. (*1-56944-041-7*) Terrell Missouri.

— Trails Plowed Under: Stories of the Old West. LC 96-8324. xxxiv, 221p. 1996. pap. 13.00 (*0-8032-8961-8*, Bison Books) U of Nebr Pr.

Russell, Charles M., jt. auth. see Peterson, Larry L.

Russell, Charles T. The Finished Mystery. (Studies in the Scriptures: Vol. VII). 608p. 1985. reprint ed. pap. 8.95 (*1-883858-28-3*) Witness CA.

Russell, Charles W. The Memoirs of Colonel John S. Mosby. 414p. 1987. reprint ed. 35.00 (*0-942211-27-8*) Olde Soldier Bks.

Russell, Charles W. & Bowhay, Robert W. Income Taxation of Natural Resources. 920p. 1988. 41.50 (*0-13-453689-4*, Busn) P-H.

***Russell, Charlie & Crawford, Sharon.** Microsoft Windows 2000 Server Administrator's Companion. LC 99-48555. 1520p. 2000. 69.99 incl. cd-rom (*1-57231-819-8*) Microsoft.

Russell, Charlotte M. Cook up a Crime. Schantz, Tom & Schantz, Enid, eds. 160p. 1998. reprint ed. pap. 13.00 (*0-915230-18-6*) Rue Morgue.

***Russell, Cheryl.** Americans & Their Homes: Demographics of Homeownership. LC 98-168798. 336p. 1998. 79.95 (*1-885070-16-0*) New Strategist.

Russell, Cheryl. The Baby Boom: Americans Aged 35 to 54. 2nd rev. ed. 369p. 1999. 69.95 (*1-885070-22-5*) New Strategist.

— Color: A Thematic Unit. (Thematic Units Ser.). (Illus.). 80p. 1993. student ed. 9.95 (*1-55734-279-2*) Tchr Create Mat.

— The Hundred Dresses. (Literature Units Ser.). 48p. (J). (gr. 3-5). 1997. pap. 7.95 (*1-57690-136-X*) Tchr Create Mat.

— The Master Trend: How the Baby Boom Generation Is Remaking America. LC 93-11511. (Illus.). 284p. (C). 1993. 23.95 (*0-306-44507-7*, Plenum Trade) Perseus Pubng.

***Russell, Cheryl.** Racial & Ethnic Diversity: Asians, Blacks, Hispanics, Native Americans, & Whites. 2nd rev. ed. LC 98-168181. 728p. 1998. 94.95 (*1-885070-15-2*) New Strategist.

Russell, Cheryl, ed. American Women: Who They Are & How They Live. LC 97-170085. 416p. 1997. 89.95 (*1-885070-08-X*) New Strategist.

Russell, Cheryl & Mitchell, Susan. Best Customers: Demographics of Consumer Demand. 730p. 1999. 89.95 (*1-885070-26-8*) New Strategist.

Russell, Ching Y. Child Bride. LC 98-73070. 136p. (J). (gr. 3-7). 1999. 15.95 (*1-56397-748-6*) Boyds Mills Pr.

— A Day on a Shrimp Boat. Littlejohn, Beth, ed. LC 93-8899. (Illus.). 57p. (J). (gr. 3-6). 1993. 12.95 (*0-87844-120-4*) Sandlapper Pub Co.

— First Apple. LC 93-74360. (Illus.). 128p. (J). (gr. 4-7). 1994. 13.95 (*1-56397-206-9*) Boyds Mills Pr.

— Moon Festival. LC 97-70583. (Illus.). 32p. (J). (ps-4). 1997. 15.95 (*1-56397-596-3*) Boyds Mills Pr.

Russell, Ching Yeung. First Apple. (J). 1996. 9.09 (*0-606-08518-1*, Pub. by Turtleback) Demco.

***Russell, Chris.** The Final Buzzer. 128p. 2000. pap. 9.95 (*1-886028-45-1*, Pub. by Savage Pr) Bookmen Inc.

Russell, Christina. Lichee Tree. LC 96-84678. (Illus.). 128p. (YA). (gr. 5 up). 1997. 14.95 (*1-56397-629-3*) Boyds Mills Pr.

— Water Ghost. LC 94-74534. (Illus.). 192p. (J). (gr. 3-7). 1995. 14.95 (*1-56397-413-4*) Boyds Mills Pr.

Russell, Christopher T., jt. ed. see Kivelson, Margaret G.

Russell, Chuck. Right Person - Right Job Guess or Know: The Breakthrough Technologies of Performance Information. 2nd ed. LC 95-74751. 114p. (Orig.). 1996. pap. 12.95 (*0-9647793-0-7*) Johnson & James.

Russell, Clifford. Sorting Out Spelling. (Illus.). 68p. (Orig.). (C). 1997. pap., teacher ed., ring bd. 48.00 (*0-9657270-2-5*) Germane Pubs.

— Star Science Program. (Illus.). (C). 1997. teacher ed., ring bd. 48.00 (*0-9657270-1-7*) Germane Pubs.

Russell, Clifford, et al. A Literature-Based Reading/Language Arts Implementation Guide. 3rd unabridged ed. (Illus.). 122p. (Orig.). (C). 1997. pap., ring bd. 52.00 (*0-9657270-0-9*) Germane Pubs.

— Mathematics Instruction: A Model Program for Elementary Teachers. unabridged ed. 468p. (C). 1998. ring bd. 62.00 (*0-9657270-3-3*) Germane Pubs.

Russell, Clifford S. Residuals Management in Industry: A Case Study of Petroleum Refining. LC 72-12367. (Resources for the Future Ser.). (Illus.). 208p. 1973. 18.00 (*0-8018-1497-9*) Johns Hopkins.

— Residuals Management in Industry: A Case Study of Petroleum Refining. LC 72-12367. (Illus.). 211p. reprint ed. pap. 65.50 (*0-608-18097-1*, 203216300078) Bks Demand.

Russell, Clifford S., ed. Collective Decision Making: Applications from Public Choice Theory. LC 79-16614. 296p. 1979. 26.00 (*0-8018-2320-X*) Resources Future.

— Ecological Modeling in a Resource Management Framework: The Proceedings of a Symposium. LC 75-15108. (Resources for the Future, RFF Working Papers: QE-1). 406p. reprint ed. pap. 125.90 (*0-608-12546-6*, 202381300034) Bks Demand.

— Safe Drinking Water: Current & Future Problems: Proceedings of a National Conference in Washington D. C. LC 78-19840. (Resources for the Future Research Paper Ser.). 1978. pap. 30.00 (*0-8018-2181-9*) Johns Hopkins.

Russell, Clifford S. & Nicholson, Norman K., eds. Public Choice & Rural Development. LC 80-8775. (Resources for the Future Research Paper: R-21). (Illus.). 312p. 1981. pap. text 15.00 (*0-8018-2600-4*) Johns Hopkins.

Russell, Clifford S. & Shogren, Jason F., eds. Theory, Modeling, & Experience in the Management of Nonpoint-Source Pollution. LC 92-36253. 368p. 1993. lib. bdg. 157.50 (*0-7923-9307-4*) Kluwer Academic.

Russell, Clifford S. & Vaughan, William J. Steel Production: Processes, Products, & Residuals. LC 75-36945. 328p. 1976. 26.50 (*0-8018-1824-9*) Resources Future.

Russell, Clifford S., et al. Drought & Water Supply: Implications of the Massachusetts Experience for Municipal Planning. LC 72-123861. 232p. 1970. 21.00 (*0-8018-1183-X*) Resources Future.

— Enforcing Pollution Control Laws. LC 85-43554. 231p. 1986. text 25.00 (*0-915707-25-X*) Resources Future.

Russell, Clifford S., jt. auth. see Vaughan, William J.

Russell, Colin. Cross Currents: Interactions Between Faith & Science. 134p. 1993. reprint ed. pap. 21.95 (*1-57383-021-6*) Regent College.

Russell, Colin A. Cross-Currents: Interactions Between Science & Faith. LC 85-10199. 272p. reprint ed. pap. 84.40 (*0-608-17883-7*, 203274500080) Bks Demand.

— Edward Frankland: Chemistry, Controversy & Conspiracy in Victorian England. (Illus.). 555p. (C). 1996. text 115.00 (*0-521-49636-5*) Cambridge U Pr.

— Lancastrian Chemist: The Early Years of Sir Edward Frankland. 192p. 1986. 69.00 (*0-335-15175-2*) OpUniv Pr.

***Russell, Colin A.** Michael Faraday. (Oxford Portraits in Science Ser.). (Illus.). 144p. (YA). 2000. lib. bdg. 22.00 (*0-19-511763-8*) OUP.

Russell, Conrad. Academic Freedom. LC 92-30810. 128p. (C). 1993. pap. 20.99 (*0-415-03715-8*, B0409) Routledge.

— The Causes of the English Civil War. (Ford Lectures 1987-1988). 252p. 1990. pap. text 22.00 (*0-19-822141-X*) OUP.

— The Crisis of Parliaments: English History, 1509-1660. (Short Oxford History of the Modern World Ser.). 450p. 1971. reprint ed. pap. text 29.95 (*0-19-913034-5*) OUP.

Russell, Conrad. The Fall of the British Monarchies, 1637-1642. 570p. 1995. pap. text 29.95 (*0-19-820588-0*) OUP.

Russell, Conrad. Unrevolutionary England, 1603-42. 343p. 1990. 60.00 (*1-85285-025-6*) Hambledon Press.

Russell, Craig H. Santiago de Murcia's "Codice Saldivar No. 4" A Treasury of Secular Guitar Music from Baroque, Vol. 1. 320p. 1995. text 59.95 (*0-252-02083-9*) U of Ill Pr.

— Santiago de Murcia's "Codice Saldivar No. 4" A Treasury of Secular Guitar Music from Baroque Mexico, 2 vols. (Music In American Life Ser.). 1995. text 85.00 (*0-252-02093-6*) U of Ill Pr.

— Santiago de Murcia's "Codice Saldivar No. 4" Vol. 2: A Treasury of Secular Guitar Music from Baroque Mexico, Vol. 2. (Music in American Life Ser.). 328p. 1995. text 39.95 (*0-252-02092-8*) U of Ill Pr.

Russell, Cynthia K., jt. auth. see Gregory, David M.

***Russell, Cynthia Stanley.** Mim & the Klan: Atbosier Quaker Farm Family's Story. LC 99-65568. (Illus.). 108p. 1999. 18.95 (*1-57860-036-7*) Guild Pr IN.

Russell, D. Criticism in Antiquity. 2nd ed. (Classical Paperbacks Ser.). 229p. 1995. pap. 27.95 (*1-85399-452-9*, Pub. by Brist Class Pr) Focus Pub-R Pullins.

— The Principles of Computer Networking. (Cambridge Computer Science Texts Ser.). 513p. (C). 1990. pap. text 44.95 (*0-521-33992-8*) Cambridge U Pr.

Russell, D. A. Classical Literary Criticism. (Oxford World's Classics Ser.). 270p. 1998. pap. 8.95 (*0-19-283900-4*) OUP.

Russell, D. A., compiled by. An Anthology of Greek Prose. (Illus.). 328p. 1991. text 65.00 (*0-19-814498-9*); pap. text 29.95 (*0-19-872122-6*) OUP.

Russell, D. A., compiled by. An Anthology of Latin Prose. 288p. 1990. text 80.00 (*0-19-814746-5*); pap. text 26.00 (*0-19-872121-8*) OUP.

Russell, D. A., ed. Antonine Literature. 256p. 1990. text 65.00 (*0-19-814057-6*) OUP.

Russell, D. A., ed. see Chrysostomus, Dio.

Russell, D. C. Our Nation's Capitol. LC 97-113690. 64p. (J). 1997. pap. 11.95 (*0-590-59929-1*) Scholastic Inc.

Russell, D. G., jt. auth. see Matthews, C. S.

Russell, D. H. Experimental Mass Spectrometry. (Illus.). 326p. (C). 1994. text 95.00 (*0-306-44457-7*, Kluwer Plenum) Kluwer Academic.

— Gas Phase Inorganic Chemistry. (Modern Inorganic Chemistry Ser.). (Illus.). 428p. (C). 1989. text 110.00 (*0-306-42972-1*, Kluwer Plenum) Kluwer Academic.

Russell, D. S. Between the Testaments. LC 77-74742. 182p. 1960. pap. 16.00 (*0-8006-1856-4*, 1-1856, Fortress Pr) Augsburg Fortress.

— Daniel. 248p. 1993. pap. 22.00 (*0-7152-0464-5*) St Mut.

— Daniel: An Active Volcano Reflections on the Book of Daniel. 144p. 1993. pap. 22.00 (*0-7152-0632-X*) St Mut.

— Divine Disclosure: An Introduction to Jewish Apocalyptic. LC 92-9523. 186p. 1992. 19.00 (*0-8006-2698-2*, 1-2698) Augsburg Fortress.

— El Periodo Intertestamentario.Tr. of Between the Testaments. (SPA.). 176p. 1997. pap. 7.50 (*0-311-03654-6*) Casa Bautista.

— Poles Apart: The Gospel in Creative Tension. 160p. (Orig.). 1993. text 25.00 (*0-7152-0646-X*, Pub. by St Andrew) St Mut.

Russell, D. S., ed. Poles Apart: The Gospel in Creative Tension. 160p. (Orig.). (C). 1991. pap. text 59.00 (*86-15-30646-X*, Pub. by St Andrew) St Mut.

Russell, D. W. Engineered Software Systems: Proceedingss of the International Sym. 284p. 1993. text 95.00 (*981-02-1549-5*) World Scientific Pub.

Russell, Daina E. The Secret Trauma: Incest in the Lives of Girls & Women. LC 85-43107. (Illus.). 464p. 1999. pap. 18.00 (*0-465-07596-7*, Pub. by Basic) HarpC.

Russell, Dale. Colour in Industrial Design. (Illus.). 96p. (C). 1991. pap. 22.95 (*0-85072-283-7*, Pub. by Gower) Ashgate Pub Co.

— Hell Above, Deep Water Below. 210p. 1995. text 24.95 (*0-9643849-9-X*) D Russell.

— The Pastels Book: The Designer's Ultimate Guide to Working with Color. (Illus.). 144p. 1998. reprint ed. text 25.00 (*0-7881-5885-6*) DIANE Pub.

Russell, Dale, jt. auth. see Acorn, John.

Russell, Dale, jt. auth. see Glossop, Jennifer.

Russell, Dale A. An Odyssey in Time: The Dinosaurs of North America. (Illus.). 256p. 1992. pap. text 24.95 (*0-8020-7718-8*) U of Toronto Pr.

Russell, Dale A. & Acorn, John. The Tiny Perfect Dinosaur Book, Bones, Egg & Poster: Presenting Leptoceratops. (Illus.). 32p. (Orig.). (J). 1991. pap. 12.95 (*0-8362-4213-0*) Andrews & McMeel.

— The Tiny Perfect Dinosaur Book, Bones, Egg & Poster Kits: Presenting Brachiosaurus. (Illus.). 32p. (J). 1994. pap. 12.95 (*0-8362-4234-3*) Andrews & McMeel.

— Tyrannosaurus Rex. (Illus.). 32p. Date not set. pap. 12.95 (*0-8362-4216-5*) Andrews & McMeel.

Russell, Dale A. & Glossup, Jennifer. The Tiny Perfect Dinosaur Book, Bones, Egg & Poster: Stegosaurus. (Illus.). 32p. (J). 1995. pap. 12.95 (*0-8362-0646-0*) Andrews & McMeel.

Russell, Dale R. Eighteenth-Century Western Cree & Their Neighbours. (Mercury Ser.: ASC No. 143). (Illus.). 248p. 1991. pap. 20.95 (*0-660-12915-9*, Pub. by CN Mus Civilization) U of Wash Pr.

***Russell, Dan.** Drug War: Covert Money, Power & Policy. LC 99-94065. (Illus.). 671p. 2000. pap. 34.95 (*0-9650253-4-9*) Kalyx.com.

Russell, Dan. Jack Russell & His Terriers. 112p. 1990. pap. 21.00 (*0-85131-276-4*) Trafalgar.

— Shamanism & the Drug Propaganda: Patriarchy & the Drug War. annot. unabridged ed. LC 98-91312. (Illus.). 357p. (Orig.). 1998. pap. 24.95 (*0-9650253-1-4*) Kalyx.com.

— Shamanism & the Drug Propaganda: The Demonization of the Ecstatic. 272p. (C). 1995. pap. 29.95 (*0-9650253-0-6*) Kalyx.com.

Russell, Dan M. Dove Shooters Handbook. (Illus.). 256p. (Orig.). 1997. pap. write for info. (*0-937866-55-5*) Atlantic Pub Co.

Russell, Daniel. Emblematic Structures in Renaissance French Culture. (Romance Ser.). (Illus.). 352p. 1995. text 75.00 (*0-8020-0616-7*) U of Toronto Pr.

Russell, Daniel, jt. auth. see Daly, Peter M.

Russell, Daniel M. Political Organizing in Grassroots Politics. LC 89-22757. 170p. (Orig.). (C). 1990. pap. text 22.50 (*0-8191-7619-2*); lib. bdg. 39.00 (*0-8191-7618-4*) U Pr of Amer.

Russell, Daniel S. The Emblem & Device in France. LC 85-80418. (French Forum Monographs: No. 59). (Illus.). 245p. (Orig.). 1985. pap. 17.95 (*0-917058-60-7*) French Forum.

Russell, Daniel S., jt. auth. see Bath, Michael.

Russell, Dava L. A Family's Heritage: Stories from Main Street, Jonesborough, Tennessee. (Illus.). 1996. pap. 10.00 (*0-9652940-4-8*) Wilco Pub.

Russell, Dave. Popular Music in England, 1840-1914: A Social History. 2nd ed. (Illus.). 368p. 1998. pap. 29.95 (*0-7190-5261-0*, Pub. by Manchester Univ Pr) St Martin.

— Popular Music in England, 1840-1914: A Social History. 2nd ed. (Illus.). 368p. 1998. 79.95 (*0-7190-5310-2*, Pub. by Manchester Univ Pr) St Martin.

— Popular Music in England, 1840-1914. 320p. 1987. 65.00 (*0-7735-0541-5*, Pub. by McG-Queens Univ Pr) CUP Services.

Russell, David. It's a Disaster: How to Protect the Things You Own Against the Forces of Nature. (Illus.). 340p. 1998. pap. 19.95 (*1-56343-172-6*, Pub. by Silver Lake) Natl Bk Netwk.

— Remediation Manual for Petroleum-Contaminated Sites. LC 91-67570. 200p. 1992. pap. text 69.95 (*0-87762-876-9*) Technomic.

Russell, David & Bazerman, Charles, eds. The Activity of Writing/The Writing of Activity: A Special Issue of Mind, Culture, & Activity. 96p. 1997. pap. write for info. (*0-8058-9849-2*) L Erlbaum Assocs.

Russell, David, et al. Reading Aids Through the Grades: A Guide to Materials & 501 Activities for Individualizing Reading Instruction. 4th rev. ed. Mueser, Anne M., ed. LC 75-15639. 320p. 1981. pap. text 19.95 (*0-8077-2609-5*) Tchrs Coll.

Russell, David, jt. auth. see Sakai, Kunlyasu.

Russell, David, jt. ed. see Ison, Ray.

Russell, David A. Superbike. 180p. (J). (gr. 4-7). 1993. 3.95 (*1-883174-00-7*) High Octane.

Russell, David G., ed. Methods in Cell Biology Vol. 45: Microbes As Tools for Cell Biology. (Illus.). 389p. 1995. pap. 48.00 (*0-12-604040-0*); text 84.00 (*0-12-564146-X*) Acad Pr.

Russell, David H. & Russell, Elizabeth F. Listening Aids Through the Grades: 232 Listening Activities. enl. ed. LC 79-607. 191p. 1979. reprint ed. pap. 59.30 (*0-608-02758-8*, 206382100007) Bks Demand.

Russell, David H., et al. Reading Aids Through the Grades: A Guide to Materials & 501 Activities for Individualizing Reading Instruction. LC 80-23048. (Illus.). 327p. 1981. reprint ed. pap. 101.40 (*0-608-04166-1*, 206489900011) Bks Demand.

Russell, David L. Literature for Children. 160p. (C). 1991. pap. text 20.95 (*0-8013-0673-6*, 78660) Longman.

— Literature for Children. 3rd ed. 288p. (J). 1996. pap. 42.00 (*0-8013-1773-8*) Longman.

***Russell, David Lee.** The American Revolution in the Southern Colonies. (Illus.). 368p. 2000. 55.00 (*0-7864-0783-2*) McFarland & Co.

Russell, David M. The New Heavens & New Earth: Hope for the Creation in Jewish Apocalyptic & the New Testament. LC 96-60935. (Studies in Biblical Apocalyptic Literature Ser.: Vol. 1). 266, vip. (Orig.). 1996. pap. 18.00 (*1-896400-17-5*, SBAL-1) Visionary Press.

Russell, David M., jt. auth. see Gondolf, Edward W.

Russell, David O. Flirting with Disaster & Spanking the Monkey. LC 97-161345. (Illus.). 208p. (Orig.). 1997. pap. 15.95 (*0-571-19071-5*) Faber & Faber.

Russell, David R. Writing in the Academic Disciplines, 1870-1990: A Curricular History. 208p. (C). 1991. 24.95 (*0-8093-1596-3*); pap. 16.95 (*0-8093-1597-1*) S Ill U Pr.

Russell, David R., jt. ed. see Bazerman, Charles.

Russell, Dean. Government & Legal Plunder: Bastiat Brought up to Date. 116p. 1985. pap. 6.95 (*0-910614-70-9*) Foun Econ Ed.

Russell, Debbie S. Make Known His Deeds: Among the People. 190p. (Orig.). 1996. pap. 7.95 (*1-57502-373-3*, P01193) Morris Pubng.

Russell, Debby, ed. see Feuerstein, Steven.

Russell, Debby, ed. see Feuerstein, Steven, et al.

Russell, Debby, ed. see Garfinkel, Simson & Schwartz, Alan.

Russell, Debby, ed. see Kline, Kevin, et al.

Russell, Debby, ed. see Murray, James.

Russell, Debby, ed. see Theriault, Marlene & Heney, William.

Russell, Deborah, jt. auth. see Powers, Paul.

Russell, Deborah, ed. see Adams, Steve.

Russell, Deborah, ed. see Burleson, Donald K.

Russell, Deborah, ed. see Chapman, D. Brent & Zwicky, Elizabeth.

Russell, Deborah, ed. see Dye, Charles.

Russell, Deborah, ed. see Feuerstein, Steven.

Russell, Deborah, ed. see Garfinkel, Simson.

Russell, Deborah, ed. see Garfinkel, Simson & Spafford, Gene.

Russell, Deborah, ed. see Gennick, Jonathan.

Russell, Deborah, ed. see Greenwald, Rick, et al.

Russell, Deborah, ed. see Kreines, David C. & Laskey, Brian.

Russell, Deborah, ed. see Murray, James D.

Russell, Deborah, ed. see Murray, James D. & VanRyper, William.

Russell, Deborah, ed. see Odewahn, Andrew.

Russell, Deborah, ed. see Walsh, Norman.

Russell, Deborah, ed. see Zwicky, Elizabeth D., et al.

Russell, Deborah F. & Gangemi, G. T., Sr. Computer Security Basics. (Computer Science). 464p. (Orig.). 1991. pap. 29.95 (*0-937175-71-4*) Thomson Learn.

Russell, Denise. Women, Madness, & Medicine. 1995. 58.95 (*0-7456-1260-1*); pap. 26.95 (*0-7456-1261-X*) Blackwell Pubs.

Russell, Dennis. Interim Management. LC 98-11397. 320p. 1998. pap. text 46.95 (*0-7506-3977-6*) Buttrwrth-Heinemann.

Russell, Diana E. Against Pornography: The Evidence of Harm. LC 93-92610. (Illus.). 169p. 1994. pap. 12.95 (*0-9634776-1-7*) Russell CA.

— Behind Closed Doors in White South Africa. Campling, Jo, ed. LC 96-52854. 208p. 1997. pap. 19.95 (*0-312-17375-X*); text 65.00 (*0-312-17374-1*) St Martin.

— The Politics of Rape: The Victim's Perspective. LC 73-90697. 312p. 1984. pap. 10.95 (*0-8128-1860-1*, Scrbrough Hse) Madison Bks UPA.

— Rape in Marriage. enl. rev. ed. LC 89-24650. (Illus.). 462p. 1990. 39.95 (*0-253-35055-7*); pap. 16.95 (*0-253-20563-8*, MB-563) Ind U Pr.

— Rebellion, Revolution, & Armed Force: A Comparative Study of Fifteen Countries with Special Emphasis on Cuba & South Africa. LC 74-7205. (Studies in Social Discontinuity). 224p. 1974. reprint ed. pap. 69.50 (*0-608-05389-9*, AU0048800006) Bks Demand.

Russell, Diana E., ed. Exposing Nuclear Phallacies. LC 88-39941. (Athene Ser.). 352p. (C). 1989. text 40.00 (*0-08-036476-4*, Pergamon Pr); pap. text 17.95 (*0-08-036475-6*, Pergamon Pr) Elsevier.

— Exposing Nuclear Phallacies. (Athene Ser.). 352p. (C). 1989. pap. text 19.95 (*0-8077-6224-5*) Tchrs Coll.

— Making Violence Sexy: Feminist Views on Pornography. 320p. 1993. pap. 2.00 (*0-335-19200-9*) OpUniv Pr.

— Making Violence Sexy: Feminist Views on Pornography. LC 92-41999. (Athene Ser.). 320p. (C). 1993. text 46.00 (*0-8077-6269-5*); pap. text 19.95 (*0-8077-6268-7*) Tchrs Coll.

Russell, Diana E. & Van deVen, Nicole, eds. Crimes Against Women: Proceedings of the International Tribunal. LC 84-8165. (Illus.). 320p. 1984. reprint ed. pap. 7.95 (*0-9603628-5-1*) Frog in Well.

Russell, Diana E., et al. Lives of Courage: Women for a New South Africa. LC 89-42525. (Illus.). 409p. reprint ed. pap. 126.80 (*0-608-09162-6*, AU0050100005) Bks Demand.

— The Secret Trauma: Incest in the Lives of Girls & Women. LC 85-43107. 444p. reprint ed. pap. 137.70 (*0-608-09161-8*, AU00500) Bks Demand.

Russell, Diana E., jt. auth. see Radford, Jill.

R

Russell, Diana E., jt. ed. see Radford, Jill.
Russell, Diane. Jackie's Treasures. 1996. 20.00 (*0-614-19835-6*) C Potter.
Russell, Diane E. Dangerous Relationships: Pornography, Misogyny, & Rape. LC 98-8897. 1998. write for info. (*0-7619-0524-3*) Sage.
***Russell, Diane E.** Dangerous Relationships: Pornography, Misogyny, & Rape. LC 98-8897. 1998. pap. 34.94 (*0-7619-0525-1*) Sage.
Russell, Diane E. Sexual Exploitation. LC 84-6950. 319p. 1984. 59.95 (*0-8039-2354-6*) Sage.
Russell, Diane H. & Durie, Brian G. Polyamines As Biochemical Markers of Normal & Malignant Growth. fac. ed. LC 75-43340. (Progress in Cancer Research & Therapy Ser.: No. 8). (Illus.). 192p. pap. 59.60 (*0-7837-7352-8*, 204716100005) Bks Demand.
Russell, Dianne. Jackie's Treasures. Date not set. pap. 0.00 (*0-609-80204-6*) Crown Pub Group.
Russell, Dick. Black Genius & the American Experience. LC 97-34048. (Illus.). 512p. 1998. 27.50 (*0-7867-0455-1*); pap. 15.95 (*0-7867-0573-6*) Carroll & Graf.
Russell, Dinah & Sharratt, Anita. Academic Recovery after Head Injury. (Illus.). 110p. (C). 1992. text 26.95 (*0-398-05788-5*) C C Thomas.
Russell, Don. Campaigning with King: Charles King, Chronicler of the Old Army. Hedren, Paul L., ed. LC 90-12335. (Illus.). 241p. 1991. reprint ed. pap. 74.80 (*0-7837-8912-2*, 204962300002) Bks Demand.
Russell, Don, jt. auth. see Brunner, Helen M.
Russell, Donald. Humanity Affections. (Orig.). 1997. pap. 8.95 (*0-533-12253-8*) Vantage.
Russell, Donald, tr. from GRE. Selected Essays & Dialogues. LC 92-18159. (World's Classics Ser.).Tr. of Moralia. 460p. 1993. pap. 10.95 (*0-19-283094-5*) OUP.
Russell, Donald A. & Winterbottom, Michael, eds. Ancient Literary Criticism: The Principal Texts in New Translations. 624p. 1988. pap. text 39.95 (*0-19-814360-5*) OUP.
Russell, Donald A., ed. see Longinus.
Russell, Donald A., ed. see Menander.
Russell, Donald B. The Lives & Legends of Buffalo Bill. LC 60-13470. (Illus.). 1979. pap. 22.95 (*0-8061-1537-8*) U of Okla Pr.
Russell, Donald E., jt. auth. see Savage, Donald E.
Russell, Donna L., ed. see Crawford, Ann C. & Crawford, William R.
Russell, Donna L., ed. see Crawford, William R. & Crawford, Ann C.
Russell, Donna L., ed. see Crawford, William R. & Crawford, Lela A.
Russell, Donna L., ed. see Hopenwasser, Susan.
Russell, Donna V. Allegany & Garrett Counties, Maryland, Genealogical Research Guide. (Illus.). 64p. (Orig.). 1996. pap. 12.00 (*0-914385-15-1*) Catoctin Pr.
— Frederick County, Maryland, Genealogical Research Guide. 2nd ed. (Illus.). 68p. 1992. pap. 14.00 (*0-914385-05-4*) Catoctin Pr.
Russell, Donna V., ed. see Myers, Margaret E.
Russell, Dora, jt. auth. see Russell, Bertrand.
Russell, Douglas A. Costume History & Style. (Illus.). 576p. 1982. 70.00 (*0-13-181214-9*) P-H.
Russell, Douglas A., ed. An Anthology of Austrian Drama. LC 76-19836. 450p. 1982. 49.50 (*0-8386-2003-5*) Fairleigh Dickinson.
Russell, Douglas S. The Orders, Decorations & Medals of Sir Winston Churchill. Langworth, Richard M., ed. (Educational Ser.: No. 3). (Illus.). 108p. 1990. pap., per. 10.00 (*0-943879-06-X*) Churchill Ctr.
Russell, E. S. Dead Easy. 202p. 1992. 19.95 (*0-8027-3214-3*) Walker & Co.
Russell, E. S. Death of a Cloudwalker. 192p. 1991. 18.95 (*0-8027-5784-7*) Walker & Co.
Russell, E. S. Form & Function: A Contribution to the History of Animal Morphology. LC 82-8575. (Phoenix Fiction Ser.). xlii, 384p. (C). 1992. pap. text 12.00 (*0-226-73173-1*) U Ch Pr.
— Interpretation of Development & Heredity: A Study in Biological Method. LC 70-39699. (Select Bibliographies Reprint Ser.). 312p. 1977. reprint ed. 19.95 (*0-8369-9943-6*) Ayer.
Russell, E. W. & Lal, Rattan, eds. Tropical Agricultural Hydrology: Watershed Management & Land Use. LC 80-41590. (Wiley-Interscience Publications). 518p. reprint ed. pap. 160.60 (*0-7837-3226-0*, 204324300007) Bks Demand.
Russell, E. W., jt. auth. see Shafritz, Jay M.
Russell Editorial Project Group, Mc Master Univers. Contemplation & Action, 1902-1914. (Collected Papers of Bertrand Russell: Vol. 12). 654p. (C). (gr. 13). 1988. text 178.00 (*0-04-920078-X*, A9420) Routledge.
Russell, Edward J. Science & Modern Life. LC 70-117833. (Essay Index Reprint Ser.). 1977. reprint ed. 17.95 (*0-8369-2440-1*) Ayer.
— World Population & World Food Supplies. LC 76-23307. (Illus.). 513p. 1976. reprint ed. lib. bdg. 35.00 (*0-8371-8997-7*, RUWP, Greenwood Pr) Greenwood.
Russell, Edward R. & Standing, P. C. Ibsen on His Merits. LC 79-181000. (Studies in European Literature: No. 56). 1972. reprint ed. lib. bdg. 49.95 (*0-8383-1370-1*) M S G Haskell Hse.
***Russell, Edward T.** Africa to the Alps: Army Air Forces in the Mediterranean Theater. 35p. 1999. pap. 2.25 (*0-16-061386-8*) USGPO.
— Leaping the Atlantic Wall: Army Air Forces Campaigns in Western Europe, 1942-1945. 36p. 1999. pap. 2.00 (*0-16-061384-1*) USGPO.
Russell, Edward W. Prospects of Eternity: Debunking Death. 164p. (Orig.). pap. 16.95 (*0-8464-4274-4*) Beekman Pubs.
— Report on Radionics. 110p. 1974. pap. 19.95 (*0-85435-002-0*, Pub. by C W Daniel) Natl Bk Netwk.
— Report on Radionics. 6th ed. (Illus.). 256p. pap. 26.95 (*0-8464-4283-3*) Beekman Pubs.
Russell, Eleanor, jt. auth. see Rowley, Ian.
Russell, Eleanor, ed. see Vasquez, Juan.
Russell, Eleanor J., jt. auth. see McManus, Francis.
Russell, Elena. The Golden Edge: Growing up in Russian Alaska. 224p. 1996. pap. 19.95 (*0-224-04061-8*, Pub. by Jonathan Cape) Trafalgar.
Russell, Elizabeth. Adaptable Stage Costume for Women. LC 73-75920. (Illus.). 1975. pap. 14.95 (*0-87830-567-X*, Thtre Arts Bks) Routledge.
— Adaptable Stage Costume for Women: A Hundred-in-One Costumes. 2nd ed. LC 73-75920. (Illus.). 95p. 1974. pap. 16.00 (*0-85343-558-8*, Pub. by J G Miller Ltd) Empire Pub Srvs.
— Elizabeth & Her German Garden. 190p. 1989. reprint ed. lib. bdg. 21.95 (*0-89966-635-3*) Buccaneer Bks.
Russell, Elizabeth F., jt. auth. see Russell, David H.
Russell, Elliot. Conversation Made Easy. 1979. pap. 5.00 (*0-87980-024-0*) Wilshire.
Russell, Elmer B. The Review of American Colonial Legislation by the King in Council. Helmholz, R. H. & Reams, Bernard D., Jr., eds. LC 80-84869. (Historical Writings in Law & Jurisprudence Ser.: No. 21, Bk. 31). 230p. 1981. reprint ed. lib. bdg. 42.00 (*0-89941-083-9*, 302370) W S Hein.
***Russell, Emily, ed.** Art at Work: Forty Years of The Chase Manhattan Collection. (Illus.). 336p. 2000. 65.00 (*0-9635340-2-5*) Chase Manhattan.
Russell, Emily, ed. see Phillips, Lisa.
Russell, Emily W. People & the Land Through Time: Linking Ecology & History. LC 96-37098. (Illus.). 320p. 1997. 40.00 (*0-300-06830-1*); pap. 17.00 (*0-300-07730-0*) Yale U Pr.
Russell, Emily W., jt. ed. see Collins, Beryl R.
Russell, Enid. A History of the Law in Western Australia & Its Development from 1829-1979. Robinson, F. M. & Nichols, P. W., eds. 413p. 1994. 34.95 (*0-85564-171-1*, Pub. by Univ of West Aust Pr) Intl Spec Bk.
Russell, Eric Frank. Men, Martians & Machines. 1993. reprint ed. lib. bdg. 18.95 (*0-89968-360-6*, Lghtyr Pr) Buccaneer Bks.
Russell, Eric Frank, jt. auth. see Foster, Alan Dean.
Russell, Eric J., et al. Neuroradiology Test & Syllabus Second Series: Test & Syllabus, Vol. 42, Series 2. LC 98-3648. (Professional Self-Evaluation Program Ser.: Vol. 42). (Illus.). 600p. 1998. 220.00 (*1-55903-042-9*) Am Coll Radiology.
Russell, Eric William. Wheels & Things: 1930s, 1940s, Places, Transport, Friends, People, Adverts, Events. LC 97-122289. 56p. (Orig.). 1996. pap. write for info. (*1-85858-093-5*) Brewin Bks.
Russell, Etta M. Basic Principles of Constitutional Money: A Textbook for High Schools & the General Public on the Federal Reserve Conspiracy. 1980. lib. bdg. 59.95 (*0-8490-3096-X*) Gordon Pr.
***Russell, Evan, et al.** Data-Driven Methods for Fault Detection & Diagnosis in Chemical Processes. LC 00-27317. (Advances in Industrial Control Ser.). (Illus.). xiii, 192p. 2000. 84.00 (*1-85233-258-1*) Spr-Verlag.
Russell, F. E., jt. auth. see Nagabhushanam, Rachakonda.
Russell, F. S. Advances in Marine Biology, Vol. 21. (Serial Publication Ser.). 1984. text 99.00 (*0-12-026121-9*) Acad Pr.
Russell, F. S., ed. Advances in Marine Biology, Vol. 16. (Serial Publication Ser.). 1979. text 99.00 (*0-12-026116-2*) Acad Pr.
Russell, Findlay. Snake Venom Poisoning. rev. ed. LC 83-3134. (Illus.). 576p. 1983. text 57.50 (*0-87936-015-1*) Scholium Intl.
Russell, Ford. Northrop Frye on Myth: An Introduction. LC 97-18441. (Theorists of Myth Ser.: Vol. 10). (Illus.). 245p. 1998. text 47.00 (*0-8240-3446-5*, H1166) Garland.
Russell, Frances. Three Studies in Twentieth Century Obscurity: Joyce, Kafka, Gertrude Stein. LC 68-658. (Studies in Comparative Literature: No. 35). (C). 1969. reprint ed. lib. bdg. 75.00 (*0-8383-0678-0*) M S G Haskell Hse.
Russell, Francine, jt. auth. see Chaiet, Donna.
Russell, Francis. The Secret War: World War II. Constable, George, ed. (Illus.). 208p. 1998. text 30.00 (*0-7881-5632-2*) DIANE Pub.
— Three Studies in Twentieth Century Obscurity. 1973. lib. bdg. 200.00 (*0-87968-046-6*) Gordon Pr.
Russell, Francis & Time-Life Books Editors. The Secret War LC 81-9382. (World War II Ser.). 208p. 1981. write for info. (*0-8094-2549-1*) Time-Life.
Russell, Francis G., tr. see Gill, A. L. & Gill, Joyce.
Russell, Frank. Explorations in the Far North. LC 74-5873. reprint ed. 43.50 (*0-404-11682-5*) AMS Pr.
Russell, Frank, ed. Terry Farrell: An Academy Architectural Monograph. (Illus.). 120p. 1985. pap. 24.95 (*0-312-79286-7*) St Martin.
Russell, Frank A. American Pilgrimage. LC 72-167408. (Essay Index Reprint Ser.). 1977. reprint ed. 25.95 (*0-8369-2715-X*) Ayer.
Russell, Frank C. Carving Folk Figures with Power. LC 95-11074. (Illus.). 64p. (Orig.). 1995. pap. 12.95 (*0-88740-854-0*) Schiffer.
— Carving Realistic Animals with Power. LC 94-66201. (Illus.). 64p. (Orig.). 1994. pap. 12.95 (*0-88740-637-8*) Schiffer.
— Carving Vermont Folk Figures, Bk. 1. (Illus.). 80p. (Orig.). 1989. pap. 8.95 (*0-685-29438-2*) Stonegate Studios.
Russell, Frank M. Theories of International Relations. LC 72-4297. (World Affairs Ser.: National & International Viewpoints). 658p. 1972. reprint ed. 44.95 (*0-405-04588-3*) Ayer.
***Russell, Frank S.** Information Gathering in Classical Greece. LC 99-47317. (Illus.). 280p. 2000. text 49.50 (*0-472-11064-0*, 11064) U of Mich Pr.
Russell, Frazier. Fweivel: The Day Will Come. 40p. (Orig.). 1996. pap. text 8.00 (*1-56439-059-4*) Ridgeway.
Russell, G., ed. Computer Aided Tools for VLSI System Design. (Computing Ser.: No. 9). 208p. 1987. write for info. (*0-86341-093-6*, CM009) INSPEC Inc.
Russell, G., jt. ed. see Taylor, G. E.
Russell, G. Hugh & Black, Kenneth, Jr. Human Behavior & Life Insurance. 262p. pap. text 40.00 (*1-57974-062-6*, Pub. by Life Office) PBD Inc.
Russell, G. L. & Mann, K. Introductory AC Circuit Theory. 208p. pap. 21.95 (*0-86840-073-4*, Pub. by New South Wales Univ Pr) Intl Spec Bk.
Russell, G. W. An Account of Some of the Descendants of John Russell, Who Came to Boston, 1635: Together with Some Sketches of the Allied Families of Wadsworth, Tuttle, & Beresford. Welles, E. S., ed. (Illus.). 318p. 1989. reprint ed. pap. 47.50 (*0-8328-1041-X*); reprint ed. lib. bdg. 57.50 (*0-8328-1040-1*) Higginson Bk Co.
Russell, Gardner H. The Effective Entrepreneur: How to Make Bad Guys Finish Last. LC 98-9688. 211p. 1999. pap. 14.95 (*0-9668238-0-X*) Advantage Pubg.
Russell, Garfield B. Alternate-Site Anesthesia: Clinical Practice Outside the Operating Room. LC 97-11403. 472p. 1997. text 78.50 (*0-7506-9817-9*) Buttrwrth-Heinemann.
Russell, Garfield B. & Rodichok, Lawrence D. Primer of Intraoperative Neurophysiologic Monitoring. LC 95-12875. 331p. 1995. text 69.95 (*0-7506-9553-6*) Buttrwrth-Heinemann.
Russell, Garfield B., jt. auth. see Blackburn, Terri W.
***Russell, Garrison R.** The Book of Isaiah: Collated by Chronological Topic. (Illus.). 128p. 1999. pap. write for info. (*0-9660131-2-3*) Xulon Pub.
Russell, Garrison R. Sonplacing: A Handbook for Warriors. rev. ed. LC 98-90252. (Illus.). 768p. (Orig.). 1998. pap. write for info. (*0-9660131-1-5*) Xulon Pub.
Russell, Garth S. Care of the Low Back: A Patient Guide. 1991. 19.95 (*0-9625923-0-7*) G S Russell.
Russell, Gary. Business Unusual. (Doctor Who Ser.). 1998. pap. 5.95 (*0-563-40575-9*) BBC.
— Dead Fall. (Orig.). 1997. mass mkt. 5.95 (*0-426-20513-8*, Pub. by Virgin Bks) London Brdge.
— Divided Loyalties. 1999. mass mkt. 6.95 (*0-563-55578-5*) BBC.
— Placebo Effect. 1998. pap. 5.95 (*0-563-40587-2*) BBC.
Russell, Gary, jt. auth. see Roberts, Gareth.
Russell, Gene H. Handcrafted Cachets, the Make Your Own Cachet & Envelope Handbook. 3rd ed. 110p. (Orig.). 1993. pap. 13.95 (*1-879390-15-9*) AFDCS.
Russell, Geoff. Legends of the Fairway: Great Women Golfers Tell How to Play the Game. 1997. 22.00 (*0-671-54510-8*) PB.
Russell, Geoffrey. Offshore Helicopter Operations. (Illus.). 360p. 1997. pap. 162.00 (*1-870945-87-5*) Oilfield Publns.
Russell, George. World Regional Geography Readings. (C). 1993. pap. text 17.29 (*1-56870-083-0*) RonJon Pub.
Russell, George & Kane, George, eds. Piers Plowman: The C Version. LC 96-45499. 1997. 155.00 (*0-520-21058-1*, Pub. by U CA Pr) Cal Prin Full Svc.
Russell, George E. Moravian Families of Carroll's Manor, Frederick County, Maryland. 2nd ed. (Illus.). 150p. (Orig.). 1996. pap. 19.00 (*0-914385-07-0*) Catoctin Pr.
— Powell Family of Allegany County, Maryland: Descendants of William Powell & Ann (Chambers) Powell of Timsbury, Somersetshire, England. (Illus.). 117p. (Orig.). 1990. pap. 16.00 (*0-914385-12-7*) Catoctin Pr.
— Washington County, Maryland, Genealogical Research Guide. (Illus.). 48p. 1993. pap. 11.00 (*0-914385-14-3*) Catoctin Pr.
Russell, George K. Vivisection & the True Aims of Education in Biology. 3rd ed. 14p. (gr. 8-12). 1971. pap. 0.75 (*0-913098-30-2*) Orion Society.
Russell, George L. Map of American Indian Nations. 3rd ed. (J). (gr. 6 up). 1993. pap. 15.00 (*1-881933-02-4*) Russell Pub AZ.
Russell, George M. The Collector's Guide to Civil War Period Bottles & Jars. 2nd ed. (Illus.). 96p. 1993. pap. 15.95 (*1-880365-27-8*) Prof Pr NC.
Russell, George W. Afterthoughts. LC 68-16975. (Essay Index Reprint Ser.). 1977. reprint ed. 23.95 (*0-8369-0843-0*) Ayer.
— The Ascending Cycle. (Sangam Texts Ser.). 105p. (Orig.). 1983. pap. 12.75 (*0-88695-013-9*) Concord Grove.
— Descent of the Gods: The Mystical Writings of G. W. Russell - A. E. Iyer, Nandini, ed. LC 88-51545. 780p. 1989. 75.00 (*0-900675-44-6*, Pub. by Smyth) Dufour.
— The Descent of the Gods: The Mystical Writings of G. W. Russell - A.E. Iyer, Raghavan N. & Iyer, Nandini, eds. LC 88-51545. 780p. 1988. 85.00 (*0-901072-44-3*, Pub. by Smyth) Dufour.
— Half-Lengths. LC 71-128309. (Essay Index Reprint Ser.). 1977. 23.95 (*0-8369-1849-5*) Ayer.
— Matthew Arnold. LC 71-130250. (English Literature Ser.: No. 33). 1970. reprint ed. lib. bdg. 75.00 (*0-8383-1140-7*) M S G Haskell Hse.
— Politics & Personalities, with Other Essays. (Essay Index Reprint Ser.). 1977. 23.95 (*0-8369-0844-9*) Ayer.
— Portraits of the Seventies. LC 73-117834. (Essay Index Reprint Ser.). 1977. 24.95 (*0-8369-1717-0*) Ayer.
Russell, George W., ed. see Arnold, Matthew.
***Russell, Gillean.** Finding the Right Retreat for You. 64p. 1999. pap. 22.00 (*1-85608-118-4*, Pub. by Hunt GBR) St Mut.
Russell, Gillian. The Theatres of War: Performance, Politics & Society, 1793-1815. (Illus.). 224p. 1995. text 55.00 (*0-19-812263-2*) OUP.
***Russell, Ginny.** The Money Boot. (First Flight Ser.). (Illus.). 64p. (J). 1999. pap. 3.95 (*1-55041-370-8*) Fitzhenry & W Ltd.
Russell, Glenn. The Plantings. (Illus.). 47p. (Orig.). 1989. pap. 3.00 (*0-926935-34-8*) Runaway Spoon.
Russell, Gordon W. The Social Psychology of Sport. LC 92-34893. (Illus.). 336p. 1994. 48.95 (*0-387-97792-9*) Spr-Verlag.
Russell, Graham. Essential Psychology for Nurses & Other Health Professionals. LC 98-36107. 1999. 75.00 (*0-415-18888-1*); pap. 24.99 (*0-415-18889-X*) Routledge.
Russell, Graham, et al, eds. Plant Canopies: Their Growth, Form & Function. (Society for Experimental Biology Seminar Ser.: No. 31). 188p. (C). 1990. pap. text 29.95 (*0-521-39563-1*) Cambridge U Pr.
Russell, Grahame. Unearthing the Truth: Exhuming a Decade of Terror in Guatemala. Kee, Sarah & Butwell, Ann, eds. (Illus.). 48p. (Orig.). 1996. pap. 5.00 (*0-918346-16-9*) EPICA.
Russell, Greg. Hans J. Morgenthau & the Ethics of American Statecraft. LC 90-5675. (Political Traditions in Foreign Policy Ser.). 288p. 1990. text 42.50 (*0-8071-1618-1*) La State U Pr.
— John Quincy Adams & the Public Virtues of Diplomacy. 304p. 1994. text 42.50 (*0-8262-0984-X*) U of Mo Pr.
Russell, Gregory D. The Death Penalty & Racial Bias: Overturning Supreme Court Assumptions, 75. LC 93-25069. (Contributions in Legal Studies: No. 75). 184p. 1993. 55.00 (*0-313-28889-5*, GM8889, Greenwood Pr) Greenwood.
Russell, Gregory D., jt. auth. see Conser, James A.
Russell, H. Diane. Eva-Ave: Woman in Renaissance & Baroque Prints. LC 90-15521. 240p. 1990. pap. 29.95 (*1-55861-040-5*) Feminist Pr.
— Eva-Ave: Woman in Renaissance & Baroque Prints. LC 90-15521. (Illus.). 238p. 1990. pap. 7.95 (*0-89468-157-5*) Natl Gallery Art.
— Eva/Ave: Woman in Renaissance & Baroque Prints. LC 90-15521. 240p. 1990. 59.95 (*1-55861-039-1*) Feminist Pr.
Russell, Hannah. Songs about the Sky. rev. ed. (Illus.). 18p. (J). 1988. reprint ed. pap. 4.50 (*0-9614089-2-8*) Avitar Bks.
Russell, Hanon W., tr. see Tal, Mikhail.
Russell, Harold E. & Beigel, Allan. Understanding Human Behavior for Effective Police Work. 3rd ed. LC 90-80676. 464p. 1990. pap. 42.00 (*0-465-08859-7*, Pub. by Basic) HarpC.
Russell, Harry K., et al, eds. Literature in English. LC 73-132139. (Play Anthology Reprint Ser.). 1977. 51.95 (*0-8369-8218-5*) Ayer.
Russell, Helen. Pediatric Drugs & Nursing Intervention. (Illus.). 1979. text 20.95 (*0-07-054298-8*) McGraw.
Russell, Helen D. Come in This House. 230p. (J). (gr. 6-12). 1982. lib. bdg. 15.95 (*0-934188-07-6*) Evans Pubns.
Russell, Helen R. Ten Minute Field Trips. 3rd ed. LC 90-63468. (Illus.). 176p. 1998. reprint ed. pap. text 19.95 (*0-87355-098-6*, PB020X) Natl Sci Tchrs.
Russell, Henry G., ed. High-Strength Concrete. LC 85-71930. (American Concrete Institute, Publication: No. SP-87). (Illus.). 288p. 1985. reprint ed. pap. 89.30 (*0-7837-9999-3*, 206072600006) Bks Demand.
***Russell, Herbert K.** Edgar Lee Masters: A Biography. LC 00-9471. 2001. write for info. (*0-252-02616-0*) U of Ill Pr.
Russell, Herbert K. A Southern Illinois Album: Farm Security Administration Photographs, 1936-1943. LC 89-6241. (Illus.). 160p. (C). 1990. pap. text 19.95 (*0-8093-1589-0*) S Ill U Pr.
Russell, Herbert K., ed. see Earle, Mary T.
Russell, Herbert K., ed. see Horrell, C. William.
Russell, Hilary. Giving up the House. (Illus.). 28p. (Orig.). 1993. pap. 10.00 (*0-944156-08-8*) Mad River MA.
— Giving up the House. deluxe ed. (Illus.). 28p. (Orig.). 1993. pap. 20.00 (*0-685-71065-3*) Mad River MA.
— The Portable Writer. 2nd ed. 128p. (YA). (gr. 9-12). 1998. pap. text 9.33 (*1-877653-47-0*) Wayside Pub.
Russell, Hilary, ed. The Anthology of American Poetry: Colonial to Contemporary. Orig. Title: The Longman Anthology of American Poetry. (Illus.). 328p. (YA). (gr. 10-12). 1992. reprint ed. pap. text 18.60 (*1-877653-49-7*) Wayside Pub.
***Russell, Horace O.** The Missionary Outreach of the West Indian Church: Jamaican Baptist Missions to West Africa in the Nineteenth Century. (Research in Religion & Family Ser.: Vol. 3). 344p. 2000. pap. text 38.95 (*0-8204-3063-3*) P Lang Pubng.
Russell, Howard S. Indian New England Before the Mayflower. LC 79-63082. (Illus.). 296p. 1980. pap. 19.95 (*0-87451-255-7*) U Pr of New Eng.
— A Long, Deep Furrow: Three Centuries of Farming in New England. abr. ed. Lapping, Mark, ed. & abr. by. LC 81-51605. (Illus.). 394p. 1982. pap. 24.95 (*0-87451-214-X*) U Pr of New Eng.
— A Long, Deep Furrow: 3 Centuries of Farming in New England. LC 73-91314. 688p. reprint ed. 200.00 (*0-608-16641-3*, 202753400055) Bks Demand.
— Parrots. 64p. Date not set. 12.95 (*0-7938-0329-2*) TFH Pubns.
Russell, I., jt. auth. see Stewart, G. G.
Russell, I. F., jt. ed. see Lyons, G.
Russell, I. John, jt. auth. see Fransen, Jenny.
Russell, I. Jon, ed. Clinical Overview & Pathogenesis of the Fibromyalgia Syndrome, Myofascial Pain Syndrome, & Other Pain Syndromes. LC 96-7347. (Journal of Musculoskeletal Pain Ser.: Vol. 4, No. 1/2). 254p. (C). 1996. 39.95 (*1-56024-833-5*, Hawrth Medical) Haworth Pr.
— Myopain '95: Abstracts from the 3rd World Congress of

An Asterisk (*) at the beginning of an entry indicates that the title is appearing for the first time.

R

Myofacial Pain & Fibromyalgia, San Antonio, Texas, U. S. A. July 30-August 3, 1995. LC 95-23108. 1995. 35.00 (*0-7890-0000-8*, Hawrth Medical) Haworth Pr.

Russell, I. Willis, ed. see McMillan, James B.

Russell, Ian, jt. auth. see Povey, Glenn.

Russell-Ides, Isabella. Getting Dangerously Close to Myself. 90p. (Orig.). 1987. pap. 7.95 (*0-941720-39-X*); lib. bdg. 13.95 (*0-941720-40-3*) Slough Pr TX.

Russell, Ina Dillard. Roots & Ever Green: The Selected Letters of Ina Dillard Russell. Russell, Sally, ed. LC 99-25068. (Illus.). 376p. 1999. 34.95 (*0-8203-2138-9*) U of Ga Pr.

Russell, Ingrid, jt. ed. see Kumar, Amruth.

Russell, Isaac F. Outline Study of Law. 2nd ed. LC 97-28836. xii, 280p. 1997. reprint ed. 45.00 (*0-8377-2584-4*, Rothman) W S Hein.

Russell, Isabel. Katharine & E. B. White. 1990. pap. 8.95 (*0-393-30638-0*) Norton.

Russell, J. Performance & Stability of Aircraft. LC 96-207392. 294p. 1996. pap. 64.95 (*0-470-23598-5*) Wiley.

Russell, J. A., et al, eds. Industrial Operations under Extremes of Weather. (Meteorological Monograph: Vol. 2, No. 9). (Illus.). 121p. 1957. pap. 17.00 (*0-933876-04-1*) Am Meteorological.

Russell, J. A., et al. The Blank Page. LC 97-65798. 140p. (Orig.). 1997. pap. 10.95 (*0-9654194-1-X*) Oasis in Print.

Russell, J. B. Dissent & Order in the Middle Ages. (Twayne's Studies in Intellectual & Cultural History). 200p. (Orig.). (C). 1992. pap. 14.95 (*0-8057-8628-7*, Twyne); text 22.95 (*0-8057-8603-1*, Twyne) Mac Lib Ref.

Russell, J. H. A Pictorial Record of Great Western Absorbed Engines. 288p. 1986. 65.00 (*0-902888-74-9*) St Mut.

Russell, J. K., jt. ed. see Nicholls, J.

Russell, J. M., jt. auth. see Alvarez-Leefmans, F. J.

Russell, J. P. Quality Management Benchmark Assessment. 2nd ed. 171p. 1995. spiral bd. 24.00 (*0-87389-332-8*, H0890) ASQ Qual Pr.

— Quality Management Benchmark Assessment. 2nd rev. ed. 192p. 1995. spiral bd. 24.00 (*0-527-76295-4*) Productivity Inc.

Russell, J. P., ed. The Quality Audit Handbook. LC 96-47516. 218p. 1997. 45.00 (*0-87389-374-3*, H0939) ASQ Qual Pr.

Russell, J. P. & Regel, Terry. After the Quality Audit: Closing the Loop on the Audit Process. 230p. 1996. 38.00 (*0-87389-365-4*, H0927) ASQ Qual Pr.

***Russell, J. P. & Regel, Terry.** After the Quality Audit: Closing the Loop on the Audit Process. 2nd ed. LC 00-26672. 2000. write for info. (*0-87389-486-3*) ASQ Qual Pr.

***Russell, J. P. & Russell, Janice.** Puzzling Auditing Puzzles. LC 00-21479. 2000. write for info. (*0-87389-478-2*) ASQ Qual Pr.

Russell, J. P. & Russell, Janice. Puzzling Quality Puzzles. (Illus.). 200p. 1998. pap. 10.00 (*0-87389-425-1*, H0993) ASQ Qual Pr.

Russell, J. S. & Isbell, R. F., eds. Australian Soils: The Human Impact. LC 85-16514. (Illus.). 522p. 1987. text 50.00 (*0-7022-1968-1*, Pub. by Univ Queensland Pr) Intl Spec Bk.

Russell, J. Stephen. Chaucer & the Trivium: The Mindsong of the Canberbury Tales. LC 98-42118. 224p. 1998. 49.95 (*0-8130-1637-1*) U Press Fla.

Russell, J. Stuart. The Parousia: The New Testament Doctrine of Our Lord?s Second Coming. 608p. (Orig.). (C). (gr. 8 up). 1999. reprint ed. pap. 24.99 (*0-8010-7725-7*) Baker Bks.

Russell, J. Thomas & Lane, W. Ronald. Kleppner's Advertising Procedure. 12th ed. LC 92-25490. 752p. 1992. teacher ed. write for info. (*0-13-517574-7*) Prntice Hall Bks.

Russell, J. Thomas, jt. auth. see Lane, W. Ronald.

***Russell, Jack.** Streetwise Subbie. 2nd ed. 80p. 2000. pap. 17.95 (*0-7506-5029-X*, Newnes) Buttrwrth-Heinemann.

Russell, Jack M. Symbols Unveiled. 275p. 1996. pap. 12.00 (*0-9664102-0-3*) Jack Russell.

— Symbols Unveiled. 1998. pap. text. write for info. (*0-9664102-2-X*) Jack Russell.

— Victory over the Inner Conflict. 28p. 1965. pap. 3.00 (*0-9664102-1-1*) Jack Russell.

Russell, Jack P. Business Programming Logic & Design. LC 93-43817. 768p. (C). 1997. pap. text 80.00 (*0-673-46840-2*) Addson-Wesley Educ.

Russell, Jacqui, ed. File on Coward. (Methuen Writer-Files Ser.). 96p. (C). 1988. pap. write for info. (*0-413-58600-6*, A0094, Methuen Drama) Methn.

Russell, James. Autism as an Executive Disorder. LC 97-37721. (Illus.). 328p. 1998. text 90.00 (*0-19-852349-1*) OUP.

— God of Miracles: Your Miracle Begins. 228p. 2001. pap. 34.95 (*0-916367-16-9*, GOM) James Russell.

***Russell, James.** Intelligent Internet Marketing: Developing a Powerful Selling Website. (Illus.). 180p. 2001. pap. 34.95 (*0-916367-21-5*, IIM) James Russell.

— Internet Address Book & Back up Files: What Every Computer User Needs. 70p. 2000. pap. 12.95 (*0-916367-20-7*) James Russell.

— Joey: A Comedy Screenplay of a Dysfunctional Family. 118p. 1999. pap. 34.95 (*0-916367-30-4*, JOEYMOVIE) James Russell.

Russell, James. Marx-Engels Dictionary. LC 80-786. (Illus.). 140p. 1980. lib. bdg. 59.95 (*0-313-22035-2*, RME/, Greenwood Pr) Greenwood.

— Museums, Vol. 1. (Twentieth-Century Ser.). 1999. 19.95 (*0-7148-3878-0*) Phaidon Pr.

— Museums, Vol. 2. (Twentieth-Century Ser.). 1999. 19.95 (*0-7148-3879-9*) Phaidon Pr.

***Russell, James.** Mystic Forest: A Fantasy Quest Screenplay for Children. 118p. 1999. pap. 34.95 (*0-916367-27-4*, MF) James Russell.

— Places of Worship. (Architecture 3s Ser.). 1999. 19.95 (*0-7148-3877-2*) Phaidon Pr.

Russell, James. Precision Shooting - The Trapshooter's Bible. (Illus.). 220p. 1998. pap. 34.95 (*0-916367-10-X*, PS) James Russell.

***Russell, James.** Revenge of the Grannies: A Comedy Screenplay of Military Power. 118p. 1999. pap. 34.95 (*0-916367-25-8*, ROG) James Russell.

Russell, James. Screen & Stage Marketing Secrets: Selling Your Screen Play. (Illus.). 180p. 2000. pap. text 34.95 (*0-916367-11-8*, SS) James Russell.

***Russell, James.** Stage Play: A Theatrical Comedy Play of Couples Seeking Marriage. 130p. 1999. pap. 34.95 (*0-916367-34-7*, SP) James Russell.

Russell, James. Steam & Diesel Power Plant Operators Examinations: For Stationary Engineers. 3rd rev. ed. (Illus.). 110p. 1997. pap. 34.95 (*0-916367-08-8*, SD) James Russell.

***Russell, James.** Tough Beat: A Prison Screenplay Based on True Events. 118p. 1999. pap. 34.95 (*0-916367-29-0*, TBT) James Russell.

Russell, James. Trap Shooting Secrets. (Illus.). 182p. 1997. pap. 34.95 (*0-916367-09-6*, TSS) James Russell.

***Russell, James.** True Bums: A Comedy Screenplay about the Railroads. 118p. 1999. pap. 34.95 (*0-916367-26-6*, T-BUMS) James Russell.

— Vortex: A Movie Script of Government Corruption. 110p. 1999. pap. 34.95 (*0-916367-28-2*, Vortex Movie) James Russell.

Russell, James, jt. auth. see Corinchock, Drew.

Russell, James, jt. ed. see Zinkel, Duane F.

Russell, James, ed. & illus. see Rossi, Luca S.

Russell, James A., ed. Everyday Conceptions of Emotion: An Introduction to the Psychology, Anthropology & Linguistics of Emotion. LC 95-13602. (NATO ASI Ser., Series D, Behavioural & Social Sciences). 1995. lib. bdg. 276.00 (*0-7923-3479-5*) Kluwer Academic.

Russell, James A. & Fernandez-Dols, Jose-Miguel, eds. The Psychology of Facial Expression. LC 96-36250. (Studies in Emotion & Social Interaction). (Illus.). 413p. (C). 1997. text 74.95 (*0-521-49667-5*); pap. text 29.95 (*0-521-58796-4*) Cambridge U Pr.

Russell, James A. & Walley, Keith R., eds. Acute Respiratory Distress Syndrome: A Comprehensive Clinical Approach. LC 98-46408. (Illus.). 336p. (C). 1999. pap. text 49.95 (*0-521-65410-6*) Cambridge U Pr.

Russell, James C. The Germanization of Early Medieval Christianity: A Sociohistorical Approach to Religious Transformation. LC 92-13182. 272p. (C). 1994. text 60.00 (*0-19-507696-6*) OUP.

— Tom, the Orphan Cat. (Illus.). (J). (gr. 3-5). 1996. 7.95 (*0-533-11445-4*) Vantage.

Russell, James D. The Audio-Tutorial System. Langdon, Danny G., ed. LC 77-25454. (Instructional Design Library). (Illus.). 80p. 1978. 27.95 (*0-87778-107-9*) Educ Tech Pubns.

Russell, James D., ed. see Hughes, Leonard V., Jr.

Russell, James E. Methods & Materials of Residential Construction. (Illus.). 368p. (C). 1985. text 29.00 (*0-685-09097-3*) P-H.

Russell, James M. Atlanta, 1847-1890: City Building in the Old South & the New. LC 87-29946. (Illus.). xiii, 314p. 1988. text 42.50 (*0-8071-1413-8*) La State U Pr.

Russell, James O. & Smelser, Georgia. The Coal Miner Preacher: A Testimony of Faith, Healings, Miracles, Angels, & Prophecies. LC 93-23506. 150p. (Orig.). 1993. pap. 7.99 (*1-56722-014-2*) Word Aflame.

Russell, James R. Zoroastrianism in Armenia. LC 87-18147. (Harvard Iranian Ser.: No. 5). (Illus.). 584p. (Orig.). 1988. pap. 39.95 (*0-674-96850-6*) HUP.

Russell, James R., ed. Matean Voghberkowtean: The Book of Lamentations, Gregory Narekatzi. LC 81-6177. 416p. 1982. 50.00 (*0-88206-029-5*) Caravan Bks.

Russell, James S. The Parousia: A Critical Inquiry into the New Testament Doctrine of Our Lord's Second Coming. 561p. (Orig.). 1996. reprint ed. pap. 16.95 (*0-9621311-3-X*) Intl Preterist Assn.

***Russell, James S.** Studios Architecture: The Power of the Pragmatic. 2000. pap. 40.00 (*88-7838-056-3*) L'Arca IT.

Russell, James W. After the Fifth Sun: Class & Race in North America. LC 93-38544. 216p. 1994. pap. text 38.80 (*0-13-036237-9*) P-H.

Russell, James W. Introduction to Macrosociology. 2nd ed. LC 95-8748. 271p. (C). 1995. pap. text 26.00 (*0-13-228230-5*) P-H.

Russell, Jan J. & Smith, Cathy. San Antonio: A Cultural Tapestry. LC 98-6742. (Urban Tapestry Ser.). (Illus.). 208p. 1998. 44.95 (*1-881096-55-6*) Towery Pub.

Russell, Jan Jarboe. Lady Bird: A Biography of Mrs. Johnson. LC 99-27544. (Lisa Drew Book Ser.). 352p. 1999. 25.50 (*0-684-81480-3*) S&S Trade.

***Russell, Jan Jarboe.** Lady Bird: A Biography of Mrs. Johnson. large type ed. LC 99-57106. (Biography Ser.). 632p. 2000. 26.95 (*0-7862-2359-6*, MML06500-171537) Thorndike Pr.

Russell, Jane. James Starkey-Seumas O'Sullivan: A Critical Biography. LC 85-45951. (Illus.). 152p. 1987. 29.50 (*0-8386-3265-3*) Fairleigh Dickinson.

***Russell, Jane.** Marilyn Monroe & the Camera. (Illus.). 245p. 2000. pap. 35.00 (*3-8238-5467-4*) te Neues.

Russell, Janice. Goldilocks. LC 95-83166. (Illus.). 32p. (J). (ps up). 1997. 8.95 (*1-56397-430-4*) Boyds Mills Pr.

— Out of Bounds: Sexual Exploitation in Counselling & Therapy. (Illus.). 160p. (C). 1993. text 69.95 (*0-8039-8533-9*); pap. text 22.95 (*0-8039-8534-7*) Sage.

Russell, Janice, jt. auth. see Russell, J. P.

Russell, Jaqueline E., ed. Satellite Remote Sensing of Clouds & the Atmosphere III. LC 99-218324. (Europto Ser.: Vol. 3495). 1998. 99.00 (*0-8194-2954-6*) SPIE.

***Russell, Jaqueline E., ed.** Satellite Remote Sensing of Clouds & the Atmosphere IV. 1999. pap. text 103.00 (*0-8194-3462-0*) SPIE.

Russell, Jay S. Booty Boys. 1999. pap. text 10.95 (*0-352-33446-0*) London Brdge.

— Burning Bright. LC 98-14721. 288p. 1998. text 23.95 (*0-312-18545-6*) St Martin.

***Russell, Jay S.** Waltzes & Whispers. 305p. 1999. 28.00 (*1-901914-16-X*, Pub. by Pumpkin Bks) Firebird Dist.

Russell, Jean, jt. ed. see Batten, Margaret.

Russell, Jeffrey B. The Devil: Perceptions of Evil from Antiquity to Primitive Christianity. LC 77-3126. (Illus.). 288p. 1987. pap. text 15.95 (*0-8014-9409-5*) Cornell U Pr.

— Dissent & Reform in the Early Middle Ages. LC 78-63178. (Heresies of the Early Christian & Medieval Era Ser.: Second Ser.). 344p. reprint ed. 36.00 (*0-404-16196-0*) AMS Pr.

— A History of Heaven. 1999. pap. 14.95 (*0-691-00684-9*, Pub. by Princeton U Pr) Cal Prin Full Svc.

— A History of Heaven: The Singing Silence. LC 96-41002. 252p. 1997. 24.95 (*0-691-01161-3*, Pub. by Princeton U Pr) Cal Prin Full Svc.

— A History of Witchcraft: Sorcerers, Heretics & Pagans. 1983. 26.50 (*0-8446-6052-3*) Peter Smith.

— A History of Witchcraft: Sorcerers, Heretics & Pagans. (Illus.). 1982. pap. 15.95 (*0-500-27242-5*, Pub. by Thames Hudson) Norton.

— Inventing the Flat Earth: Columbus & Modern Historians. 160p. 1997. pap. 15.95 (*0-275-95904-X*, Praeger Pubs) Greenwood.

— Lucifer: The Devil in the Middle Ages. LC 84-45153. (Illus.). 356p. 1986. pap. text 16.95 (*0-8014-9429-X*) Cornell U Pr.

— Mephistopheles: The Devil in the Modern World. LC 86-47648. (Illus.). 352p. 1990. reprint ed. pap. text 16.95 (*0-8014-9718-3*) Cornell U Pr.

— The Prince of Darkness: Radical Evil & the Power of Good in History. LC 88-47744. (Illus.). 304p. 1992. pap. 14.95 (*0-8014-8056-6*) Cornell U Pr.

— Satan: The Early Christian Tradition. LC 81-66649. (Illus.). 258p. 1981. text 42.50 (*0-8014-1267-6*) Cornell U Pr.

— Satan: The Early Christian Tradition. LC 81-66649. (Illus.). 258p. 1987. pap. 14.95 (*0-8014-9413-3*) Cornell U Pr.

— Witchcraft in the Middle Ages. LC 72-37755. 394p. 1984. text 47.50 (*0-8014-0697-8*); pap. text 16.95 (*0-8014-9289-0*) Cornell U Pr.

Russell, Jeffrey B., jt. auth. see Berkhout, Carl T.

Russell, Jeffrey B., jt. auth. see Ferreiro, Alberto.

***Russell, Jeffrey Burton & Lumsden, Douglas W.** A History of Medieval Christianity: Prophesy & Order. LC 99-29432. 216p. (C). 2000. pap. text 26.95 (*0-8204-4511-8*) P Lang Pubng.

Russell, Jeffrey S. Constructor Prequalification: Choosing the Best Constructor & Avoiding Constructor Failure. 208p. 1996. 30.00 (*0-614-16821-X*) Am Soc Civil Eng.

— Constructor Prequalification: Selecting the Most Qualified Constructor & Avoiding Constructor Failure. LC 95-47745. 208p. 1996. 32.00 (*0-7844-0052-0*) Am Soc Civil Eng.

***Russell, Jeremy L.** Dharamsala: Tibetan Refuge. (Illus.). 96p. 2000. 19.95 (*0-89346-920-3*) Heian Intl.

Russell, Jeremy L. Geopolitics of Natural Gas. LC 83-2670. 208p. 1983. text 32.00 (*0-88410-610-1*, HarpBusn) HarpInfo.

Russell, Jerry L. 1876 Facts about Custer & the Battle of the Little Bighorn. (Facts about History Ser.: Vol. 3). (Illus.). 264p. 1999. pap. 11.95 (*1-882810-34-1*) Savas Pub.

***Russell, Jewel.** Jewels Gems. 1999. pap. write for info. (*1-58235-292-5*) Watermrk Pr.

Russell, Jill F., jt. auth. see Pratzner, Frank C.

Russell, Jim, jt. auth. see Watson, Ed.

Russell, Joan. Teach Yourself Swahili Complete Course. 2nd rev. ed. (SWA., Illus.). 324p. 1996. pap. 14.95 (*0-8442-3709-4*) NTC Contemp Pub Co.

— The Woman's Day Book of Soft Toys & Dolls. 1980. pap. 6.95 (*0-686-61050-4*, 25403, Fireside) S&S Trade Pap.

Russell, Joan & Gregg, Joan Y. Past, Present, & Future: A Reading-Writing Text. 4th ed. (College ESL Ser.). 375p. (J). 1996. mass mkt. 28.95 (*0-8384-5282-5*) Heinle & Heinle.

Russell, Joan, jt. auth. see Gregg, Joan Y.

Russell, Joan M., jt. auth. see Russell, Alanson E.

***Russell, Joe.** Exploring the Marquesas Islands. LC 99-53080. 2000. 39.95 (*0-938665-64-2*) Fine Edge Prods.

***Russell, Joe & Shelley, Kate.** Baltimore Postcards. (Images of America Ser.). (Illus.). 128p. 1999. pap. 18.99 (*0-7385-0242-1*) Arcadia Publng.

Russell, John. Erich Kleiber: A Memoir. LC 80-29369. (Illus.). ix, 256p. 1981. reprint ed. lib. bdg. 35.00 (*0-685-55649-2*) Da Capo.

— Francis Bacon. LC 85-51434. (World of Art Ser.). (Illus.). 192p. 1985. 19.95 (*0-500-18170-5*, Pub. by Thames Hudson) Norton.

— Francis Bacon. 2nd rev. ed. LC 93-60306. (World of Art Ser.). (Illus.). 208p. 1993. pap. 14.95 (*0-500-20271-0*, Pub. by Thames Hudson) Norton.

— Hamlet & Narcissus. LC 94-22486. 248p. 1995. 38.50 (*0-87413-533-8*) U Delaware Pr.

— Honey Russell: Between Games, Between Halves. 1986. 14.95 (*0-931848-64-4*); pap. 9.95 (*0-931848-65-2*) Dryad Pr.

— London. LC 94-1528. (Illus.). 256p. 1994. 49.50 (*0-8109-3570-8*) Abrams.

— Matisse: Father & Son. LC 98-29571. (Illus.). 464p. 1999. 39.95 (*0-8109-4378-6*, Pub. by Abrams) Time Warner.

–Mill Creek Memories. (Illus.). 104p. 1995. pap. 7.00 (*0-87012-533-8*) McClain.
The history of Mill Creek, West Virginia, is told by the author with the aid of maps & photos to give the reader an in-depth look at the small town & its heritage. *Publisher Paid Annotation.*

***Russell, John.** Reciprocities in the Nonfiction Novel. 2000. 35.00 (*0-8203-2202-4*) U of Ga Pr.

Russell, John. Seurat. (World of Art Ser.). (Illus.). 286p. 1985. pap. 14.95 (*0-500-20032-7*, Pub. by Thames Hudson) Norton.

— Where the Pavement Ends. LC 73-144170. (Short Story Index Reprint Ser.). 1977. reprint ed. 21.95 (*0-8369-3785-6*) Ayer.

Russell, John & Arkava, Mort. The Bitterroot Marathon. LC 87-50939. (Illus.). 472p. 1987. boxed set 10.95 (*0-9611596-7-7*) Wilderness Adventure Bks.

Russell, John, jt. auth. see Cotter, William R.

Russell, John, ed. see Fox, Charles J.

Russell, John, tr. see Beer, Johann.

Russell, John, tr. see Kuhnau, Johann.

Russell, John, tr. see Martin du Gard, Roger.

Russell, John, tr. & intro. see Goethe, Johann Wolfgang Von.

Russell, John A., jt. ed. see Ivell, Richard.

***Russell, John C.** Spreadsheet Activities in Middle School. 2nd ed. (Illus.). 24p. 1998. pap. 21.95 (*0-87353-462-X*) NCTM.

— Stupid Kids. pap. 5.95 (*0-8222-1698-1*) Dramatists Play.

Russell, John D. Style in Modern British Fiction: Studies in Joyce, Lawrence, Forster, Lewis, & Green. LC 77-22477. 208p. reprint ed. pap. 64.50 (*0-608-07336-9*, 206756400009) Bks Demand.

Russell, John H. The Free Negro in Virginia, Sixteen Nineteen to Eighteen Sixty-Five. LC 78-63945. (Johns Hopkins University. Studies in the Social Sciences. Thirtieth Ser. 1912: 3). reprint ed. 32.50 (*0-404-61194-X*) AMS Pr.

***Russell, John J. & Spencer, Thomas S., eds.** Art on Campus: The College Art Association's Official Guide to American College & University Art Museums & Exhibition Galleries. (Illus.). 440p. 2000. pap. 24.95 (*0-9667144-0-7*, Pub. by Friars Lantern Inc) IPG Chicago.

Russell, John L., III. Involuntary Repossession or In the Steal of the Night. (Illus.). 64p. 1980. pap. 12.00 (*0-87364-233-3*) Paladin Pr.

Russell, John M. The Final Sack of Nineveh: The Discovery, Documentation & Destruction of Sennacherib's Palace at Nineveh, Iraq. LC 98-15067. 192p. 1998. 60.00 (*0-300-07418-2*) Yale U Pr.

— Sennacherib's "Palace Without Rival" at Nineveh. (Illus.). 358p. 1991. 51.95 (*0-226-73175-8*) U Ch Pr.

— The Writing on the Wall: Studies in the Architectural Context of Late Assyrian Palace Inscriptions. LC 99-14100. (Mesopotamian Civilizations Ser.: Vol. 9). (Illus.). xii, 340p. 1999. text 52.50 (*0-931464-95-1*) Eisenbrauns.

Russell, John M., et al. From Nineveh to New York: The Strange Story of the Assyrian Reliefs in the Metropolitan Museum & the Hidden Masterpiece at Canford School. LC 96-45444. (Illus.). 240p. 1997. 40.00 (*0-300-06459-4*) Yale U Pr.

Russell, John R., jt. auth. see Ruplin, Ferdinand A.

Russell, John R., tr. see Von Loen, Johann M.

Russell, John R., tr. see Von Thummel, Moritz A. & Nicolai, Friedrich.

Russell, John R., tr. & intro. see Kerth, Thomas & Gottsched, Luise.

Russell, John R., tr. & intro. see Moritz, Karl P.

Russell, John T., jt. auth. see Hildebrand, Peter E.

Russell, Johnston E., jt. auth. see Beer, Ferdinand Pierre.

***Russell, Jonathan.** The Daisy Chain. 310p. 2000. pap. write for info. (*0-7541-1034-6*, Pub. by Minerva Pr) Unity Dist.

Russell, Jonathan. The Sea Cries over My Shoulder. LC 91-70968. 1991. 12.95 (*0-8158-0472-5*) Chris Mass.

Russell, Jonathan, ed. see Rutlidge Institute Staff.

***Russell-Jones, Neil.** The Business Planning Pocketbook. 112p. 1999. pap. 8.95 (*1-870471-58-X*, Pub. by Mngmnt Pocketbks) Stylus Pub VA.

— The Managing Change Pocketbook. 112p. 1999. pap. 8.95 (*1-870471-31-8*, Pub. by Mngmnt Pocketbks) Stylus Pub VA.

Russell, Joseph, ed. The New Prayer Book Guide to Christian Education. rev. ed. 225p. (Orig.). 1996. pap. 15.95 (*1-56101-121-5*) Cowley Pubns.

Russell, Joseph J. Analysis & Dialectic. 1984. text 256.50 (*90-247-2990-4*) Kluwer Academic.

Russell, Joseph P. The Daily Lectionary - Years One & Two, 4 vols. Incl. Advent Through Eastertide, Year One. 136p. (Orig.). 1986. pap. 3.95 (*0-88028-057-3*, 854); Advent to Eastertide, Year Two. 144p. (Orig.). 1987. pap. 3.95 (*0-88028-068-9*, 905); Weekly Guide for Daily Bible Readings, the Sundays after Pentecost, Year One. 136p. (Orig.). 1987. pap. 3.95 (*0-88028-060-3*, 866); Weeks after Pentecost, Year Two. 120p. 1988. pap. 3.95 (*0-88028-069-7*, 906); 1988. Set pap. 14.00 (*0-88028-184-7*, 938) Forward Movement.

— Sharing Our Biblical Story: A Guide to Using Liturgical Readings As the Core of Church & Family Education. rev. ed. LC 88-8399. 336p. 1988. reprint ed. pap. 15.95 (*0-8192-1425-6*) Morehouse Pub.

An Asterisk (*) at the beginning of an entry indicates that the title is appearing for the first time.

Russell, Joseph P., ed. Weekday Readings: A Daily Eucharistic Lectionary for the Weekdays Following the First Sunday After Epiphany & the Feast of Pentecost, a Lectionary Authorized for Study & Evaluation. 53p. 1995. pap. 10.95 (0-89869-249-0) Church Pub Inc.

***Russell, Josh.** Yellow Jack. 2000. pap. 13.95 (0-393-32110-X) Norton.

Russell, Josh. Yellow Jack: A Novel. LC 99-21657. 224p. 1999. 23.95 (0-393-04768-7) Norton.

Russell, Josiah C. The Control of Late Ancient & Medieval Population. LC 83-71298. (Memoirs of the American Philosophical Society Ser.: Vol. 160). 288p. reprint ed. pap. 89.30 (0-7837-0543-3, 204087100019) Bks Demand.

— Medieval Demography: Essays by Josiah Cox Russell. LC 86-47837. (Studies in the Middle Ages: No. 12). 37.50 (0-404-61442-6) AMS Pr.

— Twelfth Century Studies. LC 77-83792. (Studies in the Middle Ages: No. 1). 34.50 (0-404-16022-0) AMS Pr.

Russell, Josiah C., ed. see Henry Of Avranches.

Russell, Joyce E., jt. auth. see Bernardin, John H.

Russell, Joyce R., ed. Preservation of Library Materials: Proceedings of a Seminar Sponsored by the Library Binding Institute & the Princeton-Trenton Chapter of Special Libraries Association Held at Rutgers University, July 20-21, 1979. LC 80-20706. (Illus.). 104p. reprint ed. pap. 32.30 (0-8357-7538-0, 203626100001) Bks Demand.

Russell, Joycelyne G. Diplomats at Work: Three Renaissance Studies. (Illus.). 160p. (C). 1992. text 49.95 (0-7509-0032-6, Pub. by Sutton Pub Ltd) Intl Pubs Mktg.

Russell, Judith, ed. The Wood-Engravings of Gertude Hermes: Survey & Catalogue. (Illus.). 132p. 1993. 131.95 (0-85967-888-1, Pub. by Scolar Pr) Ashgate Pub Co.

Russell, K. C. Phase Stability under Irradiation. (Illus.). 206p. 1985. pap. 83.00 (0-08-032722-2, Pergamon Pr) Elsevier.

Russell, K. C. & Aaronson, H. I., eds. Precipitation Processes in Solids: Proceedings of a Symposium Sponsored by the TMS-AIME Heat Treatment Committee at the 1976 TMS Fall Meeting at Niagara Falls, New York, September 20-21. LC 78-66760. 324p. reprint ed. pap. 100.50 (0-608-11267-4, 202276900029) Bks Demand.

Russell, Katheryn K. The Color of Crime. LC 97-33806. 203p. 1998. text 45.00 (0-8147-7471-7) NYU Pr.

— The Color of Crime. (Critical America Ser.). 1999. pap. 16.95 (0-8147-7532-2) NYU Pr.

Russell, Kathleen F. & Wall, Larry C. Achieve Your Dreams. 160p. (Orig.). 1994. pap. 7.95 (0-9635176-3-5) Walrus Prods.

— Money Now You Have It. Now You Don't. LC 95-117798. 160p. (Orig.). 1994. pap. 7.95 (0-9635176-4-3) Walrus Prods.

— The Road to Success Is Always under Construction. 160p. 1992. pap. 7.95 (0-9635176-0-0) Walrus Prods.

Russell, Kathy E., et al. The Color Complex: The Politics of Skin Color among African Americans. LC 93-13294. (Illus.). 208p. 1993. pap. 12.95 (0-385-47161-0, Anchor NY) Doubleday.

Russell, Keith, et al. Sex & Fly Fishers: A Delightful & Insightful Celebration of Fly Fishing. LC 92-62020. (Illus.). 336p. 1993. 29.95 (0-913276-61-8) Stone Wall Pr.

***Russell, Keith A.** The Disappearance of J. D. Sinclair. LC 99-71774. 173p. 1999. pap. 14.95 (0-9672684-0-0) LaVonKeish Pubs.

Russell, Keith A. In Search of the Church: New Testament Images for Tomorrow's Congregations. LC 93-74583. (Once & Future Church Ser.). 115p. (Orig.). 1994. pap. 12.25 (1-56699-123-4, AL149) Alban Inst.

***Russell, Keith A.** When Doves Cry. Francis, Faith, ed. 120p. (YA). 2000. pap. 13.00 (0-9672684-1-9) LaVonKeish Pubs.

Russell, Keith P. & Niebyl, Jennifer R. Eastman's Expectant Mother. 8th rev. ed. 1989. 9.95 (0-318-41368-X, Little Brwn Med Div) Lppncott W & W.

Russell, Ken. Complaints Against the Police: A Sociological View. 4th rev. ed. 152p. 1994. pap. 12.00 (0-9504906-7-9, Pub. by Milltak Ltd) Chivers N Amer.

***Russell, Ken.** Directing Films: The Director's Art from Script to Cutting Room. (Illus.). 176p. 2000. pap. text. write for info. (0-7134-8554-X, Pub. by B T B) Bks Intl VA.

— How to Succeed with IQ Tests: How Smart Are You? 2000. 7.99 (1-57866-090-4) Galahad Bks.

Russell, Ken. 120 Modern Crossword Puzzles. 1997. pap. text 9.95 (0-572-02289-1, Pub. by W Foulsham) Trans-Atl Phila.

***Russell, Ken.** Test Your IQ. 2000. pap. 10.95 (0-7494-3299-3) Kogan Page Ltd.

— Test Your IQ. 2000. pap. 11.95 (0-572-02484-3) W Foulsham.

Russell, Ken & Carter, Philip. Check Your IQ: The Mensa UK Puzzle Editors. (Illus.). 176p. (Orig.). 1997. pap. 11.95 (0-572-02347-2, Pub. by W Foulsham) Trans-Atl Phila.

— Victorian Conundrums: A 19th Century Puzzler. (Illus.). 167p. 1998. pap. 9.95 (1-85479-294-6) Trans-Atl Phila.

Russell, Ken, jt. auth. see Carter, Philip.

Russell, Ken A. Number Puzzles. 224p. 1994. pap. 7.95 (0-572-01890-8, Pub. by W Foulsham) Trans-Atl Phila.

— Pic Puzzles. (MENSA Ser.). 224p. 1995. pap. 7.95 (0-572-01889-4, Pub. by Foulsham UK) Assoc Pubs Grp.

Russell, Ken A. & Carter, Philip J. Challenging IQ Puzzles. (Illus.). 96p. 1996. pap. 5.95 (0-8069-9481-9) Sterling.

— The Complete Guide to Word Games & Word Play. 320p. 1995. pap. 12.99 (0-572-01979-3, Pub. by Foulsham UK) Assoc Pubs Grp.

— Getting Better at IQ Tests for Ages 11-13, Nos. 11-13. (Illus.). 160p. (Orig.). 1994. pap. 10.95 (0-572-01972-6, Pub. by W Foulsham) Trans-Atl Phila.

— Getting Better at IQ Tests for Ages 14-16. (Illus.). 160p. (Orig.). 1994. pap. 10.95 (0-572-01973-4, Pub. by W Foulsham) Trans-Atl Phila.

— Test Your IQ. (Illus.). 128p. 1992. pap. 5.95 (0-7063-7059-7, Pub. by WrLock) Sterling.

Russell, Ken A., jt. auth. see Carter, Philip J.

Russell, Kenneth. Intelligence Book. LC 98-28481. (Illus.). 64p. 1998. pap. 7.95 (0-8069-0463-1) Sterling.

Russell, Kenneth & Carter, Philip. Challenging IQ Tests. LC 97-50488. (Illus.). 96p. 1998. pap. 6.95 (0-8069-0461-5) Sterling.

Russell, Kenneth A., jt. auth. see Carter, Philip J.

Russell, Kenneth C., ed. see Minerals, Metals & Materials Society Staff.

Russell, Kenneth L., jt. auth. see Russell, Margaret.

Russell, Kenneth V., jt. ed. see Mckay, Ronald D.

Russell, L. Mark & Grant, Arnold E. The Life Planning Workbook: A Hands-on Guide to Help Parents Provide for the Future Security & Happiness of Their Child with a Disability after Their Death. 300p. (Orig.). 1995. pap. text 24.95 (0-9635780-7-3) Amer Pub IL.

Russell, L. Mark, et al. Planning for the Future: Providing a Meaningful Life for a Child with a Disability after Your Death. LC 95-187250. 430p. 1993. pap. 24.95 (0-9635780-0-6) Amer Pub IL.

Russell, Lao. Character. Lombardi, Emilia L., ed. 20p. 1991. pap. text 2.00 (1-879605-35-X) U Sci & Philos.

— God Will Work with You but Not for You. (Illus.). 266p. 1981. reprint ed. text 7.00 (1-879605-20-1) U Sci & Philos.

— Love. (Illus.). 207p. 1980. reprint ed. text 4.00 (1-879605-21-X) U Sci & Philos.

— Love Ye One Another. 45p. 1996. pap. 2.00 (1-879605-46-5) U Sci & Philos.

— Why You Cannot Die! The Continuity of Life. (Illus.). 253p. 1972. text 5.00 (1-879605-18-X) U Sci & Philos.

— You Create Your Own Destiny. Lombardi, Emilia L., ed. 20p. 1991. pap. text 3.00 (1-879605-34-1) U Sci & Philos.

Russell, Lao, jt. auth. see Russell, Walter.

Russell, Lawrence. Age of Empires: The Official Strategy Guide. LC 97-66003. 312p. 1997. per. 16.99 (0-7615-1053-2) Prima Pub.

— F-15 Strike Eagle III: The Official Strategy Guide. (Illus.). 368p. (Orig.). 1993. pap. 24.95 (1-55958-197-2) Prima Pub.

— Mystery of the Pig Killer's Daughter: Four Plays. LC 75-12079. 134p. 1975. pap. 6.95 (0-914580-03-5) Angst World.

— The Twenty-Fifth Hour. (Illus.). 48p. (Orig.). 1981. pap. 5.95 (0-914580-11-6) Angst World.

Russell, Lawrence P. It's Fun to Win. LC 99-159040. (Illus.). 80p. 1998. pap. 6.95 (0-9662767-0-1) Gaming Res.

***Russell, Lawrence T.** Flying Nightmares 2: The Official Strategy Guide. 240p. 1998. per. 19.99 (0-7615-1107-5) Prima Pub.

Russell, Lawrence T. Joint Strike Fighter: The Official Strategy Guide. LC 97-75926. 216p. 1998. per. 19.99 (0-7615-1426-0) Prima Pub.

Russell, Lee. Labyrinth. (Illus.). 1977. 4.94 (0-940244-03-9) Flying Buffalo.

— The U. S. Marine Corps since 1945. (Elite Ser.: No. 2). (Illus.). 64p. pap. 12.95 (0-85045-574-X, 9401, Pub. by Ospry) Stackpole.

Russell, Lee & Mendez, M. Albert. Grenada, 1983. (Men-at-Arms Ser.: No. 159). (Illus.). 48p. 1985. pap. 11.95 (0-85045-583-9, 9091, Pub. by Ospry) Stackpole.

Russell, Lee, jt. auth. see Katz, Samuel M.

***Russell, Lee Ann.** How to Write Poetry: Ballad to Villanelle. 3rd rev. ed. xv, 143p. 2000. spiral bd. 10.00 (0-9701290-0-9) Night Owl MO.

Russell, Lee E. Armies of the Vietnam War, Vol. 2. (Men-at-Arms Ser.: No. 143). (Illus.). 48p. pap. 11.95 (0-85045-514-6, 9075, Pub. by Ospry) Stackpole.

Russell, Leslie. The Orphans. LC 96-90982. 222p. 1998. 17.95 (0-533-12526-X) Vantage.

Russell, Letty M. Church in the Round: Feminist Interpretation of the Church. 272p. (Orig.). 1993. pap. 22.95 (0-664-25070-X) Westminster John Knox.

— Household of Freedom: Authority in Feminist Theology. LC 86-18992. Vol. 1986. 114p. (Orig.). 1987. pap. 12.95 (0-664-24017-8) Westminster John Knox.

Russell, Letty M., ed. Feminist Interpretation of the Bible. LC 84-17342. 166p. (Orig.). 1985. pap. 16.95 (0-664-24639-7) Westminster John Knox.

Russell, Letty M, et al, eds. Inheriting Our Mothers' Gardens: Feminist Theology in Third World Perspective. LC 88-10051. 182p. 1988. pap. 18.95 (0-664-25019-X) Westminster John Knox.

Russell, Letty M. & Clarkson, J. Shannon, eds. Dictionary of Feminist Theologies. LC 95-49454. 351p. 1996. 39.00 (0-664-22058-4) Westminster John Knox.

Russell, Lewis. Russell's Thru the Years: And How We Relate to Our Community Both Locally & Globally. LC 99-174617. (Illus.). 200p. 1998. pap. 16.95 (1-882063-43-0, Heritage Hse) Cottage Pr MA.

***Russell, Linda & Stephens, Shirley.** My Daughter Susan Smith. (Illus.). 304p. 2000. pap. 16.95 (0-615-11644-2) Authors Bk Nook.

— My Daughter Susan Smith. (Illus.). 304p. 2000. pap. 16.95 (0-9701076-1-7) Authors Bk Nook.

Russell, Linda W., ed. see Armstrong, William H.

Russell, Linda W., ed. see Christison, Randall B., et al.

Russell, Linda W., ed. see Henley, Victoria B. & Needham, Henry E., Jr.

Russell, Linda W., ed. see Kennedy, Raoul D. & Martin, James C.

Russell, Linette H. & Hayat, Alan, eds. The French Publication Index: A Directory of French Educational Materials. (Illus.). 320p. (Orig.). 1990. pap. 20.00 (0-9626800-0-1) Continental Bk.

Russell, Lisa. Child Maltreatment & Psychological Distress among Urban Homeless Youth. LC 97-35335. (Children of Poverty Ser.). xx, 400p. 1998. 75.00 (0-8153-3016-2) Garland.

Russell, Lisa H. The Tenor: Every Woman's Dream. LC 93-91096. 138p. 1994. pap. 10.00 (0-9643892-0-7) Banner Pubng.

Russell, Lonnie, et al. Enjoy Southern Illinois: A Complete Recreational Guide. LC 93-90943. (Illus.). 648p. (Orig.). 1993. pap. 17.95 (0-9627422-4-4) Cache River Pr.

Russell, Lonnie, jt. auth. see Clark, David.

Russell, Lonnie, jt. auth. see Trovillion, Ned.

Russell, Lonnie D. & Ettlin, Robert A. Histological & Histopathological Evaluation of the Testis. Hikim, Amiya P. & Clegy, Eric D., eds. (Illus.). 286p. (C). 1990. 62.50 (0-9627422-0-1) Cache River Pr.

Russell, Lonnie D. & Griswold, Michael D., eds. The Sertoli Cell. (Illus.). 802p. (C). 1993. 137.50 (0-9627422-1-X) Cache River Pr.

Russell, Lonnie D., jt. auth. see Bozzola, John J.

Russell, Lonnie D., ed. see Payne, Anita, et al.

Russell, Loris S. A Heritage of Light: Lamps & Lighting in the Early Canadian Home. LC 68-140801. (Illus.). 349p. reprint ed. pap. 108.20 (0-608-11332-8, 201439400093) Bks Demand.

Russell, Louise B. The Accelerated Learning Fieldbook: Making the Instructional Process Fast, Flexible & Fun. LC 99-6756. 304p. 1999. pap. text 39.95 (0-7879-4639-7) Jossey-Bass.

— The Baby Boom Generation & the Economy. LC 82-70890. (Studies in Social Economics). 183p. 1982. 32.95 (0-8157-7628-4); pap. 12.95 (0-8157-7627-6) Brookings.

Russell, Louise B. Comparison of Two Surveys of Hospitalization: National Hospital Discharge Survey & Epidemiologic Followup Study. 20p. 1997. pap. 2.00 (0-16-051476-7) USGPO.

Russell, Louise B. Educated Guesses: Making Policy About Medical Screening Tests. LC 93-8768. 1994. pap. 12.95 (0-520-08366-0, Pub. by U CA Pr) Cal Prin Full Svc.

— Evaluating Preventive Care: Report on a Workshop. LC 87-9304. 107p. 1987. 26.95 (0-8157-7626-8); pap. 9.95 (0-8157-7625-X) Brookings.

— Is Prevention Better Than Cure? LC 85-21250. (Studies in Social Economics). 134p. 1986. 32.95 (0-8157-7632-2); pap. 12.95 (0-8157-7631-4) Brookings.

— Medicare's New Hospital Payment System: Is It Working? 120p. 1989. 32.95 (0-8157-7624-1); pap. 12.95 (0-8157-7623-3) Brookings.

— Technology in Hospitals: Medical Advances & Their Diffusion. LC 79-10737. (Studies in Social Economics). 180p. 1979. 34.95 (0-8157-7630-6); pap. 14.95 (0-8157-7629-2) Brookings.

Russell, Louise B. & Burke, Carol S. Technological Diffusion in the Hospital Sector. LC 75-37308. 240p. 1976. 8.00 (0-89068-007-8) Natl Planning.

Russell, Louise B., et al. Comparison of Two Surveys of Hospitalization: The NHDS & the NHEFS. National Health & Nutrition Examination Survey Sta, ed. LC 97-36313. (Vital & Health Statistics Ser.: Series 2, No. 123). 1997. write for info. (0-8406-0530-7) Natl Ctr Health Stats.

Russell, Lynn. Montana Christmas. (Stolen Moments Ser.). 1993. pap. 1.99 (0-373-83288-5, 1-83288-0) Harlequin Bks.

Russell, Lynn, jt. auth. see Henderson, Carolyn.

Russell, Lynn A., jt. auth. see Fichtner, Sandy.

Russell, Lynn D. & Adebiyi, George A. Classical Thermodynamics. (Illus.). 944p. (C). 1993. text 87.95 (0-03-032417-3); pap. text, teacher ed. write for info. (0-03-075488-7) OUP.

***Russell, Lynne.** How to Win Friends & Kick Ass. LC 99-36061. 1999. text 23.95 (0-312-24403-7) St Martin.

Russell, M. A Is for Attitude. 2001. 12.00 (0-06-093233-3, Quil) HarperTrade.

— Land of Enchantment: Memoirs of Marian Russell along the Santa Fe Trail. LC 80-54564. 163p. 1985. reprint ed. pap. 14.95 (0-8263-0805-8) U of NM Pr.

— Palestine. 400p. 1985. 300.00 (1-85077-053-0, Pub. by Darf Pubs Ltd) St Mut.

Russell, M. Thomas. Beating Boredom, Creating Interest. LC 97-69145. (Fastback Ser.: No. 419). 46p. 1997. pap. 3.00 (0-87367-619-X, FB#419) Phi Delta Kappa.

Russell, M. W., tr. see Guyon, Jeanne.

Russell, Malcolm B. The First Modern Arab State: Syria under Faysal, 1918-1920. (Studies in Middle Eastern History: Vol 7). 1983. 30.00 (0-88297-030-5) Bibliotheca.

— The Middle East & South Asia, 1996. 30th ed. 251p. 1996. pap. 11.50 (1-887985-00-X) Stryker-Post.

— The Middle East & South Asia, 1998. 32nd ed. (World Today Ser.). 1998. pap. 11.50 (1-887985-14-X) Stryker-Post.

***Russell, Malcolm B.** Middle East & South Asia, 99. 33rd ed. 1999. pap. 11.50 (1-887985-21-2) Stryker-Post.

Russell-Manning, Betsy. Malathion: Toxic Time Bomb. LC 90-85143. (Illus.). 265p. 1991. spiral bd. 19.95 (0-930165-49-7) Greensward Pr.

— Self Treatment for AIDS: Oxygen Therapy. rev. ed. 1989. per. 16.95 (0-930165-12-8) Greensward Pr.

Russell-Manning, Betsy, ed. Candida, Silver (Mercury) Fillings & the Immune System. rev. ed. LC 85-80413. 1990. pap. 16.95 (0-930165-10-1) Greensward Pr.

— How Safe Are Silver (Mercury) Fillings? Hidden Health Facts. rev. ed. LC 84-90431. 1985. pap. 39.95 (0-930165-00-4) Greensward Pr.

— Wheatgrass Juice - Gift of Nature. rev. ed. 1988. pap. 2.95 (0-930165-06-3) Greensward Pr.

Russell, Marcia L. Fair Housing. LC 94-42601. 1995. pap. text 59.00 (0-7931-1331-8, 1520-3501, Real Estate Ed) Dearborn.

***Russell, Margaret & Russell, Kenneth L.** The "How" in Parliamentary Procedure. 6th ed. LC 98-75495. viii, 70 p. 2000. 4.00 (0-8134-3165-4) Interstate.

Russell, Margarita A. Paintings & Textiles of the Bass Museum of Art: Selections from the Collection. LC 90-82402. (Illus.). 176p. 1991. 40.00 (1-880511-02-9); pap. 25.00 (1-880511-03-7) Bass Museum.

Russell, Margo. African Freeholders: A Study of Individual Tenure Farms in Swazi Ownership. (Research Paper Ser.: Vol. 103). (Illus.). xiii, 85p. (C). 1990. pap. 7.00 (0-934519-13-7, RP103) U of Wis Land.

Russell, Mariann. Melvin B. Tolson's Harlem Gallery: A Literary Analysis. LC 80-50306. 153p. reprint ed. pap. 47.50 (0-7837-2359-8, AU0042400006) Bks Demand.

Russell, Marie, jt. auth. see Russell, Bert.

Russell, Marjorie H. The Arcadia Story. LC 85-40651. (Illus.). 190p. 1986. pap. 7.98 (0-938232-83-5) Arcadia Ministry Pubns.

— Handbook of Christian Meditation. LC 77-90859. 118p. 1978. pap. 7.98 (0-8159-5713-0) Arcadia Ministry Pubns.

— Oneness of All Life. 2nd ed. LC 84-50765. (Illus.). 203p. 1984. 3.48 (0-87159-123-5) Arcadia Ministry Pubns.

— Revelation: Your Future Prophesied. (Illus.). 80p. (Orig.). 1985. pap. 7.98 (0-9614745-0-5) Arcadia Ministry Pubns.

— The Whip-Poor-Will's Song. 120p. (Orig.). (J). 1995. pap. 5.75 (0-9614745-2-1) Arcadia Ministry Pubns.

Russell, Marjorie H., ed. & illus. see Fuller, Joy.

Russell, Mark. Golf Rules Plain & Simple. LC GV971.R97 1999. 144p. 1999. pap. 10.95 (0-06-273668-X) HarpC.

***Russell, Mark & Young, James.** Film Music, Set. 192p. 2000. pap. 39.95 incl. cd-rom (0-240-80441-4, Focal) Buttrwrth-Heinemann.

Russell, Mark, jt. auth. see Farrar, John H.

Russell, Marlou. Adoption Wisdom: A Guide to the Issues & Feelings of Adoption. LC 96-96069. 204p. (Orig.). 1996. pap. 14.95 (1-888511-12-5) Broken Branch.

Russell, Marta. Beyond Ramps: Disability at the End of the Social Contract. LC 97-16590. 256p. (Orig.). 1998. pap. 18.95 (1-56751-106-6); lib. bdg. 29.95 (1-56751-107-4) Common Courage.

Russell, Martin. A Domestic Affair. 192p. 1985. 13.95 (0-8027-5633-6) Walker & Co.

Russell, Mary. The Blessings of a Good Thick Skirt: Women Travellers & Their World. 240p. 1994. mass mkt. 14.95 (0-00-654748-6, Pub. by HarpC) Trafalgar.

Russell, Mary. Please Don't Call It Soviet Georgia. (Illus.). 268p. (Orig.). 1992. pap. 16.99 (1-85242-216-5) Serpents Tail.

***Russell, Mary.** Vortex: The End of History. 1999. pap. 23.95 (1-86163-083-2, Pub. by Capall Bann Pubng) Holmes Pub.

Russell, Mary D. Children of God. 436p. 1999. pap. 12.95 (0-449-00483-X) Fawcett.

— The Sparrow. 416p. 1997. pap. 12.00 (0-449-91255-8) Fawcett.

Russell, Mary N. Clinical Social Work: Research & Practice. (Sourcebooks for the Human Services Ser.: Vol. 14). (Illus.). 192p. (C). 1990. text 56.00 (0-8039-3782-2); pap. text 26.00 (0-8039-3783-0) Sage.

— Confronting Abusive Beliefs: Group Treatment for Abusive Men. LC 96-35124. (Interpersonal Violence: the Practice Ser.: Vol. 12). 12p. 1995. 48.00 (0-8039-5807-2); pap. 21.50 (0-8039-5808-0) Sage.

Russell, Mary T. 16PF Couple's Counseling Report User's Guide. 66p. (C). 1995. pap. 25.00 (0-918296-24-2) Inst Personality & Ability.

— The Teamwork Development Report User's Guide. (Illus.). 77p. (C). 1998. pap. 28.00 (0-918296-31-5) Inst Personality & Ability.

Russell, Mary T. & Karol, Darcie L. The Sixteen PF Fifth Edition: Administrator's Manual. 162p. (Orig.). 1994. pap. 40.00 (0-918296-21-8) Inst Personality & Ability.

Russell, Mattie U., jt. auth. see Godbold, E. Stanly, Jr.

Russell, Maureen. Days of Our Lives: A Complete History of the Long-Running Soap Opera. LC 95-35873. (Illus.). 286p. 1995. lib. bdg. 32.50 (0-7864-0112-5) McFarland & Co.

— Highlander: The Complete Watcher's Guide. LC 98-17609. (Illus.). 224p. 1998. mass mkt. 13.99 (0-446-67435-4, Pub. by Warner Bks) Little.

Russell-McCloud, Patricia. A is for Attitude: An Alphabet For Living. LC 99-32824. 256p. 1999. 21.95 (0-06-019429-4) HarpC.

Russell Meerdink Company, Ltd. Research Staff. Equifacts: The Complete Horse Record Organizer. (Illus.). 140p. 1986. ring bd. 25.00 (0-929346-00-9) R Meerdink Co Ltd.

Russell Meerdink Company Staff. Equifacts: The Complete Horse Record Organizer. 1997. pap. text 16.95 (0-929346-27-0) R Meerdink Co Ltd.

***Russell, Meg.** Reforming the House of Lords: Lessons from Overseas. LC 99-87215. 384p. 2000. text 35.00 (0-19-829831-5) OUP.

Russell, Melvia, ed. see Easter, Marvin L.

Russell, Michael. History & Present Condition of the Barbary States. 1835. 59.00 (0-403-00304-0) Scholarly.

— Nubia & Abyssinia. 440p. 1990. 135.00 (1-85077-052-2, Pub. by Darf Pubs Ltd) St Mut.

Russell, Michael, ed. see Spottiswood, John.

R

*Russell, Michael J., ed. Data Resources of the National Institute of Justice (1993) 6th ed. 300p. 1999. reprint ed. pap. text 45.00 (0-7881-7000-7) DIANE Pub.

*Russell, Michael S. The Chemistry of Fireworks. (Illus.). 117p. 2000. pap. 39.95 (0-85404-598-8, Pub. by Royal Soc Chem) Spr-Verlag.

Russell, Michel. Strange Lands. 118p. 1986. 39.00 (0-7212-0756-1, Pub. by Regency Pr GBR) St Mut.

Russell, Mike & Russell, Carolyn. How to Build Almost Anything: Starting with Practically Nothing. (Illus.). 176p. 1993. pap. 18.95 (0-921820-77-1) Firefly Bks Ltd.

*Russell, Miles. Neolithic Flint Mines in Britain. (Illus.). 176p. 2000. 32.50 (0-7524-1481-X, Pub. by Tempus Pubng) Arcadia Publng.

Russell, Milton & Toenjes, Laurence. Natural Gas Producer Regulation & Taxation: Interaction Between Federal Producer Regulation & State Severance Taxation. LC 78-635475. (MSU Public Utilities Papers: Vol. 1971). (Illus.). 95p. reprint ed. pap. 30.00 (0-608-20511-7, 207176300002) Bks Demand.

Russell, Milton, jt. auth. see Bohi, Douglas R.

Russell, Milton, jt. auth. see Bohi, Douglas R.

Russell, Morris C. Uncle Dudley's Odd Hours: Western Sketches, Indian Trail Echoes. LC 73-104558. (Illus.). 255p. reprint ed. lib. bdg. 25.00 (0-8398-1768-1) Irvington.

*Russell, N. Legislative History of Recent Primary Safety Belt Laws. 76p. 1999. per. 6.00 (0-16-049930-5) USGPO.

*Russell, N., et al. Legislative History of Recent Primary Safety Belt Laws. 62p. (C). 2000. pap. text 20.00 (0-7881-8857-7) DIANE Pub.

Russell, N. J., jt. auth. see Frantz, D. G.

Russell, N. J., jt. auth. see Harwood, J. L.

*Russell, Naomi. Guess Who's in the Jungle: Flip-the-Flap. LC 98-73378. (Illus.). (J). 1999. pap. 3.99 (0-7636-0759-2) Candlewick Pr.

Russell, Naomi. Guess Who's on the Farm? LC 95-67990. (Flip-the-Flap Book Ser.). (Illus.). 1995. write for info. (1-56402-710-4) Candlewick Pr.

*Russell, Naomi. Guess Who's on the Farm: A Flip-the-Flap Book. LC 98-73244. (Illus.). 32p. (J). (ps). 1999. pap. text 3.99 (0-7636-0689-8, Pub. by Candlewick Pr) Penguin Putnam.

Russell, Naomi. Nikki, Rooster & Chick-a-Biddy. (Illus.). 100p. (J). 1998. 15.00 (0-89904-761-0); pap. 10.00 (0-89904-762-9) Crumb Elbow Pub.

Russell, Neville. Tolley's Form & Content of Financial Statements. 270p. (C). 1994. 90.00 (0-85459-883-9, Pub. by Tolley Pubng) St Mut.

Russell, Nicholas, jt. ed. see Gacesa, Peter.

*Russell, Norman. Cyril of Alexandria. (Early Church Fathers Ser.). 2000. pap. 25.99 (0-415-18251-4) Routledge.

Russell, Norman. The Novelist & Mammon: Literary Responses to the World of Commerce in the Nineteenth Century. (Illus.). 288p. 1986. 65.00 (0-19-812851-7) OUP.

Russell, Norman, jt. auth. see Cyril.

Russell, Norman, jt. auth. see Ramfos, Stelios.

Russell, Norman, jt. tr. see Ward, Benedicta.

Russell, Norman H. From Star to Leaf: Selected Poems of Norman H. Russell. Davies, Robert A. & Gogol, John M., eds. (Illus.). 28p. (Orig.). 1995. pap. text 10.00 (0-932191-11-8) Mr Cogito Pr.

— Night Dog & Other Poems. (Orig.). 1971. pap. 1.00 (0-685-30029-3) Cottonwood KS.

Russell, Norman L. Suicide Charlie. Grad, Doug, ed. 256p. 1995. mass mkt. 6.50 (0-671-52279-5) PB.

— Suicide Charlie: A Vietnam War Story. LC 92-29817. 216p. 1993. 35.00 (0-275-94521-9, C4521, Praeger Pubs) Greenwood.

Russell, Oland D. House of Mitsui. LC 70-109836. 328p. 1971. reprint ed. lib. bdg. 38.50 (0-8371-4327-6, RUHM, Greenwood Pr) Greenwood.

Russell, Osborne. Journal of a Trapper. Haines, Aubrey L., ed. (Illus.). 256p. 1997. 7.98 (1-56731-173-3, MJF Bks) Fine Comms.

— Journal of a Trapper. Haines, Aubrey L., ed. LC 56-52. (Illus.). xxii, 241p. 1965. pap. 9.95 (0-8032-5166-1, Bison Books) U of Nebr Pr.

Russell, P. Efflorescence & the Discoloration of Concrete. 44p. (C). (gr. 13). 1998. pap. text 65.00 (0-86310-011-2, Pub. by Palladian) Scholium Intl.

Russell, P. Craig. Fairy Tales of Oscar Wilde, Vol. 2. (J). (gr. 3-7). 1994. 15.95 (1-56163-085-3) NBM.

— Fairy Tales of Oscar Wilde Vol. 3: The Birthday of the Infanta. (Illus.). 32p. (J). (gr. 3-6). 1998. 15.95 (1-56163-213-9) NBM.

— Fairy Tales of Oscar Wilde Vol. 3: The Birthday of the Infanta. limited ed. (Illus.). 32p. (J). (gr. 3-6). 1998. 50.00 (1-56163-214-7) NBM.

— The Jungle Book. LC 98-181056. (Illus.). 88p. 1997. 16.95 (1-56163-152-3) NBM.

Russell, P. Craig. Fairy Tales of Oscar Wilde, Vol. 1. LC 93-229468. 48p. (J). (gr. 1-7). 1992. 15.95 (1-56163-056-X) NBM.

*Russell, P. E. Prince Henry "the Navigator" A Life. LC 99-49569. (Illus.). 464p. 2000. 35.00 (0-300-08233-9) Yale U Pr.

Russell, P. E., ed. Spain: A Companion to Spanish Studies. (Illus.). 608p. 1983. pap. 25.00 (0-416-84110-4, NO. 3908) Routledge.

Russell, P. W., ed. Unjustified Enrichment: A Comparative Study of the Law of Restitution. LC 97-161359. 96p. 1997. pap. 17.50 (90-5383-478-8, Pub. by VUB Univ Pr) Paul & Co Pubs.

Russell, Patricia C. Bible Beginnings - & It Was Good! Old Testament Lessons for Little Listeners. 300p. (J). 1999. pap. 19.95 (1-889015-27-X) Explrs Bible.

— Bible Discovery: In the Beginning - Genesis. Constance, Nellie E., ed. 258p. (J). (gr. 3-6). 1996. pap., wbk. ed. 18.95 (1-889015-04-0) Explrs Bible.

— Bible Discovery - God's People, God's Land - Exodus-Joshua: Student Workbook. Constance, Nellie E. & Eades, Lois, eds. 231p. (J). (gr. 3-6). 1996. pap., student ed., wbk. ed. 18.95 (1-889015-08-3) Explrs Bible.

— Bible Discovery - Promises Fulfilled - Luke & Acts: Student Workbook. Constance, Nellie E. & Eades, Lois, eds. 262p. (J). (gr. 3-6). 1997. pap., student ed., wbk. ed. 18.95 (1-889015-13-X) Explrs Bible.

— Bible Foundations - New Testament Overview: Student Workbook. Constance, Nellie E., ed. 169p. (Orig.). (J). (gr. 1-2). 1996. pap., wbk. ed. 14.95 (1-889015-02-4) Explrs Bible.

— Bible Foundations - Old Testament Overview: Student Workbook. Constance, Nellie E., ed. 140p. (Orig.). (J). (gr. 1-2). 1996. pap., wbk. ed. 14.95 (1-889015-00-8) Explrs Bible.

Russell, Paul. Boys of Life. 320p. 1992. pap. 12.95 (0-452-26837-0, Plume) Dutton Plume.

— Coming Storm. LC 99-32207. 1999. text 24.95 (0-312-20514-7) St Martin.

*Russell, Paul. Coming Storm. 384p. 2000. pap. 13.95 (0-312-26303-1) St Martin.

Russell, Paul. Freedom & Moral Sentiment: Hume's Way of Naturalizing Responsibility. 216p. 1995. text 49.95 (0-19-509501-4) OUP.

— Gay One Hundred: A Ranking of the Most Influential Gay Men & Lesbians, Past & Present. (Illus.). 384p. 1994. 22.50 (0-8065-1591-0, Citadel Pr) Carol Pub Group.

— The Gay One-Hundred: A Ranking of the Most Influential Gay Men & Lesbians, Past & Present. LC 94-12607. 1994. 22.50 (1-55972-242-8, Birch Ln Pr) Carol Pub Group.

— The Gay 100: A Ranking of the Most Influential Gay Men & Lesbians, Past & Present. (Illus.). 416p. Date not set. pap. 19.95 (0-8065-1783-2, Citadel Pr) Carol Pub Group.

— An Introduction to the Celtic Languages. LC 94-44203. (Linguistics Library). 1995. pap. text. write for info. (0-582-10081-X, Pub. by Addison-Wesley) Longman.

— An Introduction to the Celtic Languages. LC 94-44203. (Linguistics Library). 1995. boxed set. write for info. (0-582-10082-8, Pub. by Addison-Wesley) Longman.

*Russell, Paul. Salt Point. (Stonewall Inn Editions Ser.). 224p. 2000. pap. 12.95 (0-312-26769-X) St Martin.

Russell, Paul, jt. auth. see Trilling, Diana.

Russell, Paul A., jt. ed. see Memrino, Marcia L.

Russell, Paul L. History of Western Oil Shale. LC 80-66410. (Illus.). 176p. 1980. 49.50 (0-86563-000-3) Ctr Prof Adv.

— Oil Shales of the World: Their Origin, Occurrence & Exploitation. LC 89-48957. (Illus.). 736p. 1990. 337.00 (0-08-037240-6, Pub. by Pergamon Repr) Franklin.

Russell, P.E. Portugal, Spain & the African Atlantic, 1343-1490: Chivalry & Crusade from John of Guant to Henry the Navigator & Beyond. (Collected Studies). 344p. 1995. 108.95 (0-86078-474-6, Pub. by Variorum) Ashgate Pub Co.

Russell, Peggy B. Confessions of a Transplant. (Illus.). 50p. 1990. reprint ed. pap. 6.95 (0-9625237-0-4) Transplant Pubns.

Russell, Penny. A Wish of Distinction: Colonial Gentility & Femininity. LC 94-189315. 244p. 1994. pap. 24.95 (0-522-84552-5, Pub. by Melbourne Univ Pr) Paul & Co Pubs.

Russell, Penny, ed. For Richer, for Poorer: Early Colonial Marriages. LC 94-156041. 250p. 1994. pap. 24.95 (0-522-84551-7, Pub. by Melbourne Univ Pr) Paul & Co Pubs.

Russell, Penny, jt. ed. see White, Richard.

Russell, Peter. All for the Wolves: Selected Poems, 1947-1975. Jay, Peter, ed. (Literary Ser.). 151p. 1984. 25.00 (0-933806-20-5) Black Swan CT.

— Attitudes to Social Structure & Mobility in Upper Canada 1815-1840. LC 89-34205. (Canadian Studies: Vol. 6). 211p. 1989. lib. bdg. 89.95 (0-88946-193-7) E Mellen.

— Brain Book. 1984. pap. 13.95 (0-452-26723-4, Plume) Dutton Plume.

Russell, Peter. The Duller Olive. 135p. pap. write for info. (3-7052-0622-2, Pub. by Poetry Salzburg) Intl Spec Bk.

Russell, Peter. The Elegies of Quintilius. LC 97-154809. 112p. 1997. pap. 17.95 (0-85646-277-2, Pub. by Anvil Press) Dufour.

Russell, Peter. Elf Rock: A Tale of Coincidence. (Illus.). 80p. 1996. pap. 12.00 (1-928586-02-3) P Russell.

Russell, Peter. Examination of Ezra Pound: A Collection of Essays by T. S. Eliot & Others. enl. rev. ed. LC 71-150418. 273p. 1973. reprint ed. 50.00 (0-87752-141-7) Gordian.

Russell, Peter. A False Start: London Poems 1959-1963. 228p. pap. write for info. (3-7052-0927-2, Pub. by Poetry Salzburg) Intl Spec Bk.

— From Science to God: The Journey of a Devout Skeptic. (Illus.). 192p. 1999. pap. 16.95 (1-928586-03-1) P Russell.

— Future of Social Democracy: Views of Leaders from Around the World. 2000. pap. text 19.95 (0-8020-8066-9) U of Toronto Pr.

— The Global Brain Awakens: Our Next Evolutionary Leap. (Illus.). 2000. pap. 16.95 (1-86204-713-8, Pub. by Element MA) Penguin Putnam.

Russell, Peter. The Global Brain Awakens: Our Next Evolutionary Leap. St. John, Gloria et al, eds. (Illus.). 352p. 1995. 22.00 (1-885261-05-5) Global Brain.

Russell, Peter. The Image of Woman As a Figure of the Spirit. 97p. pap. write for info. (3-7052-0213-8, Pub. by Poetry Salzburg) Intl Spec Bk.

Russell, Peter. Key to the Constitution: Can the Canadians Become a Sovereign People? 200p. (Orig.). 1992. text 35.00 (0-8020-2851-9); pap. text 14.95 (0-8020-7730-7) U of Toronto Pr.

— Omens & Elegies; Descent; Visions & Ruins; Agamemnon in Hades. 102p. 1997. pap. 15.95 (3-7052-0112-3, Pub. by Poetry Salzburg) Intl Spec Bk.

— Paysages Le'Gendaires & Acts of Recognition. LC 99-462689. 109p. 1997. pap. 14.95 (3-7052-0106-9, Pub. by Poetry Salzburg) Intl Spec Bk.

Russell, Peter. Poetic Asides 1. 121p. pap. write for info. (3-7052-0205-7, Pub. by Poetry Salzburg) Intl Spec Bk.

— The Pound Connection. 77p. pap. write for info. (3-7052-0203-0, Pub. by Poetry Salzburg) Intl Spec Bk.

Russell, Peter. Selected Sonnets. 72p. (Orig.). 1996. pap. 10.00 (0-944920-16-0) Bellowing Ark Pr.

Russell, Peter. Venice Poems, 1965. 332p. pap. write for info. (3-7052-0946-9, Pub. by Poetry Salzburg) Intl Spec Bk.

Russell, Peter. Waking up in Time: Finding Inner Peace in Times of Accelerating Change. rev. ed. LC 98-19130. Orig. Title: The White Hole in Time. (Illus.). 216p. 1998. pap. 16.95 (1-57983-002-1) Origin Pr CA.

Russell, Peter, ed. Ezra Pound: A Collection of Essays. LC 67-31288. 268p. (C). 1968. reprint ed. lib. bdg. 75.00 (0-8383-0791-4) M S G Haskell Hse.

Russell, Peter & Bannatyne, Patricia. Surgical Pathology of the Ovaries. (Illus.). 539p. 1989. text 199.00 (0-443-03535-0) Church.

Russell, Peter & Evans, Roger. The Creative Manager: Finding Inner Vision & Wisdom in Uncertain Times. LC 91-44415. (Management Ser.). 192p. 1992. text 32.95 (1-55542-413-9) Jossey-Bass.

Russell, Peter & Farnsworth, Annabelle. Surgical Pathology of the Ovaries. 2nd ed. LC 97-9201. 1997. text 175.00 (0-443-05384-7) Church.

Russell, Peter & Jay, Peter. All for the Wolves: Selected Poems, 1947-1975. 152p. 1984. 25.00 (0-85646-095-8, Pub. by Anvil Press) Dufour.

— All for the Wolves: Selected Poems 1947-1975. 152p. 1984. pap. 17.95 (0-85646-096-6, Pub. by Anvil Press) Dufour.

Russell, Peter E. His Majesty's Judges: Provincial Society & the Superior Court in Massachusetts, 1692-1774. LC 90-46697. (Distinguished Studies in American Legal & Constitutional History: Vol. 22). 330p. 1990. reprint ed. text 25.00 (0-8240-2527-X) Garland.

Russell, Peter H. Constitutional Odyssey: Can Canadians Be a Sovereign People? 2nd ed. 250p. 1993. pap. text 18.95 (0-8020-6997-5) U of Toronto Pr.

*Russell, Peter J. Fundamentals of Genetics. 2nd ed. LC 99-43584. 528p. (C). 1999. pap. 77.00 (0-321-03626-3) Addison-Wesley.

Russell, Peter J. Genetics. 5th ed. LC 97-29688. 805p. (C). 1997. 92.00 (0-321-00038-2); pap. text, student ed. 28.00 (0-321-00452-3) Addson-Wesley Educ.

Russell, Philip. Body & Blood. LC 98-14595. 220p. 1998. pap. 14.95 (1-886157-15-4) BkMk.

— Mexico: From Conquest to NAFTA. Date not set. pap. 24.95 (0-9639223-2-7) Mexico Res Ctr.

— Mexico under Salinas. LC 93-81213. (Illus.). x, 486p. (C). 1994. pap. text 14.95 (0-9639223-0-0) Mexico Res Ctr.

— Mouse Droppings Book of Macintosh Hints: What Apple Didn't Tell You about Your Macintosh Computer. 100p. 1986. spiral bd. 8.95 (0-318-22782-7) Macintosh Users Group.

— Mouse Droppings Second Book of Macintosh Hints. 116p. 1988. spiral bd. 8.95 (0-318-32989-1) Macintosh Users Group.

Russell, Philip & Hemmer, Joe. Energy-Smart Building for Increased Quality, Comfort, & Sales. Lamberton, Sharon & Soble, Carol E., eds. LC 93-20754. (Illus.). 150p. (Orig.). 1993. pap. 20.00 (0-86718-387-X) Home Builder.

Russell, Philip L. El Salvador in Crisis. (Illus.). 168p. 1984. pap. 9.95 (0-931302-02-1) Colo River Pr.

Russell, Phillip L. Mexico in Transition. (Illus.). 176p. 1977. pap. 7.95 (0-931302-01-3) Colo River Pr.

Russell, Phillips. Harvesters. LC 73-156713. (Essay Index Reprint Ser.). 1977. reprint ed. 23.95 (0-8369-2295-6) Ayer.

— These Old Stone Walls. unabridged ed. LC 73-151830. (Illus.). 154p. 1983. reprint ed. pap. 6.95 (0-940715-03-1) Chapel Hill Hist.

Russell-Pineda, Diana, tr. see Duran, Luis H.

Russell-Pineda, Diane, tr. see Agosin, Marjorie.

Russell, Preston & Hines, Barbara. Savannah: A History of Her People since 1733. LC 91-45219. 1993. pap. 18.00 (0-913720-81-X) Beil.

Russell, Pugh, jt. auth. see Flower, Mary.

*Russell, R. A. Un Lugar Preparado para Ti...Tr. of A Place Prepared for You. (SPA.). 10p. 1998. 1.00 (1-56722-251-X) Word Aflame.

— A Place Prepared for You. (Illus.). 10p. 1998. 1.00 (1-56722-250-1) Word Aflame.

Russell, R. Andrew. Odour Detection by Mobile Robots. LC 98-52909. 217p. 1999. 42.00 (981-02-3791-X) World Scientific Pub.

Russell, R. B., ed. Guide to First Edition Prices, 1998/9. 288p. 1997. pap. 24.95 (1-872621-29-5, Pub. by Tartarus Pr) Firebird Dist.

*Russell, R. B., ed. Guide to First Edition Prices, 2000/1. (Illus.). 327p. 1999. pap. 29.95 (1-872621-45-7, Pub. by Tartarus Pr) Firebird Dist.

Russell, R. B., tr. see Alain-Fournier.

Russell, R. Dana. The Pughs of Bayou Lafourche. 100p. 1985. 10.00 (0-911051-25-2) Plain View.

*Russell, R. G., ed. Novel Approaches to Treatment of Osteoporosis. Vol. 25. (Illus.). 264p. 1999. 99.00 (3-540-64813-5) Spr-Verlag.

Russell, R. G. & Dieppe, P. A. Osteoarthritis: Current Research & Prospects for Pharmacological Intervention. 232p. (C). 1991. 300.00 (1-85271-093-4, Pub. by IBC Tech Srvs) St Mut.

Russell, R. L. From Nightingale to Now: Nurse Education in Australia. 256p. 1990. pap. text 44.00 (0-7295-0338-0, Pub. by Harcourt) Saunders.

— Language in Psychotherapy: Strategies of Discovery. LC 87-2511. (Emotions, Personality, & Psychotherapy Ser.). (Illus.). 368p. (C). 1987. text 80.00 (0-306-42422-3, Kluwer Plenum) Kluwer Academic.

Russell, R. Robert & Wilkinson, Maurice. Microeconomics: A Synthesis of Modern & Neoclassical Theory. LC 78-17175. 476p. reprint ed. pap. 147.60 (0-7837-3501-4, 205783400008) Bks Demand.

*Russell, Ralph. An Anthology of Urdu Literature. 320p. 2000. pap. 19.95 (1-85754-468-4, Pub. by Carcanet Pr) Paul & Co Pubs.

Russell, Ralph. Hidden in the Lute: An Anthology of Two Centures of Urdu Literature. 320p. 1995. 47.50 (1-85754-117-0, Pub. by Carcanet Pr) Paul & Co Pubs.

— How Not to Write the History of Urdu Literature: And Other Essays on Urdu & Islam. LC 99-938562. 244p. 1999. text 26.50 (0-19-564749-1) OUP.

— The Pursuit of Urdu Literature: A Select History. LC 92-12331. 320p. (C). 1993. text 65.00 (1-85649-028-9, Pub. by Zed Books) St Martin.

Russell, Ralph & Islam, Khurshidul, eds. Ghalib, 1797-1869: Life & Letters. (Oxford India Paperbacks Ser.). (Illus.). 404p. 1995. pap. text 13.95 (0-19-563506-X) OUP.

Russell, Randy. Billy the Kid: The Story - The Trial. LC 94-74143. (Illus.). (Orig.). 1995. pap. 15.95 (0-9644476-3-0) Crystal Pr NM.

— Five Minutes Late. 32p. (Orig.). 1988. pap. 1.50 (0-944388-01-9) TBS Pubns.

— Universe City. 48p. (Orig.). 1987. pap. 3.00 (0-944388-00-0) TBS Pubns.

Russell, Randy & Barnett, Janet. Mountain Ghost Stories & Curious Tales of Western North Carolina. LC 88-19380. 109p. 1988. 11.95 (0-89587-064-9) Blair.

Russell, Randy & Warren, Van R. The Gxdere Principle: Self Actrualization for Those Who Dare to Color Outside the Lines. LC 98-70587. 208p. 1998. pap. 15.95 (0-9644476-7-3) Crystal Pr NM.

Russell, Randy, jt. auth. see Barnett, Janet.

Russell, Ray. Absolute Power. deluxe limited ed. 256p. 1992. 49.00 (0-940776-27-8) Maclay Assoc.

— Case Against Satan. 1962. 10.95 (0-8392-1008-6) Astor-Honor.

— Haunted Castles: The Complete Gothic Tales of Ray Russell. LC 85-61370. 192p. 1985. 12.95 (0-940776-20-0) Maclay Assoc.

— The Miracle of Personal Leadership: Revolutionary New Personal Leadership Secrets to Energize & Empower Your Work & Life. LC 95-77750. 304p. 1995. boxed set 26.95 (0-7872-0603-2) Kendall-Hunt.

Russell, Raymond. Utopia in Zion: The Israeli Experience with Worker Cooperatives. LC 94-19576. (SUNY Series in Israeli Studies). 330p. (C). 1995. text 59.50 (0-7914-2443-X); pap. text 19.95 (0-7914-2444-8) State U NY Pr.

Russell, Raymond & Rus, Veljko, eds. International Handbook of Participation in Organizations Vol. 2: Ownership & Participation. (International Handbook of Participation in Organizations Ser.: No. II). (Illus.). 384p. 1991. text 140.00 (0-19-828702-X) OUP.

Russell, Raymond, jt. auth. see Perry, Stewart E.

Russell, Raymond M., jt. auth. see Coleman, Ronny J.

Russell Reerdink Company Staff. Horse Buyer's Notebook. 1996. pap. 15.95 (0-929346-44-0) R Meerdink Co Ltd.

Russell, Rex. What the Bible Says about Healthy Living: Three Biblical Principles That Will Change Your Diet & Improve Your Health. (Illus.). 128p. 1999. 14.99 (0-8007-1768-6) Revell.

Russell, Richard. The Alchemical Works of Geber. 308p. Date not set. 24.95 (0-8488-2384-2) Amereon Ltd.

— The Dow Theory Today. LC 81-68858. 119p. 1981. reprint ed. pap. 12.00 (0-87034-061-1) Fraser Pub Co.

— Insomnia. (Illus.). 29p. 1991. pap. 10.00 (0-932526-36-5) Nexus Pr.

Russell, Richard & Brewer, Doug. Leader Lore: The Book. (Illus.). 200p. 1993. write for info. (0-9634786-4-8) Mass Media Dist.

Russell, Richard, jt. auth. see Frost, A. J.

Russell, Richard, jt. auth. see Hoffman, Kenneth.

Russell, Richard, jt. auth. see Holmyard, E. J.

Russell, Richard, tr. see Geber.

Russell, Richard, tr. see Geber the Arabian.

Russell, Richard A. Project Hula: Secret Soviet-American Cooperation in the War Against Japan. 50p. 1998. pap. 5.50 (0-16-049376-5) USGPO.

— Project Hula: Secret Soviet-American Naval Cooperation in the War Against Japan. LC 97-7022. (U. S. Navy in the Modern World Ser.). 1997. write for info. (0-945274-35-1) Naval Hist Ctr.

Russell, Richard J. River & Delta Morphology. LC 67-29343. (Louisiana State University Studies, Coastal Studies Ser.: No. 20). 63p. reprint ed. pap. 30.00 (0-608-14409-6, 205168800004) Bks Demand.

Russell, Richard L. George F. Kennan's Strategic Thought: The Making of an American Political Realist. LC 98-33625. 208p. 1999. 55.00 (0-275-96402-7, Praeger Pubs) Greenwood.

Russell, Rinaldina. Italian Women Writers: A Bio-Bibliographical Sourcebook. LC 93-49535. 512p. 1994. lib. bdg. 105.00 (0-313-28347-8, Greenwood Pr) Greenwood.

Russell, Rinaldina, ed. The Feminist Encyclopedia of Italian Literature. LC 96-35353. 416p. 1997. lib. bdg. 85.00 (0-313-29435-6, Greenwood Pr) Greenwood.

An Asterisk (*) at the beginning of an entry indicates that the title is appearing for the first time.

Russell, Rinaldina, tr. see D'Aragona, Tullia.

Russell, Robert. The Answer Will Come. 91p. 1981. reprint ed. pap. 6.95 (*0-87516-440-4*) DeVorss.

— The Fun Bus. (Technical Notes Ser.: No. 15). 43p. (Orig.). 1977. pap. 2.00 (*0-932288-42-1*) Ctr Intl Ed U of MA.

— Russian Drama of the Revolutionary Period. 192p. 1987. 50.50 (*0-389-20757-8*) B&N Imports.

Russell, Robert, ed. see Gould, Peter & Stearns, Stephen.

Russell, Robert A. Dry Those Tears. 133p. 1975. reprint ed. pap. 6.95 (*0-87516-203-7*) DeVorss.

— Making the Contact. 90p. 1980. reprint ed. pap. 6.95 (*0-87516-391-2*) DeVorss.

— You Too Can Be Prosperous. 162p. 1975. reprint ed. pap. 8.95 (*0-87516-205-3*) DeVorss.

Russell, Robert H. & Patterson, Margaret J., eds. Behind the Lines: Case Studies in Investigative Reporting. 350p. 1986. text 48.50 (*0-231-06058-0*) Col U Pr.

Russell, Robert H., tr. see Galdos, Benito Perez.

Russell, Robert J., et al, eds. Chaos & Complexity: Scientific Perspectives on Divine Action. 416p. (C). 1996. pap. text 21.95 (*0-268-00812-4*) U of Notre Dame Pr.

— Evolutionary & Molecular Biology. (Scientific Perspectives on Divine Action Ser.: Vol. 3). 552p. 1999. pap. 24.95 (*0-268-02753-6*, Pub. by U of Notre Dame Pr) Chicago Distribution Ctr.

— Quantum Cosmology & the Laws of Nature: Scientific Perspectives on Divine Action. (C). 1994. pap. text 21.95 (*0-268-03976-3*) U of Notre Dame Pr.

***Russell, Robert John, et al, eds.** Neuroscience & the Person. (Scientific Perspectives on Divine Action Ser.). 500p. 2000. pap. 26.95 (*0-268-01490-6*, Pub. by U of Notre Dame Pr) Chicago Distribution Ctr.

Russell, Robert L., ed. Reassessing Psychotherapy Research. LC 94-8548. 240p. 1994. lib. bdg. 40.00 (*0-89862-755-9*, C2755) Guilford Pubns.

Russell, Robert L., jt. auth. see Shirk, Steven R.

Russell, Robert P., tr. see Augustine, Saint.

Russell, Robert R. Economic Aspects of Southern Sectionalism, 1840-1861. LC 72-11346. (American South Ser.). 1973. reprint ed. 30.95 (*0-405-05062-3*) Ayer.

— Improvement of Communication with the Pacific Coast as an Issue in American Politics, 1783-1864. Bruchey, Stuart, ed. LC 80-1341. (Railroads Ser.). (Illus.). 1981. reprint ed. lib. bdg. 30.95 (*0-405-13813-X*) Ayer.

Russell, Roberta. Report on Effective Psychotherapy: Legislative Testimony. Smith, Suzanne, ed. LC 81-90112. 81p. (C). 1981. 30.00 (*0-940106-00-0*) Hillgarth Pr.

— Report on Effective Psychotherapy: Legislative Testimony & Recommendations for Therapeutic Relationships in a Caring World. rev. ed. Smith, Suzanne, ed. 120p. pap. text 14.95 (*0-940106-54-X*) Hillgarth Pr.

Russell, Roberta & Laing, R. D. R. D. Laing & Me: Lessons in Love. Smith, Suzanne, ed. LC 92-70905. (Illus.). 292p. 1992. 25.95 (*0-940106-61-2*); pap. 16.95 (*0-940106-50-7*) Hillgarth Pr.

***Russell, Roberta & Taylor, Bernard.** Operations Management with Multimedia CD. 3rd ed. 900p. 1999. 97.33 (*0-13-030346-1*, Prentice Hall) P-H.

***Russell, Roberta S. & Taylor, Bernard W.** Operations Management. 3rd ed. LC 99-25011. 879p. 1999. text 96.00 incl. audio compact disk (*0-13-013092-3*) P-H.

Russell, Robin, et al, contrib. by. Pain Relief in Labour. 252p. 1997. pap. 43.00 (*0-7279-1009-4*, Pub. by BMJ Pub) Login Brothers Bk Co.

***Russell, Robin, ed.** Anaesthesia in Obstetrics & Gynaecology. (Fundamentals of Anaesthesia & Acute Medicine Ser.). 369p. 2000. pap. text 62.95 (*0-7279-1276-3*, Pub. by BMJ Pub) Login Brothers Bk Co.

Russell, Robin I., ed. Elemental Diets. LC 80-25869. 280p. 1981. 155.00 (*0-8493-5671-7*, RM229, CRC Reprint) Franklin.

Russell, Robyn. Drawn Together. (Black Lace Ser.). 1998. mass mkt. 6.95 (*0-352-33269-7*, Pub. by BLA4) London Brdge.

— Ginger Root. (Orig.). 1997. mass mkt. 5.95 (*0-352-33152-6*, Pub. by BLA4) London Brdge.

***Russell, Roger.** The Darker Side of Glory. 48p. 2000. pap. 8.95 (*0-935931-32-5*, Gray Matter Pubg) Iberian Pub.

Russell, Roger W., ed. see National Research Council, U. S. National Committe.

Russell, Ronald. Cambridgeshire & Cambridge. (Country Guide Ser.: Vol. 23). (Illus.). 72p. write for info. (*0-85263-954-6*, Pub. by Shire Pubns) Lubrecht & Cramer.

— Discovering Antique Prints. 1989. pap. 25.00 (*0-85263-587-7*, Pub. by Shire Pubns) St Mut.

***Russell, Ronald.** Vast Enquiring Soul: Explorations Into the Further Reaches of Consciousness. 2000. pap. 13.95 (*1-57174-153-4*) Hampton Roads Pub Co.

Russell, Ronald, ed. Using the Whole Brain: Integrating the Right & Left Brain with Hemi-Sync Sound Patterns. 264p. 1993. pap. 14.95 (*1-878901-86-9*) Hampton Roads Pub Co.

Russell, Ronald & Medcalf, Donald. Hawaiian Money Standard Catalog, 1991. 2nd ed. (Illus.). 160p. 1990. 25.00 (*0-9623263-0-5*) R Russell.

***Russell, Rosemary.** Making Sense of Standards & Technologies for Serials Management: A Guide. 192p. 2000. pap. 85.00 (*1-85604-338-X*, LAP338X, Pub. by Library Association) Bernan Associates.

Russell, Ross. Bird Lives! The High Life & Hard Times of Charlie (Yardbird) Parker. LC 95-43925. (Illus.). 431p. 1996. reprint ed. pap. 15.95 (*0-306-80679-7*) Da Capo.

Russell, Roy E. Life, Mind & Laughter: A Theory of Laughter. LC 87-91652. (Illus.). 128p. (Orig.). (C). 1987. pap. 8.50 (*0-9619162-0-6*) Russell WV.

Russell, Russ. Managing the Curriculum Effectively. (Managing Colleges Effectively Ser.: No. 3). 224p. 1996. pap. write for info. (*0-7507-0549-3*, Falmer Pr) Taylor & Francis.

Russell, Rusty, jt. auth. see Russell, Bob.

Russell, Ruth. Lake Front. LC 74-22811. (Labor Movement in Fiction & Non-Fiction Ser.). (Illus.). reprint ed. 45.00 (*0-404-58467-5*) AMS Pr.

***Russell, Ruth.** Pastimes. (C). 1999. pap. 50.00 (*0-07-240030-7*) McGrw-H Hghr Educ.

Russell, Ruth V. Pastimes: The Context of Contemporary Leisure. 480p. (C). 1995. text. write for info. (*0-697-22725-1*) Brown & Benchmark.

Russell, Ruth V., jt. auth. see Riddick, Carol.

Russell, S., ed. see Hamilton, Elizabeth.

Russell, Sallie J. Dynamic Dimensional Designs. LC 98-137161. (Illus.). 78p. 1997. pap. 16.95 (*1-883777-02-X*) SJR Sew.

— Pockets Zippers Colors: Clothing Designs for Kids. (Illus.). 44p. (Orig.). 1992. pap. 8.95 (*1-883777-00-3*) SJR Sew.

— Which Stitch? (Illus.). 28p. 1997. pap. 6.00 (*1-883777-01-1*) SJR Sew.

Russell, Sally, ed. see Russell, Ina Dillard.

Russell, Sandi. Render Me My Song: African-American Women Writers from Slavery to the Present. 230p. 1998. pap. text 15.00 (*0-7881-5234-3*) DIANE Pub.

Russell, Scott & Sanders, Scott R. Terrarium. 288p. (Orig.). 1996. pap. 12.95 (*0-253-21021-6*) Ind U Pr.

***Russell, Scott R.** North American Clone Brews: Homebrew Recipes for Your Favorite American & Canadian Beers. LC 00-26599. (Illus.). 192p. 2000. pap. 14.95 (*1-58017-246-6*) Storey Bks.

Russell, Sean. Beneath the Vaulted Hills. 1997. 21.95 (*0-614-27886-4*) DAW Bks.

— Beneath the Vaulted Hills, Vol. 1. (River Into Darkness Ser.). 1998. mass mkt. 6.99 (*0-88677-794-1*, Pub. by DAW Bks) Penguin Putnam.

— Beneath Vaulted Hill. LC 97-190865. 576p. 1997. pap. 24.95 (*0-88677-745-3*, Pub. by DAW Bks) Penguin Putnam.

— Compass of the Soul. (River Into Darkness Ser.). 416p. 1999. mass mkt. 6.99 (*0-88677-933-2*, Pub. by DAW Bks) Penguin Putnam.

— Compass of the Soul, Vol. 2. (River Into Darkness Ser.). 400p. 1998. 24.95 (*0-88677-792-5*, Pub. by DAW Bks) Penguin Putnam.

— Gatherer of Clouds. 528p. (Orig.). 1992. mass mkt. 6.99 (*0-88677-536-1*, Pub. by DAW Bks) Penguin Putnam.

— The Initiate Brother, Bk. 1. 480p. (Orig.). 1991. mass mkt. 6.99 (*0-88677-466-7*, Pub. by DAW Bks) Penguin Putnam.

— Sea Without a Shore. (Moontide & Magic Rise Ser.: Vol. 2). 608p. 1996. mass mkt. 5.99 (*0-88677-665-1*, Pub. by DAW Bks) Penguin Putnam.

— World Without End. (Moontide & Magic Rise Ser.: No. 1). 608p. (Orig.). 1995. pap. 5.99 (*0-88677-624-4*, Pub. by DAW Bks) Penguin Putnam.

Russell, Shannon D. & Russell, Toni N. The Polaris Writings. 187p. (Orig.). 1997. pap. 12.95 (*0-9657274-0-8*) Nrth Star Pub.

Russell, Sharman. Frederick Douglass: Abolitionist Editor. Huggins, Nathan I., ed. (Black Americans of Achievement Ser.). (Illus.). 124p. (Orig.). (YA). (gr. 5 up). 1987. lib. bdg. 19.95 (*1-55546-580-3*) Chelsea Hse.

— Frederick Douglass: Abolitionist Editor. Huggins, Nathan I., ed. (Black Americans of Achievement Ser.). (Illus.). 124p. (Orig.). (YA). (gr. 5 up). 1989. pap. 9.95 (*0-7910-0204-7*) Chelsea Hse.

Russell, Sharman A. Kill the Cowboy: A Battle of Mythology in the New West. (Illus.). 256p. 1993. 20.00 (*0-201-58123-X*) Addison-Wesley.

— Songs of the Fluteplayer: Seasons of Life in the Southwest. (Illus.). 176p. 1992. pap. 10.00 (*0-201-60821-9*) Addison-Wesley.

***Russell, Sharman Apt.** The Last Matriarch. LC 99-6657. 198p. 2000. 19.95 (*0-8263-2131-3*) U of NM Pr.

— Writing Down the River into the Heart of the Grand Canyon. LC 98-11528. (Illus.). 134p. 1998. 29.95 (*0-87358-709-X*) Northland AZ.

Russell, Sharon A. A Guide to African Cinema. LC 97-27560. (Reference Guides to the World's Cinema Ser.). 208p. 1998. lib. bdg. 75.00 (*0-313-29621-9*, Greenwood Pr) Greenwood.

— Semiotics & Lighting: A Study of Six Modern French Cameramen. Kirkpatrick, Diane, ed. LC 81-3377. (Studies in Photography & Cinematography: No. 2). 185p. 1981. reprint ed. pap. 57.40 (*0-8357-1189-7*, 207021500064) Bks Demand.

— Stephen King: A Critical Companion. LC 95-50460. (Critical Companions to Popular Contemporary Writers Ser.). 192p. 1996. 29.95 (*0-313-29417-8*, Greenwood Pr) Greenwood.

Russell, Sharon S. & Teitelbaum, Michael. International Migration & International Trade. LC 92-12848. (Discussion Paper Ser.: Vol. 160). 96p. 1992. pap. 22.00 (*0-8213-2116-1*, 12116) World Bank.

Russell, Sheldon. Empire. 204p. 1993. 18.95 (*0-934188-39-4*) Evans Pubns.

***Russell, Sheldon.** Requiem at Dawn. 2000. mass mkt. 5.99 (*0-7860-1103-3*, Pinncle Kensgtn) Kensgtn Pub Corp.

Russell, Sheldon. The Savage Trail. 320p. 1998. pap. 4.99 (*0-7860-0540-8*, Pinncle Kensgtn) Kensgtn Pub Corp.

Russell, Sirley J. A New Vision in Poetry. 45p. 1995. pap. write for info. (*0-9643885-1-0*) Personal Profiles.

Russell, Stella. Art in the World. 4th ed. LC 92-70938. (Illus.). 550p. (C). 1992. pap. text. write for info. (*0-03-276543-6*) Harcourt Coll Pubs.

Russell, Stella P. Art in the World. 3rd ed. (Illus.). (C). 1989. pap. text 42.75 (*0-03-028672-7*) Harcourt Coll Pubs.

Russell, Stella Pandell. ART IN THE WORLD 4E. 4th ed. (C). 1993. pap. text 70.00 (*0-03-076543-9*) Harcourt Coll Pubs.

Russell, Stephen. The Barefoot Doctor's Guide to the Tao: A Spiritual Handbook for Urban Warriors. LC 98-50259. 224p. 1999. pap. 13.00 (*0-8129-3158-0*, Times Bks) Crown Pub Group.

Russell, Stephen & Kolb, Jurgen. The Tao of Sexual Massage. (Illus.). 192p. 1992. per. 15.00 (*0-671-78089-1*, Fireside) S&S Trade Pap.

Russell, Stephen M. & Monson, Gale. The Birds of Sonora. LC 97-33938. (Illus.). 490p. 1998. 75.00 (*0-8165-1635-9*) U of Ariz Pr.

Russell, Steven. Jewish Identity & Civil Processes. 192p. 1996. text 64.00 (*0-312-15878-5*) St Martin.

***Russell, Steven J.** Being Nice at a Price: Emotional Domination, Depression & the Search for Autonomy. McCoy, Lisa, ed. LC 99-60583. 160p. 1999. pap. 17.95 (*0-9660092-4-X*) Puget Sound.

Russell, Storm J., jt. ed. see Curtis, James E.

Russell, Stuart & Wefald, Eric H. Do the Right Thing: Studies in Limited Rationality. (Artificial Intelligence Ser.). 224p. 1991. 31.50 (*0-262-18144-4*) MIT Pr.

Russell, Stuart, jt. auth. see Cook, Stephen.

Russell, Stuart H. Resource Recovery Economics: Methods for Feasibility Analysis. (Pollution Engineering & Technology Ser.: Vol. 22). (Illus.). 312p. 1982. text 155.00 (*0-8247-1726-0*) Dekker.

Russell, Stuart J. The Use of Knowledge in Analogy & Induction. 1989. pap. text 34.95 (*1-55860-089-2*) Morgan Kaufmann.

Russell, Stuart J. & Norvig, Peter. Artificial Intelligence: A Modern Approach. LC 94-36444. 912p. 1994. 73.00 (*0-13-103805-2*) P-H.

Russell, Susan, jt. auth. see Flynn, Robert.

Russell, Susan D., ed. Ritual, Power & Economy: Upland-Lowland Contrasts in Mainland Southeast Asia. (Occasional Papers: No. 14). 143p. (C). 1989. pap. 12.95 (*1-877979-14-7*) SE Asia.

Russell, Susan D. & Cunningham, Clark E., eds. Changing Lives, Changing Rites: Ritual & Social Dynamics in Philippine & Indonesian Uplands. LC 88-63412. (Michigan Studies on South & Southeast Asia: No. 1). 201p. (Orig.). 1989. pap. 16.95 (*0-89148-058-7*) Ctr S&SE Asian.

Russell, Susan D., jt. ed. see Aragon, Lorraine V.

Russell, Susan J. & Mokros, Jan. Combining & Comparing: Addition & Subtraction. Cory, Beverly et al, eds. (Investigations in Number, Data, & Space Ser.). (Illus.). 121p. (Orig.). 1994. pap., teacher ed. 22.95 (*0-86651-805-3*, DS21243) Seymour Pubns.

Russell, Susan J. & Rubin, Andee. Landmarks in the Hundreds: The Number System. Samii, Priscilla C. & Cory, Beverly, eds. LC 94-214850. (Investigations in Number, Data, & Space Ser.). (Illus.). 98p. (Orig.). 1994. pap., teacher ed. 22.95 (*0-86651-796-0*, DS21236) Seymour Pubns.

— Landmarks in the Thousands: The Number System. Samii, Priscilla C. et al, eds. (Investigations in Number, Data, & Space Ser.). (Illus.). 110p. (Orig.). 1994. pap., teacher ed. 22.95 (*0-86651-812-6*, DS21250) Seymour Pubns.

— Landmarks in the Thousands: The Number System. rev. ed. Anderson, Catherine & Cory, Beverly, eds. (Investigations in Number, Data, & Space Ser.). (Illus.). 110p. (Orig.). (YA). (gr. 4 up). 1997. pap. text 22.95 (*1-57232-746-4*, 43893) Seymour Pubns.

Russell, Susan J., et al. Does It Walk, Crawl, or Swim? Sorting & Classifying Data. Anderson, Catherine et al, eds. (Investigations in Number, Data, & Space Ser.). (Illus.). 156p. (Orig.). (J). (gr. 2). 1996. pap., teacher ed. 22.95 (*1-57232-216-0*, DS21647) Seymour Pubns.

— Does It Walk, Crawl, or Swim? Sorting & Classifying Data. rev. ed. Anderson, Catherine et al, eds. LC 97-196102. (Illus.). 159p. (Orig.). (J). (gr. 2 up). 1997. pap. text 22.95 (*1-57232-655-7*, 43802) Seymour Pubns.

— Implementing the Investigations in Number, Data, & Space Curriculum: Grades 1 & 2. rev. ed. Anderson, Catherine et al, eds. (Investigations in Number, Data, & Space Ser.). (Illus.). 50p. 1997. pap. text, teacher ed. 5.95 (*1-57232-222-5*, 21653) Seymour Pubns.

— Implementing the Investigations in Number, Data, & Space Curriculum: Grades 3 & 4. Samii, Priscilla C. et al, eds. (Investigations in Number, Data, & Space Ser.). 48p. (Orig.). 1994. pap., teacher ed. 12.95 (*0-86651-892-4*, DS21294) Seymour Pubns.

— Implementing the Investigations in Number, Date, & Space Curriculum: Grades 3, 4, & 5. rev. ed. Anderson, Catherine et al, eds. (Investigations in Number, Data, & Space Ser.). 60p. 1996. pap., teacher ed. 12.95 (*1-57232-380-9*, DS21663) Seymour Pubns.

— Mathematical Thinking at Grade 3: Introduction. Samii, Priscilla C. et al, eds. (Investigations in Number, Data, & Space Ser.). (Illus.). 144p. (Orig.). 1994. pap., teacher ed. 22.95 (*0-86651-800-2*, DS21238) Seymour Pubns.

— Quilt Squares & Block Towns: 2-D & 3-D Geometry. Anderson, Catherine & Cory, Beverly, eds. (Investigations in Number, Data, & Space Ser.). (Illus.). 238p. (J). (gr. 1 up). 1997. pap. text 32.95 (*1-57232-469-4*, 43705) Seymour Pubns.

— The Shape of Data: Statistics. rev. ed. Anderson, Catherine & Cory, Beverly, eds. (Investigations in Number, Data, & Space Ser.). (Illus.). 105p. (YA). (gr. 4 up). 1997. pap. text 22.95 (*1-57232-748-0*, 43895) Seymour Pubns.

— The Shape of the Data: Statistics. Samii, Priscilla C. et al, eds. LC 94-214866. (Investigations in Number, Data, & Space Ser.). (Illus.). 97p. (Orig.). 1994. pap., teacher ed. 22.95 (*0-86651-814-2*, DS21252) Seymour Pubns.

Russell, Susan J., jt. auth. see Economopoulos, Karen.

Russell, Susan J., jt. auth. see Kliman, Marlene.

***Russell, Susan Jo, et al.** Mathematical Thinking at Grade 3: Introduction. LC 97-172739. (Illus.). 1998. write for info. (*1-57232-694-8*) Seymour Pubns.

Russell, T. Conan, jt. ed. see Stich, Rodney.

Russell, T. F., et al, eds. Computational Methods in Water Resources IX, 2 vols., Set. LC 92-70436. (Computational Methods in Water Resources Ser.: Vol. 9). 1594p. 1992. 548.00 (*1-56252-098-9*, 1983) Computational Mech MA.

Russell, T. P., et al, eds. Scattering, Deformation & Fracture in Polymers. (MRS Symposium Proceedings Ser.: Vol. 79). 1987. text 17.50 (*0-931837-44-8*) Materials Res.

Russell-Taylor, Elisabeth, et al. Mother Country. 167p. 1993. 32.00 (*0-7206-0848-1*, Pub. by P Owen Ltd) Dufour.

— Pillion Riders. 165p. 1993. 29.00 (*0-7206-0890-2*, Pub. by P Owen Ltd) Dufour.

Russell, Terence. The Built Environment: A Subject Index, 1800-1960, 4 vols., Set. 4450p. 1990. text 700.00 (*0-576-40006-8*) Ashgate Pub Co.

Russell, Terence & Thornton, Ann-Marie. Gardens & Landscapes in the Encyclopedie of Diderot & D'Alembert: The Letterpress Articles & Selected Engravings, 2 vols. LC 98-46723. (Illus.). 624p. 1999. text 131.95 (*1-85928-138-9*, Pub. by Ashgate Pub) Ashgate Pub Co.

Russell, Terence M. The Encyclopaedic Dictionary in the 18th Century: Architecture, Arts & Crafts, 5 vols. Incl. Ephraim Chambers: Encyclopedia. LC NA2540.R88. 400p. 1997. text 78.95 (*1-85928-063-3*, Pub. by Scolar Pr); John Harris & the Lexicon Technician: Incorporating the Works of Sir Francis Bacon & Sir Henry Wotton. LC 96-54482. 256p. 1997. text 69.95 (*1-85928-062-5*, Pub. by Scolar Pr); Samuel Johnson: A Dictionary of the English Language. LC 96-54482. 250p. 1997. text 69.95 (*1-85928-064-1*, Pub. by Scolar Pr); Society of Gentlemen: Encyclopedia Britannia. LC 96-54482. 256p. 1997. text 69.95 (*1-85928-065-X*, Pub. by Scolar Pr); Vol. 3. Builder's Dictionary. LC 96-54482. 288p. 1997. 69.95 (*1-85928-409-4*, Pub. by Scolar Pr); LC NA2540.R88. 299.95 (*1-85928-416-7*, Pub. by Scolar Pr) Ashgate Pub Co.

Russell, Terence M. & Ashworth, Ann-Marie. Architecture in the Encyclopedia of Diderot & D'Alembert: The Letterpress Articles & Selected Engravings. 224p. 1993. 96.95 (*0-85967-857-1*, Pub. by Scolar Pr) Ashgate Pub Co.

Russell, Terry & Harlen, Wynne. Assessing Science in the Primary Classroom: Practical Tasks. (Assessing Science in the Primary Classroom Ser.). (Illus.). 136p. 1990. pap. (*1-85396-078-0*) Corwin Pr.

Russell, Thomas, et al. Kleppner's Advertising Procedure. 4th ed. LC 98-17851. 716p. 1998. 90.67 (*0-13-908575-0*) P-H.

Russell, Thomas J. Pioneer Reminiscences of Jefferson County. Boody, Bertie H., ed. LC 86-62792. 160p. 1987. reprint ed. 28.00 (*0-318-22096-2*); reprint ed. pap. 20.00 (*0-318-22097-0*) SE Tex G&H.

Russell, Thomas J., jt. ed. see Schen, Michael A.

Russell, Thyra K. Job Sharing: An Annotated Bibliography. LC 93-45475. 221p. 1994. 32.50 (*0-8108-2826-X*) Scarecrow.

Russell, Tim. Effective Feedback Skills. 128p. (C). 1994. pap. 45.00 (*0-7494-1000-0*, Pub. by IPM Hse) St Mut.

— Effective Feedback Skills. 2nd ed. 128p. 1998. pap. 25.00 (*0-7494-2569-5*, Kogan Pg Educ) Stylus Pub VA.

Russell, Tim, tr. see Konig, Klaus-Peter & Hugo, Martin.

Russell, Timothy. Adversaria. 87p. 1993. 25.00 (*0-8101-5027-1*, TriQuart); pap. 10.95 (*0-8101-5002-6*, TriQuart) Northwestern U Pr.

Russell, Timothy, et al. Pavement Saw 3. (Illus.). 64p. 1996. pap. 4.00 (*1-886350-02-7*) Pavement Saw.

***Russell, Tom.** Brain Death: Philosophical Concepts & Problems. (New Critical Thinking in Philosophy Ser.). 194p. 2000. text 65.95 (*0-7546-1210-4*, Pub. by Ashgate Pub) Ashgate Pub Co.

Russell, Tom. Magic, Step-by-Step. LC 96-3019. (Illus.). 80p. (J). 1997. 17.95 (*0-8069-9533-5*) Sterling.

— Magic Step-by-Step. (J). (gr. 3-7). 1997. 17.95 (*0-614-29117-8*) Sterling.

— Magic Step by Step. (Illus.). 80p. 1998. 6.95 (*0-8069-9548-3*, Chapelle) Sterling.

Russell, Tom & Korthagen, Fred, eds. Teachers Who Teach Teachers: Reflections on Teacher Education. LC 95-16665. 202p. 1995. 75.00 (*0-7507-0465-9*, Falmer Pr); pap. 24.95 (*0-7507-0466-7*, Falmer Pr) Taylor & Francis.

Russell, Tom & Munby, Hugh, eds. Teachers & Teaching: From Classroom to Reflection. 224p. 1992. 89.95 (*0-7507-0020-3*, Falmer Pr); pap. 34.95 (*0-7507-0021-1*, Falmer Pr) Taylor & Francis.

Russell, Tom & Tyson, Sylvia, eds. And Then I Wrote. 244p. 1996. pap. 16.95 (*1-55152-023-0*, Pub. by Arsenal Pulp) LPC InBook.

Russell, Toni N., jt. auth. see Russell, Shannon D.

Russell, Tony. Blues: From Mississippi to the Millennium. 1997. 75.00 (*0-02-864862-5*) S&S Trade.

— The Complete Country Music Discography, 1922-1942. 1997. write for info. (*0-915608-07-3*) Country Music Found.

Russell, Travis. Signaling System, No. 7. LC 94-49007. (Series on Computer Communications). 1995. 65.00 (*0-07-054991-5*) McGraw.

— Signaling System, No. 7. 2nd ed. LC 98-4157. 500p. 1998. 65.00 (*0-07-058032-4*) McGraw.

***Russell, Travis.** Signaling System #7, No. 7. 3rd ed. (Telecommunications Ser.). 600p. 2000. 69.00 (*0-07-136119-7*) McGraw-Hill Prof.

Russell, Travis. Telecommunications Basics. LC 97-17358. (Telecommunications Ser.). (Illus.). 400p. 1997. pap. 44.95 (*0-07-057695-5*) McGraw.

Russell, Travis, jt. auth. see Agosta, John.

Russell, Trusten W. Voltaire, Dryden & Heroic Tragedy. LC 46-5389. reprint ed. 20.00 (*0-404-05467-6*) AMS Pr.

R

R

Russell, Victor L., ed. Forging a Consensus: Historical Essays on Toronto. 368p. 1984. pap. 14.95 (*0-8020-3410-1*); text 35.00 (*0-8020-3409-8*) U of Toronto Pr.

Russell, Virginia, jt. auth. see Farrar, Janet.

Russell, Virginia L., ed. see Williams, Kay, et al.

Russell, Vivian. Edith Wharton's Italian Gardens. LC 97-73771. (Illus.). 192p. 1998. 37.50 (*0-8212-2397-6*, Pub. by Bulfinch Pr) Little.

***Russell, Vivian.** Monet's Landscapes. (Illus.). 160p. 2000. 35.00 (*0-8212-2672-X*) Bulfinch Pr.

Russell, Vivian. Monet's Water Lilies, Vol. 1. LC ND553.M7A4 1998b. (Illus.). 88p. 1998. 24.95 (*0-8212-2553-7*, Pub. by Bulfinch Pr) Little.

Russell, W. C. Molecular Biology of Multiple Sclerosis. LC 96-9436. 320p. 1997. 175.00 (*0-471-96966-4*) Wiley.

Russell, W. Clark. The Frozen Pirate, 2 vols. LC 74-16518. (Science Fiction Ser.). 606p. 1975. reprint ed. 47.95 (*0-405-06311-3*) Ayer.

— The Yarn of Old Harbour Town. LC 99-46438. (Classics of Nautical Fiction Ser.). 255p. 1999. reprint ed. pap. 14.95 (*0-935526-65-X*, Pub. by McBooks Pr) LPC InBook.

Russell, W. M. & Burch, R. L. The Principles of Humane Experimental Technique. 238p. 1992. pap. 100.00 (*0-900767-78-2*, Pub. by Univs Fed Animal Welfare) St Mut.

Russell, W. R. Multiple Sclerosis: Control of the Disease. 84p. 1976. pap. text 18.25 (*0-08-021002-3*, Pergamon Pr) Elsevier.

Russell, Walter. The Book of Beauty. 1998. pap. 4.00 (*1-879605-57-0*) U Sci & Philos.

— The Book of Desire. 28p. 1997. pap. 4.00 (*1-879605-47-3*) U Sci & Philos.

— The Book of Early Whisperings. (Illus.). 103p. 1977. reprint ed. text 6.00 (*1-879605-17-1*) U Sci & Philos.

— The Book of Healing. 30p. 1998. pap. 4.00 (*1-879605-56-2*) U Sci & Philos.

***Russell, Walter.** The Book of Love. 50p. 1998. pap. 4.00 (*1-879605-53-8*) U Sci & Philos.

Russell, Walter. The Book of Rest. 20p. 1998. pap. 4.00 (*1-879605-54-6*) U Sci & Philos.

— Caring for Your Physical & Spiritual Health. 68p. 1994. pap. 3.00 (*1-879605-40-6*) U Sci & Philos.

— The Dawn of a New Day in Human Relations. Lombardi, Emilia L., ed. 20p. 1991. pap. text 2.00 (*1-879605-32-5*) U Sci & Philos.

— The Divine Iliad, 2 vols., Set. (Illus.). 524p. 1971. reprint ed. text 15.00 (*1-879605-24-4*) U Sci & Philos.

— The Divine Iliad, Vol. 1. (Illus.). 286p. 1971. reprint ed. text 10.00 (*1-879605-22-8*) U Sci & Philos.

— The Divine Iliad, Vol. 2. (Illus.). 238p. 1971. reprint ed. text 10.00 (*1-879605-23-6*) U Sci & Philos.

— The Electric Nature of the Universe. 1991. 3.00 (*1-879605-00-7*) U Sci & Philos.

— The Fifth Kingdom Man. 1991. 3.00 (*1-879605-01-5*) U Sci & Philos.

***Russell, Walter.** Fiftieth Anniversary Edition of Message of the Divine Iliad. large type ed. 130p. 1999. 35.00 (*1-879605-59-7*) U Sci & Philos.

Russell, Walter. Genius Inherent in Everyone. Lombardi, Emilia L., ed. 53p. 1994. pap. 3.00 (*1-879605-36-8*) U Sci & Philos.

— The Immortality of Man. Lombardi, Emilia L., ed. 20p. 1992. pap. text 3.00 (*1-879605-33-3*) U Sci & Philos.

— The Meaning & Acquisition of Wealth. 25p. 1993. pap. 2.00 (*1-879605-41-4*) U Sci & Philos.

— A New Concept of the Universe: A Brief Treatise on the Russell Cosmogony. (Illus.). 178p. 1989. reprint ed. pap. text 15.00 (*1-879605-13-9*) U Sci & Philos.

***Russell, Walter.** Playing with Fire: How the Bible Ignites Change in Your Soul. LC 00-25318. 2000. pap. 14.00 (*1-57683-142-6*) NavPress.

Russell, Walter. The Quest of the Grail. 1991. 2.00 (*1-879605-02-3*) U Sci & Philos.

— The Russell Periodic Chart of the Elements I. 1991. 5.00 (*1-879605-27-9*) U Sci & Philos.

— The Russell Periodic Chart of the Elements I, II, 2 vols., Set. 1991. 10.00 (*1-879605-29-5*) U Sci & Philos.

— The Russell Periodic Chart of the Elements II. 1991. 5.00 (*1-879605-28-7*) U Sci & Philos.

— Scientific Explanation of Sex. 1991. 5.00 (*1-879605-16-3*) U Sci & Philos.

— The Sculptor Searches for Mark Twain's Immortality. 21p. 1991. pap. 2.00 (*1-879605-31-7*) U Sci & Philos.

— The Secret of Light. (Illus.). 288p. 1974. text 17.00 (*1-879605-44-9*) U Sci & Philos.

— The Secret of Working Knowingly with God. 66p. 1993. pap. 2.00 (*1-879605-38-4*) U Sci & Philos.

— The Self-Multiplication Principle. 29p. 1993. pap. 2.00 (*1-879605-39-2*) U Sci & Philos.

— Space & the Hydrogen Age. 1991. 1.00 (*1-879605-05-8*) U Sci & Philos.

— The Universal One. (Illus.). 266p. 1974. reprint ed. text 50.00 (*1-879605-08-2*) U Sci & Philos.

— Who Am I? 30p. 1998. pap. 2.00 (*1-879605-55-4*) U Sci & Philos.

— Your Day & Night. 23p. 1946. 1.00 (*1-879605-09-0*) U Sci & Philos.

Russell, Walter & Binder, Timothy. In the Wave Lies the Secret of Creation. (Illus.). 25.00 (*1-879605-45-7*) U Sci & Philos.

***Russell, Walter & Russell, Lao.** The Art of Knowing & Thinking. Lindo, Laara, ed. 24p. 1999. pap. text 4.00 (*1-879605-60-0*) U Sci & Philos.

Russell, Walter & Russell, Lao. Atomic Suicide? (Illus.). 304p. 1981. reprint ed. text 5.00 (*1-879605-11-2*) U Sci & Philos.

***Russell, Walter & Russell, Lao.** Creative Process. Lindo, Laara, ed. (Home Study Course Theme Units Ser.). 49p. 1998. pap. text 6.00 (*1-879605-51-1*) U Sci & Philos.

Russell, Walter & Russell, Lao. The Electrifying Power of Man-Woman Balance. (Illus.). 93p. 1988. reprint ed. text 5.00 (*1-879605-14-7*) U Sci & Philos.

— The Home Study Course in Universal Law, Natural Science & Living Philosophy, 12 units, Set. (Illus.). 933p. 1951. pap. text 150.00 (*1-879605-06-6*) U Sci & Philos.

Russell, Walter & Russell, Lao. Meditation. Lindo, Laara, ed. 44p. 1997. pap. text 6.00 (*1-879605-49-X*) U Sci & Philos.

— The Nature of Energy. Lindo, Laara, ed. 40p. 1998. pap. text 6.00 (*1-879605-52-X*) U Sci & Philos.

— Prayer. Lindo, Laara, ed. 39p. 1997. pap. text 6.00 (*1-879605-48-1*) U Sci & Philos.

Russell, Walter & Russell, Lao. Scientific Answer to Human Relations: A Blueprint for Harmony in Industry. (Illus.). 68p. 1978. text 5.00 (*1-879605-15-5*) U Sci & Philos.

— Where Do I Go When I Die? 34p. 1992. pap. 2.00 (*1-879605-37-6*) U Sci & Philos.

Russell, Walter B., 3rd. The Flesh - Spirit Conflict in Galatians. LC 97-17070. 304p. (C). 1997. 56.00 (*0-7618-0797-7*); pap. 36.50 (*0-7618-0798-5*) U Pr of Amer.

Russell, Wayne. In My Heart... On My Mind. Whittington, Joy, ed. x, 105p. 1998. pap. 12.00 (*0-9673033-0-3*) Griffiths Pubng.

— Watcom C - C++ Unleashed. 900p. Date not set. 49.99 (*0-672-30893-2*) Sams.

Russell, Wiley. Our Day Out & Other Plays. 160p. 1989. pap. 11.95 (*0-09-172882-7*) Dufour.

Russell, Willey. Our Day Out. 56p. (C). 1988. pap. 7.95 (*0-413-54870-8*, A0201) Heinemann.

Russell, William. Broadcasters. LC 93-44982. (J). 1994. lib. bdg. 14.60 (*1-57103-054-9*) Rourke Pr.

— California Mental Health Is Going Down. 24p. (Orig.). 1995. pap. write for info. (*1-885206-03-8*, Iliad Pr) Cader Pubng.

— Farmers. LC 93-42481. (Careers Ser.). (J). 1994. lib. bdg. 14.60 (*1-57103-057-3*) Rourke Pr.

— Fishermen. LC 93-42482. (Careers Ser.). (J). 1994. lib. bdg. 14.60 (*1-57103-055-7*) Rourke Pr.

— Fishermen. (Careers Discovery Library). 24p. (J). (gr. k-4). 1994. lib. bdg. 10.95 (*0-86625-055-7*) Rourke Pubns.

— The Florida Keys. LC 93-48334. (Islands in the Sea Discovery Library). 24p. (J). (gr. k-4). 1994. lib. bdg. 15.93 (*1-55916-032-2*) Rourke Bk Co.

— Fossils. LC 94-2402. (From This Earth Discovery Library). 24p. (J). (gr. k-4). 1994. lib. bdg. 10.95 (*0-86593-358-8*) Rourke Corp.

— The Galapagos Islands. LC 93-48335. (Islands in the Sea Discovery Library). 24p. (J). (gr. k-4). 1994. lib. bdg. 15.93 (*1-55916-031-4*) Rourke Bk Co.

— Gold & Silver. LC 94-504. (From This Earth Discovery Library). 24p. (J). (gr. k-4). 1994. lib. bdg. 10.95 (*0-86593-359-6*) Rourke Corp.

— Hawaii. LC 93-49340. (Islands in the Sea Discovery Library). 24p. (J). (gr. k-4). 1994. lib. bdg. 15.93 (*1-55916-034-9*) Rourke Bk Co.

— Iceland. LC 93-49326. (Islands in the Sea Discovery Library). 24p. (J). (gr. k-4). 1994. lib. bdg. 15.93 (*1-55916-036-5*) Rourke Bk Co.

— Mountains & Canyons. LC 94-505. (From This Earth Discovery Library). 24p. (J). (gr. k-4). 1994. lib. bdg. 10.95 (*0-86593-360-X*) Rourke Corp.

— Oil, Coal & Gas. LC 94-2401. (From This Earth Discovery Library). 24p. (J). (gr. k-4). 1994. lib. bdg. 10.95 (*0-86593-357-X*) Rourke Corp.

— Pilots. LC 93-45009. (J). 1994. lib. bdg. 14.60 (*1-57103-059-X*) Rourke Pr.

— Precious Stones. LC 94-506. (From This Earth Discovery Library). 24p. (J). (gr. k-4). 1994. lib. bdg. 10.95 (*0-86593-361-8*) Rourke Corp.

— Rocks & Minerals. LC 94-507. (From This Earth Discovery Library). 24p. (J). (gr. k-4). 1994. lib. bdg. 10.95 (*0-86593-362-6*) Rourke Corp.

— Taiwan. LC 93-48341. (Islands in the Sea Discovery Library). 24p. (J). (gr. k-4). 1994. lib. bdg. 15.93 (*1-55916-033-0*) Rourke Bk Co.

— Truckers. LC 93-42484. (Careers Ser.). (J). 1994. lib. bdg. 14.60 (*1-57103-058-1*) Rourke Pr.

— The West Indies. LC 93-49339. (Islands in the Sea Discovery Library). 24p. (J). (gr. k-4). 1994. lib. bdg. 15.93 (*1-55916-035-7*) Rourke Bk Co.

Russell, William C. The Death Ship: A Strange Story, 2 vols. Reginald, R., ed. LC 75-46306. (Supernatural & Occult Fiction Ser.). 1976. reprint ed. lib. bdg. 70.95 (*0-405-08166-9*) Ayer.

— Honour of the Flag & Other Stories. LC 70-103528. (Short Story Index Reprint Ser.). 1977. 17.95 (*0-8369-3270-6*) Ayer.

— Horatio Nelson & the Naval Supremacy of England. LC 73-14467. (Heroes of the Nations Ser.). reprint ed. 30.00 (*0-404-58285-0*) AMS Pr.

— Wreck of the Grosvenor. LC 98-38970. (Classics of Nautical Fiction Ser.). 320p. 1998. pap. 13.95 (*0-935526-52-8*) McBooks Pr.

Russell, William F. Classic Myths to Read Aloud. 272p. 1992. pap. 11.00 (*0-517-58837-4*, Crown) Crown.

— Classics to Read Aloud to Your Children. 320p. 1992. pap. 12.00 (*0-517-58715-7*, Crown) Crown Pub Group.

— Family Learning: How to Help Your Children Succeed in School by Learning at Home. LC 97-60548. (Illus.). 368p. (Orig.). 1997. pap. 26.95 (*0-9657752-9-1*) First Word.

***Russell, William F.** How to Choose & How to Use a Dictionary. LC 99-71309. (Family Learning Guidebooks Ser.). 120p. 2000. pap. 8.95 (*0-9657752-8-3*, Pub. by First Word) IPG Chicago.

Russell, William F. More Classics to Read Aloud to Your Children. 272p. 1994. pap. 10.00 (*0-517-88227-2*, Crown) Crown Pub Group.

Russell, William G. What I Know about Winchester. 212p. 1953. write for info. (*0-318-64323-5*) Winchester-Frederick Cty Hist Soc.

Russell, William H., jt. auth. see Berwanger, Eugene H.

Russell, William L. The New York Hospital: A History of the Psychiatric Service, 1771-1936. LC 73-2414. (Mental Illness & Social Policy; the American Experience Ser.). 1973. reprint ed. 40.95 (*0-405-05224-3*) Ayer.

***Russell, William O., ed.** History of Yolo County, California, Its Resources & Its People. fac. ed. 579p. 1999. reprint ed. 62.00 (*0-8328-9987-9*) Higginson Bk Co.

Russell, William R. Luther's Theological Testament: The Schmalkald Articles. 224p. 1995. 33.00 (*0-8006-2660-5*, 1-2660, Fortress Pr) Augsburg Fortress.

Russell, William R., et al. Macroeconomic Activity & Income Inequality in the United States. LC 89-42429. (Contemporary Studies in Economic & Financial Analysis: Vol. 55). 191p. 1989. 78.50 (*1-55938-003-9*) Jai Pr.

Russell, William R., ed. see Forell, George W.

Russell, Willy. Blood Brothers. 82p. 1989. pap. 11.95 (*0-7487-0182-6*) Dufour.

— Blood Brothers. (Illus.). 68p. 1993. pap. 19.95 (*0-7119-2221-7*, AM79476) Music Sales.

— Educating Rita. Adams, Richard, ed. (Study Texts Ser.). 1985. pap. text 5.72 (*0-582-33182-X*, 72068) Longman.

— Educating Rita, Stage, Hens, Blood Brothers. 240p. (C). 1986. pap. write for info. (*0-413-41110-9*, A0079, Methuen Drama) Methn.

— Willy Russell: Plays One, Vol. 1. LC 97-153162. 1996. pap. 15.95 (*0-413-70220-0*, Methuen Drama) Methn.

— Shirley Valentine & One for the Road. 106p. (C). 1988. pap. 9.95 (*0-413-18950-3*, A0335, Methuen Drama) Methn.

Russell-Wood, A. J. Fidalgos & Philanthropists: The Santa Casa de Misericordia of Bahia, 1550-1755. LC 68-55798. 455p. reprint ed. pap. 141.10 (*0-608-15830-5*, 203131500074) Bks Demand.

— The Portuguese Empire, 1415-1808: A World on the Move. LC 98-3736. (Illus.). 289p. 1998. reprint ed. pap. 16.95 (*0-8018-5955-7*) Johns Hopkins.

— Society & Government in Colonial Brazil, 1500-1822. (Collected Studies: No. 382). 352p. 1992. 115.95 (*0-86078-333-2*, Pub. by Variorum) Ashgate Pub Co.

Russell-Wood, A. J., et al. From Colony to Nation: Essays on the Independence of Brazil. LC 74-24381. (Johns Hopkins Symposia in Comparative History Ser.: Vol. 6). 279p. reprint ed. pap. 86.50 (*0-608-06138-7*, 206647100008) Bks Demand.

***Russell-Woods, A. J. R., ed.** Government & Governance of Empires, 1450-1800, 2 vols. LC 99-51620. (An Expanding World Ser.: Vol. 21). 864p. 2000. text 240.95 (*0-86078-530-0*, Pub. by Ashgate Pub) Ashgate Pub Co.

— Local Government in European Overseas Empires, 1450-1800. LC 99-28908. (An Expanding World Ser.: 23). 832p. 1999. text 240.95 (*0-86078-529-7*, Pub. by Ashgate Pub) Ashgate Pub Co.

Russello, Gerald J., ed. see Dawson, Christopher.

Russen, David. Iter Lunare. LC 76-14908. 150p. 1976. 25.00 (*0-8398-2343-6*) Ultramarine Pub.

Russer, P., jt. auth. see Luy, J. F.

Russett. World Politics. 6th ed. Date not set. write for info. (*1-57259-752-6*) Worth.

Russett, Alan. George Chambers 1803-1840: His Life & Work. LC 96-223963. (Illus.). 200p. 1996. 59.50 (*1-85149-233-X*) Antique Collect.

Russett, Bruce M. Community & Contention: Britain & America in the Twentieth Century. LC 82-20952. 252p. 1983. reprint ed. lib. bdg. 65.00 (*0-313-23792-1*, RUCC, Greenwood Pr) Greenwood.

— Controlling the Sword: The Democratic Governance of National Security. (Illus.). 208p. 1990. 32.50 (*0-674-16990-5*) HUP.

— Grasping the Democratic Peace. 184p. 1993. pap. text 14.95 (*0-691-00164-2*, Pub. by Princeton U Pr) Cal Prin Full Svc.

— Grasping the Democratic Peace: Principles for a Post-Cold War World. LC 93-16274. 192p. 1993. text 37.50 (*0-691-03346-3*, Pub. by Princeton U Pr) Cal Prin Full Svc.

— International Regions & the International System. LC 73-16608. (Illus.). 252p. 1975. reprint ed. lib. bdg. 59.75 (*0-8371-7191-1*, RUIR, Greenwood Pr) Greenwood.

— No Clear & Present Danger: A Skeptical View of the U. S. Entry into World War II. 112p. (C). 1997. pap. 17.00 (*0-8133-3195-1*, Pub. by Westview) HarpC.

— Test Bank. (C). 1992. pap. text 16.00 (*0-7167-2375-1*) W H Freeman.

— What Price Vigilance? The Burdens of National Defense. LC 75-119475. (Yale Fastback Ser.: No. YF-5). (Illus.). 274p. reprint ed. pap. 85.00 (*0-608-30020-9*, 202203600024) Bks Demand.

— World Politics. 4th ed. (C). 1992. pap. text 29.60 (*0-7167-2290-9*) W H Freeman.

— World Politics: Printed Test Bank. 5th ed. (C). 1996. suppl. ed. 48.00 (*0-7167-2939-3*) W H Freeman.

Russett, Bruce M. & Starr, Harvey. World Politics: The Menu for Choice. 5th ed. LC 88-28780. (C). 1995. pap. text 51.95 (*0-7167-2820-6*) W H Freeman.

Russett, Bruce M., et al. World Handbook of Political & Social Indicators. LC 77-13514. (Tools & Methods of Comparative Research Ser.: No. 1). (Illus.). 373p. 1977. reprint ed. lib. bdg. 75.00 (*0-8371-9857-7*, RUWH, Greenwood Pr) Greenwood.

Russett, Cynthia. Sexual Science: The Victorian Construction of Womanhood. LC 88-24521. 272p. 1989. text 36.50 (*0-674-80290-X*) HUP.

— Sexual Science: The Victorian Construction of Womanhood. 256p. 1991. pap. text 16.50 (*0-674-80291-8*, RUSSEY) HUP.

Russett, Cynthia E., jt. auth. see Levy, William T.

Russett, Margaret. De Quincey's Romanticism: Canonical Minority & the Forms of Transmission. LC 96-52445. (Studies in Romanticism: Vol. 25). 312p. (C). 1998. text 59.95 (*0-521-57236-3*) Cambridge U Pr.

Russett, Robert & Starr, Cecile. Experimental Animation: Origins of a New Art. (Quality Paperbacks Ser.). (Illus.). 224p. 1988. reprint ed. pap. 14.95 (*0-306-80314-3*) Da Capo.

Russev, R. Bulgarian-English Dictionary. 1990. lib. bdg. 39.95 (*0-8288-2627-7*) Fr & Eur.

— Bulgarian-English Dictionary. (BUL & ENG.). 43.95 (*0-87557-006-2*) Saphrograph.

Russevelt, P. Superinsulation. (C). 1987. 130.00 (*0-7855-4205-1*, Pub. by Interntl Solar Energy Soc) St Mut.

Russi, Karen, compiled by. Hein's State Report Checklist. 2nd rev. ed. LC 87-35689. Bk. 2. 1991. lib. bdg. 65.00 (*0-89941-628-4*, 305940) W S Hein.

***Russia (Federation) Staff, et al.** Russian Company Law: Basic Legislation. 3rd ed. LC 00-37068. (Illus.). 2000. write for info. (*1-898029-52-0*, Kluwer Plenum) Kluwer Academic.

Russian Academy of Sciences, The Institute of Russian History Staff. The Economics of the Gulag & Its Part in the Development of the Soviet Union in the 1930s: A Documentary History. LC 99-28898. (Russian Documents, Bibliography, & Memoirs Ser.: Vol. 2). (RUS.). 176p. 1999. reprint ed. text 79.95 (*0-7734-3182-9*) E Mellen.

— Russia & West: The Development of Foreign Policy Stereotypes in the Consciousness of the Russian Society of the First Half of 20th Century. LC 99-27447. (Studies in Russian Politics, Sociology, & Economics: Vol. 2). (RUS.). 340p. 1999. reprint ed. pap. 99.95 (*0-7734-3188-8*) E Mellen.

Russian-American Geography Partnership Staff, et al. Beyond Borders: How Russia & the United States from Astonishing Mirror Images. (Illus.). 256p. 1996. 24.95 (*0-02-861348-1*, Pub. by Macmillan) S&S Trade.

Russian Day Committee Staff. The Orthodox Prayer Book. (ENG & SLA.). 606p. 1991. 14.95 (*1-878997-16-5*); 14.95 (*1-878997-29-7*) St Tikhons Pr.

Russian Info & Business Center, U. S. A. Staff. Grants for Russia, NIS & Baltics: U. S. Foundations with Interest in Russia, NIS & Baltics. Oleynik, Igor S. & Alexeyeva, Natalia, eds. (Illus.). 300p. 1997. lib. bdg. 99.00 (*1-57751-146-8*) Intl Business Pubns.

— Russian Hotels in Regions Directory. Oleynik, Igor S. & Alexeyeva, Natalia, eds. 300p. 1996. lib. bdg. 99.00 (*1-57751-150-6*) Intl Business Pubns.

— Russian Political Parties, Unions & Membership Organizations. Oleynik, Igor S. & Alexeyeva, Natalia, eds. 250p. 1996. lib. bdg. 99.00 (*1-57751-147-6*) Intl Business Pubns.

— U. S. Government & International Officials Working with Russia & NIS. Oleynik, Igor S. & Alexeyeva, Natalia, eds. (Illus.). 105p. 1996. lib. bdg. 49.00 (*1-57751-148-4*) Intl Business Pubns.

Russian Information & Business Center, Inc. Staff. Adygey Republic: Economy, Industry, Government, Business. 2nd rev. ed. (Russian Regional Business Directories Ser.). (Illus.). 200p. 1997. pap. 99.00 (*1-57751-350-9*) Intl Business Pubns.

— Aginskiy-Buryat Autonomous Okrug: Economy, Industry, Government, Business. 2nd rev. ed. (Russian Regional Business Directories Ser.). (Illus.). 200p. 1997. pap. 99.00 (*1-57751-433-5*) Intl Business Pubns.

— ALBANIA Business Law Handbook-98. (World Business Law Library-98). (Illus.). 350p. 1998. pap. 99.00 (*1-57751-812-8*) Intl Business Pubns.

— Albania Economic & Business Guide: Strategic & Business Information for Corporate Executives. (Eastern European Business Library). 200p. 1997. pap. 69.00 (*1-57751-236-7*) Intl Business Pubns.

— Algeria Business & Investment Opportunities Yearbook, 1998: Business, Investment, Export-Import. (Business & Investment Opportunities Library, '98). (Illus.). 1998. pap. 99.00 (*1-57751-986-8*) Intl Business Pubns.

— Altay Kray (Territory) Economy, Industry, Government, Business. 2nd rev. ed. (Russian Regional Business Directories Ser.). (Illus.). 200p. 1997. pap. 99.00 (*1-57751-373-8*) Intl Business Pubns.

— Altay Republic: Economy, Industry, Government, Business. 2nd rev. ed. (Russian Regional Business Directories Ser.). (Illus.). 200p. 1997. pap. 99.00 (*1-57751-356-8*) Intl Business Pubns.

— Amur Oblast: Economy, Industry, Government, Business. 2nd rev. ed. (Russian Regional Business Directories Ser.). (Illus.). 200p. 1997. pap. 99.00 (*1-57751-379-7*) Intl Business Pubns.

— ANTILLES Business Law Handbook-98. (World Business Law Library-98). (Illus.). 350p. 1998. pap. 99.00 (*1-57751-824-1*) Intl Business Pubns.

— ARGENTINA Business Law Handbook-98. (World Business Law Library-98). (Illus.). 350p. 1998. pap. 99.00 (*1-57751-825-X*) Intl Business Pubns.

— Arkhangelsk Oblast: Economy, Industry, Government, Business. 2nd rev. ed. (Russian Regional Business Directories Ser.). (Illus.). 200p. 1997. pap. 99.00 (*1-57751-380-0*) Intl Business Pubns.

— Armenia Business Law Handbook: Basic Export-Import, Investment & Business Laws. (NIS Business Law Library). (Illus.). 200p. 1997. pap. 99.00 (*1-57751-288-X*) Intl Business Pubns.

An Asterisk (*) at the beginning of an entry indicates that the title is appearing for the first time.

— Armenia Business Law Handbook, '98. (World Business Law Library, '98). (Illus.). 1998. pap. 99.00 (*1-57751-697-4*) Intl Business Pubns.
— Armenia Investment & Business Guide Vol. 2: Economy, Export-Import, Business & Investment Climate, Business Contacts. (Russia, NIS & Emerging Markets Investment & Business Library). (Illus.). 350p. 1998. pap. 99.00 (*1-57751-566-8*) Intl Business Pubns.
— Astrakhan Oblast: Economy, Industry, Government, Business. 2nd rev. ed. (Russian Regional Business Directories Ser.). (Illus.). 200p. 1997. pap. 99.00 (*1-57751-381-9*) Intl Business Pubns.
— Azerbaijan Business Land Handbook, '98. (World Business Law Library, '98). (Illus.). 1998. pap. 99.00 (*1-57751-689-3*) Intl Business Pubns.
— Azerbajan Business Law Handbook: Basic Export-Import, Investment & Business Laws. (NIS Business Law Library). (Illus.). 200p. 1997. pap. 99.00 (*1-57751-287-1*) Intl Business Pubns.
— Bahrain Business & Investment Opportunities Yearbook, 1998: Business, Investment, Export-Import. (Business & Investment Opportunities Library, '98). (Illus.). 1998. pap. 99.00 (*1-57751-987-6*) Intl Business Pubns.
— Bangladesh Business Law Handbook-98. (World Business Law Library-98). (Illus.). 350p. 1998. pap. 99.00 (*1-57751-846-2*) Intl Business Pubns.
— BARBADOS Business Law Handbook-98. (World Business Law Library-98). (Illus.). 350p. 1998. pap. 99.00 (*1-57751-826-8*) Intl Business Pubns.
— Bashkortostan Republic: Economy, Industry, Government, Business. 2nd rev. ed. (Russian Regional Business Directories Ser.). (Illus.). 200p. 1997. pap. 99.00 (*1-57751-351-7*) Intl Business Pubns.
— Belarus Business Law Handbook: Basic Export-Import, Investment & Business Laws. (NIS Business Law Library). (Illus.). 200p. 1997. pap. 99.00 (*1-57751-289-8*) Intl Business Pubns.
— Belarus Business Law Handbook, '98. (World Business Law Library, '98). (Illus.). 1998. pap. 99.00 (*1-57751-690-7*) Intl Business Pubns.
— Belarus Investment & Business Guide Vol. 4: Economy, Export-Import, Business & Investment Climate, Business Contacts. (Russia, NIS & Emerging Markets Investment & Business Library). (Illus.). 350p. 1998. pap. 99.00 (*1-57751-568-4*) Intl Business Pubns.
— Belgorod Oblast: Economy, Industry, Government, Business. 2nd rev. ed. (Russian Regional Business Directories Ser.). (Illus.). 200p. 1997. pap. 99.00 (*1-57751-382-7*) Intl Business Pubns.
— BELIZE Business Law Handbook-98. (World Business Law Library-98). (Illus.). 350p. 1998. pap. 99.00 (*1-57751-827-6*) Intl Business Pubns.
— BOLIVIA Business Law Handbook-98. (World Business Law Library-98). (Illus.). 350p. 1998. pap. 99.00 (*1-57751-828-4*) Intl Business Pubns.
— BOSNIA Business Law Handbook-98. (World Business Law Library-98). (Illus.). 350p. 1998. pap. 99.00 (*1-57751-813-6*) Intl Business Pubns.
— Bosnia Economic & Business Guide: Business & Strategic Information for Corporate Executives, 31 vols. (Eastern European Business Library). 200p. 1997. pap. 69.00 (*1-57751-238-3*) Intl Business Pubns.
— BRAZIL Business Law Handbook-98. (World Business Law Library-98). (Illus.). 350p. 1998. pap. 99.00 (*1-57751-829-2*) Intl Business Pubns.
— Brunei Business & Investment Opportunities Yearbook, 1998: Business, Investment, Export-Import. (Business & Investment Opportunities Library, '98). (Illus.). 1998. pap. 99.00 (*1-57751-988-4*) Intl Business Pubns.
— Bryansk Oblast: Economy, Industry, Government, Business. 2nd rev. ed. (Russian Regional Business Directories Ser.). (Illus.). 200p. 1997. pap. 99.00 (*1-57751-383-5*) Intl Business Pubns.
— BULGARIA Business Law Handbook-98. (World Business Law Library-98 Ser.). (Illus.). 350p. 1998. pap. 99.00 (*1-57751-800-4*) Intl Business Pubns.
— Bulgaria Economic, Investment & Business Guide: Everything You Need for Successful Business in Bulgaria. (Eastern European Business Library). 200p. 1997. pap. 69.00 (*1-57751-237-5*) Intl Business Pubns.
— BURMA Business Law Handbook-98. (World Business Law Library-98). (Illus.). 350p. 1998. pap. 99.00 (*1-57751-847-0*) Intl Business Pubns.
— Buryat Republic: Economy, Industry, Government, Business. 2nd rev. ed. (Russian Regional Business Directories Ser.). (Illus.). 200p. 1997. pap. 99.00 (*1-57751-352-5*) Intl Business Pubns.
— CAMBODIA Business Law Handbook-98. (World Business Law Library-98). (Illus.). 350p. 1998. pap. 99.00 (*1-57751-848-9*) Intl Business Pubns.
— Capital for Russia, NIS & Baltics: Where to Find Money & Strategic Contacts for Successful Business in Russia. Oleynik, Igor S. & Alexeyeva, Natalia, eds. 300p. (Orig.). 1997. pap. 99.00 (*1-57751-145-X*) Intl Business Pubns.
— CHECH REPUBLIC Business Law Handbook-98. (World Business Law Library-98 Ser.). (Illus.). 350p. 1998. pap. 99.00 (*1-57751-802-0*) Intl Business Pubns.
— Chech Republic Economic & Business Guide: Strategic & Business Information for Corporate Executives. (Eastern European Business Library). 200p. 1997. pap. 69.00 (*1-57751-240-5*) Intl Business Pubns.
— Chelyabinsk Oblast: Economy, Industry, Government, Business. 2nd rev. ed. (Russian Regional Business Directories Ser.). (Illus.). 200p. 1997. pap. 99.00 (*1-57751-384-3*) Intl Business Pubns.
— Chile Business Law Handbook-98. (World Business Law Library-98). (Illus.). 350p. 1998. pap. 99.00 (*1-57751-830-6*) Intl Business Pubns.
— CHINA Business Law Handbook-98. (World Business Law Library-98). (Illus.). 350p. 1998. pap. 99.00 (*1-57751-849-7*) Intl Business Pubns.
— Chita Oblast: Economy, Industry, Government, Business. 2nd rev. ed. (Russian Regional Business Directories Ser.). (Illus.). 200p. 1997. pap. 99.00 (*1-57751-385-1*) Intl Business Pubns.
— Chukotka Autonomous Okrug: Economy, Industry, Government, Business. 2nd rev. ed. (Russian Regional Business Directories Ser.). (Illus.). 200p. 1997. pap. 99.00 (*1-57751-434-3*) Intl Business Pubns.
— Chuvash Republic: Economy, Industry, Government, Business. 2nd rev. ed. (Russian Regional Business Directories Ser.). (Illus.). 200p. 1997. pap. 99.00 (*1-57751-354-1*) Intl Business Pubns.
— Columbia Business Law Handbook-98. (World Business Law Library-98). (Illus.). 350p. 1998. pap. 99.00 (*1-57751-831-4*) Intl Business Pubns.
— COSTA RICA Business Law Handbook-98. (World Business Law Library-98). (Illus.). 350p. 1998. pap. 99.00 (*1-57751-832-2*) Intl Business Pubns.
— CROATIA Business Law Handbook-98. (World Business Law Library-98 Ser.). (Illus.). 350p. 1998. pap. 99.00 (*1-57751-801-2*) Intl Business Pubns.
— Croatia Economic & Business Guide: Strategic & Business Information for Corporate Executives. (Eastern European Business Library). (Illus.). 200p. 1997. pap. 69.00 (*1-57751-239-1*) Intl Business Pubns.
— CYPRUS Business Law Handbook-98. (World Business Law Library-98). (Illus.). 350p. 1998. pap. 99.00 (*1-57751-814-4*) Intl Business Pubns.
— Dagestan Republic: Economy, Industry, Government, Business. 2nd rev. ed. (Russian Regional Business Directories Ser.). (Illus.). 200p. 1997. pap. 99.00 (*1-57751-355-X*) Intl Business Pubns.
— DOMINICAN REPUBLIC Business Law Handbook-98. (World Business Law Library-98). (Illus.). 350p. 1998. pap. 99.00 (*1-57751-833-0*) Intl Business Pubns.
— Egypt Business & Investment Opportunities Yearbook, 1998: Business, Investment, Export-Import. (Business & Investment Opportunities Library, '98). (Illus.). 1998. pap. 99.00 (*1-57751-989-2*) Intl Business Pubns.
— El Salvador Business Law Handbook-98. (World Business Law Library-98). (Illus.). 350p. 1998. pap. 99.00 (*1-57751-835-7*) Intl Business Pubns.
— Employment & Business Opportunites with International & Private Investment Funds & Banks Interested in Russia, NIS & Baltics. (Employment & Business Opportunities Library: No. 97). 300p. 1997. pap. 39.00 (*1-57751-181-6*) Intl Business Pubns.
— Employment & Business Opportunites with Major U. S. Corporations with Business & Investment Projects in Russia, NIS & the Baltics. (Employment & Business Opportunities Library: No. 97). 300p. 1997. pap. 39.00 (*1-57751-180-8*) Intl Business Pubns.
— Employment & Business Opportunites with U. S. A. Contractors on Russia, NIS, Baltics & Eastern Europe. (Employment & Business Opportunities Library: No. 97). 300p. 1997. pap. 39.00 (*1-57751-187-5*) Intl Business Pubns.
— Employment & Business Opportunites with U. S. & International Law & Consulting Companies Doing Business in Russia & NIS. (Employment & Business Opportunities Library: No. 97). 300p. 1997. pap. 39.00 (*1-57751-182-4*) Intl Business Pubns.
— Employment & Business Opportunities with International & Private Investment Funds & Banks Interested in Russia, NIS Baltics. (Employment & Business Opportunities Library). 250p. 1998. pap. 39.00 (*1-57751-577-3*) Intl Business Pubns.
— Employment & Business Opportunities with International Companies Doing Business in Russia, NIS & Baltics (Telecommunication, Oil & Gas Transportation) (Employment & Business Opportunites Library: No. 97). 300p. 1997. pap. 39.00 (*1-57751-184-0*) Intl Business Pubns.
— Employment & Business Opportunities with International Companies Doing Business in Russia, NIS, Baltics (Telecom, Oil & Gas, Transportation) (Employment & Business Opportunities Library). 250p. 1997. pap. 39.00 (*1-57751-580-3*) Intl Business Pubns.
— Employment & Business Opportunities with International Organizations & Companies with Foreign Assistance Projected in Russia & NIS. (Employment & Business Opportunities Library: No. 97). 300p. 1997. pap. 39.00 (*1-57751-185-9*) Intl Business Pubns.
— Employment & Business Opportunities with International Organizations & Companies with Foreign Assistance Projects in Russia & NIS. (Employment & Business Opportunities Library). 250p. 1998. pap. 39.00 (*1-57751-581-1*) Intl Business Pubns.
— Employment & Business Opportunities with Largest U. S. Companies & Non Profits with International Operations Located in California. (Employment & Business Opportunities Library). 250p. 1998. pap. 39.00 (*1-57751-590-0*) Intl Business Pubns.
— Employment & Business Opportunities with Largest U. S. Companies with International Operations Located in Washington DC, VA, MD. (Employment & Business Opportunities Library). 250p. 1998. pap. 250.00 (*1-57751-591-9*) Intl Business Pubns.
— Employment & Business Opportunities with Major U. S. Corporations with Business & Investment Projects in Russia, NIS & Baltics. (Employment & Business Opportunities Library). 250p. 1998. pap. 39.00 (*1-57751-576-5*) Intl Business Pubns.
— Employment & Business Opportunities with U. S. Agency of International Development Contractors on Russia, NIS Eastern Europe. (Employment & Business Opportunities Library). 250p. 1997. pap. 39.00 (*1-57751-582-X*) Intl Business Pubns.
— Employment & Business Opportunities with U. S. Aid Contractors on Russia, NIS, Baltics & Eastern Europe. (Employment & Business Opportunities Library: No. 97). 250p. 1997. pap. 39.00 (*1-57751-186-7*) Intl Business Pubns.
— Employment & Business Opportunities with U. S. & International Law & Consulting Companies Doing Business in Russia, NIS, Baltics. (Employment & Business Opportunities Library). 250p. 1998. pap. 39.00 (*1-57751-578-1*) Intl Business Pubns.
— Employment & Business Opportunities with U. S. & International Oil & Gas Companies Interested in Russia & NIS. (Employment & Business Opportunities Library). 250p. 1998. pap. 39.00 (*1-57751-588-9*) Intl Business Pubns.
— Employment & Business Opportunities with U. S. Companies Located in Russia & NIS. (Employment & Business Opportunities Library: No. 97). 250p. 1997. pap. 39.00 (*1-57751-179-4*) Intl Business Pubns.
— Employment & Business Opportunities with U. S. Companies Located in Russia & NIS. (Employment & Business Opportunities Library). 250p. 1998. pap. 39.00 (*1-57751-575-7*) Intl Business Pubns.
— Employment & Business Opportunities with U. S. Information Agency Contractors on Russia, NIS, Eastern Europe. (Employment & Business Opportunities Library). 250p. 1998. pap. 39.00 (*1-57751-583-8*) Intl Business Pubns.
— Employment & Business Opportunities with U. S. Non-Profit Organizations Interested in Russia, NIS & Eastern Europe. (Employment & Business Opportunities Library: No. 97). 300p. 1997. pap. 39.00 (*1-57751-183-2*) Intl Business Pubns.
— Employment & Business Opportunities with U. S. Nonprofits Interested in Russia, NIS, Baltics. (Employment & Business Opportunities Library). 250p. 1998. pap. 39.00 (*1-57751-579-X*) Intl Business Pubns.
— Employment & Business Opportunities with 1000 Largest Russian Banks with International Operations. (Employment & Business Opportunities Library). 250p. 1998. pap. 39.00 (*1-57751-584-6*) Intl Business Pubns.
— Employment & Business Opportunities with 1000 New York City Companies with International Operations. (Employment & Business Opportunities Library). 250p. 1998. pap. 39.00 (*1-57751-587-0*) Intl Business Pubns.
— Employment & Business Opportunities with 500 Largest U. S. Companies with International Operations. (Employment & Business Opportunities Library). 250p. 1998. pap. 39.00 (*1-57751-585-4*) Intl Business Pubns.
— Employment & Business Opportunities with 500 Largest World Companies with International Operations. (Employment & Business Opportunities Library). 250p. 1998. pap. 39.00 (*1-57751-586-2*) Intl Business Pubns.
— Employment Opportunities with U. S. Companies Located in Russia & NIS. 2nd rev. ed. (Russian Business Library). 400p. 1997. pap. 39.00 (*1-57751-328-2*) Intl Business Pubns.
— EQUADOR Business Law Handbook-98. (World Business Law Library-98). (Illus.). 350p. 1998. pap. 99.00 (*1-57751-834-9*) Intl Business Pubns.
— Equador Investment & Business Guide: Economy, Export-Import, Business & Investment Climate, Business Contacts. (Russia, NIS & Emerging Markets Investment & Business Library). (Illus.). 350p. 1998. pap. 99.00 (*1-57751-891-8*) Intl Business Pubns.
— Estonia Business Law Handbook-98. (World Business Law Library-98). (Illus.). 350p. 1998. pap. 99.00 (*1-57751-803-9*) Intl Business Pubns.
— Evenkiyskiy Autonomous Okrug: Economy, Industry, Government, Business. 2nd rev. ed. (Russian Regional Business Directories Ser.). (Illus.). 200p. 1997. pap. 99.00 (*1-57751-435-1*) Intl Business Pubns.
— Finland Business Law Handbook-98. (World Business Law Library-98). (Illus.). 350p. 1998. pap. 99.00 (*1-57751-815-2*) Intl Business Pubns.
— Foreign Banks & Representations in Russia. 2nd rev. ed. (Russian Business Library). 400p. 1997. pap. 99.00 (*1-57751-311-8*) Intl Business Pubns.
— Foreign Companies in Russia: (Business Representations & Offices) 2nd rev. ed. (Russian Business Library). 400p. 1997. pap. 99.00 (*1-57751-310-X*) Intl Business Pubns.
— Georgia Business Law Handbook: Basic Export-Import, Investment & Business Laws. (NIS Business Law Library). (Illus.). 200p. 1997. pap. 99.00 (*1-57751-290-1*) Intl Business Pubns.
— Georgia Business Law Handbook, '98. (World Business Law Library, '98). (Illus.). 1998. pap. 99.00 (*1-57751-691-5*) Intl Business Pubns.
— Georgia Investment & Business Guide Vol. 5: Economy, Export-Import, Business & Investment Climate, Business Contacts. (Russia, NIS & Emerging Markets Investment & Business Library). (Illus.). 350p. 1998. pap. 99.00 (*1-57751-569-2*) Intl Business Pubns.
— Grants for Russia: U. S. Foundations with Interest in Russia & NIS. 2nd rev. ed. (Russian Business Library). 400p. 1997. pap. 99.00 (*1-57751-306-1*) Intl Business Pubns.
— Greece Business Law Handbook-98. (World Business Law Library-98 Ser.). (Illus.). 350p. 1998. pap. 99.00 (*1-57751-816-0*) Intl Business Pubns.
— Guatemala Business Law Handbook-98. (World Business Law Library-98). (Illus.). 350p. 1998. pap. 99.00 (*1-57751-836-5*) Intl Business Pubns.
— Honduras Business Law Handbook-98. (World Business Law Library-98). (Illus.). 350p. 1998. pap. 99.00 (*1-57751-837-3*) Intl Business Pubns.
— Hong Kong Business Law Handbook-98. (World Business Law Library-98). (Illus.). 350p. 1998. pap. 99.00 (*1-57751-645-1*) Intl Business Pubns.
— Hungary Business Law Handbook-98. (World Business Law Library-98). (Illus.). 350p. 1998. pap. 99.00 (*1-57751-804-7*) Intl Business Pubns.
— Hungary Economic & Business Guide: Strategic & Business Information for Corporate Executives. (Eastern European Business Library). 1997. pap. 69.00 (*1-57751-241-3*) Intl Business Pubns.
— Iceland Business Law Handbook-98. (World Business Law Library-98). (Illus.). 350p. 1998. pap. 99.00 (*1-57751-818-7*) Intl Business Pubns.
— India Business Law Handbook-98. (World Business Law Library-98). (Illus.). 350p. 1998. pap. 99.00 (*1-57751-646-X*) Intl Business Pubns.
— Indonesia Business Law Handbook-98. (World Business Law Library-98 Ser.). (Illus.). 350p. 1998. pap. 99.00 (*1-57751-647-8*) Intl Business Pubns.
— Ingush Republic: Economy, Industry, Government, Business. 2nd rev. ed. (Russian Regional Business Directories Ser.). (Illus.). 200p. 1997. pap. 99.00 (*1-57751-357-6*) Intl Business Pubns.
— International Banks Interested in Russia & NIS. 100p. 1997. pap. 99.00 (*1-57751-234-0*) Intl Business Pubns.
— International Financial Organizations & U. S. Agencies with Russian Projects. 2nd rev. ed. (Russian Business Library). 400p. 1997. pap. 99.00 (*1-57751-312-6*) Intl Business Pubns.
— International Oil & Gas Companies Interested in Russia & NIS. 200p. 1997. pap. 99.00 (*1-57751-231-6*) Intl Business Pubns.
— International Telecommunication Companies Interested in Russia & NIS. 250p. 1997. pap. 99.00 (*1-57751-233-2*) Intl Business Pubns.
— International Transportation Companies Interested in Russia & NIS. 1997. pap. 99.00 (*1-57751-235-9*) Intl Business Pubns.
— Iran Business & Investment Opportunities Yearbook, 1998: Business, Investment, Export-Import. (Business & Investment Opportunities Library, '98). (Illus.). 1998. pap. 99.00 (*1-57751-990-6*) Intl Business Pubns.
— Irkutsk Oblast: Economy, Industry, Government, Business. 2nd rev. ed. (Russian Regional Business Directories Ser.). (Illus.). 200p. 1997. pap. 99.00 (*1-57751-386-X*) Intl Business Pubns.
— Israel Business Law Handbook-98. (World Business Law Library-98). (Illus.). 350p. 1998. pap. 99.00 (*1-57751-817-9*) Intl Business Pubns.
— Ivanova Oblast: Economy, Industry, Government, Business. 2nd rev. ed. (Russian Regional Business Directories Ser.). (Illus.). 200p. 1997. pap. 99.00 (*1-57751-387-8*) Intl Business Pubns.
— Jamaica Business Law Handbook-98. (World Business Law Library-98). (Illus.). 350p. 1998. pap. 99.00 (*1-57751-838-1*) Intl Business Pubns.
— Jordan Business & Investment Opportunities Yearbook, 1998: Business, Investment, Export-Import. (Business & Investment Opportunities Library, '98). (Illus.). 1998. pap. 99.00 (*1-57751-991-4*) Intl Business Pubns.
— Kabardin-Balkar Republic: Economy, Industry, Government, Business. (Russian Regional Business Directories Ser.). (Illus.). 200p. 1997. pap. 99.00 (*1-57751-358-4*) Intl Business Pubns.
— Kaliningrad Oblast: Economy, Industry, Government, Business. 2nd rev. ed. (Russian Regional Business Directories Ser.). (Illus.). 200p. 1997. pap. 99.00 (*1-57751-388-6*) Intl Business Pubns.
— Kalmykiya-Khalmg-Tangeh Republic: Economy, Industry, Government, Business. 2nd rev. ed. (Russian Regional Business Directories Ser.). (Illus.). 200p. 1997. pap. 99.00 (*1-57751-359-2*) Intl Business Pubns.
— Kaluga Oblast: Economy, Industry, Government, Business. 2nd rev. ed. (Russian Regional Business Directories Ser.). (Illus.). 200p. 1997. pap. 99.00 (*1-57751-389-4*) Intl Business Pubns.
— Kamchatka Oblast: Economy, Industry, Government, Business. 2nd rev. ed. (Russian Regional Business Directories Ser.). (Illus.). 200p. 1997. pap. 99.00 (*1-57751-390-8*) Intl Business Pubns.
— Karachay-Cherkess Republic: Economy, Industry, Government, Business. 2nd rev. ed. (Russian Regional Business Directories Ser.). (Illus.). 200p. 1997. pap. 99.00 (*1-57751-360-6*) Intl Business Pubns.
— Karelia Republic: Economy, Industry, Government, Business. 2nd rev. ed. (Russian Regional Business Directories Ser.). (Illus.). 200p. 1997. pap. 99.00 (*1-57751-361-4*) Intl Business Pubns.
— Kazakhstan Business Law Handbook, '98. (World Business Law Library, '98). (Illus.). 1998. pap. 99.00 (*1-57751-692-3*) Intl Business Pubns.
— Kemerovo Oblast: Economy, Industry, Government, Business. 2nd rev. ed. (Russian Regional Business Directories Ser.). (Illus.). 200p. 1997. pap. 99.00 (*1-57751-391-6*) Intl Business Pubns.
— Khabarovsk Kray: Economy, Industry, Government, Business. 2nd rev. ed. (Russian Regional Business Directories Ser.). (Illus.). 200p. 1997. pap. 99.00 (*1-57751-374-6*) Intl Business Pubns.
— Khakass Republic: Economy, Industry, Government, Business. 2nd rev. ed. (Russian Regional Business Directories Ser.). (Illus.). 200p. 1997. pap. 99.00 (*1-57751-362-2*) Intl Business Pubns.
— Khauty-Mansi Autonomous Okrug: Economy, Industry, Government, Business. 2nd rev. ed. (Russian Regional Business Directories Ser.). (Illus.). 200p. 1997. pap. 99.00 (*1-57751-436-X*) Intl Business Pubns.
— Kirov Oblast: Economy, Industry, Government, Business. 2nd rev. ed. (Russian Regional Business Directories Ser.). (Illus.). 200p. 1997. pap. 99.00 (*1-57751-392-4*) Intl Business Pubns.
— Komi-My Republic: Economy, Industry, Government, Business. 2nd rev. ed. (Russian Regional Business Directories Ser.). (Illus.). 200p. 1997. pap. 99.00 (*1-57751-363-0*) Intl Business Pubns.
— Komi-Permyak Autonomous Okrug: Economy, Industry,

R

Government, Business. 2nd rev. ed. (Russian Regional Business Directories Ser.). (Illus.). 200p. 1997. pap. 99.00 (*0-614-30773-2*) Intl Business Pubns.

— Korea Business Law Handbook-98. (World Business Law Library-98 Ser.). (Illus.). 350p. 1998. pap. 99.00 (*1-57751-648-6*) Intl Business Pubns.

— Koryak Autonomous Okrug: Economy, Industry, Government, Business. 2nd rev. ed. (Russian Regional Business Directories Ser.). (Illus.). 200p. 1997. pap. 99.00 (*1-57751-438-6*) Intl Business Pubns.

— Kostroma Oblast: Economy, Industry, Government, Business. 2nd rev. ed. (Russian Regional Business Directories Ser.). (Illus.). 200p. 1997. pap. 99.00 (*1-57751-393-2*) Intl Business Pubns.

— Krasnodar Kray: Economy, Industry, Government, Business. 2nd rev. ed. (Russian Regional Business Directories Ser.). (Illus.). 200p. 1997. pap. 99.00 (*1-57751-375-4*) Intl Business Pubns.

— Krasnoyarsk Kray: Economy, Industry, Government, Business. 2nd rev. ed. (Russian Regional Business Directories Ser.). (Illus.). 200p. 1997. pap. 99.00 (*1-57751-376-2*) Intl Business Pubns.

— Kurgan Oblast: Economy, Industry, Government, Business. 2nd rev. ed. (Russian Regional Business Directories Ser.). (Illus.). 200p. 1997. pap. 99.00 (*1-57751-394-0*) Intl Business Pubns.

— Kuwait Business & Investment Opportunities Yearbook, 1998: Business, Investment, Export-Import. (Business & Investment Opportunities Library, '98). (Illus.). 1998. pap. 99.00 (*1-57751-992-2*) Intl Business Pubns.

— Kyrgyzstan Business Law Handbook, '98. (World Business Law Library, '98). (Illus.). 1998. pap. 99.00 (*1-57751-693-1*) Intl Business Pubns.

Russian Information & Business Center Inc. Staff. Latvia Business Law Handbook-98. (World Business Law Library-98). (Illus.). 350p. 1998. pap. 99.00 (*1-57751-805-5*) Intl Business Pubns.

Russian Information & Business Center, Inc. Staff. Lebanon Business & Investment Opportunities Yearbook, 1998: Business, Investment, Export-Import. (Business & Investment Opportunities Library, '98). (Illus.). 1998. pap. 99.00 (*1-57751-993-0*) Intl Business Pubns.

— Leningrad Oblast: Economy, Industry, Government, Business. 2nd rev. ed. (Russian Regional Business Directories Ser.). (Illus.). 200p. 1997. pap. 99.00 (*1-57751-415-7*) Intl Business Pubns.

— Liberia Business Law Handbook-98. (World Business Law Library-98). (Illus.). 350p. 1998. pap. 99.00 (*1-57751-839-X*) Intl Business Pubns.

— Lipetsk Oblast: Economy, Industry, Government, Business. 2nd rev. ed. (Russian Regional Business Directories Ser.). (Illus.). 200p. 1997. pap. 99.00 (*1-57751-396-7*) Intl Business Pubns.

— Lithuania Business Law Handbook-98. (World Business Law Library-98). (Illus.). 350p. 1998. pap. 99.00 (*1-57751-806-3*) Intl Business Pubns.

— MACAU Business Law Handbook-98. (World Business Law Library-98 Ser.). (Illus.). 350p. 1998. pap. 99.00 (*1-57751-649-4*) Intl Business Pubns.

— Macedonia Business Law Handbook-98. (World Business Law Library-98). (Illus.). 350p. 1998. pap. 99.00 (*1-57751-807-1*) Intl Business Pubns.

— Magadan Oblast: Economy, Industry, Government, Business. 2nd rev. ed. (Russian Regional Business Directories Ser.). (Illus.). 200p. 1997. pap. 99.00 (*1-57751-397-5*) Intl Business Pubns.

— Mariy-El Republic: Economy, Industry, Government, Business. 2nd rev. ed. (Russian Regional Business Directories Ser.). (Illus.). 200p. 1997. pap. 99.00 (*1-57751-364-9*) Intl Business Pubns.

— Marshall Islands Business Law Handbook-98. (World Business Law Library-98). (Illus.). 350p. 1998. pap. 99.00 (*1-57751-840-3*) Intl Business Pubns.

— MEXICO Business Law Handbook-98. (World Business Law Library-98). (Illus.). 350p. 1998. pap. 99.00 (*1-57751-841-1*) Intl Business Pubns.

— Moldova Business Law Handbook, '98. (World Business Law Library, '98). (Illus.). 1998. pap. 99.00 (*1-57751-694-X*) Intl Business Pubns.

— Moldova Business Law Handbook: Basic Export-Import, Investment & Business Laws. (NIS Business Law Library). (Illus.). 200p. 1997. pap. 99.00 (*1-57751-293-6*) Intl Business Pubns.

— Moldova Investment & Business Guide Vol. 7: Economy, Export-Import, Business & Investment Climate, Business Contacts. (Russia, NIS & Emerging Markets Investment & Business Library). (Illus.). 350p. 1998. pap. 99.00 (*1-57751-571-4*) Intl Business Pubns.

— Mordovia Republic: Economy, Industry, Government, Business. 2nd rev. ed. (Russian Regional Business Directories Ser.). (Illus.). 200p. 1997. pap. 99.00 (*1-57751-365-7*) Intl Business Pubns.

— Morocco Business & Investment Opportunities Yearbook, 1998: Business, Investment, Export-Import. (Business & Investment Opportunities Library, '98). (Illus.). 1998. pap. 99.00 (*1-57751-994-9*) Intl Business Pubns.

— Moscow: Economy, Industry, Government, Business. 2nd rev. ed. (Russian Regional Business Directories Ser.). (Illus.). 200p. 1997. pap. 99.00 (*1-57751-371-1*) Intl Business Pubns.

— Moscow Oblast: Economy, Industry, Government, Business. 2nd rev. ed. (Russian Regional Business Directories Ser.). (Illus.). 200p. 1997. pap. 99.00 (*1-57751-398-3*) Intl Business Pubns.

— Murmansk: Economy, Industry, Government, Business. 2nd rev. ed. (Russian Regional Business Directories Ser.). (Illus.). 200p. 1997. pap. 99.00 (*1-57751-399-1*) Intl Business Pubns.

— Nenets Autonomous Okrus: Economy, Industry, Government, Business. 2nd rev. ed. (Russian Regional Business Directories Ser.). (Illus.). 200p. 1997. pap. 99.00 (*1-57751-428-9*) Intl Business Pubns.

— Newly Independent States (NIS) Industrial Directories Vol. 1: 500 Largest Companies. 200p. 1997. pap. 99.00 (*1-57751-202-2*) Intl Business Pubns.

— Newly Independent States (NIS) Industrial Directories Vol. 2: 1000 Largest Companies. 1997. pap. 99.00 (*1-57751-203-0*) Intl Business Pubns.

— Newly Independent States (NIS) Industrial Directories Vol. 3: Automobile Industry. 200p. 1997. pap. 99.00 (*1-57751-204-9*) Intl Business Pubns.

— Newly Independent States (NIS) Industrial Directories Vol. 4: Building Materials Industry. 200p. 1997. pap. 99.00 (*1-57751-205-7*) Intl Business Pubns.

— Newly Independent States (NIS) Industrial Directories Vol. 5: Chemical, Pharmaceutical & Microbiology Industry. 200p. 1997. pap. 99.00 (*1-57751-206-5*) Intl Business Pubns.

— Newly Independent States (NIS) Industrial Directories Vol. 6: Clothing Industry. 200p. 1997. pap. 99.00 (*1-57751-207-3*) Intl Business Pubns.

— Newly Independent States (NIS) Industrial Directories Vol. 7: Coal Mining & Peat Industry. 200p. 1997. pap. 99.00 (*1-57751-208-1*) Intl Business Pubns.

— Newly Independent States (NIS) Industrial Directories Vol. 8: Consumer Goods, Household & Cultural Foods. 200p. 1997. pap. 99.00 (*1-57751-209-X*) Intl Business Pubns.

— Newly Independent States (NIS) Industrial Directories Vol. 9: Electrical Engineering. 200p. 1997. pap. 99.00 (*1-57751-210-3*) Intl Business Pubns.

— Newly Independent States (NIS) Industrial Directories Vol. 10: Fishing & Fish Processing. 200p. 1997. pap. 99.00 (*1-57751-211-1*) Intl Business Pubns.

— Newly Independent States (NIS) Industrial Directories Vol. 11: Food & Food Processing Industry. 200p. 1997. pap. 99.00 (*1-57751-212-X*) Intl Business Pubns.

— Newly Independent States (NIS) Industrial Directories Vol. 12: Footwear & Tanning Industry. 200p. 1997. pap. 99.00 (*1-57751-213-8*) Intl Business Pubns.

— Newly Independent States (NIS) Industrial Directories Vol. 13: Forestry & Timber Processing. 200p. 1997. pap. 99.00 (*1-57751-214-6*) Intl Business Pubns.

— Newly Independent States (NIS) Industrial Directories Vol. 14: High-Tech Products, PC, Research & Design. 1997. pap. 99.00 (*1-57751-215-4*) Intl Business Pubns.

— Newly Independent States (NIS) Industrial Directories Vol. 15: Machine-Building Industry. 200p. 1997. pap. 99.00 (*1-57751-201-4*) Intl Business Pubns.

— Newly Independent States (NIS) Industrial Directories Vol. 16: Medical Equipment Industry. 200p. 1997. pap. 99.00 (*1-57751-216-2*) Intl Business Pubns.

— Newly Independent States (NIS) Industrial Directories Vol. 17: Metal-Working Industry. 200p. 1997. pap. 99.00 (*1-57751-200-6*) Intl Business Pubns.

— Newly Independent States (NIS) Industrial Directories Vol. 18: Metallurgy. 200p. 1997. pap. 99.00 (*1-57751-217-0*) Intl Business Pubns.

— Newly Independent States (NIS) Industrial Directories Vol. 19: Mining (Building Materials) 200p. 1997. pap. 99.00 (*1-57751-218-9*) Intl Business Pubns.

— Newly Independent States (NIS) Industrial Directories Vol. 20: Oil & Gas Industry. 200p. 1997. pap. 99.00 (*1-57751-219-7*) Intl Business Pubns.

— Newly Independent States (NIS) Industrial Directories Vol. 21: Oil Refining & Gas Processing. 200p. 1997. pap. 99.00 (*1-57751-220-0*) Intl Business Pubns.

— Newly Independent States (NIS) Industrial Directories Vol. 22: Gold Mining & Mining. 200p. 1997. pap. 99.00 (*1-57751-221-9*) Intl Business Pubns.

— Newly Independent States (NIS) Industrial Directories Vol. 23: Power Industry. 200p. 1997. pap. 99.00 (*1-57751-222-7*) Intl Business Pubns.

— Newly Independent States (NIS) Industrial Directories Vol. 24: Publishing & Printing. 200p. 1997. pap. 99.00 (*1-57751-223-5*) Intl Business Pubns.

— Newly Independent States (NIS) Industrial Directories Vol. 25: Pulp & Paper Industry. 200p. 1997. pap. 99.00 (*1-57751-224-3*) Intl Business Pubns.

— Newly Independent States (NIS) Industrial Directories Vol. 26: Radio-Electronic Industry. 200p. 1997. pap. 99.00 (*1-57751-225-1*) Intl Business Pubns.

— Newly Independent States (NIS) Industrial Directories Vol. 27: Rubber & Plastic Industry. 200p. 1997. pap. 99.00 (*1-57751-226-X*) Intl Business Pubns.

— Newly Independent States (NIS) Industrial Directories Vol. 28: Scrap & Waste Processing. 200p. 1997. pap. 99.00 (*1-57751-227-8*) Intl Business Pubns.

— Newly Independent States (NIS) Industrial Directories Vol. 29: Textile Industry. 200p. 1997. pap. 99.00 (*1-57751-228-6*) Intl Business Pubns.

— Newly Independent States (NIS) Industrial Directories Vol. 30: Tobacco Industry. 200p. 1997. pap. 99.00 (*1-57751-229-4*) Intl Business Pubns.

— Newly Independent States (NIS) Industrial Directories Vol. 31: Transport & Civil Engineering. 200p. 1997. pap. 99.00 (*1-57751-230-8*) Intl Business Pubns.

— Nicaragua Business Law Handbook-98. (World Business Law Library-98). (Illus.). 350p. 1998. pap. 99.00 (*1-57751-842-X*) Intl Business Pubns.

— Nizniy Novgorod Oblast: Economy, Industry, Government, Business. 2nd rev. ed. (Russian Regional Business Directories Ser.). (Illus.). 200p. 1997. pap. 99.00 (*1-57751-400-9*) Intl Business Pubns.

— North Osetia Republic: Economy, Industry, Government, Business. 2nd rev. ed. (Russian Regional Business Directories Ser.). (Illus.). 200p. 1997. pap. 99.00 (*1-57751-366-5*) Intl Business Pubns.

— Novgorod Oblast: Economy, Industry, Government, Business. 2nd rev. ed. (Russian Regional Business Directories Ser.). (Illus.). 200p. 1997. pap. 99.00 (*1-57751-401-7*) Intl Business Pubns.

— Novosibirsk Oblast: Economy, Industry, Government, Business. 2nd rev. ed. (Russian Regional Business Directories Ser.). (Illus.). 200p. 1997. pap. 99.00 (*1-57751-402-5*) Intl Business Pubns.

— Oman Business & Investment Opportunities Yearbook, 1998: Business, Investment, Export-Import. (Business & Investment Opportunities Library, '98). (Illus.). 1998. pap. 99.00 (*1-57751-995-7*) Intl Business Pubns.

— Omsk Oblast: Economy, Industry, Government, Business. 2nd rev. ed. (Russian Regional Business Directories Ser.). (Illus.). 200p. 1997. pap. 99.00 (*1-57751-403-3*) Intl Business Pubns.

— 1000 U. S. Corporate Executives Interested in Russia. 2nd ed. (Russian Business Library). 400p. 1997. pap. 99.00 (*1-57751-327-4*) Intl Business Pubns.

— Orenburg Oblast: Economy, Industry, Government, Business. 2nd rev. ed. (Russian Regional Business Directories Ser.). (Illus.). 200p. 1997. pap. 99.00 (*1-57751-404-1*) Intl Business Pubns.

— Oryol Oblast: Economy, Industry, Government, Business. 2nd rev. ed. (Russian Regional Business Directories Ser.). (Illus.). 200p. 1997. pap. 99.00 (*1-57751-405-X*) Intl Business Pubns.

— Penza Oblast: Economy, Industry, Government, Business. 2nd rev. ed. (Russian Regional Business Directories Ser.). (Illus.). 200p. 1997. pap. 99.00 (*1-57751-406-8*) Intl Business Pubns.

— Perm Oblast: Economy, Industry, Government, Business. 2nd rev. ed. (Russian Regional Business Directories Ser.). (Illus.). 200p. 1997. pap. 99.00 (*1-57751-407-6*) Intl Business Pubns.

— Peru Business Law Handbook-98. (World Business Law Library-98). (Illus.). 350p. 1998. pap. 99.00 (*1-57751-843-8*) Intl Business Pubns.

— Poland Business Law Handbook-98. (World Business Law Library-98). (Illus.). 350p. 1998. pap. 99.00 (*1-57751-808-X*) Intl Business Pubns.

— Poland Economic & Business Guide: Strategic & Business Information for Corporate Executives. (Eastern European Business Library). (Illus.). 200p. 1997. pap. 69.00 (*1-57751-285-5*) Intl Business Pubns.

— PORTUGAL Business Law Handbook-98. (World Business Law Library-98). (Illus.). 350p. 1998. pap. 99.00 (*1-57751-820-9*) Intl Business Pubns.

— Primorskiy Kray: Economy, Industry, Government, Business. 2nd rev. ed. (Russian Regional Business Directories Ser.). (Illus.). 200p. 1997. pap. 99.00 (*1-57751-377-0*) Intl Business Pubns.

— Pskov Oblast: Economy, Industry, Government, Business. 2nd rev. ed. (Russian Regional Business Directories Ser.). (Illus.). 200p. 1997. pap. 99.00 (*1-57751-408-4*) Intl Business Pubns.

— Qatar Business & Investment Opportunities Yearbook, 1998: Business, Investment, Export-Import. (Business & Investment Opportunities Library, '98). (Illus.). 1998. pap. 99.00 (*1-57751-996-5*) Intl Business Pubns.

— Romania Business Law Handbook-98. (World Business Law Library-98). (Illus.). 350p. 1998. pap. 99.00 (*1-57751-809-8*) Intl Business Pubns.

— Romania Economic & Business Guide: Business & Strategic Information for Corporate Executives. (Eastern European Business Library). (Illus.). 200p. 1997. pap. 69.00 (*1-57751-286-3*) Intl Business Pubns.

— Rostov Oblast: Economy, Industry, Government, Business. 2nd rev. ed. (Russian Regional Business Directories Ser.). (Illus.). 200p. 1997. pap. 99.00 (*1-57751-409-2*) Intl Business Pubns.

— Russia: A Country Study Guide - History, Economy, Government, People, Culture. (Illus.). 300p. 1997. pap. 49.00 (*1-57751-249-9*) Intl Business Pubns.

— Russia: Joint-Ventures in Moscow. 2nd rev. ed. (Russian Business Library). 400p. 1997. pap. 99.00 (*1-57751-314-2*) Intl Business Pubns.

— Russia: Joint-Ventures in Russian Regions. 2nd rev. ed. (Russian Business Library). 400p. 1997. pap. 99.00 (*1-57751-315-0*) Intl Business Pubns.

— Russia & NIS: Beer Production. 1997. pap. 99.00 (*1-57751-164-6*) Intl Business Pubns.

— Russia & NIS Distilling & Wine Production. 400p. 1997. pap. 99.00 (*1-57751-163-8*) Intl Business Pubns.

— Russia Business Law Handbook, '98. (World Business Law Library, '98). (Illus.). 1998. pap. 99.00 (*1-57751-695-8*) Intl Business Pubns.

— Russia Investment & Business Guide Vol. 8: Economy, Export-Import, Business & Investment Climate, Business Contacts. (Russia, NIS & Emerging Markets Investment & Business Library). (Illus.). 350p. 1998. pap. 99.00 (*1-57751-572-2*) Intl Business Pubns.

— Russian Advertising Directory. 2nd rev. ed. (Russian Business Library). 400p. 1997. pap. 99.00 (*1-57751-317-7*) Intl Business Pubns.

— Russian Banks & Financial Institutions Directory. 2nd rev. ed. (Russian Business Library). 400p. 1997. pap. 99.00 (*1-57751-324-X*) Intl Business Pubns.

— Russian Business & Investment Services Directory. 2nd rev. ed. (Russian Business Library). 400p. 1997. pap. 99.00 (*1-57751-319-3*) Intl Business Pubns.

— Russian Business Bible: Complete Package of Strategic & Business Information for Corporate Executives. 250p. 1997. pap. 49.00 (*1-57751-246-4*) Intl Business Pubns.

— Russian Business Law Handbook: Basic Export-Import, Investment & Business Laws. (NIS Business Law Library). (Illus.). 200p. 1997. pap. 99.00 (*1-57751-299-5*) Intl Business Pubns.

— Russian Business Survival Guide. 2nd rev. ed. (Russian Business Library). 400p. 1997. pap. 99.00 (*1-57751-309-6*) Intl Business Pubns.

— Russian Charity, Religions & Non-Profit Organizations. 2nd rev. ed. (Russian Business Library). 400p. 1997. pap. 99.00 (*1-57751-318-5*) Intl Business Pubns.

— Russian Economic Atlas: Geography, Economy, Industry. 2nd rev. ed. 1997. pap. 149.00 (*1-57751-174-3*) Intl Business Pubns.

— Russian Emergency Services Directory. 2nd rev. ed. (Russian Business Library). 400p. 1997. pap. 99.00 (*1-57751-325-8*) Intl Business Pubns.

— Russian Executive Government Directory. 100p. 1997. pap. 99.00 (*1-57751-168-9*) Intl Business Pubns.

— Russian Export-Import & Business Directory. 2nd rev. ed. (Russian Business Library). 400p. 1997. pap. 99.00 (*1-57751-300-2*) Intl Business Pubns.

— Russian Hotel Directory. 2nd rev. ed. (Russian Business Library). 400p. 1997. pap. 99.00 (*1-57751-320-7*) Intl Business Pubns.

— Russian Industry: Major Telecom Equipment Producers & Services Providers. 250p. 1997. pap. 99.00 (*1-57751-245-6*) Intl Business Pubns.

— Russian Industry-97: Automobile Industry. 3rd ed. (Russian Industrial Directories Ser.: Vol. 3). 400p. 1997. pap. 99.00 (*1-57751-252-9*) Intl Business Pubns.

— Russian Industry-97: Building Materials Industry. 3rd ed. (Russian Industrial Directories Ser.: Vol. 4). 400p. 1997. pap. 99.00 (*1-57751-253-7*) Intl Business Pubns.

— Russian Industry-97: Chemical, Pharmaceutical & Microbiology Industry. 3rd ed. (Russian Industrial Directories Ser.: Vol. 5). 400p. 1997. pap. 99.00 (*1-57751-254-5*) Intl Business Pubns.

— Russian Industry-97: Clothing Industry. 3rd ed. (Russian Industrial Directories Ser.: Vol. 6). 400p. 1997. pap. 99.00 (*1-57751-255-3*) Intl Business Pubns.

— Russian Industry-97: Coal Mining & Peat Industry. 3rd ed. (Russian Industrial Directories Ser.: Vol. 7). 400p. 1997. pap. 99.00 (*1-57751-256-1*) Intl Business Pubns.

— Russian Industry-97: Consumer Goods, Household & Cultural Foods. 3rd ed. (Russian Industrial Directories Ser.: Vol. 8). 400p. 1997. pap. 99.00 (*1-57751-257-X*) Intl Business Pubns.

— Russian Industry-97: Defence Industry. 3rd ed. (Russian Industrial Directories Ser.: Vol. 28). 400p. 1997. pap. 99.00 (*1-57751-277-4*) Intl Business Pubns.

— Russian Industry-97: Electrical Engineering. 3rd ed. (Russian Industrial Directories Ser.: Vol. 9). 400p. 1997. pap. 99.00 (*1-57751-258-8*) Intl Business Pubns.

— Russian Industry-97: Fishing & Fish Processing. 3rd ed. (Russian Industrial Directories Ser.: Vol. 10). 400p. 1997. pap. 99.00 (*1-57751-259-6*) Intl Business Pubns.

— Russian Industry-97: Food & Food Processing. 3rd ed. (Russian Industrial Directories Ser.: Vol. 11). 400p. 1997. pap. 99.00 (*1-57751-260-X*) Intl Business Pubns.

— Russian Industry-97: Footwear & Tanning Industry. 3rd ed. (Russian Industrial Directories Ser.: Vol. 12). 400p. 1997. pap. 99.00 (*1-57751-261-8*) Intl Business Pubns.

— Russian Industry-97: Forestry & Timber Industry. 3rd ed. (Russian Industrial Directories Ser.: Vol. 13). 400p. 1997. pap. 99.00 (*1-57751-262-6*) Intl Business Pubns.

— Russian Industry-97: Gold Mining & Mining Industry. 3rd ed. (Russian Industrial Directories Ser.: Vol. 14). 400p. 1997. pap. 99.00 (*1-57751-263-4*) Intl Business Pubns.

— Russian Industry-97: High-Tech Products, PC, Research & Design. 3rd ed. (Russian Industrial Directories Ser.: Vol. 15). 400p. 1997. pap. 99.00 (*1-57751-264-2*) Intl Business Pubns.

— Russian Industry-97: Machine-Building. 3rd ed. (Russian Industrial Directories Ser.: Vol. 16). 400p. 1997. pap. 99.00 (*1-57751-269-3*) Intl Business Pubns.

— Russian Industry-97: Medical Equipment. 3rd ed. (Russian Industrial Directories Ser.: Vol. 17). 400p. 1997. pap. 99.00 (*1-57751-266-9*) Intl Business Pubns.

— Russian-Industry, '97: Metal-Working. 3rd ed. (Russian Industrial Directories Ser.: Vol. 19). 400p. 1997. pap. 99.00 (*1-57751-268-5*) Intl Business Pubns.

— Russian-Industry, '97: Metallurgy. 3rd ed. (Russian Industrial Directories Ser.: Vol. 18). 400p. 1997. pap. 99.00 (*1-57751-267-7*) Intl Business Pubns.

— Russian Industry-97: Mining (Building Materials) 3rd ed. (Russian Industrial Directories Ser.: Vol. 20). 400p. 1997. pap. 99.00 (*0-614-30774-0*) Intl Business Pubns.

— Russian Industry-97: Oil & Gas Industry. 3rd ed. (Russian Industrial Directories Ser.: Vol. 21). 400p. 1997. pap. 99.00 (*1-57751-270-7*) Intl Business Pubns.

— Russian Industry-97: Oil Refining & Gas Processing. 3rd ed. (Russian Industrial Directories Ser.: Vol. 22). 400p. 1997. pap. 99.00 (*1-57751-271-5*) Intl Business Pubns.

— Russian Industry-97: Power Industry. 3rd ed. (Russian Industrial Directories Ser.: Vol. 23). 400p. 1997. pap. 99.00 (*1-57751-272-3*) Intl Business Pubns.

— Russian Industry-97: Publishing & Printing Industry. 3rd ed. (Russian Industrial Directories Ser.: Vol. 25). 400p. 1997. pap. 99.00 (*1-57751-274-X*) Intl Business Pubns.

— Russian Industry-97: Pulp & Paper Industry. 3rd ed. (Russian Industrial Directories Ser.: Vol. 27). 400p. 1997. pap. 99.00 (*1-57751-276-6*) Intl Business Pubns.

— Russian Industry-97: Radio-Electronic Industry. 3rd ed. (Russian Industrial Directories Ser.: Vol. 26). 400p. 1997. pap. 99.00 (*1-57751-275-8*) Intl Business Pubns.

— Russian Industry-97: Rubber & Plastic Industry. 3rd ed. (Russian Industrial Directories Ser.: Vol. 29). 400p. 1997. pap. 99.00 (*1-57751-278-2*) Intl Business Pubns.

— Russian Industry-97: Scrap & Waste Processing. 3rd ed. (Russian Industrial Directories Ser.: Vol. 32). 400p. 1997. pap. 99.00 (*1-57751-282-0*) Intl Business Pubns.

— Russian Industry-97: Textile Industry. 3rd ed. (Russian Industrial Directories Ser.: Vol. 24). 400p. 1997. pap. 99.00 (*1-57751-273-1*) Intl Business Pubns.

— Russian Industry-97: Tobacco Industry. 3rd ed. (Russian Industrial Directories Ser.: Vol. 30). 400p. 1997. pap. 99.00 (*1-57751-279-0*) Intl Business Pubns.

— Russian Industry-97: Transport & Civil Engineering. 3rd ed. (Russian Industrial Directories Ser.: Vol. 31). 400p. 1997. pap. 99.00 (*1-57751-280-4*) Intl Business Pubns.
— Russian Industry-97: 1000 Largest Companies. 3rd ed. (Russian Industrial Directories Ser.: Vol. 2). 400p. 1997. pap. 99.00 (*1-57751-251-0*) Intl Business Pubns.
— Russian Industry-97: 500 Largest Companies. 3rd ed. (Russian Industrial Directories Ser.: Vol. 1). 400p. 1997. pap. 99.00 (*1-57751-250-2*) Intl Business Pubns.
— Russian Law & Legal Services Directory: Justice Departments, Courts, Law Firms, Bar Associations. 250p. 1997. pap. 99.00 (*1-57751-166-2*) Intl Business Pubns.
— Russian Mass Media Directory. 2nd rev. ed. (Russian Business Library). 400p. 1997. pap. 99.00 (*1-57751-316-9*) Intl Business Pubns.
— Russian Medical Services & Recreation Facilities Directory. 2nd rev. ed. (Russian Business Library). 400p. 1997. pap. 99.00 (*0-614-30776-7*) Intl Business Pubns.
— Russian Parliament Directory. 2nd ed. 250p. 1997. pap. 99.00 (*1-57751-167-0*) Intl Business Pubns.
— Russian Political Atlas. 300p. 1997. pap. 149.00 (*1-57751-171-9*) Intl Business Pubns.
— Russian Political Parties, Unions & Membership Organizations Directory. 2nd ed. (Russian Business Library). 400p. 1997. pap. 99.00 (*1-57751-321-5*) Intl Business Pubns.
— Russian Regional Economic & Business Atlas. 2nd rev. ed. 600p. 1997. pap. 149.00 (*1-57751-172-7*) Intl Business Pubns.
— Russian Regional Government Directory. 400p. 1997. pap. 99.00 (*1-57751-170-0*) Intl Business Pubns.
— Russian Regional Investment & Business Guide. 2nd rev. ed. (Russian Business Library). 400p. 1997. pap. 99.00 (*1-57751-308-8*) Intl Business Pubns.
— Russian Research Institutions & Scientists Directory. 2nd ed. (Russian Business Library). 400p. 1997. pap. 99.00 (*1-57751-323-1*) Intl Business Pubns.
— Russian Telecommunication Directory. 2nd rev. ed. (Russian Business Library). 400p. 1997. pap. 99.00 (*1-57751-302-9*) Intl Business Pubns.
— Russian Trade Directory: 1000 Largest Wholesale Companies in Russian Regions. 2nd ed. (Russian Business Library). 400p. 1997. pap. 99.00 (*1-57751-301-0*) Intl Business Pubns.
— Russian Transportation Directory. 2nd rev. ed. (Russian Business Library). 400p. 1997. pap. 99.00 (*1-57751-303-7*) Intl Business Pubns.
— Russian Universities Directory. 2nd rev. ed. (Russian Business Library). 400p. 1997. pap. 99.00 (*1-57751-322-3*) Intl Business Pubns.
— Ryazan Oblast: Economy, Industry, Government, Business. 2nd rev. ed. (Russian Regional Business Directories Ser.). (Illus.). 200p. 1997. pap. 99.00 (*1-57751-410-6*) Intl Business Pubns.
— St. Petersburg: Economy, Industry, Government, Business. 2nd rev. ed. (Russian Regional Business Directories Ser.). (Illus.). 200p. 1997. pap. 99.00 (*1-57751-372-X*) Intl Business Pubns.
— Sakha (Yakut) Republic: Economy, Industry, Government, Business. 2nd rev. ed. (Russian Regional Business Directories Ser.). (Illus.). 200p. 1997. pap. 99.00 (*1-57751-367-3*) Intl Business Pubns.
— Sakhalin Oblast: Economy, Industry, Government, Business. 2nd rev. ed. (Russian Regional Business Directories Ser.). (Illus.). 200p. 1997. pap. 99.00 (*1-57751-411-4*) Intl Business Pubns.
— Samara Oblast: Economy, Industry, Government, Business. 2nd rev. ed. (Russian Regional Business Directories Ser.). (Illus.). 200p. 1997. pap. 99.00 (*1-57751-412-2*) Intl Business Pubns.
— Saratov Oblast: Economy, Industry, Government, Business. 2nd rev. ed. (Russian Regional Business Directories Ser.). (Illus.). 200p. 1997. pap. 99.00 (*1-57751-413-0*) Intl Business Pubns.
— Saudi Arabia Business & Investment Opportunities Yearbook, 1998: Business, Investment, Export-Import. (Business & Investment Opportunities Library, '98). (Illus.). 1998. pap. 99.00 (*1-57751-997-3*) Intl Business Pubns.
— Slovak Republic Business Law Handbook-98. (World Business Law Library-98). (Illus.). 350p. 1998. pap. 99.00 (*1-57751-810-1*) Intl Business Pubns.
— Slovakia Economic & Business Guide: Strategic & Business Information for Corporate Executives. (Eastern European Business Library). (Illus.). 200p. 1997. pap. 69.00 (*1-57751-242-1*) Intl Business Pubns.
— Slovenia Business Law Handbook-98. (World Business Law Library-98). (Illus.). 350p. 1998. pap. 99.00 (*1-57751-811-X*) Intl Business Pubns.
— Smolensk Oblast: Economy, Industry, Government, Business. 2nd rev. ed. (Russian Regional Business Directories Ser.). (Illus.). 200p. 1997. pap. 99.00 (*1-57751-414-9*) Intl Business Pubns.
— Spain Business Law Handbook-98. (World Business Law Library-98). (Illus.). 350p. 1998. pap. 99.00 (*1-57751-821-7*) Intl Business Pubns.
— Stavropol Kray: Economy, Industry, Government, Business. 2nd rev. ed. (Russian Regional Business Directories Ser.). (Illus.). 200p. 1997. pap. 99.00 (*1-57751-378-9*) Intl Business Pubns.
— Surinam Business & Investment Opportunities Yearbook, 1998: Business, Investment, Export-Import. (Business & Investment Opportunities Library, '98). (Illus.). 1998. pap. 99.00 (*1-57751-982-5*) Intl Business Pubns.
— Sverdlovsk Oblast: Economy, Industry, Government, Business. 2nd rev. ed. (Russian Regional Business Directories Ser.). (Illus.). 200p. 1997. pap. 99.00 (*1-57751-427-0*) Intl Business Pubns.
— SWEDEN Business Law Handbook-98. (World Business Law Library-98). (Illus.). 350p. 1998. pap. 99.00 (*1-57751-822-5*) Intl Business Pubns.
— Syria Business & Investment Opportunities Yearbook, 1998: Business, Investment, Export-Import. (Business & Investment Opportunities Library, '98). (Illus.). 1998. pap. 99.00 (*1-57751-998-1*) Intl Business Pubns.
— Tadjikistan Business Law Handbook: Basic Export-Import, Investment & Business Laws. (NIS Business Law Library). (Illus.). 200p. 1997. pap. 99.00 (*1-57751-294-4*) Intl Business Pubns.
— Tadzhikistan Business Law Handbook, '98. (World Business Law Library, '98). (Illus.). 1998. pap. 99.00 (*1-57751-696-6*) Intl Business Pubns.
— Tadzhikistan Investment & Business Guide Vol. 9: Economy, Export-Import, Business & Investment Climate, Business Contacts. (Russia, NIS & Emerging Markets Investment & Business Library). (Illus.). 350p. 1998. pap. 99.00 (*1-57751-573-0*) Intl Business Pubns.
— Taiwan Business & Investment Opportunities Yearbook, 1998: Business, Investment, Export-Import. (Business & Investment Opportunities Library, '98). (Illus.). 1998. pap. 99.00 (*1-57751-983-3*) Intl Business Pubns.
— Tambov Oblast: Economy, Industry, Government, Business. 2nd rev. ed. (Russian Regional Business Directories Ser.). (Illus.). 200p. 1997. pap. 99.00 (*1-57751-416-5*) Intl Business Pubns.
— Tatarstan Republic: Economy, Industry, Government, Business. 2nd rev. ed. (Russian Regional Business Directories Ser.). (Illus.). 200p. 1997. pap. 99.00 (*1-57751-368-1*) Intl Business Pubns.
— Taymyrskiy Autonomous Okrug: Economy, Industry, Government, Business. 2nd rev. ed. (Russian Regional Business Directories Ser.). (Illus.). 200p. 1997. pap. 99.00 (*1-57751-429-7*) Intl Business Pubns.
— Tomsk Oblast: Economy, Industry, Government, Business. 2nd rev. ed. (Russian Regional Business Directories Ser.). (Illus.). 200p. 1997. pap. 99.00 (*1-57751-417-3*) Intl Business Pubns.
— Tula Oblast: Economy, Industry, Government, Business. 2nd rev. ed. (Russian Regional Business Directories Ser.). (Illus.). 200p. 1997. pap. 99.00 (*1-57751-419-X*) Intl Business Pubns.
— Turkey Business Law Handbook-98. (World Business Law Library-98). (Illus.). 350p. 1998. pap. 99.00 (*1-57751-823-3*) Intl Business Pubns.
— Turkmenistan Business Law Handbook: Basic Export-Import, Investment & Business Laws. (NIS Business Law Library). 200p. 1997. pap. 99.00 (*1-57751-296-0*) Intl Business Pubns.
— Turkmenistan Business Law Handbook, '98. (World Business Law Library, '98). (Illus.). 1998. pap. 99.00 (*1-57751-688-5*) Intl Business Pubns.
— Turkmenistan Investment & Business Guide Vol. 10: Economy, Export-Import, Business & Investment Climate, Business Contacts. (Russia, NIS & Emerging Markets Investment & Business Library). (Illus.). 350p. 1998. pap. 99.00 (*1-57751-574-9*) Intl Business Pubns.
— Tver Oblast: Economy, Industry, Government, Business. 2nd rev. ed. (Russian Regional Business Directories Ser.). (Illus.). 200p. 1997. pap. 99.00 (*1-57751-420-3*) Intl Business Pubns.
— Tyumen Oblast: Economy, Industry, Government, Business. 2nd rev. ed. (Russian Regional Business Directories Ser.). (Illus.). 200p. 1997. pap. 99.00 (*1-57751-421-1*) Intl Business Pubns.
— Tyva Republic: Economy, Industry, Government, Business. 2nd rev. ed. (Russian Regional Business Directories Ser.). (Illus.). 200p. 1997. pap. 99.00 (*1-57751-369-X*) Intl Business Pubns.
— U. S. Companies in Russia & NIS. 2nd rev. ed. (Russian Business Library). 400p. 1997. pap. 99.00 (*0-614-30775-9*) Intl Business Pubns.
— U. S. Economic Assistance to Russia & NIS: U. S. Aid Contractors, U. S. Non-Profits, Investment Funds. 2nd rev. ed. (Russian Business Library). 400p. 1997. pap. 99.00 (*1-57751-304-5*) Intl Business Pubns.
— U. S. Government Officials Working with Russia & NIS. 2nd rev. ed. (Russian Business Library). 400p. 1997. pap. 99.00 (*1-57751-307-X*) Intl Business Pubns.
— U. S. Oil & Gas Companies Interested in Russia & NIS. 250p. 1997. pap. 99.00 (*1-57751-232-4*) Intl Business Pubns.
— Udmurt Republic: Economy, Industry, Government, Business. 2nd rev. ed. (Russian Regional Business Directories Ser.). (Illus.). 200p. 1997. pap. 99.00 (*1-57751-370-3*) Intl Business Pubns.
— Ukraine Business Law Handbook: Basic Export-Import, Investment & Business Laws. (NIS Business Law Library). 200p. 1997. pap. 99.00 (*1-57751-297-9*) Intl Business Pubns.
— Ukraine Business Law Handbook, '98. (World Business Law Library, '98). (Illus.). 1998. pap. 99.00 (*1-57751-698-2*) Intl Business Pubns.
— Ukraine Investment & Business Guide Vol. 13: Economy, Export-Import, Business & Investment Climate, Business Contacts. (Russia, NIS & Emerging Markets Investment & Business Library). (Illus.). 350p. 1998. pap. 99.00 (*1-57751-565-X*) Intl Business Pubns.
— Ulyanovsk Oblast: Economy, Industry, Government, Business. 2nd rev. ed. (Russian Regional Business Directories Ser.). (Illus.). 200p. 1997. pap. 99.00 (*1-57751-422-X*) Intl Business Pubns.
— United Arab Emirates Business & Investment Opportunities Yearbook, 1998: Business, Investment, Export-Import. (Business & Investment Opportunities Library, '98). (Illus.). 1998. pap. 99.00 (*1-57751-999-X*) Intl Business Pubns.
— URUGUAY Business Law Handbook-98. (World Business Law Library-98). (Illus.). 350p. 1998. pap. 99.00 (*1-57751-844-6*) Intl Business Pubns.
— Ust-Ordynskiy Autonomous Okrug: Economy, Industry, Government, Business. 2nd rev. ed. (Russian Regional Business Directories Ser.). (Illus.). 200p. 1997. pap. 99.00 (*0-614-30771-6*) Intl Business Pubns.
— Uzbekistan Business Law Handbook, '98. (World Business Law Library, '98). (Illus.). 1998. pap. 99.00 (*1-57751-599-0*) Intl Business Pubns.
— Uzbekistaw Business Law Handbook: Basic Export-Import, Investment & Business Laws. (NIS Business Law Library). 200p. 1997. pap. 99.00 (*1-57751-298-7*) Intl Business Pubns.
— Venezuela Business Law Handbook-98. (World Business Law Library-98). (Illus.). 350p. 1998. pap. 99.00 (*1-57751-845-4*) Intl Business Pubns.
— Vietnam Business & Investment Opportunities Yearbook, 1998: Business, Investment, Export-Import. (Business & Investment Opportunities Library, '98). (Illus.). 1998. pap. 99.00 (*1-57751-985-X*) Intl Business Pubns.
— Vladimir Oblast: Economy, Industry, Government, Business. 2nd rev. ed. (Russian Regional Business Directories Ser.). (Illus.). 200p. 1997. pap. 99.00 (*1-57751-423-8*) Intl Business Pubns.
— Volgograd Oblast: Economy, Industry, Government, Business. 2nd rev. ed. (Russian Regional Business Directories Ser.). (Illus.). 200p. 1997. pap. 99.00 (*1-57751-418-1*) Intl Business Pubns.
— Vologda Oblast: Economy, Industry, Government, Business. 2nd rev. ed. (Russian Regional Business Directories Ser.). (Illus.). 200p. 1997. pap. 99.00 (*1-57751-424-6*) Intl Business Pubns.
— Voronezh Oblast: Economy, Industry, Government, Business. 2nd rev. ed. (Russian Regional Business Directories Ser.). (Illus.). 200p. 1997. pap. 99.00 (*1-57751-425-4*) Intl Business Pubns.
— Western Companies Interested in Doing Business in Russia. 2nd ed. (Russian Business Library). 400p. 1997. pap. 99.00 (*1-57751-313-4*) Intl Business Pubns.
— Yamalo-Nenets Autonomous Okrug: Economy, Industry, Government, Business. 2nd rev. ed. (Russian Regional Business Directories Ser.). (Illus.). 200p. 1997. pap. 99.00 (*0-614-30772-4*) Intl Business Pubns.
— Yaroslavl Oblast: Economy, Industry, Government, Business. 2nd rev. ed. (Russian Regional Business Directories Ser.). (Illus.). 200p. 1997. pap. 99.00 (*1-57751-426-2*) Intl Business Pubns.
— Yevreyskaya Autonomous Oblast: Economy, Industry, Government, Business. 2nd rev. ed. (Russian Regional Business Directories Ser.). (Illus.). 200p. 1997. pap. 99.00 (*1-57751-432-7*) Intl Business Pubns.

Russian Information & Business Center, Inc. Staff, contrib. by. Albania Business & Investment Opportunities Yearbook-98: Business, Investment, Export-Import. (Business & Investment Opportunity Library-98). (Illus.). 350p. 1998. pap. 99.00 (*1-57751-954-X*) Intl Business Pubns.
— Albania Investment & Business Guide Vol. 1: Economy, Export-Import, Business & Investment Climate, Business Contacts. (Russia, NIS & Emerging Markets Investment & Business Library). (Illus.). 350p. 1998. pap. 99.00 (*1-57751-599-4*) Intl Business Pubns.
— Algeria Investment & Business Guide: Economy, Export-Import, Business & Investment Climate, Business Contacts. (Russia, NIS & Emerging Markets Investment & Business Library-98). (Illus.). 350p. 1998. pap. 99.00 (*1-57751-908-6*) Intl Business Pubns.
— Antilles Investment & Business Guide: Economy, Export-Import, Business & Investment Climate, Business Contacts. (Russia, NIS & Emerging Markets Investment & Business Library-98). (Illus.). 350p. 1998. pap. 99.00 (*1-57751-881-0*) Intl Business Pubns.
— Argentina Investment & Business Guide: Economy, Export-Import, Business & Investment Climate, Business Contacts. (Russia, NIS & Emerging Markets Investment & Business Library-98). (Illus.). 350p. 1998. pap. 99.00 (*1-57751-882-9*) Intl Business Pubns.
— Armenia Business & Investment Opportunities Yearbook-98: Business, Investment, Export-Import. (Business & Investment Opportunity Library-98). (Illus.). 350p. 1998. pap. 99.00 (*1-57751-942-6*) Intl Business Pubns.
— Azerbaijan Business & Investment Opportunities Yearbook-98: Business, Investment, Export-Import. (Business & Investment Opportunity Library-98). (Illus.). 350p. 1998. pap. 99.00 (*1-57751-943-4*) Intl Business Pubns.
— Bahrain Investment & Business Guide: Economy, Export-Import, Business & Investment Climate, Business Contacts. (Russia, NIS & Emerging Markets Investment & Business Library-98). (Illus.). 350p. 1998. pap. 99.00 (*1-57751-909-4*) Intl Business Pubns.
— Bangladesh Business & Investment Opportunities Yearbook-98: Business, Investment, Export-Import. (Business & Investment Opportunity Library-98). (Illus.). 350p. 1998. pap. 99.00 (*1-57751-966-3*) Intl Business Pubns.
— Bangladesh Investment & Business Guide: Economy, Export-Import, Business & Investment Climate, Business Contacts. (Russia, NIS & Emerging Markets Investment & Business Library-98). (Illus.). 350p. 1998. pap. 99.00 (*1-57751-862-4*) Intl Business Pubns.
— Barbados Investment & Business Guide: Economy, Export-Import, Business & Investment Climate, Business Contacts. (Russia, NIS & Emerging Markets Investment & Business Library-98). (Illus.). 350p. 1998. pap. 99.00 (*1-57751-883-7*) Intl Business Pubns.
— Belarus Business & Investment Opportunities Yearbook-98: Business, Investment, Export-Import. (Business & Investment Opportunity Library-98). (Illus.). 350p. 1998. pap. 99.00 (*1-57751-944-2*) Intl Business Pubns.
— Belize Investment & Business Guide: Economy, Export-Import, Business & Investment Climate, Business Contacts. (Russia, NIS & Emerging Markets Investment & Business Library-98). (Illus.). 350p. 1998. pap. 99.00 (*1-57751-884-5*) Intl Business Pubns.
— Bolivia Investment & Business Guide: Economy, Export-Import, Business & Investment Climate, Business Contacts. (Russia, NIS & Emerging Markets Investment & Business Library-98). (Illus.). 350p. 1998. pap. 99.00 (*1-57751-885-3*) Intl Business Pubns.
— Bosnia-Hertzegovina Business & Investment Opportunities Yearbook-98: Business, Investment, Export-Import. (Business & Investment Opportunity Library-98). (Illus.). 350p. 1998. pap. 99.00 (*1-57751-955-8*) Intl Business Pubns.
— Bosnia-Herzegovina Investment & Business Guide: Economy, Export-Import, Business & Investment Climate, Business Contacts. (Russia, NIS & Emerging Markets Investment & Business Library-98). (Illus.). 350p. 1998. pap. 99.00 (*1-57751-923-X*) Intl Business Pubns.
— Brazil Investment & Business Guide: Economy, Export-Import, Business & Investment Climate, Business Contacts. (Russia, NIS & Emerging Markets Investment & Business Library-98). (Illus.). 350p. 1998. pap. 99.00 (*1-57751-886-1*) Intl Business Pubns.
— Brunei Investment & Business Guide: Economy, Export-Import, Business & Investment Climate, Business Contacts. (Russia, NIS & Emerging Markets Investment & Business Library-98). (Illus.). 350p. 1998. pap. 99.00 (*1-57751-910-8*) Intl Business Pubns.
— Bulgaria Business & Investment Opportunities Yearbook-98: Business, Investment, Export-Import. (Business & Investment Opportunity Library-98). (Illus.). 350p. 1998. pap. 99.00 (*1-57751-930-2*) Intl Business Pubns.
— Bulgaria Investment & Business Guide: Economy, Export-Import, Business & Investment Climate, Business Contacts. (Russia, NIS & Emerging Markets Investment & Business Library-98). (Illus.). 350p. 1998. pap. 99.00 (*1-57751-850-0*) Intl Business Pubns.
— Burma Business & Investment Opportunities Yearbook-98: Business, Investment, Export-Import. (Business & Investment Opportunity Library-98). (Illus.). 350p. 1998. pap. 99.00 (*1-57751-967-1*) Intl Business Pubns.
— Burma Investment & Business Guide: Economy, Export-Import, Business & Investment Climate, Business Contacts. (Russia, NIS & Emerging Markets Investment & Business Library-98). (Illus.). 350p. 1998. pap. 99.00 (*1-57751-863-2*) Intl Business Pubns.
— Cambodia Business & Investment Opportunities Yearbook-98: Business, Investment, Export-Import. (Business & Investment Opportunity Library-98). (Illus.). 350p. 1998. pap. 99.00 (*1-57751-968-X*) Intl Business Pubns.
— Carbodia Investment & Business Guide: Economy, Export-Import, Business & Investment Climate, Business Contacts. (Russia, NIS & Emerging Markets Investment & Business Library-98). (Illus.). 350p. 1998. pap. 99.00 (*1-57751-864-0*) Intl Business Pubns.
— Chech Republic Business & Investment Opportunities Yearbook-98: Business, Investment, Export-Import. (Business & Investment Opportunity Library-98). (Illus.). 350p. 1998. pap. 99.00 (*1-57751-932-9*) Intl Business Pubns.
— Chech Republic Investment & Business Guide: Economy, Export-Import, Business & Investment Climate, Business Contacts. (Russia, NIS & Emerging Markets Investment & Business Library-98). (Illus.). 350p. 1998. pap. 99.00 (*1-57751-852-7*) Intl Business Pubns.
— Chile Investment & Business Guide: Economy, Export-Import, Business & Investment Climate, Business Contacts. (Russia, NIS & Emerging Markets Investment & Business Library-98). (Illus.). 350p. 1998. pap. 99.00 (*1-57751-887-X*) Intl Business Pubns.
— China Business & Investment Opportunities Yearbook-98: Business, Investment, Export-Import. (Business & Investment Opportunity Library-98). (Illus.). 350p. 1998. pap. 99.00 (*1-57751-969-8*) Intl Business Pubns.
— China Investment & Business Guide: Economy, Export-Import, Buisness & Investment Climate, Business Contacts. (Russia, NIS & Emerging Markets Investment & Business Library-98). (Illus.). 350p. 1998. pap. 99.00 (*1-57751-865-9*) Intl Business Pubns.
— Columbia Investment & Business Guide: Economy, Export-Import, Business & Investment Climate, Business Contacts. (Russia, NIS & Emerging Markets Investment & Business Library-98). (Illus.). 350p. 1998. pap. 99.00 (*1-57751-888-8*) Intl Business Pubns.
— Costa Rica Investment & Business Guide: Economy, Export-Import, Business & Investment Climate, Business Contacts. (Russia, NIS & Emerging Markets Investment & Business Library-98). (Illus.). 350p. 1998. pap. 99.00 (*1-57751-889-6*) Intl Business Pubns.
— Croatia Business & Investment Opportunities Yearbook-98: Business, Investment, Export-Import. (Business & Investment Opportunity Library-98). (Illus.). 350p. 1998. pap. 99.00 (*1-57751-931-0*) Intl Business Pubns.
— Croatia Investment & Business Guide: Economy, Export-Import, Business & Investment Climate, Business Contacts. (Russia, NIS & Emerging Markets Investment & Business Library-98). (Illus.). 350p. 1998. pap. 99.00 (*1-57751-851-9*) Intl Business Pubns.
— Cyprus Business & Investment Opportunities Yearbook-98: Business, Investment, Export-Import. (Business & Investment Opportunity Library-98). (Illus.). 350p. 1998. pap. 99.00 (*1-57751-956-6*) Intl Business Pubns.
— Cyprus Investment & Business Guide: Economy, Export-Import, Business & Investment Climate, Business Contacts. (Russia, NIS & Emerging Markets Investment & Business Library-98). (Illus.). 350p. 1998. pap. 99.00 (*1-57751-922-1*) Intl Business Pubns.
— Dominican Republic Investment & Business Guide: Economy, Export-Import, Business & Investment

R

R

Climate, Business Contacts. (Russia, NIS & Emerging Markets Investment & Business Library-98). (Illus.). 350p. 1998. pap. 99.00 (*1-57751-890-X*) Intl Business Pubns.

— Egypt Investment & Business Guide: Economy, Export-Import, Business & Investment Climate, Business Contacts. (Russia, NIS & Emerging Markets Investment & Business Library-98). (Illus.). 350p. 1998. pap. 99.00 (*1-57751-911-6*) Intl Business Pubns.

— El Salvador Investment & Business Guide: Economy, Export-Import, Business & Investment Climate, Business Contacts. (Russia, NIS & Emerging Markets Investment & Business Library-98). (Illus.). 350p. 1998. pap. 99.00 (*1-57751-892-6*) Intl Business Pubns.

— Estonia Business & Investment Opportunities Yearbook-98: Business, Investment, Export-Import. (Business & Investment Opportunity Library-98). (Illus.). 350p. 1998. pap. 99.00 (*1-57751-933-7*) Intl Business Pubns.

— Estonia Investment & Business Guide: Economy, Export-Import, Business & Investment Climate, Business Contacts. (Russia, NIS & Emerging Markets Investment & Business Library-98). (Illus.). 350p. 1998. pap. 99.00 (*1-57751-853-5*) Intl Business Pubns.

— Finland Business & Investment Opportunities Yearbook-98: Business, Investment, Export-Import. (Business & Investment Opportunity Library-98). (Illus.). 350p. 1998. pap. 99.00 (*1-57751-957-4*) Intl Business Pubns.

— Finland Investment & Business Guide: Economy, Export-Import, Business & Investment Climate, Business Contacts. (Russia, NIS & Emerging Markets Investment & Business Library-98). (Illus.). 350p. 1998. pap. 99.00 (*1-57751-929-9*) Intl Business Pubns.

— Gana Investment & Business Guide: Economy, Export-Import, Business & Investment Climate, Business Contacts. (Russia, NIS & Emerging Markets Investment & Business Library-98). (Illus.). 350p. 1998. pap. 99.00 (*1-57751-903-5*) Intl Business Pubns.

— Georgia Business & Investment Opportunities Yearbook-98: Business, Investment, Export-Import. (Business & Investment Opportunity Library-98). (Illus.). 350p. 1998. pap. 99.00 (*1-57751-945-0*) Intl Business Pubns.

— Greece Business & Investment Opportunities Yearbook-98: Business, Investment, Export-Import. (Business & Investment Opportunity Library-98). (Illus.). 350p. 1998. pap. 99.00 (*1-57751-958-2*) Intl Business Pubns.

— Greece Investment & Business Guide: Economy, Export-Import, Business & Investment Climate, Business Contacts. (Russia, NIS & Emerging Markets Investment & Business Library-98). (Illus.). 350p. 1998. pap. 99.00 (*1-57751-924-8*) Intl Business Pubns.

— Guatemala Investment & Business Guide: Economy, Export-Import, Business & Investment Climate, Business Contacts. (Russia, NIS & Emerging Markets Investment & Business Library-98). (Illus.). 350p. 1998. pap. 99.00 (*1-57751-893-4*) Intl Business Pubns.

— Honduras Investment & Business Guide: Economy, Export-Import, Business & Investment Climate, Business Contacts. (Russia, NIS & Emerging Markets Investment & Business Library-98). (Illus.). 350p. 1998. pap. 99.00 (*1-57751-894-2*) Intl Business Pubns.

— Hong Kong Business & Investment Opportunities Yearbook-98: Business, Investment, Export-Import. (Business & Investment Opportunity Library-98). (Illus.). 350p. 1998. pap. 99.00 (*1-57751-970-1*) Intl Business Pubns.

— Hong Kong Investment & Business Guide: Economy, Export-Import, Business & Investment Climate, Business Contacts. (Russia, NIS & Emerging Markets Investment & Business Library-98). (Illus.). 350p. 1998. pap. 99.00 (*1-57751-866-7*) Intl Business Pubns.

— Hungary Business & Investment Opportunities Yearbook-98: Business, Investment, Export-Import. (Business & Investment Opportunity Library-98). (Illus.). 350p. 1998. pap. 99.00 (*1-57751-934-5*) Intl Business Pubns.

— Hungary Investment & Business Guide: Economy, Export-Import, Business & Investment Climate, Business Contacts. (Russia, NIS & Emerging Markets Investment & Business Library - 98). (Illus.). 350p. 1998. pap. 99.00 (*1-57751-854-3*) Intl Business Pubns.

— Iceland Business & Investment Opportunities Yearbook-98: Business, Investment, Export-Import. (Business & Investment Opportunity Library-98). (Illus.). 350p. 1998. pap. 99.00 (*1-57751-960-4*) Intl Business Pubns.

— Iceland Investment & Business Guide: Economy, Export-Import, Business & Investment Climate, Business Contacts. (Russia, NIS & Emerging Markets Investment & Business Library-98). (Illus.). 350p. 1998. pap. 99.00 (*1-57751-926-4*) Intl Business Pubns.

— India Business & Investment Opportunities Yearbook-98: Business, Investment, Export-Import. (Business & Investment Opportunity Library-98). (Illus.). 350p. 1998. pap. 99.00 (*1-57751-971-X*) Intl Business Pubns.

— India Investment & Business Guide: Economy, Export-Import, Business & Investment Climate, Business Contacts. (Russia, NIS & Emerging Markets Investment & Business Library-98). (Illus.). 350p. 1998. pap. 99.00 (*1-57751-867-5*) Intl Business Pubns.

— Indonesia Business & Investment Opportunities Yearbook-98: Business, Investment, Export-Import. (Business & Investment Opportunity Library-98). (Illus.). 350p. 1998. pap. 99.00 (*1-57751-972-8*) Intl Business Pubns.

— Indonesia Investment & Business Guide: Economy, Export-Import, Business & Investment Climate, Business Contacts. (Russia, NIS & Emerging Markets Investment & Business Library-98). (Illus.). 350p. 1998. pap. 99.00 (*1-57751-868-3*) Intl Business Pubns.

— Iran Investment & Business Guide: Economy, Export-Import, Business & Investment Climate, Business Contacts. (Russia, NIS & Emerging Markets Investment & Business Library-98). (Illus.). 350p. 1998. pap. 99.00 (*1-57751-912-4*) Intl Business Pubns.

— Israel Business & Investment Opportunities Yearbook-98: Business, Investment, Export-Import. (Business & Investment Opportunity Library-98). (Illus.). 350p. 1998. pap. 99.00 (*1-57751-959-0*) Intl Business Pubns.

— Israel Investment & Business Guide: Economy, Export-Import, Business & Investment Climate, Business Contacts. (Russia, NIS & Emerging Markets Investment & Business Library-98). (Illus.). 350p. 1998. pap. 99.00 (*1-57751-925-6*) Intl Business Pubns.

— Jamaica Investment & Business Guide: Economy, Export-Import, Business & Investment Climate, Business Contacts. (Russia, NIS & Emerging Markets Investment & Business Library-98). (Illus.). 350p. 1998. pap. 99.00 (*1-57751-895-0*) Intl Business Pubns.

— Japan Business & Investment Opportunities Yearbook-98: Business, Investment, Export-Import. (Business & Investment Opportunity Library-98). (Illus.). 350p. 1998. pap. 99.00 (*1-57751-973-6*) Intl Business Pubns.

— Japan Investment & Business Guide: Economy, Export-Import, Business & Investment Climate, Business Contacts. (Russia, NIS & Emerging Markets Investment & Business Library-98). (Illus.). 350p. 1998. pap. 99.00 (*1-57751-869-1*) Intl Business Pubns.

— Jordan Investment & Business Guide: Economy, Export-Import, Business & Investment Climate, Business Contacts. (Russia, NIS & Emerging Markets Investment & Business Library-98). (Illus.). 350p. 1998. pap. 99.00 (*1-57751-913-2*) Intl Business Pubns.

— Kazakhstan Business & Investment Opportunities Yearbook-98: Business, Investment, Export-Import. (Business & Investment Opportunity Library-98). (Illus.). 350p. 1998. pap. 99.00 (*1-57751-946-9*) Intl Business Pubns.

— Korea Business & Investment Opportunities Yearbook-98: Business, Investment, Export-Import. (Business & Investment Opportunity Library-98). (Illus.). 350p. 1998. pap. 99.00 (*1-57751-974-4*) Intl Business Pubns.

— Korea Investment & Business Guide: Economy, Export-Import, Business & Investment Climate, Business Contacts. (Russia, NIS & Emerging Markets Investment & Business Library-98). (Illus.). 350p. 1998. pap. 99.00 (*1-57751-870-5*) Intl Business Pubns.

— Kuwait Investment & Business Guide: Economy, Export-Import, Business & Investment Climate, Business Contacts. (Russia, NIS & Emerging Markets Investment & Business Library-98). (Illus.). 350p. 1998. pap. 99.00 (*1-57751-914-0*) Intl Business Pubns.

— Kyrgyzstan Business & Investment Opportunities Yearbook-98: Business, Investment, Export-Import. (Business & Investment Opportunity Library-98). (Illus.). 350p. 1998. pap. 99.00 (*1-57751-947-7*) Intl Business Pubns.

— Latvia Business & Investment Opportunities Yearbook-98: Business, Investment, Export-Import. (Business & Investment Opportunity Library-98). (Illus.). 350p. 1998. pap. 99.00 (*1-57751-935-3*) Intl Business Pubns.

— Latvia Investment & Business Guide: Economy, Export-Import, Business & Investment Climate, Business Contacts. (Russia, NIS & Emerging Markets Investment & Business Library-98). (Illus.). 350p. 1998. pap. 99.00 (*1-57751-855-1*) Intl Business Pubns.

— Lebanon Investment & Business Guide: Economy, Export-Import, Business & Investment Climate, Business Contacts. (Russia, NIS & Emerging Markets Investment & Business Library-98). (Illus.). 350p. 1998. pap. 99.00 (*1-57751-915-9*) Intl Business Pubns.

— Liberia Investment & Business Guide: Economy, Export-Import, Business & Investment Climate, Business Contacts. (Russia, NIS & Emerging Markets Investment & Business Library-98). (Illus.). 350p. 1998. pap. 99.00 (*1-57751-896-9*) Intl Business Pubns.

— Lithuania Business & Investment Opportunities Yearbook-98: Business, Investment, Export-Import. (Business & Investment Opportunity Library-98). (Illus.). 350p. 1998. pap. 99.00 (*1-57751-936-1*) Intl Business Pubns.

— Lithuania Investment & Business Guide: Economy, Export-Import, Business & Investment Climate, Business Contacts. (Russia, NIS & Emerging Markets Investment & Business Library-98). (Illus.). 350p. 1998. pap. 99.00 (*1-57751-856-X*) Intl Business Pubns.

— Macau Business & Investment Opportunities Yearbook-98: Business, Investment, Export-Import. (Business & Investment Opportunity Library-98). (Illus.). 350p. 1998. pap. 99.00 (*1-57751-975-2*) Intl Business Pubns.

— Macau Investment & Business Guide: Economy, Export-Import, Business & Investment Climate, Business Contacts. (Russia, NIS & Emerging Markets Investment & Business Library-98). (Illus.). 350p. 1998. pap. 99.00 (*1-57751-871-3*) Intl Business Pubns.

— Macedonia Business & Investment Opportunities Yearbook-98: Business, Investment, Export-Import. (Business & Investment Opportunity Library-98). (Illus.). 350p. 1998. pap. 99.00 (*1-57751-937-X*) Intl Business Pubns.

— Macedonia Investment & Business Guide: Economy, Export-Import, Business & Investment Climate, Business Contacts. (Russia, NIS & Emerging Markets Investment & Business Library-98). (Illus.). 350p. 1998. pap. 99.00 (*1-57751-857-8*) Intl Business Pubns.

— Madagascar Business & Investment Opportunities Yearbook-98: Business, Investment, Export-Import. (Business & Investment Opportunity Library-98). (Illus.). 350p. 1998. pap. 99.00 (*1-57751-976-0*) Intl Business Pubns.

— Madagascar Investment & Business Guide: Economy, Export-Import, Business & Investment Climate, Business Contacts. (Russia, NIS & Emerging Markets Investment & Business Library-98). (Illus.). 350p. 1998. pap. 99.00 (*1-57751-872-1*) Intl Business Pubns.

— Malaysia Business & Investment Opportunities Yearbook-98: Business, Investment, Export-Import. (Business & Investment Opportunity Library-98). (Illus.). 350p. 1998. pap. 99.00 (*1-57751-977-9*) Intl Business Pubns.

— Malaysia Investment & Business Guide: Economy, Export-Import, Business & Investment Climate, Business Contacts. (Russia, NIS & Emerging Markets Investment & Business Library-98). (Illus.). 350p. 1998. pap. 99.00 (*1-57751-873-X*) Intl Business Pubns.

— Malta Business & Investment Opportunities Yearbook-98: Business, Investment, Export-Import. (Business & Investment Opportunity Library-98). (Illus.). 350p. 1998. pap. 99.00 (*1-57751-961-2*) Intl Business Pubns.

— Malta Investment & Business Guide: Economy, Export-Import, Business & Investment Climate, Business Contacts. (Russia, NIS & Emerging Markets Investment & Business Library-98). (Illus.). 350p. 1998. pap. 99.00 (*1-57751-927-2*) Intl Business Pubns.

— Marshall Islands Investment & Business Guide: Economy, Export-Import, Business & Investment Climate, Business Contacts. (Russia, NIS & Emerging Markets Investment & Business Library-98). (Illus.). 350p. 1998. pap. 99.00 (*1-57751-897-7*) Intl Business Pubns.

— Mauritius Investment & Business Guide: Economy, Export-Import, Business & Investment Climate, Business Contacts. (Russia, NIS & Emerging Markets Investment & Business Library-98). (Illus.). 350p. 1998. pap. 99.00 (*1-57751-906-X*) Intl Business Pubns.

— Mexico Investment & Business Guide: Economy, Export-Import, Business & Investment Climate, Business Contacts. (Russia, NIS & Emerging Markets Investment & Business Library-98). (Illus.). 350p. 1998. pap. 99.00 (*1-57751-898-5*) Intl Business Pubns.

— Moldova Business & Investment Opportunities Yearbook-98: Business, Investment, Export-Import. (Business & Investment Opportunity Library-98). (Illus.). 350p. 1998. pap. 99.00 (*1-57751-948-5*) Intl Business Pubns.

— Mongolia Business & Investment Opportunities Yearbook-98: Business, Investment, Export-Import. (Business & Investment Opportunity Library-98). (Illus.). 350p. 1998. pap. 99.00 (*1-57751-978-7*) Intl Business Pubns.

— Mongolia Investment & Business Guide Vol. 12: Economy, Export-Import, Business & Investment Climate, Business Contacts. (Russia, NIS & Emerging Markets Investment & Business Library). (Illus.). 350p. 1998. pap. 99.00 (*1-57751-598-6*) Intl Business Pubns.

— Morocco Investment & Business Guide: Economy, Export-Import, Business & Investment Climate, Business Contacts. (Russia, NIS & Emerging Markets Investment & Business Library-98). (Illus.). 350p. 1998. pap. 99.00 (*1-57751-916-7*) Intl Business Pubns.

— Nicaragua Investment & Business Guide: Economy, Export-Import, Business & Investment Climate, Business Contacts. (Russia, NIS & Emerging Markets Investment & Business Library-98). (Illus.). 350p. 1998. pap. 99.00 (*1-57751-899-3*) Intl Business Pubns.

— Nigeria Investment & Business Guide: Economy, Export-Import, Business & Investment Climate, Business Contacts. (Russia, NIS & Emerging Markets Investment & Business Library-98). (Illus.). 350p. 1998. pap. 99.00 (*1-57751-904-3*) Intl Business Pubns.

— Oman Investment & Business Guide: Economy, Export-Import, Business & Investment Climate, Business Contacts. (Russia, NIS & Emerging Markets Investment & Business Library-98). (Illus.). 350p. 1998. pap. 99.00 (*1-57751-917-5*) Intl Business Pubns.

— Pakistan Business & Investment Opportunities Yearbook-98: Business, Investment, Export-Import. (Business & Investment Opportunity Library-98). (Illus.). 350p. 1998. pap. 99.00 (*1-57751-979-5*) Intl Business Pubns.

— Pakistan Investment & Business Guide: Economy, Export-Import, Business & Investment Climate, Business Contacts. (Russia, NIS & Emerging Markets Investment & Business Library-98). (Illus.). 350p. 1998. pap. 99.00 (*1-57751-874-8*) Intl Business Pubns.

— Peru Investment & Business Guide: Economy, Export-Import, Business & Investment Climate, Business Contacts. (Russia, NIS & Emerging Markets Investment & Business Library-98). (Illus.). 350p. 1998. pap. 99.00 (*1-57751-900-0*) Intl Business Pubns.

— Philippines Investment & Business Guide: Economy, Export-Import, Business & Investment Climate, Business Contacts. (Russia, NIS & Emerging Markets Investment & Business Library-98). (Illus.). 350p. 1998. pap. 99.00 (*1-57751-875-6*) Intl Business Pubns.

— Phillippines Business & Investment Opportunities Yearbook-98: Business, Investment, Export-Import. (Business & Investment Opportunity Library-98). (Illus.). 350p. 1998. pap. 99.00 (*1-57751-980-9*) Intl Business Pubns.

— Poland Business & Investment Opportunities Yearbook-98: Business, Investment, Export-Import. (Business & Investment Opportunity Library-98). (Illus.). 350p. 1998. pap. 99.00 (*1-57751-938-8*) Intl Business Pubns.

— Poland Investment & Business Guide: Economy, Export-Import, Business & Investment Climate, Business Contacts. (Russia, NIS & Emerging Markets Investment & Business Library-98). (Illus.). 350p. 1998. pap. 99.00 (*1-57751-858-6*) Intl Business Pubns.

— Portugal Business & Investment Opportunities Yearbook-98: Business, Investment, Export-Import. (Business & Investment Opportunity Library-98). (Illus.). 350p. 1998. pap. 99.00 (*1-57751-962-0*) Intl Business Pubns.

— Qatar Investment & Business Guide: Economy, Export-Import, Business & Investment Climate, Business Contacts. (Russia, NIS & Emerging Markets Investment & Business Library-98). (Illus.). 350p. 1998. pap. 99.00 (*1-57751-918-3*) Intl Business Pubns.

— Romania Business & Investment Opportunities Yearbook-98: Business, Investment, Export-Import. (Business & Investment Opportunity Library-98). (Illus.). 350p. 1998. pap. 99.00 (*1-57751-939-6*) Intl Business Pubns.

— Romania Investment & Business Guide: Economy, Export-Import, Business & Investment Climate, Business Contacts. (Russia, NIS & Emerging Markets Investment & Business Library-98). (Illus.). 350p. 1998. pap. 99.00 (*1-57751-859-4*) Intl Business Pubns.

— Russia Business & Investment Opportunities Yearbook-98: Business, Investment, Export-Import. (Business & Investment Opportunity Library-98). (Illus.). 350p. 1998. pap. 99.00 (*1-57751-949-3*) Intl Business Pubns.

— Saudi Arabia Investment & Business Guide: Economy, Export-Import, Business & Investment Climate, Business Contacts. (Russia, NIS & Emerging Markets Investment & Business Library-98). (Illus.). 350p. 1998. pap. 99.00 (*1-57751-919-1*) Intl Business Pubns.

— Singapore Business & Investment Opportunities Yearbook-98: Business, Investment, Export-Import. (Business & Investment Opportunity Library-98). (Illus.). 350p. 1998. pap. 99.00 (*1-57751-981-7*) Intl Business Pubns.

— Singapur Investment & Business Guide: Economy, Export-Import, Business & Investment Climate, Business Contacts. (Russia, NIS & Emerging Markets Investment & Business Library-98). (Illus.). 350p. 1998. pap. 99.00 (*1-57751-876-4*) Intl Business Pubns.

— Slovak Republic Business & Investment Opportunities Yearbook-98: Business, Investment, Export-Import. (Business & Investment Opportunity Library-98). (Illus.). 350p. 1998. pap. 99.00 (*1-57751-940-X*) Intl Business Pubns.

— Slovakia Investment & Business Guide: Economy, Export-Import, Business & Investment Climate, Business Contacts. (Russia, NIS & Emerging Markets Investment & Business Library-98). (Illus.). 350p. 1998. pap. 99.00 (*1-57751-860-8*) Intl Business Pubns.

— Slovenia Business & Investment Opportunities Yearbook-98: Business, Investment, Export-Import. (Business & Investment Opportunity Library-98). (Illus.). 350p. 1998. pap. 99.00 (*1-57751-941-8*) Intl Business Pubns.

— Slovenia Investment & Business Guide: Economy, Export-Import, Business & Investment Climate, Business Contacts. (Russia, NIS & Emerging Markets Investment & Business Library-98). (Illus.). 350p. 1998. pap. 99.00 (*1-57751-861-6*) Intl Business Pubns.

— South Africa Investment & Business Guide: Economy, Export-Import, Business & Investment Climate, Business Contacts. (Russia, NIS & Emerging Markets Investment & Business Library-98). (Illus.). 350p. 1998. pap. 99.00 (*1-57751-905-1*) Intl Business Pubns.

— Spain Business & Investment Opportunities Yearbook-98: Business, Investment, Export-Import. (Business & Investment Opportunity Library-98). (Illus.). 350p. 1998. pap. 99.00 (*1-57751-963-9*) Intl Business Pubns.

— Suriname Investment & Business Guide: Economy, Export-Import, Business & Investment Climate, Business Contacts. (Russia, NIS & Emerging Markets Investment & Business Library-98). (Illus.). 350p. 1998. pap. 99.00 (*1-57751-877-2*) Intl Business Pubns.

— Sweden Business & Investment Opportunities Yearbook-98: Business, Investment, Export-Import. (Business & Investment Opportunity Library-98). (Illus.). 350p. 1998. pap. 99.00 (*1-57751-964-7*) Intl Business Pubns.

— Syria Investment & Business Guide: Economy, Export-Import, Business & Investment Climate, Business Contacts. (Russia, NIS & Emerging Markets Investment & Business Library-98). (Illus.). 350p. 1998. pap. 99.00 (*1-57751-920-5*) Intl Business Pubns.

— Tadzhikistan Business & Investment Opportunities Yearbook-98: Business, Investment, Export-Import. (Business & Investment Opportunity Library-98). (Illus.). 350p. 1998. pap. 99.00 (*1-57751-950-7*) Intl Business Pubns.

— Taiwan Investment & Business Guide: Economy, Export-Import, Business & Investment Climate, Business Contacts. (Russia, NIS & Emerging Markets Investment & Business Library-98). (Illus.). 350p. 1998. pap. 99.00 (*1-57751-878-0*) Intl Business Pubns.

— Thailand Investment & Business Guide: Economy, Export-Import, Business & Investment Climate, Business Contacts. (Russia, NIS & Emerging Markets Investment & Business Library-98). (Illus.). 350p. 1998. pap. 99.00 (*1-57751-879-9*) Intl Business Pubns.

— Turkey Business & Investment Opportunities Yearbook-98: Business, Investment, Export-Import. (Business & Investment Opportunity Library-98). (Illus.). 350p. 1998. pap. 99.00 (*1-57751-965-5*) Intl Business Pubns.

— Turkey Investment & Business Guide: Economy, Export-Import, Business & Investment Climate, Business Contacts. (Russia, NIS & Emerging Markets Investment & Business Library-98). (Illus.). 350p. 1998. pap. 99.00 (*1-57751-928-0*) Intl Business Pubns.

— Turkmenistan Business & Investment Opportunities

Yearbook-98: Business, Investment, Export-Import. (Business & Investment Opportunity Library-98). (Illus.). 350p. 1998. pap. 99.00 (*1-57751-951-5*) Intl Business Pubns.

— Ukraine Business & Investment Opportunities Yearbook-98: Business, Investment, Export-Import. (Business & Investment Opportunity Library-98). (Illus.). 350p. 1998. pap. 99.00 (*1-57751-952-3*) Intl Business Pubns.

— United Arab Emirates Investment & Business Guide: Economy, Export-Import, Business & Investment Climate, Business Contacts. (Russia, NIS & Emerging Markets Investment & Business Library-98). (Illus.). 350p. 1998. pap. 99.00 (*1-57751-921-3*) Intl Business Pubns.

— Uruguay Investment & Business Guide: Economy, Export-Import, Business & Investment Climate, Business Contacts. (Russia, NIS & Emerging Markets Investment & Business Library-98). (Illus.). 350p. 1998. pap. 99.00 (*1-57751-901-9*) Intl Business Pubns.

— Uzbekistan Business & Investment Opportunities Yearbook-98: Business, Investment, Export-Import. (Business & Investment Opportunity Library-98). (Illus.). 350p. 1998. pap. 99.00 (*1-57751-953-1*) Intl Business Pubns.

— Uzbekistan Investment & Business Guide: Economy, Export-Import, Business & Investment Climate, Business Contacts. (Russia, NIS & Emerging Markets Investment & Business Library-98). (Illus.). 350p. 1998. pap. 99.00 (*1-57751-597-8*) Intl Business Pubns.

— Venezuela Investment & Business Guide: Economy, Export-Import, Business & Investment Climate, Business Contacts. (Russia, NIS & Emerging Markets Investment & Business Library-98). (Illus.). 350p. 1998. pap. 99.00 (*1-57751-902-7*) Intl Business Pubns.

— Vietnam Investment & Business Guide: Economy, Export-Import, Business & Investment Climate, Business Contacts. (Russia, NIS & Emerging Markets Investment & Business Library-98). (Illus.). 350p. 1998. pap. 99.00 (*1-57751-880-2*) Intl Business Pubns.

— Zambia Investment & Business Guide: Economy, Export-Import, Business & Investment Climate, Business Contacts. (Russia, NIS & Emerging Markets Investment & Business Library-98). (Illus.). 350p. 1998. pap. 99.00 (*1-57751-907-8*) Intl Business Pubns.

Russian Informations & Business Center, Inc. Staff. Azerbaijan Investment & Business Guide Vol. 3: Economy, Export-Import, Business & Investment Climate, Business Contacts. (Russia, NIS & Emerging Markets Investment & Business Library). (Illus.). 350p. 1998. pap. 99.00 (*1-57751-567-6*) Intl Business Pubns.

Russian Numismatic Society Staff, ed. see Ilyin, A. A.

Russian Orthodox Greek Catholic Church of America, tr. from RUS. The Divine Liturgy According to St. John Chrysostom with Appendicies. 2nd ed. 1977. 10.00 (*1-878997-17-3*); 10.00 (*1-878997-30-0*); 16.95 (*1-878997-18-1*) St Tikhons Pr.

Russianoff, Leon. Clarinet Method, Bk. I. (Illus.). write for info. (*0-318-56700-8*) Macmillan.

— Clarinet Method, Bk. II. (Schirmer Book Ser.). (Illus.). 14.95 (*0-685-05965-0*) Macmillan.

Russianoff, Penelope. When Am I Going to Be Happy? 304p. 1997. mass mkt. 6.99 (*0-553-28215-8*) Bantam.

Russianoff, Penelope, ed. Women in Crisis. LC 80-29492. (Sponsored by Women in Crisis, Inc. Ser.). 319p. 1981. 43.95 (*0-89885-051-7*, Kluwer Acad Hman Sci) Kluwer Academic.

Russia's Goostroy Staff. Fire Safety of Buildings & Structures: Snip 21-01-97. Snip Register Inc. Staff, ed. (Building Codes of Russia Ser.). (Illus.). iv, 34p. 1998. pap. 299.95 (*1-57937-051-9*, 52100197) Snip Register.

— Heating, Ventilating & Air Conditioning Systems: Snip 2.04.05-91. 2nd ed. Snip Register Inc. Staff, ed. (Building Codes of Russia Ser.). (Illus.). iv, 113p. 1998. ring bd. 599.95 (*1-57937-058-6*, S4100591) Snip Register.

Russia's Gosstroy Staff. Concrete & Reinforced Concrete Structures: Snip 2.03.01-84. 2nd rev. ed. Snip Register Inc. Staff, ed. & tr. by. from RUS. (Building Codes of Russia Ser.). (Illus.). iv, 135p. 1997. ring bd. write for info. (*1-57937-049-7*, Snip Bldg) Snip Register.

— Construction in Seismic Areas: Snip 11-7-81. Snip Register, Inc. Staff, ed. Snip Register Inc. Staff, tr. from RUS. (Building Codes of Russia Ser.). (Illus.). iv, 76p. 1998. ring bd. 399.95 (*1-57937-059-4*, S2200781) Snip Register.

— Energy Conservation Code: Snip II-3-79. Snip Register Inc. Staff, ed. & tr. by. from RUS. (Building Codes of Russia Ser.). (Illus.). iv, 35p. 1998. ring bd. write for info. (*1-57937-054-3*, Snip Bldg) Snip Register.

— Fire Prevention Code: Snip 2.01.02-85. 2nd ed. Snip Register Inc. Staff, ed. (Building Codes of Russia Ser.). (Illus.). iv, 27p. 1998. ring bd. 99.95 (*1-57937-055-1*, S2100185) Snip Register.

— Fire Safety of Buildings & Structures: Snip 21-01-97. Snip Register Inc. Staff, ed. & tr. by. from RUS. (Building Codes of Russia Ser.). (Illus.). iv, 34p. 1998. pap. write for info. (*1-57937-053-5*, Snip Bldg) Snip Register.

— Foundation Beds: Snip 2.02.01-87. Snip Register Inc. Staff, ed. & tr. by. from RUS. (Building Codes of Russia Ser.). (Illus.). iv, 81p. (Orig.). 1997. ring bd. write for info. (*1-57937-025-X*, Snip Bldg) Snip Register.

— Pile Foundations: Snip 2.02.03-85. Snip Register, Inc. Staff, ed. & tr. by. from RUS. (Building Codes of Russia Ser.). (Illus.). iv, 75p. 1998. ring bd. 399.95 (*1-57937-056-X*, S5000385) Snip Register.

— Public Buildings & Structures: Snip 2.08.02-89. 2nd rev. ed. Snip Register Inc. Staff, ed. & tr. by. from RUS. (Building Codes of Russia Ser.). (Illus.). iv, 78p. 1998. ring bd. write for info. (*1-57937-052-7*, Snip Bldg) Snip Register.

— Public Sewage Disposal Systems & Structures: Snip 2.04.03-85. Snip Register, Inc. Staff, ed. & tr. by. from RUS. (Building Codes of Russia Ser.). (Illus.). iv, 120p. 1998. ring bd. 599.95 (*1-57937-062-4*, S4000385) Snip Register.

— Public Water Supply Systems & Structures: Snip 2.04.02-84. Snip Register, Inc. Staff, ed. & tr. by. from RUS. (Building Codes of Russia Ser.). (Illus.). iv, 120p. 1998. ring bd. 599.95 (*1-57937-061-6*, S4000284) Snip Register.

— Roads & Highways: Snip 2.05.02-85. Snip Register, Inc. Staff, ed. Snip Register Inc. Staff, tr. from RUS. (Building Codes of Russia Ser.). (Illus.). iv, 120p. 1998. ring bd. 599.95 (*1-57937-060-8*, S3200285) Snip Register.

— Steel Structures: Snip II-23-81. Snip Register Inc. Staff, ed. & tr. by. from RUS. (Building Codes of Russia Ser.). (Illus.). iv, 167p. 1997. ring bd. write for info. (*1-57937-050-0*, Snip Bldg) Snip Register.

— Storage Buildings: Snip 2.11.01-85. Snip Register, Inc. Staff, ed. & tr. by. from RUS. (Building Codes of Russia Ser.). (Illus.). iv, 12p. 1998. ring bd. 199.95 (*1-57937-057-8*, S3100185) Snip Register.

Russia's Minstroy Staff. Gas Supply: Snip 2.04.08-89. (Snip Building Codes of Russia Ser.). (Illus.). iv, 75p. (Orig.). 1996. ring bd. 1999.95 (*1-57937-040-3*) Snip Register.

— Industrial Buildings: Snip 2.09.02-89. (Snip Building Codes of Russia Ser.). (Illus.). iv, 15p. (Orig.). 1996. ring bd. 399.95 (*1-57937-016-0*) Snip Register.

— Internal Automatic Fire Protection Systems: Snip 2.04.09-84. (Snip Building Codes of Russia Ser.). (Illus.). iv, 15p. (Orig.). 1996. ring bd. 399.95 (*1-57937-034-9*) Snip Register.

— Internal Plumbing Systems: Snip 3.05.01-85. (Snip Building Codes of Russia Ser.). (Illus.). iv, 32p. (Orig.). 1996. ring bd. 999.95 (*1-57937-031-4*) Snip Register.

— Internal Water Supply & Sewage Water Systems: Snip 2.04.01-85. (Snip Building Codes of Russia Ser.). (Illus.). iv, 96p. 1996. ring bd. 1499.95 (*1-57937-037-3*) Snip Register.

— Loads & Stresses: Snip 2.01.07-89. (Snip Building Codes of Russia Ser.). (Illus.). iv, 66p. (Orig.). 1996. ring bd. 1999.95 (*1-57937-028-4*) Snip Register.

— Measurement Units for Use in Construction: Snip 528-80. (Snip Building Codes of Russia Ser.). (Illus.). iv, 40p. (Orig.). 1996. ring bd. 399.95 (*1-57937-022-5*) Snip Register.

— Residential Buildings: Snip 2.08.01-89. (Snip Building Codes of Russia Ser.). (Illus.). iv, 22p. (Orig.). 1996. ring bd. 499.95 (*1-57937-013-6*) Snip Register.

— Site Development, Landscaping & Amenities Provision: Snip III-10-75. (Snip Building Codes of Russia Ser.). (Illus.). iv, 48p. (Orig.). 1996. ring bd. 999.95 (*1-57937-019-5*) Snip Register.

— The System of Regulatory Documents in Construction Principal Provisions: Snip 10-01-94. (Snip Building Codes of Russia Ser.). (Illus.). iv, 40p. 1996. ring bd. 499.95 (*1-57937-001-2*) Snip Register.

— Urban Development, Planning & Development of Urban & Rural Settlements: Snip 2.07.01-89. (Snip Building Codes of Russia Ser.). (Illus.). iv, 63p. (Orig.). 1996. ring bd. 1999.95 (*1-57937-007-1*) Snip Register.

Russin, Robert, jt. auth. see Russin, Robin.

Russin, Robin & Downs, William M. Screenplay: Writing the Picture. 1999. text 33.50 (*0-15-507444-X*) Harcourt.

Russin, Robin & Russin, Robert. Robert Russin: A Wyoming Master. 48p. 1991. write for info. (*0-9630869-0-1*) U of WY Art Mus.

Russin, Suzanne S., ed. see Sturmthal, Adolph.

Russkaia, Pravoslavna. The Great Book of Needs: Expanded & Supplemented. LC 98-21715. 1998. 30.00 (*1-878997-57-2*) St Tikhons Pr.

Russman, Edna. Nubian Kingdoms. LC 97-29389. (African Civilizations Ser.). 64p. (J). 1998. 22.00 (*0-531-20283-6*) Watts.

Russman, Thomas A. A Prospectus for the Triumph of Realism. LC 86-28646. 208p. (C). 1987. 24.95 (*0-86554-232-5*, MUP-H205) Mercer Univ Pr.

Russman, Thomas A., ed. Thomistic Papers V, Vol. V. LC 83-73623. 104p. (C). 1990. 24.50 (*0-268-01875-8*); pap. 13.00 (*0-268-01876-6*) Ctr Thomistic.

Russmann, Edna R. & Finn, David. Egyptian Sculpture: Cairo & Luxor. (Illus.). 242p. 1989. 50.00 (*0-292-70402-X*) U of Tex Pr.

Russo. Great Treasure Hunt II. (J). (gr. 3 up). 1995. 12.00 (*0-671-73351-6*) S&S Trade.

Russo, ed. Introductory Chemistry. (C). 1999. pap. text, student ed. write for info. (*0-321-01526-6*) Addson-Wesley Educ.

— Introductory Chemistry. 610p. (C). 1999. pap. text 78.66 (*0-321-01525-8*) Addson-Wesley Educ.

Russo & Perla, Georges. French for Business & Finance. (ENG & FRE.). 237p. (C). 1985. pap., student ed. 29.16 (*0-669-05349-X*); audio 32.76 (*0-669-05351-1*) HM Trade Div.

Russo, jt. auth. see Bourne, Lyle E., Jr.

Russo, jt. auth. see Filkins.

Russo, A. D. The Assertive Formula. (Human Resources Book Ser.). 95p. 1982. pap. 4.00 (*0-9610708-0-3*) Twenty Fst CT.

— Assertiveness Is. (Illus.). 108p. (Orig.). 1985. pap. 4.00 (*0-9610708-1-1*) Twenty Fst CT.

Russo, Albert. Zapinette Video. LC 98-86006. 325p. 1998. 25.00 (*0-7388-0014-7*) Xlibris Corp.

Russo, Alexander. Profiles on Women Artists. LC 84-27015. 258p. 1985. lib. bdg. 59.95 (*0-313-27049-X*, U7049, Greenwood Pr) Greenwood.

— Vingettes. 100p. (Orig.). 1996. pap. 10.00 (*1-57502-231-1*) Morris Pubng.

Russo, Andy Lo, see Lo Russo, Andy.

Russo, Anne, jt. auth. see Fusco, Ann.

Russo, Anthony & Russo, Dorothy. A Bibliography of James Whitcomb Riley. LC 72-1267. (American Literature Ser.: No. 49). 351p. 1972. reprint ed. lib. bdg. 75.00 (*0-8383-1418-X*) M S G Haskell Hse.

Russo, Barbara. Elegant Pasta. 93p. 1994. write for info. (*1-57215-002-5*) World Pubns.

Russo, C. Russ & Russo, Tracy C. Interpreting ISO 9000 for Services: Solutions from Registered Organizations. LC 98-22825. 213p. 1998. 40.00 (*0-527-76336-5*) Productivity Inc.

Russo, C. W. ISO 9000 & Malcolm Baldrige in Training & Education: A Practical Application Guide. 360p. 1995. 49.95 (*0-9646992-5-7*) Charro Pubs.

Russo, Carlo F. & Wren, Kevin. Aristophanes: An Author for the Stage. LC 93-34433. 296p. (C). (gr. 13). 1994. 85.00 (*0-415-01082-9*, B3715) Routledge.

Russo, Carol. Three-D Hidden Pictures Activity Book. 16p. (J). 1991. pap. write for info. (*1-56156-012-X*) Kidsbks.

Russo, Carolyn & Cochrane, Dorothy. Women & Flight: Portraits of Contemporary Women Pilots. LC 96-9541. 192p. 1997. pap. 24.95 (*0-8212-2368-2*) Little.

— Women & Flight: Portraits of Contemporary Women Pilots. LC 96-9541. 192p. (gr. 8). 1997. 40.00 (*0-8212-2168-X*) Little.

Russo, Charles J. The Yearbook of Education Law, 1995. annuals LC 52-2403. 391p. 1995. 50.00 (*1-56534-090-6*) Ed Law Assn.

Russo, Charles J., ed. Case Citations No. 17: Violence & School Safety. 1994. pap. 30.00 (*1-56534-065-5*) Ed Law Assn.

— Case Citations (1992) No. 14: Discrimination. 53p. 1992. 30.00 (*1-56534-078-7*) Ed Law Assn.

— The Yearbook of Education Law, 1996. LC 52-2403. Orig. Title: The Yearbook of School Law. 381p. 1996. text 50.00 (*1-56534-092-2*) Ed Law Assn.

— The Yearbook of Education Law, 1997. 421p. 1997. 50.00 (*1-56534-095-7*) Ed Law Assn.

— The Yearbook of Education Law, 1998. 1998. 50.00 (*1-56534-098-1*) Ed Law Assn.

***Russo, Charles J., ed.** Yearbook of Education Law 1999. 400p. 1999. text 50.00 (*1-56534-099-X*) Ed Law Assn.

— The Yearbook of Education Law 2000. 400p. 2000. text 55.00 (*1-56534-100-7*) Ed Law Assn.

Russo, Charles J., et al. The Law of Home Schooling. 74p. 1994. 26.00 (*1-56534-061-2*) Ed Law Assn.

Russo, Charles J., jt. auth. see Gurst, Lyndon G.

Russo, Charles J., jt. auth. see Thomas, Stephen B.

Russo, Charles J., ed. see Cursio, Joan, et al.

Russo, D. C. & Kedesdy, J. H. Behavioral Medicine with the Developmentally Disabled. LC 88-17953. (Illus.). 308p. (C). 1988. 56.50 (*0-306-42884-9*, Plenum Trade) Perseus Pubng.

Russo, Daniel G. Town Origins & Development in Early England, c.400-950 A. D., 58. LC 96-35354. (Contributions to the Study of World History Ser.: Vol. 58). 328p. 1998. 65.00 (*0-313-30079-8*, Greenwood Pr) Greenwood.

Russo, David A. Around the World: The Great Treasure Hunt. LC 96-232619. (Illus.). 32p. (J). (gr. 2-5). 1995. per. 13.00 (*0-689-80281-1*) S&S Childrens.

— Go for It! A Mazemaster Sports Book. (Illus.). 32p. (J). (gr. 2-6). 1996. 14.00 (*0-689-80516-0*) S&S Bks Yung.

— Great Treasure Hunt. (Illus.). 32p. (J). (gr. k up). 1991. pap. 12.00 (*0-671-73349-4*) S&S Trade.

— Mazemaster 3: The Mazemaster Returns. 96p. 1993. pap. 9.95 (*0-671-73020-7*, Fireside) S&S Trade Pap.

Russo, David A., jt. ed. see Dagan, Gedeon.

Russo, David Anson. Go for It! Sports Treasure Hunt. (J). 1998. pap. 7.95 (*0-671-86804-7*) Aladdin.

***Russo, David J.** American History from a Global Perspective: An Interpretive Text. LC 99-54650. 456p. 2000. write for info. (*0-275-96896-0*) Greenwood.

Russo, David J. Clio Confused: Troubling Aspects of Historical Study from the Perspective of U. S., 163. LC 95-7909. 176p. 1995. 55.00 (*0-313-29682-0*, Greenwood Pr) Greenwood.

— Keepers of Our Past: Local Historical Writing in the United States, 1820s-1930s, 129. LC 88-36095. (Contributions in American History Ser.: No. 129). 295p. 1988. 59.95 (*0-313-26236-5*, RKP/, Greenwood Pr) Greenwood.

Russo, Dennis C., et al. Behavioral Pediatrics: Research & Practice. LC 82-3799. 432p. 1982. 65.00 (*0-306-40961-5*, Plenum Trade) Perseus Pubng.

Russo, Dorothy, jt. auth. see Russo, Anthony.

Russo, Ed, et al. Springfield Community Service: A Pictorial History. (Illinois Pictorial History Ser.). (Illus.). 160p. 1998. write for info. (*0-943963-62-1*) G Bradley.

Russo, Edward J. Springfield: Prairies of Promise. 1983. 19.95 (*0-89781-084-8*) Am Historical Pr.

Russo, Edward J. & Schoemaker, Paul J. Decision Traps: The Ten Barriers to Decision-Making & How to Overcome Them. 304p. 1990. per. 12.00 (*0-671-72609-9*) S&S Trade.

Russo, Elena. Skeptical Selves: Empiricism & Modernity in the French Novel. LC 95-18188. 244p. 1996. 39.50 (*0-8047-2465-2*); write for info. (*0-8047-2466-0*) Stanford U Pr.

Russo, Elena, ed. Yale French Studies, 92: Exploring the Conversible World: Text & Sociability from the Classical Age to the Enlightenment. Vol. 92. 1997. pap. 18.00 (*0-300-07329-1*) Yale U Pr.

Russo, Enzo & Cove, David. Genetic Engineering: Dreams & Nightmares. LC 98-5081. (Illus.). 264p. 1998. reprint ed. pap. 18.95 (*0-19-262925-5*) OUP.

***Russo, Ethan B., ed.** Handbook of Psychotropic Herbs: A Scientific Analysis of Herbal Remedies for Psychiatric Conditions. LC 00-38294. 350p. (C). 2000. 69.95 (*0-7890-0718-5*, Haworth Herbal Pr); pap. text 29.95 (*0-7890-1088-7*, Haworth Herbal Pr) Haworth Pr.

Russo, Eva M. & Shyne, Ann W. Coping with Disruptive Behavior in Group Care. LC 79-23739. 74p. (Orig.). (C). 1980. pap. 13.50 (*0-87868-137-X*, 1370) Child Welfare.

Russo, Gia, jt. auth. see Adams, Michele.

Russo, Gloria & Perla, Georges. French for Communication. (ENG & FRE.). 231p. (C). 1985. pap. text, student ed. 29.16 (*0-669-05347-3*); 2.66 (*0-669-05352-X*); audio 32.76 (*0-669-05350-3*) HM Trade Div.

Russo, Greg. Cosmik Debris: The Collected History & Improvisations of Frank Zappa. LC 99-171106. (Illus.). 232p. 1998. pap. 22.95 (*0-9648157-4-5*) Crossfire NY.

— Flying Colours: The Jethro Tull Reference Manual. (Illus.). 224p. 1999. pap. 22.95 (*0-9648157-6-1*) Crossfire NY.

— Mannerisms: The Five Phases of Manfred Mann. (Illus.). 275p. (Orig.). 1995. pap. 22.95 (*0-9648157-1-0*) Crossfire NY.

— Time of the Season: The Zombies Collector's Guide. (Illus.). 96p. 1999. pap. 13.95 (*0-9648157-5-3*) Crossfire NY.

— Yardbirds: The Ultimate Rave-Up. LC 98-217155. (Illus.). 160p. 1997. pap. 19.95 (*0-9648157-3-7*) Crossfire NY.

Russo, Gus. Live by the Sword: How the Kennedy's Secret War Against Castro Triggered JFK's Assassination & America's Longest Coverup. LC 98-72307. (Illus.). 617p. 1998. 26.95 (*1-890862-01-0*) Bancroft MD.

Russo, J., et al. Championship Baseball: Techniques, Fundamentals, & Drills. 228p. (C). 1985. text 27.95 (*0-13-126178-9*) P-H.

Russo, J. Robert. Serving & Surviving As a Human-Service Worker. 2nd ed. 182p. (C). 1993. pap. text 17.50 (*0-88133-691-2*) Waveland Pr.

Russo, Jane C., jt. auth. see Grippo, Nick.

Russo, Jean B. Free Workers in a Plantation Economy: Talbot County, Maryland, 1690-1759. (Outstanding Studies in Early American History). 498p. 1989. reprint ed. 30.00 (*0-8240-6195-0*) Garland.

Russo, Jean B., ed. Unlocking the Secrets of Time: Maryland's Hidden Heritage. (Illus.). 106p. (Orig.). 1991. pap. 10.95 (*0-938420-43-7*) MD Hist.

Russo, Jean M., jt. auth. see Campbell, Donald T.

Russo, Joe, et al. Planet of the Apes Revisited. (Illus.). 212p. (Orig.). (YA). (gr. 9-12). 1991. pap. 12.95 (*0-9627508-2-4*) Retro Vision.

Russo, Joe, jt. auth. see Landolphi, Donald.

Russo, Joe, jt. auth. see Prochnicky, Jerry.

Russo, John. Living Things. 288p. 1988. mass mkt. 3.95 (*0-445-20666-7*, Mysterious Paperbk) Warner Bks.

Russo, John A. The Awakening. 357p. mass mkt. 5.99 (*1-55197-512-2*) Picasso Publ.

— Hell's Creation. 305p. mass mkt. 6.99 (*1-55197-060-0*) Picasso Publ.

Russo, John A. How to Make Your Own Feature Movie for $10,000 or Less. LC 94-24252. 208p. 1994. pap. 19.00 (*0-935016-10-4*, Pub. by Zinn Pub Grp) Empire Pub Srvs.

Russo, John A. Limb to Limb. mass mkt. 5.99 (*1-55197-505-X*) Picasso Publ.

Russo, John A. Making Movies: The Inside Guide to Independent Movie Production. 320p. 1989. pap. 15.95 (*0-440-50046-X*) Dell.

Russo, John P. Alexander Pope: Tradition & Identity. LC 70-188354. 255p. 1972. 36.50 (*0-674-01520-7*) HUP.

— I. A. Richards: His Life & Work. 832p. 1989. text 60.00 (*0-8018-3417-1*) Johns Hopkins.

Russo, John P., ed. see Richards, Ivor A.

Russo, Jose. Tumor Diagnosis by Electron Microscope, Vol. 3. 1989. 75.00 (*0-938607-22-7*) Field & Wood Inc Medical.

Russo, Jose, ed. Immunocytochemistry in Tumor Diagnosis. (Developments in Oncology Ser.). 1985. text 152.50 (*0-89838-737-X*) Kluwer Academic.

Russo, Joseph A., et al, eds. A Commentary on Homer's Odyssey, Vol. 3, Bks. 17-24. (Illus.). 460p. 1993. reprint ed. pap. text 28.00 (*0-19-814953-0*) OUP.

Russo, Joseph M. Sing-a-Long for All Occasions. 62p. (Orig.). 1988. pap. 6.95 (*0-685-29095-6*) Mid-West Music.

— Sing-a-Longs for All Occasions. 62p. (Orig.). 1988. pap. 6.95 (*0-9624214-0-5*, PA-394-638) Mid-West Music.

***Russo, Karen.** There Is More to Football Than a Tight End: How to Watch Football with the Guys. Willoughby, Susan, ed. 63p. 2000. pap. 12.95 (*0-9672688-0-X*, 110) Beach Pr Pub.

***Russo, Kurt W.** Finding the Middle Ground: Insights & Applications of the Value Orientations Method. LC 99-48807. 2000. write for info. (*1-877864-76-5*) Intercult Pr.

Russo, Linda V. O Going Out. 46p. 1998. 7.00 (*0-937013-86-2*, Pub. by Potes Poets) SPD-Small Pr Dist.

Russo, Louis La, see La Russo, Louis, II.

Russo, M., ed. Stimulated Effects in Josephson Devices. 332p. (C). 1990. text 92.00 (*981-02-0050-1*) World Scientific Pub.

Russo, M., jt. auth. see Di Chiara, A.

***Russo, Marco.** Fuzzy Learning & Applications. (International Series on Computational Intelligence). 2000. 89.95 (*0-8493-2269-3*) CRC Pr.

Russo-Marie, Francoise, et al, eds. Advances in Inflammation Research Vol. 10: 1986. LC 85-25802. (Illus.). 461p. 1986. reprint ed. pap. 143.00 (*0-7837-9249-2*, 204715600010) Bks Demand.

Russo, Marisabina. Grandpa Abe. LC 95-2260. (Illus.). 32p. (J). (ps-3). 1996. 15.00 (*0-688-14097-1*, Grenwillow Bks); lib. bdg. 14.93 (*0-688-14098-X*, Grenwillow Bks) HarpC Child Bks.

R

— Hannah's Baby Sister. LC 97-31412. (Illus.). 32p. (J). (ps-3). 1998. 15.00 (0-688-15831-5, Grenwillow Bks) HarpC Child Bks.

*Russo, Marisabina. Hannah's Baby Sister. LC 97-31412. (Illus.). 32p. (J). (ps-3). 1998. 14.93 (0-688-15832-3, Grenwillow Bks) HarpC Child Bks.

Russo, Marisabina. I Don't Want to Go Back to School. LC 93-5479. 32p. (J). (gr. k-3). 1994. 16.00 (0-688-04601-0, Grenwillow Bks) HarpC Child Bks.

Russo, Marisabina. I Don't Want to Go Back to School. LC 93-5479. (Illus.). 32p. (J). (ps-3). 1994. 15.89 (0-688-04602-9, Grenwillow Bks) HarpC Child Bks.

Russo, Marisabina. The Line-Up Book. LC 85-24907. (Illus.). 24p. (J). (ps-1). 1986. 15.00 (0-688-06204-0, Grenwillow Bks) HarpC Child Bks.

— Mama Talks Too Much. LC 98-17695. (J). 1999. lib. bdg. write for info. (0-688-16412-9, Grenwillow Bks) HarpC Child Bks.

— Mama Talks Too Much. LC 98-17695. (Illus.). 32p. (YA). (ps-3). 1999. 16.00 (0-688-16411-0, Grenwillow Bks) HarpC Child Bks.

— Trade-in Mother. LC 91-47681. (Illus.). 32p. (J). (ps up). 1993. 14.00 (0-688-11416-4, Grenwillow Bks) HarpC Child Bks.

— Under the Table. LC 96-7145. (Illus.). 32p. (J). (ps up). 1997. 15.00 (0-688-14602-3, Grenwillow Bks) HarpC Child Bks.

Russo, Marisabina. Under the Table. LC 96-7145. (Illus.). 32p. (J). (ps up). 1997. lib. bdg. 14.93 (0-688-14603-1, Grenwillow Bks) HarpC Child Bks.

Russo, Marisabina. A Visit to Oma. LC 89-77716. (Illus.). 32p. (J). (ps up). 1991. lib. bdg. 13.88 (0-688-09624-7, Grenwillow Bks) HarpC Child Bks.

— When Mama Gets Home. LC 96-46617. (Illus.). 32p. (J). (gr. k-2). 1998. lib. bdg. 14.93 (0-688-14986-3, Grenwillow Bks) HarpC Child Bks.

— When Mama Gets Home. LC 96-46617. (Illus.). 32p. (J). (ps-3). 1998. 15.00 (0-688-14985-5, Grenwillow Bks) HarpC Child Bks.

*Russo, Mark F. & Echols, Martin M. Automating Science & Engineering Laboratories with Visual Basic. LC 98-30703. (Interscience Series on Laboratory Automation). 384p. 1999. pap. 49.95 (0-471-25493-2) Wiley.

Russo, Mary. The Female Grotesque: Risk, Excess & Modernity. 250p. (C). 1994. pap. 22.99 (0-415-90165-0, A3541) Routledge.

— The Female Grotesque: Risk, Excess & Modernity. 250p. (C). (gr. 13). 1994. 75.00 (0-415-90164-2, A3537) Routledge.

Russo, Mary J., jt. auth. see Allen, Beverly.

Russo, Mary J., jt. auth. see Fondell, Joan.

Russo, Michael. New User's Guide to the Sun Workstation. 203p. 1990. 53.95 (0-387-97249-8) Spr-Verlag.

— Yats in Movieland. LC 94-76900. 330p. 1995. pap. 14.95 (1-878044-22-2) Mayhaven Pub.

Russo, Michele. The World of Russo. 110p. (Orig.). 1981. pap. 12.95 (0-938996-00-2) Bigoni Bks.

*Russo, Monica. Creatures of the Night Dot-to-Dot. (Illus.). 2000. pap. 5.95 (0-8069-2491-8) Sterling.

Russo, Monica. Creepy Crawlies Dot to Dot. (Illus.). 64p. (J). pap. write for info. (0-8069-0465-8) Sterling.

— Dinosaur Dots. (Illus.). 96p. (J). 1991. pap. 5.95 (0-8069-7388-9) Sterling.

— Endangered Animals Dot-to-Dot. (Illus.). 80p. (J). 1994. pap. 5.95 (0-8069-0520-4) Sterling.

— Giant Book of Dot to Dot: Costco Edition. (J). 1997. 19.95 (0-8069-5721-2) Sterling.

— Mythical Animals Dot-to-Dot. 1997. pap. text 59.50 (0-8069-9883-0) Sterling.

— Mythical Animals Dot-to-Dot. (Illus.). 64p. (J). 1997. pap. 5.95 (0-8069-9716-8) Sterling.

— Watching Nature. LC 97-51572. (Illus.). 96p. 1998. 19.95 (0-8069-9515-7) Sterling.

— Wildlife Dot-to-Dot. (Illus.). 80p. (J). 1994. pap. 5.95 (0-8069-0638-3) Sterling.

Russo, N., et al, eds. Chemistry & Properties of Biomolecular Systems Vol. II: Proceedings of the Second Joint Greek-Italian Meeting on Chemistry & Biological Systems & Molecular Chemical Engineering, Cetraro, Italy, October 1992. LC 93-44247. (Topics in Molecular Organization & Engineering Ser.: Vol. 11). 432p. (C). 1994. text 204.50 (0-7923-2666-0) Kluwer Academic.

Russo, Nancy. Psychology: Discipline Analysis, Vol. 7N. (Women in the Curriculum Ser.). 39p. (Orig.). 1997. pap. 7.00 (1-885303-21-1) Towson St Univ.

Russo, Nancy F. & O'Connell, Agnes N. Models of Achievement Vol. 2: Reflections of Eminent Women in Psychology. 400p. (C). 1988. 79.95 (0-8058-0083-2); pap. text 39.95 (0-8058-0322-X) L Erlbaum Assocs.

Russo, Nancy F., jt. auth. see Bourne, Lyle E.

Russo, Nancy F., ed. see American Psychological Association, Women & Health & Organizations for Professional Women Staff.

Russo, Nancy F., jt. ed. see O'Connell, Agnes N.

*Russo, Nick. Metallica: Legendary Licks 1983-1988. 88p. 2000. pap. 19.95 incl. audio compact disk (1-57560-281-4, Pub. by Cherry Lane) H Leonard.

Russo, Nino, ed. Metal-Ligand Interactions - Structure & Reactivity: Proceedings of the NATO Advanced Study Institute, Cetraro, Italy, September 4-16, 1994. (NATO Advanced Science Institutes Ser.: Series C). 568p. (C). 1995. text 279.50 (0-7923-3833-2) Kluwer Academic.

*Russo, Nino & Salahub, Dennis R. Metal-ligand Interactions in Chemistry, Physics & Biology. 468p. 1999. pap. 72.00 (0-7923-6126-1) Kluwer Academic.

Russo, Nino, jt. ed. see Salahub, Dennis R.

Russo, Paul S, ed. Reversible Polymeric Gels & Related Systems. LC 87-20305. (Symposium Ser.: No. 350). (Illus.). x, 324p. 1987. 71.95 (0-8412-1415-8) Am Chemical.

Russo, Paul S., ed. Reversible Polymeric Gels & Related Systems. LC 87-20305. (ACS Symposium Ser.: Vol. 350). 304p. 1987. reprint ed. pap. 94.30 (0-608-03873-3, 206432000008) Bks Demand.

Russo, Peter. Die Problematik Mangelnder Preistransparenz im Bargeldlosen Zahlungsverkehr & Moglichkeiten der Problemlosung. (GER., Illus.). 260p. 1996. 51.95 (3-631-30595-8) P Lang Pubng.

Russo, Philip A., jt. ed. see Paul, Ellen F.

Russo, Phyllis, jt. auth. see May, Cecilia.

Russo, Raffaella. Venetian Palaces. (Pocket Archives Ser.). 1998. pap. 12.95 (2-85025-607-2) Hazan.

Russo, Remigio, ed. Mathematical Problems in Elasticity. LC 95-48843. 200p. 1996. write for info. (981-02-2576-8) World Scientific Pub.

Russo, Renzo, jt. auth. see Kottegoda, Nathabandu T.

Russo, Riccardo, jt. auth. see Roberts, Maxwell J.

Russo, Richard. Mohawk. 1994. pap. 13.00 (0-679-75382-6) Vin Bks.

— Nobody's Fool. 1994. pap. 14.00 (0-679-75333-8) Knopf.

— The Risk Pool. 1994. pap. 14.00 (0-679-75383-4) Vin Bks.

— Straight Man. 416p. 1998. pap. 13.00 (0-375-70190-7) Vin Bks.

Russo, Richard A., ed. Dreams Are Wiser Than Men. 320p. 1987. pap. 14.95 (0-938190-94-6); text 30.00 (0-938190-95-4) North Atlantic.

Russo, Richard M. & Stark, Robert R. Colorado Limited Liability Company Forms & Practice Manual. LC 96-1124. 636p. 1996. ring bd. 219.90 (1-57400-014-4) Data Trace Pubng.

Russo, Richard P. Carlucci's Edge. 304p. (Orig.). 1995. mass mkt. 5.99 (0-441-00205-6) Ace Bks.

— Carlucci's Heart. 1997. mass mkt. 6.50 (0-441-00485-7) Ace Bks.

*Russo, Richard Paul. Terminal Visions. LC 00-25902. 237p. 2000. 23.95 (0-9655901-3-5, Pub. by Golden Gryphon) IPG Chicago.

Russo, Rick, ed. see Rucker, Bronwyn.

Russo, Robert, jt. auth. see Smith, Christopher A.

Russo, Robert D., Jr., jt. auth. see Sorgen, Richard A.

Russo, Ron. Hawaiian Reefs: A Natural History Guide. LC 94-234570. (Illus.). 176p. (Orig.). 1994. pap. text 16.95 (0-9635696-0-0) Wavecrest Pubns.

— Mountain State Mammals: A Guide to Mammals of the Rocky Mountain Region. (Illus.). 136p. 1991. pap. 5.25 (0-912550-21-X) Nature Study.

— Pacific Coast Fish: A Guide to Marine Fish of the Pacific Coast of North America. (Illus.). 112p. 1990. pap. 5.75 (0-912550-19-8) Nature Study.

Russo, Ron & Olhausen, Pam. Pacific Coast Mammals: A Guide to Mammals of the Pacific Coast States, Their Tracks, Skulls & Other Signs. (Illus.). 96p. 1987. pap. 4.25 (0-912550-16-3) Nature Study.

— Pacific Intertidal Life: A Guide to Organisms of Rocky Reefs & Tide Pools from Alaska to Baja California, Vol. 1. (Illus.). 1981. pap. 3.00 (0-912550-10-4) Nature Study.

Russo, Ruthan. Seven Steps to HIM Compliance. LC 98-230630. (Illus.). 146p. 1998. pap. text 97.00 (1-57839-043-5) Opus Communs.

*Russo, Ruthann. A Guide to Auditing Health Care Billing Practices. 1999. ring bd. 306.00 (0-929156-59-5) Atlantic Info Services Inc.

Russo, S., jt. auth. see Aggarwal, S. L.

Russo, Salvatore, jt. auth. see Kuhn, Lesley.

Russo-Stark, Marisabina. The Big Brown Box. LC 99-14871. (Illus.). 32p. (J). (ps-3). 2000. 15.95 (0-688-17096-X, Grenwillow Bks) HarpC Child Bks.

*Russo-Stark, Marisabina. Come Back, Hannah! (J). 2001. 15.95 (0-688-17383-7, Grenwillow Bks); lib. bdg. 15.89 (0-688-17384-5, Grenwillow Bks) HarpC Child Bks.

Russo, Steve. Halloween: What's a Christian to Do? LC 98-5765. 130p. 1998. pap. 7.99 (1-56507-851-9) Harvest Hse.

— Introductory Chemistry. (C). 2000. pap. text, student ed. 25.00 (0-321-03763-4) Addison-Wesley.

— Keeping Christ in Christmas: Helping Families Find Their Focus. LC 99-21978. 140p. 1998. pap. 7.99 (0-7369-0166-3) Harvest Hse.

Russo, Steve, jt. auth. see Anderson, Neil T.

Russo, Steve, jt. auth. see Phillips, Bob.

*Russo, Steven. Introductory Chemistry: Brief Edition. 1999. pap. text. write for info. (0-321-04632-3) Addison-Wesley.

Russo, Thomas A. Regulation of the Commodities, Futures & Options Markets, 2 vols. LC 83-431. (Securities Law Publications). 1598p. 1983. text 210.00 (0-07-054348-8) Shepards.

Russo, Thomas J. Biomicro. 98p. (YA). (gr. 10 up). 1995. lab manual ed. 39.00 (1-888167-02-5) Theta Tech.

— Consumer Microchemistry. 110p. (YA). (gr. 10 up). 1995. lab manual ed. 39.00 (1-888167-03-3) Theta Tech.

— Microchemistry 1. 165p. (YA). (gr. 10 up). 1995. lab manual ed. 39.00 (1-888167-00-9) Theta Tech.

— Microchemistry 2. 120p. (YA). (gr. 10 up). 1995. lab manual ed. 39.00 (1-888167-01-7) Theta Tech.

Russo, Tom. MicroChemistry for Physical Sciences. (Illus.). 120p. (Orig.). 1996. pap. text, lab manual ed. 40.00 (1-888167-04-1) Theta Tech.

*Russo, Tom. Office Collectibles: One Hundred Years of Business Technology. (Illus.). 240p. 2000. 39.95 (0-7643-1177-8) Schiffer.

Russo, Tracy C., jt. auth. see Russo, C. Russ.

*Russo, V. E., et al, eds. Development: Genetics, Epigenetics & Environmental Regulation. LC 99-21042. 550p. 1999. 89.95 (3-540-62754-5) Spr-Verlag.

Russo, V. E., et al, eds. Development - the Molecular Genetic Approach. (Illus.). xxxv, 605p. 1993. 103.95 (0-387-54730-4) Spr-Verlag.

Russo, Valeria E, ed. see Addis, Elisabetta, et al.

Russo, Vincent J., jt. auth. see Pohl, Amelia E.

Russo, Vincenzo E., et al, eds. Epigenetic Mechanisms of Gene Regulation. LC 96-85974. (Monographs: Vol. 32). (Illus.). 672p. (C). 1996. text 129.00 (0-87969-490-4) Cold Spring Harbor.

Russo, Vito. The Celluloid Closet: Homosexuality in the Movies. rev. ed. LC 86-45684. (Illus.). 384p. 1987. pap. 16.00 (0-06-096132-5, PL 6132, Perennial) HarperTrade.

*Russo, William. Another Sunny Day. LC 99-6516. 330p. 1999. pap. 19.95 (1-892183-14-5) DTTN.

Russo, William. Composing for the Jazz Orchestra. 96p. 1973. pap. text 10.95 (0-226-73209-6, P552) U Ch Pr.

— Jazz Composition & Orchestration. LC 67-20580. (Illus.). 844p. 1975. pap. text 35.00 (0-226-73213-4) U Ch Pr.

— Jazz Composition & Orchestration. 1996. pap. text 44.95 incl. audio compact disk (0-226-73208-8) U Ch Pr.

— Jazz Composition & Orchestration. LC 67-20580. (Illus.). 843p. 1997. lib. bdg. 48.00 (0-226-73212-6) U Ch Pr.

*Russo, William. Junior Bad Guys. LC 00-100065. (Illus.). 280p. 2000. pap. 19.95 (1-892183-27-7) DTTN.

— Mal-Tempo. LC 99-90728. 160p. 1999. pap. 15.95 (1-892183-13-7) DTTN.

— A Thinker's Damn: Audie Murphy, Vietnam & the Making of the Quiet American. (Illus.). 230p. 1999. pap. 19.95 (1-892183-15-3, Lukeion) DTTN.

*Russo, William, ed. Classic Erotica: Deva Dasi & Satyricon. LC 00-190506. (Illus.). 337p. 2000. pap. 19.95 (1-892183-32-3) DTTN.

Russo, William & Hyams, Reid. Workbook for Composing for the Jazz Orchestra. LC 61-8642. 1979. pap. text 6.95 (0-226-73214-2) U Ch Pr.

— Workbook for Composing for the Jazz Orchestra. LC 72-91409. 126p. reprint ed. pap. 39.10 (0-608-09566-4, 205436800005) Bks Demand.

Russo, William, et al. Composing Music: A New Approach. LC 87-30243. (Illus.). x, 240p. 1988. pap. text 20.00 (0-226-73216-9) U Ch Pr.

Russolo, Luigi. The Art of Noises. Brown, Barclay, tr. from ITA. LC 85-28413. (Monographs in Musicology: No. 6).Tr. of L'arte dei Rumore. 87p. 1987. lib. bdg. 54.00 (0-918728-57-6) Pendragon NY.

Russom, Geoffrey. "Beowulf" & Old Germanic Metre. LC 97-13720. (Studies in Anglo-Saxon England: No. 23). 248p. (C). 1998. text 69.95 (0-521-59340-9) Cambridge U Pr.

Russon. Personality Development for Work. 5th ed. (CA - Career Development Ser.). 1981. text 25.95 (0-538-11420-7) S-W Pub.

— Simpler German Course. Date not set. pap. text. write for info. (0-582-36168-0, Pub. by Addison-Wesley) Longman.

*Russon, Anne E. Orangutans: Wizards of the Rain Forest. LC QL737.P96R87 1999. (Illus.). 224p. 2000. 29.95 (1-55209-453-7) Firefly Bks Ltd.

Russon, Anne E., et al, eds. Reaching into Thought: The Minds of the Great Apes. LC 97-13442. (Illus.). 476p. (C). 1996. text 89.95 (0-521-47168-0) Cambridge U Pr.

— Reaching into Thought: The Minds of the Great Apes. (Illus.). 480p. (C). 1999. pap. text 39.95 (0-521-64496-8) Cambridge U Pr.

Russon, Beulah W. Banyan. Our Banyan Tree. (Illus.). 571p. 1997. reprint ed. pap. 83.50 (0-8328-7369-1); reprint ed. lib. bdg. 93.50 (0-8328-7368-3) Higginson Bk Co.

*Russon, Craig & Russon, Karen. The Annotated Bibliography of International Programme Evaluation. LC 00-35657. 2000. write for info. (0-7923-8426-1) Kluwer Academic.

Russon, Jacqueline. Face Painting. LC 96-37361. (Illus.). 24p. (J). (gr. 1-4). 1997. 17.27 (1-57505-099-4, Carolrhoda) Lerner Pub.

— Face Painting. (Illus.). 32p. (J). (gr. 2-4). 1994. lib. bdg. 5.00 (1-56847-197-1) Raintree Steck-V.

— Making Faces Book & Kit. (Illus.). 48p. 1995. 19.95 (0-8069-4351-3) Sterling.

— Making Faces (Relist Kit) (Illus.). 48p. (J). 1996. pap. 9.95 (0-8069-0932-3) Sterling.

Russon, John. The Self & It's Body in Hegel's Phenomenology of Spirit. (Toronto Studies in Philosophy). 192p. 1996. text 65.00 (0-8020-0919-0) U of Toronto Pr.

Russon, John & Sallis, John, eds. Retracing the Platonic Text. LC 99-58613. 216p. 1999. pap. 24.95 (0-8101-1703-7) Northwestern U Pr.

Russon, Karen, jt. auth. see Russon, Craig.

*Russon, Kath. Handmade Silk Paper. 1999. pap. text 19.95 (0-85532-893-2) Srch Pr.

Russon, Robb. Letters to a New Elder: The Melchizedek Priesthood, Its Duty & Fulfillment. pap. 3.95 (0-89036-144-4) Liahona Pub Trust.

Russon, S., jt. auth. see Kershaw, F.

Russow, Lilly-Marlene & Curd, Martin. Principles of Reasoning. LC 88-60527. 372p. (C). 1988. pap. text 24.00 (0-312-17506-X) St Martin.

Russwum, Mary Ann, ed. Home Care for Older Adults: A Guide for Families & Other Caregivers: Instructor's Manual Lesson Plan. 176p. 1998. 19.95 (0-8261-1232-3) Springer Pub.

Russwy, William E., tr. see Schutt, Hans-Werner, ed.

Rust, A. D. Record of the Rust Family, Embracing the Descendants of Henry Rust, Who Came from England & Settled in Hingham, Mass., 1634-1635. (Illus.). 544p. 1989. reprint ed. pap. 81.50 (0-8328-1043-6); reprint ed. lib. bdg. 89.50 (0-8328-1042-8) Higginson Bk Co.

Rust, Allen F., ed. see Rust, Ann O'Connell.

Rust, Ann O. Dessa. 254p. 1996. 19.95 (1-883203-03-1); pap. 14.95 (1-883203-02-3) Amaro Bks.

— The Floridians, 5 bks. 1994. pap. 49.95 (0-9620556-4-6) Amaro Bks.

— The Floridians, 5 vols., Set. 1994. 69.95 (1-883203-01-5) Amaro Bks.

— Kissimmee. LC 90-82837. (Floridians Ser.: Vol. III). 250p. (Orig.). 1990. pap. 12.95 (0-9620556-2-X); pap. 17.50 (0-9620556-3-8) Amaro Bks.

— Monticello, Vol. IV. LC 91-72853. (Floridians Ser.). 250p. 1991. 17.50 (0-9620556-6-2); pap. 12.95 (0-9620556-5-4) Amaro Bks.

— Pahokee, Vol. V. LC 92-97012. (Floridians Ser.). 275p. 1992. 17.50 (0-9620556-8-9); pap. 12.95 (0-9620556-9-7) Amaro Bks.

— Palatka. LC 89-84402. (Floridians Ser.). 235p. (Orig.). 1989. pap. 12.95 (0-9620556-1-1) Amaro Bks.

— Palatka, Vol. II. LC 89-84402. (Floridians Ser.: Vol. 2). 231p. (Orig.). 1994. pap. text 17.50 (1-883203-00-7) Amaro Bks.

— Punta Rassa. (Floridians Ser.). 275p. (Orig.). 1988. pap. 12.95 (0-9620556-0-3) Amaro Bks.

— Punta Rassa. LC 88-70994. (Floridians Ser.). 275p. (Orig.). 1991. pap. text 17.50 (0-9620556-7-0) Amaro Bks.

— Walking with Irma. LC 99-94675. 248p. 1999. pap. 14.95 (1-883203-05-8) Amaro Bks.

Rust, Ann O'Connell. Nonie of the Everglades, Vol. 1. Rust, Allen F., ed. LC 98-74242. 72p. (J). (gr. 4-7). 1998. pap. 7.95 (1-883203-04-X) Amaro Bks.

Rust, Brian. The American Record Label Book: From the Mid-19th Century Through 1942. LC 83-18921. (Roots of Jazz Ser.). (Illus.). 336p. 1983. reprint ed. lib. bdg. 49.50 (0-306-76211-0) Da Capo.

— Brian Rust's Guide to Discography, 4. LC 79-6827. (Discographies Ser.: No. 4). (Illus.). 133p. 1980. lib. bdg. 42.95 (0-313-22086-7, RGD/, Greenwood Pr) Greenwood.

— The Columbia Master Book Discography Vol. II: Principal U. S. Matrix Series, 1910-1924, Vol. 2. LC 99-12630. (Discographies Ser.: Vol. 78). 680p. 1999. lib. bdg. 135.00 (0-313-30822-5, Greenwood Pr) Greenwood.

— The Columbia Master Book Discography Vol. III: Principal U. S. Matrix Series, 1924-1934, Vol. 3. LC 99-12630. (Discographies Ser.: Vol. 78). 840p. 1999. lib. bdg. 175.00 (0-313-30823-3, Greenwood Pr) Greenwood.

Rust, Brian, compiled by. Discography of Historical Records on Cylinders & 78s. LC 78-60530. 327p. 1979. lib. bdg. 72.95 (0-313-20561-2, RRC/, Greenwood Pr) Greenwood.

Rust, Brian & Brooks, Tim. The Columbia Master Book Discography, 78. LC 99-12630. (Discographies Ser.: 78). 2128p. 1999. lib. bdg. 395.00 (0-313-21464-6, Greenwood Pr) Greenwood.

— The Columbia Master Book Discography: U.S. Twelve-Inch Matrix Series, 1906-1931, Vol. 4. LC 99-12630. 78. 336p. 1999. lib. bdg. 85.00 (0-313-30824-1, Greenwood Pr) Greenwood.

Rust, Brian & Debus, Allen. The Complete Entertainment Discography from 1897 to 1942. 2nd ed. (Roots of Jazz Ser.). 790p. 1988. reprint ed. lib. bdg. 125.00 (0-306-76210-2) Da Capo.

Rust, Damon, jt. auth. see Linton, Steven J.

Rust, David, contrib. by. Since Statehood: Twelve Oklahoma Artists. 1996. pap. 10.00 (0-614-13529-X) Okla City Art.

Rust, David M., ed. Missions to the Sun, Vol. 2804. 314p. 1996. 85.00 (0-8194-2192-8) SPIE.

Rust-D'Eye, George H. Cabbagetown Remembered. (Illus.). 144p. pap. 10.00 (0-919783-00-7, Pub. by Boston Mills) Genl Dist Srvs.

Rust, Diane, jt. auth. see Rust, Val D.

Rust, E. Gardner. The Music & Dance of the World's Religions: A Comprehensive, Annotated Bibliography of Materials in the English Language, 54. LC 96-18212. (Music Reference Collection: Vol. 54). 504p. 1996. lib. bdg. 89.50 (0-313-29561-1, Greenwood Pr) Greenwood.

Rust, Ellsworth M. Rust of Virginia: Genealogical & Biographical Sketches of the Descendants of William Rust, 1654-1940. (Illus.). 462p. 1992. reprint ed. pap. 83.00 (0-8328-2487-9); reprint ed. lib. bdg. 73.00 (0-8328-2486-0) Higginson Bk Co.

Rust, Eric. Naval Officers under Hitler: The Story of Crew 34. LC 90-43918. 248p. 1991. 55.00 (0-275-93709-7, C3709, Praeger Pubs) Greenwood.

Rust, Eric C. Religion, Revelation & Reason. LC 81-2760. vi, 192p. (C). 1981. pap. 12.50 (0-86554-058-6, MUP-P009) Mercer Univ Pr.

Rust, Eric C., tr. see Topp, Erich.

Rust, Frances O. Changing Teaching, Changing Schools: Bringing Early Childhood Practice into Public Education: Case Studies from Kindergarten. LC 93-17378. (Early Childhood Education Ser.). 144p. (C). 1993. text 32.00 (0-8077-3286-9); pap. text 17.95 (0-8077-3285-0) Tchrs Coll.

Rust, Frances O. & Williams, Leslie, eds. The Care & Education of Young Children: Expanding Contexts, Sharpening Focus. 168p. (C). 1989. pap. text 17.95 (0-8077-2984-1) Tchrs Coll.

Rust, Graham. Decorative Designs: Over 100 Ideas for Painted Interiors, Furniture & Decorated Objects. LC 96-84781. (Illus.). 192p. 1996. 40.00 (0-8212-2329-1, Pub. by Bulfinch Pr) Little.

*Rust, Graham. Decorative Designs: Over 100 Ideas for Painted Interiors, Furniture & Decorated Objects. (Illus.). 184p. 2000. pap. 29.95 (0-8212-2657-6, Pub. by Bulfinch Pr) Little.

Rust, Graham. Graham Rust Needlepoint Designs: Over 20 Original Patterns from Pincushion to Seashell Rug. LC 98-20308. (Illus.). 135p. 1998. 35.00 (0-8109-3783-2, Pub. by Abrams) Time Warner.

An Asterisk (*) at the beginning of an entry indicates that the title is appearing for the first time.

R

An Asterisk (*) at the beginning of an entry indicates that the title is appearing for the first time.

Rustomji, R. Registration Act. 4th ed. (C). 1989. 265.00 (0-7855-3677-9) St Mut.

***Ruston, David, et al.** Orthokeratology: A Practical Approach. (Illus.). 224p. 2000. pap. 52.50 (0-7506-4007-3) Buttrwrth-Heinemann.

Ruston, John, jt. auth. see Denison, Richard.

Ruston, Roger. A Say in the End of the World: Morals & British Nuclear Weapons Policy, 1941-1987. 282p. 1989. text 32.50 (0-19-827565-X) OUP.

***Ruston, Sharon, ed.** Influence & Anxiety of the British Romantics: Spectres of Romanticism. LC 99-16083. (Salzburg Studies in English Literature: Vol. 153). 276p. 1999. text 89.95 (0-7734-7999-6) E Mellen.

Rustow, Dankwart A. Turkey: America's Forgotten Ally. rev. ed. 174p. 1989. pap. 14.95 (0-87609-065-X) Coun Foreign.

— A World of Nations: Problems of Political Modernization. LC 67-26139. 320p. 1967. reprint ed. pap. 99.20 (0-608-00491-X, 206131000007) Bks Demand.

Rustum, Y. & McGuire, J. J., eds. Expanding Role of Folates & Fluoropyrimidines in Cancer Chemotherapy. LC 88-38105. (Illus.). 346p. 1989. 79.50 (0-306-43100-9, Plenum Trade) Perseus Pubng.

Rustum, Y. M. Novel Approaches to Selective Treatments of Human Solid Tumors: Laboratory & Clinical Correlation. (Advances in Experimental Medicine & Biology Ser.: Vol. 339). (Illus.). 332p. (C). 1994. text 95.00 (0-306-44592-1, Kluwer Plenum) Kluwer Academic.

Rusva, Mirza M. Umrao Jan Ada. Matthews, David, tr. LC 96-901911. (C). 1996. 9.00 (81-7167-311-2, Pub. by Rupa) S Asia.

Rusz, Joe. Porsche Sport 73. LC 73-89096. (Illus.). 1974. pap. 5.95 (0-393-60017-3) Norton.

— Porsche Sport 72. LC 72-97717. (Illus.). 1973. pap. 4.95 (0-393-60016-5) Norton.

— Porsche Sport, 1974/1975 LC 75-663. 104 p. 1975. 7.95 (0-9600832-1-9) Ruszkiewicz Publishing.

Ruszczynsk, Johnson, jt. auth. see Ruszczynsk, S.

***Ruszczynsk, S. & Ruszczynsk, Johnson.** Psychoanalytic Psychotherapy in the Kleinian Tradition. 216p. 1999. pap. 30.00 (1-85575-175-5, Pub. by H Karnac Bks Ltd) Other Pr LLC.

Ruszczynski, A., tr. see Shor, N. Z.

Ruszczynski, Stanley, ed. Psychotherapy with Couples: Theory & Practice at the Tavistock Institute of Marital Studies. 256p. 1993. pap. text 30.00 (1-85575-045-7, Pub. by H Karnac Bks Ltd) Other Pr LLC.

Ruszczynski, Stanley & Fisher, James, eds. Intrusiveness & Intimacy in the Couple. 175p. 1995. pap. text 28.00 (1-85575-114-3, Pub. by H Karnac Bks Ltd) Other Pr LLC.

Ruszczynski, Stanley, jt. auth. see Johnson, Sue.

***Ruszkiewicz, John J.** Bookmarkes for Public Writing. LC 99-34699. 355p. (C). 1999. spiral bd. 26.53 (0-321-02393-5) Addison-Wesley.

Ruszkiewicz, John J. Scott Foresman Writer. LC 98-18681. 350p. (C). 1998. spiral bd. 35.00 (0-321-00354-3) Addison-Wesley Educ.

Ruszkiewicz, John J., jt. auth. see Corder, Jim W.

Ruszkiewicz, John J., jt. auth. see Hairston, Maxine C.

Ruszkiewicz, John J., jt. auth. see Walker, Janice R.

Rusznak, Michael. Excusious Within the Heartland Mind. 80p. 1998. pap. text 9.95 (1-889534-28-5) Jay St Pubs.

Ruta, Suzanne, tr. see Sepulveda, Luis.

Ruta, Tina, jt. ed. see Richardson, Dorothy.

Rutan, ed. Proceedings of the 22nd Annual Simulation Symposium. 194p. 1989. pap. 48.00 (0-685-66803-7, ANS22-1) Soc Computer Sim.

Rutan, Alan, ed. Proceedings, 24th Annual Simulation Symposium. LC 71-149514. 338p. 1991. pap. 58.00 (0-8186-2169-9, ANSS-24) Soc Computer Sim.

Rutan, Catherine. Changes in Position. 1983. pap. 6.00 (0-911623-00-0) I Klang.

Rutan, Debbie. Big Promises for Little People. (Illus.). (J). (gr. 1-3). 1991. pap. 3.95 (0-9624777-2-9) Green & White Pub.

Rutan, J. Scott & Stone, Walter N. Psychodynamic Group Psychotherapy. 2nd ed. LC 93-15055. 274p. 1993. lib. bdg. 35.00 (0-89862-096-1) Guilford Pubns.

***Rutan, J. Scott & Stone, Walter N.** Psychodynamic Group Psychotherapy. 3rd ed. 388p. 2000. lib. bdg. 45.00 (1-57230-518-5, C0518) Guilford Pubns.

Rutayuga, John B., jt. auth. see Murphy, John D.

Rutberg, Becky. Mary Lincoln's Dressmaker: Elizabeth Keckley's Remarkable Rise from Slave to White House Confidante. LC 94-45839. (Illus.). 176p. (YA). (gr. 5 up). 1995. 15.95 (0-8027-8224-8); lib. bdg. 16.85 (0-8027-8225-6) Walker & Co.

Rutberg, Donald Paul. Running Through Kenya. LC 99-72734. (Illus.). 40p. (J). (gr. 3-8). 1999. pap. text 8.95 (1-58521-011-0) Bks Black Chldn.

Rutberg, Jack, intro. The Prints of Kathe Kollwitz. 20p. 1996. pap. 10.00 (1-880566-12-5) J Rutberg Fine Arts.

Rutberg, Jack V. Hans Burkhardt: 1950-1960. (Illus.). 42p. 1987. pap. 15.00 (1-880566-03-6) J Rutberg Fine Arts.

Rutberg, Jack V., intro. Edward Glauder: Sculpture, 1980-88. 48p. 1989. pap. 15.00 (1-880566-06-0) J Rutberg Fine Arts.

— Patrick Graham. (Illus.). 28p. 1989. pap. 25.00 (1-880566-05-2) J Rutberg Fine Arts.

Rutberg, Sidney. The History of Asset-Based Lending. 1994. 24.95 (0-9667943-1-1) Comm Finan.

Rutebeuf. Poemes de l'Infortune et Autres Poemes (Medieval & Modern French) (Poesie Ser.). (FRE.). 308p. 1986. pap. 13.95 (2-07-032378-1) Schoenhof.

Rutecki, Randall J. Computing Against the Odds: The Beginner's Guide to Sports Handicapping with a Personal Computer. (Orig.). 1995. pap. 29.95 (0-9646727-0-7) Cybersource.

Rutemiller, Brent T. Below the Surface: How to Survive & Succeed in Building a Competitive Swim Club. LC 97-69781. 121p. 1997. write for info. (0-9647782-0-3) Sports Pubns.

Rutenbar, R. A., jt. ed. see Antao, B.

Rutenbar, Rob A., jt. auth. see Setliff, Dorothy E.

Rutenberg, A., ed. Earthquake Engineering: Proceedings of the 17th European Regional Seminar, Haifa, 5-10 September 1993. (Illus.). 300p. (C). 1994. text 104.00 (90-5410-391-4, Pub. by A A Balkema) Ashgate Pub Co.

***Rutenberg, Michael Elliot, tr.** Oedipus of Lucius Annaeus Seneca. 1999. 20.00 (0-86516-463-0) Bolchazy-Carducci.

Rutenberg, Michael Elliot, tr. & adapted by see Seneca, Lucius Annaeus.

Rutenfranz, Joseph, ed. see International Congress on Pediatric Work Physiolog.

Rutenfranz, Joseph, ed. see International Congress on Pediatric Work Physiology (11th, 1983, Papendal, Netherlands) Staff.

Ruter, Horst, jt. auth. see Dresen, L.

Ruterbories, Shavaun. The Family Investment. 196p. (Orig.). 1995. pap. 12.95 (0-9646012-0-6) L & S Ruterbories.

Rutford, Robert H. & Plummer, Charles C. Physical Geology with Interactive Plate Tectonics. 7th ed. 224p. (C). 1996. text, lab manual ed. write for info. (0-697-29324-6, WCB McGr Hill) McGrw-H Hghr Educ.

***Rutgeerts, P., et al, eds.** Advances in Inflammatory Bowel Diseases. (Falk Symposium Ser.: Vol. 106). 316p. 1999. 190.00 (0-7923-8750-3) Kluwer Academic.

Rutgers, I., ed. see Africanus, Sextus J.

Rutgers, Leonard V. The Jews in Late Ancient Rome: Evidence of Cultural Interaction in the Roman Diaspora. LC 95-5743. (Religions in the Graeco-Roman World Ser.: Vol. 126). 283p. 1995. 95.50 (90-04-10269-8) Brill Academic Pubs.

Rutgers, M., tr. see Paulis, L.

Rutgers University Staff. Communication Theory: A Reader. LC 98-175376. 432p. (C). 1998. per. 37.95 (0-7872-4659-X) Kendall-Hunt.

— Copper-Containing Composites. 74p. 1970. 11.10 (0-317-34502-8, 65) Intl Copper.

— Current Moral & Social Issues. 406p. (C). 1996. pap. text, per. 27.95 (0-7872-2787-0) Kendall-Hunt.

— Current Moral & Social Issues. 308p. (C). 1998. per. 20.50 (0-7872-4713-8) Kendall-Hunt.

Rutgers University Staff & Balliet. Georgia State Politics: The Constitutional Foundation. 3rd ed. LC 98-221409. 375p. (C). 1998. per. 28.95 (0-7872-5335-9) Kendall-Hunt.

***Ruth.** Design Standard Children Enviroment. LC 99-29058. 1998. pap. text 59.95 (0-07-057809-5) McGrw-H Hghr Educ.

***Ruth, Amy.** Jane Austen. LC 00-9315. (A&E Biography Ser.). (Illus.). 2001. lib. bdg. write for info. (0-8225-4992-1) Lerner Pub.

Ruth, Amy. Louisa May Alcott: American Storyteller. LC 97-47283. (A&E Biography Ser.). 128p. (J). (gr. 4-7). 1998. lib. bdg. 17.95 (0-8225-4938-7, Lerner Publctns) Lerner Pub.

— Mother Teresa. LC 98-23315. (A&E Biography Ser.). 112p. (YA). (gr. 6-9). 1999. 25.26 (0-8225-4943-3) Lerner Pub.

***Ruth, Amy.** Queen Latifah. LC 99-50945. (A&E Biography Ser.). (Illus.). 128p. (YA). (gr. 4-7). 2000. lib. bdg. 25.26 (0-8225-4988-3, Lerner Publctns) Lerner Pub.

Ruth, Amy. Wilma Rudolph. LC 99-28291. (Biography Ser.). (Illus.). 128p. (J). (gr. 4-7). 1999. 25.26 (0-8225-4976-X, Lerner Publctns) Lerner Pub.

Ruth, Amy, jt. auth. see Meisner, James, Jr.

***Ruth, Andy.** Concise Guide to Windows 2000 Dynamic DNS. 400p. 2000. pap. 34.99 (0-7897-2335-2) Que.

— Fast Track MCSE SQL Server & Administration. LC 98-89437. (MCSE Fast Track Ser.). (Illus.). 265p. 1999. pap. text 29.99 (0-7357-0041-9) New Riders Pub.

— MCSE Guide to Microsoft Proxy Server 2.0. 560p. per. 60.95 (0-7600-1144-3, Pub. by Course Tech) Thomson Learn.

Ruth, Andy, jt. auth. see Hudson, Kurt.

Ruth, Anita, ed. see Line, Lorie.

Ruth, Annie. Embracing Charity. LC 96-92510. (Illus.). 104p. (Orig.). 1996. pap. 10.00 (0-9656306-0-9) A Ruth Creations.

***Ruth, Annie.** He's Got Yo' Back. 32p. 1999. pap. 2.50 (0-9656306-5-X) A Ruth Creations.

Ruth, Annie. Little Angels Coloring & Activity Book: The Special Gift. large type ed. (Illus.). 24p. (J). (gr. k-3). 1999. 3.50 (0-9656306-2-5) A Ruth Creations.

— No! Not on the Pews. large type ed. (Illus.). 20p. (J). (gr. k-3). 1999. 2.50 (0-9656306-1-7) A Ruth Creations.

— Reflection: A Collection of Straight Talk & Inspirational Narratives. large type ed. LC 98-92018. (Illus.). 200p. 1999. 20.95 (0-9656306-3-3) A Ruth Creations.

***Ruth, Annie.** This Is Your Season. 40p. 1999. pap. 2.50 (0-9656306-4-1) A Ruth Creations.

Ruth, Babe. Home Run King - How Pep Pindar Won Title. 20.95 (0-8488-1586-6) Amereon Ltd.

Ruth, Bonnie. November Days: A Love Story. 299p. (Orig.). 1995. pap. 12.95 (0-9645378-7-7) F Scott Pr.

Ruth, Byron E., ed. Evaluation & Prevention of Water Damage to Asphalt Pavement Materials-STP 889. LC 85-26783. (Illus.). 160p. 1985. text 46.00 (0-8031-0460-X, STP899) ASTM.

Ruth, Corinna S. MaxNotes - King Lear. (MaxNotes Ser.). 144p. 1999. pap. text 3.95 (0-87891-989-9) Res & Educ.

— MaxNotes - Paradise Lost. (MaxNotes Ser.). 128p. 1995. pap. text 3.95 (0-87891-992-9) Res & Educ.

Ruth, Dan, ed. see Kee, Joyce L. & Marshall, Sally M.

Ruth, Dan, ed. see Pinnell, Norma L.

***Ruth, David E.** Confronting Death. 1999. 29.00 (0-226-73219-3) U Ch Pr.

Ruth, David E. Inventing the Public Enemy: The Gangster in Amerian Culture, 1918-1934. LC 95-22480. (Illus.). 200p. 1996. pap. text 17.00 (0-226-73218-5) U Ch Pr.

— Inventing the Public Enemy: The Gangster in American Culture, 1918-1934. (Illus.). 200p. 1996. lib. bdg. 42.50 (0-226-73217-7) U Ch Pr.

Ruth, Eddie. How Do the Ducks Know? (Illus.). 28p. (Orig.). (J). (gr. 1-4). 1981. pap. 2.50 (0-911826-18-1, 5448) Am Atheist.

Ruth, G. Lamar, jt. auth. see Klaus, Tom.

Ruth, George. Analyzing Financial Statements. (Illus.). (C). 1998. write for info. (0-89982-069-7) Am Bankers.

Ruth, George E. Commercial Lending. 2nd ed. Johns, Rebecca B., ed. (Illus.). 454p. 1990. text 57.00 (0-89982-363-7) Am Bankers.

Ruth, George H. Babe Ruth's Own Book of Baseball. 323p. Date not set. 24.95 (0-8488-2385-0) Amereon Ltd.

— Babe Ruth's Own Book of Baseball. LC 91-38383. (Illus.). xxii, 333p. 1992. reprint ed. pap. 12.00 (0-8032-8939-1) U of Nebr Pr.

Ruth-Heffelbower, Duane. The Anabaptists Are Back: Making Peace in a Dangerous World. LC 91-6668. 144p. (Orig.). 1991. pap. 8.99 (0-8361-3552-0) Herald Pr.

— The Christian & Jury Duty. LC 91-13624. (Peace & Justice Ser.: Vol. 14). 104p. (Orig.). 1991. pap. 6.99 (0-8361-3562-8) Herald Pr.

***Ruth-Heffelbower, Duane.** Conflict & Peacemaking Across Cultures: Training for Trainers. (Illus.). 164p. 1999. pap. 25.00 (0-9673075-0-3) Ctr for Peacemaking & Conflict.

Ruth-Heffelbower, Dwayne. A Technical Manual for Church Planters. Martin, Melba et al, eds. (Illus.). 80p. 1989. pap. 5.00 (0-317-93801-0) MB Missions.

Ruth, Herrman Siress. Working Woman's Communications Survival Guide. (C). 1996. text 7.50 (0-13-440439-4, Macmillan Coll) P-H.

Ruth, Irene, jt. auth. see Carlson, Dale.

Ruth, Jamee. Grill Pan Cookbook: Great Recipes for Stovetop Grilling. LC 98-48789. (Illus.). 108p. 1999. pap. 16.95 (0-8118-2417-0) Chronicle Bks.

Ruth, Jamee, et al. The Politically Correct 'Twas the Night Before Christmas. (Illus.). 20p. (Orig.). 1995. pap. 2.95 (0-9648745-0-4) Stickman Prods.

Ruth, Jeffrey S., tr. & intro. see De Gois, Damiao.

***Ruth, John L.** Conrad Grebel, Son of Zurich. 162p. 1999. pap. 18.00 (1-57910-308-1) Wipf & Stock.

Ruth, John L. A Quiet & Peaceable Life. (People's Place Book Ser.: No. 2). (Illus.). 96p. 1997. pap. 6.95 (1-56148-232-3) Good Bks PA.

— Twas Seeding Time: A Mennonite View of the American Revolution. LC 76-41475. 225p. reprint ed. pap. 64.20 (0-608-06028-3, 2066359) Bks Demand.

Ruth, Kent. Landmarks of the West: A Guide to Historic Sites. LC 85-29014. (Illus.). 319p. 1986. reprint ed. pap. 98.90 (0-608-02677-8, 206333000004) Bks Demand.

— Oklahoma Travel Handbook. LC 76-62517. (Illus.). 1979. pap. 14.95 (0-8061-1539-4) U of Okla Pr.

— Touring the Old West. LC 86-19305. (Illus.). x, 218p. 1987. text 40.00 (0-8032-3881-9) U of Nebr Pr.

Ruth, Kent, jt. auth. see Argo, Burnis.

Ruth, Kim, jt. auth. see Gowdy, Jim.

Ruth, Larry. M I Carbine. pap. 19.95 (0-88227-020-6) Gun Room.

Ruth, Leo & Murphy, Sandra. Designing Writing Tasks for the Assessment of Writing. Farr, Marcia, ed. LC 87-19688. (Writing Research Ser.). 336p. 1998. text 73.25 (0-89391-339-1) Ablx Pub.

Ruth, Lester. Accompanying the Journey: A Handbook for Sponsors. LC 96-86587. 80p. 1997. pap., suppl. ed. 14.95 (0-88177-176-7, DR176) Discipleship Res.

***Ruth, Lester.** A Little Heaven Below: Worship at Early Methodist Quarterly Meetings. 256p. 2000. pap. 25.00 (0-687-09024-5) Abingdon.

Ruth, M., ed. see Feurzeig, W. & Roberts, Nancy.

Ruth, Maria M. The Deserts of the Southwest. LC 97-49842. (Ecosystems of North America Ser.). (Illus.). (YA). (gr. 6 up). 1998. lib. bdg. 27.07 (0-7614-0899-1, Benchmark NY) Marshall Cavendish.

— A Rain Forest Pop-Up: Poster & Story. (Illus.). (J). (ps-3). 1995. 16.95 (0-671-51080-0) Little Simon.

Ruth, Marianne & Locke, Raymond F. Cruel City. LC 90-52813. (Illus.). 240p. (J). 1991. 19.95 (0-915677-48-2) Roundtable Pub.

Ruth, Matthias. Integrating Economics, Ecology & Thermodyanamics. LC 93-24816. (Ecology, Economy & Environment Ser.). 264p. 1993. text 174.50 (0-7923-2377-7) Kluwer Academic.

Ruth, Matthias & Hannon, Bruce M. Modeling Dynamic Economic Systems. LC 96-38303. (Modeling Dynamic Systems Ser.). (Illus.). 312p. 1997. 59.95 (0-387-94849-X) Spr-Verlag.

Ruth, Matthias, jt. auth. see Hannon, Bruce M.

Ruth, Merle. Convenants in the Plan of God. 40p. 1996. pap. 1.75 (0-7399-0218-0, 2179) Rod & Staff.

— Dying to Live with Christ. 79p. 1989. pap. 3.75 (0-7399-0196-6, 2226) Rod & Staff.

— Dying to Live with Christ. Barrantes, Kanier, tr. (Cornerstone Ser.). (SPA.). 80p. 1996. pap. 3.45 (0-7399-0197-4, 2226.1) Rod & Staff.

— The Significance of the Christian Women's Veiling. (SPA.). 30p. 1979. pap. 1.25 (0-7399-0201-6, 2385.1) Rod & Staff.

— The Significance of the Christian Women's Veiling. 24p. 1980. pap. 1.50 (0-7399-0200-8, 2385) Rod & Staff.

— Triumphant in Suffering. (Cornerstone Ser.). 78p. 1991. pap. 3.50 (0-7399-0195-8, 2409) Rod & Staff.

***Ruth, Michael.** Shadow Work: A New Guide to Spiritual & Psychological Growth. rev. ed. LC 99-71757. 243p. 1999. pap. 14.00 (0-9668083-5-5) Growth Solutions.

Ruth, Monty, jt. auth. see Bowen, Mary.

Ruth, Nancy. Soul's Love: The Evolution of the Human Species. 75p. 1999. pap. 10.00 (0-7392-0146-8, PO3085) Morris Pubng.

Ruth, Phil J. A North Penn Pictorial. (Illus.). 176p. 1988. 29.95 (0-9619350-0-6) P J Ruth.

— Seeing Souderton: The Borough's Story in Photographs, 1887-1987. (Illus.). 192p. (C). 1987. 29.95 (0-9619350-1-4) P J Ruth.

Ruth, Philip. Of Pulleys & Ropes & Gear: The Gravity Railroads of the Delaware & Hudson Canal Company & the PA Coal Company. 2nd ed. LC 97-61456. (Illus.). 75p. 1997. reprint ed. pap. 15.00 (0-9659540-0-5) Wayne Cty Hist.

Ruth, Philippa. The Trials of Ada Adams. write for info. (0-318-58991-5) World Pr Ltd.

Ruth, Ralph P., ed. see U. S. Workshop on the Physics & Chemistry of Mercu.

Ruth, Richard, jt. auth. see Blotzer, Mary Ann.

Ruth, Romy, jt. auth. see Neumann, Jeff.

***Ruth, Sean, ed.** Irish Liberation Policy. 16p. 1999. pap. 2.00 (1-58429-043-9) Rational Isl.

Ruth, Sheila. Issues in Feminism: An Introduction to Women's Studies. 4th ed. LC 97-10243. xvi, 613p. 1997. pap. text 37.95 (1-55934-936-0, 1936) Mayfield Pub.

— Take Back the Light: A Feminist Reclamation of Spirituality & Religion. LC 93-6061. (New Feminist Perspectives Ser.). 240p. (Orig.). (C). 1994. text 58.50 (0-8476-7879-2); pap. text 14.95 (0-8226-3031-1) Rowman.

Ruth Stiles Gannett, jt. auth. see Sharmat, Marjorie Weinman.

Ruth, Susan, jt. auth. see Ruth, Trevor.

Ruth, Trevor & Ruth, Susan. Drawing My View. LC 93-11827. (Illus.). (J). 1994. 4.95 (0-383-03730-1) SRA McGraw.

***Ruth, Virginia Moulton.** Messages of Friendship & Love. 2000. 12.95 (0-533-13275-4) Vantage.

Ruth, W. Lexikon der Schulphysik: Optik und Relativitaet, Vol. 4. (GER.). 85.00 (3-7614-0109-4, M-7226) Fr & Eur.

— Lexikon der Schulphysik Vol. 4: Optik und Relativitaet. (GER.). 85.00 (0-8288-7975-3, M7226) Fr & Eur.

Ruthberg, Z. G., et al. System Development Auditor. 130p. 1991. 313.00 (1-85617-116-7, Pub. by Elsvr Adv Tech) Elsevier.

Ruthberg, Zella, jt. ed. see Tipton, Hal.

Ruthberg, Zella G. & Tipton, Harold F., eds. Handbook of Information Security Management. 773p. 142.00 (0-7913-1636-X) Warren Gorham & Lamont.

— Handbook of Information Security Management: 1994-95 Handbook. LC 95-113543. 427p. 1995. pap. 142.00 (0-7913-2073-1) Warren Gorham & Lamont.

Ruthchild, Rochelle G., ed. Women in Russia & the Soviet Union. 1992. lib. bdg. 40.00 (0-685-59685-0, Hall Reference) Macmillan.

— Women in Russia & the Soviet Union: An Annotated Bibliography. (Reference Ser.). 203p. 1994. 45.00 (0-8161-8989-7, G K Hall & Co) Mac Lib Ref.

Ruthen, Marlene L. Daniel & the Silver Flute: An Old Hassidic Tale. 32p. 1986. 11.95 (0-317-55242-2) United Synagogue.

Ruthen, Marlene Lobell. My Bar Mitzvah. 36p. 1995. 13.00 (0-8074-0542-6, 510010) UAHC.

— My Bat Mitzvah. 36p. 1995. 13.00 (0-8074-0543-4, 510020) UAHC.

Ruthenberg, Stephen J. Golf Fore Beginners: The Fundamentals. LC 91-67566. 200p. (Orig.). 1992. pap. 9.95 (0-9631514-1-X) RGS Pub.

— Golf Fore Kids. 96p. (J). (gr. 3 up). 1996. 9.95 (0-9631514-2-8) RGS Pub.

— Golf Fore Kids. 96p. (J). (gr. 3). 1997. pap. 9.95 (0-9631514-3-6) RGS Pub.

Rutheny, Eugene P. Anatomy & Physiology Notebook. 272p. (C). 1993. text. write for info. (0-697-20349-2, WCB McGr Hill) McGrw-H Hghr Educ.

Ruther, W., ed. The Elbow: Endoprosthetic Replacement & Non-Endoprosthetic Procedures. (Illus.). 240p. 1995. 165.00 (3-540-59245-8) Spr-Verlag.

Rutherfoord, Andrea. Basic Communication Skills for Electronics. 304p. 1988. pap. text 36.60 (0-13-970617-8) P-H.

Rutherfoord, Andrea J. Basic Communication Skills Technology. 368p. 1990. pap. text 36.60 (0-13-058660-9) P-H.

***Rutherfoord, Andrea J.** Basic Communications Skills for Technology. 2nd ed. 416p. 2000. pap. 35.00 (0-13-087822-7) P-H.

Rutherfoord, G. Stuart & Hewlett, R. H. Atlas of Correlative Surgical Neuropathology & Imaging. LC 94-11237. (Current Histopathology Ser.: Vol. 24). 206p. (C). 1994. text 318.50 (0-7923-8951-4) Kluwer Academic.

***Rutherford.** Complete Book of Mini Rugby. 2000. 15.95 (1-85225-196-4, Pub. by Transworld Publishers Ltd) Trafalgar.

— Identity. 2nd ed. 1998. pap. text 19.50 (0-85315-871-1) Lawrence & Wishart.

Rutherford. Project Phsyics. 1981. text 67.00 (0-03-055141-2) Holt R&W.

Rutherford, ed. Identity: Community Culture Difference. (C). 1990. pap. 19.95 (0-85315-720-0, Pub. by Lawrence & Wishart) NYU Pr.

— Male Order: Unwrapping Masculinity. (C). 1988. pap. 19.50 (0-85315-690-5, Pub. by Lawrence & Wishart) NYU Pr.

Rutherford, Adam. Iceland's Great Inheritance. 40p. 1990. pap. 4.00 (0-934666-41-5) Artisan Pubs.

Rutherford, Andrew. Byron: A Critical Study. xiii, 253p. 1961. pap. 13.95 (0-8047-0072-9) Stanford U Pr.

An Asterisk (*) at the beginning of an entry indicates that the title is appearing for the first time.

Rutherford, Andrew, ed. Criminal Policy Making. LC 96-35395. (International Library of Criminology, Criminal Justice & Penology). (Illus.). 584p. 1997. text 179.95 (*1-85521-782-1*, Pub. by Dartmth Pub) Ashgate Pub Co.
— Kipling's Mind & Art: Selected Critical Essays. x, 278p. 1964. pap. 14.95 (*0-8047-0213-6*) Stanford U Pr.
Rutherford, Andrew, jt. ed. see Craven, Peter.
Rutherford, Andrew, ed. see Kipling, Rudyard.
Rutherford, Anna & Peterson, Kirsten H., eds. Chinua Achebe: A Celebration. (Studies in African Literature). 165p. (C). 1991. pap. 17.50 (*0-435-08060-1*, 08060) Heinemann.
Rutherford, Anna, jt. ed. see Peterson, Kirsten H.
***Rutherford, Anne.** Boadicea & Her Sisters: Women of Wales. 59p. 1999. pap. 8.75 (*1-889298-54-9*) Rhwymbooks.
Rutherford, Anne, ed. see Brewster, John.
Rutherford, Anne, ed. see Lightfoot, Susanna & Thomas, Martha.
Rutherford, Barry. Parent & Community Involvement in Education. LC 97-174276. 142p. 1997. pap. 11.00 (*0-16-048890-7*) USGPO.
Rutherford, Brett. Anniversarium: The Autumn Poems of Brett Rutherford. 3rd ed. 72p. 1988. 6.00 (*0-318-64089-9*) Poets Pr.
— At Lovecraft's Grave. 64p. 1988. write for info. (*0-318-64097-X*) Poets Pr.
— City Limits. 1970. write for info. (*0-318-64106-2*) Poets Pr.
Rutherford, Brett. Poems from Providence. (Illus.). 180p. 1991. pap. 10.00 (*0-922558-06-X*) Poets Pr.
Rutherford, Brett. Prometheus on Fifth Avenue. 62p. 1987. 6.00 (*0-318-64165-8*) Poets Pr.
— The Pumpkined Heart. 40p. 1973. 5.00 (*0-318-64162-3*) Poets Pr.
— Songs of the I & Thou. 1969. write for info. (*0-318-64143-7*) Poets Pr.
Rutherford, Brett, ed. Last Flowers: The Romance Poems of Edgar Allan Poe & Sarah Helen Whitman. (Illus.). 1987. 10.00 (*0-318-64156-9*) Poets Pr.
— The Lost Children. 1988. 4.50 (*0-318-64155-0*) Poets Pr.
— May Eve: A Festival of Supernatural Poems. 1975. 5.00 (*0-318-64158-5*) Poets Pr.
Rutherford, Brett & Robertson, John, eds. Piper. 1987. 4.50 (*0-318-64157-7*) Poets Pr.
Rutherford, Brett & Vanderbeck, Pieter. Twilight of the Dictators: Poems of Tyranny & Liberation. (Illus.). 83p. 1992. pap. 9.95 (*0-922558-10-8*) Poets Pr.
Rutherford, Brett, jt. ed. see Holland, Barbara A.
Rutherford, Brett, ed. see Poe, Edgar Allan & Whitman, Sarah Helen.
Rutherford, Brian & Wearing, Robert. Cases in Company Financial Reporting. (C). 1988. pap. 45.00 (*0-06-318371-4*, Pub. by P Chapman) St Mut.
— Cases in Company Financial Reporting. (C). 1988. student ed. 45.00 (*0-7855-2384-7*) St Mut.
Rutherford, Brian, et al. Cases in Public Sector Accounting. 224p. 1992. pap. 29.95 (*1-85396-072-1*, Pub. by P Chapman) Taylor & Francis.
Rutherford, Brinton L., jt. auth. see Turner, Rufus P.
Rutherford, Bruce. The Impeachment of Jim Ferguson. (Illus.). 166p. 1983. 11.95 (*0-89015-386-8*) Sunbelt Media.
***Rutherford, C., et al, eds.** Secondary Neoplasias after Organ Transplants & Radiotherapy. (Contributions to Oncology Ser.: 55). (Illus.). viii, 340p. 2000. 143.50 (*3-8055-7116-X*) S Karger.
Rutherford, Clarence. No Escape from Greatness. LC 89-85364. (Orig.). (C). 1989. pap. 12.95 (*0-9622704-1-5*) Xylo Prods.
Rutherford, Clarice & Loveland, Cherylon. Retriever Puppy Training: The Right Start for Hunting. LC 88-3015. (Illus.). 120p. 1988. pap. 11.95 (*0-931866-38-3*) Alpine Pubns.
***Rutherford, Clarice & Neil, David H.** How to Raise a Puppy You Can Live With. 3rd ed. LC 99-34985. 1999. pap. 9.95 (*1-57779-022-7*) Alpine Pubns.
Rutherford, Constance. American Water Spaniel. (Illus.). 96p. 1997. 19.95 (*0-7938-0759-X*, RX-109) TFH Pubns.
— The Art of Making Paper Flowers: Full Size Patterns & Instructions for 16 Realistic Blossoms. (Illus.). 48p. (Orig.). 1983. pap. 5.95 (*0-486-24378-8*) Dover.
***Rutherford, Darel A.** So, Why Aren't You Rich? The Prosperity Secret of the Rich. 303p. 1998. pap. 19.95 (*0-9670540-0-1*) DAR Pubg.
— The Why Aren't You Rich Workbook: How to Win the Game of Life. (Illus.). 72p. 1999. wbk. ed. 15.00 (*0-9670540-1-X*) DAR Pubg.
Rutherford, Denney G. Hotel Management & Operations. 2nd ed. 462p. 1995. pap. 48.95 (*0-442-01496-1*, VNR) Wiley.
Rutherford, Denney G., ed. Hotel Management & Operations. 2nd ed. (Hospitality, Travel & Tourism Ser.). 462p. 1994. pap. 59.95 (*0-471-28568-4*, VNR) Wiley.
Rutherford, Donald. Classical Economics. LC 98-25256. 1999. 700.00 (*0-415-15740-4*) Routledge.
— Leibniz & the Rational Order of Nature. 317p. (C). 1995. text 64.95 (*0-521-46155-3*) Cambridge U Pr.
— Leibniz & the Rational Order of Nature. 317p. 1998. pap. text 19.95 (*0-521-59737-4*) Cambridge U Pr.
— Routledge Dictionary of Economics. (Illus.). 552p. (C). 1995. pap. 20.99 (*0-415-12291-0*, C0460) Routledge.
Rutherford, Donald, ed. Classical Economics: The Critical Reviews, 1802-1852, 4 vols., Set. LC 94-23101. 2176p. (C). (gr. 13). 1995. text, boxed set 700.00 (*0-415-11270-2*) Routledge.
Rutherford, Donald, intro. Collected Works of Nassau William Senior: Rare Edition. 2388p. Date not set. 795.00 (*1-85506-617-3*) Thoemmes Pr.
Rutherford, Douglas. A Game of Sudden Death. large type ed. 1990. 27.99 (*0-7089-2144-2*) Ulverscroft.
— Stop at Nothing. large type ed. 1989. 27.99 (*0-7089-2109-4*) Ulverscroft.
***Rutherford, Edward, pseud.** The Forest. large type ed. LC 99-88998. 1116p. 2000. 26.95 (*0-375-41037-6*, Crown) Crown Pub Group.
Rutherford, Edward, pseud & Center for Learning Network Staff. Sarum: Curriculum Unit. (Novel Ser.). 76p. (YA). (gr. 9-12). 1996. spiral bd. 18.95 (*1-56077-326-X*) Ctr Learning.
***Rutherford, Elizabeth L.** Joyous Stress Free Holidays. (Illus.). 125p. 1999. 18.00 (*0-9676281-0-5*) E Rutherford.
Rutherford, Erica. An Island Alphabet. LC 94-189296. (Illus.). 32p. (J). (ps up). 1994. 14.95 (*0-921556-44-6*, Pub. by Gynergy-Ragweed) U of Toronto Pr.
Rutherford, Ernest & Boltwood, Bertram B. Rutherford & Boltwood: Letters on Radioactivity. Badash, Lawrence, ed. LC 78-81411. (Yale Studies in the History of Science & Medicine: No. 4). (Illus.). 402p. reprint ed. pap. 124.70 (*0-8357-9490-3*, 201678700005) Bks Demand.
Rutherford, F. James & Ahlgren, Andrew. Science for All Americans. (Illus.). 272p. 1991. pap. text 14.95 (*0-19-506771-1*) OUP.
Rutherford, G. K. The Physical Environment of the Faeroe Islands. 1982. text 135.00 (*90-6193-099-5*) Kluwer Academic.
Rutherford, H. C., ed. Certainly, Future: Selected Writing by Dimitrije Mitrinovic. 471p. 1987. text 82.50 (*0-88033-118-6*, 222, Pub. by East Eur Monographs) Col U Pr.
***Rutherford, H. Richard.** Honoring the Dead: Catholics & Cremation Today. LC 00-30651. 2000. write for info. (*0-8146-2714-5*) Liturgical Pr.
Rutherford, Ian. Canons of Style in the Antonine Age: Idea-Theory & Its Literary Context. LC 96-45145. (Oxford Classical Monographs). 192p. 1999. text 55.00 (*0-19-814729-5*) OUP.
— Pindar's Paeans: A Reading of the Fragments with a Survey of the Genre. 544p. (C). 2000. text 110.00 (*0-19-814381-8*) OUP.
Rutherford, J. C. River Mixing. LC 93-33033. 362p. 1994. 175.00 (*0-471-94282-0*) Wiley.
***Rutherford, Jack.** Skills, Drills & Strategies for Tennis. Pellett, Tracy L. & Blackman, Claudia, eds. LC 98-35650. (Teach, Coach, Play Ser.). (Illus.). 90p. (C). 1999. pap. 14.00 (*1-890871-14-1*) Holcomb Hath.
Rutherford, Jack, ed. see Pellett, Tracy L. & Lox, Curt.
Rutherford, Jack, ed. see Stephens, Kenneth P. & Stephens, Joni M.
Rutherford, John. The Troubadours: Their Loves & Their Lyrics with Remarks on Their Influence, Social & Literary. 1977. lib. bdg. 59.95 (*0-8490-2771-3*) Gordon Pr.
Rutherford, John, compiled by. An Annotated Bibliography of the Novels of the Mexican Revolution of 1910-1917 in English & Spanish. LC 73-150334. (ENG & SPA.). x, 180p. 1972. 40.00 (*0-87875-015-0*) Whitston Pub.
Rutherford, John A. From Pigskin to Saddle Leather: The Films of Johnny Mack Brown. unabridged ed. LC 96-61207. (Illus.). 212p. (Orig.). 1996. pap. 19.95 (*0-936505-13-3*) World Yesterday.
Rutherford, John A. & Smith, Richard B., 3rd. More Cowboy Shooting Stars. rev. ed. LC 92-74737. (Illus.). 214p. 1992. 18.00 (*0-944019-11-0*) Empire NC.
Rutherford, John D., ed. Unstable Angina. (Fundamental & Clinical Cardiology Ser.: Vol. 4). (Illus.). 328p. 1991. text 135.00 (*0-8247-8618-1*) Dekker.
Rutherford, John D., jt. auth. see Antman, Elliott M.
Rutherford, Johnathan. Forever England. LC 98-108738. 1997. pap. 18.50 (*0-85315-828-2*, Pub. by Lawrence & Wishart) NYU Pr.
***Rutherford, Johnny.** Lone Star, Jr. The Autobiography of Racing Legend Johnny Rutherford. LC 00-36422. (Illus.). 300p. 2000. 24.95 (*1-57243-353-1*) Triumph Bks.
Rutherford, Jonathan. Men's Silences: Predicaments in Masculinity. LC 92-2801. (Male Orders Ser.). 224p. (C). (gr. 13). 1992. text 89.95 (*0-415-07543-2*, A7650) Routledge.
— Young Britain. (Soundings Ser.: Vol. 6). 1997. pap. 19.50 (*0-85315-845-2*, Pub. by Lawrence & Wishart) NYU Pr.
Rutherford, Joseph F. Angels. 64p. 1987. reprint ed. pap. 2.95 (*1-883858-31-3*) Witness CA.
— Millions Now Living Will Never Die! 128p. 1985. reprint ed. pap. 5.95 (*1-883858-29-1*) Witness CA.
Rutherford, Kay M. And I Don't Mean Christmas! A Children's Photo Journal. (Illus.). 70p. (Orig.). 1996. pap. 9.95 (*0-9652742-0-9*) Aavery Pr.
Rutherford, Kim, jt. auth. see Ahrens, Thomas.
Rutherford, L. John Peter Zenger, His Press, Trial Plus Bibliography: Includes Repr. of First Edition of the Trial, 1904-1990. (Illus.). 275p. 1991. pap. 35.00 (*0-87556-800-9*) Saifer.
Rutherford, Leonard W. The Role of Chiropractic. 324p. (Orig.). 1989. text 30.00 (*0-9625065-1-6*) Hlth Educ Pub.
— The Role of Chiropractic. (Illus.). 324p. (Orig.). 1989. pap. text 22.50 (*0-9625065-0-8*) Hlth Educ Pub.
Rutherford, Lyn. Traditional Country Cooking. LC 93-37196. (Creative Cook Ser.). 64p. 1993. 16.95 (*1-56426-652-4*) Cole Group.
Rutherford, Lyn, jt. auth. see Newdick, Jane.
Rutherford, Mac S., II. Luckee's Elbow Room. (Illus.). 249p. (Orig.). 1988. pap. 4.95 (*0-922510-00-8*) Lucky Bks.
Rutherford, Malcolm. Institutions in Economics: The Old & the New Institutionalism. (Historical Perspectives on Modern Economics Ser.). 239p. (C). 1994. text 64.95 (*0-521-45189-2*) Cambridge U Pr.
— Institutions in Economics: The Old & the New Institutionalism. (Historical Perspectives on Modern Economics Ser.). 239p. 1996. pap. text 21.95 (*0-521-57447-1*) Cambridge U Pr.
Rutherford, Malcolm & Samuels, Warren J., eds. Classics in Institutional Economics II, 5 vols. LC 98-4176. 2400p. 1998. text 650.00 (*1-85196-515-7*, Pub. by Pickering & Chatto) Ashgate Pub Co.
— John R. Commons: Selected Essays, 2 vols., Set. LC 95-39288. 576p. (C). 1997. 180.00 (*0-415-13733-0*) Routledge.
— John R. Commons: Selected Essays, Vol. 1. LC 95-39288. 1996. write for info. (*0-415-14438-8*) Routledge.
— John R. Commons: Selected Essays, Vol. 2. LC 95-39288. 1996. write for info. (*0-415-14439-6*) Routledge.
Rutherford, Malcolm, jt. auth. see History of Economics Society Staff.
Rutherford, Malcolm, jt. auth. see Samuels, Warren J.
Rutherford, Mark. Clara Hopgood. 320p. 1996. pap. 7.95 (*0-460-87771-2*, Everyman's Classic Lib) Tuttle Pubng.
Rutherford, Mark, jt. auth. see Bourke, Glenn.
Rutherford, Michael. The Tale & Its Master. 68p. (Orig.). 1986. pap. 6.50 (*0-935891-00-5*) Spring Harbor.
Rutherford, Michael, photos by. Timeless Ireland: Faces & Places of the Emerald Isle. LC 98-23997. (Illus.). 1p. 1998. 19.98 (*1-56799-680-9*, MetroBooks) M Friedman Pub Grp Inc.
Rutherford, Mildred L. The South in History & Literature. 1972. 59.95 (*0-8490-1093-4*) Gordon Pr.
— Truths of History: A Historical Perspective of the Civil War Written from the Southern Viewpoint. Segars, J. H., ed. LC 98-60454. (Illus.). 192p. 1998. reprint ed. pap. 14.00 (*0-9662454-0-7*) Southern Lion.
***Rutherford-Moore, Richard.** The Legend of Robin Hood. LC 99-488071. (Illus.). 1999. pap. 21.95 (*1-86163-069-7*, Pub. by Capall Bann Pubng) Holmes Pub.
Rutherford, Nancy G., jt. auth. see Saputo, Helen N.
Rutherford, Noel. Shirley Baker & the King of Tonga. (Pasifika Press Ser.). 1996. pap. 19.95 (*0-8248-1856-3*) UH Pr.
Rutherford, P. H., jt. auth. see Goldston, R. J.
Rutherford, Pat. Crumb Crunchers Cooky Book. (Illus.). 92p. 1999. pap. write for info. (*1-57579-124-2*) Pine Hill Pr.
Rutherford, Paul. The New Icons? The Art of Television Advertising. (Illus.). 270p. (C). 1994. text 55.00 (*0-8020-2928-0*); pap. text 19.95 (*0-8020-7428-6*) U of Toronto Pr.
— A Victorian Authority: The Daily Press in Late Nineteenth-Century Canada. LC 82-190489. (Illus.). 305p. reprint ed. pap. 94.60 (*0-7837-4288-6*, 204398000012) Bks Demand.
— When Television Was Young: Primetime Canada, 1952-1967. 638p. 1990. pap. 29.95 (*0-8020-6647-X*); text 65.00 (*0-8020-5830-2*) U of Toronto Pr.
Rutherford, Paula. Instruction for All Students. (Illus.). 298p. 1997. pap. text 29.95 (*0-9663336-0-8*) JustAsk Pubns.
Rutherford, Peter. Elephant & Frog. (You Can Read It Ser.). 24p. (J). (ps-1). 1996. 3.49 (*1-85854-419-X*) Brimax Bks.
— Smile, Please! (You Can Read It Ser.). 24p. (J). (ps-1). 1996. 3.49 (*1-85854-420-3*) Brimax Bks.
— Teddy's Tail. (You Can Read It Ser.). 24p. (J). (ps-1). 1996. 3.49 (*1-85854-469-6*) Brimax Bks.
— Where Is Giraffe? (You Can Read It Ser.). 24p. (J). (ps-1). 1996. 3.49 (*1-85854-468-8*) Brimax Bks.
Rutherford, R. B. The Art of Plato: Ten Essays in Platonic Interpretation. LC 94-41991. 352p. (C). 1995. 48.95 (*0-674-04811-3*) HUP.
— The Meditations of Marcus Aurelius: A Study. (Oxford Classical Monographs). 300p. 1991. reprint ed. pap. text 35.00 (*0-19-814755-4*) OUP.
Rutherford, R. B., ed. see Homer.
Rutherford, R. B., tr. see Aurelius, Marcus.
Rutherford, Richard. The Death of a Christian: The Order of Christian Funerals. 224p. 1991. pap. 14.95 (*0-8146-6040-1*, Pueblo Bks) Liturgical Pr.
Rutherford, Robert B. Atlas of Vascular Surgery: Basic Techniques & Exposures. (Illus.). 288p. 1993. text 91.00 (*0-7216-2956-3*, W B Saunders Co) Harcrt Hlth Sci Grp.
— Vascular Surgery, 2 Vols. 5th ed. LC 98-52324. 1999. text. write for info. (*0-7216-8078-X*, W B Saunders Co) Harcrt Hlth Sci Grp.
Rutherford, Robert B., ed. Vascular Surgery, 2. 4th ed. LC 93-40051. (Illus.). 2033p. 1995. 260.00 (*0-7216-3837-6*, W B Saunders Co) Harcrt Hlth Sci Grp.
Rutherford, Robert B., jt. auth. see Ouriel, Kenneth.
Rutherford, Robert B., Jr., jt. auth. see Quinn, Mary M.
Rutherford, Robert D. How to Get from No to Go: The Magic of Negotiating Winning Agreements. LC 98-93070. 196p. 1998. pap. 22.50 (*0-9664327-0-3*) Hayden Alxndr.
Rutherford, Ronald K. Complete Guide to Managing a Portfolio of Mutual Funds. LC 97-36926. 300p. 1998. 45.00 (*0-7863-1138-X*, Irwn Prfssnl) McGraw-Hill Prof.
Rutherford, Sally D., jt. auth. see Riphagen, Dean.
Rutherford, Samuel. Letters of Samuel Rutherford. 206p. 1997. reprint ed. pap. 4.99 (*0-85151-163-5*) Banner of Truth.
— Lex Rex. 1992. pap. 19.99 (*0-87377-951-7*) GAM Pubns.
— Loveliness of Christ. 54p. 1990. 3.00 (*1-882840-04-6*) Comm Christian.
***Rutherford, Samuel.** Quaint Sermons. 384p. 1999. 27.95 (*1-57358-101-1*) Soli Deo Gloria.
***Rutherford, Scott.** The American Roller Coaster. (Illus.). 156p. 2000. 29.95 (*0-7603-0689-3*, 129828AP, Pub. by MBI Pubg) Motorbooks Intl.
Rutherford, Scott. On the Move in Japan: Useful Phrases & Common Sense for the Traveler. (JPN.). 176p. 1995. pap. text 8.95 (*4-900737-14-3*, Pub. by Yen Bks) Tuttle Pubng.
Rutherford, Scott, ed. see Featly, John.
Rutherford, Scott, ed. see Stone, Scott C.
***Rutherford, Stuart, ed.** The Poor & Their Money: Essays on Financial Services for Poor People. 100p. 2000. text 10.95 (*0-19-565255-X*) OUP.
Rutherford, Susan. A Study of American Deaf Folklore. (Dissertation Ser.). 156p. (C). 1993. pap. text 19.95 (*0-932130-17-8*, LP304) Linstok Pr.
Rutherford, Todd, ed. see Zeiss, Tony.
Rutherford, Tom A., ed. see Zeiss, Tony.
Rutherford, Ward. Celtic Mythology: The Nature & Influence of Celtic Myth- from Druidism to Arthurian Legend. (Illus.). 160p. (Orig.). 1995. pap. 15.00 (*0-85030-551-9*) Sterling.
Rutherford, William. Second Language Grammar. (C). 1989. pap. text 39.37 (*0-582-55375-X*) Addison-Wesley.
Rutherford, William E. Modern English, Vol. 1. 2nd ed. 349p. (C). 1975. pap. text 14.00 (*0-15-561059-7*) Harcourt Coll Pubs.
Rutherford, William E., ed. Language Universals & Second Language Acquisition. LC 84-9387. (Typological Studies in Language: No. 5). ix, 264p. 1984. pap. 34.95 (*0-915027-10-0*) J Benjamins Pubng Co.
Rutherford, William E., ed. see Celce-Murcia, Marianne & Hilles, Sharon L.
Rutherford, William E., ed. see Silberstein, Sandra.
Rutherford, William G., comment. Phrynichus (Arabius) The New Phrynichus Being a Revised Text of the Ecloga of the Grammarian Phrynichus. xii, 539p. 1968. reprint ed. write for info. (*0-318-72064-7*) G Olms Pubs.
Rutherfurd, Edward. The Forest. LC 00-22219. 598p. 2000. 26.95 (*0-609-60382-5*, Crown) Crown Pub Group.
***Rutherfurd, Edward.** The Forest, Set. abr. ed. 2000. audio 25.00 (*0-375-40960-2*) Random.
Rutherfurd, Edward. London. LC 97-10176. (YA). 1997. 25.95 (*0-517-59181-2*) Crown Pub Group.
— London. 1998. mass mkt. 7.99 (*0-449-00263-2*, Crest) Fawcett.
— Russka: The Novel of Russia. 945p. 1992. mass mkt. 7.99 (*0-8041-0972-9*) Ivy Books.
— Sarum: The Novel of England. 1997. pap. 14.95 (*0-449-00072-9*) Fawcett.
— Sarum: The Novel of England. 1035p. 1992. mass mkt. 7.99 (*0-8041-0298-8*) Ivy Books.
— Sarum: The Novel of England. 1994. 6.99 (*0-09-952730-8*) Random.
— Sarum: The Novel of England. 1993. reprint ed. lib. bdg. 45.95 (*1-56849-114-X*) Buccaneer Bks.
Rutherfurd, Livingston. John Peter Zenger: His Press, His Trial & a Bibliography of Zenger Imprints. LC 77-125713. (American Journalists Ser.). (Illus.). 1971. reprint ed. 26.95 (*0-405-01694-8*) Ayer.
Ruthern, Marlene L. My Bar/Bat Mitzvah. 36p. (YA). 1994. 10.00 (*0-8074-0200-1*, 510000) UAHC.
Ruthrof, Horst. The Body in Language. LC 99-19274. (Illus.). 192p. 1999. 31.95 (*0-304-70580-2*) Continuum.
— Pandora & Occam: On the Limits of Language & Literature. LC 91-26539. (Advances in Semiotics Ser.). (Illus.). 304p. 1992. text 14.95 (*0-253-34995-8*) Ind U Pr.
Ruthstrom. Information System Casebook. Date not set. pap. text, teacher ed. write for info. (*0-314-00740-7*) West Pub.
Ruthstrom, Carl R. & Dykman, Charlene A. Information Systems for Managers: Casebook. Burvikovs, ed. 200p. (C). 1992. pap. text 19.00 (*0-314-00113-1*) West Pub.
Ruthstrom, Stephen. How to Save Thousands of Mortgage Interest Dollars: Six-Easy Methods. (Illus.). 82p. (Orig.). 1995. pap. 14.95 (*0-9650440-0-9*) Home Mortg Sav.
Ruthven, Beverly & Rogers, Sue, eds. Beacham's Desktop Guide to Literature for Intermediate Students. 600p. 1995. lib. bdg. 45.00 (*0-933833-37-7*) Beacham Pub Corp.
Ruthven, D. M. & Farooq, S. Pressure Swing Adsorption. 376p. 1993. 165.00 (*0-471-18818-2*, Wiley-VCH) Wiley.
Ruthven, Douglas M. Principles of Adsorption & Adsorption Processes. LC 83-16904. 464p. 1984. 175.00 (*0-471-86606-7*) Wiley.
Ruthven, Douglas M., ed. Encyclopedia of Separation Technology, 2 Vols. LC 96-46795. 1776p. 1997. 399.00 (*0-471-16124-1*) Wiley.
Ruthven, Douglas M. & Karger, Jorg. Diffusion in Zeolites: And Other Microporous Solids. LC 90-47915. 640p. 1992. 215.00 (*0-471-50907-8*) Wiley.
Ruthven, Douglas M., et al. Pressure Swing Absorption. LC 93-33965. 1993. 95.00 (*1-56081-517-5*, Wiley-VCH) Wiley.
Ruthven, Ian, ed. see British Computer Society Staff.
Ruthven, Ianthe. The Irish Home. LC 98-65889. (Illus.). 176p. 1998. 45.00 (*0-8478-2119-6*, Pub. by Rizzoli Intl) St Martin.
***Ruthven, Ianthe.** The Scottish House: Eclectic & Unique Interiors. 2000. 45.00 (*1-85585-805-3*, Pub. by Collins & Br) Sterling.
Ruthven, John. The Earl of Gowries Conspiracies Against the Kings Majestie of Scotland. LC 76-26080. (English Experience Ser.: No. 182). 1969. reprint ed. 20.00 (*90-221-0182-7*) Walter J Johnson.
Ruthven, John, jt. auth. see Simons, Paul.
Ruthven, Jon. On the Cessation of the Charismata: A Critique of the Protestant Polemic on Postbiblical Miracles. (JPT Supplement Ser.: No. 3). 271p. 1993. pap. 21.95 (*1-85075-405-5*, Pub. by Sheffield Acad) CUP Services.
Ruthven, K. K. Feminist Literary Studies: An Introduction. (Canto Book Ser.). 160p. (C). 1990. pap. 9.95 (*0-521-39852-5*) Cambridge U Pr.

R

— A Guide to Pound's Personae (1926) 291p. 1969. pap. 12.95 (*0-520-04960-8*, Pub. by U CA Pr) Cal Prin Full Svc.

Ruthven, Ken. Nuclear Criticism. (Interpretations Ser.). 144p. (Orig.). 1993. pap. 19.95 (*0-522-84491-X*, Pub. by Melbourne Univ Pr) Paul & Co Pubs.

Ruthven, Ken, ed. see Brewster, Anne.

Ruthven, Kenneth, ed. see NATO Advanced Research Workshop on Mathematics Education.

Ruthven, Leslie, jt. auth. see Goldstein, Gerald.

***Ruthven, Malise.** Islam in the World. 2nd ed. LC 99-56010. (Illus.). 448p. 2000. pap. 18.95 (*0-19-513841-4*) OUP.

Ruthven, Suzanne. Whittlewood. 1997. pap. 14.95 (*0-9522689-2-2*, Pub. by Ignotus Pr) Intl Spec Bk.

Rutigliano, Antonio. Lorenzetti's Golden Mean: The Riformatori of Siena, 1368-1885. LC 91-19614. (American University Studies: History: Ser. IX, Vols. 101). 200p. (C). 1992. text 48.95 (*0-8204-1456-5*) P Lang Pubng.

Rutishauser, Heinz. Lectures on Numerical Mathematics. 568p. 1990. 60.50 (*0-8176-3491-6*) Birkhauser.

Rutishauser, Heinz, et al, eds. Vorlesungen Uber Numerische Mathematik, 2 vols. Incl. Vol. 2. Differentialgleichungen und Eigenwertprobleme. 228p. 1980. 78.00 (*0-8176-0850-8*); (Mathematische Reihe Ser.: Nos. 50 & 57). write for info. (*0-318-51090-1*) Birkhauser.

Rutishauser, Rolf. Blattstellung und Sprossentwicklung bei Bluetenpflanzen unter Besonderer Beruecksichtingung der Nelkengewaechse. (Dissertationes Botanicae Ser.: Vol. 62). (GER., Illus.). 200p. 1981. pap. text 27.50 (*3-7682-1304-8*) Lubrecht & Cramer.

Rutishauser, Sigrid. Physiology & Anatomy: A Basis for Nursing & Health Care. LC 94-27137. (C). 1994. pap. text 39.95 (*0-443-04151-2*) Church.

Rutizer, Barry, jt. auth. see Celi, Louis J.

Rutka, John, et al. Temporal Bone Malignancy: Anatomy, Pathology, & Treatment. LC 94-23526. (Self-Instructional Package Ser.). (Illus.). 73p. (Orig.). 1994. pap. text 25.00 (*1-56772-016-1*) AAO-HNS.

Rutka, M. J. Integrated Sensor Bus. 150p. (Orig.). 1994. pap. 52.50 (*90-6275-966-1*, Pub. by Delft U Pr) Coronet Bks.

Rutkevich, Igor M., jt. auth. see Lagarkov, A. N.

Rutkevich, Igor M., jt. auth. see Lagrakov, Andrei N.

Rutkiewic, jt. ed. see Kuznicki.

Rutkin, A. H. Family Law & Practice, 4 vols. 1985. 800.00 (*0-8205-1371-7*) Bender.

Rutkoff, Peter M., jt. auth. see Scott, William B.

Rutkoff, Peter M., jt. ed. see Hall, Alvin D.

Rutkoski, Thomas. Apostles of the Last Days: The Fruits of Medjugorje. (Illus.). 285p. (Orig.). 1992. pap. 10.00 (*0-9633667-7-7*) Gospa Missions.

Rutkosky, Nita H. Corel Wordperfect 7. LC 96-37497. 1997. write for info. (*1-56118-919-7*) Paradigm MN.

— Corel WordPerfect 7. LC 96-37497. 1997. pap. write for info. (*1-56118-920-0*) Paradigm MN.

— Corel WordPerfect 8. LC 97-38548. 1998. 44.00 (*0-7638-0134-8*); 44.00 (*0-7638-0135-6*) Paradigm MN.

— Mastery Approach to Microsoft Word, Version 5.0. 446p. (C). 1990. pap. text 32.95 (*1-56118-109-9*) Paradigm MN.

— Mastery Approach to Microsoft Word, Version 5.0. 352p. (C). 1990. pap. text, teacher ed. 19.00 (*1-56118-108-0*) Paradigm MN.

— Mastery Approach to Microsoft Word, Version 5.0: Short Course. 208p. 1990. text 22.95 (*1-56118-112-9*) Paradigm MN.

— Mastery Approach to WordPerfect for Windows, Version 5.1. 688p. 1993. pap. text 33.95 (*1-56118-469-1*) Paradigm MN.

— Mastery Approach to WordPerfect for Windows, Version 5.1: Short Course. 348p. 1993. pap. text 22.95 (*1-56118-470-5*) Paradigm MN.

— Mastery Approach to WordPerfect for Windows, Version 5.2. LC 93-48952. 720p. 1993. pap. text 33.95 (*1-56118-650-3*) Paradigm MN.

— Mastery Approach to WordPerfect for Windows, Version 5.2. 720p. 1993. pap. text, teacher ed. 19.00 (*1-56118-651-1*) Paradigm MN.

— Mastery Approach to WordPerfect, Version 5.0: Short Course. 208p. (C). 1990. pap. text 17.80 (*1-56118-077-7*) Paradigm MN.

— Mastery Approach to WordPerfect, Version 5.0: Short Course. 208p. (C). 1990. pap. text, teacher ed. 7.10 (*1-56118-078-5*) Paradigm MN.

— Mastery Approach to WordPerfect, Version 5.0 with 5.1 Update. 587p. (C). 1989. pap. text 27.95 (*1-56118-075-0*) Paradigm MN.

— Mastery Approach to WordPerfect, Version 5.0 with 5.1 Update. 587p. (C). 1989. teacher ed. 19.00 (*1-56118-076-9*) Paradigm MN.

— Mastery Approach to WordPerfect, Version 5.1. 600p. (C). 1991. teacher ed. 19.00 (*1-56118-083-1*); pap. text 32.95 (*1-56118-082-3*) Paradigm MN.

— Microsoft Excel 97. LC 97-20570. 1997. write for info. (*0-7638-0089-9*); pap. write for info. (*0-7638-0090-2*) Paradigm MN.

Rutkosky, Nita H. Microsoft Office 97 Professional: Instructor's Guide. 24.00 (*0-7638-0066-X*) EMC-Paradigm.

Rutkosky, Nita H. Microsoft Office Professional: Version 7. LC 96-39680. 1997. write for info. (*0-7638-0001-5*) Paradigm.

Rutkosky, Nita H. Microsoft Office Professional, Version 7: Instructor's Guide. 460p. 24.00 (*0-7638-0002-3*) EMC-Paradigm.

Rutkosky, Nita H. Microsoft Office 2000. LC 99-10805. 2000. text. write for info. (*0-7638-0255-7*) Paradigm MN.

Rutkosky, Nita H. Microsoft Office 2000: Instructor's Guide, CD Rom Package. 69.00 incl. cd-rom (*0-7638-0256-5*) EMC-Paradigm.

— Microsoft Powerpoint 2000: Core Certification LC 99-35151. (Benchmark Ser.). 1999. write for info. (*0-7638-0336-7*) Paradigm MN.

Rutkosky, Nita H. Microsoft Word 97. LC 97-20994. 1997. write for info. (*0-7638-0094-5*); pap. write for info. (*0-7638-0095-3*) Paradigm MN.

Rutkosky, Nita H. Microsoft Word 97: Instructor's Guide. 24.00 (*0-7638-0071-6*) EMC-Paradigm.

— Microsoft Word 7: Instructor's Guide. 24.00 (*1-56118-890-5*) EMC-Paradigm.

— Microsoft Word 7 Essentials: Instructor's Guide. 24.00 (*1-56118-894-8*) EMC-Paradigm.

— MICROSOFT WORD7 ESS WIND95 3.5 TXT: Text with Data Disk, 3.5. 425p. text 36.95 incl. 3.5 hd (*1-56118-893-X*) EMC-Paradigm.

Rutkosky, Nita H. Microsoft Word 7 for Windows 95: Essentials. LC 96-10898. 1996. pap. text 31.95 (*1-56118-892-1*) Paradigm MN.

— Microsoft Word 6.0 for Windows. LC 94-5236. 1995. pap. text 38.95 (*1-56118-738-0*) Paradigm MN.

— Microsoft Word 6.0 for Windows: Text with disk, 3.5. LC 94-5236. 1994. pap. text 38.95 (*1-56118-732-1*) Paradigm MN.

Rutkosky, Nita H. Microsoft Word 2000: Instructor's Guide, CD Rom Package. 848p. 78.95 (*0-7638-0251-4*) EMC-Paradigm.

— Microsoft Word 2000 Essentials. LC 99-37718. (Signature Ser.). 2000. text. write for info. (*0-7638-0278-6*) Paradigm MN.

— Microsoft Word 2000 Essentials: Text with CD ROM. 568p. 69.00 (*0-7638-0279-4*) EMC-Paradigm.

Rutkosky, Nita H. Microsoft Word 7 for Windows 95. LC 96-13304. 1996. pap. text. write for info. (*1-56118-888-3*); pap. text. write for info. (*1-56118-889-1*) Paradigm MN.

— Nita Hewitt Rutkosky's WordPerfect 6.0 for Windows. LC 94-9731. 1994. pap. text 35.95 (*1-56118-685-6*) Paradigm MN.

— Nita Hewitt Rutkosky's WordPerfect 6.0 for Windows. 1994. pap. text 19.00 (*1-56118-687-2*) Paradigm MN.

— Nita Hewitt Rutkosky's WordPerfect Version 6.0 for DOS Essentials. LC 94-15026. 1994. pap. text 24.95 (*1-56118-737-2*) Paradigm MN.

— WordPerfect Essentials: Version 6.0 for DOS. 368p. 1994. text 26.95 incl. 5.25 hd (*1-56118-750-X*) Paradigm MN.

— WordPerfect Essentials: Version 6.0 for DOS. 368p. 1994. pap. text 19.00 (*1-56118-727-5*) Paradigm MN.

— WordPerfect Essentials: Version 6.0 for DOS. 5th ed. 368p. 1994. pap. text 26.95 (*1-56118-728-3*) Paradigm MN.

— WordPerfect Essentials: 6.1 for Windows. LC 95-21963. 1995. pap. text 25.95 (*1-56118-795-X*) Paradigm MN.

Rutkosky, Nita H. WordPerfect 9: Instructor's Guide, CD Rom Package. 69.00 incl. cd-rom (*0-7638-0261-1*) EMC-Paradigm.

— WordPerfect 7: Instructor's Guide. 24.00 (*1-56118-921-9*) EMC-Paradigm.

Rutkosky, Nita H. WordPerfect 6.1 for Windows. LC 95-11473. 1995. 35.95 (*1-56118-833-6*) Paradigm MN.

Rutkosky, Nita H. WordPerfect 6.1 for Windows: Instructor's Guide. 24.00 (*1-56118-836-0*) EMC-Paradigm.

— WordPerfect 6.1 for Windows: Essentials: Instructor's Guide. 19.00 (*1-56118-798-4*) EMC-Paradigm.

— WordPerfect 6.1 for Windows: Essentials: Text with Data Disk, 3.5. 392p. 35.95 (*1-56118-796-8*) EMC-Paradigm.

Rutkosky, Nita H. & Arford, Joanne Marschke. Advanced Microsoft Word 97: Desktop Publishing: Instructor's Guide. 24.00 (*0-7638-0107-0*) EMC-Paradigm.

Rutkosky, Nita H. & Bruns, Cheryl L. Mastery Approach to Microsoft Word Version 5.5. 544p. 1993. pap. text 32.95 (*1-56118-464-0*) Paradigm MN.

— Mastery Approach to Microsoft Word, Version 5.5: Short Course. 256p. 1993. pap. text 22.95 (*1-56118-465-9*) Paradigm MN.

— Mastery Approach to Microsoft Word 2.0 for Windows. 608p. 1993. text 33.95 (*1-56118-489-6*) Paradigm MN.

— Mastery Approach to Microsoft Word 2.0 for Windows: Short Course. 300p. 1993. text 22.95 (*1-56118-490-X*) Paradigm MN.

Rutkosky, Nita H. & Ebert, Dineen K. Advanced WordPerfect 6.0: Desktop Publishing. 1995. pap. text 14.00 (*1-56118-714-3*) Paradigm MN.

— Advanced WordPerfect 6.0: Desktop Publishing. 5th ed. 384p. 1994. pap. text 35.95 (*1-56118-712-7*) Paradigm MN.

— Nita Hewitt Rutkosky's Advanced WordPerfect Desktop Publishing: Version 6.0 for DOS. LC 94-43778. 1994. pap. text 32.95 (*1-56118-711-9*) Paradigm MN.

***Rutkosky, Nita H. & Flynn, Meredith.** Microsoft Access 2000. LC 99-35407. (Benchmark Ser.). 1999. text 64.20 (*0-7638-0240-9*) Paradigm MN.

Rutkosky, Nita H. & Yasui, Holly. A Mastery Approach to Advanced WordPerfect Version 5.1, Desktop Publishing. (C). 1991. pap. text 31.95 (*1-56118-425-X*); pap. text, teacher ed. 14.00 (*1-56118-373-3*) Paradigm MN.

Rutkosky, Nita H., et al. Advanced Microsoft Word 7: Desktop Publishing. LC 96-25140. 1996. pap. text. write for info. (*1-56118-901-4*); pap. text. write for info. (*1-56118-902-2*) Paradigm MN.

— Advanced Microsoft Word '97 Desktop Publishing. LC 97-40893. 1998. spiral bd. 41.00 (*0-7638-0105-4*) Paradigm MN.

— Advanced Microsoft Word '97 Desktop Publishing. LC 97-40893. 1998. spiral bd. 41.00 (*0-7638-0106-2*) Paradigm MN.

Rutkosky, Nita H., et al. Advanced WordPerfect: Desktop Publishing 6.1 for Windows. teacher ed. 24.00 (*1-56118-784-4*) EMC-Paradigm.

Rutkosky, Nita H., et al. Advanced WordPerfect: Desktop Publishing 6.1 for Windows. LC 95-24393. 1995. pap. text 35.95 (*1-56118-782-8*) Paradigm MN.

Rutkosky, Nita H., jt. auth. see Flynn, Meredith.

***Rutkosky, Nita Hewitt.** Microsoft Excel 2000. LC 99-32175. (Benchmark Ser.). 1999. write for info. (*0-7638-0332-4*) Paradigm MN.

— Microsoft Word 2000: Expert Certification LC 99-35240. (Benchmark Ser.). 1999. write for info. (*0-7638-0342-1*) Paradigm MN.

— Microsoft Word 2000. LC 99-31328. 2000. text. write for info. incl. cd-rom (*0-7638-0250-6*) Paradigm MN.

— NITA HEWITT RUTKOSKY'S WORDPERFECT 6.0 FOR DOS: Textbook with disk, 3.5. text 43.95 (*1-56118-641-4*) EMC-Paradigm.

— WordPerfect 6.1 for Windows: Text with data disk, 3.5. 682p. 42.95 incl. 3.5 hd (*1-56118-834-4*) EMC-Paradigm.

— NITA HEWITT RUTKOSKY'S WORDPERFECT 6.0 FOR WINDOWS: Text with data disk, 3.5. 752p. text 43.95 (*1-56118-688-0*) EMC-Paradigm.

***Rutkosky, Nita Hewitt & Seguin, Denise.** Microsoft Access 2000. LC 99-57581. (Marquee Ser.). 2000. write for info. (*0-7638-0368-5*) Paradigm MN.

— Microsoft PowerPoint 2000. LC 99-57582. (Marquee Ser.). 2000. write for info. (*0-7638-0369-3*) Paradigm MN.

Rutkosky, Nita Hewitt, et al. Advanced Microsoft Word 7: Desktop Publishing for Windows Instructor's guide. text, teacher ed. 24.00 (*1-56118-903-0*) EMC-Paradigm.

Rutkovsky, Paul. Commodity Character. LC 82-51222. (Artists' Books Ser.). 72p. (Orig.). 1982. pap. 8.95 (*0-89822-030-0*) Visual Studies.

— I Am, Siam. LC 85-50043. (Artists' Books Ser.). (Illus.). 72p. (Orig.). 1985. pap. 8.95 (*0-89822-038-6*) Visual Studies.

Rutkovsky-Ruskin, Mary. The Nighttime Quests of Irwin Botski. 18p. (Orig.). 1994. pap. text 8.95 (*1-885902-02-6*) Printable Arts.

Rutkow, Ira M. American Surgery: An Illustrated History. LC 97-17654. (Illus.). 611p. 1997. text 79.00 (*0-316-76352-7*) Lppncott W & W.

— History of Surgery in the United States 1775-1900 Vol. II: Periodical & Pamphlet Literature. (Bibliography & Surgery Ser.: Nos. 5 & 4). (Illus.). 434p. 1992. 175.00 (*0-930405-48-X*) Norman SF.

— The History of Surgery in the United States 1775-1990 Vol. I: Textbooks, Monographs, & Treatises. LC 87-62662. (Bibliography & Surgery Ser.: No. 2). (Illus.). 514p. 1988. 145.00 (*0-930405-02-1*) Norman SF.

— Surgery: An Illustrated History. LC 93-9820. (Illus.). 560p. (C). (gr. 13). 1993. text 135.00 (*0-8016-6078-5*, 06078) Mosby Inc.

Rutkow, Ira M., jt. intro. see Moore, Samuel P.

Rutkowski. Digital Electronics Applications. (Electronics Technology Ser.). 1996. teacher ed. 14.00 (*0-8273-6438-5*); text 58.95 (*0-8273-6437-7*) Delmar.

Rutkowski, Anthony M. Integrated Services Digital Networks. LC 84-73277. (Artech House Telecommunications Library). (Illus.). 348p. 1985. reprint ed. pap. 107.90 (*0-7837-9692-7*, 206042200005) Bks Demand.

Rutkowski, Anthony M., jt. auth. see Codding, George A.

Rutkowski, Bogdan. Cult Places in the Aegean. LC 85-40469. (Illus.). 320p. 1986. 62.00 (*0-300-02962-4*) Yale U Pr.

Rutkowski, George B. Basic Electricity for Electronics: A Text Laboratory Manual. 323p. (Orig.). (C). 1984. pap. text. write for info. (*0-672-98488-1*); write for info. (*0-672-98489-X*) Macmillan.

— Integrated-Circuit Operational Amplifiers. 2nd ed. (Illus.). 320p. (C). 1984. text 52.00 (*0-13-469007-9*) P-H.

— Operational Amplifiers, Integrated & Hybrid Circuits. LC 92-20592. 357p. 1993. 135.00 (*0-471-57718-9*) Wiley.

— Solid-State Electronics. LC 77-131132. 1972. 17.90 (*0-672-20801-6*, Bobbs) Macmillan.

— Solid-State Electronics. 4th ed. LC 91-43358. 104.25 (*0-02-800665-8*) Glencoe.

Rutkowski, George B. Solid-State Electronics. 4th ed. 64p. 1992. teacher ed. 10.20 (*0-02-800667-4*) Glencoe.

Rutkowski, George B., jt. auth. see Olesky, J.

Rutkowski, Hank. Air Distribution Basics for Residential & Small Commerical Buildings, Manual T. (Illus.). 85p. Date not set. pap. 34.00 (*1-892765-06-3*) Air Conditioning Cont.

— Comfort Air Quality, & Efficiency by Design Manual RS: The Whole House. (Illus.). 176p. Date not set. pap. 70.00 (*1-892765-04-7*) Air Conditioning Cont.

— Commercial Load Calculation, Manual N. 4th ed. 119p. 1988. pap. 38.00 (*1-892765-11-X*) Air Conditioning Cont.

— Commercial Low Pressure, Low Velocity Duct System Design, Manual Q. (Illus.). 316p. Date not set. pap. 68.00 (*1-892765-02-0*) Air Conditioning Cont.

— Commerical Applications, Systems, & Equipment, Manual CS. (Illus.). 380p. Date not set. pap. 68.00 (*1-892765-05-5*) Air Conditioning Cont.

— Heat Pump Systems, Principles & Applications, Manual H. 2nd ed. (Illus.). 69p. Date not set. pap. 38.00 (*1-892765-07-1*) Air Conditioning Cont.

— Psychrometrics Manual P: Theory & Applications. (Illus.). 55p. Date not set. pap. 38.00 (*1-892765-08-X*) Air Conditioning Cont.

— Residential Duct Systems, Manual D. 2nd ed. (Illus.). 298p. Date not set. pap. 44.00 (*1-892765-00-4*) Air Conditioning Cont.

— Residential Equipment Selections, Manual S. 2nd ed. (Illus.). 115p. Date not set. pap. 46.00 (*1-892765-03-9*) Air Conditioning Cont.

— Residential Load Calculation, Manual J. 7th ed. (Illus.). 126p. Date not set. pap. 45.00 (*1-892765-01-2*) Air Conditioning Cont.

Rutkowski, Hank. Selection of Distribution Systems, Manual G. 23p. Date not set. pap. 23.00 (*1-892765-12-8*) Air Conditioning Cont.

Rutkowski, Hank. What Makes a Good Air Conditioning System?, Manual C. (Illus.). 40p. Date not set. pap. 22.00 (*1-892765-13-6*) Air Conditioning Cont.

Rutkowski, Hank, ed. Installation Techniques for Perimeter Heating & Cooling, Manual 4. 11th ed. (Illus.). 21p. Date not set. pap. 23.00 (*1-892765-09-8*) Air Conditioning Cont.

Rutkowski, Jan J. Changes in the Wage Structure During Economic Transition in Central & Eastern Europe. LC 96-34973. (Technical Papers: No. 340). 72p. 1996. pap. 22.00 (*0-8213-3750-5*) World Bank.

— Welfare & the Labor Market in Poland: Social Policy During Economic Transition. LC 98-27896. (Technical Paper Ser.: No. 417). 111p. 1998. pap. 22.00 (*0-8213-4318-1*, 14318) World Bank.

Rutkowski, Jaroslaw, jt. ed. see Rogalski, Antoni.

Rutkowski, Joanne & Runfola, Maria, compiled by. Tips: The Child Voice. 44p. 1997. pap. 8.50 (*1-56545-105-8*) MENC.

***Rutkowski, Johnnie.** Indian Legends. 2000. pap. 6.95 (*1-56794-207-5*) Star Bible.

Rutkowski, Kenneth M., ed. Happy Between Relationships: How You Can Be Very Happy When Not Involved with a Partner for 1 Hour or 10 Years. LC 98-65324. 260p. 1999. pap. 14.95 (*0-9662933-3-9*) McAlpine Pr.

Rutkowski, Marek, jt. auth. see Musiela, Merek.

Rutkowski, Nancy B. Holiday Blessings in Poem & More. 1997. pap. 56.95 (*1-57553-623-4*) Watermrk Pr.

Rutkowski, Thaddeus. Basic Training. Bixby, Robert, ed. LC 97-157248. 40p. 1996. pap. 6.00 (*1-882983-29-7*) March Street Pr.

— Roughhouse. 176p. 1999. pap. 10.95 (*1-885030-26-6*) Kaya Prod.

— Sex-Fiend Monologues. 33p. 1994. pap., per. 4.00 (*1-886206-11-2*) Venom Pr.

Rutland. Abracadabra Clarinet Repertoire. 32p. (J). (gr. k-3). 1998. pap. 9.95 (*0-7136-3332-8*, Pub. by A & C Blk) Midpt Trade.

— The Wedding Trap. 1998. per. 3.25 (*0-373-15736-3*) Harlequin Bks.

Rutland, Anne S., ed. see Zunz, Edward A., Jr. & Kraus, Alan E.

Rutland, David. Behind the Front Panel: The Design & Development of 1920's Radios. LC 94-60507. (Illus.). 186p. (Orig.). 1994. pap. 18.95 (*1-885391-00-5*) Wren Pubs.

— Why Computers Are Computers: A Personal Account of How an Early Computer Was Like Today's PC. LC 94-62225. 208p. 1995. 24.95 (*1-885391-05-6*) Wren Pubs.

Rutland, David W. Manual for Determining Physical Properties of Fertilizer. 2nd ed. LC 93-3133. (Reference Manual Ser.: No. R-10). (Illus.). 115p. (Orig.). 1993. pap. text 30.00 (*0-88090-101-2*) Intl Fertilizer.

***Rutland, Eva.** Almost a Wife. (Romance Ser.: Vol. 3621). 2000. mass mkt. 3.50 (*0-373-03621-3*, 1-03621-9) Harlequin Bks.

— Almost a Wife. large type ed. (Large Print Ser.: Vol. 467). 2000. mass mkt. 3.50 (*0-373-15867-X*, Harlequin) Harlequin Bks.

Rutland, Eva. A Child's Christmas. (Superromance Ser.: No. 769). 1997. per. 3.99 (*0-373-70769-X*, 1-70769-4) Harlequin Bks.

— Foreign Affair. (Romance Ser.). 1993. per. 2.99 (*0-373-03283-8*, 1-03283-8) Harlequin Bks.

— Fugue en Robe Blanche. (Horizon Ser.: Vol. 468). (FRE.). 1998. mass mkt. 3.50 (*0-373-39468-3*, 1-39468-3) Harlequin Bks.

***Rutland, Eva.** Her Own Prince Charming. 1999. per. 3.50 (*0-373-03550-0*, 1-03550-0, Harlequin) Harlequin Bks.

Rutland, Eva. Heritier par Amour. (Horizon Ser.: Vol. 503). (FRE.). 1999. mass mkt. 3.50 (*0-373-39503-5*, 1-39503-7) Harlequin Bks.

— Un Hombre en Casa: Foreign Affair. (SPA.). 1997. per. 3.50 (*0-373-33396-X*, 1-33396-2) Harlequin Bks.

— Marriage Bait. 1997. per. 3.25 (*0-373-03439-3*, 1-03439-6) Silhouette.

— Marriage Bait. large type ed. (Simply the Best Ser.). 1997. per. 3.25 (*0-373-15685-5*) Harlequin Bks.

— The Million-Dollar Marriage: Whirlwind Weddings. (Romance Ser.: Vol. 3518). 1998. per. 3.50 (*0-373-03518-7*, 1-03518-7) Harlequin Bks.

— The Million-Dollar Marriage: Whirlwind Weddings. large type ed. (Larger Print Ser.: Vol. 364). 1998. per. 3.50 (*0-373-15764-9*, 1-15764-3) Harlequin Bks.

— Miradas Ardientes: Burning Look, Vol. 419. (Harlequin Bianca Ser.). (SPA.). 1997. per. 3.50 (*0-373-33419-2*, 1-33419-2) Harlequin Bks.

***Rutland, Eva.** No Crystal Stair. 480p. 2000. per. 5.99 (*1-55166-519-0*, 1-66519-9, Mira Bks) Harlequin Bks.

Rutland, Eva. Private Dancer. (Romance Ser.). 1996. per. 3.25 (*0-373-03412-1*, 1-03412-3) Harlequin Bks.

— Private Dancer. large type ed. (Mills & Boon Large Print Ser.). 288p. 1996. 23.99 (*0-263-14580-8*, Pub. by Mills & Boon) Ulverscroft.

— The Wedding Trap. (Romance Ser.: No. 3490). 1998. per. 3.25 (*0-373-03490-3*, 1-03490-9) Harlequin Bks.

Rutland, John H. Rutland Papers Original Documents Illustrative of the Courts & Times of Henry Seven & Henry Eight. Jerden, William, ed. LC 17-1204. (Camden Society, London. Publications, First Ser.: No. 21). reprint ed. 35.00 (*0-404-50121-4*) AMS Pr.

An Asterisk (*) at the beginning of an entry indicates that the title is appearing for the first time.

Rutland, Jonathan. Abracadabra Clarinet: Way to Learn. 64p. (J). (gr. k-3). 1998. pap. 7.95 (*0-7136-5619-0*, Pub. by A & C Blk) Midpt Trade.
— Abracadabra Saxophone. 64p. (J). (gr. k-3). 1998. pap. 10.95 (*0-7136-3661-0*, Pub. by A & C Blk) Midpt Trade.
Rutland, Julia Dowling, jt. auth. see Dosier, Susan.
Rutland, Marion. Teaching Food Technology in Secondary School. LC 97-152645. (Roehampton Teaching Studies). 144p. 1996. pap. 24.95 (*1-85346-426-0*, Pub. by David Fulton) Taylor & Francis.
***Rutland, Mark.** God of the Valleys: Heaven's High Purpose for Your Lowest Times. 220p. 2000. pap. 11.99 (*1-56955-175-8*) Servant.
Rutland, Mark. Streams of Mercy: Receiving & Reflecting God's Grace. LC 98-32193. (Illus.). 1999. pap. 10.99 (*0-89283-998-8*) Servant.
Rutland, Peter. The Politics of Economic Stagnation in the Soviet Union: The Role of Local Political Organs in Economic Management. (Cambridge Russian, Soviet & Post-Soviet Studies: No. 88). (Illus.). 320p. (C). 1992. text 69.95 (*0-521-39241-1*) Cambridge U Pr.
Rutland, Peter, ed. Business & the State in Contemporary Russia. (John M. Olin Critical Issues Ser.). 256p. 1999. 60.00 (*0-8133-3656-2*) Westview.
Rutland, Peter, ed. see EastWest Institute (EWI) Staff.
Rutland, Peter, ed. & intro. see EastWest Institute Staff.
Rutland, Robert A. A Boyhood in the Dust Bowl, 1926-1934. (Illus.). 144p. 1995. 22.50 (*0-87081-416-8*) Univ Pr Colo.
— A Boyhood in the Dust Bowl, 1926-1934. LC 97-23463. 152p. 1997. pap. 17.50 (*0-87081-485-0*) Univ Pr Colo.
— The Democrats: From Jefferson to Clinton. rev. ed. LC 95-21252. (Illus.). 304p. (C). 1995. pap. 19.95 (*0-8262-1034-1*) U of Mo Pr.
— The First Great Newspaper Debate: The Constitutional Crisis of 1787-88. 20p. (C). 1987. reprint ed. pap. 4.00 (*0-912296-97-6*) Am Antiquarian.
Rutland, Robert A. George Mason: Reluctant Statesman. LC 79-24328. xvi, 128p. 1980. pap. 10.95 (*0-8071-0696-8*) La State U Pr.
Rutland, Robert A. James Madison: The Founding Father. LC 97-20591. (Illus.). 312p. 1997. pap. 19.95 (*0-8262-1141-0*) U of Mo Pr.
— James Madison & the American Nation, 1751-1836: An Encyclopedia. LC 94-12322. 1995. 100.00 (*0-13-508425-3*) S&S Trade.
— James Madison & the Search for Nationhood. LC 81-607967. (Illus.). 174p. 1981. 18.00 (*0-8444-0363-6*, 030-000-00133-8) Lib Congress.
— The Ordeal of the Constitution: The Anti-Federalists & the Ratification Struggle of 1787-1788. LC 83-19295. 342p. 1983. reprint ed. pap. text 17.95 (*0-930350-50-2*) NE U Pr.
— The Presidency of James Madison. LC 89-70419. (American Presidency Ser.). xiv, 234p. 1990. 29.95 (*0-7006-0465-0*) U Pr of KS.
— The Republicans: From Lincoln to Bush. LC 96-23180. (Illus.). 296p. (C). 1996. pap. 19.95 (*0-8262-1090-2*) U of Mo Pr.
— Well Acquainted with Books: The Founding Framers of 1787: With James Madison's List of Books for Congress. LC 87-2805. 95p. 1987. 6.95 (*0-8444-0561-2*) Lib Congress.
Rutland, Robert A., ed. see Madison, James.
Rutland, Robert A., ed. see Mason, George.
***Rutland, Robert Allen.** Clio's Favorites: Leading Historians of the U. S., 1945-2000. 216p. 2000. 29.95 (*0-8262-1316-2*) U of Mo Pr.
***Rutledge.** Macromolecular Symposia 133: Molecular Modeling of Polymers. 120p. 1999. 69.95 (*3-527-29801-0*) Wiley.
Rutledge, Aaron L. & Gass, Gertrude Z. Nineteen Negro Men: Personality & Manpower Retraining. LC 67-13277. (Jossey-Bass Social & Behavioral Science Ser.). 228p. reprint ed. 70.70 (*0-8357-9341-9*, 201383100088) Bks Demand.
Rutledge, Adam. Sons of Liberty. large type ed. (General Ser.). 318p. 1992. pap. 16.95 (*0-8161-5495-3*, G K Hall Lrg Type) Mac Lib Ref.
Rutledge, Albert & Molnar, Donald J. Anatomy of a Park: The Essentials of Recreation Area Planning & Design. 2nd ed. (Illus.). 189p. (C). 1992. reprint ed. text 32.95 (*0-88133-699-8*) Waveland Pr.
Rutledge, Archibald. Bird Dog Days, Wingshooting Ways. Casada, Jim, ed. LC 98-28769. (Illus.). 192p. 1998. 35.00 (*1-885106-68-8*) Wild Adven Pr.
— Home by the River. LC 88-18532. 1983. reprint ed. 16.95 (*0-87844-003-8*) Sandlapper Pub Co.
— Hunting & Home in the Southern Heartland: The Best of Archibald Rutledge. Casada, Jim, ed. LC 91-43713. 274p. 1992. 24.95 (*0-87249-822-0*) U of SC Pr.
— Life's Extras. 2nd ed. (Illus.). 56p. 1987. reprint ed. 8.95 (*0-87844-080-1*) Sandlapper Pub Co.
— Tales of Whitetails: Archibald Rutledge's Great Deer-Hunting Stories. Casada, Jim, ed. LC 92-20100. 290p. 1992. 24.95 (*0-87249-860-3*) U of SC Pr.
— Tom & I on the Old Plantation. LC 72-4643. (Black Heritage Library Collection). (Illus.). 1977. reprint ed. 18.95 (*0-8369-9124-9*) Ayer.
Rutledge, Archibald H., jt. ed. see Casada, Jim.
Rutledge, Carol, jt. auth. see Rieck, Sondra.
Rutledge, Carol B. Dying & Living on the Kansas Prairie: A Diary. LC 94-13492. 176p. 1994. 15.95 (*0-7006-0649-1*) U Pr of KS.
***Rutledge, Cynthia.** Undercover Angel. (Love Inspired Ser.). 2000. mass mkt. 4.50 (*0-373-87129-5*, 1871292) Harlequin Bks.
— Unforgettable Faith. (Love Inspired Ser.: Vol. 102). 2000. per. 4.50 (*0-373-87108-2*) Harlequin Bks.
Rutledge, D. N., ed. Signal Treatment & Signal Analysis in NMR. (Data Handling in Science & Technology Ser.: Vol. 18). 566p. 1996. text 324.25 (*0-444-81986-X*) Elsevier.
Rutledge, David. The Electronics of Radio. LC 98-39967. (Illus.). 448p. (C). 1999. text 100.00 (*0-521-64136-5*); pap. text 44.95 (*0-521-64645-6*) Cambridge U Pr.
Rutledge, David. Reading Marginally: Feminism, Deconstruction & the Bible. Vol. 21. (Illus.). X, 234p. 1996. text 84.00 (*90-04-10564-6*) Brill Academic Pubs.
Rutledge, David W. Humans & the Earth: Toward a Personal Ecology. LC 93-18800. XIV, 210p. 1993. 39.95 (*0-8204-2212-6*) P Lang Pubng.
Rutledge, Devallis. Courtroom Survival: The Officer's Guide to Better Testimony. 2nd ed. LC 87-70528. (Illus.). 188p. (C). 1998. reprint ed. pap. 14.95 (*0-942728-15-7*) Copperhouse.
— Criminal Interrogation: Law & Tactics. 3rd ed. LC 86-71973. (Illus.). 167p. (C). 1997. pap. 19.95 (*0-942728-62-9*) Copperhouse.
***Rutledge, Devallis.** Criminal Procedure, California. 4th ed. 369p. 2000. pap. 31.95 (*0-942728-97-1*) Copperhouse.
Rutledge, Devallis. The New Police Report Manual. 4th ed. LC 84-70351. (Illus.). 172p. (C). 1996. pap. 14.95 (*0-942728-12-2*) Copperhouse.
— The Officer Survival Manual. 2nd ed. (Illus.). 351p. (C). 1988. pap. 19.95 (*0-942728-36-X*) Copperhouse.
***Rutledge, Devallis.** The Search & Seizure Handbook. 6th ed. LC 95-72123. (Illus.). 195p. 1999. pap. 19.95 (*0-942728-95-5*) Copperhouse.
Rutledge, Don, jt. auth. see Rankin, Jerry.
Rutledge, Don, jt. auth. see Robinson, Rita.
Rutledge, Douglas F., ed. Ceremony & Text in the Renaissance. LC 95-41393. (Illus.). 240p. (C). 1996. 36.50 (*0-87413-573-7*) U Delaware Pr.
Rutledge, Fleming. The Bible & the New York Times. 243p. 1999. pap. 15.00 (*0-8028-4701-3*) Eerdmans.
Rutledge, Fleming. Condemned into Redemption: The Meaning of the Crucifixion of Jesus for Today's World. write for info. (*0-8028-3890-1*) Eerdmans.
— Help My Unbelief. 256p. 2000. 22.00 (*0-8028-3895-2*) Eerdmans.
***Rutledge, Gene P.** Prudhoe Bay, Discovery to Recovery! LC 98-60598. 1998. write for info. (*0-932571-03-4*) Wolfe Business Services.
Rutledge, H. L. To Be Mature. LC 74-76988. 250p. 1974. reprint ed. pap. 5.00 (*0-914520-03-2*) Insight Pr.
***Rutledge Hill Press Staff.** Christmas Photograph Album. (Illus.). 1999. write for info. (*1-55853-699-X*) Rutledge Hill Pr.
— Large Horizontal Country Cottage Collection Photo Album. (Montague House Photograph Albums Ser.). (Illus.). 1999. write for info. (*1-55853-634-5*) Rutledge Hill Pr.
— Large Vertical Country Cottage Collection Photo Album. (Montague House Photograph Albums Ser.). (Illus.). 1999. write for info. (*1-55853-635-3*) Rutledge Hill Pr.
— Large Vertical Floral Victorian Design Photo Album. (Montague House Photograph Albums Ser.). (Illus.). 1999. write for info. (*1-55853-508-X*) Rutledge Hill Pr.
Rutledge Hill Press Staff. Our Family History & Album Waterlane Edition, 2 vols. 1999. boxed set 19.99 (*1-55853-708-2*) Rutledge Hill Pr.
***Rutledge Hill Press Staff.** Plaid Tidings to You Floor Display. 1999. pap. text. write for info. (*1-55853-723-6*) Rutledge Hill Pr.
— Small Horizontal Floral Victorian Design Photo Album. (Illus.). 1999. write for info. (*1-55853-507-1*) Rutledge Hill Pr.
— Small Vertical Floral Victorian Design Photo Album. (Montague House Photograph Albums Ser.). (Illus.). 1999. write for info. (*1-55853-506-3*) Rutledge Hill Pr.
Rutledge Hill Press Staff, ed. Seventies Party. 1999. pap. 14.95 (*1-55853-764-3*) Rutledge Hill Pr.
Rutledge, J. D., ed. see Cameron, Chris & Ledford, Cawood.
Rutledge, J. D., jt. ed. see Henderson, Pay.
Rutledge, Jennifer M. Building Board Diversity. 50p. 1994. 19.00 (*0-925299-40-5*) Natl Ctr Nonprofit.
Rutledge, John. A Cracker Crumbles. (Illus.). 40p. 1996. pap. 7.99 (*0-9665521-0-5*) Dead End St.
Rutledge, John, ed. see Hardin, Valerie.
Rutledge, Katherine B. Le Bon Temps. 88p. 1982. pap. 4.95 (*0-9608282-0-6*) YWCO.
Rutledge, Keith. The Business Case for Java. (Illus.). 178p. (Orig.). 1999. pap. 24.95 (*0-9663375-3-0*) AS-Four Hundr Pr.
Rutledge, L. Hytime: A Standard for Hypermedia Document Systems. 1995. 59.00 (*0-387-58260-6*) Spr-Verlag.
Rutledge, L. & Buford, J. F. HyTime: A Standard for Hypermedia Document Systems. (Illus.). 350p. 1997. 59.00 (*3-540-58260-6*) Spr-Verlag.
Rutledge, Larry. Tomes of Delphi: WIN32 Graphics Programming. 1999. pap. 49.95 (*1-55622-722-1*) Wordware Pub.
Rutledge, Lee A. Campaign Clothing: Field Uniforms of the Indian War Army 1866-1871. (Military Collectors Guide Ser.). (Illus.). 1997. pap. 12.95 (*1-882391-20-9*) N Cape Pubns.
Rutledge, Lee A. Campaign Clothing: Field Uniforms of the Indian War Army 1872-1886. (Military Collectors Guide Ser.). (Illus.). 80p. 1997. pap. 14.95 (*1-882391-09-8*) N Cape Pubns.
Rutledge, Leigh. Cat Love Letters. 1999. pap. 9.95 (*0-452-27149-5*, Plume) Dutton Plume.
***Rutledge, Leigh.** Cat's Little Instruction Book. 2000. 6.99 (*1-57866-083-1*) Galahad Bks.
Rutledge, Leigh. Diary of a Cat. 128p. 1999. pap. 8.95 (*0-452-27554-7*, Plume) Dutton Plume.
***Rutledge, Leigh.** Lighthouse the Cat & the Sea: A Tropical Tale. LC 99-25119. 128p. 1999. 17.95 (*0-525-94349-8*, Dutton Child) Peng Put Young Read.
Rutledge, Leigh. Would I Lie to You? LC 98-11097. 272p. 1998. pap. 10.95 (*0-452-27931-3*, Plume) Dutton Plume.
***Rutledge, Leigh & Hancock, Gregory R., eds.** Too Much of a Good Thing... Quotes You Can't Get Enough Of. 136p. 2000. pap. 10.95 (*1-55583-413-2*, Pub. by Alyson Pubns) Consort Bk Sales.
Rutledge, Leigh W. Dear Tabby. 1999. pap. 9.95 (*0-452-27363-3*, Plume) Dutton Plume.
— Dear Tabby. 1999. 11.00 (*0-453-00934-4*, NAL Bks) NAL.
— Diary of a Cat: True Confessions & Lifelong Observations of a Well-Adjusted House Cat. 1999. 6.99 (*1-57866-053-X*) Galahad Bks.
— The Left-Hander's Book of Days. LC 98-54340. (Illus.). 320p. 1999. 16.95 (*0-525-94348-X*) NAL.
***Rutledge, Leigh W.** The Lighthouse, the Cat, & the Sea: A Tropical Tale. large type ed. LC 00-24257. (Americana Series). 2000. 26.95 (*0-7862-2528-9*) Thorndike Pr.
Rutledge, Leigh W. The New Gay Book of Lists. 2nd rev. ed. LC 96-19267. 208p. 1996. pap. text 11.95 (*1-55583-359-4*) Alyson Pubns.
— When My Grandmother Was a Child. 1999. pap. 8.95 (*0-452-27438-9*, Plume) Dutton Plume.
Rutledge, Leigh W., ed. Nice Girls Don't Wear Cha Cha Heels: Camp Lines from Classic Films. LC 99-36926. 196p. 1999. pap. 10.95 (*1-55583-440-X*, Pub. by Alyson Pubns) Consort Bk Sales.
Rutledge, Leigh W. & Donley, Richard. The Left-Hander's Guide to Life. (Illus.). 128p. (Orig.). 1992. pap. 9.95 (*0-452-26845-1*, Plume) Dutton Plume.
***Rutledge, Len.** Fiji. (Maverick Guides Ser.). 1998. pap. 9.95 (*1-85315-116-8*) Pelican.
— Maverick Guide to Australia. 12th ed. (Maverick Guides Ser.). (Illus.). 416p. 2000. pap. 17.95 (*1-56554-772-1*) Pelican.
Rutledge, Len. Maverick Guide to Hong Kong, Macau, & South China. LC 95-190277. (Maverick Guides Ser.). (Illus.). 296p. (Orig.). 1995. pap. 15.95 (*1-56554-071-9*) Pelican.
— The Maverick Guide to Malaysia & Singapore. 2nd ed. (Maverick Guides Ser.). (Illus.). 488p. 1994. pap. 14.95 (*0-88289-990-2*) Pelican.
— The Maverick Guide to Thailand. 3rd ed. (Illus.). 384p. 1999. pap. 15.95 (*1-56554-288-6*) Pelican.
— Maverick Guide to the Great Barrier Reef. LC 97-135064. (Illus.). 224p. 1997. pap. 14.95 (*1-56554-193-6*) Pelican.
— Maverick Guide to Vietnam, Laos, & Cambodia. 3rd rev. ed. (Maverick Guides Ser.). (Illus.). 392p. 1999. pap. 17.95 (*1-56554-126-X*) Pelican.
Rutledge, M. J. Survey of Chatham Island Indigenous Freshwater Fish LC 92-217417. 21p. 1992. write for info. (*0-478-01341-8*, Pub. by Manaaki Whenua) Balogh.
***Rutledge, Margie & Cowan, Maxine.** The Great Laundry Adventure. (Illus.). 176p. (YA). (gr. 5-8). 1999. pap. 7.95 (*0-929141-67-9*) Napoleon Publ.
Rutledge, Marilyn, et al. Guide to Accounting for Income Taxes. 1997. ring bd. 140.00 (*0-7646-0327-2*) Prctnrs Pub Co.
— Guide to Accounting for Income Taxes. 1998. ring bd. 154.00 (*0-7646-0610-7*) Prctnrs Pub Co.
***Rutledge, Marilyn, et al.** Guide to Accounting for Income Taxes. 1999. ring bd. 154.00 (*0-7646-0944-0*) Prctnrs Pub Co.
— Guide to Auditor's Reports, 2 vols. 1999. ring bd. 164.00 (*0-7646-0856-8*) Prctnrs Pub Co.
Rutledge, Marilyn, et al. Guide to Auditor's Reports, 2 vols., 1. 1992. write for info. (*1-56433-217-9*) Prctnrs Pub Co.
— Guide to Auditor's Reports, 2 vols., 1. 1993. ring bd. write for info. (*1-56433-363-9*) Prctnrs Pub Co.
— Guide to Auditor's Reports, 2 vols., 2. 1992. write for info. (*1-56433-218-7*) Prctnrs Pub Co.
— Guide to Auditor's Reports, 2 vols., 2. 1993. ring bd. write for info. (*1-56433-364-7*) Prctnrs Pub Co.
— Guide to Auditor's Reports, 2 vols., Set. 1992. ring bd. 115.00 (*1-56433-216-0*) Prctnrs Pub Co.
— Guide to Auditor's Reports, 2 vols., Set. 1993. ring bd. 115.00 (*1-56433-362-0*) Prctnrs Pub Co.
— Guide to Auditor's Reports, 2 vols., Set. rev. ed. 950p. 1991. ring bd. 115.00 (*1-56433-041-9*) Prctnrs Pub Co.
***Rutledge, Marilyn, et al.** Guide to Auditor's Reports, Vol. 1. 1999. ring bd. write for info. (*0-7646-0857-6*) Prctnrs Pub Co.
Rutledge, Marilyn, et al. Guide to Auditor's Reports, Vol. 1. rev. ed. 450p. 1991. write for info. (*1-56433-042-7*) Prctnrs Pub Co.
***Rutledge, Marilyn, et al.** Guide to Auditor's Reports, Vol. 2. 1999. ring bd. write for info. (*0-7646-0858-4*) Prctnrs Pub Co.
Rutledge, Marilyn, et al. Guide to Auditor's Reports, Vol. 2. rev. ed. 500p. 1991. write for info. (*1-56433-043-5*) Prctnrs Pub Co.
***Rutledge, Marilyn Z., et al.** Guide to Homeowners' Associations & Other Common Interest Realty Associations, 3 vols. 1999. ring bd. 164.00 (*0-7646-0810-X*) Prctnrs Pub Co.
Rutledge, Marilyn Z., et al. Guide to Homeowners Associations & Other Common Interest Realty Associations, 3 vols. Incl. Vol. 1. 1996. ring bd. (*1-56433-969-6*); Vol. 2. 1996. ring bd. (*1-56433-970-X*); Vol. 3. 1996. ring bd. (*1-56433-971-8*); 150.00 (*1-56433-968-8*) Prctnrs Pub Co.
— Guide to Homeowners' Associations & Other Common Interest Realty Associations, 3 vols. Incl. Vol. 1. 1997. ring bd. (*0-7646-0269-1*); Vol. 2. 1997. ring bd. (*0-7646-0270-5*); Vol. 3. 1997. ring bd. (*0-7646-0271-3*); 156.00 (*0-7646-0268-3*) Prctnrs Pub Co.
— Guide to Homeowners' Associations & Other Common Interest Realty Associations, 2 vols., 1. 1992. write for info. (*1-56433-226-8*) Prctnrs Pub Co.
— Guide to Homeowners' Associations & Other Common Interest Realty Associations, 3 vols., 1. 1993. write for info. (*1-56433-341-8*) Prctnrs Pub Co.
— Guide to Homeowners' Associations & Other Common Interest Realty Associations, 2 vols., 2. 1992. write for info. (*1-56433-227-6*) Prctnrs Pub Co.
— Guide to Homeowners' Associations & Other Common Interest Realty Associations, 3 vols., 2. 1993. write for info. (*1-56433-342-6*) Prctnrs Pub Co.
— Guide to Homeowners' Associations & Other Common Interest Realty Associations, 3 vols., 3. 1993. write for info. (*1-56433-343-4*) Prctnrs Pub Co.
— Guide to Homeowners' Associations & Other Common Interest Realty Associations, 2 vols., Set. 1992. ring bd. 115.00 (*1-56433-225-X*) Prctnrs Pub Co.
— Guide to Homeowners' Associations & Other Common Interest Realty Associations, 3 vols., Set. 1993. ring bd. 115.00 (*1-56433-340-X*) Prctnrs Pub Co.
***Rutledge, Marilyn Z., et al.** Guide to Homeowners' Associations & Other Common Interest Realty Associations, Vol. 1. 1999. ring bd. write for info. (*0-7646-0811-8*) Prctnrs Pub Co.
— Guide to Homeowners' Associations & Other Common Interest Realty Associations, Vol. 2. 1999. ring bd. write for info. (*0-7646-0812-6*) Prctnrs Pub Co.
— Guide to Homeowners' Associations & Other Common Interest Realty Associations, Vol. 3. 1999. ring bd. write for info. (*0-7646-0813-4*) Prctnrs Pub Co.
Rutledge, Maurice D. Churn 'Em & Burn 'Em. 250p. (Orig.). 1992. pap. 7.95 (*0-9633311-0-8*) Rutledge Pub.
Rutledge, Patrice-Ann. Access 2000 Fast & Easy. LC 98-68146. (Fast & Easy Ser.). 360p. 1999. pap. 16.99 (*0-7615-1404-X*, Prima Tech) Prima Pub.
Rutledge, Patrice-Anne. Access 97 Fast & Easy. LC 97-75515. (Fast & Easy Ser.). 400p. 2000. pap. 16.99 (*0-7615-1363-9*) Prima Pub.
***Rutledge, Patrice-Anne.** Sams Teach Yourself Quicken 2000 in 24 Hours. (Teach Yourself... in 24 Hours Ser.). (Illus.). 1999. pap. 19.99 (*0-672-31762-1*) Sams.
Rutledge, Patrice-Anne, et al. Using Microsoft PowerPoint 2000 With CDROM. Que Staff, ed. (Using ... / Que Ser.). (Illus.). 765p. 1999. pap. 39.99 (*0-7897-1904-5*) Que.
Rutledge, Patti. Guide to Owning a Boxer: AKC Rank #13. (Guide to Owning Ser.). (Illus.). 64p. 1995. pap. 6.95 (*0-7938-1861-3*, RE-311) TFH Pubns.
Rutledge, Paul. The Role of Religion in Ethnic Self-Identity: A Vietnamese Community. (Illus.). 140p. (Orig.). (C). 1985. lib. bdg. 41.00 (*0-8191-4505-X*) U Pr of Amer.
Rutledge, Paul J. The Vietnamese Experience in America. LC 91-26520. (Minorities in Modern America Ser.). (Illus.). 192p. 1992. text 31.50 (*0-253-34997-4*) Ind U Pr.
Rutledge, Rachel. The Best of the Best in Basketball. LC 98-25631. (Women of Sports Ser.). (Illus.). 64p. (YA). (gr. 4-12). 1998. lib. bdg. 22.90 (*0-7613-1301-X*, Copper Beech Bks) Millbrook Pr.
— The Best of the Best in Basketball. LC 98-25631. (Women of Sports Ser.). (Illus.). 64p. (J). (gr. 5 up). 1998. pap. 6.95 (*0-7613-0443-6*, Copper Beech Bks) Millbrook Pr.
— The Best of the Best in Figure Skating. LC 98-25634. (Women of Sports Ser.). (Illus.). 64p. (J). (gr. 5 up). 1998. pap. 6.95 (*0-7613-0444-4*, Copper Beech Bks); lib. bdg. 22.90 (*0-7613-1302-8*, Copper Beech Bks) Millbrook Pr.
— The Best of the Best in Gymnastics. LC 98-51657. (Women of Sports Ser.). (Illus.). 64p. (YA). (gr. 5 up). 1999. pap. 6.95 (*0-7613-0784-2*, Copper Beech Bks); lib. bdg. 22.90 (*0-7613-1321-4*, Copper Beech Bks) Millbrook Pr.
— The Best of the Best in Soccer. LC 98-25635. (Women of Sports Ser.). (Illus.). 64p. (J). (gr. 5 up). 1998. pap. 6.95 (*0-7613-0782-6*, Copper Beech Bks); lib. bdg. 22.90 (*0-7613-1315-X*, Copper Beech Bks) Millbrook Pr.
***Rutledge, Rachel.** The Best of the Best in Soccer. rev. ed. (Women of Sports Ser.). (Illus.). 64p. (J). (gr. 5). 2000. pap. 7.95 (*0-7613-1392-3*, Copper Beech Bks) Millbrook Pr.
Rutledge, Rachel. The Best of the Best in Tennis. LC 98-25260. (Women of Sports Ser.). (Illus.). 64p. (YA). (gr. 4-12). 1998. lib. bdg. 22.90 (*0-7613-1303-6*, Copper Beech Bks) Millbrook Pr.
— The Best of the Best in Tennis. LC 98-25260. (Women of Sports Ser.). (Illus.). 64p. (YA). (gr. 5 up). 1998. pap. 6.95 (*0-7613-0445-2*, Copper Beech Bks) Millbrook Pr.
— The Best of the Best in Track & Field. LC 98-51645. (Women of Sports Ser.). (Illus.). 64p. (YA). (gr. 5 up). 1999. pap. 6.95 (*0-7613-0446-0*, Copper Beech Bks); lib. bdg. 22.90 (*0-7613-1300-1*, Copper Beech Bks) Millbrook Pr.
***Rutledge, Rachel.** Marion Jones: Fast & Fearless. LC 00-30514. (Track & Field's New Wave Ser.). (Illus.). (YA). 2000. lib. bdg. write for info. (*0-7613-1870-4*) Millbrook Pr.
— Mia Hamm: Striking Superstar. (Soccer's New Wave Ser.). 48p. (J). 2000. 20.90 (*0-7613-1802-X*) Millbrook Pr.
— Mia Hamm: Striking Superstar. (Soccer's New Wave Ser.). (Illus.). 2000. pap. 6.95 (*0-7613-1381-8*) Millbrook Pr.
Rutledge, Samuel A. The Development of Guiding Principles for the Administration of Teachers Colleges & Normal Schools. LC 77-177221. (Columbia University. Teachers College. Contributions to Education Ser.: No. 449). reprint ed. 37.50 (*0-404-55449-0*) AMS Pr.
Rutledge, Sarah. The Carolina Housewife. annuals 18th ed. LC 79-120677. xxvi, 262p. 1979. 24.95 (*0-87249-383-0*) U of SC Pr.

R

An Asterisk (*) at the beginning of an entry indicates that the title is appearing for the first time.

Rutledge-Smalls, Lucinda. Private Thoughts, Deadly Secrets. Seebass, Diane B., ed. 512p. (Orig.). 1997. pap. 10.95 (*0-9652072-6-9*) Melano Pub.

Rutledge, Thom. Earning Your Own Respect: A Handbook of Personal Responsibility. LC 98-66706. 160p. 1998. pap. 12.95 (*1-57224-151-9*) New Harbinger.

— If I Were They: A Handbook of Practical Recovery Wisdom. 132p. (Orig.). 1993. pap. 6.95 (*0-9627963-3-6*) T W Rutledge.

— The Self-Forgiveness Handbook: A Practical & Empowering Guide. LC 97-66077. 192p. (Orig.). 1997. pap. 12.95 (*1-57224-083-0*) New Harbinger.

— Simple Truth: Ideas & Experiences for Humans from Less-Than-Perfect Families. 105p. 1994. pap. 8.95 (*0-9627963-0-1*) T W Rutledge.

Rutledge, Wiley. Declaration of Legal Faith. LC 74-114563. (American Constitutional & Legal History Ser). 1970. reprint ed. lib. bdg. 17.95 (*0-306-71921-5*) Da Capo.

Rutler, George & Rutler, George W. Beyond Modernity. LC 86-82636. 227p. pap. 24.95 incl. audio (*0-89870-135-X*, 109) Ignatius Pr.

Rutler, George W. Adam Danced: The Cross & the Seven Deadly Sins. 64p. (Orig.). 1989. pap. 6.95 (*0-931888-34-4*) Christendom Pr.

— The Brightest & Best. LC 97-76849. 1998. pap. text 15.95 (*0-89870-671-8*) Ignatius Pr.

— Christ & Reason: An Introduction to Ideas from Kant to Tyrrell. 212p. 1990. pap. 10.95 (*0-931888-38-7*) Christendom Pr.

— A Crisis of Saints: "The Real Danger to Society Is Not Merely a Lack of Virtue..." LC 94-75669. 204p. (Orig.). 1995. pap. 11.95 (*0-89870-556-8*) Ignatius Pr.

— The Cure D'Ars Today: St. John Vianney. LC 87-82978. 273p. 1988. pap. 9.95 (*0-89870-180-5*) Ignatius Pr.

— The Impatience of Job. 1981. pap. 6.95 (*0-89385-014-4*) Sugden.

— The Seven Wonders of the World: Meditations on the Last Words of Christ. LC 92-71940. 168p. 1993. pap. 10.95 (*0-89870-417-0*) Ignatius Pr.

Rutler, George W., jt. auth. see Rutler, George.

***Rutlidge Institute Staff.** 2000 National Renovation & Insurance Repair Estimator. 5th ed. Russell, Jonathan, ed. (Illus.). 560p. 1999. pap. 49.50 (*1-57218-085-4*) Craftsman.

Rutman, Anita H., jt. auth. see Rutman, Darrett B.

Rutman, Darrett B. A Militant New World, 1607-1640. Kohn, Richard H., ed. LC 78-22416. (American Military Experience Ser.). 1980. lib. bdg. 63.95 (*0-405-11890-2*) Ayer.

Rutman, Darrett B. & Rutman, Anita H. Small Worlds, Large Questions: Explorations in Early American Social History, 1600-1850. LC 94-7440. 448p. (C). 1994. pap. 19.50 (*0-8139-1530-9*) U Pr of Va.

Rutman, Leonard. Planning Useful Evaluations: Evaluability Assessment. LC 79-24116. (Sage Library of Social Research: No. 96). 208p. reprint ed. pap. 64.50 (*0-7837-1131-X*, 204166100022) Bks Demand.

Rutman, Leonard & Mowbray, George. Understanding Program Evaluation, Vol. 31. 112p. 1983. pap. 18.95 (*0-8039-2093-8*) Sage.

Rutman, Shereen G. My Book of Opposites. (J). 1997. pap. text, wbk. ed. 2.25 (*1-56293-951-3*, McClanahan Book) Learn Horizon.

— My Busy Day. (LTFT Toddler Time Ser.). (Illus.). 16p. (J). (ps). 1994. wbk. ed. 2.95 (*1-56293-464-3*, McClanahan Book) Learn Horizon.

— Numbers. (Toddler Time Ser.). (Illus.). 16p. (J). 1992. pap., student ed. 2.95 (*1-56293-191-1*, McClanahan Book) Learn Horizon.

— Observing. (Toddler Time Ser.). (Illus.). 16p. (J). 1992. pap., student ed. 2.95 (*1-56293-189-X*, McClanahan Book) Learn Horizon.

— Rhyming Words. (J). 1997. pap. text, wbk. ed. 2.25 (*1-56293-955-6*, McClanahan Book) Learn Horizon.

— Shapes. (Toddler Time Ser.). (Illus.). 16p. (J). 1992. pap., student ed. 2.95 (*1-56293-188-1*, McClanahan Book) Learn Horizon.

— Sorting. (Toddler Time Ser.). (Illus.). 16p. (J). (ps). 1992. pap., student ed. 2.95 (*1-56293-186-5*, McClanahan Book) Learn Horizon.

— What Belongs? (J). 1997. pap. text, wbk. ed. 2.25 (*1-56293-956-4*, McClanahan Book) Learn Horizon.

Rutman, Shereen G. & Speirs, John. Time to Tell Time. (Illus.). 14p. 1992. 5.99 (*0-307-14019-9*, 14019) Gldn Bks Pub Co.

Rutman, Shereen G., jt. auth. see Speirs, John.

***Rutman, Shereen Gertel.** The Amazing Game Board Book. (Illus.). 36p. (YA). (gr. 1 up). 2000. 19.99 (*1-58476-020-6*) Innovative Kids.

Rutnagar, Dicky. Khans Unlimited: A History of Squash in Pakistan. LC 97-930673. (The Jubilee Ser.). (Illus.). 234p. (C). 1997. text 45.00 (*0-19-577805-7*) OUP.

Rutner, Emile, et al, eds. Condensation & Evaporation of Solids. xviii, 708p. 1964. text 888.00 (*0-677-00740-X*) Gordon & Breach.

***Rutowska, Jolanta, et al, eds.** Liquid Crystals Vol. 3318: Physics, Technology & Applications. LC 98-172296. 556p. 1998. 99.00 (*0-8194-2759-4*) SPIE.

Rutsala, Vern. Backtracking. (Poetry Ser.). 66p. (Orig.). 1985. 14.00 (*0-934257-01-9*); pap. 6.95 (*0-934257-00-0*) Story Line.

— Little-Known Sports. LC 93-34630. 72p. 1994. pap. 9.95 (*0-87023-918-X*); lib. bdg. 20.00 (*0-87023-917-1*) U of Mass Pr.

— The New Life. LC 97-31167. 1978. pap. 2.00 (*0-932264-20-4*) Trask Hse Bks.

— Ruined Cities. LC 86-72300. (Poetry Ser.). 72p. (C). 1987. pap. 11.95 (*0-88748-041-1*) Carnegie-Mellon.

— Selected Poems of Vern Rutsala. LC 90-52857. 281p. 1991. 21.95 (*0-934257-52-3*); pap. 16.95 (*0-934257-61-2*) Story Line.

— Walking Home from the Ice-House. LC 80-70566. (Poetry Ser.). 1981. 20.95 (*0-915604-47-7*); pap. 11.95 (*0-915604-48-5*) Carnegie-Mellon.

Rutsch, Bettina. Leiblichkeit der Sprache Sprachlichkeit des Leibes: Wort, Gebarde, Tanz Bei Hugo von Hofmannsthal. (Europaische Hochschulschriften Ser.: Reihe 1, Bd. 1675). 312p. 1998. 51.95 (*3-631-33306-4*) P Lang Pubng.

Rutsch, Edward S. Smoking Technology of the Aborigines of the Iroquois Area of New York State. LC 73-92558. 252p. 1975. 39.50 (*0-8386-7568-9*) Fairleigh Dickinson.

Rutsche, Johannes. Das Leben Aus der Schrift Verstehen. 480p. 1999. 61.95 (*3-906761-83-5*) P Lang.

Rutschke, Erich. Der Kormoran. Biologie, Wiederausbreitung, Konflikte (Cormorants. Biology, Conservation, Conflicts) (Illus.). 264p. 1997. 25.00 (*3-8263-8487-3*, Pub. by Blckwell Wissenschafts) Balogh.

— Wildgaense. Lebensweise - Schutz - Nutzung (Wild Geese - Biology, Protection, & Uses) (Illus.). 260p. 1997. 39.00 (*3-8263-8478-4*, Pub. by Blckwell Wissenschafts) Balogh.

Rutschman, Mary E. Goals Bingo: A Program for Middle Junior HS Senior HS for Setting & Accomplishing Goals. LC 93-81083. 32p. (Orig.). (YA). (gr. 6-12). 1993. pap. 13.95 (*1-884063-16-0*) Mar Co Prods.

— Know Yourself: Self Exploration Program Relating to Career Awareness. LC 96-77636. (Illus.). 24p. (Orig.). (J). (gr. 5-7). 1996. pap. 6.95 (*1-884063-90-X*) Mar Co Prods.

***Rutsky, Joshua.** Beyond the Bard: Fifty Plays for Use in the English Classroom. 112p. 2000. pap. 18.00 (*0-205-30809-0*) Allyn.

Rutsky, R. L. High Techne: Art & Technology from the Machine Age to the Posthuman. LC 99-31609. (Electronic Mediations Ser.: Vol. 2). 192p. 1999. pap. 17.95 (*0-8166-3356-8*, Pub. by U of Minn Pr); lib. bdg. 44.95 (*0-8166-3355-X*, Pub. by U of Minn Pr) Chicago Distribution Ctr.

Rutstein & Daum, Kent Michael. Anomalies of Binocular Vision: Diagnosis & Management. LC 97-14847. (Illus.). 384p. (C). (gr. 13). 1997. text 64.95 (*0-8016-6916-2*, 06916) Mosby Inc.

Rutstein, Charles B. Windows NT Security: A Practical Guide to Securing Windows NT Servers & Workstations. LC 96-37593. (Illus.). 332p. 1997. pap. 34.95 (*0-07-057833-8*) McGraw.

Rutstein, Nathan. Corinne True: Faithful Handmaid of 'Abdu'l Baha. (Illus.). 272p. 1987. 19.95 (*0-85398-263-5*); pap. 12.95 (*0-85398-264-3*) G Ronald Pub.

— He Loved & Served: The Story of Curtis Kelsey. (Illus.). 208p. 1982. pap. 9.50 (*0-85398-121-3*) G Ronald Pub.

— Healing Racism in America: A Prescription for the Disease. 184p. (Orig.). 1993. pap. 12.95 (*0-9633007-1-7*) Whitcomb MA.

— The Invisible Hand: Shaping the New World Order. Morgan, Michael & Robbins, Carroll, eds. 114p. (Orig.). 1992. pap. 9.95 (*0-9633007-0-9*) Whitcomb MA.

— Racism: Unraveling the Fear. 256p. 1997. pap. 16.95 (*0-9659945-0-3*) Global Classrm.

— Teaching the Baha'i Faith: Spirit in Action. 192p. 1984. pap. 9.50 (*0-85398-176-0*) G Ronald Pub.

— A Way Out of the Trap: An Innovative & Unique Ten-Step Program for Spiritual Growth. Hinshaw, Beth, ed. LC 92-63009. 176p. (Orig.). 1995. pap. 11.95 (*0-9633001-2-1*) Whitcomb MA.

Rutstein, Nathan & Morgan, Michael, eds. Healing Racism: Education's Role. 353p. (Orig.). 1996. pap. 24.95 (*0-9633007-3-3*) Whitcomb MA.

***Rutstrum, Calvin.** North American Canoe Country: The Classic Guide to Canoe Technique. (Fesler-Lampert Minnesota Heritage Bks.). (Illus.). 2000. pap. write for info. (*0-8166-3660-5*) U of Minn Pr.

— Wilderness Route Finder: The Classic Guide to Finding Your Way in the Wild. (Illus.). 2000. pap. 14.95 (*0-8166-3661-3*) U of Minn Pr.

Rutsula, Vern. The Mystery of Lost Shoes. LC 85-160. 37p. 1985. 5.00 (*0-89924-046-1*) Lynx Hse.

Rutt, August. Surgery of the Leg & Foot. (Hackenbroch Ser.). 1980. text 142.00 (*0-7216-4446-5*, W B Saunders Co) Harcrt Hlth Sci Grp.

Rutt, Joan. Lee Wade's Korean Cookery. (Illus.). 64p. 1995. 16.95 (*0-930878-45-0*) Hollym Intl.

Rutt, Richard. A History of Hand Knitting. LC 87-46353. 248p. 1988. 24.95 (*0-934026-35-1*) Interweave.

— The Zhou Yi: A New Translation with Commentary of the Book of Changes. (Durham East Asia Ser.). 320p. (C). 1996. text 65.00 (*0-7007-0467-1*, Pub. by Curzon Pr Ltd) UH Pr.

Rutt, Richard, ed. from KOR. The Bamboo Grove: An Introduction to Sijo. LC 98-234693. (Ann Arbor Paperbacks Ser.). (ENG & KOR.). 200p. 1998. pap. text 15.95 (*0-472-08558-1*, 08558) U of Mich Pr.

Ruttan, Vernon W. Agricultural Research Policy. LC 81-16396. (Illus.). 384p. reprint ed. pap. 119.10 (*0-8357-6537-7*, 203589900097) Bks Demand.

— The Economic Demand for Irrigated Acreage: New Methodology & Some Preliminary Projections 1954-1980. (Resources for the Future Ser.). (Illus.). 152p. 1965. 14.00 (*0-8018-0571-6*) Johns Hopkins.

— The Economic Demand for Irrigated Acreage: New Methodology & Some Preliminary Projections 1954-1980. LC 65-13930. 152p. reprint ed. pap. 47.20 (*0-608-17390-8*, 203021900067) Bks Demand.

— United States Development Assistance Policy: The Domestic Politics of Foreign Economic Aid. LC 95-6422. (Studies in Development). 568p. 1995. text 65.00 (*0-8018-5051-7*) Johns Hopkins.

Ruttan, Vernon W., ed. Agriculture, Environment, & Health: Sustainable Development in the 21st Century. LC 93-8527. 384p. (C). 1994. pap. 21.95 (*0-8166-2292-2*); text 54.95 (*0-8166-2291-4*) U of Minn Pr.

— Why Food Aid? LC 92-25476. 320p. 1993. pap. text 16.95 (*0-8018-4472-X*) Johns Hopkins.

Ruttan, Vernon W., jt. auth. see Hayami, Yujiro.

Ruttan, Vernon W., jt. auth. see Thirtle, Colin G.

Rutte, Erwin & Wilczewski, Norbert. Mainfranken und Rhoen. 3rd rev. ed. (Sammlung Geologischer Fuehrer Ser.: Band 74). (GER., Illus.). viii, 232p. 1982. spiral bd. 29.00 (*3-443-15067-5*, Pub. by Gebruder Borntraeger) Balogh.

Rutte, Theophile De, see De Rutte, Theophile.

Ruttedge, Len. The Maverick Guide to Australia. 11th rev. ed. (Maverick Guides Ser.). (Illus.). 416p. 1999. pap. 17.95 (*1-56554-151-0*) Pelican.

Rutten & Van Venrooij. Telescope Optics - Evaluation & Design. 1988. 24.95 (*0-943396-18-2*) Willmann-Bell.

Rutten, J., jt. auth. see De Bakker, J. W.

Rutten, Joshua. Erosion. LC 97-34542. (Illus.). 32p. (J). 1998. lib. bdg. 22.79 (*1-56766-508-X*) Childs World.

— Forests. LC 97-36022. (Illus.). 32p. (J). 1998. lib. bdg. 22.79 (*1-56766-486-5*) Childs World.

— Red Pandas. LC 97-33250. (Nature Books Ser.). (Illus.). 32p. (J). (gr. 2-6). 1998. lib. bdg. 22.79 (*1-56766-473-3*) Childs World.

Rutten, M. Asian Capitalists in the European Mirror. LC 94-207964. 65p. 1994. pap. 16.00 (*90-5383-270-X*, Pub. by VU Univ Pr) Paul & Co Pubs.

Rutten, Mario. Farms & Factories: Social Profile of Large Farmers & Rural Industrialists in West India. LC 95-903633. (Illus.). 420p. 1995. 29.95 (*0-19-563299-0*) OUP.

Rutten, Mario & Upadhya, Carol, eds. Small Business Entrepreneurs in Asia & Europe: Towards a Comparative Perspective. LC 97-11575. 336p. 1997. 38.00 (*0-8039-9381-1*) Sage.

***Rutten, Robert J.** Map, Compass, GPS: An Introduction. (Illus.). 110p. (YA). (gr. 7 up). 2000. pap. write for info. (*0-9678156-0-6*) Outdoor Comm Co.

Rutten, Robert J., ed. Solar Surface Magnetism: Proceedings of the NATO Advanced Research Workshop, Soesterberg, the Netherlands, November 1-5, 1993. (NATO Advanced Science Institutes: C Mathematical & Physical Sciences Ser.). 552p. (C). 1994. text 326.50 (*0-7923-2845-0*) Kluwer Academic.

Rutten, Robert J. & Severino, Giuseppe, eds. Solar & Stellar Granulation. (C). 1989. text 320.50 (*0-7923-0122-6*) Kluwer Academic.

Rutten, Thomas. Demokrit - Lachender Philosoph und Sanguinischer Melancholiker: Eine Pseudohippokratische Geschichte. LC 91-36808. (Mnemosyne Ser.: Supplement 118). (GER.). xiv, 274p. 1991. 107.00 (*90-04-09523-3*) Brill Academic Pubs.

Rutten, Tim, jt. auth. see Cochran, Johnnie L.

Rutten, Tim, jt. auth. see Cochran, Johnnie L., Jr.

Ruttenbaum, Steven R. Mansions in the Clouds: The Skyscraper Palazzi of Emery Roth. (Illus.). 224p. 1986. 48.00 (*0-917439-09-0*) Balsam Pr.

Ruttenber, E. M. History of the Town of Newburgh, NY. (Illus.). 322p. 1993. reprint ed. lib. bdg. 39.00 (*0-8328-2858-0*) Higginson Bk Co.

— Indian Tribes of Hudson's River II: 1700-1850. 240p. 1992. reprint ed. pap. 12.95 (*0-910746-09-5*, IT002) Hope Farm.

— Indian Tribes of Hudson's River to 1700. (Illus.). 200p. 1998. reprint ed. pap. 12.95 (*0-910746-98-2*, IT001) Hope Farm.

Ruttenber, E. M. & Clark, L. H. History of Orange County, New York, with Illustrations & Biographical Sketches of Many of Its Prominent Men & Pioneers. (Illus.). 820p. 1992. reprint ed. lib. bdg. 59.00 (*0-8328-2368-6*) Higginson Bk Co.

Ruttenber, E. M. & Clark, L. H., compiled by. History of Orange County, New York, 1881, 2 vols., Set. (Illus.). 820p. 1980. reprint ed. 55.00 (*0-9604116-0-7*) Orange County Genealog.

Ruttenber, Edward M. History of the Town of New Windsor, Orange County. (Illus.). 213p. 1997. reprint ed. lib. bdg. 29.00 (*0-8328-6182-0*) Higginson Bk Co.

Ruttenber, James, jt. ed. see Blumenthal, Daniel S.

Ruttenber, Tim. The Complete Lunchbox: The Life & Works of Deacon Lunchbox, a Cornucopia of Southern Culture. Roarty, Robert S., ed. & intro. by. 189p. (Orig.). 1994. pap. text 19.95 (*1-878749-01-3*) Drewry Lane Bkmakers.

Ruttenberg, Nancy. Democratic Personality: Popular Voice & the Trial of American Authorship. LC 97-42315. 1998. 65.00 (*0-8047-3096-2*); pap. 19.95 (*0-8047-3097-0*) Stanford U Pr.

Rutter, jt. auth. see Barksdale.

Rutter, tr. see Martignoni, M. & Schonenberger.

Rutter, Bob. A Century of Caring: A History of the Guelph Humane Society. (Illus.). 96p. (Orig.). 1993. pap. 11.95 (*1-879260-13-1*) Evanston Pub.

Rutter, Bryce G. & Dainoff, Marvin J. The Ergonomic Office: Standards, Specifications, Design Guidelines. Becka, Anne Marie, ed. LC 94-78633. (Illus.). 250p. 1995. ring bd. 145.00 (*0-9643187-0-9*) Metaphase Pub.

Rutter, Carol. Clamorous Voices: Shakespeare's Women Today. Evans, Faith, ed. 1998. pap. 29.95 (*0-7043-4145-X*) Womens Press.

Rutter, Carol, et al. Clamorous Voices: Shakespeare's Women Today. Evans, Faith, ed. (Illus.). 131p. 1989. 39.95 (*0-87830-036-8*, A3685, Thtre Arts Bks); pap. 13.95 (*0-87830-037-6*, A3689, Thtre Arts Bks) Routledge.

Rutter, Carol, ed. & intro. see Harrison, Tony.

Rutter, D. R. & Quine, Lyn. Social Psychology & Health: European Perspectives. 232p. 1994. 67.95 (*1-85628-562-6*, Pub. by Avebry) Ashgate Pub Co.

Rutter, Derek R. & Argyle, Michael. Communicating by Telephone. LC 87-8275. (International Series Experimental Social Psychology: Vol. 15). 200p. 1987. 90.00 (*0-08-031324-8*, Pub. by Pergamon Repr) Franklin.

Rutter, E. H., jt. ed. see Knipe, R. J.

Rutter, E. Jane. The Self-Sustaining Nonprofit: Planning for Success: A Common Sense Guide from Start-Up Through Year 3. LC 97-94430. 117p. 1997. pap. 50.00 (*0-9631907-5-X*, SSNPI) Grants Link.

— The Self-Sustaining Nonprofit Workbook: 10 Tools to Stimulate Organizational Planning. (Illus.). 23p. 1997. pap., wbk. ed. 10.00 (*0-9631907-9-2*, SSNP-WB) Grants Link.

Rutter, E. Jane, et al, eds. Corporate Funders Operating in Illinois. (Orig.). 1996. pap. 99.00 (*0-9631907-3-3*) Grants Link.

— Corporate Funders Operating in Missouri. 3rd ed. 1996. pap. 60.00 (*0-9631907-1-7*) Grants Link.

— Corporate Funders Operating in Oklahoma, Kansas & Arkansas: The Proven Resource for Securing Funds. 170p. 1997. pap. 99.00 (*0-9631907-8-4*, CFOKA) Grants Link.

— Corporate Funders Operating in Texas. (Orig.). 1996. pap. 99.00 (*0-9631907-4-1*) Grants Link.

— Corporate Funders Operating in Texas: The Proven Resource for Securing Funds. 2nd ed. 264p. 1997. pap. 99.00 (*0-9631907-6-8*, CFOTX2) Grants Link.

Rutter, Eldon. The Holy Cities of Arabia, 2 vols., Set. LC 78-63477. reprint ed. 97.50 (*0-404-16543-5*) AMS Pr.

Rutter, Frank V. Dante Gabriel Rossetti: Painter & Man of Letters. LC 78-148295. (Illus.). reprint ed. 31.50 (*0-404-05468-4*) AMS Pr.

Rutter, James. Hiking Trails III: Central & Northern Vancouver Island. rev. ed. (Illus.). 128p. 1996. pap. 15.95 (*0-9697667-1-8*) Orca Bk Pubs.

Rutter, Jeremy B. The Pottery of Lerna IV. LC 75-324986. (Lerna Ser.: Vol. 3). (Illus.). xxxvi, 781p. 1995. 120.00 (*0-87661-303-2*) Am Sch Athens.

Rutter, Jill. Jewish Migrations. (Migrations Ser.). (Illus.). 48p. (J). 1994. lib. bdg. 5.00 (*1-56847-236-6*) Raintree Steck-V.

***Rutter, Jill.** Refugee Children in the Classroom: A Handbook for Teachers. 2nd ed. 228p. 2000. pap. 29.95 (*1-85856-185-X*) Stylus Pub VA.

Rutter, John, ed. Folk Songs for Choirs, 2 vols., Vol. 1. 86p. (Orig.). 1985. pap. 15.95 (*0-19-343718-X*) OUP.

— Folk Songs for Choirs, 2 vols., Vol. 2. 86p. (Orig.). 1985. pap. 15.95 (*0-19-343719-8*) OUP.

— Oxford Choral Classics: European Sacred Music. (Oxford Choral Classics). 360p. 1996. pap. 15.95 (*0-19-343695-7*) OUP.

Rutter, John & Bartlett, Clifford, eds. Opera Choruses for Male Voices. (Oxford Choral Classics Ser.). 72p. 1996. text 7.95 (*0-19-343701-5*) OUP.

— Oxford Choral Classics: Opera Choruses. 384p. 1995. pap. 15.95 (*0-19-343693-0*) OUP.

— Oxford Choral Classics: Opera Choruses. (Oxford Choral Classics Ser.). (C). 1995. pap. 16.50 incl. audio (*0-19-343699-X*); 27.95 (*0-19-343700-7*) OUP.

Rutter, John, jt. auth. see Willcocks, David.

Rutter, John, jt. ed. see Willcocks, David.

***Rutter, John W.** Geometry of Curves. LC 99-88667. (Chapman & Hall Mathematics Ser.). (Illus.). 2000. 59.95 (*1-58488-166-6*, Chap & Hall CRC) CRC Pr.

Rutter, John W. Spaces of Homotopy Self-Equivalences: A Survey, Vol. 166. LC 97-24992. (Lecture Notes in Mathematics Ser.). ix, 170p. 1997. pap. write for info. (*3-540-63103-8*) Spr-Verlag.

Rutter, M. Child & Adolescent Psychology. 3rd ed. 1995. pap. text 102.95 (*0-632-02821-1*) Blackwell Sci.

— Helping Troubled Children. LC 76-25475. (Illus.). 376p. (C). 1975. 55.00 (*0-306-30969-6*, Plenum Trade) Perseus Pubng.

Rutter, Mark. The Farmhouse Voices. Hunting, Constance, ed. 35p. (Orig.). 1992. pap. 8.95 (*0-913006-50-5*) Puckerbrush.

Rutter, Michael. Camping Made Easy: A Manual for Beginners with Tips for the Experienced. LC 98-181807. (Made Easy Ser.). (Illus.). 240p. (Orig.). 1997. pap. 17.95 (*0-7627-0043-2*) Globe Pequot.

— Changing Youth in a Changing Society: Patterns of Adolescent Development & Disorder. LC 82-242973. (Illus.). 333p. 1980. 37.95 (*0-674-10875-2*) HUP.

— Conquering the Internet. LC 95-46594. 1995. mass mkt. 31.95 (*0-538-65873-8*) S-W Pub.

— Fly Fishing for the Compleat Idiot: A No-Nonsense Guide to Fly Casting. Ort, Kathleen, ed. LC 95-6709. (Illus.). 200p. (Orig.). 1995. pap. 15.00 (*0-87842-313-3*) Mountain Pr.

***Rutter, Michael.** Fun with the Family in Utah: Hundreds of Ideas for Day Trips with the Kids. 2nd ed. (Fun with the Family Ser.). (Illus.). 288p. 2000. pap. 12.95 (*0-7627-0646-5*) Globe Pequot.

Rutter, Michael. Genetics of Criminal & Antisocial Behaviour. (Ciba Foundation Symposium Ser.: Vol. 194). 292p. 1996. 134.95 (*0-471-95719-4*) Wiley.

— Introduction to Pagemaker. LC 97-174544. (Short Course Texts Ser.). (Illus.). (Orig.). 1996. pap. 25.00 (*1-56243-336-9*, AB-16) DDC Pub.

Rutter, Michael. Maternal Deprivation. 1991. pap. 19.95 (*0-14-013526-X*, Pub. by Pnguin Bks Ltd) Trafalgar.

Rutter, Michael. Utah: Off the Beaten Path: A Guide to Unique Places. 2nd ed. LC 99-15497. (Illus.). 225p. (Orig.). 1999. pap. text 12.95 (*0-7627-0463-2*) Globe Pequot.

Rutter, Michael, ed. Developmental Psychiatry. LC 86-32058. 386p. 1987. pap. text 18.95 (*0-88048-271-0*, 8271) Am Psychiatric.

— Psychosocial Disturbances in Young People: Challenges for Prevention. (Illus.). 583p. (C). 1995. text 47.95 (*0-521-46187-1*) Cambridge U Pr.

Rutter, Michael, et al, eds. Depression in Young People: Developmental & Clinical Perspectives. LC 85-870. 568p. reprint ed. pap. 176.10 (*0-7837-1206-5*, 204173800023) Bks Demand.

***Rutter, Michael & Baumgarten, J. Alan.** Spin Casting Brilliantly. (Illus.). 232p. 2000. pap. 18.00 (*0-87842-416-4*) Mountain Pr.

Rutter, Michael & Card, Dave. Fly Fishing Made Easy: A Manual for Beginners with Tips for the Experienced. 2nd rev. ed. LC 97-49827. (Made Easy Ser.). (Illus.). 192p. 1997. pap. 17.95 (*0-7627-0055-6*) Globe Pequot.

***Rutter, Michael & Card, David.** Fly-Fishing Made Easy. 3rd ed. (Illus.). 2000. pap. 17.95 (*0-7627-0750-X*) Globe Pequot.

Rutter, Michael & Casaer, Paul, eds. Biological Risk Factors for Psychosocial Disorders. (European Network on Longitudinal Studies on Individual Development). 384p. (C). 1991. text 90.00 (*0-521-40103-8*) Cambridge U Pr.

Rutter, Michael & Hay, Dale F., eds. Development Through Life: A Handbook for Clinicians. (Illus.). 632p. 1994. 175.00 (*0-632-03693-1*, Pub. by Blckwll Scitfc UK) Blackwell Sci.

Rutter, Michael & Jones, Robin R., eds. Lead Versus Health: Sources & Effects of Low Level Lead Exposure. LC 82-16020. (Wiley-Medical Publication). (Illus.). 395p. reprint ed. pap. 122.50 (*0-8357-8644-7*, 203506800092) Bks Demand.

Rutter, Michael & Schopler, Eric, eds. Autism: A Reappraisal of Concepts & Treatment. LC 77-26910. (Illus.). 552p. 1978. 49.50 (*0-306-31096-1*, Kluwer Plenum) Kluwer Academic.

Rutter, Michael & Yule, William, eds. Language Development & Disorders. LC 65-80542. (Clinics in Developmental Medicine Ser.: No. 101-102). (Illus.). 482p. (C). 1991. text 85.00 (*0-521-41219-6*, Pub. by Mc Keith Pr) Cambridge U Pr.

Rutter, Michael, et al. Antisocial Behavior by Young People. LC 98-36581. (Illus.). 385p. (C). 1998. 59.95 (*0-521-64157-8*); pap. 18.95 (*0-521-64608-1*) Cambridge U Pr.

— Fifteen Thousand Hours: Secondary Schools & Their Effects on Children. LC 78-23382. (Illus.). 293p. 1979. pap. 15.50 (*0-674-30026-2*) HUP.

— Fifteen Thousand Hours: Secondary Schools & Their Effects on Children. 288p. 1994. pap. 24.95 (*1-85396-281-3*, Pub. by P Chapman) Taylor & Francis.

— A Neuropsychiatric Study in Children. (Clinics in Developmental Medicine Ser.: Vols. 35 & 36). (Illus.). 272p. (C). 1991. text 49.95 (*0-521-41198-X*, Pub. by Mc Keith Pr) Cambridge U Pr.

Rutter, Michael, jt. ed. see Robins, Lee N.

Rutter, Michael E. & Smith, David J., eds. Psychosocial Disorders in Young People: Time Trends & Their Causes. LC 95-1906. (Series in Clinical Psychology). 864p. 1995. 255.00 (*0-471-95054-8*) Wiley.

Rutter, Michael F. The Applicable Law in Singapore & Malaysia. 748p. 1989. boxed set 320.00 (*0-614-05484-2*, SI, MICHIE) LEXIS Pub.

— Damages for Personal Injuries & Death in Singapore & Malaysia. 1000p. 1988. 233.00 (*9971-70-060-3*, MICHIE) LEXIS Pub.

— Handbook on Damages for Personal Injuries & Death in Singapore & Malaysia. 2nd ed. 826p. 1993. boxed set 290.00 (*0-409-99638-6*, SI, MICHIE) LEXIS Pub.

— Occupiers' Liability in Singapore & Malaysia. 320p. 1986. 99.00 (*0-409-99513-4*, MICHIE) LEXIS Pub.

Rutter, Michael F. & Hay, Dale F., eds. Development Through Life: A Handbook for Clinicians. (Illus.). 640p. 1996. pap. text 54.95 (*0-632-04192-7*) Blackwell Sci.

Rutter, Micheal, ed. Psychological Disturbances in Y. 425p. 1997. pap. text 24.95 (*0-521-59873-7*) Cambridge U Pr.

Rutter, N. K. Greek Coinage. 1989. pap. 25.00 (*0-85263-635-0*, Pub. by Shire Pubns) St Mut.

Rutter, Owen. British North Borneo: An Account of Its History, Resources & Native Tribes. LC 77-87001. reprint ed. 37.50 (*0-404-16775-6*) AMS Pr.

— The Pagans of North Borneo. (Illus.). 298p. 1986. 32.50 (*0-19-582627-2*) OUP.

— The Pagans of North Borneo. LC 77-87003. (Illus.). reprint ed. 37.50 (*0-404-16776-4*) AMS Pr.

***Rutter, Owen.** The Scales of Karma. LC 99-76090. 304p. 2000. write for info. (*1-893766-09-8*) Aeon Pub Co.

Rutter, Owen. Through Formosa. (Illus.). 288p. 1989. reprint ed. 30.00 (*957-9482-15-2*) Oriental Bk Store.

Rutter, Owen, ed. The Court-Martial of the "Bounty" Mutineers. (Notable British Trials Ser.). x, 202p. 1995. reprint ed. 64.00 (*1-56169-128-3*, 14626) Gaunt.

Rutter, P. A. & Martin, A. S., eds. Management of Design Offices. 99p. 1990. pap. text 28.00 (*0-7277-1383-3*, Pub. by T Telford) RCH.

Rutter, Richard R., tr. see Neugebauer, Peter.

Rutter, S. M., et al, eds. Proceedings of the 29th International Congress of the International Society for Applied Ethology. 250p. 1995. pap. 100.00 (*0-900767-92-8*, Pub. by Univs Fed Animal Welfare) St Mut.

Rutter, Thad. Where the Heart Longs to Go: A New Image for Pastoral Ministry. LC 97-18090. 1998. 10.00 (*0-8358-0849-1*) Upper Room Bks.

Rutter, Virginia, jt. auth. see Schwartz, Pepper.

Rutter, Virginia B. Celebrating Girls. 208p. 1998. pap. 6.98 (*1-56731-269-1*) Fine Comms.

— Celebrating Girls: Nurturing & Empowering Our Daughters. 208p. (Orig.). 1996. pap. 10.95 (*1-57324-053-2*) Conari Press.

— Embracing Persephone: How to Be the Mother You Want for the Daughter You Cherish. LC 99-47927. 256p. 2000. 22.00 (*1-56836-295-1*) Kodansha.

Rutter, Virginia B. & Schwartz, Pepper. The Love Test: Romance & Relationship Self-Quizzes Developed by Psychologists & Therapists. LC 97-33452. 240p. 1998. pap. 12.00 (*0-399-52403-7*, Perigee Bks) Berkley Pub.

Rutterford. Financial Strategy. 360p. 1999. pap. 46.50 (*0-471-98349-7*) Wiley.

— Financial Strategy. 2000. text 84.00 (*0-471-98348-9*) Wiley.

Rutterford, Janette, et al, eds. Handbook of U. K. Corporate Finance. 2nd ed. 326p. 1992. pap. 72.00 (*0-406-00495-1*, UK, MICHIE) LEXIS Pub.

Ruttinger, George, jt. auth. see Fuchigami, Harry H.

Ruttkowski, W. & Blake, R. Literaturwoerterbuch: Dictionary of Literature. (ENG, FRE & GER.). 68p. 1969. pap. 24.95 (*0-8288-6605-8*, M-7543) Fr & Eur.

Ruttley, Hilary L., et al, eds. Commercial Law in the Middle East. LC 95-20802. 1995. lib. bdg. 144.00 (*1-85966-113-0*) Kluwer Law Intl.

***Ruttley, Philip, et al, eds.** Liberalisation & Protectionism in the World Trading System: 2nd Yearbook of the WTLA. 1999. 100.00 (*1-874698-92-9*, Pub. by Cameron May) Gaunt.

Ruttley, Philip, et al, eds. The WTO & International Trade Regulation. 270p. 1998. pap. 108.00 (*1-874698-12-0*, Pub. by Simmonds & Hill Pubng) Gaunt.

Ruttner, F. Biogeography & Raxonomy of Honeybees. (Illus.). 290p. 1987. 163.95 (*0-387-17781-7*) Spr-Verlag.

Ruttner, Franz. Fundamentals of Limnology. 3rd ed. Frey, D. G. & Fry, F. E. J., trs. LC 64-919. 323p. reprint ed. pap. 100.20 (*0-608-17105-0*, 202644100049) Bks Demand.

Ruttner, John, jt. ed. see Willcocks, David.

Ruttner-Kolisko, Agnes. Plankton Rotifers: Biology & Taxonomy, Band XVI. Kolisko, G., tr. (Binnengewaesser Ser.). (Illus.). vii, 146p. 1974. pap. text 28.00 (*3-510-40735-0*, Pub. by E Schweizerbartsche) Balogh.

Rutyna, Richard A. & Stewart, Peter. The History of Freemasonry in Virginia. LC 98-7593. 568p. 1998. 30.00 (*0-7618-1130-3*) U Pr of Amer.

Rutz, James H. The Open Church. LC 92-81563. 182p. (C). pap. text 8.95 (*0-940232-50-2*) Seedsowers.

Rutz, Miriam, jt. auth. see Romberg, Jenean.

Rutz, Werner. Cities & Towns in Indonesia: Their Development, Current Positions & Functions with Regard to Administration & Regional Economy. Tietze, W., ed. (Urbanization of the Earth Ser.; Vol. 4). 292p. 1987. lib. bdg. 90.00 (*3-443-37006-3*, Pub. by Gebruder Borntraeger) Balogh.

— Die Staedte Indonesiens: Staedte und Andere Nich-Landwirtschaftliche Siedlungen, Ihre Entwicklung und Gegenwaertige Stellung in Verwaltung und Wirtschaft. (Urbanisierung der Erde Ser.: Vol. 4). (GER., Illus.). 286p. 1985. lib. bdg. 72.80 (*3-443-37005-5*, Pub. by Gebruder Borntraeger) Balogh.

Rutzky. Science See Throughs That Teach: See Through Reproducible Mini Posters That Give an Inside Look. (Illus.). 48p. 1998. 8.95 (*0-590-60343-4*, 863123Q, Scholastic Ref) Scholastic Inc.

Rutzler, Klaus, ed. New Perspectives in Sponge Biology. LC 90-9996. (Illus.). 544p. (C). 1991. text 59.95 (*0-87474-784-8*) Smithsonian.

Rutzler, Klaus, jt. auth. see Boury-Esnault, Nicole.

Ruud. Prelude to Calculus. (Mathematics Ser.). 1990. student ed. 15.75 (*0-534-10291-3*) Brooks-Cole.

Ruud & Shell. College Algebra. 1997. student ed. 59.00 (*1-57259-473-X*) W H Freeman.

Ruud, Alice. Design Your Own Life: From High School to Career. 1989. student ed. 9.95 (*1-56117-000-3*) Telesis CA.

***Ruud, Anita E.** Handling Claims Against Government Entities: Winter 2000 Action Guide. Piatt, Norma, ed. 60p. 2000. pap. 58.00 (*0-7626-0416-6*) Cont Ed Bar-CA.

— Handling Claims Against Government Entities - Action Guide - Winter 1997. Tindel, Kay E., ed. 64p. 1997. pap. 58.00 (*0-7626-0081-0*, CP-11293) Cont Ed Bar-CA.

Ruud, C. O., et al. Nondestructive Characterization of Materials IV. (Illus.). 528p. (C). 1992. 174.00 (*0-306-44047-4*, Plenum Trade) Perseus Pubng.

Ruud, Charles A. Fighting Words: Imperial Censorship & the Russian Press, 1804-1906. LC 82-190787. 335p. reprint ed. pap. 103.90 (*0-7837-0528-X*, 204085400019) Bks Demand.

— Russian Entrepreneur: Publisher Ivan Sytin of Moscow, 1851-1934. (Illus.). 304p. (C). 1990. text 65.00 (*0-7735-0773-6*, Pub. by McG-Queens Univ Pr) CUP Services.

Ruud, Charles A. & Stepanov, S. A. Fontanka 16: The Tsars' Secret Police. LC 98-901352. (Illus.). 424p. 1997. 29.95 (*0-7735-1787-1*) McG-Queens Univ Pr.

Ruud, Clayton, ed. Practical Applications of Residual Stress Technology: Proceedings of the Third International Conference Held May 15-17, 1991, Indianapolis, IN. LC 91-74086. (ASM International Conference Proceedings Ser.). (Illus.). 189p. 1991. reprint ed. pap. 58.60 (*0-608-02648-4*, 206330700004) Bks Demand.

Ruud, Even. Music Therapy: Improvisation, Communication & Culture. LC 99-163042. 204p. (C). 1998. pap. text 26.00 (*1-891278-04-5*) Barcelona Pubs.

Ruud, Inger M., compiled by. Minoan Religion: A Bibliography. (Studies in Mediterranean Archaeology & Literature: No. 141). 124p. (Orig.). 1996. pap. 42.50 (*91-7081-162-8*, Pub. by P Astroms) Coronet Bks.

Ruud, Jaime S. Nutrition & the Female Athlete. LC 96-11966. (Nutrition in Exercise & Sport Ser.). 176p. 1996. boxed set 69.95 (*0-8493-7917-2*) CRC Pr.

Ruud, Judith S. Emerging Electronic Methods for Making Retail Payments. 76p. (Orig.). 1996. pap. 5.00 (*0-16-048706-4*, Congress) USGPO.

Ruud, Judith S. & Webre, Philip. Emerging Electronic Methods for Making Retail Payments. (Illus.). 50p. (Orig.). (C). 1996. pap. text 30.00 (*0-7881-3365-9*) DIANE Pub.

Ruud, Martin B. Thomas Chaucer. LC 78-174797. reprint ed. 21.50 (*0-404-05469-2*) AMS Pr.

— Thomas Chaucer. (BCL1-PR English Literature Ser.). 131p. 1992. reprint ed. lib. bdg. 69.00 (*0-7812-7176-2*) Rprt Serv.

***Ruud, Paul A.** An Introduction to Classical Econometric Theory. LC 99-89456. (Illus.). 976p. (C). 2000. text 85.00 (*0-19-511164-8*) OUP.

Ruud, Ronald C. & Woodford, Joseph J. Supervisor's Guide to Documentation & File Building for Employee Discipline. LC 83-72064. 72p. 1981. pap. 9.00 (*0-913406-06-5*) Advisory Pub.

Ruud, Warren L. Prelude to Calculus. 3rd ed. (Mathematics Ser.). 1999. text 63.95 (*0-534-94848-0*) PWS Pubs.

Ruud, Warren L. & Shell, Terry L. College Algebra. LC 96-61160. 624p. 1996. text 52.40 (*1-57259-244-3*) Worth.

— College Algebra. 1997. pap. text, student ed. 12.80 (*1-57259-246-X*) Worth.

Ruurs, Margriet. Emma's Eggs. unabridged ed. (Illus.). 24p. (J). (ps-3). 1997. 13.95 (*0-7737-2972-0*) STDK.

— A Mountain Alphabet. LC 96-60349. (Illus.). 32p. (J). (gr. 3 up). 1996. 19.95 (*0-88776-374-X*) Tundra Bks.

— A Mountain Alphabet. LC 96-931266. (Illus.). 32p. (J). (gr. 3 up). 1996. pap. 8.95 (*0-88776-384-7*) Tundra Bks.

***Ruurs, Margriet & Spurll, Barbara.** Emma & the Coyote. large type ed. (Illus.). 24p. (J). (ps-3). 1999. 15.95 (*0-7737-3140-7*) Genl Dist Srvs.

Ruurs, Rob. Saenredam: The Art of Perspective. LC 86-32669. (OCULI Studies in the Arts of the Low Countries Vol. 1). (Illus.). 228p. 1987. 76.00 (*1-55619-015-8*) J Benjamins Pubng Co.

Ruuth-Backer, Karin. En Litterar Resa Genom Det Suarta Afrika: En Bibliografisk Vagledning Till Afrikansk Skonlitteratur. 64p. 1981. write for info. (*91-7106-194-0*, Pub. by Nordic Africa) Transaction Pubs.

Ruuth, Marianne. Bill Cosby, Entertainer: Entertainer. (Black American Ser.). (Illus.). 192p. (YA). 1993. mass mkt. 3.95 (*0-87067-596-6*, Melrose Sq) Holloway.

— Eddie: Eddie Murphy from A to Z. 192p. (Orig.). (J). 1985. mass mkt. 2.95 (*0-87067-717-9*) Holloway.

Ruuth, Marianne. Frederick Douglass: Patriot & Activist. (Black American Ser.). (Illus.). 192p. (Orig.). (YA). (gr. 6-12). 1995. mass mkt. 4.95 (*0-87067-773-X*, BH773-X, Melrose Sq) Holloway.

Ruuth, Marianne. Nat King Cole: Singer & Jazz Pianist. (Black American Ser.). (Illus.). 192p. (YA). 1992. mass mkt. 3.95 (*0-87067-593-1*, Melrose Sq) Holloway.

— Oprah Winfrey: Entertainer. (Black American Ser.). (Illus.). 208p. (Orig.). (YA). (gr. 6-12). 1996. mass mkt. 4.95 (*0-87067-796-9*, BH-796-9, Melrose Sq) Holloway.

— Sarah Vaughan: Singer. (Black American Ser.). (Illus.). 208p. (Orig.). (YA). 1994. mass mkt. 3.95 (*0-87067-592-3*, Melrose Sq) Holloway.

— The Supremes: Triumph & Tragedy. rev. ed. (Illus.). 256p. 1995. mass mkt. 4.95 (*0-87067-749-7*, BH749-7) Holloway.

Ruuth, Marianne, tr. see Bergman, Ingmar.

Ruuth, Marianne, tr. see Fant, Kenne.

Ruvalcaba, Carlos. La Mariposa Bailarina. (SPA.). 1995. pap. text 8.95 (*1-56014-617-6*) Santillana.

Ruven, et al. Polycyclic Aromatic Hydrocarbons in Water Systems. 200p. 1981. 117.00 (*0-8493-6255-5*, QD341, CRC Reprint) Franklin.

Ruvinsky, A., jt. ed. see Fries, R.

Ruvinsky, A., jt. ed. see Rothschild, M. R.

Ruvinsky, Anatoly, jt. auth. see Bowling, Ann T.

Ruvinsky, Anatoly, jt. ed. see Piper, Laurie.

***Ruvinsky, Morrie.** Dream Keeper: A Novel of Myth & Destiny in the Pacific Northwest. 272p. 2000. 23.95 (*1-57061-167-X*) Sasquatch Bks.

Ruvituso, Donna, ed. see Huggan, John.

Ruvituso, Donna, ed. see Watson, Tom & Seitz, Nick.

***Ruvolo, Carol.** Faith at Work: Studies in the Book of James. 400p. 2000. pap. 14.95 (*0-9658804-3-5*) Deo Volente.

Ruvolo, Carol. James on Trials: How Faith Matures in the Storms of Life. LC 98-209938. (Faith at Work Ser.). 144p. (Orig.). 1998. pap. 7.95 (*0-9658804-0-0*) Deo Volente.

***Ruvolo, Carol.** James on Wisdom: How Faith Produces Sensible Living. (Faith at Work Ser.: Vol. 3). 160p. 1999. pap. 7.95 (*0-9658804-2-7*) Deo Volente.

Ruvolo, Carol. James on Works: How Faith Is Revealed in Pure & Undefiled Religion. (Faith at Work Ser.: Vol. 2). 1998. pap. 7.95 (*0-9658804-1-9*) Deo Volente.

Ruvolo, Carol J. Before the Throne of God: Focus on Prayer. LC 99-26104. (Light for Your Path Ser.). 180p. 1999. pap. 9.99 (*0-87552-630-6*) P & R Pubng.

***Ruvolo, Carol J.** A Believer's Guide to Spiritual Fitness: Focus on His Strength. (Light for Your Path). 208p. 2000. pap. 9.99 (*0-87552-633-0*) P & R Pubng.

Ruvolo, Carol J. A Book Like No Other: What's So Special about the Bible. LC 98-9905. (Light for Your Path Ser.). 160p. 1998. pap. 7.99 (*0-87552-627-6*) P & R Pubng.

— God with Us: Light from the Gospels. LC 98-20122. (Light for Your Path Ser.). 176p. 1998. pap. 8.99 (*0-87552-629-2*) P & R Pubng.

***Ruvolo, Carol J.** His Witnesses to the World: Light from Acts. LC 99-46637. (Light for Your Path Ser.). 216p. 1999. pap. 9.99 (*0-87552-631-4*) P & R Pubng.

Ruvolo, Carol J. The Light for Your Path Series Leader's Guide. LC 98-15493. (Light for Your Path). 32p. 1998. pap., teacher ed. 2.99 (*0-87552-628-4*) P & R Pubng.

— Turning on the Light: Discovering the Riches of God's Word. LC 98-14475. (Light for Your Path Ser.). 144p. 1998. pap. 7.99 (*0-87552-626-8*) P & R Pubng.

Ruvolo, Francine L., ed. see Pokras, Sandy.

Ruwart, Mary J. Healing Our World: The Other Piece of the Puzzle. (Illus.). 320p. (Orig.). (C). 1992. pap. 14.95 (*0-9632336-0-2*) SunStar Pr.

— Healing Our World: The Other Piece of the Puzzle. rev. ed. LC 92-35338. (Illus.). 320p. (Orig.). (C). 1993. pap. 14.95 (*0-9632336-2-9*) SunStar Pr.

***Ruwe, J.** Basic Blues Etudes in all Twelve Keys. 60p. 1998. pap. 12.95 (*0-7935-9599-1*) H Leonard.

— Major Blues Tunes in All Twelve Keys. 64p. 1997. pap. 12.95 (*0-7935-8662-3*) H Leonard.

***Ruwe, Jordan.** Velocity Exercises & Etudes for the Jazz Musician. 48p. 2000. pap. 12.95 (*0-634-01351-3*) H Leonard.

Ruwell, Mary E. Eighteenth Century Capitalism: The Formation of American Marine Insurance Companies. LC 92-40359. 200p. 1993. text 20.00 (*0-8153-0969-4*) Garland.

Ruwell, Mary E., et al. A Guide to the University Museum Archives. 72p. 1984. pap. 4.95 (*0-934718-65-2*) U Museum Pubns.

Ruwet, Nicholas, jt. auth. see Kiefer, Ferenc.

Ruwet, Nicolas. Syntax & Human Experience. Goldsmith, John, ed. & tr. by. LC 90-23535. (Studies in Contemporary Linguistics). 362p. 1991. pap. text 29.00 (*0-226-73222-3*) U Ch Pr.

— Syntax & Human Experience. Goldsmith, John, ed. & tr. by. LC 90-23535. (Studies in Contemporary Linguistics). 362p. 1996. lib. bdg. 70.00 (*0-226-73221-5*) U Ch Pr.

***Ruwisch, Silke.** Angewandte Multiplikation: Klassenfest, Puppenhaus Und Kinderbowle: Eine Qualitative Empirische Studie Zum Losungsverhalten Von Grundschulkindern Beim Bearbeiten Multiplikativer Sachsituationen. (Illus.). 336p. 1999. 51.95 (*3-631-34148-2*) P Lang Pubng.

Rux, Bruce. Architects of the Underworld: Unriddling Atlantis, Anomalies on Mars, & the Mystery of the Sphinx. LC 96-814. (Illus.). 575p. (Orig.). 1996. pap. 18.95 (*1-883319-46-3*) Frog Ltd CA.

— Hollywood vs. the Aliens: The Motion Picture Industry's Participation in UFO Disinformation. LC 96-37579. (Illus.). 200p. 1998. 19.95 (*1-883319-61-7*) Frog Ltd CA.

Rux, Carl Hancock. Pagan Operetta. LC 98-13535. 140p. 1998. pap. 14.95 (*0-9639585-8-5*) Fly By Night.

Ruxin, Robert H. An Athlete's Guide to Agents. 208p. 1993. pap. text 28.75 (*0-86720-779-5*) Jones & Bartlett.

Ruxton, George F. Life in the Far West. 330p. 1972. 20.00 (*0-87380-098-2*) Popular E Commerce.

— Life in the Far West. Hafen, LeRoy R., ed. (American Exploration & Travel Ser.: Vol. 14). (Illus.). 1979. pap. 14.95 (*0-8061-1534-3*) U of Okla Pr.

Ruxton, Ian C., ed. see Satow, Ernest M.

Ruxton, Kathy B. Executive Pay, 1997: Chief Executive Officer Compensation at S&P Super 1,500 Companies As Reported in 1997. LC 99-176344. 65p. 1998. pap. 395.00 (*1-879775-60-3*) IRRC Inc DC.

Ruxton, William E. Doing Things Right. 249p. 1985. text 49.95 (*0-910399-33-6*) Natl Tool & Mach.

Ruy-Sanchez, Alberto M. Mogador. Schafer, Mark, tr. from SPA. 124p. (Orig.). 1992. pap. 7.95 (*0-87286-271-2*) City Lights.

Ruybal, Jay D. The Drug Hazed War in Southeast Asia: A Soldier's Extraordinary Experience in the Killing Fields of South Vietnam. (Illus.). 288p. 1998. pap. 14.95 (*1-880047-59-4*); pap. 29.95 (*1-880047-61-6*) Creative Des.

Ruyer, Francois. Farm Animals. 6p. (J). (ps). 1992. pap. 9.49 (*1-881445-11-9*) Sandvik Pub.

Ruyet, Jake, jt. auth. see Lyon, Richards.

Ruymann, Frederick B., jt. auth. see Maurer, Harold M.

Ruymar, Lorene, ed. The Hawaiian Steel Guitar & Its Great Hawaiian Musicians. (Illus.). 208p. (Orig.). (C). 1996. pap. 29.95 (*1-57424-021-8*, 00000189) Centerstream Pub.

Ruymgaart, P. A. & Soong, T. T. Mathematics of Kalman-Bucy Filtering. (Information Sciences Ser.: Vol. 14). (Illus.). 190p. 1985. 35.00 (*0-387-13508-1*) Spr-Verlag.

— Mathematics of Kalman-Bucy Filtering. (Information Sciences Ser.: Vol. 14). (Illus.). 180p. 1988. 53.95 (*0-387-18781-2*) Spr-Verlag.

Ruys, Pieter H., jt. ed. see Gilles, Robert P.

Ruysbroeck, Jan Van, see Van Ruysbroeck, Jan.

Ruysbroeck, John. The Seven Steps of the Ladder of Spiritual Love. 1990. pap. 7.95 (*1-55818-130-X*) Holmes Pub.

Ruysbroeck, Willem Van, see Van Ruysbroeck, Willem.

Ruysseveldt, Doris Van, see Harzing, Anne-Wil, ed.

Ruysseveldt, Doris Van, see Harzing, Anne-Wil & Van Ruysseveldt, Doris, eds.

Ruysseveldt, Doris Van, see Harzing, Anne-Wil, ed.

Ruysseveldt, Doris Van, see Harzing, Anne-Wil & Van Ruysseveldt, Doris, eds.

Ruysseveldt, Doris Van, see Van Ruysseveldt, Doris.

Ruyter, Kitty De, see De Ruyter, Kitty.

Ruyter, Nancy L., jt. auth. see Dunin, Elsie I.

Ruyter, Nancy Lee Chalta. The Cultivation of Body & Mind in Nineteenth-Century American Delsartism, 56. LC 99-10076. (Contributions to the Study of Music & Dance Ser.: Vol. 56). 200p. 1999. 55.00 (*0-313-31042-4*) Greenwood.

Ruzdjak, V., et al, eds. Dynamics of Quiescent Prominences: Proceedings of IAU Colloquium No. 117 Held in Hvar, SR Croatia, Yugoslavia, 25-29 September 1989. (Lecture Notes in Physics Ser.: Vol. 363). xii, 304p. 1990. 54.95 (*0-387-52973-X*) Spr-Verlag.

Ruzek, Raymond P., jt. auth. see Parkinson, Kenneth L.

Ruzek, Rhonda. He's Mine. 1995. mass mkt. 4.99 (*1-896329-50-0*) Picasso Publ.

Ruzek, Sheryl B., et al. Women's Health: Complexities & Differences. LC 96-34047. (Women & Health Ser.). 689p. 1997. text 55.00 (*0-8142-0704-9*); pap. text 21.95 (*0-8142-0705-7*) Ohio St U Pr.

Ruzena, Skerlj, jt. auth. see Komac, Dasa.

Ruzer, Lev. Aerosol Research & Development in the Soviet Union: The Measurement of Main Parameters. (Illus.). 160p. (Orig.). 1989. pap. 75.00 (*0-685-35188-2*) Delphic Associates.

Ruzgis, Patricia, jt. ed. see Sternberg, Robert J.

Ruzhnikov, Andre & Harlow, Ann. Icons & Easter Eggs of Imperial Russia. (Illus.). 16p. 1995. pap. 9.95 (*1-886091-10-2*) Hearst Art Gal.

Ruzic, jt. auth. see Huizenga.

Ruzic, Neil. The Shallow Sea. 544p. 1995. 19.95 (*0-9632357-0-2*) St Clair Pr.

Ruzich, Christian. World Series Stars & Stats. McClusky, Mark, ed. 32p. (Orig.). (J). 1999. pap. 3.99 (*1-886749-66-3*, Pub. by SI For Kids) Scholastic Inc.

Ruzicho, Andrew J. & Jacobs, Louis A. Employment Practices Manual: A Guide to Minimizing Constitutional, Statutory & Common Law Liability. rev. ed. 1994. write for info. (*0-614-32073-9*) West Group.

— Equal Employment Compliance Manual. 1992. 350.00 (*0-685-14551-4*) West Group.

— Litigating Age Discrimination Cases. LC 86-11736. 1992. 140.00 (*0-685-14016-4*) West Group.

— Litigating Age Discrimination Cases. annuals 1992. suppl. ed. write for info. (*0-318-60923-1*) West Group.

Ruzicka, Jaromir. Flow Injection Analysis. 2nd ed. LC 87-18772. (Chemical Analysis Ser.). 528p. 1988. 175.00 (*0-471-81355-9*) Wiley.

Ruzicka, Jiri. Lieferung, Vol. 1. (Desmidiaceen Mitteleuropas Ser.: Band I). (GER., Illus.). viii, 292p. 1977. 82.00 (*3-510-65078-6*, Pub. by E Schweizerbartsche) Balogh.

— Lieferung, Vol. 2. (Desmidiaceen Mitteleuropas Ser.: Band I). (GER., Illus.). ix, 444p. 1981. 116.00 (*3-510-65103-0*, Pub. by E Schweizerbartsche) Balogh.

Ruzicka, Joseph. French Posters & Prints: The Gutglass Collection. (Illus.). 28p. 1997. pap. 8.95 (*0-944110-63-0*) Milwauk Art Mus.

— Ink on Paper: The Quad Collection, 1971-1966. Mills, Charlene, ed. LC 96-77777. (Illus.). 180p. 1996. pap. 24.95 (*0-944110-52-5*) Milwauk Art Mus.

Ruzicka, Lado, et al, eds. Differential Mortality: Methodological Issues & Biosocial Factors. (International Studies in Demography). (Illus.). 272p. 1989. text 75.00 (*0-19-828651-1*) OUP.

— Differential Mortality: Methodological Issues & Biosocial Factors. (International Studies in Demography). (Illus.). 268p. 1995. reprint ed. pap. text 21.00 (*0-19-828882-4*) OUP.

Ruzicka, Molly B., ed. see Meech-Pekarik, Julia.

Ruzicka, Nancy H. Embarrassingly Simple: Recipes from the Jamison Inn Bed & Breakfast. Edge, Lynn, ed. & photos by by. LC 98-89538. (Illus.). xii, 196p. 1998. write for info. (*0-9668306-0-1*) R & R Assocs.

Ruzicka, Rudolf. Control in Grammar & Pragmatics: A Cross-Linguistic Study. LC 99-22394. (Linguistik Aktuell/Linguistics Today Ser.: Vol. 27). x, 206p. 1999. 65.00 (*1-55619-911-2*) J Benjamins Pubng Co.

Ruzicka, Stephen. Politics of a Persian Dynasty: The Hecatomnids in the Fourth Century B. C. LC 92-54138. (Oklahoma Series in Classical Culture: Vol. 14). 256p. 1992. 42.50 (*0-8061-2460-1*) U of Okla Pr.

Ruzicka, T., et al, eds. Handbook of Atopic Eczema. (Illus.). 496p. 1991. 185.00 (*0-387-52992-6*) Spr-Verlag.

Ruzicka, T., jt. ed. see Eckertova, L.

Ruzicka, Thomas, ed. Eicosanoids & the Skin. 224p. 1990. lib. bdg. 229.00 (*0-8493-6032-3*, RL96) CRC Pr.

Ruzicka, William J. The Nightmare of Success: The Fallacy of the Super-Success Dream. LC 73-90028. 155p. 1973. 6.95 (*0-914372-01-7*) Peninsula Pubns.

Ruzicka, William T. Faulkner's Fictive Architecture: The Meaning of Place in the Yoknapatawpha Novels. LC 87-10799. (Studies in Modern Literature: No. 67). 165p. 1987. reprint ed. pap. 51.20 (*0-8357-1788-7*, 207064900012) Bks Demand.

Ruzicki, Dorothy A. & Ruzicki, Gerald M. In Search of Ancient Scotland: A Guide for the Independent Traveler. LC 99-63546. (Illus.). 336p. 2000. pap. 17.95 (*0-9664496-0-6*) Aspen Grove Pub.

Ruzicki, Gerald M., jt. auth. see Ruzicki, Dorothy A.

Ruzin, Steven E. Plant Microtechnique & Microscopy. LC 98-40910. (Illus.). 336p. (C). 1999. pap. text 45.00 (*0-19-508956-1*) OUP.

Ruzkova, Milena, tr. see Nickerson, Dan.

Ruzmailin, A. A., et al. Magnetic Fields of Galaxies. (C). 1988. text 215.00 (*90-277-2450-4*) Kluwer Academic.

Ruzow, Daniel A., jt. auth. see Gerrard, Michael B.

Ruzsa, I. & Szabolcsi, A. Logic & Language: Proceedings of the '87 Debrecen Symposium Held from August 25 to 28, 1987. 252p. (C). 1987. 40.00 (*963-462-238-0*, Pub. by Akade Kiado) St Mut.

Ruzyllo, J. & Novak, R. E., eds. Cleaning Technology in Semiconductor Device Manufacturing: 4th International Symposium. LC 95-61593. (Proceedings Ser.: Vol. 95-20). (Illus.). 626p. 1996. 79.00 (*1-56677-115-3*) Electrochem Soc.

Ruzyllo, Jerzy, ed. see International Symposium on Cleaning Technology in.

Ruzzante, Angelo B. L' Anconitana: The Woman from Ancona. LC 93-35922. (Biblioteca Italiana Ser.). (ENG & ITA.). 1994. 45.00 (*0-520-08525-6*, Pub. by U CA Pr); pap. 16.95 (*0-520-08526-4*, Pub. by U CA Pr) Cal Prin Full Svc.

RV Actualiza Staff. Spanish Bible Actualizada. (SPA.). 1989. 16.99 (*0-311-48785-8*) Baptist Spanish.

***RV Consumer Group Staff & Gallant, JD.** RV Rating Book: 1999 Models with the Language of RVing with. 408p. 1999. per. 48.00 (*1-890049-08-5*) R V Consumer Grp.

RV Consumer Group Staff, jt. auth. see Gallant, J. D.

RV Consumer Group Staff, jt. auth. see Gallant, JD.

RVer, Annie. Bread & Scripture: Trailer Folks Favorite Recipe, Chapter & Verse. (Illus.). 96p. 1985. pap. 8.50 (*0-9613607-1-2*) RVer Annie.

RVer Annie. Cooking on Wheels: Trailer Folks Favorite Recipes. Mitchell, Joyce S., ed. LC 84-90601. 96p. 1984. pap. 8.50 (*0-9613607-0-4*) RVer Annie.

Rwebangira, Magdalena K. The Legal Status of Women & Poverty in Tanzania. (Scandinavian Institute of African Studies: No. 100). 58p. (Orig.). 1996. pap. 20.00 (*91-7106-391-9*) Coronet Bks.

Rwebangira, Magdalena K., jt. ed. see Liljestrom, Rita.

Rwegasira, Kami. Problems of Financial Analysis in Institutional Lending Operations: Some Lessons from Tanzania. LC 92-33657. 200p. 1992. 82.95 (*1-85628-299-6*, Pub. by Avebry) Ashgate Pub Co.

Rwelamira, M. The Role of Law in Transition. LC 97-132589. 1996. pap. write for info. (*0-409-05114-4*, MICHIE) LEXIS Pub.

Rwelamira, Medard. Refugees in a Chess Game: Reflections on Botswana, Lesotho & Swaziland Refugee Policies. (Research Report Ser.: No. 88). 64p. 1990. write for info. (*91-7106-306-4*, Pub. by Nordic Africa) Transaction Pubs.

Rweyemamu, M., et al. Quality Control Testing of Rinderpest Cell Culture Vaccine - Standard Operating Procedure. LC 95-131051. (Animal Production & Health Papers: No. 118). 112p. 1994. pap. 15.00 (*92-5-103444-3*, F34443, Pub. by FAO) Bernan Associates.

***Rwomire, Apollo, ed.** African Women & Children: Crisis & Response. LC 00-27435. 260p. 2000. 64.00 (*0-275-96218-0*) Greenwood.

— Social Problems in Africa: New Visions. 2001. write for info. (*0-275-96343-8*, Praeger Pubs) Greenwood.

Ry, Meredith Van, see Van Ry, Meredith.

Rya, Aniruddha, jt. auth. see Arasaratnam, Sinnappah.

Ryabchikov, D. & Col'Braikh, E. Analytical Chemistry of Thorium. LC 63-10065. (International Series of Monographs on Analytical Chemistry: Vol. 10). 1963. 144.00 (*0-08-013737-7*, Pub. by Pergamon Repr) Franklin.

Ryabeo, V. R. Welding & Surfacing Reviews: Welding of Composite Materials, Vol. 4. (Welding & Surfacing Reviews Ser.). 193p. 1995. pap. text 77.00 (*3-7186-5758-9*) Gordon & Breach.

Ryabov, E. A. Laser Chemisty in Russia. 86p. 1993. text 237.00 (*3-7186-5373-7*) Gordon & Breach.

***Ryabov, V. R.** Welding of Aluminum Alloys to Steels Issue 3, Vol. 9. 142p. 1998. pap. text 50.00 (*90-5702-330-X*, Harwood Acad Pubs) Gordon & Breach.

***Ryabov, V. R. & Batyshev, A. I.** Welding of Dissimilar Metals: Solidification of Metals & Alloys Under Pressure. 350p. 1999. boxed set 150.00 (*1-898326-67-3*, Pub. by CISP) Balogh.

***Ryabov, V. R. & Deev.** Surface Phenomena in Welding & Surfacing Issue 3, Vol. 10 120p. 1998. pap. text 71.00 (*90-5702-426-8*, Harwood Acad Pubs) Gordon & Breach.

***Ryabov, Vladimir R. & Ryazantsev, Vladmir.** Arc Welding of Aluminum & Magnesium Alloys. (Illus.). 160p. 1999. 139.95 (*0-9644311-7-3*) Backbone Pubng.

Ryaboy, Vladislav. Upper Mantle Structure Studies by Explosion Seismology in the U. S. S. R. Nobel, Erika D., ed. (Illus.). 141p. (Orig.). 1989. pap. text 75.00 (*1-55831-091-6*) Delphic Associates.

Ryall, M. Q., jt. ed. see Holyoake, George J.

Ryall, Michael. Tapestry Reading: Level 2. LC 99-57604. (C). 2000. pap. text 25.95 (*0-8384-0056-6*) Thomson Learn.

Ryall, R., et al. Urolithiasis 2: Proceedings of the International Symposium on Urolithiasis, 7th, Cairns, Australia, Held August 1992. (Illus.). 726p. 1994. 165.00 (*0-306-44727-4*, Kluwer Plenum) Kluwer Academic.

Ryall, R. W. Mechanisms of Drug Action on the Nervous System. 2nd ed. (Illus.). 256p. (C). 1989. text 64.95 (*0-521-25424-8*); pap. text 22.95 (*0-521-27437-0*) Cambridge U Pr.

Ryall, Rhiannon. Celtic Lore & Druid Ritual. 1994. pap. 22.95 (*1-898307-24-5*, Pub. by Capall Bann Pubng) Holmes Pub.

— Symbols of Ancient Gods. (Illus.). (Orig.). 1998. pap. 21.95 (*1-86163-008-5*, Pub. by Capall Bann Pubng) Holmes Pub.

— Weaving a Web of Magic: A Potpourri of Rituals, Chants, Dances, Webs, Cords, Runes, Talismans, & Magical Information. (Illus.). (Orig.). 1996. pap. 19.95 (*1-898307-92-X*, Pub. by Capall Bann Pubng) Holmes Pub.

— West Country Wicca. (Illus.). 104p. 1990. pap. 8.95 (*0-919345-98-0*) Phoenix WA.

— West Country Wicca - A Journal of the Old Religion. 1994. pap. 17.95 (*1-898307-02-4*, Pub. by Capall Bann Pubng) Holmes Pub.

Ryall, Tom. Alfred Hitchcock & the British Cinema. 2nd ed. LC 96-204231. 208p. (C). 1986. pap. 25.00 (*0-485-12122-0*, Pub. by Athlone Pr) Humanities.

— Blackmail. (Illus.). 64p. 1994. pap. 10.95 (*0-85170-356-9*, Pub. by British Film Inst) Ind U Pr.

Ryalls, Jack. A Basic Introduction to Speech Perception. LC 96-7531. (Speech Science Ser.). (Illus.). 162p. (Orig.). (C). 1996. pap. text 34.95 (*1-56593-617-5*, 1284) Thomson Learn.

Ryals, Clyde D. Browning's Later Poetry, 1871-1889. LC 75-16927. 288p. 1975. text 42.50 (*0-8014-0964-0*) Cornell U Pr.

— The Collected Letters of Thomas & Jane Welch Carlyle, Vols. 13-15. Fielding, Kenneth J., ed. LC 71-101132. 1988. text 49.95 (*0-8223-0702-2*); text 49.95 (*0-8223-0703-0*); text 49.95 (*0-8223-0704-9*); lib. bdg. 49.95 (*0-318-61460-X*) Duke.

Ryals, Clyde D. & Fielding, Kenneth J., eds. The Collected Letters of Thomas & Jane Welsh Carlyle Vol. 19: January to September, 1845. LC 71-101323. 263p. 1993. text 49.95 (*0-8223-1286-7*) Duke.

— The Collected Letters of Thomas & Jane Welsh Carlyle Vol. 20: October 1845 to July 1846. LC 71-101323. 269p. 1993. text 49.95 (*0-8223-1287-5*) Duke.

— The Collected Letters of Thomas & Jane Welsh Carlyle Vol. 21: August 1846 to June 1847. LC 71-101323. 285p. 1993. text 49.95 (*0-8223-1288-3*) Duke.

— The Collected Letters of Thomas & Jane Welsh Carlyle Vol. 22: July 1847 to March 1848. LC 71-101132. 288p. 1995. text 49.95 (*0-8223-1608-0*) Duke.

— The Collected Letters of Thomas & Jane Welsh Carlyle Vol. 23: April 1848 to March 1849. LC 71-101132. 288p. 1995. text 49.95 (*0-8223-1609-9*) Duke.

— The Collected Letters of Thomas & Jane Welsh Carlyle Vol. 24: April to December 1849. LC 71-101132. 336p. 1995. text 49.95 (*0-8223-1610-2*) Duke.

Ryals, Clyde D., et al. The Collected Letters of Thomas & Jane Welsh Carlyle, Vol. 16. Campbell, Ian et al, eds. LC 71-101132. 424p. (Orig.). 1990. text 49.95 (*0-8223-0919-X*) Duke.

— The Collected Letters of Thomas & Jane Welsh Carlyle, Vol. 17. Campbell, Ian et al, eds. LC 71-101132. 384p. (Orig.). 1990. text 49.95 (*0-8223-0924-6*) Duke.

— The Collected Letters of Thomas & Jane Welsh Carlyle, Vol. 18. Campbell, Ian et al, eds. LC 71-101132. 384p. (Orig.). 1990. text 49.95 (*0-8223-0936-X*) Duke.

— The Collected Letters of Thomas & Jane Welsh Carlyle, Vols. 16-18. Campbell, Ian et al, eds. (Orig.). 1990. lib. bdg. write for info. (*0-318-65458-X*) Duke.

Ryals, Clyde D., ed. & intro. see Ward, Mary A.

Ryals, E. C., 3rd. It's Party Time. 304p. (Orig.). pap. 17.95 (*0-9651957-0-8*) L Ryals & Assocs.

Ryals, Mary J. A Messy Job I Never Did See a Girl Do: Stories. 144p. 1999. pap. 9.95 (*0-942979-59-1*); lib. bdg. 19.95 (*0-942979-60-5*) Livingston AL.

Ryals, Mary J. & Decker, Donna, eds. North of Wakulla: An Anhinga Anthology. (Illus.). 160p. (Orig.). 1989. pap. 12.50 (*0-938078-30-5*) Anhinga Pr.

Ryan. Anatomy for Diagnostic Imaging. (C). 1994. pap. text 57.00 (*0-7020-1447-8*) Harcourt.

***Ryan.** Bond Markets: Structure & Yield Calculations. 200p. 1998. pap. text 45.00 (*1-57958-087-4*) Fitzroy Dearborn.

Ryan. Career Adventure. 1990. mass mkt. 21.75 (*0-314-76554-9*) West Pub.

— Career Choices. Date not set. pap. text, teacher ed. 13.95 (*0-314-84242-X*) West Pub.

— Career Preparation. (CA - Career Development Ser.). (C). 1998. mass mkt. 16.25 (*0-314-12993-6*) S-W Pub.

— Career Success Continuing Education. 1996. mass mkt. 11.00 (*0-314-07136-9*) West Pub.

— Career Success Inventory. 1996. pap. text 38.50 (*0-314-06796-5*) West Pub.

— Career Success Occupation Handbook. 1996. mass mkt. 19.00 (*0-314-07139-3*) West Pub.

— Career Success Test Book. Date not set. pap. text. write for info. (*0-314-08329-4*) West Pub.

— Computer-Aided Kinetics for Machine Design. (Mechanical Engineering Ser.: Vol. 7). (Illus.). 288p. 1981. text 95.00 (*0-8247-1421-0*) Dekker.

— Lobbying from Below: Civil Liberty. 208p. 1996. 59.95 (*1-85728-255-8*, Pub. by UCL Pr Ltd); pap. 19.95 (*1-85728-256-6*, Pub. by UCL Pr Ltd) Taylor & Francis.

— Managing Your Personal Finances. (OX - Home Economics Ser.). 1984. mass mkt. 46.95 (*0-538-08030-2*) S-W Pub.

— Managing Your Personal Finances. 2nd ed. (HM - Consumer Education Ser.). 1989. mass mkt. 49.95 (*0-538-60084-5*); mass mkt., wbk. ed. 16.95 (*0-538-60085-3*) S-W Pub.

— Managing Your Personal Finances. 3rd ed. (OX - Home Economics Ser.). 1996. mass mkt., wbk. ed. 16.95 (*0-538-62897-9*) S-W Pub.

— Managing Your Personal Finances. 3rd ed. (HM - Consumer Education Ser.). 1996. mass mkt. 56.95 (*0-538-62896-0*) S-W Pub.

— Managing Your Personal Finances. 3rd ed. (HM - Consumer Education Ser.). 1997. text, teacher ed. 16.95 (*0-538-63399-9*) S-W Pub.

Ryan. Managing Your Personal Finances. 3rd ed. 1997. pap. 45.25 (*0-538-68336-8*) Thomson Learn.

Ryan. Managing Your Personal Finances: Tests. 2nd ed. (HM - Consumer Education Ser.). 1989. 3.95 (*0-538-60086-1*) S-W Pub.

— Occupational Orientation. Date not set. pap. text, teacher ed. write for info. (*0-314-09470-9*) West Pub.

— Personal Business Management. 2nd ed. (OX - Home Economics Ser.). 1990. mass mkt., wbk. ed. 14.95 (*0-538-60379-8*) S-W Pub.

— Plotting Course Act. 1997. mass mkt., wbk. ed. 20.50 (*0-314-06792-2*) West Pub.

***Ryan.** Shakespeare: Texts & Contexts. 2000. text 59.95 (*0-312-23035-4*) St Martin.

Ryan. Shakespeare: The Last Plays. LC 98-30637. 312p. (C). 1998. pap. 36.93 (*0-582-27573-3*); text 65.95 (*0-582-27574-1*) Longman.

— Small Business: An Entrepreneur's Plan. 4th ed. (C). 1995. pap. text, teacher ed. 30.00 (*0-03-017613-1*) Harcourt Coll Pubs.

— Small Business: An Entrepreneurv. 5th ed. (C). 1998. pap. text 64.00 (*0-03-022593-0*, Pub. by Harcourt Coll Pubs) Harcourt.

— Small Business: Entrepreneurs. 4th ed. (C). 1995. pap. text 64.00 (*0-03-012894-3*) Harcourt Coll Pubs.

— Strategic Accounting for Management. 1998. pap. 22.99 (*1-86152-462-5*) Thomson Learn.

— War & Peace in Ireland: Britain & the IRA in the New World Order. LC 94-8049. (C). 71.95 (*0-7453-0923-2*, Pub. by Pluto GBR); pap. 25.95 (*0-7453-0924-0*, Pub. by Pluto GBR) Stylus Pub VA.

Ryan & Reynolds. Canterbury Tales: Big Sister's Talep. (Illus.). (J). mass mkt. 7.95 (*0-340-71450-6*, Pub. by Hodder & Stought Ltd) Trafalgar.

— Canterbury Tales: Little Brother Talep. (Illus.). (J). mass mkt. 7.95 (*0-340-71451-4*, Pub. by Hodder & Stought Ltd) Trafalgar.

— Canterbury Tales: Little Sister Tale. (Illus.). (J). mass mkt. 7.95 (*0-340-71452-2*, Pub. by Hodder & Stought Ltd) Trafalgar.

Ryan & Robinson. CA Compensation Cases, 54 vols. 1989. write for info. (*0-8205-1979-0*) Bender.

Ryan & Scapens. Research Method & Methodology in Finance & Accounting. 1998. pap. 29.95 (*1-86152-460-9*) Thomson Learn.

Ryan, et al. Media & Society. LC 98-25986. 255p. 1998. pap. text 40.00 (*0-205-17400-0*, Longwood Div) Allyn.

Ryan, jt. auth. see Guile, A. E.

Ryan, jt. auth. see Kistners, Robert W.

Ryan, jt. auth. see Miller.

Ryan, jt. auth. see Ropelewski.

Ryan, A. H. Weekend Gold Miner. rev. ed. Shepherd, Robin, ed. 1991. 5.50 (*0-935182-46-2*) Gem Guides Bk.

Ryan, Alan. Bertrand Russell: A Political Life. 240p. 1993. pap. 12.95 (*0-19-508634-1*) OUP.

— John Dewey: And the High Tide of American Liberalism. LC 94-36064. (Illus.). 448p. 1995. 30.00 (*0-393-03773-8*) Norton.

— John Dewey: And the High Tide of American Liberalism. 416p. 1997. pap. 17.00 (*0-393-31550-9*) Norton.

— Liberal Anxieties & Liberal Education. LC 97-38930. 199p. 1998. 22.00 (*0-8090-6539-8*) Hill & Wang.

— The Reader's Companion to Ireland. LC 98-23354. (Illus.). 352p. (C). 1999. pap. 16.00 (*0-15-600559-X*, Harvest Bks) Harcourt.

— The Reader's Companion to South Africa. LC 98-19327. (Illus.). 352p. 1999. pap. 16.00 (*0-15-600558-1*, Harvest Bks) Harcourt.

Ryan, Alan, ed. Haunting Women. 224p. (Orig.). 1988. pap. 3.95 (*0-380-89881-0*, Avon Bks) Morrow Avon.

— Justice. LC 92-35200. (Oxford Readings in Politics & Government Ser.). 206p. 1993. pap. text 16.95 (*0-19-878038-9*) OUP.

— Latin American Short Stories. 1999. 29.95 (*0-670-83632-X*) Viking Penguin.

— The Penguin Book of Vampire Stories. 640p. 1989. pap. 14.95 (*0-14-012445-4*, Penguin Bks) Viking Penguin.

— The Reader's Companion to Alaska. LC 96-47184. 395p. (C). 1997. pap. 16.00 (*0-15-600368-6*, Harvest Bks) Harcourt.

— Reader's Companion to Cuba. LC 96-47363. 352p. 1997. pap. 16.00 (*0-15-600367-8*) Harcourt.

— The Reader's Guide to Mexico. 400p. 1995. pap. 16.00 (*0-15-676021-5*) Harcourt.

Ryan, Alan, jt. auth. see Metzger, Linda.

Ryan, Alan, ed. see Mill, John Stuart, et al.

Ryan, Alan, jt. ed. see Rogers, G. A.

Ryan, Alan, ed. & selected by see Mill, John Stuart.

Ryan, Allan. Property. LC 87-25538. (Concepts in Social Thought Ser.). 143p. (Orig.). 1988. pap. 13.95 (*0-8166-1670-1*) U of Minn Pr.

Ryan, Allan A., Jr. & United States Department of Justice Staff. Klaus Barbie & the United States Government: The Report, with Documentary Appendix, to the Attorney General of the United States. LC 83-23466. (Foreign Intelligence Book Ser.). 541p. 1984. lib. bdg. 55.00 (*0-313-27013-9*, U7013) Greenwood.

***Ryan, Allan J.** The Trickster Shift: Humour & Irony in Contemporary Native Art LC 99-17663. (Illus.). 320p. 1999. 60.00 (*0-295-97816-3*) U of Wash Pr.

Ryan, Allan J. & Stephens, Robert E. The Dancer's Complete Guide to Healthcare & a Long Career. (Illus.). 224p. 1988. 11.95 (*0-933893-76-0*) Bonus Books.

Ryan, Amanda, jt. auth. see Ross, Carol.

Ryan, Angela S., ed. Social Work with Immigrants & Refugees. LC 92-32667. (Journal of Multicultural Social Work: No. 2-1). (Illus.). 157p. 1993. lib. bdg. 39.95 (*1-56024-354-6*) Haworth Pr.

— Social Work with Immigrants & Refugees. LC 92-32667. (Journal of Multicultural Social Work: No. 2-1). (Illus.). 157p. 1993. pap. 19.95 (*1-56024-355-4*) Haworth Pr.

Ryan, Angela S., jt. ed. see Parry, Joan K.

Ryan, Anne, ed. see Solkoff, Jerome I.

***Ryan, Arliss.** Kingsley House. LC 99-89772. 432p. 2000. text 25.95 (*0-312-24209-3*) St Martin.

Ryan, Arthur N., ed. Uniquely Gloucestor: A Literary Presentation for Gloucester's 375th Anniversary. 35p. (Orig.). 1998. pap. 9.95 (*1-892839-02-4*) Curious Traveller Pr.

Ryan, Barbara. Feminism & the Women's Movement: Dynamics of Change in Social Movement Ideology & Activism. (Perspectives on Gender Ser.). (Illus.). 272p. (C). (gr. 13). 1992. pap. 22.99 (*0-415-90599-0*, A8189) Routledge.

— Women's Movement. 1996. 45.00 (*0-8161-7254-4*, G K Hall & Co) Mac Lib Ref.

Ryan, Barbara F. & Joiner, Brian L. Minitab Handbook. 3rd ed. 448p. 1994. pap. 31.95 (*0-534-21240-9*) Wadsworth Pub.

***Ryan, Barbara F. & Joiner, Brian L.** Minitab Handbook. 4th ed. LC 00-39732. 2000. pap. write for info. (*0-534-37093-4*) Brooks-Cole.

Ryan, Barbara F., et al. Minitab Handbook: With Release 8. 2nd rev. ed. 409p. 1992. pap. 24.50 (*0-534-93366-1*) Wadsworth Pub.

— Minitab Handbook (revised) 2nd ed. (Statistics Software). 379p. 1988. pap. 20.25 (0-534-91579-5) Wadsworth Pub.
— Minitab Student Handbook. LC 75-41977. (C). 1976. pap. 14.25 (0-87150-359-X) PWS Pubs.
Ryan, Barbara S. Living Each Day by the Power of Faith: Thirty Meditations to Deepen Your Trust in God. rev. ed. 144p. 1997. pap. 8.95 (1-878718-39-8, Resurrection Pr) Catholic Bk Pub.
Ryan, Barbara S., et al. To Heal As Jesus Healed. rev. ed. 112p. 1997. pap. 7.95 (1-878718-36-3, Resurrection Pr) Catholic Bk Pub.
Ryan, Bernard, Jr. Community Service for Teens: Increasing Neighborhood Service. Ferguson Publishing Company Staff, ed. LC 97-34971. (Illus.). 96p. (YA). 1998. 15.95 (0-89434-233-9) Ferguson.
— Helping Your Child Start School: A Practical Guide for Parents. LC 97-155555. 224p. 1996. pap. text 10.95 (0-8065-1798-0, Citadel Pr) Carol Pub Group.
— Helping Your Child Start School: A Practical Guide for Parents. 242p. 1999. reprint ed. 27.95 (0-7351-0114-0) Replica Bks.
Ryan, Bernard, Jr., jt. auth. see Lewin, Elizabeth.
Ryan, Betsy. Secret Love. LC 90-24058. (Hampstead High Ser.). 128p. (J). (gr. 5-9). 1991. pap. text 2.95 (0-8167-1913-6) Troll Communs.
Ryan, Betsy A. Gertrude Stein's Theatre of the Absolute. Beckerman, Bernard, ed. LC 84-191. (Theater & Dramatic Studies: No. 21). 246p. reprint ed. 76.30 (0-8357-1548-5, 207076300004) Bks Demand.
Ryan, Beverly A., jt. auth. see Burgess, Michael.
Ryan, Bill. Making Capital from Culture: The Corporate Form of Capitalist Cultural Production. (Studies in Organization: No. 35). xii, 290p. (C). 1991. lib. bdg. 54.95 (3-11-012548-X, 236-91) De Gruyter.
Ryan, Bill & Schrader, Richard. An Ounce of Pollution Prevention: Analysis & Rating of Ten State Pollution Prevention Laws. 60p. 1990. 15.00 (0-685-56588-2) CPA Washington.
Ryan, Bob. AmigaWorld AmigaDos 2 Companion. LC 90-84500. 407p. 1995. 24.95 (1-878058-09-6) IDG Bks.
Ryan, Bob, jt. auth. see Bird, Larry.
Ryan, Bob, jt. auth. see Ryan, Gary.
Ryan, Bryan, ed. Major 20th-Century Writers: A Selection of Sketches from Contemporary Authors, 4 vols. 3300p. 1990. 295.00 (0-8103-7766-7) Gale.
— Major Twentieth-Century Writers: A Selection of Sketches from Contemporary Authors, 5 vols. 2nd ed. LC 98-39995. 3124p. 1998. 315.00 (0-8103-8450-7) Gale.
Ryan, Bryan, jt. auth. see Wilson, Kathleen.
Ryan, Bryce. Caste in Modern Ceylon: The Sinhalese System in Transition. (C). 1993. reprint ed. text 32.00 (81-7013-106-5, Pub. by Navarang) S Asia.
Ryan, Bryce F. Social & Cultural Change. LC 79-84081. 506p. reprint ed. pap. 156.90 (0-608-30705-X, 201253400081) Bks Demand.
Ryan, C., et al. Phosgene & Related Carbonyl Halides. LC 96-1172. (Topics in Inorganic & General Chemistry Ser.: No. 24). 978p. 1996. text 463.00 (0-444-82445-6) Elsevier.
Ryan, C. L., et al. Ryan, Savla & Scanlan: A Guide to the Criminal Procedure & Investigations Act 1996. (Butterworths Annotated Legislation Service Ser.). 1996. pap. write for info. (0-406-99249-5, AMGC1996, MICHIE) LEXIS Pub.
Ryan, Caitlin & Futterman, Donna. Lesbian & Gay Youth: Care & Counseling. 256p. 1998. 47.50 (0-231-11190-8); pap. 22.50 (0-231-11191-6) Col U Pr.
Ryan, Caitlin, jt. auth. see Rowe, Mona.
***Ryan, Carol.** Star Island: A Minnesota Summer Community. LC 99-67281. (Illus.). 232p. 2000. pap. 19.95 (1-880654-18-0, Pub. by Pogo Pr) SCB Distributors.
Ryan, Carol A., et al. How to Get the Best Public School Education for Your Child. 224p. 1993. mass mkt. 4.50 (0-8217-4038-5, Zebra Kensgtn) Kensgtn Pub Corp.
— How to Get the Best Public School Education for Your Child: A Parent's Guide for the Nineties. 224p. 1991. 21.95 (0-8027-1156-1); pap. 12.95 (0-8027-7355-9) Walker & Co.
Ryan, Carrie-Anne, ed. see Ryan, Marlene A.
Ryan, Cary, ed. see Alcott, Louisa May.
Ryan, Cathy E., jt. auth. see Senelick, Richard C.
Ryan, Celeste. The Dream Quilt. LC 99-24665. (Illus.). 48p. (J). (ps-2). 1999. 12.95 (1-57856-223-6) Waterbrook Pr.
Ryan, Charles. Basic Electricity: A Self-Teaching Guide. 2nd ed. LC 86-11114. 304p. 1986. pap. 19.95 (0-471-85085-3) Wiley.
— Black Eagle - Black Eagle: Operative's Kit. (Illus.). 64p. (Orig.). 1992. pap. 14.95 (0-9628748-3-3) Chameleon Eclectic.
— Code Black. 304p. 1997. mass mkt. 5.99 (0-380-79131-5, Avon Bks) Morrow Avon.
— Millennium's End: Contemporary & Near-Future Role-Playing Game. 2nd ed. (Illus.). 192p. (Orig.). 1993. pap. 20.00 (0-9628748-5-X) Chameleon Eclectic.
— The Millennium's End GM Screen & 1999 Datasource. (Illus.). 32p. (Orig.). 1992. pap. text 11.95 (0-9628748-2-5) Chameleon Eclectic.
— Millennium's End GM's Companion. (Illus.). 144p. (Orig.). 1995. pap. 15.00 (0-9628748-7-6) Chameleon Eclectic.
— Nightwalker - The Villee Affair: Three Assignments for the Millenniums End Contemporary Roleplaying Game System. (Illus.). 88p. (Orig.). 1991. pap. text 11.95 (0-9628748-1-7) Chameleon Eclectic.
— Track of the Bengal. 304p. 1999. mass mkt. 6.50 (0-380-79132-3, Avon Bks) Morrow Avon.
***Ryan, Charles.** Triamore: The Covenant at Lucien's Folly. (Ars Magica Ser.). (Illus.). 144p. 2000. pap. 20.95 (1-887801-85-5) Trident MN.
Ryan, Charles. Ultramodern Firearms. (Illus.). 176p. (Orig.). 1993. pap. 20.00 (0-9628748-4-1) Chameleon Eclectic.
Ryan, Charles & Fletcher, John. Psychosis: Ship of Fools. (Illus.). 170p. (Orig.). 1995. pap. 15.00 (0-9628748-9-2) Chameleon Eclectic.
Ryan, Charles, ed. & illus. see Smedman, Lisa, et al.
Ryan, Charles J. H. P. Blavatsky & the Theosophical Movement. rev. ed. Knoche, Grace F., ed. LC 75-4433. (Illus.). 376p. 1975. pap. 13.95 (0-911500-80-4) Theos U Pr.
— H. P. Blavatsky & the Theosophical Movement. 2nd rev. ed. Knoche, Grace F., ed. LC 75-4433. (Illus.). 376p. 1975. 20.95 (0-911500-79-0) Theos U Pr.
— H. P. Blavatsky & the Theosophical Movement: With 7 Appendixes. Small, W. Emmett & Todd, Helen, eds. (Illus.). 484p. 1975. reprint ed. pap. 12.00 (0-913004-25-1) Point Loma Pub.
— What Is Theosophy? A General View of Occult Doctrine. rev. ed. Small, W. Emmett & Todd, Helen, eds. (Theosophical Manual Ser.: No. 1). 92p. 1975. pap. 5.00 (0-913004-18-9) Point Loma Pub.
Ryan, Charles J., jt. auth. see Ross, Lydia.
Ryan, Charles W., jt. auth. see Drummond, Robert J.
Ryan, Charlotte. Prime Time Activism: Media Strategies for Grassroots Organizing. 295p. 1991. 30.00 (0-89608-402-7) South End Pr.
Ryan, Cheli D. Hildilid's Night. (Illus.). 32p. (J). (ps-3). 1996. mass mkt. 4.99 (0-689-80538-1) Aladdin.
Ryan, Chris. The One That Got Away: My SAS Mission Behind Iraqi Lines. LC 97-40358. (Illus.). 252p. 1998. reprint ed. pap. 17.95 (1-57488-156-6) Brasseys.
— Recreational Tourism: A Social Science Perspective. 272p. (C). (gr. 13). 1991. pap. 27.95 (0-415-05424-9, A5702) Routledge.
— Researching Tourist Satisfaction: Issues, Concepts, Problems. LC 94-7224. 320p. (Orig.). (C). 1994. pap. 19.99 (0-415-10158-1, B4756) Thomson Learn.
— Researching Tourist Satisfaction: Issues, Concepts, Problems. LC 94-7224. 320p. (Orig.). (C). (gr. 13). 1994. pap. 81.95 (0-415-10157-3, B4752) Thomson Learn.
Ryan, Chris, ed. The Tourist Experience: A New Introduction. (Studies in Tourism). (Illus.). 192p. 1996. pap. 37.95 (0-304-33806-0); text 89.50 (0-304-33807-9) Continuum.
***Ryan, Chris & Page, Stephen.** Tourism Management. LC 99-47662. (Advances in Tourism Research Ser.). 2000. write for info. (0-08-043589-0, Pergamon Pr) Elsevier.
Ryan, Chris A., jt. ed. see Crotts, John C.
Ryan, Christopher. Michelangelo. 1998. pap. text 3.50 (0-460-87963-4, Everyman's Classic Lib) Tuttle Pubng.
— The Poetry of Michelangelo. LC 97-50387. 352p. 1998. 47.50 (0-8386-3802-3) Fairleigh Dickinson.
— SWOT Criminal Law. 4th ed. 286p. 1995. pap. 22.00 (1-85431-339-8, Pub. by Blackstone Pr) Gaunt.
— SWOT Criminal Law. 5th ed. 301p. 1998. pap. 24.00 (1-85431-780-6, Pub. by Blackstone Pr) Gaunt.
Ryan, Christopher & Scanlan, Gary. SWOT Criminal Law. 238p. (C). 1990. 80.00 (1-85431-034-8, Pub. by Blackstone Pr) St Mut.
Ryan, Christopher, jt. auth. see Scanlan, Gary.
Ryan, Christopher, ed. see Grice-Hutchinson, Marjorie.
Ryan, Christopher J. Metacomet-Monadnock Trail Guide: A Trail Guide with Maps of the 117 Mile Long Distance Foot Path Through the 3 County-Pioneer Valley Region of Western Massachusetts & the Monadnock Region of S. W. New Hampshire. 9th rev. ed. (Illus.). 89p. 1999. per. 8.95 (1-889787-03-5) NE Cartographics.
Ryan, Christopher J., ed. see Scofield, Bruce.
Ryan, Clarence, ed. see DuPont - UCLA Symposium on Molecular Strategies fo.
Ryan, Colleen. Beyers Naude: Pilgrimage of Faith. 248p. (C). 1990. 49.95 (0-86543-193-0); pap. 19.95 (0-86543-190-6) Africa World.
— Beyers Naude: Pilgrimage of Faith. LC 90-82835. (Illus.). 246p. 1990. reprint ed. pap. 76.30 (0-7837-8092-3, 204784600008) Bks Demand.
Ryan, Concetta D. Authentic Assessment. (Professional's Guide Ser.). 80p. 1995. pap., teacher ed. 9.95 (1-55734-838-3) Tchr Create Mat.
— The Black Pearl: A Literature Unit. (Literature Units Ser.). (Illus.). 48p. (Orig.). (gr. 3-5). 1992. student ed. 7.95 (1-55734-410-8) Tchr Create Mat.
— Charlie & the Chocolate Factory: A Literature Unit. (Literature Units Ser.). (Illus.). 48p. (Orig.). 1993. pap., student ed. 7.95 (1-55734-420-5) Tchr Create Mat.
— My Grammar Dictionary. Rogers, Kathy, ed. (Illus.). 32p. 1999. pap., teacher ed., wbk. ed. 1.99 (1-56472-611-8) Edupress Inc.
— The Secret Garden: A Literature Unit. (Literature Units Ser.). (Illus.). 48p. (Orig.). 1992. student ed. 7.95 (1-55734-414-0) Tchr Create Mat.
Ryan, Concetta D. & Teacher Created Materials Staff. Learning Through Literature: U. S. History. (Learning Through Literature Ser.). 144p. (J). (gr. 3-5). 1997. pap. 14.95 (1-55734-472-8) Tchr Create Mat.
***Ryan, Constance Doti.** Quick-Flip Activities for Multiple Intelligences. Rogers, Kathy, ed. 1998. 3.99 (1-56472-490-5) Edupress Inc.
— Quick-Flip Ideas for Writing Domains. Rogers, Kathy, ed. 1998. 3.99 (1-56472-491-3) Edupress Inc.
— Quick Flip Reference for Phonics. Rogers, Kathy, ed. 1998. 3.99 (1-56472-492-1) Edupress Inc.
Ryan, Constance M. & Emery, L. Jean. Meeting the Challenge of HIV Infection in Family Foster Care. 96p. 1991. pap. 10.95 (0-87868-449-0) Child Welfare.
Ryan, Cornelius. A Bridge Too Far: The Classic History of the Greatest Airborne Battle of World War II. 1995. per. 15.00 (0-684-80330-5, Touchstone) S&S Trade Pap.
— The Last Battle: The Classic History of Battle for Berlin. (Illus.). 576p. 1995. per. 16.00 (0-684-80329-1) S&S Trade Pap.
— The Longest Day: The Classic Epic of D-Day. 352p. 1994. pap. 12.00 (0-671-89091-3, Touchstone) S&S Trade Pap.
***Ryan, Courtney.** Absolute Beginners. large type ed. LC 00-21592. (Thorndike Romance Ser.). 2000. 25.95 (0-7862-2489-4) Thorndike Pr.
Ryan, Courtney. For Love of Mike. large type ed. LC 99-18676. 195p. 1999. 22.95 (0-7838-8572-5, G K Hall & Co) Mac Lib Ref.
Ryan, Craig. The Pre-Astronauts: Manned Ballooning on the Threshold of Space. (Illus.). 368p. 1995. 31.95 (1-55750-732-5) Naval Inst Pr.
Ryan, D. The Catholic Parish. 1990. pap. 80.00 (0-7220-1576-3); pap. 140.00 (0-7220-1575-5) St Mut.
Ryan, D. H., ed. Recent Progress in Random Magnets. LC 92-16899. 300p. 1992. text 98.00 (981-02-0885-5) World Scientific Pub.
Ryan, D. W. Current Practice in Critical Illness, Vol. 2. (Illus.). 160p. 1997. text 39.50 (0-412-61800-1, Pub. by E A) OUP.
Ryan, D. W., jt. auth. see Park, G.
Ryan, Dale & Ryan, Juanita. Life Recovery Guides, 10 vols., Set. (Orig.). 1990. pap., wbk. ed. 49.90 (0-8308-1150-8, 1150) InterVarsity.
— Recovery from Abuse. (Life Recovery Guides Ser.). 64p. 1990. pap., wbk. ed. 4.99 (0-8308-1158-3, 1158) InterVarsity.
— Recovery from Depression. (Life Recovery Guides Ser.). 64p. (Orig.). 1993. pap., wbk. ed. 4.99 (0-8308-1161-3, 1161) InterVarsity.
— Recovery from Family Dysfunctions. (Life Recovery Guides Ser.). 64p. 1990. pap., wbk. ed. 4.99 (0-8308-1151-6, 1151) InterVarsity.
— Recovery from Loss. (Life Recovery Guides Ser.). 64p. (Orig.). 1990. pap., wbk. ed. 4.99 (0-8308-1157-5, 1157) InterVarsity.
***Ryan, Dale & Ryan, Juanita.** The Twelve Steps-A Spiritual Kindergarten: Christian Perspectives on the Twelve Steps. 144p. 1999. pap. 12.95 (0-941405-23-0) RPI Pubng.
Ryan, Daniel, ed. CAD-CAE Descriptive Geometry. 224p. 1991. lib. bdg. 59.95 (0-8493-4273-2, TA345) CRC Pr.
Ryan, Daniel B., ed. Pretrial Release & Detention & Pretrial Services. 80p. (Orig.). (C). 1993. pap. text 30.00 (1-56806-350-4) DIANE Pub.
Ryan, Daniel J. Civil War Literature of Ohio. Date not set. lib. bdg. 59.95 (0-8488-1713-3) Amereon Ltd.
— The Job Search Handbook for People with Disabilities. 220p. 1999. pap. 16.95 (1-56370-665-2) Park Ave.
— Privatization & Competition in Telecommunications: International Developments. LC 96-36358. (Privatizing Government Ser.). 232p. 1997. 65.00 (0-275-95813-2, Praeger Pubs) Greenwood.
Ryan, Daniel L. Computer-Aided Architectural Graphics. LC 83-7433. (Illus.). 445p. reprint ed. pap. 138.00 (0-608-08980-X, 206961500005) Bks Demand.
— Computer-Aided Graphics & Design. 3rd expanded rev. ed. LC 93-46012. (Computer Aided Engineering Ser.: Vol. 4). (Illus.). 280p. 1994. text 79.75 (0-8247-9164-9) Dekker.
— Graphical Displays for Engineering Documentation. LC 87-5309. (Illus.). 279p. reprint ed. pap. 86.50 (0-608-08981-8, 206961600005) Bks Demand.
— Principles of Automated Drafting. (Mechanical Engineering Ser.: Vol. 28). (Illus.). 336p. 1984. text 99.75 (0-8247-7175-3) Dekker.
— Robotic Simulation. LC 93-17598. 336p. 1993. boxed set 104.95 (0-8493-4468-9, TJ211) CRC Pr.
***Ryan, David.** U. S. Foreign Policy in World History. LC 00-36888. (New International History Ser.). 2000. pap. write for info. (0-415-12345-3) Routledge.
Ryan, David. U. S.-Sandinista Diplomatic Relations: Voice of Intolerance. LC 95-14923. 250p. 1995. text 59.95 (0-312-12821-5) St Martin.
***Ryan, David.** United States & Decolonization. LC 99-59274. 224p. 2000. text 59.95 (0-312-23158-X) St Martin.
Ryan, David D. Cornbread & Maggots, Cloak & Dagger, Union Prisoners & Spies in Civil War Richmond. 1994. 24.95 (0-87517-083-8) Dietz.
— Richmond Illustrated: Unusual Stories of a City. (Illus.). 94p. 1993. 16.95 (0-87517-071-4) Dietz.
— Urbanna, Virginia: A Port Town since 1860. (Illus.). 1995. pap. 12.00 (0-87517-074-9) Dietz.
Ryan, David D., ed. A Yankee Spy in Richmond: The Civil War Diary of "Crazy Bet" Van Lew. (Illus.). 176p. 1996. 22.95 (0-8117-0554-4) Stackpole.
Ryan, David L. Kansas Administrative Law with Federal References. 1991st ed. LC 85-80208. 125.00 (0-942357-25-6) KS Bar.
Ryan, David S. America: A Guide to the Experience. (Illus.). 144p. 1989. pap. 17.95 (0-905116-17-8) Seven Hills Bk.
— India: A Guide to the Experience. (Illus.). 125p. 1989. pap. 17.95 (0-905116-11-9) Seven Hills Bk.
— Taboo. 191p. 1984. pap. 8.95 (0-905116-14-3) Seven Hills Bk.
***Ryan, Dennis.** A Journey Through Boston's Irish History. (Images of America Ser.). (Illus.). 128p. 1999. pap. 18.99 (0-7524-1397-X) Arcadia Publng.
Ryan, Dennis. Two Nineteenth Century Versions of the New Testament: Translated by JNO & by Wk, with Comments on Text & Translation from the Works of William Kelly of Blackheath. 766p. 1995. 45.00 (0-9640037-9-1) Pres Truth.
Ryan, Dennis, jt. auth. see Shine, Joseph W.
Ryan, Dennis P., ed. Einstein & the Humanities, 32. LC 86-19444. (Contributions in Philosophy Ser.: No. 32). 229p. 1987. 59.95 (0-313-25380-3, RYA/, Greenwood Pr) Greenwood.
Ryan, Desmond. Michael Collins. 2nd ed. 160p. 1994. reprint ed. pap. 13.95 (0-947962-83-2, Pub. by Anvil Books Ltd) Irish Bks Media.
Ryan, Desmond, ed. The 1916 Poets. LC 79-18768. 224p. 1980. reprint ed. lib. bdg. 59.50 (0-313-22100-6, RYNI, Greenwood Pr) Greenwood.
Ryan, Desmond, ed. see Pearse, Patrick, et al.
Ryan, Donald D. Complete Idiot's Guide to Lost Civilizations. LC 97-80967. (Complete Idiot's Guides (Lifestyle) Ser.). (Illus.). 350p. 1999. pap. 16.95 (0-02-862954-X) Macmillan Gen Ref.
Ryan, Donna F. The Holocaust & the Jews of Marseille: The Enforcement of Anti-Semitic Policies in Vichy France. LC 95-50221. (Illus.). 280p. (C). 1996. text 39.95 (0-252-02227-0); pap. text 17.95 (0-252-06530-1) U of Ill Pr.
Ryan, Donna H. Mycotoxins, Cancer, & Health. Bray, George A., ed. LC 90-13706. (Pennington Center Nutrition Ser.: Vol. 1). (Illus.). 352p. 1991. text 50.00 (0-8071-1679-3) La State U Pr.
Ryan, Donna H., jt. ed. see Bray, George A.
Ryan, Dorothy. Philip Boileau: Painter of Fair Women. (Illus.). (Orig.). 1980. pap. 9.95 (0-910664-47-1) Gotham.
Ryan, Dorothy & Ryan, Louis J., compiled by. The Kennedy Family of Massachusetts: A Bibliography. LC 81-6672. 200p. 1981. lib. bdg. 49.95 (0-313-23189-3, RKF/, Greenwood Pr) Greenwood.
Ryan, Dorothy, jt. auth. see Davis, Jack.
Ryan, Douglas A. Business Aspects of Catering. 1989. pap. text. write for info. (0-582-01852-8, Pub. by Addison-Wesley) Longman.
Ryan, D.W. Current Practice in Critical Illness, Vol. 3. (Illus.). 226p. 1999. text 49.95 (0-412-79300-8, Pub. by E A) OUP.
Ryan, E. Davis, jt. auth. see Swencionis, Charles.
Ryan, E. P. Optimal Relay & Saturating Control System Synthesis. (Control Engineering Ser.: No. 14). 352p. 1982. boxed set 145.00 (0-906048-56-7, CE014) INSPEC Inc.
***Ryan, E. Scott.** The Theology of Crime: The Masonic Writings of Dr. E. Scott Ryan. deluxe ed. Roberts, Kenneth D., ed. LC 00-102240. 156p. 2000. 22.95 (0-935633-20-0) Anchor Comm.
Ryan, Edward. Paper Soldiers: Illustrated History of Printed Paper Armies. LC 99-199545. (Illus.). 528p. 1995. 225.00 (0-904568-96-2, Pub. by Golden Age Edits) Pincushion Pr.
Ryan, Edward, jt. ed. see Castagnera, James O.
***Ryan, Edward A.** The Last Knight of Camelot. 220p. 2000. pap. 14.95 (0-7414-0361-7) Buy Books.
***Ryan, Edward W.** Liberty, Virtue, & Happiness: The Story of Economic Freedom in America. LC 98-37418. 1998. 34.00 (1-56072-620-2) Nova Sci Pubs.
Ryan, Edward W., ed. In the Words of Adam Smith. LC 90-93270. 1990. 15.95 (0-913878-49-9); pap. text 8.95 (0-913878-48-0) T Horton & Dghts.
Ryan, Elizabeth. How to Build a Better Vocabulary. LC 91-3136. (Student Survival Power Ser.). 112p. (J). (gr. 5-9). 1997. pap. 3.95 (0-8167-2461-X) Troll Communs.
— How to Write Better Book Reports. LC 91-3134. (Student Survival Power Ser.). 80p. (J). (gr. 5-9). 1992. lib. bdg. 10.50 (0-8167-2458-X) Troll Communs.
Ryan, Elizabeth A. How to Write Better Book Reports. (Student Survival Power Ser.). (J). 1992. 9.15 (0-606-02676-2, Pub. by Turtleback) Demco.
Ryan, Elizabeth A. Straight Talk about Drugs & Alcohol. rev. ed. (Straight Talk Ser.). 160p. (YA). (gr. 6-12). 1995. 19.95 (0-8160-3249-1) Facts on File.
— Straight Talk about Drugs & Alcohol. rev. ed. (Straight Talk Ser.). 160p. (YA). (gr. 6-12). 1996. pap. 9.95 (0-8160-3549-0) Facts on File.
— Straight Talk about Parents. (Straight Talk Ser.). 144p. (YA). (gr. 6-12). 1989. 19.95 (0-8160-1526-0) Facts on File.
— Student Thesaurus. LC 89-20305. (Illus.). 160p. (J). (gr. 2-8). 1990. lib. bdg. 20.65 (0-8167-1914-4) Troll Communs.
— Student Thesaurus. LC 89-20305. (Illus.). 160p. (J). (gr. 2-8). 1997. pap. 7.95 (0-8167-1856-3) Troll Communs.
Ryan, Ellish. Rosemary Haughton: Witness to Hope. LC 97-20332. 240p. 1997. pap. 15.95 (1-55612-860-6, LL1860) Sheed & Ward WI.
***Ryan, Emer & Newman, Clive, eds.** From Two Islands: The Best of Irish-Australian Writers with New Fiction for Younger Readers. 167p. 2000. pap. 12.95 (1-86368-282-1, Pub. by Fremantle Arts) Intl Spec Bk.
Ryan, F. W. Usury & Usury Laws. 1977. lib. bdg. 200.00 (0-8490-2791-8) Gordon Pr.
Ryan, Fergus. Siege of Mt. Nevermind. (DragonLance Ser.). 312p. 1999. pap. 5.99 (0-7869-1381-9, Pub. by TSR Inc) Random.
Ryan, Frances & Rybolt, John E., eds. Vincent de Paul & Louise de Marillac: Rules, Conferences, & Writings. LC 95-3447. (Classics of Western Spirituality Ser.). 1995. 24.95 (0-8091-0471-7); pap. 18.95 (0-8091-3564-7) Paulist Pr.
Ryan, Frank. The Forgotten Plague: How the Battle Against Tuberculosis Was Won - & Lost. 1994. pap. 15.95 (0-316-76381-0, Little Brwn Med Div) Lppncott W & W.
— Tiger, Tiger. large type ed. 1990. 27.99 (0-7089-2287-2) Ulverscroft.
— The Verve of Passion & Peril. 1997. pap. write for info. (1-57553-497-5) Watermrk Pr.
— Virus-X: Tracking the New Killer Plagues Out of the Present & into the Future. LC 96-30495. (Illus.). 448p. 1997. 24.95 (0-316-76383-7) Little.
— Virus-X: Tracking the New Killer Plagues Out of the Present & into the Future. 448p. 1998. pap. 15.00 (0-316-76306-3) Little.

Ryan, Frank, jt. ed. see Krueger, Merle.

***Ryan, Frank W.** Socrates' Justice from Ancient Greece: How We Evolve to Nonviolence, Brotherhood & Lasting Peace. (Illus.). 125p. 2000. pap. text 16.00 (*1-55605-296-0*) Wyndham Hall.

***Ryan, Frank X. & Madden, Edward H., eds.** The Evolutionary Philosophy of Chauncey Wright, 3 vols. (Foundations of American Evolutionism Ser.). 1190p. 2000. 295.00 (*1-85506-849-4*) Thoemmes Pr.

Ryan, G. Jeremiah & Smith, Nanette J., eds. Marketing & Development for Community Colleges. 252p. 1989. 20.00 (*0-89964-270-5*, 23901) Coun Adv & Supp Ed.

Ryan, Gail. FrameMaker 5.5 Made Easy. LC 99-13251. 194p. 1999. 48.95 (*1-881795-14-4*, Z253) Bellwether-Cross.

— Web of Meaning: A Developmental-Contextual Approach in Sexual Abuse Treatment. LC 98-30615. 192p. 1999. pap. 22.00 (*1-884444-50-4*, WP065) Safer Soc.

Ryan, Gail D. & Lane, Sandy L. Juvenile Sexual Offending: A Handbook of Causes, Consequences & Correction. LC 96-50209. 1997. pap. 41.95 (*0-7879-0843-6*) Jossey-Bass.

Ryan, Garry D. & Nenninger, Timothy K., eds. Soldiers & Civilians: The U. S. Army & the American People. LC 86-21664. (Illus.). 210p. 1987. text 25.00 (*0-911333-52-5*, 10011) National Archives & Recs.

Ryan, Gary & Ryan, Bob. Ryan & Ryan's Thots That Stick to the Roof of Your Mind. Lindsay, Karen, ed. 192p. (Orig.). 1994. pap. text 7.95 (*0-9644687-0-0*) R&R Creat Adv.

Ryan, George. Reclaiming Male Sexuality: A Guide to Potency, Vitality, & Prowess. LC 96-34928. 256p. (Orig.). 1997. pap. 14.95 (*0-87131-809-1*) M Evans.

Ryan, George, jt. auth. see Fensin, Alan.

Ryan, George, jt. auth. see Lipper, Arthur, III.

Ryan, George, jt. auth. see Sosin, Allan E.

Ryan, George E. A Life of Bandmaster Richard Willis. LC 99-74474. (Illus.). 256p. 2000. 34.95 (*0-8158-0540-3*) Chris Mass.

Ryan, Gerald D. Radiographic Positioning of Small Animals. LC 80-26069. 159p. reprint ed. pap. 49.30 (*0-7837-1476-9*, 205717100023) Bks Demand.

Ryan, Gerry, jt. auth. see Hecht, Ellen.

***Ryan, Gig.** Pure & Applied. 92p. 1999. pap. text 11.95 (*0-9586482-6-3*, Paper Bark) Gordon & Breach.

Ryan, Gordon. Conflict, 1898-1919. LC 97-49436. (Spirit of Union Ser.). x, 400 p. 1998. write for info. (*1-57345-284-X*) Deseret Bk.

— Dangerous Legacy. LC 94-26638. iv, 379p. 1994. 14.95 (*0-87579-905-1*, Shadow Mount) Deseret Bk.

***Ryan, Gordon.** Heritage, 1919-1940 LC 99-34053. (Spirit of Union Ser.). 1999. write for info. (*1-57345-577-6*) Deseret Bk.

Ryan, Gordon. Spirit of Union: Destiny. LC 96-27285. 354p. 1996. 16.95 (*1-57345-215-7*) Deseret Bk.

— Threads of Honor. LC 96-33821. xv, 80p. 1996. pap. 6.95 (*1-57345-169-X*, Shadow Mount) Deseret Bk.

Ryan, Gordon G. The Top Five Percent: How to Save & Invest While Minimizing Taxes. 140p. (Orig.). 1988. pap. 12.95 (*0-9621442-0-7*) Mntnview Pub WA.

Ryan, Greg & Beyer, Sally. The Twin Cities, Naturally! A Pictorial Tour of the Minneapolis-St. Paul Metropolitan Area. LC 93-34642. (Illus.). 96p. 1994. pap. 16.95 (*0-89658-232-9*) Voyageur Pr.

Ryan, Gregory, ed. The Burning Heart: Reading the New Testament with John Main. 96p. (Orig.). 1997. pap. 8.95 (*0-8091-3724-0*) Paulist Pr.

Ryan, H. M., ed. High Voltage Engineering & Testing. (IEE Power Ser.: No. 17). 450p. 1994. 99.00 (*0-86341-293-9*, Pub. by Peregrinus) Dist Unknown.

Ryan, H. M. & Jones, G. R. SF6 Switchgear. (Power Ser.: No. 10). 202p. 1989. 99.00 (*0-86341-123-1*, PO010) INSPEC Inc.

Ryan, Halford. Classical Communication for the Contemporary Communicator. LC 91-21417. xi, 244p. (C). 1992. pap. text 38.00 (*1-55934-033-9*, 1033) Mayfield Pub.

Ryan, Halford R. Contemporary American Public Discourse: A Collection of Speeches & Critical Essays. 3rd ed. (Illus.). 384p. (C). 1992. pap. text 21.95 (*0-88133-629-7*) Waveland Pr.

— Franklin Roosevelt's Rhetorical Presidency, 206. LC 87-31778. (Contributions in Political Science Ser.: No. 206). 209p. 1988. 57.95 (*0-313-25567-9*, RFR/, Greenwood Pr) Greenwood.

— Harry Emerson Fosdick: Persuasive Preacher, 2. LC 88-25101. (Great American Orators: Critical Studies, Speeches & Sources: No. 2). 200p. 1989. 52.95 (*0-313-25897-X*, RHF/, Greenwood Pr) Greenwood.

— Harry S. Truman: Presidential Rhetoric, 17. LC 92-18350. (Great American Orators Ser.: No. 17). 232p. 1993. lib. bdg. 55.00 (*0-313-27908-X*, RHU, Greenwood Pr) Greenwood.

— Henry Ward Beecher: Peripatetic Preacher, 5. LC 89-38228. 179p. 1990. lib. bdg. 52.95 (*0-313-26389-2*, RHY/, Greenwood Pr) Greenwood.

Ryan, Halford R., ed. The Inaugural Addresses of Twentieth-Century American Presidents. LC 92-34950. (Series in Political Communication). 352p. 1993. 65.00 (*0-275-94039-X*, C4039, Praeger Pubs) Greenwood.

— Oratorical Encounters: Selected Studies & Sources of Twentieth-Century Political Accusations & Apologies, 9. LC 87-23662. (Contributions to the Study of Mass Media & Communications Ser.: No. 9). 354p. 1988. 69.50 (*0-313-25568-7*, ROR/) Greenwood.

— U. S. Presidents As Orators: A Bio-Critical Sourcebook. LC 94-43039. 408p. 1995. lib. bdg. 99.50 (*0-313-29059-8*, Greenwood Pr) Greenwood.

Ryan, Halford R., jt. ed. see Duffy, Bernard K.

Ryan-Hayes, Karen, ed. Venedikt Erofeev's Moscow - Petushki: Critical Perspectives. LC 96-34896. (Middlebury Studies in Russian Languages & Literature: Vol. 14). (ENG & RUS.). X, 231p. (C). 1997. text 47.95 (*0-8204-3666-6*) P Lang Pubng.

Ryan-Hayes, Karen L. Contemporary Russian Satire: A Genre Study. (Studies in Russian Literature). 303p. (C). 1996. text 69.95 (*0-521-47515-5*) Cambridge U Pr.

— Russian Publicistic Satire under Glasnost: The Journalistic Feuilleton. LC 93-30736. 212p. 1993. text 89.95 (*0-7734-9348-4*) E Mellen.

Ryan, Henry B. The Fall of Che Guevara: A Story Of Soldiers, Spies, & Diplomats. (Illus.). 256p. 1999. pap. 17.95 (*0-19-513100-2*) OUP.

— The Fall of Che Guevera: A Story of Soldiers, Spies, & Diplomats. (Illus.). 256p. (C). 1998. 35.00 (*0-19-511879-0*) OUP.

Ryan, Henry B., ed. USIA: New Directions for a New Era. (ISD Reports). 56p. (Orig.). 1993. pap. text 3.00 (*0-934742-76-6*) Geo U Inst Dplmcy.

Ryan, Herbert, ed. The Final Report of the Anglican-Roman Catholic International Commission. 128p. 1982. reprint ed. pap. 10.00 (*0-88028-014-X*, 1423) Forward Movement.

Ryan, Hugh F. Ancestral Voices. 208p. 1994. 19.95 (*0-918339-32-4*) Vandamere.

Ryan, Hugh W. Practical Guide to Client/Server Computing 1999. 99th ed. 19p. 1998. boxed set 95.00 (*0-8493-9967-X*) CRC Pr.

Ryan, Hugh W., et al. Practical Guide to Client/Server Computing. 98th ed. LC 97-209141. 816p. 1997. boxed set 160.00 (*0-8493-9951-3*) CRC Pr.

Ryan, I. M. It's All So Damn Simple: Solving Nation's Problems. 250p. 1998. 17.95 (*0-9623535-6-6*) Remco Inc.

Ryan, Irwin M. JODI: Genghis Khan's DNA Progeny Invades Washington. write for info. (*0-9623535-3-1*) Remco Inc.

— The Last Congress, Vol. 1. 464p. 1989. 17.95 (*0-9623535-0-7*) Remco Inc.

Ryan, J. A Background Study of the Non-Admitted Insurance Market. LC 79-93288. 71p. 1980. pap. 25.00 (*0-317-35009-9*) Nat Assn Insurance.

***Ryan, J.** DIRAC Operators in Analysis. (Research Notes in Mathematics Ser.: Vol. 394). (Illus.). 1998. pap. text 59.95 (*0-582-35681-4*) Addison-Wesley.

Ryan, J. A. The Town of Milan. (Illus.). 96p. 1997. reprint ed. pap. 17.50 (*0-8328-5745-5*) Higginson Bk Co.

Ryan, J. Atticus, jt. ed. see Mullen, Christopher A.

Ryan, J. G. Building on Success: Agricultural Research, Technology & Policy for Development. 1987. pap. 42.00 (*0-949511-50-1*, Pub. by ACIAR) St Mut.

— East Africa Consultation on Agricultural Research. 242p. 1984. pap. 78.00 (*0-949511-01-3*, Pub. by ACIAR) St Mut.

Ryan, J. G., jt. auth. see Nuru, Saka.

Ryan, J. R. & Baker, L. O., eds. Recent Concepts in Sarcoma Treatment. (Developments in Oncology Ser.). (C). 1988. text 191.00 (*0-89838-376-5*) Kluwer Academic.

Ryan, J. W. Guns, Mortars & Rockets. (Brassey's Battlefield Weapons Systems & Technology Ser.: Vol. 2). (Illus.). 236p. 1982. text 30.00 (*0-08-028324-1*, P110, Pergamon Pr); pap. text 19.25 (*0-08-028325-X*, Pergamon Pr) Elsevier.

Ryan, Jack. John Sayles, Filmmaker: A Critical Study of the Independent Writer-Director; With a Filmography & a Bibliography. LC 98-29150. (Illus.). 279p. 1998. lib. bdg. 42.50 (*0-7864-0529-5*) McFarland & Co.

Ryan, Jacqueline, jt. auth. see Clayson, Alan.

Ryan, Jake & Sackrey, Charles. Strangers in Paradise: Academics from the Working Class. 2nd ed. 328p. (Orig.). (C). 1995. pap. text 34.00 (*0-7618-0142-1*); lib. bdg. 59.00 (*0-7618-0141-3*) U Pr of Amer.

***Ryan, James.** Earl Browder: The Failure of American Communism. 144p. 2000. pap. text 19.95 (*0-8173-1013-4*) U of Ala Pr.

Ryan, James. Picturing Empire: Photography & the Visualization of the British Empire. LC 97-26401. 272p. 1998. 38.00 (*0-226-73233-9*) U Ch Pr.

***Ryan, James.** Race & Ethnicity in Multi-Ethnic Schools. LC 99-12740. (Language & Education Library: Vol. 15). 218p. 1999. 79.00 (*1-85359-447-4*, Pub. by Multilingual Matters) Taylor & Francis.

Ryan, James. Race & Ethnicity in Multiethnic Schools: A Critical Case Study LC 99-12740. (The Language & Education Library). 1999. 24.95 (*1-85359-446-6*) Multilingual Matters.

— Screenwriting from the Heart: The Technique of the Character-Driven Screenplay. LC 99-87771. (Illus.). 192p. 1999. pap. 16.95 (*0-8230-8419-1*) Watsn-Guptill.

— The Young Girl & the Monsoon. 1998. pap. 5.25 (*0-8222-1650-7*) Dramatists Play.

Ryan, James, ed. Sinews of the Heart: A Book of Men's Writings. 164p. (Orig.). (YA). (gr. 12). 1995. pap. 14.98 (*0-907123-41-4*, Pub. by Five Leaves) AK Pr Dist.

Ryan, James, jt. auth. see Naylor, Simon.

Ryan, James F., et al. Australasian Radiology: A History. LC 97-179437. (Illus.). 150p. 1995. text. write for info. (*0-07-470207-6*) McGraw-Hill HPD.

Ryan, James G. Earl Browder: The Failure of American Communism. LC 96-25763. 296p. 1997. text 39.95 (*0-8173-0843-1*) U of Ala Pr.

— Irish Records: Sources for Family & Local History. rev. ed. LC 97-11624. 668p. 1997. 49.95 (*0-916489-76-0*) Ancestry.

Ryan, James G., jt. auth. see Walker, T. S.

Ryan, James M., et al, eds. Ballistic Trauma: Clinical Relevance in Peace & War. LC 96-53122. (An Arnold Publication). (Illus.). 312p. (C). 1997. text 149.50 (*0-340-58114-X*, Pub. by E A) OUP.

Ryan, James M. & Vestrand, W. Thomas. High Energy Solar Phenomena: A New Era of Spacecraft Measurements. (AIP Conference Proceedings Ser.: No. 294). 500p. 1994. text 245.00 (*1-56396-291-8*) Am Inst Physics.

Ryan, James M., jt. ed. see McConnell, Mark L.

Ryan, James P. & Tuma, Ronald F., eds. Physiology. 9th ed. (Basic Sciences: Pretest Self Assessment & Review Ser.). (Illus.). 291p. 1998. pap. 18.95 (*0-07-052691-5*) McGraw-Hill HPD.

Ryan, James W. Camerone: The French Foreign Legion's Greatest Battle. LC 95-43726. 144p. 1996. 52.95 (*0-275-95490-0*, Praeger Pubs) Greenwood.

Ryan, James W., jt. auth. see Crehan, Herbert F.

Ryan, James W., jt. auth. see Enright, Joseph F.

Ryan, James W., jt. auth. see O'Connell, Lenahan.

Ryan, Janie. Illustrated Guide to Knitting. 1986. 12.98 (*0-671-08306-6*) S&S Trade.

Ryan, Jeanette M. Another Chance. 128p. 1985. pap. 2.50 (*0-380-89705-9*, Avon Bks) Morrow Avon.

Ryan, Jeff, jt. auth. see Starkey, Chad.

Ryan, Jeffrey M., jt. auth. see Knight, Stephen A.

Ryan, Jenna. The Arms of the Law. (Intrigue Ser.: Vol. 488). 1998. per. 3.99 (*0-373-22488-5*, 1-22488-0) Harlequin Bks.

— Belladonna (Her Protector) (Intrigue Ser.). 251p. 1996. per. 3.75 (*0-373-22364-1*, 1-22364-3) Harlequin Bks.

— Bittersweet Legacy. (Intrigue Ser.). 1993. pap. 2.89 (*0-373-22221-1*, 1-22221-5) Harlequin Bks.

— Midnight Masque. (Intrigue Ser.). 1993. per. 2.99 (*0-373-22251-3*, 1-22251-2) Harlequin Bks.

***Ryan, Jenna.** The Stroke of Midnight, No. 543. (Harlequin Intrigue Ser.). 1999. per. 3.99 (*0-373-22543-1*) Harlequin Bks.

Ryan, Jenna. Sweet Revenge. 1996. per. 3.75 (*0-373-22393-5*, 1-22393-2) Harlequin Bks.

— The Visitor. (Intrigue Ser.). 1993. per. 2.99 (*0-373-22239-4*, 1-22239-7) Harlequin Bks.

— When Night Falls. (Intrigue Ser.). 1994. per. 2.99 (*0-373-22265-3*, 1-22265-2) Harlequin Bks.

— The Woman in Black. (Intrigue Ser.: No. 450). 1998. per. 3.75 (*0-373-22450-8*, 1-22450-0) Harlequin Bks.

Ryan, Jerry & Ryan, Roberta. Preparing for Career Success. LC 95-37416. 1995. pap. 48.00 (*0-314-04883-9*) West Pub.

Ryan, Jillian & Ryan, Joseph A. Please, Somebody Love Me! Surviving Abuse & Becoming Whole. 160p. (YA). (gr. 10). 1996. mass mkt. 5.99 (*0-8007-8640-8*, Spire) Revell.

Ryan, Jim. Mobilizing Illinois: Governor's Commission on Gangs Final Report. (Illus.). 126p. (C). 1998. pap. text 25.00 (*0-7881-7440-1*) DIANE Pub.

***Ryan, Jim.** Rhythmic Aerobics - Drumset Beats & Fills - Todays Musician. 104p. 1999. 14.95 (*0-7866-3317-4*, 96938) Mel Bay.

Ryan, Joal. Katherine Hepburn: A Stylish Life. 1999. text 27.95 (*0-312-24649-8*) St Martin.

***Ryan, Joal.** Puffy, Xena, Quentin, Uma & 10,000 Other Names for Your New Millenium Baby. LC 98-50403. 432p. 1999. pap. 13.95 (*0-452-28091-5*, Plume) Dutton Plume.

Ryan, Joal. Totally Unauthorized Brandy. 1998. pap. 8.95 (*0-345-43375-0*) Ballantine Pub Grp.

***Ryan, Joan.** Little Girls in Pretty Boxes: The Making & Breaking of Elite Gymnasts & Figure Skaters. 2000. pap. write for info. (*0-446-67682-9*) Warner Bks.

Ryan, Joan. Little Girls in Pretty Boxes: The Making & Breaking of Elite Gymnasts & Figure Skaters. rev. ed. 228p. 1996. mass mkt. 12.99 (*0-446-67250-5*, Pub. by Warner Bks) Little.

Ryan, Joan, jt. auth. see VanDerveer, Tara.

Ryan, Joan A. Lessons from Dad: A Tribute to Fatherhood. 200p. 1997. pap. 10.95 (*1-55874-479-7*) Health Comm.

— Lessons from Mom: A Tribute to Loving Wisdom. 200p. 1996. pap. 10.95 (*1-55874-386-3*, 3863) Health Comm.

***Ryan, Joan Aho.** Lessons from Our Children: A Tribute to the Wisdom of Kids. LC 99-31723. 200p. 1999. pap. 10.95 (*1-55874-691-9*) Health Comm.

Ryan, Joan S., jt. auth. see Lawrence, Michael D.

Ryan, Joanna & Thomas, Frank. The Politics of Mental Handicap. 190p. (C). 1987. pap. 14.50 (*0-946960-92-5*, Pub. by Free Assoc Bks) NYU Pr.

Ryan, Joanna, jt. auth. see O'Connor, Noreen.

Ryan, Joanne. Lindsay: A Woman of Courage. LC 97-90084. 179p. (Orig.). 1997. pap. 12.95 (*0-533-12281-3*) Vantage.

Ryan, Joe. Coming Full Circle: A Journey of Self Discovery & Growth. LC 94-71175. 128p. (Orig.). 1994. pap. 12.95 (*0-9640860-8-5*) CFC Prodns.

Ryan, John. Giant-Killer. (Illus.). 32p. (J). (gr. 1-4). 1995. 5.99 (*0-7459-3379-3*) Lion USA.

— Irish Monasticism. 512p. 1993. 45.00 (*1-85182-112-0*, Pub. by Four Cts Pr); pap. 30.00 (*1-85182-111-2*, Pub. by Four Cts Pr) Intl Spec Bk.

— Psychotherapy, Religion & the Teilhardian Visions. (Teilhard Studies: No. 34). 1997. pap. write for info. (*0-89012-076-5*) Am Teilhard.

— Pugwash Aloft. (Illus.). 32p. (J). (gr. k-2). 1994. 19.95 (*0-370-00692-5*, Pub. by Bodley Head) Trafalgar.

— Pugwash the Smuggler. (Illus.). 32p. (J). (gr. k-2). 1994. 19.95 (*0-370-10786-1*, Pub. by Bodley Head) Trafalgar.

— Very Hungry Lions. LC 97-185817. (J). 1997. pap. text 5.99 (*0-7459-3723-3*) Lion USA.

Ryan, John, ed. Clifford Algebras in Analysis & Related Topics: A Proceedings of the Conference "Clifford Algebras in Analysis" Held at Fayetteville, Arkansas, 8-10th April 1993. 384p. 1995. boxed set 99.95 (*0-8493-8481-8*, 8481) CRC Pr.

Ryan, John, jt. auth. see Castagnera, James O.

Ryan, John A. Declining Liberty, & Other Papers. LC 68-8491. (Essay Index Reprint Ser.). 1977. 23.95 (*0-8369-0845-7*) Ayer.

— Declining Liberty & Other Papers. LC 73-159802. (Civil Liberties in American History Ser.). 350p. 1972. reprint ed. lib. bdg. 42.50 (*0-306-70253-3*) Da Capo.

— Distributive Justice. 1978. 40.95 (*0-405-10849-4*, 11852) Ayer.

— Economic Justice: Selections from Distributive Justice & a Living Wage. Beckley, Harlan R., ed. & intro. by. LC 96-398. (Library of Theological Ethics). 256p. 1996. pap. 29.00 (*0-664-25660-0*) Westminster John Knox.

— Living Wage: Its Ethical & Economic Aspects. LC 72-156422. (American Labor Ser., No. 2). 1971. reprint ed. 24.95 (*0-405-02939-X*) Ayer.

— Questions of the Day. LC 67-26779. (Essay Index Reprint Ser.). 1977. 23.95 (*0-8369-0846-5*) Ayer.

Ryan, John B. & Lodato, Francis J. Creating Your Christian Engagement. LC 94-76020. 144p. (Orig.). 1994. pap. 6.95 (*0-89243-575-5*) Liguori Pubns.

Ryan, John C. Hazardous Handouts: Taxpayers Subsidies to Environment Destruction. LC 95-68006. (New Reports). 56p. 1995. pap. text 8.00 (*1-886093-01-6*) NW Environ Watch.

— Life Support: Conserving Biological Diversity. 70p. (Orig.). 1992. pap. 5.00 (*1-878071-09-2*) Worldwatch Inst.

— Over Our Heads: A Local Look at Global Climate. Chu, Ellen W., ed. LC 97-76494. (New Report: No. 6). (Illus.). 80p. 1997. pap. 9.95 (*1-886093-06-7*) NW Environ Watch.

***Ryan, John C.** Seven Wonders 1999. pap. (*0-679-78313-X*) Random Hse Chldrns.

Ryan, John C. Seven Wonders: Everyday Things for a Healthier Planet. LC 99-22858. 98p. 1999. pap. 12.95 (*1-57805-038-3*, Pub. by Sierra) Random.

***Ryan, John C.** State of the Northwest, 2000 Edition. 2nd rev. ed. Chu, Ellen W., ed. (New Reports: Vol. 9). (Illus.). 100p. 2000. pap. 12.50 (*1-886093-10-5*) NW Environ Watch.

Ryan, John C. & Durning, Alan T. Stuff: The Secret Lives of Everyday Things. Chu, Ellen, ed. LC 97-177001. (Illus.). 88p. (Orig.). (C). 1997. pap. 9.95 (*1-886093-04-0*) NW Environ Watch.

Ryan, John C. & Northwest Environment Watch Staff. State of the Northwest. LC 94-61323. (New Reports: No. 1). 80p. (Orig.). 1995. pap. 9.95 (*1-886093-00-8*) NW Environ Watch.

Ryan, John Duncan. Expressions - 1988-1999. 47.50 (*0-9700069-0-X*) J D Ryan.

Ryan, John J. The Apostolic Conciliarism of Jean Gerson. LC 98-21363. (AAR the Religions Ser.). 96p. 1998. 24.95 (*0-7885-0464-9*) OUP.

— The Nature, Structure & Function of the Church of William of Ockham. LC 78-2891. (American Academy of Religion. Studies in Religion: No. 16). 69p. reprint ed. pap. 30.00 (*0-7837-5483-3*, 204524800005) Bks Demand.

Ryan, John K. Heirs & Ancestors. LC 74-171872. (Studies in Philosophy & the History of Philosophy: No. 6). 301p. reprint ed. pap. 93.40 (*0-608-17240-5*, 202949700061) Bks Demand.

— Introduction to the Devout Life. rev. ed. 320p. 1972. pap. 12.95 (*0-385-03009-6*, Image Bks) Doubleday.

— John Duns Scotus, 1265-1965. Bonansea, Bernardine M., ed. LC 61-66336. (Studies in Philosophy & the History of Philosophy: Vol. 3). 392p. reprint ed. pap. 121.60 (*0-608-30589-8*, 202258400028) Bks Demand.

Ryan, John K., ed. Studies in Philosophy & the History of Philosophy, Vol. 2. LC 61-66336. 266p. 1963. reprint ed. pap. 82.50 (*0-608-08399-2*, 202950500002) Bks Demand.

— Studies in Philosophy & the History of Philosophy, Vol. 4. LC 61-66336. 238p. 1969. reprint ed. pap. 73.80 (*0-8357-9057-6*, 201727900004) Bks Demand.

— Studies in Philosophy & the History of Philosophy: Ancients & Moderns, Vol.5. LC 61-66336. 374p. reprint ed. pap. 116.00 (*0-608-08400-X*, 201728000007) Bks Demand.

Ryan, John K. & Benard, Edmond, eds. American Essays for the Newman Centennial. LC 47-30528. 258p. reprint ed. pap. 80.00 (*0-8357-5367-0*, 200537900053) Bks Demand.

Ryan, John L., jt. ed. see Morrison, Donald C.

Ryan, John P. Fort Stanton & Its Community, 1855-1896. (Frontier Forts & People Ser.: No. 2). (Illus.). 176p. 1998. 25.00 (*1-881325-26-1*); pap. 14.95 (*1-881325-28-8*) Yucca Tree Pr.

Ryan, Jon R., jt. auth. see Wallin, Desna L.

Ryan, Jona. Artistic Angels. 44p. (Orig.). 1996. pap. 11.95 (*1-879825-28-7*) Jones Publish.

***Ryan, Joseph.** Check Him Out! The American Woman's Guide to Background Investigations. 95p. 2000. pap. 19.95 (*0-937801-14-3*) Wash Res Assocs.

Ryan, Joseph. Employment Opportunities U. S. A. LC 85-51246. 260p. 1997. ring bd. 184.00 (*0-937801-11-9*) Wash Res Assocs.

***Ryan, Joseph, ed.** Employment Opportunities, U. S. A. 17th ed. LC 85-51246. 300p. 2000. 184.00 (*0-937801-15-1*) Wash Res Assocs.

— Employment Opportunities, U. S. A: A Career News Service. 16th ed. 250p. 1999. 184.00 (*0-937801-13-5*) Wash Res Assocs.

***Ryan, Joseph & Davies, Jill Rosemary.** Healing Herbs: Ginger: A Step-by-Step Guide. (In a Nutshell Ser.). 2000. 7.95 (*1-86204-708-1*, Pub. by Element MA) Penguin Putnam.

Ryan, Joseph, ed. see MacDonnell, Joseph F.

Ryan, Joseph A. Loving Again. 160p. 1991. pap. 7.99 (*0-310-53631-6*) Zondervan.

Ryan, Joseph A., jt. auth. see Ryan, Jillian.

An Asterisk (*) at the beginning of an entry indicates that the title is appearing for the first time.

Ryan, Joseph N. & Edwards, Marc, eds. Critical Issues in Water & Wastewater Treatment: Proceedings of the 1994 National Conference on Environmental Engineering, Boulder, CO, July 11-13, 1994. LC 94-20431. 824p. 1994. 76.00 (0-7844-0031-8) Am Soc Civil Eng.

Ryan, Joyce. America's Best Cheesecakes: 150 Delicious & Easy-to-Prepare Recipes. LC 97-31656. 128p. 1998. pap. 12.95 (0-939077-06-X) Butterfly Bks.

— Calligraphy: Elegant & Easy. LC 94-94049. (Illus.). 104p. (Orig.). 1994. pap. 12.95 (0-939077-04-3) Butterfly Bks.

— Drawing at Home: Learn How to Draw in the Comfort & Privacy of Your Home. LC 95-83835. (Illus.). 112p. (Orig.). 1996. pap. text 14.95 (0-939077-05-1) Butterfly Bks.

— The Happy Camper's Gourmet Cookbook: The Complete Guide to Camper-RV Cooking. LC 92-70449. (Illus.). 200p. (Orig.). 1992. pap. 11.95 (0-939077-03-5) Butterfly Bks.

— Traveling with Your Sketchbook: A Step-by-Step Guide to Travel Sketching with Emphasis on Pen-&-Ink. LC 90-83216. (Illus.). 200p. (Orig.). 1990. pap. 19.95 (0-939077-02-7) Butterfly Bks.

Ryan, Juanita. Psalms II: Heart Cries to God. (LifeGuide Bible Studies Ser.). (Orig.). 1995. pap., wbk. ed. 4.99 (0-8308-1038-2, 1038) InterVarsity.

Ryan, Juanita, jt. auth. see Ryan, Dale.

***Ryan, Judith.** Rilke, Modernism & Poetic Tradition. LC 99-11717. (Cambridge Studies in German). 240p. (C). 1999. 64.95 (0-521-66173-0) Cambridge U Pr.

Ryan, Judith. The Uncompleted Past: Postwar German Novels & the Third Reich. LC 83-6744. 184p. reprint ed. pap. 57.10 (0-608-16063-6, 203319400084) Bks Demand.

— The Vanishing Subject: Early Psychology & Literary Modernism. LC 90-27330. 278p. 1991. 34.50 (0-226-73226-6) U Ch Pr.

Ryan, Judith, tr. see Goethe, Johann Wolfgang Von.

Ryan, Judith H. The Birthplace of New Scotland: An Illustrated History of Pictou County, Canada's Cradle of Industry. (Illus.). 128p. 1997. pap. 16.95 (0-88780-292-3, Pub. by Formac Publ Co) Formac Dist Ltd.

Ryan, Judy L. Angel Poems. (Illus.). 32p. (Orig.). (J). (gr. 1-12). 1995. pap. 5.00 (0-9649316-0-5) J L Ryan.

Ryan, Julie. The Last Night at Patty's Saloon. (Illus.). (Orig.). 1996. pap. 4.50 (0-942186-05-2) Paperbacks Plus.

— Perennial Gardens for Texas. LC 97-4692. (Illus.). 400p. 1998. 50.00 (0-292-78106-7); pap. 27.95 (0-292-77089-8) U of Tex Pr.

Ryan, Julie-Anne. Natural Way HIV & AIDS: A Comprehensive Guide to Effective Treatment. LC 99-19663. 128p. 1999. pap. 5.95 (1-85230-854-0, Pub. by Element MA) Penguin Putnam.

Ryan, K. W., ed. International Law in Australia. 2nd ed. xliii, 523p. 1984. pap. 85.00 (0-455-20269-9, Pub. by LawBk Co) Gaunt.

***Ryan, Karen.** Twentieth Century Russian Literature. 2000. text 69.95 (0-312-23418-X) St Martin.

Ryan, Karen-Lee. 40 Great Rail-Trails in New York & New England. (Illus.). 220p. (Orig.). 1996. pap. 14.95 (0-925794-12-0) Rails Trails.

— 40 Great Rail-Trails in the Mid-Atlantic. (Illus.). 290p. (Orig.). 1995. pap. 14.95 (0-925794-10-4) Rails Trails.

Ryan, Karen-Lee & Wincerich, Julie, eds. Secrets of Successful Rail-Trails: An Acquisition & Organizing Manual for Converting Rails into Trails. (Illus.). 192p. (Orig.). 1990. 19.95 (0-925794-05-8) Rails Trails.

Ryan, Karen-Lee, jt. auth. see Smith, Greg.

Ryan, Karlene K. To Find Hope: Simple Wisdom for Those Who Grieve. LC 97-15027. 64p. (Orig.). 1997. pap. 7.95 (0-8091-3735-6, 3735-6) Paulist Pr.

Ryan, Kate. Old Boston Museum Days. LC 77-131822. (Illus.). 1971. reprint ed. 49.00 (0-403-00709-7) Scholarly.

Ryan, Katherine E., jt. auth. see Ory, John C.

Ryan, Kathleen. Clan Novel Ravnos. (Illus.). 288p. 1999. pap. 5.99 (1-56504-808-3, 11106) White Wolf.

— Clan Novel Setite. (Vampire Ser.). (Illus.). 288p. 1999. pap. 5.99 (1-56504-804-0, 11103, Wrld of Darkness) White Wolf.

— Doll Artists at Work, Vol. 1. (Illus.). 136p. (Orig.). 1995. pap. 9.95 (1-888076-01-1) Infodial.

Ryan, Kathleen & Brucato, Phil. Beyond the Barrier: Book of Worlds. (Mage Ser.). (Illus.). 1996. pap. 22.00 (1-56504-434-7, 4007) White Wolf.

Ryan, Kathleen D. Courageous Messenger: How to Successfully Speak up at Work. 1996. 25.00 (0-7879-0268-3) Jossey-Bass.

***Ryan, Kathleen D. & Oestreich, Daniel K.** Driving Fear Out of the Work Place: Creating the High-Trust, High-Performance Organization. 2nd ed. LC 97-49000. 272p. 1998. pap. 20.00 (0-7879-3968-4) Jossey-Bass.

Ryan, Kathleen D. & Oestreich, Daniel K. Driving Fear Out of the Workplace: How to Overcome the Invisible Barriers to Quality, Productivity, & Innovation. LC 90-47648. (Management Ser.). 283p. 1993. pap. 19.00 (1-55542-509-7) Jossey-Bass.

Ryan, Kathleen J. & Share, Bernard, eds. Irish Traditions. (Illus.). 192p. 1990. 39.95 (0-8109-1109-4); pap. 19.98 (0-8109-8096-7, Pub. by Abrams) Time Warner.

Ryan, Kathleen J., et al. Ranching Traditions: Legacy of the American West. (Illus.). 296p. 1993. 22.98 (0-89660-032-7, Artabras) Abbeville Pr.

***Ryan, Kathleen Jo.** Deep in the Heart of Texas: Texas Ranchers in Their Own Words. LC 99-11726. (Illus.). 160p. 1999. pap. 24.95 (1-58008-101-0) Ten Speed Pr.

***Ryan, Kathleen Jo & Kelton, Elmer.** Texas Cattle Barons: Their Families, Land & Legacy. LC 99-11727. (Illus.). 208p. 1999. 49.95 (1-58008-100-2) Ten Speed Pr.

Ryan, Kathleen S. & Ryan, Kathleen S. The Narrow Cage: An American Family Saga. LC 80-687. 320p. 1980. 12.95 (0-672-52655-7, Bobbs) Macmillan.

Ryan, Kathleen S., jt. auth. see Ryan, Kathleen S.

Ryan, Kathryn, jt. auth. see Mohnach, Mary Beth E.

Ryan, Kathryn H., ed. see Barilleaux, Rene P. & Heartney, Eleanor.

Ryan, Kay. Dragon Acts to Dragon Ends. LC 82-51255. 64p. (Orig.). pap. 4.95 (0-911407-00-6) Taylor Street.

— Elephant Rocks. 96p. 1996. 18.00 (0-8021-1586-1, Grove) Grove-Atltic.

— Elephant Rocks: Poems. 96p. 1997. pap. 12.00 (0-8021-3525-0, Grove) Grove-Atltic.

— Flamingo Watching. LC 94-14755. 63p. (Orig.). 1994. pap. 9.95 (0-914278-64-9) Copper Beech.

***Ryan, Kay.** Say Uncle: Poems. LC 00-26454. 80p. 2000. pap. 13.00 (0-8021-3717-2, Grove) Grove-Atltic.

Ryan, Keith. Found Money: How to Consciously Win the Lottery. 105p. 1998. pap. 12.95 (0-9683922-0-2) KR Pub.

Ryan, Ken. Computer Anxiety? Instant Relief! An Easy-to-Read Introduction to IBM PCs, Compatibles & Clones. 2nd ed. Hansen, Laurie A., ed. LC 92-71577. (Illus.). 128p. 1992. pap. 9.95 (1-879925-05-2) Castle Mnt Pr.

Ryan, Kenneth. Catholic Questions, Catholic Answers. 212p. (Orig.). (C). 1990. pap. 10.99 (0-89283-663-6, Charis) Servant.

Ryan, Kenneth J. Sherris Medical Microbiology. 3rd ed. (Illus.). 890p. (C). 1999. pap. text 62.00 (0-8385-8541-8, A8541-3, Apple Lange Med) McGraw.

— Sherris Medical Microbiology. 4th ed. 1999. 74.95 (0-8385-8529-9, Medical Exam) Appleton & Lange.

Ryan, Kenneth J., et al. Kistner's Gynecology & Women's Health. 7th ed. (Illus.). 760p. (C). 1999. text. write for info. (0-323-00201-3) Mosby Inc.

Ryan, Kevin. The Illustrated Guide to Snowboarding. LC 97-31314. (Illus.). 336p. (Orig.). 1997. pap. 16.95 (1-57028-144-0, 81440H, Mstrs Pr) NTC Contemp Pub Co.

— Kaleidoscope, 7 vols. LC 94-76549. (C). 1994. pap. 41.16 (0-395-71246-7) HM.

— Those Who Can, Teach, 7 vols. LC 94-76550. (C). 1994. pap. 63.96 (0-395-71242-4) HM.

— Those Who Teach, 6 vols. 6th ed. (C). 1991. pap. text, teacher ed. 3.96 (0-395-60158-4) HM.

Ryan, Kevin & Lickona, Thomas, eds. Character Development in Schools & Beyond. enl. ed. LC 92-10115. (Cultural Heritage & Contemporary Change Series VI: Foundations of Moral Education,: Vol. 3). 350p. 1992. pap. 17.50 (1-56518-059-3) Coun Res Values.

— Character Development in Schools & Beyond. 2nd enl. ed. LC 92-10115. (Cultural Heritage & Contemporary Change Series VI: Foundations of Moral Education,: Vol. 3). 350p. 1992. 45.00 (1-56518-058-5) Coun Res Values.

Ryan, Kevin & Pollack, Pam, eds. Tails of Terror. (Super Adventures of Wishbone Ser.: No. 4). (Illus.). 256p. (J). (gr. 3-6). 1999. mass mkt. 3.99 (1-57064-480-2, Big Red) Lyrick Pub.

Ryan, Kevin & Ryan, Marilyn. Why I Am Still a Catholic. LC 97-32061. 224p. 1998. 13.00 (1-57322-677-7, Riverhd Trade) Berkley Pub.

Ryan, Kevin & Sutcliffe, F. E., eds. AI & Cognitive Science, 1992: University of Limerick, 10-11 September, 1992. LC 93-26018. (Workshops in Computing Ser.). 1993. 85.95 (0-387-19799-0) Spr-Verlag.

Ryan, Kevin & Sutcliffe, R. F., eds. AI & Cognitive Science, 1992. (Workshops in Computing Ser.). (Illus.). 385p. 1993. pap. write for info. (3-540-19799-0) Spr-Verlag.

Ryan, Kevin, jt. auth. see Friedman, Michael J.

Ryan, Kevin, jt. auth. see Wynne, Edward A.

Ryan, Kevin, ed. see Asherman, Allan.

Ryan, Kevin, ed. see Boyle, Randall.

Ryan, Kevin, ed. see Butcher, Nancy.

Ryan, Kevin, ed. see Cabeci, Anne.

Ryan, Kevin, ed. see Capeci, Anne.

Ryan, Kevin, ed. see Carter, Carmen.

Ryan, Kevin, ed. see Crispin, A. C.

Ryan, Kevin, ed. see David, Peter.

Ryan, Kevin, ed. see Dillard, J. M.

Ryan, Kevin, ed. see Duane E., Diane.

Ryan, Kevin, ed. see Friedman, Michael J.

Ryan, Kevin, ed. see Friedman, Michael & Kupperberg, Paul.

Ryan, Kevin, ed. see Gantt, Leticia.

Ryan, Kevin, ed. see Glaf, L. A.

Ryan, Kevin, ed. see Holder, Nancy.

Ryan, Kevin, ed. see Hugh, Daffyd A.

Ryan, Kevin, ed. see Jablonski, Carla.

Ryan, Kevin, ed. see Longyear, Barry B.

Ryan, Kevin, ed. see Mosley, Walter.

Ryan, Kevin, ed. see Neason, Rebecca V.

Ryan, Kevin, ed. see Peel, John.

Ryan, Kevin, ed. see Quark & Behr, Ira S.

Ryan, Kevin, ed. see Reeves-Stevens, Judith & Reeves-Stevens, Garfield.

Ryan, Kevin, ed. see Sathre, Vivian.

Ryan, Kevin, ed. see Steele, Alexander.

Ryan, Kevin, ed. see Steele, Anthony.

Ryan, Kevin, ed. see Steele, Michael A.

Ryan, Kevin, ed. see Steele, Michael Anthony.

Ryan, Kevin, ed. see Strickland, Brad & Fuller, Thomas.

Ryan, Kevin, ed. see Strickland, Brad & Strickland, Barbara.

Ryan, Kevin, ed. see Tilton, Lois.

Ryan, Kevin, ed. see Wright, Susan.

Ryan, Kevin A. & Bohlin, Karen E. Building Character in Schools: Strategies for Bringing Moral Instruction to Life. LC 98-25497. (Education Ser.). 208p. 1998. 25.00 (0-7879-4344-4) Jossey-Bass.

Ryan, Kiernan. Ian McEwan. (Writers & Their Work Ser.). 95p. (Orig.). 1996. pap. text 13.00 (0-7463-0742-X, Pub. by Northcote House) U Pr of Miss.

— New Historicism & Cultural Materialism: A Reader. 232p. 1996. pap. text 19.95 (0-340-61458-7, Pub. by E A) OUP.

Ryan, Kiernan. Shakespeare. 2nd ed. LC 95-5834. 176p. (C). 1995. pap. text 16.95 (0-13-355546-1) P-H.

— Shakespeare: Texts & Contexts. LC 99-52644. 2000. pap. 24.95 (0-312-23036-2) St Martin.

Ryan, Kiernan, ed. New Historicism & Cultural Materialism: A Reader. 232p. 1996. 65.00 (0-340-66307-3, Pub. by E A) OUP.

Ryan, Kiernan, ed. see Shakespeare, William.

Ryan, Kirk R. Pharmacologic Intervention in the Treatment of AIDS. 1992. pap. 9.00 (0-9623535-4-X) Remco Inc.

Ryan, L. Blood Lines. 1995. mass mkt. 13.95 (0-340-62456-6, Pub. by Hodder & Stought Ltd) Trafalgar.

— Note of Parting. 1996. mass mkt. 13.95 (0-340-62458-2, Pub. by Hodder & Stought Ltd) Trafalgar.

— Taste of Freedom. mass mkt. 13.95 (0-340-67211-0, Pub. by Hodder & Stought Ltd) Trafalgar.

Ryan, Larry, ed. see Getz, Frank.

Ryan, Larry, ed. see Sloop, Joseph G.

Ryan, Lawrence V. Roger Ascham. viii, 352p. 1963. 42.50 (0-8047-0149-0) Stanford U Pr.

— Roger Ascham. fac. ed. LC 63-10735. 364p. 1963. reprint ed. pap. 30.00 (0-7837-7912-7, 204766800008) Bks Demand.

***Ryan, Lawrie.** Advanced Chemistry for You. (Illus.). 448p. (YA). 2000. pap. 62.50 (0-7487-5297-8, Pub. by S Thornes Pubs) Trans-Atl Phila.

Ryan, Lawrie. Chemistry for You: Teacher's Support Pack. 300p. 1998. pap., teacher ed. 135.00 (0-7487-2757-4, Pub. by S Thornes Pubs) Trans-Atl Phila.

Ryan, Lee F. The Natural Classical Guitar: Principles of Effortless Playing. (Illus.). 291p. 1990. reprint ed. pap. 27.95 (0-933224-40-0, T037) Bold Strummer Ltd.

Ryan, Leigh. The Bedford Guide for Writing Tutors. 2nd ed. LC 99-462581. 90p. 1997. pap. text 13.95 (0-312-16732-6) St Martin.

Ryan, Leland B. The Editor's Toolbox: A Reference Guide for Beginners & Professionals. 2nd rev. ed. O'Donnell, Michael, ed. (Illus.). 144p. (C). 1995. pap. text 25.00 (1-888559-01-2, 95001202) Pug Pubng.

***Ryan, Leland B. & O'Donnell, Michael.** The Editor's Toolbox: Reference Guide for Beginners & Professionals. (Illus.). 368p. 2000. 39.95 (0-8138-1129-5) Iowa St U Pr.

Ryan, Leland B. & O'Donnell, Michael. Wordwise: A Guide to the Language for Journalists. 2nd rev. ed. LC 95-1201. 132p. (Orig.). (C). 1995. pap. text 25.00 (1-888559-00-4) Pug Pubng.

***Ryan, Leo V.** Business Students Focus on Ethics. (Praxiology Ser.: Vol. 8). 2000. 49.95 (0-7658-0037-3) Transaction Pubs.

Ryan, Leo V., jt. auth. see Hunter, Richard J.

Ryan, Lisa G. Insect Musicians & Cricket Champions: A Cultural History of Singing Insects in China & Japan. (Illus.). 88p. 1996. 21.95 (0-8351-2576-9) China Bks.

Ryan, Liz. Blood Lines. 640p. 1995. text 35.00 (0-340-62455-8, Pub. by Hodder & Stought Ltd) Trafalgar

Ryan, Liz. Cics Primer LC 85-11941. xiii, 326p. 1986. write for info. (0-574-21940-4) SRA.

Ryan, Lorna. Reading "The Prostitute" Appearance, Place, & Time in British & Irish Press Stories of Prostitution. LC 97-70892. (Illus.). 288p. 1997. text 73.95 (1-85972-539-2, Pub. by Ashgate Pub) Ashgate Pub Co.

Ryan, Louis J., jt. compiled by see Ryan, Dorothy.

Ryan, Luke, jt. auth. see Ryan, Mike.

Ryan-Lush, Geraldine. Hairs on Bears. (Illus.). 24p. (J). (ps-1). 1994. pap. 4.95 (1-55037-352-8, Pub. by Annick); lib. bdg. 14.95 (1-55037-351-X, Pub. by Annick) Firefly Bks Ltd.

— Poils, Poils et Repoils - Hairs on Bears. (FRE., Illus.). 32p. (J). 1996. pap. 5.95 (1-55037-980-1, Pub. by Annick); lib. bdg. 14.95 (1-55037-981-X, Pub. by Annick) Firefly Bks Ltd.

Ryan, Lyndall. Aboriginal Tasmanians. 2nd ed. LC 96-174090. (Illus.). 416p. 1997. pap. text 24.95 (1-86373-965-3, Pub. by Allen & Unwin Pty) Paul & Co Pubs.

Ryan, M. Politics of Penal Reform. Date not set. pap. text. write for info. (0-582-29539-4, Pub. by Addison-Wesley) Longman.

Ryan, M., ed. Illustrated Archaeology of Ireland. (Illus.). 224p. 1991. write for info. (0-946172-25-0, Pub. by Cntry Hse) Roberts Rinehart.

Ryan, M., jt. auth. see Huth, M.

Ryan, M. J. Attitudes of Gratitude: How to Give & Receive Joy Every Day of Your Life. LC 98-49656. 180p. 1999. pap. 9.95 (1-57324-149-0) Conari Press.

***Ryan, M. J.** Attitudes of Gratitude: How to Give & Receive Joy Every Day of Your Life. 208p. 1999. 6.98 (1-56731-372-8, MJF Bks) Fine Comms.

— Attitudes of Gratitude: How to Give & Receive Joy Every Day of Your Life. gift ed. 2000. 14.95 (1-57324-511-9) Conari Press.

— The Fabric of the Future: Women Visionaries Illuminate the Path to Tomorrow. 464p. 2000. pap. text 18.95 (1-57324-197-0) Conari Press.

— The Giving Heart: Unlocking the Transformative Power of Generosity in Your Life. 208p. 2000. pap. 11.95 (1-57324-521-6) Conari Press.

Ryan, M. J. A Grateful Heart: Daily Blessings for the Evening Meal from Buddha to the Beatles. (Illus.). 280p. 1994. 14.95 (0-943233-84-4) Conari Press.

***Ryan, M. J.** 365 Health & Happiness Boosters. LC 99-88973. 384p. 2000. pap. 14.95 (1-57324-500-3) Conari Press.

Ryan, M. J., ed. The Fabric of the Future Vol. 1: Women Visionaries Illuminate the Path to Tomorrow. LC 98-8504. 300p. 1998. 25.00 (1-57324-129-6) Conari Press.

— A Grateful Heart. 288p. 1997. 7.98 (1-56731-194-6, MJF Bks) Fine Comms.

Ryan, M. Stanley. Parliamentary Procedure: Essential Principles. LC 83-45012. 232p. 1985. 14.95 (0-8453-4771-3, Cornwall Bks) Assoc Univ Prs.

Ryan, Marah E. The Druid Path. LC 73-130071. (Short Story Index Reprint Ser.). (Illus.). 1977. 20.95 (0-8369-3652-3) Ayer.

— The Druid Path. 324p. 1996. reprint ed. pap. 19.95 (1-56459-623-0) Kessinger Pub.

— A Flower of France: A Story of Old Louisiana. LC 72-2930. (Black Heritage Library Collection). 1977. reprint ed. 29.95 (0-8369-9078-1) Ayer.

Ryan, Marc, jt. auth. see Haskins, Clem.

***Ryan, Marcus.** The Thesis: Adventures in Academia. 200p. 2000. pap. 18.00 (0-7388-2040-7) Xlibris Corp.

Ryan, Margaret. How to Give a Speech. (Speak Out, Write On! Ser.). (Illus.). 96p. (YA). (gr. 7-12). 1994. lib. bdg. 24.00 (0-531-11199-7) Watts.

— How to Give a Speech. rev. ed. (Speak Out, Write On! Ser.). (Illus.). 143p. (YA). (gr. 7-12). 1996. pap. 7.95 (0-531-15804-7) Watts.

— How to Write a Poem. (Speak Out, Write On! Ser.). 128p. (YA). (gr. 7-12). 1996. pap. 7.95 (0-531-15788-1); lib. bdg. 24.00 (0-531-11252-7) Watts.

Ryan, Margaret. Puffling in a Pickle. pap. 7.95 (0-14-037062-5, Pub. by Pnguin Bks Ltd) Trafalgar.

Ryan, Margaret. The Samoyed Book. deluxe ed. (Illus.). 300p. 1995. 55.00 (0-614-04549-5) Donald R Hoflin.

Ryan, Margaret O., jt. auth. see Zukow, Bud.

Ryan, Margaret O., ed. see Erickson, Milton H.

Ryan, Margaret O., jt. auth. see Wolinsky, Stephen.

Ryan, Marie-Laure. Cyberspace Textuality: Computer Technology & Literary Theory. LC 98-43225. (Illus.). 304p. 1998. 39.95 (0-253-33465-9); pap. 17.95 (0-253-21242-1) Ind U Pr.

***Ryan, Marie-Laure.** Narrative as Virtual Reality: Immersion & Interactivity in Literature & Electronic Media. (Parallax Ser.). (Illus.). 352p. 2000. 45.00 (0-8018-6487-9) Johns Hopkins.

— Narrative as Virtual Reality: Immersion & Interactivity in Literature & Electronic Media. LC 00-8955. (Parallax Ser.). 2001. pap. write for info. (0-8018-6488-7) Johns Hopkins.

Ryan, Marie-Laure. Possible Worlds, Artificial Intelligence, & Narrative Theory. LC 91-6825. (Illus.). 308p. 1992. 14.95 (0-253-35004-2) Ind U Pr.

Ryan, Marilyn, jt. auth. see Ryan, Kevin.

***Ryan, Mark.** Ask the Teacher: A Practitioner's Guide to Teaching & Learning in the Diverse Classroom. (C). 2000. pap., student ed. 56.25 (0-07-242013-8) McGrw-H Hghr Educ.

Ryan, Mark, jt. auth. see Chamberlain.

Ryan, Mark, jt. auth. see Lee, Paul A.

Ryan, Mark A. Chinese Attitudes Toward Nuclear Weapons: China & the United States during the Korean War. LC 89-4158. 256p. (gr. 13). 1990. text 74.95 (0-87332-530-3, East Gate Bk) M E Sharpe.

Ryan, Marleigh G. Japan's First Modern Novel: "Ukigumo" of Futabatei Shimei. LC 83-12764. 381p. 1983. reprint ed. lib. bdg. 65.00 (0-313-24128-7, RYJA, Greenwood Pr) Greenwood.

Ryan, Marleigh G., tr. from JPN. Japan's First Modern Novel: "Ukigumo" of Futabatei Shimei. LC 90-1371. (Michigan Classics in Japanese Studies: No. 1). xiv, 381p. 1990. reprint ed. pap. text 15.95 (0-939512-44-0) U MI Japan.

***Ryan, Marlene A.** If You Believe in...True Love! Ryan, Carrie-Anne, ed. (Illus.). 160p. 1999. pap. write for info. incl. cd-rom (1-929327-00-5) Ashly Pubns.

Ryan, Martin. The Last Resort: A Study of Consumer Bankrupts. 320p. 1995. 82.95 (1-85972-010-2, Pub. by Avebry) Ashgate Pub Co.

— Social Work & Debt Problems. 180p. 1996. text 63.95 (1-85972-011-0, Pub. by Avebry) Ashgate Pub Co.

Ryan, Mary. The Children Act, 1989: Putting It into Practice. 252p. 1994. 28.95 (1-85742-192-2, Pub. by Arena) Ashgate Pub Co.

***Ryan, Mary.** The Children Act, 1989: Putting It into Practice. 2nd ed. LC 99-204958. 272p. 1999. pap. 28.95 (1-85742-433-6, Pub. by Ashgate Pub) Ashgate Pub Co.

Ryan, Mary. Glenallen. 1993. 24.95 (0-312-28797-6) St Martin.

— Mask of the Night. large type ed. LC 98-41388. 1998. 30.00 (0-7838-0380-X, G K Hall Lrg Type) Mac Lib Ref.

— The Promise. LC 99-24818. 1999. text 22.95 (0-312-20571-6) St Martin.

***Ryan, Mary.** Song of the Tide. 2000. 24.95 (0-312-26648-0) St Martin.

— The Song of the Tide. large type ed. 472p. 1999. 31.99 (0-7089-4163-X) Ulverscroft.

Ryan, Mary, ed. see Wehmann, Howard H. & DeWhitt, Benjamin.

Ryan, Mary, tr. see Sertillanges, A. G.

Ryan, Mary C. Frankie's Run. (J). (gr. 3-7). 1987. 12.95 (0-316-76370-5) Little.

— Frankie's Run. (J). 1988. pap. 2.50 (0-380-70537-0, Avon Bks) Morrow Avon.

R

R

— Ghosts, Gadgets & Great Ideas. 96p. (Orig.). (J). (gr. 3). 1993. pap. 3.50 (*0-380-76537-3*, Avon Bks) Morrow Avon.
— Me Two. 192p. (J). 1993. pap. 3.50 (*0-380-71826-X*, Avon Bks) Morrow Avon.
— My Friend, O'Connell. 112p. (Orig.). (J). (gr. 3-4). 1991. pap. 2.95 (*0-380-76145-9*, Avon Bks) Morrow Avon.
***Ryan, Mary C.** The Secret in the West Woods. 115p. (J). (gr. 4-6). 2000. pap. 7.95 (*0-9678115-0-3*) Dragonseed Pr.
Ryan, Mary C. The Voice from the Mendelsohns' Maple. LC 89-31569. (Illus.). 132p. (J). (gr. 5-7). 1990. 13.95 (*0-316-76360-8*) Little.
— The Voice from the Mendelsohns' Maple. 144p. (J). (gr. 5). 1992. pap. 3.50 (*0-380-71140-0*, Avon Bks) Morrow Avon.
— Who Says I Can't? 160p. (YA). (gr. 12 up). 1988. 12.95 (*0-316-76374-8*) Little.
— Who Says I Can't? 160p. (YA). (gr. 12 up). 1990. mass mkt. 2.95 (*0-380-70804-3*, Avon Bks) Morrow Avon.
Ryan, Mary C., et al. Serving Job Seekers & Career Changers: A Planning Manual for Public Libraries. LC 92-38870. (Public Library Development Ser.). (Illus.). 125p. (C). 1993. pap. text 25.00 (*0-8389-3419-6*) ALA.
Ryan, Mary C., jt. ed. see Smith, Nancy Kegan.
Ryan, Mary C., jt. ed. see Smith, Nancy K.
Ryan, Mary E. Alias. LC 96-34184. 160p. (YA). (gr. 7 up). 1998. per. 4.99 (*0-689-82264-2*) Aladdin.
— Alias. LC 96-34184. 176p. (J). (gr. 5-9). 1997. 16.00 (*0-689-80789-9*) S&S Bks Yung.
— Alias. (YA). (gr. 7 up). 1997. 16.00 (*0-614-29066-X*) S&S Childrens.
— Me, My Sister, & I. LC 92-368. 160p. (YA). (gr. 5-9). 1992. pap. 15.00 (*0-671-73851-8*) S&S Bks Yung.
— The Trouble with Perfect. (J). 15.00 (*0-671-86586-2*) S&S Bks Yung.
Ryan, Mary E., jt. auth. see Cochrane, Willard W.
Ryan, Mary J. & Thompson, William P. CQI & the Renovation of an American Health Care System: A Culture under Construction. LC 97-3243. 216p. 1997. 27.00 (*0-87389-417-0*, H0960) ASQ Qual Pr.
Ryan, Mary K. & Shattuck, Arthur. Treating AIDS with Chinese Medicine. LC 93-85212. 384p. 1993. pap. 29.95 (*1-881896-07-2*) Pacific View Pr.
Ryan, Mary P. Civic Wars: Democracy & Public Life in the American City During the Nineteenth Century. LC 96-25630. (Illus.). 389p. 1997. 40.00 (*0-520-20441-7*, Pub. by U CA Pr) Cal Prin Full Svc.
— Civic Wars: Democracy & Public Life in the American City During the Nineteenth Century. (Illus.). 394p. 1998. pap. 17.95 (*0-520-21660-1*, Pub. by U CA Pr) Cal Prin Full Svc.
— Cradle of the Middle Class: The Family in Oneida County, New York, 1790-1865. LC 80-18460. (Interdisciplinary Perspectives on Modern History Ser.). (Illus.). 321p. 1983. pap. text 18.95 (*0-521-27403-6*) Cambridge U Pr.
— The Empire of the Mother: American Writing about Domesticity, 1830-1860. LC 82-15631. (Women & History Ser.: Nos. 2 & 3). 170p. 1982. text 49.95 (*0-86656-133-1*) Haworth Pr.
— The Empire of the Mother: American Writing about Domesticity 1830-1860. LC 85-5818. 170p. 1985. reprint ed. pap. 24.95 (*0-918393-18-3*, Harrington Park) Haworth Pr.
— Women in Public: Between Banners & Ballots, 1825-1880. LC 89-32863. (Symposia in Comparative History Ser.). (Illus.). 208p. 1990. text 37.95 (*0-8018-3908-4*) Johns Hopkins.
Ryan, Matthew. Andrea's Arm. LC 97-61046. (Aesop's Fables Running Start Ser.). (Illus.). 32p. (J). (gr. 2-4). 1997. pap. 4.95 (*1-890570-20-6*) Huckleberry CT.
— Pass the Ball. LC 97-61043. (Aesop's Fables Running Start Ser.). (Illus.). 32p. (J). (gr. 1-3). 1997. pap. 4.95 (*1-890570-18-4*) Huckleberry CT.
Ryan, Maura A. & Whitmore, Todd D. The Challenge of Global Stewardship: Roman Catholic Responses. LC 97-5311. 1997. pap. 15.00 (*0-268-00822-1*) U of Notre Dame Pr.
Ryan, Maureen. Innocence & Estrangement in the Fiction of Jean Stafford. LC 87-2780. 181p. 1987. pap. 56.20 (*0-7837-8517-8*, 204932600011) Bks Demand.
Ryan, Meda. Michael Collins & The Women in His Life. LC 97-116359. (Illus.). 208p. 1997. pap. 12.95 (*1-85635-166-1*, Pub. by Mercier Pr) Irish Amer Bk.
Ryan, Meda C. The Day Michael Collins Was Shot. LC 89-82488. 240p. 1996. pap. 14.95 (*1-85371-041-5*, Pub. by Poolbeg Pr) Dufour.
— Real Chief. 1986. pap. 13.95 (*0-85342-764-X*) Dufour.
***Ryan, Michael.** A Difficult Grace: On Poets, Poetry & Writing. LC 00-26110. 2000. write for info. (*0-8203-2231-8*) U of Ga Pr.
— A Difficult Grace: On Poets, Poetry, & Writing. 200p. 2000. 40.00 (*0-8203-2264-4*) U of Ga Pr.
Ryan, Michael. Golden Years - Golden Words. (Illus.). 168p. (Orig.). 1993. pap. 5.95 (*1-56245-027-1*) Great Quotations.
— Golf Forever Work... Whenever. 366p. (Orig.). 1993. pap., spiral bd. 8.95 (*1-56245-047-6*) Great Quotations.
— Gulliver. 175p. Date not set. 7.00 (*0-936756-19-5*) Autonomedia.
— Inspirations: Compelling Food for Thought. Caton, Patrick, ed. 168p. (Orig.). 1996. pap. 5.95 (*1-56245-243-6*) Great Quotations.
— Literary Theory: A Practical Introduction. LC 98-28722. 512p. 1999. 59.95 (*0-631-17275-0*); pap. 27.95 (*0-631-17276-9*) Blackwell Pubs.
— Marxism & Deconstruction: A Critical Articulation. LC 81-48185. 272p. (C). 1982. pap. 14.95 (*0-8018-3248-9*) Johns Hopkins.
— Metal Craftsmanship in Early Ireland. (Treasures of the National Museum of Ireland Ser.). (Illus.). 48p. (Orig.). 1995. pap. 7.95 (*0-946172-37-4*, Pub. by Town Hse) Roberts Rinehart.
— The "O" Book: The Other Sixteen Hours: The Social & Emotional Problems of Dyslexia. (Orton Emeritus Ser.). 1994. pap. 5.00 (*0-89214-008-9*) Intl Dyslexia.
— The Philosophy of Marriage, in Its Social, Moral, & Physical Relations. LC 73-20638. (Sex, Marriage & Society Ser.). 400p. 1974. reprint ed. 33.95 (*0-405-05815-2*) Ayer.
— Politics & Culture: Working Hypotheses for a Post-Revolutionary Society. LC 88-31746. (Parallax). 280p. 1989. text 42.00 (*0-8018-3827-4*) Johns Hopkins.
— Reformers: Living History. (C). 1988. 59.00 (*0-946139-52-0*) St Mut.
— Run Like You Was Bein' Shot At: And Other Adventures. 208p. 1994. pap. 9.95 (*0-9631695-2-1*) Whist & Jugg.
— Secret Life. 1996. pap. 14.00 (*0-679-76776-2*) Vin Bks.
— 201 Best Things Ever Said. 168p. (Orig.). 1993. pap. 5.95 (*1-56245-079-4*) Great Quotations.
— Votes for Women: Living History. (C). 1990. 65.00 (*0-946139-91-1*, Pub. by Elm Pubns) St Mut.
— Who Really Said. 78p. (Orig.). 1993. pap. 7.95 (*1-56245-032-8*) Great Quotations.
Ryan, Michael, ed. Apple a Day. 366p. (Orig.). 1993. pap., spiral bd. 8.95 (*1-56245-080-8*) Great Quotations.
— Hollywords: Great Quotes from Great Stars. (Illus.). 168p. 1993. pap. 5.95 (*1-56245-026-3*) Great Quotations.
— How to Hypnotize a Chicken: (Plus Thirty Other Ways to Liven up Your Life) A Guide to Creative Living for Regular Folks. 158p. (Orig.). 1991. pap. 9.95 (*0-9631695-1-3*) Whist & Jugg.
— Irish Archaeology Illustrated. rev. ed. (Illus.). 224p. (C). 1995. pap. 21.95 (*1-57098-035-7*) Roberts Rinehart.
— Reflections. 168p. (Orig.). 1993. pap. 5.95 (*1-56245-033-6*) Great Quotations.
Ryan, Michael, tr. Social Trends in Contemporary Russia: A Statistical Source-Book. LC 93-7913. 1993. text 59.95 (*0-312-10070-1*) St Martin.
Ryan, Michael & Kellner, Douglas M. Camera Politica: The Politics & Ideology of Contemporary Hollywood Film. LC 86-45477. (Illus.). 346p. (Orig.). 1988. 49.95 (*0-253-31334-1*) Ind U Pr.
— Camera Politica: The Politics & Ideology of Contemporary Hollywood Film. LC 86-45477. (Illus.). 346p. (Orig.). 1990. pap. 17.95 (*0-253-20604-9*, MB-604) Ind U Pr.
Ryan, Michael & Weatherley, Michael. Move into Work. 138p. (C). 1987. 80.00 (*0-946139-56-3*, Pub. by Elm Pubns) St Mut.
Ryan, Michael, et al. AT&T & Triad Policies Toward HDTV. (Pew Case Studies in International Affairs). 50p. (C). 1995. pap. text 3.50 (*1-56927-705-2*, GU Schl Foreign) Geo U Inst Dplmcy.
— AT&T's Strategy for Market Entry into the European Market for Telecommunications Services. (Pew Case Studies in International Affairs). 50p. (C). 1995. pap. text 3.50 (*1-56927-706-0*, GU Schl Foreign) Geo U Inst Dplmcy.
— Clean Technology, Cummins Engine, & Pollution Regulation As Competitive Advantage. (Pew Case Studies in International Affairs). 50p. (C). 1995. pap. text 3.50 (*1-56927-711-7*, GU Schl Foreign) Geo U Inst Dplmcy.
— Export Controls & Cray's Battle for Supercomputer Supremacy. (Pew Case Studies in International Affairs). 50p. (C). 1995. pap. text 3.50 (*1-56927-720-6*, GU Schl Foreign) Geo U Inst Dplmcy.
— Fairchild & Fujitsu Confront National Security. (Pew Case Studies in International Affairs). 50p. (C). 1996. pap. text 3.50 (*1-56927-708-7*, GU Schl Foreign) Geo U Inst Dplmcy.
— Harley-Davidson & Adjusting to the Costs of Free Trade. (Pew Case Studies in International Affairs). 50p. (C). 1995. pap. text 3.50 (*1-56927-715-X*, GU Schl Foreign) Geo U Inst Dplmcy.
— The Marlboro Man & Japanese Import Policy Toward Cigarettes. (Pew Case Studies in International Affairs). 50p. (C). 1995. pap. text 3.50 (*1-56927-719-2*, GU Schl Foreign) Geo U Inst Dplmcy.
— Motorola University & the Learning Organization. (Pew Case Studies in International Affairs). 50p. (C). 1995. pap. text 3.50 (*1-56927-714-1*, GU Schl Foreign) Geo U Inst Dplmcy.
— NAFTA: Honda Motor Company or Free Trade in the Real World. (Pew Case Studies in International Affairs). 50p. (C). 1995. pap. text 3.50 (*1-56927-718-4*, GU Schl Foreign) Geo U Inst Dplmcy.
— Negotiation Simulation: Drugs, Books, & Videos--U. S.-Korea Dispute Over Intellectual Property Rights. (Pew Case Studies in International Affairs). 50p. (C). 1995. pap. text 3.50 (*1-56927-710-9*, GU Schl Foreign) Geo U Inst Dplmcy.
— SIA, Japanese Electronics Giants, & Global Competition in Semiconductors. (Pew Case Studies in International Affairs). 50p. (C). 1995. pap. text 3.50 (*1-56927-707-9*, GU Schl Foreign) Geo U Inst Dplmcy.
— Smith Kline-Beecham Collaborates with NIH. (Pew Case Studies in International Affairs). 50p. (C). 1995. pap. text 3.50 (*1-56927-712-5*, GU Schl Foreign) Geo U Inst Dplmcy.
— Tecumseh, Matsushita, & Refrigeration Compression Subsidies in Singapore. (Pew Case Studies in International Affairs). 50p. (C). 1995. pap. text 3.50 (*1-56927-716-8*, GU Schl Foreign) Geo U Inst Dplmcy.
— Turning Swords into Plowshares: Defense Conversion. (Pew Case Studies in International Affairs). 50p. (C). 1995. pap. text 3.50 (*1-56927-713-3*, GU Schl Foreign) Geo U Inst Dplmcy.
— Will the Real American Company Please Stand Up: Brother's Antidumping Counterattack on Smith Corona. (Pew Case Studies in International Affairs). 50p. (C). 1995. pap. text 3.50 (*1-56927-717-6*, GU Schl Foreign) Geo U Inst Dplmcy.
— World-Wide Pharmaceutical in China: Investing in & Bargaining with a Socialist State in Transition. (Pew Case Studies in International Affairs). 50p. (C). 1995. pap. text 3.50 (*1-56927-709-5*, GU Schl Foreign) Geo U Inst Dplmcy.
Ryan, Michael, jt. auth. see Anderson, Mac.
Ryan, Michael, jt. auth. see Enck, John.
Ryan, Michael, jt. auth. see Riehl, Dan.
Ryan, Michael, ed. see Davis, Kathy.
Ryan, Michael, ed. see Minow, Martha.
Ryan, Michael, jt. ed. see Rivkin, Julie.
Ryan, Michael, tr. see Guattari, Felix & Negri, Toni.
Ryan, Michael D., ed. Human Responses to the Holocaust: Perpetrators, Victims, Bystanders & Resisters. LC 81-38331. (Texts & Studies in Religion: Vol. 9). 278p. 1981. lib. bdg. 89.95 (*0-88946-901-6*) E Mellen.
Ryan, Michael E. Fundamentals of Polymerization & Polymer Processing Technology. (Special Issue of the Journal Chemical Engineering Communications). 144p. 1983. text 161.00 (*0-677-06525-6*) Gordon & Breach.
Ryan, Michael E., jt. ed. see Rumer, Ralph R.
Ryan, Michael G., et al. Research Natural Areas in Colorado, Nebraska, North Dakota, South Dakota, & Parts of Wyoming. (Illus.). 68p. 1997. reprint ed. 17.00 (*0-89904-608-8*, Bear Meadows Resrch Grp); reprint ed. pap. 11.00 (*0-89904-609-6*, Bear Meadows Resrch Grp) Crumb Elbow Pub.
Ryan, Michael J. The Tungara Frog: A Study in Sexual Selection & Communication. LC 84-24110. (Illus.). xvi, 230p. 1992. pap. text 14.95 (*0-226-73229-0*) U Ch Pr.
— The Tungara Frog: A Study in Sexual Selection & Communication. LC 84-24110. (Illus.). xvi, 230p. 1994. lib. bdg. 33.00 (*0-226-73228-2*) U Ch Pr.
— The Tungara Frog: A Study in Sexual Selection & Communication. LC 84-24110. (Illus.). 246p. reprint ed. pap. 76.30 (*0-608-09520-6*, 205432200005) Bks Demand.
Ryan, Michael J., ed. Your Future Career in Education. LC 96-70242. 62p. 1996. pap. 7.00 (*0-87367-491-X*) Phi Delta Kappa.
Ryan, Michael P. Knowledge Diplomacy: Global Competition & the Politics of Intellectual Property. LC 98-8966. 249p. 1998. pap. 16.95 (*0-8157-7653-5*) Brookings.
— Knowledge Diplomacy: Global Competition & the Politics of Intellectual Property. LC 98-8966. 249p. 1998. text 39.95 (*0-8157-7654-3*) Brookings.
— Playing by the Rules: American Trade Power & Diplomacy in the Pacific. LC 94-32278. 320p. 1995. 42.50 (*0-87840-579-8*) Georgetown U Pr.
— Tomen Assesses Chemical Export Opportunities in Latin America. (Pew Case Studies in International Affairs). 50p. (C). 1996. text 3.50 (*1-56927-723-0*) Geo U Inst Dplmcy.
Ryan, Michael P., ed. Magmatic Systems. (International Geophysics Ser.: No. 57). (Illus.). 401p. 1994. text 73.00 (*0-12-605070-8*) Acad Pr.
Ryan, Michael W. Executorship & Administration. 171p. 1986. 150.00 (*1-85190-003-9*, Pub. by Fourmat Pub) St Mut.
— Executorship & Administration. 3rd ed. Demby, B., ed. 300p. 1995. pap. 210.00 (*0-85459-049-8*, Pub. by Tolley Pubng) St Mut.
Ryan, Michael W. & Aldridge, Lester. Executorship & Administration. 2nd ed. 269p. 1992. 84.00 (*1-85190-139-6*, Pub. by Tolley Pubng) St Mut.
Ryan, Mick & Ward, Tony. Privatization & the Penal System: The American Experience & the Debate in Britain. 176p. 1989. 45.00 (*0-335-09916-5*); pap. 14.99 (*0-335-09915-7*) OpUniv Pr.
***Ryan, Mike & Oliver, David.** Warplanes of the Future. (Illus.). 176p. 2000. 24.95 (*0-7603-0904-3*, 130303AP, Pub. by MBI Pubg) Motorbooks Intl.
Ryan, Mike & Ryan, Luke. It's Where You Played the Game: How Youth Baseball Determines the Personality of the American Male. 88p. 1995. 20.00 (*0-8050-4661-5*) H Holt & Co.
Ryan, Mildred G. Quilting Made Easy. LC 87-6854. (Illus.). 308p. 1987. 16.95 (*0-87131-523-8*) M Evans.
Ryan, Milo. View of a Universe: A Love Story of Ann Arbor at Middle Age. (Illus.). 211p. (Orig.). 1985. pap. 9.95 (*1-882574-02-8*) Ann Arbor Hist.
Ryan, Miriam P. Riverside. 341p. 1994. 15.95 (*0-9645678-0-6*) Vincent Pub.
Ryan-Mitlyng, Theresa A., jt. auth. see Micklitsch, Christine N.
Ryan, Monique. Complete Guide to Sports Nutrition. LC 99-13746. (Ultimate Training Series From Velo Press). (Illus.). 240p. 1999. pap. 16.95 (*1-884737-57-9*) VeloPress.
Ryan, N. Jesse. Junebug Prophecy. 32p. (Orig.). 1997. pap. 6.00 (*1-877801-33-X*) Still Waters.
***Ryan, Nan.** Amor Sin Fronteras. (SPA.). 368p. 2000. pap. 9.50 (*0-553-06128-3*) Bantam.
Ryan, Nan. Cloudcastle. (Love Spell Ser.). 384p. 1999. reprint ed. mass mkt. 5.50 (*0-505-52310-8*, Love Spell) Dorchester Pub Co.
***Ryan, Nan.** The Countess Misbehaves. 2000. mass mkt. 6.50 (*1-55166-591-3*, 1-66591-8, Mira Bks) Harlequin Bks.
Ryan, Nan. Desert Storm. 432p. 1987. mass mkt. 3.95 (*0-373-97038-2*) Harlequin Bks.
— Wanting You. 1999. per. 5.99 (*1-55166-521-2*, Mira Bks) Harlequin Bks.
***Ryan, Nan.** Wayward Lady. 448p. 1999. mass mkt. 5.50 (*0-505-52298-5*, Love Spell) Dorchester Pub Co.
Ryan, Nan. You Belong to My Heart. large type ed. LC 96-14350. (Large Print Bks.). 1996. pap. 22.95 (*1-56895-333-X*) Wheeler Pub.
Ryan, Nancy, jt. auth. see Eureka, William E.
Ryan, Nancy, jt. auth. see McMahon, James P.
Ryan, Nancy, jt. auth. see Soules, Aline.
Ryan, Nancy E., ed. Taguchi Methods & QFD: Hows & Whys for Management. LC 88-22182. (Illus.). 110p. 1988. 16.50 (*0-941243-04-4*) ASI Pr.
Ryan, Nancy E., jt. auth. see Eureka, William E.
Ryan, Nancy R. Louisiana's New Garde. Miller, Carolyn, ed. LC 94-76410. (Illus.). 162p. 1994. 29.95 (*0-929714-63-6*); pap. 24.95 (*0-929714-64-4*) Great Chefs TV.
Ryan, Nigel, tr. see Simenon, Georges.
Ryan, Nolan. Miracle Man. 314p. 1993. mass mkt. 5.99 (*0-8499-3507-5*) Word Pub.
Ryan, Nolan & Frommer, Harvey. Throwing Heat. 288p. 1990. mass mkt. 5.99 (*0-380-70826-4*, Avon Bks) Morrow Avon.
Ryan, Nolan & House, Tom. Nolan Ryan's Pitcher's Bible: The Ultimate Guide to Power, Precision, & Long-Term Performance. LC 90-39634. (Illus.). 176p. (Orig.). 1991. per. 12.00 (*0-671-70581-4*, Fireside) S&S Trade Pap.
Ryan, Nolan & Jenkins, Jerry. Miracle Man: Nolan Ryan, the Autobiography. large type ed. LC 92-33582. 333p. 1993. 16.95 (*0-8161-5606-9*, G K Hall & Co) Mac Lib Ref.
Ryan, Nolan, et al. Nolan Ryan: The Road to Cooperstown. LC 99-49223. (Illus.). 112p. 1999. 26.95 (*1-886110-82-4*, Pub. by Addax Pubng) Midpt Trade.
Ryan, P. & Sennett, Christ, eds. Formal Methods in Systems Engineering: Proceedings of the 2nd Formal Methods Workshop, Held in Drymen, Scotland, 24 - 27 September, 1991. (Illus.). xi, 195p. 1993. pap. 59.00 (*0-387-19751-6*) Spr-Verlag.
Ryan, P., et al. Nuclear Medicine in Clinical Practice: 100 Self-Assessment Case Studies. LC 97-67752. (Illus.). 224p. 1997. pap. text 29.95 (*0-412-45830-6*, Pub. by E A) OUP.
Ryan, P., jt. ed. see MacNiocaill, C.
Ryan, P. A., et al. Durability of Cladding: A State of the Art Report. LC 95-117925. 126p. 1994. 12.00 (*0-7277-2012-0*) Am Soc Civil Eng.
Ryan, P. D. Buddhism & the Natural World: Towards a Meaningful Myth. 144p. 1998. pap. 13.95 (*1-899579-00-1*) Weatherhill.
Ryan, Paddy. The Snorkeller's Guide to the Coral Reef: From the Red Sea to the Pacific Ocean. (Illus.). 1994. pap. 19.95 (*0-8248-1605-6*) UH Pr.
Ryan, Pam, jt. auth. see Pallotta, Jerry.
Ryan, Pam, jt. auth. see Read Martin, Jane.
Ryan, Pam, ed. see Cage, Cheryl A.
Ryan, Pam, ed. see Tarver, Judy A.
***Ryan, Pam Mudnoz.** Esperanza Rising. LC 00-24186. (Illus.). 208p. (YA). (gr. 4-9). 2000. 15.95 (*0-439-12041-1*) Scholastic Inc.
Ryan, Pam Munoz. Amelia & Eleanor Go for a Ride. LC 98-31788. (Illus.). 40p. (J). (gr. k-4). 1999. 16.95 (*0-590-96075-X*, Pub. by Scholastic Inc) Penguin Putnam.
— Armadillos Sleep in Dugouts & Other Places Animals Live. LC 96-35931. (Illus.). 32p. (J). (gr. k-3). 1997. lib. bdg. 14.89 (*0-7868-2222-8*, Pub. by Hyprn Child) Little.
— California Aqui Vamos! LC 95-34693.Tr. of Along the California Trail. (SPA., Illus.). 32p. (J). (ps-3). 1997. pap. 6.95 (*0-88106-883-7*) Charlesbridge Pub.
— California Aqui Vamos!Tr. of Along the California Trail. 1997. 12.15 (*0-606-13236-8*, Pub. by Turtleback) Demco.
— California, Here We Come! 1997. 12.15 (*0-606-13240-6*, Pub. by Turtleback) Demco.
— California Here We Come! LC 95-9471. (Illus.). 32p. (J). (ps-3). 1997. 16.95 (*0-88106-881-0*); pap. 6.95 (*0-88106-880-2*) Charlesbridge Pub.
Ryan, Pam Munoz. Crayon Counting Book. (Illus.). (J). 1996. 12.40 (*0-606-18024-9*) Turtleback.
— Doug Counts Down. LC PZ7.R9553Do 1998. (Doug Picture Bks.). (Illus.). 32p. (J). (gr. k-4). 1998. pap. 8.95 (*0-7868-3141-3*, Pub. by Disney Pr) Time Warner.
— Doug's Treasure Hunt. (Doug Ser.). 10p. 1999. 8.99 (*0-7364-0012-5*, Pub. by Mouse Works) Time Warner.
Ryan, Pam Munoz. The Flag We Love. LC 95-6619. (Illus.). 32p. (J). (ps-3). 1996. 16.95 (*0-88106-845-4*) Charlesbridge Pub.
— The Flag We Love. LC 95-6619. (Illus.). 32p. (J). 2000. pap. 7.95 (*0-88106-844-6*) Charlesbridge Pub.
— Funnie Family Vacation. (Doug Chronicles: No. 10). 64p. (J). (gr. 2-4). 1999. pap. 3.99 (*0-7868-4298-9*, Pub. by Disney Pr) Time Warner.
— Hello, Ocean. LC 98-15983. (Illus.). (J). Date not set. write for info. (*0-88106-987-6*) Charlesbridge Pub.
— One Hundred Is a Family. (Illus.). 24p. (J). 1998. 5.95 (*0-7868-0405-X*, Pub. by Hyperion) Time Warner.
— One Hundred Is a Family. LC 93-30914. (Illus.). 32p. (J). (ps-3). 1996. pap. 4.95 (*0-7868-1120-X*, Pub. by Hyprn Ppbks) Little.
— One Hundred Is a Family. LC 93-30914. (J). 1996. 10.15 (*0-606-09715-5*, Pub. by Turtleback) Demco.
— Riding Freedom. LC 97-18040. (Illus.). 144p. (J). (gr. 3-7). 1998. 15.95 (*0-590-95766-X*) Scholastic Inc.
***Ryan, Pam Munoz.** Riding Freedom. (Illus.). 144p. (J). (gr. 3-7). 1999. pap. 4.99 (*0-439-08796-1*, Pub. by Scholastic Inc) Penguin Putnam.
Ryan, Pam Munoz & Pallotta, Jerry. The Crayon Counting Book. LC 96-946. (Illus.). 32p. (J). (ps-3). 1996. 16.95 (*0-88106-954-X*); pap. 6.95 (*0-88106-953-1*) Charlesbridge Pub.

An Asterisk (*) at the beginning of an entry indicates that the title is appearing for the first time.

Ryan, Pam Munoz, et al. A Pinky Is a Baby Mouse & Other Baby Animal Names. LC 95-25396. (Illus.). 32p. (J). (ps-3). 1997. lib. bdg. 14.89 (0-7868-2190-6, Pub. by Hyprn Child) Time Warner.

Ryan, Pamela Munoz. Mud Is Cake. 32p. Date not set. text 14.99 (0-7868-0501-3, Pub. by Hyprn Child) Little.

— Mud Is Cake. 32p. 2005. lib. bdg. 15.49 (0-7868-2434-4, Pub. by Hyprn Child) Little.

Ryan, Pat. China. LC 96-13903. (Faces & Places Ser.). (Illus.). 32p. (J). (gr. 2-6). 1997. lib. bdg. 22.79 (1-56766-276-5) Childs World.

***Ryan, Pat.** Egypt. LC 97-46183. (Illus.). 32p. (J). 1998. lib. bdg. 22.79 (1-56766-514-4) Childs World.

Ryan, Pat. Indonesia. LC 96-7524. (Faces & Places Ser.). (Illus.). 32p. (J). (gr. 2-6). 1997. lib. bdg. 22.79 (1-56766-275-7) Childs World.

***Ryan, Pat.** Ireland. LC 98-45689. (Illus.). 32p. 1999. lib. bdg. 22.79 (1-56766-599-3) Childs World.

Ryan, Pat. Kenya. LC 97-32647. (Illus.). 32p. (J). 1998. lib. bdg. 22.79 (1-56766-516-0) Childs World.

— New Zealand. LC 98-11692. (Illus.). 32p. (J). 1999. lib. bdg. 22.79 (1-56766-577-2) Childs World.

— Rock Climbing. LC 98-33683. (World of Sports Ser.). (Illus.). 32p. (YA). (gr. 4 up). 2000. lib. bdg. 22.60 (1-887068-57-0) Smart Apple.

— South Korea. LC 97-50299. (Illus.). 32p. (J). 1998. lib. bdg. 22.79 (1-56766-517-9) Childs World.

Ryan, Pat & Ryan, Rosemary. Lent Begins at Home: Family Prayers & Activities. 64p. 1978. pap. 3.95 (0-89243-101-6) Liguori Pubns.

Ryan, Pat, jt. auth. see Lund, Bill.

Ryan, Patric J. Organized Crime. LC 95-12100. (Contemporary World Issues Ser.). 297p. (YA). (gr. 10 up). 1995. lib. bdg. 39.50 (0-87436-746-8) ABC-CLIO.

Ryan, Patricia. All of Me. (Temptation Ser.: Bk. 764). 216p. 2000. per. 3.75 (0-373-25864-X, 1-25864-9) Harlequin Bks.

— A Burning Touch. LC 96-3676. (Temptation Ser.). 219p. 1996. per. 3.25 (0-373-25671-X, 1-25671-8) Harlequin Bks.

— For the Thrill of It! (Temptation Ser.). 1996. per. 3.50 (0-373-25702-3, 1-25702-1) Harlequin Bks.

— In Hot Pursuit: (Hero for Hire) (Temptation Ser.: Vol. 701). 1998. per. 3.75 (0-373-25801-1, 1-25801-1) Harlequin Bks.

— Pas d'Amour Entre Nous. (Rouge Passion Ser.). (FRE.). 1997. pap. 3.50 (0-373-37432-1, 1-37432-1) Harlequin Bks.

— The Return of the Black Sheep: (Rebels & Rogues) LC 95-13563. (Temptation Ser.). 218p. 1995. per. 3.25 (0-373-25640-X, 1-25640-3) Harlequin Bks.

— Secret Thunder. 1997. mass mkt. 5.99 (0-614-27798-1, Topaz) NAL.

— Silken Threads. 320p. 1999. mass mkt. 5.99 (0-451-40827-6, Topaz) NAL.

***Ryan, Patricia.** The Sun & the Moon. 352p. 2000. mass mkt. 5.99 (0-451-20032-2, Sig) NAL.

Ryan, Patricia. Twice the Spice. 1997. per. 3.50 (0-373-25731-7, 1-25731-0) Harlequin Bks.

— Urban Development Law & Policy. cxiii, 473p. 1987. 129.50 (0-455-20750-X, Pub. by LawBk Co); pap. 84.00 (0-455-20749-6, Pub. by LawBk Co) Gaunt.

— Wild Wind. 1998. mass mkt. 5.99 (0-451-40826-8, Onyx) NAL.

Ryan, Patricia, jt. auth. see Burford, Pamela.

Ryan, Patricia K., jt. auth. see Kling, M. Terry.

Ryan, Patrick. India. rev. ed. LC 98-44245. (Illus.). 32p. (J). 1999. lib. bdg. 22.79 (1-56766-579-9) Childs World.

***Ryan, Patrick.** Poland LC 99-37426. 2000. write for info. (1-56766-716-3) Childs World.

Ryan, Patrick J. Bond Markets: Structure & Yield Calculations. LC 00-551713. 150p. 1998. 45.00 (0-8144-0473-1) AMACOM.

— The Coming of Our God: Scriptual Reflections for Advent, Christmas & Epiphany. LC 99-30275. 224p. 1999. pap. 12.95 (0-8091-3880-8) Paulist Pr.

— Euclidean & Non-Euclidean Geometry: An Analytic Approach. (Illus.). 240p. 1986. pap. text 26.95 (0-521-27635-7) Cambridge U Pr.

Ryan, Patrick J. & Rush, George E., eds. Understanding Organized Crime: A Reader. LC 97-21083. 224p. 1997. 55.00 (0-7619-0981-8); pap. 24.95 (0-7619-0982-6) Sage.

Ryan, Patrick M. South Africa. LC 96-30664. (Countries Ser.). (Illus.). 32p. (J). (gr. k-3). 1997. lib. bdg. 22.79 (1-56766-373-7) Childs World.

Ryan, Patti, jt. auth. see Voyer, Royer.

Ryan, Paul. Birth & Death & Cybernation: Cybernetics of the Sacred. xiv, 176p. 1973. text 101.00 (0-677-04320-1) Gordon & Breach.

— Video Mind, Earth Mind: Art, Communications, & Ecology. LC 92-4840. (Semiotics & the Human Sciences Ser.: Vol. 4). 437p. 1993. 54.95 (0-8204-1871-4) P Lang Pubng.

Ryan, Paul, ed. International Comparisons of Vocational Education & Training. 250p. 1991. pap. 39.95 (1-85000-900-7, Falmer Pr) Taylor & Francis.

Ryan, Paul, et al, eds. Estimating Woody Biomass in Sub-Saharan Africa. LC 93-23481. 208p. 1994. pap. 25.00 (0-8213-2306-7, 12306) World Bank.

— Estimating Woody Biomass in Sub-Saharan Africa. (FRE.). 232p. 1994. pap. 25.00 (0-8213-2507-8, 12507) World Bank.

Ryan, Paul, jt. auth. see Grubb, W. Norton.

Ryan, Paul, tr. see Plato.

Ryan, Paul B. The Panama Canal Controversy: U. S. Diplomacy & Defense Interests. LC 77-20643. (Publication Ser.: No. 187). (Illus.). 1978. pap. 2.78 (0-8179-6872-5) Hoover Inst Pr.

Ryan, Paul R. Khmer Rouge End Game. LC 98-65062. x, 236p. 1998. pap. 16.95 (0-9662707-4-6) Munewata Pr.

— Khmer Rouge End Game: A Novel. LC 98-65062. xvi, 192 p. 1998. write for info. (0-9662707-3-8) Munewata Pr.

***Ryan, Paul Ryder.** Bangladesh 2000: On the Brink of Civil War. unabridged ed. (Illus.). 152p. 2000. pap. 13.95 (0-9662707-6-2) Munewata Pr.

Ryan, Paula L. Bounce Back from Bankruptcy: Step-by-Step Guide to Getting Back on Your Financial Feet. 2nd rev. ed. 224p. 1998. pap. 14.95 (1-889605-01-8) Pellingham Casper.

Ryan, Pauline, jt. auth. see Rabushka, Alvin.

Ryan, Penelope. Contemporary Catholics in Conflict. 1995. pap. 12.95 (0-8050-4664-X) H Holt & Co.

Ryan, Penelope J. Practicing Catholic: The Search for a Liveable Catholicism. LC 97-51624. 256p. 1995. 22.95 (0-8050-4663-1) H Holt & Co.

Ryan, Perry T. A Biography of Maurice F. O'Connell: The Story of an American Hero. LC 96-92109. (Illus.). 68p. (Orig.). 1996. pap. 5.00 (0-9625504-7-7) P T Ryan.

— A Biography of Maurice F. O'Connell (Biographie de Maurice F. O'Connell) The Story of an American Hero (Histoire d'un Heros Americain) Bodin, Philippe, tr. LC 96-92109. (FRE., Illus.). 1998. pap. 5.00 (0-9625504-8-5) P T Ryan.

— The Last Public Execution in America. LC 92-91052. (Illus.). 272p. (Orig.). 1992. pap. 12.95 (0-9625504-4-2) P T Ryan.

— Legal Lynching: The Plight of Sam Jennings. LC 89-92805. (Illus.). 230p. (Orig.). 1989. pap. 9.95 (0-9625504-2-6) P T Ryan.

— The Ryan Family of Breckinridge County, Kentucky. LC 83-62918. (Illus.). 528p. 1989. reprint ed. 30.00 (0-9625504-0-X) P T Ryan.

Ryan, Phil. The Fall & Rise of the Market in Sandinista Nicaragua. LC 96-185945. 352p. 1995. 65.00 (0-7735-1347-7, Pub. by McG-Queens Univ Pr); pap. 19.95 (0-7735-1359-0, Pub. by McG-Queens Univ Pr) CUP Services.

Ryan, Philip B. Noel Purcell: A Biography. (Illus.). 203p. 1993. 35.00 (1-85371-197-7, Pub. by Poolbeg Pr) Dufour.

Ryan, Philip M. & Intrator, Thomas, eds. Radio Frequency Power in Plasmas: 12th Topical Conference. (AIP Conference Proceedings: Vol. 403). (Illus.). 512p. 1997. 120.00 (1-56396-709-X) Am Inst Physics.

Ryan, Phyllis. The Company I Kept: Revelations from the Life of Ireland's Most Distinguished & Independent Theatrical Manager. LC 97-101878. (Illus.). 296p. 1996. 34.95 (1-86059-025-X, Pub. by Town Hse) Roberts Rinehart.

Ryan, R. & Shahinpoor, Mo, eds. Vibrations & Dynamics of Robotic & Multibody Structures. LC 93-72633. (DE Ser.: Vol. 57). 132p. 1993. 45.00 (0-7918-1174-3, G00818) ASME.

***Ryan, R. J.** Keepers of the Ark: An Elephants View of Captivity. LC 99-91227. 1999. 25.00 (0-7388-0688-9); pap. 25.00 (0-7388-0689-7) Xlibris Corp.

Ryan, R. M. The Golden Rules: An Adventure Story. 272p. 1998. pap. 16.00 (1-57650-093-4) Hi Jinx Pr.

Ryan, R. M., jt. auth. see Deci, E. L.

Ryan-Ranson, Helen, ed. Imagination, Emblems & Expressions: Essays on Latin American, Caribbean, & Continental Culture & Identify. LC 93-70305. 365p. (C). 1993. 45.95 (0-87972-580-X); pap. 16.95 (0-87972-581-8) Bowling Green Univ Popular Press.

Ryan, Ray. Basic Digital Electronics. 2nd ed. (Illus.). 250p. 1990. pap. 16.95 (0-8306-3370-7) McGraw-Hill Prof.

— Basic Digital Electronics: Understanding Number Systems, Boolean Algebra & Logical Circuits. LC 74-14326. (Illus.). 1975. pap. 11.95 (0-8306-3728-1, 728P) McGraw-Hill Prof.

***Ryan, Ray.** Writing in the Republic: Literature Culture Politics in the Republic. 2000. text 69.95 (0-312-23153-9) St Martin.

Ryan, Ray & Doyle, Lisa A. Digital Electronics. rev. ed. LC 92-34443. (Tech Ser.). Orig. Title: Basic Digital Electronics. 1992. pap. write for info. (0-02-801306-9) Glencoe.

Ryan, Reade H. & Field, Arthur. Legal Opinions in Corporate Transactions. Vol. C6. text 82.00 (0-8205-2412-3) Bender.

Ryan, Regina, jt. auth. see LaRouche, Janice.

***Ryan, Regina S.** After Surgery: 10-Steps to Mind-Body-Spirit Health in Recuperation. LC 99-23646. 240p. 1999. pap. 14.95 (0-934252-95-5) Hohm Pr.

Ryan, Regina S., intro. In Praise of Japanese Love Poetry. LC 94-77025. 96p. (Orig.). 1994. pap. 10.00 (0-934252-44-0, Pub. by Hohm Pr) SCB Distributors.

— In Praise of Rumi. LC 90-4017. 80p. (Orig.). (C). 1989. pap. 9.95 (0-934252-23-8, Pub. by Hohm Pr) SCB Distributors.

Ryan, Regina S., jt. auth. see Travis, John.

Ryan, Regina S., jt. auth. see Travis, John W.

Ryan, Regina S., ed. see Lozowick, Lee.

Ryan, Regina S., ed. see Santillo, Humbart.

Ryan, Regina Sara. The Woman Awake: Feminine Wisdom for Spiritual Life. LC 97-51495. (Illus.). 520p. 1998. pap. 19.95 (0-934252-79-3, Pub. by Hohm Pr) SCB Distributors.

***Ryan, Rex & Walker, Jeff.** Coaching Football's 46 Defense. (Illus.). 196p. 1999. pap. 16.95 (1-57167-371-7) Coaches Choice.

Ryan, Richard. Funnelweb. LC 97-221199. 339p. 1997. write for info. (0-7329-0888-4) Macmill Educ.

***Ryan, Richard.** Master of the Blade: Secrets of the Deadly Art of Knife Fighting. (Illus.). 176p. 1999. pap. 20.00 (1-58160-048-8) Paladin Pr.

Ryan, Rick & Newton, Dave. Worship & Music Ministry. Smith, Chuck, ed. (Calvary Basics Ser.). 109p. 1995. pap. 3.50 (0-936728-63-9) Word for Today.

***Ryan, Rob.** Dancing on the Edge of Chaos. 2001. write for info. (0-06-662066-X) HarpC.

Ryan, Robert E. The Strong Eye of Shamanism: A Journey into the Caves of Consciousness. LC 98-47208. (Illus.). 320p. 1999. pap. 19.95 (0-89281-709-7) Inner Tradit.

Ryan, Robert M. Keats: The Religious Sense. LC 76-3019. 246p. 1976. reprint ed. pap. 76.30 (0-608-03295-6, 206381300007) Bks Demand.

— The Romantic Reformation: Religious Politics in English Literature 1789-1824. (Studies in Romanticism: Vol. 24). 304p. (C). 1997. text 59.95 (0-521-57008-5) Cambridge U Pr.

Ryan, Robert M. & Sharp, Ronald A., eds. The Persistence of Poetry: Bicentennial Essays on Keats. LC 98-7840. 232p. 1998. 29.95 (1-55849-175-9) U of Mass Pr.

Ryan, Robert P. Toxicology Desk Reference: The Toxic Exposure & Medical Monitoring Index. 5th ed. 1999. 550.00 (1-56032-855-X); 450.00 (1-56032-795-2) Taylor & Francis.

Ryan, Robert P. & Terry, Claude E., eds. Toxicology Desk Reference: The Toxic Exposure & Medical Monitoring Index, 3 vols. 4th ed. 2200p. 1997. pap. 450.00 (1-56032-615-8) Hemisp Pub.

Ryan, Robert S. Pennsylvania Zoning Law & Practice, 2 vols. 1993. ring bd. 195.00 (1-887024-67-0) Bisel Co.

Ryan, Roberta, jt. auth. see Ryan, Jerry.

***Ryan, Robin.** 60 Seconds & Youre Hired. LC 99-37216. 2000. pap. 10.95 (0-14-028903-8) Penguin Putnam.

Ryan, Robin. Winning Career Moves. (Robin Ryan the Career Coach Ser.). 215p. 1997. pap. 10.95 (0-471-19066-7) Wiley.

Ryan, Robin. Winning Cover Letters. LC 97-204888. (Robin Ryan the Career Coach Ser.). 189p. 1997. pap. 10.95 (0-471-19063-2) Wiley.

Ryan, Robin. Winning Resumes. LC 97-204889. (Robin Ryan the Career Coach Ser.). 224p. 1997. pap. 10.95 (0-471-19064-0) Wiley.

Ryan, Rod, ed. American Cinematographer Manual. 7th ed. (Illus.). 619p. 1993. 49.95 (0-935578-11-0) ASC Holding.

Ryan, Ronald J. Yield-Curve Dynamics: State-of-the-Art Techniques for Modeling, Trading, & Hedging. (Glenlake Business Monographs). 300p. 1998. 65.00 (1-884964-74-5) Fitzroy Dearborn.

— Yield-Curve Dynamics: State-of-the-Art Techniques for Modeling, Trading, & Hedging. 232p. Date not set. 65.00 (1-888998-06-7) Glenlake Pub.

Ryan, Rosalie & Wolkerstorfer, John C. More Than a Dream: Eighty-Five Years at the College of St. Catherine. LC 92-72011. 168p. 1992. 24.95 (0-9633553-0-9) Coll St Catherine.

Ryan, Rosemary, jt. auth. see Ryan, Pat.

***Ryan, S.** Boys in Green. 1998. text 35.00 (1-85158-939-2, Pub. by Mainstream Pubng) Trafalgar.

Ryan, S., jt. auth. see Alsop, A.

Ryan, Sally E. The Combined Volume: COTA & Practice Issues in Occupational Therapy. 2nd ed. (Illus.). 770p. 1995. pap. 50.00 (1-55642-290-3, 32903) SLACK Inc.

Ryan, Sally E., ed. The Certified Occupational Therapy Assistant: Principles, Concepts & Techniques. 2nd ed. LC 92-50395. (Illus.). 304p. (C). 1992. pap. 30.00 (1-55642-178-8, 31788) SLACK Inc.

— Practice Issues in Occupational Therapy: Intraprofessional Team Building. LC 92-50459. (Illus.). 408p. 1993. pap. 30.00 (1-55642-179-6) SLACK Inc.

***Ryan, Sally E. & Sladyk, Karen.** COTA 3rd Edition & Practice Issues 2nd Edition. 600p. (C). 2000. pap. text 45.00 (1-55642-407-8) SLACK Inc.

***Ryan, Sarah.** Drug Therapy in Rheumatology Nursing, 1. 1999. pap. text 34.95 (1-86156-114-8) Whurr Pub.

Ryan, Scott, jt. auth. see Kashiwagi, Dean T.

Ryan, Scott B. Business Basic - What Do You Say after It Says Ready? READY: How to Develop & Maintain "Plain Vanilla"-Transportable Business BASIC Application Software. 2nd ed. Ryan, Starla J., ed. 360p. (C). 1991. reprint ed. pap. 65.00 (0-9621699-1-9) Busn Basic Servs.

Ryan, Sean. Hypnography for Men. 1999. audio 11.95 (1-886233-27-8) Passion Pr.

— Hypnography for Women. 1999. audio 16.95 (1-886233-28-6) Passion Pr.

Ryan, Selwyn D. Race & Nationalism in Trinidad & Tobago: A Study of Decolonization in Multiracial Society. LC 70-185735. 525p. reprint ed. pap. 162.80 (0-608-15422-9, 202934800060) Bks Demand.

Ryan, Shawn. Brethren. 336p. (Orig.). 1993. mass mkt. 4.99 (0-671-79243-1) PB.

— Nocturnas. Tobias, Eric, ed. 448p. (Orig.). 1995. mass mkt. 5.50 (0-671-88270-8) PB.

Ryan, Sheila & Hallaj, Muhammad. Palestine Is, but Not in Jordan. (Information Papers: No. 24). 36p. (Orig.). 1983. pap. text 3.50 (0-937694-60-6) Assn Arab-Amer U Grads.

Ryan, Sheila, jt. auth. see Will, Donald.

Ryan, Shelagh, jt. auth. see Schackman, Lynn.

Ryan, Shelia, jt. auth. see Will, Donald.

Ryan, Shirley, ed. see Thompson, Linda & Ebbens, Joan.

Ryan, Shirley V., ed. see Lindberg, Karen.

Ryan, Simon. The Cartographic Eye: How Explorers Saw Australia. (Illus.). 247p. 1996. pap. text 21.95 (0-521-57791-8) Cambridge U Pr.

— The Cartographic Eye: How Explorers Saw Australia. (Illus.). 247p. (C). 1996. text 64.95 (0-521-57112-X) Cambridge U Pr.

Ryan, Simon, jt. ed. see Dale, Leigh.

Ryan, Starla J., ed. see Ryan, Scott B.

Ryan, Stephen. Ethnic Conflict & International Relations. 2nd ed. 304p. 1995. 72.95 (1-85521-650-7, Pub. by Dartmth Pub) Ashgate Pub Co.

***Ryan, Stephen.** Exceptional Plants: 100 Tree & Shrubs to Give Your Garden the Edge. (Illus.). 2000. 32.95 (1-86447-075-5) Hyland Hse.

— The United Nations & International Politics LC 99-37894. (Studies in Contemporary History). 2000. pap. 19.95 (0-312-22825-2) St Martin.

— The United Nations & International Politics. LC 99-37894. (Studies in Contemporary History). 2000. 55.00 (0-312-22824-4) St Martin.

Ryan, Stephen J., ed. Retina. 2nd ed. LC 93-40452. (Illus.). 2800p. (C). (gr. 13). 1994. text 440.00 (0-8016-8032-8, 08032) Mosby Inc.

***Ryan, Stephen J., et al.** Retina. 3rd ed. (Illus.). 2912p. (C). 1999. text. write for info. (0-323-00804-6) Mosby Inc.

Ryan, Stephen J., jt. auth. see Sloan, Louise L.

Ryan, Steve. Challenging Pencil Puzzlers. (Illus.). 96p. (J). (gr. 6-10). 1992. pap. 5.95 (0-8069-8752-9) Sterling.

— Great Rebus Puzzles. LC 99-15854. 1999. pap. text 6.95 (0-8069-1811-X) Sterling.

— Mystifying Math Puzzles. (Illus.). 96p. 1996. pap. 5.95 (0-8069-1304-5) Sterling.

— Pencil Puzzlers. (Illus.). 96p. (YA). (gr. 7-12). 1992. pap. 5.95 (0-8069-8542-9) Sterling.

— Test Your Word Play IQ. (Illus.). 96p. 1993. pap. 5.95 (0-8069-0412-7) Sterling.

***Ryan, Steve & American Mensa Limited Staff.** Mighty Mini Rhyming Picture Puzzles. LC 99-86833. 2000. 4.95 (0-8069-2893-X) Sterling.

Ryan, Steven W. & Molyneux, Elizabeth. Acute Pediatrics. (Illus.). 240p. 1996. pap. text 34.95 (0-86542-624-4) Blackwell Sci.

***Ryan, Sue & McKay, Beth.** Thinking & Reasoning in Therapy: Narratives from Practice. (Illus.). 224p. 1999. pap. 28.95 (0-7487-3717-0) Standard Pub.

Ryan, Susan. Student Loan Default Remedies. (Illus.). 16p. (Orig.). 1996. pap. 3.00 (1-884241-62-X, PO317) Energeia Pub.

Ryan, Susan, ed. see Crane, Dick.

***Ryan, Susan E. & Indiana, Robert.** Robert Indiana. LC 99-37076. (Illus.). 288p. 2000. 45.00 (0-300-07957-5) Yale U Pr.

Ryan, Susan E., ed. & intro. see Hartley, Marsden.

***Ryan, Susan Elizabeth, et al.** The Sight of Time: Robert Cahen Video at LSU. (Illus.). 48p. 2000. pap. 10.00 (0-9678327-0-5) Schl of Art.

Ryan, Susan M. Downloading Democracy: Government Information in an Electronic Age. LC 95-44811. (C). 1995. pap. text 28.50 (1-57273-049-8) Hampton Pr NJ.

— Downloading Democracy: Government Information in an Electronic Age. LC 95-44811. (C). 1996. text 72.50 (1-57273-048-X) Hampton Pr NJ.

Ryan, Suzanne, jt. auth. see Tabor, Richard.

Ryan, T. Analysis for Drugs of Abuse. (Illus.). Date not set. text. write for info. (0-8247-9853-8) Dekker.

Ryan, T. & Walker, R. Making Life Story Books. (C). 1989. 65.00 (0-903534-60-6, Pub. by Brit Ag for Adopt & Fost) St Mut.

Ryan, Tammy. Pig. LC 98-222981. 1998. pap. 5.25 (0-8222-1600-0) Dramatists Play.

Ryan, Taylor. Beauty & the Beast. 1996. per. 4.99 (0-373-28942-1, 1-28942-0) Harlequin Bks.

— Birdie. (Historical Ser.). 1996. per. 4.50 (0-373-28912-X, 1-28912-3) Harlequin Bks.

— The Essential Wife. (Historical Ser.: No. 368). 1997. per. 4.99 (0-373-28968-5, 1-28968-5) Harlequin Bks.

— Love's Wild Wager: March Madness. LC 95-7081. (Historical Ser.). 296p. 1995. per. 4.50 (0-373-28862-X, 1-28862-0) Harlequin Bks.

Ryan, Terence J. The Management of Leg Ulcers. 2nd ed. (Illus.). 110p. 1987. pap. 19.95 (0-19-261663-3) OUP.

Ryan, Terry. The Toolbox for Remodeling Your Problem Dog. LC 97-30072. 208p. 1997. 19.95 (0-87605-049-6) Howell Bks.

Ryan, Thomas. American Hit Radio: A History of Popular Singles 1955-Present. 672p. 1995. pap. text 19.95 (0-7615-0230-0) Prima Pub.

— Jimmy Buffett Trivia Book: 501 Questions & Answers for Parrotheads. LC 97-41402. (Illus.). 128p. 1997. pap. text 9.95 (0-8065-1922-3, Citadel Pr) Carol Pub Group.

— Parrot Head Companion: An Insider's Guide to Jimmy Buffett. LC 98-27639. (Illus.). 176p. 1998. pap. 10.95 (0-8065-2015-9) Carol Pub Group.

— Recollections of an Old Musician. (Music Reprint Ser.). 290p. 1979. reprint ed. lib. bdg. 37.50 (0-306-79521-3) Da Capo.

— The Sacristy Manual. Philippart, David, ed. LC 93-29863. (Illus.). 278p. 1993. pap. 18.00 (0-929650-92-1, SACMNL) Liturgy Tr Pubns.

***Ryan, Thomas.** Thomas Aquinas as Reader of the Psalms: The Postilla Super Psalmos. LC 00-36416. (Studies in Spirituality & Theology: Vol. 6). 222p. 2000. 40.00 (0-268-02003-5) U of Notre Dame Pr.

Ryan, Thomas A. Intentional Behavior, an Approach to Human Motivation. LC 79-110391. 602p. (C). reprint ed. 186.70 (0-8357-9522-5, 201236200081) Bks Demand.

— One More Try, a Story of Entreprenurial Passion. 288p. (Orig.). 1993. pap. write for info. (0-9638573-3-9) T A Ryan.

Ryan, Thomas A., ed. see Gartner Group, Inc. Staff.

Ryan, Thomas E. Hoelderlin's Silence. (Studies in Modern German Literature: Vol. 17). VIII, 366p. 1988. 44.00 (0-8204-0551-5) P Lang Pubng.

Ryan, Thomas E. & Monostory, Denes, eds. Word & Deed: German Studies in Honor of Wolfgang F. Michael. LC 91-28432. 296p. (C). 1992. text 69.95 (0-8204-1101-9) P Lang Pubng.

Ryan, Thomas P. Disciplines for Christian Living. LC 92-42596. (Interfaith Perspectives Ser.). 1993. pap. 12.95 (0-8091-3380-6) Paulist Pr.

R

— Modern Regression Methods. LC 96-6368. (Series in Probability & Statistics, Applied Probability & Statistics). 515p. 1996. 84.95 (*0-471-52912-5*) Wiley.

— Prayer of Heart & Body: Meditation & Yoga As Christian Spiritual Practice. LC 94-32996. (Illus.). 336p. 1995. pap. 12.95 (*0-8091-3523-X*) Paulist Pr.

***Ryan, Thomas P.** Statistical Methods for Quality Improvement. 2nd ed. LC 99-15784. 564p. 2000. 89.95 (*0-471-19775-0*) Wiley.

Ryan, Thomas P., ed. Surgical Applications of Energy, Vol. 3249. LC 98-171723. 288p. 1998. 69.00 (*0-8194-2688-1*) SPIE.

***Ryan, Thomas P. & Society of Photo-Optical Instrumentation Engineers Staff.** Matching the Energy Source to the Clinical Need: Proceedings of a Conference Held 23-24 January, 2000, San Jose, California. LC 99-59974. (Critical Reviews of Optical Science & Technology Ser.). 2000. pap. write for info. (*0-8194-3512-0*) SPIE.

***Ryan, Thomas P. & Wong, Terence Z., eds.** Thermal Treatment of Tissue with Image Guidance. 244p. 1999. pap. text 62.00 (*0-8194-3064-1*) SPIE.

Ryan, Thomas R. Orestes A. Brownson: The Pope's Champion in America. 1984. 49.50 (*0-8290-0333-9*); pap. 10.95 (*0-8290-1608-2*) Irvington.

Ryan, Tim. Whole Again Resource Guide. LC 83-641044. 380p. 1986. pap. 24.95 (*0-915051-01-X*) SourceNet.

Ryan, Tim & Miles, Douglas G. Macintosh Book of Fonts: A Desktop Publishing Handbook for Font Lovers. LC 87-9607. 400p. 1988. pap. 24.95 (*0-915051-02-8*) SourceNet.

Ryan, Tim, ed. see Cierzniak, Mark.

Ryan, Timothy, jt. auth. see Mercuro, Nicholas.

Ryan, Timothy W. Distributed Object Technology: Concepts & Applications. LC 96-32744. 224p. (C). 1996. pap. text 50.00 (*0-13-348996-5*) P-H.

Ryan, Tony, ed. Managing Crisis & Risk in Mental Health Nursing. (Illus.). 224p. 1999. pap. 28.95 (*0-7487-3336-1*) Standard Pub.

***Ryan, Tony & Heaner, Martica.** Cross Training for Dummies. 384p. 2000. pap. 19.99 (*0-7645-5237-6*) IDG Bks.

Ryan, Tony & Walker, Rodger. Life Story Work. 68p. 1993. pap. 50.00 (*1-873868-10-3*) BAAF.

Ryan, Tracey, ed. Federal Regional Staff Directory. 1998. pap. 99.00 (*0-87289-138-0*) C Q Staff.

— Federal Regional Staff Directory. 1998. pap. 99.00 (*0-87289-148-8*) C Q Staff.

— Municipal Staff Directory. 1998. pap. 99.00 (*0-87289-139-9*) C Q Staff.

— State Staff Directory. 1998. 99.00 (*0-87289-137-2*) C Q Staff.

— State Staff Directory. 1998. pap. 99.00 (*0-87289-144-5*) C Q Staff.

— State Staff Directory. 1998. pap. 99.00 (*0-87289-147-X*) C Q Staff.

Ryan, Tracy. Slant. 29p. 1997. spiral bd. 12.00 (*1-901361-03-9*, Pub. by Rem Pr) SPD-Small Pr Dist.

Ryan, Tracy. Vamp. LC 97-163030. 187p. 1997. pap. 16.95 (*1-86368-172-8*, Pub. by Indra Pub) Intl Spec Bk.

***Ryan, Tracy.** The Willing Eye. 80p. 2000. pap. 15.95 (*1-85224-506-9*, Pub. by Bloodaxe Bks) Dufour.

Ryan, Tracy. The Willing Eye. 88p. 1999. pap. 16.95 (*1-86368-239-2*, Pub. by Fremantle Arts) Intl Spec Bk.

Ryan, Una S., ed. Endothelial Cells, Vol. I. 208p. 1988. lib. bdg. 195.00 (*0-8493-4990-7*, QP88) CRC Pr.

— Endothelial Cells, Vol. II. 288p. 1988. lib. bdg. 229.00 (*0-8493-4991-5*, 4991) CRC Pr.

— Endothelial Cells, Vol. III. 288p. 1988. lib. bdg. 229.00 (*0-8493-4992-3*, QP88) CRC Pr.

— Pulmonary Endothelium in Health & Disease. (Lung Biology in Health & Disease Ser.: Vol. 32). (Illus.). 520p. 1987. text 255.00 (*0-8247-7758-1*) Dekker.

Ryan, Una S. & Rubanyi, Gabor M., eds. Endothelial Regulation of Vascular Tone. (Illus.). 416p. 1991. text 199.00 (*0-8247-8578-9*) Dekker.

Ryan, Vernon N. Human Stress & Distress - Psychological & Medical Therapy: Index of New Information with Authors & Subjects. 180p. 1993. 47.50 (*1-55914-888-8*); pap. 44.50 (*1-55914-889-6*) ABBE Pubs Assn.

Ryan, Victoria, jt. auth. see Marsh, Arthur I.

Ryan, Vincent. Advent Epiphanty. 96p. 1989. pap. 45.00 (*0-86217-136-9*, Pub. by Veritas Pubns) St Mut.

— Eastertime & Feasts of the Lord. 98p. 1989. pap. 21.00 (*0-86217-164-4*, Pub. by Veritas Pubns) St Mut.

— The Shaping of Sunday: Sunday & Eucharist in the Irish Tradition LC 98-148154. 111p. 1997. pap. write for info. (*1-85390-352-3*) Veritas Pubns.

— Welcome to Sunday. 96p. 1989. pap. 22.00 (*0-86218-000-7*, Pub. by Veritas Pubns) St Mut.

Ryan, Vincent J. Ireland Restored: The New Self-Determination. LC 90-44856. (Illus.). 494p. (C). 1991. pap. text 29.50 (*0-932088-59-7*); lib. bdg. 54.00 (*0-932088-60-0*) Freedom Hse.

Ryan, Virginia & Wilson, Kate. Case Studies in Non-Directive Play Therapy. 258p. 1996. pap. text 36.95 (*0-7020-1830-9*, Pub. by W B Saunders) Saunders.

Ryan, W. Properties of Ceramic Raw Materials. 2nd ed. (Illus.). 120p. (C). 1992. reprint ed. 55.00 (*1-878907-29-8*) TechBooks.

Ryan, W., et al, eds. Proceedings of the International Heat Pump Absorption Conference: New Orleans, Louisiana - January 19-21, 1994. LC 94-74375. (AES Ser.: Vol. 31). 544p. 1994. 75.00 (*0-7918-0698-7*, I00361) ASME.

Ryan, W., jt. auth. see Pogorzelski, H.

Ryan, W. Carson. Studies in Early Graduate Education. LC 73-165729. (American Education Ser, No. 2). 1972. reprint ed. 12.95 (*0-405-03718-X*) Ayer.

***Ryan, W. F.** The Bathhouse at Midnight: An Historical Survey of Magic & Divination in Russia. LC 99-28362. 1999. pap. 22.50 (*0-271-01967-0*) Pa St U Pr.

Ryan, W. F. Penguin Russian Dictionary: English-Russian, Russian-English. LC 96-212668. 1152p. 1996. pap. 22.95 (*0-14-051067-2*, Viking) Viking Penguin.

Ryan, W. Michael. Lieutenant-Colonel Charles A. Court Repington: A Study in the Interaction of Personality, the Press & Power. (Modern European History Ser.). 248p. 1987. text 15.00 (*0-8240-7830-6*) Garland.

Ryan, Wendy, jt. auth. see Rowell, Bruce.

Ryan, Will. Grundo Beach Party. Becker, Mary, ed. (Teddy Ruxpin Adventure Ser.). (Illus.). 26p. (J). (ps). 1986. 9.95 (*0-934323-35-6*); audio. write for info. (*0-318-60971-1*) Alchemy Comms.

— Lost in Boggley Woods. Becker, Mary, ed. (Teddy Ruxpin Adventure Ser.). (Illus.). 26p. (J). (ps). 1986. 9.95 (*0-934323-38-0*); audio. write for info. (*0-318-60973-8*) Alchemy Comms.

***Ryan, Will.** Northern Pike. LC 99-54423. (Illus.). 2000. 35.00 (*1-58574-044-6*) Lyons Pr.

Ryan, Will. Smallmouth Strategies for the Fly Rod. (Illus.). 240p. 1996. 25.00 (*1-55821-343-0*, 13430) Lyons Pr.

Ryan, Will G. Endocrine Disorders: A Pathophysiologic Approach. 2nd ed. Myers, Jack D. & Rogers, David E., eds. LC 79-22635. (Illus.). 164p. reprint ed. pap. 50.90 (*0-608-18481-0*, 203300000082) Bks Demand.

Ryan, Will H. Counterpoint for Death. 160p. (Orig.). 1995. pap. 12.95 (*1-56474-137-0*) Fithian Pr.

— Nile Nightmare: A Novel of Suspense. 288p. (Orig.). 1993. pap. 12.95 (*1-56474-049-8*) Fithian Pr.

Ryan, William. Blaming the Victim. 320p. 1976. pap. 9.95 (*0-394-72226-4*) Vin Bks.

— Equality. 234p. 1981. 6.95 (*0-394-42359-3*) Pantheon.

— To Die in Latin. LC 94-10673. 1994. 19.95 (*0-89924-089-5*); pap. 9.95 (*0-89924-088-7*) Lynx Hse.

Ryan, William, et al. High Performance Nonprofit Organizations: Managing Upstream for Greater Impact. LC 98-24240. (Nonprofit Law, Finance, & Management Ser.). 224p. 1998. 29.95 (*0-471-17457-2*) Wiley.

Ryan, William, jt. auth. see Pitman, Walter.

***Ryan, William B. F. & Pitman, Walter C.** Noah's Flood: The New Scientific Discoveries about the Event That Changed History. LC 98-45384. 320p. 2000. per. 13.00 (*0-684-85920-3*, Touchstone) S&S Trade Pap.

Ryan, William E., jt. auth. see Bivins, Thomas H.

Ryan, William F. Culture, Spirituality & Economic Development: Opening a Dialogue. LC 97-701232. ix, 80p. 1995. pap. 12.00 (*0-88936-782-5*, Pub. by IDRC Bks) Stylus Pub VA.

Ryan, William F. & Tyrrell, Bernard J., eds. A Second Collection: Bernard Lonergan. 320p. 1996. pap. text 22.95 (*0-8020-7943-1*) U of Toronto Pr.

Ryan, William G., tr. see De Voragine, Jacobus.

Ryan, William J., jt. auth. see Pogorzelski, Henry A.

Ryan, William L., ed. Cold Regions Engineering: Proceedings. 488p. 1986. 72.00 (*0-87262-513-3*) Am Soc Civil Eng.

Ryan, William L. & Crissman, Randy D., eds. Cold Regions Hydrology & Hydraulics. LC 90-41156. 840p. 1990. pap. text 78.00 (*0-87262-773-X*) Am Soc Civil Eng.

Ryan, William M. Eating the Heart of the Enemy. LC 83-23868. 105p. 1984. pap. 7.00 (*0-89924-041-0*) Lynx Hse.

Ryan, William R. Personal Adventures in Upper & Lower California in 1848-9. LC 72-9466. (Far Western Frontier Ser.). (Illus.). 822p. 1973. reprint ed. 53.95 (*0-405-04994-3*) Ayer.

***Ryan, Yoni.** Supervising Post-Graduates from Non-English Speaking Backgrounds. LC 98-45151. 1999. 105.00 (*0-335-20372-8*) Taylor & Francis.

Ryan, Yoni & Zuber-Skerritt, Ortrun, eds. Supervising Post-Graduates from Non-English Speaking Backgrounds. LC 98-45151. (Illus.). 193p. 1999. pap. 36.95 (*0-335-20371-X*) OpUniv Pr.

***Ryang, Sonia.** Koreans in Japan: Critical Voices from the Margin. LC 99-39943. (Studies in Asia's Transformations). 240p. 2000. 90.00 (*0-415-21999-X*) Routledge.

Ryang, Sonia. North Koreans in Japan: Language, Ideology & Identity. (Transitions: Asia & Asian America Ser.). (C). 1996. pap. text 26.00 (*0-8133-3050-5*, Pub. by Westview) HarpC.

Ryans, Adrian B., et al. Winning Market Leadership In High-tech Businesses. 288p. 2000. 29.95 (*0-471-64430-7*) Wiley.

Ryans, Briceida. American New World Dictionary of Dream Language Interpretations. unabridged ed. 650p. 1997. write for info. (*0-9657194-6-4*); lib. bdg. write for info. (*0-9657194-5-6*); mass mkt. write for info. (*0-9657194-8-0*) Goldenland.

— American New World Dictionary of Dream Language Interpretations. unabridged ed. 650p. 1999. pap. 24.94 (*0-9657194-0-5*) Goldenland.

Ryans, Cynthia C., ed. The Card Catalog: Current Issues. LC 81-720. 336p. 1981. 26.50 (*0-8108-1417-X*) Scarecrow.

Ryans, Cynthia C. & Shanklin, William L. Strategic Planning, Marketing & Public Relations, & Fund-raising in Higher Education: Perspectives, Reading, & Annotated Bibliography. LC 86-3871. 280p. 1986. 29.50 (*0-8108-1891-4*) Scarecrow.

Ryans, John K., et al, eds. China, the U. S. S. R., & Eastern Europe: A U. S. Trade Perspective. LC 74-79995. 208p. reprint ed. pap. 64.50 (*0-608-17134-4*, 202730700055) Bks Demand.

Ryans, John K., Jr. & Rau, Pradaeep A. Marketing Strategies for the New Europe: A North American Perspective in 1992. LC 89-18279. 202p. 1990. 29.95 (*0-87757-203-8*) Am Mktg.

Ryans, John K., Jr., jt. auth. see Shanklin, William L.

Ryans, John K., Jr., jt. ed. see Paliwoda, Stanley J.

Ryant, Carl. Profit's Prophet: Garet Garrett, 1878-1954. LC 88-43110. (Illus.). 128p. 1989. 28.50 (*0-945636-04-0*) Susquehanna U Pr.

Ryant, Cynthia. Something Permanent. LC 93-3861. (Illus.). 64p. (YA). (gr. 9 up). 1994. 18.00 (*0-15-277090-9*) Harcourt.

Ryant, Granger, tr. see Couturier, M. A.

Ryavec, Karl W. United States & Soviet Relations. 2nd ed. (C). 1996. pap. text. write for info. (*0-8013-0688-4*) Addison-Wesley.

Ryavec, Karl W., ed. Soviet Society & the Communist Party. LC 78-53179. 240p. (C). 1978. 30.00 (*0-87023-258-4*) U of Mass Pr.

Ryavec, Karl W., ed. see Vali, Ferenc A.

Ryazanova-Clarke, Larissa, jt. auth. see Wade, Terence Leslie Brian.

Ryazanskaya, S., tr. see Marx, Karl & Engels, Friedrich.

Ryazantsev, Vladimir, jt. auth. see Ryabov, Vladimir R.

Ryazhsky, A. Uchjebnik Tserkovnago Penija.Tr. of Textbook of Sacred Singing. 105p. 1966. reprint ed. pap. 5.00 (*0-317-30382-1*) Holy Trinity.

Ryba, Alexander J., jt. auth. see Kruse, Robert L.

Ryba, Raymond. Education, Democracy & Development. 152p. 1997. pap. text 57.00 (*0-7923-4552-5*) Kluwer Academic.

Ryba, Thomas. The Essence of Phenomenology & Its Meaning for the Scientific Study of Religion. (Toronto Studies in Religion). (Illus.). XVII, 269p. (C). 1991. text 47.95 (*0-8204-0742-9*) P Lang Pubng.

Rybacek, V., ed. Hop Production. (Developments in Crop Science Ser.: No. 16). 286p. 1991. 143.25 (*0-444-98770-3*) Elsevier.

Rybach, L. & Muffler, L. J., eds. Geothermal Systems: Principles & Case Histories. LC 80-40290. (Illus.). 373p. reprint ed. pap. 115.70 (*0-8357-7545-3*, 203626700001) Bks Demand.

Rybach, L., jt. ed. see Cermak, V.

Ryback, David. Look 10 Years Younger, Live 10 Years Longer: A Man's Guide. 1999. 9.99 (*1-57866-061-0*) Galahad Bks.

— Look 10 Years Younger, Live 10 Years Longer: A Man's Guide. LC 95-34064. 318p. (C). 1995. text 24.95 (*0-13-079344-2*) P-H.

— Look 10 Years Younger, Live 10 Years Longer: A Man's Guide. LC 95-34064. 318p. (C). 1995. pap. text 13.95 (*0-13-079336-1*); pap. text 14.95 (*0-13-079310-8*) P-H.

— Look 10 Years Younger, Live 10 Years Longer: A Woman's Guide. 1999. 9.99 (*1-57866-062-9*) Galahad Bks.

— Look 10 Years Younger, Live 10 Years Longer: A Woman's Guide. LC 95-35882. 368p. (C). 1995. text 24.95 (*0-13-079328-0*) P-H.

— Putting Emotional Intelligence to Work, Successful Leadership Is More Than IQ: The New Ethic of Self-Management. LC 97-15319. 224p. 1997. pap. text 17.95 (*0-7506-9956-6*) Buttrwrth-Heinemann.

Ryback, Jeffrey W. Eugene O'Neill: Dancing with the Devil (Playscript) LC 89-43703. 1991. pap. 6.00 (*0-88734-224-8*) Players Pr.

— The Many Faces of William Shakespeare. Landes, William-Alan, ed. LC 97-20145. 51p. (Orig.). 1997. pap. 6.00 (*0-88734-245-0*) Players Pr.

Ryback, Stephaine, contrib. by. Breakthrough French: The Quick & Easy Way to Speak & Understand French, Set. (Breakthrough Ser.). (FRE & ENG.). 256p. 1997. pap. 59.95 incl. audio (*0-8442-0241-X*) NTC Contemp Pub Co.

— Breakthrough German: The Quick & Easy Way to Speak & Understand German, Set. (Breakthrough Ser.). (GER & ENG.). 256p. 1997. pap. 59.95 incl. audio (*0-8442-0255-X*, 0255X) NTC Contemp Pub Co.

— Breakthrough Italian: The Quick & Easy Way to Speak & Understand Italian, 4 vols. (Breakthrough Ser.). (ITA & ENG.). 256p. 1997. pap. 59.95 incl. audio (*0-8442-0269-X*, 0269X) NTC Contemp Pub Co.

— Breakthrough Spanish: The Quick & Easy Way to Speak & Understand Spanish, Set. (Breakthrough Ser.). (SPA & ENG.). 256p. 1997. pap. 59.95 incl. audio (*0-8442-0238-X*) NTC Contemp Pub Co.

Ryback, Stephanie. Just Listen 'n Learn French. (FRE.). (C). 1984. 17.95 (*0-8442-1600-3*, VF1600-3) NTC Contemp Pub Co.

— Just Listen 'n Learn French: Beginning. (FRE.). (C). pap., teacher ed. 8.40 (*0-8442-9613-9*, VF9613-9) NTC Contemp Pub Co.

— Just Listen 'n Learn French Plus: For Improving Your French & Communicating More Effectively. 1995. pap. 17.95 (*0-8442-1610-0*, Passprt Bks) NTC Contemp Pub Co.

— Just Listen 'n Learn French Plus: Intermediate. (FRE.). (C). pap., teacher ed. 8.40 (*0-8442-9573-6*, VF9573-6) NTC Contemp Pub Co.

***Ryback, Timothy W.** The Last Survivor: In Search of Martin Zaidenstadt. 2000. pap. 12.00 (*0-679-75826-7*) Knopf.

Ryback, Timothy W. The Last Survivor: In Search of Martin Zaidenstadt. LC 98-52319. 160p. 1999. 21.00 (*0-679-43971-4*) Pantheon.

Rybacki, Donald J., jt. auth. see Rybacki, Karyn C.

Rybacki, Donald Jay, jt. auth. see Rybacki, Karyn Charles.

Rybacki, James J. Essential Guide to Prescription Drugs, 1999. (Illus.). 1120p. 1999. pap. 20.00 (*0-06-273635-3*) HarpC.

***Rybacki, James J.** Essential Guide to Prescription Drugs 2000: Everything You Need to Know for Safe Drug Use, Vol. 1. LC 87-657561. (Essential Guide Ser.). (Illus.). 1216p. 2000. 50.00 (*0-06-271613-1*, HarpRes) HarpInfo.

Rybacki, James J. & Long, James W. The Essential Guide to Prescription Drugs 1998: Everything You Need to Know for Safe Drug Use. 1152p. 1997. 50.00 (*0-06-271606-9*, Harper Ref) HarpC.

Rybacki, Karyn C. & Rybacki, Donald J. Communication Criticism: Approaches & Genres. 381p. (C). 1990. 39.50 (*0-534-14118-8*) Wadsworth Pub.

Rybacki, Karyn Charles & Rybacki, Donald Jay. Advocacy & Opposition. 4th ed. LC 99-13970. 292p. (C). 1999. pap. text 55.00 (*0-205-29583-5*, Longwood Div) Allyn.

***Rybaczyk, Peter.** Cisco Router Troubleshooting Handbook. 528p. 2000. pap. text 29.99 (*0-7645-4647-3*) IDG Bks.

Rybaczyk, Peter. Novell's Internet Plumbing Handbook. LC 97-77540. 336p. 1998. pap. 34.99 (*0-7645-4537-X*) IDG Bks.

Rybaczyk, Peter, jt. auth. see Fortino, Andres.

Rybak, B., ed. Advanced Technobiology. 712p. 1979. text 183.00 (*90-286-0299-2*) Kluwer Academic.

— Bio-Informatics & Bio-Process Studies in the Physiology of Communication. (Health Communications & Informatics Biosciences Communications Ser.: Vol. 4, No. 3). (Illus.). 1978. 16.75 (*3-8055-2856-6*) S Karger.

Rybak, Bob. I Love a Mystery. (Illus.). 176p. (J). (gr. 3-7). 1992. 14.99 (*0-86653-655-8*, GA1388) Good Apple.

— I Love an Adventure. (Illus.). 176p. (J). (gr. 3-7). 1992. 14.99 (*0-86653-656-6*, GA1389) Good Apple.

Rybak, Deborah C. & Phelps, David. Smoked: The Inside Story of the Minnesota Tobacco Trial. Mason, Tom, ed. (Illus.). 480p. 1998. pap. 17.95 (*0-9641908-4-2*) MSP Communs.

Rybak, Rywka. Rywka Rybak: A Survivor of the Holocaust. LC 93-60965. 88p. (Orig.). 1993. pap. 10.95 (*0-9638507-0-9*) Prologue Pubns.

Rybak, Sharon. ABC Clip & Copy. 208p. (J). 1991. 15.99 (*0-86653-586-1*, GA1301) Good Apple.

— Cooperative Learning Throughout the Curriculum. (Illus.). 144p. 1992. 10.99 (*0-86653-664-7*, GA1396) Good Apple.

— Good Apple Lesson Organizer. 128p. (J). (gr. k-6). 1990. 19.99 (*0-86653-563-2*, GA1149) Good Apple.

— Launching a Great Year. 144p. (J). (ps-2). 1989. 13.99 (*0-86653-507-1*, GA1093) Good Apple.

— Teach Smarter, Not Harder. 128p. (J). (gr. k-6). 1991. 12.99 (*0-86653-620-5*, GA1339) Good Apple.

Rybak, Stephanie. Breakthrough French: The Quick & Easy Way to Speak & Understand French, Vol. 1. (Breakthrough Self-Guided Language Courses Ser.). 256p. 1999. pap. 59.95 incl. audio, cd-rom (*0-8442-2735-8*, Passprt Bks) NTC Contemp Pub Co.

***Rybak, Stephanie.** Breakthrough French 2: The Successful Way to Speak Read & Understand French. (Breakthrough Ser.). (ENG & FRE.). 224p. 2000. pap. 59.95 (*0-658-00509-X*, 00509X) NTC Contemp Pub Co.

Rybak, Tom, jt. auth. see Schwarz, Ted.

Rybakin, A., ed. Dictionary of English Personal Names. 222p. (C). 1989. 50.00 (*0-7855-6429-2*, Pub. by Collets) St Mut.

Rybakov, Boris V. & Sidorov, V. A. Fast Neutron Spectroscopy: 1958 Edition. Vlasov, N. A., ed. LC 60-8723. (Soviet Journal of Atomic Energy: No. 6). 131p. reprint ed. pap. 40.70 (*0-608-31007-7*, 202064900018) Bks Demand.

Rybakov, V., ed. see Sesemann, Dimitri.

Rybakov, Vladimir V. Admissibility of Logical Inference Rules. LC 96-6560. (Studies in Logic & the Foundations of Mathematics Ser.: Vol. 136). 622p. 1997. 152.50 (*0-444-89505-1*) Elsevier.

Rybakowski, K. P. The Homotopy Index Theory on Metric Spaces with Applications to Partial Differential Equations. (Universitext Ser.). (Illus.). ix, 208p. 1987. 59.95 (*0-387-18067-2*) Spr-Verlag.

Rybalka. Boris Vian. (Bibliotheque des Lettres Modernes Ser.). (FRE.). 256p. 1984. pap. 19.95 (*0-7859-1553-2*, 2852102048) Fr & Eur.

Rybalka, Maya, tr. see De La Mettrie, Julien O.

Rybalka, Michel & Contat, Michel, eds. Sartre: Bibliography, 1980-1992. (Bibliographies of Famous Philosophers Ser.). 247p. 1993. 40.00 (*0-912632-96-8*) Philos Document.

Rybalka, Michel, ed. see Sartre, Jean-Paul.

Rybarczyk, Bruce & Bellg, Albert. Listening to Life Stories: A New Approach to Stress Intervention in Health Care. 168p. 1997. 36.95 (*0-8261-9570-9*) Springer Pub.

Rybash. Adult Development & Aging. 5th ed. 2000. pap. text 37.75 (*0-697-36202-7*) McGraw.

Rybash, et al. Adult Development. 3rd ed. 1995. teacher ed. 14.68 (*0-697-10504-0*) McGraw.

— Adult Development & Aging. 4th ed. LC 98-41408. xi, 660 p. 1999. write for info. (*0-697-25301-5*) Bus & Educ Tech.

Rybash, John M., et al. Adult Development & Aging. 3rd ed. 624p. (C). 1994. text. write for info. (*0-697-10503-2*) Brown & Benchmark.

Rybczyk, Mark L. San Antonio Uncovered. LC 91-20146. (Illus.). 304p. 1991. pap. 16.95 (*1-55622-145-2*, Seaside Pr) Wordware Pub.

***Rybczyk, Mark L.** San Antonio Uncovered. 2nd ed. LC 99-22234. 1999. pap. write for info. (*1-55622-735-3*, Rep of TX Pr) Wordware Pub.

Rybczynski, Witold. City Life: Urban Expectations in a New World. 256p. (C). 1998. text 23.00 (*0-7881-5517-2*) DIANE Pub.

— City Life: Urban Expectations in a New World. 1995. 22.50 (*0-684-81302-5*) S&S Trade.

— City Life: Urban Expectations in a New World. 256p. 1996. per. 12.00 (*0-684-82529-5*) S&S Trade.

An Asterisk (*) at the beginning of an entry indicates that the title is appearing for the first time.

*Rybczynski, Witold. A Clearing in the Distance: Frederich Law Olmstead & America in the Nineteenth Century. (Illus.). 480p. 2000. per. 15.00 (0-684-86575-0) S&S Trade.

Rybczynski, Witold. A Clearing in the Distance: Frederick Law Olmsted & America in the Nineteenth Century. LC 99-18094. (Illus.). 480p. 1999. 29.50 (0-684-82463-9) Scribner.

— Home: A Home History of an Idea. (Illus.). 272p. 1987. pap. 13.95 (0-14-010231-0, Penguin Bks) Viking Penguin.

— Looking Around: A Journey Through Architecture. 320p. 1993. reprint ed. pap. 12.95 (0-14-016889-3, Penguin Bks) Viking Penguin.

— The Most Beautiful House in the World. (Illus.). 240p. 1990. pap. 12.95 (0-14-010566-2, Penguin Bks) Viking Penguin.

*Rybczynski, Witold. One Good Turn: A Natural History of the Screwdriver & the Screw. (Illus.). 176p. 2000. 22.00 (0-684-86729-X) Scribner.

Rybczynski, Witold. A Place for Art: The Architecture of the National Gallery of Canada. (FRE & ENG., Illus.). 97p. 1993. pap. text 25.00 (0-88884-620-7) U Ch Pr.

Rybczynski, Witold, et al. McGill: A Celebration. (Illus.). 224p. (C). 1991. text 49.95 (0-7735-0795-7, Pub. by McG-Queens Univ Pr) CUP Services.

Rybczynski, Witold, jt. auth. see Walker, Lester.

Rybek, Stephanie. Easy French Exercises: Practice for Beginners. (Easy Exercises Ser.). (FRE., Illus.). 96p. 1996. pap. 7.95 (0-8442-1606-2, 16062, Passprt Bks) NTC Contemp Pub Co.

Ryberg, J., jt. ed. see Choppin, Gregory R.

Ryberg, J., jt. ed. see Choppin, G.

Rybicki, Edmund F. & Benzley, Steven E., eds. Computational Fracture Mechanics: Presented at the 2nd National Congress on Pressure Vessels & Piping, San Francisco, CA, June 23-27, 1975. LC 75-149. 222p. reprint ed. pap. 68.90 (0-608-30655-X, 201685900006) Bks Demand.

Rybicki, Edmund F., ed. see ASME Pressure Vessels & Piping Conference Staff.

Rybicki, George B. & Lightman, Alan P. Radiative Processes in Astrophysics. 400p. 1985. pap. 74.95 (0-471-82759-2) Wiley.

Rybicki, John. Traveling at High Speeds. (New Issues Press Poetry Ser.). 64p. 1996. pap. 12.00 (0-932826-45-8) New Issues MI.

Rybicki, K., jt. ed. see Rozanska, M.

Rybickl, Richard. Body Symbolism. 200p. (Orig.). 1985. pap. 5.95 (0-9614341-1-2) Future Dream Pr.

Rybolt, John E. Sirach. Bergant, Dianne, ed. (Collegeville Bible Commentary - Old Testament Ser.). 1994. pap. 4.95 (0-8146-1478-7) Liturgical Pr.

— Wisdom. (Collegeville Bible Commentary - Old Testament Ser.). 64p. 1986. pap. 4.95 (0-8146-1477-9) Liturgical Pr.

Rybolt, John E., jt. ed. see Ryan, Frances.

Rybolt, Richard. No Chairs Make for Short Meetings: And Other Business Maxims from Dad. 128p. 1994. 12.95 (0-525-93873-7) NAL.

Rybolt, Thomas R. & Mebane, Robert C. Environmental Experiments about Air. LC 92-26297. (Science Experiments for Young People Ser.). (Illus.). 96p. (YA). (gr. 4-9). 1993. lib. bdg. 19.95 (0-89490-409-4) Enslow Pubs.

— Environmental Experiments about Land. LC 93-15581. (Science Experiments for Young People Ser.). (Illus.). 96p. (YA). (gr. 4-9). 1993. lib. bdg. 19.95 (0-89490-411-6) Enslow Pubs.

— Environmental Experiments about Life. LC 93-15582. (Science Experiments for Young People Ser.). (Illus.). 96p. (YA). (gr. 4-9). 1993. lib. bdg. 19.95 (0-89490-412-4) Enslow Pubs.

— Environmental Experiments about Renewable Energy. LC 93-48543. (Science Experiments for Young People Ser.). (Illus.). 96p. (YA). (gr. 4-9). 1994. lib. bdg. 19.95 (0-89490-579-1) Enslow Pubs.

— Environmental Experiments about Water. LC 92-41235. (Science Experiments for Young People Ser.). (Illus.). 96p. (YA). (gr. 4-9). 1993. lib. bdg. 19.95 (0-89490-410-8) Enslow Pubs.

— Science Experiments for Young People Series, 3 bks. (Illus.). (YA). (gr. 4-9). 1993. lib. bdg. 54.85 (0-89490-448-5) Enslow Pubs.

Rybolt, Thomas R., jt. auth. see Mebane, Robert C.

Rybolt, William E. Mechanical Design Data Book. 4th rev. ed. (Illus.). 60p. (C). 1999. pap. 8.95 (0-941801-17-9) Rybolt Pubns.

Rybowski, Lisa, ed. see Goldman, Janlori & Hudson, Zoe.

*Rybski, Melinda. Kinesiology for Occupational Therapy. (C). 2001. pap. text 32.00 (1-55642-491-4) SLACK Inc.

Ryburn, Donald & Gould, Robin. Poetry Pathology. 87p. (Orig.). 1996. pap. text 7.95 (1-888406-00-3) Phoenix Access.

Ryburn, Murray. Contested Adoptions: Research, Law, Policy & Practice. 232p. 1994. 69.95 (1-85742-187-6, Pub. by Arena); pap. 35.95 (1-85742-188-4, Pub. by Arena) Ashgate Pub Co.

— Open Adoption: Research, Theory & Practice. 240p. 1994. 66.95 (1-85628-692-4, Pub. by Avebry) Ashgate Pub Co.

RYC, Inc. Staff. DB2 Answers! Certified Tech Support. (Answers! Ser.). 512p. 1999. 29.99 (0-07-211914-4) Osborne-McGraw.

Rycaut, Paul. Present State of the Greek & Armenian Churches. LC 75-13321. reprint ed. 45.00 (0-404-05476-5) AMS Pr.

— Present State of the Ottoman Empire. LC 76-135845. (Eastern Europe Collection). 1971. reprint ed. 17.95 (0-405-02787-7) Ayer.

Ryce, C. J. Napsha, the Miracle Dragon. LC 96-69587. (Illus.). 64p. (Orig.). (J). (gr. 1-5). 1997. per. 13.95 (0-9653695-2-8) Spellbound Pub.

Ryce, Karen. Parenting for the New Millennium: Friendly Families Through the Power of Respect. Stasa, Suzanne, ed. (Illus.). 210p. (Orig.). 1996. pap. 14.95 (0-9651103-0-3) HU Enterprises.

Ryce-Menuhin, Joel. Naked & Erect: Male Sexuality & Feeling. LC 96-25222. 152p. (Orig.). 1996. pap. 14.95 (1-888602-00-7, 007) Chiron Pubns.

— The Self in Early Childhood. (Free Association Bks.). 288p. 1988. 55.00 (1-85343-002-1) St Martin.

Ryce-Menuhin, Joel, ed. Jung & the Monotheisms: Judaism, Christianity, & Islam. LC 93-8077. 288p. (C). 1994. pap. 29.99 (0-415-10414-9) Routledge.

Ryce, Michael. Why Is This Happening to Me... Again?! And What You Can Do About It. 1996. pap. 15.00 (1-886562-29-6) M Ryce. James Redfield, author of THE CELESTINE PROPHESY, says IN THE INTRODUCTION, "A new & original understanding of relationship dynamics...an amazing journey through the world of inner healing...Michael has the gift of being able to synthesize the many diverse elements of human experience & bring them into a clear picture...a coherent system for change!" A synthesis of the ancient Aramaic language & culture that integrates physics, psychology, Naturopathic Medicine & theology into a profound, life-changing event! The techniques taught are easy to grasp & assimilate--& they work! A dialogue between Michael & the troubled Richard is fast paced & enlightening. You will be gripped by the way Richard unravels the blocks that keep him from the love for which he yearns, & rebuilds his understanding of life & relationships. The deep, heartfelt learning that happens for Richard becomes available to the reader through the insights & the wisdom he gains. This unusually intimate conversation between two men covers topics equally illuminating for both sexes including: * Communication * The Cause of Health * How the Mind Works * The Cause of Pain * The Human Energy System * Healing Inherited Patterns * How to: - Truly Forgive, - Form & Maintain Healing Relationships, - Heal Guilt, Blame, Fear & Other Wounds. Available for product support such as booksingings & workshops, also a wide variety of tapes. Contact dr. michael ryce at Heartland 417-273-4838. We want to be on your team! Website: www.whyagain.com, E-mail: mail@whyagain.com
Publisher Paid Annotation.

Ryce, Rodney. To the Deacon. 90p. 1995. write for info. (0-9648514-0-7); write for info. (0-9648514-1-5) PRO-FAN.

Ryce, Victoria. By Me, about Me: Writing Your Life. LC 96-910699. 160p. 1997. pap. 11.95 (1-55192-064-6) Raincoast Bk.

— Marketwise. (Illus.). 170p. 1988. pap. 18.95 (0-7737-5143-2) Genl Dist Srvs.

Rycenga, Jennifer, jt. auth. see Waller, Marguerite R.

Rychener, Hans. Freude am Wort. Gutes Deutsch: Guter Stil. (GER.). 282p. 1982. 9.00 (3-261-04984-7) P Lang Pubng.

Rychetnik, Joe. Alaska's Sky Follies: The Funny Side of Flying in the Far North. (Illus.). 160p. 1995. pap. 13.95 (0-945397-44-5) Epicenter Pr.

*Rychetnik, Joseph. Joe Rychetnik Reflects on Guns, Hunting & Days Gone By. (Illus.). 256p. 1999. pap. 17.95 (0-9670948-1-X) Precision Shootg.

Rychkun, Ed A. Guide to Salmon Fishing. 96p. 1992. pap. 8.95 (0-88839-305-9) Hancock House.

— 195 Lakes of the Fraser Valley, Vol. 1. 500p. 1995. pap. 17.95 (0-88839-339-3) Hancock House.

— Trout Fishing: The Tactical Secrets of Lake Fishing. 120p. 1994. pap. 11.95 (0-88839-338-5) Hancock House.

Rychkun, Ed A., jt. auth. see Peck, Ted.

Rychlak, Joseph F. In Defense of Human Consciousness. LC 97-3877. (Illus.). 351p. 1997. text 29.95 (1-55798-421-2, 431-6880) Am Psychol.

Rychlak, Joseph F. Introduction to Personality & Psychotherapy, 2 vols. 2nd ed. LC 80-68141. (Illus.). 800p. (C). 1981. text 83.56 (0-395-29736-2) HM.

Rychlak, Joseph F. Logical Learning Theory: A Human Teleology & Its Empirical Support. LC 93-49664. xix, 387p. 1994. text 45.00 (0-8032-3904-1) U of Nebr Pr.

— The Psychology of Rigorous Humanism. LC 76-54838. (Illus.). 561p. reprint ed. pap. 174.00 (0-608-10674-7, 201988900015); reprint ed. pap. 159.90 (0-608-30559-6, 2019889) Bks Demand.

Rychlak, Joseph F., contrib. by. The Psychology of Rigorous Humanism. LC 76-54838. (Illus.). 561p. reprint ed. pap. 159.90 (0-608-30299-6) Bks Demand.

Rychlak, Joseph F., ed. Dialectics: Humanistic Rationale for Behavior & Development. (Contributions to Human Development Ser.: Vol. 2). 150p. 1976. 42.75 (3-8055-2288-6) S Karger.

Rychlak, Joseph F., jt. auth. see Cameron, Norman.

*Rychlak, Ronald J. Hitler, the War & the Pope. 2000. 26.95 (1-58571-006-7, Pub. by Genesis Press) BookWorld.

— Real & Demonstrative Evidence: Applications & Theory. 577p. 1995. 100.00 (0-327-12338-9) LEXIS Pub.

Rychlak, Ronald J. Real & Demonstrative Evidence: Applications & Theory. 577p. 1995. 95.00 (0-614-05953-4, MICHIE); 100.00 (1-55834-220-6, 66800-10, MICHIE) LEXIS Pub.

— Real & Demonstrative Evidence: Applications & Theory. LC 95-75265. 160p. 1998. write for info. (0-327-00231-X, 66801-12) LEXIS Pub.

*Rychlak, Ronald J. Real & Demonstrative Evidence, 1999 Cumulative Supplement: Applications & Theory: Pocketpart. 160p. 1999. suppl. ed. write for info. (0-327-01686-8, 6680113) LEXIS Pub.

Rychlewska, ed. Turpilii. (LAT.). 1971. 17.95 (3-322-00215-2, T1926, Pub. by B G Teubner) U of Mich Pr

Rychlik, Otmar & Paoletti, John T. Arnulf Rainer: Drawing on Death. Longhauser, Elsa, ed. LC 89-8229. (Illus.). 35p. 1990. pap. 25.00 (1-58442-038-3) Galleries at Moore.

Rychlik, Reinhard. Business English for the Pharmaceutical Industry: English-German, German-English. (ENG & GER.). 407p. 1993. 150.00 (0-7859-9982-5) Fr & Eur.

Rychner, Jean, ed. see Villon, Francois.

Rychner, Lorenz M. The Classic Yamaha DX7. 93p. (C). 1987. pap. 19.95 (0-939067-05-6) Alexander Pub.

— Roland Alpha Juno I: Getting the Most Out of Yours. Alexander, Peter L., ed. (Roland Juno Support Ser.). (Illus.). 65p. (C). 1987. pap. text 16.95 (0-939067-11-0) Alexander Pub.

— Roland Alpha Juno II: Getting the Most Our of Yours. Alexander, Peter L., ed. (Roland Juno Support Ser.). (Illus.). 65p. (C). 1987. pap. text 16.95 (0-939067-43-9) Alexander Pub.

— Yamaha DX100 Working Musicians Guide. 67p. (C). 1987. pap. 14.95 (0-939067-38-2) Alexander Pub.

— Yamaha DX7IIFD, Vol. 1. 152p. (C). 1987. pap. 24.95 (0-939067-36-6) Alexander Pub.

— Yamaha DX21: Getting the Most Out of Yours. Alexander, Peter L., ed. (Yamaha DX Support Ser.). (Illus.). 84p. (C). 1987. pap. text 19.95 (0-939067-02-1) Alexander Pub.

— Yamaha TX802. Alexander, Peter L., ed. (Illus.). 110p. (C). 1988. pap. text 19.95 (0-939067-23-4) Alexander Pub.

— Yamaha TX81Z. Alexander, Peter L., ed. (Illus.). 104p. (C). 1987. pap. text 19.95 (0-939067-22-6) Alexander Pub.

Rychner, Lorenz M. & Mead, Charles. The Korg DSS-One Sampler. Alexander, Peter L., ed. (Illus.). 209p. (C). 1987. pap. text 34.95 (0-939067-41-2) Alexander Pub.

Rychner, Lorenz M., jt. auth. see Alexander, Peter L.

Rychner, Lorenz M., jt. auth. see Carr, Beau.

Rychner, Lorenz M., jt. auth. see Frankfurt, Scott.

Rychnofsky, Ray. San Francisco Bay Fishing Guide. (Illus.). 109p. 1999. pap. 18.95 (1-57188-174-3) F Amato Pubns.

Rychnovska, Milena, ed. Structure & Functioning of Seminatural Meadows. LC 92-11732. (Developments in Agricultural & Managed-Forest Ecology Ser.). 386p. 1993. 224.75 (0-444-98669-3) Elsevier.

Rychnovsky, Ray. The Trollers Handbook: For All American Fish Species. LC 99-177289. (Illus.). 92p. 1998. pap. 12.95 (1-57188-122-0) F Amato Pubns.

Ryckbost, D., jt. auth. see Bocken, Hubert.

Ryckbost, D., jt. ed. see Brocken, H.

Ryckewaert, A., jt. auth. see De Seze, S.

Ryckman. Theories of Personality. (Psychology Ser.). 1978. mass mkt. 18.50 (0-534-27107-3); mass mkt., teacher ed. 1.75 (0-534-27109-X) Brooks-Cole.

— Theories of Personality. 2nd ed. (Psychology Ser.). 1982. text. write for info. (0-534-02168-9) Brooks-Cole.

— Theories of Personality. 3rd ed. (Psychology Ser.). 1985. teacher ed. write for info. (0-534-04915-X) Wadsworth Pub.

— Theories of Personality. 7th ed. 1999. 10.00 (0-534-25111-0) Wadsworth Pub.

Ryckman, Richard M. Theories of Personality. 3rd ed. LC 84-23287. (Psychology Ser.). 544p. (C). 1985. mass mkt. 34.50 (0-534-04914-1) Brooks-Cole.

— Theories of Personality. 4th ed. 550p. (C). 1988. mass mkt. 45.50 (0-534-09996-3) Brooks-Cole.

— Theories of Personality. 5th ed. LC 92-2646. 560p. (C). 1993. text 43.25 (0-534-16644-X) Brooks-Cole.

— Theories of Personality. 6th ed. LC 96-5593. (Psychology Ser.). 635p. (C). 1996. mass mkt. 42.50 (0-534-33976-X) Brooks-Cole.

*Ryckman, Richard M. Theories of Personality. 7th ed. LC 99-24491. (Psychology Ser.). 689p. 1999. mass mkt. 72.95 (0-534-34898-X) Brooks-Cole.

Ryckman, Richard M. Theories of Personality: Test Items. 6th ed. 1997. write for info. (0-534-34248-5) Brooks-Cole.

Rycraft, Carol & Rowton, Paul, eds. The Rycraft Cookie Stamp Collector's Handbook: A Price Guide & History of the Cookie Stamps Grandma Used. 30th anniversary ed. (Illus.). 64p. 1998. pap. 5.95 (0-9641345-2-7) Rycraft.

Rycraft, Carol, jt. auth. see Rycraft, Robin.

Rycraft, Joan R., jt. ed. see Mech, Edmund V.

Rycraft, Robin & Rycraft, Carol. The Art of Clay Casting with Rycraft Ceramic Stamps. (Illus.). 32p. (Orig.). 1996. pap. 7.00 (0-9641345-1-9) Rycraft.

— The Art of Paper Casting: With Rycraft Ceramic Stamps. (Illus.). 32p. 1994. pap. 7.00 (0-9641345-0-0) Rycraft.

*Rycroft, A. A Colour Handbook of Dermatology. 220p. 1999. pap. 45.00 (0-8385-1622-X, Apple Lange Med) McGraw.

Rycroft, A. & Jordaan, B. Guide to South African Labour Law. 2nd ed. 384p. 1992. pap. 42.00 (0-7021-2806-6, Pub. by Juta & Co) Gaunt.

Rycroft, Charles. Anxiety & Neurosis. 166p. 1988. reprint ed. pap. text 25.00 (0-946439-52-4, Pub. by H Karnac Bks Ltd) Other Pr LLC.

— A Critical Dictionary of Psychoanalysis. 256p. 1995. pap. 14.95 (0-14-051310-8, Penguin Bks) Viking Penguin.

— The Innocence of Dreams. 200p. 1996. pap. 40.00 (1-56821-783-8) Aronson.

— Psychoanalysis & Beyond. 316p. (C). 1995. pap. text 15.00 (0-226-73289-4) U Ch Pr.

— Rycroft on Analysis Creativity. 192p. (C). 1992. pap. text 19.50 (0-8147-7428-8) NYU Pr.

Rycroft, D. K. & Ngcobo, A. B., eds. The Praises of Dingana. (Killie Campbell Africana Library Publication). (Illus.). 272p. 1988. 23.00 (0-86980-629-7, Pub. by Univ Natal Pr) Intl Spec Bk.

Rycroft, D. W., jt. ed. see Smith, K. V.

Rycroft, David, ed. & tr. see Dube, J. L.

Rycroft, David W., jt. auth. see Smedema, Lambert K.

Rycroft, Michael J. Space Research Vol.20: Proceedings of the Open Meetings of the Working Groups on Physical Sciences of the Twenty-Second Plenary Meeting of the Committee on Space Research, Bangalore, India, 29 May- 9 June 1979. LC 79-41359. (Illus.). 294p. 1980. 70.00 (0-08-024437-8, Pergamon Pr) Elsevier.

Rycroft, Michael J., ed. Proceedings of the 21st Plenary Meeting of COSPAR, Innsbruck, Austria, May-June 1978. (Advances in Space Research Ser.: Vol. 19). 642p. 1979. 145.00 (0-08-023417-8, Pergamon Pr) Elsevier.

— Space Research, Vol. 13. 1977. 115.00 (0-08-021787-7) Elsevier.

— Space Research, Vol. 14. 1977. 140.00 (0-08-021788-5) Elsevier.

— Space Research, Vol. 15. 1977. 115.00 (0-08-021789-3) Elsevier.

— Space Research, Vol. 17. 1977. 115.00 (0-08-021636-6) Elsevier.

— Space Research, Vol. 18. 1978. 140.00 (0-08-022021-5) Elsevier.

Rycroft, Michael J., et al, eds. Upper Atmosphere Models & Research: Proceedings of Workshops X, XI, & of the Topical Meeting of the COSPAR Interdisciplinary Scientific Commission C (Meeting C1) of the COSPAR 27th Plenary Meeting Held in Espoo, Finland, 18-29 July, 1988. (Advances in Space Research Ser.: Vol. 10). (Illus.). 318p. 1989. pap. 95.00 (0-08-040167-8, Pergamon Pr) Elsevier.

Rycroft, Michael J., jt. auth. see Haskell, G.

Rycroft, Michael J., jt. auth. see Houston, A.

Rycroft, Michael J., jt. ed. see Cook, M. V.

Rycroft, Richard J. & Menne, Torkil. Textbook of Contact Dermatitis. LC 92-2195. (Illus.). xxiv, 839p. 1992. 243.00 (0-387-54562-X) Spr-Verlag.

Rycroft, Robert, jt. auth. see Dietz, Thomas.

Rycroft, Robert W. & Kash, Don E. The Complexity Challenge: Technological Innovation for the 21st Century. LC 76-15644. (Science, Technology & the International Political Economy Ser.). 224p. 2002. 75.00 (1-85567-608-7); pap. 25.95 (1-85567-611-7) Continuum.

Rycroft, Robert W., jt. auth. see Kash, Don E.

Rycroft, Robert W., jt. auth. see Regens, James L.

Rycus, Judith S. & Hughes, Ronald C. Developmental Disabilities & Child Welfare. LC 98-205311. 1998. pap. text 8.95 (0-87868-734-3, 7343, CWLA Pr) Child Welfare.

— Field Guide to Child Welfare, 4 vols. Incl. Vol. 1. Field Guide to Child Welfare. LC 98-4701. 1998. pap. (0-87868-617-7, 6223, CWLA Pr); Vol. 2. Field Guide to Child Welfare. LC 98-4701. 1998. pap. (0-87868-618-5, 6223, CWLA Pr); Vol. 3. Field Guide to Child Welfare. LC 98-4701. 1998. pap. (0-87868-619-3, 6223, CWLA Pr); Vol. 4. Field Guide to Child Welfare. LC 98-4701. 1998. pap. (0-87868-620-7, 6223, CWLA Pr); 1998. Set pap. 139.95 (0-614-31368-6) Child Welfare.

— Field Guide to Child Welfare: Foundations of Child Protective Services, Vols. I-IV. 1144p. 1998. pap. text 139.95 (0-87868-622-3, 6223, CWLA Pr) Child Welfare.

Rycus, Judith S., jt. auth. see Hughes, Ronald C.

*Ryczek, Bill. Crash of the Titans: The Early Years of the New York Jets & the AFL. (Illus.). 224p. (J). 2000. 23.95 (1-892129-27-2) Total Sprts.

Ryczek, William J. When Johnny Came Sliding Home: The Post Civil War Baseball Boom, 1865-1870. LC 98-34783. (Illus.). 323p. 1998. lib. bdg. 35.00 (0-7864-0514-7) McFarland & Co.

Rydberg, Denny. Building Community in Youth Groups. (Illus.). 179p. (Orig.). 1985. pap. 15.99 (0-931529-06-9) Group Pub.

— Creative Bible Studies for Young Adults: 20 Studies for 18-to-35-Year-Olds. 204p. (YA). 1990. pap. 16.99 (0-931529-99-9) Group Pub.

— Twentysomething: Life Beyond College. 192p. 1991. pap. 7.99 (0-310-53571-9) Zondervan.

— Youth Group Trust Builders: 71 Activities to Develop Community in Your Youth Group. Parolini, Stephen, ed. LC 92-40663. 137p. 1993. pap. 15.99 (1-55945-172-6) Group Pub.

Rydberg, Denny, jt. auth. see Rohrbach, Mike.

Rydberg, Jan & Musikas, Claude, eds. Principles & Practices of Solvent Extraction. (Illus.). 576p. 1992. text 225.00 (0-8247-8668-8) Dekker.

Rydberg, Ulf, et al, eds. Alcohol & the Developing Brain: Third International Berzelius Symposium. LC 85-18467. 239p. 1985. reprint ed. pap. 74.10 (0-608-03444-4, 206414500008) Bks Demand.

Ryde, Nils. Atoms & Molecules in Electric Fields. (Illus.). 455p. 1976. 96.50 (0-685-13587-X) Coronet Bks.

— Development of Ideas in Physics. 196p. 1994. pap. 52.50 (91-22-01649-X) Coronet Bks.

R

An Asterisk (*) at the beginning of an entry indicates that the title is appearing for the first time.

Ryde, Peter. A Good Start, Considering. 288p. 1999. pap. 14.95 (0-85449-281-X) LPC InBook.

Ryde, Peter, ed. Mostly Golf: A Bernard Darwin Anthology. rev. ed. (Illus.). 206p. 1989. 28.00 (0-940889-12-9) Classics Golf.

Rydel, Beverlee, jt. auth. see Tesden, Kathleen.

Rydell, C. Peter, jt. auth. see Everingham, S. M.

Rydell, C. Peter, jt. auth. see Stevens, Benjamin H.

Rydell, Katy. Wind Says Good Night. 32p. (J). (ps). 1994. 16.00 (0-395-60474-5) HM.

***Rydell, Katy.** Wind Says Good Night. (Illus.). 32p. (J). (ps-3). 2000. pap. 5.95 (0-618-08585-8) HM.

Rydell, Mirelle G., jt. tr. see Williams, Harry F.

Rydell, Richard L., jt. auth. see Bria, William F.

Rydell, Robert, et al. In the People's Interest: A Centennial History of Montana State University. (Illus.). 344p. 1992. 40.00 (0-9635114-0-8) Montana St U.

Rydell, Robert W. All the World's a Fair: Visions of Empire at American International Expositions, 1876-1916. LC 84-2674. (Illus.). 320p. 1985. 27.50 (0-226-73239-8) U Ch Pr.

— All the World's a Fair: Visions of Empire at American International Expositions, 1876-1916. LC 84-2674. (Illus.). x, 338p. (C). 1987. pap. text 19.00 (0-226-73240-1) U Ch Pr.

***Rydell, Robert W.** Reason Why the Colored American Is Not in the World's Columbian Exposition: The Afro-American's Contribution to Columbian Literature: The Afro-American's Contribution to Columbian Literature. LC 98-58021. 136p. 1999. pap. text 14.95 (0-252-06784-3) U of Ill Pr.

Rydell, Robert W. World of Fairs: The Century-of-Progress Expositions. LC 92-45690. (Illus.). 280p. 1993. pap. 17.95 (0-226-73237-1) U Ch Pr.

— World of Fairs: The Century-of-Progress Expositions. LC 92-45690. (Illus.). 280p. 1996. lib. bdg. 49.95 (0-226-73236-3) U Ch Pr.

Rydell, Robert W. & Gwinn, Nancy E., eds. Fair Representations: World's Fairs & the Modern World. (European Contributions to American Studies: Vol. 27). 253p. 1995. pap. 32.50 (90-5383-282-3, Pub. by VU Univ Pr) Paul & Co Pubs.

***Rydell, Robert W., et al.** Fair America: World's Fairs in the United States. (Illus.). 176p. 2000. 29.95 (1-56098-968-8); pap. 15.95 (1-56098-384-1) Smithsonian.

Rydell, Robert W., ed. & intro. see Penn, Irvine Garland.

Rydell, Sierra. Homeward Bound. 1994. per. 3.50 (0-373-09900-2, 1-09900-1) Harlequin Bks.

— The Road Back Home. (Special Edition Ser.: No. 1044). 1996. per. 3.99 (0-373-24044-9, 1-24044-9) Silhouette.

Rydell, Wendy. Instant Sewing Handbook: A Complete Guide for the Home Sewer. LC 72-89526. (Illus.). 320p. 1984. 6.95 (0-911744-12-6) Career Pub IL.

Ryden, David K. Representation in Crisis: The Constitution, Interest Groups, & Political Parties. LC 95-39220. (SUNY Series in Political Party Development). 309p. (C). 1996. text 65.50 (0-7914-3057-X); pap. text 23.95 (0-7914-3058-8) State U NY Pr.

***Ryden, David K., ed.** The U. S. Supreme Court & the Electoral Process. LC 00-26366. 328p. 2000. text 65.00 (0-87840-805-3); pap. text 23.95 (0-87840-806-1) Georgetown U Pr.

Ryden, George H. Letters to & from Caesar Rodney. LC 75-107417. (Era of the American Revolution Ser.). 1970. reprint ed. lib. bdg. 55.00 (0-306-71881-2) Da Capo.

Ryden, Hope. ABC of Crawlers & Flyers. LC 95-45676. (Illus.). 32p. (J). (gr. k-3). 1996. 14.95 (0-395-72808-8, Clarion Bks) HM.

***Ryden, Hope.** America's Last Wild Horses. LC 99-43321. 1999. pap. 18.95 (1-55821-976-5) Lyons Pr.

Ryden, Hope. Backyard Rescue. LC 93-11683. (Illus.). (J). 1994. 15.00 (0-688-12880-7, Wm Morrow) Morrow Avon.

— Backyard Rescue. LC 93-11683. (Illus.). 128p. (J). (gr. 3-7). 1997. mass mkt. 4.95 (0-688-15496-4, Wm Morrow) Morrow Avon.

— Backyard Rescue. (J). 1997. 10.05 (0-606-11088-7, Pub. by Turtleback) Demco.

— God's Dog: The North American Coyote. (Illus.). 321p. 1979. reprint ed. pap. 17.95 (1-55821-046-6, 1046-6) Lyons Pr.

Ryden, Hope. Joey: The Story of a Baby Kangaroo. LC 93-15419. (Illus.). 40p. (J). 1994. 14.93 (0-688-12745-2, Wm Morrow) Morrow Avon.

Ryden, Hope. Lily Pond: Four Years with a Family of Beavers. LC 96-28176. 256p. 1997. pap. 16.95 (1-55821-455-0) Lyons Pr.

— The Little Deer of the Florida Keys. rev. ed. (Illus.). 64p. (Orig.). (J). (gr. 5 up). 1986. reprint ed. pap. 8.95 (0-912451-14-9) Florida Classics.

— The Little Deer of the Florida Keys. rev. ed. (Illus.). 64p. (Orig.). (YA). (gr. 5 up). 1986. reprint ed. 13.95 (0-912451-13-0) Florida Classics.

— Wild Horse Summer. 160p. (J). 1999. pap. 3.99 (0-440-41548-9) BDD Bks Young Read.

— Wild Horse Summer. LC 96-14221. (Illus.). 160p. (J). (gr. 4-9). 1997. 15.00 (0-395-77519-1, Clarion Bks) HM.

— Wild Horses I Have Known. LC 97-49021. (Illus.). 96p. (YA). (gr. 4 up). 1999. 18.00 (0-395-77520-5, Clarion Bks) HM.

Ryden, Kent C. Mapping the Invisible Landscape: Folklore, Writing, & the Sense of Place. LC 92-46529. (American Land & Life Ser.). (Illus.). 362p. 1993. text 39.95 (0-87745-406-X); pap. text 17.95 (0-87745-414-0) U of Iowa Pr.

Ryden, Lars, jt. auth. see Janson, Jan-Christer.

Ryden, Lars G., jt. ed. see Janson, Jan-Christen.

Ryden, Lennart, ed. The Life of St. Andrew the Fool, 2 vols., Set. LC 96-164247. (Studia Byzantina Upsaliensia Ser.: No. 4, Nos. 1-2). 741p. 1995. pap. 137.50 (91-554-3651-X, Pub. by Uppsala Univ Acta Univ Uppsaliensis) Coronet Bks.

Ryden, Lennart & Rosenqvist, Jan O., eds. Aspects of Late Antiquity & Early Byzantium. (Illus.). 173p. (Orig.). 1993. pap. 48.50 (91-86884-05-0) Coronet Bks.

Ryden, Mats, ed. see Kyto, Merja.

Ryden, Michael. Dyslexia: How Would I Cope? 3rd ed. LC 97-121356. 64p. 1996. pap. text 9.95 (1-85302-385-X, Pub. by Jessica Kingsley) Taylor & Francis.

Ryden, Ruth. The Golden Path. 200p. (Orig.). 1993. pap. 11.95 (0-929385-43-8) Light Tech Pubng.

— Living the Golden Path. 186p. (Orig.). 1994. pap. 11.95 (0-929385-65-9) Light Tech Pubng.

Ryden, Tom K., ed. Managing Urban Transportation with Limited Resources. 108p. 1983. pap. 5.00 (0-87262-363-7) Am Soc Civil Eng.

Ryden, Vassula. My Angel, Daniel: Early Dawn of True Life in God. (True Life in God Ser.: Vol.). 314p. 1995. pap. 9.95 (1-883225-17-5) Trinitas.

— True Life in God. (True Life in God Ser.: Vol. 2). 199p. (Orig.). 1991. pap. 9.95 (0-9631193-4-6) Trinitas.

— True Life in God. (True Life in God Ser.: Vol. 3). 208p. (Orig.). 1991. pap. 9.95 (0-9631193-5-4) Trinitas.

— True Life in God. (True Life in God Ser.: Vol. 4). 191p. (Orig.). 1991. pap. 9.95 (0-9631193-6-2) Trinitas.

— True Life in God. (True Life in God Ser.: Vol. 5). 80p. (Orig.). 1992. pap. 6.75 (0-9631193-7-0) Trinitas.

— True Life in God. (True Life in God Ser.: Vol. 6). 105p. (Orig.). 1993. pap. 8.50 (0-9631193-9-7) Trinitas.

— True Life in God. (True Life in God Ser.: Vol. 7). 92p. (Orig.). 1994. pap. 8.50 (1-883225-16-7) Trinitas.

— True Life in God. (True Life in God Ser.: Vol. 8). 558p. (Orig.). 1995. pap. 12.00 (1-883225-18-3) Trinitas.

— True Life in God, Vol. 1. 216p. (Orig.). 1991. pap. write for info. (0-9631193-3-8) Trinitas.

— The Two Witnesses: Extracts from "True Life in God" 295p. 1996. pap. 10.00 (1-890137-34-0) One Hund-One Fnd.

Ryden, Vassula, contrib. by. True Life in God Vol. 9: Original Handwriting Edition. 547p. (Orig.). (YA). 1997. pap. 12.00 (1-883225-20-5) Trinitas.

Ryden, Wendy A. & Horowitz, Emily. Spirits - Legacies: One Story Each. (Orig.). 1989. pap. 3.75 (0-9621918-0-9) Red Wine Pr.

Ryden, William. Christmas Duets for All: Bb Clarinet/Bass Clarinet. Proctor, Thom, ed. 24p. (C). 1995. pap. text 5.95 (0-7692-1758-3, EL9556) Wrner Bros.

— Christmas Duets for All: Horn in F. Proctor, Thom, ed. 24p. (C). 1995. pap. text 5.95 (0-7692-1757-5, EL9560) Wrner Bros.

— Christmas Quartets for All: Alto Saxophone. Proctor, Thom, ed. 24p. (C). 1995. pap. text 5.95 (0-7692-1753-2, EL9581) Wrner Bros.

— Christmas Quartets for All: Cello/Bass. Proctor, Thom, ed. 24p. (C). 1995. pap. text 5.95 (0-7692-1756-7, EL9588) Wrner Bros.

— Christmas Quartets for All: Violin. Proctor, Thom, ed. 24p. (C). 1995. pap. text 5.95 (0-7692-1752-4, EL9586) Wrner Bros.

— Christmas Trios for All: Bb Clarinet/Bass Clarinet. Proctor, Thom, ed. 24p. (C). 1995. pap. text 5.95 (0-7692-1754-0, EL9568) Wrner Bros.

— Christmas Trios for All: Flute/Piccolo. Proctor, Thom, ed. 24p. (C). 1995. pap. text 5.95 (0-7692-1755-9, EL9567) Wrner Bros.

Ryder, jt. auth. see Elrod.

Ryder, Alan. Alfonso the Magnanimous: King of Aragon, Naples, & Sicily, 1396-1458. (Illus.). 480p. 1990. 98.00 (0-19-821954-7) OUP.

Ryder, Alex. Pasion de Una Noche (Passion of a Night) (SPA.). 1999. mass mkt. 3.50 (0-373-33494-X, 1-33494-5) Harlequin Bks.

***Ryder, Andrew.** Following Christ. LC 99-36301. 108p. 1999. 12.95 (1-58051-068-X) Sheed & Ward WI.

***Ryder, Anthony.** The Artist's Complete Guide to Figure Drawing: A Contemporary Master Reveals the Secrets of Drawing the Human Form. LC 99-22843. (Illus.). 160p. 1999. pap. text 24.95 (0-8230-0303-5) Watsn-Guptill.

Ryder, Arthur W., tr. Panchatantra. 1994. pap. text 15.00 (0-226-73249-5) U Ch Pr.

Ryder, Arthur W., tr. see Dandin.

Ryder, Brent. The Alpha Book on Cancer & Living: For Patients, Family & Friends. 1993. pap. 18.95 (0-9632360-9-1) Alpha Inst.

Ryder, Brent G. Alpha Book on Cancer & Living: For Patients, Family & Friends. 1993. 24.95 (0-9632360-8-3) Alpha Inst.

— Alpha Book on Cancer & Living: For Patients, Family, & Friends. rev. ed. LC 93-71332. (Illus.). 448p. 1993. reprint ed. 24.95 (0-9632360-0-8) Alpha Inst.

Ryder, Brent G., jt. auth. see Alpha Institute Staff.

Ryder, Charles. Help! I Want to Work for Myself. 96p. 1999. pap. 6.95 (1-84024-064-4, Pub. by Summers) Seven Hills Bk.

Ryder, Daniel. Cover-up of the Century: Satanic Ritual Crime & World Conspiracy. LC 96-92385. 248p. 1996. pap. 13.95 (0-7880-0693-2, Fairway Pr) CSS OH.

Ryder, Daniel & Ryder, Liz. This Present Darkness: Live! A Case Study. LC 96-92224. 74p. 1996. pap. 6.95 (0-7880-0680-0, Fairway Pr) CSS OH.

Ryder, Donald G. The Inside Story: Living & Learning Through Life's Storms. LC 85-27780. (Illus.). 56p. 1985. 16.00 (0-935973-38-9) Ryder Pub Co.

Ryder, Edward F. The Art of Entering Sweepstakes & Winning Consistently. (Orig.). 1997. pap. 7.95 (0-934650-00-4) Sunnyside.

Ryder, Edward F., see Ingalls, Harold, pseud.

Ryder, Edward F., see Nash, M. A., pseud.

Ryder, Edward J. Lettuce, Endive & Chicory. LC 98-34438. (Crop Production Science in Horticulture Ser.). 224p. 1999. 50.00 (0-85199-285-4) OUP.

***Ryder, Esther.** Vision & Fantasy. 1999. pap. write for info. (1-58235-076-0) Watermrk Pr.

Ryder, Frank, ed. see Goethe, Johann Wolfgang Von.

Ryder, Frank, ed. & tr. see Goethe, Johann Wolfgang Von.

Ryder, Frank G. German Romantic Stories. LC 82-18263. (German Library: Vol. 35). 320p. (C). 1987. pap. 19.95 (0-8264-0313-1) Continuum.

Ryder, Frank G., tr. Song of the Nibelungs: A Verse Translation from the Middle High German Nibelungenlied. LC 82-17432. 436p. 1963. pap. text 17.95 (0-8143-1192-X, WB15) Wayne St U Pr.

Ryder, Frank G. & Browning, Robert, eds. German Literary Fairy Tales. LC 82-12550. (German Library: Vol. 30). 320p. 1982. 39.50 (0-8264-0276-3) Continuum.

Ryder, Frank G. & McCormick, E. Allen. Lebendige Literatur, 3 vols. 3rd ed. LC 85-81205. 448p. (C). 1985. pap. 41.56 (0-395-35959-7) HM.

Ryder, Frank G., ed. see Brentano & Eichendorff.

Ryder, Frank G., ed. see Keller, Gottfried.

Ryder, Frank G., ed. see Von Kleist, Heinrich & Paul, Jean.

Ryder, G. H. & Bennett, M. D. Mechanics of Machines. 2nd ed. (Illus.). 350p. 1990. 42.95 (0-8311-3030-X) Indus Pr.

Ryder, George & Allen, Charles. Guitar Chord Progression Made Easy. (Illus.). 1974. pap. 4.95 (0-934286-25-6) Kenyon.

***Ryder, George & Steinberg, David.** Sing You Seniors. LC 99-61094. 96p. 1999. pap. 13.95 (0-88739-259-8) Creat Arts Bk.

Ryder, Graham, ed. Proceedings of the 20th Lunar & Planetary Science Conference. LC 87-643480. (Illus.). 533p. 1990. 50.00 (0-942862-04-X) Lunar & Planet Inst.

Ryder, Graham, et al, eds. The Cretaceous-Tertiary Event & Other Catastrophes in Earth History. LC 96-28012. (Special Papers: No. 307). (Illus.). 1996. pap. 149.00 (0-8137-2307-8) Geol Soc.

Ryder, Graham & Sharpton, Virgil L., eds. Proceedings of Lunar & Planetary Science, Vol. 21. (Illus.). 738p. 1991. 50.00 (0-942862-05-8) Lunar & Planet Inst.

— Proceedings of Lunar & Planetary Science, Vol. 22. (Illus.). 481p. (C). 1992. 50.00 (0-685-51793-4) Lunar & Planet Inst.

Ryder, H. & Slafter, Edmund F. Colonial Coins of Vermont, 2 bks. in 1. (Illus.). 52p. 1981. pap. 12.00 (0-915262-65-7) S J Durst.

Ryder, Hillyer. Copper Coins of Massachusetts. (Illus.). 1981. reprint ed. pap. 7.00 (0-915262-66-5) S J Durst.

Ryder, J. D. & Fink, Donald G. Engineers & Electrons: A Century of Electrical Progress. LC 83-22681. 272p. 1984. 34.95 (0-87942-172-X, PC01669) Inst Electrical.

Ryder, James F. Voightlander & I. LC 72-9235. (Literature of Photography Ser.). 1973. reprint ed. 23.95 (0-405-04940-4) Ayer.

Ryder, Jim. Honda's V-Force. LC 98-72322. (Illus.). 160p. 1998. pap. 21.95 (1-85960-421-8, Pub. by J H Haynes & Co) Motorbooks Intl.

Ryder, Joan. The Snail's Spell. (Illus.). (J). (gr. 3-8). 1988. pap. 5.99 (0-14-050891-0, PuffinBks) Peng Put Young Read.

Ryder, Joanne. Bear Out There. (Illus.). 32p. (J). (ps-3). 1995. 15.00 (0-689-31780-8) Atheneum Yung Read.

— Dancers in the Garden. LC 89-10555. (Illus.). 32p. (J). (gr. k-3). 1992. 15.95 (0-87156-578-1, Pub. by Sierra Club Childrens) Little.

— Each Living Thing. LC 98-51832. (Illus.). 32p. (J). 2000. 16.00 (0-15-201898-0, Gulliver Bks) Harcourt.

— Earthdance. (Illus.). 32p. (J). (gr. k-5). 1995. 16.95 (0-8050-2678-9) H Holt & Co.

***Ryder, Joanne.** Earthdance. (ps-3). 1999. pap. text 6.95 (0-8050-6231-9) H Holt & Co.

— Fawn in the Grass. 2000. text 15.95 (0-8050-6236-X) St Martin.

Ryder, Joanne. Fireflies. LC 76-58695. (I Can Read Science Bks.). (Illus.). 64p. (J). (ps-3). 1977. 9.95 (0-06-025153-0) HarpC Child Bks.

— First Grade Elves. LC 93-25543. (First Grade Is the Best! Ser.). (Illus.). 32p. (J). (ps-2). 1993. lib. bdg. 15.85 (0-8167-3010-5) Troll Communs.

— First Grade Elves. LC 93-25543. (First Grade Is the Best! Ser.). (Illus.). 32p. (J). (ps-2). 1996. pap. 3.95 (0-8167-3011-3) Troll Communs.

— Hello, First Grade. LC 93-9041. (First Grade Is the Best! Ser.). (Illus.). 32p. (J). (ps-2). 1993. lib. bdg. 15.85 (0-8167-3008-3) Troll Communs.

— Hello, First Grade. LC 93-9041. (First Grade Is the Best! Ser.). (Illus.). 32p. (J). (ps-2). 1997. pap. 3.95 (0-8167-3009-1) Troll Communs.

***Ryder, Joanne.** A Just for a Day Book: Tyrannosaurus Time. LC 98-45236. (Just for a Day Bks.). 32p. (J). 1999. 15.95 (0-688-13682-6, Wm Morrow); 15.89 (0-688-13683-4, Wm Morrow) Morrow Avon.

Ryder, Joanne. Lizard in the Sun. LC 89-33886. (Illus.). 32p. (J). (ps up). 1994. mass mkt. 4.95 (0-688-13081-X, Wm Morrow) Morrow Avon.

Ryder, Joanne. Lizard in the Sun. LC 89-33866. (Just for a Day Bks.). 1994. 10.15 (0-606-06543-1, Pub. by Turtleback) Demco.

— Mouse Tail Moon. 2001. text 16.95 (0-8050-6404-4) St Martin.

Ryder, Joanne. My Father's Hands. LC 93-27116. (Illus.). 32p. (J). (ps up). 1994. 16.95 (0-688-09189-X, Wm Morrow) Morrow Avon.

— My Father's Hands. LC 93-27116. (Illus.). 32p. (YA). (ps up). 1994. lib. bdg. 15.93 (0-688-09190-3, Wm Morrow) Morrow Avon.

— Night Flight. (Illus.). 32p. (J). (ps-3). 1998. per. 5.99 (0-689-82150-6) S&S Childrens.

— Night Gliders. (Illus.). 32p. (J). (ps-2). 1997. pap. 4.95 (0-8167-3821-1) Troll Communs.

— Osos Por Aji. Dorros, Sandra M., tr.Tr. of Bears Out There. (SPA., Illus.). 32p. (J). (ps-3). 1995. 15.00 (0-689-31982-7) Atheneum Yung Read.

— Rainbow Wings. LC 98-47038. (Illus.). 40p. (J). (gr. k-3). 2000. 15.95 (0-688-14128-5, Wm Morrow) Morrow Avon.

— Rainbow Wings. LC 98-47038. (Illus.). 40p. (J). (gr. k-5). 2000. 15.89 (0-688-14129-3, Wm Morrow) Morrow Avon.

— Shark in the Sea. LC 96-16963. (Just for a Day Bks.). (Illus.). 32p. (J). 1997. 16.00 (0-688-14909-X, Wm Morrow) Morrow Avon.

Ryder, Joanne. Shark in the Sea. LC 96-16963. (Just for a Day Bks.). (Illus.). 32p. (J). 1997. lib. bdg., lab manual ed. 15.93 (0-688-14910-3, Wm Morrow) Morrow Avon.

Ryder, Joanne. Snail's Spell. (Picture Puffin Ser.). (J). 1988. 11.19 (0-606-03924-4, Pub. by Turtleback) Demco.

— Walt Disney's Bambi's Forest: A Year in the Life of the Forest. LC 93-72551. (Illus.). 32p. (J). (gr. k-3). 1994. 11.95 (1-56282-643-3, Pub. by Disney Pr); lib. bdg. 11.89 (1-56282-698-0, Pub. by Disney Pr) Little.

— Where Butterflies Grow. LC 88-37989. (Illus.). 32p. (J). (ps-3). 1989. 15.99 (0-525-57284-2, Dutton Child) Peng Put Young Read.

— Where Butterflies Grow. (Illus.). 32p. (J). (ps-3). 1996. pap. 5.99 (0-14-055858-6, PuffinBks) Peng Put Young Read.

— Where Butterflies Grow. LC 88-37989. 1996. 10.19 (0-606-10059-8, Pub. by Turtleback) Demco.

***Ryder, Joanne.** Wild Birds. LC 99-42218. 2001. write for info. (0-06-027738-6); write for info. (0-06-027739-4) HarpC Child Bks.

— Winter Whale. (Just for a Day Bks.). 1994. 10.15 (0-606-06885-6, Pub. by Turtleback) Demco.

Ryder, Joanne. Winter Whale. Cohn, Amy, ed. LC 90-19174. (Illus.). 32p. (J). (gr. k up). 1994. reprint ed. pap. 4.95 (0-688-13110-7, Wm Morrow) Morrow Avon.

— Winter White. LC 95-35387. (Illus.). 32p. (J). 1997. 16.00 (0-688-12992-7, Wm Morrow) Morrow Avon.

— Without Words. (Illus.). 32p. (J). (gr. k-3). 1995. 15.95 (0-87156-580-3, Pub. by Sierra Club Childrens) Little.

Ryder, Joanne, adapted by. Walt Disney's Bambi. LC 92-54875. (Sketchbook Ser.) (Illus.). 64p. (J). (gr. 2-6). 1993. pap. 2.95 (1-56282-444-9, Pub. by Disney Pr) Little.

Ryder, Joanne, ed. Sea Elf. LC 92-27608. (Just for a Day Book). (Illus.). 32p. (J). (gr. k up). 1993. 15.00 (0-688-10060-0, Wm Morrow) Morrow Avon.

Ryder, Joanne & Rothman, Michael. A Just for a Day Book: Jaguar in the Rainforest. LC 94-16646. (Just for a Day Bks.). (Illus.). 32p. (J). (gr. k-3). 1996. 15.89 (0-688-12991-9, Wm Morrow) Morrow Avon.

Ryder, Joanne & Rothman, Michael. A Just for a Day Book: Jaguar in the Rainforest. LC 94-16646. (Just for a Day Bks.). (Illus.). (J). (gr. 1-3). 1996. 16.00 (0-688-12990-0, Wm Morrow) Morrow Avon.

Ryder, John. The Case for Legibility. (Illus.). 1979. 8.50 (0-89679-002-9) Moretus Pr.

— Interpreting America: Russian & Soviet Studies of the History of American Thought. LC 98-58118. (Vanderbilt Library of American Philosophy). 416p. (C). 1999. 44.95 (0-8265-1334-4) Vanderbilt U Pr.

— Printing for Pleasure. (Illus.). 144p. 1976. reprint ed. 20.00 (0-370-10443-9, Pub. by Bodley Head) Oak Knoll.

Ryder, John, ed. American Philosophic Naturalism in the Twentieth Century. LC 94-18813. 566p. (C). 1994. 36.95 (0-87975-894-5) Prometheus Bks.

Ryder, John D. Electronic Fundamentals & Applications: Integrated & Discrete Systems. 5th ed. (Illus.). 640p. (C). 1976. text 67.00 (0-13-251371-4) P-H.

Ryder, Judith & Campbell, Lesley. Balancing Acts in Personal, Social & Health Education: A Practical Guide for Teachers' 320p. (C). 1988. lib. bdg. 55.00 (0-415-00537-X, A2468) Routledge.

Ryder, Judy. Turning Your Great Idea into a Great Success: How to Develop, License, Protect, & Promote Your Product Idea. LC 94-45493. 256p. (Orig.). 1995. pap. 14.95 (1-56079-462-3, Petersons Pacesetter) Petersons.

Ryder, Julia, ed. Library Services to Household People. LC 90-223190. (Illus.). 233p. Date not set. reprint ed. pap. 72.30 (0-608-20731-4, 207182900002) Bks Demand.

***Ryder, Julian.** Carl Fogarty: The Complete Racer. 2nd ed. (Illus.). 160p. 1999. pap. text 29.95 (1-85960-641-5, 129515AE, Pub. by Haynes Manuals) Motorbooks Intl.

Ryder, Julian. Carl Fogarty - the Complete Racer. (Illus.). 160p. 1997. pap. 24.95 (1-85960-408-0) Haynes Manuals.

— Ten Years of Superbike. LC 97-61071. (Illus.). 160p. 1998. pap. 24.95 (1-85960-404-8, Pub. by J H Haynes & Co) Motorbooks Intl.

***Ryder, Julian.** World Superbike Winners. (Illus.). 160p. 2000. 29.95 (1-85960-678-4, 130667AE, Pub. by Haynes Manuals) Motorbooks Intl.

Ryder, Laura. A Conversation with Laura Ryder: Laura Ryder Interviewed by Harry Burrus. (Illus.). 1995. 3.00 (1-884185-12-6) O Zone.

— Exchanging Gifts: Poems & Prose. LC 90-306. (Illus.). 112p. (Orig.). Date not set. pap. 12.50 (0-941749-09-6) Black Tie Pr.

— Exchanging Gifts: Poems & Prose. deluxe limited ed. LC 90-306. (Illus.). 112p. (Orig.). 1990. pap. 15.00 (0-941749-10-X) Black Tie Pr.

— You Can't Hide on Leather Seats. limited ed. (Codex Booklet Ser.). (Illus.). 12p. 1993. pap. 10.00 (1-884185-02-9) O Zone.

Ryder, Laura, jt. auth. see Beining, Guy.

Ryder, Lewis H. Elementary Particles & Symmetries. rev. ed. Lx, 296p. 1975. text 195.00 (*0-677-05130-1*) Gordon & Breach.
— Quantum Field Theory. 2nd ed. (Illus.). 505p. (C). 1996. text 125.00 (*0-521-47242-3*); pap. text 42.95 (*0-521-47814-6*) Cambridge U Pr.
Ryder, Liz, jt. auth. see Ryder, Daniel.
Ryder, M. H., et al, eds. Improving Plant Productivity with Rhizosphere Bacteria. LC 96-141769. (Illus.). 288p. 1994. pap. 60.00 (*0-643-05396-4*, Pub. by CSIRO) Accents Pubns.
Ryder, M. L. The Production & Properties of Wool & Other Animal Fibres. 63p. 1975. 85.00 (*0-7855-7218-X*) St Mut.
Ryder, Mary E. Ordered Chaos: The Interpretation of English Noun-Noun Compounds. LC 94-9527. 1994. 55.00 (*0-520-09777-7*, Pub. by U CA Pr) Cal Prin Full Svc.
Ryder, Mary R. Willa Cather & Classical Myth: The Search for a New Parnassus. LC 90-34815. (Studies in American Literature: Vol. 11). 312p. 1990. lib. bdg. 99.95 (*0-88946-113-9*) E Mellen.
Ryder, Nora L. In the Wild. LC 96-15416. (J). 1995. 11.95 (*0-8050-1775-5*) H Holt & Co.
Ryder, Norman B. The Cohort Approach: Essays in the Measurement of Temporal Variations in Demographic Behavior. Zuckerman, Harriet & Merton, Robert K., eds. LC 79-9023. (Dissertations on Sociology Ser.). 1980. lib. bdg. 21.95 (*0-405-12991-2*) Ayer.
Ryder, Norman B. & Westoff, Charles F. The Contraceptive Revolution. LC 76-27840. 397p. 1977. reprint ed. pap. 123.10 (*0-7837-9438-X*, 206018000004) Bks Demand.
— Reproduction in the United States, 1965. LC 78-120760. 423p. reprint ed. pap. 131.20 (*0-7837-0244-2*, 204055300017) Bks Demand.
Ryder, Nova, jt. auth. see Melia, Trevor.
Ryder, O. A. & Byrd, M. L., eds. One Medicine: A Tribute to Kurt Benirschke. (Illus.). xiv, 373p. 1984. 86.95 (*0-387-13275-9*) Spr-Verlag.
Ryder, R. A. & Edwards, C. J., eds. A Conceptual Approach for the Application of Biological Indicators of Ecosystem Quality in the Great Lakes Basin: A Joint Effort of the International Joint Commission & the Great Lakes Fishery Commission, Report to the Great Lakes Science Advisory Board. fac. ed. LC 92-123616. (Illus.). 199p. pap. 61.70 (*0-7837-8626-3*, 207523800007) Bks Demand.
***Ryder, R. E. J., et al.** An Aid to the MRCP Short Cases. 2nd ed. LC 98-42252. (Illus.). 400p. 1999. pap. 49.95 (*0-632-03067-4*) Blackwell Sci.
***Ryder, Randall.** Reading & Learning in Content Areas. 2nd ed. (Illus.). 400p. 1998. pap., teacher ed. 52.95 (*0-471-36558-0*) Wiley.
Ryder, Randall & Graves, Michael F. Literacy & Learning in Content. 2nd ed. LC 97-22988. 385p. 1997. pap. text 48.00 (*0-13-267774-1*) P-H.
Ryder, Randall J. & Hughes, Tom. Internet for Educators. 2nd ed. LC 97-45603. 198p. 1997. spiral bd. 26.00 (*0-13-699075-4*, Merrill Coll) P-H.
Ryder, Randall J., et al. Easy Reading: Book Series & Periodicals for Less Able Readers. LC 89-7642. (Reading Aids Ser.). (Illus.). 96p. reprint ed. pap. 30.00 (*0-7837-4586-9*, 204430500002) Bks Demand.
***Ryder, Richard.** Animal Revolution: Changing Attitudes Toward Speciesism. (Illus.). 224p. 2000. pap. 19.50 (*1-85973-330-1*, Pub. by Berg Pubs) NYU Pr.
— Animal Revolution: Changing Attitudes Toward Speciesism. rev. ed. (Illus.). 256p. 2000. 65.00 (*1-85973-325-5*, Pub. by Berg Pubs) NYU Pr.
Ryder, Richard. Global Telecommunications: Researching the Communications Revolution. 192p. 1999. boxed set 900.00 (*1-85573-324-2*, Pub. by Woodhead Pubng) Am Educ Systs.
Ryder, Richard D. The Political Animal: The Conquest of Speciesism. LC 98-19445. (Illus.). 157p. 1998. lib. bdg. 32.00 (*0-7864-0530-9*) McFarland & Co.
Ryder, Robert G. The Realistic Therapist: Modesty & Relativism in Therapy & Research. LC 86-1765. 205p. 1987. reprint ed. pap. 63.60 (*0-608-00819-2*, 206160700010) Bks Demand.
Ryder, Robert T., et al. Seismic Models of Sandstone Stratigraphic Traps in Rocky Mountain Basins. LC 81-52315. (Methods in Exploration Ser.). 124p. reprint ed. pap. 38.50 (*0-7837-3972-9*, 204380100011) Bks Demand.
Ryder, Stephanie. The Christmas Story. 32p. (J). (ps-2). 1995. 3.98 (*0-86112-891-5*) Brimax Bks.
— Katy's & Sam's ABC. (Die-Cut Board Bks.). 20p. (J). (ps). 1996. bds. 5.98 (*1-85854-361-4*) Brimax Bks.
— Mis Primeras 500 Palabras.Tr. of My First 500 Words. (ENG & SPA.). 64p. (J). (ps-1). 1995. 7.98 (*1-85854-340-1*) Brimax Bks.
— My First 100 Words. 20p. (J). (ps). 1997. bds. 5.98 (*1-85854-547-1*) Brimax Bks.
— The Night Before Christmas. 32p. (J). (ps-2). 1995. 3.98 (*0-86112-892-3*) Brimax Bks.
— Tell the Time at the Farm. (Clock Bks.). 12p. (J). (ps-1). 1996. bds. 5.98 (*1-85854-378-9*) Brimax Bks.
Ryder, Stephen M. Dinner Behind the Lines. 150p. 1997. pap. 18.95 (*0-9654867-1-0*) Bennington NY.
— Minstrel: And Selected Poems. Ganz, Anna L., ed. 85p. (Orig.). 1997. pap. 12.95 (*0-9654867-0-2*) Bennington NY.
Ryder, Stuart A. The D-Stem in Western Semitic. (Janua Linguarum, Ser. Practica: No. 131). 173p. 1974. pap. text 93.10 (*90-279-2669-7*) Mouton.
Ryder, Sue. Child of My Love: An Autobiography. LC 98-178436. (Illus.). 672p. 1998. 32.00 (*1-86046-432-7*, Pub. by Harvill Press) FS&G.
Ryder, Thomas. Coson Carriage Collection at Beechdale. Morrow, Rodger, ed. (Illus.). 175p. (Orig.). 1989. pap., boxed set 30.00 (*1-880499-03-7*) Carriage Museum.
Ryder, Tim. Health Professionals Abroad. 1997. pap. 17.95 (*1-85458-172-4*, Pub. by Vac Wrk Pubns) Petersons.
— Health Professionals Abroad. 2nd rev. ed. 256p. 2000. pap. 17.95 (*1-85458-227-5*, Pub. by Vac Wrk Pubns) Seven Hills Bk.
— Working with the Environment. 272p. 1997. pap. 17.95 (*1-85458-148-1*, Pub. by Vac Wrk Pubns) Seven Hills Bk.
***Ryder, Tim.** Working with the Environment. 2nd ed. (Illus.). 2000. pap. 19.95 (*1-85458-243-7*) Vac Wrk Pubns.
Ryder, Tracie R. How Can It Look So Good & Feel So Bad. 1990. student ed. 9.95 (*0-317-91191-0*); audio 9.95 (*0-317-91192-9*); VHS 39.95 (*0-317-91193-7*); disk 49.95 (*0-317-91194-5*) Positive Prod.
— How Can It Look So Good & Feel So Bad? Your Guide to Inner Peace. MacStravic, Sue, ed. LC 88-28093. (Illus.). 232p. 1989. pap. text 14.95 (*0-929656-18-0*) Positive Prod.
Ryder, Verdene. Parents & Their Children. annuals LC 98-48864. 544p. 2000. text 45.28 (*1-56637-517-7*) Goodheart.
Ryder, Verdene & Harter, Marjorie B. Contemporary Living. rev. ed. LC 99-11551. (Illus.). 684p. 2000. 47.96 (*1-56637-640-8*) Goodheart.
Ryder, Verdene & Smith, Peggy B. Human Sexuality: Responsible Life Choices. LC 97-52767. (Illus.). 197p. (J). (gr. 8-12). 1998. pap. text 26.60 (*1-56637-455-3*) Goodheart.
Ryder, Virginia P. Travels of an Olive Eater from Pit to Pit Plus How to Cure an Olive. (Illus.). 57p. (Orig.). 1991. pap. 15.95 (*0-935098-03-8*) Amigo Pr.
Ryder, Willet. The Art Experience, Grades 4-6. 1991. pap. 12.95 (*0-673-46353-2*, GoodYrBooks) Addson-Wesley Educ.
— Celebrating Diversity with Art: Thematic Projects for Every Month of the Year. 128p. (Orig.). 1995. pap. 8.95 (*0-673-36170-5*, GoodYrBooks) Addson-Wesley Educ.
Rydesky, Mary & DeVaughn, Tanya, eds. Patient Education Sourcebook. 547p. 1986. 50.00 (*0-318-20441-X*) Health Sci Comm.
Rydholm, C. Fred. Superior Heartland: A Backwoods History, 2 vols., Set, Vols. I & II. 1600p. 1989. 65.00 (*0-9639948-2-4*) Superior Hrtland.
— Superior Heartland: A Backwoods History, Vol. I. LC 89-90710. 850p. 1989. write for info. (*0-9639948-0-8*) Superior Hrtland.
— Superior Heartland: A Backwoods History, Vol. II. 750p. 1989. write for info. (*0-9639948-1-6*) Superior Hrtland.
Rydholm, Fred, jt. auth. see Burrows, Russell E.
Rydin, Y., jt. auth. see Mazza, L.
Rydin, Yvonne. The Environmental Impact of Land & Property Management. LC 96-1950. 208p. 1996. 120.00 (*0-471-96612-6*) Wiley.
— Residential Development & the Planning System: A Study of the Housing Land System at the Local Level. (Illus.). 70p. 1985. pap. 22.00 (*0-08-032742-7*, Pub. by PPL) Elsevier.
Rydin, Yvonne, jt. auth. see Brindley, Tim.
Rydin, Yvonne, jt. auth. see Myerson, George.
Ryding & Pechefsky. A World Elsewhere: The Life of Bruno Walter. 400p. 2000. 35.00 (*0-02-864848-X*) S&S Trade.
Ryding, Erik S. In Harmony Framed: Musical Humanism, Thomas Campion, & the Two Daniels. LC 92-21689. (Sixteenth Century Essays & Studies: Vol. 21). 223p. 1992. text 40.00 (*0-940474-22-0*, SCJP) Truman St Univ.
Ryding, J., jt. auth. see Patterson, K. D.
Ryding, Karin C. Formal Spoken Arabic: A Basic Course. 434p. 1996. pap. 16.95 (*0-614-21643-5*, 1388) Kazi Pubns.
— Formal Spoken Arabic: Basic Course. LC 90-2823. 434p. (Orig.). (C). 1990. pap. 19.95 (*0-87840-279-9*) Georgetown U Pr.
— Formal Spoken Arabic: Basic Course, Set. LC 90-2823. 434p. (Orig.). (C). 1990. audio 95.00 (*0-87840-283-7*) Georgetown U Pr.
— Formal Spoken Arabic: Fast Course. 244p. 1996. pap. 14.95 (*0-614-21644-3*, 1387) Kazi Pubns.
Ryding, Karin C., ed. Early Medieval Arabic: Studies on Al-Khalil Ibn Ahmed. LC 97-37420. 160p. 1998. 39.95 (*0-87840-663-8*) Georgetown U Pr.
Ryding, Karin C. & Nydell, Margaret K. Saudi Arabic Familiarization Course. 80p. 1990. pap. text 24.95 incl. audio (*0-9628410-1-3*) DLS VA.
Ryding, Karin C. & Zaiback, Abdelnour. Formal Spoken Arabic FAST Course. (ARA & ENG.). 158p. (Orig.). (C). 1993. pap. text 21.95 (*0-87840-284-5*); audio 95.00 (*0-87840-285-3*) Georgetown U Pr.
Ryding, Sven-Olof. Environmental Management Handbook. 750p. 1994. 63.00 (*1-56670-123-6*, IOL123) Lewis Pubs.
— The Environmental Management Handbook Vol. 2: The Holistic Approach from Problems to Strategies. LC 94-77311. 797p. (YA). (gr. 12). 1994. pap. 55.00 (*90-5199-171-1*) IOS Press.
Ryding, Sven-Olof, ed. Environmental Management Handbook. 797p. (gr. 12). 1992. 125.00 (*90-5199-062-6*, Pub. by IOS Pr) IOS Press.
Ryding, William W. Structure in Medieval Narrative. LC 72-154531. (De Proprietatibus Litterarum, Ser. Major: No. 12). 177p. 1971. text 34.65 (*90-279-1795-7*) Mouton.
Rydjord, John. Indian Place Names: Their Origin, Evolution, & Meanings Collected in Kansas from the Siouian, Alogonguin, Shoshonean, Caddoan, Iroquoian, & Other Tongues. LC 68-10303. (Illus.). 380p. 1982. pap. 19.95 (*0-8061-1763-X*) U of Okla Pr.
Rydlova-Erlich, Marcela, ed. Treasury of Czech Love Poems, Quotations & Proverbs. LC 97-45856. 128p. 1997. 11.95 (*0-7818-0571-6*) Hippocrene Bks.
Rydlun, Judith, ed. see Mikal, Elizabeth J.
Rydlun, Judith, ed. see Waring, Cynthia.
Rydnik, V. J., et al. Dictionary of Physics: In Russian, English, German & French. (ENG, FRE, GER & RUS.). 392p. 1989. 197.75 (*0-444-70490-6*, North Holland) Elsevier
— Dictionary of Physics in Russian, German, English & French. (ENG, FRE, GER & RUS.). 392p. 1989. 250.00 (*0-8288-9318-7*) Fr & Eur.
Rydon, Joan. The Federal Legislature: The Austrian Federal Parliament, 1901-1980. 250p. 1986. 39.95 (*0-19-554689-X*) OUP.
Rydqvist, Kristian. Pricing of Shares with Different Voting Power & the Theory of Oceanic Games. Stockholm School of Economics Staff, ed. 178p. (Orig.). 1986. pap. text 65.00 (*91-7258-211-1*) Coronet Bks.
Rydving, Hakan. The End of Drum Time: Religious Change among the Lule Saami, 1670s-1740s. 2nd ed. (Historia Religionum Ser.: No. 12). (Illus.). 213p. (Orig.). 1995. pap. 46.50 (*91-554-3580-7*) Coronet Bks.
Rydz, John S. Common Sense Approach to Manufacturing Management: Excellence from the Shop Floor to the Executive Suite. 208p. 1990. 24.95 (*0-88730-211-4*, HarpBusn) HarpInfo.
— Commonsense Manufacturing Management: Excellence from the Shop Floor to the Executive Suite. 1991. pap. 14.95 (*0-88730-494-X*, HarpBusn) HarpInfo.
Rydzeski, Justine. Radical Nostalgia in the Age of "Piers Plowman" Economics, Apocalypticism & Discontent. LC 98-30631. (Studies in the Humanities: Vol. 48). 172p. 1999. text 42.95 (*0-8204-4273-9*, 42739) P Lang Pubng.
Rye. Making Cult Connections. 1994. pap. text, teacher ed. 2.09 (*0-312-08072-7*) St Martin.
Rye, Colin. The Change Management Action Kit: A Practical Guide to Managing Change. 160p. pap. 17.95 (*0-7494-1845-1*) Kogan Page Ltd.
***Rye, Colin.** Change Management Action Kit: The 5 Step Action Kit. 2nd ed. 2000. pap. 27.00 (*0-7494-3380-9*) Kogan Page Ltd.
Rye, David E. How to Start & Operate a Successful Business: Winning the Entrepreneurial Game. 304p. 1998. pap. 9.95 (*1-58062-006-X*) Adams Media.
— 1001 Ways to Get Promoted. LC 99-30192. 288p. 1999. pap. 15.99 (*1-56414-430-5*) Career Pr Inc.
— 1001 Ways to Inspire Your Organization, Your Team & Yourself. LC 97-46188. 272p. 1998. pap. 15.99 (*1-56414-348-1*) Career Pr Inc.
***Rye, David E.** 1,001 Ways to Save, Grow & Invest Your Money. LC 98-55719. 288p. 1999. pap. 15.99 (*1-56414-404-6*) Career Pr Inc.
Rye, David E. The Vest Pocket Entrepreneur: Everything You Need to Start & Run Your Own Business. 400p. (C). 1994. 19.95 (*0-13-158510-X*) P-H.
Rye, David E. & Hickman, Craig R. Starting Up: Do You Have What It Takes to Make It in Your Own Business? 336p. 1998. pap. text 14.00 (*0-7352-0028-9*) PH Pr.
Rye, Edgar. Colleen, the Mountain Maid: A Story of War & Feud in Kentucky. Linck, Charles E., ed. 1994. write for info. (*0-9617714-7-X*) Cow Hill Pr.
***Rye, Edgar.** The Quirt & the Spur: Vanishing Shadows of the Texas Frontier. 2000. pap. 17.95 (*0-89672-441-7*) Tex Tech Univ Pr.
Rye, Graham. The James Bond Girls. rev. ed. LC 98-137655. (Illus.). 1997. pap. text 16.95 (*0-8065-1958-4*, Citadel Pr) Carol Pub Group.
Rye, Howard W., jt. auth. see Marks, Anthony.
Rye, Jennifer. Look . . . What Do You See? LC 90-40231. (First Science Ser.). (Illus.). 32p. (J). (gr. k-3). 1991. pap. 3.95 (*0-8167-2123-8*); lib. bdg. 17.25 (*0-8167-2122-X*) Troll Communs.
Rye, Jennifer, jt. auth. see Wood, Nicholas.
Rye, Kerry-Anne, jt. ed. see Barter, Philip J.
Rye, Linda N. How Many Diamond Rings. 62p. 1972. 3.95 (*0-913976-01-6*) Discovery Bks.
Rye, Owen S. Pottery Technology: Principles & Reconstruction. LC 80-53439. (Manuals on Archeology Ser.: No. 4). (Illus.). xi, 150p. 1981. 18.00 (*0-9602822-2-X*) Taraxacum.
Rye, Owen S. & Evans, Clifford. Traditional Pottery Techniques of Pakistan: Field & Laboratory Studies. LC 75-619168. (Smithsonian Contributions to Anthropology Ser.: no. 21). 301p. reprint ed. pap. 93.40 (*0-608-13597-6*, 202031400016) Bks Demand.
***Rye, Phil D., et al, eds.** ISOBM TD-3 International Workshop on Monoclonal Antibodies Against Prostate-Specific Antigen. (Tumor Biology Ser.: Vol. 20, Suppl. 1). (Illus.). vi, 94p. 1999. pap. 34.00 (*3-8055-6983-1*) S Karger.
Rye, Phil D. & Price, Michael R., eds. ISOBM TD-4 International Workshop on Monoclonal Antibodies Against MUC1: Workshop, San Diego, Calif., November 1996. (Tumor Biology Ser.: Vol. 19, Suppl. 1, 1998). (Illus.). vi, 152p. 1997. pap. 48.75 (*3-8055-6597-6*) S Karger.
***Rye, Terry L.** Creative Wedding Florals You Can Make. (Illus.). 128p. 2000. pap. 19.99 (*1-55870-560-0*, Betrwy Bks) F & W Pubns Inc.
— Creative Wedding Keepsakes You Can Make. (Illus.). 128p. 2001. pap. 19.99 (*1-55870-559-7*, Betrwy Bks) F & W Pubns Inc.
Rye, W. A. Glossary of Words Used in East Anglia: Founded on That of Forby. (English Dialect Society Publications: No. 75). 1969. reprint ed. pap. 30.00 (*0-8115-0493-X*) Periodicals Srv.
Rye, William B., ed. England As Seen by Foreigners in the Days of Elizabeth & James the First. LC 66-12288. 1972. reprint ed. 215.45 (*0-405-08903-1*) Ayer.
Ryecart, Guy, jt. auth. see Attwood, David.
R'Yehoshua Leib Diskin. Tales of the Heavenly City. 112p. 1992. pap. 6.95 (*1-56062-133-8*) CIS Comm.
Ryely, Robert M., ed. see Fearing, Kenneth.
Ryen, Dag. Traces: The Story of Lexington's Past. (Illus.). 177p. (J). (gr. 4 up). 1987. text 13.95 (*0-912839-08-2*) Lexington-Fayette.
Ryen, Dag, et al. The ABCs of World Trade: A Handbook for State Officials on International Trade & Export Promotion. LC 98-189096. 46 p. 1997. write for info. (*0-87292-934-5*) Coun State Govts.
Ryer. Dynamis. Rohou, ed. (Exeter French Texts Ser.: Vol. 82). (FRE.). 108p. Date not set. pap. text 19.95 (*0-85989-376-6*, Pub. by Univ Exeter Pr) Northwestern U Pr.
Ryer, Du, see Du Ryer.
***Ryer, Francine.** Feelings. 1999. pap. write for info. (*1-58235-234-8*) Watermrk Pr.
Ryer, Jeanne C. Healthnet: Your Essential Resource for the Most Up-to-Date Medical Information Online. LC 96-9503. 240p. 1997. pap. 16.95 (*0-471-13769-3*) Wiley.
Ryer, Jeanne C. & LaQuey, Tracy L. The Internet Companion Plus. LC 93-35647. 208p. 1993. pap. text 19.95 (*0-201-62719-1*) Addison-Wesley.
Ryer, John. A Husband's Guide to Quilt Appreciation. LC 98-103175. (Illus.). 32p. 1997. 15.95 (*0-9658286-1-1*) Calico.
Ryerson, A. E. Loyalists of America & Their Times, 1620-1816, 2 Vols. LC 68-31273. (American History & Americana Ser.: No. 47). 1969. reprint ed. lib. bdg. 150.00 (*0-8383-0195-9*) M S G Haskell Hse.
Ryerson, Edward. Dailies System Manual: How to Fix Your Head to Make It in the 21st Century. 130p. 1994. pap. 7.95 (*0-9638570-1-0*) Pali Pubng.
Ryerson, Florence & Clements, Colin. First Person Singular. 110p. 1937. 5.00 (*0-573-60066-X*) French.
Ryerson, Florence, jt. auth. see Clements, Colin.
Ryerson, Margery A., ed. see Henri, Robert.
***Ryerson, Marilyn.** Revelations from Heaven's Doorway. 2000. pap. 10.97 (*1-883906-40-7*) Kingdom Prods.
Ryerson, Marilyn. The Years the Locusts Have Eaten. (Illus.). 80p. (Orig.). 1997. pap. 18.95 (*0-9658025-0-7*) TRIAGE Inc.
Ryerson, Richard A., et al, eds. Adams Family Correspondence, Vols. 5 & 6: October 1782-December 1785, Vol. 5. (Adams Papers: No. 2). (Illus.). 960p. 1992. text 114.50 (*0-674-00406-X*) HUP.
Ryerson, Susan & Levit, Kathryn. Movement Disorders: A Contemporary Model for Stroke Rehabilitation. LC 96-48529. 1996. text 90.00 (*0-443-08913-2*) Church.
***Ryersson, Scot D. & Yaccarino, Michael Orlando.** Infinite Variety: The Life & Legend of the Marchesa Casati. LC 99-70826. (Illus.). 256p. 1999. 27.95 (*0-9670527-2-6*) Viridian Bks.
***Ryf.** Range of Motio-AO ASIF Neutral-O Method. (Illus.). 264p. 2000. pap. 49.00 incl. cd-rom (*0-86577-824-8*) Thieme Med Pubs.
Ryf, Robert S. Henry Green. LC 67-27360. (Columbia Essays on Modern Writers Ser.: No. 29). 1967. pap. text 12.00 (*0-231-02897-0*) Col U Pr.
— Joseph Conrad. LC 74-110599. (Essays on Modern Writers Ser.: No. 49). (Orig.). 1970. pap. text 12.00 (*0-231-03264-1*) Col U Pr.
Ryfa, Juras T. The Problem of Genre & the Quest for Justice in Cheknov's "The Island of Sakhalin" LC 98-52446. (Studies in Slavic Language & Literature Ser.: Vol. 13). 252p. 1999. text 89.95 (*0-7734-8172-9*) E Mellen.
***Ryfa, Juras T., ed.** Collected Essays in Honor of the Bicentennial of Alexander Pushkin's Birth. LC 99-88985. (Slavic Studies: Vol. 4). 288p. 2000. text 89.95 (*0-7734-7785-3*) E Mellen.
Ryff, Carol D. & Marshall, Victor W., eds. The Self & Society in Aging Processes. LC 99-25933. (Illus.). 504p. 1999. text 52.95 (*0-8261-1267-6*) Springer Pub.
Ryff, Carol D. & Seltzer, Marsha M., eds. The Parental Experience in Midlife. LC 96-12012. (Illus.). 688p. 1996. 39.95 (*0-226-73251-7*) U Ch Pr.
Ryff, Peter F. Electric Machinery. 2nd ed. LC 93-44578. 320p. (C). 1994. text 61.60 (*0-13-475625-8*) P-H.
Ryff, Peter F., et al. Electrical Machines & Transformers: Principles & Applications. (Illus.). 480p. 1987. text 34.95 (*0-685-14917-X*) P-H.
Ryff, Walther H., jt. auth. see Rivius, Gualtherus H.
Ryffel, Bernhard, et al, eds. International Review of Experimental Pathology: Cytokine-Induced Pathology, Inflammatory Cytokines, Receptors, & Disease, Vol. 34, Pt. B. (Illus.). 232p. (C). 1993. text 94.00 (*0-12-364935-8*) Acad Pr.
— International Review of Experimental Pathology Vol. 34, Pt. A: Cytokine-Induced Pathology, Interleukins & Hemopoietic Growth Factors. (Illus.). 252p. (C). 1993. text 94.00 (*0-12-364934-X*) Acad Pr.
Ryffel, Heinrich. Wandel der Staatsverfassungen. LC 72-7904. (Greek History Ser.). (GER.). 1973. reprint ed. 25.95 (*0-405-04800-9*) Ayer.
Ryffel, Henry H., jt. auth. see Jones, Franklin.
Ryffel, Henry H., jt. auth. see Norton, Holbrook.
Ryfle, Steve. Japan's Favorite Mon-Star: The Unauthorized Biography of the Big "G" (Illus.). 300p. 1998. pap. 16.95 (*1-55022-348-8*, Pub. by ECW) LPC InBook.
Ryga & Gregory. The Athabasca Ryga. LC 90-189505. (NFS Canada Ser.). 224p. 1990. pap. 14.95 (*0-88922-276-2*, Pub. by Talonbks) Genl Dist Srvs.
Ryga, George. Ballad of a Stonepicker. LC 77-369514. 144p. 1976. pap. 6.95 (*0-88922-110-3*, Pub. by Talonbks) Genl Dist Srvs.
— The Ecstasy of Rita Joe. 128p. (Orig.). 1970. pap. 11.95 (*0-88922-000-X*, Pub. by Talonbks) Genl Dist Srvs.
— Hungry Hills. LC 78-5493. 168p. 1974. reprint ed. pap. 6.95 (*0-88922-134-0*, Pub. by Talonbks) Genl Dist Srvs.
— Night Desk. 128p. reprint ed. pap. 6.95 (*0-88922-089-1*, Pub. by Talonbks) Genl Dist Srvs.
Ryga, George. Ploughmen of the Glacier. 80p. 1977. pap. 9.95 (*0-88922-118-9*, Pub. by Talonbks) Genl Dist Srvs.

An Asterisk (*) at the beginning of an entry indicates that the title is appearing for the first time.

R

Ryga, George. Seven Hours to Sundown. 112p. 1977. per. 11.95 (*0-88922-124-3*, Pub. by Talonbks) Genl Dist Srvs.

Ryga, George & Kujundzic, eds. Summerland. LC 93-136820. 448p. 1992. pap. 26.95 (*0-88922-313-0*, Pub. by Talonbks) Genl Dist Srvs.

Rygaard, J. & Spang-Thomsen, M., eds. Immune-Deficient Animals in Biomedical Research. (Illus.). xvi, 420p. 1987. 232.25 (*3-8055-4385-9*) S Karger.

Rygelski, Jim, jt. auth. see Castle, George.

***Rygg, Kristin.** Masqued Mysteries Unmasked: Early Modern Music Theater & Its Pythagorean Subtext. LC 00-23699. (Interplay Ser.). 2000. write for info. (*1-57647-035-0*) Pendragon NY.

Rygg, Pernille. The Butterfly Effect. 256p. 1998. 26.00 (*1-86046-311-8*) Harvill Press.

— The Butterfly Effect. Tate, Joan, tr. from NOR. 256p. 1998. pap. 11.00 (*1-86046-433-5*) Harvill Press.

Rygh, George T., tr. see Rosenius, Carl O.

Rygiel, Mary A. Shakespeare among School Children: Approaches for the Secondary Classroom. 135p. 1992. pap. 11.95 (*0-8141-4381-4*) NCTE.

Rygle, Kathy J. & Pedersen, Stephen F. Northeast Treasure Hunter's Gem & Mineral Guide: Where & How to Dig, Pan & Mine Your Own Gems & Minerals. LC 99-39215. (Illus.). 1999. pap. 14.95 (*0-943763-27-4*) GemStone Pr.

— Northwest Treasure Hunter's Gem & Mineral Guide: Where & How to Dig, Pan & Mine Your Own Gems & Minerals. LC 99-39215. (Illus.). 176p. 1999. pap. 14.95 (*0-943763-24-X*) GemStone Pr.

— Southeast Treasure Hunter's Gem & Mineral Guide: Where & How to Dig, Pan & Mine Your Own Gems & Minerals. LC 99-39215. (Illus.). 192p. 1999. pap. 14.95 (*0-943763-26-6*) GemStone Pr.

— Southwest Treasure Hunter's Gem & Mineral Guide: Where & How to Dig, Pan & Mine Your Own Gems & Minerals. LC 99-39215. (Illus.). 208p. 1999. pap. 14.95 (*0-943763-25-8*) GemStone Pr.

Ryglewicz, Hilary & Pepper, Bert. Lives at Risk. 256p. 1996. 29.95 (*0-684-82807-3*) Free Pr.

Ryglewicz, Hilary, jt. auth. see Pepper, Bert.

Ryglewicz, Hilary, jt. ed. see Pepper, Bert.

Rygmyr, David, jt. auth. see Halvorson, Michael.

Ryhn, Douglas & Reed, David, eds. Twenty-Seventh Street Storefronts. (Publications in Architecture & Urban Planning: No. R89-5). (Illus.). iii, 52p. (C). 1989. 3.00 (*0-938744-68-2*) U of Wis Ctr Arch-Urban.

Ryholt, K. S. B. & Bulow-Jacobsen, Adam. The Political Situation in Egypt During the Second Intermediate Period, C. 1800-1550 B.C. LC 98-198517. (CNI Publications). xiv, 463 p. 1997. write for info. (*87-7289-421-0*) Mus Tusculanum.

***Ryholt, Kim.** The Story of Petese Son of Petetum Seventy Other Good & Bad Stories (P. Petese) (Carlsberg Papyri Ser.: Vol. 4). (Illus.). 130p. 1999. 52.00 (*87-7289-527-6*, Pub. by Mus Tusculanum) Intl Spec Bk.

Rykalin, N., et al. Laser Machining & Welding. (Illus.). 1978. 147.00 (*0-08-022724-4*, Pub. by Pergamon Repr) Franklin.

Ryken, Leland. How to Read the Bible as Literature. 200p. (Orig.). (C). 1984. pap. 16.99 (*0-310-39021-4*, 11158P) Zondervan.

— The Liberated Imagination: Thinking Christianly about the Arts. (Wheaton Literary Ser.). 283p. 1989. pap. 12.99 (*0-87788-495-1*, H Shaw Pubs) Waterbrook Pr.

— Realms of Gold: The Classics in Christian Perspective. (Wheaton Literary Ser.). 240p. (Orig.). (C). 1991. pap. 14.99 (*0-87788-717-9*, H Shaw Pubs) Waterbrook Pr.

— Redeeming the Time: A Christian Approach to Work & Leisure. LC 95-18568. 304p. 1995. pap. 17.99 (*0-8010-5169-X*) Baker Bks.

— Windows to the World: Literature in Christian Perspective. 176p. 1985. pap. 11.95 (*0-310-32451-3*, 11059P) Zondervan.

***Ryken, Leland.** Windows to the World: Literature in Christian Perspective. 192p. 2000. pap. 20.00 (*1-57910-340-5*) Wipf & Stock.

Ryken, Leland. Wordly Saints: The Puritans As They Really Were. 272p. 1986. 18.95 (*0-310-32500-5*, 11070) Zondervan.

— Words of Delight: A Literary Introduction to the Bible. 2nd ed. LC 92-42603. 546p. (gr. 10). 1993. pap. 29.99 (*0-8010-7769-9*) Baker Bks.

Ryken, Leland, et al, eds. Dictionary of Biblical Imagery. LC 98-16945. 1072p. 1998. 39.99 (*0-8308-1451-5*, 1451) InterVarsity.

Ryken, Leland & Longman, Tremper, III, eds. A Complete Literary Guide to the Bible. 592p. 1993. 32.99 (*0-310-51830-X*) Zondervan.

Ryken, Leland, jt. auth. see Wilhoit, Jim.

Ryken, Leland, jt. ed. see Walhout, Clarence.

Ryken, Philip G. Courage to Stand: Jeremiah's Battle Plan for Pagan Times. LC 98-18646. 176p. 1998. pap. 10.99 (*1-58134-012-5*) Crossway Bks.

— Discovering God in Stories from the Bible. LC 99-31124. 176p. 1999. pap. 10.99 (*1-58134-113-X*) Crossway Bks.

Ryken, Philip G. & Boice, James M. The Heart of the Cross. LC 98-47905. 192p. 1999. 14.99 (*1-58134-039-7*) Crossway Bks.

***Ryken, Philip Graham.** Is Jesus the Only Way? LC 99-36909. (Today's Issues Ser.). 48p. 1999. pap. 4.99 (*1-58134-119-9*) Crossway Bks.

— Jeremiah & Lamentations: From Sorrow to Hope. (Preaching the Word Ser.). 880p. 2000. 34.99 (*1-58134-167-9*) Crossway Bks.

— When You Pray: Making the Lord's Prayer Your Own. 208p. 2000. pap. 12.99 (*1-58134-194-6*) Crossway Bks.

***Ryken, Philip Oraham.** Thomas Boston as Preacher of the Four Fold State. (Rutherford Studies in Historical Theology). 357p. 1999. pap. 9.99 (*0-946068-72-0*, Pub. by Rutherford Hse) OM Literature.

Ryker, Breck, jt. auth. see Whitener, Angela.

Ryker, Lori, ed. Mockbee Coker: Thought & Process. (Illus.). 128p. (Orig.). 1995. pap. 27.95 (*1-56898-042-6*) Princeton Arch.

Rykert, Liz, jt. auth. see James, Maureen.

Rykken, Jessica J., jt. auth. see Hanson, Trish.

Rykov, Vladimir V., jt. auth. see Kitaev, Mikhail U.

Rykovich, Robert. Diagnosis Cancer: A Prescription for Creating Your Own Life-Saving Miracle, 1. 2000. pap. 17.95 (*1-58501-006-5*) CeShore Pubg.

***Ryks, Tracy.** God Loves You Today! (Illus.). 28p. (J). (ps-3). 2000. pap. 9.95 (*0-9677367-0-6*) Devoted to You Bks.

***Rykunov, L.** The 1996 Eruptions in the Karynsky Volcanic Centre & Related Events. 120p. 1998. pap. text 112.00 (*90-5699-197-3*, Harwood Acad Pubs) Gordon & Breach.

Rykwert, Joseph. The Dancing Column: On Order in Architecture. (Illus.). 616p. 1998. reprint ed. pap. text 40.00 (*0-262-68101-3*) MIT Pr.

— The Dancing Column: On Order of Architecture. LC 95-35555. (Illus.). 616p. 1996. 80.00 (*0-262-18170-3*) MIT Pr.

— The Idea of a Town: An Anthropology of Urban Form in Rome, Italy & the Ancient World. 2nd ed. (Illus.). 242p. 1988. reprint ed. pap. text 22.00 (*0-262-68056-4*) MIT Pr.

— On Adam's House in Paradise: The Idea of the Primitive Hut in Architectural History. 2nd ed. (Illus.). 240p. (C). 1981. reprint ed. pap. text 17.50 (*0-262-68036-X*) MIT Pr.

***Rykwert, Joseph.** Palladian Ideal. (Illus.). 228p. 2000. 85.00 (*0-8478-2158-7*, Pub. by Rizzoli Intl) St Martin.

Rykwert, Joseph. Seduction of Place: The City in the Twenty-First Century & Beyond. (Illus.). 320p. 2000. 27.50 (*0-375-40048-6*) Pantheon.

***Rykwert, Joseph.** The Villa: From Ancient to Modern. (Illus.). 224p. 2000. 60.00 (*0-8109-3944-4*, Pub. by Abrams) Time Warner.

Rykwert, Joseph, compiled by. Richard Meier, Architect. LC 83-42911. (Illus.). 412p. 1990. 65.00 (*0-8478-0496-8*, Pub. by Rizzoli Intl) St Martin.

— Richard Meier, Architect. LC 83-42911. (Illus.). 412p. 1991. pap. 49.50 (*0-8478-0497-6*, Pub. by Rizzoli Intl) St Martin.

Rykwert, Joseph, jt. contrib. by see Frampton, Kenneth.

Rykwert, Joseph, tr. see Alberti, Leon Battista.

Rylaarsdam, J. Coert, ed. see Habel, Norman C.

Rylaarsdam, J. Coert, ed. see Tucker, Gene M.

Rylaarsdam, John C. Revelation in Jewish Wisdom Literature. LC BS1455.R9. (Midway Reprint Ser.). 140p. reprint ed. pap. 43.40 (*0-608-12600-4*, 202406500035) Bks Demand.

Rylah, Lindsey T., ed. Critical Care of the Burned Patient. (Illus.). 222p. (C). 1992. text 74.95 (*0-521-39495-3*) Cambridge U Pr.

Rylance, Dan, jt. auth. see Fritz, Chester.

***Rylance, Rick.** Victorian Psychology & British Culture 1850-1880. (Illus.). 368p. 2000. text 74.00 (*0-19-812283-7*) OUP.

Rylance, Rick, ed. Debating Texts: Readings in 20th Century Literary Theory & Method. 310p. 1987. text 35.00 (*0-8020-5768-3*) U of Toronto Pr.

Rylance, Rick W., ed. Debating Texts: A Reader in Twentieth-Century Literary Theory & Method. 304p. 1987. 37.50 (*0-335-09006-0*) OpUniv Pr.

— Debating Texts: A Reader in Twentieth-Century Literary Theory & Method. 304p. 1987. pap. 10.99 (*0-335-09005-2*) OpUniv Pr.

Ryland, Cynthia. Scarecrow. LC 96-7652. (Illus.). 40p. (J). (ps-2). 1998. 16.00 (*0-15-201084-X*) Harcourt.

— The Van Gogh Cafe. 64p. (J). (gr. 3-7). 1998. pap. 3.99 (*0-590-90717-4*) Scholastic Inc.

Ryland, G. J. & Menz, Kenneth M., eds. Bulk Handling of Paddy & Rice in Malaysia: An Economic Analysis. 1989. pap. 44.00 (*0-949511-86-2*, Pub. by ACIAR) St Mut.

Ryland, John S., jt. ed. see Hayward, Peter J.

***Ryland, Philip, ed.** Pocket Investor. LC 98-40637. (Economist Ser.). 215p. 1998. pap. 14.95 (*0-471-29597-3*) Wiley.

Ryland, Stephen. Deep Treasure & Cache Location with the Fisher Gemini-3. 64p. 1993. 7.00 (*1-883170-04-4*) FRL.

Rylander, Edith. Dancing Back the Cranes. 80p. 1993. pap. 9.95 (*0-87839-084-7*) North Star.

— Rural Routes: Essays on Living in Rural Minnesota. LC 93-4854. 1993. pap. 9.95 (*0-87839-079-0*) North Star.

Rylander, Kristina, ed. Att Studera Afrika: En Litteraturvagledning. 110p. 1995. write for info. (*91-7106-367-6*, Pub. by Nordic Africa) Transaction Pubs.

Rylander, Michael K., jt. auth. see Bolen, Eric G.

Rylander, Paul N., ed. Hydrogenation Methods. (Best Synthetic Methods Ser.). 193p. 1990. reprint ed. spiral bd. 65.00 (*0-12-605366-9*) Acad Pr.

Rylander, Paul N., et al, eds. Catalysis of Organic Reactions. LC 87-36855. (Chemical Industries Ser.: Vol. 33). (Illus.). 461p. reprint ed. pap. 143.00 (*0-608-08589-8*, 206911200002) Bks Demand.

Rylander, Ranner. Organic Dusts: Exposure, Effects, & Prevention. 320p. 1994. lib. bdg. 99.95 (*0-87371-699-X*, L699) Lewis Pubs.

Rylands, Anthony B. The Status of Conservation Areas in the Brazilian Amazon. LC 92-232849. 156p. (Orig.). 1991. pap. 48.40 (*0-608-04963-8*, 206554200004) Bks Demand.

Rylands, Ljiljana. Some of Us. (Dinosaur Ser.). (Illus.). (J). 1985. pap. 2.95 (*0-85122-744-9*) Parkwest Pubns.

Rylands, Philip. Palma Vecchio. (Studies in the History of Art). (Illus.). 402p. (C). 1992. text 139.95 (*0-521-37332-8*) Cambridge U Pr.

— Stuart Davis. (Illus.). 207p. 1998. 40.00 (*0-8212-2517-0*, Pub. by Bulfinch Pr) Little.

Rylant, Cynthia. All I See. LC 88-42547. (Illus.). 32p. (J). (gr. k-2). 1988. 17.95 (*0-531-05777-1*) Orchard Bks Watts.

— All I See. LC 88-42547. (Illus.). 32p. (J). (gr. k-2). 1994. pap. 6.95 (*0-531-07048-4*) Orchard Bks Watts.

— All I See. 1988. 12.15 (*0-606-08686-2*, Pub. by Turtleback) Demco.

— An Angel for Solomon Singer. LC 91-15957. (Illus.). 32p. (J). 1996. pap. 6.95 (*0-531-07082-4*) Orchard Bks Watts.

Rylant, Cynthia. An Angel for Solomon Singer. (J). 1996. 11.15 (*0-606-10741-X*, Pub. by Turtleback) Demco.

Rylant, Cynthia. Appalachia: The Voices of Sleeping Birds. LC 90-36798. (Illus.). 32p. (J). (ps up). 1991. 17.00 (*0-15-201605-8*) Harcourt.

— Appalachia: The Voices of Sleeping Birds. LC 90-36798. (Illus.). 32p. (J). 1998. pap. 6.00 (*0-15-201893-X*) Harcourt.

— Appalachia: The Voices of Sleeping Birds. 1998. 11.20 (*0-606-13146-9*, Pub. by Turtleback) Demco.

— Bear Day. LC 96-40090. (Illus.). 23p. (C). (ps-1). 1998. 12.00 (*0-15-201090-4*) Harcourt.

— Best Wishes. LC 92-7796. (Meet the Author Ser.). (Illus.). 32p. (J). (gr. 2-5). 1992. 14.95 (*1-878450-20-4*, 702) R Owen Pubs.

— The Bird House. LC 97-25415. (Illus.). 32p. (J). (gr. 1-4). 1998. 15.95 (*0-590-47345-X*, Pub. by Scholastic Inc) Penguin Putnam.

— Birthday Presents. LC 87-5485. (Illus.). 32p. (J). (ps-1). 1991. pap. 5.95 (*0-531-07026-3*) Orchard Bks Watts.

Rylant, Cynthia. Birthday Presents. LC 87-5485. 1987. 11.15 (*0-606-09079-7*, Pub. by Turtleback) Demco.

Rylant, Cynthia. Bless Us All: A Child's Yearbook of Blessings. LC 98-4395. (Illus.). 32p. (J). 1998. per. 14.00 (*0-689-82370-3*) S&S Childrens.

— A Blue-Eyed Daisy. LC 84-21554. 112p. (J). (gr. 5-7). 1985. lib. bdg. 15.00 (*0-02-777960-2*, Bradbury S&S) S&S Childrens.

— The Blue Hill Meadows. LC 95-52260. (Illus.). 48p. (J). (gr. 3-5). 1997. 16.00 (*0-15-201404-7*) Harcourt.

— The Blue Hill Meadows & the Much-Loved Dog. LC 93-40538. (Illus.). (J). (gr. 3-7). 1994. 14.95 (*0-15-253155-6*) Harcourt.

— The Bookshop Dog. LC 95-26169. (Illus.). 40p. (J). (ps-3). 1996. 14.95 (*0-590-54331-8*, Blue Sky Press) Scholastic Inc.

— Bunny Bungalow. LC 97-43707. (Illus.). 32p. (J). (ps-1). 1999. 13.00 (*0-15-201092-0*) Harcourt.

Rylant, Cynthia. But I'll Be Back Again. LC 93-16188. (Illus.). 80p. (YA). (gr. 7 up). 1993. mass mkt. 6.95 (*0-688-12653-7*, Wm Morrow) Morrow Avon.

Rylant, Cynthia. But I'll Be Back Again. (J). 1993. 10.15 (*0-606-05774-9*, Pub. by Turtleback) Demco.

— Cat Heaven. LC 96-49501. (Illus.). 40p. (J). 1997. 15.95 (*0-590-10054-8*) Scholastic Inc.

— Children of Christmas: Stories for the Season. LC 87-1690. (Illus.). 48p. (J). (gr. 3 up). 1993. pap. 6.95 (*0-531-07042-5*) Orchard Bks Watts.

— Children of Christmas: Stories for the Season. (J). 1993. 11.15 (*0-606-05785-4*, Pub. by Turtleback) Demco.

— The Cobble Street Cousins. (J). 2000. mass mkt. 4.50 (*0-689-81712-6*) S&S Childrens.

***Rylant, Cynthia.** The Cobble Street Cousins: A Little Shopping. LC 97-20996. (Cobble Street Cousins Ser.). (Illus.). 64p. (J). (gr. k-5). 1998. per. 14.00 (*0-689-81710-X*) S&S Childrens.

Rylant, Cynthia. The Cobble Street Cousins: In Aunt Lucy's Kitchen. LC 97-20995. (Cobble Street Cousins Ser.). (Illus.). 54p. (J). (gr. k-5). 1998. per. 14.00 (*0-689-81711-8*) S&S Childrens.

— The Cobble Street Cousins Book 3: Special Gifts. LC 98-19563. (Illus.). 64p. (J). (gr. 2-5). 1999. per. 15.00 (*0-689-81714-2*) S&S Childrens.

— The Cobble Street Cousins Book 4: Some Good News. LC 98-19568. (Illus.). 64p. (J). (gr. 2-5). 1999. per. 15.00 (*0-689-81715-0*) S&S Childrens.

— The Cookie-Store Cat. LC 98-5714. 40p. (J). (ps-3). 1999. 15.95 (*0-590-54329-6*, Blue Sky Press) Scholastic Inc.

— A Couple of Kooks: And Other Stories about Love. LC 90-30646. 112p. (J). (gr. 7 up). 1990. 16.95 (*0-531-05900-6*) Orchard Bks Watts.

— Dog Heaven. LC 94-40950. (Illus.). 32p. (J). (ps-3). 1995. 14.95 (*0-590-41701-0*, Blue Sky Press) Scholastic Inc.

— Every Living Thing. LC 88-19359. (Illus.). 96p. (YA). (gr. 5 up). 1988. mass mkt. 3.95 (*0-689-71263-4*) Aladdin.

— Every Living Thing. LC 85-7701. (Illus.). 96p. (J). (gr. 5-7). 1985. lib. bdg. 14.00 (*0-02-777200-4*, Bradbury S&S) S&S Childrens.

Rylant, Cynthia. Every Living Thing. (J). 1985. 9.05 (*0-606-03780-2*, Pub. by Turtleback) Demco.

Rylant, Cynthia. An Everyday Book. (J). (ps-k). 1997. bds. 12.95 (*0-614-29058-9*) S&S Childrens.

— An Everyday Book. LC 96-68858. (Illus.). 32p. (J). (ps up). 1997. per. 12.95 (*0-689-81255-8*) S&S Childrens.

— The Everyday Books: Everyday Children. LC 92-40932. (Everyday Bks.). (Illus.). 14p. (J). (ps-k). 1993. mass mkt. 4.95 (*0-02-778022-8*, Bradbury S&S) S&S Childrens.

— The Everyday Books: Everyday Garden. LC 92-40542. (Everyday Bks.). (Illus.). 14p. (J). (ps-k). 1993. mass mkt. 4.95 (*0-02-778023-6*, Bradbury S&S) S&S Childrens.

— The Everyday Books: Everyday House. LC 92-40943. (Everyday Bks.). (Illus.). 14p. (J). (ps-k). 1993. mass mkt. 4.95 (*0-02-778024-4*, Bradbury S&S) S&S Childrens.

— The Everyday Books: Everyday Pets. LC 92-40934. (Everyday Bks.). (Illus.). 14p. (J). (ps-k). 1993. mass mkt. 4.95 (*0-02-778025-2*, Bradbury S&S) S&S Childrens.

— The Everyday Books: Everyday Town. LC 92-40541. (Everyday Bks.). (Illus.). 14p. (J). (ps-k). 1993. bds. 4.95 (*0-02-788026-5*, Bradbury S&S) S&S Childrens.

— Everyday Town. LC 92-40541. (Everyday Bks.). (Illus.). 14p. (J). (ps-k). 1993. mass mkt. 4.95 (*0-02-778026-0*, Bradbury S&S) S&S Childrens.

— A Fine White Dust. LC 86-1003. (J). (gr. 6-8). 1996. pap. 3.95 (*0-689-80462-8*) Aladdin.

— A Fine White Dust. LC 86-1003. 120p. (J). (gr. 6-8). 1986. lib. bdg. 16.00 (*0-02-777240-3*, Bradbury S&S) S&S Childrens.

— A Fine White Dust. (J). 1998. per. 2.65 (*0-689-82166-2*) S&S Childrens.

— A Fine White Dust. LC 86-1003. 1996. 9.05 (*0-606-09274-9*, Pub. by Turtleback) Demco.

***Rylant, Cynthia.** Fine White Dust. (Illus.). 2000. per. 16.00 (*0-689-84087-X*) S&S Childrens.

Rylant, Cynthia. Give Me Grace: A Child's Daybook of Prayers. LC 98-49368. (Illus.). 32p. (J). (ps-3). 1999. per. 12.00 (*0-689-82293-6*) S&S Bks Yung.

— Gooseberry Park. LC 94-11578. (Illus.). 112p. (J). (gr. 3-7). 1995. 15.00 (*0-15-232242-6*, Harcourt Child Bks) Harcourt.

— Gooseberry Park. (Illus.). 133p. (J). (gr. 3-7). 1998. pap. 3.99 (*0-590-94715-X*) Scholastic Inc.

***Rylant, Cynthia.** Gooseberry Park. (Apple Signature Edition Ser.). (Illus.). (J). 1999. 9.09 (*0-606-15554-6*) Turtleback.

— The Heavenly Village: A Novel. LC 98-48063. 96p. (J). (gr. 5-9). 1999. 15.95 (*0-439-04096-5*, Pub. by Scholastic Inc) Penguin Putnam.

Rylant, Cynthia. Henry & Mudge: The First Book of Their Adventures. (Henry & Mudge Ser.). (J). (gr. k-3). 1990. pap. 9.48 (*0-395-55143-9*) HM.

— Henry & Mudge: The First Book of Their Adventures. (Henry & Mudge Ser.). (J). (gr. k-3). 1992. pap. 9.48 (*0-395-61769-3*) HM.

— Henry & Mudge: The First Book of Their Adventures. (Henry & Mudge Ser.). (J). (gr. k-3). 1992. 79.80 (*0-689-71659-1*) S&S Trade.

— Henry & Mudge: The First Book of Their Adventures. (Henry & Mudge Ser.). (Illus.). 40p. (J). (gr. 1-4). 1996. per. 14.00 (*0-689-81004-0*) S&S Trade.

— Henry & Mudge: The First Book of Their Adventures. (Henry & Mudge Ser.). (J). (gr. k-3). 1990. 9.19 (*0-606-03444-7*, Pub. by Turtleback) Demco.

— Henry & Mudge & a Very Merry Christmas. LC 98-20940. (Henry & Mudge Ser.). (J). (gr. k-3). 2000. 14.00 (*0-689-81168-3*) S&S Childrens.

***Rylant, Cynthia.** Henry & Mudge & Annie's Good Move. (Henry & Mudge Ser.). 48p. (J). (gr. k-3). 2000. per. 3.99 (*0-689-83284-2*) Aladdin.

— Henry & Mudge & Annie's Good Move. LC 97-2723. (Henry & Mudge Ser.). (Illus.). 40p. (J). (gr. k-3). 1998. 14.00 (*0-689-81174-8*) S&S Childrens.

Rylant, Cynthia. Henry & Mudge & Annie's Perfect Pet. LC 98-20017. (Henry & Mudge Ser.). 48p. (J). (gr. k-3). 2000. 15.00 (*0-689-81177-2*) S&S Childrens.

— Henry & Mudge & Mrs. Hopper's House. (Henry & Mudge Ser.). (J). (gr. k-3). Date not set. 12.95 (*0-689-81320-1*) S&S Childrens.

— Henry & Mudge & Mrs. Hopper's House. LC 98-20937. (Henry & Mudge Ser.). (J). (gr. k-3). 2001. 14.00 (*0-689-81153-5*) S&S Childrens.

— Henry & Mudge & the Bedtime Thumps. (Henry & Mudge Ser.). (Illus.). 40p. (J). (gr. k-3). 1996. per. 3.99 (*0-689-80162-9*) Aladdin.

— Henry & Mudge & the Bedtime Thumps. (Henry & Mudge Ser.). (Illus.). 40p. (J). (gr. k-3). 1996. per. 14.00 (*0-689-81011-3*) S&S Childrens.

— Henry & Mudge & the Bedtime Thumps. LC 89-49529. (Henry & Mudge Ser.). (J). (gr. k-3). 1996. 9.19 (*0-606-09403-2*, Pub. by Turtleback) Demco.

— Henry & Mudge & the Best Day of All. (Henry & Mudge Ser.). (Illus.). 40p. (J). (gr. k-3). 1997. per. 5.99 (*0-689-81469-0*) Aladdin.

— Henry & Mudge & the Best Day of All. (Henry & Mudge Ser.). (Illus.). 40p. (J). (gr. k-3). 1997. per. 3.99 (*0-689-81385-6*) S&S Childrens.

— Henry & Mudge & the Best Day of All. (Henry & Mudge Ser.). (Illus.). 40p. (J). (gr. k-3). 1996. 14.00 (*0-689-81006-7*) S&S Trade.

— Henry & Mudge & the Best Day of All. (Henry & Mudge Ser.). (J). (gr. k-3). 1997. 9.19 (*0-606-12723-2*, Pub. by Turtleback) Demco.

Rylant, Cynthia. Henry & Mudge & the Best Day of All. unabridged ed. (Henry & Mudge Ser.). (J). (gr. k-3). 1997. boxed set 22.24 incl. audio (*0-7887-1820-7*, 40600) Recorded Bks.

— Henry & Mudge & the Big Sleep Over. LC 98-20935. (Henry & Mudge Ser.). (J). (gr. k-3). 2001. 14.00 (*0-689-81171-3*) S&S Childrens.

Rylant, Cynthia. Henry & Mudge & the Careful Cousin. LC 92-12851. (Henry & Mudge Ser.). (Illus.). 48p. (J). (gr. k-3). 1997. per. 3.99 (*0-689-81386-4*) Aladdin.

— Henry & Mudge & the Careful Cousin. LC 92-12851. (Henry & Mudge Ser.). (Illus.). 48p. (J). (gr. k-3). 1994. text 14.00 (*0-02-778021-X*, Bradbury S&S) S&S Childrens.

— Henry & Mudge & the Careful Cousin. (Henry & Mudge Ser.). (Illus.). 48p. (J). (gr. k-3). 1999. per. 15.00 (*0-689-81007-5*) S&S Trade.

An Asterisk (*) at the beginning of an entry indicates that the title is appearing for the first time.

— Henry & Mudge & the Careful Cousin. (Henry & Mudge Ser.). (J). (gr. k-3). 1997. 9.19 (*0-606-11456-4*, Pub. by Turtleback) Demco.

***Rylant, Cynthia.** Henry & Mudge & the Careful Cousin. unabridged ed. (Henry & Mudge Ser.). (J). (gr. k-3). 1999. 24.95 incl. audio (*0-87499-529-9*); pap. 15.95 incl. audio (*0-87499-528-0*) Live Oak Media.

— Henry & Mudge & the Forever Sea. (Henry & Mudge Ser.). (Illus.). 48p. (J). (gr. k-3). 1996. 14.00 (*0-689-81016-4*) S&S Trade.

Rylant, Cynthia. Henry & Mudge & the Forever Sea. (Henry & Mudge Ser.). (Illus.). 48p. (J). (gr. k-3). 1997. per. 3.99 (*0-689-81017-2*) S&S Trade.

— Henry & Mudge & the Forever Sea. (Henry & Mudge Ser.). (J). (gr. k-3). 1993. 9.19 (*0-606-02669-X*, Pub. by Turtleback) Demco.

— Henry & Mudge & the Forever Sea. LC 92-28646. (Henry & Mudge Ser.). (Illus.). 48p. (J). (gr. k-3). 1993. reprint ed. pap. 3.95 (*0-689-71701-6*) Aladdin.

— Henry & Mudge & the Funny Lunch. LC 98-20939. (Henry & Mudge Ser.). (J). (gr. k-3). 1999. 14.00 (*0-689-81178-0*) S&S Childrens.

***Rylant, Cynthia.** Henry & Mudge & the Great Grandpas. LC 98-18317. (Henry & Mudge Ser.). (J). (gr. k-3). 2005. 14.00 (*0-689-81170-5*) S&S Childrens.

Rylant, Cynthia. Henry & Mudge & the Happy Cat. LC 93-10797. (Henry & Mudge Ser.: Vol. 8). (Illus.). 48p. (J). (gr. 1-4). 1994. pap. 3.99 (*0-689-81013-X*) Aladdin.

— Henry & Mudge & the Happy Cat. (Henry & Mudge Ser.). (Illus.). 48p. (J). (gr. k-3). 1997. 14.00 (*0-689-81012-1*) S&S Trade.

— Henry & Mudge & the Happy Cat. (Henry & Mudge Ser.). (J). (gr. k-3). 1994. 9.19 (*0-606-05870-2*, Pub. by Turtleback) Demco.

— Henry & Mudge & the Long Weekend. LC 90-26799. (Henry & Mudge Ser.). (Illus.). 40p. (J). (gr. k-3). 1992. 13.00 (*0-02-778013-9*, Bradbury S&S) S&S Childrens.

— Henry & Mudge & the Long Weekend. (Henry & Mudge Ser.). (J). (gr. k-3). 1996. 9.19 (*0-606-10840-8*, Pub. by Turtleback) Demco.

— Henry & Mudge & the Long Weekend. rev. ed. LC 90-26799. (Henry & Mudge Ser.). (Illus.). 40p. (J). (gr. k-3). 1996. per. 3.99 (*0-689-80885-2*) S&S Childrens.

— Henry & Mudge & the Long Weekend. rev. ed. LC 90-26799. (Henry & Mudge Ser.). (Illus.). 40p. (J). (gr. 1-3). 1997. per. 14.00 (*0-689-81009-1*) S&S Childrens.

***Rylant, Cynthia.** Henry & Mudge & the Sneaky Crackers. LC 96-44986. (Henry & Mudge Ser.). (Illus.). 48p. (J). (gr. k-3). 1999. per. 3.99 (*0-689-82525-0*) Aladdin.

Rylant, Cynthia. Henry & Mudge & the Sneaky Crackers. LC 96-44986. (Henry & Mudge Ser.). 40p. (J). (gr. k-3). 1998. per. 14.00 (*0-689-81176-4*) S&S Childrens.

— Henry & Mudge & the Snowman Plan. LC 98-7042. (Henry & Mudge Ser.). (Illus.). 40p. (J). (gr. k-3). 1999. 14.00 (*0-689-81169-1*) S&S Bks Yung.

— Henry & Mudge & the Starry Night. LC 96-44443. (Henry & Mudge Ser.). (Illus.). 48p. (J). (gr. k-3). 1999. mass mkt. 3.99 (*0-689-82586-2*, 076714003996) Aladdin.

— Henry & Mudge & the Starry Night. LC 96-44443. (Henry & Mudge Ser.). (Illus.). 40p. (J). (gr. 1-3). 1998. per. 14.00 (*0-689-81175-6*) S&S Childrens.

***Rylant, Cynthia.** Henry & Mudge & the Tall Treehouse. LC 98-20938. (Henry & Mudge Ser.). (J). (gr. k-3). 2000. 14.00 (*0-689-81173-X*) S&S Childrens.

Rylant, Cynthia. Henry & Mudge & the Tumbling Trip. LC 98-20936. (Henry & Mudge Ser.). (J). (gr. k-3). 2002. 14.00 (*0-689-81180-2*) S&S Childrens.

***Rylant, Cynthia.** Henry & Mudge & the Wild Goose Chase. LC 98-7043. (Henry & Mudge Ser.). (J). (gr. k-3). 2001. 14.00 (*0-689-81172-1*) S&S Childrens.

Rylant, Cynthia. Henry & Mudge & the Wild Wind. (Henry & Mudge Ser.). (Illus.). 40p. (J). (gr. k-3). 1996. per. 3.99 (*0-689-80838-0*) Aladdin.

Rylant, Cynthia. Henry & Mudge & the Wild Wind. LC 91-12644. (Henry & Mudge Ser.). (Illus.). 40p. (J). (gr. k-3). 1993. mass mkt. 13.00 (*0-02-778014-7*, Bradbury S&S) S&S Childrens.

Rylant, Cynthia. Henry & Mudge & the Wild Wind. (Henry & Mudge Ser.). (Illus.). 40p. (J). (gr. k-3). 2000. pap. 14.00 (*0-689-81008-3*) S&S Trade.

— Henry & Mudge & the Wild Wind. (Henry & Mudge Ser.). (J). (gr. k-3). 1996. 9.19 (*0-606-09404-0*, Pub. by Turtleback) Demco.

— Henry & Mudge Get the Cold Shivers. LC 93-45588. (Henry & Mudge Ser.). (Illus.). 48p. (J). (gr. k-3). 1994. pap. 3.95 (*0-689-71849-7*) Aladdin.

— Henry & Mudge Get the Cold Shivers. LC 88-18854. (Henry & Mudge Ser.). (Illus.). 48p. (J). (gr. k-3). 1989. text 12.95 (*0-02-778011-2*, Bradbury S&S) S&S Childrens.

— Henry & Mudge Get the Cold Shivers. (Henry & Mudge Ser.). 48p. (J). (gr. k-3). 1996. per. 3.99 (*0-689-81015-6*) S&S Trade.

— Henry & Mudge Get the Cold Shivers. (Henry & Mudge Ser.). (Illus.). 48p. (J). (gr. k-3). 1996. 14.00 (*0-689-81014-8*) S&S Trade.

***Rylant, Cynthia.** Henry & Mudge in Puddle Trouble. (Henry & Mudge Ser.). (Illus.). (J). (gr. k-3). 1998. pap., teacher ed. 29.95 incl. audio (*0-87499-443-8*) Live Oak Media.

Rylant, Cynthia. Henry & Mudge in Puddle Trouble. (Henry & Mudge Ser.). (J). (gr. k-3). 1996. mass mkt. 3.99 (*0-689-81003-2*) S&S Trade.

— Henry & Mudge in Puddle Trouble. (Henry & Mudge Ser.). (Illus.). 48p. (J). (gr. k-3). 1996. 14.00 (*0-689-81002-4*) S&S Trade.

— Henry & Mudge in Puddle Trouble. (Henry & Mudge Ser.). (J). (gr. k-3). 1987. 9.19 (*0-606-03443-9*, Pub. by Turtleback) Demco.

— Henry & Mudge in Puddle Trouble. unabridged ed. (Henry & Mudge Ser.). (Illus.). (J). (gr. k-3). 1998. 24.95 incl. audio (*0-87499-442-X*); pap. 15.95 incl. audio (*0-87499-441-1*) Live Oak Media.

— Henry & Mudge in the Family Trees. LC 96-19964. (Henry & Mudge Ser.). (Illus.). 48p. (J). (gr. k-3). 1998. per. 3.99 (*0-689-82317-7*) Aladdin.

— Henry & Mudge in the Family Trees. LC 96-19964. (Henry & Mudge Ser.). (Illus.). 40p. (J). (gr. k-3). 1997. 14.00 (*0-689-81179-9*) S&S Childrens.

— Henry & Mudge in the Green Time. LC 86-26386. (Henry & Mudge Ser.). (Illus.). 48p. (J). (gr. k-3). 1987. text 12.95 (*0-02-778003-1*, Bradbury S&S) S&S Childrens.

— Henry & Mudge in the Green Time. (Henry & Mudge Ser.). 48p. (J). (gr. k-3). 1996. per. 3.99 (*0-689-81001-6*) S&S Trade.

— Henry & Mudge in the Green Time. (Henry & Mudge Ser.). (J). (gr. k-3). 1998. pap. 14.00 (*0-689-81000-8*) S&S Trade.

— Henry & Mudge in the Green Time. (Henry & Mudge Ser.). (J). (gr. k-3). 1992. 9.19 (*0-606-01591-4*, Pub. by Turtleback) Demco.

***Rylant, Cynthia.** Henry & Mudge in the Green Time. unabridged ed. (Henry & Mudge Ser.). (J). (gr. k-3). 1999. 24.95 incl. audio (*0-87499-422-5*) Live Oak Media.

Rylant, Cynthia. Henry & Mudge in the Sparkle Days. (Henry & Mudge Ser.). (Illus.). 48p. (J). (gr. k-3). 1996. 14.00 (*0-689-81018-0*) S&S Trade.

— Henry & Mudge in the Sparkle Days. LC 92-42535. (Henry & Mudge Ser.). (Illus.). 48p. (J). (gr. k-3). 1997. per. 3.99 (*0-689-81019-9*) S&S Trade.

— Henry & Mudge in the Sparkle Days. (Henry & Mudge Ser.). (J). (gr. k-3). 1993. 9.15 (*0-606-05871-0*, Pub. by Turtleback) Demco.

— Henry & Mudge Take the Big Test. (Henry & Mudge Ser.). (Illus.). 40p. (J). (gr. k-3). 1996. pap. 3.99 (*0-689-80886-0*) S&S Bks Yung.

— Henry & Mudge Take the Big Test. (Henry & Mudge Ser.). (Illus.). 40p. (J). (gr. k-3). 1997. 14.00 (*0-689-81010-5*) S&S Trade.

Rylant, Cynthia. Henry & Mudge Take the Big Test. (Henry & Mudge Ser.). (J). (gr. k-3). 1996. 9.19 (*0-606-10841-6*, Pub. by Turtleback) Demco.

Rylant, Cynthia. Henry & Mudge under the Yellow Moon. (Henry & Mudge Ser.). (Illus.). (J). (gr. k-3). 1998. pap., teacher ed. 29.95 incl. audio (*0-87499-447-0*) Live Oak Media.

— Henry & Mudge under the Yellow Moon. LC 86-26390. (Henry & Mudge Ser.). (Illus.). 48p. (J). (gr. k-3). 1987. text 12.95 (*0-02-778004-X*, Bradbury S&S) S&S Childrens.

— Henry & Mudge under the Yellow Moon. (Henry & Mudge Ser.). 48p. (J). (gr. k-3). 1996. per. 3.99 (*0-689-81021-0*) S&S Trade.

— Henry & Mudge under the Yellow Moon. (Henry & Mudge Ser.). (J). (gr. k-3). 1992. 9.19 (*0-606-01592-2*, Pub. by Turtleback) Demco.

— Henry & Mudge under the Yellow Moon. rev. ed. LC 86-26390. (Henry & Mudge Ser.). 48p. (J). (gr. k-3). 1997. lib. bdg. 14.00 (*0-689-81020-2*) S&S Childrens.

— Henry & Mudge under the Yellow Moon. unabridged ed. (Henry & Mudge Ser.). (Illus.). (J). (gr. k-3). 1998. 24.95 incl. audio (*0-87499-446-2*); pap. 15.95 incl. audio (*0-87499-445-4*) Live Oak Media.

— Henry y Mudge: El Primer Libro. Ada, Alma F., tr. (Ready-to-Read Ser.). (SPA., Illus.). (J). (gr. 1-3). 1996. 14.00 (*0-614-15780-3*) Aladdin.

— Henry y Mudge: El Primer Libro. Ada, Alma F., tr. LC 95-36439. (Ready-to-Read Ser.). (SPA., Illus.). 40p. (J). (gr. 1-3). 1996. mass mkt. 3.99 (*0-689-80684-1*) Aladdin.

— Henry Y. Mudge: El Primer Libro De Sus Aventuras. LC 95-36439. (SPA., Illus.). (J). (gr. 1-3). 1999. 13.00 (*0-689-80685-X*) Atheneum Yung Read.

— Henry Y. Mudge: El Primer Libro De Sus Aventuras. (SPA.). 1996. 9.19 (*0-606-09406-7*, Pub. by Turtleback) Demco.

— Henry y Mudge con Barro Hasta el Rabo. (Henry & Mudge Ser.).Tr. of Henry & Mudge in Puddle Trouble. (SPA., Illus.). 48p. (J). (gr. k-3). 1996. mass mkt. 5.99 (*0-689-80687-6*) Aladdin.

— Henry y Mudge con Barro Hasta el Rabo. (Henry & Mudge Ser.).Tr. of Henry & Mudge in Puddle Trouble. (SPA.). (J). (gr. k-3). 1998. 13.00 (*0-689-80686-8*) Aladdin.

— Henry y Mudge Con Barro Hasta El Rabo; El Segundo Libro de Sus Aventuras. 1996. 11.19 (*0-606-10427-5*, Pub. by Turtleback) Demco.

— Henry y Mudge y El Mejor Dia del Ano/Henry & Mudge & the Best Day of All. (Listos-Para-Leer Ser.). 1997. 11.19 (*0-606-12724-0*, Pub. by Turtleback) Demco.

— The High-Rise Private Eyes: The Case of the Climbing Cat. LC 99-44210. 48p. (J). 2000. 14.89 (*0-688-16309-2*, Grenwillow Bks) HarpC Child Bks.

— The High-Rise Private Eyes: The Case of the Climbing Cat. LC 99-44210. Vol. 2. (Illus.). 48p. (J). (gr. 1-4). 2000. 14.95 (*0-688-16310-6*, Grenwillow Bks) HarpC Child Bks.

— The High-Rise Private Eyes: The Case of the Missing Monkey. LC 99-16878. 48p. (J). (gr. 1 up). 2000. 14.95 (*0-688-16306-8*, Grenwillow Bks) HarpC Child Bks.

— The High-Rise Private Eyes: The Case of the Puzzling Possum. (J). 2001. 14.95 (*0-688-16308-4*, Grenwillow Bks); lib. bdg. 14.89 (*0-688-16307-6*, Grenwillow Bks) HarpC Child Bks.

— The High-Rise Private Eyes: The Case of the Troublesome Turtle. (J). 2001. 14.95 (*0-688-16312-2*, Grenwillow Bks); lib. bdg. 14.89 (*0-688-16311-4*, Grenwillow Bks) HarpC Child Bks.

— High-Rise Private Eyes, The: The Case of the Missing Monkey. LC 99-16878. (Illus.). 48p. (J). (gr. 1-4). 2000. 14.89 (*0-688-16305-X*, Grenwillow Bks) HarpC Child Bks.

— I Had Seen Castles. LC 92-42325. 112p. (YA). (gr. 7 up). 1993. 10.95 (*0-15-238003-5*) Harcourt.

— I Had Seen Castles. LC 92-42325. 112p. (YA). (gr. 7 up). 1995. pap. 5.00 (*0-15-200374-6*) Harcourt.

— I Had Seen Castles. 1995. 9.10 (*0-606-07683-2*, Pub. by Turtleback) Demco.

— In November. LC 98-22276. (Illus.). 32p. (J). (ps-3). 2000. 16.00 (*0-15-201076-9*, Harcourt Child Bks) Harcourt.

***Rylant, Cynthia.** The Islander. 112p. (YA). (gr. 6-12). 1999. reprint ed. pap. 4.99 (*0-440-41542-X*) Bantam.

Rylant, Cynthia. A Kindness. (Sky Bks.). Date not set. pap. text. write for info. (*0-582-08106-8*, Pub. by Addison-Wesley) Longman.

— A Little Shopping. LC 97-20996. (Cobble Street Cousins Ser.: Vol. 2). (Illus.). 55p. (J). (gr. 2-5). 2000. per. 4.50 (*0-689-81709-6*) Aladdin.

— Margaret, Frank, & Andy: Three Writers' Stories. LC 95-45526. (Illus.). 56p. (J). 1996. 15.00 (*0-15-201083-1*) Harcourt.

— Missing May. 96p. (YA). (gr. 7 up). 1993. pap. 5.50 (*0-440-40865-2*) Dell.

— Missing May. LC 91-23303. 96p. (YA). (gr. 6 up). 1992. 14.95 (*0-531-05996-0*); lib. bdg. 15.99 (*0-531-08596-1*) Orchard Bks Watts.

— Missing May. (J). 1992. 9.60 (*0-606-05468-5*, Pub. by Turtleback) Demco.

— Mr. Putter & Tabby Bake the Cake. LC 94-9557. (Illus.). 44p. (J). (gr. 1-5). 1994. 12.00 (*0-15-200205-7*) Harcourt.

— Mr. Putter & Tabby Bake the Cake. LC 94-9557. (J). 1994. 10.15 (*0-606-09640-X*, Pub. by Turtleback) Demco.

— Mr. Putter & Tabby Bake the Cake, Vol. 3. LC 94-9557. (Illus.). 44p. (J). (gr. 1-5). 1994. pap. 5.95 (*0-15-200214-6*) Harcourt.

— Mr. Putter & Tabby Books. (J). 1994. 19.80 (*0-15-201279-6*) Harcourt.

— Mr. Putter & Tabby Fly the Plane. LC 95-48786. (Illus.). 44p. (J). (gr. 1-5). 1997. pap. 5.00 (*0-15-201060-2*) Harcourt.

— Mr. Putter & Tabby Fly the Plane. LC 95-48786. (Illus.). 44p. (J). 1997. 11.00 (*0-15-256253-2*) Harcourt.

— Mr. Putter & Tabby Fly the Plane. 1997. 10.20 (*0-606-12773-9*, Pub. by Turtleback) Demco.

***Rylant, Cynthia.** Mr. Putter & Tabby Paint the Porch. (Illus.). 44p. (J). (gr. 1-4). 2000. 13.00 (*0-15-201787-9*, Harcourt Child Bks) Harcourt.

Rylant, Cynthia. Mr. Putter & Tabby Pick the Pears. LC 94-11259. (Mr. Putter & Tabby Ser.). (Illus.). 44p. (J). (gr. 1-5). 1995. pap. 6.00 (*0-15-200246-4*, Harcourt Child Bks) Harcourt.

— Mr. Putter & Tabby Pick the Pears. LC 94-11259. (J). 1995. 11.20 (*0-606-09641-8*, Pub. by Turtleback) Demco.

— Mr. Putter & Tabby Pick the Pears. abr. ed. LC 94-11259. (Mr. Putter & Tabby Ser.). (Illus.). 44p. (J). (gr. 1-5). 1995. 12.00 (*0-15-200245-6*, Harcourt Child Bks) Harcourt.

— Mr. Putter & Tabby Row the Boat. LC 93-41832. (Illus.). 44p. (C). 1997. pap. 6.00 (*0-15-201059-9*, Harcourt Child Bks) Harcourt.

— Mr. Putter & Tabby Row the Boat. LC 93-41832. (Illus.). 44p. (J). 1997. 11.00 (*0-15-256257-5*) Harcourt.

— Mr Putter & Tabby Take the Train. LC 97-23471. (Illus.). 44p. (J). (ps-2). 1998. 13.00 (*0-15-201786-0*) Harcourt.

***Rylant, Cynthia.** Mr. Putter & Tabby Take the Train. (Early Chapter Bks.). (Illus.). 44p. (J). (gr. 1-4). 2000. pap. 6.00 (*0-15-202389-5*, Harcourt Child Bks) Harcourt.

Rylant, Cynthia. Mr. Putter & Tabby Toot the Horn. LC 96-41768. (Illus.). 44p. (J). (gr. k-2). 1998. 13.00 (*0-15-200244-8*) Harcourt.

— Mr. Putter & Tabby Toot the Horn. LC 96-41768. (Illus.). 44p. (J). 1999. pap. 5.95 (*0-15-200247-2*, Voyager Bks) Harcourt.

— Mr. Putter & Tabby Walk the Dog. LC 93-21467. (Illus.). 44p. (J). (gr. 1-6). 1994. 13.00 (*0-15-256259-1*) Harcourt.

— Mr. Putter & Tabby Walk the Dog. LC 93-21467. (Illus.). 44p. 1994. pap. 6.00 (*0-15-200891-8*) Harcourt Bindery Inc.

— Mr. Putter & Tabby Walk the Dog. LC 93-21467. 1994. 11.20 (*0-606-06585-7*, Pub. by Turtleback) Demco.

— Mr. Griggs' Work. LC 88-1484. (Illus.). 32p. (J). (ps-2). 1993. pap. 6.95 (*0-531-07037-9*) Orchard Bks Watts.

— Mr. Griggs' Work. (J). 1989. 11.15 (*0-606-05482-0*, Pub. by Turtleback) Demco.

***Rylant, Cynthia.** Mr. Putter & Tabby Feed the Fish. 2001. write for info. (*0-15-202408-5*) Harcourt.

Rylant, Cynthia. Mr. Putter & Tabby Pour the Tea. LC 93-21470. (Illus.). 44p. (C). (gr. 1-5). 1994. 13.00 (*0-15-256255-9*) Harcourt.

— Mr. Putter & Tabby Pour the Tea. LC 93-21470. (Illus.). 44p. (J). (gr. 1-5). 1994. pap. 5.95 (*0-15-200901-9*, Harcourt Child Bks) Harcourt.

Rylant, Cynthia. Mr. Putter & Tabby Pour the Tea. LC 93-21470. (J). 1994. 10.15 (*0-606-06584-9*, Pub. by Turtleback) Demco.

Rylant, Cynthia. Night in the Country. LC 85-70963. (Illus.). 32p. (J). (ps-1). 1986. lib. bdg. 14.95 (*0-02-777210-1*, Bradbury S&S) S&S Childrens.

— Night in the Country. (J). 1991. 10.15 (*0-606-04760-3*, Pub. by Turtleback) Demco.

— Night in the Country. LC 90-1043. (Illus.). 32p. (J). (ps-2). 1991. reprint ed. mass mkt. 4.95 (*0-689-71473-4*) Aladdin.

— The Old Woman Who Named Things. LC 93-40537. (Illus.). 32p. (C). (ps-3). 1996. 16.00 (*0-15-257809-9*) Harcourt.

— The Old Woman Who Named Things. (Illus.). 32p. (ps-3). 2000. pap. 6.00 (*0-15-202102-7*, Harcourt Child Bks) Harcourt.

— Poppleton. LC 96-3365. (Illus.). 56p. (J). (ps-2). 1997. 13.95 (*0-590-84782-1*, Blue Sky Press); pap. 3.99 (*0-590-84783-X*, Blue Sky Press) Scholastic Inc.

— Poppleton. 1997. 9.19 (*0-606-11760-1*, Pub. by Turtleback) Demco.

— Poppleton & Friends. LC 96-3366. (Illus.). 48p. (J). (ps-2). 1997. pap. 3.99 (*0-590-84788-0*, Blue Sky Press) Scholastic Inc.

— Poppleton & Friends. LC 96-3366. (Illus.). 72p. (J). (ps-2). 1997. 13.95 (*0-590-84786-4*, Blue Sky Press) Scholastic Inc.

— Poppleton & Friends. 1998. 9.19 (*0-606-13716-5*, Pub. by Turtleback) Demco.

***Rylant, Cynthia.** Poppleton Display. (J). 1999. pap. text 95.76 (*0-439-05990-9*) Scholastic Inc.

Rylant, Cynthia. Poppleton Everyday. LC 97-933. (Illus.). 48p. (J). (ps-2). 1998. 14.95 (*0-590-84845-3*, Blue Sky Press); pap. 3.99 (*0-590-84853-4*) Scholastic Inc.

— Poppleton Everyday. 1998. 9.44 (*0-606-13717-3*) Turtleback.

— Poppleton Forever. (Illus.). 56p. (J). (ps-2). 1998. pap. 3.99 (*0-590-84844-5*) Scholastic Inc.

— Poppleton Forever. LC 97-14047. (Illus.). 56p. (J). (ps-2). 1998. 14.95 (*0-590-84843-7*, Blue Sky Press) Scholastic Inc.

— Poppleton Forever. 1998. 9.19 (*0-606-13718-1*, Pub. by Turtleback) Demco.

***Rylant, Cynthia.** Poppleton Has Fun. (Illus.). 56p. (J). (ps-2). 2000. pap. 3.99 (*0-590-84841-0*) Scholastic Inc.

Rylant, Cynthia. Poppleton in Fall. LC 98-31791. (Illus.). 56p. (J). (ps-2). 1999. 14.95 (*0-590-84789-9*, Pub. by Scholastic Inc); pap. 3.99 (*0-590-84794-5*, Pub. by Scholastic Inc) Penguin Putnam.

— Poppleton in Spring. LC 98-12858. (Illus.). 48p. (ps-2). 1999. pap. 3.99 (*0-590-84822-4*) Scholastic Inc.

— Poppleton in Spring. LC 98-12858. (Poppleton Ser.). (Illus.). 48p. (J). (ps-2). 1999. 15.95 (*0-590-84818-6*, Blue Sky Press) Scholastic Inc.

— The Relatives Came. LC 85-10929. (Illus.). 32p. (J). (ps-2). 1985. lib. bdg. 16.00 (*0-02-777220-9*, Bradbury S&S) S&S Childrens.

— The Relatives Came. (J). 1993. 11.19 (*0-606-05565-7*, Pub. by Turtleback) Demco.

— Silver Packages: An Appalachian Christmas Story. LC 96-53876. (Illus.). 32p. (J). (gr. k-3). 1997. 16.95 (*0-531-30051-X*); lib. bdg. 17.99 (*0-531-33051-6*) Orchard Bks Watts.

— Soda Jerk. LC 89-35654. (Illus.). 48p. (YA). (gr. 7 up). 1990. lib. bdg. 16.99 (*0-531-08464-7*) Orchard Bks Watts.

Rylant, Cynthia. Soda Jerk. LC 89-35654. (Illus.). 48p. (YA). (gr. 7 up). 1990. 15.95 (*0-531-05864-6*) Orchard Bks Watts.

Rylant, Cynthia. A Story of E. B. White. (J). 1996. 16.00 (*0-689-80152-1*) S&S Bks Yung.

— A Story of L. Frank Baum. LC 94-48813. (J). 1996. 16.00 (*0-689-80153-X*) S&S Bks Yung.

— A Story of Margaret Wise Brown. LC 94-48812. (Illus.). (J). 1996. 16.00 (*0-689-80151-3*) S&S Bks Yung.

— Thimbleberry Stories. LC 98-20043. (Illus.). 64p. (J). (gr. k-3). 2000. 15.00 (*0-15-201081-5*, Harcourt Child Bks) Harcourt.

— This Year's Garden. (J). 1998. pap. 4.95 (*0-87628-397-0*) Ctr Appl Res.

***Rylant, Cynthia.** This Year's Garden. (Illus.). (ps-3). 1999. pap. 12.20 (*0-8085-9240-8*) Econo-Clad Bks.

Rylant, Cynthia. This Year's Garden. LC 86-22224. (Illus.). 32p. (J). (ps-3). 1987. reprint ed. mass mkt. 4.95 (*0-689-71122-0*) Aladdin.

— The Ticky-Tacky Doll. LC 97-20281. (Illus.). (J). 2001. write for info. (*0-15-201078-5*) Harcourt.

— Tulip Sees America. LC 96-54267. (Illus.). 32p. (J). (ps-3). 1998. 15.95 (*0-590-84744-9*, Blue Sky Press) Scholastic Inc.

— The Van Gogh Cafe. LC 94-43348. (Illus.). 64p. (J). (gr. 3-7). 1995. 14.00 (*0-15-200843-8*) Harcourt.

— The Van Gogh Cafe. 1998. 9.44 (*0-606-13098-5*) Turtleback.

— Waiting to Waltz: A Childhood. LC 84-11030. (Illus.). 48p. (J). (gr. 6-8). 1984. text 16.00 (*0-02-778000-7*, Bradbury S&S) S&S Childrens.

— The Whales. LC 95-15298. (Illus.). 40p. (J). (ps-3). 1996. 14.95 (*0-590-58285-2*, Blue Sky Press) Scholastic Inc.

***Rylant, Cynthia.** The Whales. (Illus.). 40p. (J). (ps-3). 2000. mass mkt. 5.99 (*0-590-61560-2*) Scholastic Inc.

Rylant, Cynthia. When I Was Young in the Mountains. LC 81-5359. (Unicorn Paperbacks Ser.). (Illus.). 32p. (J). (ps-3). 1982. 15.99 (*0-525-42525-X*, 0966-290, Dutton Child) Peng Put Young Read.

— When I Was Young in the Mountains. (Reading Rainbow Bks.). 1985. 10.19 (*0-606-00879-9*, Pub. by Turtleback) Demco.

— Winter Gifts. (Cobble Street Cousins Ser.). (J). 2000. mass mkt. 4.50 (*0-689-81715-0*) S&S Childrens.

***Rylant, Cynthia.** The Wonderful Happens. LC 99-31241. (J). 2000. 16.00 (*0-689-83177-3*) S&S Childrens.

Rylant, Cynthia, ed. Children of Christmas & Every Living Thing, Set. unabridged ed. (Young Adult Cassette Library). 38p. (J). (gr. 4-6). 27.98 incl. audio (*0-8072-7325-2*, YA8185SP) Listening Lib.

***Rylant, Cynthia & Bowers, Tim.** Little Whistle. LC 99-12650. 2000. 20.01 (*0-15-201087-4*) Harcourt.

Rylant, Cynthia & Bowers, Tim. Little Whistle's Dinner Party. LC 99-12383. 2001. 20.01 (*0-15-201079-3*) Harcourt.

R

R

Rylant, Cynthia & Distribution Media. The Relatives Came. (J). 1986. 14.00 incl. audio (0-676-31727-8) Random.

Rylant, Cynthia & Halperin, Wendy Anderson. In Aunt Lucy's Kitchen: A Little Shopping. LC 97-20995. (Cobble Street Cousins Ser.: Vol. 1). (Illus.). 64p. (J). (gr. 2-5). 2000. per. 4.50 (0-689-81708-8) Aladdin.

***Rylant, Cynthia & Halperin, Wendy Anderson.** Let's Go Home: The Wonderful Things about a House. LC 99-22574. 2000. 20.01 (0-689-82326-6) S&S Childrens.

Rylant, Cynthia & Jackson, Richard. The Islander. LC 97-36059. (YA). (gr. 5-8). 1998. 14.95 (0-7894-2490-8) DK Pub Inc.

Rylant, Cynthia & Stevenson, Sucie. Henry & Mudge: The First Book of Their Adventures. (Henry & Mudge Ser.). (Illus.). 40p. (J). (gr. k-3). 1996. per. 3.99 (0-689-81005-9) S&S Trade.

***Rylant, Cynthia & Teague, Mark.** Poppleton Through & Through. LC 99-29039. (J). 2000. 15.95 (0-590-84839-9, Blue Sky Press) Scholastic Inc.

Rylatt, Alastair. Learning Unlimited: Practical Strategies & Techniques for Transforming Learning in the Workplace. 295p. (Orig.). 1999. pap. text 29.95 (1-875680-11-X) Woodslane.

Rylatt, Alastair & Lohan, Kevin. Creating Training Miracles. 2nd ed. LC 96-50924. 368p. 1997. 44.95 (0-7879-0992-0, Pfffr & Co) Jossey-Bass.

Rylatt, R. M. Surveying the Canadian Pacific: Memoir of a Railroad Pioneer. (Illus.). 272p. 1991. pap. 25.95 (0-7748-0568-4) U of Wash Pr.

Ryle, R. C. Alive or Dead. unabridged ed. 20p. 1996. reprint ed. pap. 2.50 (1-58339-171-1, E8) Triangle Press.
— Duties of Parents. unabridged ed. 38p. 1993. reprint ed. pap. 2.50 (1-58339-170-3, E7) Triangle Press.
— Home Truths, Vol. 1. unabridged ed. 252p. 1996. reprint ed. pap. 19.95 (1-58339-172-X, E9) Triangle Press.
— Home Truths, Vol. 2. unabridged ed. 255p. 1996. reprint ed. pap. 19.95 (1-58339-173-8, E9) Triangle Press.

Ryle, Anthony. Cognitive Analytical Therapy & Borderline Personality Disorder: The Model & the Method. LC 97-8657. 206p. 1997. 79.50 (0-471-97617-2); pap. 48.50 (0-471-97618-0) Wiley.

Ryle, Anthony, ed. Cognitive Analytic Therapy: Developments in Theory & Practice. LC 94-45112. (Wiley Series in Psychotherapy & Counselling). 210p. 1995. pap. 59.95 (0-471-94355-X) Wiley.

Ryle, Anthony, et al. Cognitive-Analytic Therapy: Active Participation in Change - A New Integration in Brief Psychotherapy. 282p. 1992. reprint ed. pap. 95.00 (0-471-93069-5) Wiley.

Ryle, E. Brown. FW-190D Walk Around. LC 97-171836. (Walk Around Ser.: No. 10). (Illus.). 80p. (Orig.). 1997. pap. 14.95 (0-89747-374-4, 5510) Squad Sig Pubns.

***Ryle, E. Brown & Laing, Malcolm.** FW190A Walk Around. (Walk Around Ser.: Vol. 22). (Illus.). 80p. 2000. pap. 14.95 (0-89747-414-7, 5522) Squad Sig Pubns.

Ryle, George. The Forest Service: First Forty Five Years of the Forestry Commission of Great Britain. LC 69-11237. (Illus.). 340p. 1969. 29.95 (0-678-05675-7) Kelley.

Ryle, Gilbert. Aspects of Mind. Meyer, Rene, ed. LC 92-21759. 256p. 1993. 55.95 (0-631-18489-9) Blackwell Pubs.
— Collected Papers Critical Essays & Collected Essays 1929-68: 1971 Edition, 2 vols., Set. 808p. 1996. reprint ed. 100.00 (1-85506-024-8) Bks Intl VA.
— The Concept of Mind. LC 83-24147. 334p. (C). 1984. pap. text 15.00 (0-226-73295-9) U Ch Pr.
— Dilemmas. 138p. (C). 1954. pap. text 20.95 (0-521-09115-2) Cambridge U Pr.
— Plato's Progress. LC 66-15278. 319p. reprint ed. pap. 91.00 (0-608-10014-5, 2013248) Bks Demand.
— Plato's Progress: 1966 Edition. (Key Texts Ser.). 320p. 1996. reprint ed. pap. 29.95 (1-85506-321-2) Bks Intl VA.

Ryle, J. C. Are You Born Again. pap. 0.06 (0-87377-126-5) GAM Pubns.
— Assurance. 5.99 (0-614-11444-6, Pub. by Christian Focus) Spring Arbor Dist.
— Assurance. large type ed. 5.99 (1-871676-05-3, Pub. by Christian Focus) Spring Arbor Dist.
— Boys & Girls Playing: Addresses to Children. large type ed. Kistler, Don, ed. LC 97-105622. 128p. (J). (ps-5). 1996. 16.95 (1-57358-046-5) Soli Deo Gloria.
— A Call to Prayer: An Urgent Plea to Enter into the Secret Place. 43p. (Orig.). 1996. pap. 2.95 (1-879737-20-5) Calvary Press.

***Ryle, J. C.** Caminando con Dios: Un Tratado Sobre las Implicaciones Practicas del Cristianismo. abr. ed. Montgomery, Thomas & Negrete, Omar Ibanez, trs. Orig. Title: Walking with God. (SPA.). 134p. 1999. pap. 2.98 (1-928980-02-3) Pub Faro.

Ryle, J. C. Christian Leaders of the Eighteenth Century: Includes Whitefield, Wesley, Grimshaw, Romaine, Rowlands, Berridge, Venn, Walker, Harvey, Toplady, & Fletcher. 1978. pap. 11.99 (0-85151-268-2) Banner of Truth.
— Churches Beware: Warnings to the Churches. 1998. 12.99 (0-85234-415-5, Pub. by Evangelical Pr) P & R Pubng.
— Daily Readings from J. C. Ryle Vol. 1: Matthew, Mark, Luke. 352p. 1982. pap. 11.95 (0-85234-164-4) Ballantine Pub Grp.
— Expository Thoughts on John, 3 vols., Vol. 1. (Expository Thoughts on the Gospel Ser.). 448p. 1987. reprint ed. pap. 9.99 (0-85151-504-5) Banner of Truth.
— Expository Thoughts on John, 3 vols., Vol. 2. (Expository Thoughts on the Gospel Ser.). 448p. 1987. reprint ed. pap. 9.99 (0-85151-505-3) Banner of Truth.
— Expository Thoughts on John, 3 vols., Vol. 3. (Expository Thoughts on the Gospel Ser.). 552p. 1987. reprint ed. pap. 9.99 (0-85151-506-1) Banner of Truth.
— Expository Thoughts on the Gospels, 7 vols., Set. 1990. pap. 65.99 (0-85151-629-7, RYL1) Banner of Truth.
— Five English Reformers. rev. ed. 160p. (Orig.). 1981. reprint ed. pap. text 6.99 (0-85151-138-4) Banner of Truth.
— Foundations of Faith. LC 87-72750. (Faith Pocket Classics Ser.). Orig. Title: Old Paths. 300p. 1988. mass mkt. 5.99 (0-88270-642-X) Bridge-Logos.
— Heaven. large type ed. Date not set. 5.99 (1-871676-75-4, Pub. by Christian Focus) Spring Arbor Dist.
— Holiness. 1979. pap. 16.99 (0-85234-136-9, Pub. by Evangelical Pr) P & R Pubng.

***Ryle, J. C.** Light from Old Times: Protestant Facts & Men. deluxe ed. (Illus.). 432p. 2000. 29.95 (0-9677603-0-5) C Nolan.

Ryle, J. C. Luke. abr. ed. LC 97-17281. (Classic Commentaries Ser.). 304p. 1997. pap. 17.99 (0-89107-955-6) Crossway Bks.
— Luke. (Expository Thoughts on the Gospel Ser.: Vol. 1). 390p. 1986. reprint ed. pap. 9.99 (0-85151-497-9) Banner of Truth.
— Luke. (Expository Thoughts on the Gospel Ser.: Vol. 2). 530p. 1986. reprint ed. pap. 9.99 (0-85151-498-7) Banner of Truth.
— Mark. abr. ed. LC 92-45785. (Classic Commentaries Ser.). 288p. 1993. pap. 15.90 (0-89107-727-8) Crossway Bks.
— Mark. 370p. 1984. reprint ed. pap. 9.99 (0-85151-441-3) Banner of Truth.
— Matthew. (Expository Thoughts on the Gospel Ser.). 368p. 1986. reprint ed. pap. 9.99 (0-85151-483-9) Banner of Truth.
— Matthew, Vol. 1. abr. ed. LC 92-47006. (Classic Commentaries Ser.). 320p. 1993. pap. 15.99 (0-89107-726-X) Crossway Bks.
— Neuva Vida. (SPA.). 220p. 1990. 5.99 (0-85151-413-8) Banner of Truth.
— Old Paths. 521p. 1999. reprint ed. pap. text 11.99 (0-85151-760-9) Banner of Truth.
— Practical Religion: Being Plain Papers on Daily Duties, Experience Dangers, & Privileges of Professing Christianity. 495p. 1998. pap. text 11.99 (0-85151-743-9) Banner of Truth.
— Prophecy. Date not set. 8.99 (1-871676-64-9, Pub. by Christian Focus) Spring Arbor Dist.
— Shall We Know One Another in Heaven. 1997. pap. 7.99 (1-898787-82-4) Emerald House Group Inc.
— Thoughts for Young Men. 95p. 1999. pap. text 5.95 (1-879737-18-3) Calvary Pr.
— Thoughts for Young Men. rev. ed. 96p. (YA). (gr. 9 up). 1993. pap. 5.95 (1-879737-09-4) Calvary Press.
— The Two Bears. unabridged ed. (Children's Heritage Ser.). 134p. (J). (gr. 4-6). 1996. pap. 6.98 (1-58339-105-3, D5) Triangle Press.
— Warnings to the Churches. 176p. 1992. pap. 4.99 (0-85151-043-4) Banner of Truth.

Ryle, J. C., et al. Christian Life Classics. deluxe ed. Green, Jay P., Sr., ed. (Fifty Greatest Christian Classics Ser.: Vol. III). 768p. 1990. 24.95 (1-878442-52-X) Sovreign Grace Pubs.

Ryle, J. Charles. Certeza. large type ed.Tr. of Assurance. (SPA.). 144p. 1988. pap. 3.50 (1-56063-340-9, 494022) Editorial Unilit.
— El Cielo. large type ed.Tr. of Heaven. (SPA.). 45p. 1991. pap. 2.99 (1-56063-342-5, 494025) Editorial Unilit.

Ryle, James. A Dream Come True: A Biblical Look at How God Speaks Through Dreams & Visions. LC 95-68489. 1995. pap. 11.99 (0-88419-394-2) Creation House.
— Hippo in the Garden: A Non-Religious Approach to Having a Conversation with God. LC 93-71207. 294p. (Orig.). 1993. pap. 10.99 (0-88419-340-3) Creation House.

Ryle, John A. Changing Disciplines: Lectures on the History, Method & Motives of Social Pathology. 123p. (C). 1994. pap. 21.95 (1-56000-746-X) Transaction Pubs.

Ryle, John C. Holiness. Phillips, Tom, ed. (Collection of Classics Ser.). 59p. 1996. pap. text 2.95 (1-879089-24-6) B Graham Ctr.

Ryle, Juan C. El Secreto de la Vida Cristiana. (SPA.). 252p. 1988. reprint ed. pap. 7.99 (0-85151-412-X) Banner of Truth.

Ryle, Martin. Ecology & Socialism. 1989. pap. 9.95 (0-09-182247-5, Pub. by Hutchinson) Trafalgar.
— Journeys in Ireland: Literary Travellers, Rural Landscapes, Cultural Relations. LC 98-42862. (Illus.). 1p. 1999. text 69.95 (1-85928-200-8, Pub. by Ashgate Pub) Ashgate Pub Co.

Ryle, Martin, tr. see Canfora, Luciano.

Ryle, Martin, tr. see Pallottino, Massimo.

Ryles, A. P., et al. Essential Organic Chemistry for Students of the Life Sciences. LC 78-31504. (Illus.). 320p. reprint ed. pap. 99.20 (0-608-20231-2, 207149000012) Bks Demand.
— Worked Examples in Essential Organic Chemistry. LC 80-42022. 171p. reprint ed. pap. 53.10 (0-8357-6945-3, 203900400009) Bks Demand.

Rylestone, Anne L. Prophetic Memory in Wordsworth's "Ecclesiastical Sonnets" LC 89-26352. 160p. (C). 1991. 21.95 (0-8093-1643-9) S Ill U Pr.

Ryley, J. F., ed. Chemotherapy of Fungal Diseases. (Handbook of Experimental Pharmacology Ser.: Vol. 96). (Illus.). 560p. 1990. 348.95 (0-387-52232-8) Spr-Verlag.

Ryley, J. Horton, ed. see Fitch, Ralph.

Ryley, Nancy. The Forsaken Garden: Four Conversations on the Deep Meaning of Environmental Illness. LC 98-15996. (Illus.). 256p. 1998. pap. 16.00 (0-8356-0771-2, Pub. by Theos Pub Hse) Natl Bk Netwk.

Ryley, Thomas W. Gilbert Hitchcock of Nebraska-Wilson's Floor Leader in the Fight for the Versailles Treaty. LC 97-49130. (Studies in American History: Vol. 18). 404p. 1998. text 109.95 (0-7734-8476-0) E Mellen.

Ryley, Thomas W., jt. auth. see Kaplan, Edward S.

Ryll, Wolfgang. Litigation & Settlement in a Game with Incomplete Information: An Experimental Study. LC 96-20401. (Lecture Notes in Economics & Mathematical Systems Ser.). 174p. 1996. pap. 52.00 (3-540-61304-8) Spr-Verlag.

Rymam, Geoff. 253: The Print Remix. LC 98-28602. 384p. 1998. pap. 14.95 (0-312-18295-3) St Martin.

Ryman. Population Genetics & Fisheries. Utter, Fred, ed. 488p. 1987. 35.00 (0-295-96435-9) U of Wash Pr.

***Ryman.** Shalimar. 1999. mass mkt. write for info. (0-312-97150-8) St Martin.

Ryman, Anne. Myst Strategies & Secrets: For DOS. LC 95-67585. 112p. 1995. pap. 12.99 (0-7821-1678-7, Strategies & Secrets) Sybex.

Ryman, Daniele. Aromatherapy: The Complete Guide to Plant & Flower Essences for Health & Beauty. LC 92-22869. 384p. 1993. pap. 13.95 (0-553-37166-5) Bantam.
— Aromatherapy Handbook. 103p. 1989. pap. 11.95 (0-85207-215-5, Pub. by C W Daniel) Natl Bk Netwk.
— The Aromatherapy Handbook: The Secret Healing Power of Essential Oils. 196p. (Orig.). 1990. pap. 19.95 (0-8464-1338-8) Beekman Pubs.
— Aromatherapy in Your Diet: How to Enjoy the Health Benefits of Aromatherapy without Using Essential Oils. 288p. 1997. mass mkt. 6.50 (0-425-15978-7) Berkley Pub.
— Marguerite Maury's Guide to Aromatherapy. 108p. 1989. pap. 17.95 (0-85207-163-9, Pub. by C W Daniel) Natl Bk Netwk.

Ryman, Daniele, ed. Marguerite Maury's Guide to Aromatherapy. 3rd ed. 240p. pap. 26.95 (0-8464-4249-3) Beekman Pubs.

Ryman, Geoff. The Child Garden. 400p. 1994. pap. 13.95 (0-312-89023-0) Orb NYC.

Ryman, Geoff. The Child Garden. 1993. mass mkt. 3.99 (0-8125-1998-1) Tor Bks.

Ryman, Geoff. Was. LC 92-46237. 384p. 1993. pap. 13.95 (0-14-017872-4, Penguin Bks) Viking Penguin.

Ryman, Rebecca. Shalimar. LC 99-22078. 512p. 1999. text 26.95 (0-312-20361-6) St Martin.

Ryman, Rhonda. Dictionary of Classical Ballet Terminology: Royal Academy of Dancing. 2nd ed. 92p. 1998. reprint ed. pap. 16.95 (0-9524848-0-3, Pub. by Royal Acad Dancing) Princeton Bk Co.
— Intermediate Labanotation Assignments. 34p. (Orig.). (C). 1991. pap. text 9.00 (0-614-16919-4) Dance Notation.

Ryman, Rhonda S. Intermediate Labanotation Assignments. 50p. 1996. pap. 9.00 (0-614-24954-6) Princeton Bk Co.

Rymar, Cyndy, ed. see Baker, Cozy.

Rymaszewski, Eugene J., jt. ed. see Tummala, Rao R.

Rymaszewski, Michael. Caesar II: The Official Strategy Guide. LC 95-70976. 1995. pap. 19.95 (0-7615-0360-9) Prima Pub.
— Command & Conquer: Red Alert, Unauthorized Advanced Strategies. LC 96-72317. 224p. 1997. per. 19.99 (0-7615-1055-9) Prima Pub.
— Command & Conquer: Secrets & Solutions: The Unauthorized Edition. 1996. pap. text 14.95 (0-7615-0047-2) Prima Pub.

Rymaszewski, Michael. Command & Conquer Secrets & Solutions: The Unauthorized Edition. rev. ed. 272p. 1996. pap., per. 16.99 (0-7615-0800-7) Prima Pub.
— Computer Strategy Games Bible Unauthorized. LC 96-69123. 336p. 1996. pap., per. 22.99 (0-7615-0846-5) Prima Pub.

Rymaszewski, Michael. Conquest of the New World: The Official Strategy Guide. LC 95-70956. 1996. pap. text 19.99 (0-7615-0170-3) Prima Pub.
— Marco Polo Official Secrets & Solutions. 1995. pap. text 14.95 (0-7615-0262-9) Prima Pub.
— Unlock the Secrets of Deadlock 2: The Exclusive Game Guide. (Unlock the Secrets of Ser.). 1997. pap. text 12.95 (1-56893-952-3) GT Interactive Software.
— Wages of War: The Official Strategy Guide. LC 96-71320. 192p. 1996. pap. 19.99 (0-7615-0983-6) Prima Pub.
— War of the Worlds. 1998. pap. 19.95 (1-56893-910-8) GT Interactive Software.

Rymer. Gynaecology Color Guide. 2nd ed. (Illus.). 114p. (C). 1998. pap. text 16.95 (0-443-05878-4) Church.
— Picture Tests in Obstetrics. 1994. pap. text 16.95 (0-443-04950-5, W B Saunders Co) Harcrt Hlth Sci Grp.

Rymer, Alta M. Beep-Bap-Zap-Jack. LC 74-20428. (Tales of Planet Artembo Ser.: Bk. 1). (Illus.). 48p. (J). (gr. 5-7). 1974. pap. 20.00 (0-9600792-0-3) Rymer Bks.
— Captain Zomo. LC 79-67651. (Tales of Planet Artembo Ser.: Bk. 2). (Illus.). 48p. (Orig.). (J). (gr. 5-7). 1993. pap. 20.00 (0-9600792-2-X) Rymer Bks.
— Coping with the Grief Syndrome: A Small Treatise, Written with Love, for All Who Are Suffering. (Illus.). 24p. 1998. pap. 9.95 (0-934723-10-9) Rymer Bks.
— Hobart & Humbert Gruzzy. LC 85-61860. (Tales of Planet Artembo Ser.: Bk. 5). (Illus.). 28p. (Orig.). (J). (gr. 5-7). pap. 20.00 (0-9600792-6-2) Rymer Bks.
— Love Never Forgets: A Small Books of Verse. (Illus.). 32p. 1998. pap. 9.95 (0-934723-09-5) Rymer Bks.
— Oopletrump's Odyssey, Bk. 4. LC 85-61861. (Tales of Planet Artembo Ser.). (Illus.). 48p. (Orig.). (J). (gr. 5-7). pap. text 20.00 (0-9600792-5-4) Rymer Bks.
— Stars of Obron: Chambo Returns. (Tales of Planet Artembo Ser.: Bk. 3). (Illus.). 56p. (Orig.). (J). (gr. 5-7). pap. text 20.00 (0-9600792-3-8) Rymer Bks.
— Up from Uzam. (Tharma Lo Fairyland Ser.: Story 1). (Illus.). 28p. (Orig.). (J). (gr. 2-4). pap. 20.00 (0-9600792-8-9) Rymer Bks.

Rymer, Cyndy, ed. see Carlson, Susan E.

Rymer, Cyndy, ed. see Cory, Pepper.

Rymer, Cyndy, ed. see Gilbert, Jennifer.

Rymer, Cyndy, ed. see Oroyan, Susanna.

Rymer, Cyndy, ed. see Phalen, Diane.

Rymer, Cyndy, ed. see Sienkiewicz, Elly.

Rymer, Cyndy, ed. see Slusser, Donna Ingram & Magaret, Patricia Maixner.

Rymer, Janice. Gynaecology. (Colour Guide Ser.). (Illus.). 122p. 1992. pap. text 19.95 (0-443-04513-5) Harcrt Hlth Sci Grp.
— Preparation & Revision for the Diploma of the Royal College of Obstetricians & Gynaecologists. 2nd ed. LC 97-18740. 1998. write for info. (0-443-05097-X) Church.

Rymer, Janice, et al. Gynaecology. 2nd ed. LC 97-16821. (Colour Guide Ser.). 1997. write for info. (0-443-05775-3) Harcrt Hlth Sci Grp.
— Preparation & Revision for DRCOG. (Illus.). 258p. 1990. pap. text 43.00 (0-443-04248-9) Church.

Rymer, John R. The Seven Steps in Architecting Client/Server Applications (Illus.). 81p. 1995. pap. write for info. (1-892815-15-X) Patricia Seybold.

Rymer, Michael. Angel Baby: The Screenplay. 1997. pap. 17.95 (0-86819-457-3, Pub. by Currency Pr) Accents Pubns.

Rymer, Michael J., jt. ed. see Andersen, David W.

Rymer, Russ. American Beach: A Saga of Race, Wealth, & Memory. LC 98-230257. (Illus.). 352p. 1998. 25.00 (0-06-017483-8) HarpC.
— American Beach: How "Progress" Robbed a Black Town--and Nation--of History, Wealth, & Power. (Illus.). 352p. 2000. pap. 14.00 (0-06-093089-6) HarpC.
— Genie: A Scientific Tragedy. LC 92-53327. 256p. 1994. pap. 12.50 (0-06-092465-9, Perennial) HarperTrade.

***Rymer, Suzanne A.** Preserving Dignity for People in Your Care. (Illus.). 79p. 2000. pap. 29.95 (1-888343-32-X) Hartman Pub.

Rymer, Thomas. Short View of Tragedy. LC 79-118069. 1968. reprint ed. 29.50 (0-404-05478-1) AMS Pr.
— Short View of Tragedy. 184p. 1971. reprint ed. 26.00 (0-7146-2519-1, Pub. by F Cass Pubs) Intl Spec Bk.

Rymes, Thomas K., ed. Keynes's Lectures, 1932-35, Notes of a Representative Student: A Synthesis of Lecture Notes Taken by Students at Keynes's Lectures in the 1930s Leading up to the Publication of The General Theory. LC 89-4776. (Illus.). 212p. 1990. text 60.00 (0-472-10131-5, 10131) U of Mich Pr.

Rymes, Thomas K., jt. auth. see Cas, Alexandra.

Rymeszewski, Michael. Sid Meier's Civilization: Advanced Strategies, No. II. 144p. 1996 pap., per. 16.99 (0-7615-0917-8) Prima Pub.

Rymill, Linda. Good Knight. LC 97-18665. (Illus.). 32p. (J). 1998. 15.95 (0-8050-4129-X) H Holt & Co.

Rymkiewicz, Jaroslaw M. The Final Station: Umschlagplatz. Taylor, Nina, tr. LC 93-39631. 327p. 1994. text 27.50 (0-374-15495-3) FS&G.

***Rymland, Lizbeth.** Fugue States. 180p. 2000. pap. 20.00 (0-930829-49-2) Lumen Inc.

Rymniak, Paul. Mystery of Healing. 256p. (Orig.). 1996. pap. write for info. (0-614-14973-8) P Rymniak.

Rymut, Kazimierz. Slownik Nazwisk Wspolczesnie W Polsce Uzywanych, 10 vols. (POL.). 1994. pap. 400.00 (83-85579-25-7) Szwede Slavic.

Ryn, August Van, see Van Ryn, August.

Ryn, Claes G. Democracy & the Ethical Life: A Philosophy of Politics & Community. LC 77-9505. 245p. 1990. pap. 14.95 (0-8132-0711-8) Cath U Pr.
— The New Jacobinism: Can Democracy Survive? LC 91-2774. 102p. (Orig.). 1991. pap. 9.95 (0-932783-03-1) Natl Human Inst.
— Will, Imagination, & Reason. LC 86-6588. 392p. (Orig.). 1986. 15.00 (0-89526-579-6); pap. 7.95 (0-89526-807-8) Regnery Pub.
— Will, Imagination, & Reason: Babbitt, Croce, & the Problem of Reality. LC 96-38939. 240p. (Orig.). 1997. pap. text 19.95 (1-56000-918-7) Transaction Pubs.

Ryn, Claes G., jt. ed. see Panichas, George A.

Ryn, Van, see Van Ryn.

Ryna, Leo, jt. ed. see Gasparski, Wojciech.

Rynaenen, S. S., jt. ed. see Lindroth, S. E.

***Rynard, Paul & Shugarman, David, eds.** Cruelty & Deception: The Problem of Dirty Hands in Politics. 248p. 1999. pap. 19.95 (1-55111-196-9) Broadview Pr.

Rynard, Thomas. Insurance & Risk Management for State & Local Government, Vol. 1. 1991. 145.00 incl. cd-rom (0-8205-1386-5) Bender.

Rynbrandt, Linda J. Caroline Bartlett Crane & Progressive Reform: Social Housekeeping As Sociology. LC 98-39886. (Women & Sociological Theory Ser.: Vol. 1). 192p. 1998. 52.00 (0-8153-2982-2, SS1177) Garland.

Ryndak, Diane L. & Alper, Sandra K. Curriculum Content for Students with Moderate & Severe Disabilities in Inclusive Settings. LC 95-6135. 416p. 1995. 82.00 (0-205-14667-8) Allyn.

Rynders, John E. & Horrobin, J. Margaret. Down Syndrome: Birth to Adulthood (Giving Families an Edge) LC 94-76444. 356p. 1996. pap. 37.95 (0-89108-236-0) Love Pub Co.

Ryne, Robert. Computational Accelerator Physics. (AIP Conference Proceedings Ser.: No. 297). 640p. 1994. text 111.00 (1-56396-222-5) Am Inst Physics.

Rynearson, Rhoda. Harvest Waiting: Reaching Out to the Deaf. LC 95-161961. 39p. 1995. write for info. (0-570-09939-0) Concordia.

Rynell, A. The Rivalry of Scandinavian & Native Synonyms, in Middle English Especially "Taker" & "Nimen" With an Excursus on "Nema" & "Tuka" in Old Scandinavian. (Lund Studies in English: Vol. 13). 1974. reprint ed. pap. 50.00 (0-8115-0556-1) Periodicals Srv.

An Asterisk (*) at the beginning of an entry indicates that the title is appearing for the first time.

Rynell, Alarik. Antedatings & Additions for the Oxford English Dictionary from the Catalogue of Prints of Political & Personal Satire in the British Museum. (Stockholm Studies in English: No. LXXII). 184p. (Orig.). 1987. pap. text 40.00 (91-22-00872-1) Coronet Bks.

Rynerson, Fred. Exploring & Mining for Gems & Gold in the West, Vol. 1. (Illus.). 204p. 1970. pap. 8.95 (0-911010-60-2) Naturegraph.

***Rynes, S. & Gerhart, Barry A.** Compensation in Organizations: Current Research & Practice. LC 00-21238. (Frontiers of Industrial & Organizational Psychology Ser.). (Illus.). 544p. 2000. 46.95 (0-7879-5274-5) Jossey-Bass.

Ryneveld, Edna C. Menopause: A Gentle, Natural Approach. 2nd ed. LC 98-5984. (Illus.). 240p. 1999. pap. text 12.95 (1-56718-595-9) Llewellyn Pubns.

— Secrets of a Natural Menopause: A Positive, Drug-Free Approach. LC 94-33401. (Illus.). 240p. 1994. pap. 12.95 (1-56718-596-7) Llewellyn Pubns.

***Ryniak, Steven.** Dear Alice: Rejected Letters to Advice Columns from Completely Insane Idiots, 1. 104p. (C). 2000. 10.95 (1-930213-00-X) Muse World Media.

Rynk, Robert, et al. On-Farm Composting Handbook. (Illus.). 186p. 1992. pap. text 20.00 (0-935817-19-0, NRAES-54) NRAES.

Rynn, Maria, jt. auth. see Bohl, Marilyn.

***Rynn, Midori Yamanouchi.** Listen to the Voices from the Sea: Writings of the Fallen Japanese Students. LC 00-37418. 2000. pap. write for info. (0-940866-85-4) U Scranton Pr.

Rynne, Colin. The Archaeology of Cork City & Harbour: From the Earliest Times to Industrialisation. 110p. 1993. pap. 12.95 (0-9516036-8-X) Dufour.

***Rynne, Colin.** At the Sign of the Cow: The Cork Butter Market, 1770-1924. LC 98-215075. 118 p. 1998. 16.95 (1-898256-60-8) Collins Press.

Rynne, Stephen. Green Fields: A Journey of Irish Country Life. 256p. 1995. reprint ed. pap. 15.95 (0-86322-203-X, Pub. by Brandon Bk Pubs) Irish Bks Media.

Rynne, Terrence J. Competitive Market Strategies in Healthcare: Meeting the Marketing Challenges in an Integrated Delivery System. 225p. (C). 1995. text 45.00 (1-55738-635-8, Irwn Prfssnl) McGraw-Hill Prof.

Rynne, Xavier. Vatican Council II. 616p. 1999. reprint ed. pap. 28.00 (1-57075-293-1) Orbis Bks.

Rynning, Ole. Ole Rynning's True Account of America. Blegen, Theodore C., ed. & tr. by. LC 70-160992. (Select Bibliographies Reprint Ser.). 1977. reprint ed. 16.95 (0-8369-5827-6) Ayer.

Rynone, William. Linear Active Circuits: Design & Analysis. LC 85-73317. (Illus.). 613p. 1986. reprint ed. pap. 190.10 (0-7837-9772-9, 206050100005) Bks Demand.

Ryntz, Rose A. Adhesion to Plastics: Molding & Paintability. (Illus.). 300p. 1997. 84.95 (1-890086-02-9) Global Pr MN.

***Ryntz, Rose A.** Plastics & Coatings: Durability, Stabilization, Testing. LC 00-39564. 2000. write for info. (1-56990-290-9) Hanser-Gardner.

Ryntz, Rose Ann. Painting of Plastics. (Illus.). 32p. 1994. pap. 30.00 (0-934010-36-6) Fed Soc Coat Tech.

Ryo Sakaizumi. Introduction to Marker Drawing. (Easy Start Guide Ser.). (Illus.). 112p. 1992. 37.95 (4-7661-0624-5, Pub. by Graphic-Sha) Bks Nippan.

Ryokan. Between the Floating Mist: Poems of Ryokan. Maloney & Oshiro, trs. from JPN. 88p. (Orig.). 1992. pap. 12.00 (1-877800-01-5) Springhse Editions.

Ryon, Roderick N. West Baltimore Neighborhoods: Sketches of Their History, 1840-1960. LC 93-60361. (Orig.). 1993. pap. write for info. (0-9636930-0-X) R N Ryon.

Ryou, Daniel H. Zephaniah's Oracles Against the Nations: A Synchronic & Diachronic Study of Zephaniah 2:1-3:8. LC 95-1102. (Biblical Interpretation Ser.: Vol. 13). 1995. 117.00 (90-04-10311-2) Brill Academic Pubs.

Ryp, Ellen. Deadly Bonds. 1989. mass mkt. 4.95 (0-446-35133-4) Warner Bks.

Ryp, Wolff. The Fury. (Midnight Secrets Ser.). 1996. pap. 3.50 (0-8167-3544-1) Troll Communs.

— The Temptation. (Midnight Secrets Ser.: No. 01). 224p. (YA). 1996. pap. 3.50 (0-8167-3542-5) Troll Communs.

— The Thrill. (Midnight Secrets Ser.: No. 02). 224p. (YA). 1996. pap. 3.95 (0-8167-3543-3) Troll Communs.

Rypins, Harold & Frohlich, Edward D. Rypins' Basic Sciences Review. 17th ed. LC 96-34954. 848p. 1996. pap. text 34.95 (0-397-51488-3) Lppncott W & W.

— Rypins' Clinical Sciences Review. 17th ed. LC 96-36162. 400p. 1996. pap. text 32.95 (0-397-51544-8) Lppncott W & W.

Rypins, S., ed. Three Old English Prose Texts. (EETS, OS Ser.: No. 161). 1974. reprint ed. 45.00 (0-527-00158-9) Periodicals Srv.

Rypinski, Arthur. Voluntary Reporting of Greenhouse Gases (1995) (Illus.). 75p. (Orig.). (C). 1997. pap. text 30.00 (0-7881-3730-1) DIANE Pub.

Rypinski, Richard R. Eminent Domain: A Practical Guide. (Orig.). 1998. pap. text 25.00 (0-923956-37-9) Solano Pr.

Rypka, J., et al. History of Iranian Literature. enl. rev. ed. Jahn, Karl, ed. Van Popta-Hope, P., tr. from GER. 928p. 1968. lib. bdg. 239.50 (90-277-0143-1) Kluwer Academic.

Rypstat, Craig. This Book Won't Help You! 120p. 1997. pap. 7.95 (0-9654436-2-0) Honey Creek WI.

Ryrie, Charles C. Acts of the Apostles. (Everyman's Bible Commentaries Ser.). pap. 9.99 (0-8024-2044-3, 485) Moody.

— Apocalipsis. (Comentario Biblico Portavoz Ser.). Orig. Title: Revelation. (SPA.). 128p. 1980. pap. 6.99 (0-8254-1625-6, Edit Portavoz) Kregel.

— Balancing the Christian Life: 25th Anniversary Edition. LC 96-112534. pap. 11.99 (0-8024-0887-7, 83) Moody.

— Las Bases de la Fe Premilenial. Orig. Title: The Basis of the Premillennial Faith. (SPA.). 224p. 1984. mass mkt. 5.99 (0-8254-1626-4, Edit Portavoz) Kregel.

— Basic Theology: A Popular Systemic Guide to Understanding Biblical Truth. LC 99-216002. 1999. 29.99 (0-8024-2734-0) Moody.

— The Basis of the Premillennial Faith. 160p. 1954. pap. 8.99 (0-87213-741-4) Loizeaux.

— Biblical Answers to Contemporary Issues. pap. 9.99 (0-8024-1077-4, 91) Moody.

— Biblical Theology of the New Testament. LC 98-10549. 1998. pap. 14.99 (0-87213-743-0) Loizeaux.

— Dispensacionalismo Hoy. Orig. Title: Dispensationalism Today. (SPA.). 208p. 1974. pap. 7.99 (0-8254-1627-2, Edit Portavoz) Kregel.

— Dispensationalism. expanded rev. ed. 224p. pap. 11.99 (0-8024-2187-3, 129) Moody.

— Equilibrio en la Vida Cristiana. Orig. Title: Balancing the Christian Life. (SPA.). 256p. 1974. pap. 8.99 (0-8254-1628-0, Edit Portavoz) Kregel.

— El Espiritu Santo. Orig. Title: The Holy Spirit. (SPA.). 152p. 1978. pap. 6.99 (0-8254-1629-9, Edit Portavoz) Kregel.

— First & Second Thessalonians. (Everyman's Bible Commentaries Ser.). pap. 9.99 (0-8024-2052-4, 491) Moody.

— La Gracia de Dios. Orig. Title: The Grace of God. (SPA.). 160p. 1979. mass mkt. 5.99 (0-8254-1630-2, Edit Portavoz) Kregel.

— Los Hechos de los Apostoles. (Comentario Biblico Portavoz Ser.). Orig. Title: Acts of the Apostles. (SPA.). 112p. 1981. pap. 6.99 (0-8254-1631-0, Edit Portavoz) Kregel.

— The Holy Spirit. expanded rev. ed. LC 97-206844. 224p. (Orig.). 1997. pap. 10.99 (0-8024-3578-5, 165) Moody.

— The Miracles of Our Lord. LC 88-16608. 186p. 1988. reprint ed. 14.99 (0-87213-742-2) Loizeaux.

— Nailing Down a Board: Serving Effectively on the Not for Profit Board. LC 98-50471. 1999. pap. 5.99 (0-8254-3649-4) Kregel.

— Nuevo Testamento de Estudio.Tr. of Ryrie Study New Testament. (SPA.). 512p. 1996. 9.99 (0-8254-1647-7, Edit Portavoz) Kregel.

— Object Lessons: 100 Lessons from Everyday Life. expanded rev. ed. pap. 5.99 (0-8024-6029-1, 234) Moody.

— Primera y Segunda Tesalonicenses. (Comentario Biblico Portavoz Ser.). Orig. Title: First & Second Thessalonians. (SPA.). 104p. 1981. pap. 6.99 (0-8254-1634-5, Edit Portavoz) Kregel.

— Revelation. LC 96-207807. (Everyman's Bible Commentaries Ser.). 152p. 1996. pap. 9.99 (0-8024-7108-0, 499) Moody.

— Sintesis de Doctrina Biblica. (SPA.). 216p. 1979. pap. 8.99 (0-8254-1636-1, Edit Portavoz) Kregel.

— So Great Salvation. 168p. 1990. pap. 9.99 (0-89693-127-7, 6-1127, Victor Bks) Chariot Victor.

— So Great Salvation: What It Means to Believe in Jesus Christ. 160p. 1997. pap. 11.99 (0-8024-7818-2, 13) Moody.

— A Survey of Bible Doctrine. LC 72-77958. 192p. (C). pap. 10.99 (0-8024-8438-7, 293) Moody.

— Teologia Basica.Tr. of Basic Theology. (SPA.). 1993. 21.99 (1-56063-194-5, 498473) Editorial Unilit.

— Teologia Biblica.Tr. of Basic Theology. (SPA.). 625p. 1993. pap. write for info. (0-614-27144-4) Editorial Unilit.

— Teologia Biblica del Nuevo Testamento. (SPA.). 364p. 1979. pap. 10.99 (0-8254-1637-X, Edit Portavoz) Kregel.

— Ven Pronto, Senor Jesus: Lo Que Necesita Saber Acerca del Arrebatamiento de la Iglesia. (SPA.). 112p. 1997. pap. 6.99 (0-8254-1638-8, Edit Portavoz) Kregel.

Ryrie, Charles C., et al, eds. Countdown to Armageddon: A Comprehensive Look from Today's Prophecy Experts. LC 98-47206. 350p. 1999. pap. 11.99 (0-7369-0014-4) Harvest Hse.

Ryrie, Charlie. The Healing Energies of Water. (Illus.). 1999. pap. 17.95 (1-885203-72-1) Tuttle Pubng.

Ryrie, William. First World, Third World. 240p. 1997. pap. 18.95 (0-312-17279-6) St Martin.

Rys, F. S. & Gyr, A., eds. Physical Processes & Chemical Reactions in Liquid Flows. LC 99-496414. (IAHR Monograph Ser.). (Illus.). 244p. (C). 1998. text 95.00 (90-5410-700-6, Pub. by A A Balkema) Ashgate Pub Co.

Rys, Frans S., jt. ed. see Gyr, Albert.

Rys, Janet Van, see Van Rys, Janet.

Rys, Paul, jt. auth. see Zollinger, Heinrich.

Rysavy, B. & Ryzhikov, K. M., eds. Helminths of Fish Eating Birds of the Palaearctic Region: Volume 1, Nematoda. (Illus.). 1978. text 155.50 (90-6193-551-2) Kluwer Academic.

Ryscavage, Paul. Income Inequality in America: An Analysis of Trends. LC 98-23186. 244p. (gr. 13). 1998. pap. text 25.95 (0-7656-0234-2) M E Sharpe.

— Income Inequality in America: An Analysis of Trends. LC 98-23186. (Issues in Work & Human Resources Ser.). (Illus.). 244p. (C). (gr. 13). 1998. text 59.95 (0-7656-0233-4) M E Sharpe.

Ryschkewitsch, George E. Chemical Bonding & the Geometry of Molecules. LC 62-20784. (Selected Topics in Modern Chemistry Ser.). 129p. reprint ed. pap. 40.00 (0-608-10293-8, 200579400060) Bks Demand.

Ryscroft, John. The A-Z of Chess. 1994. pap. 29.95 (1-85744-007-2, Pub. by Cadgn Bks) Macmillan.

***Rysdyk, Evelyn C.** Modern Shamanic Living: New Explorations of an Ancient Path. LC 99-22633. 128p. 1999. pap. 9.95 (1-57863-125-4) Weiser.

***Ryser, Elliot T. & Marth, Elmer H.** Listeria, Listeriosis & Food Safety. 2nd expanded ed. LC 98-50963. (Food Science & Technology Ser.). (Illus.). 1030p. 1999. text 195.00 (0-8247-0235-2) Dekker.

Ryser, Fred A., Jr. Birds of the Great Basin: A Natural History. LC 84-25763. (Max C. Fleischmann Series in Great Basin Natural History). (Illus.). 642p. (Orig.). 1985. pap. 39.95 (0-87417-080-X) U of Nev Pr.

Ryser, Frieder. Reverse Paintings on Glass: The Ryser Collection. (Illus.). 192p. 1992. pap. 9.95 (0-87290-127-0) Corning.

Ryser, Gail, jt. auth. see McConnell, Kathleen.

Ryser, Herbert J. Combinatorial Mathematics. LC 65-12288. (Carus Mathematical Monograph: No. 14). 154p. 1963. 18.00 (0-88385-014-1, CAM-14) Math Assn.

Ryser, Herbert J., jt. auth. see Brualdi, Richard A.

Ryser, Otto E. & Brown, James R. A Manual of Tumbling & Apparatus Stunts. 8th ed. 272p. (C). 1989. text. write for info. (0-697-10418-4) Brown & Benchmark.

Ryser, Rudolph C. Anti-Indian Movement on the Tribal Frontier. rev. ed. (Occasional Papers). (Illus.). 56p. 1995. pap. 15.00 (1-893710-01-7) Ctr for World Studies.

— Indian Self-Government Process Evaluation: Preliminary Findings October 1, 1995. (Illus.). 12p. 1995. pap. 10.00 (1-893710-03-3, DayKeeper Pr) Ctr for World Studies.

— Solving Intergovernmental Conflicts: Tribes & States in Conflict: A Tribal Solution. (Occasional Papers: Vol. 20). (Illus.). 20p. 1992. pap. 7.00 (1-893710-05-X) Ctr for World Studies.

— Whose Law in This Land: A Case Study: Indian National Governments & Washington State Government in the Northwest United States of America. (Occasional Papers). (Illus.). 20p. 1986. pap. 3.50 (1-893710-02-5, DayKeeper Pr) Ctr for World Studies.

Ryser, Rudolph C. & Griggs, Richard A. Fourth World Geopolitical Reader I: International Relations & Political Geography Between Nations & States. (Illus.). 68p. pap. 15.00 (1-893710-06-8, DayKeeper Pr) Ctr for World Studies.

Ryser, Rudolph C. & Korn, Leslie E. Indian Self-Government Process Evaluation: Final Report March 1, 1996. (Fourth World Documentation Ser.). 46p. 1996. pap. 15.00 (1-893710-04-1) Ctr for World Studies.

Ryser, Rudolph C., jt. auth. see Morris, Glen T.

Ryserson, Andre, jt. ed. see Fonte, John.

***Ryskamp, Charles.** Works of John Chalkhill. (Illus.). 220p. 2000. 195.00 (0-691-06994-8) Princeton U Pr.

Ryskamp, Charles, et al. Art in the Frick Collection: Paintings, Sculpture, Decorative Arts. LC 95-48353. 1996. pap. 17.25 (0-8109-2668-7) Abrams.

— Art in the Frick Collection: Paintings, Sculpture, Decorative Arts. LC 95-48353. (Illus.). 208p. 1996. 60.00 (0-8109-1972-9, Pub. by Abrams) Time Warner.

Ryskamp, Charles, ed. see Cowper, William.

Ryskamp, George R. Finding Your Hispanic Roots. LC 96-77405. 306p. 1997. pap. 19.95 (0-8063-1517-2) Genealog Pub.

Ryskamp, John. Nature Studies. LC 98-37014. 300p. 1998. pap. 12.95 (1-57366-039-6) Fiction Coll.

Ryskin, Grigorii. Osen' Na Vindzorskoi Doroge: Zapiski Massazhista. LC 86-9773. (RUS.). 164p. 1986. pap. 8.50 (0-938920-71-5) Hermitage Pubs.

Ryskin, Iurii D., ed. Sovetskoe Literaturovedenie I Kritika, 1917-1925, Bibliograficheskii Ukazetel' Literatury Na Russkom Iazyke - Soviet Studies in Literature & Literary Criticism, 1917-1925 Vols. 1-3, Vol. 1. (RUS.). xii, 266p. 1994. lib. bdg. write for info. (0-88354-367-2) N Ross.

Ryskov, S. S., ed. The Geometry of Positive Quadratic Forms. LC 82-24328. (Proceedings of the Steklov Institute of Mathematics Ser.: No. 152). 258p. 1983. pap. 119.00 (0-8218-3070-8, STEKLO/152) Am Math.

Ryskov, S. S. & Baranovskii, E. P. C-Types of N-Dimensional Lattices & Five- Dimensional Primitive Parallelohedra with Application to the Theory of Coverings. LC 78-21923. (Proceedings of the Steklov Institute of Mathematics Ser.). 140p. 1978. pap. 83.00 (0-8218-3037-6, STEKLO/137) Am Math.

Ryssel, H. & Pichler, P., eds. Simulation of Semiconductor Devices & Processes, Vol. 6. 516p. 1995. 174.95 (3-211-82736-6) Spr-Verlag.

Ryssel, Heiner. Ion Implantation Techniques, Berchtesgaden, FRG, 1982. (Electrophysics Ser.: Vol. 10). (Illus.). 372p. 1982. 64.95 (0-387-11878-0) Spr-Verlag.

Ryssel, Heiner & Ruge, Ingolf. Ion Implantation. fac. ed. Buckman, Jerome-Allan, tr. LC 84-3723. 477p. reprint ed. pap. 147.90 (0-7837-8272-1, 204905300009) Bks Demand.

Rysso, Henry B. Health Risks, Risk-Taking Behavior, Assessments & Management: Index of New Information with Authors, Subjects & References. 150p. 1996. 47.50 (0-7883-1290-1); pap. 44.50 (0-7883-1291-X) ABBE Pubs Assn.

Rysstad, Jean. Home Fires. 160p. 1997. pap. 16.95 (1-55017-159-3) Harbour Bks.

Ryst, Marie. Handmade Books & Albums: The Pleasures of Creative Hand-Bookbinding. (Illus.). 80p. 1998. pap. text 18.95 (1-55821-570-0) Lyons Pr.

Rystedt, Eva. Acquarossa Vol. 4: Early Etruscan Akroteria from Acquarossa & Poggio Civitate (Murlo) (Acta Instituti Romani Regni Sueciae, Series in 4 Degrees: Vol. XXXVIII:IV). (Illus.). 200p. 1983. pap. 79.50 (91-7042-095-5, Pub. by JCB Mohr) Coronet Bks.

Rystedt, Eva, ed. The Swedish Cyprus Expedition - The Living Past. LC 96-216836. (Museum of Mediterranean & Near Eastern Antiquities: Memoir 9). (Illus.). 777p. (Orig.). 1994. pap. 32.50 (91-7192-939-8, Pub. by P Astroms) Coronet Bks.

Rystedt, Eva, et al, eds. Deliciae Fictiles: Proceedings of the First International Conference on Central Italic Architectural Terracottas at the Swedish Institute in Rome, 10-12 December, 1990. (Acta Instituti Romani Regni Sueciae Ser.: Series 4, L). (Illus.). 311p. (Orig.). 1993. pap. 87.50 (91-7042-143-9, Pub. by P Astroms) Coronet Bks.

Rystrom, Kenneth. The Why, Who & How of the Editorial Page. 3rd ed. LC 98-26946. (Illus.). 376p. 1999. pap. text 33.75 (1-891136-01-1) Strata Pub Co.

Rytand, David A., ed. Annual Review of Medicine, Vol. 6. LC 51-1659. 1955. 40.00 (0-8243-0506-X) Annual Reviews.

Rytand, David A., et al, eds. Annual Review of Medicine: Selected Topics in the Clinical Sciences, Vol. 11. LC 51-1659. 1960. text 40.00 (0-8243-0511-6) Annual Reviews.

— Annual Review of Medicine: Selected Topics in the Clinical Sciences, Vol. 12. LC 51-1659. 1961. text 40.00 (0-8243-0512-4) Annual Reviews.

— Annual Review of Medicine: Selected Topics in the Clinical Sciences, Vol. 13. LC 51-1659. 1962. text 40.00 (0-8243-0513-2) Annual Reviews.

Rytel, Michael J. Rapid Diagnosis in Infectious Diseases. 224p. 1979. pap. 129.00 (0-8493-5535-4, RC112, CRC Reprint) Franklin.

Ryter, Derek. Mountain Biking Colorado's la Platas: Great Rides Between Durango & Telluride. LC 95-3520. (Illus.). 129p. 1995. pap. 16.95 (0-87108-860-6) Pruett.

Ryter, Derek & Ryter, Jarral. Mountain Biking Colorado's Front Range: Great Rides in & Around Fort Collins, Denver & Boulder. LC 98-23659. (Illus.). 197p. 1998. pap. 16.95 (0-87108-890-8) Pruett.

Ryter, Jarral, jt. auth. see Ryter, Derek.

***Ryter, Jon Christian.** What Ever Happened to America. Hallberg, Charles, ed. 512p. 2000. 29.95 (0-87319-049-1) Hallberg Pub Corp.

Rytlewski, Ralf, jt. ed. see Berg-Schlosser, Dirk.

Rytov, S. M., et al. Principles of Statistical Radiophysics, No. 1. (Illus.). 260p. 1987. 111.95 (0-387-12562-0) Spr-Verlag.

— Principles of Statistical Radiophysics, No. 2. (Illus.). 240p. 1988. 126.95 (0-387-16186-4) Spr-Verlag.

— Principles of Statistical Radiophysics, No. 3. (Illus.). 255p. 1989. 135.95 (0-387-17829-5) Spr-Verlag.

— Principles of Statistical Radiophysics, No. 4. (Illus.). 200p. 1989. 108.95 (0-387-17828-7) Spr-Verlag.

Rytter, Wojciech, jt. auth. see Crochemore, Maxime.

Rytter, Wojciech, jt. auth. see Gibbons, Alan.

Rytter, Wojciech, jt. auth. see Karpinski, Marek.

Rytting, Gloria W., ed. Christmas Recipes from the Lion House. LC 89-35572. (Illus.). 214p. 1989. 12.95 (0-87579-255-3) Deseret Bk.

Ryu, Akira, ed. The Best Use of Landscape Items in Architectural Rendering. (Illus.). 144p. 1995. pap. text 49.95 (4-7661-0771-3, Pub. by Graphic-Sha) Bks Nippan.

Ryu, Chen-Chel. Die Urkundendelikte Im Deutschen und Koreanischen Strafrecht. XIII, 190p. 1997. 44.95 (3-631-32069-8) P Lang Pubng.

Ryu, Chi S., jt. auth. see Lee, Pong K.

Ryu, Dean P., tr. from KOR. Korean Criminal Code. (American Series of Foreign Penal Codes: Vol. 2). x, 145p. 1960. 20.00 (0-8377-0022-1, Rothman) W S Hein.

Ryu, Dewey D. Proceedings of Biotechnology: KSEA Series in Advances in Science & Engineering. Lee, Sang S. & Han, Moon H., eds. (KSEA Series in Advances in Science & Engineering: Vol. I). (ENG & KOR., Illus.). xiv, 323p. (Orig.). 1997. pap. text 100.00 (1-889495-00-X) U CA Biochem.

Ryu, Dewey D., jt. ed. see Furusaki, S.

Ryu, H. K. & Slottje, D. J., eds. Measuring Trends in U. S. Income Inequality: Theory & Applications. LC 98-3099. (Lecture Notes in Economics & Mathematical Systems Ser.: Vol. 459). (Illus.). xi, 195p. 1998. pap. 61.00 (3-540-64229-3) Spr-Verlag.

Ryu, Paul K., jt. auth. see Silving, Helen.

Ryu, Shiro. Coherent Lightwave Communication Systems. LC 94-23490. 294p. 1994. 37.00 (0-89006-612-4) Artech Hse.

Ryugo, Kay. Fruit Culture: Its Arts & Science. LC 88-5540. 352p. 1988. text 99.95 (0-471-89191-6) Wiley.

Ryuichi, Tamura. Dead Languages: Selected Poems 1946-1984. Fitzsimmons, Thomas, ed. Drake, Christopher, tr. & intro. by. LC 84-12621. (Asian Poetry in Translation Ser.: No. 5). (ENG & JPN.). 336p. 1985. pap. 20.00 (0-942668-06-5) Katydid Bks.

Ryuijie. Ryuijie Photographs. (Illus.). 100p. 1991. 50.00 (0-9627927-0-5); pap. 25.00 (0-9627927-1-3) Freshsilver.

Ryumin, A. Decorative Metal-Work of the Urals, 18th-19th Centuries. (ENG, FRE, GER & RUS.). 205p. 1982. 200.00 (0-7855-1585-2) St Mut.

Ryun, Anne, ed. see Ryun, Ned & Ryun, Drew.

Ryun, Drew, jt. auth. see Ryun, Ned.

Ryun, Ned & Ryun, Drew. It's a Lifestyle Vol. 1: An Appeal to Common Sense. Ryun, Anne, ed. 125p. 1996. lib. bdg. 8.95 (0-9651723-0-9) Silver Clarion.

Ryunosuke, Akutagawa. Cogwheels & Other Stories. 74p. 1994. 9.95 (0-88962-176-4) Mosaic.

Ryusen, Miyahara. Buddhist Paintings - Japanese National Treasures: Restored Copies. 127p. 1981. 65.00 (4-333-01039-X, Pub. by Kosei Pub Co) Tuttle Pubng.

Ryvarden, Leif. Genera of Polypores. Nomenclature & Taxonomy. (Synopsis Fungorum Ser.: No. 5). 363p. 1991. pap. 95.00 (82-90724-10-1, Pub. by Fungi-Flora) Lubrecht & Cramer.

— The Polyporaceae of North Europe, 2 vols., Set. (Illus.). 1988. pap. text. write for info. (0-945345-13-5) Lubrecht & Cramer.

Ryvarden, Leif, jt. auth. see Eriksson, J.

Ryvarden, Leif, jt. auth. see Gilbertson, R. L.

Ryvarden, Leif, jt. auth. see Hjortstam, K.

Ryvarden, Leif, jt. auth. see Johansen, Inger.

R

R

Ryves, Thomas. The Poore Vicars Plea. Declaring That a Competencie of Means Is Due to Them Out of the Tithes..Notwithstanding the Impropriations. LC 79-84135. (English Experience Ser.: No. 953). 164p. 1979. reprint ed. lib. bdg. 20.00 (*90-221-0953-4*) Walter J Johnson.

***Ryvkin, Kostya, et al.** Internetworking with Microsoft TCP/IP on Microsoft Windows NT 4.0: Exam: 70-088. (MCSE Ser.). (Illus.). 432p. 1999. pap. text 49.99 (*0-13-011251-8*) P-H.

— Network + Certification. LC 99-56523. 500p. 1999. 49.99 (*0-13-016895-5*) P-H.

Ryvkina, Rozalina, jt. auth. see Brym, Robert J.

Rywater, Murray A. B-25's Target Kyushu. 2nd ed. (Illus.). 297p. (C). 1995. 27.50 (*0-9639575-0-3*) B Twenty Five.

Rywell, Martin. Sharps Rifle: The Gun That Shaped American Destiny. 160p. 1956. 7.00 (*0-913150-21-5*) Pioneer Pr.

***Rywick, Robert, et al, eds.** Federal Tax Handbook, 2000. rev. ed. 854p. 2000. pap. 45.00 (*0-7811-0219-7*) Res Inst Am.

— Individual Tax Return Guide, 2000. rev. ed. 160p. 2000. pap. 16.50 (*0-7811-0240-5*) Res Inst Am.

— 1999 Fiduciary Tax Return Guide. 160p. 2000. pap. 16.50 (*0-7811-0237-5*) Res Inst Am.

— Tax Guide, Vols. 1 & 2. rev. ed. 3008p. 2000. pap. 215.00 (*0-7811-0241-3*) Res Inst Am.

Rywkin, Michael. Moscow's Lost Empire. LC 93-29308. (Illus.). 230p. (C). (gr. 13). 1994. text 74.95 (*1-56324-236-2*) M E Sharpe.

Rywkin, Michael. Moscow's Lost Empire. LC 93-29308. (Illus.). 230p. (C). (gr. 13). 1994. pap. text 35.95 (*1-56324-237-0*) M E Sharpe.

Rywkin, Michael. Moscow's Muslim Challenge: Soviet Central Asia. rev. ed. LC 89-29825. 202p. (gr. 13). 1990. text 66.95 (*0-87332-613-X*) M E Sharpe.

Rywkin, Michael. Moscow's Muslim Challenge: Soviet Central Asia. rev. ed. LC 89-29825. 202p. (gr. 13). 1990. pap. text 42.95 (*0-87332-614-8*) M E Sharpe.

Rywkin, Michael. Soviet Society Today. LC 89-4192. 256p. (gr. 13). 1989. text 85.95 (*0-87332-444-7*) M E Sharpe.

Rywkin, Michael. Soviet Society Today. LC 89-4192. 256p. (gr. 13). 1989. pap. text 38.95 (*0-87332-445-5*) M E Sharpe.

Rywkin, Michael, ed. Russian Colonial Expansion to 1917. LC 84-71094. (Issue Studies (U. S. S. R. & East Europe): No. 4). xviii, 274p. 1988. 30.00 (*0-7201-1867-0*) Assn Study Nat.

Ryzenkov, A. V. Unfolding the Eco-Wave. LC 99-37218. 150p. 2000. 103.00 (*0-471-60792-4*) Wiley.

Ryzhikov, K. M., jt. ed. see Rysavy, B.

Ryzhjk, J. M., jt. auth. see Gradshteyn, J. S.

Ryzin, Robert R. Van, see Van Ryzin, Robert R.

Ryzkova, et al. Precvicme Si Pravopis, Vol. 6. (SLO.). 80p. 1996. write for info. (*80-08-01761-9*, Pub. by Slov Pegagog Naklad) IBD Ltd.

— Precvicme Si Pravopis, Vol. 7. (SLO.). 80p. 1996. write for info. (*80-08-01770-8*, Pub. by Slov Pegagog Naklad) IBD Ltd.

— Precvicme Si Pravopis, Vol. 8. (SLO.). 96p. 1996. write for info. (*80-08-01771-6*, Pub. by Slov Pegagog Naklad) IBD Ltd.

— Ucime Sa Pravopis, Vol. 2. (SLO.). 58p. 1997. write for info. (*80-08-02589-1*, Pub. by Slov Pegagog Naklad) IBD Ltd.

— Ucime Sa Pravopis, Vol. 3. (SLO.). 72p. 1997. write for info. (*80-08-02590-5*, Pub. by Slov Pegagog Naklad) IBD Ltd.

— Ucime Sa Pravopis, Vol. 4. (SLO.). 80p. 1997. write for info. (*80-08-02591-3*, Pub. by Slov Pegagog Naklad) IBD Ltd.

— Ucime Sa Pravopis, Vol. 5. (SLO.). 80p. 1997. write for info. (*80-08-02588-3*, Pub. by Slov Pegagog Naklad) IBD Ltd.

Ryzuk, Mary S. The Circle Repertory Company: The First Fifteen Years. LC 88-13704. (Illus.). 327p. 1989. reprint ed. pap. 101.40 (*0-608-00141-4*, 206092200006) Bks Demand.

— Thou Shalt Not Kill. 1990. mass mkt. 4.95 (*0-445-21043-5*, Pub. by Warner Bks) Little.

Rzach, ed. Hesiodi. (GRE.). 1992. reprint ed. pap. 22.95 (*3-519-01418-1*, T1418, Pub. by B G Teubner) U of Mich Pr.

Rzayev, G., ed. English - Azerbaijan Dictionary, 2 vols. (AZE & ENG.). 484p. (Orig.). (C). 1994. pap. 59.95 (*0-8285-5349-1*) Firebird NY.

***Rzchowski, M., et al, eds.** Magnetoresistive Oxides & Related Materials Vol. 602: Materials Research Society Symposium Proceedings. 2000. text 93.00 (*1-55899-510-2*) Materials Res.

Rzecki, Catherine. Surfing the Blues: Understanding & Coping with Mood Disorders. 1998. pap. 13.95 (*0-207-18866-1*) HarpC.

Rzeczkoski, Matthew, tr. see Aquinas, Thomas, Saint.

Rzempoluck, Edward J. Neural Network Data Analysis Using Simulnet. LC 97-16666. (Illus.). 216p. 1997. 39.95 incl. cd-rom (*0-387-98255-8*) Spr-Verlag.

***Rzepa, Henry.** Electronic Conference on Heterocyclic Chemistry. 1998. 38.00 (*1-86094-183-4*) Imperial College.

Rzepecki, Arnold. Book Review Index to Social Science Periodicals, 4 vols., Set. LC 78-51070. 1982. 275.00 (*0-685-73413-7*) Pierian.

— Book Review Index to Social Science Periodicals, 4 vols., Vol. 1: 1978. LC 78-51070. 1978. 75.00 (*0-87650-026-2*) Pierian.

— Book Review Index to Social Science Periodicals, 4 vols., Vol. 2: 1979. LC 78-51070. 1982. 75.00 (*0-87650-110-2*) Pierian.

— Book Review Index to Social Science Periodicals, 4 vols., Vol. 3: 1980. LC 78-51070. 1980. 75.00 (*0-87650-049-1*) Pierian.

— Book Review Index to Social Science Periodicals, 4 vols., Vol. 4: 1982. LC 78-51070. 1982. 75.00 (*0-87650-114-5*) Pierian.

Rzepecki, Arnold N., compiled by. Literature & Language Bibliographies from the American Yearbook, 1910-1919: The Predecessor of the MLA Bibliography. (Cumulated Bibliography Ser.: No. 1). 1970. 29.50 (*0-87650-013-0*) Pierian.

Rzepecki, Edward L., ed. Packaging & Environmental Issues. (Illus.). (C). 1991. pap. text 65.00 (*0-9624229-4-0*) St Thomas Tech.

Rzepecki, Edward L. & Swenson, Linda K., eds. Responsible Packaging. (Illus.). 513p. (C). 1998. per. 79.95 (*1-887199-03-9*) St Thomas Tech.

Rzepka, Charles J. Sacramental Commodities: Gift, Text, & the Sublime in De Quincey. LC 94-38875. 360p. (C). 1995. pap. text 19.95 (*0-87023-962-7*); lib. bdg. 55.00 (*0-87023-961-9*) U of Mass Pr.

— The Self As Mind: Vision & Identity in Wordsworth, Coleridge, & Keats. 298p. 1986. 37.50 (*0-674-80085-0*) HUP.

***Rzepka, Jane R.** Thematic Preaching. 256p. 2000. pap. 26.99 (*0-8272-3653-0*) Chalice Pr.

Rzepnicki, Tina L. & Stein, Theodore J. Decision Making in Child Welfare Services: Intake & Planning. 1984. lib. bdg. 88.50 (*0-89838-138-X*) Kluwer Academic.

Rzeppa, Anna M., jt. auth. see Bywalec, Gloria L.

Rzeswski, Theodore S. & Rzeszewski, Theodore S. Digital Video: Concepts & Applications Across Industries. LC 94-33543. 608p. 1995. 79.95 (*0-7803-1099-3*, PC4523) Inst Electrical.

Rzeszewski, Theodore S., jt. auth. see Rzeswski, Theodore S.

Rzetelny, Harriet & Mellor, Joanna. Support Groups for Caregivers of the Aged: A Training Manual for Facilitators. LC 84-167188. 72p. (Orig.). 1981. pap. 7.50 (*0-88156-008-1*) Comm Serv Soc NY.

Rzevski, G., et al, eds. Applications of Artifical Intelligence in Engineering IX. 632p. 1994. 299.00 (*1-85312-284-X*) Computational Mech MA.

Rzevski, G., et al, eds. Applications of Artificial Intelligence: Expert Sytems, Robots & Vision Systems, Fuzzy Logic & Neural Networks. LC 96-83657. (AIENG Ser.: Vol. 11). 134p. 1996. 299.00 incl. cd-rom (*1-85312-410-9*, 4109) Computational Mech MA.

Rzevski, George. Perception, Cognition & Execution - Mechatronics: Designing Intelligent Machines, Vol. 1. LC 95-210719. 336p. 1995. pap. text 42.95 (*0-7506-2404-3*) Buttrwrth-Heinemann.

Rzevski, George, ed. Artificial Intelligence in Design. LC 89-61419. (AIENG Ser.: Vol. 4). 564p. 1989. 152.00 (*0-945824-20-3*) Computational Mech MA.

— Artificial Intelligence in Manufacturing. LC 89-61419. (AIENG Ser.: Vol. 4). 476p. 1989. 132.00 (*0-945824-22-X*) Computational Mech MA.

Rzevski, George, jt. ed. see Adey, Robert A.

Rzevski, George, jt. ed. see Gero, J. S.

Rzheshevsky, Oleg A. War & Diplomacy: The Making of a Grand Alliance. (History of Russia Ser.: Vol. 2). 325p. 1996. text 37.00 (*3-7186-5790-2*, Harwood Acad Pubs) Gordon & Breach.

Rzhevsky, Nicholas, ed. An Anthology of Russian Literature from Earliest Writings to Modern Fiction: Introduction to a Culture. LC 95-42684. (Illus.). 608p. (C). (gr. 13). 1996. 82.95 (*1-56324-421-7*); pap. 36.95 (*1-56324-422-5*) M E Sharpe.

— The Cambridge Companion to Modern Russian Culture. LC 98-3850. (Cambridge Companions to Culture Ser.). (Illus.). 320p. (C). 1999. 54.95 (*0-521-47218-0*); pap. 19.95 (*0-521-47799-9*) Cambridge U Pr.

Rzhevsky, V. Opencast Mining Technology & Integrated Mechanisation. 495p. (C). 1987. 110.00 (*0-685-46641-8*, Pub. by Collets) St Mut.

Rzoska, Julian. On the Nature of Rivers: With Case Stories of the Nile, Zaire, & Amazon. 1978. text 44.00 (*90-6193-589-X*) Kluwer Academic.

Rzoska, Julian, ed. Euphrates & Tigris: Mesopotamian Ecology & Destiny. (Monographiae Biologicae: No. 38). (Illus.). 122p. 1980. text 99.50 (*90-6193-090-1*) Kluwer Academic.

An Asterisk (*) at the beginning of an entry indicates that the title is appearing for the first time.